T0315798

INTERNATIONAL WHO'S WHO IN MUSIC AND MUSICIANS' DIRECTORY

INTERNATIONAL WHO'S WHO IN MUSIC
and Musicians' Directory

PUBLISHER:
Nicholas S. Law

SENIOR EDITOR:
Sean Tyler

CONSULTING EDITOR:
David M. Cummings

PRODUCTION MANAGER:
Jocelyn Timothy

EDITORIAL ASSISTANTS:
Barbara Cooper
Janine Lawrence

All communication to: International Biographical Centre,
Cambridge CB2 3QP, England

INTERNATIONAL WHO'S WHO IN MUSIC AND MUSICIANS' DIRECTORY

(IN THE CLASSICAL AND LIGHT CLASSICAL FIELDS)

SIXTEENTH EDITION

1998/1999

EDITOR
DAVID M. CUMMINGS

Routledge
Taylor & Francis Group

LONDON AND NEW YORK

©1998 by Melrose Press Ltd, Cambridge, England

ALL RIGHTS RESERVED. No part of this publication may be reproduced, stored in a retrieval system or transmitted in any form or by any means, electronic, mechanical, photocopying or otherwise without prior written permission of the publisher.

This edition re-issued 2014 by Routledge
2 Park Square, Milton Park, Abingdon, Oxon OX14 4RN
711 Third Avenue, New York, NY, 10017, USA

Routledge is an imprint of the Taylor & Francis Group, an informa business

First Published
1935
Second Editon
1937
Third Edition
1950
Fourth Edition
1962
Fifth Edition
1969
Sixth Edition
1972
Seventh Edition
1975
Eighth Edition
1977
Ninth Edition
1980
Tenth Edition
1985
Eleventh Edition
1988
Twelfth Edition
1990
Thirteenth Edition
1992
Fourteenth Edition
1994
Fifteenth Edition
1996
Sixteenth Edition
1998

ISBN: 978-0-948875-92-2 (hbk)

FOREWORD BY THE EDITOR

In the Fifteenth Edition of the *International Who's Who in Music, 1996,* it was my intention to provide a comprehensive record of achievement in the classical and light classical fields. For this, the *Sixteenth Edition,* I have been responsible for some 2,000 new or largely new entries, while the remaining 6,000 entries have nearly all been revised. The result is a fuller, more accurate and more up-to-date source for contemporary musicians than any other book published so far.

As before, every biographee was sent a typescript of his or her entry for amending and approval, and the necessary corrections and updates have been incorporated in the final copy. Even in a book with such a wide scope as the *International Who's Who in Music* it is not possible to include in each case all the information which is submitted. If the Honours and Memberships sections have been pruned it will be appreciated that more space is made available to provide essential career information (e.g. works in the case of composers, or repertory for performers). While every care is taken to ensure accuracy, it is inevitable that some detail will have 'fallen under the table'. I must bear the responsibility for such errors but if I am written to care of the publishers I will put matters right in the next edition.

I am now solely responsible for the biographical section of the *International Who's Who in Music,* and have developed the invaluable work of Dennis McIntire for the Appendices; these include full details of orchestras, opera houses, festivals and competitions from around the world. The first two of these now contain phone and fax numbers for the first time.

While it is always a pleasure to record the achievement of young musicians, there is also sadness in having to delete those of earlier generations who have died. Perhaps the greatest loss since the last edition is that of Michael Tippett; other losses have been sustained by the deaths of such musicians as Sviatoslav Richter, Klaus Tennstedt and Georg Solti.

It only remains for me to thank all those who have helped to produce the *Sixteenth Edition*: the Publisher Nicholas Law has once again allowed me to act as editor and I am particularly grateful to Sean Tyler and his staff for their patience, cooperation and efficiency.

David Cummings

David Cummings
Editor

April 1998

INTERNATIONAL BIOGRAPHICAL CENTRE
RANGE OF REFERENCE TITLES

From one of the widest ranges of contemporary biographical reference works published under any one imprint, some IBC titles date back to the 1930's. Each edition is compiled from information supplied by those listed, who include leading personalities of particular countries or professions. Information offered usually includes date and place of birth; family details; qualifications; career histories; awards and honours received; books published or other creative work; other relevant information including postal address. Naturally there is no charge or fee for inclusion.

New editions are freshly compiled and contain on average 80-90% new information. New titles are regularly added to the IBC reference library.

Titles include:

Dictionary of International Biography

Who's Who in Australasia and the Pacific Nations

Who's Who in Western Europe

Dictionary of Scandinavian Biography

International Who's Who in Art and Antiques

International Authors and Writers Who's Who

International Leaders in Achievement

International Who's Who in Community Service

International Who's Who in Education

International Who's Who in Engineering

International Who's Who in Medicine

International Who's Who in Music and Musicians' Directory - Volume One - Classical and Light Classical

International Who's Who in Music - Volume Two - Popular Music

Men of Achievement

The World Who's Who of Women

The World Who's Who of Women in Education

International Youth of Achievement

Foremost Women of the Twentieth Century

International Who's Who in Poetry and Poets' Encyclopaedia

2000 Outstanding People of the 20th Century

Enquiries to:
International Biographical Centre
Cambridge CB2 3QP
England

CONTENTS

A

AADLAND Eivind, b. 19 Sept 1956, Bergen, Norway. Violinist. Education: Norwegian State Music Academy, Oslo with Camilla Wicks; International Menuhin Music Academy, Switzerland with Alberto Lysy and Yehudi Menuhin; Masterclasses with Sandor Vegh. Career: Formerly Concertmaster, Bergen Philharmonic Orchestra; Music Director, European Community Chamber Orchestra, 1988-; Has appeared in major halls and festivals worldwide including Musikverein, Vienna, Concertgebouw, Amsterdam, Salle Pleyel, Paris and Gewandhaus, Leipzig. Recordings: 12 CDs. Address: Arupsgate 10, 0192 Oslo, Norway.

AAQUIST JOHANSEN Svend, b. 1948, Denmark. Composer; Conductor; Computer Programmer. Education: University of Copenhagen; The Royal Danish Academy of Music, Copenhagen; International courses; Teachers include Elisabeth Klein, Arne Hammelboe, Michel Tabachnik. Debut: 1969. Career includes: Conductor for numerous choirs, chamber ensembles and orchestras, 1969-, High School Teacher, 1969-75; Teacher of Conducting, Royal Danish Academy of Music and State Academy of Music at Esbjerg; Numerous workshops and seminars for musical and conducting courses; Chief Conductor and Artistic Director, Esbjerg Symphony Orchestra; Artistic Adviser, Esbjerg Ensemble, 1984-; Appeared in many concerts, festivals, on radio and TV recordings, in Denmark and abroad; Concerts given with many orchestras including Odense Symphony Orchestra; Concert tours with West German Chamber Orchestra, Ensemble Modern, 1981, 1982, 1984. Compositions include: Pentagram, 1969; Salut-Salut, 1970; Ke-Tjak, 1973; Unite, 1974; Sinfonia Sisyphus, 1976; Malinche, 1979; Sun, 1983; Hymn With Dances, 1985. Recordings: Numerous. Memberships: Co-founder of LUT and LYT; Danish State Music Council; NOMUS, 1971-76; President, 1973-74, Nordic Composers' Council; Board Member, Society for Publication of Danish Music, 1974-84; Chairman, 1973-74, Danish Composers' Society; Chairman, 1980-84, DUT Danish ISCM. Address: Rialtovej 7, DK-2300 Copenhagen, Denmark.

ABAJAN Maria, b. 1950, Eriwan, Armenia. Singer (Soprano). Education: Studied at Eriwan and Tchaikovsky Conservatory in Moscow; Further studies at Los Angeles. Career: Moved to USA in 1977; Successful at singing competitions in New York, San Francisco, Italy and Mexico; Appeared in Europe, 1985-, notably as Turandot in Liège, Abigaille in Nabucco, (Brussels, 1987) and Aida in Zurich; Has sung Leonora in Trovatore and Elisabeth de Valois at Hamburg, Tosca and Amelia in Ballo in Maschera in Essen; Appeared as Tosca with Scottish Opera, Glasgow, in 1990. Address: c/o Scottish Opera, 39 Elmbank Crescent, Glasgow, G2 4PT, Scotland.

ABBADO Claudio, b. 26 June 1933, Milan, Italy. Conductor. Education: Giuseppe Verdi Conservatory, Milan; Academy of Music, Vienna, with Hans Swabarowsky. Debut: La Scala, Milan, 1960, in concert celebrating tercentenary of A Scarlatti; Salzburg Festival, 1965, local premiere of G Manzoni's opera Atomtod. Career: Conducted opening of La Scala season, 1967; Music Director, La Scala, 1968-86; Covent Garden debut, 1968 (Don Carlos); Has conducted the Vienna Philharmonic Orchestra from 1972; Tour of USA with Cleveland and Philadelphia Orchestras, 1972; Tour with La Scala company to Munich, 1972; USSR, 1974; London 1976 (Simon Boccanegra); USA, 1976; Japan, 1981; Tour with the Vienna Philharmonic to Japan and China, 1973; Founder, European Community Youth Orchestra, 1978; Musical Director, London Symphony Orchestra, 1979-88 (series of concerts, Mahler, Vienna and the 20th Century, 1985); Principal Conductor, Chamber Orchestra of Europe, 1981; Founder of La Filharmonica della Scala, 1982; Principal Guest Conductor of Chicago Symphony Orchestra, 1982-85; Debut at the Vienna State Opera, 1984; Director, 1986-91; Founder, Gustav Mahler Jugendorchester, Vienna, 1986; Conductor, New Year's Eve concerts, Vienna, 1988 and 1990; Appointed Musical Director and Principal Conductor, Berlin Philharmonic Orchestra, 1989; Promenade Concerts, London, 1991, with the Gustav Mahler Jugendorchester (5th Symphony) and the Berlin Philharmonic (Brahms 2nd Piano Concerto and Mahler 4); Conductor, The House of the Dead, Salzburg Festival, 1992; Bruckner's 5th Symphony with the Gustav Mahler Youth Orchestra, Promenade Concerts, 1993; La Scala, 1994, Il Barbiere di Siviglia; Artistic Director, Salzburg Easter Festival, 1994; Engaged to conduct Tristan und Isolde at Salzburg, 1999. Recordings include: Operas by Rossini and Verdi, Mussorgsky, Berg, Schubert (Fierabras); Music by Berg and Nono; Complete Symphonies of Mahler, Schubert, Mendelssohn, Beethoven and Tchaikovsky; Mozart Piano Concertos with Rudolf Serkin; Brahms Piano Concerto No 1, with Brendel and Vivaldi's Four Seasons, with Viktoria Mullova; Works of Haydn and Prokofiev, Bartók, Ravel, Debussy; currently working on cycle of complete Bruckner symphonies. Publication: La Casa Del Suoni: Book for Children about Music. Honours include: Mozart Medaille; Premio Abbiati; Officier of the French Légion d'Honneur; Koussevitzky Prize (Tanglewood); Winner, Mitropoulos Conducting Competition. Address: Harold Holt Ltd, 31 Sinclair Road, London W14 0NS, England.

ABBADO Marcello, b. 7 Oct 1926, Milan, Italy. Musician. Education: Diploma in Piano, 1944, and Composition, 1947, Milan Conservatory. Career: Soloist and Conductor in Europe, America, Africa, Asia, 1944-; Specialised in Debussy and piano concertos of Mozart; Professor of Piano at Conservatories of Cagliari, Venice, Milan and of Composition at Parma and Bologna, 1950; Director, Liceo Musicale, Piacenza, 1958; Director, Rossini Conservatory, Pesaro, 1966; Director, Verdi Conservatory, Milan, 1972. Compositions include: Scena Senza Storia, ballet; Orchestral: Concerto for Orchestra, Hommage à Debussy, Costruzioni for 5 Small Orchestras, Risonanze for 2 Pianos and Chamber Orchestra, Cantata Ebraica for Vocal Soloists, Choir and Orchestra, Seven Ricercari for 6 Intermezzi, Violin and Orchestra; Chamber: 15 Poesie T'ang for Voice and 4 Instruments, Ciapo for Voice and 9 Instruments, Three Quatuor, Duo for Violin and Cello, Fantasian 2 for 4 Instruments and 31 Percussionists, Riverberazioni for Wind Instruments and Piano, Concertante for Piano and Instrument, Sonata for Flute, Lamento for the Mother's Death for Clavicordo, Aus dem Klavier for Piano, Responsorio for Choir and Organ, Sarà Sara for Guitar; Quadruplo Concerto for Piano, Violin, Viola, Cello and Orchestra, 1970; L'Idea fissa for Violin "Scordato" and Percussion Orchestra, 1994; Doppio Concerto for Flute, Guitar and Orchestra, 1995. Memberships: Administrative Council, Teatro alla Scala; Fondazione Curci, Naples; Fondazione Puccini, Lucca and Verdi Conservatory, Milan; President of juries of national and international competitions of chamber music, composition, conducting, piano and others. Address: Via Conservatorio 12, 20122 Milano, Italy.

ABBADO Roberto, b. 1954, Milan, Italy. Conductor. Education: Studied at Pesaro and Milan Conservatories with Franco Ferrara in Rome and at Teatro La Fenice, Venice. Debut: With Orchestra of Accademia Santa Cecilia in 1977. Career: Operatic debut in 1978 with a new production of Simon Boccanegra at Macerata; Festival appearances at Edinburgh, 1982, Israel, 1984, Lille and Munich, 1989; Chief Conductor of Munich Radio Orchestra, 1991; Engagements with Staatskapelle Dresden, Bamberg Symphony, Orchestre National de France, RAI Turin, the Orchestra of Saint Luke's in New York, Maggio Musicale Fiorentino Orchestra; Opera engagements at La Scala with world premiere of Flavio Testi's Il Sosia and Riccardo III and a new production of Don Pasquale; Vienna State Opera with a new production of La Cenerentola, Bayerische Staatsoper, Munich with a new production of La Traviata, 1993 and Adriana Lecouvreur, Manon Lescaut, Don Pasquale; Conducted La Forza del Destino at San Francisco, and appeared at Rome, Florence, Bologna, Venice, Berlin Deutsche Oper, Zurich, Barcelona, and Tokyo with Teatro Comunale Bologna, 1993; Conducted Adriana Lecouvreur at the Metropolitan in New York, 1994; Opera Bastille debut, Lucia di Lammermoor, 1995; Houston Grand Opera debut, Norma, 1996; Engaged for Aida at the 1997 Munich Festival. Recordings: Many. Honours: Echo Klassic Deutscher Schallplattenpreis by the Deutsche Phono Akademi for recording of Rossini's Tancredi at the 1997 Best Opera Production of the Year.Address: c/o M L Falcone, Public Relations, 155 West 68th Street, Suite 1114, New York, NY 10023, USA.

ABDEL-RAHIM Gamal, b. 25 Nov 1924, Cairo, Egypt. Composer; Professor. m. Samha El-Kholy, 8 Dec 1959, 1 daughter. Education: BA, History, University of Cairo, 1945; Composition study with H Genzmer at the Staatliche Hochschule für Musik, Freiburg, Germany, 1950-57; Diploma in Composition, 1957. Career: Assistant Professor, 1959-71, Professor, 1971-84, Vice Dean, 1978-81, Founder and Chairman of Composition Department (1st in Arab region), 1970s-84, Professor Emeritus, 1984-, State Conservatory, Cairo; Visiting Professor, University of South Florida, Tampa, 1987-. Compositions include: Orchestral: Suite for Orchestra; Symphonic Variation On An Egyptian Theme; Jubiland Dance; Lotus Pond for Flute, Oboe and Orchestra; Echoes for Flute and Orchestra; Awakening, cantata for Baritone, Choir and Orchestra; Egyptian Aspects On 4 Folktunes for Choir and Orchestra; Ballet Music: Osiris, 5 scenes, for Percussion, Harp and Chamber Ensemble; Hassan and Maima, 3 scenes, Chamber Music: Sonata for Violin and Piano; Improvisations for Unaccompanied Cello; Variations for Piano; Many songs, a capella choral work, and incidental music for theatre, film and TV. Recordings: All works recorded on Egyptian Radio and TV. Hobbies: Anthroposophy and Zen-Buddhism Readings; Languages (self taught). Address: 13044 Leverington Street, Tampa, FL 33624, USA.

ABDRASAKOV Askar, b. Ufa, Urals, Russia. Singer (bass). Education: Studied at the Ufa Conservatoire and with Irina Arkipova in Moscow. Career: Soloist with the Bashkirian Opera from 1990, as Sobakin (The Tsar's Bride), Konchak in Prince Igor, Gremin, Zuniga, Sparafucile and Rossini's Don Basilio; Recital with Arkhipova at the Wigmore Hall, 1994 and Rimsky's Invisible City of Kitezh at the Bregenz Festival, 1995; In recital at the Châtelet, Paris, the Bonze in Stravinsky's Nightingale under Pierre Boulez in Paris and London, Rimsky's Tsar Saltan at Florence and the Grand Inquisitor in Don Carlos at Bologna, 1996-97; Concerts include the Verdi Requiem, Puccini Messa di Gloria; Russian and French songs and Lieder. Honours include: Prizewinner at the 1991 Glinka Competition; Winner, Chaliapin Bass Competition at Kazan, 1994; Grand Prix, Maria Callas Competition in Athens, 1995. Address: c/o Lies Askonas Ltd, 6 Henrietta Street, Lonodn WC2E 8LA, England.

ABEL Yves, b. 1968, Canada. Conductor. Career: Conducted a revival of Wagner's Das Liebesverbot at the Wexford Festival, 1994; Metropolitan Opera debut with La Traviata 1995, returning for Carmen, 1997; Rossini Festival at Pesaro, with Il Cambiale di Matrimonio, Matilde di Shabran and Il Barbiere di Siviglia, 1995-97; As Music Director of L'Opera Français de New York has led productions of Chabrier's L'Etoile, Bizet's Docteur Miracle, Cherubini's Médée and Gluck's Iphigénie en Aulide and Orphée et Euridice; Further engegments with San Francisco Opera for Thomas' Hamlet, Netherlands Opera (Les Dialogues des Carmélites) and Nice (Massenet's Thaïs); French opera debut with Faust at the Opera Bastille, Paris, 1996; Season 1995-96 with Roméo et Juliette for Florida Grand Opera, and La Cenerentola at Seattle; Glyndebourne debut with Le Comte Ory, 1998. Recordings include: Thaïs, with Renée Fleming and Thomas Hampson. Address: c/o Harold Holt Ltd, 31 Sinclair Road, London W14 0NS, England.

ÅBERG Thomas Harald Georg, b. 15 Feb 1952, Stockholm, Sweden. Composer; Concert Organist. m. Solveig Hansen, 16 Jan 1986. Education: Piano with Märta Söderberg; Piano and Organ with Tore Nilson, 1973-75; Composition with Stig Gustav Schönberg, 1981-83. Debut: As Composer, Stockholm, 1978. Career: Began composing for church organ, 1976; Leader, Skeppsholm Group contemporary music quartet, 1978-81; Concert Organist (soloist), mainly own works, 1981-; 1st solo concert, Stockholm, 1981; 1st performances, Switzerland, 1983, Denmark (recital), 1984, Stockholm Concert Hall, 1984, Russia, 1988, Japan, 1989; 5 concerts, Stockholm, May 1984; Toured Norway, 1990; Lectured at Sibelius Academy, Helsinki, 1990; Stockholm Concert Hall, 1991; Played digital organ at outdoor concerts, Stockholm, 1992-93; 6 concerts in Stockholm Cathedral during Stockholm Water Festival, 1994; Toured USA, 1996; His works represented at organ festivals, Varazze International (Italy), 1983, Åland (Finland), 1986, 1989, Flensburg International (Germany), 1986, Fromborker International (Poland), Norrköping (Sweden), Japan International, 1991, also New Sweden Festival, New York, 1988. Compositions: Fantasy for solo cello; Klockklang, Christmas hymn; Sommarpsalm, summer hymn; Suite for cello and piano; Organ works include: Toccata Nos 1-12; 2 Suites; Tre korta fantasistycken; Fantasy in A minor; Legends No 1-5; Nocturne; Suite for small organ. Recordings: Various. Honours: Scholarships, Swedish Performing Right Society, 1987, 1990, Arts Grants Committee, 1993, Swedish Composers' Association, 1995. Memberships: Swedish Composers' Association; Swedish Performing Right Society, Staff 1981-. Hobby: Living outdoor life with his dogs. Address: Näsby Hästhagen, 740 10 Almunge, Sweden.

ABESHOUSE Warren, b. 8 May 1952, Sydney, New South Wales, Australia. Composer. Education: Diploma, State Conservatoire, New South Wales, 1977. Career: ABC Radio and Television, 1975-87; Office Manager, 1994-. Compositions include: Five Bagatelles for Piano, 1972; Two Piano Sonatas, 1975, 1986; Psalm 70 for Chorus and organ, 1975; Four Characteristic Pieces for Clarinet, 1976; Two Bagatelles for Cello, 1976; Lemmata, Essay for Orchestra, 1977; On Love for Tenor and Piano, 1980; Shadow Darkly for Oboe and Strings, 1990; The Christopher Sonatina for Piano, 1991; Womblemov for Horn, Cello and Timpani, 1993; Lament for Piano, 1993. Honours include: First Prize, Original work for solo instrument, City of Sydney Eisteddford, 1990. Address: c/o APRA, 1A Eden Street, Crows Nest, NSW 2065, Australia.

ABRAHAMSEN Hans, b. 23 Dec 1952, Copenhagen, Denmark. Composer. Education: Studied horn, theory, and music history at Royal Danish Conservatory, Copenhagen, 1969-71; Composition with Pelle Gudmundsen- Holmgreen and Per Norgard at Jutland Academy of Music, Aarhus. Compositions: Orchestral: Foam, 1970; Symphony in C, 1972; Symphony No 1, 1974; Stratifications, 1973-75; Nach und Trompeten, 1981; Marchenbilder for 14 players, 1984; Cello Concerto, 1987; Chamber: Fantasy Pieces After Hans Jorgen Nielsen for Flute, Horn, Cello and Piano, 1969, revised, 1976; October for Piano Left Hand, 1969, revised 1976; Round And In Between for Brass Quintet, 1972; 2 Woodwind Quintets: No 1, Lanscapes, 1972, No 2, Walden, 1978; Nocturnes for Flute and Piano, 1972; Flowersongs for 3 Flutes, 1973; Scraps for Cello and Piano, 1973; 2 String Quartets: No 1, 10 Preludes, 1973, No 2, 1981; Flush for Saxophone, 1974, revised, 1979; Double for Flute and Guitar, 1975; Winternacht for 7 instruments, 1976-79; Canzone for Accordion, 1978; Geduldspiel for 10 instruments, 1980; 6 Pieces for Violin, Horn and Piano, 1984; 10 Studies for Piano, 1983-87; Vocal: Herbst for Tenor, Flute, Guitar and Cello, 1970-72, revised, 1977; Universe Birds for 10 Sopranos, 1973; Songs of Denmark for Soprano and 5 Instruments, 1974, revised 1976; Aria for Soprano and 4 Instruments, 1979. Address: c/o PRS Ltd, (Mbr Registration, Denmark), 29-33 Berners Street, London, W1.

ACCARDO Salvatore, b. 26 Sep 1941, Turin, Italy. Violinist; Conductor. Education: Studied with Luigi d' Ambrosio at Naples Conservatory, diploma in 1956; Postgraduate study with Yvonne Astruc at the Accademia Chigiana, Sienna. Career: Has toured extensively as solo violinist and latterly as conductor in Europe and America; Founded the Turin L'Orchestra da Camera Italiana in 1968; Soloist with the ensemble I Musici, 1972-77 and Semaines Musicales of Chamber Music at Naples; Repertory includes Bach, Vivaldi and Paganini; Works composed for him include Fantasia for Violin and Orchestra by Walter Piston, Argot for Solo Violin by Franco Donatoni, and Dikhtas by Iannis Xenakis, 1980; Conducted Rossini's opera L'Occasione fa il Ladro at the 1987 Pesaro Festival; Plays several Stradivarius violins and a Guarnerius del Gesu of 1733; Took part in a performance of Schoenberg's String Trio at the Elizabeth Hall in London in 1990. Publication: L'Arte del Violino, 1987. Recordings include: Paganini's 24 Caprices and the Six Concertos. Address: c/o Accademia Musicale Chigiana, Via di Citta 89, 53100 Sienna, Italy.

ACHUCCARO Joaquin, b. 1 Nov 1936, Bilbao, Spain. Concert Pianist. Education: Studied at the Accademia Chigiana and with Walter Gieseking. Career: Many solo and concert performances worldwide from 1959, including appearances with the Berlin and New York Philharmonic, London Symphony and Philharmonia Orchestras, Orchestre National de France and Warsaw National Orchestra; Has also featured as soloist-conductor with chamber orchestras in Britain, Italy, Germany and Spain; from 1989 teacher at Southern Methodist University Dallas; BBC recitals on tour, 1997. Recordings include: Albums of Granados, Falla, Schubert, Ravel, Debussy and Brahms. Honours include: Winner, 1959 Liverpool International Competition. Address: Olivia Ma Management, 28 Sheffield Terrace, London W8 7NA, England.

ACKER Dieter, b. 3 Nov 1940, Sibiu-Hermannstadt, Romania. Composer; Teacher. Education: Studied piano, organ, theory with Fr Xav Dressler, Sibiu, 1950-58; Composition with Sigismund Todutá, Cluj Conservatory, 1959-64. Career: Teacher of Theory and Composition, Cluj Conservatory, 1964-69; Teacher, Robert Schumann Conservatory, Düsseldorf, 1969-72; Teacher of Theory and Composition, 1972-76, Professor of Composition, 1976-, Munich Hochschule für Musik. Compositions include: Symphoniy No 1, 1977-78; Eichendorff-Sonate for clarinet and piano, 1983; Mörike-Sonata for violin cello and piano, 1978; Bassoon Concerto, 1979-80; Violin Concerto No 1, 1981; Piano Concerto, 1984; Piano Trio No 2, 1984; Piano Trio No 2, 1984; String Trio No 3, 1987; String Quartet No 5, 1990-95; Music for Two Horns and Strings, 1991; Symphony No 3, 1992; Sinfonia Breve for brass, 1993; Notturno, for string orchestra, 1994; Violin Concerto No 2, 1994-95; Sonata for two pianos, 1993; Sonata for Piano No 2, 1993; Trinklieder for vocal quartet and piano, 1994; Sonata for Bassoon and Piano, 1996; Vocal music; Organ Music. Recordings include: Nachtstücke for two flutes; Piano Trio Stigmen, CD; Rilke Sonate for violin and piano, CD. Honours include: Recipient of numerous prizes for his works including: Prag 1996 Prize for String Quartet No I; Johann-Wenzel-Stamitz-Prize, Stuttgart, 1970; Lions Club International Prize for String Quartet No IV, Dusseldorf, 1973; Prix Henriette Renié for Music for Strings and Harp, Paris, 1988; Johann-Wenzel-Stamitz-Prize, Mannheim, 1990. Address: Kleiststrasse 12, D-85521 Munich-Ottobrunn, Germany.

ACS Janos, b. 23 Mar 1952, Hungary. Conductor. Divorced, 1 son, 2 daughters. Education: Diplomas in Flute, Pianoforte and Composition from Bela Bartok Institute, F Liszt Academy, Budapest; Organ Diploma from Verdi Conservatorio, Milan. Debut: In Fidelio at Teatro Carlo Felice, Genoa in 1979. Career: Appearances: Idomeneo at Opera di Roma, Tancredi at La Fenice, Falstaff, I Capuleti, Amico Fritz at Arena di Verona, Offenbach at Comunale di Firenze, La Bohème at Frankfurt, Symphonic Programmes in Tokyo, Manon, Pagliacci, La Traviata, and Otello in Denver, Carmen, Il Trovatore, and Tristan und Isolde in Pretoria, Faust in Hong Kong, and Luciano Pavarotti recital in Budapest; One of Pavarotti's conductors; Principal Conductor, Pact Theater, Pretoria, 1983-88; Principal Conductor at Opera Colorado in Denver, USA, 1985-91. Recordings: Bellini Overtures; Donizetti Overtures; I Puritani; Carmen, video of Pact Theater in Pretoria; Respighi's Gli Uccelli, Trittico Botticelliano. Honour: Respighi Memorial Concert and Prize, 1985. Membership: Co-Director, Franz Liszt Society of Germany. Hobbies: Swimming; Riding. Address: Durener Str 33-A, 518 Eschweiler, Germany.

AD-EL Shalev, b. 14 Jan 1968, Ramat-Gan, Israel. Musician. Education: Musc High School, Israel; Graduate, Royal Conservatory of the Hague, The Netherlands. Career: Conducted Polish Baroque Orchestra; Musica Viva Amsterdam; Kibbutz Chamber Orchestra; Norwegian Baroque; Halle Chamber Orchestra; Taught Course in Jerusalem Early Music Workshop, Brno Summer Academy, Radovlijca Summer Courses, Rheinsberg Academy of Music, Dresden Hochschule für Music, Dresdner Akademie, Conservatory of Lodz, Notenbalck, Holland, Rostock, Tage Alter Music, Charles University, Prague, Valtice Summer Courses, Israel Recorder Society. Recordings include: Chandos (cembalo toccatas and gamba sonatas by J S Bach, with Richard Boothby); Koch International (Mira Zakai Recital); Vlcek (Mozart flute quartets with continuo/Rameau pieces de Clavecin/Benda cembalo sonatas); Ramovs (Pepush cantatas); Metrix (Handel oboe sonatas/christmas record for the Marktkirche). Honours: 1st Prize, Francois Shapira Comp of the Israel-American Cultural Foundation; Honour Citizen of the City of Radovlijca. Current Management: CK Art Management, PO Box 3062, Herzliya 46104, Israel. Address: Navigatoru 27, 16100 Praha 6, Israel.

ADAM Theo, b. 1 Aug 1926, Dresden, Germany. Singer (Bass Baritone); Producer. Education: Sang in Dresden Kreuzchor and studied with Rudolf Dietrich in Dresden and in Weimar. Debut: Dresden in 1949 as the Hermit in Der Freischütz. Career includes: Berlin State Opera from 1952; Bayreuth debut in 1952 as Ortel in Meistersinger, later sang Wotan, Gurnemanz, King Henry, Pogner, Sachs and Amfortas; Covent Garden debut in 1967 as Wotan, Metropolitan Opera debut in 1969 as Sachs; Guest appearances include Hamburg, Vienna, Budapest and Chicago with roles including Berg's Wozzeck and Verdi's King Philip; Sang in and produced the premiere production of Dessau's Einstein at Berlin State Opera in 1974; Sang at Salzburg Festival, 1981, 1984 in premieres of Cerha's Baal and Berio's Un Re in Ascolto; In 1985 sang at reopened Semper Opera House, Dresden, in Der Freischütz and as Ochs in Der Rosenkavalier; Sang Don Alfonso at Tokyo in 1988 and La Roche in Capriccio at Munich Festival, 1990; Staged Graun's Cesare e Cleopatra for the 250th Anniversary of the Berlin State Opera, 1992; Sang Schigolch in Lulu at the Festival Hall in London, 1994 and at the Berlin Staatsoper, 1997; Sang in Henze's Bassarids at Dresden, 1997. Publication: Seht, hier ist Tinte, Feder, Papier..., autobiography, 1983. Recordings: Bach Cantatas; Freischütz; Parsifal; Meistersinger; Die Zauberflöte; Cosi fan tutte; Der Ring des Nibelungen; St Matthew Passion; Fidelio; Krenek's Karl V; Baal; Dantons Tod; Rosenkavalier; Die schweigsame Frau. Address: Schillerstrasse, D-8054 Dresden, Germany.

ADAMENKO Michail, b. 26 November 1954, Kiev, Soviet Union. m. Vira Starcenko, 28 April 1979, 1 son, 1 daughter. Education: Academy of Music, Kiev, 1981. Debut: As Edwin in Csardaskirállyné, Kiev, 1985. Career: Die Fledermaus, 1986; Der Zigeunerbaron, 1987; Die Lustige Witwe, 1990; Die Nacht in Venedig, Slovakia, 1991; Pimpinone, State Theatre-opera Kosice, 1991; Il Barbiere di Sevigliam, 1992; Manon Lescaut, 1992; Il Pagliacci, 1994; Carmen, 1997; Recitals of folk songs of Ukraine; Il Barbiere, Opera Festival Zvolen Slovakia, 1992; Light classical music on TV and Radio, Kosice. Hobbies: Woodcutting; Gardening. Address: Janigova 11, 040 01 Kosice, Slovakia.

ADAMIS Michael, b. 19 May 1929, Piraeus, Greece. Composer; Choral Director. m. Pany Carella, 30 Jul 1973, 2 sons. Education: Theology Degree, Athens University, 1954; Byzantine Music Degree, Piraeus Conservatory, 1955; Composition Degree, Hellenicon Conservatory, 1959; Graduate studies in composition, electronic music, Byzantine Paleography, Brandeis University, Boston, USA, 1962-65. Career includes: Founder and Director of Hellenic Royal Palace Boys Choir, 1950-67 and Athens Chamber Chorus, 1958-61; Taught Byzantine Music, directed choir, Greek Orthodox College of Theology, Boston, USA, 1961-63; Founder of 1st Electronic Music Studio in Athens, Greece in 1968; Head of Music Department, Choir Director, Pierce College, Athens, 1968-; Many festival commissions including: Hellenic Weeks of Contemporary Music, 1967-72, English Bach Festival, 1971, 1973; Worldwide performances of works include: ONCE Festival, USA, 1962, Barcelona, 1973, Leicester, 1976, Greek Month in London, 1975, 1989, Art Weeks throughout Europe, Middle and Far East; Many international Radio and TV broadcasts; Toured Europe and the Americas with ballet piece Genesis, 1973. Compositions include: Epallelon for Orchestra; Anakyklesis; Hirmos for Voices; Kratema. Recordings: Genesis; Apocalypsis; Minyrismos; Metallic Sculptures; Byzantine Passion; Psalmic Ode. Membership: President, Supreme Council for Music, Ministry of Culture, 1993. Address: Gravias 43, 15342 Ayia Paraskevi, Athens, Greece.

ADAMS Byron, b. 9 Mar 1955, Atlanta, Georgia, USA. Composer; Conductor; Author; Teacher. Education: BM, Jacksonville University, 1977; MM, University of Southern California, 1979; DMA, Cornell University, 1984. Career: Commposer-in-Residence, Music Center, University of the South, 1979-84; Guest Composer, 26th Warsaw Autumn Festival, 1983, and San Francisco Conservatory, 1986; Lecturer, Cornell University, New York City, 1985-87; Assistant Professor, currently Associate Professor, University of California at Riverside. Compositions: Quintet for piano and strings, 1979; Concerto for trumpet and string orchestra, 1983; Sonata for trumpet and piano, 1983; Concerto for violin and orchestra, 1984; Go Lovely Rose for male chorus, 1984; Missa brevis, 1988; Three Epitaphs, 1988. Recordings: Nightingales, 1979; Serenata aestiva, 1986. Contributions to: The Instrumentalist; Musical quarterly; Notes. Honours: Grand Prize, Delius Festival Composition Competition, 1977; American Society of Composers, Authors and Publishers Raymond Hubbell Award, Cornell University, 1984; Medly P Ray Composition Award, 1985; Vaughan Williams Research Fellowship, Carthusian Trust, 1985. Hobbies: Reading; Travel; Hiking. Address: Department of Music, University of California at Riverside, Riverside, CA 92521, USA.

ADAMS David, b. 19 Apr 1949, Box Hill, Victoria, Australia. Composer; Conductor; Librettist. Education: BA, Canberra School of Music, 1976. Career: Lowther Hall Anglican Girls Grammar School, 1977-81; Scotch College, 1978-83; Melbourne College of Advanced Education, 1985-87; Commissions from Sydney Dance Company, Australian Musicians Guild and the British Musical Society, 1987. Compositions include: Memories of the Future for guitar and harpischord, 1979; Strangers, ballet, for string quartet, oboe, horn and percussion, 1981; being divinely for soprano, percussion and strings, 1983; Variations for oboe and guitar, 1983; In Memoriam, for soprano and ensemble, 1984; Fan Fare for chorus, orchestra, soprano and viola, 1985; Time Locked in his Tower, music theatre for flutes, guitar and percussion, 1987; In My Craft of Sullen Art for soprano and viola, 1994; lunar aspects, song cycle for soprano and guitar, 1996. Honours include: Winner, Australian Composition Sections at Geelong Eisteddfod, also Bandigo Eisteddfod, 1981-83. Address: c/o APRA, 1A Eden Street, Crows Nest, NSW 2065, Australia.

ADAMS John (Coolidge), b. 15 Feb 1947, Worcester, MA, USA. Composer; Conductor. Education: Studied clarinet with father and Felix Viscuglia; BA, 1969, MA, 1971, Harvard College; Studied composition with Leon Kirchner, David Del Tredici and Roger Sessions. Career: Appearances as clarinettist and conductor; Head, Composition Department, San Francisco Conservatory, 1971-81; Adviser on New Music, 1978, Composer-in-Residence, 1982-85, San Francisco Symphony Orchestra; Conducted Nixon in China at 1988 Edinburgh Festival; Creative Adviser, St Paul Chamber Orchestra, MN, 1988-89; The Death of Klinghoffer premiered at Brussels, Lyon and Vienna, 1991; I Was Looking at the Ceiling performed at Berkeley, New York, Paris, Edinburgh and Hamburg, 1995. Compositions: Operas: Nixon in China, 1987, The Death of Klinghoffer, 1991; Musical, I Was Looking at the Ceiling and then I Saw the Sky, 1995; Orchestral: Common Tones In Simple Time, 1979, Harmonium for Chorus and Orchestra, 1980, Grand Pianola Music for 2 Sopranos, 2 Pianos and Small Orchestra, 1981-82, Shaker Loops for String Orchestra, 1983, Harmonielehre, 1984-85, Fearful Symmetries, 1988, The Wound-Dresser for Baritone and Orchestra, 1989, Eros Piano for Piano and Orchestra, 1989; Liszt La Lugubre Gondola, and, Wiegenlied arranged for orchestra, 1989; Violin Concerto, 1993; Gnarly Buttons, 1996; Slonimsky's Earbox, 1996; Chamber: Piano Quintet, 1970, American Standard for Unspecified Ensemble, 1973, Grounding for 3 Solo Voices, Instruments and Electronics, 1975, Onyx for Tape, 1976; Piano: Ragamarole, 1973, China Gates, 1977, Phrygian Gates, 1977. Honour: Guggenheim Fellowship, 1982. Address: c/o Boosey & Hawkes Ltd, 295 Regent Street, London W1R 8JH, England.

ADASKIN Murray, b. 28 Mar 1906, Toronto, Ontario, Canada. Composer. m. (1) Frances James, 16 Jul 1931 (dec 22 Aug 1988), (2) Asta Dorothea Larsen, 7 May 1989. Education: Royal Conservatory of Music, Toronto; Paris, France; Music Academy of the West, CA; Aspen School of Music, CO; LLD, University of Lethbridge, 1970; DMus, Brandon University, 1972; DMus, University of Windsor, 1977; LLD, University of Saskatchewan, 1984; DMus, University of Victoria, 1984. Career: Professor, Head, Department of Music, 1952-66, First Composer in Residence, 1966-73, University of Saskatchewan; Member, Canada Council, 1966-69; Violinist, Toronto Symphony Orchestra for 10 years; 2 Hour broadcast, Profile of Murray Adaskin at 65, CBC, 1971; 6 Hour broadcast, Murray Adaskin - A Canadian Music Retrospective, CBC, 1989, 1990; Premiere, Concerto for Orchestra, dedicated to Myfanwy Pavelic, 1990; Radio broadcast, Murray Adaskin Retrospective Week, 1993. Compositions: Over 120 Vocal, Solo, Chamber and Orchestral works including: Centennial Opera, Grant Warden of the Plains; Many commissioned works including: Of Man and The Universe; Coronation Overture; Algonquin Symphony; Concerto for Solo Viola and Orchestra, 1991, dedicated to Rivka Golani, Violist; Woodwind Quintet No 2, 1993; Quartet No 2, 1994; La Cadenze, dedicated to Lafayette String Quartet; String Quartet, written for and dedicated to Lafayette String Quartet and Gary Karr, Bass, 1995; Concerto No 2 for Viola and Orchestra, 1995; Travelling Musicians for Narrator/Singer, Soprano and Tenor and Chamber Orchestra, 1997. Recordings: CDs; Adaskin Collection. Publications: 73 works published. Honours: Lifetime Award,

Excellence in the Arts, Saskatchewan Arts Board, 1991; Honoured by Saskatchewan Music Festival Association as Distinguished Canadian Composer, 1994. Address: 3020 Devon Road, Victoria, British Columbia, Canada, V8R 6C9.

ADDENBROOKE David, b. 1 Feb 1947, Exmouth, Devon, England. Double Bass and Violin Player. Education: BSc, University of Exeter, 1968; Musical education, Dartington College of Arts, Totnes, 1966, and subsequent private study with Robin McGee, 1989. Career: Public performances in London area under conductors David Atherton, Nicholas Braithwaite, Andrew Davis, John Lubbock, Roger Norrington, Nicholas Kraemer, Paul Steinitz, Guy Woolfenden, John Poole and John Gardiner. Hobbies: Sea fishing (rowing-boat and shore); Cycling with violin on handlebars. Address: 19 Anchor Park, Snettisham, Norfolk PE31 7QH, England.

ADDISON John, b. 16 Mar 1920, West Chobham, Surrey, England. Composer; Conductor. m. Pamela Druitt, 15 Dec 1951, 2 sons, 2 daughters. Education: Royal College of Music, London, 1938-40, 1946-50; ARCM. Career: Professor of Composition and Theory, Royal College of Music, 1950-56; Conducted London Symphony, Royal Philharmonic and BBC Symphony Orchestras in performances of own music; Also film music concerts with American orchestras including San Francisco and Detroit Symphonies; Works commissioned by Sadler's Wells Ballet, English Opera Group, BBC, National Youth Orchestra, and Farnham Festival. Compositions: Orchestral includes: Three Terpsichorian Studies; Concerto for Trumpet, Strings and Percussion; Carte Blanche, ballet suite; Partita for Strings; Wellington Suite; Concertino for Orchestra, 1993; Chamber includes: Serenade for Wind Quintet and Harp; Conversation Piece for 2 Soprano Voices, Harpsichord/Chamber Organ and Harp; Divertimento for Wind Quintet; Bagatelles for brass quintet; celebrations for 2 oboes, bassoon and harpsichord; Theatre Music: Cranks, revue; The Entertainer and Luther, John Osborne, St Joan of the Stockyards, Brecht, Hamlet, National Theatre, The Workhouse Donkey, John Arden; Musicals: The Amazons at Nottingham Playhouse, Popkiss at Globe Theatre in London; Films include: Seven Days to Noon, Private's Progress, Reach for the Sky, Tom Jones, The Charge of The Light Brigade, Torn Curtain, Sleuth, A Bridge Too Far. Recordings: Numerous. Hobbies: Tennis; Skiing; Walking. Current Management: Gorfaine and Schwartz Agency. Address: c/o Gorfaine and Schwartz Agency, 3301 Barham Boulevard, Suite 201, Los Angeles, CA 90068, USA.

ADES Thomas, b. 1971, London, England. Composer; Pianist. Education: Guildhall School of Music, with Paul Berkowitz and Robert Saxton; King's College, Cambridge; Courses at Dartington (1991) and Aldeburgh (1992). Career: From 1992 as Memer of the Composers Ensemble and as solo recitalist: PLG Young Concert Artists Platform concert at the Purcell Room, 1993; Composer in Association with the Hallé Orchestra, 1993 (The Origin of the Harp); London Rostrum; Opera, Powder Her Face, commissioned by Almeida Opera and premiered at Cheltenham, 1995; Compositions include: Aubade for soprano, 1990; Five Eliot Landscapes, 1990; Chamber Symphony, 1990; Catch for clarinet, piano, cello and violin, 1991; Darkness Visible for piano, 1992; Still Sorrowing for piano, 1992; Under Hamelin Hill for chamber organ, 1992; Fool's Rhymes for chorus and ensemble, 1992; Life Story for soprano and ensemble, 1993; Living Toys for chamber ensemble, 1993; Sonata da Caccia for ensemble, 1993.... but all shal be well, for orchestra, 1993; The Origin of the Harp for chamber ensemble, 1994; Arcadiana for string quartet, 1994; Powder Her Face, chamber opera, 1995; Traced Overhead for piano, 1996; These Premises are Alarmed, for orchestra, 1996; Asyla, for orchestra (City of Birmingham SO under Simon Rattle), 1997. Honours include: Lutine Prize, GSM, 1986; Runner-up, 1989 BBC Young Musician of the Year (piano class), 1989; Winner, 1994 Paris Rostrum, for best piece by composer under 30. Address: c/o Faber Music Ltd, 3 Queen Square, London WC1N 3AU, England.

ADEY Christopher, b. 1943, Essex, England. Conductor. Education: Royal Academy of Music, London, principally as violinist with Manoug Parikian. Career: Violinist until 1973 mainly with Halle and London Philharmonic Orchestras; Debut as Conductor in 1973; Became Associate Conductor for BBC Scottish Symphony Orchestra, 1973-76; Frequent guest appearances throughout Britain and with the leading London orchestras; Associate Conductor with Ulster Orchestra, 1981-84; Has worked in most European countries, Middle and Far East, Canada and USA; Frequent broadcasts for BBC and abroad; Extensive repertoire covering symphonic and chamber orchestra works of all periods and including choral works and opera; Professor of Conducting at Royal College of Music, 1979-92; Orchestral Trainer in demand at conservatoires throughout Britain and maintains a large commitment to guest conducting with county, national and international youth orchestras; Cycle of the complete Martinu symphonies for BBC, 1992. Honours include: ARAM, 1979; Commemorative Medal of Czech Government,

1986; FRCM, 1989. Address: c/o Richard Haigh, Performing Arts, 6 Windmill Street, London, W1P 1HF, England.

ADKINS Cecil D(ale), b. 30 Jan 1932, Red Oak, IA, USA. Musicologist. Education: BFA, University of Omaha, 1953; MM, University of South Dakota, 1959; PhD, University of Iowa, 1963. Career: Assistant Conductor and Arranger, Fourth Armoured Division Band, Fort Hood, TX, 1954-55; Director of Instrumental Music, Paullina, IA, 1955-60; Graduate Assistant, University of Iowa, 1960-63; Instructor, Music department, Mount Mercy College, Cedar Rapids, IA, 1960-63; Professor of Music, University of North Texas, Denton, 1963-; Regents Professor, 1988-; Chairman, International Musicological Society's Center for Musicological Works in Progress, 1969-; President, American Musical Instrument Society, 1987-91. Publications: Editor, Doctoral Dissertations in Musicology, 5th edition, 1971, 7th edition, 1984, with A Dickinson, 8th edition, 1989; The A Berg Positive Organ: Basle, Historical Museum 1927-28, Description and Technical Drawing, 1979; A Trumpet by Any Other Name: A History of the Trumpet Marine, with A Dickinson, 1987; Four Historical Trumpet Marines, Description and Technical Drawings, 1987. Contributions: Articles in many journals and reference works. Memberships: American Musicological Society; International Musicological Society; American Musical Instrument Society; Dansk Selskab for Musikforskning. Address: c/o School of Music, University of North Texas, Denton, TX 76203, USA.

ADLER Larry (Lawrence Cecil), b. 10 Feb 1914, Baltimore, MD, USA. Harmonica Player. m. (1) Eileen Walser, 1938, dissolved 1961, 1 son, 2 daughters, (2) Sally Cline, 1969, dissolved 1977, 1 daughter. Education: Baltimore City College. Debut: First stage appearance in New York, 1928. Career: Appeared in various revues; First solo engagement with Sydney Symphony Orchestra, 1939; Command performances for various heads of state; Tours throughout the USA, Europe and the Far East; Radio and TV appearances; Nightclub engagements, recordings. Compositions: Composer of film scores and other works. Publication: It Ain't Necessarily So, autobiography, 1984. Honour: Winner, Maryland Harmonica Championship, 1927. Address: c/o Michael Bakewell, 118 Tottenham Court Road, London, W1, England.

ADLER Samuel (Hans), b. 4 Mar 1928, Mannheim, Germany. Composer; Conductor; Music Professor. m. (1) Carol Ellen Stalker, divorced 1988, 2 daughters, (2) Emily Freeman Brown, 1992. Education: BM, Boston University, 1948; MA, Harvard University, 1950; Studied composition with Herbert Fromm, Boston, 1941-46, with Hugo Norden, Walter Piston, Randall Thompson, Paul Hindemith and Aaron Copland; Musicology with Karl Geiringer; Conducting with Serge Koussevitzy, Berkshire Music Centre, Tanglewood. Career: Founder-First Conductor, 7th Army Symphony Orchestra, 1952; Director of Music, Temple Emanu-El, Dallas, 1963-66; Conductor, Dallas Lyric Theatre, 1955-57; Professor of Composition, North Texas State University, Denton, 1957-66; Professor of Composition, 1966-; Chairman, Composition Department, 1973-, Eastman School of Music, Rochester, New York; Guest Conductor, symphony orchestras and opera companies worldwide; Guest Lecturer in USA and other countries. Compositions include: Operas: The Outcasts of Poker Flat, 1959; The Lodge of Shadows, 1973; Orchestral works include: 6 Symphonies, 1953-85; Rhapsody for Violin and Orchestra, 1961; Elegy for String Orchestra, 1962; Requiescat in Pace, in memory of President John F Kennedy, 1963; Concerto for Orchestra, 1971; Sinfonietta, 1971; Much chamber music including: 8 string quartets, 1945, 1950, 1953, revised 1964, 1963, 1969, 1975, 1981, 1990; Organ Pieces. Publications include: Anthology for the Teaching of Choral Conducting, 1971, 2nd edition, 1985. Contributions to: Numerous journals. Honours include: Recipient of several honorary degrees; Music Award, American Academy and Institute of Arts and Letters. Memberships: Professional organisations. Address: 54 Railroad Mills Road, Pittsford, NY 14534, USA.

ADNI Daniel, b. 6 Dec 1951, Haifa, Israel. Concert Pianist. Education: Paris Conservatoire, 1968-69. Debut: London, 1970. Career: Since debut played as soloist with most orchestras in UK, Israel, Holland, Germany, USA, Far East and Japan; Solo recitals in many major cities and festivals; Also played chamber music at such festivals as Kuhmo, Finland; Numerous broadcasts on various radio stations including BBC; Joined The Solomon Trio in 1994. Recordings: Over 21 records including: works by Chopin and Debussy, Complete Songs Without Words by Mendelssohn, Complete Grieg Lyric Pieces, Piano Music by John Ireland and Percy Grainger, Mendelssohn Preludes and Fugues op 35, Schubert Sonatas, Concertos by Saint-Saëns and Mendelssohn, and Rhapsody in Blue by Gershwin. Honours: Winner of many prizes for piano, Solfège and sight reading, Paris Conservatoire, 1969; Winner, Young Concert Artists, New York, 1976; Winner, Phillip M Fanuett Prize, New York, 1981. Hobbies: Cinema; Theatre; Bridge; Walking. Address: 64A Menelik Road, London, NW2 3RH, England.

ADOLPHE Bruce, b. 31 May 1955, New York City, USA. Composer. Education: Studied at the Juilliard School, NY until 1976. Career: Has taught at New York University Tisch School, 1983 and at Yale University, 1984-85; Composer-in-Residence at 92nd Street Y School Concert Series, 1988-90, and Santa Fe Chamber Music Festival, 1989; His operas have been performed in Boston and New York. Compositions include: The Tell-Tale Heart, one act opera after Edgar Allan Poe, 1982; Mikhoels The Wise, opera in 2 acts, 1982; The False Messiah, opera in 2 acts, 1983. Address: c/o ASCAP, ASCAP Building, One Lincoln Plaza, New York, NY 10023, USA.

ADORJAN András, b. 26 Sep 1944, Budapest, Hungary. Flautist. Education: Dentist Diploma, Copenhagen, 1968; Musical Studies with Jean-Pierre Rampal and Aurèle Nicolet. Career: Principal with the orchestra of the Royal Opera, Stockholm, 1970-72, Gurzenich Orchestra, Cologne, 1972-73, Sudwestfunk Baden-Baden, 1973-74 and Bavarian Radio Symphony Orchestra, 1974-88; Teacher at the Nice Summer Academy from 1971; Professor at the Musikhochschule at Cologne, Germany from 1987 and the Musikhochschule München from 1996; Gave the 1981 premiere of Ground, concerto for Flute and Orchestra by Sven-Erik Werner; Dedication of Moz-Art à la Mozart by Alfred Schnittke, 1990; Concerto for Flute and Harp by Edison Denisov, 1995. Recordings: Over 90 including the first complete recording of all 14 flute concertos by François Devienne. Address: Musikhochschule München, Arcisstr 12, 80333 Munich, Germany.

ADRIANO, b. 10 July 1944, Fribourg, Switzerland. Composer; Conductor; Producer. Education: Conservatory of Music; Mainly self-taught. Career includes: Active as stage director and language coach; Performs as Concert Narrator; Specialised conductor of unknown music and Ottorino Respighi specialist; Writer and director of classical music videos. Compositions: Piano pieces and songs; Concertino for Celesta and Strings; Orchestrations of piano pieces and song cycles by Respighi, Mussorgsky, Ibert, Wolf and Schoek and editing of many classic film scores. Recordings: As conductor: 20 recordings of Respighi, Ibert, Lazzari, Auric, Honegger, Khatchaturian, Waxman, Herrmann; As producer: 10 items with many world premiere recordings. Publications: An International Respighi Discography; Ottorino Respighi, Discography 1919-1996. Contributions to: Articles on Ibert, Wolf and Schoeck and Ottorino Respighi to various publications. Honours: Gold Medal, Italian Respighi Foundation. Address: Sihlberg 22, CH-8022 Zurich, Switzerland.

AFANASSIEV Valery, b. 1947, Moscow, Russia. Pianist. Education: Studied at the Moscow Conservatory with Emil Gilels. Career: Performances throughout Eastern Europe after winning 1969 Bach Competition at Leipzig; Settled in Brussels, 1974, Versailles thereafter; Chamber musician with violinist Gidon Kremer. Honours include: Winner, Queen Elisabeth of the Belgians Competition, Brussels, 1972. Address: c/o Gidon Kremer, Terry Harrison Management, The Orchard, Market Street, Charlbury, Oxfordshire OX7 3PJ, England.

AFANASYEVA Veronika, b. 1960, Moscow, Russia. Violinist. Education: Studied at Central Music School, Moscow. Career: Co-Founder of Quartet Veronique in 1989; Many concerts in Russia notably in the Russian Chamber Music Series and 150th birthday celebrations for Tchaikovsky in 1990; Masterclasses at Aldeburgh Festival in 1991; Concert tour of Britain in season 1992-93; Repertoire includes works by Beethoven, Brahms, Tchaikovsky, Bartók, Shostakovich and Schnittke. Recordings include: Schnittke's 3rd Quartet. Honours include: With Quartet Veronique: Winner, All-Union String Quartet Competition at St Petersburg, 1990-91, 3rd Place, International Shostakovich Competition at St Petersburg, 1991. Address: c/o Sonata (Quartet Veronique), 11 Northgate Street, Glasgow, G20 7AA, Scotland.

AGACHE Alexandru, b. 16 Aug 1955, Cluj, Romania. Baritone. Education: Studied in Cluj. Debut: As Silvano in Ballo in Maschera, Cluj, 1979. Career: Has sung Sharpless, Don Giovanni, Malatesta and Verdi's Posa, Luna, Nabucco and Germont at Cluj; Further appearances in Dresden, Budapest and Ankara; Sang Don Giovanni at Livorno and Toulon, 1987, Renato at Covent Garden followed by Enrico Ashton in Lucia di Lammermoor and Simon Boccanegra in a new production of Verdi's opera in 1991; La Scala debut as Belcore in L'Elisir d'Amore, 1988; Marquis di Posa in Hamburg, 1988 and La Fenice, Venice in 1992; Sang Renato in Ballo in Maschera in Zurich and Dusseldorf, 1989, Marcello in La Bohème at Lyon Opera in 1991 and Renato at Opera Bastille in Paris in 1992; Sang Amonasro at Covent Garden, 1994 returning 1997 for Simon Boccanegra. Recordings include: Golem The Rebel by Nicolas Bretan; Video of Covent Garden performance of Simon Boccanegra under Solti. Address: c/o Stafford Law Associates, 6 Barham Close, Weybridge, Surrey, KT13 9PR, England.

AGAY Karola, b. 30 Mar 1927, Budapest, Hungary. Soprano. Education: Studied in Budapest. Career: Sang first in choir of Hungarian Army; Stage debut in Budapest in 1955 as the Queen of Night; Other roles include Gilda, Constanze, Lucia di Lammermoor, Mélisande and Zerbinetta; Metropolitan Opera in 1969 as Lucia; Guest engagements in Vienna, East Berlin, France, Moscow and Prague; Many song recitals with her husband, the guitarist L Szendrey-Karper.

AGAZHANOV Artyom (Artyomovich), b. 3 Feb 1958, Moscow, Russia. Composer; Pianist. Education: Piano and composition at Moscow Central Music School, 1965-76; Further study at Moscow State Tchaikovsky Conservatoire. Career: Teacher at Moscow Central Music School, 1983-; Concert appearances as composer and pianist in Russia, Bulgaria, Italy, Germany, including festivals: Moscow autumne, 1986, 1987, 1989 and 1994, Moscow Stars, 1989, and International Music Festival, 1988. Compositions include: Pax in terra for Orchestra, 1983; Kolobrod, music for film, 1990; Incite to Rebellion The City, music for film, 1992. Recordings: Vision for Violin and Piano, 1988; Sonata for Violoncello and Piano, 1989; Gust, overture for Orchestra, 1989; Since 3 til 6 for Piano, 1989; Variations on Theme by Chopin for Piano, 1992; 6 Japanese Hokku for Soprano and Piano, 1993; Poet's Way, vocal symphony poem for Tenor, Mixed Choir and Full Orchestra, 1994. Publication: Without Colouring The Truth, 1993. Honours: All Union Competition of Young Composers, 1981. Memberships: Union of Russian Composers. Address: Nezhdanova 8-10 Apt 55, Moscow 103009, Russia.

AGNEW Paul, b. 1964, Glasgow, Scotland. Tenor. Education: Chorister at St Chad's Cathedral, Birmingham; Lay-Clerkships at Birmingham and Lichfield Cathedrals; Choral Scholar at Magdalen College, Oxford. Career: Tours with the Consort of Musicke to Germany, Switzerland, Holland, Italy, Spain, Austria, Sweden and Australia; Handel songs in the National Gallery, London with the Parley of Instruments; Promenade Concerts debut in 1989 in The Judgement of Paris; Has sung the Evangelist in the St Matthew Passion for the London Handel Orchestra; South Bank debut at the Purcell Room celebrating the centenary of Ivor Gurney's birth; Engaged for the St John Passion with the Schola Cantorum of Basle and for Les Noces in Zurich; Tour of the USA with the Festival of Voices directed by Paul Hillier; Sang in Monteverdi Madrigals with the Consort of Musicke at Promenade Concerts in 1993; Sang with New London Consort at the Purcell Room, London, 1997. Recordings include: Monteverdi Madrigals. Address: c/o Hazard Chase Ltd, Richmond House, 16-20 Regent Street, Cambridge CB2 1DB, England.

AGOLLI Lejla, b. 4 Oct 1950, Korce, Albania. Composer. Education: Studied at the Tirana Conservatory. Career: From 1974 teacher at the Jordan Misja Art Lyceum, Tirana. Compositions include: Symphony, 1973; 2 cantatas; 2 piano concertos, 1973, 1984; 2 violin concertos (2nd 1983); 2 Albums for violin and piano, 20 pieces in all. Address: c/o The Albanian New Music Rr, Mine Peca 87sh 3-21, Tirana, Albania.

AGUDELA Graciela, b. 7 Dec 1945, Mexico City, Mexico. Composer; Pianist. Education: Studied at the Universidad Nacional Autonoma de Mexico and at the National Music Conservatory. Career: Teacher of the Yamaha system from 1967; Participated in first seminar of electronic music in Mexico, 1974. Compositions: Sonata, andante and 17 Preludes for piano, 1970-73; Cancrizante, electronic, 1972; String quartet, 1971; Variaciones for flute, viola and piano; Voyagers of the Twilight for clarinet, bassoon and piano, 1993. Address: c/o SACM, Mayorazgo No 129, Col Xoco, 03330 Mexico DF, Mexico.

AGUERA Luc-Marie, b. 1960, France. Violinist. Education: Studied at the Paris Conservatoire with Jean-Claude Pennetier and with members of the Amadeus and Alban Berg Quartets. Career: Member of the Ysaye String Quartet from 1985; Many concert performances in France, Europe, America and the Far East; Festival engagements at Salzburg, Tivoli, Bergen, Lockenhaus, Barcelona and Stresa; Many appearances in Italy notably with the "Haydn" Quartets of Mozart; Tours of Japan and USA in 1990 and 1992. Recordings: Mozart Quartet K421 and Quintet K516; Ravel, Debussy and Mendelssohn Quartets. Honours: Grand Prix Evian International String Quartet Competition, 1988; Special Prizes for Best Performances of a Mozart Quartet, the Debussy Quartet and a contemporary work; 2nd Prize, Portsmouth International String Quartet Competition, 1988. Address: c/o Artist Management International Ltd, 12-13 Richmond Buildings, Dean Street, London, W1V 5AF, England.

AHLIN Sven Åke, b. 6 Apr 1951, Sundsvall, Sweden. Composer. m. Emma Rosendal, 1 July 1989, 1 son, 1 daughter. Education: Composition, 1974-77, Music Theory Pedagogy, 1977-80, Royal College of Music, Stockholm; Composition, 1982, Indiana University, USA, 1982. Debut: Stockholm, 1977. Career: Numerous performances of his choir music and chamber music in Sweden, including trombone concerto with Christian Lindberg as soloist in Jönköping; Broadcasts include 3 first performances by the Swedish Radio Choir, and piano concerto with Mats

Widlund as soloist; Performances abroad in Norway, Iceland, Russia, France and Spain. Compositions: Al Fresco, piano concerto; Narratives, trombone concerto; Across for orchestra; Ritual for Huitzilopochtli; Choral music including Dream of Elysium; Clashing Worlds; I have a dream; Concertos: Al fresco (piano); Narratives (trombone); Numerous pieces of chamber music. Membership: Society of Swedish composers. Hobby: Studying languages. Address: Ålstorp, Mossehus, 312 94 Laholm, Sweden.

AHLSTEDT Douglas, b. 16 Mar 1945, Jamestown, NY, USA. Tenor. Education: Studied at State University, New York and Eastman School, Rochester. Debut: As Ramiro in La Cenerentola, Western Opera Theater, San Francisco, 1971. Career: Sang at Metropolitan Opera from season 1974-75, with debut as Italian Singer in Rosenkavalier, then as Fenton in Falstaff; Member of Deutsche Oper Dusseldorf, 1975-84 and guest appearances in Vienna, Hamburg, Zurich and Karlsruhe; Returned to New York in 1983 and sang Iopas in Les Troyens, Almaviva in Barbiere di Siviglia and Debussy's Pelléas, 1988; Salzburg Festival as Anfinoma in the Henze-Monteverdi Il Ritorno di Ulisse, 1985; Teatro San Carlo in Naples as Orestes in Ermione by Rossini, 1988; Other engagements in Dallas, Philadelphia, Santiago as Don Ottavio, Genoa, Avignon and Rome as Idreno in Semiramide, 1982; Other roles include Tamino, Jacquino in Fidelio, Narcisio in Il Turco in Italia, the Fox in Cunning Little Vixen and Peter Quint in The Turn of the Screw; Sang Dorvil in La Scala di Seta in Stuttgart, 1991; Zurich Opera as Flamand in Capriccio, 1992. Recordings include: Video of Il Ritorno di Ulisse, Salzburg, 1985. Address: c/o Staatstheater Stuttgart, Oberer Schlossgarten 6, 7000 Stuttgart, Germany.

AHNSJO Claes Haakon, b. 1 Aug 1942, Stockholm, Sweden. Tenor. m. Helena Jungwirth. Education: Studied in Stockholm with Erik Saeden, Aksel Schiotz and Max Lorenz. Debut: Royal Opera Stockholm in 1969 as Tamino. Career: Sang in Stockholm until 1973, then with the Munich Opera notably in operas by Mozart and Rossini; Drottningholm Opera from 1969; Bayreuth Festival, 1973; Kennedy Music Center, NY, 1974 in Die Jahreszeiten by Haydn; Guest appearances in Frankfurt, Cologne, Tokyo, Hamburg, Stuttgart and Nancy; Concert tours of Italy and Spain; Sang at Munich in 1985 as the Painter in Lulu, and in the premiere of Le Roi Bérenger by Sutermeister; Sang at Berlin in 1987 as Ramiro in La Cenerentola by Rossini; Sang Wolfgang Capito in Mathis der Maler and the Abbé in Adriana Lecouvreur, 1989; Munich Festival in premiere of Penderecki's Ubu Rex in 1991. Recordings: Bastien und Bastienne; Orlando Paladino, La Vera Costanza and L'Infedeltà Delusa by Haydn; Betulia Liberata by Mozart; Die Lustigen Weiber von Windsor; Bruckner's Te Deum. Address: c/o Bayerische Staatsoper, Postfach 745, D-8000 Munich 1, Germany.

AHO Kalevi, b. 9 Mar 1949, Forssa, Finland. Composer; Teacher; Writer on Music. Education: Diploma, Sibelius Academy, Helsinki, 1971; Studied composition with Einojuhani Rautavaara, Boris Blacher at Staatliche Hochschule für Musik und Darstellende Kunst, Berlin, 1971-72. Career: Lecturer on Music, University of Helsinki, 1974-88; Professor of Composition at Sibelius Academy, Helsinki, 1988-93; Free artist in Helsinki since 1993. Compositions include: Stage: Avain, dramatic monologue, 1978-79, Ennen Kuin Me Kaikki Olemme Hukkuneet, opera in 2 acts, 1995-96; Orchestra: Symphony No 1, 1969, No 5, 1975-76, No 8, 1993, No 9, 1993-94, Chamber Symphony No 1 for String Orchestra, 1976, No 2, 1991-92, Pergamon, 1990; Solo Instrument and Orchestra: Concerto for Violin and Orchestra, 1981, Symphony No 8 for Organ and Orchestra, 1993, Symphony No 9 for Trombone and Orchestra, 1993-94; Chamber: String Quartet No 3, 1971, Quintet for Bassoon and String Quartet, 1977, Inventions for Oboe and Cello, 1986, Nuppu for Flute and Piano, 1991, Epilogue for Trombone and Organ, 1994; Solo Instrument: Sonata for Violin, 1973, Piano Sonata, 1980, In Memoriam for Organ, 1980, Solo III for Flute, 1990-91, Three Interludes for Organ, 1993; Vocal: Mysteerio for Female Choir, 1994; Several orchestrations and arrangements including Matti Rautio: Divertimento No 2, 1990. Recordings include: Symphony No 9; Concerto for Cello and Orchestra. Publications include: Author of articles, essays, treatises and three books including: Einojuhani Rautavaara Sinfonikkona, text in Finnish, German and English, 1988, and The Tasks of The Artist in Postmodern Society, in Finnish, 1992. Address: Taivaskalliontie 15, FIN-00600 Helsinki, Finland.

AHRENS Sieglinde, b. 19 Feb 1936, Berlin, Germany. Composer; Organist. Education: Studied with Blacher at the Berlin Hochschule für Musik and with Messiaen and Milhaud at the Paris Conservatoire. Career: Organist from 1947, with tours throughout Germany and in France and Holland; Professor of organ at the Folkswanghochschule, Essen, from 1970. Compositions: Three Pieces, Fantasia, Rhapsody and Suite In fletu solatium for organ; Sonata for violin and organ, 1957; Three songs for bass and organ; Five Pieces for string trio. Publications include: Das Orgelwerk Olivier Messiaens, with H-D Moller and A Rossler,

1976. Address: c/o GEMA, Postfach 80 07 67, D-81607 Munich, Germany.

AHRONOVITCH Yuri, b. 13 May 1933, Leningrad, Russia. Conductor. m. Tamar Sakson, 1973. Education: Graduated, Leningrad Conservatory of Music, 1954. Career: Debuts with Leningrad Philharmonic Orchestra, Bolshoi Theatre, Moscow; Professor of Music, 1958-; Principal Conductor and Music Director, Moscow Radio Symphony Orchestra, 1964-72; Guest Conductor for London Symphony Orchestra, Vienna Symphony Orchestra, Jerusalem Symphony Orchestra, Rome St Cecilia Orchestra, New York Philharmonic Orchestra, Berlin, Hamburg and Munich Radio Orchestras, and Teatro alla Scala, Milan, French Radio in Paris, Israel Philharmonique, Tonhalle Zürich; Guest Opera Conductor with Royal Opera House, Covent Garden, London, Lyric Opera House, Chicago, Main Italian Opera Houses, Stockholm Royal Opera House, and Munich State Opera House; Principal Conductor and Music Director, Cologne Philharmonic Orchestra, Gurženich, 1975-86; Principal Conductor, Stockholm Philharmonic Orchestra, 1982-87. Recordings include: Tchaikovsky's Manfred Symphony; Rachmaninov's Piano Concertos with Vasary LSO; Prokofiev's Violin Concertos; Shostakovich's 1st and 5th Symphony; Sorochintsy Fair by Mussorgsky; As well as works by Dvorak, Wagner, Tanyev, Grieg, Liszt, Nielsen, Prokokiev, Brahms and others. Honours: Prize for Best Opera Production, German Music Journal, 1977; Commander, The Royal Order of the Polar Star by the King of Sweden, 1987; Israeli Etinger Prize for the Arts, 1988; Prize of Arca d'ro by leading newspaper La Stampa and the University of Turin, 1991. Memberships: Elected Member, Royal Swedish Academy of Music, 1984-. Address: Kunstlersecretariat Schoerke, Mönckebergalle 41, 30153 Hannover 91, Germany.

AIKIN Laura, b. 1965, Buffalo, USA. Singer (Soprano). Education: Studied at Buffalo, New York and Indiana University; Vocal studies withReri Grist in Munich. Career: Appearances at the Staatsoper Berlin and elsewhere in Europe as Amenaide in Tancredi (Zurich), 1996, the Queen of Night, Adele and Gretel; Deutsche Oper Berlin debut as Mdme Herz in Mozart's Schauspieldirektor; Schwetzingen Festival in L'Opera Seria by Florian Gassman, under René Jacobs; Salzburg Festival recital with Maurizio Pollini, in Schubert's Hirt auf den Felsen, 1996; Strauss's Zerbinetta at the Vienna Staatsoper and a Jonathan Miller production of Ariadne auf Naxos at Florence, 1997; Recitals at Carnegie Hall and elsewhere, with appearances in Berlin as Rosina, Gilda, Musetta, Lulu and Silvia in Haydn's L'Isola diabitata; Further concerts include Schoenberg's oratorio Die Jakobslieter under Michael Gielen, Beethoven's Christus am Olberg with Daniel Barenboim in Jerusalem and Chicago, and Pierre Boulez 70th birthday celebrations at Carnegie Hall; Season 1998 engaged as Nannetta in the Jonathan Miller production of Falstaff, Zerbinetta in the original version of Ariadne auf Naxos and Met debut as the Queen of Night. Honours include: Winner, Geneva International Competition. Address: Ingpen & Williams Ltd, 26 Wadham Road, London SW15 2LR, England.

AIMARD Pierre-Laurent, b. 9 Sept 1947, Lyon, France. Pianist. Education: Studied at the Lyon Conservatoire from 1954, Paris Conservatoire, 1972; Further study with Yvonne Loriod. Career: Many appearances in France and elsewhere as solo pianist; Soloist with the Ensemble InterContemporain, from 1976. Honours: Chamber music prize at the Paris Conservatoire, 1973; Prizewinner at the 1973 Olivier Messiaen Competition, Royan. Address: c/o Ensemble InterContemporain, 9 Rue d'Echelle, F-75001 Paris, France.

AINSLEY John Mark, b. 9 July, 1963, Crewe, England. Singer (Tenor). Education: Studied at Oxford Univerity. Career: Many concert performances from 1985 with the Taverner Consort, the New London Consort and London Baroque; Appearances in Mozart Masses at The Vienna Konzerthaus with Heinz Holliger, Handel's Saul at Göttingen with John Eliot Gardiner and the Mozart Requiem under Yehudi Menuhin at Gstaad and Pulcinella at the Barbican under Jeffrey Tate; Other concerts with the Ulster Orchestra and the Bournemouth Sinfonietta; US Debut at Lincoln Center in the B minor Mass with Christopher Hogwood; Opera debut at the Innsbruck Festival in Scarlatti's Gli Equivoci nel Sembiante; English National Opera in 1989 in The Return of Ulysses; Title role in Méhul's Joseph for Dutch Radio, Handel's Acis in Stuttgart and Solomon for Radio France, under Leopold Hager; Has sung Mozart's Tamino for Opera Northern Ireland and Ferrando for Glyndebourne Touring Opera; Engaged in Falstaff for Scottish Opera and Idomeneo for Welsh National Opera; Sang Ferrando at Glyndebourne Festival in 1992, and Don Ottavio in 1994, Haydn's The Seasons with the London Classical Players; Promenade Concerts in London, 1993; Stravinsky concert under Andrew Davis at the Festival Hall, 1997. Recordings include: Handel's Nisi Dominus, under Simon Preston and Purcell's Odes with Trevor Pinnock; Mozart's C minor Mass with Hogwood and Great Baroque Arias with the King's Consort; Acis and Galatea; Saul. Address: c/o Glyndebourne Festival Opera, Lewes, Sussex, England.

AITKEN Hugh, b. 7 Sept 1924, NY, USA. Composer; Teacher. Education: Studied composition with Wagenaar, Persichetti and Ward at the Juilliard School; MS, 1950. Career: Taught privately and at the Juilliard Preparatory Division, 1950-65; Faculty, Juilliard School, 1960-70; Professor, William Paterson College, 1970-. Compositions: Stage: Felipe, opera, Fables, chamber opera, and dance scores; Other: 3 Violin Concertos, 1984, 1988, Oratorio, The Revelation Of St John The Divine, 1953-90, 10 Solo Cantatas, In Praise Of Ockeghem for Strings, Rameau Remembered for Flute and Chamber Orchestra, Happy Birthday, overture; Opus 95 Revisited for String Quartet, unaccompanied works for various instruments, Duo for Cello and Piano, Trios for 11 Players, Quintet for Oboe and String Quartet. Recordings include: Piano Fantasy and 2 Cantatas. Publications: Various. Honours: National Academy of Arts and Letters, 1988; Several grants, National Endowment for the Arts. Address: Music Department, William Paterson College of New Jersey, Wayne, NJ 07470, USA.

AITKEN Robert M(orris), b. 28 Aug 1939, Kentville, Nova Scotia, Canada. Flautist; Teacher; Composer. m. Marion I Ross. Education: Studied flute as child in Pennsylvania, later with Nicholas Fiore, Royal Conservatory of Music, Toronto, 1955-59; Composition with Barbara Pentland, University of British Columbia, and with John Weinzweig; Electronic music with Myron Schaeffer; Flute with various teachers, 1964-65; MMus, University of Toronto, 1964. Career includes: Principal Flautist with Vancouver Symphony Orchestra, 1958-59, Stratford Festival Orchestra, Ontario, 1962-64; Soloist with orchestras and chamber music player with many tours abroad; Artistic Director of Music Today, Shaw Festival, Niagara-on-the-Lake, 1970-72, and New Music Concerts, Toronto, 1971-; Advanced studies in music programme, 1985-89; Professor of Flute, Staatliche Hochschule für Musik, Freiburg im Breisgau, 1988-. Compositions include: Rhapsody for Orchestra, 1961; Music for Flute and Electronic Tape, 1963; Concerto for 12 Solo Instruments, 1964; Kebyar for Flute, Clarinet, 2 Double Basses, Percussion and Tape, 1971; Shadows III, Nira for Solo Violin, Flute, Oboe, Viola, Double Bass, Piano and Harpsichord, 1974-88; Icicle for Flute, 1977; Folia for Woodwind Quintet, 1980. Recordings: Various compositions recorded; Many discs as soloist and chamber music artist. Address: 14 Maxwell Avenue, Toronto, Ontario, Canada, M5P 2B5.

AJMONE-MARSAN Guido, b. 24 Mar 1947, Turin, Italy. Orchestral Conductor. m. Helle Winkelhorn, 14 Aug 1971. Education: Bachelor Degree cum laude, Conducting and Clarinet, Eastman School of Music, New York, USA, 1968; Study with F Ferrara at Conservatory of St Cecilia, Rome, Italy, 1968-71. Career: Chief Conductor of the Gelders Orchestra, Arnhem, Netherlands, 1982-86; Music Advisor and Principal Conductor of the Orchestra of Illinois at Chicago, USA, 1982-87; Music Director of Opera House, Essen, Germany, 1986-90; Guest Conductor for many international orchestras and opera houses including: Jerusalem Symphony, Philharmonia, London Symphony, Covent Garden Opera, NHK Japan, Welsh National Opera, Spoleto Festival, La Scala Orchestra, Metropolitan Opera and English National Opera. Recordings: Many for Radio broadcast with radio orchestras in Czechoslovakia, UK, Germany, Japan, Australia, Netherlands, Denmark, Italy and France. Honours: Many Prizes, Cantelli Competition, Milan, 1969, Mitropoulos, NY, 1970, Winner, Rupert Foundation Conducting Competition, with one year assistantship to London Symphony, 1973, Winner, G Solti Competition, Chicago, 1973; The Deane Sherman Performing Arts Award, MD, USA, 1992. Current Management: ICM Artists, New York, USA; Christopher Tennant, London. Address: 57 Wood Vale, London, N10 3DL,England.

AKIYAMA Kazuyoshi, b. 2 Jan 1941, Tokyo, Japan. Conductor. Education: Studied conducting with Hideo Saito, Toho School of Music, Tokyo. Debut: Tokyo Symphony Orchestra, 1964. Career: Music Director of the Tokyo Symphony Orchestra, 1964; Conductor, Japanese Orchestras; Music Director, American Symphony Orchestra, New York, 1973-78; Resident Conductor and Music Director, Vancouver Symphony Orchestra, BC, 1972-85; Music Director, Syracuse Symphony Orchestra, NY, 1985-. Recordings: Various. Address: c/o Syracuse Symphony Orchestra, 411 Montgomery Street, Syracuse, NY 13202, USA.

AKL Walid, b. 13 July 1945, Bikfaya, Lebanon. Pianist. Education: Studied at the Academy Marguerite Long, Paris, from 1963, then the Ecole Normale de Musique, with Yvonne Lefebure and Jacques Février. Career: Many engagements in France and throughout the Middle East. Recordings include: Complete piano music of Haydn and Borodin; Liszt's transcription of Beethoven's Eroica Symphony; Complete piano music of Nietzsche. Address: c/o Ecole Normale de Musique, 1/4 bis Boulevard Malesherbes, F-75017 Paris, France.

AKOKA Gérard, b. 2 Nov 1949, Paris, France. Conductor. Education: Studied at the Paris Conservatoire, at the Accademia di Santa Cecilia and with Jean Martinon, Igor Markevitch, Sergiu Celibidache and Franco Ferrara. Career: Former assistant to Daniel Barenboim and Leonard Bernstein; Assistant to Boulez at Orchestre de Paris (1977) and musical director of the Lorraine Philharmonic, 1983-84; Recent engagements in Taiwan and elsewhere in the Far East. Address: c/o Tapei City Symphony Orchestra, 25 Pa Teh Road, Sec 3, Taipei 10560, Taiwan, China.

ALÉN RODRIGUEZ Olavo, b. 23 Dec 1947. Musicologist. m. Carmen Corral, 1 son. Education: Introduction to music and piano with his father; Middle Level studies, 1962-69, Graduated as pianist, 1969, at the Escuela Nacional de Arte; Musicology lectures with Dr Argeliers Léon, Havana, 1974-77; Estudies musicology at the Humboldt-University, Berlin, 1974-77; PhD, Humboldt-University, Berlin, Germany, 1977-79. Career: Music Teacher, National School of Dance, 1969-71; Music Advisor, National Council for Culture, 1971-73; Director of the Center for Research and Development of Cuban Music, 1978-; Professor at the High Level Art Institute, 1900-93. Publications: Combinaciones instrumentales y vocales de Cuba, La Habana, Ed Min Educaión, 1973; Géneros de la Música Cubana, La Habana, Ed Pueblo y Educación, 1976; La Música en las sociedades de tumba francesa en Cuba, La Habana, Ed Casa de las Américas, 1987; De lo Afrocubano a la Slasa, San Juan, Ed Cubanacán, Puerto Rico, 1992, 2nd edition, 1994. Contributions to: Articles include those for several important Music Dictionaries: The New Grove Dictionary of Music and Musicians, 1994, 1996; Diccionario Enciclopédico de la Musica Espanola e Hispanoamericana, 1997; Musik in Geshichte und Gegewart (MGG), 1995, 1996. Honours: Premio Musicologia, Casa de las Américas, Havana, 1979; Distinción por I Culture Nacional, Ministry of Culture, Cuba, 1983; Humboldt Prize, Berlin, 1997. Membership: Union de Escritoires y Artistes de Cuba (UNEAC); Liason Officer for Cuba, International Council for Traditional Music ICTM, 1986-94. Hobbies: Films; Dogs; Gardens. Address: Arellano no 302 e/Luz y C, Lawton, 10de octobre, C Habana, Cuba.

ALAGNA Roberto, b. 7 Jun 1963, Clichy-sur-Bois, France. Singer (Tenor). m. Angela Gheorghiu, 1996. Education: Studied in France and Italy. Debut: Plymouth, 1988, as Alfredo in La Traviata for Glyndebourne Touring Opera. Career: Sang Rodolfo at Covent Garden (1990) and has returned for Gounod's Roméo and Don Carlos, 1994-96; sang Donizetti's Roberto Devereux at Monte Carlo (1992) and the Duke of Mantua at the Vienna Staatsoper (1995); Sang Don Carlos at the Théâtre du Châtelet, Paris, 1996; American appearances at Chicago and New York (debut at Met 1996, as Rodolfo); Alfredo at La Scala, Milan. Recordings include: video of Gounod's Roméo et Juliette (Pioneer); La Traviata, from La Scala (Sony) and Don Carlos, Paris. Honours include: Winner, 1988 Pavarotti Competition. Address: c/o Royal Opera House, Covent Garden, London WC2.

ALAIMO Simone, b. 3 Feb 1950, Villabate, Palermo, Italy. Bass Baritone. m. Vittorio Mazzoni, 30 Apr 1988, 1 son, 1 daughter. Education: Literary studies at University of Palermo; Scuola di Perfezionamento Teatro alla Scala di Milano per Giovani Lirici. Debut: In Don Pasquale at Pavia, 1977. Career: Appearances at La Scala, Teatro dell Opera, Rome, Teatro Comunale, Florence, Teatro San Carlo, Naples, Chicago, San Francisco, Dallas, Vienna, Monaco, Paris, Madrid, Barcelona, Lisbon and Marseilles; Radio and TV appearances in Luisa Miller, Cavalleria Rusticana and Zaira; Sang Mustafà in L'Italiana in Algeri at San Francisco in 1992 followed by Dulcamara, Rossini's Don Basilio at Genoa in 1992; Appeared in film of Il Barbiere di Siviglia. Recordings: La Cenerentola; Don Giovanni; Il Turco in Italia; Maria Stuarda; I Masnadieri; L'Ebreo; Torquato Tasso; L'Esule di Roma; Convenienze Teatrali; Barbiere di Siviglia; (Bongiovanni). Honours: Lions Prize, 1977; Voce Verdiane di Busseto International Competition, 1978; Beniamino Gigli di Macerata International Competition, 1978; Maria Callas International Competition, 1980. Hobbies: Antiquities; Gardening; Cookery; Football. Address: Via Pacevecchia, Parc Conim, 82100 Benevento, Italy.

ALAIN Marie Claire, b. 10 Aug 1926, Saint Germain-en-Laye, France. Organist. m. Jacques Gommier, 1950, 1 s, 1 d. Education: Institut Notre Dame, Saint Germain-en-Laye, Conservatoire National Supérieur de Musique, Paris. Career: Organ Teacher, Conservatoire de Musique de Paris; Lecturer, Summer Academy for Organists, Haarlem, Netherlands, 1956-72; Numerous concerts throughout the world, 1955-; Lecturer at numerous universities worldwide; Expert on organology to Minister of Culture. Recordings: Over 300 records including complete works of J Alain, CPE Bach, J S Bach, C Balbastre, G Böhm, N Bruhns, D Buxtehude, L N Clerambault, F Couperin, L C Daquin, C Franck, N De Grigny, J A Guilain, G F Handel, J Haydn, F Mendelssohn and A Vivaldi and others. Honours: Honorary DHL, CO State University; Honorary DMus, Southern Methodist University, Dallas; Commandeur de la Légion d'Honneur; Honorary Doctorate, Sibelius Academy, Helsinki; Numerous prizes for recordings and performances including: Buxtehudepreis, Lübeck, Germany; Leonie Sonning Prize, Copenhagen, Denmark; Prix Franz Liszt, Budapest; Officier des Arts et Lettres, Commandeur dans l'Ordre du Merite, Chevalier du Daneborg. Address: 4 Rue Victor Hugo, 78230 Le Pecq, France.

ALARIE Pierrette M(arguerite), b. 9 Nov 1921, Montreal, Canada. Soprano; Teacher. m. Leopold Simoneau, 1946. Education: Studied voice and acting with Jeanne Maubourg and Albert Roberval; Voice with Salvator Issaurel, 1938-43, with Elisabeth Schumann, Curtis Institute of Music, Philadelphia, 1943-46. Debut: Operatic debut at Montreal in 1943. Career: Metropolitan Opera debut as Oscar in Un Ballo in Maschera, 1945; European debut in Paris, 1949; Sang in opera, concert and recital in leading North American and European music centres; Retired from operatic stage in 1966, with farewell appearance as soloist in Handel's Messiah with Montreal Symphony Orchestra, 1970; Taught voice. Recordings: Numerous including album of Mozart arias with husband. Honours: Winner, Metropolitan Opera Auditions of the Air, 1945; Officier of the Order of Canada, 1967; Winner, Grand Prix du Disque, 1961.

ALBANESE Cecilia, b. 26 Nov 1937, Caracas, Venezuela. Soprano. Education: Studied at Giuseppe Verdi Conservatory, Milan and with Ettore Campogalliani. Debut: Gilda in Rigoletto at Reggio Emilia. Career: Many appearances in Italy at La Scala, Milan, Teatro San Carlo, Naples and in Rome; Overseas engagements at Hamburg, Barcelona, New York City Opera, with Scottish Opera, and Welsh National Opera; Repertoire has included Bellini's Amina, Donizetti's Lucia and Norina, Rosina, The Queen of Night, Verdi's Nannetta and Violetta and Puccini's Musetta. Honours: Prizewinner at competitions at Macerate, Vercelli and Parma. Address: c/o Teatro La Scala, Via Filodrammatici 2, 20121 Milan, Italy.

ALBANESE Licia, b. 22 July 1913, Bari, Italy Singer (soprano, retired). m. Joseph Gimma, 7 Apr 1945. Education: Studied voice with Emanuel De Rosa, Bari and Giuseppina Baldassare-Tedeschi, Milan. Debut: Operatic debut as Butterfly, Teatro Lirico, Milan, 1934. Career: Formal operatic debut, New York as Cio-Cio San, 1940 and sang there until 1966; Appeared in concerts; Taught; Roles included Butterfly, Violetta, Zerlina, Desdemona, Susanna, Manon, Tosca, Gounod's Marguerite, Mimi. Recordings: NBC radio broadcasts under Toscanini. Honours: Order of Merit of Italy; Lady Grand Cross of the Equestrian Order of the Holy Sepulchre. Address: Nathan Hale Drive, Wilson Point South, Norwalk, CT 06854, USA.

ALBERGA Eleanor, b. 30 Sept 1949, Kingston, Jamaica. Composer. Education: Studied at the Royal Academy of Music, London, from 1970. Career: Has performed with an African dance company and played piano for the London Contemporary Dance Theatre. Compositions: Mobile I for orchestra, 1983; Jamaican Medley for piano, 1983; Clouds piano quintet, 1984; Ice Flow for piano, 1985; Stone Dream for prepared piano and tape, 1986; Suite for piano 4 hands, 1986; Mobile II for ensemble, 1988; Whose Own for prepared piano and sound processor, 1988; Sun Warrior for orchestra, 1990; Dancing with the Shadows for ensemble, 1991; Jupiter's Fairground for orchestra, 1991. Address: 166 Bethnall Green Road, London E2 6DL, England. Street, London.

ALBERMAN David, b. 1959, London, England. Violinist. Education: Private tuition with Mary Long, Emanuel Hurwitz, Sheila Nelson, Vera Kantrovich, Igor Ozim in Cologne; LRAM, 1975; MA in Greats, Classical Languages and Literature, Merton College, Oxford, 1981. Career: Leader of the National Youth Orchestra of Great Britain, 1977; Has performed with the London Mozart Players, Royal Philharmonic Orchestra, London Symphony, Associate Member, 1983-85, and the Academy of St Martin-in-the-Fields; Former leader of the Chamber Orchestra of Europe; Has performed music by Lutoslawski, Penderecki, Osborne and Bainbridge with such groups as the Ballet Rambert and Divertimenti; Member, Arditti Quartet, 1986-94; Many performances at festivals across Europe and North America; Resident string tutor at the Darmstadt Fereinkurse for New Music from 1986; Music in camera programme for BBC Television, 1987; Cycle of Schoenberg's Quartets Purcell Room, London, November 1988; recital in the Russian Spring Series at South Bank, May 1991; Engaged to perform in all the quartets of Berg, Webern and Schoenberg at Antwerp, Cologne, Frankfurt, London and Paris, 1991-93; Took part in the premieres of quartets by Böse, No 3, 1989; Bussotti, 1988; John Cage, Music for 4, 1988, 4, 1989; Ferneyhough, Nos 3 and 4; Gubaidulina, No 3, 1987; Harvey, No 2; Kagel, No 3, 1987; Nancarrow, No 3, 1988; Pousseur, No 2, 1989; Rihm, Nos 6 and 8; Xenakis, Akea Piano Quintet, 1986, Tetora, 1991, Isang Yun, Flute Quintet, 1987; Premiere of Nono's Hay que caminar sonando for violin duo, with Irvine Arditti, Violin, 1989. Recordings include: Elliott Carter's Quartets; Quartets by Ferneyhough, Address: 14 Fairmead Road, London N19 4DF, England.

ALBERT Donnie Ray, b. 1950, Louisiana, USA. Singer (Bass-baritone). Career: Sang Gershwin's Porgy at Houston (1976) and sang there regularly until 1990; Guest appearances at the New York City Opera (Scarpia, 1978), Washington Opera

(Amonasro, 1990), Boston, San Francisco and elsewhere in the USA; Appearances in Berlin and Florence as Porgy; Other roles include Carlos in Ernani, Monterone, Nabucco, Iago, Jack Rance, Jochanaan, Escamillo, Varlaam, and the title role in Gruenberg's Emperor Jones; Concert engagements in New York, Los Angeles and Chicago. Address: c/o Houston Grand Opera, 510 Preston Avenue, Houston, TX 77002, USA.

ALBERT Werner Andreas, b. 1935, Weinheim, Germany. Conductor. Education: Studied at the Mannheim Hochschule and at Heidelberg University; Conducting studies with Herbert von Karajan and Hans Rosbaud. Career: Conducted the Heidelberg Chamber Orchestra, 1961-63; Principal Conductor of the North West German Philharmonic, 1963-71 and Gulbenkian Orchestra, Lisbon, 1971-74; Musical Director of the Nuremberg Symphony Orchestra and the Bavarian Youth Orchestra from 1974; Lecturer at Nuremberg Academy of Music, 1977-. Recordings include: Oboe Concertos by Leclair, Haydn and Dittersdorf; Beethoven's 9th Symphony; Rossini's Petite Messe Solennelle; Cello Concertos by Sutermeister; Mozart's Clarinet Concerto and Horn Concerto K447; Puccini's Messa di Gloria. Address: c/o Nürnberger Symphoniker, Bayernstrasse 100, W-8500 Nurnberg 44, Germany.

ALBERY Tim, b. 5 May 1952, Harpenden, England. Stage Director. Career: Has produced plays for Liverpool Playhouse, Liverpool Everyman, Contact Theatre, Manchester, The Half Moon, ICA and Almeida Theatres, London; Has directed plays in Germany and Netherlands; Was Director of ICA Theatre, London, 1981-82; Has directed Schiller at Greenwich Theatre and at Royal Shakespeare Company; Shakespeare for the Old Vic and Racine at the National Theatre; Debut as Opera Director with The Turn of the Screw at Batignano, Italy, 1983; Other work includes The Midsummer Marriage, Don Giovanni and La Finta Giardiniera for Opera North, The Trojans for Opera North, Scottish Opera, Welsh National Opera and Opéra de Nice; The Rape of Lucretia at Gothenburg, 1987; La Wally at Bregenz, 1990; Billy Budd, Beatrice and Benedict, Peter Grimes and Lohengrin for English National Opera, 1988, 1990, 1991 and 1993; Berlioz's Benvenuto Cellini in Amsterdam, 1991; Don Carlos for Opera North, 1993; Chérubin for Royal Opera House and Fidelio for Scottish Opera, 1994; Engaged by ENO for From the House of the Dead, 1997. Address: c/o Harriet Cruikshank, 97 Old Lambeth Road, London SW8 1XU, England.

ALBIN Roger, b. 30 Sep 1920, Beausoleil, France. Conductor; Cellist. Education: Studied with Umberto Benedetti at Monte Carlo from 1926; Paris Conservatoire with Henri Busser, Milhaud and Olivier Messiaen. Career: Played cello at Monte Carlo, The Paris Opera and at the Société des Concerts du Conservatoire; Duo partnership with pianist Claude Helffer, 1949-57; Studied further with Roger Desormiére, Carl Schuricht and Hans Rosbaud and conducted from 1957 with chorus at the Opéra Comique, Paris; Musical Director at Nancy, 1960-61, Toulouse, 1961-66 and French Radio Orchestra at Strasbourg, 1966-75; Cellist with the French National Orchestra, 1978-81, also a member of the orchestra's String Sextet; Professor of Chamber Music at the Strasbourg Conservatory, 1981-87. Recordings: As cellist: Prokofiev's Concerto and Ravel's Trio; Fauré's Fantasie and the Fantasie for Piano and Orchestra by Debussy; Ibert's Diane Poitiers. Honours include: Premier Prix in cello class at the Paris Conservatoire, 1936.

ALBRECHT Georg-Alexander, b. 15 Feb 1935, Bremen, Germany. Conductor. Education: Studied violin, piano and composition, 1942-54. Debut: As conductor, 1949. Career: Chief Conductor at the Bremen Opera, 1958-61, Hanover Opera from 1961; Guest Conductor with the Dresden Staatskapelle, the Berlin Philharmonic and other German orchestras; Professor at the Hanover Conservatory. Repertory includes the 1st Symphony of Wolfgang Rihm (premiere, 1984). Address: c/o Hochschule für Musik Hannover, Emmichplatz 1, 3000 Hannover 1, Germany.

ALBRECHT Gerd, b. 19 Jul 1935, Essen, Germany. Conductor. Education: Studied conducting with Wilhelm Bruckner-Ruggenerg, Hamburg Hochschule für Musik and musicology at Universities of Kiel and Hamburg. Career: Repetiteur and Conductor, Wurttenberg State Theater, Stuttgart, 1958-61; First Conductor, Mainz, 1961-63; Generalmusikdirektor, Lubeck, 1963-66 and Kassel, 1966-72; Chief Conductor, Deutsche Oper, West Berlin, 1972-79 and Tonhalle Orchestra, Zurich, 1975-80; Guest Conductor with Vienna State Opera, 1976-; Conducted the premieres of Henze's Telemanniana in Berlin in 1967, Fortner's Elisabeth Tudor in Berlin in 1972, Henze's Barcarola in Zurich in 1980 and Reimann's Troades in Munich in 1986; Guest appearances with various European and North American Opera companies and orchestras; Conductor, Der fliegende Holländer at Covent Garden in 1986; Chief Conductor, Hamburg State Opera and Philharmonic State Orchestra, 1988-; Conducted Schreker's Der Schatzgräber at Hamburg. 1989-90 followed by Idomeneo and Tannhäuser; Conducted Tchaikovsky's Maid of Orleans at the 1990 Munich Festival, with Waltraud Meier; Chief Conductor of the Czech Philharmonic Orchestra 1992-94; Hamburg State Opera from 1995; Season 1992 with Dvorák's Dimitri at Munich, Reimann's Troades at Frankfurt and Tannhäuser at Barcelona; premiere of Schnittke's Historia von D Johann Fausten at Hamburg, 1995. Recordings include: CD of Der Schatzgräber. Honours: Winner, Besançon, 1957; Conducting Competitions, Hilversum, 1958. Address: c/o Hamburg State Opera, Postfach 302448, 2000 Hamburg 36, Germany.

ALBRECHT Theodore (John), b. 24 Sep 1945, Jamestown, New York, USA. Orchestra Conductor; Musicologist. m. Carol Padgham, 16 Aug 1976. Education: BME, St Mary's University, 1967; MM, 1969, PhD, 1975, North Texas State University. Career includes: Assistant Professor, Appalachian State University, 1975-76; Conductor, German Orchestra of Cleveland, 1977-80; Music Director, Northland Symphony Orchestra, Kansas City, Missouri, 1980-87; Professor, Park College, 1980-92; Music Director, Philharmonia of Greater Kansas City, 1987-92; Associate Professor, Kent State University, Kent, Ohio, 1992-; Notable performances include, US premieres of Bruckner Dialog by Gottfried von Einem, 1982, Symphony in C, op 46 by Hans Pfitzner, 1983, Ludi Leopoldini by Gottfried von Einem, 1984; 1st American conductor to conduct all 9 Dvorak symphonies; World premiere of Song of the Prairie by Timothy Corrao, 1987. Publications: Editor, Dika Newlin, Friend and Mentor: A Birthday Anthology, 1973; Translations of Felix Weingartner's On the Performance of the Symphonies of Mozart, 1985, Schubert and Schumann, 1986; Editor, Thayer, Salieri, Rival of Mozart, 1989; Letters to Beethoven and Other Correspondence, 3 volumes, 1996; Beethoven: A Research Guide, 1998. Contributions to: Editor, Journal of Musicology, Journal of Musicological Research, Beethoven Newsletter and Beethoven Forum; Notes; Musical Quarterly; American Choral Review; The Opera Journal; The Clarinet; Symposium. Honour: ASCAP/Deems Taylor Award, 1997. Hobbies: Photography; Walking; Cultural Geography; Local History. Address: 1635 Chadwick Drive, Kent, OH 44240, USA.

ALBRIGHT William H(ugh), b. 20 Oct 1944, Gary, IN, USA. Pianist; Organist; Teacher; Composer. Education: Studied piano with Rosetta Goodkind, theory with Hugh Aitken, Juilliard Preparatory Department, NY, 1959-62, composition with Ross Lee Finney, George Rochberg, Olivier Messiaen, Paris Conservatory, 1968 and organ with Marilyn Mason, University of Michigan, 1963-70. Career: Teacher, 1970-82, Professor of Music, 1982-, Associate Director, Electronic Music Studio, Chair, Composition Department, University of Michigan; Concert tours as pianist and organist throughout USA, Canada and Europe. Compositions include: Multimedia and stage: Cross Of Gold, music theatre, 1975, incidental music to Yeat's play, 1978; Orchestral: Alliance, suite, 1967-70, Gothic Suite for Organ, Strings and Percussion, 1973; Chamber: Amerithon for Variable Ensemble, 1966-67, Peace Pipe for 2 Bassoons, 1976, Halo for Organ and Metal Percussion Instruments, 1978, Brass Tacks, rag march, for Brass Quintet, 1983; Piano and Organ: Vocal Mass in D for Chorus, Organ, Percussion and Congregation, 1974, Pax In Terra for Soprano, Tenor and Chorus, 1981, A Song To David, oratorio, 1983, Take Up The Song for Soprano, Chorus and Piano, 1986, Deum De Deo for Choir and Organ, 1988, Concerto for Harpsichord and String Orchestra, 1991, Flights Of Fancy, ballet for Organ, 1992; Rustles of Spring, chamaber ensemble, 1994; Fantasy Etudes for saxophone quartet, 1993. Recordings: As performer and composer. Honours: Guggenheim Fellowship, 1976, 1987; Composer in Residence, American Academy, Rome, 1979; Many commissions and awards; Composer of the Year, American Guild of Organists, 1993. Current Management: Karen McFarlane Artists Inc, 12429 Cedar Road, Cleveland, OH 44106, USA. Address: c/o Music Department, University of Michigan, Ann Arbor, MI 48109, USA.

ALCANTARA Theo, b. 16 Apr 1941, Cuenca, Spain. Conductor. m. Susan Alcantara. Education: Madrid Conservatory and Salzburg Mozarteum. Career: Conductor, Frankfurt am Main, 1964-66; Director of orchestras, University of Michigan, Ann Arbor, 1968-73; Music Director, Grand Rapids Symphony Orchestra, MI, 1973-78; Music Director, Phoenix Symphony Orchestra, 1978-89; Artistic Director, Music Academy of the West, Santa Barbara, CA, 1981-84; Principal Conductor, Pittsburgh Opera, 1987-; Conducted Elektra at Pittsburgh, 1989. Honours: Silver Medal, Mitropoulos Competition, 1966. Address: c/o ICM Artists Ltd, 40 West 57th Street, New York, NY 10019, USA.

ALDEN David, b. 16 Sept 1949, New York City, USA. Stage Director. Career: Has directed the premieres of Stephen Burton's The Duchess of Malfi, Wolf Trap, 1978, Pasatieri's Washington Square and Conrad Susa's Don Perlimpin at San Francisco, Fidelio and Wozzeck at the Metropolitan Opera, and Rigoletto, Wozzeck and Mahagonny for Scottish Opera; Productions of The Rake's Progress for Netherlands Opera and at the Israel Festival, Werther at Nancy and the US premiere of Judith by Siegfried Matthus at Sante Fe in 1990; English National Opera with Mazeppa, Simon Boccanegra, A Masked Ball and double bill of Oedipus Rex and Duke Bluebeard's Castle in 1991; Staged Tristan and Isolde for ENO, 1996; Affiliations with opera at the Academy, New York, with La Calisto and New Israel Opera with Les Contes d'Hoffmann, La Bohème and the world premiere of Noam Sheriff's The Sorrows of Job; Monteverdi's Poppea for the Bavarian State Opera, 1997. Address: c/o English National Opera, St Martin's Lane, London, WC2, England.

ALDULESCU Radu, b. 17 Sept 1922, Piteasca-Pasares, Rumania. Concert Cellist. Education: Studied at the Bucharest Conservatory. Debut: Played for Bucharest Radio, 1941. Career: Soloist with the Georges Enescu Philharmonic, Bucharest, and with the Orchestra of the Accademia di Santa Cecilia, Rome; Assistant to Gaspar Cassado from 1964 and formed string trio with Salvatore Accardo and Luigi Bianchi, 1972; Chamber recitals with Carlo Zecchi. Address: c/o Conservatorui de Mukica, Str Stirbei Voda 33, 70732 Bucharest, Rumania.

ALER David, b. 26 Apr 1959, Stockholm, Sweden. Baritone. Education: Studied in Gothenburg with Jacqueline Delman until 1987; Further studies with Geoffrey Parsons, Janet Baker, Kim Borg and Galina Vishnevskaya. Career: Sang at Landestheater Coburg and in Sweden, 1988- as Don Giovanni, Guglielmo and Tarquinius in The Rape of Lucretia; Appeared in Vadstena and Reykjavik, 1988-89 in the premiere production of Someone I Have Seen by Karolina Eriksdottir; Stora Theater in Gothenburg as Schaunard in La Bohème, 1989; Concert engagements in Stockholm with Drottningholm Baroque Ensemble and Chapelle Royale of Versailles. Address: c/o M & M Lyric Artists, 140 Battersea Park Road, London, SW11 5NY, England.

ALER John, b. 4 Oct 1949, Baltimore, MD, USA. Singer (Tenor). Education: Bachelor and Master degrees in Voice Performance, School of Music, Catholic University of America, 1972; Juilliard School of Music, American Opera Center and Opera Training Department, 1972-75; Studied with Oren Brown and Martin Isepp. Career: Has sung in opera, oratorio and recitals in USA, Canada, UK and most of Europe; Many appearances including Tanglewood, Glyndebourne and Aix-en-Provence Festivals, Salzburg Festival, La Scala and London Proms; Has sung with major national and international orchestras; Vienna Staatsoper debut 1982; Toured Japan with Royal Opera, Covent Garden, 1986; Toured Taiwan with Ludwigsburg Festival Chorus and Orchestra, 1987; Sang Eumolpus in Stravinsky's Persephone at Promenade Concerts, London, 1993. Recordings include: Handel's Messiah, 1986; Bizet's Les Pêcheurs des Perles, 1989; Songs and Duos of Saint-Saëns, with John Ostendorf and John van Buskirk, 1989; Enesco's Oedipe; Semele, with Kathleen Battle, 1990; Title role in Gazzaniga's Don Giovanni; Orfeo, 1990; Stravinsky works with London Sinfonietta, 1990; Rossini's Songs of My Old Age, 1991; Handel's Joshua, 1991; Gounod's Mors et Vita with Orchestre du Capitole de Toulouse under Michel Plasson, 1992; Dvorák's Stabat Mater with New Jersey Symphony, 1994; Merry Widow, Glyndebourne company in concert, 1994; Songs We Forgot to Remember, 1996. Honours: Grammy Award for Best Classical Vocal Soloist for Berlioz Requiem, 1985; Featured on 2 Grammy winning albums, Best Classical Album for Bartók - Cantata Profana and Best Opera Recording for Handel - Semele, 1994. Current Management: Herbert Barrett Management. Address: c/o Mary Lynn Fixler, Herbert Barrett Management, 1776 Broadway, Suite 1610, New York, NY 10019, USA.

ALEXANDER Carlos, b. 15 Oct 1915, Utica, NY, USA. Bass Baritone. Education: Studied in Berlin and with Friedrich Schorr in New York. Debut: St Louis in 1941 as Masetto. Career: Sang widely in North and South America; Founded an opera society at Salt Lake City in 1948; Moved to Germany in 1955 and sang first at Munster, Hanover and Krefeld; Cologne, 1958-61, and Stuttgart Opera from 1961; Glyndebourne Festival in 1961 as Gregor Mittenhofer in the first British performance of Henze's Elegy for Young Lovers; Guest appearances in Dusseldorf and Munich; Maggio Musicale Florence in 1961 as Mandryka in Arabella; Bayreuth Festival, 1963-65 as Beckmesser in Die Meistersinger; Stuttgart, 1968 in the premiere of Prometheus by Orff; Teacher at the Salzburg Mozarteum. Recordings: Antigonae by Orff; Don Giovanni.

ALEXANDER Christian (David), b. 15 Jan 1964, Liverpool, England. Composer. Education: BA, Honours, 1986, MMus, 1991, Bristol University; Studied composition with Robert Saxton; Studied with: Maxwell Davies, Steve Martland at Hoy Summer School, 1990. Career: Music written and performed for BBC documentary, The Zoo, 1986; Works performed by: BBC Singers, Op 5 and 25, Bournemouth Sinfonietta, Op 23, Jennifer Stinton, Op 36; Works performed at: Wigmore Hall, Op 36, Purcell Room, Op 21, St John's, Smith Square, Op 14, Keele University, Tread Softly Op 40, by English Guitar Quartet; Composer-in-Residence, Radley College, 1991-96; Trustee on the Finzi Trust, 1996-; Associate Composer at Sedbergh School, 1996-97. Compositions: 6 Published works, ensemble, instrumental and vocal music; Other works include: February Afternoon, Op 5 for Choir and Vibraphone, 1987, Child of Treblinka, Op 11 for Chamber Ensemble, 1988, Garden of Love, Op 21 for Soprano and Piano, 1990, New Earth, Op 23 for Chamber Orchestra, 1990, Madrigal, Op 25 for Choir, 1990, Caol Ila, Op 34 for Viola and Orchestra, 1992, Tread Softly, Op 40, 1994, How Hearts May Beat, Op 38, 1994; Sonata No 4 Op 44 for piano; Stella Celi for clarinet and guitar, 1997; Catch, Snatch, Maggot and Dump, op 49, for two guitars, 1997. Recording: How Hearts May Beat, Op 38 recorded for broadcast on BBC Radio 3. Publications: Organ Fantasia Op 2; Divertimento No 1 Op 3; Tears Op 4; Have I Been Gazing on the Western Sky? Op 7; Quintet Op 8; Piano Prelude Op 9. Memberships: Performing Rights Society; Association of Professional Composers. Hobbies: Cooking; Cycling. Address: 26 New Road, Kingham, Oxfordshire OX7 6YP, England.

ALEXANDER Haim, b. 9 Aug 1915, Berlin, Germany. Composer. m. 6 January 1941, 2 sons. Education: Sternsches Conservatory, Berlin; Graduated, Palestine Conservatory and Academy of Music, 1945; Higher Studies, Freiburg, Germany. Career: Teacher of Piano and Theory, 1945-; Associate Professor, Composition and Theory, Head, Department of Theoretical Subjects, Rubin Academy of Music, Jerusalem, 1971-82; Associate Professor, 1972-76, Full Professorship, 1976-, Theoretical Subjects, Department of Musicology, University of Tel-Aviv; Retired 1982, but continuing part-time work. Compositions include: Miscellaneous works for piano, 2 pianos, chamber music, pieces based on Oriental Folklore, choral music, songs for voice and piano, works for orchestra; Metamorphoses on a theme by Mozart, Piano solo, 1990; Piano Sonata, 1994; 3 Ballads by Goethe for 4 women's voices, 1997; Late Love for chamber orchestra, 1997. Publications: Improvisation am Klavier (two parts and two cassettes), in German, 1986. Contributions to: Encyclopaedia Hebraica. Honour: Golden Feather Prize for Lifetime Achievement from ACUM, 1996. Hobbies: Gymnastics; Swimming; Bridge. Address: 55 Tschernichowsky Street, 92587 Jerusalem, Israel.

ALEXANDER Leni, b. 8 June 1924, Breslau, Germany. Composer. m. Ernst Bodenhöfer, 24 Dec 1941, divorced, 2 s, 1 d. Emigrated to Chile from Hamburg in 1939. Education: Real-Gymnasium Hamburg, 1939; Diploma Montessori, University of Chile, 1945; Piano, Violoncello, Composition with Fre Focke; Conservatoire de Paris with Olivier Messiaen and composition studies with René Leibowitz, 1954. Career: Public concerts of symphonique works in: Santiago de Chile, Buenos Aires, Paris, Rome, New York, Cologne (Chamber Music), Venice, Toulouse, Tokyo and Stuttgart; Film Music, ballet music in Santiago; Special broadcast commission, San Francisco. Compositions include: Cuarteto para Cuerdas, 1957; Cantata From Death to Morning; Equinoccio; 2..ils se sont perdus dans l'espace etoile..., 1975; Aulicio II, 1985; Time and Consumation; Tessimenti; Adras; Par Quoi? A Quoi? Pour Quoi?; Maramoh; Los Disparates; Sous le quotidien, decelez l'inexplicalbe; ..Est-ce donc si doux cette vie?..; Ballet Music: Soon we shall be one, 1959, Les trois visages de la lune, 1966, Un medecin de campagne, Schigan for Organ, 1989, Dishona for Voice, Saxophone and 3 Percussions, 1988. Contributions to: Music and Psychoanalysis; Alban Berg; The Music Which Freud Never Heard; Psychoanalytic Variations about a theme by Gustav Mahler. Honours: Fellowship of the French Government, 1953; Cantata From Death to Morning, chosen as best work by RAI Italy, 1960; Festival of The ISMC, Köln, only work selected and played from Latin America; Guggenheim Fellowship, 1969; Various commissions by the Ministere de la Culture, France and Radio France. Address: c/o Beatrice Bodenhofer, Arzobispo Casanova, 24 Bellavista, Santiago de Chile.

ALEXANDER Roberta, b. 3 Mar 1949, Lynchburg, VA, USA. Soprano. Education: Studied at the University of Michigan and with Herman Woltman at the Royal Conservatory, The Hague. Career: European debut as Rossini's Fanny, La Cambiale di Matrimonio, Netherlands Opera in 1975; Sang Pamina at Houston in 1980 and Strauss's Daphne at Santa Fe in 1981; Covent Garden debut as Mimi in La Bohème; Metropolitan debut in 1983 as Zerlina and returned to New York as Jenufa, Mimi, Vitellia, Countess and Gershwin's Bess; Sang at Netherlands Opera as Vitellia, Fiordigili and Violetta, Vienna State Opera as Donna Elvira, Jenufa, and Hamburg State Opera as Elettra in Idomeneo, Donna Elvira and Countess; Glyndebourne debut in 1989 as Jenufa; Sang Mozart's Vitellia at Zurich in 1989 and Elettra, Idomeneo at the Hamburg Staatsoper in 1990; Sang Vitellia at Glyndebourne 1995; Concert appearances include Strauss Four Last Songs with Los Angeles Philharmonic under Previn, and San Francisco Symphony, Mahler No 4 with Boston Symphony under Ozawa, Concertgebouw under Haitink, Cleveland under Ashkenazy, and Mahler No 8 at the Salzburg Festival under Maazel; Concerts with Concentus Musicus Wien under Harnoncourt. Recordings: Mahler No 4; Porgy and Bess excerpts; St John Passion; Giulio Cesare excerpts; Don Giovanni; Telemann Cantatas; Songs by Ives, Strauss, Mozart, Bernstein, Barber and Puccini. Address: c/o IMG Artists Europe, Media House, 3 Burlington Lane, Chiswick, London W4 2TH, England.

ALEXANDRA Liana, b. 27 May 1947, Bucharest, Rumania. Composer. Education: Studied at the Bucharest Conservatory, 1965-71, and at Weimar and Darmstadt. Career: Reader at the Bucharest Academy. Compositions include: The Snow Queen, opera, 1980; The Little Siren, ballet, 1983; In the Labyrinth, opera, 1987; 7 symphonies, 1971-93; Clarinet concerto, 1974; Concerto for viola, flute and chamber orchestra, 1980; Ierusalim, symphonic poem, 1991; 2 wind quintets, 1977 and 1983, and other chamber music; Cantatas and ballads for mixed chorus. Address: Bucharest Academy of Music, Bucharest, Romania.

ALEXASHKIN Sergei, b. Saratov, Russia. Singer (Bass). Education: Studied at the Saratov Conservatoire and at La Scala. Career: Member of the Kirov Opera from 1984, including tours to the Edinburgh Festival, 1991, and New York Metropolitan, 1992; Roles have included Mussorgsky's Boris, Rangoni and Dosifei, Sobakin in The Tsar's Bride, Ivan Susanin, Glinka's Ruslan and Farlaf, Kutuzov in War and Peace and Rimsky's Ivan the Terrible; Engagements at Frankfurt and Salzburg in Boris Godunov, at Vienna in Prince Igor and The Damnation of Faust at Rome; Other roles include Verdi's Philip II, Fiesco, Ramfis and Procida, Gounod's Mephistopheles, Sarastro, and Don Giovanni; Concerts include Shostakovich's 13th Symphony with the Chicago SO, 1995, Mussorgsky's Songs and Dances of Death (UK debut with the BBC PO under Solti, 1996), and Shostakovich's 14th Symphony, at the Vienna Konzerthaus and Ferrara Musica. Recordings include: The Fiery Angel and Sadko. Address: c/o Lies Askonas Ltd, 6 Henrietta St, London, WC2E 8LA, England.

ALEXEEV Dmitri, b. 10 Aug 1947, Moscow, Russia. Pianist. m. Tatiana Sarkissova, 1 daughter. Education: Piano Studies from age of 5; Entered Central Music School, Moscow Conservatory, aged 6; Postgraduate Studies, Dmitri Bashkirov, Moscow. Debut: London, 1975, Vienna, 1975, Chicago 1976, New York, 1978, Paris. Career includes: Numerous appearances, great orchestras worldwide; English recitals include: Major music societies and festivals (Aldeburgh, Edinburgh); Regular performances throughout Russia, Europe, USA, Japan, Australia; Solo appearances; Concerts with soprano Barbara Hendricks (London, Stockholm, Frankfurt, Munich, Milan, Florence and TV Russia, France). Recordings include: Piano concertos by Schumann, Grieg, Rachmaninov, Prokofiev, Shostakovich, Scriabin, Medtner and solo works by Brahms, Rachmaninov, Schumann, Chopin and Liszt; Spirituals with Barbara Hendricks; Chopin Waltzes; Chopin Preludes; Grieg and Schumann Concertos with Yuri Temirkanov and Royal Philharmonic Orchestra Scriabin - Prometheus/ Philadelphia Orchestra (R Muti); Schumann's Kreisleriana and Etudes Symphoniques, Shostakovich Concertos with the English Chamber Orchestra, Classics for Pleasure; Hyperion, Medtner, Piano Concerto & Piano Quintet, BBC Symphony; BMG Rachmaninov, Paganini Rhapsody, St Petersburg Philharmonic; Rachmaninov Double CD Complete Preludes and Moments Musicaux. Honours: Top Honours at the Marguerite Long Competition, Paris, 1969, the George Enescu Competition, Bucharest, 1970 and at the Tchaikovsky Competition in Moscow in 1974; First Prize, Leeds International Piano Competition, 1975; Edison Award, 1994. Current Management: IMG Artists. Address: c/o IMG Artists Europe, Media House, 3 Burlington Lane, Chiswick, London W4 2TH, England.

ALEXEYEV Anya, b. Moscow, Russia. Concert Pianist. Education: Studied with Dmitri Bashkirov at the Moscow Conservatoire and at the Royal College of Music, with Irina Zarits-Kaya, 1990-. Career: Frequent appearances in Russia and at the major London venues: Barbican Centre, South Bank and St John's Smith Square; Wigmore Hall recital, 1994; Tour of South America 1993 and with the Lithuanian SO on tour to the UK, in Concerto no 2 by Shostakovich; Rachmaniniv 2 with the Philharmonia and Beethoven 4 in South Africa; Season 1994-95 with recitals in Ireland and at Festivals in Belgium, Spain, France and Finland; Schumann's Concerto with the Bournemouth SO, the Grieg Concerto with the Royal Scottish National Orchestra, UK tour with the Moscow State Orchestra and recitals at the Bath and Brighton Festivals. Honours include: Winner, Newport International Piano Competition, 1991. Address: c/o Harrison/Parrott Ltd, 12 Penzance Place, London W11 4PA, England.

ALI-ZADEH Franghiz, b. 29 May 1947, Azerbaijan, Russia. Composer; Pianist. Education: Studied at the Baku Conservatory, 1970-76. Career: Teacher at the Baku Conservatory from 1977. Compositions include: The Legend about White Horseman, rock opera, 1985; Piano concerto, 1972; Symphony, 1976; Concerto for chamber orchestra, 1986; Songs about the Motherland, oratorio, 1978; Ode for chorus and orchestra, 1980; 2 piano sonatas, 1970, 1990; String quartet, 1974, and other chamber music; Crossings for chamber ensemble, 1992; Songs. Address: c/o RAO, Bolchaia Bronnai 6-a, Moscow 103670, Russia.

ALIBERTI Lucia, b. 1957, Sicily, Italy. Soprano. Education: Studied at the Messina Conservatory. Debut: Teatro Sperimentale, Spoleto in 1978 as Amina in La Sonnambula. Career: Spoleto Festival in 1979 as Amina, Wexford Festival in 1979 in Crispino e la Comare by the brothers Ricci; Returned in 1980 in Un Giorno di Regno and in 1983 as Linda di Chamounix; Sang at Piccola Scala Milan in 1980 as Elisa in Il Re Pastore by Mozart, then in Handel's Ariodante, at Glyndebourne Festival in 1980 as Nannetta and also at La Scala Milan in 1981; Sang at the Teatro Bellini Catania in 1982 as Elvira in I Puritani and Olympia in Les Contes d'Hoffmann; Deutsche Oper Berlin and Munich Opera in 1983 as Lucia and Gilda; Cologne and Zurich in 1985 and 1986 as Violetta; Sang title role in Rossini's La Donna del Lago followed by Norma at Catania in 1990. Recordings include: La Buona Figliuola by Piccinni; CD of L'Arte del Belcanto. Address: Oper der Stadt Bonn, Am Boselagerhof 1, D-5300 Bonn, Germany.

ALLANBROOK Douglas (Phillips), b. 1 Apr 1921, Melrose, MA, USA. Composer; Teacher. Education: Studied with Nadia Boulanger, Longy School of Music, Cambridge, MA, 1941-42; Paris, 1948-50; BA, Harvard College, 1948; With Walter Piston; Studied harpsichord and early keyboard music with Ruggero Gerlin, Naples, 1950-52. Career: Teacher, St John's College, Annapolis. Compositions include: Operas: Ethan Frome, 1950-52; Nightmare Abbey, 1960-62; Orchestral: Concerto for Harpshichord and Small Orchestra, 1949-50; Violin Concerto, 1959; Serenade for Piano and Orchestra, 1978; 7 Symphonies including: Five Heroic Attitudes, 1979; Chamber: 4 String Quartets, 1955, 1956, 1958, 1972; Partita for Cello, 1958; Night and Morning Music for Brass Quintet, 1978; Invitation to the Side Show for Brass Quintet, 1985; Piano: 2 Bagatelles, 1959; 40 Changes, 1967; 5 Night Pieces, 1986; Harpsichord Music; Choral: The Seven Last Words for 2 Soloists, Chorus and Orchestra, 1968; An English Mass for Chorus and Organ, 1974; Moon Songs for Children's Chorus and Orchestra, 1986-87; Vocal: Songs to Petrarch Sonnets, 1948; 3 Love and Death Songs for High Voice, Oboe, 2 Clarinets and 3 Strings, 1981; Latest: Quintet for Strings, 1991; 5 New American Preludes, 1994. Recordings: Numerous keyboard music. Publication: 20th Century Music, Great Ideas Today. Honours: Fulbright Fellowship; American Academy of Arts and Letters, 1986. Memberships: ASCAP; Director of Corporation of YADDO. Address: 6 Revell Street, Annapolis, MD 21401, USA.

ALLARD Maurice, b. 25 May 1923, Sin-le-Noble, France. Concert Bassoonist. Education: Graduated from the Paris Conservatoire, 1940. Career: Soloist with the Concerts Lamoureux (1942) and played with the Orchestra of the Paris Opéra from 1949; Professor at the Paris Conservatoire from 1957; Premieres include works by Henri Tomasi, Landowski, Jacques Rivier and André Jolivet. Honours include: Winner of the Geneva International Competition, 1949. Address: c/o Conservatoire National, 14 Rue de Madrid, F-75000 Paris, France.

ALLDIS John, b. 10 Aug 1929, London, England. Conductor. m. Ursula Mason, 23 Jul 1960, 2 s. Education: Felsted School, 1943-47; Choral Scholar, King's College, Cambridge, 1949-52; ARCO, 1954; MA, 1957. Career: Founder and Conductor, John Alldis Choir, 1962-; Professor, Guildhall School of Music, 1966-77; Founder and Conductor, London Symphony Chorus, 1966-69; Conductor of London Philharmonic Choir, 1969-82; Conductor of Danish Radio Choir, 1972-77; Musical Director, Groupe Vocal de France, 1978-83. Recordings: Over 50 various recordings with John Alldis Choir, of contemporary music and opera; CDs of Beethoven's Missa Solemnis (Klemperer), Elgar's The Dream of Gerontius (Boult), Berlioz's Grande Messe des Morts, (Colin Davis) and L'Enfance du Christ, Ives Symphony No 4, (Serebrier), Mozart's Die Entführung, (Davis), Puccini's Turandot, (Mehta), Tchaikovsky's Eugene Onegin, (Solti) and Vivaldi's Sacred Choral Works, Negri. Honours: Various awards and Grammy nominations; Gold Disc with London Philharmonic Choir, 1977; FGSM, 1976; Fellow, Westminster Choir College, Princeton, NJ, USA, 1978; Chevalier des Arts et des Lettres, 1984. Current Management: Allied Artists. Address: 3 Wool Road, Wimbledon, London, SW20 0HN, England.

ALLEMANDI Antonio, b. 20 Mar 197, Milan, Italy. Conductor. Education: Studied at the Milan Conservatory with Gianluigi Gelmetti, with Franco Ferrara and with Bernstein and Ozawa at Tanglewood. Debut: Florence, 1978, with the premiere of Corghi's ballet with voices, Actus III. Career: Assistant to Abbado at La Scala, Milan, notably with Nono's Prometeo, 1985; Guest Conductor at opera houses in France, Italy and elsewhere in Europe. Address: c/o Teatro alla Scala, Via Filadrammatici 2, 20121 Milan, Italy.

ALLEN Betty, b. 17 Mar 1930, Campbell, OH, USA. Mezzo-Soprano; Teacher; Administrator. m. Ritten Edward Lee III, 17 Oct 1953, 1 son, 1 daughter. Education: Wilberforce University, 1944-46; Certificate, Hartford School of Music, 1953; Private vocal studies with Sarah Peck More, Zinka Milanov, Paul Ulanowsky, Carolina Segrera Holden; Berkshire Music Center, Tanglewood. Career: Soloist, Bernstein's Jeremiah Symphony, Tanglewood, 1951; Appeared in Thomson's Four Saints in Three Acts, New York 1952; Debut at New York City Opera in Kern's Queenie, 1954; Toured Europe under auspices of the US State Department, 1955; New York recital debut at Town Hall n 1958; Formal operatic debut at Teatro Colon, Buenos Aires as Jocasta in Oedipus Rex, 1964; USA operatic debut at San Francisco, 1966 and Metropolitan Opera debut in 1973; Appearances with other USA opera companies; Many concert engagements; Teacher at Manhattan School of Music in New York, 1969, North Carolina School of the Arts at Winston-Salem, 1978-87 and Philadelphia Musical Academy, 1979; Executive Director, Harlem School of the Arts, 1979-; Teacher of masterclasses in voice at Teatro Colon, Buenos Aires, 1985-86 and Curtis Institute of Music, Philadelphia, 1987-. Recordings: Various. Honours: Marian Anderson Award, 1953-54; LHD, Wittenberg University, 1971; DMus, Union College, 1981; DFA, Adelphi University, 1990; American Eagle Award, National Music Council. Memberships: NAACP, Urban League; Various musical organizations. Address: c/o Harlem School of the Arts, 645 St Nicholas Avenue, New York, NY 10030, USA.

ALLEN Ross (Clearman), b. 16 Dec 1921, Kirksville, MO, USA. Opera Director; Teacher. Education: Studied at Indiana University. Debut: Staged the choral sequences in Britten's Billy Budd at its US (student) premiere, 1952. Career: Joined faculty of Indiana University in 1953; Has staged over 150 works including Candide by Bernstein in 1958; US premieres of Christmas Eve by Rimsky Korsakov and Martinu's Greek Passion; Staged Aida at the opening of Jones Hall, Houston, 1966; World premiere of John Eaton's Myshkin (after The Idiot by Dostoyevsky), Indiana, 1973; Has also assisted in the direction of 16th century Italian entertainments. Honours include: Peabody Award for television production of Elegy for Young Lovers by Henze, 1969. Address: Indiana University Opera Theater, School of Music, Bloomington, IN 47405, USA.

ALLEN Thomas (Boaz), b. 10 Sep 1944, Seaham Harbour, County Durham, England. Singer (Baritone). m. (1) Margaret Holley, 30 Mar 1968, (2) Jeannie Lascelles, 12 Mar 1988, 1 son. Education: Studied at Royal College of Music, London. Debut: Welsh National Opera, 1969; Covent Garden, 1971. Career: Sang many roles with Welsh National Opera, 1969-72, and at Royal Opera in London 1971-, notably as Mozart's Count and Guglielmo, Rossini's Figaro and Britten's Billy Budd; Has sung many roles at various festivals including his first appearance at Glyndebourne Festival as Papageno in 1973; Has appeared in Paris, Florence, Buenos Aires, Geneva, and Metropolitan Opera House, NY; In 1985 sang the title role in Henze's realization of Monteverdi's Il Ritorno d'Ulisse at Salzburg Festival; In 1986 sang title role in first British stage performance of Busoni's Doktor Faust, ENO London Coliseum; In 1987 as Don Giovanni at La Scala; Sang Mozart's Count at Los Angeles in 1990 and Salzburg in 1991; Sang Malatesta in Don Pasquale at Covent Garden in 1990 followed by Forester in a new production of The Cunning Little Vixen, Eisenstein at the Metropolitan; Chicago Lyric Opera debut in 1990 as Figaro; Sang Don Giovanni at Covent Garden in 1991 and Count Almaviva at the Salzburg Festival, 1993; Sang Morone in Palestrina for the Royal Opera, 1997; Prince Consort Professor at Royal College of Music, 1994-. Recordings include: Carmina Burana; Peter Grimes; King Priam; Eugene Onegin; Werther; Wolf Italian Song Book; War Requiem; Duruflé Requiem; Vaughan Williams Songs of Travel. Publication: Foreign Parts, A Singer's Journal, 1992. Honours: Honorary MA, University of Newcastle upon Tyne, 1986; Honorary DMus, University of Durham, 1988; Honorary FRAM, 1988; Honorary FRCM, 1988; CBE, 1988; ARCM, 1988. Hobbies: Painting; Ornithology; Golf. Address: c/o Lies Askonas Ltd, 6 Henrietta Street, London WC2E 8LA, England.

ALLERS Franz, b. 6 Aug 1905, Czechoslovakia. Conductor. m. Janne Furch, 30 May 1963, 1 daughter. Education: Diploma in conducting, composition, violin and piano, Academy of Music, Berlin, 1926; Musicology, University of Berlin, 1926; Member of Berlin Philharmonic, 1924-26. Debut: Fledermaus with Richard Tauber, Carlsbad, Czechoslovakia in 1926. Career includes: Conductor with repertoire including Hindemith's Cardillac and Berg's Wozzeck, Wuppertal, Germany; Conductor for Ballet Russe de Monte Carlo, London and tours of USA; Has conducted most major symphony orchestras in USA. Compositions include: Innumerable arrangements and transcriptions. Recordings include: La Vie Parisienne by Offenbach, prizewinner. Contributions to: Music magazines. Honours: Grand Cross of Merit 1st Class in recognition of performing Austrian music with Vienna Tonkuenstler Orchestra on 2 tours in USA, Austrian Government. Memberships: American Conductors' Guild; American Symphony League; Bohemians; New York Musicians Club. Hobbies: Reading Non-Fiction; Hiking; Travel; Swimming. Current Management: Judie Janowski, Columbia Artists Management. Address: Columbia Artists Management, 165 West 57th Street, New York, NY 10019, USA.

ALLIK Kristi, b. 6 Feb 1952, Toronto, Ontario, Canada. Composer; Teacher. Education: Studied at Toronto University, at Princeton, and with Milton Babbitt at the University of Southern California. Career: Teacher at Queen's University, Kingston, Ontario, from 1988; Co-founder of electronic music studio at Queen's. Compositions include: Loom Sword River, opera, 1982; Of all the People for voices and ensemble, 1983, Skyharp, sound sculpture, 1991; Multi-media works with electronics Electronic Zen Garden (1983), Rondeau (1985), Cometose (1986), Rhythm and Culture (1986), Till Rust do us Part (1988), Vitamin B-52 (1989); Piano trio, 1979; Lend me your Harp for chorus and chamber orchestra, 1981; Zone Two for ensemble, 1984; Rohan for cello and chamber orchestra, 1988; Trio for clarinet, piano and low voice, 1989. Address: c/o Queen's University, School of Music, Kingston, Ontario, Canada K7L 3N6.

ALLIOT-LUGAZ Colette, b. 20 Jul 1947, Notre-Dame-de-Bellecombe, France. Soprano. Education: Studied at Bonneville with Magda Fonay-Besson in Geneva and at the Opera Studio Paris with Rene Koster and Vera Rozsa; Further study at the Lyon Conservatoire. Career: Has sung widely in France and elsewhere as Mozart's Pamina, Cherubino and Zerlina; Engagements as Messager's Véronique, Rosina and Weber's Aennchen and in operas by Monteverdi, Haydn and Rameau; Has often appeared as Debussy's Mélisande notably at the Lyon Opera in 1980; Festival performances at Aix and Glyndebourne and at the Paris Opéra and the Théâtre de la Monnaie, Brussels; Modern repertory includes La Passion de Gilles by Boesmans, creation 1983, and Berio's opera; Sang Ascanius in Les Troyens at the opening of the Opéra Bastille, Paris in 1990; Appeared as Lully's Alceste at the Théâtre des Champ-Elysées, 1992. Recordings include: Pelléas et Mélisande, conducted by Charles Dutoit; Fragoletto in Les Brigands by Offenbach; Campra's Tancrède. Address: Les Frasses, Notre Dame de Bellecombe, 73590 France.

ALLISTER Jean (Maria), b. 26 Feb 1932, Northern Ireland. Singer. m. (1) Edgar Fleet, 5 Oct 1955, 1 son, (2) René Atkinson, 20 Feb 1974. Education: LRAM, 1954, FRAM, 1968, Royal Academy of Music, London; FGSM, 1976; FGSM Emeritus, 1979. Debut: Royal Albert Hall, London, 1954. Career: Many oratorio and recital performances, England and abroad, 1954-80; Henry Wood Promenade Concerts, 1959-70; Premiere, In Terra Pax, 1960; Three Choirs Festivals, 1961-77; Appeared as Italian Girl in Algiers, Camden Festival, 1961; Sadler's Wells Opera debut, 1962; Sang at Glyndebourne, 1962-68; British premiere, Henze's Novae de Infinito Laudes, Leeds, 1965; Alexander Nevsky, Festival Hall, 1968; L'Ormindo, Munich, 1969; Covent Garden debut as Page in Salome, 1970; Scipio, Handel Opera Society, Herrenhausen and Drottningholm, 1970; Premiere, John Gardner's The Visitors, 1972; Delius's Koanga, Sadler's Wells Opera, 1972; British Premiere, F Martin's Requiem, 1975; Final appearances before retiring from public performance, Jenufa, Opera North, 1980. Recordings: Stravinsky Mass (L'Oiseau Lyre) conducted by C Davis; Pirates of Penzance, Ruddigore, D'Oyly Carte; Gilbert and Sullivan Selection, RCA Victor; Koanga, Groves; Cavalli L'Ormindo, Leppard; The Mikado, Sadler's Wells Orchestra. Publication: Editor, Sing Solo Soprano, 1985. Honour: Minnie Hauk Prize, 1953. Hobbies: Cooking; Bridge; Golf. Address: Little Paddock, Elm Crescent, Charlbury, Oxfordshire OX7 3PZ, England.

ALLMAN Robert, b. 8 June 1927, Melbourne, Australia. Baritone. Education: Studied with Horace Stevens, at the Melbourne Conservatory, with Marjorie Smith in Sydney and with Dominique Modesti in Paris, 1955-57. Career: Sang with the Victoria National Opera Company, 1952, and Royal Opera House, Covent Garden in 1956 as Escamillo; Guest appearances at Sadler's Wells and at Berlin Staatsoper, Hamburg as Iago, Frankfurt, Munich and Cologne until 1967; Appearances in Australia from 1960 as Rigoletto, Jochanaan in Salome, Macbeth, Escamillo, Scarpia, Belcore and Valentine; Sang Don Giovanni, Iago and Nabucco, 1970-71 with the Elizabethan Opera Company; Further guest engagements at Stuttgart, Dusseldorf, Kassel, Zurich and Strasbourg as Macbeth and Simon Boccanegra; Glyndebourne Festival in 1979 as Pizarro; Member of the Australian Opera at Sydney from 1971; Sang Amonasro in Aida at Brisbane in 1988; Many concert performances notably in Messiah. Address: c/o Lyric Opera of Queensland, PO Box 677, South Brisbane, Queensland 4101, Australia.

ALMASI Istvan, b. 8 Dec 1934, Cluj-Napoca, Romania. Ethnomusicologist. m. 24 July 1965, 1 son, 1 daughter. Education: Graduate, Academy of Music, Cluj-Napoca, 1956; DMus, 1989. Career: Researcher, 1957-69, Senior Researcher, 1970-, Folklore Archives, Romanian Academy; Collector of over 6000 folk songs and instrumental melodies. Publications include: Anthology of Hungarian Folk Songs, 1972; 245 Folk Dance Melodies; Hungarian Folk Music From the Szilagy Region; Folk Poetry From the Village Magyargyeromonostor. Honours: Cultural Order, 1970; Ciprian Porumbescu Prize, Romanian Academy, 1981. Memberships: Hungarian Ethnographical Society; Hungarian Kodaly Society; Transylvanian Museum Association; World Federation of Hungarian Musicians & Dancers; Society of Hungarian Musicians in Romania. Hobbies: Gardening; Excursions. Address: Str Unirii 3/42, RO-3400 Cluj-Napoca, Romania.

ALMEIDA Laurindo, b. 2 Sept 1917, Sao Paulo, Brazil (Naturalized US Citizen, 1961). Guitarist; Composer; Music Publisher. m. (1) Maria M Ferreira, 20 May 1944, deceased 1970. m. (2) Deltra Eamon, 3 Aug 1971. Education: Escola Nacional de Musica do Rio de Janeiro. Career: Performed on the Radio and led his own orchestra at the Casino da Urca in Rio de Janeiro; Settled in the US, 1947; Was soloist with Stan Kenton's Orchestra, 1947-50; Performed in and composed for films; Was Founder-Director, Brazilliance Music Publishing Company, 1952-; Toured widely as a Recitalist and as a Soloist with Symphony Orchestras; Toured Japan for a month as soloist in Concerto de Aranguey with the Modern Jazz Quartet, 1991; Performed with the Modern Jazz Quartet, Carnegie Hall, 1991; Toured major cities of New Zealand and played with the Symphony in Auckland, 1993; Performed as Brazilian Reflection in Wigmore Hall with Deltra Eamon, his wife, 1993. Compositions: First Concerto for Guitar and Orchestra. Recordings: First Concerto for Guitar and Orchestra (soloist Laurindo Almeida), 1980; Outra Vex, (L Almeida Trio), 1992. Address: 4104 Wtizel Drive, Sherman Oaks, California 91423, USA.

ALONSO Odon, b. 28 Feb 1925, La Baneza, Leon, Spain. Conductor. Education: Studied at the Madrid Conservatoire and in Siena and Vienna. Career: Choral Director of the Madrid Soloists, 1952, specializing in Music of the Spanish Renaissance and Baroque; Conducted the Spanish National Orchestra, 1952-56, Madrid Philharmonic, 1956-58; Directed the Zarzuela Theatre at Madrid, 1956-57; Conducted the Spanish Radio and Television Orchestra from 1968; Guest engagements at the Vienna Volksoper, New York City Opera, Teatro Liceo Barcelona and the Madrid Opera. Recordings include: Guitar Concertos by Vivaldi and Rodrigo, with Narcisco Ypes; Turina's Rapsodia Sinfonica.

ALONSO-CRESPO Eduardo, b. 18 Mar 1956, Tucuman, Argentina. Composer; Conductor. Education: Civil Engineer, National University of Tucuman; Professor of Piano, School of Musical Arts, National University of Tucuman; MFA, Conducting, Carnegie Mellon University, Pittsburgh. Debut: Conducting: Carnegie Mellon Philharmonic in Ginastera, USA, 1987; Tucuman Symphony in Alonso-Crespo, Mozart, Brahms, Argentina, 1988. Career: Assistant Conductor, Pittsburgh Civic Orchestra, 1988-90; Associate Conductor, Carnegie Mellon Philharmonic, 1989-91; Music Director, Tucuman Symphony Orchestra and Carnegie Mellon Contemporary Ensemble, 1989-; Orquesta de Tucuman, seasons 1991, 1992; Carnegie Mellon Wind Ensemble, 1991-92; Conductor-in-Residence, Carnegie Mellon University, 1991-92; Guest conducting, Argentina, USA. Compositions include: Gorbachev, 2-Act Opera; Juana, La Loca, 1-Act Opera; Putzi, 1-Act Opera; Medea, Ballet, for Chorus and Orchestra; Piano Concerto N 1, Commentaries on Three Waltzes by Alberdi; Two Stories of Birds for Orchestra; Sinfonietta for String Orchestra. Hobbies: Books on Linguistics and Sociology. Address: Marcos Paz 250, Tucuman 4000, Argentina.

ALOTIN Yardena, b. 19 Oct 1930, Tel Aviv, Israel. Composer. Education: Studied at the Israel Academy of Music with Oedoen Partos. Career: Commissions from the Tel Aviv Foundation and James Galway (for Yefei Nof, 1978); Pianist and piano teacher. Compositions include: Cantata for unaccompanied choir, 1956; A Painful Exile for mezzo and orchestra, 1958; Cello sonata, 1976; Yefei Nof for flute, 1978; Festive Song for chorus, 1984. Address: c/o ACUM Ltd, PO Box 14220, Acum House, Rothschild Boulevard 118, Tel-Aviv 61140, Israel.

ALPENHEIM Ilse Von, b. 11 Feb 1927, Innsbruck, Austria. Pianist. m. Antal Dorati, 16 Dec 1969, deceased 1988. Education: Studied with Franz Ledwinka and Winfried Wolf, Salzburg Mozarteum. Career: Soloist with major European and USA Orchestras; Many engagements as Recitalist and Chamber-Music Player. Recordings: For Desto; Turnabout; Vox, Philips & Pantheon; Haydn Piano Music Complete, Schubert Chamber Music with Piano Complete.

ALPERIN Yoram, b. 1945, Romania. Cellist. Education: Studied with Uzi Wiezel, Rubin Academy of Music, Tel Aviv. Career: Member and solo appearances with Israel Philharmonic, 1971-; Co-founded Jerusalem String Trio, 1977, giving many concerts, Israel and Europe, 1981-; Repertoire includes String Trios by Beethoven, Dohnanyi, Mozart, Reger, Schubert and Tanyev, Piano Quartets by Beethoven, Brahms, Dvorak, Mozart and Schumann; Concerts with Radu Lupu and Daniel Adni. Recordings: Several albums. Address: c/o Anglo Swiss Management, Suite 35-37, Morley House, 320 Regent Street, London W1R 5AD, England.

ALSOP Marin. Education: Yale University; Master Degree, Juilliard School. Career: Creative Conductor Chair, St Louis Symphony, 1995; Principal Conductor, Colorado Symphony, since 1993. Honours include: Prize-Winner, Leopold Stokowski Conducting Competition, American Symphony Orchestra, 1989; Awarded Leonard Bernstein Conducting Fellowship, Tanglewood Music Center, 1988, 1989. Address: Hebbelstrabe 61, 50968 Koln, Germany.

ALSTED Birgitte, b. 15 June 1942, Odense, Denmark. Composer; Violinist. Education: Violin Studies, Royal Danish Academy of Music; Music Academy, Warsaw, Poland; Composition Seminars with Per Norgard, Copenhagen. Career: Performer of new music in, Det unge Tonekunstnerselskab; Kvinder i Musik; Danmarks Radio, TV Acting Musician, experimental Theatre; Teacher, Compositions performed in DUT, Radio, TV, KIM, Paris, Rome, New York, Mexico City, Berlin, Stockholm, London; Commissions, Contemporary Dance Theatre, London, Nordiske Forum 88, Danmarks Radio. Compositions include: Klumpe, 1972; Stykke 2, 1973; 12 toner i Zoo, 1973; Smedierne i Granada, 1976; Strygekvartet i CD, 1977; Konkurrence, 1979; Haiku-Sange, 1979; Solen og jeg, 1981; Gentagne Gange, 1980; Solen på Moddingen, 1982; Phasing Moon Facing Changing, 1983; Antigone, 1983; Kaere Allesammen, 1984; På Afstand af Bolgen, 1984-85; Om Natten, 1985; Skiftetid, 1985; Kindleins Schlaflied, 1986; Frokost i det Gronne, 1985; Nostalgisk Extranummer, 1985; Extra Nostalgisk nr 2, 1986; Espressione Emotionale, 1987; Fatsy, 1987; Dromme-spil, 1988; Opbrud, 1988; Vakst, 1989; Lyst, 1990; 2 sange til Doden, 1990; Episoder til Thomas, 1991; Havet ved Forår, 1991; Karen's Å, 1992; Unoder, 1992; Natterdag, 1992; Berceuse Neptunoise, 1993; Spring I, 1994; Stelle, 1995; Sorgsang, 1995; Hojsang, 1995. Recordings: Antigone; Frokost i det Gronne; Vakst; Natterdag; To Sange til Doden; Sorgsang. Honours: Komponistforemingens Jubilaeumslegat, 1985; Gustav Enna's Mindelegat, 1988; Several grants, Art Foundation of Danish State, including 3 years, 1980-83. Memberships: Dansk Komponistforening; Kvinder i Musik; Det Unge Tonekunstnerselskab. Hobbies: Tea Drinking; Talking; Psychology; Meditation. Address: Dansk Komponistforening, Grabrodretorv 16, DK-1154 Kobenhavn K, Denmark.

ALTENA Marius van, b. 10 Oct 1938, Amsterdam, Netherlands. Singer (Counter-Tenor). m. Marianne Syses, 2 sons. Education: Piano Diploma A&B, Singing Diploma A&B, Conservatory of Music, Amsterdam. Debut: Germany, 1970. Career: Concerts throughout Europe and the US with early music groups; Further tours to Japan and Australia; Holland Festival, 1974, in Eumelio by Agazzari and in Seelewig by Staden; Returned 1980, for Gluck's L'Isle de Merlin; Performed with Vienna-based group Spectaculum, 1980-84, in stage works by Fux, Leopold I and Conti; Later turned to conducting. Recordings include: Leopold I's Il figliuol prodigo; Madrigals by Monteverdi (RCA); Bach Concertos with Harmoncourt and Gustav Leonhardt, 1985; Hodges Ensemble with Paul V Nevel, 1990-97; Camerata Trajectina, 1988-97. Hobbies: Tennis; Billiards; Walking; Reading. Address: Bloemberg 8, 7924 PW Veeningen, Netherlands.

ALTENBURGER Christian, b. 5 Sept 1957, Heidelberg, Germany. Violinist. Education: Graduated Vienna Academy of Music, 1973; Graduated, Juilliard School, New York, 1978; Studied Violin with father and Dorothy DeLay. Debut: First appearance in 1964; Formal debut, Recital, Musikverein, Vienna, 1976. Career: Soloist with various major orchestras in Europe and the USA; With Bruno Canino played the Sonata by Strauss, Schoenberg's Fantasy and Bartók's 2nd Sonata, Salzburg Festival, 1990. Recordings: For Arabesque; ProArte.

ALTMEYER Jeannine, b. 2 May 1948, La Habra, California, USA. Soprano. Education: Studied with Martial Singher and Lotte Lehmann in Santa Barbara, California; Attended the Salzburg Mozarteum. Career: Operatic debut as the Heavenly Voice in Don Carlos, Metropolitan Opera, New York, 25 September 1971; Appeared with the Chicago Lyric Opera, 1972, in Salzburg, 1973 and at Bayreuth, 1979; Member of the Wurttemberg State Theatre, Stuttgart, 1975-79; Then sang throughout Europe, achieving success as a Wagnerian; Roles: Elsa, Eva, Sieglinde, Isolde, Elisabeth, Gutrune and Brünnhilde; Sang Isolde at Bayreuth, 1986; Paris Opéra and Los Angeles, 1987 as Chrysothemis, Isolde; Brünnhilde in Götterdämmerung at the Zurich Opera, 1989; Sang Leonore at La Scala, 1990. Recordings: Sang Brünnhilde in The Ring under Janowski; Video of Die Walküre, in production from Bayreuth. Address: c/o Theateragentur Dr Germinal Hilbert, Maximilianstrasse 22, D-8000 Munich 22, Germany.

ALTMEYER Theo(dor Daniel), b. 16 Mar 1931, Eschweiler, Aachen, Germany. Singer (Tenor). Education: Studied in Cologne with Clemens Glettenberg, 1953-56. Career: Sang at the Städtische Oper Berlin, 1955-60, notably in the 1958 premiere of Diary of a Madman by Searle; Sang at Hanover from 1960, in operas by Rossini, Lortzing and Mozart, and as Pfitzner's Palestrina; Sang in Stuttgart from 1958; Vienna from 1969; Many concert appearances, often as the Evangelist in the Passions of Bach; Guest engagements in France, Austria, Italy, Belgium, England, Switzerland and Holland; Festivals of Venice, Lucerne, Montreux, Ansbach, Vienna, Florence and Naples; Professor at the Hannover Musikhochschule from 1974. Recordings: St Matthew and St John Passions of Bach, Dettinger Te Deum by Handel, Beethoven and Haydn Masses, Bach Cantatas; Evangelist in the St Luke Passion by Telemann and the St John Passion by Schütz; Schütz St Matthew Passion. Address: Hochschule für Musik und Theater Hannover, Emmichplatz 1, 3 Hannover, Germany.

ALTWEGG Raffaele, b. 17 Nov 1938, Tettenhall, England. Musician. m. Barbara von Schulthess, 17 Aug 1968, 1 son, 1 daughter. Education: MB, St Thomas's Hospital, University of London, 1961; Master Classes with Pablo Casals and Paul Grummer. Career: Soloist, 1957-; Leader, Cello Section, Tonhalle Orchestra, Zurich, Tonhalle Quartet, 1958-60; Founder Member, Ensemble Die Kammermusiker, Zurich, 1960-; Professor, Zurich Academy of Music, 1960-75; Conductor, Master Classes for Cello, 1963-; Called upon by Australian Government to help build up the new National Music School in Canberra, 1968-70; Professor, Basle Academy of Music, 1970-75; State Expert for all Music Diplomas, 1976-; Director, Music School, Zollikon, 1979-; Founder, Conductor, Zollikon Orchestra, 1985-95. Recordings: Numerous. Honours: Recipient of many honours and awards. Memberships: Schweizerischer Tonkünstlerverein; Schweizerischer Musikpädagogischer Verband. Hobbies: Reading; Gardening. Address: Schlossbergstrasse 27, CH-8702 Zollikon, Zurich, Switzerland.

ALVA Luigi, b. 10 Apr 1927, Lima, Peru. Singer (Tenor). Education: Studied with Rosa Moarales in Lima and with Emilio Ghiradini and Ettore Campogalliani in Milan. Debut: Sang at Lima in the Zarauela Luisa Fernanda, 1949; Beppe in Pagliacci, 1950. Career: Sang Paolino in Cimarosa's Il matrimonio segreto at La Scala, 1955; Salzburg Festival, 1957-58, as Fenton in Falstaff and Fernando in Cosi fan tutte; Sang Rossini's Almaviva more than 300 times, starting with La Scala, 1956; Returned to Milan in 1958 for the local premiere of Janácek's The Cunning Little Vixen and world premieres of Una domanda di matrimonio by Luciano Chailly and Malipiero's La donna e mobile; appeared in Holland Festival in 1959 in Il mondo della luna by Haydn and made his Covent Garden debut in 1960; Glyndebourne Festival, 1961-62, as Nemorino in L'elisir d'amore; Aix-en-Provence from 1960, Vienna Staatsoper from 1961; Metropolitan Opera, 1964-76 as Ernesto in Don Pasquale, Almaviva, Lindoro in L'Italiana in Algeri and Mozart's Tamino; Other appearances in Hamburg, Berlin, Moscow, Edinburgh, Stockholm, Lisbon, Venice, Florence and Mexico City; Artistic Director of Prolirica in Lima from 1982; Retired as singer, 1989. Recordings include: Il Barbiere di Siviglia, Il matrimonio segreto and Falstaff (Columbia); La Cenerentola (Deutsche Grammophon); Handel's Alcina, L'Italiana in Algeri and Mozart's Il re pastore (Decca); Haydn's L'Isola disabitata (Philips); Alfonso und Estrella by Schubert (Melodram). Address: Via Moscova 46/3, 20121 Milan, Italy.

ALVARES Eduardo, b. 10 June 1947, Rio de Janeiro, Brazil. Singer (Tenor). Career: Stated career in Europe, (debut as Don José) Linz, Frankfurt, Vienna and Stuttgart, returned to Brazil and then sang Des Grieux (Manon Lescaut) at Metropolitan, and Netherlands Opera (also Dick Johnson in Fanciulla del West), Manrico in Il Trovatore for Opera North and Calaf in Turandot for Scottish Opera; English National Opera as Radames in Aida, 1985; Teatro Municipal Rio de Janeiro, 1987-88, as Don José and Bacchus; Other roles include Alfredo, Gabriele Adorno, Don Carlos, Faust, Werther and Alva in Lulu; Wexford Festival, 1983-84, in Hans Heiling and The Kiss. Address: c/o English National Opera, London Colisseum, St Martin's Lane, London WC2, England.

ALVAREZ Carlos, b. 1963, Malaga, Spain. Singer (Baritone). Education: Studied at the Malaga Conservatory. Career: Sang Morales in Carmen with Luis Lima and gave concert with him at the Teatro Arriga in Bilbao; Further appearances at the Teatro La Zarzuela, Madrid, Teatro Colon Buenos Aires, Vienna Staatsoper, La Scala Milan and Royal Opera, Covent Garden; Operas have included Eugene Onegin (at Madrid), La Boheme, Il Barbiere di Siviglia (Zürich), La Traviata and Fedora (London), Don Carlos (Mannheim) and Madama Butterfly (Milan); Frequent appearances with Placido Domingo, including Il Guarnay by Gomes at Bonn and concerts in Tokyo, Berlin, Madrid and Seville; Les Troyens with the London Symphony at the Barbican Hall, under Colin Davis, 1993; Guest engagements in New York, Geneva and Washington. Address: c/o Opernhaus Zürich, Falkenstrasse 1, CH-8008 Zürich, Switzerland.

ALWYN Kenneth, b. 28 July 1928, Croydon, England. Conductor. m. Mary Law, 2 daughters. Education: Graduate, Royal Schools of Music, London, 1951; Associate, Royal Academy of Music, London, 1958. Debut: London. Career: Conductor, Royal Choral Union, New Zealand; Sadler's Wells Theatre Ballet; Royal Ballet, Royal Opera House, Covent Garden; BBC Staff Conductor; Radio and television presenter. Compositions: Various concert radio and television commissions. Recordings: Major recordings with leading orchestras; Conductor of first stereophonie recordings by Decca with London Symphony Orchestra, 1958, Tchaikovsky's 1812 Overture; Complete recording, Hiawatha, with Welsh National Opera for Decca, 1991. Honour: Mann's Prize for Conducting, 1951. Memberships: Incorporated Society of Musicians; BBC's Central Music Advisory Committee. Hobby: Flying. Address: Horelands, Broadford Bridge, Billingshurst, Sussex RH14 9EA, England.

AM Magnar, b. 9 Apr 1952, Trondheim, Norway. Composer. Education: Studied Organ and Composition, Bergen Conservatory, 1971; Advanced training in composition, Lidholm, Stockholm, 1971-72. Compositions include: Prayer for soprano chorus and string orchestra, 1972; Song for brass and percussion, 1974; Dance for harp, guitar and harpsichord, 1977; Octet, 1977; Point Zero for soprano, alto, chorus, children's chorus and amateur orchestra, 1979; 2 alternative versions; Ajar, double-bass concerto, 1981; A Cage-bird's Dream, multimedia piece, 1981; Inconceivable Father for Child Soprano, children's chorus, bass clarinet, timpani, double bass and organ, 1982; My Planet, My Soul, symphony, 1982; Piano pieces; Like a Leaf on the River, for guitar, 1983; Omen, for violin, horn, piano, 1983; Conqilia for violin, horn, piano, recitor, 1984; Right Through All This, for orchestra, 1985; Freetonal Conversations, for violin, cello and piano, 1986; Hovering depths for double bass, 1986; A Miracle and a Tear, for mixed chorus, 1987; If We Lift As One, for orchestra, 1988; Tonebath, experience room, 1989; And Let the Boat Slip Quietly Out, for orchestra, 1989;...And Life, an oratorio, 1990; Quiet Ruby, for choir, 1992; Glimpses of an Embrace, for trumpet, horn and mountain echoes, 1994; Among Mirrors, for violin, cello and piano, 1995; Be Quiet, My Heart, for orchestra, 1995; The Silver Thread for string quartet, 1996; On the Wings of the Ka-bird, for choir, 1996; The Wondering and the Wonder, for orchestra and dolphins, 1996; You are Loved, for soprano, choir (SSA), two horns and harp, 1997. Recordings: Hovering Depths; Study on a Norwegian Hymn; Point Zero; Like a Leaf on the River. Address: Vevendelvegen 46, 6100 Volda, Norway.

AM BACH Rudolf, b. 6 June 1919, Trogen, Switzerland. Pianist; Professor. m., 2 children. Education: Music Conservatory, 3 years; Private student of Professor Emil Frey, Zürich; Teacher's Diploma (Piano), 1938; Soloist's Diploma summa cum laude, 1939; Studies with Professor Frédéric Lamond (student of Franz Liszt), London, 1940. Career: Teacher of Piano, Collegium, Winterthur, 1939-87; Piano recitals, Zürich, 1941-43, 1945, 1948-73; Concert tours and recitals, UK, 1951, 1956, 1958, France, Germany, Austria, Spain, Canada (1967); Radio recitals including Radio London, 1958 (Swiss compositions); Radio Zürich; Works performed include 3 Siècles de Pianoforte; 47 Concertos and various works by F Busoni, R Strauss, Scriabin, Ravel, Prokofiev. Recordings include: Anthologie Schweizer Musik; Gustav Weber, Idyll on Faust op 9, pieces for piano; Frank Martin, Petite Symphonie Concertante; Felix Mendelssohn, Songs without Words and Works by Franz Liszt Années de Pèlerinage, Switzerland; Bach; Mozart; Mendelssohn Fantasy op 28; De Falla 4 piezas espagnoles; Ottorino Respighi piano works. Hobby: Playing chamber music in trio. Address: Agnesstrasse 8, CH-8004 Zürich, Switzerland.

AMADUCCI Bruno, b. 5 Jan 1935, Viganello-Lugano, Switzerland. Conductor. Education: Conservatorio Giuseppe Verdi, Milan, Italy; Ecole normale de Musique, Paris, France. Career: 1st Concert, Mozart Requiem, Swiss Radio Monteceneri, 1951; 1st Public Concert with Alfred Cortot and Orchestra, Pomeriggi Musicali, Milan, 1951; Former Conductor, Metropolitan Opera, Vienna State Opera, Vienna Symphony Orchestra, Paris Opera, Deutsche Oper, Berlin; Member of Jury, Concorso Voci Verdiane, Busseto, Italy and Concours Internationale, Geneva. Publications: L'Amfiparnaso de Orazio Vecchi par rapport au dévéloppement de l'expression du langage musicale, 1951; La Musica nella Svizzera Italiana e La Presenzadella Radio-Orchestra, 1973; The Puccini Dynasty, 1973. Address: Casella Postale, Lugano, CH-6901, Switzerland.

AMARA Lucine, b. 1 March 1925, Hartford, Connecticut, USA. Singer (Soprano). Education: Studied voice with Stella Eisner-Eyn in San Francisco; Attended the Music Academy of West Santa Barbara, 1947 and the University of Southern California, Los Angeles, 1949-50. Career: Member, San Francisco Opera Chorus, 1945-46; Concert debut, San Francisco Opera, sang at the Hollywood Bowl, 1948; Metropolitan Opera debut, 1950; Regular Appearances there in subsequent seasons; Sang at the Glyndebourne Festival, 1954-58, as Strauss's Ariadne and Mozart's Donna Elvira; Edinburgh Festival 1954, Vienna State Opera 1960, Russia 1965, China 1983; Major Roles, Gluck's Euridice, Verdi's Aida and Leonora (Il Trovatore), Puccini's Mimi and Leoncavallo's Nedda; Sang Mère Marie in Dialogues des Carmélites at the Met, 1987; Sang with the Metropolitan Opera for 41 years. Recordings: Bohème as Musetta, Beecham conducting; Lohengrin as Elsa, Leinsdorf conducting; Verdi Requiem, Ormandy conducting. Honour: 1st Prize, Atwater Kent Auditions, 1948. Memberships: Sigma Alpha Iota. Address: 260 West End Avenue, Suite 7A, New York, NY 10023, USA.

AMBACHE Diana (Bella), b. 18 June 1948, Kent, England. Pianist. m. Jeremy Polmear, 12 Feb 1982. Education: Bedales School; Royal Academy of Music, 1966-67; Diploma, LRAM Performers, 1967, BA, Honours, 1970, Sheffield University,

1967-70. Debut: Purcell Room, 1979. Career: Founder and Musical Director, Mozart Chamber Orchestra, 1977-83; Founder and Musical Director, Ambache Chamber Orchestra, 1984-; Concert tours in India and Nepal, 1977; International tourinmg to 30 different countries; First performances of Complete Version in Modern Times of Mozart, Rondo in D, K386, 1980; Dussek Piano Concerto in G Minor Opus 49, 1981; Fantasy for Piano by Francis Shaw, 1982; Many UK premieres of piano concertos and chamber music by G Taillefere, Clara Schumann, Fanny Mendelssohn, Kozeluch, Benda, Michael Haydn and others; Concert series Women of Note, from 1995; Played Mozart's Concerto K271 at the South Bank, London, 1997. Recordings: Numerous including: Mozart Pianos Concertos K453 and K459 on Teldec's Academy Collection; Sweet Melancholy: 20th Century oboe and piano English Collection on Unicorn; Artistic Director of Women of Note concert series in major London venues. Honours: Gold Medal, Associated Board, 1966; Scholarship to Royal Academy of Music, 1967; Exhibition from Sheffield University, 1970. Hobbies: Travel; Cycling; Walking. Address: 9 Beversbrook Road, London N19 4QG, England.

AMECHER Maryanne, b. 25 Feb 1942, Kates, Pennsylvania, USA. Composer; Performer; Mixed-Media Artist. Education: Studied composition with George Rochberg at the University of Pennsylvania, BFA 1964; Studies with Karlheinz Stockhausen and at the Universities of Pennsylvania and Illinois (Computer Science). Career: Taught in the Experimental Music Studio at the School of Engineering, University of Illinois, 1964-66; Creative Associate at the Center of Creative and Performing Arts, State University, New York, 1966-67; Fellow at the Massachusetts Institute of Technology, 1972-76; Fellow at Radcliffe College, Harvard, 1978-79; Sound experiments with John Cage and Merce Cunningham; Has initiated various projects with natural sound experiments in the local environemnt. Compositions include: City Links, performed in New York, Buffalo, Paris and Chicago, 1967-79; Lecture on the Weather, collaboration with Cage, 1975; Remainder, dance music for Merce Cunningham, for Tape and Electronics, 1976; Mixed Media works include Sound-Joined Rooms, 1980-82; Close Up; Intelligent Life, 1982; Music for the Webern Car. Honours include: Multi-Media Award from New York State Council of Arts, 1978-79; Composition Award from the National Endowment of the Arts, 1978-79; Beard Arts Fund, 1980. Address: ASCAP, ASCAP Building, One Lincoln Plaza, New York, NY 10023, USA.

AMES Richard, b. 20 Aug 1931, Cleveland, Ohio, USA. Singer (Tenor). Education: Studied with Mario Basiola in Milan; Studied with Max Lorenz, 1966-68. Career: Sang first as Baritone, debut in New Orleans, 1958, as Masetto; Further appearances, Philadelphia and Boston, then sang Don Giovanni in Munster, 1961; Wuppertal, 1962-65, as Iago, Amfortas, and Nick Shadow in The Rake's Progress; Debut as tenor as Siegmund in Die Walküre, Oldenburg, 1967; With Graz Opera, 1968-, notably as Palestrina, Florestan, Otello and Lohengrin; Appeared in premiere of Schwertsik's Der Lange Weg zur grossen Mauer, Lucerne, 1975; Sang as Herod in Salome, in Rome, Monte Carlo and Brussels; Further engagements in Leipzig, Budapest, Zagreb, Dortmund, Mannheim and Basle as Mime, the Captain in Wozzeck and Aegisthus in Elektra; Herod at Augsburg, 1988. Address: c/o Deutsches Tourneetheater, Dambor Strasse 11, 8900 Augsburg, Germany.

AMIRKHANIAN Charles (Benjamin), b. 19 Jan 1945, Fresno, California, USA. Composer. Education: BA, English Literature, California State University, Fresno, 1967; MA, Interdisciplinary Creative Arts, San Francisco State University, 1969; MFA, Mills College, Oakland, California, 1980; Studied electronic music and sound recording techniques with David Behrman, Robert Ashley and Paul de Marinis. Career: Composer-in-Residence, Ann Halprin's Dancers Workshop Company, 1968-69; Music Director, KPFA Radio, Berkeley, California, 1969-; Lecturer, San Francisco State University, 1977-80. Compositions: Live-Performance: Canticle No 1 for Percussion Quartet, 1963; Canticle No 2 for Flute and Timpani, 1963; Canticle No 3 for Percussion Trio, 1966; Canticle No 4 for Percussion Quartet, 1966; Ode to Gravity, Theatre Piece, 1967; Spoilt Music, Theatre Piece, 1979; Text-Sound (Tape): Oratora Konkurso Rezulto: Autoro de la Jara (Portrait of Lou Harrison), 1970; Each'll, 1971; If In Is, 1971; Sound Nutrition, 1972; Heavy Aspirations (Portrait of Nicolas Slonimsky), 1973; Seatbelt Seatbelt, 1973; She She and She, 1974; Mahogany Ballpark, 1976; Dutiful Ducks, 1977; Audience, 1978; Dreams Freud Dreamed, 1979; Hypothetical Moments (in the Intellectual Life of Southern California), 1981; Dog of Stravinsky, 1982; The Real Perpetuum Mobile, 1984. Address: c/o ASCAP, One Lincoln Plaza, New York, NY 10023, USA.

AMMANN Raymond, b. 7 April 1957, Basel, Switzerland. Ethnomusicologist. m. Lisette Babois, 2 May 1959, 1 son, 1 daughter. Education: University of Basel; Doctoral Dissertation, University of Bern; Habilitation, University of Innsbrück. Career: Field Research Bering in the Strait Region, and in Melanesia; Director of Ethnmusicological and Ethnochoreological Research at Agence de Developpement de la Culture, Kanak, New Caledonia, 1992-97. Recordings: 3 Musical Cassettes of Traditional Music of the Loyalty Islands; 1 CD of Traditional Music of New Caledonia. Publications: Les danses kanak, une introduction, 1994; Kanak Dance and Music, 1997. Honour: Dr phil, University of Berne. Memberships: International Council For Traditional Music; European Seminary in Ethnomusicology. Hobby: Triathlon. Address: c/o Agence de Development de la Culture Kanak, BP 378, 98848 Nouméa, New Caledonia.

AMOYAL Pierre, b. 22 Jun 1949, Paris, France. Violinist. Education: Studied at the Paris Conservatoire and with Jascha Heifetz between 1966 and 1971. Debut: Paris 1971, in the Berg Concerto, with the Orchestre de Paris. Career: Appearances with the BBC Symphony Orchestra, Hallé Orchestra, London Philharmonic, Philharmonia, Berlin Philharmonic, Boston Symphony, Cleveland Orchestra, Philadelphia Orchestra and Orchestras in Canada and France; Conductors include Karajan, Ozawa, Boulez, Dutoit, Sanderling, Maazel, Solti, Prêtre, Masur and Rozhdestvensky; Plays Concertos by Berg, Schoenberg and Dutilleux, in addition to the standard repertory; Played Brahms Concerto with the Royal Philharmonic Orchestra, 1995; Artist in Residence at Beaumaris Festival in Wales, 1995; Recitals at St John's Smith Square for the BBC; New York Carnegie Hall debut 1985; Professor at the Paris Conservatoire from 1977; Currently Professor at the Lausanne Conservatoire. Recordings: Concertos by Dutilleux, Respighi and Saint Saëns with the Orchestre National conducted by Charles Dutoit; Chamber music (sonatas by Brahms, Fauré and Franck) with Pascal Rogé; Schoenberg Concerto with the London Symphony Orchestra conducted by Boulez. Honours include: Ginette Neveu Prize, 1963; Paganini Prize, 1964; Enescu Prize, 1970. Address: c/o Marks Management Ltd, 14 New Burlington Street, London W1X 1FF, England.

AMRAM David, b. 17 Nov 1930, Philadelphia, Pennsylvania, USA. Composer; Conductor; Multi-Instrumentalist. m. Lora Lee, 7 Jan 1979, 1 son, 2 daughters. Education: Ba, George Washington University. Career includes: Pioneer of the French horn in jazz and Latin music during the late 1940's; World tours as a jazz player, multi-instrumentalist, folklorist, composer and conductor; Director of Music, New York Shakespeare Festival, 1956-67; Director of Music, Lincoln Center Theater, 1963-65; Director of Music, Peoples Concerts and Parks Concerts, Brooklyn Philharmonic, 1971-; Guest Conducts annually with 14 orchestras including Montreal, Toronto, Grant Park and Milwaukee Orchestras. Compositions: Over 100 orchestral, choral, operatic and chamber works including American Dance Suite (all published by C F Peters); Commissioned work to celebrate the opening of the Jefferson Wing of the Library of Congress, 1995; A Little Rebellion: Thomas Jefferson, for narrator and orchestra. Recordings: Over 40 recordings of his own compositions; 15 albums as soloist, and as feature performer with Lionel Hampton, Charlie Mingus, Oscar Pettiford, Mary Lou Williams, Kenny Durham. Publication: Vibrations: The Musical Times of David Amram, 1968. Symphonic Works performed by New York Philharmonic, Boston Symphony, Philadelphia Orchestras, one of US 20 most performed composers of concert music, since 1974. Memberships: BMI. Hobbies: Farming; Raising his family. Current Management: Barnd Ostentag, New York, USA. Address: c/o Ostentag, 501 5th Avenue, New York City, NY 10017, USA.

AMSELLEM Norah, b. 1970, Paris, France. Singer (Soprano).Education: Studied in New York; Participant in Met's Young Artist Development Program. Debut: Michaela at the Metropolitan in Opera, 1995. Career: Concert debut at Alice Tully Hall, New York; Opera appearances as Michaela at the Opera Bastille, Paris, and Lyon; Liu at the Met and Mozart's Countess at the 1997 Glyndebourne Festival; Season 1997-98 as Michaela at the Met, under James Levine and with Placido Domingo, Liu in debut at the San Francisco Opera; Norina (Don Pasquale) and Gounod's Juliette at the Grand Theatre, Bordeaux; Manon of Massenet at La Scala, Milan and in Toulouse and Bordeaux; Michaela in Monte Carlo and Japan. Address: c/o Metropolitan Opera, Lincoln Center, New York, NY 10023, USA.

AMY Gilbert, b. 29 Aug 1936, Paris, France. Conductor; Music Educator; Composer. Education: Studied piano with Loriod and composition with Mihaud and Messiaen at the Paris Conservatory, attended Boulez's courses in new music at Darmstadt. Career: Commenced conducting 1962; Director, Domaine Musical, Paris, 1967-73; Founder-Conductor, Nouvel Orchestre Philharmonique de Radio France, Paris, 1976-81; Taught analysis and composition, Yale University, 1982; Director, Lyons Conservatory, 1984-. Compositions: Orchestral: Mouvements, 1958; Diaphonies, 1962; Antiphonies for 2 orchestras, 1964; Triade, 1965; Chant, 1968-69, revised 1980; Refrains, 1972; Orchestrale, 1985; Chamber: Piano Sonata, 1957-60; Epigrammes for piano, 1961; Inventions for ensemble, 1959-61; Alpha-Beth for wind sextet, 1963-64; Cycle for percussion sextet; 7 Bagatelles for organ, 1975; Quasi scherzando for cello, 1981; Vocal: Cantata breve for soprano and 3 instruments, 1957; D'un Espace deploye for soprano, 2 pianos and 2 orchestral groups, 1973; Strophe for soprano and orchestra, 1965-77; Une saison en enfer for soprano, piano, percussion and tape; Messe for soloists, chorus and orchesta, 1982-3; Ecrits sur toiles for reciter and small ensemble, 1983; Posauren for four trombones, 1986; Choros for soloists, chorus and orchestra, 1989; String Quartet, 1992. Address: c/o Conservatoire National superieur de Musique de Lyon, 3 rue de l'Angile, 69005 Lyon, France.

ANCONA Solange, b. 14 Aug 1943, Paris, France. Composer. Education: Studied with Messiaen at the Paris Conservatoire, and with Boulez, Maderna, Stockhausen and Pousseur in Darmstadt and Cologne; Electroacoustic music at the Schola Cantorum in Paris, 1968-69. Compositions: Maiamoi for 5 voices and ensemble, 1967; Chtaslivi for ensemble and tape, 1971; Slantzo III for soprano and orchestra, after Dante, 1975; All'eterno dal tempo for organ, 1982; Preludio for 2 violas, 1989. Address: c/o SACEM, 225 avenue Charles de Gaulle, 92521 Neuilly sur Seine Cedex, France.

ANDERSEN Bo, b. 10 Nov 1963, Denmark. Composer; Organist; Musicologist. Education: Department of Musicology and Nordic Philology, University of Copenhagen, 1984-99; Composition with Ib Norholm, 1988-95, music theory with Yngve Trede and orchestration with Erik Norby, Royal Danish Academy of Music, Copenhagen; Examination as Organist at the Royal Academy, Copenhagen, 1990, after private studies. Career: Numerous performances of most of his works, many commissions from ensembles and soloists. Compositions: Main Works: Vier Stücke im alten Stil, for string quartet, 1989; Drei kleine Stücke für das Pianoforte, 1989; Annähernd eine Sonate, for cello and klavier, 1989-90; Pezzo Concertante, 4 accordians and 2 percussionists, 1991; Serenade for 3 woodwinds, flute, clarinet and bassoon, 1991; Invocation for solo flute, 1993; Forthcoming works: Three Flowersongs for soprano, viola and guitar, texts ny Kirsten Ahlemann; Growth, chamber opera with text by Sanne Bjerg; Concerto for trumpet and orchestra; Symphony, Roaring Dragon and Singing Phoenix. Recordings: Serenade; Invocation for solo flute. Honours: Several grants from Danish Composers' Association and Danish Arts Council; Astrid and Aksel Agerby Memorial Grant, 1993. Membership: Danish Composers' Association; Society for Publication of Danish Music; Musica Nova. Hobbies: Modern art exhibitions; Poetry; Motorcycling. Address: c/o S E Mielche, Frederiksberg Allé 78 1.mf, Dk-1820 Frederiksberg C, Denmark.

ANDERSEN Karsten, b. 16 Feb 1920, Kristiania (now Oslo), Norway. Conductor; Violinist. Education: Studied in Norway and Italy. Career: Violinist and Conductor; Music Director, Stavanger Symphony Orchestra, 1945-65; Bergen Symphony Orchestra, 1965-85; Iceland Symphony Orchestra, 1973-80; Guest Conductor of Orchestras in Europe and the USA. Recordings: For Composers Recording Inc: Norskkultturrads Klassikerserie; Philipps, including Svendsen's Concertos for Violin and Cello and Egge's Symphony No 1.

ANDERSEN Stig Fogh, b. 24 Feb 1950; Horsholm, Denmark. Singer (Tenor). m. Tina Kibert. Education: Studied at the Aarhus and Copenhagen Conservatories. Career: Sang at Aarhus from 1978 and made debut at Royal Opera Copenhagen, 1980, as Macduff in Macbeth; Many appearances in Copenhagen and elsewhere as guest, singing Tamino (1985), Sergei in Shostakovich's Lady Macbeth (1990), Don José (1992), Leander in Maskarade, Don Carlos, Lensky, Otello and Florestan; sang Siegfried at Arhus, 1994; Cardinal Albrecht in Mathis der Maler at Covent Garden, 1995. Address: c/o Det Kongelige Teater, Box 2185, DK-1017 Copenhagen, Denmark.

ANDERSON Avril, b. 10 June 1953, Southsea, Hampshire, England. Composer. Education: Studied at the Royal College of Music with Humphrey Searle, 1972-76, at the New England Conservatory and with Jonathan Harvey at Sussex University. Career: Co-founded the modern music group Sounds Positive, 1987. Compositions: Mono-staus for 3 clarinets, 1975; Où allons nous? for soprano and orchestra, 1976; Edward II, opera in 1 act, 1978; Black Eyes in an Orange Sky for soprano and piano, 1979; Private Energy for soprano and ensemble, 1983; Dynamics of Matter for piano, 1989. Address: 28 Cavendish Avenue, London N3 3QN, England.

ANDERSON Beth, b. 3 Jan 1950, Lexington, Kentucky, USA. Composer; Performance Artist. Education: Studied with Larry Austin and Jon Cage at Davis, California, and with Terry Riley and Robert Ashley at Mills College, Oakland. Career: Founded Ear Magazine in New York, 1975; Solo performer as vocalist and piano accompanist at dance studios. Compositions include: Queen Christina, opera, 1973; Riot Rot, text-sound piece, 1984; Joan, oratorio, 1974; Elizabeth Rex and Soap Tuning, music theatre; Revel for orchestra, 1985; Rosemary Swale for string quartet, 1986; Brass Swale for brass quintet, 1989; German Swale for tape, 1990; The Fat Opera, musical, 1991. Address: c/o

ASCAP, ASCAP House, One Lincoln Center, New York, NY 10023, USA.

ANDERSON David Maxwell, b. 1964, Scotland. Singer (Tenor). Education: Studied at the Glasgow Academy and Queen's College, Cambridge; Royal College of Music from 1986, National Opera Studio, 1989. Debut: Rinuccio in Gianni Schicchi for Opera North, 1990. Career: Has sung Rinuccio for English National Opera; Rodolfo in La Bohème for Scottish Opera and Glyndebourne Touring Opera, Pinkerton in Madama Butterfly for Opera North, the Duke of Mantua in Rigoletto for Opera North and the Teatro di Pisa, Alfredo in La Traviata for the Teatro di Pisa and Opera North; Other roles include Steva in Jenua (English National Opera) and Oronte in I Lombardi (Opera North); Concert engagements include the Verdi Requiem (David Willcocks), Vaughan Williams Serenade to Music (Vernon Handley), Bruckner Te Deum (Alexander Gibson and John Eliot Gardiner), and the Rossini Stabat Mater (Raphael Frühbeck de Burgos). Address: 26 Aberdare Gardens, London NW6 3QA, England.

ANDERSON (Evelyn) Ruth, b. 21 May 1928, Kalispell, Montana, USA. Composer; Flautist. Education: Studied at the University of Washington and at Columbia and Princeton Universitites with Earl Kim and Ussachevsky; Further studies with Nadia Boulanger, Darius Milhaud and Jean-Pierre Rampal. Career: Flautist with the Totenberg Instrumental Ensemble, the Portland and Seattle Symphony Orchestras and the Boston Pops Orchestra during the 1950's; Orchestrator for NBC Television and Broadway shows; Teacher of Composition and Electronic Music at Hunter College, New York, from 1966. Compositions include: Tape: The Pregnant Dream, 1968; DUMP, Collage, 1970; 3 Studies, 1970; State of the Union Message, Collage, 1973; Conversations, 1974; Dress Rehearsal, 1976; I Come Out of your Sleep, 1979; Mixed Media: Centering, Dance, for 4 performers and live electronics, 1979; Sound Sculptures: Sound Environment, 1975; Time and Tempo, 1984. Recordings include: 1750 Arch, 1977; Opus One, 1981; CRI, 1997, 1998; XI, 1998. Honours include: Five MacDowell Colony Fellowships, 1957-73; Fulbright Scholarships, 1958, 1959; Martha Baird Rockefeller Fund; Alice M Ditson Fund. Address: c/o ASCAP, ASCAP Building, One Lincoln Plaza, New York, NY 10023, USA.

ANDERSON Julian, b. 1967, London, England. Composer. Education: BMus, Royal College of Music, London; Further study with Tristan Murail in Paris, Alexander Goehr at Cambridge and with Oliver Knussen; Attendance at the Dartington International Summer School, the Britten-Pears School (1992) and Tanglewood (1993). Career: Freelance Composer, with performances at the 1996 International Rostrum of Composers (Paris), at the Brighton, Huddersfield Contemporary Music and Cambridge Elgar Festivals; Further performances at the 1995 Ars Musica Festival, Brussels, London Proms, Tanglewood and 1996 Warsaw Festival; Professor of Composition RCM. Compositions include: Diptych, 2 movements for orchestra, 1991-95; Khorovod for 15 players, 1994; The Bearded Lady, for oboe, clarinet and piano, 1994; The Colour of Pomegranates for alto flute and piano, 1994; Scherzo with Trains for four clarinets, 1989-93; Tiramisu for ten players, 1994-95; I'm Nobody who Are You for tenor, violin and piano, 1995; Three Parts off the Ground for 13 players, 1995; Piano Etudes Nos 1 & 2, 1995-96; The Crazed Moon for orchestra, 1995-96; Past Hymns for 15 solo strings, 1996; Poetry Nearing Silence, Divertimento for 7 instruments, 1997; BBC Commission for the 1998 Promenade Concerts. Address: c/o Faber Music, 3 Queen Square, London, WC1N 3AU, England.

ANDERSON June, b. 30 Dec 1952, Boston, USA. Singer (Soprano). Education: Won Rockefeller Foundation Scholarship to the Metropolitan Opera, New York in 1970. Career: New York City Opera, 1978-84; Appearances in Italy, Palermo, Florence, La Scala, Milan, Venice, Rome, Bologna; Debut Vienna State Opera, 1987, Naples, 1988; Other European appearances, Hamburg, Geneva, Bordeaux, Paris, Madrid, Nice, Prague Festival, Pesaro, Aix-en-Provence Festival, 1988; Metropolitan Opera, 1989 (debut as Gilda); Royal Opera House, London (debut 1986) as Semiramide in a concert performance of Rossini's opera; Other roles include Gilda and Giulietta in Bellini's I Capuleti at La Scala; Lucia di Lammermoor and Isabella in Robert le Diable, Paris Opera; Rossini's Armida at Pesaro and Desdemona at San Francisco; Sang in concert at opening of the Bastille Opera Paris, 1989; Luciano Pavarotti 30th Anniversary Gala at Reggio Emilia, 1991; TV appearances in Beethoven's Ninth Symphony, Berlin, Bernstein, and title role in Lusia Miller, Lyons Opera; Bellini's Elvira in a new production of I Puritani at Covent Garden, May 1992; Sang Zoraide in Rossini's Ricciardo e Zoraide at Pesaro, 1990; Giovanna d'Arco at Covent Garden, 1996. Recordings include: Mosè in Egitto, La Jolie Fille de Perth, Le Postillon de Longjumeau, La Fille du Régiment, Maometto II, La Muette de Portici. Address: Patricia Greenan Artists Management, 19B Belsize Park, London NW3.

ANDERSON Laurie, b. 5 June 1947, Chicago, Illinois, USA. Performance Artist; Composer. Education: Studied Violin; BA, Art History, Barnard College, 1969; MFA, Sculpture, Columbia University, 1972; Studied Painting with Sol LeWitt. Career: Taught Art History, City College of the City University, New York, 1973-75; Performance Artist; Composer; Regular tours of the USA and Europe; Created several instruments for own use. Compositions: From songs to epic performance-art work, USA, 1983-; New York Social Life; O Superman (for Massenet), 1981; United States, 1983; Empty Places, 1989. Honours: Guggenheim Fellowship, 1983. Address: c/o Liz Rosenberg, Warner Brothers Records, 3 East 54th Street, New York, NY 10022, USA.

ANDERSON (Leonard) Mark, b. 8 Oct 1963, Eureka, California, USA. Pianist. Education: BMus, Honours, San Jose State University, 1987; LRAM, London, 1988; PPRNCM, with distinction, Royal Northern College of Music, Manchester, 1989. Debut: New York, 1988; San Francisco, 1988; Tokyo, 1992; Toronto, 1993; London, 1994; Zurich, 1994; Alice Tully Hall, New York, 1994. Career: Performances at major venues worldwide with leading orchestras and conductors. Recordings: Various solo piano works of Liszt, Brahms and Schumann; Brahms First Piano Concerto with the Hungarian State Symphony Orchestra, Adam Fischer conducting; Liszt Recital, 1996; Brahms Variations, op 118 and 119, 1997. Contributions to: Piano Quarterly; Keyboard Stylist. Honours: Winner, Leeds Pianoforte Competition, 1993; 1st Prize, William Kapell International Piano Competition, Washington DC, 1994. Address: 253 Tomas Way, Pleasanton, CA 94566, USA.

ANDERSON Lorna, b. 1962, Glasgow, Scotland. Singer (Soprano). Education: Royal Scottish Academy of Music, with Patricia MacMahon; Royal College of Music, London. Career: Concerts with the Bach Choir, the English Concert under Trevor Pinnock, and the Scottish Chamber Orchestra; Tour of Spain and Poland and appearances at the Kings Lynn, City of London, Brighton, Edinburgh and Aldeburgh Festivals; In 1988 sang with London Baroque under Charles Medlam, with the London Mozart Players under Andrew Parrott and the Bournemouth Sinfonietta under Roger Norrington; Promenade concert debut 1988; Further concerts with the London Classical Players, the Orchestra of the Age of Enlightenment and the Scottish National Orchestra, under Matthias Bamert; Sang Innocenza in the first modern revival of Marazzoli's La Vita Humana, for Scottish Early Music Consort, Glasgow, 1990; The Fairy Queen with the Sixteen at the Elizabeth Hall, 1990; Les Noces with Pierre Boulez and Ensemble Intercontemporain, 1990 and 1992; Morgana in Alcina, Halle Handel Festival and Innsbruck Festival, 1992; Mozart Mass in C minor, with Scottish Chamber Orchestra under Charles Mackerras, 1992; Sang in Bach's St John Passion at the Festival Hall, 1997; Opera: Clorinda in Il Combattimento di Tancredi e Clorinda, Netherlands Opera, 1991 and 1993. Major Recordings: The Fairy Queen with Harry Christophers/The Sixteen, Linley Shakespeare Ode with The Parley of Instruments; CD no 22 in Hyperion Complete Schubert Edition; Complete Britten Folksongs for Hyperion. Honours: First Prize in Peter Pears and Royal Overseas League Competition, 1984; Purcell-Britten Prize for Concert Singers, Aldeburgh, 1986. Address: c/o Lies Askonas Limited, 6 Henrietta Street, London WC2E 8LA, England.

ANDERSON Robert (David), b. 20 Aug 1927, Shillong, Assam, India. Conductor; Writer; Editor. Education: MA, Gonville and Caius College, Cambridge, England, 1954. Career: Assistant Editor, Record News, 1954-56; Assistant Master and Director of Music, Gordonstoun School, Scotland, 1956-62; Conductor, Moray Choral Union; Assistant Conductor, Spoleto Festival, 1962; Conductor, St Bartholomew's Hospital Choral Society, 1965-90; Associate Editor, The Musical Times, 1967-85; Critic, The Times, 1967-72; Contributor to British Broadcasting Corporation Music Weekly and other programmes; Coordinating Editor, Elgar Complete Edition; Television programme on Paganini, BBC2, 1971. Recordings: Mozart Sacred Music; Elgar Church Music. Publications: Catalogue of Egyptian Antiquities in the British Museum, III, Musical Instruments, 1976; Wagner, 1980; Wagner, in Heritage of Music III, 1989; Elgar in Manuscript, 1990; Elgar, 1993. Honours: Liveryman, Worshipful Company of Musicians, 1977; Fellow, Society of Antiquaries, 1983; DMus (Hon), City University, 1985. Memberships: Egypt Exploration Society; Royal Musical Association. Hobby: Modulating from music to Egyptology. Address: 54 Hornton Street, London W8 4NT, England.

ANDERSON Sylvia, b. 1938, Denver, Colorado, USA. Singer (Mezzo-Soprano). m. Matthias Kuntzsch. Education: Studied at the Eastman School with Anna Kaskas and at the Cologne Musikhochschule with Ellen Bosenius. Debut: Cologne 1962, as Fyodor in Boris Godunov. Career: Sang at the Hamburg Staatsoper, 1965-69, notably as Ophelia in the 1968 premiere of Searle's Hamlet; Bayreuth Festival, 1970-71; Salzburg Festival, 1973, in the premiere of De Temporum fine Comoedia by Orff; Guest appearances in Zurich, Stuttgart, Frankfurt, Dusseldorf, Brussels, Barcelona, Trieste and Amsterdam; US engagements at the Metropolitan and New York City Operas, and in San Francisco, Washington and Santa Fe; Repertoire includes Operas by Gluck, Purcell, Rossini, Verdi, Wagner and modern composers; Many concert appearances. Recordings: Schubert Masses; De Temporum fine Comoedia.

ANDERSON T(homas) J(efferson) Jr, b. 17 August 1928, Coatesville, Pennsylvania, USA. Composer; Music Educator. m. 3 children. Education: BMus, West Virginia State College, 1950; MEd, Pennsylvania State University, 1951; Studied Composition with Scott Huston, Cincinnati Conservatory of Music, 1954; PhD, University of Iowa, 1958; With Philip Bezanson and Richard Hervig; With Darius Milhaud, Aspen School of Music, 1964. Career: Teacher, Instrumental Music, High Point, North Carolina Public Schools, 1951-54; Instructor, West Virginia State College, Institute, West Virginia, 1955-56; Professor of Music, Chairman of Music Department, Langston (Oklahoma) University, 1958-63; Professor of Music, Tennessee State University, Nashville, 1963-69; Composer-in-Residence, Atlanta, Georgia, 1971-72; Professor of Music, Chairman, Music Department 1972-80, Chair, Austin Fletcher Professor of Music 1976-90, Emeritus 1990, Tufts University, Medford, Massachusetts; Doctor of Music, Honoris Causa, Bridgewater State College, 1991; Scholar-in-Residence, The Rockefeller Foundation, Study and Conference Centre, Bellagio, Italy, 1984, 1994; fellowship, John Simon Guggenheim Foundation, 1988; Fellow, National Humanities Centre, Research Triangle Park, North Carolina, 1996-97. Compositions include: Stage, The Shell Fairy, operetta, 1976-77; Re-Creation for 3 Speakers, Dancer and 6 Instruments, 1978; Soldier Boy, Soldier, opera, 1982; Orchestral, Introduction and Allegro, 1959; Classical Symphony, 1961; 6 Pieces for Clarinet and Chamber Orchestra, 1962; Symphony in 3 Movements, 1964; Songs of Illumination, song cycle, 1990; Whatever Happened to the Big Bands, 1991; Bahia, Bahia, for chamber orchestra, 1991; Walker, chamber opera with words by Derek Walcott, 1992; Spirit Songs commissiond by Yo Yo Ma, for cello and piano, 1993; Here in the Flesh, hymn, 1993; 7 Cabaret Songs, for jazz singer, 1994; Flute, viola, cello and piano, Broke Baroque for violin and piano, 1996; Shouts, 1997. Recordings: Chamber Symphony: London Philharmonic Orchestra, James Dixon conductor; Variations on a Theme by M B Tolson; Contemporary Chamber Ensemble, Arthur Weisberg conductor; Squares: Baltimore Symphony Orchestra, Paul Freeman conductor; Intermezzi, Videmus, Vivian Taylor, Artistic Director. Honours: Honorary DMA, College of the Holy Cross, 1983 and St Augustines College, 1996; Honorary DM, West Virginia State College, 1984 and Bridgewater State College, 1991. Address: 111 Cameron Glen Drive, Chapel Hill, NC 27516, USA.

ANDERSON Valdine, b. 1965, Canada. Singer (Soprano). Career: Appearances with Edmonton Opera as Mozart's Blonde and Pamina, and with Vancouver Opera as Micaela; Contemporary repertory includes Lutoslawski's Chatefleurs et Chantefables (composer conducting), Michael Torke's Book of Proverbs, Gorecki's Symphony of Sorrowful Songs (Vancouver SO) and the Maid in Powder Her Face by Thomas Ades (premiere, at the Cheltenham Festival); Varese Offrandes with the BBC Scottish SO, Berg's Altenberlieder, Benjamin's A Mind of Winter, Kurtag's The Sayings Season 1997 with Carmina Burana (Edmonton SO), Messiah in Winnipeg and a Maxwell Davies premiere with Vancouver New Music; Other repertory includes Britten's Spring Symphony (Aldeburgh), 1995; Beethoven's Ninth (Toronto SO) and Ein Deutsches Requiem. Address: Ingpen & Williams Ltd, 26 Wadham Road, London SW15 2LR, England.

ANDERSON-JAQUEST Tommie (Crowell), b. 22 Feb 1941, USA. Singer; University Lecturer. m. Gordon N Jaquest, 14 Aug 1993. Education: BMus, 1962; MMus, 1964; DMus (coursework), 1968; Studied Singing under Audrey Langford; MA, Sociology, 1987; MA, International Relations, 1989. Career: Freelance Musician (voice and piano) and University Lecturer; Various professional solo recitals, concerts and operatic appearances, USA; Has sung with the Chicago Lyric Opera and San Francisco Opera; Major roles include Lady Billows (Albert Herring), Countess (Marriage of Figaro), title role in Suor Angelica, Nedda (Pagliacci), Magda (The Consul), Pamina (The Magic Flute), title role in Medea, Antonia (Tales of Hoffmann), Marschallin (Der Rosenkavalier); Lecturer, University of Maryland (UK); Currently writing in the field of international relations and lecturing in music; Teaching international relations. Honours: Pi Kappa Lambda, 1968. Memberships: American Guild of Musical Artists; Incorporated Society of Musicians. Address: 16 Vincent Road, Cobham, Surrey KT11 3JB, England.

ANDERSSON Laila, b. 30 Mar 1941, Losen, Blekinge, Sweden. Singer (Soprano). m. Ulf Palme, 1984. Education: Studied with Sylvia Mang-Borenberg, Ragnar Hulten, and Hjordis Schymberg in Stockholm. Career: Royal Opera Stockholm from 1964, as Susanna, Leonore (Il Trovatore), Mathilde (Guillaume Tell), Madama Butterfly, Jenůfa and Sophie; Sang in the premieres of Herr von Hancken by Blomdahl 1965 and Granskibbutzen by Karkoff, 1975; Sang the title role in Berg's Lulu, 1977; Frequent visits to the Drottningholm Festival from 1967 (Gustaf Adolf och Ebba Brahe by the Abbé Vogler, 1973); Guest engagements at the Edinburgh Festival 1974, Copenhagen, Wiesbaden, Helsinki and Oslo; Sang Tosca at Stockholm and Bonn, 1977, Salome at the Metropolitan (debut,

1981), Gelsenkirchen, Vienna, Rio de Janeiro, Berlin and Montreal, 1985; Sang Brünnhilde at Arhus, Denmark, 1987; Fidelio at Washington and Montreal, 1988; Sang Tiresias in the premiere of Backanterna by Daniel Börtz, 1992; as Elektra, Stockholm Opera, 1993; Member of the Nya Bjorling Vocal Quartet. Honours: Singer of the Royal Court, 1985; Litteris et Artibus, 1992. Address: Köpmantorget 10, S-111 31 Stockholm, Sweden.

ANDERSZEWSKI Piotr, b. 4 Apr 1969, Warsaw, Poland. Concert Pianist. Education: Studied at the Conservatories of Lyon and Strasbourg, University of Southern California in Los Angeles; Chopin Academy, Warsaw. Career: recitals in Poland, United States and France; Wigmore Hall, London debut, Feb 1991; Further British engagements include the Harrogate Festival, 1991 and concerts with the Royal Liverpool Philharmonic and Hallé Orchestras; Festival Hall debut with the London Philharmonic conducted by Franz Welser-Möst; Recordings for Polish radio and television; European recital tour, Autumn 1992; Regular duo partner with violinist Viktoria Mullova, 1992-93 season; Edinburgh Festival debut in recital, 1994; Concert performances with CBSO, Sept 1994, Ulster Orchestra, Feb 1995, Lahti Symphony, Oct 1994 and National Symphony Orchestra of Ireland, May 1995. Recordings: Recital disc with Viktoria Mullova for Philips Classics; Prokofiev, Sonata and Piano No 1 Op 80; Debussy, Sonata for Violin and Piano; Janacek, Sonata for Violin and Piano. Honours: Chosen as one of five internationally-known young pianists to receive International Piano Foundation Scholarship at IPF on Lake Como, Italy, 1994-95. Current Management: Harold Holt Limited. Address: 31 Sinclair Road, London W14 0NS, England.

ANDONIAN Andrea, b. 1950, Colorado, USA. Singer (Mezzo-Soprano). Education: Studied at Florida and Ohio Universities and Operastudio in Cologne. Career: Sang at Cologne Offenbach Theatre, 1977-78; Engaged at Krefeld-Monchengladbach, 1978-85; Has sung with Deutsche Oper Berlin, 1986-; Guest appearances, Germany and elsewhere in repertory including Cherubino, Dorabella, Ramiro in Mozart's Finta Giardiniera, Idamante in Idomeneo and Annio in La Clemenza di Tito; Humperdinck's Hansel, Siebel in Faust, the Prince in Massenet's Cendrillon, and Britten's Lucretia and Hermia; Sang Urbain in Les Huguenots with Deutsche Oper, 1987, and at Covent Garden, 1991; Paris Opéra-Comique, 1992, in Rossini's L'Occasione fa il Ladro, La Scala di Seta, La Cambiale di Matrimonio and Il Signor Bruschino. Recordings include: Schumann's Requiem. Address: Deutsche Oper Berlin, Richard Wagnerstrasse 10, 1000 Berlin 10, Germany.

ANDRADE Levine, b. 1954, Bombay, India. Violist. Education: Studied Violin at the Yehudi Menuhin School with Robert Mastres; Studied with Menuhin and Nadia Boulanger; Viola studies with Patrick Ireland; Royal Academy of Music from 1969 with Frederick Grinke, Max Gilbert, Sidney Griller and Colin Hampton. Career includes: Co-founded the Arditti String Quartet, 1974 and member until 1989; Frequent concerts with the London Symphony Orchestra, Royal Philharmonic, Academy of St Martin-in-the-Fields, the London Sinfonietta and the London Mozart Players; Guest Professor at the Royal Academy of Music; Many concerts with the Arditti Quartet in Europe and North America; Festival engagements at Aldeburgh, Bath, BBC Proms, Berlin, Budapest, Paris, Venice Biennale, Vienna and Warsaw; Music in Camera programme, BBC Television, 1987; Series of seven recitals for Radio 3, 1987; Played in all Schoenberg's quartets in a single recital, Elizabeth Hall, London, November, 1988; Took part in the premieres of quartets by Georges Aperghis, 1985; Berio, Divertimento for Trio, 1987; Böse, No 3, 1989; Britten, Quartettino, 1983; Gavin Bryars, 1985; Bussotti, 1988; John Cage, Music for 4, 1988; Davies, 1983; Ferneyhough, Numbers 2 and 3; Gubaidulina No 3, 1987; Harvey, Numbers 1 and 2; Hindemith Quartet 1915, 1986; Kagel, 1987; Nancarrow, No 3, 1988; Ohana, No 2, 1982; Pousseur, No 2, 1989; Premiered quartets by Michael Finnissy, Michael Nyman and Tim Souster. Recordings include: Henze's Five String Quartets; 25 CDs. Honours include: Deutsche Schallplattenpreis for Henze Quartets, 1987. Address: 80 Whellock Road, London W4 1DJ, England.

ANDRADE Rosario, b. 6 Apr 1951, Veracruz, Mexico. Singer (Soprano). Education: Studied in Veracruz and Accademia di Santa Cecilia, Rome. Debut: As Madame Butterfly, Mexico City, 1974. Carerr: Sang at Glyndebourne Festival as Donna Elvira in Don Giovanni, 1977-78; Many guest appearances in Europe and North America, Brussels, 1978, Lyon (in Cavalli's La Calisto), 1979, Warsaw, 1981-82, Connecticut, 1987, Pittsburgh and Mississippi Opera Company, 1988; Metropolitan Opera debut, 1982, as Antonia in Les Contes d'Hoffmann, returning as Manon, 1986; Other roles include Mimi, Micaela, Marguerite, Donna Anna, Aida and Maddalena in Andrea Chenier; Concert repertory includes Marguerite in La Damnation de Faust. Address: c/o Metropolitan Opera, Lincoln Center, New York, NY 10023, USA.

ANDRASOVAN Tibor, b. 3 Apr 1917, Slovenska, Lupca, Slovakia. Conductor; Composer. m. (1) Ivanka Dimitrová, 16 July 1948, 1 son, 2 daughters, (2) Mária Kutejová, 21 Oct 1973. Education: Pedagogic University; Pupil of E Suchon and A Moyses at the Bratislava Conservatory; The Master School of Music, Prague. Career: Professor, 1941; Conductor since 1945; Repetiteur, Slovak National Theatre, 1946-57; Artistic Director, Slovak Folk Artistic Ensemble, 1955-58, 1969-74. Compositions: Stage: Gelo the Joker, 1957; The Quadrille, Operatta, 1960; The White Disease, Music Drama, 1967; The Gamekeeper's Wife, Opera, 1973-74; The King of Fools, Musical, 1982; Ballets: Orpheus and Euridice, 1948; The Song of Peace, 1949; The Festival of Solstice, 1985; Orchestral: Little Goral, Overture, 1961; Concerto for Cembalo and Strings, 1977; Chamber: String Quartet, Folklorica, 1976; Partita Romantica for Piano, 1983; Vocal: Tokajik, Cantata for Soprano, Chorus and Orchestra, 1975; The Echoes of the Uprising Mountains, Song Cycle for Narrator, Soprano, Tenor and Piano, 1979; The Recruit Songs, Song Cycle, 1973; The Pines Whispered, Song Cycle for Soprano and Piano, 1976; The Woman and Muse, Song Cycle for Bass-Baritone and Piano, 1978; Also Incidental Music, Film Scores and Music for Folk Ensembles. Publication: Tonalic System of Slovak Music, 1996. Contributions to: Magazines and journals in USA, Japan, Mongolia and the Soviet Union. Honours: Numerous awards; Dr Honoris Causa "Science of Music", National Prize of Slovakia, 1949; State Prize of Slovakia, 1953; The Prize of NHK Radio, Tokyo; Made a Merited Artist of the Czechoslovak Socialist Republic, 1971. Membership: Union of Slovak Composers and Musicians. Address: Hlboká 12, Bratislava 81104, Slovak Republic.

ANDRASSY Gabor, b. 1951, Transylvania, Romania. Singer (Bass). Career: Sang at the Berne Opera, 1979-81, then at Krefeld, 1981-87; Karlsruhe, 1988-90, with guest appearances at Geneva, Théâtre des Champs-Elysées Paris, as Fafner in The Ring and at Seattle (1989) as Wagner's Daland; Has performed widely in France as King Marke at Nantes, Hunding and Hagen at Nice, and Fafner, Boris Godunov and Ivan Khovansky at Strasbourg (1991-92); Seattle Opera in The Ring and as Rocco in Fidelio; Other roles include the Commendatore in Don Giovanni, Boris Godunov and King Philip, King Henry and Grand Inquisitor. Address: c/o Merle Hubbard Management, 133 West 71st Street, Apt 8a, New York, NY 10023, USA.

ANDRÉ Martin, b. 10 Dec 1960, West Wickam, England. Conductor. Education: Studied at the Yehudi Menuhin School, the Royal College of Music and Cambridge University. Career: Played with the National Youth Orchestra as Percussionist from 1970; Founded the Mozart Chamber Ensemble at Cambridge and was appointed conductor of the University Orchestra and Chorus, and the University Chamber Orchestra; Conducted his edition of Purcell's King Arthur at Cambridge and the Minack Theatre, Cornwall, 1982; Has worked with the Welsh National Orchestra from 1982, leading Aida, Jenůfa, Ernani, Rigoletto, Madame Butterfly, Un Ballo in Maschera, Eugene Onegin and Il Barbiere di Siviglia; Vancouver Opera from season 1986-87 with Janacek's From the House of the Dead and Cunning Little Vixen, Ariadne auf Naxos, La Traviata and La Bohème; Seattle Opera 1987, Carmen; London concert debut January 1987, with the English Chamber Orchestra at the Barbican; Further concerts with the Scottish Chamber Orchestra and the Northern Sinfonia; Scottish Opera from 1989, The Merry Widow and La Clemenza di Tito; Conducted the Love of Three Oranges at the English National Opera, 1990 and at Teatro Sao-Carlos, Lisbon, 1991; Madame Butterfly for Opera North; World premiere, The Bacchae by John Buller for ENO, 1992; Music Director, English Touring Opera, 1993; Recent notable debuts include Verdi's Un Ballo in maschera at the Royal Opera House Covent Garden; Conducted the UK premiere of Matthus' Cornet Christoph Rilke's Song of Love and Death for Glyndebourne Touring Opera; The Makropoulos Case for GTO in 1997; Engagements with the New Israeli Opera include conducting Don Pasquale and Love of Three Oranges. Address: c/o Ingpen & Williams Limited, 14 Kensington Court, London W8 5DN, England.

ANDRÉ Maurice, b. 21 May 1933, Ales, France. Trumpeter. Education: Studied with his father and with Sabarich at the Paris Conservatoire. Career: Soloist with the Concerts Lamoureuz, 1953-60, L'Orchestre Philharmonique of ORTF (French Radio), 1953-62, and the orchestra of the Operé-Comique, Paris, 1962-67; Many concert performances in Europe; North American Professor at the Paris Conservatoire, 1967-78; Composers who have written for him include Boris Blacher (Concerto 1971), Charles Chaynes, Marcel Landowski, Jean-Claude Eloy, Harold Genzmer, Bernhard Krol, Jean Langlais (Chorals for trumpet and organ), Henri Tomasi and André Jolivet (Arioso barocco, 1968). Honours: First prizes at International Competitions in Geneva, 1955 and Munich 1963.

ANDREAE Marc (Edouard), b. 8 Nov 1939, Zurich, Switzerland. Conductor. Education: Zurich Conservatory; University of Zurich; Study with Nadia Boulanger in Paris, with Franco Ferrara in Rome. Career: CHief COnductor, Broadcasting Orchestra of Italian Switzerland, Lugano, 1969-90; Regular Guest, numerous European and Japanese symphony orchestras and at festivals, Paris, Berlin, Lucerne, Vienna, Salzburg, Ascona, Brescia; Numerous concerts and operas for television including Eurovision; Music and Artistic Director of the Angelicum in Milan, Italy, 1990-93. Recordings: With NDR Hamburg, Hamburg Philharmonic Orchestra, Munich Philharmonic, Cologne Radio Symphony Orchestra, Bamberg Symphony, National Orchestra of France. Publications: Music of Weber, Rossini, Donizetti, Schumann, Lortzing, Tchaikovsky and Liszt. Honours: 1st Prize, Swiss National Competition. 1966; 2 Grand Prix, Italian Record Critics, 1974; LP Techno Distinction, Tokyo, 1975. Memberships: Swiss Music Edition, President. Current Management: Valmalete, Paris, France. Address: Via Moretto 6, 6924 Sorengo, Switzerland.

ANDREESCU Horia, b. 18 October 1946, Brasov, Rumania. Conductor. Education: Studied at the Brasov School of Music and the Bucharest Conservatoire; Further study with Hans Swarowsky in Vienna and Sergiu Celibidache in Munich. Career: Chief Conductor of Ploiesti Philharmonic, 1974-87; Permanent Guest Conductor, Mecklenburgische Staatskapells Schwerie, 1979-90; Permanent Guest Conductor, Radio Symphony Orchestra, Berlin, 1981-91; Permanent Guest Conductor, Dresden Philharmonia, 1983-91; Joint Artistic Director of the George Enescu Philharmonic at Bucharest, 1987-; Professor, Academy of Music, 1988-90; Conductor, Virtuosi of Bucharest Chamber Orchestra; Conductor, Bucharest George Enescu Philharmonic Orchestra; Chief Conductor and General Music Director, Bucharest National Radio Orchestra, 1992-. Recordings: Recorded over 30 LP's and CD's, including, the First Integral orchestral work of George Enescu; Recorded for Radio Bucharest, Radio East Berlin (Haydn, Brahms, Wagner, Stravinsky, Hindemith, Prokofiev), Radio Leipzig (Bartok), BBC (Haydn, Mozart, Beethoven, Tchaikovsky), Radio Madrid, Radio Copenhagen and Radio Suisse Romande. Honours: Prize Winner at Geneva and Copenhagen Competitions. Address: c/o Radio Romania, Directia Formatilor Muzicale, Str General Berthelot 62-68, Bucharest, Romania.

ANDREEV Andrei, b. 1950, Crimea, USSR. Violinist. Career: Co-founded Rachmaninov Quartet under auspices of Sochi State Philharmonic Society, Crimea, 1974; Many concerts in former Soviet Union; From season 1975-76 tours to Switzerland, Austria, Bulgaria, Norway and Germany; Participation in Shoshtakovich Chamber Music Festival, Vilnius, 1976 and festivals in Moscow and St Petersburg; Repertoire includes works by Haydn, Mozart, Beethoven, Bartók, Brahms, Schnittke, Shostakovich, Boris Tchaikovsky, Chalayev and Meyerovich. Honours include: With Rachmaninov Quartet: Prizewinner at First All-Union Borodin String Quartet Competition, 1987. Current Management: Sonata, Glasgow, Scotland. Address: 11 North Park Street, Glasgow, G20 7AA, Scotland.

ANDREW Donald, b. 26 May 1920, Barnstaple, North Devon, England. Oboist; Organist. Education: The Choristers' School, Exeter, Devon; Exeter Cathedral Choir; Royal Military School of Music, Kneller Hall, Twickenham; Royal Academy of Music, London. Debut: BBC Bristol, 1945. Career: BBC Soloist, 1945-77; Has played for all leading London orchestras; Principal Oboe: Liverpool Philharmonic Orchestra, Sadler's Wells Opera Orchestra, BBC Revue Orchestra, Leighton Licas Chamber Orchestra, Ballet Rambert, Old St Paul's Musical Society, Edinburgh; Member, Wind Band, Royal Shakespeare Theatre, Stratford-upon-Avon; Organist, St Margaret's Parish Church, Northam, North Devon, 1990-91; Gave first broadcast performance of the Haydn Oboe Concerto with Reginald Redman and West of England Studio Orchestra, also played the Haydn and Goossens concertos with Sir Malcolm Sargent and Liverpool Philharmonic Orchestra; BBC broadcasts include many 9-o'clock recitals and others with piano; Concertos from Bristol, Cardiff, Birmingham, Glasgow and Music at Night, several in Musician in Scotland including first broadcast performance of Shaun Dillon's Sonata for oboe and piano and Hans Gal's Sonata for oboe and piano. Honours: FIBA, 1978. Memberships: Incorporated Society of Musicians; Royal College of Organists. Address: 132 Bay View Road, Northam, Bideford, Devon EX39 1BY, England.

ANDREW Jon, b. 1936, New Zealand. Singer (Tenor). Education: Studied in Auckland. Debut: As Don José in Carmen, Auckland, 1982. Career: Sang with Sadler's Wells Opera, 1963-68, as Ricardo, Radames, Don José, and Agrippa in the British premiere of the Fiery Angel (New Opera Company); Sang in Germany, 1969-, notably in Karlsruhe, Mannheim and Dusseldorf in Wagner roles including Siegmund in Die Walküre; Glyndebourne Festival as the Italian Singer in Rosenkavalier, 1965; Covent Garden, 1967 and 1974, as Froh in Das Rheingold and Dimitri in Boris Godunov; Further appearances with Welsh National Opera, Handel Opera Society, 1967, and at San Diego as Siegmund and Otello, 1975-76; Also sang Siegmund at Madrid, Berlin Staatsoper, and with English National Opera, 1975; Wexford Festival as Pedro in Tiefland, 1978; Further engagements at La Scala, Milan, and Nice and Santiago, 1981; Other roles have included Turiddu, Erik in Fliegende Holländer, Max in Der Freischütz, Laca in Jenůfa, and Bob Boles in Peter

Grimes. Address: c/o English National Opera, St Martin's Lane, London WC2, England.

ANDREW Ludmilla, b. 1939, Vancouver, Canada. Singer (Soprano). Debut: With Vancouver Opera as Donna Elvira. Career: Has sung in San Francisco in Aida and Der Rosenkavalier; British debut with Sadler's Wells Opera as Madama Butterfly; Later roles have been Senta, Aida and Tosca; Covent Garden in The Ring and as Elektra, Leonora (La Forza del Destino), Arabella and Tosca; Glyndebourne 1968, as Anna Bolena; Scottish Opera as Donna Anna, and Miss Jessel (The Turn of the Screw); With Welsh National Opera has sung Abigaille, Giorgetta (Il Tabarro), Rosalinda, Aida and Tosa; Venus with Chelsea Opera Group, in a concert performance of Tannhäuser; Title roles in Donizetti's Maria di Rudenz and Rosmunda d'Inghilterra, and Mayr's Medea in Corinto, at the Elizabeth Hall; Other roles include Ellen Orford (Buenos Aires and Rio de Janeiro); the Marschallin and Mozart's Electra (Brussels); Norma (Dublin); Ursula in Mathis der Maler, Jenůfa, Turandot (New Zealand); Countess Almaviva (Vancouver); Sieglinde; Sang Anaide in Leoncavallo's Zaza, Wexford Festival, 1990; Frequent recitals with Geoffrey Parsons in the French, German and Russian repertoire; Concert performances with leading British orchestras in the Requiems of Mozart and Verdi, the Choral Symphony and Sibelius songs conducted by Rozhdestvensky. Recordings include: Video of Macbeth (Glyndebourne); Songs by Bernard Van Dieren. Address: c/o Korman International Management, 24a Burnaby Gardens, London W4 3DP, England.

ANDRIASOVA Marta, b. 23 Jan 1941, Moscow, Russia. Musicologist. m. Iosif Andriasov, 7 Apr 1963, 1 son, 1 daughter. Education: Graduate Degree, 1964, Postgraduate Degree, 1966, Moscow State P I Tchaikovsky Conservatory. Publications: The Concertos of Eugeny Golubev; The Oratorio and the Cantata; Forword to the Score of Iosif Andriasov's First Symphony; Forward to the Score of Eugeny Golubev's Fifth String Quartet; The Instrumental Works of Eugeny Golubev; The Six Concerti Armonici Are Returned to Their Genuine Author, The Great Italian Composer-Violinist Pietro Locatelli; the Symphonies of Dmitry Shostakovich; International and National Tendencies in Music; Numerous Publicity Notes for the Following Compositions of Iosif Andriasov: The First Symphony, The Second Symphony, Concertino for Trumpet and Orchestra, Concertino for Clarinet and Orchestra, Cantata To The Mother Earth and The Spring, Written for various performing groups. Honours: Music Research in Milan, Italy, Italian Government, 1990. Membership: American Musicological Society. Address: 251 West 92nd Street, Apt #9D, New York, NY 10025, USA.

ANDRIESSEN Jurriaan, b. 15 Nov 1925, Haarlem, The Netherlands. Composer. Education: Studied composition with father, Hendrik Andriessen; Graduated at Utrecht Conservatory, 1947; Studied conducting with Willem van Otterloo, Film music in Paris and Composition with Aaron Copland at Berkshire Music Center, Tanglewood, 1949-50. Compositions include: Stage: Kalchas, opera, 1959; Orchestral: Piano Concertino, 1943, Piano Concerto, 1948, 12 Symphonies including No 1, Berkshire Symphonies, 1949, also as the ballet Jones Beach, 1950 and No 5, Time Spirit, 1970, Cymbeline, overture, 1954, Thai, 1960, Trelleborg Concerto for Harpsichord and 3 Orchestral Groups, 1969, Pasticcio-Finale for Orchestra, Dixieland Band and Tape, 1974, Les Branles Gaulois for Accordion and Chamber Orchestra, 1978, Time Suspended, 1984; Chamber: Hommage a Milhaud for 11 Instruments, 1945 also for Flute and String Quartet, 1948, Octet Divertissement for Winds, 1948, 5 Trios, 1955-59, Duo for 2 Violins, 1958, Trio for Clarinet, Cello and Piano, 1965, Antifono e Fusione for Wind Quintet, Brass Quartet and Timpani, 1966, Summer Dances for 7 Percussionists, Harp and Guitar, 1966, The Cave for Cello, 12 Winds, 4 Keyboard Instruments and Electronics, 1976, Entrata della regina for Brass Ensemble, 1980, Sextet, 1985, Due canzone di Don Chisciotte for Violin and Harp, 1985, Music for Harpsichord, 1987, Piano pieces and vocal music, Ballade for Guitar and Harp, 1990, Reflections for Violin Solo, 1990, Aspetti di HFA for Organ, 1990, Quartet for Flute, Violin, Viola and Cello, 1992. Address: BUMA/STERMA Huis, Postbus 725, 1180 AS Amstelveen, Netherlands.

ANDRIESSEN Louis, b. 6 Jun 1939, Utrecht, The Netherlands. Composer. Education: Studied with his father, Hendrik Andriesson, and with Kees van Baaren, Royal Conservatory of Music, The Hague, 1957-62; with Luciano Berio, Milan, 1962-63. Compositions: Stage: Reconstructie, Opera, 1968-69, in collaboration with 4 colleagues; Matthew Passion, 1976; Orpheus, 1977; George Sand, 1980; Orchestral: What it's Like for live Electronic Improvisers and 52 Strings, 1970; Uproar for 16 Winds, 6 Percussionists and Electronic Instruments, 1970; The 9 Symphonies of Beethoven for Promenade Orchestra and Ice Cream Bell, 1970; Symphony for Open Strings, 1978; Velocity, 1983; De Stijl, 1985; Chamber: Flute Sonata, 1956; Percosse for Flute, Trumpet, Bassoon and Percussion, 1958; A Flower Song I for Violin, 1963, II for Oboe, 1963; and III for Cello, 1964; Double for Clarinet and Piano, 1965; Souvenirs d'enfance for Piano and Tape, 1966; The Persistence for Piano and Winds, 1972; Felicitatie for 3 Trumpets, 1979; Disco for Violin and Piano, 1982; Overture to Orpheus for Harpsichord, 1982; Piano Pieces; Vocal: Nocturne for Soprano and Chamber Orchestra, 1959; Il Principe for 2 Choirs, Winds, Piano and Bass Guitar, 1974; The State for 4 Women's Voices and 27 Instruments, 1972-76; Mausoleum for 2 Baritones and Chamber Ensemble, 1979, revised 1981; Time for Choir and Orchestra, 1981; Madrigal Concerto for Choir, 1984; Collaboration with Peter Greenaway in 1991 TV Series Not Mozart: M is for Man, Music, Mozart; Rosa, a horse drama, 1994. Address: c/o BUMA, Postbus 725, 1180 AS Amstelveen, Netherlands.

ANDSNES Leif Ove, b. 7 Apr 1970, Karmooy, Norway. Pianist. Education: Studied at the Music Conservatory of Bergen with Jiri Hlinka. Debut: Oslo, 1987; British debut, Edinburgh Festival with the Oslo Philharmonic, Mariss Jansons, 1989; US Debut, Cleveland Symphony, Neeme Järvi. Career: Appearances include: Schleswig-Holstein Festival and with orchestras such as Los Angeles Philharmonic, Berlin Philharmonic, London Philharmonic, Philharmonia, City of Birmingham Symphony Orchestra, Royal Scottish National Orchestra, BBC Philharmonic Orchestra for his debut at the Proms, 1992 and Chicago Symphony Orchestra; Artistic Director, Risor Festival; Recitals at Teatro Communale, Bologna, Wigmore Hall, Barbican Hall, London, Herkulesaal, Munich, Concertgebouw, Amsterdam, Konzerthaus Vienna and Glasgow Royal Concert Hall. Recordings include: Grieg: A Minor and Liszt A Major concerti; Janacek, Solo Piano Music; Chopin, Sonatas and Grieg, Solo Piano Music; Brahmns and Schumann works for piano and viola with Lars Anders Tomter. Honours: First Prize at the Hindemith Competition in Frankfurt; Norwegian Critics' Prize; Dorothy Chandler Award in Los Angeles; Deutschen Schallplaten Award. Current Management: IMG Artists (Europe), Chiswick, London, England. Address: C/O Kathryn Enticott, IMG Artists (Europe), Media House, 3 Burlington Lane, Chiswick, London W4 2TH, England.

ANFUSO Nella, b. 5 Oct 1942, Alia, Palermo, Sicily, Italy. Singer (Soprano). Education: Studied at the Cherubini Conservatory, Florence and the Accademia Santa Cecilia, Rome. Debut: Florence, 1971, in a recital of songs by Caccini. Career: Has appeared widely in music by 17th century Italian composers and has produced operas from the same period (Monteverdi's Combattimento in Switzerland, 1974); Has researched early music performance practice and toured with a Florence-based group from 1985; Professor of Literature at the Boccherini Conservatory, Lucca.

ANGAS Richard, b. 1942, Surrey, England. Singer (Bass). Education: Studied in Vienna and London. Debut: With Scottish Opera as Fafner in The Ring. Career: Appearances with the Welsh National Opera and at Covent Garden; Performances in Germany as King Mark and King Henry, Baron Ochs, Osmin, Rocco and Mephistopheles; Engagements throughout Europe, Israel, Australia and South America in Oratorio and Recital; English National Opera as Monteverdi's Seneca and Pluto, Basilio in Il Barbiere di Siviglia, Pimen (Boris Godunov), Daland (The Flying Dutchman) and Jupiter (Orpheus in the Underworld); The Mikado, 1990, and Bartolo in Figaro; The Doctor in a new production of Wozzeck, 1990; Has sung in the world premiere of Birtwistle's The Mask of Orpheus, 1986 and the British premiere of The Making of the Representative for Planet 8 by Philip Glass, 1988; Sang in The Love for Three Oranges with Opera North, Leeds; Debut in Paris, Opera Garnier, as Pontius Pilate in Höller's Master and Marguerite, 1991; Debut in USA as Rocco in Fidelio, 1994; Tosca and The Mikado for ENO, 1994; Mulhouse, 1996, as the Commandant in From the House of the Dead. Address: c/o English National Opera, St Martins Lane, London WC2, England.

ANGEL Marie, b. 3 June 1953, Pinnaroo, South Australia. Singer (Soprano). m. David Freeman. Career: Has sung with Opera Factory London and Opera Factory Zurich in Cosi fan tutte (Fiordiligi, also televised); The Knot Garden (Denise); Birtwistle's Punch and Judy (Pretty Polly); Aventures by Ligeti; Mahagonny Songspiel; Gluck's Iphigenia operas (title role); Donna Anna and Mozart's Countess, 1991; Other roles include Euridice in Monteverdi's Orfeo and the Oracle of the Dead in the premiere of The Mask of Orpheus, 1986 for the English National Opera; Mozart's Queen of Night for Welsh National Opera; Musetta for Opera North; Sang Berio's Recital at South Bank and Jo-Ann for Glyndebourne Touring Opera in Tippett's New Year; Created the role of Morgana Le Fay in the premiere of Birtwistle's Gawain at Covent Garden, May 1991; Sang Monteverdi's Poppea in a new production by Opera Factory, 1992; Has also sung Donna Anna for Victoria State Opera and appeared with Houston Grand Opera and at the New York City Opera; Created the role of Esmerelda in Rosa, the opera by Peter Greenaway and Louis Andriessen at the Music Theatre, Amsterdam, 1994; Sang Hecate in The Mask of Orpheus at the Festival Hall, London, 1996. Current Management: Allied Artists Agency, London. Address: 42 Montpelier Square, London SW7 1JZ, England.

ANGEL Ryland, b. 22 November 1966, England. Singer (Countertenor). Education: Vocal studies with David Mason and Gerald Lesne in London. Career: Appearances in Handel's Amadigi at the Karlsruhe Festival, 1996-97, Purcell's Dido and Aeneas, Blow's Venus and Adonis with René Jacobs at De Vlaamse Opera; Peri's Euridice with Opera Normandie, the medieval Play of Daniel in New York and a staged production of Caldara's oratorio La Santissima Annunziata with Le Parlement de Musique at the Louvre, Paris; Settings of Orfeo by Monteverdi and Gluck with English National Opera and English Touring Opera, Purcell Fairy Queen with the English Bach Festival and for ENO, 1998; Further concerts with La Chapelle Royale, Le Concert Spirituel and Les Jeunes Solistes; Festival appearances at Lucerne, BBC Proms, Athens, Lufthansa Baroque Festival (London) and Venice International Contemporary Music Festival; Solo recitals in Paris, with Bach's Cantata 54, Vivaldi's Stabat Mater and Salve Regina; Season 1997 as Anfinomo in Il Ritorno d'Ulisse with ENO, Messiah in Prague and a Buxtehude programme with Christophe Coin. Address: c/o English National Opera, St Martin's Lane, London WC2, England.

ANGELO Mariana, b. 1954, Sofia, Bulgaria. Singer (Soprano). Education: Studied at Conservatoire of Sofia. Career: Sang at the Komische Oper Berlin, 1978-84; Berne Opera, 1984-86; Has appeared at the Nationaltheater Mannheim, 1987-, and has sung as guest at Dresden, Karlruhe, Sofia, Graz, Nancy, Paris, Ghent and Antwerp; Lausanne Opera, 1989, as Liu in Turandot; Other roles include Verdi's Leonora (Il Trovatore and La Forza del Destino), Amelia Boccanegra, Aida, Violetta and Desdemona; Puccini's Mimi, Manon Lescaut and Madame Butterfly; Nedda, Tatiana and Mathilde in Guillaume Tell. Address: c/o Music International, 13 Ardilaun Road, London N5 2QR, England.

ANGERER Paul, b. 16 May 1927, Vienna, Austria. Conductor; Violist; Composer. m. Anita Rosser, 18 Jun 1952, 2 s, 2 d. Education: Studies, Theory, Piano, Violin and Organ, Hochschule für Musik, Vienna and at Vienna Conservatory, 1941-46. Career: Violist, 1947, Principal Violist, 1953-56, Vienna Symphony Orchestra; Violist, Zurich Tonhalle Orchestra, 1948, Orchestre de la Suisse Romande, Geneva, 1949-52; Director, Chief Conductor, Vienna Chamber Orchestra, 1956-63; Composer, Conductor, Burgtheater, Vienna, 1960-64; Principal Conductor, Bonn City Theatre, 1964-66; Permanent Guest Conductor, Haydn Symphonic Orchestra of Bolzano and Trento, 1960-90; Musical Opera Director, Ulm Theatre, 1966-68, Salzburg Landestheater, 1968-72; Artistic Director, Hellbrunn Festival, 1970-71; Director, SW German Chamber Orchestra, 1972-82; Professor, Hochschule für Musik, Vienna, 1983-92; Numerous tours as Guest Conductor; Leader, Concilium Musicum; Editor, Baroque and Pre-Classical Music and works by Joseph Lanner; Moderator, ORF, Austrian Radio. Compositions include: Orchestral pieces; Chamber works; Viola and Piano Concertos; A Dramatic Cantata; Television Opera; Works for Organ, Harp, Viola, Harpsichord. Recordings: Numerous recordings as soloist, conductor and instrumentalist. Honours: Medal Winner, Geneva Music Competition, 1948; 1st Prize for Composition, Organ Competition, Haarlem, 1954; Austrian State Prize, 1956; Theodor Korner Prize, 1958; 1st Prize, Salzburg Opera Competition, 1959; Vienna Cultural Prize, 1983; Cultural Prize, Lower Austria, 1987; Mozart Prize, for Musikwissenschafliche Arbeit, 1994. Hobbies: Joinery; Masonry. Address: Esteplatz 3, A-1030 Vienna, Austria.

ANGERMÜLLER Rudolph (Kurt), b. 2 Sept 1940, Bielefeld, Germany. Music Editor; Music Librarian. m. Hannelore Johannböke, 1 son, 1 daughter. Education: MA; PhD 1970; Graduate, Försterling Conservatory of Music, Bielefeld. Career: Assistant, Musicology Institute, University of Salzburg; Chief Editor, New Mozart Edition, and Librarian, International Mozarteum Foundation, 1972-; Chief of Research Department International Mozarteum Foundation, 1981-; General Secreatry, International Mozarteum Foundation, 1988; Professor, 1993. Publications: Untersuchungen zur Geschichte des Carmen-Stoffes, 1967; Antonio Salieri, Sein Leben und seine weltichen Werke unter besonderer Berücksichtigung seiner grossen Opern, 3 Volumes, 1971, 1972, 1974; W A Mozarts Musikalische Umwelt in Paris, 1977-78, Eine Dokumentation, 1982; Mozart's Operas, 1988; Ich johannes chrisostomus Amadeus Wolfgangus sigismundus Mozart, 1991; Mozarts Reisen in Italien, 1994; Franz Xaver Wolfgang Mozart, Reisetagebuch 1819-1821, 1994; Mozart auf der Reise nach Prag, Dresden, Leipzig und Berlin, 1995. Contributions to: Bulletin of the International Mozarteum Foundation; Mozart-Jahrbuch; Haydn-Jahrbuch; Die Musikforschung; Österreichische Musikzeitschrift; Wiener Figaro; Musical Times; Deutsches Jahrbuch für Musikwissenschaft; Numerous other professional journals and books. Memberships: International Musicological Society; Society for Music Research; Austrian Musicological Society. Hobby: Collecting Old Books and Copperplate Engravings. Address: 92a Moosstrasse, 5020 Salzburg, Austria.

ANHALT Istvan, b. 12 Apr 1919, Budapest, Hungary. Composer; Author; Educator. Education: Royal Hungarian

Academy of Music; Conservatoire National de Musique de Paris, France; Composition with Zoltan Kodaly and Nadia Boulanger; Instruction in conducting from Louis Fourestier and Piano with Soulima Stravinsky. Career: Appointed to Faculty of Music, McGill University, Montreal, Canada, 1949; Carried out experimentation and compositional work at electronic music laboratory of National Research Council, Ottawa, Columbia-Princeton Electronic Music centre and Bell Telephone Laboratories, Anhalt installed electronic music studio and appointed Director and Member of the Senate, McGill University, 1964; Appointed Slee professorship, New York State University at Buffalo, 1969; Head of Music, Queen's University, Kingston, Ontario, 1971-81. Compositions include: Dramatic Works: Arc en Ciel, 1951; Cycle of 4 musico-dramatic (operatic) works: La Tourangelle: A Musical Tableau, 1975, Winthrop: A Musical Pageant, 1983, Traces (Tikkun): A Pluri-drama for solo lyric baritone and orchestra, 1995, Millennial Mall (Lady Diotima's Walk): A Voice-Drama for the Imagination for solo lyric soprano, choir and orchestra, 1998; Orchestral: Interludium, 1950; Symphony No 1, 1958; Symphony of Modules, (Symphony No 2), 1967; Simulacrum, 1987; Sparkskraps, 1988; Sonance Resonance (Welche Töne? 1989; Chorus: The Bell-Man, 1954, revised, 1980; Three Songs of Death, 1954; Journey of the Magi, 1951; Traces, for baritone and orchestra, 1994; Chamber Music: Funeral Music, 1951; Sonata for Violin and Piano, 1954; Sonata for Piano, 1951; Electronic Tape: Electronic Composition No 1-4, 1959-62. Recordings: Numerous including: Cento; Fantasia for Piano; Foci; Sonata for Violin and Piano; Trio for violin, cello and piano. Publication: Alternative Voices, 1984. Honours: DMus, honoris causa, McGill University, 1982; Professor Emeritus, 1984, Honorary LLD, 1992, Queen's University. Address: 274 Johnson Street, Kingston, Ontario K7L 1Y4, Canada.

ANHORN Carmen, b. 5 Aug 1956, Lucerne, Switzerland. Singer (Mezzo-Soprano). Education: Studied at Zurich Musikhochschule, with Brigitte Fassbaender in Munich and Leonore Kirchstein in Augsburg. Career: Member of Bayerische Staatsoper, Munich, 1982-88; Sang first as Coloratura Soprano, then as Mezzo; Guest appearances, Hamburg, Dusseldorf, Frankfurt, Milan, Salzburg, Barcelona and Bordeaux; Appeared in Parsifal at Bayreuth, 1989, as Cherubino at Vienna Volksoper, 1990; Other roles have included Mozart's Zerlina, Despina and Papagena, Woglinde in Das Rheingold, Musetta in La Bohème and Amor in Orfeo ed Euridice; Sang in Wagner's Das Liebesverbot at Palermo, 1991; Concert engagements at the Bach-Wochen in Ansbach and in Leipzig, Munich, Madrid and Vienna. Recordings include: Nuri in d'Albert's Tiefland; Iphigénie en Tauride and Egk's Peer Gynt. Address: c/o Teatro Massimo di Palermo, Piazza Verdi, 90138 Palermo, Italy.

ANIEVAS Agustin, b. 11 June 1934, New York, USA. Pianist; Teacher. Education: Commenced piano lessons at age 4 with his mother; was a pupil of Steuermann, Samaroff and Marcus at the Juilliard School of Music, New York. Career: Formal debut as soloist with the Little Orchestra Society, New York, 1952; Later toured North and South American, Australia and the Far East; Professor of Piano, Brooklyn College of the City University of New York, 1974-. Recordings: For Angel-EMI and Seraphim, notably of music by Bartok, Prokofiev, Rachmaninov, Chopin and Liszt. Honours: Concert Artists Guild Award, 1959; First Prize, Dimitri Mitropoulos Competition, 1961. Address: c/o Music Department, Brooklyn College of the City University of New York, Brooklyn, NY 11210, USA.

ANISIMOV Alexander, b. Krasnoyarsk, Russia. Singer (Bass). Education: Studied with Ekaterina Yofel in Krasnoyarsk. Career: Joined the Bolshoi Theatre Moscow and sang major roles in Glinka's Ivan Susanin and Tchaikovsky's Iolanta; Season 1992 as the Grand Inquisitor in Don Carlos at La Scala and the Old Prisoner in Lady Macbeth of the Mtsensk District at the Opéra Bastille, Paris; Prince Gremin in Eugene Onegin, at the Théâtre du Châtelet; Season 1993-94 as the Commendatore at La Scala, Sparafucile in Rigoletto at the Berlin Staatsoper and the Glagolitic Mass with the London Philharmonic; US debut at the New York Met in Lady Macbeth; Season 1995-96 as Lodovico in Otello and Sparafucile at the Met, King Dodon in The Golden Cockerel at Nice and the Verdi Requiem in Tel Aviv; Further engagements as Timur in Turandot at Chicago and Pimen in Boris Godunov at Frankfurt. Recordings include: Don Carlos; Eugene Onegin. Address: c/o Lies Askonas Ltd, 6 Henrietta St, London WC2E 8LA, England.

ANISIMOVA Tanya, b. 15 Feb Moscow Conservatory, 1989-90; Studied with George Neikrug, Artist's Diploma, Boston University, 1990-92; Graduate Studies with Aldo Parisot, Yale University School of Music, 1992-. Career: Solo Recitals, Russia, Massachusetts, Virginia, Washington DC, and Soloist with Orchestras, Young Performers Series, Moscow, Minsk, Gorky, Ulianovsk, Lugansk and local Philharmonic Orchestras, Russia, and Central Massachusetts Symphony, USA, 1985-91; With Glazunov String Quartet, Russia, Poland, Greece, Japan, Germany; Artist-in-Residence, Banff Music Festival, 1993. Recordings: Moscow State Radio, 1987; With Glazunov String Quartet, Athens Radio, Greece, 1989; WBGH Public Radio, Boston, Massachusetts, 1991; WCUW Radio, Worcester, Massachusetts, 1992. Contributions to: Magazines, Reviews, Journals. Honours: 1st Prize, Concertino Praha International Competition, Prague, 1981; 1st Prize, All-Union String Quartet Competition, Voronezh, Russia, 1987. Hobbies: Singing (mezzo-soprano); Playing the Piano (Bach, Mozart, Chopin). Address: 265 College Street, Apt 6B, New Haven, CT 06510, USA.

ANISSIMOV Alexander, b. 1947, Russia. Conductor. Education: Graduated from the St Petersburg Conservatory, 1970; Moscow Conservatory, 1977. Career: Chief Conductor of the Belorussian Opera from 1980, giving many premieres of Russian, Italian and French works; Led the Soviet premiere of Prokofiev's Fiery Angel, 1984, Maddalena, 1989; Followed with Khovanshchina, Eugene Onegin, Otello, The Queen of Spades and War and Peace; Guest conductor with Kirov Opera St Petersburg, Genoa (Don Carlos), Rotterdam (from 1994) and Utrecht; Season 1995 with Boris Godunov at La Fenice, Venice, Teatro Colon Buenos Aires, Wexford Festival, Chere Vichki, The Demon by Rubinstein, and the Opéra Bastille (Eugene Onegin); Season 1996 as Chief Conductor of the Belorussian State Philharmonic and Principal Guest with the RTE National Symphony Orchestra of Ireland, Dublin; Prince Igor in San Francisco and Rimsky Korsakov's Tale of Tsar Saltan at the Florence Opera; Concerts with such artists as Montserrat Caballé (at the Kremlin Palace), Galina Gorchakova (Hong Kong Festival) and Maxim Vengerov. Recordings include: The Demon, and Rachmaninov Symphonies, Glazunov Symphony and Raymonda. Address: c/o Lies Askonas Ltd, 6 Henrietta St, London WC2E 8LA, England.

ANNEAR Gwynneth, b. 1939, Tailenbend, South Australia. Singer (Soprano and Mezzo-Soprano). Education: Studied at the University of Adelaide and at the Royal College of Music, London. Debut: Sang in Amahl and the Night Visitors while at the Royal College of Music, 1964. Career: Sang the title role in Anna Bolena by Donizetti at the 1965 Glyndebourne Festival; Tour of Italy with Italian Company, 1968, in Fidelio and Così fan tutte; Has sung at the Camden Festival and with opera companies in Australia; Frequent broadcasts and concert engagements; Glyndebourne Festival 1970 and 1973, First Lady in Die Zauberflöte. Address: c/o Australian Opera, Sydney Opera House, Sydney, New South Wales, Australia.

ANSELL Gillian, b. 1968, Auckland, New Zealand. Violist. Education: Studied at Royal College of Music, London, and with Igor Ozim and the Amadeus Quartet in Cologne. Career: Played with Kent Opera Orchestra, Chamber Orchestra of Europe and Philharmonia, 1984-; Co-Founded New Zealand String Quartet, under auspices of Music Federation of New Zealand, 1987; Debut Concert, Wellington, May 1988; Concerts at Tanglewood School, USA, Banff International Competition, Canada; Performances with Lindsay Quartet at International Festival of the Arts, Wellington, 1990; Soloist with New Zealand Symphony Orchestra; Artist-in-Residence, Victoria University, Wellington; Tour to Australia for Musica Viva Australia, 1990; New Zealand tours, 1992; Concerts in New York, 1993. Recordings include: Several albums. Address: c/o Ingpen & Williams Limited, 14 Kensington Court, London W5 5DN, England.

ANTHONY Charles, b. 15 July 1929, New Orleans, Louisiana, USA. Singer (Tenor). Education: Studied voice with Dorothy Hulse at Loyola University; Continued training with Riccardo Picozzi and Giuseppe Ruisi in Italy. Career: Won Metropolitan Opera Auditions of the Air, 1952; Metropolitan debut 1954, as Missail in Boris Godunov; Later sang Ernesto in Don Pasquale, Almaviva in Il Barbiere di Siviglia, David in Die Meistersinger and Nemorino in L'Elisir d'Amore; Sang nearly 2000 performances with Metropolitan company; Also sang as guest in Dallas, Santa Fe and Boston; Sang Eisslinger in a new production of Die Meistersinger at the Metropolitan, 1993. Address: c/o Metrolpolitan Opera House, Lincoln Center, New York, NY 10023, USA.

ANTHONY James (Raymond), b. 18 Feb 1922, Providence, Rhode Island, USA. Professor; Musicologist. m. Louise MacNair, 24 May 1952, 1 son, 2 daughters. Education: BS, 1946, MA, 1948, Columbia University, New York; Diploma, Sorbonne, University of Paris, France, 1961; PhD, University of Southern California, USA, 1964. Career includes: Professor of Musicology, University of Arizona. Publications: French Baroque Music, 1974, 2nd Edition, 1978, Paperback, 1981, revised expanded version, 1993; Book III of Montéclair's Sonatas (with D Akmajian), 1979; La Musique en France à l'époque baroque, 1981; De profundis, M R Delalande, 1981. Contributor to: Church Music in France, 1661-1750 (with N Dufourcq) in New Oxford History of Music, 1975; Over 40 articles in New Grove Dictionary of Music and Musicians, 1981; New Grove Dictionary of Opera, 1990; MQ; Journal of the American Musicological Society; Notes; Early Music; Acta Musicologica; Recherches; Others. Honours: Grants from ACLS, American Philosophical Society; Festschrift: Studies on Jean-Baptise Lully and French Baroque Music in honor of James R Anthony, 1987; Chevalier de l'Ordre des Arts et des Lettres, 1995. Memberships: American Musicological Society (Council Member 1975-77, 1983-85); Société Française de Musicologie; American Associate of University Professors. Hobbies: Reading; Travel; Hiking. Address: 800 North Wilson Avenue, Tucson, Arizona, AZ 85719, USA.

ANTOINE Bernadetta, b. 8 Mar 1940, Nancy, France. Singer (Soprano). Education: Studied at the Conservatories of Nancy and Paris. Debut: Theatre Region Parisienne 1967, as Musetta. Career: Has sung at the Grand Opéra and the Opéra-Comique, Paris and in Lyon, Marseille, Toulouse, Rouen, Hamburg, Brussels, Lisbon and Geneva; ORTF, Radio France, in the 1972 premiere of Don Juan ou l'amour de la geometrie by Semenov; Strasbourg 1974, in the premiere of Les Liaisons Dangereuses by Prey; Repertoire includes works by Gluck, Mozart, Puccini, Berloiz, Debussy, Poulenc, Britten and Prokofiev; Many concert appearances.

ANTOKOLETZ Elliott, b. 3 Aug 1942, Jersey City, NJ, USA. Musicologist. m. Juana Canabal, 28 May 1972, 1 s. Education: Violin, Juilliard School of Music, 1960-65; BA, Musicology, 1968, MA, Musicology, Hunter College, 1970, PhD, Musicology, Graduate Center, 1975, City University of New York. Career: Instructor, Violin, Chamber, Brearley School, 1970-76; Lecturer, Theory Chamber Music, Faculty String Quartet, Queens College, City University of New York, 1973-76; Professor, Musicology, University of TX, Austin, 1976-; Editor, International Journal of Musicology. Publications: Books include: The Music of Bela Bartók: A Study of Tonality and Progression in Twentieth-Century Music, 1984; Bela Bartók, A Guide to Research, 1988; Twentieth Century Music, 1992; 3 Chapters in The Bartok Companion; George Perle: A Bio-Bibliography; Musical Symbolism in the Operas of Debussy and Bartok Dukas; Editor of the International Journal of Music, 1992-. Contributions to: Journal of the American Musicological Society; Musica - Realta; Musik und Dichtung; Studia Musicologica; Tempo. Honours: Béla Bartók Plaque and Diploma from the Hungarian Government, 1981; PhD Alumni Award from City College of the University of New York, 1987. Memberships: Sonneck Society; American Musicological Society; International Musicological Society; College Music Society. Hobby: Oil paintings. Address: School of Music, University of Texas at Austin, Austin, TX 78712, USA.

ANTONACCI Anna Caterina, b. 5 Apr 1961, Ferrara, Italy. Singer (Soprano). Education: Studied in Bologna. Debut: Sang Rossini's Rosina at Arrezzo, 1986. Career: Appeared as Elizabeth I in Maria Stuarda in Bari, 1988, then as Horatia in Cimarosa's Gli Orazi ed i Curiazi in Rome and Lisbon; Further engagements in Venice, Macerata, Catania, Savona and Bergamo as Paisiello's Elfrida, Adalgisa and Fiordiligi; Other roles in Manfroce's Hecuba (Polyxena) and Mayr's La Rosa Bianca e La Rosa Rossa; Rossini roles include Dorliska (Torvaldo e Dorliska), Ninetta, Semiramide, and Ermione in British concert premiere of Rossini's Opera, London, 1992; Appeared as Anais in Moise in Bologna, 1991; Rossini's Elisabetta in Naples, 1992, and Elena in La Donna del Lago, Amsterdam Concertgebouw; Sang the title role in Gluck's Armide at the opening of the 1996-97 La Scala season. Honours include: Prizewinner at Pavarotti and Callas Competitions; sang Ermione at Glyndebourne, 1995. Address: c/o Teatro Massimo Bellini, Via Perrotta 12, 95131 Cantania, Italy.

ANTONIOU Theodore, b. 10 Feb 1935, Athens, Greece. Composer; Conductor; Teacher. Education: Studied violin, voice and theory, National Conservatory, Athens, 1947-58; Composition with Yannis Papaioannou, Hellenic Conservatory, 1956-61; Composition and Conducting with Gunter Bialas, Munich Hochschule für Musik, 1961-65; Attended the Darmstadt Summer Courses, 1963-65. Career: Active as a Conductor with various contemporary music groups; Teacher of Composition and Orchestration, Stanford University, 1969-70, University of Utah, 1970, Philadelphia Music Academy 1970-75, Berkshire Music Center, Tanglewood, 1975, University of Pennsylvania, 1978, Boston University, 1979-. Compositions: Stage Periander, opera, 1977-79; Ballets, Bacchae, 1980, and The Magic World, 1984; Music Theatre pieces; Mixed media scores; Incidental music to various dramas; Film Scores; Orchestral, Concerto for clarinet, trumpet, violin and orchestra, 1959; Antithese, 1962; Piano Concertino, 1962; Jeux for cello and strings, 1963; Micrographies, 1964; Violin Concerto, 1965; Kinesis ABCD for 2 string orchestras, 1966; Threnos for wind ensemble, piano, percussion and double bass, 1972; Double Concerto for percussion and orchestra, 1972; Double Concerto for percussion and orchestra, 1977; The GBYSO Music, 1982; Various Choral Works, Solo Vocal Pieces and Chamber Music with Tape. Recordings: As Conductor of his own works and of works by other contemporary composers. Honours: Many commissions and awards. Address: c/o Music Department, Boston University, Boston, MA 02215, USA.

ANTONIOZZO Alfonso, b. 1963, Italy. Singer (Bass-Baritone). Education: Studied with Sesto Bruscantini. Career: Sang at the Montepulciano Festival from 1986, Florence and Torre del Festival, 1987, Bologna, 1988; Has appeared widely in Italy in Turandot (as Ping), Rossini's L'occasione fa il ladro, Adina and Il barbiere di Siviglia; San Francisco, 1992, as Taddeo in L'Italiana in Algeri; Other roles include Pistol in Falstaff, Bizet's Don Procopio, Schaunard in La Bohème and Patroclus in Paer's Achille. Recordings include: Don Procopio and Cimarosa's I traci amanti (Bongiovanni). Address: c/o San Francisco Opera, War Memorial Opera House, San Francisco, CA 94102, USA.

ANTONSEN Ole (Edvard), b. 25 Apr 1962, Ringsaker, Norway. Trumpeter. Education: Studied with Harry Kvaebek at the Norwegian State Academy of Music, Diploma 1982. Career: Played with the Oslo Philharmonic 1982-90; Solo career from 1990; Concerto appearances with Atlanta Symphony, Dresdner Philharmonie, Stuttgart Chamber Orchestra. I Fiamminghi Chamber Orchestra, Wurtembergisches Kammerorchester, Swedish Radio Symphony Orchestra, Oslo and Bergen Philharmonic Orchestras in Sweden, Kioi Sinfonietta, Tokyo, Israel Chamber Orchestra, Orchestre de la Suisse Romande, Leipzig Radio Orchestra, Prague Symphony, London Festival Orchestra, Royal Swedish Chamber Orchestra and Cantilena (Scotland); Tour of 15 different countries 1989, including Russia and Brazil; Season 1990 with Paris debut (Oslo Philharmonic) and engagements in Spain, USA (New York and Washington recitals), West Germany and Switzerland; Plays jazz and contemporary music as well as the standard classics; 1995-96 included a recital debut with Wayne Marshall at the Royal Festival Hall, London; Appearances for the Istanbul International, City of London and Bermuda Festivals, concerts in Germany, Switzerland, Scandinavia and Austria and a 6th tour of Japan; 1997 included a return to the 1997 Schleswig-Holstein Festival, a tour with Dmitri Sitkovsky and the New European String Orchestra and engagements in Europe, North America and the Far East. Recordings include: Recital with the Norwegian Chamber Orchestra, conducted by Iona Brown; with Wayne Marshall and the ECO, 1992; Berlin Philharmonic Orchestra with M Jansons and M Rudy for EMI. Recordings include: Tour de Force, 1993; Trumpet and piano recital disc with Wolfgang Sawallisch in 1996. Honours: First prize at the 1987 CIEM-Competition in Geneva; Laureat of the 1989 UNESCO Competition in Bratislava; Norwegian Grammy; Arets, Spillemann, for his Norwegian recording, Tour de Force, 1992. Address: Pro Arte International, Artists Management, Fosswinckelsgt 9, N-5007 Bergen, Norway.

ANTONUCCI Stefano, b. 1955, Italy. Singer (Baritone). Education: Studied at the Genoa Conservatory and in Alessandria. Career: Sang Enrico in Donizetti's Il Campanelllo at Alessandria, 1986; Maggio Musicale Florence, 1987, in Monteverdi's Ulisse; La Scala Milan from 1989, notably in La Bohème and Pergolesi's Lo frate 'nnamorato; Savona, 1990, as Duca d'Orbaco in Rossini's Torvaldo and Dorliska; Further appearances at Parma (Marcello, 1989), Rome, Monte Carlo, Martina Franca (Mercadante's Il Bravo, 1990) and the Staatsoper Berlin (Germont, 1992); Other roles include Rossini's Figaro, Eugene Onegin and Guglielmo. Address: c/o Teatro alla Scala, Via Filodrammatici 2, 20121 Milan, Italy.

ANTUNES Jorge, b. 23 Apr 1942, Rio de Janeiro, Brazil. University Professor; Composer; Conductor; Violinist. m. Mariuga Lisboa Antunes, 12 Mar 1969, 3 sons. Education: Physics, Master of Composition and Violin, University of Brazil; Master of Composition, Instituto Torcuato di Tella, Buenos Aires; Electronic and Electroacoustic Music courses; Doctorate, Sorbonne, Paris, France, 1977. Career: Professor of Composition, Director of Electronic Music Laboratory, Coordinator of Composition and Conducting, General Coordinator of Nucleus for Studies and Researches in Sonology, University of Brasilia; TV and radio appearances. Compositions: Cromorfonetica, 1969; Tartina MCMLXX, 1970; Para Nascer Aqui, 1970-71; Macroformobiles 1, 1972-73; Catastrophe Ultra-Violette, 1974; Plumbea Spes, 1976; Congadasein, 1978; Elégie Violette pour Monseigneur Romero, 1980; Qorpo-Santo, opera, 1983; Sinfonia das Directas, 1984; Dramatic Polimaniquexixe, 1985; Modinha para Mindinha, 1986; Serie Meninos, for young violinist and tape, 1986-87; Amerika 500, 1992; Olga, opera, 1993; Rimbaudiannisia MCMXCV, for children's choir, lights, masks and orchestra, 1994; Ballade Dure, electroacoustic music, 1995. Recordings: Numerous including: Jorge Antunes - Musica Eletronica, 1975; Jorge Antunes Com A Orquestra Sinfonica Brasileira, 1978; No Se Mata La Justicia - Jorge Antunes, 1982; Musica Eletronica 70's - I, 1994; Musica Eletronica 70's - II, 1995. Publications: Books: Sobre a correspondência entre os sons e as cores, 1982; Notaçao na música contemporânea, 1989. Honours include: 1st Prize Premio Angelicum, di Milano, 1971; Premio Vitae, Brazil, 1991; Premio APAC, 1992; Prix Musica Criativa, 1994; Member, Academia Brasileira de Música, 1994. Hobby: Painting. Address: Universidad de Brasilia, Depto de Musica, 70910 Brasilia, DF Brazil.

ANTUNES DE OLIVEIRA Glacy, b. 15 Oct 1943, Goiania, Goias, Brazil. Concert Pianist. Education: Graduated, Conservatory of Music, Federal University of Goias; Master's Degree, National School of Music, Federal University of Rio de Janeiro; PhD, Institute of Arts, Federal University of Goias; Postgraduate work, Rio de Janeiro and USA; Has worked under Professor Jose Kliass, Sao Paulo, and at Brigham Young University, Utah. Career: Recitals, Solo and Chamber Music, all over Brazil, North and South America, Germany, Switzerland, Austria; Founder, Director, Musika Centro de Estudos, Goiania; President, National Piano Competition, Coordinator, Postgraduate Diploma Course in Music, Institute of Arts, Federal University. Recordings: 3 as Soloist with Orquestra de Camara de Blumenau. Hobbies: Poetry; Musicals; Soccer Championships. Address: Rua 19 No 32 S Oeste, Goiania, Goias 740001-970, Brazil.

ANZAGHI Davide, b. 29 Nov 1936, Milan, Italy. Composer; Teacher. Education: Graduated, Milan Conservatory, 1957; Studied Composition with E Pozzoli, A Maggioni, G Ghedini and F Donatoni. Career: Teacher of Composition, Milan Conservatory. Compositions: Orchestral: Limbale, 1973; Ausa, 1973; Egophonie, 1974; Aur'ore for Chorus and Orchestra, 1975-76; Ermosonio, 1978; Anco, 1987; First Piano Concerto, 1987-88; Chamber: Limini for String Trio, 1971; In-Chiostro for 2 Violins and Viola, 1975, revised 1982; Alena for 10 Wind Instruments, 1976; Remota for 7 Players, 1977; Alia for Bass Clarinet and Piano, 1980; Oiseau Triste for Piccolo and Piano, 1980; Soavodia for Clarinet and Piano, 1980; Eco for Cello and Piano, 1980; Onirama for Soprano and Piano, 1980; Tornelli for Oboe and Piano, 1981; Labia for String Quartet, 1982; Ricrio for Brass Octet, 1982; Soliludio for Flute, Clarinet, Violin, Cello and Piano, 1982; Mitofania for Flute, Clarinet, Violin, Cello, Piano and Percussion, 1982; For Four for String Quartet, 1983; Airy for Clarinet, 1983; Halpith for Flute, 1984; Elan for 9 Instruments, 1984; Pri-ter for String Quartet, 1985; Queen That for Wind Quintet, 1985; Apogeo for 5 Instruments, 1987; Tremes for Viola and Piano, 1988; Viol-Once-All, 3 Pieces for Cello, 1988; Piano Pieces; Second Concerto, for Piano and Orchestra, 1990-91; Variazioni for Piano, Concerto Breve for Clarinet and Orchestra, 1990-91; Settimino for Clarinet, Horn, Bassoon, Piano, Violin, Viola and Cello, 1992; Concerto for Violin and Orchestra, 1992; Third Piano Concerto for Piano and Orchestra, 1993; Tuveuzione, Schizzo, Variazioni for Guitar, 1994; Elea for Violin and Piano, 1994; Rituzgia for Two Recitant Voices, Chorus and Orchestra, 1994; Chitattro I and II for Guitar, 1995; Suite for Cello and Piano, 1995. Memberships: President of Novurgia (Associazione Italiana per L'Arte, Lo Spettacolo, La Culture, Oggi). Address: Via Previati 37, 20149 Milan, Italy.

APERGHIS Georges, b. 23 Dec 1945, Athens, Greece. Composer. Education: Studied with Y Papaioannous, Athens; With I Xenakis, Paris, 1963. Career: Founder-Director, Atelier Théâtre et Musique, Bagnolet, France, 1976-91, Nanterre, 1992-. Compositions: Many musical theatre pieces and operas including: Pandemonium, opera, 1973; Jacques le Fataliste, opera, 1975; La Bouteille à la mer, for actors (or amateur musicians) and 4 instruments, 1976; Histoire de loups, opera, 1976; Je vous dis que je suis mort, opera, 1978; Les sept crimes de l'amour, for voice, clarinet and percussion, 1979; Liebestod, opera, 1981; L'écharpe rouge, opera, 1984; Conversations, for 2 actors and percussion, 1985; Enumerations, for 6 actor-musicians, 1988; Jojo, for 7 actor-musicians, 1990; H, Litanie musicale et égalitaire, for 1 soprano, 3 percussions and 4 actors, 1992; Sextuor, for 5 female voices and violoncello, 1993; Other works: Vesper, oratorio, 1972; De la nature de l'eau, for 6 singers, 2 actors, percussion and piano, 1974; Il Gigante Goglia, for soprano and 11 instruments, 1975; 14 recitations for solo voice, 1978; Le corps à corps, for solo percussion, 1978; Triangle carré, for string quarter and percussion trio, 1989; Tingel-Tangel, for voice, accordion and percussion, 1990; Declamations, for orchestra, 1990; Ritournelles, for 2 baritones, piccolo, clarinet, piano, mandolin, guitar, harp, marimba, violoncello and double bass, 1992; L'Adieu, for orchestra, 1994. Recordings: Récitations; Sextuor. Publication: Georges Aperghis, le corps musical, 1990. Address: c/o Théâtre des Amandies, 7 av Pablo Picasso, 92022 Nanterre Cedex, France.

APIVOR Denis, b. 14 Apr 1916. Composer. 1 son, 1 daughter. Education: Chorister, Christ Church Oxford and Hereford Cathedrals, 1925-30; University College, London, 1934 seq; Studied Pianoforte, Organ, Clarinet; Private Composition Pupil, Professor Patrick Hadley and Alan Rawsthorne, 1937-39. Debut: 1st London Concert, Wigmore Hall, April 1947. Career: Works performed: BBC Concert, Broadcasting House, 1950; Royal Ballet, Covent Garden, 1952; Royal Ballet, Sadlers Wells Theatre, 1953; BBC-ICA Concert, 1956; London Proms, 1958; BBC, Camden Theatre, 1960; Düsseldorf and Copenhagen, 1960; Volksoper, Vienna, 1962; Pollitzer Trust, Wigmore Hall, 1967; Cheltenham Festival, 1968; BBC Television, 1968; BBC Invitation Concert, 1973; Royal Northern College, Manchester, 1983; Other occupations, translator of Lorca's verse, sculpture, oriental philosophy. Compositions: The Hollow Men, 1951; A Mirror for Witches; Blood Wedding, Ballet; Tamar and Amnon for Chorus and Orchestra; Piano Concerto; Yerma, Opera, Sadler's Wells commission; Corporal Jan, TV ballet; Guitar Concerto, 1962; One Man Concert; Triple Concerto for Strings; Lorca Songs with Guitar, 1972; Neumes, Orchestral variations; 5 Symphonies (1952-91); Violin concerto, 1975; Cello Concerto, 1977; In the Landscape of Spring septet, 1993; T S Eliot Songs for voice and piano, 1994; Five Songs of F Garcia Lorca, for voice and pianoforte; "Lamentaciones", works from El poemo del Canto Jondo, 1994. Publications include: Serialism for Guitarists, 1983. Contributions to: Setting T S Eliot to Music, (T S Eliot Symposium), 1958; Chapter in Rupert Hart Davis; A Musician's Role in Ballet, to Dancing Times; On Peter Warlock and on Bernard Van Dieren, to Music Review, 1980's. Memberships: Composers Guild; Performing Right Society. Address: 9 Ashurst Avenue, Saltdean, East Sussex BN2 8DR, England.

APONTE-LEDÉE Rafael, b. 15 Oct 1938, Guayama, Puerto Rico. Composer; Teacher. Education: Studies in piano, harmony, counterpoint and composition at Madrid Conservatory, 1957-64 with Cristobal Halffter; Further study with Alberto Ginastera at the Latin American Institute of Higher Musical Studies, Di Tella Institute, Buenos Aires, diploma in 1966. Career: Teacher of theory and composition, University of Puerto Rico, 1968-73, and the Puerto Rico Conservatory of Music, 1968-; Promoter of avant-garde music festivals. Compositions include: Orchestral: Elejia, 1965, revised, 1967, Impulsos, in memoriam Julia de Burgos, 1967, Dos Cuentos Para Orquesta, 1987, Canción De Albada Y Epitafio, 1991; Orchestra and Soloist: Cantata, 1988; Chamber Orchestra: A Flor De Piel with 2 singers; Chamber Opera: El Passo De Buster Keaton; Solo Instruments: Tres Bagatelas for Guitar, Tema Y Seis Diferencias for Piano; Chamber: Dialogantes for Flute and Viola, 1965; Piano pieces, many other works for various instruments, tape; Canción de Albada for orchestra, 1991. Recordings: Musica de Cámara, 1976; La Canción De Arte Puertorriquena with Margarita Castro, 1989; La Musica De Rafael Aponte Ledée. Publications: Tema y seis diferencias; Sombras, Zona de Carga y Descarga; La Ventana Abierta. Memberships: Musical Director of Latin American Foundation for Contemporary Music. Honours: ASCAP, 1989, 1990, 1991. Address: c/o Conservatorio de Musica de Puerto Rico, Apartdo 41227, Minillas Station, Santurce, Puerto Rico 00940.

APPEL Andrew, b. 8 June 1951, New York City, USA. Harpsichordist. Education: Duke University, 1969-71; Doctorate, Juilliard School, 1983. Debut: Carnegie Recital Hall, 1977. Career: Solo recitals in Europe and USA; Director of Four Nations Ensemble; Festival participation at Spoleto, Aston Magna; Teacher at Temple University, Juilliard, Princeton; Mostly Mozart. Recordings: Bach, Works for Harpsichord, 1983; Couperin, Works for Harpsichord, 1989; JB Bach-Bridge, 1987; Couperin, 1991. Publication: Gaspard Le Roux - Complete Works, 1989. Honour: 1st Prize, Erwin Bodkey Competition, 1977. Memberships: American Musical Society; Early Music America; South Eastern Historical Keyboard Society. Hobbies: History; Cinema. Address: 39 Plaza Street, Brooklyn, NY 11217, USA.

APPELGREN Curt, b. 1945, Sweden. Bass Baritone Opera Singer. Career: Began as a violinist and later made his debut as a singer at the Drottningholm Court Theatre as Dulcamara in L'Elisir d'Amore; Sang Pogner in Götz Freidrich's production of Die Meistersinger at the Royal Opera in Stockholm; Other Swedish roles include Cimarosa's Maestro di Capella, Jokanaan in Salome and Leporello in Don Giovanni; Sang Oxenstierna in the premiere of Christina by Hans Gefors, 1986; Perugia Festival in Spontini's La Vestale; Sung at Glyndebourne as Rocco and Bottom, and in Peter Hall's productions of Fidelio and A Midsummer Night's Dream; Sang Bottom at the Hong Kong Festival and Rossini's Basilio at Glyndebourne; Appearances with the London Choral Society and the London Philharmonic Orchestra at the Festival Hall; Sang Johann in a revival of Vogler's Gustaf Adolf och Ebba Braha at Drottningholm, 1990; King Mark in Tristan und Isolde at the Festival Hall, London, 1993. Address: c/o Lies Askonas, 6 Henrietta Street, London, WC2, England.

ARAD Atar, b. 1943, Israel. Violist. Career: Member of the Cleveland Quartet, 1980-87; Regular tours of USA, Canada, Europe, Japan, South America and the Middle East; Faculty of Indiana University, Bloomington; Concerts in Paris, Lyon, London, Bonn, Prague, Brussels and Houston; Appeared at Salzburg, Edinburgh, Aspen, Mostly Mozart and Lucern festivals; In addition to standard repertory performs works by John Harbison, Samuel Adler, Christopher Rouse, Toru Takemitsu and Solo Sonata for Viola by Atar Arad. Recordings: Repertoire from Mozart to Ravel; Recordings in collaboration with Cleveland Quartet, Emanuel Ax and Yo Yo Ma. Address: 1657 Bellemeade Avenue, Bloomington, IN 47401, USA.

ARAGALL Giacomo, b. 6 June 1939, Barcelona, Spain. Tenor. Education: Studied with Francesco Puig in Barcelona and with Vladimir Badiali in Milan. Debut: La Fenice, Venice, 1963 in the first modern performance of Verdi's Jerusalem. Career: La

Scala Milan in 1963 as Mascagni's Fritz; In 1965 sang in Haydn's Le Pescatrici with Netherlands Opera and at the Edinburgh Festival; Vienna Staatsoper debut in 1966 as Rodolfo in La Bohème; Covent Garden debut in 1966 as the Duke of Mantua; Metropolitan Opera debut in 1968; Guest appearances in Berlin, Italy, San Francisco and at the Lyric Opera Chicago; Sang at San Carlo Opera Naples in 1972 in a revival of Donizetti's Caterina Cornaro; Festival appearances at Bregenz and Orange in 1984 as Cavaradossi and Don Carlos; Sang Gabriele Adorno at Barcelona in 1990 and Don Carlos at the Orange Festival in 1990; Sang Rodolfo at Barcelona in 1991 and Don Carlos at the Deutsche Oper Berlin, 1992; Sang Cavaradossi at the Opéra Bastille, 1994. Other roles include Pinkerton, Romeo in I Capuleti e i Montecchi, Werther and Gennaro in Lucrezia Borgia. Recordings: La Traviata; Lucrezia Borgia; Faust; Rigoletto; Simon Boccanegra; Madama Butterfly. Address: c/o Stafford Law Associates, 6 Barham Close, Weybridge, Surrey KT13 9PR, England.

ARAIZA (Jose) Francisco, b. 4 Oct 1950, Mexico City, Mexico. Singer (Tenor). Divorced, 2 sons, 2 daughters. Education: University of Mexico City; Vocal studies with Irma Gonzalez and Erika Kubacsek (Repertory). Debut: As First Prisoner in Beethoven's Fidelio, Mexico City, 1970. Career: With Karlsruhe Opera, 1974-78; Permanent member of Zurich Opera House, 1978-; Guest appearances in Vienna, Munich, Hamburg, Berlin, Covent Garden London, Opera Bastille Paris, La Scala of Milan, Rome, Parma, Barcelona, Madrid, San Francisco, Chicago, Buenos Aires and Japan; Also at the international festivals of Aix-en-Provence, Orange, Bayreuth, Salzburg (debut in 1980 under Von Karajan), Edinburgh, Rossini Festival Pesaro, Schubert Festival Hohenems, Richard Strauss Festival, Garmisch; Operatic repertoire ranges from Mozart and Rossini in 1983 to dramatic Italian and French repertory to Wagner roles such as Lohengrin in Venice 1990 and Walter in Die Meistersinger Von Nürnberg with Metropolitan Opera in New York, 1993; Sang Faust in a new production of Gounod's opera, Zurich, 1997; Renowned Lieder and Concert Singer, Festival Orange. Recordings include: Die schöne Müllerin; All major Mozart roles including Tamino, Belmonte, Ferrando, Don Ottavio and Idomeneo; Il Barbiere di Siviglia, Faust, Les Contes d'Hoffmann, La Bohème, Hagenbach in La Wally, Der Freischütz; Das Lied von der Erde, Beethoven's 9th Symphony, Die Schöpfung and Mozart's Requiem; Arias and Lieder; Several videos including: La Cenerentola; The Abduction from the Seraglio. Honours: Deutscher Schallplattenpreis; Orphee d'Or; Mozart Medal, Mexico; Otello d'Oro: Goldener Merkur, Best Performer's Award, 1996. Hobbies: Tennis; Curling; Breeding Thoroughbreds. Address: c/o Kunstlermanagement, M Kursidem, Tal 15, 80331 Munich, Germany.

ARBONELLI Guido, b. 26 Feb 1962, Perugia, Italy. Teacher; Clarinettist. m. Genderian Cinzia, 15 Sept 1986, 1 daughter. Education: Conservatory F Morlacchi, Perugia. Debut: Perugia, 1977. Career: Appearances at Malta Festival, Sweden Fylkingen, The Netherlands - Gavdeamus, Belgrade Festival, Italian Radio, Siena, Venice Theatre - Italy, Laudamo, Bologna - Accademia, Florence, Gamo, Vienna, Ancona Festival, Fiesole Festival, Perugia Sagra Music and others. Compositions: Images From Auschwitz. Recordings: Several CD's. Publication: Images From Auschwitz, 1997. Honours: 13 1st Prizes, Rome, Genova, Caserta, Udine, Stresa, Sorrento; Gaudeamus Prize, Rotterdam, 1995. Address: Via Del Frumento 57, 06070 Pila, Perugia, Italy.

ARCHER Neill, b. 31 Aug 1961, Northampton, England. Singer (Tenor). Education: Studied at the University of East Anglia and the Brevard Music Centre in North Carolina. Career: Concert engagements with the London Philharmonic, BBC Symphony, English Baroque Soloists and the Junge Deutsche Philharmonie; Promenade Concerts debut in 1983 with Babylon The Great is Fallen, by Alexander Goehr; Festival Hall debut in Mozart's Requiem followed by Schoenberg's Moses und Aron under John Pritchard; Sang in Bach's St John Passion at the Accademia di Santa Cecilia in Rome, the St Matthew Passion in Stavanger and Schumann's Das Paradies und die Peri at Paris Opéra; Season 1987-88 with Tamino for Kent Opera, Ferrando for Scottish Opera and Don Ottavio with Welsh National Opera; Teatro Regio Turin in 1988 in Testi's Riccardo III; Returned to Italy as Andres in Wozzeck at Parma; Buxton Festival in 1988 as Ubaldo in Haydn's Armida followed by Carmina Burana at the Edinburgh Festival; Sang Ferrando in Cosi fan tutte for Opera Factory, also televised; Season 1989-90 included Almaviva in Oslo and for Opera North; Sang at English National Opera and Covent Garden in 1991 as Tamino and Jacquino; Sang Pylade in Iphigénie en Tauride at Basle in 1991; Season 1991-92 included Don Ottavio in New Zealand and Pelléas with WNO in a Pierre Boulez/Peter Stein presentation of Debussy's opera; Sang the Steersman in a new production of Der fliegende Holländer at Covent Garden in 1992; Season 1994 as Tamino for ENO and Almaviva at Garsington. Address: c/o Athole Still Ltd, Foresters Hall, 25-27 Westow Street, London SE19 3RY, england.

ARCHER Richard Donald, b. 3 July 1947, Leicester, England. Teacher. Education: BA, University of Durham; PGCE, Christs College of Education, University of Liverpool; MusB, Trinity College, Dublin; MMus, University of Sheffield; FRCO; ADCM; FTCL; LRAM; ARCM. Career: Organist, Recitals Locally, Solo Organist at Concerts; Organist, Leicester Philharmonic Society; Radio Broadcasts, Conductor, Hinckley Choral Union & City of Leicester Singers; Guest Conductor, Accompanist, Director of Music, St John the Baptist, Leicester. Compositions: Works for Local Choirs in Manuscript, including 2 Sonnets, Fire of the Spirit. Recording: Fire of the Spirit. Honours: Prizes, Organ Playing Competitions. Memberships: Incorporated Society of Musicians; Hymn Society of Great Britain and Ireland; Methodist Church Music Society; Leicester and District Organists Association. Hobbies: Walking; Reading. Address: 11 Frampton Avenue, Leicester LE3 0SG, England.

ARCHER Violet (Balestreri), b. 24 Apr 1913, Montreal, Canada. Composer; Teacher; Performer; Adjudicator. Education: Teacher's Licence, 1934, BMus, 1936, McGill University; Associate, Royal Canadian College of Organists, 1938; BMus, 1948, MMus, 1949, Yale University, USA. Debut: With own composition, Scherzo Sinfonia, Montreal Symphony Orchestra, 1940. Career: Faculty of McGill University, 1943-47, North Texas State College, 1950-53, University of OK, 1953-61, University of Alberta, 1962-78; Visiting Lecturer or Professor, Resident Composer at various other universities and colleges in USA and Canada. Compositions: Numerous works for piano, voice, violin, organ, choir, orchestra, harp, trumpet, oboe, saxophone and combinations; Commissions include Piano Sonata No 2, 1979, 4 Duets for Violin and Cello, 1979, Song Cycle, 1979, Whatsoever Things Are True, film score, 1980, Sonata for Bassoon and Piano, 1980, Psalm 145, a cappella, 1981, Sonata for Solo Cello, 1981, Sololoquies in B Flat and A for Clarinets, 1982, 2 Fanfares For A Festive Day, for Brass Quintet, 1989, most works published and performed worldwide; The Owl Queen for High Voice and Piano, 1990; Variations for Violin and Piano; Improvisation for Solo Snare Drum, 1990; Dancing on the Seashore for piano, 1991. Recordings: Numerous and Varied. Honours: Scholarships, fellowships, awards and honorary degrees. Hobbies: Reading; Hiking; Theatre; Films. Address: 10805 85th Avenue, Edmonton, Alberta, Canada, T6E 2L2.

ARCHIBALD Ann, b. 1967, Scotland. Singer (Soprano). Education: Studied at the Royal Scottish Academy of Music and Drama with Elizabeth Izatt. Career: Concert debut with the City of Glasgow Philharmonic at Glasgow Royal Concert Hall; Concert repertory includes Carmina Burana, Handel and Bach Cantatas (Göttingen Festival), Beethoven's Ninth (with the Royal Scottish National Orchestra) and Mahler's 4th Symphony; Opera debut 1992, as Papagena with Scottish Opera; Further appearances as Second Niece in Peter Grimes, Mozart's Barbarina and Mrs Honor in Tom Jones by Philidor (Drottningholm Festival, 1995); Season 1995-96 as Musetta and the Sandman in Hansel and Gretel for Scottish Opera, and in Monteverdi's Orfeo for English National Opera. Honours include: Numerous prizes with the Royal Scottish Academy. Address: c/o Lies Askonas Ltd, 6 Henrietta St, London WC2E 8LA, England.

ARCO Annie d', b. 28 Oct 1920, Marseilles, France. Pianist. Education: Studied at the Marseilles Conservatory and in Paris with Marguerite Long, 1934-38. Career: Pianist at the Paris Conservatoire, 1938-43; Concert debut with the Lamoureux Orchestra, followed by concerts in France and throughout Europe: Accompanist to such soloists as Pierre Pierlot (oboe), Henryk Szeryng, Jean-Pierre Rampal and André Navarra; Teacher at the Ecole Normale de Musique in Paris from 1966. Honours include: Prizewinner at the 1946 Geneva International Competition. Address: c/o Ecole Normale de Musique, 1/4 bis Boulevard Malesherbes, F-75017 Paris, France.

ARDAM Elzbieta, b. 22 Sept 1959, Kielczewo, Poland. Singer. m. Udo gefe, 24 May 1991, 1 son. Education: Consevatory of Poznan, 1985. Debut: Santuzza, 1983. Career: Orfeo, Poppea, Reign, World Premier, Orfeo, La Scala di Milan, Otello, Chicago Symphony & New York Carnegie Hall. Recordings: Janacek Diary; Boesmans Reigen; Emilia in Otello. Honours: Silver Medal, Geneva, 1981; Tschaikovsky Bronze Medal, Moscow, 1982; R Vinas Bronze Medal, Barcelona, 1984. Memberships: Teatr Wieki, Poznan, 1982-87. Hobby: Reading Books. Address: Gartenstrasse 38, D-60596 Frankfurt, Germany.

ARDEN-GRIFFITH Paul, b. 18 Jan 1952, Stockport, England. Singer (Tenor). Education: Royal Manchester and Colleges of Music; GRSM (Teachers), Piano, Singing; ARMCM (Teachers), Piano, Singing; ARMCM (Performers), Singing; Cantica Voice Studio, London; Current Vocal Coach, Anthony Hocking. Debut: Puck in Benjamin Britten's Midsummer Night's Dream, Sadler's Wells Theatre, London, 1973. Career includes: Has sung UK, abroad; Franz Lehar's Merry Widow with English National Opera, London Coliseum; World premiere, Henze's We Come to the River, Covent Garden, 1976; UK premiere, Britten's Paul Bunyan, Aldeburgh Festival, 1976; Carlisle Floyd's Of Mice and Men, Wexford Festival, 1980; Carl Orff's Carmina Burana, Singapore Festival of the Arts, 1984; World concert tours, Hong Kong, Singapore, Sydney, 1983, 1985; Greenwich Festival, 1986-87; World premiere, Phantom of the Opera, London, 1986; Mobil Concert Season; Founder Member, Arts Council Opera 80 UK Touring Company; Guest Soloist, Royal Artillery Orchestra; Prokofiev's The Duenna, Wexford Festival, 1989; Count Almaviva in Rossini Bicentennial UK Tour of Barber of Seville, 1992; Opera Gala Nights Series aboard Cunard QE2, 1993; Puccini's Il Tabarro, Barezzi Opera, 1993; Esplorando!, Costa Lines Cruising Show, Miami, 1994-95; Rossini's Count Ory, White Horse Opera, England, 1996; Lloyd Webber's Sunset Boulevard, Wiesbaden, Germany, 1997-98; Frequent Guest Soloist with the Royal Artillery Orchestra. Recordings: Debut Record-Paul Arden-Griffith - The Song is You, 1986; Phantom of the Opera, original cast; An Evening with Alan Jay Lerner; Minstrel Magic, cast album; Nessum Dorma: The Classic Collection; Encore!; A Minstrel on Broadway; Accolade!; Video: On Stage Please at the Hackney Empire. Honours: Gwilym Gwalchmai Jones Scholarship for Singing, Royal Manchester College of Music, 1974. Memberships: Musicians' Union; British Actors Equity Association; Performing Arts Media Association. Address: c/o Ken Spencer Personal Management, 138 Sandy Hill Road, Woolwich, London SE18 7BA, England.

ARDITTI Irvine, b. 8 Feb 1953, London, England. Violinist. m. Jenny Whitelegg, 3 sons. Education: Royal Academy of Music with Clarence Myerscough and Manoug Parikian, 1969-74. Career: Concert Violinist; Co-Founder, Leader, Arditti String Quartet with many 20th Century performances worldwide, 1974-; Co-leader, London Symphony Orchestra, 1976-80; Engagements, major festivals in cities throughout Europe including Aldeburgh, Bath, BBC Proms, Berlin, Budapest, Paris, Venice Biennale, Vienna and Warsaw and USA; Resident String Tutor, Darmstadt Ferienkurse for New Music, 1982-; BBC Television Music in Camera, Radio 3 series of 7 recitals, 1987; All Schoenberg's quartets in single recital, Elizabeth Hall, London, November, 1988; Solo appearances in Turin, Brussels, Berlin, Belgian and Turin Radio Symphony Orchestras, London Sinfonietta, Spectrum and Ensemble Cologne; World Premiere, solo works by various composers including J Dillon, J Harvey and Xenakis; With Arditti Quartet has given complete quartets of Berg, Webern and Schoenberg and numerous other composers; Promenade concert debut with United Kingdom premiere of L Francesconi's Rita Neurali in 1993. Recordings: Complete Kurtag Quartets, Lachemann, Dutilleux, and Nono; Rihm, Harvey Quartets; La Lontanza for violin and tape. Publications: Premiere of New Work for Violin and Orchestra by Liebermann, 1994. Honours: Gold Medal. Worshipful Society of Musicians, 1994; Chamber Music Award, Royal Philharmonic Society. Address: c/o Lorraine Lyons, 12 Chatteris Avenue, Harold Hill, Romford, Essex RM3 8JX, England.

ARENA Maurizio, b. 13 Mar 1935, Messina, Italy. Conductor. Education: Studied in Palermo and with Franco Ferrara. Career: assistant to Tulio Serafin and Antonio Votto; Music Director of the Palermo Opera, 1963-69; Guest appearances in Italian opera houses and throughout Europe; Operas by Zandonai and Anton Rubinstein for the Italian Radio, RAI. Address: c/o Teatro Massimo di Palermo, Piazza Verdi, 90138 Palermo, Italy.

ARENS Rolf-Dieter, b. 16 Feb 1945, Zinnwald, Germany. Pianist. Education: Studied at the Leipzig Musikhochschule, 1963-68. Career: Many appearances in Germany and elsewhere in Europe as soloist and chamber musician; Soloist with the Berlin Symphony Orchestra, from 1986; Teacher at the Leipzig Hochschule from 1970, Franz Liszt Hochschule, Weimar, 1976. Honours include: Prizewinner at the Budapest International Competition (1966), Bach International at Leipzig (1968) and Long-Thibaud Competition at Paris (1971). Address: c/o Hochschule für Musik Franz Liszt, Platz der Demokratie 2-3, 5300 Weimar, Germany.

AREVALO Octavio, b. 1963, Mexico City. Singer (Tenor). Education: Studied at the Verdi Conservatoire, Milan, 1984-85; Further study with Ernst Haefliger and James King in Munich. Career: Concert appearances in Switzerland, in Bach's Christmas Oratorio and Mozart's C Minor Mass; Stage debut as Paolino in Il Matrimonio Segreto at the Gärtnerplatz Theatre, Munich, 1989; Sang Tamino at Mexico City, 1990; Stadttheater Lucerne, as Mozart's Belmonte, Tamono and Don Ottavio, Nemorino, Rodolfo and Pinkerton, 1991-; Vienna Staatsoper debut as Nemorino, 1992; Season 1994-95 as Rinuccio in Gianni Schicchi at the Komische Oper Berlin, Ferrando (Cosi fan tutte) at Mexico City, Verdi's Fenton in Madrid and Polyceute in Donizetti's Les Martyrs at Nancy; Season 1996-97 in Le Roi Arthus by Chausson at the Bergenz Festival, Orombello in Beatrice di Tenda at the Deutsche Oper Berlin and Leicester in Maria Stuarda at the Herkulessahl, Munich; Further concert repertory includes Dvorák's Stabat Mater (in Zurich), the Verdi Requiem (Moscow) and Bruckner's Te Deum (Madrid, 1997). Recordings include: Rossini's Il Signor Bruschino and Semiramide. Address: c/o Lies Askonas Ltd, 6 Henrietta St, London WC2 8LA, England.

ARGENTA Nancy, b. 17 Jan 1957, Nelson, British Columbia, Canada. Soprano. Education: Graduated, University of Western Ontario, 1980; Vocal study in West Germany and with Peter Pears and Gerard Souzay; Further study with Vera Rosza. Career: Appearances at the Vienna and Schwetzingen Festivals with London Baroque; Sang in Scarlatti's La Giuditta in Italy, Mozart Mass in C minor with the English Chamber Orchestra, Handel's Messiah and Giulio Cesare in Canada; Concerts with the Songmakers' Almanac; Opera engagements as Susanna with Welsh National Opera, Haydn's L'Infedeltà Delusa in Paris, Brussels and Cologne, Astreia in Handel's Tamerlano at the Opéra de Lyon, La Chasseuresse in Rameau's Hippolyte et Aricie and Purcell's King Arthur at Aix-en-Provence; Sang the title role in L'Incoronazione di Poppea, on South Bank, London; Purcell's Dido in Utrecht, Paris, Beaune and Saintes; Further concerts in the Schoenberg Reluctant Revolutionary series on South Bank and Cupid in Venus and Adonis by Blow at the 1989 Promenade Concerts; Sang Vespina in Haydn's L'Infedeltà Delusa, Antwerp, 1990; Rossanne in the North American premiere of Floridante, Toronto, 1990; Sang Clärchen's songs in Beethoven's Egmont at the Festival Hall, 1991; Mozart's Requiem at the 1991 Proms, conducted by Roger Norrington; Debut in 1996 at the Salzburg, Flanders and Budapest Festivals, singing Euridice from Gluck's Orfeo ed Euridice with Ivan Fischer and the Budapest Festival Orchestra; Also performed Tafelmusik in Toronto, the National Arts Centre Ottawa, the Scottish Chamber Orchestra, Ensemble Baroque de Limoges, the Orchestra of the Age of enlightenment, Academy of Ancient Music and at the Ansbach, Halle and Spitalfields Festivals; Mahler's 2nd Symphony at the Festival Hall, 1997. Recordings include: Handel's Solomon and the Magnificat by Bach; Bach B Minor Mass, St John Passion and Christmas Oratorio; Monteverdi's Orfeo; Handel's Tamerlano; Barbarina in Le Nozze di Figaro. Address: c/o Ron Gonsalves Management, 10 Dagnan Road, London, SW12 9LQ, England.

ARGENTO Dominick, b. 27 Oct 1927, York, PA, USA. Composer; Teacher. Education: Studied with Nicolas Nabokov and Hugo Weisgall at the Peabody Conservatory of Music, Baltimore, BA, 1951; Piano with Pietro Scarpini and composition with Luigi Dallapiccola at the Florence Conservatory, 1951-52; Studied composition with Bernard Rogers, Howard Hanson and Alan Hovhaness at the Eastman School of Music, PhD, 1957. Career: Teacher of theory and composition, 1958-, Regents Professor, 1979-, University of Minnesota; Compositions include: Operas: The Boor, 1957, Christopher Sly, 1962-63, The Shoemaker's Holiday, 1967, The Voyage of Edgar Allan Poe, 1975-76, Casanova's Homecoming, 1980-84; The Aspern Papers, 1988; The Dream of Valentino, 1993; Monodramas: A Water Bird Talk, 1974; Ballets: The Resurrection Of Don Juan, 1955, Incidental music to plays; Orchestral: Ode To The West Wind, concerto for Soprano and Orchestra, 1956, Bravo Mozart!, 1969, In Praise Of Music, 1977, Le Tombeau d'Edgar Poe, 1985; Chamber: Divertimento for Piano and Strings, 1954; Vocal: Songs About Spring for Soprano and Piano or Chamber Orchestra, 1954, The Revelation Of St John The Divine for Tenor, Men's Voices, Brass and Percussion, 1966, Letters From Composers for Tenor and Guitar, 1968, To Be Sung Upon The Water, song cycle for High Voice, Clarinet and Piano, 1972, From The Diary Of Virginia Woolf, song cycle for Mezzo-Soprano and Piano, 1974, I Hate And I Love, song cycle for Chorus and Percussion, 1981, Te Deum for Chorus and Orchestra, 1987. Honours: Fulbright Fellowship, 1951-52; Guggenheim Fellowships, 1957, 1964; Pulitzer Prize in Music, 1975; Numerous commissions; Honorary Doctorates. Memberships include: Institute of Arts and Letters, 1980. Address: c/o School of Music, University of Minnesota, MN 55455, USA.

ARGERICH Martha, b. 5 June 1941, Buenos Aires, Argentina. Pianist. Education: Studied with V Scaramuzza in Argentine and with Freidrich Gulda, Madeleine Lipatti, Nikita Magaloff and Michelangeli in Europe. Debut: 1946. Career: Gave recitals in Buenos Aires, 1949, 1952; Moved to Europe in 1955; London debut in 1964; Soloist with the world's leading orchestras; Often heard in Chopin, Liszt, Schumann, Prokofiev and Bartók; Duo partnership with the violinist Gidon Kremer; London recital in 1988 with sonatas by Schumann, Franck and Bartók; Played Beethoven's 3rd Concerto with Chamber Orchestra of Europe at the Barbican Hall, London, 1991. Honours include: Winner, International Music Competition, Geneva, 1957; Winner, Busoni Competition, Bolzano, 1957; 1st Prize, Seventh Warsaw International Chopin Competition, 1965; Polish Radio Prize, 1965.

ARGIRIS Spiros, b. 24 Aug 1948, Athens, Greece. Conductor. Education: Studied piano with Alfons Kontarsky, conducting with Hans Swarowsky; With Nadia Boulanger in Paris. Career: Conducted at opera houses in Berlin, Hamburg, Cologne and elsewhere in Germany; Has led concerts at the Venice Biennale and at the Maggio Musicale, Florence; Musical Director of the Festival of Two Worlds, Spoleto-Charleston, 1986; Conducted Salome in 1989; Musical Director of the Trieste Opera, 1987, leading The Queen of Spades in 1988 and Il Barbiere di Siviglia and Parsifal in 1989; Conducted Elektra at the Teatro Nuovo, Spoleto, 1990; Parsifal and Le nozze di Figaro at Charleston; Modern repertoire includes Henze's El Rey de Harlem, premiere 1980, and Hans Jurgen von Böse's Die Nacht aus Blei, premiere 1981; Appointed Musical Director of the Opera and Orchestre Philharmonique at Nice, 1988. Address: Orchestre Philharmonique de Nice, Opera de Nice, Rue Saint Francois de Paule, F-06300 Nice, France.

ARHO Anneli, b. 12 Apr 1951, Helsinki, Finland. Composer. Education: Studied at the Sibelius Academy, Helsinki, and with Klaus Huber and Brian Ferneyhough at Freiburg. Career: Teacher at the Sibelius Academy from 1979. Compositions: Minos for harpsichord, 1978; Answer for mezzo, horn and string quartet, 1978; Once upon a Time for wind quintet, 1979; Par comparison for 3 cellos, 1981; Les temps emboîtés for 3 cellos, 1987. Address: c/o Sibelius Academy of Music, Töölönkatu 28, SF-00260 Helsinki, Finland.

ARIOSTINI Armando, b. 30 Mar 1951, Milan, Italy. Singer (Baritone). Education: Studied in Alessandria. Career: Sang Schaunard at Trieste in 1981, Fabrizio in Rossini's Pietra del Paragone at Piccola Scala (1982), returning for Gluck's Rencontre Imprévue; Has sung widely in Italy at such centres as Bologna, Savona, Treviso and Venice; Sang in Paisiello's Barbiere di Siviglia at Bordeaux and has appeared further in Naples, Florence, Paris and Zurich; Other roles include Filippo in La Gazza Ladra and Bellini's Beatrice di Tenda, Sharpless, Ford, Olivier in Capriccio and Massenet's Lescaut. Recordings include: L'Italiana in Londra, by Cimarosa (Bongiovanni). Address: c/o Teatro Comunale di Trieste, Riva Novembre 1, 34121 Trieste, Italy.

ARISTO Giorgio, b. 28 Dec 1950, New York City, USA. Singer (Tenor). Education: Studied at Manhattan School of Music and in Milan and Zurich. Career: Sang at Passau, 1979-81, as the Duke in Rigoletto, Rodolfo in La Bohème and Rossini's Count Almaviva; Engaged in Essen, 1981-83, Hanover, 1983-; Guest appearances in Dusseldorf as Done José, Vienna as Massenet's Werther, Munich in The Bartered Bride and Copenhagen as Cavaradossi; Season 1988-89 as Calaf in Nantes and Andrea Chenier in Toulon and Liège; Other roles include Alfredo and Turiddu; Many concert appearances. Address: C/O Opéra Royale de Wallonie, 4 Leopoldstrasse, B-1000 Brussels, Belgium.

ARKADIEV Mikhail, b. 1958, Moscow, Russia. Pianist; Composer. Education: Graduated from the Tchaikovsky Conservatoire, Moscow, 1978; Gnessin Institute, 1988. Career: Solo performances throughout Russia and recital accompanist to baritone Dmitri Hvorostovsky, 1990-; Tours to Europe, America, East Asia and the Pacific Music Festival; Solo debut in Berlin, 1990; Chair of the Piano Department at the Academy of Choral Art in Moscow. Compositions include: Mass For Choir And Organ; Vocal and chamber works. Publications include: The Temporal Structures of New European Music; An Essay in Phenomenological Study, 1992. Address: c/o Lies Askonas Ltd, 6 Henrietta St, London WC2E 8LA, England.

ARKHIPOVA Irina (Konstantinova), b. 2 Dec 1925, Moscow, USSR. Singer (Mezzo-Soprano). Education: Studied with Leonid Savranski at the Moscow Conservatory. Career: Sang at Sverdlovsk 1954-56; Member of the Bolshoi Opera, Moscow from 1956; Has sung Azucena, Marina, Marfa (Khovanshchina), Amneris, Eboli and Charlotte; Further Russian repertoire includes Lyubasha (The Tsar's Bride), Polina and Lyubov (The Queen of Spades), and parts in the Bolshoi premieres of War and Peace and The Story of a Real Man by Prokofiev, Khrennikov's The Mother and Shchedrin's Not Love Alone; Teatro San Carlo Naples 1960, as Carmen; La Scala Milan 1964 as Helen in War and Peace (with the Bolshoi Company); 1967-71, as Marfa and Marina; Orange and Covent Garden 1972 and 1975, as Azucena; San Francisco 1972, as Amneris; Savonlinna Festival, Finland, 1989 as Marfa in Khovanshchina; Sang Ulrica at Covent Garden, 1988; Appeared with the Kirov Opera at the Metropolitan, (the Countess in The Queen of Spades), 1992; and as the Nurse in Eugene Onegin at the Théâtre du Châtelet, 1992. Recordings: War and Peace, Khovanshchina, Boris Godunov, The Snow Maiden, The Queen of Spades, Mazeppa (Melodya), Alexander Nevsky by Prokofiev (Decca). Honours include: People's Artist of the USSR, 1966.

ARMENGUARD Jean-Pierre, b. 17 June 1943, Clermont-Ferrand, France. Pianist. Education: Studied at the Ecole Normale and the Sorbonne, Paris, and with Jacques Février. Career: Has performed throughout France and elsewhere in Europe in a wide repertory, including 20th century music; Founded the Sainte-Baume music festival and co-founded (1970) a trio with clarinet and piano; French cultural ambassador to Sweden (1982-85) and to Greece (1985-88). Publications include: History of Music from the time of Beethoven.

ARMER Elinor, b. 6 Oct 1939, Oakland, California, USA. Composer; Pianist. Education: Studied at Mills College and at Berkeley and San Francisco, with Milhaud and Leon Kirchner. Career: Teacher at the San Francisco Conservatory of Music from 1976 (currently head of composition). Compositions: Uses of Uttermost Parts 1-8, 1986-93, series of varied pieces with Ursula K Le Guin; String quartet, 1983; A Season of Grief for low voice and piano, 1987; Pearl for orchestra, 1986. Address: San Francisco Conservatory of Music, 1201 Ortega Street, San Francisco, CA 94122, USA.

ARMILATO Fabio, b. 1963, Genoa, Italy. Singer (Tenor). Education: Paganini Conservatoire and the Academia Virgiliana, Mantua. Debut: Teatro Pergolesi di Jesi, 1986, as Licinio in La Vestale. Career: Appearances at La Scala and throughout Italy as Faust in Mefistofele, Alfredo, Edgardo, Turiddu, Pinkerton and Gabriele Adorno; Vlaamse Opera Antwerp as Don Carlos, Rodolfo, Des Grieux and Cavaradossi; North American debut at the New York City Opera as Don José; Metropolitan Opera as Radames, Gabriele, Turiddu, Manrico and Loris in Fedora; San Francisco Opera from 1994, as Manrico and Radames, 1997; Further engagements with the Houston Opera as Pinkerton, at Pittsburgh as Don José, Buenos Aires as Andrea Chenier and in Paris as Cavaradossi. Honours include: Winner, 1986 Tito Schipa Competition. Address: c/o Music International, 13 Ardilaun Road, London, N5 2QR, England.

ARMITSTEAD Melanie, b. 1957, England. Soprano. Education: Studied at Guildhall School of Music. Debut: Frasquita and Micaela in Carmen for Scottish Opera. Career: Appearances with Kent Opera, 1987-, as Venus in Pygmalion, First Lady in The Magic Flute, and Minerva in The Return of Ulysses; Scottish Opera debut as Titania in Eugene Onegin in 1988 returning as Fiordigili; English National Opera and Opera North debuts in 1990 as Nicoletta in The Love for Three Oranges and Mélisande in Ariane et Barbe-Bleue; Returned to Leeds as Xenia in Boris Godunov in 1992; Created the Niece in Fenelon's Le Chevalier Imaginaire, Théâtre du Châtelet, Paris, 1992; Concert performances with Liverpool Philharmonic, the Halle and Royal Philharmonic; Season 1989-90 included Vivaldi's Gloria with English Chamber Orchestra, Messiah with Tokyo Philharmonic, St John Passion in The Netherlands, and Bach's Magnificat at the Barbican Hall; Recitalist at the Wigmore Hall (Debut 1987), Purcell Room and Elizabeth Hall; Appearances with the pianist Julian Drake and oboist Nicholas Daniel. Address: c/o Opera North, The Grand Theatre, 46 New Briggate, Leeds, Yorkshire, LS1 6NU, England.

ARMSTRONG Karan, b. 14 Dec 1941, Horne, Montana, USA. Soprano. m. Götz Friedrich. Education: Studied in Minnesota with Thelma Halverson, California with Lotte Lehmann and Fritz Zweig. Debut: Metropolitan Opera in 1969 in Hansel and Gretel. Career includes: Appearances with opera companies in Houston, Seattle, Cincinnati and Portland; Roles include Donizetti's Norina, Puccini's Butterfly, Verdi's Alice Ford and Wagner's Eva; Sang at New York City Opera, 1975-78 as Minnie, Tosca, Concepcion and the Queen of Shemakha; European debut at Strasbourg in 1976 as Salomé; Guest appearances in Munich, Frankfurt, Geneva, Oslo and Vienna; Bayreuth debut in 1979 as Elsa; World premiere performances in Von Einem's Jesu Hochzeit, Vienna in 1980, Sinopoli's Lou Salomé at Munich in 1981 and Berio's Un Re in Ascolto at Salzburg in 1984; Covent Garden in 1981 as Lulu in the first British performance of the 3 act version of Berg's opera; Other roles include Berg's Marie and the Woman in Schoenberg's Erwartung; Sang Katerina Ismailova at Berlin in 1988 and Elena Makropoulos and Regina in Mathis der Maler, 1990; Weisbaden Festival in 1989 as Katya Kabanova, Alice Ford at Los Angeles in 1990 followed by Leonore; Sang Wagner's Sieglinde and Gutrune at Covent Garden in 1991, Janácek's Emilia Marty at Los Angeles in 1992, and Megara in the premiere of Desdemona und Ihre Schwestern by Siegfried Matthus at Schwetzingen Festival in 1992; Concert appearances in the Four Last Songs of Strauss, Zemlinsky's Lyric Symphony and the Bruchstücke from Wozzeck; Sang Schoenberg's Woman at the Deutsche Oper Berlin, 1994; Floyd's Susannah in 1997. Recordings include: Elsa in Lohengrin from Bayreuth. Address: c/o Harrison Parrott Ltd, 12 Penzance Place, London, W11 4PA, England.

ARMSTRONG Richard, b. 1 July 1943, Leicester, England. Conductor. Education: Studied at Cambridge University. Career: Member of Music Staff at Royal Opera Covent Garden, 1966-68; Music Director of Welsh National Opera, 1973-86; Covent Garden debut in 1982 with Billy Budd, returning for Andrea Chénier, Un Ballo in Maschera and Don Carlos, 1989; Conducted Elektra, Die Frau ohne Schatten, Wozzeck, operas by Janáček, The Midsummer Marriage and Peter Grimes; Led the Welsh company in The Ring at Covent Garden in 1986; Guest engagements with Netherlands Opera in Elektra, Komische Oper Berlin in Peter Grimes, Frankfurt in Der fliegende Hôllander, and new productions of Elektra and Araidne auf Naxos and at Geneva in Don Carlos; Conducted the premiere of John Metcalf's Tornrak for WNO, 1990 followed by Otello and House of The Dead; Music Director of Scottish Opera from 1993; Conducted Moses und Aron and La Voix Humaine at the 1992 Edinburgh Festival; Werther at Toulouse, 1997. Honours include: CBE, 1992 Address: c/o

Ingpen and Williams Ltd, 26 Wadham Road, London SW15 2LR, England.

ARMSTRONG Sheila, b. 13 Aug 1942, Ashington, England. Soprano Singer. Education: Royal Academy of Music. Career: Sang Despina in Così fan Tutte at Sadler's Wells, 1965; Belinda, in Dido and Aeneas, Glyndebourne, 1966; Returned as Mozart's Pamina and Zerlina and Fiorila in Rossini's Il Turco in Italia; Sang in the premiere of John McCabe's Notturni ed Alba, at 1970 Three Choirs Festival; New York Debut, 1971 with New York Philharmonic; Sang with Los Angeles Philharmonic under Mehta; Covent Garden Debut, 1973, as Marzelline in Fidelio; Donizetti's Norina and Mozart's Donna Elvira for Scottish Opera; Concert engagements include Messiah at the Concertgebouw, tour of the Far East with Bach Choir, Britten's Spring Symphony conducted by Previn, Strauss's Four Last Songs with Royal Philharmonic; Also heard in Elgar's Oratorios and the Sea Symphony by Vaughan Williams; Conductors include Barenboim, Bernstein, Boult, Giulini, Haitink, Leppard and Mackerras; Song recitals in UK and abroad. Recordings: Samson, Dido and Aeneas, Mozart's Requiem, Carmina Burana, Elgar's Apostles, The Pilgrim's Progress, Cantatas by Bach, Haydn's Stabat Mater, Beethoven's Ninth Symphony and Mahler's 2nd and 4th. Honours: Winner, Kathleen Ferrier Memorial Award; Mozart Prize, RAM; FRAM, 1973; Honorary MA, 1979; Honorary DMus, 1991. Membership: Royal Philharmonic Society. Address: Harvesters, Tilford Road, Hindhead, Surrey, GU26 6SQ, England.

ARNAULD Serge, b. 16 Nov 1944, Geneva, Switzerland. Composer; Scholar. m. Christiane Wirz, 16 Jan 1965, 3 sons, 1 daughter. Education: Maitrise, Philosophy with Professor Vladimir Jankelevitch, Sorbonne, Paris, 1973; Studied composition with Darius Milhaud, Marcel Landowski, Adrienne Clostre and Louis Saguer. Career: Radio: Swiss selection for Paul Gibson Prize and Prix Italia with Pugilat, 1979, and miniopera, Masculin-Singulier, 1987; Films: Jean-Luc Godard's Sauve qui Peut (La Vie) et Passion, participated as actor; Musicology: Les Manuscrits de Carpentras, 1979, Scenes de la Vie Judeo-Comtadine, 1980; Founder and Artistic Director for International Music Festival from the Academies of Rome, 1984-88; Collaborator a la Dramaturgie au Grand Théâtre de Genève, 1989. Compositions: Le Jeu De La Tarasque, ballet-pantomime, 1985; L'Esprit De Genève, produced by Jean-Louis Martinoty, 1986, to commemorate 450th anniversary of the Reformation in Geneva; Guillaume Tell en Jacobin, to commemorate the bicentenary of the French Revolution and for 700th anniversary of the Swiss Confederation, 1991. Recordings: Cantates Ambivalentes; Requiem de Pâques; L'Amour. Publications: La Coronalité and Le Systeme Hexacordal, Paris, 1968-69. Honour: Member, Institut Suisse, Rome, 1983. Hobby: Asian Travel. Address: 6 Rue de la Mairie, 1207 Geneva, Switzerland.

ARNELL Richard (Anthony Sayer), b. 15 Sept 1917, Hampstead, London, England. Composer. m. Joan Heycock, 1992. Education: Hall School, University College School, London; Royal College of Music. Career: Music Consultant, BBC North American Service, 1943-46; Lecturer, Royal Ballet School, 1958-59; Editor, The Composer, 1961-64; Chairman, Composers Guild of Great Britain, 1964, 1974-75, Vice President, 1992-; Visiting Fulbright Professor, Bowdoin College, Maine, 1967-68. Hofstra University, New York, 1968-70; Music Director, Board Member, London International Film School, 1975-88; Music Director, Ram Filming Ltd, 1980-85; Vice President, Friends of Trinity College of Music Junior Department, 1987-; Founder Chairman, Tadcaster Civic Society Arts Committee, 1988-91; Founder Chairman, Saxmundham Music and Arts, 1992-95, Resident, 1995-. Compositions: Operas: Love in Transit; Moonflowers; Ballets: Punch and the Child, Beecham/RPO Sony CD SMK 46683; Great Detective, Composer/Pro Arte, EMI CD 7647182; Harlequin in April; The Great Detective; The Angels; Orchestral: 6 Symphonies; 2 Concertos for Violin; Concerto for Harpsichord; 2 Concertos for Piano; Symphonic Portrait Lord Byron; Landscapes and Figures; Robert Faherty; Impression; Ode to Beecham, 1986; Xanadu, 1992; Chamber: 6 String Quartets; 2 Quintets; Piano Trio; Piano Works; Music for Wind Instruments; Brass Instruments; Electronic Music; Song Cycles; Numerous film scores. Publications: Technique of Film Music (co-editor). Honours: Tadcaster Town Council Merit Award, 1990. Memberships: Composers Guild of Great Britain; BETC Union; Savage Club. Address: c/o Composers Guild of Great Britain, 34 Hanway Street, London W1P 9DE, England.

ARNESTAD Finn (Oluf Bjerke), b. 23 Sept 1915, Oslo, Norway. Composer; Music Critic. Education: Studied violin and piano at Oslo, composition with Bjarne Brustad, African and Oriental Folk Music in Paris, 1952. Career: Music Critic in Oslo. Compositions: Orchestral: Constellation, 1948, Conversation for Piano and Orchestra, 1950, Meditation, 1952, INRI, 2 suites from a symphonic mystery play, 1952-55, Violin Concerto, 1957, Aria Appassionata, 1962, Cavatina Cambiata, 1965, Overture, 1970, Toccata, 1972, Arabesque, 1975, Piano Concerto, 1976, Mouvement Concertant for Double Bass and Orchestra, 1978; Chamber: String Quartet, 1947, Sextet for Flute, Clarinet,

Bassoon, Violin, Cello and Piano, 1959, Quintet for Flute and Strings, 1962, Suite In Old Dance Rhythms for Flute, Oboe, Harpsichord and Strings, 1966, Trombone Sonata, 1971, Solo Violin Sonata, 1980, Solo Double Bass Sonata, 1980, Piano Music; Several vocal works.

ARNOLD David (Charles), b. 1949, Atlanta, Georgia, USA. Opera and Concert Singer (Baritone). Debut: Metropolitan Opera as Enrico in Lucia; English National Opera as Escamillo in Carmen; New York City Opera as Zurga in Les Pêcheurs de Perles; Escamillo in Carmen, Komische Oper Berlin. Career: Performances of many world premieres including: John Harbison's Full Moon in March and his Winter's Tale, David Diamond's Ninth Symphony for Baritone and Orchestra, Leonard Bernstein conducting at Carnegie Hall, Charles Fussell's Specimen Days; 2 guest appearances at the White House singing Berlioz's L'Enfance du Christ and performance of American Song repertoire; Performances of Amonasro in Aida with Opera Company of Boston, L'Opera de Montréal and Opera Omaha and Le nozze di Figaro with L'Opéra de Québec; Performances with most leading orchestras including: the Boston Symphony for 6 seasons, St Louis Symphony, Atlanta Symphony, American Symphony Orchestra, San Francisco Symphony, Chicago Symphony, Buffalo Philharmonic and with the Spoleto Festivals. Recordings: Schoenberg's Gurrelieder, Boston Symphony; Harbison's Full Moon in March; Judith Lang's Zaimont's Magic World; Mendelssohn's Walpurgisnacht; Beethoven's 9th Symphony, 1993; Mozart's Requiem, 1995; Haydn's Lord Nelson Mass, 1997; Cherubini's Médée, 1997; Elijah, 1998. Current Management: William Knight. Address: William Knight, Grant House, 309 Wood Street, Burlington, NJ 08016, USA.

ARNOLD Malcolm (Henry) (Sir), b. 21 Oct 1921, Northampton, England. Composer. 2 sons, 1 daughter. Education: Studied Trumpet with Ernest Hall, Piano with Hurst Bannister, Composition with Gordon Jacob, Royal College of Music, London. Career: First Trumpet Player, London Philharmonic Orchestra, 1942-49 (apart from break for military service, and short spell with BBC Symphony Orchestra); Numerous appearances on concert platform as soloist in Haydn, Goedicke, Riisager and other concertos; Mendelssohn Scholarship for study in Italy, 1948; Composer of wide range of concert music, and nearly 120 film scores; Omnibus - 70th Birthday, 1991. Compositions include: Two operas, The Dancing Master, 1951 and The Open Window, 1956; Ballets, Homage to the Queen, for the 1953 Coronation, Rinaldo and Armida, 1955 and Electra, 1963; Orchestral, 9 Symphonies, 1951, 1953, 1954, 1960, 1961, 1967, 1973, 1979, 1987; 10 Overtures, including Beckus the Dandipratt, 1948 and Tam O'Shanter, 1955; Toy Symphony, 1957; Concertos for clarinet, 1951 and 1974, oboe 1952, flute 1954 and 1972, harmonica 1954, guitar 1961, horn 1947 and 1956, viola 1971, two violins 1962; Trumpet Concerto commissioned by the Royal College of Music in celebration of its foundation in 1988; Recorder Concerto for Michala Petri, 1988; Cello Concerto commissioned by the Royal Philharmonic Society for Julian Lloyd Webber, first performance Royal Festival Hall, London, 1989; Two Brass Quintets 1961 and 1988 and Two String Quartets, 1951 and 1975; Children's pieces include music for The Turtle Drum for BBC Television; Film music includes The Bridge on the River Kwai (awarded Hollywood Oscar, 1958); The Inn of the Sixth Happiness; Whistle Down the Wind; Wind Octet, 1989; Four Welsh Dances, 1989; Flourish for a Battle for RAF Battle of Britain, 1990; Robert Kett Overture, 1990; Manx Suite, 1990; Fantasy for Recorder and String Quartet, 1991. Recordings: Chandos, string quartets; Film Suites; Conifers Symphonies 6, 7, 8 and Cancenta's Hyperium Chamber music; Reference, Ceventuries. Publications: Music of Malcolm Arnold, Faber, Hugo Cole, Novello, Lenenick. Honours: Commander of the British Empire, 1970; Bard of the Cornish Gorsedd, 1969; W W Cobbett Prize, 1941; Honorary Doctorates of Music, Exeter University 1969, Durham University 1982, Leicester University 1983; Honorary Member, Royal Academy of Music, London; Ivor Novello Award for Outstanding Services to British Music, 1985; Wavendon All Music Composer of the Year, 1987; Doctor of Arts and Humane Letters, Miami University, Oxford, USA, 1990; FTCL, 1992; Knights Batchelor, 1993. Current Management: Anthony Day. Address: 26 Springfields, Attleborough, Norfolk NR17 2PA, England.

ARONOFF Josef, b. 13 June 1932, Budapest, Hungary. Violinist; Violist; Conductor. m. Astrid Gray, 3 sons, 1 daughter. Education: Franz Liszt Academy of Music, Budapest; Guildhall School of Music, London; MBC (UK); AGSM; LRAM. Career: Radio and TV appearances, Hungary, Austria, UK, Portugal, France, Germany, USA, Hong Kong, Australia; Professor, Royal Manchester College of Music, England, 1965-70; Head of String Department, Queensland Conservatorium of Music, Australia, 1970-75; Musical Director, Conservatorium Chamber Orchestra, 1970-75; Musical Director, Artemon Ensemble and Orchestra, 1971-; Concertmaster, Director of Instrumental Studies, Darling Downs Institute of Advanced Education, 1975-77; Conductor, Allegri Players, 1975-77; Senior Lecturer, Adelaide College of Arts, 1977-79; Musical Director, South-Western Symphony

Orchestra, 1977-79; Professor, Guildhall School of Music and Drama, England, 1979-88; Professor, Birmingham School of Music, 1979-88; Senior Examiner, Australian Music Examination Board, 1988-. Recordings: On CD, Viola Concerto 1989 by C Reichard-Gross; Memories of Sunny Days for Violin and Orchestra by C Reichard-Gross, with Hungarian Northern Symphony Orchestra, soloist Josef Aronoff (viola/violin), conductor Laszlo Kovacs. Contributions to: Music and Musicians; Strad Magazine; International Music Magazine. Honours: London's Lord Mayor Sheriff Prize, 1959; Alfred Gibson Prize, 1960; Louis Pecskay Prize, 1960. Memberships: Incorporated Society of Musicians; Society of Contemporary Music; European String Teachers' Association. Hobbies: Sailing; Swimming; Current Management: Camerata Artists, UK; Austral Artists, Australia. Address: 40 Isabella Street, Tarragindi, Brisbane, Queensland 4121, Australia.

ARROYO Martina, b. 2 Feb 1936, Harlem, NY, USA. Soprano. Education: BA, Hunter College of the City University of New York, 1956. Career: Sang in the US premiere of Pizzetti's Assassinio nella Cattedrale, NY, 1958; Metropolitan Opera debut as the Heavenly Voice in Don Carlos, 1959; Appeared in Europe from 1963 singing at the Vienna State Opera, Berlin State Opera, Zurich Opera, Covent Garden London and Paris Opera; Sang major roles at the Metropolitan Opera from 1965 with debut as Aida; Sang several Verdi roles as well as Wagner's Elsa and Mozart's Donna Anna; Concert performances in music by Varèse, Dallapiccola and Stockhausen; Metropolitan Opera in Aida, (Santuzza, 1986-87) and Seattle Opera in 1988 in Turandot. Recordings: Various. Honours: Winner, Metropolitan Opera Auditions of the Air, 1958; Honorary DHL, Hunter College, CUNY, 1987. Address: c/o Thea Dispeker Inc, 59 East 54th Street, New York, NY 10022, USA.

ARTAUD Pierre-Yves, b. 13 July 1946, Paris, France. Flautist. Education: Studied at the Paris Conservatoire, graduated 1970. Played the piccolo in the Orchestre Philharmonique, Ile-de-France, 1964-68, and flute with the Orchestra Laetitia Musica, 1971; Directed contemporary flute studies at Sainte-Baume, 1973-80; Visiting Professor at Pecs and Csingrad in Hungary from 1978; Responsible for instrumental research at IRCAM, Paris, Electronic Music Studio, 1981; Professor at Darmstadt, 1982; Performer in recital groups including Arcadie, quartet of flutes, 1964, Da Camera, wind quintet, 1970-72, and the Albert Roussel Quintet, 1973-74; Collaboration with harpist Sylvie Beltrando and harpsichordist Pierre Bouyer; Has premiered works by Brian Ferneyhough, Betsy Jolas, Tristan Murail, Franco Donatoni, Maurice Ohana and André Boucourechliev; Professor of Chamber Music at Paris Conservatoire from 1985 and of Flute from 1987. Publication: La Flute, 1987. Honours: 1st Prize at the Conservatoire, 1969 and 1970; Medal Of Arts, Sciences and Letters, 1978; Grand Prix of French Contemporary Music Interpretation, 1982; Prix de l'Academie du Disque Français, 1984; Prix Charles Inos, 1985. Address: 209 Avenue Jean Jaurès, 75079 Paris, France.

ARTYOMOV Vyacheslav, b. 29 June 1940, Moscow, Russia. Composer. Education: Studied composition with Pirumov and Sidelnikov; Graduated, Moscow Conservatory, 1968. Compositions: Piano Concerto, 1961; 2 Clarinet Sonatas, 1966, 1971; Variations, Nestling Antsali for Flute and Piano, 1974; Capriccio For New Years Eve for Soprano, Saxophone, Baritone Saxophone and Vibraphone, 1975; Totem for Percussion Group, 1976; A Symphony Of Elegies, 1977; Way To Olympus for Orchestra, 1984; In Memoriam, symphony for Violin Solo and Orchestra, 1968-84; Tristia for Orchestra, 1983; Invocations for Soprano and Percussion Group, 1981; Moonlight Dreams, cantata, for Soprano (mezzo-soprano), Alto Flute, Cello and Piano, 1982; Hymns Of Sudden Wafts for Ensemble, 1985; Gurian Hymns for 3 Violins and Orchestra, 1986; Requiem for Soloists, 2 Choirs and Orchestra, 1988; Sola Fiole (By Faith Alone), ballet, 1987; Various works for different instruments. Address: c/o RAO, Bolchaia Bronnai 6-1, Moscow 103670, Russia.

ARTZT Alice (Josephine), b. 16 Mar 1943, Philadelphia, Pennsylvania, USA. Classical Guitarist. Education: BA, Columbia University, 1966; Studied guitar with Ida Presti and Alexandre Lagoya, France; Julian Bream, England; Composition with Darius Milhaud; Graduate work in composition and musicology, Columbia University. Career: Teacher of Guitar: Mannes College of Music, New York City, 1966-69; Trenton State University, New Jersey, 1977-80; Performer, 1969-; Appearances throughout North America; Many tours: Europe; South and Central America; The Caribbean; Mexico; Performed in: Africa; Near East; Japan; Korea; Singapore; Taiwan; Hong Kong; Australia; New Zealand; Soloist with orchestras, Europe, Near East, USA; Premiered 3 new concertos; Duo concerts with harpsichordist Igor Kipnis. Recordings: LP albums: Alice Artzt Classic Guitar; Alice Artzt Classic Guitar; Alice Artzt Plays Original Works; Bach and His Friends; Guitar Music by Fernando Sor; Guitar Music by Francisco Tarrega; 20th Century Guitar Music; English Guitar Music; The Music of Manuel Ponce; Virtuoso Romantic Guitar;

Musical Tributes; Variations, Passacaglias and Chaconnes; American Music of the Stage and Screen by The Alice Artzt Trio. Publications: The Art of Practising, 1978; Editor, The GFA International Guitarist's Cookbook, 1986; Rhythmic Mastery, 1997; Numerous articles and reviews to professional journals in music and film. Contributions to: Composer and performer in TV and Film scores. Honours: Various Critics Choice Awards. Memberships: Former Chairman, Board of Directors, Guitar Foundation of America. Hobbies: Travel; Hi-Fi; Films; Researching Charlie Chaplin. Address: 51 Hawthorne Avenue, Princeton, NJ 08540, USA.

ARUHN Britt Marie, b. 11 Nov 1943, Motala, Sweden. Soprano. Education: Studied at the Stockholm Academy of Music. Debut: Stockholm in 1974 in Les Contes d'Hoffmann. Career: Has sung at Stockholm and the Drottningholm Festival as Norina, Zerbinetta, Gilda, Mélisande, Musetta and Adina; Staatsoper Dresden in 1976 as Gilda and Sophie; Covent Garden in 1978 and Hamburg Staatsoper in 1983; Sang at Brussels in 1984 in Lucio Silla by Mozart; Sang Sandrina in La Finta Giardiniera at Brussels and Gluck's Elena at Drottningholm, 1987; Sang First Lady in a film version of The Magic Flute, arranged by Ingmar Bergman; Frequent concert appearances. Recordings include: Brahms's Ein Deutsches Requiem. Address: Kungliga Teatern, PO Box 16094, S-10322 Stockholm, Sweden.

ASAWA Brian, b. 1966, USA. Singer (Countertenor). Education: Studied in New York. Career: Season 1995 as Britten's Oberon with the London Symphony Orchestra, Endimione in La Calisto at Brussels, Arsamenes in Hancel's Xerxes at the Cologne Opera and a Wigmore Hall recital with Melvyn Tan; Season 1996-97 in Handel's Semele at the Berlin Staatsoper, Monteverdi's Orfeo in Amsterdam and Lyon and Orlofsky in Die Fledermaus for San Francisco Opera; Seattle and Göttingen debuts as Arsamenes, Opera Bastille and Covent Garden debuts as Tolomeo in Giulio Cesare; Season 1997-98 in Mozart's Mitridate for Lyon Opera and Monteverdi's Nero for Australian Opera, and Dallas Opera debut in Handel's Ariodante; Recitals at Lincoln Center, the Geneva opera, Sydney Festival and on tour to Japan. Recordings include: A Midsummer Night's Dream; Solo recitals for BMG Classics USA. Honours include: Winner, Metropolitan Opera Auditions, 1991; Richard Tucker Foundation grant, 1993; Prize winner, Placido Domingo Operalia Competition, 1994. Address: c/o Lies Askonas Ltd, 6 Henrietta St, London WC2E 8LA.

ASAZUMA Fumiki, b. 23 Aug 1931, Tokyo, Japan. Professor of Viola; Conductor; Viola d'Amore Player. m. Michiko Nagamatsu, 19 Jun 1957, 1 son, 2 daughters. Education: BMus, Tokyo National University of Fine Arts and Music, 1956; Viola and Viol d'Amore studies at Vienna Academy, 1966-67. Career: Violist, NHK Symphony Orchestra, Tokyo, 1956-62; Professor of Viola, Tokyo National University of Fine Arts and Music, 1962-; Director and Conductor, Tokio Akademiker Ensemble (Kammerorchester) Tokyo, 1968-; Many TV and radio appearances, NHK and especially on FM-Tokyo, 1968-85. Recordings: With Tokio Akademiker Ensemble: 3 Divertimentos by Mozart, 1972, Stamitz, Bach, Mozart, 1975, Flute Concertos by Vivaldi with Christian Larde, 1975, Mozart with Christian Larde and Marie Claire Jamet, 1977, Doppler, Fauré, Gluck, Kreisler, Genin, with Paula Robison, 1984. Publications: Translator, The Interpretation of the Music of the XVII and XVIII Centuries by Arnold Dolmetsch, 1966. Memberships: President, Japan Viola Research Society; The Dolmetsch Foundation; Japan Musicology Society; Nippon Conductors Association; Rotary Club. Hobbies: Painting; Driving. Address: 13-17 Hachiyama, Shibuya-ku, Tokyo 150, Japan.

ASBURY Stefan, b. 2 July 1965, Dudley, West Midlands, England. Conductor. Education: Oxford University; Royal College of Music with Oliver Knusen; Tanglewood Music Centre, 1990. Career: Engagements with the BBC Symphony Orchestra, City of Birmingham Symphony Orchestra, London Symphony and the Philharmonia, English Chamber Orchestra, Bournemouth Sinfonietta, National Orchestra of Spain, City of London Sinfonia, Britten-Pears Orchestra and I Pomeriggi Musicali, Italy; Co-director of the Oxford Contemporary Music Festival and collaboration with Stockhausen at the 1995 Holland Festival; Chamber concerts with the Schoenberg Ensemble (Holland), Capricorn, Endymion Ensemble and London Sinfonietta; Appearances with the Berlin SO, ASKO Ensemble and Netherlands Dance Theatre, 1996; Opera Engagements include the premiere of Freeze by Rob Zuidam at the Munich Biennale and the 1994 Holland Festival, H K Gruber's Gloria for Opera North, Oliver Knussen Double Bill at the 1996 Helsinki Festival, and Britten's Paul Bunyan at the Aldeburgh Festival; Season 1997-98 with ASKO Ensemble, London Sinfonietta, Birmingham Contemporary Music Group, New World Symphony, Britten Sinfonia, Philharmonia, BRTN, Rundfunk Sinfonie, Ensemble Intercontemporain, Orchestra Berlin. Honours include: Leonard Bernstein Fellowship, Tanglewood, 1990. Address: c/o Harrison/Parrott Ltd, 12 Penzance Place, London W11 4PA, England.

ASCHENBACH Hans, b. 1965, Idaho, USA (Swedish and German arents). Singer (Tenor). Education: Studid in Idaho and with Sir Neville Marriner. Career: Engagements at the New Orleans Opera, Lyric Opera of Queensland, New York Metropolitan, English National Opera and Connecticut Opera; Sang Schoenberg's Aron with the Leipzig Opera and in concert with the Philharmonic Orchestra at the Festival Hall, London, 1996; Other roles include Alwa in Lulu, Nuremberg Opera, 1996; Concerts at Carnegie Hall and throughout Europe. Address: c/o Stadtische Buhnen Numberg, Richard Wagner Platz 2-10, D-8500 Nurnberg 70, Germany.

ASHE Rosie, b. 1953, England. Singer (Soprano). Education: Studied at the Royal Academy and the London Opera Centre. Career: Sang in the premiere of Tavener's Thérèse at Covent Garden (1979) and for English National Opera has sung Papagena, Esmeralda (Bartered Bride), Fiakermilli (Arabella) and Venus (Orpheus in the Underworld); Other roles include the Queen of Night (Opera North), Despina (Cosi fan Tutte on BBC tv), Frasquita (Earl's Court and Japan), Musetta, Violetta, and Offenbach's Helen (Sadler's Wells); Season 1994/95 as Shakespeare's Hermia at Barbados and in Brand's Maschinist Hopkins in Amsterdam; Many appearances in musicals. Address: Helen Sykes Management, Fourth Floor, Parkway House, Sheen Lane, East Sheen, London SW14 8LS, England.

ASHER Nadine, b. 1957, Chicago, Illinois, USA. Singer (Contralto). Education: Studied at Indiana University and Juilliard, New York. Career: Sang at first in concert, then opera engagement at Kiel from 1984; Guest appearances at Heidelberg, Munster and Lucerne, as Bostania in Cornelius's Barbier von Bagdad; Zurich Opera from 1987, as Wagner's Flosshilde and Grimgerde, Edwige in Guillaume Tell and Ulrica (Ballo in maschera). Address: c/o Opernhaus Zurich, Falkenstrasse 1, CH-8008 Zurich, Switzerland.

ASHKENASI Shmuel, b. 1940, Israel. Violinist. Education: Studied with Ilona Feher in Israel and with Efrem Zimbalist at the Curtis Institute in Philadelphia. Career: Concert tours of the US, Europe, Russia and Japan; Co-founded the Vermeer String Quartet at the Marlboro Festival in 1970; Performances in all major US centres and in Europe, Israel and Australia; Festival engagements at Tanglewood, Aspen, Spoleto, Edinburgh, Mostly Mozart in New York, Aldeburgh, South Bank, Sante Fe, Chamber Music West and the Casals Festival; Resident Quartet for Chamber Music Chicago; Master classes at the Royal Northern College of Music, Manchester; Member of the Resident Artists Faculty of Northern Illinois University. Recordings: Paganini Concertos with the Vienna Symphony Orchestra; Mozart Concerto K219 and Beethoven Romances; Quartets by Beethoven, Dvorák, Verdi and Schubert; Brahms Clarinet Quintet with Carl Leister. Honours: Winner, Merriweather Post Contest, Washington DC; Finalist of Queen Elisabeth Competition, Brussels; 2nd Prize, Tchaikovsky International Competition, Moscow. Address: Caecilia, 5 Place de la Fustene, 1204 Geneva, Switzerland.

ASHKENAZY Dimitri, b. 1969, New York, USA. Clarinettist. m. Ariane Haering. Education: Studied at the Lucerne Conservatory with Giambattista Sisini. Career: Founder member of the European Soloists Ensemble, 1992, with appearances in London, Paris, Munich and Geneva; Duo recitals with Vladimir Ashkenazy in Rome, Florence, Zürich, Milan and Toronto; Further concerts in 1992/93 at the Hollywood Bowl and with the Royal Philharmonic in London (Mozart's Concerto); Tour of Japan 1993, followed by Maxwell Davies's Strathclyde Concerto no 4 with the composer conducting; 1994 premiere of Marco Jutino's concerto at La Scala; Recent tours of Russia and Italy and chamber concerts with the Kodály Quartet and European Soloists Ensemble; Season 1996-97 with the premiere of Filippo del Corno's Concerto and concerts in Japan with the European Soloists Ensemble; Season 1997-98 includes a tour with the Swiss Youth Symphony Orchestra, a further tour with the Kodaly Quartet and dates in Warsaw (with the Warsaw Philharmonic), Salzburg (Festspiele) and Milan (Serate Musicali). Recordings include: Rossini Variations in C; Richard Strauss Duet-Concertino; Stravinsky Ebony Concerto; Stravinsky Chamber Music. Hobbies: CD's; Postcards; Coins; Swimming. Address: Rue des Parcs 159, CH-2000 Neuchâtel, Switzerland.

ASHKENAZY Vladimir, b. 6 July 1937, Gorky, USSR. Pianist; Conductor. m. Thorunn Sofia Johannsdottir, 25 Feb 1961, 2 sons, 3 daughters. Education: Moscow Central Music School, 1945-55; Moscow Conservatory, 1955-63. Career: Concert appearances throughout the world, solo recitals and with major orchestras; Conductor of major orchestras especially the Philharmonia, the Concertgebouw (Amsterdam) and the Cleveland Orchestras; Music Director, the Royal Philharmonic Orchestra, 1987-94; Music Director, the Berlin Radio Symphony Orchestra (now called Deutsches Symphonie Orchester Berlin), 1989-; Conducted at the Prokofiev Centenary Celebrations at the Festival Hall, London, 1991; Promenade Concerts, London, 1991, with the European Community Youth Orchestra; La Mer, 8th Symphony by Shostakovich, and the Royal Philharmonic, Tippett's Concerto for Double String Orchestra and Walton's 1st Symphony, conducted works by Walton (Henry V, Cello Concerto and Belshazzar's Feast) at the Festival Hall, London, 1993; Conducted the Deutsches Symphony Orchestra in Mahler's 8th Symphony, 1996 (tour of South America 1997 and engaged for the 1998 Salzburg Festival); Music Director of the Czech Philharmonic, 1998-. Recordings: Over 100 including works by Mozart, Prokofiev, Beethoven, Liszt, Chopin, Schumann and Brahms. Honours: 2nd Prize, Chopin International Competition, 1955; 1st Prize, Queen Elisabeth of Belgium Competition, Brussels, 1965; 1st Prize, Tchaikovsky Competition, 1962. Current Management: Harrison Parrott Ltd, 12 Penzance Place, London W11 4PA, England. Address: Käppelistra 15, 6045 Meggen, Switzerland.

ASHKENAZY Vovka, b. 1961, Moscow, Russia. Pianist. (Son of preceding). Education: Early piano studies in Iceland with Rögnvaldur Sigurjonsson; Moved to England 1977 and completed studies at Royal Northern College of Music, 1983. Debut: Barbican Hall, London, 1983 in The Tchaikovsky 1st Piano Concerto with London Symphony Orchestra. Career: Concerts in Germany, Italy, Holland, France and Canada; Appearances with most London orchestras in concertos by Brahms, Schumann, Grieg, Tchaikovsky and Rachmaninov; US debut with Los Angeles Philharmonic, at Hollywood Bowl; Recital tour of Israel and tours of Australia and Japan; Appearances in many countries including: Austria, Australia, Belgium, Canada, Denmark, France, Greece, Guatemala, Germany, Holland, Iceland, Italy, Ireland, Japan, Malta, Norway, New Zealand, Finland, Russia, Israel, Switzerland and Spain. Recordings: Arensky and Tchaikovsky Piano Trios; Bartók Sonata for Two Pianos and Percussion. Current Management: Jens Gunnar Becker, Grünstrasse 13, D-58313 Herdecke, Germany. Address: Rilkestrasse 86, D-53225 Bonn, Germany.

ASHLEY Robert (Reynolds), b. 28 Mar 1930, Ann Arbor, MI, USA. Composer. Education: Studied theory at University of Michigan, Ann Arbor, BMus in 1952, Piano and composition at Manhattan School of Music, NY, MMus in 1952; Postgraduate studies in acoustics and composition at University of Michigan, 1957-60. Career: Active with Milton Cohen's Space Theater, 1957-64, the ONCE Festivals and ONCE Group, 1959-69, and the Sonic Arts Union, 1966-76; Toured with these groups in the US and Europe; Director, Center for Contemporary Music, Mills College, Oakland, CA, 1969-81. Compositions include: Operas: That Morning Thing, 1967, Atlanta (Acts Of God), 1982; Various electronic music theatre pieces including Heat, 1961, Public Opinion Descends Upon The Demonstrators, 1961, Kittyhawk: An Antigravity Piece, 1964, Night Train, 1965, The Trial Of Anne Opie Wehrer And Unknown Accomplices For Crimes Against Humanity, 1968, Fancy Free, 1970, It's There, 1970; Films, videotapes; Video Operas: Music With Roots In The Aether, 1976, Title Withdrawn, 1976, The Lessons, 1981, Atlanta Strategy, 1984; Commission from Florida Grand Opera for opera on thje Cuban 'Rafters', 1997 Instrumental pieces including Fives for 2 Pianos, 2 Percussion and String Quintet, 1962, In Memoriam...Kit Carson, opera, 1963, Odalisque, 1985, Superior Seven, 1988; Piano pieces. Address: 10 Beach Street, New York, NY 10013, USA.

ASHMAN Mike, b. 16 Apr 1950, Hertford, England. Opera Director. Career: Major Productions include: Das Rheingold, 1993, Die Walküre, 1994, Siegfried, 1995 and Der fliegende Holländer, 1989 for Den Norske Opera, Oslo; Parsifal, 1983 and world premiere of John Metcalf's Tornrak, 1990 for Welsh National Opera; Der fliegende Holländer, 1986 and Médée, 1989 for Royal Opera House, Covent Garden; Spanish premiere of Peter Grimes, 1991 for Teatro Lirico de la Zarzuela, Madrid; Has also directed for Scottish Opera Go-Round, Dublin Grand Opera, Banff Centre Alberta, Opera de Nice, Teatro Regio Turin and Opéra Comique, Paris; Associate Producer for London Royal Schools of Music Opera Department directing 8 productions; Production of Wagner's Ring for the Norwegian Opera, Oslo, brought to the Theatre Royal, Norwich, 1997; Has made performing translations of The Bartered Bride and Weill's Der Jasager. Address: North House, Stansteadbury, Ware, Hertfordshsire SG12 8JZ, England.

ASHWORTH Valerie (Grace), b. 12 Sep 1956, Sale, Cheshire, England. Pianist. m. Vincent Pirillo, 2 daughters. Education: Chetham's School of Music, Manchester, 1969-75; Studied with Kendall Taylor at Royal College of Music, London, 1975-79; Masterclasses in solo repertoire with Sir William Glock, Albert Ferber, Rudolf Firkusny, Hochschule für Musik, Vienna, 1979-81; ARCM, Piano Performer, 1971; LLRAM, Piano Performer, 1974; ARCM, Teacher's Diploma, 1977. Debut: Radio debut, Young Artists, 1969. Career: Soloist, chamber musician and accompanist in England, France, Switzerland, Italy, Denmark, Germany, Japan, Hungary and Austria; TV debut on John Amis Music On Two, 1972 and Austrian TV debut in 1982; American debut at Carnegie Hall in 1989; Official accompanist including Jacqueline du Pré masterclasses, England, 1979, Summer

Academy, Nice, France, 1980, Irwin Gage in Zurich, 1984-86, Carinthia Summer 1984 and Summer Academy at Salzburg in 1991; Teaching Contract: Coach, String Department, 1982-87, Vocal Department, 1987-89, Hochschule für Musik und Vienna; Taught piano at University of Osnabruck, 1989-93. Honours: Finalist, National Junior Piano Playing Competition, 1969, and Commonwealth Competition, 1972; 1st Prize, Kathleen Long Chamber Music Competition, 1978, and Duo Chamber Music Competition, Finale Liguria, Italy, 1985. Memberships: ISM; EPTA. Hobbies: Languages; Travel; The Arts. Current Management: Wilhelm Hansen, Denmark.

AST Margharete, b. 1932, Guben, Germany. Mezzo-Soprano. Education: Studied at Berlin Musikhochschule. Career: Sang in the premiere of Krenek's Pallas Athene Weint, Hamburg, 1955; Appeared at Kassel from 1958, notably in premieres of Barnstable by Francis Burt in 1969, and Ein Menschentraum by PM Hamel in 1981; Guest engagements at Vienna Festival, 1962, and Vienna Staatsoper, 1965-68; Other roles in Austria and Germany: Gluck's Orpheus, Wagner's Magdalene, Erda, Waltraute and Flosshilde, Strauss's Herodias, Composer, Clytemnestra and Adelaide, Verdi's Amneris, Eboli and Mistress Quickly, Marina in Boris Godunov, Tchaikovsky's Maid of Orleans, Kabanicha in Jenufa, Berg's Countess Geschwitz and Charlotte in Die Soldaten by Zimmermann; Many concert appearances. Address: c/o Staatstheater, Freidrichplatz, 3500 Kassel, Germany.

ASTON Peter (George), b. 5 Oct 1938, Birmingham, England. Composer; Conductor; University Teacher m. Elaine Veronica Neale, 13 Aug 1960, 1 son. Education: Birmingham School of Music; DPhil, University of York; GBSM; FTCL; FCI; ARCM; Hon RCM; Hon FGCM; FRSA. Career: Lecturer in Music, 1964-72, Senior Lecturer, 1972-74, University of York; Professor, Head of Music, 1974-, Dean, School of Fine Arts and Music, 1981-84, University of East Anglia, Norwich; Director, The Tudor Consort, 1959-65; Conductor, English Baroque Ensemble, 1967-70; Aldeburgh Festival Singers, 1974-88; Principal Guest Conductor, Sacramento Bach Festival, USA, 1993-; Incontri Corali, Italy, 1996; Series Editor, UEA Recordings, 1979-; Joint and Founder Artistic Director, Norwich Festival of Contemporary Church Music, 1981-. Compositions: Chamber Music; Opera; Church music; Numerous choral and orchestral works; Editions of Baroque music including complete works of George Jeffreys. Recordings: Mellers' Life Cycle; Jeffrey's Anthems and Devotional Songs; Choral music by Holst and Britten; Numerous choral and orchestral works. Publications: The Music of York Minster, 1972; Sound and Silence, co-author, 1970, German edition, 1972, Italian edition, 1980, Japanese edition, 1981; Music Theory in Practice, 3 volumes, 1992-93. Address: 9 Bourne Close, Long Stratton, Norwich NR15 2RW, England.

ASTRAND (Karl) Hans (Vilhelm), b. 5 Feb 1925, Bredaryd, Sweden. Music Historian; Perpetual Secretary Emeritus, Royal Swedish Academy of Music. m. Birgitta Helga Margareta Örle, 25 Mar 1972, 1 son. Education: Filosofie Licentiatexamen Romance Languages, Lund University, 1958; Studied organ for 2 years with Gunnar Ek, double bass for 4 years with Sune Pettersson and Violoncello for 3 years with Gunnar Berggren. Debut: Choir Conductor, Malmö, 1953. Career: Perpetual Secretary, Royal Swedish Academy of Music, 1973-90; Chief Editor, Sohlman's Dictionary of Music, 5 volumes, 1975-79; Music Critic, Kvällsposten. Publications: Chief Editor, Sohlman's Dictionary of Music, 5 volumes, 1975-79; Bird's Eye Perspectives on American Music Life, 1983; J G Naumann als Opernkomponist - heute, 1991; Joseph Martin Kraus, The Great Exception, 1992. Contributions to: Nutida Musik; Artes; Mientras cantan las cuerdas, on contemporary Spanish music, in Revista de Occidente, 1991. Honours: PhD, honoris causa, Lund University, 1985; Palmes Académiques, France, 1979; Medalla de Plata de las Bellas Artes, Spain, 1991. Memberships: Royal Swedish Academy of Music; Corresponding Member, Real Academia de Bellas Artes de San Fernando, Spain. Address: Mästarbacken 145, S-12940 Hägersten, Sweden.

ATHERTON David, b. 3 Jan 1944, Blackpool, England. Conductor. m. Ann Gianetta Drake, 1 son, 2 daughters. Education: MA (Cantab); LRAM; LTCL; LGSM. Debut: Royal Opera House, Covent Garden, 1968. Career: At Aldeburgh Festival conducted Birtwistle's Punch and Judy world premiere, 1968, Crosse's Grace of Todd, 1969; Resident Conductor, Royal Opera House, 1968-80; Il Trovatore, Don Giovanni, The Rake's Progress and Henze's We Come to the River world premiere; Founder, 1968, Music Director, 1968-73, 1989-91, London Sinfonietta; Principal Conductor, 1980-83, Principal Guest Conductor, 1983-86, Royal Liverpool Philharmonic Orchestra; Music Director, Principal Conductor, San Diego Symphony, 1980-87; Principal Guest Conductor, BBC Symphony Orchestra, 1985-89; Music Director, Hong Kong Philharmonic Orchestra, 1989-; Guest Conductor, orchestras in UK, Iran, Lebanon, Western Europe, Iceland, Canada, Russia, Japan, Korea, Hong Kong, USA, Sweden, Finland, Australia, New Zealand, Yugoslavia, Israel, Czechoslovakia; Founder, Music Director, Mainly Mozart Festival, Southern California, 1989-; Conducted Wozzeck at Toronto, 1990, Tippett's The Ice Break at the London Proms; New production of Peter Grimes, London Coliseum, 1991; 1991 Proms, with the National Youth Orchestra of Great Britain, Walton Viola Concerto, Shostakovich 7th Symphony, and the BBC Symphony, Ravel Piano Concerto and Vaughan Williams 2nd Symphony; New production of Les Huguenots, Covent Garden, 1991; Il barbiere di Siviglia at the Met, 1995; Der Rosenkavalier for English National Opera, 1997. Recordings include: Complete works for chamber ensemble by Schoenberg and Janácek; Works by Mozart, Schubert, Weill and Stravinsky; Numerous recordings with London Symphony, London Philharmonic and English Chamber Orchestras, London Sinfonietta, Philharmonia, Berlin Radio Symphony Orchestra. Publications: Editor, Pandora Suite and Don Quixote Suite, Gerhard; Arranger, Pandora (for Royal Ballet), Gerhard; Editor, The Complete Instrumental and Chamber Music of Arnold Schoenberg and Roberto Gerhard, 1973. Contributions to: Revised Musical Companion; Grove's Dictionary of Music and Musicians. Honours: Edison Award, Grand Prix du Disque; International Record Critics Award, Cecilia Prize; Special Award, Composers' Guild; Conductor of the Year, 1981; Koussevitsky Award. Membership: Incorporated Society of Musicians. Hobbies: Squash; Reading; Travel. Current Management: Harold Holt Ltd. Address: c/o Harold Holt Ltd, 31 Sinclair Road, London W14 0NS, England.

ATHERTON Michael, b. 17 Feb 1950, Liverpool, England (Australian Citizen). Composer; Musician; Author. Education: MA (Hon), University of New South Wales, 1977; Musicology Studies, University of Sydney; Ethnomusicology studies, University of New England. Career includes: Artist in Residence, Australian Museum, 1993; Foundation Professor of Music, University of Western Sydney, 1993-; Performer of classical, early music, folk and Asia Pacific instruments in various groups internationally. Compositions include: The Mahogany Ship for choir, strings and percussion, 1993; Exhortation for double choir and percussion, 1996; Namatjira for choir, 1995; Songs for Imberombera for choir, strings and percussion, 1997; Theme for Children's Hospital, Australian Broadcasting Corporation Television, 1997. Publications include: Australia Made...Australian Played - handcrafted musical instruments from didjeridu to synthesizer. Honours include: Australian Guild of Screen Writers Award for Best Music for a Documentary, 1992. Address: School of Contemporary Arts, University of Western Sydney Nepean, P O Box 10 Kingswood, New South Wales 2747, Australia.

ATKINSON Ann, b. 1965, Corwen, Clwyd, Wales. Singer (Mezzo-soprano). Education: Studied in Wales, with Kenneth Bowen at the Royal Academy of Music and with Ryland Davies. Career: Many concert performances throughout Wales, notably as conductor of the Bro Glyndwr Male Voice Choir, 1984-90; Recent singing engagements in the Saint-Saëns Christmas Oratorio and Diabelli's Pastoral Mass with the Limburg SO, Messiah at Ely Cathedral, Mozart's Requiem, Haydn's Nelson Mass and Beethoven's Ninth; Appearances with Scottish Opera from 1992 and Glyndebourne Festival and Tour from 1994. Address: Helen Sykes Management, Fourth Floor, Parkway, Sheen Lane, East Shane, London SW14 8LS, England.

ATKINSON Lynton, b. 1962, England. Tenor. Education: Studied under George Guest at Cambridge and in London with David Mason and Gita Denise. Career: Concert appearances in festivals at Innsbruck, Utrecht, Malta, Brighton and Edinburgh; Sang at cathedrals of Canterbury, Wells, Durham and Birmingham, at King's College Cambridge and the Sheldonian Theatre in Oxford; Has sung in Bach's St John Passion on tour to Spain, the St Matthew Passion in Bad Homburg and L'Incoronazione di Poppea at the Spitalfields Festival; Vienna in 1989 with Handel's Susanna under Martin Haselbrock; Sang Alfredo in a production of La Traviata in Mauritius; Handel's Belshazzar with Concerto Köln in Germany and Italy; Sang at Edinburgh Festival and in Poland with the City of London Sinfonia under Richard Hickox; Covent garden, 1990-91 as First Prisoner in Fidelio and Ywain in the world premiere of Birtwistle's Gawain; Sang at Buxton Festival and Spitalfields in 1991 in Il Sogno di Scipione by Mozart and Acis and Galatea; Season 1992 as Nathaniel in Hoffmann and Zefirino in Il Viaggio a Reims at Covent Garden. Recordings include: L'Incoronazione di Poppea; Video of Covent Garden Fidelio as First Prisoner. Honours include: Prizewinner, Alfredo Kraus International Singing Competition, Las Palmas, 1990.

ATLANTOV Vladimir, b. 19 Feb 1939, Leningrad, USSR. Singer (Tenor). Education: Studied with N Bolotina at the Leningrad Conservatory and at the La Scala opera school, Milan. Career: Sang at the Kirov Theatre, Moscow from 1963, Bolshoi Theatre from 1967, roles include Lenski, Hermann, Don Carlos, Radames, Done José, Alfredo, Cavaradossi and Canio; Vienna Staatsoper 1971; Vladimir in Prince Igor with the Bolshoi company at La Scala, 1973; Deutsche Oper Berlin 1974, as Cavaradossi; Has also sung baritone roles from 1977, notably Posa in Don Carlos; Munich 1980, as Otello; Covent Garden 1989 as Canio in Pagliacci (also at Kenwood, Lakeside); Sang Samson at Berlin, Deutsche Opera, 1989; Otello at Covent Garden, 1990 followed by Hermann at La Scala and Canio at the Caracalla Festival, Rome; Sang Samson for Opera Pacific at Costa Mesa, 1992 and Otello there in 1997; Concert tours of Canada, Europe and Japan. Recordings: Prince Igor, Eugene Onegin, Francesca da Rimini by Rachmaninov, Iolanta by Tchaikovsky, Ruslan and Ludmila, The Stone Guest by Darghomyzhsky. Honours include: People's Artist of the RSFSR, 1972. Address: c/o Allied Artists Agency, 42 Montpellier Square, London SW7 1JZ, England.

ATLAS Allan W(arren), b. 19 Feb 1943, New York, USA. Musicologist. Education: BA, Hunter College of the City University of New York, 1964; MA, 1966, PhD, 1971, New York University. Career: Faculty, Brooklyn College, 1971-; Visiting Professor, New York University, 1971, 1984, 1986; Executive Officer, PhD and DMA Programs in Music, Graduate School, City University of New York. Publications: The Cappella Giulia Chansonnier: Rome, Biblioteca Apostolica Vaticana, CG XIII 27, 2 volumes, 1975-76; Music at the Aragonese Court of Naples, 1985; The Wheatstone English Concertina in Victorian England, 1996; Renaissance Music, 1998; Anthology of Renaissance Music, 1998. Contributions to: Articles in the New Grove Dictionary of Music and Musicians and in various journals. Address: 945 Cedar Lane, Woodmere, NY 11598, USA.

ATTROT Ingrid, b. 1961, Canada. Soprano. Education: Graduated, University of Toronto's Opera School, 1985; Britten-Pears School at Aldeburgh; National Opera Studio, 1986-87. Career: Has appeared as Mozart's Countess and Donna Anna and Meg Page in Sir John In Love by Vaughan Williams, Ibert's Angélique and Respighi's Maria Egiziaca; Sang Madeline in Debussy's Fall of the House of Usher at Elizabeth Hall, 1989; Wigmore Hall and Purcell Room recitals in 1989; Handel's Ode to St Cecilia with Charles Dutoit and the Montreal Symphony; Bach's B minor Mass in Montreal; Vivaldi's Gloria in Ottawa and New York under Trevor Pinnock; Mendelssohn's Midsummer Night's Dream under Neville Marriner at the Festival Hall; Season 1989-90 with Carmina Burana and the Petite Messe Solennelle; Szymanowski recital at the Purcell Room; Handel's Floridante in Canada and California; Stravinsky's Les Noces in Antwerp and Elgar's The Kingdom; Tour of Russia with English National Opera productions of Macbeth and The Turn of The Screw; Season 1992 as Mathilde in Guillaume Tell for Haddo House Opera and the Governess in The Turn of the Screw for Pimlico Opera; Sang Donna Anna at Belfast, 1994. Honours include: Winner, Eckhardt-Gramatte Competition for Contemporary Music, Canada; Awards from Canada Council, University of Toronto, the Canadian Aldeburgh Foundation and the Friends of Covent Garden. Address: Juggs Cottage, Forebridge, Little Bedwyn, Marlborough, Wiltshire SN8 3JS, England.

ATZMON Moshe, b. 30 July 1931, Budapest, Hungary. Conductor. Education: Studied cello in Hungary and continued musical training in Israel where he studied horn and piano; Further studies at the Tel Aviv Academy of Music, 1958-62; Composition studies at the Guildhall School of Music, London. Career: Played horn in Israel Symphony and opera orchestras; Chief Conductor, Sydney Symphony Orchestra, 1969-71, Basle Symphony Orchestra, 1972-77, North German Radio Symphony Orchestra, Hamburg, 1972-76 and Tokyo Metropolitan Symphony Orchestra, 1978-82; Co-Principal Conductor of American Symphony Orchestra, NY, 1982-84; Chief Conductor of Nagoya Philharmonic Orchestra, 1986-92; Director of the Dortmund Orchestra in 1991, conducting Siegfried, Buenos Aires Filarmónica concert, 1996. Recordings include: Mendelssohn Overtures; Liszt's Piano Concertos with Garrick Ohlsson; Brahms's Double Concerto and Serenade Op 11; Bach's E major and A minor Violin Concertos with Schneiderhan; CD of works for piano and orchestra by Addinsell, Litolff, Gottschalk and Rachmaninov. Honours: 1st Prize, Conducting, Guildhall School of Music, 1963; 1st Prize, Liverpool International Conductors' Competition, 1964. Address: PGM, Top floor, 59 Lansdowne Place, Hove, East Sussex BN3 1FL, England.

AUBERSON Jean Marie, b. 2 May 1920, Chavorney, Vaud, Switzerland. Conductor. Education: Studied at the Lausanne Conservatory; Studied conducting with Van Kampen at Sienna and with Gunther Wand in Cologne, 1950-51. Career: Played violin with the Lausanne Chamber Orchestra, 1943-46, and Suisse Romande Orchestra, 1946-49; Conducted the Lausanne Chamber Orchestra, then the Radio Beromunster Orchestra at Zurich, the Suisse Romande Orchestra and the Zurich Tonhalle; Ballet evenings at the Geneva Opera and the Hamburg Staatsoper; Further career with Orchestra of Radio Basle and of Ville de Saint-Gall; Conducted the premieres of the ballet Paris by Henri Sauguet in 1964, Ginastera's Piano Concerto in 1977 and La Follie de Tristan by Schibler in 1980. Recordings include: Mozart C minor Mass with the Vienna Philharmonic; Handel's Organ Concertos with Lionel Rogg and the Geneva Baroque Orchestra; Tchaikovsky's Violin Concerto with Tibor Varga; Oboe Concertos by CPE Bach, Marcello and Bellini, with Heinz Holliger.

Address: c/o Grand Théâtre de Genève, 11 Boulevard du Théâtre, CH-1211 Geneva 11, Switzerland.

AUDI Pierre, b. 1957, Beirut, Lebanon. Stage Director. Education: Studied at Exeter College, Oxford, 1975-78. Career: Founded the Almeida Theatre, Islington, London, 1979; Director of theatre and annual contemporary music festival until 1989; Artistic Director of Netherlands Opera from 1988, productions include Schoenberg's Die Glückliche Hand, Feldman's Neither and Monteverdi's Il Ritorno di Ulisse, part of a complete cycle; Directed stage works by Wolfgang Rihm, Michael Finnissy (The Undivine Comedy) and John Casken (Golem) for the Almeida Theatre; Opera North 1990 with the British stage premiere of Verdi's Jerusalem; Produced Birtwistle's Punch and Judy for Netherlands Opera in 1993; Staged premiere of Henze's Venus and Adonis at Munich, 1997. Honours include: Lesley Boosey Award, 1990. Address: c/o Ingpen and Williams Ltd, 14 Kensington Court, London, W8 5DN, England.

AUGUIN Philippe, b. France. Conductor. Education: Studied in Vienna and Florence. Career: Musical assistant to Herbert von Karajan, 1986-; Associated with Georg Solti at the Salzburg Festival; La Scala Milan, with Don Giovanni, La Damnation de Faust, Die Zauberflöte and Figaro, 1993-; Covent Garden with La Traviata and Un Ballo in Maschera, 1994; Music Director of the Braunschweig Opera leading Tristan und Isolde, Parsifal, Salome, Pelléas et Mélisande and Wozzeck, 1994-; Mahler and Schoenberg cycles with Czech and Royal Philharmonics, Dresden State Orchestra and Orchestre National de France; Principal Conductor of the Staatstheater Stuttgart, with Tannhäuser, Elektra, Lohengrin, Rosenkavalier and Ariadne; Otello at the Hamburg Staatsoper, Der Fliegende Holländer at Leipzig and La Sonnambula at Cologne; Salzburg Festival, 1991-; with Fidelio, 1996; Season 1996-97 with Figaro at La Scala, Tannhäuser for Australian Opera, Le Roi Arthus in Cologne and concerts with the Royal Scottish National. Address: Lies Askonas Ltd, 6 Henrietta St, London WC2E 8LA, England.

AUSTBÖ Hakon, b. 22 Oct 1948, Kongsberg, Norway, Pianist. Education: Studied in Norway and at the Paris Conservatoire aand Ecole Normale de Musique, 1966-71; Juilliard School, New York, USA, 1971-72; Staatliche Hochschule für Musik, Munich, Germany, 1972-74; Private studies in London. Career:Played with Bergen Philharmonic Orchestra,1963; First Oslo recital, 1964; Concert and solo engagements throughout Scandinavia and Europe; Piano duo with Marina Horak, and chamber concerts with Trio du Nord until 1985; Numerous radio and television performances. Honours: Winner of the 1971 Messiaen Competition at Royaun and prizewinner at the Skriabin Competition, Oslo (1972) and the Ravel Competition at Paris (1975); Professor at the University of Utrecht from 1979. Address: c/o Utrechts Conservatorium, Mariaplaats 28, 3511 LL Utrecht, Netherlands.

AUSTIN Elizabeth (Scheidel), b. 15 July 1938, Baltimore, Maryland, USA. Composer. m. (1) Rolf D Scheidel, 2 sons, 1 daughter, (2) Gerhard Austin, 28 October 1989. Education: Studied with Nadia Boulanger, Conservatoire Americaine, Fontainebleau, France, summer 1958; BA with High Honours, Goucher College, Towson, Maryland, 1960; MMus, Composition, Hartt School of Music, University of Hartford, 1982; PhD, Music, University of Connecticut, 1987. Career: Compositions performed in USA and Europe; 2 Portrait Concerts sponsored by Die Staatliche Hochschule für Musik, Heidelberg-Mannheim and GEDOK, held in Mannheim, Germany, 1989, 1991; Performed own work, Lighthouse 1 for harpsichord, American Music Week, Storrs, Connecticut, 1989; Composer in Residence, David Lipscomb College, Nov 1992; Currently Assistant Director, Mannheim Programme for Mansfield Center, Connecticut. Compositions: Christ Being Raised, SATB, 1959; Klavier Double for piano and tape, 1983; Wilderness Symphony for 2 reciters and orchestra, 1987; Sonnets from the Portuguese for soprano and piano, 1989. Recordings: Klavier Double performed by Jerome Reed (Capstone label); Sonate fuer Blockfloete, performed by Stefanie Grundmann, 1991; Sonnets from the Portuguese performed by Melinda Liebermann and Cornelius Witthoeft, 1993; Wilderness Symphony, 1994; CD of Chamber Works, 1994, published byArsis Press, Peter Tonger Verlag. Address: 9 Eastwood Road, Storrs, CT 06268, USA.

AUSTIN Larry (Don), b. 12 Sept 1930, Duncan, OK, USA. Composer; Music Educator. m. Edna Navarro, 31 Oct 1953, 2 sons, 3 daughters. Education: BME, 1951, MM, 1952, University of North Texas, Denton; Studied with Darius Milhaud, Mills College, Oakland, CA, 1955; Seymour Shifrin and Andrew Imbrie, University of California, Berkeley, 1955-58; Computer music workshops, Stanford University, 1969; Massachusetts Institute of Technology, 1978. Career: Professor, 1958-72, Director of University's bands, 1958-72, Co-director, New Music Ensemble, 1963-68, University of California, Davis; Publisher and Owner, Source and Composer/Performer Edition, 1966-; University of South Florida, Tampa, 1972-78, University of North Texas, 1978-. Compositions include: Woodwind Quintet, 1949; Mass for Chorus and Orchestra, 1955-58; Quartet Three, electronic music on tape, 1971; Quadrants, 1-11; Catalogo Sonoro-Narcisso for Viola and Tape, 1978; Protoforms, hybrid musics for 3 Sopranos and Computer, 1980; Euphonia: A Tale Of The Future, opera, 1982; Sonata Concertante for Pianist and Computer, 1983-84; Violet's Invention for Piano, 1988; A Universe Of Symphony: The Earth, Life Pulse And Heavens, 1974-93; Accidents Two: Sound Projections for Piano with Computer Music, 1992. Recordings: Several. Publication: Learning to Compose: Modes, Materials and Models of Musical Invention, with Thomas Clark, 1988. Contributions to: Articles in various publications. Honours: Numerous grants and commissions; Several awards. Address: 2109 Woodbrook, Denton, TX 76205, USA.

AUSTIN William Weaver, b. 18 Jan 1920, Lawton, Oklahoma, USA. Professor Emeritus. m. Elizabeth Jane, 2 daughters. Education: 1936-41, PhD, 1942-50, Harvard University; Studies in Sciences and Philosophy, Cornell University, 1947-; Early study with pianist teachers; Harvard studies included, theory, history, composition, using piano for choruses, assistant teaching; Cornell, experience with organ, some conducting many kinds of teaching; Paris, London; US Navy service, 1941-45. Publications: Music in the 20th Century, 1966; New Looks at Italian Opera, 1968; Susanna...Foster..., 1975, 2nd edition, 1987; Esthetics of Music, translation from Carl Dahlhaus, 1967, 1982. Memberships: American Musicological Society; International Musicological Society; American Society of Arts and Sciences; College Music Society; Sonneck Society of American Music. Address: 301 Savage Farm Drive, Ithaca, NY 14850, USA.

AUSTIN-PHILIPS Eric, b. 12 Oct 1947, Melbourne, Victoria, Australia. Composer; Conductor. Education: BMus, University of Melbourne; Composition with John McCabe and conducting with Roger Norrington, 1975. Career: Faculty Member, The University High School, 1972-; Conductor, Music Critic. Compositions include: Portraits of my Friends and Others, for flute, oboe, clarinet, bassoon and piano, 1973; Nirthanjali for mandolin and orchestra, 1973; Into the Air for piano, 1976; Macavity: The Mystery Cat, for choir, 1981; Comfits and Joys for soprano, choir and strings, 1982; The Black Swan, for choir, 1984; Sinfonietta No 2 for plectra ensemble, 1986; Commissions from the British Music Society (1972), Melbourne Mandolin Orchestra and The Melbourne Chronicle (1982). Honours include: Dorian Le Gallienne Prize, 1972. Address: c/o APRA, 1A Eden Street, Crows Nest, NSW 2065, Australia.

AVDEYEVA Larisa (Ivanova), b. 21 June 1925, Moscow, Russia. Mezzo-Soprano. m. Evgeny Svetlanov. Education: Studied at the Stanislavsky Opera Studio, 1946. Career: Sang at the Stanislavsky Music Theatre, Moscow from 1947 as Offenbach's La Perichole, Susuki in Madame Butterfly and in Khrennikov's Into The Storm and Molchanov's The Stone Flower; Bolshoy Theatre in Moscow from 1952 as Olga in Eugene Onegin, Marina in Boris Godunov, Lehl in The Snow Maiden by Rimsky-Korsakov, Konchakovna in Prince Igor, Akhrosimova in Prokofiev's War and Peace, Carmen and the Sorceress in the opera by Tchaikovsky; Has toured as opera and concert singer in Canada, Europe, USA and the Far East. Honours include: People's Artist of RSFSR, 1964. Address: c/o Bolshoy Theatre, Pr Marxa 8-2, 103009 Moscow, Russia.

AVELING Valda, b. 16 May 1920, Sydney, Australia. Harpsichordist. Education: Performers and Teachers Diplomas, New South Wales Conservatorium of Music, 1936. Debut: Town Hall, Sydney, with Sir Malcolm Sargent, 1938. Career: Appearances with all leading orchestras and at all Music Festivals in the United Kingdom; Frequent concert and record collaboration with Richard Bonynge and Joan Sutherland; Numerous recitals as Duo with Evelyn Barbirolli (oboe); Numerous tours of Europe, Canada and Far East including tour of Germany as joint soloist with Yehudi Menuhin; Performances at Rome Harpsichord Festival, Italy, 1971, 1972; Four visits to Australia for Australian Broadcasting Commission, lates 1976; Recital, University of Indiana, USA, 1976. Recordings include: Scarlatti Sonatas for harpsichord, for EMI, 1976; Chio Mi Scordi di Te, Mozart; Harpsichord Pieces, Thomas Morley; The Collection of Historic Instruments at the Victoria and Albert Museum, London; Music for Four Harpsichords; Harpsichord Continuo. Contributor to: Music and Musicians. Honours: Honorary FTCL; Awarded OBE, 1982; Elected Honorary Member of the Art Workers Guild, 1985. Memberships: Elected Member of Jury, Chairman, Sir Yehudi Menuhin International Violin Competition, held in Paris, sponsored by the City of Paris, 1985. Hobbies: Cooking; Gardening; Reading. Address: 15 Priory Road, London NW6 4NN, England.

AVGERINOS Yannis, b. 30 Apr 1949, Alexandria, Egypt. Music Teacher; Conductor; Composer. Education: Diploma, Department of Ancient Greek Philology, Athens University; Piano and Composition at Athens National Conservatoire; Conducting, Piano and Composition at Trinity College of Music, London. Debut: Athens, Greece. Career: Conductor, Greek premieres of various 20th Century works; Theatre music for A Midsummer Night's Dream; Music for TV documentary on Concentration Camps; Temporary Orchestrator and Producer, Greek Radio Corporation; Founder, Director, Composition Teacher and Principal, Athinaikon Conservatoire; World premiere of Antonin Tucapsky's Concertino for piano and strings. Compositions: Several for Piano Solo, Violoncello Solo, Voice for Greek and French Poetry; Suite for Small Orchestra; One-Movement sinfonietta; Arrangements of other composers' works for choir, orchestra and different combinations. Recordings: Video tapes for Greek Radio and TV: De Falla's Concertino for Harpsichord and Greek Premiere of Spiro Mazi's Anaplassis for Chamber Orchestra, first videography for TV. Contributions to: Various lectures on music. Memberships: Patron, British Music Society, London; Founder, Society for Music Analysis, London. Hobbies: Theatre; Cinema; Books; Travel. Address: 87 Ionias Avenue, GR-10445 Athens, Greece.

AVIDOM Menahem, b. 6 Jan 1908, Stanislau, Galicia. Composer. m. 31 Jan 1935, 2 daughters. Education: BA, American University, Beirut, 1928; Paris, 1934. Compositions: 10 Symphonies, 7 operas, 20 chamber music works, 4 string quartets, 2 woodwind quartets and several vocal works. Recordings: Cassettes of all compositions in Israel. Publications: Several. Contributions to: Music Critic, Jerusalem Post, 1958-72. Honours: Recipient of many honours including Honorary DMus, London Institute for Appointed Research, Knight of the Lofsenis Ursinos Order. Memberships: Honorary President, Israel Composers' League; Israel State Prize Laureate; Qualifying Jury, Leonardo Da Vinci Award, World Cultural Council; Maison International des Intellectuals, Paris. Hobbies: Painting; Chess. Address: 1 Mazeh St, Herzliya 46408, Israel.

AVNI Tzvi (Jacob), b. 7 Sept 1927, Saarbrucken, Germany (living in Israel since 1935). Composer; Music Educator. m. Hanna Avni, 26 Aug 1979, 1 s, 1 d. Education includes: Diploma in Theory and Composition, Israel Music Academy, Tel Aviv, 1958; Further studies in USA, 1962-64. Career includes: Director, AMLI Central Music Library, Tel Aviv, 1961-75; Director, Electronic Music Studio, 1977-, Professor of Music Theory and Composition, Rubin Academy, Jerusalem, 1971-; North Eastern University, Boston, 1993-94; Queens College, New York, 1994-95. Compositions include: Two String Quartets, Wind Quintet, Five Pantomimes for 8 Players; Works for choir, various electronic pieces, works for ballet, art films and radio plays; Vitrage for Harp Solo, 1990; Desert Scenes, symphony in 3 movements, 1990; Three Lyric Songs on P Celan Poems for Mezzo Soprano, English Horn and Harp, 1990; Fagotti Fugati for 2 Bassoons, 1991; Variations on a Sephardic Tune for Recorder Ensemble, 1992; Haleluyah for Mixed Choir, 1993; Triptych for Piano, 1994; The Three Legged Monster, musical legend, for Narrator, Piano and Small Orchestra with text by Hanna Avni, 1994; Anthropomorphic Landscapes, No 1 Flute Solo, No 2 Oboe Solo, No 3 Clarinet Solo for mixed choir, in memory of Itzhak Rabin, 1996-97; Songs and Melodies. Recordings include: Love Under a Different Sun, CD of Chamber - Vocal Works; Program Music 1980 with Israel Philharmonic and Mehta CD; Piano Sonata No 1, CD; String Quartet No 1 (Summer Strings), Israeli String Quartet, CD; 5 Variations for Mr "K", for percussion and Tape, CD. Publications include: An Orchestra is Born; Editor of Gittit, Israel,1966-80. Contributions include: Dictionary of 20th Century Music; Music in Israel. Honours include: Lieberson Prize for String Quartet No 2, 1969; Engel - Tel Aviv Prize for Holiday Metaphors, 1973; Küstermeyer Prize, 1990. Memberships include: Israel Composers League, Chairman 1978-80; Chairman of Israel Jeunesses Musicales. Hobbies: Wood Carving; Art (Contemporary). Current Management: Electronic Music Studio, Rubin Academy of Music, Jerusalem. Address: 54 Bourla Street, Tel Aviv 69364, Israel.

AVSHALOMOV Jacob (David), b. 28 Mar 1919, Tsintao, China. Conductor; Composer. Education: Studied with his father, Aaron Avshalomov in Peking, with Ernst Toch in Los Angeles, 1938, at Reed College in Portland, OR, 1939-41 and with Bernard Rogers at Eastman School of Music, Rochester, NY, 1941-43. Career: Teacher, 1947-54, Conductor of Chorus and Orchestra, Columbia University; Conductor of Portland Junior Symphony Orchestra, 1954-78 and Portland Youth Philharmonic, 1978-. Compositions include: The Taking of T'Ung Kuan for Orchestra, 1943, revised, 1953; Slow Dance for Orchestra, 1945; Sinfonietta, 1946; Evocations for Clarinet and Chamber Orchestra, 1947; Sonatine for Viola and Piano, 1947; Prophecy for Cantor, Chorus and Organ, 1948; How Long, O Lord, cantata, 1948-49; Tom O'Bedlam for Chorus, 1953; The Plywood Age for Orchestra, 1955; Psalm 100 for Chorus and Wind Instruments, 1956; Inscriptions At The City Of Brass for Female Narrator, Chorus and Orchestra, 1956; Phases Of The Great Land for Orchestra, 1959; Symphony: The Oregon, 1959-61; City Upon The Hill for Narrator, Chorus, Orchestra and Liberty Bell, 1965; The Thirteen Clocks for 2 Storytellers and Orchestra, 1973; Raptures for Orchestra, 1975; Quodibet Montagna for Brass Sextet, 1975; Praises From The Corners Of The Earth for Chorus and Orchestra, 1976; Songs for Alyce, 1976; The Most Triumphant Bird, chorus, piano and viola concertante, text Emily Dickinson, 1986; Glorious The Assembled

Fires for Chorus and Orchestra, 1990; Songs in Season, full orchestra, 1993. Recordings: 4 CDs of contemporary American music on Composers Recordings Inc, New York. Publication: The Concerts Reviewed, 65 Years of the Portland Youth Philharmonic, 1989. Address: c/o Portland Youth Philharmonic, 1119 South West Park Avenue, Portland, OR 97205, USA.

AWAD Emil, b. 2 Aug 1963, Mexico. Composer; Conductor. Education: BM, Manhattan School of Music; PhD Composition, Harvard University, 1995. Career: Dudley Orchestra, Harvard, 1989-93; Conductor, Ensamble de las Rosas, 1994-96; Guest Conductor: Manhattan Contemporary Ensemble, Harvard Contemporary Ensemble; Orquesta de Camara de Bellas Artes; Artistic Director, over 50 premieres in Mexico, 1994-, including works by Martino, Davidovsky, Carter and Kim; Guest Lecturer, lectures on tonal system and 12-tone system; Chairman, Composition Faculty, Conservatorio de las Rosas. Compositions: Zazil for Orchestra; Piedras Sueltas, text by Octavio Paz, for flute, violin, viola, cello, piano and soprano; Guitar Solo; Sextet Flute, Guitar, Vibraphone, HnF, Viola, Double Bass; Sonatitas for piano. Contributions to: Curriculum Study for Composition, 1997. Honours: Harvard Grant; Manhattan School of Music Merit Scholarship; Juilliard School of Music Composition Prize. Memberships: Organos Historicos de Mexico. Hobby: Mountaineering. Address: Mangles 37, Bosques de las Lomas, Mexico DF 11700, Mexico.

AX Emanuel, b. 8 June 1949, Lwow, Poland. Pianist. m. Yoko Nozaki, 23 Nov 1974, 1 son, 1 daughter. Education: BA, Columbia University, NY, USA, 1970; Postgraduate Diploma, Juilliard School of Music, 1972. Career: Concert Pianist, 1974-; Appearances in USA and abroad; Performances with major orchestras including the New York Philharmonic, Philadelphia Orchestra, Chicago Symphony Orchestra, Los Angeles Orchestra, and London Philharmonic; Played Beethoven's 2nd Concerto with London Philharmonic at the Festival Hall in 1991, and Brahms 1st Concerto at Promenade Concerts in 1991; Mozart's D minor Concerto at the 1994 Proms. Recordings: With Philadelphia Orchestra, Chicago Symphony, Cleveland Quartet and Guarneri Quartet. Honours: 1st Prize, Arthur Rubenstein International Piano Master Competition, 1974; Record of the Year Award, Stereo Review, 1977; 1 of 5 Best Records of the Year Award, Time Magazine, 1977; Avery Fisher Award, 1979. Memberships: Advisory Board, Plam Beach Festival; Chopin Society. Current Management: ICM Artists Ltd. Address: c/o ICM Artists Ltd, 40 West 57th Street, New York, NY 10019, USA.

AXERLIS Stella, b. 5 Mar 1944, Alexandria, Greece. Soprano. Education: Studied at the University of Melbourne, Australia. Debut: Hagen in Germany in 1968 as Aida. Career: Sang at the Deutsche Oper am Rhein, Dusseldorf, 1970-85 as Leonore, Elisabeth de Valois, Lady Macbeth, Senta, Venus, Sieglinde, Gutrune, Tatiana, Marina, the Marschallin, Jenufa, Santuzza and Madama Butterfly; Guest appearances in Hamburg, Cologne, Kassel, Amsterdam, Paris, Sydney and Covent Garden in London; Zurich Opera in 1986 as the Kostelnicka in Jenufa; Sang Ortrud in Lohengrin at Sydney, 1987. Address: Deutsche Oper am Rhein, Heinrich Heine Allee, Dusseldorf, Germany.

AYDIN Özgür, b. 4 June 1972, Boulder, Colorado, USA. Pianist. Education: Studied at the Ankara Conservatory and the Royal College of Music, London; Currently studying at the Hannover Musikhochschule. Career: Appeared at the 1994 Salzburg Festival and the 1995 Schleswig-Holstein Musik Festival; Concerts broadcast by Classic FM, London, 1993, ABC Sydney, 1996, North German Radio, 1997; Played Brahms's piano concerto with the Bavarian Radio Symphony Orchestra, Herkules-Saal München, live broadcast by Bavarian Radio and television, 1997. Honours: Winner of the 46th International Music Competition of the ARD, Munich, 1997; Nippon Music Award, Tokyo, 1997. Address: Roscherstrasse 3, D-30161 Hanover, Germany.

AYKAL Gurer, b. 1942, Turkey. Music Director; Conductor. Widower, 3 sons. Education: Degrees in Violin and Composition, Ankara State Conservatory, 1969; Diploma in Conducting, Guildhall School of Music, London, 1971; Resident Conductor under direction of Franco Ferrera, Accademia Santa Cecilia, receiving Diploma in Conducting, Rome, 1973; Studied Gregorian choir music and Renaissance polyphony with Dominico Bartolucci, Pontifical Institute of Sacred Music; Also studied under Andre Previn and George Hurst in London. Career: Appointed Permanent Conductor of Presidential Symphony Orchestra, Turkey; Founder, Ankara Chamber Orchestra; Toured Russia as Conductor of Moscow State Symphony Orchestra, 1984; Toured South American and Caribbean Islands as Conductor of English Chamber Orchestra; Music Director and Conductor, Lubbock Symphony Orchestra, TX, 1987-93; Conducted Istanbul Symphony Orchestra, 1989; Principal Guest Conductor of Amsterdam Concertgebouw Chamber Orchestra, 1989; Music Director and Conductor, El Paso Symphony Orchestra, TX, 1992-. Recordings: CD of works with London Philharmonic Orchestra. Honours: Title of State Artist, Turkish Government, 1981;

Selected for National Music Museum, London, for distinguished contribution to the music profession. Address: El Paso Symphony Orchestra, 10 Civic Center Plaza, El Paso, TX 79901, USA.

AYO Felix, b. 1 July 1933, Sestao, Spain (Italian citizen). Violinist. Education: Studied in Paris and Rome, gaining his performance diploma, 1947. Career: Founder member and lead of I Musici, 1952-67; Co-founded Quartetto Beethoven, with Marcello Abbado (piano) and others, 1968; Teacher at the Accademia di Santa Cecilia at Rome from 1972; Plays a Gennaro Gagliano violin (Naples, 1768). Recordings: Many works from the Italian Baroque, including Vivaldi's Four Seasons, with I Musici. Address: c/o Conservatorio Santa Cecilia, Via dei Greci 19, I-00187 Rome, Italy.

AYRTON Norman (Walter), b. 25 Sept 1924, London, England. International Theatre and Opera Director; Dean of British American Drama Academy, London. Education: Acting under Michael Saint Denis at Old Vic Theatre School, London, 1947-48. Career includes: War Service, RNVR, 1939-45; Member, Old Vic Company, 1949, Festival Season, 1951; Repertory at Farnham and Oxford, 1949-50; Staff Member, Old Vic Theatre School, 1949-52; Opened own teaching studio in 1952; Began dramatic coaching for Royal Opera House, Covent Garden, 1953; Assistant Principal, 1954-66, Principal, 1966-72, London Academy of Music and Dramatic Art; Taught at Shakespeare Festival, Stratford, Ontario, Canada and Royal Shakespeare Theatre, England, 1959-62; GHQ Drama Adviser to Girl Guide Movement, 1960-74; Dean, World Shakespeare Study Center, Bankside, 1972; Guest Teacher at Loeb Drama Center, Harvard, 1974; Directed: Artaxerxes for Handel Opera Society, Camden Festival, 1963, La Traviata at Covent Garden, 1963, Manon at Covent Garden, 1964, Sutherland-Williamson Grand Opera Season, Australia, 1965, Twelfth Night for Dallas Theater Center, TX, 1967, The Way of the World, NY, 1976, Lakmé for Australian Opera, 1976, Der Rosenkavalier for Australian Opera Centre, 1983; Guest Director for many international productions, 1973-84 including: Faculty, Juillard School of Music, NY, 1974-85, Melbourne Theatre Co, 1974-, Hartford Stage Company and American Stage Festival, 1978-, Spoleto Festival, USA, 1984, Utah Shakespeare Festival, 1994 and Cornell University, NY, 1995; Director of Opera, Royal Academy of Music, 1986-90. Honour: Honorary RAM, 1989. Hobbies: Reading; Music; Travel; Gardening. Address: 40A Birchington Road, London, NW6, England.

AZKOUL Jad, b. 8 June 1948, New York City, USA. Concert Guitarist. m. Clarissa Whitaker, 27 Dec 1984, 2 sons. Education: BA, 1969, MA, Psychology, 1971, American University, Beirut; Arranging and Composition at Berklee School of Music, Boston, 1971-73; Composition and Analysis with Nadia Boulanger and Pierre Petit in Paris, 1973-75; Guitar with Alberto Ponce, Ecole Normale de Musique, Paris, 1976-78 and with Abel Carlevaro, Montevideo, 1978-81; Masterclasses. Career includes: Recitals, chamber music, orchestra soloist in North and South America, Europe and the Middle East and at many international festivals; Radio and TV appearances in many countries; Professor, Conservatoire Poplulaire de Musique, Geneva, 1984-91 and Music Faculty, American University, Washington DC, 1993-; Catholic University, Washington DC, 1995-; D'Addario concert series, 1992-93; International workshops and masterclasses and jury member for guitar competitions. Compositions: Piano and guitar pieces and film music. Recording: CD, Latin Illustrations For Guitar, France, 1992. Publications: Translator of books by Abel Carlevaro including School of Guitar, into French and English. Contributions to: Various publications. Honours include: Fellowships: French Government, 1974-78, Uruguayan Government, 1979; Winner, Affiliate Artists USA Competition, 1985; Order of the Cedar, Lebanon, 1988. Memberships include: College Music Society; American University of Beirut Alumni Association; American String Teachers Association; Societé de Pédagogie Suisse. Hobbies: Reading; Tennis; Theatre; Languages. Address: 2711 Welcome Drive, Falls Church, VA 22046, USA.

AZUMA Atsuko, b. 11 Dec 1939, Osaka, Japan. Soprano. Education: Studied with Fumiko Yotsuya in Tokyo, Giulia Tess in Milan and Ettore Campogalliani in Parma. Debut: Reggio Emilia in 1963 as Suzel in L'Amico Fritz. Career: Has sung with the Fujiwara Opera Company and at La Scala, Milan, State Operas of Hamburg and Vienna, 1970 and 1971, Metropolitan Opera in 1972, and State Operas of Dresden and Berlin in 1973 and 1976; Further appearances in Buenos Aires, Belgrade, Strasbourg, Washington, Prague, Munich, Copenhagen, Barcelona, Boston, Cincinnati, Miami, Naples and Venice; Roles include Madama Butterfly, Iris in the opera by Mascagni, Mimi, Micaela, Violetta and parts in operas by Mozart and Strauss.

AZZI María Susana, b. 12 Oct 1952, Buenos Aires, Argentina. Social Anthropologist. Education: Licenciada en Ciencias Antropológicas, Universidad de Buenos Aires, 1987; Columbia University, New York, 1986; MBA, Escuela Superior de Economía y Administración de Empresas, Buenos Aires; Piano

Lessons with Teresa Eichelbaum, 1984-92, Vera Anosova, 1992-95. Career: Professor, Board Member, Academia Nacional del Tango, Buenos Aires; Lecturer on the Tango and Astor Piazzolla in Argentina, USA, Europe, Australia, Mexico & Korea; TV and Radio Appearances in Argentina, London; Consulted by New York USA, Sony Classical; Dance Perspectives Foundation and Metropolitan Museum of Art; Metropolitan Museum of Art, Musical Instruments Department; Washington, DC Smithsonian Institution; Buenos Aires, Argentina: Fundación Astor Piazzolla, Instituto Nacional de Antropología. Publications include: Italian Immigration and Their Impact on the Tango in Argentina, 1997; Tango Album by Yo-Yo Ma, 1997; Tango Argentino, 1998; Memberships include: Academia Nacional del Tango; Society for Ethnomusicology; American Anthropological Association; International Council for Traditional Music; International Association for the Study of Popular Music. Hobby: Golf. Address: Posadas 1612 8, Buenos Aires 1112, Argentina.

B

BABAK Renate, b. 4 Feb 1939, Kharkov, Ukraine. Opera Singer (Mezzo-Soprano). Education: Rimsky-Korsakov Conservatory, Leningrad, 1955-58; P I Tchaikovsky Conservatory, Kiev, Ukraine, 1958-61; Diploma, Opera Singer, 1961. Debut: As Princess in Dargomizhsky's The Mermaid, Leningrad State Opera, 1958. Career: With Lvov State Opera, Ukraine, 1961-64; With Bolshoi Theatre Opera, Moscow, 1964-73; Roles: Carmen, Amneris, Eboli in Don Carlos, Azucena, Charlotte in Werther, Ortrud in Lohengrin, Marina in Boris Godunov, Marfa in Khovanshchina, Lubasha in Tsar's Bride, Lubov in Mazeppa, Olga in Eugene Onegin, Pauline in The Queen of Spades, Ratmir in Ruslan and Ludmilla, Princess in The Mermaid; Roles in USA, 1973-; Ulrica in Un Ballo in Maschera, Santuzza in Cavalleria Rusticana, Amneris, Azucena, Leonora in La Forza del Destino; Concert tours, North America and Europe; Head, Vocal Department and Opera Workshop, Washington Conservatory of Music, 1983-. Recordings: Renata Babak, Golden Age Stereo 1006; Renata Babak Sings Ukrainian Songs and Arias by Puccini and Verdi. Honours include: Honorary Degrees from Brandeis University, 1991, Princeton University, 1991; William Schuman Award of Columbia University, 1992.

BABBITT Milton (Byron), b. 10 May 1916, Philadelphia, PA, USA. Composer; Music Educator; Music Theorist. m. Sylvia Miller, 27 Dec 1939, 1 daughter. Education: Studied violin, clarinet and saxophone in childhood; Mathematics, University of PA; BA, New York University, 1935; MFA, Princeton University, 1942; Studied music with Marion Bauer and Philip James and privately with Roger Sessions. Career: Teacher, Music Faculty, 1938-42, 1948-84, Mathematics Faculty, 1942-45, William Shubael Conant Professor, 1966-84, Professor Emeritus, Princeton University; Director, Columbia-Princeton Electronic Music Center, 1959-84; Member, Composition Faculty, Juilliard School, NY, 1972-; Guest Lecturer, many USA and European colleges and universities; PhD, Princeton Univeresity, 1992. Compositions include: Orchestral: Fabulous Voyage, 1946, Ars Combinatoria, 1981, Piano Concerto, 1985; Chamber: 5 String Quartets, 1948-82, Woodwind Quartet, 1953, Sextets for Violin and Piano, 1966, My Ends Are My Beginnings for Clarinet, 1978, Dual for Cello and Piano, 1980, Groupwise for 7 Instruments, 1983, Sheer Pluck for Guitar, 1984, Fanfare for Double Brass Sextet, 1987, Whirled Series for Saxophone and Piano, 1987, The Crowded Air for 11 Instruments, 1988; None but the Lonely Flute, 1991; Septet, But Equal, 1992; Around the Horn, 1993; No Longer Very Clear, for soprano and four instruments, 1994; Trial, clarinet, viola and piano, 1994; Solo piano pieces, choruses, songs and tape pieces. Publication: Milton Babbitt: Words about Music, the Madison lectures, 1987. Contributions to: Articles in various journals. Honours include: American Academy and Institute of Arts and Letters Gold Medal in Music, 1988. Memberships include: President, 1951-52, International Society of Contemporary Music. Hobbies include: Analytical Philosophy. Address: 222 Western Way, Princeton, NJ 08540, USA.

BABYKIN Anatol, b. 1944, Tscheljabinsk, Russia. Singer (Bass). Education: Studied at the Astrakan Conservatory until 1976. Career: Member of the Bolshoi Opera at Moscow from 1976; Roles have included King René (Iolanthe), Gremin (Eugene Onegin), Leporello in The Stone Guest by Dargomizhsky and Don Alfonso (Così fan tutte); Sang with the Bolshoi at the Edinburgh Festival in 1991, operas by Tchaikovsky and Rimsky-Korsakov. Address: c/o Bolshoi Opera, 103009 Moscow, Russia.

BACELLI Monica, b. 1964, Italy. Singer (Mezzo-Soprano). Education: Studied in Rome and Milan. Career: Spoleto Festival from 1987, as Bessie in Weill's Mahagonny and Dorabella in Così fan tutte; Netherlands Opera, 1989, as Rosina, and Rome, 1990, as Zerlina in Don Giovanni; US debut, San Francisco, 1991, as Cecilio in Lucio Silla by Mozart; Other roles include Isaura in Rossini's Tancredi (at Bologna) and Cherubino (Salzburg, 1992). Recordings include: Mozart's La Finta Giardiniera (Teldec). Address: c/o Teatro dell'Opera, Piazza B Gigli 8, 00184 Rome, Italy.

BACH Andreas, b. 29 July 1968, Dennbach, Germany. Pianist. Education: First music lessons, 1973-80; Studied with Professor Karl-Heinz Kammerlung, Hanover. Debut: Alte Opera, Frankfurt in 1984. Career: Appearance in Eurovision Competition, 1984; 1st tour to USA with debuts at New York, San Francisco and Washington DC, 1987 and to Japan, 1988; Several further tours to USA and appearances in France, England, Switzerland, Italy and Portugal. Recordings: Schumann Op 6, Op 7, 1989; Beethoven Op 7, Op 31, No 2, Op 126, Novalis, 1990. Honours: Winner, several Youth Competitions, 1975-84; Bernhard Sprengel Prize for Music, 1985; Kulturpreis von Rheinland-Pfalz, 1990. Hobbies: Reading German Literature; Photography; Swimming; Biking. Current Management: Concerto Winde-stein, Munich, Germany. Address: Ringstrasse 20, 5430 Montabaur, Germany.

BACH Jan (Morris), b. 11 Dec 1937, Forrest, Illinois, USA. Composer; Educator. m. Dalia Zakaras, 20 August 1971, 2 daughters. Education: BMus 1959, MMus 1961, DMA 1971, Composition, University of Illinois, Urbana-Champaign. Career: Assistant 1st Horn, United States Army Band, 1962-65; Instructor in Music, University of Tampa, Florida, 1965-66; Professor of Music, Northern Illinois University, Dekalb, 1966-. Compositions include: Four Two-Bit Contraptions, 1967; Skizzen, 1967; Burgundy Variations, 1968; Woodwork, 1970; Eisteddfod, 1972; The System, 1973; Piano Concerto, 1975; The Eve of St Agnes, for antiphonal wind ensemble, 1976; Praetorius Suite, 1977; Hair Today, 1977; Canon and Caccia, for five French horns, 1977; Happy Prince, 1978; Quintet for Tuba and Strings, 1978; Gala Fanfare, 1979; The Student from Salamanca, 1979; Rounds and Dances, 1980; Sprint, 1982; French Suite, for unaccompanied horn, 1982; Horn Concerto, 1983; Dompes & Jompes, 1986; Harp Concerto, 1986; Concerto for Trumpet and Wind Ensemble, 1987; Concerto, for Euphonium and Orchestra, 1990; Anachronisms, for string quartet. 1991; People of Note, 1993; Concerto for Steel Drum and Orchestra, 1994; The Last Flower, 1995; Foliations, 1995; Concertino for Bassoon and Strings, 1996; Pilgrimage, 1997; Variations on a theme of Brahms, 1997. Recordings include: Laudes for Brass Quintet; Skizzen for Woodwind Quintet; Four Two-Bit Contraptions; Eisteddfod, 1972; Concert Variations, for Euphonium and Piano, 1977; Fanfare and Fugue for Five Trumpets, 1979; Rounds and Dances, 1980; Triptych, for Brass Quintet, 1989. Honours: First Prize, BMI Student Composers Contest, 1957; First Prize, Mannes (New York) Opera Competition, 1974; First Prize, New York City Opera Competition, 1980; Distinguished Research Professor, Northern Illinois University, 1982. Memberships: Broadcast Music Inc; TUBA Society. Hobbies: Bicycling; Crossword puzzles; Jigsaw puzzles; Caricature cartooning; Collecting old radio programmes; Playing French horn. Address: PO Box 403, Wasco, IL 60183, USA.

BACHLUND Gary, b. 1958, New York City, New York, USA. Singer (Tenor). Education: Studied in New York. Career: Sang Parsifal at Carnegie Hall and appeared in operas by Mussorgsky, Wagner (Das Rheingold) and Gounod (Roméo et Juliette) at the Metropolitan Opera: Sang Strauss's Bacchus with Minnesota Opera, Florestan for Boston Opera and Don José for Scottish Opera at Glasgow (European debut, 1986); Other roles include Agrippa in The Fiery Angel, Jimmy in Mahagonny and Aegisthus in Elektra (all at Los Angeles); Enée in Les Troyens at the Opera Bastille, Paris (1990) and Wagner's Erik at Cologne (1992). Address: c/o Oper der Stadt Köln, Offenbachplatz, W-5000 Cologne 1, Germany.

BACHMANN Rhonda, b. 24 Oct 1952, Chicago, Illinois, USA. Soprano. m. Arthur Hammond, 24 Aug 1986, dec 1991. Education: Conservatoire National Superior de Musique de Paris, 1972-76; Concours de Maitres du Chant, Paris, 1973, 1st Prize; Institut de Musicologie, Sorbonne, Paris, 1971-72, Licence es Lettres, 1976; Master of Music in Applied Voice 1978, Northwestern University, Evanston, Illinois, 1977-78; Further private study with Jan Keizer, Amsterdam, 1983-87. Career: Chicago Opera Theatre, 1979-80; Theatre de la Porte St Martin, Paris, 1981, title role, Rose Marie; Theatre du Rhin, Strasbourg, 1981-84; Centre France Lyrique, Paris, 1982-83; Concerts include, Radio France 1980; 1979, 1993 Marie Antoinette Bicentennial, Naantali Festival, Finland, 1981; Salle Gaveau, Paris, 1981; Buffalo, New York, 1985; Royal Opera House, Friends of Covent Garden Christmas Gala, 1985; Institut Francais London, 1986; Pavillon Dauphine, Paris, 1986; Some 40 recitals and chamber music concerts in Paris, Germany, Italy, including the music of Vivaldi, Bach, Handel, Mozart, Schubert, Spohr, Brahms, Schoenberg, Ravel and Dowland; Many appearances in theatres and on television, New York, Paris, Marseilles; Acted in 3 films, 1974-76; Leading role, Harriet Smithson, The Life of Berlioz; Toured extensively with recital in 18th Century Costume as Queen Marie Antoinette, Songs for the Queen, Songs for the Revolution, 150 performances, 5 programmes of which 73 in the Grand Trianon, Versailles, 1988-93; Tours to America, England, Scotland, Ireland, Bulgaria, Austria. Recordings: Cassettine: Quand tu étais petit, Lieder in French translation by Mozart, Schubert and Brahms; Record, Excerpts from the production of Rose-Marie at the Theatre de la Porte St Martin, 1981. Address: 47 Floral Street, London WC2, England.

BACIU Ion, b. 21 June 1931, Brateiu, Rumania. Conductor. Education: Studied at the Bucharest Conservatory, with Constantin Silvestri, 1950-55. Career: Chief conductor of the Ploesti Philharmonic, 1955-62; Musical director of the Moldavian Philharmonic at Iasi, 1962-87; First tour of the USA, 1967, and returned to the Ploiesti Philharmonic, 1987. Address: c/o Conservatoriul de Muzica, Str Closca 9, 6600 Iasi, Rumania.

BACK Andrée, b. 1950, England. Soprano. Education: Studied at the Royal College of Music. Career: Has sung in oratorios, recitals and symphony concerts with appearances in most major European and American cities; Frequent engagements in Switzerland, Norway, Austria, Belgium and the Netherlands (Radio Symphony Orchestra, Rotterdam); Has sung in Carmina Burana at Liège, Siegen and Edinburgh, Berlioz's La Mort de Cléopâtre with Berlin Symphony Orchestra, Mozart's Requiem and Coronation Mass in Marienstatt with the Bonn Bach Choir, and Mozart Concert Arias with the Schwabische Symphony Orchestra; Sang in Mahler's 4th Symphony at Cheltenham Festival and in A Child of Our Time at Bury St Edmunds, Telemann Cantatas in Hamburg and Haydn's Berenice and Strauss' Four Last Songs with the Billings Symphony Orchestra, 1989; Other concert repertoire includes Bach's Mass in B minor, Magnificat, Passions and Christmas Oratorio, Beethoven's Missa Solemnis, Mass in C and Choral Symphony, Requiems by Brahms, Fauré, Britten and Verdi, Handel's Messiah, Judas Maccabeus, Jephtha, Joshua, Acis and Galatea, Hercules, Israel in Egypt, Samson, Saul and Chandos Anthems, Janácek's Glagolitic Mass, Mahler's 2nd and 8th Symphonies, Rückert Lieder, Schubert's Salve Regina, Masses, Vivaldi's Gloria and Magnificat, Wagner's Wesendonck Lieder. Address: Mancroft Towers, Oulton Broad, Lowestoft, Suffolk, NR32 3PS, England.

BACQUIER Gabriel, b. 17 May 1924, Beziers, France. Baritone. Education: Studied at the Paris Conservatoire. Debut: Sang in Landowski's Le Fou at Nice in 1950. Career: Sang in Brussels, 1953-56 and at the Opéra Comique, Paris, 1956-58; Appeared at the Paris Opéra from 1958 as Escamillo, Valentin, Rigoletto, Simon Boccanegra and Boris Godunov; Aix-en-Provence in 1960 as Don Giovanni, Glyndebourne Festival in 1962 as Mozart's Count, and Covent Garden in 1964 as Riccardo in I Puritani and Scarpia; US debut in 1962 at Chicago as the High Priest in Samson et Dalila; Metropolitan Opera, 1964-79 as Don Pasquale, the Villains in Les Contes d'Hoffmann, Iago, Leporello, Golaud and Rossini's Bartolo; Holland Festival in 1972 as Falstaff; Teatro Fenice, Venice, 1973-74; Teacher at the Paris Conservatoire until 1987; Sang Sancho Panza in Massenet's Don Quichotte at Florence and Monte Carlo, 1992; Debussy's Arkel at Lille, 1996. Recordings include: Guillaume Tell; Gounod's Mireille and Roméo et Juliette; La Belle Hélène; Lakmé; Les Huguenots; Don Giovanni; Les Contes d'Hoffmann; Così fan tutte; Le nozze di Figaro; Don Quichotte; La Favorite by Donizetti; Thais by Massenet; Ariane et Barbe-Bleue by Dukas. Address: Marks Management, 4 Highgate High Street, London N6 5JL, England.

BACULEWSKI Krzysztof Jan, b. 26 Dec 1950, Warsaw, Poland. Composer. m. Agnieszka Dmowska, 20 Dec 1979. Education: MA, Academy of Music, Warsaw, 1974; Postgraduate Studies, Conservatoire National Supérieur de Musique, Paris, 1976-77; PhD, Warsaw University, 1982. Debut: Warsaw, 1975. Career: Many Compositions Performed at Warsaw Autumn International Festival of Contemporary Music and Abroad, including USA, France, Germany, Finland, Hungary, South America. Compositions: Vivace e Cautileua for Chamber Ensemble, 1975; Epitaphim for Orchestra, 1973; Ground for Orchestra, 1981; Concerto for Orchestra, 1983; A Walking Shadow for Orchestra, 1990; Antitheton I, for Piano Trio, 1989; Antitheton II, for Baroque instruments, 1996. Recordings: Sonata for Percussion, Rilke-Lieder for Choir a Cappella, Nox Ultima, Motet for Choir a Cappella, The Profane Anthem to Anne, text by John Donne, a Cantata, A Walking Shadow for Orchestra. Contributions to: Ruch Muzyczny; Studio. Honours: Many Prizes at Polish Competitions. Memberships: Polish Composers Union; ISCM; Authors Society Zaiks. Hobbies: Skiing; Yachting; Travel. Address: ul Ludwika Hirszfelda 8 m 42, 02-776 Warszawa, Poland.

BADER Hans-Dieter, b. 16 Feb 1938, Stuttgart, Germany. Tenor. Education: Studied with Rudolf Gehrung and in Stuttgart. Debut: Stuttgart Staatsoper in 1960 as Arturo in Lucia di Lammermoor. Career: Sang at Brunswick, Karlsruhe, Essen, Cassel and Mannheim; Appeared in Hannover, 1965-84 as Rodolfo in La Bohème, Faust at Nuremberg, Hamburg, Dusseldorf, Strásbourg and Vienna Volksoper; Other roles include Ferrando in Così fan tutte and the Duke of Mantua. Recordings include: Reger's Requiem; Sly by Wolf-Ferrari; Strauss's Feuersnot.

BADER Roland, b. 24 Aug 1938, Wangen, Germany. Conductor; Choral Director. Education: Studied at the Stuttgart Musikhochschule. Career: Chief Conductor at Oberhausen, 1970-74, and Director of the Folkwanghochschule at Essen; Choral Director at St Hedvig's Cathedral at Berlin, 1974, and guest conductor in Australia, the USA and the Far East; Chief guest with the Cracow Philharmonic and Choral Director at NDR, Hamburg, from 1983; Regular choral concerts at the Salzburg Festival, from 1984. Address: c/o NDR Sinfonieorchester (Chorus), Rothenbaumehaussee 132, W-2000 Hamburg 13, Germany.

BADIAN Maya, b. 18 Apr 1945, Bucharest, Romania. Settled in Montreal, Canada since 1987. Composer; Musicologist; Doctor of Music. m. Lucian Munteanu, 1 son (deceased 1989). Education: MMus, Composition, Music Academy of Bucharest, Bucharest; DMus, Composition, Montreal University, Montreal, Canada. Debut: Symphonic Movement, Romania in 1968. Career:

Musical Director for RTV, Bucharest, 1968-72; Professor of Composition and Keyboard, Bucharest, 1972-87; Teacher at the Montreal University since 1990; Musicology writings; Lecturer at international contemporary music festivals and congress in Europe and Canada; Concerts in Europe, USA and Canada; Member of various international juries. Compositions: Over 50 works including: Symphonic: Holocaust - In Memoriam, symphony; Concertante music: Concertos for Piano, for Violin, for Guitar, for Cello, for Marimba and Vibraphone for Clarinet and Saxaphone for 4 Timpanis (To Mircea Badian); Vocal-Orchestral works: Canada 125 - Cantata Profana, Towards The Pinnacle, poem for Soprano; Chamber: Concerto for Horn and Percussion, Solos, duos, trios and other chamber ensembles. Recordings: ST-ECE 02331, Maya Badian, Romania, 1977; CD, Towards The Pinnacle, Canada, 1994, LB CD-1001-94. Publications: All compositions published in Lucian Badian Editions, Canada. Contributions to: Various musical periodicals; RTV interviews. Honour: All her archival documents and manuscripts are deposited at the Manuscript Collection, Music Division, National Library of Canada, Ottawa. Address: 2001 - 1140 Fisher Avenue, Ottawa, Ontario K1Z 8M5, Canada.

BADINSKI Nikolai, b. 19 Dec 1937, Sofia, Bulgaria. Composer; Violinist; Pedagogue. Education: Diploma, Academy of Music, Sofia, 1956-61; Masterclass, Composition, Academy of Arts, East Berlin, 1967-70; Scholarship for Masterclasses, Accademia Musicale, Siena, Italy, 1975, 1976. Career: Active as Composer, University Teacher in Berlin, Sofia, Halle; Concert Violinist; Concertmaster; Special Advisor for Music Education, String Quartet, German Democratic Republic; Active in the Darmstadt International Courses for New Music, 1974-78; Guest Professor, Universitites of Stockholm and Copenhagen; Assistant to Max Deutsch, Sorbonne and Ecole Normale de Musique, Paris, 1982; Living in Paris (Scholar of the French Government), 1985-86; Composer-in-Residence (California); Appearances at various Festivals;. Numerous performances, Radio and TV Broadcaster. Compositions: Numerous compositions including 3 Symphonies, Several Concertos for Instruments and Orchestra; Widerspiegelungen der Weisheir for S, B, Choir and Orchestra, Ballets, Music for Orchestra, Chamber Music; 3 Espressioni, for Soprano and Tape, 1981; Cantico di S Francesco, for Baritone and Tape, 1981-82; Vocal, Organ Music; Electroacoustic Music; Schwendes Berl Märchen, Traumvisionen, Dostoevsky Reflections, Homage to Kafka, Rotation (in Memory of a Cosmonaut), Phoenixe, Sevtopolis; Watermusic, 1980; Musik mit Papier; Luftmusik, 1980-81; Musicvisuel Correspondence P, 1980-82; Six Capricii for baritone and piano, 1991; Seven Memorial Stones, In memorium of the Holocaust Victims - A Requiem. Recordings: 6 LP's and several CD's with Compositions by Aban-Abt and by pro Viva. Contributor to: Freelance Contributor to the BBC, London. Honours: 1st Place Prize, 28th International Competition for Composition, Viotti, Italy, 1997; International competition for Composers, Stockhausen, Italy, 1978; Internal Trieste Prize for symphonic music, Italy, 1979; Prix de Rome, 1979. Membership: Corresponding Member, European Academy of Arts, Sciences and Humanities, Paris. Address: Landgrafenstrasse 8, D-10787 Berlin, Germany.

BADOREK Wilfried, b. 1936, Germany. Singer (Tenor). Career: Sang first in Karlsruhe, 1960-62, then Aachen, Essen and Gartnerplatz, Munich, 1965-67; Later engaged in Mannheim and Cologne, 1977-82; Sang in Innsbruck, 1979-83; Staatsoper Vienna and Bregenz Festival, 1973, as Erik in Fliegende Holländer; Venice as Max in Der Freischütz, 1974, Rome and Lisbon as Florestan, 1977; Further guest appearances in Tehran, 1976, Ottawa, 1977, and Brussels including as the Drum Major in Wozzeck, 1981; Other roles have included Verdi's Duke and Gabriele Adorno, Pinkerton, Andrea Chenier and Turiddu; Wagner's Lohengrin, Walter and Parsifal; Strauss's Bacchus and Emperor, and title role in La Damnation de Faust. Recordings include: Highlights from Die Zauberflöte. Address: c/o Théâtre Royale de la Monnaie, 4 Rue Leopold, B-1000 Brussels, Belgium.

BADURA-SKODA Eva, b. 15 Jan 1929, Munich, Germany. Musicologist. m. Paul Badura-Skoda, 4 children. Education: Universities of Heidelberg, Vienna and Innsbruck; PhD, 1953; 3 years study, Hochschule für Musik, Vienna. Career: Freelance Lecturer and Writer, until 1962; Summer School Lecturer, Mozarteum Salzburg; Professor, University of Wisconsin, 1964-74; Guest Professor, University of Boston, 1976; Queen's University, Kingston, Canada, 1979; McGill University, Montreal, Canada, 1981-82, Winter-term; Universitat Goettingen, 1982-83. Publications: Mozart Interpretation, 1957; Interpretating Mozart on the Keyboard, 1961; Mozart's C Minor Piano Concerto, 1971; An Unknown Singspiel by Joseph Haydn, 1972; Schubert Studies, 1982; Internationaler Joseph Haydn Kongress Wien 1982 Congress Report, Henle Verlag Munich, 1985. Contributions to: Musical Journals; New Grove Dictionary of Music and Musicians, 1980; More than 100 scholarly articles on History of Viennese Classical Music and History of the Fortepiano. Honours: Austrian Decoration: Honorary Cross Litteris et Artibus; 3 University Grants. Memberships: International Musicological Society; Haydn Institute, Cologne; Zentralinstitut für Mozart-Forschung des Mozarteums, Salzburg. Address: Zuckerkandlgasse 14, 1190 Vienna, Austria, & 5802 Julia Street, Madison, WI 53705, USA.

BADURA-SKODA Paul, b. 6 Oct 1927, Vienna, Austria. Pianist. m. Eva Badura-Skoda, 4 children. Education: Studied Conducting and Piano at State Conservatory, Vienna; Master class of Edwin Fischer, Lucerne. Career: Concert Pianist from 1948, notably in works by Mozart, Beethoven and Schubert; NewYork debut 1953; Tokyo, 1959; Moscow debut, 1964; Duets with violinist D Oistrakh; Held annual master classes, formerly in Edinburgh and Salzburg, latterly at Siena Festival; Artist-in-Residence, University of Wisconsin, 1966-71; Premieres of Martin's 2nd Piano Concerto, 1970 and Fantasie sur des rhythmes flamencos, 1973; Numerous recordings. Compositions: Mass in D; Sonata romantique for flute and piano, 1994; Cadenzas to piano and violin concertos by Mozart and Haydn. Publications: Mozart Interpretation 1957 (with wife); The Piano Sonatas of Beethoven (with Jorg Demus) 1970; Interpreting Bach at the Keyboard, 1988; Editions of works by Schubert, Mozart and Chopin. Honours include: Chevalier de la Legion d'Honneur, France, 1992; Cross of Honour, Austria, 1977. Address: c/o 3116 Live Oak Street, Dallas, TX 75204, USA.

BAERG Theodore, b. 1953, Toronto, Canada. Singer (Baritone). Debut: Canadian Opera Company, 1978, as Monterone in Rigoletto. Career: Sang in the Canadian premiere of Tchaikovsky's The Maid of Orleans (1980) and in Lulu, The Merry Widow and Die Zauberflöte (Papageno); Other roles include Mozart's Count (Hamilton Opera, 1984), Rossini's Figaro (Vancouver) and Ramiro in L'Heure Espagnole (Glyndebourne, 1988); Guested as Marcello in La Bohème at San Diego (1990) and Papageno at Washington (1991); Toronto, 1992, in the premiere of Mario and the Magician by Harry Somers. Address: c/o Canadian Opera Company, 227 Front Street East, Toronto, Ontario, Canada M5A 1E8.

BAEVA Vera, b. 18 Mar 1930, Burgas, Bulgaria. Composer; Pianist. Education: Graduated Sofia State Academy, 1953. Career: Conducted the chorus of Radio Sofia, from 1954; Lecturer at the Sofia State Academy from 1986; Teacher of chamber music at the Open Society Foundation, 1993. Compositions: Five Impressions for piano, 1973; Four Songs, 1975; 2 Preludes for cello, 1984; Nostalgichno for chamber ensemble, 1986; Sonata for piano 4 hands, 1988; Butterfly for female voices and ensemble, 1989; Tristezza for violin, 1990; Dance around the Fire of the God Tangra for male voices and ensemble, 1991. Address: c/o MUSICAUTOR, 63 Tzar Assen Street, 1463 Sofia, Bulgaria.

BAGINSKI Zbigniew, b. 19 Jan 1949, Stettin, Poland. Composer; Teacher. m. Alicja, 23 August 1988, 2 daughters. Education: MA, High School of Music, Warsaw, 1972. Career: Many performances of compositions in Germany, Great Britain, Denmark, Sweden, USA, USSR, Holland, Hungary, Cuba; Assistant Professor, 1978-88, Associate Professor 1988-; Vice-Dean, Faculty of Composition, Conducting and Music Theory, 1987-90, Academy of Music Frederic Chopin, Warsaw. Compositions: Sinfonia Notturna, 1984; Concert for Harpsichord and Orchestra, 1985; Oh, Sweet Baroquel Suite for String Orchestra, 1985; Symphony in Seven Scenes, 1988; Canons, Scherzos and Epigrams, 1987; Nocturne-Berceusee, 1989; Trio with Coda, 1983; Piano Quartet, 1990; Refrain for 2 Pianos, 1975; Acho for Organ, 1974; Expeditions on the Other Side, 1973. Memberships: Polish Composers Union, Vice-President of Warsaw Branch, 1985-89, General Secreatry, 1989. Hobbies: Tennis; Skiing. Address: ul Schillera 8m5, 00-248 Warsaw, Poland.

BAGLIONI Bruna, b. 8 Apr 1947, Frascati, Italy. Mezzo-Soprano. Education: Studied with Gina Maria Rebori and Walter Castaldi-Tassoni in Rome. Debut: Spoleto 1970, as Maddalena in Rigoletto. Career: Has sung at major theatres in Milan, Venice, Naples, Trieste, Rome, Bologna and London (at Covent Garden as Eboli in Don Carlos); Other roles include Verdi's Amneris, Ulrica and Azucena; La Cieca in La Gioconda; Marina in Boris Godunov; Leonore in Donizetti's La Favorite and Giovanna Seymour in Anna Bolena; Charlotte in Werther by Massenet; Sang Amneris at Dallas, Laura in La Gioconda at Rome, 1992; Eboli and Amneris at the Verona Arena, 1992; Many concert appearances. Recordings include: Don Carlos from Covent Garden. Address: Arena di Verona, Piazza Bra 28, 37121 Verona, Italy.

BAGRATUNI Suren, b. 17 Mar 1963, Yerevan, Armenia. Cellist. m. Natalia Khoma, 5 July 1986. Education: Yerevan State Komitas Conservatory; Moscow State Tchaikovsky Conservatory; New England Conservatory, Boston; Central Music School (Yerevan). Debut: Solo in Yerevan, 1974; With an orchestra in Yerevan, 1978. Career: Solo recitals in Grand Hall, Moscow Conservatory; Carnegie (Weill), New York; Jordan and Symphony Halls, Boston; Gasteig-Munchen; Gaveau-Paris; Alice Tully; Merkin, New York; Tonhalle, St Gallen, Switzerland; Professor of Cello, University of Illinois, Urbana-Champaign; Concertos and recitals throughout the world. Recordings: Solo Cello and Two Cellos, 1995; Shostakovich, Prokoviev - Sonatas, 1997; Trios by Beethoven (op 1 no3) Brahms (Op 8), Tchaikovsky, Rachmaninov, 1997; Babajanian, Trio, 1997; Short Pieces for cello and piano, 1997. Honours: First Prize, Armenia National, 1980; First Prize, Trancaucasus, 1981; Winner, USSR National, 1981; Silver Medal, Tchaikovsky, 1986; First Prize, Vittorio Gui, 1988. Member: Moscow Conservatory Trio (based in New York). Current Management: Curzon and Kedersha; ICM (Trio). Address: 4106 Englewood Drive, Champaign, IL 61821, USA.

BAHK Jehi, b. 26 June 1971, Vienna, Austria. Violinist. Education: Vienna Academy for Music and Performing Arts. Debut: Konzerthaus, Vienna, 1995. Career: Founding Member, Leader, Hugo Wolf Quartet, 1995-; Salzburg Mozarteum, Schubertiade Feldkirch, Carinthian Summer, 1996; Munchen Herkules-Saal, Numberg kaiserburg, Prague, Rudolfinum, 1997; Edinburgh Festival, Carnegie Hall, New York, 1998. Honour: 1st Prize, 5th International Competition for String Quartets, Cremona, Italy, 1995. Address: Paulanergasse 3/15, A 1040 Wien, Austria.

BAILES Anthony (James), b. 18 June 1947, Bristol, England. Lutenist. m. Anne Van Royen. Education: Bulmershe College of Further Education; Studies with Michael Watson (Bristol), Diana Poulton (London), Gusta Goldschmidt (Amsterdam), Eugen M Dombois (Schola Cantorum Basiliensis). Debut: Purcell Room, 1971. Career: Solo Concerts and Tours throughout Europe and Scandinavia; Many Recordings both solo and in ensemble; Professor of Lute. Recordings: Numerous recordings and broadcasts. Publications: An Introduction to 17th Century Lute Music, 1983; Lessons for the Lute (with A Van Royen), 1983; 32 Easy Pieces for Baroque Lute, 1984. Contributions to: Criticism for various journals and magazines and some articles. Hobbies: Reading. Address: Hollenweg 3A, 4144 Arlesheim, Switzerland.

BAILEY Judith (Margaret), b. 18 July 1941, Camboume, England. Composer; Conductor. Education: Studied at the Royal Academy of Music, 1959-63. Career: Conductor and lecturer from 1971. Compositions: Trencrom, symphonic poem, 1978; 2 symphonies, 1981, 1982; Seascape for women's chorus, woodwind trio and orchestra, 1985; Penwith, overture, 1986; Fiesta for orchestra, 1988; Concerto for clarinet and strings, 1988; Chamber music. Address: c/o British Music Information Centre, 10 Stratford Place, London W1N 9AE, England.

BAILEY Norman (Stanley), b. 23 Mar 1933, Birmingham, England. Operatic and Concert Baritone. m. (1) Doreen Simpson, 1957 (divorced 1983), 2 s, 1 d, (2) Kristine Ciesinki, July 1985. Education: Rhodes University, South Africa; BMus, Vienna State Academy, Austria; Performers and Teachers Licenciate in Singing; Diplomas in Opera, Lieder and Oratorio. Debut: Linz, 1960. Career: Principal Baritone, Sadler's Wells Opera, London, 1967-71; Regular engagements at world's major opera houses and festivals including: La Scala, Milan, Royal Opera House, Covent Garden; 1st British Hans Sachs in Meistersinger, 1969 at Bayreuth Wagner Festival, also sang Amfortas there; Sang at: Vienna State Opera, Metropolitan Opera, NY, Paris Opera, Edinburgh Festival, Hamburg State Opera, Munich State Opera, English National Opera, Scottish Opera; In 1985 sang in the world premiere of Goehr's Behold The Sun; Performances for BBC include: Falstaff in La Traviata, The Flying Dutchman, Macbeth; Has also sung: Sharpless with Scottish Opera, Britten's Theseus for Opera London, Sadler's Wells and Stromminger in La Wally for Bregenz Festival, 1990; Sang in Reginald Goodall's Memorial Concert, Wahnmonolog, Festival Hall, 1991; Season 1992 as Sharpless in Madame Butterfly for ENO and King René in Tchaikovsky's Yolanta for Opera North; Sang Oroveso in Bellini's Norma for Opera North, 1993; Glyndebourne debut, as Schigolch in Lulu, 1996 (also televised); Sang Landgrave in Tannhäuser for Opera North, 1997. Recordings include: The Ring, Goodall; Meistersinger; Der fliegende Holländer, Solti; Walküre, Klemperer. Honours: Commander Of The Order of the British Empire, 1977; Honorary RAM, 1981; Honorary Doctor of Music, 1986. Membership: Baha'i World Community. Hobbies: Chess; Notaphily; Golf; Microcomputing. Address: 84 Warham Road, South Croydon, Surrey, CR2 6LB, England.

BAILLIE Alexander, b. 6 Jan 1956, Stockport, Lancashire, England. Concert Cellist. Education: Studied with Jacqueline du Pré, at the Royal College of Music and with André Navarra in Vienna. Career: Many performances with leading British Orchestras; Concerts in Europe and North America include the first Canadian performance of Penderecki's 2nd Concerto; Tour of Britain with the Budapest String Orchestra, 1991, followed by tour of the Far East; Promenade Concert appearances include the Concerto by Colin Matthews, 1984, Henze's Sieben Liebeslieder, Takemitsu's Orion and Pleiades 1989, Schumann Concerto, 1990 and the Delius Concerto, 1993; Has premiered works by Lutoslawski (Grave), Schnittke (Sonata for Cello and Piano), Gordon Crosse (Wave-Songs) and Takemitsu (Orion and Pleiades); Principal Guest Artist with the East of England Orchestra; Concerts with the Villiers Piano Quartet; Recital debut at the Kennedy Center in Washington, 1992; Season 1993 with

US Concerto debut, Boston Philharmonic, and visits to the Edinburgh and Harrogate Festivals; Recital of unaccompanied works at the Wigmore Hall, London, 1997; Professor at the Royal Academy of Music. Recordings include: Tippett Triple Concerto with Ernst Kovacic and Gerard Causse; Concertos by Elgar, Matthews and Bernard Stevens; Frank Bridge's Oration, the Britten Cello Suites and Sonata; Sonatas by Rachmaninov, Shostakovich, Prokofiev and Schnittke. Honours: Prize winner in competitions at Budapest (Casals) and Munich (ARD). Address: c/o TBM, 3 Brunswick Place, Julian Road, Bath BA1 2RQ, England.

BAILLIE Peter, b. 1938, New Zealand. Singer (Tenor). Education: Studied in Australia and New Zealand. Career: Sang with New Zealand Opera and the Elizabethan Opera Trust at Sydney, from 1963; Roles included Tamino, Ferrando, Jacquino (Fidelio) and Gounod's Faust; Member of the Vienna Volksoper, 1967-88, in such character roles as Mozart's Bartolo and Monostatos, Albert Herring and Nando in Tiefland; Also appeared in The Bartered Bride, From the House of the Dead and Zemlinsky's Kleider machen Leute; Glyndebourne debut, 1968, as Hervey in Anna Bolena, Wexford, 1968 (Mozart's Titus) and Salzburg, 1971 (first modern revival of Mozart's Mitridate); Other roles include Ernesto in Don Pasquale, Malcolm in Macbeth and Svatopluk Cech in The Excursions of Mr Broucek; Sang Mozart's Basilio for Wellington City Opera, 1995. Address: c/o Volksoper, Währingerstrasse 78, A-1090 Vienna, Austria.

BAINBRIDGE Elizabeth, b. 28 Mar 1936, Lancashire, England. Singer (Mezzo-Soprano). Education: Studied at Guildhall School with Norman Walker. Debut: Glyndebourne 1963 in Die Zauberflöte. Career: Sang in British premiere of Rossini's La Pietra del Paragone, London 1963; Member of Covent Garden Opera from 1965, in Butterfly (Suzuki), The Midsummer Marriage, Falstaff (Mistress Quickly), Les Troyens, Un Ballo in Maschera (Arvidson), Troilus and Cressida and Lulu, Erda, (Rheingold, Siegfried), Amelia, Otello, Jenufa (Grandmother), Onegin (Nurse), Aida (Amneris); Tours to La Scala Milan, 1976; Far East, 1979; Los Angeles; Athens Festival; Guest appearances with English National Opera, Scottish Opera, Welsh National Opera; US debut, Chicago, 1977 in Peter Grimes; Buenos Aires debut, 1979; Israel Jenufa, 1993, 1995; Covent Garden, First Maid in Elektra, Innkeeper's Wife in the Cunning Little Vixen, 1990; Peter Grimes, Dublin Grand Opera Society; Widow Sweeney in The Rising of the Moon, Wexford Festival; Sang the Hostess in the Covent Garden premiere of Prokofiev's The Fiery Angel, 1992. Recordings include: Dido and Aeneas, Sorceress; Sir John in Love, Mistress Ford; The Rape of Lucretia, Bianca; Peter Grimes, Auntie; Cendrillon, Dorothée, Filipyevna in Eugene Onegin for EMI. Address: Buckleys, Forestside, Rowlands Castle, Hants PO9 6ED, England.

BAINBRIDGE Simon (Jeremy), b. 30 Aug 1952, London, England. Composer; Conductor. m. Lynda Richardson, 17 July 1980, 1 daughter. Education: Central Tutorial School for Young Musicians (now Purcell School), 1965-66; Highgate School, 1966-69; Royal College of Music, 1969-72; Studied Composition with John Lambert at the Berkshire Music Center, Tanglewood, Massachusetts, USA, 1973-74, with Gunther Schuller. Career: Freelance Composer, 1972-; His music performed extensively in UK, USA, Europe, Australia; Has worked as Conductor with BBC Symphony Orchestra, BBC Scottish Symphony Orchestra, Bournemouth Symphony Orchestra, London Sinfonietta, Northern Sinfonia, Nash Ensemble, Composer's Ensemble, Capricorn and Divertimenti; Teaches composition at Royal College of Music and Guildhall School of Music and Drama. Compositions include: Wind Quintet; String Quartet; String Sextet; Clarinet Quintet; Works for small and large Chamber Ensembles, with and without voice; Choral Music; Works for large orchestra; Dance Score for Rambert Dance Company; Music for 2 Madame Tussaud Exhibitions, London and Amsterdam; Double Concerto for oboe, clarinet and chamber orchestra, 1990; Clarinet Quintet, 1993. Recordings: Music of Simon Bainbridge: Fantasia for Double Orchestra-BBC Symphony Orchestra/Composer, Viola Concerto-London Sinfonietta/Michael Tilson Thomas-Walter Trampler Viola, Concertante in moto perpetue-composer's ensemble/composer-Nicholas Daniel oboe. Honours: Margaret Lee Crofts Fellowship, USA, 1973; Leonard Bernstein Fellowship, USA, 1974; Forman Fellowship, 1976; USA-UK Bicentennial Fellowship, 1978; Published by United Music Publishers, Novello-Music Sales. Memberships: Executive Committees: Society for the Promotion of New Music; International Society for Contemporary Music; Association of Professional Composers. Hobbies: Cooking; Walking; Swimming; Travel; Movies; Reading. Address: 38 Constantine Road, London NW3 2NG, England.

BAIRD Julianne, b. 10 Dec 1952, Stateville, North Carolina, USA. Singer (Soprano). Education: Studied at Eastman School with Masako Ono Toribara and at Stanford University; Further study with Walter Berry and Harnoncourt, and at Salzburg Mozarteum. Career: Sang in New York with Waverly Consort and Concert Royal; Stage debut in Handel's Il Pastor Fido; Later appearances in Santa Fe, Washington DC, Philadelphia and Los

Angeles in operas by Gluck, Mozart, Purcell, Charpentier and Gagliano; Concert engagements in sacred music by Bach and French Baroque music; Sang in Dido and Aeneas with Academy of Ancient Music at the Barbican Hall, London, 1992; Teacher at Rutgers University. Recordings included: Handel's Imeneo, Acis and Galatea, Joshua and Siroe; Cantatas by Bach, Telemann and Clerambault; Bach's Magnificat and B Minor Mass; J C Bach's Amadis de Gaule; La Serva Padrona by Pergolesi and Monteverdi's Orfeo. Contributor to: Journals such as Continuo and Early Music. Address: c/o Washington Opera, John F Kennedy Center for the Performing Arts, Washington DC 20566, USA.

BAKELS Kees, b. 14 Jan 1945, Amsterdam, Netherlands. Conductor. Education: Studied at the Amsterdam Conservatory and at the Accademia Chigiana in Siena with Franco Ferrara and Bruno Rigacci; Further study with Kiril Kondrashin. Career: Associate Conductor of the Amsterdam Philharmonic and Principal Guest Conductor of the Netherlands Chamber Orchestra; Tours to England, Belgium, Spain and the USA; Has led all the major Dutch Orchestras and has guested with the Warsaw Philharmonic, BBC Philharmonic, BBC Welsh, San Diego, Quebec and Oregon Symphony Orchestras; New Belgian Chamber Orchestra; Ulster Orchestra; Scottish Chamber; Bournemouth Sinfonietta; Royal Liverpool Philharmonic; Appeared with the National Youth Orchestra at the 1985 Promenade Concerts; Currently Chief Guest Conductor with the Bournemouth Symphony and Principal Conductor of Netherlands Radio Symphony Orchestra, 1993-; Has worked with the soloists Yehudi Menuhin, Claudio Arrau, Pierre Fournier, Paul Tortelier, David Oistrakh and Ruggiero Ricci; Appearances with Netherlands Opera in Nabucco, Ariadne auf Naxos, Carmen, Lucia di Lammermoor, Idomeneo and I Puritani; San Diego Opera Oberto and Madama Butterfly; Vancouver Opera Carmen, Così fan tutte, Le nozze di Figaro and Die Zauberflöte; Conducted the Lyon Opera in Cinderella (also on tour to Poland); Welsh National Opera with Die Zauberflöte, La Bohème and Carmen; At English National Opera has led Aida and Fidelio; Conducted Carmen at San Diego, 1992; Season 1992/93 with engagements in Britain, the Netherlands and Denmark; US appearances with the Florida Symphony, Oregon Symphony and Calgary Philharmonic; Concert performance of Robert Deveraux with Netherlands Radio Symphony at the Concertgebouw; Four concerts with Tokyo Metropolitan Symphony Orchestra; Future engagements include concerts with l'Orchestre Philharmonique de Monte-Carlo, Saarbrucken Radio and teh BBC Symphony Orchestra. Recordings: Vaughan Williams Symphonies with the Bournemouth Symphony; Complete Nelson Concerti with the Bournemouth Symphony Orchestra. Address: Unit 2, 39 Tadema Road, London SW10 0PY, England.

BAKER Gregg, b. 7 Dec 1955, Chicago, Illinois, USA. Singer (Baritone). Education: Studied at Northwestern University and with Andrew Smith. Career: Sang on Broadway in such musicals as The Wiz, Timbuktu and Raisin; Metropolitan Opera debut, as Crown in Porgy and Bess, 1985, appearing later as Escamillo and the High Priest in Samson and Delilah; Has also sung Crown at Glyndebourne, 1985, and in Helsinki and Tulsa; Concert performance of Porgy and Bess at the Elizabeth Hall, London, 1989; Other roles include Ford in Falstaff, Count Almaviva and Marcello in La Bohème; Old Vic Theatre, London in Carmen Jones, 1991; Sang Crown in Porgy and Bess at Covent Garden, London and Savonlinna Festival, Finland, 1992; Italian debut as Escamillo, at the 1996 Verona Festival. Recordings include: Porgy and Bess. Address: c/o Harrison Parrott Limited, 12 Penzance Place, London W11 4PA, England.

BAKER Israel, b. 11 Feb 1921, Chicago, Illinois, USA. Violinist. Education: Studied with Adolf Pick, Chicago Conservatory, Louis Persinger at Juilliard School of Music in New York, Jacques Gordon and Bronislaw Huberman. Career: Soloist with various orchestras; Concertmaster; Many chamber music appearances including 2nd violinist, Heifetz-Piatigorsky Chamber Concerts; Often heard in Schoenberg's Concerto and Berg's Chamber Concerto; Member of Pacific Art Trio; Professor of Music at Scripps College, Claremont, CA. Recordings: Various as soloist and chamber music player, including works by Ives, Antheil, Kubik and Stravinksy. Address: c/o Scripps College, Claremont, California, USA.

BAKER Janet (Abbott) (Dame), b. 21 Aug 1933, Hatfield, Yorkshire, England. Singer (Mezzo-Soprano). m. James Keith Shelley, 1957. Education: The College for Girls, York; Vocal Studies with Helene Isepp and Meriel St Clair in London. Debut: Oxford University Opera Club, 1956, as Roza in The Secret by Smetana. Career: Sang in concert, and in opera as Gluck's Orpheus, London 1958, and Pippo in La Gazza Ladra at the 1959 Wexford Festival; Sang Eduige in Handel's Rodelinda, London 1959 and the title roles in Tamerlano, Ariodante, Orlando and Admeto, Birmingham, 1962-68; Rameau's Hippolyte et Aricie, 1965; Sang in Mahler's Resurrection Symphony at the 1961 Edinburgh Festival; English Opera Group from 1962, as Dido, Polly in The Beggar's Opera and Lucretia; Sang in the premieres of Britten's Owen Wingrave, 1971 and Phaedra, 1976; New York

concert debut, 1966; Scottish Opera debut 1967, as Dorabella, followed by Dido in The Trojans, Octavian, and the Composer in Ariadne auf Naxos; Glyndebourne Festival, 1965-72, as Dido, Diana-Jupiter in La Calisto and Penelope in Il Ritorno d'Ulisse; Covent Garden, 1966-74, as Hermia in A Midsummer Night's Dream, Dido, Kate in Owen Wingrave and Vitellia in La Clemenza di Tito; With English National Opera appeared as Poppea, 1971, Mary Stuart, 1973, Charlotte, 1976 and Julius Caesar; Concert repertory includes works by Mahler, Elgar, Britten, Brahms and Bach; Lieder by Schubert and French and English Songs; Retired from opera 1982, singing Gluck's Orpheus at Glyndebourne and Alceste at Covent Garden; Sang Orpheus in a concert performance at Carnegie Hall and retired 1989; Appointed Chancellor of University of York, 1991; Trustee, Foundation for Sport and the Arts, 1991. Recordings include: The Angel in The Dream of Gerontius; Dido and Aeneas; La Calisto; Mozart's Requiem; I Capuleti e i Montecchi; Maria Stuarda; The Rape of Lucretia and Owen Wingrave; Duets with Dietrich Fischer-Dieskau; Handel's Messiah, Judas Maccabeus and Ariodante; La Clemenza di Tito; Verdi Requiem; Orfeo ed Euridice; Labels include Erato, Deutsche Grammophon, EMI and Philips. Publications: Full Circle, Autobiography, 1982. Honours include: CBE, 1970; DBE, 1976; Shakespeare Prize, Hamburg, 1971; Honorary Fellow, St Anne's College, Oxford, 1975; Copenhagen Sonning Prize, 1979; Honorary DMus from Birmingham, Leicester, London, Hull, Oxford, Leeds, Lancaster and York Universities; Honorary MusD, Cambridge, 1984; Honorary Fellow, Downing College, Cambridge, 1985; Gold Medal, Royal Philharmonic Society, 1990. Membership: Fellow of the Royal Society of Arts, 1979. Hobbies: Reading; Walking. Address: c/o TRANSART (UK) Limited, 8 Bristol Gardens, London WC 2JG, England.

BAKER Julius, b. 23 Sept 1915, Cleveland, Ohio, USA. Flautist; Teacher. Education: Studied with William Kincaid at the Curtis Institute. Career: Member of the Cleveland Orchestra, 1937-41; Principal flautist of the Pittsburgh Symphony Orchestra, 1941-43, CBS Synmphony Orchestra, 1943-50, and the Chicago Symphony Orchestra, 1951-53; Performed with the Bach Aria Group, 1946-64; Member of Faculty, Juilliard School of Music from 1954; Gave the US premieres of the flute concertos by Ibert (1947) and Imbrie (1979); Principal flautist of New York Philharmonic Orchestra, 1964-83; Joined faculty of the Curtis Institute, Philadelphia, 1980; Graduate of Curtis Institute of Music; Faculty of Carnegie Mellon University since 1991. Recordings: For several labels. Publications include: Editions of flute solos from sacred music by Bach, 1972. Address: c/o Curtis Institute of Music, 1826 Locust Street, Rittenhouse Square, Philadelphia, PA 19103, USA.

BAKER Mark, b. 1949, Tulsa, Oklahoma, USA. Singer (Tenor). Education: Studied at the New England Conservatory, 1970. Career: Metropolitan Opera from 1986, as Paris in Roméo et Juliette (debut role), Narraboth in Salome, Froh in Das Rheingold and Melot in Tristan und Isolde; Glimmerglass Opera, 1987, as Lensky in Eugene Onegin, Santa Fé, 1988 (Erik in Fliegende Holländer), Glyndebourne Touring Opera, 1990, as Florestan; Sang Steva in Jenufa and Ferrando in Così fan tutte at 1989 Glyndebourne Festival; Nantes, 1991, as Monteverdi's Ulisse, Théâtre du Châtelet, Paris, 1992 and Met, 1997, as the Drum Major in Wozzeck. Recordings include: Jenufa, from Glyndebourne (Virgin Classics). Address: c/o Metropolitan Opera, Lincoln Plaza, New York, NY 10023, USA.

BAKER Michael (Conway), b. 13 Mar 1937, West Palm Beach, Florida, USA (became Canadian Citizen in 1970). Composer; Lecturer. m. Penny Anne Baker. Education: BMus, University of British Columbia, 1966; MA, Western Washington State College, 1972. Career: Active career as film and concert composer; Over period of almost 25 years has taught and developed music programmes for children of all ages, adult education and university students; Taught two courses at University of British Columbia as well as one extension course at Simon Fraser University; Was also Composer-in-Residence for Vancouver School Board, now retired. Compositions include: Counterplay for Viola and Strings, 1971; Concerto for Flute and Strings, 1974; Sonata for Piano, 1974; Concerto for Piano and Orchestra, 1976; Symphony No 1, Highland, 1977; Washington Square, 60 minute ballet for orchestra, 1978; Evocations for Flute, Quartet and Orchestra, 1982; Seven Wonders: A Song Cycle for Soprano and Piano, 1983; Chanson Joyeuse for Orchestra, 1987; Intermezzo for Fute and Harp, 1988; Through the Lions' Gate: Tone Poems for Orchestra, 1989; Capriccio for Clarinet and Orchestra, 1991; Cinderella - Frozen in Time, 90 minute ice ballet, 1993; Century Symphony (# 2), 1994; Summit Concorde for Trumpet and Orchestra, 1995; Vancouver Variations, 1996; Music for films, such as The Grey Fox, One Magic Christmas and John and the Missus; His Fanfare to Expo 86 opened the proceedings of Expo 86 in Vancouver; Recordings: Washington Square; Hope's Journey; Greater Vancouver music album - Music from Treetop Lane; 120 concert works and film projects. Publications: Subject of article in Classical Music Magazine, 1997. Honours: Juno, Best Classical Composition, 1991; Order of British

Columbia, 1997. Membership: ALCM. Address: 2440 Treetop Lane, North Vancouver, British Columbia, Canada V7H 2K5.

BAKER Reginald, b. Carshalton, England. Concert Pianist. Education: Trinity College of Music, London; Goldsmiths College, London University; Private Studies with Frank Merrick. Debut: Recital, Wigmore Hall, 1971; Concerto, MSO London, 1966; Chamber Music, Fairfield Hall. Career: Britain and Abroad. Memberships: Associate, Incorporated Society of Musicians. Hobbies: All the Arts; Philosophy; Christianity. Address: 30 White Lodge Close, Christchurch Park, Sutton SM2 5TQ, England.

BAKER Richard (Douglas James), b. 15 June 1925, Willesden, London, England. Radio and Television Broadcaster; Author. m. Margaret Celia Baker, 2 sons. Education: MA, Peterhouse, Cambridge. Debut: Actor, 1948, As BBC Announcer, 1950. Career: Actor, 1948-49; Teacher, 1949-50; BBC Television Newsreader, 1954-82; Panellist on BBC Television's Face the Music, 1964-79; Presenter of television concerts, 1960-; Presenter of numerous radio programmes including: These You Have Loved, Radio 4, 1972-77; Baker's Dozen, Radio 4, 1977-78; Melodies For You, Radio 2, 1988-; Richard Baker Compares Notes, Radio 4, 1989-; Music for A While, World Service, 1990-91; In Tune, Radio 3, 1992; Classic FM from 1995; Sound Stories, Radio 3, from 1998; Numerous concert appearances as narrator and compere. Recordings: As Narrator of Peter and the Wolf; Young Person's Guide to the Orchestra; Façade, with Susana Walton. Publications: The Magic of Music, 1975; Richard Baker's Music Guide, 1979; Mozart, 1982, new illustrated edition, 1991; Richard Baker: Companion to Music, 1993. Memberships; Garrick; Governor, National Youth Orchestra; Director, Youth and Music; Trustee, D'Oyly Carte Opera. Honours: Officer of the Order of the British Empire, 1976; Reserve Decoration, 1979; Honorary FLCM; Honorary RCM. Hobbies: Gardening; Sailing. Current Management: Stephannie Williams Artists. Address: 12 Central Chambers, Wood Street, Stratford Upon Avon, CV37 6QJ, England.

BAKHCHIEV Alexander, b. 27 July 1930, Moscow, USSR. Pianist. m. Elena Sorokina, 28 Nov 1962, 1 daughter. Education: MA, Performance, 1953, completed postgraduate courses, 1956, Moscow Conservatory. Debut: Solo programme, Liszt, Beethoven Hall, Bolshoi Theatre, Moscow, 1954. Career: State, TV, radio, over 35 years; Solo, with orchestra, in chamber music ensembles, with singers; Regular duo with wife; Played with orchestras conducted by Rozhdestvensky. Svetlanov, Kondrashin, Chaikin, with V Popov (bassoon), A Korneyev (flute), others; Performed, France, 1954; TV chamber music concerts, 1970s; Many educational TV and radio series; Concerts all over USSR, including Moscow State Conservatory and with Leningrad Philharmonic; Duets, Soviet and British modern music, England, 1989; International festivals including Mozart Festival, Tokyo, 1991; Teaching Chamber Ensemble, Moscow State Conservatory, 1990-; 8 programmes, all Schubert piano duets (with wife); Piano duo festivals, Novosibirsk, Ekaterinburg, 1993-95; Piano Duet lecture series for teachers and students, Russia; Music dedicated to him and wife by Boyarsky, Lubovksy, Fried, Moore; Gubaidulina's concerto Introitus written for him. Recordings: About 70; Solo discs include Haydn, Liszt, Bach, Handel, Rubinstein, Arensky, Liadov, Lyapunov, Mussorgsky, Borodin; Ensembles: All sonatas, flute, harpsichord, Bach, Handel; Vivaldi (with A Korneyev); With Valery Popov: Masterpieces of Baroque; Czechoslovakian music, bassoon, piano; Series: Early Mozart, solo, ensembles; Duets with wife: Schubert, all Mozart, Rachmaninov, Russian Salon Piano Music; Music of France; Albums: Music of Old Vienna; J S Bach, his family and pupils; Music for 6 and 8 hands (with wife, Rozhdestvensky, Postnikova); Music and paintings, with wife, orchestra conducted by Rozhdestvensky. Honours: Honoured Artist of Russia, 1982; Kodama Prize, International Piano Duo Association, 1994. Memberships: Mozart and Schubert Societies, Moscow. Current Management: Vadim Dubrovitsky Producer Firm, Ramenki Gallery, Ramenki Str 6-2, 117607 Moscow, Russia. Address: 4-32 Koshkin str, Moscow 115409, Russia.

BAKKE Ruth, b. 2 Aug 1947, Bergen, Norway. Composer; Organist. Education: Studied at the Bergen Conservatory and Oslo University and in the USA. Career: Organist at the Storetveit Church, Bergen, from 1973. Compositions: Organ sonata, 1970; Colour Clouds for orchestra, 1972; Rumus for chamber orchestra, 1976; Bonn for organ, soprano and guitar, 1976; Trollsuite for string quartet, 1981; Into the Light for violin and organ, 1982; Meditation for horn and organ, 1986; Noncense for solo voice, 1990; Sphaerae for organ, 1992; Suite ACD for Renaissance instruments, 1992; Psalm 2000 for organ and tuba, 1993. Address: c/o TONO, 4 Galleri Oslo, Toyenbekken 21, Postboks 9171, Gronland, 0134 Oslo 1, Norway.

BAKST Lawrence, b. 1955, Washington, District of Columbia, USA. Singer (Tenor). Education: Studied in America and Europe. Career: Sang Radames with Opera Delaware and Kentucky Operas; Verdi's Don Carlos at several Italian centres; Macduff in New Jersey, Barcelona and Marseilles; Gabriele Adorno, Riccardo, Manrico, Canio, Calaf and Faust in Mefistofeles; Appearances at the New York City Opera, Zagreb, Wexford, Detmold, Wuppertal and the Opera Forum in Holland; Season 1990-91 as Faust, Cavaradossi and Edgar (Lucia di Lammermoor) in Wuppertal; Bob Boles in Peter Grimes at Marseilles and Pylade in Iphigénie en Tauride at the Opéra de Bastille, Paris; Sang Pylade with the Tanztheater of Wuppertal at Rome, 1992. Honours: Winner, Metropolitan Opera National Council Auditions Competition; Premier Grand Prix and Best Tenor Award in the Vinas Competition, Barcelona; Concours International de Chant, Toulouse; 1st Prize, G B Viotti Competition, Vercelli. Address: c/o Music International, 13 Ardilaun Road, London N5 2QR, England.

BALADA Leonardo, b. 22 Sept 1933, Barcelona, Spain. Composer; Professor. m. (1) 1 son, (2) Joan Winer, 28 July 1979. Education: Studied Piano at Barcelona Conservatory; New York College of Music, 1956-57; Juilliard School of Music, 1958-60; Mannes College of Music, 1961-62; Principal teachers: Copland, Tansman, Persichetti for composition and Markevitch for conducting. Career: Teacher, United Nations International School, 1963-70; Faculty, 1970-75, Professor, 1975-90, University Professor, 1990-, Carnegie-Mellon University. Compositions include: Opera: Christopher Columbus, 1987, premiered in 1989, Barcelona Opera, with Jose Carreras and Monserrat Caballé singing leading roles; Orchestral: Piano Concerto, 1964, Guitar Concerto, 1965, Guernica, 1966, Bandoneon Concerto, 1970, Steel Symphony, 1972, Ponce de Leon for Narrator and Orchestra, 1973, Homage to Casals, 1975, Sardana, 1979, Quasi un Pasodoble, premiered with New York Philharmonia and Sarasate, 1981, Alegrias for Flute and String Orchestra, 1988, Symphony No 4, The Lausanne Chamber Orchestra, 1992, Music for Oboe and Orchestra, Lorin Maazel and the Pittsburgh Symphony Orchestra, 1993, Shadows, Cincinnati Symphony Orchestra, 1995, Morning Music, premiered by Julius Baker flute, and Carnegie Mellon Philharmonic, 1995; Concierto Magico, for guitar and orchestra, 1997; No-Res, revised, 1997; Cantata, with Barcelona Symphony Orchestra and National Chorus of Spain, 1997; Many solo pieces and choral works. Recordings include: Steel Symphony with Pittsburgh Symphony Orchestra under Lorin Maazel; Torquemada, cantata; Concerto for Piano, Winds and Percussion; Music for Oboe and Orchestra; Maria Sabina, Cantata with Louisville Orchestra. Honour: Winner of National Composition Prize of Catalonia, Barcelona, 1993. Hobbies: Theatre; Travel. Address: c/o Music Department, Carnegie Mellon University, Pittsburgh, PA 15213, USA.

BALASSA Sándor, b. 20 Jan 1935, Budapest, Hungary. Composer; Teacher of Orchestration. m. (1) Irene Balogh, 18 Aug 1957, 1 son, 1 daughter, (2) Marianne Orosz, 1994. Education: Studied Choral Leadership, Bela Bartok Conservatory, Budapest; Composer Diploma, Liszt Academy, Budapest. Debut: 1965. Career: Radio broadcasts including Legend (21 stations), 1971; Requiem for Lajor Kassak (30 stations), 1972-73; Xenia (BBC), 1974; Works performed abroad; Commissions, including from Koussevitzky Music Foundation; Teacher of Orchestra, Academy of Music, Budapest; Retired in 1996. Compositions include: The Chant of Glarus, full orchestra; Man Outside, opera in 5 movements; Motet, mixed choir; The Last Shepherd, cello; Quintet for brass; Kyrie, female choir; Karl and Anna, opera in 3 acts, 1988-92; Damjanich's Prayer, mixed choir, 1992; Tündér Ilona, orchestra, 1992; Prince Csaba, string orchestra, 1993; Bölcskei Concerto, string orchestra, 1993; Szonatina, harp, 1993; Divertimento, 2 cimbalons, 1993; John's Day Music, violin solo, 1993; Little Garland, trio for flute, viola, harp, 1993; Dances of Mucsa, orchestra, 1994; String Quartet, 1995; A nap fiai, for orchestra, 1995; Nyirbatori harangok, for brass, 1996; Preludiums and Fantasia, for organ, 1997; Four Portraits, for orchestra, 1996; 301-s parcella, for orchestra, 1997. Commissions: Calls and Cries (Boston Symphonic Orchestra Centennial); The Day Dreamer's Diary, orchestra (Elizabeth Sprague Coolidge Foundation, Washington); Three Fantasies (BBC Philharmonic Orchestra); The Third Planet, opera-cantata, text by composer (Hungarian Radio). Recordings: Antinomia, trio for soprano, clarinet, cello; Xenia, nonet; Requiem for Lajos Kassak; Iris, orchestra; Cantata Y; Lupercalia, orchestra; Tabulae, chamber orchestra; The Island of Everlasting Youth, orchestra. Publication: Hajta viragai, subject of book by Ede Terenyi, in Hungarian. Membership: Vice-President, Hungarian Art Academy; Hobbies: Nature; Mountains. Address: Sumegvar u.18, 1118 Budapest, Hungary.

BALAZS-CZICZER Adrienne, b. 18 April 1951, Lucenec, Slovakia. Pianist; Accompanist; Soloist; Professor. m. Andras Cziczer, 25 July 1980, 1 daughter. Education: School of Music, 1956-65; Piano, Conservatory of Music, 1965-71; Academy of Music, Korsakov, 1971-76; International Master Course of george Cziffra, Keszthely, Hungary, 1986. Debut: Frist Independent Recital, age 14 years, Lucenec, Slovakia. Career: Piano Concert Festival, Prague, 1956; Radio Appearance, Bratislava, 1963; First Orchestral Evening, Beethoven Piano Concerto in G Major, Bratislava, 1970; Television Appearance, Report and Interview, Bratislava, 1971; Recital, Bratislava, 1971, Leningrad, Russia, 1976; Radio Appearance, Riga, 1974; Trio Debut Recital, Trento, 1990. Publication: Keszthely, 1986. Contributions to: Journals and magazines. Honours: Winner, National Music Competitions, 1956-65; 1st Prize, Who What Knows? Talent Scouting Competition, 1963. Memberships: Slovak Pianists; Association of the Hungarian Music Artists. Hobbies: Gardening; Needlework; Painting; Family. Address: Conservatory of Bartok Bela, Bartok Bela Ter 1, 3501 Miskolc, Hungary.

BALATSCH Norbert, b. 10 Mar 1928, Vienna, Austria. Chorus Master. Education: Studied at the Vienna Music Academy; Private studies in cello and piano. Career: Sang with the Vienna Boys' Choir as a child, then directed after graduation; Directed the Vienna Mens' Chorus, then from 1952 the chorus of the Vienna Staatsoper (Chorus Master 1978-84); Director of the Bayreuth Festival Chorus from 1972 together with the Philharmonic Chorus, London (1974-79); Chorus of Accademia di Santa Cecilia, Rome from 1984; Has directed sacred works by Mozart, Haydn and others at the chapel of the Viennese Court; Led the chorus in Der fliegende Holländer at Bayreuth, 1990. Address: Festspielhaus, D-8580 Bayreuth, Germany.

BALDWIN Dalton, b. 19 Dec 1931, Summit, New Jersey, USA. Pianist. Education: Juilliard School of Music, New York; BM, Oberlin College Conservatory of Music; Studies with Nadia Boulanger, Madeleine Lipatti, Paris; Special coaching from Sibelius, Barber, Poulenc, et al. Career: Toured extensively as Accompanist including: Gerard Souzay, Elly Ameling, Marilyn Horne and Jessye Norman; Took part with Souzay in the premiere of Rorem's War Scenes, 1969. Recordings: Numerous recordings including the complete songs of Fauré, Debussy, Ravel and Poulenc. Address: c/o Columbia Artists Management, 165 West 57th Street, NY 10019, USA.

BALKIND Jonathan (Paul Brenner), b. 6 July 1946, Los Angeles, California, USA. Impresario. Education: Cambridge University; Architectural Association, London. Career: Historic Buildings Inspector by GLC/English Heritage with special responsibility for Spitalfields, 1974-88; Board Member, Advisor, Endymion Ensemble, 1980-; General and Artistic Director, Opera London, 1988-; Director, Songbird Films (Music and Arts); Artistic Advisor, City of London Sinfonia, 1988-91; Chairman, Collegium Music '90; Project Director, Bosnia, for AIM/UNHCR (construction of refugee shelters in northern Bosnia), 1993; Founder, Spitalfields Festival and Director, 1976-82; Festivals of Handel, 1977, Early Music, 1978, English Music, 1979, Young Mozart, 1980; Produced Mozart Lucio Silla, last performances by Janet Baker of Dido and Aeneas and many other concerts and first performances; Produced operas for stage in Spitalfields and other festivals, Barbican, South Bank and Sadler's Wells, including Gluck's Armide, 1982, broadcast BBC, Handel's Alcina, restaged in Los Angeles, Monteverdi's L'Incoronazione di Poppea, and Britten's A Midsummer Night's Dream (all 4 recorded); Produced extensive music theatre with Endymion Ensemble, including Birtwistle's Punch and Judy with Opera Factory; Directed operas by Gluck, Mozart and Mussorgsky; Music Advisor: BBC TV films Janet Baker - Full Circle, 1982, Jessye Norman - Singer, 1986, and dance documentaries for Channel 4; Beethoven in Love for BBC. Contributions to: Frequently to various publications; Notes for concerts by Endymion Ensemble and City of London Sinfonia; Editor, festival and opera programmes. Honours: Nominee, ABSA/Daily Telegraph Orb Award, 1991. Hobbies: Cooking for friends; Restoring houses; Reading; Travel. Address: 45 Chalcot Road, London NW1 8LS, England.

BALKWILL Bryan (Havell), b. 2 July 1922, London, England. Conductor. m. Susan Elizabeth Roberts, 23 July 1949, 1 son, 1 daughter. Education: FRAM, Royal Academy of Music. Debut: New London Opera Company, 1947. Career: Conductor, New London Opera, 1947-49; Glyndebourne, Wexford Festivals, 1950-64; Sadler's Wells, English National Opera, Royal Opera House, Covent Garden, 1957-78; Toured USSR and Portugal with the English Opera Group, conducting Albert Herring and A Midsummer Night's Dream; Gave premiere of Bennett's A Penny for a Song at Sadler's Wells, London, 1967; Musical Director, Welsh National Opera, 1963-67; Freelance, opera and concerts in the United Kingdom, Europe, USA and Canada; Professor of Conducting, Indiana University, USA, 1977-92. Recordings: Madam Butterfly Highlights, Sadlers Wells Opera; Recital with Geraint Evans and Suisse Romande Orchestra. Honours: Fellow, Royal Academy of Music; Life Member, Royal Philharmonic Society. Address: 8 The Green, Wimbledon Common, London SW19 5AZ, England.

BALLARD Louis, b. 8 July 1931, Miami, Oklahoma, USA. Composer. Education: Studied at Oklahoma and Tulsa Universities; MM, 1962; Further study with Milhaud, Castelnuovo-Tedesco and Carlos Surinach. Career: Programme Director, Bureau of Indian Affairs, Washington, District of Columbia, 1979-79. Compositions include: Koshare, ballet on Indian themes, 1966; The God will Hear, cantata, 1966; The Four Moons, ballet, 1967; Ritmo Indio for wind instruments, 1968; Katcin Dances for cello and piano, 1970; Desert Trilog for winds, strings and percussion, 1971; Cacega Ayuwipi for percussion ensemble, 1973; Devil's Promenade for orchestra, 1973; Incident at Wounded Knee for orchestra, 1974; Thus Spake Abraham, cantata, 1976; City of Fire for piano; Companion of Talking God for orchestra, 1982; Fantasy Aborigine III for orchestra, 1984. Publications include: My Music Reaches to the Sky, 1973; Music of North American Indians, 1974. Address: c/o ASCAP, ASCAP Building, One Lincoln Plaza, New York, NY 10023, USA.

BALLEYS Brigitte, b. 18 June 1959, Martigny, Walis, Switzerland. Singer (Mezzo-soprano). Education: Studied at the Bern Conservatory, 1978-82 with Jakob Stämpfli; Further study with Elisabeth Schwarzkopf. Career: Sang in concert from 1976, notably in sacred music by Bach, the Brahms Alto Rhapsody, Masses by Mozart, Haydn, Schubert, Bruckner, Dvorak and Rossini; Schumann's Paradies und die Peri and Mahler Lieder; Appearances in Switzerland, West Germany, Austria, Italy, France, Portugal, Spain, South America, USA, Czechoslovakia; Festival engagements at Zurich, Lucerne, Florence and Siena; Recitalist in songs by de Falla, Shostakovich, Schoeck and Wolf-Ferrari, as well as French chansons and German songs; Sang in opera at Freiburg, 1985, with guest appearances at Zurich, Geneva, Avignon, Schwetzingen, Lausanne, and Montepellier; Vienna Staatsoper 1987, as Cherubino conducted Leinsdorf; Sang Octavian in Bern, Montepellier, Toulouse, 1990; Season 1992 as Fragoletto in Offenbach's Les Brigands at Amsterdam and Ramiro in Jean-Claude Malgoire's Vivaldi pasticcio Montezuma at Monte Carlo; Sang Nerone in Monteverdi's Poppea at Amsterdam, 1996; Other roles include Jocasta in Oedipus Rex (at Palermo), Gluck's Orpheus, Ottavia in Coronation of Poppea, Charlotte in Werther of Massenet, Meg Page and Orlofsky. Recordings include: La Demoiselle Elue by Debussy and Janacek's Diary of One who Disappeared (Deutsche Grammophon); Mendelssohn's St Paul and Die Zauberflöte, as Second Lady (Erato); Zelenka's Requiem (Claves). Honours: First Prize, Benson and Hedges in London, 1983 and Special Prize for Lied. Address: c/o Stadttheater Bern, Mageligasse 1, CH-3011 Bern, Switzerland.

BALLIF Claude (Andre Francois), b. 22 May 1924, Paris, France. Composer; Teacher; Writer on music. Education: Bordeaux Conservatory; Courses in Composition with Aubin, Galon and Messiaen, Paris Conservatory and Blacher and Rufer, Berlin Hochschule für Musik. Career: Worked with the Groupe de Recherches Musicales of the French Radio and Television, Paris, 1959-63; Professor, Rheims Conservatory, 1964-71; Professor of Analysis, 1971-, Associate Professor of Composition, 1982-, Paris Conservatory; Professor of Analysis and Composition, Sevran Conservatory, October 1990. Compositions include: Orchestral: Lovecraft, 1955; Voyage de mon oreille, 1957; Fantasio, 1957, revised 1962; Ceci et cela, 1959-65; A cor et a cri, 1962; Ivre moi immobile for clarinet and orchestra, 1976; Chamber pieces for various instruments entitled Imaginaire; 4 Quintets, 1952-60; 5 String Quartets, 1955, 1958, 1959, 1987, 1989; Violin Sonata, 1957; Quintet for Flute, Oboe and String Trio, 1958; Double Trio for Flute, Oboe and Cello and Violin, Clarinet and Horn, 1961; Poemes de la felicité for 3 Women's Voices, Guitar and 2 percussion, 1977; Clarinet Sonata, 1978; 4 organ sonatas, 1956; 15 pieces for various solo instruments entitled Solfeggietto, 1961-82; Le Livre du Seugneur, for three choruses, baritone and orchestra; Il suffit d'un Peu d'air, opera, 1992; La Transfiguration de l'Univers, 1993; 6 piano sonatas, 1994. Recordings: Numerous. Publications: Introduction a la metatonalite, 1956; Berlioz, 1968; Voyage de mon oreille, 1979; Economie musicale Souhaits entre symboles, 1979. Address: Conservatoire de Sevran, 28 Ave du General Leclerc, Parc Louis Armand, 93270 Sevran, France.

BALLISTA Antonio, b. 30 Mar 1936, Milan, Italy. Pianist. Education: Studied piano and composition Milan Conservatory, graduated 1955. Career: Toured widely as a soloist, also many duo recitals with the pianist Bruno Canino; Took part in the premieres of Rapsodia (1984), by Davidee Anzaghi, Concerto for two pieces by Berio (1973), Tableaux Vivants (1964), by Berio, Foglio d'album (1969), by Bussotti, Couplets (1979), by Castiglioni, B.A.C.H. (1970) and Piano Concerto (1976), by Aldo Clementi, Estratto (1969), by Donatoni and De La Nuit 1971, by Sciarrino; Professor at Giuseppe Verdi Conservatory from 1964. Recordings: Several recordings of contemporary works. Address: Consercatoiro Giuseppe Verdi, Via Conservatorio 12, 20122 Milan, Italy.

BALLO Pietro, b. 2 Oct 1952, Palermo, Italy. Singer (Tenor). Education: Studied at the school of La Scala, Milan, and with Gina Cigna. Debut: Pavia, 1977, as Ernesto in Don Pasquale. Career: Sang in opera at Venice from 1981, Genoa, 1982, Florence, 1983, and Turin, 1984; La Scala, 1984-86, as Ernesto, and Elvino in La Sonnambula; Glyndebourne Touring Opera, 1980 (Rodolfo), Festival, 1982 (Italian Singer in Der Rosenkavalier); Sang in Capriccio at Salzburg (1985) and guested at Hamburg (1984-88), Deutsche Oper Berlin (1988-89) and the 1987 Edinburgh Festival (Duke of Mantua); Other roles include Leicester in Donizetti's Maria Stuarda (Bergamo, 1989), Nemorino, Fenton, and Edgardo; US appearances at Dallas (1986) and elsewhere. Address: c/o Deutsche Oper Berlin, Bismarckstrasse 35, W-1000 Berlin, Germany.

BALOGH Endre, b. 1954, Los Angeles, California, USA. Violinist. Education: Attended Yehudi Menuhin's School, England, at age 9; Violin studies with Joseph Piastro, Manuel Compinsky and Mehli Mehta. Debut: New York Town Hall, 1971. Career: Played 1st concerto with orchestra at age 6; Recital, Los Angeles, at age 15; 1st European tour including concerts in Berlin and London, 1973; Performed in Austria, Netherlands and Italy; Recital for BBC, London, and on-the-air, Amsterdam; Appearances with various orchestras including Los Angeles Philharmonic and Washington, Seattle, Honolulu and other Symphony Orchestras; Numerous recitals in key US cities; Performed with Berlin Philharmonic, Rotterdam Philharmonic, Frankfurt Symphony, Tonhalle Orchestra of Zurich, Basel Symphony; As soloist with orchestra under conductors Zubin Mehta, Lawrence Foster, Henry Lewis, Vladimir Golschmann, Milton Katims, Hirouko Iwaki, Edo de Waart; Numerous appearances with American Youth Symphony, under Mehli Mehta; Played many benefits for State of Israel, United Nations, Philosophical Research Society and others; Violinist, Pacific Trio, throughout USA and Canada. Recordings: CD, Pacific Trio, 1990; Brahms C major and Shostakovich E major trios. Hobbies: Psychology; Comparative religion; Philosophy; Semantics; Designing and executing stained glass windows; Collecting Oriental carpets; Travel; Meeting new people. Address: 318 Detroit Street, Los Angeles, CA 90036, USA.

BALSACH PEIG Llorenç, b. 16 Apr 1953, Sabadell, Barcelona, Spain. Composer; Music Theorist. m. Sedes Garcia-Cascon, 12 Apr 1991. Education: Mathematics, University of Barcelona, 1975-80; Music Theory, Harmony, Sabadell and Barcelona Conservatories of Music, 1973-81; Composition with composer Josep Soler, 1978-80. Career: Freelance Composer, 1976-; Commissions, Baden-Baden Südwestfunk Orchestra, 1979, Associació Catalana de Compositors, 1983, 1991, CDMC, Barcelona City Council, 1991, VallèsSymphony Orchestra, 1991, Spanish Ministry of Culture, 1992, Radio Nacional de España, 1993, 1994, film Entreacte, 1985, and stage works; Creator, pioneer music software in GADIN Company, 1983-87; Editor, LA MA DE GUIDO Music Publishing House editions, 1986-; Consultant, Phonos, Pompeu Fabra University, 1994-. Compositions include: Orchestral: Gran Copa especial, 1979; Poema Promiscu, 1981; Visions grotesques, 1992; Quatre dibuixos per a guitarra i cordes, 1994; Chamber: De Caldetes a Moià, 1978; Suite Gàstrica, 1979; Rondó, 1983; Musica-Màgica, 1992; Trio per a cordes, 1992; Vocal: Música groga, 1980; Sis cançons breus, 1982; Olis d'olimpia, 1991; Tres converses per a 10 instruments, 1997. Recordings: Gran Copa Especial; Variaciones per a 20 dits; De Caldetes a Moià; Suite Gàstrica; Dos contes; L'arlequí; La negra, lliscosa; Peça gomosa; Lleu; Trio per a cordes; Sis cançons breus; Música Vironera; Visions grotesques; Rondo; Musica-Magica. Publications: La Convergència Harmònica, book, 1994; Sheet music of most compositions; Numerous historical unpublished music works (editor); Article: Application of virtual pitch theory in music analysis, Journal of New Music Research, 1997. Honours: Chosen by international jury as a young composer to represent Spain with a work in the 1985 European Music Year; Simolog Prize, Madrid, 1986. Memberships: Catalan Composers' Society; Spanish Musicology Society; Society for Music Theory; Acoustic Creation Area; Catalan Cinema Institute. Hobby: Science. Address: Les Planes 37, E-08201 Sabadell, Barcelona, Spain.

BALSLEV Lisbeth, b. 21 Feb 1945, Abenraa, Germany. Singer (soprano). Education: Vestjysk Conservatory in Esbjerg, Denmark; Royal Opera School, Copenhagen. Debut: Copenhagen, 1976, as Jaroslavna in Prince Igor. Career: Sang Mozart's Fiordiligi, Leonore in Il Trovatore and Wagner's Senta in Copenhagen; Bern Opera, 1977, as Electra in Idomeneo; Bayreuth from 1978, as Senta in Der fliegende Holländer; Hamburg Opera debut, 1979, as Elsa in Lohengrin; Munich Staatsoper, 1979, in the title role of Iphigénie en Tauride by Gluck; Guest appearances in Dresden, Amsterdam, Berlin, Stuttgart, Cologne and Frankfurt; La Scala, Milan, 1987, as Salome; Lisbon and Berne, 1987, Senta and Elisabeth; Turin and Florence, 1988, as Wagner's Isolde; Leonore in Fidelio with Cologne Opera, Hong Kong, 1989; Isolde in a concert performance of Tristan und Isolde with Jutland Opera, Edinburgh Festival, 1990. Recordings include: Senta in Der fliegende Holländer from Bayreuth. Address: Ingpen and Williams Ltd, 26 Wadham Road, London SW15 2LR, England.

BALTHROP Carmen (Arlen), b. 14 May 1948, Washington DC, USA. Soprano. Education: Studied at the University of Maryland, College Park and the Catholic University of America. Debut: Washington DC in 1973 as Virtue in L'Incoronazione di Poppea, and as Minerva in the US premiere of Il Ritorno di Ulisse, 1974. Career: Sang the title role in Scott Joplin's Treemonisha at Houston Opera in 1975; In 1977 sang in Cavalli's L'Egisto at Wolf Trap and made her Metropolitan debut as Pamina; Sang at New York City Opera in 1978 as Roggiero in Rossini's Tancredi; Innsbruck Early Music Festival in 1980 as Monteverdi's Poppea, in the edition by Alan Curtis; Sang Poppea at Spoleto in 1979 and Santa Fe in 1986; Sang in Venice as Gluck's Euridice and Poppea in Handel's Agrippina, 1982-83; Michigan Opera Theater as Treemonisha and Pamina, 1982-84; Sang Gretel at Milwaukee, 1995. Recordings include: Treemonisha. Honours include: Winner, Metropolitan Opera Auditions, 1975. Address: c/o Santa Fe Opera, PO Box 2408, Santa Fe, NM 878504, USA.

BALTSA Agnes, b. 19 Nov 1944, Lefkas, Greece. Singer (mezzo-soprano). m. Gunter Missenhardt, 1974. Education: Study in Athens with Nunuka Fragia-Spilopoulos; Frankfurt with Herbert Champian. Debut: Frankfurt Opera, 1968, as Cherubino in Figaro. Career: Octavian in Der Rosenkavalier at the Vienna Staatsoper, 1969; Guest appearances in Hamburg, Athens, Berlin, Munich, Barcelona and Belgrade; US debut, 1971, with Houston Opera, as Carmen; Concert tour of USA, 1976, with Karajan; Salzburg Festival from 1970, in Bastien et Bastienne and as Herodias in Salome, Eboli in Don Carlos and as Octavian; Covent Garden debut, 1976; Returned to London as Giulietta in Les Contes d'Hoffmann, Adalgisa in Norma, as Romeo in I Capuleti e i Montecchi, 1984, as Isabella in L'Italiana in Algeri, 1987, and as Eboli in Don Carlos, 1989; Metropolitan Opera debut, 1979, as Octavian; Returned to New York, 1987, as Carmen; Sang Santuzza, Vienna Staatsoper, 1989; Cenerentola and Dalila, Covent Garden, 1990-91; Season 1992-93 as Elisabeth in Maria Stuarda at Barcelona and Azucena at the Vienna Staatsoper; Sang Dalila at Zurich, 1996; Other roles include Berlioz's Dido, Gluck's Orfeo and Mozart's Dorabella. Recordings: Roles in Salome, Don Carlos, Aida, Orfeo ed Euridice, Così fan tutte, Les Contes d'Hoffmann, I Capuleti e i Montecchi, Mitridate, Die Zauberflöte, Rosenkavalier, Don Giovanni, Ascanio in Alba, Le nozze di Figaro. Address: c/o Staatsoper, Opernring, Vienna, Austria.

BALUN Frantisek, b. 13 Sept 1948, Chrinianska Navá Ves. Soloist of the opera ensemble (Baritone). m. Velánia Halúnová, 3 sons, 1 daughter. Education: The State Conservatory in Brno, Czech Republic (with Professor Richard Novák). Debut: Theater of the Jená Záborsky Persov, 1968. Career: Slovak National Theatre, 1972-77; The State Theatre, Kosice, 1977-; Tchaikovsky's Iolanta; Ravel, The Spanish Hour; Sang Nabucco in Paris, 1994; Sang in Germany: Tetere, Bettelstudent, 1996, Carmen, 1997; Sang in Austria: Nabucco, and Carmen, 1997; In Czech Republic: Il Trovatore, Madam Butterfly; Opera and operetta arias; Folk songs for Slovak Radio. Honours: Prize of the Musical Fund for Tosca (Scarpia), Il Trovatore (Luna); Annual Prize of the Musical Fund and the Ministry of Culture for the performance of Mr Scrooge. Memberships: Ján Cikker. Current Management: Opera Director, East Slovak State Theatre, Kosice. Address: Dvorkinova 6, 040 22 Kosice, Slovak Republic.

BALZANI Vincenzo, b. 1965, Milan, Italy. Concert Pianist. Education: Studied at the Giuseppe Verdi Conservatory in Milan with Alberto Mozzati. Debut: Has performed in public from age 14. Career: Italian engagements at La Fenice Venice, the Comunale of Bologna, the Verdi Theatre in Trieste and the Academia Filarmonica Romana; Further appearances in France, Germany and Spain; London recital debut at the Purcell Room in 1989 playing Scarlatti Sonatas, Brahms Paganini Variations, Gaspard de la Nuit, Chopin Etudes Op 10 and Liszt Rigoletto Paraphrase. Recordings include: Music by Liszt, Mozart and Hummel; Chopin Etudes Op 10. Honours include: Liszt Prize at the Maria Canals Competition in Barcelona.

BAMBERGER David, b. 14 Oct 1940, Albany, New York, USA. Opera Director and Producer. m. Carola Beral, 1 son. Education: Yale University School of Drama; Université de Paris, France; BA, Swarthmore College. Career: Stage Director/Producer: The Barber of Seville, The Magic Flute, Der Rosenkavalier, New York City Opera; Rigoletto, Lucia di Lammermoor, National Opera, Santiago, Chile; Madame Butterfly, Don Pasquale, Cincinnati Opera; Don Pasquale, Pittsburgh Opera; The Flying Dutchman, Harford Opera Company; Producer/Director, Don Giovanni, Four Saints in Three Acts, Madame Butterfly; Così Fan tutte; The Gondoliers, Die Fledermaus, Menotti's Tamu-Tamu (1st production after world premiere), Oberlin Music Theatre, Ohio; General Director, Cleveland Opera, 1976-, 50 productions including La Traviata, La Bohème, Daughter of the Regiment, Tosca, Aida, Faust, Falstaff, The Medium, The Secret Marriage, The Merry Widow, Holy Blood and Crescent Moon (world premiere); Artistic Director, Toledo (Ohio) Opera, 1983-85, staged Faust, Don Pasquale, Aida, Barber of Seville; Non-operatic productions include 1st major New York production of Sophocles Oedipus at Colonus and American tour of Much Ado About Nothing, National Shakespeare Company. Address: 1422 Euclid Avenue, Cleveland, OH 44115, USA.

BAMERT Matthias, b. 5 July 1942, Ersigen, Switzerland. Conductor; Composer. m. Susan Bamert, 2 children. Education: Studied in Bern and Paris; Principal composition teachers: Jean Rivier and Pierre Boulez. Career: First oboist, Mozarteum

Orchestra, Salzburg, 1965-69; Assistant conductor, American Symphony Orchestra, New York, 1970-71; Joined the conducting staff of the Cleveland Orchestra, 1971; Music director, Basle Radio Symphony Orchestra, 1977-83; Principal guest conductor, Scottish National Orchestra, Glasgow, and Director, Musica Nova, Glasgow, 1985-90; Conducted Schoenberg's Violin Concerto, 1988; Conducted Ulster Orchestra, Belfast, 1991 in Nielsen's Helios Overture, Sibelius's 2nd Symphony and works by Sandström and Saariaho; Promenade concerts, London, 1991, with BBC Symphony in Liszt's Hunnenschlacht, Alexander Nevsky, premiere of Martin Butler's O Rio; Conducted the National Youth Orchestra in music by Mussorgsky and Birtwistle (Gawain's Journey) at the 1993 Proms; Led the BBC Philharmonic in the premiere of Roberto Gerhard's 1930s ballet, Soirées de Barcelone, 1996; Principal conductor of the London Mozart Players from 1993; Toured Switzerland with the Royal Philharmonic, and Japan with the London Mozart Players; Engagements for the 1997-98 season include: 1997 Luzern Festival, Orchestre de Paris, tours to Holland, Spain and Switzerland with the LMP; North American concerts with the Cleveland Orchestra, Houston and Pittsburgh symphonies; Conducted world premieres of Takemitsu, Denisov, Holliger, Erb, Huber, Casken, Dillon and Rihm. Compositions: Concertino for English horn, string orchestra and piano, 1966; Septuria Lunaris for orchestra, 1970; Rheology for string orchestra, 1970; Mantrajana for orchestra, 1971; Once upon an Orchestra for narrator, 12 dancers and orchestra, 1975; Ol-Okun for string orchestra, 1976; Keepsake for orchestra, 1979; Circus Parade for narrator and orchestra, 1979. Recordings: Pelleas et Melisande with Scottish National Orchestra; Complete symphonies of Hubert Parry with the London Philharmonic; 5-disc series of Frank Martin; Contributed to Contemporaries of Mozart with London Mozart Players; Recordings with BBC Philharmonic of Stokowski's transciptions and Korngold. Honours include: Received the first George Szell Memorial Award, 1971. Address: c/o Scottish National Orchestra, 3 La Belle Place, Glasgow G3 7LH, Scotland.

BAMPTON Rose E, b. 28 Nov 1909, Cleveland, Ohio, USA. Retired Concert and Opera Singer (Soprano). m. Wilfred Pelletier. Education: BMus, Curtis Institute of Music, Philadelphia; LHD, Drake University, Iowa. Debut: Metropolitan Opera, New York City, 1932, as Laura in La Gioconda. Career: Metropolitan Opera, New York, 1932-50, notably as Leonora (Il Trovatore), Sieglinde, Kundry and Donna Anna; Covent Garden, London, England, 1937; As Amneris, Teatro Colon, Buenos Aires, Argentina, 1945-50; Sang Daphne in the first American performance of the Opera by Strauss, 1948; Chicago Opera, San Francisco Opera; Voice faculty, Manhattan School of Music, 1962-82, Juilliard School of Music, 1974-. Recordings: Gurrelieder, Stokowski; Fidelio, Toscanini; Operatic Arias, Wilfred Pelletier. Honours: LHD, Holart and William Smith Colleges, Geneva and New York, 1978. Hobbies: Tennis; Riding; swimming; Collecting antique earrings. Address: 322 East 57th Street, New York, NY 10022, USA.

BANDELLI Antonella, b. 1955, Italy. Singer (Soprano). Debut: Florence, 1976, in Henze's Il Re Cervo. Career: Bologna, 1984, as Sabina in Cimarosa's Gli Orazi ed i Curiazi; Sang in Pergolesi's Il Flaminio at Naples (1985), Rosina at Florence, Massenet's Sophie at Catania (1987) and Xenia in Boris Godunov. Recordings include: Giannetta in L'Elisir d'amore (DGG). Address: c/o Teatro Massimo Bellini, Via Perrotta 12, 95131 Catania, Italy.

BANDITELLI Gloria, b. 1954, Italy. Singer (Mezzo-Soprano). Career: Sang first in Sacchini's Fra'Donato, for RAI, Naples; Siena, 1980, in Cavalieri's La Rappresentazione; Teatro Vale Rome, 1982, in Gagliano's Dafne, Innsbruck Festival, 1983, as Cesti's Tito, followed by Handel's Rodrigo, Medea in Cavalli's Giasone, Teodota in Handel's Flavio and Amastris in Serse; Bologna, 1984 and 1991, in Gluck's Armide and as Maria in Mosè in Egitto; La Scala, Milan, 1988, in Jommelli's Fetonte, Utrecht Festival, 1988, in Giasone and Montpellier, 1989, as Gluck's Orpheus; Concerts include Mozart's Requiem in Vienna, on 200th anniversary of his death; Sang the Messenger in Monteverdi's Orfeo at Palermo, 1996. Recordings include: Le Cinesi by Gluck (Harmonia Mundi), Pergolesi's Adriano in Siria (Bongiovanni) and Penelope in Monteverdi's Ulisse (Nuova Era). Address: c/o Tiroler Landestheater, Rennweg 2, A-6020 Innsbruck, Austria.

BANDOVA-STOLFOVA Hana, b. 3 Sept 1948, Prostejov, Czech Republic. Singer. m. Marian Banda, 1 June 1952. Education: Economic Academy, 1963-67; University of Musical Arts, Bratislava, 1972-76; Postgraduate Study, Tchaikowsky Concervatory, Moscow, 1977-78; PhD Study, University of Musical Arts, Bratislava, 1982-85. Debut: Vocal Concert by Mozart, Brahms, Dvorak, Slovak Philharmonic Orchestra, Bratislava, 1976. Career: Solo Recitals and Orchestra Soloist, Mezzosoprano and Contralto, Mostly by Bach, handel, Mozart, Beethoven, Verdi, Dvorak, Mahler; Singer, Italy, Austria, France, Germany, Uruguay, Argentina. Recordings: Dvorak, Stabat Mater; Beethoven, IX Symphony; Handel, Messiah; Dvorak, Requiem; Mozart, Requiem; Honegger, Jean D'Arc; Saint-Saens, Nöel Oratorio. Honours: Slovak Musical Fund Prize, 1975, 1976; Bratislava Antonin Dvorak Prize, 1976; Carls Bad Fritz Kafenda Prize, 1995. Membership: Slovak Musical Union. Hobby: Painting. Current Management: ARS Koncert, Brno, Czech Republic. Address: Zochova 16/V11, 81103 Bratislava, Slovak Republic.

BANFIELD Stephen (David), b. 15 July 1951, Dulwich, London, England. Professor of Music. Education: FRCO, 1969; Clare College, Cambridge, 1969-72; BA Cantab, 1st Class Honours, 1972; St John's College, Oxford, 1972-75; DPhil (Oxon), 1980; Harvard University, 1975-76. Career: Lecturer in Music, 1978-88, Senior Lecturer, 1988-92, Keele University; Elgar Professor of Music, Head of School of Performance Studies, University of Birmingham, 1992-. Publications: Sensibility and English Song, 1985; Sondheim's Broadway Musicals, 1993; Editor, The Blackwell History of Music in Britain, volume VI, 1995. Contributions to: Various articles, chapters and reviews. Memberships: Royal Musical Association; Sonneck Society for American Music; Fellow, Royal Society of Arts; Viola da Gamba Society; Kurt Weill Foundation, member of Kurt Weill Edition Advisory Board; Member, Editorial Committee, Musica Britannica; Founder Member, Stephen Sondheim Society. Hobbies: Architecture; Literature; Travel. Address: 6 King's Court, 108 Livery Street, Birmingham, B3 1RR, England.

BANIEWICZ Vera, b. 1949, Russia. Singer (mezzo-soprano). Education: Studied in Warsaw. Career: Sang first at chamber operas of Warsaw and Cracow; Engaged at Dortmund, 1976, and sang Flosshilde, Olga in Eugene Onegin, Octavian, Carmen and Concepcion in L'Heure Espagnole; Hannover, 1985-87, notably as Renata in The Fiery Angel; State Operas of Hamburg and Munich as Eboli in Don Carlos; Further guest appearances, Berlin, Stuttgart, Brunswick as Kundry, 1989, and Barcelona as Herodias, 1989; With Deutsche Oper am Rhein Dusseldorf has sung Lady Macbeth, Preziosilla in La Forza del Destino, Azucena, Maddalena, and Brangaene in Tristan und Isolde; Sang Mistress Quickly in Falstaff at the Komische Oper Berlin, 1996. Address: c/o Deutsche Oper am Rhein, Heinrich Heine Allée 16, 4000 Dusseldorf, Germany.

BANKS Barry, b. 1960, England. Singer (Tenor). Education: Studied at Royal Northern College of Music with Josef Ward. Career: Sang Tamino and Don Ottavio at Royal Northern College of Music; Covent Garden debut as Beppe in Pagliacci, 1989; English National Opera as Rossini's Almaviva, Fenton, the Novice in Billy Budd and Brighella in Ariadne auf Naxos; Tamino and in Britten's Flute for Glyndebourne Touring Opera; Appearances with Opera North as Mozart's Basilio, Arturo in Lucia di Lammermoor, Iopas in Les Troyens and in the Griffiths/Mozart pasticcio The Jewel Box; Has sung Pedrillo in Die Entführung with Netherlands Opera with performances of Il Signor Bruschino and Peri's Euridice in Paris and Tamino in Leipzig; Concert showings in France, Germany, Italy and Belgium and at Festivals at Cheltenham, Buxton and Aldeburgh; Messiah with Tokyo Philharmonic and Liverpool Philharmonic; Season 1991 with Tamino in Brussels, debut with BBC Symphony and Mozart's Mitridate with English Chamber Orchestra under Jeffrey Tate at the Barbican; Sang Gianetto in The Thieving Magpie for Opera North, 1992; Sang Tom Rakewell with Glyndebourne Touring Opera; Recent performances: Edgardo, WNO, 1994, and title role of Candide with Chicago Lyric Opera, 1994; Engaged for Lucio Silla at the 1997 Salzburg Festival; Other roles include Nemorino and Argirio in Tancredi (both at Frankfurt) and Britten's Flute (Met debut, 1996). Honours include: Peter Moores Foundation Scholarship, 1983. Current Management: Harrison Parrott Ltd. Address: c/o Harrison Parrott Ltd, 12 Penzance Place, London, W11 4PA, England.

BANNATYNE-SCOTT Brian, b. 4 Nov 1955, Edinburgh, Scotland. Singer (Bass). m. Frances Stewart Leaf, 23 Apr 1979, 1 son, 1 daughter. Education: St Andrew's University; Guildhall School of Music; Further study with Norman Bailey. Career: Debuts at La Fenice Venice, 1981, and the Rome Opera, 1982; Scottish Opera from 1982, as Colline, Don Fernando (Fidelio), Nourabad (The Pearl Fishers) and the Speaker in The Magic Flute; English National Opera from 1987 as Monterone (Rigoletto), Pogner and the Commendatore (1991); Varlaam (Boris Godunov), Opera North and BBC Prom, 1992; Banquo, ENO, 1993; Sang Fafner and Hagen in the City of Birmingham Touring Opera version of The Ring; Tour of Europe as Cold Genius in Purcell's King Arthur; Salzburg Festival debut, 1991, as Polyphemus in Acis and Galatea; Bermuda Festival, 1991, as Don Alfonso in Così fan tutte; Concert engagements with leading British orchestras; Has sung Christus in the St John Passion settings of Bach and Arvo Pärt (in Italy, Germany and Japan); Stravinsky's Les Noces with London Sinfonietta and Simon Rattle, 1993; Aldeburgh masterclasses with Galina Vishnevskaya (also televised) and recital at 1990 Prom Concert; Appearances: The Trojans, LSO, 1993, 1994; Swallow in Peter Grimes, Nantes; Bastille Opera, Tosca; Gurrelieder, CBSO; Flander's Festival, Handel's Chandos Anthems; Liège, Der Kaiser von Atlantis; 1995: Bartolo in Figaro, Bermuda Festival; Sarastro in Magic Flute, Nantes; Purcell's King Arthur in Europe and Buenos Aires; Sang Araspe in Handel's Tolomeo at Halle, 1996. Recordings include: King Arthur; Poppea; Dioclesian and Timon of Athens; The Wreckers; A Midsummer Night's Dream; Tolomeo. Hobbies: Reading; Politics; Sport; Travel. Address: Magenta Music International, 4 Highgate High Street, London N6 5JL, England.

BANSE Juliane, b. 1969, Germany. Soprano Singer. Education: Trained as ballet dancer in Zurich; Vocal Studies in Zurich and with Brigitte Fassbaender and Daphne Evangelatos in Munich. Debut: Sang Pamina in Harry Kupfer's production of Die Zauberflöte at Komische Oper Berlin, 1989. Career: Engagements at Komische Oper as Ilia and Susanna, 1991-92; Pamina in Stuttgart and Brussels; Sophie in Rosenkavalier at Landestheater Salzburg and Zerlina at Glyndebourne, 1994, 1995; Sophie, Susanna, Pamina and Zdenka; Contract with Vienna State Opera, 1994-96; Concert repertoire includes all major oratorio repertoire; European concert performances with Orchestre de Bastille, Paris, Mahler's 4th Symphony with Vienna Philharmonic Orchestra under Claudio Abbado; Many Lieder recitals throughout Europe; US debut in 1995 in St Louis and Indianapolis; Sang in Henze's Raft of the Medusa at the Festival Hall, London, 1997. Recordings include: Lieder by Schoeck; Bach's Christmas Oratorio with the Windsbacher Knabenchor, TV Tape and CD; Berg's Lulu Suite and Altenberg Lieder with Vienna Philharmonic Orchestra, Claudio Abbado; Mendelssohn's Paulus with H Rilling. Honours: Winner, Kulturforum Competition, Munich, 1989; Schubert Award, Vienna, 1993. Current Management: IMG Artists. Address: c/o IMG Artists, Media House, 3 Burlington Lane, London, W4 2TH, England.

BÄR Olaf, b. 19 Dec 1957, Dresden, Germany. Singer (baritone). Career: Studied in Dresden, sang in Dresden Kreuzchor, 1966-75, and was a principal member of Dresden State Opera until 1991; UK debut, Nov 1983, at Wigmore Hall; Returned summer 1985; Covent Garden debut, 1985, as Harlekin in Ariadne auf Naxos; Aix-en-Provence Festival, 1986, in Ariadne; Die Zauberflöte at La Scala; Glyndebourne Festival, 1987, as the Count in Capriccio; Aix, 1988, as Guglielmo in Così fan tutte, conducted by Jeffrey Tate; Concert performances, Europe and USA; USD debut, 1987, as Christus in the St Matthew Passion with the Chicago Symphony Orchestra conducted by Solti; Tours of Australia, 1989, 1993, Japan, 1989, 1992; Created roles in premieres of operas by Matthus, 1985, and Mayer, 1989; At Covent Garden Opera sang Papageno, 1991; Glyndebourne as Don Giovanni, 1991; Sang in Britten's War Requiem; Oliver in Capriccio, Opernhaus Zurich, 1992; Marcello in La Bohème, Staatsoper Dresden, 1992; Count in Le nozze di Figaro, Netherlands Opera Amsterdam, 1993; Operatic debut, USA as Papageno, Chicago, 1996; Sang in Schubert's Alfonso und Estrella at the 1997 Vienna Festival. Recordings: Schumann Dichterliebe Op 48 and Liederkreis Op 39, Kerner-Lieder Op 35 and Liederkreis Op 24; Schubert Die schöne Müllerin, Die Winterreise and Schwanengesang; Wolf Möricke Lieder; Brahms Lieder; Beethoven Lieder; Mozart Arien; Bach Christmas Oratorio with John Eliot Gardiner and the Monteverdi Choir; Christus in the St Matthew-Passion (Arias), conductor J E Gardiner; St Matthew-Passion (Christus), conductor Georg Solti; St John-Passion (Arias), conductor Peter Schreier; Fauré and Duruflé Requiems; Further recordings include Papageno in Mozart's Die Zauberflöte; Adam in Haydn's Creation and Harlekin in Strauss's Ariadne auf Naxos. Current Management: IMG Artists Vocal Division, Media House, 3 Burlington Lane, Chiswick, London W4 2TH, England. Address: Steglichstr 6, 01324 Dresden, Germany.

BAR-ILLAN David (Jacob), b. 7 Feb 1930, Haifa, Palestine (now Israel). Pianist; Teacher. Education: Graduate, Haifa Music Institute; Juilliard School of Music; Mannes College of Music. Debut: Professional debut as soloist with Palestine Broadcasting Service Orchestra, 1946. Career: British debut, Wigmore Hall, London, England; First US tour, 1954; Appearances as soloist with many of the world's major orchestras and as a recitalist; Teacher of Piano, Mannes College of Music, 1980-. Recordings: For two labels. Contributions to: Articles to several journals. Address: c/o Mannes College of Music, 150 West 85th Street, New York, NY 10024, USA.

BARAB Seymour, b. 9 Jan 1921, Chicago, Illinois, USA. Composer; Cellist. Education: Studied the cello with Gregor Piatigorsky and Edmund Kurtz. Career: Performed first as church organist in Chicago; Played the cello in symphony orchestras of Indianapolis, Cleveland, Portland and San Francisco, 1940-60; Assisted in the organisation of the Composers Quartet and the New York Pro Musica; Has taught at Rutgers, the State University of New Jersey and the New England Conservatory. Compositions include: Operas: Chanticleer, after Chaucer, Aspen, 1956; A Game of Chance, Illinois, 1957; Little Red Riding Hood, New York, 1962; The Toy Shop, New York, 1978; A Piece of String, Colorado, 1985; The Maker of Illusion, New York, 1985; Song settings of A Child's Garden of Verses and Songs of Perfect

Propriety. Address: c/o ASCAP, ASCAP Building, One Lincoln Plaza, New York, NY 10023, USA.

BARABAS Sari, b. 14 Mar 1918, Budapest, Hungary. Soprano. m. Franz Klarwein. Education: Studied in Budapest. Debut: Budapest in 1939 as Gilda in Rigoletto. Career: Member of the Hamburg Staatsoper from 1949; Sang in San Francisco in 1950 as the Queen of Night, Glyndebourne, 1953-57 as Constanze in Die Entführung, Adèle in Le Comte Ory and Zerbinetta in Ariadne auf Naxos, and at Florence Maggio Musicale in 1955; Guest appearances in Germany and Austria in operettas; Sang in London in 1969 in The Great Waltz. Recordings include: Le Comte Ory from the Glyndebourne Festival, 1956; Excerpts from works by Johann Strauss, Gasparone, Telefunken.

BARAN Peter, b. 16 Mar 1950, Bratislava, Czechoslovakia. Musician (Cellist). m. Beata Baranova, 15 Aug 1975, 2 sons. Education: Music School, Bratislava, 1956-65; Conservatory, Bratislava, 1965-72; Hochschule für Musik und Darstellende Kunst, Vienna, 1979-83. Debut: Haydn's Cello Concerto in D major, 1972. Career: Member: Slovak Philharmonic Orchestra, 1972-; Suchon Quartet, 1973-77; Bratislava Chamber Harmony, 1973-80; Capella Istropolitana Chamber Orchestra, 1982-89; Bratislava String Trio, 1985-; Kontrapunkte, ensemble of 20th century music, Vienna, 1988-; Concertmaster, Slovak Philharmonic Orchestra, 1989-; Soloist and Member, Orchestra Ensemble Kanazawa, Japan, 1992-; Major performances, solo: Concerto for 2 Celli (Handel) with Slovak Philharmonic Orchestra, 1984; Symphonia Concertante (Haydn) with Slovak Chamber Orchestra, 1985; Cello Concerto op 33 (Saint-Saëns) with Slovak Philharmonic Orchestra, 1985; Concerto for String Trio and Orchestra (C Stamitz), 1987; Quatuor pour la fin du temps (Messiaen) at BHS Festival, 1987; Concerto in A minor for violin, cello and orchestra, op 102 (Brahms) and Sonata da Camera and Orchestra (Martinu), both with Slovak Philharmonic Orchestra, 1993; Don Quixote with Slovak Philharmonic, 1997; Currently, Cellist, Kyoto Symphony Orchestra; Slovak and Austrian Radio performances: Jagdquartet (Haydn); Cello Concerto in C major (Haydn); TV: Sonata in F major, op 99 (Brahms); String Trio Serenade (Dohnányi); Divertimento (Mozart); Trio in G major (Hummel); Little Trio (A Moyzes); Ernest Bloch, Schelomo, Hebraic Rhapsody for Violoncello and orchestra. Recordings: Vivaldi: Cello Concerto in A minor, Concerto in G minor for 2 celli; Beethoven: Septet, op 20; String Trio in G major by Hummel; Clarinet Quartet E flat, J N Hummel and Concerto for string trio and orchestra, C Stamitz, CD on Slovak Records. Memberships: Slovak Music Union; Musicians' Union, Japan. Hobbies: Chamber music; Family. Address: Medena 35, 81102 Bratislava, Slovakia.

BARANTSCHIK Alexander, b. 1953, Leningrad, USSR. Violinist. Education: Studied at the Leningrad Conservatory, 1960-72, with Professor Waiman, 1972-77. Career: Gave concerts in Russia, then emigrated, 1979, becoming leader of the Bamberg Symphony Orchestra; Leader of the Radio Philharmonic Orchestra of the Netherlands, 1982; Solo engagements with leading orchestras in Germany, Netherlands, Britain and Hungary; Appearances in Russia with the Kazan Symphony and the Leningrad Philharmonic; Performed the Sibelius Concerto with the London Symphony in Spain, 1987, Prokofiev's 1st in the USA and London, 1989-90; Leader of the London Symphony Orchestra from 1989, played the Tchaikovsky Concerto with the orchestra, Mar 1991, Bach on tour to the USA, Aug 1991; Brahms Double Concerto at the Barbican, 1997. Honours include: Winner, International Violin Competition at Sion, 1980. Address: c/o London Symphony Orchestra, Barbican Centre, London EC2Y 8DS, England.

BARBACINI Paolo, b. 1963, Reggio Emilia, Italy. Singer (Tenor). Career: Has sung throughout Italy in operas by Mozart and Rossini, notably Don Giovanni, Il Re Pastore, Cenerentola, Il Turco in Italia, Adina and Aureliano in Palmira; La Scala Milan from 1980, in Falstaff and Figaro and on tour to Tokyo and Sofia; Has sung in La Pietra del Paragone for the Israel Festival, Il Turco in Italia in Aix and Rossini's Elisabetta in Turin and on tour to the USA; Modern repertory includes Manzoni's Doctor Faustus (premiere, at La Scala, 1985), Wozzeck, Orff's Catulli Carmina and the premiere of Bussotti's L'Ispirazione (Florence, 1988); Sang Pang in Turandot at Macerata, 1996. Address: c/o Atholl Still Ltd, Foresters Hall, 25-27 Westow St, London SE19 3RY, England.

BARBAUX Christine, b. 1955, Saint-Mande, France. Singer (soprano). Education: Studied at Paris Conservatory. Debut: Strasbourg, as Despina, 1977. Career: Sang Barbarina in Le nozze di Figaro in Paris, 1978, Vienna and Salzburg under Karajan; Further engagements in Geneva in The Love of Three Oranges, 1984; Théâtre de la Monnaie, Brussels, as Servilia in La Clemenza di Tito and Sophie in Rosenkavalier, 1982, 1986, Aix-en-Provence as Sophie, Amsterdam as Norina, 1988, Salzburg Festival as Servilia, 1988; Other roles include Ophelia in Hamlet by Thomas, Gilda, and Blanche Force in Les Dialogues des Carmélites; Sang Alice Ford in Falstaff in Bonn, 1991. Recordings include: Werther and Pelléas et Mélisande; Fauré's Pénélope; Le nozze di Figaro. Address: c/o Oper der Stadt Bonn, Am Boselagerhof 1, 5300 Bonn, Germany.

BARBER Graham (David), b. 30 Dec 1948, London, England. Musician (Organist). m. Dianne Mackay, 20 July 1990. Education: BA, 1st Class Honours, 1970, MMus, 1971, University of East Anglia; Royal Northern College of Music; ARNCM Piano, 1974; Piano Accompaniment. distinction, 1975. debut: Royal Festival Hall, London, 1978. Career: International Concert Organist; Musical Director, Chorus Master, Harpsichordist, Piano Accompanist, Coach; Frequent BBC Radio appearances as Organist, mainly featuring German Baroque music and Max Reger; Lecturer in Music, University of Leeds, 1981-; Chorus Master, Leeds Philharmonic Society. 1983-92; Curator, Historic Schulze Organ, St Bartholomew's Church, Armley, 1986-; Chorus Master, Sheffield Philharmonic Chorus, 1987-; Chorus Master, Leeds Philharmonic Society, 1981-90; Tutor in Organ Studies, The Royal Northern College of Music, 1995-. Recordings: Numerous including: Johann Gottfried Walther Organ Works, Reid Concert hall, Edinburgh; Franz Schmidt: Organ Works; English Romantic at Truro Cathedral; Bach Neumeister Chorales and Early Organ Works, Volume 1 and 2; Organ Music from Salisbury Cathedral; The Sandtner Organ at Villingen, Munster; The Klais Organ at Altenberg Dom. Contributions to: Musical Times, 1984. Honours: Limpus and F J Reed Prizes, FRCO Exams, 1969. Memberships: Fellow, Royal College of Organists; Trustee, Percy Whitlock trust; Incorporated Society of Musicians; BIOS; ABC; Karg Elert Society; Incorporated Association of Organists. Hobbies: Gardening; 1930s Ceramics. Address: 37 Chapel Lane, Armley, Leeds LS12 2BY, England.

BARBER Kimberley, b. 1961, Canada. Singer (Mezzo-soprano). Debut: Sang Hansel in Hansel and Gretel for Calgary Opera, 1985. Career: Has sung widely in Canada and in Europe in travesti roles by Mozart, Rossini and Strauss; Also sings Massenet's Cendrillon, Nicklausse in Les Contes d'Hoffmann and Lazuli in L'Etoile; Frankfurt Opera from 1989, as the Composer, Hermia, Ramiro (La finta giardiniera), Dorabella, Cherubino and Rosina; Sang Pauline in The Gambler for English National Opera and has appeared in concert with the Chicago, Toronto and Cincinnati Symphonies; New York and Wigmore Hall concert debuts, 1994. Address: Atholl Still Ltd, Foresters Hall, 25-27 Westow Street, London SE19 3RY, England.

BARBIERI Fedora, b. 4 June 1920, Trieste, Italy. Opera Singer (mezzo-soprano); Stage Director. m. Luigi Barlozetti, 23 Sept 1943 (dec.), 2 sons. Education: Conservatory of Trieste. Debut: As Fidelma in Matrimonio Segreto and Azucena in Il Trovatore, Nov 1940. Career: Appearances in all major opera-houses world wide including New York Metropolitan, San Francisco Metropolitan, Covent Garden London, La Scala Milan, Salzburg Festival and Vienna Staatsoper, Berlin Opera, Geneva Opera, Madrid, Barcelona, Paris, Lisbon, Buenos Aires, Sao Paulo; Her 90 opera roles included Carmen, L'Italiana in Algieri, Amneris, Eboli in Don Carlo, Ortrud in Lohengrin, Delilah; Film roles in Cavalleria Rusticana with Zeffirelli, Rigoletto with Ponnelle, Il Trovatore with Bastianni and Del Monaco; TV films of Adriana Lecouvreur and Falstaff; Has worked with Toscanini, Bernstein, von Karajan, Serafin, Abbado and others; Staged Cavalleria Rusticana at Lodz (Poland), 1991, Norma at Warsaw, 1992. Recordings: Verdi Requiem; 2 Aida; 2 Ballo in Maschera; 3 Il Trovatore; La Favorita; La Gioconda; Suor Angelica; 2 Medea; Falstaff; Orfeo; Solo album of Arie Antiche; Numerous live recordings. Honours: Winner, International Competition, Maggio Musicale, Florence, 1940; Metropolitan Gold Award, 1963; Commendation from the Italian President, 1964; Oscar della Lirica, 1965; La Maschera di Argento di Roma, 1965; San Valentino d'Oro, 1972; Trovatore Prize for the Verdi Centennial, 1973; Mario del Monaco Gold Plaque, 1986. Memberships: International Juries at Singing Competitions; Amici della Lirica. Hobbies: Taking care of her animals and plants; Reading; Cooking. Address: Viale Belfiore 9, 50144 Firenze, Italy.

BARBIROLLI Evelyn, b. 24 Jan 1911, Wallingford, England. Musician; Adjudicator; Lecturer; Master Class Giver; Ex-Oboist. m. Sir John Barbirolli CH, 5 July 1939. Education: Downe House School, Newbury, England; Royal College of Music, London. Career: Scottish, London Symphony, Glyndebourne Festival Opera Orchestras, 1932-39; Soloist and Chamber Music Player later. Compositions: Oboe Technique; The Oboist's Companion; Many arrangements and editions for oboe. Recordings: Many recordings for EMI, some now on CD, including concertos by Haydn, Mozart, Corelli, Handel, Pergolesi, Cimarosa; Also recordings for Pye, Concertos by Albinoni, Marcello. Publications: Oboe Technique, 1953, 3rd edition, 1987; translated into Japanese and Norwegian; The Oboist's Companion, 3 volumes; A Tune for Oboe; A Book of Scales for The Oboe. Contributions to: Many articles for various magazines. Honours: OBE, 1984; DMus; MA; FRCM; RAM; FRNCM; RTCL. Membership: Incorporated Society of Musicians, Ex-President. Hobbies: Gardening; Photography. Address: 15a Buckland Crescent, Londn NW3 5DH, England.

BARBIZET Pierre, b. 20 Sept 1922, Arica, Chile. (French citizen). Pianist. Education: Graduated Paris Conservatoire, 1944. Career: Many performances as soloist and chamber musician, notably with violinist Christian Ferras; Frequent performances of Chabrier, and director of the Marseilles Conservatory from 1963. Recordings include: Complete Beethoven violin sonatas, with Christian Ferras. Honours include: Prizewinner at the Long-Thibaud Competition. Address: Conservatoire National de Marseille, 2 Place Carli, F-13001 Marseille, France.

BARCE Ramon, b. 16 Mar 1928, Madrid, Spain. Composer. m. Elena Martin, 22 June 1984. Education: Conservatory of Madrid, 1950-54; PhD, 1956. Career: Foundation Member, Group Nueva Musica, 1958; Foundation Member, Group Zaj, 1964; Foundation Member, Group Sonda, 1967; Editor of the magazine "Sonda" of contemporary music, 1967-74; Musical Critic Paper "Ya", 1971-78; Foundation Member Asociacion de Compositores Sinfonicos Españoles and First President, 1976-88. Compositions: five Symphonies 1975, 1982, 1983, 1984, 1995; Concert for Piano, 1974; Nine Conciertos de Lizara, 1973-88; Forty Eight Preludios for Piano, 1973-83; Ten String Quartets, 1958-94; Coral hablado, 1966; Melodramas Oleada and Hacia mañana hacia hoy, 1982, 1987; Nuevas polifonias I-II, 1971, 1985; Parabola, 1963 and Travesia 1979 for brass quintet. Recordings: Canada-Trio 1970 and 1993; Twenty Four Preludios, 1987; Obertura fonética, 1977, 1979 and 1994; Siala, 1973; Estudio de valores for piano, 1992; Sonata No 3 for violin and piano, 1990; Sintesis de Siala, 1993; Musica funebre, 1979, 1994; Tango para Yvar, 1995. Publications: Fronteras de la musica, 1985; Tiempo de tinieblas y algunas sonrisas, 1992; Boccherini en Madrid, 1992; Translations of Harmonielehre of Schoenberg 1974, Alois Haba 1984 and Schenker 1990. Contributions to: 12 advertencias para una sociologia de la musica in Coloquio Artes 72, Lisboa 1987; La vanguardia y yo in Revista Musical Catalana 59, Barcelona, 1989. Honours: National Prize of Music, 1973; Prize of Comunidad de Madrid, 1991; Medalla de Oro al mérito en las Bellas Artes, 1996. Memberships: Asociacion de Compositores Sinfonicos Españoles;Sociedad Espanola de Musicologia; Sociedad General de Autores y Editores. Address: Valdevarnes 35, 28039 Madrid, Spain.

BARCZA Peter, b. 23 June 1949, Stockholm, Sweden. Singer (Baritone). Education: Graduated Toronto University, 1971. Career: Sang with Canadian Touring Opera, 1972-73, notably as Guglielmo (Così fan tutte), Papageno, Enrico (Lucia di Lammermoor), Marcello and Germont; Guest appearances at Memphis (1981), New Orleans (from 1985), Seattle and the New York City Opera (from 1990); European appearances include Monteverdi's Ulisse at Bad Hersfeld; Other roles include Rossini's Figaro, Malatesta (Don Pasquale), Luna, Ping (Turandot), Valentin (Faust), and Rangoni in Boris Godunov. Address: c/o New York City Opera, Lincoln Center, New York, NY 10023, USA.

BARDON Patricia, b. 1964, Ireland. Singer (mezzo-soprano). Career: Concert engagements have taken her to France, Belgium, Spain, Netherlands, Hungary, Japan and Switzerland; US debut with the Cincinnati Symphony in Beethoven's Missa Solemnis; Has sung in Verdi's Requiem in Brussels, Mendelssohn's Elijah in Madrid and Janácek's Diary of One Who Disappeared in Barcelona; With Welsh National Opera has appeared as Flosshilde in the Ring and Olga in Eugene Onegin; Anna in Les Troyens for Opera North and Scottish Opera (also as guest at Covent Garden, 1990); Other roles include Gluck's Orfeo (Spain and Dublin), Maddalena in Rigoletto, Royal Opera House and Opera North; Suzuki (Madama Butterfly), Opera North, Edwige (Guillaume Tell, and in La Fanciulla, at Covent Garden); Helen (King Priam), Opera North, and Third Lady in Die Zauberflöte, Verona, 1991; Featured in BBC TV programme on her work; Arsace in Semiramide at La Fenice, Venice; Sang Maddalena in Rigoletto for English National Opera, 1992; Helen in Tippett's King Priam aat Antwerp, 1996. Recordings include: Olga in Eugene Onegin; Giovanna in Rigoletto. Honours include: Prize winner, Cardiff Singer of the World Competition, 1983. Address: 846 Tyrwhitt Road, Brockley, London SE4 1QB, England.

BARENBOIM Daniel, b. 15 Nov 1942, Buenos Aires, Argentina. Pianist; Conductor. m. (1) Jacqueline Du Pré, 1967 (dec. 1987), (2) Elena Bashkirova, 1988, 2 sons. Education: Studied with father; Accademia di Santa Cecilia, Rome; Conducting, Salzburg, 1954. Debut: Buenos Aires, 1949. Career: Played at Salzburg Mozarteum, 1951; Israel Philharmonic, 1953-; UK debut, 1955; Played a Mozart concerto, Festival Hall, 1956, with Royal Philharmonic; New York debut, conducted by Stokowski, 1957; Berlin Philharmonic, 1963-; New York Philharmonic, 1964-; Many appearances with London Philharmonic and Chicago Symphony; Conducting debut, Israel, 1962, then tour of Australia; Conductor, Pianist, English Chamber Orchestra, 1964-; Tours, Latin America, Far East; Directed South Bank Summer Music Festival, London, 1968-70; Premiere of Goehr's Piano Concerto, Brighton, 1972; Conducted Don Giovanni and Figaro, Edinburgh Festival, 1973, 1975; Music Director, Orchestra de Paris, 1975-89; Conducted Tristan und

Isolde, Bayreuth, 1981, Der Ring des Nibelungen, 1988-90; Concert, Bayreuth Festspielhaus, 1986, for centenary of Liszt's death; Tristan at the 1995 Bayreuth Festival; Artistic Director, Mozart Festival, Paris, 1983-, Don Giovanni, Così fan tutte, Figaro, 1986; Accompanied Janet Baker and Dietrich Fischer-Dieskau in Lieder; Chamber music with Pinchas Zukerman and Itzhak Perlman; Many complete cycles of Beethoven Piano Sonatas, notably TV series from historic houses in Vienna; Music Director, Chicago Symphony, Berlin Staatsoper, 1991-; Concerts with Berlin Philharmonic in London, 1990 (Bruckner 7th, Beethoven 3rd, Schubert 8th); Conducted Parsifal excerpts, Chicago, 1990; Played Brahms D minor Concerto, Festival Hall, Philharmonia, 1991; Mozart 200 Festival, English Chamber Orchestra, Barbican (K183, K543, K271); Conducted the Vienna Philharmonic in Mozart and Bruckner, Festival Hall, 1997; Engaged to conduct Busoni's Doktor Faust at the Berlin Staatsoper, 1998. Recordings include: Berlioz cycle; Beethoven Concertos as soloist and conductor; Mozart Concertos, English Chamber Orchestra; Don Giovanni; Le nozze di Figaro; Complete Mozart Piano Sonatas; Liszt Cycle, sound and video; Tristan und Isolde (Teldec), 1995. Honours include: Beethoven Medal, 1958; Paderewski Medal, 1963; Beethoven Society Medal, 1982. Address: 5 Place de la Fusterie, 1204 Geneva, Switzerland.

BARGIELSKI Zbigniew, b. 21 Jan 1937, Lomza, Poland. Composer. Education: Studied at Warsaw Conservatory with Szeligowski and at Katowice with Boleslaw Szabelski; Further study with Boulanger in Paris and at Graz. Compositions include: The Little Prince, musical tale, 1970; Danton, or some scenes from the History of the Great French Revolution, opera, 1968-69; Alice in Wonderland, youth opera, 1972; Phantoms do not Lie, comic opera, 1981; Parades for orchestra, 1965; Percussion Concerto, 1975; Espace étrapé for orchestra, 1973; Violin Concerto, 1975; Ballads for wind and percussion, 1976; Three Sonnet-Capriccios for clarinet, 1976; Impromptu for percussion, 1976; String Quartet, 1976. Address: c/o ZAIKS, 2 rue Hipoteczna, 00 092 Warsaw, Poland.

BARHAM Edmund, b. 22 March 1950, Beckenham, England. Singer (tenor). Education: Studied at the Trinity College of Music, London, and the London Opera Centre. Career: Sang leading lyric roles in Wuppertal, then became a member of the company of the Theater am Gärtnerplatz, Munich; Many appearances at leading German opera houses; English National Opera from 1985, as Jenik in The Bartered Bride, Turiddu, Narroboth in Salome, Pinkerton, Cavaradossi, Gabriele Adorno, and Vakula in the first British production of Rimsky-Korsakov's Christmas Eve, 1988; Engagements with Opera North as Don José, Boris in Katya Kabanova and Dimitri in Boris Godunov; Sang in the Gounod Grande Messe Solenelle for BBC television; Sang Alfredo, English National Opera, 1990, and Macduff in a new production of Macbeth (also on tour to USSR); Sang Manrico at St Gallen, 1991; Don Carlos, English National Opera, 1992; Overseas appearances include The Rise and Fall of Mahagonny and Adriana Lecouvreur in Switzerland, Howard Blake's Benedictus in Norway, and Don José at the Bregenz Festival; Engaged as Otello for the Victoria State Opera, 1993; Manrico in Il Trovatore for Opera North, 1994; Don José for Welsh National Opera, 1997. Recordings: First Armed Man in Die Zauberflöte; 18th Century English Songs for orchestra and chorus; Rossini's Petite Messe Solonelle. Address: c/o Stafford Law Associates, 6 Barham Close, Weybridge, Surrey KT13 9PR, England.

BARK Jan, b. 19 Apr 1934, Harnosand, Sweden. Composer. Education: Studied in Stockholm with Larsson, Blomdahl and Ligeti; Further study in Far East. Career: Worked at Tape Music Center, San Francisco, and with Swedish Broadcasting Service; Co-Founder, Culture Quartet (4 trombones) with Folk Rabe. Compositions include: Piano Sonata, 1957; 2 string quartets, 1959, 1962; Metakronismer for orchestra, 1960; Lamento for ensemble, 1962; Boca Chica for chamber ensemble, 1962; Pyknos for orchestra, 1962; Missa Bassa for small orchestra with 7 conductors, 1964; Nota for mixed chorus, 1964; Bar, electronic music; Light Music for chorus a cappella, 1968; Lyndon Bunk Johnson, 1968; Irk-Ork for chamber ensemble, 1970; Memoria in memoria for chamber ensemble, 1974; Utspel for band, 1978; Malumma for tuba and band, 1984; Concerto for orchestra, 1985; Theatre and film music. Address: c/o STIM, Sandhamnsgatan 79, PO Box 27372, S-102 54 Stockholm, Sweden.

BARKAUSKAS Vytautas (Pranas Marius), b. 25 Mar 1931, Kaunas, Lithuania. Composer; Professor. m. (1) Elena Tverjonaite, 27 July 1954, (2) Tiina Vabrit, 20 Dec 1984, (3) Svetlana Cherniavska, 15 Feb 1991, 1 son, 1 daughter. Education: Lithuanian State Conservatory, Vilnius, 1953-59. Career: Accompanist, Vilnius College of Music, 1954-58; Instructor, House of the People's Creative Work of the Republic, 1958-61; Professor, Theory, Composition, Lithuanian State Academy of Music, Vilnius, 1961-. Compositions include: Variations for 2 pianos, 1957; 5 symphonies, 1962, 1971, 1979, 1984, 1986; Word About Revolution, cantata-poem, narrator, men's chorus, orchestra, 1967; Intimate Composition for oboe and 12 string, 1968; Three Aspects for symphony orchestra, 1969; Partita for solo violin, 1967; Contrast Music for flute, cello and 2 percussion, 1969; Monologue for solo oboe, 1970; string quartets, 1972, 1983; Gloria Urbi, organ, 1972; Prelude and Fugue, chorus, 1974; Legend About Love, opera, 1975; Salute Your Land, oratorio-mystery, 1976; Sonatas for violin and piano, No 1 Sonata subita, 1976, No 2 Dialogue, 1978, No 3, 1984; Open Window, mezzo-soprano, 5 instruments, 1978; Rondo capriccioso, bassoon, piano, 1981; Concerto for Viola and Chamber Orchestra, 1981; The Sun, symphonic picture, 1983; Duo Sonata, violin, viola, 1984; Sonata for 2 pianos and 3 performers, 1984; Sextet, 2 violins, viola, cello, double bass, piano, 1985; Cantus Amores, cantata, 1986; Sonata for double bass and piano, 1987; Hope, oratorio, 1988; The Second Legend of Ciurlionis, piano, 1988; Credo, organ, 1989; Concerto for Piano and Orchestra, 1992; Konzertstück für Orchester No 1, 1992; Concert Suite, cello, piano, 1993; Reminiscence, cembals, 1993; Intimate Music, op 100, flute, percussion, 1993; Divertimento, piano 6-hands, 1993; The Third Legend of Ciurtionis, piano, 1993; Inspiration, organ, 1994; Konzertstück für Orchester No 2, 1994; Trio a déux, violin, viola, cello, 1995; Allegro Brillante for two pianos, 1996; Modus vivendi for violin, cello and piano, 1996; Scherzo for violin and chamber orchestra, 1996; Duo for guitar and piano, 1997. Recordings: Ars vivendi, 1992; Cavalli, 1993; Proud Sound, 1995; Lithuanian New Music series, 1997. Contributions to: articles in music journals. Membership: Union of Composers, Lithuania. Hobbies: Skiing; Swimming; Lawn tennis. Address: Saltiniu Street 11/15 b.44, Vilnius 2006, Lithuania.

BARKER Jennifer Margaret, b. 6 May 1965, Glasgow, Scotland. Composer. Education: BMus, honours, University of Glasgow; MMus, Piano Performance, MMus, Composition, Syracuse University, USA; AM, PhD, Composition, University of Pennsylvania. Career: Director of Theory and Composition, Music Director of Opera Workshop and Musicals, Christopher Newport University; Artist-in-Residence, WHRO/FM Norfolk Public Radio. Compositions: The Enchanted Glen. Recordings: Geodha; The Enchanted Glen; Earthtones; Nyvaigs; Three Highbrows We; Nobody Told Me. Honours: Helen L Weiss Prize in Composition, 1993; Winner, Cambridge Contemporary Music Festival Composition Competition, 1996; Meet the Composer Grant Winner, 1998. Memberships: Society of Composers Inc; National Association of Composers, USA; International Alliance of Women in Music; American Society of Composers, Authors & Publishers. Address: 2 Kirkhouse Avenue, Blanefield, Glasgow G63 9BT, Scotland.

BARKER Noelle, b. 28 Dec 1928, Aberdeen, Scotland. Soprano. m. Christopher Peake, 3 children. Education: MA, Aberdeen University, 1948; Dartington Hall; Amsterdam Conservatory; Munich Academy; Studied with Hans Hotter. Debut: Royal Festival Hall, London. Career: Oratorio, lieder and contemporary music with leading choral societies and ensembles; Appearances with three choirs and at various festivals; Sang with the English Opera Group, London Sinfonietta and Dreamtiger Ensemble; Broadcasts on BBC and European stations; Professor, Guildhall School of Music and Drama, Royal Academy, London and Conservatoire National, Paris; Private teaching in London and Paris; Masterclasses worldwide and Jury Member of various international competitions; Director of British Youth Opera. Recordings: Complete solo vocal works of Messiaen; Jazz Songs. Publications: Co-Editor of Pathodia Sacra e Profana; Editor of The Junior Recitalist. Honours: FGSM, 1974; OBE, 1985. Hobbies: Chamber Music; Skiing; Tennis; Breadmaking; Dressmaking; Swimming. Address: Brontë Cottage, 89 South End Road, London, NW3 2RJ, England.

BARKER Paul (Alan), b. 1 Jul y1956, Cambridge, England. Composer. m. (1) Christine Susan Barker, 3 Sep 1977, divorced 1991, (2) Maria Huesca, 23 May 1992. Education: Guildhall School of Music, 1974-78; GGSM 1st Class; MMus, Durham University, 1983-85. Career includes: Visiting Lecturer, City University, 1978-83; Musical Director of Dancers Anonymous, 1979-86; Associate Lecturer, Kingsway-Princeton College, 1984-90; Artistic Director of Modern Music Theatre Troupe, 1985-94; Kingsway-Princeton College, 1984-90; Composer in Residence, West Sussex, 1991-93; Composer in Association, London Mozart Players, 1993-; Lecturer, Hertfordshire University, 1997-. Compositions include: Operas: The Marriages Between Zones 3, 4 and 5, The Place, 1985, Phantastes, Camden Festival 1986, The Pillow Song, 1988, La Malinche, 1989, Albergo Empedocle, 1990, Dirty Tricks, 1997, at London International Opera Festival and Prologue at Festival del Centro Historico, Mexico City, 1992; 10 Contemporary dance scores for European companies; Orchestral works include Fantasy on Four Notes, 1978; Instrumental ensemble, vocal, choral and chamber works; Music for Theatre; Children's Operas and educational music; Three Songs for Sylvia, commissioned by London Festival Orchestra, Bristol Cathedral, 1994; Concerto for 8, for London Mozart Players, Henley Festival, 1995; Concerto for Violin and Orchestra for Tasmin Little and London Mozart Players 1996. Recordings: Barbican Fanfare, 1979; The Pied Piper of Hamelin, 1980. Honour: Royal Philharmonia Society Prize for Composition, 1978. Memberships: Executive Committee, APC; Honorary Associate Member, OMTF; PCS Committee of ISM. Hobbies: Literature; Theatre; Travel. Current Management: Modern Music Theatre Troupe. Address: Flat 3, 33 Hopton Road, London SW16 2EH, England.

BARKIN Elaine R(adoff), b. 15 Dec 1932, New York, New York, USA. Composer; Music Educator; Writer on Music. m. George J Barkin, 28 November 1957, 3 sons. Education: BA, Music, Queens College, 1954; MFA, Composition 1956, PhD, Composition and Theory 1971, Brandeis University; Certificate in Composition and Piano, Berlin Hochschule für Musik, 1957; Studied with Karol Rathaus, Irving Fine, Boris Blacher, Arthur Berger and Harold Shapero. Career: Assistant to Co-Editor, Perspectives of New Music, 1963-85; Lecturer in Music, Queens College, 1964-70; Sarah Lawrence College, 1969-70; Assistant, Associate Professor of Music Theory, University of Michigan, 1970-74; Visiting Assistant Professor, Princeton University, 1974; Associate Professor 1974-77, Professor 1977-97, Composition and Theory, University of California, Los Angeles; Guest Lecturer at various colleges and universities. Compositions: String Quartet, 1969; Sound Play for violin, 1974; String Trio, 1976; Plein Chant, alto flute, 1977; Ebb Tide, 2 vibraphones 1977; ...the Supple Suitor... for soprano and 5 players, 1978; De Amore, chamber mini-opera, 1980; Impromptu for violin, cello and piano, 1981; Media Speak, theatre piece, 1981; At the Piano, piano, 1982; For String Quartet, 1982; Quilt Piece, graphic score for 7 instruments, 1984; On the Way to Becoming, for 4-track Tape Collage, 1985; Demeter and Persephone for violin, tape, chamber ensemble and dancers, 1986; 3 Rhapsodies, flutes and clarinet, 1986; Encore for Javanese Gamelan Ensemble, 1988; Out of the Air for Basset Horn and Tape, 1988; To Whom It May Concern, 4-track Tape Collage, Reader and 4 Players, 1989; Legong Dreams, Oboe, 1990 (and since 1980 many improvised group and duo sessions on tape); Gamélange, harp and mixed gamelan band, 1992; Five Tape Collages, Open Space CD #3, 1993; For My Friends' Pleasure, for soprano and harp, 1993; Touching All Bases, electric bass, percussion, Balinese gamelan, 1996. Publication: e: An Anthology, music text and graphics, 1997. Honours: Fulbright Award, 1957; NEA Awards, 1975, 1979; Rockefeller Foundation, 1980; Meet the Composer, 1994. Address: Department of Music, 405 Hilgard Avenue, University of California, Los Angeles, CA 90095, USA.

BARKL Michael Laurence Gordon, b. 9 Aug 1958, Sydney, New South Wales, Australia. Composer. m Sharyn Lee, 25 Jan 1986, 1 daughter. Education: BMus, New South Wales State Conservatorium of Music, 1981; FTCL, Trinity College of Music, London, 1982; MMus, University of New England, 1986; DipEd, Sydney College of Advanced Education, 1986; PhD, Deakin University, 1995. Career: Tutor, University of New England, 1982; Head Teacher of Music at the Illawarra Institute of Technology, 1987-; Commissions from Seymour Group, Synergy, Elision, Duo Contemporain, Manly Art Gallery and Orange City Council. Compositions include: The Time, The Time, for choir, 1981; Voce di Testa and Voce di Petto, for orchestra, 1981-82; Chroma for harpsichord, 1981; Drumming for piano, 1983; Psychonaut for chorus, 1983; Iambus for wind quintet and strings, 1983; Cabaret for orchestra, 1985; Expressive and Ferocious, for string quartet, 1985; Backyard Swing for concert band, 1986; Blues for clarinet and marimba, 1986; Rondo for chamber orchestra, 1988; Disco for percussion quartet, 1989. Honours include: Segnalata, Valentino Bucchi competition for Composition, Italy, 1981. Address: 119 Combermere Street, Goulburn, NSW 2580, Australia.

BARLOW Clara, b. 28 July 1928, Brooklyn, New York, USA. Singer (Soprano). Education: Studied with Cecile Jacobson in New York. Debut: Berne Opera 1962, as Venus in Tannhäuser. Career: Sang at Oberhausen, 1963-65, Kiel 1965-66; Komische Oper Berlin 1967, as Donna Anna; Engaged at Wiesbaden 1967-69, Zurich 1969-70; Guest appearances at the Spoleto Festival (as Isolde, 1968), San Diego (1969) and the Metropolitan Opera (as Leonore 1970); Returned to New York 1974, as Isolde; Deutsche Oper Berlin 1970, Vienna Staatsoper 1973; Sang Fata Morgana in The Love of Three Oranges at La Scala 1974; Appearances as Brünnhilde at Seattle (1970-72 and 1976) and Dallas (1981); Scottish Opera 1973, as Isolde; Further appearances at Dresden, Stuttgart, Hamburg, Munich, Chicago (1976-77), Houston, Copenhagen, Toronto, Budapest and Mexico City; Stadttheater Bremen 1985-86, as Elektra and Leonore; Other roles have included the Dyer's Wife (Die Frau ohne Schatten), Agathe, Senta, Elsa, Elisabeth, Ariadne, Salome, Aida, Elisabeth de Valois, Jenufa, Marina (Boris Godunov) and Giulietta in Les Contes d'Hoffmann. Address: c/o Bremer Theater, Postfach 101046, D-2800 Bremen, Germany.

BARLOW Stephen, b. 30 June 1954, Seven Kings, Essex. Conductor. m. Joanna Lumley. Education: Studied in Canterbury, at Trinity College, Cambridge, and Guildhall School of Music. Career: Founded New London Chamber Group, based at the Riverside Studios, Hammersmith; Guest conductor of opera at the Guildhall School, notably Falstaff and Maw's The Rising of the

Moon; Glyndebourne Festival and Tour, 1979-85, leading Die schweigsame Frau, Der Rosenkavalier, Arabella, Oliver Knussen double bill, Cosi fan tutte, Gluck's Orfeo, The Rake's Progress and Love of Three Oranges; For English National Opera has conducted The Flying Dutchman, Carmen, Abduction from the Seraglio, The Damnation of Faust, La Cenerentola, The Italian Girl in Algiers, Barber of Seville; Scottish Opera from 1983, with Hansel and Gretel, The Bartered Bride, Intermezzo; Has conducted Opera 80 from its inception, Musical Director from 1987, leading Marriage of Figaro, The Masked Ball, The Rake's Progress, The Merry Widow, 1989-90; Covent Garden debut, 1989, with Turandot, returning for Die Zauberflöte in 1991; San Francisco Opera, 1990, Capriccio; Has also worked for Opera North and Vancouver Opera; Australian debut, Melbourne, in Die Zauberflöte, 1991; Conducted Faust for Opera Northern Ireland, 1992; Conducted Capriccio in Catonia, Marriage of Figaro at Garsington, Carmen in Adelaide; Madama Butterfly at Auckland, 1994; Madama Butterfly in Belfast, 1997; Concert engagements with the English Chamber Orchestra, City of London Symphonia, London Sinfonietta, City of Birmingham Symphony, Royal Liverpool Philharmonic, Scottish Chamber Orchestra, BBC Scottish and Bournemouth Sinfonietta; Concerts in Spain, Netherlands, Germany; BBC National Orchestra of Wales, Radio Philharmonic Orchestra, Hilversum; New Zealand, Vancouver, Melbourne and Detroit Symphony Orchestras, BBC Philharmonic. Address: c/o Robert Gilder and Co, Enterprise House, 59-65 Upper Ground, London SE1 9PQ, England.

BARLOW Wayne (Brewster), b. 6 Sept 1912, Elyria, Ohio, USA. Composer; Music Educator; Organist; Choirmaster. Education: BM, theory, composition, 1934, MM, composition, 1935, PhD, music (composition), 1937, Eastman School of Music, with Howard Hanson and Bernard Rogers; Studied composition with Arnold Schoenberg, University of Southern California, Los Angeles, 1935; Seminar, electronic music with Myron Schaeffer, University of Toronto, 1963-64; Fulbright postdoctoral research grant, Universities of Brussels, Ghent and Utrecht, 1964-65. Career: Faculty member, 1937-78, Director of Graduate Studies, 1955-57, Chairman, Composition Department, 1968-73, Director, Electronic Music Studio, 1968-78, Dean of Graduate Studies, 1973-78, Emeritus Professor of Composition, 1978-, Eastman School of Music, Rochester, New York; Guest lecturer, composer, colleges and universities; Organist, choirmaster, St Thomas Episcopal Church, Rochester, 1946-76; Christ Episcopal Church, Rochester, 1976-78. Compositions: Orchestral: De Profundis, 1934; False Faces, ballet suite, 1935; Sinfonietta, 1936; The Winter's Passed, oboe, strings, 1938; Lyrical Piece, clarinet, strings, 1943; Nocturne, chamber orchestra, 1946; Rondo-Overture, 1947; Sinfonietta, 1950; Lento and Allegro, 1955; Night Song, 1958; Rota, chamber orchestra, 1959; Images, harp, orchestra, 1961; Sinfonia da Camera, chamber orchestra, 1962; Vistas, 1963; Concerto for Saxophone and Band, 1970; Hampton Beach, overture, 1971; Soundscapes, orchestra, tape, 1972; Divertissement, flute, chamber orchestra, 1980; Frontiers, band, 1982; Vocal: Mass, chorus, orchestra; Cantatas Wait for the Promise of the Father and Voices of Faith; Organ music including 4 volumes of Hymn Voluntaries for the Church Year, 1963-81; The Seven Seals, oratorio, text from Bible (Book of Revelations), large chorus, full symphony, soloists, 1991; Requiem and Alleluia, ensemble of 100 trombones. Address: 1600 East Avenue Apt 301, Rochester, NY 14610-1625, USA.

BARNARD Trevor (John), b. 3 Jan 1938, London, England. Concert Pianist; Lecturer in Music. m. Helen Richmond, 28 Aug 1974. Education: Royal Academy of Music, London; Royal College of Music, London; Herbert Fryer; Harold Craxton; Institute of Musical Instrument Technology, London, 1946-60; ARCM, 1954; Graduate, MIMIT, 1960. Career: Pianist-in-Residence, Boston University Radio, 1967-71; Faculty, New England Concervatory of Music, Boston, MA, 1968-72; Piano Tutor, Monash University, Australia, 1972-74; Lecturer in Music, Melbourne College of Advanced Education, 1974-88; Lecturer in Music, The University of Melbourne and Examiner, Australian Music Examinations Board, 1989-; Many appearances as pianist, BBC and ABC; Music-in-the-Round Chamber Music Festivals; Many orchestras, music societies. Recordings: An Introduction to Piano Music; Bliss Piano Concerto; J S Bach transcriptions and piano music from Australia. Publications: Pedalling and Other Reflections on Piano Teaching, 1991; A Guide to the Study of Solo Piano Repertoire at Tertiary Level, 1996; Contributions to: Reviews in Australian Music Teacher, 1992-. Honour: Full Scholarship, Royal College of Music, 1955. Membership: Honorary Secretary, Australian Musicians Guild, 1982-93; President, Camberwell Music Society, 1990-. Hobbies: Golf; Swimming; Yoga. Address: 10 Grosvenor Road, Glen Iris, Victoria 3146, Australia.

BARNES Milton, b. 16 Dec 1931, Toronto, Ontario, Canada. Composer; Conductor. Education: Composition with John Weinzweig and Ernst Krenek; Conducting with Victor Feldbrill, Boyd Neel, Walter Susskind; Piano with Samuel Dolin, Royal Conservatory of Music, Toronto, 1952-55; Conducting at Accademia Chigiana and Berkshire Music Center; Graduated, Vienna Academy of Music, 1961. Career: Music Director, Composer, Crest Theatre, 1961-63; Founder-Conductor, Toronto Repertory Orchestra, 1964-73; Conductor: St Catherine's (Ontario) Symphony Orchestra and Chorus, 1964-72, Niagara Falls (New York) Philharmonic and Chorus, 1965-73; Composer, Conductor in residence, Toronto Dance Theatre, 1968-73. Compositions include: 3 symphonies, 1964, 1973, 1987; Children's Suite, 1966; Pinocchio, symphonic poem, 1967; Psalms of David, soprano, baritone, chorus, orchestra, 1973; The Spiral Stairs Septet, Ballet Suite, 1973; Concerto Grosso Sextet, 1973; Shebetim, tableau, string orchestra, 1975; Concerto, violin, strings, 1975; Madrigals Female Chorus, for 2 trumpets and 2 trombones, 1975; Shir Hashirim (Song of Songs), for soprano, and tenor soloists, female chorus and seven solo instruments, 1975; Concerto, viola, orchestra, 1975; Maid of the Mist, symphonic poem, 1977; Channukah Suite #1, for symphony orchestra or chamber orchestra, 1977; The Dybbuk, masque for dancing, 1977; Divertimento, harp or string quartet, 1978; String Quartet #2, 1978; Serenade for String Quartet and String Orchestra, 1979; Anerca 1, for solo Bassoon or Solo String Bass, 1979; Octet, 1985; Double Concerto, 2 guitars, string orchestra, 1986; Three French Canadian Legends for Orchestra, 1986; Papageno Variations, (after the Magic Flute of Mozart) string bass, piano or string orchestra, 1988; The Odyssey: A Symphonic Tale, 1990; Song of the Bow: Concerto, string bass, orchestra, 1991; Rites of Passage, Requiem for Rene Highway Male Chorus (tenors, basses) with piano, 1991; Harbord Street Suite for flute, viola and harp, 1991; La Rosa Variations, for solo cello, 1992; Fantasy of Jewish Folk Themes for solo tenor, Chorus and Klezmer band, 1993; Adioses Cantata, for mezzo soprano female chorus, flute, cello, piano and percussion, 1994; Vocal music; Many music theatre and multi-media works. Recordings include: Lamentations of Jeremiah, 1959; Variations, Solo Harp, 1976; Divertimento, Harp and Strings, 1978; Ballade, Solo Viola, 1979; Annexus, Percussion Ensemble, 1982; Three French Canadian Legends for Orchestra, 1986; Papageno Variations (after The Magic Flute of Mozart), for string bass and string orchestra, 1988. Publications: Lamentations on Jeremiah, for solo viola, 1959; Fantasy for Guitar, 1975; Channukah Suite #1, for chamber orchestra, 1977; Anerca 1, for solo bassoon, 1979; O Clap Your Hands, Psalm 47, accapella chorus, 1987; Papageno Variations, piano version, 1988; Contributions to: books, newspapers and journals. Honours: Nominated for Juno Award; Best Classical Composition, Divertimento for Harp and String Quartet, 1993; Certificate of Appreciation and Honorary Membership, American Harp Society. Memberships: SOCAN; Society of Composers, Authors and Music Publishers of Canada; Founding Member, Society of Canada Film Composers. Address: 99 Heddington Avenue, Toronto, Ontario M5N 2K9, Canada.

BARNETT John M(anley), b. 3 Sept 1917, New York, USA. Conductor. Education: Studied piano and conducting at the Manhattan School of Music; Further studies with Bruno Walter, Nikolai Malko, Felix Weingartner and George Enescu in Europe. Career: Worked under Leon Barzin with the National Orchestral Association; Staff Conductor with the WPA Federal Music Project of New York, 1939-42; Assistant to Otto Klemperer with the Federal Knickerbocker Orchestra and worked with the New York Symphony Orchestra and the Stamford Symphony Orchestra; Associate Conductor of the Los Angeles Philharmonic, 1948-58 with a tour of the Far east in 1956; Organized and trained the Japan-American Philharmonic Orchestra; Musical Director of the National Orchestral Association, 1958-70; Music Director, Philharmonic Symphony Orchestra of Westchester, NY, 1961-71; Artistic Consultant to the National Endowment of the Arts, 1972-78; Music Director of the Puerto Rico Symphony Orchestra from 1979.

BAROLSKY Michael, b. 19 July 1947, Vilnius, Lithuania. Composer. Education: Studied piano, music theory and ethnology in Lithuania; Further studies with Witold Lutoslawski in Warsaw and Edison Denisov and Alfred Schnittke in Moscow. Career: Music Adviser to Lithuanian Radio, 1969-71; Emigrated to Germany, 1971, and attended seminars led by Ligeti, Stockhausen and Kagel at Darmstadt; Taught in Tel Aviv, 1974-77; Settled in Cologne and worked on electronic music with Humpert at the studio there. Compositions include: Violin Sonata, 1964; String Trio, 1964; Concertino, 1967; Telefonoballade for baritone, 6 narrators and ensemble, 1969; Exodus for orchestra, 1970; Scriptus after Kafka, 1972; Dakar for percussion and electronics, 1972; Melos for mezzo-soprano and ensemble, 1975; Sublimato for ensemble and tape, 1975; Cries and Whispers for ensemble and electronics, 1975; Blue Eye, Brown Eye, chamber opera, 1976; Apocalypse, song cycle, 1976; Pranah for violin and tape, 1976; Sternegesang for chamber orchestra, 1977; The Book of Emanations for orchestra, 1978; Ein Stück aus der Nacht for actor and electronics, 1978; Tonus for synthesizer, 1979; Seelekalender for mezzo and piano, 1982; The Book of Changes for piano; Stück-Mund-Stück for trombone and tape, 1983; Piccolostück, 1983; Rainbow Music for 6 recorders, 1984; Triotrio for violin, cello and tape, 1984. Address: c/o GEMA, Herzog Wilhelm Strasse 28, 8000 Munich, Germany.

BAROVA Anna, b. 1932, Plzen, Czechoslovakia. Singer (Mezzo-Soprano). Education: Studied at the Prague Academy. Career: Sang at the Leipzig Opera from 1959-69, notably in the 1961 German premiere of Prokofiev's War and Peace, as Sonia; Guested widely in former East Germany and sang at the Janacek Opera, Brno, from 1969; Roles have included Suzuki, Rosina, Ulrica, Dorabella, Ramiro in La Finta Giardiniera, Olga, and Pauline (The Queen of Spades); Concert repertory includes Beethoven's Ninth, the Verdi Requiem and Das Lied von Erde. Recordings include: The Devil and Kate by Dvorak, Eva and Sarka by Foerster, Jenufa and Osud by Janacek (Supraphon). Address: Sosnova 26, 63700 Brno, Czech Republic.

BARRAUD Henry, b. 23 Apr 1900, Bordeaux, France. Composer. m. Denise Parly, 3 children. Education: Studied at Paris Conservatoire, 1926-27; Later study with Dukas and Aubert. Career: In charge of music at Paris International Exposition, 1937; Former Musical Director and Director, National Programme, French Radio, 1944-65. Compositions: Finale dans le mode rustique, 1932; Poème for orchestra, 1934; Concerto da Camera, 1936; Le diable à la Kermesse, ballet, 1943; Le Mystère de Saints Innocents, oratorio, 1944; Piano Concerto, 1946; Offrande à une Ombre, 1946; La Farce du Maître Pathelin, 1948; Symphonie de Numance, 1950; Concertino for piano and 4 winds, 1953; Numance, opera, 1955; Te Deum, 1955; Symphony for Strings, 1955; Symphony No 3, 1958; Rapsodie dionysienne, 1961; Lavinia, opera, 1961; Divertimento, 1962; Flute Concerto, 1963; Symphonie Concertante for trumpet and orchestra, 1965; 3 Etudes for orchestra; Une Saison en enfer, symphonic suite after Rimbaud, 1969; La Divine Comédie for 5 solo voices and orchestra, 1972; Operas, Le roi Gordogne (1979) and Tête d'or (1981). Publications: La France et la Musique Occidentale; Berlioz, 1955, 1966; Pour Comprendre les Musiques d'Aujourd'hui, 1968; Les Cinq Grands Opéras, 1972. Honours: Légion d' Honneur; Commander, Ordre des Arts et des Lettres; Grand Prix Nationale de la Musique, 1959. Address: 20 Rue Jean Daudin, 75015 Paris, France.

BARREAU Gisele, b. 28 Feb 1948, Cueron, France. Composer. Education: Studied at the Paris Conservatoire with Messiaen and others; Further study with the Groupe de Recherches Musicales. Career: Assistant to Morton Feldman in New York; Composer-in-residence at the Villa Medici, Rome. Compositions: Rituel for men's chorus and ensemble, 1974; Profile for female voices and ensemble, 1975; Oceanes for 2 orchestras, 1976; Submarines for 2 pianos and percussion, 1977; Tlaloc for 2 percussion, 1988; Cendres for 8 voices and ensemble, 1978; Clameurs for 2 choruses and orchestra, 1978; Inside for ensemble, 1989; Quartet for clarinet and strings, 1991. Honours: Koussevitsky Prize, 1977; Prix Chapelier-Clergue, 1988. Address: c/o SACEM, 225 avenue Charles de Gaulle, 92521 Neuilly sur Seine Cedex, France.

BARRELL David, b. 1962, England. Singer (Baritone). Education: London University and the Royal Academy of Music; Opera Center at the Juilliard School, New York. Career: Sang Gounod's Ourrais (Mireille) and Don Giovanni at Juilliard; Appearances at the Spoleto Festivals (Italy and USA) 1986; Wexford Festival 1987 and Britten's Demetrius at the Bloomsbury Festival; Welsh National Opera as Ottokar in Der Freischütz, The Speaker in Die Zauberflöte, Don Carlos (Ernani) and Germont; Season 1992-93 as Rossini's Figaro and Alfonso in La Favorita, with WNO at Covent Garden; Sang 'I' in the British premiere production of Schnittke's Life with an Idiot (English National Opera, 1994); Siskov in House of the Dead in Nice; Wolfram in Tannhaüser for Chelsea Opera Group and Thaos in Iphigenie en Tauride at the 1996 Edinburgh Festival; Season 1996-97 with Germont for Opera Northern Ireland, Major Haudy in Zimmermann's Die Soldaten for ENO, Puccini's Marcello, The Forester in The Cunning Little Vixen and Balstrode in Peter Grimes, for Scottish Opera; Concerts include: The Brahms Requiem, Carmina Burana, Elijah and Elgar's The Kingdom; Premiere of Tippett's Tempest Suite, season 1995-96. Honours include: Winner, New York Oratorio Society International Soloist Competition, Carnegie Hall; Associate of Royal Academy of Music. Address: AlliedArtists, 42 Montpellier Square, London SW7 1JZ, England.

BARRERA Giulia, b. 28 Apr 1942, Brooklyn, New York, USA. Singer (soprano). Education: Studied in New York with Dick Marzollo. Debut: New York City Opera, 1963, as Aida. Career: Sang in Baltimore, New Orleans, Pittsburgh, Washington and Seattle; Member of New York City Opera: Roles include Verdi's Amelia and Leonora (Il Trovatore), Santuzza, Don Giovanni, Sieglinde in Die Walküre, Tosca, Manon Lescaut, Venus in Tannhäuser and Monteverdi's Euridice; Guest appearances in Copenhagen, Rome, Parma, Cardiff, Montreal and Nuremburg. Recordings include: The Mother in Dallapiccola's Il Prigioniero.

BARRIERE Françoise, b. 12 June 1944, Paris, France. Composer. Education: Studied at the Versailles and Paris Conservatoires. Career: Co-founded the Groupe de Musique Experimentale de Bourges, 1970. Compositions include:

Electronic pieces Ode à la terre marine, 1970; Java Rosa, 1972; Au paradis des assassins, 1973; Ritratto di Giovane, with piano, 1973; Aujourd'hui, 1975; Scènes des voyages d'Ulysse, 1981; Chant des consonnes, 1987; Le tombeau de Robespierre, 1989; Conversations enfatines, 1991; Nos petits montres musiciens, 1992. Address: c/o SACEM, 225 rue Charles de Gaulle, 92521 Neuilly sur Seine Cedex, France.

BARRIERE Jean-Baptiste (Marie), b. 2 Jan 1958, Paris, France. Composer; Director of Musical Research. m. Kaija Saariaho, 26 May 1984. Education: Licence, Mathematical Logic, 1980, DEA Philosophy, 1981, Doctorate in Philosophy, 1987, University of Paris I, Panthéon Sorbonne. Career: Member of the Synthesizer Ensemble of the Centre Européen pour la Recherche Musicale, Metz, 1976-77; Researcher, Composer, 1981-84, Director of Musical Research, 1984-, Institut de Recherche et de Coordination Acoustique Musique, Paris. Compositions: Pandémonium: Ville Ouverte, 1975; Pandémonium: Non, Jamais l'Esperance, 1976; Sophistic Variations, 1980; Chreode I, 1983; Collisions, 1984; Epigénèse, 1986; Hybris, 1987. Recordings: Pandémonium: Ville Ouverte, 1977; Pandémonium: Non, Jamais l'Esperance, 1978. Publications: Le Timbre: Métaphores pour la Composition, 1987-88; Actes du Symposium Systèmes Personnels et Informatique Musicale, 1987. Contributions to: Chreode I: A Path to a New Music with the Computer, for Contemporary Music Review No 1, 984; Mutations de l'Escriture, Mutations du Matériau, for Inharmoniques No 1, 1987. Honours: Digital Music Prize in the Electro-Acoustic Music Competition, Bourges, France, 1983. Membership: Collectif pour la Recherche en Information Musicale. Address: IRCAM, 31 Rue St Merri, Paris 75004, France.

BARRON Angela, b. 9 May 1949, Birmingham, England. Composer; Musician; Author; Music Teacher. Education: Moseley School of Art; Birmingham School of Contemporary Pop and Jazz. Career: Freelance Percussionist, Birmingham Symphony Orchestra; Theatre, Caberet Musician with Top Entertainers including Bruce Forsyth, Des O'Connor, Leslie Crowther, Val Doonican; Part-time Lecturer, Percussion and Composition, City and County of Coventry and Warwickshire, for Coventry Centre of Performing Arts and Warwickshire College of Technology and Art. Compositions: TV Signature Tunes, Shut That Door (also released as a single) and Where Are They Now; Commissioned by Chappel Library for Album, Short Pieces as Jingles, Theme, Incidental Music for TV, Radio, Films (distributed worldwide); Collaboration with Boosey and Hawkes Music Publishers on Albums, including Album Recorded by Royal Philharmonic Orchestra; Also Wrote for Their Educational Catalogue under Pseudonyms: Chris Barron, Christine Barron. Publications: 2 Comprehensive Tutors with Cassettes for Learn As You Play Series: Learn As You Play Drums; Learn as You Play Tuned Percussion and Timpani; Learn as You Play Drums Cassette. Memberships: Association of Professional Composers; British Academy of Songwriters, Composers and Authors Hobbies: Art; Swimming; Travel. Current Management: Boosey and Hawkes Music Publishers Ltd. Address: 27 Madeira Croft, Coventry CV5 8NX, England.

BARRON Bebe, b. 16 June 1927, Minneapolis, Minnesota, USA. Composer. Education: Studied at the Universities of Minnesota and Mexico and in New York with Riegger and Cowell. Career: With husband Louis Barron (1920-89) co-founded electro-acoustic music studio in New York, 1949; Secretary of the Society for Electro-Acoustic Music from 1985. Compositions (with Louis Barron): Dramatic Legend, 1955; Ballet, 1958; Heavenly Menagerie, 1952; For an Electronic Nervous System, 1954; Music of Tomorrow, 1960; Spaceboy, 1971; The Circe Circuit, 1982; Elegy for a Dying Planet, 1982; Film scores, including Forbidden Planet, 1956, and Cannabis, 1975. Address: c/o ASCAP, ASCAP House, One Lincoln Plaza, New York, NY 10023, USA.

BARROSO Sergio, b. 4 Mar 1946, Havana, Cuba. Composer; Synthesist. Education: Composition; Piano; Organ; Theory; National Conservatory, Havana, 1950-66; Postgraduaget, Prague Superior Academy of Music; Orchestral Conducting, University of Havana; Computer Music, CCRMA, Stanford University, USA. Career: Professor; Composition; Institute of Arts, Havana; Performances include: Monte Carlo Theatre, 1972; Warsaw Autumn Festivals, 1972, 1985; Budapest Opera, 1976; Teatro de la Zarzuela, Madrid, 1976; MET-Lincoln Center, New York, 1977-78; San Francisco Opera, 1977; Bratislava Philharmonic Hall, 1979; ISCM Festival, Belgium, 1980, Oslo, 1990; IRCMA, Paris, 1980; Array, Toronto, 1981; Utrecht Conservatorium, Netherlands, 1982; Manuel de Falla Festival, Granada, 1985; Wired Society, Toronto, 1986; ACREQ, Montreal, 1987; Museo Tamaya, Mexico City, 1988; National Arts Centre, Ottawa, 1988; South Bank Centre, London, 1989; Toronto New Music Concerts, 1990; Sub-Tropics Festival, Miami, 1991; LIEM, Centro Reina Sofia, Madrid, 1991; ICMC, Montreal, 1991; New Music Across America, Seattle, 1992; Others. Compositions: 2 ballets; Plasmasis, 1970; La Casa de Bernarda Alba, 1975; Oboe Concerto, 1968; Yantra IV flute, tape, 1982; Ireme, voice, percussion, tape, 1985; En Febrero Mueren las Flores, violin,

tape, 1987; Tablao, guitar, tape, 1991; Concerto for violin & orchestra, 1992; Synthesizers: Soledad, 1987; Canzone, 1988; La Fiesta, synthesizers, tape, 1989; La Fiesta Grande, synthesizers, orchestra, 1990; Cronicas de Ultrasueno, oboe, synthesizers, 1992; Sonatada, 1992. Address: c/o CMC, 200-2021 West Avenue, Vancouver, British Columbia, Canada, V6J 1N3.

BARRUECO Manuel, b. 16 Dec 1952, Santiago de Cuba, Cuba. (American citizen). Guitarist. Education: Studied at the Estevan Salas Conservatory, Santiago de Cuba and the Peabody Conservatory, Maryland. Debut: New York, 1974. Career: Many concert appearances as soloist; Faculty Member at the Peabody Conservatory and assisted in the creation of a faculty for guitar at the Manhattan School of Music; Gave the US premiere of Takemitsu's guitar concerto, 1985; Numerous recordings, both solo and with artists such as Placido Domingo. Recordings: Rodrigo, with Placido Domingo; Bach Sonatas; Albeniz Turina, solo. Honours include: Winner of the Concert Artists' Guild Award, 1974. Address: M B General Management, P O Box 4466, Timonium, MD 21094-4466, USA.

BARRY Gerald, b. 1952, Ireland. Composer. Education: Studied in Cologne with Stockhausen and Kagel; Studied organ with Piet Kee in Amsterdam. Compositions: Principal works include: Chevaux de frise for orchestra (performed at the 1988 Proms); The Intelligence Park, opera (ICA commission, first performed at the 1990 Almeida Festival; The Triumph of Beauty and Deceit (Channel 4 TV commission, 1992, 1993); The Conquest of Ireland, vocal and orchestral work (BBC Symphony Orchestra commission). Recordings: Piano and Chamber music - Noriko Kawai, piano, with the Nua Nos ensemble. Contributions to: The Intelligence Park, to Contemporary Music Review, Vol 5; Irish Wit, to The Musical Times, Sept 1993; Bob's Your Uncle, to The Musical Times, Apr 1995. Current Management: Oxford University Press. Address: Oxford University Press, 3 Park Road, London NW1 6XN, England.

BARSHAI Rudolf, b. 28 Sept 1924, Labinskaya, USSR. Conductor. m. (1) 3 sons, (2) Elena Raskova. Education: Conducting course under Ilya Musin, Leningrad; Violin and Viola studies with Lev Zeitlin, Moscow Conservatory. Career: Solo Violinist, Moscow Philharmonic Quartet, Member, Borodin and Tchaikovsky Quartets, Founder and Conductor, Moscow Chamber Orchestra, Guest Conductor, Moscow Philharmonic, State Orchestra of USSR, USSR Radio Orchestra, 1955-77; Guest Conductor, New Israel Orchestra, 1977-, also London Symphony, London Philharmonic and Royal Philharmonic Orchestras, BBC London, Philharmonia, English Chamber Orchestra, Scottish National Orchestra, City of Birmingham Symphony Orchestra, BBC Philharmonic, Vienna Symphony, Orchestre National de France, Orchestre de Paris, Mozarteum Salzburg, Tokyo Philharmonic, Yomiuri and NHK Orchestras, RAI Turin, Pittsburgh Symphony, Swiss Radio Orchestra, Bavarian Radio Symphony Orchestra, Munich, Radio Symphony Orchestra, Hamburg, Radio Symphony Orchestra, Cologne, Tonhalle Orchestra Zurich; Principal Conductor, Bournemouth Symphony, 1982-88; Music Director, Vancouver Symphony, 1985-88; Principal Guest Conductor, Orchestre National de France, 1987-88. Compositions: Arrangements of Bach; Art of the Fugue; Musical Offering; Shostakovich: Chamber Symphony op 49a, op 110a, op 83a, Symphony for Strings op 118a, Symphony for Woodwinds and Strings, op 73a; Prokofiev: Visions Fugitives, others. Recordings: Many including works by Bach, Vivaldi, Corelli, Mozart, Haydn, Beethoven, Schubert, Brahms, Mahler, Stravinsky, Bartók, Shostakovich, Tchaikovsky, Tippett, Prokofiev, for various labels. Honours: Grand Prix du Disque; Honorary Doctorate, University of Southampton, 1985. Membership: President, International Toscanini Conductor's Competition, 1986-93. Current Management: Lies Askonas Ltd, 6 Henrietta Street, London WC2E 8LA, England; Concerto Winderstein, Leopoldstrasse 25, Munich 80802, Germany.

BARSOV Victor N, b. 2 Feb 1928, Poltava, Ukraine. Conductor. m. Masitova Galima, 1 Jan 1984, 2 sons. Education: Pianist, Kharkov Conservatoire, Ukraine, 1950; Conductor, Lvov Conservatoire, Ukraine, 1952. Debut: Minsk, Belorussia, 1958. Career: Conductor of Belorussian Philharmonic, 1958-65; Chief Conductor of Irkutsk Symphony Orchestra, East Siberia, 1965-70; Professor of Urals Conservatory, 1970-72; Conductor, Yaroslavl, 1972-84; Music Director, Kuzbass Symphony, 1984-95. Compositions: Regular appearances on TV, Radio, conducted concerts in major cities of FSU, France, Belgium, Spain, Malta, Hungary, Czechoslavkia, Switzerland, Yugoslavia. Recordings: All-union Radio, Moscow; Czechoslovakian Radio. Publications: Regular pieces for violin and orchestra, Moscow, 1990-. Honours: Czechoslovakian Composers' Union Medal of Smetana, 1979; Honoured Artist of RSFSR, 1979. Membership: Union of the Workers of Culture. Hobbies: Photography; Travelling; Kuzbass Symphony Orchestra.

BARSTOW Josephine (Clare), (Dame), b. 27 Sept 1940, Sheffield, Yorkshire, England. Opera Singer. m. (1) Terry Hands, (2) Ande Anderson, 25 Oct 1969. Education: BA Hons, English,

Birmingham University; London Opera Centre, one year. Debut: 1964, Opera for All. Career: Has appeared with all major British Opera Companies; In world premieres of The Knot Garden and The Ice Break by Tippett and We Come to the River by Henze at Covent Garden; The Story of Vasco at ENO; Summer, 1986, at Salzburg Festival in leading role in Penderecki's Die schwarze Maske; Has sung in all major houses in USA, Germany, including Bayreuth, France, Switzerland, Italy, Buenos Aires, Africa and Russia, at the Bolshoi; Main Roles in Verdi and Strauss, frequently Salome and Janacek, Mozart, Puccini, Beethoven and Wagner; Role of Kate in Kiss Me Kate; Sang Odabella in a new production of Attila at Covent Garden; Amelia in Un Ballo in Maschera at Salzburg, 1990; Ellen Orford in a new production of Peter Grimes, ENO, 1991; Sang Leonara in a new production of La Forza del Destino for ENO, 1992; Chrysothemis in Elektra at Houston, 1993; Elizabeth I in Gloriana for Opera North at Covent Garden, 1994; the Kostelnicka for Opera North, 1995, returned 1997, as Elizabeth I. Recordings: The Knot Garden by Michael Tippett; Recital of Verdi Arias and Ballo in Maschera under Karajan; Four Opera Finales; Gloriana, title role; Kiss Me Kate; Albert Herring. Honours: Critics Prize, Berliner Zeitung; Best Debut, Buenos Aires; Honorary doctorate of Music, Birmingham University, CBE, 1985; Fidelio Medal; DBE, 1995. Hobby: Runs Arabian Stud Farm in Sussex. Current Management: Robert Clarke at Lies Askonas. Address: 6 Henrietta Street, London WC2E 8LA, England.

BARTA Ales, b. 30 Aug 1960, Rychnov, Czechoslovakia. Organist. m. 25 Feb 1984. Education: Conservatoire in Brno; Academy of Music, Prague. Debut: With Prague Symphony Orchestra, Prague Spring Festival, 1984. Career: Foreign tours of Denmark, 1979, Austria, 1983, Hungary, 1984, 1985, Turkey, 1985, Germany, 1986, 1990, France, 1987, Russia, 1988; USA debut at concert of Czech music, New York, 1990; Festival appearances: Recitals at Prague Spring Festival, 1984, 1988 and 1991, Avignon Festival, 1987, Istanbul Festival, 1985, Leipzig Festival, 1986; Debut with Prague Radio Symphony Orchestra, Berlin Festival, 1987. Recordings: Organ recital, Bach, Reger and Flosman, 1986; Organ recital, Bach, 1991; Organ recital, Live recording, Bach, Reger, Sokola, 1992. Honours: 1st Prize, Anton Bruckner International Organ Competition, Linz, 1982; 1st Prize, Czech Organists Competition, 1984; 1st Prize, Prague Spring International Organ Competition, 1984. Hobbies: Football; Driving. Address: Nuselska 6, 14000 Prague 4, Czech Republic.

BARTA Jiri, b. 19 June 1935, Sumice, Czechoslovakia. Composer. m. Jindra Bartova, 1 Feb 1964, 1 daughter. Education: Conservatoire; Janacek Academy of Music and Dramatic Arts, Brno, Czechoslovakia. Debut: Concerto for Orchestra, 1962. Career: Music Theory teacher, Conservatory, Brno, 1968-. Compositions: Lyric Variations for Violin and Piano; Melancholy and Defiance for Violin, Cello and Piano; Concerto da Camera per Pianoforte ed Archi; Reliefs for Orchestra, Music for Strings: In Memoriam Miloslav Istvan, Chitra-Chamber Opera. Recordings: CD, Camerata Brno Live I (2 Impromptus for Piano), Czech Radio. Honours: Prize, Union of Czech Composers, 1986; Prize, Czech Musical Fund, 1986, 1990. Memberships: Association of Composers and Music Publicists, Camerata Brno. Address: Solnicni 5-9, 602 00 Brno, Czech Republic.

BARTA Michael (Mihaly), b. 6 Feb 1954, Budapest, Hungary. Violinist; University Professor. m. Irene Barta, 3 May 1980, 1 son. Education: Béla Bartók Conservatory, 1964-69; F Liszt Academy, Budapest, 1969-75; Post-Graduate study with Arthur Grumiaux, -1975. Career: Concerts, Wigmore Hall, London; Tokyo, Frankfurt, Carnegie Recital Hall, New York, Detroit Art Institute; Radio: Radio France, Scottish BBC, Radio Bremen, Berlin, Hungarian Radio, WDR Köln, PBS USA; Concerts in Sofia Conservatory, La Valetta,(Malta), Budapest (Franz Liszt Academy); Hungarian Television, PBS-USA. Recordings: Suite for Violin and Piano; Prokofiev: Sonata for Two Violins; Numerous recordings for major labels and national and international radio stations. Honours: 2nd Prize, Joseph Szigeti International Competition, Budapest, 1973; Gold Medal, Belgian Eugene Ysaye Society, 1973; Special Prize, finals, Tchaikovsky International Competition, Moscow, 1974. Hobbies: Travel; Cycling; Chess. Address: 45 Twin Creeks Lane, Murphysboro, IL 62966, USA.

BARTELINK Bernard G M, b. 24 Nov 1929, Enschede, Netherlands. Musician; Organist; Composer. m. Rina Stolwyk, 23 Apr 1955, 2 sons. Education: Diploma, Composition, 1955, Prix d'excellence, organ, 1954, Amsterdam Conservatory. Career: Recitals in major concert halls and cathedrals in the United Kingdom, Europe and USA; Radio appearances in many countries; Professor of organ at Sweelinck Conservatory, Amsterdam until 1989; Organist at St Bavo Cathedral, Haarlem; Organist for Concertgebouw Orchestra, Amsterdam. Compositions: The Beatitudes for voice and organ; Works for organ, choir and chamber music, commissioned by Dutch Government, City of Amsterdam. Recordings: Several solo LPs and CDs. Honours: First prize, International Organ Improvisation Contest, Haarlem, 1961; Knight in the Papal Order of St

Sylvester; Silver Medal of the Academic Society, Arts, Sciences and Letters, Paris. Address: Leeghwaterstraat 14, 2012 GD Haarlem, The Netherlands.

BARTHA Clarry, b. 1958, Sweden. Singer, Soprano. Education: Studied at the Accadamia di Santa Cecilia, Rome, with Maria Teresa Pediconi and George Favaretto; Further study with Vera Rozsa in London. Debut: Donna Anna at Drottningholm, Sweden, 1981. Career: Has sung Donna Anna in Catania, at the Montepulciano Festival and at Brighton Festival with the Drottningholm Company; At Marseilles has sung Lisa in The Queen of Spades, Fiordiligi and Margherita in Mefistofele; Basle Opera as Agathe, Tatiana in Eugene Onegin and Mozart's Countess; Performances of Gluck's La Danza at Bologna, season 1986-87; Frankfurt Opera, 1987-88 as Iphigénie en Tauride, Desdemona and Fiordiligi; She sang Mozart's Countess at Rome in 1989; Sang Katya Kabanova at Basle, 1991; Concert commitments at the Prague Spring, Monteale, Palermo and Ravello Festivals; Has sung with the Italian Radio, RAI, in Rome, Naples and Milan; Accademia di Santa Cecilia in Rome and the Maggio Musicale in Florence; Mozart's Vespers and Mendelssohn's Elijah in Stockholm; Tour of Israel with Gary Bertini. Honours: Prizewinner at the Beniamino Gigli; Vincenzo Bellini competitions. Address: c/o Ingpen and Williams Ltd, 26 Wadham Road, London SW15 2LR, England.

BARTHA Denes, b. 2 Oct 1908, Budapest, Hungary. Musicologist; Music Educator. Education: PhD, University of Berlin, 1930; Studied with Wolf, Albert, Blume, Sachs, Hornbostel and Schering. Career: Librarian, Music Division, Hungarian National Museum, Budapest, 1930-32; Lecturer, Franz Liszt Academy of Music, Budapest, 1935-; Privatdozent, University of Budapest; Visiting Professor, Smith College, 1964; Harvard University 1964, 1965; Cornell University 1965-66; University of Pittsburgh, 1966-67; Andrew W Mellon Professor, University of Pittsburgh, 1969-78. Publications: Benedictus Ducis und Appenzeller, 1930; Das Musklehrbuch einer ungarischen Klosterschule aus 1490, 1934; Lehrbuch der Muskgeschichte, 1935; Franz Liszt, 1936; Die ungarische Musik, with Zoltan Kodaly, 1943; Antologie der Musikgeschichte, 1948; J S Bach, 1956, 2nd edition 1960; Beethoven kilenc szimfoniaja, 1956, 5th edition revised 1975; Haydn als Opernkapellmeister, with Laszlo Somfai, 1960; Edited Joseph Haydn: Gesammelte Briefe und Aufzeichnungen, 1965; Edited Zenei Lexikon 2nd edition revised, 1965-66. Address: Attila ut 87 III 14, H-1012, Budapest, Hungary.

BARTHOLOMÉE Pierre, b. 5 Aug 1937, Brussels, Belgium. Conductor. Education: Studied at the Brussels Conservatoire, 1953-58, and with Wilhelm Kempff and Henri Pousseur. Career: Founded Musiques Nouvelles, 1962; Conductor of the Liège Philharmonic from 1977 and has premiered works by Berio (Cena, 1979), Boesmans (La Passion de Gilles, 1983), Marius Constant, York Höller and Pousseur (Déclaration d'orage, 1989); Professor of analysis at the Brussels Conservatoire. Address: c/o Conservatoire de Musique, 30 Rue de la Régence, B-1000 Brussels, Belgium.

BARTKIEWICZ Urszula, b. 28 Jan 1952, Bielsko-Biala, Poland. Harpsichordist. m. Jerzy Kozub, 13 Sept 1987, 1 son. Education: Certificate of Maturity, 1971; Studies at the Academy of Music in Cracow headed by Kryzsztof Penderecki, 1971-75; Graduation with distinction; Studies at Conservatoire National de Bobigny, Paris, 1976-77; Harpsichord Class of Huguette Dreyfus; International Master Courses: with Zuzana Ruzickova, Rafael Puyana and Kenneth Gilbert; Doctor's Thesis in Musicology at Polish Academy of Sciences in preparation. Career: Numerous concerts in Poland, eg International Festivals, Warsaw Autumn; Wratislavia Cantans; Lancut Chamber Festival; Concerts in France, Czechoslovakia, Germany, Russia, Switzerland, Belgium, Austria, Great Britain and USA; Co-operation with the Polish National Philharmony, Jerzy Maksymiuk's Polish Chamber Orchestra; Several appearances on television and radio in Poland and USA; Master Class and recital for students of Wayne State University, Department of Music, Detroit, Jan 1988. Recordings: Regular recordings for Polish Radio 1975-90; International & Polish harpsichord music from XVI-XX centuries, solo & chamber music; Records with Polish National Philharmony and Jerzy Maksymiuk's Polish Chamber Orchestra, basso continuo. Hobbies: Philosophy; Literature; Psychology; Sociology; Cycling; Sailing; Walking. Address: ul Bacha 10 m 301, 02-743, Warsaw, Poland.

BARTLE Graham Alfred Reginald, b. 6 Nov 1929, Australia. University Lecturer, Retired. m. Ruth Marian Walker, 11 May 1963, 1 son, 3 daughters. Education: BA, 1952, Dip Ed, 1953, University of Melbourne; FTCL, Organ; BMus, 1964, MMus, 1971, University of Melbourne. Appointments: Teacher, Yallourn High School, 1954-57, University High School, Melbourne, 1955-61; Lecturer, Music, Secondary Teachers College, Melbourne, 1962-65; Lecturer, Senior Lecturer, 1966-, Deputy Dean, Deputy Head, 1978-93, Faculty of Music, University of Melbourne; Retired, 1993. Publications: Music in Australian Schools; International Directory of Music Education; International Directory of Music and Music Education Institutions. Contributions to: Australian Journal of Music Education; International Journal of Music Education. Honours: Ormond Exhibition, University of Melbourne, 1958; Composition Prize, Faculty of Music, University of Melbourne, 1960. Memberships: Australian Society of Music Education; International Society of Music Education; Incorporated Society of Musicians; International Kodály Society; Music Educators National Conference. Hobbies: Gardening; Walking. Address: 10 Chaucer Crescent, Canterbury, Victoria 3126, Australia.

BARTLETT Clifford (Alfred James), b. 15 Aug 1939, London, England. Practical Musicologist; Music Writer. m. Elaine King, 16 Aug 1975, 1 son, 1 daughter. Education: Dulwich College; Magdalene College, Cambridge University. Career: Deputy Music Librarian, BBC, 1970-82; Keyboard Player for Ars Nova, 1969-75; Freelance Writer and Publisher, 1983-; Director, Early Music Centre Festival, 1987-88. Publications: Monteverdi; Orfeo; Vespers; Ulisse and Poppea; Blow's Venus and Adonis; Purcell's Dido and Aeneas; Handel's Alcina, Partenope, Scipione, La Resurrezione and Coronation Anthems; Arne's Artaxerxes. Contributions to: Monthly surveys in Early Music News, 1977-; Editor, Brio, 1974-85; Contributor of numerous programme notes for major record companies & festivals. Memberships: Chairman, Eastern Early Music Forum; Council of Early Music Centre; Committee, Early Music Network. Address: Redcroft, Banks End, Wyton, Huntingdon, Cambridgeshire, PE17 2AA, England.

BARTLETT Ian James, b. 20 Sept 1934, London, England. Lecturer. m. Anne Verne Lucas, 3 Aug 1960, 1 son, 2 daughters. Education: BA, 1956, MA, 1960, Brasenose College, Oxford; ARCM, 1957, LRAM, 1961, Royal Academy of Music; PGCE, Institute of Education, University of London, 1957-58; MMus, 1974, King's College, University of London. Career: Director of Music, Bilborough Grammar School, Nottingham, 1958-62; Lecturer in Music, Bretton Hall College of Education, Yorkshire, 1962-65; Director of Music, North Oxon Junior Music School, 1966-70; Director of Music, Banbury School, 1965-70; Senior Lecturer in Music, Goldsmiths College, University of London, 1970-77; Principal Lecturer, 1977-89, Acting Head of Music, 1980-83; Dean of Faculty of Music, University of London, 1982-86; Freelance Lecturer, Writer, Musician, Piano Teacher and Accompanist 1989-; Visiting Lecturer, Goldsmiths College, 1989; Visiting Lecturer, Trinity College of Music, 1995-. Compositios: Arrangements. Recordings: BBC, Editor of Works by William Boyce. Publications: Editor, William Boyce's Solomon, Musica Britannica, 1996. Contributions to: Music Teacher; The Musical Times; Music and Letters; RMA Research Chronicle; New Grove. Memberships: Royal Musical Association; Royal Society of Musicians; Society for Research in Psychology of Music and Music Education; Curwen Institute. Hobbies: Athletics; Theatre. Address: 463 Footscray Road, New Eltham, London SE9 3UH, England.

BARTO Tzimon, b. 2 Jan 1963, Eusto, Florida, USA. Conductor; Composer; Musician (Pianist). Education: Studied piano with Adele Markus, studied conducting and repetiteur for opera, Juillard School, New York, USA. Debut: Spoleto Festival of Two Worlds, Italy, 1985. Career: Conducted opera by Gian Carlo Menotti, The Saint of Bleecker Street, for 75th birthday celebration; Series of concerts in Europe and USA; Concerts at Vienna Musikverein, at the invitation of von Karajan, and Salzburg Music Festival; Lincoln Centre, New York, as soloist with Houston Symphony Orchestra; Varied repertoire of classical and jazz improvisational pieces. Recordings: Ravel's Concerto in G Major; Prokofiev's 3rd Concerto; Gershwin's Rhapsody in Blue; Rachmaninoff's 3rd Piano Concerto; Bartók's 2nd Piano Concerto. Honours: Best Conductor of his Class, Tanglewood Institute, 1980; Winner, Gina Bachauer Memnorial Competition, 1982-83. Current Management: Astrid Schoerke. Address: c/o Monckebergallee 41, 30453 Hannover, Germany.

BARTOLETTI Bruno, b. 10 June 1926, Sesto Fiorentino, Italy. Conductor. m. Rosanna Bartoletti, 2 children. Education: Studied flute at Cherubini Conservatory, Florence; Received training in piano & composition. Debut: Conducting, Dec 1953, with Rigoletto; Symphonic debut, Maggio Musicale Fiorentino, 1954, resident conductor, 1957-64; US Debut, Lyric Opera of Chicago, 1956. Career: Played flute in orchestra of the Teatro Comunale, Florence; Assistant conductor from 1949, working with Rodzinski, Mitropoulos, Gui and Serafin; Led the premieres of Rocca's Antiche iscrizioni, 1955 and Malipiero's Il figluol prodigo and Venere prigioniera, 1957 at Florence; Mortari's La scuola delle mogli, 1959, at La Scala and Ginastera's Don Rodrigo at the Teatro Colon Buenos Aires, 1964; Italian premieres of Egk's Der Revisor and The Nose by Shostakovich; Conducted Italian opera at The Royal Opera, Copenhagen, 1957-60; Co-artistic director, 1975- Artistic Director, Rome Opera, 1965-69; Artistic adviser 1986-87; Artistic Director, Teatro Comunale Florence, 1987-92, conducted Madama Butterfly and I Puritani in Florence, 1988-89; Lyric Opera, Chicago 1988-89 with La Traviata and Tancredi; Guest conductor with many opera houses in Europe, USA and South America; Grand Théâtre Geneva, 1991, Peter Grimes; Conducted I Quattro Rusteghi at Geneva, 1992; Norma at Genoa, 1994; Conducted Simon Boccanegra at Rome, 1996. Recordings: Il Barbiere di Siviglia; Vivaldi's Gloria and Credo, Deutsche Grammophon; Manon Lescaut; Un Ballo in Maschera. Address: c/o Chicago Lyric Opera, 20 North Wacker Drive, Chicago, IL 60606, USA.

BARTOLI Cecilia, b. 4 June 1966, Rome, Italy. Singer (Mezzo-Soprano). Education: Studied at the Accademia di Santa Cecilia, Rome. Debut: Verona, 1987. Career: Sang in concert at Rome; Florence; Moderna; Bologna; Appearances at the Staatsoper Berlin; Nantes; Warsaw, 1987; Sang Handel arias in the pasticcio Donna abandonata at Nancy, 1987; Best known as Rossini's Rosina which she sung at Cologne, Catania and Schwetzingen, 1988; Zurich Opera, 1989, as Rosina and Cherubino; Pesaro Festival, 1988, in La Scala di Seta; Teatro San Carlo Naples, 1990, as Giannetta in Le Cantatrice villane, by Fioravanti; Also sings Mozart's Dorabella; Song recital at Wigmore Hall, London, 1989; Featured artist, South Bank Show, London Weekend Television, 1992; Sang Cheubino at Orchestra Hall, Chicago, 1992; Sang Haydn's Euridice at the 1994 Vienna Festival; Engaged as Elena in La Donna del Lago, Zurich, 1995; Met debut as Despina, 1996. Recordings: Il Barbiere di Siviglia, La Cenerentola and arias by Rossini, conducted by Giuseppe Patanè; Mozart's Cherubino, Dorabella and Cecilio in Lucio Silla; Concepcion in L'Heure espagnole, Haydn's Orfeo ed Euridice (Decca), 1997. Address: c/o Decca (UK), 22 St Peters Square, London W6 9NW, England.

BARTOLINI Lando, b. 11 Apr 1937, Casale di Prato, Florence, Italy. Opera Singer (Tenor). m. Deanna Mungai, 26 Jan 1966, 2 daughters. Education: 5-year scholarship to Academy of Vocal Arts, Philadelphia, USA, 1968-73; Vocal instruction with Nicola Moscona; Graduated, 1973. Debut: In Iris of Mascagni at the Gran Liceo of Barcelona, Oct 1973. Career: American debut in Cavalleria Rusticana, New York City Opera, 1976; Appeared at special events including: Concert with Philadelphia Orchestra; New Production of Ernani with Chicago Lyric; Manon Lescaut with Vienna State Opera in Tokyo; Simon Boccanegra at Festival d'Orange; New Production of Turandot at Munich State Opera; Turandot with La Scala, Milan; In Seoul during Olympic Games; Has sung in many other major venues around the world including La Scala, Arena di Verona, Paris Opéra, Metropolitan Opera, Covent Garden, Vienna, Budapest, Buenos Aires, Santiago del Chile, South Africa, Canada, Lisbon, Boston and Cleveland with Metropolitan Opera; Wide repertoire includes: Aida, Tosca, La Boheme, Il Trovatore, Don Carlo, Macbeth, Forza del Destino, Il Tabarro, Mephistopheles and Rigoletto; Sang Manrico in Il Trovatore at the Orange Festival, 1992; Radames for Opera Pacific, 1994; Sang Des Grieux in Manon Lescaut at Torre del Lago, 1996. Recordings: I Cavalieri Di Ekebu, with director Gianandrea Gavazzeni; Hungaroton, 1992; Respighi's La Semirama, 1st recording; Hungaroton, 1991 Solo Tenor Arias; Turandot Last Duet Alfano original, first time on record, 1990. Publications: La Follia Di New York, 1989; Orpheus Berlin, 1990; Das Opern Glas Germany, 1990; Opera News New York, 1991-93. Hobbies: Pool; Golf; Darts. Current Management: ICM Artists, New York. Address: Via Bargo 12, 50047 Casale di Prato, Firenze, Italy.

BÄRTSCHI Werner, b. 1 Jan 1950, Zürich, Switzerland. Musician; Pianist; Composer. Education: Volksschule and Gymnasium Zürich; Studied as pianist, composer and conductor in Zürich and Basel. Career: Concerts as pianist in 35 countries in 5 continents; TV appearances in various countries; Film Actor in Justiz, by Geissendörfer; Initiation and realisation of the Satie-Saison, 1980-81, and the Ives-Zyklus, 1985-86, both in Zürich; President of Music Committee of City of Zürich, 1990-92; Artistic Advisor of 1991 June Festival in Zürich; Artistic Director of various concert series in Switzerland; Performances of his compositions in over 30 countries, several broadcasts and recordings. Compositions include: Over 20 works: Orchestral music, chamber music, vocal music, piano music; several transcriptions: Rossini, Fauré, Schoeck, Schnebel. Recordings: Over 30 recordings including music of over 40 composers; 10 films for Swiss TV. Publications: Die unvermeidliche Musik des John Cage, 1969; Musik der Entfremdung-entfremdete Musik, 1981-82; Ratio und Intuition in der Musik, Kunst und Wissenschaft, 1984; Italian translation, 1989, Zu meinem Klavierstück in Trauer und Prunk, 1989; Leistung und Plausch im Musikuntericht, 1989; German editions of selected writings by Erik Satie, 1980 and Charles Ives, 1985; Music Editions of works by Zdenek Fibich, 1988, and Wladimir Vogel, 1989. Honour: Grand Prize, Academie du disque française, 1983. Memberships include: Schweizerischer Tonkünstlerverein; Schweizerischer Musikpädagogischer Verband; Komponistensekretariat Zürich. Hobby: Mountain Climbing. Address: Zolliker Strasse 97, CH-8702 Zollikon, Switzerland.

BARTZ Ingrid, b. 1960, Aachen, Germany. Singer (Mezzo-soprano). Education: Studied in Cologne and Berne with Juliette Bise-Delnon, Edith Mathis and Brigitte Fassbaender. Career: Sang at Aachen Opera, from 1982, including Britten's

Hermia; Opera-studio at Düsseldorf Opera, with Hänsel, 1986-87; Karlsruhe Opera, as Cherubino, Octavian, the Composer in Ariadne auf Naxos, Suzuki, Flora, Rosina, Mignon and Sesto in Handel's Giulio Cesare, from 1988; Guest appearances include major roles at Dusseldorf, Liège, Luxembourg, Strasbourg, Zürich, Lucerne, Frankfurt, Mannheim, Essen; Concert engagements with most German radio and TV stations and abroad; Bonn Opera, including several premieres and debuts: Nicklausse, Zerlina, Orlofsky, Fenena, from 1993. Recordings include: Lieder by Mahler (Rückert and Wunderhorn Lieder), Brahms (Zigeunerlieder) and Wagner (Wesendoncklieder). Address: c/o NWB Apollon & Hermes, Künstleragentur Management Production, Im Flögerhof 12, D-53819 Neunkirchen-Wolperath, Germany.

BARRYLLI Walter, b. 16 June 1921, Vienna, Austria. Violinist. Education: Vienna Hochschule; Violin study with F von Reuter, Munich. Debut: Munich, 1936. Career: Concert tours throughout Europe and overseas; Member, Vienna State Opera Orchestra and Vienna Philharmonic, 1938-; Formerly, leader of both orchestras; Leader Barylli Quartet, 1945-; Professor of Violin, Vienna Conservatory, 1969. Honours include: Kreisler Prize (twice won). Address: Rennweg 4-14, A-1030 Vienna, Austria.

BARZUN Jacques, b. 30 Nov 1907, Creteil, Seine, France. Historian; Educator. m. (1) Mariana Lowell, 1936 (dec 1979), 2 sons, 1 daughter, (2) Marguerite Dsvenport, 1980. Education: AB, 1927, PhD, 1932, Columbia University, New York. Career includes: Dean of Faculties and Provost, 1958-67, Seth Low Professor of History, 1960-67, Columbia University, New York City, USA. Publications include: Darwin, Marx, Wagner: Critique of a Heritage, 1941, 2nd edition revised, 1958; Berlioz and the Romantic Century, 1950, 3rd edition revised, 1969; The Use and Abuse of Art, 1974; The Culture We Deserve, 1989; Begin Here, 1992; Publications include: Articles to various journals. Honours: Legion d'Honneur, France; Lecturer, Glimmerglass Opera, New York, 1992-. Memberships: American Philosophical Association; American Academy of Arts and Letters, President 1972-75, 1977-78; Phi Beta Kappa; Extraordinary Fellow, Churchill College, Cambridge; Fellow, Royal Society of Arts; Royal Society of Literature. Address: 18 Wolfeton Way, San Antonio, TX 78218, USA.

BASELT Franz (Bernhard), b. 13 Sept 1934, Halle, Saale, Germany. Professor of Musicology. m. Elfried Kalisch, 3 Oct 1962, 1 son, 1 daughter. Education: Abitur, 1953; Hochschule für Musik Halle; Martin-Luther-Universität Halle, Dipl phil, 1958; Dr Phil, 1963; Dr sc phil, 1975. Career: Freeland, 1958-59; Assistant Professor, 1959-76; Professor of Musicology, 1977-82; Full Professor of Musicology, 1983; Chief Editor, Hallische Handel-Ausgabe, 1989; University Halle-Wittenburg; President, Georg-Friedrich-Handel-Gesellschaft, 1991; Editor, Handel-Jahrbuch, 1991. Publications: Handel-Handbuch vol I-III, 1978-86; G F Handel, Leipzig, 1988; Editions of operas by G Ph Telemann, Ch W Gluck, G F Handel, 1967, 1969, 1970, 1988; Editions of Handel's Oreste, Kassel 1991; Telemann's Don Quixote, Madison, 1991. Contributions to: Handel-Jahrbuch; Musical Times; Veroff der Intern; Handel-Akademie Karlsruhe; Music & Letters. Address: Reilstrasse 83, D-04020, Halle Saale, Germany.

BASHMET Yuri, b. 24 Jan 1953, Rostov, USSR. Concert Violist. Education: Moscow Conservatoire, from 1971 with Vadim Borvisovky and Feodor Druzhinin. Debut: UK, Tour Oct 1988 Chamber music recitals. Career: Appearances with Sviatoslav Richter, Oleg Kagan, Natalia Gutman, Borodin Quartet, Wigmore Hall, Jan 1989; London Promenade Concert, 1989. Career: 1976, won 1st prize in Munich International Viola Competition; Appearances with the Vienna Symphony; Bavarian Radio; Dresden Staatskapelle Orchestras; Conductors include Abbado, Kubelik, Colin Davis, Rozhdestvensky and Mariss Yansons; In 1986 formed chamber orchestra Moscow Soloists; Tours to Germany, Italy and France; Many performances of contemporary music, including the premiere of the Schnittke Concerto with the Concertgebouw Orchestra, 1986; Repeated the work with the BBC Philharmonic at the 1987 Lichfield Festival; Made a Channel 4 TV programme, with the London Sinfonietta and Esa-Pekka Salonen; Bartók's Concerto at the Barbican Hall, 1989; Four concerts at Sydney Opera House, 1990, at the 1991 Promenade Concerts; Played Bartók's Concerto and conducted Moscow Coloists, Barbican Hall, 1991; Subject of profile LWT's South Bank Show, 1990; Bartók Concerto at the 1993 Prom Concerts, London and premiered the concerto by Rouders, 1995; World premiere of Sofia Gubaidulina's Viola Concerto, Chicago, 1997; Followed by European premiere, BBC Prom concert, 1997. Address: c/o Van Walsum Management Ltd, 4 Addison Bridge Place, London W14 8XP, England.

BASINSKAS Justinas, b. 22 Jan 1923, Mazoji Trakiske, Lithuania. Composer. m. Vyliute Sofija-Jurate Igno, 12 July 1976, 1 son, 2 daughters. Education: Specialised Music School, Kaunas, 1945-50; Lithuanian State Conservatory, Vilnius, 1955-55. Compositions: The Accursed Monks, ballet, 1982; 8 Symphonies including No 4: The Bells, 1973; Being, 1977; The Lamentations, 1979; In the Whirlpools, 1983 and No 8 The Call of the Earth, 1986; Chamber Symphony, 1984; The Call of the Earth, 1986; Cantatas: A Tale About Soldier's Bread, 1961; Requiem, 1969; Morning, 1974; Mother's Hands, 1978; Chamber works: Piano Sonata, 1979; Sonata for Violin and Piano, 1979; Sonata for Piano, 4-hands, 1979; String Quartet, 1980; Sonata for Solo Viola, 1983; Vocal cycles for voice and piano: The Animals in Winter, 1968; The Autumn, 1969; The Hour of the Eagle-Owl, 1985; Choruses; Solo songs. Recordings: Discs of: The Bells; Being; The Lamentations; Sonata for Violin and Piano. Honours: National Prize, Lithuanian SSR, 1983; Received title of Merited Cultural Worker of the Lithuanian SSR, 1983. Membership: Lithuanian Composers' Union. Hobby: Enjoying nature. Address: Traidenio Street 34-6, 2004 Vilnius, Lithuania.

BASSETT Leslie (Raymond), b. 22 Jan 1923, Hanford, California, USA. Composer. m. Anita Denniston, 21 Aug 1949, 2 sons, 1 daughter. Education: BA, Fresno State College, Now California State University, Fresno, 1947; MMus, Composition, 1949; AMusD, Composition, 1956, University of Michigan, 1949; Fulbright Fellow, Ecole Normale de Musique, Paris, 1950-51; Pupil of Ross Le Finney, Nadia Boulanger, Arthur Honegger, Roberto Gerhard. Career: Henry Russel Lecturer, University of Michigan, 1984; Albert A Stanley Distinguished University Professor of Music Emeritus. Compositions: Variations for Orchestra; Echoes from an Invisible World, orchestra; Concerto for Orchestra, 1991; From a Source Evolving, orchestra; Concerto Lirico, trombone and orchestra; Fantasy for Clarinet and Wind Ensemble; Sounds, Shapes and Symbols, band; Colors and Contours, band; Sextet for Piano and Strings; Fourth String Quartet, 1978; Arias for Clarinet and Piano; Dialogues for Oboe and Piano; Narratives for Guitar Quartet. Honours: Pulitzer Prize for Variations for orchestra, 1966; Rome Prize, American Academy in Rome, 1961-63; Koussevitsky Foundation Commissions, 1971, 1990; Guggenheim Fellow, 1973, 1980; Naumberg Recording Award, 1974; Distinguished Artist Award, State of Michigan, 1981. Memberships: American Academy of Arts and Letters. Address: 1618 Harbal Drive, Ann Arbor, MI 48105, USA.

BASTIAN Hanns, b. 30 Jan 1928, Pforzheim, Germany. Singer (Tenor). Education: Studied in Karlsruhe with Karl Hartlieb and in Coburg and Pforzheim. Career: Sang first in Pforzheim, 1946-53, then at Coburg; Engaged at Basel Opera, 1955-80, notably in premiere of Titus Feuerfuchs by Sutermeister, 1966, and in buffo and character roles; Guest appearances in Zurich, Berne, Darmstadt and Bergenz. Other roles included Florestan, Mozart's Pedrillo and Monostatos, David in Die Meistersinger, and many parts in operetta. Address: c/o Theater Basel, Theaterstrasse 7, CH-4010 Basel, Switzerland.

BASTO Carla, b. 1956, Lourenco Marques, Mozambique. Singer (Soprano). Education: Studied at the Lisbon Conservatory and in Milan. Debut: Bogota (Colombia), 1982, as Lucia di Lammermoor. Career: Sang widely in South America and appeared at La Scala, Milan, from 1982, notably as Anita Garibaldi in the premiere of Addio Garibaldi by Arrigo; Florence, 1987, as Anna Bolena, Lucca, 1985, as Dejanice in the opera by Catalani; Turin from 1987, as Penelope in Ulisse, Massenet's Thais and Pamina; Also admired as Violetta. Recordings include: Catalani's Dejanice (Bongiovanni), Address: c/o Teatro Regio di Torino, Piazza Castello 215, 10124 Turin, Italy.

BATE Jennifer (Lucy), b. 11 Nov 1944, London, England. Musician (Organist). Education: BA Honours in Music, Bristol University; Early Music with Carl Dolmetsch; Composition with Eric Thiman and Arthur Pritchard; LRAM; ARCM; FRCO. Career: Shaw Librarian, LSE, 1966-69; Full-time concert career, 1969-; Organizer of several teaching programmes; Designed portable pipe organ with N P Mander Ltd, 1984, and a prototype computer organ, 1987. Compositions: Toccata on a Theme of Martin Shaw; Introduction and Variations on an old French carol; 4 Reflections for Organ; Homage to 1685, 4 studies; Lament; An English Canon; Variations on a Gregorian Theme. Recordings include: Complete Works of Messiaen in 7 volumes; Complete Works of Franck in 3 volumes; An English Choice; Virtuoso French Organ Music; Panufnik: Metasinfonia; Vivaldi Double and Triple Concertos; Jennifer Bate and Friends; Jennifer Plays Vierne. Contributions include: Grove's Dictionary of Music and Musicians; Organist's Review. Honours: F J Read Prize, Royal College of Organists, 1972; Grand Prix du Disque for World Première Recording of Livre du Saint Sacrement; Personality of Year, France, 1989; One of the Women of the Year, 1990, 1991, 1993, 1994, 1995, 1997. Memberships include: Incorporated Society of Music; British Music Society; Royal Philharmonic Society. Hobbies: Reading; Gardening; Cooking; Philately. Current Management: Bureau de Concerts Maurice Werner. Address: 35 Collingwood Avenue, Muswell Hill, London N10 3EH, England.

BATIZ Enrique, b. 4 May 1942, Mexico City, Mexico. Pianist; Conductor. m. 1965, divorced 1982, 1 son, 1 daughter. Education: Bachelor's Degree, Mexico University Centre, 1959; Southern Methodist University, Dallas, USA, 1960-62; Juilliard School of Music, New York, studied piano with Adele Marcus; Conducting with Jorge Mester, 1963-66; Postgraduate work, Warsaw Conservatory. Debut: Mexico City, 1969. Career includes: Founder-Conductor, Orquesta Sinfonica del Estado de Mexico, 1971-73, 1990-; Appointed Guest Conductor, Royal Philharmonic Orchestra, London, England, 1984-; Guest COnductor with 150 orchestras woorldwide; Conductor, Royal Philharmonic Orchestra tour in Mexico, 1988. Composition: Es Tiempo de Paz, symphonic poem, 1976. Recordings include: Over 115 recordings including 41 with the Royal Philharmonic, 29 with the State of Mexico Symphony Orchestra and 19 with the Mexico City Philharmonic orchestra. Contributions to: Joaquin Rodrigo, His Life, in Epoca, 1993. Memberships: IAPA; Club de Clubes; Club Cambridge, Mexico City. Current Management: Mrs C A Ross, 6 Petersfield Crescent, Coulsdon, Surrey CR5 2JQ, England. Address: Plaza Fray Andres de Castro, Edificio "C", Primer Piso, Toluca, Estado de Mexico CP 5000.

BATJER Margaret, b. 17 Feb 1959, San Angelo, TX, USA. Violinist. m. Joel McNeely, 14 Apr 1985. Education: Interlochen Academy; Studied with Ivan Galamian & David Cerone at Curtis Institute of Music. Debut: Solo appearance in Violin Concerto by Menotti with Chicago Symphony, aged 15; Appeared as Soloist with Philadelphia Orchestra at Academy of Music, with Dallas and Seattle Symphonies in Mendelssohn's Concerto at the St Louis Symphony; Chamber Orchestra of Europe; Prague Chamber Orchestra; Berlin Symphony Orchestra; New York String Orchestra at Carnegie Hall; Radio Telefis Dublin, with Prokofiev's 2nd Concerto; Concerts at the Marlboro Music Festival, Vermont and US tour with Music of Marlboro Ensemble; Tour of Germany, 1984. Recordings: Bach Concerto for Two Violins with Salvatore Accardo and the Chamber Orchestra of Europe; Mozart Concertone with Salvatore Accardo and the Prague Chamber Orchestra; Verdi and Borodin String Quartets, Mozart Complete Viola Quintets. Honours: Winner, G B Dealey Competition, Dallas, 1979. Current Management: Del Rosenfield Associates, 714 Ladd Road, Bronx, NY 10471, USA. Address: 5971 Lubao Ave, Woodland Hills, CA 91367, USA.

BATTEL Giovanni (Umberto), b. 11 Dec 1956, Portoguaro, Venice, Italy. Pianist. m. Mariangela Zamper, 15 June 1985. Education: Liceo in Classical Studies, 1975; Conservatory Tartini, Trieste, 1977; National Music Academy St Cecilia, Rome, 1984. Career: S Remo Theatre, 1980; RAI Radio 3, 1981; Stresa Festival, 1981; With symphony orchestra, Auditorium RAI Rome, 1982; RAI 1, 1982, 1983, 1984; Alghero Festival, 1983; Mater Festival, 1983; Trondheim Symphony Orchestra, 1983; With Scarlatti Orchestra, Auditorium RAI Naples, 1983; Trieste Theatre, 1985; Auditorium Caglian, 1985; Musik Halle Hamburg, 1986; Lubeck, Bonn, 1986; Athens, Salonika, Greece, 1986; San Francisco, Los Angeles, USA; Paris, Nantes, Lille, France, 1987; Todi Festival, 1988; London, 1988. Recordings: Miroirs and Valses Nobles et Sentimentales, Ravel; Busoni's Piano Concerto. Honours: 1st Prize National competitions: La Spezia, 1975; Trieste, 1978; Taranto, 1979; Albenga, 1979; International competition: 2nd prize, Vercelli, 1978; 2nd prize, Seregno, 1979; 4th prize, Bolzano, 1980; 1st prize, Enna, 1982. Hobbies: Photography. Address: via Valle 23, 30026 Portogruaro, Venice, Italy.

BATTLE Kathleen (Deanna), b. 13 Aug 1948, Portsmouth, Ohio, USA. Soprano. Education: BMus, 1970; MMus 1971, University of Cincinnati-College Conservatory of Music; Studied with Franklin Bens and Italo Tajo. Debut: Professional debut, soloist, Brahms Requiem, Spoleto Festival, 1972. Career: Operatic debut as Rosina, Michigan Opera Theatre, Detroit, 1975; Metropolitan Opera, NY, 1978-1994; Appearances with many other major opera houses of the world, including Covent Garden, debut 1985 as Zerbinetta in Ariadne auf Naxos; Soloist with leading orchestras; Recitalist various music centres; Operatic roles include Susanna, Cleopatra, Zerbinetta, Sophie, Adina, Zerlina, Blonde, Nannetta and Despina; Sang Norina in Don Pasquale at Covent Garden, London, 1990; Contract at NY Met terminated, 1994. Recordings: For Deutsche Grammophon, Angel-EMI, Decca-London, Musicmasters, RCA and Telarc; In Mozart's Requiem, Cosí fan tutte, Coronation Mass, Don Giovanni and Die Zauberflöte; L'Italiana in Algeri; Ein Deutsches Requiem; Mahler 4th Symphony; Il Barbiere di Siviglia, Abbado; Handel Arias, Marriner; Semele; Videos of Il Barbiere di Siviglia and Die Zauberflöte from the Metropolitan, DGG. Address: c/o Columbia Artists Managements Inc, 165 West 57th Street, NY 10019, USA.

BATURIN Sergei, b. 1952, Moscow, Russia. Violinist. Education: Studied at Moscow Conservatoire with Fjodor Druzhinin. Career: Co-founded Amistad Quartet, 1973, changed named to Tchaikovsky Quartet in 1994; Many concerts in former Soviet Union and Russia, with repertoire including works by Haydn, Mozart, Beethoven, Schubert, Brahms, Tchaikovsky, Borodin, Prokofiev, Shostakovich, Bartók, Bucci, Golovin and Tikhomirov; recent concert tours to Mexico, Italy and Germany. Recordings: Recitals for US-Russian company Arts and Electronics; By Tchaikovsky Quartet for Great Hall CD Company.

Honours include: With Amistad Quartet: Prizewinner at Bela Bartók Festival, 1976 and Bucchi Competition, Rome, 1990; Series in commemoration of Tchaikovsky in Moscow. Current Management: Sonata, Glasgow, Scotland. Address: 11 North Park Street, Glasgow G20 7AA, Scotland.

BAUDO Serge, b. 16 July 1927, Marseille, France. Conductor. m. Madelein Reties, 16 June 1947, 1 son, 1 daughter. Education: Student, Conservatory of Paris. Career: Director, Radio Nice, France, 1957-59; Conductor, Paris Orchestra, 1968-70; Music Director, Opéra de Lyon, 1969-71; Music Director, Orchestra of Lyon, 1971-; Conductor of many international Orchestras including Tonhalle Orchestra, Zurich, Orchestre de la Suisse Romande, Berlin Philharmonic, Royal Philharmonic, London Philharmonic, NHR Orchestra, Leningrad Philharmonic, Stockholm Philharmonic, La Scala, Metropolitan Opera (debut 1970 Les Contes d'Hoffmann), Dallas Orchestra and Deutsche Oper, Berlin; Has conducted premieres of Messiaen's Et exspecto at Chartres 1965 and La Transfiguration at Lisbon, 1969; Milhaud's La Mêre Coupable, Geneva, 1966; Dutilleux's Cello Concerto, Aix, 1970; Fastes de l'imaginaire by Nigg, 1974; Ohana's Le Livre des Prodiges, 1979; Daniel-Leseur's Dialogues dans le nuit, 1988; Founder, Berloiz Festival, Lyon, 1979; Conducted Roméo et Juliette at Zurich, 1990; Samson et Dalila ar Zurich, 1996. Honours: Decorated, Chevalier Ordre National du Merité; Officer des Arts et des Lettres; Recipient, Grand Prix due Disque, 1976; Chevalier de la Legion D'Honneur Disque D'or. Address: Orchestre National de Lyon Hotel de Ville, 69000 Lyon, France.

BAUER Hartmut, b. 1939, Kassel, Germany. Singer (Bass). Education: Studied at the Frankfurt Musikhochschule. Career: Sang at Augsburg Opera, 1965-68, Coburg, 1968-70, Wuppertal from 1970-90, notably as Creon in the 1972 German premiere of Milhaud's Médée; Bayreuth Festival, 1973-75, as Fafner and Hans Schwarz; Other appearances as Ariodeno in Cavalli's L'Ormindo, Mozart's Bartolo and Commendatore, Ramphis (Aida), Colline (La Bohème), Pimen, Schigolch (Lulu) and Cornelius' Abu Hassan; Guest at Cologne, Frankfurt, Barcelona and Hanover; Sang in the premiere of V D Kirchner's Erinys, Wuppertal, 1990; Gurnemanz in Parsifal, 1994. Address: c/o Wuppertaler Buhnen, Opernhaus, Spinnstrasse 4, W-5600 Wuppertal 2, Germany.

BAULD Alison (Margaret), b. 7 May 1944, Sydney, New South Wales, Australia. Composer. m. Nicholas Evans, 4 Apr 1978, 1 son, 1 daughter. Education: Diploma, National Institute of Dramatic Art, Sydney; BMus, Sydney University; Composition Studies with Elisabeth Lutyens and Hans Keller; DPhil, York University, 1974; Studied Piano with Sverjensky, New South Wales Conservatorium. Career: Professional Actress, Shakespeare and Australian Television; Finalist, Radcliffe Competition, 1973; Musical Director, Laban Cente for Dance, Goldsmiths' College, University of London, 1975-78; Composer-in-Residence, New South Wales Conservatory, Sydney, 1978; Currently teaches part-time for University of Delaware, Hollins College and Pepperdine University, London; Works performed and broadcast, London, also Aldeburgh, York and Edinburgh Festivals, several European countries, Australia. Compositions include: On the Afternoon of the Pigsty for speaker and ensemble, 1971; Humpty Dumpty for tenor, flute and guitar, 1972; In a Dead Brown Land, music theatre, 1972; Mad Moll for solo soprano, 1973; Dear Emily, for soprano and harp, 1973; One Pearl for soprano and string quartet, 1973; Concert for piano and tape, 1974; Exiles, music theatre, 1974; Van Diemen's Land for choir, 1976; One Pearl II for soprano, flute and strings, 1976; I Loved Miss Watson for soprano, piano and tape, 1977; Banquo's Buried for soprano and piano, 1982; Richard III for voice and string quartet, 1985; Monody for solo flute, 1985; Copy Cats for violin and piano, 1985; Once Upon a Time, music theatre, 1986; Nell, Ballad opera, 1988; My Own Island for clarinet and piano, 1989; Farewell Already for string quartet, 1993; Shakespeare Songs. Recordings include: Banquo's Buried, CD; CD, Farewell Already, string quartet and soprano. Publications: Play Your Way, piano and composition tutor, 1993; Shakespeare Songs for soprano and piano. Honours: Gold Medal, Piano, New South Wales, 1959; Paris Rostrum, composition, 1973. Memberships: Association of Professional Composers; Musician's Union. Hobbies: Has written book on Mozart's sister. Address: 7 Suffold Road, Barnes, London SW13, England.

BAUMANN Hermann, b. 1 Aug 1934, Hamburg, Germany. Horn Player. Education: Studied at the Hamburg Musikhochschule. Career: First horn with the Stuttgart Radio Symphony from 1961, Professor at the Folkswanghochschule, Essen, from 1967; Many appearances throughout Europe as soloist, notably in the concertos of Mozart; Performances of baroque music with Nicholas Harnoncourt and Gustav Leonhardt. Address: c/o Hochschule für Musik Ruhr, Abtei 43, 4300 Essen 16, Germany.

BAUMEL Herbert, b. 30 Sept 1919, New York, New York, USA. Violinist; Conductor; Composer. m. (1) Rachael Bail, 17 Oct 1949, div Nov 1970, 1 son, 2 daughters, 1 dec, (2) Joan Patricia French, 11 July 1971. Education: Violin study with Pasquale Pagliucca, Louis Persinger, Paul Stassevich, Vlado Kolitsch, Lea Luboshutz, Nathan Milstein; Mannes School of Music, 1932-34; Diploma, Curtis Institute of Music, 1942; Santa Cecilia, Accademia Chigiana, Rome and Siena, 1954-56. Career: Violinist, Concertmaster, Conductor, orchestras, chamber groups, Broadway shows, jazz ensembles, ballets, operas, worldwide, 1939-; Violin Soloist: Samuel Barber Violin Concerto, Curtis Symphony, Philadelphia Orchestra, 1939-40; New York City Ballet, Fort Wayne Philharmonic, WQXR Orchestra, Radio Italiana, Radio Nacional Venezuela, 1945-; 1st Violin, Philadelphia Orchestra, 1942-45; Member, Baumel-Booth Duo, 1968-; Baumel-Booth-Smith Trio, 1969-72; Violinist and Storyteller, 1969-; Concertmaster: Philadelphia, New York City and San Carlo Operas, Orquesta Sinfonica Venezuela, Broadway musicals including Fiorello, 1959, She Loves Me, 1963, Fiddler on the Roof, 1964, A Little Night Music, 1973; Presidential Gala Orchestra, Washington DC and New York, 1961-65; Conductor: Fort Wayne Civic and Corvallis Symphonies, Chamber Music Associates Orchestra, Alessandro Scarlatti Orchestra (Naples), Oregon State University Chamber Players, 1945-. Hobbies: Photography; Tennis; Gardening; Reading; Chess. Address: Baumel Associates, 86 Rosedale Road, Yonkers, NY 10710, USA.

BAUMGARTNER Rudolf, b. 14 Sept 1917, Zurich, Switzerland. Violinist; Conductor; Administrator. Education: University of Zurich; Zurich Conservatory; Violin studies with Stefi Geyer, Carl Flesch and Wolfgang Schneiderhan. Career: Appearances as a violin soloist and in chamber music ensembles; Co-Founder with Wolfgang Schneiderhan of Lucerne Festival Strings, 1956; Subsequently served as its director; Took it on numerous tours abroad; Several arrangements, including Bach's Musical Offering & Art of Fugue; Appointed Director, Lucerne Conservatory, 1960 and Lucerne Festival, 1968; Concerts at the 1995 Festival. Recordings: For Denon, Deutsche Grammophon, Eurodisc, Finlandia, RCA; Notably music by Bach & Mozart; Bach Brandenburg Concertos, Ein musikalisches Opfer, Harpsichord & Violin Concertos; The Four Seasons by Vivaldi with Wolfgang Schneiderhan; Mozart Divertimenti; Piano Concertos with Margit Weber, Clara Haskil and Horsowski; Flute Concertos with Hans-Martin Linde and James Galway; Horn Concertos; Telemann Viola Concerto; Deutsche Grammophon, Archiv. Address: c/o Lucerne Conservatory of Music, Lucerne, Switzerland.

BAVERSTAM Asa, b. 1958, Sweden. Singer (Soprano). Education: Studied at the Conservatory of Jutland in Aarhus, Denmark and at the Royal Opera Academy, Copenhagen. Debut: Royal Opera in Copenhagen, 1990, as Despina. Career: Has performed Susanna and Sophie in Der Rosenkavalier with the Opera Academy; Sang in the premiere of Life is a Bed of Roses by Arne Melinas, 1989; Theater Basel from 1990 as Xenia in Boris Godunov, Adina; Zerlina (1992); Has sung in masses and oratorios by Bach, Haydn, Handel, Mozart and Schubert in Denmark and Sweden; Concerts with the baroque orchestra La Stravaganza and as a member of the renaissance quartet Ensemble Charneyron. Honours: Fourth round, Cardiff Singer of the World Competition, 1989. Address: Kaye Artists Management Ltd, Barratt House, 7 Chertsey Road, Woking, Surrey GU21 5AB, England.

BAVICCHI John (Alexander), b. 25 Apr 1922, Boston, Massachusetts, USA. Composer; Conductor; Teacher. Education: Studied Business Engineering and Administration, Massachusetts Institute of Technology, 1940-42; Civil Engineering, Newark College of Engineering, 1942-43; Cornell University, 1943; BM, New England Conservatory of Music, 1952; Studied Music with Carl McKinley, Francis Judd Cooke; Theory with Archibald T Davison; Composition with Walter Piston; Musicology with Otto Gombosi, Harvard University Graduate School, 1952-55. Career: Many teaching positions including: South End Music School, 1950-64; Boston Center for Adult Education, 1952-55; Cape Cod Conservatory of Music, 1956-58; Cambridge Center for Adult Education, 1960-73; Professor, Composition, Berklee College of Music, 1964-; Various conducting positions including: American Festival Ballet Company, 1962-65; Arlington Philharmonic Orchestra, 1968-82. Compositions: Orchestral: Concerto for clarinet and string orchestra, 1954; Suite No 1, 1955; A Concert Overture, 1957; Fantasy for harp and chamber orchestra, 1959; Concertante for oboe, bassoon and string orchestra, 1961; Fantasia on Korean Folk Tunes, 1966; Caroline's Dance, 1974-75; Mont Blanc, overture, 1976-77; Music for small orchestra, 1981; Fusions for trombone and orchestra, 1984-85; Pyramid, 1986; Canto I for string orchestra, 1987; Songs of Remembrance, 1990; Quintet for Clarinet and String Quartet, 1995; Band: Summer Incident, 1959; Suite No 2, 1961; Festival Symphony, 1965; JDC March, 1967; Spring Festival Overture, 1968; Suite No 3, 1969; Concertante No 2, 1972-75; Band of the Year, 1975; Symphony No 2, 1975-77; Fantasy, 1979; Concord Bridge, 1982-83; Concerto for clarinet and wind ensemble, 1984; Large Ensemble: Suite No 2 for clarinet ensemble, 1961; Fireworks, 1962; Music for mallets and percussion, 1967; Ceremonial Music, 1978-82; Concerto for 2 pianos and percussion, 1985; Concerto for Tuba and concert Band, 1988; Chamber Music; Piano Pieces; Organ Music; Choruses; Solo Songs. Honours: Award, National Institute of Arts and Letters, 1959; Featured composer, Cardiff Festival, Wales, 1981. Address: 26 Hartford Street, Newton, MA 02161, USA.

BAVOUZET Jean-Efflam, b. 1962, France. Concert Pianist. Education: Studied at the Paris Conservatoire with Pierre Sancan; Master classes with Paul Badura-Skoda, Nikita Magaloff, Menahem Pressler, György Sandor. Career: Recitals in major concert halls worldwide, including the Kennedy Center, Lincoln Center, Kaufmann Hall, New York and the Salle Gaveau, Paris; Tours of Japan and USA; British engagements from 1987; Has appeared as concerto soloist with such conductors as Marek Janowski, Andrew Litton, Jorge Meste and Michel Plasson; Engagements in Germany, Holland, Japan, France and USA; Ravels Left Hand Concerto with the Solingen Philharmonica and the Bournemouth Symphony, 1991. Recordings: Haydn 4 Sonatas and Fantaisie; Harmonic Records HCD 9141. Contribution: Interview with Zoltan Kocsis for Le Monde de la Musique. Honours: Finalist at the 1987 Leeds International Competition; Prize Winner at the Young Concert Artists Competition, 1986, USA; Tomassoni-Beethoven Cologne, 1986; Special Jury Prize, Santander, Spain; Guilde Française des Artistes Solistes; First Prize, Paris Conservatoire, for Piano & Chamber Music; Chamber Music Prize, 1989. Address: c/o Robert Gilder and Co. Enterprise House, 59-65 Upper Ground, London, SE1 9PQ, England.

BAWDEN Rupert, b. 1958, London. Composer; Conductor; Violinist. Education: Studied at Cambridge University with Robin Holloway. Debut: Conductor at the 1986 Aldeburgh Festival. Career: Plays violin and viola with various ensembles, including London Sinfonietta and the English Concert; Performances of works by Birtwistle, Goehr, Harvey, Weir and Hoyland, including several world premieres; TV recordings of works by Gruber, Holloway and Kagel; Michael Nyman's The Man who Mistook his Wife for a Hat for BBC Radio; Engagements with the Bath, King's Lynn and London International Opera Festivals; BBC Symphony and Scottish Chamber Orchestra; Works have been performed in USA, Australia, Far East, Britain and France; 1989 performances by the London Sinfonietta and at the Promenade Concerts; Ballet commission from Munich Biennale 1990. Compositions: Railings for flute and piano 1980; Three-part Motet for soprano, mezzo, baritone and orchestra 1980; Passamezzo di Battaglia for oboe, horn and harpsichord, 1984; Sunless for ensemble 1984; Seven Songs from the House of Sand for brass quintet 1985; Le Livre de Fauvel for soprano, mezzo and ensemble 1986; The Angel and the Ship of Souls for 19 players 1983-87; Souvenirs de Fauvel for 2 pianos 1987; Dramatic Cantata on the Legend of Apollo & Daphne for violin, cello & 13 players 1989; Ultima Scena; Commissioned by Henry Wood Promenade Concerts 1989; Ballet Le Livre de Fauvel 1990. Address: c/o Novello & Company, 8 Lower James Street, London W1R 3PL, England.

BAYLE François, b. 27 Apr 1932, Tamatave, Madagascar. Composer; Music Administrator. Education: Studied with Olivier Messiaen, Paris; Pierre Schaeffer, Groupe de Recherches Musicales, Paris, 1958-60; Darmstadt summer courses in new music, Karlheinz Stockhausen, 1959-62. Career: Director, Groupe de Recherches Musicales, 1966; Institut National de l'Audiovisuel, 1975-97. Compositions: Principal works include: Trois Portraits d'un Oiseau qui n'existe pas, 1962; l'Archipel, 1963; Pluriel, 1963; Espaces inhabitables, 1967; Jeita ou Murmure des Eaux, 1969-70; L'Experience Acoustique, 1969-72; Trois Reves d'Oiseau, 1972; Vibrations Composees, 1973; La Divine Comedie, 1972-74; Grande Polyphonie, 1974; Camera oscura, 1976; Erosphere, 1978-80; Les Couleurs de la Nuit, 1982; Son Vitesse-Lumiere, 1980-83; Aeroformes, 1982-84; Motion-Emotion, 1985-86; Aer, 1987; Theatre d'Ombres, 1988-89; Fabulae, 1990-91; La Main Vide, 1992-95; Morceaux de ciels, 1996-97. Recordings: Various compositions recorded. Publications: Musique Acousmatique, propositions..positions, Ed. Buchet; Chstel, 1993. Contributions: Encyclopaedia Universal, 1984, 1990. Honours: Ordre du Merite, 1976-97; Commandeur des Arts et Lettres, 1986; ARS Electronica, 1989; Legion d'Honneur, 1990; Grand Prix de la Ville de Paris, 1996. Address: c/o Magison, 31 Rue de la Harpe, 75005 Paris, France.

BAYLEY Clive, b. 15 Nov 1960, Manchester, England. Singer, Bass. m. Paula Bradley, 15 July 1989. Education: Studied at the Royal Northern College of Music & at the National Opera Studio. Debut: With Opera North. Career: Sang in The Rape of Lucretia, Il Barbiere di Siviglia and Billy Budd, Claggart, while at the RNCM; Professional debut as Schwarz in Die Meistersinger for Opera North, followed by the King in Aida, Colline in La Bohème, Don Basilio, Banquo, Bartolo in Le nozze di Figaro and in British premiere of Verdi's Jerusalem; English National Opera debut 1987, as Pietro in Simon Boccanegra, followed by appearances in Bill Budd, Un ballo in Maschera, Don Giovanni, Doctor Faust and The Return of Ulysses; Netherlands Opera 1989, as Trufaldino in Ariadne auf Naxos; December 1989 in a concert performance of Bernstein's Candide, conducted by the composer; Sang in the premiere of Birtwistle's Gawain at Covent Garden, May 1991; Concert repertory includes the Verdi Requiem, Elgar's Dream of Gerontius and Apostles, the Brahms Requiem, Handel's Messiah, Israel in Egypt, the Choral Symphony, Rossini's Petite Messe Solenelle and Christus in the St Matthew Passion; Roles at ROH with parts in Fidelio, The Fiery Angel, Die Meistersinger, Colline in La Bohème; Further roles at Opera North include: Sparafucile, The Monk in Don Carlos and Raleigh in Gloriana; Sang Ferrando in Il Trovatore for Opera North, 1994; Mozart's Figaro for Opera North, 1996. Recordings: Candide, DGG. Honours: Curtis Gold Medal for Singing; The Robin Kay Memorial Prize for Opera, RNCM. Hobbies: Most Sport, especially Football; Cricket; Rugby; Weight Training; Walking; Reading; CD Collection; Hi-Fi; 2 Persian Cats; Boris & Lennie. Current Management: Tom Graham, IMG Artists. Address: IMG Artists, Media House, 3 Burlington Lane, Chiswick, London W4 2IH, England.

BAYO Maria, b. 1964, Spain. Singer (Soprano). Career: Won prizes at the Francisco Vines and Maria Callas Competitions and has appeared from 1988 at Lucerne (Lucia di Lammermoor) and St Gallen (Amina in La Sonnambula); Sang Susanna at Madrid and Marseille (1990), Micaela at Monte Carlo (1991) and Musetta in La Bohème (debut role at La Scala, 1991); Season 1991/92 as Susanna at the Opéra Bastille, Paris, Norina in Don Pasquale at Hamburg, Amenaide in Tancredi at Schwetzingen and Rosina at Strasbourg; Concert repertory includes Rossini's Stabat Mater and Mahler's 2nd Symphony. Address: c/o Teatro alla Scala, Via Filodrammatici 2, 20121 Milan, Italy.

BAZOLA François, b. 1965, Paris, France. Singer (Bass). Education: Studied at the Paris Conservatoire, with William Christie. Career: Has sung with Les Arts Florissants in Lully's Atys (in Paris and New York), Rameau's Les Indes Galantes and Castor et Pollux, Purcell's Fairy Queen (Aix-en-Provence) and Charpentier's Le malade imaginaire; Sang Arcas in Médée by Charpentier in Paris, Lisbon and New York (1993) and Pan in King Arthur by Purcell (Paris and London, 1995); Assistant to William Christie with the choir of Les Arts Florissants, from 1994. Address: c/o Les Arts Florissants, 10 Rue de Florence, F-75008 Paris, France.

BEACH David (Williams), b. 5 Sept 1938, Hartford, CT, USA. Professor of Music Theory; Administrator. m. Marcia Francesca Salemme, 20 June 1964, 1 son, 1 daughter. Education: BA, Brown University, 1961; MMus, 1964; PhD, 1974, Yale University. Career: Academic; Assistant Professor, Yale University, 1964-71; Assistant Professor, Brooklyn College, City University of New York, 1971-72; Associate Professor, 1974-85; Chairman, Theory Department, 1981-90, 1995-96; Professor, 1985-, Eastman School of Music; Chairman, Theory Department, 1981-90; University Dean of Graduate Studies, University of Rochester, 1991-1995; Professor and Dean, Faculty of Music, University of Toronto, 1996-. Publications: The Art of Strict Musical Composition by J P Kirnberger, translated by D Beach and J Thym with introduction and explanatory notes by Beach, 1982; Aspects of Schenkerian Theory, Editor, 1983; Music Theory in Concept and Practice, co-editor, 1997. Contributions: Acta Musicologia; Music Analysis; Journal of Music Theory; Music Theory Spectrum; Theory & Practice; Journal of Musicological Research Integral; Journal of Music Theory Pedagogy. Honour: Deems Taylor Award ASCAP, 1983. Memberships: Society for Music Theory, Executive Board, 1984-87; Chairman, Publications Committee, 1979-84; American Musicological Society. Address: Faculty of Music, University of Toronto, 80 Queens Park, Toronto, Ontario M5S 2C5, Canada.

BEAMISH Sally, b. 26 Aug 1956, London, England. Composer; Violist. m. Robert Irvine 2 Apr 1988, 2 sons, 1 daughter. Education: Trinity College of Music; Studied at the Royal Northern College of Music; Staatliche Hodischule für Musik Detmold. Debut: BBC Proms Debut, Viola Concerto, 1995. Career: Viola player until 1989; Professional Composer from 1990; Performances by: Academy of St Martin, Nash Ensemble, LPO, RSNO, BBC Scottish Symphony Orchestra, LMP, SCO, Philharmonia. Compositions include: Symphony no 1, 1992; Tam Lin for oboe and orchestra, 1993; Maagnificat, for 2 sopranos and ensemble, 1993; Violin Concerto, 1994; Monster, 1996; 1st Cello Concerto, 1997; Between Earth and Sea for ensemble, 1997; Symphony No 2, 1998. Recording: Tuscan Lullaby NMC in Dreaming. Honours: GRNCM, 1978; Arts Council Composers Bursary, 1989; Paul Hamlyn Foundation Award, 1993. Memberships: SPNM, APC. Hobbies: Art, Gardening. Current Management: Scottish Music Information Centre. Address: c/o SMIC, 1 Bowmont Gardens, Glasgow G12 9LR, Scotland.

BEAN Hugh (Cecil), b. 1929, Beckenham, England. Violinist. m. Mary Harrow. Education: Fellow of Royal College of Music; Studies with Albert Sammons and André Gertler. Career: Professor, Royal College of Music, 1954; Leader, Philharmonia and New Philharmonia Orchestras, 1957-68; Associate Leader, BBC Symphony Orchestra, 1967; Returned to the Philharmonia as Co-Leader, 1991. Recordings include: Elgar's Violin Concerto and Violin Sonata; Vaughan Williams' Lark Ascending; Vivaldi's Concerti Opus 8, 1-4; Various recordings with David Parkhouse and Music Group of London. Honours: Commander of the British Empire; Cobbett Gold Medal; Double Premier Prize, Brussels Conservatory. Hobbies: Model Aircraft; Model Railways. Address: 30 Stone Park Avenue, Beckenham, Kent BR3 3LX, England.

BEARDSLEE Bethany, b. 25 Dec 1927, Lansing, Michigan, USA. Singer (Soprano). m. (1) Jacques-Louis Monod, (2) Godfrey Winham, 1956. Education: Michigan State University; Juilliard School. Debut: New York, 1949. Career: Concerts with Jacques-Louis Monod, giving the US premieres of works by Berg, Stravinsky, Webern, Krenek and Schoenberg; Concerts of Medieval and Renaissance music with the New York Pro Musica, 1957-60; Commissioned & performed Babbitt's Philomel 1964; Performed Schoenberg's Pierrot Lunaire with members of the Cleveland Orchestra 1972; Taught at Westminster Choir College from 1976; Partnership with pianist Richard Goode 1981; Professor of singing at University of Texas, Austin, 1981-82; Brooklyn College, City University of New York, from 1983. Recordings: Pierrot Lunaire, conducted by Robert Craft; Works by Babbitt, George Perle, Mel Powell, Bach, Haydn and Pergolesi. Honours: Laurel Leaf from American Composers Alliance, 1962; Ford Foundation Grant 1964; Honorary Doctorate, Princeton University, 1977.

BEAT Janet Eveline, b. 17 Dec 1937, Streetly, Staffordshire, England. Composer. Education: BMus, 1960, MA, 1968, Birmingham University. Career: Freelance horn player, 1962-65; Lecturer in Music, Madeley College of Education, 1965-67; Lecturer in Music, Worcester College of Education, 1967-71; Lecturer, Royal Scottish Academy of Music and Drama, 1972-96; Lecturer, Music Department (part-time), University of Glasgow, 1996-98. Compositions include: Brass: Hunting Horns are Memories, 1977; Fireworks, 1987; Chard Fanfare, 1992; Bold As Brass!, 1996; Keyboard: Pentad, 1969; Piangam, 1978-89; Sonata no 1, 1985-87; Cross Currents and Reflections, 1981-82; Alexa's Comet, 1984; Orchestra: Synchronism, 1977; Strings: Le Tombeau de Claude, 1973; The Leaves of My Brain, 1974; Circe, 1974; After Reading "Lessons of War", 1977; "Vincent" Sonata, 1979-80; A Willow Swept By Rain, 1982; Arabesque, 1985; Cat's Cradle for the Nemurineko, 1991; Convergencies, 1992; Scherzo Notturno, 1992; Joie de Vivre, 1994; Equinox Rituals, 1996; Violin Sonata No 2, 1997; Vocal: Summer Poem no V, 1970; The Fiery Sunflower, 1972; Landscapes, 1976-77; Premiers Désirs, 1978; Mitylene Mosics, 1983-84; Nomoi Aulodiki, 1984; Sylvia Myrtea, 1985; Aztec Myth, 1987; Cat's Cradle for the Nemurineko, 1991; Aspara Music 1, 1994; Woodwind: Apollo and Marysas, 1972-73; Inventions for Woodwind, 1974; Seascape With Clouds, 1978; Mitylene Mosaics, 1983-84; Nomoi Aulodiki, 1984; Electronic: Aztec Myth, 1987; A Springtime Pillow Book, 1990; Beating Around the Bush, 1990; Not Necessarily: As She Opened Her Eyes, 1990; Lydian Mix, 1990; Mandala, 1990; Memories of Java, 1990; The Song of The Silkie, 1991; Fêtes Pour Claude, 1992; Der Regenplast, 1993. Honour: G D Cunningham Award, 1963. Address: The Scottish Music Information Centre, 1 Bowmont Gardens, Glasgow G12 9LR, Scotland.

BEATH Betty, b. 19 Nov 1932, Bundaberg, Queensland, Australia. Composer; Pianist. Education: Queensland and New South Wales Conservatories (DipMus). Career: Lecturer and Accompanist, Queensland Conservatory, 1967-. Compositions include: Strange Adventures of Marco Polo, 1 act opera, 1972; Francis, 1 act opera 1974; Songs from the Beasts' Choir for soprano and piano, 1978; Poems from the Chinese for soprano, clarinet, cello and percussion, 1979; Piccolo Victory, 1982; Black on White for piano left hand, 1983; Points in a Journey for soprano, flute and piano, 1987; Abigail and the Mythical Beast, music theatre, 1985; River Songs for soprano and piano, 1992; Lagu Lagu Manis for cello and piano, 1994; Asmaranda for orchestra, 1994; Journeys: An Indonesian Triptych for chamber orchestra, 1994; Indonesian Diptych, 1994; Golden Hours for chamber orchestra, 1995; Dreams and Visions, 1996; From a Quiet Place, 1997; Commissions from the Queensland Opera (1973) and Philharmonic (1995). Recordings: Indonesian Diptych on Music from Six Continents, 1995; Lagu Lagu Manis, Music from Six Continents, 1996. Memberships: International Alliance for Women in Music; Australian Music Centre; Fellowship of Australian Composers. Address: 8 St James Street, Highgate Hill, Queensland 4101, Australia.

BEAUCHAMP Michael (John), b. 2 June 1949, London, England. Opera and Theatre Director; Teacher. Education: University College, Durham; Trained, Glyndebourne Opera, 1971-74. Career: Staff Producer, Sadler's Wells and English National Opera, 1973-75; Resident Producer, Australian Opera, 1975-80; Freelance, 1980-; Productions: Happy End, Adelaide; Simon Boccanegra; HMS Pinafore; La Bohème; Australian Opera; La Bohème, National Opera of New Zealand and Glyndebourne Touring Opera; Rake's Progress, Brisbane and Sydney; Rigoletto, Perth, Western Australia and Melbourne; Lucia di Lammermoor, Songs from Sideshow Alley, Perth; Tancredi, Wexford; Once a Catholic, Whyalla, South Australia; The Happy Prince, Dunstan and The Devil, Morley Opera; Director, gala premieres for Australian Bicentennial, New South Wales Directorate; Teaching; NIDA, Sydney; New South Wales Conservatorium; Flinders University; Elder Conservatorium, Adelaide; Kelvin Grove College of Adult Education, Brisbane; Queensland Conservatorium, Brisbane; Victorian College of Arts; Western Australia Academy of Performing Arts; Guildhall School of Music and Drama, London; Royal Academy of Music, London, Birmingham School of Music; South Warwickshire College; Morley College. Hobbies: Cricket; Driving; Wine. Address: 40A Regents Park Road, London, NW1 7SX, England.

BEAUDRY Jacques, b. 10 Oct 1929, Sorel, Quebec, Canada. Symphony and Opera Conductor. m. Pauline Bonneville. Education: BA, University of Montreal; Royal Conservatory of Music, Brussels, Belgium; Studied with René Defossez, Paul Van Kempen, Willem Van Otterloo. Career: Professor of Orchestral Conducting, University of Montreal; Toured Europe as conductor: Montreal Symphony, Opéra Comique, Paris Opera House, and New York Metropolitan Opera; Radio performances in Canada, Belgium, Holland, Italy, Czechoslovakia, Norway, Luxembourg and France; Concerts in Russia, Poland, Guatemala, Switzerland, Greece, Monaco and USA; Television appearances in Canada and France. Honour: Recipient of Golden Medal of Quebec Lieutenant Governor, 1958. Current Management: Beaudry Concerts, Montreal. Hobbies: Skiing; Swimming; French wines and cuisine. Address: 235 Sherbrooke O P2, Montreal, Quebec H2X 1X8, Canada.

BEAVEN Peter Richard, b. 17 Jan 1954, Plymouth, Devon, England. Conductor; Singer; Organist. m. Juliet Felicity Forbes Ames-Lewis, 16 Aug 1997. Education: Trinity College of Music. Career: Senior Conducting Clinician, St Pauls Experience, 1995-; Assistant Director, The Wren Singers of London; Director, Pms Network. Compositions: St Pauls Evening Service, 1996; Wren Evening Service, 1996. Recordings: Conductor, Ashford Choral Society and Carlo Curley (Christmas Music), Joy To The World, 1997. Contributions to: Organists Review; Choir and Organ. Memberships: ISM; RCO; Equity. Hobbies: Travel; Food. Current Management: Pms Concert Management & Promotion. Address: 181 Nursery Road, Sunbury on Thames, Middlesex TW16 6LX, England.

BEBBINGTON Warren (Arthur), b. 25 Apr 1952, Melbourne, Australia. Musicologist; Conductor; Pro-Vice-Chancellor. m. (1) 1981, (div 1990), (2) Barbara neé Watson, 1991, 1 son. Education: BMus 1974, MMus 1977, University of Melbourne; MA, Queens College, New York, USA, 1978; MPhil 1979, PhD 1983, Cith University of New York. Career: Tutor, University of Melbourne, 1974-76; Research Assistant to Professor Gustave Reese, 1977; Lecturer, Canberra School of Music, 1979-85; Conductor, Canberra Chamber Choir and Youth Orchestra, 1981-84; Guest Conductor, Queensland Theatre Orchestra, 1985-86; Director, 2 National Choral Festivals in Australia; Professor of Music, Dean, Faculty of Music, University of Queensland, 1985-91; Ormond Professor, Dean, Faculty of Music, University of Melbourne, 1991-95; Pro-Vice-Chancellor, University of Sydney, 1995-. Publications: Editor, Musicology Australia, 1984-92; Studies in Music, 1988-; Symphonies of J G and C H Graun, 1985; String Trio V 10 of Haydn, 1986; Adviser to Encyclopaedia Britannica; Contributor to Orchestras of the World: Selected Profiles, 1986. Contributions to: Various articles in Australian Dictionary of Biography; Journal of the American Musicological Society. Hobbies: Swimming; Sailing; Flying. Address: Office of the Pro-Vice-Chancellor, University of Sydney, Sydney 2006, Australia.

BECCARIA Bruno, b. 4 July 1957, Rome, Italy. Singer (Tenor). Debut: Bologna, 1986, as Edgardo in Lucia di Lammermoor. Carer: Sang at La Scala, Milan, 1986-87, as Ismaele and Pinkerton; Philadelphia Opera, 1986 and 1988, Vienna Staatsoper from 1987, New York Metropolitan debut, 1987, as Rodolfo; Verona Arena from 1988, as Enzo in La Gioconda, Radames and Turiddu; Teatro La Fenice Venice, 1990, as Ernani; Other roles include Gabriele Adorno (Catania, 1992), Andrea Chenier (San Francisco Opera), Faust, Don Carlos, and Maurizio in Adriana Lecouvreur. Recordings include: Beethoven's Mass in C (Decca). Address: c/o Teatro La Fenice, Campo S Fantin 1965, 30124 Venice, Italy.

BECERRA Gustavo, b. 26 Aug 1925, Temuco, Chile. Composer. Education: Studied at Santiago Conservatory, with Pedro Allende and with Domingo Santa Cruz. Career: Cultural Attache to Chilean Embassy in Bonn, 1968-70; Freelance composer. Compositions: La Muerte de Don Rodrigo, opera, 1958; Three Symphonies, 1955, 1958, 1960; La Araucuna and Lord Cochrane, oratorios, 1965, 1967; Violin Concerto, 1950; Flute Concerto, 1957; Piano Concerto for oboe, clarinet, bassoon & strings, 1970; Three Violin Sonatas; Viola Sonata; Three Cello Sonatas; Sonata for double bass & piano; Choral music. Honours: Premio Nacional de Arte, 1971. Address: c/o SCD, Condell 346, Providencia, Santiago, Chile.

BECHLY Daniela, b. 1958, Hamburg, Germany. Singer (Soprano). Education: Opera Diploma at the Hamburg Hochschule fur Musik, 1984. Debut: Vienna Kammeroper, 1984; Wexford Festival 1986, as Humperdinck's Goose Girl in Königskinder. Career: Sang at Brunswick Opera, 1983-; Appeared with the Krefeld Mönchengladbach company, 1985-87; Member of the Deutsche Oper Berlin, 1987-; Has also sung Susanna, Aennchen, Pamina, Anna in Die Lustige Weiber von Windsor, Gretel, Sandrina in La Finta Giardiniera, Elvira in Don Giovanni (Bern, 1991); Malwina in Der Vampyr by Marschner (Wexford, 1992) and Haydn's L'Incontro Improvviso; Concert engagements in Ireland, Denmark, Norway, France, Italy, Austria. Recordings: Blumenmädchen in Parsifal recording under Barenboim. Honours: 1st prize, Hamburg Singing Contest, 1980; Finals Vienna Belvedere Competition, 1984; 2nd prize, Bordeaux Festival International de Jeunes Solistes. Address: Music International, 13 Ardilaun Road, London N5 2QR, England.

BECHT Hermann, b. 19 Mar 1939, Karlsruhe, Germany. Singer (Baritone). Education: Studied with E Wolf-Dengel in Karlsruhe & with Josef Greindl. Career: Sang at Brunswick and Wiesbaden; Deutsche Oper am Rhein, Dusseldorf, from 1974; Roles include Strauss's Mandryka, Falstaff, Amfortas and Pfitzner's Borromeo; Bayreuth Festival from 1979, as Alberich and Kurwenal; Covent Garden Opera in The Ring; Sang Alberich in Festival Hall, London in a concert performance of Das Rheingold; Guest appearances in New York, Stuttgart, Vienna and Staatsoper Munich 1986, in the premiere of V D Kirchner's Belshazzar; Waldner in Arabella, Teatro Liceo Barcelona, 1989; Sang Kurwenal at Nantes, 1989 and Alberich in Das Rheingold, Bonn, 1990; Sang in the premiere production of Mayer's Sansibar, Munich, 1994. Recordings: Alberich in Ring cycle from Bayreuth. Address: c/o Ingpen & Williams Ltd, 14 Kensington Court, London, W8 5DN, England.

BECKER Günther (Hugo), b. 1 Apr 1924, Forbach, Baden, Germany. Composer; Music Educator. Education: Studied conducting with Gerhard Nestler, Badische Hoschschule für Musik, Karlsruhe, 1946-49; Composition with Wolfgang Fortner, 1948-56; Choral conducting with Kurt Thomas, 1953-55, North West German Academy of Music, Detmold. Career: Music Teacher, Greek National School Anavryta, Athens, 1956-58; Music Advisor, Goethe Institute, Athens, 1957-68; Music Teacher, German Dörpfeld Gymnasium, Athens, 1957-68; Founded, Mega-Hertz, live electronic music group, Germany, 1969; Teacher, International Summer Courses for New Music, Darmstadt, 1967, 1968, 1970; Lecturer, Musikhochschule Rheinland, Robert Schumann Institute, Düsseldorf, 1973; Professor of Composition and Live Electronics, Hochschule für Musik, Düsseldorf, 1974-89. Compositions: Orchestral: Nacht-und Traumgesänge for Chorus and Orchestra, 1964; Stabil-instabil, 1965; Corresponances I for Clarinet and Chamber Orchestra, 1966; Griechische Tanzsuite, 1967; Caprices concertants, 1968; Transformationen for Orchestra, Live Electronic Ensemble and Tape, 1970; Attitude, 1972-73; Konzert for Electronic Modulated Oboe and Orchestra, 1973-74; Ihre Bösheit wird die ganze Erde zu einer Wüste machen, sacred concerto for Speaker, Alto, Chorus, Organ, Instrumental Ensemble and Tape, 1978; Magnum Mysterium-Zeugenaussagen zur Auferstehung, scenic oratorio, 1979-80; Psychogramme for Trombone, Accordian and Percussion, 1993; Pieces for various instruments and electronics; 3 String Quartets, 1963, 1967, 1988. Membership: International Society for Contemporary Music, President German Section, 1971-74. Address: Schillerstrasse 46, 40237 Düsseldorf, Germany.

BECKER Heinz, b. 26 June 1922, Berlin, Germany. Musicologist; Music Educator. Education: Trained in clarinet, piano, conduting & composition, Berlin Hochschule fur Musik; PhD, Humboldt University, Berlin, 1951; Habilitation, University of Hamburg, 1961. Career: Assistant Lecturer, Institute of Musicology, University of Hamburg, 1956-66; Professor of Musicology, Ruhr University, Bochum, 1966-87. Publications: Der Fall Heine-Meyerbeer, 1958; Edited, Giacomo Meyerbeer; Briefwechsel und Tagebucher, 4 volumes, 1960-85; Geschichte der Instrumentation, 1964; Beitrage zur Geschichte der Musikkritik, 1965; Studien zur Entwicklungsgeschichte der antiken und mittelalterlichen Rohrblattinstrumente, 1966; Beitrage zur Geschichte der Opera, 1969; Die Couleur locale in der Oper des 19 Jahrhunderts, 1976; Giacomo Meyerbeer in Selbstzeugnissen und Bilddokumenten, 1980; Giacomo Meyerbeer; Ein Leben in Briefen, with G Becker, 1983, English edition with supplements, 1989; Johannes Brahms, 1993. Contributions: Articles in various music journals & other publications; uber 400 Einzelveroffentlichungen. Honours: Festschrift published in honour of 60th birthday, 1982; Meyerbeeriana, Festschrift in honour of 70th birthday, 1992, ed Sieghart Dohring & Jurgen Schlader. Memberships: Gesellschaft fur Muskforschung since 1951. Address: c/o Music Department, Ruhr University, Bochum, Germany.

BECKER Rolf, b. 1935, Germany. Singer (Bass). Career: Sang with Cologne Opera, 1959-62, Hanover, 1962-92; Roles have included Mozart's Sarastro and Commendatore, Rocco, Daland, Fafner, Hunding, Gurnemanz, and Mephistopheles; Has also sung such modern repertory as Wesener in Die Soldaten by Zimmermann and buffo roles, including Basilio, Osmin, Kecal and Bartolo; Concert engagements in Spain, France and Italy. Address: c/o Niedersachsische Staatstheater, Opernhaus, Opernplatz 1, W-3000 Hannover 1, Germany.

BECKMANN Judith, b. 10 May 1935, Jamestown, North Dakota, USA. Singer (Soprano). m. Irving Beckmann. Education: Studied in Los Angeles and with Lotte Lehmann in Santa Barbara; Further study in Hamburg and Dusseldorf. Debut: Brunswick 1962, as Fiordilgi in Cosi fan Tutte. Career: Sang widely in Germany; Member, Deutsche Oper am Rhein, Dusselforf, 1964; Hamburg Saatsoper, 1967; Guest appearances in Brussels, Nancy, Geneva, Venice, Florence, London; Turin 1986, as the Marschallin in Der Rosenkavalier; Arabella, Munich Staatsoper, 1988; Ariadne, Dortmund Opera, 1988; Sang the Marschallin at Hanover and Munich, 1990; Concert engagements in music by Bach. Recordings include: Cantatas by Bach. Address: c/o Hochschule für Musik Hamburg, Harvestehuderweg 10, 20148 Hamburg, Germany.

BECKMANN Thomas (Riemke), b. 18 Apr 1957, Dusseldorf, Germany. Concert Soloist; Cellist. Education: Philosophy, Classical Latin and Greek, Universities of Dusseldorf & Cologne; Examination, Music High School, Dusseldorf; Pupil of Pierre Fournier, Geneva, 1980-86. Debut: TV Concert, ZDF, 1986. Career: Over 100 TV appearances; 100 concerts yearly, 1986-; Appearances in all important German concert halls including Berlin Philharmonic; Cologne Philharmonic; Hamburg Musikhalle; Munich Herkules-Saal. Recordings: OH! That Cello, Play That Cello, Encore, Thomas Beckmann-Charlie Chaplin. Honours: Prize, German Record Critics. Memberships: Violoncello Society, New York. Hibbies: Jogging. Current Management: Jaro, Bremen, Germany. Address: c/o Jaro, Bismarkstr 83, 28203 Bremen, Germany.

BECKWITH Daniel, b. 1954, Chicago, USA. Conductor. Education: Studied at Westminster Choir College, Princeton. Career: Opera Conductor; Recent engagements with Il Matrimonio Segreto and Falstaff at Wolf Trap, Cosí fan tutte for the Lyric Opera of Chicago, Geétey's Zemire et Azor at Houston; Giulio Cesare, The Rape of Lucretia and Turandot at Edmonton; The Coronation of Poppea and Mozart's Il Re Pastore for Canadian Opera; Other appearances include Don Giovanni at the Metropolitan (1995, 1997), Figaro at Vancouver and Il Barbiere di Siviglia in Florida; L'Italiana in Algeri for Cleveland Opera; Season 1997 with Theodora at the Glyndebourne Festival, L'Elisir d'Amore at Fort Worth, Handel's Xerxes in Seattle and Rinaldo for the Geneva Opera; Magic Flute at Washington DC; Il Barbiere di Siviglia at England's Opera North. Address: IMG Artists, 420 West 45th Street, New York, NY 10036, USA.

BECKWITH John, b. 9 Mar 1927, Victoria, British Columbia, Canada. Composer; Teacher; Writer; Pianist. Education: MusB, 1947; MusM, 1961, University of Toronto, Faculty of Music; Private Piano studies, Alberto Guerrero, Royal Conservatory of Music, Toronto, 1945-50; Private composition studies, Nadia Boulanger, Paris, 1950-51. Career: Public Relations Director, Royal Conservatory of Music, Toronto, 1948-50; Staff writer for radio music continuity, Canadian Broadcasting Corporation, Toronto, 1953-55; Freelance Radio programmer & writer, 1955-70; Reviewer & columnist, Toronto Daily Star, 1959-62, 1963-65; Special lecturer, part-time, University of Toronto, 1952-53, Lecturer, 1954-60; Assistant Professor, 1960-66; Associate Professor, 1966-70; Dean, 1970-77; Professor, 1977-90; Director, Institute for Canadian Music, 1984-90. Compositions: Night Blooming Cereus, 1958; Concerto Fantasy, 1960; Flower Variations & Wheels, 1962; Canada Dash, Canada Dot, 1967; All the Bees & All the Keys, 1973; The Shivaree, 1978; Keyboard Practice, 1979; A Little Organ Concert, 1981; Mating Time, 1981; 6 Songs to poems by E E Cummings, 1982; A Concert of Myths, 1983; Arctic Dances, 1984; Crazy to Kill, 1988; Peregrine, 1989; Round & Round, 1992; Taptoo!, 1994; Eureka, 1996. Published Compositions: 4 songs to poems of E E Cummings, 1950; Fall Scene & Fair Dance, 1956; Jonah, 1963; Sharon Fragments, 1966; Circle, with Tangents, 1967; Gas!, 1969; Taking a Stand, 1972; Musical Chairs, 1976; 3 Motets on Swan's China, 1981; Sonatina in 2 movements, 1981; Harp of David, 1985. Publications: The Modern Composer & His World, 1961; Contemporary Canadian Composers, 1975; Canadian Composers Series, 1975-91; Canadian Consultant, The New Grove, London, 1980; The Canadian Musical Heritage, volume 5, 1986, volume 18, 1995; Musical Canada, 1987; Music Papers, 1997. Honour: Member, Order of Canada, 1987. Address: 121 Howland Avenue, Toronto, Canada, M5R 3B4.

BECZALA Piotr, b. 1965, Poland. Singer (Tenor). Education: Studied at the Katowice Music Academy and in Weimar, Krakow and Villecrose: Sena Jurinac has been among his teachers. Career: Sang at the Linz and Salzburg Landestheater, as Mozart's Ferrando and Tamino, Gaston in Krenek's Schwergewicht, Cassio, Werther and Belmonte, 1992-; Zurich Opera debut as Rinuccio in Gianni Schicchi (company member from 1998), 1996; Further appearances as Alfredo, Lensky and Don Ottavio at Linz and as Alfred in Fledermaus; Concerts include Bruckner's Te Deum with the Vienna Philharmonic under Giulini and Schubert's E flat Mass under Muti; Further engagements at the Vienna Musikverein, and in Milan, Leipzig and Dresden; Théâtre de la Monnaie, Brussels, as Rinuccio, 1997. Address: c/o Opernhaus Zurich, Falkenstrasse 1, CH-8008 Zurich, Switzerland.

BEDFORD David, b. 4 Aug 1937, London, England. Composer. m. 1. Maureen Parsonage, 1958, 2 daughters; 2. Susan Pilgrim, 1969. Education: Royal Academy of Music & Trinity College, London, LTCL; ARAM. Career: Porter, Guy's Hospital, London, 1956; Teacher, Whitefield School, Hendon, 1965; Teacher, 1968-80; Composer-in-residence, 1969-81, Queen's College, London; Associate Visiting Composer, Gordonstoun, Scotland, 1983-86. Composer in Association, English Sinfonia, 1987-. Compositions: School operas, The Rime of the Ancient Mariner, 1975-76; The Death of Baldur, 1979; Fridiof's Saga, 1980; The Ranarok, 1982-83; Symphony 1981; Sun Paints Rainbows on the Vast Waves, 1982; Snakes and the Giant, 1982; Star Clusters, Nebulae and places in Devon for chorus and orchestra, 1971; Pancakes with Butter, Maple Syrup, and Bacon and The Weatherman for brass quintet, 1973; instrumental music; Diafone, flute and vibraphone, 1986; Seascapes, string quintet & voices, 1986; For Tess, brass quintet, 1985; Into thy Wondrous House, soprano chorus & orchestra, 1987; Gere curam mei finis, vocal soloists and harmonizer, 1987; Erkenne Mich, ensemble, 1988; Odysseus, Children's Opera, 1988; The Transfiguration; A Meditation, Chamber orchestra, 1988; Fireworks, 1990; The OCD Band; The Minotaur, soprano & ensemble, 1990; Touristen Dachau, 1991; Allison's Concerto, 1992; The Goddess of Mahi River, 1993; A Charm of Grace, 1994; Recorder Concerto, 1995. Recordings: Numerous. Memberships: Director, Performing Rights Society; Director, Youth Music English Sinfonia, 1987; Chairman, Association Professional Composers, 1991. Hobbies: Squash; Table Tennis; Cricket; Astronomy; Ancient History; Philosophy. Address: 39 Shakespeare Road, Mill Hill, London, NW7 4BA, England.

BEDFORD Steuart (John Rudolf), b. 31 July 1939, London, England. Pianist; Conductor. m. (1) Norma Burrowes, 1969, (2) Celia Harding, 1980, 2 daughters. Education: BA, Lancing College, Oxford; Royal Academy of Music; FRCO; FRAM. Debut: Oxford Chamber Orchestra, 1964. Career: Glyndebourne Festival Opera, 1965-67; Debut with The Beggar's Opera, 1967; English Opera Group; English Music Theatre, Aldeburgh and London, 1967-73; At Aldeburgh conducted the world premieres of Britten's Death in Venice, 1973, and Phaedra, 1976; Artistic Director and Resident Conductor, English Music Theatre and Aldeburgh Festival, 1975-; Chief Conductor, English Sinfonia Orchestra, 1981-; Freelance Conductor at home and abroad, including Metropolitan Opera New York, Santa Fe, Buenos Aires, Rio de Janeiro, Canada, France, Germany, Austria, Australia and New Zealand; Royal Opera House Covent Garden, English National Opera, Welsh National Opera, Opera North; Conducted Noyes Fludde at Aldeburgh, 1994; Season 1997-98 with Billy Budd at the Met, A Midsummer Night's Dream for ENO and Martinu's Julietta for Opera North. Recordings include: Death in Venice; Phaedra; Beggar's Opera; Collins Britten series. Honours: Medal, Worshipful Company of Musicians; Organ Scholarship. Hobbies: Skiing; Golf. Current Management: Harrison/Parrott, 12 Penzance Place, London W11, England. Address: 76 Cromwell Avenue, London N6 5HQ, England.

BEECROFT Norma, b. 11 April 1934, Oshawa, Ontario, Canada. Composer. Education: Studied with John Wienzweg in Toronto, 1952-58, at Tanglewood with Foss and Copland, at Darmstadt with Maderna and in Rome with Petrassi; Further studies in Electronic Music at the University of Toronto and Columbia-Princeton Electronic Music Center. Career: Worked in Toronto, 1965-73, Co-founding the New Music Concerts, 1971, President and General Manager until 1989. Compositions include: Improvisazioni Concertanti I-III, 1961, 1971, 1973; From Dreams of Brass for Narrator, Soprano, Chorus, Orchestra and Tape, 1964; Piece Concertante for Orchestra, 1966; Undersea Fantasy, Puppet Opera for Tape, 1967; The Living Flame of Love for chorus, 1967; Rsasa I-III for Chamber Ensemble, 1968, 1973, 1974; Collage '76 for Ensemble, 1976; Consequences for Five, 1977; Collage '78 for Bassoon, Piano, 2 Percussion and Tape; Hedda, Ballet for Orchestra and Tape, 1983; The Dissipation of Purely Sound, Radiophonic Opera for Tape, 1988; Accordion Play, 1989; Requiem Mass for Soloists, Chorus and Orchestra, 1990. Address: SOCAN (Canada), 41 Valleybrook Drive, Don Mills, Ontario M3B 2S6, Canada.

BEESLEY Mark, b. 1961, Harrogate, Yorkshire, England. Singer (Bass). Education: Studied at Sussex University (MSc) and with Dennis Wicks and Laura Sarti. Career: Appearances with

New Sussex Opera, the City of Birmingham Touring Opera, Opera North, Opera 80 and at the Batignano Festival; Member of the Royal Opera Covent Garden, 1989-, in Idomeneo (Voice of Neptune), Arabella, Fidelio, Capriccio, Samson et Dalila, Turandot (Timor), La Bohème (Colline), I Capuleti, Otello (Lodovico), and La Damnation de Faust (Brander, 1993); Other engagements in Poppea at the City of London Festival, Tosca (Angelotti) in Hong Kong and Midsummer Night's Dream (Theseus) at Aix-en-Provence; Sang in La Traviata and Don Carlos at Covent Garden, 1996; Concert repertoire includes the Verdi Requiem (at Seville) and Beethoven's Ninth (Brussels Philharmonic). Current Management: Portland Wallis, 50 Great Portland Street, London. Address: Portland Wallis, 50 Great Portland Street, London W1N 5AH, England.

BEESON Jack (Hamilton), b. 15 July 1921, Muncie, Indiana, USA. Composer; Educator; Writer. m. Nora Beate Sigerist, 1 son (deceased), 1 daughter. Education: BMus, 1942, MMus, 1943, Eastman School of Music, Rochester University; Graduate Study, and Columbia University; Studied Piano, Cello and Clarinet and Percussion and composition privately with Béla Bartók. Debut: As actor in own opera, My Heart's In The Highlands, NET, 1970. Compositions: Over 60 published including: Jonah; Hello Out There; The Sweet Bye and Bye; Lizzie Borden; My Heart's in the Highlands; Captain Jinks of The Horse Marines; Dr Heidegger's Fountain of Youth; Cyrano; Sorry, Wrong Number (operas); Symphony No 1 in A. Contributions to: Journals and Grove's Dictionary, 6th Edition. Honours: Rome Prize, 1948-50; Fulbright Fellowship, 1949; Guggenheim Fellowship, 1958-59; Marc Blitzstein Award, National Institute of Arts and Letters, 1968; Gold Medal National Arts Club, 1976; Great Teacher Award, Columbia University, 1978; Alumni Achievement Award, University of Rochester, 1985. Memberships: Alice M Ditson Fund, Music Publishing Committee, Columbia University Press; Co-acting President, 1975-76, Honorary Trustee, CRI Incorporated; Advisory Board, Composer's Forum; American Academy of Arts and Letters, Treasurer, 1980-83, 1988-91, Vice President, 1984-87; Member of Board, ASCAP, 1990-95; Trustee, 1975-84, Trustee Emeritus, 1993-, American Academy in Rome. Hobby: Swimming. Address: 404 Riverside Drive, New York, NY 10025, USA.

BEGG Heather, b. 1 Dec 1932, Nelson, New Zealand. Opera Singer (Mezzo-Soprano). Education: Vocal studies with Dame Sister Mary Leo, Auckland, 1950-53; Gertrude Narev, Auckland, 1953-54; Marianne Mathy, Sydney, 1955-56; Florence Norberg, London, 1958-84; National School of Opera, London, 1957-. Debut: Auckland, New Zealand, 1954, as Azucena in Il Trovatore. Career: National Opera of Australia, 1954-56; J G Williams Italian Opera, Australia, 1955; Carl Rosa Opera, London, 1960; Resident, Sadlers Wells Opera, London, 1961-64; New Zealand Opera, 1964-66; English National Opera Guest Artist, 1968-72; Royal Opera, Covent Garden, Guest Artist, 1959-72, Resident, 1972-76; Resident, Australian Opera, 1976-; Guest Artist in Edinburgh, Salzburg and Orange Festivals, Strasbourg, Bordeaux, Milan, Vancouver, Chicago, San Francisco, San Diego, Singapore and Barcelona; Concert Artist and Recitalist for radio and TV in UK, New Zealand and Australia; Concert artist and recitalist for radio and TV in UK, New Zealand and Australia; Operatic repertoire of over 100 principal mezzo-soprano roles; Film and video appearances include Adriana Lecouvreur, Die Fledermaus, Dialogues of the Carmelites, La Fille du Régiment, The Mikado, Patience, Le Nozze di Figaro. Recordings include: Les Troyens; La Traviata; I Lombardi; La Sonnambula (Lyric); Mefistofele; I Puritani; The Little Sweep; Southern Voices; Video recordings include: Die Fledermaus; Adriana Lecouvreur; Dialogues of the Carmelites; La fille du Régiment; The Mikado; Voss; Gipsy Princess; Patience; Le Nozze di Figaor. Honours: Sydney Sun Aria Winner, 1955; Recipient, New Zealand Government Music Bursary, 1956; Countess of Munster Scholarship, 1959; Order of the British Empire, 1978. Hobbies: Needlepoint; Photography; Gardening. Address: c/o Opera Australia, 480 Elizabeth Street, Surry Hills, NSW 2010, Australia.

BEGLARIAN Eve, b. 22 July 1958, Ann Arbor, Michigan, USA. Composer; Record Producer. Education: BA, Princeton University; MA, Columbia University. Career: Music performed at Washington Ballet, Kennedy Center, May 1991; Anthony de Hare, Kennedy Center, May 1990; New York New Music Ensemble, June 1988; Dinosaur Annex, Boston, 1989, 1990; Monday Evening Concerts, Los Angeles, 1990, 1991; Weil Recital Hall, April 1987. Compositions: Eloise (Electric Cello and Tape); The Beginning of Terror (Electronic Tape); Making Sense of It (Flute, Cello, Violin, Violoncello, Pianoforte, Percussion, Tape); Miranda's Kiss (Piano solo); A Big Enough Umbrella (Viola, Tape). Recordings: Space 1986; Needful Things - Stephen King Audio Book, 1991; Born Dancin'/Eloise, 1991. Publications: Mikrokosmos, Bartok, corrected edition 1989.

BEGLARIAN Grant, b. 1 Dec 1927, Tiblisi, Georgia, Russia. Composer; Consultant. m. Joyce Ellyn Heeney, 2 Sep 1950, 1 s, 1 d. Education: BM, Composition, 1950, MM, Composition, 1961, DMA, 1958, University of Michigan, Ann Arbor, USA; Berkshire Music Center with Aaron Copland, 1960. Career: Director, Contemporary Music Project, The Ford Foundation, New York and Washington, 1960-69; Dean, Professor of Music, School of Performing Arts, University of Southern CA, Los Angeles, 1969-82; President of National Foundation for Advancement in the Arts, Miami, 1982-91; Consultant in the Arts and Education, 1991-; International Co-ordinator, Think Quest, Armenk, New York. Compositions include: Duets for Violins, 1955; First Portrait for Band, 1959; Sinfonia for Orchestra, 1961; A Short Suite for String Orchestra, 1968; Fables, Foibles and Fancies for Narrator and Cellist, 1971; Diversions for Viola, Cello and Orchestra, 1972; To Manitou for Soprano and Orchestra, 1976; Partita for Orchestra, 1986. Publications: Film-Video as an Artistic Discipline, editor, 1978; The Arts in Shaping the American Experience, 1979; The Professional Education and Career Entry of Artists, 1982. Honours: George Gershwin Prize, 1959; Ysaye Medal, 1973; Distinguished Service Award, Music Teachers National Association, 1991. Memberships: ASCAP; International Council of Fine Arts Deans. Hobbies: Reading; Travel; Amateur Bridge. Address: 141 River Road, Scarborough, NY 10510, USA.

BEGLARISHVILI Jemal, b. 1940, Gori, Georgia. Music Teacher. m. Grdzelishvili Lali, 1967, 1 son, 1 daughter. Education: Graduated, Tbilisi Conservatoire, Georgia, 1967. Debut: Tbilisi, 1971. Career: Music for Theatrical & TV Performances. Compositions: Concerto, for Orchestra, 1967; Cantata "Perished Heroes Are Speaking", 1979; Cantata "Long Live Peace", for Mixed Chorus & Symphony Orchestra; Vocal Cycle "Two Monologues"; Vocal Cycle "The Frescos", for Mezzo-Soprano, Piano & Percussion Instruments; String Quartet; Chorus Compositions; Nursery Songs; Vocal Cycle, for Soprano, Reader, Violoncello & Piano; Concerto, for Symphony Orchestra; Chorus Compositions, for Mixed, Womens & Childrens Chorus. Contributions to: Sabchota Khelovneba. Honours: Prizes, Music Society of Georgia, 1971, 1977, 1978; Prize, Union of Composers, 1985. Membership: Union of Composers, Georgia. Hobbies: Wood Engraving; Gardening. Address: Guramishvili St 70, Ap 17, 363501 Gori, Georgia.

BEGLEY Kim, b. 1955, Birkenhead, Merseyside, England. Singer (Tenor). Education: Guildhall School of Music, 1980-82; National Opera Studio, 1982-83. Career: Royal Opera House Covent Garden from 1983 as Andres in Wozzeck; Lysander in A Midsummer Night's Dream; The Prince in Zemlinsky's Florentine Tragedy; Achilles in King Priam and Froh in Das Rheingold; Other appearances include Boris in Katya Kabanova, Pellegrin in Tippett's New Year and Laca in Jenůfa for Glyndebourne Festival; Dancing Master in Ariadne and Male Chorus in Rape of Lucretia for ENO; Shuisky in Boris Godunov, Fritz in the British premiere of Der Ferne Klang, 1992, and Lohengrin and Alfred, Die Fledermaus in Frankfurt; Narraboth at the 1993 Salzburg Festival; Sang in Pfitzner's Palestrina at Covent Garden, 1997; Concert appearances include Die Fledermaus, Alfred, with Andre Previn at the Royal Philharmonic Orchestra; Elgar's Dream of Gerontius with the Philharmonia under Vernon Handley, Tippett's New Year with the London Philharmonic Orchestra and Janacek's From the House of the Dead with the BBC Symphony Orchestra. Address: IMG Artists Europe, Media House, 3 Burlington Lane, Chiswick W4, England.

BEHAGUE Gerard (Henri), b. 2 November 1937, Montpellier, France; Musicologist. Education: Studied Piano and Composition at the National School of Music, University of Brazil, and at the Brazilian Conservatory of Music, Rio de Janeiro; Studied further at the Institute de Musicologie at the University of Paris, with Chailley; Musicology with Gilbert Chase at Tulane University, PhD 1966. Career: Joined faculty of University of Illinois and was appointed Professor of Music at the University of Texas, 1974; Associate Editor of the Yearbook for Inter-American Musical Research, 1969-75; Editor, Music Section of the Handbook of Latin American Studies, 1970-74; Editor of Ethnomusicology, 1974-78, and Latin American Music Review, from 1980; Editorial Adviser and major contributor to the New Grove Dictionary of Music and Musicians, 1970-80. Publications include: The Beginnings of Musical Nationalism in Brazil (Detroit 1971); Music in Latin America: An Introduction, 1977; Heitor Villa-Lobos: The Search of Brazil's Musical Soul, 1994. Address: c/o New Grove Dictionary, 4 Little Essex Street, London WC2, England.

BEHLE Renate, b. 1953, Graz, Austria. Singer (Soprano). Education: Studied at the University and Music Academy of Graz. Career: Sang as mezzo-soprano at Gelsenkirchen, 1979-82; Hanover State Opera, 1982-, as Minnie, Mozart's Elettra, Leonore in Fidelio, Sieglinde, Tosca, the Marschallin and Ariadne; Other Strauss roles include the Dyer's Wife in Die Frau ohne schatten, 1993-, and Chrysothemis (at Barcelona, 1997); Guest engagements at Hamburg, Cologne, La Scala Milan (as Salome) and Los Angeles (Isolde, 1997); 20th Century repertory includes Agaue in Henze's Bassarids, Shostakovich's Katarina and Montezuma in Rihm's Die Eroberung vom Mexico, all at Hamburg; Katya Kabanova; Concerts include the Shostakovich 14th Symphony in Leipzig and Beethoven's Ninth in Granada, 1997. Recordings include: Zemlinsky's Der Kreidekreis and Spohr's Jessonda. Address: Haydn Rawstron Ltd, 36 Station Road, London SE20 7BQ, England.

BEHNKE Anna-Katharina, b. 1964, Austria. Singer (Soprano). Education: Studied at the Munich Musikhochschule. Debut: Vienna Kammeroper, 1986, as Mozart's Susanna. Career: Sang at the Munich Festival in Die wundersame Schusterfrau, by Udo Zimmermann, and guested in Germany, Austria and France; National Theatre Prague as Lucia di Lammermoor, Lulu at Detmold and sang at Bonn in Butterfly, Adriana Lecouvreur, Das Rheingold, Rossini's La Donna del Lago and Martinu's The Marriage (1989); Sang Lulu at Basle, 1994. Address: c/o Oper der Stadt Bonn, Am Boeselgerhof 1, W-5300 Bonn, Germany.

BEHR Randall, b. 1958, USA. Conductor; Pianist. Career: Conducted Peter Hall's production of Salome at Los Angeles Music Center, 1989; Has returned to Los Angeles for La Traviata, Tosca (with Maria Ewing and Placido Domingo) and Peter Hall's production of Die Zauberflöte, 1993; Other repertory includes the Oliver Knussen Double Bill, Orfeo ed Euridice, Nixon in China, Cosí fan tutte, Die Frau ohne Schatten, La Bohème and Vivaldi's Orlando Furioso; Music Director of Long Beach Opera, California; Peter Brook's La Tragédie de Carmen on Broadway; Conducted La Traviata at the Liceu, Barcelona, 1992; Die Walküre in Valencia and Tancredi at Bilbao, with Marilyn Horne; Vienna Staatsoper debut, 1993-94, Madama Butterfly; Appearance as pianist with Maria Ewing at Covent Garden and at the Teatro Comunale Florence, Théâtre du Châtelet Paris, the Vienna Konzerthaus and the Opéra de Lyon. Address: c/o Harold Holt Limited, 31 Sinclair Road, London W14 0NS, England.

BEHRENS Hildegard, b. 9 Feb 1937, Varel, Oldenburg, Germany. Singer (Soprano). m. Seth Scheidman. Education: Freiburg Music Academy with Ines Leuwen. Debut: Freiburg 1971, as Mozart's Countess. Career: Sang in Dusseldorf and Frankfurt as Fiordiligi, Marie (Wozzeck), Agathe (Der Freischütz), Elsa and Katya Kabanova; Covent Garden debut 1976, as Leonore in Fidelio; Metropolitan Opera from 1976, as Giorgetta (Il Tabarro), Donna Anna, Tosca, Mozart's Electra and Wagner's Sieglinde, Isolde and Brünnhilde; Salzburg 1977, Salome; Guest appearances in Munich, Vienna and Lisbon; Bayreuth from 1983, sang Brünnhilde in a new production of The Ring, directed by Harry Kupfer, 1988 and in New York, 1988-90; Marie in Wozzeck, Metropolitan, 1990; Salome at Munich Concert and at Covent Garden, Sept 1990; Sang Elektra at Athens and the New York Metropolitan, 1991 and at ovent Garden, 1997; Isolde at the reopening of the Prinzregenten-theater, Munich, 1996. Recordings include: Salome, conducted by Karajan (HMV); Fidelio (Decca); Les Nuits d'Eté and Ravel's Shéhérazade (Decca); Tristan und Isolde (Philips); Brünnhilde in The Ring, conducted by James Levine, also in Video; Video of Wozzeck, from Vienna conducted by Abbado (Virgin Classics). Address: c/o Royal Opera House, Covent Garden, London WC2, England.

BEHRMAN David, b. 16 Aug 1937, Salzburg, Austria. Composer. Education: Studied privately in New York with Wallingford Riegger and at Princeton with Walter Piston; European studies with Henri Pousseur and Karlheinz Stockhausen. Career: From 1966 toured widely in the US with the Sonic Arts Union, giving performances of electronic music; Associated with John Cage, David Tudor and Gordon Mumma at the Merce Cunningham Dance Company, 1970-76; Formerly Artist-in-Residence at Mills College, Oakland serving as Co-Director of the Center for Contemporary Music. Compositions include: Players with Curtains, 1966; Wave Train, 1966; Runthrough, 1967; For Nearly an Hour, 1968; A New Team Takes Over, 1969; Pools of Phase-locked Loops, 1972; Cloud Music, 1974-79; Figure in a Clearing, 1977; On the Other Ocean, 1977; Touch Tones, 1979; Indoor Geyser, 1979-81; Singing Stick, 1981; She's Wild, 1981; Sound Fountain, 1982; 6-Circle, 1984; Orchestral Construction Set, 1984; Interspecies Smalltalk, 1984; Installation for La Villett, 1985. Recordings include: Many albums of experimental music. Address: c/o ASCAP, ASCAP Building, One Lincoln Plaza, New York, NY 10023, USA.

BEILMAN Douglas, b. 1965, Kansas, USA. Violinist. Education: Studied at Juilliard and the New England Conservatory, with Dorothy Delay. Career: Co-founded the Sierra Quartet and performed at the Olympic Music Festival; Co-founded the New Zealand String Quartet, 1987, under the auspices of the Music Federation of New Zealand; Debut concert in Wellington, May 1988; Concerts at the Tanglewood School in USA, Banff International Competition in Canada and performances with the Lindsay Quartet at the 1990 International Festival of the Arts, Wellington; Soloist with New Zealand Symphony Orchestra and Artist-in-Residence at Victoria University, Wellington; Tour to Australia, 1990, for Musica Viva Australia; Tours of New Zealand, 1992, and concerts in New York, 1993. Recordings include: Several Albums. Address: c/o Ingpen and Williams Limited, 14 Kensington Court, London W5 5DN, England.

BEKKU Sadao, b. 24 May 1922, Tokyo, Japan. Composer. Education: Studied with Milhaud, Rivier and Messiaen at the Paris Conservatoire, 1951-54. Career: Teacher in Tokyo and President of the Japanese Branch of International Society for Contemporary Music, 1968-73. Compositions: Operas: A Story of Three Women, Tokyo, 1965; Prince Arima, Tokyo, 1967; Aoi-no-ue, Tokyo, 1981; Two Japanese Suites, 1955, 1958; String Quartet, 1955; Two Prayers for Orchestra, 1956; Symphonies for Strings, 1959; 4 Symphonies, 1962, 1977, 1984, 1991; Piano Sonatina, 1965; Kaleidoscope for Piano, 1966; Violin Sonata, 1967; Violin Concerto, 1969; Three Paraphrases for Piano, 1968; Sonata in Classical Style for Piano, 1969; Viola Concerto, 1972; Piano Concerto, 1981. Publications include: The Occult in Music, 1972. Address: JASRAC, Jasrac House 7-13, 1-Chome Nishishimbashi, Minato-ku, Tokyo 105, Japan.

BEKMAN Lazar, b. 26 Feb 1930, Leningrad, Russia. Pianist. m. Valentina Berman, 28 December 1968, 1 son. Education: Central Musical School, Moscow Conservatory, 1939-48; Musical School, Leningrad Conservatory. Career: Concerts in Russia, US, England. Recordings: Numerous. Honours: Best Recording, Liszt Competition; Premio Muses Florence, 1997. Address: Tintori 23, Florence 50122, Italy.

BELAMARIC Miro, b. 9 Feb 1935, Sibenik, Dalmatia. Composer; Conductor. Education: Studied with Milan Horvat and Stjepan Sulek at the Zagreb Academy of Music; Lovro von Matacic in Salzburg; Sergiu Celibidache in Siena. Career: Conductor of the Symphony Orchestra of Zagreb Radio from 1959; Chief Conductor of the Komedija Theatre and from 1978 Chief Conductor of Zagreb Opera; Assistant to Karajan at Salzburg Festival, 1965-68, to Karl Böhm, 1975-77. Compositions include: Operas: The Love of Don Perlimplin, Zagreb, 1975; Don Juan - ein Rebell fur alle Zeiten, 1983. Honours include: Winner, Vienna State Opera Competition for Don Juan, 1983. Address: c/o Vienna Staatsoper, Opernring 2, A-1010 Vienna, Austria.

BELCOURT Emile, b. 1934, Saskatchewan, Canada. Singer (Tenor). Education: Academy of Music, Vienna; Paris with Pierre Bernac and Germaine Lubin. Career: Early opera appearances in Germany and France; Paris Opéra Comique as Pelléas; Sang in Debussy's opera for Scottish Opera, 1962; Covent Garden 1963, as Gonzalez in L'Heure Espagnole; Sadler's Wells/English National Opera from 1963, in Die Fledermaus, Orpheus in the Underworld, Bluebeard, The Violins of St Jacques, Patience, Salome and Lucky Peter's Journey, Loge in The Ring; Sang in premieres of Bennett's A Penny for a Song, 1967; Hamilton's The Royal Hunt of the Sun, 1977; Blake's Toussaint l'ouverture, 1977; Lead in stage musicals Man of La Mancha and Kiss me Kate; Canadian Opera debut in Heloise and Abelard, 1973; San Francisco, 1982, as Herod in Salome; Sang in the Covent Garden premiere of Berg's Lulu, 1981. Recordings include: Loge in The Ring Cycle, conducted by Reginald Goodall. Address: c/o English National Opera, London Coliseum, St Martin's Lane, London WC2N 4ES, England.

BELKIN Boris, b. 26 Jan 1948, Sverdlovsk, USSR. Violinist. Education: Began Violin studies aged six; Central Music School, Moscow, then Moscow Conservatory with Yankelevitz and Andrievsky. Career: Public appearances from 1955; Won Soviet National Competition for Violinists, 1972 and emigrated 1974; Debut in West, 1974 with Zubin Mehta and the Israel Philharmonics; Orchestras with whom he has appeared include, Berlin Philharmonic, Concertgebouw, Israel Philharmonic, Los Angeles Philharmonic, Philadelphia and Cleveland; Conductors include, Muti, Bernstein, Maazel, Haitink, Mehta, Ashkenazy and Steinberg; Season 1987-88 with London Philharmonic and Cleveland Orchestras and recitals in Spain, Italy, Finland, and Portugal; Season 1988-89 with the Pittsburgh, Royal Philharmonic, Concertgebouw and Tokyo Philharmonic Orchestras. Recordings: Paganini Concerto No 1 with the Israel Philharmonic; Tchaikovsky and Sibelius Concertos with the Philharmonia Orchestra; Prokofiev's Concertos with the London Philharmonic; Brahms Concerto with the London Symphony; Shostakovich Concerto No 1 with the Royal Philharmonic; Brahms Sonatas with Dalberto. Address: T Harrison Artists, The Orchard, Market Street, Charlbury, Oxfordshire OX7 3PJ, England.

BELL Christopher, b. 1961, Belfast. Conductor. Career: Chorusmaster of the Edinburgh Royal Choral Union, 1987-90; Regular Concerts with the Scottish Chamber Orchestra from 1988, notably in West Side Story and Porgy and Bess, and a five concert tour of the Highlands; Chorus Master of the Royal Scottish Orchestra Chorus and from 1989 Associate Conductor of the BBC Scottish Symphony; Barbican Hall, London, debut 1989 with the London Concert Orchestra; Has also conducted the Royal Philharmonic, the Basle Symphony, the Brabants Orkest and the Nordhollands Orkest; Gave Tosca with Opera Northern Ireland and Dublin Grand Opera, 1990; Edinburgh Festival 1991 and debut with the City of London Sinfonia; Music in education includes Chorister Training Scheme at Palmerston Place Church, Edinburgh (Director of Music); Ulster Orchestra, Royal Scottish National Orchestra, Essex Philharmonic; Associate Conductor BBC, 1989-91; Artistic Director, Edinburgh Royal Choral Union, 1993-. Current Management: Robert Gilder & Co. Address: Enterprise House, 59-65 Upper Ground, London SE1 9PQ, England.

BELL Donald (Munro), b. 19 June 1934, Burnaby, Canada. Professor; Baritone. Education: Royal College of Music, 1953-55; Berlin, 1955-60; Presented paper at Memorial University's Phenomenon of Singing, Using Digital Technology via Voice Lesson, 1997. Debut: Wigmore Hall, 1958; Bayreuth, 1958, the Herlad in Lohengrin, 1960. Career: CBC, BBC, NOS TV Holland; Appeared at Glyndebourne in 1963 as the Speaker in Die Zauberflöte, Geneva, London Royal Festival Hall, Royal Albert Hall, at opening of Lincoln Center, and Carnegie Hall. Honours: Recipient of various honours and awards. Memberships: Governor, NATS; Rotary Club; Strike Gov, NOA. Hobbies: Fishing; Archery. Address: University of Calgary, Department of Music, 2500 University Drive NW, Calgary, Alberta T2N 1N4, Canada.

BELL Elizabeth, b. 1 Dec 1928, Cincinnati, Ohio, USA. Composer. m. (1) Frank D Drake, 7 Mar 1953, 3 sons, (2) Robert E Friou, 16 Apr 1983. Education: BA, Music, Wellesley College, Wellesley, Massachusetts, 1950; BS, Composition, Juilliard School of Music, New York City, 1953; Studied under Peter Mennin and Vittorio Giannini; Later studied privately with Paul Alan Levi. Career: Performances throughout USA, also Russia, Ukraine, Bulgaria, Armenia, Japan, Australia, Canada, South America; 4 retrospective concerts: Ithaca, New York, Jan 1973, Cincinnati, Apr 1985, New York City, October 1991 and May 1998; Radio and television interviews. Compositions: Variations and Interludes for Piano, 1952; String Quartet, 1957; Songs of Here and Forever, 1970; Fantasy Sonata for Cello and Piano, 1971; Symphony No 1, 1971; 2nd Sonata for Piano, 1972; Soliloquy for Solo Cello, 1980; Loss-Songs for Soprano and Piano, 1983; Perne in a Gyre for Clarinet, Violin, Cello and Piano, 1984; Duovarios for 2 Pianos, 1987; Millennium for Soprano, Clarinet and Piano, 1988; Spectra for 11 instruments, 1989; Night Music for Piano, 1990; River Fantasy for Flute and String Trio, 1991; Andromeda for Piano, String Orchestra and Percussion, 1993; Les Neiges d'Anton, Sonata for violin and piano, 1998. Recordings: 2nd Sonata; Perne in a Gyre; Millennium; Andromeda; Variations and Interludes. Contributions to: Music reviews for Ithaca Journal, 1969-75. Honours: 1st Prize for Perne, 1986, Grand Prize for Spectra, 1994, Utah Composers Competition; Delius Prize for Duovarios, Jacksonville, Florida, 1994; Commissions from New York State Council on the Arts, Inoue Chamber Ens, Max Lifchitz, Vienna Modern Masters, others. Memberships include: Broadcast Music Inc; American Music Center; American Composers Alliance; New York Women Composers; Society of Composers Inc; International Alliance of Women in Music; American Composers Forum. Hobbies: Family; Poetry; Photography. Current Management: American Composers Alliance. Address: 21 Beech Lane, Tarrytown, NY 10591-3001, USA.

BELL Joshua, b. 1967, Indiana, USA. Musician (Violinist). Education: Studied with Josef Gingold. Career: Concert with Philadelphia Orchestra, 1981; Season 1993-94, performed Nicholas Mair's Violin Concerto with the Philharmonia Orchestra, conducted by Leonard Slatkin, and at the Proms with London Philharmonic Orchestra and Roger Norrington, 1996; Season 1997-98, performances with orchestras such as New York Philharmonic, Boston Symphony, Cleveland Orchestra, Los Angeles Philharmonic, Pittsburgh and Dallas Symphony Orchestras and many European Orchestras; Performed at Salzburg Music Festival; Annual Joshua Bell Chamber Music Festival, Wigmore Hall, London, 1997-; Guest Professor, Royal Academy of Music, London, 1997-; Has worked with many great conductors including Vladimir Ashkenazy, John Eliot Gardiner, Christoph von Dohnanyi, Lorin Maazel, André Previn, Richard Hickox, Leonard Slatkin and Sir Neville Marriner; Numerous appearances on TV and video. Recordings: Nicholas Mair's Violin Concerto; Violin concertos of Mendelssohn and Bruch; Tchaikovsky's A Minor Lalo; Symphonie Espagnole, Saint-Saens; Mozart, Symphonies No 3 and 5; Chamber music recitals with the Takacs Quartet; Film music for The Red Violin, forthcoming; John William's transcription of Porgy and Bess, forthcoming. Current Management: Astrid Schoerke. Address: c/o Monckebergallee 41, 30453 Hannover, Germany.

BELLAI Judit, b. 12 Oct 1968, Kaposvar, Hungary. Opera Singer. Education: Music High School, Pecs, Hungary; Diploma, Voice and Violin Cello, Music Academy, Pecs, Hungary. Debut: As Sylva Varescu, The Czardas Queen, Operette Theatre, Budapest. Career: Budapest Operette Theatre, Major Operette Leading Roles: The Czardas Queen, The Gypsy Baron, The Bat, Gypsy Love, Countess Maricza, Merry Widow, Girditta, The Ciras Princess; Regular Tours with Operette Theatre Budapest Worldwide; Regular Appearances on Television and in Films in Hungary. Honours: Finalist, Competition, Vienna, 1995; 1st Prize, Operette Interpretation, International Singing Competition, 1996. Current Management: Promonti-Sause, Vocal Management, Lucerne. Address: c/o Promouti-Sauser Vocal Management, PO Box 4051, CH-6002 Lucerne, Switzerland.

BELLING Susan, b. 3 May 1943, Bronx, New York, USA. Opera Singer; Educator. Education: Chatham Square Music School, 1958-60; Kathryn Long School, 1965-67; Metropolitan Opera Studio, 1964-67; Manhattan School of Music, 1960-63. Career: Masterclasses and workshops at Stanford University, California, 1978, University of Houston, 1978, and Manhattan School of Music, 1984; Faculty, New School of Social Research, 1986-; Over 100 American and world premieres; Sang title role in Reimann's Melusine for Santa Fe Opera, and Kirchner's Lily with New York City Opera; Performance of Arnold Schoenberg's Second Quartet with Erich Leinsdorf and the Boston Symphony; Sang Belinda in Dido and Aeneas for Metropolitan Opera's Premiere Season of the Forum Opera, Lincoln Center; Performed on numerous occasions with conductor James Levine in such roles as Zerlina in Don Giovanni at Hollywood Bowl, Papagena in Magic Flute with Cleveland Concert Associates, as soprano soloist in Midsummer Night's Dream and the Mahler Fourth Symphony with the Chicago Symphony, and with Atlanta Symphony in Marriage of Figaro; Debut in Europe, Baroque Festival of Venetian Music, Castelfranco, Veneto and Teatro Olimico, Italy, 1977; Numerous other performances include Haydn's Lord Nelson Mass with Minnesota Orchestra, Neville Marriner conducting, and Pamina in The Magic Flute. Address: c/o Allied Artists Bureau, Michael Leavitt, 195 Steamboat Road, Great Neck, NY 11024, USA.

BELLU Cristina, b. 7 Feb 1968. Cellist. m. James A Holzwarth, 29 Feb 1992. Education: Diploma, Violoncelle, 1991; Chicago Musical College, Roosevelt University, 1994. Career: Member, Civic Orchestra of Chicago. Appearances with Orchestra da Camera Fiorentina, Orchestra Lirico-Sinfonica del Teatro del Giglio di Lucca, University of Chicago Symphony Orchestra; Chicago Chamber Orchestra; Orchestra del Maggio Musicale Fiorentino; Numerous performances worldwide; Co-founder, Operacion Tango group. Address: 16 Rue Courriard, 74100 Annerasse, France.

BELLUGI Piero, b. 14 July 1924, Florence, Italy. Conductor. m. (1) Ursula Herzberger, 1954 (divorced), (2) Margherita Vivian, 1960, 5 children. Education: Conservatorio Cherubini, Florence; Accademia Chigiana, Siena; Akademie des Mozarteums, Salzburg and Tanglewood, MA, USA. Career: Musical Director, Oakland, California, Portland, Oregon Symphony Orchestras, 1955-61; Permanent Conductor, Radio Symphony Orchestra, Turin, 1967; Professor of courses for orchestral players and conductors, Italian Youth Orchestra, 1981-; Guest Conductor including La Scala, Milan; debut 1961 with Handel's Serse; Vienna State Opera; Rome Opera; Aix-en-Provence Festival; Berlin Radio; Paris; Rome S Cecilia; Chicago; San Francisco Operas; Conducted L'Elisir d'Amore at Pisa, 1995; Concert repertory includes music by Mahler, Berg, Schoenberg and Webern; Conducted the premieres of Milhaud's 10th Symphony, 1961 and Settimo Concerto by Petrassi, 1965. Address: 50027 Strada in Chianti, Florence, Italy.

BELOHLAVEK Jiri, b. 24 Feb 1946, Prague, Czechoslovakia. Conductor. Education: Studied at the Prague Academy of Arts with Sergiu Celibidache. Career: Assistant Conductor with the Czech Philharmonic; Conductor of the Brno State Philharmonic, 1971-77; Chief Conductor of the Prague Symphony Orchestra, 1977-90; Artistic Director and Principal Conductor of the Czech Philharmonic Orchestra from 1990-92; Extensive tours with the Prague Symphony and the Czech Philharmonic in Europe, the USA and Japan; Guest appearances with the Berlin Philharmonic, New York Philharmonic, the Boston, Toronto and Vienna Symphony Orchestras, Leipzig Gewandhaus, Stockholm Philharmonic, NHK Philharmonic (Tokyo) and the USSR State Symphony Orchestra; Edinburgh Festival, 1990, with the Prague Symphony Orchestra; Further British engagements with the City of Birmingham Symphony, the BBC Philharmonic, Scottish National, Royal Liverpool Philharmonic and BBC Welsh Symphony Orchestras; Principal guest with the BBC SO, 1995; Recent concerts with the St Louis, Bavarian Radio, Washington National Dresden Philharmonic, Deutsche Kammerphilharmonie and Tonhalle (Zurich) Orchestras; Conducted the BBC Philharmonic in music by Brahms, Zemlinsky (Maeterlinck Songs) and Mahler (1st Symphony) at the 1993 Promenade Concerts. Recordings include: Works by Martinu and Janacek, with the Czech Philharmonic. Honours include: Finalist, Herbert von Karajan International Conducting Competition, 1971.

BELOIU Nicolae, b. 9 May 1927, Ocnita, Romania. Composer; Professor. m. Victoria-Sonia Sabau, 1 Feb 1956. Education: Architecture and Mathematics, Bucharest, 1948-51; Academy of Music, Bucharest, 1949-54. Career: Musical Director, Radio Bucharest, 1960-72; Professor, 1970-, Rector, 1990-92, Academy of Music, Bucharest, 1970-. Compositions: Divertimento per archi, 1953, revised, 1971; Divertissement for 2 violas, 1953, revised, 1971; Ben Jonson's Volpone, theatre music, 1956;

Chamber concerto for 2 violins and viola, 1959; Concerto for 18 strings, 1959, revised, 1971; 2 symphonies, 1967, 1977; Towns Rhythms, 1970; Jubilations and Lamento, 1978; Settimino Scenico, 1972; String Quartet, 1982; Sonata for solo violin, 1984; Sonata for Solo Violoncello, 1993; Sonata for Solo Viola, 1997. Recordings: Symphony in Two Movements (No 1); Symphony No 2. Honours: Prizes, Romanian Composers, 1955, 1972, 1978, 1979, 1985, 1987; Grand Prix, International Musical Competition, Queen Elisabeth of Belgium 1969; Prize, Romanian Ministry of Culture, 1971; Prize, Romanian Academy, 1978. Membership: Union of Romanian Composers. Hobbies: Sport; Fine arts. Current Management: Musical Edition of the Union of Romanian Composers, Calea Victoriei No 141, 71102 Bucharest 1, Romania. Address: Strada Olari No 7, 70317 Bucharest II, Romania.

BELSKAYA Nina, b. 1960, Moscow, Russia. Violist. Education: Studied at Moscow Conservatoire with Professor Strakhovos. Career: Member of the Prokofiev Quartet, founded at the Moscow Festival of World Youth and the International Quartet Competition at Budapest; Many concerts in the former Soviet Union and on tour to Czechoslovakia, Germany, Austria, USA, Canada, Spain, Japan and Italy; Repertoire includes works by Haydn, Mozart, Beethoven, Schubert, Debussy, Ravel, Tchaikovsky, Bartok and Shostakovich. Current Management: Sonata, Glasgow, Scotland. Address: 11 North Park Street. Glasgow G20 7AA, Scotland.

BELTON Ian, b. 1959, England. Violinist. Education: Studied at the Royal Northern College of Music; Diploma and degrees, BMus, Manchester University; GRNCM; PPRNCM. Career: Founder member of the Brodsky String Quartet; Resident at Cambridge University for 4 years and later residencies at Dartington International Summer School, Devon; Concert engagements include the Shostakovich Quartets at the Elizabeth Hall in London and performances at the Ludwigsburg and Schleswig-Holstein Festivals; New York debut at the Metropolitan Museum; Tours of Italy, North America, Australia, Poland, Czechoslovakia, Istanbul and Japan; Complete quartets of Schoenberg for the BBC; French concerts include Théâtre du Châtelet, Paris; Concert in Amsterdam and performances at Berlin Festival, Carnegie Hall; Tour of Australia in 1993. Recordings include: Quartets of Elgar and Delius; Schubert A minor and Beethoven Op 74; Complete Quartets of Shostakovich; Borodin Quartet No 2; Tchaikovsky Quartet No 3; Collaboration with Elvis Costello entitled Juliet Letters. Address: c/o Brodsky Quartet, 21-22 Old Steine, Brighton, BN1 1EG, England.

BELTRAN Tito, b. 1969, Chile. Singer (Tenor). Education: Studied at the Gothenburg Academy. Career: Has sung Nemorino for Gothenburg Opera, Rodolfo and the Italian Tenor at Covent Garden, the Duke of Mantua in Monte Carlo and Geneva, Ruggero in La Rondine for Opera North (1994) and Macduff for Toulouse Opera further appearances as Rodolfo at San Francisco and Toulouse London concert debut 1993; Sang in opening gala at new opera house at Detroit, 1996. Honours include: Finalist, 1993 Cardiff Singer of the World Competition. Recording: Arias and songs (Silva Screen Records). Address: c/o Harold Holt Ltd. 31 Sinclair Road, London W14 0NS, England.

BELYAEV Yevegeni, b. 1950, Crimea, Russia. Violinist. Career: Co-Founder, Rachmaninov Quartet, 1974, under auspices of the Sochi State Philharmonic Society, Crimea; Many concerts in the former Soviet Union and from 1975-76 tours to Switzerland, Austria, Bulgaria, Norway and Germany; Participation in the 1976 Shostakovich Chamber Music Festival at Vilnius and in festivals in Moscow and St Petersburg; Repertoire has included works by Haydn, Mozart, Beethoven, Bartók, Schnittke, Shostakovich, Boris Tchaikovsky, Chalayev and Meyerovich. Honours include: With the Rachmaninov Quartet: Prizewinner, First All-Union Borodin String Quartet Competition, 1987. Current Management: Sonata, Glasgow, Scotland. Address: 11 North Park Street, Glasgow G20 7AA, Scotland.

BEN-YOHANAN Asher, b. 22 May 1929, Kavala, Greece. (Israeli citizen). Composer; Music Educator. m. Shoshana Zwibel, 1 s, 1 d. Education: Studied oboe and piano; Composition studies with Paul Ben-Haim, Israel, Aaron Copland, USA and Luigi Nono in Italy; Studies with Gustave Reese and Jan La Rue, New York University Music Department, NY, USA; MMus, University of Michigan. Career: Compositions performed in Israel, Europe, USA and South America; Head of Music Department, Thelma Yellin Music and Arts School, Tel-Aviv, Israel, 1966-75; Professor of Music, Department of Musicology, Bar-Ilan University. Compositions include: Two Movements for Orchestra, 1959; String Quartet, 1962-64; Music for Orchestra, 1967; Chamber Music for 6, 1968; Quartetto Concertato, 1969; Mosaic, 1971; Concerto for String Orchestra, 1973; Four Summer Songs, 1974; Impressions for Piano, 1976; Soliloquy for Violin, 1977; Desert Winds for Flute, 1979; Three Songs without Titles, 1983; Episode for Trombone, 1984; Woodwind Quintet, 1985; Divertimento for Brass Trio, 1988-89; Hidden Feelings for Harp, 1990; Meditations for chamber orchestra, 1992. Publications: Music In Israel, A Short Survey, 1975; Music Notation, 1983. Honours: Morse Fellowship in Composition from University of Cincinnati, USA, 1971; Pi Kappa Lambda. Membership: Chairman of the Israel Composers' League, 1989-92. Hobby: Photography. Address: 4 Bloch Street, Tel-Aviv 64161, Irsael.

BENACKOVA Gabriela, b. 25 Mar 1944, Bratislava, Czechoslovakia. Soprano. Education: Bratislava Academy with Janko Blaho and Tatiana Kiesakova. Debut: Prague National Theatre, 1970 as Natasha in War and Peace; Returned as Mimi, Marenka in The Bartered Bride, Jenufa and Libuse in Smetana's opera, 1983; Appeared at Covent Garden in 1979 as Tatiana in Eugene Onegin, Cologne Opera in 1983 as Maddalena in Andrea Chénier, Vienna Staatsoper, 1985 as Marguerite in a new production of Faust directed by Ken Russell, San Francisco in 1986 as Jenufa, Vienna Staatsoper in 1987 as Rusalka; Sang Desdemona at Stuttgart in 1990, Leonore at 1990 Salzburg Festival, Katya Kabanova at the Metropolitan in 1991; Season 1992 as Fidelio at Covent Garden; Sang Maddalena in Andrea Chenier at Zurich, 1994; Sang Wagner's Senta at Hamburg, 1996. Recordings: Janácek's Jenufa and The Cunning Little Vixen; The Bartered Bride; Libuse; Rusalka; Soloist in Janácek's Glagolitic Mass; Dvorák's Requiem. Honours: Prize winner, Janácek Competition, Luhacovice in 1962; Winner, Dvorák Competition, Karlovy Vary in 1963; Czech National Artist in 1985. Address: c/o Lies Askonas Ltd, 6 Henrietta Street, London, WC2E 8LA, England.

BENARY Barbara, b. 7 Apr 1946, Bay Shore, NY, USA. Composer; Gamelan Performer. Education: BA, 1968, Sarah Lawrence College; PhD in Ethnomusicology, Wesleyan University, 1973. Career: Has played the violin and has performed on various stringed instruments of India, China and Bulgaria; In 1974 formed the Gamelan Son of Lion, an ensemble of Javanese instruments; Assistant Professor at Livingstone College, Rutgers University, New Jersey, 1973-80. Compositions include: Music Theatre: Three Sisters Who Are Not Sisters, 1967, The Only Jealousy Of Emer, 1970, The Interior Castle, 1973, The Gauntlet, 1976, Sanguine, 1976, The Tempest, 1981; Gamelan: Convergance, 1975, Braid, 1975, No Friends In An Auction, 1976, In Time Enough, 1978, Sleeping Braid, 1978, The Zen Story, 1979, In Scroll Of Leaves, 1980, Moon Cat Chant, 1980, Singing Braid, 1980, Solkattu, 1980, Sun Square, 1980, Exchanges, 1981, Hot-Rolled Steel, 1984; Dance Scores: Night Thunks, 1980, A New Pantheon, 1981, Engineering, 1981. Address: c/o ASCAP, ASCAP Building, One Lincoln Plaza, New York, NY 10023, USA.

BENCZÉNÉ Mezö, b. 16 May 1933, Szeghalom, Hungary. Professor; Teacher. m. Bencze László, 24 Jan 1953, 2 sons, 1 daughter. Education: Doctorate of Ethnography, Kossuth Lajos University, Debrecen, 1983; Musical Secondary School of Békés-Tarhos; Liszt Ferenc Academy of Music, Budapest; Choirmaster Diploma as student of Zoltán Vásáhelyi, 1956. Career: Collecting folk music, 1952-, following Kodály's and Jardanyi's lead; Learnt notation from Laszlo Lajtha; Broadcasts on Hungarian radio for several folk music, folk dance groups; Makes folk music programmes and writes up folk songs; Scientific and educational lectures and gives continuation courses; Professor and Teacher at Conservatoire of Debrecen, 1956-; Professor and Deputy Headmaster of Institute of Debrecen of the Liszt Academy of Music, 1966-; Professor of the Teachers' Training Institute of Debrecen, 1982-. Recordings: Radio lectures about folk music and 4 folk song suites for singing voice and folk music orchestra; Hungarian Zither Music; Hungarian Instrumental Folk Music. Publications include: Dr Nagy József sárreti nepdalgjüjtése, folksongs of Sárrét, 1981; A ladanyi torony tetejebe, folk songs of Hortobagy, 2nd edition, 1982; Szivarvanyos az eg alja, folksongs of Bihar, 2nd edition, 1982; Folk Music and Folk Dance in Békés, 1983; The Monograph of Village Csépa, 1984; Barand, 1985. Contributions to: Hungarian Academy of Folkmusic Department. Hobbies: Travel; Grandchildren.

BENEDICT Roger, b. 1962, England. Violist. Education: Studied with Patrick Ireland and Eli Goren at the Royal Northern College of Music. Career: Principal violist of the Philharmonia Orchestra and guest in Strauss's Don Quixote at the Edinburgh Festival and Festival Hall, London; Vaughan Williams Flos Campi with the New London Orchestra and premiere of Michael Berkeley's Concerto, with Philharmonia Orchestra, 1994; Also plays concerto works by Mozart, Bartók, Walton and Berlioz; Member of the Bell'Arte Ensemble with performances at Symphony Hall, Birmingham. Address: c/o Hazard Chase, Richmond House, 16-20 Regent Street, Cambridge CB2 1DB, England.

BENELLI Ugo, b. 20 Jan 1935, Genoa, Italy. Tenor. Education: Studied with assistance of La Scala stipendium. Debut: Piccola Scala, 1960. Career: Guest appearances in Wiesbaden, Buenos Aires, Barcelona, Mexico City and Rio de Janeiro; Appeared at Wexford Festival, 1966, Glyndebourne Festival, 1970 in Il Turco in Italia; Covent Garden debut in 1974 as Ernesto in Don Pasquale; Appeared in Turin in 1975 in Die drei Pintos by Weber/Mahler; Further engagements in Edinburgh, Moscow and San Francisco; Appeared at Théâtre de la Monnaie, Brussels in 1986 as Podestà in La Finta Giardiniera; Roles include Rossini's Almaviva, Lindoro, Don Ramiro and Giannetto, Bellini's Elvino, Donizetti's Nemorino and Tonio, Bizet's Nadir and Massenet's Des Grieux and Werther; Season 1992 as Conte Riccardo in I Quattro Rusteghi at Geneva, Don Anchise in La Finta Giardiniera at the Salzburg Festival and Mozart's Basilio at Florence; Sang Hauk in The Makropoulos Case at Turin, 1993. Recordings include: Il Barbiere di Siviglia and La Cenerentola; Don Pasquale and La Fille du Régiment. Address: c/o Théâtre Royal de la Monnaie, 4 Léopoldstrasse, B-1000 Brussels, Belgium.

BENES Jirí, b. 24 Sept 1928, Komarno, Czechoslovakia. Viola Player; Musicologist. m. (1) 1 son, (2) Zdenka Bubenickova, 1 daughter. Education: PhD, University of Brno, 1952; Graduate, Conservatory of Brno, 1953; Diploma, Janácek Academy of Musical Arts, 1958. Debut: As Viola Player, Brno, 1952. Career: State Philharmonic Orchestra, Brno, 1951-69; Moravian Quartet, 1965-92; Dramaturg, 1992-, including Brno International Music Festival (Moravian Autumn), 1993- Appearances on radio and television with Moravian Quartet, Czechoslovakia, Germany, Sweden, Italy; Tours of most European countries; Teacher: Janácek Academy, 1968-74, Conservatory of Brno, 1969-82. Recordings: Numerous chamber music records. Contributions to: Professional journals; Radio programme notes; Record sleeve notes; Other publications. Honours: Italian Quartet Prize, 1965; Janácek Medal, 1978; Prize, Novecento Musicale Europeo, Naples, 1988. Membership: Czech Musical (Janácek) Society. Hobbies: Running; Sledging. Address: Filipova 19, 63500 Brno, Czech Republic.

BENES Juraj, b. 2 Mar 1940, Trnava, Slovakia. Composer. Education: Piano with R Rychlo, Bratislava Conservatory, 1954-60; Composition under Jan Cikker, Academy of Music, Bratislava, 1960-66. Career: Repetiteur, Slovak National Theatre Opera, 1964-74; Lecturer, Music Theory: University of Bratislava, 1974-83; Academy of Music and Theatre, Bratislava, 1984-. Compositions include: Operas: Emperor's New Clothes, 1969; Petrified, 1974; The Feast, 1980; The Players (Hamlet), 1994; Orchestral: Allegro, 1974; Memoire, chamber orchestra, 1977; Music for trumpet, percussion, strings, 1978; In memorium Pavel Raska per archi, 1981; Music for orchestra, 1982; Preludium, 1983; Music for J S, 1985; Music for trombone and orchestra, 1989; When Music..., 1991; Musica D'Inverno, 1992; Chamber: 3 String Quartets, 1977, 1984, 1989; Quartetto d'archi, No 3, 1989; Chanson Triste vn cl pf, 1996; Préférence, ensemble, 1974; Musique pour Grock No 1, flute, guitar, No 2, clarinet, violin, trombone, No 3, violin, viola, cello, 1975; Waltz for Colonel Brumble, ensemble, 1975; Intermezzo No 1, 6 flutes, 1976, No 2, 12 cellos, 1979, No 3, 2 pianos, 1987; Canzona, wind quintet, 1977; Instrumental: Sonatas for piano, No 1-6, 1971, 1976, 1977, 1978, 1979, 1985; Matrimonial music, 2 pianos, 1976; Populacijó Hajkeles, pipe organ, 1976, Sonata, solo violin, 1976; Lamento, solo violin, 1969; Sonata per un clarinetto solo, 1981; Old Boys Anthology, piano suite, 1983; Sonata, solo cello, 1985; For Instance Black Pony, per corno di bassetto, 1992; Five Nocturnes, for piano, 1989, 1992, 1997. Vocal: Various choral works and songs; Symphony vn and 12 singers, 1974; 14 song cycles including Three Monodies, 1979, O Virtú mia, 1983, Il Sogno di Poppea, 1984; Temptation of St Anthony, for King's Singers, 1981; Requiem, 1986; Cantata no 1, Eating, 1992; Cantata no 2, Déjeuner, 1995. Honours: Prize for Three Monodies, Slovak Music Foundation, 1983; Prize for The Feast, Minister of Culture, 1984; Prize for Quartetto d'archi No 3, Slovak Music Foundation, 1989. Memberships: Slovak Composers Union; Chairman and Founder, ISCM, Slovak Section. Address: Palisady 18, 81106 Bratislava, Slovakia.

BENESTAD Finn, b. 30 Oct 1929, Kristiansand, Norway. Music Educator; Musicologist. Education: Violin lessons with Ernst Glaser, 1947-50; Music courses at University of Oslo; MA, 1953; PhD, 1961. Career: Teacher, 1950-59; Music Critic, 1953-61; Professor of Musicology at University of Trondheim, 1961-64, University of Oslo, 1965-; Chairman, Collected Works of Grieg. Publications: Johannes Haarklou: mannen og vberket, 1961; Waldemar Thrane: en pioner i norsk musikkliv, 1961; Musikklaere, 1963, 5th edition, 1977; Musikkhistorisk oversikt, 1965, 3rd edition, 1976; Editor, Norsk musikk: Studier i Norge, volume 6, 1968; Editor, Skolens visebok, 1972; Co-author, Edvard Grieg: Mennesket og kunstneren, 1980, English edition as Edvard Grieg: The Man and The Artist, 1987; Co-author, Johan Svendsen: Mennesket og kunstneren, 1990 and Edvard Grieg, Chamber Music, 1993. Contributions to: Articles in various journals and in other publications. Honours: Fulbright Scholar, University of California, Los Angeles, 1968-69; Elected Member, Norwegian Academy of Sciences and Letters, 1979. Address: Guldbergs vei 13B, 0375 Oslo 3, Norway.

BENFALL Stephen McRae, b. 9 May 1957, Perth, Western Australia. Composer; Session Musician. Education: BMus (Hons), University of Western Australia, 1982; Further study with John Exton and Roger Smalley. Career: Australian Department of

Defence, 1975-88; Western Australia Ministry of Education, 1988-; Commissions from Perth Saxophone Quartet, Roger Smalley, Nova Ensemble and the Festival of Perth. Compositions include: Rock Music, for tape, 1987; Saxophone Quartet, 1988; Hammers, for piano, 1990; Rough Cut, for percussion quartet, 1992; Shadows, for saxophone and ensemble, 1993; Empathy for flute, violin and cello, 1994. Honours include: Sounds Australian Award, 1990. Address: c/o APRA, 1A Eden Street, Crows Nest, NSW 2065, Australia.

BENGL Volker, b. 19 July 1960, Ludwigshafen, Germany. Singer (Tenor). Education: Mannheim-Heidelberg Musikhochschule in Munich. Career: Staatstheater am Gaertnerplatz, Munich; Guest, Vienna, Berlin, Wiesbaden; Sang at Saarbrucken from 1985; Guest appearances in Essen, Brunswick, Karlsruhe and Heidelberg; Sang Hans in The Bartered Bride at Kaiserslautern, 1990; Other roles include Max in Der Freischütz, Tamino, Belfiore in La Finta Giardiniera, Don José, Pinkerton and parts in operetta; As concert singer appeared in New York, 1989, Berlin (Bruckner F minor Mass and Te Deum) and elsewhere in Europe; Other Repertoire includes Bach Christmas Oratorio and Dvorak Requiem. Composition: Wiegenlied, words and music, 1997. Address: Marschalls h-6, 80802 Munich, Germany.

BENGTSSON Erling Blondal, b. 1932, Copenhagen, Denmark. Cellist. Education: Studied with Piatgorsky at Curtis Institute, USA. Debut: First public concert at age 4. Career: First concerto with orchestra at age 10; Professor of Cello, Curtis Institute, USA; Played with most of Europe's leading orchestras; Broadcasts for the BBC and various European radio stations; Played in North America with such conductors as Monteux, Kletzki, Schmidt-Isserstedt, Sargent, Lutoslawski, Pritchard, Blomstedt, Dorati, Gibson, Groves, Ehrling and Berglund; Masterclasses at Aldeburgh and in Switzerland; Professor of Cello at Royal Danish Conservatory and State Academy in Cologne. Recordings: Beethoven and Brahms Sonatas; Bach Suites for Solo Cello; Haydn Concerto in D; Stravinsky Suite Italienne; Vivaldi Concertos.

BENGUEREL Xavier, b. 9 Feb 1931, Barcelona, Spain. Composer. Education: Studied in Santiago and Barcelona with Cristobal Taltabull. Compositions include: 2 Violin Sonatas, 1953, 1959; String Quartet, 1955; Concerto for Piano and Strings, 1955; Concerto for 2 Flutes and Strings, 1961; Sinfonia Continua, 1962; Successions for Wind Quartet, 1960; Duo for Clarinet and Piano, 1963; Nocturno for Soprano, Chorus and Orchestra, 1963; Violin Concerto, 1965; Sinfonia Per A Un Festival, 1966; Sinfonia for Small Orchestra, 1967; Paraules De Cada Dia for Voice and Chamber Orchestra, 1967; Musica for 3 Percussionists, 1967; Sinfonia for Large Orchestra, 1969; Dialogue Orchestrale, 1969; Musica Riservata for Strings, 1969; Crescendo for Organ, 1970; Organ Concerto, 1971; Arbor, cantata, 1972; Verses for Guitar, 1973; Destructio for Orchestra. 1973; Capriccio Stravagante for Ensemble, 1974; Thesis for Chamber Group; Concerto for Percussion and Orchestra, 1976. Honours include: Winner, Composition Prize of the Barcelona Juventudes Musicales, 1955; Represented Spain at ISCM Festival, 1960. Address: c/o SGAE, Fernando VI 4, Apartado 484, 28080 Madrid 4, Spain.

BENJAMIN George, b. 31 Jan 1960, London, England. Composer; Conductor; Pianist. Education: Peter Gellhorn, 1974-76; With Oliver Messiaen at the Paris Conservatoire, 1976-78; With Alexander Goehr at King's College, Cambridge, 1978-82; Research at IRCAM, Paris, 1984-87; Composition Masterclasses in Avignon, Rome, Beijing, Stravanger, Bombay. Debut: Redcliffe Concert, Purcell Room, London, 1979. Career: Youngest Composer ever played at the BBC Promenade Concerts, 1980; Works performed frequently at International Festivals and by such orchestras as London Sinfonietta, London Philharmonic, BBC Symphony, Concertgebouw, New York Philharmonic, Toronto Symphony, Ensemble Modern and Ensemble Intercontemporain; BBC Television documentary profile, Omnibus, 1987; Artistic Director and Conductor of contemporary music festivals with San Francisco Symphony, 1992; Opéra Bastille, 1992; South Bank, 1993; Prince Consort Professor of Composition, Royal College of Music; Principal Guest Artist, Hallé Orchestra, 1993-; Featured Composer, 1993 Salzburg Festival; conducted the London Sinfonietta in Boulez and Stravinsky at South Bank, 1997. Compositions: Orchestral: Ringed by the Flat Horizon, 1979-80; A Mind of Winter, 1981; At First Light, 1982; Jubilation, 1985; Antara (with electronics), 1985-87; Sudden Time, 1989-93; 3 inventions for chamber orchestra, 1995; Chamber: Violin Sonata, 19756-77; Octet, 1978; Flight for flute, 1979; Duo for cello and piano, 1980; Piano Sonata, 1977-78; Sortileges, 1981; 3 Studies: Fantasy on Iambic Rhythm, Meditation on Haydn's Name Relatively Rag, 1982-85; Upon Silence, mezzo and 5 viols, 1990; mezzo and string ensemble, 1991; Sometime Voices for baritone, chorus and orchestra, 1996. Recordings: Majority of works recorded on Nimbus CDs. Honours: Lili Boulanger Award, Boston, 1985; Koussevitsky International Record Award, New York, 1987; Grand Prix Charles Cros du Disque, Paris, 1988; FRCM, 1994. Current Management: Harold Holt, 31 Sinclair Road, London W14 0NS. Address: c/o Faber Music, 3 Queens Square, London WC1N 3AU, England.

BENNETT Elinor, b. 17 Apr 1943, Llanidloes, Wales. Harpist. m. Dafydd Wigley, 26 Aug 1967, 3 sons, 2 deceased, 1 daughter. Education: LLB Hons, University College of Wales; Royal Academy of Music, London; Recital Diploma. Debut: Wigmore Hall, London. Career: Freelance Harpist with London Symphony Orchestra, Philharmonia, English Chamber Orchestra, 1967-71; Soloist and Recitalist, BBC Radio 3; HTV, A Day in the Life of Elinor Bennett; BBC, At Home (Richard Baker); Soloist; Recitalist; Chamber music player; Director of festivals; Dedicatee of many new works. Recordings: Two Harps; With Harp and Voice; The Harp of Wales; Portrait of the Harp, 1988; Nimbus: Images and Impressions, with Judith Hall (flute); Lorelt: Sea of Glass, 1994; Nimbus: Mathias, Santa Fe Suite and other 20th century classics, 1995; Sain: Harps and Songs, Portrait of the Harp, The Harp of Wales, Two Harps; Victorian Harp Music. Publication: Living Harp. Honours: Countess of Munster Musical Trust, 1964-66; Idloes Owen Prize; Incorporated Society of Musicians Prize, 1982; Churchill Fellow, 1985; Associate of the Royal Academy of Music, 1992; Fellow of the University of Wales, Aberystwyth, 1996. Membership: Incorporated Society of Musicians, Solo Section; Musician's Union; Governor, Welsh College of Music and Drama, 1996-; Arts Council of Wales, 1997-. Hobbies: Politics; Swimming; Cycling; Art appreciation; Poetry reading. Current Management: Audrey Ellison, International Artists Management. Address: c/o Audrey Ellison International Artists Management, 135 Stevenage Road, London SW6 6PB, England.

BENNETT Richard Rodney, b. 29 Mar 1936, Broadstairs, Kent, England. Composer. Education: Royal Academy of Music, London; French Government Scholarship to study with Pierre Boulez in Paris, 1957-59. Career: Commissioned to write 2 operas by Sadler's Wells, 1962; Professor of Composition at Royal Academy of Music, 1963-65; Vice-President of Royal College of Music, 1983-; International Chair of Composition at the Royal Academy of Music, London, 1995. Compositions include: The Approaches of Sleep, 1959; The Ledge, 1961; Nocturnes, 1962; Jazz Calendar, 1964; Symphony No 1, 1965, No 2, 1967, No 3, 1987; Piano Concerto, 1968; Oboe Concerto, 1970; Guitar Concerto, 1971; Viola Concerto, 1973; Spells, choral in 1975; Violin Concerto, 1975; Serenade for Youth Orchestra, 1977; Acteon, for Horn and Orchestra, 1977; Sonnets To Orpheus, for Cello and Orchestra, 1979; Anniversaries, 1982; Sinfonietta, 1984; Love Songs, for Tenor and Orchestra, 1984; Moving Into Aquarius; Reflections On A Theme Of William Walton, for 11 solo strings, 1985; Clarinet Concerto, 1987; Saxophone Concerto, 1988; Percussion Concerto, 1990; Partita for orchestra, 1995; Chamber and incidental music; Opera: The Mines of Sulphur, 1964; A Penny For A Song, 1966; Victory, 1969; All The King's Men (for children), 1969; Isadora, ballet, 1981; Film and TV music. Honours: Arnold Bax Society Prize for Commonwealth Composers, 1964; Anthony Asquith Memorial Award for Murder On The Orient Express film music, Society of Film and TV Awards, 1974. Membership: General Council, Performing Rights Society, 1975-. Hobbies: Cinema; Modern Jazz. Address: c/o London Management, Regent House, 235-241 Regent Street, London, W1, England.

BENNINGSEN Lillian, b. 17 July 1924, Vienna, Austria. Singer, (Contralto). Education: Studied in Vienna with Anna Bahr-Mildenburg. Debut: Salzburg Landestheater, 1948. Career: Sang with Cologne Opera, 1950-52; Munich Staatsoper from 1951; As Eboli in Don Carlos, Fricka, Carmen, Amneris, Octavian and Dorabella; Marcellina in Le nozze di Figaro; Covent Garden, 1953 in the British premiere of Strauss's Die Liebe der Danae, with the Munich Company; Salzburg Festival, 1955, in the premiere of Egk's Irische Legende; Schwetzingen Fesitval, 1961, in the premiere of Henze's Elegie für junge Liebende; Widely heard in recital and concert. Recordings: Le nozze di Figaro; Magdalene in Die Meistersinger conducted by Keilberth; Ariadne auf Naxos; Die tote Stadt by Korngold.

BENOIT Jean-Christophe, b. 18 Mar 1925, Paris, France. Singer, (Bass-Baritone). Education: Studied at the Paris Conservatoire. Career: Sang in the French provinces, then at the Paris Opéra & Opéra-Comique; Guest appearances in Geneva for the premieres of Monsieur de Pourceaugnac by Martin, 1963; Milhaud's La Mère Coupable, 1966; Aix-en-Province Festival, 1954-57; Salzburg Festival, 1956; La Scala Milan, 1958; Further engagements at the Holland Festival, Monte Carlo and Brussels; Best known as Mozart's Guglielmo and Antonio; Rossini's Basilio; Rambaud in Le Comte Ory; Somarone in Béatrice et Bénédict; Boniface in Le Jongleur de notre Dame; Torquemada in L'Heure Espagnole; Professor of Singing at the Paris Conservatoire. Recordings: Carmen; Platée; Lakmé; Les Contes d'Hoffmann and Il Barbiere di Siviglia; Les Indes Galantes; Paer's Le Maître de Chapelle. Address: c/o Conservatoire National de Musique, 14 Rue de Madrid, F-75008, Paris, France.

BENOLIEL Bernard, b. 25 Sept 1943, Detroit, USA. Composer. Education: University of Michigan, 1961-64; Private Tuition, Stefan Wolpe, 1968-69. Career: Administrator, Secretary, Ralph Vaughan Williams Trust, 1978-; Director, RVW Limited, 1983-. Compositions: Op 1, Eternity Junctions for chorus; Op 2, The Black Tower; Op3, Two Movements for Piano after Thomas Mann's Doktor Faustus; Op 4, The After-War; The Into Light for chorus & organ; Op 5, Symphony; Op 6, With St Paul in Albion for amplified cello and organ; Op 7, String Quartet; Op 8, Infinity-Edge, amplified violin, organ, chorus, orchestra; Op 9, Three Movements for Piano after Gericault's Fragments Anatomiques; Op 10 Eternity-Junctions second sequence for small chorus and five instruments. Contributions to: Tempo; Music & Musicians. Hobbies: Psychology; Philosophy; Lieterature; Visual Arts; Travel. Address: Flat 2, 13 Nevern Square, London, SW5, England.

BENSON Clifford (George), b. 17 Nov 1946, Grays, Essex, England. Concert Pianist. m. 1 September 1973, 2 daughters. Education: ARCM Performance Diploma, 1964; Studied Piano with Lamar Crowson and Cyril Smith, Royal College of Music, London; Private Studies with George Malcolm, 1964-69; Studied Composition with Herbert Howells. Debut: Royal Festival Hall, London, 1970. Career: Performed Recordings and Broadcasts, BBC Radio 3, 1969-; Soloist, Royal Albert Hall Promenade Concerts, 1975; Travelled extensively playing at many major music festivals; Numerous recitals, solo and chamber music, also concertos; Duos with Thea King, William Bennett and Levon Chilingirian. Compositions: 3 Pieces for Piano, 1983; Mozart Goes to Town (piano duet), 1985. Recordings: CRD; Deutsche Grammophon; CBS; Hyperion. Honours: Chopin Sonata Prize, Royal College of Music, 1966; Tagore Gold Medal, Royal College of Music, 1969; BBC Beethoven Duo Competition, 1969, Munich International Duo Competition, 1971 (with violnist Levon Chilingirian); Martin Musical Scholarship, NPO, 1968. Memberships: Incorporated Society of Musicians; Royal College of Music Union. Hobbies: Swimming; Tennis; Snooker; Yoga. Address: 76 Quarry Hill Road, Tonbridge, Kent TN9 2PE, England.

BENSON Joan, b. 1935, St Paul, Minnesota, USA. Concert Artist, on clavichord and fortepiano; Lecturer. Education: Masters of Music, University of Illinois; Performer's award, University of Indiana; Protégéé of Edwin Fischer, Switzerland; Studies in clavichord music, with Fritz Neumeyer, Germany; Santiago Kastner, Portugal; Advanced study in Vienna, Paris, Italy and Germany. Career: Concerts, lectures, appearances in Festivals; On TV, Radio, throughout USA; Europe; Near and Far East; Lecturer in Music, Stanford University, 1970-76; Assistant Professor of Music, 1976-82; Adjunct Professor, 1982-87, University of Oregon. Recordings: Music by Kuhnau and CPE Bach, 1988; Haydn and Pasquini, Boston Museum of Fine Arts clavichords, 1982; CPE Bach on clavichord and fortepiano, 1972; Music for Clavichord, 1962. Publications: Haydn and the Clavichord, 1982; The Clavichord in 20th Century America, 1992; Bach and the Clavier, 1996. Contributions to: Articles: Haydn and the Clavicord, Vienna, 1982; Gulbenkian Society, Portugal; The Clavichord in 20th Century America, 1989; American Liszt Society Journal; Edwin Fischer, 1985; Clavier Magazine, Bach and the Clavier, 1990; Kate Neal Award for Performance. Hobbies: Sea; Mountains. Current Management: Marla Lowen. Address: 2795 Central Boulevard, Eugene, OR 97403, USA.

BENT Ian (David), b. 1 Jan 1938, Birmingham, England. University Teacher. m. Caroline Coverdale, 27 Aug 1979, 2 s, 1 d. Education: ARCO, 1958; St John's College, Cambridge, 1958-65; BA, 1st Class, Music Tripos, 1961; BMus, 1962; MA, 1965; PhD, 1969. Career: Lecturer in Music, King's College, University of London, 1965-75; Senior Consulting Editor, The New Grove Dictionary of Music, 1970-80; Professor of Music, University of Nottingham, 1975-87; Visiting Professor, Harvard University, USA, 1982-83; Visiting Professor, Columbia University, 1986-87; Professor, Columbia University, 1987-. Publications: The Early History of the English Chapel Royal, 1066-1327, 1969; Source Materials and the Interpretation of Music; A Memorial Volume to Thurston Dart, 1981; Analysis, 1987; Music Analysis in the Nineteenth Century, 2 volumes, 1994. Contributions to: Journal of the American Musicological Society; Music Analysis; Musical Times; Music and Letters; Proceedings of the Royal Musical Association; Theoria; General Editor, Cambridge Studies in Music Theory and Analysis. Memberships: American Musicological Society; Royal Musical Association; Society for Music Theory; International Musicological Society. Hobbies: Gardening; Reading. Address: Columbia University, New York, NY 10027, USA.

BENT Margaret (Hilda), b. 23 Dec 1940, St Albans, England. Musicologist. m. Ian Bent. Education: Studied at Girton College, Cambridge, PhD, 1969. Career: Taught at Cambridge, King's College London, 1965-75; Goldsmiths' College, from 1972; Teacher at Brandeis University, 1975-81; Princeton, from 1981; Researched Old Hall MS under Thurston Dart at Cambridge, published study with Andrew Hughes. Publications: The Old Hall

Manuscript in the Corpus Mensurabilis Musicae series, XLVI, 1969-73; Dunstaple, London, 1981; Articles on John Dunstable, Notation, Old Hall MS; Leonel Power and Square in the New Grove Dictionary of Music and Musicians, 1980. Memberships: President, American Musicological Society, 1983. Address: c/o Grove's Dictionaries, 4 Little Essex St, London WC2.

BENTLEY Andrew, b. 30 June 1952, Fleetwood, England. Composer; Computer Music Researcher. m. Anna-Kaarina Kiviniemi, 9th Aug 1975, 2 sons. Education: BA, Honours; DPhil, Composition, University of York, England. Career: Designer; Electronic Music Studio; Finnish Radio Experimental Studio, 1976-84; Teacher, Sibelius Academy, Helsinki, 1981-82; Studio Director, Helsinki University, 1982-84; Lecturer, Salford College of Technology, 1985-86; Director, Composers Desktop Project, York, 1986-; Leverhulme Computer Music Fellow, University of Nottingham, 1987-; Bowing, 1979; Portrait, 1979; Modulo, 1979; Contact with Bronze, 1979; Zoologic, 1980; Winter Winters, 1980; Aerial Views, 1981; Time for Change, 1981; Divertimento, 1983; Small Print, 1983. Contributions to: Electronic Music for Schools, 1984; Professional Journals. Honours: Bourges International EAM Competition, 1979; Luigi Russolo Competition, 1979; Address: Leankatu 4 B 13, Helsinki 00240, Finland.

BENTZON Niels Viggo, b. 24 Aug 1919, Copenhagen, Denmark. Composer. Education: Piano tuition from his mother, Karen Bentzon; Royal Danish Conservatoire. Debut: Pianist from Soloist Class, Royal Danish Conservatoire, 1943. Career: Notable pianist performing in Denmark and throughout Europe. Compositions include: Opera Faust III, 1964; 7 Ballets including Duell, 1977; 23 Piano Sonatas; The Tempered Clavier, numbers 1-6; Tocata for Piano; Woodcuts for Piano; Kaleidoscope for Piano; 10 Small preludes; Paganini Variations for Piano; Prelude, Intermezzo and Fugue for Organ; Mimosas for Organ; Pezzo for 12 Pianos; Concertino for 2 Pianos; Chamber Music: Sonata for Cello Solo; Variations of the Volga Boatmen; 16 String Quartets, 1940-76; Sonata No 7; Square Root 3 for Violin and Piano; Maximilian 1, suite for Violin and Piano; Suite for Cello and Piano; Sextet for Flute, Oboe, Clarinet, Horn, Bassoon and Piano; Quartetto Sonare for Recorder, Oboe, Gamba and Spinet; Sonata for 12 Instruments; In The Zoo for Accordion Solo; Orchestra: 24 Symphonies, 1942-91; Symphonic Variations; Pezzi Sinfonici; 5 Mobiles; Eastern Gasworks No 2; Concertos: 8 for Piano, 1947-82; 4 for Violin, 1951-76; 3 for Cello, 1956, 1973, 1982; Flute Concerto No 2; Oboe Concerto; Clarinet Concerto; 5 Operas. Recordings: Much of his work recorded including Piano and Chamber Music. Publication: Kompositioner, 1980. Honours: Carl Nielsen Prize; Aucyer Prize. Address: c/o KODA, Rosenvaengets Hovedvej 14, 2100 Copenhagen, Denmark.

BENZA Georgina, b. 1959, Russia (of Hungarian parentage). Singer (Soprano). Education: Studied in Kiev and Budapest and in Munich with Wilma Lipp. Career: Has sung at the Munich Staatsoper from 1983, in such roles as Adina, Lauretta, Sophie, Pamina and Fiordiligi; More recent repertory includes Violetta, Tosca, Tatiana, Suor Angelica, Madama Butterfly, Marguerite and Aida; Guest engagements in Berlin (Deutsche Oper and Staatsoper), Frankfurt, Copenhagen, Leipzig, Bonn, Dresden and Barcelona; Bielefeld Opera as Tosca and Amelia in Un Ballo in Maschera. Honours include: Winner of Mozart Prizes in Vienna and Salzburg. Address: c/o Athole Still Ltd, 25-27 Westow Street, London SE19 3RY, England.

BENZI Roberto, b. 12 Dec 1937, Marseilles, France. Conductor. m. Jane Rhodes. Education: Studied music from age of 3; Baccalaureat, Sorbonne, Paris; Studied with André Cluytens, 1947-50; Debut: Bayonne, 1948. Career: Conducted the Concerts Colonne in Paris. 1948; Appeared in films Prélude a la Gloire, 1949; L'Appel du Destin, 1950; Debut as opera conductor, 1954; Conducted Carmen at the Paris Opéra, 1959; Tours to Japan, 1961; Central Europe; North and South America; US Debut, 1971; Metropolitan Opera, 1972, Faust; Musical Director of the Orchestra Regional de Bordeaux-Aquitaine, 1973-87; Artistic Advisor of Gelders Orchestra, Arnhem, 1989. Compositions: Orchestrations of the Brahms Variations Op 23 and Op 24, 1970, 1973. Recordings: Many works with the London Symphony Orchestra, Lamoureux Orchestra, Paris Opera, Hague Philharmonic and Budapest Philharmonic, including Beethoven and Rossini overtures; Chopin's 1st Piano Concerto and with Magaloff, Bizet's Symphony, Liszt's Faust Symphony; Cello Concertos by Lalo and Saint-Saëns with Maurice Gendron. Honours: Chevalier de l'Ordre National; Chevalier de la Legion d'Honneur. Hobbies: Cycling; Zoology.

BERBIÉ Jane, b. 6 May 1934, Ville-franche-de-Lauraguais, Toulouse, France. Singer (Mezzo-Soprano). Education: Studied at the Toulouse Conservatory. Career: After debut in 1958, sang at La Scala 1960, in L'Enfant et les Sortilèges, Glyndebourne Festival, 1969-71, 1983-84, as Despina in Così fan tutte; London Coliseum in the British premiere (concert) of Roussel's Padmavati, Aix-en-Provence, 1969-70; Salzburg Festival, 1974, as Marcellina in Le nozze di Figaro; Paris Opera from 1975, as Zerlina and in Das Rheingold and Jenufa; Guest appearances in Tokyo, Munich, London, Cologne and Milan, Rosina in Il Barbiere di Siviglia; Other roles include Concepcion in L'Heure Espagnole, Orsini in Lucrezia Borgia, Cherubino and Ascanio in Benvenuto Cellini; Salzburg Festival, 1988 as Mozart's Marcellina; Sang Annina in Der Rosenkavalier at the Théâtre des Champs Elysées, Paris, 1989; Teatro San Carlos, Lisbon, as the Marquise in La Fille du Regiment, 1989. Recordings: Benvenuto Cellini, conducted by Colin Davis; Così fan tutte; L'Enfant et les Sortilèges; Il Turco in Italia; Massenet's Cendrillon. Honours: Grand Prix; Toulouse Conservatory. Address: c/o Théâtre des Champs Elysées, 15 Avenue Montaigne, F-75008, Paris, France.

BERCZELLY Istvan, b. 1938, Budapest, Hungary. Singer (Baritone). Education: Studied in Budapest. Debut: Debrecen, 1967, as Don Giovanni. Career: Sang at Debrecen until 1970; Budapest National Theatre from 1970, notably as Verdi's Renato, Basilio in La Fiamma by Respighi, Valentin (Faust), Bellini's Capulet, Wagner's Gunther, and the title role in Samson by Szokolay; Budapest, 1987, in the premiere of Szokolay's Ecce Homo. Address: c/o Hungarian State Opera, Nepoztarsasag utja 22, 1061 Budapest, Hungary.

BERENS Barbara, b. 25 Apr 1966, St Ingbert, Germany. Singer (Soprano). Education: Studied with Erika Koth and Josef Metternich, and in London with Vera Rozsa. Career: Sang with the Deutsche Oper am Rhein at Dusseldorf from 1988, notably as Susanna, Fiordiligi, Pamina, Elvira in I Puritani, Liu and Hanna Glawari; Guest engagements in Cologne (as Gretel), Saarbrucken (Mme Cortese in Il Viaggio a Reims) and elsewhere in Germany; Also a noted recitalist. Address: c/o Deutsche Oper am Rhein, Heinrich Heine-Allee 16a, W-4000 Dusseldorf, Germany.

BERESFORD Hugh, b. 17 Dec 1925, Birkenhead, England. Singer; (Baritone and Tenor). Education: Royal College of Music, Manchester; Vienna Music Academy; Studied with Dino Borgioli and Alfred Piccaver. Debut: Linz, 1953, as Wolfram in Tannhäuser. Career: Sang at Deutsche Oper am Rhein, Dusseldorf, from 1960; Sang in Graz, Augsburg and Wuppertal; Guest appearances at Covent Garden, Vienna, Munich, Stuttgart, Cologne, Brussells and Paris; Holland Festival, 1963, 1966; Venice, 1966, as Mandryka in Arabella; Sang further as Rigoletto, Posa in Don Carlos and Don Giovanni; Later career as tenor with Otello and Florestan at the Vienna Staatsoper, 1973; Tannhäuser at Bayreuth, 1972-73; Cologne Opera, 1981 as Florestan and Erik in Der fliegende Holländer. Address: c/o Oper der Stadt Koln, Offenbachplatz, D-5000 Cologne, Germany.

BEREZOVSKY Boris, b. Russia. Concert Pianist. Education: Studied at the Moscow Tchaikovsky Conservatoire. Career: Many concerts and recitals in Russia, Europe, Far East and the USA, 1990-; Appearances with the Royal Philharmonic and Philharmonia Orchestras, BBC Orchestra, London, the NDR Hamburg Symphony, the New York Philharmonic and the Moscow Philharmonic; Solo recitalist major international concert halls and festivals; Partnership with violinist Vadim Repin. Recordings include: Rachmaninov and Liszt Concertos; Chopin, Schumann, Ravel and Rachmaninov solos. Honours include: Gold Medal, International Tchaikovsky Competition, Moscow, 1990. Address: c/o IMG Artists, Media House, 3 Burlington Lane, London W4 2TH, England.

BERG Nathan, b. 1968, Saskatchewan, Canada. Singer (Baritone). Education: Augustana University, Alberta; University of Western Ontario; Maitrise Nationale de Versailles; Guildhall School with Vera Rozsa. Debut: Recital at Wigmore Hall, London. Career: Sang Thesée in Rameau's Hippolyte, Peter Quince, Dr Falke and Eustachio in Donizetti's L'assedio di Calais at the Guildhall School; Guglielmo and Mozart's Figaro with British Youth Opera; Various appearances & recordings with William Christie, Colin Davis, Yan Pascal, Tortellier and John Lubbock; Futher appearances in Monteverdi's Poppea at the Netherlands Opera; Schaunard at Canadian Opera Company; Various Oratorio & Recital Work. Honours: Prize Winner, Peter Pears, Kathleen Ferrier, Walter Gruner and Royal Overseas League Competitions. Address: IMG Artists, Media House, 3 Burlington Lane, London, W4 2TH, England.

BERGANZA Teresa, b. 16 March 1935, Madrid, Spain. Singer (mezzo-soprano). m. (1) Felix Lavilla, 1957, (2) Jose Rifa, 1986, 1 son, 2 daughters. Education: Bachillerato, Conservatorio, Madrid. Debut: Aix-en-Provence, France, 1957, as Mozart's Dorabella. Career: Appeared in Cosi fan Tutte and Le Nozze di Figaro, Mozart; La Cenerentola, Italiana in Algeri, Barbiere di Siviglia by Rossini; Carmen, Bizet; Werther, Massenet; Orpheo-Gluck; British debut Glyndebourne, 1958, as Mozart's Cherubino; At Covent Garden she has appeared as Rossini's Rosina and Cinderella and Bizet's Carmen; Sang in the opening concert of Bastille Opera at Paris, 13 July 1989; Carmen at the Palais Omnisports, Paris, 1989; Sang Carmen at Madrid, 1992; Recital at the Wigmore Hall, London, 1997; Film, Don Giovanni, directed by Losey. Recordings: About 120 records by various record companies, including Le Nozze di Figaro, Il Barbiere di Siviglia, Alcina, La Clemenza di Tito and L'Italiana in Algeri (HMV/EMI); La Finta Semplice by Mozart; Don Giovanni (CBS). Publications: Meditaciones de Una Cantante, Madrid, 1985. Honours: Medalla de Oro Merito Bellas Artes; Commandeur aux Arts et Letres; Grand Prix de Disque, 6 times; Grand Prix Rossini; First Elected Woman and Singer since 250 years in the Spanish Royal Academy of Arts, 1995. Hobbies: Montanismo; Cycling; Biographical Books; Japanese Culture. Current Management: Musiepana, c/Zurbamo, 34, 28101 Madrid, Spain. Address: Apdo 137, 28200 SLD Escorial, Madrid, Spain.

BERGASA Carlos, b. 1966, Spain. Singer (Baritone). Career: Many engagements at opera houses in Spain and elsewhere in Europe, notably in Donizetti's La Favorita, Mozart's Così fan tutte (as Guglielmo) and Gounod's Faust (as Valentin); Also sings the Mörické-Lieder by Wolf; Contestant at the 1995 Cardiff Singer of the World Competition. Address: Fernan Gonzales 17, Madrid 28009, Spain.

BERGE Sigurd, b. 1 July 1929, Vinstra, Norway. Composer. Education: Studied with Thor Lief Eken at the Oslo Conservatory, also with Finn Mortensen, Course in Electronic Music, Stockholm, Utrecht. Career: Tutor, Sagene College of Education, from 1959. Compositions: Episode for violin, piano, 1958; Divertimento for violin, viola, cello, 1956; For strings, Percussion, 1961; Pezzo rochestrale, 1958; Tamburo piccolo for strings, percussion, 1961; Chroma for Orchestra, 1963, A for Orchestra, 1965, B for Orchestra, 1966; Yuan Guan for wind quintet, 1967; Ballet for 2 dancers, percussion, 1968, 1970; Horn Call, 1972; Between Mirrors for violin, chamber orchestra, 1977; Juvenes, amateur string orchestra, 1977; Music for Orchestra, 1978; Gudbrandsdalsspelet, music drama, 1980; Wind Ballet, 1981; Music for 4 horns, 1984; Electronic pieces. Memberships: Chairman, Norwegian composers Union, 1985-88. Address: c/o PRS Ltd (Norway), 29-33 Berners Street, Member Registration, London,W1P 4AA, England.

BERGEL Erich, b. 1 June 1930, Rosenau, Romania. Conductor. Education: Sibiu and Cluj Conservatories. debut: US Houston Symphony Orchestra, 1975. Career: Played flute in the Sibiu Philharmonic Orchestra, 1945-48; Studied further in Cluj with Ciolan, 1950-55 and was conductor of the Oradea Philharmonic, 1955-59, Cluj Philharmonic, 1959-72; Musical Director of the Nordwestdeutsche Philharmonie, 1972-74; Principal Guest Conductor, Houston Symphony Orchestra, 1979-81; Directed the BBC Welsh Symphony Orchestra at Cardiff and has been Professor of Conducting at the Berlin Hochschule für Musik. Publications include: Bach's Art of Fugue, volume 1, Bonn, 1979. Address: c/o BBC Natl Symph Orch of Wales, Broadcasting House, Landaff, Cardiff, CF5 2YQ

BERGEN Beverly, b. 1950, New Zealand. Singer; Soprano; Mezzo-Soprano. Education: Studied at London Opera Centre. Career: Has appeared as guest artist at the Deutsche Oper Berlin, also in Hamburg, Dusseldorf and elsewhere in Germany; Sang in premiere of Maderna's Hyperion at Brussels; Operatic roles include Constanze, Jenufa, Strauss's Countess, Katherina in Lady Macbeth of Mtsensk, Senta, Luisa Miller, Violetta, Musetta and Lucia di Lammermoor; Has performed throughout Australia in Messiah, Beethoven's Ninth and Das Klagende Lied by Mahler; Other repertoire includes Mozart's Requiem, The Trojans, Bruckner's Te Deum, with the Sydney Symphony Orchestra and Judas Maccabeus with St Hedwig's Cathedral Choir, Berlin; Changed to mezzo-soprano repertoire, 1989, appeared as Amneris in Aida; Engagements with Opera Factory, London. Address: c/o Opera Factory, London Sinfonietta, 8a The Leather Market, Weston Street, London, SE1 3ER, England.

BERGER Arthur, b. 15 May 1912, New York, New York, USA. Composer; Critic; Teacher. Education: New York and Harvard Universities; Further studies in Paris with Nadia Boulanger and at the Sorbonne. Career includes: Teacher at Mills College, 1939-43, and Brandeis University, 1953-80 retiring as Irving Fine Professor of Music Emeritus, currently teaching at New England Conservatory; Music Critic for New York Sun from 1943 and New York Herald Tribune from 1946-1953. Compositions include: Orchestral: Serenade Concertante, 1944, revised 1951, for CBS, Polyphony, 1956, for Louisville Orchestra, and Ideas of Order, 1952, for Dimitri Mitropoulos; Perspectives II, 1985; Chamber Music: Quartet in C Major for Winds, 1941; Chamber Music for 13 Players, 1956, Quintet for Woodwinds, 1984, for Harvard Musical Association; String Quartet, 1958; Septet, 1966; Trio for Violin, Guitar and Piano, 1972; Trio for Guitar, Cello and Piano, 1980; Diptych for chamber ensemble, 1990; Collage III, 1992, revised 1994 for chamber ensemble; Piano Music: Partita for Piano, 1947; Five pieces for Piano, 1969; Perspectives II, for four hands, 1982; Two Episodes, 1933, 2 Birthday Pieces, Improvisation for AC for Aaron Copland, 1980 and For Elliott at 75 for Elliott Carter, 1983; Vocal, Choral: Words for Music, Perhaps, 1939; Five Settings of European Poets for Tenor and Piano, 1978-79, Love, Sweet Animal for Chamber Chorus and Piano 4-Hands, 1982; Ode of Ronsard, 1987. Recordings include: (Two) Episodes with Robert Helps; Polyphony; String Quartet; Serenade Concertante; Five Pieces for

Piano, Septet; Three pieces for two pianos; Chamber music for 13 players. Publications: Numerous critical and analytical articles; Seminal study, Problems of Pitch Organization in Stravinsky; Wrote about Charles Ives and was first to write a book on the music of Aaron Copland, 1953, reprinted 1990. Honours include: Award from Council of Learned Societies, 1933; Also from Guggenheim and other foundations, the NEA, League of Composers; Fellow of American Academy of Arts and Letters and American Academy of Arts and Sciences. Current Management: Verna Fine, Rosalie Calabrese Management. Address: PO Box 20580, Park West Station, New York, NY 10025-1521, USA.

BERGER Roman, b. 9 Aug 1930, Cieszyn, Poland. Composer. m. Ruth Strbova, 6 July 1968. Education: Academy of Musical Arts, Katowice, 1949-52; Academy of Musical Arts Bratislava, 1952-56, 1960-65. Career: Professor of Piano, Conservatoire, Bratislava, 1955-66; Fellow, TV sound laboratory, 1966-67; Secretary, Union of Slovak composers, 1967-69; Lecturer on theory of composition, contemporary music and electronic music, Academy of musical arts, Bratislava,1969-71, 1983-85; Contracted to Musicological Institute of the Slovak Academy of Sciences, 1977-91. Compositions: Transformations, 4 symphonic pieces, 1965; Memento for orchestra, 1974; Epitaph to Copernicus for electronics, 1973; De Profundis for bass, cello and electronics, 1980; Exodus for organ, 1982. Publications: On Music Integration, 1976; System Theory and Musical Communication, 1981; Museum and Utopy, 1985; Theory Wrongly Present, 1989; Velvet Revolution and Music, 1990. Honours: Prize in composition at Bourges, 1974; Herder Prize, 1988; Prize of Czechosl Critics, 1967, 1990. Memberships: International Society for Contemporary Music, Slovac Section; European Culture Club, Slovac Section; Team for Interdisciplinary Semiotics, Prague; Czech Association for the Club of Rome. Address: Bazovského 11/17, SR 841 01, Bratislava, Slovak Republic.

BERGER-TUNA Helmut, b. 7 May 1942, Vienna, Austria. Singer, (Bass). Education: Studied in Vienna with Franz Schuch-Tovini. Debut: Linz 1969, as Lodovico in Otello. Career: Sang at Graz from 1972; Guest engagements in Vienna; Frankfurt; Karlsruhe; Barcelona; Stuttgart 1981, as Ochs in Der Rosenkavalier; Sang at the Salzburg Festival 1981, in the premiere of Cerha's Baal; Hamburg 1983, in a concert performance of Rudi Stephan's Die ersten Menschen; Paris Opera 1984, as Ochs; Often heard in operas by Mozart, Rossini, Donizetti, Verdi, Smetana and Strauss; Sang Baron Ochs and Kecal in the Bartered Bride at the Zurich Opera 1988; Don Magnifico in La Cenerentola at Stuttgart 1989, followed by Kecal in 1990; Sang the Priest in Lady Macbeth of the Mtsensk District, 1992; Other roles include Osmin at La Scala, Paris, Frankfurt and Japan; Hunding at Covent Garden; Rocco, Leporello, Daland and Sarastro in Berlin; Sang Baron Ochs at Los Angeles, 1994 and Mustafa in L'Italiana in Algeri, 1996. Recordings: Zar und Zimmermann, BASF; Die schweigsame Frau; Baal, Amadeo; Der Corregidor by Wolf, Schwann. Address: c/o Staatsheater Stuttgart, Oberer Schlossgarten 6, D-7000 Stuttgart, Germany.

BERGLUND Ingela, b. 1959, Sweden. Singer (Soprano). Education: Studied viola at Stockholm College of Music, 1974-79; State Opera School, Stockholm, 1985-88, with Kerstin Meyer and Elisabeth Söderström. Debut: Royal Opera Stockholm, 1988, as Donna Anna. Career: Member of Royal Stockholm Philharmonic Orchestra, 1979-84; Sang Mozart's Countess and the woman in La Voix Humaine at Stockholm, 1988; Salzburg Landestheater, 1989-92 as Donna Anna, Musetta, Tatiana, Fiordiligi and Hanna Glawari in Die Lustige Witwe; As Beatrice in Boccaccio by Suppé at Royal Opera, Stockholm; Guest appearances at Semper Opera, Dresden and in Austria, USA, Spain and Japan. Recordings: Radio and television in Sweden. Current Management: IM Audio and Music AB, Stockholm. Address: Asogatan 67 VI 5-118 29 Stockholm, Sweden.

BERGLUND Paavo (Allan Englebert), b. 14 April 1929, Helsinki, Finland. Conductor. m. Kirsti Kiveskas, 1958, 1 son, 2 daughters. Education: Sibelius Academy, Helsinki. Debut: 1965, Bournemouth Symphony Orchestra. Career: Violinist, Finnish Radio Symphony Orchestra, 1949-56; Conductor, 1956-62; Principal Conductor, 1962-71, Bournemouth Symphony Orchestra, 1972-79; Helsinki Philharmonic Orchestra, 1975-79; Principal Conductor of Stockholm Philharmonic Orchestra, 1987-91; Principal Conductor of Royal Danish Orchestra, 1993-96; Conducted the London Philharmonic at the Festival Hall, Lodnon, 1997; Maskarade by Nielsen at Copenhagen, 1996. Recordings: Complete Sibelius symphonies including first recording of Kullervo Symphony, 1971-77; Ma Vlast by Smetana, Shostakovich symphonies 5, 6, 7, 10, 11, and many other recordings including CD of Mozart and Strauss Oboe Concertos with Douglas Boyd; Chamber Orchestra of Europe, ASV. Publications: A comparative study of the printed score and the Manuscript of the Seventh Symphony of Sibelius 1970. Address: Munkkiniemenranta 41, 00330 Helsinki 33, Finland.

BERGMAN Erik (Valdemar), b. 24 Nov 1911, Nykarleby, Finland. Composer. m. Solveig von Schoultz, 7 July 1961. Education: Literature and Aesthetics, Musicology, University of Helsinki, 1931-33; Composition Diploma, Sibelius Academy, Helsinki, 1939; Studied Composition in Berlin with Heinz Tiessen and in Switzerland with Wladimir Vogel. Debut: Helsinki, 1940. Career: Conductor, Helsinki University Chorus, 1950-69; Professor of Composition at the Sibelius Academy, Helsinki, 1963-76; Concerts in Washington DC and New York, 1981, 1991, London, 1986, Leningrad, 1989, St Petersburg, 1992, Stockholm, 1993; Works performed at several international festivals. Compositions: The Singing Tree, opera (1995); Works for orchestra, concertos for soloists and orchestra, works for soloists, choir and orchestra, works for solo instruments, chamber music. Recordings: The Singing Tree; Concerto for violin and Orchestra; Birds in the Morning, flute and orchestra; Chamber works, works for piano, guitar, choral and vocal works. Honours: Pro Finlandia Medal, Sibelius International Prize, 1965; DPhil, hc, 1978, 1982; Royal Swedish Academy of Music; Honorary Member, Society of Finnish Composers; Commander, Order of the White Rose of Finland; Commander, Order of the Lion of Finland; The State's Music Prize, 1989; The Nordic Council Music Prize, 1994; Finland Prize, 1997. Membership: Academy of Finland, 1982. Address: Berggatan 22 C 52, SF-00100 Helsinki, Finland.

BERGONZI Carlo, b. 13 July 1924, Busseto, Parma, Italy. Opera Singer (Tenor). m. Adele, 2 children. Education: Parma Conservatory. Career: Debut (as baritone) as Figaro (Il Barbiere di Siviglia) at Lecce, 1949; Debut as Tenor in title role of Andrea Chénier, Teatro Petruzzelli, Bari, 1951; Subsequently appeared at various Italian opera houses including La Scala, Milan; US debut in Il Tabarro and Cavalleria Rusticana, Lyric Opera, Chicago, 1955; Appeared at Metropolitan Opera, New York in Aida (as Radames) and Il Trovatore (as Manrico), 1955-56; London Debut Stoll Theatre, 1953 as Alvaro in La forza del destino; At Covent Garden he sang Verdi's Riccardo, Radames and Manrico and Puccini's Cavaradossi; Appeared at all the major opera houses in Europe and also in USA and South America; Repertoire included many Verdi roles as well as roles in operas by Donizetti, Boito, Leoncavallo and Mascagni; Sang Edgardo at Covent Garden, 1985; Metropolitan Opera 1956-83, in 249 performances of 21 roles, including Canio, Andrea Chénier, Cavaradossi, Riccardo, Nemorino, Macduff, Rodolfo, Alfredo, Pollione, Enzo and Manrico; Metropolitan Gala (25th anniversary), 4 Dec 1981; Sang Edgardo at the Vienna Staatsoper, 1988; Nemorino for New Jersey State Opera, 1989; Farewell Recital at Covent Garden, 1992. Address: c/o Harold Holt Ltd, 31 Sinclair Road, London W1A 0NS, England.

BERINI Bianca, b. 20 Dec 1928, Trieste, Italy. Mezzo-Soprano. Education: Studied in Trieste and Milan. Debut: Teatro Nuovo Milan, 1963 as Suzuki in Madama Butterfly. Career: Has sung throughout Italy and in Vienna, Berlin, Amsterdam, Brussels, Marseilles, Nice, Toulouse and London; Metropolitan Opera debut in 1978 as Amneris, returning to New York as Eboli, Amneris, Santuzza, Dalila, Ulrica, Azucena and Frederica in Luisa Miller; Further engagements in Dallas, Philadelphia, Baltimore, San Francisco, Lisbon, Barcelona and Zurich; Other roles include Adalgisa in Norma, Laura in La Gioconda, Ortrud in Lohengrin, Charlotte in Werther and Jane Seymour in Anna Bolena. Recordings include: Verdi's Requiem. Address: c/o Metropolitan Opera, Lincoln Center, New York, NY 10023, USA.

BERIO Luciano, b. 24 Oct 1925, Oneglia, Italy. Composer. m. 1. Cathy Berberian, 1950, dissolved 1964, 1 daughter; 2. Susan Oyama 1964 dissolved 1971, 1 son, 1 daughter; 3. Talia Packer, 1977, 1 son. Education: Liceo Classico and Conservatorio G Verdi, Milan; Further study with Dallapiccola in USA. Career: Founder of Studio Fonologia Musicale, Italian Radio; Teacher of Composition and Lecturer at Mills College, California, Darmstadt 1954-59 and Harvard University; Professor of Composition at the Juilliard School from 1965; Has worked with Boulez at the studios of IRCAM, Paris. Compositions: Dramatic: Allez-Hop mimed story, 1959, rev. 1968; Passagio, mesa in scena, 1963; Laborintus II 1970; Opera 1970, rev 1979; Recital 1, For Cathy, 1972; I Trionfi di Petraca, ballet 1974; Linea, ballet 1974; La Vera Storia, opera 1982; Un Re in Ascolto, opera 1984; Naturale, ballet, 1986; Orchestral: Variazioni 1954; Nones 1954; Divertimento, with Maderna, 1958; Chemins I-IV 1965-75; Tempi Concertati 1959; Bewegung 1971; Concerto for 2 pianos & orchestra 1973; Still 1973; Eindrucke 1974; Points on the curve to find, for piano and 20 instruments 1974; Il Ritorno degli Snovidenia for cello and orchestra 1977; Piano Concerto 1977; Entrata 1980; Accordo for 4 wind bands 1981; Corale for violin and orchestra 1982; Voci for viola and orchestra, 1984; Requies, 1984; Formazioni 1986; Festum, 1989; Schubert Rendering, sketches, 1989; Brahms-Berio Op 120 No 1, 1986; Shofar, 1995; Clarinet Concerto, 1997. Vocal: Quattro canzoni Populari 1947; Opus Number Zoo for speaker and wind quintet, 1952, rev 1970; Chamber Music, Joyce 1953; Circles (Cummings), with harp and 2 percussion 1960; Epifanie for female voice and orchestra, 1961; Sinfonia 1968-69; Questo vuol dire che, for solo voices, small chorus, instruments and tape 1969; Ora, Virgil, 1971; Bewegung II for baritone and orchestra 1971; Cries of London for 8 solo voices 1973; 11 Folk songs for mezzo and orchestra 1975; Calmo, In Memorian Bruno Maderna, for soprano and ensemble 1974; Coro for 40 voices & orchestra 1976; Duo for baritone, 2 violins, chorus and orchestra 1982; Mahler-Berio, Funf Frühe Lieder and Sechs Frühe Lieder, 1986-87; Ofanim, 1988; Canticum Novissimi Testamenti 1989; Chamber and Instrumental: Suite for piano 1948; String Quartet 1956; Serenata for flute and 14 instruments 1957; Differences for ensemble 1959; Sincronie for string quartet 1964; Wasserklavier and Erdenklavier for piano 1964, 1970; Memory for 2 pianos & percussion 1970, rev. 1973; Musica Leggera for flute, viola, cello, 1974; Sequenze I-XI for solo flute, harp, voice, piano, trombone, viola, oboe, violin, clarinet, trumpet, guitar, 1958-88; Duette per due violini 1979-82; Luftklavier 1985; Ricorrenze per Quintetto a Fiati 1987; String Quartet 1986-90. Feuerklavier, 1989; Electronic Mutazioni 1955; Perspectives 1957. Thema, Omaggio a Joyce, 1958; Momenti 1960, Visage 1961. Chants Paralleles 1975. Address: 11 Colombaio, Radicondoli, Siena, Italy.

BERKELEY Edward (Charles), b. 18 Jan 1945, New York, USA. Education: Career: Co-General Director, Aspen Opera Theatre Centre; Faculty The Juilliard School; Director of the Juilliard Opera Theatre; Faculty of Circle in the Square Theatre's Professional Workshop; Co-Founder and Artistic Director, The Willow Cabin Theater Company; Beyond Manhattan, he has served as Artistic Director of the Musical Theater Lab at the John F Kennedy Center; Has directed at Wolf Trap; The Library of Congress in Washington DC; Opera Festival of New Jersey; Williamstown Theater Festival; Berkshire Theatre Festival; Long Beach Opera; San Diego's Old Globe Theatre; The Eastman School and Brooklyn College; At Aspen Music Festival had directed many unusual and acclaimed productions; Co-Teaches a unique Opera Scenes Master Class; Notable productions include the American Stage premiere of Milhaud's Christophe Colomb; Macbeth and The Tempest at Lincoln Center; The American Stage premiere of Mark Neikrug's Los Alamos; A premiere workshop of Jacob Druckman's Medea; Falla's El Retablo de Maese Pedro; Milhaud's Le Pauvre Matelot and Les Malheurs d'Orphée. Address: 1150 Park Avenue, New York, NY 10128, USA.

BERKELEY Michael, b. 29 May 1948, London, England. Composer. Education: Westminster Cathedral Choir School; Royal Academy of Music; Further study with Lennox Berkeley and Richard Rodney Bennett. Career: BBC Radio 3 Announcer, 1974-79; Programme Presenter, BBC2 TV; Composer-in-Residence, London College of Music, 1987-88; Opera, Baa Baa Black Sheep premiered at 1992 Cheltenham Festival; Artistic Director, Cheltenham International Festival of Music, 1995-; Co-Artistic Director, Spitalfields Festival, 1995-. Compositions: Meditations for Strings, 1976; Oboe Concerto, 1977; Fantasia Concertant for Chamber Orchestra, 1977; String Trio, 1978; The Wild Winds for Soprano and Chamber Orchestra, 1978; Cello Sonata, 1978; Violin Sonata, 1979; Organ Sonata, 1979; At The Round Earth's Imagin'd Corners for Soprano, Baritone, Chorus and Organ, 1980; Uprising Symphony, 1980; Chamber Symphony, 1980; 4 String Quartets, , 1981, 1984, 1988, 1995; Wessex Graves for Tenor and Harp, 1981; Flames for Orchestra, 1981; Suite, Vision of Piers The Ploughman, 1981; Gregorian Variations for Orchestra, 1982; Cello Concerto, 1982; Oratorio, Or Shall We Die?, 1982; Guitar Sonata, 1982; Clarinet Quintet, 1982; Songs of Awakening Love, 1986; Organ Concerto, 1987; Bastet, 1988; Music for a Ballet; Keening for Saxophone and Piano, 1988; Quartet Study, 1988; Coronach for String Orchestra, 1988; The Red Macula for Chorus and Orchestra, 1989; Fierce Tears for Solo Oboe, 1990; Stupendous Stranger for Chorus and Brass, 1990; Entertaining Master Punch for Chamber Orchestra, 1991; Opera, Baa Baa Black Sheep, 1992; Clarinet Concerto, 1992; Elegy for flute and strings, 1993; Viola Concerto, 1994. Address: c/o Oxford University Press, Music Department, 3 Park Road, London, NW1 6XN, England.

BERKES Kalman, b. 1952, Budapest, Hungary. Clarinettist. Education: Studied Music from the age of 4; Bela Bartók Conservatory, 1966-70; Ferenc Liszt Academy of Music, 1977. Career: Principal Clarinettist, Budapest State Opera Orchestra and Budapest Philharmonic, 1972; Budapest Chamber Ensemble and Jeunesses Musicales Wind Quintet, 1973; Extensive Guest Performances throughout Europe including: Austria,France, Germany, Netherlands, Italy and Switzerland; Played Trios by Beethoven, Brahms and Zemlinsky at St John's, London, 1997. Recordings: Has made a number of records including Bartók's Contrasts. Honours: Silver Medal, Geneva International Musical Concours, 1972. Address: c/o St John's, Smith Square (Artists' Contracts), London SW1P 3HA, England.

BERKOWITZ Paul, b. 1 Oct 1948, Montreal, Canada. Concert Pianist. Education: McGill University and Curtis Institute with Serkin and Horszowski. Debut: London, 1973 (resident in London, 1973-93, Santa Barbara, California, 1993-); New York Solo Debut, Alice Tully Hall, 1978. Career: Recitalist, Wigmore and Queen Elizabeth Halls, London; Tivoli, Copenhagen and throughout Europe and North America; Soloist with majaor orchestras in Britain and North America; Festival engagements in Belgium, Denmark, England, France, Italy, Scotland and Spain; Frequent solo radio broadcasts and recitals for BBC and CBC; Barcelona Festival with the Endellion Quartet and the Albion Ensemble; Beethoven duets with Richard Goode at the Wigmore Hall, 1990-91; Appearances with the BBC Scottish Symphony and English Sinfonia; Professor, Guildhall School, 1975-93; Professor, University of California, Santa Barbara, 1993-; Masterclasses at McGill University, University of British Columbia, Queens University, Royal Conservatory of Music, Toronto, in Canada and Yehudi Menuhin School and elsewhere in Britain, France and Barcelona; Repertoire includes sonatas and other major works by Schubert, Beethoven, Brahms, Mozart, Schumann, Chopin and Bartok; The Brahms Handel Variations and Klavierstücke op 76 and opp 116-119 and Schumann's Kreisleriana and C major Fantasy. Recordings include: Complete Sonatas of Schubert (7 volumes); Schumann's Kreisleriana and Davidsbündlertänze, Brahms Piano Pieces Opp 116-118. Honours include: Fellow of the Guildhall School of Music, 1988; Canada Council Grants, 1989-91; BBC Record Review and BBC Magazine First Choice Award for recording of Schumann's Kreisleriana, 1993. Address: Department of Music, University of California, Santa Barbara, CA 93106-6070, USA.

BERL Christine, b. 22 July 1943, New York City, USA. Composer. 2 sons. Education: BS in Piano, Mannes College of Music, 1961-64; MA in Composition, Queen's College, 1968-70. Career: Performances by Emanuel Ax in Highland Park, Ravinia, 1988; Commissioned by Peter Serkin for 1989-90, The Chamber Music Society of Lincoln Center for their 20th Anniversary Season with Frederica von Stade as guest artist, 1989, Cornell University Chorus, 1989; Concert devoted to Berl's works on Distinguished Artists Series of 92nd Street Y, 1990; Commissioned work for Peter Serkin, Emmanuel Ax for 2 Pianos; Other participants: Patricia Spence, Matt Haimovitz, Richard Stoltzman, Richard Goode, Andre-Michel Schub, 1994; World premiere by French violinist Pierre Amoyal and Jeremy Menuhin of Masmoudi, a violin sonata commissioned by Radio France; New York premiere of Masmudi at Merkin Concert Hall, 1994. Compositions: Elegy for Piano Solo, 1974; Three Pieces for Chamber Ensemble, 1975; Ab La Dolchor for Soprano, Female Chorus and Orchestra, 1979; Sonata for Piano, 1986-87; Dark Summer for Mezzo Soprano, Piano and String Trio; The Lord of the Dance, for Peter Serkin; The Violent Bear It Away for Orchestra, 1988; Cantilena for Cello and Piano, for Matt Haimovitz. Recordings: Three Pieces for Chamber Ensemble, 1975, with Arthur Weisburg and members of the Contemporary Chamber Ensemble and Speculum Musicae, Ursula Oppens, Piano; Elegy, The Lord of The Dance on CD; Piano Sonata by Edipan. Address: 250 West 85th Street, No 12D, New York, NY 10024, USA.

BERMAN Boris, b. 3 Apr 1948, Moscow, Russia. Concert Pianist; Professor of Piano. m. Zina Tabachnikova, 1975, 1 son, 1 daughter. Education: BA, MA, Moscow Tchaikovsky Conservatory, 1971. Debut: Moscow, 1965. Career: Performances in over 30 countries, appeared with Concertgebouw, Philharmonia, Royal Scottish, Detroit, Minnesota, Houston, Atlanta, Toronto, Israel Philharmonic, Moscow Philharmonic, St Petersburg Philharmonic and many others; Festivals include Bergen, Ravina, Israel, Marlboro; Numerous radio and TV appearances around the world; Former Professor of Piano at Tel-Aviv University, Indiana University, Bloomington, Boston University; Currently at Yale School of Music; Music Director, Music Spectrum concert series, Tel-Aviv, 1975-84; Music Director, Yale Music Spectrum, USA, 1984-97; Director, Summer Piano Institute at Yale, 1990-92; Director, International Summer Piano Institute, Hong Kong, 1995-97; Played Beethoven and Debussy at St John's, London, 1997. Recordings: All solo piano works by Prokofiev in 9 vols, Stravinsky Concerto with Orchestre de la Suisse Romande, N Järvi, Prokofiev Concertos 1,4,5 with Concertgebouw Orchestra, N Järvi, Shostakovich, Scriabin all Sonatas in 2 vols; Recitals or works by Debussy, Stravinsky, Shostakovich, Schnittke; Numerous Chamber Recordings. Honour: Edison Classic Award, 1990, Holland. Memberships: Juror at various national, international piano competitions. Current Management: Columbia Artists, New York; Lies Askonas, England. Address: Yale School of Music, PO Box 208246, New Haven, CT 06520, USA.

BERMAN Lazar, b. 26 Feb 1930, Leningrad, Russia. Pianist. m. Valentina Berman, 28 Dec 1961, 1 s. Education: Graduated, Moscow Conservatory, 1953; Student of Masterclasses, 1953-57. Debut: In concert, 1934. Career: Orchestral debut, Moscow Philharmonic, playing Mozart's C major Concerto, K503, 1940; Professional Concert Pianist, 1957-; US debut at Miami University, Oxford, OH, also with American Orchestra, 1976; Appearances at Carnegie Hall with New Jersey Symphony Orchestra, 1971. Recordings: Recording artist in music by Beethoven, Liszt, Prokofiev, Scriabin and Tchaikovsky's 1st Piano Concerto with Karajan, 1976. Honours: 1st Prize, International Youth Festival, East Berlin; 4th Place, Queen Elisabeth of Belgium Contest, Brussels, 1951. Memberships: Philharmonic Society of Moscow; Founder, Russia-Belgium Friendship Society. Address: c/o Jacques Leister Artists Management, Corchester Towers, 165 West 6th Street, New York, NY 10023 USA.

BERNARD André, b. 6 Apr 1946, Gap, France. Conductor; Trumpeter. Education: Diplome Superieur of Conducting, Paris; 1st Place for Trumpet, Paris Superior Conservatory; Laureat Concours International Trumpet, Geneva, Switzerland, 1968; Studied German romantic repertory with Carlo Maria Giulini and Italian opera with Bruno Bartoletti, Sienna, Italy. Career: Guest Conductor for many international orchestras including London Philharmonic, London Symphony Orchestra, and Mozarteum Salzburg; Opera conducting in Strasbourg, Lille, Sienna, Geneva; TV appearances in France, Germany and Japan; Radio appearances in USA, Canada, Japan, Germany, Italy and France; Solo appearances including Salzburg Festival, Berlin Philharmonie, Carnegie Hall and Lincoln Center in New York, Paris, Tokyo, London, Rome, Prague, Madrid, Venice, and Washington; Appearances with world's leading orchestras; 31 Concerts on tour conducting Philharmonia Hungarica, including Carnegie Hall and Los Angeles, 1986; Contract for concert series in London, tours in France and Italy and recordings with New Symphony Orchestra of London and London Chamber Orchestra, 1982-87. Recordings: 20 with Academy of St Martin-in-the-Fields, English Chamber Orchestra, and Ensemble Instrumental de France. Current Management: Columbia Artists Management, NY, USA. Address: 19 Rue Joliot Curie, 93100 Montreuil, Paris, France.

BERNARD Annabelle, b. 1938, New Orleans, Louisana, USA. Singer (Soprano). Education: Studies, Xavier University, New Orleans; The New England Conservatory. Debut: Sang Susanna in Le Nozze di Figaro, conducted by Boris Goldovsky, 1958. Career: Appeared as Butterfly in Stuttgart, 1959; Lieder recitals with Hermann Reutter; Vienna Staatsoper debut as Aida, conducted by Karajan; Sang at the Deutsche Oper Berlin from 1962, debut as Aida; Salzburg Festival, 1973, as Electra in Idomeneo, conducted by Karl Böhm; Visits with the Deutsche Oper to Japan as Fiordiligi and in The Ring, 1987; Washington Opera, 1986, as Fiordiligi; New Orleans Opera as Maddalena in Adrea Chénier; Sang in the stage premiere of Musorgsky's Salambo at San Carlo, Naples; Modern repertory includes the premieres on Montezuma by Sessions, 1964 and Dallapiccola's Ulisse, 1968; Concert appearances with the Cleveland Orchestra conducted by Lorin Maazel at Carnegie Hall, the Berlin Philharmonic Orchestra. Honours: Berliner Kammersängerin, 1970; MD, Honoris Causa, Xavier University, 1976. Address: c/o Deutsche Oper Berlin, Richard Wagnerstrasse 10, D-1000 Berlin, Germany.

BERNARDI Mario, b. 20 Aug 1930, Kirkland Lake, Ontario, Canada. Conductor; Pianist. m. Mona Kelly, 12 May 1962, 1 daughter. Education: Diplomas in Piano; Organ; Composition, B Marcello Conservatory, Venice, 1947; Piano with Lubka Kolessa, Toronto. Career: Sadler's Wells Opera, 1963-69, with many performances of operas by Verdi; San Francisco Opera 1967, 1968, 1982; New York City Opera, 1970-86; Metropolitan Opera, 1984; Several major orchestras including Chicago, Pittsburgh, San Francisco, Toronto, Montreal, BBC; 13 years with National Arts Centre Orchestra, Ottawa, 1969-82, giving many premieres of works by Canadian Composers; Music Director, Calgary Philharmonic; Season 1987-88, with Cendrillon at Washington and Don Giovanni at Montreal; Conducted Lucia di Lammermoor at Washington 1989; Gave the Verdi Reqieum at the 1988 Olympic Arts Festival; Conducted Fidelio at Toronto, 1991; Massenet's Chérubin at Covent Garden, 1994; Recordings: Numerous recordings for EMI; RCA; CBC with Sadler's Wells Company; National Arts Centre Orchestra, Toronto, Vancouver Symphonies, CBC Radio Orchestra; Recordings include Hansel and Gretel, with Sadler's Wells Company; Mozart Symphony K551 and Concerto K219, with Steven Staryk; Haydn arias and symphony No 85; Brahms Serenade Op 11. Honours: Companion of the Order of Canada; Several honorary doctorates. Memberships: Savage Club, London; Ranchmen's Club, Calgary. Hobbies: Chess; Mountain hiking. Current Management: Columbia Artists Management, New York. Address: 248 Warren Road, Toronto, Ontario M4V 2S8, Canada.

BERNARDINI Alfredo, b. 30 Oct 1961, Rome, Italy. Oboist. 2 sons, 1 daughter. Education: Studies, Royal Conservatory, The Hague, Netherlands, 1982-; Soloist diploma, 1987; Diploma, University of Oxford, 1985. career: Performs with major European ensembles such as Hesperion XX, Les Arts Florissants, La Petite Bande, Capella Coloniensis, Amsterdam Baroque Orchestra, Collegio Strumentale Italiano, La Grande Ecurie, Concerto Armonico Budapest and Concerto Italiano. Recordings: With EMI, D&GM, Astrée and Bongiovanni. Contributions to: Articles on Il Flauto Dolce; Early Music; Journal of the American Musical Instruments Society. Hobbies: Research on history of woodwind instruments in Italy; Making of 18th Century oboes, copies. Address: via Sebenico 2, 00198 Roma, Italy.

BERNAS Richard, b. 21 Apr 1950, New York, USA. Conductor. m. 1. Deirdre Busenberg, div; 2. Beatrice Harper, 2 sons. Debut: As pianist, Kent University, 1966; As conductor, London, England, 1976. Career: Warsaw Autumn Festival, 1977; Vienna Festival, 1984; Opéra de Lyons and Paris Opéra, 1985; London Sinfonietta, England, 1986; Edinburgh Festival, Scotland, 1986; The Royal Helsinki Philharmonic, 1988; Royal Ballet, Covent Garden, BBC Symphony Orchestra, 1989; Holland Festival, 1989; Aldeburgh Festival Opera, Suffolk, England, 1990; English National Opera, London, 1990; Netherlands Opera, Amsterdam and The Hague, 1991; Ars Musica Festival, Brussels, 1991; Orchestre National de Belgique, Brussels, 1993; Netherlands Radio Symphony Orchestra, 1994; Opera de Bastille, 1995; Musique Oblique, Paris, 1995; Conductor, Saltarello Choir, 1976-80; Conductor, Music Projects, London, 1978-; Conductor in Residence, Sussex University, 1979-82. Recordings: Factory Classics; Virgin Classics; Continum; NMC; Decca-Argo. Current Mangement: Robert Gilder and Co. London, England. Address: 73 Avenue Gardens, London, W3 8HB, England.

BERNASCONI Silvano, b. 16 Oct 1950, Chiasso, Switzerland. Pianist; Composer. m. Irene Cairoli Alessandra, 20 June 1984, 1 son. Education: Conservatoire de Lausanne; Piano with Francesto Zaza; Composition with Andor Kovach; Electronic music with Rainer Bosch; Conservatorio Santa Cecilia in Rome; Composition with Vieri Tosatti, Gregorian song with Domenico Bartolucci; Organ with Ferdinando Germani; Electronic music with Franco Evangelisti. Debut: Rome, 1974. Career: Pianist and composer, 1980-85; Executions of music commissioned by Musica Ticinensis, 1982 and Television. Compositions: Sounds and Crystals for two Vibraphones, 1982; Psallite, four lines for organ, 1974; Tourbillon, for violin & Orchestra, 1993. Recordings: Sounds and Crystals, transparencies for two vibraphones and piano; Sounds Am Bach, for piano played by the composer. Publications: Didactics compositions in the European year of Music, 1985; Contributor to Musica & Teatro magazine. Honours: Invitation by UNCM to found a European Composers Union, 1991. Memberships: Association of Swiss Musicians; European Composers Union. Hobbies: Abstract painting; New fables; Natural sculpture. Address: Casa Am Bach, 6803 Famignolo-Lugana, Switzerland.

BERNATHOVA Eva, b. 4 Dec 1922, Budapest, Hungary. Concert Pianist; Senior Lecturer. m. Joseph Bernath, 20 Feb 1947. Education: Gymnasium, Budapest; Professor Diploma, 1949; Performing Artist Diploma, 1950; Franz Liszt Academy of Music, Budapest. Debut: Prague, 1948. Career: Has toured in Europe, USA, Canada, Far East, India, Japan, Australia and New Zealand; Soloist with many world famous orchestras including Berlin Philharmonic, Czech Philharmonic, Orchestre de la Suisse Romande, Royal Philharmonic Orchestra, Gewandhaus Orchestra; Senior Lecturer at Trinity College of Music, London. Recordings include: Solo works by J H Vorisek, Franz Liszt, M Balakirev, J Suk, Mozart; Janácek's Concertino for Piano and Chamber Orchestra; Franck's Symphonic Variations; Ravel's Concerto in G; Bartók's Concerto No 3; Chamber Music: Dvorák's Piano Quintet in A, Brahms's Piano Quintet in F minor, Franck's Piano Quintet in F minor, Shostakovich's Piano Quintet in G minor. Hobbies: Literature; Languages; Table Tennis. Address: 8 Purley Avenue, London, NW2 1SJ, England.

BERNATIK Rudolf, b. 6 Mar 1937, Sumbark, Czech Republic. University Professor; Pianist. m. Vlasta Ryskova, 3 June 1961, 1 son. Education: School of Music, 1951; Conservatoire in Ostrava, 1956; Academy of Arts in Prague, 1961. Debut: Piano Recital, Ostrava and CZ Republic Radio, 1955. Career: Stage Appearances, Praha, Moskva, Nagoy, Venezia, Berlin, Sophia, Oslo, Göteborg, Haag, Buenos Aires, Tokyo; Television Appearances, Praha, Ostrava, Haag; Radio Appearances, Czech, Swedish, Norwegian, Germany. Compositions: Cantata, Golden Gate, for Children and Piano; Cantata, Joy of the Earth, for Mixed Choir and Piano. Recordings: J A Stepan, Hindemith, Krenek, Millhaud, Slavicky, Dadak, Chopin, Beethoven, Kraus, Brahms. Contributions to: Moravskoslezsky den. Honour: International Competition of Pianists, Moscow, 1957. Memberships: International Jury Piano Competition, Hradec, Praha, Brno, Marianské, Lazne, Katowice. Hobbies: Music; Social Activities. Address: Vozacska 8, 710 00 Slezska Ostrava, Czech Republic.

BERNDTSON Berndt Richard, b. 29 Nov 1938, Gothenburg, Sweden. Producer; Editor. m. Eva, 1 daughter. Education: Music, Music Engineering, Stockholm. Career: Music Engineering, Swedish National Radio, 1968-79; Light Music Producer, Editor, Weekly Radio Program Experimental and Electronic Music, 1979-96. Honours: Monaco Radio Prize, 1973, 1976; FST, Swedish Composers Society. Memberships: Artistic Board, Stockholm Electronic Music Festival; Board Member, ICEM; International Confederation of Electroacoustic Music; DEGEM, Germany. Hobbies: Literature; Films; Art; Gardening; Travel. Current Management: Production Enterprise. Address: c/o Modern Music & Media Stockholm, Ryttmastarvagen 126, S-16270 Vallingby, Sweden.

BERNEDE Jean-Claude, b. 19 Sept 1935, Angers, France. Conductor; Violinist. Education: Studied at the Paris Conservatoire with Pierre Dervaux and Igor Markevitch. Career: Soloist with the Ensemble de Musique Contemporain from 1958; Founded the Bernede string quartet, 1965, and was director of the Chamber Orchestra of Rouen, 1973-82; Artistic advisor of the Concerts Lamoureux from 1977 and director of the Rennes City Orchestra, 1981-85; Chief conductor of the Concerts Lamoureux from 1983 and professor of chamber music at the Paris Conservatoire, 1984. Address: c/o Association des Concerts Lamoureux, 252 Rue du Faubourg St Honoré, F-75008 Paris, France.

BERNET Dietfried, b. 14 May 1940, Vienna, Austria. Conductor. m. Johanna Lonsky. Education: Studied in Vienna at the Academy of Music and Performing Arts with Hans Swarowsky and Dimitri Mitropoulos. Debut: Orchestral concerts in Austria. Career: Conducted at major opera houses and guested with leading orchestas since 1962; Permanent Conductor at both Austrian State Opera Houses, 1964-; General Director of Music, City of Mainz and Conductor, Vienna State and Volksoper; Appearances with the Vienna and Chicago Symphonies, London Philharmonic and Philharmonia; RAI Orchestras in Italy, Berlin Philharmonic, Munich Radio and Philharmonia Hungarica; Festival engagements at Salzburg, Vienna, Spoleto, Glyndebourne, Budapest and Turin; repertoire includes works by Brahms, Bruckner, Mahler, Wagner, Verdi, Puccini and composers of the 20th century; Season 1991-92 with Die Meistersinger at Marseille, Don Giovanni at the Mozart Festival Schoenbrunn, Vienna; 1992-93 with Les Contes d'Hoffmann and Der Freischütz at the Volksoper; Idomeneo at Pretoria; 1994 concerts at Teatro Colon, Buenos Aires; Clemenza di Tito at Marseille; 1995 Tannhäuser at Copenhagen; Pearlfishers at Leeds, with Opera North; Guest with Royal Danish Opera at Covent Garden with The Love of Three Oranges; Verdi Requiem with RPO at Royal Albert Hall; Meistersinger at Torino; Chief Guest Conductor of the Royal Danish Opera, 1995-; 1996, Entführung at Geneva; House of the Dead, at Strasbourg; Arabella at Glyndebourne Festival; Don Giovanni at Covent Garden; 1997, Boris at Torino; Cosí fan tutte at Covent Garden (BBC live transmission); Mahler 3rd Symphony and Arabella at Copehagen; Berlioz's Romeo and Juliette with Theatre de la Monnaie, Brussels; Merry Widow with Royal Opera, London; Has also conducted opera at Munich, Hamburg, Cologne, Stuttgart, Naples, Barcelona, Venice, Palermo and Trieste. Recordings: Albums recorded on major labels. Honours include: Winner, International Conductor's Competition at Liverpool, 1962; Granted title of Professor by the Austrian State President for merits for the republic of Austria, 1995. Current Management: Athole Still International Management. Address: Foresters Hall, 25-27 Westow Street, London SW19 3RY, England.

BERNHEIMER Martin, b. 28 Sept 1936, Munich, Germany. Music Critic. m. 1. Lucinda Pearson, 30 Sept 1961, div 1989, 1 son, 3 daughters; 2. Linda Winer, 27 Sept 1993. Education: MusB, 1958-59; MA, New York University, 1961; Studied musicology with Gustave Reese. Career: Teacher, New York University, 1959-62; Contributing critic, New York Herald-Tribune, 1959-62; Contributing Editor, Musical Courier, 1961-64; Temporary Music Critic, New York Post, 1961-65; Assistant to the music editor, Saturday Review, 1962-65; Managing editor, Philharmonic Hall Programme, New York, 1962-65; New York correspondent 1962-65, Los Angeles Correspondent 1965-97; Opera; Music Editor and Chief Music Critic, Los Angeles Times, 1965-96; Teacher, University of Southern California, Los Angeles, 1966-71; University of California at Los Angeles, 1969-75; California Institute of the Arts, 1975-82; California State University, Northridge, 1978-81; Music Critic for New York Sidewalk (Microsoft), 1997-. Contributions: Articles in New Grove Dictionary of Music & Musicians; Articles and reviews in various journals; Liner notes for recordings; New Grove Dictionary of American Music; New Grove Dictionary of American Opera; Regular panelist, moderator, essayist on Metropolitan Opera Broadcasts; Frequent guest on CBC broadcasts. Honour: Winner of Pulitzer Prize in Criticism, 1981. Memberships: Pulitzer Prize Music Jury, 1984, 1986, 1989. Address: 245 East 87 Street #6C, New York, NY 10128, USA.

BERNSTEIN Elmer, b. 4 Apr 1922, New York City, USA. Composer; Conductor. m. (1) Pearl Glusman, 21 Dec 1946, 2 s, (2) Eve Adamson, 25 Oct 1965, 2 d. Education: Studied composition with Israel Citkowitz, Roger Sessions, Ivan Langstroth and Stefan Wolpe; Studied at New York University. Career: US Army Air Corps, arranger and composer for the Armed Forces Radio Service; Concert Pianist, 1946-50; Composer and Conductor for Films; Founder of Film Music Collection, 1974. Compositions: How Now, Dow Jones, musical, 1967; 3 Orchestral suites; Chamber music and songs; Many film scores including: The Man with The Golden Arm, 1955, The Ten Commandments, 1956, Desire Under the Elms, 1958, The Magnificant Seven, 1960, Walk on the Wild Side, 1963, To Kill a Mocking Bird, 1963, Hawaii, 1966, Thoroughly Modern Millie, 1967, The Bridge at Remagen, 1969, The Trial of Billy Jack, 1974, Airplane!, 1980, Ghostbusters, 1984, My Left Foot, 1989, The Grifters, 1991, The Age Of Innocence, 1993. Search and Destroy, 1995, Devil in a Blue Dress, 1995, Bulletproof, 1996, Buddy, 1997, Hoodlum, 1997 and The Rainmaker, 1997. Honour: Received his star on the Hollywood Walk of Fame, 1996. Memberships: Academy of Motion Picture Art and Sciences, first vice-president, 1963-73; Composers and Lyricists Guild of America, president, 1970-82; Film Music Society, President, 1995-. Address: c/o ASCAP, ASCAP Building, 1 Lincoln Plaza, New York, NY 10023, USA.

BERNSTEIN Lawrence F, b. 25 Mar 1939, New York City, USA. Musicologist; University Professor. Education: BS, Hofstra University, 1960; PhD, New York University, 1969. Career: Instructor, 1965-66; Assistant Professor, 1966-70; Music & Humanitites, University of Chicago; Associate Professor 1970-81; Chairman Department of Music, 1972-73, 1974-77; Professor of Music, 1981-, University of Pennsylvania; Visiting Lecturer, Columbia University, Graduate School of Arts & Sciences, 1979; Visiting Associate Professor, Princeton University, 1980; Visiting Professor, Rutgers University, 1982-83; Supervising Editor, Masters & Monuments of the Renaissance, 1970-; Editor-in-Chief, Journal of the American Musicological Society, 1975-77. Publications: Ihan Gero; Madrigali italiani et canzoni francese a due voci, with James Haar, 1980; La Couronne et fleur des chansons a troys, 1984; The French Secular Chanson in the Sixteenth Century. Contributions to: Articles in New Grove Dictionary of Music & Musicians, 1980; Articles & reviews in journals & other publications. Address: c/o Department of Music, University of Pennsylvania, 201 S 34th Street, Philadelphia, PA 19104-6313, USA.

BÉROFF Michel, b. 9 May 1950, Epinal, France. Pianist. Education: Conservatories of Nancy and Paris, with Yvonne Loriod. Debut: Paris, 1966. Career: Has appeared on TV and at Festivals in Portugal and Iran, 1967, also at Royal and Oxford Bach Festivals; Has lectured and given recitals and concerts in various European and South American countries; Appearances with the London Symphony Orchestra, Concerts Colonne, Orchestre de Paris, New York Philharmonic and BBC Symphony Orchestras; Toured Japan and South Africa. Recordings include: Prokofiev's Visions Fugitives; Messiaen's Quatuor pour le fin du Temps and Vingt Regards sur L'Enfant Jesus; Debussy's Preludes, Estampes and Pour le Piano; Music by Bartok, Stravinsky and Mozart. Honours: First Prize and Excellnet Prize, Nancy Conservatory, 1962, 1963; First Prize, Paris Conservatory, 1966; First Prize, Oliver Messiaen Competition, Royan. Address: 114 rue de Dames, Paris 17, France.

BERRY Walter, b. 8 Apr 1929, Vienna, Austria. Baritone. m. 1. Christa Ludwig, 1957, divorced 1970, 1 son; 2. Brigitte Hohenecker, 1973. Education: Vienna School of Engineering; Vienna Music Academy. Career: Student Member, Vienna State Opera, 1950-53; Ordinary Member, 1953-; Roles have included Mozart's Count, Leporello and Papageno; Awarded title Kammersaenger by Austrian Government, 1963; Guest singer at openings of opera houses in Vienna, Munich, Berlin, Tokyo and New York, Metropolitan Opera; At Festivals in Munich, Aix-en-Provence, Lucerne, Netherlands, Stockholm and Saratoga; Salzburg Festival, from 1952, created roles in the premieres of Liebermann's Penelope, Egk's Irische Legende and Einem's Der Prozess; Also frequently appeared as Mozart's Guglielmo; Appearances in New York, Chicago, Buenos Aires, Tokyo, London, Paris, Berlin and Munich; Covent Garden debut 1976, as Strauss's Barak; Other roles include Berg's Wozzeck, Wagner's Telramund and Wotan and Beethoven's Pizarro; Sang Waldner in Arabella at Covent Garden, 1986; Klingsor at San Francisco, 1988; Salzburg Festival, 1988, as Don Magnifico in Cenerentola, also on video; Vienna Staatsoper, 1990, in Zimmermann's Die Soldaten; Concert Artist in works by Bach, Beethoven, Mozart, and others. Honours: Prizes from Music Concourses in Vienna; Verviers; Geneva. Hobbies: Listening to and taping music; Yachting; Swimming; Archaeology; Photography. Address: c/o Vienna Staatsoper, Operning 2, A-1010 Vienna, Austria.

BERTA Mariana, b. 16 Jan 1956, Montevideo, Uruguay. Oboist; Researcher. m. Franco Simini. Education: Based on Arts and Languages (German, French, English, Italian, Spanish); Music with Daniel Viglietti and Miguel Marozzi at Núcleo de Educación Musical, NEMUS; Musicology and Oboe Studies at Universidad de la República Oriental del Uruguay and Escuela Municipal de Música de Montevideo; Advanced Oboe Studies at the Collegium Musicum of Buenos Aires with Pedro Cocchiararo and with David Walter in Paris, France; Harmony and Analysis with Héctor Tosar; Instrumentation, Composition and Electracoustics with Graciela Paraskevaidis and Coriún Aharonián; 4th, 5th, 6th, 7th and 8th Cursos Latinoamericanos de Música Contemporánea. Debut: Contemporary Music Concert (Núcleo de Música Nueva). Career: Active in contemporary music performance and diffusion with Núcleo Música Nueva, Montevideo, 1976-; 1st Oboe with Orquesta de Cámara del MEC, 1988-; Orquesta del SODRE, 1988 and 1995; Ensemble International de Paris, 1988; Banda Sinfónica Municipal, 1993-; Soloist (Oboe/Recorder) with Conjunto Barroco, 1982 and 1983; Banda Sinfónica Municipal, 1995; Orquesta de Cámara del MEC, 1985, 1988, 1990 and 1996; Live Mega Concerts with José Carreras, 1995, Placido Domingo, 1996 and Fito Páez, 1996 as English Horn and 1st Oboe; Chamber Groups: Conjunto Barroco, Wind Quintet of JJMM "KAIROS" (baroque quintet). Recordings: With Leo Masliah, 1983, Rubén Olivera, 1983, Numa Moraes, 1986 and 1995, Compositores del Uruguay, 1987 and 1992, Fernando Cabrera, 1990, Daniel Viglietti, 1993, Héctor Tosar, 1994, Mauricio Ubal, 1995, Graciela Paraskevaidis, 1996. Honours: Scholarships from French Government for Advanced Oboe Studies and Musik för Ungdom, Sweden, for Chamber Music, 1987. Address: Av A Ricaldoni 2529 Apt 601, 11600 Montevideo, Uraguay.

BERTHOLD Beatrice, b. 11 Sept 1964, Wiesbaden, Germany. Concert Pianist. Education: Academies of Music, Vienna & Cologne; Academy of Music, Detmold. Debut: Wiesbaden National Theatre, 1983. Career: Solo Recitals & Concerts with Renowned Orchestras in Europe: Lucerne Music Festival, Berlin (Concerthaus Philharmonie), Hamburg (Musikhalle), Cologne (Philharmonie), London, 1983-; Several Concert Tours to South America: Porto Alegre, Caracas, 1996-; TV & Radio Appearances. Compositions: Beethoven Piano Concerto No 5; Rakhmaninoff Piano Sonata No 1 & 2; Granados, Goyescas; Brahms, Fantasias op 116; Rhapsodies op 78; Scriabin, Fantasia op 28; Villa-Lobos, Ciclo Brasilieiro. Recordings: The Young Rakhmaninoff, 1990; Tchaikowsky/Rakhmaninoff/Scriabin: Early Piano Works, 1992; Granados: Goyescas + El Pelele, 1992; Hommage au Piano, 1994. Honours: German Record Prize, 1990; Hans-Romney Memorial Prize, IYCAC, Tunbridge Wells; 1st Prize, GEDOK Competition. Membership: German Music Council. Hobbies: Flamenco; Fashion Design; Movie History; Musical, Chanson Jazz; Cooking. Current Management: Konzertagentur Jens Gunnar Becker. Address: Grunstrasse 13, D-58313 Herdecke, Germany.

BERTI Marco, b. 1961, Turin, Italy. Singer (Tenor). Education: Studied at the Verdi Conservatory in Milan. Career: Sang widely in Italy as Jim in Mahagonny by Weill; Sang Pinkerton in Consenza (1990) and Don Ottavio at Macerata, 1991; Frankfurt, 1991, as Guevara in a concert performance of Franchetti's Cristoforo Colombo; Strasbourg, 1992, as Alfredo. Recordings include: Cristoforo Colombo (Koch); Don Giovanni (Koch); Manon Lescaut (Sony). Address: c/o Opéra du Rhin, 19 Place Broglie, F-67008 Strasbourg, France.

BERTINI Gary, b. 1 May 1927, Brichevo, Bessarabia, Russia. Composer; Conductor. m. Rosette Berengole, 21 Oct 1956, 2 children. Education: Diploma, Tel Aviv Conservatorio Verdi, Milan, 1948; Diploma, Tel Aviv Music College, 1951; Conservatoire National Superieur, Paris, 1954; Ecole ormale de Musique, 1954; Institut de Musicologie, Sorbonne, Paris, 1955. Career: Music Director, Rinat Chamber Chorus, 1955-72; Music Director, Israel Chamber Ensemble Orchestra, 1965-75; Principal Guest Conductor, Scottish National Orchestra, 1971-81; Music Director, Jerusalem Symphony Orchestra, 1977-86; Chief Conductor, Cologne Radio-Symphony Orchestra, 1983-91; Intendant and General Music Director, Frankfurt Opera, 1987-91; Guest Conductor, Principal Orchestras and Opera Houses, Europe, USA, Japan; Artisitc Advisor, Israel Festival, 1976-83; Conducted Dukas' Ariane et Barbebleue at the Paris Opera in 1975; Has given the premieres of 4 operas by Josef Tal, Ashmedai 1971, Masada 1967, (1973), Die Versuchung 1977 and Josef, 1995; Boris Godunov at the opening of the New Israel Opera 1994; Music Director, Israel Opera from 1994; Conducted Weber's Die drei Pintos at the 1997 Vienna Festival; Carmen at the Opéra Bastille, Paris; Professor, Tel Aviv University, 1976. Compositions: Symphonic, Chamber, Incidental Music for theatre and radio. Publications: Contributor to musical journals of articles in the field of music. Honours: Recipient, Israel State Prize, 1978. Membership: Israel League of Composers. Address: Konzertgesellschaft, PO Box, CH-4002 Basel, Switzerland.

BERTOLINO Mario (Ercole), b. 10 Sept 1934, Palermo, Italy. Singer, Bass-Baritone. Education: Studied in Palmero & with Mario Basiola in Milan; Giuseppe Danise in New York. Debut: Teatro Nuovo Milan, 1955; Marcello in La Bohème. Career: Sang at La Scala, in Rome, Palermo, Munich, Lyon and Mexico City; Moved to Forest Hills, NY, sang widely in the US at Boston, Cincinnati, Pittsburgh, San Antonio, Washington and New York City Opera; Roles have included Verdi's Amonasro, Renato, Macbeth, Iago, Germont and Luna; Donizetti's Dulcamara, Don Pasquale and Enrico; Gerard in Andrea Chénier; Puccini's Sharpless and Iago; Lescaut; Also sang in concert.

BERTOLO Aldo, b. 1951, Italy. Singer (Tenor). Debut: Sang Mozart's Ferrando at Susa, 1978. Career: Many appearances in Italy; South America; Europe, in the lyric repertoire; Among his best roles are Donizetti's Edgardo, Tonie and Ernesto; Pylades, in Piccinni's Iphigénie en Tauride; Rossini's Lindoro; Adalbert in

Adelaide di Borgogna and Don Ottavio; Season 1985 sang Arturo in I Puritani at Martina Franca; Ramiro in La Cenerentola, in Santiago; At Valle d'Itria 1986, sang Thoas in the first modern revival of Traetta's Ifigenia en Tauride; Elvino in La Sonnambula at Piacenza, 1986; Teatro Carlo Felice, Genoa 1988, as Narciso in L'Italiana in Algeri; Other roles include the Fisherman in Guillaume Tell, Lorenzo in Fra Diavolo and Verdi's Alfredo; Season 1991, as Ernesto at Pisa and Narciso at Trieste. Address: c/o Teatro Carlo Felice, 1-16100 Genoa, Italy.

BERTON Liliane, b. 1929, Lille, France. Singer (Soprano). Education: Studied at the Lille and Paris Conservatories. Debut: Paris Opéra-Comique, 1952, in the premiere of Dolores by Michel-Maurice Levy. Career: Many appearances in Paris and elsewhere in France as Cherubino, Susanna, Rosina, Eurydice and Marguerite; Operetta roles have included the title role in Noces de Jeannette by Massé; Sang Constance in the premiere of Dialogues des Carmélites by Poulenc, 1957.

BESA Alexander, b. 28 Feb 1971, Havana, Cuba. Czech Musician - Violist. Education: Music School, Znojmo, Czech Republic, 1978-84; State Conservatory, Brno, Czech Republic, 1985-91; International Menuhin Music Academy, Switzerland, 1991-93; Music Akademie Basel, 1993-96. Debut: Mozart Symphony Concertante K 364 with Moravian Chamber Orchestra, Brno, 1990. Career: Appeared as Viola Solist with Camerata Bern, Kurphälzisches Kammerorchester, Camerata Lysy, Basle Symphony and Radio Orchestra, Janácek Philharmonic, Ostrava, B Martinu Philharmonic, Zlin, Lucerne Symphony Orchestra, State Philharmonic, Kosice; Principal Violist. Lucerne Symphony Orchestra and Camerata Bern. Recordings: A Lysy, Camerata Lysy - Mendelssohn, 1992; T Zehetmair, Camerata Bern - Vivaldi, 1995; H Holliger, Camerata Bern - Bach, 1996; Ensemble Tiramisu - Quintets from Brahms and Herzogenberg, Octets by Mendelssohn and Gage, 1996, 1997; Viola Recital, 1997. Honours: Winner, Beethoven International Viola Competition, Czech Republic, 1994; Winner, H Schaeuble Viola Competition, Lausanne, 1995; Morris Maddrell Prize, L Tertis Viola Competition, Isle of Man, UK, 1997. Current Management: Agentura Sinfonietta, Brno, Czech Republic. Address: Sonmattstrasse 4, CH-6206 Neuenkirchen, Switzerland.

BESCH Anthony (John Elwyn), b. 5 Feb 1924, London, England. Opera and Theatre Director. Education: Worcester College, Oxford; MA (Oxon); FGSM. Career: Director, various operas and theatres, 1950-; Produced the world premiere of Birtwistle's Punch and Judy (Aldeburgh 1968) and the British premieres of Shostakovich's The Nose and Ginastera's Bomarzo; Royal Opera House, Covent Garden, London; Glyndebourne Opera, from 1951 produced Mozart's Der Schauspieldirektor there in 1957; English National Opera, London Coliseum; Scottish Opera; New Opera Company, London; Handel Opera Society; Edinburgh Festival; Wexford Festival; Deutsche Oper, Berlin; Royal Netherlands Opera; Théâtre de la Monnaie, Brussels, Belgium; Teatro Colon, Buenos Aires, Argentina; New York City Opera; San Francisco Opera; Canadian Opera Company; National Arts Centre, Canada; Australian Opera; State Opera, South Australia; Victoria State Opera; Head of Opera Studies, Guildhall School of Music & Drama, Barbican, London, Jan 1987-89; Tosca Scottish Opera 1980; Staged Rota's Silent Night for Morley Opera, 1990; Other work has included Il Trovatore at Brisbane and Martinu's Julietta for ENO/New Opera Company; Staged Il Barbiere di Siviglia for the Canadian Opera Company at Toronto, 1992; 1993 included, Madame Butterfly at the Opera Forum, Holland; Haydn's L'Infedeltà Delusa, Garsington Opera; Tosca, Scottish Opera. Honour: FGSM, 1990. Address: 201 Hammersmith Grove, London W6 0NP, England.

BESRODNY Igor, b. 7 May 1930, Tblisi, Russia. Conductor; Violinist. Education: Graduated Moscow Conservatoire, 1955. Career: Many appearances in Russia and elsewhere from 1948, after winning the Prague International Competition; Teacher at the Moscow Conservatoire from 1957 (professor, 1972); Debut as conductor, 1970, directing the Moscow Chamber Orchestra, 1977-83; Premiered the first Concerto by Kabalevsky, 1948. Address: c/o Moscow Conservatoire, ul Gertzena 13, 103009 Moscow, Russia.

BESSEL Annemarie, b. 1935, Germany. Singer (Soprano and Mezzo-Soprano). Career: Sang at Heidelberg, 1956-58, Wuppertal, 1958-63, Cologne, 1964-72; Among her best roles have been Ottavia in Poppea, Venus in Tannhäuser, Brangaene (Tristan), Lady Macbeth, Amneris, Amelia (Un Ballo in Maschera), Kundry and Emma in Khovanshchina; La Scala, 1964-65, as The Woman in Erwartung and Mary in Fliegende Holländer; Further guest appearances at Wiesbaden, Karlsruhe and San Francisco (Ortrud in Lohengrin, 1965). Address: c/o Oper der Stadt Köln, Offenbachplatz, W-5000 Cologne 1, Germany.

BEST Jonathan, b. 1958, England. Singer (Bass). Debut: Sang Sarstro with Welsh National Opera, 1983. Career: Many leading roles in the bass repertory, with Welsh National Opera, Scottish Opera, Dublin Grand Opera, Kent Opera and Opera North; Appearances at Covent Garden in Die Meistersinger, Otello, Don Carlos and King Arthur (as Grimbauld, with Les Arts Florissants, 1995); Season 1994-95 in The Rake's Progress at Salzburg, in The Queen of Spades at Glyndebourne and The Fairy Queen for English National Opera; Other roles include Don Alfonso in Così fan tutte (Opera North, 1997); Sang Trulove in The Rake's Progress for Welsh National Opera, 1996. Address: c/o Music International, 13 Ardilaun Road, London N5 2QR, England.

BEST Matthew, b. 6 Feb 1957, Farnborough, Kent, England. Singer (Bass); Conductor. m. Rosalind Mayes, 1983. Education: Sevenoaks School; Choral Scholar at King's College, Cambridge, MA, Hons in Music; Studied under Otakar Kraus and at National Opera Studio, 1979-80; Subsequently with Robert Lloyd and Patrick McGuigan. debut: Seneca in Coronation of Poppaea, Cambridge University Opera Society, 1978. Career: Principal Bass, Royal Opera House, 1980-86; Regular guest artist with Welsh National Opera, Opera North, also Alte Oper, Frankfurt & Glyndebourne Touring Opera; Extensive concert career; Founder and Director of the Corydon Singers, 1973-; Has also worked frequently, as conductor, with English Chamber Orchestra; Guest appearances with City of London Sinfonia, BBC Singers and London Mozart Players. Compositions: Opera Alice, work performed Aldeburgh Festival 1979; Sang the Archbishop in a concert performance of Szymanowski's King Roger at the Festival Hall, 1990; Wesver in Milhaud's Les Malheurs d'Orphée at the Elizabeth Hall, 1990; Appearances with Opera North 1992, as Fernando in The Thieving Magpie and as Pimen in Boris Godunov at the London Proms; Sang Pizarro in Beethoven's Leonore at the 1996 Salzburg Festival. Recordings: As singer: include, Rossini Il Barbiere di Siviglia; Stravinsky The Rake's Progress; Verdi Don Carlo, video; Saint-Saëns Samson et Dalila, video; As conductor: Duruflé Requiem; Bruckner Mass in E Minor, Motets and Requiem; Fauré Requiem; Works by Britten, Vaughan Williams, Bernstein and Copland, all with Corydon Singers and English Chamber Orchestra. Honours: SE Arts Association; Friends of Covent Garden, Bursary, 1980; Decca-Kathleen Ferrier Prize, 1982. Address: c/o Harrison-Parrott Limited, 12 Penzance Place, London W11 4PA, England.

BEST Roger, b. 28 Sept 1938, Liverpool, England. Violist; College Professor. m. Bronwen Naish, 5 children. Education: Royal Manchester College of Music. Debut: Manchester 1955. Career: With Hallé Orchestra, 1958-60; Principal Viola, Northern Sinfonia Orchestra, 1961-73; Gave world premieres of viola concertos by Malcolm Arnold, 1972 and Richard Rodney Bennett, 1973; Professor, Royal College of Music. Honours: Open Scholarship, RMCM, 1955; Hiles Gold Medal, 1958; Barber Trust Scholarship to Birmingham University, 1960. Hobbies: Painting; Golf. Address: 9 Granard Road, Wandsworth Common, London SW12, England.

BESTOR Charles, b. 21 Dec 1924, NY, USA. Composer; Educator. m. Ann N Elder, 1 Nov 1952, 3 sons, 3 daughters. Education: BA, Swarthmore College, 1948; BMus, Juilliard School of Music, 1951; MMus, University of Illinois, 1952; DMA, University of Colorado, 1974. Career: Assistant Dean, Juilliard School of Music, 1951-59; Assistant Professor, University of Colorado, 1959-64; Dean, Willmette University, 1964-71; Head of Music: University of Alabama, 1971-73; University of Utah, 1973-77; University of Massachusetts, 1977-88, Professor since 1977. Compositions: Chaconne for Chamber Orchestra; Times Arrow; Incantations and Dances; Soliloquies; In Memoriam Bill Evans; Stations of the Night; Pathways from the Dream Spell Series; Cycles; Overture to a Romantic Comedy; Three Portraits; Three Ways of Looking at the Night, 1995. Recordings: JB Suite; Suite for Sax and Percussion; More Sort of Love Songs; Cello Sonata; Lyric Variations; Piano Sonata; Duo Variations; Second Moon of Venus; Overture to a Romantic Comedy; Variations for Orchestra; In Memoriam Bill Evans; Chaconne for Chamber Winds; Three Portraits. Honours: National Endowment for The Arts Composer's Fellowship, 1993; Omaha Symphony International Composition Competition, 1994; Musica Nova 96, International Composition Competition, 1996. Hobby: Cycling. Address: Department of Music and Dance, University of Massachusetts, Amherst, MA 01003, USA.

BESUTTI Paola, b. 18 Apr 1960, Mantova, Italy. Researcher. m. Roberto Giuliani, 16 July 1992. Education: Musicological studies at Parma University; Pianoforte at Conservatory of Music in Mantova. Career: Professor at Pesaro Conservatory of Music; Member of editorial staff of Rivista Italiana di Musicologia; Professor, Researcher, Institute of Musicology of Parma University, 1990-. Recordings: Collaborated with Parrott, Vartolo, Savall, Gini; BBC, RAI, Radio France, RSI. Publications include: La corte musicale di Ferdinando Carlo Gonzaga, Mantova Areari, 1989; Hildegard von Bingen, Ordo Virtutum, Sa musique et son idée de théatre, in Actes de la Societé Internationale pour l'étude du théatre médiéval, Barcelona, Institut del Teatro, 1997; Ave maris stella: la tradizione mantovana nuovamente posta in musica da Monteverdi in Claudio Monteverdi, Studi e prospettive, Firenze, Olschki, 1997; Tasso contra Guarini: una Rappresentazione con intermedi degli Intrichi d'amore (1606) in Torquato Tasso e la cultura estense, Firenze, Olschki, 1997; La figura professionale del cantante d'opera: Quaderni storici, XXXII n 2 agosto, 1997; Giostre e tornei a Mantova Parma e Piacenza fra Cinque e Seicento in Musica e tornei nel Seicento Italiano, Lucca, LIM. Contributions to: Music reviews and publications including: Atlas Mondiale du Baroque, Dizionario degli Editori Musicali Italiani, The New Grove, The New Grove Dictionary of Opera. Memberships: American Musicological Society; International Musicological Society; Società Italiana di Educazione Musicale; Società Italiana di Musicologia. Address: Piazzale Vittorio Veneto 1, 46100 Mantova, Italy.

BETKO Milos, b. 27 May 1964, Bratislava, Slovakia. Composer; Recording Producer. Education: Composition, Violin, Conservatoire National, Bratislava; Composition, Conservatoire National de Region de Boulogne-Billancourt; Composition, Academy of Music, Bratislava; Composition, Conservatoire National Supérieur de Musique et de Danse, Paris. Compositions: Walter in Baden, 1989; Concert for 14 Clarinets, 1990; Quintet for Orchestra, 1991; Wer Ist? Binich! und Was Willst?, 1994; Personal Relations, 1997; Office on the Road, 1997. Recordings: A. Adam: Giselle, 1994; L. Delibes: Coppelia, 1995; L. Delibes: Sylvia, 1995; A Glasunow: The Piano Concertos, 1995; World's National Anthems, 1995-97; E Chabrier: Gwendoline, 1996. Address: Sibirska 16, 831 02 Bratislava, Slovakia.

BEVAN Maurice (Guy Smalman), b. 10 Mar 1921, London, England. Singer. m. Anne Alderson, 1 d. Education: Magdalen College, Oxford; BMus Cantuar, 1990; FTCL; ARCM. Career: Vicar Choral, St Paul's Cathedral, 1949-89; Founder Member, The Deller Consort; Oratorio and Recitals, BBC; Soloist in Britain, Europe, USA, Israel and Brazil. Publications: Editions of English vocal music of the 17th and 18th Centuries. Recordings include: Purcell's Fairy Queen; Handel's Acis and Galatea. Contributions to: Journal of the American Musicological Society; Die Musik in Geschichte und Gegenwart; Grove's Dictionary of Music and Musicians. Hobby: Cooking. Address: 45 Court Way, Twickenham, Middlesex, TW2 7SA, England.

BEYER Frank (Michael), b. 8 Mar 1928, Berlin, Germany. Composer; Professor. Education: Studied Sacred Music, Berlin; Studied Composition with Ernst Pepping, Berlin Staatliche Hochschule für Musik. Career: Assistant Professor, Berlin Kirchenmusikschule, 1953-62; Assistant Professor, Berlin Hochschule für Musik, 1960-68; Professor of Composition, Berlin Hochschule für Musik, 1968-93; Founder-Director, Musica Nova Sacra Concert Series, Berlin; Director, Contemporary Music Section, Berlin Akademie der Kunste; Mitglied: Bayerische Akademie der Sdiönen küunste. Compositions: Ballet: Geburt des Tanzes, 1987; Orchestral: Flute Concerto, 1964; Versi for Strings, 1968; Rondeau Imaginaire, 1972; Concertino a Tre for Chamber Orchestra, 1974; Diaphonie, 1975; Streicherfantasien to a Motive by J S Bach, 1977, also for String Quintet, 1978; Griechenland for 3 String Groups, 1981; Deutsche Tänze for Cello, Double Bass and Chamber Orchestra, 1982, arranged from Deutsche Tänze for Cello and Double Bass, 1980; Notre-Dame-Musik, 1983-84; Mysteriensonate for Viola and Orchestra, 1986; Architettura per Musica, 1989; Concerto for Oboe and Strings, 1986; Klangtore for orchestra; Chamber: Biblische Szenen for soprano, tenor and 4 instruments, 1956; 3 String Quartets, 1957, 1969, 1985; Concerto for Organ and 7 Instruments, 1966-69, 1968; Chaconne for Violin, 1970; Wind Quintet, 1972; Sonata for Violin and Piano, 1977; De Lumine for 7 Players, 1978; Trio for Oboe, Viola and Harp, 1980; Fantasia Concertante for 2 Violins, 1982; Melos for Viola, 1983; Passacaglia Fantastica for Violin, Cello and Piano, 1984; Echo for Bass Flute, 1986; Sinfonien for 8 Players, 1989; Sanctus for Saxophone Quartet, 1989; Organ Music; Piano Pieces; Vocal; Major Angelis for Soprano, Women's Chorus and 6 Instruments, 1970; Canticum Mose et Agni for 8 Voice Double Chorus, 1976; Musik der Frühe for Violin and Orchestra, 1993; Persephone-Hades-Persephone for chamber ensemble, 1995. Recordings: Several Compositions recorded. Address: Akademie der Künste, Hanseatenweg 10, 10557 Berlin, Germany.

BIANCHI Lino, b. 14 May 1920, Vedano Olona, Vasese, Italy. Musicologist; Composer. m. Gabriella Limentani. Education: Diploma in Composition, G Rossini Conservatory, Pesaro, 1945. Career: Artistic Director, Centro Oratorio Musicale, Rome, 1949-63; Edition de Santis, Rome, 1960-; GP da Palestrina Foundation, 1973-; Numerous broadcasts on Palestrina, Carissimi and other early composers; Italian Radio & TV, 1952-. Compositions: Il Principe Felice, 1-act opera; Uruel, 3-act dramatic commentary. Recordings: As conductor, works by Carissimi, Stradella, A Scarlatti and D Scarlatti. Publications: Editions of complete works of G Carissimi and GP de Palestrina; Complete oratorios of A Scarlatti, 1964-; A Stradella, 1969; Musical encyclopedias & Journals. Address: Circonvallazione Clodia 82, 00195 Rome, Italy.

BIANCONI Lorenzo (Gennaro), b. 14 Jan 1946, Minusio/Muralto, Switzerland. Musicologist. m. Giuseppina La

Face, 2 June 1979, 2 sons. Education: PhD, University of Heidelberg, Germany, 1974; Studied Music Theory with Luciano Sgrizzi, Lugano, Switzerland. Career: Collaborator, Répertoire International des Sources Musicales, Italy, 1969-70; Member, German Institute, Venice, 1974-76; Guest Assistant, German Historical Institute, Rome, 1976; Guest Professor, Princeton University, USA, 1977; Professor of Musical Dramaturgy, Bologna University, Italy, 1977-; Professor of the History of Music, Siena University, Arezzo, Italy, 1980-83; Co-Editor, Rivista Italiana di Musicologia, 1973-79; Editor, Acta Musicologica, 1987-91; Head of Programme Committee, 14th International Musicological Congress, Bologna, 1987; Co-Editor, Musica e Storia, 1993-; Co-Founder, Il Saggiatore Musicale, 1994-. Publications: B Marcello, Sonates pour clavecin (editor with Luciano Sgrizzi), 1971; P M Marsolo, Madrigali a 4 voci (1614), 1973; A Il Verso, Madrigali a 3 e a 5 voci (1605-19), 1978; Il Seicento, 1982, English Edition, 1987; La Drammaturgia Musicale, 1986; Storia dell'Opera Italiana, 1987, Anglo-American edition forthcoming; I Libretti Italiani di G F Händel, 1992; Il Teatro d'Opera in Italia, 1993. Honours: Dent Medal of the Royal Musical Association, 1983; Premio Imola per la Critica, 1994. Memberships: International and American Musicological Society; Gesellschaft für Musikforschung. Address: Via Murri 89, I-40137 Bologna, Italy.

BIBBY Gillian, b. 31 Aug 1945, Lower Hutt, New Zealand. Composer. Education: Studied at the University of Otago and at Victoria University with Douglas Lilburn; Further study in Berlin and Cologne, with Aloys Kontarsky, Kagel and Stockhausen. Career: Teacher in New Zealand, and editor of Canzona, 1982-84. Compositions include: Lest you be my enemy, ballet, 1976; Synthesis for tape, 1977; In Memoriam for 8 voices, organ and percussion, 1979; Marama Music, music-theatre, 1978; 11 Characters in Search of a Composer, for military band and percussion. Address: c/o New Zealand Music Centre, PO Box 10042, Level 13, Brandon Street, Wellington, New Zealand.

BIBLE Frances, b. 26 Jan 1927, Sacketts Harbour, New York, USA. Singer (Mezzo-Soprano). Education: Studied at the Juilliard School with Queena Mario. Debut: New York City Center Opera 1948, in Tosca. Career: Appeared in New York until 1977 as Adalgisa, Cherubino, Octavian, Nicklausse, Siebel, Amneris, Cenerentola; Glyndebourne 1955, 1962, as Cherubino and in L'Incoronazione di Poppea; Sang in the premieres of The Ballad of Baby Doe, Central City 1956; Robert Ward's The Crucible, New York 1961; Metropolitan Opera 1967, as Octavian. Recordings: L'Incoronazione di Poppea; Euryanthe.

BICKERSTAFF Robert, b. 26 July 1932, Sydney, Australia. Singer, (Baritone); Teacher, Voice. m. Ann Howard. Education: Studied at the New South Wales Conservatorium with Lyndon Jones; Melbourne Conservatorium with Henry Portnoj; Paris with Dominique Modesti. Debut: Marseilles 1962, as Thoas in Iphigénie en Tauride. Career: Sang in Nice, Bordeaux and Marseille; Principal Baritone Sadler's Wells and English National Opera, 1964-70; Roles included: Amonasro, Escamillo, Macbeth, Boccanegra, Scarpia, Wotan, Mozart's Count and Eugene Onegin; Guest appearances with Pittsburgh Opera, Welsh National Opera and at Covent Garden; Over 60 roles in Opera; Other roles include Wagner's Dutchman, Ezio in Attila, Luna, Renato in Un Ballo in Maschera, Enrico in Lucia di Lammermoor and Massenet's Herode; Boris in Lady Macbeth of Mtsensk by Shostakovich, Adelaide Festival; Oratorio and recital performances; Appearances on BBC radio and TV; Previously Professor of singing at the Royal Academy in Music; London and Tutor of Singing at King's College, Cambridge. Recordings: La Juive, Raritas; Society of Musicians, London. Hobbies: Reading; Golf; Outdoor Activities. Address: 8 William Street, North Sydney, 2060 Australia.

BICKETT Harry, b. Liverpool, England. Conductor; Harpsichordist. Education: Royal College of Music and Oxford University. Career: Posts as organist, including Westminster Abbey; Harpsichordist with the English Concert, Monteverdi Orchestra, Philharmonia Orchestra and City of Birmimgham Symphony (The Creation under Rattle); Chorus Master of English National Opera, conducting Monteverdi's Orfeo and Combattimento and Handel's Ariodante; Operas by Monteverdi, Cesti, Gluck, Mozart and Massenet for Scottish Opera, Batignano Festival, Opera North, Buxton Festival and ENO (Don Quichotte); Conducted Monteverdi's Ulysses at the Buxton Festival, 1996, Handel's Theodora at Glyndebourne and on tour; L'Incoronazione di Poppea for Florida Grand Opera, 1997; Season 1997-98 with Figaro at New York City Opera, Giulio Cesare for Australian Opera and Rodelinda on the Glyndebourne Tour; Guest conducting with CLS, Sydney Symphony Orchestra and NACO; Season 1998-99 to include Semele with English National Opera; Television work includes My Night With Handel, Channel 4, 1996. Address: c/o Harold Holt Ltd, 31 Sinclair Road, London W14 ONS, England.

BICKLEY Susan, b. 1966, Liverpool, England. Singer (Mezzo-soprano). Education: City University, London, and the Guildhall School of Music. Debut: As Proserpina in Monteverdi's Orfeo, at Florence. Career: Opera roles include Baba the Turk and Ulrica for Opera 80, Mozart's Marcellina and Elvira, Janacek's Kabanicha and Kostelnicka for the Glyndebourne Tour; Britten's Florence Pike, Hippolyta and Mrs Sedley at the Glyndebourne Festival; Dorabella and Andromache in King Priam for English National Opera, Feodor in Boris Godunov at Covent Garden; Further engagements as Kabanicha and a Flowermaiden at the Opera Bastille (1997), Octavian at the Hong Kong Festival and Herodias in Salome at San Francisco; Concerts include Ligeti's Requiem at the 1994 Salzburg Festival and the Missa Solemnis on tour with Les Arts Florissants to Vienna and in France, 1995; Season 1995-96 with El Amor Brujo in Rome and Stravinsky's Faun and Shepherdess in Hong Kong; Further concerts with the London Symphony, Philharmonia, LPO, London Sinfonietta, London Classical Players and Allegri and Brodsky Quartets; Season 1996-97 included Messiah with the Hallé Orchestra, Stravinsky with the BBC SO and Das Lied von der Erde with the BBC National Orchestra of Wales. Recordings include: Socrate by Satie, Monteverdi's Il Ballo delle Ingrate, Dido and Aeneas, and The Fairy Queen (EMI); Other labels include Hyperion, Nimbus and DGG. Address: Allied Artists, 42 Montpellier Square, London SW7 1JZ, England.

BICKNELL Robert David, b. 7 Dec 1957, St Helier, Jersey, Channel Islands. Singing Teacher. Education: Redroofs Theatre School; Goldsmiths University of London; Singers' Workshop, Amsterdam and at Pineapple Studios, London. Career includes: Tosca, Aida, Carmen, Hello Dolly, Rocky Horror Show, Godspell, Many Pantos; TV includes: Robin Hood, Lenny Henry Show, Doctor Who, Saturday Night Live; TV as Singing Coach including appearances on the Big Breakfast Show, 6 months, O-Zone, This Morning; Radio work for Eclipse FM and GLR; Musical Director, Royal Albert Hall, Wembley Arena; Also pop music work for record companies. Recordings: Love Can Build A Bridge; Film, The Matchmaker. Contributions to: Daily Mail; The Stage; Television Today. Honour: BMus, London. Memberships: Equity; British Voice Association; Incorporated Society of Musicians. Hobbies: Horseriding; Gym training. Address: 69 Lower Flat, Acre Lane, London SW2 5TN, England.

BIDDINGTON Eric (Wilhelm), b. 19 Oct 1953, Timaru, New Zealand. Composer. m. Elizabeth Ann Biddington, 4 July 1989. Education: BA, MA (Hons), BSc, MusB, MusB (Hons), ATCL, University of Canterbury, Christchurch. Debut: Christchurch Arts Centre, Christchurch. Career: Major recitals of chamber music, Christchurch, 1985-97, Lower Hutt, 1988, Hamilton, 1989; Premiere performance of Concerto for Two Violins and String Orchestra at Tempe, Arizona, USA, 1989. Compositions: Mainly chamber music and some orchestral works, including Suite for Violin and Piano, 1985; Three Pieces for Cello and Piano, 1986; Scherzetto, for Clarinet and Piano, 1986; Autumn Music for Viola and Piano, 1987; Music for Friends for piano trio, 1988; Suite for Oboe and Piano, 1989; Two Dances for Alto Saxophone and Piano, 1989; Four Piano Preludes, 1990; Three Bagatelles for Flute and Piano, 1990; Haere Ra - A Song for 2-part Treble Voices and Piano; Introduction for Clarinet and Piano, 1993; Concertos for Flute, Oboe, Alto Saxophone, Two Violins; Sinfonietta; Overtures; Sonatinas for Violin and Pianoforte, Tenor Saxophone and Piano, Oboe and Piano, Clarinet and Piano, Treble Recorder and Piano, Flute and Piano, Trumpet and Piano; Beauty and The Beast, ballet, 1994; Divertimento for Orchestra, 1996. Recordings: The Chamber Music of Eric Biddington; Music for Friends. Publications: 10 publications of chamber music with Nota Bene Music; 20 private publications, chamber music; Pastorale for Clarinet and Piano, 1994; Introduction and Allegro for Alto Saxophone and Piano, 1994; Two Amourettes for Oboe and Piano, 1995. Honour: Award, Composers Association of New Zealand Trust Fund, 1989. Memberships: Composers Association of New Zealand; APRA. Hobbies: Reading; Gardening. Address: 27 Torrens Road, Hillmorton, Christchurch 2, New Zealand.

BIEL Ann-Christin, b. 1958, Sweden. Singer (Soprano). Education: Studied at the Royal Music Academy, Stockholm with Birgit Sternberg & with Daniel Ferro, in New York. Debut: Drottningholm 1981, as Cherubino. Career: Has appeared at the Summer festival at Drottningholm, Stockholm, as Pamina 1982, 1989; Fiordiligi, 1984-85; Ilia, 1986, 1991; Susanna 1987; Serpetta in La Finta Giardiniera, 1988, 1990; Royal Opera Stockholm 1985, L'arbore di Diana by Martín y Soler; 1986 as Oscar in Un Ballo in Maschera; Sang Konstanze in the Berne, 1986, world premiere of Armin Schibler's Mozart und der graue Bote, Mozart's last days; Toured as Micaela in the Peter Brook version of Carmen, Paris, Hamburg, New York and Tokyo, 1982-86; Théâtre des Champs-Elysées, Paris 1986, as Barbarina in Le nozze di Figaro; Sang Julie in the world premiere of Miss Julie at Stockholm 1990; (music by Margareta Hallin, the part of Julie written for Ms Biel); Sang Gluck's Orpheus at Drottningholm, 1992; Concert appearances in Stockholm, New York, Paris, Amsterdam, Parma, Verona, Milan and Copenhagen: repertoire includes Bach's Passions, Die Schöpfung, Mozart's Vespers and Requiem. Monteverdi's Vespers and Ein Deutsches Requiem. Recordings: Videos of Mozart operas from Drottningholm, directed by Goran Järvefelt, conducted by Arnold Östman. Address: Drottningholms Slottstheater, PO Box 27050, S-102 51 Stockholm, Sweden.

BIELAWA Herbert, b. 3 Feb 1930, Chicago, Illinois, USA. Composer. Education: BM; MM; BA at University of Illinois; DMA, University of Southern California; Studied with Gordon Binkerd, Burrill Phillips, Ingolf Dahl, Halsey Stevens, Ellis Kohs. Career: Professor of Music & Director of Electronic Music Studio at San Francisco State from 1966-91; Now retired. Compositions: A Bird in the Bush, Chamber Opera 1962; Spectrum for Band & Tape, 1965; Divergents, for Orchestra, 1969; A Dickinson Album for Choir, Synthesized Sound; Piano; Guitar, 1972; Dreams, for SSAA Chorus, 1984; Rants 1 & 11, for SATB and Violin, 1988; Song Cycles, The Snake and Other Creatures, for Sopranio and Piano, 1991; Quodlibet SF42569 for Organ and Tape, 1981; Duo for Violin and Harpsichord, 1984; Ants for Soprano, Violin and Piano 1985; Through Thick and Thin, for Flute, Clarinet, Viola & Piano, 1991; Undertones, for Organ, 1980; Monophonies, for Organ, 1979; Organ Booklet for Organ, 1992; Pentarcs, for Piano, 1982; Expressions, for Piano, 1992. Address: c/o ASCAP, ASCAP Building, One Lincoln Plaza, New York, NY 10023, USA.

BIERHANZL Petr, b. 27 July 1952, Prague, Czech Republic. Guitarist. m. Jana Bierhanzlova, 17 June 1977, 1 son. Education: Conservatory of Prague, Czech Republic. Debut: Prague, 1975. Career: Member, Guitar duo with Jana Bierhanzlova. Concerts: Czech Republic, 1975-97; Poland, 1986, 1990, 1994; Germany, 1995, 1997; Radio: Poland, 1990; Czech Republic, 1992, 1993, 1995, 1996, 1997; Television: German TV, 1978; Czech TV, 1992, 1993, 1994, 1996, 1997; Repertoire includes: J Dowland's Lachrimae Pavan, Welcome Home, A Michna's Czech Lute, J S Bach's Preludes and fugues, Scarlatti's Sonata K 380, A Vivaldi's Concerto op 3 Nr 6, A Soler's Sonatas, W A Mozart's Divertimento KV 439 b, F Sor's L'Encouragement op 34, F Carulli's Duo op 34 Nr 2, E Granados' Danzas Espanolas; I Albeniz's Granada, Sevilla, A Dvorak's Sonatina op 100, Educational activity: Professor at the Jezek Conservatory of Prague, 1980-. Recordings: The European Guitar Duets (Czech Guitar Duo), Scarlatti, Carulli, Sor and Truhlar (the first Czech CD with recordings of a guitar duo) 1992; English Renaissance Music (Czech Guitar Duo), Dowland, Byrd, Johnson and Bull. Membership: Intergram, Prague. Hobbies: Travelling; Reading. Current Management: Art Agency Sarka, Prague. Address: V Sareckem Udoli 2, 160 00 Praha 6, Czech Republic.

BILASH Olexander (Ivanovych), b. 6 Mar 1931, Hraduzk, Ukraine, Russia. Composer. Education: Studied at the Kiev Conservatory. Career: Freelance composer of songs, choral works, orchestral music and play and film music; Director of the Composers Union of the Ukraine, 1989. Compositions include: Stage works Haydamaky, 1965; Ballad of War, 1971; The Clear Well, operetta, 1975; The Legend of Kieve, operetta, 1983; The Russian Bell, operetta, 1984; The Standard Bearers, 1985. Address: Composers Union of the Ukraine, Kiev, Ukraine, CIS.

BILGRAM Hedwig, b. 31 Mar 1933, Memmingen, Germany. Organist; Harpsichordist. Education: Studied with Karl Richter and Friedrich Wührer. Career: Teacher at the Munich Hochschule für Musik from 1961, professor, 1964; Many performances under Karl Richter in Munich and elsewhere, in the Baroque repertory; Appeared also with trumpeter Maurice André; Premieres of works by André Jolivet, Henri Tomasi and Harald Genzmer. Address: c/o Hochschule für Musik, Areisstrasse 12, 8000 Munich 2, Germany.

BILINSKA Jolanta, b. 1 Mar 1951, Rzeszów, Poland. Musicologist. Education: Diploma with Honours, Musicology Department, Jagiellonian University, Krakow, 1976. Career includes: Secretary of the Warsaw International Festival of Contemporary Music, 1979-95; Currently, Director of Polish Radio Music Recording Department. Publications: Opery Mozarta na scenach polskich w latach 1783-1830 (Mozart's Operas on Polish Stages from 1783-1830); Musikbiliothek und Musikleben am Hof der Fuerstin Izabella Lubomirska in Lancut 1791-1816, Musik des Ostens, Bd 11, 1989; Recepcja dziel Mozarta w Polsce 1783-1830 (Reception of Mozart's Works in Poland 1783-1830), 1991, German edition, 1992. Contributions to: Ruch Muzyczny, a bi-weekly music magazine; Polish Music, quarterly. Hobbies: Opera; Theatre; History, enlightenment. Address: Osowska 23 m 5, 04 312 Warsaw, Poland.

BILSON Malcolm, b. 24 Oct 1935, Los Angeles, California, USA. Concert Pianist. Education: Studied at Bard College, BA, 1957; The Vienna State Academy, Reifezeugnis, 1959; Ecole Normale de Musique, Paris, Licence Libre, 1960; University of Illinois, MM 1962, DMA 1968. Career: Assistant Professor at Cornell University, 1968; Associate 1970; Full Professor, 1975; Frederick J Whiton Professor of Music, 1990; Acquired five-octave fortepiano by Philip Belt in 1969 and has given many concerts in the USA and abroad with late 18th century keyboard music; Concertos by Mozart and other composers with the Los Angeles Philharmonic, Milwaukee and Chicago Symphony, Vienna Tonkunstler, CBC Vancouver, Smithsonian Chamber

Ensemble, Academy of Ancient Music, English Baroque Soloists, Philadelphia Chamber Orchestra and St Paul Chamber Orchestra; Music Director of the series On Original Instruments at Merkin Hall; New York; Recent performances of late 19th century repertoire on historic 6 and 61/2 octave Viennese pianos; Solo recitals in season 1990-91, with works by Beethoven, Schubert, Schumann and Chopin, on original 1825 Alois Graf piano; Mozart Bicentennial 1991, with the Mozart piano sonatas in four recitals throughout the USA; European tour with John Eliot Gardiner and The English Baroque Soloists; Orchestra of the 18th century under Frans Brueggen, also appears with Nicholas McGegan; Co-director of 8 Mozart concerts on original instruments at Lincoln Center, 1991-92; Has presented fortepiano workshops and master classes at the University of California, Oberlin, Eastman, Juilliard, the Sibelius Academy in Helsinki, the Utrecht Early Music Festival and the Franz Liszt Academy in Budapest. Recordings: Mozart Complete Concertos for fortepiano and orchestra, with the English Baroque Soloists; The Piano Quartets, Deutsche Grammophon; Mozart Fortepiano-violin sonatas, with Sergiu Luca; Beethoven fortepiano-cello sonatas, with Anner Bylsma, Mozart music for 2 fortepianos and sonatas for fortepiano four hands, Nonesuch; Haydn English Canzonettas, with Adrienne Csengery, Hungaroton; 7 Haydn sonatas for fortepiano, Titanic. Address: c/o Judith Handershott Arts Management, 4 Bennett Park, Blackheath, London, SE3 9RB, England.

BIMBERG Guido, b. 14 Mar 1954, Halle, Germany. Musicologist; Professor. m. Christiane Bimberg, 11 Apr 1981, 1 son. Education: Studied Musicology, Music Education, Piano, Literature, Art History, Theatre, University of Halle, Hochschule für Musik, Leipzig and Felsenstein-Seminar, Berlin; PhD, 1979; Research Fellowship, Baltic, Central Asian, Caucasian, Russian, Siberian and Ukrainian Archives, 1979-80; Habilitation, 1981, Facultas docendi for Musicology and Music Education, 1983, Martin Luther University, Halle. Career: Lecturer, 1979, Reader, 1982, Associate Professor, Music History, 1985-95, Halle University, then Dortmund, 1995-; Visiting Professor, Havanna University, 1983-86; Guest Lecturer, All European Countries and Australia, Canada, China, Cuba, Hong Kong, Japan, Kenya, New Zealand, Philippines, Singapore, South Africa, South Korea, Taiwan, USA; Program Consultant, MRI Inc, 1993-. Publications include: Opera in 18th Century Russia, 1981; Dramaturgy of the Handel Operas, 1985; Anatoli Lunacharsky: Essays on Music, 1985; Schütz-Bach-Handel, 1989; Mozart's Entführung aus dem Serail, 1990; Music of Russian and German Composers, 1990; Fasch and the music in 18th Century Europe, 1995; Co-author: Andreas Werckmeister; Die musicalische Temperatur, 1996; Music in 18th Century European Society, 1997; Perspectives in musicology and education for the 21st century, 1997; Music in Canada/La Musique au Canada, 1997; Music Sources from the Westfalian Music Archive, 1997; Co-editor of numerous works; Music books for children. Contributions to: Symmetry Quarterly; English Studies; History of European Ideas; RITMO; Shakespeare Yearbook; Shakespeare Jahrbuch; Deutsche Literaturzeitung; Musik in der Schule; Musik des Ostens; Kirchemusikalisches Jahrbuch. Honours: Modest Musorgsky Prize, 1990; Gold Crown Medal, Hong Kong Music Association, 1995; Prize, Musica Westfalia, 1997. Memberships: President, German Handel Society; Vice-President, German Fasch Society; Vice-President, Werckmeister Society; President, Westfalian Music Society; International Musicological Society; International Society for Music Education; American Musicological Society; Royal Musical Association. Current Management: Hochschule für Musik, Dortmund. Address: Im Grund 25, D-58313 Herdecke, Germany.

BIMBERG Siegfried (Wolfgang), b. 5 May 1927, Halle, Saale, Germany. Musicologist; Psychologist; Composer; Conductor. m. Ortrud Rummler, 19 June 1953, 1 son. Education: Musicology and Psychology, Martin Luther University, Halle; Diploma Degree, BA; PhD, 1953, Dr paed habil, 1956, DrSc phil, 1982. Debut: Martin Luther University, Halle. Career: Lecturer of Musicology, Halle University, 1952-1962-; Lecturer of Musicology, Humboldt University, Berlin, 1956-62; Ordinary Professor of Musicology and Music Education, 1964-92; Head of Department for Musikdidatik, Martin Luther University, Halle-Wittenberg, 1962-90; Conductor and Leader, Chamber Choir, Halle University Hallenser Madrigalistyen, 1963-80; Concert tours throughout Europe; Records, radio and television. Compositions include: Opera, The Singing Horse, 1961; Eulenspiegels Brautfahrt, 1987; Cantatas; Songs; Ballads. Recordings: Own compositions (choir works); Interpretation of own works and works of other composers. Publications include: Einfuehrung in die Musikpsychologie, 1957; Vom Singen zum Musikverstehen, 1957, 1969; Methodisch-didaktische Grundlagen der Musikerziehung, 1968, 1973; Handbuch der Musikaesthetik, editor, 1979; Kontrast als musikaesthetische Kategorie, 1981; Handbuch der Chorleitung, editor, 1981; Lieder lernen-Lieder singen, 1981; Ferruccio Busoni: Von der Macht der Toene, editor, 1983; Musik-Erleben-Lernen, 1995; Nachhall 1 and 2, 1996; Musikwissenschaft und Musikpädgogik Perspektiven für das 21 Jahrhundert, 1997. Memberships: Freie deutsche Akademie der Künste und Wissenschaften, Bonn; Landesverband Sachsen-Anhalt, Deutscher Komponisten. Address: Ernestusstrasse 24, 06114 Halle, Germany.

BINGHAM Judith, b. 21 June 1952, Nottingham, England. Composer; Singer. m. Andrew Petrow, 20 Dec 1985. Education: Royal Academy of Music, London. Career: Studied with Hans Keller. Commissions from Peter Pears; King's Singers; BBC Singers; Songmakers' Almanac; Omega Guitar Quartet; New London Consort; TV and Radio scores; Singing debut at penultimate night of the Proms, 1984 in Strauss's Deutsche Motette; Appearances with Taverner Consort, Combattimento. Compositions: Cocaine Lil, Soprano and Piano, 1975; A Divine Image, Harpsichord, 1976; Chopin, Piano, 1979; A Falling Figure for Baritone, Clarient, Piano; BBC Commission, 1979; Mercutio for Baritone, Piano, 1980; Iago, Bass-Baritone, Piano, 1980; Clouded Windows, Mezzo, Piano, 1980; The Ruin, SATB, 1981; A Midsummer Night's Dream, Mezzo, Piano, 1981; Into the Wilderness, Organ, 1982; Pictured Within, Piano, 1982; Ferrara, Tenor, Piano, 1982; A Hymn Before Sunrise in the Vale of Chamounix, 24 SATB-BBC Singers, 1982; Cradle Song of the Blessed Virgin, SSATB, 1983; Mass Setting; Sterna Paradisaea, SATB and Organ, 1984; A Winter Walk at Noon, 27 solo voices, BBC Commission, 1984; Just Before Dawn, SSAA, 1986; Chartres, Orchestra, 1987. Recordings: Cradle Song of the Blessed Virgin. Honours: Principal's Prize for Composition, 1971; BBC Young Composer, 1976. Membership: ISM. Hobbies: Birdwatching; Photography; Sailing. Address: c/o Novello, 8 Lower James Street, London, W1, England.

BINI Carlo, b. 1947, Naples, Italy. Singer, Tenor. Education: Studied at the Naples Conservatory. Debut: Teatro San Carlo Naples, 1969, as Pinkerton. Career: Sang in Italy and at the Deutsche Oper Berlin; State Opera Houses of Munich and Stuttgart; Hamburg Staatsoper, 1974, as Alfredo in La Traviata and Rodolfo; Sang further in Brussels, Paris, Marseille, Rio de Janeiro and New York City Opera; Metropolitan Opera, 1982, as Enzo in La Gioconda; La Scala, 1984, in I Lombardi; Sang Arrigo in I Vespri siciliani at Santiago, 1990; Avito in Montemezzi's L'amore dei tre re at Palermo, 1990; Other roles include, Rodolfo in Luisa Miller, Don Carlos, Gabrielle Adorno, Don José, Laca in Jenufa and Tchaikovsky's Vakula. Recordings: Verdi Requeim; Eine Nacht in Venedig; Video of I Lombardi. Address: c/o Teatro Massimo, 1-90100, Palermo, Italy.

BINKERD Gordon, b. 22 May 1916, Lynch, Nebraska, USA. Composer. Education: Studied at the South Dakota Wesleyan University with Gail Kubik, BMus 1937; Eastman School, Rochester, with Bernard Rogers; Harvard University with Walter Piston and Irving Fine, MA 1952. Career: Professor of Music, University of Illinois, 1949-71; Commissions from the St Louis Symphony Orchestra, the McKim Fund of the Library of Congress and the Ford and Fromm Foundations. Compositions include: 3 Symphonies, 1955, 1957, 1959; A Part of Heaven for violin and orchestra, 1972; The Battle for brass and percussion, 1972; Movement for orchestra, 1972; Choral, Autumn Flowers 1968, To Electra 1968-73, In a Whispering Gallery 1969, Nocturne 1969, A Christmas Carol 1970, A Scotch Mist 1976, Sung Under the Silver Umbrella 1977, Requiem for Soldiers Lost in Ocean Transports 1984, House at Dusk 1984, Dakota Day 1985; Instrumental, Cello Sonata 1952, 4 Piano Sonatas 1955, 1981-83, 2 String Quartets 1958, 1961, Violin Sonata 1977, String Trio 1979; Songs. Honours include: Guggenheim Fellowship, 1959; National Institute of Arts and Letters Award, 1964. Address: c/o ASCAP, ASCAP Building, 1 Lincoln Plaza, NY 10023, USA.

BINKLEY Thomas, b. 26 Dec 1931, Cleveland, Ohio, USA. Musician; Teacher. m. Raglind Herrel, 3 sons. Education: BMus cum laude, University of Illinois, 1952-56. Career: Director, Studio der Fruhen Musik, Munich, 1957-79; Teacher and Performer, Medieval Program, Schola Cantorum Basiliensis, Switzerland, 1973-77; Visiting Professor, Stanford University, 1977, 1979; Professor of Music and Director, Early Music Institute, Indiana University, 1979-. Recordings include: In excess of fifty from 1962, including Adam de la Hall, Robin et Marion, 1991; Hildegard of Bingen, 1991; Guillaume Dufay, Misse la face ay pale, 1988; Music in Medieval Europe 1&2, 1988; Andalusische Musik, 1984; L'Agonie de Languedoc, 1976; Camino de Santiago I, 1973. Publications: Editor, Music Scholarship and Performance; Publications of the Early Music Institute; Focus Recordings; Collected Articles and Reviews, 1986-89; Translation of Fritz Winckel, Music, Sound and Sensation, 1967; Contributor to Alte Musik Praxis und Reflection, 1983; Companion to Medieval and Renaissance Music, 1991; Neues Handbuch der Musikwissenschaft, ed Carl Dahlhaus; vol II, Musikalisch & Interpretation: Die Musik des Mittelalters, Laaber, 1992. Address: c/o Early Music Institute, School of Music, Indiana University, Bloomington, IN 47405, USA.

BINNS Malcolm, b. 29 Jan 1936, Nottingham, England. Concert Pianist. Education: Bradford Grammar School, 1948-52; ARCM Royal College of Music, 1952-56; Chappell Medal, 1956. Debuts: London, 1957; Henry Wood Proms, 1960; Royal Festival Hall, 1961, in the first British performance of Prokofiev 4th Piano Concerto, with the Royal Philharmonic Orchestra. Career: Appearances, London Philharmonic Orchestra International series; Royal Festival Hall, 1969-; Concerts at the Aldeburgh Festival, Leeds Festival and Three Choirs Festival, 1975; Regular appearances at Promenade concerts; Formed a duo partnership with the violinist Manoug Parikian in 1966; Toured with Scottish National Orchestra and Limbourg Orchestra, 1988. Recordings: 1st complete recording of Beethoven piano sonatas on original instruments, 1980; Over 30 recordings for Decca, EMI and Chandos; Recordings of four concertos by William Sterndale Bennett with LPO and Philharmonia Orchestra released on Lyrita, 1990. Honours: Recipient of Chappel Gold Medal; Medal of Worshipful Company of Musicians; Royal College of Music. Hobbies: Collecting Antique Gramophone records. Current Management: Melanie Turner Management. Address: c/o Melanie Turner Management, Suite 408, Parkway House, Sheen Lane, London, SW14 8LS, England.

BIRET Idil, b. 21 Nov 1941, Ankara, Turkey. Concert Pianist. Education: Studied at the Paris Conservatoire with Alfred Cortot and Nadia Boulanger; Further studies with Wilhelm Kempff. Debut: Played Mozart's Concerto K365 with Kempff in Paris, 1953. Career: Worldwide concerts with major orchestras including the conductors Monteux, Scherchen, Leinsdorf, Boult, Kempe, Sargent, Rozhdestvensky, Groves, Mackerras, Keilberth and Pritchard; US debut in 1962 playing Rachmaninov's 3rd Concerto with the Boston Symphony; London Symphony in 1963 under Monteux; Istanbul Festival in 1973 playing Beethoven's Violin Sonatas with Yehudi Menuhin; Frequent tours of Russia (with Leningrad Philharmonic 1984); Tours of Australia in 1980 and 1984; 85th Birthday celebration concert for Wilhelm Backhaus and 90th Birthday for Wilhelm Kempff; Festival engagements at Montreal, Persepolis, Royan, La Rochelle, Athens, Berlin and Gstaad; Symphonies of Beethoven arranged by Liszt at the Montpellier Festival in 1986; Ravel Gaspard de la Nuit and Beethoven's 6th Symphony at the Wigmore Hall in 1989; Member of juries at the Queen Elizabeth Competition, Belgium, The Van Cliburn in USA and the Busoni Competition, Italy. Recordings include: World premiere of Beethoven's Symphonies transcribed by Liszt, 1986; Complete works of Chopin, 1992; Complete piano solo works of Brahms, 1995. Honours include: Lily Boulanger Memorial Fund, Boston, 1954, 1964; Harriet Cohen/Dinu Lipatti Gold Medal, London, 1959; Polish Artistic Merit Award, 1974; Chevalier de l'Ordre du Merite, France, 1976; State Artist of Turkey. Address: c/o M Sefik B Yuksel, 51 Avenue General de Gaulle, B-1050 Bruxelles, Belgium.

BIRKELAND Oystein, b. 1958, Norway. Cellist. Education: Norwegian State Academy of Music; Studied in Basel with Heinrich Schiff, in London with William Pleeth and Ralph Kirshbaum. Career: Has worked with Frans Helmersson, Arto Noras, Erling Blondal Bengtsson and Jacqueline du Pré; Member, 1982-, Principal Cellist, 1985-, Norwegian Chamber Orchestra; Performances as soloist, Norway, UK, Germany, Switzerland, in concertos by Haydn, Boccherini, Vivaldi and others; Has played with Oslo Philharmonic, Trondheim Symphony Orchestra and Norwegian Radio Orchestra; Recent debut with Academy of St Martin-in-the-Fields, playing the Haydn Concerto in C major in Oslo, Helsinki and Stockholm; Recent festival appearances include Bergen International Music Festival, the Contemporary Music Festivals Platform, London, and Schleswig Holstein Music Festival; Plays a cello by Francesco Ruggiere (Cremona, 1680). Recordings: For BBC with pianist Joanna McGregor; With pianist Havard Gimse; 3 Russian sonatas with Ian Brown. Current Management: Diana Walters Artists Management, England. Address: c/o Diana Walters Artists Management, Ivy Cottage, 3 Main Street, Keyham, Leicestershire LE7 9JQ, England.

BIRKS Ronald, b. 1945, England. Violinist. Education: Studied with Sidney Griller at the Royal Academy of Music, with Sandor Vegh at the University of Keele; With Vilmos Tatrai in Budapest. Career: Member of the Lindsay String Quartet from 1972; Regular tours of Europe, Britain, USA, From 1974, quartet in residence at Sheffield University, then Manchester University, 1979; Premiered the 4th Quartet of Tippett at the 1979 Bath Festival and commissioned Tippett's 5th Quartet, 1992; Chamber Music Festival established at Sheffield, 1984; Regular concerts at the Wigmore Hall, including Haydn series, 1987; Plays Campo Selice Stradivarius of 1694. Recordings: Complete cycles of Bartók; Tippett and Beethoven; CDs of Haydn quartets Live from the Wigmore Hall, ASV. Honours: Prize Winner, with members Lindsay Quartets, at Liège International Competition, 1969; Gramophone Chamber Award for late Beethoven quartets, 1984. Address: c/o Ingpen and Williams Ltd, 14 Kensington Court, London, W8 5DN, England.

BIRNSTEIN Renate, b. 17 Nov 1946, Hamburg, Germany. Composer. Education: Studied with Ligeti at the Hamburg Musik Hochschule. Career: Teacher at the Lubeck Hochschule, 1973-80, Hamburg from 1979 (professor, 1988). Compositions include: Imaginations for orchestra, 1972; Heptagon for piano, 1976; Five Pieces for strings, 1980; Sextet for six orchestral ensembles, 1981; String quintet, 1982; String quartet, 1986; Septet, 1988;

Kurwenal for cello, 1990. Address: c/o GEMA, Postfach 80 07 67, D-81607 Munich, Germany.

BIRTWISTLE Harrison (Sir), b. 15 July 1934, Accrington, Lancashire, England. Composer. m. Sheila Birtwistle, 3 sons. Education: Royal Manchester College of Music; Royal Academy of Music. Career: Director of Music, Cranborne Chase School, 1962-65; Visiting Fellow, Princeton University (Harkness International Fellowship), 1966; Cornell Visiting Professor of Music, Swarthmore College, Pennsylvania, 1973-74; Slee Visiting Professor, New York State University, Buffalo, 1975; Associate Director, National Theatre, 1975; Works widely performed at major festivals in Europe including Venice Biennale, ISCM Festivals in Vienna and Copenhagen, Warsaw Autumn Festival and at Cheltenham, Aldeburgh and Edinburgh; With Peter Maxwell Davies founded the Pierrot Players, 1975 (later The Fires of London); The Mask of Orpheus premiered at London Colisuem, 1986, Gawain at Covent Garden, 1991; Featured composer at the 1991 Aldeburgh Festival. Compositions include: Stage: Monodrama for soprano, speaker, ensemble, 1967; Down by the Greenwood Side, dramatic pastoral, 1969; Incidental music for National Theatre productions of Hamlet, 1975, The Oresteia, 1981; Ballet Frames, Pulses and Interrupttions, 1977; Bow Down, music theatre, 1977; Operas: Punch and Judy, 1-act opera, 1968; The Mask of Orpheus, 1973-75, 1981-84; Yan Tan Tethera, TV opera, 1986; Gawain, 1988-91; The Second Mrs Kong, 1992-94; Orchestral: Chorales, 1960-63; 3 Movements with Fanfares, 1964; Nomos, 1968; An Imaginary Landscape, 1971; The Triumph of Time, 1972; Grimethorpe Aria for Brass Band, 1973; Melencolia I, 1976; Silbury Air for small orchestra, 1977; Still Movement for 13 solo strings, 1984; Earth Dances, 1985; Endless Parade for trumpet, vibraphone, strings, 1987; Ritual Fragment, 1990; Gawain's Journey, 1991; Panic, 1995; Vocal: Monody for Corpus Christi for soprano and ensemble, 1959; Narration: A Description of the Passing Year for chorus, 1963; Entr'actes and Sappho Fragments for soprano and ensemble, 1964; Carmen Paschale for chorus and organ, 1965; Ring a Dumb Clarion for soprano, clarinet, percussion, 1965; Cantata for soprano and ensemble, 1969; Nenia on the Death of Orpheus for soprano and ensemble, 1970; The Fields of Sorrow for 2 sopranos, chorus, ensemble, 1971-72; Meridian for mezzo, chorus, ensemble, 1970-71; Epilogue: Full Fathom Five for baritone and ensemble, 1972; ...agm...for 16 solo voices and 3 instruments, 1979; On the Sheer Threshold of the Night for 4 solo voices and 12-part chorus; White and Light for soprano and ensemble, 1989; Four Poems by Jaan Kaplinski for soprano and ensemble, 1991; Instrumental: Refrains and Choruses for wind quintet, 1957; The World is Discovered for ensemble, 1960; Tragoedia for ensemble, 1965; Verses for Ensembles, 1969; Ut heremita solus, arr of Ockeghem, 1969; Hoquetus David, arr of Machaut, 1969; Medusa for ensemble, 1970, revised, 1980; Chronometer for 8-track tape, 1971; Chorales from a Toyshop, 1967-74; Carmen Arcadiae Mechanicae Perpetuum for ensemble, 1977; For O, For O, the Hobby Horse is Forgot for 6 percussion, 1976; Clarinet Quintet, 1980; Salford Toccata for brass band and bass drum, 1988; An Uninterrupted Endless Melody for Oboe and Piano, 1991; Antiphonies for Piano and Orchestra, 1992; Five Distances for Five Instruments, 1992; Tenebrae for Soprano and Ensemble, 1992; Night for Soprano and Ensemble, 1992; Movement for String Quartet, 1992. Recordings include: Gawain (Chandos); Punch and Judy; Music for Wind and Percussion; Earth Dances; Triumph of Time, Gawain's Journey; Melencolia I, Ritual Fragments. Honours include: Granemeyer Award, USA, for The Mask of Orpheus, 1986; KBE, 1987. Address: c/o Universal Edition (London) Ltd, Warwick House, 9 Warwick Street, London W1R 5RA, England.

BISATT Susan, b. 1963, England. Singer (Soprano). Career: Frequent festival engagements, including Almeida Contemporary Opera (Isabelle Rimbaud in The Man Who Strides the Wind by Kevin Volans) and Edinburgh (Salome in the opera by Strauss); Roles with Opera Restor's in Britain and Abroad, in Dido and Aeneas, The Death of Dido (Pepusch) and Pyramus and Thisbe (Lampe); Other appearances with Opera North (as Papagena) and elsewhere as Violetta, Donna Elvira, Lucia di Lammermoor, Gilda, Norina and the soprano leads in Les Contes d'Hoffmann; Gluck's Eurydice, Mozart's Countess, and Rosina; Tours of Britain, Ireland and Finland with Opera Circus; Opera workshops with Opera North, Compact Opera, Theatre de Complicité and the David Glass Ensemble; Television includes: The Singing Voice, for Channel 4. Recordings include: English Baroque Opera (Hyperion); Scenes from operas by Charles Dibdin; Purcell Songs (Naxos). Address: c/o C&M Craig Services Ltd, 3 Kersley Street, London SW11 4PR, England.

BISCARDI Chester, b. 19 Oct 1948, Kenosha, WI, USA. Composer; Teacher. Education: BA, English Literature, 1970, MA, Italian Language, 1972, MM, Composition, 1974, University of WI, Madison; Studies at: Universita di Bologna; Conservatorio di Musica, G B Martini; MMA, 1976, DMA, Composition, Yale University School of Music, 1980. Career includes: Teacher, University of WI, 1970-74; Yale University, 1975-76; Music Faculty, Sarah Lawrence College, Bronxville, NY, 1977-; Currently, Chairman of Music Department, 1st William Schuman Chair in Music, Sarah Lawrence College, Bronxville, NY. Compositions include: Tight-Rope, chamber opera, 1985; Piano Sonata, 1986, revised, 1987; Traverso, for Flute and Piano, 1987; Netori, 1990; The Gift of Life, for Soprano and Piano, 1990-93; Music for an Occasion, for Brass, Piano and Percussion, 1992; Nel giardinetto della villa, for Piano 4 hands, 1994. Recordings include: Piano Sonata; Mestiere; Trasumanar; Traverso; The Gift of Life; Companion Piece; Incitation to Desire, tango; Tenzone; At The Still Point. Address: 542 Avenue of the Americas 4R, New York, NY 10011-2011, USA.

BISCHOF Rainer, b. 20 June 1947, Vienna, Austria. Composer. Education: PhD, University of Vienna, 1973; Studied composition privately with Hans Apostel, 1967-72. Compositions: Sonatine for Clarinet, 1969; Sonatine for Horn, 1970; Duo for Flute and Clarinet, 1970; Theme and 7 variations for Oboe and Cello, 1970; Quartet for Flute, Oboe, Horn and Bassoon, 1971; Grave for Violin and Piano, 1970-71; Deduction for Strings, 1973-74; Characteristic Differences for Violin and Piano, 1974; In Memoriam Memoriae, song cycle for Mezzo-soprano, Speaker, Vibraphone, Celesta, Bass, Clarinet and Cello, 1975-77; Orchesterstücke, 1976-82; Flute Concerto, 1978-79; Studies from the Flute Concerto for solo flute, 1978; Concerto for Violin, Cello and Orchestra, 1979-80; Variations for Organ, 1981; Viola Tricolor, 32 variations for Viola, 1982; Music for 6 Recorders, 1982-83; String Sextet, 1990; Studie in PP, 1991. Address: AKM, 111 Baumstr 8-10, 1031 Wien, Austria.

BISPO Antonio (Alexandre), b. 17 Mar 1949, Sao Paulo, Brazil; Came to Germany, 1974; Musicologist. Education: Diploma, Architecture, University of Sao Paulo, 1972; Licence, Music Education, Institute Musical de Sao Paulo, 1972; Licence, Conducting, 1973; Doctor of Musicology, University of Cologne, Germany, 1979. Career: Director, Conservatorio Jardim America, Sao Paulo, 1971-72; Lecturer, Ethnomusicology and Aesthetics of Music, 1972-74; Researcher, Institut für Hymnologische und Musikethnologische Studien Maria Laach, Germany, 1979-; Director, Musikschule der Stadt Leichlingen, Germany, 1981-84. Publications: Die katholische Kirchenmusik in der Provinz Sao Paulo, 1979; Collectanea Musicae Sacrae Brasiliensis, 1981; Grundlagen christlicher Musikkultur in der aussereuropäishen Welt der Neuzeit, 1989; Leben und Werk von Martin Braunwieser, 1991-92; Christliche Volkstraditonen and Synkretismus in Brasilien, 1989-90; Die Musikkulturen der Indianer Brasiliens, 1994-95; Editor, Correspondencia Musicológica, 1989-. Contributions to: Musices Aptatio, 1980, 1982, 1984-85; Editor, Leichlinger Musikforum, 1981-84; Boletim da Sociedade Brasileira de Musicologia, 1981-86; Articles, professional journals. Memberships: Consociato Internationalis Musicae Sacrae, Rome, 1979-; Sociedade Brasileira de Musicologia, Board, 1981-94; Academia Paulistana de Historia, 1981-; Associaçao Brasileira de Folclore, 1981-; Gesellschaft für Musikforschung, 1984-; Gesellschaft zur Erforschung und Förderung der Blasmusik, 1984-; Ordem Nacional dos Bandeirantes, 1981-; Institut für Studien der Musikkultur des portugiesischen Sprachraumes, 1985-. Address: Theodor-Heuss-Ring 14, 50668 Cologne 1, Nordrhein-Westphalen, Germany.

BISSON Yves, b. 31 May 1936, Mostaganem, Algeria. Baritone. Education: Studied at Paris Conservatoire with Renee Gilly-Musy and Louis Noguera. Career: Sung at the Paris Opera, and the Opéra Comique, notably in Manon, Faust, Platée, La Bohème, Werther, Romeo et Juliette, and Les Pêcheurs de Perles (all televised); Festival engagements at Aix-en-Provence as Rodolphe in Les Fêtes Vénitiennes by Campra, Avignon, Carpentras and Orange; Has sung in France, New York, Washington, Amsterdam, Brussels, Covent Garden London, Lisbon, Geneva, Zurich, Barcelona, Madrid, Vienna, Naples and Russia; Other roles include Lescaut in Auber's Manon Lescaut, Escamillo, Nilakantha in Lakmé, Mercutio, Sander in Zemire et Azor by Grétry, Massenet's Lescaut, Albert and Caoudal in Sapho, Mozart's Figaro and Masetto, Rangoni in Boris Godunov, Puccini's Marcello, Schaunard, Sharpless and Lescaut, Rameau's Oromases in Zoroastre and Citeron in Platée, Verdi's Posa, Germont and Ford; Sang Françoise in Le Chemineau by Leroux at Marseilles, 1996. Address: Place de l'Opéra, 36 Rue Ballu, 75009 Paris, France.

BISWAS Anup (Kumar), b. 1957, West Bangal, India. Composer; Concert Cellist. Education: Studied in India with Rev T Mathieson, at Royal College of Music; Further study with Pierre Fournier in Geneva, and Jacqueline du Pre in London. Career: Concerts throughout UK, including St James and Lambeth Palaces; Elizabeth and Wigmore Halls; Grays Inn and Riverside Studios; Festival engagements at Cleveland; Belfast; Greenwich; Hereford; Masterclassed at the Dartington Summer School and concerts in Germany, Finland and Norway; JS Bach Tercentenary concerts in cathedrals and churches in the UK, featuring the suites for unaccompanied cello; Artistic Director of the Dante Alighieri Orchestra, from 1989; Royal Albert Hall, 1992, performing Celebration from his own ballet Ten Guineas under the Banyan Tree; Purcell Room Concert, 1993, playing Beethoven, Shostakovich, Walton and Brahms. Compositions: Music for Thetre Taliesin, Wales, 1986 production of Tristan and Essylt, featured by BBC Wales. Address: East West Arts Limited, 93b Cambridge Gardens, London, W10 6JE, England.

BJONER Ingrid, b. 8 Nov 1927, Kraakstad, Norway. Opera and Concert Singer (Soprano). Education: Conservatory of Music, Oslo, with Gudrun Boellemose; Hochschule für Musik, Frankfurt, with Paul Lohmann; Further study with Ellen Repp in New York; Graduate Pharmacist, University of Oslo, 1951. Career: Sang Third Norn and Gutrune in Norwegian radio recording of Götterdämmerung, 1956; Stage Debut, Oslo, 1957, as Donna Anna; Drottningholm Opera, 1957, as Handel's Rodelinda; Member, Wuppertal Opera, Germany, 1957-59; Deutsche Oper am Rhein Dusseldorf, 1959-61; Bayreuth Festival 1960, as Freia, Helmvige and Gutrune; Has sung with Bayerische Staatsoper Munich from 1961, notably as the Empress in Die Frau ohne Schatten 1963 and as Isolde, in the centenary production of Tristan and Isolde, 1965; Metropolitan Opera debut 1961, as Elsa in Lohengrin; Covent Garden from 1967, as Senta, Sieglinde and Leonore (Fidelio); Salzburg Festival, 1969-1970, Leonore; Sang the Duchess of Parma in the US premiere of Doktor Faust by Busoni, Carnegie Hall, 1974; Oslo and Copenhagen, 1985-86, as Elektra; Further appearances at La Scala, Vienna, Hollywood Bowl, Hamburg, Deutsche Oper Berlin, Cologne Opera, Warsaw and Vancouver; Season 1986-87 sang Isolde at Bayreuth and the Kostelnicka in Jenufa at Karlsruhe; Staatsoper Munich 1988, as the Dyer's Wife in Die Frau ohne Schatten; Oslo Opera, 1989, Senta; Concert appearances worldwide, often in the songs of Grieg; Professor at Royal Academy of Music, Copenhagen, 1991-; Professor at Royal Academy of Music, Oslo, 1992-. Recordings include: Götterdämmerung, Decca; Die Frau ohne Schatten, DGG; Wagner's Wesendonck Lieder; Songs by Sibelius. Honours include: Order of St Olav, Norway, 1964; Bavarian Order of Merit. Address: Gregers Grams vei 33, 0382 Oslo 3, Norway.

BJORLIN Ulf, b. 21 May 1933, Stockholm, Sweden. Composer; Conductor. Education: Studied with Igor Markevitch in Salzburg and Nadia Boulanger in Paris. Career: Director of Royal Dramatic Theatre, Stockholm, 1963-68; Freelance Composer; Conductor of leading orchestras in Sweden and elsewhere in Scandanavia. Compositions: Pinochhio, children's musical, 1966; Ekon for orchestra, 1967; In Five Years, opera for actors and chamber ensemble, 1967; Epitah for Lars Gorling, for orchestra, 1967; Of Melancholy, choreographic oratoria, 1970-; The Bit Theatre, opera, 1972; The Ballad of Kasper Rosenrod, opera, 1972; Karlekin till Belisa, radio opera, 1981; Wind Quintet, 1983; Tillfalle gor Tiufven, opera buffa, 1983; Den Frammande Kvinnan, opera, 1984. Address: c/o STIM, Sandhamnsgatan 79, PO Box 27372, S-102 54 Stockholm, Sweden.

BJORLING Rolf, b. 25 Dec 1928, Jonkoping, Sweden. Singer, Tenor. m. Gunnel Eklund. Education: Studied at the Stockholm Music Academy, 1953-54, with Dimitri Onofrei in San Francisco. Debut: Stockholm 1960, in concert. Career: Stage debut Gothenburg, 1962 as Pinkerton; Guest appearances in Berlin, Hamburg, Munich, Helsinki, Oslo and San Francisco; Appearances at Drottningholm Opera House; Roles include Florestan, Manrico, Cavaradossi, Calaf, Radames and Don José; Founded the Nyla Bjorling Vocal Quartet, 1971; Tours of Scandinavia and North America. Memberships: Royal Opera Stockholm, from 1969.

BJORNSON Maria, b. Paris, France (Norwegian and Rumanian parentage). Stage Designer. Career: Worked for various theatre companies, including the Royal Shakespeare, Stratford; Designs for Scottish Opera include Die Zauberflöte, The Golden Cockerel, Die Meistersinger and a Janácek cycle shared with Welsh National Opera; The Queen of Spades, Die Walkure, The Gambler and Carmen for the English National Opera; Covent Garden designs include the British premiere of Stockhausen's Donnerstag aus Licht, 1985; Der Rosenkavalier and Les Contes d'Hoffman (costumes); Mahagonny for the 1990 Maggio Musicale; Così fan Tutte at Glyndbourne, 1991; Katya Kabanova and The Sleeping Beauty for Covent Garden, 1994; Further designs at the Wexford Festival, Komische Oper Berlin, Houston, Geneva, Sydney and Amsterdam; Musicals include pieces by Stephen Sondheim and Andrew Lloyd Webber. Honours include: Gold Medal from the Prague Biennale. Address: c/o Lies Askonas Ltd, 6 Henrietta St, London WC2E 8LA, England.

BJORNSSON Sigurd, b. 19 Mar 1932, Hafnarfjordur, Iceland. Singer (Tenor). Education: Studied with Gerhard Husch in Munich. Debut: Stuttgart, 1962, as Arturo in Lucia di Lammermoor. Career: Sang at Stuttgart until 1968, Kassel, 1968-72, Graz, 1972-75, and Theater am Gärtnerplatz Munich until 1977; Among his best roles were Mozart's Belmonte, Ferrando and Tamino, Lionel in Martha, Nicolai's Fenton, Wagner's Froh and Steuermann, Bellini's Riccardo and Rinuccio in Gianni Schicchi; Guest appearances at the Deutsche Oper Berlin, Munich, Hamburg, the Vienna Volksoper and the Bregenz and Schwetzingen Festivals. Address: c/o Staatstheater am Gärtnerplatz, Gärtnerplatz 3, W-8000 Munich 5,Germany.

BLACK Jeffrey, b. 1964, Australia. Singer (Baritone). Debut: European, Harlekin in Ariadne auf Naxos at Monte Carlo, 1986. Career: Sang with Australian Opera from 1985 as Mercutio, Schaunard, Papageno, Dr Falke, Dandini, Rossini's Figaro and Ottone in Poppaea; Glyndebourne Festival, from 1986, as Sid in Albert Herring, Demetrius and the Count in Figaro and Capriccio; Covent Garden appearances as well as engagements at Los Angeles as Guglielmo and Marcello, 1993, Opéra Bastille in Paris, Puccini's Lescaut, Geneva Opera, Fieramosca in Benvenuto Cellini, San Francisco, Rossini's Figaro; Lyric Opera of Chicago and 1993 Salzburg Festival as Guglielmo, Teatro Colon, (Buenos Aires) as Dandini, Don Giovanni in Antwerp, Count (Le nozze di Figaro) in Washington, Figaro (Barbiere) at the Met, New York and in Munich, Valentin (Faust) in Geneva and Eugene Onegin at San Diego; Returned to Australia to appear with Lyric Opera of Queensland and Victoria State Opera, Melbourne; Sang Britten's Demetrius for New Israeli Opera, 1994; Mozart's Count at the Metropolitan, 1997; Concerts include tour of Australia with Geoffrey Parsons and the ABC Orchestras, Carmina Burana with the London Philharmonic and Christus in the St Matthew Passion under Franz Welser-Möst. Recordings include: Carmina Burana. Address: IMG Artists, Media House, 3 Burlington Lane, London W4 2TH, England.

BLACK Lynton, b. 1960, England. Bass-Baritone. Education: Studied at the Royal Academy of Music. Career: Appearances with the English Touring Opera, English Bach Festival and at Aix-en-Provence and Salzburg Festivals (Mozart's Le Nozze di Figaro in 1995); Other roles include Handels' Polyphemus, Mozart's Don Alfonso, Luca in Walton's Bear and Deadeye in HMS Pinafore; Concerts with Scottish Chamber Orchestra and Northern Sinfonia; Principal Bass, D'Oyly Carte Opera Company, 1994-; Sang in Haydn's L'Incontro Improvviso, Garsington, 1994 and Budd in Albert Herring, 1996. Address: Ron Gonsalves Management, 7 Old Town, Clapham, London, SW4 0JT, England.

BLACK Stanley, b. 14 June 1913, London, England. Conductor; Composer; Pianist; Arranger. m. Edna Kaye, 2 children. Education: Matthay School of Music. Career: Conductor of BBC Dance Orchestra, 1944-52; Musical Director of Associated British Pictures Corporation, Elstree Studios, 1958-63; BBC Television appearances; Guest Conductor in New Zealand, Australia, Canada, Japan, Korea, USA, Netherlands, Belgium and UK; Associate Conductor, Royal Philharmonic Orchestra, 1967; Principal Conductor of BBC Northern Ireland Orchestra, 1968-69; Associate Conductor for Osaka Philharmonic Orchestra, 1971; Principal Conductor for New Zealand Proms, 1972 and 1974; Concerts with Royal Philharmonic Orchestra, Bournemouth Symphony Orchestra, English Northern Philharmonia, National Philharmonic Orchestra and BBC Festival of Light Music. Compositions include: Over 100 film scores. Recordings: Numerous. Honours: Various Gold Records; Order of the British Empire in 1986 New Year's Honours List; Gold Award, British Academy of Songwriters, Composers and Authors, 1987; Freedom of The City of London, 1988. Hobbies: Theatre; Riding. Address: 8 Linnell Close, London, NW11, England.

BLACK Virginia, b. 1950, England. Harpsichordist. m. Howard Davis. Career: London concerts in the Wigmore Hall, Purcell Room and Queen Elizabeth Hall; Appearances at major festivals in the UK; Recordings for the BBC and the Westdeutsche Rundfunk; Television performance of Bach's 5th Brandenburg Concerto, with the English Chamber Orchestra; Tours to Europe, the USA, Australia and New Zealand; Concerts with Howard Davis, violin; Other repertoire includes: Sonatas by Soler and Scarlatti; Bach's Chromatic Fantasy and Fugue, Concertos in E and C Minor, Fantasie and Fugue in A minor, Toccata in D and Partitas; Pieces by Rameau, Dandrieu, Duphly and Forqueray; Falla's Harpsichord Concerto; Professor of Harpsichord at the Royal Academy of Music. Address: Manygate Management, 13 Cotswold Mews, 12-16 Battersea High Street, London SW11 3JB, England.

BLACK William (David), b. 23 Feb 1952, Dallas, TX, USA. Concert Pianist. Education: BM, Oberlin College, 1974; MM 1976, DMA 1979, The Juilliard School. Debut: New York, 1977; London, England, 1979. Career: Solo and orchestral engagements across the USA, Canada, England, France, Holland, Belgium, Germany, Iceland, Japan, China and Italy; Television appearances in the USA and numerous USA and European radio broadcasts including worldwide broadcasts of the Voice of America. Recordings: Works of David Diamond; World premiere recording of the original version of the 4th Piano Concerto of Sergei Rachmaninov; Hunter Johnson Piano Sonata; Gershwin, Rhapsody in Blue. Contributions to: Keyboard Classics. Honours: Pi Kappa Lambda, 1974; Concert Artists Guild Award; Morris Loeb Award, The Juilliard School; Solo Recitalist Grant, National Endowment for The Arts, 1991. Memberships: Bohemians, New York Musicians Club; European Piano Teachers' Association.

BLACKBURN Bonnie J, b. 15 July 1939, Albany, NY, USA. Musicologist. m. (1) Edward E Lowinsky, 10 Sep 1971, deceased 1985, (2) Leofranc Holford-Strevens, 6 Jan 1990. Education: BA, Wellesley College, 1961; MA 1963, PhD 1970, University of Chicago. Career: Research Assistant, Department of Music, 1963-76, Visiting Associate Professor, 1986, University of Chicago; Lecturer, School of Music, Northwestern University, 1987; Visiting Associate Professor, State University of New York, Buffalo, 1989-90; General Editor of Monuments of Renaissance Music, 1993-. Publications: Music for Treviso Cathedral in the Late Sixteenth Century: A Reconstruction of the Lost Manuscripts, 29 and 30, 1987; Josquin des Prez: Proceedings of The International Josquin Festival Conference, 1976, edited with E Lowinsky; Edited Johannis Lupi Opera omnia, 3 volumes, 1980-89; Edited, Music in the Culture of the Renaissance and Other Essays by Edward E Lowinsky, 1989; Editor with E Lowinsky and C A Miller, A Correspondence of Renaissance Musicians, 1991. Contributions to: Musical Quarterly; Journal of The American Musicological Society; Musica Disciplina; Early Music History; The New Grove Dictionary of Music and Musicians; Early Music; Studi Musicali; Journal of Musicology; Die Musik in Geschichte und Gegenwart. Address: 67 St Bernard's Road, Oxford, OX2 6EJ, England.

BLACKBURN Olivia, b. 1960, London, England. Singer (Soprano). Education: Studied at Trinity College, London, and at the Pears-Britten School. Career: Regular concert on South Bank, London, in Die Schöpfung by Haydn, Vivaldi's Magnificat and Handel's Jephtha; German requiem by Brahms at the Barbican with the Philharmonia and the St Matthew Passion with the Steinitz Bach Players; European performances in the Bach B Minor Mass, Haydn's Paukenmesse (Missa in tempore belli), Messiah and the Mozart Requiem; Opera debut in The Poisoned Kiss by Vaughan Williams at the Bloomsbury Theatre; Wexford Festival, 1987; With Cologne Opera has sung Naiad in Ariadne auf Naxos, Siebel in Faust, Sandrina (La Finta Giardiniera), Helena in A Midsummer Night's Dream and Pamina; Song recitals in Paris, Dublin, London, and Cambridge; Appearances with the Songmakers' Almanac in London and at the Nottingham and Buxton Festivals; Season 1989-90 in Ode to the West Wind by Arnell, Aci in Handel's Aci, Galatea e Polifemo with London Baroque at the Beaune Festival and Mendelssohn's Lobgesang conducted by Richard Hickox; Mozart's C Minor Mass in Scotland and in France with Malgoire and Portugal with Brüggen conducting; Covent Garden debut, 1992, as a Young Nun in The Fiery Angel; TV recording of Handel's Roman Vespers in Vienna. Recordings include: Bach B Minor Mass. Address: c/o Ron Gonsalves Management, 10 Dagnan Road, London SW12 9LQ, England.

BLACKHAM Joyce, b. 1 Jan 1934, Rotherham, Yorkshire, England. Singer (Soprano). m. Peter Glossop (div). Education: Studied at the Guildhall School of Music with Joseph Hislop. Debut: Sadler's Wells Opera 1955, as Olga in Eugene Onegin. Career: Covent Garden debut as Esmeralda in The Bartered Bride; Best known as Carmen, also sang Dorabella, Mimi, Norina, Rosina and roles in operettas by Offenbach, Johann, Strauss and Lehar; Guest appearances Berlin, New York and New Zealand, with Welsh National Opera sang Rosina, Amneris and Cherubino; Sang Maddalena in Rigoletto at Covent Garden, 1974.

BLACKWELL Harolyn, b. 1960, Washington, District of Columbia, USA. Singer (Soprano). Education: Studied at the Catholic University of America and with Carlo Bergonzi and Renata Tebaldi in Italy. Career: Has sung Jemmy in Guillaume Tell at the San Antonio Festival, Papagena in Cleveland, Oscar in Hamburg, Gilda with the Miami Opera, Sister Constance in Dialogues des Carmélites for Canadian Opera and Clara in Porgy and Bess at the 1986 Glyndebourne Festival; Symphonic engagements with the National Symphony, St Louis Philharmonic, Cincinnati Symphony, Minnesota Orchestra and Buffalo Philharmonic; Carnegie Hall as Xanthe in Die Liebe der Danae by Strauss; Recitals in Buffalo, Denver, Dallas and New York (debut 1987); Season 1986-87 with debuts at Chicago as Oscar (Un Ballo in Maschera) and at the Metropolitan as Pousette in Manon; Xenia in Boris Godunov, conducted by James Conlon; Season 1987-88 with concert performance of Porgy and Bess under Simon Rattle, Nannetta in Falstaff at Nice and the Princess in L'Enfant et les Sortilèges at Glyndebourne; Season 1988-89 included Schubert's A-flat Mass in Detroit, Barbarina and Sophie (Werther) at the Met, Olga in Giordano's Fedora at Carnegie Hall and Zdenka (Arabella) at Glyndebourne; Season 1989-90 with Adele at the Met and Marie (La Fille du Régiment) in Seattle; Blondchen in Die Entführung at Aix-en-Provence; Season 1990-91 highlights were Oscar at the Met, Mahler's 4th Symphony in Florida and Charleston, Bach and Handel with the New York Chamber Symphony, Mozart's Il Re Pastore with the Nice Opera and Le nozze di Figaro (Susanna) in Toronto. Recordings include: Porgy and Bess. Address: c/o Columbia Artists Management Inc, 165 West 57th Street, New York, NY 10019, USA.

BLACKWOOD Easley, b. 21 Apr 1933, Indianapolis, Indiana, USA. Composer; Pianist; Music Educator. Education: Received piano training in Indianapolis; Studied composition, Berkshire Music Center, Tanglewood, Massachusetts, summers, 1948, 1949 (with Messiaen), 1950, with Heiden, Indiana University School of Music, Bloomington; With Hindemith, Yale University, MA, 1954, and with Boulanger in Paris, 1954-56. Career: Appeared as soloist with the Indianapolis Symphony Orchestra, 1947; Concerts throughout North American and Europe; Faculty member, 1958-68, Professor, 1968-, University of Chicago; Retired, 1997. Compositions: Orchestral: Symphony No 1, 1954-55, No 2, 1960, No 3, 1964, No 4, 1977, No 5, 1992; Chamber Symphony, 1954; Clarinet Concerto, 1964; Symphonic Fantasy, 1965; Oboe Concerto, 1965; Violin Concerto, 1967; Flute Concerto, 1968; Piano Concerto, 1970; Chamber: Viola Sonata, 1953; 2 string quartets, 1957, 1959; Concerto for 5 instruments, 1959; 2 violin sonatas, 1960, 1973; Fantasy for Cello and Piano, 1960; Pastorale and Variations for Wind Quintet, 1961; Sonata for Flute and Harpsichord, 1962; Fantasy for Flute, Clarinet and Piano, 1965; Symphonic Episode for Organ, 1966; Piano Trio, 1967; 12 Microtonal Etudes for Synthesizer, 1982; Piano pieces; Vocal: Un voyage à Cythère for soprano and winds, 1966; 4 Letter Scenes from Gulliver's Last Voyage for mezzo-soprano, baritone and tape, 1972; Sonatina for Piccolo Clarinet and Piano, 1994; Sonata for Piano, 1996. Recordings: Piano works of Casella, Szymanowski; Ives, Copland, Prokofiev, Stravinsky, Berg, Nielsen and Alain. Publication: The Structure of Recognizable Diatonic Tunings, 1986; Honours: Fulbright Scholarship, 1954-56; 1st Prize, Koussevitzky Music Foundation, 1958; Creative Arts Award, Brandeis University, 1968; Several commissions. Current Management: Magna Carta Management, 3359 Kelly Lane SW, Roanoke, VA 24018, USA. Address: 5300 S Shore Drive #44, Chicago, IL 60615, USA.

BLADES James, b. 9 Sept 1901, Peterborough, England. Orchestral Timpanist; Tutor; Lecturer; Author. m. Joan Goossens, 1 child. Career: Apprenticed as engineer; Played in orchestras for silent films; Joined London Symphony Orchestra as principal percussionist, 1940; Played with most British orchestras and many chamber ensembles; Associated with the English Opera Group in the premieres of Britten's Church Parables; Professor of Timpani and Percussion at the Royal Academy of Music, 1960; Many lectures and broadcasts. Recordings: Blades on Percussion, 1973; Discourses, 1974. Publications: Percussion Instruments and Their History, 1970-75. Contributions to: Saturday Book, 1969. Honours include: Order of the British Empire, 1972. Hobby: Mechanics. Address: 191 Sandy Lane, Cheam, Surrey SM2 7EU, England.

BLADIN Christer, b. 1947, Stockholm, Sweden. Singer (Tenor). Education: Studied in Freiburg and Stockholm. Career: Sang at the Freiburg Opera, 1972-76, Berne, 1976-78, Darmstadt, 1978-84, and at the Bonn Opera from 1986; Guest appearances at Perugia (Salieri's Les Danaides, 1984), Vaison-la-Romaine (Haydn's Orfeo, 1985) and Aix-en-Provence (Rossini's Armida, 1988); Other roles include Froh in Das Rheingold (Barcelona, 1986), Mozart's Belmonte and Tamino, Admète in Lully's Alceste and Ernesto in Don Pasquale; Has also appeared at La Scala, Milan, Nantes, Ghent and Marseille. Address: c/o Oper der Stadt Bonn, Am Boeselagerhof 1, W-5300 Bonn, Germany.

BLAHA Ivo, b. 14 Mar 1936, Litomysl, Czechoslovakia. Composer; Teacher. Education: Pupil of Ridky and Sommer, graduated 1958, postgraduate studies with Hlobil, 1965-70, Prague Academy of Music; Training in electronic music from Kabelac and Herzog, Plzen Radio. Career: Teacher, Praguer Academy of Music, 1964-; Docent, Film and Television Faculty, 1967-, Head, Department of Sound Creation, FAMU. Compositions: 3 string quartets, 1957, 1966, 1983; Concerto for Orchestra, 1957; 3 Movements for Violin and Piano, 1961; Spring Plays for Wind Quintet, 1962; Concerto for Percussion and Orchestra, 1964; Solitude, sonata for solo violin, 1965; Music for Wind Quintet, 1965; Violin Concerto, 1968; Music to Pictures of a Friend for flute, oboe and clarinet, 1971; Cello Sonata, 1972; 2 Inventions for Solo Flute, 1974; Duo for Bass Clarinet and Piano, 1975; Cet amour for speaker, wood instruments and tape, 1975; Rays for Piano, 1976; Per archi: Sinfonia, 1977; The Violin for Solo Instrument, 1979; Hymn for Organ, 1980; Sonata transparenta for flute and piano, 1982; Moravian Lullabies for soprano, flute and piano, 1982; Zoolessons I for guitar, 1984, II, 1987; Vaults for Organ, 1986; Imaginations for violin and piano, 1988; Sonata introspecta for viola, 1989; Infant Jesus, Christmas Cantata for children's choir and instrumental ensemble, 1997. Recording: 3rd String Quartet, CD. Publication: Sound Dramaturgy of Audio-visual Work, 1995. Honours: Front position, International Rostrum of Composers, UNESCO, 1991; Annual Prize of CHF Prague, 1993. Membership: Association of Musicians and Musicologists, Prague. Address: Jablonecká 418, 190 00 Prague 9, Czech Republic.

BLAHA Vladislav, b. 22 Aug 1957, Brno, Czech Republic. Concert Guitarist; Professor. m. Alice Blahova, 9 Oct 1981, 1 son, 1 daughter. Education: Conservatory, Brno; Hochschule für Musik, Weimar, Germany; Masterclasses with John W Duarte, G Crosskey, C Cotsiolis and A Carlevaro.Debut: Besedni Hall, Brno,

1976. Career: Concerts in 28 cities worldwide: Los Angeles, Chicago, Prague, Vienna, Berlin, Jakkarta, Havana, London, Dallas, Portland, Valencia, Saigon, Hanoi, Budapest, Moscow, Paris; Has had works dedicated to him by 18 international composers. Recordings: Concerts for guitar and orchestra by Ponce and Kohaut; Blaha Plays Suites by Bach and Weiss; Blaha: The Spanish Guitar; Blaha Plays Czech Guitar Works; Masters of Czech Classical Guitar. Contributions to: Classical Guitar Magazine, 1996-. Honours: 4 1st Prizes, Competitions in Greece, Hungary, Czech Republic and Germany; Honorary Citizenship, City of Dallas, USA, 1996. Memberships: President, Czech Classical Guitar Society; Director, International Guitar Festival, Czech Republic, 1992-. Address: Pellicova 5d, 60200 Brno, Czech Republic.

BLAHOVA Eva, b. 1 Dec 1944, Skalica, Slovakia. University Professor; Singer. div, 1 son, 1 daughter. Education: Music Academy, Bratislava, 1962-68; Music Academy, Wien, Austria, 1968-71; Master Class, Professor D Ferro and Professor E Werba. Debut: Slovak Philharmonie, 1965. Career: Sang in Concert Festivals: Music Festival, Bratislava; BHS, Cracow; Easter Festival, Poland; The Prague Spring Festival; Czech Republic; Carin Thian Summe F Ossiach, Austria; Montreal, Canada; Parma; Trento; Italy; France; Wien, Austria; Professor of Singing, European Mozart Foundation, 1992-. Recordings: Nine Germany Arias, 1979; Haydn, Mozart, Beethoven Koncert Ariac, 1983; Romantic Songs, 1997. Contributions to: Music Life; Slovak Reviews. Honour: Prize, Slovak Music Foundation, 1973. Memberships: President, Slovak Musicians, 1997; President, Slovak-Canadian Musicians; President, Singing Competition M Schneidertrnavsky, Slovakia. Address: Lermontouova 16, 81105 Bratislava, Slovakia.

BLAHUSIAKOVA Magdalena, b. 1947, Czechoslovakia. Singer (Soprano). Education: Studied in Sofia and Bratislava. Career: Member of the Brno Opera, 1969-82, notably as Santuzza, Aida, Donna Anna and Donna Elvira, Fiordiligi, Tatiana and Amelia (Simon Boccanegra) and Un Ballo in Maschera; Guest appearances in Barcelona (1980), Genoa (as Jenufa), and Lausanne (Rusalka); Concert engagements in The Spectre's Bride by Dvorak, Vienna, 1984, the Requiems of Dvorak and Mozart and Beethoven's Ninth; Concert tour of the USA, 1985. Address: c/o Janacek Opera, Dvorakoáva 11, 65770 Brno, Czech Republic.

BLAIR James, b. 1940, Stirling, Scotland. Conductor. Education: Studied at Trinity College, London, and with Adrian Boult; Won Ricordi Conducting Prize and an Italian Government Scholarship to study with Franco Ferrara in Siena and Venice. Career: Artistic Director and Principal Conductor, Young Musicians' Symphony Orchestra, 1971-; Many performances of Mahler, Messiaen and Strauss; Engagements with all leading British orchestras and works with Opera North, Dublin Grand Opera and Athens Opera; US debut, 1984, with the Delaware Symphony; Later conducted Colorado Springs and Kansas City Symphony Orchestras; Many Young Musicians' Symphony Orchestra concerts given on BBC, including Mahler's 8th Symphony. Recordings: Late Romantic repertory. Address: c/o Anglo-Swiss Artists Management Ltd, 35-37 Morley House, 320 Regent Street, London W1R 5AD, England.

BLAKE David, b. 2 Sept 1936, London, England. Composer; Professor of Music. m. Rita Muir, 24 Sept 1960, 2 s, 1 d. Education: BA, MA, Gonville and Caius College, Cambridge, 1957-60; Deutsche Akademie der Künste, 1960-61. Career includes: Lecturer in Music, 1964-71, Senior Lecturer, 1971-76, Professor of Music, 1976-, University of York. Compositions include: Variations for Piano, 1960; Three Choruses to Poems of Robert Frost, 1964; What is the Cause for Chorus; Fulke Greville, 1967; Nonet for Wind, 1971; Violin Concerto, BBC Proms, 1976; Toussaint, libretto Anthony Ward, premiere London Coliseum, 1977, opera in 3 acts, 1974-77; Clarinet Quintet, 1980; Scherzi ed Intermezzi for Orchestra, 1984; Seasonal Variants for 7 Players, 1985; Pastoral Paraphrase for Bassoon and Small Orchestra, 1988; The Plumber's Gift, libretto John Birtwhistle, premiere, London Coliseum, 1989; A Little More Night Music, for Saxophone Quartet, 1990; Mill Music for Brass Band, 1990; Cello Concerto, 1992; Three Ritsos Choruses, 1992; The Griffin's Tale for Baritone and Orchestra, text by John Birtwhistle, 1994; The Fabulous Adventures of Alexander the Great, for soloists, chorus and orchestra of young people, text by John Birtwhistle, 1996. Recordings: Violin Concerto, In Praise of Krishna; Variations for Piano; The Almanack. Current Management: University of York Music Press. Address: Mill Gill, Askrigg Nr Leyburn, North Yorkshire, DL8 3HR, England.

BLAKE Howard, b. 28 Oct 1938, London, England. Composer. Education: Royal Academy of Music with Harold Craxton and Howard Ferguson. Career: Pianist, conductor, orchestrator and composer, London, 1960-70; From 1971 freelance composer; Benedictus performed at Manchester, Llandaff and St Alban's Cathedrals, Perth and Three Choirs Festivals, by the Bach Choir in London (1988) and with the Philharmonia RFH, 1989; Barbican concerts for children; Director of Performing Right Society and Executive Director, 1978-87; Visiting Professor of Composition at Royal Academy of Music, 1992. Compositions: The Station, comic opera, 1987; Orchestral: Toccata, 1976; The Annunciation (ballet); Concert Dances, 1984; Clarinet Concerto, 1984; Diversions for cello and orchestra, 1985; Vocal: Three Sussex Songs, 1973; Two Songs of the Nativity, 1976; The Song of St Francis, 1976; A Toccata of Galuppi's for baritone and harpsichord, 1978; Benedictus, dramatic oratorio, 1979; The Snowman for narrator, boy soprano and orchestra, 1982; Festival Mass for double choir a capella, 1987; Shakespeare Songs for tenor and string quartet, 1987; Instrumental: Piano Quartet, 1974; The Up and Down Man, children's suite, 1974; Penillion for violin and harp, 1975; Eight Character Pieces for piano, 1976; Dances for 2 pianos, 1976; Prelude for solo viola, 1979; Sinfonietta for 10 brass, 1981; Piano Concerto, Philharmonia commission to celebrate 30th birthday of HRH Princess of Wales, 1991; Violin Concerto, world premiere; Leeds City Council commission for their Centenary; Also many scores for films, theatre, ballet. Recordings: Diversions for cello and orchestra, Toccata, 1991; Snowman; Benedictus; Clarinet and Piano Concertos; Granpa. Publications: Many. Honours: Fellow, Royal Academy of Music, 1989; OBE, services to music, 1994. Memberships: MU; APC; Incorporated Society of Musicians; Garrick Club. Address: c/o Faber Music Ltd, 3 Queen Square, London WC1N 3AU, England.

BLAKE Rockwell (Robert), b 10 Jan 1951, Plattsburgh, New York, USA. Tenor. m. Deborah Jeanne Bourlier, 25 Aug 1973. Education: Studied voice with Renata Booth in high school; State University of New York, Fredonia; Catholic University of America, Washington DC. Career: Soloist: US Navy Band; Washington DC, Opera, 1976; Hamburg State Opera, 1977-79; Vienna State Opera, 1978; New York City Opera, 1979-81; Metropolitan Opera, New York, 1981-83, 1986, 1988, as Lindoro in L'Italiana in Algeri, Almaviva, Don Ottavio and Arturo in I Puritani; Chicago Lyric Opera, 1983, 1987; Rossini Opera Festival, Pesaro, 1983-85, 1987-88; San Francisco Opera, 1984; Paris Opera, 1985; Naples San Carlo, 1985-88; Opéra-Comique, Paris, 1987; Bavarian State Opera, Munich, 1987; Rome Opera, 1988-89; Sang James V in La Donna del Lago at Bonn, 1990; Arturo in I Puritani at Barcelona, 1990; Tonio (La Fille du Régiment) at Santiago; Concert performance of Meyerbeer's Il Crociato in Egitto at the 1990 Montpellier Festival; Rossini cantatas at Martina Franca; Title role in Il Pirata at Lausanne, 1992; Season 1992 as Rossini's Almaviva at Genoa, Selim in Rossini's Adina at Rome, James V in La Donna del Lago at La Scala, Mozart's Ferrando at Dallas; Almaviva at the 1992 Caracalla Festival; Sang in Semiramide at the 1994 Pesaro Festival; Aix Festival 1996, as Jupiter in the French premiere of Handel's Semele; Various concert engagements. Recordings: The Rossini Tenor; The Mozart Tenor; Encore Rossini; Alina la Regina di Golconda; Il Barbiere di Siviglia; Video of Rossini's Barber from the Metropolitan. Honours: First winner, Richard Tucker Award, 1978; National Opera Institute Grantee, 1975, 1976; Honorary DMus, State Orchestra. Hobbies: Musicological research; Computers; Designing jewellery; Making furniture; Woodworking. Address: c/o Columbia Artists Management Inc, 165 West 57th Street, New York, NY 10019, USA.

BLANC Ernest (Marius Victor), b. 1 Nov 1923, Sanary-sur-Mer, France. Singer (baritone). m. Eliane Guiraud. Education: Studied at the Toulon Conservatory, 1946-49. Debut: Marseilles, 1950, as Tonio in Pagliacci. Career: Paris Opera from 1954, debut as Rigoletto; Sang in Paris until 1976, in operas by Puccini, Wagner, Offenbach and Verdi; Bayreuth Festival, 1958-59, as Telramund; La Scala Milan, 1960; Glyndebourne, 1960, as Don Giovanni and as Riccardo in I Puritani; Guest appearances in Naples, New York, Barcelona, Lisbon, Tel Aviv, Florence and Amsterdam. Recordings: Faust, Carmen, Iphigénie en Tauride, Les Contes d'Hoffmann, Les Pêcheurs de Perles. Hobby: Mechanics.

BLANC Jonny, b. 10 July 1939, Lessebo, Sweden. Singer (Tenor). Education: Studied at the Stockholm Conservatory with Kathe Sundstrom and with Clemens Kaiser-Breme in Essen. Career: Sang as baritone, 1962-67; Tenor debut, Stockholm, 1967, as Dmitri in Boris Godunov; Sang in the premieres of operas by Braein and Werle and as Florestan, Siegmund, Eisenstein in Die Fledermaus, Don Carlos, Don José, Cavaradossi and Riccardo in Un Ballo in Maschera; Sang in a revival of the Abbé Vogler's Gustaf Adolf och Ebba Brahe at Drottningholm, 1973; Sang Steva in the Stockholm Opera production of Jenufa at the Edinburgh Festival, 1974; Guest appearances with Scottish Opera and in Malmö, Oslo, Frankfurt, Copenhagen, Miami, Lisbon and Helsinki; Well-known as concert singer; Artistic Manager, Malmö City Theatre, 1986; Opera Manager, Royal Opera Stockholm, 1991-; Principal, University College of Opera, Stockholm, 1994. Address: University College of Opera, Strandvägen 82, 11527 Stockholm, Sweden.

BLANCK Kirsten, b. 1965, Germany. Singer (Soprano). Education: Studied in Hamburg with Judith Beckmann and in Kiel and Lubeck. Debut: Saarbrucken, 1986. Career: Sang at the Lubeck and Kiel Operas from 1990, notably as Mozart's Queen of Night, and in Dresden, Berlin Stuttgart and Frankfurt; Other roles include Donna Anna, Gilda, Sophie in Der Rosenkavalier, Zerbinetta, and Lulu; Many concert appearances. Address: c/o Buhnen der Hansestadt Lubeck, Fischergrube 5-21, W-2400 Lubeck, Germany.

BLANK Allan, b. 27 Dec 1925, New York, New York, USA. Composer. Education: High School of Music and Art in New York; Juilliard, 1946-47, Washington Square College; MA, University of Minnesota, 1950; University of Iowa. Career: Violinist, Pittsburgh Symphony Orchestra, 1950-52; Teacher, Western Illinois University, 1966-68, Patterson State College, 1968-70, Lehmann College, 1970-77, and Virginia Commonwealth University at Richmond, 1978-; Music Director of the Richmond Community Orchestra, 1986-89. Compositions include: Operas Aria da Capo, 1960; Excitement at the Circus, children's opera, Patterson, 1969; The Magic Bonbons, 1983; The Noise, Richmond, 1986; Incidental music for Othello, 1983, and Measure for Measure, 1984; 2 String Quartets, 1958, 1981; Concert Piece for band, 1963; Music for Orchestra, 1967; Wind Quintet, 1970; An American Medley, 1976; Music for Tubas, 1977; Divertimento for tuba and band, 1979; Kreutzer March for band, 1981; Concertino for bassoon and strings, 1984; Concert for 5 players, 1986; Concertino for string orchestra, 1987; Forked Paths, suite of 11 miniatures for trumpet, 1988; Overture for a Happy Occasion, 1986; Polymorphics, 1988; String Quartet, 1989; Concerto for clarinet and string orchestra, 1990; Songs from the Holocaust, 1996; Concert for Violin and Orchestra, 1995; Concerto for Contrabass and String Orchestra, 1996; Songs. Honours: George Eastman Competition, 1983; National Endowment for the Arts, 1983; Virginia Music Teachers Association Commission, 1979, 1988, 1991. Address: 2920 Archdale Road, Richmond, VA 23235, USA.

BLANKENBURG Heinz (Horst), b. 15 Oct 1931, New York City, New York, USA. Opera Baritone; Stage Director. m. (1) 2 sons, 1 daughter, (2) Gayle Cameron-McComb, 14 Dec 1986. Education: Local universities, Los Angeles. Debut: San Francisco Opera, 1955. Career: Leading baritone, Glyndebourne Festival Opera, 1957-70, roles there included Mozart's Papageno and Figaro, Rossini's Raimbaud and Busoni's Arlecchino; Hamburg State Opera, 1959-73, San Francisco Opera, 1955-66; As Beckmesser, Schaunard, Fra Melitone (Forza del Destino) and Paolo in Simon Boccanegra; Sang with the Hamburg Staatsoper in the British premiere of Die Frau ohne Schatten, Sadler's Wells Theatre, 1966; Guest baritone with opera companies of Munich, Berlin, Vienna, Paris, Frankfurt, Metropolitan, Amsterdam, Rome, Brussels, Lausanne, Basle, Strasbourg, Naples, Venice, New Zealand, St Louis, Portland, Vancouver, Seattle, Los Angeles; Faculty, University of California, Los Angeles and California State University, Los Angeles. Recordings: Discs, 2 labels; TV and radio recordings for BBC, RAI and ZDF. Honours: Kammersänger, Hamburg State Opera, 1966; Maori Welcome, New Zealand, 1971; Honorary Doctor of Performing Arts, California State University, Los Angeles, 1977, University of California, Los Angeles, 1986; Maori Welcome, New Zealand, 1971. Address: Opera Theatre, California State University, 5151 State University Drive, Los Angeles, CA 90032, USA.

BLANKENHEIM Toni, b. 12 Dec 1921, Cologne, Germany. Singer (bass-baritone). Education: Studied with Paul Lohmann in Frankfurt and with Res Fischer in Stuttgart. Debut: Frankfurt, 1947, as Mozart's Figaro. Career: Sang at Frankfurt until 1950, then at Hamburg; Bayreuth Festival, 1954-59, as Kothner, Klingsor and Donner; Darmstadt, 1965-68; Stuttgart from 1968; Sang at Hamburg in the premieres of operas by Mihalovici, Martinu, Henze, Krenek, Von Einem, Goehr, Searle, Kelemen and Constant; Performances of works by Berg, Stravinsky, Liebermann and other modern composers; Sang Schigolch at the Paris Opéra in the 1979 premiere of Berg's Lulu; Guest appearances in Vienna, Berlin, Munich, Milan, Paris, Mexico City, San Francisco and New York; Sang in the first local performance of The Birthday by Kalevi, at Hamburg, 1982; Many concert appearances. Recordings: Bastien et Bastienne by Mozart; Lulu; Donner in Das Rheingold, Bayreuth, 1957; Klingsor in Parsifal, Bayreuth, 1956.

BLANKENSHIP Rebecca, b. 24 Mar 1954, New York, USA. Singer (Soprano). Education: Studied voice in New York with Judith Oas. Career: Sang two seasons at Ulm as a Mezzo Soprano; Sang Ariadne at Berlin Staatsoper, 1986; Appeared in Basle 1986-88 as Mozart's Elettra and First Lady, Leonora in Il Trovatore, Katharina in Lady Macbeth of Mtsensk; Season 1988-90: Martha, in Tiefland in Berlin and Vienna Volksoper, Leonore in Fidelio in Stuttgart and with Opera Forum in Netherlands, Elsa in Liège and Senta at Bregenz Festival; Marie in Wozzeck with Vienna Staatsoper, 1990-92; Regular appearances in Vienna, 1991-; Other roles include Female Chorus, in The Rape of Lucretia, Agathe in Der Freischütz, Hanna Glawari in Die Lustige Witwe; Sang Sieglinde at the San Francisco Opera, 1990, and at the Wiener Staatsoper, 1991,

Marie in Wozzeck, La Fenice, Venice, 1992, Lady Macbeth of Mtsensk, Katarina at the Wiener Volksoper, 1992-, Erwartung by Schoenberg for Canadian Opera at Toronto, and Edinburgh Festival, 1993, Erwartung at the Le Grand Théâtre Genève, 1995. Address: Music International, 13 Ardilaun Road, London, N5 2QR, England.

BLANZAT Anne-Marie, b. 24 Nov 1944, Neuilly, France. Soprano. Education: Studied in Paris. Career: Sang Yniold in Debussy's Pelléas et Mélisande at Aix-en-Provence, 1966, and Glyndebourne, 1969; Returned to Glyndebourne, 1976, as Mélisande, and sang the role many times in France and elsewhere (Nantes, 1974); Also successful as Susanna, Juliette (Strasbourg, 1983) and Manon; Sang also in modern repertory by Prodromidès, Poulenc and Prey, and in Rameau's Hippolyte et Aricie. Address: c/o Opéra du Rhin, 19 Place Broglie, F-67008 Strasbourg Cedex, France.

BLASIUS Martin, b. 5 June 1956, Schwelm, Westphalen, Germany. Bass Singer. Education: Studied at the Folkwang-Musikhochschule, Essen. Career: Sang at first in concert, notably for Austrian and Italian Radio, at the Bach-Woche Ansbach, the Göttingen Handel Festival and at the Frankurt Festival; Opera debut as Dulcamara, Gelsenkirchen, 1983; Moved to Hannover in 1987 and Dusseldorf in 1989; Guest appearances in opera and concert throughout Germany; Appeared in a new production of Henze's The Bassarids, Duisburg, 1991 and sang the Grand Inquisitor in Don Carlos at Dusseldorf. Recordings include: Der Traumgörge by Zemlinsky; Saint-Saëns's Christmas Oratorio; Golgotha by Martin; Kreutzer's Das Nachtalger von Granada, and Notturni. Address: c/o Deutsche Oper am Rhein, Heinrich Heine Allee 16, 4000 Dusseldorf, Germany.

BLATNY Pavel, b. 14 Sept 1931, Brno, Czechoslovakia. Composer; Conductor. Education: Brno Conservatory, 1950-55, and with Borkovec in Prague, 1955-58; Further study in jazz piano at the Berklee College of Music, USA. Career: More than 2000 recitals of piano music, often in a third-stream mode, mixing jzz and classical techniques; Conductor of many concerts in Czechoslovakia; Chief of the music division on Brno television, 1971; Teacher, Janácek Academy of Musical Arts, Brno, 1979-. Compositions include: Forest Tales, The Well and Little House, television operas for children, 1975; Cantatas with orchestra: The Willow Tree, 1980, Christmas Eve, 1982, and The Midday Witch, 1982; Third Stream Music; Music for Piano and Orchestra, 1955; Concerto for Orchestra, 1956; The Bells, symphonic movement, 1981; Hommage à Gustav Mahler for orchestras, 1982; Music for wind instruments; Piano music. Address: OSA, CS Armady 20, 160 56 Prague 6, Bubenec, Czech Republic.

BLAUKOPF Kurt, b. 15 Feb 1914, Czernowitz, Austria. Musicologist. Education: Studied with Stefan Wolpe and Herman Scherchen in Vienna, 1932-37; Music History at Jerusalem, 1940-42. Career: Editor of Phono, 1954-65; Lecturer in Music Sociology, 1962, Professor, 1968, Vienna Academy of Music; Honorary Professor, Vienna University, 1974; Member of Executive Board of UNESCO, 1972-76; Editor of Hi-Fi Stereophonie, Vienna, 1965-. Publications: Musiksoziologie, Cologne, 1952 and in Spanish as Sociologia de la Musica, 1988, 2nd edition, 1972; Grosse Dirigenten, 1953; Grosse Vituosen, 1954; Gustav Mahler, oder der Zeitgenosse der Zukunft, Vienna, 1969 and in English, 1973 and 1985; Die Wiener Philharmoniker: Wesen, Werden, Wirken eines Grossen Orchesters, with H Blaukopf, Vienna, 1986, 2nd edition, 1992; Editor, Gustav Mahler Sein Leben, sein Werk unde seine Welt in Zeitgenossischen Bildern und Texten, Vienna, 1976, 2nd edition Stuttgart, 1994 and in English as Gustav Mahler: A Documentary Study, 1976, 2nd edition, 1991; Musik im Wandel der Gesellschaft: Grundzuge der Musiksoziologie, Munich, 1982, Darmstadt, 1996; Musical Life in a Changing Society: Aspects of Music Sociology, Portland, OR, USA, 1992; Pioniere empiristischer Musikforschung, Vienna, 1995; Die Aesthetik Bernard Bolzanos, Sankt Augustin, 1996. Honour: Honorary Doctorate, University of Vienna, 1994. Address: Institut für Musiksoziologie, Hochschule für Musik, Schubertring 14, A-1010 Wien, Austria.

BLAUSTEIN Susan (Morton), b. 22 Mar 1953, Palo Alto, California, USA. Composer. Education: Studied with Pousseur in Liège, and at Yale with Jacob Druckman and Betsy Jolas. Career: Former Junior Fellow at Harvard University; Assistant professor at Columbia University, New York, 1985-90. Compositions include: Commedia for 8 players, 1980; To Orpheus, 4 sonnets, 1982; String Quartet, 1982; Sextet, 1983; Concerto for cello and chamber orchestra, 1984; Song of Songs for mezzo, tenor and orchestra, 1985. Honours include: Commissions from the Koussevitsky and Fromm Foundations. Address: c/o ASCAP, ASCAP House, One Lincoln Plaza, New York, NY 10023, USA.

BLAZE Robin, b. 1971, England. Singer (Counter-tenor). Education: Studied at Magdalen College Oxford and the Royal College of Music. Career: Solo engagements with the King's Consort throughout Europe and South America and with the BBC, the Edinburgh Choral Union and Chandos Baroque Players; has sung Bach with Northern Sinfonia, Purcell with the Collegium Vocale, Ghent, and Zelenka with the RIAS chamber choir, Berlin; Unulfo in Rodelinda. Recordings include: Blow Anthems, with the Parley of Instruments; Unulfo in Rodelina for Hyperion. Address: Ron Gonsalves Management, 7 Old Town, Clapham, London SW4 0JT, England.

BLAZEKOVIC Zdravko, b. 13 May 1956, Zagreb, Yugoslavia. Musicologist. Education: BA, Musicology, 1980, MA, Musicology, 1983, University of Zagreb. Career: Assistant, 1980-81, Researcher, 1984-91, Institute for Musicological Research, and Yugoslav Academy of Sciences and Arts, Zagreb; Librarian at Croatian Music Institute, Zagreb, 1985-87; Research Associate, Research Center for Music Iconography, Répertoire International d'Iconographie Musical, City University of New York, USA, 1990-; Associate Editor, RILM Abstracts of Music Literature, New York, 1989; Editor of RIdIM/RCMI Newsletter, New York, 1989-. Publications: Catalogue of music manuscripts and prints in the collections of the Historical Archives and the Museum of the City of Dubrovnik, volume 1 of series, Indices Collectorum Musicarum Tubulariorumque in SR Croatia, 1988. Contributions to: International Review of the Aesthetics and Sociology of Music; Arti Musices; Current Musicology; Musica Periodica; Rad JAZU, Zvuk. Memberships: International Musicological Society; Croatian Composers' Society; American Musicological Society; International Council for Traditional Music.

BLECH Harry, b. 2 Mar 1910, London, England. Conductor. m. (1) Enid Lessing, 1935, divorced 1957, 1 son, 2 daughters, (2) Marion Manley, 1957, 1 son, 3 daughters. Education: Central London Foundation, Trinity College of Music and Manchester College of Music. Career: Violin Soloist, 1928-30; With BBC Symphony Orchestra, 1930-36; Founder Member, Blech Quartet, 1933-50; London Wind Players, 1942; London Mozart Players, 1949-84; Haydn-Mozart Society, 1949; London Mozart Choir, 1952; Conductor, Royal Academy of Music Chamber Orchestra, 1961-65. Recordings include: Mozart's mature symphonies, Posthorn Serenade, Sinfonia Concertante (with Norbert Brainin and Peter Schidlof), Piano Concertos K453 and K503 (Matthews), K491 (Kentner) and K488 (Roll), Bassoon Concerto, Mass K317, Violin Concerto K219 (Milstein) and Divertimento K251. Honours: CBE; Honorary Member, Royal Academy of Music; Fellow, Royal Manchester College of Music, Trinity College of Music. Hobby: Reading. Address: The Owls, 70 Leopold Road, Wimbledon, London SW19 7JQ, England.

BLEGEN Judith, b. 27 Apr 1941, Missoula, Montana, USA. Opera and Concert Singer (Soprano). m. (1) Peter Singher, 1976, div. 1975, 1 son, (2) Raymond Gniewek, 1977. Education: Curtis Institute of Music, Philadelphia, Pennsylvania; Music Academy of the West, Santa Barbara, California. Career: Leading soprano, Nuremberg Opera, 1965-68, as Donizetti's Lucia and Strauss's Zerbinetta; Staatsoper, Vienna, 1968-70; Metropolitan Opera, New York, 1970-, debut as Mozart's Papagena; Vienna roles include Zerbinetta (Ariadne auf Naxos), Rosina (The Barber of Seville), Aennchen (Der Freischütz), Norina (Don Pasquale); Numerous performances at Metropolitan include Marzelline (Fidelio), Sophie (Werther), Sophie (Der Rosenkavalier), Adina (L'Elisir d'Amore), Juliette (Roméo et Juliette); Other appearances include Susanna (The Marriage of Figaro), San Francisco, title role in Manon, Tulsa Opera, Gilda (Rigoletto), Chicago, Despina (Così fan tutte), Covent Garden, Blondchen (Die Entführung), Salzburg Festival, Mélisande (Pelléas et Mélisande), Spoleto Festival, Susanna (The Marriage of Figaro), Edinburgh Festival, Sophie, Paris Opera; Has sung and played the violin in Menotti's Help, Help, the Globolinks! (premiere, Hamburg). Recordings: Numerous including La Bohème (Puccini), Carmina Burana (Orff), Symphony No 4 (Mahler), Harmonienmesse (Haydn), The Marriage of Figaro (Mozart), A Midsummer Night's Dream (Mendelssohn), Lord Nelson Mass (Haydn), Gloria (Poulenc), Peer Gynt Suite (Grieg), Lieder recital (Richard Strauss and Hugo Wolf), Baroque music recital. Honours: Fulbright Scholarship; Grammy Awards. Address: c/o Thea Dispeker, 59 East 54th Street, New York, NY 10022, USA.

BLINKHOF Jan, b. 10 July 1940, Leiden, Netherlands. Singer (tenor). Education: Studied in Amsterdam, with Joseph Metternich in Cologne and with Luigi Ricci in Rome. Debut: With Netherlands Opera, 1971, as Arturo in Lucia di Lammermoor. Career: Holland Festival, 1971, in the premiere of Spinoza by Ton de Kruyf; Amsterdam, 1974, in the premiere of Dorian Gray by Kox; Geneva Opera, 1985, as Tristan; Nice, 1986, as Herman in The Queen of Spades; Sang Laca in Jenufa at the Zurich Opera, 1986; Other roles include Ismaele in Nabucco; Boris in Katya Kabanova, and roles in Wozzeck, The Rape of Lucretia, The Gambler by Prokofiev and Henze's Der Junge Lord; Sang Tristan at Nice, 1986-87, Laca at Covent Garden, 1988; Deutsche Oper Berlin, 1988, as Sergei in Lady Macbeth of the Mtsensk District; Sang Boris in Katya Kabanova at Geneva and Florence, 1989; Albert Gregor in The Makropoulos Case at Berlin, 1990, followed by Sergei in Hamburg and Laca (Jenufa) at Barcelona; Season 1994 as Florestan at Lisbon and Sergei at Florence; Season 1996 as Luca in From the House of the Dead at Nice and Florestan in Fidelio at Rome. Address: c/o Deutsche Oper Berlin, Richard Wagnerstrasse 10, D-1000 Berlin, Germany.

BLISS Anthony, b. 19 Apr 1913, New York, USA. Manager. Education: Studied at Harvard University, BA 1936 and the University of Virginia. Career: Practised Law on Wall Street; Member of the Board of Directors of the Metropolitan Opera Association, 1949; President of MOA, 1956-57, Executive Director, 1974-81, General Manager, 1981-85; Established the Metropolitan National Company in 1965; Administrative or Board Positions with the Jeffrey Ballet, the American Arts Alliance, National Endowment of the Arts and the New York Foundation of the Arts. Address: c/o Metropolitan Opera, Lincoln Center, New York, NY 10023, USA.

BLOCH Augustyn, b. 13 Aug 1929, Grudziadz, Poland. Composer. Education: Studied composition with Tadeusz Szeligowski and organ with Felik Raczkowski at Warsaw Conservatory. m. Halina Lukomska. Career: Music Consultant to the Polish Radio Theatre from 1954. Compositions include: Opera: Jeptha's Daughter, 1968; Children's Opera-Pantomime: Sleeping Princess, 1974; Musical: Tale of The Violin Soul, 1978; Ballet: Voci, 1967, Gilgamesh, 1968, The Looking Glass, 1975; Orchestral: Meditations for Soprano, Organ and Percussion, 1961, Dialogues for Violin and Orchestra, 1963, Enfiando for Orchestra, 1970, A Poem About Warsaw for Narrator, Chorus and Orchestra, 1974, Oratorio for Organ, Strings and Percussion, 1982, Abide with Us, Lord, for Orchestra, 1986, Exaltabo Te for Mixed Choir, 1988, Ostra Brama Litany for Choir and Orchestra, 1989, Trio for Violin, violoncello and Piano, 1992, Upwards for Orchestra, 1993, Scared Out, song for Baritone, Viola, Cello and Piano to a text by Else Lasker-Schüler. Recordings: Bloch Plays Bloch; Thou Shalt Not Kill; Chamber Music. Honours: Cavalier's and Officer's Cross of The Rebirth of Poland, 1969 and 1979; Polish Composers Union Prize, 1981; Brighton Festival Prize, 1989. Memberships: Polish Composers Union. Address: Wybieg 14, 00 788 Warsaw, Poland.

BLOCHWITZ Hans Peter, b. 28 Sept 1949, Garmisch-Partenkirchen, Germany. Singer (Tenor). Education: Studied at Darmstadt, Mainz and Frankfurt. Career: Sang at first in concert, notably as the Evangelist in the St Matthew Passion and in Lieder recitals (Die Schöne Müllerin by Schubert); Opera debut Frankfurt 1984, as Lensky; Sang in the Scala-staged version of the St Matthew Passion at San Marco, Milan, 1985; Théâtre de la Monnaie Brussels and Geneva 1986, as Don Ottavio and Lensky; Guest appearances in Hamburg, Amsterdam and London (Ferrando in Cosí fan tutte, 1989); Aix-en-Provence Festival 1987-89, as Belmonte and Ferrando; Sang Idamante in Idomeneo at San Francisco, 1989; Don Ottavio in the Metropolitan Opera, 1990; Sang in the Choral Symphony at the 1993 Prom Concerts, London; Title role in Henze's Der Junge Lord, Munich, 1995. Recordings include: St Matthew Passion; Mozart Requiem and Schuldigkeit des Ersten Gebotes, Mendelssohn St Paul; Christmas Oratorio by Bach, Mendelssohn's 2nd Symphony, Cosí fan tutte; Die Zauberflöte conducted by William Christie, 1996; Davidde Penitente; Don Giovanni; Selected Lieder, Schubert. Current Management/Address: Artists Management/Künstlersekretariat, Peter G Alferink, Apollolaan 181, 1077 AT Amsterdam, The Netherlands.

BLOCKEEL Dirk, (Jacob Baert), b. 29 June 1955, Roeselare, Belgium. Teacher; Organist; Composer; Writer. m. Marijke Deconinck, 6 May 1983, 1 son, 2 daughters. Education: Dutch, German and English language studies, 2 years; Diploma as Teacher; Studied at Conservatory of Ghent, with 1st prizes in Harmony, Counterpoint, Fugue, History of Music, Organ and Cembalo. Career: Teacher of Organ, Harpsichord and Analysis; Organist, principal church of Kortrijk, Nov 1992-; Writes and composes as Jacob Baert. Compositions include: (As Jacob Baert), Ein Ring für Rainer Maria Rilke, 12 Lieder for oboe, violoncello and percussion, 1994; Ognissanto illuminato for soprano, violin, violoncello and organ, 1996; Saint Martin cantata, 1997; Many songs cycles based on Flemish, French and German poetry including works of Rimbaud and Silesius. Recordings: Several for Radio 3, Brussels; Piano piece on CD of contemporary music. Contributions to: Articles about music composers and literary authors, in 2 arts periodicals. Hobbies: Riding his bicycle; Reading. Address: Grote Noordstraat 18, 8830 Hooglede, Belgium.

BLOMSTEDT Herbert (Thorson), b. 11 July 1927, Springfield, Massachusetts, USA (Swedish citizen). Music Director; Conductor. m. Waltraud Regina Petersen, 29 May 1955, 4 daughters. Education: Diplomas: Music Education, 1948, Organist/Cantor, 1950, Orchestra Conductor, 1950, 1950, Royal Academy of Music, Stockholm; Philosophy candidate, University of Uppsala, Sweden, 1952. Career: Music Director, Norrköping Symphony Orchestra, Sweden, 1954-61; Professor of Conducting, Royal Academy of Music, Stockholm, 1961-70; Permanent Conductor, Oslo Philharmonic, 1962-68; Music

Director: Danish Radio Symphony Orchestra, Copenhagen, 1967-77, Dresden Staatskapelle, 1975-85, Swedish Radio Symphony, 1977-82, San Francisco Symphony, 1985-95; Conducted Nielsen's 4th Symphony at 1990 Edinburgh Festival; Music Director, NDR Symphony Orchestra, Hamburg, 1996-98, Leipzig Gewandhaus Orchestra, Leipzig, 1998-. Recordings: Conductor, over 120 titles including CDs of Bruckner's 4th and 7th Symphonies (Staatskapelle Dresden), Nielsen's 1st, 6th, 4th (San Francisco Symphony); Strauss Ein Heldenleben; Hindemith Mathis Maler Symphony, Trauermusik and Metamorphosis. Publications: Till Kännedomen om J C Bach Symfonier, dissertation, 1951; Lars Erik Larsson och hans concertinor (co-author), book, 1957; Numerous articles; Editor, musical score of Franz Berwald's Sinfonie Singulière, 1965. Honours include: Jenny Lind Scholarship, Royal Academy of Music, Stockholm, 1950; Music Prize, Expressen, Stockholm, 1964; Knight, Royal Order of North Star, Sweden, 1971; Knight, Royal Order of Dannebrogen, Denmark, 1978; Honorary DMus, Andrews University, Michigan, 1978; Litteris et Artibus Gold Medal, Sweden, 1979; National Academy of Recording Arts and Sciences Grammy Award, 1996. Membership: Royal Academy of Music, Stockholm. Current Management: KuenstlerSekretaariat am Gasteig. Address: c/o Rosenheimer Str. 52, D-81669 Munich, Germany.

BLOOMFIELD Arthur (John), b. 3 Jan 1931, San Francisco, California, USA. Music Critic; Food Writer. m. Anne E Buenger, 14 July 1956, 1 son, 2 daughters. Education: BA, Music, Stanford University, 1951. Publications: Fifty Years of the San Francisco Opera, 1972; The San Francisco Opera 1922-78, 1978; Arthur Bloomfield's Restaurant Book, 1987. Contributions to: Music critic for San Francisco Examiner, 1965-79; San Francisco correspondent for Opera, 1964-89; Program notes, Music and Arts records, 1996. Hobby: Cooking. Address: 2229 Webster Street, San Francisco, CA 94115, USA.

BLOOMFIELD Theodore (Robert), b. 14 June 1923, Cleveland, Ohio, USA. Conductor. Education: Studied conducting with Maurice Kessler, piano training, BM, 1944, Oberlin College Conservatory of Music; Conducting with Edgar Schenkman, Juilliard Graduate School, New York; Piano with Claudio Arrau; Conducting with Pierre Monteux. Debut: New York Little Symphony Orchestra, 1945. Career: Apprentice conductor to George Szell and Cleveland Orchestra, 1946-47; Conductor, Cleveland Little Symphony Orchestra, Cleveland Civic Opera Workshop, 1947-52; Music Director, Portland (Oregon) Symphony Orchestra, 1955-59, Rochester (New York) Philharmonic Orchestra, 1959-63; First Conductor, Hamburg State Opera, 1964-66; General Music Director, Frankfurt-am-Main, 1966-68; Chief Conductor, (West) Berlin Symphony Orchestra, 1975-82. Recordings: For several labels. Address: c/o Das Sinfonie Orchester Berlin, Kurfurstendamm 225, D-1000 Berlin, Germany.

BLUMENFELD Harold, b. 15 Oct 1923, Seattle, WA, USA. Composer; Writer; Linguist. Education: BM, 1948, MM, 1949, Yale School of Music; Zürich Konservatorium, Winter, 1948. Career: Professor of Music at Washington University, St Louis, MO, 1951-; Director, Opera Theatre of St Louis, 1964-68; Co-Founder of New Music Circle. Compositions include: War Lament for Chorus after Siegfried Sassoon, 1970; Eroscapes, 1971; Rilke for Voice and Guitar, 1975; Circle Of The Eye, song cycle, 1975; La Vie Antérieure, spatial cantata after Baudelaire, 1976; Voyages, after Hart Crane, 1977; Silentium, song cycle after Mandelstam, 1979; La Voix Reconnue, cantata for Tenor, Soprano and Chamber Ensemble, after Verlaine, 1980; Charioteer Of Delphi, after James Merrill, 1985; Fourscore: An Opera Of Opposites, 1980-86; Fields Of Emerald And Iron...Diluvium: Orchestral Evocations Of Rimbaud for Large Orchestra, 1988; Seasons in Hell, opera based on Rimbaud and Verlaine, 1996. Recordings: Voyages, 1977; Rilke, 1978; War Lament, 1983. Publications: English translation of Michael Praetorius, Syntagma Musicum, volume II, 1980; All musical works published in USA. Contributions to: Musical Quarterly; Perspectives of New Music; Opera; Opera Journal. Honours: American Academy and Institute of Arts and Letters Composition Award, 1977; National Endowment for Arts Opera Award, 1979. Memberships: ASCAP; ASUC; National Opera Association; Fellow of Yaddo; President, River Styx Literary Association, 1987-89.

BLUMENTHAL Daniel, b. 23 Sept 1952, Landstuhl, Germany. (American citizen). Pianist. Education: Studied at the University of Michigan and at Juilliard, New York, 1975-77. Career: Many performances in Europe and elsewhere in the solo and chamber repertory, notably French and American music; With the Piano Trio of the Monnaie, Brussels, premiered the G minor Trio of Debussy, 1985; Other partners include Pierre Amoyal, Barry Tuckwell and the Orlando Quartet; Professor at the Flemish Conservatory, Brussels, from 1985. Address: Helen Jennings Concert Agency, 2 Hereford House, Links Road, London W3 0HX, England.

BLUNT Marcus, b. 31 Dec 1947, Birmingham, England. Composer; Teacher. m. Maureen Ann Marsh, 9 Apr 1988. Education: BMus, honours, University College of Wales, 1970. Career: Compositions Performed in at Least 10 Countries and BBC Radio 3, Classic FM; Woodwind Teacher, 1976-. Compositions: Symphony; The Rings of Saturn for Orchestra; Piano Concerto; Once in A Western Island... for Violin and Orchestra; Concerto Pastorale for Oboe d'Amore and Strings; Aspects of Saturn for Strings; Capricorn for 12 Wind; Venice Suite for Brass Ensemble; The Throstle-Nest in Spring for Octet; Cerulean for Wind Quintet; 2 String Quartets; A Celebration of Brahms and Joachim for Piano Trio; Lorenzo the Much Travel'd Clown for Bassoon and Piano; The Life Force for Piano. Memberships: Composers Guild of Great Britain; Performing Right Society; Incorporated Society of Musicians. Hobbies: Photography; Gardening. Address: Craigs Cottage, Lochmaben, Lockerbie, Dumfrieshire DG11 1RW, Scotland.

BLYTH Alan, b. 27 July 1929, London, England. Music Critic and Editor. m. Ursula Zumloh. Education: MA, Oxford University. Career: Contributor as Critic, The Times, 1963-76; Associate Editor, Opera, 1967-84; Music Editor, Encyclopaedia Britannica, 1971-76; Critic, Daily Telegraph, 1976-89. Publications: The Enjoyment of Opera, 1969; Colin Davis, A Short Biography, 1972; Opera on Record (editor), 1979; Remembering Britten, 1980; Wagner's Ring: An Introduction, 1980; Opera on Record 2 (editor), 1983; Opera on Record 3 (editor), 1984; Song on Record (editor), Volume 1, 1986, Volume 2, 1988; Choral Music on Record, 1990; Opera on CD, 1992; Opera on Video, 1995. Contributions to: Gramophone; BBC; Memberships: Critics' Circle; Garrick Club. Hobbies: Gardening; Wine; Collecting 78 rpm vocal records. Address: 22 Shilling Street, Lavenham, Suffolk CO10 9RH, England.

BLYTON Carey, b. 14 Mar 1932, Beckenham, Kent, England. Composer; Arranger; Author; Music Editor; Lecturer. m. Mary Josephine Mills, 2 sons. Education: University College, London University, 1950-51; TCM, 1953-57; AMusTCL, LTCL (TTD), FTCL (Composition), BMus (London); Royal Danish Academy of Music, Copenhagen, 1957-58. Career: Music Editor, Mills Music Limited, 1958-63; Freelance Composer and Arranger, 1963-; Member, Professorial Staff, Trinity College of Music, 1963-73; Music Editor, Faber Music Limited, 1963-74, editorial work for Benjamin Britten, 1963-70; Professor of Composition for Film, Television and Radio, Guildhall School of Music, 1972-83. Compositions: (Published), Numerous Orchestral and Instrumental Works including: Cinque Port, The Hobbit, On Holiday; Music for Solo Guitar; Numerous Vocal works include: Carols, Madrigals, Children's Songs. Recordings: CD Series: Complete Music for Saxophone Quartet; 1 & 2 Guitars; Solo and Duet Piano; Folksong Arrangements. Publications: Faber Book of Nursery Songs, with D Mitchell; Bananas in Pyjamas. Contributions to: Numerous professional journals. Honours: Sir G Bantock Prize for Composition, Trinity College of Music, 1954; Sir W Churchill Endowment Fund Scholarship, 1957. Memberships include: Performing Right Society; Mechanical-Copyright Protection Society; CGGB. Hobbies: Tropical fish keeping. Address: "Howans", Pytches Road, Woodbridge, Suffolk IP12 1EY, England.

BO Sonia, b. 27 Mar 1960, Lecco, Italy. Composer. Education: Graduated, Milan Conservatory, 1985, and studied further with Donatoni in Rome. Career: Teacher of composition at the Piacenza Conservatory. Compositions: Concerto for chamber orchestra, 1984; Come un'allegoria for soprano and ensemble, 1986; D'Iride for ensemble, 1988; Polittico, five songs with ensemble, 1992. Honours include: Winner, 1985 Guido d'Arezzo International Competition. Address: c/i SIAE, Via della Letteratura n 30, 00100 Rome, Italy.

BOATWRIGHT Helen, b. 17 Nov 1916, Sheboygen, Wisconsin, USA. Soprano; Teacher. m. Howard Boatwright 1943. Education: Pupil of Anna Shram Imig; Studied with Marion Sims, Oberlin College. Debut: Ann, Die Lustigen Weiber von Windsor, Berkshire Music Center, Tanglewood, Massachusetts, 1942. Career: Appeared with Austin (Texas) and San Antonio (Texas) Operas, 1943-45; Sang with many orchestras and choral groups in the USA; Taught voice, New Haven, Connecticut, 1945-64; Adjunct Professor of Voice, Syracuse University, New York; Professor of Voice, Eastman School of Music, Rochester, 1972-79; Professor of Voice, Peabody Conservatory of Music, Baltimore, 1987-89; Professor of Voice, Summers of 1969-88; Masterclass, Glimmerglass Opera; University of Massachusetts; University of North Carolina and Washington University, 1989; Professor of Voice, Eastman, Syracuse University, Peabody Conservatory and Cornell University. Recordings: CDs: Songs of Charles Ives and Ernst Bacon. Address: c/o Music Department, Syracuse University, Syracuse, NY 13210, USA.

BOATWRIGHT Howard (Leake) Jr, b. 16 Mar 1918, Newport News, Virginia, USA. Violinist; Conductor; Music Educator; Composer. m. Helen Boatwright, 1943. Education: Studied Violin with Israel Feldman, Norfolk, Virginia; Composition with Paul Hindemith, Yale University, 1945-48. Debut: Violin Soloist, Richmond Symphony Orchestra, Virginia, 1935. Career: Teacher, University of Texas, Austin, 1943-45; Yale University, 1948-64; Music Director, St Thomas; Church, New Haven, 1949-64; Concertmaster, New Haven Symphony Orchestra, 1950-52; Dean, School of Music, 1964-72, Teacher, 1972-, Syracuse University; Professor Emeritus, 1983-. Compositions: Variation for Chamber Orchestra, 1949; Symphony, 1976; 2 String Quartets, 1947, 1975; Serenade for 2 String Instruments and 2 Wind Instruments, 1952; Clarinet Quartet, 1958; 12 Pieces for Violin, 1977; Clarinet Sonata, 1980; Mass, 1958; The Passion According to St Matthew for Chorus, 1962; Choral Works; Songs. Publications: Books: Introduction to the Theory of Music, 1956; Essays Before a Sonata and Other Writings (Charles Ives), editor, 1962; Chromaticism: Theory and Practice, 1994. Address: c/o School of Music, Syracuse University, Syracuse, NY 13210, USA.

BOATWRIGHT McHenry, b. 29 Feb 1928, Tennille, GA, USA. Singer (Bass-Baritone). Education: Studied at the New England Conservatory; BM, 1950-54. Debut: Jordan Hall, Boston, 1956. Career: New York Town Hall debut in 1958; New England Opera Theater, 1958 as Arkel in Pelléas et Mélisande; Concert appearances with Charles Munch, Leonard Bernstein and other leading conductors; Sang with the Hamburg Staatsoper in contemporary works, notably in the 1966 premiere of Schuller's The Visitation at the Metropolitan Opera, 1967; Concert tour of the Far East and Europe in 1966; Sang at the funeral of Duke Ellington; Well known in Negro Spirituals. Recordings: La Damnation de Faust; Porgy and Bess. Honours: Marian Anderson Award, 1953, 1954; Winner, Arthur Fielder Voice Contest; Winner, National Federation of Music Clubs Competition, 1957.

BOBESCO Lola, b. 9 Aug 1921, Craiova, Rumania. Violinist. Education: Studied with her father, Professor Aurel Bobescu. Career: Many solo appearances from 1934, appearing with such conductors as Kempe, Klemperer, Böhm and Ansermet; Chamber musician, and until 1979 leader of the Eugene Ysaÿe string orchestra; Professor at the Brussels Conservatoire. Honours include. Prize winner at the 1937 Eugene Ysaÿe Competition. Address: Conservatoire de Musique, 30 Rue de la Régence, Brussels, Belgium.

BOBOC Nicolae, b. 26 Sept 1920, Ilia, Romania. Conductor; Composer. m. Maria Giurguit, 7 May 1953, 2 daughters. Education: Graduate Diploma, Faculty of Philosophy and Letters, Bucharest University, 1946; High School Diploma, Pedagogy, Conducting, Composition, Bucharest Music Academy, 1946. Career: Professor, Harmony, Counterpoint, Conservatoire ARAD, Romania, 1947-53; Chief Conductor and Manager, State Philharmonic Orchestra, ARAD, 1948-59; Chief Conductor, State Philharmonic Orchestra, Timisoara, 1959-82; Chief Conductor and Manager, State Opera, Timisoara, 1963-74; Chief Conductor, State Philharmonic Orchestra, ARAD, 1982-90; Guest Conductor: Bucharest Festival; Nice Festival; Pleven Festival; Marijanske Lazne Festival; Brasov Festival; Vienna ORF Orchestra; Bucharest Philharmonic; Bucharest RTV Orchestra; Belgrade Symphony Orchestra; Havana, Haifa, Greensboro (North Carolina), Skopje, Thessaloniki, Wroclaw, Erfurt, Poznan, Rostock, Jena, Schwerin, Cluj, Leeuwarden Iassy, Mulhouse, Lausanne Symphonies (Chamber) Orchestras; Operas in: Cairo, Bonn, Basel, Bucharest, Copenhagen, Plovdiv, Odessa, Bratislava, Gdansk, Sarajevo, Szeged, Klagenfurt, and Ankara; Conductor Opera, Ankara, 1990; Professor History of Music, Academy for Music, Timisoara, 1990-93. Compositions: Divertimento in Classical Style (Chamber Orchestra), 1951; Halmagiu Land (Tara Halmagiulu), (Great Symphonic Orchestra), 1953; Triptych of Hunedoara (for chorus, soloists and Great Symphonic Orchestra), 1980; Colinde (Winter-Solstice Songs) of Hunedoara (Mixed Chorus and Percussion Instruments), 1979; Ballad (mixed chorus and orchestra), 1989. Recordings: 20 Records from 1968-88 including: W A Mozart, Requiem; A Bruckner, Symphony no 1; F Mendelssohn, Symphony no 3 and 5; R Schumann; Symphony no 2; J Haydn, Symphony no 82 (The Bear) and no 92 (Oxford); Recordings for RTV in Romania, Austria, Czechoslovakia, Cuba, Switzerland, Yugoslavia. Address: 3 Mihai Eminescu Boulevard, 1900 Timisoara, Romania.

BOCHKOVA Irina, b. 2 Nov 1938, Moscow, Russia. Violinist. Education: Studied in Kazan and at the Moscow Conservatoire, 1957-62. Career: Many appearances in Russia and Europe from 1962, notably as chamber music partner with Vladimir Krainev (piano) and Natalia Gutman (cello); Teacher at the Moscow Conservatory from 1978. Honours include: Silver Medal, 1962 Tchaikovsky Competition, Moscow; Winner, 1963 Long-Thibaud Competition, Moscow. Address: c/o Moscow Conservatory, ul Gertzena 13, 103009 Moscow, Russia, CIS.

BODE Hannelore, b. 2 Aug 1941, Berlin, Germany. Singer (soprano). m. Heinz Feldhoff. Education: Studied with Ria Schmitz-Gohr in Berlin, at the Salzburg Mozarteum, Fred Husler, Lugano, and Karl-Heinz Jarius, Frankfurt. Career: Sang in Bonn from 1964; Basle, 1967-68; Deutsche Oper am Rhein Düsseldorf from 1968, notably as Weber's Agathe, Wagner's Elsa, Eva, Elisabeth and Sieglinde; Kammersängerin, Nationaltheater, Mannheim, 1971-; Appearances in London, Buenos Aires,

Washington, Vienna, Munich, Berlin; Bayreuth, 1969-80, as Elsa, Eva and in The Ring. Recordings: Parsifal; Die Meistersinger conducted by Solti; Die Meistersinger, conducted by Varviso; Trionfo d' Afrodite by Orff. Address: c/o Nationaltheater Mannheim, Goethestraße, D-68161 Mannheim, Germany.

BODIN Lars-Gunnar, b. 15 July 1935, Stockholm, Sweden. Composer. Education: Studied with Lennart Wenstrom, 1956-60, and visited Darmstadt, 1962. Career: Composer-in-residence, Mills College, Oakland, 1972; Director of the Electronic Music Studio, Stockholm Conservatory, 1978-; Collaboration with Bengt Emil Johnson in text-sound compositions. Compositions include: Dance pieces, Place of Plays, 1967, and...from one point to any other point, 1968; Music for brass instruments, 1960; Arioso for ensemble, 1962; Semi-Kolon: Dag Knutson in Memoriam for horn and ensemble, 1962; Calendar Music for piano, 1964; My World in Your World for organ and tape, 1966; Primary Structures for bassoon and tape, 1976; Enbart for Kerstin for mezzo and tape, 1979; Anima for soprano, flute and tape, 1984; Diskus for wind quintet and tape, 1987; Electronic: Winter Events, 1967; Toccata, 1969; Traces I and II, 1970-71; Memoires d'un temps avant la destruction, 1982; For Jon II Retrospective Episodes, 1986; Text-sound pieces. Address: c/o STIM, Sandhamnsgatan 79, PO Box 27327, S-102 54 Stockholm, Sweden.

BODLEY Seoirse, b. 4 Apr 1933, Dublin, Republic of Ireland. Composer. Education: Studied at the Royal Irish Academy and in Stuttgart with Johann Nepomuk David. Career: Associate Professor of Music at University College, Dublin. Compositions: 5 symphonies, 1959, 1980, 1981, 1990, 1991; 2 chamber symphonies, 1964, 1982; Violin sonata, 1957; Scintillae for 2 harps, 1968; Two String quartets, 1969, 1992; Choruses and incidental music. Address: c/o University College, Faculty of Music, Dublin, Republic of Ireland.

BODOROVÁ Sylvie, b. 31 Dec 1954, Česke Budějovice, Czechoslovakia. Composer. m. Jiři Štilec, 10 Aug 1984. Education: Studied in Brno, Bratislava and Prague; Further study with Franco Donatoni in Siena. Career: Performances of works in London, Dresden and at the Prague Spring Festival; Teaching in CCM Cincinnati, Ohio, 1995-96. Compositions include: Passion Plays for viola and orchestra, 1982; Pontem video for organ, percussion and strings, 1983; Canzoni for Guitar and Strings, 1985; Messagio, violin concerto, 1989; Magikon for oboe and strings, 1990; Panamody for flute and strings, 1992; Vocal and instrumental music, including Una volta prima vera, violin sonata, 1992; Dona Nobis Lucem, 1995; Concerto dei Fiori, 1996; Terezin Ghetto Requiem, 1997. Recordings: Prague Guitar Concertos; Pontem Video. Membership: QUATTRO, Prague. Hobbies: History; Literature; Countryside. Address: Valentova 1731, 149 00 Prague 4, Czech Republic.

BODY Jack, b. 7 Oct 1944, Te Aroha, New Zealand. Composer; Ethnomusicologist. Education: Studied at the University of Auckland.Career: Taught at Indonesian Music Academy, 1976-77, and at Victoria University, Wellington, from 1980. Compositions include: All genres including instrumental music, electroacoustic music, music for dance and mixed media installations. Publications include: Editor, Waiteata Music Press, 1980-; Recordings of traditional music of Indonesia and China. Address: c/o School of Music, Victoria University of Wellington, PO Box 600, Wellington, New Zealand.

BOEHMER Konrad, b. 24 May 1941, Berlin, Germany. Composer. Education: Studied at Cologne University, 1961-66. Career: Scientific Assistant, Utrecht Institute of Sonology, 1966-68; Former Music Editor, Vrij Nederland; Teacher, Royal Conservatory, The Hague, 1971; Director, The Hague Institute of Sociology, 1993. Compositions include: Dr Faustus, Paris Opera, 1985; Woutertje Pieterse, Stadsschouwburg Rotterdam, 1988 (premiere). Address: Royal Conservatory of Music and Drama, Juliana van Stolberglaan 1, 2595 CA The Hague, Netherlands.

BOESCH Christian, b. 27 July 1941, Vienna, Austria. Baritone. Education: Studied at the Vienna Hochschule für Musik. Debut: Berne in 1966. Career; Sang in Saarbrucken, Lucerne and Kiel; Joined Vienna Volksoper in 1975; Sang at Salzburg Festival in 1978 as Papageno in Die Zauberflöte, Metropolitan Opera from 1979 as Papageno, Masetto and Wozzeck, and as Papageno at the Théâtre des Champs Elysées, Paris in 1987; Often heard in modern repertoire; Sang in Wolf-Ferrari's Le Donne Curiose at the Cuvilliés Theatre in Munich, 1989; Sang Wozzeck at Buenos Aires in 1989. Recordings: Die Zauberflöte; Il Prigioniero by Dallapiccola; Haydn's Die Feuersbrunst. Address: c/o Volksoper, Wahringerstrasse 78, A 1090 Vienna, Austria.

BOESE Ursula, b. 27 July 1928, Hamburg, Germany. Singer (mezzo-soprano). Education: Studied at the Musikhochschule, Hamburg. Career: Began career as concert soloist; Bayreuth Festival, 1958-65, in Parsifal and Der Ring des Nibelungen; Hamburg Opera from 1960, notably in Handel's Giulio Cesare, with Joan Sutherland, 1969; San Francisco, 1968, in Oedipus Rex; Guest appearances in Milan, Rome, Buenos Aires, London, Paris and New York; Opera roles have included Gluck's Orpheus, Handel's Cornelia, Dalila, Gaea in Daphne, Jocasta, Verdi's Ulrica and Azucena and Wagner's Fricka, Erda, Waltraute and Magdalene; Often sang Bach in concert. Recordings: Christmas Oratorio by Bach; Der Evangelimann by Kienzl; Salome and Lulu; Parsifal and The Devils of Loudun. Honours: Kammersängerin, 1969. Address: c/o Hamburgische Staatsoper, Grosse-Theaterstraße 34, D-20354 Hamburg, Germany.

BOESMANS Phillipe, b. 17 May 1936, Tongeren, Belgium. Composer. Education: Studied composition with Froidebise and Pousseur at Liège Conservatory, 1954-62. Career: Music producer for Belgian radio from 1961; Worked at Liège electronic music studios, Centre de Recherches Musicales de Wallonie, from 1971; Pianist with the Ensemble Musique Nouvelle. Compositions: Etude 1 for piano, 1963; Sonance for 2 pianos, 1964; Sonance II for 3 pianos, 1967; Impromptu for 23 instruments, 1965; Correlations for clarinet and 2 instrumental groups, 1967; Explosives for harp and 10 instrumentalists, 1968; Verticles for orchestra, 1969; Blocage for voice, chorus and chamber ensemble, 1970; Upon La, Mi for voice, amplified horn and instrumental group, 1970; Fanfare for 2 pianos, 1971; Intervalles I for orchestra, 1972, II for orchestra, 1973, III for voice and orchestra, 1974; Sur Mi for 2 pianos, electric organ, crotale and tam-tam, 1974; Multiples for 2 pianos and orchestra, 1974; Element-Extensions for piano and chamber orchestra, 1976; Doublures for harp, piano, percussion and 4 instrumental groups, 1977; Attitudes, musical spectacle for voice, 2 pianos, synthesizer and percussion, 1977; Piano Concerto, 1978; Violin Concerto, 1979; Conversions for orchestra, 1980; La Passion de Gilles, opera, 1983; Ricercar for organ, 1983; Reigen, opera, 1993. Honours: Italia Prize, 1971. Address: SABAM, Rue d' Arlon 75-77, B-1040 Brussels, Belgium.

BOETTCHER Wolfgang, b. 1940, Berlin, Germany. Cellist. Education: Hochschule der Kunste, Berlin. Career: Soloist, Berlin Philharmonic until 1976; Co-founder, Brandis String Quartet, 1976, with chamber music appearances in Munich, Hamburg, Milan, Paris, London and Tokyo including concerts with the Wiener Singverein and the Berlin Philharmonic; Festival engagements at Salzburg, Lucerne, Vienna, Florence, Tours, Bergen and Edinburgh; Co-premiered Helmut Eder's Clarinet Quintet, 1984, the 3rd Quartet of Gottfried von Einem, 1981, and the 3rd Quartet of Giselher Klebe, 1983; Founding member of the Philharmonische Solisten, Berlin; Concerto appearances with such conductors as Celibidache, Fischer-Dieskau, Lutoslawski, Karajan and Menuhin; Professor at the Hochschule der Kunste, Berlin. Recordings include: Albums in the standard repertoire from 1978, recent releases include quartets by Beethoven, Weill, Schulhoff and Hindemith and the String Quintet by Schubert. Honours include: Prizewinner, International ARD Competition in Munich. Address: c/o Anglo Swiss Management, Suite 35-37 Morley House, 320 Regent Street, London W1R 5AD, England.

BOEYKENS Walter, b. 6 Jan 1938, Bornem, Belgium. Clarinettist. Education: Studied at the Brussels Conservatoire. Career: From 1964 soloist with the Belgian Radio Symphony and has appeared with many other leading orchestras throughout Europe; Chamber engagements with the Amadeus, Grumiaux and Via Nova Quartets; Premiered Domains by Boulez and works by Philippe Boesmans and Marcel Poot; From 1969 Teacher at Conservatories in Anvers and Utrecht. Address: c/o Utrecht Conservatorium, Mariaplaats 28, 3511 LL Utrecht, Netherlands.

BOFILL LEVI Ana, b. 25 Apr 1944, Barcelona, Spain. Composer. Education: Studied in Barcelona, with Luigi Nono and in Paris with Xenakis. Compositions include: Esclat for ensemble, 1971; Suite for harpsichord, 1977; Septet de set sous, 1978; Trio for piano, violin and tape, 1981; Urfaust, scenography, with tape, 1983; Fills d'un Deu Menor for tape, 1984. Address: c/o SGAE, Fernando VI 4, Apartado 484, 28080 Madrid 4, Spain.

BOGACHEV Vladimir, b. 1960, Moscow, Russia. Singer (Tenor). Many appearances at the Bolshoi, Moscow and in Europe as Radames, Cavaradossi, Don José, Dmitri in Boris Godunov and Otello; Lensky in Eugene Onegin and Herman in the Queen of Spades, Montreal, 1990; Season 1993 with Otello at Orlando, Florida, Radames in Liège and Don Carlos in Portland; sang in Tchaikovsky's Iolanata at Dresden, staged by Peter Ustinov; Sang Aeneas in Les Troyens with the London Symphony Orchestra under Colin Davis at the Barbican Hall, London, 1993, repeated at La Scala, 1996; Season 1996 as Otello in Amsterdam, Calaf at the Macerata Festival and in Khovanshchina at Brussels; Many appearances on Russian broadcasting services. Hobbies include: Fishing. Address: c/o Theatre Royal de la Monnaie, 4 Leopoldstrasse, 8-1000 Brussels, Belgium.

BOGACZ Pavel, b. 6 Mar 1957, Bohumin, Czechoslovakia. Violinist. m. Daniela Kruschberska, 15 August 1981, 4 daughters. Education: Ostrava Conservatory; Academy of Music, Prague; Masterclass with N Milstein-Zurich. Career: Member of Prague Chamber Soloists, 1978-81; Concert Master, Slovak Philharmonic Orchestra, Bratislava, 1981-91; Member and Soloist, Chamber Orchestra Capella Istropolitana; Leader, Bratislava String Trio; Teacher of Academy of Music Art, Bratislava; Regular appearances with various orchestras, foreign concert tours and international festivals to Europe, Japan, Australia and Asia; First Concert Master of Orchestra Ensemble Kanazawa, 1991-. Recordings: Bach, Brandenburg Concertos; Romantic Violin Mimiatures; Hummel, String Trio G Major; Parik, Nocturno; Berger, Violin Sonata Adagio; Schnittke, Concerto Grosso. Honours: Best record, Record Academy of Japan, 1993. Address: Zapadny Rad 43, 81104 Bratislava, Slovakia.

BOGART Jean-Paul, b. 17 Sept 1952, USA. Singer (Bass). Education: Studied at Princeton, Yale and the Juilliard School. Career: Sang as child in production of Die Zauberflöte at the Metropolitan Opera; Sang at Santa Fe, Miami and Philadelphia; Dallas Opera as First Nazarene in Salome; La Scala Milan as Basilio in Il Barbiere di Siviglia; Vienna Staatsoper as Ramphis, Sarastro, Raimondo, Sparafucile and Colline; Basle Opera, 1984-85 as Mozart's Figaro and as La Roche in Capriccio; Paris Opéra Comique in 1985 in The Stone Guest by Dargomizhsky; Théâtre Châtelet Paris in I Masnaderi by Verdi; Chicago Lyric Opera as Masetto in Don Giovanni; Baltimore Opera as Gremin in Eugene Onegin; Sang in the premiere of Célestine by Maurice Ohana at the Paris Opéra in 1988; Milwaukee in 1989 as Gounod's Mephistopheles; Lodovico in Otello at Lisbon in 1989; Bonn Opera 1994, as Alonso in Il Guarany by Gomes; Also heard as concert singer. Recordings: Zuniga in Carmen; Turandot; Chichester Psalms; L'Esule di Roma by Donizetti.

BOGATSCHOVA Irina, b. 1943, Russia. Singer (Mezzo-Soprano). Education: Studied at the Leningrad Conservatory. Career: Sang at the Kirov Theatre, Leningrad, from 1965, and guested at the Bolshoi, Moscow, and abroad as Marina (Boris Godunov) and in Prokofiev's War and Peace (San Francisco, 1991); Sang the Countess in The Queen of Spades at Hamburg (1990), La Scala, Théâtre des Champs Elysées, Paris, and elsewhere. Recordings: Several issues on Melodiya. Address: c/o Kirov Theatre, St Petersburg, Russia.

BOGIANCKINO Massimo, b. 10 Nov 1922, Rome, Italy. Opera Director. m. Judith Matthias, 1950. Education: Conservatory of Music and Santa Cecilia Academy, Rome; University of Rome; PhD. Career: Musicologist and Concert Pianist; Director, Enciclopedia dello Spettacolo, 1957-62; Director, Accademia Filarmonica, Rome, 1960-63; Director, Teatro dell'Opera, Rome, 1963-68; Artistic Director, Festival of Two Worlds, Spoleto, 1968-71; Director of Concert Programmes, Accademia di Santa Cecilia, Rome, 1970-71; Artistic Director, La Scala, Milan, 1971-74; General Manager, Teatro Comunale, Florence, 1974-82; Adminstrator General, Paris Opera, 1982-85; In 1985 became Mayor of Florence. Publications: L'arte clavicembalistica di D Scarlatti, 1956; Aspetti del Teatro musicale in Italia e in Francia nell'eta Barocca, 1968; Le canzonette e i madrigali di V Cossa, 1981. Honours: Bundesverdienstkreuz, Federal Republic of Germany. Address: Théâtre National d'Opéra, Paris, France.

BOGUSLAWSKI Edward, b. 22 Sept 1940, Chorzow, Poland. Composer; Teacher. Education: Studied composition with Szabelski in Katowice and with Haubenstock-Ramati in Vienna. Career: Teacher at the State College in Katowice from 1963, currently head of composition department. Compositions: Intonazioni for 9 instruments, 1962; String Quartet, 1963; Apocalypse for reciter, choir and ensemble, 1965; Sketch for oboe and piano, 1965; Signals for orchestra, 1966; Intonazioni II for orchestra, 1966; Canti for soprano and orchestra, 1967; Metamorphosis for ensemble, 1967; Oboe Concerto, 1968; Sinfonia for choir and Orchestra, 1969; Musica per ensemble, MW-2, 1970; Trio for flute, oboe and guitar, 1970; Capriccioso notturno for orchestra, 1972; Impromptu for flute, viola and harp, 1973; L'Etre for soprano and ensemble, 1973; Musica Notturna, 1973; Pro Varsovia for orchestra, 1974; Evocation for baritone and orchestra, 1974; Beelzebub's Sonata, chamber opera, 1977; Prelude and Cadenza for solo violin, 1979; Music Concertante for alto saxophone and orchestra, 1980; Piano Concerto, 1981; Symphony Concertante for violin and chamber orchestra, 1982; Polonia, symphonic poem for violin and orchestra, 1984; The Game of Dreams, musical drama after Strindberg, 1985; Concerto for accordion, percussion and strings, 1985; Lacrimosa for soprano and piano, 1991; Concerto per chitana and orchestra, 1991; Dies inae for choir and instruments, 1992; Trio for violino, violoncello and piano, 1993; Second String Quartet, 1995. Address: c/o ZAIKS, 2 rue Hipoteczna, 00 092 Warsaw, Poland.

BOHAC Josef, b. 25 Mar 1929, Vienna, Austria. Composer. Education: Pupil of Petrzelka, Janacek Academy of Music, Brno, 1951-56. Career: Director, Panton publishing concern, 1968-71; Head, Department of Music Broadcasts, Czech Television; Secretary, Union of Czech Composers, 1979-; Rumcajs, 1985. Compositions: Operas: The Wooing, 1967; The Eyes, 1973; Goya, 1971-76; Golden Wedding, 1981; Orchestral: Symphonic

Overture, 1964; Fragment, 1969; Elegy for Cello and Chamber Orchestra, 1969; Dramatic Suite for Strings and Kettledrums, 1969-70; Blue and White, suite, 1970; February Overture, 1973; Piano Concerto, 1974; Concerto for Violin and Chamber Orchestra, 1978; Concertino Pastorale for 2 Horns and Orchestra, 1978; Concerto for Orchestra, 1983; Dramatic Variants for Viola and Orchestra, 1983; Chamber: String Trio, 1965; Sonetti per Sonatori for Flute, Bass Clarinet, Harpsichord, Piano and Percussion, 1974; Sonata Giovane for Piano, 1983; Vocal: My Lute Resounds, monodrama for Tenor, Soprano and Nonet or Piano, 1971; 2 cantatas, 1976, 1979; Sonata Lirica for Soprano, Strings and Vibraphone, 1982. Address: c/o 14700 Prague 4, Ustavni 39, Czech Republic.

BOHAN Edmund, b. 5 Oct 1935, Christchurch, New Zealand. Singer (Tenor); Writer. m. Gillian Margaret Neason, 18 Nov 1968, 1 son, 1 daughter. Education: Singing with Godfrey Stirling, (Sydney), Eric Green and Gustave Sacher (London). Debut: Oratorio, 1956, Opera, 1962, New Zealand. Career: Repertoire of over 170 operas and major works including Opera, Oratorio, Concerts in England, Europe and Australasia and Brazil; Opera, English Opera Group, Dublin Grand Opera, London Chamber Opera, State Opera of South Australia, Canterbury Opera New Zealand; Wexford Festival, New Zealand International Festival of the Arts, Aldeburgh Festival, Norwich Triennial, Adelaide Festival; Wellington City Opera, New Zealand; Television includes Australian Broadcasting, BBC Proms, ABC, and New Zealand Radio; Film, Barber of Seville; Venues include Royal Festival Hall, Queen Elizabeth Hall and other major halls with RPO, London Concert, BBC Concert and Ulster Orchestras; Oratorio Soloist with British, Australian and New Zealand Choral Societies. Recordings: A Gilbert and Sullivan Spectacular; When Song is Sweet; Sweet and Low; Gilbert and Sullivan with Band and Voice; The Olympians (Bliss) Intaglo. Publications: The Writ of Green Wax, 1971; The Buckler, 1972; Edward Stafford: New Zealand's First Statesman, 1994; The Opawa Affair, 1996; The Story So Far: A Short History of New Zealand, 1997; The Dancing Man, 1997. Contributions to: New Zealand Dictionary of Biography, 1991, 1993. Memberships: British Incorporated Society of Musicians; New Zealand Association of Singing Teachers. Hobbies: Gardening; Reading. Address: 5 Vincent Place, Opawa, Christchurch, New Zealand.

BÖHM Ludwig, b. 5 July 1947, Munich, Germany. Music Archivist; Author; Editor. Education: Universities of Munich and Würzburg. Career: Secondary School Teacher, English, French, Spanish, Munich, 1981-83; Founder: Theobald Böhm Archives, 1980, and Theobald Böhm Society, 1990; Organiser, Commemorative Concerts, 1981 and 1994 in Munich. Publications: Complete Musical Works for Flute by Theobald Böhm (editor), 15 volumes, 1999; Documentation about Theobald Böhm in 10 volumes (author, vols 1 and 4-7, editor, vols 2, 3 and 8-10): vol 1 - Commemorative Publication on the Occasion of Th Böhm's 200th Birthday; vol 2 - Letters to and Articles about Th Böhm concerning Flute Construction; vol 3 - Letters to and Articles about Th Böhm not concerning Flute Construction; vol 4 - Catalogue of the Concerts by and with Th Böhm (ca 120); vol 5 - Catalogue of the Musical Works of Th Böhm (47 works with opus numbers and 37 arrangements without opus numbers); vol 6 - Catalogue of the still existing Flutes of Th Böhm; vol 7 - The Estate of Th Bohm in the Municipal Archives in Munich; vol 8 - Complete Letters and Articles by Th Böhm; vol 9 - Five Publications on Flute Construction by Th Böhm; vol 10 - Biographies of Th Böhm by Karl von Schafhäutl, Marie Böhm and Karl Böhm. Contributions to: Articles to flute and music journals worldwide include: On the Trail of Th Böhm, 1981; Spelling Th Böhm or Th Boehm, 1984; Th Böhm's Comment on the closed G Sharp Key, 1984. Memberships: President, Theobald Böhm Society; German Flute Society; French Flute Association; British Flute Society; National Flute Association, USA; Honorary Life Member, Victorian Flute Guild, Australia. Hobbies: Flute playing; Tennis; Skiing; Mountaineering. Address: Asamstrasse 6, D-82166 Gräfelfing, Germany.

BOHMAN Gunnel, b. 4 Mar 1959, Stockholm, Sweden. Singer (soprano). Education: Studied at the Opera School, Stockholm. Career: Engaged by Lorin Maazel for the Vienna Staatsoper; Sang at the Mannheim Opera as Pamina, Fiordiligi and Marenka in The Bartered Bride; Sang Pamina at the Bregenz Festival and appeared further in Vienna, Zurich, Houston and Hamburg as Mozart's Countess, Agathe, Micaela, Mimi and Lola; Sang in the Jussi Björling Memorial Concert in Stockholm, 1985, with Birgit Nilsson, Elisabeth Söderström, Nicolai Gedda and Robert Merrill; Bregenz Festival, 1985-86, as Pamina, Vienna Volksoper from 1987 (as Fiordiligi), Staatsoper from 1988; Zurich and Parma, 1987, as Smetana's Marenka and Gluck's Euridice; Glyndebourne Festival, 1989, as the Countess in Figaro (also at the Albert Hall); Sang Elisabeth in Tannhäuser at the 1996 Savonlinna Festival; Concert repertoire includes Bach's Passions, B minor Mass and Christmas Oratorio; Ein Deutsches Requiem and Requiems of Mozart and Dvorák; Haydn Die Schöpfung and Die Jahreszeiten; Strauss Vier Letzte Lieder and Wagner Wesendonck Lieder. Honours include: Jenny Lind Fellowship,

1978. Address: Svenska Konsertbyrån AB, Schonfelds grand 1, Box 2058 S-10312 Stockholm, Sweden.

BOIS Rob du, b. 28 May 1934, Amsterdam, Netherlands. Composer. Education: Received training in piano and jurisprudence; Self-taught in composition. Compositions: Orchestral: Piano Concerto, 1960, revised, 1968; Cercle for Piano, 9 Winds and Percussion, 1963; Simultaneous, 1965; Breuker Concerto for 2 Clarinets, 4 saxophones and 21 strings, 1968; A Flower Given to My Daughter, 1970; Le Concerto pour Hrisanide for piano and orchestra, 1971; Allegro for strings, 1973; 3 Pezzi, 1973; Suite No 1, 1973; Violin Concerto, 1975; Skarabee, 1977; Zodiak, 1977; Concerto for 2 violins and orchestra, 1979; Sinfonia da camera for wind orchestra, 1980; Luna, for alto flute and orchestra, 1988; Chamber: 7 Pastorales, 1960-64; Trio for flute, oboe and clarinet, 1961; Rondeaux pour deux for piano and percussion, 1962, 2nd series for piano 4-hands and percussion, 1964; Chants et contrepoints, for wind quintet, 1962; Espaces à remplir for 11 musicians, 1963; Oboe Quartet, 1964; String Trio, 1967; Symposium for oboe, violin, viola and cello, 1969; Trio Agitate for horn, trombone and tuba, 1969; Reflexions sur le jour ou Perotin le Grand ressuscitera for wind quintet, 1969; Fusion pour deux for bass clarinet and piano, 1971; Tracery for bass clarinet and 4 percussionists, 1979; Sonata for violin and piano, 1980; Elegia for oboe d'amore, violin, viola and cello, 1980; String Quartet No 3, 1981; Sonata for Solo Viola, 1981; Ars aequi for 2 double basses and piano, 1984; Autumn Leaves for guitar and harpsichord, 1984; Hyperion for clarinet, horn, viola and piano, 1984; Forever Amber for 2 guitars, 1985; Das Liebesverbot for 4 Wagner tubas; On a Lion's Interlude for alto flute, 1986; Symphorine for flute, 1987; 4 String Quartets,1960-90. Address: Professor J Bronnerlaan 7, 2012PM Haarlem, Netherlands.

BOISSY Nathalie, b. 1963, Beaune, Côte d'Or, France. Singer (Soprano). Education: Studied at Colmar, Strasbourg, Paris and the Oberlin Conservatory, USA. Career: Sang at the Linz Opera from 1988, as Frau Fluth (Nicolai), Marzelline, the Countess in Romeo et Juliette, Mimi, Romilda in Xerxes, Micaela, Leila in Les Pêcheurs de Perles and the Infantin in Der Zwerg by Zemlinsky; Sang Micaela at Bregenz (1991) and in Mendelssohn's Elijah at Linz, 1991. Address: c/o Landestheater, Promenade 39, A-4010 Linz, Austria.

BOKANOWSKI Michèle, b. 9 Aug 1943, Cannes, France. Composer. Education: Studied in Paris with Pierre Schaeffer; Computer music in Vincennes. Career: Has researched sound synthesis with the Groupe de Recherches Musicales. Compositions include: Salome, ballet, 1985; Hamlet, incidental music, 1986; L'eclipse de la balle, 1987; Musique concrète, including Phone Variations, 1988; Film music. Address: c/o SACEM, 225 avenue Charles de Gaulle, 92521 Neuilly sur Seine Cedex, France.

BOKES Vladimir, b. 11 Jan 1946, Bratislava, Czechoslovakia. Composer. m. Klara Olejárová, 11 July 1970, 2 sons, 1 daughter. Education: Secondary Music School, Konzervatorium, 1960-65; High Music School, Vysoka skola muzickych umeni, Music Academy, 1965-70. Career: Teacher in Conservatory, Bratislava, 1971-75; Assistant, High Music School, Bratislava, 1975-; Docent, 1988, Professor, 1993. Compositions: Symphony No 1, 1970, No 2, 1978, No 3, 1980, No 4, 1982, No 5, 1987; Piano Concerto No 1, 1976, No 2, 1984; Chamber and piano works; Vocal cycles, Sposob ticha, The way of silence, 1977, and Na svoj sposob, In its own way. 1978; 12 preludes and fugues for piano, 1989; Missa Posoniensis for 4 soli, choir, organ and orchestra, 1991. Recordings: Variations on a Theme from Haydn for Piano, 1975; 1st Piano Concerto, 1978; 3rd Symphony, 1989; Sonata for Viola and Piano, 1992. Contributions to: Biennale Zagreb, 1977; Hudobny zivot, Bratislava, 1977; Communicativity in Music, essay in Hudobny zivot, 1988; Slovenska hudba, Bratislava, 1991, 1995; Essays, 1992. Memberships: Union of Slovak Composers; Slovak Music Society; President, International Festival of the Contemporary Music Melos-Ethos Bratislava, 1993-95/ Address: Svoradova 5, 811 03 Bratislava, Slovakia.

BOLCOM William, b. 26 May 1938, Washington, USA. Composer. m. (1) Fay Levine, div 1967, (2) Katherine Agee Ling, div 1969, (3) Joan Morris, 28 Nov 1975. Education: BA, University of Washington, 1958; MA, Mills College, 1961; Paris Conservatoire de Musique, 1959-61, 1964-65; DMusArt, Stanford University, 1964; Piano studies with Berthe Poncy Jacobson; Composition studies with John Verrall, Leland Smith, Darius Milhaud, George Rochberg. Career: Acting Assistant Professor of Music, University of Washington, 1965-66; Lecturer, Assistant Professor of Music, Queen's College, City University of New York, 1966-68; Visiting Critic in Music Theatre Drama School, Yale University, 1968-69; Composer in Residence, New York University, School of the Arts, 1969-71; Assistant Professor, 1973, Associate Professor, 1977, Professor, 1983-, Ross Lee Finney Distinguished Professor of Composition, 1993; School of Music, University of Michigan. Compositions include: 4 Violin Sonatas, 1956-94; 6 Symphonies, 1957-97; Concertos for piano,

violin, clarinet; 10 String Quartets, 1950-88; Fantasy Sonata for Piano, 1961-62; 12 New Etudes for piano, 1977-86; Sonata for Cello and Piano, 1989; Casino Paradise, musical, 1990; McTeague, opera, 1992. Publication: Reminiscing with Sissle and Blake, 1973. Contributions to: Grove's Dictionary; Contributing Editor, Annals of Scholarship. Honours include: Kurt Weill Award for Composition, 1963; Guggenheim Foundation Fellow; Rockefeller Foundation Awards; NEA Grants; Pulitzer Prize for Music, 1988; American Academy of Arts and Letters, 1993; Henry Russel Lectureship, 1997. Memberships: Board, American Music Center; Charles Ives Society; American Composers' Alliance. Address: 3080 Whitmore Lake Road, Ann Arbor, MI 48105, USA.

BOLDYREV Vladimir, b. 1955, Ukraine. Baritone. Education: Studied at the Kharkov Institute of Arts. Career: Principal at the Kharkov Opera from 1985, notably as Don Giovanni, Germont, Rossini's Figaro, Escamilo, Eugene Onegin, Yeletsky, Silvio and Samson; Further opera and recital engagements in the USA, Germany, France and Italy; Repertoire includes songs by Rachmaninov, Glinka and Tchaikovsky, and Lieder by Mahler, Schubert and Schumann. Honours include: Prizewinner at the 1987 All-Union Glinka Song Competition. Address: Sonata Ltd, 11 North Park Street, Glasgow, G20 7AA, Scotland.

BOLGAN Marina, b. 20 Mar 1957, Mestre, Venice, Italy. Singer (soprano). Education: Studied at Conservatories in Venice, Siena and Rome. Debut: Sang Rosina in various Italian cities, 1981. Career: Sang Nannetta in Falstaff at the Teatro della Zarzuela, Madrid, 1982, and Gilda at Toulouse; Adina in L'Elisir d'Amore, Venice, 1984; Bellini's Elvira at the Bregenz Festival, 1985; Paisiello's Nina at Catania; Annetta in Crispino e la comare by the brothers Ricci at Teatro La Fenice Venice and Théâtre des Champs Elysées, Paris; Elvira and Lucia, Zurich Opera, 1987, 1989; at the Hamburg Staatsoper, sang Adina and elsewhere in Donizetti's La Romanziera and Betly; Further appearances at Bologna, Verona and the Vienna Staatsoper (Lucia, 1988); Sang Selinda in Vivaldi's Farnace at the Valle d'Istria Festival, Martina Franca, 1991.

BOLLIGER Phillip John, b. 2 May 1963, Sydney, New South Wales, Australia. Composer; Classical Guitarist. Education: Vienna Hochschule, 1986; Siena and Basle, 1990-91; Graduated, University of Sydney, 1992; Study with Peter Sculthorpe, 1992-93. Career: Freelance guitarist and private teacher; Composer of film music, 1991-. Compositions include: Inventions for guitar, 1986; The Birds of My Gully for flute, 1988; Sailing Song for piano, 1990; Four Greek Dances for two guitars, 1990; Romance for flute and orchestra, 1990; Three Preludes for guitar, 1992; Benedictus Balaenarum for trombone and piano, 1993; Requiem Chernobyl for choir and orchestra, 1993; Zagorsk for string quartet and piano, 1993; Monsoon for flute, 1997. Honours include: First Prize, City of Sydney Eisteddfod, 1987; First Prize, Warringah Eisteddfod, 1992. Address: c/o APRA, 1A Eden Street, Crows Nest, NSW 2065, Australia.

BOLTON Andrea, b. 1960, England. Singer (soprano). Education: Studied at the Royal Northern College of Music and at the National Opera Studio. Career: While a student sang Gilda, Rosina, Susanna, Adina (L'Elisir d'Amore), Amina (La Sonnambula), Sophie and Zerbinetta; Welsh National Opera from 1985, as Despina, Oscar, Susanna, Adele in Fledermaus, Blondchen (Die Entführung) and Echo in Ariadne auf Naxos; Musica nel Chiostro in Battignano, 1986, as Lisetta in Paisiello's Il re Teodoro in Venezia; Season 1987-88 with debuts at Opera North as Valencienne in The Merry Widow and with Scottish Opera as Cunegonde in Bernstein's Candide; Wexford Festival, 1988, as Donna Elvira in Gazzaniga's Don Giovanni, televised by RTE and British Sky Broadcasting; Scottish Opera, 1990, as Ascanius in Les Troyens; Concert repertory includes Mendelssohn's A Midsummer Night's Dream (Royal Liverpool Philharmonic); Haydn's Creation (RTE in Ireland); Sacred music by Handel, Caldara and Charpentier (Holst Singers at St John's Smith Square). Recordings include: Albums in Opera Rara's One Hundred Years of Italian Opera series. Address: c/o Korman International Management, Crunnells Green Cottage, Preston, Herts SG5 7UQ, England.

BOLTON Ivor, b. 17 May 1958, Lancashire, England. Conductor. Education: Clare College, Royal College of Music, National Opera Studio. Career: Conductor, Schola Cantorum of Oxford; Glyndebourne, 1982-92; Conductor, Gluck's Orfeo, Glyndebourne, 1989, has led Il Barbiere di Siviglia, Die Zauberflöte, The Rake's Progress and La Bohème for the Touring Company; Music Director, Glyndebourne Touring Opera, La Clemenza di Tito, 1993-94; Founded St James Baroque Players, 1984, and directs annual Luthansa Festival of Baroque Music at St James, Piccadilly; Music Director of English Touring Opera, 1990-93, leading Don Giovanni, Figaro, Lucia di Lammermoor, Così fan tutte, Die Zauberflöte, La Cenerentola and Carmen; Così fan tutte at the Aldeburgh Festival; English National Opera debut, with Xerxes, 1992; La Gazza Ladra for Opera North and Monteverdi's Poppea in Bologna, 1993; Season 1997 with Giulio

Cesare, Serse and Poppea at the Munich Festival; Chief Conductor of the Scottish Chamber Orchestra from Aug 1994, regular concerts with the London Mozart Players, English Chamber Orchestra, Scottish Symphony, Bournemouth Sinfonietta and BBC Symphony. Recordings include: Bach's concertos for Harpsichord; Purcell's Dido and Aeneas; Brahms and Mendelssohn Violin Concertos; Vivaldi's Stabat Mater. Address: c/o Ingpen & Williams Ltd, 20 Wadham Road, London SW15 2LR, England.

BONALDI Clara, b. 9 Mar 1937, Dombasle-sur-Meurthe, France. Violinist. Education: Studied at the Paris Conservatoire (first prize for violin, 1955). Career: Many appearances at major festivals in France and elsewhere in Europe; Has edited for performance the sonatas of Francouer and Tartini and partnered harpsichordist Luciano Sorizzi (pianist Noel Lee from 1980). Honours include: Prize winner at the 1955 Long-Thibaud Competition and at the 1963 Munich International (as piano duettist). Address: c/o Noel Lee, 4 Villa Laugier, F-75017 Paris, France.

BONAZZI Elaine, b. 1936, Endicott, New York, USA. Singer (Mezzo-Soprano). Education: Studied at the Eastman School of Music, Rochester, and at Hunter College, New York. Career: Santa Fe Opera from 1959, notably as Meg Page in Falstaff and in the 1961 US premiere of Hindemith's Neues vom Tage; Appearances in Cincinnati, Houston, Dallas, Pittsburgh, Mexico City, Vancouver and New York (City Opera); Caramoor Festival New York in Semele,1969; Often heard in operas by Rossini and in contemporary music; sang the Marquise in La Fille du Régiment at St Louis, 1990; Sang Linfea in La Calisto for Glimmerglass Opera, 1996; Many engagements as concert singer; Taught at Peabody Conservatory, Baltimore. Recordings: La Pietra del Paragone by Rossini (Vanguard); Le Rossignol by Stravinsky (CBS). Address: c/o Opera Theater of St Louis, PO Box 13148, St Louis, MO 63119, USA.

BONCOMPAGNI Elio, b. 8 May 1933, Arezzo, Italy. Conductor. Education: Violin and Composition, Florence and Padua; Conducting in Perugia and Hilversum. Debut: Bologna, 1962, Don Carlos. Career: Conductor at opera houses in Europe, including Théâtre de la Monnaie, Brussels, from 1974; British debut, 1983, Cherubini's Medée at the Barbican Hall, London; Un Ballo in Maschera for Opera Montreal, 1990; conducted José Carreras concert at the Scottish Exhibition Centre, Glasgow, 1991. Honours include: Prize, Italian Radio International Competition, 1961, and Mitropoulos Competition, New York, 1967. Address: c/o Opéra de Montreal, 1157 Rue Sainte Catherine E, Montreal, Quebec Province, Canada H2L 2G8.

BOND Timothy M, b. 21 July 1948, Mullion, Cornwall, England. Concert Organist; Lecturer. Education: BMus, FRCO, ARCM, Royal College of Music, London, England. Debut: Westminster Cathedral, 1974. Career: British Premiere, Schoenberg's Sonata Fragment, 1974; Premieres at Henry Wood Proms of: Ligeti - Two Studies, 1976; Schoenberg-Variations on a Recitative, 1979; Messiaen-L'Ascension, 1981; Schoenberg Festival, Royal Festival Hall, 1989; Appearances at Festivals including: Aldeburgh, Huddersfield, Southampton, City of London, Normandy; TV: Ceremonies and Rituals, broadcast of Messiaen's L'Ascension; Many broadcasts of Modern Organ Music including: Schoenberg, Messiaen, Stockhausen, Berio, Pousseur, Goehr, J Lambert, A Anderson, D Sutton-Anderson; British Premiere of original version of Schoenberg's Variations on a Recitative, 1974. Recordings: Messiaen: L'Ascension; Quatre Méditations Symphoniques. Creative works: Commission and Premieres of works specially written: Uccelli by John Lambert, 1992; Echo Toccata by John Lambert, 1993; The Grass is Sleeping by Avril Anderson, 1979; Concerto for Organ and Orchestra: Crossing The Great Water, by David Sutton-Anderson, 1992. Contribution to: Musical Times, 1978. Honours: SPNM Young Artists and Twentieth Century Music, 1975. Hobbies: Modern British Art; Modern architecture. Address: 25 York Avenue, Hove, Sussex BN3 1PJ, England.

BOND Victoria, b. 6 May 1945, Los Angeles, CA, USA. Conductor; Composer; Music Director. m. Stephan Peskin, 27 Jan 1974. Education includes: BMA, University of Southern CA, 1968; MMA, 1975; DMA, 1977; Juilliard School; Teachers include: Conducting: Ehrling; Herbert von Karajan; Composition: Roger Sessions; Darius Milhaud. Career: Assistant Conductor, 1972-77: Juillard Orchestra; Juilliard Contemporary Music Ensemble; American Opera Centre; Cabrillo Music Festival, CA, 1974; White Mountains Music Festival, NH, 1975; Aspen Opera, CO, 1976; Colorado Philharmonic, 1977; Exxon, Arts Endowment Conductor, Pittsburgh Symphony (Previn), 1978-80; Music Director: Pittsburgh Youth Symphony Orchestra, 1978-80; New Amsterdam Symphony, 1978-80; Southeastern Music Centre, GA, 1983-85; Empire State Youth Orchestra, Albany, 1982-86; Conducting staff, Albany Symphony, 1983-85; Artistic Director, Bel Canto Opera Company, NYC, 1982-88; Music Director, Roanoke Symphony Orchestra, VA, 1986-95; Artistic Director, Opera Roanoke, 1989-95; Guest Conducting includes: Houston Symphony; Richmond Symphony; Anchorage, Alaska; Radio Telefis Eirann, Ireland; Shanghai Symphony, China. Compositions include: Old New Borrowed Blues for Chamber Ensemble; From an Antique Land for Voice and Piano; Molly Manybloom; Urban Bird, saxophone concerto; Thinking Like a Mountain for Narrator and Orchestra; Dreams of Flying for String Quartet; Travels, opera. Recordings include: Delusion of the Fury; Notes from Underground; An American Collage. Publications: The Orchestra at the Time of Mozart, 1977. Hobbies: Horseback Riding; Sailing; Hiking. Address: 256 West 10th Street, New York, NY 10014, USA.

BONDARENKO Alexander, b. 1950, Crimea, Russia. Violinist. Career: Co-Founder, Rachmaninov Quartet, 1974, under the auspices of the Sochi State Philharmonic Society, Crimea; Concerts in the former Soviet Union and from 1975-76 tours to Switzerland, Austria, Bulgaria, Norway and Germany; Participant in 1976 Shostakovich Chamber Music Festival at Vilnius, and in festivals in Moscow and St Petersburg; repertoire has included works by Haydn, Mozart, Beethoven, Bartok, Schnittke, Shostakovich, Boris Tchaikovsky, Chalayev and Meyerovich. Honours include: Prize, First All-Union Borodin String Quartet Competititon with the Rachmaninov Quartet, 1987. Current Management: Sonata, Glasgow, Scotland. Address: 11 North Park Street, Glasgow G20 7AA, Scotland.

BONELL Carlos (Antonio), b. 23 July 1949, London, England. Guitarist. m. Pinuccia Rossetti, 2 sons. Education: Royal College of Music. Debut: Wigmore Hall, London. Career: Soloist with all the major British orchestras and many orchestras overseas; Founded, Carlos Bonell Ensemble, 1983; Frequent broadcaster. Compositions: Spanish Folk Songs and Dances; 20 First Pieces, 1984. Recordings: Fandango, 1976; Rodrigo Concerto de Aranjuez with Montreal Symphony Orchestra and Charles Dutoit, 1981; 20th Century Music for Guitar, 1987; The Sea in Spring, 1997. Publications: Airs and Dances of Gasper Sanz, 1977; The Romantic Guitar and The Classical Guitar, 1983; Tarrega: Fantasia and Purcell: 3 Pieces from the Fairy Queen; Masterclass on Playing The Guitar, 1983; 3 Spanish Folk Songs for 3 Guitars, 1984; The Technique Builder, 1997. Contributions to: Guitar Magazine. Honours: Honorary, Associate, Royal College of Music, 1978; Nomination for Best Chamber Music Performance for Record, John Williams and Friends, American National Academy of Recording Arts and Sciences, 1978; Nominated for Grammy Award; Hon RCM. Membership: Musicians Union; ISM. Hobbies: Reading; Walking. Current Management: Upbeat. Address: Sutton Business Centre, Restmor Way, Wallington, Surrey SM6 7AH, England.

BONETTI Antoni (Robert), b. 6 Nov 1952, London, England. Violinist; Conductor. m. Ruth Back, 16 Mar 1974, 3 sons. Education: AMusA, DSCM, New South Wales Conservatorium, 1973; ARCM, 1978. Career: Violinist, Principal 2nd Violin, 1968-72, Australian Youth Orchestra; Tour to Japan, 1970, South East Asia, 1974; Freelance Violinist, London, 1975-76, appearing with Royal Philharmonic Orchestra, New Philharmonia Orchestra, London Mozart Players; Concertmaster, Norrlands Opera Orchestra, Sweden, 1976-77; Stockholm Ensemble, 1977-78; Conductor, Musik Sällskap, Umeå, 1978; Baroque Violin with Gammerith Consort, Austria, 1978; Member of Kurpfalzisches Kammerorchester, Federal Republic of Germany, 1979-81; Concertmaster, Queensland Theatre Orchestra, 1981-84; Lecturer, Queensland Conservatorium of Music, 1982-92; Head of Orchestral Studies, St Peter's Lutheran College, 1985-; Conductor, Baroque Orchestra of Brisbane, Brisbane Christian Chamber Orchestra, 1986-89, Concert Society Orchestra, 1987-90; Extensive tours with Divertimento Bonetti ensemble throughout Europe; Various conducting engagements with Redcliffe City Choir, Cleveland Symphony Orchestra, Ipswich Youth Orchestra, 1989; Drector and Founder, Brisbane Sinfonia, 1990-; Adjudicator, various Eisteddfods. Composition: Jacaranda for orchestra, 1992. Honours: Fellowship, Australian Council for the Arts, 1974. Hobbies: Birdwatching; Gardening.

BONIS Ferenc, b. 17 May 1932, Miskolc, Hungary. Musicologist. m. Terézia Csajbók. Education: DMus, Ferenc Liszt Academy of Music, Budapest. Career: Music Producer, Hungarian Radio, 1950-70; Scientific Collaborator, Musicological Institute of Hungarian Academy of Sciences, 1961-73; Professor, Musicological Faculty, Ferenc Liszt Academy of Music, 1972-; Editor, Magyar Zenetudomány (Hungarian Musicology), 1959-; Editor, Magyar Zenetöténeti Tanulmányok (Studies on History of Hungarian Music), 1968-; Editor, Complete Edition of B Szabolcsi's Works, 1977-; Leader, Music Department for Children and Youth, Hungarian Radio, 1970-94; Leading Music Producer, Hungarian Radio, 1994-. Recordings: Editor, Early Hungarian Chamber Music; Works by P Wranitzky and L Mozart; Béla Bartók - As We Saw Him (recollections); Zoltán Kodály - As We Saw Him (recollections). Publications include: Mosonyi Mihály, 1960; G Mahler und F Erkel, 1960; Zoltán Kodály, A Hungarian Master of Neoclassicism, 1982; Tizenhárom találkozás Ferencsik Jánossal (Meeting J Ferencsik), 1984; International Kodaly Conference (with E Szönyi and L Vikár), 1986; Harmichárom óra ifjabb Bartók Bélával (33 hours with B Bartók Jr), 1991; Hódolat Bartóknak és Kodálynak (Devotion to Bartók and Kodály), 1992; Bartók-Lengyel, A csodálatos mandarin, 1993; Himnusz (Hungarian National Anthem), facsimile edition, 1994; Igy láttuk Kodályt (3rd enlarged edition), 1994; Igy láttuk Bartókot (2nd enlarged edition), 1995; A Himnusz születése és másfél százada (The Birth of the Hungarian National Anthem and its 150 Years), 1995. Honours: Ferenc Erkel Prize, 1973; Officer's Cross of Order of the Hungarian Republic, 1992. Memberships: Gesellschaft für Musikforschung; President, Hungarian Kodály Society; President, Ferenc Erkel Society. Address: Belgrad rakpart 27 I 5, Budapest H-1056, Hungary.

BONISOLLI Franco, b. 1938, Rovereto, Italy. Singer (tenor). Education: Studied privately. Career: Spoleto, 1961, as Ruggero in La Rondine. Career: Spoleto, 1963, in The Love of Three Oranges; Amsterdam, 1965, as Des Grieux in Manon Lescaut; US debut, San Francisco, 1969, as Alfredo; La Scala Milan, 1969, in L'Assedio di Corinto by Rossini; Metropolitan Opera from 1971, as Rossini's Almaviva, Nemorino, Faust, the Duke of Mantua, Alfredo and Cavaradossi (1986); Guest appearances in London, Vienna, Rome, Toulouse, Dallas, Philadelphia, Hamburg and Brussels; Other roles include Rodolfo, Alvaro in La Forza del Destino and Pinkerton; Deutsche Oper Berlin, 1982, in La Fanciulla del West; Verona Arena, 1985, as Manrico; Sang Calaf at Covent Garden, 1987, Enzo in La Gioconda at the Verona Arena, 1988 (Radames, 1989). Recordings: La Traviata; Tosca; Il Trovatore, Pagliacci; Rigoletto; Gluck's Iphigénie en Aulide and Paride ed Helena; L'Assedio di Corinto. Address: Allied Artists Agency, 42 Montpelier Square, London SW7 1JZ, England.

BONNER Tessa, b. 1955, England. Singer (soprano). Education: Studied at Leeds University and the Guildhall School of Music. Career: Solo singer and consort member of such groups as the Tallis Scholars, the New London Consort, the Lute Group, Gabrieli Consort, Taverner Consort and the Early Opera Project; Frequent appearances with Musica Secreta, notably at the Early Music Centre Festival, the Lufthansa Festival of Baroque Music, and at the National Gallery; Early Music Network Tour of Britain, Nov 1991, with programme Filiae Jerusalem (sacred music for women's voices by Monteverdi, Carissimi, Cavalli, Viadna, Grandi and Marco da Gagliano); Other repertoire includes works by Marenzio, Luzzaschi, Wert, Luigi Rossi and the women composers Francesca Caccini and Barbara Strozzi; Participation in lecture-recitals and workshops on performance practice and ornamentation. Address: Robert White Management, 182 Moselle Avenue, London N22 6EX, England.

BONNEY Barbara, b. 14 April 1956, Montclair, New Jersey, USA. Singer, Soprano. m. Hakan Hagegard. Education: Studied in Canada and at the Salzburg Mozarteum with Walter Raninger. Debut: Darmstadt 1979, in Die Lustigen Weiber von Windsor. Career: Sang Blondchen in Die Entführung, Cherubino in Le nozze di Figaro, Nathali in Henze's Der Prinz von Homburg and Massenet's Manon; Appeared at Frankfurt, Hamburg and Munich 1983-84; Covent Garden 1984; As Sophie in Der Rosenkavalier: Returned as Blondchen, 1987; La Scala Milan 1985, as Pamina; Schwetzingen Festival 1985 in Handels Semele; Season 1987-88 as Sophie in Monte Carlo, Pamina at Geneva, Adina at Lausanne and Susanna at Zurich; Metropolitan 1989-90, as Adele in Fledermaus, Sophie in Der Rosenkavalier, 1991; Chicago Lyric Opera debut 1989, as Adele; Concert appearances include the Monteverdi Vespers at Copenhagen, 1990; Sang in Mozart Bicentenary Gala at Covent Garden, 1991; Mozart's Coronation Mass and Solemn Vespers at the 1993 Prom Concerts, London; Mozart's Susanna at the Metropolitan, 1997; Soloist in centenary performance of the Brahms Requiem, Vienna Musikverein, 1997. Recordings: Moses und Aron by Schoenberg and Haydn's Lord Nelson Mass; Lortzing's Zar und Zimmermann; Video of Messiah. Address: IMG Artists, Media House, 3 Burlington Lane, London, W4 2TH.

BONYNGE Richard, b. 29 Sept 1930, Sydney, New South Wales, Australia. Opera Conductor. m. Joan Sutherland, 1954, 1 son. Education: Trained as pianist; Specialist in bel canto repertoire. Debut: As Conductor, with Santa Cecilia Orchestra, Rome, 1962. Career: Conducted first opera, Faust, Vancouver, 1963; Has conducted in most world leading opera houses and at Edinburgh, Vienna and Florence Festivals; Has been Principal Conductor and Artistic/Musical Director of companies including Sutherland/ Williamson International Grand Opera Company, 1965, Vancouver Opera, 1974-78, Australian Opera, 1976-86; Conducted Les Huguenots for Australian Opera, 1989 (Joan Sutherland's Farewell), Maria Stuarda at Sydney, 1992; Conducted La Fille du Régiment at Monte Carlo, 1996. Recordings: Opera including: Bellini's Beatrice di Tenda, Norma, I Puritani, La Sonnambula; Delibes' Lakmé; Donizetti's L'Elisir d'Amore, La Fille du Régiment, Lucia di Lammermoor, Lucrezia Borgia, Maria Stuarda; Gounod's Faust; Handel's Alcina and Giulio Cesare; Léhar's Merry Widow; Leoni's L'Oracolo; Massenet's Esclarmonde, Le Roi de Lahore and Thérèse; Meyerbeer's Les Huguenots; Mozart's Don Giovanni; Offenbach's

Les Contes d'Hoffmann; Puccini's Suor Angelica; Rossini's Semiramide; Strauss's Die Fledermaus; Thomas's Hamlet; Verdi's I Masnadieri, Rigoletto, La Traviata and Il Trovatore; Ballet including: Adam's Le Diable à Quatre, Giselle; Auber's Marco Spada; Burgmuller's La Péri; Chopin's Les Sylphides; Delibes' Coppelia, Sylvia; Massenet's Le Carillon, La Cigale; Offenbach's Le Papillon; Rossini-Respighi's La Boutique Fantasque; Strauss's Aschenbrödel; Tchaikovsky's The Nutcracker, Sleeping Beauty, Swan Lake; Others include recital discs with Sutherland, Tebaldi, Tourangeau and Pavarotti and many orchestral and ballet anthologies. Address: c/o Ingpen and Williams, 26 Wadham Road, London SW15 2LR, England.

BOOGAARTS Jan, b. 10 May 1934, Helmond, Netherlands. University Lecturer; Docent; Choir Director; Organist; Organ Specialist. m. Dorine Sniedt, 26 Dec 1964, 2 s, 1 d. Education: Conservatory Tilburg; Royal Conservatory, The Hague (Piano, organ, direction, schools); Institute of Musicology, University Utrecht. Career: Radio recordings for BBC, various Dutch Radio stations, Sud Deutscher Rundfunk, ORTF, France, Culture France, Radio DDR, Radio Warsaw, Poland, Belgian Radio; Television: NOS KRO (Holland Festival), Warsaw Poland; Docent Choir Direction, Royal Conservatory, The Hague; Lecturer at University Utrecht; Visiting Professorships throughout Europe and America. Recordings: 30 including Plainsong, Holy Week, Ordo Missae Instauratus Concilii Vaticani II, Vespers, Compline, Famous Hymni and Sequentiae; Renaissance Music: Madrigals and Chansons with texts Petrach and Ronsard; Works of R White, Josquin, Lassus, Isaak, Senfl and others. Publications: Many articles in period Festschrift and small publications. Contributions to: Many magazines and journals. Honours: Price Radio Warsaw, 1977; Comphaneiro Bandeiro Bandeirante of the Ordem Nacional dos Bandeirantes, Sao Paulo, 1981; Knight, Order of St Gregory, Rome, 1983. Memberships: Consociation Internationalis Musicae Sacrae; Vereniging voor Latijnse Liturgie; Advisor to the Monuments Commission of Gelderland on the Restoration of Historic Organs. Hobby: Gardening. Address: Haveza The, Duiven, Gelderland, The Netherlands.

BOOKSPAN Martin, b. 30 Jul 1926, Boston, MA, USA. Broadcaster; Writer. m. Janet S Sobel, 24 Oct 1954, 1 s, 2 d. Education: Boston Music School, 1936-42; Harvard College, 1947. Career: Host and Commentator: Radio Broadcasts of Boston Symphony Orchestra, 1957-67; Radio Broadcasts of Pittsburgh Symphony, National Symphony and American Symphony Orchestra, 1967-69; Live from Studio 8H telecasts, 1980-; Radio and TV Voice of New York Philharmonic, 1975-; Commentator, Live from Lincoln Center, 1976-; Host and Commentator, Chamber Music Radio Broadcasts Spoleto Festival, USA, 1982-. Publications: New York Times Guide to Recorded Music, 1967; 101 Masterpieces of Music and Their Composers, 1968; Consumer Reports Reviews Classical Records, 1971; Zubin - The Zubin Mehta Story, 1978; André Previn: A Biography, 1981. Contributions to: Contributing editor, Stereo Review Magazine, 1958-74; Record Critic, Consumer Reports, 1962-78; Contributing editor, Ovation Magazine, 1980-86; Classical Music Expert, Prodigy Interactive Computer Service, 1991-. Honours: Medal of Honor, National Arts Club, 1984; Lifetime Achievement Award, Concert Artists Guild, 1986; Honorary Doctor of Music, Mannes College, 1991; Honrary DHL, Suffolk University, 1995. Memberships: The Bohemians, New York Musicians Club, 1958-; Board, The Musicians Foundation, 1982-. Hobbies: History; Politics; Spectator Sports.

BOONE Charles, b. 21 June 1939, Cleveland, Ohio, USA. Composer. Education: Pupil of Karl Schiske, Vienna Academy of Music, 1960-61; Received private instruction from Ernst Krenek and Adolph Weiss, Los Angeles, 1961-62; Studied theory at the University of Southern California, Los Angeles, BM, 1963 and composition at San francisco State College, MA 1968. Career: Chairman, San Francisco Composers' Forum; Coordinator, Mills College Performing Group and Tape Music Center; Composer-in-Residence, Berlin, under the sponsorship of the Deutscher Akademischer Austauchdienst, 1975-77; Writer and Lecturer on contemporary music. Compositions: 3 Motets for Chorus, 1962-65; Oblique Formation for Flute and Piano, 1965; Starfish for Flute, Clarinet, 2 Percussions, 2 Violins and Piano, 1966; A Cool Glow of Radiation for Flute and Tape, 1966; The Edge of the Land for Orchestra, 1968; Not Now for Clarinet, 1969; Zephyrus for Oboe and Piano, 1970; Vermilion for Oboe, 1970; Quartet for Clarinet, Violin, Cello and Piano, 1970; Chinese Texts for Soprano and Orchestra, 1971; First Landscape for Orchestra, 1971; Vocalise for Soprano, 1972; Second Landscape for Chamber Orchestra, 1973, also for Orchestra, 1979; String Piece for String Orchestra, 1978; Streaming for Flute, 1979; Little Flute Pieces, 1979; Springtime for Oboe, 1980; Winter's End for Soprano, Countertenor, Viola da Gamba, and Harpsichord, 1980; Slant for Percussion, 1980; The Watts Tower for 1 Percussion, 1981; Trace for Flute and 10 Instruments, 1981-83; Solar One for Flute and Trumpet, 1985; The Timberline and Other Pieces for Carillon, 1987; Morphosis for Percussion Quartet, 1991. Honours: National Endowment for the Arts Grants, 1968, 1975, 1983; Commissions. Address: 37003 Gravstark Street, Houston, TX 77006, USA.

BOOTH Juliet, b. 1961, London, England. Singer (Soprano). m. William Symington, 1 June 1996. Education: Studied at Bristol University and the Guildhall School of Music. Career: Opera North from 1987, Frasquita (debut role), Ninetta in The Love for Three Oragnes, Xenia in Boris Godunov; Pusette in Manon, Arminda in La Finta Giardiniera, Norina in Don Pasquale and Lauretta; Has also sung Mélisande at Aldeburgh, Virtu and Valletto in Opera London's L'Incoronazione di Poppea and Mozart's Countess for Welsh National Opera; Aix-en-Provence, 1991, as Helena in A Midsummer Night's Dream; Concert appearances at the South Bank and the Barbican, in France, Belgium and Singapore; Handel's Solomon in Berlin and Carmina Burana at the Edinburgh Festival under Neeme Järvi; Television appearances include Dennis O'Neill and Friends on BBC2 season 1990-91 with The Kingdom (Elgar), Haydn's Nelson Mass and Creation, Salieri's Prima la Musica with the City of London Sinfonia; Concert arias with the English Chamber Orchestra; Messiah; Gilda in Rigoletto, Opera North, 1992; Countess in Figaro, Glyndebourne Touring Opera, 1992; Morgana in Alcina, Covent Garden debut, 1992; Musetta and Mimi in La Bohème, Opera North, 1993; Alexina in Le Roi malgré Lui, 1994. Recordings include: L'Incoronazione di Poppea conducted by Richard Hickox (Virgin Classics); Bruckner Mass in F, Hyperion, 1992. Honours: Gold Medal for Singers, Schubert Prize for Lieder and the Ricordi Opera Prize, at the Guildhall School. Current Management: IMG Artists Europe. Address: Media House, 3 Burlington Lane, Chiswick, London W4 2TH, England.

BOOTH Philip, b. 6 May 1942, Washington, DC, USA. Singer (bass). Education: Sang with US Army Chorus, then studied further at the Eastman School of Music, with Julius Huehn, and with Todd Duncan in Washington. Career: Kennedy Center, Washington, 1971, in Ariodante; Many appearances as concert singer; Engagements at the opera houses of San Diego, Houston and San Francisco; Metropolitan Opera from 1973, as Pimen in Boris Godunov, Ramphis, Fasolt and Fafner in Der Ring des Nibelungen, Basilio and Osmin; Sang in the US premiere of Mascagni's Le Maschere, with Westchester Opera, 1989. Address: c/o Metropolitan Opera, Lincoln Center, New York, NY 10023, USA.

BOOTH-JONES Christopher, b. 1943, Somerset, England. Singer (baritone). Education: Royal Academy of Music, London. Career: Toured with Welsh National Opera for All as Mozart's Figaro and Rossini's Bartolo, 1972-73; Welsh National Opera, Figaro in Mozart's Marriage and Bohème; Glyndebourne Festival and Touring Opera; English National Opera from 1982 in Roméo et Juliette, Patience, Cosi fan Tutte, Pagliacci, La Bohème, War and Peace, Osud, Akhnaten and Xerxes; Sang Claudio in a new production of Beatrice and Benedict, 1990; Mr Astley in a revival of The Gambler; English Music Theatre in Tom Jones, La Cenerentola and The Threepenny Opera; Die Zauberflöte; Opera North in Der Freischütz, A Midsummer Night's Dream and Beatrice and Benedict; Kent Opera as Monostatos in Die Zauberflöte; Season 1992 with English National Opera in the premiere of Bakxai by John Buller and as the Music Master in Ariadne auf Naxos; Demetrius in A Midsummer Night's Dream, 1996. Recordings: Julius Caesar and Pacific Overtures; Videos of The Gondoliers, Rusalka, Xerxes and Billy Budd. Address: c/o Music International, 13 Ardilaun Road, Highbury, London N5 2QR, England.

BOOTHBY Richard, b. 1955, England. Viola da Gamba Player; Cellist. Career: Member of the Purcell Quartet, debut concert at St John's Smith Square, London, 1984; Extensive tours and broadcasts in France, Belgium, Netherlands, Germany, Austria, Switzerland, Italy and Spain; Tours of the USA and Japan, 1991-92; British appearances include 4 Purcell concerts at the Wigmore Hall, 1987, later broadcast on Radio 3; Repertoire includes music on the La Folia theme by Vivaldi, Corelli, C P E Bach, Marais, A Scarlatti, Vitali and Geminiani; Instrumental works and songs by Purcell, music by Matthew Locke, John Blow and Fantazias and Airs by William Lawes; 17th century virtuoso Italian music by Marini, Buonamente, Gabrieli, Fontana, Stradella and Lonati; J S Bach and his forerunners - Biber, Scheidt, Schenk, Reinken and Buxtehude; Member of Fretwork, debut concert at the Wigmore Hall, 1986; Appearances in the Renaissance and Baroque repertoire in Sweden, Austria, Belgium, Netherlands, France and Italy; Tour of Soviet Union, Sept 1989, Japan, June 1991; Gave George Benjamin's Upon Silence at the Elizabeth Hall, 1990; Wigmore Hall concerts, 1990-91, with music by Lawes, Purcell, Locke and Byrd; Other repertory includes In nomines and Fantasias by Tallis and Parsons, dance music by Holborne and Dowland (including Lachrimae), London Cries by Gibbons and Dering, Resurrection Story and Last Seven Words by Schütz. Recordings include: With the Purcell Quartet: 6-record set on the La Folia theme; Purcell Sonatas for 2 violins, viola da gamba and continuo; Sonatas by Vivaldi and Corelli; Series of 10 recordings with Fretwork. Address: Wigmore Hall (Contracts), Wigmore St, London, W1.

BOOZER Brenda (Lynn), b. 25 Jan 1948, Atlanta, Georgia, USA. Mezzo-soprano. m. Robert Martin Klein, 29 Apr 1973. Education: BA, Florida State University, Tallahassee, 1970; Postgraduate studies, Juilliard School, New York, 1974-77. Career: Chicago Lyric Opera, 1978; Festival of Two Worlds, Spoleto, Italy, 1978, 1979; Greater Miami Opera, 1979; Houston Grand Opera, 1979; Metropolitan Opera, New York, 1979-83, 1985, as Hansel, Meg Page, the Composer (Ariadne auf Naxos), Octavian and Orlofsky; Netherlands Opera, Amsterdam, 1981; Paris Opera, 1982-83; Falstaff, at Covent Garden, 1983; Spoleto Festival, 1989, as Nicklausse in Les Contes d'Hoffmann; Concerts; Television appearances. Honours: Recording of Falstaff with the Los Angeles Philharmonic was nominated for a Grammy Award in 1984. Address: c/o Columbia Artists Management Inc, 165 West 57th Street, New York, NY 10019, USA.

BORDAS Ricard, b. 1965 Barcelona, Spain. Singer (Countertenor). Education: Studied with Charles Brett at the Royal Academy of Music. Career: Proms debut in the St Matthew Passion under Joshua Rifkin, 1994; Carmina Burana at La Scala and the Granada Festival and Bach's Magnificat at the Barbican, London; London Handel Festival as Siroe and in Alexander's Feast; Ottone in Handel's Agrippina for Midsummer Opera and Scarlatti's Mitridate at the Schwetzingen Festival, 1996; Jonathon Miller's staged St Matthew Passion, tour of Dido and Aneas in Mexico and Monteverdi's Poppea with Netherlands Opera; Season 1996-97 as Selino in Cesti's L'Argia at Innsbruck, the Monteverdi Vespers in Ripon Cathedral and Handel's Israel in Egypt at Bristol; Music Director of Camerata Hispanica in London and the Group Vocal Odarum in Barcelona; Guest teacher at major Lopndon colleges. Honours include: Shinn Fellowship, at the RAM.

BORETZ Benjamin (Aaron), b. 3 Oct 1934, New York City, New York, USA. Composer; Music Theorist; Teacher; Writer on Music. Education: Piano and cello study; Training, conducting from Julius Rudel, harpsichord from Erwin Bodky; BA, Brooklyn College, 1954; Manhattan School of Music, New York; MFA, Brandeis University, 1957; Aspen Music School; University of California, Los Angeles; MFA, 1960, PhD, 1970, Princeton University; Composition teachers included Irving Fine, Harold Shapero, Arthur Berger, Darius Milhaud, Lukas Foss, Roger Sessions. Career: Consultant, Writer, Fromm Music Foundation, 1960-70; Founding Co-Editor, 1961-64, Editor, 1964-84, Perspectives of New Music; Music Critic, The National, 1962-70; Teacher, including New York University, 1964-69, Columbia University, 1969-72, Bard College, 1973-; Distinguished Visiting Professor, University of California, Los Angeles, 1991; Visiting Professor, University of California, Santa Barbara, 1991; Invited, Interdisciplinary Conference, Calgary, 1991. Compositions include: Concerto grosso, string orchestra, 1956; Violin concerto, 1956; Divertimento, 5 instruments, 1957; String Quartet, 1958; Group Variations I, orchestra, 1967, II, computer, 1971; Liebeslied, piano, 1974; ...my chart shines high where the blue milk's upset..., piano, 1978; Passage for Roger Sessions, piano, 1979; Language, as a Music, 6 Marginal Pretexts for Composition, speaker, piano, prerecorded tape, 1980; Soliloquy I, piano, 1981; Soundscore works; Scores for Composing series, 1991-93; Camille, video piece, 1997. Recordings include: An Experiment in Reading, 1981; One (exercise) 8 piano solo sound sessions, Open Space 4CDs, 1992; Open Space CD, 1993. Publications include: Edited with Edward T Cone: Perspectives on Schoenberg and Stravinsky, 1968, 2nd edition, 1972; Perspectives on American Composers, 1971; Perspectives on Contemporary Music Theory, 1972; Perspectives on Notation and Performance, 1976; Open Space, 1991. Contributions to: Professional magazines and journals. Address: c/o Music Department, Bard College, Annandale-on Hudson, NY 12504, USA.

BOREYKO Andrey, b. 22 July 1957, Saint Petersburg, Russia. Conductor; Teacher; Composer. m. Julia Wolk, 1 February 1990, 1 daughter. Education: Graduated summa cum laude, Conducting with Elisabeta Kudriavzeva and Alexander Dimitriev, Composition, Rimski-Korsakov Conservatory. Debut: As conductor, aged 20. Career: Founder, Director, Res Facta early music group, Leningrad, 1977; Founder, Director, Barocco Consort, Leningrad, 1984; Conductor, St Petersburg Theatre of Music, 1985-86; Principal Conductor, State Symphony Orchestra of Ulyanovsk, Russia, and Chamber Music Theatre, 1987-89; General Musical Director, Ural Philharmonic Orchestra, Yekaterinenburg, 1990-92; Artistic Director, Chief Conductor of Poznan Philharmonic Orchestra, Poland, 1992-95; International guest performances and concerts with Leningrad Philharmonic, Moscow Symphony, RPHO and RSO of NOS (Netherlands); RTL-Luxemburg, Bergen Symphony Orchestra; Concerts in Tchaikovsky Hall, Moscow Conservatorium, Schauspielhaus, Berlin, Concertgebouw Amsterdam, Big Hall of Leningrad Philharmonic Society; 12 Performances of Stravinsky's Soldier's Tale, Salzburg Festival, 1994; Debut with Deutsches Symphonie-Orchester, Berlin Philharmonie with works by Hermann, Shostakovich and Philip Glass; Conducted Deutsches Symphonie-Orchester with Brahms' Piano Concerto No 1 with Yefim Bronfman, Mussorgsky's Pictures at an Exhibition;

International Interdisciplinary Festival, New York, 1997; Music Summer Gstaad, 1997; Currently, Chief Conductor, Jenaer Philharmonic, Germany, 1998-; Has worked closely with composers such as Pärt, Gorecki and Silvestrov; Work with noted soloists including Gidon Kremer, David Geringas and Leon Fisher; Guest at numerous important festivals including Dresden Music Festival, Flanders Festival and Salzburg Festival; Forthcoming engagements include concert tours with the New Russian Philharmonic and the Russian National Orchestra; Engaged to conduct the Deutsches Symphonie-Orchester, Berlin, 1998; Music Festival Bratislava, October 1998; Tour of USA with Gil Shaham as soloist; Tours of Poland, Germany, Netherlands and France. Recordings: Silvestrov, Monadia, Sinfonie No 4, 1992; Silvestrov, Sinfonie No 5, 1992; A Ginastera, Ballettmusik, Philharmonie Poznan, 1993; Takemitsu, Nostalghia für Violine und Orchester, 1998. Honours: Diplomas and prizes, Grzegorz Fitelberg conductors' competition, Katowice, 1987; 3rd Prize, K Kondrashin Competition, Hilversum, Amsterdam, Netherlands, 1989; 4th Prize, XII Fitelbberg Competition, Poland, 1987. Current Management: Monica Ott, Berliner Konzertagentur, Berlin. Address: ul Uisia Uszatka 10, Poznan, Poland.

BORG Kim, b. 7 Aug 1919, Helsinki, Finland. Professor; Singer (Baritone); Composer. m. Ebon Ringblom, 10 February 1950, 1 son, 1 daughter. Education: MSc, Chemistry, Institute of Technology, Helsinki; Studied Singing Privately in Finland, Sweden, Denmark, Italy, Austria, USA; Musical Theory and Composition in Finland and Sweden. Debut: Helsinki, 1945. Career: Professional Singer, 1949-; Opera and Concerts in Europe, North and South America, Asia, Australia and Africa including longer periods with the Metropolitan Opera (debut 1959 as Mozart's Count); State Opera, Hamburg; Royal Opera, Stockholm; Royal Opera, Copenhagen; National Opera, Helsinki; At Glyndebourne he sang Don Giovanni, 1956, Beethoven's Pizarro, 1959, Tchaikovsky's Gremin, 1968; Other roles included Boris Godunov, Hans Sachs and King Philipp; Guest Appearances in Vienna and Moscow; Professor, The Royal Academy of Music, Denmark, 1972-89. Compositions: East Karelian Songs; Songs from Saimaa; Concerto for trombone; 7 Kivi-Songs; Ironical Songs to Fröding Poems; Diatonic Quintet for Wood Winds; Concerto for double bass and strings; Sinfonietta for strings; Symphony for full orchestra; Symphony No 2, Sinfonia da camera, 1992. Recordings: German, Scandinavian and Russian Songs, Oratorios and Operas. Publications: Suomalainen laulajanaapinen, 1972; Many articles in books about music and singing in several countries; Muistelmia (Memoirs), 1992. Honours: Cross of Liberty Class 4 (Finland); Knight of White Rose Class 1 (Finland); Pro Finlandia-Medaille (Finland); Commander of North Star (Sweden); Knight of Dannebrog, Denmark; Honorary Cross of Arts and Sciences Class 1, Austria; Commander of Finnish Lion; Finnish Cultural Foundations Honorary Prize. Membership: Det danske Sangselskab, Chairman, 1972-82. Current Management: Lies Askonas Ltd, London. Address: Osterbrogade 156, DK2100 Copenhagen, Denmark.

BORG Matti, b. 1956 Copenhagen, Denmark. Composer. Opera Singer (baritone). m. Gitta-Maria Sjoberg, 1 July 1989, 1 son. Education: Theory of Music, University of Copenhagen, 1974-78; Diploma in Composition, 1983, Diploma in Solo Singing, 1987, Royal Conservatory of Denmark. Debut: Copenhagen, 1987. Career: Appeared as soloist in concerts in Scandinavia and on TV and radio; Opera debut in Sweden, Norrlandsoperan; Works performed in Sweden, Norway and Denmark. Compositions: Choral works, chamber music and songs, music for theatre, musicals; Symboise for mixed choir and solo instruments, 1979; Thirteen ways of looking at a blackbird, trio for soprano, flute and piano, 1981; Recollection, string quartet, 1983; Musicals: What are we dreaming of, 1986; Irene and her men, 1991; Fabliau, for female voice and 12 celli, 1995; Poems by Mörike, for mixed choir, 1997. Membership: Danish Composers' Society. Hobby: Painting. Address: Obdams Allé 24, DK 2300 Copenhagen S, Denmark.

BORGIR Tharald, b. 27 Dec 1929, Gjerpen, Norway. Musicologist (Keyboard). m. 5 Sept 1951, 3 sons, 1 daughter. Education: Music Conservatory, Oslo, 1951; MM, Yale University, USA, 1960; PhD, University of California, Berkeley, 1971. Debut: Piano, Oslo, 1957. Career: Teaching, 1967-93, Professor, 1987-, Chair, 1987-92, Oregon State University, Corvallis, USA; Numerous appearances on piano, harpsichord, fortepiano. Publications: The Performance of the Basso Continuo in Italian Baroque Music, 1987, paperback, 1988. Memberships: Greenberg Award Committee, American Musicology Society; College Music Society; Early Music America. Address: Department of Music, Oregon State University, Corvallis, OR 97331, USA.

BORISENKO Vera, b. 16 Jan 1918, Goel, Russia. Singer (mezzo-soprano). Education: Studied in Gomel and at the Minsk Conservatory; Further study in Kiev with Evtushenko and in Moscow and Sverdlovsk. Career: Sang at Sverdlovsk, 1941-45, Kiev, 1945-46, Bolshoi Theatre, Moscow, 1946-65, notably as Lyubava in Sadko, Lyubasha in The Tsar's Bride and Bonny Spring in The Snow Maiden; Other roles included Marfa in Khovanshchina and Carmen; Gave concert performances from the 1960s. Recordings include: The Snow Maiden, Prince Igor, Dargomizhsky's Rusalka, Tchaikovsky's The Enchantress, Rimsky's May Night, Carmen (title role) and Rigoletto (Maddalena). Address: c/o Bolshoi Theatre, Pr Marxa 8/2, 103009 Moscow, Russia, CIS.

BORISOVA Rosa, b. 1960, Moscow, Russia. Cellist. Education: Central Music School, Moscow. Career: Co-Founder, Quartet Veronique, 1989; Concerts in Russia, including Russian Chamber Music Series and the 150th birthday celebrations for Tchaikovsky, 1990; Masterclasses at the Aldeburgh Festival, 1991; Concert tour of Britain in season, 1992-93; Repertoire includes works by Beethoven, Brahms, Tchaikovsky, Bartók, Shostakovich and Schnittke; Resident Quartet, Milwaukee University, USA, 1993-94. Recordings include: Schnittke's 3rd Quartet. Honours include: With the Quartet Veronique: Winner, All-Union String Quartet Competition in St Petersburg, 1990-91; Third Place, 1991 International Shostakovich Competition at St Petersburg; Participated in Evian and London Quartet Competitions, 1994. Current Management: Sonata, Glasgow, Scotland. Address: 11 North Park Street, Glasgow G20 7AA, Scotland.

BORK Hanneke van, b. 1935, Amsterdam, Netherlands. Singer (soprano). Career: Sang in Solothurn-Biel, 1959-60, Innsbruck, 1960-61, and Brunswick, 1961-62; Member of the Basle Opera, 1962-66; Glyndebourne Festival, 1968-69, in Cavalli's L'Ormindo and as Fiordiligi in Così fan tutte; Wexford Festival, 1968, Holland Festival, 1971-72; Sang with Netherlands Opera, 1972-74, and in 1973 appeared as Elsa in Lohengrin at Mainz; Other roles included Mozart's Vitellia and Pamina, Gluck's Euridice, Mélisande, Ellen Orford and Sicle in L'Ormindo. Recordings include: Die Zauberflöte and L'Ormindo; Scarlatti's Stabat Mater. Address: c/o Staatstheater, Gutenplatz 7, 6500 Mainz, Germany.

BORK Robert, b. 1959, Chicago, Illinois, USA. Singer (Baritone). Education: Studied at Wheaton College, Illinois, and at the Cologne Opera Studio. Career: Sang at Cologne from 1987, notably as Hummel in Reimann's Gespenstersonate, as Tarquinius in The Rape of Lucretia, Papageno, Belcore, Escamillo, Tsar Peter (Lortzing) and Schaunard in La Bohème; Guest appearances at Hamburg (Brander in La Damnation de Faust, 1989) and Bonn (Masetto and Paolo in Simon Bocanegra). Address: c/o Oper der Stadt Köln, Offenbachplatz, W-5000 Cologne 1, Germany.

BORKH Inge, b. 26 May 1917, Mannheim, Germany. Soprano. m. Alexander Welitsch. Education: Studied first as an actress in Vienna; Vocal studies with Muratti in Milan, and at the Salzburg Mozarteum. Debut: Lucerne in 1940 as Agathe. Career: Sang in Switzerland until 1952, notably as Magda Sorel in The Consul by Menotti; Bayreuth in 1952 as Freia and Sieglinde; US debut at San Francisco in 1953 as Elektra; Guest appearances in Vienna, Hamburg, Stuttgart, Barcelona, Lisbon and Naples; Florence in 1954 as Eglantine in Euryanthe; Salzburg Festival in 1955 in the premiere of Irische Legende by Egk; La Scala Milan debut in 1955 as Silvana in La Fiamma by Respighi; Cincinnati in 1956 in Britten's Gloriana; Metropolitan Opera in 1958 and 1961 as Salome and Elektra; Covent Garden in 1959 and 1967 as Salome and the Dyer's Wife in Die Frau ohne Schatten; Academy of Music in New York 1968 in the US premiere of Orff's Antigonae; Other roles have included Lady Macbeth by Verdi and Bloch, and Turandot; Resumed career as an actress in 1977 appearing at the Hamburg Schauspielhaus. Recordings: Turandot; Antigonae; Die Frau ohne Schatten; Elektra; Salome; Das Rheingold; Euryanthe.

BORKOWSKI Marian, b. 17 Aug 1934, Pabianice, Poland. Teacher; Composer. Education: MA, Academy of Music, Warsaw, 1959-65; MM, Warsaw University, 1959-66; Postgraduate studies with Nadia Boulanger and Olivier Messiaen, Paris Conservatory; Musicology with Jacques Chailley and Barry S Brook, Paris University; Philosophy with Jean Hyppolite and - Jules Vuillemin, Sorbonne and Collège de France, 1966-68; Master's courses: International Courses of New Music, Darmstadt, 1972, 1974; Accademia Musicale Chigiana, Siena, 1973, 1975, studied with France Donatoni, Diploma with distinction, 1975. Career: Assistant Lecturer and Senior Assistant Lecturer, Department of Composition, 1967-71, Assistant Professor of Composition, 1971-76, Associate Professor, 1976-, Vice-Dean, Faculty of Composition, Conducting and Music Theory, 1975-78, Vice-Rector, 1878-81, 1987-, Artistic Director, Laboratory of New Music, 1985-, Chopin Academy of Music, Warsaw; Concert, radio and television performances; Performances at numerous international festivals. Compositions include: Spectra, 1980; Dynamics, 1981; Mater mea for mixed choir a cappella, to words by Krzysztof K Baczynski, 1982; Apasionate, 1983, Avante, 1984; Concerto, 1985-86; Pax in terra I, 1987, II, 1988. Recordings: Numerous. Contributions to: Numerous critiques in magazines and newspapers. Address: ul Galczynskiego 5 m 17, 00-362 Warsaw, Poland.

BORNEMANN Barbara, b. 8 Mar 1955, Dingelstadt, Germany. Singer (mezzo-soprano). Education: Studied in Weimar and at the Hans Eisler Musikhochschule Berlin, with Hannelore Kuhse. Debut: Halberstadt, 1978, as Olga in Eugene Onegin. Career: Sang at Halberstadt until 1981, at Schwerin, 1981-86; Member of the Berlin Staatsoper from 1986; Further appearances in Dresden, Leipzig, Czechoslovakia, Poland and Japan; Bayreuth Festival, 1990, as Mary in Der fliegende Holländer; Geneviève in Pelléas et Mélisande in Berlin, 1991; Sang Gaea in Strauss's Daphne, concert performance Rome, 1991; Other roles include Mozart's Marcellina, Verdi's Ulrica and Mistress Quickly, Wagner's Magdalene and Fricka; Concert repertoire includes Bach's Christmas Oratorio and St John Passion, the Mozart and Verdi Requiems, Mendelssohn's Elijah and St Paul, Mahler's Kindertotenlieder. Address: c/o Deutsche Staatsoper Berlin, Unter den Linden 7, 1087 Berlin, Germany.

BORODINA Olga, b. 29 July 1963, Minsk, Russia. Singer (mezzo-soprano). Education: Studied in St Petersburg and San Francisco. Career: Tours with the Mariinsky Opera, St Petersburg, to Europe and the USA, including Marfa in Khovanshchina and Konchakovna at the 1991 Edinburgh Festival and in Rome, 1992; Appearances at the Mariinsky Theatre, St Petersburg, in Boris Godunov and War and Peace, both televised in the West, as Carmen and as Lyubasha in Rimsky-Korsakov's A Bride for the Tsar; Merida Festival, Spain, 1991, in Mussorgsky's Salammbo and in the final scene of Carmen, with Placido Domingo; Further engagements at San Francisco, as the Opera Bastille, Paris, and in Bologna as Marina; Covent Garden, 1992-94, as Dalila, Marguerite in La Damnation de Faust and Cenerentola; Concert performances of Damnation de Faust with Valeri Gergiev in St Petersburg; Further engagements in Vienna, Berlin, Edinburgh and San Francisco; Engaged as Marina in Boris Godunov, Salzburg Festival and the Metropolitan, 1997-98. Recordings: Songs by Tchaikovsky; Roméo et Juliette; Il Barbiere di Siviglia; La Cenerentola. Address: c/o Lies Askonas Ltd, 6 Henrietta Street, London WC2, England.

BORONKAY Antal, b. 5 Feb 1948, Budapest, Hungary. Musicologist; Music Critic. m. Eva Verbenyi, 15 June 1974, 2 sons. Education: Conducting and Piano, 1967-69, Diploma in Musicology, 1969-74, Liszt Ferenc Academy of Music, Budapest. Career: Music Critic, Muzsika (Hungarian Musical Monthly), 1976-; Editor, Musical book department, 1974-; Deputy Chief Executive, Editio Musica Budapest, 1987-; Editor, Hungarian Music Quarterly. Publications: Editor: New Liszt Edition, volume I/5, 1983, Hungarian Licence Edition, Brockhaus-Riemann Dictionary of Music, in 3 volumes, 1983-85. Honour: Prize for activities as a music critic, Hungarian Ministry of Culture, 1979. Memberships: Association of Hungarian Musicologists and Music Critics. Hobby: Regatta Sailing (past Hungarian champion). Address: 1114 Budapest, Ulaszlo u 22, Hungary.

BOROWSKA Joanna, b. 1956, Warsaw, Poland. Singer (soprano). Education: Studied in Warsaw, and at the Opera studio of Vienna Staatsoper, 1980-82. Debut: Romilda in Serse and Micaela in Carmen at Warsaw, 1980. Career: Member of Vienna Staatsoper from 1982, notably as Marenka in The Bartered Bride and as Mozart's Fiordiligi, Susanna and Marzelline, Gluck's Iphigénie en Aulide, (1987), Mimi, 1988, and Marguerite in Faust; Further engagements at Klagenfurt (Countess in Figaro), Bregenz (in Zeller's Der Vogelhändler, 1984), Barcelona and Covent Garden, London, Marenka at Bonn, 1991. Recordings include: Emma in Khovanshchina, Vienna Staatsoper, 1989, and Maidservant in Elektra, conducted by Abbado. Address: c/o Oper der Stadt Bonn, Am Boselagerhof 1, 5300 Bonn, Germany.

BORRIS Kaja, b. 8 Jan 1948, Den Haag, Netherlands. Singer (Mezzo-Soprano). Education: Studied in Cologne and at the Opera Studio of the Deutsche Oper Berlin. Career: Member of the Deutsche Oper Berlin from 1973, singing Verdi's Mistress Quickly and Ulrica, Annina in Rosenkavalier, Azucena and Emilia (Othello), Geneviève in Pelléas et Mélisande, 1984, and Marthe in Faust, 1988; Appeared in the premiere of Reimann's Gespenstersonate, 1984; Salzburg Easter Festival, 1982-83, as Mary in Fliegende Holländer; Further engagements at Munich, Hamburg, Vienna and Schwetzingen and in the concert hall; Sang the Sphinx in Enescu's Oedipe at the Deutsche Oper, 1996. Recordings include: Der fliegende Holländer; Feuersnot by Strauss; Die Lustige Witwe; Der Corregidor by Wolf; Schmidt's Notre Dame and Midwife in Zemlinsky's Der Kreidekreis. Address: c/o Deutsche Oper Berlin, Richard Wagnerstrasse 10, 1000 Berlin 10, Germany.

BORROFF Edith, b. 2 Aug 1925, New York City, New York, USA. Musicologist; Composer. Education: Studied at the Oberlin Conservatory and the American Conservatory of Music in Chicago; PhD, University of Michigan, 1958. Career: Teacher at Milwaukee Downer College, 1950-54, Hillsdale College, Michigan, 1958-62, University of Wisconsin, 1962-66, Eastern Michigan

University, 1966-72, and the State University of New York at Binghamton, 1973-92. Compositions include: String Trio, 1943; Clarinet Quintet, 1948; Sonata for cello and piano, 1949; Spring over Brooklyn, musical, 1954; IONS for flute and piano, 1968; The Sun and the Wind, musical fable, 1976; Game Pieces for woodwind quintet, 1980; Concerto for marimba and small orchestra, 1981; The Elements, sonata for violin and cello, 1987; Music for piano and organ; Choral music; Songs. Publications include: Elisabeth Jacquet de la Guerre, 1966; The Music of the Baroque, 1970; Music in Europe and the United States, A History, 1971, 1989; Music in Perspective, 1976; Three American Composers (co-author), 1987. Address: 65 Forest at Duke Drive, Durham, NC 27705, USA.

BORST Danielle, b. 27 Jan 1946, Geneva, Switzerland. Singer (soprano). m. Philippe Huttenlocher. Education: Studied at Geneva Conservatoire and with Juliette Bisse and Philippe Huttenlocher. Career: Former member of the Ensemble Vocale de Lausanne, under Michel Corboz; Opera appearances in Geneva, Lausanne, Biel-Solothurn, Aix-en-Provence, Montpellier and Vienna (Staatsoper); Paris Opera, 1988, as Eurydice in Orphée aux Enfers; Mezières, 1988, as Gluck's Euridice; Sang Urbain in Les Huguenots at Montpellier, 1990; Hero in Béatrice et Bénédict at Toulouse, Pamina at Monte Carlo and Vitellia in Gluck's La Clemenza di Tito at Lausanne, 1991; Other roles include Mozart's Despina, Susanna, Sandrina and Illia, Gounod's Juliette, Dalinda (Ariodante), Rameau's Aricie, Micaela and Aennchen in Der Freischütz; Sang Mitrena in Vivaldi's Montezuma (pasticcio) at Monte Carlo, 1992; Gounod's Mireille at Lausanne, 1994; Sang Rosalinde at Lyons, 1995-96; Concerts include: Haydn's Schöpfung and Jahreszeiten, Berlioz L'Enfant du Christ, Honegger's Roi David, Passions and Oratorios by Bach, works by Monteverdi, Pergolesi, Handel and Mahler. Recordings include: Fauré's Pénélope, Armide by Lully, Monteverdi's Orfeo, Dido and Aeneas; Iphigénie en Tauride; Title role in L'Incoronazione de Poppea, conducted by René Jacobs. Address: c/o Opera de Lausanne, PO Box 3972, CH-1002 Lausanne, Switzerland.

BORST Martina, b. 13 Jan 1957, Aachen, Germany. Singer, (Mezzo-Soprano). Education: Studied with Elsa Cavelti in Frankfurt and with Carla Castellani in Milan. Career: Sang at the National Theater Mannheim, from 1981, notably as Annius in La Clemenza di Tito, Cherubino, Dorabella, Rosina, Cenerentola, Orpheus and the Composer in Ariadne auf Naxos; Ludwigsburg Festival, 1982, 1984 as Annius and as Juno in Semele; Vienna Volksoper; 1987, as Dorabella; Bregenz Festival, 1988 as Nicklausse in Les Contes d'Hoffmann; Liège and Nantes, 1989; As Bersi in Andrea Chenier; Sang Octavian at Hanover, 1990; Schwetzingen Festival, 1995 as Timante in Demofoonte by Jommelli; Many concert hall appearances, including Mahler's Kindertotenlieder. Recordings: Così fan tutte, Harmonia Mundi.

BÖRTZ Daniel, b. 8 Aug 1943, Osby, Sweden. Composer. Education: Studied with Hilding Rosenberg, with Blomdahl and Lidholm at the Stockholm Music High School; Electronic Music, University of Utrecht. Debut: Voces for orchestra, Concert Hall, Stockholm, 1968. Career: Freelance Composer, 1968-; Opera Backanterna performed at the Royal Opera, Stockholm in production by Ingmar Bergman, 1991. Compositions include: 3 string quartets, 1966, 1971, 1987; 11 symphonies, 1973-94; Concerto Grosso No 2 for wind band, 1981; Violin Concerto, 1985; Oboe Concerto, 1986; Parodos for orchestra, 1987; Intermezzo for orchestra, 1989-90; Backanterna opera after Euripides, 1991; Songs about Death, for soprano and orchestra. 1992-94; Ballad for alto guitar, 1992-94; Strindberg Suite for orchestra, 1993-94; Variations and Intermezzi for strings, 1994; Sonata for piano, 1994; Songs and danses, trumpet concerto, 1994-95; Songs and Shadows, Violin concerto no 2, 1995-96; Marie Antoinette, opera, 1996-97. Recordings include: Parodos Symphonies Nos 1 and 7, Strindberg Suite with Stockholm Royal Philharmonic Orchestra and Gennady Rozhdestvensky; Symphony No 6, chamber and choir works, with Stockholm Royal Philharmonic Orchestra, Hugh Wolff, Eric Ericson chamber choir; The Bacchae opera; Oboe Concerto. Honours: Christ Johnson Music Prize, Stockholm, 1987; International Rostrum of Composers, Paris, 1989. Membership: Royal Swedish Academy of Music, 1989-. Address: c/o Carl Gehrmans, Box 6005, S-10231 Stockholm, Sweden.

BORUP-JORGENSEN Alex, b. 22 Nov 1924, Hjorring, Denmark. Composer. Education: Studied Piano with Rachlew and Orchestration with Schierbeck and Jersild, Royal Conservatory, Copenhagen, 1946-51; Darmstadt, 1959, 1962. Career: Piano Teacher, Else Printz Music School, Copenhagen, 1950-64, then privately. Compositions: Partita viola, 1954; Improvisations quartet, 1955; Music for percussion and Viola, 1956; Duino Elegies by Rilke for mezzo, flute, violencello, 1956; Mikrooranglsma quarter, 1956; Sommasvit, string orchestra, 1957; Several songs with piano or other instruments, 1957-60; Sonatina, 2 violin, 1958; Winter Pieces, piano, 1961; Cantata, Rilke Herbsttag, alto, 7 instruments, 1963; Many songs for mezzo and piano, also for several voices, mostly Rilke and Th. Storm; Schlusztuck, Rilke, choir, 5 instruments, 1964; 5 String Quartets, 1950-65; Nordic Summer pastoral small orchestra, 1964; Torso quartet and tape, 1965; Wintereleige, Holderlin, 3 voices, 9 instruments; Marin Orchestra, 1970; Mirrors; Soprano; Marimba; Guitar, 1974; Works for speaking choir, 1971-72; Tagebuch im Winter, flute, quartet, 1974; Praembula, guitar, 1976; Morceaux, guitar, 1974; Deja vu, concerto for guitar and string orchestra, 1983; Coast of sirens, 7 instruments and multivoice, tape, 1985; Thalatta, Piano, 1988; Several works for recorder instruments, solo or with harpsichord. Address: Fredsholmvej 11, DK 3460 Birkerod, Denmark.

BOSABALIAN Luisa, b. 24 Mar 1936, Marseilles, France. Singer (Soprano). Education: Studied in Beirut, Milan, with Vittorio Ruffo. Debut: Théâtre de la Monnaie Brussels as Micaela, 1964. Career: Sang at Brussels as Mini, Donna Anna, Donna Elvira, Desdemona and Giulietta and Antonia in Les Contes d'Hoffmann; Concert appearances at Edinburgh and the Holland Festival, conducted by Giulini. Metropolitan Opera, 1966, as Jenufa; Guest appearances in London, Dusseldorf, Frankfurt, Rome, Moscow, Oslo, Milan and Vienna; Strasbourg 1974, in Les Indes Galantes by Rameau; Concert appearances in contemporary works; Music by Bach; Gave Lieder recital in Stuttgart, 1988; Concerts for Armenian relief at Munich, 1988-89; Sang at the Hamburg Staatsoper, 1965-73.

BOSCHKOVA Nelly, b. 1954, Bulgaria. Singer (Mezzo-Soprano). Education: Studied in Sofia and with Ghena Dimitrova and Nicolai Ghiaurov. Career: Sang at the Sofia Opera from 1976, notably as Cherubino, Siebel, Olga, Marina, and Feodor in Boris Godunov; Komische Oper Berlin from 1981, as Baba the Turk and Monteverdi's Ottavia; Bremen Opera, 1984-90, as Santuzza, Rosina, Amneris, Ortrud and Bellini's Romeo; Guest appearance at Zurich (Azucena, 1991), and the Vienna Staatsoper (Marfa in Khovanshchina, 1992). Address: c/o Bremen Theater, Pf 101046, W-2800 Bremen, Germany.

BÖSE Hans-Jurgen von, b. 24 Dec 1953, Munich, Germany. Composer. Education: Hoch Conservatory, Frankfurt am Main, 1969-72; Pupil in composition of Hans Ulrich Engelmann; In piano of Klaus Billing, Hochschule für Musik, Frankfurt am Main, 1972-75; Opera 63; Dream Palace performed at Munich, 1990; Slaughterhouse Five premiered at the 1996 Munich Festival; Compositions: Stage; Blutbund, chamber opera, 1974; Das Diplom, chamber opera, 1975; Die Nacht aus Blei, kinetic action, 1980-81; Die Leiden des jungen Werthers, lyrical scenes, 1986; 63: Dream Place, 1990; Slaughterhouse Five, 1995; Orchestra: Morphogenesis, 1975; Symphony No 1, 1976; Musik fur ein Haus voll Zeit, 1977; 3 Songs for Tenor and Chamber Orchestra, 1977; Travesties in a Sad Landscape for Chamber Orchestra, 1978; Symphonic Fragment for Tenor, Baritone, Bass, Chorus; Orchestra, 1980; Variations for 15 strings, 1980; Idyllen, 1983; Sappho-Gesänge for Mezzo-Soprano and Chamber Orchestra, 1982-83; Labyrinth I, 1987; Oboe Concerto, 1986-87; 5 Children's Rhymes for Alto and 5 Instrumentalists, 1974; Threnos-Hommage à Bernd Alois Zimmermann for Viola and Cello, 1975; Solo Violin Sonata, 1977; Variations for Cello, 1978-79; Vom Wege abkommen for viola, 1982; Guarda el Canto for Soprano & String Quartet, 1982; Studie I for Violin and Piano, 1986; Lorca-Gesänge for Baritone and 10 instruments, 1986; Wind Sextet, 1986. Address: c/o GEMA, Herzog-Wilhelm Strasse 38, 8000 Munich 2, Germany.

BOSQUET Thierry, b. 1932, Belgium. Stage and Costume Designer. Education: National School of Architecture, Art and Design, Brussels. Career: From 1959 sets and costumes for more than 70 operas and ballets at the Theatre Royale de la Monnaie, Brussels; Many other stagings in France, Italy, Switzerland, Germany, Canada, South America and Australia; Rigoletto and Otello in Liège, La Belle Hélène for Canadian Opera; New York City Opera with Werther, Die Zauberflöte and La Traviata; San Francisco Opera from 1980, with costumes for Aida, Carmen, Fledermaus and Capriccio; Realizations of original designs and costumes for Ruslan and Lyudmilla (1995), Der Rosenkavalier (original Alfred Roller designs) and Tosca (San Francisco premiere, 1932); Pelléas et Mélisande at San Francisco, 1997. Address: c/o San Francisco Opera, War Memorial House, Van Ness Avenue, San Francisco, CA 94102, USA.

BOSSIN Jeffery Alan, b. 1 July 1950, Santa Monica, CA, USA. Education: BA, Music, University of California at Riverside, 1972; Reid School of Music, University of Edinburgh, 1971-72; Masters in Musicology, Technische Universität, Berlin, 1984. Debut: Carillonneur Riverside, California, 1971. Career: Carillon concerts in Europe and the US, 1971-97, including at international festivals in Barcelona, Springfield, Illinois, Klaipeda, Lithuania, performance of electronic music compositions at the Hochschule der künste and Akademie der Künste Berlin 1977 and Bourges Electronic Music Festival in France, 1978; Carillon concerts in Berlin for the World Bank meeting, 1988; Official ceremony for reunification of Germany in Berlin, 1990; Christos Wrapped Reichstag, 1995, weekly concerts from the beginning of May until end of September in Berlin, 1988-97; Consultant of Carillon at construction of Carillon at Congresshall in Berlin, 1987. Publications: Die Carillons von Berlin und Potsdam, 1991; Masters Thesis: Social Function and Musical Technique in the Early Piano Sonatas of Muzio Clementi, 1983. Contributions: Articles in Jahrbuch der Glockenkunde and Glocken in Geschichte und Gegenwart lectures in Europe and USA. Honour: Positions: Carillonneur for city of Berlin, since 1987. Memberships: Founding Member, Russian Association of Companological Arts; Delegate of Germany in European carillon organization Eurocarillon. Address: Handjerystr 37, 12159 Berlin, Germany.

BOSTOCK (Nigel) Douglas, b. 11 June 1955, Northwich, Cheshire, England. Conductor. Education: Clarinet, Northern School of Music; BMus Honours, MMus, University of Sheffield; Private pupil of Sir Adrian Boult, London; Conducting masterclass of Professor Dr Francis Travis and Higher Artistic Diploma, Freiburg Hochschule für Musik, Germany. Career: Musikdirektor, Konstanz, Germany, 1979-93; Regular Guest Conductor, Southwest German Philharmonic; Principal Conductor and Music Director, Karlovy Vary Symphony Orchestra, Czech Republic, 1991-; Principal Guest Conductor, Chamber Philharmonic of Bohemia, 19910; Guest conducting appearances with major orchestras throughout Europe, America and Japan; Conducted for TV, Radio and CDs; Guest artist at many international music festivals. Recordings: Many CDs with music by Dvorak, Fibich, Smetana, Novak, Mozart, Brahms, Bellini, other composers; Series of rare French music, 3 volumes; The British Symphony with Munich Symphony Orchestra; CDs in Czech Republic, UK with Royal Philharmonic, Germany, Japan, baroque music in Italy, Germany, Japan. Publication: Hans Pfitzner - the last Romantic, 1979. Honours: Fontainbleau Medal, France, 1988; Martinu Medal Policka, 1990; Medal, Martinu Foundation, Prague, 1995. Memberships: Americal Symphony Orchestra League; Hans Pfitzner Gesellschaft; Brahms Gesellschaft; Martinu Society; Dvorak Society, UK. Hobbies: Cooking; Nature. Current Management: Various including Manygate, UK. Address: Seestrasse 68, D-78479 Reichenau, Germany.

BOSTRIDGE Ian, b. 1965, England. Singer (Tenor). Education: Studied at Cambridge and Oxford (doctorate 1990). Career: Wigmore Hall debut, 1993, Winterreise at the Purcell Room and Aldeburgh Festival concert, 1994; Further concerts include the Bach B minor Mass in Ottawa under Pinnock, Handel's Resurrezione in Berlin, Britten's Serenade at the Schleswig-Holstein Festival, Schumann's Scenes from Faust with the LPO and Hylas in Les Troyens under Colin Davis with the LSO; Opera debut, London, 1994, as Britten's Lysander; Covent Garden 1995 in Salome, ENO 1996 as Tamino and Lysander; Season 1995 with War Requiem in London and Hamburg, Britten's Spring Symphony at Aldeburgh, the St Matthew Passion under Charles Mackerras and Bach's Magnificat at the London Proms; Sang Schubert's Schöne Müllerin in bicentenary concert at the Wigmore Hall, 1997. Recordings include: Rossini Messa di Milano, War Requiem and St Matthew Passion under Frans Bruggen (Philips); Purcell's Music for Queen Mary (Hyperion); Britten Holy Sonnets of John Donne. Address: Lies Askonas Ltd, 6 Henrietta Street, London WC2E 8LA, England.

BOTES Christine, b. 1964, England. Mezzo Soprano Singer. Education: Studied with Frederic Cox at the Royal Northern College of Music and at the National Opera Studio. Career: Sang with Glyndebourne Chorus then with the RSC in The Tempest; Appearances with Scottish Opera as Iolanthe and Second Lady in The Magic Flute; Opera Factory as Diana in La Calisto, Thea in Knot Garden and Dorabella, also televised; Mozart roles include Cherubino at Sadler's Wells, Donna Elvira in the Netherlands and Belgium; With English National Opera has sung as Hansel on tour to Russia in 1990 and as the Fox in The Cunning Little Vixen, 1991; For ENO sang Cherubino in Figaro's Wedding, 1991; Sang in the Mikado, 1991, Proserpina in Orfeo, 1992, Minerva in Return of Ulysses in 1992; Concert engagements with the Royal Philharmonic in Elgar's Sea Pictures and the London Sinfonietta, City of London Sinfonia and The Hanover Band; Bach's B Minor Mass in France and Poland and Messiah with the Orchestre de Liège and the City of Birmingham Choir; Concerts in Cologne and Lisbon with the Ensemble Modern of Frankfurt; Sang Herodias in Stradella's San Giovanni Battista, Batignano, 1996. Current Management: Robert Gilder and Co, 59-65 Upper Ground, London, SE1 9PQ, England. Address: Magenta Music International, 4 Highgate High Street, London, N6 5JL, England.

BOTHA Johan, b. 1965, Rustenberg, South Afirca. Singer (Tenor). Education: Studied in Pretoria. Career: Sang at Pretoria from 1988, in the premiere of Hofmeyer's The Fall of the House of Usher and other works; Europe from 1990 (concerts in Warsaw and Moscow); Kaiserslautern, 1991, as Gustavus in Un Ballo in Maschera, Dortmund Opera as the Prince in The Love for Three Oranges; Other roles include Max (Der Freischütz), Florestan (at Bonn), Pinkerton, Cassio (Otello), Pedro in Tiefland and Theo in Rautavaara's Vincent; Royal Opera, Covent Garden, 1995 as Rodolfo; Sang Turiddu at Bonn, 1996. Address: c/o Stadtische Buhnen, Kuhstrasse 12, W-4600 Dortmund, Germany.

BOTNEN Geir, b. 27 Feb 1959, Norheimsund, Norway. Pianist. m. Heidi, 3 sons, 1 daughter. Education: Private Lessons with György Kurtag; Conservatory of Music, Bergen, with Jiri Hlinka, 1978-83. Debut: Oslo, 1988; London, 1993; Belgium, 1996. Career: Bergen Philharmonic, Norway, 1997; Bergen International Festival of Music, Tours in Europe, USA and Far East. Recordings: E Grieg, Norwegian Folktunes & Peasant Dances, 1993; 20th Century Flute Music with Ingela Ien, 1994; G Tveitt, Solo Piano Pieces, 1995; G Tveitt, Fifty Folktunes from Hardanger, double CD, 1996; Grieg in Hardanger, 1996. Publication: High Performance Review, 1995; Fanfare, 1996. Address: Furuflaten 17, 5600 Norheimsund, Norway.

BOTT Catherine, b. 11 Sept 1952, Leamington Spa, England. Singer (Soprano). Career: Many appearances with leading early music ensembles, notably the New London Consort; Appearances at major concert halls in Europe, Latin America and USSR; British engagements include Early Music Network Tours; Festival concerts at Bath, Edinburgh and City of London; Mediaeval Christmas Extravaganza on the South Bank and concerts for the South Bank's 21st anniversary; Season 1988-89 with visits to Israel, Spain, Holland and Italy; French debut as Salome in Stradella's San Giovanni Battista at Versailles; Solo recitals at Flanders and Utrecht Festivals, Sadler's Wells Theatre and the Kings Singers Summer Festival at the Barbican; Promenade Concert, London, 1990, with The Bonfire of the Vanities (Medici Wedding Celebration of 1539); Season 1991 with concerts and recordings in France, recitals in Holland and Belgium and tour of Japan; Sang Mozart's Zaide at Queen Elizabeth Hall, 1991; Purcell's Dido at the Barbican, 1992; Sang in Michael Nyman concert on South Bank, 1996; Oswald von Wolkenstein concert, 1997. Recordings include: Monteverdi Vespers and Orfeo; Virtuoso Italian vocal music: de Rore, Rasi, Cavalieri, Luzzaschi, G and F Caccini, Gagliano, Marini, Rossi, Frescobaldi, Monteverdi, Barnardi and Carissimi (Il Lamento di Maria Stuarda); Cantigas de Amigo by Martin Codax and Cantigas di Santa Maria, anon (all with the New London Consort); Vaughan Williams Sinfonia Antartica, with the London Symphony Orchestra; English canzonets and Scotch songs, with Melvyn Tan; English restoration theatre music: mad songs by Purcell and by Eccles and Weldon; Walton film music, with the Academy of St Martin-in-the-Fields. Address: c/o Hazard Chase Ltd, Richmond House, 16-20 Regent Street, Cambridge CB2 1DB, England.

BOTTI Patrick, b. 27 July 1954, Marseilles, France. Conductor. m. Catherine Fuller, 2 daughters. Education: Conservatoire National Supérieur de Musique, Paris; École Normale de Musique, Paris; Université de Paris, Sorbonne, Paris; New England Conservatory of Music, Boston, USA; Boston University, Boston; Conservatoire National de Marseille; Université de Droit et Sciences Politiques, Aix en Provence. Debut: As a pianist, Palais des Festivals, Cannes, France, 1967; As a conductor, Marseilles, 1974. Career: Conducted in France, England, Italy, Canada, United States; Music Director, Concilium Musicum of Paris, 1977-82; Artistic Advisor and Principal Guest Conductor, Concilium Museum of Paris, 1982-; Music Director, Conductor, French Symphony of Boston, since season 1984-85; Artistic Director, Conductor, New Hampshire Philharmonic Orchestra, since season 1993-94; Principal Guest Conductor, Central Massachusetts Symphony Orchestra, since season 1993-94; As Guest Conductor appearances included Colorado Springs Symphony Orchestra, Boston Philharmonic, New Hampshire Philharmonic Orchestra, New England Conservatory Symphony Orchestra, Paris Conservatory Orchestra, Marseilles Conservatory Orchestras; Sorrento Orchestra; Saskatoon Symphony Orchestra (Canada); Concilium Musicum of Paris; Boston Youth Symphony Orchestras; New England Chamber Orchestra; Jamaica Plain Symphony; Other orchestras: Royal College of Music, London, Greater Boston Youth Symphony Orchestra, Tanglewood Orchestra, Echo du Futur Symphony (Marseilles). Recordings: Producer of major recordings, Paris, Boston, 1989-; Two CD recordings of French music, conducting the French Symphony at Boston, to be released, 1998-99. Honours: Analysis Prize, Paris Conservatory, 1980; Fulbright Scholarships to study at New England Conservatory and at Boston University, 1982. Membership: American Symphony Orchestra League. Hobbies: Computers; Aeroplanes; Sailing. Address: Conductor's Cooperative Management, 1208 Massachusetts Avenue, Suite #8, Cambridge, MA 02139, USA.

BOTTOMLEY Sally Ann, b. 18 May 1959, Yorkshire, England. Concert Pianist; Educator. Education: Chetham's School of Music; Royal Northern College of Music, PPRNCM. Debut: Concert debut with City of Birmingham Symphony, 1980; London recital debut, Purcell Room, 1981. Career: Appearances with Royal Philharmonic, London Symphony, City of Birmingham, Hallé, RLPO, Scottish National; Conductors include, Skrowaczewski, Järvi, Groves, Downes, Litton, Tortelier; Two Piano Partnerships with John Gough; Lecturer, Huddersfield University and Chethams School of Music; Several TV appearances and advertisements and radio performances. Address: Dale Cottage, Sheardale Park, Honley, Huddersfield HD7 2NH, Yorkshire, England.

BOTTONE Bonaventura, b. 19 Sept 1950, England. Singer (Tenor). Education: Studied at the Royal Academy of Music with Bruce Boyce. Debut: Covent Garden, as Italian Singer in Der Rosenkavalier, conducted by Haitink; Returned in Capriccio by Strauss; US debut as Pedrillo in Die Entführung, at Houston Opera. Career: Has sung with English National Opera as David in Die Meistersinger, the Duke of Mantua, Beppe, Nanki Poo in Jonathan Miller's production of The Mikado, Sam Kaplan in Weill's Street Scene, Truffaldino in the Love for Three Oranges, 1989 and Alfredo in La Traviata, 1990; Scottish Opera, 1989, as Governor General in Candide and Loge in Das Rheingold; Appearances at the Wexford and Batignano Festivals; Sang the Italian Tenor in Capriccio at Glyndebourne, 1990; Season 1992, as Verdi's Fenton at the London Coliseum and Conte di Libenskof in Il Viaggio a Reims at Covent Garden; Sang the Berlioz Faust with ENO, 1997; Frequent broadcaster in a wide range of BBC programmes. Recordings: The Mikado; Orpheus in the Underworld. Address: c/o Stafford Law Associates, 6 Barham Road, Weybridge, Surrey KT13 9PR, England.

BOUCHARD Antoine, b. 22 Mar 1932, St Philippe-de-Neri, Quebec Province, Canada. Organist; Professor of Organ. Education: BA, LTh, Laval University, Quebec. Career: Concerts and festivals, Quebec City, Montreal, Paris; Concerts, Canada and USA; Radio performances, CBC and ORTF; Series of concerts on 20 European Historical Organs, Radio Canada; Organ Professor and Director, 1977-80, School of Music, Laval University, Quebec. Compositions: Prelude and In Paradisum, for organ, in Le Tombeau de Henri Gagnon. Recordings: Music by Dandrieu and Buxtehude; Noels français du 18e Siècle; Bach and Pachelbel; Anthologie de l'organiste, volumes I, II, III; The Early Pipe Organs of Quebec, volumes II, IV, VII; On CD, The 18 Chorals, by J S Bach; Oeuvres de Gaston Litaize, on CD; L'Orgue Français classique en Nouvelle-France; 7 historical organs of North-western Germany; Nicolas Lebegue. Publication: L'Organiste, 3 volumes, 1982. Contributions to: The Organ Yearbook, Netherlands; L'Orgue, Paris; Musicanada; L'Encyclopédie de la musique au Canada. Bulletin des Amis de l'Orgue. Address: 908 rue du Belvédère, St-Nicolas-Est, Quebec G7A 3V3, Canada.

BOUCHER (Charles) Gene, b. 6 Dec 1933, Tagbilaren, Bohol, Philippines. Singer (Baritone). Education: BA, Westminster College, Fulton, MO, 1955; Diplome de Chant, Conservatoire de Lille, 1956. Debut: Teatro Nuovo, Milan, Italy, 1958. Career: Metropolitan Opera, NY, USA, 1965-85; Guest artist with American opera companies; Concerts given. Honour: Winner, American Opera Auditions, 1958. Membership: President, 1977-82, National Executive Secretary, 1983-88, American Guild of Musical Artists. Address: 239 West 76th Street, New York, NY 10023, USA.

BOUCOURECHLIEV André, b. 28 July 1925, Sofia, Bulgaria. Composer; Writer. Education: Sofia State Academy, 1946-49; Ecole Normale de Musique, Paris, 1949-51; Saarbrucken Conservatory, 1955, piano with Walter Gieseking. Career: French citizen from 1956, resident in Paris from 1949; Research at radio stations in Milan, Paris; Teacher of piano at Ecole Normale de Musique, 1954-60; Music critic in France from 1957. Compositions: Piano Sonata, 1959; Texte I & II for tape, 1959, 1960; Archipel Series: No 1 for 2 pianos, 2 percussionists, 1967; No 2 for string quartet, 1969; No 3 for piano & 6 percussionists, 1969; No 4 for piano, 1970; No 5 for 6 instruments, 1970; Ombres, Hommage a Beethoven for string orchestra, 1970; Faces for orchestra, 1972; Threne, for tape & 2 speakers, Piano concerto, 1975; Grodek for soprano & 3 percussion groups; Orion series, 1979-83; Lit de Neige, 1984. Publications: Biography of Schumann, 1957; Pictorial Biography of Chopin, 1962; 2 Monographs on Beethoven, 1963; Revised Edition of Stravinsky, 1987. Address: c/o SACEM,225 avenue Charles de Gaulle, 92521 Neuilly sur Seine Cedex, France.

BOUE Georgi, b. 16 Oct 1918, Toulouse, France. Singer (Soprano). m. Roger Bourdin, dec 1973. Education: Studied at the Toulouse Conservatory, in Paris with Henri Busser and Reynaldo Hahn. Debut: Toulouse, 1935, as Urbain in Les Huguenots. Debut: Mireille in the opera by Gounod. Career: Sang at Toulouse as Siebel in Faust, Hilda in Reyer's Sigurd, Mathilde in Guillaume Tell and Bizet's Micaela; Paris Opéra-Comique from 1938; Paris Opéra from 1942, notably in Les Indes Galantes by Rameau, 1953; Guest appearances in Arles, Brussels, Nice, Barcelona, Germany, Mexico City and Italy; La Scala Milan as Debussy's Mélisande; Tour of Russia as Tatiana in Eugene Onegin and Madama Butterfly; Théâtre de la Monniae Brussels, 1960, in La Belle Hélène; Die Lustige Witwe; Appeared as Malibran in the film by Sacha Guitry. Recordings: Thais, Urania; Faust conducted by Beecham; Les Contes d'Hoffmann; L'Aiglon.

BOUGHTON William (Paul), b. 18 Dec 1948, Birmingham, England. Conductor. m. Susan Ann Cullis, 8 Aug 1981. Education: Guildhall School of Music, London; Prague Academy; AGSM; Honorary Associate, Janacek Academy. Career: Founder, Director, English String Orchestra; Principal Conductor, English Symphony Orchestra and Jyvaskyla Sinfonia, Finland, 1986-93; Artistic Director, Malvern Festival, 1983-88; Guest conducting with Philharmonia, Royal Philharmonic Orchestra, London Philharmonic Orchestra and London Symphony Orchestra. Recordings: Numerous on Nimbus label including 1st recordings of Finzi's Love's Labours Lost and Parry's 1st Symphony and Death to Life. Honours: Jyvaskyla City Award; Hon DLitt. Memberships: Royal Overseas League. Hobbies: Reading; Walking; Skiing; Sailing. Current Management: Anglo-Swiss Artists Management Ltd, England. Address: c/o Eleanor Hope, 9 Southwood Hall, Wood Lane, London N6 5UF, England.

BOUKOV Yuri, b. 1 May 1923, Sofia, Bulgaria. (French citizen). Pianist. Education: Studied in Bulgaria. Debut, Sofia, 1938. Career: Studied further at the Paris Conservatoire, where he received first prize, 1946; Many appearances throughout Europe in post-war period, with tour to China, 1956; Often heard in the sonatas of Prokofiev and premiered works by Menotti and Wissmer.

BOULEYN Kathryn, b. 3 May 1947, Maga Vita, Maryland, USA. Singer (Soprano). Education: Studied at Indiana University anmd the Curtis Institute. Debut: San Diego, 1978, as Nannetta in Falstaff. Career: Miami, 1978, as Desdemona; New York City Opera from 1979; Spoleto Festival at Charleston in Haydn's La Vera Costanza, St Louis, 1981, in the US premiere of Fennimore and Gerda by Delius (as Fennimore); European debut, 1981, as Janacek's Fox (The Cunning Little Vixen) with Netherlands Opera; Other appearances as Gutrune at San Francisco (1985), Mozart's Countess at San Diego (1986), Tatiana in Eugene Onegin for Welsh National Opera (1988), Vitellia in La Clemenza di Tito (Scottish Opera), Donna Elvira, Elisabeth de Valois, Mimi, Manon Lescaut, Micaela and Venus in Tannhäuser. Address: c/o New York City Opera, Lincoln Center, Nw York, NY 10023, USA.

BOULEZ Pierre, b. 26 Mar 1925, Montbrison, France. Composer; Conductor. Education: Paris Conservatoire, studied with Messiaen, Vaurabourg-Honegger and Leibowitz. Career: Director of Music to Jean-Louis Barrault Theatre, 1948; Aided by Barrault and Madeleine Renaud Barrault founded the Concerts Marigny which later became the Domaine Musical, Paris; Principal Guest Conductor, Cleveland Symphony Orchestra; Principal Conductor, BBC Symphony Orchestra, 1971-75, with the orchestra gave many performances of music by Bartók, Berg, Messiaen, Debussy, Schoenberg and Stravinsky; Musical Director, New York Philharmonic, 1971-77; Director, Institute de Recherches et de Co-ordination Acoustique/Musique, 1975-91; Conducted the centenary production of Wagner's Ring, Bayreuth, 1976-80; Conducted Pelléas et Mélisande for Welsh National Opera, 1992; 70th birthday concerts in London, Paris and New York, 1995; Inaugurated the BBC Series Sounding the Century, Festival Hall, 1997, Stravinsky's Nightingale and The Rite of Spring. Compositions include: Le Marteau sans Maître (cantata for voice and instruments to text by René Char); Structures (2 pianos), 1952-61; Third Piano Sonata, 1957; Improvisations sur Mallarmé (soprano and chamber ensemble); Poesie pour Pouvoir (orchestra), 1958; Pli selon Pli, 1957-89; Figures-doubles-prismes, 1963-68, Eclat and Eclat Multiples; Domaines, 1968; Explosante/Fixe, 1993. Recordings include: Numerous, videos and professional recordings. Publications: Relevés d'apprenti (essay), 1966; Par volonté et par hasard, 1975; Points de repère; Jalons, 1989; Le pays fertile: Paul Klee, 1989; Correspondence P Boulez/John Cage, 1991. Honours include: Honorary Doctorate, Leeds, Oxford, Cambridge, Bristol and University of Southern California. Address: c/o IRCAM, 1 place Igor-Stravinsky, 75004 Paris, France.

BOULTON Timothy, b. 1960, England. Violist. Education: Studied with Nicholas Roth in London. Career: Academy of St Martin-in-the-Fields; Teacher at GSM, Junior Department; Performances in a portable white geodesic domus on informal locations in Europe and Australia; Public Workshops; Discussion groups; Open Rehearsals in a wide repertoire; Frequent performances in London at the Wigmore Hall, on the South Bank; Throughout the UK; Radio 3; Festival engagements at Bath, Cheltenham, Salisbury, Sheffield and City of London; Tours of South America, Canada, Spain, Italy, Germany, Ireland and Norway; 1991 tours of the Netherlands and New Zealand. Recordings: Piano Quartets by Fauré, Dvorak, Brahms, Mozart and Mendelssohn; Schubert's Trout Quintet and Adagio & Rondo Concertante, with pianist Chi-chi Nwanoku; Works by Martinu, Suk, Kodaly and Dohnanyi for Hyperion & Virgin Classics. Honours: Deutsche Schallplattenpreis, 1986; Gramophone Magazine Award for Best Chamber Music Record of 1986 for Fauré, Piano Quartets. Memberships: Domus from 1985. Address: Christopher Tennant Artists' Management, Unit 2 39 Tadema Road, London, SW10 OPY, England.

BOUMAN Hendrik, b. 29 Sept 1951, Dordrecht, The Netherlands. Harpsichordist; Fortepianist; Conductor; Profess. 1

Son. Education: Teaching certificate, 1977, Harpsichord solo performance diploma, 1978; Sweelinck Conservatorium, Amsterdam. Debut: Conducting, Basilica of Notre Dame, Montreal, Canada, premier of Tu me cherches by Alain Pierard; Mass for orchestra; Several hundred Choristers; International Year of Youth, 1985. Career: Harpsichordist of Musica Antiqua Koln, 1976-83; Extensive Tours throughout Europe; Festivals in Berlin; London; Holland; Flanders; Besancon; Festival de Paris; World Tours of South America, 1980; North America, 1981; Asia, including India and Japan, 1982; Regular radio recordings for all major European stations; Founder; Director; Ensemble Les nations de Montreal, 1986; Professor, University of Laval, Quebec, 1987; University of Concordia, 1985-; Master classes & Lectures, 1979-. Compositions: Several transcripts for harpsichord duo. Recordings: Numerous. Publications: Basso Continuo realisations for Marais; Sonnerie; Maresienne; Mancini; Recorder Concerto; Figured Bass & Harpsichord Improvisation. Honours: Diapason d'Or, 1982, for Giles; Diapasond'Or, 1982 for Monteverdi; Deutscher Schallplattenpreis, 1982; Early Music Award, 1982. Memberships: CAPAC. Hobbies: Yoga; Childcare; Cartoon making; Travelling.

BOUR Ernest, b. 20 Apr 1913, Thionville, France. Conductor. Education: Studied piano, organ and theory at Strasbourg Conservatoire, with Fritz Munch; Further study with Hermann Scherchen, 1933-34. Career: Chorus master at Radio Geneva, Musical Director of the Radio Strasbourg Orchestra, 1935-39; Professor of piano at the Strasbourg Conservatory, 1940-41; Musical director of the Mulhouse orchestra, 1941-47; Director of the Conservatoire there from 1945; Director of the Orchestre Municipal at Strasbourg Opera from 1955; Conductor of the South West German Radio Symphony Orchestra at Baden-Baden, 1964-79; Conductor of the Chamber Orchestra of Netherlands Radio at Hilversum from 1979; Conducted the premieres of works by Andre Jolivet, Cosmogonie, 1947; Jean Rivier, 5th Symphony, 1951; György Ligeti, Apparitions, 1960; Jean Claude Eloy, Etude III, 1962; Aribert Reimman, Monumenta, 1963; Isang Yung, Reak, 1966; Wolfgang Fortner, Immagini, 1970; Dieter Schnebel, Diapason; Kazimierz Serocki, Fantasia Elegiaca, 1972; Brian Ferneyhough, Epicycle, 1974; Sylvano Bussotti, Opus Cygne, 1979; Wolfgang Rihm, Andere Schatten, 1985; Iannis Xenakis, Alax, 1985; Conducted the French premieres of Hindemith's Mathis der Maler, Duke Bluebeard's Castle and The Rake's Progress. Recordings: L'Enfant et les Sortilèges; Stravinsky's Violin Concerto, with Arthur Grumiaux; Cello Concertos by Hindemith and B A Zimmermann with Siegfried Palm; Ligeti's Atmosphères, Lontano and Ramifications; Lutoslawski's 2nd Symphony; Saint-Saëns's 3rd Symphony, Telefunken. Address: c/o Radio Kamerorkest, PO Box 10, 1200 JB, Hilversum, Holland.

BOURGEOIS Derek, b. 16 Oct 1941, Kingston on Thames, England. Director of Music. m. Jean Berry, 21 Aug 1965. Education: MA Cantab, 1962, DMus, Cantab, 1971, Magdalene College, Cambridge; Royal College of Music, 1963-65. Career: Lecturer in Music, Bristol University, 1971-84; Director of Music, National Youth Orchestra of Great Britain, 1984-93; Founder, National Youth Chamber Orchestra of Great Britain, 1989-93; Director of Music, St Paul's Girls' School, London, 1994-. Compositions include: 150 works including: Six Symphonies; Concertos for double bass, clarinet, trombone, tuba, organ, Euphonium, 3 trombones, percussion; 3 Concertos for Brass Band; 2 Symphonies for Wind Orchestra; Symphonic Fantasy the Astronauts; 6 works for chorus and orchestra; One Opera. Memberships: Composers Guild of Great Britain, Chairman, 1980-83; APC; Royal Society of Musicians. Hobbies: Fine Wine; Computing; Golf. Address: The Vines, Hewelsfield, Lydney, Glos GL15 6XE, England.

BOURGUE Daniel, b. 12 Jan 1937, Avignon, France. Horn Player. Education: Avignon Conservatoire & Paris Convertoire. Career: Concerts with the Musica wind quintet, 1961-67; Horn Soloist, Garde Republicaine Orchestra, 1963; At Concerts Pasadeloup, 1964; Opéra-Comique, 1967; Paris Opéra from 1969; The Ensemble Intercontemporain; Ensemble Orchestral de Paris; Has premired works by Messiaen, (Appel Interstellaire), Francaix (Divertimento); Xenakis (Anaktoria, 1965) and Delerue, Concerto; Professor of Chamber Music at the Champigny Conservatoire; Teacher in Belgium; Italy; USA. Recordings: Music by Dukas, Charbrier, Corrette, Breval, d'Indy and Gounod. Memberships: Paris Octet, 1965-82. Address: c/o Ensemble Orchestral de Paris, Salle Pleyle, 252 Rue du Faoubourg St, Honore, F-75008, Paris, France.

BOURGUE Maurice, b. 6 Nov 1939, Avignon, France. Oboist. Conductor. Education: Studied at the Paris Conservatoire. Career: Principal of the Basle Orchestra, 1964-67, Orchestre de Paris 1967-79; Solo appearances with the Israel CO, I Solisti Veneti, I Musici, Lucerne Festival Strings and all the major French orchestras; UK debut at the Wigmore Hall, 1979; Engagements with the ECO, Chamber Orchestra of Europe, Royal Philharmonic, and the LSO under Abbado; Premieres have included Chemins IV by Berio (1974), Les Citations by Dutilleux (1991) and Messiaen's Concerts á Quatre (1994); Founded the Ensemble á Vent Maurice Bourgue 1972 and has conducted the Oslo PO, Ensemble Orchestral de Paris, Israel CO and Orchestras in Lyon, Montpellier, Nancy and the Auvergne; Tour of the UK with the Bournemouth Sinfonietta, 1995. Honours include: Winner of Competitions at Birmingham (1985), Prague (1968) and Budapest (1970). Address: c/o Ingpen & Williams Ltd, 26 Wadham Road, London SW15 2LR, England.

BOUSKOVA Jana, b. 27 Sept 1970, Prague, Czech Republic. Harpist (Solo, Chamber). m. Jiri Kubita, 3 Sept 1993. Education: Prague Conservatory; Ostrava University; Indiana University; Teachers: Libuse Vachalova; Susann McDonald. Career: Concert Harpist, solo, chamber, concerts in USA, Japan, Germany, France, Italy, Spain, Greece, Canada, Czech Republic, Slovakia, The Netherlands, Switzerland; Recital at Lincoln Centre, 1993; Concert at the Berliner Philharmony Hall; Many recordings for TV and radio; Teacher at the Prague Conservatory Concerte at the World Harp Congresses (Vienna, Paris, Copenhagen, Seattle). Recordings: Harp Recital (Scarlatti, Bach, Tournier, etc); Harp Recital (J L Dussek); Harp Recital (J F Fischer); Harp Concertos (Händel, Krumpholz, Boieldieu); Harp Concertos (J C H Bach); Harp Concertos (J K Krumpholz No 1-6); Harp Recital (Bach, Fischer); Harp-Violin (Kreutzer-Nocturnos); Harp-Flute (Spohr, Ravel); Jana Bouskova Plays Encores (Chopin, Liszt, Falla). Honours: Maria Damm Prize, USA International Harp Competition, 1989; 1st Prize, The Indiana University Harp Concerto Competition, 1991; 1st Prize, Gold Medal, USA International Harp Competition, 1992; 2nd Prize, International Harp Contest, 1992; The Music Views Journal Prize, The Best Interpretation of the International Music Festival, Youth Stage, 1993; The Czech Music Foundation Prize for the CD Recording of Harp Concertos, 1993; Prize, Classic Talent of the Year, 1997; Chairman of the Artistic Committee for the Seventh World Harp Congress in Prague, 1999. Address: Chodovicka 544/22, 19300 Prague 9, Czech Republic.

BOVINO Maria, b. 1960, England. Singer (Soprano). Education: Studied at Sheffield University and the Guildhall School of Music and Drama. Debut: At King's College in London, as Bella in Schubert's Die Verschworenen. Career: Sang Fiorella in Offenbach's Les Brigands with the Intermezzi Ensemble; Opera 80 from 1982 as Adele in Die Fledermaus, Despina in Cosi fan Tutte and Elvira in L'Italiana in Algeri; Season 1984-85 as Emmie in Albert Herring at Glyndebourne and Tytania in A Midsummer Night's Dream for Glyndebourne Tour; Sang First Boy in The Magic Flute for English National Opera in 1986 followed by the Queen of Night in 1988; With Scottish Opera from 1987 as Blondchen in Die Entführung and Papagena; English Bach Festival in Gluck's Orfeo and Dido and Aeneas in London, Granada and Athens; Covent Garden debut in 1989 in Albert Herring; Performances with Travelling Opera in season 1990-91 as Mimi and Gilda; Also sings Gilbert and Sullivan with the London Savoyards; Sang Susanna with Crystal Clear Productions in 1991; Sang Gilda with English Touring Opera, 1996. Address: c/o English National Opera, St Martin's Lane, London, WC2, England.

BOWATER Helen, b. 16 Nov 1952, Wellington, New Zealand. Composer. Education: Studied with Gwyneth Brown and at Victoria University, Wellington. Career: Resident composer at Nelson School of Music, 1992; Mozart Fellow at University of Otago, 1993. Compositions include: Black Rain for soprano and cello, 1985; Songs of Mourning for baritone and string quartet, 1989; Stay Awake Ananda for 5 percussionists, 1990; The Bodhi Tree, string quartet, 1991; Witch's Mine for tape, 1991; Magma for orchestra, 1992. Address: c/o New Zealand Music Centre, PO Box 10042, Level 13, Brandon Street, Wellington, New Zealand.

BOWDEN Pamela, b, 1934, Lancashire, England. Singer (Contralto). m. Derrick Edwards, 1 son, 1 daughter. Education: Royal Manchester College of Music. career: Concert and opera engagements from 1954 throught United Kingdom and Europe; Tours of West Indies, Middle East, Scandinavia; Festival appearances and seasons with the English Opera Group; Lieder recitals worldwide and concerts with leading orchestra in Britain and Europe, including the Concertgebouw, Suisse Romande and Israel Philharmonic; Conductors include Ansermet, Paul Sacher, Scherchen, Krips, Boult, Boulez, Sargent, Pritchard, Solti, Gui, Mackerras, Rattle and Charles Groves; Many Promenade Concerts and broadcasts; Well known in works of Handel and Bach and as the Angel in The Dream of Gerontius; Premiered works include Malcolm Arnold's Five William Blake Songs; Sang Larina in Eugene Onegin for Glyndebourne Festival Opera and Royal Opera House, Covent Garden; Head of Singing, London College of Music, Visiting Professor, Royal Scottish Academy of Music and Drama. Recordings include: Tippett A Child of Our Time; Berkeley Four Poems of St Teresa; Britten A Charm of Lullabies. Memberships: President, Incorporated Society of Musicians, 1988; Fellow, RMCM; Honorary Fellow, LCM; Fellow, RSA. Address: 11 Wickliffe Avenue, London N3, England.

BOWEN Geraint (Robert Lewis), b. 11 Jan 1963, London, England. Organist; Conductor. m. Lucy Dennis, 1987, 2 sons. Education: BA, Cambridge, 1986; MA, 1989; MusB, Trinity College, Dublin, 1987; Study with Christopher Herrick, John Scott and Stephen Cleobury. Career: Organ Scholar, Jesus College, Cambridge, 1982-85; TV and Radio broadcasts as organ accompanist and conductor, 1984-; Assistant Organist at Hampstead Parish Church, St Clement Danes Church, 1985-86, St Patrick's Cathedral, Dublin, 1986-89 and Hereford Cathedral, 1989-94; Assistant Conductor and Accompanist, Hereford Choral Society, 1989-94; Festival Organist at Hereford Three Choirs Festival, 1991, 1994; Recital venues include King's College, Cambridge, St John's College, Cambridge, Southwark Cathedral, Queen's College, Oxford and Three Choirs Festival; Organist and Master of the Choristers at St Davids Cathedral, Wales, 1995-; Artistic Director, St Davids Cathedral Festival, 1995-; Founder and Conductor, St Davids Cathedral Festival Chorus, 1996-. Recordings: Aeternae laudis lilium; The Psalms of David, volume 1; Te Deum and Jubilate, volume 3; The Sound of St Davids. Honour: Selected for Gramophone Magazine's Critics' Choice, 1985. Membership: FRCO, 1987. Hobbies: Gardening; Railways; Typography; Walking. Address: The Organist's Lodgings, Cathedral Close, St Davids, Pembrokeshire SA62 6PE, Wales.

BOWEN John, b. 1968, England. Tenor. Education: Studied at the Royal College of Music. Career: Appearances with Bath and Wessex Opera, Garsington Festival, City of Birmingham Touring Opera and Opera Factory Zurich; Roles include Ugone in Flavio and Pan in La Calisto; Concerts with the English Chamber Orchestra, Royal Liverpool Philharmonic Orchestra, London Mozart Players, and the King's Consort in The Indian Queen and Judas Maccabeus; Sang in the premiere of Taverner's Apocolypse at the London Proms in 1994 and tour of Bach's B minor Mass with René Jacobs; Sang Soliman in Mozart's Zaide at the 1996 Covent Garden Festival. Recordings include: Rachmaninov's Vespers; Messiah; Monteverdi's Vespers. Address: Ron Gonsalves Management, 7 Old Town, Clapham, London, SW4 0JT, England.

BOWEN Kenneth (John), b. 3 Aug 1932, Llanelli, Wales. Singer; Conductor; Teacher; Broadcaster. m. Angela Mary Bowen, 31 Mar 1959, 2 sons. Education: BA, University of Wales; MA, MusB, St John's College, Cambridge; Institute of Education, University of London. Debut: Tom Rakewell, New Opera Company, Sadler's Wells, 1957. Career: Flying Officer, Education Branch, RAF, 1958-60; Professor of Singing, 1967-, Head of Vocal Studies, 1987-91, RAM; Conductor of London Welsh Chorale, 1983- and London Welsh Festival Chorus; Former concert and operatic tenor, retired in 1988; Appeared at Promenade Concerts, Aldeburgh, Bath, Swansea, Llandaff and Fishguard Festivals, throughout Europe, Israel, North American and the Far East; Performed at Royal Opera House, ENO, WNO, Glyndebourne Touring Opera, English Opera Group, English Music Theatre, Kent Opera, and Handel Opera Society; Frequent broadcasts, numerous first performances and many recordings. Honours: Prizes in Geneva, s'Hertogenbosch, Liverpool and Munich International Competition (1st) and Queens Prize; Honorary RAM, John Edwards Memorial Award, GPWM. Memberships: Fellow, Royal Society of Arts; Vice President, Guild for the Promotion of Welsh Music; Gorsedd of Bards, Royal National Eisteddfod of Wales; Council, British Youth Opera; Chairman, 1990-91, Association of Teachers of Singing; Association of English Singers and Speakers; British Voice Association; Incorporated Society of Musicians; President, RAM Club, 1991; Royal Society of Musicians. Hobbies: Golf; Cinema; Theatre; Books and Paintings; Walking. Address: 12 Steele's Road, London, NW3 4SE, England.

BOWERS Evan, b. 1960, New York, USA. Singer (Tenor). Career: Sang Alfredo and Gounod's Tybalt for Texas Opera Theatre, Ernesto in San Francisco and for the Metropolitan Opera Guild; Ferrando and the Duke of Mantua for Israeli Vocal Arts Institute; European debut 1992, as Don Ottavio for the Wiener Kammeroper; Engagement with the Nuremberg Opera as Tamino, Oberon, Leopold in La Juive, Andres in Wozzeck and Rossini's Almaviva; Guest as Fenton at Innsbruck and Nemorino at the Salzburg Landestheater; Leipzig Opera from 1994, as Rodolfo, Lensky and Don Ottavio; Graz Opera debut as Tamino; Season 1996-97 as Beethoven's Jacquino, Don Ottavio at the Schonbrunn Festival and Gratiano in The Merchant of Venice for Portland Opera; Concerts include: The Missa Solemnis, Haydn's Creation and Seasons, Requiems of Verdi and Mozart; Venues include: France, Germany and the USA. Address: Athole Still Ltd, Foresters Hall, 25-27 Westow Street, London SE19 3RY, England.

BOWERS-BROADBENT Christopher (Joseph), b. 13 Jan 1945, Hemel Hempstead, England. Organist; Composer. m. Deirdre Cape, 17 Oct 1970, 1 son, 1 daughter. Education: Chorister, King's College Choir School, 1954-58; RAM; FRAM, Royal Academy of Music, 1962-66. Career includes: Organ recitals; Organist, West London Synagogue and Gray's Inn; Professor, Organ, Royal Academy of Music, 1976-92.

Compositions include: The Seacock Bane, teenagers' opera; The Last Man, comic opera; Worthy is the Lamb, oratorio; The Hollow Men, cantata; Te Deum; Collected Church Pieces, 1972. Recordings: Passio; Miserere; Trivium. Membership: Royal College of Organists. Hobby: Painting. Current Management: Magenta Music International, 64 Highgate High Street, London N6 5HX, England. Address: 94 Colney Hatch Lane, London N10 1EA, England.

BOWLES Edmund (Addison), b. 24 Mar 1925, Cambridge, MA, USA. Musicologist; Specialist in Mediaeval Musical Instruments and Performance Practices; Musical Iconography; Timpanist; Musical Iconography; MusicalEnsembles in court festivals of state. m. Marianne von Recklinghausen, 1 son, 1 daughter. Education: BA, Swarthmore College; PhD, Yale University; Diploma, Berks Music Center, Tanglewood, MA. Career includes: Instructor in Humanities, Massachusetts Institute of Technology; Publicity Staff, Bell Telephone Laboratories; Manager of Professional Activities, University Relations; Senior Programme Administrator, IBM Corporation, 1959-88; Retired. Publications include: Computers in Humanistic Research: Readings and Perspectives, 1967; Musikleben des 15 Jahrunderts, 1976; Musical Performance in The Late Middle Ages La Pratique Musicale au Moyen-Age, 1983; Musical Ensembles in Festival Books: An Iconography and Documentary Survey, 1988; The Timpani: A History in Pictures and Documents, 1992. Recording: Handel's Messiah, 1984. Contributions to: Various professional journals; Dictionary of The Middle Ages; Encyclopaedia Britannica; The New Grove Dictionaries; The New Harvard Dictionary of Music. Honours: Bessaraboff Prize, 1991; Curt Sachs Award, American Musical Instrument Society, 1997. Hobbies: Orchestral Playing; Baroque Timpani. Address: 3210 Valley Lane, Falls Church, VA 22044, USA.

BOWLES Garrett H, b. 3 Feb 1938, San Francisco, CA, USA. Music Librarian. 1 son, 1 daughter. Education: BA, Music, University of California, Davis, 1960; MA, Music Composition, San Jose State University, 1962; MLS, University of California, Berkeley, 1965; PhD, Musicology, Stanford University, 1978. Career: Head Music Cataloguer, Stanford University, 1965-79; Head Music Librarian, 1979-, Assistant Adjunct Professor of Music, 1980-, University of California, San Diego; Visiting Lecturer at University of Exeter, England, 1983. Compositions include: Festklang for Ernst Krenek, in Perspectives of New Music, 1985. Publications: Directory, Music Library Automation Projects, 1973, 1979; Ernst Krenek, Bio-bibliography, 1989; Editor, Ernst Krenek Newsletter, 1990-. Contributions to: Journal of Association for Recorded Sound Collectors; Notes; Forte Artis Musicae. Address: Music Library 0175-Q, University of California at San Diego, 9500 Gilman Drive, La Jolla, CA 92093-0175, USA.

BOWLES Paul (Frederick), b. 30 Dec 1910, NY, USA. Composer. m. Jane Auer, 21 Feb 1938. Education: Studied composition with Aaron Copland and Virgil Thomson. Career includes: Music Critic for New York Herald-Tribune for 4 years. Compositions: Various chamber works, songs and piano pieces published and recorded. Recordings: Concerto for 2 Pianos, Winds and Percussion; Music For A Farce; The Wind Remains, one-act opera excerpts; Scenes d'Anabase; Songs and piano music; Sonata for Two Pianos; A Picnic Cantata; Sonata for Flute and Piano. Honours: Guggenheim Fellowship, 1941; Rockefeller Grant to record Moroccan music for the Library of Congress, Washington, 1959. Membership: American Society of Composers, Authors and Publishers. Address: 2117 Tanger Socco, Tangier, Morocco.

BOWMAN James (Thomas), b. 6 Nov 1941, Oxford, England. Counter-Tenor. Education: Cathedral Choir School; Kings School, Ely, Cambridgeshire; New College, Oxford; DipEd, 1964, MA(Oxon), History, 1967. Career includes: Sang with English Opera Group, 1967-, with debut as Britten's Oberon, and Early Music Consort, 1967-76; Operatic performances include: Sadler's Wells Opera, 1970-, Glyndebourne Festival Opera, 1970-, Opéra Comique, Paris, 1979-, Geneva, 1983, and Dallas and San Francisco Operas, USA; Operatic roles include: Endymion in La Calisto, The Priest in Taverner in the world premiere at Covent Garden in 1972, Apollo in Death in Venice, and Astron in The Ice Break in the 1977 premiere; Title roles include: Handel's Giulio Cesare, Tamerlano, and Scipione; Appearances include La Scala, Milan in 1988 as Jommelli's Fetonte, English National Opera in 1989 as Amphinomous in The Return of Ulysses, and Promenade Concerts in 1991 in Purcell's Ode for St Cecilia's Day; Sang Britten's Oberon at Aix-en-Provence in 1992, Barak in Handel's Deborah at 1993 Prom Concerts in London; Other roles include: Goffredo in Rinaldo, Lidio in Cavalli's Egisto, and Ruggiero in Vivaldi's Orlando; Sang Herod in Fux's La Fede Sacrilega in Vienna and Monteverdi's Ottone as Poppea at the Spitalfields Festival in London; Bach's St John Passion at St John's, London, 1997; Daniel in Handel's Belshazzar at the 1996 Göttingen Festival. Recordings: Oratorio; Mediaeval and Renaissance vocal music. Hobbies: Ecclesiastical Architecture; Collecting Records. Address: 19a Wetherby Gardens, London, SW5 0JP, England.

BOWYER Kevin (John), b. 9 Jan 1961, Essex, England. Organist. m. Ursula Steiner, 27 Aug 1981, 2 sons, 2 daughters. Education: Royal Academy of Music with Douglas Hawkridge and Christopher Bowers-Broadbent, 1979-82; Studied with David Sanger. Debut: Royal Festival Hall in 1984. Career: Concerts throughout Europe and North America, specializing in unusual and contemporary repertoire; Performances of Kaikhosru Sorabji's Organ Symphony in London, 1987, Aarhus, 1988 and Linz in 1992; Broadcasts for BBC Radio 3 include works by Ligeti, Hugh Wood, Malcolm Williamson, Berio, Henze, Brian Ferneybough, Charles Camilleri, Niccolo Castiglioni; Numerous broadcasts for other networks. Recordings: A Late Twentieth Century Edwardian Bach Recital; Alkan Organ Works; Brahms Complete Organ Works; Reubke's 94th Psalm Sonata; Schumann's 6 Fugues on Bach; Organ Works by Dupre, Langlais, Hindemith, Pepping, Arnold Schoenberg; Complete Organ Works of J S Bach; Messiaen Organ Works, in 2 volumes; Sorabji Organ Symphony No 1; Works by Busoni, Ronald Stevenson, Alistair Hinton. Publications: Articles on Sorabji for The Organ and Organists Review. Honours: Grant, Countess of Munster Musical Trust; 1st Prize, St Albans International Organ Festival, 1983; 1st Prizes at international organ festivals in Dublin, Paisley, Odense and Calgary, 1990. Hobbies: Reading; Malt Whiskeys; Obscure Cinema. Address: 2 Kingston Barn College, Kingston Farm, Chesterton, Leamington Spa, CV33 9LH, England.

BOYD Anne (Elizabeth), b. 10 Apr 1946, Sydney, Australia. Composer; University Music Teacher; Music Critic. 1 daughter. Education: BA, 1st Class Honours, University of Sydney; DPhil, University of York; NSW Conservatorium of Music; Composition Teachers: Peter Sculthorpe, Wilfrid Mellers, Bernard Rands. Debut: Adelaide Festival of Arts, 1966. Career: Festival performances include: Adelaide in 1966, 1968, and 1976; Opening Season Festival of Sydney Opera House, 1973; Appearances at Edinburgh Windsor Festival, 1974, Aldeburgh Festival, 1980, and Hong Kong Arts Festival, 1985; Lecturer in Music, University of Sussex, 1972-77; Founding Head and Reader, Department of Music at University of Hong Kong, 1981-. Compositions include: String Quartets 1 and 2; The Voice Of The Phoenix for Solo Piano, Guitar, Harp, Harpsichord and Full Orchestra; As It Leaves The Bell for Piano, 2 Harps and 4 Percussion; Goldfish Through Summer Rain, Red Sun, Chill Wind And Cloudy Mountain for Flute and Piano. Recordings: Several. Contributions to: Founding Managing Editor, Music Now; Musical Times; Miscellanea Musicologica; Australian Journal of Music Education. Hobbies: Swimming; Squash; Photography; Reading; Chinese Calligraphy. Address: c/o Faber Music London Ltd, 3 Queen Square, London WC1N 3AU, England.

BOYD Douglas, b. 1960, Glasgow, Scotland. Oboist. Education: Studied with Janet Craxton at the Royal Academy and with Maurice Bourge in Paris. Career: Solo engagements in works by Strauss and Mozart, in Europe, The Far East and USA; Conductors have included Abbado, Berglund, Menuhin, Alexander Schneider and Michael Tilson Thomas; Co-Founder of the Chamber Orchestra of Europe as Principal Oboist, and leading member of the Wind Soloists of the Chamber Orchestra of Europe; Played in the Lutoslawski Concerto for Oboe and Harp, Glasgow, 1991; World premiere of Sally Beamish's Oboe Concerto written for him at the Queen Elizabeth Hall, London, 1993; During 1993-94 season performed with the Basle Radio Symphony Orchestra under Rudolph Barshai, National Arts Centre Orchestra of Ottawa under Nicholas McGegan, Hong Kong Philharmonic under David Atherton, BBC Scottish Symphony Orchestra under Alun Francis, and Budapest String Soloists; Has also appeared at the Bath and Boxgrove Festivals and Glasgow's Mayfest; Concertos with various orchestras and tours of the USA with Jeffrey Kahane and the Ridge Ensemble; Invitations to the Perth, Vancouver and Prague Autumn Festivals; In 1997 he made his first tour of Japan. Recordings: Bach Concertos with Salvatore Accardo; Beethoven Music for Wind Instruments; Dvorák Serenade in D minor; Haydn Sinfonia Concertante; Vivaldi and Strauss Concertos; Mozart Concerto, Concertante K297b, Quartet K370, Serenades in E flat and C minor, Serenade (Gran partita), K361; Schumann recital with Maria Joao Pires. Address: c/o Sue Lubbock Concert Management, 25 Courthorpe Road, London, NW3 2LE, England.

BOYD James, b. 1960, England. Violist. Education: Studied at the Yehudi Menuhin School, Guildhall School of Music and the Menuhin Academy in Gstaad. Debut: South Bank, London premiere of Robert Simpson's 13th Quartet; BBC Radio 3 debut in 1991. Career: Frequent tours with the Rafael Ensemble; Co-founder of Vellinger String Quartet in 1990; Participated in masterclasses with the Borodin Quartet at the Pears-Britten School, 1991; Concerts at the Ferrar Musica Festival in Italy; Season 1992-93 concerts in London, Glasgow, Cambridge, Davos Festival, Switzerland and the Crickdale Festival in Wiltshire; Played at Wigmore Hall with works by Haydn, Gubaidulina and Beethoven, and at Purcell Room with Haydn's Last Seven Words. Recordings include: Elgar's Quartet and Quintet, with Piers Lane. Honour: Joint Winner of the Bernard Shore Viola Prize, 1988. Address: Vellinger String Quartet, c/o Georgina Ivor Associates, 66 Alderbrook Road, London, SW12 8AB, England.

BOYD Malcolm, b. 24 May 1932, Newcastle-upon-Tyne, England. Lecturer in Music. m. Beryl Gowen, 2 s. Education: BMus; MA; ARCO. Career: National Service; Teacher; Lecturer, University College, Cardiff, retired in 1992. Publications: Harmonizing Bach Chorales, 1967; Bach's Instrumental Counterpoint, 1967; Palestrina Style, 1973; William Mathias, 1978; Grace Williams, 1980; Bach, 1983; Domenico Scarlatti, Master of Music, 1986; Bach: The Brandenburg Concertos, 1993. Contributions to: Musical Times; Music and Letters; The Music Review; Tempo; La Musica; Sohlman's Musiklexikon; The New Grove Dictionary of Music and Musicians. Memberships: Royal Musical Association; RCO. Hobby: Gardening. Address: 211 Fidlas Road, Llanishen, Cardiff, CF4 5NA, Wales.

BOYDE Andreas, b. 13 Nov 1967, Oschatz, Germany. Pianist. Education: Spezialschule & Musikhochschule, Dresden; Guildhall School of Music & Drama, London; Musikfestwocher Luzerh. Debut: With Berlin Symphony Orchestra, 1989. Career: Concerts with Dresden Philharmonic Orchestra, 1992, 1996; Recital, Munich Philharmonic Hall, Gasteig, 1992; Festival La Roque d'Antheron, France, 1993; Concert with Transylvanian State Orchestra, Romania, 1994; Concert, Zurich Tonhalle with Zurich Chamber Orchestra, 1994; Concerts with Freiburg Philharmonic Orchestra, 1994, 1997, Dresden State Orchestra, 1994, 1995; Recitalist in Schumann Cycle Dusseldorf, 1995; South American Debut, Recital in teatro Municipal Santiago, Chile, 1996; Concert, Munich Herkulessaal with Munich Symphony, 1997; Concert Tour with Northwest German Philharmonic Orchestra, 1997; Recital, Munich Prinzregenten Theatre, 1997; Concert Tour with Odessa Philharmonic Orchestra, 1997. Recordings: Rachmonino, Francaik, Hindemith, Schubert, Schumann, Liszt, Ravel, Davorak Piano Concerto & Tchaikovsky 2nd Piano Concerto; Beethoven, Chopin, Debussy. Address: Zulpicher Strabe 355, 50935 Koln, Germany.

BOYDELL Brian (Patrick), b. 17 Mar 1917, Dublin, Ireland. Musicologist; Composer; Retired University Professor of Music. m. Mary Jones, 6 June 1944, 3 sons, 1 deceased. Education: BA, Natural Science, Clare College, Cambridge, England; Royal College of Music, London, 1938-39; BA ad eundem, 1939, MusB, 1942, MusD, 1959, University of Dublin, Ireland; Licentiate in Singing, Royal Irish Academy of Music, 1941. Career: Adjudicator for numerous music festivals, including the Canadian Chain and Hong Kong; Over 900 broadcasts on musical subjects; Conductor, Dublin Orchestral Players, 1942-68; Director, Dowland Consort, 1958-69; Guest Conductor, RTE Symphony Orchestra and other orchestras; Professor of Music, University of Dublin, 1962-82. Compositions include: Violin Concerto; 4 String Quartets; Orchestral, symphonic, chamber, vocal, choral and film music. Recordings include: String Quartet No 1; Symphonic Inscapes; Megalithic Ritual dances; Dance for an Ancient Ritual; String Quartet No 2, 1994; In Memorian Mahatma Gandhi; Violin Concerto; Megalithic Ritual Dances; Masai Mara, 1997. Publications: Four Centuries of Music in Ireland, Editor, 1979; A Dublin Musical Calendar 1700-1776, 1988; Rotunda Music in 18th Century Dublin, 1992. Contributions to: New Grove, 1980; New History of Ireland Volume IV, 1986; Proceedings of Royal Musicological Association; Dublin Historical Record. Honours: DMus, Honoris Causa, NUI, 1974; Commendatore della Republica Italiana, 1983; FRIAM, Honoris Causa, 1990. Memberships: President, Dublin Orchestral Players; Honorary President, Association of Irish Composers. Hobbies: Gardening; Fishing; Travel. Address: Trinity College, Dublin 2, Republic of Ireland.

BOYKAN Martin, b. 12 Apr 1931, New York, USA. Composer. m. (1) Constance Berke, June 1964, divorced, (2) Susan Schwalb, Nov 1983, 2 daughters. Education: Berkshire Music Center, Tanglewood, 1949-50; University of Zurich, 1951-52; BA, Harvard University, 1951; MM, Yale University, 1953. Compositions: Psalm 128, 1965; String Quartets Nos 1, 2, 3; Concerto for 13 Players, 1971; Piano Trio, 1976; Elegy for soprano and 6 instruments, 1982; Epithalamion, 1985; Shalom Rav, 1987; Fantasy-Sonata for piano, 1987; Symphony No 1, 1989; Piano sonata No 2, Nocturne for cello, piano and percussion; Eclogue for 5 instruments, 1991; Echos of Petrarch, for flute, clarinet and piano, 1992; Voyages for Soprano and pf, 1992; Sonata for cello and piano, 1992; Sea-Gardens for soprano and piano, 1993; Impromptu for violin solo, 1993;Three Psalms for soprano and pf, 1993; Pastorale for piano, 1993; Sonata for violin and piano, 1994; Maiyiv Settings for chorus and organ, 1995; City of Gold for flute solo, 1996; String Quartet No 4, 1996; 3 Shakespeare's Songs for Women's Chorus, 1996; Piano Trio No 2, 1997; Psalm 121, for soprano and string quartet, 1997; Usurpations for piano solo, 1997. Recordings: String Quartets Nos 1 and 2; Elegy and Epithalamion; String Quartet No 4. Publications: C.F Peters: Quartets, #1, #3, #4, 1987; Fantasy-Sonata, 1992; Piano Sonata #2, 1995; Sonata for cello; Echoes of Petrarch; Impromptu for violin solo; Sonata for violin and piano; City of Gold; Psalm 128; String Quartet No 2; Piano

Trio No 1. Contributions to: Perspectives of New Music; Journal of the American Society of University Composers; Musical Quarterly; Notes. Honours: Jeunesses Musicales, 1967; Martha Baird Rockefeller, 1974; Fromm Foundation Commission, 1976; Yaddo Foundation, 1981-92; MacDowell, 1982, 1989, 1992; NEA, 1983; League-ISCM Prize, 1983, Guggenheim, 1984; Koussevitsky Commission, 1985; 2 Awards, American Academy of Arts and Letters, 1986, 1988; Virginia Center for Creative Arts, 1992; Senior Fulbright Fellowship, 1994. Address: 10 Winsor Avenue, Watertown, MA 02172, USA.

BOYLAN Orla, b. Sept 1971, Dublin, Ireland. Singer (Soprano). Education: Dublin and Milan (masterclasses with Leyla Gencer, Graziella Sciutti and Renata Scotto). Career: Concerts include: Mozart's Requiem, Coronation Mass and Mass in C minor, Messiah, Verdi's Requiem and Rossini's Petite Messe; RTE production of Mendelssohn's A Midsummer Night Dream and Strauss's Four Last Songs with the Wexford Symphonia; Song recitals at the Salle Cortot, Paris, and throughout Ireland; Season 1996-97 with Mozart's Fiordiligi in Milan, the C Minor Mass in Liverpool and Dublin and concerts with the RTE Concert orchestra. Honours include: Prize Winner, European Operatic Singing Competition, La Scala, 1996; Belvedere International Singing Competition, Vienna, 1996. Address: c/o Harrison/Parrott Ltd, 12 Penzance Place, London W11 4PA, England.

BOYLAN Patricia, b. 1945, London, England. Singer (Mezzo-Soprano). Education: Trinity College of Music; National Opera School; London Opera Centre. Career: English Opera Group with tours in Britten's operas under the composer to Russia; Appearances with Scottish Opera in Peter Grimes and Die Walküre, concerts and oratorios throughout Britain, including the Aldeburgh and Edinburgh Festivals; After raising her family returned to the concert hall in such works as Beethoven's Ninth and Mass in C, Mozart's C minor Mass and Requiem, the Verdi Requiem and Mahler's Kindertotenlieder; Sang in El Amor Brujo at the Manuel de Falla Festival in Seville; Operatic appearances as Larina in Eugene Onegin in Lisbon, Azucena in Madrid, Orpheus, Carmen and Amneris at Managa; Sang Clytemnestra in Elektra for Welsh National Opera in 1992 and Auntie in Peter Grimes for Scottish Opera, 1993. Address: IMG Artists, Media House, 3 Burlington Lane, London, W4 2TH, England.

BOYLE Alison Julie, b. 5 Aug 1963, Chorley, Lancashire, England. Financial Consultant; Piano Teacher. Education: Financial Studies, Preston Polytechnic; Associate, London College of Music; Studies with Mary Engel, Margaret Heylings. Honour: ALCM, 1991. Memberships: Lancashire Schools Symphonic Wind Band; Incorporated Society of Musicians. Hobbies: Music; Psychology. Address: 23 Linacre Road, Eccleshall, Staffs ST21 6DZ, England.

BOZARTH George S, b. 28 Feb 1947, Trenton, NJ, USA. Historical Musicologist. Education: MFA 1973, PhD 1978, Princeton University. Career: Professor of Music, University of Washington; Director of Brahms Archive, Seattle, WA; Director of International Brahms Conference, Washington DC, 1983; Performer on historical pianos of late 18th through mid-19th centuries; Member of The Classical Consort; Co-Artistic Director of Gallery Concerts in Seattle. Publications: Editions: Johannes Brahms, Orgelwerke, The Organ Works, Munich, G Henle, 1988, J S Bach, Cantata, Ach Gott vom Himmel sieh darein, BWV2, Neue Bach Ausgabe, 1/16, 1981, 1984; The Brahms Keller Correspondance, 1996; Facsimile editions of Brahms's manuscripts; Editor of Brahms Studies: Analytical and Historical Perspectives, 1990. Contributions to: Numerous articles on Brahms's Lieder and Duets, the genesis and chronology of Brahms's works, Brahms's piano sonatas and First Piano Concerto, editorial problems and questions of authenticity, Brahms's pianos and piano music. Honours: Fulbright-Hayes Scholarship to Austria, 1975-77; ACLS Fellowship for Recent Recipient of the PhD, 1982; NEH Research Conference Grant, 1983. Memberships: American Brahms Society, Executive Director; American Musicological Society; Early Music America. Address: School of Music, Box 353450, University of Washington, Seattle, WA 98195-3450, USA.

BOZAY Attila, b. 11 Aug 1939, Balatonfüzfő, Hungary. Composer; Teacher. Education: Bela Bartók Conservatory, Budapest, 1954-57; Pupil of Ferenc Farkas at Budapest Academy of Music, 1957-62. Career: Music Producer, Hungarian Radio, 1963-66; Teacher of composition and orchestration at Budapest Academy of Music. Compositions: Operas: Queen Kungisz, 1968-69, Csongor and Tunde, 1978-84, Hamlet, 1984; Orchestral: Pezzo Concertato for Viola and Orchestra, 1965, Pezzo Sinfonico, 1967, Pezzo D'Archi, 1968-74, Pezzo Concertato No 2 for Zither and Orchestra, 1974-75, Pezzo Sinfonico No 2, 1975-76, Children's Songs for 18 Strings, 1976, Variazioni, 1977; Chamber Group: Series, 1970, The Mill, 1972-73; Chamber: Duo for 2 Violins, 1958, Episodes for Bassoon and Piano, 1959, Trio Per Archi for Violin, Viola and Cello, 1960, revised 1966, Wind Quintet, 1962, 2 String Quartets, 1964, 1971, 2 Movements for Oboe and Piano, 1970, Improvisations No 2 for Recorders and String Trio, 1976, Mirror for Zither and Cimbalom, 1977; Many pieces for solo instruments; Vocal Pieces and Choruses. Honours: Erkel Prize, 1968, 1979; Merited Artist, Hungarian People's Republic, 1984; Bartók-Pásztory Award, 1988. Address: ARTISJUS, Vorosmarty ter 1, PB 67, H-1364 Budapest, Hungary.

BOŽIČ Darijan, b. 29 Apr 1933, Slavonski brod, Croatia. Composer. Education: Composition and Conducting, Ljubljana Academy of Music, 1958, 1961; Further study in London and Paris. Career: Conductor and Director of Studies, Slovene Opera, 1968-70; Conductor and Artistic Director, Slovena Philharmonic, 1970-74; Professor, University of Ljubljana, 1980-94, University of Maribor, 1988-95; Director of SNG Opera, Ljubljana, 1995. Compositions include: Stage Works: La Bohème, 57, Opera, 1958; La Putain Respecteuse, Opera Fater Sartre, 1960; Jago, Happening for 8 performers and tape after Shakespeare, 1968; Ares-Eros Musical Drama after Aristophanes, 1970; Lizistrata 75, Operatic Farce after Aristophanes; Kralj Lear, Music Drama after Shakespeare, 1985; Telmah, Music Drama after Shakespeare; Bolt's a Man for All Seasons, 1990. Address: c/o Slovensko Narodno Gledaslišče, Župančičeva 1, 61000 Ljubljana, Slovenia.

BOZIWICK George E, b. 23 Aug 1954, Rockville Centre, New York, USA. Composer; Librarian. m. Stephanie Doba, 26 July 1986, 2 daughters. Education: BA, State University of New York, College at Oneonta, 1976; MA, Composition, Hunter College, 1981; MLS, Columbia University School of Library Service, 1987. Career: Librarian, Hunter College Music Department, 1978-85; Music Librarian, Circulating Music Collection, 1986-88, Music Division, 1988-91, Curator, American Music Collection, 1991-, The New York Public Library for the Performing Arts. Compositions: Boats Against the Current, 1990; Fabliau of Florida, 1994; Out of the Blues, for Toy Piano, 1996; Emily Dickinson: Then and Now, 1998; Mass, 1998. Recordings: Red Skies at Night, 1988; First Dance, Beyond the Last Thought and Boats Against the Current, 1993; Out of the Blues, 1996. Contributions to: Music Library Association Reviews, 1982-83, 1989; New Grove Dictionary of Music and Musicians, revised edition; New Grove Dictionary of Jazz, 2nd edition. Honours: Graduate Assistantship, Hunter College, 1978-81; Scholarship, Columbia University School of Library Service, 1985-86; Grants: Meet the Composer, 1990, 1996, Mary Flagler Cary Charitable Trust, 1992, American Music Center, 1993, 1995, 1996. Memberships: Music Library Association; International Association of Music Libraries; Sonneck Society for Studies in American Music; American Music Center; American Composers Forum; Broadcast Music Inc; American Composers Alliance; National Association of Composers, USA. Hobbies: Baseball Card Collecting; Professional Blues Harmonica Player. Address: 614 10th Street, Brooklyn, NY 11215-4402, USA.

BRABBINS Martyn, b. 1961, England. Conductor. Education: Goldsmiths' College, London, and Leningrad Conservatoire with Ilya Musin. Career: From 1988 appearances with most leading chamber and symphony orchestras in Britain, including all the BBC Orchestras (BBC Scottish at the 1997 Edinburgh Festival); Further festival engagements at Lichfield (Philharmonia Orchestra), Windsor, Cheltenham, Bath, Aldeburgh and Three Choirs; Guest with the St Petersburg PO, North German Radio SO and Orchestra of Gran Canaria; Tour with Australia Youth Orchestra, 1995; Tour of Russia with Sinfonia 21 (1996) and Contemporary Music Network tour of Britain, 1997; Opera includes Don Giovanni at the Kirov, Magic Flute for English National Opera, Schreker's Der ferne klang for Opera North and Aida for Opera Northern Ireland (season 1997-98); The Olympians by Bliss, Tchaikovsky's Cherivichki, and Tannhäuser for Chelsea Opera Group; Associate Principal Conductor of the BBC Scottish SO, Principal Conductor of Sinfonia 21 and Conducting Consultant at the Royal Scottish Academy; Premiere recording of Die Kathrin by Korngold with BBC Concert Orchestra, 1997. Honours include: Winner, 1988 Leeds Conductors' Competition. Address: Allied Artists, 42 Montpellier Square, London SW7 1JZ, England.

BRABEC Lubomir, b. 21 May 1953, Pilsen, Czechoslovakia. Guitarist (Solo Concert Guitarist). Education: Conservatoire Pilsen, 1968-72; Conservatoire Prague, 1972-74; Royal Academy of Music, 1980-81; Early Music Centre, 1980-81; Career: Regular appearances with Prague Orchestras; Has performed throughout Europe, USSR, North and Latin America; Many TV and Radio appearances, including two one-hour TV Recitals. Recordings: Baroque Music: Bach, Handel, Weiss, Jelinek; Spanish Music: Torroba, Falla, Albeniz; Turina, Rodrigo; A Vivaldi - Guitar Concertos with Prague Chamber Orchestra and with Violist L Maly and Guitarist M Myslivecek; F Tarrega - Guitar Works and Arrangements; H Villa-Lobos - 5 Preludes, 12 Etudes; J Obrovska - Concerto for Two Guitars with M Zelenka; S Bodorova - Tre Canzone de Suonare; Transformations I - Bach, Lennon/McCartney, Myers, Satie, Falla, Prokofiev; Transformation II - Bach, Janacek, Musorgsky, Marcello; Lubomir Brabec Live at Prague Spring Festival - Dowland, Bach, Villa-Lobos; Viola and Guitar, Italian Music with Lubomir Maly. Honours: Title, Laureate of the Concours International de Guitare, Paris, 1974; H Villa-Lobos Medal, 1987, from Brazilian Government. Membership: SAI. Hobbies: White Water Canoeing; Trekking. Current Management: Pragokoncert. Address: Pragokoncert, Maltezske nam 1, 11813 Praha-1, Czech Republic.

BRACANIN Philip (Keith), b. 26 May 1942, Kalgoorlie, Western Australia. Composer. Education: MA, 1966, PhD, 1970, University of Western Australia. Career: Faculty of University of Queensland, 1970- (currently Associate Professor); Commissions from University of Queensland and Queensland SO. Compositions include: With and Without for small orchestra, 1975; Trombone Concerto, 1976; Selections from the Omar Khayyam for choir and strings, 1979; Heterophony for orchestra, 1979; Rondellus for string orchestra, 1980; Because We Have No Time, song cycle for low voice and orchestra, 1981; Clarinet Concerto, 1985; Concerto for Orchestra, 1985; Throw Me a Heaven Around a Child, for baritone and chamber orchestra, 1986; Concerto for Orchestra no 2, 1987; Dance Poem for chamber orchestra, 1990; Guitar Concerto, 1991. Honours include: Australasian Performing Right Association, 1995. Address: c/o APRA, 1A Eden Street, Crows Nest, NSW 1065, Australia.

BRACHT Roland, b. 1952, Munich. Singer (Bass). Education: Studied at the Munich Musikhochschule; Studied at the Munich Music College, under Professor Blaschke. Career: Debut at the National Theatre in Verdi's Don Carlos; Sang at the Munich Opera Studio from 1971; Member of the Stuttgart Opera from 1973, notably as the Commendatore, in the production of Don Giovanni which reopened the Staatsoper, 1984; Ludwigsburg, 1978 as Masetto; Schwetzingen Festival, 1983, in the premiere of The English Cat by Henze; San Francisco, 1985 in Der Ring des Nibelungen; Debut in the War Memorial Opera House in San Francisco, June 1985; Debut in the Metropolitan Opera in New York, playing the part of King Heinrich, 1986; sang Pogner in Die Meistersinger at the opening of the new Essen Opera, 1988; King Heinrich at Pretoria, 1989; Sang Colline in La Bohème at Stuttgart, 1991 and Mustafa in L'Italiana in Algeri, 1996. Recordings: Don Giovanni; Die Entführung; Das Rheingold; Die Zauberflöte; Oedipus Rex; Alceste by Gluck; Die Feen by Wagner; Video of Der Freischütz. Address: c/o Staatstheater Stuttgart, Oberer Schlossgarten 6, D-7000 Stuttgart, Germany.

BRADBURY Colin, b. 1935, England. Clarinettist. Education: Studied at the Royal College of Music with Frederick Thurston, graduating in 1956. Career: Principal Clarinettist of the BBC Symphony, 1968-93; Performances of Concertos by Mozart, Weber, and Nielsen at the London Prom Concerts and director of the RCM Wind Ensemble; Duo partnership with pianist, Oliver Davies from 1978 with performances and recordings of Italian operatic fantasias, sonatas by Reger, Victorian music and The Art of The Clarinettist; Tutor with the National Youth Orchestra of Great Britain. Address: Manygate Management, 13 Cotswold Mews, 30 Battersea Square, London, SW11 3RA, England.

BRADLEY Gwendolyn, b. 12 Dec 1952, New York City, USA. Soprano. Education: North Carolina School of the Arts, Winston-Salem, North Carolina; Curtis Institute of Music, Philadelphia; Academy of Vocal Arts, Philadelphia. Debut: Nannetta, Falstaff, Lake George Opera, New York, 1976. Career: Metropolitan Opera debut, Nightingale, L'Enfant et les Sortilèges, 1981; Appearing as Blondchen, Gilda and Offenbach's Olympia; European debut, Corfu Festival, Greece, 1981; Gueat appearances with opera companies in Cleveland, Philadelphia, Central City, Amsterdam, Glyndebourne, Hamburg, Berlin, Monte Carlo, Nice; Sang Rodelinda with Netherlands Opera, 1983-84 (also Sophie in Der Rosenkavalier); Paris Opéra 1986, Zerbinetta; Appeared as the Fiakermilli in Arabella at the 1987 Glyndebourne Festival; Deutsche Oper Berlin, 1989, as Musetta; Sang Gilda at the Wiesbaden Festival, 1990, with the company of the Deutsche Oper; Sang the Heavenly Voice in Don Carlos at the Deutsche Oper, 1992; Mozart's Blonde at Los Angeles, 1995; Many engagements as soloist with leading USA orchestras; Recitals. Address: c/o Columbia Artists Management Inc, 165 West 57th Street, New York, NY 10019, USA.

BRADSHAW Claire, b. 1970, Hull, England. Singer (Mezzo-soprano). Education: Studied at the Royal Northern College of Music and with Barbara Robotham. Career: Appearances from 1994 with Scottish Opera-Go-Round and Scottish Opera as Euridice, Cherubino and Hansel; Concerts throughout the north of England at King's College Cambridge (Messiah), with the Hallé Orchestra and in Western Australia and Provence; Season 1997 with Susuki in concert (Royal Liverpool PO) and recitals throughout the UK and Australia. Honours include: Webster Booth/ESSO Award and James Gulliver Prize, Scotland. Address: Harrison/Parrott Ltd, 12 Penzance Place, London W11 4PA, England.

BRADSHAW Merrill, b. 18 June 1929, Wyoming, USA. Composer. Teacher. Education: Brigham Young University, University of Illinois, DMA, 1962. Career: Teacher, Brigham Young University from 1957; Executive Director, Barlow Endowment for Music Composition. Compositions: Dialogue for

Flute and Horn, 1956; 2 String Quartets, 1957, 1969; Violin Sonata, 1957; Suite for Viola, 1967; Brass Quintet, 1969; 5 Symphonies, 1957-79; Piano Concerto, 1955; Faces for Orchestra, 1965; Feathers for Orchestra, 1968; The Restoration, Oratorio, 1974; Four Mountain Sketches, and Nocturnes and Revels for Orchestra, 1974; Nocture for 2 Horns and Strings, 1977; The Title of Liberty, Musical, 1975; Viola Concerto, 1979; Violin Concerto, 1981; Love and Death, 4 Elizabethan Lyrics for Viola, Soprano and Strings, 1982; Christ Metaphors, 1989; Visionscape, 1990; Requiem Music, 1991; Museum Piece, 1993; Double Concerto, 1994; Piano Music. Address: 248 E 3140 North, Provo, UT 84604, USA.

BRADSHAW Murray (Charles), b. 25 Sept 1930, Illinois, USA. Professor of Musicology. m. 2 sons, 1 daughter. Education: MMus, American Conservatory of Music, 1955, Piano 1958, Organ; PhD, Musicology, University of Chicago, 1969. Compositions: Several organ compositions in The Organists Companion. Publications: The Origin of the Toccata, 1972; The Falsobordone, 1978; Francesco Severi, 1981; Girolamo Diruta Il Transilvano, 1984; Giovanni Luca Conforti, 1985; Gabriele Fattorini, 1986; Emilio de'Cavalieri, 1990. Contributions to: Journal of Musicology; Performance Practice Review; The Music Quarterly; The Music Review; Studi Musicali; Musica Antiqua; Musica Disciplina; Tijdschrift. Honours: American Philsophical Society, 1987. Memberships: International and American Musicological Societies; American Guild of Organists. Hobbies: Jogging; Bridge; Yoga; Latin. Address: Department of Musicology, UCLA, Los Angeles, CA 90024, USA.

BRAEM Thuering L M, b. 10 Apr 1944, Basel, Switzerland. Conductor; Composer. Education: Basel University; Heidelberg University; Piano Diploma, degree in Conducting, Academy of Music, Basel; MA, Composition, University of California, Berkeley; Studied Conducting, Curtis Institute of Music, Philadelphia. Career: Director, Music School, Basel, 1973-87; Director, Lucerne Conservatory, 1987-; Music Director, Ragio-Choir, Basel and Junge Philharmonie Zentralschweiz; President, Jeunesses Musicales, Switzerland, 1984-90; Principal Guest Conductor, Bohemian Chamber Philharmony Pardubic and others. Compositions: Lettres de Cezanne; Alleluja for Voice; Ara for Flute Ensemble (all Nepomuk-Verlag, AARAU); Chamber Music, Choral Music; Ombra for VI, Va and String Orchestra, 1991; Torrenieri for Horn and Strings, 1992; Concerto for Piano Trio and Orchestra, 1992. Recordings: Children's Songs of the American Indians; Fauré's Requiem; Music for Violincello and Orchestra by Martinu, Fauré, Dvorak and Tchaikovsky; Panton, Orch Music with Young Philharmonic of Central Switzerland. Publications: Musik und Raum, Basel, 1986; Series, Information und Versuche, 1975-90, 20 Issues; Bewahren and Oeffnen, Aarau, 1992; Research and Development in Future Institutions of Higher Learning in Music, 1997. Contributions to: Articles in newspapers and journals. Honour: Edwin Fischer Prize, 1992. Address: Lerchenstr 56, CH-4059 Basel, Switzerland.

BRAININ Norbert, b. 12 Mar 1923, Vienna, Austria. Violinist. m. Kathe Kottow, 7 Apr 1948, 1 daughter. Education: Studies with Professor Ricardo Odnoposoff, Konservatorium, Vienna; Professor Rosa Hochmann-Rosenfeld, Vienna; Professor Carl Flesch and Professor Max Rostal, London. Career: Debut with Amadeus Quartet and for forty years all over the world; Professor of annual Amadeus Quartet Course at the Royal Academy of Music, London; Professor of Violin Playing at Scuola di Musica di Fiesole, 1980; Professor of Quartet Playing at Reichenau, Austria; Professor of Violin Playing at Hochschule für Musik Franz Liszt, Weimar, 1995. Recordings: Amadeus Quartet of almost the entire classical romantic and modern repertoire for string quartet and or strings and piano and strings; Also works with clarinet, oboe and flute. Honours: OBE; DHC, University of London; DHC, Österreichisches Unterrichtministerium; Das Grosse Verdienstkreuz der Bundesrepublik Deutschlands, First Class. Memberships: Royal Academy of Music, London; Hochschule für Musik, Cologne. Address: 19 Prowse Avenue, Bushey Heath, Hertfordshire, England.

BRAITHWAITE Nicholas (Paul Dallon), b. 26 Aug 1939, London, England. Musician; Conductor. m. Gillian Agnes Haggarty, 24 August 1985, 1 son, 1 daughter. Education: Royal Academy of Music; Festival Masterclasses in Bayreuth and with Hans Swarowsky, Vienna. Career: Chief Conductor, Adelaide Symphony Orchestra, 1987-91; Principal Guest Conductor, 1977-84, Principal Conductor, 1984-91, Manchester Camerata; Chief Conductor, Tasmanian Symphony Orchestra; Permanent Guest Conductor, Norwegian State Radio Orchestra; Associate Conductor to Constantin Silvestri with Bournemouth Symphony Orchestra; Frequent Guest Conductor for all major orchestras in the UK; Toured Japan and Korea as Associate Conductor to Georg Solti with London Philharmonic Orchestra; Appearances with ORTF Orchestra, Paris; Oslo Philharmonic; Bergen Harmonien Symphony Orchestra; Odensee Symphony Orchestra; New Zealand Symphony Orchestra; Melbourne Symphony Orchestra; Sydney Symphony Orchestra; Danish Radio Orchestra; Bergen Festival; Symphony Nova Scotia, Halifax; Musical Director and Chief Conductor, Stora Teater Opera and Ballet Companies, Gothenberg, 1981-84; Musical Director, Glyndebourne Touring Opera, 1976-80; Associate Principal Conductor, English National Opera Company, 1970-74; Dean of Music, Victorian College of the Arts, 1988-91; Conducted Tosca at Elder Park, Adelaide, 1990; Francesca da Rimini for Chelsea Opera Group, 1994; Fledermaus for Scottish Opera, 1997. Recordings: Numerous. Honour: FRAM. Memberships: ISM; MU. Hobbies: Computers; Model Aircraft. Current Management: Christopher Tennant. Address: Taringa Park, Mount Barker Road, Mahndorf, South Australia 5245.

BRANDIS Thomas, b. 1935, Hamburg, Germany. Violinist. Education: Studied with Eva Hauptmann at the Musikhochschule Hamburg, 1952-57 and with Max Rostal in London. Career: Leader, Berlin Philharmonic Orchestra, 1962-63; Co-Founder, Brandis Quartet, 1976; Many Chamber engagements in Europe and Tokyo, with the Wiener Singverein and the Berlin Philharmonic; Festival appearances at Salzburg, Florende, Vienna, Edinburgh, Tours and Bergen; Has co-premiered the Clarinet Quintet Helmut Eder, 1984, and the 3rd Quartets of Gottfried von Einem and Giselher Klebe, 1981, 1983; Solo Concerto work under such conductors as Karajan, Böhm, Solti, Abbado, Schmidt-Isserstedt, Keilberth, Jochum, Tennstedt, and Albrecht. Recordings: As soloist: Albums with Karajan and Böhm; With the Brandis Quartet: Complete quartets of Schubert and Beethoven with other repertoire for the EMI/Electrola, Teldec, Orfeo, Nimbus and Harmonia Mundi labels. Honours: Prize, German Hochschulen Competition, 1946; International ARD Competition in Munich, 1947. Address: c/o Anglo Swiss Management, Suite 35-37, Morley House, 320 Regent Street, London W1R 5AD, England.

BRANDSTETTER John, b. 2 Oct 1949, Wayne, Nebraska, USA. Singer (Baritone). Education: Studied at the University of Nebraska and with Richard Hughes in New York. Debut: Minnesota Opera, 1976, as Ben in Conrad Susa's Black River. Career: Sang at Minneapolis in the premiere of Argento's, The Voyage of Edgar Allan Poe, 1976; Has also sung in the premieres of Bernstein's, A Quite Place, 1983, repeated in Vienna, 1986, as Josuke in Miki's Joruri, St Louis, 1985, and in The Balcony by Di Domenica, Boston, 1990; Season 1986-87 appeared as Enrico (Lucia di Lammermoor) at Seattle, Silvio (Pagliacci) in Detroit and as the Beast in the US premiere of Stephen Oliver's Beauty and the Beast, at St Louis; Sang Egberto in Verdi's Stiffelio at Sarasota, 1990, and the High Priest in Alceste at the Chicago Lyric Opera; Other roles include Mozart's Almaviva and Papageno, Figaro, Germont and Falke; Has also appeared at Dusseldorf, the City Opera New York, Miami and Philadelphia.

BRANSCOMBE Peter (John), b. 7 Dec 1929, Sittingbourne, Kent, England. University Teacher; Musicologist. m. Marina Elizabeth Riley, 14 Dec 1967, 2 sons, 1 daughter. Education: Dulwich College, London, 1944-48; MA, Worcester College, Oxford, 1956; PhD, Bedford College, London, 1977. Career: Appearances on BBC radio and television, Austrian Radio; Scottish television; Lecturer, German, 1959-69, Senior Lecturer, 1970-79, Professor of Austrian Studies, 1979-, University of St Andrews. Publications: Translator, Mozart and His World in Contemporary Pictures, 1961; Co-translator, Mozart, A Documentary Biography, 1965, revised 1966, revised third edition, 1990; Part Author, Co-Editor, Schubert Studies: Problems of Style and Chronology, 1982; Author, Mozart, Die Zauberflöte, 1991. Contributions to: New Grove Dictionary of Music and Musicians, approximately 120 articles, 1980; New Grove Dictionary of Opera, approximately 120 articles, 1992; Various professional journals. Honours: Governor, Royal Scottish Academy of Music, 1967-73; Music Committee, Scottish Arts Council, 1974-81; Scottish Arts Council, 1976-79; Chairman, Conference of University Teachers of German in Scotland, 1983-85. Memberships: Advisory Committee, Scottish Early Music Consort, 1981-89; Royal Musical Association; Modern Humanities Research Association; English Goethe Society; International Nestroy Society; Internationales Franz Schubert Institut; Schubert Institute, United Kingdom; Haydn Society of Great Britain; Whauden Society. Hobbies: Walking; Natural History. Address: 32 North Street, St Andrews, Fife KY16 9AQ, Scotland.

BRANT Henry (Dreyfus), b. 15 Sept 1913, Montreal, Quebec, Canada. Composer. Education: Studied at McGill Conservatorium, Montreal, 1926-29, the Institute of Musical Art and The Juilliard School in New York, 1932-34; Private study with Wallingford Riegger, Aaron Copland, George Antheil and Fritz Mahler. Career: Worked for Radio, Films, Jazz Groups and Ballets as Composer, Conductor and Arranger; Commercial music in Hollywood and Europe; Teacher at Columbia University, 1945-52, The Juilliard School, 1947-54 and Bennington College, 1957-80; Performer on Wind and Percussion Instruments; Music has employed spatial separation with variously contrasted instrumental and vocal groups. Compositions include: Antiphony I for 5 Orchestral Groups, 1953, revised 1968; Ceremony, Triple Concerto for violin, oboe and cello with voices, 1954; Labyrinth I (strings) and II for winds, 1955; The Grand Universal Circus, spatial opera, 1956; Conclave for Mezzo, Baritone and Instrumental ensemble, 1955; On the Nature of Things, for chamber orchestra, 1956; The Children's Hour for Voices, Brass, Organ and Percussion, 1958; Atlantis, Antiphonal Symphony, 1960; Violin Concerto with Lights, 1961; Fire in Cities, for 2 choirs and 2 instrumental ensembles, 1961; Odyssey - Why Not? for 2 Flutes and 4 small orchestral groups, 1965; Verticals Ascending for 2 wind ensembles, 1967; Windjammer for 5 Wind Instruments, 1969; An American Requiem, for wind orchestra, 1973; Divinity: Dialogues in the Form of Secret Portraits, spatial chamber music, 1973; Six Grand Pianos Bash Plus Friends, 1974; Solomon's Gardens for Voices, 24 Handbells and 3 Instruments. 1974; Homage to Ives, for baritone and orchestral groups, 1975; American Commencement for 2 Brass and percussion groups; Antiphonal Responses, for 3 bassoons and orchestra, 1978; Cerberus, for double bass and piccolo, 1978; The $1,000,000 Confessions for 2 Trumpets and 3 Trombones, 1978; Trinity of Spheres for 3 orchestral groups, 1978; Orbits for 80 Trombones, Soprano and Organ, 1979; The Glass Pyramid, spatial fantasy, 1980; Inside Track, spatial piano concerto, 1980; The Secret Calendar, spatial chronicle, 1980; Horizontals Extending, for 2 wind ensembles and jazz drummer, 1982; Desert Forests for orchestral groups, 1983; Litany of Tides for Solo Violin, 2 orchestras and 4 Voices, 1983; Meteor Farm, spatial oratorio, 1983; Fire under Water, multiple improvisations, 1983; Burning Brant on the Amstel, mobile spatial aquatic spectacle, 1984; Western Springs for 2 orchestras, 2 choruses and 2 jazz combos, 1984; More recent compositions include: Pathways to Security, ambulant spatial cantata, 1990; Prisons of the Mind, spatial symphony for 8 orchestral groups, 1990; Skull and Bones, spatial oratorio, 1991; Hidden Hemisphere, spatial assembly for 4 concert bands, 1992; Fourscore, 4 spatial string quartet including tenor-cello, 1993; Homeless People, spatial string quartet with percussion inside piano, 1993; Trajectory, spatial cantata with silent film, 1994; Dormant Craters, for spatial percussion orchestra, 1995; Plowshares and Swords, total symphonic orchestral environment in 74 individual parts, 1995. Address: 1607 Chino Street, Santa Barbara, CA 93101-4757, USA.

BRAUCHLI Bernard, b. 5 May 1944, Lausanne, Switzerland. Clavichord Player. Education: Piano Studies in Lausanne and Vienna, 1963-69; Studied Musicology at the New England Conservatory with Julia Sutton; Researched Iberian keyboard music at Lisbon, 1977. Debut: Fribourg, Switzerland, 1972; US debut at Marlboro College, Vermont, 1973; Numerous tours of Europe and North America with keyboard works of the 16-18th Centuries, including works by Portuguese and Spanish Composers; Has given summer courses in Austria and Spain, 1978-82; Lecturer at the Boston Museum of fine Arts, 1978-83; Professor of Clavichord at the New England Conservatory from 1983.

BRAUN Russell, b. 1968, Frankfurt, Germany. Singer (Baritone). Education: Studied in Frankfurt and Toronto. Career: Appearances with Canadian Opera as Mozart's Guglielmo and Papagaeno, Rossini's Figaro and in concert performances of Henri VIII by Saint-Säens and Massenet's Cendrillon; New York City Opera 1992, as Morales in Carmen, Pacific Opera 1993 as Britten's Demetrius; Concerts include Messiah in Montreal, Belshazzar's Feast with the Hartford SO and at Salzburg in Mozart concert arias; Season 1995-96 as Mozart's Count in Monte Carlo and at the Paris Opéra-Comique. Address: Harrison/Parrott Ltd, 12 Penzance Place, London W11 4PA, England.

BRAUN Victor, b. 4 Aug 1935, Windsor, Ontario, Canada. Singer (Baritone). Education: Studied at the Toronto Conservatory and in Vienna. Career: Sang first with the Canadian Opera Company in Montreal and Vancouver; Sang in Germany from 1964, notably at Frankfurt (Escamillo), Cologne, Dusseldorf and Hamburg; Bayerische Staatsoper, Munich from 1968; La Scala, Milan, 1969, as Wolfram in Tannhäuser; Sang Hamlet in the Covent Garden premiere of Searle's opera, and returned to London as Don Giovanni and Mozart's Count, Germont, Posa (Don Carlos) and Eugene Onegin; Salzburg, 1970, as Mozart's Count; Boston, 1977, in the US premiere of Glinka's Ruslan and Ludmilla; Santa Fe, 1983-84, as Mandryka in Arabella by Strauss and in Henze's We Come to the River; Nice, 1986, as Hans Sachs in Die Meistersinger; Maggio Musicale Florence, 1987, in Benvenuto Cellini, Debussy's Golaud, 1989; Sang in Doktor Faust by Busoni at Amsterdam, 1987; Chicago Lyric Opera as Wozzeck; Hans Sachs at the opening of the new Essen Opera, 1988, Don Alfonso for Netherlands Opera, 1990; Sang Holofernes in the US premiere of Judith by Siegfried Matthus, Santa Fe, 1990; Hans Sachs with the Canadian Opera Company at Toronto, 1992; Sang Gunther in a new production of Götterdämmerung at Brussels, 1991; Amfortas in Parsifal at Essen, 1992; Sang Debussy's Golaud at Frankfurt, 1994 and at the 1997 Salzburg Festival. Recordings include: Tannhäuser. Honours include: First Prize, International Mozart Competition, Vienna. Address: Ingpen and Williams Limited, 26 Wadham Road, London SW15 2LR, England.

BRÄUNINGER Jürgen, b. 13 Sept 1956, Stuttgart, West Germany. Composer, Electronic Instruments. m. Brigitte Keck, 1985. Education: MA, San Jose State University, San Jose, California, 1983; Staatliche Hochschule für Musik und darstellende Kunst, Stuttgart, 1992. Career: Tutor, 1977-82; Musical Director, Theatre Tri Buehne, Stuttgart, 1980-82; Member of Musica Nova, Society for New Music and New Jazz, Board of Directors, 1981-85; Co-Organiser, New Music Concert Series, Media, 1984-85; Lecturer, Staatliche Akademie der bildenden Künste, Stuttgart, 1984-85, Staatliche Hochschule für Musik und darstellende Kunst, Stuttgart, 1984-85; Lecturer in Composition and Director Electronic Music Studio, 1985-, Senior Lecturer, 1991-, Associate Professor, 1997-, University of Natal; Distinguished Visiting Composer, San Jose State University, California, 1988-89. Compositions: The Tam Tam Tape, Elektronische Musik, Oranment, 1982; Saxomanie, D-Art S and Bass-Auf, all 1984, on Vibraphony-Saxonomie Ornament; Xherone, 1986; .... anywhere far, 1991; Ahimsa-Ubuntu, 1995. Recordings: As a Synthesist, Wir spielen Märchen Otto Maier, Ravensburg, 1980; Traumspiel, Sandra, 1980; Contributing composer and complete score realization motion picture soundtrack: The Lawnmower Man, New Line Cinema Corporation, USA, 1991; Orchestration and additional music motion picture soundtrack: The Dead Pit, Skouras Picture, USA, 1989; Publications: As Producer: Mandela Peace Rally, 1990; Music for Liberation, 1990; Celebrating Oral Tradition: Bandlululondini, 1992; Art Gecko, 1993; Gathering Forces I, 1994; Old World, New World, Third World Studios, proceedings of the International Computer Music Conference, San Jose, California, 1992. Membership: GEMA. Address: University of Natal, Department of Music, Private Bag X10, Dalbridge 4014, South Africa.

BRAUSS Helmut F, b. 19 Oct 1930, Milan, Italy. Concert Pianist. Education: German Arbitur, 1950; Handel Conservatory, Munich, Hochschule für Musik, Heidelberg; Private study with Hans Ehlers, Elly Ney, Edwin Fischer. Debut: Munich, 1952. Career: Numerous Recitals, Broadcasts and Solo Appearances with Orchestras in Europe, USA, Japan, China and Korea; Appearances in Canada with Saskatchewan Festival Orchestra, Edmonton Symphony, Vancouver and Winnipeg CBC Orchestras and in most major centres; Initiator and Coordinator, Beethoven Festival, Sasketchewan, 1970; Specialist in Music of Beethoven, Brahms and Schumann; Currently, Professor of Music, University of Alberta. Recordings: Works by Mozart, Beethoven, Schubert, Schumann, Brahms, Chopin, Pfitzner, Khachaturian on PBS West Germany and Poulenc, on CBS Canada. Publications: Musik Aus Zweiter Hand (article); Max Reger's Music for Solo Piano, 1993. Honours: Killam Professor, University of Alberta, 1993. Hobbies: Swimming; Chess. Address: Department of Music, University of Alberto, Edmonton, Alberta T6G 2C9, Canada.

BRAUTIGAM Ronald, b. 1 Oct 1954, Haarlemmermeer, Netherlands. Pianist. m. Mary Elizabeth Jane Cooper, 14 Dec 1995. Education: Sweelinck Conservatory, Amsterdam; RAM, London; Rudolf Serkin, USA. Debut: Concertgebouw Amsterdam, 1979. Career: Appearances with all major orchestras in the Netherlands; Foreign engagements include Oslo Philharmonic Orchestra, Bavarian Radio Symphony Orchestra München, English Chamber Orchestra. Recordings: Shostakovich, Concerto No 1 (Concertgebouw Orchestra/Chailly, Decca); Hindemith, 2nd Kammer Musik (Concertgebouw Orchestra/Chailly, Decca); Mendelssohn, piano concertos. (Nieuw Sinfonietta Amsterdam, Markiz). Honour: Dutch Music Prize, 1984. Memberships: Ronald Stevenson Society, Edinburgh; Frank Martin Society, Holland. Hobbies: Reading; Cooking; Collecting Rare 19th Century Piano Music. Current Management: Marianne Brinks. Address: c/o Marianne Brinks, Graaf Willemlaan 52, 1191 EH Amstelveen, The Netherlands.

BRAZDA Josef, b. 1939, Babice u Rosic, Brno, Czech Republic. Musician. m. Vlasta Brazdova, 8 June 1974, 2 daughters. Education: Private Artistic School, Brno; State Conservatorium, Brno; Janácek's Akademie of Musical Arts, Brno. Debut: State Philharmonic Orchestra, Brno. Career: Prague Akademic, Wind Quintet; Prague Chamber Orchestra; Nusici d' Praga-Chamber Orchestra; Haydn Sinfonietta Vienna; Horn Instructor; Solo Concertos; Sonatas. Compositions: Instructive Compositions for 2,3,4 Horns. Recordings: Richard Strauss, Second Horn Concerto; Paul Hindemith, Hornkonzert; Franz Danzi, Hornkonzert E Major; P Hindemith, both Sonatas; Haydn, Hornkonzert D Major Hob VII; Haydn, Divertimenti; Haydn Sinfonietta Vienna. Honours: Several Prizes. Hobby: Painting. Address: Roklanska 1095, 25101 Ricany u Prahy, Czech Republic.

BRAZZI Jean, b. 30 May 1936, Troyes, France. Singer (Tenor). Education: Troyes and at the Conservatoire National in Paris. Debut: Stage: Besancon 1961, as Alfredo in Traviata. Career: Sang in Concert from 1961; Appearances in Bordeaux, Rouen, Marseilles, Lyon and Lille; Wexford Festival, 1967, as Gounod's Romeo, Glyndebourne, 1966, 1969, as Werther; Paris Opéra 1968 and 1980; Appeared as Charpentier's Julien at Monte Carlo 1970, as Phaedon in the French premiere of Satie's Socrate, Marseilles, 1972; Barcelona 1980 as Hoffmann; Other roles include Massenet's Des Grieux and Jean (Herodiade), Don José, Turiddu, Cavaradossi, Pinkerton, Maurizio in Adriana Lecouvreur, Steva (Jenufa) and Paco (La Vida Breve). Recordings include: Highlights from Werther; Herodiade; Les Beatitudes by Franck. Address: c/o Gran Teatro del Liceu, Barcelona, Spain.

BREAM Julian, b. 15 July 1933, London, England. Guitarist and Lutenist. Education: Royal College of Music. Debut: Began Professional Career, Cheltenham, 1947; Wigmore Hall, London, 1950. Career: Tours in Europe, America, Japan, Australia, India and Far East; Appeared at festivals at Aldeburgh, Bath, Edinburgh, Three Choirs, King's Lynn, Holland, Ansbach, Berlin and Stratford (Canada); Research into Elizabethan Lute Music which led to revival of interest in that instrument; Has encouraged contemporary English compositions for the guitar (including works by Britten, Walton and Tippett); Henze has composed Royal Winter Music (2 Sonatas after Shakespeare) for him; Formed Julian Bream Consort, 1960; Inaugurated Semley Festival of Music and Poetry, 1971; Season 1990-91 included concerts with Scottish Chamber Orchestra and tours of Italy and Britain (including 40th Anniversary Concert at the Wigmore Hall); Spring tours of Germany and the USA; Promenade Concerts, London with Malcolm Arnold's Guitar Concerto, 1991; Season 1992-93 included 60th Birthday Concert at the Wigmore Hall, Summer Festivals and BBC Proms. Recordings include: CD of Villa-Lobos Concerto; Five Preludes and 12 Preludes. Honours: DUniv, Surrey, 1968; ARAM, 1969; FRCM, 1981; FRNCM, 1983; Exclusive Contract with EMI Classics since 1990; OBE, 1964; Villa-Lobos Gold Medal, 1976; CBE, 1985. Hobbies: Playing the Guitar; Cricket; Table Tennis; Gardening; Backgammon. Address: c/o Hazard Chase Ltd, Richmond House, 16-20 Regent Street, Cambridge CB2 1DB, England.

BRECKNOCK John, b. 29 Nov 1937, Long Eaton, Derbyshire, England. Singer (Tenor). Education: Birmingham Music School with Frederic Sharp and Dennis Dowling. Debut: Alfred in Die Fledermaus, Sadler's Wells, London, 1967; Later repertoire includes Rossini's Almaviva and Comte Ory, Mozart's Belmonte and Ottavio and Verdi's Duke of Mantua; With the English National Opera at the London Coliseum sang in the UK stage premieres of Prokofiev's War and Peace, 1972, and Henze's The Bassarids, 1974, and in the world premiere of Gordon Crosse's The Story of Vasco, 1974; Covent Garden debut 1974, as Fenton in Falstaff; Glyndebourne debut 1971; Has sung at the Metropolitan Opera and toured Canada in 1973; At the Teatro Regio Parma, 1985, sang Almaviva in Il Barbiere di Siviglia; Season 1985-86 sang Rossini roles in Paris. Recordings include: Alfredo in an English language Traviata, opposite Valerie Masterson. Address: c/o English National Opera, St Martin's Lane, London WC2, England.

BREDEMEYER Reiner, b. 2 Feb 1929, Velez, Colombia. Composer. Education: Studied with Karl Hoeller in Munich, 1949-53, and with Wagner-Regeny at the Akademie der Kunste in East Berlin, 1955-57. Career: Conductor of the German Theatre in East Berlin since 1961; Teacher, Akademie der Kuenste from 1978. Compositions include: Leben des Andres, Opera, 1971; Die Galoschenoper, 1978; Orchestral: Integration, 1961; Variante, 1962; Schlagstück 3, for Orchestra and 3 Percussion Groups; Bagatellen für B, for Piano and Orchestra, 1970; Piano und ... 1970; Symphony, 1974; Double Concerto for Harpsichord, Oboe and Orchestra, 1974; Auftakte for 3 Orchestral Groups, 1976; Concerto for Oboe and Orchestra, 1977; 9 Bagatelles for Strings, 1984; Chamber includes: 4 Quintets, 1956, 1958, 1969, 1991; 3 String Quartets, 1962, 1968, 1983; 3 Septets, 1980, 1987, 1990; Vocal: Cantata, 1961; Wostock for Choir and Orchestra, 1961; Karthago for Chorus and Chamber Ensemble, 1961; Zum 13.7 fur Schoenberg, for Female Voice and Ensemble, 1976; Cantata 2 for 16 Voices and 16 Instruments, 1977; Das Alltaegliche for Soprano, Tenor and Orchestra, 1980; Die Winterreise for Baritone, Piano and Horn, 1984; Die Schoene Muellerin for Baritone, String Quartet and Horn Quartet, 1986; Operas: Candide, 1981-82; Der Neinsager, 1990; Songs; Piano Music. Address: GEMA, Postfach 80 07 67, D-81607 Munich, Germany.

BREHM Alvin, b. 8 Feb 1925, New York, USA. Composer; Conductor; Double Bass Player. Education: Studied with Zimmermann and Giannini at Juilliard, 1942-43 and with Walingford Reigger at Columbia University, MA, 1951. Career: Played double bass with the Pittsburgh Symphony Orchestra, 1950-51; The Contemporary Chamber Ensemble, 1969-73; The Group for Contemporary Music, 1971-73; The Philomusica Chamber Music Society, 1973-83; The Chamber Music Society of Lincoln Center, 1984-89; Conductor of Contemporary Music from 1947; Founder-Conductor of the Composers' Theater Orchestra, 1967; Teacher, State University of Stony Brook, 1968-75; Manhattan School of Music, 1969-75; and SUNY at Purchase from 1982; Dean of Purchase, State University of New York Music Division, 1982-92; Head of Composition, Purchase, 1992-; Member of Fulbright Composition Panel, 1992-95. Compositions include: Divertimento for Trumpet, Horn and Trombone, 1962; Dialogies for Bassoon and Percussion, 1964; Brass Quintet, 1967; Cello Sonata, 1974; Concertino for Violin and Strings, 1975; Quarks for flute, Bassoon, String Quartet and Piano, 1976; Sextet for Piano and Strings, 1976; Piano Concerto, 1977; Double Bass Concerto, 1982; Tuba Concerto, 1982; Sextet for Woodwind Quintet and Piano, 1984; Children's Games for Flute, Clarinet, String Trio and Piano, 1985; Cialles for Russian Town, piano, 1993; Metamorphy, European Tour, piano. Recordings: Cycle of Songs to Poems of Lorea, for soprano and 10 instruments; Quintet for Brass; Bassoon Quartet; 3 works for piano. Contributions to: Clavier magazine, cover articles; American Record Guide, reviews. Honours: Grants: Naumburg Foundation, NEA, New York State Arts Council. Address: 8 Oakwood Drive, Weston, CT 06883, USA.

BRELL Mario, b. 1937, Hamburg, Germany. Singer (Tenor). Education: Studied at Hamburg. Career: Sang operetta at Hof, 1963-65; Lucerne, 1965-67; Oldenburg, 1967-71; Krefold, 1971-73; At Gelsenkirchen, 1973-82; Sang such repertory as Lohengrin, Parsifal, Zemlinsky's Zwerg, Hofmann in Les Contes d'Hoffmann; Member of the Deutsche Oper am Rhein Dusseldorf from 1982, singing Diomedes in Penthesilea by Schoeck, 1986; Guest appearances in Zurich, Frankfurt, Karlsruhe and Wiesbaden (premiere of Kirchner's Belshazar, 1986); Amsterdam, 1987, as Busoni's Mephisto, Bielefield, 1990, as Bacchus in Ariadne auf Naxos; Other roles include the Count in Schreker's Irrelohe and Max in Der Freischütz; Sang the major in Einem's Besuch der alten Dame, Gelsenkirchen 1991. Recordings include: Der Zar lässt sich photographieren by Weill. Address: c/o Deutsche Oper am Rhein, Heinrich-Heine Allee 16, 4000 Dusseldorf, Germany.

BREM Peter, b. 1948, Munich, Germany. Violinist. Education: Graduate, Richard Strauss Conservatory, Munich, 1970. Career: Berlin Philharmonic Orchestra, 1970-76; Co-Founder, Brandis String Quartet, 1976, with concerts in Tokyo, London, Hamburg, Munich, Paris and Milan and engagements with the Wiener Singverein and the Berlin Philharmonic; Festival appearances at Salzburg, Edinburgh, Lucerne, Tours, Bergen, Florence and Vienna; Has Co-Premiered the 3rd Quartets of Gottfried von Einem and Giselher Klebe, 1981, 1983, and the Clarinet Quintet of Helmut Eder, 1984; Solo concerts with such orchestras as the Radio-Sinfonieorchester Berlin. Recordings incl: Albums in the standard repertoire from 1978 with the EMI/Electrola, Teldec, Orfeo and Harmonia Mundi labels; Recent releases of Beethoven, Weill, Schulhoff and Hindemith and the Schubert String Quintet with Nimbus. Honours: Prizewinner at the Deutsche Hochschulewettbewerb. Address: c/o Anglo Swiss Management, Suite 35-37 Morley House, 320 Regent Street, London W1R 5AD, England.

BREMERT Ingeborg, b. 1930, Germany. Singer (Soprano). Career: Sang at Pforzheim, 1953-55, Zurich Opera, 1955-57; Member of the Munich Opera, 1960-67; Schwetzingen Festival, 1961, as Elizabeth in the premiere of Henze's Elegy for Young Lovers; Many guest appearances as Mozart's Arminda (La finta giardiniera) and Cherubino, Eva, the Composer (Ariadne auf Naxos), Isabella in Krenek's Karl V and Regina in Mathis der Maler by Hindemith. Address: c/o Bayerische Staatsoper, Max Joseph-Platz, W-8000 Munich 1, Germany.

BRENDEL Alfred, b. 5 Jan 1931, Wiesenburg, Austria. Pianist; Writer. m. (1) Irish Heymann-Gonzala, 1960, div. 1972, (2) Irene Semler, 1975, 1 son, 3 daughters. Education: Piano under Sofija Dezelic (Zagreb), Loduvika v Kaan (Graz), Edwin Fischer (Lucerne), Paul Baumgartner (Basel), Eduard Steuermann (Salzburg), Composition under A Michl (Graz), Harmony under Franjo Dugan (Zagreb). Debut: 1948, Musikverein, Graz. Career: Extensive concert repertoire from Bach to Schoenberg; Important in establishing Schubert piano sonatas, and Schoenberg Piano Concerto in the concert repertoire; 1992-96, performed last complete series of Beethoven Sonatas throughout Europe and USA; Regular guest with leading orchestras worldwide; Recitals performed at major musical centres and festivals. Recordings: Extensive repertoire on disc; First pianist to record Beethoven's complete piano works; Recorded third complete series of Beethoven Sonatas. Publications: Musical Thoughts and Afterthoughts, 1976; Nachdenken über Musik, 1977; Musik beim Wort genommen, 1992; Humerous works: Fingerzeig, 1996; Störendes Lachen während Des Jaworts, 1997. Honours: Grand Prix du Disque, 1965, 1984, Edison Prize, 1973, 1981, 1984, 1987, Deutscher Schallplattenpreis, 1976, 1977, 1981, 1982, 1984, Wiener Flötenuhr, 1976, 1977, 1979, 1982, 1984, 1987, Gramophone Award, 1977, 1978, 1980, 1981, 1982, 1983, 1984, Japanese Record Academy Award, 1977, 1978, 1980, 1982, 1984, 1992, Franz Liszt Prize, 1979, 1982, 1983, 1987, Preis der deutschen Schallplattenkritik, 1992; Hon DMus, London, 1978, Oxford, 1983, Warwick, 1991, Yale, 1992; Hon DLitt, Sussex, 1981; Hon KBE, 1989; Diapason d'Or Award, 1992; Several other prizes and honours. Current Management: Thomas Hull, Ingpen and Williams. Address: c/o Ingpen and Williams Ltd, 26 Wadham Road, London SW15 2LR, England.

BRENDEL Wolfgang, b. 20 Oct 1947, Munich, Germany. Singer (Baritone). Education: Studied in Munich. Career: Sang Don Giovanni in Kaiserslautern, 1970, then became a member of the Bayersische Staatsoper Munich; Roles include Papageno, Germont and Pelléas; Guest appearances in Hamburg, Dusseldorf and Karlsruhe; Metropolitan Opera dubut 1975, as Mozart's Count; Sang Verdi's Miller with the Chicago Lyric Opera, 1983; Bayreuth Festival, 1985, as Wolfram in Tannhäuser; Covent Garden debut 1985, as Luna in Il Trovatore; Eugene Onegin and Donizetti's Enrico, 1988; Metropolitan Opera and Bayreuth Festival, 1989, as Germont and Wolfram; Teatro, San Carlos, Lisbon, 1989, as Amfortas; Chicago 1990, as Eugene Onegin; Other roles include Puccini's Marcello and Strauss's Mandryka; Season 1991-92 as Amfortas in Parsifal at La Scala and as Count Luna at Munich; Sang Verdi's Renato, 1994; Wagner'sDutchman at the Deutsche Oper Berlin, 1997. Recordings: Die Lustigen Weiber von Windsor, Paer's Leonora and Der Freischütz (Decca); Die Zauberflöte, La Bohème and Zar und Zimmermann (HMV); Ein Deutsches Requiem (Deutsche Grammophon). Address: c/o Ingpen & Williams, 26 Wadham Road, London SW15 2LR, England.

BRENET Thérèse, b. 22 Oct 1935, Paris, France. Composer. Education: Studied at the Paris Conservatoire. Career: Professor at the Conservatoire from 1970. Compositions include: Moires, for 6 ondes martenots and strings, 1985; Incandescence for baritone, saxophone and piano, 1986; Vibration for celtic harp and strings, 1984; Oceanides for piano left hand, 1986; Plus souple que l'eau for ondes martenot and percussion, 1986. Honours include: Prix de Rome, 1965. Address: c/o SACEM, 225 avenue Charles de Gaulle, 92521 Neuilly sur Seine Cedex, France.

BRENNEIS Gerd, b. 3 Jan 1936, Nienhegen, Mecklenburg, Germany. Singer (Tenor). Debut: Essen, 1960, as Curzio in Figaro. Career: Sang at Augsburg from 1965 as Verdi's Manrico and Gabriele Adorno, Idomeneo, Abdre Chenier, Lensky and Dmitri (Boris Godunov) and in operas by Wagner; Bayreuth Festival, 1973-74, as Walther and Siegmund; Deutsche Oper Berlin from 1974 as Wagner's Parsifal, Lohengrin and Tannhäuser, Strauss's Bacchus and the Emperor in Die Frau ohne Schatten; Huon in Oberon, 1986; Metropolitan Opera, 1976, as Walther; Has sung Tristan at Pretoria, South Africa, 1985, in Tokyo with the company of the Vienna Staatsoper, 1986, and Turin, 1987; Has also sung in Munich, Cologne, Florence and Milan; New York, 1976-81, as the Emperor; Nice Opera, 1988, as Siegfried; Television appearances include the title role in Wagner's Rienzi, with the Wiesbaden Opera. Address: Deutsche Oper Berlin, Richard Wagnerstrasse 10, D-1000 Berlin, Germany.

BRESNICK Martin, b. 13 Nov 1946, NY, USA. Composer. m. Anna Barbara Broell, 21 Jun 1969, 1 d. Education: BA in Music Composition, Hartt School of Music, University of Hartford, 1967; MA, 1968 and DMA, 1972 in Music Composition, Stanford University; Akademie für Musik, Vienna, Austria, 1969-70. Compositions: Trio for 2 Trumpets and Percussion, 1966; Introit, 1969; Ocean of Storms, 1970; Intermezzi, 1971; Musica, 1972; B's Garlands, 1973; Wir Weben, Wir Weben, 1978; Conspiracies, 1979; Der Signal, 1982; High Art, 1983; String Quartet No 2 Bucephalus; One, 1986; Lady Neil's Dumpe, 1987; Trio, 1988; Pontoosuc, 1989; Musica Povera, Nos 1-3, 1991; String Quartet No 3, 1992. Recordings: B's Garlands; Conspiracies; 3 Intermezzi; String Quartet No 2 Bucephalus; Wir Weben, Wir Weben; Lady Neil's Dumpe, CD; Piano Trio; Just Time, CD. Publication: How Music Works. Contributions to: Mosaic; Yale Journal of Music Theory. Address: Yale School of Music, 96 Wall Street, New Haven, CT 06520, USA.

BRESNIG Ulla, b. 1939, Germany. Singer (Mezzo-Soprano). Education: Studied at the Graz Conservatory. Career: Sang at the St Gallen Opera, 1964-65, Trier, 1967-69, and Kiel from 1969 (notably in the German premiere of Milhaud's La Mère Coupable); Hanover Opera, 1969-76; Among her best roles have been Mozart's Marcellina, Erda, the Countess in Lortzing's Der Wildschütz, Octavian, Verdi's Fenena and Azucena, and Orzse in Kodály's Háry Janos; Many concert appearances.

BRESS Hyman, b. 30 June 1931, Cap, Canada. Violinist. Education: Studied at the Curtis Institute and with Heifetz at Tanglewood. Career: Soloist with the Montreal Symphony, 1956-60, and has given many concertos and solo engagements in North America and Europe; Bach's D Minor partita at the Wigmore Hall, London; Premiered the Virtuose Musik by Blacher, 1968. Recordings include: Solo violin works by Ysaÿe. Publications include: An Introduction to Modern Music.

BRETT Charles, b. 27 Oct 1941, Maidenhead, Berkshire, England. Singer (Countertenor). m. Brigid Barstow, 1 Aug 1973, 1 s, 1 d. Education: Choral scholar, King's College, Cambridge. Career: Leading performer with early and Baroque music ensembles led by Munrow, Harnoncourt, Leonhardt, Hogwood, Gardiner, Herreweghe and Malgoire; Recent engagements in US, France, Switzerland, Germany, Spain and Norway; Handel's Theodora, in Oslo; Israel in Egypt, and Geneva; Bach's Christmas Oratorio in Versailles; Bach's St John Passion in Cambridge and London; B Minor Mass with Collegium Vocale Gent at Lourdes, Paris and Lyon; Many concerts with Le Grande Ecurie et la Chambre du Roy, conducted by Malgoire; Opera debut, 1984, in Angelica Vincitrice di Alcina by Fux, at Graz; Handel's Semele at Ludwigsburg; Tour of France with La Clemenza di Tito by Gluck; Aachen Opera, 1987, as Oberon; Founder and Director, Amaryllis Consort, vocal group specializing in Renaissance repertoire; Professor, Royal Academy of Music; Master class in Canada, Belgium, Germany, Spain, Mexico, France; Conductor: Performances of works by various composers in France; Dido and Aeneas for Cervantino Festival, Mexico, 1995. Recordings: Handel's Dixit Dominus, Rinaldo, Messiah, The Triumph of Time and Truth; Bach's B Minor Mass; Lambert: Leçons de Ténèbres; Mozart Masses; Bach: Cantatas; Burgon: Canciones de Alma; Italian and English madrigals with Amaryllis Consort; Vivaldi's Nisi Dominus and Stabat Mater. Honour: Honorary RAM, 1991. Membership: ISM. Address: 4 Lebanon Court, Twickenham, TW1 3DA, England.

BRETT Kathleen, b. 4 Sept 1962, Campbell River, Canada. Singer (Soprano). Career: Appearances with the Canada Opera Ensemble and elsewhere in Canada as Susanna, Bizet's Leila (Manitoba Opera), Adina (Calgary Opera) and Pamina (Edmonton Opera); European debut as Dorinda in Handel's Orlando at Antwerp, followed by Mozart's Barbarina at Covent Garden, Susanna at Monte Carlo and Amor in Gluck's Orphée et Euridice with L'Opera Française in New York; Other repertory includes Kristina in The Makropoulos Case (San Francisco), Drusilla in Monteverdi's Poppea (Dallas Opera), Despina (Vancouver Opera), Zerlina, and Amarilli in Handel's Pastor Fido (at Toronto); Concerts include Messiah at Montreal, the Fauré Requiem with the Vancouver SO, and A Midsummer Night's Dream by Mendessohn; Season 1997-98 with Sophie in Der Rosenkavalier at Seattle, Pamina at Dallas, Nannetta in Falstaff at Los Angeles, Mozart's Servilia at Antwerp and Iris in Semele for Opera Pacific. Honours include: Best Canadian Singer at the 1991 International Mozart Competition; Sullivan Award winner; Canadian Council Career Development Grant. Address: c/o IMG Artists, Media House, 3 Burlington Lane, London W4 2TH, England.

BRETT Philip, b. 17 Oct 1937, Edwinstowe, England. Musicologist; Conductor. Education: Studies, King's College, Cambridge, PhD 1965; University of California, Berkeley. Career: Researched English Madrigal Composers with Thurston Dart, Cambridge; Assistant Lecturer, Music, Fellow, King's College, Cambridge, 1963-66; Assistant Professor, 1966-71, Associate Professor, 1971-78, Professor, 1978-, University of California, Berkeley; Professor of Music, University of California, Riverside, 1991-. Recordings: Lou Harrison, La Koro Sutro, New Albion; Morton Feldman, Rothko Chapel, New Albion; Handel's Susanna, Harmonia Mundi (prepared chorus). Publications include: Consort Songs, 1969; William Byrd, Consort Songs for Voice and Viols, 1970; William Byrd, Madrigals, Songs and Canons, 1976; William Byrd, The Masses, 1981; William Byrd, Gradualia, 1990-97; Benjamin Britten, Peter Grimes (Cambridge Opera Handbooks, 1983); Queering the Pitch: The New Gay and Lesbian Musicology, edited with Elizabeth Wood and Gary C Thomas, 1994; General Editor, The Byrd Edition. Contributions to: Numerous professional journals and bulletins. Honours: Archibald T Davison Medal for Musicology, 1969; Noah Greenberg Award, American Musicological Society, 1980; Grammy Nomination for Handel's Susanna Recording, Choral Class, 1991. Memberships: Board Member, American Musicological Society, 1984-86; Royal Musicological Association; Society for Ethnomusicology. Address: 17341 Ranchero Road, Riverside, CA 92504, USA.

BREUL Elisabeth, b. 25 Aug 1936, Gea, Germany. Singer (Soprano). Education: Studied at the Musikhochschule of Gera and Dresden. Debut: Gera 1958, as Donna Anna. Career: Member of the Dresden Opera from 1960; Guest appearances in Berlin, Brussels, Brno, Lodz, Budapest, Genoa and Wiesbaden and music centres in Russia, France, Rumania and Spain; Other roles include Tatiana in Eugene Onegin, Natasha in War and Peace, Marguerite, Tosca, Agathe and Mozart's Countess and Susanna; Many appearances in the concert hall, in music by Bach and Handel; Teacher at the Musikhochschule of Dresden and Leipzig.

BREVIG Per A, b. 7 Sept 1936, Halden, Norway. Conductor. m. Berit Brevig, 22 April 1959, 2 sons, 2 daughters. Education: Diploma 1966, Postgraduate Diploma 1967, Bachelor of Arts Degree 1968, Doctor of Musical Arts 1971, The Juilliard School; Conducting Studies: Bergen, Norway, 1963, 1964; Norrkoping Sweden, 1963, 1965; Hilversum, Holland, 1964; The Juilliard School, New York, USA, 1966-68; Leopold Stokowski Symposium for Young Conductors, New York, 1966-68. Debut: Soloist with Bergen Philharmonic Orchestra, 1961. Career: Principal Trombonist: Detroit Symphony Orchestra, Detroit, 1966; Bergen Philharmonic Orchestra, Bergen, Norway, 1957-65; American Symphony Orchestra, New York, 1966-70; Metropolitan Opera Orchestra, New York, 1968-94; Music Director and Conductor, Empire State Opera Company, New York, 1990-; Conductor, Island Lyric Opera, New York, 1993-. Commissions and Dedications include: Roger Smith: Sonata for Trombone and Piano, 1965; Alcides Lanza: Acufenos for Trombone and Four Instruments, 1966; Egil Hovland: Concerto for Trombone and Orchestra; Noel Da Costa: Four Preludes for Trombone and Piano, 19 73; Vincenet Persichetti: Parable for Solo Trombone, 1978; Robert Starer: Serenade for Trombone, Vibraphone and Strings, 1982; Paul Turok: Canzona Concertante No 2, 1982; Walter Ross: Trombone Concerto No 2 for Trombone and Orchestra, 1984; Melvyn Broiles: The Great Northern Posaune for Trombone and Brass Ensemble, 1989; Arne Nordheim: Return of the Snark for Trombone and Electronic Tape, 1989. Publications include: Avant Garde Techniques in solo Trombone Music, Problems of Notation and Execution, 1974; Losing One's Lip and Other Problems of Embouchure, 1990; Edvard Grieg and the Edvard Grieg Society, 1993; Medical Problems of Musicians, 1995. Honours: XIV International Music Competition, Prague; Henry B Cabot Award, Boston Symphony Orchestra, Mass; Elsie and Walter B Naumburg Fellowship, The Juilliard School; Royal Medal of St Olav by King Olav V of Norway; Scandinavian of the Month, Norwegian-American Chamber of Commerce, 1995; Neill Humfeld Award for Excellence in Teaching, 1995; Honored by New York Brass Conference, 1996. Memberships include: National Society of Literature and the Arts; International Trombone Association, Advisory Board; Norwegian Church, New York, Cultural Committee; Musikphysiologie und Musikermedizin, Stuttgart, Germany. Address: 118 Constitution Drive, Orangeburg, NY 10962, USA.

BREVIK Tor, b. 22 Jan 1932, Oslo, Norway. Composer; Conductor; Music Critic. Education: Studied violin, viola and theory, Oslo Conservatory; Also Sweden. Career: Founded Youth Chamber Orchestra, Oslo, 1958; Music critic. Compositions: Opera, Da kongen kom til Spilliputt, 1973; Adagio and Fugue for Strings, 1958; Overture, 1958; Serenade for Strings, 1959; Chaconne for Orchestra, 1960; Concertino for Clarinet and Strings, 1961; Music for Violin, 1963; Canto Elegiaco for Orchestra, 1964; Contrasts, chamber ballet, 1964; Elegy for Soprano, Viola, Double bass and Percussion, 1964; Divertimento for wind quintet, 1964; Adagio Religioso for Horn, 1967; String de Quartet, 1967; Concertino for Strings, 1967; Music for 4 strings, 1968; Intrada for orchestra, 1969; Romance for Violin and Orchestra or Piano, 1972; Andante Cantabile for Violin and Strings, 1975; Septet, 1976l; Fantasy for Flute, 1979; Light of Peace, Christmas play for children, 1980; Viola Concerto, 1982; Sinfonietta, 1989; Choral music; Songs; Sinfonia Brevik, 1991; The Singing Raft, cantata for soprano, mixed chorus, children's chorus and strings, 1992; Music for Orchestra, 1993; Serenade for 10 Winds, 1994; On Request!, music for band, 1994. Recordings: String Quartet, Divertimento for Wind Quintet; Septet and Elegy for Soprano. Membership: The Society of Norwegian Composers. Address: Nebbaveien 53, NB 1433 Vinterbro, Norway.

BREWER Aline, b. 14 Sept 1963, Shropshire, England. Harpist. Education: Royal College of Music with Marisa Robles. Debut: Wigmore Hall, 1990. Career: Principal Harp with the Royal Philharmonic Orchestra; Former member of the European Community Orchestra and the Britten-Pears Orchestra; Solo appearances with the London Mozart Players, Primavera and the Britten-Pears Orchestra; Duo recitals with flautist Jennifer Stinton; Member of the Britten-Pears Ensemble, with performances throughout Britain and the USA. Recordings include: Romantic music for Flute and Harp; Mozart's Concerto K299, with Jennifer Stinton and the Philharmonia Orchestra. Honours include: Joint Winner, South East Arts Young Artists Platform. Address: c/o Owen White Management, 14 Nightingale Lane, London N8 7QU, England.

BREWER Bruce, b. 12 Oct 1941, San Antonio, Texas, USA. Singer (Tenor). m. Joyce Castle. Education: Studied with Josephine Lucchese at University of Texas, Austin, and with Richard Bonynge in New York and London; Further study with Nadia Boulanger and Rosalyn Tureck. Career: Sang as first in concert, notably in Baroque and early music; Opera debut San Antonio 1970, as Don Ottavio; Camden Festival, London, in Donizetti's Torquato Tasso, 1974; Sang at Opera Houses in Boston, San Francisco, Berlin, Paris, Toulouse, Spoleto and London, Covent Garden 1979; Aix-en-Provence Festival in revival of music by Campra; La Scala Milan 1980, in L'Enfance de Christ by Berlioz; Rossini's Le Comte Ory, 1991; Often heard in Bach and Mozart; Sang Lord Puff in Henze's English Cat in Paris, and in the premieres of Ballif's Dracula and Denisov's L'écume des jours; Paris Opéra, 1988, in the premiere of La Célestine by Maurice Ohana; Sang Fatty in Weill's Mahagonny at the Maggio Musicale, Florence, 1990; Truffaldino in Busoni's Turandot at Lyon, 1992. Recordings: Les Indes Galantes by Rameau; Rameau's Platée and Les Paladins; Messiaen's St François d'Assise; Rameau's Zoroastre; Boulevard Solitude by Henze; Beethoven's 9th Symphony; Berlioz's works for Soloists and Chorus; Les Nuits d'été; Gretry's L'Amant Jaloux; Liszt's

Complete Songs for Tenor; Lully's Alceste; Offenbach's Orphée aux Enfers. Address: 1 rue du Courier, 53250 Couptrain, France.

BREWER Christine, b. 1960, USA. Singer (Soprano). Education: Studies in the USA with Bigit Nilsson. Career: Appearances with the Opera Theatre of St Louis as Ellen Orford in Peter Grimes, Ariadne, Donna Anna (also for Vancouver Opera, 1994); Sang Sifare in Mozart's Mitridate at the 1992 Mostly Mozart Festival in New York, Lady Billows in Albert Herring at San Diego and Vitellia in La Clemenza di Tito; Concert engagements include Szymanowki's Stabat Mater in Cleveland, the Vaughan Williams Benedicte in Louisville and Poulenc's Stabat Mater with the Leipzig Gewandhaus Orchestra; Beethoven's Ninth Symphony in Colombus and the Missa Solemnis in Washington DC and San Diego; Mendelssohn's Elijah with the Houston and Honolulu Symphonies; Recent engagements include the Mozart and Dvorak Requiems in Toronto, the Janacek Glagolitic Mass in Atlanta and at the Mann Music Center with the Philadelphia Orchestra under Charles Dutoit; Gretchen in Schumann's Faust at the Caramoor Festival. Honour: Winner, Metropolital Opera National Council Auditions, 1989. Address: c/o IMG Artists, Media House, 3 Burlington Lane, London W4 2TH, England.

BREZINA Ales, b. 17 Sept 1965, Teplice, Czech Republic. Director; Musicologist; Secretary. m. Jarmila Brezinova, 22 April 1988. Education: Violin, Piano, Music Academy, Pilsen, 1979-85; MA, Department of Musicology, Charles University, Prague, 1989; Postgraduate Studies, 1989-95, Doctorate, 1992-, Department of Musicology, University Basle. Appointments: Director, Martinu Foundations Study Center, Prague; Secretary, Bohuslav Martinu Foundation, Prague. Publications: Die Martinu-Manuskripte in der Paul Sacher Stiftung Basel; Schweizer Jahrbuch für Musikwissenschaft, 1994; Prager Musikleben zu Beginn des 20, 1997. Memberships: Czech Music Society; Czech Society for Musicology; Swiss Society for Musicology. Hobby: Music. Address: c/o Bohuslav Martinu Foundation, Besedni 3, CZ-118 00 Prague 1, Czech Republic.

BRICCETTI Thomas (Bernard), b. 14 Jan1936, Mount Kisco, New York, USA. Conductor; Composer. Education: Studied Piano with Jean Dansereau, Composition with Samuel Barber, Peter Mennin and Alan Hovhaness; Eastman School of Music, Rochester, New York, 1955. Career: Music Director, St Petersburg Symphony Orchestra, 1963-68; Florida Sun Coast Poera, 1964-68; Associate Conductor, Indianapolis Symphony Orchestra, 1968-72; Music Director, Fort Wayne Philharmonic Orchestra, 1971-78; Cleveland Institute of Music University Circle Orchestra, 1972-75; Omaha Symphony Orchestra, 1975-83; Nebraska Sinfonia, 1975-83; Principal Guest Conductor, Stavanger Symphony Radio Orchestra, 1986-87; Artistic Director, Orchestra Stabile, Bergamo, 1988-; Guest Conductor with various orchestras in North America, South America and Europe. Compositions: Opera, Eurydice; Symphony No 1; Violin Concerto; The Fountain of Youth, overture; Illusions, symphonic poem; Some Chamber Music including a String Quartet; Flute Sonata; Piano Sonata; Choral Pieces; Songs; Cennina Concertino, 1992; Cello Concerto, 1993; Symphony (No 1) No 2, 1994; French Toast, 1994. Recordings: With the Indiana Chamber Orchestra, Nebraska Sinfonia, Louisville Orchestra, Orchestra Stabile di Bergano, Symphonia Perusina, Virtuosi di Prague. Honours: ASCAP Special Awards Grants, 1960-88; Ford Foundation Composers Fellowships, 1961-63; Yaddo Foundation Residence Grant, 1963; Pulitzer Prize in Music Nomination for Illusions, 1985; Various commissions. Current Management: Columbia Artists Management, New York City, Address: Via Eburnea 1, 06123 Perugia, Italy.

BRIDEOAKE Peter, b. 23 April 1945, Adelaide, South Australia. Composer. Education: MMus, Adelaide University, 1971; Study with Richard Meale, 1969-71. Career: Faculty Member, Elder Conservatory, 1975-; Commissions from the Australian Chamber Orchestra, Seymour Group and Victoria String Quartet. Compositions include: Composition for Winds, 1971; Music for Flute and Percussionists, 1972; Gedatsu for guitar, 1972; Chiaroscuro, 1978; String Quartet, 1980; Interplay for 2 clarinets and harp, 1981; Imagery for string orchestra, 1981; Shifting Reflections for chamber ensemble, 1982; Canto for Clarinet Alone, 1987; A Poet's Lament for soprano and piano, 1988. Honours include: John Bishop Memorial Prize, 1976. Address: c/o APRA, 1A Eden Street, Crows Nest, NSW 2065, Australia.

BRIDGES Althea, b. 11 Jan 1936, Sydney, Australia. Singer (Soprano). Education: Studied at the Sydney Conservatory. Career: Member of the Australian Opera Company, 1961-64; Sang in Europe from 1964, at first in Austria (Graz); Vienna, Theater an der Wien, in the premiere of Hauer's Die Schwarze Spinne, 1966; Stuttgart, 1968, in the premiere of Orff's Prometheus; Landestheater Linz, 1971-83; Sang Tosca at Frankfurt and Donna Anna at the Glyndebourne Festival; Bari, Italy, as Ortrud in Lohengrin; Other roles include Strauss's Elektra and Marschallin, Marguerite in Faust and Azucena in Il Trovatore; Sang in the premeiere of Michael Kohlhaas by Karl Kögler at Linz, 1989. Address: c/o Landestheater, Promenade 39, A-4010 Linz, Austria.

BRIGGS Sarah, b. 1972, England. Concert Pianist. m. 19 Nov 1994. Education: Studied with Denis Matthews at Newcastle, with John Lill, and Chamber Music with Bruno Giuranna at Blonay, Switzerland. Debut: Fairfield Hall, Beethoven's 2nd Piano Concerto with New Symphony Orchestra. Career: Many recitals and concerto performances throughout England and Scotland, Germany, Switzerland, Austria, France and USA; International radio and television recordings; Chester Summer Festival, 1989, with world premiere of posthumous pieces by Benjamin Britten; London concerto debut at the Barbican, 1989, playing Mozart K453; Also plays Mozart's other 20 original concertos; Further engagements with the Royal Liverpool Philharmonic, Northern Sinfonia, English Chamber Orchestra, Royal Philharmonic, Northern Chamber Orchestra; Ulster Orchestra, Scottish Chamber Orchestra, Manchester Camerata and the London Soloists Chamber Orchestra; US debut, July 1991, in the San Francisco Stern Grove Festival with the Midsummer Mozart Festival Orchestra, conducted by George Cleve; Further visits to USA for concertos and recitals; Returned to Midsummer Mozart Festival, 1993; Queen Elizabeth Hall debut, 1992, performing 2 Mozart piano concertos with Manchester Camerata; Chamber music concerts including recent series at the Royal College of Music, Manchester. Honours include: 1st Prize, Surrey Young Pianist of the Year Competition; 3rd Prize, BBC Young Musician of the Year, 1984; 1st Prize, Yorkshire Television Young Musicians' Awards, 1987; Hindemith Scholarship, 1987; Joint Winner, International Mozart Competition, Salzburg, 1988 (leading to engagement with Austrian Radio Symphony under Michael Gielen). Address: Lime Kiln Farm, Coneysthorpe, York YO6 7DD, England.

BRIGHT Colin (Michael), b. 28 June 1949, Sydney, New South Wales. Composer; Music Lectuer. Education: Studied with Mary Egan Linden Sands, Christopher Nicols and Ton de Leeuw (composition, 1982). Career: Lecturer for High School Music Teachers, from 1987; Commissions from Synergy, Seymour Group, Southern Crossings and Sydney Symphony Orchestra. Compositions include: Percussion Quartet, 1980; Earth Spirit for orchestra, 1982; The Dreamtime for baritone and ensemble, 1982; Earth, Wind and Fire for saxophone quartet, 1982; Long Reef for string quintet and wind quintet, 1984; Midnight Tulips song cycle for soprano and large ensemble, 1985; The Sinking of the Rainbow Warrior, 1 act opera; Tulpistick Talk for percussion, 1985; Red Earth for flute and ensemble, 1985; Music for contrabass octet and didjeridoo, 1986; Sun is God, string quartet, 1989; The Journey, opera, 1991; The Butcher' Apron for four percussion, 1991; Young Tree Green: Double Bass Concerto, 1993; War and Peace, vocal sextet, 1994. Honours include: 1 Act Opera Award, Australian Music Centre, 1986. Address: c/o APRA, 1A Eden Street, Crows Nest, NSW 2065, Australia.

BRILIOTH Helge, b. 7 May 1931, Lund, Sweden. Singer (Tenor). Education: Studied at the Royal Academy and the Opera School in Stockholm; Academia di Santa Cecilia, Rome; Mozarteum Salzburg. Career: In 1960 at Drottningholm sang the Baritone role of Bartolo in Paisiello's Il Barbiere di Siviglia; Bielefeld, 1962-64; Tenor debut as Don José, Stockholm, 1966; Bayreuth, 1969-75 as Siegmund and Tristan; Salzburg Easter Festival 1970 as Siegfried, under Karajan; Covent Garden 1970- as Siegmund, Siegfried, Tristan and Parsifal; Metropolitan Opera debut 1971, as Parsifal; Glyndebourne 1971, as Bacchus in Ariadne auf Naxos; Drottningholm 1972, in the title role of Cavalli's Scipione Affricano; At the Royal Opera Stockholm, 1975 sang the Emperor in the Swedish premiere of Die Frau ohne Schatten; Sang at Stockholm in the 1986 premiere of Christina by Hans Gefors. Recordings include: Siegfried in Götterdämmerung. Address: Birger Jarlsgatan 79, 11356 Stockholm, Sweden.

BRILOVA Elena, b. 9 Feb 1961, Moscow, Russia. Singer (Soprano). Education: Graduate, Moscow Conservatoire, 1986. Career: Sang in Concert, 1986-88; Bolshoi Opera Moscow from 1988 as the Queen of Shemakha, Antonida (A Life for the Tsar), Traviata, Rosina and other leading roles; Concert appearances as Constanze, Sophie, Oscar, Norina, Lucia, Amina and Leila (Les Pêcheurs de perles); Further engagements as the Queen of Night at Cologne and Vienna, Gilda in Oslo and Vienna; Palmide in Il Crociato in Egitto at the 1991 Ludwigsburg Festival; British debut, 1992, as the Queen of Shemakha with the London Symphony Orchestra; Season 1993 as Gilda at the Bergen Festival and in concert performances of Rigoletto at Tel Aviv, conducted by Zubin Mehta; Concert engagements at Brussels and Frankfurt and with such conductors as Bashmet, Simonov, Rostropovitch, Rozhdestvensky and Svetlanov. Current Management: Athole Still International Management Limited. Address: Foresters Hall, 25-27 Westow Street, London SE19 3RY, England.

BRINDUS Nicolae, (Nicolae Brandus), b. 16 Apr 1935, Bucharest, Romania. Composer. m. Ioana Teronim, 22 Oct 1982, 2 sons, 1 daughter. Education: Graduate in Piano, 1956, Composition, 1964, Academy of Music, Bucharest; PhD, Cluj-Napoca Academy of Music, 1981. Debut: Pianist, George Enescu Philharmony of Bucharest, 1955. Career: Piano Soloist, 1958-75; Concert performances in Romania and abroad; Soloist, Ploiesti Philharmonic Orchestra, 1959-69; Professor, Academy of Music, Bucharest, 1969-81; Editor, Muzica Review, Bucharest, 1981-; Professor, Academy of Music, Bucharest, 1992-; Compositions printed, recorded, played and broadcast on radio and television, Bucharest and abroad. Compositions: Edited and recorded: Pieces for piano, 1966, 1984; 7 Psalms, 1969, 1981; Mamsell Hus, 1977, 1981; Edited: 8 Madrigals for choir a capella, 1968; Sonata for 2 pianos, 1978; The Betrothal, opera, 1981; Languir me fais, 1986; Dialo(va)gos, concerto for piano and orchestra, 1988; Rhythmodia, 1989. Recordings include: Vagues. 1990; Kitsch-N, 1984; Antifonia, 1986; Soliloque I, 1986; Soliloque II (Reverberations), 1986; With the Gipsy Girls, opera, 1988. Publication: Inter-relations, musical studies, 1984. Contributions to: Numerous magazines and journals. Honours include: Order of Cultural Merit, Bucharest, 1968; Prize, Romanian Composers and Musicologists Union, 1974; George Enescu Prize, Romanian Academy, 1977. Memberships include: Romanian Composers and Musicologists Union; SACEM, Paris; President, Romanian Section, International Society of Contemporary Music. Hobbies: Literature; Theatre; Gastronomy. Address: Str Dr Felix 101 bl 19, Sc A Apt 42, 78153 Bucharest, Romania.

BRINKMANN Bodo, b. 7 Dec 1942, Binder, Brunswick, Germany. Singer (Baritone). Education: Studied at the Berlin Musikhochschule with Karl-Heinz Lohmann. Debut: Kaiserslautern, 1971; Member of the National Theatre Mannheim from 1974; Staatsoper Hamburg in Lohengrin; Munich Staatsoper, notably as Escamillo, 1984 and in the 1986 premiere of Reimann's Troades; Guest appearances in Berlin, Paris and Strasbourg; Deutsche Oper am Rhein 1987, as Telramund; Munich Olympia Hall, 1987, as Prince Igor; Bayreuth Festival 1987-92, Kurwenal, Donner and Gunther; Sang Jochanaan in Salome at Barcelona, 1989; Cologne Opera 1990, as Wotan in Die Walküre; Recordings include: Video of The Ring from Bayreuth (Teldec). Address: c/o Oper der Stadt Köln, Offenbachplatz, D-5000 Cologne, Germany.

BRITTON Rhodri, b. 1961, Hwlfford, Wales. Singer (Bass-Baritone). Education: Studied at Christ's Hospital, Balliol College, Oxford, and at the Royal Academy of Music. Career: While at the Royal Academy of Music sang in The Cunning Little Vixen, Cosi fan Tutte, Orpheus in the Underworld, Gianni Schicchi and Les Boréades (Adamas in the British stage premiere of Rameau's opera, conducted by Roger Norrington, 1985); Welsh National Opera from 1987 in Les Troyens, Il Barbiere di Siviglia, Salome, Don Giovanni (Masetto) and Tosca (Angelotti); Sang Gremin (Eugene Onegin) and Mozart's Figaro with Opera 80, 1989; Performances of Henze's The English Cat in Gütersloh and Berlin, 1989; Scottish Opera debut 1990, as Gremin; Currently Principal Bass-Baritone at the Landestheater, Eisenach; Concert repertory includes Schubert's Winterreise (At Balliol and the Royal Academy of Music), the Brahms Requiem (Rennes, France) and Bach's St John Passion at Southwell Minster. Address: c/o Korman International Management, Crunnells Green Cottage, Preston, Herts SG4 7UQ, England.

BRIZZI Aldo, b. 7 June 1960, Alessandria, Italy. Conductor; Composer. Education: Bologna University; Milan Conservatorio. Debut: 1st appearance as Conductor, 1978. Career: Conducted concerts in Europe, Israel, USA, Central and South America; Principal performances with Berlin Philharmonic Chamber Ensemble, The Cluj Philharmonic Orchestra; Santa Cecilia Chamber Orchestra of Rome, The Haydn Orchestra of Bolzano; Musical Conductor of the Ensemble of Ferienkurse, Darmstadt; Permanent Conductor of E M Ferrari Orchestra, Alessandria and Akabthos Ensemble. Compositions: Works performed by numerous European orchestras, ensembles and soloists including, Ecyo, Danish Radio Orchestra, Montepulciano Festival Orchestra, New Philharmonic Orchestra of Paris, Ens de Cuivres et Percussion de l'InterContemporian; Works broadcast by 21 European Radio Stations, 2 USA and Israeli State Radio. Recordings: Salabert conducting the Arditti String Quartet Consort; Electrecord conducting the Bacau Symphony Orchestra; Edipan with Composition of A Brizzi. Publications: Proposte Musicali, 1980; La Musica, Le Idée, Le Cose, 1981. Contributions to: numerous magazines. Honours: Venezia Opera Prima, 1981; Stipendiendpzies, Darmstadt, 1984; Young Generation in Europe, Venice, Paris, Cologne, 1985; Franco Evangelisti, Rome, 1986; Young Composers' Forum, Cologne, 1989; Artistic Director of Scelsi Foundation, Rome. Hobbies: Walking; Overseas Travel; Skiing. Address: Via Boves 6, 15100 Alessandria, Italy.

BRKANOVIC Zeljko, b. 20 Dec 1937, Zagreb, Croatia. Composer; Conductor; Professor. m. Ivanka Brkanovic, 27 Sept 1964, 1 son, 1 daughter. Education: Music School, 10 years; Zagreb Music Academy (piano); Skopje Music Academy (composition); Academia Chigiana Siena (Italy); High School Stuttgart (Germany). Debut: First string quartet in Zagreb, 1974. Appointments: Conductor, Croatian National Theatre Opera, Split and Zagreb, 1963-69; Musical Editor on radio and television, 1969-80; Professor on Music Academy in Zagreb, 1980-. Compositions: Nomos, Suite for Strings; Ricercari, Two Symphonies; Concert for violin; Concert for Piano and Orchestra; Chamber; Piano; Organ music. Recordings: Tonal Sonata, 1977; Divertimento For Strings, 1977; Concerto For Piano And Orchestra, 1981; Concerto For Violin, 1983; Antependium, 1989; Second Symphony, 1991; Figures, 1995; Song Book, 1996; Authors, CD, 1996. Publications; Professor Dr E Karkoschka, Stuttgart, 1991; Bilten/Croatian Composer Society, 1992. Contributions to: Schweinfurtische Nachrchten, Vjesnik Zagreb, Piano Journal No 49 London, p 46, 1992. Honours: Josip Slavenski Prize, for Concert for Piano and Orchestra, 1983; Prize of the Ministry of Culture, for Concerto for Percussion and Clarinet, 1997. Membership: Croatian Composers Society. Hobbies: Sport; Reading. Current Management: Professor, Zagreb Music Academy. Address: TRG Kralja Tomislava 18, Croatia.

BROADBENT Graeme, b. Halifax, England. Singer (Bass). Education: Studied at the Royal College of Music with Lyndon Vanderpump; Moscow Conservatoire with Evgeny Nesterenko. Career: Has sung Thanatos in Gluck's Alceste at Covent Garden with the English Bach Festival; Monteverdi's Nettuno and Mozart's Osmin and Sarastro for regional companies; English National Opera 1989 as Hans Schwartz in Mastersingers and Ribbing in A Masked Ball; Opera North 1990 as the Emir in the British stage premiere of Verdi's Jerusalem; Don Fernando in Fidelio for Scottish Opera; Concert repertoire includes the Monteverdi Vespers, the Mozart Requiem and Schoenberg's Serenade Op 24; Solo recital at the Rachmaninov Hall, Moscow, 1991; English National Opera: Ceprano (Rigoletto), 1992; Guron (Princess Ida), 1993; Opera North: Nikitich (Boris Godunov), also in Promenade Concert, Royal Albert Hall, 1992; Colline (La Bohème), 1993; Theseus (A Midsummer Night's Dream) in Paris, Lyon and Montpellier; Plutone (L'Orfeo) at Covent Garden with the EBF, 1994; Sang Caronte (L'Orfeo) in Lugano, Winter/Hymen (The Fairy Queen) in Athens, Granada and Covent Garden with the EBF in 1995; Le Muphti in Le Bourgeois Gentilhomme, 1996; Season 1997 in Salome at Covent Garden and in Pfitzner's Palestrina with the Royal Opera at the New York Met. Current Management: Harold Holt Limited. Address: c/o Robert Clarke, 31 Sinclair Road, London W14 0NS, England.

BROADSTOCK Brenton (Thomas), b. 12 Dec 1952, Melbourne, Victoria, Australia. Composer. m., 3 children. Education: BA, Monash University, 1975; Education: MMus, Memphis State University, USA; Diploma in Composition, University of Sydney; Composition with Peter Sculthorpe; AMusTCL, Trinity College of Music; DMus, University of Melbourne. Career: Tutor in Music, 1982-84, Senior Tutor in Music, 1984-87, Senior Lecturer in Music, 1989, then Associate Professor, Faculty of Music, University of Melbourne; Inaugural Composer-in-residence, Melbourne Symphony Orchestra, 1988; Performances: Melbourne Summer Music Festival, 1985; Stroud Festival, England, 1985; Adelaide Festival, 1986; Spoleto Festival, Melbourne, 1986; Nova Festival, Brisbane, 1987; Music Today Festival, Tokyo, 1988; International Society for Contemporary Music World Days, Hong Kong, 1988, Oslo, 1990. Compositions: Symphony No 3; 4 String Quartets; The Mountain for orchestra; Tuba Concerto; Piano Concerto; Battlements for orchestra; Woodwind Quartet; Aureole 104 for flute and piano; Solo Bass Clarinet; Oboe and Piano; Solo Piano; Beast from Air for trombone and percussion; Many works for brass band; Symphony No 1, 1988; Symphony No 2, 1989; Bright Tracks, soprano and string trio, 1994; Celebration for chamber ensemble, 1995; Saxophone Concertino, 1995. Recordings: Many works performed, recorded and broadcast by ABC; Fahrenheit 451, opera, 1992. Honours: Paul Lowin Prize, 1994. Hobbies: Basketball; Reading; Films. Current Management: G Schirmer, Australia. Address: 20 Simmons Street, Box Hill North, Victoria 3129, Australia.

BROADWAY Kenneth, b. 1950, USA. Duo Pianist. Education: Studied at the Cleveland Institute of Music with Vronsky and Babin. Career: Formed Piano Duo partnership with Ralph Markham and has given many recitals and concerts in North America and Europe; BBC debut recital, 1979 and further broadcasts on CBC TV, Radio France Musique, the Bavarian Radio and Radio Hilversum in Holland; Stravinsky's Three Dances from Petrushka at the Theatre des Champs Elysees, Paris, 1984; Season 1987-88 included 40 North American recitals, concert with the Vancouver Symphony and New York debut on WQXR Radio; Season 1988-89 included the Concertos for Two Pianos by Mozart and Bruch in Canada and a recital tour of England and Germany; Recent performances of the Bartók Sonata for Two Pianos and Percussion, with Evelyn Glennie and a 1990-91 tour of North America, Europe and the Far East; Festival appearances include Newport USA 1988 (releases on CD). Recordings include: Duos by Anton Rubenstein; Vaughan Williams Concerto for Two Pianos; Bartók Sonata for Two Pianos and Percussion. Honours include: Young Artist of the Year, Musical America Magazine, 1989 (with Ralph Markham). Address: c/o Anglo-Swiss Management, Suite 35-37, Morley House, 320 Regent Street, London W1R 5AD, England.

BROADWAY Michael, b. 5 Dec 1947, London, England. Pianolist. m. Frances Robertson, 20 Oct 1979. Education: Organ, Harpsichord, London College of Music; Early Music with Nathalie Dolmetsch; ALCM, 1969; GLCM, 1971. Debut: Purcell Room, 1989. Career: Pianola Debut, Rome, 1990; Concert Tour, Rome, Prague, Budapest, 1991; BBC Radio 3 First Broadcast Performance of Herbert Howells Phantasy Minuet for Pianola and Trois Pieces pour Pianola by Alfredo Casella, 1992; Concert Tour of Treviso and Bolzano, 1993; Other Venues include Bath, Spitalfields, Royal Concert Hall in Nottingham. Recordings: Trois Pieces pour Pianola; Alfredo Casella Tre Improvvisi per Pianola; G F Malipiero Fonotipia FT. Publication: Le Magicien Prodigieux, 1998; Le Magicien Prodigieur, performing edition in preparation. Membership: Liveryman, Worshipful Company of Glaziers; Fellow, Royal Society of Arts. Address: 39 Sydner Road, Stoke Newington, London N16 7UF, England.

BRÖCHELER John, b. 21 February 1945, Vaals, Limbourg, Holland. Singer (Baritone). Education: Studied with Leo Ketelaars in Maastrict and with Pierre Bernac in Paris. Career: Sang at first in Concert, notably in the Bach Passions, the Choral Symphony and the Brahms Requiem; Berlin Festival in the premieres of Die Erprobung de Petrus Hebraicus by Henri Pousseur, 1974 and Mare Nostrum by Kagel, 1975; San Diego Opera as Sharpless in Madama Butterfly, Ford in Falstaff, and in the 1979 premiere of Menotti's La Loca, with Beverly Sills; Netherlands Opera as Germont, Don Giovanni and Marcello and in Donizetti's Maria Stuarda with Joan Sutherland; Frankfurt Opera 1983, as Amfortas in Parsifal; Glyndebourne 1984, as Mandryka in Arabella; Los Angeles Opera as Nabucco; La Scala Milan 1985, as Jochanaan in Salome and Golaud in Pelléas et Mélisande; Stuttgart 1985, in Henze's König Hirsch; Other appearances in Toronto, New York and Paris, Vienna 1988 - Golaud in Pelléas and Mélisande, Bonn 1989; Wolfram, Tannhäuser, Munich 1989; Mathis der Maler, Hindemith; Sang Orestes in Elektra at Barcelona, 1990; Hindemith's Mathis and Von Einem's Danton at the 1990 Munich Festival; Sang Barak in Die Frau ohne Schatten for Netherlands Opera, 1992; Wozzeck, Stuttgart, 1993; Simon Boccanegra, Frankfurt, 1993; Wanderer in Siegfried, 1994; (Dr Schön) Lulu, Salzburger Festspiele, 1995 and at the Berlin Staatsoper, 1997. Recordings: Dichterliebe; Handel's Dettinger Te Deum and Judas Maccabeus; Kindertotenlieder, Mahler; Des Knaben Wunderhorn (Mahler); Lucrezia Borgia; Das Paradies und Die Peri. Address: c/o Bayerische Staatsoper, Postfach 745, D-8000 Munich 1, Germany.

BROCKLESS Brian, b. 21 Jan 1926, London, England. Conductor; Composer; Organist; Teacher. m. (1) 1 son, (2) Jennifer Wright, 1 son. Education: BMus, ARCM; ARCO; Hon ARAM. Career: Concerts with English Chamber Orchestra, Royal Philharmonic Orchestra, Northern Sinfonia; Italian Tours with London Schubert Orchestra; Concerts in Romania, Palermo, Stockholm, Brussels, Venezuela, Denmark; Choral and Orchestral Performances for BBC, Belgian, Swedish and Danish radio; Director, Music, St Bartholonew the Great Priory, London, 1961-71, 1979-; Senior Lecturer, University of Surrey; Festival Adjudicator, retired, 1991. Compositions: Prelude, Toccata and Chaconne; Introduction, Passacaglia and Coda; Fantasia, Adagio and Fugue, organ; Toccata for an Occasion, 1982, commissioned for Peterborough Organ Festival; English Elegy for String Orchestra; Church Music, Songs and Chamber Music; Toccatina, 1995. Recordings: English Church Music, ALPHA ACA 522 Elgar, Britten Brockless; Organ Mixtures, PRIORY PRC 239; Darke, Alcock, Willan, Jackson, Brockless, MSV CD 92002. Honours: Conducting Prize, Sienna, Italy, 1963; Honorary Academician, RAM, 1982. Memberships: Director, Dolmetsch Foundation; Herbert Howells Society; Royal Academy of Music Club. Hobbies: Reading; Ornithology; Cricket. Address: 2 Grove Health North, Ripley, Surrey GU23 6EN, England.

BRODARD Michael, b. 1 April 1946, Fribourg, Switzerland. Singer (Bass-Baritone). Education: Fribourg Conservatoire, 1965-74. Career: Concert Singer in France and Switzerland; Opera Engagements at Geneva, Lusanne, Lucerne, Nancy and Metz; Further concerts at Brussels, Marseilles, Frankfurt, Barcelona, Lisbon, Buenos Aires, Madrid and Warsaw; Repertoire ranges from Baroque to Modern Works. Recordings include: L'Enfant et les Sortilèges, Pelléas et Mélisande, Bach's Christmas Oratorio, Haydn's St Theresa Mass, Madrigals and Vespers by Monteverdi, Schubert's E-flat Mass and Vivaldi's Psalm 110; Stravinsky's Renard and Les Noces, Masses by Mozart. Address: c/o Erato (Contracts), WEA Records, 59 Alperton Lane, Wembley, Middlesex HA0 1FJ, England.

BROKAW James Albert II, b. 4 February 1951, Princeton, New Jersey, USA. Historical Musicologist. m. Mollie Sandock, 27 June 1984. Education: BA, German Literature, Kenyon College, 1973; Studies in Music History and Theory, Baldwin Wallace Conservatory, 1977-78; PhD, Musicology, University of Chicago, 1986. Career: Assistant Professor of Music, Northeastern Illinois University, 1989-; Lecturer in Music, Chicago State University, 1986-; Lecturer in Music, University of Chicago Open Programme, 1987-; Advisory Board Member, Riemenschneider Bach Institute, 1982-86; Judge, Mu Phi Epsilon Music History Competition, 1988. Publication: The Genesis of the Prelude in C Major, in Bach Studies, Cambridge University Press, 1989; Techniques of Expansion in the Preludes and Fugues of Johann Sebastian Bach, dissertation; Programme Notes: The Chicago Symphony Orchestra/Performances for Peace, 1984-88; Music of the Baroque, 1984, 1987. Contributions to: Reviews of scholarly editions of keyboard music of J S Bach, C P E Bach and Louis Couperin, in Notes, 1985, 1986, 1989; Recent Research on the Genesis and Sources of Bach's Well-Tempered Clavier, II, in Bach: The Quarterly Journal of the Reimenschneider Bach Institute, 1985. Honours: 1st Alternate, Whiting Dissertation Fellowship in the Humanities, 1984; NEH Summer Seminar for College Teachers on Mozart's Operas, Cornell University, 1988. Memberships: American Musicological Society; New Bach Society; College Music Society. Address: Box 125 Ogden Dunes, Portage, IN 46368, USA.

BROKMEIER Willi, b. 8 Apr 1928, Bochum, Germany. Singer (Tenor). Education: Studied in Mainz. Debut: Stadttheater Mainz, 1952. Career: Appearances in lighter operatic roles at the Deutsche Oper am Rhein Dusseldorf; Many engagements in operetta, notably at the Theater am Gärtnerplatz, Munich, and elsewhere in Germany; Cologne Opera, 1965, in the premiere of Zimmermann's Die Soldaten; Munich Festival, 1973; as Pedrillo in Die Entführung. Recordings: Gräfin Mariza; Lehar's Lustige Witwe and Land des Lächelns; Die Kluge by Orff; Korngold's Die Tote Stadt (RCA); Feuersnot by Strauss (Acanta).

BRONDER Peter, b. 1953, England. Singer (Tenor). Education: Studied at the Royal Academy of Music with Joy Mammen and at the National Opera Studio. Career: Principal Tenor with the Welsh National Opera from 1986-90; Covent Garden debut as Arturo in Lucia di Lammermoor in 1986, also Major Domo in Der Rosenkavalier; Youth in Die Frau ohne Schlatten, 1992; First Jew in Salome, 1995; Sang Kudryash in Katya Kabanova in 1989 and Andres in Wozzeck in 1990 with the English National Opera; Shepherd in Oedipus Rex, 1991; Almaviva in 1992-93; Alfred in Die Fledermaus and Italian Tenor in Der Rosenkavalier, 1993; Further appearances include: Netherlands Opera as Ernesto, 1989 and the Prince in Les Brigands, 1992; Glyndebourne Festival, 1990; For Welsh National Opera performances in New York, 1989, Milan, 1989 and Tokyo, 1990; Debut at the Bavarian State Opera, Munich, as Mazal in The Adventures of Mr Broucek, also Narraboth, 1994; Invitations for Pedrillo in Die Entführung at Covent Garden, also Istanbul; Sang Pylades in Gluck's Iphigenia auf Tauris, Edinburgh, 1996; Concert appearances in London, Paris, Vienna, Lisbon and for the Australian Broadcasting Company, Perth. Recordings include: Kiri te Kanawa recital, Turco in Italia (Phonogram); Adriana Lecouvreur (Decca); Osud, Beethoven 9 (EMI); La Traviata, Ballo in Maschera (Teldec). Honours: Associate, Royal Academy of Music, 1989. Current Management: Allied Artists, London. Address: c/o Allied Artists, 42 Montpelier Square, London SW7 1JZ, England.

BRONFMAN Yefim, b. 10 Apr 1958, Tashkent, Russia. Pianist. Education: Juilliard School of Music, New York, USA; Curtis Institute, Philadelphia, Pennsylvania; Private studies with Rudolf Serkin and Arie Vardi. Debut: Israel Philharmonic with Kostalanetz, 1974. Career: As Soloist with: Montreal Symphony Orchestra; Philadelphia; Los Angeles Philharmonic; New York Philharmonic; Minnesota Orchestra; Mostly Mozart Orchestra; English Chamber Orchestra; St Louis Symphony Orchestra; Scottish Chamber Orchestra; Vancouver Symphony Orchestra; Pittsburgh Symphony Orchestra; London Philharmonia; St Paul Chamber Orchestra; Houston Symphony Orchestra; Toronto Symphony Orchestra; Goteborg Symphony Orchestra; Royal Philharmonic; San Francisco Symphony Orchestra; Berlin Philharmonic; Chicago Symphony Orchestra; Baltimore Symphony Orchestra; Rotterdam Philharmonic; Bournemouth Symphony Orchestra; Cleveland Orchestra; National Symphony Orchestra; Rochester Philharmonic; Jerusalem Symphony Orchestra; Winnipeg Symphony Orchestra; Richmond Symphony Orchestra; New Jersey Symphony; Partnered Joshua Bell in Mozart-Tchaikovsky Festival at the Wigmore Hall, London, 1997. Recordings: Deutsche Grammophon: All Fauré disc and Prokofiev Violin Sonatas with Shlomo Mintz; Musical Heritage, Brahms Sonata in F minor and Scherzo Op 4; Music Masters: Mozart Sonatas for violin and piano with Robert Mann; CBS Masterworks: Prokofiev Piano Sonatas 7 and 8; Sony Classical, 1991, Mussorgsky, Pictures at an Exhibition, Stravinsky, 3 scenes from Petrushka; Rachmaninoff: Piano Concertos 2 and 3, with Esa-Pekka Salonen and Philharmonia Orchestra, Sony Classical, 1992; Prokofiev: Piano Concertos 1, 3 and 5, with Zubin Mehta and Israel Philharmonic, Sony Classical, 1993. Honours: American-Israel Cultural Foundation Scholarship, 1974; Winner of Avery Fisher Prize, 1991. Current Management: ICM Artists. Address: 40 West 57 Street, New York, NY 10019, USA.

BRONHILL June, b. June 1930, Broken Hill, New South Wales, Australia. Singer (Soprano). m. Richard Finney. Education: Studied in London. Debut: Adele in Fledermaus, Sadler's Wells, London, 1954. Career: Sang such roles in London as Zerbinetta, Gilda and Norina in Don Pasquale; Successful also as Hanna Glawari in Die Lustige Witwe, the Queen of Night, Lucia (Covent Garden Company) and in the title role of the British premiere of Janácek's Cunning Little Vixen (Sadler's Wells 1961); Blonde in Die Entführung at the Sydney Opera House and Magda in La Rondine with the English Opera Group, 1974. Honours include: OBE, 1976. Address: c/o Australian Opera, PO Box 291, Strawberry Hills, NSW 2012 Australia.

BROOK Barry, b. 1 Nov 1918, New York, USA. Musicologist. Education: MA, Studied at the City College of New York and Columbia University, 1942; Doctorate from the Sorbonne, Paris, 1959. Career: On faculty of Queens College New York from 1945; Professor of Music and Executive Officer of the PhD Programme, City University of New York, 1967-89; Director of CUNY Center for Music Research and Documentation from 1989; Has also taught at the Institut de Musicologie at the University of Paris, 1967-68, the Eastman School of Music, 1973, University of Adelaide, 1974, Juilliard from 1977, the Centre National de la Recherche Scientifique in Paris, 1983 and the University of Alabama, 1987. Publications: La Symphonie Française dans le seconde moitié du XVII siècle, 1962; The Breitkopf Thematic Catalogue, 1762-1787, 1966; Editor in Chief, Répertoire International de Littérature Musicale, Abstracts of Music Literature from 1966; The Symphony 1720-1840, 1979-86; French Opera in the 17th and 18th centuries, 1984-; Joint editor of Giovanni Battista Pergolesi Complete Works, 1986-; Editor: Musicology and the Computer; Musicology 1960-2000: A Practical Program, 1970; Thematic catalogues in Music: An Annotated Bibliography, 1972. Honours: Guggenheim Fellowships; Ford Foundation Fellowships; Dent Medal, Royal Musical Association, 1965; Chevalier of the Order of Arts and Letters, 1972; Smetana Medal, Czechoslovakia, 1978; President, International Music Council of UNESCO, 1981-82; Member, Royal Swedish Academy, 1989.

BROOK Peter, b. 21 Mar 1925, London, England. Stage and Film Director. Education: Studied at Oxford. Career: Director of productions at Covent Garden, 1948-50, with Boris Godunov, Salome (designs by Salvador Dali) and the premiere of the Olympians by Bliss, The Marriage of Figaro, 1949; Filmed The Beggar's Opera by Gay/Pepusch with Laurence Olivier, 1953; Metropolitan Opera, 1953 and 1957, Faust and Eugene Onegin; His reduction of Carmen, La tragédie de Carmen, was produced at the Paris Bouffes du Nord in the season 1981-82 and was seen on tour in Europe and the USA (New York), 1983; A much reduced version of Pelléas et Mélisande (Impressions of Pelléas) was performed in 1992-93; Engaged for Don Giovanni at Aix-en-Provence, 1998. Address: c/o Théâtre des Bouffes du Nord, 37 bis Bd de la Chapelle, 75010 Paris, France.

BROOKS Darla, b. 1957, West Virginia, USA. Singer (Soprano). Education: Studied in the USA and at Graz. Career: Sang throughout the USA in opera and concert, notably in Chicago and Cincinnati; European debut with Lucerne Opera, 1985, followed by engagements at Wurzburg and Cologne; Roles have included Norina in Don Pasquale, Blondchen, Zerlina, Zerbinetta, Adele in Die Fledermaus and Adina in L'Elisir d'amore (at the Deutsche Oper Berlin); Other venues include the Teatro Liceu Barcelona, and the State Operas of Munich and Vienna. Address: c/o Oper der Stadt Köln, Offenbachplatz Pf 180241, W-5000 Cologne 1, Germany.

BROPHY Gerard, b. 1953, Sydney, Australia. Composer. Education: Master classes with Turibio Santos, 1976; Composition seminar, Mauricio Kagel, Basel, Switzerland; Studied with Richard Toop, NSW State Conservatorium of Music, 1981; Studied with Franco Donatoni, Italy; Graduated, Accademia Nazionale de Santa Cecilia, Rome, 1983; Composition course, Accademia Chigiana di Siena, 1983. Career: Composer in Residence, Musica Viva Australia, 1983; Australian Chamber Orchestra, 1986; Queensland Conservatorium of Music, 1987; Pittsburgh New Music Ensemble, 1988; Queensland Conservatorium of Music, 1989. Compositions include: Orchestral Works: Orfeo, 1982; Le Reveil de L'Ange, 1987; Matho, 1987; Ensemble Works: Lace, 1985; Mercurio, 1985; Spur, 1988; Head, 1988; Séraphita, 1988; Forbidden Colours, 1988; Frisson, 1989; Vocal Works: Flesh, 1987; Shiver, 1989; Vorrei Bacierti, for baritone and chamber ensemble, 1991; Instrumental Works: Chiarissima, 1987; Pink Chair Light Green Violet Violent FLASH, 1990; Vorrei Baciarti, for Baritone and Chamber Ensemble, 1991; Tweak, for Piccolo, 1991; Pluck It!, for Solo Guitar, 1992; Twist, for Solo Clarinet, 1993; Recent works include: Tudo Liquido, for Wind and Percussion, 1994; Colour Red...Your Mouth...Heart, for Orchestra, 1994; Es, for Solo Flute, 1994; Bisoux, for English Horn and Bass Clarinet, 1994; Umbigada, Obrigado!, for Percussion Quartet, 1995. Recordings include: 8 CDs including: Forbidden Colours, Queensland Symphony Orchestra; November Snow; Angelicon, Lisa Moore. Honours: Numerous grants and fellowships including: Composer Fellowship, Australia Council Music Board, 1982, 1983; Italian Government Scholarship. Address: 37 Montpelier Street, Wilston, Queensland 4051, Australia.

BROS José, b. 1963, Barcelona, Spain. Singer (Tenor). Education: Barcelona Conservatory with Jaime Francisco Puig. Debut: Carmina Burana at Palma, 1987. Career: From 1992 many performances in leading roles at major opera houses; Ernesto and Don Ottavio at Sabadelli, Spain; Duke of Mantua at Palma and Nadir in Les Pêcheurs de Perles, followed by Percy in Anna Bolena, at Barcelona; Further leads in La Favorita at Las Palmas, Falstaff and I Capuleti at Lisbon, Lucia di Lammermoor at Zurich, Don Pasquale and Così fan tutte at Bilbao and L'Elisir d'Amore (Nemorino, Covent Garden, 1997); Further recent engagements at Hamburg, Vienna, Rome, Naples, Munich, Florence (Edgardo, under Zubin Mehta, at the Maggio Musicale), Bologna and Marseilles; Recitals and concerts throughout Europe and in London. Address: c/o Bayersiche Staatsoper, Max-Joseph Platz, Pf 100148, D-8000 Munich 1, Germany.

BROSTER Eileen, b. 23 Jun 1935, London, England. Pianist. m. R Chaplin, 6 May 1972, 1 son. Education: Studied with Frank Merrick and Cyril Smith at The Royal College of Music. Debut: Wigmore Hall. Career: Performed on BBC Radio and TV; Appeared in all South Bank Halls; Toured extensively as soloist in recitals and concerti; Performances at Wigmore Hall. Memberships: Incorporated Society of Musicians; EPTA. Address: 199 Beehive Lane, Gants Hill, Ilford, Essex, England.

BROTT Alexander, b. 14 Mar 1915, Montreal, Canada. Musical Director; Conductor; Professor of Music. m. Lotte Goetzel, 27 Mar 1933, 2 sons. Education: Lic Mus, McGill University Faculty of Music, 1932; Laureat degree, Quebec Academy of Music, 1933; Postgraduate Diploma, Performer, Composer and Conductor, Juilliard School of Music, NY, USA, 1933-38; DMus, Chicago University, 1960; LLD, Queen's University, Canada, 1973; DMus, McGill University, 1979. Career: Professor and Conductor in Residence at McGill University since 1939; Concertmaster and Assistant Conductor, Montreal Symphony Orchestra; Founder and Musical Director, McGill Chamber Orchestra; Conductor of Montreal Pops Concert; Conductor and Musical Director of Kingston Symphony Orchestra and Kingston Pops Concerts. Compositions: 18 Symphonies (13 Commissioned); 25 Solo and Chamber Music (12 Commissioned); 8 Vocal works (5 Commissioned), 1938-71; Songs and Orchestrations (11 Commissioned), 1971-78. Recordings: 15 many with McGill Chamber Orchestra including own compositions and works by Mozart, Haydn, Schubert and Bach; CD of Alexander Brott's Compositions, 1994. Honour: Elected "Great Montrealer" in 1994. Hobby: Gemmology. Address: 5459 Earnscliffe Avenue, Montreal, Quebec, Canada, H3X 2P8.

BROTT Boris, b. 14 Mar 1944, Montreal, Quebec, Canada. Conductor. m. Ardyth Webster, 2 sons, 1 daughter. Education: Conservatoire de Musique, Montreal; McGill University, Montreal; Studied conducting with Pierre Monteux, Igor Markevitch, Leonard Bernstein, Alexander Brott. Debut: As violinist with Montreal Symphony, 1949. Career: Founder, Conductor, Philharmonic Youth Orchestra, Montreal, 1959-61; Assistant Conductor: Toronto Symphony Orchestra, 1963-65; New York Philharmonic, 1968-69; Music Director: Northern Sinfonia Orchestra, England, 1964-69; Royal Ballet, Covent Garden, 1966-68, including the Covent Garden premiere of Stravinsky's The Soldier's Tale; Lakehead University, Thunder Bay, Ontario,1967-72; Regina Symphony, 1970-73; Conductor, Music Director: Hamilton Philharmonic Orchestra, 1969-90; Ontario Place Pops Orchestra, 1983-91; Chief Conductor: BBC Welsh Symphony Orchestra, 1972-77; CBC Symphony, 1976-83; President, Great Music Canada,1977-; Artistic Director, Stratford Summer Music Festival, Ontario, 1982-84; Conductor, McGill Orchestra, Montreal, Quebec, 1989-; Artistic Director, Boris-Brott Summer Music Festival, Hamilton, Ontario, 1988-95; Conductor and MD, New West Symphony, Los Angeles, 1995-; Conductor and Music Director, Ventura County Symphony, Ventura, California, 1992-; Guest Conductor, All British orchestras, all major Canadian orchestras, USA, Korea, Japan, Germany, France, Sweden, Israel, Mexico, Salvador, Italy, Denmark; Principal Guest Conductor and Music Advisor, Symphony Nova Scotia, 1981-; Guest Conductor, Sadler's Wells Opera, Canadian Opera Company, Edmonton Opera; Writer, Host, Conductor, over 100 TV programmes, UK, USA, Canada; Appeared in film and radio. Recordings: Numerous for CBC, Septre-Mace, Mercury, including suites from operas by Handel; Dvorák's Serenade op 44; Symphonies by Richter, Holzbauer and Cannabich; Sibelius Pelléas; Ravel Le Tombeau de Couperin. Address: 301 Bay Street South, Hamilton, Ontario L8P 3JZ, Canada.

BROTT Denis, b. 9 Sept 1950, Quebec, Canada. Cellist. m. 27 Aug 1976, 1 s, 3 d. Education: Studied with Gregor Piatigorsky, University of Southern California, USA. Career: Festivals include Marlboro, Aspen, Hampden-Sydney, Orford and Sitka; Artistic Director, Festival of the Sound, Ontario, 1991; Faculty of the Music Academy of the West, Santa Barbara, 1993 & 1994 summer season, performing chamber music at festivals in Hampden-Sydney, Virginia and Sitka Alaska; Jury member, Evian International String Quartet Competition in France, also recitalist, chamber artist and soloist with orchestra; Currently, Professor of Cello and Chamber Music at Conservatoire de Musique de Montreal, Canada; In 1995 established a two-week Festival de Musique de Chambre de Montréal, a celebration of chamber music in the Chateau de Belvedere atop Mont Royal; On jury for the 1993 Evian International String Quartet Competition in France and the 1996 Munich String Quartet Competition; One of 3 invited guest lecturers for the Piatigorsky Seminar for Cellists, University of Southern California in Los Angeles, 1997. Publications include: Article, Schelome: The Message of King Solomon, Violoncello Society and Canadian Jewish News Viewpoints, 1993. Recordings include: 20 chamber music works including the complete string quartets of Beethoven with the Orford String Quartet and Hommage to Piatigorsky, a solo CD; Works of his father, Alexander Brott, featuring Arabesque for Cello & Orchestra, 1993. Contributions to: Numerous articles including The Message of King Solomon in Strad magazine, 1994. Honours: Two Juno Awards for Best Classical Recording by a Chamber Ensemble; Grand Prix du Disque, 1987; Winner, Munich International Cello Competition. Hobbies: Photography; Skiing; Gardening; Swimming. Current Management: Davis Joachim, Les Concerts Davis Joachim Inc, 201 Brock Avenue North, Montreal, Quebec H4X 2G1, Canada. Address: 201 Brock Avenue North, Montreal, Quebec H4X 2G1, Canada.

BROUWENSTYN Gre, b. 26 Aug 1915, Den Helder, The Netherlands. Singer (Soprano). Education: Amsterdam. Career: Joined and subsequently became First Soprano, Amsterdam Opera; Has appeared in London, Berlin, Stuttgart, Brussels, Copenhagen, Paris, Vienna, Bayreuth (1954-56), Barcelona, and Buenos Aires; Covent Garden debut 1951, as Aida, and appeared as Elisabeth de Valois in 1958; Repertoire included roles in Forza del Destino; Tosca; Aida; Otello; Un Ballo in Maschera; Tannhäuser; Die Walküre; Die Meistersinger; Le nozze de Figaro; Jenufa; Il Trovatore; Cavalleria Rusticana; Don Carlos; retired in 1971, after singing Beethoven's Leonore with Netherlands Opera. Honour: Order of Orange-Nassau. Address: 3 Bachplain, Amsterdam, The Netherlands.

BROUWER Leo, b. 1 March 1939, Havana, Cuba. Composer; Guitarist. Education: Studied at the Juilliard School, New York, with Stefan Wolpe and Vincent Persichetti; Hartt College with Isadore Freed. Debut: 1956. Career: Teacher at the National Conservatory, Havana, 1961-67; Director of experimental department of Cuban film music from 1967; Many tours as guitar soloist; Guitar Competition founded in his honour, Japan, 1984. Compositions include: Sonograms for prepared piano, 1963; Tropos for orchestra, 1967; Hexahedron for six players, 1969; Flute concerto, 1972; Homenaja a Lenin for electronics; 3 guitar concertos, 1972-86; Many smaller pieces for guitar. Address: c/o ACDAM, Calle 6 No 313 entre 13 y 15, Vedado 10400, Havana, Cuba.

BROWN A Peter, b. 30 Apr 1943, Chicago, Illinois, USA. Professor of Musicology. m. Carol Vanderbilt, 21 Mar 1968, 1 daughter. Education: BM, 1965, MM, 1966, PhD, 1970, Northwestern University; Domaine School for Conductors, Hancock, Maine, 1965; Postdoctoral work, New York University, 1970. Career: Professor of Musicology, University of Hawaii, 1969-74; Professor of Musicology, Indiana University, Bloomington, 1974-. Publications: Joseph Haydn in Literature: A Bibliography, 1974; Carlo d'Ordonez: A Thematic Catalogue, 1978; Carlo d'Ordonez, 7 Symphonies, 1979; String Quartets Op 1, 1980; Performing Haydn's The Creation, 1986; Joseph Haydn's Keyboard Music: Sources and Style, 1986; The French Music Publishers Guera of Lyon, 1987; Haydn, The Creation (editor), 1995; The Symphonic Repertoire, 5 volumes. Contributions to: Acta Musicologica; Journal of American Musicological Society; Music Review; Music and Letters; Musical Times; Haydn Yearbook; Haydn-Studien; Haydn-Studies; Mozart Jahrbuch; Musical Quarterly; Journal of Musicology; Journal of Musicological Research; The New Grove; The Heritage of Music; Caldara Essays; American Scholar; American Historical Review. Address: School of Music, Indiana University, Bloomington, IN 47405, USA.

BROWN Christopher (Roland), b. 17 June 1943, Tunbridge Wells, Kent, England. Composer. m. (1) Anne Smillie, 29 Mar 1969, 1 son, 1 daughter, (2) Fiona Caithness, 28 Dec 1985, 1 son. Education: Westminster Abbey Choir School, 1952-57; Dean Close School, Cheltenham, 1957-62; King's College, Cambridge, 1962-65; BA, 1965, MA, 1968; Royal Academy of Music, London, 1965-67; Hochschule für Musik, Berlin, Germany, 1967-68. Career: Freelance Composer, 1968-; Member, Professorial Staff, Royal Academy of Music, 1969-; Conductor, Huntingdonshire Philharmonic, 1976-91, 1994-95; Composer-in-Residence, Nene College, Northampton, 1986-88; Conductor, Dorset Bach Cantata Club, 1988-; Conductor, New

Cambridge Singers, 1997-. Compositions: Regularly performed worldwide including: Triptych; The Sun: Rising; Organ Concerto; Festive Prelude; Festival Variations; 4 Operas; 2 String Quartets; Chamber Music for 5 instruments; Images; Ruscelli d'oro; La Légend de L'Etoile; Choral works include: David; A Hymn to the Holy Innocents; Three Medieval Lyrics; Magnificat; Chauntecleer; The Vision of Saul; The Snows of Winter; Hodie Salvator Apparuit; Tres cantus Sacri; landscapes; the Circling Year; Numerous songs, carols, church music; Mass for 4 voices, 1991; Christmas Cantata, 1992; The Ship of Fools, 1992; Star Song I, 1994; Summer Winds, 1995; Star Song III, 1996; Brown the Bear, 1997. Recordings include: laudate Dominum, Dean Close School Choir; Laudate Dominum, Canterbury Cathedral Choir; 'Tis Christmas Time, Huntingdonshire Philharmonic and Canticum. Publications: Numerous. Honours include: Guiness Prize for Composition, 1974, 1976; Prince Pierre of Monaco Prize, 1976; Washington International Composition Prize, 1976; Fellow, RAM, 1993. Memberships include: Association of Professional Composers; Composers Guild of Great Britain; Royal Society of Musicians. Current Management: J & W Chester Limited, London. Address: 6 Station Road, Catworth, Huntingdon, Cambridgeshire PE18 0PE, England.

BROWN David, b. 8 Jul 1929, Gravesend, Kent, England. Professor of Musicology; University Teacher; Writer on Music; Broadcaster. m. Elizabeth Valentine, 24 Dec 1953, 2 d. Education: Sheffield University, 1947-52, BA 1950, BMus 1951, DipEd 1952, MA 1960; PhD, Southampton University, 1971; LTCL. Career: Schoolmaster, 1954-59; Music Librarian, London University, 1959-62; Lecturer in Music, 1962-, Professor of Musicology, 1983-89, Southampton University. Publications: Thomas Weelkes, 1969; Mikhail Glinka, 1973; John Wilbye, 1974; Tchaikovsky, 4 volumes, vol 1 1840-74, 1978, vol 2 1874-78, 1982, vol 3 1878-85, 1986 and vol 4 1885-93, 1991; Tchaikovsky Remembered, 1993. Contributions to: Music and Letters; Musical Times; Music Review; Monthly Musical Record; Listener; Survey. Honours: Derek Allen Prize of The British Academy, for Tchaikovsky volume 2, 1982; Yorkshire Post Music Book Award, for Tchaikovsky volume 4, 1991. Memberships: Royal Musical Association; Royal Society of Arts; Member of Editorial Committee of Musica Britannica. Hobby: Walking. Address: Braishfield Lodge West, Braishfield, Romsey, Hampshire, SO51 0PS, England.

BROWN Donna, b. 15 Feb 1952, Renfrew, Ontario, Canada. Singer (Soprano). Education: Studied in Canada and with Edith Mathis in Switzerland. Career: Sang at first in concert and made opera debut at the Paris Opéra-Comique (1985) as Rameau's Aricie; Has sung further as Amina in La Sonnambula and Morgana in Alcina (Paris), Fata Morgana in The Love for Three Oranges (Vancouver), Poppea in Agrippina (Vienna) and Belinda in Dido and Aeneas (Brussels); Other roles include Mozart's Susanna, Blondchen and Despina, Gilda, Zerbinetta and Olympia in Les Contes d'Hoffmann; Season 1996-97 with British operatic debut as Sophie in Der Rosenkavalier (ENO); Almirena in Rinaldo at Geneva and Mozart's Requiem on tour. Recordings include: Leclair's Scylla et Glaucus (Erato), Handel's Saul (Philips) and Messiah (Hanssler). Address: c/o Harrison/Parrott Ltd, 12 Penzance Place, London W11 4PA, England.

BROWN Earle, b. 26 Dec 1926, Lunenburg, Massachusetts, USA. Composer. Education: Studied at the Schillinger House School of Music, Boston (1946-50) and with Rosalyn Brogue Henning. Career: Worked with John Cage on magnetic tape music project in New Yorik, 1952-55; Commissions from Pierre Boulez, Merce Cunningham, Luigi Nono, Lukas Foss and the Rome Radio Orchestra; Teacher at Cologne Conservatory 1966; Guest Professor, Basle Conservatory, 1975; Visiting Professor, UCLA, 1978; Composer-in-Residence, California Institute of the Arts, 1974-83; President of the American Music center, 1986-89. Compositions: Perspectives for Piano 1952; Folio 1952-53; 25 Pages, for any number of pianos, 1953; Octet I for tapes 1953; Indices for chamber orchestra 1954; Pentathis for ensemble 1957; Hodograph for ensemble 1959; Available Forms 1961; Light Music 1961; Available Forms II for 98 musicians and 2 conductors 1962; Corroboree for 3 pianos 1964; String Quartet 1965; Chef d'Orchestre/Calder Piece 1967; Syntagam for 8 instruments 1970; New Piece Loops 1971; Time Spans for Orchestra 1972; Sign Sounds for ensemble 1972; Centring for violin and ensemble 1973; Cross Sections and Color Fields for orchestra 1975; Patchen for chorus and orchestra 1979; Windsor Jams for soprano and chamber orchestra; Folio II 1981; Sounder Rounds for orchestra 1982; Tracer for ensemble and 4-track tape 1984. Honours include: Guggenheim Fellowship 1965-66; National Institute of Arts and Letters Award 1972; Brandeis University Creative Arts Award 1977. Address: c/o ASCAP, ASCAP Building, One Lincoln Plaza, New York, NY 10023, USA.

BROWN Ian, b. 1955, England. Pianist; Conductor. Career: Originally began as a bassoonist, then became Pianist-in-residence, Southampton University; Concerto soloist with many leading British orchestras including BBC Symphony Orchestra, BBC Welsh Orchestra, Bournemouth Symphony Orchestra, performing in major European and Scandinavian countries, the Middle East, North and South America, Singapore, Hong Kong and Japan; Pianist with Nash Ensemble from 1978, playing in the annual Wigmore series and at all major British festivals; Has appeared in duo with Mstislav Rostropovich, Henryk Szeryng, Ruggiero Ricci, Elisabeth Söderström, Felicity Lott, Ralph Kirshbaum, Gyorgy Pauk, James Galway and others; Soloist in Messiaen's Oiseaux Exotiques at the Proms; Toured Germany with BBC Philharmonic Orchestra in concerts celebrating Hans Werner Henze's 60th birthday; Recent appearances as conductor with Northern Sinfonia, the City of London Sinfonia, Scottish Chamber Orchestra and Bournemouth Symphony Orchestra and Sinfonietta; London conducting debut at the Barbican (Mahler's Resurrection Symphony with the Salomon Orchestra and London Choral Society). Recordings: Extensive recordings of chamber music from Haydn to the present day, with the Nash Ensemble. Current Management: Diana Walters Artists Management, England. Address: c/o Diana Walters Artists Management, Ivy Cottage, 3 Main Street, Keyham, Leicestershire LE7 9JQ, England.

BROWN Iona, b. 7 Jan 1941, Salisbury, Wiltshire, England. Violinist; Conductor. Education: Studied in Rome, Brussels, Vienna and Paris, notably with Henryk Szeryng. Career: Member, London Philharmonic Orchestra 1963-66; Solo career from 1966; Violinist and conductor with the Academy of St Martin in the Fields from 1974; Artistic Director of the Norwegian Chamber Orchestra 1981; Director of the City of Birmingham Symphony with reduced size forces 1985; Artistic Director of the Los Angeles Chamber Orchestra 1987-; Played the Beethoven Concerto at the 1988 Schleswig-Holstein Festival; Directed the Norwegian Chamber Orchestra at the 1991 Promenade Concerts: Britten Frank Bridge Variations, Strauss Metamorphosen and the Haffner Serenade. Recordings include: CDs with the Academy of St Martin in the Fields of The Lark Ascending by Vaughan Williams and Mozart's Haffner Serenade (as soloist); Poulenc's Organ Concerto and 19th Century Guitar Concertos (as conductor). Address: Academy of St Martin in the Fields, 109 Boundary Road, London NW8 0RG, England.

BROWN John, b. 1943, Yorkshire, England. Violinist. Education: Royal Manchester College of Music, with Endre Wolf and Gyorgy Pauk, and at Salzburg Mozarteum. Career: Co-leader, 1968, Leader, 1973, London Symphony Orchestra; Leader of the Orchestra of the Royal Opera House, Covent Garden, from 1976; Solo appearances with the BBC Scottish, BBC Symphony and London Symphony Orchestras; Plays a Stradivarius violin. Honours include: Prizewinner of the BBC Violin Competition, 1966; Order of the British Empire, 1987. Address: c/o Royal Opera House Orchestra, Covent Garden, London WC2, England.

BROWN John Gracen, b. 7 Oct 1936, Martinsburg, West Virginia, USA. Education: BS, 1961, MS, 1962, Southern Illinois University. Publications: Variation in Verse, 1975; A Sojourn of the Spirit, 1981; Passages in the Wind, 1985; Eight Dramas, 1991; The Search, 1994. Honours: Lyrics from poetry and drama used worldwide by over 150 composers. Membership: American Society of Composers. Hobbies: Outdoor activities. Address: 430 Virginia Avenue, Martinsburg, WV 25401, USA.

BROWN Justin, b. 1962, England. Conductor. Education: Studied at Trinity College, Cambridge, and at Tanglewood with Rozhdestvensky Ozawa and Bernstein. Career: Appearances with the LSO, RPO, BBC SO and Scottish SO, Bournemouth SO, Ulster Orchestra, Orchestre National du Capitole du Toulouse, Gothenburg SO, St Petersburg PO, Melbourne SO and Orchestre Internazionale d'Italia; Engagements with English National Opera, Scottish Opera and at the Maggio Musicale, Santa Fe, Lisbon, Stuttgart, Strasbourg and La Monnaie (Brussels) opera houses; Season 1996-97 with debut at Norwegian and Nantes Opera. Recordings: Bernstein, Candide, Scottish Opera; Taverner, The Protecting Veil, Wallfisch RPO. Honours include: Winner, London Mozart Players Best Young Conductor, 1990. Address: c/o IMG Artists, Media House, 3 Burlingtn Lane, London W4 2TH, England.

BROWN Rayner, b. 23 Feb 1912, Des Moines, Iowa, USA. Organist; Teacher; Composer. Education: BMus 1938, MMus 1947, University of Southern California, Los Angeles; Studied with Ingolf Dahl, Hanns Eisler and Lucien Cailliet. Career: Organist, Wilshire Presbyterian Church, Los Angeles, 1941-77; Professor of Music, Biola University, California, 1950-77; Emeritus Professor, Biola University, 1977-; Dean of Los Angeles Chapter, American Guild of Organists, 1961-63. Compositions include: Orchestral, 6 symphonies, 1952-82; Variations on a Hymn, 1957; 7 Organ Concertos, 1959-86; Concerto for Organ and Band, 1960; Symphony for Clarinet Choir, 1968; Concerto for Clarinet and Wind Orchestra, 1979; Organ, Sirist, Monologues, Variations, 1993; Organ with Instruments, Sonata for flute, cello and organ, 1994; Sonata for organ and string quartet, 1995; Organ Duets, Wamzipthe, Eight Impromptus, 1993; Piano, Quatre Skizzen, Intermezzi, Preludes, 1993; Piano four Hands, Scherzi, Ylfete, 1993; Chamber Music, Iris for flute, 1993. Recordings: Symphony for Clarinet Choir; Concerto for Two Pianos, Brass and Percussion; Fantasy-Fugue for Brass Ensemble; Sonata Breve for Piano; Sonata for Flute and Organ; Concertino for Piano and Band; Five Pieces for Organ, Harp, Brass and Percussion; Brass Quintet No 2; Concertino for Harp and Brass Quintet; The Craigheads at Asbury. Honours: Member of ASCAP with many annual awards for contributions to American Music; Ford Foundation Grants; Honorary Member, Sigma Alpha Iota. Current Management: Church Music Supply, 2755 West Broadway, Los Angeles, CA 90041, USA. Address: 2423 Panorama Terrace, Los Angeles, CA 90039, USA.

BROWN Robert (Stephen), b. 11 Feb 1952, Cookeville, Tennessee, USA. Managing Director of Opera Centre. m. Susan Johnson Morse, 24 July 1982, 1 daughter. Education: BS, Music Education (Composition and Piano), Tennessee Technological University, Cookeville, 1977; MM, Theory, Opera Conducting, Western Michigan University, Kalamazoo, 1977; Postgraduate study in Opera Stage Direction, School of Music, Indiana University, Bloomington, 1977. Career: Freelance director of musical theatre, 1977-; Production Stage Manager and Assistant Director: Fort Worth Opera, 1978-80; New Orleans Opera, 1978-79; San Diego Opera, 1979-81, 1983; Assistant Director and Stage Manager, Opera Theater of St Louis, 1978; Lyric Opera of Chicago, 1980-81; Executive Stage Manager, Lyric Opera of Chicago, 1983-84; Managing Director, 1984-, Stage Director, 1985-, Lyric Opera Center for American Artists, Chicago. Address: 1438 Lake Avenue, Wilmette, IL 60091, USA.

BROWNE Sandra, b. 27 July 1947, Point Fortin, Trinidad, West Indies. Singer (Mezzo-Soprano). Education: BA Modern Languages, Vassar College, USA; Brussels Conservatory with Mina Bolotine; Royal Manchester College of Music with Frederic Cox. Debut: With Welsh National Opera in Nabucco, 1972. Career: Sang in the premiere of Alun Hoddinott's The Beach of Falsea, 1974; Kent Opera as Monteverdi's Poppea, English National Opera from 1974, as Octavian, Rosina, Monteverdi's Poppea Dido and Carmen; Guest appearances in Toulouse, Marseille, Nancy and Florence as Carmen; Verona 1978, in a revival of Vivaldi's Orlando Furioso; La Scala Milan 1981 in Ariodante; Aix-en-Provence 1983, in Mozart's Mitridate; Other engagements in Pergolesi's Adriano in Siria (Florence), Dido and Aeneas (New York City Opera), Salome (Welsh National Opera), Radamisto and Ottone (Handel Opera Society); Concerts with most leading British orchestras, and in Norway, Portugal, France, Italy, Latin America and Australia; Regular Prom concert appearances. Recordings: Offenbach, Robinson Crusoe; Songs by Barber and Copland; Songs by Falla, Rodrigo, Granados and Montsalvatge; Rossini, Mosè in Egitto (Philips); Albinoni, Il Nascimento dell'Aurora (Erato); Vivaldi, Serenata a tre, Mio Cor Povero Cor (Erato). Honours: Kathleen Ferrier Memorial Scholarship 1971; RMCM Gold Medal for Voice 1972; Nominated for Lawrence Olivier Award, 1991. Hobbies: Lighting Bonfires; Letter Writing; The Garden; Lying on Tropical Beaches; Good Company. Address: New Zealand Cottages, Barnham, Thetford, Norfolk IP24 2PL, England.

BROWNER Alison, b. 22 September 1958, Dublin, Ireland. Singer. m. Wilhelm Gries, 1 son, 1 daughter. Education: BA, Trinity College, Dublin; School of Music, Dublin; Private Studies, Hans Hotter, Munich. Debut: Ludwigsburger Schlob Festspiele. Career: National Theatre, Mannheim; Appeared at Bayreuth Stuttgart, Zurich, Brussels, Antwerp, Covent Garden, Wexford Opera Festival, Staatsoper Berlin; Roles include La Cenerentola, Rosina (Barbiere), Cherubino, Hansel, Sesto, Idamante. Recordings: Oberto (Verdi) Christmas Oratorio, B Minor Mass, St Matthew Passion (Bach), Hugo Wolf Orchestral Songs with Choir. Current Management: Music International. Address: Kauterstr 14, D-65549 Limburg.

BROWNING John, b. 23 May 1933, Denver, Colorado, USA. Concert Pianist. Education: Juilliard School of Music. Debut: With New York Philharmonic, Carnegie Hall, New York City, 1956. Career: Appearances with numerous orchestras, USA Europe, USSR, Mexico; Recitalist worldwide; Pianist for World Premiere of Samuel Barber's Piano Concerto with Boston Symphony; Pianist with Cleveland Orchestra State Department; Toured USSR, 1965. Honours: Hollywood Bowl Young Artists Competition Award, National Federation of Music Clubs, 1954; Edgar M Leventritt Award, 1955; Queen Elizabeth International Concours Award, 1956; Honorary DMus, Occidental College; Honorary DMus, Ithaca College. Recordings: The complete Piano Concertos of Prokofiev, with Erich Leinsdorf and the Boston Symphony Orchestra, and music by Mozart and Rachmaninov; 6 concert length CD's, Rachmaninov, Liszt, Mussorgsky, Batber, Chopin and Scarlatti. Honours: Grammy Award, Best Instrumental Soloist with Orchestra, 1992; Best Soloist Without Orchestra, 1993. Current Management: Laurence Tucker, Columbia Artists Management, Incorporated. Address: c/o Shirley Kirshbaum & Associates, 711 West End Avenue, No 5KN, New York, NY 10025, USA.

BROWNRIDGE Angela (Mary), b. 14 Oct 1944, North Humberside, England. Concert Pianist. m. Arthur Johnson, 12 Oct 1968. 1 son. Education: Piano Scholar, Edinburgh University; Private study with Dorothy Hesse, Guido Agosti and Maria Curcio. Debut: Wigmore Hall, London, 1970. Career: Appearances in major London concert halls and with major orchestras in England and Abroad; Regular Broadcaster with Radio 3 and stations worldwide; Extensive recital tours in England, America, Canada, Far East and Europe. Compositions to: Piano pieces, aged 7. Recordings: Solo piano repertoire by Camilleri, Satie, Barber Tchaikovsky, Scriabin, Schumann, Gershwin and Liszt; First ever completed collections of solo works by Barber and Gershwin, Barber and Satie voted Records of the Month; Concerto with Royal Philharmonic Orchestra. Honours: Scholarship to Edinburgh University, 1963; Tovey Prize for Performance, 1965; Frazer Scholarship, 1966; Vaughan Williams Trust Fund, 1972; Arts Council Award, 1972. Memberships: Incorporated Society of Musicians; Musicians Union; EPTA. Hobbies: Skiing; Horse Riding; Keeping Fit; Gourmet Cookery. Current Management: Karen Durant Management. Address: 118 Audley Road, Hendon, London NW4 3HG, England.

BROZAK Daniel, b. 13 Apr 1947, Písek, Czechoslovakia. Composer; Theoretician; Violinist. Education: Prague Conservatory; Royal Conservatory in the Hague; Institute for Sonology at Utrecht State University. Debut: In Prague with own works for solo violin, 1973. Appointments: Leader of Prague Chamber Studio until 1969; Musica Intuitiva until 1975; Theoretic Research in the field of 12 tone harmony, 1975-84; Elektronic and computer music, 1985-94. Compositions: Les Voiles, 1977; Slunovrat, 1978; Equinox, 1978; The Seasons, 1981; Concerto da Chiesa, 1984; Diseased Society, 1988; Requiem, 1991. Recordings: Fresky, 1974; Rigorosym, 1975; Ave, 1978; In Manus Tuas, 1987; In A, 1988; In The Middle of Nowhere, 1988-90; Poetische Stunde, 1989; Dopisy Olze, 1990; Zbytecná Hudbe, 1992; Necas Trhovcu, 1994; Katolické Radovánky, 1996; Privat Sky, 1997. Publications: Interval Keys, 1977; Structural Harmony, 1988; Pathology of Music, 1991; Music and the Church of Saaldorf, 1997. Contributions to: Interval Keys and Structural Harmony (with D Pandula) la Accademia Cristiana, Roma, Studie 110-11, 1987. Honours: Wieniauski, composition competition (Sonata for solo violin, op 52), 1980. Memberships: IG-Komponisten Salzburg; SEAH Prague; SPNMS; SNH 39815; Artistic Initiative-EKVNM. Hobbies: Poetry; Painting. Current Management: Donemus, Adau, Netherlands. Address: Leustetten, Paulus Potterstraat 16, 1071 CZ, Amsterdam.

BRUA Claire, b. 1970, France. Singer (Soprano). Education: Studied with Albert Lance at the Nice Conservatoire; Paris Conservatoire with Rachel Yakar, Gundula Janowitz and William Christie. Career: Many performances in France and abroad with such conductors of Baroque music as René Jacobs and Jean-Claude Malgoire; Appearances with William Christie and Les Arts Florissants include Purcell's Dido, in Paris and Rome; Repertory includes Handel, Mozart and Rossini, and recitals of French song; Sang Pulcheria in Handel's Riccardo Primo, with Les Talens Lyriques under Christophe Rousset, Fontevraud, 1995; Sang many Mozart roles, Dorabella in Cosi fan tutte, Cherubino in Le nozze di Figaro, Zerlina in Don Giovanni, Annio in La Clemenza di Tito, Zweite Dame in Die Zauberflöte. Recordings include: Riccardo Primo. Address: 1 Rue de Chantilly, 75009 Paris, France.

BRUCE Margaret, b. 28 June 1943, Vancouver, British Columbia, Canada. Musician; Pianist. m. The Hon H L T Lumley-Savile, 26 July 1972, 3 sons (triplets). Education: ARCM (Performers and Teachers); Royal College of Music, London. Debut: Wigmore Hall, 1968, Career: Performances at Wigmore Hall, 1968, 1979; Purcell Room, 1970, 1975, 1978, 1980, 1983; Barbican, 1983, 1985; Royal Concert Huddersfield, 1982; Italian debut, 1983; Tours: Czechoslovakia, 1968, 1981, Canada, 1984, 1987, 1989; Originator, new concert series at St John's, Smith Square, London, Canadians and Classics, 1986, 1988, 1989, 1990; Many other concerts at St John's, including solo and duet; With Royal Philharmonic Orchestra, Barbican, 1985; Bulgarian debut, 1992; Chomé Piano Trio debut, Barbican; Many concerts and recordings to follow, 1993; Bruce-Colwell Duo, Edinburgh Festival debut, 1994. Compositions: CBC Recordings, Canada, 1969, 1982, 1984. Recordings: Premiere recording of Dvorák's From the Bohemian Forest, Op 68, with Peter Gellhorn; Solo recording, 1983. Honours: Royal College of Music, 1962; Sir James Caird Scholarship, 1966. Hobbies: Learning Italian; Studying; Art history. Current Management: c/o Lyttelton, Via dei Pandolfini 27, Florence 50122, Italy. Address: 7 Denbigh Gardens, Richmond, Surrey TW10 6EN, England.

BRUCE Neely, b. 21 Jan 1944, Memphis, Tennessee, USA, Composer; Pianist; Conductor. Education: Studied Piano with Roy McAllister, University of Alabama; Piano and Composition with Soulima Stravinsky and Ben Johnston, University of Illinois. Career: Teacher, Wesleyan University, 1974-, and Conductor, American Music/Theater Group; Piano performances of much American music including premieres of works by Cage, Duckworth, Farwell, Brant; New York debut, 1968, at the Electric Circus; European debut, Warsaw, 1972, in songs by Ives; Directed scenes from American operas at Holland Festival, 1982; Member, Editorial Committee, New World Records, 1974-79; Chairman, New England Sacred Harp Singing, 1976, 1979, 1982; Senior Research Fellow, Institute for Studies in American Music, Brooklyn College, 1980. Compositions include: Pyramus and Thisbe, chamber opera, 1965; The Trials of Psyche, opera, 1971; Concerto for violin and chamber orchestra, 1974; Americana, or, A New Tale of the Genii, opera, 1983; The Blades O' Blue Grass Songbook, solo voices, piano, 1984-95; Atmo-Rag, chamber orchestra, 1987; Santa Ynez Waltz, chamber orchestra, 1990; Orion Rising, First Album for orchestra, 1991; Barnum's Band, large wind ensemble, 1992; Tanglewood, oratorio, 1993; Trio for Bands, 3 rock bands, 1994; Hugomotion, oratorio on texts of Hugo Grotius, 1995; Instrumental, chamber, choral and vocal works. Recordings: Eight Ghosts, The Dream of the Other Dreamers, The Plague: A Commentary on the Work of the Fourth Horseman, composed for Electric Phoenix vocal quartet with electronics, 1992; CD: Perfumes and Meaning, Illinois Contemporary Chamber Singers with William Brooks, conductor, Stanzas for Shep and Nancy, Linda Hirst, mezzo-soprano, composer at piano, For Tom Howell, John Fonville, flautist, 1992. Current Management: Jonathan Wentworth Associates, Mt Vernon, New York, USA. Address: 440 Chamberlain Road, Middleton, CT 06457, USA.

BRUDERHANS Zdenek, b. 29 July 1934, Prague, Czechoslovakia. Flautist; University Reader. m. Eva Holubarova, 19 April 1962, 1 son, 1 daughter. Education: Bacalaureat, Akademicke Gymnasium, Prague; Distinction Diploma, Prague Conservatorium of Music; MMus, Prague Academy of Music. Debut: Prague, 1957. Career: Assistant Principal Flautist, Prague National Theatre, 1955-59; Principal Flutist, Prague Radio Symphony Orchestra, 1960-68; Flute Professor, Sweden, 1969-73; Lecturer, Senior Lecturer, Reader, Dean of Music, 1987-88, Adelaide University, South Australia, 1973-97; Flute Soloist in Czechoslovakia and 14 European Countries, USA, England, Australia and Asia on Radio (recitals, concertos) and in Festivals. Recordings: 10 recordings including 6 LP recitals released by numerous labels of works by Bach, Mozart, Haydn, Hindemith, Martinu, Messiaen, Berio, Debussy, Varèse, Ravel and Feld; Zdenek Bruderhaus Almanacs, CD; Sonatas by Martinu, Feld, Prokofiev. Publication: Music, Tectonics and Flute Playing, 1997. Contributions to: Miscellania Musicologica; The Instrumentalist; Pan and the Flute. Honour: Grand Prize, International Competition of Wind Instruments, Prague Spring Festival, 1959. Hobby: Swimming. Address: 2 McLaughlan Avenue, Brighton 5048, South Australia.

BRUEGGEN Frans, b. 30 Oct 1934, Amsterdam, Netherlands. Conductor; Musicologist. Education: Musieklyceum, Amsterdam; Recorder with Kees Otten; Awarded recorder diploma; Musicology at University of Amsterdam. Career: Many engagements as performer and conductor, in early and modern music; Played original 18th century flutes and recorders or copies; Member of avant-garde ensembles, including SourCream; Has commissioned many works (Berio's Gesti, 1966); Erasmus Professor of late Baroque music at Harvard University, 1972-73; Regent's Professor, University of California, Berkeley, 1974; Professor of recorder and early 18th century music at the Royal Conservatory, The Hague; Frequent concerts with cellist Anner Bylsma and harpsichordist Gustav Leonhardt; From 1981 has conducted symphonic music; Founder and Conductor of the Orchestra of the Eighteenth Century (concerts with the orchestra and Malcolm Bilson for the Mozart Bicentenary, 1991); Conducted Idomeneo for Netherlands Opera, 1991; Principal Guest Conductor of the Orchestra of the Age of Enlightenment from 1992, leading it at the 1993 Promenade Concerts in Haydn's London and Beethoven's Ninth Symphonies. Recordings include: CDs of Mozart's Piano Concertos K466 and K491 (John Gibbons), Symphony K550 and Beethoven's 1st Symphony; Haydn Symphonies Nos 90 and 93; Rameau Suites from Dardanus and Les Boréades; Vivaldi Flute Concertos. Publications: Various editions of early music, published in London, Tokyo or Amsterdam. Current Management: c/o Felix Warnock. Address: Orchestra of the Age of Enlightenment, 26 St Anne's Court, Dean Street, London W1V 3AW, England.

BRUHN Siglind, b. 11 Oct 1951, Hamburg, Germany. Concert Pianist; Music Analyst. m. Gerhold Becker, 20 Aug 1985. Education: MA, Romance Literature, Philosophy, University of Munich; MA, Piano Performance, Piano Pedgogy, Musikhochschule Hamburg and Stuttgart; Master classes with Wladimir Horbowski, Hans Leygraf, Nikita Magaloff; DrPhil, Music Analysis, Musikhochschule and University of Vienna, 1985. Debut: 1965. Career: Head of Community Music School, Munich, 1978-82; Head, Institute for Musical Interpretation, 1982-87; Director, Pianists' Academy, Ansbach, 1984-87; Director of Studies, University of Ansbach, 1984-87; Director of Studies, University of Hong Kong, 1987-94; Guest Professor, Beijing Central Conservatory of Music, 1990; Visiting Scholar, University of Michigan, Ann Arbor, 1993-97; Permanent Research Associate, Institute for Humanities, University of Michigan, 1977-; Performances in all major West German cities, Zurich, London, Paris, Lisbon, Venice, Athens, Beirut, Rio de Janeiro, Quito, Johannesburg, Cape Town, Hong Kong, Manila, Beijing, Shanghai, Melbourne, Adelaide; TV and radio appearances on most German stations and for British, French, Swiss, Italian, Lebanese and South African, Australian broadcasting corporations; Adjudicator Hong Kong Music Festival 1987, Taiwan International Mozart Competition 1990; Japan Mozart Competition 1991. Recordings: Ravel, Moussorgsky, 1984; Dvorak, 1986; Hindemith, duo sonatas, 1997; Hindemith, piano solo, 1997. Publications: Die Kunst musikalischer Gestaltung am Klavier, 1981; Die musikalische Darstellung psychologischer Wirklichkeit in Alban Bergs Wozzeck 1986; Guidelines to Piano Interpretation, 1989; How to Play J S Bach's Little Piano Pieces, 1990; Analysis and Interpretation in J S Bach's Well-Tempered Clavier, 1993; Musikalische Symbolik in Olivier Messiaens Weihnachtsvignetten, 1997; Images and Ideas in Modern French Piano Music, 1997; Alban Berg's Music as Encrypted Speech, editor, 1997; The Temptation of Paul Hindemith: Mathis der Maler as a Spiritual Testimony, 1998; Messiaen's Language of Mystical Love, editor, 1998. Contributions to: Scholarly journals, handbooks and collections in Europe, Asia and USA. Hobbies:Romance and South-East Asian Languages; Travel. Address: 1308 Broadway, Ann Arbor, MI 48105, USA.

BRUK Fridrich, b. 18 Sept 1937, Kharkov, Ukraine. Composer. m. Nadezhda Mislavskaya, 10 Sept 1959, 1 son. Education: School for Gifted Children, Kharkov; Diploma, Composition, Conservatory Rimsky-Korsakov, Leningrad, 1961. Debut: Opera 41, 1961. Career: Composer, Chamber and Orchestral Works, Music for Theatre and films; Popular songs/singers: Arja Saijonmaa, Eino Grön, records. Compositions include: String Quartet No 1, 1983; Music for Children: Spring, 1982; Snowdrop, 1983; Sleigh Bells, 1984; Summer, 1985; Golden Autumn, 1988; Winter, 1988; Sunflecks, suite for orchestra, 1987; Five duets for clarinet (B) and violoncello or bassoon, 1983; Lyrical Images, suite for piano, 1985; Variations for Piano on the Karelian song Strawberry, 1985; Concert Variations on the old Kalevala Song, for violoncello and piano, 1985; The Steppe, suite for woodwind quartet; Variations on a Finnish Shepherd's Song for Young Pianists, 1986; 7 Songs for 3 Voice choir, 1986; Sonata for Cantele, 1986; String Quartet N2 1987; Concertino for 2 violins and string orchestra or piano, 1987; Sonata for 2 violins, 1988; Sonata for violoncello, 1989; Sonata for 2 trumpets, 1989; Sonatina for piano no 2, 1989; Woodwind Quintet, 1989; Music to tv-films, 1988, 1989; Four pieces for flute and piano; Sonata for Viola, I, II, III, 1990; Sonata for Clarinet, (B), 1991; Sonata for Piano, 1994; Seven Dialogues for Oboe and Viola, 1995; Trio for Clarinet (B), Viola and Violoncello, 1996. Recordings: On CD: Compositions by Fridrich Bruk, 1993; Lyrical Images, 1994; From Kallvala, 1994; The Snowdrop, 1996; Dialogues, 1996. Honour: Decoration of Finnish Lion Knight's Cross for Service from the President of Finland, 1988. Address: Papinkatu 18 A 41, Tampere, 33200 Suomi, Finland.

BRUMAIRE Jacqueline, b. 5 Nov 1921, Herbley, France. Singer (Soprano). Education: Studied at the Paris Conservatoire. Debut: Paris Opéra-Comique, 1946, as The Countess in Le Nozze di Figaro. Career: Sang in Paris as Mimi in La Bohème, Micaela, Manon, Antonia in Les Contes d'Hoffmann and Fiordiligi; Opera-Comique 1951, in the premiere of Madame Bovary by Bondeville; Paris Opéra 1962, as Donna Elvira in Don Giovanni; Visited Peking 1981, to sing Carmen. Recordings: Opera arias, Philips; Milhaud's Les malheurs d'Orphée and Le Pauvre Matelot; Le Roi d'Yvetot by Ibert.

BRUMBY Colin (James), b. 18 June 1933, Melbourne, Victoria, Australia. Composer; Lecturer; Conductor. Education: BMus, 1957; DMus, 1972; Conservatorium of Music, University of Melbourne. Career: Lecturer in Music, Kelvin Grove Teachers College, 1960-62; Head of Music Department, Greenford Grammar School, Middlesex, 1962-64; Lecturer in Music, 1964-65; Senior Lecturer, 1966-71; Associate Professor of Music, 1976-; University of Queensland. Compositions: Flute Concerto; The Phoenix and the Turtle; Festival Overture on Australian Themes; Charlie Bubbles Book of Hours; Three Italian Songs for High Voice and String Quartet; Guitar Concerto; Violin Concerto 1 and 2; Piano Concerto; South Bank Overture; Symphony No 1 (The Sun); The Vision and The Gap (Cantata); Bassoon Concerto; Bassoon Sonata; Clarinet Sonatina; Flute Sonatina; Haydn Down Under (Bassoon Quintet); Victimae Paschali (SATB and Strings); Stabat Mater (Cantata); Piano Quartet; Christmas Bells, 1986; A Service of Rounds, 1985; Four Australian Christmas Carols, 1986; Operas: Fire on the Wind; Summer Carol; Borromeo Suite for flute and guitar; Viola Concerto, Tre aspetti di Roma; Trumpet Concerto; Symphony No 2, Mosaics of Ravenna. Publications: Missa Canonica, 1991; Harlequinade, 1987; Of a Rose, a Lovely Rose, 1994. Honour: Advance Australia Award (Music), 1981. Memberships: University of Queensland Staff Association; Australian Performing Rights Association. Hobbies: Reading; Travelling; Eating. Current Management: Australia Music Centre, PO Box N690 Grosvenor

Place, Sydney, NSW 2000, Australia. Address: 9 Teague Street, Indooroopilly, Queensland 4068, Australia.

BRUNELLE Philip, b. 1 July 1943, Minnesota, USA. Conductor; Artistic Director. m. Carolyn Olsen, 11 September 1965, 2 sons, 1 daughter. Education: University of Minnesota. Debut: Conducting: Europe, Aldeburgh Music Festival; Sweden, Gothenburg Opera, 1985. Career: Artistic Director and Founder, Plymouth Music Series of Minnesota, 1969-; Music Director, Minnesota Opera, 1968-85; Minnesota Orchestra, 1963-68; Guest Conductor of Opera and Orchestra, 1985-, throughout the USA and Europe; Organist, Choirmaster, Plymouth Congregational Church, Minneapolis, 1969-. Recordings: Virgin Classics: Paul Bunyan, Britten; The Tender Land, Copland; The Company of Heaven, Britten; Mass in D, Smyth; Te Deum and Masque of Night, Argento; Songs of a Cat, Garrison Keilor; Soloman II, Kraus; Serenade for a Christmas Night, Susa; Pro Arte; In a Winter Garden, Larsen; CRI: Jonah and the Whale, Argento; Witness, Collins Classics; Now It Is Christmas Again, Angel/EMI; Welcome Christmas!, RCQA Victor. Publications: Monthly Column in the American Organist, 1982-. Contributions to: The Musical Times. Honours: Kodaly Medal, 1982; Stikkan Anderson Prize, 1988; Order of the Polar Star, King of Sweden, 1989; Hon PhD, St Olaf College, 1988; Gramophone Prize, Best Opera Recording, 1988; Hon PhD, Gustavus Adolphus College, 1993. Hobbies: French Cooking; Hiking. Current Management: Norman McCann Limited. Address: 4211 Glencrest Road, Golden Valley, MN 55416, USA.

BRUNNER Eduard, b. 14 July 1939, Basle, Switzerland. Clarinettist. Education: Studied in Basle and Paris. Career: Chamber musician in Germany and Switzerland, from 1959; Soloist with the Bavarian Radio Symphony Orchestra, from 1963; Collaborations with such musicians as violinist Gidon Kremer (at Lockenhaus), Heinz Holliger (oboe) and Aurèle Nicolet (flute); Has premiered works by Francaix and Isang Yun (Concerto, 1982, Quintet, 1984). Address: c/o Rundfunkorchester des Bayerischen Rundfunks, Rundfunkplatz 1, W-8000 Munich 2, Germany.

BRUNNER Evelyn, b. 17 Dec 1949, Lausanne, Switzerland. Singer, Soprano. Education: Studied at the Lausanne Conservatory with Paul Sandoz, in Milan and with Herbert Graf in Geneva. Career: Sang with the Ensemble Vocal de Lausanne under Michael Corboz and with the Orchestre de Chambre de Lausanne under Victor Desrazens; Appearances at the Grand Théâtre de Genève as Micaela in Carmen, Marguerite in Faust and Cimarosa's Il Matrimonio Segreto, 1971; Sang Mozart's Countess at the Paris Opéra and in Hamburg and Berlin; Opéra du Rhin, Strasbourg, as Elsa in Lohengrin, 1986; Engagements at opera houses in Lyons, Toulouse, Avignon and Nantes; Other roles include Mozart's Fiordiligi and Donna Anna, Liu in Turandot and Verdi's Elisabeth de Valois and Violetta; Many concerts with the Collegium Academicum de Genève. Recordings: Rossini's Il Signor Bruschino, conducted by Robert Dunand.

BRUNNER Richard, b. 1953, Ohio, USA. Singer (Tenor). Education: Studied at the Opera School of Toronto and the Academy of Vocal Arts in Pittsburgh. Career: Sang Ramiro in Cenerentola with Philadelphia Opera (1978), Mime in Das Rheingold (Cincinnati and Dallas, 1981-82), Steva in Jenufa at the Spoleto Festival, Florestan with Scottish Opera (1991) and roles such as Elemer (Arabella), Narraboth (Salome) and Cassio (Otello) at the Vienna Staatsoper; Denver Opera, 1992, as Walther von Stolzing; Other roles include Melot, Sellem (The Rake's Progress) and Eisenstein in Die Fledermaus. Address: c/o Opera Colorado, 695 South Colorado Boulevard, Suite 20, Denver, CA 80222, USA.

BRUNNER Vladislav, b. 10 Nov 1943, Brno, Czechoslovakia. Flautist. m. E Illesova, 19 Jan 1963, 2 sons. Education: Music Conservatory, Bratislava. Debut: Cimarosa Flute Concerto with Philharmonic Orchestra Ostrava, 1963. Career: Solo Flautist Radio Symphony Orchestra Bratislava, 1963; Solo Flautist Slovak Philharmonic Orchestra, Bratislava, 1977; Solo Flautist, Radio Symphony Orchestra, Frankfurt, 1978; Major Festivals include Vienna, Salzburg, Prague Spring and Jerusalem; European Flautist Festival Frankfurt. Recordings: Flute concertos of Stamitz, Benda, Bach, Romberg and FX Richter. Honours: Honorable mention, Slovakian Ministry of Education; Silver Medal, International Music Competition, Geneva, 1973; Honorary Professor, Music Conservatory, Frankfurt. Hobbies: Chess. Current Management: Radio Symphony Orchestra, Frankfurt. Address: Leerbachstrasse 120, D-6000 Frankfurt am Main 1, Germany.

BRUNO Joanna (Mary), b. 1944, Orange, New Jersey, USA. Singer (Soprano). Education: Studied with Katherine Eastment in New Jersey, at the Juilliard School with Jennie Tourel and with Luigi Ricci in Rome. Debut: Spoleto Festival 1969, in The Medium by Menotti. Career: Sang in Santa Fe, Houston, Chicago, Fort Worth, City Opera, New York notably in the 1971 premiere of Menotti's The Most Important Man; European engagements in Trieste, Paris, Amsterdam and for Scottish Opera; Other roles include Mozart's Despina, Susanna and Pamina; Anne Trulove in The Rake's Progress, Micaela, Verdi's Nannetta; Puccini's Butterfly; Musetta; Mimi.

BRUSA Elisabetta (Olga Laura), b. 3 Apr 1954, Milan, Italy. Composer; Professor. m. Gilberto Serembe, 3 May 1997. Education: Diploma, Composition, Conservatorio of Milan with Bruno Bettinelli & Azio Corghi, 1980; Further studies with Hans Keller, London. Debut: First Composition performed, Piccola Scala, 1982. Career: TV Programme on Young Italian Composers, 1983; Various commissions, performances; Radio and TV Broadcasts in Italy, England, USA, Canada, Australia, Korea, and Albania with Orchestras such as the BBC Philharmonic, BBC Scottish Symphony Orchestra, CBC Vancouver Orchestra, Boris Brott Festival Orchestra, Radio and TV Symphony Orchestra of Tirana, London Chamber Symphony, New England Philharmonic, Tanglewood Music Center Orchestra, Alea III Ensemble, Contemporary Music Forum; Professor, Composition at: Conservatorio of Vicenza, 1980-82; Conservatorio of Mantova, 1982-84; Conservatorio of Brescia, 1984-85; Conservatorio of Milan, 1985-. Compositions include: Belsize String Quartet, 1981; Fables for Chamber Orchestra, 1983; Marcia Funebre for Piano, 1984; Suite Concertante for Orchestra, 1986; Nittemero Symphony for Chamber Orchestra, 1988; Symphony No 1 for Large Orchestra, 1990; Sonata for Piano; Sonata Rapsodica for Violin and Piano, 1991; La Triade for large Orchestra, 1992; Firelights for large Orchestra, 1993; Requiescat for Mezzo Soprano and large Orchestra, 1995; Fanfare for large orchestra, 1996; Adagio for string orchestra, 1996; Wedding Song for large orchestra, 1997; Florestan for large orchestra, 1997. Recordings: CD with Edipan Editions. Address: Via Pisacane 36, 20129 Milan, Italy.

BRUSCANTINI Sesto, b. 10 Dec 1919, Porto Civitanova, Macerata, Italy. Singer (Bass-Baritone). Education: Studied Law at first, then singing with Luigi Ricci in Rome. Debut: As Colline in La Bohème, Civitanova 1946; La Scala Milan from 1949, debut in Cimarosa's Il Matrimonio Segreto; US 1961, Chicago. Career: Sang Selim opposite Maria Callas in Il Turco in Italia, Rome 1950; Glyndebourne 1951-60 as Mozart's Guglielmo, Figaro and Leporello; Rossini's Raimbaud, Dandini and Figaro; Strauss's Music Master and Verdi's Ford; At Salzburg, 1953; Covent Garden, 1974, sang Malatesta in Don Pasquale; Sang the Magistrate in Werther at Rome, 1990; Don Alfonso at the 1990 Macerata Festival; Other roles include Verdi's Falstaff, Posa, Germont, Iago, Renato and Rigoletto. Recordings: La Fille du Regiment, L'Elisir d'Amore and Don Pasquale by Donizetti; Le Cantatrice villane by Fioravanti; Un Giorno di Regno, La Traviata and I Masnadierei, Verdi; 2 Versions of Rossini's La Cenerentola; Orlando Furioso by Vivaldi; Così fan tutte; Le Nozze di Figaro; La Ceccina by Piccinni; Griselda by A Scarlatti. Honours: Lyons Club Award, 1970. Hobbies: Photography; Amateur Film Making. Address: Via dei Sansovino 6, Rome, Italy.

BRUSILOW Anshel, b. 14 Aug 1928, Philadelphia, Pennsylvania, USA. Violinist; Conductor; Teacher. Education: Studied with Efrem Zimbalist, Curtis Institute of Music, Philadelphia, 1943; Jani Szanto, Diploma, Philadelphia Musical Academy, 1947; Conducting, Pierre Monteux, 1944-54. Debut: Violinist, Philadelphia Orchestra, 1944. Career: Concertmaster, New Orleans Symphony Orchestra, 1954-55; Associate Concertmaster, Cleveland Orchestra, 1955-59; Concertmaster, Philadelphia Orchestra, 1959-66; Founder; Conductor, Philadelphia Chamber Orchestra, 1961-65; Chamber Symphony of Philadelphia, 1966-68; Resident Conductor, 1970-71, Executive Director & Conductor, 1971-73; Dallas Symphony Orchestra; Teacher, Southern Methodist University, Dallas, 1982-89; College of Music, University of North Texas, 1989-. Recordings: Columbia; Composers Recordings Inc. Honours: Honorary Doctorate of Music, Capitol University, Columbus, OH, 1968. Address: College of Music, University of North Texas, Denton, TX 76203, USA.

BRUSON Renato, b. 13 Jan 1936, Este, Italy. Singer (Baritone). Education: Studied in Padua, Italy. Debut: Spoleto Festival, 1961. Career: Has appeared at all major Italian Opera Houses including La Scala, Milan, Debut 1972; Specialising in Verdi and Donizetti operas in Attila, La Traviata, La Favorita and Lucia di Lammermoor; Other opera houses include Vienna, Hamburg, Berlin, Paris, Brussels etc; Covent Garden debut 1976, as Renato in Un Ballo in Maschera; Appearances in USA include Chicago, New York Metropolitan Opera and San Francisco; Debut as Enrico at the Metropolitan, 1969; Has sung at the Verona Arena 1975-76, 1978-82, 1985; Los Angeles and Covent Garden, 1982, as Falstaff; Also at Parma, 1986; Munich, 1985, as Macbeth; Sang Iago at La Scala, 1987; Don Giovanni at the Deutsche Oper Berlin, 1988; Carnegie Hall, New York, 1990, as Montfort in Les Vêpres Siciliennes; Sang Carlos in Ernani at Parma, 1990, Germont at Turin, Carlos at La Fenice, Venice; Sang Enrico in Lucia di Lammermoor at La Scala, 1992, Germont at the 1992 Macerata Festival and at Covent Garden, 1995; Sang Macbeth at Monte Carlo, 1997. Recordings: Luisa Miller; Falstaff; Samson and Delilah etc. Films & TV include Don Carlos, La Scala and Luisa Miller, Covent Garden. Address: Teatro Alla Scala, Via Filodrammatici 2, Milano, Italy.

BRUYNEL Ton, b. 26 Jan 1934, Utrecht, The Netherlands. Composer. Education: Piano at Utrecht Conservatory. Career: Associated with Electronic Music Studio, University of Utrecht; Established own electronic music studio in 1957. Compositions include: Mostly with sound tracks; Resonance I, ballet, 1960-62; Reflexes for Birma Drum, 1961; Relief for Organ, 1964; Mobile, 1965; Milieu, 1965-66; Mekaniek for Wind Quintet, 1967; Decor, ballet, 1967; Signs for Wind Quintet and Video Projection, 1969; Intra 1 for Bass Clarinet, 1971; Elegy for Female Voices, 1972; Looking Ears for Bass Clarinet and Grand Piano, 1972; Soft Song for Oboe, 1975; Dialogue for Bass Clarinet, 1976; Translucent II for String Orchestra, 1978; From the Tripod for Loudspeakers, Women and Listeners, 1981; John's Lullaby for Chorus and Tape, 1985; Continuation for Chorus and Tape, 1985; Adieu petit Prince for Voice, 1983; Denk Mal das Denkmal for Man's Voice, 1984; Chicharres text, 1986; Toccare for Clavecimbalo, 1987; Ascolta for Chorus and Soloist, 1989; Nocturnes en Pedraza for Flute and Soundtrack, 1988; Kolom for Organ, 1987; Non Sono un Cello for Tenor and Bass Baritone; La Dernière pavane for Small Mixed Choir, 1989; La Cadulta for Tenor Bass Baritone; Tropico for Tenor Bass Baritone, 1990; Dust for Small Organ, 1991; Tarde for Cello, 1992; Le Jardin for Alto Flute, Harpsichord and Woman's Voice. Address: Fen Have 13, NL-7983 KD, Wapse Diever, The Netherlands.

BRUZDOWICZ Joanna, b. 17 May 1943, Warsaw, Poland. Composer; Music Critic. Education: Piano with Irena Protasewicz and Wanda Losakiewicz; Composition with Kazimierz Sikorski, MA, Warsaw Conservatory, 1966; Composition with Nadia Boulanger, Olivier Messiaen, Pierre Schaeffer, Paris, 1968-70. Career: Groupe de Recherches Musicales, French Radio and TV, Paris; Groupe International de Musique Electroacoustique de Paris; IPEM; Electronic studios, University of Ghent, Belgian Radio and TV; Founder, Jeunesses Musicales, Poland; Founder President, Frédéric Chopin and Karol Szymanowski Society, Belgium; Vice President, International Federation of Chopin Societies; Music criticism; Advocate of contemporary music. Compositions: Operas: In der Strafkolonie, or La Colonie Pénitentiaire, 1972, revised, 1986, 1995; Les Troyennes, 1973; The Gates of Paradise, 1987; Tides and Waves, opera, musical, 1992; Ballet: Le Petit Prince, 1976; Many film and theatre scores; Orchestral including: Piano Concerto, 1974; Symphony, 1975; Violin Concerto, 1975; Aquae Sextiae for winds, 1978; Double Bass Concerto, 1982; Four Seasons' Greetings, 4 concertos for violins, pianos, flute, marimba, string orchestra, 1989; The Cry of the Phoenix for cello and symphony orchestra, 1994; Chamber including: Trio dei Due Mondi for violin, cello, piano, 1980; Dum Spiro Spero for flute and tape, 1981; Para y contra for double bass and tape, 1981; Trio per Trio for flute, violin, harpsichord, 1982; Dreams and Drums for percussion, 1982; Oracle for bassoon and tape, 1982; Aurora Borealis for harp and organ, 1988; String Quartet No 1, La Vita, 1983, No 2, Cantus Aeterna with speaker, 1988; Spring in America, violin-piano sonata, 1994; Cantata: Urbi et Orbi for tenor, children's choir, 2 trumpets, 2 trombones, organ, 1985; The Cry of the Phoenix, cello concerto, 1994; Piano pieces; Organ music; Electronic and electroacoustic pieces. Recordings: Several CDs. Address: Roelandsheide 38, B-3080 Tervuren, Belgium.

BRYAN John (Howard), b. 24 Feb 1952, Ilford, Essex, England. Performer on Early Instruments; Lecturer. 1 son, 2 daughters. Education: BA, Honours; BPhil, University of York, 1970-74. Debut: 1973. Career: Co-Director, Landini Consort; Director, Rose Consort of Viols; Artistic Adviser, York early Music Festival; Principal Lecturer, University of Huddersfield; Also plays with Consort of Musicke and Musica Antiqua of London. Recordings: Nowell, Landini Consort; Songs and Dances of Fourteenth Century Italy, Landini Consort; The Play of Daniel, Landini Consort and Pro Cantione Antiqua; Elizabethan Christmas Anthems, Rose Consort of Viols; Dowland, Lachrimae, Rose Consort of Viols; Born is the Babe, Ah, dear Heart, Rose Consort of Viols; John Jenkins, Consort Music, Rose Consort of Viols; William Byrd, Consort music, songs and anthems, Rose Consort of Viols; Orlando Gibbons, Consort music, songs and anthems, Rose Consort of Viols. Contributions to: Music in Education; Compendium of Contemporary Musical Knowledge, 1992. Memberships: North East Early Music Forum; National Early Music Association. Hobbies: Opera; Theatre; Walking. Current Management: Karen Durant Management. Address: 28 Wentworth Road, Scarcroft Hill, York YO2 1DG, England.

BRYAN Paul. Professor of Music Emeritus. Education: BMus, 1941, MMus, 1949, PhD, Musicology, 1956, University of Michigan. Career: Professor of Music and Conductor of Duke Wind Symphony, Duke University, 1951-89; Instructor and Visiting Professor of Theory at the University of Michigan, 1948-51, 1954-55; Conductor and Head of Theory Instruction at Brevard Music Center, 1949-57; Conductor of Workshops and Clinics in Universities, Colleges, High Schools in Several States in USA,

Canada and Austria; Organizer and Conductor of Duke Wind Symphony's Semester-long Programs in Vienna; Concerts performed in Austria, Italy, Hungary, Germany and Czech Republic. Publications: The Symphonies of Johann Vanhal, 1956; Articles in Haydn Jahrbuch, Haydn Studien, Alta musica; Johann Vanhal, Viennese Symphonist: His Life and Musical Environment, 1997. Contributions to: Fontes Artis Musicae; CBDNA Journal; Journal of Band Research. Honours include: Recognition as Outstanding Conductor, School Musician Magazine; Phi Beta Mu. Memberships: Chairman, American Bandmasters Association Research Center Committee; College Band Directors National Association; North Carolina Train Host Association. Address: 1108 Watts Street, Durham, NC 27701, USA.

BRYARS (Richard) Gavin, b. 16 Jan 1943, Goole, Yorkshire, England. Composer. Education: BA, Honours in Philosophy, Sheffield University, 1964; Northern School of Music, 1964-66; Private musical composition studies with Cyril Ramsey, 1959-61, George Linstead, 1963-66 and Benjamin Johnston in USA, 1968. Career includes: Lecturer in Liberal Studies, Northampton College of Technology, 1966-67; Lecturer in Music, Portsmouth College of Art, 1969-70; Senior Lecturer of Music, Leicester Polytechnic, 1970-83; Principal Lecturer, 1983-85, Professor of Music, De Montfort University, 1985-96. Compositions include: The Sinking of The Titanic, 1969; Jesus's Blood Never Failed Me Yet, 1971; My First Homage, for 2 Pianos, 1978; Medea, opera premiered in Paris in 1984; By The Vaar for Double Bass and Ensemble, 1987; Glorious Hill, capella, 1988; Cadman Requiem, 1989; Four Elements, commissioned by Rambert Dance Company, 1990; The Black River for Soprano and Organ, 1991; The War in Heaven, commissioned by the BBC for Chorus and Orchestra, 1993; The North Shore for Solo Viola and Small Orchestra, 1994; Epilogue from "Wonderlawn" for 4 Players, 1994; Cello concerto, 1995; Aanan Songbook, 1996; Dr Ox's Experiment, opera commission from ENO, 1998. Recordings: Numerous including CDs: The Archangel Trip, The Green Ray, String Quartet No 1, Sub Rosa, Three Elegies for Nine Clarinets, The South Downs, A Man in a Room Gambling. Publication: Lors Berner's Exhibition Catalogue, 1979. Contributions to: Music and Musicians; Studio International; Art and Artists; Contact. Honours: British Ambassador for the Foundation Erik Satie; ISCM British Representation, 1977 and 1988. Memberships: College Pataphysique, 1974-; Oulipopo, 1974-; Association of Professional Composers, 1985-. Current Management: Erica Bolton and Jane Quinn Ltd. Address: c/o Erica Bolton and Jane Quinn Ltd, 8 Pottery Lane, London W11 4LZ, England.

BRYDEN John, b. 16 June 1947, Edinburgh, Scotland. Pianist. m. Margaret Greenlaw, 7 April 1973, 2 daughters. Education: Emmanuel College, Cambridge, 1965-68; Piano Studies with Mary Moore, Peter Katin, Guido Agosti, Claudio Arrau. Debut: Purcell Room, London, 1971. Career: Concerts at the Purcell Room and Wigmore Hall, London, and all over the United Kingdom as well as France and Italy; Member, Dartington and Roxburgh Trios, (chamber music); Local TV, Radio3 and Radio Scotland; Senior Lecturer in Music, Dartington College of Arts, 1982-91; Director of Music, St Christopher's School, Staverton; Visiting Piano Teacher, Sherborne School for Girls, Dartington College of Arts, The Abbey School, Torquay. Recordings: Martinu Chamber Music. Memberships: National Youth Orchestra of Great Britain, 1963-65; ISM; EPTA. Hobbies: Walking; Reading. Address: 35 St Marychurch Road, Torquay, Devon TQ1 3LF, England.

BRYDENFELT Michael, b. 3 April 1966, Roskilde, Denmark. Trumpet Soloist. m. Carol Conrad Brydenfelt, 3 November 1993, 1 son. Education: RoyalDanish Conservatory; Paris Conservatoire Superiore; Private Studies with Bo Nilsson, Philip Smith, Edward Tarr. Debut: Copenhagen, 1994. Appointments: Soloist, 90 Appearances Per Year. Recordings: Channel Classics Records; The Trumpet Player; Michael Brydenfelt. Honours: 1st Prize, Danish National Trumpet Guild Competition; 4th Prize, 44th International Music Competition, Prague Spring Festival; 1st Prize, Euro-ITG Competition for Young Artists; 3rd Prize & Prize for Exceptional Performance, 18th International Concours pour Instruments au Vent, Toulon, France; 3rd Prize, Bernard Soustrot's Prestige de la Trompette Competition, Alsace, France; Gladsaxe Music Prize; Carl Nielsen Grant; Special Soloist Award, Danish Radio Symphony Orchestra. Current Management: Tivoli Festival Management, Denmark. Address: Hollaendervej 16, 2791 Dragor, Denmark.

BRYDON Roderick, b. 1939, Edinburgh, Scotland. Conductor. Education: Daniel Stewart's College, Edinburgh; BMus Edinburgh University; Chigiana Academy, Siena. Debut: Covent Garden, 1984, with A Midsummer Night's Dream. Career: Close association with Sadler's Wells Opera and Scottish Opera in operas by Janacek (From the House of the Dead), Stravinsky, Mozart, Puccini, Debussy and Cavalli, (L'Egisto); Formerly General Music Director Lucerne Opera, conducting Carmen, Don Giovanni, Albert Herring and Fidelio; Musical Director of Berne Opera, 1988-90, leading A Village Romeo and Juliet, Capriccio and Peter Grimes; Guest engagements in Hannover, Copenhagen, Karlsruhe (Handel's Alcina); Bordeaux, (Così fan tutte) and Geneva (Death in Venice, The Rake's Progress and La Clemenza di Tito); Mozart's Mitridate and Rossini's Otello in Venice; Death in Venice at the 1983 Edinburgh Festival; La Traviata; The Rake's Progres with Opera North; Artistic Director of the Scottish Chamber Orchestra for the first 9 years of its existence including concerts at the Aix and Edinburgh Festivals; Promenade Concerts, 1982; Further concerts in Munich, Paris and Venice; Conducted Parsifal at the City Theatre Berne, 1989; Concert performances of The Cunning Little Vixen, 1990; Conducted Albert Herring at Los Angeles, 1992, followed by A Midsummer Night's Dream; The Rake's Progress, at the 1992 Aldeburgh Festival; Lucia di Lammermoor at Sydney, 1996. Address: c/o Music International, 13 Ardilaun Road, London N5 2QR, England.

BRYMER Jack, b. 27 Jan 1915, South Shields, County Durham, England. Clarinettist. m. 21 Oct 1939, 1 s. Education: Goldsmiths' College, London; Also privately. Debut: BBC Recital, 1947. Career: Principal Clarinet with Royal Philharmonic, 1947-63, BBC Symphony, 1963-71 and London Symphony, 1971-86; Member of Prometheus, Wigmore and London Baroque Ensembles; Directed London Wind Soloists. Recordings: Mozart Concerto; Mozart and Brahms Quintets; Siegmeister Concerto; Mozart Trio; Complete Wind Works of Mozart, Hadyn, J S Bach, Beethoven, Brahms Sonatas, Weber Duo, Stanford Sonata; Krommer Concerto; Debussy Rhapsody, Weber Concertino and Bärmann Adagio. Publications: The Clarinet; From Where I Sat, autobiography; In The Orchestra, autobiography. Contributions to: Regular articles in woodwind magazines. Honours: Honorary RAM, 1956; OBE, 1960; FGSM, 1970; Honorary MA, Newcastle University, 1973; FGCL, 1986; FRNCM, 1989; Honorary DMus, Kingston, 1993. Memberships: President of ISM and CASS. Hobbies: Golf; Swimming; Gardening. Address: Underwood, Ballards Farm Road, South Croydon, Surrey, CR2 7JA, England.

BRYN-JONES Delmé, b. 29 March 1935, Brynamman, Wales. Singer (Baritone). m. Carolyn Bryn-Jones, 1 son, 1 daughter. Education: Studied at the Guildhall School of Music and at the Vienna Academy of Music. Debut: With the New Opera Company, 1959, in The Sofa by Elizabeth Maconchy. Career: Sang at Covent Garden from 1963 in operas by Mozart, Verdi, Puccini, Bizet and Britten; Glyndebourne Festival 1963-64, 1972 as the Speaker in Die Zauberflöte, Nick Shadow and Macbeth; Appearances at the Aldeburgh and Edinburgh Festivals, and with the Welsh National Opera and Scottish Opera; US debut San Francisco 1967; Many engagements as concert singer; Broadcasts include British premiere of Henze's The Bassarids and 1-hour documentary on life and career by HTV, 1973. Recordings: Billy Budd by Britten. Contributions: Artists in Wales, 1975. Memberships: Gorsedd by Bards, Royal National Eisteddod, Wales. Hobbies: Rugby. Address: 57 Elm Avenue, Eastcote, Ruislip, Middlesex HA4 8PE, England.

BRYN-JULSON Phyllis, b. 5 Feb 1945, Bowdon, North Dakota, USA. Singer, Soprano. Education: Studied singing at the Berkshire Music Center and at Syracuse University. Debut: With the Boston Symphony in Berg's Lulu Suite, 1966. Career: Has given performances of works by George Crumb, David Del Tredici, Lukas Foss, Ligeti, Berg, Webern and Schoenberg (Pierrot Lunaire); Appearances at the Berlin, Edinburgh, Lucerne and Aldeburgh Festivals; British debut 1975, in Pli selon Pli by Boulez, conducted by the compser; Boulez 60th birthday celebrations at Baden-Baden 1985; Orchestras with whom she has appeared include the New York Philharmonic, the Boston Symphony, Chicago Symphony, Berlin Philharmonic under Abbado; First operatic role as Malinche in Montezuma by Roger Sessions, US premiere, Boston 1976; Sang in Stravinsky's Nightingale and Ravel's L'Enfant et les Sortilèges at Covent Garden, season 1986-87; Tours of Australia, New Zealand, USSR with Boulez; Ensemble InterContemporain; Tours of the US with the Los Angeles Philharmonic and of Europe with the BBC Symphony; Gave master classes at the Moscow Conservatoire in 1987 and took park in the 80th birthday celebrations for Olivier Messiaen and Elliott Carter, 1988; Sang in Carter's A Mirror on Which to Dwell, at London's Elizabeth Hall, Feb 1991. Honours: Distinguished Alumni Award, Syracuse University; Amphion Foundation Award. Recordings: A Mirror on which to Dwell; Le Visage Nuptial; Le Soleil des Eaux by Boulez, Erato. Address: c/o Ingpen & Williams Limited, 26 Wadhgam Road, London SW15 2LR, England.

BRYSON Roger, b. 1944, London, England. Singer (Bass). Education: Guildhall School, London; London Opera Centre with Walther Gruner and Otakar Kraus. Career: Glyndebourne Festival and Touring Opera from 1978 as Neptune in Il Ritorno di Ulisse, Quince and Bottom in A Midsummer Night's Dream, Osmin in Die Entführung, Rocco in Fidelio and Leporello in Don Giovanni; Kent Opera in Rigoletto, Die Zauberflöte and Don Giovanni; English National Opera in the British premiere of Ligeti's Le Grand Macabre, 1982; Opera North in Die Meistersinger, Werther, La Fanciulla del West and Love of Three Oranges; Scottish Opera as Schigolch in Lulu and Don Alfonso in Così fan tutte; Sang at Nancy in the French premiere of Tippett's King Priam and on TV in the Midsummer Marriage, 1989; As Alvise in La Gioconda for the Chelsea Opera Group, Mephistopheles in Faust for New Sussex Opera, 1989, Swallow in Peter Grimes, Don Pasquale for Opera North, Bartered Bride for New Tel Aviv Opera; Sang in concert performances of Ligeti's Le Grand Macabre at the Festival Hall, 1989, Don Pasquale for Opera North, 1990, Premieres of Europeras 3 and 4 by John Cage at the 1990 Almeida Festival, London; Sang Quince in A Midsummer Night's Dream, Sadler's Wells, Dikoi in Katya Kabanova for Glyndebourne Touring Opera, 1992, Flint in Billy Budd, 1992, Claggart in Billy Budd for Opera de Nancy, 1993, Don Basilio in Barber of Seville for Opera Northern Ireland, Calandro in L'Incontro Improvviso by Hadyn, for Garsington Festival, and Don Alfonso in Così fan tutte for ENO. Address: c/o Music International, 13 Ardilaun Road, Highbury, London, N5 2QR, England.

BUCCI Mark, b. 26 Feb 1924, New York City, USA. Composer. Education: St John's University, New York, 1941-42; Composition with Tibor Serly, 1942-45; Frederick Jacobi & Vittorio Giannini, BS, Juilliard School of Music, New York, 1951; Aaron Copland, Berkshire Music Center, Tanglewood. Compositions: Operas: The Boor, 1949; The Dress, 1953; Sweet Betsey from Pike, 1953; Tale for a Deaf Ear, 1957; The Hero, 1965; Midas, 1981; Musicals: Caucasian Chalk Circle, 1948; The Thirteen Clocks, 1953; The Adamses, 1956; Time and Again, 1958; The Girl from Outside, 1959; Chain of Jade, 1960; Pink Party Dress, 1960; The Old Lady Shows Her Medals, 1960; Cheaper by the Dozen, 1961; Johnny Mishuga, 1961; Our Miss Brooks, 1961; The Best of Broadway, 1961; Ask Any Girl, 1967; Second Coming, 1976; Incidental music to several plays; Film sscores; Concerto for Kazoo & Orchestra, 1959 renamed Concerto for a Singing Instrument; Flute Concerto; Choral pieces; Songs. Honours: Piatigorsky Award, 1949; MacDowell Colony Fellowships, 1952, 1954; Guggenheim Fellowships, 1953-54 and 1957-58; National Instituten of Arts and Letters grant, 1959; Co-winner, Prix Italia, 1966. Address: c/o ASCAP, ASCAP Building, One Lincoln Plaza, New York, NY 10023, USA.

BUCHAN Cynthia, b. 1960, Edinburgh, Scotland. Singer (Mezzo-Soprano). Education: Royal Scottish Academy of Music. Career: Has appeared widely in Britain and Europe as Mozart's Cherubino and Dorabella, Massenet's Charlotte, Rossini's Rosina, Verdi's Preziosilla, Tchaikovsky's Olga and as Carmen; In 1987 sang in L'Enfant et les Sortilèges at Glyndebourne, Carmen for Opera North and Mistress Quickly in Peter Stein's production of Falstaff for the Welsh National Opera; Guest appearances in Madrid, Munich, Paris as Rosina, Frankfurt as Babette in Henze's English Cat, Adelaide, Hamburg as Miranda in Cavalli's L'Ormindo and Amsterdam as Vavara in Katya Kabanova; Glyndebourne 1989 as Hermia in A Midsummer Night's Dream; Sang Despina in Così fan tutte for New Israeli Opera, 1994; Maddalena in Rigoletto for WNO, 1997; Concert appearances in London, Munich, Paris and Lyon; Conductors include Gielen, Andrew Davis, Rattle, Ivan Fischer, Knussen, Del Mar, Bernstein and Bertini. Recordings include: Video of Bersi in Andrea Chénier, at Covent Garden in 1985. Address: c/o Lies Askonas Ltd, 6 Henrietta Street, London, WC2, England.

BUCHANAN Alison, b. England. Singer (Soprano). Education: Studied at the Guildhall School of Music and the Curtis Institute, Philadelphia. Career: Appearances as Clara in Porgy and Bess at the Barbican, in Messiah at Chichester Cathedral, Mozart's Requiem and Bach's Christmas Oratorio at Chelmsford Cathedral and Strauss's Four Last Songs at Curtis Hall; Debut with the San Francisco Opera with Western Opera Theatre as Mozart's Countess; Season 1995-96 at San Francisco as Mimi, Juliana in Argento's The Aspern Papers, and Micaela; Season 1996-97 with Porgy and Bess excerpts in Bruges and Paris and appearances in Elektra, Death in Venice and Rigoletto at San Francisco; Other roles include Rosalinde, Mathilde in Guillaume Tell, Helena in a A Midsummer Night's Dream and Madame Cortese in Il Viaggio a Reims. Honours include: First Prize, Washington International Competition, 1995; Pavarotti Competition in Philadelphia, 1995. Address: c/o San Francisco Opera, Van Ness Avenue, San Francisco, CA, USA.

BUCHANAN Dorothy (Quita), b. 28 Sept 1945, Christchurch, New Zealand. Composer. Education: Graduated, University of Canterbury, 1967. Career: Founded music workshops at Christchurch, 1973; Music educationalist from 1977; Composer-in-residence at New Zealand Film Archives, Wellington, 1984. Compositions include: Five Vignettes of Women for flute and female chorus, 1987, and other vocal music; Sinfoniette in 5 Movements, 1989; Due concertante for violin, cello and orchestra, 1991; Music for stage and screen; Chamber music, including Echoes and Reflections for clarinet, guitar, violin and cello, 1993. Address: c/o New Zealand Music Centre, Level 13, Brandon Street, Wellington, New Zealand.

BUCHANAN Isobel (Wilson), b. 15 Mar 1954, Glasgow, Scotland. Soprano. m. Jonathan King (otherwise Jonathan Hyde, actor), 1980, 2 daughters. Education: Royal Scottish Academy of Music and Drama. Debut: Glyndebourne, 1978 as Pamina; Vienna Staatsoper, 1978, as Micaela; Santa Fe, USA, 1979, as Zerlina and Adina; Chicago, 1979; New York, 1979; Cologne, Germany, 1979; Aix-en-Provence, France, 1981. Career: Australian Opera Principal Singer, 1975-78; Freelance Singer, 1978-; Performances with Scottish Opera, Covent Garden, Munich Radio, Belgium, Norway and others; Other roles include Fiordiligi, Susanna and Donna Elvira; Sang Dorabella at the 1987 Glyndebourne Festival; In recent years has devoted career to concert appearances. Recordings: Various operatic and vocal recordings. Hobbies: Reading; Gardening; Cooking; Dressmaking; Knitting; Tennis. Current Management: Marks Management Limited, London. Address: 14 New Burlington Street, London W1X 1FF, England.

BUCHBINDER Rudolf, b. 11 Feb 1946, Leitmeritz, Austria. Pianist. Education: Studied piano with Bruno Seidlhofer. Career: Extensive repertoire of concert pieces, both classical and modern; Has performed works rarely played including The Diabelli Variations, a collection from 50 Austrian composers; Has performed a cycle of all 32 Beethoven Sonatas; Performances in many major cities in Europe, USA, South America, Australia and Japan; Regular guest at major music festivals; Has played with all important leading conductors. Recordings: The Diabelli Variations; Collection of Joseph Haydn piano works; Over 80 recordings. Honour: Grand Prix du Disque, for Haydn's piano works. Hobbies: Literature; Collecting modern paintings and graphics; Amateur painting. Current Management: Astrid Schoerke. Address: c/o Monckebergallee 41, 30453 Hannover, Germany.

BUCHLA Donald F(rederick), b. 17 Apr 1937, Southgate, CA, USA. Electronic Instrument Designer and Builder; Composer; Performer. Education: BA, Physics, University of CA, Berkeley, 1961. Career: Installed first Buchla synthesizer, San Francisco Tape Music Center, 1966; Founder of Buchla Associates, Berkeley, 1966; Designed and manufactured various electronic instruments; Designed electronic music studios including Royal Academy of Music, Stockholm, and IRCAM in Paris; Co-Founder of Electric Weasel Ensemble in 1975; Co-Director, Artists Research Collective, Berkeley, 1978-. Compositions: Various pieces with electronic instruments including Cicada Music for some 2,500 Cicadas, 1963; 5 Video Mirrors for Audience of 1 or More, 1966; Anagnorisis for 1 Performer and 1 Voice, 1970; Harmonic Pendulum for Buchla Series 200 Synthesizer, 1972; Garden for 3 Performers and 1 Dancer, 1975; Keyboard Encounter for 2 Pianos, 1976; Q for 14 Instruments, 1979; Silicon Cello for Amplified Cello, 1979; Consensus Conduction for Buchla Series 300 Synthesizer and Audience, 1981. Honours: Guggenheim Fellowship, 1978; National Endowment for the Arts Grant, 1981. Address: Music Department, University of California, Berkeley, California, USA.

BUCHNER Eberhard, b. 6 Nov 1939, Dresden, Germany. Tenor. Education: Studied at the Carl Maria Von Weber-Musikhochschule, Dresden, 1959-64. Debut: Schwerin in 1964 as Tamino. Career: Staatsoper Dresden from 1966, and Staatsoper Berlin from 1968, notably in operas by Struass, Mozart and Wagner; Sang Schubert's Die Schöne Mullerin, in Vienna, 1972; Appeared at the Vatican in 1973 in a concert conducted by Bernstein; Sang at Metropolitan Opera in 1974, Covent Garden in 1975, Hamburg Staatsoper in 1983 in a revival of Amadis de Gaule by JC Bach, Théâtre de la Monnaie in Brussels and Salzburg Festival in 1985 and 1990 as Flamand in Capriccio, and Royal Opera Copenhagen in 1986 as Wagner's Lohengrin; Sang Adolar in Euryanthe at the Berlin Staatsoper, 1986; La Scala Milan in 1988 as Erik in Der fliegende Holländer and sang Lohengrin at Lisbon in 1990; Sang Dionysus in The Bassarids at Hamburg, 1994. Recordings: Die schweigsame Frau by Strauss; Froh in Das Rheingold; Bach Cantatas; Bach's B minor Mass; Sacred Music by Mozart; Beethoven's 9th Symphony.

BUCHT Gunnar, b, 5 August 1927, Stocksund, Sweden. Composer. m. Bergljot Krohn, 12 April 1958. Education: PhD, Musicology; Studied Composition with Karl Birger-Blomdahl, Carl Orff, Goffredo Petrassi, Max Deutsch; Piano with Yngve Flyckt. Debut: Composer and Pianist, 1949. Career: Chairman, Society of Swedish Composers, 1963-69; Teacher, Stockholm University, 1965-69; Vice President, International Society for Contemporary Music, 1969-72; Cultural Attache to the Swedish Embassy at Bonn, 1970-73; Professor of Composition, State College of Music, 1975-85, Director, 1987-93. Compositions include: Opera, The Pretenders, after Ibsen, 1966; Symphonies, 1952-97; 2 Cello Concertos, 1955-90; La fine della diaspora for tenor, chorus and orchestra, 1957; Lutheran Mass, 1973; Journées oubliées, 1975; Au delá, 1977; Violin Concerto, 1978; The Big Bang - And After, 1979; Georgica (Quasimodo), 1980; En Clairobscur for chamber orchestra, 1981; Fresques mobiles, 1986; Tönend bewegte Formen for orchestra, 1987; Chamber Music including String Quintet, 1950, 3 String Quartets, 1951, 1959, 1997, Sonata for piano and percussion, 1955, Symphonie pour la musique libérée for tape, 1969, Blad från mitt gulsippeänge for clarinet and piano, 1985; Unter Vollem Einsatz for organ and 5 percussionists, 1987; One Day I Went Out Into The World, novel for orchestra, 1983-84; Piano Concerto, 1994. Recordings: Symphony 7, Violin Concerto, Piano Concerto, Georgica Cantata, Quatre pièces pour le pianiste. Publications: Electronic Music in Sweden, 1977; Europe in Music, 1996; Född på Krigsstigen (Born on the War Path), autobiography, 1997. Contributions to: Swedish Journal of Musicology. Honours: Litteris et artibus, Royal Medal. Membership: Royal Academy of Music. Address: Burge Hablingbo, S-62011 Havdhem, Sweden.

BUCK Peter, b. 18 May 1937, Stuttgart, Germany. Cellist. Education: Stuttgart's Conservatory with Ludwig Hoelscher. Career: Former member of Karl Munchinger's Stuttgart Chamber Orchestra in Heilbronn; Co-Founder of Melos Quartet of Stuttgart, 1965; Represented Germany at the Jeunesses Musicales in Paris, 1966; International concert tours from 1967; Bicentenary concerts in the Beethoven Haus at Bonn in 1970; Toured Russia, Eastern Europe, Africa, North and South America, The Far East and Australia; British concerts and festivals from 1974; Cycle of Beethoven quartets at Edinburgh Festival, 1987; Played at Wigmore Hall, St John's Smith Square and Bath Festival in 1990; Associations with Rostropovich in the Schubert Quintet and the Cleveland Quartet in works by Sophr and Mendelssohn; Teacher at the Stuttgart Musikhochschule. Recordings include: Complete Quartets of Beethoven, Schubert, Mozart and Brahms; Quintets by Boccherini with Narcisco Ypes, and by Mozart with Franz Beyer. Honours include: With Melos Quartet, Grand Prix du Disque and Prix Caecilia, from Academie du Disque in Brussels. Address: Melos Quartet, c/o Ingpen and Williams Ltd, 14 Kensington Court, London, W8 5DN, England.

BUCKEL Ursula, b. 11 Feb 1926, Lauscha, Germany. Soprano; Teacher. Education: Studied with Hans Hoefflin in Freiburg and with Ria Ginster in Zurich. Career: Sang in Bach's Johannes Passion at Kreuzlingen, Switzerland; Based in Geneva from 1954; Many performances of cantatas and Passions by Bach, notably at the Bach-Festwochen at Schaffhausen and Ansbach; Tours of Switzerland, England, Finland, Austria, France, Germany and Italy; Far East tour with the Deutsche Bach-Solisten under Helmut Winschermann; Further tours to Athens and to Israel; Performances of music by Frank Martin; Teacher of Voice at the Geneva Conservatory from 1971. Recordings: Mendelssohn's Elijah; Bach Cantatas; Christmas Oratorio by Schütz; L'Incoronazione di Poppea by Monteverdi.

BUCKLEY Richard E(dward), b. 1 Sep 1953, New York City, USA. Conductor. Education: BM, North Carolina School of the Arts, Winston-Salem, 1973; MMus, Catholic University of America, Washington DC, 1974; Aspen School of Music, CO, 1974; Salzburg Mozarteum, 1977. Career: Assistant Conductor and Chorusmaster, Washington Opera Society, 1973-74; Assistant Associate, Resident, and Principal Guest Conductor at Seattle Opera, 1974-75; Music Assistant to Conductor at Seattle Symphony Orchestra, 1974-85; Music Director, Oakland Symphony Orchestra, CA, 1983-86; Guest Conductor, New York Philharmonic Orchestra, Philadelphia Orchestra, Houston Symphony Orchestra, San Antonio Symphony Orchestra, Oregon Symphony Orchestra, Los Angeles Philharmonic Orchestra, Minnesota Orchestra, Indianapolis Symphony Orchestra, BBC Symphony Orchestra, Royal Philharmonic Orchestra, Royal Liverpool Philharmonic Orchestra, Chicago Lyric Opera, Los Angeles Opera, New York City Opera, Houston Grand Opera, Canadian Opera, Netherlands Opera, and Hamburg State Opera; Recent operatic premieres include Paulus' The Postman Always Rings Twice with Miami Opera and The Woodlanders at St Louis; US premiere of Sallinen's The King Goes Forth to France, for Sante Fe Opera; Other projects include Les Contes d'Hoffmann with Los Angeles Music Center Opera, Aida at Chicago and Rossini's Il Viaggio a Reims at St Louis; Conducted Il Barbiere di Siviglia for Miami Opera in 1990, and Dvorák's The Devil and Kate at St Louis; Season 1996 with Butterfly at Los Angeles and Aida at Philadelphia. Honours: Prize Winner, Besançon Competition in 1979; Rupert Foundation Competition in 1982. Address: c/o Herbert Barrett Management Inc, 1776 Broadway, New York, NY 10019, USA.

BUCQUET Marie-Francoise, b. 28 Oct 1937, Montvilliers, France. Pianist; Teacher. Education: Studied at the Vienna Music Academy, The Paris Conservatoire and with Wilhelm Kempff, Alfred Brendel and Leon Fleisher. Debut: Marguerite Long School in 1948. Career: Attended course by Eduard Steuermann at Salzburg to study music of Schoenberg and followed courses by Pierre Boulez at Basle; Sylvano Bussotti, Betsy Jolas and Iannis Xenakis have written for her; Performs works by Bach, Haydn, Stockhausen, Schoenberg and standard repertory music; Professor of Accompaniment and Piano Pedagogy at the Paris Conservatoire from 1986. Address: c/o Conservatoire de Paris, 209 Avenue Jean Jaurés, Paris 75019, France.

BUCZEK (BUCZKOWNA) Barbara (Kazimiera Zofia), b. 9 Jan 1940, Cracow, Poland. Composer. Education: Certificate with Distinction, Secondary School of Music, Cracow, 1959; Piano studies with Maria Bilinska-Reigerowa; Diploma in Piano, State College of Music, Cracow, 1965, with L Stefanski; Diploma with Distinction in Composition, under Boguslaw Schaeffer, 1974. Debut: Performance of Anekumena in Warsaw, 1975. Career includes: Major premieres: Warsaw in 1975, Cracow in 1980, Danzig in 1984, Rome in 1984, Basel in 1984, Salzburg in 1985, Vienna in 1985, Cracow in 1985, Radio Uno, Italy in 1986, and Cracow in 1989; Teacher at Music Academy in Cracow, 1972-. Compositions include: 2 Impressions for Orchestra; Anekumena Concerto; Concerto for Cello, Choir and Orchestra; Hipostaza; Motet; Primus Inter Pares; Vocal Concerto for 12 Solo Voices; Music for G Zechberger, 1991; Fantasmagorie for chamber orchestra, 1992. Recordings include: Transgressio for String Quartet. Publications include: Wielosc Jednosé w Muzyce Sakralnej B Schaeffera. Contributions include: Artur Malawski: A Drama of Unfulfilment; Boguslaw Schaeffer's Creative Works. Honours include: Distinction, Young Composers' Competition, Warsaw, 1976, Lancut, 1980; Gold Cross of Merit for 20 Years Distinguished Service in Field of Education, 1985. Memberships: Artistic Society Cracow Group, Art Gallery Krzysztofory; Polish Composers' Union; Internationaler Arbeitskreis Frau und Musik. Hobbies: Nature; Excursions, especially in mountains; Literature; Philosophy of Art. Address: Brodowicza 22 m 1, 31-518 Cracow, Poland.

BUCZYNSKI Walter, b. 17 Dec 1933, Toronto, Canada. Composer; Pianist. Education: Studied Composition with Milhaud, 1956 and Nadia Boulanger, 1960-62 at Toronto Conservatory. Career: Teacher of Piano and Theory at Royal Conservatory of Toronto, 1962, and Theory at University of Toronto from 1970. Compositions include: Piano Trio, 1954; Suite for Wind Quintet, 1955; Divertimento for Violin, Cello, Clarinet and Bassoon, 1957; Children's operas Mr Rhinoceros And His Musicians, 1957 and, Do Re Mi, 1967; Squares In A Circle for Flute, Violin, Cello and Strings, 1967; Four Movements for Piano and Strings, 1969; Zeroing In, 5 pieces for various vocal and instrumental groups, 1971-72; Three Against Many for Flute, Clarinet, Bassoon and Orchestra, 1973; Concerto for Violin, Cello and Orchestra, 1975; Olympics '75 for Brass Quintet; From The Buczynski Book Of The Dead, chamber opera, 1975; Naked At The Opera, 1979; Piano Concerto, 1979; Piano Quintet, 1984; The August Collection, 27 preludes, 1987; Litanies for Accordion and Percussion, 1988; Songs and piano music. Address: SOCAN, 41 Valleybrook Drive, Don Mills, Ontario M3B 2S6, Canada.

BUDAI Livia, b. 23 Jun 1950, Esztergom, Hungary. Mezzo-Soprano. Education: Franz Liszt Academy Budapest with Olga Revheggi. Debut: Sofia in 1973 as Carmen. Career: Member of Hungarian State Opera, 1973-77; Concert appearances with the Hungarian Philharmonic and on Budapest Radio; Guest engagements in Austria, Bulgaria, Finland, France, Germany and Russia; Member of Gelsenkirchen Opera, 1977; Covent Garden debut in 1978 as Azucena, returning as Eboli in Don Carlos in 1983; US debut in San Francisco in 1979 as Eboli; Munich Staatsoper from 1980; Bologna in 1983 as Brangaene in Tristan und Isolde; Appearances in Berlin, Brussels, Vienna, Barcelona, Florence and Madrid as Elisabetta in Maria Stuarda, Marguerite in The Damnation of Faust, Wagner's Venus and Fricka, and Verdi's Amneris, Preziosilla and Azucena; Other roles include Gluck's Orfeo, Saint-Saëns's Dalila, Bartók's Judith and the Composer in Ariadne auf Naxos; Aix-en-Provence in 1987 as Mistress Quickly, Marseilles in 1989 as Cassandre in Les Troyens; Sang Amneris at Bonn in 1990, Ortrud at Brussels, and the Princess in Adriana Lecouvreur for L'Opéra de Montréal; Appeared as Marfa in Dvorák's Dimitrij at Munich in 1992; Kundry in Parsifal with RAI at Turin in 1992; Sang Clytemnestra in Elektra at Frankfurt, 1994. Recordings: Stabat Mater and Lange Mala Umbrae Terrores. Address: c/o Ingpen and Williams Ltd, 26 Wadham Road, London SW15 2LR, England.

BUDD Harold, b. 24 May 1936, Los Angeles, CA, USA. Composer. m. Paula Katzman, 26 Jun 1960, 2 sons. Education: Los Angeles City College, 1957-59; BA, San Fernando State College, 1963; MM, University of Southern California, 1966. Career: Composition Faculty, California Institute of the Arts, 1971-76. Compositions and Recordings: The Pavilion Of Dreams, 1978; The Plateaux Of Mirror, with Brian Eno, 1980; The Serpent (In Quicksilver), 1981; The Pearl, with Brian Eno, 1984; Abandoned Cities, 1984; The Moon And The Melodies, with The Cocteau Twins, 1986; Lovely Thunder, 1986; The White Arcades. Honours: National Endowment for The Arts, Composer Fellowship, 1974, 1979. Current Management: Opal Ltd. Address: c/o Opal Ltd, 330 Harrow Road, London, W9 2HP, England.

BUDDEN Julian, b. 9 Apr 1924, Hoylake, Merseyside, England. Musicologist; BBC Producer. Education: Queen's College, Oxford, 1942-43; MA (Oxon); Royal College of Music, London, 1948-50; BMus (London); FBA, 1987. Career: Music Library Clerk, BBC Radio, 1951, became successively Music Presentation Assistant, 1955, Music Producer, 1956, Chief Producer of Opera, 1970, External Services Music Organiser, 1976; Retired, 1983. Publications: The Operas of Verdi, Volume I, 1973, Volume 2, 1978, Volume 3, 1981; Verdi (The Master

Musicians), 1985. Contributions to: Numerous professional journals including: Music and Letters; Musical Times; The Listener. Honours: Yorkshire Post Award for Best Music Book, 1979; Derek Allen Prize for work on Verdi, British Academy, 1980; Premio Diego Fabbri, 1989; OBE, 1991. Membership: Editorial Committee, Critical Edition of the Works of G Verdi. Address: 94 Station Road, Finchley, London N3 2SG, England.

BUDIN Jan, b. 20 May 1950, Prague, Czech Republic. Clarinettist. m. Vlasta Budínová, 5 July 1973, 1 son, 1 daughter. Education: Academy of Arts, Prague. Career: Concert performances in European countries; TV performances in the Czech Republic, Poland, Germany, Sweden, Denmark. Compositions: Some compositions for various chamber ensembles. Recordings: Frantisek Vincenc Kramár - Quartet B flat major, Op 21, No 1; Quartet E flat major, Op 21, No 2; Quintet B flat major, OP 95 - Jan Budín with Panocha Quartet; Johannes Brahms - Quintet B minor, Op 115 - Jan Budín with Panocha Quartet; More recordings (especially early Czech music for Czech radio). Contributions: Editor-in-Chief of Musical Journal for Blind. Honour: First Prize in the International Competition of Blind Musicians, Prague, 1975. Hobbies: Cycling; Travelling. Address: 11 Dusní Street, 110 00 Prague 1, Czech Republic.

BUFKENS Roland, b. 26 Apr 1936, Ronse, Belgium. Singer (Tenor); Singing Professor. m. Simone Deboelpaepe, 25 Apr 1961, 1 d. Education: Brussels Conservatoire; Proficiency Course in Germany under Clemens Glettenberg. Debut: In Germany. Career: German concerts specialising in Bach tradition and also the St John and St Matthew Passion; Performances with several German orchestras conducted by Kurt Thomas, Karl Richter, Kurt Redel and Nikolaus Harnoncourt; International career: notably a performance of Berlioz's Romeo and Juliet in a tour of Japan and later in Paris' Théâtre des Champs Elysées, both conducted by Lorin Maazel; Other performances include: Stravinsky's Mavra, in the Concertgebouw of Amsterdam; Martin's Mystère de la Nativité, Madrid; All these performances were broadcast; Manuel de Falla's Vida Breve conducted by R F de Burgos in Brussels; Participated several times in the Holland Festival, Biennale of Zagreb, Festival of Lourdes, Schwetzinger Festspiele, Festival van Vlaanderen; Professor at Brussels Conservatoire and Lemmens Institute, Leuven. Recordings: Works by Schubert, Grétry, Gossec, Lully, Schütz, Bach, Dumont and Carl Orff; Compositions by Belgian composers Andre Laporte and Willem Kersters. Contributor to: Lemmensinstitute Adem; Articles for Dutch Singers Association ANZ. Honours: 1st Prize at Brussels Conservatoire, 1959; Chevalier de l'Ordre de la Couronne, 1978; Cecilia Prize, Belgium, 1974 for Zemire et Azor, F M Grétry. Hobbies: Connoisseur of Wines; Travel; Ecomonics. Address: 25 Avenue Georges Leclerq, 1080 Brussels, Belgium.

BUGHICI Dumitru, b. 14 Nov 1921, Iasi, Rumania. Composer; Teacher. Education: Studied with Salmanov, Iasi Conservatory; Schnitke, Leningrad Conservatory, 1950-55. Career: Faculty, Bucharest Conservatory. Compositions include: Orchestral: Simfonie-Poem, 1961, No 3, Ecouri De Jazz, 1965-66, Simfonia Bucegilor, 1978-79, Simfonie Lirico-Dramatica-In Memoriam for String Orchestra, 1984, Simfonia Aspiratillor, 1985; Sinfoniettas: Simfonieta Tinertii, 1958, Muzica De Concert, Simfonieta III, 1969; Other works: Filimon Sarbu, 1959, Poemul Bucuriei, 1962, Monumentul, 1964, Omagiu, 1967, Balada Concertana for Violin and Orchestra, 1969, Sinfonietta Da Camera, 1970, Cello Concerto, 1974, Trumpet Concerto, 1975, Jazz Concerto, 1982-83; Flute Concerto, 1985; Chamber: Suite for Violin and Piano, 1953, Scherzo for Cello and Piano, 1954, Fantasia for Trumpet and Piano, 1960, Violin Sonata, 1963, Fantasia Quartet, 1969, Five String Quartets, 1954-78, Fantasy for Xylophone and Double Bass, 1980; Piano Pieces. Address: Conservatorui de Muzica Ciprian Porumbescu, Str Stirbei Voda 33, 70732 Bucharest, Romania.

BUJARSKI Zbigniew, b. 21 Aug 1933, Muszyna, Poland. Composer. Education: Studied composition with Wiechowicz and conducting with Wodiczko at the Kracow State College of Music. Compositions include: Burning Bushes for Soprano and Chamber Ensemble, 1958; Triptych for String Orchestra and Percussion, 1959; Synchrony I for Soprano and Chamber Ensemble, 1959, II for Soprano, Chorus and Orchestra, 1960; Zones for Chamber Ensemble, 1961; Kinoth for Orchestra, 1963; Chamber Composition for Voice and Ensemble, 1963; Contraria for Orchestra, 1965; El Hombre for Vocal Soloists, Chorus and Orchestra, 1969-73; Musica Domestica for 18 Strings, 1977; Concert for Strings, 1979; Similis Greco, symphonic cycle, 1979-83; Quartet On The Advent, 1984; Quartet For The Resurrection, 1990. Address: c/o ZAIKS, 2 rue Hipoteczna, 00 092 Warsaw, Poland.

BUJEVSKY Taras, b. 23 June 1957, Kharkov, Ukraine. m. Jekaterina Tarakanova, 8 June 1991. 1 son. Education: Composer, 1989; Postgraduate Course, Moscow State Conservatoire, 1991. Career: Musical Editor, Russian TV, 1993-; Lecturer, Russian Theatre Academy, 1995-; His music is frequently heard on Russian Radio and TV, including 5 large broadcasts devoted to his life and music, 1991-95. Compositions: Symphony, 1989; Repercussions of the Light for string orchestra, 1992; Foreshortenings, chamber symphony for percussion, trumpet, two pianos and mechanical devices, 1993; Post Scriptum for symphony orchestra, 1994; Breathing of Stillness for chamber orchestra, 1995; Music for Chamber Ensembles and Solo Instruments includes: Sensus Sonoris for flute and percussion, 1990; Silver Voices for four trumpets, 1991; Pathes of Phonosphere for clarinet; Voice of Loneliness for tenor saxophone, 1993; Mosaics, Suite for grand piano, 1994; Ciao Antonio for flute, oboe, voilin, cello, cembalo and tape; Für Isabella for sextet, 1995; Electronic Music, music for old silent films: House on Trubnaja Square, 1994; Bear Wedding, 1995; Music to television performances: Soul is Dying, after M. Gorky's The Latters, 1994; To Live Up to Fear and Pain, devoted to S. Jesenin, 1995; Participant in international festivals: Moscow, Autumn 1990-95; 5 Capitals, Kiev, 1993; Festival of Contemporary Russian Music in Helsingborg, Sweden, 1994; Festival of Electronic Music, Synthesis-95, Bourges, France. Honours: All-Union Competition of Young Composers Laureate, USSR, 1987; Grant Soros, 1994; Berlin Academy of Arts Scholarship Programme, Moscow Berlin, 1995. Memberships: Moscow Composers' Union. Address: Miusskaja Square 5, Apt 105, 125047 Moscow, Russia.

BUJIC Bojan, b. 6 October 1937, Sarajevo, Bosnia and Herzegovina. Musicologist. m. Alison Warwick, 30 June 1979, 1 son, 1 daughter. Education: BA, English Literature, 1961; BA, Musicology, Sarajevo University, Bosnia and Herzegovina, 1963; DPhil, Music, Lincoln College, Oxford University, England, 1967. Career: Lecturer in History of Music, Sarajevo Academy of Music, 1968-69; Lecturer in Music, Reading University, England, 1969-78; University Lecturer in Music, Fellow of Magdalen College, Oxford, 1978-; Visiting Fellow, The Society for the Humanities, Cornell University, Ithaca, New York, USA, 1971. Publications: Music in European Thought 1851-1912, 1988. Contributions to: Acta Musicologica; Arti Musices; The British Journal of Aesthetics; Erasmus; International Review of the Aesthetics and Sociology of Music; Music and Letters; Early Music History; The Italianist; The New Grove Dictionary; The New Oxford Companion to Music. Memberships: Royal Musical Association; British Society of Aesthetics. Hobbies: Travel; Photography. Address: Magdalen College, Oxford, England.

BUKETOFF Igor, b. 29 May 1915, Hartford, CT, USA. Conductor. Education: University of Kansas, 1931-32; BS, 1935, MS, 1941, Juilliard School of Music, NY; Los Angeles Conservatory. Career: Teacher at Juilliard School of Music, 1935-45, Chautauqua School of Music, 1941-47, Columbia University, 1943-47, Butler University, 1953-63, and University of Houstoun, 1977-79; Music Director, Chautauqua Opera, 1941-47, New York Philharmonic Young People's Concerts, 1948-53, Fort Wayne Philharmonic, 1948-66, Iceland Symphony Orchestra, 1964-66, St Paul Opera, Minnesota, 1968-74, and Texas Chamber Orchestra, 1980-81; Founder of World Music Bank for International Exchange and Promotion of Contemporary Music, 1957; Director, Contemporary Composers Project, Institute of International Education, 1967-70; Conducted the premiere of Rachmaninov's fragmentary opera, Mona Vanna, at Saratoga Arts Center, 1984, with the Philadelphia Orchestra. Recordings: Various contemporary works. Honours: First Alice M Ditson Award for Young Conductors, 1942; Honorary Doctorate, Los Angeles Conservatory.

BUKOWSKI Miroslaw (Andrzej), b. 5 Jan 1936, Warsaw, Poland. Composer; Conductor. m. Hanna Burzynska, 20 Aug 1966, 1 daughter. Education: MA, Composition, Academy of Music, Poznan, 1959; MA, Conducting, Academy of Music at Gdansk and Poznan, 1963. Debut: Polish Students' Music Festival in Poznan, 1957. Career: Assistant, 1963-67, Lecturer, 1967-80, Assistant Professor, 1980-88, Professor, 1988-, Academy of Music, Poznan; Conductor, Wielkopolska Symphony Orchestra, 1971-75; Professor, Pedagogical College in Zielena Gora, 1984-. Compositions include: Requiem for Solo Voices, Mixed Choir and Orchestra, based on Akhmatova's poem; Pastourelle, Interferances for Symphony Orchestra; Concerto for Cello and Orchestra; Ostinato and Mobile for Percussion Ensemble; Swinging Concerto; Symphonic Allegro for Symphony Orchestra; 4 Piano Sonatas; Sonatina for Piano; Expression for Piano; Three Sleepy Poems for Mixed Choir; 2 Cycles of Songs, Znikomosc, Stances. Memberships: Association of Polish Composers; Authors' Association ZAIKS. Hobbies include: Travel. Address: Osiedle Pod Lipami 5-182, 61-632 Poznan, Poland.

BULJUBASIC Mileva, b. 17 Aug 1937, Sarajevo, Yugoslavia. Soprano. Education: Studied in Sarajevo, Italy and Austria. Career: Features as Concert Artist since 1960; Stage career from 1970, with guest appearances in Italy, Germany, England, Russia, Japan and Czechoslovakia; Member of the Deutsche Oper am Rhein, Dusseldorf from 1979; Sang at Seattle in 1975; Roles have included Butterfly, Mimi, Marenka in the Bartered Bride, Rusalka, Beethoven's Leonore and Verdi's Amelia in Ballo in Maschera and Leonora in Il Trovatore. Honours: Prize for Interpretation; Modern Yugoslavian Musik Prize; Prix des Concours, Madama Butterfly, Japan, 1973. Address: Sertoriusring 7, 55126 Mainz, Germany.

BULJUBASIC Sead, b. 10 Oct 1942, Cazin, Bosnia. Tenor; Professor of Opera Singing. m. Mileva Buljubasic, 17 Feb 1973. Education: BA, Italian Language and Literature; Musical Faculty of Art and Magisterium-Belgrade Conservatorio Giuseppe Verdi Milano; Mozarteum Salzburg. Debut: National Theatre Opera Stage Belgrade, Eugene Onegin, Lenski. Career: Opera Houses: Yugoslavia, Romania, Austria, Germany, USA; RTV Belgrade, RTV Sarajevo, until 1988, Duke of Mantua, Manrico, Alfred Germont, Rodolfo, Mario Cavaradossi, Pinkerton, Calaf, Count Almaviva, Radames, Werther, Don José, Jenik, Prince (Rusalka), Lenski, Turiddu, Bluebeard, Faust, Edgardo. Recordings. TV and Radio, Sarajevo, Belgrade, opera arias and songs; Concert Repertoire Songs: Schumann, Schubert, Strauss, Debussy, De Falla, Turina, Tchaikovsky, Rachmaninov. Hobbies: Reading; Listening to Music. Address: Sertorius Ring 7, 55126 Mainz, Germany.

BULL Edvard (Hagerup), b. 10 Jun 1922, Bergen, Norway. Composer. m. Anna Kvarme, 1955, 2 daughters. Education: Examination, Oslo University, 1944; Organ Diploma, Oslo Conservatory, 1947; Studied organ, composition and piano with Sandvold, Irgens Jensen, Brustad, Riefling and Wester; Pupil of Charles Koechlin, 1947-49; Composition with Darius Milhaud and Jean Rivier; Analysis with Olivier Messaien; Diploma and Prize for Musical Composition, Conservatoire National Superieur de Musique, Paris, France, 1948-53; Pupil of Boris Blacher and Josef Rufer at Hochschule für Musik, Berlin, 1958-60. Debut: Philharmonic Orchestra, Paris. Career: Formerly Teacher of Theory, Oslo Klaverakademi and Oslo Musikkonservatorium; Performances in over 30 countries; Many commissions from French Radio and TV, Ministry of Culture, Quatuor Instrumental de Paris, Ensemble Moderne de Paris, Trio Daraux de Paris, Trio de France, Quatuor des Clarinettes de Belgique, Norske Blåse-Kvintett. Compositions include: 5 Symphonies, 1955-72; 6 Concertos; Le Soldat De Plomb, ballet, 1949; Portrait Münchhausen, ballet, 1961; Le Jeu Du Feu, one act opera, 1974; Lamentation Pour Un Cygne Maudit, Hommage A Israel, opera, 1972-77; Chamber, instrumental and vocal works. Address: Kringsjavn 6, 1342 Jar, Norway.

BULLER John, b. 7 Feb 1927, London, England. Composer. Education: Studied with Anthony Milner from 1959; BMus, London University, 1964. Career: Joined the McNaughton Concerts Committee, 1965, Chairman, 1971-72; Gained attention in 1970s with series of works based on Finnegans Wake; Proenca and The Theatre of Memory commissioned by the BBC, Promenade Concerts, 1977 and 1981; Composer-in-Residence, University of Edinburgh, 1975-76; Composer-in-Residence, Queens University, Belfast, 1985-86. Compositions include: The Cave for ensemble, 1970; 2 Night Pieces from Finnegans Wake for soprano and ensemble, 1970; Finnegan's Floras for chorus, percussion and piano, 1972; The Mime of Mick, Nick and The Magpies, for soprano, tenor, baritone chorus and orchestra, 1975-76; Proenca for mezzo, electric guitar and orchestra, 1977; Music for Film: Correction Please, Arts Council, 1979; The Theatre of Memory for orchestra, 1980-81; Of Three Shakespeare Sonnets for mezzo, flute, clarinet, harp and string quartet, 1983; A la fontana, for Hilliard Ensemble, 1983; Bakxai, opera, for English National Opera, 1991-92; Bacchae Metres, BBC Proms, 1993; Mr Purcell's Maggot, for Spitalfields Festival, 1994. Recordings: Unicorn Aanchana; Proenca and The Theatre of Memory. Honours include: Arts Council Bursary, 1978; Proenca and The Theatre of Memory selected by International Rostrum of Composers, Paris. Membership: Association of Professional Composers. Address: c/o Oxford University Press, 3 Park Road, London NW1 6XN, England.

BULLOCK Susan, b. England. Singer (Soprano). Education: Studied at Landa University, the Royal Academy of Music and the National Opera Studio, London. Career: Roles with English National Opera have included Donna Anna, Marguerite in Faust, Alice Ford, Butterfly, Ellen Orford and Princess Natalie in Henze's Prince of Homburg, 1996; Glyndebourne debut as Jenufa, followed by Katya Kabanova and Lisa in the Queen of Spades; Guest appearances with New Israeli Opera and Flanders Opera (in Tippett's King Priam); 1996 American debut, as Butterfly at Portland and the title role in the British premiere of Die Agyptische Helena by Strauss, at Garsington; Season 1997-98, Butterfly at Houston, Bonn, and Tosca at Portland, Jenufa at Charleston, South Carolina, and also Desdemona in Otello with ENO; Concerts include La Mort de Cléopâtre by Berlioz, with the BBC Philharmonic Orchestra; Rachmaninov's The Bells; Mahler's 4th Symphony with the Royal Liverpool Philharmonic and Hindemith's Sancta Susanna with the BBC; Beethoven's Missa Solemnis with Les Arts Florissants on tour to Vienna, Paris and Aix-en-Provence. Recordings include: Sancta Susanna and Hindemith Songs. Address: Harrison/Parrott Ltd, 12 Penzance Place, London W11 4PA, England.

BUMBRY Grace, b. 4 Jan 1937, St Louis, MO, USA. Soprano and Mezzo-Soprano. Education: Boston University; Morthwestern University; Music Academy of the West under Lotte Lehmann; Paris with Pierre Bernac. Debut: Paris Opera in 1960 as Amneris in Aida. Career: Sang at the Stadttheater Basle until 1964; Bayreuth Festival, 1961-63 as Venus in Tannhäuser; Brussels Opera in 1961 as Carmen; Chicago Lyric Opera in 1963 as Ulrica in Un Ballo in Maschera; Covent Garden from 1963 as Eboli, Amneris, Salome and Tosca; Salzburg Festival, 1964-67 as Lady Macbeth and Carmen; Metropolitan Opera debut in 1965 as Eboli, later singing in New York as Carmen, Tosca, Venus, Gioconda and Gershwin's Bess in 1985; Has sung soprano roles from 1970 as Elisabeth de Valois, Santuzza in Vienna, 1970, Jenufa at La Scala, 1974 and Ariane in Ariane et Barbe-Bleue by Dukas at Paris Opera in 1975; Mezzo roles include Fricka, Azucena, Orpheus and Dalila; Appearances in Frankfurt, Budapest, Lisbon, Munich, Hamburg and Verona; Sang Aida at Luxor and Massenet's Herodiade at Nice in 1987; Marseilles in 1989 as Didon in Les Troyens; Sang Cassandre at the opening of the Opéra Bastille in Paris, 1990; Arena di Verona in 1990 as Carmen; Sang Cherubini's Medea at Athens, 1995. Recordings include: Israel in Egypt; Messiah; Don Carlos; Tannhäuser; Aida; Film of Carmen in 1968. Honours include: Richard Wagner Medal, 1963; Honorary Doctorates from Rust College, Holy Spring, MS, Rockhurst College, Kansas City, University of Missouri at St Louis. Hobbies: Tennis; Sewing; Body Building; Entertaining. Address: c/o Bruce Zemsky, Columbia Artists Management, 165 West 57th Street, New York, NY 10019, USA.

BUNDSCHUH Eva-Maria, b. 16 Oct 1941, Brunswick, Germany. Singer (Soprano). Education: Studied in Chemitz and Leipzig. Debut: Bernburg 1967, as Humperdinck's Hansel. Career: Sang at Chemnitz, 1969-74, Potsdam, 1974-77; Associated with the Staatsoper Berlin from 1976, the Komische Oper from 1981; Sang first as mezzo, as Dorabella, Carmen and Eboli then soprano repertory from 1978; Olympia and Antonia in Les Contes d'Hoffmann, Wagner's Eva and Freia, Violetta, Mussetta and Donna Anna; Recent Berlin Staatsoper roles have included the title part in the premiere of Judith by Siegfried Matthus, 1985, Jenufa, 1986, and Isolde, 1988; Komische Oper, 1987-88, as Donna Anna and Salome; Bayreuth Festival, 1988, as Gutrune; Further engagements at Amsterdam, Salzburg, Wiesbaden, Bucharest and Moscow; Sang Chrysothemis in a new production of Elektra for Welsh National Opera, 1992; Elektra in a new production at Netherlands Opera, 1996. Address: c/o Welsh National Opera (Contracts), John Street, Cardiff, Wales CF1 4SP.

BUNIN Victor (Vladimirovich), b. 2 Mar 1936, Voroezh, Russia. Pianist; Professor of Music; Writer on Music. m. Svetlana Eruhimovna Beskina, 7 Feb 1958, 1 son. Education: Student, 1956-61, Postgraduate, 1961-64, Moscow Conservatoire; Study with S E Feinberg and V K Merzhanov. Career: Regular appearances with Moscow and provincial orchestras including Moscow Philharmonic Orchestra, Soviet TV and Radio Large Symphony Orchestra; Participated in 3 films for Union TV, and several TV concert programmes; Many radio recordings for Radio Fund, 1967-. Recordings: 12 albums including Rubinstein's Concerto No 4, 1978, 1st performance of A N Alexandrov's Concerto-Symphony, 1981, Feinberg's original compositions by composers former students, double record, 1981, Feinberg's transcriptions of JS Bach, double record, 1986. Publications: Pedagogic Principles of S E Feinberg. Current management: Souz-Conzert, Moscow Music Association. Address: Prospekt Mira 116 B, Apt 105, Moscow 12926, Russia.

BURA Corina, b. 15 Feb 1948, Cluj, Romania. Violinist; Professor. m. Mihai Constantinescu, 17 Apr 1981. Education: Bachelorship: Lyceum Emil Racovitza, Cluj, 1967, and Music Lyceum, Cluj, 1967; Diploma, Conservatory of Music, Bucharest, 1973. Debut: Soloist with The Philharmonia, Cluj, 1967. Career: Recitals and concerts with Philharmonics in Romania; Recitals in Germany; TV appearances; Radio recordings of Bach, Handel, Telemann, Corelli, Pergolesi, Rameau, Tchaikovsky, Paganini, Szymanowsky, Bartók and Romanian Music. Recordings: 2 records of Handel. Contributions to: Studies About Modern Music and Aesthetics published in The Conservatory's Publications. Honours: Diploma of Chief Promotion, The Music Lyceum, 1965, 1966, 1967; Diploma of Chief Promotion, The Conservatory of Bucharest, 1972. Membership: The Professorial Association of The Conservatory of Bucharest. Hobbies: Literature; Theatre; Plastic Arts; Animals. Address: Str Ecaterina Teodoroiu No 17, 78108 Bucharest, Romania.

BURCHINAL Frederick, b. 7 Dec 1948, Wichita, KS, USA. Baritone. Education: Studied at the Empoira State University and the Juilliard School. Career: Worked with the Metropolitan Opera Studio and made European debut in Floyd's of Mice and Men, at Amsterdam, 1976; Sang Scrooge in the 1979 premiere of Musgrave's A Christmas Carol, Virginia Opera; New York City Opera, State Theater, 1978-88; Metropolitan Opera from 1988 as Macbeth and Rigoletto; Other US appearances for the San Francisco Opera, Miami, Houston, New Orleans and San Diego Opera; Deutsche Oper am Rhein, Dusseldorf from 1988; Title role in Simon Boccanegra with the Cologne Opera in 1990; Has also sung in London, Zurich, Berlin and Frankfurt; Other roles include Rossini's Figaro, Iago, Jack Rance, Tonio, Di Luna, Scarpia, Falstaff and Nick Shadow; Sang Posa in Don Carlos at Dusseldorf in 1991; Boccanegra at the Opéra Bastille, Paris, 1994. Address: c/o Metropolitan Opera, Lincoln Center, New York, NY 10023, USA.

BURCHULADZE Paata, b. 12 Feb 1951, Tblisi, Russia. Bass Singer. Education: Studied at the Tblisi Conservatory. Debut: Tblisi in 1975 as Mephistopheles in Faust. Career: Sang in Russia and Milan; Studied further in Italy and began international career after winning competitions, 1981-82; Roles include Basilio in Il Barbiere di Siviglia, Leporello, King Rene in Iolantha, Gremin in Eugene Onegin and Boris Godunov; Guest appearances at the Bolshoy in Moscow; British debut in 1983 at the Lichfield Festival, in The Dream of Gerontius by Elgar; Covent Garden debut in 1984 as Ramfis in Aida; Salzburg Festival appearances as the Commendatore in Don Giovanni under Karajan; Sang Rossini's Basilio at the Metropolitan in 1989, and Khan Konchak in a new production of Prince Igor at Covent Garden in 1990; Sang Boris Godunov in a revival of Mussorgsky's opera, 1991, the Inquisitor in Prokofiev's The Fiery Angel in 1992; Sang King Philip in Don Carlos at Santiago, 1994; Sang Zaccaria in Nabucco at the Verona Arena in 1996. Recordings include: Scenes from operas by Mussorgsky and Verdi; Don Giovanni; Fiesco in Simon Boccanegra; Sparafucile in Rigoletto; Ramfis in Aida; Samson et Dalila. Current Management: Artist Management International. Address: Artist Management International, 12-13 Richmond Buildings, London, W1V 5AF, England.

BURDA Pavel, b. 7 Apr 1942, Bohemian Budweis. University Professor; Conductor; Timpanist; Percussionist. Education: Started Studying the Piano at an early age followed by some Winds and Strings, later Timpani/Percussion and Conducting; Graduate Diploma, Prague Conservatory of Music; MMus, State University of New York, USA; Postgraduate Studies, State Academy of Music, Hamburg, Federal Republic of Germany. Career includes: Performances in major European Cities; Toured Eastern and Western Europe and North Africa; Solo Timpanist with Brazilian Symphony Orchestra, Rio de Janeiro; Principal Timpanist/Percussionist with Orchestra Da Camera, New York; Solo Timpanist with Casals Festival Orchestra and Puerto Rico Symphony Orchestra in San Juan; Conducting includes various ensembles in San Juan, Europe, New York, Milwaukee; Developed The Music-with-Percussion Ensemble, University of Wisconsin-Milwaukee; Founded The Milwaukee 20th Century Ensemble, 1979; Commissioned and conducted premieres of numerous works; TV and Radio broadcasts. Compositions: Song-Cycle for Voice and Chamber Ensemble for a Radio Series; Incidental Music. Recordings: Several for major record companies and several films. Honour: The Fromm Tanglewood Fellowship, 1970. Hobby: Travel. Address: 3003 North Farwell Avenue, Milwaukee, WI 53211, USA.

BURDEN William, b. Florida, USA. Singer (Tenor). Education: Studied at Indiana University. Career: Appearances with the San Francisco Opera as Belmonte, Count Lerma in Don Carlos and the title role in Bernstein's Candide; European debut as Rodolfo for Opera North (returned as Tamino); Further appearances as Rossini's Almaviva with Opera Northern Ireland, Janek in the Makropoulos Case at San Francisco, Ali (L'Incontro Improvviso by Haydn) at Nice, Ramiro (Cenerentola) in South Africa and Ubalo in Haydn's Armida, at St Louis; Season 1995-96 with New York Met debut as Janek, and Tybalt in Roméo et Juliette; Mozart's La Finta Giardiniera for Glimmerglass Opera; Season 1997-98 as Tom Rakewell at Genoa, Tamino for Florida Opera, Ali in Bourdeaux and Cimarosa's Il Matrimonio Segreto in Lausanne; Concert repertoire from Bach to Bernstein, with Messiah under William Christie. Address: c/o Harold Holt Ltd, 31 Sinclair Road, London W14 ONS, England.

BURGANGER Judith, b. Buffalo, New York, USA. Concert Pianist; Professor of Music; Artist-in-Residence. m. 3 daughters. Education: Artist Diploma, 1961, Graduate Certificate (MM), 1965, State Conservatory of Music, Stuttgart, Germany. Debuts: Solo recital, Buffalo; Orchestral, with Amherst Symphony. Career: Early performances, 1946-60: Soloist with Buffalo Philharmonic, Toronto Symphony, National Symphony (Washington DC), Marlboro Festival (Vermont); Later performances, 1960-: Soloist, symphony orchestras throughout USA, Germany, Austria, Netherlands, Scandinavia, Italy, Switzerland, Japan; Conductors include Steinberg, Previn, Commissiona, Dixon, Fiedler, Krips, Solti, Haitink, Tilson-Thomas, Conlon, Akiyama; International guest performances, chamber music; Teaching: Artist Teacher, Cleveland Institute of Music; Associate Professor, Artist-in-Residence, Texas Tech University; Artist Teacher, Carnegie Mellon University; Associate Professor, 1980, Professor, 1984-, Director of Conservatory of Music, College of Liberal Arts, Florida Atlantic University; Created an annual Brahms Festival, all chamber music compositions and works for 4 hands at 1 piano and songs performed, and now in 2nd decade includes masterpieces from Friends of Brahms; Founder, FAU Chamber Soloists, 1987, ensemble performing subscription series throughout Florida and works for all combinations of instruments and voice. Recording: CD by Burganger and Leonid Treer, The Art of Four Hands at One Piano, 1997. Address: Conservatory of Music, College of Liberal Arts, Florida Atlantic University, Davie, FL 33314, USA.

BURGER Ernst (Manfred), b. 26 Mar 1937, Munich, Germany. Pianist; Writer on Music; Leading Researcher for Chopin and Liszt. m. Dorothea Maillinger, 20 Sept 1972, 1 son. Education: Liberal Arts High School; Staatliche Hochschule für Musik, Munich; Künstlerische Staatsprüfung, 1964; Pädagogische Staatsprüfung, 1965. Publications: Franz Liszt, A Chronicle of His Life in Pictures and Documents, Munich, 1986, Paris, 1988, New York, 1989; Frédéric Chopin, A Chronicle of His Life in Pictures and Documents, Munich, 1990; Carl Tausig, Bonn, 1990; Robert Schumann, A Chronicle of His Life in Pictures and Documents, 1998. Contributions to: Die Musik in Geschichte und Gegenwart (MGG); Commentaries for recorded music. Honours: Grand Prix de Littérature Musicale, 1988; Ordre du Mérite en faveur de la culture polonaise, 1991. Hobbies: Reading; Museums; Skiing. Address: Erhardtstrasse 6, 80469 Munich, Germany.

BURGESS Brio, b. 27 Apr 1943, San Francisco, USA. Composer; Dramatist; Poet; Jazz Singer. Education: Self taught on recorder, guitar, piano, clarinet and other instruments; BA, Sociology, Russell Sage College, 1995. Career: Various clerical positions at Federal, state, city and county agencies, 1972-; Performances, Saratoga Springs, NY, San Francisco, San Mateo, CA, Albany, NY, and Troy, NY, of music and words (original works) in various formats; Presentation of Street Kids on Radio WRPI, NY and Play with Music, 1992, Radio Free America Broadcast. Compositions: Suite for Picasso; Escape, ballet, for Piano, Harp, Feet and Chains; Girl on a Ball, Childrens Dance and Toys, piano tunes; Sound Dreams, piano music; Space Visions, including The Painter's Song; Hippy Children's Concentration Camp Blues, for Piano, Harp and Words; Tin Angel Blues, 1990; Purple Hood Suite, 1991-92. Recordings: Tape: Music and words published on 10 audiocassettes, 1978-84; Clear, 1978; Briomindsound, 1979; Ulyses Dog No 9, 1980; Gathered Hear, 1980; Still, 1981; Ringade, 1982; Grate, 1982; Ether, 1982; Zen Meditations, 1987. Publications: Poems, in Poetalk Publications and BAPC Anthologies, 1989-95; Outlaw Blues, 8 song-poems, 1992; Poem in Open Mic: The Albany Anthology, 1994; Street Kids and Other Plays, 4 opera-musical libretto, 1995. Contributions to: The New Penguin Dictionary of Music; The New Penguin Dictionary of Musical Performers. Honours: Edward Arlington Robinson Fellowship, 1969; Standard Annual Awards, ASCAP, 1992-95. Memberships: ASCAP, 1973-; The Dramatists' Guild, 1983-. Current Management: c/o Gail G Tolley, 5 Cuyler Street, Albany, NY 12202, USA. Address: c/o ASCAP, ASCAP Building 1 Lincoln Plaza, New York, NY 10023, USA.

BURGESS Grayston, b. 7 Apr 1932, Cheriton, Kent, England. Conductor; Countertenor. m. Katherine Mary Bryan, 3 daughters. Education: MA, King's College, Cambridge. Career: Sang with Westminster Abbey Choir, 1955-69; Sang Oberon in Britten's A Midsummer Night's Dream at Covent Garden; Dowland TV programme; Performances with Handel Opera Society and the Henry Wood Promenade Concerts; Numerous radio broadcasts; Founder and Director of The Purcell Consort of Voices, 1963; Debut as Conductor at the 1963 Aldeburgh Festival; Concerts and recordings with the Purcell Instrumental Ensemble, the Elizabeth Consort of Voices, Musica Reservata, the London Sackbut Ensemble, the Philip Jones Brass Ensemble and the Jaye Consort of Voices. Recordings include: Josquin's Deploration sur le Morte de Johan; Dunstable's Laudi; Ockeghem's Vive le Roy and Ave Maria; Machaut's La Messe de Notre Dame; William Byrd's Church Music; Richard Davy's St Matthew Passion; Music by Schütz, Schein and Scheidt; Doulce Memoire; 16th Century French Chansons; English Madrigals from the Reign of Queen Elizabeth; English Secular Music of the Late Renaissance; The Eton Choir Book; The Triumphs of Oriana; High Renaissance Music in England.

BURGESS Sally, b. 9 Oct 1953, Durban, South Africa. Singer (Mezzo- Soprano). Education: Royal College of Music, with Hervey Alan and Marion Studholm. Career includes: Engaged by English National Opera and sang Zerlina (Don Giovanni), Cherubino, Pamina, Mimi, Micaela, the Composer in Ariadne, Massenet's Charlotte and Mrs Thatcher as Public Opinion in David Pountney's production of Orpheus in the Underworld; Covent Garden debut, 1983 as Siebel in Faust; Glyndebourne, 1983, in The Love of Three Oranges; Cavalli's Eritrea for the Camden Festival, 1985; Sang Carmen in a new production by English National Opera, 1986; Amneris for Opera North; Other roles include Sextus in Julius Caesar and Orlofsky in Die Fledermaus; Sang Minerva in The Return of Ulysses at the London Coliseum, 1989; Julie La Verne in Show Boat for RSC-Opera North (Gluck's Orpheus, 1990, Carmen, 1991); Fricka in Die Walküre for Scottish Opera, 1991; Amneris in Aida for Scottish Opera, 1992; Sang Judith in new production of Duke

Bluebeard's Castle at the Coliseum, 1991; Sang in the premiere of Paul McCartney's Liverpool Oratorio, co-written by Carl Davis; Sang Carmen at Bregenz, 1991-92, London Coliseum, 1993, Zurich and Berlin, 1994; Sang Dalila at Nantes, 1994 and Carmen, New Zealand; Engaged to sing Widow Begbick in Mahagonny by Kurt Weill, 1995 and Herodias in Salome by Richard Strauss, 1996, for the English National Opera; Isabella, The Voyage, Met, 1996; Engaged for ENO, Dulcinée (Don Quixote) 1996 and Carmen in Munich; Concert appearances include Elgar's Dream of Gerontius; Verdi's Requiem; Songs of the Auvergne by Canteloube; Premiere of Twice Through the Heart by Mark-Antony Turnage at the 1997 Aldeburgh Festival. Recordings include: The King and I (TER); 5 Irish Folk Songs, Howard Ferguson (Chandos). Current Management: IMG Artists Europe. Address: Media House, 3 Burlington Lane, London W4 2TH, England.

BURGON Geoffrey (Alan), b. 15 Jul 1941, Hambledon, Hampshire, England. Composer. m. (1) Janice Elizabeth Garwood, 1963, marriage dissolved, 1 son, 1 daughter, (2) Jacqueline Krofchak, 1992. Education: GGSM. Career: Composer, Trumpeter, 1964-71; Composer, Conductor, 1971-; As Trumpeter performed at Royal Opera House, with Northern Sinfonia Orchestra, Philomusica, London Mozart Players and others; Session work at theatres and jazz bands; As Conductor for film and TV works. Compositions include: Many scores for dance including London Contemporary Dance Theatre, Ballet Rambert, London Festival Ballet and Royal Ballet; Over 40 scores for film, TV and radio including: Tinker Tailor Soldier Spy, Brideshead Revisited, Bleak House, Life of Brian, Turtle Diary, The Chronicles of Narnia and The Children of The North; Choral and Orchestral Music: Gending, Acquainted With Night, Think On Dreadful Doomsday, Canciones Del Alma, Requiem, Veni Spiritus, The World Again, Revelations, Title Divine, The Trials Of Prometheus, Trumpet Concerto, 1993, Hard Times, opera. Recordings: Cathedral Music of Geoffrey Burgon; Brideshead Revisited; Music for Counter Tenor. Publications: Over 30 scores. Contributions to: Various professional journals. Honours: Prince Pierre of Monaco Award, 1969; Ivor Novello Awards, 1979, 1981; Gold Disc for Brideshead Revisited, 1982. Hobbies include: Jazz; Cricket. Address: c/o Chester Music, 8-9 Frith Street, London, W1V 5TZ, England.

BURMESTER Pedro, b. 9 Oct 1963, Oporto, Portugal. Pianist. Education: Oporto Musical Conservatory; Private studies with Helena Costa, Sequeria Costa, Leon Fleisher and Dmitri Paperno; Teaching, Oporto High School of Music. Debut: 1972. Career: Solo recitalist; Guest Soloist with orchestras in Portugal, Spain, Austria, France, Germany, Italy and USA; TV appearances in Portugal; Various musical festivals in Portugal and Macau; Radio appearances in Portugal and the USA. Recordings: Several. Honours: 1st Prize, 9th International Vianna da Mota Piano Competition, Lisbon, 1983; Jury Discretionary Award, 8th Van Cliburn International Piano Competition, Fort Worth. Hobby: Music. Current Management: Liliane Weinstadt, Bureau de Concerts, Rue Langeveld 69, 1180 Brussels, Belgium. Address: Rua do Souto 283, 4470 Porto, Portugal.

BURNS James Milton, b. 22 February 1922, Coal City, Indiana, USA. Music Educator. m. Thomasiala Ciofalo, 22 August 1970. Education: BMus, Manhattan School of Music, 1949; MMus, French Horn Performance, Manhattan School of Music, 1953; DEd, Fairleigh Dickinson University, 1984. Memberships: Over 20 Professional Associations. Address: 7 Nordic Drive, Petersburg, NJ 08270, USA.

BURNSIDE Iain, b. 1950, Glasgow, Scotland. Pianist. Education: Studied in Oxford, London and Warsaw. Career: Recital accompanist to Margaret Price, Victoria de Los Angeles, Sarah Walker, Nancy Argenta, Thomas Allen and Stephen Varcoe; Chamber Music performances with the Brodsky and Delmé Quartets, Douglas Boyd and Shmuel Ashkenasi; Appearances at the major British festivals and recitals in Europe, USA, Canada and Japan; Devised song series for Schoenberg, The Reluctant Revolutionary concert series on South Bank, London, 1988-89; Further contributions to the French Revolution Festival and Hermann Prey's Schubertiade, 1989; Artistic Director of series of vocal and chamber concerts at St John's Smith Square, London, 1989-; Recitals featuring Karol Szymanowski on South Bank. Recordings include: Gurney's Ludlow and Teme with Adrian Thompson and the Delmé Quartet. Address: c/o Ron Gonsalves, 10 Dagnan Road, London, SW12 9LQ, England.

BURROUGHS Bruce (Douglas), b. 12 Nov 1944, Hagerstown, Maryland, USA. Operatic Baritone; Pedagogue; Writer. Education: AB, English Literature, University of California, Los Angeles, 1966; MM, Voice and Vocal Pedagogy, New England Conservatory of Music, 1971. Debut: Papageno, in Magic Flute, Los Angeles Guild Opera, 1965. Career: Metropolitan Opera debut in Einstein on the Beach, 1976; More than 40 roles including title roles of Monteverdi's Orfeo, Mozart's Don Giovanni, Busoni's Arlecchino, Menotti's Bishop of Brindisi; Editor-in Chief, The Opera Quarterly; Music Critic, Los Angeles Times. Recordings: Several. Publications: Author of biographical essays in International Dictionary of Opera, 1996; Author, chapters in Metropolitan Opera Guide to Opera, on video, 1997; Contributor, Collier's Encyclopaedia, 1998. Contributions: Articles, features and reviews to Music Journal and Opera News. Honours: Deems Taylor Award, American Society of Composers, Authors and Publishers, 1991. Membership: American Guild of Musical Artists. Address: 14832 Hart Street, Van Nuys, CA 91405, USA.

BURROWES Norma (Elizabeth), b. 24 Apr 1944, Bangor, County Down. Opera and Concert Singer (Soprano). m. Steuart Bedford, 1969, divorced 1980. Education: Queen's University, Belfast, Northern Ireland; Royal Academy of Music. Debut: Glyndebourne Touring Opera as Zerlina in Don Giovanni, 1969; Debut with Royal Opera House as Fiakermili in Arabella, 1976. Career: Roles included Blondchen in Die Entführung, Oscar in Un Ballo in Maschera, Despina in Così fan tutte, Woodbird, Siegfried, Sophie in Der Rosenkavalier, Cunning Little Vixen, Manon, Titania in Midsummer Night's Dream, Nannetta in Falstaff, Gilda in Rigoletto, Marie in Daughter of the Regiment, Juliet, Adina in L'Elisir d'Amore, Susanna in Nozze di Figaro, and Lauretta, Gianni Schicchi; Sang regularly with Glyndebourne Opera, Scottish Opera, at Aldeburgh Festival, English National Opera, and Welsh National Opera among others; Sang at Salzburg, Paris, Aix-en-Provence, Avignon, Ottawa, Montreal, New York, Chicago and Buenos Aires; Metropolitan Opera from 1979 as Blondchen, Oscar and Sophie; Sang with all the principal London orchestras and on BBC Radio and TV retiring in 1982. Recordings: Made numerous recordings including Die Schöpfung, The Fairy Queen, Hansel and Gretel, Acis and Galata, Ariodante, Die Entführung, Haydn's Armida, Israel in Egypt and Semele, and Riders to the Sea by Vaughan Williams. Honours: Honorary DMus, Queen's University, Belfast; Order of Worshipful Company of Musicians. Hobbies: Gardening; Embroidery. Address: 56 Rochester Road, London, NW1 9JG, England.

BURROWS Donald (Donwald) James, b. 28 Dec 1945, London, England. Lecturer; Conductor; Organist; Harpsichordist. m. Marilyn Jones, 23 July 1971, 3 sons. Education: BA, 1968, CertEd, 1969, MA, 1971, Trinity Hall, Cambridge University; PhD, Open University, 1981. Career: Director of Music, John Mason School, Abingdon, 1970-81; Lecturer in Music, Open University, 1982-89; Senior Lecturer in Music, 1989-95, Professor of Music, 1995-, Head of Music Department, 1991-; Conductor, Abingdon and District Music Society, 1972-83; Conductor, Oxford Holiday Orchestra, 1978-; Organist and Choirmaster, St Nicholas Church, Abingdon, 1972-82; Master of the Music, St Botolph's, Aspley Guise, 1985-95; Member, Redaktionskollegium, Hallische Händel-Ausgabe, 1984-; Founder Member, Handel Institute, 1985-; Member of Vorstand, Georg Friedrich Händel-Gesellschaft, 1987-; Member of Advisory Board, Maryland Handel Festival, USA, 1988-. Recordings: Insert notes for recordings of Handel's Water Music, Anthems, Utrecht Te Deum, Ode for St Cecilia's Day, Israel in Egypt, Organ Concertos and Messiah. Publications include: Handel Alexander's Feast; The Anthem on the Peace; Foundling Hospital Anthem, Violin Sonatas, Messiah, As Pants the Hart, Songs for Soprano and Continuo, Belshazzar also Elgar pieces for violin and piano, (all as Editor); A Catalogue of Handel's Musical Autographs; Handel (Master Musicians Biography); Handel's Messiah. Contributions to: The Musical Times; Music and Letters; Early Music; Göttinge Händel-Beiträge. Honours: Studentship, Merton College, Oxford University, 1979; British Academy Research Grant, 1979. Memberships: Royal Musical Association; Royal College of Organists. Hobbies: Steam locomotives; Model railways. Address: 126 High Street, Cranfield, Bedford MK43 0DG, England.

BURROWS John, b. 3 Aug 1941, Newcastle under Lyme, England. Conductor. m. Melinda Whiting, 26 Dec 1994, 1 s, 1 d, from previous marriage. Education: GRSM; ARMCM; Royal Manchester College of Music, 1959-62; BMus, Manchester University, 1959-62; London Opera Centre, 1962-64. Career: Music Staff, Sadler's Wells (later English National) Opera, 1965-70; Prompter, Ring Cycle, English National Opera, 1970-73; Musical Director, Cowardy Custard, Mermaid Theatre, 1973-74; Musical Director, Cole, Mermaid Theatre, 1965-76; Musical Director, A Chorus Line, Theatre Royal, Drury Lane, 1977-78; Musical Director, London Savoyards, Royal Albert Hall, London, Kennedy Center, Washington, USA and tours of: UK; USA; Canada; Holland; Belgium; Germany, 1979-86; Professor of Opera, Southern Methodist University, Dallas, TX, 1980-83; Professor of Opera, Temple University, Philadelphia, 1983-86; Artistic Director, The Lyric Opera of Dallas, 1983-92; Guest Conductor: National Symphony Orchestra of America, 1986; Opera Theatre of San Antonio, 1988; Shreveport Opera, 1988, 1988-89; Opera Omnia, 1989; Fort Worth Opera, 1991; American Music Theatre Festival, 1992; Opera Northeast, 1992-93; Chorus Master: PA Opera Theatre, 1992; Opera Delaware, 1993; Opera Theatre of Connecticut, 1994; Washington Savoyards, 1994; Faculty, Academy of Vocal Arts, Philadelphia, 1993-94; Faculty, University of the Arts, Philadelphia, 1994-95. Compositions: Composer and Arranger, BBC TV. Current Management: Warden Associates Inc, 127 West 72nd Street, Ste 2R, New York, NY 10023, USA. Address: 1538 Naudain Street, Philadelphia, PA 19146-1627, USA.

BURROWS Stuart, b. 7 Feb 1933, Pontypridd, Wales. Tenor. m. Enid Lewis, 1 son, 1 daughter. Education: Trinity College, Carmarthen. Career: Sang in concerts at first; Stage debut with Welsh National Opera in 1963 as Ismaele in Nabucco; Don Ottavio in Don Giovanni, Jenek in Bartered Bride, Ernesto Pasquale, Rodolfo in Bohème; Athens in 1965 as Oedipus Rex with Stravinsky; Covent Garden from 1967 as Beppe in Pagliacci, Tamino in Magic Flute, Ottavio in Don Giovanni, Fenton in Falstaff, Elvino in La Sonnambula, Lensky in Onegin, Ernesto in Don Pasquale, Alfredo in Don Pasquale, Pinkerton in Butterfly, Alfredo in Traviata, Idomeneo, Titus in La Clemenza di Tito, Faust; US debut in 1967 as Tamino, Lensky, Pinkerton, Ottavio, Des Grieux; Vienna Staatsoper in 1970 as Tamino and Ottavio, Faust, Pinkerton, Salzburg Festival from 1970 in Mozart Roles; Metropolitan Opera from 1971 as Ottavio, Tamino, Pinkerton, Faust, Alfredo and Belmonte; Paris Opéra, 1975 Ottavio, Belmonte; Appearances at Aix-en-Provence and Orange Festivals, and at Hamburg, Geneva, Houston, (Des Grieux), Santa Fe, (Tamino, Alfredo) and Boston; Many concert appearances notably in music by Bach and Handel; BBC TV films of Faust, La Bohème and Rigoletto. Recordings: Maria Stuarda by Donizetti; Die Zauberflöte; Don Giovanni; Beethoven's 9th Symphony; Eugene Onegin; La Clemenza di Tito; Don Giovanni; Die Entführung. Honours include: Blue Riband, National Eisteddfod of Wales, 1959; Honorary Doctorate, Carmarthen, 1989 and University of Wales, Aberystwyth, 1992. Address: c/o Harrison Parrot Ltd, 12 Penzance Place, London, W11 4PA, England.

BURT Francis, b. 28 Apr 1926, London, England. Composer; Professor. m. Lina Burt. Education: Royal Academy of Music, 1948-51; Hochschule für Musik, Berlin, 1951-54. Career: Professor of Composition, Hochschule für Musik und darstellende Kunst, Vienna, 1973-93. Compositions include: Iambics, for orchestra, Opus 5; Volpone, opera, Opus 9; Espressione Orchestrale, Opus 10; Der Golem, ballet, Opus 11; Fantasmasgoria, for orchestra, Opus 12; Barnstable, opera, Opus 13; Unter den blanken Hacke des Monds, for baritone and orchestra; Und Gott der Herr sprach, for solo voices, 2 choruses and orchestra; Morgana, for orchestra; Echoes, for 9 players; Hommage à Jean-Henri Fabre, for 5 players; 2 String Quartets; Blind Visions, for oboe and orchestra. Recordings: Classic Amadeo; Francis Burt, CD. Honours: Associate, Royal Academy of Music, 1957; Mendelssohn Scholarship, 1954; Körner Prize, 1973; Würdigungspreis für Musik, Austrian Federal Ministry of Education and Art, 1978; City of Vienna Prize for Music, 1981; Grosses Silbernes Ehrenzeichen für Verdienste um die Republik Österreich, 1992. Hobbies: Reading; Sheep farming; Eating; Drinking; Good friends. Address: Mayerhofgasse 12/20, A-1040 Vienna, Austria.

BURT Michael, b. 1943, Farnham, Surrey, England. Singer (Bass baritone). Education: Studied with Richard Federicks in new York. Debut: Caracas, 1977, as Monterone and Sparafucile in the same performance of Rigoletto. Career: Concert soloist in North America, including Bach's Christmas Oratorio and B minor Mass at Carnegie Hall; Covent Garden, London, 1979, as Second Armed Man in Die Zauberflöte; Further appearances at Frankfurt as Pizarro in Fidelio and at New Orleans as King Henry in Lohengrin; Zaccaria and the Hoffmann villains at Hannover, 1986-87; King Philip in Don Carlos and Wotan in Der Ring des Nibelungen at Graz, 1988; Adolfo in Schubert's Alfonso und Estrella, 1991; Sang Wagner's Dutchman at Montpellier, 1992, Jochanaan in Salome at Barcelona, 1991. Address: c/o Vereinigte Buhnen, Kaiser Josef Platz 10, A-8010 Graz, Austria.

BURT Robert, b. 22 May 1962, England. Tenor. Education: Graduated from the Guildhall School in 1989. Career: Appearances with Oper 80 as Monostatos and Don Ottavio, Dancing Master in Ariadne auf Naxos directed by Jonathan Miller with Chelsea Opera Group as Kleontes in Daphne and Mid-Wales Opera as Goro in Butterfly; Sang Don Jerome in the British premiere of Prokofiev's The Duenna, at the Guildhall School under Rostropovich, 1991; Glyndebourne Festival debut in 1992 as Tchaplitsky in The Queen of Spades, repeated at the Promenade Concerts, London; Sang Don Curzio in Figaro with Glyndebourne Touring Opera in 1992 and Janácek's From The House of the Dead, at the Barbican Hall, 1993; Young Servant in Elektra at opening night of BBC Proms, 1993; Recitals and oratorios include Carmina Burana at Snape, Vaughan Williams' Serenade to Music at the Barbican, and the Easter Oratorio by Bach and Mozart's Requiem in Munich; Festival engagements at Bath, Sully-sur-Loire and Dijon. Address: Owen White Management, 14 Nightingale Lane, Hornsey, London, N8 7QU, England.

BURT Warren (Arnold), b. 10 Oct 1949, Baltimore, Maryland, USA. Composer. Education: MA, University of California at San Diego, 1975; Study with Robert Erickson and Kenneth Gaburro, 1971-75. Career includes: Australian Centre for

Arts and Technology, 1994; Resident, Mills College, Oakland, 1995; Multi-Media Artist; Writer. Compositions (many with visuals and electronics) include: Nighthawk, 1973-76; Aardvarks IV, 1975; Moods, 1978-79; The Wanderer: Pocket Calculator Music II, 1983; Woodwind Quintet, 1985; Meditations, 1986; Voice, Tuning Fork and Accordion, 1986; Samples III, 1987; String Quartet no 4, 1987; Chaotic Research Music, 1990; Some Kind of Seasoning, 1990-91; Dense Room, 1994.Recordings include: Aardvarks V, 1978; Song Dawn Chords, 1981; Four Pieces for Synthesizer, 1981; Almond Bread Harmonies II, 1985; Chaotic Research Music, 1989-90; Three Inverse Genera, 1990; Parts of Speech, 1992. Publications: Music Talks; 24 Pamphlets written of edited, 1982-85, Council of Adult Education, Melbourne; Writings from a Scarlet Aardvark - 15 Essays on Music and Art. Honours include: Sounds Australian Award. Hobby: Nature Studies. Address: PO Box 2154, St Kilda West, Victoria 3182, Australia.

BURTON Humphrey (McGuire), b. 25 Mar 1931, Trowbridge, England. Television Producer and Presenter. 2 sons, 3 daughters. Education: BA (Cantab); Honours degree, Music and History, Cambridge. Career: Head of Music and Arts, BBC TV, 1965-67, 1975-81; Editor, Presenter, Aquarius, ITV, 1970-75; Presenter, Concerts, Opera and Ballet, BBC, 1975-94; Presenter, Young Musician of the Year, 1978-94; Chairman, EBU TV Music Working Party, 1976-86; Artistic Director, Barbican Centre, 1988-90; Director, Tender is the North, Festival of Scandinavian Arts, Barbican Centre, 1992; Television direction, 1995 includes: Ermione at Glyndebourne, Channel 4, Cardiff Singer of the World BBC2. Recordings: Mozart Harpsichord Duet K9A, with Erik Smith. Publications: Leonard Bernstein, biography, USA, UK, Germany, Japan, 1994. Contributions to: The Sunday Times; Evening Standard; Columnist, Classic FM, the Magazine; Other publications. Memberships: RPS; Honorary Fellow, Chartered Society of Designers. Hobbies: Tennis; Playing duets. Address: 123 Oakwood Court, London W14 8LA, England.

BURTON Stephen,b. 24 Feb 1943, Whittier, California, USA. Composer. Education: Studied at the Oberlin Conservatory, Vienna Concservatory, 1957-60; Salzburg Mozarteum, 1962-65; Further study with Hans Werner Henze, 1962-66. Career: Director of the Munich Kammerspiel, 1963-64; Teacher, Heritage Chair in Music, George Mason University, Fairfax, VA, 1974-. Compositions include: Concerto Da Camera, 1963; Ode To A Nightingale for Soprano and Ensemble, 1963; Symphony No 1, 1968; No Trifling With Love, opera, 1970; Stravinskiana for Flute and Orchestra, 1972; Dithyramb, 1972; 6 Hebrew Melodies, after Byron, 1973; String Quartet, 1974; Piano Trio, 1975; Songs Of The Tulpehocken for Tenor and Orchestra, 1976; Six Songs for Voice and 13 Instruments, 1977; Ballet Finisterre, 1977; The Duchess Of Malfi, opera after Webster, 1978; Symphony No 2, after Sylvia Plath poems, for Mezzo, Baritone and Orchestra, 1979; Variations On A Theme Of Mahler for Chamber Orchestra, 1982; Violin Concerto, 1983; Aimee, opera, 1983; I Have A Dream, cantata for Narrator, Soprano and Orchestra, 1987; An American Triptych, 3 one-act operas after Crane's Maggie, Hawthorne's Dr Heidegger's Experiment and Melville's Benito Cereno, 1989; From Noon to Starry Night for chorus and chamber orchestra, 1989; Brotherhood, Music Theatre, 1992. Address: GMU, 4400 University Drive, Fairfax, VA 22030, 4444, USA.

BURY Edward, b. 18 Sep 1918, Gniezno, Poland. Composer; Conductor. Education: Studied composition with Sikorski, and conducting at the Warsaw Conservatory, 1937-44. Career: Teacher, Krakow Conservatory, 1945-54; Freelance Composer from 1948. Compositions include: Czech Fantasy for Piano and Orchestra, 1948; Little Suite for Orchestra, 1950; Triptych for Orchestra, 1952; Violin Concerto, 1954; Suita Giocosa for Orchestra, 1956; The Millenium Hymn for Chorus and Orchestra, 1956; 8 Symphonies, 1960-80; Chamber music and piano pieces. Publications include: The Principles of Conducting, 1961; The Technique of Reading Scores, 1971. Address: c/o ZAIKS, 2 rue Hipoteczna, 00 092 Warsaw, Poland.

BURY Grzegorz (Piotr Michal), b. 17 Nov 1961, Katowice, Poland. Composer. Education: K Szymanowski Academy of Music, Katowice, Theory of Music, 1981-86, Composition, 1986-89, MA in Art, 1990. Debut: Festival of Fascinating Music in Katowice, 1983. Compositions include: Solo instruments: Suite for Flute, Lament Songs (Treny) for Piano, Sonata With Air-Hammer for Piano, Little Prince, suite, for Piano, Echo, Clouds And Mountains for Piano: Pieces for solo instrument and piano: Walo, lullaby, for Viola and Piano, Gabeag, folk dance, for Violin and Piano, Polonaise, Goliwogs War, Largo Cantabile e Finale for Bassoon and Piano, Sheheresade for Oboe and Piano, Dialogues for Viola and Bassoon, Trio for Clarinet, Basson and Piano; Symphonic: Crux, from texts from The Bible, for Boy Soprano, Tenor, Bass, Reciter, Mixed Choir and Orchestra, Concerto for Piano and Orchestra, Symphony for Jazz Band or Soloist improvising and Symphonic Orchestra, Missa Pro Defunctis, Requiem, for Voices, Choir and Orchestra; Chamber Music: Imitations for Flute, Oboe, Basson and Percussion, Oberek for Brass Quintet, In The Circus for 2 Pianos, Songs On The Lapse Of Time for Bass/Baritone/Oboe and Percussion, Classic Quartet for String, Black And White for 2 String Orchestras, Happy Sorrow for 5 Musicians, Rapsody, in suite form, for Percussion, Piano and Percussion Group, Variations for Violin and Cello, Dialogues for Viola and Bassoon, Trio for Clarinet, Bassoon and Piano, Alarm for Voice, Dock and Chamber Ensemble, Elegia for Voice and Piano, 1993. Hobbies: Travel; Nature; Chess; Tennis; Skiing; Kayaking; Films. Address: 40-866 ul Piastow 7-3, Osiedle 1000 lecia, Katowice, Poland.

BUSCHING Rainer, b. 1943, Halle, Germany. Bass Singer. Education: Studied at the Mendelssohn Musikhochschule, Leipzig, 1967-71. Career: Guest appearances in Germany then engaged at Dessau, 1973-85; Member of the Dresden Staatsoper from 1985 notably as Wagner's Daland, Landgrave and King Henry, Verdi's Zaccaria, Ramphis and Padre Guardiano, Mozart's Sarastro and Commendatore, Weber's Lysiart and Kaspar, Basilio in Il Barbiere di Siviglia, Handel's Giulio Cesare and Gremin in Eugene Onegin; Guest appearances in Italy, Poland and Russia; Concert repertory includes St John and Matthew Passions by Bach, Messiah, Die Schöpfung and Jahreszeiten by Haydn, and Schubert's Winterreise. Address: c/o Dresden Staatsoper, 01069 Dresden, Germany.

BUSH Geoffrey, b. 23 Mar 1920, London, England. Composer; Pianist; Musicologist; University Lecturer. m. Julie McKenna, 15 Apr 1950, 2 sons. Education: Salisbury Cathedral Choir School; Lancing College; MA, DMus, Balliol College, Oxford. Debut: As Composer, Winter Ballet, Bath, 1934. Career: Lecturer, Oxford University, 1947-52; Staff Tutor, 1952-64, Senior Staff Tutor, 1964-80, London University; Visiting Professor, King's College, London, 1969-89; Music Adviser, John Ireland Trust, 1969-; Honorary fellow, University College of Wales, Aberystwyth, 1986-91. Compositions: 2 Symphonies; Overture Yorick; Christmas Cantata; Summer Serenade; In Praise of Mary; Concertante Works for Trumpet, Piano, Oboe and Cello; Operas: If The Cap Fits, The Equation, Lod Arthur Savile's Crime; Violin Sonata; Wind Quintet; Trio; Dialogue for Oboe and Piano; 2 Piano Sonatinas; A Menagerie, Farewell Earth's Bliss, Herrick Songs; Song Cycles; Sang Aegisthus in Elektra at Seattle, 1996. Recordings: Anthems, Canticles and Carols (Abbey); Symphonies No 1 and 2, Overture Yorick, Music for Orchestra (Lyrita); A Little Love Music (songs), Quintet, Trio, Dialogue (Chandos); In Praise of Mary (Unicorn-Kanchana); Christmas Cantata (Saydisc); Piano Sonatino No 1; Summer Serenade (Chandos). Publications: Musical Creation and the Listener, 1954; Left, Right and Centre, 1983; Editor, Music Britannica, volume 37, 1972, volume 43, 1979, volume 49, 1982, volume 52, 1986; An Unsentimental Education, 1990. Contributions to: Musical Times; Music and Letters; Music and Musicians; Composer. Honour: Philharmonic Prize for Overture Yorick, 1949. Memberships include: Composers Guild of Great Britain, Chairman, 1957; Royal Music Association. Address: 43 Corringham Road, London NW11 7BS, England.

BUSSE Barry, b. 18 Aug 1946, Gloversville, NY, USA. Tenor. Education: Studied at Oberlin College and the Manhattan School of Music. Career: Has sung as tenor from 1977 in Carlisle Floyd's Of Mice and Men at Houston; Created Bothwell in Musgrave's Mary Queen of Scots for Virginia Opera in 1977 and repeated the role at the New York City Opera in 1980; Sang at Sant Fe in 1979 as Alwa in the US premiere of the 3 act version of Lulu; European debut in 1982 as Don José for Netherlands Opera; Further appearances in Toulouse, San Francisco, Santa Fe and Miami; Seattle Opera in 1985 as Siegmund in Die Walküre; Sang Tichon in Katya Kabanova at Florence in 1988 and at Geneva in 1989; Sang Mephistopheles and Agrippa in Prokofiev's Fiery Angel at the Holland Festival in 1990; Other roles include Florestan, Cavardossi, Canio, Parsifal at Toulouse in 1987, Peter Grimes, Narraboth, Apollo in Daphne, Pollione and Massenet's Des Grieux; Created the title role in Nosferatu by Randolph Peters, Toronto, 1995. Recordings include: CD of Mary Queen of Scots. Address: c/o Seattle Opera Association, PO Box 9248, Seattle, WA 98109, USA.

BUSSI Francesco, b. 14 Sept 1926, Piacenza, Italy. Musician; Musicologist. m. Maria Villa, 20 July 1957, 1 son, 1 daughter. Education: Laurea in Lettere Classiche, 1948; Diploma di Pianoforte, 1949; Diploma di Paleografia Musicale, 1953; Diploma di Musica Corale, 1955. Career: Docente di Storia ed Estetica Musicale at Conservatorio di Parma, 1955-59; Docente di Storia ed Estetica Musicale at Conservatorio di Piacenza e Bibliotecario, 1959-. Recordings: Francesco Cavalli, Missa Pro Defunctis (Requiem) a 8 Voci, con il responsorio Libera me, Domine a 5 Voci, 1985; Gasparo Villami, Gratiarum actiones a 20 Voci, 1993. Publications: Antifonario-Graduale di S Antonino in Piacenza; Umanità e Arte di G Parabosco; Catalogo dell' Archivio Musicale del Duomo di Piacenza; La Musica Sacra di F Cavalli in rapporto a Monteverdi; Storia, Tradizione e Arte nel' Requiem di Cavalli; L'Opera Veneziana dalla Morte di Monteverdi alla Fine del '600 and many others. Contributions to: Jone di Chio; Il Cantore Spagnolo Pedro Valenzuela; Le "Toscanelle" di Gabriele Villani; La Musica Strumentale di J Brahms; Mutti i hieder di J Brahms; Altro Cavalli Sacro Restituito; New Grove Dictionary of Music and Musicians; New Grove Dictionary of Opera; MGG; DEUMM and many others; Moderna Edizione Critica di Pezzi di Girolamo Parabosco, del Requiem di Cavalli, delle Toscanelle e delle Gratiarum Actiones di Villani, di Altri Pezzi Sacri di e dei 3 Vesperi Cavalli; Edizione Italiana dei Voll 2, 4 and 5 della New Oxford History of Music. Honours: S Antonino d'oro, 1990; Premio internazionale, L'Illica, 1991-. Memberships: SIDM; AIBM; AMS; Membro Effettivo della Deputazione di Storia Patria per le Province Parmensi. Address: Strada Guastafredda, 45-29100 Piacenza, Italy.

BUSSOTTI Sylvano, b. 1 Oct 1931, Florence, Italy. Composer; Painter; Film Director; Stage Designer. Education: Florence Conservatory, 1940-45, with Dallapiccola, Maglioni and Lupi; Private composition studies, 1949-56; Studied with Deutsch in Paris; Darmstadt courses with Cage; USA, 1964-65 on Rockefeller Foundation Grant. Career: Appearances at music festivals from 1958; Co-Founder of the exhibition Musica e Segno, seen in Europe and USA, 1962; Exhibited his own paintings in Italy, US, Japan, France and Germany; Director and Designer of stage works including his own; Professor of Music Drama at the L'Aquila Academy of Fine Arts Scuola di Musica di Fierole, 1971-74; Director of the Teatro La Fenice, Venice, 1975; Bussothoperaballet, Scuola Spattacole, 1984-92. Compositions include: Stage: Tema-Variazioni, Geographie Francaise, 1956, Raramente, mystery play, 1971, Bergkristall, ballet, 1974, Nottetempo, lyric drama, 1976, Le Racine, 1980, Fedra, lyric tragedy, 1988; L'Ispirazione, 1988; Concert: El Carbonero for 5 Voices, 1957, Breve for Ondes Martenot, 1958, Sette Folgi, 1959, Phrase A Trois for String Trio, 1960, Torso for Solo Voices and Orchestra, 1960-63, Rara for Guitar and String Trio, 1964-67, Julio Organum Julii for Speaker and Organ, 1968, I Semi Di Gramsci for String Quartet and Orchestra, 1962-71, Novelletta for Piano, 1962-73, Opus Cygne for Orchestra, 1979; Concerto a L'Aquila for piano and 9 instruments, 1986; Furioso, for mezzo and orchestra, 1994. Honours include: First Prize, Italian Section ISCM, 1965, 1972; DAAD, Berlin, 1972; Commandeur l'Ordre des Arts et Les Lettres. Address: Via di Colle Marta 1, 2, 00030 Genazzano (RM), Italy.

BUSWELL James Oliver (IV), b. 4 Dec 1946, Fort Wayne, IN, USA. Violinist; Conductor; Teacher. Education: BA, Harvard College, 1970; Studied violin with Ivan Galamian at Juilliard School of Music, NY. Debut: Violinist, St Louis in 1963; New York recital debut at Philharmonic Hall in 1967. Career: Soloist with various orchestras, recitalist and chamber music player; Appearances as conductor; Visiting Professor at University of Arizona, Tucson, 1972-73; Teacher, Indiana University School of Music, Bloomington, 1974-86, and New England Conservatory of Music, Boston, 1986-; Former Member, Buswell Parnas Luvisi Trio; TV Host for Stations of Bach on PBS Television. Recordings: Various. Current Management: Michael Schmidt Artists, New York. Address: c/o New England Conservatory of Music, 290 Huntington Avenue, Boston, MA 02115, USA.

BUTLER Mark, b. 5 Feb 1949, Canada, now British Citizen. Violinist. Education: Studied at Royal College of Music with Leonard Hirch. Career: Co-Leader of Ulster Orchestra, 1970-71; BBC debut in 1971, London debut in 1972; Solo recitals in UK and Canada; Second Violinist of the Chilingirian Quartet, 1971; Resident Quartet of Liverpool University, 1973-76, Sussex University, 1978-, and Royal College of Music, 1986-; Annual series of concerts at the Elizabeth Hall and Wigmore Hall; Performances at the Edinburgh, Bath and Aldeburgh Festivals; Played at Munich Herkulessaal, Amsterdam Concertgebouw, Zurich Tonhalle, Vienna Konzerthaus, and Stockholm Konserthuset; New York debut in 1976; Annual coast-to-coast tours of USA and Canada; Represented Britain at the New York International Festival Quartet Series; Tours of Australia, New Zealand, South America and the Far East; TV and radio appearances throughout Europe on National Public Radio in USA, and the BBC. Recordings: All Great Mozart Quartets; Late Schubert Quartets; Debussy and Ravel Quartets; Elgar Quartet and Piano Quintet; Schubert Cello Quintet and Octet; Mozart Clarinet Quintet; Complete Quartets of Bartók and Dvorák; Bartók Piano Quintet. Address: c/o Intermusica Artists' Management. 16 Duncan Terrace, London, N1 8BZ, England.

BUTLER Martin, b. 1 Mar 1960, Hampshire, England. Lecturer; Composer. Education: Winchester School of Art, 1976-78' University of Manchester, 1978-81; Royal Northern College of Music, 1978-82; Princeton University, USA, 1983-87; BMus, Honours, PPRNCM, MFA. Publications include: From an Antique Land for ensemble, 1982; Concertino for chamber orchestra, 1983; Dance Fragments for ensemble, 1984; Cavalcade for orchestra, 1985; Tin Pan Ballet, 1986, arranged as Ballet con Salsa, 1987; Bluegrass Variations for violin, 1987; Piano Piano for 2 pianos and tape, 1988; Graffiti for tape, 1989; Jazz Machines for ensemble, 1990; O Rio, for full orchestra, 1990; Chaconne, for solo oboe, 1991; Down Hollow Winds, for wind quintet, 1991; American Dream, for string quartet and electronic tape, 1991; Going with the Grain, for solo marimba and ensemble, 1992; On the Rocks, for solo piano, 1992; Still

Breathing, for wind orchestra, 1992; Craig's Progress, opera, 1995. Recording: Tin Pan Ballet. Publication: Craig's Progress, 1994. Honour: Fellow, RNCM, 1994. Address: Oxford University Press, 3 Park Road, London NW1 6XN, England.

BUTTERLEY Nigel (Henry), b. 13 May 1935, Sydney, Australia. Composer; Pianist. Compositions include: Chamber Music: String Quartets No 1, 1965, No 2, 1974, No 3, 1979, No 4, 1995; Trio for Clarinet, Cello and Piano, 1979; Forest I for Viola and Piano, 1990; The Wind Stirs Gently, for flute and cello, 1992; Forest II, for trumpet and piano, 1993; Radiophonic: Watershore, 1978; Piano: Uttering Joyous Leaves, 1981; Lawrence Hargrave Flying Alone, 1981; Il Gubbo, 1987; Vocal: The Owl, 1983; There came a Wind like a Bugle, Emily Dickinson, 1987; The Woven Light for Soprano and Orchestra, Kathleen Raine, 1994; Spring's Ending, Du Fu, 1997; Orchestral: Meditiations of Thomas Traherne, 1968; Violin Concerto, 1970; Symphony, 1980; Goldengrove, 1982; In Passing, 1982; From Sorrowing Earth, 1991; Opera: Lawrence Hargrave Flying Alone, 1988. Recordings: Laudes, 1963; In the Head the Fire, 1966; Explorations for Piano and Orchestra, 1970; Violin Concerto, 1970; Letter from Hardy's Bay, 1971; First Day Covers with Barry Humphries, 1973; Fire in the heavens, 1973; Sometimes With One I Love, 1976; String Quartet No 3, 1979; CDs: Violin Concerto; Meditations of Thomas Traherne; Goldengrove; From Sorrowing Earth; The Owl. Honours: Italia Prize for radiophonic composition for In the Head the Fire, 1966; Appointed Member of the Order of Australia, 1991; Australian Artists Creative Fellowship, 1992-95; Sounds Australian Award, Best Work by Australian Composer, 1992; Hon DMus, Newcastle University, 1996. Current Management: Tall Poppies Management, PO Box 373, Glebe, NSW 2037, Australia. Address: 57 Temple Street, Stanmore, New South Wales, Australia 2048.

BUUWALDA Sytse, b. 28 Sep 1964, Holland. Counter-Tenor. Education: Studied at the Stwelinck Conservatory with Canne-Meyer and Paul Hameleers. Career: Appearances in Holland and in Europe in a repertoire ranging from Monteverdi to Britten; Concert performances of Messiah, Handel's Theodora and the Masses of Bach; Engagements with the Netherlands Chamber Choir from 1989, featuring a tour of Europe with music by Bach accompanied by the Orchestra of the Eighteenth Century under Frans Bruggen; Opera roles include Gluck's Orpheus. Recordings include: Te Deums by Blanchard and Caldara. Address: Anglo-Swiss Management, Suite 35-37 Morley House, 320 Regent Street, London W1R 5AD, England.

BUZA'S Pal, b. 3 Mar 1939, Cluj, Romania. Piano Teacher; Pianist; Editor. m. 30 Mar 1974, div 21 Dec 1978, 1 daughter. Education: Piano, High School of Music, Cluj-Napoca, Romania, graduated 1956; Piano, Academy of Music Gheorghe Dima, Cluj-Napoca, graduated 1962. Career: Solo concerts; Chamber music concerts in major towns in Romania, Hungary and France. Recordings: At television and radio studios, DUNA television, Budapest and at Cluj and Bucharest. Publications: Csillagzatok (Stars), 1993; Buzas Family Community in Kalotaszeg, 1995. Contributions to: Kalotaszeg Huedin, magazine, 1991-98; Music Criticism magazines in Romania. Honour: Liszt Prize, Hungary, 1986. Memberships: Hungarians from Romania Music Society; Pro Kalotaszeg Cultural Union; Hungarian Journalists' Romanian Union. Hobby: Amateur chorus conductor. Address: Str Amurg Nr 20 Ap 2, 3400 Cluj-Napoca, Romania.

BYBEE Luretta, b. 1965, Midland, Texas, USA. Singer (Mezzo-contralto). Career: Has sung widely in the USA and Europe as Isabella (Cologne and Dublin), Cherubino, Falliero in the US premiere of Rossini's Bianca e Falliero, Meg Page, Farnaces in Mozart's Mitridate at Wexford, Orlofsky, Nicklausse and Maddalena (New Orleans); Season 1993-94 as Dalila with Indianapolis Opera; Recent engagements as Carmen for Dayton Opera (following earlier appearances in Peter Brook's La Tragédie de Carmen), Amneris, Laura (La Gioconda), Venus and Waltraute; Concerts include the Verdi Requiem at Carnegie Hall, Messiah in Texas and the Mozart Requiem at Anchorage, Alaska. Address: c/o Atholl Still Ltd, Foresters Hall, 25-27 Westow Street, London SE19 3RY, England.

BYCHKOV Semyon, b. 30 Nov 1952, Leningrad, Russia. Conductor. m. Tatiana Rozina, 3 Jul 1973, 1 son, 1 daughter. Education: Diploma of Honour, Glinka Choir School, Leningrad, 1970; Studied with Ilya Musin and graduated from Leningrad Conservatory in 1974; Artistic Diploma, Mannes College of Music, New York, 1976. Career: Music Director, Bonch-Bruyevich Institute Chorus, Leningrad, 1970-72; Conductor of Leningrad Conservatory Symphony and Opera Orchestra, 1972-74; Associate Conductor, Music Director, Mannes College of Music Orchestra, 1976-80; Music Director, Grand Rapids Symphony Orchestra, 1980-85; Associate Conductor, 1980-81, Principal Guest Conductor, 1981-85, Music Director, 1985-89, Buffalo Philharmonic Orchestra; Music Director, Orchestre de Paris, 1987, 1989; Guest Conductor with major world orchestras; Led the Orchestre de Paris at the 1991 Promenade Concerts in London; Conducted Beethoven's 5th Piano Concerto, 10th

Symphony of Shostakovich and 2nd by Dutilleux, Dances of Galanta and also Sprach Zarathustra; Parsifal at Florence, 1997, (Idomoneo, 1996); Principal Guest Conductor of the Orchestra of the Maggio Musicale Fiorentino, 1992; Conducted Eugene Onegin at the Théâtre du Châtelet in 1992; Lady Macbeth of Mtsensk at Florence, 1994; Principal Guest Conductor of St Petersburg Philharmonic Orchestra, 1992. Recordings: Various. Honour: 1st Prize, Rachmaninoff Conducting Competition, 1973. Address: c/o Orchestre de Paris, 252 Rue du Faubourg St Honore, F-75008 Paris, France.

BYERS Reginald, b. 5 Dec 1934, Sydney, Australia. Tenor. Education: Sydney Conservatory and in Austria. Debut: As Cavaradossi with Australian Opera at Sydney. Career: Guest appearances in New York City Opera and with Scottish Opera in Glasgow; Many engagements with opera companies in Australia; Other roles have included Verdi's Radames, Ismaele in Nabucco, Gabriele Adorno, Riccardo, Alfredo and Don Carlos, Faust, Turiddu, Rodolfo, Dick Johnson, Calaf, Steva in Jenufa and Bacchus in Ariadne auf Naxos; After retirement from stage, gave concerts and taught in Sydney. Address: c/o Sydney Opera House, Sydney, New South Wales, Australia.

BYLES Edward, b. 1949, Ebbw Vale, Wales. Tenor. Career: Toured with Opera For All and sang with major companies including Royal Opera and in Europe, Russia, Australia and Ireland; Joined English National Opera in 1974 with roles including Monstatos, Mime, Missail in Boris Godunov and Vitek in The Makropoulos Case; Has sung in Tosca, War and Peace, Madama Butterfly, Orpheus in The Underworld and Pacific Overtures; In 1988 took part in the first British performance of Rimsky Korsakov's Christmas Eve; Season 1992 with English National Opera as the Broomstick-maker in Königskinder and Trabuco in The Force of Destiny; Spoletta in Tosca for ENO, 1994. Address: c/o English National Opera, London Coliseum, St Martin's Lane, London, EC2, England.

BYLSMA Anner, b. 17 Feb 1934, The Hague, The Netherlands. Cellist; Teacher. Education: Studied with Carel Boomkamp, Royal Conservatory of Music, The Hague. Career: Principal Cellist, Concertgebouw Orchestra, Amsterdam, 1962-68; Toured throughout the world as Soloist with orchestras; Recitalist and Chamber-music player; Many trio appearances with Frans Brüggen and Gustav Leonhardt; Teacher, Royal Conservatory of Music, The Hague; Sweelinck Conservatory, Amsterdam; Erasmus Scholar, Harvard University, 1982; Played Cello Suites by Bach, BBC Lunchtime Concert, 1992. Recordings: Numerous recordings including Angel-EMI; Das Alte Werk; Decca London; Harmonia Mundi; Philips; Pro Arte; RCA; Teldec; Telefunken. Honours: Winner, Pablo Casals Competition, Mexico City, 1959; Prix d'excellence, Royal Conservatory of Music, 1957. Address: c/o Byers Schwalbe & Associates Inc, One Fifth Avenue, New York, NY 10003, USA.

BYRNE Connell, b. 1936, Australia. Singer (Tenor). Education: Studied in Australia, Italy and London. Career: Sang in such small London companies as Group Eight and Philopera Circle, from 1961; Member of the Brunswick Opera, 1963-64, Mannheim Opera from 1965; Appearances at Graz and Berne from 1969 and at Bremen until 1980; Member of the Deutsche Oper am Rhein at Dusseldorf, 1976-82; Guest appearances at Sadler's Wells, London, 1968, as Walther in The Mastersingers, at Barcelona (Aegisthus, 1970), Turin (Tristan, 1976), the Vienna Staatsoper (Laca and Cavaradossi) and Dublin; Other roles include Erik, Lohengrin, Rienzi, Tannhäuser, Parsifal, Bacchus, Don Carlos and Don José. Address: c/o Deutsche Oper am Rhein, Heinrich-Heine-Allee 16a, W-4000 Dusseldorf 1, Germany.

BYRNES-HARRIS Aleicia, b. Toronto, Ontario, Canada. Singer (Soprano). Education: Studied in California, at Aspen and the San Diego Opera Studio. Career: Sang at first in San Diego and Los Angeles as Santuzza, Magda in The Consul and Mme Lidoine in The Carmelites; European engagements from 1981, notably at Oldenburg, Wiesbaden, Nürnberg and Hamburg as Butterfly, Desdemona, Marie in Wozzeck, Irene in Rienzi, Amelia in Ballo in Maschera, Leonore, the Dyer's Wife, Kundry and Isolde; Tosca, Senta, Elektra (Elektra), Ariadne, Rosalinde Appeared at Zurich and Munich National Theatre. Address: Sonnenfelsgasse 11/7c, A-1010 Vienna, Austria.

BYRON Michael, b. 7 Sep 1953, Chicago, IL, USA. Composer. Education: Studied at the California Institute of the Arts with Mario Guarneri, Thomas Stevens and Joe Higgins; Further studies at York University, Ontario, BA, 1974. Career: Active on behalf of other US composers; Works in collaboration with the performance art group, Maple Sugar. Compositions include: Song Of The Lifting Up Of The Head for Piano, 1972; Starfields for Piano 4 Hands, 1974; Morning Glory for Percussion, 1975; Marimbas, 1976; A Living Room At The Bottom Of A Lake for Orchestra, 1977; Music for 1 Piano, 1978; Three Mirrors for Percussion Ensemble, 1979; Music Of Steady Light; 158 Pieces for Strings, 1979-82; Tidal for Ensemble, 1981; Double String Quartet, 1984. Honours include: Grants from York University, the

Ontario Arts Council, The National Endowment for The Arts and The New York State Council of The Arts. Address: c/o ASCAP, ASCAP Building, One Lincoln Plaza, New York, NY 10023, USA.

C

CAAMANO Roberto, b. 7 Jul 1923, Buenos Aires, Argentina. Composer; Pianist; Professor. m. Maria Teresa Stafforini, 11 Feb 1956, 3 sons, 1 daughter. Education: National Conservatory, Buenos Aires, 1939-46. Career: Piano concerts in Latin America, USA and Europe, 1944-61; Professor of Piano, Universidad Nacional del Litoral, 1949-52; Professor of Piano, National Conservatory, Buenos Aires, 1956-79; Artistic Director, Teatro Colon, 1961-64; Professor of Composition, Orchestration and Harmony, 1964-, Dean, Facultad de Artes y Ciencias Musicales, 1966-, Universidad Catolica, Argentina; Member, Board of Directors of the National Arts Fund, 1980-83; Commissioned by Louisville Philharmonic Society, Elizabeth Coolidge Foundation, Interamerican Music Council, and Music Division of the Organization of American States. Compositions include: Works for chorus and orchestra: Magnificat, Cantata De La Paz, Canto A San Martin, Te Deum; Soloist and Orchestra: 2 Piano Concerti, Guitar Concerto, Harp Concerto; Works for chorus a cappella, chamber music, and vocal music. Publications: Historia del Teatro Colón, 3 volumes, 1969; Apuntes Para la Formación del Pianista Profesional, 1978. Hobby: Gardening. Address: Juan B Alberdi 1275, 1406 Buenos Aires, Argentina.

CABALLÉ Monserrat, b. 12 Apr 1933, Barcelona, Spain. Soprano Opera Singer. m. Bernabé Marti, 1 son. Education: Conservatorio del Liceo; Studied under Eugenia Kemeny, Conchita Badia and Maestro Annovazi. Debut: Mimi in La Bohème, State Opera of Basel, 1956. Career: North American debut, Manon, Mexico City in 1964; US debut in Lucrezia Borgia at Carnegie Hall, 1965; Appeared at Glyndebourne Festival as the Marschallin in Der Rosenkavalier and the Countess in the Marriage of Figaro, 1965; Metropolitan Opera debut as Marguerite in Faust, 1965; Appeared frequently at Metropolitan Opera and other US opera houses; Has performed in most leading opera houses in Europe including Gran Teatro del Liceo, La Scala, Vienna Staatsoper, Paris and Rome Operas; Covent Garden debut in 1972 as Violetta; Had repertoire of over 40 roles; Sang Hypermestra in Salieri's Les Danaides at Perugia, 1983; Rome Opera in 1986 in title role of Spontini's Agnes di Hohenstaufen; Pesaro and Barcelona in 1987 as Rossini's Ermione and Pacini's Saffo; Vienna Staatsoper in 1988 as Mme Cortese in Il Viaggio a Reims; Barcelona in 1989 in La Fiamma by Respighi and the premiere of Cristobal Colón by Balada; Sang Mme Cortese in a new production of Il Viaggio a Reims at Covent Garden in 1992; Llangollen International Festival, 1997. Recordings: Lucrezia Borgia; La Traviata; Salome; Aida. Honours: Most Excellent and Illustrious Dobna and Cross of Isabella the Catholic. Current Management: Columbia Artists Management Inc. Address: c/o Columbia Artists Management Inc, 165 West 57th Street, New York, Ny 10019, USA.

CABLE Margaret, b. 1950, England. Mezzo-Soprano. Career: Appearances in Europe, Scandinavia, Israel and the USA; Festival engagements at the Bath and Three Choirs Festivals; Promenade Concerts in London; Performances in Baroque repertoire with ensembles, using original instruments, including Bach's St Matthew Passion under Andrew Parrott and Messiah at the 1985 Lucerne Festival under Christopher Hogwood; Broadcasts include Handel's Belshazzar, Tippett's A Child of Our Time, works with orchestra by Arthur Bliss and Robin Holloway; Stage roles with Kent Opera included Mrs Grose in The Turn of The Screw, Dorabella, and Marcellina in Le Nozze di Figaro, also at the 1986 Vienna International Festival; Sang Juno in Handel's Semele at York Early Music Festival in 1991; Sang in Bach's St John Passion at the Festivall Hall, London, 1997. Recordings include: Haydn Masses with the Academy of Ancient Music; Madrigals directed by Peter Pears; Works by Mozart and Scarlatti directed by George Guest; Glazunov Songs and Lux Aetrena by William Mathias, with the Bach Choir; Handel's Carmelite Vespers and Messiah with Andrew Parrott and The Taverner Players.

CACERES German, b. 9 July 1954, San Salvador, El Salvador. Composer; Conductor. m. Ana Maria Espinosa, 15 Feb 1992, 1 son. Education: Diploma, The Juillard School, New York, 1977; Postgraduate Diploma, The Juillard School, 1978; Doctor of Musical Arts, University of Cincinnatti, Ohio, 1989. Debut: Carnegie Recital Hall, New York, 1978; Lincoln Center Washington, 1982; Cleveland Museum of Art, 1986. Career: Director of Music of Our Time, Radio Clasica, San Salvador. Compositions include: Fanfare to San Salvador, for 4 trumpets, 4 horns, 3 trombones and tuba, 1996; Villancico del Calendario, for a capella choir, 1996; Tiento, for chamber orchestra, 1996; Tiento II, for solo clarinet, 1997; Tiento III, for solo cello, 1997; 8 Variations upon an 8 note set, for solo guitar, 1997; Lo que dice el Caracol, for soprano and orchestra (poem by Salarrue), 1997. Publications: Sonata for Piano, 1984; Diferencias, 1988; Laconicas, for Piano, 1993; Contributions to: Music in El Salvador, 1993; Beethoven, 1995; Cultural Identity, 1997; Ars Magazine, San Salvador; Many articles for El Diario de Hoy (journal), San Salvador. Honours include: National Prize of Culture, San Salvador, 1982; International Gertrud Ramdhor Prize, Hamburg, Germany, 1986; Best Fulbright Fellow of the Year, San Salvador, 1990; L'Ordre des Arts et Lettres (Chevalier), Government of France, 1992; XX Century Music Category Prize, Latin-American Musical Tribune, Rosario, Argentina, 1997. Memberships: Ateneo de El Salvador; Instituto Sanmartiniano; Centro Cultural Salvadoreno. Hobby: Reading (Literature, History). Address: Apartado Postal, 2979 Correo Central, San Salvador, El Slavador.

CACHEMAILLE Gilles, b. 25 Nov 1951, Orbe, Switzerland. Bass-Baritone. Education: Studied at the Lausanne Conservatoire with Juliette Bise. Career: Concert hall appearances from 1978 at the Aix and Salzburg Festivals, at Paris, Lyon, Buenos Aires, Madrid, Strasbourg, Lisbon and Tokyo; Repertoire has included the Passions of Bach, L'Enfance du Christ by Berlioz, Franck's Les Beatitudes, Haydn's Schöpfung and Jahreszeiten, works by Monteverdi and songs by Duparc, Poulenc, Schubert and Strauss; Debut as member of the Lyon Opera in the stage premiere of Rameau's Les Boréades at Aix, 1982; Lausanne Opera as Guglielmo, Simone in La Finta Semplice, Mozart's Figaro and Papageno, and Belcore in L'Elisir d'Amore, 1988; Mezieres in 1988 as Gluck's Orpheus, Leoporello at the Hamburg Staatsoper in 1987 and Vienna in 1989; Sang in Martinu's Les Trois Souhaits at Lyons in 1990, and Leporello at Houston in 1991; Sang Don Giovanni at Glyndebourne, 1994; Merlin in Chausson's Le Roi Arthus, at the 1996 Bregenz Festival. Recordings include: L'Enfance du Christ; Chausson's Le Roi Arthus; Iphigénie en Aulide; Les Boréades; Gluck's La Rencontre Imprévue; Dominic in Arabella; Golaud in Pelléas et Mélisande; Guglielmo in Così fan tutte under Harnoncourt; Claudio in Beatrice et Benedict. Address: c/o Balmer and Dixon Management AG, Granitweg 2, CH-8006 Zurich, Switzerland.

CADDY Ian (Graham), b. 1 Mar 1947, Southampton, England. Singer (Bass-Baritone). m. Kathryn Dorothy Ash, 29 Sept 1979, divorced 28 Apr 1994, 1 son, 2 daughters. Education: Royal Academy of Music, 1965-70, LRAM, ARCM. Debut: London in 1974. Career: Sang with Opera For All, Kent Opera, New Opera Company, Phoenix Opera, Glyndebourne, Scottish Opera, Welsh National Opera, Royal Opera Covent Garden, and English National Opera; Houston Grand Opera, Nantes Opera, Vancouver Opera; Opera, oratorio, festivals and recitals throughout Britain also in Austria, Canada, at Wexford and Versailles Festivals, in Denmark, Eire, France, Germany, Hong Kong, Iceland, Netherlands, Spain, USA and Yugoslavia; Houston Grand Opera; Vancouver Opera; Edited, published, performed and broadcast with works by J S Mayr and Donizetti; Staging director of baroque opera in strict period style; Numerous TV and radio broadcasts worldwide; Sang Plutone in Peri's Euridice, St James's Church, Piccadilly, 1994; Bach's B Minor Mass at the Queen Elizabeth Hall, London, 1997; Runs own publishing title, Caddy Publishing. Recordings include: Edited and Recorded: Songs and Canatas by Mayr and Donizetti; L'Amor Coniugale by Mayr; Jigs - Reels and Songs of the Bottle, Holbrooke; Vivaldi's Dixit Dominus; Rameau's Princesse de Navarre and Nais; Schoeck's Notturno; Wallace's Maritana; Video of Macbeth, The Beggar's Opera, Nais, Castor et Pollux, La Fanciulla del West; Intermezzo. Honours include: Ricordi Prize, 1967; Vaughan Williams Trust Award, 1969; Countess of Munster Musical Trust Award, 1970; Royal Academy of Music President's Prize, 1970; Associate of the Royal Academy of Music, 1984. Memberships: Co-founder of The Mayr-Donizetti Collaboration, 1985. Current Management: Music International, 13 Ardilaun Road, London, N5 2QR, England. Address: Convent Lodge, Andover Down, Hampshire SP11 6LR, England.

CADOL Christine, b. 1956, France. Singer (Mezzo-Soprano). Education: Studied at the Paris Conservatoire, where she won a prize for her interpretation of Carmen. Career: Appearances from 1978 as Dalila at Nantes, Britten's Lucretia at Rouen, Anita in La Navarraise by Massenet at Marseilles, and Suzuki in Madama Butterfly; Further guest engagements at Liège, Limoges and Saint-Cere; Other roles include Meg Page, Waltraute and Marguerite in La Damnation de Faust; Many concert appearances. Address: 164 Avenue de la Capelette, 13010 Marseille, France.

CADUFF Sylvia, b. 7 Jan 1937, Chur, Switzerland. Conductor; Professor of Conducting and Orchestral Studies. Education: Studied at the Conservatoire of Lucerne; Further studies with Karajan at the Berlin Conservatory and with Kubelik, Matacic and Van Otterloo. Debut: With the Tonhalle Orchestra, Zurich. Career: Guest Conductor in all the European countries, USA, Japan, South Korea; Appearances with New York Philharmonic, Munich and Berlin Philharmonics, Radio Orchestra Berlin, Royal Philharmonic London; Assistant to Bernstein at the New York Philharmonic, 1966-67; As Music Director in Solingen, 1977-86, was first woman to be appointed Music Director in Europe; Taught conducting at the Berne Conservatory, 1972-77. Honours include: 1st Prize, Mitropoulos Competition, New York, 1966. Memberships: Swiss Musicians Association; Swiss Conductors Union. Address: Belleriverstrasse 29, 6006 Lucerne, Switzerland.

CAETANI Oleg, b. 1956, Lausanne, Switzerland. Conductor. Education: Studied with Nadia Boulanger, Igor Markevitch (his father), in Rome with Frano Ferrara, in Moscow with Kyrill Kondrashin and in Leningrad with Ilia Mussin. Career: Assistant to Otmar Suitner at the Staatsoper Berlin, 1981-84; Deutsche Nationaltheater Weimar, 1984-87; Kapellmeister at the Städtische Buhnen Frankfurt am Main; Music Director at Wiesbaden, leading the Ring, Tristan und Isolde, La Forza del Destino, Otello, Rimsky's Invisible City of Kitezh and Bluebeard's Castle, 1992-95; Guest engagements with Semiramide in Vienna, Les Vêpres Siciliennes in Nice, Lucia di Lammermoor and Tosca at Trieste and Verdi's Falstaff at Stuttgart, in season 1996-97; Zurich Opera with Rigoletto, The Nutcracker, La Bohème and Norma; Concert repertory includes music by Beethoven, Schubert, Schumann and Shostakovich, with soloists such as Martha Argerich, Viktoria Mullova, Shlomo Mintz and Sviatoslav Richter. Honours include: Winner of the 1979 RAI Competition in Turin; Prize winner at the 1982 Herbert von Karajan Competition. Address: c/o Opernhaus Zurich, Falkenstrasse 1, CH-8008 Zurich, Switzerland.

CAFORIO Armando, b. 1956, Civitavecchia, Italy. Singer (Bass). Education: Studied in Alessandria and the USA. Debut: Genoa, 1982, as Count Rodolfo in La Sonnambula. Career: Florence, 1983, as Colline in La Bohème, Turin and Martina Franca from 1984; Guest appearances, 1984-85, in Dublin, Geneva, 1987; Torre del Lago and Maggio Musicale Festivals from 1987; Savona, 1990, in L'Ebreo by Apollini; Other roles include Rossini's Don Magnifico and Basilio, the Grand Inquisitor, and Loredano in Verdi's Due Foscari. Address: c/o Teatro Comunale, Via Solferino 15, 50123 Florence, Italy.

CAGLI Bruno, b. 2 June 1942, Narni, Italy. Administrator; Writer on Music. Education: Studies at Rome University. Career: Writer for the Theatre and for Broadcasting Companies; Music Criticism in Journals and Newspapers; Librettist of L'Ombre di Banquo, 1976 and Le Campanule, 1981 by Renosto; Director of the Fondazione Rossini at Pesaro from 1971, collaborating in the new critical edition of Rossini's Works with Philip Gossett and others; Artistic Director of the Teatro dell'Opera at Rome, 1987-90; Teacher at Naples and Urbino Universities and at the Rome Conservatoires; President, National Academy of Santa Cecilia, 1990-. Publications includes: Studies of Donizetti, Verdi and Rossini (including the literary sources of Rossini's libretti); Storia di San Carlo, 1989; Lettere e documenti di G Rossini, 1992. Honour: Winner, Premio Italia with Una Vendetta in Musica, 1981. Address: c/o Accademia Nationale di Santa Cecilia, via Vittoria 6-, 00186 Roma, Italy.

CAHILL Teresa (Mary), b. 30 July 1944, Maidenhead, Berkshire, England. Singer (Lyric Soprano). Divorced. Education: Associate, Guildhall School of Music, Piano; Licentiate, Royal Academy of Music, Singing. Debut: Covent Garden, 1970; Glyndebourne, 1970, First Lady in Die Zauberflöte. Career: Glyndebourne, the English National Opera; Scottish Welsh Opera; Covent Garden; Debut at Santa Fe Opera, 1972; La Scala, Milan, 1976, Philadelphia Opera, 1981, roles include Strauss's Sophie, Verdi's Alice Ford and Mozart's Donna Elvira; Sang at Covent Garden, 1970-77 as Zerlina, Sophie and Barbarina, and in the 1976 premiere of Henze's We Come to the River; ENO, 1977, as Pauline Le Clerc in the premiere at Toussaint L'overture by David Blake; Sang the title role in Strauss's Daphne, Chelsea Opera, 1990; Concerts include: Edinburgh Festival, Proms, Chicago Symphony Orchestra, Vienna Festival, Berlin Festival, Hallé Orchestra, Frankfurt Radio Orchestra, Danish Radio Orchestra, Stockholm Philharmonic, BBC Orchestras, English Chamber Orchestra, Royal Liverpool Philharmonic, Houston Symphony Orchestra, Brussels Radio Orchestra, RAI Turin Orchestra, London Sinfonietta and Hamburg Philharmonie; Numerous television & radio performances; Professor, Royal Northern College of Music, Trinity College of Music, London and Guildhall School; Masterclasses, Lecturer & Private voice consultant; Vocal Consultant to the University of Yor and Oxford University, 1995-96; Examiner and Adjudicator at major vocal competitions. Recordings: King Olaf by Elgar, EMI; Mahler's Eighth Symphony, Denon; Strauss, Lieder Recital; Spirit of England and Coronation Ode by Elgar, both on Chandos; Elgar War Music on Pearl Label. Honours: Silver Medal, Worshipful Company of Musicians, 1966; John Christie Award, Glydebourne, 1970. Memberships: Incorporated Society of Musicians; Equity; Royal Overseas League. Hobbies: Photogrphy; Arts; Cooking; Going to sales, from car boots to Sothebys. Address: 65 Leyland Road, London, SE12 8DW.

CAHOVA Monika, b. 20 June 1966, Prague, Czech Republic. Singer (Soprano). Education: The State Conservatory, Prague. Debut: Sang Inez in Il Trovatore at the National Theatre, Prague, 1988. Career: Many appearances at the Opera Theatre Liberec and also sings in the National Theatre of Prague; Roles in opera include: Marenka in Smetana's The Bartered Bride; Blazenka in The Secret; Vendulka in The Kiss; Dalibor; Dvorak's

Rusalka and Terinka in Jakobin; Elisabeta in Don Carlo, Leonora in Il Trovatore, and Amelia in Simone Boccanegra; Mimi in La Bohème, and Tosca; Gioconda in La Gioconda; Margarete in Faust; Micaela in Carmen; Giulietta in Les Contes d'Hoffman and Helene in La Belle Helene; Donna Elvira in Don Giovanni and the Countess; Liza in Tchaikovsky's Queen of Spades; Marica in Kalman's Dir Gräfin Marica; Liza in Das Land des Lächelns and Hana in Die Lustige Witwe; Also sang in Britten's War Requiem at the Summer Festival in Olomouc; In Zagreb, The Days of Czech Opera, sang Dvorak's Rusalka and Marenka; Sang Donna Elvira with the National Theater of Brno of Italy; Also appeared at the Teatro dell'Aquila, Fermo Teatro di Cita, Salerno; Dvorak's Stabat Mater at the Summer Festival in Marianskelazne; The Concert of Czech Music in Gmunden, Salzburg. Hobby: Painting. Address: Nadrazni 7/294, Praha 5, Smichov 15000, Czech Republic.

CAILLARD Jean-Philippe, b. 31 July 1924, Paris, France. Choral Director. Career: Formed first vocal ensemble, 1944, for the performance of then little heard Renaissance music; Recorded many albums, 1955-70, beginning with Josquin's Missa Pange Lingua; Associations with such conductors as Jean-François Paillard and Louis Fremaux in the performance of French Baroque music; Pedagogic and educational activities from 1951, and has researched early music performance. Address: c/o 23 Rue de Marly, 7860 Etang la ville, France.

CAINE Rebecca, b. 1962, Toronto, Canada. Soprano. Education: Studied at the Guildhall School of Music, London. Career: North American debut in 1991 as Lulu for Canadian Opera, returning as Despina, Micaela and Pamina; Further appearances with New Sadler's Wells Opera, Handel Opera Society, Glyndebourne and Tulsa Opera; Created L A Lola in Mason's Playing Away with Opera North in 1994, and returned to Leeds in 1995 as Thomas' Ophelia; Opera Lyra Ottawa as Gilda and English National Opera as Pamina in 1995; Opera de Nice in 1995 as Balkis in Haydn's L'Incontro Improvviso; Sang Violetta at Belfast, 1996; Season 1996-97 included Musetta and Susanna fpr English National Opera, Bernstein's Curegonde for the BBC; Engaged as Martinu's Julietta for English National Opera, 1997-98. Address: c/o Harold Holt Ltd, 31 Sinclair Road, London, W14 0NS, England.

CAIRE Patrice, b. 17 June 1949, Lyon, France. Organist. Education: Baccalaureat, 1968; Faculty of Law; Lyon Conservatory; Conservatoire National Superieur de Musique, Paris; Licence de Concert, Ecole Normale de Musique, Paris, 1975. Career: Organist, Sainte Croix Church, Lyon, 1973-83; Organist, St Bonaventure Sactuary, Lyon, 1983-; Keeper, Grandes Orgues de l'Auditorium Maurice Ravel, Lyon, 1980-; Commissioner, International Improvisation Competition, 1982-83; Teacher, Conservatoire National Superieur de Musique, Lyon, 1979-; Recitals in, France, Germany, England, Scotland, Switzerland, Sweden, Spain, Italy, Belgium, USA and Canada; Concert performances: Radio France; France Musique; France Culture; Radio Cando; Radio Suisse Romande; Spanish Radio Television; Sweden Radio; With orchestra under S Baudo, E Krivine, S Skrowaczewski, J Nelson and E Tchakarov. Recordings: 2 recitals; Ch M Widor, Symphony No 6; A Guilmant, Sonata No 1 REM; 6 Pieces; Brass; Organ; Percussion; Busser; Litaize; Dupré; Vierne: Gigout, REM; N J Lemmens; Fanfare; Priere; Sonatas No 1, 2, 3, REM; Lemmens, Lefebure Wely, REM; C Franck et l'orgue du Trocadero, REM; L Vierne, Finales of 6 Symphonies; Ch M Widor, Symphonies No 4, 5,; Ch M Widor, Symphonies, No 1 2; L Boellmann, Work for Grand Organ; C Franck, 12 Pieces for Grand Organ; Les Maitres du Trocadero; Guilmant; Widor; Lemmens; Franck; Dubois; Gigout; Saint-Saens. Memberships: Founder; Artistic Director, Les Grandes Orgues de l'Auditorium Maurice Ravel, Lyon. Current Management: North America; Ph Truckenbrod, PO Box 69, West Hartford, CT 06107, USA. Hobbies: Sport; Cinema; Reading. Address: 73 Rue Pierre Corneille 69006, Lyon, France.

CAIRNS Christine, b. 11 Feb 1959, Ayrshire, Scotland. Singer (Mezzo-Soprano). Education: Royal Scottish Academy of Music and Drama, Glasgow; Further study with Neilson Taylor. Career: Concerts with André Previn and the Los Angeles Philharmonic 1985; Prokofiev's Alexander Nevsky in Los Angeles and with the Cleveland & Philadelphia Orchestras; Royal Philharmonic Orchestra 1988, in Mahler's Kindertotenlieder; Tour of the US with Mahler's 4th Symphony; Festival Hall London, 1988, in Schoenberg's Songs Op 22; Promenade Concerts London, 1989, in Mozart's Coronation Mass, returned 1990; Guest appearances throughout the British Isles, Athens, Basle, Tokyo, Berlin, San Francisco and Dortmund; Touring throughout Spain; Guest engagements in Paris, Madrid, Rome, Zurich, Singapore and Rio de Janiero; Staged performances of Monteverdi's Orfeo in Valencia; Concerts with Ashkenazy in Berlin and London, 1990; Mahler with Simon Rattle and Yuri Temirkanov in LA, 1991; Season 1996-97 with Beethoven's Mass in C at the Bath Mozart Festival and Elijah with the Ulster Orchestra. Recordings: Mendelssohn's Midsummer Night's Dream, Previn, Vienna Philharmonic; Prokofiev Alexander Nevsky, Previn, LA Philharmonic; Die Erste Walpurgisnacht, Dohnányi, Cleveland Orchestra. Current Management: c/o Harrison Parrott Ltd, 12 Penzance Place, London, W11 4PA, England.

CAIRNS David (Adam), b. 8 June 1926, Loughton, Essex. Critic; Writer. Education: Oxford University, 1945-48; Princeton University, 1950-51. Career: Co-founded Chelsea Opera Group, 1950; Music Critic, Spectator, 1958-62; Financial Times, 1962-67; New Statesman, 1967-70; Sunday Times, 1973-; Succeeded Desmond Shawe-Taylor as chief music critic, 1983; Has also written reviews for the Observer, Evening Standard. Publications include: Translation of the Berlioz Memoirs, 1969, revised, 1977; Collection of essays, Responses, 1973-80; First volume of biography of Berlioz, 1989. Contributions to: Beethoven and Berlioz in Viking Opera Guide, 1993. Honours include: CBE, 1997. Address: c/o Sunday Times, 1 Pennington Street, London EC2, England.

CAIRNS Janice, b. 1955, Ashington, Northumberland, England. Singer (Soprano). Education: Studied at the Royal Scottish Academy, with John Hauxvell and with Titto Gobbi in Rome. Debut: Sang Verdi's Desdemona at the Thessaloniki Festival, directed by Gobbi. Career: London Debut as Odabella in Attila, for University College Opera; Appearances with Kent Opera as Alice Ford and Donna Anna; Manon Lescaut and Leonora in La Forza del Destino for Chelsea Opera Group; With English National Opera has sung Musetta, Ariadne, Eva, Maria in Mazeppa, Lisa, Maria Boccanegra, Tosca and Amelia; Scottish Opera as Rezia in Oberon, Leonara (Il Trovatore), Aida and Madama Butterfly; For Opera North has sung Aida, Leonore and Helen in the British stage premiere of Verdi's Jerusalem, 1989; Italian debut with Scottish Opera at La Fenice, Venice, as Rezia; Concert engagements include the Verdi Requiem with the LSO, Odabella at the Concertgebouw, Rachmaninov's The Bells at the Proms and Britten's War Requiem at the Norwich Festival. English National Opera, 1992, as Anna in Street Scene and as Ariadne; Sang Turandot for Welsh National Opera, 1994; Tosca for English National Opera, 1996; Season 1997 with Korngold's Violanta for Opera North and at the London Proms. Address: c/o Harold Holt Ltd, 31 Sinclair Road, London, W14 0NS, England.

CALCAFUOCO Angelo, b. 19 May 1957, Ontario, Canada. Concert Violinist. m. Claudia Carolina Calcafuoco, 2 sons. Education: BMus, Performance, University of Toronto, teachers included Steven Staryk and Sydney Harth. Debut: Sault Ste Marie, 1974. Career: Former Director, Algoma Music Camp; Former Director, Founder, Summer Performance Academy, Oakville, Ontario; Former Director, Royal Conservatory Chamber Orchestra; Teacher, Former Chairman, Royal Conservatory of Music, University of Toronto String Department; Former Director, Royal Conservatory Chamber Orchestra; Concert Master, Royal Conservatory Heritage Orchestra; Concert Master, Canadian Chamber Orchestra; Formerly Head of Strings, Appleby College, and Director, Appleby Centre for the Arts; Project Manager, Architect Royal Conservatory Strings Syllabus and Graded Book Series; Currently Visiting Artist, Etobicoke School for the Arts; Active Concert Violinist; Formerly on Board of Examiners of Royal College of Music. Publication: Scale System for Violinists, 1995. Honours: Scholarships from University of Toronto, 1976-81; Banff Centre, 1980. Memberships: Toronto Musicians' Association; Chamber Music America. Hobbies: Collecting ceramics; Carpentry; Gardening.

CALDWELL Sarah, b. 6 Mar 1924, Maryville, USA. Conductor. Opera Impresario; Opera Director. Education: University of Arkansas; Hendrix Colelge; Violin with Richard Burgin, New England Conservatory of Music; Viola with Georges Fourel; Apprenticeship with Boris Goldovsky. Career: Assistant to Boris Coldovsky, Opera Dept, New England Conservatory of Music; Director, Boston University Opera Workshop, 1952-60; Founder; Director, Opera Group, Boston, 1958, which became Opera Company of Boston, 1965; Conducted or Produced the US Premieres of Prokofiev's War and Peace, Nono's Intolleranza, Moses and Aron and Montezuma by Roger Sessions: Producer of the original versions of Boris Godunov and Don Carlos; Guest Conductor, Various orchestras including New York Philharmonic, Pittsburgh Symphony, Boston Symphony and Indianapolis Symphony. Honours: 1st Woman to appear as a Conductor with the Metropolitan Opera, New York, 1976, La Traviata. Address: c/o Opera Company of Boston, PO Box 50, Boston, MA 02112, USA.

CALE Bruce (William), b. 17 Feb 1939, Leura, New South Wales, Australia. Composer; Arranger; Jazz Musician. Career: Founder of the Bruce Cale Quartet and Orchestra. Compositions include: Brass Quintet, 1984; Violin Concerto, 1984, Enigma Soft Yet Bold, 1988; Cello Concerto, 1988; Bridal Veil for harp and orchestra, 1987; Breeze in the Chimes of the Time, 1991; Symphony No 1 Intercession for soprano, tenor, baritone, chorus and orchestra, 1991; Coalesce for piano, 1992; Double Bass Concerto, 1994; Commissions from Frederick Dutton, David Pereira, Gordon Webb, Michael Cleary and Ian Shanahan. Honours include: Fellowship of Australian Composers Prize, 1992; Jean Bogan Prize for Coalesce; Adolf Spivakovsky Prize for Cullenbenbong; Composer Fellowship of Australian Council, 1993 Address: c/o APRA, 1A Eden Street, Crows Nest, NSW 2065, Australia.

CALLEO Riccardo, b. 1947, Endicot, New York, USA. Singer (Tenor). Education: Studies at Yale, the Verdi Conservatory in Milan and at the Curtis Institute; Further study with Ken Neate in Stuttgart. Career: Sang at Bonn Opera, 1974-77, Innsbruck, 1977-79, and at the New York City Opera from 1979; Guest engagements at Cincinnati, Washington (Edgardo, 1983), Houston, Miami, Baltimore and Portland; Nantes Opera, 1989, Dorset Opera, 1991, as Boito's Faust; Other roles include Manrico, Turiddu, Radames, Rodolfo, Nemorino, Percy in Anna Bolena, the Duke of Mantua and Riccardo (Gustavus). Address: c/o New York City Opera, Lincoln Center, New York, NY 10023, USA.

CALLIGARIS Sergio, b. 1941, Rosario, Argentina. Composer; Pianist; Professor of Piano. Career includes: Concerts in Europe, the Americas and South Africa, 1954-; Chair, Piano, Cleveland Institute of Music, OH, USA and California State University, Los Angeles, 1969; Teacher at Conservatories in Italy from 1974; Arts Director of American Academy of the Arts in Europe; Jury member of national and international piano competitions in Italy and abroad; Musical profile as composer and pianist, Società Aquilana dei Concerti, 40th Anniversary Concert Cycle, 1986; His works performed on TV internationally; Commissioned works: Concerto, for strings, Istituzione Sinfonica Abruzzese, 1989 and Danze Sinfoniche, Omaggio a Bellini, Teatro Massimo Bellini, Catania, 100th Anniversary, 2nd Festival Bellinano, 1990; Continuous and regular performances of his works in the major centers and musical institutions worldwide. Compositions include: Published and recorded works: 24 Studi, 1978, 1979, 1980, Il Quaderno Pianistico di Renzo, for piano, 1978, Tre Madrigali, 1979; Published works: Scherzo, 1957, Sonata op 9, for cello and piano, 1978, Passacaglia, 1983, Due Danze Concertanti, 1986, Suite op 28 for solo cello, 1992, Suite da Requiem op 17a, for violin, horn and piano, 1983, Scene Coreografiche, op 30 for 2 Pianos (or Piano 4-Hands) and String Orchestra, 1994, Sonata Fantasia, op 31 for Trumpet and Piano, 1994, and op 32 for Solo Piano, 1994, Preludio, Corale e Finale, op 33 for Accordion, 1994; Clarinet Quartet No 1, op 34, 1995; Strings Quartet No 2, op 35, 1995; Toccatra, Adagio and Fugue, op 36, for strings orchestra, 1995; Double Concerto, op 37, for piano, violin and strings orchestra, 1996; Sonata, op 38, for clarinet and piano, Sonata op 39, for viola and piano, Sonata op 40, for violin and piano, 1997; Recorded works: Ave Maria, 1978, Seconda Suite di Danze Sinfoniche, op 27 for Large Orchestra, 1990, Concerto for Piano and Orchestra, op 29, 1992. Recordings include: Concerts for Union Europeènne Radiodiffusion, 1977, 1985, 1987, 1994; Sergio Calligaris, recital; CD dedicated to him of works by Chopin, Rachmaninoff, Vitalini and Calligaris, 1993; Piano Concerto op 29, Second Suite of Symphonic Dances, op 27 and Sonata Fantasia for piano op 32, CD, 1996. Contributions to: CD Classica, 1995; Piano Time, 1996; Musica, 1996; Amadeus, 1997; Il Giornale della Musica, 1997. Current Management: Nuova Carisch, Sp A. Milan, Italy. Address: Viale Libia 76, 00199 Rome, Italy.

CALM Birgit, b. 1959, Lubeck, Germany. Singer (Mezzo-soprano). Education: Studied in Lubeck and Hamburg. Career: Sang first at the Kiel Opera, then Osnabruck, 1984-85; Appearances at the Bayerische Staatsoper from 1984 have included Humperdinck's Hansel, Alkmene in Die Liebe der Danae and Carlotta in Die schweigsame Frau; Guest appearances in concert & opera in Germany and abroad. Recordings: Sacred music by Dittersdorf, Harmonia Mundi; Third Maid in Elektra, conducted by Sawallisch. Address: c/o Bayerische Staatsoper, Postfach 100148, 8000 Munich 1, Germany.

CAMANI Adrianna, b. 27 Mar 1936, Padua, Italy. Singer (Mezzo-Soprano). Education: Studied at the Padua Conservatory with Sara Sforni Corti. Debut: Naples 1968, as the Nurse in L'Incoronazione di Poppea. Career: Has sung widely in Italy, notably in Genoa, Turin, Trieste, Venice and Naples; Sang in the Scala premiere of Dallapiccola's Ulisse; Major roles include La Cieca in La Gioconda, Ulrica in Un Ballo in Maschera, Eboli in Don Carlos and parts in Madama Butterfly; Andrea Chénier, Francesca da Rimini and Il Quattro Rusteghi. Address: Teatro alla Scala, Via Filodrammatici 2, Milan, Italy.

CAMBRELING Sylvain, b. 2 July 1948, Amiens, France. Conductor. Education: Conservatoire National Superieur de Musique de Paris. Career: Assistant Conductor, Orchestre de Lyon, 1975-81; First Guest Conductor, Ensemble Intercontemporain, Paris, 1976-81; Musical Director, Theatre de la Monnaie Brussels, 1981-92; Guest Conductor: Salzburg and Glyndebourne Festivals, Festival d'Aix-en-Provence, Hamburg Opera, Scala Milan, Paris Opéra, Metropolitan Opera, New York, Grand Theatre at Geneva, Berlin Philharmonic, Munich State Orchestra, Vienna Symphony, Academia Santa Cecilia Rome, Museum Orchestra at Frankfurt, Gurzenich Orchestra Cologne,

Cincinnati Symphony, St Paul Chamber Orchestra, Hallé Orchestra and Royal Liverpool Philharmonic; Conducted The Rake's Progress at the 1989 Glyndebourne Festival; Premiere of Des Glas in Kopf Wird Vom Glas by Eugeniusz Knapik at Antwerp, 1990; Lohengrin and From the House of the Dead at Brussels, 1990; New Production of Simon Boccanegra, 1990-91 season; Director of the Frankfurt Opera from 1993, Wozzeck, From the House of the Dead and Elektra; Engaged for Lucio Silla at the 1997 Salzburg Festival. Recordings: La Clemenza di Tito, Lucio Silla, Louise-Charpentier, Semiramide, The Tales of Hoffmann, Le Sacre du Printemps; Sapho-Gounod; L'Histoire du Soldât, Requiem by Fauré and La Finta Giardiniera. Management: DARSA SA Michael Rainer, Paris; Askonas Ltd, London; Concerto Winderstein Munich; ICM New York. Address: c/o Lies Askonas Ltd, 6 Henrietta Street, London W1, England.

CAMDEN Anthony, b. 26 Apr 1938, London, England. Oboist. m. (1) Diane, div, 1 son, 1 daughter, (2) Lily, 1 daughter. Career: Founder Member, London Virtuosi, 1972-; Principal Oboe, London Symphony Orchestra, 1973-88; Chairman, LSO, Board of Directors, 1975-87; Professor, Director and Provost of Queensland Conservatorium of Music, 1988-93, (Griffith University); Dean of Music, Academy of Performing Arts, 1993-; Honorary Professor, Shanghai Conservatory, China. Recordings: Bach Concerto for Violin and Oboe, with Yehudi Menuhin; 16 Albinoni Oboe Concertos for Naxos with London Virtuosi, Grace Williams Oboe Concerto LSO; Mozart Oboe Quartet, Telemann Concerto for Flute and Oboe, with James Galway; Complete Handel Oboe Concertos; CD of Italian Oboe Concertos; The Art of the Oboe; The Mozart Oboe Concerto. Hobbies: Cricket; Swimming. Address: c/o Academy of Performing Arts, 1 Gloucester Road, Wanchai, Hong Kong.

CAMERON Fiona (Mary), b. 4 Mar 1931, London, England. Musician (Pianist). m. Derek Simpson, 10 Apr 1954, div, 2 sons, 1 daughter. Education: Royal Academy of Music, London, with Harold Craxton; 2 months in Paris with Yvonne Léfébure. Debut: Piano with Derek Simpson, cello, Recital Room, Royal Festival Hall, 24 June 1953. Career: Broadcasting with Derek Simpson, cello, 1955-62, and Carl Pini, violin, 1962-64; Concerts at music clubs and Wigmore Hall until 1971, including Purcell Room with Diana Cummings, piano, Apr 1968; Taught Piano, Royal Academy of Music and Royal Ballet School, 1974-86; Head of Piano, St Paul's Girls' School, London, 1987-92. Recording: Mendelssohn Sonata in D major for cello and piano, with Derek Simpson. Honours: Fellow, Royal Academy of Music, 1983. Memberships: Incorporated Society of Musicians; Royal Society of Musicians. Hobbies: Gardening; Photography; Cooking. Address: Cremona, 19 Willowhayne Avenue, East Preston, Littlehampton, West Sussex BN16 1PE, England.

CAMERON John, b. 20 Mar 1918, Coolamon, New South Wales, Australia. Lecturer; Teacher; Singer (Baritone). m. Patricia Lawrie, 29 Mar 1961, deceased. Education: Sydney Technical College; NSW Conservatorium of Music, Australia. Debut: Covent Garden, as Germont, 1949. Career: Sang with Australian Elizabethan Trust Opera, 1949-74, notably as Mozart's Figaro, Guglielmo and Papageno; Glyndebourne Festival, 1953-54; Soloist with Sadler's Wells Opera in premiere of Benjamin's The Tale of Two Cities, 1957; Dallapiccola's Prigioniero and the premiere of Bennett's The Mines of Sulphur, 1965; New Opera Company, 1970 and British premiere of Goehr's Arden must Die, 1974; Concert appearances at the Festival Hall and on tour to India; Throughout Europe; Sang Punch in the premiere of Birtwistle's Punch and Judy, Aldeburgh Festival, 1968; BBC engagements include series My Songs Go Round The World; Principal Lecturer, Fellow, Royal Northern College of Music, Manchester, 1976-; Numerous television performances and radio recitals. Recordings: Macheath in the Beggar's Opera, conducted by Sargent; King Arthur and Elijah; Claudio in Béatrice et Bénédict; Applausus by Haydn, with Joan Sutherland; Other pressings with Boult, Beecham and Stokowski. Membership: Incorporated Society of Musicians. Hobbies: Reading; Travel. Address: 13 Stamford Road, Altrincham, Cheshire WA14 2JT, England.

CAMERON Patricia, b. 1970, Canada. Singer (Soprano). Education: Studied at the Royal Northern College of Music. Career: Appearances with D'Oyly Carte Opera as Sullivan's Yum Yum, Edith and Josephine; Title role in Donzetti's Mary Stuart in Scottish Opera's Opera-Go-Round; Royal Opera House, Covent Garden, in Die Walküre, The Cunning Little Vixen, Die Frau ohne Schatten, Death in Venice, Turandot and Elektra; Servant in Rigoletto, 1997. Honours include: Arts Council Grant to study at the RNCM. Address: c/o Scottish Opera (Opera-Go-Round), 39 Elmbank Crescent, Glasgow, Scotland, G2 4PT.

CAMILLERI Charles, b. 7 Sept 1931, Hamrun, Malta. Composer. m. 22 Sept 1957, 1 son, 1 daughter. Education: Lyceum, Malta; Toronto University, Canada. Career: Conductor, CBC; Visiting Professor in numerous institutions. Compositions: Missa Mundi; Piano Concerto No 1; Stone Island Within; Piano Trio; Taqsim; Piano Concertos Nos 2 & 3; Organ Concerto; Unum Deum, Cantata; Missa Brevis; 3 operas; Oratorio; Chamber Works. Publications: The Music of The Mediterranean, 1986. Address: 24 Orchard Avenue, Finchley, London, N3 3NL, England.

CAMPANELLA Bruno, b. 6 Jan 1943, Bari, Italy. Conductor. Education: Studied Conducting with Piero Bellugi, Hans Swarowsky and Thomas Schippers; Composition with Dallapiccola. Debut: Spoleto Festival, 1967. Career: From 1971, has conducted nineteenth century Italian at La Scala Milan, elsewhere in Italy and in Europe and North America; Conducted Rossini's Le Comte Ory at Montreal 1989; Don Pasquale at Covent Garden; Piccinni's La Cecchina at the 1990 Martina Franca Festival; Conducted L'Italiana in Algeri at the Teatro Regio Turin, 1992; 1992 at La Scala, Le Comte Ory and Fra Diavolo; Direttore stabile, Teatro Regio, Turin, 1992-; Conducted La Fille du Régiment in San Francisco, 1993; Returned to Covent Garden for Cenerentola in 1994. Recordings: Il Barbiere di Siviglia; La Fille du Régiment; DGG recording of bel canto arias with Kathleen Battle. Address: c/o Patricia Greenan, 19/b Belsize Park, London NW3 7QU, England.

CAMPBELL David, b. 15 Apr 1953, Hemel Hempstead, Hertfordshire, England. Clarinettist. m. 7 Nov 1981, 1 son. Education: Barton Peveril, Hampshire, 1964-71; Royal College of Music, 1971-75; GRSM; ARCM; LRAM. Debut: Wigmore Hall, April 1975. Career: Solo clarinettist, recitalist & chamber music; Has played in 40 countries; Concertos with Royal Philharmonic Orchestra, English Chamber Orchestra, City of London Sinfonia, London Mozart Players, BBC Concert and BBC Scottish; BBC Welsh, BBC Philharmonic, Bournemouth Sinfonietta, Quebec Symphony, Bilbao Symphony and San Sebastian Symphony; Professor and Head of Woodwind, London College of Music. Recordings: Mozart Clarinet Concerto with City of London Sinfonia under Hickox on Pickwick; Steptoe Quintet and Complete Chamber Music for Clarinet by Brahms on Phoenix; Ravel Introduction and Allegro, Virgin Classics; Beethoven and Brahms Trios on Pickwick; Schubert Octet; Messiaen Quartet for the End of Time, Collins. Publications: Regular contributor to Allegro magazine. Honours: Mozart Memorial Prize, 1976; Martin Musical Scholarship, 1976. Memberships: Incorporated Society of Musicians; Clarinet & Saxophone Society. Hobbies: Walking; Bird Watching. Current Management: Janet Hughes, Manager, 76 Cross Oak Road, Berkhamsted, HP4 3HZ, Hertfordshire. Address: 83 Woodwarde Road, Dulwich, London, SE22 8UL, England.

CAMPBELL Ian (David), b. 21 Dec 1945, Brisbane, Queensland, Australia. General Director of Opera and Stage Director. m. Ann Spira, 1 Sept 1985, 2 sons. Education: Voice studies with Godfrey Stirling, Sydney, 1964-72; BA, University of Sydney, 1967. Debut: Australian Opera, Sydney, 1967. Career: Principal Tenor, Australian Opera, 1967-74; Senior Music Officer, Australia Council, 1974-76; General Manager, State Opera of South Australia, 1976-82; Assistant Artistic Administrator, Metropolitan Opera, New York City, USA, 1982-83; General Director, San Diego Opera, California, 1983-; Producer and Host, At The Opera, 1985-97, San Diego Opera Radio Program, 1985-97, both on Radio KFSD-FM, San Diego; New series of San Diego Opera Radio Program on X-BACH-AM, 1997-; Master classes, Music Academy of the West, Santa Barbara, California, 1991-96; Stage Director, La Bohème, 1981, Les contes d'Hoffmann, 1982, State Opera of South Australia. Recording: War and Peace, television, opening of Sydney Opera House, 1973. Honours: Peri Award for services to California opera, 1983; San Diego Press Club Headliner of Year, 1991. Memberships: Associate Fellow, Australian Institute of Management; Kona Kai Club, San Diego; Board Member, Opera America, 1985-93, 1997-. Hobbies: Squash; Golf; Surfing. Address: San Diego Opera, PO Box 988, San Diego, CA 92112-0988, USA.

CAMPBELL Margaret, b. London, England. Author; Lecturer on Musical Subjects. m. Richard Barrington Beare, 2 sons, 1 daughter. Education: Art Scholarship, London. Career: Talks and Interviews on BBC Radio; Cleveland Radio; Voice of America; USA; CBC Canada; BBC & Southern Television; Lectures at Cornell; Oberlin; Indiana; Oklahoma and Southern Methodist Universitites; Manhattan School of Music, New York; Rice University; University of Texas at Austin; University of Southern California USA; Cambridge, Guildford and Bath Universitites; Guildhall School of Music and Drama; Purcell School, England; Festivals at Bergen and Utrecht, Holland; Editor, Journal of British Music Therapy, 1974-90. Publications: Dolmetsch: The Man and His Work, London & USA in 1975; The Great Violinists, London & USA in 1981, Germany 1982; Japan 1983 and China; The Great Cellists, 1988, Chinese; Henry Purcell: Glory of His Age, London 1993, paperback 1995. Contributions: The New Grove Dictionary of Music, 1980. Hobbies: Swimming; Walking; Reading biography. Address: 71 Shrublands Avenue, Berkhamsted, Herts, HP4 3JG, England.

CAMPBELL Richard, b. 1960, England. Violin Player. Career: Member of Fretwork, first London concert at the Wigmore Hall, London, July, 1986; Appearances in the Renaissance and Baroque repertoire in Sweden, France, Belgium, Holland, Germany, Austria, Switzerland and Italy; Radio broadcasts in Sweden, Holland, Germany and Austria; Televised concert on ZDF, Mainz, Tour of Soviet Union Sept 1989; Japan June 1991; Festival engagements in Britain; Repertory includes in Nomines and Fantasias by Tallis, Parsons and Byrd; Dance music by Holborne and Dowland, including Lachrimae; Six-part consorts by Gibbons and William Lawes; Songs and instrumental works by Purcell; Colloborations with vocal group Red Byrd in verse anthems by Byrd and Tomkins, London Cries by Gibbons and Dering; Resurrection Story and Seven Last Words by Schütz; Gave George Benjamin's Upon Silence at the Elizabeth Hall, Oct 1990; Wigmore Hall concerts 1990-91 with music by Lawes, Purcell, Locke, Dowland and Byrd. Recordings: Heart's Ease, late Tudor and Early Stuart; Armada, Courts of Philip II and Elizabeth I; Night's Black Bird, Downland & Byrd; Cries and Fancies, Fantasias, In Nomines and The Cries of London; Go Nightly Cares, Consort songs, dances and In Nomines by Byrd & Dowland; All on Virgin Classics Veritas label. Address: c/o Virgin Classics Ltd, 64 Baker Street, London W1M 1DJ, England.

CAMPION Joanna, b. 1965, England. Singer (Mezzo-soprano). Education: Choral Scholar, Trinity College, Cambridge, England; Royal College of Music, Guildhall School, Britten Pears School and the National Opera Studio. Debut: Ursula in Beatrice et Benedict, for Cambridge Operatic Society. Career: Other roles include title part in Prokofiev's The Duenna, Mrs Page in The Merry Wives of Windsor, Britten's Hermia, and Carmen (British Youth Opera, 1992); Baba the Turk in The Rake's Progress at Glyndebourne, Cenerentola for Welsh National Opera and Rosina for English Touring Opera; Concerts include Messiah on tour with Les Arts Florissants (1994) Mozart's C minor Mass at St Martin in the Fields, Bach's Passions at St John's Smith Square, Dream of Gerontius, Elijah and the Verdi Requiem at the Royal Albert Hall; Mahler Lieder, Elgar Sea Pictures and the Brahms Alto Rhapsody; Birthday celebrations for Yehudi Menuhin at Buckingham Palace, 1996; Engaged as Feodor in Boris Godunov for Welsh National Opera, 1998. Address: Athole Still Ltd, Foresters Hall, 25-27 Westow Street, London SE19 3RY, England.

CAMPORA Giuseppe, b. 30 Sept 1923, Tortona, Italy. Singer (Tenor). Education: Studied in Genoa & Milan. Debut: Bari 1949, as Rodolfo in La Bohème. Career. La Scala Milan from 1951; Debut as Maurizio in Adriana Lecouvreur; Buenos Aires and Rio de Janeiro, 1952; Metropolitan Opera 1954, as Rodolfo; Guest engagements in Verona, Florence, Brussels, Paris, Hamburg, Lisbon, Zurich, Geneva, Monte Carlo, Baltimore and Cincinnati; La Scala 1952 in the premiere of Rocca's Uragano; Bregenz 1964, in Das Land des Lächelns; Italian TV appearances as Radames, Pinkerton and Enzo in La Gioconda. Recordings: La Forza del Destino; La Gioconda; Madama Butterfly; Zaza by Leoncavallo; Scenes from Conchita by Zandonai. Address: Teatro alla Scala, Via Filodrammatici 2, 1-20121 Milan, Italy.

CAMPOS Anisia. Concert Pianist; Pedagogue. m. Remus Tzincoca. Education: Graduate, Ecole Normale de Musique de Paris and Mozarteum Academy of Music, Salzburg, Austria; Studied with K Leimer, Reine Gianoli, Alfred Cortot and Claudio Arrau. Career: Recitals in Brazil, Portugal, Romania, France, Germany, England, Canada and Austria; Soloist with many orchestras including: Brazilian Symphony Orchestra in Rio de Janeiro, Brazil, the Bucharest George Enescu Philharmonic, Radio TV Orchestra in Bucharest, Cluj Philharmonic and Timisoara Philhamronic; Gave the first audition of Enescu's Sonata No 1 in many cities; Collaborated with Remus Tzincoca in the discovery and reconstruction of the original version, in Romanian language, of Bartok's Cantata Profana, 1980s; Full Professor for Piano and Head of Clavier Section (Piano, Organ, Harpsichord), Conservatoire de Musicque of Montreal (State Conservatory); Professor for Interpretation, Ecole Supérieure de Musique, Vincent d'Indy, Montreal and University of Ottawa for several years; Held summer courses at the Orford Arts Centre. Memberships: Co-Founder, President, Canadian Enescu Foundation; Jury Member, Ecole Normale de Musique de Paris, France. Address: 632 Avenue Hervé-Beaudry, Laval, Quebec H7E 2X6, Canada.

CAMUS Raoul F, b. 5 December 1930, Buffalo, New York, USA. Musicologist. Conductor; Education: BA, Queens College, City University of New York, 1952; MA, Columbia University, 1956; PhD, New York University, 1969. Career: Queensborough Community College, City University of New York, 1969-95; Professor Emeritus; Founder and Director, Queens Symphonic Band, 1970-96; Bandmaster, 42nd Infantry (Rainbow) Division Band, NYARNG, 1957-74. Publications: Military Music of the American Revolution, 1976, reprinted 1993; Military Band in the United States Army Prior to 1834, 1969; Early American Wind and Ceremonial Music, 1636-1836, 1989; American Wind & Percussion Music, 1992. Contributor to: Grove's Dictionary of American Music; Grove's Dictionary of Music; Journal of Band Research; Notes; American Music. Honours: NEH Summer

Fellowship, 1978; Research Fellowship, 1990; Research Grant, 1982, 1986. Memberships: Sonneck Society, President, 1981-85, Treasurer, 1977-81; Book Review Editor, 1984-89; American Musicological Society; College Band Directors National Association; World Association for Symphonic Bands and Ensembles; International Military Music Society; Internationale Gesellschaft zur Erforschung und Förderung der Blasmusik. Hobbies: Musical Performance and Research. Address: 14-34 155 Street, Whitestone, NY 11357, USA.

CANARINA John (Baptiste), b. 19 May 1934, New York, USA. Conductor. Education: BS, 1957; MS, 1958, Juilliard School; Conducting with Pierre Monteux and Jean Morel, Piano with Arthur Lloyd & Double Bass with Frederick Zimmermann. Career: Conductor, 7th US Army Symphony Orchestra, 1959-60; Assistant conductor, New York Philharmonic, 1961-62; Music Director, Jacksonville Symphony Orchestra, Florida, 1962-69; Director of Orchestral Activities, Drake University, 1973-; Guest Conductor: Royal Philharmonic; Philharmonia Orchestra; Bournemouth Symphony; BBC Welsh and Scottish Symphonies; Belgian Radio Orchestra; Slovak Radio Symphony Bratislava. Publications: Contributor to Tempo, High Fidelity, Opus and Keynote. Honours: Ford Foundation Grant, 1964; Berkshire Music Centre Fellowship, 1965. Memberships: Conductors Guild; American Symphony Orchestra League; Delius Association of Florida. Hobbies: Films; Baseball; Theatre. Address: 3663 Grand Avenue, Apt 903, Des Moines, IA 50312, USA.

CANAT DE CHIZY Edith, b. 26 Mar 1950, Lyon, France. Composer. Education: Studied with Maurice Ohana and Ivo Malec at the Paris Conservatoire, 1978-84. Career: Director of a conservatory in Paris from 1986. Compositions include: String sextet, 1982; Luceat for 10 solo violins, 1983; Livre d'heures for solo voices and ensemble, 1984; Yell for orchestra, 1985; Kyoran for ensemble, 1987; De noche for orchestra, 1991; Hallel for string trio, 1991; Siloel for strings, 1992; Canciones for 12 solo voices, 1992. Address: c/o SACEM, 225 avenue Charles de Gaulle, 92521 Neuilly sur Seine Cedex, France.

CANELLAKIS Martin, b. 10 Jan 1942, Tientsin, China. Conductor; Music Director; Professor. m. Sheryl Swint, 2 Jan 1968, 1 s, 1 d. Education: Lycée Carnot, Paris, France, 1956-60; Ecole Normale de Musique (Piano Prize), 1956-60; Bachelor and Master of Science in Piano, Juilliard School of Music, USA, 1965; Professional Diploma, Columbia University Teachers College, 1967; Doctoral studies, Conducting Program, Peabody Conservatory of Music, 1966-67; Postgraduate Diploma in Conducting, Mannes College of Music, 1968. Debut: Alice Tully Hall, Lincoln Center, New York City, 1978. Career: Founder and Conductor of Peabody Chamber Orchestra, 1966-67; Guest Conductor, Baltimore Symphony in Rockefeller Projects for American Music, 1967; Music Director of Brooklyn Symphony Orchestra, 1968-77, Queensborough Orchestra, 1971-, Queens College Orchestral Society, 1975-85, Westchester Symphony Orchestra, 1982-91; Guest Conductor of Southern Vermont Music Festival, 1978 and 1979, Jerusalem Symphony Orchestra, 1978, Long Island String Festival, 1988; Professor of Music at City University of New York, 1971-. Recording: Sonnet for Orchestra by Max Stern with the Jerusalem Symphony Orchestra, CD, 1995. Honours include: Conducting Fellowships; Aspen Music Festival, 1966, 1968, 1969; Meadow Brook Music Festival, 1965; National Orchestral Association, 1970-71; Piano Assistantship at PeabodyConservatory, 1966; Perera Award, Mannes College of Music, 1968; Laureate Conductor, Westchester Symphony Orchestra, 1991-. Address: 452 Riverside Drive, New York, NY 10027, USA.

CANGALOVIC Miroslav, b. 3 Mar 1921, Glamoc, Yugoslavia. Singer (Bass). Education: Studied in Belgrade. Debut: Belgrade 1946, as Pimen in Boris Godunov. Career: Sang in Belgrade and elsewhere in Yugoslavia as Philip II, Mephistopheles; Leporello, Sarastro, Kecal and in The Bartered Bride; Guest appearances in Basel, Zurich and Geneva as Boris, Dosifey and Prince Igor; Edinburgh Festival, 1962 with the Belgrade Opera and further appearances at Vienna, Leipzig, Berlin and Florence; Other roles have included Konchak and Galitzky in Prince Igor; Gremin and Mefistofele. Recordings: Boris Godunov, Khovanshchina, Prince Igor, Eugene Onegin, The Snow Maiden and Don Quichotte. Address: Narodno Pozoriste, Francuska 3, 11000 Belgrade, Serbia.

CANIHAC Jean-Pierre, b. 16 Apr 1947, Toulouse, France. Cornet Player. m. Michele Chauzy, 17 Aug 1968, 1 son, 1 daughter. Education: Baccalaureat, 1966; Conservatoire de Toulouse; Conservatoire de Versailles; Conservatoire National Superieur de Musique, Paris. Career: Founder, Saqueboutiers de Toulouse; Professor, CNR, Toulouse; Professor, Conservatoire National Superior de Musique, Lyon; Member of Hesperion XX, La Grande Ecurie et la Chambre du Roy, La Chapelle Royale, Clemencic Consort. Recordings: L'Art de Cornet, Arion; Schütz, Symphoniae Sacrae, Erato; 7 Last Words of Christ, H Mundi; Siècle d'or â Venise, Adda; Six Marian Vespers of Monteverdi, Malgoire; and other music conducted by Parrott, Herreweghe and Corboz. Contributions: Brass Bulletin; Blue Brass. Honours: 1st Prize, Conservatoire de Toulouse, 1966; 1st prize, Conservatoire de Versailles, 1968; 1st prize Conservatoire National Superieur, Paris, 1970. Address: 8 rue Maran, 31400 Toulouse, France.

CANIN Stuart V, b. 5 Apr 1926, New York City, USA. Violinist; Educator. m. Virginia Yarkin, 8 June 1952, 2 sons. Education: Juilliard School of Music, 1946-49. Career: Professor, Violin, State University of Iowa, 1953-60, Oberlin Conservatory of Music, 1960-66; Concertmaster, Chamber Symphony of Philadelphia, 1966-68; Concertmaster, San Francisco Symphony, 1970-80; Concertmaster, San Francisco Opera, 1969-72; Artist Faculty, Aspen Colorado Music Festival, 1960-63; Artist Faculty, Music Academy of the West, Santa Barbara, 1983-; Senior Visiting Lecturer, University of California, Santa Barbara, 1983-; Concertmaster, Casals Festival, San Juan, Puerto Rico, 1974-75, Mostly Mozart Festival, New York City, 1980. Honours: 1st Prize, Paganini International Violin competition, Genoa, 1959; Fulbright Professor to Freiburg, Germany Staatliche Hochschule für Musik, 1956-57. Address: 1302 Holmby Avenue, Los Angeles, CA 90024, USA.

CANINO Bruno, b. 30 Dec 1935, Naples, Italy. Pianist; Composer. Education: Studied at the Milan Conservatory with Calace and Bettinelli. Career: Piano Duo partner from 1953 with Antonio Ballista; Career as soloist from 1956, notably in works by Bussotti, Donatoni and Castiglioni; Professor of Music at the Milan Conservatory from 1961; Played in premieres of Rapsodia, by Davide Anzaghi, 1984; Played Ode by Castiglioni, 1966, Tableaux Vivants by Bussoti, 1964, Concerto for 2 Pianos and Orchestra by Berio, 1973; Member of the Trio di Milano; Accompanist to instrumentalists and singers including Cathy Berberian until 1983. Compositions include: Chamber and Instrumental Music. Honours: Prizes at Piano Competitions of Bolzano and Darmstadt, 1956-60. Address: Conservatorio Giuseppe Verdi, Via Conservatorio 12, 20122 Milan, Italy.

CANN Claire and Antoinette, twins, b. 1963, England. Duo-Pianists. Education: Studied with Phyllis Sellick at the Royal College of Music, first class honours in solo and duo piano performance. Debut: First major concert aged 13. Career: Many appearances in Europe, Canada and USA; New Zealand; Far East; Extensive tours of Britain, including concerts at the Festival Hall, London premiere of the Max Bruch Concerto, Fairfield Hall, St David's Hall Cardiff; Glasgow Royal Concert Hall; London orchestras include the Philharmonic; Royal Philharmonic; BBC Concert; Mozart Players and Philomusica; Television engagements in Britain; Japan; USA; New Zealand; Season 1992-93 with three concerts at the Festival Hall with the LPO; Gala opening of the Ohji Concert Hall Tokyo; Recital at St John's Smith Square in Brahms, Lutoslawski, Ravel and Liszt. Recordings: Albums titled Gemini; La Danse; Rhapsody. Honours: Park Lane Group Series Prize; Countess of Munster Trust Awards; RCM President's Rose Bowl. Address: Gwen Howell Management, 7 Gurlings Close, Haverhill, Suffolk, CB9 OEG, England.

CANNAN Phyllis, b. 1945, Paisley, Scotland. Singer (Soprano). Career: Sang as soprano with most major companies in Britain; Soprano repertoire from 1983; First Major role in Vivaldi's Griselda, Buxton Festival 1983; Sang Gluck's Alceste at the Elizabeth Hall; Kostelnicka in Jenufa and Katerina in The Greek Passion for Welsh National Opera; Santuzza, Tosca, Rusalka and Goneril, in the British premiere of Reimann's Lear, for English National Opera; Appearances in Der Rosenkavalier and King Priam at Covent Garden; Senta in Der fliegende Holländer at the 1987 Hong Kong Festival; Gerhilde in Die Walküre at the 1989 Promenade Concerts; Concert engagements include Britten's War Requiem in Belgium; Sang the Overseer in Elektra at the First Night of the 1993 London Proms. Address: c/o Lies Askonas Ltd, 6 Henrietta Street, London WC2, England.

CANNE MEIJER Cora, b. 11 Aug 1929, Amsterdam, The Netherlands. Singer (Mezzo-Soprano); Coach; Voice Teacher. Education: Amsterdam Conservatory with Jan Keizer & Re Koster; Studied further with Noemie Perugia in Paris and Alfred Jerger in Vienna. Debut: With Netherlands Opera, Amsterdam, 1951. Career: Glyndebourne, 1956, as Cherubino and in Die Zauberflöte and Cenerentola; Salzburg, 1959, in Haydn's Il Mondo della Luna; Zurich Opera, 1960-62; Regular appearances at the Holland Festival; Has sang at many major opera houses including, Vienna, Frankfurt, Brussels, Munich and Hamburg; Performed over 65 roles including: Dorabella, Isolier, Rosina, Isabella, Octavian, Marina in Boris Godunov and Carmen; In world premiere of Milhaud's La Mère Coupable, Geneva, 1966; Was also widely demanded as Lied, concert & Oratorio singer, repertory including works by Stravinsky and Berlioz, Bach's St Matthew Passion, Verdi's Requiem; Appeared on TV as Carmen and Rosina; For over 20 years has taught at Amsterdam Sweelinck Conservatorium and giving master classes at home and abroad; Produced and Directed open air production of Mozart's Zauberflöte, summer 1989; Frequent Jury Member, International vocal competitions. Recordings: Les Noces by Stravinsky; Der Tag des Gerichts by Telemann; Comte Ory from Glyndebourne; Spanish Folksongs; French and Spanish Songs; Diary of one who Disappeared by Janacek. Address: Weteringstraat 48, 1017 SP Amsterdam, The Netherlands.

CANNON Philip, b. 21 Dec 1929, Paris, France. Composer. m. Jacqueline Laidlaw, 1950, 1 daughter. Education: Dartington Hall Devon; Royal College of Music, London. Career: Lecturer in Music, Sydney University, 1958-60; Professor of Composition, Royal College of Music, 1960-. Compositions: 3 Operas, 2 Symphonies, including Son of Man commissioned by the BBC to mark Britain's entry to the EC; Choral works, Lord of Light, large scale requiem; Chamber Music, all broadcast & performed internationally. Recordings: Commissions: BBC; RF; BBCTV; Three Choirs Festival; Gulbenkian Foundation; Chromatica USA. Publications: Biographical & critical articles in various magazines. Honours: Grand Prix; Critics Prize, Paris, 1965; FRCM, 1970; Te Deum, Commissioned by & dedicated to HM The Queen, 1975. Memberships: RMA; RPS; ISM; NFMS; PRS; MCPS. Hobbies: Meeting People; Philosophy; Art. Address: 25 Andsell Street, London, W8 5BN, England.

CANONICI Corrado, b. 26 Mar 1961, Ancona, Italy. Double Bass Soloist. Education: Studied Double Bass and Composition, Rossini Conservatory, Pesaro; Double Bass masterclasses with Franco Petracchi and Gary Karr; Composition masterclasses with Hans Werner Henze and Brian Ferneyhough. Career: Recitals in Italy, UK, Ireland, USA, Luxembourg, Portugal, Spain, Switzerland, Sweden, Germany, Romania; Chamber music with Ensemble Modern, Cambridge New Music Players, others; Appearances, Italian Radio, Romanian Television, German Radio, French Radio, USA Radio in Los Angeles, Russian National Television in short film of Dec 1996 US tour; Masterclasses, New York University, Harvard University, Boston University, universities in Los Angeles and Manhattan School of Music, New York; Double bass version of solo work by Stockhausen dedicated to Canonici and premiered in London, 4 Oct 1997; Artistic Director, Musica 2000 Festival, Italy. Recordings: Contrabass, including world premiere recording of Luciano Berio's solo bass piece, 1995. Contribution to: New Notes magazine, 1997. Honours: Xenakis Award, Paris, 1992; Darmstadt Award, 1992; International New Music Consortium Award, 1993, 1997; Performer in Residence, New York University, 1996. Membership: Musicians Union. Hobby: Reading. Current Management: Lyons Management. Address: 35 Yerbury Road, London N19 4RN, England.

CANONICI Luca, b. 1961, Tuscany, Italy. Singer (Tenor). Education: Studied in Rome with Tito Gobbi and at Pesaro. Debut: Teatro Sociale Mantua, 1986, as the Duke of Mantua. Career: Sang the Duke in Rome, 1986; Appearances in various Italian theatres, including Bologna and Florence, notably in the Italian premiere of Monteverdi's Ulisse in the version by Henze; Appeared as Rodolfo in the 1987 film version of La Bohème; Other roles include Nemorino and Ernesto, Fernando in Donizetti's Il Furioso all isola di San Domingo; Frederico in L'Arlesiana; Almaviva and Werther; Bergamo 1990, in Mayr's La rose bianca e la rosa rossa; Season 1991 as Fenton in Falstaff at Bonn; Pilade in Rossini's Ermione at Rome; Leading role in La Cambiale di Matrimonio at the Pesaro Festival; Sang Max in Leoncavallo's La Reginetta della Rose, Palermo, 1992; Idreno in Semiramide at Zurich and Tonio in La Fille du Régiment at Rome. Address: c/o Teatro dell'Opera, Piazza B Gigli 8, 00184, Rome, Italy.

CANTELO April, b. 2 Apr 1928, Purbrook, Hampshire, England. Singer (Soprano); Singing Coach; Teacher; Adjudicator. Education: Studied at London with Julian Kimbell and at Dartington with Imogen Holst. Debut: Sang Barbarina in Figaro and Echo in Ariande auf Naxos with the Glyndebourne Company at Edinburgh, 1950. Career: Glyndebourne Festivals, 1953, 1963, as Blondchen and Marzelline; English Opera Group, 1960-70, notably as Helena in the premiere of a Midsummer Night's Dream and as Emmeline in Purcell's King Arthur; At Sadler's Wells Theatre, 1962-66, sang in the premieres of Williamson's Our Man in Havana and The Violins of St Jacques; British premieres of Henze's Boulevard Solitude and Weill's Aufstieg und Fall der Stadt Mahogonny; Also created roles in Williamson's The Happy Prince, 1965, and Julius Cesar Jones, 1966; Directed Purcell's The Fairy Queen in New Zealand, 1972; Frequent concert appearances. Recordings: The Indian Queen; Albert Herring and The Little Sweep; Beatrice et Bénédict; 18th Century Shakespeare Songs; Berlioz Irelande; Haydn Masses with St Johns College Choir, Cambridge. Memberships: Equity; ISM; AOTOS. Address: 1 The Coalyard, All Saints Lane, Sutton Courtenay, Oxon OX14 4AG, England.

CANTRELL Derrick (Edward), b. 2 June 1926, Sheffield, England. Cathedral Organist. m. Nancy Georgina Bland, 4 children. Education: MA; BMus, Oxford University; FRCO. Career: Organist, Manchester Cathedral, 1962-77; Lecturer, Royal Northern College of Music. Recordings: Manchester Cathedral Organ. Honours: Recipient of Sawyer & Limpus Prizes, Royal

College of Organists. Address: 36 Parsonage Road, Manchester, M20 9PQ, England.

CAPDEVILLE Constance, b. 16 Mar 1937, Barcelona, Spain. Composer. Education: Studied at the Lisbon Conservatory. Career: Teacher in Lisbon, with performances of her music at Royan, Warsaw and Zagreb festivals. Compositions include: Music theatre pieces (Uma hora com Igor Stravinsky, 1980); Ballets, scenic and film music; Et maintenant, écoute la lumière for orchestra, 1990; Chamber and solo instrumental music; Multi-media music theatre works, including Avec Picasso, ce matin, 1984, and Um quadrado em rador de Simbad, 1986. Address: c/o SGAE, Fernando VI 4, Apartado 484, 28080 Madrid 4, Spain.

CAPECCHI Renato, b. 6 Nov 1923, Cairo, Egypt. Singer (Baritone); Producer. Education: Studied with Ubaldo Carrozzi in Milan. Debut: Italian Radio 1948. Career: Stage debut 1949, as Amonasro at Reggio Emilia; Sang in the premiere of Ghedini's Billy Budd, 1949 at Venice; La Scala Milan from 1950, debut in the premiere of Mailipiero's Allegra Brigata; Metropolitan Opera debut, 1951, as Germont; Returned to New York 1975; Sang at Milan in the premieres of Tosatti's Guidizio Universale, Napoli's Un Curioso accidente, Chailly's Domanda di matrimonio and Malipiero's La Donna e Mobile; Florence 1953, in the stage premiere of Prokofiev's War and Peace; Covent Garden debut 1962, as Melitone in La Forza del Destino; Holland Festival 1970, in Haydn's La Fedeltà Premiata; Schönbrunn, Vienna, in Il Barbiere di Siviglia by Paisiello, 1976; Glyndebourne Festival 1977, 1980, as Falstaff; Sang at Verona Arena, 1953-83; Genoa Opera as Dulcamara, 1989; Three Week Workshop, Australian Opera, 1989; Production, Il Barbiere di Siviglia; Sang Geronte in Manon Lescaut at Modena, 1990; Guest appearances at Drottningholm; Moscow; the Paris Opéra, Strasbourg, Berlin, Munich, Stuttgart, Montreal and Tel Aviv; Sang Mozart's Don Alfonso at the Metropolitan, 1991; Gianni Schicchi at Toronto, 1996. Recordings: L'Elisir d'Amore, La Forza del Destino, I Puritani; Rigoletto; Don Pasquale; Gianni Schicchi; Le Nozze di Figaro; Il Barbiere di Siviglia; La Cenerentola, Deutsche Grammophon; La Bohème. Address: Teatro Carlo Felice, 1-16100 Genoa, Italy.

CAPLAT Moran, b. 1 Oct 1916, Herne Bay, Kent, England. General Administrator. m. Diane Downton, 29 May 1943, 1 son, 2 daughters. Education: Royal Academy of Dramatic Art. Career: Actor; Yachtsman; Naval Officer; Opera Administrator; General Administrator, Glyndebourne, 1949-81. Publication: Dinghies to Divas, autobiography, 1985. Contributions to: Glyndebourne Programme Book; Sundry articles in professional journals and magazines. Honour: Commander of the British Empire, 1968. Hobbies: Sailing; Gardening; Conviviality. Address: Mermaid Cottage, 6 Church Road, Newick, Lewes, East Sussex, England.

CAPOBIANCO Tito, b. 28 Aug 1931, La Plata, Argentina. Stage Director; Producer; Set & Lighting Designer; Educator. m. Elena Denda, 2 sons. Career: Producer & Technical Director, 1964, Producing Director, Technical Director and Set Designer, 1958, Teatro Colon, Buenos Aires; Artistic Director of Santiago Opera Festival; Stage Director of National Ballet of Chile; Professor of Acting and Interpretation at University of Chile, 1956; Stage Director & Lighting Designer of SODRE National Ballet & Opera; Stage Director of SODRE, Montevideo, Uruguay 1957; Artistic Director of Teatro Argentino; Producing Director & Stage Director of National Drama Company of Buenos Aires, 1959; Artistic Director, Cincinnati Opera and Summer Festival; Director of Opera Productions throughout the USA, 1961-65; Producer & Director, International Opera Festival, Mexico City, 1963-65; Founder & General Director of American Opera Centre, Juilliard School of Music, NY 1968-71; Created Opera Department of College of Performing Arts, Philadelphia, 1972; Artistic Director, 1975; General Director 1977; Created Verdi Festival 1978; Young American Conductor's Programme 1980; San Diego Opera; Vice-President & General Director, Pittsburgh Opera, 1983; Professor, Opera Department, Yale University 1983. Compositions: Libretto of Zapata. Publications: The Merry Widow, Franz Lehar, Translation. Honours: Cavaliere della Republica, Italy, 1979; Officier dans l'Ordre des Arts et Lettres, France, 1984; Doctor of Music, Duquesne University, 1988; Doctor of Letters, Indiana University of Pennsylvania, 1988; Doctor of Humane Letters, La Roche College, 1989. Hobbies: Reading; Sports. Address: Pittsburgh Opera, 711 Penn Avenue, Pittsburgh, PA 15222, USA.

CAPOIANU Dumitru, b. 19 Oct 1929, Bucharest, Romania. Composer. Education: Studied at the Bucharest Conservatory 1941-53. Career: Manager of the George Enescu Philharmonic Orchestra, 1959-73. Compositions: Wind Quintet, 1950; Viola Sonata, 1952; 2 Suites for orchestra, 1953, 1954; 2 String Quartets, 1954, 1959; Divertisement for string orchestra and 2 clarinets, 1956; Violin concerto 1957; Cosmos 60, ballet scene 1960; Cinematographic Variations for Orchestra, 1965; Steel, ballet 1965; String Trio 1968; Curte domneasca, The Princely Courtyard, spectacle of sound and light, 1969; Moto perpetuo for

violin & orchestra, 1972; Chemari 77 for orchestra; Muzica de ambianta for orchestra 1980; Valses ignobles et sentimentales du tout for mezzo and strings, 1986; Two musicals, Dragostei Printesei, 1982 and Censareasa 1984; Choral Music. Address: Association of Romanian Composers, Bucharest, Romania.

CAPOLONGO Paul, b. 17 Mar 1940, Algiers, Algeria. (French citizen). Conductor. Education: Studied at the Algiers and Paris Conservatories. Career: Director of the Quito Symphony, 1963-67, and Director of the Quito Conservatory, 1963-66; Assistant to Leonard Bernstein at the New York Philharmonic, 1967-68, and conductor of Rhine Symphony Orchestra at Mulhouse, 1975-85. Honours include: Winner of the 1967 Mitropoulos Competition. Address: c/o Orchestre Symphonique du Rhin-Mulhouse, 38 Passage du Théâtre, F-68100 Mulhouse, France.

CAPPELLETTI Andrea, b. 21 May 1961, Italy. Violinist. Education: Diploma cum laude, Naples Conservatory, Parallel course, Liceo Linguistico. Career: 1st Violin, ECYO, 1977; Debut, Israel, 1984; Debut, RFH, 1986; Queen Elizabeth Hall, 1988; Regular appearances with leading orchestras, Italy; France; Germany; Scandinavia; Regular appearances in Europe; Australia; USA; Appointed Art Director, United Nations Concerts for the Disabled, 1990. Recordings: Exclusive contract, Koch International with 5 Mozart violin concertos, Italian Baroque Concerti, Respighi Concerti and Tartini sonatas for violin solo; For UNICEF Haydn Concerti. Honours: Vittorio Veneto, 1975; Kiefer Balitzel, 1977-78; Fordergemeinschaft, 1986. Hobbies: Archery; Swimming. Current Management: Robert Kirp Corporation. Address: Via della Ripa 77, 50075 Montespertoli, Ripa F1, Italy.

CAPPUCCILLI Piero, b. 9 Nov 1929, Triest, Italy. Singer (Baritone). Education: Studied in Trieste with Luciana Doaggio. Debut: Teatro Nuovo Milan 1957, as Tonio in Pagliacci; Metropolitan Opera debut 1960, as Germont; La Scala Milan from 1964, debut as Ashton in Lucia di Lammermoor; Covent Garden debut 1967, as Germont; Returned to London as Iago, Renato in Un Ballo in Maschera and Simon Boccanegra, with the company of La Scala, 1976; Verona Arena 1968, 1970, as Posa in Don Calos and as Luna in Il Trovatore; Chicago Lyric Opera 1969, in I Due Foscari; Salzburg Festival, 1975-77, as Posa and Boccanegra; Paris Opera 1978; Arena di Verona, 1988, 1989, Amonasro and Nabucco; Stuttgart Opera, 1990, as Scarpia; Sang Simon Boccanegra at Barcelona, 1990; Luciano Pavarotti 30th Anniversay Gala, Reggio Emilia, 1991; Other roles include Nabucco; Macbeth; Rigoletto and Escamillo. Recordings: Lucia di Lammermoor, La Wally, I Puritani, Cavalleria Rusticana, Aida, Don Carlos, Il Pirata, Macbeth, Nabucco and Rigoletto, (Deutsche Grammophon); I Masnadieri, I Due Foscari. Address: SA Gorlinsky Ltd, 33 Dover Street, London, W1X 4NJ, England.

CAPRIOLI Alberto, b. 16 Nov 1956, Bologna, Italy. Composer; Conductor; Musicologist. Education: Studied Composition with F Margola, C Togni (Parma Conservatory), B Schaeffer (Salzburg Mozarteum); Conducting with O Suitner, Vienna Academy of Music; Humanities with E Raimondi, C Ginzburg; U Eco (Bologna University). Career: Guest Conductor, several European orchestras and new music festivals; Professor, Bologna Conservatory of Music. Compositions: Frammenti dal diario, piano, 1974; Abendlied, soprano and orchestra, 1977; Sonata in memorian Alban Berg, piano, 1982; Canto, orchestra, 1983; Sonetti di Shakespeare, child reciter and 10 instruments, 1983; Trio, piano, violin and cello, 1984; Del celeste confine, string quartet, 1985; Serenade per Francesca, 6 players, 1985; A la dolce ombra, piano trio, 1985; Dialogue, solo contrabass and 2 string quartets, 1986; Per lo dolce silentio de la notte, piano and computer music tape, 1987; Due Notturni d'oblio, 10 players, 1988; Symphoniae I, II, III, violin, 1988-89; Il vostro pianto aurora o luna, 5 players, 1989; Intermedio I, flute and computer music tape, 1989; Vor dem singenden Oden, quintet, 1990; Kyrie per Dina Campana, soli, choir and 29 instruments, 1991; John Cage Variations, quintet, 1991; A quinze and, cello, 1992; Anges, G-flute, viola and harp; Folâtre (Notturno di rosa), 2 guitars, 1993; L'ascesa degli angeli ribelli, reciter and 13 players, 1994; Dittico baciato, choir and orchestra, 1994. Recordings: 3 CDs. Publications include: Philarmonia, Guida alle capitali dell'Europa musicale, 1993; L'Italia nell'Europa Romantica, 1993. Contributions to: Comparatistica, 1989-93; Shakespeare Yearbook, 1994; Others. Membership: Board of Directors, Italian Society for Comparative Literature, Florence. Address: D Guglielmini 7, I-40137 Bologna, Italy.

CAPRONI Bruno, b. 1960, England. Singer, Baritone. Education: Studied at the Royal Northern College of Music and the National Opera Studio. Career: Sang in Menotti's The Consul, Madame Butterfly and Rigoletto while in college; Appearances with Opera Northern Ireland, Dublin Grand Opera, Wexford and Glyndebourne festivals; Royal Opera House Covent Garden from 1988 in Madame Butterfly; Don Carlos, Rigoletto, Der Freischütz, Otello, Die Meistersinger and Turandot; Sang Ezio in Verdi's Attila in a concert performance conducted by Edward Downes; Other roles include Marcello in La Bohème; Belcore; Ottokar in Der

Freischütz; Verdi's Germont, Posa and Amonasro; Sang Schaunard in La Bohème at Covent Garden, 1996. Honours: Vaughan Williams; Frederick Cox award, 1987; Ricordi Prize for Opera 1988. Address: c/o Harrison Parrott Ltd, 12 Penzance Place, London W11 4PA, England.

CARACCIOLO Franco, b. 29 Mar 1920, Bari, Italy. Conductor. Education: Studied at the Naples and Rome Conservatories. Career: Has conducted widely in Italy from 1944, leading the Alessandro Scarlatti Orchestra of Naples, 1949-64; Conducted the orchestra of RAI (Italian Radio) at Milan, 1964-71, before returning to Naples, 1971-87; Has revived many major works of the Baroque repertory, including Handel's Dettingen Te Deum. Address: c/o Orchestre della RAI, Via Marconi 5, 80125 Naples, Italy.

CARBONARI Virgilio, b. 1927, Italy. Singer (Bass). Career: Sang in Bergamo and Brussels from 1956, La Scala Milan from 1959, notably in operas by Verdi, Puccini, Giordano and Mascagni; Verona Arena, 1969-69, as Marullo in Rigoletto and Alcindoro in La Bohème; Other appearances in Parma, Genoa, Bologna, Barcelona and Vienna; Other roles include Melitone (Forza del Destino), Mesner (Tosca) and Benoit (Bohème). Recordings include: Operas by Verdi on Decca. Address: c/o Arena di Verona, Piazza Bra 28, 37121 Verona, Italy.

CARD June, b. 10 Apr 1942, Dunkirk, New York, USA. Singer, (Soprano). Education: Studied at Mannes College, New York. Career: Sang on Broadway from 1959, with New York City Opera from 1963; European engagements at Munich, two titles of Kammersangerin from Frankfurt and Munich; Gartnerplatzheater, from 1967; Member of the Frankfurt Opera 1969-; Appearances in Hamburg, London, Paris, Barcelona, Vienna, Cologne, Met New York, San Carlo (Naples); Roles include Violetta, Jenufa, Madama Butterfly, Minnie in La Fanciulla del West and Marie in Die Soldaten by Zimmermann; Has sang Janacek's Vixen, Katya and Emilia Marty, Magda in La Rondine, and roles in Schreker's Die Gezeichneten, Henze's Der Junge Lord and Bassarids and The Rake's Progress; Sieglinde and Katerina Ismailova; Frankfurt, 1988 in Poulenc's La Voix Humaine; Holland Festival in The Orestia by Milhaud; Produced La Clemenza di Tito at Giessen, 1988; Fidelio, in France. Recordings: Traviata, Gezeichneten. Current Management: Agentur Schulz, PO 802, Martiustrasse 3, Munich, Germany. Address: Arabellastrasse 5-1411, 81925 Munich, Germany.

CARDEN Joan (Maralyn), b. 9 Oct 1937, Richmond, Victoria, Australia. Opera and Concert Singer. m. W Coyne, 31 Aug 1962, divorced 1980, 2 daughters. Education: Trinity College of Music, London, Piano; Theory of Music Voice; Thea Phillips, Melbourne; Henry Portnoj, Melbourne; Vida Harford, London, 1961-91; London Opera Centre, 1967. Debut: New Opera Company in world premiere of Malcolm Williamson's Our Man in Havana, Sadler's Wells Theatre, 1963. Career: Australian Opera, 1971; Glyndebourne Opera, 1977; Scottish Opera, 1977 and Houston Grand Opera, 1977 as Vitellia in Clemenza di Tito and the Marschallin in Der Rosenkavalier; Elisabetta, Maria Stuarda, Sydney, 1992; Médée, 1995; Tosca, Victoria State Opera, 1995; Metropolitan Opera Tour, 1978; Miami Opera, 1981; Kennedy Center, Washington, 1980; Singapore Festival, 1983; Adelaide Festival, 1984; Other roles include Liu, Fiordiligi, Mozart's Countess, Donna Elvira, Pamina, Violetta, Gilda, Marguerite, Natasha in War and Peace and Leonora (La Forza del Destino), Sydney, 1988; Sang Gounod's Marguerite at Brisbane, 1991; The Marschallin 1991; Wagner's Eva at Melbourne in 1994; Sang Liu and Cherubini's Médée for the Australian Opera, 1995. Recordings: Joan Carden Sings Mozart; Stars of Australian Opera Sing Verdi; Music for Australia Day ABC, CD; Video; Mozart Selection, T.A.O.; La Traviata, T.A.O., Video. Honours: Stuyvesant Scholar, London Opera Centre, 1967; A.O. 1988, for services to opera; OBE, for services to Opera, 1980; Dame Joan Hammond Award, 1987. Current Management: J Eddy, Opera; Classical Concert, Non-Australasian Opera; Avere Artists Management, 26 Oxley Drive, Bowral, NSW 2576, Australia. Address: The Australian Opera, PO Box 291, Strawberry Hills, NSW 2012, Australia.

CARDI Mauro, b. 22 July 1955, Rome, Italy. Composer; Teacher; Conservatory of Music. Education: Diploma Composition, Diploma, Choral Music & Direction, Rome Conservatory of Music; Diploma, Postgraduate composition studies, National Academy, St Cecilia. Career: Various Broadcasts, own works, Italy, France, Halland, Belgium, East Germany, Argentina. Compositions: Melos; Soprano & Orchestra; Trama; Violin; Les Masques; Flute; Viola; Guitar; String Quartet; Filigrana; 8 performers; Promenade, 7 performers; Bianco, guitar; Texture, 2 guitars; Silete Venti, guitar 8 performers; RIBES female voice; Trio, le clair sillage. Recordings: EdiPan; RCA; Broadcasts. Contributions: Many essays on contemporary music published, newspapers, magazines, reviews. Honours: Prizes, International Composition Competitions: V Bucchi Prize, 1982; Gaudeamus Prize, 1984; Selection, Gaudeamus Music Week, 1984, 1985, 1986. Memberships: Nuova Consonanza Association, Rome.

Hobbies: Photography; Computers. Address: Via Latisana 8. 00177 Rome, Italy.

CARDY Patrick (Robert Thomas), b. 22 Aug 1953, Toronto, Ontario, Canada. Composer; Professor of Music. Education: BMus, Honours, Theory and Composition, University of Western Ontario, 1975; MMA in Composition, 1976, DMus, Composition, 1981, McGill University. Career: Professor, School for Studies in Art and Culture, Carleton University, Ottawa, 1977-; 9 Ontario Arts Council Commissions, 9 Canada Council Commissions, 4 Canadian Broadcasting Corporation commission, 11 private commissions, 2 canada Council Doctoral Fellowships, 3 Canada Council Grants; Performances in Canada, USA and Europe. Compositions include: Golden Days, Silver Nights, 1977; Vox Humana, 1977; Jig, 1984; Mirages, 1984; Outremer: The Land Beyond the Sea, 1985; Mimesis, 1987; Qilakitsoq: The Sky Hangs Low, 1988; Tango!, 1989; Tombeau, 1989; The Little Mermaid, 1990; Avalon, 1991; Serenade, 1992; Chaconne, 1992; Autumn, 1992; "Dulce et decorum est...", 1993; Danses folles et amoureuses, 1993; Et in Arcadia ego, 1994; Fhir a Bhata: The Boatman, 1994; Silver and Shadow, 1994; Te Deum, 1995; Dreams of the Sídhe, 1995; La Folia, 1996; Sans Souci, 1996; Bonavista, 1997; The Return of the Hero, 1997. Recordings include: Virelai, CD; Numerous on major labels. Address: 29 Morgan's Grant Way, Kanata, Ontario K2K 2G2, Canada.

CAREWE John (Maurice Foxall), b. 24 Jan 1933, Derby, England. Conductor. 2 daughters. Education: Guildhall School of Music and Drama, London; Conservatoire National, Paris. Career: Founded Music Today, New Music Ensemble, 1958; Principal Conductor, BBC Welsh Orchestra, 1966-71; Musical Director, Principal Conductor, Brighton Philharmonic Society, 1974-87; Principal Conductor, Fires of London, 1980-94; General Music Director of the Opera and the Robert Schumann Philharmonic, Chemnitz, 1993-96. Recordings: Stravinsky, Histoire du Soldât; Milhaud, Création du Monde; Bennett, Calendar; Maxwell Davies, Leopardi Fragments; Bedford, Music for Albion Moonlight; Debussy, Ibéria; Falla, Interlude and Dance, La Vida Breve; Bridge, Enter Spring and Oration; Colin Matthews, Landscape and Cello Concerto; Muller-Siemens, Under Neon Light I; Leyendecker, Cello Concerto; Debussy, Pelléas et Mélisande; Dvorák, Symphony No 8; Brahms, Tragic Overture. Honours: Bablock Prize, 1960. Hobbies: Photography; Cooking. Current Management: Jürgen Erlebach, Hamburg. Address: c/o Jürgen Erlebach, Grillparzerstrasse 24, 22085 Hamburg 76, Germany.

CAREY Thomas, b. 29 Dec 1931, Bennetsville, Connecticut, USA. Singer (Baritone). Education: Studied at the Henry Street Music School, New York, and with Rose Bampton; Further study at the Stuttgart Musikhochschule and with Hans Hotter. Debut: Netherlands Opera, Amsterdam, as Germont, 1964. Career: Sang in Lisbon, Nice, Paris, Stockholm, Basle, Zagreb, Venice and Belgrade; Guest singer at the State Operas of Munich, Hamburg, Stuttgart and Berlin; Covent Garden, 1970, as Mel in the premiere of Tippett's The Knot Garden; US engagements in Boston, Memphis and New Orleans; Many concert appearances; Teacher of Voice at the University of Oklahoma, Norman. Recordings include: The Knot Garden. Address: c/o University of Oklahoma, Catlett Music Center, Norman, OK 73019, USA.

CARIAGA Marvellee, b. 11 Aug 1942, California, USA. Singer (Mezzo-soprano). Education: Studied at California State University. Career: Sang with San Diego Opera from 1971; Fricka in performances of Der Ring des Nibelungen for Seattle Opera, 1975-81; Guest appearances at Vancouver, 1975-78, San Francisco, 1981, and Pittsburgh, Portland and Los Angeles, 1987-88; Rio de Janeiro, 1979, as Santuzza; Netherlands Opera, 1979 and 1982; Other roles have included Wagner's Venus, Ortrud, Waltraute, Brünnhilde (Siegfried), Isolde and Magdalene; Donna Anna, Amelia (Ballo in Maschera), Herodias and Kostelnicka in Jenufa; Colorado, 1986, in the premiere of Pasatieri's The Three Sisters; Los Angeles Music Center Opera, 1991, as Mrs Grose in The Turn of the Screw; Mrs Herring at the Dorothy Chandler Pavilion, Los Angeles, 1992. Recordings include: The Three Sisters. Address: Los Angeles Music Center Opera, 135 North Grand Avenue, Los Angeles, CA 90012, USA.

CARIDIS Miltiades, b. 9 May 1923, Gdansk (Greek Citizen). Conductor. m. Dr Sonja Dengel, 1 d. Education: Diploma in Conducting, Music Academy, Vienna, Austria, 1947. Career: Permanent Conductor, Opera in Graz, Cologne, Vienna (State Opera); Permanent Conductor, Danish Radio Symphony Orchestra, Copenhagen, 1962-69; Conductor in Chief, Philharmonia Hungarica, 1960-67; Artistic and Music Director, Philharmonic Society, Oslo, 1969-75; Conductor in Chief, Duisburg Symphony Orchestra, Germany, 1975-81; Artistic and Music Director, Tonkünstler-Orchester, Vienna, 1979-85; Guest Conductor to over 100 orchestras and 80 choirs since 1995; Artistic and Music Director, Radio Symphony Orchestra, Athens. Address: Himmelhofgasse 10, A-1130 Vienna, Austria.

CARL Eugene (Gene) Marion Jr, b. 8 Nov 1953, Los Angeles, California, USA. Composer; Pianist. Education: BA cum laude, Pomona College, USA, 1971-75; Freiburg im Breisgau, Germany, 1974; Institute for Sonology, Utrecht State University, Netherlands, 1975-76; Royal Conservatory, The Hague, 1976-81; Piano studies with John Ritter, 1971-74, Geoffrey Madge, 1976-81, master classes with Padolsky, Voorhies, Kontarsky; Composition with Karl Kohn, 1971-75, Konrad Lechner, 1974, Jan van Vlymen and Jan Boerman, 1976-81, master classes, Darmstadt, 1976. Debut: Beethoven Piano Concerto No 1, with Sepulveda Orchestra, 1968. Compositions include: Scratch, violin solo, 1985; Gagarin for double orchestra, mixed choir, 2 solo voices, children's choir, synthesizers, tape, 1986-89; Leonardo, Leonardo for violin, electric guitar, tuba, drum-kit, synthesizers, tape, voice, 1986; Hommage à Tarkovski for 2 saxophones, violin, synthesizers, percussion, tape, 1987; Claremont Concerto for Bb clarinet, piano and string quartet, 1987; Roscoe Boulevard for 2 saxophones (doubling bass clarinet and clarinet) and ensemble, 1988. Recorded: 2 albums as member of Hoketus Ensemble; Pianist with 5 UUs; Motor Totemist Guild; Double LP Balans, with Hoketus; Own works: Gray Matter, Hommage à Tarkovski, Slierten, Leonardo's Doek, Panorama City, Roscoe Boulevard. Contributions to: Co-editor, E 1976-78; Journal of the Schoenberg Institute; Key Notes, Amsterdam. Address: c/o Donemus, Paulus Potterstraat 14, 1071 CZ Amsterdam, Netherlands.

CARL Jeffrey, b. 1961, Canada. Singer (Baritone). Education: BMus, Hons, Voice Performance, McGill University; CON DIP/OPDIP, University of Toronto, with Louis Quilico, at Stena and the Britten-Pears School. Career: Nick Shadow in Stravinsky's The Rake's Progress, Vancouver Opera; Ford in Falstaff at the Aldeburgh Festival; Verdi's Germont di Luna, Macbeth; Puccini's Sharpless, Marcello, Scarpia; Tchaikovsky's Onegin, Mozart's Don Giovanni, Guglielmo; Donizetti's Enrico, Luisignano; Riccardo, Gounod's Valentin, Thomas's Hamlet, Bizet's Escamillo as well as Henry VIII (Saint-Saëns), Genoveva (Schumann), Brandenburgers in Bohenia (Smetana) and Gershwin's Blue Monday which was his Italian debut in 1997; Concerts include: His most standard repertoire under Sir David Wilcocks with the Montreal Symphony, Sir Simon Rattle with the Royal Liverpool Philharmonic and Michael Tippett: Messiah, Carmina Burana, Verdi's Requiem, Beethoven's Ninth, Bach Passions, The Creation, Belshazzar's Feast; Future engagements include: La Gioconda in Toronto, Carmen in Portugal, Child of Our Time in Singapore, IRIS in Italy, Ballo in Maschera in Italy, Falstaff (Ford) in London, Mahler op 8 and Scarpia in Verona. Recordings: Firebrand of Florence with Thomas Hampson; La Boheme (Alagna, Ramey, Vaduva, Pappano conducting); The Czarevich with Hadley/Gustafson and Guiditta with Hadley/Reidel conducted by Richard Bonynge; Future recordings include: Caterina Cornaro, Donizetti, CD with Richard Bonynge. Address: c/o Franco Silvestri, Via Marconi 2, 37011 Bardolina, Italy.

CARLOS Wendy (Walter), b. 14 Nov 1939, Pawtucket, Rhode Island, USA. Organist; Performer on Electronic Instruments; Composer. Education: Pupil of Ron Nelson, Brown University; AB, 1962; MA, 1965. Career: Associated with Robert Moog in perfecting the Moog Synthesizer, 1964; Pioneer in utilising the resources of the synthesizer. Compositions: Noah, opera, 1964-65; Various pieces for synthesizer and tape or orchestra; Film scores; Chamber music. Recordings: Switched On Bach, 1968; The Well Tempered Synthesizer, 1969; Timesteps, 1970; Pompous Circumstances, 1974-75; Digital Moonscapes, 1985. Address: c/o ASCAP, ASCAP Building, One Lincoln Plaza, New York, NY 10023, USA.

CARLSEN Toril, b. 1954, Oslo, Norway. Singer (Soprano). Education: Studied in Oslo and Budapest. Career: Appearances at the National Theatre, Oslo, from 1979, notably as Fiordiligi, Pamina, Adina, Musetta, Micaela and Zdenka; Guest at the Berlin Staatsoper from 1989 (Mélisande, 1991); Many concert appearances. Recordings include: Peer Gynt by Grieg (Unicorn). Address: c/o Den Norske Opera, PO Box 8800, Youngstorget, N-0028 Oslo, Norway.

CARLSON Claudine, b. 26 Feb 1950, Mulhouse, France. Mezzo-soprano. Education: Vocal training in California; Pupil of Gertrude Gruenderg, Jennie Tourel and Esther Andreas, Manhattan School of Music, New York. Career: Numerous appearances as soloist with major orchestras, including Boston Symphony, Detroit Symphony, New York Philharmonic, Minnesota Philharmonic, Los Angeles Philharmonic, St Louis Symphony, National Symphony, London Symphony Orchestra, Orchestre de Paris, Israel Philharmonic; Many festival appearances; Recitalist worldwide. Recordings: Various labels. Honours: 1st Prize, National Federation of Music Clubs Singing Competition; Martha Baird Rockefeller Award. Address: c/o ICM Artists Ltd, 40 West 57th Street, New York, NY 10019, USA.

CARLSON Lenus (Jesse), b. 11 Feb 1945, Jamestown, North Dakota, USA. Baritone; Teacher. m. Linda Kay Jones, 20 Aug 1972. Education: BA, 1967; Postgraduate studies with Oren Brown, Juilliard School, 1970-73. Career: Apprentice Artist, Central City (Colorado) Opera, 1965-66; Debut as Demetrius, Midsummer Night's Dream, Minnesota Opera, 1968; Sang with opera companies in Dallas, 1972-73, San Antonio, 1973, Boston, 1973, Washington DC, 1973, New York (Metropolitan Opera, debut as Purcell's Aeneas, 23 Feb 1973), Amsterdam, 1974, others; British debut, Scottish Opera, Edinburgh Festival, 1975; Covent Garden debut, London, as Valentin, 1976; Sang at the Deutsche Oper Berlin as Paul in Die tote Stadt by Korngold, 1983; Nevers in Les Huguenots, 1987, Arcesias in Die toten Augen by d'Albert, 1987; Premiere of Oedipus by Wolfgang Rihm, 1988; Sang the Acrobat in Lulu at the Festival Hall, London, 1994; Creon in Enescu's Oedipe at the Deutsche Oper, 1996; Various concert engagements; Teacher, Voice, Minneapolis, 1965-70, New York, 1970-. Address: c/o Columbia Artists Management Inc, 165 West 57th Street, New York, NY 10019, USA.

CARLYLE Joan (Hildred), b. 6 Apr 1931, Wirral, Cheshire, England. Soprano. 2 daughters. Education: Studied with Bertha Nicklass Kempner. Career: Principal Lyric Soprano, Covent Garden; Major roles sung in UK include: Oscar, Ballo in Maschera, 1957-58; Sophie, Der Rosenkavalier, 1958-69; Nedda, Pagliacci, Zeffirelli production, 1959; Mimi, La Bohème, 1960; Titania, Midsummer Night's Dream, Britten (Gielgud production), 1960; Pamina, Magic Flute, 1962, 1966; Countess, Marriage of Figaro, 1963; Zdenka, Arabella (Hartmann production), 1964; Suor Angelica, 1965; Desdemona, Otello, 1965; Arabella, 1967; Marschallin, Der Rosenkavalier, 1968; Jenifer, Midsummer Marriage, 1969; Donna Anna, 1970; Reiza, Oberon, 1970; Adrianna Lecouvreur, 1970; Russalka, Elisabetta, Don Carlos, 1975; Major roles sung abroad include Oscar, Nedda, Mimi, Pamina, Zdenka, Micaela, Donna Anna, Arabella, Elisabetta and Desdemona; Debuts at Salzburg, Metropolitan Opera, New York, and Teatro Colón, Buenos Aires, 1968; Currently teaching and promoting young singers. Recordings: Several including Karajan's production of Pagliacci as Nedda and Midsummer Marriage as Jenifer. Hobbies: Gardening; Travel; Preservation of the countryside; Interior design; Cooking. Address: Laundry Cottage, Hanmer, Clywdd, North Wales.

CARMICHAEL John Russell, b. 5 October 1930, Melbourne, Victoria, Australia. Composer. Education: Mus Dip (Hons), University of Melbourne, 1951; Paris Conservatoire, 1954; Study with Arthur Benjamin 1955-57 and Anthony Milner, 1957-60; Commission from Friends of the Victorian Opera, 1995. Compositions include: Concierto Folklorico, for piano and strings, 1970; Trumpet Concerto, 1975; Fantasy Concerto for flute and orchestra, 1982; Lyric Concerto for cornet and piano, 1982; A Country Flair for clarinet and orchestra, 1989; Fetes Champetres for clarinet, 1989; Monotony for 2 pianos, 1990; When Will the Sun for soprano and piano, 1990; Bravura Waltzes for 2 pianos, 1990; Saxophone Concerto, 1990; Dark Scenarios for 2 pianos, 1994; From the Dark Side for piano, 1995. Address: c/o APRA, 1A Eden Street, Crows Nest, NSW 2065, Australia.

CARNEGY Patrick, b. 23 Sep 1940, Leeds, England. Writer; Lecturer; Broadcaster. Education: Rugby School, 1953-58; MA, Trinity Hall, Cambridge, 1960-63. Career: The Times Educational Supplement, 1964-69; Course Director, Bayreuth Youth Festival from 1968; Assistant Editor with special responsibility for music, The Times Literary Supplement, 1969-78; Editor of music books, Faber and Faber, 1978-88; Director of Faber Music, 1979-88; Writer, lecturer and broadcaster on music and literature; Founding Member of Bayreuth International Arts Centre; Member of BBC Central Music Advisory Committee, 1986-89; Dramaturg of the Royal Opera House, 1988-92; Member of BBC General Advisory Council, 1990-. Publication: Faust as Musician: A Study of Thomas Mann's Novel Doctor Faustus, 1973. Contributions include: The Times and Its Supplements; London Review of Books; Opera; The Musical Times; Art International. Hobbies: Mountains; Wine. Address: 5 The Causeway, Elsworth, Cambridge, CB3 8HT, England.

CAROSIO Margherita, b. 7 June 1908, Genoa, Italy. Singer (Soprano). Education: Studied with her father, Natale Carosio, and at the Paganini Conservatory, Genoa. Debut: Novi Ligure, 1927, as Lucia di Lammermoor. Career: Covent Garden, 1928, as Musetta and as Feodor in Boris Godunov; La Scala Milan, 1929-55, notably in the premieres of Mascagni's Nerone (1935) and Wolf-Ferrari's Il Campiello (1936) and in the first local performances of operas by Rimsky-Korsakov, Strauss (Die schweigsame Frau) and Menotti; Buenos Aires, 1937, in Le Coq d'Or; Salzburg Festival, 1939, as Rosina; Teatro San Carlo, Naples, 1942, in the premiere of Beatrice Cenci by Pannain; Guest appearances in Barcelona, Antwerp, Vienna, Berlin and Nice; Sang in London, 1946, as Violetta (with the San Carlo Company) and in 1950 as Adina in L'Elisir d'Amore, with La Scala. Recordings include: L'Elisir d'Amore; Amelia al Ballo by Menotti.

CARR Colin (Michael), b. 25 Oct 1957, Liverpool, England. Cellist. Education: Yehudi Menuhin School, 1966-74; Associate (Honours), Royal College of Music, 1972. Career: Soloist throughout Europe, North America, Australia and Far East with major orchestras including: The Royal Philharmonic Orchestra, Concertgebouw Orchestra, British Broadcasting Corporation Symphony, Philharmonic, Chicago Symphony, National Symphony Washington, English Chamber Orchestra, Scottish Chamber Orchestra, CBSO, Philadelphia Orchestra, Montreal Symphony; Recitals, London, Amsterdam, Paris, New York, Washington, Boston, Los Angeles, television and radio recordings, throughout both continents; Faculty Member, New England Conservatory, Boston, USA, 1983-. Recordings: Sonatas by Debussy and Franck; Elegie, Romance and Papillon by Fauré; Complete Schubert works for Piano Trio; Complete Mendelssohn works for Piano Trio; Complete Brahms Trios with Golub, Kaplan, Carr Trio. Honours: Martin Music Scholarship, Gulbenkian Fellowship, Lambeth Music Award, 1st Prize Royal Overseas League Competition, 1974-; Winner, Young Concert Artists Competition, New York, USA, 1978; Piatigorsky Prize, 1981; Naumburg Competition Winner, 1981; Grand Prize Winner, Rostropovitch Competition, Paris. Hobbies: Vegetarian and Indian cooking; Soccer; Tennis; Skiing; Squash; Running. Current Management: Clarion/Seven Muses Concert Agency, London, England; Herbert Barrett Management, New York, USA. Address: Rycote Park, Milton Common, Oxford, England.

CARR-BOYD Ann, b. 13 July 1938, Sydney, New South Wales, Australia. Composer. Education: Studied at the University of Sydney (MA, 1963) and in London with Fricker and Goehr. Career: Teacher at the University of Sydney, 1967-73. Compositions include: Symphony, 1964; 2 string quartets, 1964, 1966; Vocal music, including Home Thoughts from Abroad for mezzo and ensemble, 1987; Instrumental pieces, including Dance Suite for woodwind quintet, 1984, and Theme and Variations for organ, 1989. Address: c/o APRA, 1A Eden Street, Crows Nest, New South Wales 2065, Australia.

CARRERAS José, b. 5 Dec 1946, Barcelona, Spain. Tenor. 1 son, 1 daughter. Debut: Flavio (Norma), Gennaro (Lucrezia Borgia), Teatro Liceu, 1970-71. Career: Appeared in La Bohème, Un Ballo in Maschera and I Lombardi, Teatro Reggio Parma, Italy, after winning 1972 Verdi singing competition; US debut as Pinkerton in Madama Butterfly, New York City Opera, 1972; Metropolitan Opera House debut, 1974, as Cavaradossi; Teatro alla Scala Milan debut, 1975, Riccardo in Un Ballo in Maschera; Appeared in film and video versions of Don Carlos, Andrea Chénier, I Lombardi, La Bohème, Verdi's Requiem Mass, Stiffelio, My Life (personal life story), Turandot, West Side Story (the recording); Other appearances include Teatro Colón, Buenos Aires, Vienna Staatsoper, Royal Opera House, Covent Garden, London, Salzburg Easter and Summer Festivals, Lyric Opera House, Chicago, War Memorial Opera House, San Francisco, notably as Alfredo (La Traviata), Nemorino (L'Elisir d'Amore), Andrea Chénier, Don José (Carmen), Radames (Aida), Werther, Edgardo (Lucia di Lammermoor, Alvaro (La Forza del Destino), Manrico (Il Trovatore); Returned to concert and stage after illness, 1987; Open air concert for audience of 150,000, 1988; Sang with 2 tenors at World Cup finals concert, Rome, 1990; apperared as Loris in Fedora at Covent Garden, 1994 and at La Scala, 1996. Recordings: Un Ballo in Maschera; Tosca; Turandot; Werther; Aida; La Bohème; Don Carlo; Requiem Mass (Verdi); West Side Story; South Pacific; La Forza del Destino; Carmen; Pagliacci. Publication: Singing with the Soul, autobiography, 1989. Honours: Winner, Sir Laurence Olivier Award, 1993. Membership: Founder, President, José Carreras International Leukemia Foundation, 1988-. Current Management: Carlos Caballé, Opera Caballé, Barcelona. Address: c/o Opera Caballé, Via Augusta 59, Barcelona, Spain.

CARRINGTON Simon (Robert), b. 23 Oct 1942, Salisbury, Wiltshire, England. Musician; Teacher; Adjudicator; Bass Player; Music Director. m. Hilary Stott, 2 Aug 1969. 1 s, 1 d. Education: Christ Church Cathedral Choir School, Oxford; The King's School, Canterbury; King's College, Cambridge; New College, Oxford; MA(Cantab); Teaching Certificate (Oxon); Choral Scholar, King's College, Cambridge. Career: Co-Founder and Director of the King's Singers, 1968-93 with 3000 performances worldwide and numerous concerts, radio and television appearances; Freelance Double Bass Player with all major UK symphony and chamber orchestras; Since 1994 Professor, Artist in Residence and Director of Choral Activities at the University of Kansas; Monteverdi Vespers, 1994; Britten War Requiem, Tallis 40 part Motet, Tribute to Henry Purcell, 1995; Walton Belshazzar's Feast, Ligeti Lux Aeterna, Josquin Missa Gaudeamus, 1996; Mendelssohn Elijah (staged as an opera), Music ffrom the time of the Mexican Viceroys, Bach Motets, 1997; Director of the Graduate Degree Programs in Choral Directing; Freelance Choral Workshop Director and Choral Competition Judge in the UK, USA, France, Germany, Netherlands and Hungary; Choral Conductor worldwide including Carnegie Hall performances, 1996 and 1997. Compositions: Numerous arrangements for The King's Singers. Recordings: Numerous with various labels internationally, 1971-93 including madrigals, motets, folk songs from five centuries. Publications: The King's Singers - A Self Portrait, 1981; Video: The Art of The King's Singers. Honours: Silver Disc, 1975, Gold Disc, 1978, EMI; Grammy Nomination, 1985; Deutsche Schallplatten Preis, 1978. Memberships: ACDA; ISM; ABCD. Hobbies: Restoring French cottages. Address: Department of Music and Dance, 332 Murphy Hall, University of Kansas, Lawrence, KS 66044, USA.

CARROLI Silvano, b. 22 Feb 1939, Venice, Italy. Singer (Baritone). Education: Studied at the Opera School of La Fenice, Venice. Debut: Venice 1964, as Marcello in La Boheme. Career: Sang widely in Italy and toured North America with the company of La Scala, 1976; Verona Arena from 1973, in Samson et Dalila, as Ezio in Attila (1985) and Renato in Un Ballo in Maschera (1986); Washington Opera 1977-78, as Cavaradossi; London, Covent Garden, as Iago and in La Fanciulla del West; Chicago Lyric Opera 1978; Brussels 1980, in a revival of Donizetti's Il Duca d'Alba; Barcelona 1983, as Escamillo; Paris Opera 1984, as Nabucco and in Verdi's Jerusalem; Further appearances at the Metropolitan Opera and at the Deutsche Oper Berlin; Amonasro, Luxor, Egypt, 1987; Season 1988-89, Barnaba, Alfio at Verona, Michele in Il Tabarro at Florence, Puccini's Jack Rance at Caracalla Festival, Rome; Iago, Covent Garden, 1990; Scarpia, Arena di Verona; Season 1992, as Gerard in Andrea Chenier at Turin, Scarpia at Covent Garden, Amonasro at the Festival of Caracalla. Recordings include: Video of I Lombardi (Topaz). Address: c/o Stafford Law Associates, 6 Barham Close, Weybridge, Surrey, KT13 9PR, England.

CARROLL Joan, b. 27 July 1932, Philadelphia, USA. Singer (Soprano). Education: Studied in America, then with Margarethe von Winterfeldt in Berlin. Debut: New York Opera Company 1957, as Zerbinetta. Career: Appearances in North America and in Havanna; Santa Fe 1963, as Lulu (US premiere of Berg's opera); European engagements in Belgium, France, Denmark, Switzerland and Holland; Sang Lulu in Hamburg, Munich and Zurich during the 1960s; Member of the Deutsche Oper am Rhein Dusseldorf from 1967; Sang Mozart's Constanze, Donna Anna and Queen of Night, as well as modern repertory, in Hanover, Berlin, Stuttgart, Cologne and Nuremberg. Recordings include: Works by Gorecki and Stravinsky.

CARRON Elizabeth, b. 12 Feb 1933, New York City, New York, USA. Singer (Soprano). Education: Studied in New York. Debut: New York City Opera, 1957, as Madama Butterfly. Career: Sang in New York until 1977 and made guest appearances in Cincinnati, Chicago, Pittsburgh, San Francisco and New Orleans; Dallas, 1958, as Dirce in Cherubini's Médée, opposite Maria Callas; Edinburgh Festival, 1984, with the Washington Opera; Other roles have included Mozart's Constanze, Susanna and Zerlina, Violetta, Micaela, Mimi and Liu, Norina, Strauss's Salome and Daphne, Aithra in Die Ägyptische Helena and Birdie in Regina by Blitzstein. Recordings include: Regina. Address: c/o Washington Opera, Kennedy Center for the Performing Arts, Washington, DC 30566, USA.

CARSEN Robert, b. 23 June 1954, Toronto, Canada. Stage Director. Career: Glyndebourne Festival Opera, as Assistant Director, 1982-85; Production of Boito's Mefistofele seen at Geneva 1988 and at San Francisco, Chicago, Houston and Washington; Aix-en-Provence Festival from 1991-96, with A Midsummer Night's Dream, Handel's Orlando, Die Zauberflöte, Semele (French premiere); Salome in Lyon; Bellini's La Straniera for Wexford, A Village Romeo and Juliet for Opera North, Mozart's Finta Semplice and Finta Giardiniera for the Camden Festival, London, and Cendrillon for Welsh National Opera; Metropolitan Opera debut with Eugene Onegin, European premiere of Blitzstein's Regina for Scottish Opera; Lucia di Lammermoor at Zurich and Munich, Katya Kabanova in Canada and Figaro for Bordeaux, Paris and Israel, 1997; Seven-part Puccini cycle for the Flemish Opera, 1990-96; Falstaff and Otello in Cologne, Verdi's Jerusalem in Vienna; Lohengrin, Nabucco, Capuleti e i Montecchi and Manon Lescaut at the Opéra Bastille, Paris; Season 1997-98 with Macbeth in Cologne, Carmelites in Amsterdam, Semele at English National Opera and Antwerp, Alcina and Tales of Hoffmann for the Paris Opera, Die Frau ohne Schatten at the Vienna State Opera; The Ring in Cologne. Honours include: Carl Ebert Award for directing, 1982; Chevalier des Arts et des Lettres, 1996; Grand Prix de la Presse Musicale Internationale, 1996. Address: IMG Artists, Media House, 3 Burlington Lane, London W4 2TH, England.

CARSON Clarice, b. 23 Dec 1936, Montreal, Canada. Singer (Soprano). Education: Studied with Pauline Donalda and Jacqueline Richard in Montreal, with Julia Drobner in New York. Debut: Montreal Opera 1962, in Menotti's Amahl and the Night Visitors. Career: Many guest engagements in North America; New York City Opera 1965, as Mozart's Countess; Metropolitan Touring Opera 1967; European engagements in Barcelona, Rouen, Amsterdam and with Scottish Opera, Glasgow, 1969; Schwetzingen 1976, as Paer's Leonora; Other roles include Cassandre in Les Troyens; Mozart's Donna Anna, and Constanze; Verdi's Desdemona, Violetta, Aida, Elisabeth, Amelia and Leonora (Il Trovatore); Puccini's Tosca, Mimi, Liu, Butterfly and Musetta; Marguerite in Faust and the title role in Salome; Many concert performances. Recordings include: Leonora by Paer (MRF).

CARTER Barbara, b. Columbus, Ohio, USA. Singer (Soprano). Education: Studied at Capital University; University of Toronto with Louis Quilico; Musical Academy of the West with Martial Singher. Career: Sang Violetta and Musetta with the Canadian Opera Company on tour of the USA and Canada; European debut with the Essen Opera, then appeared as Queen of Night in Die Zauberflöte with the Covent Garden Opera on tour to the Far East; Further appearances in Berlin, Munich, Buenos Aires, Paris, Vienna, Amsterdam, La Scala, Milan, Venice, Barcelona, New York, Ottawa and Bregenz; Roles have included Lucia, Gilda, Marie in La Fille du Régiment, Zerbinetta, Sophie, Constanze, Zerlina, Rosina, Elvira in Puritani, Amenaide in Tancredi, Olympia, Nannetta and Gretel; Concert appearances in works by Bach, Mozart, Haydn, Handel, Brahms, Orff, Schubert and Charpentier; Mahler's Symphonies 2, 4 and 8; Engagements with Giuseppe Sinopoli leading the Czech Philharmonic, the Philharmonia (London) on tour in Japan, the Accademia di Santa Cecilia in Rome and the Deutsche Oper Berlin (Fiakermilli in Arabella); Recital repertoire includes German Lieder and songs in Russian, French, English, Spanish, Italian and Portuguese. Address: Balan Str 82 W, 81541 Munich, Germany.

CARTER Elliott (Cook) Jr, b. 11 Dec 1908, New York City, New York, USA. Composer; Teacher. m. Helen Frost-Jones, 6 July 1939, 1 son. Education: Piano, Longy School of Music; MA, Harvard University, 1932; Licence de contrepoint, Ecole Normale de Musique, Paris, Nadia Boulanger; Literature, languages, harmony and counterpoint with Walter Piston, orchestration, E B Hill. Career: Music Director, Ballet Caravan, 1937-39; Teacher, Music, Mathematics, Physics, Classical Greek, St John's College, Annapolis, 1939-41; Faculty: Peabody Conservatory of Music, 1946-48; Columbia, 1948-50; Yale, 1958-62; Composer in residence, American Academy, Rome, 1963; Professor at large, Cornell, 1967-68; Violin Concerto UK premiere, Carter Festival, South Bank, London, 1991. Compositions: 2 ballets: Pocahontas, 1936, The Minotaur, 1947; Symphony No 1, 1942, 1954; Chamber Elegy, cello, piano, 1943, arrangements, 1946, 1952, 1961; Holiday Overture, 1944, 1961; Piano Sonata, 1945-46; Sonata, cello, piano, 1948; Woodwind Quintet, 1948; 5 String Quartets, 1950-51, 1959, 1971, 1986, 1995; Elegy, strings, 1952; Sonata, flute, oboe, cello, harpsichord, 1952; Variations, orchestra, 1954-55; Double Concerto, harpsichord, piano, 2 chamber orchestras, 1961; Piano Concerto, 1964-65; Concerto for Orchestra, 1969-69; Canon for 3: In Memoriam Igor Stravinsky, 3 equal instruments, 1971; Duo, violin, piano, 1973-74; Brass Quintet, 1974; A Symphony of 3 Orchestras, 1976; Night Fantasies, piano, 1980; Triple Duo, violin, cello, flute, clarinet, piano, percussion, 1982-83; Changes, guitar, 1983; Esprit rude-esprit doux, flute, clarinet, 1984; Penthode, 5 instrumental quartets, 1984-85; Oboe Concerto, 1987; A Celebration of Some 100x150 Notes, 1987; Enchanted Preludes, flute, cello, 1988; Remembrance, 1988; Violin Concerto, 1990; Con leggerezza pensosa, clarinet, violin, cello, 1990; Anniversary, orchestra, 1991; Trilogy, harp, oboe, 1992; Quintet, piano, winds, 1992; Adagio Tenebroso, 1995; Clarinet Concerto, 1997; Incidental music; Choral and vocal works. Recordings: Various works. Honours: Guggenheim Fellow, 1945, 1950; American Prix de Rome, 1953; Pulitzer Prize, Music, 1960, 1973; Various honorary doctorates; National Medal of Arts, 1985; Chevalier, Ordre des Arts et des Lettres, 1990; Commendatore, Italian Order of Merit. Address: c/o Boosey & Hawkes, 24 East 21st Street, New York, NY 10010-7200, USA.

CARTER Peter (John Burnett), b. 30 January 1935, Durban, South Africa. Musician (Violinist). m. Sally Mackay, 20 December 1974, 1 son, 1 daughter. Education: Royal College of Music, London, 1952-55; Conservatoire Royale de Musique, Brussels, 1955-58; ARCM; LCRM; MMus Honoris Causa, University of Hull, 1987. Career: 2nd Violin, Dartington String Quartet, 1958-68; Director, Music, Natal Performing Arts Council, 1968-69; 1st Violin, Delmé String Quartet, Member ECO, 1969-74; Senior Lecturer, Cape Town, 1974-77; 1st Violin, Allegri String Quartet, Allegri Robles Ensemble, 1977, Melos Ensemble, 1984. Recordings: Complete Schubert Quartets, 1979-81; Brahms Quartets; Beethoven Quartets and Quintets; Ravel Septet; Stolen Gems, James Campbell, 1986; Leader Bath International Ensemble, 1988; Brahms Clarinet Quintet (James Campbell); Piano Quintet (Rian de Waal), 1992 CALA; Lombardini Sirman 6 Quartets, 1994; Bruch and Brahms 2 Viola Quintets, 1995. Honours: Doctor of Music, Nottingham University, 1994; Doctor of Music, Southampton University, 1995. Memberships: Musicians Union; Incorporated Society of Musicians. Hobbies: Tennis; Bridge; Theatre. Current Management: Magenta Music International. Address: 35 Gartmoor Gardens, London SW19 6NX, England.

CARTER Ronald, b. 1961, Texas, USA. Singer (Tenor). Career: Sang first as baritone then appeared as Don José with New Rochelle Opera, Manrico for Long Island Opera and Canio for the Metro Lyric Opera of New Jersey; Has appeared with

Augsburg Opera as Tichon (Katya Kabanova), Strauss's Emperor (1993), Turiddu and Cavaradossi; Guest appearances as Bacchus at Kaiserslautern and in Basle and Hanover. Honours include: Awards from the Jugend in Wien competition, the Pavarotti Competition and the Liederkranz Foundation. Address: c/o Atholl Still Ltd, Foresters Hall, 25-27 Westow Street, London SE19 3RY, England.

CARTERI Rosanna, b. 14 Dec 1930, Verona, Italy. Singer (Soprano). Education: Studied with Cuisnati and Nino Ederle. Debut: Rome 1949, as Elsa in Lohengrin. Career: La Scala debut 1951, in La Buona Figliuola by Piccinni; Sang in many concerts, notably in Donizetti's Requeim and in the premiere of Pizzetti's Ifigenia (Italian Radio 1950); Salzburg Festival 1952, as Desdemona, conducted by Furtwängler; Florence 1953, as Natasha in the stage premiere of Prokofiev's War and Peace; San Francisco 1954, as Mimi; Chicago Lyric Opera 1955, as Marguerite in Faust; Verona Arena 1958-59; Covent Garden 1960, Mimi; Sang in the premiere of Pizzetti's Calzare d'Argento, Milan 1961; Premiere, Gilbert Bécaud's Opera d'Aran, Théâtre des Champs-Elysées, Paris, 1952. Recordings include: La Traviata (RCA); Falstaff, Guillaume Tell, Suor Angelica, La Bohème (Cetra); Solo in the Brahms Requiem, conducted by Bruno Walter.

CARTLEDGE Nicholas Haydn, b. 18 December 1973, Chertsey, Surrey, England. Flautist. Education: Kings College School, Wimbledon, 1987-92; BMus, hons, Dip RCM, Royal College of Music, 1992-96. Debut: Queen Elizabeth Hall, London, 1988. Career: London Venues & Abroad, 1988-90; Soloist, Mozart Concertos with Chamber Orchestra of London, 1993; London Premiere of Edwin Roxburg's Star-Drift, Performed with Susan Milan, 1995; Solo Performance, Purcell Room, London Premiere, Dave Heath Concerto, Free the Spirit, 1995; Wigmore Hall Debut with Guitarists John Williams & Carlos Bonell, 1995; Concert, St James's Palace for Prince of Wales, 1996. Honours: 2nd Prize (twice), British Flute Society's Young Artist Competition, 1992, 1995; Joint Overall Winner, Royal Overseas League Competition, 1996; Tagore Gold Medal, Constant & Kit Lambert Scholarship, 1996; Malcolm Sargent Bursary, 1996. Membership: British Flute Society. Hobbies: Composing; Films; Art Galleries; Travel. Current Management: Karen Durant Management. Address: 298 Nelson Road, Whitton, Twickenham TW2 7BW, England.

CARVALHO Eleazar (de), b. 28 July 1912, Iguatu, Brazil. Conductor; Composer. Education: Studied at the National School of Music, Brazil, graduating 1934. Career: Played the tuba in the orchestra of the Teatro Municipal in Rio de Janeiro, 1930-40; Conducted the Brazilian Symphony Orchestra from 1941, Conductor for Life, 1965; Conducted the Boston Symphony Orchestra, 1947; Guest appearances in Europe and the USA; Music Director of the St Louis Symphony Orchestra, 1963, Conductor Emeritus, 1968; Conductor of the Pro Arte Symphony at Hofstra University, Hempstead, New York, 1968-73; Music Director of the Orquestra Sinfonica Estadual, Sao Paulo, 1973; Taught at the Juilliard School, New York, 1983; Conducted works by Berg, Webern and Schoenberg, as well as the standard repertory. Address: c/o Orquestra Sinfonica Estadual de Sao Paulo, Teatro de Cultura Artistica, Rua Nestor Pestona 196, 01303 Sao Paulo, Brazil.

CARVER Marilyn Joan Gassei, b. 2 Aug 1934, St Louis, USA. Assistant Professor of Music. m. Newton G Carver, 26 Sept 1973, 1 son, 1 daughter. Education: BMus, Tulsa University; MMus, DMA, University of Oklahoma; Boris Goldovsky Opera Institute; American Choral Foundation; Choral Institute of Oklahoma, Quartz Mountain; Fall Arts Institute. Appointments: Teacher, Public High School Choral Music, 1955-60, 1965-82, Voice Class, Tulsa Community College, 1981-83, Conducting, Choral, Voice, Music Education, Oral Roberts University, 1981-; Performances with Tulsa Opera Inc and Theatre Tulsa; Artist, Singer, Musical Director, ACDA Bicentennial Choir. Publications: Selected Treble Choruses From Nineteenth and Twentieth Century Operas: An Annotated Bibliography. Contributions to: ACDA Choral Journal; OCDA Sooner Style Newsletter. Honours include: OMEA Award for Excellence in Teaching, 1996. Memberships: Sigma Alpha Iota; American Choral Directors; Oklahoma Choral Directors; Music Educators National Conference; Oklahoma Music Educators Association; National Association of Teachers of Singing; Phi Kappa Phi; Phi Kappa Lambda. Hobby: Collecting Musical Boxes. Address: 3416 South 85th East Avenue, Tulsa, OK 74145, USA.

CARY Tristram (Ogilvie), b. 14 May 1925, Oxford, England. Composer; Writer; Teacher. m. Doris E Jukes, 7 July 1951 (div 1978) 2 sons, 1 daughter. Education: Dragon School, Oxford, 1928-38; Westminster School (King's Scholar), 1938-42; Christ Church, Oxford (Exhibitioner), 1942-43, 1946-47, interrupted by service in Royal Navy, BA, MA; Trinity College of Music, AMusTCL, LMusTCL, 1949-51; Hon RCM, 1972. Debut: Wigmore Hall, London, 1949. Career: Composing from age 14; Record Shop Assistant, 1951-54; 1st Electronic Music Studio, 1952; Self-employed, 1955-; Music for concerts, films, radio, TV, theatre, musical directories; Founded Electronic Studio at Royal College of Music, 1967; Senior Lecturer 1974, Reader, Dean of Music 1982, University of Adelaide; Self-employed as Composer, Teacher, Writer, Computer Music Consultant. Compositions: 345 Narcissus Trios; Sonata for Guitar Alone; Three Threes and One Make Ten; Arrangement of Bach's 6-part Ricercar, Continuum, Contours and Densities at First Hill; Peccata Mundi; Divertimento; The Songs Inside; Romantic Interiors; Steam Music; Two Songs from the Piae Cantiones; Nonet, Soft Walls; I Am Here; Family Conferece; Seeds; Trellises; Strands; String Quartet II; Sevens, The Dancing Girls, Black White and Rose, Strange Places, Earth Holds Songs; Messages, 1993; Inside Stories, 1993; The Impossible Piano, 1994; Suite - The Ladykillers, 1996. Recordings include: CDs of computer and orchestral music; Many Radio, Film, TV Score Recordings; Quatermass and the Pit, the Film Music of Tristram Cary Volume 1; The Ladykillers; Suite (music from those Glorious Ealing Films). Publications: Illustrated Compendium of Musical Technology published in USA as Dictionary of Musical Technology, 1992. Contributions to: Musical Times; Composer; The Electronic Music Review; The Guardian; Opera Australia; The Australian. Honours include: Medal of the Order of Australia, (OAM), 1991. Memberships: Council Member, Composers Guild of Great Britain; Institute of Electrical Engineers (IEng). Hobbies: Swimming; Sailing; Cycling; Snooker; Cookery; Wine; Good Conversation. Address: 30 Fowlers Road, Glen Osmond, SA 5064, Australia.

CASADESUS Gaby, b. 9 Aug 1901, Marseilles, France. Concert Pianist; Professor. m. Robert Casadesus, 16 Jul 1921 (deceased), 2 s, 1 d. Education: Paris Conservatory. Career: Soloist with major orchestras in Europe; Duo piano team with husband and performed worldwide under leading conductors, later joined by their son Jean (deceased); Master classes including Ravel Academy, summer school of Mozarteum in Salzburg, Schola Cantorum in Paris and currently Fontainebleau School; Co-founder with Grant Johannesen, Martha Joseph and Odette Valabrèque Wurzburger, Robert Casadesus International Piano Competition, Cleveland, Ohio, biannually, 1975-; Judge in international piano competitions including: Paris; Geneva; Brussels; Montreal; Bolzano; New York; London; Concert career continues with orchestra and chamber music ensembles. Recordings: Numerous recordings of 4 hand, 1, 2 and 3 piano works; Mozart concertos; Fauré; Bach; Saint-Saëns; Ravel; Compositions of Robert Casadesus; Debussy Pelléas et Mélisande. Publications: Editor of works of Ravel and of Debussy under Great Performers Edition. Contributions to: Clavier; Piano Quarterly; Musique and Concerts. Honours: 1st Prize in Piano and Prix Pagès, Paris Conservatory, 1917; Officier Legion d'Honneur, France. Membership: Founding Member, Robert Casadesus Association. Address: 54 Rue Vaneau, 75007 Paris, France.

CASADESUS Jean-Claude, b. 7 Dec 1935, Paris, France. Conductor. m. Anne Sevestre, 2 sons, 1 daughter. Education: Harmony, Counterpoint, Fugue, Composition, Percussion (1st Prize), Paris National Conservatory, 1959; Conducting (1st Prize), Ecole Normale de Musique, Paris, 1965, with Pierre Dervaux; With Pierre Boulez, Basle, 1965. Career: Solo Timpanist, Concert Colonne, 1959-68; Percussion Soloist, Domaine Musicalo with Pierre Boulez; Conductor, Paris Opéra, 1969-71; Co-Director, Orchestre Pays de Loire, 1971-76; Founder, Director, Lille National Orchestra, 1976-; Guest Conductor, USA, UK, Moscow, Leningrad, Prague, Leipzig, Dresden, Italy, Switzerland, Japan, elsewhere; Conducted Orchestra National de Lille in Revolution Revisited series, South Bank, London, 1989; Conducted Pelléas et Mélisande at Lille, 1996. Compositions include: Music for theatre and films. Recordings include: Dutilleux, 1st Symphony; Berlioz, Symphonie fantastique; Ravel, Daphnis and Chloe, Bolero, La Valse, Concertos pour piano; Wieniawski, 2 violin concertos with Gitlis; Poulenc, Bal masqué, La Voix Humaine, Groupes des Six, Les Mariés de la Tour Eiffel; Bartók, Sonata for 2 pianos and percussion; Berio, Circles; Liszt, Préludes, Mephisto Waltz; Mozart, Funeral music, Clarinet Concerto, Double Concerto for flute and harp; Beethoven, 7th Symphony, 3rd Piano Concerto, Violin Concerto; Mahler, Symphonies Nos 1, 2, 4, 5, Kindertotenlieder, Rückertlieder, Des Knaben Wunderhorn; Stravinsky, Petrushka, Firebird; Bizet, Arlesienne, Clovis et Clothilde, Carmen Suites, Roma Symphony; Richard Wagner, Musical Extracts; Debussy, La Mer, La Damoiselle Elue, Nocturnes; Prokokiev, Alexander Nevsky. Honours include: 1st Recording Prize, Académie Charles Cros; Grand Prize, Record, European Year of Music, 1985; SACEM Grand Prix, 1985; Advisor to Prime Minister, 1981-84; General Secretary, Superior Council of Music; Cross of Officer, Legion d'Honneur; Ordre des Palmes Académiques; Cross of Commander, Ordre des Arts et des Lettres; Cross of Officer, Order of Leopold; Commander: Order of Nassau, Ordre de Mérite National. Hobbiess: Skiing; Sailing; Tennis; Riding. Current Management: International Management Group, 2 rue Dufrenoy, 75116 Paris, France. Address: 2 rue de Steinkerque, Paris 75018, France.

CASAPIETRA Celestina, b. 23 Aug 1938, Genoa, Italy. Singer (Soprano). m. Herbert Kegel (dec. 1990). Education: Studied at the Milan Conservatory with Gina Cigna. Debut: Teatro Nuovo, Milan, 1961, in Mese Mariano by Giordano. Career: Sang in Genoa, San Remo, Pisa, Venice and Lyons; Sang at the Staatsoper Berlin from 1985, notably as Elsa, Constanze, Donna Anna, Agathe, Mimi, Micaela, Tatiana in Eugene Onegin and the title role in Daphne by Strauss; Salzburg Mozartwochen, 1984, as Vitellia in La Clemenza di Tito; Las Palmas, 1986, as Elisabeth in Tannhäuser; Guest engagements in London, Moscow, Helsinki, Copenhagen, Vienna and Prague; Zemlinsky's Der Kreidekreis, Hamburg, 1983, Amsterdam, 1989. Recordings include: Fiordiligi in Così fan tutte; Mozart's Masses; Orff's Trionfi. Address: c/o Deutsche Staatsoper, Unter den Linden 7, D-1086 Berlin, Germany.

CASCIOLI Gianluca, b. 1979, Turin, Italy. Concert Pianist. Education: Began piano studies 1986; Entered the Accademia Musicale in Imola, 1991; Composition classes at the Verdi Conservatory, Turin. Career: Many recital appearances throughout Italy specialising in classical and contemporary repertory, 1994-; Engagements with Orchestre della Scala, Orpheus Chamber Orchestra, Gustav Mahler Orchestra, Berliner Sinfonie-Orchestre, Orchestre Nazionale della RAI, Orchestre Sinfonica di Santa Cecilie, Orchester des Mozarteum, Salzburg; Work with the conductors Riccardo Muti, Claudio Abbado, Myung-Whum Chung; Concerts in Munich, Vienna, Berlin, Salzburg, Hannover, Frankfurt, Bremen, Hamburg, Paris, Barcelona, Lisbon, Athens, Tokyo, Beijing; Further engagements in Paris and Athens and in International Piano Series at the Queen Elizabeth Hall, London; Named Star of the Year at Munich. Recordings include: Scarlatti; Beethoven; Debussy; Prokofiev; Boulez, Ligeti, Webern and Schoenberg, 1996. Honours include: First prize, Umberto Micheli International Piano Competition, Milan, 1994. Address: c/o Ingpen & Williams Ltd, 14 Kensington Court, London W8 5DN, England.

CASELLATO Renzo, b. 18 Oct 1936, Adria, Rovigo, Italy. Singer (Tenor). Education: Studied at the Benedetto Marcello Conservatory, Venice, and with Maria Carbone. Debut: Reggio Emilia, 1963, as Nemorino. Career: Sang the title role in Mozart's La Clemenza di Tito, La Scala, 1966; Guest engagements in Vienna, Rio de Janeiro, Florence, Buenos Aires, Moscow, Copenhagen, Chicago and Dallas; Other roles include Nadir in Les Pêcheurs de Perles, Rossini's Almaviva, Alfredo in La Traviata, Fenton in Falstaff and Massenet's Werther; Sang in Galuppi's L'amante di tutte at Palermo, 1994; The Devil in Ibert's Angelique at Palermo, 1996. Recordings include: Pia de Tolomei by Donizetti; Rossini's Tancredi, with Marilyn Horne. Address: c/o Teatro alla Scala, Via Filodrammatici 2, I-20121 Milan, Italy.

CASHMORE John, b. 1960, Birmingham, England. Singer (Baritone). Education: Studied at the Birmingham School of Music and the National Opera Studio, London. Debut: Sang Guglielmo with Birmingham Music Theatre. Career: Opera engagements with English National Opera, Scottish Opera-Go-Round, Wexford Festival, Batignano and the New D'Oyly Carte Opera Company; Guglielmo for Opera Forum in Holland, 1991, Figaro in a British tour of Mozart's Opera, Marullo in Rigoletto for ENO, 1992 and roles from 1992 at Aachen including Lortzing's Zar and Don Giovanni; Opera galas at the Albert Hall, Festival Hall and in Glasgow; Oratorio engagements include Carmina Burana in Birmingham and Glasgow, Monteverdi Vespers at Coventry Cathedral and Victory's Ultima Rerum in Dublin. Current Management: Athole Still International Management Limited. Address: Athole Still Ltd, Foresters Hall, 25-27 Weston Street, London SE19 3RY, England.

CASKEL Christoph, b. 12 Jan 1932, Greifswald, Germany. Percussionist. Education: Studied in Cologne, 1949-55. Career: Many performances of modern music at Darmstadt and elsewhere, notably with the brothers Kontarsky in Bartók's Sonata for two Pianos and Percussion; Collaborations with Stockhausen (premiere of Zyklus, 1959, and Kontakte), Mauricio Kagel and keyboard player Franz-Peter Goebels; Has performed with the Capella Coloniensis and given courses at Darmstadt and Cologne. Address: c/o Hochschule für Musik Rheinland, Dagoberstrasse 38, 5000 Cologne 1, Germany.

CASKEN John, b. 15 July 1949, Barnsley, Yorkshire, England. Composer. Education: Birmingham University with Peter Dickinson and John Joubert, 1967-71; Warsaw with Dobrowolski and Lutoslawski, 1971-73. Career includes: Lecturer, Birmingham University, 1973-79; Huddersfield Polytechnic, 1979-81; Durham University, 1981-; Professor of Music at Manchester University, 1992-; Featured Composer, 1980 Bath Festival; Opera, Golem, premiered at 1989 Almeida Festival, London; Professor of Music, University of Manchester, 1992; Composer Choice Concert at the Purcell Room, London, 1997. Compositions: Music for cello and piano, 1972; Kagura for 13 wind, 1973; Jadu for 2 cellos, 1973; Fluctus for violin and piano, 1974; Music for the Crabbing Sun for quartet, 1974; Music for a Tawney-Gold Day for quartet, 1976; Arenaria for flute and ensemble, 1976; Tableaux des trois, for orchestra, 1977; Amarentos for nonet, 1978; Ligatura for organ, 1978; La Orana, Gauguin, for soprano and piano, 1978; Melanos for tuba and nonet, 1979; Firewhirl for soprano and septet, 1980; A Belle Pavine for violin and tape, 1980; Piano Concerto, 1980; String Quartet, 1982; Masque for oboe and chamber orchestra, 1982; Taerset for clarinet and piano, 1983; Erin for double bass and chamber orchestra; To Fields We Do Not Know for chorus, 1984; Orion over Farne, for orchestra, 1984; Clarion Sea for brass quintet, 1985; Vaganza for ensemble, 1985; Golem, opera, 1989; Maharal Dreaming, orchestra, 1989; Piano Quartet, 1990; Cello Concerto, 1991; A Gathering for unaccompanied chorus, 1991; Sharp Thorn for four solo voices, 1991-92; Still Mine for baritone and orchestra, 1991-92; Darting the Skiff for strings, 1993; Infanta Marina for ensemble, 1994; Concerto for Saxophone Quartet and Wind Band, 1997. Honours: 1st Britten Award for composition of opera Golem, 1990. Current Management: Schott and Company Limited. Address: H Schott Ltd, 48 Great Marlborough Street, London W1V 2BN, England.

CASOLLA Giovanna, b. 1953, Italy. Singer (Soprano). Debut: Lisbon, 1977, as Eboli in Don Carlos. Career: Sang at Turin, 1978, 1982, Trieste, 1979, Buenos Aires, 1980, Detroit, 1981; San Diego, 1982, in the America premiere of Zandonai's Giulietta e Romeo; Metropolitan Opera, 1984, as Zandonai's Francesca da Rimini (returned 1986, as Eboli); La Scala Milan, 1983 and 1986, as Giorgetta in Il Tabarro; Verona Arena, 1986 and 1988, as Maddalena in Andrea Chénier and La Gioconda; Caracalla Festival, 1987, 1989, as Tosca; Further guest appearances at Vienna and Miami, 1988, Deutsche Oper Berlin, 1989, Tosca, Stuttgart and Venice (Eboli, 1991); La Scala and Florence, 1991, as Minnie in La Fanciulla del West and Santuzza; Puccini Festival, Torre del Lago, 1991, as Giorgetta; Other roles include Fedora, Amelia (Ballo in Maschera), Adriana Lecouvreur, Manon Lescaut, Silvana in Respighi's La Fiamma, Bartok's Judith, Maria in Tchaikovsky's Mazeppa and Elena Makropoulos; Sang Santuzza at Florence, 1996; Many concert appearances. Address: c/o Teatro alla Scala, Via Filodrammatici 2, 20121 Milan, Italy.

CASONI Bianca-Maria, b. 1 Mar 1932, Milan, Italy. Singer (Mezzo-Soprano). Education: Studied at the Milan Conservatory with Bruna Jona and Mercedes Llopart. Debut: Milan 1956, as Mercedes in Carmen. Career: Sang widely in Italy after winning La Scala Competition; Salzburg 1960, as Giacinta in La Finta Semplice, 1960; Glyndebourne 1965, as Cherubino; Concert performance of Bellini's La Straniera, New York, 1969; Appearances at Covent Garden and the Festivals of Aix and Edinburgh; Monte Carlo, Geneva, Barcelona, Philadelphia and the Metropolitan Opera; Turin 1975, in the Italian premiere of Die drei Pintos, Mahler/Weber; Berlin Staatsoper 1981, as Cinderella. Recordings include: Mozart's Coronation Mass; La Straniera; Preziosilla in La Forza del Destino (EMI). Address: c/o Deutsche Staatsoper, Under der Linden 7, D-1086 Berlin, Germany.

CASSEL John (Walter), b. 15 May 1910, Council Bluffs, Iowa, USA. Baritone Singer (Opera, Recitals, Operetta, Musicals). m. (1) Nadine Blackburn, (2) Gail Manners, 27 Feb 1955, 3 sons, 2 daughters. Education: Creighton University, Nebraska; Studied voice privately with Harry Cooper, Council Bluffs; Trumpet, piano and additional voice studies in Council Bluffs; Studied voice with Frank La Forge, New York City, 17 years. Debut: Metropolitan Opera, 1943. Career: Leads in Broadway musicals, Mason Radio programmes, London Great Waltz, New York City Opera; Created role of Horace Tabor in world premiere of Ballad of Baby Doe, Central City, 1956; Leading baritone, operatic roles in Europe; With Metropolitan Opera, 1943-74, 203 performances including Strauss's Mandryka and Jochanaan and Wagner's Dutchman, Telramund and Kurwenal; Recitals throughout USA; Sang with all major US orchestras including Philadelphia Orchestra, New York Philharmonic, Boston Symphony, San Francisco Symphony; TV guest; Appeared in Warner Bros films early in career; Noted for acting; Professor of Voice and Drama, Indiana University School of Music, Bloomington, 1974-. Recordings: Tosca and Carmen, Metropolitan Opera Guild; Faust and The Ballad of Baby Doe, New York Guild; Belshazzar's Feast, with Philadelphia Orchestra; Reverence for Life (in honour of Albert Schweitzer); Great Waltz. Honours: Recipient of decoration, New York Society of Voice Teachers. Memberships: Actors Equity; AGMA, 1st Vice-President 2 years; AGVA; Screen Actors' Guild. Hobbies: Horseshoes; Riding; Swimming; Tennis; Travel. Address: Studio No 103, Indiana University School of Music, Bloomington, IN 47401, USA.

CASSELLO Kathleen, b. 1958, Delaware, USA. Singer (Soprano). Education: Dan Pressley, Delaware; Wilma Lipp, Salzburg; Sesto Bruscantini, Italy. Career: European debut as Queen of Night in Hamburg, 1985; More than 200 Queen of Night performances since in Hamburg, 1986-88, Deutsche Oper and Staatsoper, Berlin, 1986-89, Moscow, 1987, Zurich, Geneva and Salzburg, 1988, Stuttgart, 1990; Staatstheater Karlsruhe Ensemble, 1987-89; Lucia in Karlsruhe, 1989-92, Sao Paulo, 1989, Marseille, San Sebastian and Zürich, 1990, Malaga, 1992, Treviso, Rome and Palermo, 1993; Traviata in Karlsruhe, 1987-92, Oviedo, 1991, Toulouse, 1992, Festival Orange and Rome, 1993, Tokyo, 1994, and Geneva; Elvira in Puritani at

Marseille, 1991, Malaga, 1993; Gilda in Rigoletto at Marseille, 1992, Mexico City and Nice, 1993, La Scala with Riccardo Muti, 1994; Konstanze in Entführung in St Gallen, 1986-87, Vienna, 1988, Karlsruhe, 1989, Zurich, 1990, Munich National Theater, 1992, Avignon, 1993, Marseille and Hamburg, 1994-; Other roles include: Manon at the Met, 1990; Thaïs at Marseille, 1991; Pamina at Barcelona, 1991; Musetta at the Arena di Verona, 1992; Vitellia in La Clemenza di Tito in Toulouse, 1992, Athens, 1994; Amina in La Sonnambula at Messina, 1993; Elettra in Idomeneo at Venice, 1993; Giulietta in I Capuleti e i Montecchi at Parma, 1994; Amina at Rome, 1996. Address: Friedlgasse 57/2. A-1190 Vienna, Austria.

CASSIDY Paul, b. 1959, Ireland. Violist. Education: Studied at the Royal College of Music, University of California at Los Angeles and Detmold, Germany. Career: Founder member of the Brodsky Quartet (name derives from violinist Adolph Brodsky, Principal of the Royal Manchester College of Music, 1895-29); Resident at Cambridge University for 4 years and later residencies at the Dartington International Summer School, Devon; Concert engagements include the Shostakovich quartets at the Elizabeth Hall, London, and performances at the Ludwigsburg and Schleswig-Holstein Festivals; New York debut at the Metropolitan Museum; Further tours of Italy, North America, Australia, Poland, Czechoslovakia and Japan; Complete quartets of Schoenberg for the BBC, 1992; French concerts include visit to the Théâtre du Châtelet, Paris. Recordings include: Quartets of Elgar and Delius; Schubert A minor and also Schubert D minor and Crumb, Black Angels; Beethoven Op 74; Complete quartets of Shostakovich. Address: 21-22 Old Steine, Brighton, England.

CASSILLY Richard, b. 14 Dec 1927, Washington, District of Columbia, USA. Opera Singer (Tenor). m. Helen Koliopulos, 1951, 4 sons, 3 daughters. Education: Peabody Conservatory of Music, Baltimore, Maryland. Career: New York City Opera, 1955-66; Chicago Lyric, 1959-; Deutsche Oper Berlin, 1965-; San Francisco Opera, 1966-; Hamburgische Staatsoper, 1966-; Covent Garden, 1968-, debut as Janácek's Laca; La Scala Milan 1970; Wiener Staatsoper, Austria, 1970; Staatsoper München, Germany, 1970; Paris Opera, 1972; Metropolitan Opera, New York, 1973-, as Radames, Tannhäuser, Tristan, Otello, Samson and Captain Vere in Billy Budd; Kammersänger, 1973; Sang Aron in a concert performance of Schoenberg's Moses and Aron, London, 1974, conducted by Boulez; Television performances of Otello, Peter Grimes, Saint of Bleecker Street, Fidelio, Wozzeck and Die Meistersinger; Aeneas in concert performance of Les Troyens, Promenade Concerts, London, 1980; Tannhäuser, production of Wagner's opera by Peter Sellars at Chicago, 1988; Herod in Salome, Metropolitan, 1989. Recordings: Has made numerous recordings including Aeneas in Les Troyens at Carnegie Hall (1959-60) and Moses und Aron. Current Management: Robert Lombardo Associates, New York, USA. Address: c/o Robert Lombardo Associates, 30 West 60th Street, New York, NY 10023, USA.

CASSIS Alessandro, b. 1949, Italy. Singer (Baritone). Debut: Florence, 1971, in Un Ballo in Maschera. Career: Sang in the Maggio Musicale, Florence, 1974, in La Fanciulla del West; Piccola Scala Milan in La Favola d'Orfeo by Casella; Sang Germont at Turin, 1977, Amonasro at the Verona Arena, 1982; La Scala Milan, 1983, as Michele in Il Tabarro, Sharpless in Butterfly, 1985; Returned to Verona in 1986 and 1988, as Gérard (Andrea Chénier) and Barnaba (La Gioconda); Further appearances at Naples, Genoa, Geneva, Palermo, Trieste and Lisbon; Baths of Caracalla, Rome, 1991, as Amonasro; Other roles include Carlo in La Forza del Destino and Verdi's Luna, Rigoletto and Renato; High Priest in Samson et Delila. Recordings include: I Lutuani by Ponchielli; Nerone by Boito. Address: Teatro alla Scala, Via Filodrammatici 2, 20121 Milan, Italy.

CASSUTO Alvaro (Leon), b. 17 Nov 1938, Oporto, Portugal. Conductor; Composer. Education: Studied violin and piano as a child; Studied composition with Arthur Santos and Lopes Graca; Courses with Ligeti, Messiaen and Stockhausen, Darmstadt, summers 1960 and 1961; Studied conducting with Karajan, Pedro de Freitas Branco, Lisbon, and with Ferrara in Hilversum; PhD, Law, University of Lisbon, 1964; MA, Conducting, Vienna Academy of Music, 1965. Career: Assistant Conductor, Gulbenkian Orchestra, Lisbon, 1965-68; Little Orchestra, New York, 1968-70; Permanent Conductor, 1970-75, Music Director, 1975-, National Radio Orchestra, Lisbon; Lecturer, 1974-75, Professor in Music, 1975-79, Conductor, Symphony Orchestra, University of California, Irvine; Music Director, Rhode Island Philharmonic Orchestra, Providence, 1979-85; National Orchestra Association, New York, 1981-87; Nova Filarmonia Portuguesa. Compositions: In the Name of Peace, opera, 1971; Orchestral: Sinfonia breve No 1, 1959, No 2, 1960; Variations, 1961; Permutations for 2 orchestras, 1962; Concertino for piano and orchestra, 1965; Cro(mo-no)fonia for 20 strings, 1967; Canticum in Tenebris for soloists, chorus and orchestra, 1968; Evocations, 1969; Circle, 1971; To Love and Peace, symphonic poem, 1973; Homage to My People, suite for band, 1977; Return to the Future, 1985; The Four Seasons for

piano and orchestra, 1986; Chamber: String Sextet, 1962; Song of Loneliness for 12 performers, 1972. Recordings: Various. Honours: Koussevitzky Prize, Tanglewood, Massachusetts, 1969. Address: Rua da Bela Vista 172, 2750 Cascais, Portugal.

CASTEL Nico, b. 1 Aug 1931, Lisbon, Portugal. Tenor Singer. Education: Studied with: Carmen Hurtado in Caracas; Mercedes Llopart in Milan; Julia Drobner in New York. Debut: Santa Fe, 1958, as Fenton in Falstaff. Career: New York City Opera, 1965, in The Fiery Angel by Prokofiev; Currently celebrating 25 years as Principal Artist, 1970-, Metropolitan Opera: Le nozze di Figaro; Hansel and Gretel; Boris Godunov; Guillot, in the Beverly Sills recording of Manon; Appearances in Lisbon, Florence, Chicago, Houston, Baltimore and Philadelphia; Diction and Phonetics Teacher for singers; Staff diction coach, Metropolitan Opera; Adjunct Professor, Boston University; Professor at Juilliard School. Recordings include: La Bohème; Manon, Les Contes d'Hoffmann. Publications: A Singers' Manual of Spanish Lyric Diction, 1994; The Complete Puccini, Verdi and Mozart Libretti, Translated and Phoneticized, 1994. Address: 214 West 92nd Street, Apt 77E, New York City, NY 10025, USA.

CASTLE Joyce, b. 17 January 1944, Beaumont, Texas, USA. Singer (Mezzo-soprano). Education: Studied at the University of Kansas, the Eastman School and in New York. Debut: San Francisco 1970, as Siebel in Faust. Career: Debut, Metropolitan Opera, 1985; Die Fledermaus, Eugene Onegin; Puccini, Trittico; Wagner's Ring Cycle; Boris Godounov; Debut, New York City Opera, 1983, Ballad of Baby Doe, Sweeney Todd, Rake's Progress, Casanova; Regularly sings Santa Fe Opera, Seattle Opera, Houston, Dallas, Washington, Montreal; Created role of Nazimova in Argento's Valentino, 1994, Kennedy Center; 1st performance of Bernstein's Arias & Barcarolles with Bernstein at the Piano; World premieres of Weisgall's Esther, 1993, New York City; Turin 1996 as Madame de la Haltière in Messenet's Cendrillon. Recordings: Candide, Old Lady, New York City Opera Recording; Grammy Winner, Sondheim Book of the Month Recording; Vocal Music of Stefan Wolpe; Vocal Music of Joseph Fennimore. Current Management: Janice Mayer & Associates. Address: 201 W 57th Street, New York, NY 10019, USA.

CASTRO Paulo Ferreira De, b. 9 July 1959, Oporto, Portugal. Administrator; Artistic Director. Education: Architecture, Oporto, Portugal; Degree, Musicology, Strasbourg University, France; MMus, Leeds University, England; Conservatoire Training, Oporto. Career: Artistic Director, 1992-, Administrator, 1996-, Teatro Nacional De Sao Carlos; Lecturer, Universidade Nova De Lisboa, 1985-; Directed for T.N. Sao Carlos: Beethoven, Fidelio, 1994 (Restaged 1995); Stravinsky, Le Rossignol, 1997; Berlioz, Les Troyens, 1997, 1998; Programme Manager, Portuguese Arts Festival, Frankfurt Book Fair, 1997. Publication: History of Portuguese Music, 1991. Contributions to: Expresso, Lisbon, 1989-92. Memberships: Portuguese Music Council; Portuguese Musicological Association. Address: c/o Teatro nacional De Sao Carlos, Rua Serpa Pinto 9, 1200 Lisboa, Portugal.

CASTRO-ALBERTY Margarita, b. Oct 1947. Puerto Rico. Singer (Soprano). Education: Studied at the Pablo Casals Conservatory, Puerto Rico, the Accademia di Santa Cecilia, Rome, and at Juilliard, New York. Debut: Santiago, 1978, as Amelia in Un Ballo in Maschera. Career: Sang at the Teatro Colon, Buenos Aires, 1979-80; European debut, 1980, in La Vida Breve by Falla; Carnegie Hall, 1981, as Lucrezia in I Due Foscari; Metropolitan debut, 1982, as Amelia; Festival d'Orange, 1983, as Aida; Guest engagements in Venice, Berlin, Vienna, Nancy, Rome and Toronto; Other roles include Donna Anna, Amelia Grimaldi, Nedda, Butterfly, Lucrezia Borgia, Elisabeth de Valois and the Trovatore Leonora; Sang at Marseilles, 1987. Address: c/o Opéra de Marseille, 2 Rue Molière, F-13231 Marseille Cedex 01, France.

CASTRO-ROBINSON Eve de, b. 9 Nov 1956, London, England. Composer. Education: Studied at the University of Auckland (DMus, 1991). Career: Composer-in-residence with the Auckland Philharmonic, 1991; Performances of her music with the Karlheinz Company in Auckland and with UNESCO in Paris. Compositions include: Stringencies for 11 solo strings, 1986; Peregrinations, piano concerto, 1987; Concerto for 3 clarinets, 1991; Instrumental pieces, including Tumbling Strains for violin and cello, 1992, and Tingling Strings for piano, 1993. Address: c/o New Zealand Music Centre, PO Box 10042, Level 13, Brandon Street, Wellington, New Zealand.

CASULA Maria, b. 1939, Cagliari, Sardinia, Italy. Singer (Soprano). Education: Studied in Rome and Venice. Career: Sang with I Virtuosi di Roma, in concert; Vienna Staatsoper, 1967, as Vitellia in La Clemenza di Tito; Glyndebourne, 1969, Despina; Roma, 1978, in the Italian premiere of The Beggar's Opera, arranged by Britten; Cagliari, 1987, in Guillaume Tell. Recordings include: Il Barbiere di Siviglia (DGG), La Clemenza di Tito (Decca), Le nozze di Figaro (Philips), Leonora by Paer (MRF).

Address: c/o Teatro Lirico, Viale Regina Margherita 6, 09100 Cagliari, Italy.

CATHCART Allen, b. 2 Aug 1938, Baltimore, Maryland, USA. Singer (Tenor). Education: Studied at the University of California and with Boris Goldovsky in New York. Debut: Metropolitan Opera Studio, 1961, as Guglielmo in Così fan tutte. Career: European engagements in Brussels, Rome, Zurich, Cologne, Stuttgart and Kiel; Welsh National Opera in Cardiff; Paris Opéra-Comique, in The Stone Guest by Dargomyzhsky, 1985; Paris Opéra as The Drum Major in Wozzeck; Other roles include Don José, Florestan, Cavaradossi, the Emperor in Die Frau ohne Schatten, Laca in Jenufa and parts in operas by Wagner. Recordings include: Jason in Mayr's Medea in Corinto.

CAUDLE Mark, b. 1950, England. Bass Viol and Bass Violin Player; Cellist. Career: Member of The Parley of Instruments; Frequent tours in Britain and abroad, including the British Early Music Network; Performances in Spain, France, Germany, Holland, Poland and Czechoslovakia; US debut in New York, 1988; Many concerts with first modern performances of early music in new editions by Peter Holman; Numerous broadcasts on Radio 3 and elsewhere; Repertoire includes Renaissance Violin Consort Music (Christmas music by Michael Praetorius and Peter Philips, music for Prince Charles I by Orlando Gibbons and Thomas Lupo); Baroque Consort Music by Monteverdi, Matthew Locke (anthems, motets and ceremonial music), Purcell (ayres for the theatre), Georg Muffat (Armonico Tributo sonatas, 1682), Heinrich Biber (Sonate tam aris, quam aulis servientes, 1676), Vivaldi (sonatas and concertos for lute and mandolin, concertos for recorders) and J S Bach (Hunt cantata No 208), with Crispian Steele-Perkins, trumpet, and Emma Kirkby, soprano, among others. Recordings: Many albums.

CAUSSE Gérard, b. 26 June 1948, Toulouse, France. Violist. Education: Studied in Toulouse and at the Paris Conservatoire. Career: Violist of the Via Nova Quartet, 1969-71, Parrenin Quartet, 1972-80; Member of the Ensemble Inter-Contemporain from 1976; Professor at the Boulogne Conservatoire, 1980, Lyon, 1982, Paris, 1987; Chamber musician from 1982, notably with the Ivaldi Quartet. Address: c/o Conservatoire National, 14 Rue de Madrid, F-75008 Paris, France.

CAVA Carlo, b. 16 Aug 1928, Ascoli Piceno, Italy. Singer (Bass). Education: Studied in Rome. Debut: Spoleto, 1955, in L'Italiana in Algeri. Career: Netherlands Opera, Amsterdam, 1959; Glyndebourne, 1961-65, as Seneca in L'Incoronazione di Poppea, as Sarastro, Bartolo in Le nozze di Figaro, Basilio in Il Barbiere di Siviglia and Henry VIII in Anna Bolena; La Scala, 1973, as Boris Godunov; Appearances in Cairo, Amsterdam, Brussels, Frankfurt, Vienna, Munich, Berlin and Paris. Recordings include: Oroveso in Norma; Zaccaria in Nabucco; L'Incoronazione di Poppea; Il Barbiere di Siviglia; Linda di Chamounix. Address: c/o Teatro alla Scala, Via Filodrammatici 2, I-21021 Milan, Italy.

CAVALLIER Nicolas, b. 1964, France. Singer (Bass). Education: Studied at Royal Academy of Music and National Opera Studio (1988-89), with Elisabeth Söderström and with Iris dell'Acqua. Debuts: Nancy Opera, 1987, as Cascanda in The Merry Widow; Sang Achilles in Giulio Cesare conducted by Trevor Pinnock at the Royal Academy of Music. Career: Season 1988-89 in Massenet's Thaïs for Chelsea Opera Group and roles in Les Malheurs d'Orphée (Milhaud), Renard (Stravinsky) and Genévièva de Brabant (Satie) at the Elizabeth Hall; Season 1989-90 with Glass's Fall of the House of Usher in Wales, Henze's The English Cat in Berlin, Messiah with the Bournemouth Sinfonietta and John Metcalf's Tornrak at the Banff Centre in Canada; Sarastro in Die Zauberflöte at Glyndebourne; Sang Don Fernando (Fidelio) for the Glyndebourne Tour, 1990, Zuniga for Welsh National Opera and in Alcione by Marais for Les Arts Florissants in Paris; Masetto for Nancy Opera; Other roles include Don Giovanni, Narbal in Les Troyens, Don Quichotte, Sparafucile and Mozart's Bartolo and Osmin; Season 1991-92 as Masetto at Nancy, Raleigh in Roberto Devereux at Monte Carlo and Caelnus in Lully's Atys with Les Arts Florissants; 1992-93 in Hamlet by Thomas at Monte Carlo, Leporello at Metz and Mr Flint in Billy Budd at Nancy; Loredano in I Due Foscari by Verdi for Scottish Opera at the 1993 Edinburgh Festival; Sang Félix in Donizetti's Les Martyrs at Nancy, 1996; Concert repertoire includes the Verdi and Mozart Requiems, A Child of our Time, Monteverdi Vespers and Die Schöpfung. Honours include: Anne Lloyd Exhibition, Helen Eames Prize, Paton Award and Ricordi Award, Royal Academy of Music. Address: Robert Gilder & Co, Enterprise House, 59-65 Upper Ground, London SE1 9PQ, England.

CAVE Penelope, b. 17 Apr 1951, Guildford, Surrey, England. Harpsichordist. m. Michael Heale, 27 Jul 1974, 1 s, 1 d. Education: GRSM; Royal Academy of Music, 1969-74; Lessons and Masterclasses with Kenneth Gilbert, Colin Tilney, Ton Koopman and Gustav Leonhardt; LRAM. Debut: Wigmore Hall, 1980. Career: Solo recitals, major festivals in England and abroad; Played at Purcell Room and Wigmore Hall and for BBC Radio 3, Belgian Radio and Classic FM; Solo recitals at Edinburgh and Ryedale Summer Music Festivals, 1995; Accompanist at Trinity College of Music; Head of Harpsichord Studies at Morley College, London; Regular Tutor of harpsichord courses, master classes and workshops in England and abroad. Recordings: With the Camerata of London, Garth Hewitt and the Feinstein Ensemble. Contributions to: Harpsichord Fortepiano magazine. Honours: Raymond Russell Memorial Prize for Harpsichord, 1972; 1st Prize at Southport National Harpsichord Competition, 1976; Laureate Bruges International Harpsichord Competition, 1983; ARAM, 1991. Memberships: Musicians Union; Committee Chairman of Incorporated Society of Musicians. Hobby: Watercolour painting. Address: 8 Pit Farm Road, Guildford, Surrey, GU1 2JH, England.

CAVELTI Elsa, b. 4 May 1914, Rorschach, Lake Geneva, Switzerland. Singer (Mezzo-Soprano). Education: Studied in Zurich, Frankfurt and Vienna. Debut: Katowice, 1936.Career: Sang first in Dusseldorf and Dresden, then at La Scala and in Veinna; Vicenza and Vennice 1949 (L'Incoronazione di Poppea); Paris Opera and La Scala 1951 as Brangaene and in Honegger's Judith; For Rome Radio sang in the first performance of Berg's Altenberglieder, 1953; Bayreuth Festival, 1967; Guest appearances in London, Paris, Chicago and New York; Often heard in music by Bach. Recordings include: Fricka in Die Walküre; Brangaene in Tristan und Isolde; Octavian in Der Rosenkavalier.

CECCARINI Giancarlo, b. 19 July 1951, Pisa, Italy. Singer (Baritone). Education: Studied in Pisa and Rome. Debut: Spoleto 1975, as Belcore in L'Elisir d'Amore. Career: Has appeared widely in Italy as Marcello (La Bohème), Cimarosa's Maestro di Capella and Osmano in L'Ormindo by Cavalli (Venice 1976); Performances of Monteverdi's Combattimento at Terni, Bologna, Zurich, Mantua, Cremona and Frankfurt, 1980. Recordings: On Swiss Radio from 1977, including La Gazetta by Rossini; At Genoa has sung Podesta in Docteur Miracle by Bizet, and Gianni Schicchi; San Remo, 1982, as Nabucco; Ping in Turandot at Helsinki, 1991; Records include I Pazzi per Progresso by Donizetti (UORC); Turandot (Nuova Era). Address: c/o Teatro La Fenice, Campo S Fantin 1965, 30124 Venice, Italy.

CECCATO Aldo, b. 18 Feb 1934, Milan, Italy. Conductor. m. Eliana de Sabata, 1966, 2 sons. Education: Verdi Conservatory, Milan, 1948-55; Studied conducting with Albert Wolff and Willem van Otterloo, the Netherlands, 1958; Berlin Hochschule für Musik, 1959-62. Career: Appearances as jazz and concert pianist; Assistant to Sergiu Celibidache, Accademia Musicale Chigiana, Siena, 1960; Guest conducting engagements throughout Italy and Europe; USA debut, Chicago Lyric Opera, 1969; Music Director, Detroit Symphony Orchestra, 1973-77; Generalmusikdirektor, Hamburg State Philharmonic Orchestra, 1975-83; Chief Conductor, Hannover Radio Orchestra, 1985-; Bergen Symphony Orchestra, 1985-; Conducted Maria Stuarda at Bergamo, 1989. Recordings: For ABC; Angel-EMI; Arabesque; Audio Fidelity; Klavier; Philips; Supraphon; La Traviata, Maria Stuarda, The Four Seasons, Mendelssohn's Piano Concertos (John Ogdon), Music by Ravel and Liszt. Honour: 1st Prize, RAI Conducting Competition, 1964. Address: c/o Rundfunkorchester Hannover, Rudolf von Bennigsen Ufer 22, D-3000 Hannover, Germany.

CECCHELE Gianfranco, b. 25 June 1940, Galliera Veneta, Italy. Singer (Tenor). Education: Studied with Marcello del Monaco in Treviso. Career: Sang at Catania from 1964; Many appearances on the major Italian stages; Guest appearances in London, Paris, Barcelona, Hamburg, Munich, Nice, Chicago, Philadelphia and Montreal; Carnegie Hall New York 1968, as Zamoro in a concert performance of Verdi's Alzira; Best known in operas by Puccini and Verdi; Verona between 1967 and 1984; Rio de Janeiro, 1988, as Radames; Mercadante's La Vestale at Split, 1987. Recordings incl: Aroldo by Verdi; Loreley by Catalani; Alzira; Title role in Rienzi by Wagner; Decio in Mercadante's La Vestale, Bongiovanni. Address: c/o Arena di Verona, Piazza Bra 28, 1-3 7121 Verona, Italy.

CECCHI Gabriella, b. 3 Nov 1944, Ricco del Golfo, La Spezia, Italy. Composer. Education: Studied at the Lucca Institute, Genoa Conservatory, 1974-77, in Siena with Franco Donatoni and with Brian Ferneyhough. Career: Performances of her music throughout Italy and elsewhere in Europe. Compositions include: Kite for chamber orchestra, 1981; In proiezione for orchestra, 1986; Riverberi for violin and harpsichord, 1988; Parvula for 10 flutes, 1990; Il gallo rosso, small chamber opera, 1992; Doppel atmung for 4 recorders and percussion, 1993; Grig Bian Ner, ballet, for piano, saxophone and percussion, 1994. Address: c/o SIAE, Sezione Musica, Viale della Letteratura n 30, 00144 Rome, Italy.

CEELY Robert (Paige), b. 17 Jan 1930, Torrington, Connecticut, USA. Composer. m. Jonatha Kropp, 13 Jan 1962. Education: BMus, New England Conservatory, Boston, MA; MA, Mills College, CA; Graduate study at Princeton University, NJ; Major composition teachers include Darius Milhaud, Leon Kirchner, Roger Sessions and Milton Babbitt. Career: Faculty of Composition, Director of Electronic Music at New England Conservatory of Music, Boston, 1967. Compositions: String Trio, 1953; Woodwind Quintet, 1954; Composition for 10 Instruments, 1963; Stratti for Magnetic Tape, 1963; Elegia for Magnetic Tape, 1964; Vonce for Magnetic Tape, 1967; Modules for 7 Instruments, 1968; Logs for 2 Double Basses, 1968; Hymn for Cello and Bass, 1969; Beyond the Ghost Spectrum, ballet, 1969; Mitsyn for Computer Generated Tape, 1971; Slide Music for 4 Trombones, 1974; Rituals for 40 Flutes, 1978; Frames for Computer Generated Tape, 1978; Lullaby for Trombone and Soprano, 1979; Flee, Floret, Florens for 15 Solo Voices, 1979; Piano Piece, 1980; Bottom Dogs for 4 Double Basses, 1981; Roundels for Large Wind Ensemble and Tape, 1981; Piano Variations, 1982; Totems for Oboe and Tape, 1982; Dialogue for Solo Flute, 1983; Giostra for Oboe and Tape, 1984; Minute Rag for Solo Piano, 1985; Pitch Dark for Jazz Ensemble, 1985; Synoecy for Clarinet and Tape, 1986; Timeshares for Percussion Ensemble, 1988; Special K Variations for Piano, 1989; Post hoc, ergo propter hoc for Solo Bass Clarinet, 1989; Harlequin for Solo Double Bass and Tape, 1990; Hypallage for Solo Trumpet and Tape, 1990; Asyndeton for Piano and Tape, 1993; Opera from Fernando Arrabal's The Automobile Graveyard, 1994; Group Sax, for five saxophones, 1996; Music for Ten, 1996; Enchanted Cycles, for computer generated tape, 1996; Auros, for five instruments, 1997. Publication: Electronic Music Resource Book, 1979. Honours: Two Cine Golden Globes for Film Soundtracks, 1976; National Endowment for the Arts Grant, 1979; Alice M Ditson Grant, 1995; New England Conservatory Outstanding Alumnus Award, 1995. Memberships: Broadcast Music Inc; Audio Engineering Society; American Composers Society; Society for Electro-Acoustic in the US; Darius Milhaud Society; Society for Music Theory. Address: 33 Elm Street, Brookline, MA, USA.

CEGOLEA Gabriela, b. 1950, USSR. Singer, (Soprano). Education: Studied in Bucharest and at the Benedetto Marcello Conservatory, Venice; Sang at the Taormina Festival, then studied further at the School of the Royal Opera, Stockholm. Debut: Stockholm, 1977, as Tosca. Career: Appearances as Tosca at Oslo and as Manon at Venice; La Scala Milan with Placido Domingo, conducted by Georges Prêtre; Further engagements in New York, Berlin, Stuttgart, San Francisco, Naples and Rome; Tours of Australia, Brazil and South Korea; Liège, 1989, as Maddalena in Andrea Chenier.

CELLI Joseph, b. 19 Mar 1944, Bridgeport, Connecticut, USA. Composer; Oboist. Education: BME, Hartt College of Music, Hartford, Connecticut, USA, 1962-65; MM (major in oboe performance/composition), Northwestern University, Chicago, 1970-72; Performance Seminar (2 summers), Oberlin Conservatory, Ohio, Private oboe/English horn study with Ray Still (Chicago Symphony) Albert Goltzer (New York Philharmonic), Wayne Rapier (Boston Symphony Orchestra) John Mack (Cleveland Symphony Orchestra), 1970 and 1971; Fulbright Scholar, Korean Traditionl Performing Arts Center, Seoul, Korea, 1991-93. Career: Composer, videomaker, performer throughout Europe, Asia, North and South America, 1972-; Arts Consultant, Panelist, for various state arts agencies, NEA, foundations, 1972-; Executive Director, Real Art Ways (contemporary arts center), Hartford, Connecticut, 1975-86; CEO/Executive Director, New Music America Miami Festival, Florida, 1987-89; Director of Cultural Programs, Miami-Dade Community College, Miami, Florida, 1989-90; Director, OO DISCS Inc Recording company (contemporary American music), 1991-; Founder/Director, Korean Performing Arts Institute, New York/Seoul, 1993-. Compositions include: World Soundprint: Asia for radio (with Jin Hi Kim), 1993; Pink Pelvis: Music For Dance for double reeds, Korean ajeng & Brazilian percussion, 1994; Sunny's piece: Music For Dance with double reeds, Komungo, percussion, 1994; Quintet: for Kayagum, Wx-7 and three kalimba, 1995. Honours include: Numerous fellowships and grants, most recent are: Djerassi Foundation, Composer Residency, California, 1995; Rockefeller Foundation, Bellagio Center Composition Residency, Italy, 1996; Meet the Composer: Composer/Choreographer Grant, 1996; Connecticut Commission on the Arts, Composer Fellowship, 1996. Address: 261 Groovers Avenue, Black Rock, CT 06605-3452, USA.

CEMORE Alan, b. 1958, Wisconsin, USA. Singer (Baritone). Education: BM, Vocal Performance, University of Northern Iowa, 1981; MMus, Indiana University, 1985; Hochschule für Musik, Frankfurt, 1981-82; Studied Voice with Margaret Harshaw and David Smalley. Career: Leading Baritone at the Wiesbaden Opera, 1986-88, Basel Opera, 1988-90, Graz from 1990; Spoleto Festival, 1984 in Die lustige Witwe, 1985, in La Fanciulla del West; Sang Tom in Henze's English Cat at Frankfurt (1986), at Turin and at the 1987 Edinburgh Festival; Wexford as Biagio in Gazzaniga's Don Giovanni and Pantalone in Busoni's Turandot, 1988; Radio and television appearances in Europe, Asia and USA; Over 50 opera roles in the USA and Europe. Recordings include: Die grossmuetige Tomyris by Keiser; Oh wie verfuehrerisch, selections from TV show. Honours: Prizewinner, ARD International Music Competition, Munich, 1984;

Rotary International Graduate Fellowship, 1981; Cole Porter Memorial Fellowship Winner, 1984. Address: c/o Robert Lombardo Associates, One Harkness Plaza, 61 West 62nd Street, Suite 6F, New York, NY 10023, USA.

CEPICKY Leos, b. 21 August 1965, Pardubice, Czech Republic. Musician. m. Katerina Kus, 28 April 1985, 1 son, 1 daughter. Education: Prague Academy of Arts. Debut: Prague Spring Quartet Competition, 1988. Career: Member, Wihan Quartet, Music Festivals in England, Austria, Germany, France, Italy, Belgium, Spain, Portugal, Singapore, USA, Japan, Rome and on Radio France. Recordings: Popron (Suk, Dvorak, Janacek); Haydn op 64, op 71; Mozart 168, 458, 465; Dvorak, Smetana I; Janacek 1 & 2; Ravel & Britten 2; Beethoven op 59 1, 2, 3, op 14; Dvorak op 51 & op 106. Contributions to: The Strad. Honours: Prize, Prague Spring Competition, 1988; Prize, London International String Quartet Competition. Hobby: Sport. Current Management: Pragoart Music. Address: Archaeologicka 1884, 15000 Praha 5, Czech Republic.

CERHA Friedrich, b. 17 Feb 1926, Vienna, Austria. Composer. Education: Studied at the Vienna Academy, 1946-51, with Vasa Prihoda (violin) and Alfred Uhl (composistion) and at the university; Dr.phil. Career: With Kurt Schwertsik co-founded ensemble Die Reihe, 1958, with performances of contemporary music and works by the Second Viennese School; Completion of Act III of Alban Berg's Lulu performed at the Paris Opéra, 1979; Opera Baal premiered at the 1981 Salzburg Festival; Der Rattenfänger at Graz, 1987. Compositions: Espressioni fondamentali for orchestra, 1957; Relazioni fragili for harpsichord and chamber orchestra; Fasce for orchestra, 1959; Spiegel I-VII, 1960-61; Netzwerk, musical theatre, 1962-80, premiered Wiener Festwochen, 1981; Espressioni Exercises for baritone and chamber ensemble, 1962-67; Langegger Nachtmusik I and II for orchestra, 1969, 1970, III, 1991; Double Concerto for violin, cello and orchestra, 1975; Baal-Gesänge for Bariton and orchestra, 1981; Keintate I, 1981-83, II, 1984-85,for voice and 11 instruments; Requiem für Hollensteiner for bariton, choir and orchestra, 1982-83; Eine Art Chansons for voice and 3 instruments, 1985-86; Phantasiestück in C's Manier for cello and orchestra, 1989; String-Quartett I, 1989, II, 1990, III, 1992; Impulse for orchestra, 1992-93; Concerto for viola and orchestra, 1993; Concertino for violin, accordion and ensemble, 1994; Requiem for choir and orchestra, 1994. Publications: Concerto for Cello and Orchestra, 1996-97; Lichtenberg-Splitter, for baritone and ensemble, 1997. Address: Kupelwiesergasse14, 1130 Vienna, Austria.

CERMAKOVA Vera, b. 17 Mar 1961, Prague, Czech Republic. Composer; Pianist; Music teacher. m. Josef Cermák, 12 July 1984, 1 son. Education: Conservatoire in Prague: Finished piano studies with Professor Alena Poláková, 1977-83; Passed the branch of Composition with Professor Oldrich Semerák. 1986-92. Career: Teaching piano and composition at Music School in Kladno; Interpretation of piano compositions - participation in festivals; Days of contemporary music in Prague, Atelier 90; Music studio N; Recording for Czech broadcast. Compositions: The free cycle of Three String Quartets entitled The Plays of Lights, 1993; Fragments No 1-4 of symphonic orchestra, 1993; Seven Preludes for guitar solo, 1994; Three Bagatelles of Saxophone Quartets, 1996. Recordings: For Czech broadcast: Prelude And Rhythmic Fanatasia, piano solo, 1992; Fantasia, piano solo, 1993; Ostinato, Melodic No 2 piano solo, 1995; Kaleidoskop, piano solo, 1996; Seclusion Of Clarinet, clarinet solo, 1997. Memberships: Association of Musicians, Scientists and Artists, Prague; Atelier 90, Prague; Music studio N, Association of Contemporary Music. Hobbies: Travelling; History. Address: Karla Tomana 824, 272 04 Kladno, Czech Republic.

CERNY Florian, b. 1954, Germany. Singer (Baritone). Education: Studied in Australia, Vienna and Munich. Career: Solo debut with the Israel National Opera; Principal baritone of the Kiel Opera and has sung in Hamburg, Dusseldorf, Hanover and elsewhere in Europe; Geneva Opera as Biterolf in Tannhäuser; Season 1984-85 as Alfio and Tonio (Cav and Pag) with Opera North and Mozart's Figaro with English National Opera; Bayerische Staatsoper Munich 1986-, as Bretigny in Manon, Caliph in Der Barbier von Bagdad, Schaunard, and Dominic in Arabella; Other roles include Wagner's Dutchman and Kothner, Riccardo (I Puritani), Iago and Don Carlos (La Forza del Destino). Address: Music International, 13 Ardilaun Road, London N5 2QR, England.

CERNY Pavel, b. 9 October 1970, Praha, Czech Republic. Organist. Education: Academy of Music. Career: Live TV recording, 1994; Several Czech radio record of History Organ; Set of History Organ Recordings for the Dutch Radio (KRO) and Production; Concerts: Prague Philharmony (Recital, 1995); Charters (FR), Padova, Verona (IT) (Recitals, 1996); Wienna, 1994; Salzburg, 1994. Recordings: CD, Romantic Organ Repertoire for Four Hands and Four Legs, with Martin Rost (Germany), 1997; CD, Jiri Ropek, Composer and Organist. Publications: Cooperation to International Organ Dictionary -

Belgie. Contributions: Study about significant Prague Organs - Hetorgel, 1997. Honours: 1st Prize, Opava (National), 1990; 1st Prize, Ljublja, 1992; 1st Prize, Prague, 1994. Hobby: Scooter Travelling. Address: Noutonice 10, 252 64 Velké Prilepy, Czech.

CERQUETTI Anita, b. 13 Mar 1931, Montecorsaro-Macerata, Italy. Singer (Soprano). Education: Studied at the Liceo Morlacchi in Perugia. Debut: Spoleto 1951, as Aida. Career: Sang Aida and the Trovatore Leonora at Verona, 1953; Chicago Lyric Opera, 1955-56, debut as Amelia in Un Ballo in Maschera; New York 1957, in Paride ed Elena by Gluck; Milan 1958 as Abigaille in Nabucco; Other roles include Norma, La Gioconda and Elena in I Vespri Siciliani. Recordings: La Gioconda (Decca); Reiza in Oberon; Mathilde in Guillaume Tell; Elvira in Verdi's Ernani; Zoraima in Les Abencérages by Cherubini (Cetra). Address: c/o Teatra alla Scala, Via Filodrammatici 2, Milan, Italy.

CERVENA Sona, b. 9 Sept 1925, Prague, Czech Republic. Singer (Mezzo-Soprano). Education: Studied with Robert Rosner and Lydia Wegener in Prague. Career: janacek Opera Brno, 1952-58, Staatsoper Berlin, 1958-61, Deutsche Oper Berlin, 1962-64, Opera Frankfurt, 1964-90; Title, Kammersaengerin Berlin and Frankfurt; Guest appearances, Prague, Vienna, Amsterdam, Brussels, Geneva, London, Milano, Paris, Barcelona, Lisbon, San Francisco, Los Angeles, Chicago; Festivals, Bayreuth 1960-66, Salzburg 1961, Glyndebourne 1963-64, Edinburgh 1966-78. Address: Thalia Theater, Alstertor, D-20095 Hamburg, Germany.

CERVENKA Jan, b. 1940, London, England. Conductor. Education: Studied at the Royal College of Music and the Berlin Hochschule. Career: Assistant and Conductor at the Munster and Wiesbaden opera houses then returned to England to conduct Britten's Noye's Fludde; Guest with the BBC orchestras, in Venezuela with Nielsen's 4th Symphony, Holland, Bulgaria and Rumania; Further concerts at the Albert and Festival Halls, London; Music Director of Worthing Borough Council from 1979; Guest Conductor with the Belgian Radio Symphony Orchestra and Choir from 1986. Address: c/o Manygate Management, 13 Cotswold Mews, 30 Battersea Square, London, SW11 3RA, England.

CERVENKOVA Milada, b. 8 Sept 1947, Trebic, Czech Republic. Orchestra Musician. m. Stanislav Cervenka, 30 Jan 1971. Education: Conservatoire Brno - violin; Conservatoire Ostrava - composition. Debut: Violin - Brno, 1968; Composition - Ostrava, 1990. Career: Violinist, Moravian Philharmonic Orchestra Olomouc, from 1968; Performance of compositions in Prague, Brno, Ostrava, Olomouc, Plzen and Heidelberg, from 1990. Compositions: 4 recorded compositions from 22 chamber, vocal and orchestral works. Recordings: Sonata for violin and piano; String quartet; Passacaglia for big orchestra; Pastoral Suite for flute and harp. Honour: Year's Prize of Czech Music Fund, Prague, 1992. Membership: Society of Czech Composers. Hobby: Hare Krishna. Current Management: Member of Moravian Philharmonic Orchestra Olomouc. Address: Hellerova 13, 77200 Olomouc, Czech Republic.

CERVESATO Michela, b. 29 Sept 1954, Motta di L, Treviso, Italy. Pianist; Singer; Musical Paleographer. m. Walter Durigon, 28 Oct 1989, 1 son. Education: Diploma in Musical Paleography & Philology, University of Pavia; Diploma in Piano; Diploma in Singing. Career: Many TV and radio appearances; As Pianist and Singer (Italian Renaissance music), concerts in Italy and abroad. Compositions: Transcription and revision of Renaissance frottole. Recordings: Ascolta, infida, un sogno, LP, Celesta Records, 1986. Contributions to: A Collection of 19th Century Musicians' Letters in La Nuova Rivista Musicale Italiana ERI, 1985. Honour: Concorso Kolbe Prize, Naples, 1980. Hobbies: Cooking; Basketball; Travel. Address: Via Corazzin No 14, 31046 Oderzo, Italy.

CERVETTI Sergio, b. 9 November 1940, Dolores, Uruguay. Composer; Teacher. Education: E Krenek & S Grove, Peabody Conservatory of Music, Baltimore, USA, 1963-67. Career: Composer in Residence, German Artists' Programme, West Berlin, 1969; Faculty, Tisch School of the Arts, New York University, 1970-. Compositions: String Trio, 1963; Piano Sonata, 1964; 5 Sequences for Flute, Horn, Cello, Electric Guitar, Piano, Percussion, 1966; Orbitas, Orchestra, 1967; El Carro de Heno, 1967; Zinctum, 1968; Peripetia, 1970; Plexus, 1971; Madrigal III, 1976; 4 Fragments of Isadora, 1979; Enclosed Time for Electronics, 1985; Night Trippers, 1986; Leyenda, for Soprano and Orchestra, 1991; Concerto for Harpsichord and 11 Instruments, 1992. Recordings: Compositions recorded on Composers' Recordings Inc and Periodic Music Inc; Film Music, Segments of The Hay Wain used in Oliver Stone Natural Born Killers, 1994. Honours: Many commissions; Grants for NEA, New York State Council for the Arts, and Meet the Composer. Membership: Broadcast Music Inc. Address: 212 East Court Street, Doylestown, PA 18901, USA.

CHABRUN Daniel, b. 26 Jan 1925, Mayenne, France. Conductor. Education: Graduated Paris Conservatoire, 1954. Career: Many performances of modern music in France and elsewhere; Anton Webern festival with the ensemble Ars Nova, 1965, and premiere of Claude Prey's opera Jonas, 1966; Has also given works by Maurice Ohana, Lutoslawski, Xenakis, Barraud and Denisov; French premiere of Purcell's Indian Queen, 1966; Directed the orchestra of the Paris Conservatoire from 1972; Professor at the Montreal Conservatoire, 1975; Inspector with the French Ministry of Culture, 1980. Address: c/o Université de Montreal, Faculty of Music, 2900 Boulevard Edouard Montpetit, Montreal, Quebec, Canada H3C 3J7.

CHACHAVA Vazha, b. 20 April 1933, Tbilisi, Georgia. Pianist; Accompanist. Education: Graduate, 24th Male School, Tbilisi, 1951; Study, Ruslaveli Theatre College, Tbilisi, 1953-57; Graduate, Central Music School, Tbilisi, 1952; Studies, Saradzhishvili Tbilisi Concervatory, 1958-62. Debut: Solo Concert, Tbilisi Conservatory, 1952. Career: Concerts and Recitals with E Obraztsova, I Archipova, V Chernov, V Lukiyanets, S Schwets, A Papian, N Anguladze, Z Sotkilava, G Tsypola, M Amiranashvili, M Kasrashvili in many Countries of Europe, America and Asia, Among them Recitals in La Scala, Lisseo, Maryinsky Theatre and Many Famous Concert Halls; Chairman, 1st and 2nd Russian National Accompanists Competitions; Jury, 14th and 15th Glinka International Opera Singers Competitions; Many Film, Television and Radio Russian Nationwide Broadcastings and Appearances. Recordings: Melodia; R Schuman, Romances, E Obraztsova, 1979; Tchaikovsky, Romances, E Obraztsova, 1979; G Rossini Petite Messe Solennele, 1981; O Taktakishvili Vocal Poems on G Tabidze Verses, 1982; Lieder von Komitas with Hasmik Papian, 1996. Publications: Gerald Moor - Singer and Accompanist, 1987; Chamber-Vocal Music, Tchaikovsky Romances, 1988; G Sviridov Romances, Accompanist's Notes, 1995. Honours include: State Medal, Valiant Labour, 1971; Glinka Russian Opera Singer Competition, 1975. Hobbies: AMICI VERDI. Hobbies: Collecting Books; Fine Arts. Address: Bolshoi Nicolopescovsky per 3-16, Moscow 121002, Russia.

CHAILLY Luciano, b. 19 January 1920, Ferrara, Italy. Composer; Administrator; Teacher. m. Anna Maria Motta, 1 son, 2 daughters. Education: Violin Diploma, Fa, 1941; BA, University of Bologna, 1943; Diploma, Verdi Conservatory, Milan, 1945; Studied Composition with R Bossi and P Hindemith. Career: Director of Music Programming, Italian Radio and Television, 1950-67; Teacher of Composition, Perugia Conservatory, Verdi Conservatory, Milan, 1968-83; Artistic Director 1968-71, General Director 1976-, Teatro alla Scala, Milan; Artistic Director, Teatro Regio, Turin, 1972; Angelicum, Milan, 1973-75; Arena, Verona, 1975-76; Genoa Opera, 1983-85. Compositions: Operas include: Ferrovia soprelevata, 1955; Una domanda di matrimonio, 1957; Il canto del cigno, 1957; La riva delle Sirti, 1959; Procedura penale, 1959; Il mantello, 1960; Era proibito, 1963; Vassiliev, 1967; Markheim, 1967; L'Idiota, 1970; Sogno (ma forse no), 1975; La cantatrice calva, 1986; Instrumental include: Toccata for Orchestra, 1948; 12 Sonate tritematiche: No 1 for Piano, 1951; No 2 for Orchestra, 1952; No 3 for Chamber Orchestra, 1952; No 4 for Orchestra, 1953; No 5 for Cello and Piano, 1954; No 6 for Piano, 1954; No 7 for Strings, 1955; No 8 for Violin and Piano, 1955; Sequenze dell' Artide for Orchestra, 1961; Piccole serenate for Strings, 1967; Es-Kammerkonzert for Small Instrumental Group, 1983; Several chamber works; Piano pieces; Choral music; Songs. Honours: Le Muse, 1968; Legion d'oro and Rosa del Garda, 1973; Leonardo and S Francesco d'oro, 1977; L'Olifante d'oro, 1978; S Giorgio, 1981; Frescobaldi, 1983; Medaglia d'oro from the President of the Republic, 1984; Premio Lorenzo il Magnifico, 1987; Accademico di Santa Cecilia, Rome, 1990; Premio Pirandello, 1994. Address: Viale Bianca Maria 17, 20122 Milan, Italy.

CHAILLY Riccardo, b. 20 Feb 1953, Milan, Italy. Orchestral Conductor. Education: Conservatories of Giuseppe Verdi, Milan and Perugia and with Piero Guarino, Franco Caracciolo and Franco Ferrara. Career: Assistant to Conductor, La Scala, Milan, 1972-74; Debut, Chicago Opera USA 1974 with Madama Butterfly; Debut, La Scala, Milan, Italy, 1978; Debut, Covent Garden, London, England, 1979, Don Pasquale; British concert debut, London Symphony and at Edinburgh Festival, Scotland, 1979; American concert debut, Los Angeles Philharmonic, California, 1980; Metropolitan Opera debut, New York, 1982, Les Contes d'Hoffmann; Principal Guest Conductor, London Philharmonic, England, 1982-85; Chief Conductor, RSO, Berlin, 1982-90, with the orchestra gave the premiere of Schoenberg's Frühlingstod; Debut, Vienna State Opera, Austria, 1983; Salzburg Festival, 1984, Macbeth, 1985, 1986, 1988, La Cenerentola; Debut, New York Philharmonic, USA, 1985; Exclusive Recording Contract with Decca; Music Director of Bologna, Teatro Comunale, Italy, 1986-89; Principal Conductor, Concertgebouw, Amsterdam, Netherlands, 1988-; Promenade Concerts, 1990, with Beethoven's 1st, Prokofiev's 3rd, Schumann's 4th Symphonies; Conducted The Fiery Angel, Holland Festival, 1990; Rossini's Ricciardo e Zoraide at Pesaro; Concertgebouw, Bruckner's 5th

Symphony, Barbican Centre, May 1991; Conducted Otello at the 1996 Holland Festival. Recordings include: Alexander Nevsky; Carmina Burana; Bruckner's Symphonies No 3 and No 7; Rossini Overtures; William Tell; Andrea Chénier; The Rake's Progress; Tchaikovsky Symphony No 5. Honour: Decorated grand ufficiale della Repubblica Italiana. Membership: Honorary Member, Royal Academy of Music, London. Address: c/o Jacob Obrechtstraat 51, 1071 KJ Amsterdam, Netherlands.

CHAITKIN David, b. 16 May 1938, New York City, USA. Composer. m. Carol McCauley, 23 July 1960, 1 son. Education: BA, Pomona College, 1959; MA, University of California at Berkeley, 1965; Studied with Luigi Dallapiccola, Seymour Shifrin, Max Deutsch, Andrew Imbrie and Karl Kohn. Career: Early experience as a jazz pianist; Composed music for film, The Game; Commissions from Philadelphia Composers' Forum, Sylvan Winds, New Hampshire Music Festival, Da Capo Chamber Players, New York State Council on the Arts, Quintet of the Americas, Chamber Music America; Gordon Gotteib; Pomona College, in honour of its Centennial; Anders Paulsson/Gotland (Sweden) Chamber Music Festival, Francesco Trio/Koussevitzky Music Foundation; Professor of Music, Reed College, 1968-69; New York University, 1969-76. Compositions: Symphony; Summersong, for 23 wind instruments; Etudes for Piano; Concerto for Flute and Strings; Seasons Such as These for mixed chorus a cappella; Serenade for 7 players; Scattering Dark and Bright, duo for piano and percussion; Quintet, mixed chamber ensemble; Pacific Images, for chamber orchestra; Music in Five Parts, for septet; Nocturne for Woodwind Quintet; Impromptu for Piano; Song Cycle for soprano and piano, 1992; Three Dances for Piano; Rhapsody for Cello and Piano; Aria, for soprano saxophone and strings. Recordings: Etudes for piano, David Burge pianist; Serenade, New York New Music Ensemble, Black; Seasons Such as These, Cantata Singers, Harbison; Summersong, for 23 wind instruments, Sylvan Winds, Weisberg; Scattering Dark and Bright. Publications: Etudes for piano, 1979; Summersong, 1983; Nocturne, 1991; Impromptu for piano, 1993; Quintet, 1988; Prelude and Dance, Piano Solo, 1995. Honours: National Endowment for the Arts, 1981; Guggenheim Fellowship, 1985; American Academy of Arts and Letters, 1980, 1994. Current Management: Music Publishing Services, 236 West 26th Street, Suite 11-S, New York, NY 10001, USA. Address: 160 West 87th Street, New York, NY 10024, USA.

CHALIER Alexis, b. 19 March 1960, Geneva, Switzerland. Musician; Composer. m. Sabine Krogmann, 2 sons, 1 daughter. Education: Diplome de Hautbois; Licence de Concert. Debut: Geneva, Switzerland. Career: Several Concert Tours and Appearances on Radio and Television. Compositions: Trichromie, 1993; Persistance, 1994; Concertino Grosso, 1995; Le Mythe d'Orphie, 1997. Recordings: Mozart's Requiem. Honours: Several. Memberships: Association of Swiss Musicians. Hobbies: Sports; Gardening. Address: Ch des Bois 41b, 1255 Veyrier, Switzerland.

CHALKER Margaret, b. 1958, Waterloo, New York, USA. Singer (Soprano). Education: BME, Studied at Baldwin-Wallace College in Ohio; MM, Syracuse University. Career: Mostly Mozart Festival New York as Sifare in Mitridate and Giunia in Lucio Silla; Houston Opera as Pamina; Deutsche Oper am Rhein Dusseldorf from 1985, as Oscar (Ballo in Maschera), Gilda, Celia (Haydn's La Fedelta Premiata) and Lauretta in Gianni Schicchi; Zurich Opera from 1987, as Pamina, Gilda, Jemmy in Guillaume Tell, Sophie (Rosenkavalier) and Janacek's Vixen; Other roles include Mozart's Countess and Donna Anna, Micaela, Antonia in Les Contes d'Hoffmann and Helen in Gluck's Paride ed Elena; Many concert appearances, notably in works by Bach and Composers of the 20th Century. Address: c/o Opernhaus Zurich, Falkenstrasse 1, CH-8008 Zurich, Switzerland.

CHALLENGER Robert, b. 1967, South Yorkshire, England. Singer (Tenor). Education: Studied at the Guildhall School of Music; Schubert Lieder with Martin Isepp and French Melodie with Suzanne Danco and Hugues Cuenod at Aldeburgh. Career: Concert appearances as the Evangelist in Bach's Passions, Handel's Messiah and Alexander's Feast; Mozart Requiem and C Minor Mass; Haydn Creation and Mass in Time of War; Britten Rejoice in the Lamb and Cantata Accademica; Other concert repertory includes music by Palestrina, Byrd, Cage and Feldman; Operatic roles include Beppe in Pagliacci, Brack Weaver in Weill's Down in the Valley and parts in La jollie Fille de Perth and Rossini's Il Viaggio a Reims. Honours include: Scholarships to Aldeburgh; Winner, Young Songmakers' Almanac Competition (recital at St John's Smith Square); Gramophone Prize for recording of Chamber Music, 1992. Address: c/o Royal Opera House, Covent Garden, London WC2, England.

CHALLIS Philip, b. 11 Aug 1929, Huddersfield, Yorkshire, England. Pianist. m. Mary J White, 19 Nov 1955. Education: Huddersfield College; Royal Manchester College of Music, studies with Herbert Fryer, Marguerite Long, Joszef Gat and Ilona Kabos. Debut: BBC, London, 1943. Career: Many broadcasts and television appearances in England, America and Canada; Innumerable concert tours in England, America and Canada,

Europe, Scandinavia and the Far East. Recordings: Mephisto Music, Liszt; Liszt-Beethoven, Piano Transcriptions; Sonatas of John Field; Selected Piano works, Moscheles; Second Piano Concerto, Josef Holbrooke. Honour: Fellow, Royal Manchester College of Music, 1972. Membership: Incorporated Society of Musicians, Chairman of Brighton Centre, 1983-86. Hobbies: Cooking; Travel. Address: Balaton, 97 Alinora Crescent, West Worthing, Sussex BN12 4HH, England.

CHALMERS Penelope, b. 5 Oct 1946, Worcester, England. Singer (Soprano). Education: Studied at Bristol University. Career: Has sung such roles as the Marschallin (Der Rosenkavalier), Leonora (Trovatore), Turandot and Tosca with fringe opera companies; Title role in the British premiere of Bruch's Lorelei for University College Opera, Fiordiligi for Pavilion Opera and Rezia in Weber's Oberon at Haddo House, Scotland; London debut at the Prom concerts in Lambert's Rio Grande; Recent appearances as the Dyer's Wife in Die Frau ohne Schatten at Geneva, Helmwige and Ortlinde in Die Walküre at Covent Garden and Emilia Marty in The Makropoulos Case at Hagen, Germany; Donna Anna and Lady Billows in Albert Herring for Opera 1980, season 1991-92; Judith in Bluebeard's Castle, at the English National Opera, 1993; Sang title role in Salome with Scottish Opera; National Television debut as prima donna in BBC production of Stendhal's Le Rouge et le Noir, 1993. Current Management: Athole Still International Management Limited. Address: Foresters Hall, 25-27 Westow Street, London SE19 3RY, England.

CHAMPNEY Wendy, b. 23 Feb 1958, USA. Violist. Education: Studied at Indiana University, the International Menuhin Academy in Gstaad. Career: Co-Founder and Violist of the Carmina Quartet, 1984; Appearances from 1987 in Europe, Israel, USA and Japan; Regular concerts at the Wigmore Hall from Oct 1987; Concerts at the South Bank Centre, London, Amsterdam Concertgebouw, the Kleine Philharmonie in Berlin, Konzertverein Vienna; Four engagements in Paris 1990-91, seven in London; Tours in Australasia, USA, Japan; Concerts at the Hohenems, Graz, Hong Kong, Montreux, Schleswig-Holstein, Bath, Lucerne and Prague Spring Festivals; Collaborations with Dietrich Fischer-Dieskau, Olaf Bär and Mitsuko Uchida. Recordings: Albums for Ex Libris, Bayer, Claves and Denon (from 1991). Honour: Joint winner (with members of Carmina Quartet) Paolo Borciani String Quartet Competition in Reggio Emilia, Italy, 1987. Address: c/o Intermusica Artists' Management, 16 Duncan Terrace, London N1 8BZ, England.

CHANCE Michael, b. 7 Mar 1955, Penn, Buckinghamshire, England. Singer (Counter-Tenor). Career: Choral Scholar at King's College Cambridge; Appearances with the English Chamber Orchestra, Academy of Ancient Music, English Concert, Orchestra of St John's, Smith Square and the Bournemouth Sinfonietta; Handel's Messiah at the Alice Tully and Avery Fisher Halls New York; Concerts with John Eliot Gardiner and the Monteverdi Choir in New York and at the Göttingen and Aix-en-Provence Festivals; Operatic roles include Apollo in Cavalli's Jason (Buxton Festival), 1983; Andronico in Handel's Tamerlano (Lyon Opera), 1985; Otho in Handel's Agrippina (Bath Festival), Ottone in Monteverdi's L'Incoronazione di Poppea and the Military Governor in the world premiere of Judith Weir's A Night at the Chinese Opera (Kent Opera); Britten's Oberon and Voice of Apollo with Glyndebourne Opera; Paris Opera debut 1988, as Ptolomeo in Handel's Giulio Cesare; Season 1992, as Amphinomous in Monteverdi's Ulisse for ENO, Julius Caesar for Scottish Opera and Britten's Apollo at Glyndebourne; Sang in the premiere of Birtwistle's Second Mrs Kong, 1994; Concerts include Bach cantatas at the Promenade Concerts, London, Messiah at King's College, Cambridge, Royal Albert Hall and in Edinburgh; Handel's Theodora at the Paris Opera, 1987; Israel in Egypt in Stuttgart and at La Scala, Milan; Jephtha in London and Göttingen; Bach's St Matthew Passion in Spain and London, B Minor Mass with the Manchester Camerata; World premiere of Bennett's Ophelia, 1988; Apollo in Death in Venice with Glyndebourne Touring Opera at Norwich, 1989; The Fairy Queen with the Sixteen, Elizabeth Hall, 1990; Promenade Concerts, London, Britten's Cantata Misericordium, Mozart's Credo Mass, 1991; Sang the title role in Gluck's Orpheus for ENO, 1997. Recordings: Bach's St John Passion, Christmas Oratorio and St Matthew Passion, Handel's Messiah (Deutsche Grammophon); Jephtha (Philips); Cavalli's Giasone (Harmonia Mundi); Bacco and other roles, The Death of Orpheus by Stefano Landi; Handel's Tamerlano, Orfeo settings by Monteverdi and Gluck. Address: c/o IMG Artists, Media House, 3 Burlington Lane, London W4 2TH, England.

CHANCE Nancy (Laird), b. 19 Mar 1931, Cincinnati, Ohio, USA. Composer. m. 7 Sept 1950, divorced, 3 sons. Education: Magna cum laude, The Foxcroft School, 1945-49; Bryn Mawr College, 1949-50; Columbia University, part-time, 1959-68; Piano with William R Smith and Lilias McKinnon; Theory and Composition with Otto Luening and Vladimir Ussachevsky; Sundance Institute Film Composer Fellow, 1988. Career: Performances of her works by Philadelphia Orchestra, St Louis

Symphony, The Jupiter Symphony, The American Composers Orchestra, The League ISCM, The Group for Contemporary Music, The New Music Consort, Da Capo Chamber Players, Relache, Continuum, The Goldman Memorial Band and numerous others; World premiere of Planasthai with the Cleveland Chamber Symphony. Compositions: Odysseus, solo voice, percussion and orchestra; String Quartet No 1; Liturgy for orchestra; Elegy for string orchestra; Woodwind Quintet; Domine, Dominus: Motet for double chorus acapella; Duos III for violin and cello; Exultation and Lament for alto saxophone and timpani; Ritual Sounds, for brass quintet and percussion; Daysongs for alto flute and percussion; 3 Rilke Songs for soprano, flute, English horn and cello; In Paradisum, solo voice, mixed chorus, orchestra; Rhapsodia For Marimba Quartet; Ceremonial for Percussion Quartet; Planasthai, chamber orchestra, piano and percussion, 1992. Recordings: Daysongs, Ritual Sounds, Duos III and Lament all recorded on Opus One Records. Honours: Winner: ASCAP Rudolph Missim Prize for Orchestral Compositions, 1982, 1984; NEA Composer Fellowships, 1981, 1983. Address: PO Box 96, Austerlitz, New York, NY 12017, USA.

CHANG Debra (Wei Kuan), b. 23 Oct 1952, Honolulu, Hawaii, USA. Composer; Multimedia Performance Artist. Education: BA, Ethnomusicology, BMus, composition, University of Hawaii; MMus, North Texas State University; DMA, University of North Texas. Career: Co-Founder, Intermedia Ensemble with Phil Winsor; Guest Composer Residenfcies at American New Music Festivals and Universities including New Mexico State University, East Texas State University, Rice University, University of California at San Diego, University of Redlands, San Diego State University, University of New Mexico, Cleveland State University, Bowling Green State University, Del Mar College, Baylor University; Administrative Assistant, Teaching Fellow, Centre for Experimental Music & Intermedia, North Texas State University, 1983-86. Address: 109 Virginia Street, Bellingham, WA 98225, USA.

CHANG Sarah, b. 10 Dec 1980, Philadelphia, USA. Violinist. Education: Studied at the Juilliard School with Dorothy DeLay. Debut: With the New York Philharmonic, 1988. Career: Has appeared at London's Festival Hall and with the Los Angeles Philharmonic, Chicago Symphony, Leipzig Gewandhaus, Berlin Philharmonic, Concertgebouw Amsterdam, Orchestre National De France and London Symphony Orchestras. Recordings include: Concertos by Paganini and Tchaikovsky. Address: c/o ICM Artists (London) Ltd, Oxford House, 76 Oxford Street, London, W1R 1RB.

CHANG Yuan-Chih Beryl, b. 22 Dec 1962, Shanghai, China. Violinist; Business Administrator. Education: Shanghai Conservatory of Music, 1978-80; BMus, Manhattan School of Music, New York, 1987; MA, Columbia University, New York, 1991; MBA, 1997. Debut: Shanghai Symphony Hall, China, 1980. Career: Shanghai Symphony Orchestra at 15 years of age; Orchestra performances and tours with New York City Symphony Orchestra, New York City Opera, American Symphony Orchestra. Honours: Winner, 26th Annual Congress of Strings in US; Kappa Delta Pi; Numerous Music Merit Scholarships. Hobbies: Cooking; Reading. Address: 440 West End Avenue, Apt 11-D, New York, NY 10024, USA.

CHANG-YONG Liao, b. 1969, China. Singer (Baritone). Career: Many engagements in the Far and East and Europe, notably in operas by Mozart (Le nozze di Figaro) and Massenet, with chansons by Duparc, Debussy and Ravel; Contestant at the 1995 Cardiff Singer of the World Competition. Address: c/o Mr Wu Xun, Bureau of External Relations, Ministry of Culture, 2 Shatan Beijie, Beijing 100722, China.

CHAPIN Schuyler (Garrison), b. 13 Feb 1923, New York, New York, USA. Commissioner of Cultural Affairs for the City of New York; Music, Arts and Education Administrator. m. 15 Mar 1947, 4 sons. Education: Longy School of Music, 1940-41. Career: Vice-President, Programs, Lincoln Center, New York, 1963-68; Executive Producer, Amberson Productions, 1968-72; General manager, Metropolitan Opera, New York, 1972-76; Dean, School of Arts, Columbia University, 1976-87; Dean Emeritus, 1987-; Vice President. Worldwide Concert and Artist Activities, Steinway and Sons, 1990-92. Recordings: Director, Columbia Records, USA, Masterworks and later, Vice-President, Creative Services; Recorded, among others, Bernstein and the New York Philharmonic; Ormandy, Philadelphia Orchestra; Szell, Cleveland Orchestra; Stern; Serkin; Francescatti; Casadesus; Fleisher; Tucker; Farrell; Gould; Juilliard Quartet; Budapest Quartet. Publications: Musical Chairs, 1978; Leonard Bernstein: Notes From A Friend, 1992; Sopranos, Mezzos, Tenors, Bassos and Other Friends, 1995. Contributions to: New York Times; National Review; Prime Time; Horizons, and others. Honours: Gold Medal, National Arts Club; Honorary LHD, New York University, Hobart College, and William Smith College, 1974; Honorary DLitt, Emerson College, 1976; Hon Mus D, Mannes College, New School, 1990. Address: 655 Park Avenue, Apt 8c, New York, NY 10021, USA.

CHAPMAN Janice, b. 1945, Australia. Singer (Soprano); Teacher. Education: Studied at the University of Adelaide and at the Royal College of Music in London and the London Opera Centre. Career: Sang leading roles with Sadler's Wells/English National Opera, Welsh and Scottish Operas and in many European houses; Toured Russia with the English Opera Group under Benjamin Britten and worked with the composer on the roles of Miss Jesel and Mrs Grose in The Turn of the Screw; Sang Mrs Julian in the stage premiere of Owen Wingrave at Covent Garden 1973; Other Britten roles have been Ellen Orford and Lady Billows, and she has sung in operas by Mozart, Wagner, Verdi and Puccini; Concert engagements with leading orchestras; Sang with her trio The Alexandra Ensemble at the Women's Music Festival at Beersheba in Israel, 1986; Appeared as Mrs Grose for New Israel Opera, 1990, conducted by Roderick Brydon; Professor of Voice at the London College of Music. Address: c/o Korman International Management, Crunnells Green, Preston, Herts SG4 7UQ, England.

CHAPPLE Brian, b. 24 Mar 1945, London, England. Composer. Education: GRSM, LRAM, Royal Academy of Music, London. Compositions include: Scherzos for four pianos, 1970; Trees Revisited, 1970; Praeludiana, 1971; Green and Pleasant, 1973; In Ecclesiis, 1976; Piano Concerto, 1977; Cantica, 1978; Venus Fly Trap, 1979; Little Symphony, 1982; Lamentations of Jeremiah, 1984; Piano Sonata, 1986; Magnificat, 1986; In Memoriam, 1989; Berkeley Tribute, 1989; Frink Tribute, 1990; Requies, 1991; Missa Brevis, 1991; Three Motets, 1992; Songs of Innocence, 1993; Ebony and Ivory, 1995; Anthems, canticles, children's songs, piano music. Honours: BBC Monarchy 1000 Prize, 1973; UNESCO International Rostrum of Composers, 1976. Memberships: Performing Right Society; Association of Professional Composers. Hobbies: Gardening; Drawing. Current Management: Chester Music. Address: 31 Warwick Road, New Barnet, Herts EN5 5EQ, England.

CHAPUIS Gérard, b. 21 Oct 1931, Lyon, France. Singer (Bass). Education: Studied at the Lyon Conservatory. Career: Sang with the Lyon Opera, 1954-56, Paris Opéra, 1956-73; Among his best roles have been the Minister in Fidelio, Sparafucile, Ramphis, Raimondo (Lucia di Lammermoor), Pistol, Hector in Les Troyens, Zarasto (Die Zauberflöte), Commandator (Don Giovanni), Osmin (Die Entführung), Un ballo in Maschera and Barbiere di Siviglia; Other appearances at the Paris Opéra-Comique. Honour: Concours de Voix d'Or 1st Prize Caruso, 1956. Memberships: President, des Voix d'Or; President, Scine Française Address: 5 rue Lyautey, 75016 Paris, France.

CHAPUIS Michel, b. 15 Jan 1930, Dole, France. Organist. Education: Studied in Paris with Marcel Dupré. Career: Organist at Saint-Germain-l'Auxerrois, 1951, Saint-Nicolas-des-Champs, 1954; Organist at Dole from 1942, Saint-Severin from 1964, reviving music of the French Baroque era by Couperin, Marchand, de Grigny and Clérambault; Professor at the Strasbourg Conservatoire, 1956-79, Besançon, 1979, and Paris, 1986. Recordings: Complete editions of Balbastre, Dandrieu, Titelouze and Daquin. Address: c/o Conservatoire National, 14 Rue de Madrid, F-75008 Paris, France.

CHARBONNEAU Pierre, b. 1947, Canada. Singer (Bass). Career: Sang first in Canada, notably at Vancouver from 1974, and then with Canadian Opera at Toronto from 1978; Opéra de Montreal from 1983; Guest appearances with Washington Opera (1976), Opéra de Lyon from 1988; Sang Jupiter in Orphée aux Enfers at the Paris Opera (1988), Don Pasquale at Rio de Janeiro, 1989; Carnegie Hall, 1991, in Boieldieu's La Dame Blanche; Other roles include Masetto, Sparafucile, Rocco, Raimondo, Hunding, Arkel, and Timur in Turandot. Address: c/o L'Opéra de Montréal, 260 de Maisonneuve Boulevard West, Montréal, Province Québec, Canada H2X 1Y9.

CHARD Geoffrey, b. 9 Aug 1930, Sydney, Australia. Singer (Baritone). Education: Studied at the New South Wales Conservatory. Debut: Sydney 1951, in Carmen. Career: Moved to England and became a member of the English National Opera; Other appearances with Welsh National Opera and the Glyndebourne and Edinburgh Festivals; Aldeburgh Festival 1967, 1968, in the premieres of Berkeley's The Castaway and Birtwistle's Punch and Judy; London Coliseum 1973-83, in the British premiere of Penederecki's The Devils of Loudun; Ginastera's Bomarzo and Ligeti's Le Grand Macabre; Roles in operas by Gluck, Mozart, Wagner, Britten, Orff, Menotti, Shostakovich, Janacek and contemporary British composers; Many engagements as concert singer; Sang Bartolo in Il Barbiere di Siviglia for Victoria State Opera, 1989; Germont in Traviata for the Ballarat Opera Festival, 1992, Balstrode (Peter Grimes) and Pizarro at Sydney; Tonio in Pagliacci at Sydney, 1996. Address: Victoria State Opera, 370 Nicholson Street, Fitzroy, VIC 3065, Australia.

CHARLTON, David, b. 20 June 1946, London, England. Musicologist. Education: Nottingham University and at Cambridge with Hugh Macdonald; PhD, 1973; Career: Lecturer, 1970, Reader, 1991-, University of East Anglia; Reader, Royal Holloway, University of London, 1995-. Publications: Many articles and reference works including entries on French opera of the late 18th and early 19th centuries in the New Grove Dictionary of Music and the New Grove Dictionary of Opera; Grétry and the Growth of Opéra-Comique, 1986; Chapters on 19th century French Opera in the New Oxford History of Music, 1990; Editorial: ETA Hoffmann's musical writings, 1989; Hector Berlioz, Choral Works with Orchestra (New Berlioz Edition Vol 12B), 1993; Member, Editorial Board, Cambridge Opera Journal. Address: Department of Music, Royal Holloway, Egham, Surrey TW20 0EX, England.

CHARNOCK Helen, b. 1958, England. Soprano Singer. Education: Studied at the University of East Anglia, BA with Honours in Music and at Guildhall School with Laura Sarti. Career: Many performances with Opera Factory and London Sinfonietta, including the world premieres of Hell's Angels by Nigel Osborne and Birtwistle's Yan Tan Tethera, 1986; Sang in Weill's Mahagonny Songspiel, Ligeti's Aventures, Nouvelles Aventures and the British premiere of Reimann's Ghost Sonata; Workshops and performances in many venues with the London Sinfonietta's Education Programme, including Holloway Prison and the Huddersfield Contemporary Music Festival; Australian debut in 1986 as Clytemnestra in Iphigénie en Tauride; Sang in the premiere of Greek by Mark-Anthony Turnage at 1988 Munich Biennale, repeated at Edinburgh Festival in 1988 and English National Opera 1990; Has sung Britten's Governess and Mrs Coyle at Aldeburgh Festival and has appeared elsewhere as Semele, First Lady, Pamina, Micaela, Butterfly, Titania, Gretel, Adele, Despina and Musetta; Television appearances in works by Birtwistle, Ligeti and Turnage. Recording: CD of Greek by Turnage, 1993. Honours: The English Singers and Speakers Prize; 2 Royal Society of Arts Awards; Incorporated Society of Musicians Young Artists Award; Ian Fleming Bursary. Address: 21 Glengall Road, London, SE15 6NJ, England.

CHARTERIS Richard, b. 24 June 1948, Chatham Islands, New Zealand. Musicologist; Writer; Editor. Education: BA, Victoria University, Wellington, New Zealand, 1970; MA with 1st class hons, University of Canterbury, 1972; PhD 1976, Universities of Canterbury and London. Career: Rothmans Research Fellowship, University of Sydney, 1976-78; Research Fellowship, University of Queensland, 1979-80; Australian Research Council Chief Investigator, Music Department, University of Sydney, 1981-90; Australian Research Council Senior Research Fellow (Reader), Music Department, 1991-, Professor in Historical Mucisology and Australian Research Council Senior Research Fellow, Music Department, 1995-, University of Sydney. Publications include: Author of over 90 books and editions devoted to the music of Giovanni Bassaro, John Coprario, Alfonso Ferrabosco the Elder, Domenico Maria Ferrabosco, Andrea and Giovanni Gabrieli, Adam Gumpelzhaimer, Hans Leo Hassler, Thomas Lupo, Claudio Monteverdi and others, and mostly in the series Corpus Mensurabilis Musicae, Musica Britannica, Recent Researches in the Music of the Baroque Era, Boethius Editions, Fretwork Editions, King's Music Editions, Baroque Music Series; and books on composers, music and early sources in the series Boethius Editions, Thematic Catalogue Series, Musicological Studies and Documents and Alto Polo. Contributions to: Numerous journals and magazines; Music Letters; Early Music; Royal Musical Association Research Chronicle; Musica Disciplina; Chelys; The Galpin Society Journal; MLA Notes; The Huntington Library Quarterly; Studies in Music.. Honours: Fellow, Australian Academy of the Humanities, 1990. Address: Music Department, University of Sydney, NSW 2006, Australia.

CHASE Roger, b. 1958, London, England. Concert Violist. Education: Studied at Royal College of Music with Bernard Shore and in Canada with Steven Staryk. Debut: Solo with the English Chamber Orchestra, 1979. Career: Performances internationally from 1976 with such ensembles as the London Sinfonietta, The Estherhazy Baryton Trio and the Nash Ensemble; Concerts with the chamber ensemble Hausmusik, featuring works by Mendelssohn, Schubert and Hummel; Modern repertoire includes a concerto by Richard Harvey, premiere at the Exeter Festival, 1991; Toured the USA with Hanover Band, 1992 playing Mozart's Sinfonia Concertante; Professor at the Guildhall School of Music and Drama. Recordings include: Works by Mendelssohn, Mozart's Concertante and Britten's Lachrymae. Current Management: Owen/White Management. Address: c/o Owen/White Management, 14 Nightingale Lane, London, N8 7QU, England.

CHASLIN Frederic, b. 1963, Paris, France. Conductor; Pianist. Career: Assistant to Daniel Barenboim at the Orchestre de Paris 1987-87 and to Pierre Boulez at Ensemble Intercontemporain, 1989-91; Music Director of Rouen Opera and Symphonie 1991-94; Guest with the Orchestre National de France, from 1993, Orchestre de Paris (1994), Vienna SO (1993-95) RAI Milan and orchestras of Nice, Marseilles, Lyon, Dusseldorf, Stuttgart and Toho Gakuen in Tokyo; Permanent Guest at the Bregenz Festival, 1993-, with Nabucco and Fidelio; Season 1994-95 with Lakmé at the Paris Opéra-Comique, followed by Der Ring des Nibelungen at Hanover; Guest with Manchester Hallé Orchestra, 1996; Season 1997-98 with Carmen and Manon at the Paris Opéra Bastille, Samson et Dalila for Scottish Opera; Concerts in Israel include Le Marteau sans Maitre by Boulez. Address: Allied Artists, 42 Montpellier Square, London SW7 1JZ, England.

CHATEAUNEUF Paula, b. 1958, USA. Player of Lutes and Early Guitars. Education: Studied at University of Connecticut, New England Conservatory and with Patrick O'Brien in New York; Further study as Fulbright Scholar, Guildhall School of Music, London, with Nigel North. Career: Moved to London, 1982; Appearances with many early music ensembles, including the New London Consort, Taverner Consort, English Concert, Sinfonye and the Gabrieli Consort; Has worked extensively as continuo player, particularly in Baroque opera; Involved in groups and projects devoted to improvisation and early dance music; Tours of Europe and North America as Soloist and Ensemble Player, performing at major festivals and recording for radio and television. Recordings include: Video, music for San Rocco, with the Gabrieli Consort (Archiv). Address: The Garden Flat, 26 Oliver Grove, London SE25 6EJ, England.

CHATER James (Michael), b. 12 Jun 1951, Henley, England. Musicologist. Education: BA, Music, 1973, DPhil, Music, 1980, Exeter College, Oxford University. Career: Fellow, Harvard Center for Italian Renaissance Studies, Florence, Italy, 1981-82; Fellowships and Teaching positions: University of Wales, 1982-83, Washington University, St Louis, USA, 1983-84, University of Victoria, Canada, 1984-85, University of British Columbia, 1985-86; Editor, English Language Booklet, Netherlands, 1986-. Publications: Luca Marenzio and The Italian Madrigal 1577-93, 1981. Contributions to: Musical Times; Music and Letters; Journal of The American Musicological Society; Rivista Italiana di Musicologia; Studi Musicali. Memberships: Royal Musical Association; Società Italiana di Musicologia. Hobbies: Chess; Travel. Address: c/o Philips Music Group, Hobbemastraat 20, 1071 ZC Amsterdam, The Netherlands.

CHATHAM Stephen, b. 28 Feb 1950, Fairbault, Minnesota, USA. Composer. Education: Studied with Joseph Wood at the Oberlin Conservatory and with Ross Lee Finney and William Bolcom at the University of Michigan; Further study in Cologne. Career: Teacher, University of British Columbia from 1976, Associate Professor 1982. Compositions include: Two Followers of Lien for orchestra, 1973; Wild Cat for flute, 1975; Whisper, Baby, for chorus, paino and percussion, 1975; On the Contrary for clarinet and chamber ensemble, 1974; Quiet Exchange for clarinet and percussion, 1976; Occasions for orchestra, 1977; Hesitation for violin and cello, 1977; Amusements for piano, 1978; Grouse Mountain Lullaby and They all Replied, for orchestra, 1978; Gossamer Leaves for clarinet and piano, 1981; Crimson Dream for orchestra, 1983. Honours include: Fulbright Scholarship, 1974; BMI Student Composer Awards, 1974-76; Ives Award from the American Academy & Institute of Arts & Letters, 1976; Commissions from the Canadian Arts Council, the National Endowment of the Arts and Ontario Arts Council.

CHAUSSON Carlos, b. 17 Mar 1950, Saragossa, Spain. Singer (Bass-Baritone). Education: Studied in Madrid and at the University of Michigan. Debut: San Diego, 1977, as Masetto. Career: Appearances at Boston, Miami, New York City Opera and Mexico City (as Bartolo in Il Barbiere di Siviglia); Sang at Madrid from 1983, Barcelona from 1985; Vienna Staatsoper from 1986, as Paolo in Simon Boccanergra, and Don Alvaro in Il Viaggio a Reims, conducted by Abbado; Vienna Konzerthaus in Les Danaides by Salieri; Parma 1987, as Falstaff, Bologna, 1988-89, as Michonnet in Adriana Lecouvreur, Pantaleone in Le Maschere by Mascagni and Sharpless in Butterfly; Barcelona 1989, in the premiere of Cristobal Colon by Beladas, returned 1990, as Paolo; Modena 1990, as Geronte in Manon Lescaut; Sang Mozart's Figaro at Madrid, Masetto at the 1990 Vienna Festival; Grand Théâtre de Genève 1991, as Paolo; Madrid 1992, as Bartolo in the new production of Il Barbiere di Sigivlia conducted by Alberto Zedda; Sang Don Magnifico in Cenerentola at the Palais Garnier, Paris, 1996. Address: c/o Gran Teatre del Liceu, Barcelona, Spain.

CHAUVET Guy, b. 2 Oct 1933, Montlucon, Tarbes, France. Singer (Tenor). Education: Studied with Bernard Baillour in Tarbes. Career: After winning prizes at Cannes, Toulouse and Paris, sand at the Paris Opera 1959, as Tamino, returned as Faust, Cavaradossi, Florestan, Aeneas in Les Troyens and Jason in Médée; Holland Festival and Buenos Aires, 1961; Covent Garden debut as Cavaradossi, 1963; London Coliseum, 1969, in a concert performance of Roussel's Padmavati; Verona Arena 1971, as Radames; Has sung Parsifal in Brussels, Lohengrin in Berlin and Samson in Geneva; Vienna Staatsoper as Aeneas and Otello; Further appearances in New York, Metropolitan, as John of Leyden, Le Prophète, 1979; Monte Carlo, Lisbon and Dublin; Rio de Janeiro, Don José, 1981; San Francisco, Samson, 1983. Recordings: Highlights from Werther and Hérodiade by Massenet;

Scenes from Les Troyens; Sigurd by Reyer. Address: c/o San Francisco Opera, War Memorial Opera House, San Francisco,CA 94102, USA.

CHAVEZ Abraham, b. 6 Mar 1927, El Paso, Texas, USA. Music Director; Conductor. m. Lucy Villegas, 18 Nov 1945, 3 sons, 1 daughter. Education: Private Music study with Professor Edmundo J Dieguez, Mexico, 1938-43, Robert Semon, 1940-45, Noumi Fisher, 1949; Los Angeles Conservatory of Music, 1949; Texas Western College, 1955-59; BM, University of Texas, El Paso, 1955-59. Career: Member, 1940-45, Concert Master, 1947-66, El Paso Symphony Orchestra; Private Violin Teacher, 1951-59; Artist-in-Residence, 1955-66, Professor, Music, 1975-92, University of Texas at El Paso; Professor, Music, University of Colorado, 1966-75; Music Director, Conductor: El Paso Youth Symphony, 1975-82, El Paso Symphony, 1975-92, Ysleta Symphony, 1992-; Appearances with many orchestras include: European tour with All-American Symphony Orchestra, 1972; New Mexico All-State Orchestra, 1979, 1983, 1987; South Dakota, Arizona, Oregon, Oklahoma, Montana, Louisiana, Ohio and Kentucky State Orchestras; National Symphony of Mexico, Mexico City, 1987, 1988; Guadalajara Symphony Orchestra, Mexico, 1989; University of Tamaulipas Symphony Orchestra, 1990; Orquesta Sinfonica Nacional, Dominican Republic, 1991; Midwestern Music Festival Orchestra, University of Kansas, Lawrence, 19 years; Violin recitals, University of Colorado, 1961-75, Bozeman, Montana, 1970, Bellingham, Washington, 1971, with Oxana Yablonskaya, 1981. Recordings: Works by Mexican Composers: N Ponce, B Galindo, R Halfter, directing National Symphony of Mexico at Royce Hall, UCLA, 1988. Current Management: Maxim Gershunoff. Address: 4236 Park Hill Drive, El Paso, TX 79902, USA.

CHEDEL Arlette, b. 25 May 1933, Neuchatel, Switzerland. Singer (Contralto). Education: Studied in Neuchatel and at the Vienna Musikakademie with Erik Werba. Career: Concert appearances in works by Schütz, Handel, Bach, Kodály, Frank Martin and Honegger; Radio Lausanne 1974, in the premiere of Trois Visions espagnoles by Gerber; Montreux Festival, 1986, in Folie de Tristan by Schibler; Guest engagements in Vienna, Prague, Berlin, Rome and Besancon; Opera roles include Wagner's Erda, Magadalene and Mary, Mozart's Marcellina, Catherine in Jeanne d'Arc au Bucher, the Nurse in Boris Godunov and Geneviève in Pelléas et Mélisande. Recordings include: L'Enfant et les Sortilèges and Les Noces by Stravinsky (Erato). Address: c/o Grand Théâtre de Genève, 11 Blvd du Théâtre, CH-1211, Genève 11, Switzerland.

CHEEK John, b. 17 Aug 1948, Greenville, South Carolina, USA. Singer (Bass-Baritone). Education: Studied at the North Carolina School of Arts and at the Accademia Chigiana in Siena with Gino Bechi. Career: Sang at the Festivals of Ravinia and Tanglewood and elsewhere in the USA, notably in music by Mozart; Metropolitan Opera debut 1977, as the Doctor in Pelléas et Mélisande: later appeared as Pimen, Ferrando in IL Trovatore, Klingsor, Panthée in Les Troyens, Monterone and Figaro; New York City Opera 1986, as Mephistopheles in Faust; Other roles include Wurm in Luisa Miller; Attila, New York, 1988; Padre Guardiano, Toronto; Metropolitan, La Bohème, 1989; Ramphis in Aida, Cincinnati Opera, 1990; SSang Don Pasquale at Cincinnati, 1996; TV Appearances and concerts. Recordings include: Tosca (EMI); Haydn Creation (Telarc), Stravinsky The Rake's Progress, as Nick Shadow; Messiah, (RCA); César Frank, Les Béatitudes (Satan); Hänssler. Honours: Doctor of Music (Honorary), 1985; North Carolina Prize, 1987. Current Management: Thea Dispeker Artist Representative, 59 E 54th Street, New York, NY 10022, USA. Address: Thea Dispeker Artist Representative, 59 E 54th St, New York, NY 10022, USA.

CHEMPIN Beryl Margaret, b. Edgbaston, Birmingham, England. Piano Teacher; Pianist; Lecturer; Writer. m. (1) Arnold Chempin, deceased, 2 daughters, (2) Bernard While, deceased, (3) Denis Matthews, CBE, deceased, (4) Peter Gilroy Bevan, CBE. Education: Birmingham Conservatoire; Studied with Harold Craxton and Kendall Taylor, FTCL; LRAM; ARCM; LTCL; ABSM. Career: Piano Teacher, Birmingham Conservatoire (now the University of Central England in Birmingham) and Birmingham Young Musicians' Scheme; Private Teacher, Solo Performer and Accompanist; Lecturer and Adjudicator; Writer of CD sleeve notes and programme notes; Founder and Chairman, Denis Matthews Memorial Trust; Inaugurator of annual Beryl Chempin Bach Prize, Beethoven Prize and Post-graduate Keyboard Prize at Birmingham Conservatoire; Conducted Masterclasses in Australia, Hong Kong, Finland and UK. Publication: The Physiology of Piano Playing (with Professor Peter Gilroy Bevan), 1995. Contributions to: Musical Times; Music Teacher; Music Journal; EPTA Journal; Fanfare. Honours: Midland Woman of the Year, 1977; National Award for Piano Teaching, 1983. Memberships: Incorporated Society of Musicians; Royal Society of Musicians; European Piano Teachers' Association; City of Birmingham Symphony Orchestra Society; King Edward's High School Old Edwardians; British Federation of Music Festivals; Birmingham Conservatoire Association. Hobbies: Reading; Languages; Art; Cookery. Address: 10 Russell Road, Moseley, Birmingham B13 8RD, England.

CHEN Leland, b. 8 July 1965. Concert Violinist. Career: Won the Yehudi Menuhin International Competition and made London concerto debut with the London Philharmonia at the Barbican; Further concerts with the London Philharmonic Orchestra and London Symphony Orchestra; Tour of North America in 1985 with the Royal Philharmonic Orchestra; Royal Concert London in 1986 playing the Bach Double Concerto with Yehudi Menuhin; Tours of Poland and the Netherlands and a sixty-city recital tour of the USA; Played Vivaldi's Four Seasons at Kennedy Center, Washington DC, telecast by CBS; Performances at Gstaad and Schleswig-Holstein festivals; Repertoire includes works by Bartok, Beethoven, Elgar, Mozart, Mendelssohn, Sibelius and Tchaikovsky. Address: Upbeat Management, Sutton Business Centre, Restmor Way, Wallington, Surrey, SM6 7AH, England.

CHEN Pi-Hsien, b. 1950, Taiwan. Pianist. Education: Studied in Taiwan and at the Cologne Musikhochschule, Diploma 1970; further studies with Hans Leygraf and master classes with Wilhelm Kempff, Tatiana Nikolayeva and Geza Anda. Career: From 1972 has given performances in London (BBC Proms, South Bank, Barbican), Amsterdam, Zurich, Berlin, Munich,Barcelona and Tokyo; Festival appearances at Huddersfield, Lucerne, Schwetzingen, Hong Kong and Osaka; Orchestras include London Symphony, BBC Symphony, Royal Concertgebouw, Radio orchestras in Austria and Germany, the Zuricher Kammerorchester, Tonhalle Orchestra and the Collegium Musicum Zurich; Conductors include Colin Davis, Bernard Haitink, Jean Martinon, Ferdinand Leitner, Bernhard Klee, Marek Janowski, Paul Sacher, Horst Stein and Peter Eötvös; Repertory ranges from Scarlatti to Boulez; Piano Duo performances with Pierre-Laurent Aimard. Honours incl: Prize Winner, Concours Reine Elisabeth, 1972, Belgium; First Prize, Competition of the Runfunkanstalten Munich, 1972. Address: c/o Ingpen & Williams Ltd, 26 Wadham Road, London SW15 2LR, England.

CHEN Xieyang, b. 4 May 1939, Shanghai, China. Symphony Orchestra Conductor. m. Jian-Ying Wang, 6 Apr 1973. Education: Piano student, Music Middle School, Shanghai Conservatory, 1953-60; Major in Conducting, Shanghai Conservatory, 1969-65; Musical study with Otto Mueller, Yale University, USA, 1981-82. Debut: Shanghai. Career: Conductor: Shanghai Ballet Orchestra, 1965-81; Aspen Festival, Group for Contemporary Music-New York, Brooklyn Philharmonia, Honolulu Symphony, Philippine State Orchestra, Hong Kong Philharmonic, Shanghai Symphony, Central Philharmonic-Beijing, 1981-83; Vilnius Symphony, Kaunas Symphony, Novosibirsk Symphony-USSR, 1985; Tokyo Symphony, Miyagi Philharmonic, Music Festival-Scotland, 1986-88; Music Director, Principal Conductor, Shanghai Symphony Orchestra; Resident Conductor, Central Philharmonic, Beijing. Recordings: Beethoven symphonies and Chinese composition for French recording company, 1983; Rachmaninov Symphony No 2 and Szymanowski Violin Concerto No 1, 1987; Chen Gang Violin Concerto The Butterfly Lovers and Beethoven's 9 symphonies, 1988. Address: 105 Hunan Lu, Shanghai, China.

CHEN Yi, b. 4 Apr 1953, Guangzhou, China. Composer; Violinist. m. 20 Jul 1983. Education: BA, 1983, MA, 1986, Central Conservatory of Music, Beijing; DMA, 1993, Columbia University, NY, USA. Career: Concert Mistress, Beijing Opera Troup Orchestra, 1970-78; Composer in Residence, The Women's Philharmonic, Chanticleer, San Francisco, 1993-96; Member of Composition Faculty, Peabody Conservatory, Johns Hopkins University, 1996-. Compositions: Works performed and broadcast in Europe, USA and China, 1984-; Duo Ye No 2, Orchestra; Symphony No 1; Viola and Orchestra Concerto; Sprout for String Orchestra; 3 Poems from Song Dynasty for Chorus; Woodwind Quintet; Near Distance, sextet for Chamber Ensemble; As in a Dream for Soprano, Violin and Cello; Overture No 1 and No 2 for Chinese Orchestra; Piano Concerto; Symphony No 2; Song in Winter, two versions, 1993; Ge Xu (Antiphony) for Orchestra, 1994; The Linear for Orchestra, 1994; Shuo for String Orchestra, 1994; Set of Chinese Folksongs for Mixed Choir or School Choir and Strings, 1994; Tang Poems Cantata, 1995; Chinese Myths Cantata, 1996; Qi for chamber ensemble, 1997; Golden Flute for flute and orchestra, 1997; Spring Dreams for mixed chorus, 1997. Recordings: Duo Ye, A Collection of Orchestral Works by Chen Yi, 1986; Second Collection of Orchestral Works by Chen Yi, 1996; Chamber Music of Chen Yi, 1998. Honours: 1st Prize, China National Composition Competition, 1985; Lili Boulanger Award, 1994; NEA Fellowship, 1994; Goddard Lieberson Fellowship of American Academy of Arts and Letters, 1996; Guggenheim Fellowship, 1996; Sorel Medal for Excellence in Music, New York University, 1996; CalArts/Alpert Award, 1997; Koussevitzky Foundation Commission Award, 1997; Chamber Music America Commission Award, 1997. Current Management: Theodore Presser Co. Address: 728 41st 4E, Brooklyn, NY 11232, USA.

CHEN Zuohuang, b. 2 April 1947, Shanghai, China. Conductor; Pianist; Music Director. m. Zaiyi Wang, 10 September 1969, 1 daughter. Education: High School Division, Central Conservatory, Beijing, 1960-65; Central Conservatory, Beijing, 1977-80; MMus, 1982, DMA Orchestral Conducting, 1985, University of Michigan, USA. Career: Conductor, All China Trade Union Music and Dance Troupe, 1966-74; Conductor, China Film Philharmonic Orchestra, 1974-76; Associate Professor of Conducting, University of Kansas, USA, 1985-87; Conductor, Central Philharmonic Orchestra, Beijing, 1987-96; Led its US debut tour throughout America, 1987; Conductor of China Youth Symphony Orchestra, 1987-, leading its European Tour, 1987; Guest Conductor in over 20 countries with Zurich Tonhalle Orchestra, Vancouver Symphony Orchestra, Hungary State Symphony, Gulbenkian Orchestra, Tanglewood Music Festival Orchestra, Colorado Symphoyn Orchestra, Pacific Symphony Orchestra, Russian Philharmonic Orchestra, Haifa Symphony, Slovak Radio Symphony Orchestra, Hong Kong Philharmonic Orchestra, Pusan Philharmonic Orchestra, Mexico National and UNAM Symphony and the Taipei Symphony Orchestra; Music Director/Conductor, Wichita Symphony Orchestra, 1990; Music Director/Conductor, Rhode Island Philharmonic Orchestra, 1992-96; Artistic Director/Conductor, China National Symphony Orchestra, 1996-. Recordings: Recordings released by major labels. Honours: Outstanding Educator, March 1986; Hope Award, 1987; National Arts Associate, 1987. Current Managements: ICM Artists Limited, 40 W 57th Street, New York, NY 10019, USA. Address: 1506 E Kay Street, Derby KS 67037, USA.

CHENETTE Jonathan (Lee), b. 8 May 1954, Libertyville, IL, USA. Composer; Pianist; College Teacher. m. Jeanmarie Kern, 20 May 1978, 2 s, 1 d. Education: BA, Mathematics, University of Chicago, 1975; MM, Composition, Butler University, 1980; PhD in Composition, University of Chicago, 1984. Career: Galliano Trio, 1985; Performances by Galliano Trio, Mirecourt Trio, St Paul Chamber Orchestra, Netherlands Radio Chamber Orchestra (ISCM World Music Days); Members of Canadian National Orchestra, Des Moines Symphony Orchestra, Dubuque Symphony Orchestra and Cedar Rapids Chamber Orchestra; Lecturer, Japanese Conceptions of Space and Time in the Music of Takemitsu, Society of Composers National Convention, 1985; Microtonality and the Liberal Arts, Society of Composers National Convention, 1993. Compositions: Jazmines for Baritone Voice and Chamber Ensemble, 1979; Idyll for Soprano, Flute and Harp, 1982; Redolence for Harp, 1982; Fantasy and Fugue on Bach for Piano Trio, 1985; Chamber Symphony, 1983; Eric's Salvation for Baritone Voice and 12 Instruments, 1987; Liberty from the Tyranny of 12 Equal Tones, electronic, 1989; Oh Millersville! for Soprano and Piano, 1990; Oh Millersville! for Soprano and Orchestra, 1991; Music for Episcopal Worship, 1991; Duo Variations for Double Bass and Harp, 1991; Four Character Pieces for Flute and Piano, 1992; Eric Hermannson's Soul, opera, 1993; Triple Feature for Chamber Orchestra, 1994; Posthumous Orpheus for soprano and lute, 1995; Broken Ground for Chorus and Orchestra, 1996; Strings in the Earth for treble voice choir and harp, 1997; The Bright Harmonica String for treble voice choir and harp, 1997. Publications: Synthetic Scales, Charles Griffes and the Kairn of Koridwen, PhD dissertation, 1984; Edited, reorchestrated and conducted world premieres of orientalist works by Charles Griffes, 1985. Honours: ISCM World Music Days, 1985; MacDowell Fellowship, 1986; Bellagio Fellowship, 1987; Blanche Johnson Professorship in Music, Grinnell College, 1997. Memberships: Society of Composers Inc; American Composers Forum; American Music Center; College Music Society; Iowa Composers Forum. Address: Music Department, Grinnell College, Grinnell, IA 50112-0806, USA.

CHENG Edmund Chung-kei, b. 4 May 1972, Hong Kong. Pianist; Musicologist. Education: BA, Southern Illinois University, USA; MA, University of California, Los Angeles, USA; BA, Southern Illinois University, USA. Debut: Hong Kong, 1986. Career: Recording Producer, first cd recording, 1996; Orchestra for Plays, first play performed, September 1997, California State University, Los Angeles. Honour: First Prize, Gospel Song Writing Competition, Los Angeles, USA, 1996. Memberships: American Musicological Society; Music Teacher Association of California. Address: 773 Barnum Way, Monterey Park, CA 91754, USA.

CHÉREAU Patrice, b. 2 Nov 1944, Lezigne, Maine-et-Loire, France. Opera Producer. Career: Co-Director of the Théâtre National Populaire, Paris, 1979-81; Director, Théâtre des Amandiers, Nanterre, from 1982; Opera Productions include Les Contes d'Hoffmann and Lulu, 1979, for the Paris Opéra and Der Ring des Nibelungen, Bayreuth, 1976; Has produced Lucio Silla by Mozart at La Scala, Milan; Produced for Wozzeck at Paris (Châtelet), Berlin (Staatsoper) and the Lyric Opera, Chicago, 1992-93; Don Giovanni at Salzburg, 1994. Address: Festspielhaus, 8580 Bayreuth 1, Germany.

CHERICI Paolo, b. 26 Mar 1952, Naples, Italy. Lute Teacher at Milan Conservatory. Education: Milan Conservatoire and Schola Cantorum of Basel. Career: Concerts of Renaissance and Baroque music such as lute soloist and in ensemble in Italy and abroad; Appearances on radio and TV in Italy and Switzerland; Lute Teacher at summer courses in Vicenza, Monza, Moneglia, Venice, Rocchetta Nevina, Vieste, Mercogliano; Founder of the lute class at Milan Conservatoire. Recordings: Collaborations with several recordings with music from the Renaissance to Baroque period. Publications: A Piccinini, Toccata per 2 liuti, 1977; J S Bach, Opere complete per liuto, 1980; A Vivaldi, Concerto per liuto e archi in D major, 1981. Contributions to: Articles and reviews to Il Fronimo. Honours: Società Italiana del Liuto. Memberships: The Lute Society, England; The Lute Society of America. Address: Via Ciro Menotti 7, 20129 Milan, Italy.

CHERNEY Brian, b. 4 Sept 1942, Canada. Composer; Educator. Education: BMus, 1964, MMus, 1967, PhD, Musicology, 1974, University of Toronto; ARCT Piano, 1961; Studied composition with Samuel Dolin and John Weinzweig. Career: Professor, Faculty of Music, McGill University, Montreal, 1972-. Compositions: Chamber Concerto for viola and 10 players, 1974; String Trio, 1976; Dans le crépuscule du souvenir for piano, 1977-80; Adieux for orchestra, 1980; River of Fire for harp and oboe d'amore, 1983; In the Stillness of the Seventh Autumn for piano, 1983; Into the Distant Stillness for orchestra, 1984; String Quartet No 3, 1985; In Stillness Ascending for viola and piano, 1986; Illuminations for string orchestra, 1987; Shekhinah for solo viola, 1988; Oboe Concerto, 1989; Transfiguration for orchestra, 1990; Et j'entends la nuit qui chante dans les cloches, for piano and orchestra, 1990; Apparitions, for cello and 14 musicians, 1991; Doppelganger for 2 flutes, 1991; In the Stillness of September 1942 for English horn and 9 solo strings, 1992; Like Ghosts from an Enchanter Feeling, for cello and piano, 1993; Die klingende Zeit, for flute and chamber ensemble, 1993-94; Et la solitude dérive au fil des fleuves, for orchestra, 1995; Tombeau, for piano, 1996. Recordings include: Adieux; River of Fire: Into the Distant Stillness; Illuminations. Publications: Harry Somers, book, 1975; Compositions published, 1970-97. Honours: First Place, String Trio, International Rostrum of Composers, 1979; Jules Léger Prize for New Chamber Music, 1985. Memberships: Canadian League of Composers; Associate Composer, Canadian Music Center. Address: 4362 Hingston Avenue, Montreal, Quebec, Canada H4A 2J9.

CHERNOUSHENKO Vladislav, b. 14 Jan 1936, Leningrad, Russia. Conductor. Education: Studied at the Leningrad State Conservatoire. Career: Sang with the Boys Choir of the Glinka State Capella from 1944; Conducted the Karelia State Radio Orchestra, then the Leningrad Chamber Choir, 1962-74; Music Director of the Glinka State Capella, 1974-; Directed the premiere performance of Rachmaninov's complete Vespers, 1974; Re-established the Symphony Orchestra of the Glinka State Capella, 1988 and has toured with it to Germany, Holland, Switzerland, Ireland and France with a repertoire including Haydn, Shostakovich, Brahms, Bruckner, Schnittke and Mozart; Rector, Leningrad-St Petersburg State Conservatoire, 1979-. Recordings include: A wide repertoire. Address: c/o Sonata, 11 Northpark Street, Glasgow G20 7AA, Scotland.

CHERNOV Vladimir, b. 22 Sept 1953, Russia. Baritone. Education: Graduated Moscow Conservatory, 1981; Further study at La Scala, Milan. Career: Soloist with Kirov Theatre, Leningrad from 1984 as Rossini's Figaro, Germont, Valentin in Faust, Yeletzky in The Queen of Spades; Toured Britain and Ireland with the Moscow Radio Symphony Orchestra, 1985; US Debut as Marcello in La Bohème with the Opera Company of Boston in 1989; In 1990 debuts with Scottish Opera as Don Carlo in La Forza del Destino, with Los Angeles Music Center Opera as Posa in Don Carlo, with Covent Garden as Figaro and Ezio in Attila and with Seattle Opera as Prince Andrei in War and Peace; Debuts in 1991 included Metropolitan Opera and Rome Opera as Miller in Luisa Miller; At Metropolitan has sung Germont, di Luna (Trovatore), Posa, Figaro, Stankar (Stiffelio) and title-role of Simon Boccanegra; San Francisco Opera debut as Ezio (Attila) in 1992; Debut with Vienna State Opera as Figaro in 1992; Since then has sung there almost his entire repertoire, including Ford (Falstaff) which also was his Salzburg Festival debut, 1993; Chicago Lyric Opera debut in 1992 as Renato in Ballo in Machera; Deutsche Oper Berlin debut in 1993 as di Luna and Renato; Debuts in 1994 included Arena di Verona as Marcello and Posa and Paris Bastille Opera as Simon Boccanegra; La Scala debut in 1995 as Stankar; Sang Francesco in Due Foscari at Covent Garden, 1995 and Eugene Onegin at the Met, 1997. Recordings include: Rigoletto, DGG; Ballo in Maschera, Teldec. Creative Works: Several videos. Honours: Glinka Competition 2nd Prize, 1981; 3rd Prize, Tchaikovsky Competition, 1981; 2nd Prize, Voci Verdiani Competition, 1983; 1st Prize, Tito Gobbi Prize, Miriam Helin Competition, 1984. Address: CAMI, 165 West 57th Street, New York, NY 10019, USA.

CHERNYKH Pavel, b. 1960, Moscow, Russia. Singer (Baritone). Education: Studied at Tchaikovsky Music School and with Yevgeny Nesterenko at the Moscow Conservatoire. Debut: Stage Debut in season 1989-90 as Tchaikovsky's Onegin at the Bolshoy. Career: Concerts and recordings with the Maly State Symphony, the St Petersburg Philharmonic and the Moscow Radio Orchestras, 1987-; Further performances as Silvio in Pagliacci, Robert in Tchaikovsky's Iolanta, Yeletsky in The Queen of Spades and Renato (Ballo in Maschera); Sang Onegin at the Paris Opéra Comique, 1987 and for the Vlaamse Opera in Antwerp, 1990; Stars of the Bolshoi Theatre concerts in Germany and Norway, 1990; Toured with the Bolshoi as Onegin to the USA, 1990 and sang at the Wolf Trap Theatre, Washington DC; Edinburgh Festival as Onegin, 1991. Address: c/o Sonata, 11 Northpark Street, Glasgow G20 7AA, Scotland.

CHESWORTH David (Anthony), b. 31 Mar 1958, Stoke, England. Composer; Sound Designer. Education: BA (Hons), La Trobe University, 1979; National Young Composers School, 1986. Career includes: Sound Design School, 1987-92; Freelance Composer, 1993-; Commissions from Paris Autumn Festival, 1985; Melbourne Festival, 1990-91; Australian Broadcasting Corporation, 1993. Compositions include: Choral, for piano, 1982; Stories of Immitation and Corruption for orchestra and tape, 1986; Lacuna, chamber opera, 1992; Duet I for violin, cello and vibraphones, 1993; Exotica Suite for ensemble, 1993; The Soft Skin for cello, clarinet and piano, 1993; The Two Executioners, chamber opera, 1994; Focal Wall Soundscape, 1995. Honours include: Prix Ars Electronica, Austria, 1993. Address: c/o APRA, 1A Eden Street, Crows Nest, NSW 2065, Australia.

CHETINYAN Krikor (Hazaros), b. 22 June 1943, Plovdiv, Bulgaria. Conductor. Education: Graduated, Bulgarian State Academy of Music, 1970. Debuts: Sofia, 1965; Bayreuth, Germany, 1970. Career: Regular concerts with Plovdiv Philharmonic Orchestra and Plovdiv Women's Chamber Choir, Germany, England, USA, Belgium, Russia, Poland, Hungary, Greece, Israel, Netherlands, Italy, Austria, Slovenia, Japan; Numerous recordings for radio and TV, Cologne, Frankfurt, Munich, Berlin, London, Moscow, Milan, Tel-Aviv, Atlanta, Prague, Budapest, Warsaw, Sofia; Head, Conducting Department, Academy of Music and Dance, Plovdiv; Served on international juries, Italy, Netherlands, Hungary, Greece, Bulgaria. Recordings: 8 works by Bulgarian and foreign composers. Publications: Choir Songs by Bulgarian Composers, 1980; From the Choir Baroque Music, 1985; Songs for a Uniform Choir, 1991. Hobby: Football. Address: Shesti Septemvri str N158, 4000 Plovdiv, Bulgaria.

CHEW Geoffrey (Alexander), b. 23 Apr 1940, South Africa. University Lecturer. m. Jennifer Comrie, 22 Jul 1967, 1 s, 2 d. Education: Royal College of Music, 1958-61; Caius College, Cambridge, 1961-64; BA, 1963; MusB, 1964; PhD, Manchester University, 1968. Career: University Lecturer: Johannesburg, 1968-70, Aberdeen, 1970-77, Royal Holloway College, University of London, 1977-95. Contributions to: Journal of The American Musicological Society; Music Analysis; Musiktheorie; Cambridge Opera Journal. Memberships: Royal Musical Association; American Musicological Society; Gesellschaft für Musikforschung; International Musicological Society; Society for Music Theory. Address: The Mount, Malt Hill, Egham, Surrey, TW20 9PB, England.

CHIARA Maria, b. 24 Nov 1939, Oderzo, Italy. Singer (Soprano). Education: Conservatorio Benedetto Marcello in Venice, with Antonio Cassinelli. Debut: Venice Festival, 1965, as Desdemona in Otello; Sang widely in Italy, 1965-70, notably as Puccini's Liu at Verona, and Verdi's Odabella, Amelia (Ballo in Maschera) and Aida; Several debuts in Germany and Austria, 1970-71, including Munich and Vienna as Mimi and Butterfly; La Scala debut, 1972, as Micaela in Carmen; Covent Garden debut, 1973, as Liu in Turandot; Metropolitan Opera, 1977, as Violetta; Chicago Lyric Opera in Manon Lescaut; Appearances in Buenos Aires as Amelia (Simon Boccanegra) and Suor Angelica; Opened the 1985-86 season at La Scala as Aida; Australian Opera, Melbourne, 1986, in Un Ballo in Maschera; Aida at Luxor, Egypt, 1987; Amelia in Ballo in Maschera, at Bologna, Parma and Naples, 1989; Leonora in Forza del Destino, at the 1989 Spoleto and Verona Festivals; Aida at Turin, 1990; Other roles include Donizetti's Anna Bolena and Maria Stuarda, Verdi's Elisabeth de Valois and Giordano's Maddalena; Sang Leonora in Il Trovatore at Turin, 1991. Recordings include: Aida; Madama Butterfly; Video of the Scala production of Aida. Address: c/o S A Gorlinsky Ltd, 33 Dover Street, London W1X 4NJ, England.

CHIHARA Paul (Seiko), b. 9 July 1938, Seattle, Washington, USA. Composer. Education: Studied with Robert Palmer at Cornell University, with Nadia Boulanger in Paris, Ernst Pepping in Berlin and with Gunther Schuller at the Berkshire Music Center. Career: Teacher, University of California, Los Angeles, 1966; Associate Professor, UCLA until 1974; Founded and Directed the Twice Ensemble; Andrew Mellon Professor, California Institute of Technology, 1975; Teacher, California Institute of the Arts, 1976; Composer-in-Residence, San Francisco Ballet, 1980; Commissions from the Boston Symphony Orchestra and the Los Angeles Philharmonic. Compositions include: Magnificat for 6 female voices, 1965; Driftwood for string quartet, 1967; Branches for 2 bassoons and percussion, 1968; Forest Music for orchestra, 1970; Windsong for cello and orchestra, 1971; Grass for double bass and orchestra, 1972; Ceremony III for flute and orchestra, 1973; Shinju, ballet, 1975; Missa Carminum, 1975; The Beauty of the Rose is in its Passing for ensemble, 1976; String Quartet (Primavera), 1977; 2 Symphonies, 1975, 1980; Misletoe Bride, ballet, 1978; Concerto for string quartet and orchestra, 1980; Sinfonia Concertante for 9 instruments, 1980; The Tempest, ballet, 1980; Saxophone concerto, 1981; Sequoia for string quartet and tape, 1984; Film and television scores; Arrangements for musicals. Address: c/o ASCAP, ASCAP Bulding, One Lincoln Plaza, NY 10023, USA.

CHILCOTT Bob (Robert Lionel), b. 9 Apr 1955, Plymouth, Devon, England. Composer. m. Polly Ballard, 1 Aug 1981, 1 son, 3 daughters. Education: Royal College of Music, London. Compositions: Singing by Numbers, 1995; Fragments From His Dish, 1995; City Songs, 1996; Organ Dances, 1996; Friends, 1997; The Elements, 1997. Memberships: SPNM; Royal Society of Musicians. Hobbies: Football; Running. Current Management: Oxford University Press. Address: c/o Oxford University Press, New Music Promotion, 70 Baker Street, London W1M 1DJ, England.

CHILCOTT Susan, b. 1963, England. Singer (Soprano). Education: Studied at the Guildhall School and the Banff Centre of Fine Arts in Canada with Mollie Petrie. Career: Concert engagements include Mendelssohn's Elijah at the Albert Hall, Haydn's Seasons in Madrid under Neville Marriner and appearances with the Royal Scottish Orchestra and the Scottish Chamber Orchestra; Scottish Opera as Frasquite in Carmen and First Lady in The Magic Flute, 1992; Dona Luisa in the British premiere of Gerhard's The Duenna for Opera North, Ellen Orford in Brussels and Mozart's Countess for Garsington Opera, 1993; Season 1993-94 Micaela at Barcelona and Lady Rich in Britten's Gloriana for Opera North; Tatiana in A Midsummer Night's Dream for ENO, 1994; Wigmore Hall recital (Mahler and Schumann), 1997. Address: Ingpen & Williams Ltd, 14 Kensington Court, London W8 5DN, England.

CHILDS Barney (Sanford), b. 13 February 1926, Spokane, Washington, USA. Composer; Teacher. m. (div), 2 daughters. Education includes: BA, University of Nevada, 1949; BA honours, Oxford University, England, 1951; PhD, Stanford University, USA, 1959; Studied with Leonard Ratner, Carlos Chavez Aaron Copland, Elliott Carter. Career includes: Assistant Professor of English, University of Arizona, 1961-65; Dean, Deep Springs College, 1965-69; Composer-in-Residence, Wisconsin College Conservatory, 1969-71; Faculty Fellow in Music and Literature, Johnston College, 1971-73; Professor of Composition and Music Literature, University of Redlands, 1973-94; Visiting Lecturer, Goldsmith's College, University of London, 1989; Professor Emeritus, Johnston Alumni Fellow in Literature, University of Redlands, 1994-. Compositions: About 80 compositions published, 15 recorded included 8 string quartets (1951-74), two Symphonies (1954, 1956), Intrada for Saxophone Quartet, 1992. Recordings include: Clay music, A question of summer (tuba and harp); A music, that it might be (2 clarinets); Sonata for solo trombone; Music for two flute players; Mr T his fancy (solo contrabass); The edge of the world (bass clarinet and organ); Variations sur une chanson de canotier (brass quintet), A Box of Views, wind quintet and piano. Publications: Contemporary Composers on Contemporary Music, co-editor, 1967 revised edition 1995; Associate Editor, Perspectives of New Music; The New Instrumentation, co-editor, 6 volumes. Contributions to: Various books and journals. Memberships: Society of Composers; American Composers Alliance (National Advisory Committee). Hobby: Reading. Address: Johnston Center, University of Redlands, Redlands, CA 92373, USA.

CHILDS Robert (Brynley), b. 5 Apr 1957, Crickhowell, Wales. Professional Euphoniumist. m. Lorraine Childs, 3 July 1976, 1 son, 1 daughter. Education: Kettering Technical College; ARCM with honours, 1985; MMus, The University of Leeds, 1995. Debut: Duet with brother (Nicholas), Royal Albert Hall, London, 1984. Career: Solo performances in Sydney Opera House, 1981, Grieg Hall, Norway, 1986, Festival Hall, London, 1986, Carnegie Hall, New York, 1989, 1993; Principal Euphonium with Black Dyke Mills Band, Brighouse and Rastrick Band and the Hallé Orchestra; Head of Brass Studies, Hymers College, Hull. Recordings: 3 solo albums; Numerous solo performances with Black Dyke Mills Band; Mahler 7th Symphony with BBC Symphony Orchestra; Euphonium Concerto by J Horowitz, N Clarke, J Golland. Publications: Softley As I Leave You, Solo Album, 1983; Child's Choice, Solo Album, 1984; Czardas, Solo Album, 1990; Lip Flexabilities, 1991. Contributions to: Wind Player, Japan, 1990; Soloist Course, to British Bandsman, 1993; The Bridge, USA, 1994. Honours: British Euphonium Champion, 1976; International Euphonium Player of the Year, 1982-83; Various national titles as euphoniumist with Black Dyke Mills Band. Memberships: Council Member, National Youth Brass Band of Great Britain; Associate, Royal College of Music; TUBA; British Association of Symphonic Wind Bands. Hobby: Conducting amateur band and orchestra. Address: 2 Priory Close, Swanland, Hull HU14 3QS, England.

CHILINGIRIAN Levon, b. 28 May 1948, Cyprus. Violinist. Education: Royal College of Music, London. Debut: Purcell Room, 1969. Career: Duo with Clifford Benson (piano), BBC Radio and Television, German and Swiss Radio; Various festivals with Chilingirian Quartet; Proms; Cheltenham, London, Aldeburgh, Bath, Paris, New York, Berlin and Adelaide Festivals; BBC Television and Radio; Resident Ensemble Liverpool University, 1973-76; Sussex, 1978-93; Royal College of Music, 1987-. Recordings: Quartet: Works by Arriaga, Berwald, Korngold, Mozart, Haydn, Schubert, Beethoven, Schumann, Dvorak, Bartók, Debussy, Ravel, Panufnik, Tavener, Pärt, Wood, Stravinsky, Schnittke; Solo: Tippett Triple Concerto; Duo: Schubert, Mathias, Ferguson and Finzi. Honours: First prize, BBC Beethoven Competition,1969 and Munich Competition, 1971; FRCM, 1989; DMus, Sussex University, 1992. Memberships: ISM; Musician's Union; ESTA. Hobbies: Table-tennis; Talking. Current Management: Intermusica. Address: 7 Holingbourne Road, London SE24 9NB, England.

CHISSELL Joan (Olive), b. 22 May 1919, Cromer, Norfolk, England. Music Critic. Education: Royal College of Music; ARCM; GRSM. Career: Lecturer in Music for Extra-Mural Departments, London and Oxford Universities, 1943-48; Piano Teacher, Junior Department, Royal College of Music, 1943-53; Assistant Music Critic, The Times, 1948-79; Regular Broadcaster for BBC and Reviewer for The Gramophone; Jury Member, International Piano Competitions, including Milan, Leeds, Zwickau, Budapest, Dublin and Sydney, Australia. Publications: Schumann, 1948, revised 1989; Chopin, 1965; Schumann's Piano Music, 1972; Brahms, 1977; Clara Schumann, 1983. Contributions to: Benjamin Britten (A Symposium); Chamber Music; The Concerto; Numerous magazines including the Radio Times and The Listener. Honours: Robert Schumann Prize awarded by the Town of Zwickau, 1991. Memberships: Critics' Circle; Royal College of Music Society. Hobby: Boating on the River Thames. Address: Flat D, 7 Abbey Road, London NW8, England.

CHLITSIOS George, b. 25 Mar 1969, Volos, Greece. Conductor; Lecturer. Education: Studied Viola, Piano, Composition, Conducting, Epirotic Conservatory, Ioannina, Greece; Rotterdam Conservatorium and Royal (Koninklijk) Conservatorium, Hague, Netherlands; London College of Music; Thames Valley University. Debut: Conductor, Tsakalof Youth Symphony Orchestra, 1989. Career: Principal Conductor, Tsakalof Symphony Orchestra, 1993-; Guest Conductor, LCM Symphony Orchestra, 1994; Guest Conductor, Athens State Orchestra, 1997; Principal Conductor, Epirus Opera House, Greece, 1997-; Concerts in Greece, France, England, Germany; Conducted many world premieres of symphonic works; Appearances in TV and radio networks in Greece and abroad. Honours: Scholarship, Academy of Athens, 1993; Representative Conductor for Greece, VE-Day Celebrations, London, 1995; Medal, Mayor of Ioannina, Greece, 1995; Medal, Mayor of Kifisia, Greece, 1996. Memberships: Incorporated Society of Musicians; American Symphony Orchestra League; Society for the Promotion of New Music; Music Notation Modernization Association. Address: c/o Tsakalof Symphony Orchestra, Platia G, Stavrou 5, GR-454 44 Ioannina, Greece.

CHMURA Gabriel, b. 7 May 1946, Wroclaw, Poland. Conductor. m. Mareile Chmura, 1 daughter. Education: Diploma (Conducting), Vienna Academy of Music; Ecole Normale de Musique, Paris; MA, Piano and Composition, Tel Aviv University. Career: Assistant to Karajan, 1971-73; Generalmusikdirektor, Aachen, 1974-82; Bochum Symphony Orchestra, 1982-87; Music Director-Designate, 1986-87, Principal Conductor, Music Director, 1987-90, National Arts Centre Orchestra, Ottawa, Canada; Guest Conductor: Berlin Philharmonic Orchestra; Vienna Symphony Orchestra; London Symphony Orchestra; Orchestre Nationale de France, Paris; Tonhalle Orchester, Zurich; North German Radio Symphony Orchestra, Hamburg; Bavarian Radio Symphony Orchestra, Munich; South German Radio Symphony Orchestra, Stuttgart; New York Philharmonic Orchestra; Paris Opera; Bavarian State Opera, Munich; Conducted Werther at Parma, 1990; Music Director, Ottawa and American orchestras, 1991-97. Compositions: Piece pour Piano, 1968; 3 Songs for Soprano and Piano; Text James Joyce. Recordings include: Mendelssohn Overtures with London Symphony Orchestra; Schubert; Lazarus; Haydn Symphonies 5, 7, 8 with National Arts Centre Orchestra, Canada. Honours: Gold Medal, Guido Cantelli Conducting Competition, Milan, 1971; 1st Prize, Herbert von Karajan Conducting Competition, Berlin, 1971; Prix Mondial du Disque de Montreux, 1983. Address: c/o TransArt (UK) Ltd, 8 Bristol Gardens, London W9 2JG, England.

CHODOS Gabriel, b. 7 Feb 1939, White Plains, New York, USA. Pianist; Teacher. Education: BA, Philosophy, 1959, MA, Music, 1964, University of California, Los Angeles; Diploma in Piano, Akademie für Musik, Vienna, 1966. Debut: Carnegie Recital, New York City, 1970. Career: Appearances throughout USA; Numerous tours of Europe, Israel and Japan; Solo performances with Chicago Symphony Orchestra, Radio Philharmonic, Holland, Jerusalem Symphony Orchestra and

Aspen Chamber Symphony; Master Classes at Aspen Festival, Rutgers Summer Festival and Chautauqua Festival, Toho Conservatory, Kunitachi Music University, Osaka University of Arts and elsewhere throughout Japan. Recordings: Bartók's Sonata; Bloch's Visions and Prophecies; Franck's Prélude, Aria et Final; Schubert's Sonata in B-flat major; Encore Favourites by various composers, Victor/Japan; Berlinsky's Sonata for Violin and Piano. Address: 245 Waban Avenue, Waban, MA 02168, USA.

CHOJNACKA Elisabeth, b. 10 Sept 1939, Warsaw, Poland. Harpsichordist. Education: Studied in Warsaw and with Aimée Van de Wiele in Paris. Career: Many performances of modern music throughout France and Europe, notably at the Domaine Musical and Ars Nova festivals; Has premiered works by Bussotti, Marius Constant, Donatoni, Gorecki, Christobal Halffter, Ligeti (Hungarian Rock, 1978) and Xenakis (Komboi, 1981). Address: c/o Ensemble Ars Nova, 16 Rue des Fossés St Jacques, F-75008 Paris, France.

CHOMINSKI Jozef (Michal), b. 24 Aug 1906, Ostrow, Poland. Musicologist; Professor. Education: Studied composition with M Soltys, conducting with A Soltys, Lwow Conservatory, 1927-29; Musicology with Chybinski; Ethnography with Adam Fischer; MA 1931, PhD 1936, University of Lwow; habilitation, University of Poznan, 1949. Career: Professor of Music History, Poznan Music School, 1945-48; Lecturer in Music History, 1947-51, Senior Lecturer 1951-54, Reader 1954-60, Professor of Music History and Theory, 1960-76, University of Warsaw; Chairman, Music Division Art Institute, Polish Academy of Sciences, 1951-63; Editor, Studia Muykologiczne 1953-56, Rocznik Chopinowski, Annales Chopin edited with K Wilkowska-Chominska 1956-71, Muzyka 1956-71, Monumenta Musicae in Polonia edited with K Wilkowska-Chominska 1964-71. Publications: Preludia Chopina 1950; Music of the Polish Renaissance 1958; Formy muzyczne edited with K Wilkowska-Chominska: I Small instrumental forms 1983; II Large instrumental forms 1987; III Song 1974; IV Opera and Drama 1976; V, Large vocal forms, 1984; History of Harmony and Counter-point 2 volumes, 1958, 1962, 1988; Sonaty Chopina, 1960; A Dictionary of Polish Musicians, 2 volumes, 1964-67; Music in the People's Republic of Poland, 1968; Studia nad tworczoscia Karola Szymanowskiego, 1969; History of Music edited with K Wilkowska-Chominska, 1989; A Catalogue of the works of Frederick Chopin edited with T D Turlo, 1990. Address: Wyszatycka 48, 04-946 Warsaw, Poland.

CHOO David Ik-Sung, b. 10 Sept 1962, Seoul, Korea. Conductor. Education: BMus, California State University, Northridge, 1981-88; MMus, Orchestral Conducting, University of Southern California, 1988-90; Conducting studies with Frederik Prausnitz, Daniel Lewis, Murry Sidlin, Gary Pratt, Jon Robertson and Lawrence Christiansen; Violin studies with Manuel Compinsky, Miwako Watanabe and Kathleen Lenski; Piano studies with Nobuko Fujimoto. Debuts: Guest Conductor, Aspen Concert Orchestra, 1988; Central Philharmonic Orchestra of China, Beijing, 1991. Career: Conductor: US Chamber (assistant) and Symphony Orchestras (guest); Washington Central Choir and Central Orchestra; The Angeles Orchestra; The Central Philharmonic Orchestra of China (guest); The Savaria Symphony Orchestra (guest), Hungary, 1992; St Petersburg Congress Orchestra (Guest), Russia, 1995; Hradec Kralove Philharmonic (Guest), Czech Republic, 1995; Ploisti Philharmonic Orchestra, (Guest), Romania, 1994; Concerts include: Central Philharmonic Orchestra of China, Wagner: Die Meistersinger von Nurnberg Overture, Mozart: Clarinet Concerto in A Major, Tchaikovsky: Symphony No 5; Savaria Symphony Orchestra. Honours: Prize Winner, Nicolai Malko Conducting Competition, Copenhagen, 1992. Address: 204 West Fayette Street, Baltimore, MD 21201, USA.

CHOOKASIAN Lili, b. 1 Aug 1921, Chicago, Illinois, USA. Singer (Mezzo-Soprano). Education: Studied with Philip Manuel in New York and with Rosa Ponselle in Baltimore. Debut: Chicago Symphony Orchestra conducted by Bruno Walter in Mahler, 1957. Career: Stage debut Little Rock 1959, as Adalgisa in Norma; New York debut 1962, in Prokofiev's Alexander Nevsky; Metropolitan Opera debut 1962, as La Cieca in La Gioconda; Returned as Wagner's Erda and in Suor Angelica, Pelléas et Mélisande, Il Tabarro and Falstaff; New York City Opera 1963, The Medium by Menotti; Appearances at Salzburg, Bayreuth (Erda 1965), Mexico City, Hamburg and Buenos Aires; Created the Queen in Ines de Castro by Pasatieri (1976); Other roles include Amneris, Azucena, Mary in Der fliegende Holländer, Ulrica, and Madelon in Andrea Chénier; Concert engagements with major US orchestras. Recordings: Symphony No 2 by Yardumian and Mahler's Das Lied von der Erde, with the Philadelphia Orchestra; Götterdämmerung (Deutsche Grammophon); Mahler 2 (CBS); Beethoven 9 (BASF).

CHOPARD Patrice, b. 28 Mar 1953, Zurich, Switzerland. Composer; Guitarist; Teacher. Education: University of Zurich, 1973-82; Classical Guitar, 1973-77; Guitar Teacher, 1977;

Composition, Zurich, 1980-82; Royal Danish Academy of Music, 1982-83; Magister Artium (musicology and Scandinavian literature), Hamburg University, 1996. Career: Concerts and compositions; Teacher, Switzerland, 1973-82, University of Bremen, Germany, 1984-92; Cultural Management and Composer, Bremen, 1990-92; Cultural Management, Osnabruck, 1992-93; Freelance Musician, project management, musicology, 1994-97. Compositions: Augenblick aus dem Fenster, 1982; Berceuse, 1983; Pieza tocada, 1984; Wolken, 1984; O Carolan arrangements, 1984; Adaptionen, 1985; Happy Birdday Ludwig Fan, 1986; Schneelied, 1987-89; Waller Gesänge, 1992. Recordings: Land of Erin, suite, 1984; O'Carolan arrangements, 1987; Tasten im Raum, 1989; Möwen, 1994. Publications: Augenblicke aus dem Fenster (with Hans Hehlen), 1982; O'Carolan for guitar, 1984. Memberships: Swiss Musicians' Association; German Composers' Society; Swiss Society of Music Education; German Society of Musical Artists; Chairman, Composers Society of Bremen. Address: Lübberstedterstrasse 34, D-28217 Bremen, Germany.

CHORZEMPA Daniel (Walter), b. 7 December 1944, Minneapolis, Minnesota, USA. Pianist; Organist; Musicologist; Composer. Education: University of Minnesota; Fulbright Scholar, Cologne, Federal Republic of Germany, 1965-66. Career: Former Church Organist, USA; Organ Instructor, University of Minnesota, 1962-65; Extensive Piano and Organ Recitals including Germany, Denmark, Italy and UK, 1968-; in 1970 and 1971 played Beethoven's Diabelli Variations in Oxford and London. Recordings: For Philips including the major organ works of Liszt. Hobbies: Mathematics; Architecture; Poetry; Renaissance History and Literature. Address: 5000 Cologne 1, Gross Budengasse 11, Germany.

CHOWNING John (MacLeod), b. 22 Aug 1934, Salem, New Jersey, USA. Composer; Teacher. Education: BM, Wittenberg University, Springfield, Ohio, 1959; Studied with Nadia Boulanger, Paris, 1959-62; PhD, Stanford University, 1966. Career: Teacher, 1966-, Director, Computer Music and Acoustics Project, 1966-74, Center for Computer Research in Music and Acoustics (CCRMA), 1975, Professor of Music, 1979, at Stanford University; Inventor of FM sound synthesis. Compositions: Pieces for computer-generated quadrophonic sound including: Sabelithe, 1971; Turenas, 1972; Stria, 1977; Phone, 1981. Recordings: Music with Computers, John Chowning. Publications: FM Theory and Applications, 1986. Contributions to: The Simulation of Moving Sound Sources, 1972, The Synthesis of Complex Audio Spectra by Means of Frequency Modulation, 1973, both to Journal of the Audio Engineering Society. Honours: National Endowment for the Arts Grants; Commissions from Institut de Recherche et de Coordination Acoustique/Musique; Fellow, American Academy of Arts and Sciences, 1988; Awarded the Hooker Chair by the School of Humanities and Sciences at Stanford, 1993. Address: c/o Center for Computer Research in Music and Acoustics, Music Department, Stanford University, Stanford, CA 94305-8180, USA.

CHRETIEN Raphaël, b. 17 February 1972, Paris, France. Cellist. Education: National Superior Conservatory. Career: Played, Europe: Barbican Hall, 1993, Théatre des Champs Elysées, 1994; Basel Symphonic Hall, 1995; USA: Marlboro Music Festival, 1994, 1995; Japan: Touring Major Halls, 1994; Appearances with Prague Television and Radio, Philharmonic Orchestra, Dvorak, 1994, Basel Symphony Orchestra, Lalo, 1995, Cannes Philharmonic Orchestra, Tchaikovsky, 1994; Cello Teacher, Bordeaux National Conservatory. Recordings: Piatti, Caprices for Solo Cello; Brahms Trio Op.114, Dapheneo. Honours: Vienna, 1993, Prague, 1994, Trapani & Belgrade, 1995, International Cello Competitions. Address: 7 rue de Wils, 94500 Champigny, France.

CHRIBKOVA Irena, b. 22 July 1959, Bohumin. Organist. Education: Kromeriz Conservatory; Prague Academy of Music; Conservatoire National de Rueil-Malmaison, Paris; International Organ Master Classes, Rotterdam, Biarritz, Porrentruy. Debut: Prague, 1981. Career: Solo Organ Recitals at International Festivals: Olomouc, Paris, 1985; Brno, Ljubljana, 1987; Paris, 1988; Piran, Slovakia, 1992; Warsaw, Poland, Auxerre, Bourges, France, 1993; Hamburg, Germany, 1994; Prague, Czech Republic, Wisla, Warsaw, Fromborg, Poland, 1995; Swedish Premiere of Faust, for Organ and Reciter by Peter Eben, 1995; Slovak Premiere of Faust and Four Biblical Dances by Peter Ebden, 1995; Berlin, Traunstein, Germany, Monte Carlo, Bourges, Prague, 1996; Berlin, Chartres, France, Serravalle Sesia, Italy, Hannover, Germany, 1997; Television Broadcasts of Concerts in Piran, 1992 and Warsaw, 1995; Dramaturge of the International Organ Festival in St james's Basilica, Prague; Member of Juries at International Organ Competitions. Recordings: Its Organs, Composing Organists, Prague St James's Basilica, 1996. Honours: 2nd Prize, Organ Interpretation Competition, Opava, 1978; Honourable Mention, International Organ Competition Prague Spirng, 1984; Finalist, Grand Prix Bordeaux, 1987; Médaille d'Or à l'unanimité du Jury, Conservatoire National de Rueil-Malmaison, 1987. Hobbies: Hiking; Travel; Literature;

Theatre; Winter Sports. Address: Nedrazni 19, 150 00 Prague 5, Czech Republic.

CHRIST Wolfram, b. 17 October 1955, Hachenburg. Violist. Education: Studies at Freiburg. Career: Prize Winner ARD competition, Munich, 1976; Numerous solo concertos with conductors like Abbado, Metha Karajan, Maazel, Ozawa, Kubelik with Berlin Philharmonic, Munich Philharmonic, Hamburg Philharmonic, Czech Philharmonic and other orchestras throughout the world; Principal Violist, Berlin Philharmonic Orchestra, since 1978. Recordings: Bartók Viola concerto, Ozawa, BPO; Berlioz Harold in Italy, Maazel, BPO; Hindemith Viola concerto, Abbado, BPO; Mozart Sinfonia Concertante, Abbado, BPO; plays regularly at international festivals as soloist and chamber musician. Current Management: Berlin Philharmonic Orchestra. Address: Matthäikirch st, 1000 Berlin, Germany.

CHRISTENSEN Dieter, b. 17 Apr 1932, Berlin, Germany. Professor of Ethnomusicology. m. Nerthus Karger, 1 son, 1 daughter. Education: Study of Cello, Berlin State Conservatory; PhD, Musicology, Free University, Berlin, 1957. Debut: RIAS Radio, Berlin, 1949. Career: Taught at University of Berlin and Hamburg, then at Wesleyan University and City University of New York, USA. Currently Professor and Director, Center of Ethnomusicology, Columbia University, New York City; Co-Director, UNESCO project The Universe of Music, A History, until 1993; Editor, UNESCO Collection of Traditional Music, 1994-. Recordings: Lappish folk songs; Kurdish folk music; Yugoslav folk music; Traditional Arts of Oman, 1993; A Wedding in Sohar, Oman, 1993. Publications include: Die Musik der Kate und Sialum, 1957; Die Musik der Ellice-Inseln (with G Koch), 1964; Hornbostel Opera Omnia (co-editor), 1974; Der Ring des Tlalocan, 1977; Musical Traditions in Oman, 1993; Shauqi's Dictionary of Traditional Music in Oman, 1994. Contributions to: German and international professional journals; Book review editor, Journal of Society for Ethnomusicology; Editor, Yearbook for Traditional Music. Hobbies: Agriculture; Electronics. Address: Department of Music, Columbia University, New York, NY 10027, USA.

CHRISTENSEN Jesper Boje, b. 3 December 1944, Copenhagen, Denmark. Harpsichordist; Professor; Musicologist. 1 daughter. Education: Diploma, Composition, Theory, Pianoforte, Royal Danish Academy of Music, 1971. Career: Numerous Concerts & Masterclasses at Most Major Festivals & Centers of Ancient Music; Professor, Schola Cantorum, Basel, 1988-; Jury, Festival van Vlaanderen, International Harpsichord Competition, 1992. Recordings: 12 Sonatas, for Traverso & Harpsichord; A Corelli op V Sonatas, for Violin and basso continuo; Corelli op VI Concerti Grossi; G Muffat, Armonico Tributo; F A Bonporti, Invenzioni op X, for Violin and basso continuo. Publications: Der Generalbass bei Bach und Händel, 1985; Die Grundlagen des Generalbass-spiels in 18 Fahrhundert, 1992; Some Sacred Cows, 1995. Honour: Carl Nielsen Prize, Copenhagen, 1971. Hobbies: Vintage & Thoroughbred Cars; Harpsichord Building. Address: Byfangweg 43, CH-4051 Basel, Italy.

CHRISTENSEN Mogens, b. 7 Apr 1955, Laesoe, Denmark. Composer; Assistant Professor. m. Helle Kristensen. Education: Diploma in Music History and Music Theory, Royal Academy of Music, Aarhus, 1983; Teaching Certificate, Royal Academy of Music, Aarhus, 1983; Diploma in Composition, Royal Academy of Music, Aarhus, 1988; MMus, University of Aarhus, 1992; Soloist Diploma (PhD) in Composition, Royal Academy of Music, Copenhagen, 1993. Debut: As a Composer, Denmark, 1982. Career: His music has been performed in almost all European countries, in USA and South America. Being prizewinner at the UNESCO Composers International Rostrum, 1994, his piece Winter Light was broadcast all over the world; Teacher, Royal Academies of Music, Copenhagen and Aarhus, Acadmies of Music in Aalborg and Esbjerg and the Universities of Aarhus and Aalborg; Currently Assistant Professor, Academy of Music, Esbjerg. Compositions include: Orchestral, Zurvan Akarana, 1986; Dreams within Dreams, 1st violin concerto, 1990; Las flores del mar de la muerte, 2nd violin concerto, 1993; Chamber works, Orphian Fire Mountains, 1988; The Lost Poems of Princess Ateh, 1991; The Khazarian Mirrors, 1993; Vocal works, Hyperions Schicksalslied, 1982; Pessimisticum, 1993. Recordings: CD: Mogens Christensen, Vocal and Chamber Music volume I, 1991, volume II, 1993, volume III, 1995; Odriozola and Kristensen play Christensen and Odriozola (including Winter Light), 1995; 1994 Ensemble Nord (including The Lost Poems of Princess Ateh), 1992. Publications: Winter Light, 1994; 3 Works for Violin Solo, 1995. Contributions to: Betrachtungen Über den Tonalitätsbegriff bei Edvard Grieg und Carl Nielsen (from Die Gratulanten kommen, 1993). Honours: Artist Prize of the County of Bergen, 1991; Artist Scholarship of the Danish State, 1993-95; Prize Winner, UNESCO Composers International Rostrum, 1994. Membership: Danish Composers Society. Address: Stavnsholtvej 161, DK-3520 Farum, Denmark.

CHRISTESEN Robert, b. 15 Feb 1943, Washington DC, USA. Singer (Baritone). Education: Studied at the Manhattan School of Music and at Aspen School of Music with Aksel Schiotz and Jennie Tourel. Debut: Henrik in Maskarade by Nielsen at St Paul, 1972. Career: Sang with the Frankfurt and Dortmund Operas and appeared as guest Berlin (Komische Oper), Copenhagen, Budapest, Warsaw, Toulouse, Brno, Prague and in North and South America; Other roles have included Mozart's Count and Don Giovanni, Verdi's Ford, Germont and Luna, Eugene Onegin, Jochanaan, Rossini's Figaro, Kaspar in Der Freischütz and Lescaut in Henze's Boulevard Solitude. Address: c/o Stādische Buhnen, Untermainanlage 11, 6000 Frankfurt am Main, Germany.

CHRISTIE George (William Langham) (Sir), b. 31 Dec 1934, Glyndebourne, England. Chairman of Companies. m. Patricia Mary Nicholson, 1958, 3 sons, 1 daughter. Career: Assistant to Secretary of X Calouste Gulbenkian Foundation, 1957-62; Chairman of Glyndebourne Productions Limited, 1956-, and of other family companies; Has been instrumental in the widening of Glyndebourne Festival repertory to include operas by Henze, Janácek, Stravinsky, Ravel, Strauss and Gershwin; Supervised rebuilding of main auditorium at Glyndebourne (opened 1994); Founder and Chairman, The London Sinfonietta. Honours: Knight, 1984; Deputy Lieutenant, East Sussex. Address: Glyndebourne, Lewes, East Sussex, England.

CHRISTIE Michael, b. 1975, USA. Conductor. Education: Graduate, Oberlin College Conservatory of Music, 1997. Career: Conducting engagements with the Los Angeles and Buffalo Philharmonics, the Lahti Symphony and the Helsinki and Tampere (Finland) Philharmonics, Royal Scottish National Orchestra; UK debut with the City of Birmingham Symphony Orchestra, 1996; Season 1997-98, Assistant to Franz Welser-Möst at the Zurich Opera; Apprentice Conductor with the Chicago Symphony Orchestra, 1995-96. Honours include: Prize for Outstanding Potential at the First International Sibelius Conductor's Competition, Helsinki, 1995. Address: c/o IMG Artists, Media House, 3 Burlington Lane, London W4 2Th, England.

CHRISTIE Nan, b. 1950, Ayr, Scotland. Singer, Soprano. Education: Royal Scottish Academy of Music; London Opera Centre. Career: Repertoire with Scottish Opera includes Britten's Tytania, Rimsky's Queen of Shemakha, The Queen of Night and Zerbinetta in Ariadne auf Naxos; Tours to Portugal, Poland, Switzerland and Germany; Sang in Mozart's La Finta Giardiniera and the premiere of Oliver's Tom Jones, with English Music Theatre; Tytania with Opera North; Isotta in Die schweigsame Frau and Despina in Così fan tutte, at the Glyndebourne Festival; Zdenka in Arabella, the Queen of Night and Offenbach's Eurydice with English National Opera; European engagements with Netherlands Opera, Despina; Opera de Nancy as Pamina; Zurich Opera in the Ponnelle production of Lucio Silla and Frankfurt Opera as Zerbinetta, Marie in Die Soldaten and Susanna; Scottish Opera, 1990 as Despina in a new production of Così fan tutte; Birdie Hubbard in the British premiere of Blitzstein's Regina, Glasgow, 1991; Concerts at the Hong Kong Festival, Hallé Orchestra, BBC Symphony and London Symphony Orchestra, Nash Ensemble and the London Sinfonietta; TV appearances in Mozart's Schauspieldirektor and Ravel's L'Enfant et les Sortilèges; Italian debut: Mitridate by Mozart, La Fenice, Venice, and the Queen of Night in The Magic Flute for ENO, 1992; Premiere of Jonathan Harvey's Inquest of Love, English National Opera, 1993; Sang Third Official in the premiere of The Doctor of Myddfai, by Peter Maxwell Davies, Cardiff, 1996. Recordings: Videos of Glyndebourne Festival Così fan tutte; The Gondoliers, The Sorcerer and Princess Ida. Address: c/o Lies Askonas Ltd, 6 Henrietta Street, London, WC2, England.

CHRISTIE William (Lincoln), b. 19 Dec 1944, Buffalo, New York, USA. Harpsichordist; Conductor; Teacher. Education: Studied harpsichord with Igor Kipnis, Berkshire Music Center, Tanglewood; BA, Harvard University, 1966; Harpsichord with Ralph Kirkpatrick; Organ with Charles Kribaum; Musicology with Claude Palisca and Nicholas Temperley; MMus, Yale University, 1970. Career: Teacher, Dartmouth College, 1970-71; Member, Five Centuries Ensemble, France, 1971-75; Concerto Vocale, 1972-; Founder-Director, Les Arts Florissants, 1978-; Teacher, Innsbruck Summer Academy for Early Music, 1977-83; Professorship, Paris Conservatory, 1982-; Conducted Alcina at the Théâtre de Châtelet and Geneva, 1990; London debut of Les Arts Florissants at Greenwich, 1990, with Charpentier's Actéon, and Dido and Aeneas; Les Indes Galantes at Aix-en-Provence; Conducted Luigi Rossi's Orfeo at Vienna Konzerthaus, 1990; Season 1992 with Purcell's Fairy Queen at the Barbican Hall, London, Rameau's Castor et Pollux for the Baroque Festival at Versailles and Lully's Atys at Madrid; Purcell's King Arthur at Covent Garden, 1995; Hippolyte et Aricie in Paris and Rameau's Les Fêtes d'Hébé at the Barbican, London, 1996. Recordings: Many discs devoted to the masters of the French and Italian Baroque including Landi's Il Sant Alessio and Handel's Orlando, 1996-97; Rameau's Les Fêtes d'Hébé; d'India's Madrigals. Honours: Numerous awards including a number of Grand Prix du Disque of France and Prix Mondiale du Disque; First American to hold a Professorship at the Paris Conservatory; Awarded the French Légion d'Honneur, 1993. Address: Les Arts Florissants, 10 Rue de Florence, F-75008, Paris, France.

CHRISTIN Judith, b. 15 Feb 1948, Providence, Rhode Island, USA. Singer (Mezzo-Soprano). Education: Studied at Indiana University. Career: Sang at first in concert, opera from 1980; Washington Opera from 1981 and at Santa Fe in the US premieres of Weir's A Night at the Chinese Opera, Penderecki's Schwarze Maske and Judith by Matthus; Los Angeles from 1983, San Diego, 1984, Philadelphia, 1986; New York Metropolitan from 1988, in Eugene Onegin, Faust, Die Zauberflöte, Luisa Miller and Le nozze di Figaro; European career from 1987 (Netherlands Opera); Roles have included Despina (Santa Fe, 1988-90), the Hostess in Boris Godunov, Suzuki in Butterfly and Carlotta in Die schweigsame Frau. Address: c/o Metropolitan Opera, Lincoln Center, New York, NY 10023, USA.

CHRISTOFF Dimiter, b. 2 Oct 1933, Sofia, Bulgaria. Composer; Professor. Education: Studied composition with M Goleminov, State Music Academy, Sofia, 1951-56; Study tour West Germany, USA, France, The Netherlands, 1963; Dr Habil 1975. Career: Teacher 1970-76, Professor 1976-, State Music Academy; General Secretary, International Music Council, UNESCO, 1975-79. Compositions: Operas: The Game, 1978; The Golden Fish Line, 1984; Orchestral: 3 piano concertos 1954, 1983, 1994; Sinfonietta for Strings, 1956; Poem, 1957; 3 Symphonies, 1958, 1964, 1969; Overture, 1961; Symphonic Episodes, 1962; 3 Violin Concertos, 1966, 1996, 1997; Chamber Suite for Two Piccolo, Piano, Percussion and Strings, 1966; Cello Concerto, 1969; Concert Miniatures, 1970; Overture with Fanfares, 1974; Quasi una fantasia-gioco, 1981; Game for Celli and Orchestra, 1983; Perpetui mobili in pianissimi, 1987; Chamber: Suite for Brass Quartet, 1953; 2 Dances, for Trumpet and Piano, 1960; Sonata for Solo Cello, 1965; Concerto for 3 small drums and 5 instruments, 1967; String Quartet, 1970; Quartet for Flute, Viola, Harp and Harpsichord, 1973; 12 Piano sonatas; Also choruses and songs. Memberships: International Society for Music Education; Bulgarian Composers Union, vice-President, 1972-85. Address: Mavrovets 7, 1415 Sofia-Dragalevtsi, Bulgaria.

CHRISTOPHERS Harry, b. 26 December 1953, Goudhurst, Kent, England. Conductor; Choral Director. m. Veronica Mary Hayward, 2 June 1979, 2 sons, 2 daughters. Education: Studied at Canterbury Cathedral Choir School (Head Chorister), King's School Canterbury; BA, Honours, Music, Magdalen College, Oxford (Academical Clerk). Career: Founded the choral group The Sixteen, 1977 (now known as The Symphony of Harmony and Invention, 1997); Tours of Britain, Europe, Brazil and Japan, 1989; BBC debut May 1981; BBC Prom debut, 1990; Has also worked with the Deutschen Kammer-Philharmonie and with the Turku Philharmonic in Finland; Association with the RTE Concert Orchestra and Chorus, Dublin, with Messiah and Bach's St John Passion and Christmas Oratorio; Concerts in Lahti with Avanti and the Finnish Chamber Choir, in Espoo and Helsinki with the Espoo City Orchestra and the Helsinki Philharmonic; Concerts with the Scottish Chamber Orchestra, BBC Philharmonic, English Chamber Orchestra, City of London Sinfonia; Appearances with The Sixteen in the premiere of Birtwistle's Gawain at Covent Garden, May 1991; Other 1991 concerts at St John's Smith Square (Poulenc, the Eton Choir Book, Bach's Magnificat and Christmas Concerts); Perpignan, France (Purcell); Bach's B minor Mass, 1994; Stravinsky's Symphony of Psalms, 1994; Conducted Orfeo by Gluck at the San Carlos Opera, Lisbon, 1996-97. Recordings include: Handel's Messiah, Monteverdi Vespers; Handel Chandos Anthems, Bach St John Passion and Tallis Spem in Alium); John Sheppard, Church Music vol I-IV, Taverner, Festal Mass series; Teixeira Te Deum, music from the Eton Choirbook vol I-IV; Handel's Esther (1995); Handel's Samson, 1997. Honours include: Grand Prix du Disque from the Academie Charles Cros, 1986 for Messiah recording; Gramophone, Early Music Award, 1992 for The Rose and the Ostrich Feather; Deutschen Schallplattenkritik, 1992 for Handel Alexander's Feast; Diapason D'Or 1992 for Teixeira Te Deum. Hobbies include: Cooking; Football (Arsenal FC). Address: c/o Harrison/Parrott Ltd, 12 Penzance Road, London W11 4PA, England.

CHRISTOS Marianna, b. 1950, Beaverly Falls, Pennsylvania, USA. Singer (Soprano). Career: Sang with the New York City Opera, 1975-79, debut as Liu in Turandot; Has appeared widely in the USA at Pittsburgh, Washington, St Louis, Houston, Los Angeles and San Francisco; Roles have included Mimi, Gilda, Adina in L'elisir d'amore, Margharita in Mefistofele, Donna Anna, Donna Elvira, Micaela, and Antonia in Les Contes d'Hoffmann. Address: c/o New York City Opera, Lincoln Center, New York, NY 10023, USA.

CHU Wang-Hua, b. 5 September 1941, Jiangsu, China. Composer; Teacher. Education: BMus, Central Conservatory, Peking, 1963; MMus, University of Melbourne, 1985. Career:

Faculty of Central Conservatory, Peking, 1963-82; Freelance pianist and teacher in Australia, 1982-. Compositions include: Seven Preludes, and Three Piano Variations, 1961-80; Piano Sonata, 1981; String Quartet, 1983; Ash Wednesday for orchestra, 1984; The Borderland Moon for soprano and ensemble, 1984; Concerto for Chamber Orchestra, 1984; The Bamboo for piano and orchestra, 1986; Drinking Alone by Moonlight for soprano and chamber ensemble, 1985; 30 Chinese Folk Songs for piano, 1979-86; Autumn Cry for orchestra, 1988; Symphony, 1988; Sinfonia for chamber orchestra, 1988; Piano Concerto, 1989; Fantasia Symphony: The Silk Road, 1990; Eva, Beloved Mother, for piano, 1993. Address: c/o APRA, 1A Eden Street, Crows Nest, NSW 2065, Australia.

CHUCHRO Josef, b. 3 July 1931, Prague, Czechoslovakia. Cellist. Education: Studied at the Prague Conservatory, 1946-50. Career: Soloist with the Czech Philharmonic from 1961; From 1960 partnered Jan Panenka and Josef Suk in the Suk Trio; Professor at the Prague Academy of Arts from 1969; Dean of Music Faculty, 1990-97; Frequent performances as concert soloist. Address: Academy of Music and Arts in Prague. Music Faculty, Malostranské nám 13, 118 00 Prague 1, Czech Republic.

CHUCHROVA Liubov, b. 1973, Lithuania. Soprano. Career: Frequent opera and concert engagements in Lithuania and throughout Europe; Opera repertory includes Gounod's Marguerite in Faust, and Fiordiligi in Cosi fan tutte; Also sings songs by Schumann and Brahms; Participations in the International Placido Domingo Contest and the 1995 Cardiff Singer of the World Competition. Recordings include: Haydn's L'Isola Disabitata. Address: Gabijos 57-39, Vilnius 2022, Lithuania.

CHUDOVA Tatiana, b. 16 June 1944, Moscow, Russia. Composer. Education: Studied at the Moscow Central Music School and Conservatory, notably with Khrennikov. Career: Teacher in Moscow from 1970. Compositions include: Operas: The Dead Princess and the Seven Heroes, 1967, and To the Village, to Grandfather, 1978; 3 Suites for orchestra of folk instruments, 1980-82; Symphonic trilogy, 1981-82, and Symphony no 4, 1988; Choral, solo vocal and instrumental music, including 2 violin sonatas, 1974, 1987. Address: c/o RAO, Bolchaia Bronnai 6-1, Moscow 103670, Russia.

CHUNG Kyung-Wha, b. 26 Mar 1948, Seoul, Korea. m. 2 sons. Violinist. Education: Studied under Ivan Galamian, Juilliard School of Music, New York, USA. Debut: USA. Career: European debut, 1970; Has played under numerous conductors including Abbado, Barenboim, Davis, Dorati, Dutoit, Giulini, Haitink, Jochum, Kempe, Kondrashin, Leinsdorf, Levine, Maazel, Mehta, Muti, Previn, Rattle, Rozhdestvensky and Solti; Has played with major orchestras including all London Orchestras, Chicago, Boston and Pittsburgh Symphony Orchestras, New York, Cleveland, Philadelphia, Berlin, Israel and Vienna Philharmonics, and Orchestre de Paris; Has toured the world; Played at Salzburg Festival, London Symphony Orchestra, 1973; Vienna Festival, 1981, 1984; Edinburgh Festival, 1981; Played at 80th Birthday Concert of William Walton, 1982; Beethoven's Sonatas Op 30 Nos 1 and 2 and Op 96 with Stephen Kovacevich, Barbican Centre, May 1991. Recordings: Concertos by Beethoven, Bruch, Mendelssohn, Tchaikovsky, Bartók, Stravinsky, Walton, Vieuxtemps. Honours: Winner, Leventritt Competition, 1968; Hobbies: Arts. Current Management: Columbia Artists Management Inc, New York. Address: c/o Columbia Artists Management Inc, 165 West 57th Street, New York, NY 10019, USA.

CHUNG Mia, b. 9 October 1964, Madison, Wisconsin, USA. Concert Pianist; Assistant Professor of Music. Education: BA magna cum laude, Harvard University, 1986; MM, Yale University, 1988; DMA, Juilliard School of Music, 1991. Debut: Hall of the Americas, OAS Building, Washington DC, 1983. Career: Assistant Professor of Music and Artist-in-Residence, Gordon College, 1991-; Appearances with Baltimore Symphony Orchestra, 1977, 1981; Performed with National Symphony Orchestra, 1983; Performed with National Gallery Orchestra, 1987; Performed with Fort Collins Symphony Orchestra, 1990; Performed with New Haven Symphony, 1989; Solo Recitals and Chamber Performances at OAS, Alice Tully Hall, National Gallery of Art, the Kennedy Center for Performing Arts, American Academy of Arts and Sciences and other venues; Records exclusively for Channel Classics Records. Recordings: Beethoven Bagatelles, Op 126 and Sonatas No 16 in G major Op 31, No 1 and No 32 in C minor Op 111. Honours: First Prize in 1981 Johann Sebastian Bach International Competition in New York City, 1993. Hobbies: Long Distance Swimming; Art History; Cooking. Current Management: Concert Artist Guild. Address: Fine Arts Department, Gordon College, Wenham, MA 01984, USA.

CHUNG Myung-Wha, b. 19 Mar 1944, Seoul, Korea. Concert Cellist. Education: Studied with Leonard Rose at the Juilliard School and with Gregor Piatigorsky at his University of Southern California Master Class. Debut: Played with the Seoul Philharmonic before study in New York; US at San Francisco, 1967; Europe at Spoleto, 1969. Career: Has appeared widely in Europe and North America from 1971, notably in England, Italy, Denmark,Germany, Spain, Sweden, Netherlands, Belgium, France, Switzerland, Portugal, Israel and Mexico; Festival appearances at Lucerne, Flanders, Spoleto, Palma de Majorca, Birmingham, Evian and Dijon; Television programmes in the USA, England, Germany and Switzerland; Plays a 1731 Stradivarius Cello known as Braga. Recordings include: Tchaikovsky Rococco Variations with the Los Angeles Philharmonic under Charles Dutoit; Ten Piano Trio Works with the Chung Trio. Honours include: 1st Prize, Geneva International Music Competition, 1971; National Order of Cultural Merit, Korea, 1992; Serves as Goodwill Ambassador for UN Drug Control Programme since 1992; On the Cello Faculties of New York's Mannes College of Music and the Korean National Institute of Arts. Address: 142 West End Avenue (#17U), New York, NY 10023, USA.

CHUNG Myung-Whun, b. 22 Jan 1953, Seoul, Korea. Conductor; Pianist. Education: Began musical studies as a pianist; Mannes College of Music, New York, with Nadia Rosenberg and Carl Bamburger; Juilliard School 1974-78, with Sixten Ehrling. Career: Associate Conductor of the Los Angeles Philharmonic Orchestra, 1978-81; Moved to Europe 1981 and conducted the Berlin Philharmonic, Munich Philharmonic, Concertgebouw Orchestra, Orchestre de Paris, Israel Philharmonic and the major London Orchestras; Music Director and Principal Conductor of the Saarlandischer Rundfunk in Saarbrucken, 1984-89; On visits to USA has conducted the New York Philharmonic, National Symphony Washington, the Boston Symphony and the Cleveland and Chicago Orchestras; Metropolitan Opera from 1986, debut with Simon Boccanegra; Principal Guest Conductor at the Teatro Comunale in Florence; New Productions of Boris Godunov, Simon Boccanegra and Idomeneo; Has worked at opera houses in Monte Carlo and Geneva and conducted a new production of Prokofiev's The Fiery Angel at the Paris Opera; Music Director of the Opera de la Bastille, Paris, 1989-94; Conducted Les Troyens, first production, 1990; The Legend of the Invisible City of Kitezh (Rimsky-Korsakov), 1990, at the Maggio Musicale, Florence; Conducted the Orchestra of the Opera Bastille de Paris in Symphonie Fantastique at the Spoleto Festival, 1990; Season 1992 with Lady Macbeth of Mtsensk at Paris; Conducted Otello at Covent Garden, 1997 (house debut). Recordings: Nielsen Symphonies and Dvorak Symphonies 7 and 8 with the Gothenburg Symphony; Messiaen's Turangalila Symphonie; Piano Trios with his sisters Kyung-Wha and Myung-Wha Chung; Beethoven Triple Concerto with Philharmonia Orchestra. Honours: Second Prize, Tchaikovsky International Piano Competition, Moscow, 1974; Premio Abbiati for operatic work in season 1987-88. Address: Opera de Paris Bastille, 120 Rue de Lyon, 75012 Paris, France.

CHURCHES Richard (Mark), b. 20 July 1966, Caerleon, Wales. Composer; Baritone; Conductor. m. Jennifer Kathleen Hornett, 11 Aug 1990. Education: AMusLCM; London University, 1984-89; Studied Composition with Gwyn Pritchard and Brian Dennis; Singing with Jean Cannard and Brian Dennis. Debut: As Baritone, Riensei in 1st performance of Brian Dennis' opera Atsumori, 21 June 1988. Career: Compositional style influenced by Cardew school; Rejected avant-garde in favour of a controversially traditional aesthetic; Works for large and small forces; Director of Music, ACAT, Turin, 1989-91; Currently a Haberdashers' Director of Music; Founded the British Contemporary Music Anthology with Gerald Leach and Brian Dennis, 1995. Compositions: The Whole Wide World is White, songs, 1985-91; Three Pieces for Guitar, 1986; Concert Overture, piano and orchestra, 1987; Brand-A Lyric Poem for Symphony Orchestra, 1988-92; Songs from a Jade Terrace, 1992. Recordings: Songs from a Jade Terrace (Songs by Richard Churches and Brian Dennis), with Jeremy Huw Williams, baritone, and Nigel Foster, piano, Royal Academy of Music, CD and tape. Publications: Composers in Education, Composers' Guild of Great Britain project (contributor), 1990; 2 chapters in The Scratch Orchestra (1969-74), a Symposium, 1996. Honours: 3rd place, Cornelius Cardew Composition Prize, Royal Academy of Music, 1994; Holst Foundation Grant, 1995. Memberships: Composers' Guild of Great Britain; British Music Society. Address: c/o 44 Mendip Avenue, Worle, Weston-super-Mare, Avon BS22 0HW, England.

CHURGIN Bathia (Dina), b. 9 October 1928, New York, New York, USA. Musicologist. Education: BA, Hunter College, New York City, 1950; MA, Radcliffe College, 1952; PhD, Harvard University, 1963. Career: Instructor to Full Professor, Vassar College, 1952-57, 1959-71; Professor, Founding Head of Department, Bar-Ilan University, Ramat Gan, Israel, 1970-; Visiting Professor, Harvard Summer School, Northwestern University, University of North Carolina, Chapel Hill, CUNY, Queens College and Graduate Center, Tel Aviv University, The Hebrew University, Jerusalem; Rubin Academy of Music, Jerusalem. Publications: The Symphonies of G B Sammartini, vol 1: The Early Symphonies, 1968; Thematic Catalogue of the Works of Giovanni Battista Sammartini, Orchestral and Vocal Music (with Newell Jenkins), 1976; Editor, Israel Studies in Musicology II, 1980; G B Sammartini, Sonate a tre stromenti, A New Edition with Historical and Analytical Essays, 1981; G B Sammartini: Ten Symphonies, 1984; Editor, Israel Studies in Musicology VI, 1996; Beethoven's Fourth Symphony, Editor, 1997. Contributions to: Professional Journals: Francesco Galeazzi's Description (1796) of Sonata Form, JAMS XXI (1968); Beethoven and Mozart's Requiem: A New Connection, JM V, 1987; Beethoven's Sketches for his String Quintet, Op 29, LaRue Festschrift (1990); Harmonic and Tonal Instability in the Second Key Area of Classic Sonata Form, Ratner Festschrift (1992). Honours: Fellowship, American Council of Learned Societies, 1964, 1986 Memberships: Chair, Israel Musicological Society, 1994-95; American Musicological Society; International Musicological Society. Address: Department of Musicology, Bar-Ilan University, Ramat Gan, 52900 Israel.

CHUSID Martin, b. 19 Aug 1925, Brooklyn, New York, USA. Musicologist; Professor. m. Anita B Chusid, 1 son. Education: BA, 1950, MA, 1955, PhD, 1961, University of California, Berkeley. Career: Teaching Assistant, 1953-55, Associate, 1955-57, University of California, Berkeley; Instructor, 1959-62, Assistant Professor, 1962-63, University of Southern California, Los Angeles; Associate Professor, 1963-68, Professor, 1968-, Acting Chairman, Music Department, 1966-67, 1981, 1986-87, New York University; Chairman, Music Department, Washington Square College of Arts and Sciences, 1967-70; Associate Dean, Graduate School of Arts and Sciences, 1970-72; Director, American Institute for Verdi Studies, 1976-; Visiting Professor of Music: Boston University, 1975, University of British Columbia, 1979, Southern Methodist University, 1980, Princeton University, 1981, Brigham Young University, 1982; Principal Editor, Verdi Newsletter, 1981-. Publications: Schubert's Unfinished Symphony: A Monograph and Edition, 2nd edition, 1971; A Catalog of Verdi's Operas, 1974; The Verdi Companion (with W Weaver), 1979; Editions of works by Schubert and Verdi; Verdi's Middle Period, 1997; Schubert's "Schwanengesang": Facsimiles and Reprint, 1998; A Companion to Schubert's "Schwanengesang", 1998. Contributions to: Articles on Verdi, Schubert, Mozart, Haydn, Dvorák, to various publications. Honours: Honorary Doctor of Humane Letters, Centre College of Kentucky, 1977. Address: 4 Washington Square Village, New York, NY 10012, USA.

CHVALA Jiri, b. 9 May 1933, Moravec, Czech Republic. Conductor. m. Svatava Sarmova, 16 July 1971, 1 son, 1 daughter. Education: Music School, Pisek; Music Faculty, Academy of Performing Arts, Prague. Debut: Smetana Hall, Prague, 1958. Career: Conductor of Prague Philharmonic Choir, 1959-72; Artistic Director, Conductor-in-Chief, Prague Philharmonic Childrens Choir, 1967-; Professor, Academy of Performing Arts, Prague, 1986-; Conductor of Prague Philharmonic Childrens Choir at Festivals in Europe, USA, Japan; Juror, Numerous Choral Competitions in Czech Republic and Abroad; Several Radio and Television Appearances. Recordings: Jan seidel, Bethlehem Songs; Jan Krtitel Vanhal, Stabat mater; Jiri Teml, Splnilo se Pismo svaté; Rafael Kubelik, Invence a interludia; Heidenröslein, Pony Canyon; Europe's Christmas, Pony Canyon; Jakub Jan Ryba, Pastorals. Contributions to: Professional Journals. Honours: Prize, Frantisek Lysek, Czech Choral Union, Czech Music Foundation & Association of Choral Conductors. Memberships: Association of Music Artists, Prague; Association of Choral Conductors. Hobbies: Literature; Tourism. Address: Orlicka 8, 130 00 Praha 3, Czech Republic.

CHYLINSKA Teresa (Wanda), b. 20 June 1931, Wojciechowice, Poland. Musicologist; Music editor; Writer on music. m. 1957, divorced 1960, 1 son. Education: MA, Musicology, Jagiellonian University, Krakow, 1949-53. Career: Chief, Department of Polish, Polish Music Publications, Krakow, 1954-89; Lecturer, Jagiellonian University and Academy of Music, 1970s; President, The Karol Szymanowski Music Society, 1979-80; Member, Scientific Board, The Chopin Society, Warsaw, 1982-. Publications include: First critical edition of The Complete Works of Karol Szymanowski (26 volumes Polish version, 17 volumes German-English in co-edition with Universal Edition, Vienna); A Complete edition of Szymanowski's correspondence, Volume 1, 1982, volume 2, 1994, volume 3, 1997; Szymanowski's Literary Writings, 1989; Szymanowski's Days at Zakopane, 1982, 4th edition; Szymanowski and His Music, popular monograph for young readers, 1990, 3rd edition; Karol Szymanowski, His Life and Works (in English), 1993. Contributions to: New Grove Dictionary of Music and Musicians; Encyclopedia Muzyczna PWM; Pipers Enzyklopädie des Musik Theaters. Address: ul Syrokomli 16 m 10, 30-102 Krakow, Poland.

CIANI Suzanne, b. 4 June 1946, Edinburg, Indiana, USA. Composer. Education: BA, music major, Wellesley College, 1968; MA, music composition, University of California, Berkeley, 1970. Career: Has written electronic and acoustic music for films and television; Performer on synthesizer and piano with orchestra;

Composer, Arranger and producer of 10 original record albums. Recordings include: Seven Waves, 1981; The Velocity of Love, 1985; Neverland. 1988; History of My Heart, 1989; Pianissimo, 1990; Hotel Luna, 1991; The Private Music of Suzanne Ciani, 1992; Dream Suite, 1995; Film score for The Incredible Shrinking Woman, 1980; Mother Teresa, 1986; Pianissimo II, 1996; Suzanne Ciani and The Wave: Live, 1997. Honours: Grammy Nominations, 1988, 1991, 1995, 1996. Memberships: ASCAP; AES. Current management: Joe Anderson. Address: c/o Seventh Wave Productions, 20 Sunnyside Avenue, A-197, Mill Valley, CA 94941, USA.

CIANNELLA Giuliano, b. 25 Oct 1943, Palermo, Italy. Singer, Tenor. Debut: La Scala 1976, as Cassio in Otello. Career: Metropolitan Opera from 1979, as Don Carlos, Des Grieux in Manon Lescaut, Rodolfo, Pinkerton, Alfredo and Macduff; Guest engagements in San Francisco, as Don José 1984 and Munich, Don Carlos, 1985; Covent Garden debut 1986, as Manrico in Il Trovatore; Verona Arena, 1983, 1985 and 1988; Bregenz Festival 1987, as Ernani; Cologne Opera, 1988, as Don José and Puccini's Des Grieux; Riccardo in Ballo in Maschera, at Parma, 1989. Address: c/o Teatro Regio, Via Garibaldi 16, 1-43100 Parma, Italy.

CICCOLINI Aldo, b. 15 Aug 1925, Naples, Italy. Concert Pianist. Education: Studied with Paolo Denza at the Naples Conservatory. Debut: Naples 1942, in Chopin's F Minor Concerto; Professor at the Naples Conservatory from 1947; Moved to France 1949; Professor at the Paris Conservatoire from 1971; US debut 1950, with the New York Philharmonic, playing Tchaikovsky's 1st Concerto; Many concerts with the world's leading orchestras; Recital programmes include music by Fauré; Ravel, Liszt and Debussy. Honours: Santa Cecilia Prize, Rome, 1948; Marguerite Long-Jacques Thibaud Prize, Paris, 1949. Recordings: Liszt, Années de Pelèrinage and Harmonies Poetiques et Religieuses; Complete piano works of Satie; Concertos by Saint-Saëns; Piano Concerto in D by Alexis de Castillon, conducted by Georges Prêtre. Address: c/o Conservatoire National Superiuer de Musique, 14 Rue de Madrid, 75008 France.

CIESINSKI Katherine, b. 13 Oct 1950, Newark, Delaware, USA. Mezzo-Soprano. Education: Studies with Margaret Harshaw at Curtis Institute, Philadelphia. Career: Sang in the US premiere of Berg's 3 act Lulu; European debut 1976 at Aix-en-Provence; Later sang in Asia, Israel and elsewhere in Europe; In 1988 sang in premiere of Argento's The Aspern Papers at Dallas and La Celestine by Maurice Ohana, Paris; Metropolitan Opera debut 1988, as Nicklausse in Les contes d'Hoffmann, returning as Judith in Duke Bluebeard's Castle by Bartók; Other roles include Waltraute in Götterdämmerung, Strauss's Composer and Octavian, Brangaene in Tristan und Isolde, Britten's Lucretia, Laura in La Gioconda and Barber's Vanessa; Cassandre in Les Troyens for Scottish Opera and at Covent Garden; La Favorite, title role, in revival of original French version, 1991. Recordings: War and Peace by Prokofiev, Dukas' Ariane et Barbe Bleue; Sapho by Massenet; Pauline in The Queen of Spades.

CIESINSKI Kristine (Frances), b. 5 Jul 1952, Wilmington, DE, USA. Soprano. m. Norman Bailey, 1985. Education: Temple University, 1970-71; University of Delaware, 1971-72; BA in Voice, Boston University, 1974. Career: New York concert debut as Soloist in Handel's Messiah, 1977; European operatic debut as Baroness Freimann in Die Wildschütz at Salzburg Landestheater, 1979, singing there until 1981; Member of Bremen State Opera, 1985-88; Guest appearances at Cincinnati Opera, Florentine Opera, Milwaukee in 1983 and 1987, Cleveland Opera, 1985, Scottish Opera, 1985 and 1989, Canadian Opera, 1986, Opera North, Leeds, 1986 and 1988, Augsburg Opera, 1986, Mexico City, 1986, Welsh National Opera, 1987 and 1989, Bregenz Festival, 1987, Zagreb National Opera, 1988, Wexford Festival, 1988, English National Opera, 1989-93, Munich State Opera, 1989, Baltimore Opera, 1989, Winnipeg Opera, 1989 and 1991, Frankfurt State Opera, 1990 and 1993, New Orleans Opera, 1992, Leipzig Opera, 1992, and La Scala Milan in 1992; Roles include: Medea, La Wally, Eva, Senta, Donna Anna, Tosca, Aida, Ariadne, Salome, Verdi's Lady Macbeth, Shostakovich's Lady Macbeth of Mtsensk, Erwartung, Judith from Bartók's Bluebeard, Berg's Marie, Beethoven's Leonora, Tchaikovsky's Tatiana and Salome, also many concert engagements in a repertory ranging from traditional works to contemporary scores; Sang Salome in a new production of Strauss's opera, ENO, 1996. Recordings: Several. Honours: Gold Medal, Geneva International Competition, 1977; 1st Prize, Salzburg International Competition, 1977. Address: c/o Trawick Artists Management Inc, 129 West 72nd Street, New York City, NY 10023-3239, USA.

CIGNA Gina, b. 6 Mar 1900, Angere, Paris, France. Singer, Soprano. Education: Studied in Paris with Calvé, Storchio and Darclée. Debut: La Scala 1927, as Freia in Das Rheingold. Career: Sang at La Scala until 1943, notably as Turandot, La Gioconda and the leading Verdi roles; Covent Garden 1933-39, debut as Marguerite in La Damnation de Faust; Metropolitan

Opera 1937-38, as Aida, the Trovatore Leonora, Donna Elvira, Santuzza and Norma; Florence 1933, 1935, 1937, in Nabucco, Alceste and L'Incoronazione di Poppea; Venice, 1941, as the Kostelnicka in Jenufa; Guest appearances in Buenos Aires, Paris, Berlin, Vienna, Amsterdam & Brussels; Teacher at Toronto 1953-57 and at the Accademia Chigiana in Siena, 1957-65. Recordings: La Gioconda, Turandot and Norma; Labels include Columbia, Telefunken and Cetra.

CILLARIO Carlo Felice, b. 7 Feb 1915, San Rafael, Argentina. Conductor. Education: Studied at the G B Martini Conservatory and in Odessa. Career: After playing as concert violinist has conducted from 1942; Formed the Orchestra da Camera in Bologna, 1946; Formed the Symphony Orchestra of the University of Tucuman in Argentina, 1948; Resident Conductor of the Orquesta Sinfonica del Estado, Buenos Aires, 1949-51; Conductor of opera seasons at Covent Garden, Glyndebourne (1961-62, L'Elisir d'Amore), Chicago (debut, 1961, La Forza del Destino), San Francisco, Buenos Aires, Venice, Paris, Hamburg and Florence; Metropolitan Opera debut, 1972, La Sonnambula; Conducted Tosca, 1985; Royal Opera, Stockholm, from 1980, with Macbeth, La Bohème, Tosca, Médée and Falstaff; Drottningholm Theatre, 1982-84, La Cenerentola and Il Fanatico Burlato by Cimarosa; Performances of La Bohème, Il Trittico, Die Walküre, Tosca, Un Ballo in Maschera, Don Pasquale and Eugene Onegin with Australian Opera; San Francisco, 1986, Lucia di Lammermoor; Bi-centennial concerts at Sydney, 1988; Principal Guest Conductor and Music Consultant to the Australian Opera, 1988; Conducted Maria Stuarda at Stockholm, 1990; Cavalleria Rusticana and Pagliacci at Buenos Aires, 1992. Recordings include: Music by Carissimi, Monteverdi's Orfeo, Stradella's San Giovanni Battista, Leoni's La Morte di Abele and Rossi's Giuseppe, Figlio di Giacobbe; Handel's Salve Regina and Aci, Galatea e Polifemo, Mozart's Ascanio in Alba, Lucio Silla and La Betulia Liberata, with the Angelicum Orchestra of Milan. Address: c/o Kungliga Teatern, PO Box 16094, S-10322 Stockholm, Sweden.

CIMINELLI Giovanni, b. 1930, Italy. Singer (Baritone). Career: Sang at La Scala from 1959, debut as Faraone in Mose in Egitto; Further appearances at Rome (from 1966), Bari (1967), Cagliari (1969) and Venice (1970); Alfio in Cavalleria Rusticana at Trieste, 1978; Hartford Opera, USA, 1973-76; Other roles have included Escamillo, Germont, Luna, Amonasro, Simon Boccanegra and Enrico in Lucia di Lammermoor. Address: c/o Teatro Comunale, Riva Novembre 1, 34121 Trieste, Italy.

CINCERA Andreas, b. 2 Jan 1960, Zurich, Switzerland. Double-bassist. Education: Conservatory and Music High School of Zurich; Orchestral Diploma; Master's degree cum laude; Diploma in Music Education; Postgraduate studies with Gary Karr, Germany, and Duncan McTies, UK. Career: Now Soloist and Chamber Musician; Solo Bass Player, Orchestre Philharmonique Suisse; Member of Collegium Novum Zurich; Professor, Head of Seminar for Music Education, Conservatory and Music High School of Zurich. Recordings: 2 in preparation. Publication: Method for Double Bass, in preparation. Current Management: Roland Müller rel, CH-8493 Saland, Switzerland. Address: Sonnengartenstrasse 44, CH-8125 Zollikerberg, Switzerland.

CIOBANU Maya, b. 5 May 1952, Bucharest, Rumania. Composer; Education: Studied at the Bucharest Conservatory, 1971-75, and Darmstadt. Career: Teacher at the George Enescu High School, Bucharest, from 1981. Compositions include: Cantata Riddles, 1975; Symphonic movement, 1975; Violin concerto, 1980; Three sculptures for string quartet, 1982; Cantata, December in Transylvania, 1983; Symphony, 1988; Cantata, The Six Seals, 1991. Address: c/o Georges Enescu High School, Bucharest, Romania.

CIONI Renato, b. 15 Apr 1929, Portoferraio, Elba. Singer, Tenor. Education: Studied at the Florence Conservatory. Debut: Spoleto 1956, as Edgardo in Lucia di Lammermoor. Career: Italian TV 1957, as Pinkerton; La Scala Milan from 1958; Spoleto 1959, in a revival of Donizetti's IL Duca d'Alba; Appearances in San Francisco and Chicago from 1961; Palermo 1963, in I Capuleti e i Montecchi by Bellini; Covent Garden 1964-65, as Cavaradossi, with Callas; the Duke of Mantua and Gabriele Adorno; Verona Arena 1966, as Cavaradossi; Engagements in Berlin, Prague, Paris, Berlin, Copenhagen, Buenos Aires, Bucharest and Edinburgh; Metropolitan Opera 1969-70. Recordings: Rigoletto and Lucia di Lammermoor, with Joan Sutherland.

CIONI-LEONI Maria Luisa, b. 1923, Italy. Singer (Soprano). Debut: Verona, 1947, as Oscar in Un Ballo in Maschera. Career: Sang at the Zurich Opera from 1947, Gilda at the Paris Opéra; Appeared widely throughout Italy, notably as Lucia di Lammermoor; La Scala Milan, 1969-70, debut as Donizetti's Maria di Rohan; Guest appearances at Cairo (Traviata, 1963), Barcelona (Micaela, 1969), Toulouse (Elvira in Puritani, 1968) and Johannesburg (Forza Leonora, 1975); Retired, 1980; Other roles

included Giulia in Spontini's Vestale, Norma, Anna Bolena and Marguerite. Address: c/o Teatro alla Scala, Via Filodrammatici 2, 20121 Milan, Italy.

CIORMILA Mariana, b. 1956, Rumania. Singer (Mezzo-Soprano). Education: Studied in Gelsenkirchen and sang there, 1982-84. Career: Appearances at Klagenfurt Opera, 1984-85, Houston Opera, 1986 (Marina in Boris Godunov), and Montpellier, 1987 (Orsini in Lucrezia Borgia); Has sung widely in Belgium as Adalgisa, Tancredi, Eboli and the Princess in Adriana Lecouvreur; Deutsche Oper Berlin, 1991, as Sextus in La Clemenza di Tito, Monte Carlo, 1992, as Dulcinée in Don Quichotte; Other roles include Dorabella, Isabella (Rossini) and Cenerentola. Address: c/o Opéra de Monte Carlo, Place du Casino, Monte Carlo.

CIUCIURA Leoncjusz, b. 22 Jul 1930, Grodzisk Mazowiecki, Poland. Composer. m. Sylwia Grelich, 18 Jun 1967. Education: BA, Composition, Theory and Conducting, State College of Music, Warsaw, 1960. Debut: Concert at State College of Music, Warsaw. Career: Co-founder, Polish branch of Jeunesses Musicales movement, 1958-62; Founder, Editor, Carmina Academica Musical Publication; Editor, Musical Publication for Contemporary Music, 1989; Compositions performed worldwide, 1964-97 including Festival ISCM World Music Days, International Festival of Music, Warsaw Autumn; Numerous international festivals of contemporary music in Austria, Belgium, Czech Republic, Denmark, England, Germany, Greece, Finland, France, Netherlands, Italy, Mexico, Norway, Poland, Spain, Sweden, Switzerland, USA and elsewhere. Compositions: Penetrations for Orchestral Groups, 4 Conductors and Composer, 1963; Emergenza for Choirs and Orchestra, 3 Conductors and Composer, 1963; In Infinitum I, II for Optional Instrumental Set, 1964-97; In progress from 1963, Spiral Form. Publications: Spirale 1 per uno, 1964; Spirale II per uno e piu, 1964; Creatoria I, 1964-97; Creatoria I, II, 1964-97; Spirale I per uno, Spirale II per uno e piu, 1964-97; Intarsio, I, II, 1964-97; Rencontre, I, II, 1964-97; In Infinitum 1964-97 (all for optional instruments and accompaniment). Recordings: Spirale I and II. Honours include: Laureate Prize of Ministry of Culture and Art, 1960; Prize at Competition Grunwald 60 for Suite; Praize at Polish Composers' Union Competition for Canti al Fresco, 1961; Prize at International Composers Competition, Prague, for Copncertino da Camera, 1962; Television Prize for Ornament, 1961; Commemorative Gold Medal of Honour, 1991, Most Admired Man of the Decade, 1992, American Biographical Institute; Twentieth Century Award for Achievement, International Biographical Centre. Address: Zwirki and Wigury 5, 05-825 Grodzisk Mazowiecki, Poland.

CIURCA Cleopatra, b. 1954, Rumania. Singer (Mezzo-Soprano). Career: Sang in Western Europe from 1981, notably at Reggio Emilio in Il Turco in Italia, at Dublin as Carmen, in Brussels as Eboli and at the Verona Arena as Laura in La Gioconda; New York Metropolitan from 1984, as Olga in Eugene Onegin, Marina, Maddalena and Eboli; Further engagements in San Francisco, Washington, Milan (Fenena in Nabucco), Paris and Detroit; Concert appearances include the Verdi Requiem in Vancouver (1986) and Adriana Lecouvreur (as the Princess) in London, 1987. Address: c/o Metropolitan Opera, Lincoln Center, New York, NY 10023, USA.

CLAASSEN René, b. 1937, Helmond, Netherlands. Tenor Singer. Education: Amsterdam Conservatory, The Hague. Debut: Maastricht, 1960. Career: Sang at Bremerhaven from 1964, Kassel from 1968 as Wagner's Loge and Mime, Monostatos in Die Zauberflöte, Shuratov in From the House of The Dead, and the villains in Les Contes d'Hoffmann; Appeared in Der Ring des Nibelungen, 1989 and sang Aschenbach in Death in Venice; Amsterdam 1986 in Zemlinsky's Der Kreidekreis and Loge and Mime at Rotterdam; 1989; Sang Leonard in Nielsen's Maskarade at Kassel, 1994; Many concert appearances. Address: c/o Der Nederlandse Opera, Waterlooplein 22, 1011 PG Amsterdam, Netherlands.

CLAPTON Nicholas, b. 1955, Worcester, England. Singer (Counter-tenor). Education: MA, Magdalen College, Oxford, 1981; Studiedwith David Mason and Diane Forlano. Debut: Wigmore Hall, London, 1984. Career: Aldeburgh Festival, 1985; London recital debut, 1986, Purcell Room; Since then numerous appearances throughout Europe and in the Far East; Operatic roles for ENO, Opera North, Channel 4 TV, Batignano, EBF, ranging from Monteverdi and Handel to world premieres (Barry, Lefanu, Benedict Mason); Many recitals (Purcell, Rossini, Romantic song, etc) with Jennifer Partridge. Recordings: Purcell: Hail, Bright Cecilia; Duruflé: Requiem; B Marcello: Cantatas; Nicola Porpora: Cantatas. Honours: Winner, English Song Award, 1987; Winner, Heart of England International Competition for Singers, 1987; Two prizes, Concurso "Francisco Viñas", Barcelona, 1985. Membership: ISM. Current Management: Robert Gilder & Co. Address: 4 Helen Road, Oxford OX2 0DE, England.

CLARET Lluis, b. 10 Mar 1951, Andorra. Cellist. m. Anna Mora, 1 son. Education: Liceo Conservatory, Barcelona; Conservatoire European, Paris; Bloomington School of Music, USA; Teachers include Enric Casals; Radu Aldulescu; Eva Janzer; György Sebok. Debut: Boccherini Cello Concerto, Barcelona, 1968. Career: Soloist concerts with National Symphony of Washington and Moscow Philharmonic; Orchestre National de France; English Chamber Orchestra; Czech Philharmonic, under Rostropovitch, Pierre Boulez, Vaclav Neumman, Witold Lutoslawski. Played at closing ceremony of Barcelona 92 Olympics. Recordings: Bach: Complete Suites for cello solo, Auvidis Valois, 1993; Schubert: Sonata Arpeggione for cello and piano, Harmonia Mundi, 1992; Chopin: Sonata for cello and piano; Strauss: Sonata for cello and piano, Harmonia Mundi, 1991; Kodály: Sonata for cello, 1990; Schumann: Concerto for cello and orchestra, 1990; Haydn: Concerto No 1 in C for cello and orchestra; Boccherini: Concerto No 3 in G minor for cello and orchestra; Dvorak: Trio, Dumky, op. 90, Trio in F minor, 1992; Other works by Boulez, Mendelssohn and Ravel. Honours: First prize, Rostropovitch Competition, 1977; Casals Competition, 1976; Bolonia Competition, 1975. Memberships: Barcelon Trio. Hobbies: Family & Friends. Current Management: Carmen Netzel. Address: c/o Netzel, Pasaje Marimon, 10-4, 08021 Barcelona, Spain.

CLAREY Cynthia, b. 25 Apr 1949, Smithfield, Virginia, USA. Singer (Mezzo-soprano). m. Jake Gardner, 17 June 1978, 1 son. Education: BMus, Howard University, Washington DC; Postgraduate Diploma, Juilliard School. Career: Sang first with the Tri-Cities Opera Company; Has sung in The Voice of Ariadne by Thea Musgrave with the New York City Opera; Boston Opera Company in the US premiere of Tippett's The Ice Break (1979) and The Makropoulos Case (1986); Binghamton, New York, 1986, in the premiere of Chinchilla by Myron Fink; UK debut at the Glyndebourne Festival, 1984, as Monteverdi's Ottavia, followed by Serena in Porgy and Bess (1986); Wexford Festival, 1985 and 1986, as Polinesso in Ariodante and Thomas's Mignon; Has toured with Peter Brook's version of Carmen and appeared in the 1989-90 season in concert versions of Anna Bolena (Concertgebouw, as Jane Seymour), Weill's Lost in the Stars (Almeida Festival, London) and The Ice Break (as Hanna, at the Promenade Concerts, London); Has also sung in operas by Cavalli, Mozart, Verdi, Puccini, Menotti and Offenbach; Other roles include Monteverdi's Penelope, Cavalli's Diana (L'Ormindo), Handel's Rinaldo, Zerlina, Isoletta (La Straniera), Preziosilla, Dalila, Butterfly, Nicklausse and Octavian; Sang Serena in the Covent Garden premiere of Porgy and Bess, 1992, and in Weill/Grosz Concert at the 1993 London Proms; 3 roles in Berg's Lulu at the Festival Hall, London, 1994; Sang Gershwin's Bess at Cape Town, 1996; Sang with major orchestras including: Chicago Symphony, Boston Symphony, Oakland Symphony, New York Philharmonic, BBC Symphony, City of London Sinfonia, Halle Orchestra and Dallas Symphony; Numerous concert appearances. Recordings include: CD of Porgy and Bess; Tippett's The Ice Break; Duffy's A Time for Remembrance. Current management: Lies Askonas; Harold Holt Ltd. Address: 2 The Warren, Horsham Road, Handcross, West Sussex RH17 6DX, England.

CLARK Derek John, b. 22 Aug 1955, Glasgow, Scotland. Conductor; Coach; Accompanist. m. Heather Fryer, 26 Apr 1980, 1 daughter. Education: Dumbarton Academy, 1967-72; Royal Scottish Academy of Music and Drama, 1972-76, Dip MusEd (hons), DipRSAM; University of Durham, BMus, hons 1st class, 1978; London Opera Centre, 1976-77. Debut: Accompanist, Purcell Room, 1976; Conductor, Welsh National Opera, 1982. Appointments: Staff Conductor, Welsh National Opera, 1976-97; Guest Conductor, Mid Wales Opera, 1989-92; Coach, Conductor, Welsh College of Music and Drama, 1992-97; Head of Music, Scottish Opera, 1997-; Conductor's repertoire includes: Tamerlano, Samson, Marriage of Figaro, Cosí fan tutte, Il Seraglio, La finta giardiniera, Lucia di Lammermoor, Don Pasquale, Count Ory, Beatrice and Benedict, Carmen, La Traviata, Rigoletto, The Rake's Progress, Noyes Fludde and Maxwell Davies's Cinderella. Compositions: 2 One Act Operas for Young People; Songs, Choral Music & Arrangements. Honour: Worshipful Company of Musicians Silver Medal, 1976. Hobby: Reading. Address: Dalmally, 96 East King Street, Helensburgh G84 7DT, Scotland.

CLARK Graham, b. 10 Nov 1941, Littleborough, Lancashire, England. Singer, (Tenor). Education: Studied with Bruce Boyce in London and in Bologna. Career: Debut: with Scottish Opera in 1975; English National Opera from 1978-85; Sang with Welsh National Opera and Opera North in the United Kingdom; Extensive International Career, appearing at the Metropolitan Opera in New York each season from 1985-93; the Bayreuth Festival each season between 1981 and 1992, where he sang over 100 performances, as well as appearances in Paris, Vienna, Berlin, Chicago, San Francisco, Munich, Zurich, Barcelona, Turin, Nice, Rome, Toronto, Amsterdam, Stockholm, Bonn, Tel-Aviv and Vancouver. Has also sung in concert with many of the world's leading orchestras and at the festivals of

Lucerne, Edinburgh, Brussels and London Proms; Recorded with Philips, Decca, EMI, Erato, Teldec, The Met and BBC; Appears on several videos including Bayreuth performances of Die Meistersinger, Der fliegende Holländer and 1992 Ring des Nibelungen, as well as the Met's Ghosts of Versailles; Returned to New York, 1997, as the Captain in Wozzeck; Salzburg's Festival 1997 as Piet in Le Grand Macabre. Honours: Nominated three times for Outstanding Individual Achievement in Opera, including a 1993 Emmy nomination for his role of Begearss in The Ghosts of Versailles; Won Olivier Award in 1986 for his portrayal of Mephistopheles in Busoni's Doctor Faust. Address: c/o Ingpen & Wailliams Ltd, 14 Kensington Court, London W8 5DN, England.

CLARK J Bunker, b. 19 October 1931, Detroit, Michigan, USA. Musicologist. m. Marilyn Jane Slawson, 3 August 1964. Education: BMus 1954, MMus 1957, PhD 1964, University of Michigan. Career: Instructor of Organ and Theory, Stephens College, Columbia, Missouri, 1957-59; Lecturer in Music, University of California, Santa Barbara, 1964-65; Professor of Music History, University of Kansas, 1965-93; Emeritus, 1993-. Publications: Transposition in Seventeenth Century English Organ Accompaniments and the Transposing Organ, 1974; Editor, Anthology of Early American Keyboard Music, 1787-1830, 1977; Editor, Nathaniel Giles: Anthems, 1979; The Dawning of American Keyboard Music, 1988; Editor, American Keyboard Music through 1865, 1990; Series Editor, Bibliographies in American Music, 1975-84; Series Editor, Detroit Studies in Music Bibliography, 1985-; Series Editor, Detroit Monographs in Musicology/Studies in Music, 1990. Contributions to: American Organist; The Choral Journal; Music & Letters; Musica Disciplina; Journal of the American Musicological Society; American Music. Address: Music Department, University of Kansas, Lawrence, KS 66045-2279, USA.

CLARK Richard J, b. 25 April 1943, Tucson, Arizona, USA. Singer (Baritone). Education: Studied at Academy of Vocal Arts, Philadelphia, and at the Juilliard School, New York. Debut: San Francisco, as Monterone in Rigoletto. Career: Metropolitan Opera from 1981, as Verdi's Monterone and di Luna, Wagner's Amfortas and Kurwenal, Barnaba in La Gioconda, Michele in Il Tabarro and Gianciotto in Francesca da Rimini by Zandonai. Address: c/o Metropolitan Opera, Lincoln Center, New York, NY 10023, USA.

CLARKE Adrian, b. 1960, Northampton, England. Singer (Baritone). Education: Royal College of Music, London, and the London Opera Centre. Career: Appearances with Opera North in Die Fledermaus, The Mikado, Fanciulla del West, The Golden Cockerel, Faust and Carmen (as Escamillo); Don Ferdinand in the British stage premiere of Gerhard's The Duenna, 1994; Rossini's Barber for Scottish Opera and Dublin Grand Opera, Guglielmo and Taddeo in L'Italiana in Algeri for Opera 80; Nick Shadow in The Rake's Progress for New Sussex Opera; Contemporary music includes: Maxwell Davie's Martyrdom of St Magnus for Opera Factory, the premieres of Casken's Golem and Cage's Europera III (London, Berlin and Paris); Gerald Barry's Triumph of Beauty and Deceit for Channel 4 TV, the British premiere of Mason's Playing Away (Opera North), Osborne's I am Goya and Rihm's Unsungen (Glasgow and Amsterdam); Season 1995-96 with Rossini's Barber for English Touring Opera, Rigoletto for Mid-Wales Opera and La Bohème for Glyndebourne Touring Opera. Address: Musicmakers, Little Easthall, St Paul's Walden, Nr Hitchin, Herts SG4 8DH, England.

CLARKE John Michael, b. 22 Apr 1956, Grimsby, England. Composer; Lecturer. Education: BA, PhD, Durham; MTC, London. Appointments: Lecturer, Director, Electroacoustic Music Studio, 1987-, Reader, 1996-, University of Huddersfield. Compositions: Soundings, Cello and Tape, 1983; Uppvaknande, Tape, 1984; Mälarsång, Tape, 1987; Refractions, Trombone and Tape, 1989; The Hidden Sun, choir, 1991; Epicycle, Piano and Tape, 1991; Icicles, Flute, Violin, and Piano, 1992; Confluence, Cello and Synthesizer, 1995; TIM (br) E, 1996. Recordings: Refractions; Mälarsång; Epicycle; Uppvaknande. Publication: Software: FOF Synthesis Algorithm, 1988; SYnthia, 1994. Contributions to: Several journals and magazines. Honours: CIM Prize, France, 1983; Chandos Prize, 1984; European Academic Software Award, 1994; Musica Nova, Prague, 1997. Memberships: Board of Management, Huddersfield Contemporary Music Festival, 1988-. Address: 3 Crodingley Farm Court, Thong Lane, Holmfirth, Huddersfield HD7 2TY, England.

CLARKE Karin, b. 1963, New York, USA. Singer (Soprano). Education: Tri-Cities Opera, New York, and International Opera Studio, Zurich. Career: Appearances at the Trier Opera as Giulietta in Hoffmann, Marguerite, Mozart's Countess and Anne Trulove; Further engagements at Hagen, Sarrbrucken, Munster and Bielefeld notably as Fiordiligi, Saffi (Zigeunerbaron) and Rosalinde in Die Fledermaus; Guest at Brussels, Ghent, Liège and Linz, with concert appearances in New York and throughout Germany; Other roles include Agathe, Lady (Hindemith's Cardillac), Elvira in Ernani, Marenka in The Bartered Bride and the Marschallin; Sang the title role in a revival of Zemlinsky's Sarema, Trier Opera 1996 (first production this

century). Recordings include: Sarema (Koch International). Address: c/o Theater der Stadt Trier, Am Augustinerhof, D-5500 Trier, Germany.

CLARKE Paul Charles, b. 1965, Liverpool, England. Tenor. Education: Royal College of Music with Neil Mackie. Career: Many performances throughout Britain including concerts with Bournemouth Sinfonietta, London Ensemble and Scottish Chamber Orchestra; Duke in Rigoletto, Fenton, the High Priest, Idomeneo and Rodolfo with Welsh National Opera, 1990-93; Paris debut, 1991 as Fenton at Théâtre des Champs Elysées; recent engagements as Dimitri in Boris Godunov and Rodolfo for Opera North, Alfredo and Nemorino for Scottish Opera, 1993-94; Covent Garden debut, 1994-95; Cassio in Otello; Tybalt in Roméo et Juliette; Alfredo in La Traviata; USA debut with Seattle Opera singing Duke in Rigoletto, 1995; Engaged as Faust with Welsh National Opera and Rodolfo at Royal Opera House, Covent Garden, 1996; Season 1997-98 as Verdi's Macduff at Monte Carlo, Gabriele Adorno for WNO and the Duke of Mantua for Scottish Opera; Roméo at the Met and Rodolfo at Seattle. Honours: Peter Pears Scholarship and Kathleen Ferrier Memorial Prize. Current Management: Harold Holt Limited. Address: 31 Sinclair Road, London W14 0NS, England.

CLARKE Stephen (David Justin), b. 21 July 1964, Thame, Oxon, England. Conductor. m. Helen Victoria Morrison, 1 son. Education: New College, Oxford, 1977-82; MA, Music, Honours, Hertford College, organ scholarship, Oxford University; ARCO; Diploma, Guildhall School of Music and Drama. Career: Conductor, Oxford Philharmonia, 1983-85; Founder, St Michael's Sinfonia, 1981; Conductor, Oxford University Opera Club, 1983-85; Conductor, Schola Cantorum of Oxford, 1985-87; Guest Conductor, Oxford Pro Musica, 1985; Guest Conductor, St Endellion Festival Orchestra, 1987; Worked with Kent Opera, 1988, Geneva Grand Opera, 1988, Royal Scottish Academy of Music and Drama, 1988-89, British Youth Opera, 1988; Assistant Chorus Master, English National Opera, 1990; Head of Music, Scottish Opera, 1993. Honours: Ricordi Conducting Prize, 1985-86; Guildhall Diploma of Conducting, 1986. Hobbies: Sailing; Squash; Windsurfing. Address: 5 Crown Circus, Glasgow G12 9HB, Scotland.

CLARKSON Gustav, b. 20 June 1954, London, England. Musician; Violinist. m. Micaela Comberti, 15 Aug 1980. Education: Royal Academy of Music, 1971-76; Mozarteum, 1976-77; Salzburg, Austria. Career: As member of the Bochmann Quartet from 1978-83, many appearances on the South Bank, Wigmore Hall, on BBC radio, tours in the UK and abroad; Many solo appearances including, Paris and London; Past Member, the Endymion Ensemble, Schubert Ensemble; Member, Arienski Ensemble, Rossignol, Clarkson-Munro Duo. Recordings: Clarinet Quintets by Brahms and Steptoe with the Bochmann Quartet and David Campbell; Britten Oboe Fantasy with Robin Canter; Howells and Dyson Octet, Triptych and Oboe Quartet with Divertimenti. Honours: Royal Society of Arts major Award for study abroad, 1976; Awarded ARAM, 1991; Teaches violin at Royal Northern College of Music. Address: 15 Elm Park Road, London N3, England.

CLASS Sarah Jane, b. 31 May 1968, Watford, England. Composer. Education: BA, honours, Bishop Otter College, Sussex. Career: Appearances on BBC Radio 3's Music Machine with Tommy Pearson, 1997, BBC Radio Bristol, BBC Radio Plymouth at Première of Ses Trois Visages. Compositions include: Der Smaragdene Flüss; Lux Aeterna Mass; Straight From the Heart; Who's Afraid of...; Play it for Real; Illustrated Origin of Species; The Ghost of Ivy Tilsley; Grüne Inselnim Steinernen Meer. Honours: The Medina School's Young Musician of the Year, 1984; Silver Rembrandt, Holland, 1997. Memberships: PRS; MU; MCPS; Composers Guild. Hobbies: Painting; Travel. Current Management: Contact: Mary Novakovich.

CLAUSEN Jeanne, b. 16 Oct 1944, Los Angeles, California, USA. Musician (Violinist). m. John Cleveland, 2 July 1990, 1 daughter. Education: BA, Sarah Lawrence College, New York City; MMus, Cleveland Institute of Music, Ohio; Juilliard School of Music, New York City; Music Academy of the West, Santa Barbara, California; Meadowmount School of Music, New York City; Studied with Sascha Jacobsen, Dorothy Delay, Donald Weilerstein, Sigiswald Kuijken and Ivan Galamian. Career: Founder and Leader of Ensemble La Cetra of Milan, Italy; Former Member of Amsterdam Baroque Orchestra, Netherlands, and "California New Music Ensemble" of Los Angeles; Performances on the Lira da Braccia. Recordings: Numerous. Contribution: Article on the Lira da Braccia. Honours: Coleman Chamber Music Auditions in Los Angeles, 1959, 1961; Scholarship, J M Kaplan Fund, New York, 1967. Membership: International Lira Society. Hobbies: Hiking in mountains; Sailing. Address: Via Veneto 9/6, 20068 Peschiera Borromeo, Milan, Italy.

CLAYTON Laura, b. 8 Dec 1943, Lexington, Kentucky, USA. Composer; Pianist. Education: Studied with Milhaud at the Aspen School, Wuorinen at the New England Conservatory, and at the University of Michigan. Compositions include: Implosure for 2 dancers, slide and tape, 1977; Cree Songs for the Newborn for soprano and chamber orchestra, 1987; Panels for chamber ensemble, 1983; Sagarama for piano and orchestra, 1984; Clara's Sea for women's voices, 1988; Terra Lucida for orchestra, 1988. Honours include: NEA awards and Guggenheim Fellowship. Address: c/o ASCAP, ASCAP House, One Lincoln Plazxa, New York, NY 10023, USA.

CLEGG John, b. 7 Nov 1928, London, England. Concert Pianist. Education: Jesus College, Cambridge, 1946-49; Royal College of Music, Piano studies with Herbert Fryer, 1949-52. Debut: Wigmore Hall, London, 1951. Career: Has given recitals, concerts and broadcasts in most countries, with frequent tours of Africa, Middle East and Far East, and concerts in principal European centres; Regular performer on BBC radio and television; Pianist-in-Residence, Lancaster University, 1981-93. Recordings: 6 LPs of music by British composers and by Fauré, Weber, Scriabin, Ravel and Medtner; Digital tapes of music by Ravel, Fauré, Medtner and Poulenc; CD of all Alan Rawsthorne's piano music, 1996. Honours: 1st Class honours, Jesus College, 1949; Harriet Cohen International Award, 1968. Current Management: J Audrey Ellison, International Artists' Management, 135 Stevenage Road, Fulham, London SW6 6PB, England. Address: Concord, 53 Marine Drive, Hest Bank, Lancaster LA2 6EG, England.

CLELLAND Lamond, b. 19 July 1921, Gateshead, England. Flautist; Conductor; Teacher. m. Patricia Ann Susan, 5 Aug 1989. Education: Diploma, Education, Bristol; LTCL; TD. Debut: Dusseldorf Opera House with Dusseldorf Symphony Orchestra, 1945. Career, Band, Coldstream Guards, 1945-54; Freelance, London Orchestras, 1945-54; Recitals Broadcast, Duo and Vincian Trio Concertos with Bournemouth Symphony Orchestra, BBC Orchestra, 1954-66; Assistant Music Director, Hants Youth Orchestra, 1966-69; Conductor, Coach, Youth Groups; Conductor, Wessex Chamber Orchestra, Wessex Flute Band; Arrangements for Orchestras, Bands and Chamber Groups. Recording: Four Your Delight. Publication: Still the Lark. Contributions to: Making Music; BFS Pan Magazine. Memberships: Incorporated Society of Musicians; British Flute Society. Hobbies: Bridge; Chess; Harpsichord; Making gold panning; Bird Watching. Address: c/o 23 Wood Lane, Bear Cross, Bournemouth, Dorset, England.

CLEMENCIC René, b. 27 Feb 1928, Vienna, Austria. Musician; Composer; Recorder Player; Harpsichordist; Conductor. m. (1) 1 daughter, (2) Edda Rischka, 11 Apr 1968, 1 daughter. Education: PhD, University of Vienna, 1956; Old Music with J Mertin, Musical Theory with J Polnauer, Recorder with H U Staeps, L Höffer, V Winterfeld, W Nitschke, Harpsichord with Eta Harich-Schneider. Career: Clavichord player; Founder, Leader, early music ensemble Clemencic Consort, from 1968; Editor, mediaeval Carmina Burana; Baroque opera performances (1st modern including: Draghi's L'Eternita Soggetta al Tempo, Peri's Euridice, Leopold I's Il Lutto dell'Universo); TV play; Concerts worldwide. Compositions: Maraviglia III and V; Sesostris II and III; Chronos II; Bicinia Nova; Music for Ariana Mnouchkine's film Molière; Musik zum Urfaust; Tolldrastische Szenen; Stufen; Musik zum Prinzen von Homburg; Missa Mundi; Unus Mundus; Requiem pro Vivis et Mortuis; Musica Hermetica; Drachenkampf; Strukturen Musica Instrumentalis; Revolution; Opus für Flöte und Streicher, 1991; Kabbala, 1992; Kammeroper, Der Berg; Apokalypsis, 1996; Klaviertrio Jeruschalajim, 1997. Recordings: Over 100 as soloist on recorder and with consort; Numerous flute solos; Josquin: Missa Hercules Dux Ferrariae, Musica Sacra; Monteverdi: Missa da Capella, Il Combattimento, Messa a 4 voci; Mediaeval Carmina Burana; Dufay: Missa Ave Regina Coelorum, Missa Sine Nomine, Missa Caput, Missa Ecce Ancilla; Obrecht: Missa Fortuna Desperata; Ockeghem: Requiem; Marcello: Sonate a Flauto; Biber: Fidicinium; Fux: Dafne in Lauro; Carvalho: Testoride; Vivaldi: L'Olimpiade; Pergolesi: Stabat Mater; René Clemencic: Le Combat du Dragon Kabbala. Publications: Alte Musikinstrumente, 1968; Carmina Burana, 1979. Honours: Edison Award, 1981; Accademico della Filarmonica Romana; Ehrenmedaille (Gold), Vienna; Record of the Year; Several Grand Prix du Disques, Diapason d'Or, KMP, Bern; Town of Vienna Prize for Music, 1997. Hobbies: Italian literature; Collecting sculpture; Nazarener paintings. Current Management: M Werner, Paris; Kentron Musa Promotion, Bern. Address: Reisnerstrasse 26/7, A-1030 Vienna, Austria.

CLEMENT Sheree, b. 8 Dec 1955, Boston, Massachusetts, USA. Composer. Education: Studied at the Peabody Conservatory and with Mario Davidovsky at Columbia University, New York. Compositions include: Five Nocturnes for orchestra, 1976; Thresholds for tape, 1976-77; Music from a Summer Afternoon for orchestra, 1978; String quartet, 1980; Variations/Obsessions for ensemble, 1985. Honours include: Guggenheim Fellowships and American Academy awards. Address: c/o ASCAP, ASCAP House, One Lincoln Plaza, New York, NY 10023, USA.

CLEMENTI Aldo, b. 25 May 1925, Catania, Italy. Composer. Education: Studied with Pietro Scarpini in Siena, at Catania and with Petrassi in Rome, 1952-54; Summer courses at Darmstadt, 1955-62. Compositions: Concertino in forma di variazioni, 1956; Tre Studi for chamber orchestra, 1957; 7 Scenes for chamber orchestra, 1961; Collage I-III, 1961-67; Informel I-III for various instrumental combinations, 1962-63; Variante A for chorus and orchestra and B for orchestra, 1964; Silben for female voice, clarinet, violin and 2 pianos, 1966; Concerto for wind orchestra and 2 pianos, 1967; Reticolo for string quartet, 1968; Concerto for piano and 7 instruments, 1970; Replica for harpsichord, 1972; Blitz, musical action for chamber ensemble, 1973; Sinfonia da camera, 1974; Concerto for piano, 24 instruments and carillons, 1975; Clessidra for 11 instruments, 1976; Reticolo for 12 strings, 1978; Collage Jesu meine Freude, action for 8 strings, 8 winds and tape, 1979; Es, rondeau in 1 act, produced at Teatro la Fenice, Venice, 1981; AEB for 17 instruments, 1983; Finale for 4 sopranos and orchestra, 1984; O du Selige for orchestra, 1985; Concerto for piano and 11 instruments, 1986. Address: SIAE (Sezione Musica), Viale della Letteratura n 30, 00144 Rome, Italy.

CLEMENTS Joy, b. 1931, Dayton, Ohio, USA. Singer, Soprano. Education: Studied at University of Miami & in Philadelphia & New York. Debut: Miami Opera 1956 at Musetta in La Bohème. Career: Sang 1959-72 at New York City Opera and in Pittsburgh, Cincinnati, Baltimore, San Diego, Fort Worth, Hawaii; Appeared as Mary Warren in premiere of The Crucible by Robert Ward, New York, 1961; Appearances at Metropolitan from 1963; Guest engagements at Tel Aviv 1963 and Brussels 1975; Other roles have included Mozart's Despina, Pamina and Susanna; Verdi's Violetta and Gilda, Gounod's Juliette, Manon, Martha, Gershwin's Bess; Many concert appearances. Address: c/o Metropolitan Opera, Lincoln Center, NY 10023, USA.

CLEOBURY Nicholas (Randall), b. 23 June 1950, Bromley, Kent, England. Conductor. m. Heather Kay, 4 Nov 1978, 1 son, 1 daughter. Education: Worcester College, Oxford University. Career: Assistant Organist, Chichester Cathedral, 1971-72; Assistant Organist, Christ Church, Oxford, 1972-76; Chorus Master, Glyndebourne, 1976-79; Assistant Director, BBC Singers, 1977-80; Freelance Conductor with all London and BBC orchestras, all major British orchestras; Extensive work in Europe, Scandinavia, USA and Australia, 1980-; Work with English and Welsh National Operas, Opera North and Flanders Opera; Principal Opera Conductor, Royal Academy of Music, 1980-87; Artistic Director, Broomhill, 1990-94; Artistic Director, Britten Sinfonia, 1991-; Numerous broadcasts. Recordings: Numerous. Honours: Fellow, Royal College of Organists, Limpus Prize, 1968; Honorary Member, Royal Academy of Music, 1985. Memberships: Savage Club; Lodge Taverners. Hobbies: Reading; Walking; Cricket; Food; Wine. Current Management: Allied Artists, London, England. Address: c/o Allied Artists, 42 Montpelier Square, London SW7 1JZ, England.

CLEOBURY Stephen, b. 31 December 1948, Bromley, Kent, England. Conductor; Organist. 2 daughters. Education: King's School, Worcester; St John's College, Cambridge, MA, MusB; FRCM; FRCO. Career: Organist, St Matthew's, Northampton, 1971-74; Sub-Organist, Westminster Abbey, 1974-78; Master of Music, Westminster Cathedral, 1979-82; Director of Music, King's College, Cambridge, 1982-; Chief Conductor, BBC Singers, 1995-; Many Radio and Television appearances in United Kingdom and abroad with King's College Choir; Conducted Bach's B Minor Mass at St John's, London, 1997. Recordings: A wide range of music including that with King's College Choir and as Organist at Westminster Abbey and King's College. Publications: Carol arrangements. Honours: Diploma, FRCO, 1968; Honorary, FRCM, 1994. Memberships: Royal College of Organists, President 1990-92; Incorporated Society of Musicians. Current Management: Magenta (UK), McFarlane Artists, (USA). Address: King's College, Cambridge CB2 1ST, England.

CLEVE George, b. 9 July 1936, Vienna, Austria. Conductor. Education: Studied at Mannes College, New York, and with Pierre Monteux, George Szell, Franco Ferrara and Leonard Bernstein. Debut: Salzburg Festival. Career: Appearances with major American orchestras, including the New York Philharmonic and Symphony Orchestras of Chicago, Boston, Cleveland, Minnesota and San Francisco; Music Director of the San Jose Symphony and founder of the Midsummer Mozart Festival in San Francisco, 1974; Has conducted La Bohème, La Traviata, Le nozze di Figaro and Oedipus Rex; European engagements with the Northern Sinfonia, the Vienna Symphony Orchestra and the Orchestre National de France; Flanders Festival, 1990, Don Giovanni; Tour of Europe with the English Chamber Orchestra; Germany with the Stockholm Chamber Orchestra. Honours include: Officier, Ordre des Arts et des Lettres, from the French Government; Silver Medal of Honour, City of Vienna. Address: c/o Terry Harrison Artists Management, The Orchard, Market Street, Charlbury, Oxon OX7 3PJ, England.

CLIBURN Van (Harvey Lavan), b. 12 July 1934, Shreveport, Louisiana, USA. Pianist. Education: Studied with mother Rildia Bee Cliburn and at Juilliard School of Music. Debut: Shreveport, 1940; Houston Symphony Orchestra, 1952. Career: New York Philharmonic Orchestra, 1954, 1958; Concert pianist on tour, USA, 1955-56; USSR 1958; Appearances include Brussels, London, Amsterdam and Paris, notably in music by Tchaikovsky and Rachmaninov. Honours: Honorary HHD, Baylor University; Winner, 1st International Tchaikovsky Piano Competition, Moscow, USSR, 1958; In 1962 he established a Piano Competition in his name at Fort Worth, Texas. Current Management: Shaw Concerts Incorporated, 1995 Broadway, New York, NY 10023, USA. Address: 455 Wilder Place, Shreveport, LA 71104, USA.

CLINE Charles (Williem), b. 1 Mar 1937, Waleska, Georgia, USA. Professor of English; Poet; Author; Pianist; Organist. m. Sandra Williamson, 11 June 1996, div 1996, 1 son. Education: AA, Reinhardt College, 1957; BA, Peabody College of Vanderbilt University, 1960; MA, plus additional graduate study, Vanderbilt University, 1963; DLitt honorary, World University, 1981; Piano Performance Certificate and Medal, Reinhardt College, 91957; Piano Performance Scholarships, College-Conservatory of Music, University of Cincinnati, 1957, 1958, (Study with Olga Conus); Study of Piano and Organ, School of Music, Peabody College, 1959-63. Debut: First public appearance at age 11, 1948; Debut solo recital, Reinhardt Acaddemy, 1955. Career: Concert Pianist on television, 1950s; On stage in USA, England, Scotland, Australia, 1963-; Featured Piano Soloist at International Congresses on Arts and Communications, 1992-; Pianist at churches in Georgia, 1950-60; Guest Organist at First United Methodist Church, Portage, Michigan, 1987; Seminars on piano technique and interpretation, 1976-. Publication: The Gifts of Music, contributor, 1994. Honours: Medallion for Distinguished Participation, 20th International Congress on Arts and Communications, Cambridge, Massachusetts, 1993; Knight, Order of Knight Templars of Jerusalem, 1991; Knight, Order of the Holy Grail, 1996; Order of Merit, 1992; Diplôme d'Honneur en Littérature et Musique, Instut des Affaires Internationales, 1996. Address: 9866 S Westnedge Avenue, Portage, MI 49002, USA.

CLINGAN Judith, b. 19 Jan 1945, Sydney, New South Wales, Australia. Composer; Conductor. Education: Studied with Larry Sitsky at Canberra and at the Kodaly Institute, Hungary. Career: Founded Gaudeamus, 1983, for the furtherance of music education. Compositions include: Children's operas Just Looking and Marco, 1991; Choruses, including The Birds' Noel, 1990, and Kakadu, 1990; A Canberra Cycle for soprano, baritone and ensemble, 1991; Songs of Solitude for soprano and ensemble, 1991. Address: c/o APRA, 1A Eden Street, PO Box 567, Crows Nest, NSW 2065, Australia.

CLOAD Julia, b. 6 Oct 1946, London, England. Musician (Pianist). Education: Royal College of Music, London; Liszt Academy, Budapest, Hungary; Further studies with Maria Curcio and Hans Keller. Debut: Wigmore Hall. Career: Concerto performances with Royal Philharmonic Orchestra, London Philharmonic Orchestra, Halle Orchestra, Royal Liverpool Philharmonic Orchestra, under conductors including Bernard Haitink, John Pritchard, Adrian Boult, James Loughran, Christopher Seaman; Recitals, at the Wigmore Hall, Queen Elizabeth Hall, BBC and Budapest Spring Festival; Concertos: Royal Festival Hall and Radio 3. Recordings: Haydn Piano Sonatas, 3 CDs, Merriman Records; Schumann Sonatas. Hobbies: Walking; Reading. Address: 1/6 Colville Houses, Talbot Road, London W11 1JB, England.

CLOSTRE Adrienne, b. 9 Oct 1921, Thomery, France. Composer. Education: Studied at the Paris Conservatoire with Messiaen and Milhaud. Compositions include: Stage works: Nietzsche (1975), Le secret (1981), Romans (1983), L'albatross (1988) and Annapurna (1988): Melodramas: L'écriture du Dieu (1991) and Le Zaire (1992); Oboe concerto (1970) and Concerto for flute, violin and chamber orchestra (1972); Sun, lecture de Virginia Woolf par le quatuor à cordes (1991). Honours include: Prix Florence Gould, 1976. Address: c/o SACEM, 225 avenue Charles de Gaulle, 92521 Neuilly sur Seine Cedex, France.

CLOZIER Christian (Robert Adrien), b. 25 August 1945, Compiègne, France. Composer; Director. 1 daughter. Education: National Conservatory of Music, Paris; Practical School for Higher Studies, Paris. Career: Founder, Director, GMEB; Director, International Competition of Electro-acoustic Music, Bourges; President, International Confederation of Electro-acoustic Music (ICEM); Conceptor of Music Electroacoustic Instruments. Compositions include: La Discordature; Opéra, A Vie; 22 août; Loin la Lune; Symphonie pour un enfant Seul; A la Prochaine, la Taupe; Quasars; Markarian 205; Par Pangloss Gymnopède; Le Bonheur, une idée neuve en Europe, Mon nom sous le soleil est France, le Temps scintille et le songs est savoir; Eleven spectacles multi-media. Recordings: La Discordatura, Pathé Marconi; Lettre à une Demoiselle; Dichotomie, Pathé Marconi;

Symphonie pour un Enfant Seul, Edition GMEB; Quasars, Le Chant du Monde. Contributions to: Musique en Jeu No 8, 1970; Faire 2-3, 1974; Faire 4-5, 1975; Poésie Sonore Internationale, Edition J.M. Place. Honour: Chevalier des Arts et Lettes, France, 1985. Memberships: President, International Confederation of Electroacoustic Music; Administrator, Conseil National de la Musique, France. Current Management: Director of the Bourges International Institute for Electroacoustic Music. Address: Institut International de Musique Electroacoustique, Place Andre Mairaux, 18000 Bourges, France.

CLURMAN Judith, b. 11 Mar 1953, Brooklyn, NY, USA. Conductor. m. Bruce Ruben, 15 Jun 1982, 1 s. Education: Oberlin College, 1971-73; BMus, 1977, MMus, 1978, The Juilliard School. Career: Founder, Director, The New York Concert Singers, debut 1988; Founder, Director, The New York Chamber Symphony Chorus, debut, 1996; Appearances on Lincoln Center Great Performers; Carnegie Hall and PBS television; Merkin Concert Hall Series; Lincoln Center Community Programs; Faculty, The Juilliard School, 1989-; Guest Appearances: Orchestra of St Luke's, Boston Symphony Orchestra; Mostly Mozart; Classical Band; Lincoln Center Salutes the Philharmonic; Mozart Bicentennial; Voice of America; National Public Radio; WOXR Broadcasts; Conducted numerous premieres including: Music by Leonard Bernstein; William Bolcom; John Corigliano; Aaron Jay Kennis; Libby Larsen; David Diamond; Stephen Paulus; Ned Rorem; Christopher Rousa; Ellen Taaffe Zwilich. Honour: New York Concert Singers First Prize in ASCAP - Chorus America award, 1992. Membership: Chorus America. Hobby: Reading. Address: 75 East End Avenue 9L, New York, NY 10028-7915, USA.

COAD Jonathan, b. 1964, Crayford, Kent, England. Singer (Baritone). Education: Studied at the Royal College of Music, London, England. Career: Many concert appearances, including tours with the Groupe Vocale de France throughout Europe and North America; Concert soloist in England and France; Sang Pooh-bah in The Mikado for D'Oyly Carte Opera, and in Bernstein's Candide at the Old Vic, 1989; Engagements with the Royal Opera, Covent Garden, in Death in Venice, The Fiery Angel, Jenufa, Tosca, Arabella, and La Bohème, Rigoletto 1997, as Court Usher. Recordings include: Albums with Groupe Vocale de France. Address: c/o Royal Opera House (Contracts), Covent Garden, London WC2, England.

COATES Gloria, b. 10 Oct 1938, Wausau, Wisconsin, USA. Composer. Education: BMus, Composition, Voice; BA, Art, Theatre; MMus, Composition, Musicology; Studied with Otto Luening and Alexander Tcherepnin. Career: Freelance Composer, Munich, Germany, 1969-; Organiser of German-American Contemporary Music Series, Munich and Cologne, 1971-84; Demonstrated work in vocal multiphonics, International Summer Course for New Music, Darmstadt, 1972; Compositions widely performed, Europe, USA, India, including Warsaw Autumn Festival, 1978, Musica Viva Series in Munich, East Berlin Festival, 1979, 1st International Festival of New Music in Russia, Moscow, 1981; Radio recordings include for BBC-London, Swiss Romande, RAI Rome, Radio Poland, German Radio stations, Radio Johannesburg, Sweden, USA; Additional broadcasts, People's Republic of China, Finland, Spain, Portugal, Brazil, Canada, Belgium, Netherlands; Invited lectures, Harvard University, 1981, Max Mueller Bhavans, India, 1982. Compositions include: Music on Open Strings, 1974; String Quartet, commissioned by Kronos Quartet; Orchestral piece for Next Wave Festival; Piece for harp, flute and viola for Munich Festival. Recordings: Bielefelder Catalog, Music on Open Strings, String Quartets I, II and IV. Honours: Music on Open Strings cited as 1 of 12 most important recorded works by living composer, International Koussevitzsky Panel, 1986. Address: Postfach 0661, 8000 Munich 43, Germany.

COATES Leon, b. 15 June 1937, Wolverhampton, England. University Lecturer; Composer. m. 11 September 1976. Education: St Johns College, Cambridge. Career: Various Radio Appearances as Organizer, Pianist, Harpsichordist, with Scottish Baroque Ensemble; Several Broadcasts. Compositions: Song Cycle, North West Passage, 1994; Concerts for Viola & Harpsichord; Music for Concert Band & Choir. Recordings: BBC Archive Recording of Music for 2 Harpsichords. Contributions to: Tempo; Music in New Zealand. Memberships: Composers Guild; Scottish Society of Composers; Royal College of Organists. Hobby: Hill Walking. Address: 35 Comely Bank Place, Edinburgh EH4 1ER, Scotland.

COATMAN Graham Robert, b. 18 Sept 1952, Croydon, England. Composer; Musical Director; Music Education Projects Specialist. m. Julie Spencer, 23 May 1981, 1 son, 1 daughter. Education: BA, hons, Bristol University; PG Dip Advanced Composition, GSMD; AMusM, Nottingham University. Career: Musical Director, Dancers Anonymous, Arts Educational School, London, 1976-79; Musical Director, Haymarket Theatre and Phoenix Arts, Leicester, 1979-83; Director, Contraband, 1982-; Composer-in-Residence, Bretton Hall, Yorks, 1983; Lecturer, North Warks College, 1983-88; Fellow in Music, Bradford University, 1988-93; Composer-in-Residence, Leeds Festival, 1990; Composer, Director, Education Projects, Sinfonia 21, 1994-96; Education Consultant, Classical Adventures, 1996-; Performances at Many Festivals in England and Europe. Compositions include: Laxative and Letting Blood, 1988; Feste's Floorshow, 1990; Giovanni's Women, 1994. Honours: OW Memorial Prize, 1975; Prizewinner, Menuhin Composition Competition, 1979; RVW Trust Award, 1980. Address: 4 Sunny Bank, Shipley, West Yorkshire BD18 3RP, England.

COBURN Pamela, b. 29 March 1955, Dayton, OH, USA. Singer, Soprano. Education: De Pauw University, Eastman School and Juilliard. Career: Has sung at Munich Staatsoper from 1982. Vienna from 1984; Maggio Musicale Florence 1988 as Ellen Orford in Peter Grimes; Los Angeles 1990 as Ilia in Idomeneo; Sang Saffi in Der Zigeunerbaron at Zurich and Alice Ford in Falstaff for Miami Opera 1991; Salzburg and Munich Festivals 1991, as Mozart's Countess; Sang Ellen Orford in a production of Peter Grimes by Tim Albery, Munich, 1991; Engaged for Giulio Cesare and Das Rheingold at the 1997 Munich Festival; Other roles include Fiordiligi; Rosalinde in Die Fledermaus and Lauretta in Gianni Schicchi. Recordings: Honegger's King David; Siebel in Faust; Mozart's L'Oca del Cairo; Marzelline in Fidelio; Zemlinsky's Traumgörge; First Lady in Die Zauberflöte; Flowermaiden in Parsifal conducted by Barenboim. Honours: Prizewinner at ARD Competition, Munich 1980; Metropolitan Auditions of the Air 1982. Address: c/o Ingpen & Williams Ltd, 14 Kensington Court, London W8 5DN, England.

COBURN Robert (James), b. 29 Oct 1949, Montebello, California, USA. Composer; Educator. m. Jeanne N Ashby, 12 May 1974, 1 son. Education: MA, Composition, University of California at Berkeley; BMus in Composition, University of the Pacific; PhD in Composition, University of Victoria. Career: Composition Commissions: Sun River Music Festival; San Francisco New Music Ensemble; Oregon Coast Music Festival; Sound-Art Environment Comm: City of Philadelphia Avenue of Arts, 1995; Oregon Convention Centre (landscape); Henry Gallery, Seattle; Performances: Festival of New Music, Roulette, New York; Forum '82 International Festival, New York; Electronic Music Plus Festival. Compositions: Traces (Star Map I) for viola and computer sound; Staursahng for live electronic music and visual images; Cantos for chamber orchestra; Bell Circles II, permanent sound environment, Oregon Convention Center; Luminous Shadows for cello, piano, and percussion, 1993-; Songs of Solitude for chorus; Ellipse for solo flute; Shadowbox for clarinet, 1994. Contributions to: Portland Review; Prologue; Leonardo Music Journal. Honour: Oregon Artists Fellowship, 1978. Memberships: International Society for the Arts, Sciences and Technology; Computer Music Association; Founding Member, World Forum for Acoustic Ecology. Hobbies: Hiking; Cooking; Reading. Address: Conservatory of Music, University of the Pacific, Stockton, CA 95211, USA.

COCHRAN James B, b. 11 Feb 1956, DuBois, Pennsylvania, USA. Organist; Conductor. Education: BMus (Hons), Susquehanna University, Pennsylvania; MMus and DMA, Eastman School of Music, University of Rochester, New York; Architecture and Modern British Literature at University College, Oxford University, England. Career: Director of Music at Vanderbilt Presbyterian Church, Naples, Florida, where he conducts the 50-voice Chancel Choir, the Handbell Choir and a fully-graded children's choir programme; Coordinator and performer in church's 3-concert series which he inaugurated in 1991; Founder-Director of The Philharmonic Center Chorale, an 80-voice auditioned chorus which performs with The Naples Philharmonic and as a separate musical ensemble of the Center; Resident Organist of the Naples Philharmonic and Chairman of the inaugural Naples International Organ Festival in June 1993; Organ recitalist who has performed throughout the United States, Canada, Great Britain and Mexico; Pianist for German baritone Hermann Prey, tenor Seth McCoy, instrumentalists from the Naples Philharmonic and local singers; Guest Conductor of the Naples Philharmonic in the December Holiday Pops concerts with the Philharmonic Center Chorale, 1993-94. Hobbies: Aerobics; Cooking. Address: 2334 Naples Trace Circle No 7, Naples, FL 33942, USA.

COCHRAN William, b. 23 June 1943, Columbus, Ohio, USA. Singer (Tenor). Education: Studies with Martial Singher at the Curtis Institute, Philadelphia and with Lauritz Melchior and Lotte Lehmann in California. Career: Sang Wagner roles in San Francisco and Mexico; Many appearances in Europe from 1967, notably in Hamburg and Frankfurt, roles include Max in Der Freischütz, Jason in Médée, Otello, Herod in Salome and Dmitri in Boris Godunov; Concert with the New York Philharmonic 1971; Covent Garden debut 1974, as Laca in Jenufa; San Francisco 1977, as Tichon in Katya Kabanova; Appearances in operas by Busoni, Janacek, Zimmermann, Shostakovich and Stravinsky (Tom Rakewell at Frankfurt 1983); Sang Bacchus in Ariadne auf Naxos at the Metropolitan Opera 1985; Deutsche Oper Berlin, 1989 Schreker's Die Gezeichneten; Season 1988-89 at Dusseldorf; Sang Siegfried in Paris and Brussels, 1991; Zimmerman's Die Soldaten at Strasbourg and Tichon (Katya Kabanova), Los Angeles; The Councillor in The Nose by Shostakovich, Frankfurt City Opera; Title role, Otello for Welsh National Opera, May 1990; Season 1992 as Samson at Amsterdam and Schoenberg's Aron (concert performance) at the Edinburgh Festival; Sang Aegisthus in Elektra at the First Night of the 1993 London Proms; Herod in Salome at San Francisco, 1997. Recordings: Mathis der Maler and Act I of Die Walküre (EMI); Doktor Faust by Busoni (Deutsche Grammophon); Mahler's 8th Symphony (Philips). Address: c/o Welsh National Opera, John Street, Cardiff, CF1 4SP, Wales.

CODREANU-MIHALCEA Claudia, b. 1969, Rumania. Mezzo-Soprano. Career: Many concert and opera engagements in Romania and elsewhere in Europe; Repertory includes Mozart's Clemenza di Tito, Rossini's Cenerentola, and songs by Brahms and Mussorgsky; Contestant at the 1995 Cardiff Singer of the World Competition. Address: Bloc 3, SC 1, Apt 38, Sector 2, Str Doamna Ghieca nr 5, 72404 Bucharest, Romania.

COELHO Elaine, b. 1950, Rio de Janeiro, Brazil. Singer (Soprano). Education: Studied in Rio and Hanover. Career: Sang at Landestheater Detmold from 1974 as Verdi's Violetta and Nannetta, Mozart's Constanze Zdenka in Arabella and Liu in Turandot Stadttheater Bremen from 1976, as Norina in Don Pasquale, Mozart's Susanna, Euridice, Fiorilla in Il Turco in Italia and Lulu; Sang at Frankfurt am Main from 1984 and appeared as guest in Turin as Lulu; Further engagements at Aachen, the Vienna Volksoper and the Bregenz Festival, Giulietta in Les Contes d'Hoffmann, 1988; Sang Donna Anna in Don Giovanni at the Teatro Municipal, Rio de Janeiro, 1991; Vienna Volksoper 1992, as Abigaille in Nabucco. Address: Stadtische Buhnen, Untermainanlage 11, 6000 Frankfurt am Main, Germany.

COEN Massimo, b. 11 March 1933, Rome, Italy. Violinist; Composer. m. Mirella Thau, 2 sons, 1 daughter. Education: Law Degree, Rome University; Violin Diploma, St Cecilia Conservatory, Rome; Private Study, Chamber Music and Violin. Career: Founder, Chamber Music Groups; 1 Solisti di Roma, 1961 and Quartetto Nuova Musica, 1963, giving concerts and radio performances throughout Europe; Tour of USA and Canada as soloist with Cameristica Italiana, 1969; Founder, Music School, Rome; Teacher, National Academy of Dance; Discoverer, Editor and Performer of numerous ancient Italian musical MSS. Compositions: Quartetto II, 4 Temperamenti, 1987; Divertimento 1, flute and strings, 1988; Divertimento II, La Marsigliese, 1989; Violin-Concerto, Saudades de Rio, 1991; C'Era una Volta, 1979; Intergrazioni, 1980; Dosilado, 1983; Nascite, 1983; Peav Suite, 1983; Didone, 1983; La Donna Senz'ombra, 1984; Il Rovescio della Medaglia, 1984; Sophitour, 1985; Introduzione e Valzer in Do, 1985; Quartetto per Archi No 1, 1986; Quartetto per Archi No 2, 1987; Concerto Grosso per Orchestra D'Archi, 1988; 2 Divertimenti, 1988-89; Fantasia Per Oboe e Quarteito D'Archi, 1993; 3 Liriche Per Soprano and Violin, 1994. Recordings: Baroque and Contemporary Music; Massimo Coen works Edipan Rome. Contributions to: Mondo Operaio. Honour: Member, International Jury, Gaudeamus Foundation Competition, Rotterdam, 1976. Memberships: Professional Associations and Councils. Address: Via Ipponio 8, 00183 Rome, Italy.

COERTSE Mimi, b. 12 June 1932, Durban, South Africa. Singer, (Soprano). Education: Studied in Johannesburg and in Vienna, with Josef Witt. Debut: With the Vienna Staatsoper in Naples, as a Flowermaiden in Parsifal, 1955. Career: Basle 1956, as the Queen of Night; Tour of South Africa; Appearances at the Salzburg Festival as Constanze in Die Entführung, 1956; Glyndebourne Festival 1957, as Zerbinetta; Salzburg 1960, as the Queen of Night; Mahler's 8th Symphony; Guest Appearances in London, Cologne, Brussels, Frankfurt and Munich; Sang Mozart's Countess in Pretoria, South Africa, 1989. Recordings: Fiakermilli in Arabella. Memberships: Vienna Staatsoper from 1957.

COGEN Pierre, b. 2 Oct 1931, Paris, France. Organist; Composer; Music Professor. m. Michèle Vermesse, 5 July 1986. Education: Cathedral Music School for Children, 1944-51; Higher studies in Philosophy, Paris, 1957-59; Organ study with Jean Langlais, Schola Cantorum; Certificate of Competence as Professor of Organ at National Conservatories; CAPES, Music Education (Secondary). Career: Liturgical Organist, 1945-94; Director of Boys' Choir, 1952-65; Concert Organist, 1959-; Professor of Organ and Music Education, 1961-93; Assistant to Jean Langlais, Sainte Clotilde and Schola Cantorum, 1972-76; Organist, Basilique Sainte Clotilde, 1976-94. Compositions include: Pieces for Organ, published in Das neue Orgelbaum II, 1986; Pieces for Organ, in Pedals Only, 1988; Offrande, 1990; Nocturne, 1992; Deux Chorals, 1992; Various unpublished works. Recordings: Organ works of Jean Langlais, 2 recordings; Sept Chorals-Boémes pour les Sept Paroles du Christ, de Charles Tournemire. Honours: Recipient, prizes for organ and for composition. Address: 12 rue Saint-Saëns, F-75015 Paris, France.

COGHILL Harry (MacLeod), b. 14 Apr 1944, Edinburgh, Scotland. Opera and Concert Singer (Bass). m. Anna Sweeny, 9 Apr 1970, 1 son, 1 daughter. Education: Royal Manchester College of Music, studied singing with Frederick Cox, 1967-71; ARMCM, Teaching and Performing; Studied with Yvonne Rodd-Marling, 1976-82. Debut: With English National Opera, as Seneca in Monteverdi's L'Incoronazione di Poppea, 1971. Career: Concert tour of North America, 1965; Member of Glyndebourne Festival Chorus, 1970, 1971; Principal Bass, English National Opera, 1971-79; Created several roles in contemporary operas; Extensive repertoire in all periods of opera and oratorio; Freelance appearances with English Music Theatre, Handel Opera, Kent Opera, Opera 80 and other English companies, 1979-; Appearances in festivals at Aldeburgh, Belfast, Dortmund, Exeter, Munich, Vienna; Founder, A Song for Ockenden, concert series for The Ockenden Venture, in aid of refugee children, 1980; Lecturer in Singing, School of Music, University of Auckland, New Zealand, 1987. Contributions to: Educational supplements. Honours: Imperial League of Opera Prize and Ricordi Prize, Royal Manchester College of Music, 1970; Fellowship, Griffith Institute of Higher Education, Griffith University Queensland, 1996; Director, Studio Opera, Queensland Conservatorium of Music, Brisbane, 1997. Memberships: Incorporated Society of Musicians; British Actors' Equity. Hobbies: Golf; Books; Tandem riding. Address: Derryheen, Hook Heath Road, Woking, Surrey GU22 0LB, England.

COGRAM John, b. 1967, Sussex, England. Singer (Tenor). Education: Studied at the Royal College of Music, National Opera Studio and with Janice Chapman; Masterclasses with Birgit Nilsson and Luigi Alva. Career: Ulm Opera 1994-96, as M Triquet in Eugene Onegin, Wenzel in The Bartered Bride, Steersman in Fliegende Holländer, Remendado (Carmen) and Bajazet in Handel's Tamerlano; Other roles include Alfredo in La Traviata at Clonter Farm, Pinkerton with English Festival Opera and Rodolfo with English Touring Opera; Oronte in Handel's Alcina in concert performances at Cologne; Basle Opera from 1996, as Pedrillo (Entführung) and Pang in Turandot; Recitals include: Die schöne Müllerin and Dichterliebe. Honours include: Cuthbert Smith Award, RCM. Address: C&M Craig Services Ltd, 3 Kersley Street, London SW11 4PR, England.

COHEN Arnaldo, b. 22 Apr 1948, Rio de Janeiro, Brazil. Concert Pianist. 1 s, 2 step children. Education: Engineering University of Rio de Janeiro; Graduate in Piano and Violin, School of Music, Federal University of Rio de Janeiro. Debut: Royal Festival Hall, London, 1977. Career: Appearances at Albert Hall, Barbican, Queen Elizabeth Hall and Wigmore Hall in London, La Scala in Milan, Concertgebouw in Amsterdam and Musikverein in Vienna; Performed in the Amadeus Piano Trio, 1988-92; Served on the Jury of the Busoni and Liszt Competitions; Concerts under Menuhin, Tennstedt, Sanderling and Masur; Masterclasses in Europe, USA and South America. Recordings: Chopin Solo of 2nd Scherzo, 4th Ballade, Allegro de Concert, Largo and Bolero; Liszt B Minor Sonata, Dante Sonata, Scherzo and March. Recordings: TV and Radio recordings: BBC, Dutch, German, Italian and others. Memberships: Broadwood Fellow in Piano studies at Royal Northern College of Music, 1991. Honours: 1st Prize, Beethoven Competition, 1970; 1st Prize, Busoni Piano Competition, Italy, 1972; Appointed to the Broadwood Trust Fellowship, newly established at Royal Northern College of Music, 1992. Hobbies: Chess; Football. Current Management: General: Jacques Leiser Artists' Management, USA. Address: 4 Connaught Square, London, W2 2HG.

COHEN Isidore (Leonard), b. 16 Dec 1922, New York City, New York, USA. Violinist; Teacher. m. Judith Goldberg, 1 son, 1 daughter. Education: Studied violin with Ivan Galamian; Chamber music with Felix Salmond and Hans Letz; BS, Juilliard School of Music, 1948. Career: Member: Schneider String Quartet, 1952-55; Juilliard String Quartet, 1958-66; Beaux Arts Trio, 1968-; Appearances as soloist with orchestras and as a recitalist; Associated with Marlboro (Vermont) Music School and Festival, 1957-; Teacher: Juilliard School of Music, 1957-65; Mannes College of Music, 1970-88. Recordings: Numerous discs as member of Beaux Arts Trio. Honours: Various awards as member of Beaux Arts Trio; Career highlighted in N Delblanco's book The Beaux Arts Trio: A Portrait, 1985. Address: c/o Columbia Artists Management Inc, 165 West 57th Street, New York, NY 10019, USA.

COHEN Joel, b. 23 May 1942, Providence, Rhode Island, USA. Conductor; Lutenist; Writer; Lecturer. Education: BA, Composition, Musicology, Brown University, 1963; MA, Harvard University, 1965; Studied theory and composition with Nadia Boulanger, Paris, 1965-67. Career: Director, Boston Camerata, 1968-; Guest conductor at various music festivals (Aix-en-Provence, Strasbourg, Tanglewood); Lecturer, Early Music Performance at US and European universities and conservatories; Specialist in Mediaeval, Renaissance and Baroque music. Recordings: With Boston Camerata and Cambridge Consort. Honours: Grand Prix du Disque, 1989. Address: c/o The Aaron Concert Management, 729 Boylston Street, Suite 206, Boston, MA 02116, USA.

COHEN Raymond, b. 27 July 1919, Manchester, England. Musician (Violinist). m. 8 Mar 1953, 1 son, 1 daughter. Education: Fellow, Royal Manchester College of Music. Debut: As a child. Career: International soloist, having played with major orchestras in many parts of the world; Leader of many orchestras, including Royal Philharmonic Orchestra, 1959-65; Violinist, Cohen Trio; Soloist on BBC radio and television. Recordings: Violinist, Delius's Double Concerto, with Royal Philharmonic Orchestra; Soloist, Robert Farnon's Rhapsody; Saint-Saëns's Introduction and Rondo Capriccioso; Vivaldi's Concerto for 2 violins and orchestra. Honours: 1st Prize Winner, Carl Flesch International Competition, 1945; Honorary Member, Royal College of Music. Membership: Incorporated Society of Musicians. Hobbies: Antique furniture; Theatre. Address: 6 Alvanley Gardens, London NW6 1JD, England.

COHEN Robert, b. 15 June 1959, London, England. Concert Cellist. m. Rachel Smith, 1 Aug 1976. Education: Guildhall School of Music, 1975-77; Cello studies with William Pleeth, André Navarra, J Du Pré, M Rostropovich. Career: Royal Festival Hall debut, Boccherini Concerto, age 12; London recital debut, Wigmore Hall, age 17; Invited to Tanglewood Festival, USA, 1978; First tour of USA, 1979; Concerts in Europe and Eastern Europe, 1979; Concerts worldwide with major orchestras and eminent conductors, 1980; Many TV appearances and radio broadcasts; Performs on Bonjour Stradivarius cello dated 1692. Recordings: Elgar Cello Concerto; Dvorák Cello Concerto; Grieg Sonata; Rodrigo Concerto en Modo Galante; Virtuoso Cello Music; Beethoven Triple Concerto; Dvorák Complete Piano Trios with Cohen Trio; Schubert String Quartet with Amadeus Quartet; Tchaikovsky Rococo Variations; Franck Sonata. Honours: Suggia Prize, 1967-72; Young Concert Artists, New York, 1978; Piatigorsky Prize, 1978; UNESCO Prize, Czechoslovakia, 1980. Memberships: Incorporated Society of Musicians; Patron, Beauchamp Music Club; Fellow, Purcell School of Music. Hobbies: Photography; Squash; Driving fast cars (Member, Institute of Advanced Motorists); Computers. Current management: Intermusic Artists' Management. Address: Intermusic Artists' Management, Grafton House, 2/3 Golden Square, London W1R 3AD, England.

COHN Arthur, b. 6 November 1910, Philadelphia, Pennsylvania, USA. Administrator; Conductor; Publishing Executive; Writer on Music; Composer. Education: Combs Conservatory of Music, Philadelphia, 1920-28; University of Pennsylvania; Studied Composition with Rubin Goldmark, Juilliard Graduate School, New York, 1933-34; Studied with William F Happich; Violin with Sascha Jacobinoff. Career includes: Director, Edwin A Fleisher Music Collection, Free Library of Philadelphia, 1934-52; Head, Music Department, Free Library of Philadelphia, 1946-52; Executive Director, Philadelphia Settlement Music School, 1952-56; Director, serious music, MCA Music, 1966-72; Carl Fischer, 1972-; Wrote music criticism; Appearances on radio and television. Compositions: 5 string quartets, 1928-45; 5 Nature Studies for Orchestra, 1932; The Pot-bellied God for Baritone and String Quartet, 1937; Suite for Viola and Orchestra, 1937; Music for Ancient Instruments, 1938; 4 Symphonic Documents, 1939; Quintuple Concerto for 5 Ancient Instruments and Modern Orchestra, 1940; The 12 for Narrator and String Quartet, 1940; Flute Concerto, 1941; Variations for Clarinet, Saxophone and String Orchestra, 1945; Music for Bassoon, 1947; Quotations in Percussion for 103 Percussion Instruments and 6 Players, 1958; Kaddish for Orchestra, 1964; Percussion Concerto, 1970. Recording: Kaddish for Orchestra (Royal Philharmonic Orchestra). Publications: The Collector's Twentieth-Century Music in the Western Hemisphere, 1961; Twentieth-Century Music in Western Europe, 1965; Musical Quizzical, 1970; Recorded Classical Music: A Critical Guide to Compositions and Performances, 1981; Music Mind-Benders, 1992; The Literature of Chamber Music, 4 volumes, 1997. Address: c/o Carl Fisher Inc, 62 Cooper Square, New York, NY 10003, USA.

COHN James (Myron), b. 12 Feb 1928, Newark, New Jersey, USA. Composer; Musicologist; Inventor. m. Eileen B Wions, 3 Sept 1979. Education: BS, 1949, MS, 1950, Juilliard School of Music; Postgraduate study in Electronic Music, Hunter College, New York; Study of Musical Composition with Roy Harris, Wayne Barlow and Bernard Wagenaar. Career: Musicologist, American Society of Composers, Authors and Publishers, 1954-84; Inventor of various patented control devices for electronic musical instruments. Compositions include: Published works: Symphonies Nos 3-8; A Song of the Waters; Variations on The Wayfaring Stranger; Variations on John Henry; The Little Circus; Sonata for Flute and Piano; Statues in the Park, choral; 2 Concertos for Clarinet and String Orchestra. Recordings include: Concerto da camera; Quintet for Winds; Little Overture; Sonatina for clarinet and piano; Sonata for flute and piano; Serenade for flute, violin and cello; Trio for piano, violin and cello; Mount Gretna Suite for chamber orchestra; Recordings for radio, television and films. Contributions to: Book reviews to Library Journal. Honours: Queen Elisabeth of Belgium Prize for Symphony No 2, 1953; AIDEM Prize for Symphony No 4. Memberships: American Federation of Musicians; American Society of Composers, Authors and Publishers; Songwriters' Guild of America. Address: 38-62 240th Street, Little Neck, NY 11363, USA.

COHRS Gunnar, b. 1960, Hameln, Germany. Conductor. Education: Jugendmusikschule, Hameln, 1972-85; Hochschule für Künste Bremen, 1989-94; High Distinction Degrees in Conducting and Flute; Diploma in Musicology, as DAAD Scholar, University of Adelaide, 1994-95. Compositions: Choralvorspiel for Organ, 1985; Trois Pastorales for Flute and Clarinet, 1993; Berceuse pour L'Amour Perdu for Piano, 1994. Recordings: Mendelssohn's Die Hebridien; Vaughan-Williams' 5th Symphony; Sibelius' Rakastava; Martin's Sonata da Chiesa with Susanne Meier, Flute; Production of Radio Bremen, 1994. Publications: Bruckner's IX Symphony, Finale, 1993; Three unknown compositions by Honegger: Semiramis, ballet for Orchestra, The Tempest, Suite, La Nuit est si Profonde, 1992; Musical Examples of Arthur Honegger, by Harry Halbriech, 1992; Frank Martin's Sonata da Chiesa, arrangement for Flute and Strings, 1995 Universal Edition, Vienna. Contributions to: Fono-Forum, 1988; Bruckner-Jahrbuch, 1989-90, 1991-92, Wien 1993-95; Neue Zeitschrift für Musik, 1990; Lili Boulanger, Tage Bremen, 1993; Festival Catalogue, Bremen, 1993; Bruckner Klangbau, 1992; Bremer - Die Stadtillustrierte, collaborator since 1989; Several cover texts. Memberships: Internationale Bruckner Gesellschaft Wien. Hobbies: Sport; Books; Cooking; Cinema; Unknown Orchestral Works; SF; Philosophy. Address: c/o Bettina Braun-Angott, Arte Music Konzertagentur, Gabelsbergerstrasse 48B, D-80 333 München, Germany.

COKER Paul, b. 1959, London, England. Pianist. Education: Began piano studies aged 5 and entered Yehudi Menuhin School, 1967, piano with Louis Kentner. Career: Won National Federation of Music Societies' Concert Award, 1978, and soon gave several London recitals, as well as concerts in France, Germany, Belgium, Netherlands, the USA, Canada and India; Further study at Tanglewood, USA, from 1980, winning the Jackson Master Award there; Has played with most leading British orchestras and with the Berlin Philharmonic; the Grieg Concerto with the Belgian National Symphony; Many recitals with Yehudi Menuhin in Europe, the United States, Far East and Australia. Address: c/o Anglo-Swiss Ltd, 4/5 Primrose Mews, 1a Sharpleshall Street, London NW1 8YW, England.

COKU Alexandru, b. 1963, USA. Singer (Soprano). Education: Studied with Margaret Harshaw at Indiana University. Career: Has sung in Europe from 1988, notably as Euridice to the Orpheus of Jochen Kowalski at Covent Garden and as Pamina at the rebuilt Frankfurt Opera, 1991; Further engagements as Pamina at Vienna, Munich and Dusseldorf; Amsterdam, 1992, as Ismene in Mozart's Mitridate; US appearances as Anne Trulove in The Rake's Progress at Chicago (1990) and Cecilio in Lucio Silla at San Francisco (1991). Address: c/o San Francisco Opera, War Memorial House, San Francisco, CA 94102, USA.

COLBERT Brendan, b. 11 September 1956, Ballarat, Victoria, Australia. Composer. Education: Studied with Brenton Broadstock, 1983-86 Riccardo Formosa 1986-88; National Orchestral Composers School, 1991, 1995. Compositions include: Passages for alto saxophone, electric guitar, piano and percussion, 1987; Murderers of Calm for ensemble, 1987; Agite II for mandolin, 1989; Fourplay for viola, cello, clarinet and piano, 1991; Agite I for flute, 1991; Parallaxis for ensemble, 1993; Agite II for piano, 1993-95; Mirror, Picture, Echo, Shadow, Dream for cello, flute, percussion and piano, 1994; Entfernt for string orchestra, 1994; Sphinx for ensemble, 1995; Sanctuary for orchestra, 1995. Honours include: Warringah Eisteddfod Young Composers Competiton, 1985. Address: c/o APRA, 1A Eden Street, Crows Nest, NSW 2065, Australia.

COLD Ulrik, b. 15 May 1939, Copenhagen, Denmark. Singer (Bass). Education: As Singer, privately educated in Copenhagen and Aarhus; Bachelor of Laws from Copenhagen University. Career: Sang in concert from 1963, then in opera in Copenhagen; Engaged at Kassell, 1969-71; Komische Oper Berlin, 1971, as Massenet's Don Quixote; Sang Sarastro in the Bergman film version of Die Zauberflöte; Intendant of the Royal Opera Copenhagen, 1975-77; Baroque repertory concerts in France, Germany, Netherlands, Switzerland and Scandinavia; Operatic roles include: Wagner's Marke, Landgraf and Gurnemanz; Verdi's Padre Guardiano and Zaccharia; Roles in works by Handel, Monteverdi and Rameau; US debut, San Francisco, as Sarastro, 1980; Alazim in Zaide, Wexford Festival, 1981; Sang at Teatro Comunale Bologna, 1987; The General in The Gambler by Prokofiev, English National Opera. Recordings: Armide by Lully; Admeto by Handel; Rameau's Hippolyte et Aricie and Handel's Xerxes; L'Incoronazione di Poppea; St Matthew Passion by Bach; Ulrik Cold Sings Carl Nielsen; Schnittke's Faust

Cantata. Address: c/o Allied Artists Agency, 42 Montpelier Square, London SW7 1JZ, England.

COLDING-JORGENSEN Henrik, b. 21 Mar 1944, Riisskov, Denmark. Composer; Organist; Pedagogue; Choir Leader. m. (1) Birgit Nielsen, 1966-87, (2) Mette Bramso, 1992, 1 d. Education: Organist, 1966, Organ Pedagogue, Royal Danish Conservatory. Career: Organ teacher; Teacher of Musical Theory; Organist; Choir Leader; Producer of Radio and TV programmes; Composer; Chairman of Board, Holstebro Electronic Music Studio, 1977-85; Member, Musical Committee, Roskilde County, 1979-87; Member, Committee of Representatives of State Music Council, 1981-91; Member, Committee of Representatives of State Art Council, 1981-85; Member, Danish Arts Council, 1981-84. Compositions include: Ave Maria, 1974; Balances, 1974; To Love Music, 1975; Victoria Through the Forest, 1975; Boast, 1980; Dein Schweigen, 1982; Recitativ and Fuga; An Die Nachgeborenen II, 1984; Du Sollst Nicht, 1984; Sic Enim, 1985; Nuup Kangerlua, 1985; Partita, aria e minuetto, 1986; Le Alpi Nel Cuore, 1988; 2 Songs by Keats, 1988; Nunc Est, 1989; The Soul and The Butterfly, 1990; Babylon, 1991; As a Traveller, 1992; Krystal; Metamorfose, 1993; Discourse with Time, 1996; Sourires, 1997. Honours: Various bursaries, prizes and commissions; Concours International de Composition Musicale Opera et Ballet, Geneva, 1985. Memberships: Danish Composer Society, Board, 1981-91; Danish ISCM, Board until 1982; Danish Organist and Cantor Society, Board, 1992-95; Danish Choirleaders, 1996. Address: Kildehuset 2, 3.tv, DK-2670 Greve, Denmark.

COLE Maggie, b. 1952, USA. Harpsichordist; Pianist. Career: Performed widely in USA, then Europe (from 1974); Gave the 6 Partitas by Bach at the Wigmore Hall, 1985; Appeared at Bath, Cheltenham and King's Lynn Festivals; Frequent broadcasts on Radio 3; Overseas engagements at Seattle, Chicago, Bruges, Cologne, Tallinn and Moscow; Collaborations with Lisa Beznosiuk (Flute) in music by Handel, J S Bach, Locatelli, Philidor, Hummel, Clementi and Beethoven; New York debut, Mar 1991; With Simon Standage (Baroque and classical violins) in music by Corelli, J S Bach, Leclair, Mondonville, Mozart, Pinto and Beethoven: the Kreutzer Sonata at the Purcell Room, 1988; With Nigel North (lute and guitar) in music by Weber, Hummel, Diabelli, Beethoven, Giuliani and Sor, Wigmore Hall concerts and tours of Poland, Israel, the USSR; with Steven Isserlis (cello) from 1986, notably in sonatas by Boccherini. Recordings include: Scarlatti Sonatas; Poulenc's Concert Champêtre and Bach's Goldberg Variations; Boccherini Cello Sonatas; Soler Sonatas on harpsichord and fortepiano. Address: c/o Robert White Management, 182 Moselle Avenue, London N22 6EX, England.

COLE Malcolm Stanley, b. 15 Apr 1936, San Francisco, California, USA. Professor of Musicology. m. Susan Lee Cooke, 9 Aug 1969, 1 son, 1 daughter. Education: AB, University of California, Berkeley, 1958; MFA, 1960, PhD, 1964, Princeton University; Piano study with Mme E Robert Schmitz, Bernhard Abramowitsch, Adolph Baller. Career: Registrar, Dean, San Francisco Conservatory of Music, 1964-67; Music Director, St Francis' Episcopal Church, 1964-67; Assistant Professor, Associate Professor, Professor, University of California, Los Angeles, 1967-. Publications: Book: Armseelchen: The Life and Music of Eric Zeisl (with Barbara Barclay), 1984; Guided Listening (with Eleanor Hammer), 1992. Contributions to: Numerous scholarly journals; New Grove Dictionary of Music and Musicians and other reference works. Honours: Numerous fellowships as a graduate student, 1958-61; Numerous grants for musicological research from UCLA, 1969-; National Endowment for the Humanities, Summer Stipend, 1976. Memberships: American Musicological Society; American Guild of Organists; American Society for Eighteenth-Century Studies. Hobbies: Water Sports; Model Railroading. Address: 7926 Ramsgate Avenue, Los Angeles, CA 90045, USA.

COLE Steve, b. 1954, USA. Singer (Tenor). Career: Sang with Washington Opera from 1981, Aix-en-Provence (as Monostatos), 1982, and in Paris, Avignon (Henze's Boulevard Solitude), and Nice; New York Metropolitan debut, 1987, as Brighella in Ariadne auf Naxos; San Francisco Opera from 1990; Other modern repertory includes the premieres of Medea by Gavin Bryars (Lyon, 1984) and La Noche Triste by Prodromidès (Nancy, 1989); Other buffo and character roles include Bardolph in Falstaff, Pong in Turandot and Sellem in The Rake's Progress. Address: c/o San Francisco Opera, War Memorial House, Van Ness Avenue, San Francisco, CA 94102, USA.

COLE Vinson, b. 21 Nov 1950, Kansas City, Kansas, USA. Tenor. Education: Studied at the Curtis Institute, Philadelphia. Debut: Sang Werther in the opera by Massenet while still a student, 1975. Career: Sang in the premiere of Jubilee by Ulysses Kay at Jackson, Mississippi, in 1976; European debut, 1976, with Welsh National Opera, as Belmonte in Die Entführung aus dem Serail; Later appearances in Stuttgart, Naples, Salzburg, Paris and Marseilles; St Louis, 1976-80, as Tamino and Rossini's Comte Ory; New York City Opera, 1981, as Fenton in Die lustigen Weiber von Windsor; Other roles include Gennaro in Lucrezia Borgia, Nadir in Les Pêcheurs de Perles, Lenski in Eugene Onegin, Gluck's Orfeo and Gounod's Faust; Sang in Mozart's Requiem under Georg Solti at Vienna, 1991; Sang Donizetti's Edgardo at Detroit, Ferrando at Seattle, 1992; Nadir in Les Pêcheurs de Perles in Seattle, 1994; Sang Jason in Cherubini's Medea, Athens 1995; Don Carlo in the French version of Verdi's opera, Brussels, 1996; Renaud in Gluck's Armide, to open the 1996-97 Season at La Scala. Address: c/o Seattle Opera Association, PO Box 9248, Seattle, WA 98109, USA.

COLEMAN Tim, b. 30 Oct 1949, Eastbourne, Sussex, England. Stage Director. Education: Cambridge and Amsterdam Conservatory, composition. Career: Wrote incidental music for over 30 plays, then Chief Dramaturg of The Netherlands Opera; Debut as Director with Opera Northern Ireland in Die Fledermaus, 1990, returned 1991 for Le nozze di Figaro and 1992 Rigoletto; United State debut with The Beggar's Opera for the Manhattan School of Music; Season 1991-92, Tosca for Minnesota Opera and Opera Omaha, Tamerlano for Dublin Opera Theatre, and The Merry Wives of Windsor for the Guildhall School of Music; Season 1992-93, L'Italiana in Algeri for Dublin Grand Opera/Opera Ireland, Così fan tutte in Oklahoma City; Season 1993-94, Rigoletto in Hong Kong, L'Isola disabitata in New York, Tosca in Indianapolis, Le nozze di Figaro for the Kirov Opera in the Mariinsky Theatre, St Petersburg; Festivals of Mikkele, Finland, Schleswig-Holstein, Germany, and Beth Shean (Israel) Season, 1994-95; Un Giorno di Regno, Dorset Opera; La Traviata, Hong Kong; Le nozze di Figaro, The Hague, Netherlands. Current Management: Athole Still International Management Ltd. Address: Athole Still Ltd, Foresters Hall, 25-27 Westow Street, London SE19 3RY, England.

COLEMAN-WRIGHT Peter, b. 1958, Australia. Singer (Baritone). Education: Studied in London with Otakar Kraus, Joan Hammond, Paul Hamburger and Geoffrey Parsons. Career: Has sung at Glyndebourne as Gugliemo, Demetrius, Dandini, Morales in Carmen and Sid in Albert Herring; English National Opera as Neils Lynne in Fennimore and Gerda, Rossini's Barber, Schaunard, Billy Budd and Don Giovanni; Australian Opera as Mozart's Count; Covent Garden, Dandini, then Don Alvaro in Rossini's Il Viaggio a Reims and Papageno; Bordeaux Opera, Gugliemo, Masetto; Victoria State Opera, Wolfram, Papageno, Valentin in Faust; Further engagements with Netherlands Opera, the Fenice Venice and the Australian Opera; Grand Théâtre Genève; Other roles include Eisenstein and Falke in Die Fledermaus, Masetto, Rossini's Figaro, Wolfram in Tannhäuser, Zurga and the Soldier/Brother in Busoni's Doctor Faust; Lieder recitals at the South Bank, Covent Garden, Théâtre du Châtelet in Paris and the Aix and Spoleto Festivals; Brahms Requiem and Mahler Kindertotenlieder in Austria; Concerts in Holland, Spain, Germany, Finland, Iceland and for the Australian Broadcasting Commission; Premiere of Inquest of Love by Jonathan Harvey, English National Opera, 1993; Wigmore Recital, 1993; Bordeaux, Count Almaviva, 1993; Australian Opera, Don Giovanni, 1993; Staatsoper Munich, Don Giovanni; Marcello, Grande Théâtre Genève and Covent Garden in Eugene Onegin, ENO and Lyric Opera Queensland; Billy Budd, Covent Garden; Chorèbe in Les Troyens, Australian Opera; Sang Escamillo in Carmen at the Opera Bastille, Paris, 1997; Concerts with BBC Symphony including the British premiere of Hindemith's Mörder Hoffnung der Frauen. Recording: Oedipus Rex by Stravinsky, EMI. Honours include: Glyndebourne Touring Prize. Current Management: IMG Artists, Media House, 32 Burlington Lane, London W4 2TH, England.

COLES Samuel, b. 1964, England. Flautist. Education: Studied with James Galway, at the Guildhall School of Music and at the Paris Conservatoire with Jean-Pierre Rampal. Career: Solo and chamber music performances in Britain and Europe in Holland Concertgebouw and The Hague, with the Bordeaux Symphony, the Monte Carlo Orchestra and the London Soloists Chamber Orchestra; Mozart Concerto K313 with the Orchestre de Paris at Rampal's Gala Concert, Paris; Chamber recitals with members of the European Community Youth Orchestra and duet partnership with harpist Isabelle Courret; Concerto engagements with Kenneth Montgomery, Aldo Ceccato and Alain Lombard; As orchestral player has performed under Simon Rattle, Claudio Abbado and Pierre Boulez. Recordings include: Mozart Concerti with the English Chamber Orchestra under Yehudi Menuhin. Honours: Premier Prix at the Paris Conservatoire, 1987; Winner, Scheveningen International Flute Competition, Netherlands, and National Flute Association Young Artists' Competition, San Diego, USA. Address: c/o Anglo-Swiss Management, 4-5 Primrose Mews, 1a Sharpleshall Street, London NW1 8YW, England.

COLETTI Paul, b. 1959, Scotland. Concert Violist; Professor. Education: Studied at Royal Scottish Academy, International Menuhin Academy, Banff Center and Juilliard School; Teachers included Alberto Lysy, Sandor Vegh and Don McInnes. Career: Solo concerts at Elizabeth Hall, Geneva, Buenos Aires, Edinburgh, Assissi, Toulon and Harrogate Festivals; Recitals at Toronto, Chicago, Cincinnati, Belgrade and Los Angeles; NY debut recital in 1983; Member of the Menuhin Festival Piano Quartet; Chamber performances with Menuhin in Paris, London and Gstaad; Member of Chamber Society of Lincoln Center, NY; Further engagements with Camerata Lysy Ensemble and playing Bartók's Viola Concerto in Berlin; Former Professor of Viola and Chamber Music at Menuhin Academy; Former Head of Viola Department at Peabody Conservatory, Baltimore; Head of String Department at University of Washington, Seattle; Guest conducted the New Japan Philharmonic in Tokyo. Compositions: From My Heart, 1994; Viola Tango, 1994; Dream Ocean, 1995. Recordings: Chamber pieces by Mozart, Strauss and Mendelssohn; Currently 20 CDs recorded. Current Management: Tom Parker Artists. Address: c/o Tom Parker Artists, 328 Central Park Avenue No 9G, New York, NY 10025, USA.

COLGRASS Michael (Charles), b. 22 Apr 1932, Chicago, Illinois, USA. Composer. m. Ulla Damgaard, 25 Nov 1966, 1 son. Education: MusB, University of Illinois, 1956; Composition with Lukas Foss, Berkshire Music Center, Tanglewood, summers 1952, 1954; Darius Milhaud, Aspen, Colorado Music School, summer 1953; Wallingford Riegger, 1958-59, Ben Weber, 1959-62, New York. Career: Freelance solo percussionist, various New York groups, 1956-67. Compositions include: Stage: Virgil's Dream, music theatre, 1967; Nightingale Inc, comic opera, 1971; Something's Gonna Happen, children's musical, 1978; Orchestral: Auras, harp, orchestra, 1973; Concertmasters, 3 violins, orchestra, 1975; Letter from Mozart, 1976; Déjà vu, 4 percussionists, orchestra, 1977; Delta, violin, clarinet, percussion, orchestra, 1979; Memento, 2 pianos, orchestra, 1982; Demon, amplified piano, percussion, tape, radio, orchestra, 1984; Chaconne, viola, orchestra, 1984; The Schubert Birds, 1989; Snow Walker, Organ, orchestra, 1990; Arctic Dreams, symphonic band, 1991; Chamber: Wolf, cello, 1976; Flashback, 5 brass; Winds of Nagual-A Musical Fable, wind ensemble, 1985; Strangers, Variations, clarinet, viola, piano, 1886; Folklines, string quartet, 1987; Piano pieces; Vocal: The Earth's a Baked Apple, chorus, orchestra, 1969; New People, mezzo-soprano, viola, piano, 1969; Image of Man, 4 solo voices, chorus, orchestra, 1974; Theatre of the Universe, solo voices, chorus, orchestra, 1975; Best Wishes USA, 4 solo voices, double chorus, 2 jazz bands, folk instruments, orchestra, 1976; Beautiful People, chorus, 1976; Mystery Flowers of Spring, 1978; Night of the Raccoon, 1979. Recordings: Chaconne; Variations for 4 Drums and Viola; The Earth's a Baked Apple; New People; Déjà vu; Light Spirit; As Quiet As; Fantasy Variations; Concertmasters; Night of the Raccoon; Three Brothers; Many others. Contributions to: Articles to New York Times. Honours include: Guggenheim Fellow, 1964, 1968; Rockefeller Grant, 1968; Ford Foundation Grant, 1972; Pulitzer Prize in Music, 1978; Emmy Awards, 1982, 1988; Jules Léger Chamber Music Prize. Address: 583 Palmerston Avenue, Toronto, Ontario, Canada M6G 2P6.

COLIBAN Sorin, b. 1970, Romania. Singer (Bass-baritone). Education: Studied at the Bucharest Conservatory. Debut: Bartók's Bluebeard at Bucharest, 1993. Career: Season 1995-96 with Don Giovanni at Athens, Royal Opera debut as Alvaro in a concert performance of Verdi's Alzira, and the Monk in Don Carlos at the London Proms; Season 1996-97 included Colline and Verdi's Monterone at Covent Garden, and Zuniga in Carmen at the Opéra Bastille; Further Paris performances as Alidoro (Cenerentola), Masetto, Don Giovanni and Angelotti (Tosca); Other roles include Mozart's Bartolo, Baron Duphol (La Traviata) and Capellio in I Capuleti e i Montecchi and Raimondo (Lucia). Honours include: Winner of national competitions in Romania. Address: c/o Penelope Marland Artists Management, 10 Roseneath Road, London SW11 6AH, England.

COLIN Georges, b. 15 Jun 1921, Schaerbeek, Brussels, Belgium. Composer. m. Albertine De Clerck, 17 Mar 1948, 2 s, 2 d. Education: Royal Conservatory of Music, Brussels; Harmony, 1943; Counterpoint, 1948; Fugue, 1949; History of Music, 1959. Career: Teacher, Athenee and Ecole Normale de Schaerbeek, 1976; Headmaster, Academy of Music, Anderlecht, 1976-81. Compositions: Symphonie breve for Orchestra, 1950; Cinq Poèmes français de R M Rilke for Voice and Piano, 1952; Woodwind Quartet, 1955; Concertstuck La Folia, for contrebasse and orchestra, 1964; Cinq Croquis d'eleves, for piano, 1962; Sonatine for Violin and Piano, 1962; Sonate for Flute and Piano, 1965; La Porte de pierre, poem of André Doms, for baritone solo, mixed choir and orchestra, 1969; Phantasme for Harp, 1977; Sequences for Violin and Piano, 1978; Pièces brèves for piano, 1996; Lithos, atmosphères pour 14 intruments, 1997; With Jeanne Colin: Le Tombeau d'André Jolivet for 2 Pianos, 1975; Short Pieces for Harps, 1976; Flutes Quartet, 1976; Two Pieces for Flute and Harp, 1979; Cantate Pour Le Vif Des Temps, poems of André Doms, tryptique profane pour soprano and baritone solos, mixed choir and orchestra; Ryoan-Ji, 1986; Corps de feu, 1991. Publications: 9 Chants Populaire, Chants and Danses Populaires; Doucle France, flauto dolce; La Flute à bec alto (méthode en 3 volumes). Honours: Médaille Commemorative de la Guerre, 1940-45; Prix de Composition de la Province de Brabant, 1964; Lettres à un jeune compositeur, 1996. Memberships: SABAM;

CeBeDeM. Address: Haut du Village 40, B-5600 Sautour, Philippeville, Belgium.

COLLARD Jean-Philippe, b. 27 Jan 1948, Mareuil-sur-Ay, France. Concert Pianist. 3 sons, 1 daughter. Education: Studied at the Paris Conservatoire, 1959-64. Career: Performances throughout France and in Russia, Japan, Spain, Italy, Germany, Switzerland and the Netherlands; US debut in a series of concerts with the San Francisco Symphony under Seiji Ozawa; Regular appearances with the New York Philharmonic; British engagements with the London Symphony, Royal Philharmonic, Philharmonia Hallé, City of Birmingham Symphony, Scottish Chamber and BBC Symphony, Welsh and Philharmonic Orchestras; Conductors include Dorati, Previn, Mehta, Lombard, Skrowaczewski, Loughran, Rattle, Maksymiuk, Dutoit and Pritchard; Tour of Britain, 1991, with the Orchestre de Paris under Semyon Bychkov; Season 1992-93 included concerts with the New York Philharmonic under Previn, the Philadelphia Orchestra and the Royal Scottish Orchestra; Played Rachmaninov's 1st Concerto at the London Proms, 1993. Recordings: Rachmaninov Etudes Tableaux; Brahms Hungarian Dances, with Michel Béroff; Ravel Concertos with the Orchestre National de France; Saint-Saëns Complete Concertos with André Previn and the Royal Philharmonic; Franck and Magnard Violin Sonatas with Augustin Dumay; Chopin Ballades and 3rd Sonata. Honours include: Premier Prix du Conservatoire de Paris, 1964; Grand Prix du Concours National des Artistes Solistes; Prix Albert Roussel; Grand Prix du Concours International Marguérite Long/Jacques Thibaud; Record of the Year, USA, 1978, 1979; Prize, French Recording Academy, 1978, 1981, 1982; Chevalier des Arts et des Lettres. Hobbies: Squash; Windsurfing. Address: Unit 2, 39 Tadema Road, London SW10 0PY, England.

COLLIER Gilman (Frederick), b. 14 Apr 1929, New York City, New York, USA. Composer; Conductor; Pianist; Teacher. Education: AB, Harvard University, 1950; Yale School of Music, 1950-51; Mannes Music School, 1951-53; Studied theory and composition with Walter Piston, Paul Hindemith, Bohuslav Martinu, conducting with Carl Bamberger, Leonard Bernstein and Pierre Monteux, piano privately with Nadia Reisenberg. Career: Music Director, Conductor, the Monmouth Symphony Orchestra, 1964-72; Faculty Member, New School for Social Research, New York City, 1953-60; Faculty Member, Westchester Conservatory of Music, White Plains, New York, 1954-74; Faculty Member, 1969-, Assistant Director, 1975-95, Monmouth Conservatory of Music. Compositions: 3 piano sonatas and many shorter works for piano solo; Sonata for 1 piano, 4 hands; Duo sonatas for flute, oboe, English horn, clarinet, French horn, trumpet, violin, viola and cello with piano; String Quintet; Fantasy for double-reed ensemble; Trios for flute, violin, piano, violin, cello, piano and oboe, English horn and piano; 2 String Quartets; Piano quintet; 4 Chicago Psalms, SSAA; Concerto Grosso for string orchestra and piano; Almande Smedelyn and Divertimento for double reed ensemble; Songs for voice and piano. Hobbies: Photography; Horsebreeding. Address: 65 Larchwood Avenue, Oakhurst, NJ 07755, USA.

COLLINS Anne, b. 29 Aug 1943, Durham, England. Opera and Concert Contralto. Education: Royal College of Music, London; ARCM; LRAM. Debut: Governess in The Queen of Spades, SWO, Coliseum. Career: English National Opera; Covent Garden; Welsh National Opera Company; Glyndebourne Festival; Scottish Opera; Grand Théâtre Genève; Canadian Opera Company; Théâtre de la Monnaie Brussels; Châtelet Paris; Roles included Erda, Waltraute, Mrs Herring and Ulrica; Mistress Quickly, Florence Pike, Auntie, Mrs Sedley, Baba the Turk, Marcellina; Beroe and Akhrosimova in the UK stage premieres of The Bassarids and War and Peace; Sosostris (Midsummer Marriage) and Anna in Les Troyens, (Covent Garden debut, 1977), Scottish Opera, Opera North; BBC Promenade Concerts; Recordings and song recitals; Concerts with major orchestras and choral societies in UK and Europe; Toured Australia for ABC; Video films of Gilbert and Sullivan operas, Gondoliers, Mikado, Iolanthe, Patience and Princess Ida, 1983; Sang the Angel of Death in the premiere of MacMillan's Inès de Castro, Edinburgh, 1996. Recordings: Erda, Rhinegold and Siegfried (English National Opera, Goodall); Janácek Glagolitic Mass, Kempe; Vivaldi Cantatas; Elgar Coronation Ode; Third Lady in Die Zauberflöte; Mrs Peachum in Britten's version of The Beggars Opera; Dame Carruthers in Yeoman of the Guard; Mes Sedley in Peter Grimes. Current Management: c/o Lies Askonas, 6 Henrietta St, London WC2E 8LA, England.

COLLINS Kenneth, b. 21 Oct 1935, Birmingham, England. Singer (Tenor). Education: Studied with Charles Dean and Ettore Campogaliani; Debut: Camden Festival 1970, as Marcello in the British premiere of Leoncavallo's La Boheme; Career: Has sung with Welsh National Opera, Scottish Opera, Covent Garden, Aldeburgh Festival, English National Opera, Paris Opera, NY City Opera, Colon/Buenos Aires, the Australian Opera, Strasbourg, Cologne, Granada, Valence, Madrid, Florence, Los Angeles; Repertoire includes Calaf, Manrico, Alvaro, Don Carlos, Radames, Gustavus, Dick Johnson, Andrea Chenier, Ernani and Cavaradossi. Awarded Australia Medal 1993 for services to opera. Current Management: Jenifer Eddy Artists' Management, 11/596 St Kilda Road, Melbourne 3004, Australia.

COLLINS Michael, b. 27 Jan 1962, London, England. Clarinettist. Education: Began clarinet studies aged 10; Royal College of Music with David Hamilton; Further studies with Thea King. Career: BBC TV Young Musician of the Year while still at school; Other awards include Frederick Thurston Prize, 1st Prize in Leeds National Competition and Concert Artists' Guild of New York Amcon Award, 1983; Carnegie Hall debut, 1984; BBC Promenade Concert debut, 1984, with Thea Musgrave's Concerto; 1985 Proms season played the Copland Concerto and was soloist in Bernstein's Prelude, Fugue and Riffs; Appointed youngest ever Professor at the Royal College of Music, 1985; Played the Finzi Concerto with the City of London Sinfonia in 1987; Performances of Weber's 2nd Concerto conducted by Stanislaw Skrowaczewski and Esa-Pekka Salonen; Appointed principal clarinet of the Philharmonia Orchestra, 1988; Associated with the Takacs Quartet, the Nash Ensemble and the pianists Noriko Ogawa and Kathryn Stott in chamber music; Recital partnership with Mikhail Pletnev, piano; Played Malcolm Arnold's 2nd Concerto at the Last Night of the London Proms, 1993; Stravinsky's Ebony Concerto at South Bank, London, 1999. Recordings: Finzi's Concerto; Bernstein's Prelude, Fugue and Riffs and Stravinsky's Ebony Concerto; Quintets by Mozart and Brahms with the Nash Ensemble. Address: c/o Clarion/Seven Muses, 64 Whitehall Park, London N19 3TN, England.

COLLINS Michael (Augustus), b. 16 Oct 1948, Sydney, Australia. Conductor; Pianist. m. Lynette Kay Jennings, 24 Nov 1971, 2 sons. Education: CBHS, St Mary's Cathedral, Sydney (Leaving Certificate, 1965); Performers and Teachers Diploma in Piano, New South Wales State Conservatorium of Music, 1965-68; Conducting Hochschule für Musik, Vienna, 1973-74. Career: Repetiteur and Conductor, Australian Opera, 1970-73; Repetiteur, Vienna Staatsoper, 1974-77; Repetiteur and Conductor, Württembergische Staatsoper, Stuttgart, 1977-79; Musical Director, Stuttgart Ballet, 1979-84; Conductor, Bayerische Staatsoper, Munich, 1984-90; 1 Kapellmeister Staatstheater Braunschweig, Guest Conductor, Deutsche Oper, Berlin, 1990. Hobbies: Photography; Stamp Collecting. Address: c/o Deutsche Oper Berlin, Richard Wagnerstrasse 10, 1000 Berlin, Germany.

COLLINS Michael B, b. 26 July 1930, Turlock, California, USA. Professor of Musicology. Education: BA, 1957, MA, 1958, PhD, 1963, Stanford University. Career: Eastman School of Music, 1964-68; School of Music, University of North Texas, Denton, 1968-. Publications: Editor, Alessandro Scarlatti's Tigrane, 1983; Co-Editor, Opera and Vivaldi, 1984; Editor, Gioachino Rossini's Otello, 1994. Contributions to: Dramatic Theory and the Italian Baroque Libretto, Cadential Structures and Accompanimental Practices in Eighteenth-Century Italian Recitative, Brazio Bracciolo's Orlando furioso: A History and Synopsis of the Libretto, in Opera and Vivaldi; The Performance of Sesquialtera and Hemiolia in the 16th century, 1964; The Performance of Triplets in the 17th and 18th Centuries, 1966, A Re-examination of Notes inégales, 1967, In Defence of the French Trill, 1973, The Literary Background of Bellini's I Capuleti ed i Montecchi, 1982, in Journal of the American Musicological Society; A reconsideration of French Over-dotting, Music and Letters, 1969. Honour: Fulbright-Hays Grant for research in Italy, 1963-64. Memberships: American Musicological Society. Address: College of Music, University of North Texas, Denton, TX 76203, USA.

COLLINS Richard L, b. 13 October 1927, Louisville, Kentucky, USA. Baritone; Stage Director; Professor. m. Ruth Strittmatter, 25 July 1981, 1 son, 1 daughter. Education: BA, Chemistry, University of Louisville; BM, Cincinnati Conservatory, Ohio; MA, Columbia University, New York; DM, Indiana University. Debut: Punch Opera, New York City, 1952. Career: Stage Director, Opera: Birmingham Civic Opera, Alabama, 1963-80; State Opera of Florida, 1964-69; Jacksonville Opera, Florida, 1970-84; Opera Memphis, Tennessee, 1976; Baritone, over 40 roles including: Title roles in Gianni Schicchi and Rigoletto, Ford in Falstaff, Iago in Otello, Amonasro in Aida, with Lake George Opera, Birmingham Civic Opera, State Opera of Florida, and Theatre Under the Stars, Houston, Texas; Professor: Auburn University, Florida State University, Millikin University. Publication: A Study of the Musical and Dramatic Treatment of Five Baritone Roles in Operas by Verdi (doctoral thesis), 1975. Honour: Etelka Evans Award, 1948. Membership: Vice-President, President, National Opera Association. Hobbies: Antique Phonographs. Address: 8722 Reamer Street, Houston, TX 77074, USA.

COLLINS Walter (Stowe), b. 12 Jan 1926, West Hartford, Connecticut, USA. Professor Emeritus. m. Jane Katherine Reynolds, 21 June 1958, 1 son, 2 daughters. Education: AB, 1948, BMus, 1951, Yale University; MA, 1953, PhD, 1960, University of Michigan; Oxford University, England, 1957-58. Career includes: Director of Choral Music: Auburn University, 1951-55, University of Minnesota, 1958-60; Chairman, Department of Music, Oakland University, Michigan, 1960-71; Founder and Dean, Meadow Brook Festival and School of Music; Professor, Associate Dean, 1971-, Professor Emeritus, 1988-, University of Colorado; Research interest in editing early choral music, and in bibliography and literature of choral music. Publications: Author and editor, numerous articles and editions of music, 1958-; Thomas Weelkes: Collected Anthems, (co-editor), 1966; Co-author: Choral Conducting Symposium, 1973, 2nd edition, 1988; Five Centuries of Choral Music: Essays in Honor of Howard Swan, 1988; Editor: International Choral Bulletin, International Federation for Choral Music, 1981-89; Familiar Choral Masterworks in Authoritative Editions, 1981-. Honour: Distinguished Alumnus, Yale University School of Music, 1977-79. Memberships: President, College Music Society, 1971-74; President, American Choral Directors Association, 1977-79. Address: College of Music, University of Colorado, Box 301, Boulder, CO 80309-0301, USA.

COLLOT Serge, b. 27 Sept 1923, Paris, France. Violist. Education: Studied at the Paris Conservatoire, 1944-48 (composition with Arthur Honegger). Career: Co-founder and member of the Parrenin Quartet, 1944-57; French String Trio from 1960; Violist with the Domaine Musical Concerts, 1953-70, and premiered the Sequenza for viola by Berio; Teacher at the Paris Conservatoire from 1969 and violist with the orchestra of the Paris Opéra until 1986. Address: c/o Conservatoire National, 14 Rue de Madrid, F-75008 Paris, France.

COLOMBARA Carlo, b. 1964, Bologna, Italy. Singer (Bass). Career: Sang at Teatro Donizetti, Bergamo, 1985, in a Young Singers Concert; Teatro dell'Opera Rome as Silva in Ernani and Wurm in Luisa Miller; Creon in Oedipus Rex by Stravinsky at Venice, Banquo in Macbeth and Oroveso in Norma in Tokyo; Guest appearances at Vienna Staatsoper, Bolshoi Moscow, London, Berlin, Buenos Aires, Brussels and San Francisco; La Scala debut, 1989, as Procida in I Vespri Siciliani, and appeared in Moscow with the company of La Scala in Turandot and I Capuleti i Montecchi; Verdi Requiem at Festival Hall, London, 1990; Sang Assur in Semiramide at Venice, 1990, Rodolfo in La Sonnambula; Engagements with such conductors as Giulini, Colin Davis, Gianandrea Gavazzeni, Maazel, Sawallisch and Solti; Sang Raimondo in Lucia di Lammermoor at Munich, 1991, Padre Guardiano at Cremona and Colline at 1992 Verona Arena Festival; Attila in Verdi's opera at Macerata, 1996; Television appearances include Aida and Lucia di Lammermoor from La Scala. Recordings: Colline in La Bohème; Verdi Requiem; Handel's Rinaldo. Honours: Winner, G B Viotti International Competition, Vercelli, 1985. Address: c/o Teatroalla Scala, Via Filodrammatics 2, 20121 Milan, Italy.

COLOMBO Emilio, b. 1920, Buenos Aires, Argentina. Guitarist. Education: Guitar lessons with Alejandro Spinardi from age of 11; Studied solfa and theory of music with Alejandro and Carlos Spinardi; Studied harmony and counterpoint with Adolio V Luna and Alfredo Schiuma; Studied on scholarship from the Secreatariat (office) for Foreign Relations, Spain, with Andrés Segovia, in Santiago de Compostela, Spain, 1961-62. Career: Concerts include: Adolfo V Luna's Sonata for guitar and string quintet at the Teatro Cervantes, Buenos Aires, with the Proarte Quintet of the Teatro Colon, 1952; Performed same work with the Acedo quartet at SADAIC and the Arcangelo Corelli Quartet at Club Espanol; Also played in Rosario and on National Radio with pianist Alma Melgar; Teaching music: Professor, Chair of Guitar, Collegium Musicum; Professor, Athos Palma Conservatory, Buenos Aires; Honorary Professor, Instituto de Arte Guitarristico, Mexico City; Master classes in introduction to guitar technique according to Manuel Lopez Ramos School; Main presentations at: Instituto de Cultura Guitarristica, Mexico City; Schools of Music ZurichSwitzerland; Instituto Cultural Argentino de Musica Hispanica; Mar del Plata Library; Associaión Guitarristica de Salta; Athos Palma Conservatory. Honours include: Representative and Adviser for the Argentinian area for the Andres Segovia Foundation of the City of Linares and Madrid; Works dedicated to him by composers Adolfo V Luna, Oscar Rosatti and D Emilio Pujol; Diploma of Honour from Associación Argentina de Musica de Cámara, 1953. Address: Muniz 776 2do A, 1234 Buenos Aires, Argentina.

COLONELLO Attilio, b. 9 Nov 1930, Milan, Italy. Stage Director and Designer. Education: Studied architecture with Gio Ponti and Ernesto Rogers in Milan. Career: Designed Traviata for 1956 Florence Festival, Mefistofele at La Scala, 1958; Returned to Milan for Don Pasquale, 1965 and 1973, and the premiere of Pizzetti's Clitennestra, 1965; US debut at Dallas, 1962, Otello and L'Incoronazione di Poppea, 1963; Metropolitan Opera, New York, with designs for Lucia di Lammermoor, 1964, Luisa Miller, 1968, and Il Trovatore, 1969; Designs and productions at San Carlo, Naples, 1964-88, for Roberto Devereux, Adriana Lecouvreur, Samson et Dalila, Carmen, La Gioconda and I Puritani; Verona Arena, 1962-84, with Nabucco, Cavalleria Rusticana, La Bohème, Rigoletto, La Forza del Destino, Aida, Un Ballo in Maschera and I Lombardi; Teatro Margherita, Genoa, 1991, Andrea Chenier;

Directed the Italian premiere of Rossini's Le Siège de Corinthe at Genoa, 1992, Turandot at 1992 Caracalla Festival.

COLZANI Anselmo, b. 1923, Budrio, Bologna, Italy. Singer (Baritone). Education: Studied with Corrado Zambelli in Bologna. Debut: Bologna, 1947, as the Herald in Lohengrin; Verona Arena from 1952; La Scala from 1954, notably in the stage premiere of Milhaud's David; US debut, 1956, as Count Luna at San Francisco; Metropolitan Opera debut, 1960, as Boccanegra; Returned to New York for 16 seasons as Verdi's Falstaff and Amonasro, Puccini's Scarpia and Jack Rance, Gerard in Andrea Chenier and Ashton in Lucia di Lammermoor; Sang Amonasro for Houston Grand Opera, 1966. Recordings: La Gioconda; La Forza del Destino; Maria di Rohan by Donizetti; Iphigénie en Tauride, with Callas; Agnese di Hohenstaufen by Spontini, Florence, 1957; Zandonai's Francesca da Rimini. Address: c/o Metropolitan Opera, Lincoln Center, New York, NY 10023, USA.

COMAN Nicolae, b. 23 Feb 1936, Bucharest, Romania. Composer; Professor of Harmony and Composition. m. Lavinia Tomulescu, 2 July 1966. Education: Ciprian Porombescu Academy of Music; Diploma in Musical Composition, 1959. Debut: Public first performance, Piano and Violin Sonata, Athenee, Bucharest, 1957. Career: Scientific Researcher, Ethnographical Institute of Romanian Academy, 1960-63; Professor of Harmony and Composition, Ciprian Porumbescu Academy of Music, 1963-. Compositions: Over 60 musical programmes for television and radio; The Source of the Peace, lyric cantata; Piano Concerto with orchestra; 67 piano pieces; 2 piano sonatas; 65 lieder for voice and piano (piano/flute, piano/clarinet, string quartet); Sonata for piano and violin; Resonances mioritiques for violin and piano; 31 songs; Others. Recordings: Most compositions recorded; Metamorfozele cerului, 8 songs for voice, clarinet and piano on poems by Giuseppe Ungaretti; Terra Mater; Iarba; Andantino notturno for piano. Publications: 8 lieder, 1971; 10 pieces for piano, 1978; Sonata for Violin and Piano, 1979; 16 lieder for voice and piano, 1987. Contributions to: Romania Literara; Contemporanul Revista Muzica. Honours: Prize of the Romanian Composers Union, 1969; Medal, 50 years from liberation of Romania, 1974. Memberships: Romanian Composers Union; SACEM, Paris. Hobbies: Poetry; Chess. Address: Str Delea Veche nr 45, Sector 2, 73119 Bucharest, Romania.

COMENCINI Maurizio, b. 1958, Italy. Singer (Tenor). Education: Studied at the Verona Conservatory and the Scala Opera Milan. Career: After winning prizes at the Toti dal Monte and Maria Callas Competitions has sung widely in Italy, notably as Fenton in Falstaff at Parma (1986), in Monteverdi's Ulisse (Florence, 1987) and as Belfiore in Mozart's Finta Giardiniera (Alessandria, 1991); Further engagements at Palermo in Auber's Fra Diavolo, at Genoa in 1992 as Neocles in Rossini's Siège de Corinthe and at Lucca as Donizetti's Nemorino; Many radio and other concert engagements. Address: c/o Teatro Comunale, Via I Frugoni 15/6, 16121 Genoa, Italy.

COMES Liviu, b. 13 Dec 1918, Serel-Transylvania, Romania. Composer; Musicologist; Professor. m. (1) Valeria, 13 May 1943, 1 s, 1 d, (2) Alice, 22 Jun 1992. Education: Cluj-Napoca Academy of Music, 1946-50; Graduate in Composition, 1950. Career: Professor, Harmony, Counterpoint and Musical Forms, 1950-69, Pro-Rector, 1963-65, Rector, 1965-69, Cluj-Napoca Music Academy; Professor, Counterpoint, 1969-81, Pro-Rector, 1971-74, Bucharest Music Academy. Compositions: Sonatas for Piano, 1951; For Violin and Piano, 1954; For Clarinet and Piano, 1967; Wind Quintet, 1964; Wind Trio, 1981; A Song in Stone, oratorio, 1978; Salba for Orchestra, 1969; Maguri for Orchestra, 1986; Transylvanian Offer, cantata, 1987; Vocal and Choral music; String Quartet, 1989; Byzantine Mass, 1990. Publications: The Melody of Palestrina, 1971, Italian translation, 1975; Treatise on Counterpoint, 1986; The World of Polyphony, 1984. Contributions to: Articles and papers to Romanian Press. Honours: Order of Labour, 1965; Order of Cultural Merit, 1969; Prize of the Romanian Academy, 1974. Address: Str Spatarului No 42, 70241 Bucharest, Romania.

COMISSIONA Sergiu, b. 16 June 1928, Bucharest, Romania. Conductor. m. Robinne Comissiona, 16 July 1949. Education: Studied violin, piano, horn; Voice and conducting with Silverstri and Lindenberg, Bucharest Conservatory. Debut: Conducted Gounod's Faust, Sibiu, 1945. Career: Violinist, Bucharest Radio Quartet, 1946-47; Violinist, 1947-48, Assistant Conductor, 1948-50, Music Director, 1950-55, Romanian State Ensemble; Principal Conductor, Romanian State Opera, 1955-59; Music Director, Haifa Symphony, 1960-66; Founder, Music Director, Ramat Gan Chamber Orchestra, 1960-67; Music Director, Göteborg Symphony, 1966-77; Music Advisor, Northern Ireland Orchestra, Belfast, 1967-68; Music Director, Baltimore Symphony, 1969-84; Chautauqua (NY) Festival Orchestra, 1976-80; Music Advisor, Temple University Festival, 1977-80; American Symphony Orchestra, New York, 1977-82; Artistic Director, 1980-83; Music Director-Designate, 1983-84, Music Director, 1984-88, Houston Symphony, Chief Conductor, Radio Philharmonic Orchestra, Hilversum, 1982-; Music Director, New York City Opera, 1987-88; Chief Conductor, Helsinki Philharmonic, Music Director, Vancouver Symphony, Chief Conductor, Orquesta Sinfonica, RTVE, Madrid, 1990; Guest conductor, orchestras and opera companies throughout world. Recordings include: Roussel's Sinfonietta and Stravinsky's Apollon Musagète; Chopin's 2nd Piano Concerto, Nights in the Gardens of Spain (Alicia de Larrocha); Britten's Les Illuminations and Diversions; Mendelssohn's 3rd Symphony; Liszt's Works for Piano and Orchestra (Jerome Lowenthal); Rachmaninoff's Symphonic Dances. Hobbies: Mime; Films. Address: c/o Vancouver Symphony, 601 Smithe Street, Vancouver, British Columbia V6B 5G1, Canada.

COMMAND Michele, b. 27 November 1946, Caumont, France. Singer (Soprano). Education: Studied at the Conservatories of Grenoble and Paris. Debut: Lyons 1967, as Musetta in La Bohème. Career: Toulouse 1968, as Fiordiligi; Sang in Paris, at the Opera and the Opéra-Comique, as Mozart's Donna Elvira and Fiordiligi, Gounod's Mireille, Mélisande and Portia in the premiere of Reynaldo Hahn's Le Marchand de Venise; Paris Palais des Sports 1989, as Micaela in Carmen; Sang Gounod's Sapho at Saint-Etienne, 1992. Recordings: include, Pelléas et Mélisande; Ariane et Barbe-Bleue and Fauré's Pénélope; Don Quichotte by Massenet; Orphée aux Enfers by Offenbach, Siebel in Faust; Harawi by Messiaen.

COMPARONE Elaine, b. 5 Mar 1943, Lawrence, Massachusetts, USA. Harpsichordist. Education: BA, Brandeis University; Fulbright Fellowship, Academy of Music, Vienna; Private Study since 4 years old with parents Nellie and Frank. Debut: Carnegie Recital Hall, 1970. Career: Solo appearances at Alice Tully Hall, Lincoln Center; Metropolitan Museum of Art; All Major New York Halls; Library of Congress; Frick Collection; Nationwide Tours for Columbia Artists and Community Concerts; Founder, Director, Trio Bell Arte and The Queen's Chamber Band; Founder, Director, Harpsichord Unlimited. Recordings: Bach With Pluck, vol I and II; Persichetti and Scarlatti; The Bueckeburg Bach; The Entertainer. Honours: Concert Artists Guild Award, 1970; Grants, National Endowment for the Arts, 1983, 1987. Hobbies: Cats and dogs; Walking; Window boxes. Current Management: Harpsichord Unlimited. Address: 215 West 98th Street, Apt 2A, New York City, NY 10025, USA.

CONANT Robert (Scott), b. 6 Jan 1928, Passaic, New Jersey, USA. Harpsichordist. m. Nancy Lydia Jackson, 10 Oct 1959, 1 son, 1 daughter. Education: BA, Yale University, 1949; Juilliard School, 1949-50; MM, Yale School of Music, 1956; Piano with Sascha Gorodnitzki; Harpsichord with Ralph Kirkpatrick. Debuts: Town Hall, New York, 1953; Wigmore Hall, London, England, 1958. Career: Major recital series and ensemble engagements in USA and Europe, 1956-; Chicago, Denver and Philadelphia Symphony Orchestras; Founded annual Festival of Baroque Music, now held in Saratoga Springs and Greenfield Center, New York, 1959-; Assistant Professor, Yale School of Music, 1961-66; Associate Professor, Professor, 1967-86, Professor Emeritus, 1986-, Chicago Musical College, Roosevelt University; Currently Harpsichordist with: Viola da Gamba Trio of Basel; The Robert Conant Baroque Trio, with Terry King on baroque cello and Kenneth Goldsmith on baroque violin, 1986-; Nova/Antiqua, with James Ketterer, percussion, and Brian Cassier on double bass, 1986-. Recordings: Solo on old harpsichords, Yale Collection of Musical Instruments, volume 1; Solo CD: Robert Conant, Harpsichord, Foundation for Baroque Music; Ensemble performances on several labels. Publication: Twentieth Century Harpsichord Music: A Classified Catalog (with Frances Bedford), 1974. Contributions to: The Consort; Journal of the American Musicological Society; The Music Journal. Honours: Lifetime Achievement Award, Saratoga County Arts Council, New York, 1992. Memberships: College Music Society, Treasurer 1971-76; American Musical Instrument Society; American Musicological Society. Hobby: Photography. Address: 163 Wilton Road, Greenfield Center, NY 12833, USA.

CONDO Nucci, b. 1948, Trieste, Italy. Singer (Mezzo-soprano). Education: Studied in Rome. Career: Sang in Vivaldi's Juditha Triumphans at the Elizabeth Hall, London, 1972; New York Kennedy Center, 1972; Glyndebourne Festival, 1972-79, in Le nozze di Figaro, Falstaff, Il Ritorno d'Ulisse and Der Rosenkavalier; Cologne, 1984, as Lucia in La Gazza Ladra; La Scala, 1985, in a revival of Rossi's Orfeo; Guest appearances with Netherlands Opera and at the Prague and Dubrovnik Festivals; Sang as Ida in Gemma di Vergy at the Teatro Donizetti, Bergamo, 1987; Sang Mozart's Marcellina at the Teatro La Fenice, Venice, 1991; Concert tours of Yugoslavia, Austria and the USA. Recordings include: La Gazza Ladra; Rossini's Otello; Il Ritorno d'Ulisse; Mefistofele by Boito; Video of Le nozze di Figaro, Glyndebourne, 1973. Address: c/o Teatro alla Scala, Via Filodrammatici 2, 20121 Milan, Italy.

CONE Edward T(oner), b. 4 May 1917, Greensboro, NC, USA. Composer; Pianist; University Professor; Writer. Education: AB 1939, MFA 1942, Princeton University. Career: Assistant Professor, 1947-52, Associate Professor, 1952-60, Professor, 1960-85, Professor Emeritus, 1985-, Princeton University, NJ; A D White Professor at Large, Cornell University, 1979-85. Compositions: Excursions for Unaccompanied Chorus, 1955; Silent Noon for Soprano, 1964; Numerous unpublished works. Publications: Musical Form and Musical Performance, 1968; The Composer's Voice, 1974; Music: A View From Delft, 1989; Editor: Berlioz, Fantastic Symphony, 1971 and Roger Sessions on Music, 1979; Co-editor: Perspectives on Schoenberg and Stravinsky, 1968, Perspectives on American Composers, 1971, Perspectives on Contemporary Music Theory, 1972 and Perspectives on Notation and Performance, 1976; Editor, Perspectives of New Music, 1966-68 and Advisory Editor 1968-72. Contributions to: Perspectives of New Music; Musical Quarterly; 19th Century Music; Musical Times. Honours: Honorary DMus, University of Rochester, 1973; Honorary DFA, University of NC, 1983; Honorary DMus, New England Conservatory of Music, 1984; Deems Taylor - ASCAP Award, 1975 and 1990. Memberships: The Century Association; National Academy of Arts and Sciences; American Philosophical Society. Address: 18 College Road West, Princeton, NJ 08540, USA.

CONLON James (Joseph), b. 18 Mar 1950, New York City, New York, USA. Conductor. Education: High School of Music and Art, New York; BM, Juilliard School, New York, 1972; Studied conducting with Jean Morel. Debut: Formal debut conducting with Boris Godunov, Spoleto Festival, 1971. Career: Conductor, Juilliard School, 1972-75; Youngest conductor to lead a subscription concert, New York Philharmonic Orchestra, 1974; Metropolitan Opera debut, New York, with Die Zauberflöte, 1976; Guest conductor with major orchestras and opera companies in USA and Europe, including Chicago, Boston, Philadelphia, Cleveland, Pittsburgh and National Symphony Orchestras; Music Director, Cincinnati May Festival, 1979-; Chief Conductor, Rotterdam Philharmonic Orchestra, 1983-91; Principal Conductor, Cologne Opera, 1989-; General Music Director of the City of Cologne, 1991-; Principal Conductor, Opera National de Paris, 1996-; London, Covent Garden debut with Don Carlo, 1979; Opéra de Paris debut with Il Tabarro and Pagliacci in 1982, Maggio Musicale Florentino debut with Don Carlo, 1985, Chicago Lyric Opera debut in 1988 with La Forza del Destino, Milan La Scala debut with Oberon in 1993; General Music Director, City of Cologne; Led Pelléas et Mélisande at the Palais Garnier, Paris, 1997. Recordings: For 2 recording companies. Address: c/o Cologne Opera, Buhnen der Stadt Köln, Offenbachplatz, Postfach 18 02 41, 50505 Cologne, Germany.

CONNELL Elizabeth, b. 22 Oct 1946, Port Elizabeth, South Africa. Singer (Soprano). Education: London Opera Centre with Otakar Kraus; Maggie Teyte Prize, 1972. Debut: Varvara in Katya Kabanova at the 1972 Wexford Festival; Appeared with Australian Opera and sang mezzo roles with English National Opera, 1975-80, notably Verdi's Eboli and Herodias in Salome; Covent Garden debut, 1976, as Viclinda in I Lombardi; Bayreuth debut, 1980, as Ortrud in Lohengrin; Sang Lady Macbeth in Hamburg, Mozart's Vitellia at Covent Garden and Wagner's Kundry and Venus with Netherlands Opera; Soprano roles from 1983; Season 1984-85 as Electra in Idomeneo at Salzburg, Norma in Geneva and Vitellia in a new production of La Clemenza di Tito at the Metropolitan; Season 1985-86, Leonora (Trovatore) and Beethoven's Leonore at Covent Garden; Electra at Glyndebourne, 1985; Appearances at La Scala in Macbeth and I Lombardi; Sang Electra in new production of Idomeneo, Covent Garden, 1989; Lady Macbeth, Bonn, 1990, and Cologne, 1992; Sang Fidelio at Sydney, Odabella in Attila at Geneva, 1992, Senta in Der fliegende Holländer at the Bayreuth Festival; Concert performances of Mendelssohn's 2nd Symphony under Abbado and the Missa Solemnia in Paris; Sang Isolde at the Festival Hall, London, 1993 and at the Coliseum theatre, 1996; Elektra at San francisco, 1997. Recordings: I Due Foscari; Video of Covent Garden production of Luisa Miller. Address: c/o S A Gorlinsky Ltd, 33 Dover Street, London W11 4NJ, England.

CONNELL John, b. 1956, England. Singer (Bass). Education: Studied at Royal Northern College of Music and at National Opera Studio Debut: English National Opera; Roles at Royal Opera, Covent Garden: Titurel in Parsifal, Il Frate in Don Carlos, Sparafucile in Rigoletto (1985) and as Ramphis in Aida. Career: With English National Opera has sung the Commendatore, Colline, the Monk in Don Carlos, Ferrando in Trovatore, Leporello in Stone Guest, Pogner, Basilio, Banquo and Sarastro; Televised appearances in Billy Budd and Lady Macbeth by Shostakovich; Season 1990-91 in new productions of Pelléas et Mélisande and Peter Grimes, as Arkel and Swallow; Sang Banquo in Bolshoi Moscow and Kirov Leningrad, 1990, on tour with English National Opera; Welsh National Opera, Sarastro in The Magic Flute and Silva in Ernani; Opera North in Salome, The Barber of Seville and La Bohème; Other engagements as Hunding in Spain and France; Concert engagements in the Verdi Requiem at The Barbican and as Pimen in Boris Godunov; Windsor Festival, 1987, as Fidelio; Season 1992 as the father Superior in The Force of Destiny and as Sarastro for English National Opera; The Hermit in Der Freischütz, with the New York

Philharmonic and Peter Grimes with the LSO and Rostropovich; Swallow in Peter Grimes at La Monnaie, Brussels and Don Basilio for Garsington Opera, 1994; Dansker in Billy Budd for Royal Opera House, Covent Garden,1995; Don Fernando in Fidelio, ENO, 1996; Season 1997 with Mozart's Bartolo and Wagner's Daland for ENO. Recordings include: Elijah (Philips); Serenade to Music by Vaughan Williams (Hyperion). Current Management: Harold Holt. Address: c/o Harold Holt Ltd, 31 Sinclair Road, London W14 0NS, England.

CONNER Nadine, b. 20 Feb 1913, Compton, CA, USA. Singer, Soprano. Education: Studied with Horatio Cogswell and Amado Fernandez at the University of Southern California; With Florence Easton in NY, USA. Debut: Los Angeles 1940, with the California Opera Company under Albert Coates, as Marguerite in Faust. Career: Metropolitan Opera from 1941, as Mozart's Pamina, Zerlina and Susanna, Verdi's Gilda and Violetta, Marzelline in Fidelio, Mimi, Micaela, Sophie and Rosina; Sang in Europe from 1953, notably in England, France, Belgium and Italy. Recordings: Hansel und Gretel; Soprano solo in the Brahms Requeim, conducted by Bruno Walter.

CONNOLLY Justin (Riveagh), b. 11 Aug 1933, London, England. Composer. Education: Royal College of Music with Peter Racine Fricker and Adrian Boult. Career: Harkness Fellowship, 1963-65, studying with Mel Powell; Taught at Yale University, 1963-66; Professor of Theory and Composition at the Royal College of Music from 1966-89. Compositions include: Sonatina in 5 Studies for Piano; Antiphonies for orchestra; Cinquepaces for brass quintet; Poems of Wallace Stevens I and II for soprano and instruments, 1967, 1970; Anima for violin and orchestra, 1974; Diaphony for organ and orchestra, 1977; Chamber music series with titles Obbligati, Triads and Tesserae, 1966-89; Ceilidh for 4 violins, 1976; Waka for mezzo-soprano and piano, 1981; Sestina A and B for ensemble, 1978; Verse and Prose for a cappella chorus Fourfold, from The Garden of Forking Paths for 2 pianos, 1983; Ennead (Night Thoughts) for piano, 1983; Spelt from Sibyl's Leaves for 6 solo voices and ensemble, 1989; Nocturnal, flutes with piano, percussion, double-bass, 1990; Cantata, soprano and piano, 1991; Symphony, 1991. Honours: Collard Fellowship, The Musicians' Company, 1986. Memberships: Association of Professional Composers; Liveryman, Worshipful Company of Musicians. Address: c/o Novello & Co Ltd, Lower James Street, London W1, England.

CONNOLLY Sarah, b. County Durham, England. Singer (Mezzo-soprano). Education: Studied at the Royal College of Music and with David Mason and Gerald Martin Moore. Career: Concert engagements include Mozart's Requiem under Sir Neville Marriner, Bach's B Minor Mass with Philippe Herreweghe, in Berlin and Honegger's Jeanne d'Arc au Bücher with the Royal Liverpool Philharmonic at the 1997 Prom Concerts, London; Opera debut as Annina in Der Rosenkavalier for Welsh National Opera, 1994; Further roles include the Messenger in Orfeo and the Fox in the Cunning Little Vixen (English National Opera), Messenet's Charlotte for English Touring Opera and the Musician in Manon Lescaut at the Glyndebourne Festival, 1997; Season 1997-98 for ENO as Handel's Xerxes, Meg in Verdi's Falstaff; Further concerts include Bach's St Matthew Passion with the Gabrieli Consort in Spain and with Herreweghe in 1998; The Dream of Gerontius in Sydney and Mark Anthony Turnage's Twice Through the Heart, with Markus Stenz in Rome and London. Recordings include: Bach Cantatas with Philippe Herreweghe; Les Fêtes d'Hebé by Rameau with Les Arts Florissants and Juditha Triumphans, Vivaldi, with the Kings Consort. Honours include: Prizewinner, opera section of the Hertogenbosch Competition, Netherlands, 1994. Address: c/o Lies Askonas Ltd, 6 Henrietta Street, London WC2E 8LA, England.

CONRAD Barbara, b. 11 Aug 1945, Pittsburg, Texas, USA. Singer (Mezzo-soprano). Education: Studied at the University of Texas, Austin. Career: Metropolitan Opera from 1982, as Verdi's Preziosilla and Maddalena, Annina in Der Rosenkavalier and Maria in Porgy and Bess; European engagements at Frankfurt, Vienna, Brussels and Munich; Sang at Greater Miami Opera, 1989; Other roles include Wagner's Fricka and Verdi's Azucena and Eboli. Recordings include: Hamlet (Thomas) and Porgy and Bess.Address: c/o Bess Pruitt and Associates Inc, 819 East 168th Street, Bronx, NY 10459, USA.

CONSOLI Marc-Antonio, b. 19 May 1941, Italy. Composer; Conductor; Editor. Education: BMus, 1966; MMus, 1967; DMA, 1976; Studied with Ernst Krenek, Gunther Schüller, George Crumb. Career: Commissioned by Fromm and Koussevitsky Foundations, the Royan in France, Steirischer Herbst of Austria (Festivals); Works performed at International Festivals including International Society for Contemporary Music in Helsinki, 1978, Belgium, 1981; New York Philharmonic and Los Angeles Philharmonic. Compositions include: Sciuri Novi; Interactions I, II, III, IV, V, 1970-71; Isonic, 1971; Lux Aeterna, 1972; Profile, 1973; Music for Chambers, 1974; Sciuri Novi II, 1974; Canti Trinacriani, 1976; Memorie Pie, 1976; Tre Canzoni, 1976; Odefonia, 1976; Tre Fiori Musicali, 1987; Vuci Siculani, 1979; Naked Masks, 1980; Orpheus Meditation, 1981; The Last Unicorn, 1981; Afterimages, 1982; String Quartet, 1983; Ancient Greek Lyrics, 1985; Musiculi II, 1985-86; Reflections, 1986; The Light Cantata, 1986; Eyes of the Peacock, 1987; Cello Concerto, 1988; Greek Lyrics, 1988; String Quartet II, 1989; Arie Mutate, 1990; Musiculi IV, 1990, 1992; Musiculi III, 1992, 1994; Games for 2, 3 and 4, 1994, 1995; Cinque Canti, 1995; Vanie Azioni Siculi, 1995; Pensieri sospesi, 1997. Honours: Guggenheim Memorial Fellowships, 1971, 1979; Fulbright Scholarship to Poland, 1972-74; National Endowment for the Arts Grants, 1976, 1979; Prize, Competition, Monaco. Memberships: Broadcast Music Association; American Composers' Alliance. Address: 95-27 239th Street, Bellerosse, NY 11426, USA.

CONSTABLE John (Robert), b. 5 Oct 1934, Sunbury-on-Thames, Middlesex, England. Piano Accompanist; Harpsichordist. m. Katharine Ingham, 2 d. Education: Studied with Harold Craxton, Royal Academy of Music, London; Fellow, Royal Academy of Music. Career: Repetiteur, Royal Opera House, Covent Garden, London, 1960-72; Principal Keyboard Player, London Sinfonietta, since its formation; Principal Harpsichordist, Academy of St Martin-in-the-Fields, 1984-; Professor, Royal College of Music, 1985-. Recordings: Many with London Sinfonietta and Academy of St Martin-in-the-Fields, playing harpsichord continuo for operas and as accompanist on recital records. Honour: Fellow, Royal Academy of Music, 1986. Memberships: Incorporated Society of Music; Musicians Union. Hobbies: Travel; Watching Cricket. Address: 13 Denbigh Terrace, London, W11, England.

CONSTANT Franz, b. 17 Nov 1910, Montignies-le-Tilleul, Belgium; Pianist; Teacher; Composer. m. Jeanne Pellaerts. Education: Charleroi Academy of Music; Studied with M Maas, L Jongen, F de Bourguignon and J Absil, Brussels Conservatory; With H Tomasi, Paris. Career: Appearances as Pianist; Due piano recitals with wife, Teacher, Brussels Conservatory, 1947-. Compositions: Orchestral: Rhapsodie for Violin and Orchestra, 1962; Saxophone Concerto, 1965; Sinfonietta for Flute, Oboe, String Orchestra, 1968; Fantasia for Saxophone and Orchestra, 1969; Concertino for Flute and String Orchestra, 1970; Violin Concerto, 1971; Expressions for Violin, Piano, Strings, 1973; Rhapsodie, 1973; Clarinet Concertino, 1975; Ballade du sud for 2 Pianos and Orchestra, 1979; Movement rhapsodique for Double Bass and Orchestra, 1980; Préambule, 1980; Musique for Saxophone Quartet and String Orchestra, 1981; Quattro movimenti sinfonici, 1983; Eventail, 1983; Concerto for Accordion and Wind Orchestra, 1985; Concerto for Brass and Wind Orchestra, 1987; Chamber: Sonatine picturale for Clarinet and Piano, 1980; Couleur provençale for Horn and Piano, 1970; 5 Miniatures for Violin, Flute, Piano, 1971; Piano Quartet, 1971; Divertissement for Bassoon and Piano, 1972; Musique à deux for Flute and Guitar, 1973; Marée for Oboe and Piano, 1973; Musica lyrica for Flute, Violin, Piano or Harpsichord, 1976; Suite en trio for Flute, Violin, Piano, 1977; Rhapsodie d'été for Clarinet Octet and Percussion, 1977; Suite for Violin, Cello, Piano, 1978; Mouvements for Flute, Clarinet, Violin, Piano, 1978; Serenade for Violin and Piano, 1980; Odyssée for Cello and Piano, 1982; Movimento for Trumpet and Piano, 1982; Evasion for Clarinet and Piano, 1983; Ballade for Violin and Piano; Sonate à trois for 2 Violins and Piano, 1983; Triptyque for 2 Pianos and Percussion, 1984; Episodes for Alto Saxophone and Piano, 1985; String Quartet, 1985; Impromptu for Alto Saxophone and Piano, 1987; Piano pieces; Choral works; Songs. Address: c/o Conservatoire Royal de Musique, 30 rue de la Régence, Brussels, Belgium.

CONSTANT Marius, b. 7 Feb 1925, Bucharest, Rumania. Composer; Conductor. 1 son. Education: Bucharest Conservatory of Music; National Conservatory of Music, Paris. Career: Musical Director, French Radio, 1952-; Musical Director, Roland Petit Ballet and Paris Opera Ballet, 1973-78; Conductor, Ars Nova Ensemble; Regular guest conductor of leading orchestras in Europe, Canada, USA and Japan; Teaches composition at Stanford University, USA, and conducting at Hilversum, Netherlands. Compositions: Operas: Le Souper, 1969; Jeu de Sainte Agnés, 1974; La Tragédie de Carmen, (version of Bizet), 1981; Impressions de Pelléas, (version of Debussy), 1992; Sade/Teresa (original), 1996; Oratorio, Des Droits de l'Homme, 1989; Ballets: Cyrano de Bergérac, 1959; Eloge de la Folie, 1966; Paradis Perdu, 1967; Candide, 1970; Septentrion, 1975; Nana, 1976; L'Ange Bleu, 1985; Orchestral: 24 Preludes, 1959; Twilight Zone, signature tune, 1961; Turner; Chants de Maldoror, 1962; Chaconne et Marche Militaire, 1968; Candide for harpsichord and orchestra, 1971; Concerto Gli Elementi for trombone and orchestra, 1977; Symphony for Winds, 1978; Concertante for alto saxophone and orchestra, 1978; Nana-Symphony, 1980; 103 Régards dans l'Eau, 1981; Pelléas et Mélisande-Symphony, 1983; L'Inauguration de la Maison for wind band, 1985; Choruses and Interludes for French Horn and Orchestra, 1990; Hameenlinna: An Imaginary Landscape, for orchestra, 1991. Other works: Winds, 1968; 14 Stations for percussion and 6 instruments, 1970; Traits, Cadavre Exquis, aleatoric, 1971; Chamber music. Recordings: Music by Satie, Xenakis, Debussy, Varèse, Messiaen and Constant. Honours include: 1st Prize for Composition, Paris Conservatory; Officier, Légion d'Honneur; Grand Officier, Ordre du Mérite; Prix Italia, 1952; Member of the Académie de Beaux-Arts, 1993. Address: 16 rue des Fosses St Jacques, 75005 Paris, France.

CONSTANTIN Rudolf, b. 16 Feb 1935, Paris, France. Singer (Baritone). Education: Studied in Paris and Zurich. Career: Sang at Rheydt, 1958-59, Aachen, 1959-60, Berne, 1960-63, Graz, 1963-67, Cologne, 1967-69; Frankfurt am Main, 1969-83; Guest appearances at Dresden, Berlin, Amsterdam, Brussels, Vienna (Volksoper), Paris and Copenhagen; Sang Ruprecht in The Fiery Angel at Zurich, Gunther in Götterdämmerung at Covent Garden and the Villains in Les Contes d'Hoffmann at the Salzburg Festival; Other roles have included Mozart's Don Giovanni, Count and Guglielmo, Verdi's Amonasro, Luna, Germont, Nabucco, Simon Boccanegra, Rigoletto, Macbeth, Posa and Iago; Wagner's Telramund, Dutchman, Wolfram, Amfortas and Wotan (Die Walküre); Strauss's Orestes, Jochanaan, Mandryka and Faninal; Golaud in Pelléas et Mélisande and Mittenhofer in Elegy for Young Lovers by Henze: Further engagements at Geneva, Marseille, Monte Carlo, Prague and Edinburgh; Many concert appearances.

CONSTANTINE Andrew, b. 1964, England. Conductor. Education: Studied in Siena, at the Turin Opera and the St Petersburg Conservatoire. Career: Engagements from 1991 with the London Philharmonic in Prokofiev's 5th Symphony, the Hallé and English Chamber Orchestras, The Royal Philharmonic Orchestra and London Mozart Players; Assistant Conductor of English National Opera's Madama Butterfly and Principal Conductor of the Sinfonia of Birmingham; Further appearances with the St Petersburg and Sofia Philharmonics and the Komische Opera, Berlin. Honour: Winner in 1991 of the Donatella Flick Conducting Competition, London. Address: Hazard Chase, Richmond House, 16-20 Regent Street, Cambridge, CB2 1DB, England.

CONSTANTINESCU Dan, b. 10 June 1931, Bucharest, Rumania. Composer. Education: Composer's Diploma, Bucharest Conservatory of Music. Debut: Jassy Philharmonic, 1957. Career: Lecturer in Harmony and Composition, Bucharest Conservatory. Compositions include: Divertissement for string orchestra; Ballad for orchestra; Chamber Symphony; Symphony Concertante; Concerto for piano and string orchestra; Concerto for 2 pianos and small orchestra; 4 Sonatas for 2 instruments; Trio for violin, clarinet, piano and percussion; 5 Quartets; Symphony for string orchestra; Symphony for wind instruments; Concerto for harpsichord, harp and wind instruments; String sextet; Symphony for 32 voices; 5 cycles of piano music. Recordings: Piano part, various works. Honours: Georges Enescu Prize, Rumanian Academy, 1968. Membership: Rumanian Composers' Union. Address: Strada Corneliu Botez 3, Bucharest 9, Rumania.

CONSTANTINESCU Mihai, b. 22 Aug 1926, Chisinau, Russia. Violinist; Professor. m. Corina Bura, 17 Apr 1981, 1 daughter. Education: Bachelorship of the Matel Basarab High School; Diploma, Conservatoire of Music, Bucharest. Debuts: Radio Bucharest, 1941; Recital, Dalles Hall, Bucharest, 1943. Career: Soloist, George Enescu Philharmonic, Bucharest; Radio and television appearances; Tours in Russia, Czechoslovakia, Korea, China, Germany, Vietnam, Poland, Bulgaria, France, Belgium, Luxembourg, Hungary, Yugoslavia, Italy, Cuba, Spain, Venezuela, Chile, Argentina, Ecuador and elsewhere; Professor, Conservatoire of Music, Bucharest. Compositions: Cadenzas for Mozart's Third Concerto for violin and orchestra and Haydn's First Concerto for violin and orchestra. Recordings: Works by Mozart, Beethoven, Pergolesi, Handel, Sabin Dragoi, Livui Comes, Wilhelm Berger (Rumanian music); 2 Handel recordings, and Rameau, 1986. Address: Str Ecaterina Teodoriou 17, 78108 Bucharest 1, Rumania.

CONTE David, b. 20 Dec 1955, Denver, Colorado, USA. Composer; Teacher. Education: BM, Bowling Green State University, Ohio; MFA, DMA, Cornell University; Private study with Nadia Boulanger, 2 years. Career: Faculties, Cornell University, Colgate University, Interlochen Centre for the Arts, San Francisco Conservatory of Music. Compositions: Invocation and Dance for male chorus and orchestra; Requiem Triptych (im memoriam Nadia Boulanger) for male chorus and orchestra; Piano Fantasy; The Masque of the Red Death; Ballet for orchestra; Of a Summer's Evening, guitar duo; The Dreamers; 2 act Chamber Opera; Pastorale and Toccata for organ; Piano Quintet; In Praise of Music, SATB and orchestra; Ave Maria; The Gift of the Magi, one-act chamber opera; Songs of Consolation, soprano and organ. Honours: Fulbright Scholarship, 1976; Meet the Composer Grant, 1983, 1986, 1987; Ralph Vaughan Williams Fellowship. Memberships: American Society of Composers and Publishers. Current Management: E C Schirmer Music Co, 138 Ipswich Street, Boston, MA 02215, USA. Address: San Francisco Conservatory of Music, 1201 Ortega Street, San Francisco, CA 94122, USA.

CONTI Nicoletta, b. 12 July 1957, Bologna, Italy. Orchestral Conductor; Teacher. Education: Bologna Conservatory of Music; Milan Conservatory. Debut: Liszt Academy, Budapest, 1984. Career: Aspen Music Festival, 1984; Tanglewood Music Center, 1985; Appearances with Orchestra Sinfonica di Bari, Orchestra Regionale Toscana, Orchestra Simphonia Perusina, Orchestra Sinfonica Abrudiese, Orchestra Pro Musica Riminia, Danish Radio Orchestra. Honours: Concorso da Camera Stresa, 1981; Malko Competition for Young Conductors, 1986. Membership: American Symphony Orchestra League. Hobbies: Skiing; Tennis. Address: Via Palestro 7, 40123 Bologna, Italy.

CONTI Paolo, b. 1957, Perugia, Italy. Singer (Baritone). Education: Studied in Perugia and with Rodolfo Celletti. Debut: Teatro Lirico Milan, 1984, as Seid in Verdi's Il Corsaro. Career: Guest appearances at Genoa, the Festival of Martina Franca and Bologna, as Henry, Lucia di Lammermoor, Verdi's Germont, Posa, Ford and Renato and Riccardo in I Puritani; Metropolitan Opera and Valle d'Istria, 1988, as Belcore and as Chevreuse in Donizetti's Maria di Rohan; Further engagements at Cologne, Vienna, London, Covent Garden, Geneva, Florence (Riccardo), and Milan (Paolo in Simon Boccanegra); Season 1990-91 as Germont at San Francisco and Naples, Macbeth at Jesi, Posa in Turin, Onegin and Renato at Bologna and the Massenet Lescaut at Parma; Valle d'Istria in Ernani and a Meyerbeer Concert. Recordings: Manon Lescaut and Simon Boccanegra; Maria di Rohan and Alina, Regina di Golconda by Donizetti. Address: c/o Teatro Comunale di Bologn, Largo Respighi 1, 40126 Bologna, Italy.

CONTIGUGLIA John and Richard (twins), b. 13 Apr 1937, Auburn, New York, USA. Pianist. Education: Received advice from Percy Grainger; Studied with Jean Wilder and Bruce Simonds, Yale University; Dame Myra Hess, London. Debut: Duo recital at age 6. Career: Professional debut, London, 1962; Performed throughout the world as a virtuoso duo; Repertoire includes works from the past to contemporary scores; Special emphasis on the piano transcriptions of Liszt; Premiere of Liszt's Grosses Konzertstück über Mendelssohn's Lieder ohne Worte, Utrecht, 1986. Recordings: Several. Honours: Ditson Fellowship. Address: c/o ICM Artists Ltd, 40 West 57th Street, New York City, NY 10019, USA.

CONVERY Robert, b. 4 Oct 1954, Wichita, Kansas, USA. Composer. Education: Studied at Westminster Choir College, Curtis Institute and Juilliard, New York; David Diamond, Vincent Persichetti and Ned Rorem were among his teachers. Career: Resident Composer with Phillips Exeter Academy, 1988, 1991, Dickinson College, 1989-90, and the New York Concert Singers, 1991-93. Compositions: The Lady of Larkspur, opera in 1 act after Tennessee Williams, 1980; Pyramus and Thisbe, 2 scenes after Shakespeare, 1983; The Blanket, opera in 1 act, produced at Spoleto Festival, Charleston, 1988. Honours: Charles Miller-Alfredo Casella Award; Charles E Ives Award for The Blanket. Address: c/o ASCAP, ASCAP Building, One Lincoln Plaza, New York, NY 10023, USA.

CONWELL Julia, b. 1954, Philadelphia, Pennsylvania, USA. Singer (Soprano). m. Giancarlo del Monaco. Education: Studied at Curtis Institute of Music and with Margaret Harshaw. Career: Sang in various US opera houses, notably as Musetta in La Bohème for Michigan Opera; European debut with Munich Staatsoper as Musetta; Further appearances as Nedda in Pagliacci, Liu in Turandot, Dusseldorf, 1982, and Oscar in Ballo in Maschera, Frankfurt, 1984; Sang Charpentier's Louise at Nice and Zerlina at Rome, 1984; Other roles have included Paolina in Poliuto by Donizetti, Rome, 1986; Gilda and Salome at Augsburg, 1988, and Diana in Iphigénie en Tauride, Deutsche Oper Berlin; Member of the Stuttgart Staatsoper from 1985. Recordings: Sandrina in La Finta Giardiniera; Euridice in Orfeo by Gluck; Works by Henze. Address: c/o Stuttgart Staatstheater, Oberer Schlossgarten 6, 7000 Stuttgart, Germany.

CONYNGHAM Barry (Ernest), b. 27 Aug 1944, Sydney, New South Wales, Australia. Composer; Reader in Music. Education: MA, University of Sydney; Postdoctoral Studies Certificate, University of California, San Diego; DMus, University of Melbourne; Professor (Creative Arts) University of Wollongong. Career: Part-time Lecturer, Tutor, University of New South Wales and National Institute of Dramatic Art, 1968-70; Senior Tutor, University of Western Australia, 1971; Postdoctoral post, University of California, San Diego, 1972-73; Visiting Fellow, Princeton University, 1973-74; Composer and Researcher in residence, University of Aix-Marseille, 1974-75; Lecturer, 1975-79, Senior Lecturer, 1979-84, Reader, 1984-, University of Melbourne; Visiting Scholar, University of Minnesota, Visiting Fellow, Pennsylvania State University, 1982. Compositions: Crisis: Thoughts in a City, 1968; The Little Sherriff, 1969; Five Windows, 1969; Three, 1969; Five, 1970; Water..Footsteps..Time, 1970; Ice Carving, 1970; Edward John Eyre, 1971-73; Six, 1971; Playback, 1972; Without Gesture, 1973; From Voss, 1973; Snowflake, 1973; Ned, 1974-77; Mirror Images, 1975; Sky, 1977; Apology of Bony Anderson, 1978; Mirages, 1978; Bony Anderson,

1978; Concerto for Double Bass, 1979; Basho, 1980; Journeys, 1980; Viola, 1981; Imaginary Letters, 1981; Horizons: Concerto for Orchestra; Southern Cross: Concerto for Violin and Piano, 1991; Dwellings, 1982; Fly, 1982-84; Voicings, 1983; Cello Concerto, 1984; Preview, 1984; Antipodes, 1984-85; The Oath of Bad Brown Bill, 1985; Generations, 1985; Recurrences, 1986; Diamentina Ghosts, 1986; Vast I The Sea, II The Coast, III The Centre, IV The Cities, 1987; Glimpses, 1987; Bennelong, 1988; Matilda, 1988; Streams, 1988; Monuments: Piano Concerto, 1989; Waterways: Viola Concerto, 1990; Cloudlines: Harp Concerto, 1990; Decades for orchestra, 1993; Alterimages for koto and orchestra, 1994. Recordings: Many. Honours: 4 Fellowships: Churchill, 1970, Harkness, 1972-74, Australia Council, 1975, Fulbright Senior, 1982. Membership: Board, Playbox Theatre Company. Address: University of Wollongong, Wollongong, New South Wales, Australia.

COOK Billie, b. 14 Mar 1924, Mount Pleasant, Texas, USA. Musician; Violinist; Teacher. m. Chester E Cook, 8 Sept 1945, 1 son, 2 daughters. Education: Studied Violin, Southern Methodist University, Dallas; BS, English Literature, 1945; Studies, New York City National Orchestral Association, 1948-49; MFA, Comparative Arts, 1974; Graduate, Humanities, University of Texas, Dallas, 1978-85. Career: Orchestral Musician, Fort Worth Symphony and Opera Orchestra, 1958-72; Teacher, Violin, Humanities, Chamber Music, Community Colleges of Dallas County, 1980-98; Numerous Performances with Professional Orchestras. Honour: MFA, summa cum laude, 1974. Memberships: AFM Musicians Union; Board Member, Dallas Chamber Music Society; Dallas Wagner Society; Dallas Symphony Orchestra Guild; Dallas Opera Guild. Address: 4048 Lovers Lane, Dallas, TX 75225, USA.

COOK Brian (Robert) Rayner, b. 17 May 1945, London, England. Singer (Baritone). m. Angela Mary Romney, 24 Aug 1974, 1 son, 1 daughter. Education: BA, Music, University of Bristol, 1966; Postgraduate Studies, Royal College of Music, London; ARCM, Honours, Singing Performance; Studied privately with Alexander Young (vocal studies) and Helga Mott (repertoire). Debuts: Major conducting debut, opera, 1966; Professional solo singing debut, 1967. Career: Church Organist and Choir Master at age of 15; First concert at major London venue, Royal Albert Hall, conducted by John Barbirolli, 1969; Appearances as Solo Singer, oratorio, recitals and opera throughout the United Kingdom, Western and Eastern Europe, USA, Canada, South America, Middle East, Far East, North Africa; Frequent broadcasts British and European radio and television; Many first performances and broadcasts particularly works created for him by various distinguished composers; Visiting Tutor in Vocal Studies, Birmingham Conservatoire, England, 1980-, and formerly Welsh College of Music and Drama, Cardiff; Has directed a number of Singers' Workshops, taught at summer schools, served on juries of international singing competitions and given specialist adjudications. Recordings include: Opera and oratorio from Schütz, Charpentier, Adam, Fauré, Dvorak, Nielsen and Orff to Parry, Elgar, Delius, Vaughan Williams, Ferguson and Walton; Song recitals including Vaughan Williams, Butterworth, Elgar, Poston, Coates, Cruft, Holst, Rubbra, Williamson, Havergal Brian, Camilleri. Contributions to: Royal College of Music Magazine. Hobbies: Colour photography; 78rpm recordings; Laurel and Hardy films; Messing about in boats. Address: The Quavers, 53 Friars Avenue, Friern Barnet, London N20 0XG, England.

COOK Deborah, b. 6 July 1948, Philadelphia, Pennsylvania, USA. Opera and Concert Singer (Soprano); Cantor. m. Ronald Marlowe, 30 Aug 1985, 1 son. Education: Private study with Irene Williams. Debut: Operatic-Glyndebourne and Covent Garden; Glyndebourne Touring Opera, 1971, as Zerbinetta. Career: 3 years principal soprano in Bremen, 2 years Munich National Theatre; Sang in Sydney, Melbourne, Barcelona, Edinburgh, Geneva, Rome, Paris, Los Angeles, San Francisco, Leipzig, East Berlin; Appeared at Covent Garden Opera House, Hamburg State Opera, Deutsche Oper Berlin, Frankfurt Opera, Stuttgart Opera, Deutsche Oper am Rhein; Roles include Verdi's Gilda, Strauss's Zerbinetta, Donizetti's Lucia and Mozart's Queen of Night and Constanze; Created role of Rachel in Henze's We Come to the River, Covent Garden, 1976, and Angel of Bright Future in Rochberg's The Confidence Man; Sang Lucia di Lammermoor at the Buxton Festival, 1979. Recordings: Dinorah; Ariadne auf Naxos; L'Etoile du Nord. Hobby: Baking. Address: c/o Opera Rara, 25 Compton Terrace, London N1 2UN, England.

COOK Donald (Frederick), b. 22 May 1937, St John's, Newfoundland, Canada. University Professor. m. Clara June Penney, 27 Dec 1961, 1 son, 2 daughters. Education: BMus, Mount Alison University, Canada, 1957; Associate Diploma, Organ, Royal College of Music, London, England, 1958; Associate Diploma, American Guild of Organists, 1964; Master of Sacred Music, Union Theological Seminary, New York City, 1965; Choirmaster's Diploma, American Guild of Organists, 1965; PhD, Musicology, King's College, University of London, England, 1983. Career: Organ recitalist and Choral Director; Joined Faculty of Memorial University of Newfoundland, 1968; Head of Music

Department, 1975 and to Full Professor, 1983, Director of School of Music, 1985-90; Serves concurrently as Organist and Choirmaster, Newfoundland Cathedral in St John's; Left memorial University and Newfoundland Cathedral in 1992; Principal, Western Ontario Conservatory of Music, London, Ontario, 1992-. Compositions: Puer natus (SATB choral), 1970; Numerous arrangements for choir of Newfoundland folksongs, 1977-, all of which have been recorded; Two Miniatures of Sea and Land, 1988. Honours: Order of Canada, 1993; Donald F Cook Recital Hall, named at Memorial University, 1993. Hobby: Sailing. Address: Western Ontario Conservatory of Music, 645 Windermere Road, London, Ontario N5X 2P1, Canada.

COOK Jeff (Holland), b. 21 Aug 1940, Chicago, Illinois, USA. Music Director; Conductor; Composer. m. Kate Young, 12 May 1974, 1 daughter. Education: BM, Northwestern University, 1962; MA, Ohio State University, 1964; MM, New England Conservatory of Music, 1966; Studied with Pierre Boulez, John Barbirolli, Jean Fournet, Bruno Maderna, Herbert von Karajan, Erich Leinsdorf, Karlheinz Stockhausen, György Ligeti. Career: Music Director, Conductor, Wheeling Symphony Orchestra, 1973-85; Music Director, Conductor, Mansfield Symphony Orchestra, Ohio, 1976-; Associate Conductor, Pittsburgh Ballet Theatre, 1987-91; Conductor, Louisville Ballet, Kentucky, 1990-; Guest Conductor: Anchorage Symphony, Eastern Music Festival, Rhode Island Philharmonic, North Carolina Symphony, Orquesta Sinfonica Nacional (Santo Domingo), Ballet of Ljubljana (Slovenia); North Bay Music Festival (Ontario). Composition: Euripides Electra, 1972; Recordings: Broadcasts on West Virginia Public Radio, Ohio Public Radio, Canadian Broadcasting Corporation. Hobby: Travel. Address: RD 4, Box 116, Wheeling, WV 26003, USA.

COOK Terry, b. 9 Feb 1956, Plainville, Texas, USA. Singer (Bass). Education: Studied at Texas University. Career: Sang with the Chicago Lyric Opera from 1980, at Santa Fe (Festival) from 1982, and at the Metropolitan from 1983; Roles have included Dr Grenvil in Traviata, Ferrando, the King in Aida, Oroe in Semiramide and Gershwin's Porgy; Further engagements at Seattle (1985), Théâtre Châtelet, Paris (in Handel's Rinaldo), at the Grand Opéra Paris as Colline in La Bohème and the Opéra Comique as the Speaker in Die Zauberflöte; Other roles include Achillas in Giulio Cesare, Raimondo in Lucia di Lammermoor and the Minister in Fidelio; Many concert appearances. Address: c/o Metropolitan Opera, Lincoln Center, New York, NY 10023, USA.

COOK-MACDONALD Linda, b. 22 Sept 1949, Twin Falls, Idaho, USA. Singer (Soprano). Education: Studied in Cincinnati and Mainz. Debut: Krefeld, 1971, as Fiordiligi. Career: Sang at such German houses as Krefeld, Wuppertal, Essen and Darmstadt; US appearances at Memphis, Cincinnati, Pittsburgh and Portland; Sang in New York at City Opera; Roles have included Mozart's Constanze, Pamina, Queen of Night and Zerlina, Agathe, Alice Ford, Marguerite, Musetta and Zdenka; Modern repertory has included Thalmar in Leben des Orest by Krenek and Philippe in Penderecki's The Devils of Loudun; Many concert appearances.

COOKE Arnold (Atkinson), b. 4 Nov 1906, Gomersal, Yorkshire, England. Music Professor; Composer. Education: BA (Cantab), 1928; BMus (Cantab), 1929; DMus, 1948; Staatliche Akademische Hochschule für Musik, Berlin, Germany, 1929-32; Pupil of Paul Hindemith. Career: Professor, Harmony, Counterpoint and Composition, Royal Manchester College of Music, 1933-38; Professor, Harmony, Counterpoint and Composition, Trinity College of Music, London, 1947-78. Compositions: Various chamber works; Choral works; Songs and song cycles; Concertos; Orchestral works including Symphonies Nos 1-6; Operas: Mary Barton; The Invisible Duke; Jabez and the Devil, ballet. Recordings include: Symphony No 3 and Suite from Jabez and the Devil; Song Cycle, The Seamew, Suite in C for Piano; Quartet for Oboe and String Trio; Concerto for Clarinet and String Orchestra. Contributor to: Music Survey. Honours: 3rd Prize for Overture, Daily Telegraph, 1934. Memberships: Composers' Guild of Great Britain, Chairman 1953; Incorporated Society of Musicians; Performing Rights Society; MCPS; Governor, Dolmetsch Foundation; President, Tonbridge Music Club. Hobbies: Walking; Gardening. Address: c/o Mrs J Earnshaw, 94 Totley Brook Road, Sheffield, S17 3QT, England.

COOKE Mervyn (John), b. 29 Aug 1963, Dover, Kent, England. Composer; Musicologist. Education: BA, Honours, 1st Class, 1984, MPhil, 1985, MA, 1987, PhD, 1989. Junior Exhibitioner, Royal Academy of Music; King's College, Cambridge. Career: Research Fellow, Fitzwilliam College, Cambridge, 1987-93; Lecturer in Music, University of Nottingham, 1993. Compositions: Symphonic Poem Messalina, Broadcast, BBC Concert Orchestra, Radio 3, 1980; Horn Sonata, Broadcast, BBC Radio 3, 1986; Compositions performed at Purcell Room, 1979, Festival Hall, 1980, Queen Elizabeth Hall, 1986; Cambridge Greek Plays, incidental scores, 1983 and 1989. Publications: Britten and the Gamelan, in D J Mitchell, Death in Venice, 1987; Britten: Billy Budd, 1993; Britten: Letters, 1946-56, Co-editor

Donald Mitchell, 1994. Contributions to: Musical Times; Journal of Musicological Research; Journal of Royal Musical Association; Music and Letters. Address: Department of Music, University of Nottingham, NG7 2RD, England.

COOKE Richard, b. 1958, England. Conductor. Education: Chorister at St Paul's Cathedral; Choral scholar at King's College, Cambridge, under David Willcocks. Career: Conducted various University orchestras; Led the chamber ensemble in the War Requiem at the Festival Hall, 1984; Trained the London Philharmonic Choir in Mahler 8 and for The Kingdom by Elgar; Has conducted concerts at the Albert and Festival Halls and throughout South East England; Gothenburg Symphony Orchestra from 1989 in Belshazzar's Feast, the Glagolitic Mass, Dvorák 6 and the Sea Symphony by Vaughan Williams; Has also conducted the Brahms Requiem, A Child of our Time, Monteverdi's Vespers and St Nicolas in Sweden; Verdi Requiem at the Uppsala International Festival (1990) and in Boulogne and Canterbury; Conductor of the Chalmers Music Weeks in Sweden and Artistic Director of the St Columb Festival in Cornwall. Recordings include: Mahler 8th Symphony and The Kingdom, with the London Philharmonic Choir. Address:

COOP Jane (Austin), b. 18 April 1950, Saint John, New Brunswick, Canada. Concert Pianist. m. George Laverock, 22 February 1984, 1 daughter. Education: Artist Diploma, 1971, MusBac (Performance), 1972, University of Toronto; MM, Peabody Conservatory, Baltimore, 1974. Debut: St Lawrence Centre, Toronto, Canada; Wigmore Hall, London, England; Carnegie Recital Hall, New York, USA. Career: Soloist with all major Canadian Orchestras; Recitals and Concerts in Canada, USA, England, France, Poland, Holland, Yugoslavia, Hungary, Czechoslovakia, Russia; Major Tours of Hong Kong, China, Japan. Recordings: The Romantic Piano; Beethoven - Eroica variations and Sonatas Op 109 and Op 111; Bach, English Suite No 3 and Partita No 5; Haydn, 4 Sonatas; Mozart, The Piano Quartets, with members of the Orford Quartet; Piano Pieces; Piano Variations (Schumann, Schubert, Brahms); Piano Concerti, (Bartók and Prokofiev). Honours: 1st Prize, Washington International Piano Competition, 1975; Finalist, Munich International Competition, 1977; Killam Award for Career Excellence, 1989. Current Management: Joyce Maguire Arts Management, 3526 West 5th Avenue, Vancouver, British Colombia, Canada.

COOPER Anna, b. 1965, England. Singer (Mezzo-soprano). Education: Studied at the Royal Academy of Music, and at La Fenice, Venice. Career: Many appearances with leading British opera companies, including Glyndebourne, English National Opera and English Opera Group; Roles have included parts in Albert Herring, Die Walküre, Die Zauberflöte, L'Italiana in Algeri and Dido and Aeneas; Appearances with the Royal Opera, Covent Garden, as Flora, Lola, the Madrigal Singer (Manon Lescaut), Kate Pinkerton, Grimgerde, Countess Ceprano (Rigoletto) and Annina; Glasa in Katya Kabanova, 1997; Further engagements in Brussels, Saarbrucken, Milan, Athens, Korea, Strasbourg, Japan and the USA. Honours include: Winner, Kathleen Ferrier Award; Scholarship to La Fenice, Venice. Address: c/o English National Opera, St Martin's Lane, London WC2, England.

COOPER Barry (Anthony Raymond), b. 2 May 1949, Westcliff-on-Sea, Essex, England. University Lecturer. m. Susan Catherine Baynes, 7 July 1973, 4 children. Education: Gordonstoun School, 1962-66; University College, Oxford, 1966-73; MA, DPhil, FRCO, FRSA, Organ Studies with John Webster, Composition with Kenneth Leighton. Career: Lecturer in Music, St Andrews University, 1973; Research Officer, 1974, Lecturer in Music, 1978, Senior Lecturer in Music, 1989, University of Aberdeen; Senior Lecturer in Music, University of Manchester, 1990. Compositions: Oratorio, The Ascension; Song-Cycle, The Unasked Question; Wind Band, Mons Graupius; Choral, Organ and Chamber Music. Publications include: G B Sammartini, Concerto in G (editor OUP) 1976; J C Schickhardt, Sonata in D (Ed OUP) 1978; Catalogue of Early Printed Music in Aberdeen Libraries, 1978; Englische Musiktheorie im 17 und 18 Jahrhundert (in Geschichte der Musiktheorie, Band 9, 1986); Beethoven's Symphony No 10, First Movement (Realisation and Completion), Universal Edition, 1988; English Solo Keyboard Music of the Middle and Late Baroque, 1989; Beethoven and the Creative Process, 1990; L v Beethoven, Three Bagatelles (Ed Novello), 1991; The Beethoven Compendium (Ed), 1991; Beethoven's Folksong Settings, 1994. Contributions to: Musical Times; Music and Letters; Music Review; RMA Research Chronicle; Proceedings of RMA; Recherches sur la Musique Française Classique; Early Music; Acta Musicologica; Beethoven Newsletter; BBC Music Magazine. Honours: Osgood Prize, 1972; Halstead Scholarship, 1972-74; RSE Research Fellow, 1986-87. Memberships: Royal Musical Association; Royal College of Organists. Hobbies: Soccer; Drama. Address: Department of Music, University of Manchester, Denmark Road, Manchester M15 6HY, England.

COOPER Imogen, b. 28 Aug 1949, London, England. Concert Pianist. m. John Alexander Batten, 18 June 1982. Education: Premier Prix Diploma, Paris Conservatoire, 1967; Master classes, Alfred Brendel, Vienna, 1969, 1970. Career: TV debut, Promenade Concerts, London, 1973; Prom appearances since then; 1st woman pianist (and British artist), South Bank Piano Series, Queen Elizabeth Hall, London; Regular broadcasts, all major British orchestras and festivals; Performances in USA, Australia, Japan and most European countries. Recordings: Schubert: Last 6 Years, 1823-28; Mozart: Concerti for 2 and 3 Pianos, with Alfred Brendel and Neville Marriner, Academy of St-Martin-in-the-Fields; Schubert, 3-disc box, 4-hand piano music, with Anne Queffelec. Honours: Mozart Memorial Prize, 1969. Hobbies: Reading; Walking; Tandem cycling with husband; Visiting art galleries; Eating. Current Management: Mebus Artists Management, Nijkerk, Netherlands. Address: Mebus Artists Management, PO Box 355, 3860 AJ Nijkerk, Netherlands.

COOPER Joseph (Elliott Needham), b. 7 October 1912, Westbury on Trym, England. Concert Pianist; Lecturer. m. (1) Jean Greig, 1947 (dec 1973), (2) Carol Borg, 1975. Education: Organ Scholar, Keble College, Oxford University, MA Oxon; ARCM Solo Piano; Study of Piano with Egon Petri. Debut: Wigmore Hall, 1947 (postponed from 1939 due to WWII). Career: Recitals throughout England and performances with leading orchestras; Presenter of Concert Biographies; Tours of Europe, Africa, India, Canada; Regular Contributor to BBC programmes and Chairman, Face the Music, BBCTV. Compositions: Arrangement of Vaughan Williams Piano Concerto for 2 Pianos. Recordings: Standard Piano Repertoire and Hidden Melodies (own compositions of well-known tunes in styles of classical composers). Honours: Ambrose Fleming Award, Royal TV Society, 1961; OBE, 1982. Memberships: Livery, Worshipful Company of Musicians; Garrick Club; Member, Music Panel, Arts Council & Chairman, Piano Sub-Committee, 1966-71. Hobbies: Church Architecture; Walking. Address: Octagon Lodge, Ranmore, Dorking, Surrey RH5 6SX, England.

COOPER Kenneth, b. 31 May 1941, New York City, USA. Harpsichordist; Pianist; Musicologist; Conductor; Educator. m. Josephine Mongiardo, 1 June 1969, 1 son. Education: High School of Music and Art, New York City; BA, 1962, MA, Graduate faculties, 1964, PhD, Graduate Faculties, 1971, Columbia University; Harpsichord Study with Sylvia Marlowe, Mannes College of Music. Debut: Wigmore Hall, 1965; Alice Tully Hall, USA, 1973. Career: Academic Instructor, Barnard College, 1965-71; Adjunct Assistant Professor, Brooklyn College, 1971-73; Professor of Harpsichord, Director of Collegium, Mannes College, 1975-85; Visiting Specialist in Performance Practice, Montclair State College, 1977-92; Artist-in-Residence, Columbia University, 1983-; Graduate seminars in Baroque Performance Practice, Manhattan School of Music, 1984-; Director, Baroque Orchestra, Manhattan School of Music; Graduate Workshops in Performance Practice, Peabody Conservatory of Music, 1987-90; Many residencies and guest appearances and lectures; Performance: Premieres of works by Seymour Barab, Noel Lee, Ferruccio Busoni, Paul Ben-Haim, Ernst Krenek and others; Dozens of modern day revivals; Guest appearances and festivals; Harpsichordist and Pianist, Grand Canyon Chamber Music Festival, 1985-; Director, Berkshire Bach Ensemble, 1991-; Co-Director, Music at Orchard Hill, Brattleboro, Vermont, 1993-; Chairman, Harpsichord Department, Manhattan School of Music, 1984-. Recordings: Numerous including: soundtracks, Van Gogh Revisted; Every Eye Forms Its Own Beauty; Valmont; Louis Cat Orze. Publications include: Three Centuries of Music in Score. Contributions to: Professional journals. Address: 425 Riverside Drive, New York, NY 10025, USA.

COOPER Lawrence, b. 14 Aug 1946, Los Angeles, California, USA. Singer (Baritone). Education: Studied at the San Fernando State College. Career: Sang with the San Francisco Opera from 1977 and at the City Opera New York from 1983; Wexford Festival, 1981, as George in Moore's Of Mice and Men, Houston Opera, 1982, as Wozzeck; Guest engagements in Los Angeles, Chicago (Lyric Opera), Seattle and Detroit; Other roles include Ford in Falstaff, Marcello in La Bohème, Valentin (Faust) and Germont; Frequent concert appearances. Address: c/o New York City Opera, Lincoln Center, New York, NY 10023, USA.

COOPER GAY Rebecca Ann, b. 21 Dec 1943, McKinney, Texas, USA. Musician; Teacher; Singer; Conductor. m. G Errol Gay, 22 Apr 1975, 2 daughters. Education: BA in Music, Organ concentration, Austin College, Texas; MMus in Music Education, Diploma in Opera with distinction, University of Toronto; Piano, Flute and Organ studies during university; Further studies in Strings, Oboe and Conducting. Debut: Toronto Symphony Orchestra, Nov 1983. Career: Assistant Musical Director, Charlottetown Festival, 1967-69; Associate Chorusmaster, 1971-75, Music Director and Conductor, Touring Company, 1974-76, Canadian Opera Company; Guest Conductor, National Arts Centre of Ottawa, Toronto Symphony, Orchestras of Edmonton, Winnipeg, Hamilton, Regina, Saskatoon, Windsor, London, Kitchener-Waterloo and Arlington, Texas; Music Advisor and Conductor, Hart House Orchestra, University of Toronto, 1987-. Honours: Top of Graduating Class in Music Award, 1962; Canada Council Pre-Doctoral Fellowship, 1965. Memberships: Association of Canadian Orchestras; College Music Society; American Federation of Musicians. Hobbies: Trains; Travel. Address: 276 MacPherson Avenue, Toronto, Ontario, Canada M4V 1A3.

COOTE Alice, b. 10 May 1968, Frodsham, Cheshire, England. Singer (Mezzo-soprano). Education: Studied at the Guildhall School of Music and Drama, London and the National Opera Studio. Career: Concerts include Oratorio with London and Liverpool Philharmonic Orchestras, Bergen Philharmonic, London Mozart Players; Honneger's Joan of Arc at the Stake; 1997 BBC Proms; RLPO under Libor Pesek; Mahler's Symphony No 3 under Kent Nagano; Le Martyre de Saint Sebastian and La Damoiselle Elue with Philharmonic Orchestra under Esa Pekka Salonen in London, Brussels, Paris and Vienna; Recitals at Cheltenham Festival, BBC Radio 3 and Schubertiade at the Wigmore Hall; Operatic roles include Cherubino in Figaro, Dorabella in Così fan tutte, Penelope in The Return of Ulysses, Kate Pinkerton in Madam Butterfly and Suzy in La Rondine for Opera North, the Page in Salome, Ruggiero in Alcina for Staatstheater Stuttgart, Glycere in Ancreon ou l'amour fugitif in Stuttgart and Palermo, Fortuna and Valletto in Poppea for Welsh National Opera, Hanna Kennedy in Mary Stuart for Scottish Opera Go Round; Season 1998-99, debut at Opera Bastille in Parsifal; Title role, Rape of Lucretia at Nantes; Tamyris in Il Re Pastore for Opera North. Recordings include: Nancy in Hugh the Drover by Vaughan Williams; Elmira in Rossini's Ricciardo e Zoraide. Honours include: Brigitte Fassbaender Award for Lieder Interpretation; Decca-Kathleen Ferrier Prize, 1992. Address: c/o IMG Artists, Media House, 3 Burlington Lane, London W4 2TH, England.

COPE David (Howell), b. 17 May 1941, San Francisco, California, USA. Composer; Writer; Instrument Maker. Education: Studied at Arizona State University and with Halsey Stevens, Ingolf Dahl and George Perle at the University of Southern California. Career: Teacher at Kansas State College, 1968-69, California Lutheran College, the Cleveland Institute, Miami University of Ohio and the University of California, Santa Cruz, from 1977; Editor of The Composer, 1969-81. Compositions include: Tragic Overture, 1960; 4 Piano Sonatas, 1960-67; 2 String Quartets, 1961, 1963; Variations for piano and wind, 1965; Contrasts for orchestra, 1966; Music for Brass and Strings, 1967; Iceberg Meadow for prepared piano, 1968; Streams for orchestra, 1973; Spirals for tuba and tape, 1973; Requiem for Bosque Redondo, 1974; Arena for cello and tape, 1974; Re-Birth for concert band, 1975; Rituals for cello, 1976; Vectors for 4 percussion, 1976; Tenor Saxophone Concerto, 1976; Threshold and Visions for orchestra, 1977; Glassworks for 2 pianos and tape, 1979; Piano Concerto, 1980; The Way for various instruments, 1981; Corridors of Light for various instruments, 1983; Afterlife for orchestra, 1983. Address: c/o ASCAP, ASCAP Building, One Lincoln Plaza, New York, NY 10023, USA.

COPELAND Robert Marshall, b. 30 Jan 1945, Douglas, Wyoming, USA. Musicologist; Choral Conductor. m. Louise Margaret Edgar, 10 June 1966, 1 son, 2 daughters. Education: BS, Geneva College, 1966; MMus, 1970, PhD, 1974, University of Cincinnati. Appointments: Assistant Professor, Associate Professor, Music, Acting Chairman, Fine Arts, Mid America College, Kansas, 1971-81; Visiting Lecturer, Music History, University of Kansas, 1977; Professor, Music, Chairman, Department of Music, Geneva College, 1981-. Publications: Sing Up: Learning Music For Worship, 1973; The Book of Psalms for Singing, 1973; Spare No Exertions, 1986; Isaac Baker Woodbury, 1995. Contributions to: Musical Quarterly; College Music Symposium; American Music; Notes; Christian Scholars Review. Memberships: American Musicological Society; Sonneck Society for American Music; American Choral Directors Association; Society for Ethnomusicology; American Association of University Professors. Hobbies: Book Collecting; Genealogy. Address: Department of Music, Geneva College, 3200 College Avenue, Beaver Falls, PA 15010-3599, USA.

COPLEY John (Michael Harold), b. 12 June 1933, Birmingham, England. Opera Director; Producer. Education: Sadler's Wells Ballet School; Diploma, honours in Theatre Design, Central School of Arts and Crafts, London. Career: Stage Manager: Opera and ballet companies, Sadler's Wells in Rosebery Avenue, 1953-567, musicals, plays and so on, London West End; Deputy Stage Manager, 1960-63, Assistant Resident Producer, 1963-65, Associate Resident Producer, 1966-72, Resident Producer, 1972-75, Principal Resident Producer, 1975-88, Covent Garden Opera Company, productions including: Suor Angelica, 1965, Così fan tutte, 1968, 1981, Le nozze di Figaro, 1971, Don Giovanni, 1973, Faust, 1974, Benvenuto Cellini, 1976, Ariadne auf Naxos, 1976, Maria Stuarda, Royal Silver Jubilee Gala, 1977, La Traviata, Lucrezia Borgia, 1980, Semele, 1982; Other productions include: Numerous operas, London Coliseum, Athens Festival, Netherlands Opera, Belgian National Opera, Wexford Festival, Dallas Civic Opera (US debut,

1972, Lucia di Lammermoor), Chicago Lyric Opera, Greek National Opera, Australian Opera, English Opera North, Scottish Opera, English Opera Group; Vancouver Opera; Ottawa Festival, San Francisco Opera, Metropolitan Opera (New York), Santa Fe Opera, La Bohème, 1990; Houston Grand Opera, Washington Opera, San Diego Opera, London West End; Dallas production of Hansel and Gretel seen at Los Angeles, 1992; Directed local premiere of Britten's A Midsummer Night's Dream, Houston, 1993; Season 1996 with La Rondine at St Louis and Madama Butterfly at Santa Fe; Appearances include: Apprentice, Britten's Peter Grimes, Covent Garden, 1950; Soloist, Bach's St John Passion, Bremen, Germany, 1965; Co-director with Patrick Garland, Fanfare for Europe Gala, Covent Garden, 1973. Address: 9D Thistle Grove, London SW10 9RR, England.

CORAZZA Remy, b. 16 Apr 1933, Revin, Ardennes, France. Singer (Tenor). Education: Studied at the Toulouse and Paris Conservatories. Debut: Opéra-Comique, Paris, as Beppe in Pagliacci, 1959. Career: Sang Gonzalve in L'Heure Espagnole at the Paris Opéra, 1960; Many performances in Paris and elsewhere in France as Pinkerton, Rodolfo, Hoffman, Nadir and in Mozart roles; Opéra du Rhin, Strasbourg, from 1974, Salzburg from 1978, as Monastatos and the Hoffmann buffo roles; Professor at the Paris Conservatory, 1985; Glyndebourne debut, 1987, as Torquemada in L'Heure Espagnole. Address: c/o Conservatoire National, 14 Rue de Madrid, F-75008 Paris, France.

CORBELLI Alessandro, b. 21 Sept 1952, Turin, Italy. Singer (Baritone). Education: Studied with Giuseppe Valdengo. Debut: Bergamo, 1974, as Marcello in La Bohème. Career: Many appearances in the buffo repertory at opera houses in Italy, Vienna, Paris and Germany; Rossini roles include Pacuvio in La Pietra del Paragone (Picco Scala and Edinburgh, 1982), Dandini in La Cenerentola (Glyndebourne, 1985) and Gaudenzio in Il Signor Bruschino (Paris, 1986); Rome Opera, 1985-86, as Belcore (L'Elisir d'Amore) and Marcello; Covent Garden debut, 1988, as Taddeo in L'Italiana in Algeri; Season 1989-90 in Pergolesi's Lo frate 'nnamorato at La Scala, conducted by Muti, as Don Alfonso at the Salzburg Festival and as Germano in La Scala di Seta at Schwetzingen; Other roles include Papageno (Ravenna, 1986), Guglielmo, Escamillo, Malatesta and the Figaros of Mozart, Rossini and Paisiello; Fabrizio in Crispino e la Comare, Pantaleone in The Love of Three Oranges and Monteverdi's Ottone; Season 1992 as Belcore at Parma, Rossini's Martino and Germano at Cologne, the Paris Opéra-Comique and the Schwetzingen Festival; Sang Leporello at Lausanne, 1996 and Alfonso at Covent Garden, 1997. Recordings include: La Cenerentola, conducted by Abbado; L'Italiana in Algeri; Paisiello's Barbiere di Siviglia and La Buona Figliuola by Piccinni. Address: c/o Teatro alla Scala, Via Filodrammatici 2, I-20212 Milan, Italy.

CORBETT Sidney, b. 26 Apr 1960, Chicago, Illinois, USA. Composer. Education: BA with high distinction in Music Composition, 1982, further studies, 1978-82, University of San Diego, California; Studied composition principally with Pauline Oliveros, Bernard Rands, Joji Yuasa, Jean-Charles François; MM, 1984, MMA, 1985, DMA, 1989, Yale School of Music; Principal composition teachers include Jacob Druckman and Martin Bresnick; Thesis on Metaphor Structures in Contemporary Music; DAAD Fellow and member of G Ligeti Seminar, Hamburg, Germany, 1985-87. Career: Compositions performed in USA and Europe, including radio broadcasts; Active as composer in Germany, 1985-. Compositions: Arien, violin solo, 1983; Pastel Nos 1 and 2, trombone quartet, 1984, 1988; Ghost Reveille for orchestra, 1984; For Pianos, for 4 pianos, 1984; Bass Animation for contrabass with 2 percussions, 1985; Arien IV: Solo Music for Guitar, 1986; Kandinsky Romance for chamber ensemble, 1986; Cactus Flower for solo flute, 1988; Pianos' Dream, piano duo, 1989; Concerto for trombone and wind orchestra, 1989; Lieder aus der Dunkelkammer for soprano, harp and chamber orchestra, 1990; Symphony No 1 Tympan, 1991-92; Hamlet Variations (in memoriam John Coltrane) for solo euphonium, 1992; Gloucester Epiphenies for chamber ensemble, 1993. Hobbies: Reading; Sports. Address: Vogelsangstrasse 55, 7000 Stuttgart 1, Germany.

CORBOZ Michel, b. 14 Feb 1934, Marsens, Switzerland. Conductor. Education: Studied at Ecole Normale in Fribourg. Career: Chorus Master at Notre-Dame in Lausanne from 1954, leading such works as the Fauré Requiem; Accompanied singers at the organ and worked at various Lausanne churches; Founded the Ensemble Vocal et Instrumental de Lausanne, 1961, giving notable performances of Monteverdi's Orfeo; Conductor of the choirs of the Gulbenkian Foundation in Lisbon from 1969, leading works by Bach, Monteverdi and Vivaldi; Conducted Monetverdi's Il Ritorno di Ulisse at Mézières, 1989. Recordings: Monteverdi's Orfeo and Vespers, Bach's B minor Mass, Cavalli's Ercole Amante, Charpentier's David et Jonathas, works by Vivaldi and Giovanni Gabrieli. Address: c/o Erato, WEA Records, PO Box 59, Alperton Lane, Wembley, London HA0 1FJ, England.

CORDERO Roque, b. 16 Aug 1917, Panama. Composer; Conductor; Educator. m. Elizabeth L Johnson, 30 Jun 1947, 3 s. Education: BA, magna cum laude, Hamline University, 1947; Studied composition with Ernst Krenek, 1943-47 and conducting with Dimitri Mitropoulos, 1944-46, Stanley Chapple, 1946 and Leon Barzin, 1947-49. Career: Director and Professor, National Institute of Music, Panama, 1950-64; Conductor, National Orchestra of Panama, 1964-66; Guest Conductor in Colombia, Brazil, Chile, Argentina, Puerto Rico, USA, El Salvador and Guatemala; Professor of Music and Assistant Director, Latin American Music Center, IN University, USA, 1966-69; Professor of Music, IL State University, 1972-. Compositions: Over 20 published including Cinco Mensajes para Cuatro Amigos for Guitar, 1983; Cantata for Peace for Solo Baritone, Choir and Orchestra, 1979; Fourth Symphony, Panamanian, 1986; Serenata, for flute, viola, clarinet and harp, 1987. Recordings: Violin Concerto and 8 Miniatures with Detroit Symphony; 2nd Symphony; Duo, 1954; Dodecaconcerto; Cinco Mensajes para Cuatro Amigos for Guitar; Sonatina Ritmica; Permutaciones 7; Quinteto; Four Messages for flutes and piano; 8 Miniatures (Chicago Sinfonietta). Publications: Curso de Solfeo, Argentina 1963, Mexico 1975; The Music of Panama. Contributions to: Buenos Aires Musical; Revista Musical Chilena; Journal of Inter-American Studies; Grove Dictionary of Music. Honours: Caro de Boesi Award for Second Symphony, Venezuela, 1957; Koussevitsky International Recording Award for Violin Concerto, 1974; Chamber Music Award for Third String Quartet, Costa Rica, 1977. Memberships: Founder member, CIDEM; ISME. Hobby: Chess. Address: Music Department, Illinois State University, Normal, IL 61790-5660, USA.

CORDIER David (John), b. 1 May 1959, Rochester, Kent, England. Singer (Counter Tenor). m. Ursula Cordier, 27 March 1990, 1 son, 1 daughter. Education: MA, King's College, Cambridge, England; Royal College of Music, London, England. Debut: Wigmore Hall, 1989; Darmstadt (Lear-Reimann), 1990. Career: Handel Opera, Göttingen; Halle and Karlsruhe Festivals; Recital Berlin Philharmonic, 1996; Opera in Amsterdam, Munich, Dusseldorf, Dresden; Innsbruck, Salzburg and Bern; Teacher at Hanns Eisler Hochschule in Berlin (Counter Tenor). Recordings include: Bach Matthew Passion, G Leonhard; Solo recitals English song. Address: Lindlarer Str 98, D-51491 Overath, Germany.

CORELLI Franco, b. 8 Apr 1921, Ancona, Italy. Singer (Tenor). Education: Liceo Musicale, Pesaro. Debut: Spoleto, 1951, as Don José in Carmen, Career: La Scala Milan, 1954-65, as Licinio in La Vestale, Poliuto, as Raoul in Les Huguenots and as Gualtiero in Il Pirata; Covent Garden debut, 1957, as Cavaradossi in Tosca; Metropolitan Opera, 1961-74, notably as Puccini's Calaf and Rodolfo, Verdi's Ernani and Manrico, Gounod's Romeo and Massenet's Werther; Guest appearances in Paris, Berlin, Vienna, San Francisco and Florence. Recordings: Roles in Aida, Tosca, Carmen, Don Carlos, Les Huguenots, Il Trovatore, Faust and Norma. Address: c/o Teatro alla Scala, Via Filodrammatici 2, Milan, Italy.

CORGHI Azio, b. 9 Mar 1937, Cirie, Turin, Italy. Composer. Education: Studied at Turin Conservatory, Piano Diploma, 1961, and with Bruno Bettinelli at Milan Conservatory. Career: Freelance composer and teacher of composition at Conservatorio Giuseppe Verdi, Milan. Compositions: Music theatre pieces: Symbola, 1971, and Tactus, 1974; Ballets with voices: Actus III, 1978, and Mazapegul, 1986; Opera Gargantua after Rabelais, produced at Teatro Regio, Turin, 1984; Opera Blimunda, produced at Teatro Lirico, Milan, 1990; Opera Divara, produced at Städtischen Bühnen Münster, 1993. Publications: Critical editions of L'Italiana in Algeri and Tosca. Address: Conservatorio Giuseppe Verdi, Via del Conservatorio 12, I-20122 Milan, Italy.

CORIGLIANO John (Paul), b. 16 Feb 1938, New York City, New York, USA. Composer; Teacher. Education: BA, Columbia University, 1959; With Otto Luening, Vittorio Giannini, Manhattan School of Music; Privately with Paul Creston; Honorary doctorates from Manhattan School of Music, 1992 and Ithaca College, 1995. Career: Music Programmer, WQXR-FM and WBAI-FM, New York, 1959-64; Associate Producer, Musical Programmes, CBS-TV, 1961-72; Music Director, Morris Theatre, New Jersey, 1962-64; Teacher of Composition: College of Church Musicians, Washington DC, 1968-71; Manhattan School of Music, 1971-; Lehman College, City University of New York, 1973-; Distinguished Professor, 1986-; Composer-in-residence, Chicago Symphony Orchestra, 1987-89; Symphony No 1 premiere, Boston Symphony, also New York Philharmonic, Chicago Symphony, Seattle Symphony; The Ghosts of Versailles premiere, Metropolitan Opera, 1991; Fanfares to Music, Cincinnati Symphony, 1995. Compositions: Kaleidoscope, 2 pianos, 1959; Sonata, violin, piano, 1963; Elegy, orchestra, 1965; The Cloisters, 4 songs, voice, piano, 1965, voice, orchestra, 1976; Christmas at the Cloisters, chorus, organ or piano, 1966; Tournaments Overture, 1966; Piano Concerto, 1968; Poem in October, tenor, 8 instruments, 1970, tenor, orchestra, 1976; The Naked Carmen, mixed-media opera, 1970; Creations, 2 scenes from Genesis,

narrator, chamber orchestra, 1972; Gazebo Dances, band, 1973; Aria, oboe, strings, 1975; Oboe Concerto, 1975; Poem for His Birthday, 1976; Etude Fantasy, piano, 1976; Voyage, string orchestra, 1976, flute, string orchestra, 1983; Clarinet Concerto, 1977; Pied Piper Fantasy, Flute Concerto, 1981; 3 Hallucinations, 1981; Promenade Overture, 1981; Echoes of Forgotten Rites: Summer Fanfare, 1982; Fantasia on an Ostinato, orchestra, 1985; Symphony No 1, 1989-90; Opera, The Ghosts of Versailles, 1991; Incidental music for plays; Film scores. Recordings: Symphony No 1, Chicago Symphony/Barenboim; Pied Piper Fantasy; Fantasia on an Ostinato. Honours: Guggenheim Fellow, 1968-69; NEA Grant, 1976; Award, 1990, Member, 1991, American Academy and Institute of Arts and Letters; V Grawemeyer Award, 1991; Musical American Composer of the Year Winner, 1992. Memberships: American Society of Composers, Authors and Publishers. Current Management: Fine Arts Management, 291-A Sixth Avenue, Brooklyn, NY 11217, USA. Address: 365 West End Avenue, New York, NY 10024, USA.

CORNELIUS Gilbert Dale, b. 31 January 1934, Charlotte, North Carolina, USA. Teacher. Education: English, Washington-Lee University, 1956; MA, University of North Carolina, 1967; Public School of Music; Private Lessons, Composition. Compositions: Sehnsucht for String Quartets 1-5; Symphony 1-6; Piano Sonatina, Ronda 1-2, for Piano; Quilt; Violin Sonatas 1-3. Recordings: 1 String Quartet; 2 Piano Sonatina Ronda; 2 Violin Sonates. Hobby: Composing Music. Address: 1301 Reece Road, Charlotte, NC 29209, USA.

CORNWELL Joseph, b. 1959, England. Singer (Tenor). Education: BA Honours in Music, York University. Career: Sang originally with such early music groups as the Consort of Musicke and the Taverner Consort; Promenade Concert debut, 1982, in Monteverdi's Vespers under Andrew Parrott; Tours of Netherlands and France in the Bach Passions; Verdi's Requiem at the Albert Hall, conducted by David Willcocks; Bruckner's Te Deum at the Festival Hall; Appearances at the Paris, Bruges, Flanders, Three Choirs and Brighton Festivals; Conductors include Trevor Pinnock, Stephen Cleobury, Ton Koopman and Roger Norrington; Bach's B minor Mass with the London Bach Orchestra at the Barbican, Nov 1990; Has sung on ITV, Swiss television and BBC TV; Opera roles include Fenton in Falstaff, Frederic in Mignon, Jove in The Return of Ulysses (Kent Opera) and parts in Mahagonny and Let's Make an Opera; Sang title role in Monteverdi's Orfeo for Oslo Summer Opera, conducted by Andrew Parrott, and in 1993 for Boston Early Music Festival; Also sang Lurcanio in Handel's Ariodante for St Gallen Opera, in Switzerland; Arretro in Peri's Euridice in Rouen, 1992-93; Sang in King Arthur with The Sixteen, Lisbon, 1996. Recordings include: Monteverdi Christmas Vespers; Handel's Messiah; Albums for several labels; Monteverdi Vespers with Parrott; Rossini's Petite Messe Sollenelle with Jos Van Immerseel. Address: c/o Hazard Chase Ltd, Richmond House, 16-20 Regent Street, Cambridge CB2 1DB, England.

CORP Ronald, b. 4 Jan 1951, Wells, Somerset, England. Conductor. Career: Founder Conductor, New London Orchestra, 1988 and New London Children's Choir, 1991; Musical Director, London Choral Society and Conductor of Highgate Choral Society; Director, Finchley Children's Music Group, 1981-91; Broadcasts for BBC with BBC Singers, BBC Concert Orchestra, Ulster Orchestra, New London Orchestra and New London Children's Choir; Promenade Concert debut, 1990 with Britten's Noye's Fludde and further Proms with New London Orchestra in 1991 and 1995 and with BBC Concert orchestra, 1996 and 1997. Compositions: And All the Trumpets Sounded, 1989; Laudamus, 1992; Four Elizabethan Lyrics, 1994; Jubilate Deo, 1995; Cornucopia, 1997; Piano Concerto, 1997; Other choral works. Recordings: 7 discs with New London Orchestra, including British Light Music Classics I and British Light Music Classics II; Poulenc, Satie, Milhaud, Prokofiev and Virgil Thomson; Britten disc with New London Children's Choir. Publication: The Choral Singer's Companion, 1987. Memberships: ABCD; BFYC; NFMS. Hobby: Reading. Address: 41 Aberdare Gardens, London NW6 3AL, England.

CORSARO Frank (Andrew), b. 22 Dec 1924, New York City, New York, USA. Opera Director. Education: Studied at the City College of New York, the Yale University School of Drama and the Actors' Studio. Debut: New York City Opera, 1958, Floyd's Susanna. Career: City Opera productions have included Rigoletto, La Traviata, Pelléas et Mélisande, Prince Igor, Faust, Don Giovanni, A Village Romeo and Juliet and Janácek's Makropoulos Affair and Cunning Little Vixen, 1981; For Houston Opera has produced premiere productions of Pasatieri's The Seagull, 1974, and Scott Joplin's Treemonisha, 1975; Premieres of Floyd's Of Mice and Men (Seattle, 1970) and Hoiby's Summer and Smoke (St Paul, 1971); At the Glyndebourne Festival has produced Prokofiev's The Love of Three Oranges; Metropolitan Opera, 1984, Handel's Rinaldo; Season 1992 with the US stage premiere of Busoni's Doktor Faust, New York City Opera; New production of Faust for the Chicago Lyric Opera, 1996. Address:

c/o New York City Opera, Lincoln Center, New York, NY 10023, USA.

CORTE Miguel, b. 1952, Mexico. Singer (Tenor). Education: Studied in Monterrey and New York. Debut: Metropolitan Opera, 1981, as Alfredo. Career: Sang with Kentucky Opera as the Duke of Mantua, Rodolfo, Pinkerton, Fenton and Jacquino; European engagements as the Duke at Zurich (1984), Alfredo at Trieste (1985) and Werther in Mexico City (1985); Has also sung in Salzburg (Alfredo, 1983), San Francisco (as Pinkerton) and in the Verdi Requiem (at Seattle). Address: c/o Kentucky Opera, 631 South Fifth Street, Louisville, KY 40202, USA.

CORTES Gardar, b. 1950, Reykjavik, Iceland. Singer (Tenor); Conductor. Education: Studied at Royal Academy of Music and Trinity College of Music in London. Career: Has conducted choirs in Iceland and founded the Reykjavik Symphony Orchestra, 1985, leading it on a tour of Denmark; With Icelandic Opera has conducted Orpheus in the Underworld, Pagliacci and Die Fledermaus, Noye's Fludde at the International Festival in Reykjavik; Appearances as singer with Oslo Opera, Royal Swedish Opera, Seattle Opera, Windsor Festival, Opera North and Belfast Festival; Intendant of the Gothenburg Opera, Sweden; Roles have included Eisenstein, Tamino, Hoffmann, Radames, Cavaradossi, Florestan and Otello. Address: c/o John Coast Ltd, 31 Sinclair Road, London W14 0NS, England.

CORTESE Paul, b. 3 Mar 1960, Kenosha, Wisconsin, USA. Violist. m. Montserrat Vallvé, 30 Dec 1994, 1 son. Education: BM, Performers Certificate, University of Illinois, Champaign-Urbana; Curtis Institute of Music, Philadelphia; New England Conservatory of Music, Boston. Debut: Tully Hall, New York City, 1991. Career: Philadelphia Orchestra, 1984-88; Principal Viola, Teatro Alla Scala, Milan; Principal Violist, Gothenburg Symphony, Sweden, 1986-87; Principal Viola, Barcelona Orchestra, 1992. Recordings: Numerous Solo Works by Elliot Carter, George Rochberg, William Bergsma, Alan Hovaness, Max Reger, Debussy, Genzmer, Nathan Currier, Jolivet; The Complete Solo Viola Music of Paul Hindemith. Hobby: Cycling. Address: Carrrer Doctor Dou 19, #3, #2, 08001 Barcelona, Spain.

CORTEZ Viorica, b. 22 Dec 1935, Bucium, Rumania. Singer (Mezzo-soprano). m. Emmanuel Bondeville, 1974 (dec. 1987). Education: Studied at the Iasi and Bucharest Conservatories. Debut: Iasi Opera, 1960, as Dalila. Career: Sang Dalila at Toulouse, 1965; Bucharest Opera, 1965-70; Covent Garden debut, 1968, as Carmen; Italian debut, 1969, as Amneris at Naples; La Scala Milan, 1970, as Dalila; US debut, Seattle Opera, 1971; Metropolitan Opera from 1971, as Carmen, Amneris, Giulietta in Les Contes d'Hoffmann, Adalgisa in Norma and Azucena; Chicago debut, 1973, in Maria Stuarda; Sang in the premiere of Bondeville's Antoine et Cléopatre, Rouen, 1974; Paris Opera, 1980, in Bluebeard's Castle, Oedipus Rex and Boris Godunov; Sang La Cieca in La Gioconda at the Verona Arena and Barcelona, 1988; Gertrude in Hamlet, Turin, 1990, and the title role in the premiere of La Lupa by Marco Tutino at Livorno; Season 1992 as Ulrica at Genoa; Sang Rosa in Cilea's L'Arlesiana at Montpellier, 1996. Recordings: Carmen; Aida; Il Trovatore; Verdi's Oberto; Donizetti's Requiem; Rigoletto; Video of Rigoletto. Address: c/o S A Gorlinsky Ltd, 33 Dover Street, London W1X 4NJ, England.

CORY Eleanor, b. 8 Sep 1943, Englewood, NJ, USA. Composer. Education: Studied with Charles Wuorinen and others at Columbia University in New York. Career: Has taught at Yale University, Manhattan School of Music, and Sarah Lawrence College among others. Compositions include: Waking for Soprano and Ensemble, 1974; Octagons for Ensemble, 1976; Tapestry for Orchestra, 1982; String Quartet, 1985; Of Mere Being for Chorus and Brass Quintet, 1987; Fantasy for Flute, Guitar and Percussion, 1991; Canyons for Chamber Orchestra, 1991. Address: c/o ASCAP, ASCAP Building, One Lincoln Plaza, New York, NY 10023, USA.

COSMA Octavian (Lazar), b. 15 Feb 1933, Treznea, Salaj, Romania. Musicologist; Professor; Doctor. m. Elena, 15 Nov 1958, 1 s, 1 d. Education: Rimsky Korsakov Conservatory, St Petersburg, Russia, 1959. Debut: Muzica, 1954. Career: Counselor, Ministry of Culture and Education, 1959-63; Assistant Lecturer, Professor, Academy of Music, Bucharest, 1959-; Secretary, 1990, Vice President, 1992, Romanian Union of Composers and Musicologists; Editor-in-Chief of journal, Mizica, 1990. Publications: The Romanian Opera, 2 volumes, 1962; Enesco's Oedipus, 1967; The Chronicle of Romanian Music, volumes I 1973, II 1974, III 1975, IV 1976, V 1983, VI 1984, VII 1986, VIII 1988, IX 1991. Contributions to: Various professional journals. Honours: Ciprian Porumbescu Prize, Romanian Academy, 1962; Prize, Romanian Union of Composers, 1968. Memberships: Romanian Union of Composers; American Musicological Society. Current Management: Conservatorul Ciprian Porumbescu, Bucharest. Hobbies: Sport; Football; Tourism. Address: Cotroceni 5-7, Bucharest 76528, Romania.

COSMA Viorel, b. 30 Mar 1923, Timisoara, Romania. Musicologist; Professor. m. Coralia Cosma. Education: Municipal Conservatory, Timisoara; Academie of Music, Bucharest. Debut: As conductor in 1944. Career: Musicologist and Music Critic from 1946; Professor from 1950. Publications: Historiographic Works: Two Millenian of Music, in English, 1982, Musicological Exegeses, 1984; Lexicography: Romanian Musicians, Lexicon, 1970, Musicians of Romania (A-C), Lexicon, 1989; Monographs: Ion Vidu, 1956, Ciprian Porumbescu, 1957, Elena Teodorini, 1960, Nicolae Filimon, 1966, The George Enescu Philharmonic, 1968, The Madrigal Choir, 1971, Enescu Today, 1981, Dinu Lipatti, 1991; Epistolography: Bartók, 1955, Enescu, 2 volumes, 1974 and 1981. Honours: Prize, Romanian Composers, 1970, 1972, 1978, 1983, 1988, 1991; Prize, Academy of Romania, 1971. Hobby: Motoring. Address: Str Luterana 3, Bucharest, Romania.

COSSA Dominic, b. 13 May 1935, Jessup, Pennsylvania, USA. Baritone; Teacher. m. Janet Edgerton, 26 Dec 1957, 1 son, 1 daughter. Education: BS, University of Scranton, 1959; MA, University of Detroit, 1961; LhD, University of Scranton; Detroit Institute of Musical Arts, Philadelphia Academy of Vocal Arts; Principal vocal teachers: Anthony Marlowe, Robert Weede and Armen Boyajian. Debut: Operatic debut as Morales, Carmen, New York City Opera, 1961. Career: Leading baritone roles, New York City Opera; Metropolitan Opera debut, New York as Silvio in Pagliacci, 1970-76; Opéra du Rhin, Strasbourg, 1976; Teacher, Manhattan School of Music, New York; University of Maryland, Baltimore. Recordings: For Decca-London; New World Records; RCA-Victor including Achilles in Giulio Cesare, conducted by Julius Rudel. Honours: Inducted into Hall of Fame for great American Singers, Philadelphia Academy of Vocal Arts, 1993. Address: 845 Stonington Way, Arnold, MD 21012, USA.

COSSOTI Max-René, b. 1950, Italy. Singer (Tenor). Debut: Siena, 1973, in Gazzaniga's Don Giovanni. Career: Genoa, 1974, Ernesto at Spoleto (1975) and Glyndebourne from 1976, as Fenton, Ferrando, Almaviva, Eurymachos in Monteverdi's Ulisse and Fileno in Haydn's La Fedeltà Premiata; Further engagements at Innsbruck, 1983, in Cesti's Il Tito; Lisbon, 1985, as the Prince in Cenerentola and Trieste, 1992, as Zemlinsky's Zwerg; Other roles include Elvino in La Sonnambula, Alfredo, Gerald in Lakmé, Werther, and Alfred in Die Fledermaus; Sang L'Incredible in Andrea Chenier at Rome, 1996. Recordings include: Videos of Ulisse, Falstaff and Il Barbiere di Siviglia, from Glyndebourne. Address: c/o Teatro Comunale G Verdi, Riva Novembre 1, 34121 Trieste, Italy.

COSSOTTO Fiorenza, b. 22 Apr 1935, Crescentino, Italy. Singer (Mezzo-soprano). m. Ivo Vinco, 1958. Education: Turin Conservatory; Study with Ettore Campogalliani. Debut: La Scala Milan, 1957, in the premiere of Poulenc's Les Dialogues des Carmélites; Returned to Milan until 1973, notably as Verdi's Eboli, Amneris and Azucena, and in La Favorite, Les Huguenots, Il Barbiere di Siviglia and Cavalleria Rusticana; Sang Jane Seymour in Anna Bolena at Wexford in 1958; Covent Garden debut, 1959, as Neris in Cherubini's Médée; Chicago Lyric Opera, 1964, in La Favorite; Metropolitan Opera debut, 1968, as Amneris, returning for Laura in La Gioconda, Adalgisa, Norma, Carmen and Mistress Quickly (Falstaff); Sang, Verona Arena, 1960-89, notably as Amneris, which she sang at the Metropolitan, 1989; Sang Dalila at Newark, New Jersey, 1989, the Princess in Adriana Lecouvreur, Rome; Sang Santuzza, Piacenza, 1990; Ulrica at Lisbon and Amneris at Buenos Aires; Sang Ulrica at Genoa, 1992. Recordings: Roles in Andrea Chénier, Norma, Madama Butterfly, La Sonnambula, Macbeth, Don Carlos, Cavalleria Rusticana, Médée and Il Trovatore. Address: Marks Management Ltd, 14 New Burlington Street, London W1X 1FF, England.

COSSUTTA Carlo, b. 8 May 1932, Trieste, Italy. Singer (Tenor). Education: Studied in Buenos Aires with Manfredo Miselli, Mario Melani and Arturo Wolken. Career: Sang small roles at the Teatro Colon Buenos Aires from 1958; Created the title role in Ginastera's Don Rodrigo, 1964; Covent Garden debut, 1964, as the Duke of Mantua (Rigoletto); Returned to London as Verdi's Gabriele Adorno, Manrico and Otello; Metropolitan Opera debut, 1973, as Pollione in Norma; 1974 sang Radames in Moscow with the La Scala company on tour; Guest appearances in Vienna, Paris, Berlin, Munich and Hamburg from 1977; Samson, Bregenz Festival, 1988-89; Sang Radames at the National Indoor Arena, Birmingham, 1991. Recordings: Falla, La Vida Breve; Verdi Requiem; Otello.

COSTA Mary, b. 5 Apr 1932, Knoxville, Tennessee, USA. Singer (Soprano). Education: Studied with Mario Chamlee at Los Angeles Conservatory and with Ernest St John Metz. Career: Sang in concert and took small roles in opera, then appeared as Susanna at Glyndebourne, 1958; San Francisco Opera from 1959, notably in the US premiere of A Midsummer Night's Dream, 1961; Royal Opera House, 1962, as Concepcion in L'Heure Espagnole and Violetta; Metropolitan Opera from 1964, as Violetta, Vanessa, Gilda, Despina, Alice Ford, Manon, Rosalinde and Musetta; Sang at the Bolshoi Theatre, Moscow, 1970, and appeared in the film The Great Waltz, 1972; Founded the Knoxville Tennessee Opera Company, 1978, and established the Mary Costa Scholarship at the University of Tennessee, 1979; Many concert appearances. Recording: La Bohème. Address: c/o Knoxville Opera Company, PO Box 16, Knoxville, TN 37901, USA.

COSTANZO Giuseppe, b. 1958, Catania, Italy. Singer (Tenor). Debut: Bari, 1983, as Arturo in Lucia di Lammermoor. Career: Macerata Festival, 1984, as Alamaviva; Bergamo, 1984, as Ernani, Trieste and Tel Aviv, 1985, as Pinkerton; La Scala debut, 1988, as Conte Alberto in L'Occasione fa il ladro; Cologne, 1991, as Gabriele Adorno in Simon Boccanegra; Other roles include Ernesto, Rinuccio in Gianni Schicchi, Edgardo, and Alfredo (Lisbon, 1987); Many concert engagements. Address: c/o Teatro alla Scala, Via Filodrammatici 2, 20121 Milan, Italy.

COSTINESCU Gheorghe, b. 12 Dec 1934, Bucharest, Romania. Composer; Conductor; Pianist; Educator. m. Silvelin von Scanzoni, 12 Nov 1971. Education: Master's degree in Composition, Bucharest Conservatory, 1961; Courses in New Music, Darmstadt and Cologne, 1968; Postgraduate Diploma, The Juilliard School, 1971; Doctor of Musical Arts with distinction, Columbia University, 1976; Studied composition with Mihail Jora in Romania and Luciano Berio in USA; Additional studies with Nadia Boulanger, Karlheinz Stockhausen, Mario Davidovsky and Chou Wen-Chung; Studied conducting with Harold Faberman, Maurice Peress and Dennis Russell Davies in USA and with Sergiu Celibidache in Germany. Debut: As Composer and Pianist, Sonata for Violin and Piano at Shiraz-Persepolis Festival, Iran, 1967. Career: Professor, Lehman College, City University of New York; Premieres: Evolving Cycle of Two-Part Modal Inventions for Piano, Romanian Broadcast, 1964; Past Are The Years for tenor and vocal ensemble with Juilliard Chorus, Lincoln Center, New York City, 1970; Jubilus for soprano, trumpet and percussive body sounds, commissioned and broadcasted by National Public Radio, USA, 1981; Premiere of Stage work: The Musical Seminar at Tanglewood Festival, 1982; German premiere at State Opera of Stuttgart, 1989; UK premiere with Paragon Opera Project at Royal Academy of Music, Glasgow, 1992. Recordings: Composers Recordings Inc, USA; Published works: Evolving Cycle for Piano, 1964; Song to the Rivers of My Country, vocal symphonic work, 1967; Sonata for Violin and Piano, 1968. Honours: George Enescu Prize, Romanian Academy, 1965; Alexandre Gretcheaninoff Prize in Composition, Juilliard School, 1970; Music Award, American Academy and Institute of Arts and Letters, 1985; Winner, International Society for Contemporary Music National Composers' Competition, USA, 1986; 2 National Endowment for the Arts Grants, as producer, 1986, as composer, 1989; Fulbright Scholar Award, 1997-98. Memberships: Broadcast Music Inc; American Composers' Alliance; Romanian Composer's and Musicologist's Alliance; American Music Center; Conductors' Guild. Hobbies: Drawing; Tennis; Downhill Skiing. Address: 120 Riverside Drive, Apt 6E, New York, NY 10024, USA.

COTRUBAS Ileana, b. 9 June 1939, Galati, Rumania. Opera and Concert Singer. m. Manfred Ramin, 1972. Education: Conservatorul Ciprian Porumbescu, Bucharest. Debut: Yniold in Pelléas et Mélisande, Bucharest Opera, 1964. Career: Frankfurt Opera, 1968-70; Glyndebourne Festival, 1968; Salzburg Festival, 1969; Royal Opera House, Covent Garden, London, 1971, as Tchaikovsky's Tatiana; Lyric Opera of Chicago, 1973; Paris Opera, 1974; La Scala, Milan, 1975; Metropolitan Opera, New York, 1977, as Mimi in La Bohème; Operatic roles included Susanna, Pamina, Norina, Gilda, Traviata, Manon, Antonia, Tatiana, Mimi, Mélisande; Concerts with all major European orchestras; Lieder recitals at Musikverein Vienna, Royal Opera House Covent Garden, Carnegie Hall, New York, La Scala; CD of Manon, 1988; Sang Elisabeth of Valois, Florence, Marguerite at Hamburg, 1985, Amelia Boccanegra, Naples, 1986; Monte Carlo, 1987, as Alice Ford, Barcelona, 1988, as Desdemona; Sang Mélisande, Florence, 1989; Retired, 1990. Recordings: Bach Cantatas; Mozart Masses; Brahms Requiem; Mahler Symphonies Nos 2 and 8; Complete Operas including Le nozze di Figaro, Die Zauberflöte, Hansel and Gretel, Calisto, Louise, L'Elisir d'Amore, Les Pêcheurs de Perles, La Traviata, Rigoletto, Alzira. Honours: 1st Prize, International Singing Competition, 's Hertogenbosch, Netherlands, 1965; 1st Prize, Munich Radio Competition, 1966; Austrian Kammersängerin, 1981; Great Officer of the Order Sant Iago da Espada (Portugal), 1990.

COUROUPOS Yorgos, b. 1 Jan 1942, Athens, Greece. Composer. Education: Studied the piano at Athens Conservatory, and composition with Messiaen in Paris, 1968-72. Career: Administrative posts at National Lyric Theatre, Athens; Director of Calamata Municipal Conservatory from 1985. Compositions: Music theatre works, notably: Dieu le Veut, 1975; Grisélidis, 1977; Pylades, opera in 1 act with libretto by G Himonas after Sophocles and Euripides, performed at the Athens Concert Hall, 1992. Address: c/o AEPI, Fragoklisias and Samou Street 51, 151 25 Amarousio, Athens, Greece.

COUROUX Marc, b. 1970, Montreal, Canada. Pianist; Lecturer; Writer; Disseminator. Education: Humanities & Mathematics; Studies with Louis-Philippe Pelletier, McGill University, 1989-94. Career: Works include Night Fantasies by Elliott Carter, Euryali by Iannis Xenakis, 14 Etudes by György Ligeti, Other Works by Ambrosini, Cage, Donatoni, Lindberg, Messiaen, Nancarrow, Rzewski, Schoenberg, Stockhausen, Szymanski, Tippett, along with Canadian Composers Brégent, Cherney, Gonneville, Tremblay & Vivier; Premiers of Envolée by Sean Ferguson & Variations by James Harley, 1994; Premiers of Works by Michael Oesterle, USA, Marko Ciciliani, Germany, James Harley, Canada & Renaud de Putter, Belgium, 1995; Soloist, McGill Symphony Orchestra in the North American Premiere of Bengt Hambraeus' Concerto for Piano & Orchestra, 1995; Recital of Canadian & Belgian Works, ARS Musica Festival Brussels, 1995; Performed, Concerto for Piano & Orchestra by György Ligeti with CBC Vancouver Orchestra, 1996; Performed Piano Solo Pieces, Nouvel Ensemble Moderne, 1996; Artist-in-Residence, Banff Centre for the Arts, Princeton & Rutgers Universities, Domaine Forget Summer Course for New Music, St-Irénée, Quebec; Lecturer, University of New York, Stony Brook & Buffalo. Publications: Several articles in professional journals. Address: c/o Latitude 45, Arts Promotion Inc, 109 St Joseph Blvd West, Montreal, Quebec H2T 2P7, Canada.

COURTIS Jean-Philippe, b. 24 May 1951, France. Singer (Bass). Education: Studied at the Paris Conservatoire. Career: Sang first at the Paris Opéra (from 1980), then the Opéra-Comique (1983); Appearances at the Aix Festival in Werther, Semiramide, and Ariadne auf Naxos, and guest engagements throughout Europe as Henry VIII in Anna Bolena (Amsterdam, 1989), Don Giovanni (Strasbourg, 1990) and Arkel (Vienna Staatsoper, 1991); Sang Méphistophélès in Faust at the Paris Opéra, 1988, and appeared in the 1990 opening of the Opéra Bastille (Les Troyens); Other roles include the Commendatore in Don Giovanni, Don Quichotte, and Frère Bernard in Messiaen's St François d'Assise (premiere, 1983); Many concert engagements. Address: c/o Opére de la Bastille, 120 Rue de Lyon, F-75012 Paris, France.

COVELL Roger (David), b. 1 February 1931, Sydney, Australia. Musicologist; Critic; Conductor; Composer. m. Patricia Anne Brown, 10 May 1975, 3 sons, 1 daughter. Education: BA, Queensland; PhD, New South Wales. Career: Chief Music Critic, Sydney Morning Herald, 1960-; Senior Lecturer, Head, Music Department, University of New South Wales, 1966; Associate Professor, 1973, Personal Chair, 1984, Head, School of Music & Music Education; Visiting Professor, Education, 1997-. Compositions: Theatre Music & Choral Works. Recordings: Barry Conyngham's Edward John Eyre, 1974. Publications: Australia's Music: Themes of a New Society, 1967; Music in Australia, Needs & Prospects, 1970; Edward Geoghegan's Currency Lass, 1976; Folk Songs of Australia, 1987. Contributions to: Studies in Music; Australian Encyclopedia; New Grove Dictionary of Opera. Honours: Fellow, Australian Academy of the Humanities, 1983; Order of Australia, 1986. Memberships: Australia Council, 1977-83; Australia Society for Music Educators; Musicological Society of Australia. Hobbies: Cycling; Blackberry Cutting. Address: 9 Kubya Street, Blackheath, NSW 2785, Australia.

COVELLI John (Thomas), b. 12 Oct 1936, Chicago, IL, USA. Conductor; Pianist. Education: Studied at Columbia University. Debut: NY Town Hall 1957, as piano soloist. Career: Played piano with US army, 1960-62, then assisted Pierre Monteux at the London Symphony Orchestra; Conducted the Harkness Ballet and the NYC Opera in the late 1960s; St Louis Symphony 1970-71, Kansas City Philharmonic 1971-72; Led the Milwaukee Symphony 1974-76 and was music director of the Flint Symphony 1976-82 and the Binghamton Symphony, NY, USA; Has appeared as conductor and pianist with the Boston Pops Orchestra from 1979.

COVEY-CRUMP Rogers, b. 1944, England. Singer (Tenor). Education: Studied at the Royal College of Music in London; BMus, London University. Career: Concert, broadcasting and commercial recording engagements as a solo artist and as a member of the Hilliard Ensemble, Gothic Voices, the Deller and Taverner Consorts and Singcircle (Stockhausen's Stimmung); Promenade Concerts, 1984-95, Purcell's Odes, Bach's Matthew Passion; Pärt's Miserere; Turku Festival, 1985, with the Sixteen and London Baroque in Bach B Minor Mass; Returned to Finland for Haydn's Creation, Messiah and the St John Passion by Pärt; Bach B Minor Mass in Netherlands with Ton Koopman and Amsterdam Baroque Orchestra, 1986; St Matthew Passion in Madrid; Performances of St John's Passion (as Evangelist) in London, Oxford and Cambridge, 1987; Arundel Festival, 1988, in the Monteverdi Vespers; Tour of Britain, 1988, 1992, with Contemporary Music Network in Pärt's St John Passion and Miserere; Hilliard Summer Schools since 1984; Residences with the Hilliard Ensemble at the University of California at Davis, 1988, and Bucknell University, Pennsylvania, 1992; Summer schools in Finland; Lecturer and writer on aspects of vocal ensemble style; Sang Purcell's Ode for St Cecilia's Day, 1991 Promenade Concerts, London. Recordings include: Bach's B Minor Mass and St John's Passion (Evangelist and Arias), Purcell Ode to St Cecilia and Monteverdi Vespers with Andrew Parrott and the Taverner Players; Bach's St Matthew Passion with Roy Goodman and the choir of King's College, Cambridge; Purcell's Dioclesian and Timon of Athens with John Eliot Gardiner; Pärt's St John Passion and Miserere; French and English Lute Songs, with Paul O'Dette and with Jakob Lindberg. Address: c/o Hazard Chase Ltd, Richmond House, 16-20 Regent Street, Cambridge CB2 1DB, England.

COVIELLO Roberto, b. 1958, Italy. Singer (Baritone). Debut: Naples, 1983. Career: Sang Guglielmo at Bari, 1984, and Paisiello's Figaro at the 1986 Spoleto Festival; La Scala Milan from 1987, as Don Giovanni and other major baritone roles; Pesaro Festival, 1988-89, in La Scala di Seta and La Gazza Ladra; Other roles include Mozart's Figaro, Belcore, Malatesta, Valentin, Mercutio (Roméo et Juliette), Valentin and Ford in Falstaff. Address: c/o Teatro alla Scala, via Filodrammatici 2, 20121 Milan, Italy.

COWAN Richard, b. 1957, Euclid, Ohio, USA. Singer (Bass-Baritone). Debut: Chicago Lyric, 1983, in Lady Macbeth of the Mtsensk District by Shostakovich. Career: Has sung frequently in Chicago (Escamillo, 1991) and guested in Los Angeles and Miami; Maggio Musicale, Florence, 1985, as the Animal Tamer in Lulu, Aix Festival, 1986, as Masetto and Théâtre de Châtelet, Paris, 1988-89, in Der Freischütz and Fidelio; La Scala Milan debut, 1989, Metropolitan, New York from 1990, as Schaunard, Don Giovanni and Guglielmo; Further engagements in Vancouver (as Jochanaan), Rio de Janeiro, San Francisco and Santa Fe; Sang Scarpia at Montreal, 1996. Address: c/o Metropolitan Opera, Lincoln Center, New York, NY 10023, USA.

COWAN Sigmund, b. 4 Mar 1948, New York City, New York, USA. Singer (Baritone). Education: University of Miami; University of Florida; New York Institute of Finance; Scholarship, Juilliard School; Fellowship, Manhattan School of Music. Career: Appearances: New York City Opera, Deutsche Oper am Rhein; Spoleto Festival, Kennedy Center, Miami Opera, Basel, Essen, Wiesbaden, Vienna Festival, Berlin Staatstheater, Brussels, Amsterdam (Opera and Concertgebouw), Carnegie Hall, Mexico City, Dublin, and Calgary and Edmonton (Canada), Rotterdam (TV VARA), Utrecht (Radio KRO), Amsterdam (VARA Radio), Italy (RAI), USA (NBC TV), Austria (TV ORF), Germany (TV 3rd Channel); Sang with Rochester Philharmonic, National Symphony, Baltimore Symphony and at Flagstaff Festival; Appeared with National Orchestra, Mexico City, Canadian Opera, L'Opera de Montreal, Baltimore Opera; TV Live from Lincoln Center PBS Tonio in Pagliacci; Roles in Nabucco, Rigoletto, Macbeth, Il Trovatore, I Due Foscari, Un Ballo in Maschera, La Forza del Destino, La Traviata; Sang Rigoletto at Toronto, 1996. Recordings include: Die Gezeichneten with Edo de Waart. Hobbies: Cooking; Theatre; Photography. Current Management: Athole Still, London, England; Dorothy Cone, New York, USA. Address: c/o Dorothy Cone, 60E 86th Street, New York, NY 10028, USA.

COWIE Edward, b. 17 Aug 1943, Birmingham, England. Composer; Painter; Natural Scientist; Writer; Film-maker. m. Heather Jean Johns, 1995, 2 daughters by second marriage. Education: BEd, London University; BMus, DMus, Southampton University; PhD, Lancaster University. Appointments: Senior Lecturer, Lancaster University, 1973-83; Professor, Creative Arts, University of Wollongong, New South Wales, Australia, 1983-89; Granada Composer/Conductor, Royal Liverpool Philharmonic Orchestra, 1983-86; Professor, Creative Arts, James Cook University, Queensland, Australia, 1989-95; Professor and Director of Research, Dartington College of Arts, Devon, England, 1995-. Recordings: many compositions recorded. Publications: Music published in London; 41 exhibitions as painter. Honours: Many prizes won as composer. Memberships: British Ornithologists Union; Fellow, Royal Society of Arts. Hobbies: Natural Sciences; Reading; Walking; Family Life; Thinking. Address: c/o Dartington College of Arts, Totnes, Devon TQ9 6EJ, England.

COX Jean, b. 16 Jan 1922, Gadsen, Alabama, USA. Singer (Tenor). Education: University of Alabama and the New England Conservatory; With Wally Kirsamer in Frankfurt, Luigi Ricci in Rome and Max Lorenz in Munich. Debut: New England Opera Company, 1951, as Lensky in Eugene Onegin. Career: Spoleto, 1954, as Rodolfo; Sang at Brunswick, 1955-59, Mannheim from 1959; Bayreuth Festival, 1956-75, as the Steersman, Erik, Lohengrin, Parsifal, Siegfried and Walther; Hamburg Staatsoper, 1958-73; Guest appearances in Berlin, Vienna, Munich, Stuttgart and Frankfurt; Bregenz Festival, 1961, in Fra Diavolo; Chicago Lyric Opera, 1964, 1970, 1973; Paris Opera, 1971, as Siegmund; Covent Garden, 1975; Siegfried; Metropolitan Opera debut, 1976, as Walther; Further engagements in Lisbon, Stockholm, Geneva, Zurich, Mexico City, Houston and Pittsburgh; Other roles included Strauss's Herod and Bacchus; Alvaro in La Forza del Destino, Max in Der Freischütz and the Cardinal in Mathis der Maler by Hindemith; Siegfried and Walter von Stolzing, Bayreuth Festival, 1983-84; Sang Captain Vere in Billy Budd at Mannheim, 1989. Recordings include: Die Meistersinger; Jean Cox sings Wagner. Address: Nationaltheater, Postfach 102362, D-6800 Mannheim, Germany.

COX John, b. 12 Mar 1935, Bristol, England. Opera and Play Producer. Education: BA, Oxford University. Debut: L'Enfant et les Sortilèges with Sadler's Wells. Career: Assisted Gunther Rennert and Carl Ebert at Glyndebourne, Director of Productions, 1971-81; Work has included productions of Arabella, Capriccio and Intermezzo, by Strauss; General Administrator of Scottish Opera, 1981-84, Artistic Director, 1985-86 (including first local production of Berg's Lulu); Directed Il Barbiere di Siviglia at the Metropolitan, 1982; Other productions include Le Comte Ory (Nice), Don Carlo and Die Zauberflöte (San Francisco) and Daphne by Strauss (Munich); Also directed at Milan, Stockholm, Brussels, Amsterdam, Sydney, Cologne, Nuremberg, Hanover, Spoleto, Wexford, Houston, Santa Fe (La Calisto), Washington, Honolulu, Salzburg (Il Re Pastore) and Florence (Idomemeo); Extensive work in the straight theatre and with television and documentary films; Production Director at Covent Garden, 1988-; New productions of Guillaume Tell and Capriccio; Directed Die Frau ohne Schatten in London, 1992; Hamlet by Ambroise Thomas at Monte Carlo and Eugene Onegin at Covent Garden, 1993; Revived his Albert Herring production at Sydney, 1996. Recordings: Director for stereophonic sound: Coronation of Poppea/Pritchard and Otello/Barbirolli. Hobbies: Fine arts; Gardens. Address: Lies Askonas Ltd, 6 Henrietta Street, London WC2, England.

COXON Richard, b. 25 August 1968, Nottingham, England. Singer (Tenor). Education: Royal Northern College of Music, with John Mitchinson and Robert Alderson. Debut: Flavio in Norma for Scottish Opera, 1993. Career: Further roles with Scottish Opera have included Narraboth in Salome, Jacquino, Nemorino, Alfred in Die Fledermaus, Barbarigo in Verdi's Due Foscari, Don Ottavio, Alfredo, and Jiri in The Jacobin by Dvorak; Guest appearances for Opera Northern Ireland, Opera Zuid in Masstricht and English National Opera; Concerts include Mendelssohn's St Paul with the Scottish National Orchestra, Messiah with the Bergen PO and engagements with the Hallé Orchestra, BBC Concert Orchestra, BBC Scottish SO and London Pops Orchestra; Season 1997-98 with Fenton in Falstaff and Young Convict in From the House of the Dead for English National Opera; Mr By-Ends in Pilgrim's Progress for Royal Opera, Covent Garden; Brighella in Ariadne auf Naxos for Scottish Opera at the Edinburgh Festival and on tour; Edgardo in film version of Lucia di Lammermoor, directed by Don Boyd. Honours include: Webster Booth/Esso Award; Clonter Opera Prize; Ricordi Opera Prize. Address: c/o IMG Artists, Media House, 3 Burlington Lane, London W4 2TH, England.

CRAFT Robert (Lawson), b. 20 October 1923, Kingston, New York, USA. Conductor; Writer on Music. Education: BA, Juilliard School of Music, New York, 1946; Berkshire Music Centre, Tanglewood; Studied Conducting with Pierre Monteux. Career: Conductor, Evenings-on-the-Roof and Monday Evening Concerts, Los Angeles, 1950-68; Assistant to, later closest associate of Igor Stravinsky, 1948-71; Collaborated with Stravinsky in concerts and in preparing several books; Conducted first performances of various later works by Stravinsky; Conducted works ranging from Monteverdi to Boulez; US premiere of Berg's Lulu (2 act version) Santa Fe, 1963. Recordings: Many including works of Stravinsky, Webern, completed works and Schoenberg, several albums for CBS. Publications: With Stravinsky: Conversations with Igor Stravinsky, 1959; Memories and Commentaries, 1960; Expositions and Developments, 1962; Dialogues and a Diary, 1963; Themes and Episodes, 1967; Retrospections and Conclusions, 1969; Chronicle of a Friendship, 1972; Prejudices in Disguise, 1974; with Vera Stravinsky, Stravinsky in Photographs and Documents, 1976; Current Convictions: Views and Reviews, 1977; Present Perspectives, 1984; Translator and Editor, Stravinsky's Selected Correspondence, 2 volumes, 1982, 1984. Contributions to: Articles in various journals and other publications. Address: 1390 South Ocean Blvd, Pompano Beach, FL 33062, USA.

CRAFTS Edward (James), b. 11 Nov 1946, New York City, New York, USA. Singer (Bass-Baritone). Education: Studied at Curtis and Indiana University. Career: Has sung widely in the USA from 1982, notably at Houston Opera (as Dulcamara), St Louis and the City Opera New York (as Escamillo); Santa Fe, 1984, in the US premiere of Zemlinsky's Eine Florentinische Tragödie; La Scala Milan, 1984, in Bernstein's Trouble in Tahiti; Seattle, 1987, as Iago; New Jersey, 1983, in the US premiere of Wagner's Liebesverbot; Further appearances at La Scala, Covent Garden, Cleveland and Chicago; Other roles include Falstaff, Scarpia and Mephistopheles. Address: c/o New York City Opera, Lincoln Center, New York, NY 10023, USA.

CRAIG Jon, b. 30 Oct 1923, St Louis, Missouri, USA. Singer (Tenor). Education: Studied in Washington, at Juilliard and with Paul Althouse. Debut: Sang Pinkerton in 1948. Career: Sang at New York City Opera, 1952-65, notably in the 1954 premiere of The Tender Land by Copland and in US premieres of Der Prozess, 1953, Der Revisor by Egk, 1960, and The Fiery Angel, 1965; Metropolitan Opera from 1953, San Francisco from 1957; Further engagements at Pittsburgh, Chicago, Philadelphia, Mexico City and New Orleans; Other roles have included the Duke of Mantua, Fenton and Alfredo by Verdi, Cavaradossi, Don José, Turiddu, Rodolfo, Erik in Fliegende Holländer, Dimitri, Boris Godunov and Walton's Troilus. Recording: Highlights from Les Contes d'Hoffmann.

CRAIG Russell, b. 1950, New Zealand. Stage Designer. Education: Studied in New Zealand and moved to London in 1974. Career: Designs for Scottish Opera with Savitri, Hedda Gabler, Rossini double bill, Oberon and L'Elisir d'Amore, 1981-94, Welsh National Opera with Barber of Seville, Die Entführung, Ariadne and Le Comte Ory, 1986-91, and English National Opera with The Rape of Lucretia and Ariadne auf Naxos, 1983; Designs for Opera North include Cosi fan tutte, The Magic Flute, A Village Romeo and Juliet, Acis and Galatea, Showboat, and Oberto, 1983-94; La Bohème for Glyndebourne Touring Opera in 1991. Address: Performing Arts, 6 Windmill Street, London, W1P 1HF, England.

CRANE Louise, b. 1965, England. Mezzo-Soprano. Education: Studied at the Guildhall School of Music, 1982-86, and at the Royal Northern College of Music with Barbara Robotham. Career: Sang in Opera Factory's Don Giovanni and Les Carmélites for Opéra de Lyon; Further engagements as Third Lady and Mistress Quickly with English Touring Opera, in The Siege of Corinth and The Nightingale for Chelsea Opera Group, Stravinsky's Mother Goose at Aldeburgh and Mozart's Marcellina for European Chamber Opera; English National Opera debut, 1993 in the premiere of Harvey's Inquest of Love; Sang Rita in Zampa for Opera Omnibus, 1996; Concert engagements in Rossini's Stabat Mater, Messiah, Beethoven's Ninth and Missa Solemnis, The Dream of Gerontius and Das Lied von der Erde; Touring performances of Gilbert and Sullivan. Address: Helen Sykes Management, Fourth Floor, Parkway House, Sheen Lane, East Sheen, London, SW14 8LS, England.

CRASS Franz, b. 9 Dec 1928, Wipperfurth, Germany. Singer (Bass-baritone). Education: Studied at the Cologne Musikhochschule with Clemens Glettenberg. Debut: Krefeld, 1954, as the King in Aida. Career: Sang at Hanover, 1956-62; Bayreuth Festival, 1959-73, as King Henry, the Dutchman, Fasolt, Wolfram, King Marke and Gurnemanz; La Scala, 1960, as Rocco and the Commendatore; Salzburg Festival as Sarastro; London, 1960, 1964, in the Missa Solemnis and Mozart's Requiem, conducted by Klemperer; From 1964 sang in Hamburg, Munich, Frankfurt and Vienna; With Hamburg Opera sang Barak in the British premiere of Die Frau ohne Schatten, Sadler's Wells Theatre, 1966; Other roles included Philip II, Nicolai's Falstaff, Duke Bluebeard and the Hermit in Der Freischütz; Often heard in sacred music by Bach. Recordings include: Der fliegende Holländer; Lohengrin; Ein Deutsches Requiem; Die Zauberflöte; Fidelio; Parsifal; Giulio Cesare by Handel; Der Freischütz; Speaker, Second Armed Man and Second Priest in Die Zauberflöte, conducted by Klemperer, CD issued 1989. Address: EMI Classics (Artists' Contracts), 30 Gloucester Place, London W1A 1ES, England.

CRAWFORD Bruce, b. 16 Mar 1929, West Bridgewater, Massachusetts, USA. Manager. m. Christine Crawford, 1958. Education: BS, University of Pennsylvania, 1952. Career: Entered advertising, 1956; Chief Executive Officer, BBDO International, 1977-; President, Batten, Barton, Durstine and Osborn, 1978-; Joined Board of Metropolitan Opera, 1976, serving on Executive Committee, 1977-, Vice-President, 1981, President, May 1984, General Manager, Metropolitan Opera, 1985-89. Address: c/o Metropolitan Opera, Lincoln Center, New York, NY 10023, USA.

CRAWFORD John (Charlton), b. 19 Jan 1931, Philadelphia, USA. Composer; Educator. m. Dorothy Lamb, 25 Jun 1955, 1 s, 1 d. Education: BMus, 1950, MMus, 1955, Yale School of Music; PhD at Harvard University, 1963. Career: Instructor of Music, Amherst College, 1961-63; Assistant Professor, Wellesley College, 1963-70; Associate Professor of Music, 1970-75, Professor of Music, 1975-94, University of California, Riverside. Compositions include: Magnificat, 1959; Ash Wednesday, 1968; Three Shakespeare Songs, 1970; Psalm 98, 1971; Don Cristobal and Rosita, 1979; Two Shakespeare Madrigals, 1980; Prelude, Fugue and Meditation for String Quartet, 1993. Recordings: String Quartet No 2, Sequoia Quartet, CD, 1993. Publications: Translator and Essayist, Arnold Schoenberg, Wassily Kandinsky: Letters, Pictures and Documents, 1984; Co-author with Dorothy L Crawford of Expressionism in 20th Century Music, 1993. Contributions to: Musical Quarterly; Journal of Arnold Schoenberg Institute. Honours: Boott Prize in Choral Composition, Harvard University, 1956; ASCAP Serious Music Award, 1969-74 and 1994-97. Memberships: ASCAP; American Musicological Society; American Music Center. Hobbies: Tennis; Sailing; Travel. Address: 203 Lexington Street, Lexington, MA 02138, USA.

CRAWFORD Timothy (Terry), b. 11 July 1948, Farnham, Surrey, England. Lutenist; Musicologist. m. Emilia de Grey, 18 Apr 1975, 1 son, 1 daughter. Education: University of Sussex, 1966-69; Royal College of Music, 1971-75; Arts Council Research Grant for Continental Travel, 1976. Career: Founder Member of early music ensembles Ars Nova and Parley of Instruments; Frequent appearances with English Baroque Soloists, London Philharmonic Orchestra; Assistant Editor, Early Music Magazine, 1984-85; Music Coordinator for Royal Academy of Arts. Recordings: Orfeo (Conductor: J E Gardiner); Il Ritorno d'Ulisse (Conductor: R Leppard); Sacred Music of Monteverdi (with Parley of Instruments and Emma Kirkby, Ian Partridge and David Thomas). Publications: Editor: Lute Society Journal and The Lute, 1979-87; Lord Danby's Lute Book (1987), containing several unknown works by Handel; Anthology of Renaissance Lute Music, 10 volumes; Dictionary of Guitar, Lute and Related Instruments. Contributions to: Frequent to The Lute, Early Music, Chelys, Journal of the Lute Society of America. Memberships: Lute Society, Committee 1975-87; National Early Music Association, Committee 1985-86; RMA; Musicians' Union; Early Music Centre Council. Address: 40 Albion Drive, Hackney, London E8 4LX, England.

CREECH Philip, b. 1 June 1950, Hempstead, New York, USA. Singer (Tenor). Education: Studied at Northwestern University. Career: Sang with Chicago Symphony Chorus, 1973-75; Metropolitan Opera, debut 1979 as Beppe in Pagliacci; Other roles at the Metropolitan have been Mozart's Pedrillo, Edmondo in Manon Lescaut, Brighella in Ariadne auf Naxos, Hylas in Les Troyens and Rinuccio in Gianni Schicchi; Many concert appearances. Recording: Carmina Burana. Address: c/o Metropolitan Opera, Lincoln Center, NY 10023, USA.

CREED Kay, b. 19 Aug 1940, Oklahoma City, USA. Singer; Voice Teacher; Opera Coach; Lecturer. m. Carveth Osterhaus, 5 Oct 1975, 1 daughter. Education: BMus, MPA, Oklahoma City University; Study in Munich, Germany, 1965. Debut: New York City Opera, 1965. Career: Created role of Fortuna in Don Rodrigo by Ginastera; Mrs Danton in Danton's Death; Opera roles include Carmen, Cenerentola, Dorabella, Hansel, Giulietta, Sextus in Julius Caeser, Ulrica, Urbain (Les Huguenots); Solo Performances with New York Philharmonic, Chicago Symphony, Philadelphia Orchestra, Carnegie Hall, Les Huguenots; Dallas Symphony; Naumberg Orchestra, Oklahoma City Symphony; Board of Directors, Cimarron Circuit Opera, 1985; Lecturer in Opera and Voice, Cantor Classes for Catholic Litugy; Founding Member, Oklahoma City Guild of Tulsa Opera; Founding Member, Oklahoma Opera and Musical Theater Company; Founding Director, Edmond Central Historical Opera. Address: 415 W Eubanks, Oklahoma City, OK 73118, USA.

CREFFELD Rosanna, b. 1945, England. Singer (Mezzo-Soprano). m. Richard Angas. Education: Royal College of Music with Flora Nielsen; Paris with Pierre Bernac; Further study with Vera Rosza in London. Debut: Glyndebourne 1969, as Second Lady in Die Zauberflöte. Career: Glyndebourne Touring Opera 1969-70, as Dorabella, and as Olga in Eugene Onegin; Appearances at Aix-en-Provence, Amsterdam, Strasbourg, Lyons and Bremen; Scottish Opera Glasgow as Dorabella and Cherubino; Monteverdi's Orfeo with the English National Opera; Paris Opera as Cherubino and as Lucretia in The Rape of Lucretia by Britten; Engagements in San Diego 1984, and Pittsburgh 1986; Lausanne 1986, in Honegger's Antigone. Recordings incl: Matilde in Rossini's Elisabetta Regina d'Inghilterra (Philips). Address: c/o English National Opera, St Martin's Lane, London WC2, England.

CRESHEVSKY Noah, b. 31 Jan 1945, Rochester, New York, USA. Composer. Education: Studied at the Eastman School, Rochester, 1950-61 and at the Juilliard School with Berio, 1966; Further study with Nadia Boulanger in Paris and with Virgil Thomson. Career: Teacher, Juilliard and Hunter College, New York; Brooklyn College from 1969; Visiting Professor, Princeton University, 1987-88 Director, centre for Computer Music, Brooklyn College, 1992-. Compositions include: Vier Lieder, stage piece, 1966; Three pieces in the Shape of a Square for 4 performers and tape, 1967; Monogenesis for voices, chamber orchestra and tape, 1968; Variations for 4 pianists and tape, 1969; Mirrors for dancers and tape, 1970; Circuit for tape, 1971; Broadcast, 1973; Chaconne for piano or harp, 1974; Guitar, 1975; In Other Words: Portrait of John Cage, 1976; Great Performances for any 2 instruments and tape, 1977; Great Performances, 1978; Portrait of Rudy Perez, 1978; Highway, 1979; Sonata, Nightscape and Celebration for tape, 1980-83; Strategic Defense Initiative, 1986; Electric String Quartet, 1988; Talea, 1991; Private Lives, 1993. Honours include: National Endowment of the Arts Grant, 1981. Address: c/o ASCAP, ASCAP Building, One Lincoln Plaza, NY 10023, USA.

CRESPIN Regine, b. 23 Feb 1927, Marseille, France. Singer (Soprano). Education: Paris Conservatoire with Suzanne Cesbron-Viseur and Georges Jouatte. Debut: Mulhouse 1950, as Elsa. Career: Sang Elsa at the Paris Opera, 1950; Sang Desdemona, Marguerite, the Prioress in Dialogues des Carmélites and Reiza in Oberon; Paris, Tosca, Ballo in Maschera; Iphigénie en Tauride; Die Walküre; Tannhaüser; Bayreuth Festival 1958-61, as Kundry and Sieglinde; La Scala Milan 1959, as Pizzetti's Phaedra; Glyndebourne 1959-60, as the Marschallin; Covent Garden from 1960, as Tosca, Elsa and Leonore in Fidelio; US debut Chicago 1962, as Tosca, Marshallin; Metropolitan Opera from 1962, the Marschallin, Senta, Amelia in Un Ballo in Maschera, Sieglinde, Brünnhilde in Die Walküre, Charlotte, Santuzza and Carmen; Teatro Colon, Buenos Aires from 1962, as Fauré's Pénélope, Didon and Cassandre in Les Troyens, Gluck's Iphigénie (en Tauride); At the Colon Parsifal, Der Rosenkavalier; Werther; Damnation de Faust; Carmen; various concerts and recitals; Salzburg Festival 1967, as Brünnhilde in Die Walküre, conducted by Karajan; Mezzo-Soprano roles from 1971, including title roles, Offenbach's La Grand Duchesse de Gerolstein and Menotti's The Medium, San Francisco, 1983, 1986; Sang Mme de Croisy at the Metropolitan, Dialogues des Carmélites, 1987; Retired 1989 after singing the Countess in The Queen of Spades, Paris; Recitalist in Poulenc, Wolf and Offenbach; Concert repertoire included Ravel's Shéhérazade and Nuits d'Eté by Berlioz. Recordings include: Les Dialogues des Carmélites (EMI); Sieglinde in Die Walküre, Der Rosenkavalier, Don Quichotte by Massenet (Decca); Brünnhilde in Die Walküre (Deutsche Grammophon); Tosca; Iphigénie en Tauride; Pénélope; Damnation de Faust; Carmen; Les Troyens; La Grande Duchesse de Gérolstein; Le Perichole; La Vie Parisienne; Poulenc's Stabat Mater. Address: Music International, 13 Ardilaun Road, London N5 2QR, England.

CRESSWELL Lyell (Richard), b. 13 Oct 1944, Wellington, New Zealand. Composer. m. Catherine Mawson, 4 Jan 1972. Education: BMus, Honours, Victoria University of Wellington, New Zealand, 1968; MusM, University of Toronto, Canada, 1970; PhD, Aberdeen University, 1974. Career: Music Organiser, Chapter Arts Centre, Cardiff, 1978-80; Forman Fellow in Composition, Edinburgh University, 1980-82; Cramb Fellow in Composition, 1982-85; Glasgow University, 1985-; Freelance Composer. Compositions: Ylur, 1990-91; Voices of Ocean Winds; The Pumpkin Massacre; Il Suono di Enormi Distanze; A Modern Ecstasy; Cello Concerto; O!; Salm; Speak for Us, Great Sea; Passacagli; O Let the Fire Burn, Concerto for String Quartet and Orchestra (premiered 1997). Recordings: Numerous. Honours: Ian Whyte Award, 1978; APRA Silver Scroll, 1980. Memberships: APRA; Association of Professional Composers; Composers Guild of Great Britain; Composers Association of New Zealand. Hobbies: Chess; Travel. Address: 4 Leslie Place, Edinburgh, EH4 1NQ, Scotland.

CRICHTON Ronald (Henry), b. 28 December 1913, Scarorough, Yorkshire, England. Writer; Music Critic. Education: Radley College, 1927-31; BA, MA, Christ Church, Oxford, 1932-36. Career: Programme Organiser, Anglo-French Art and Travel Society, London, 1937-39; Army Service, 1940-46; British Council: Greece, Belgium, West Germany, London, 1946-67; Music Criticsm, Financial Times, 1967-78; Freelance, 1979; Governing Body, British Institute of Recorded Sound, 1973-77; Arts Council Sub-Committees: Dance Theatre, 1973-76, Opera, 1976-80. Publications: Joint Editor, A Dictionary of Modern Ballet, 1959; Manuel de Falla: A Descriptive Catalogue of His Works, 1976; Falla - BBC Music Guide, 1982; The Memoirs of Ethel Smyth, 1987, edited and abridged by Ronald Crichton. Contributions to: The New Grove Dictionary of Music & Musicians; Heritage of Music, 1989; Newspapers, reviews, periodicals, in England and abroad. Memberships: Critics Circle, Society of Authors. Address: c/o David Higham Associates Limited, 5-8 Lower John Street, London W1R 4HA, England.

CRIDER Michele, b. 1963, Illinois, USA. Singer (Soprano). Debut: Leonora in Il Trovatore at Dortmund, 1989. Career: Appearances from 1991 at La Scala, Covent Garden, Deutsche Oper Berlin and the State Operas of Hamburg, Vienna, Munich, Stuttgart and Wiesbaden; Further appearances at Florence, Zurich and Barcelona; Roles have included Aida, Luisa Miller, Butterfly, the Trovatore and Forza Leonoras, Odabella (Attila), Lucrezia (Due Foscari and Amelia (Un Ballo in Maschera); US debut as Butterfly for San Diego, followed by Elisabeth in Don Carlos and the Trovatore Leonora at the Metropolitan; Opéra Bastille, Paris as Madama Butterfly; Concert engagements at Salzburg, Maggio Musicale Florence, Orange and Ravipia Festivals, Salle Pleyel Paris and London Barbican. Recordings include: Un Ballo in Masdera, under Carlo Rizzi; Elena and Margherita in Mefistofele, conducted by Muti; Verdi Requiem, under Richard Hickox. Honours include: Finalist, 1988 Pavarotti Competition; Prize winner, 1989 Geneva International Music Competition. Address: c/o Metropolitan Opera, Lincoln Center, New York, NY 12003, USA.

CRIST Richard, b. 21 Oct 1947, Harrisburg, Pennsylvania, USA. Classical Singer (Bass); Vocal Instructor. m. (1) Assunta Ercolano, 3 Aug 1975, divorced, 1 daughter, (2) Yvonne Brennan, 21 Mar 1993, 1 son. Education: BS, Music Education, Messiah College, Grantham, Pennsylvania, 1970; MM, Voice, New England Conservatory, Boston, 1972. Deubt: Berlioz's Les Troyens, Opera Company of Boston, 1972. Career: Appearances with Opera Companies including: Santa Fe, Boston, Philadelphia, San Francisco, Memphis, Mobile, Orlando, Lake George and the Virginia and Goldovsky Opera Theatres; European debut with Opera de Lyon in the French creation of Die Soldaten by Zimmermann (1982) under Ken Russell and Serge Baudo; Opera and Oratorio appearances throughout USA and with various orchestras; Canadian debut with Toronto Mendelssohn Choir, 1984; Debut with Philippine Philharmonic Orchestra, Internationale Bamboo Organ Festival, Manila, 1984; Frequent Soloist with Pro Arte Chorale of New Hersey, Beethoven Society of New York, Rochester Oratorio Society and the Bethlehem Bach Festival; Operatic Repertoire of over 75 roles and nearly 100 Oratorio and Symphonic Works; Opera Performance of Tchaikovsky's The Queen of Spades, filmed for PBS TV, Philadelphia, 1984; Debut in La Traviata, Metropolitan Opera, 1985; Sang in Semiramide, Fidelio, Meistersinger, Der Freischütz and Ballo in Maschera, Hamburg State Opera, 1985; Debut in Contes d'Hoffmann, San Diego Opera, 1985; Debut in Pelléas and Mélisande, Philadelphia Orchestra, 1986; Appearances in Henze's The English Cat, Alte Opera, Frankfurt, Germany and Turin, Italy, 1986; First Performance in USA of Mayr's Requiem, Alice Tully Hall 1986; Sang with the Company of the Bolshoi, Moscow, at Boston, 1988 in Schedrin's Dead Souls; premiere of The Balcony by Di Domenica, Boston, 1990; other roles include Mozart's Leporello, Osmin, and Sarastro; Rocco in Fidelio, Gremin in Eugene Onegin and Samuel in Un Ballo in Maschera; Season 1991/2 in Gluck's La Rencontre Imprévue at Wexford, as Mozart's Bartolo in Dublin and in the Rossini Birthday Gala at the Barbican Hall; Sang with Bolshoi Opera, Moscow, 1991; Svertlovsk Philharmonic Orchestra, 1993. Current Management: Thea SAFIMM, Ludvig Brunner, 250 West 57th Street, New York, NY 10107, USA. Membership: American Guild of Musical Artists. Address: 484 West 43rd Street, Apartment 9-S, New York, NY 10036, USA.

CRISTESCU Constanta, b. 10 May 1959, Vatra-Dornei, Romania. Researcher. Education: Academia de Muzica George Dima, Cluj Napoca; Laboratorul de cercetari interdisciplinare al Universitatii din Cluj Napoca condus de Prof.Dr.Doc Elena Popoviciu; Liceul de Muzica, Cluj, Romania; Academia de Muzica G Dima, Cluj Napoca, Romania; Academia de Muzica, Bucharest, Romania; Assistant Researcher, Byzantine Music, Musicology, Ethnomusicology, Orthodox Monasterys. Debut: Iasi-Cluj napoca, 1982. Career: Soprano in Antifonia, Choir, 1980-84, Romania, Italy, Deutschland, Belgium; Alto and Soprano in Psalmodia, Choir, Bucharest, Romania; Researcher in Ethnomusicology Publications; Radio Appearances in Cluj Napoca, Bucherest. Recordings: Les chemins duparadis, 1997; Rethoric der Byzantine Music. Contributions to: Journals and magazines. Honours: Doctorate, Musicology and Ethnomusicology. Memberships: ICTM; IOV-UNESCO; DEMOS-REDAKTION; Comisii ale Academiei Romania; UCMR; Laboratorul interd Cluj. Address: Str Al Obregia nr 3, Bloc M2, etaj 9, ap 73, Sector 4, 75571 Bucharest, Romania.

CROCKETT Donald, b. 18 February 1951, Pasadena, California, USA. Composer; University Professor; Conductor. m. (1) divorced, 1 daughter, (2) Vicki Ray, 6 June 1988. Education: BM, 1974, MM, 1976, University of Southern California; PhD, University of California, Santa Barbara, 1981. Career: Conductor, USC Contemporary Music Ensemble, Monday Evening Concerts, regional and national premieres of music by Lutoslawski, Davies, Musgrave, Gruber, Ruders, et al; Composer-in-Residence, Pasadena Chamber Orchestra (conductor Robert Duerr), 1984-87; Professor, University of Southern California; Composer-in-Residence, Los Angeles Chamber Orchestra (conductor Christof Perick), 1991-97. Compositions: Occhi dell'alma mia (high voice & guitar), 1977; Lyrikos (tenor & orchestra), 1979; The Pensive Traveller (high voice and piano), 1982; Vox in Rama (double chorus & orchestra), 1983; Melting Voices (orchestra), 1986; The 10th Muse (soprano & orchestra), 1986; dell'alma mia (high voice & guitar), 1977; Array for String Quartet, commissioned by the Kronos Quartet, 1988; Pilgrimage for piano solo, 1988; Still Life with Bell, 14 players, commissioned by the Los Angeles Philharmonic, 1989; Celestial Mechanics, oboe and string quartet, 1990; String Quartet No 2, commissioned by the Stanford String Quartet, 1993; Roethke Preludes (orchestra), commissioned by the Los Angeles Chamber Orchestra, 1994. Recordings: Melting Voices, orchestra, Orchestra of the Americas, Paul Freeman, conductor; Celestial Mechanics (oboe & string quartet), Los Angeles Chamber Orchestra. Publications include: Still Life With Bell, 14 players, Celestial Mechanics, oboe and string quartet. Contributions to: Stucky, Hartke, Crockett; Conversations in Los Angeles, in Contemporary Music Review, 1994. Honours: Kennedy Center Friedheim Award, 2nd Prize, 1991; Goddard Lieberson Fellowship from the American Academy of Arts and Letters, 1994. Memberships: American Music Center; American Composers Forum. Hobbies: Skiing; Backpacking. Address: School of Music, University of Southern California, Los Angeles, CA 90089-0851, USA.

CROFT Richard, b. 1959, USA. Singer (Tenor). Career: Sang Nemorino at Washington and Ramiro in La Cenerentola at St Louis, season 1986-87; European engagements include Mozart's Belfiore, Achille in Gluck's Iphigénie en Aulide and Belmonte at Drottningholm; Strasbourg and Nice, 1990-91, as Don Ottavio and Ferrando; Welsh National Opera, 1989, as Belmonte (repeated at the Metropolitan, 1991); Glyndebourne, 1991, Don Ottavio; Septimus in Handel's Theodora at Glyndebourne, 1996 and Tom Rakewell at Santa Fe. Recordings include: Video of Die Entführung (Virgin). Address: c/o Metropolitan Opera, Lincoln Center, New York, NY 10023, USA.

CROLL Gerhard, b. 25 May 1927, Dusseldorf, Germany. Musicologist. Education: Studied at University of Gottingen, doctorate 1954. Career: Assistant Lecturer, University of Munster, 1958; Chair of Musicology, Salzburg from 1966; President, International Gluck-Gesellschaft from 1987. Publications: Editions of Steffani's Tassilone and Die Entführung aus dem Serail; Gluck's Le Cinesi for the complete edition, 1958, Editor-in-Chief from 1960 and Alceste 1988; Entries on Gluck and Weerbecke in The New Grove Dictionary of Music; Articles on Mozart discoveries Larghetto and Allegro in E-flat for two pianos and string quartet arrangement of a Bach fugue, K405; Member of Zentralinstitut fur Mozart-Forschung and contributor to the Neue-Mozart-Ausgabe. Address: c/o Hochschul fur Musik und Darstellende Kunst, Mozarteum Mirabellplatz 1, A-5020 Salzburg, Austria.

CRONIN Stephen (John), b. 2 September 1960, Brisbane, Queensland, Australia. Composer. Education: PhD, University of Queensland, 1995; Studied with Colin Brumby, 1978-81. Career: Faculty Member, University of Queensland, 1984, Queensland Conservatory, 1986; Commissions from Seymour Group 1993, Synergy 1993; Australian Chamber Orchestra, 1995. Compositions include: In Moments Unseen for string quartet, 1984; Requiem, for chorus, percussion, 2 pianos and harp, 1985; Duo Concertante, for clarinet, viola and strings, 1986; The Drover's Wife for narrator and orchestra, 1987; Piano Concerto, 1989; The Snake Pit for ensemble, 1990; Eros and Agape for chamber ensemble, 1990; House Songs for tenor and ensemble, 1991; Eros Reclaimed, for ensemble, 1992; Carmina Pu for chorus, 1992; Cries and Whispers, for orchestra, 1993; Eve Love can Wield a Stealthy Blade, for bass clarinet and percussion, 1993; Blow for wind octet, 1994; Kiss, for percussion quartet, 1994; Après Nuages for string orchestra, 1995. Honours include: Vienna Modern Masters Recording Project, 1992. Address: c/o APRA, 1A Eden Street, Crows Nest, NSW 2065, Australia.

CROOK Howard, b. 15 June 1947, New Jersey, USA. Singer (Tenor). Education: Studied at State University, Illinois, and appeared at first in concert. Career: Sang at the Seattle Opera, then appeared as Pelléas and Belmonte at Amsterdam; Paris Opéra-Comique, 1987, as Lully's Atys, Aix-en-Provence, 1987, as Vulcan in Lully's Psyche; Schwetzingen, 1988, in Salieri's Tarare, Versailles, 1988, in Rameau's Pygmalion; Albert Hall, London, 1989, in Daniel Purcell's The Judgement of Paris; Sang in Cesti's Orontea at the 1990 Innsbruck Festival, Rameau's Castor et Pollux at Aix (1991) and Lully's Alceste at the Théâtre des Champs-Elysées, Paris; Sang with Les Musiciens du Louvre in Lully's Acis et Galatée at Beaune, 1996. Recordings include: St Matthew Passion and Messiah (DGG); Scylla at Glaucus (Erato); Bach Magnificat and Pygmalion (Harmonia Mundi). Address: c/o Tiroler Landestheater, Rennweg 2, A-6020 Innsbruck, Austria.

CROOM James, b. 1960, North Carolina, USA. Singer (Tenor). Education: Studied with James Schwabacher. Career: Appeared for two seasons as apprentice artist with Santa Fe Opers; Has sung twenty roles with Scottish Opera, the Glasgow Grand Opera (Calaf, 1990), Western Opera Theatre and San Francisco Opera; Appearances in Simon Boccanegra, Manon Lescaut, Die Zauberflöte (Monostatos) and Die Meistersinger for Scottish Opera; Other roles include Arbace (Idomeneo), Goro (Madama Butterfly) and Mephistopheles in Busoni's Doktor Faust. Recordings include: Video of L'Africaine, from San Francisco Opera. Honours: Regional finalist, Metropolitan Opera Auditions; Regional Winner, National Association of Teachers of Singing Competition. Address: c/o Norman McCann International Artists Ltd, The Coach House, 56 Lawrie Park Gardens, London SE26 6XJ, England.

CROPPER Peter, b. 1945, England. Violinist. Education: Studied with Sidney Griller at the Royal Academy of Music, with Alexander Mo at skowsky whilst at the University of Keele and with Vilmos Tatrai in Budapest. Career: Founder Member, Lindsay String Quartet, 1986; Regular tours of Europe, England and the USA; From 1972 quartet in residence at Sheffield University, then Manchester University (1978); Premiered the 4th Quartet of Tippett at the 1979 Bath festival and commissioned Tippett's 5th Quartet, 1992; For the Chamber Music Festival established at Sheffield, 1984; Regular concerts at the Wigmore Hall, including Haydn series, 1987. Recordings include: Complete cycles of Bartók, Tippett and Beethoven; CDs of Haydn quartets Live from the Wigmore Hall (ASV). Honours: Prize Winner (with members of Lindsay Quartet) at Liège International Competition, 1969; Gramophone Chamber Award for late Beethoven Quartets, 1984; Plays Stradivarius from the Golden Period. Address: c/o Ingpen & Williams Ltd, 14 Kensington Court, London W8 5DN, England.

CROSBY John (O'Hea), b. 12 July 1926, New York City, USA. Conductor; Opera Impresario; Music Educator. Education: BA, Yale University, 1950; Studied Composition with Paul Hindemith; Conducting with Rudolph Thomas and Pierre Monteux. Career: Accompanist and Conductor, New York City, 1951-56; Founder-General Director, Santa Fe Opera Company, New Mexico, 1957-, Conducted Daphne and Butterfly there, 1996; Oversaw many USA and world premieres; President, Opera America, 1976-80; Manhattan School of Music, 1976-86; Accompanist, Coach and Conductor, New York City, 1951-56; Guest Conductor, various opera companies, Canada and USA, 1960-. Honours: LittD, University of New Mexico, 1967; MusD, College of Santa Fe, 1968; Cleveland Institute of Music, 1974; LHD, University of Denver, 1977; Honorary DFA, Yale University, 1991; National Medal of Arts, USA, 1991; Verdienstkreuz First Class Bundesrepublik, Germany, 1992. Address: PO Box 2408, Santa Fe, NM 87501, USA.

CROSS Gregory, b. 1960, USA. Singer (Tenor). Career: European debut, 1992, as Renaud in Gluck's Armide at Versailles, under Marc Minkowski; Further appearances as Rossini's Almaviva for Opéra de Nancy, Ferrando at Strasbourg, Tamino for Greater Miami Opera, Lurcano in Ariodante for Welsh National Opera and in Messiah at San Francisco; Sang Iopas in Les Troyens under Colin Davis and Leukippos in Daphne under André Previn, both with the LSO; Further concerts include Haydn's Seasons and Mozart's Requiem in Canada, and the Saint Matthew Passion and Mozart's C minor Mass at the Kennedy Center, Washington DC. Recordings include: Les Troyens, under Charles Dutoit (Decca). Address: Lies Askonas Ltd, 6 Henrietta Street, London WC2E 8LA, England.

CROSS Ronald, b. 18 Feb 1929, Ft Worth, Texas, USA. Musicologist; Keyboard, Wind & String Player;Conductor; Composer. Education: Guilmant Organ School, New York; Studied Organ with Harold Friedell, New York; Master Classes with E Power Biggs and Virgil Fox;BA, Centenary College of Louisiana, 1950; Studied Musicology with Gustave Reese and Curt Sachs; Composition with Philip James; MA 1953, PhD 1962, New York University; Studied at Venice Conservatory, University of Florence, Accademia Chigiana, Siena, University of Siena, University of Vienna, 1955-57. Career: Organist and Choirmaster, New York Churches; Concert appearances as keyboard, wind, string player and conductor; Faculty Member, Notre Dame College of Staten Island, 1958-68; Associate Professor 1968-75, Professor 1975-, Director of the Collegium Musicum, Chairman of the Music Department 1981-84, Wagner College, New York. Compositions: Many vocal and chamber pieces. Recordings: Several discs; Video, The Harpsichord Today: An Interview with Ronald Cross, 1991. Publications: Edited Matthaeus Pipelare: Opera omnia, 3 volumes, 1966-67. Honours: Performance Grants for Harpsichord Recitals, New York State Council on the Arts, 1986-97. Address: 221 Ward Avenue, Staten Island, NY 10304, USA.

CROSSE Gordon, b. 1 Dec 1937, Bury, Lancashire, England. Composer. Education: Oxford University withWellesz; Accademia di Santa Cecilia, Rome with Petrassi. Career: Birmingham University 1964-69, as Tutor in extra mural department and in music department; Fellow in Music, University of Essex, 1969-76; Visiting Professor in Composition, University of California, 1977; Freelance Composer, from 1978; Commissions from the BBC Symphony Orchestra, Royal Philharmonic Orchestra, London Symphony Orchestra and Festivals of Aldeburgh, Cheltenham and Edinburgh; The Story of Vasco premiered at the London Coliseum. Compositions: Stage Purgatory, 1-act opera after Yeats, 1966; The Grace of Todd, comedy, 1969; Wheel of the World, entertainment on Chaucer's The Canterbury Tales, 1972; The Story of Vasco, opera in 3 acts, 1974; Potter Thompson, 1-act music drama, 1975; Orchestral: Elegy, 1959; Concerto da Camera, 1962; Symphony No 1, 1964; Ceremony, 1966; 2 Violin Concertos, 1969, 1970; Some Marches on a Ground, 1970; Ariadne for oboe and ensemble, 1972; Symphony No 2, 1975; Epiphany Variations, 1976; Wildboy, 1977; Thel for ensemble, 1978; Symphony for Chamber Orchestra, 1976; Dreamsongs, 1979; Cello Concerto, 1979; Array for trumpet and orchestra, 1986; Quiet, for wind band, 1987; Vocal: Changes for soprano, baritone, chorus and orchestra, 1965; The Covenant of the Rainbow for chorus and organ; For the Unfallen for tenor, horn and strings, 1968; Memories of Morning Night for mezzo and orchestra, 1971; The New World, poems by Ted Hughes for voice and piano, 1978; Harvest Songs for chorus and orchestra, 1980; Dreamcanon I, for chorus, 2 pianos and percussion, 1981; Chamber: String Quartet, 1980; Wave Songs for cello and piano, 1983; Meet My Folks, 1964, Holly from the Bongs, 1974, and Harvest Songs, 1980 all for children. Address: Brants Cottage, Blackheath, Wenhaston, Halesworth, Suffolk IP19 9EX, England.

CROSSLEY Paul, b. 17 May 1944, Dewsbury, Yorkshire, England. Pianist. Education: Organ Scholar at Mansfield College, Oxford; Piano with Fanny Waterman; Study with Messiaen and Yvonne Loriod in Paris. Career: Won 1968 Messiaen Piano Competition at Royaun; 1973 premiered Tippett's 3rd Sonata (Bath) and Maw's Personae (London); Jan 1985 premiered Tippett's 4th Sonata in Los Angeles; 1986 presented series of six programmes for Channel 4 TV, Sinfonietta, featuring major 20th century composers; Programmes on Liszt and Ravel for BBC TV and Poulenc for Hessischer Rundfunk, Germany; Piano Soloist in British stage premiere of Janácek's Diary of One Who Disappeared, London Coliseum, 1986; Artistic Director of the London Sinfonietta, 1988-94; Season 1993-94, Debussy recital tour of Japan; Engagements with Hallé, BBC Scottish, Netherlands Radio Philharmonic and Los Angeles Orchestras; Played in the British premiere of Henze's Requiem at the 1993 London Proms; Ravel recital at the South Bank, London, 1997. Recordings: Diapason d'Or for the complete solo works of Ravel and Tippett; Prix Caecilia for the Berg Chamber Concerto with the London Sinfonietta; Grand Prix de l'Académie Française for the Fauré Violin sonatas, with Arthur Grumiaux; Recently recorded Franck and complete Debussy piano works, and Franck's Symphonic Variations with Vienna Philharmonic under Carlo Maria Guilini. Address: 26 Wadham Road, London SW15 2LR, England.

CROSSLEY-HOLLAND Peter (Charles), b. 28 Jan 1916, London, England. Composer; Professor; Ethnomusicologist. Education: BA, St John's College, Oxford; MA, 1941; BMus, 1943; Royal College of Music, London; School of Oriental and African Studies, University of London. Debut: League of Arts Concerts, London, 1938. Career: Conductor of own compositions on BBC radio and at English festivals; Appearances as Medieval Harpist, TV and Radio; Numerous broadcasts and lectures on music of Celts, Tibet and Orient; Assistant Director, Institute of Comparative Music Studies, Berlin, 1964-66; Visiting Lecturer, University of Illinois, 1966; Visiting Professor of Music, University of Hawaii, 1968-69; Professor of Music, University of California at Los Angeles, 1969-93; External Examiner in Music, University of Wales, Aberystwyth, 1987-93; Currently, Emeritus Professor. Compositions: Cantata The Sacred Dance; 2 Songs for soprano and piano; 24 Rounds of Nature; Cantata The Visions of St Godric; Des Puys d'Amors, songs for string orchestra and harp; Breton Tunes; Field Recordings mainly on Tibetan Music; Towards Phi, symphonic poem, 1990; Invocation at Midsummer, (tenor recorder) Symphony in D, 1994. Publications: Secular Medieval Music in Wales, 1942; Editor and co-author, Music in Wales, 1948; Music: A Report on Musical Life in England, 1949; The Pelican History of Music, volume 1 part 1, 1960; Musical Artefacts from Prehispanic West Mexico, monograph, 1980; Wales (Music of) in the New Grove, 1980; Musical Instruments in Tibetan Legend and Folklore, monograph, 1982. Contributions to: Learned journals; Culture is Our Destination, in Trivium vol 23, summer, 1988; Editor, Journal of the International Folk Music Council, vols XVII-XX, 1965-68; Editor, Selected Reports in Ethnomusicology, vol II No 1. Honours: Essays in Honour of Peter Crossley-Holland on his Sixty-Fifth Birthday, UCLA, 1983; Honorary Professor, University of Wales, Lampeter 1987-; Honorary Fellowships, University of Wales and Bangor. Memberships: Composers Guild; Fellow, Royal Anthropological Institute. Address: Plas Geler, Llandysul, Dyfed SA44 5AZ, West Wales.

CROSSMAN (Wallace) Bruce, b. 2 November 1961, Auckland, New Zealand. Composer. m. Colleen Anne Guild, 18 January 1986, 1 son. Education: MusB (Hons), 1983, MMus with Jack Speirs, 1985, Otago University, Dunedin; MPhil with David Blake, York University, England, 1990; Candidate for Doctor of Creative Arts degree, University of Wollongong, 1996. Career: New Zealand Queen Elizabeth II Arts Council Grants, 1983-93; Composer-in-Residence, Nelson School of Music, New Zealand, 1987; Fellow in Composition, Pacific Composers Conference, Japan, 1990; Mozart Fellow, Otago University, New Zealand, 1992; Visiting Lecturer in Music, Waikato University, 1994. Compositions: Piece Number Two for orchestra, 1984; Pezzo Languendo for solo piano, 1984; Expression in Blue for violin and piano, 1988; Dual for two violins, 1988; Dialogue for Jerusalem for clarinet and piano, 1989; A Peace in Time for 2 pianos, 1989; City of Broken Dreams for orchestra, 1989; Timbres for guitar, 1991; Colour Resonances and Dance for orchestra, 1996; Rituals for Soprano and String Quartet, 1996. Honours: Corbould Composition Competition Prize, 1996; Australian Postgraduate Award, 1996-98. Memberships: Composers Association of New Zealand; Australian Music Centre. Address: c/o Faculty of Creative Arts, University of Wollongong, Northfields Avenue, Wollongong, NSW 2522, Australia.

CROW Todd, b. 25 Jul 1945, Santa Barbara, California, USA. Pianist; Music Professor. m. Linda Goolsby, 12 Aug 1967, 1 s, 1 d. Education: BA, Univerity of California, 1967; MS, Juilliard School, 1968; Music Academy of The West. Debut: London, 1975; New York, 1981; London orchestral debut, LPO, 1986. Career: Has given numerous concerts in USA, Europe and South America; Mount Desert Festival of Chamber Music, Maine; Maverick Concerts, Woodstock, New York, Music Mountain, Connecticut; Radio appearances on BBC, National Public Radio and New York City Stations; Chairman and Professor of Music, Department of Music, Vassar College, Poughkeepsie, NY; New York orchestral debut with American Symphony Orchestra, 1992; Additional festivals include: Casals Festival and Bard Music Festival; Music Director, Mount Desert Festival of Chamber Music, Maine; Performances with St Luke's Chamber Ensemble. Recordings: Schubert Piano Sonatas; The Artistry of Todd Crow; Mozart Piano Concerto K467; Liszt E flat Piano Concerto; Berlioz/Liszt Symphonie Fantastique; Complete music for cello and piano by Mendelssohn (with Mark Shuman, cellist). Publication: Bartók Studies, 1976. Contributions to: Notes; Journal of the American Liszt Society. Hobbies: Golf; Reading. Address: Department of Music, Vassar College, Poughkeepsie, NY 12604, USA.

CROXFORD Eileen, b. 21 March 1924, Leighton Buzzard, Bucks, England. Cellist. m. Concert piaist, David Parkhouse, (deceased 1989), 2 sons. Education: Royal College of Music; Studied with Effie Richardson, Ivor James, Pablo Casals. Debut: London, Wigmore Hall; BBC Promenade Concerts, Royal Albert Hall. Career: Recitalist worldwide with husband, David Parkhouse; Concertos with leading orchestras; Trio with David Parkhouse and High Bean; Acclaimed in 1987 as world's longest standing Trio; Tours of East and West Europe, North and South America, Far East, Middle East, China and North Africa. Recordings: Beethoven, Ghost and Archduke Trios, Irish Songs; Schubert, Trout Quintet; Trios by Bush, Mendelssohn and Ravel; Cello and piano sonatas by Dohnányi, Barber, Rachmaninov, Kodály, Debussy; Vaughan Williams, 2 Quartets, On Wenlock Edge, Studies on Folk Songs; Warlock, The Curlew; Lennox Berkeley, Sextet; Elgar, String Quartet. Honours: Alexander Prize, 1945; Queen's Prize, 1948; Boise Foundation Award, 1949; Fellow, Royal College of Music, 1983; Cobbett Medal of the Worshipful Co of Musicians for services to Chamber Music, 1991; Founder, Parkhouse Award, The International Chamber Music Award for Piano based groups in memory of David Parkhouse. Membership: Founder, Member with David Parkhouse of Music Group of London. Hobbies: Family; Travelling; Writing; Teaching; Adjudicating. Address: 11 Roehampton Ct, Queens Ride, London SW13, England.

CRUMB George, b. 24 Oct 1929, Charleston, West Virginia, USA. Composer; University Professor. m. 2 sons, 1 daughter. Education: BM, Mason College of Music, 1950; MMus, University of Illinois, 1952; DMA, University of Michigan, 1959; Hochschule für Musik,Berlin, 1955-56. Career: Professor, Composition, University of Pennsylvania. Compositions: (all Recorded) include 5 Pieces for Piano; Night Music; 4 Nocturnes for violin and piano; Echoes of Time and the River; 4 Processionals for orchestra; Night of the 4 Moons; Black Angels for electric string quartet; Makrokosmos Vols 1-V, 1972-79; Lux Whale for 3 masked musicians and ensemble, 1971; Dream Sequence, violin, cello, piano and percussion, 1976; Star-Child for soprano, children's chorus and orchestra, 1977; Apparition, Whitman, for soprano and piano, 1979; A Little Suite for Christmas, 1980; Gnomic Variations for piano, 1981; Pastoral Drone for organ, 1982; Processional for piano, 1983; A Haunted Landscape, orchestra, 1984; Federico's Little Songs for soprano, flute and percussion 1986; Zeitgeist for two amplified pianos, 1987; Quest forr guitar and ensemble, 1990; Easter Dawning for Carillan, 1991. Honours: Pulitzer Prize in Music for Echoes of Time and the River, 1968; Koussevitsky International Recording Award, 1971; International Rostrum of Composers (UNESCO) Award, 1971. Membership: Broadcast Music Inc. Hobby: Reading. Address: 240 Kirk Lane, Media, PA 19063, USA.

CRUZ DE CASTRO Carlos, b. 23 Dec 1941, Madrid, Spain. Composer; Professor; Production Manager. Education: Studied Law and Social Sciences at Universidad Central de Madrid; Studied music at Royal High Conservatory of Music, Madrid, composition with Gerardo Gombau and Francisco Calés, conducting with Enrique García Asensio and composition with Milko Kélemen at Hochschule Robert Schumann in Dusseldorf and with Gunther Becker and Antonio Janigro. Career includes: Participant at the VII Biennial in Paris, representing Spain with his pieces, Menaje for Non-Conventional Instruments and, Pente for Wind Quintet, 1971; Co-Founder with Mexican pianist and composer, Alicia Urreta of the Spanish-Mexican Festival of Contemporary Music, 1973; Took part in Premio Italia representing Spanish National Radio with his work, Mixtitlan in 1975 and at the Composers' International Tribune in Paris in 1979; With 6 other composers he established the Spanish Association of Symphonic Composers in 1976; Professor of Composition, Counterpoint, Chamber Music, Musical Forms and Aesthetics at the Conservatory at Albacete, 1983; Currently Production Manager of Radio Clásica for Spanish National Radio. Compositions include: Theatre: El Momento De Un Instante II, 1973-74; Ballet: Carta A Mi Hermana Salud, 1985; Instrumental: Imagenes De Infancia for Piano; There And Back for Guitar; Concerto for Orchestra, 1984, Suite for Guitar No 1, 1993; Toccata Vieja En Tono Nuevo. Recordings include: Ida Y Vuelta; Concierto Para Guitarra Y Orquesta De Cuerda; Menaje; Morfologia Sonora No 1. Honour: Music Prize by Mexican Union of Theatre and Music Chroniclers, 1977. Membership: Spanish Association of Symphonic Composers. Hobby: Chess. Address: Clara Del Rey 46, 28002 Madrid, Spain.

CRUZ-ROMO Gilda, b. 12 Feb 1940, Guadalajara, Mexico. Opera Singer (Soprano). Education: Mexico City Conservatory, with Angel Esquivel. Debut: Mexico City 1962, in Die Walküre. Career: Metropolitan Opera from 1970 as Madame Butterfly, Puccini's Tosca, Manon and Suor Angelica; Verdi's Leonora (Trovatore and La Forza del Destino), Elisabeth de Valois, Aida, Amelia (Ballo in Maschera) and Violetta; Season 1972-73 at Covent Garden and La Scala Milan, as Aida; Appearances in Australia, South America and the Soviet Union and at the Vienna State Opera, Rome Opera, Paris Opera, New York City Opera and Chicago Lyric Opera; Concert appearances in Canada, Mexico, USA, Japan, Israel and Soviet Union; Vienna Staatsoper, 1979 as Leonora in La Forza del Destino; New Jersey and Connecticut, 1988 as Donna Anna and Cherubini's Medea; Ars Musica Chorale and Orchestra, Englewood, New Jersey, as Santuzza and Matilda in the US premiere of Mascagni's Silvana, 1988-89. Recordings include: Rossini's Stabat Mater; Video of Aida at 1976 Orange Festival. Honours include: 1st Prize, Metropolitan Opera National Award, 1970. Address: c/o Harold Holt Ltd, 31 Sinclair Road, London W14 0NS, England.

CSAMMER Alfred, b. 30 Nov 1938, Budweis, Bohemia. Violinist. Education: Started to study Violin at age of 5 with his father, Eugen, a former student of Sevcik; Studied at Music Academy in Karlsruhe with Heinz Stanske, Bronislaw Gimpel & Henri Lewkowicz; In Stuttgart with Ricardo Odnoposoff; In Zurich with Nathan Milstein. Career: Concerts, radio productions, master classes and recordings in most European countries, in the USA and Canada as a Soloist and in chamber music; Artistic Director of Karlsruhe Chamber Orchestra; Teacher of Violin at the Johannes-Gutenberg University, Mainz. Recordings: Mendelssohn Sonata in F-major; Dvorak's Romantic Pieces, Strauss Sonata in Eb-major with Pianist Sontraud Speidel. Hobbies: Drawing; Filming; Making Cartoons. Address: Seegasse 2, D-7500 Karlsruhe 41, Germany.

CSAPO Gyula, b. 26 Sept 1955, Papa, Hungary. Composer. m. Eva Botai, 10 Oct 1980, 1 son. Education: Béla Bartok Conservatory; Diploma in Composition & Music Theory, Franz Liszt Academy of Music, Budapest, 1981; Institute pour la Recherche et Coordination Acoustique/Musique, Paris, 1982; PhD, Composition, State University of New York, Buffalo, 1989. Career: Member, New Music Studio, Budapest; Extensive concert performances, radio recordings and broadcasts with, or without the Studio in Budapest, Warsaw, Torun (Poland), Vienna, Darmstadt, Milan, Rotteerdam, London, Frankfurt am Main, Edmonton (Alberta, Canada), Buffalo, New York, USA, Nedw York City; Film music scores; Assoicated with Protean Forms Collective, New York City. Compositions incl: Krapp's Last Tape, After Beckett, 1974-75; Tao Song, 1:1/2, 1974-77; Fanatritraritrana, 1977-81; Handshake After Shot, 1977; Hark, Edward..., 1979-81; Na'Conxypan, 1978-88; Phedre's Hymn to the Sun, 1981; Yagul, 1987; Infrared Notes, No 1: (Prismed Through Darkness), 1986-88. Hobbies: Maya Archaeology; Japanese & Indian Culture and Philosophy; Persian Literature; Tennis. Address: 182 Graham Avenue, Apt No 3, Brooklyn, NY 11206, USA.

CSENGERY Adrienne, b. 1950, Hungary. Singer (Soprano). Education: Studied at the Bartok Conservatory in Budapest and with Eva Kutrucz at the Franz Liszt Academy. Career: Early engagements at the Budapest State Opera and in Monteverdi's Vespers, conducted by Lovro von Matacic; Engagements in Zagreb, Dubrovnik and Palermo; Marzelline in Fidelio at the 1974 Munich Festival; Hungarian State Opera Budapest as Marguerite, Lulu and Anne Trulove; Mozart roles at Munich; Susanna, Pamina, Fiordiligi and Zerlina; Appearances at Hamburg, Bayreuth, Cologne, Amsterdam and Bern with Sawallisch, Pritchard, Haitink, Lopez-Cobos, Michael Gielen and Roderick Brydon; Glyndebourne Festival 1976-77 as Susanna and Zerlina, in productions directed by Peter Hall; Wigmore Hall recital 1980, with English Canzonettas by Haydn; Gave the world premiere of Kurtag's Messages of the Late Miss RV Troussova, with the Ensemble Intercontemporain conducted by Boulez, 1981; Later performances of the work in La Rochelle, Milan, Venice, Florence, Budapest, Bath, Edinburgh and London; Gave the British premiere of Kafka Fragments by Kurtag at the 1989 Almeida Festival, London. Recordings include: Wigmore Hall Recital 1980 (Hungaroton); Messages of the late RV Troussova (Erato). Honours include: Gramophone Record Prize, 1983;

Gramophone Contemporary Music Award, 1985. Address: c/o Christopher Tennant Artists Management, 11 Lawrence Street, London SW3 5NB, England.

CSENKI Imre, b. 7 Aug 1912, Puspokladany, Hungary. Composer; Conductor. m. Maria Sandor, 20 Aug 1938, 1 son, 1 daughter. Education: Teachers Diploma, 1932; Professor's Diploma, Singing and Music, Franz Liszt Royal Music Academy, 1942. Debut: Conductor of the Choir of Debrecen College Concerts in Hungary and Switzerland, 1946. Career: Founder, Hungarian State Folk Ensemble, 1950; Artistic Director, Chief Conductor, 1950-70; Conductor, Choir of the Hungarian Radio, 1964-66. Compositions: Gypsy Suite; Bagpipe Song; Choral Works; Rhapsody for Violin and Piano; 99 Gypsy Songs; Gypsy Ballads and Laments; Two Operas; Transylvanian Mosaic No 1 and No 2 for orchestra; 12 Choral works on poems by Sandor Weores for mixed, female and children's choir; Cantat 1988 for mixed choir and symphony orchestra; Black Torch, cycle for mixed choir; Rhapsodia Orientale for piano and symphony orchestra. Recordings: Works by Bartók, Kodály, Bardos etc; Madrigals, Romantic Composers; Grand Priz du Disques, French Academy for Folklore Records, 1955; Gypsy Rhapsody, Qualiton; Folk Songs, Hungarian vocal and instrumental arrangements by I Csenki. Publications: Gypsy Ballads and Laments; Gypsy Songs and Dances; Hungarian Folk Songs (with Gy Schiffert). Contributions to: Music Critic, Tiszantul, prior to 2nd World War. Honour: Kossuth Prize, 1952. Hobbies: Gardening; Collecting Folk Songs. Address: Parisi utca 6/a, H-1052, Budapest, Hungary.

CSERVENY Alexandra Bogdana, b. 5 Jan 1959, Tirgoviste, Romania. Composer; Pianist; Piano Teacher. m. Stefan Cserveny, 1 Aug 1970, 1 daughter. Education: Piano Diploma, 1973, Composition with Anatol Vieru and Stefan Niculuescu, Diploma, 1974; Darmstadt Summer School, 1976; Composition with Jean Balissat, Lausanne Conservatoire. Career: Played Les animaux chanteurs, Lausanne Conservatoire opening, 1990; Réminiscences at Lyceum Club International Contest, 1997; Alice at 50th Anniversary of Ecole Sociale de Musique, Lausanne, 1998; Contemporary Music Society concerts on Swiss Radio; Swiss Radio recordings. Compositions: Lamento for clarinet and 2 basset horns, 1982; String Quartet, 1983; Colind for flute, violoncello and piano, 1987; Les animaux chanteurs de Brème for solo instruments, narrator and orchestra, 1990; Rhapsodie for oboe, oboe d'amore and cor anglais, 1994; Réminiscences for violin, 1997; Alice aux pays des merveilles for solo instruments, choir and narrator, 1998. Recordings: Les animaux chanteurs de Brème, CD; Lamento; String Quartet; Colind; Rhapsodie; Réminiscences. Honour: Hemmerling Composition Prize, Lausanne Conservatoire, 1982. Memberships: Swiss Musicians Association; Swiss Music Authors Rights Society; Contemporary Music Society; Lyceum Club of Switzerland. Current Management: Ecole Social de Musique, Lausanne. Address: Bois Murat 18, 1066 Epalinges, Switzerland.

CSIKY Boldizsar, b. 3 Oct 1937, Targu-Mures, Rumania. Composer; Teacher. Education: Studied at Bolyai High School and at the Art School with Sarolta T Erkel; Music Academy, 1955-61; Studied under Sigismund Toduta. Career: Music Secretary of Tirgu Mures Philharmonic, 1961-90; Taught Chamber Music, Musical Forms, Harmony and Counterpoint at the Music High Art School, 1986; Director of Tirgu Mures Philharmonic, 1990-; His works have been performed several times in Rumania, Hungary, Germany, Italy, USA, England and elsewhere; Initation and organization of Targu Mures Musical Days, the Musica Sacra Festival and the Constantin Silvestri Festival are connected with his name. Compositions: Main works, Two Orchestral Pieces, 1965; Prelude, Fugue and Postlude for orchestra, 1969; Songs of Bravery for chamber orchestra, 1970; Old Transylvanian Songs and Dances for chamber orchestra, 1973; Four Sketches for Strings, 1976; The Mountain, symphonic poem, 1979; Holderlin-Songs for soprano and strings, 1980; Barcsai, ballad for mixed choir and symphonic orchestra, 1981; String quartet, 1988; Divertimento for winds and double-bass, 1989; Cantatas, choral works (especially to poems by Szilagyi, Weores and to folk songs), songs, piano pieces, chamber music, several stage music works for puppet theatre and many folk song adaptations. Honours: George Enescu Prize of the Romanian Academy, 1980; Bartók Prize of the Hungarian Liszt Academy, Budapest, 1986. Address: Filarmonica de stat Tirgu Mures, str G Enescu nr 2, 4300 Tirgu Mures, Rumania.

CUBAYNES Jean-Jacques, b. 14 Feb 1950, Toulouse, France. Singer (Bass-baritone). Education: Studied at the Toulouse Conservatory and the Paris Opera studio. Career: Sang at the Toulouse Opera from 1978, notably as Zuniga, Mephistopheles, Colline and Monterone; Paris Opera, 1979, as Publio in La Clemenza di Tito; Guest appearances throughout France and in Dublin, Perugia and Seville; Other roles have included Arkel in Pelléas et Mélisande, Gessler in Guillaume Tell, Sparafucile, Daland, and Rodolfo in La Sonnambula. Recordings include: Gounod's Mireille and Roussel's Padmavati (EMI). Address: c/o Théâtre de Capitole, Place du Capitole, F-31000 Toulouse, France.

CUBERLI Lella (Alice), b. 29 Sept 1945, Austin, Texas, USA. Concert and Opera Singer (Soprano). m. Luigi Cuberli, 11 Jan 1972. Education: BMus, Southern Methodist University, 1974. Debut: European Violetta in La Traviata in Hungary, 1975. Career: Debut at the Sagra Musicale Umbra in the oratorio La Betulia Liberata by Mozart, 1975; Debut at Spoleto Festival concerto da camera with music by Schubert and Beethoven, 1977; Debut at La Scala in Milan in Mozart's Abduction, 1978; Since then regular appearances in operas such as Mozart's Re Pastore, 1979, Handel's Ariodante, 1981 (Opera taken on tour by La Scala to the Edinburgh Festival, 1982), Mozart's Lucio Silla, 1984; Le nozze di Figaro, 1987 and Orfeo by Gluck, 1989; Debut at Festival Woche in Berlin with the Beethoven Missa Solemnis, conductor Herbert von Karajan, 1985, also performed in the Beethoven 9th, 1986 and the Brahms Requiem, 1987, again with Karajan conducting; 1986 debut at Salzburg Festival with Le nozze di Figaro (role of Countess) with James Levine conducting with repeats in 1987 and 1988; 1986 debut at the Mozart Festival in Paris again in Figaro with Daniel Barenboim conducting; 1987, new production of Traviata made especially for her at the Monnaie in Brussels; 1988 debut at Vienna Staatsoper in Viaggio a Reims, Claudio Abbado conducting; 1989 concert at Pesaro Opera, Festival of Beethoven's Schottische Lieder, Pianist Maurizio Pollini; Sang Mozart's Countess at Orchestra Hall, Chicago, 1992; Antonia in Les Contes d'Hoffmann at the Opera Bastille, the Countess with the Royal Opera in Japan and at Florence, 1992; Sang Donna Anna at the 1996 Salzburg Festival. Recordings include: Beethoven, Missa Solemnis, Deutsche Grammophon (Karajan), 1985; Mozart, Da Ponte operas, Erato (Barenboim) Berlin Philharmonic, 1990. Honours include: Franco Abbiati Italian Critics Award, 1981 and Premio Jorio, 1984; Le Grand Prix du Disque conferred by the Academy of Rance in Paris and Prix Rossini of Paris and the Maschera d'argento award in Campione d'Italia, 1986; Premio Paisiello in Taranto, Italy, 1987. Address: c/o Music Centre, Via Ponte Vetero 1, 20121 Milan, Italy.

CUCKSTON Alan, b. 2 July 1940, Horsforth, Yorkshire, England. Harpsichordist; Pianist; Conductor; Lecturer. m. Vivien Broadbent, 16 November 1965, 2 sons, 3 daughters. Education: Kings College, Cambridge, BMus 1963, MA 1965. Debut: Wigmore Hall, 1965. Career: BBC recitalist 1964; Solo concerts in Europe, United States; Keyboard Accompanist with Academy of St Martin in the Fields and Pro Cantione Antiqua. Recordings: Solo Piano Music of Alan Rawsthorne, William Baines, Eugene Goossens, Edward German, John Field, Sterndale Bennett, Stanford, Corder; Solo Harpsichord Music of Burnett, Kinloch, Farnaby, Tallis, Byrd, Handel, Couperin, Rameau. Publications: Reviewer, Music and Letters. Hobbies: Gardening; Local History. Address: 9 The Crescent, Ripon, North Yorkshire, HG4 2JB, England.

CUENOD Hugues, b. 26 June 1902, Corseaux-sur-Vevey, Switzerland. Singer (Tenor). Education: Studied at the Conservatories of Geneva and Basle and in Vienna. Debut: Paris 1928, in the French premiere of Krenek's Jonny spielt Auf. Career: Sang in Geneva 1930-33, Paris 1934-37; Concert tour of North America with Nadia Boulanger, 1937-39; Professor at the Geneva Conservatory, 1940-46; Widely known in French songs and in early music; Lieder recitals with Clara Haskil; Sang in the premiere of Honegger's Le Danse des Morts, Basle, 1940; Performances as the Evangelist in Bach's St Matthew Passion; Created Sellem in The Rake's Progress, Venice, 1951; Covent Garden, 1954, as the Astrologer in The Golden Cockerel; Glyndebourne, 1954-, notably as Don Basilio, in Cavalli's L'Ormindo and La Calisto, and in Le Nozze di Figaro (50th Anniversary Season, 1984); Metropolitan Opera debut 1987, as the Emperor in Turandot; Geneva Opera 1989, as Monsieur Taupe in Capriccio. Recordings: St Matthew Passion (Nixa); L'Enfant et les Sortilèges, Ariadne auf Naxos, Oedipus Rex, Les Contes d'Hoffmann, La Calisto (Decca); Le nozze di Figaro (EMI); Early Music for Erato. Address: c/o Glyndebourne Festival Opera, Lewes, Sussex, England.

CULLEN Bernadette, b. 1949, Australia. Singer (Mezzo-soprano). Career: Appearances from 1981 with Australian Opera as Maffio Orsini in Lucrezia Borgia, Nicklausse and Giulietta in Hoffman, Cherubino in Figaro, Angelina in Cenerentola, Ottavia in Poppea, the Secretary in The Consul, Charlotte in Werther and Rosina in Il Barbiere di Siviglia; Further performances include Brangaene in a new production of Tristan, Sesto in Clemenza di Tito, Donna Elvira in Don Giovanni, also for Lyric Opera of Queensland; Eboli in Don Carlos and Adalgisa in Norma for Victoria State Opera; Vitellia in concert under Christopher Hogwood, Gala Concert with Joan Sutherland and Richard Bonynge in Perth, Dorabella at Hong Kong and British debut as Isolier in Le Comte Ory for Welsh National Opera; Sang Donna Elvira at the re-opening of the Tyl Theatre, Prague, under Charles Mackerras, Leonara in La Favorita for WNO in Cardiff and at Covent Garden, Dido in Dido and Aeneas in Palermo (1994), Cassandre in La Prise de Troie for the Australian Opera, Brangaene in Tristan and Isolde for Scottish Opera; Concert repertoire includes Mahler's 8th under Charles Dutoit; Rossini Stabat Mater and Petite messe Solonelle; Verdi Requiem in Sydney under Carlo Rizzi and with the Hallé Orchestra, Liverpool Oratorio under Carl Davis, Dream of Gerontius with the Ulster Orchestra and Beethoven's Ninth. Recordings: Pulcinella with the Australian Chamber Orchestra; The Bohemian Girl, conducted by Richard Bonynge. Honours: Vienna State Opera Award, Opera Foundation Australia, 1995. Current Management: IMG Artists. Address: Media House, 3 Burlington Lane, London W4 2th, England.

CULLIS Rita, b. 25 Sept 1952, Ellesmere Port, Cheshire, England. Singer (Soprano). Education: Royal Manchester College of Music. Career: Joined the chorus Welsh National Opera, 1973; Principal on Contract, Welsh National Opera, 1976; Roles include Leila (Pearl Fishers), the Countess (Figaro), Tytania (Midsummer Night's Dream), Pamina (Magic Flute), Ellen (Peter Grimes), Donna Anna (Don Giovanni) and Lenio in Martinu's Greek Passion; Buxton Festival 1981, as Elisetta in Cimarosa's Il Matrimonio Segreto; Opera North 1985, as Jenifer in The Midsummer Marriage and as Christine in Strauss's Intermezzo; Season 1986-87 sang the Countess of Tel-Aviv Opera, Ariadne for Opera Northern Ireland and Donna Anna for her debut at the English National Opera, returned for The Fox in Janácek's Cunning Little Vixen; Concert engagements with RAI Milan, Hallé Orchestra, Ulster Radio, Royal Liverpool Philharmonic and the Bournemouth Symphony; Netherlands Opera, Freischütz, 1989-90; Other engagements as the Composer and Fiordiligi, English National Opera, the Fox in The Cunning Little Vixen, Scottish Opera, and the Countess and Donna Anna, debuts with the Canadian Opera Company and San Diego Opera, 1992; Season 1992-93 as the Composer in Ariadne for ENO and Covent Garden debut as Janácek's Fox; Sang Third Norn in Götterdämmerung at Covent Garden, 1995; Bach's St Matthew Passion at the Festival Hall, 1997; Season 1997-98 with Elisabeth in Tannhäuser for Opera North, Senta for ENO, Ellen Orford and Sieglinde for Royal Opera. Address: c/o Harold Holt Ltd, 31 Sinclair Road, London W14 0NS, England.

CULMER-SCHELLBACH Lona, b. 4 Feb 1954, Miami, Florida, USA. Singer (Soprano). Career: Prize winner at the 1985 Mozart Competition, Salzburg, and appeared in the 1986 premiere of Penderecki's Schwarze Maske, at Salzburg; Also sang the role of Europa at the Vienna Staatsoper and at Santa Fe, 1988; Sang in the premiere of Patmos by Wolfgang von Schweinitz at Munich (1990) and appeared at Kassel from 1989; Further appearances in Essen, Paris, Berlin and Dresden, as Marie in Wozzeck, Shostakovich's Lady Macbeth, Elsa, Donna Elvira and Ariadne; Frequent concert engagements. Address: c/o Staatstheater Kassel, Friedrichplatz 15, W-3500 Kassel, Germany.

CULVER (David) Andrew, b. 30 Aug 1953, Morristown, New Jersey, USA. Composer; Performer. Education: Studied composition with Bengt Hambaeus, electronic music and sound recording at McGill University, MM 1980. Career: Founder Member of SONDE, Canadian music design and performance group; Has worked at Yellow Springs Institute for Contemporary Studies, New Music Concerts Toronto, Staten Island Children's Museum, 1983 and the Children's Museum of Manhattan, 1989-91; Collaborations with John Cage 1981-92, including computer assistance with the premiere of Europeras 1 and 2 at the Frankfurt Schauspielhaus, 1987. Compositions: Stage works Viti 1981; Music with Tensegrity Sound Source No 5, 1983; Hard Lake Frozen Moon, 1989; Quasicrystals, sound sculpture, 1989. Address: 127 Willowbrook Road, Clinton Corners, NY 12514, USA.

CUMBERLAND David, b. 1945, Ohio, USA. Singer (Bass-baritone). Education: Studied at the Juilliard School, New York. Debut: Sang Pizarro in a concert performance of Fidelio under Leonard Bernstein at Lincoln Center. Career: Has appeared widely at German opera houses, notably in Frankfurt, Gelsenkirchen, Wiesbaden, Cologne, Leipzig and Freiburg; Repertoire has included Hans Sachs, the Landgrave in Tannhäuser, King Phillip in Don Carlo and the Dutchman; Has sung in the opera of Marseille and appeared in La Serva Padrona and Bastien and Bastienne at Clermont-Ferrand; Linz Opera in Der fliegende Holländer; US engagements at the Kentucky Opera, Philadelphia Opera; National Grand Opera and in Dallas; San Francisco and New York (City Opera); Spoleto Festival as Rodolfo in La Sonnambula; British debut with Opera North, 1988 as the Dutchman; Concert appearances at the Carnegie Hall, in Boston, at the Vienna Musikverein and in Santiago; Francesco Cenci in the world premiere of Beatrice Cenci, by Berthold Goldschmidt, 1994; Sang King Lycomedes in the world premiere of Wolfgang Andreas Schultz's Achill und der den Mädchen, Kassel, Germany in 1997, Pogner in Die Meistersinger von Nürnberg in the reopening of the opera house in Magdeburg, Germany and sang Alberich in Wagner's Rheingold in Magdeburg and in further performances of Wagner's Ring in 1998. Address: Weinmarkt 5, CH 6004, Luzern, Switzerland.

CUMMINGS Claudia, b. 12 Nov 1941, Santa Barbara, California, USA. Opera Singer (Soprano). m. (1) H W Cummings, 12 June 1962, (2) Jack Aranson, 26 May 1973, 1 daughter. Education: BA, Vocal Performance, San Francisco University, 1963. Debut: San Francisco Opera, 1971. Career: San Francisco, New York City, Houston, Seattle, San Diego, Minnesota, Miami, Charlotte Opera Companies; Netherlands Opera; Stuttgart Opera; Canadian Opera; Sang Countess de la Roche by B A Zimmermann, 1991 at New York City Opera; Other roles have included Violetta, Rosalinda, Lucia di Lammermoor, Lulu, Marguerite, 3 Heroines in the Tales of Hoffmann, Countess in The Marriage of Figaro. Recordings: Satyagraha, Philip Glass. Hobby: Restoring Historic Houses. Address: PO Box 4306, New Windsor, NY 12553, USA.

CUMMINGS Conrad, b. 10 Feb 1948, San Francisco, California, USA. Composer. Education: Studied with Bulent Arel and Joan Panetti at Yale University and with David Lewin at Stony Brook, New York; Further study with Mario Davidovsky and Ussachevsky at Columbia University; Summer courses at the Berkshire Music Center and Stanford University. Career: Teacher at the Columbia-Princeton Electronic Music Center, 1974-76; Electronic Music Coordinator, Brooklyn College, 1976-79; Assistant Professor, Oberlin College, 1980. Compositions incl: Operas Eros and Psyche 1983, Cassandra 1985 and Tonkin 1993; Triptych for cello 1971; Divertimento for oboe, cello and guitar 1971; Bone Songs for clarinet, trumpet and double bass 1974; Morning Music for ensemble 1974; Subway Songs for 4 trak tape, 1974; Movement for orchestra 1975; Composition for orchestra, 1977; Endangered Species, dance music 1977; Skin Songs for soprano and ensemble 1978; Tap Dancer for 6 percussion 1978; Beast Songs for soprano and ensemble 1979; Second Bassett for Times Square 1980; Summer air, nonet, tape and 14 loudspeakers 1981; Music for Starlore for stereo tape, 1982; Piece for Mean-Tone Organ 1982; Zephyr's Lesson for flute, cello, percussion and tape, 1985; After Eros and Psyche for chamber orchestra and tape, 1985. Honours incl: MacDowell Colony Fellowships; Grants from the National Endowment for the Arts and the Martha Baird Rockefeller Fund; Commission from the Smithsonian Institution and Oberlin College. Address: c/o BMI, 320 West 57th Street, New York, NY 10019, USA.

CUMMINGS David (Michael), b. 10 Oct 1942, London, England. Lexicographer. m. Anne Marie Zammit-Tabona, 1970, 2 sons, 1 daughter. Education: Dartington Hall School, 1953-60; BEd, Hons, Sidney Webb College, London, 1971-75. Career: School Teacher, 1975-; Lexicographer, Music Reference Books, 1980-. Contributions to: Baker's Biographical Dictionary of Musicians, New York, 1984 and 1992; The Oxford Dictionary of Music, Oxford, 1985 and 1994; The Grove Concise Dictionary of Music, London, 1988 (in the USA as The Norton/Grove Concise Encyclopedia of Music); Penguin Dictionary of Musical Performers, 1990; Grosses Sängerlexikon (Ergänzungsband) Berne, 1991-93, new edition, 5 volumes, 1997; New Grove Dictionary of Opera, 4 vols, 1992; Concise Oxford Dictionary of Opera, 1996; Baker's Biographical Dictionary of 20th Century Classical Musicians, 1997. Publications: New Everyman Dictionary of Music, 6th Edition, London, 1988; Editor, International Who's Who in Music, 12th-16th Editions, 1990-98; Hutchinson Encyclopaedia of Music (book and CD versions), 1995. Hobbies: Armchair Cricket; Casaubonology. Address: 7 Gerard Road, Harrow HA1 2ND, England.

CUMMINGS Diana, b. 27 Apr 1941, Amersham, Bucks, England. Violinist. m. Luciano Jorios, 2 sons, 1 daughter. Education: Recital Diploma, RAM; ARAM. Debut: Wigmore Hall. Career: Has toured throughout Britain as soloist and chamber musician; Numerous TV and radio broadcasts; Formerly leader of English Piano Quartet; Member of Cummings String Trio; With Trio, gave Haydn's Op 53 No 1, Martinu's trio and Beethoven's Op 9 No 1, for the BBC, 1991. Recordings include: Complete String Trios of Beethoven. Honours include: Prizewinner, International Paganini Competition, Genoa, 1963; International Competition A. Curci, Naples, 1967. Memberships: Musicians Union; ISM. Address: 2 Fairhazel Mansions, Fairhazel Gardens, London NW6, England.

CUMMINGS Douglas, b. 5 Oct 1946, England. Cellist. m. 2 sons. Career: Principal Cellist of the London Symphony Orchestra, 1969-92. Recordings: 2 Bach Suites for unaccompanied cello (Abbey); Swan Lake duet, with Ida Haendl (violin) and the LSO; Schubert Quintet in C, with the Lindsay Quartet. Honour: FRAM, 1977. Address: 11 St Marks Road, Ealing Common, London W5 3JS, England.

CUMMINGS Laurence, b. 1968, Sutton Coldfield, England. Harpischordist; Conductor. Education: Studied at Oxford University (Organ scholar at Christ Church) and the Royal College of Music. Career: Many concerts as harpischordist and continuo player throughout Britain with such ensembles as The Sixteen Choir, the Gabrieli Consort and Orchestra of the Age of Enlightenment; Many tours world wide, including concerts with Les Arts Florissants in Paris and New York; Senior Coach at the 1997 Glyndebourne Festival, with Handel's Theodora; Head of Historical Performance, Royal Academy of Music, 1997-. Recordings include: Louis and Francois Couperin keyboard music. Address: 81 Chetwynd Road, Dartmouth Park, London NW5 1DA, England.

CUPER Philippe, b. 25 Apr 1957, Lille, France. Clarinettist. Education: Studied at the Paris Conservatoire with Guy Deplus, Henri Druart, Guy Dangain, Jacques Lancelot and Gilbert Voisin and with Stanley Drucker at Juilliard, New York. Career includes: Soloist with the Concerts Lamoureux, 1978-87; Orchestra of the Paris Opera from 1984; Many appearances as concert soloist and as chamber musician with the Paris Wind Octet, pianists Paul Badura-Skoda and Michel Dalberto and violinist Augustin Dumay. Recordings: 25 CDs. Contributions to: Clarinette magazine; International Clarinet Society magazine; Band Journal, Tokyo; Clarinet and Saxophone Society Magazine, London. Honours include:Prizewinner, Munich International Competition, 1982, Geneva, 1979, and Prague, 1986; 1st Prize, Prague, 1986. Address: c/o Association des Concerts Lamourexu, 252 Rue du Faubourg St Honoré, F-75008 Paris, France.

CUPERS Jean-Louis (Georges Marie), b. 19 June 1946, Etterbeek, Brussels. Philologist; Musicologist; Pianist. m. Michèle Derixhon, 19 Jan 1985, 2 daughters. Education: 2nd Licentiate, Philosophy and Letters, 1968, BPhilosophy, 1971, D Literature, 1978, 1st Licentiate Musicology, 1972, Catholic University, Louvain. Career: Performing on 18th and 19th century pianofortes (Musée Instrumental de Bruxelles). Recording: Mendelssohn's Piano Concerto No 1 in G Minor, 1967. Contributions to: Revue des archéologues et historiens d'art de Louvain, 1971; International Review Aesthetics and Sociology Music, 1974; Mélanges de Musicologie, Louvain, 1974; Literature and the other Arts, 1981; Littérature et musique, 1982; Moderne Encyclopedie van de Wereldliteratuur, 1982; Revue de littérature comparée, 1987. Publications: Aldous Huxley and Music, A Little More John Sebastian Like, 1985; Euterpe and Harpocrates or the Musical Challenge to Literature, 1988; Musico-Poetics Today, Co-editor, 1997; Ouvertures sur l'art, forthcoming. Hobbies: Walking; Dancing; Playing the piano. Address: 12 Rue Jean-Hippolyte Lambotte, 1150 Brussels, Belgium.

CUPIDO Alberto, b. 19 Mar 1948, Portofino, Italy. Singer (Tenor). Education: Studied at the Giuseppe Verdi Conservatory, Milan and at the Accademia Chigiana in Siena. Debut: Geonoa 1977 as Pinkerton. Career: Sang widely in Italy and in Strasbourg, Vienna and Frankfurt; Glydndebourne 1978 as Rodolfo; Munich Staatsoper 1982 as Faust; US debut San Francisco 1983; Florence 1983 as Rinuccio in Gianni Schicchi; La Scala debut 1984 as Edgardo in Lucia di Lammermoor; Returned 1986 as Orontes in I Lombardi; Wiesbaden 1986 in Giulietta e Romeo by Zandonai; Further appearances in Cologne, Hamburg, Berlin and Montreal; Other roles include Alfredo, Fenton, the Duke of Mantua, Fernando in La Favorita and Rodolfo in Luisa Miller; Sang Edgardo at Monte Carlo, 1987; Faust at Geneva, 1988; Teatro Comunale Florence, 1989; As Faust in Mefistofele, Rodolfo at Rome, 1990; Gabriele Adorno in a new production of Simon Boccanegra at Brussels, 1990; Debut at the Verona Arena as Cavaradossi; Season 1991-92 as Boito's Faust at the Lyric Opera Chicago and as Don Carlo at Verona; Also heard in the concert hall. Honours: Prizewinner at Competitions in Parma, 1975 and Busseto, 1976. Address: Stafford Law Associates, 6 Barham Close, Weybridge, Surrey KT13 9PR, England.

CURA José, b. 1962, Rosario, Santa Fe, Argentina. Singer (Tenor). Education: Composition and conducting studies at the University of Rosario; Vocal studies at the School of Arts of the Teatro Colon, Buenos Aires; Vocal studies with Horacio Amauri in Argentina and Vittorio Terranova in Italy. Career: International appearances at leading opera houses from 1992; Season 1993-94 included Albert Gregor, Makropulos Case, in Turin; Le Villi, Martina Franca; Season 1994-95, sang Fedora in Chicago; Stiffelio in Covent Garden; Season 1995-96, sang in Iris, in Rome, Samson in Covent Garden and in the Puccini Spectacular in Australia; Season 1996-97 included Don José with San Francisco Opera; Stiffelio and Samson at Covent Garden; Cavalleria Rusticana in Ravenna; Norma in Los Angeles; Carmen in San Francisco; Tosca with the Vienna Staatsoper, in Milan in Gioconda; In Verona with Carmen; Amsterdam Concertgebouw in I Pagliacci; Otello in Turin; Season 1997-98 with Night of the Stars Royal Opera Gala at the Albert Hall, London, Loris in Fedora at the Vienna Staatsoper, Samson at Turin, and Radames in Tokyo; Further concert engagements include Puccini Arias at the Barbican Centre, London, 1998; Puccini Documentary on BBC2 in Great Composers series, 1998; Appearances at opera houses throughout Germany, 1997-98, including Hamburg, Stuttgart, Cologne, Mannheim; Further roles include Puccini's Des Grieux, and Manrico in Il Trovatore; Debut as Verdi's Otello, 1997, conducted by Claudio Abbado (also televised). Recordings include: Le Villi; Iris; Argentine Songs, forthcoming; Puccini Arias; Samson and Dalila; Otello; I Pagliacci; Manon Lescaut. Honours include: Premio Abbiati Italian Critics' Award; Premio Carrara Cultura Millenaria, 1997; XII Premio Internazionale di Arte e Cultura Cilea, 1997; Opera Now Artist of the Year 1997-98 (Sept/Oct 1997 issue). Address: c/o Royal Opera House, Covent Garden, London WC2, England.

CURLEY Carlo, b. 24 August 1952, USA. Concert Organist. Education: North Carolina School for the Arts; Privately with Virgil Fox, Robert Elmore (Philadelphia), Arthur Poister (Syracuse University) and Sir George Thalben-Ball (Temple Church, London). Career: Organist-Choirmaster and Teacher of Music, Girard College, Philadelphia; Director of Music, Druids Hills Baptist Church, Atlanta, Georgia; Artist-in-Residence, Fountain Street Church, Grand Rapids, Michigan; Organist, Alexandra Palace, London; Performances and Master classes at National Music Camp, Interlochen, Michigan; Frequent appearances on radio and television in USA, England, Australia, Canada, Japan and Denmark; Organ Consultant and Designer. Recordings: The Emperor's Fanfare, Brightly Shining, Organ Fantasia, Organ Imperial, Bach Organ Favourites, Bach Great Organ Works; The World of Carlo Curley (all for Decca). Honours: Patron, Holbrook Music Society (UK); Patron and Organ Consultant to the City of Melbourne. Hobbies: Trains; Reading; Fine Wines. Current Management: PVA Management Limited, Hallow Park, Worcester WR2 6PG, England. Address: Paul Vaughan Associates, Alpha Tower, Paradise Circus, Birmingham B1 1TT, England.

CURPHEY Margaret, b. 27 Feb 1938, Douglas, Isle of Man. Singer (Soprano). Education: Studied with John Carol Case in Birmingham and with David Galiver and Joan Cross in London. Debut: Sadler's Wells Opera 1965, as Micaela in Carmen. Career: Sang with Sadler's Wells/English National Opera in operas by Mozart, Wagner, Verdi and Puccini; Sang Eva in new production of The Mastersingers, conducted by Reginald Goodall, Sieglinde in The Valkyrie and Gutrune in The Twilight of the Gods; Camden Theatre 1967, in the British premiere of Mozart's Lucio Silla, Guest engagements in Sofia and elsewhere in Europe; Sang Brünnhilde at the London Coliseum, 1977; Many appearances as concert singer. Recordings: The Ring of the Nibelung, conducted by Reginald Goodall (EMI). Honours include: Prizewinner at 1970 International Competition, Sofia. Address: c/o English National Opera, St Martin's Lane, London WC2, England.

CURRAN Alvin, b. 13 Dec 1938, Providence, Rhode Island, USA. Composer; Performer. Education: BA, Brown University, 1960; Studied composition with Ron Nelson (Brown) and Elliott Carter (Yale), theory with Allen Forte; MMus, Yale University, 1963. Career: Co-Founder, Musica Elettronica Viva Group, Rome, 1966; Solo performances in major festivals (new music), 1973-; Large-scale environmental works for chorus, orchestra, ship's horns and fog-horns, 1980-. Compositions: Songs and Views from the Magnetic Garden; Light Flowers, Dark Flowers; The Works; Canti Illuminati; For Cornelius and Era Ora; Natural History; For Four or More, string quartet. Contributions to: EAR magazine; Musics; Almannaco Musicale; Music Works (Toronto). Honours: National Endowment for the Arts Grants, 1978, 1984; Prix Italia for Radio Works, 1985 - A Piece for Peace; DAAD Resident Composer in Berlin, 1986. Address: c/o SIAE, Viale della Letteratura n 30, 00144 Rome, Italy.

CURRIE Neil, b. 4 Dec 1955, Moose Jaw, Canada. Composer. Education: MA (Hons), University of British Columbia, Vancouver; Study with Peter Sculthorpe, Australia, 1985-88; MMus, University of Sydney, 1989. Career: Composer/Artist in Residence, Australian Broadcasting Corporation, 1990-91; Doctoral Fellowship, University of British Columbia, Vancouver, Canada, 1995-97. Compositions include: Windmill for clarinet, 2 pianos and 2 percussion, 1985; Stopping by Woods on a Snowy Evening for tenor recorder, 1985; Ortigas Avenue for ensemble, 1986; String Quartet, 1988; Dance Pieces for orchestra, 1987-89; Sons of Rhythm for viola, cello, clarinet and piano, 1989; Ballade for orchestra, 1991; Tumbling Strain, trombone concerto, 1991; Guitar Concerto, 1993; Precipitous for woodwinds, 1997; Commissions from Simon Preston, John Williams and the Seymour Group. Address: 3806 Balfour Place, Saskatoon, S7H 3Z7, Canada.

CURRIE Russell, b. 3 Apr 1954, North Arlington, New Jersey, USA. Composer. Education: Studied composition with Robert Starer at Brooklyn College. Career: Founded Orra 1988, promoting a multi-approach to musical performance; Director of the Music Theatre Programme at New York's 3rd Street School; Commissions from the Bronx Arts Ensemble. Compositions: The Cask of Amontillado, chamber opera after Poe, 1982; A Dream Within a Dream, chamber opera after Poe's The Fall of the House of Usher, 1984; Ligeia, operatic fantasy after Poe, 1987; Rimshot, music theatre, 1990. Address: c/o ASCAP, ASCAP Building, One Lincoln Plaza, NY 10023, USA.

CURRY Diane, b. 26 Feb 1942, Clifton Forge, Virginia, USA. Singer (Mezzo soprano). Career: Sang at the City Opera, New York, from 1972, Spoleto Festival from 1975 and at Graz from 1977; Other European engagements at the Deutsche Oper Berlin (1984-88), Bonn, Hamburg Staatsoper, Köln, Bonn, Brussels, Geneva, Marseille, Nice, Teatro di Bologna, 1991,

Teatro di Firenze and Maggio Musicale di Firenze, 1984, and Théâtre du Châtelet, Paris (the Mother in Dallapiccola's Prigioniero, 1992); Returned to the USA at the Metropolitan, New York (Nurse in Die Frau ohne Schatten, 1990), Ulrica, San Francisco and Seattle (Fricka and Waltraute in Wagner's Ring cycle, 1981-87); Other roles include Amneris, Azucena, Laura and Cieca in La Gioconda, Jenufa, Kostelnicka, Brangaene, Herodias, Clytemnestra, Mere Marie in Dialogues des Carmelites; Many concert appearances, notably in the Verdi Requiem; Recorded Verdi Requiem for Telarc. Honour: Grammy Award, Gramophone Award, 1988. Address: c/o Metropolitan Opera, Lincoln Cener, New York, NY 10023, USA.

CURTIN Phyllis, b. 3 Dec 1921, Clarksburg, WV, USA. Soprano Singer. Education: BA, Wellesley College; Studied at Wellesley College with Olga Avierino; Opera study with Boris Goldovsky at New England Conservatory and Tanglewood. Debut: With New England Opera Theater, 1946 as Countess in the Marriage of Figaro and Lady Billows in Albert Herring. Career includes: Sang at New York City Opera from 1953, notably in Von Einem's Der Prozess, Salome and in the premieres of Floyd's Susannah and The Passion of Jonathan Wade; Also sang Cressida in Walton's Troilus and Cressida, Giannini's The Taming of The Shrew and Poulenc's Les Mamelles de Teresias; Sante Fe in 1958 in premiere of Floyd's Wuthering Heights; Glyndebourne in 1959 as Donna Anna; Metropolitan Opera from 1961 as Fiordiligi, Rosalinde, Eva, Mozart's Countess, Violetta and Ellen Orford in Peter Grimes; New York concert performances of Pelléas et Mélisande, 1962; Guest appearances in Vienna, Buenos Aires, Frankfurt, Milan, Glasgow, Paris and Trieste; Other roles included: Salome and Alice Ford in Falstaff; Sang Rosine in the premiere of Milhaud's La Mère Coupable, Geneva, 1966; Ellen Orford at Edinburgh Festival, 1968; Retired from public singing in 1984; Teacher at Aspen School of Music and the Berkshire Music Center; Artist-in-Residence at Tanglewood, 1964-; Guest Teacher, Central Conservatory, Beijing, 1987 and Moscow Conservatory, 1989; Recitalist across USA, Canada, Australia, New Zealand and South ASmerica; Soloist with major orchestras of US and other countries; US premieres of Britten's War Requiem with Boston Symphony and Shostakovich's Symphony No 14 with the Philadelphia Orchestra; Currently Dean Emerita and Professor of Voice and Artistic Director at Opera Institute in Boston University School for the Arts; Head of Vocal Program at Tanglewood. Honour: Ambassador for The Arts by US Government. Membership: Formerly served on National Council of The Arts. Address: c/o School of The Arts, Boston University, 855 Commonwealth Avenue, Boston, MA 02215, USA.

CURTIS Alan, b. 17 Nov 1934, Mason, Michigan, USA. Harpsichordist; Conductor; Musicologist. Education: BM, Michigan University, 1955; PhD, University Illinois, 1963; Amsterdam with Gustav Leonhardt, 1957-59. Career: Joined Faculty of University of California at Berkeley, 1960; Professor, 1970-; Active as keyboard player and conductor in the USA and Europe; Productions of L'Incoronazione di Poppea, staged and designed by Filippo Sanjust, in Amsterdam, Brussels, Innsbruck, Spoleto and Venice; Handel's Ariodante at La Scala, 1980, Later productions in Innsbruck and Turin; Conducted Rameau's Dardanus at Basel, 1981; Il Sant'Alessio by Stefano Landi at Rome Opera, 1981; La Schiava Liberata by Jommelli for Netherlands Opera, 1982, and at the San Carlo, Naples, 1984; Cesti's Il Tito at Innsbruck, 1983, and Venice and Turin 1984; First production since 1707 of Handel's Rodrigo, Innsbruck, Madeira and Lisbon, 1984; Conducted a new production of Gluck's Armide, to open the restored Bibiena Theatre in Bologna, 1984; Gluck's Paride ed Elena at Vicenza, 1988; Conducted Cimarosa's Gli Orazi e i Curiazi at Rome, 1989, to mark the 200th anniversary of the French Revolution; Handel's Floridante with the Tafelmusik Baroque Orchestra at Toronto, 1990; Revival of Gli Orazi at Lisbon, 1990; Collector of early keyboard instruments by Martin Skowroneck. Recordings: Cavalli's Erismena; L'Incoronazione di Poppea (Fonit Cetra); Handel's Admeto and Rodrigo (Erato); La Schiava Liberata (Erato); La Susanna by Stradella; Goldberg Variations by Bach; CPE Bach's Rondos nebst eine Fantasie fürs Fortepiano. Publications: Sweelinck's Keyboard Music: A Study of English Elements in Seventeenth Century Dutch Composition, 1969, 1972; Edition of Jommelli's La Schiava Liberata and L'Incoronazione di Poppea, Novello, 1990. Current Management: Music International, 13 Ardilaun Road, Highbury, London N5 2QR, England.

CURTIS Mark, b. 1958, Hertfordshire, England. Singer (Tenor). Education: Studied at the Royal Northern College of Music and at the National Opera Studio; Italy with Maestro Campogalliani. Career: Appearances with Glyndebourne Touring Opera in Die Zauberflöte and as Fenton and Jacquino; At Covent Garden in Alceste, Pagliacci (Beppe), Manon Lescaut and Fidelio; Kent Opera as Don Ottavio and Monostatos and in King Priam and Carmen; With Opera North has sung The Steersman, Vasek, Stroh (Intermezzo), Don Basilio (Le Nozze di Figaro) and Arv in the British premiere of Nielsen's Maskarade; English National Opera as Amenophis in Mosè, and Don Ottavio, and in the world premiere of Birtwistle's The Mask of Orpheus, 1986; Other roles include Hylas in Les Troyens, the Madwoman in Curlew River and Nadir in Les Pêcheurs de Perles; Sang in the Mozart pasticcio The Jewel Box and King Priam (Hermes) for Opera North, 1991; Has also sung at Bath Abbey and the South Bank Halls and in Dublin, Brussels, Hanover, Berlin, Rome, Palermo, Seville, Hong Kong, Jerusalem, Helsinki and Edinburgh; Many concert appearances with English National Opera, Hilarion in Princess Ida and at Théâtre Royal de la Monnaie, Brussels, Der Soldat in world premiere of Philippe Boesmans, Reigen, 1993; English National Opera in King Priam (Hermes), 1995; Sang Goro in Butterfly for Opera North, 1996. Recordings include: Trabuco in La Forza del Destino and Yamadori in Madame Butterfly (Deutsche Grammophon). Address: Music International, 13 Ardilaun Road, London N5 2QR, England.

CURTIS Matthew, b. 2 June 1959, Embleton, Cumbria, England. Composer. Education: Worcester College, Oxford. Debut: BBC Radio, 1982. Career: Numerous Radio Broadcasts; Amateur Performances in England and USA. Compositions: Pas De Deux; Fiesta; Romanza; Autumn Song; Open Road; Improbable Centenary; Amsterdam Suite; Serenade for Strings; Outward Bound; Three Psalms for Chorus and Orchestra. Membership: Composers Guild of Great Britain. Hobbies: Conversation; Food and drink; Travel. Address: 152 Granville Road, London NW2 2LD, England.

CURTIS-VERNA Mary, b. 9 May 1927, Salem, Massachusetts, USA. Singer (Soprano). Education: Studied at Hollis College, Virginia and with Ettore Verna. Debut: Teatro Lirico Milan, 1949 as Desdemona. Career: Appearances in Vienna, Paris, Munich, Stuttgart and Florence; Returned to USA 1951 and sang in Philadelphia; San Francisco 1952, Aida and Donna Anna; New York City Opera 1954 as Donna Anna; La Scala Milan 1954 as Desdemona; Metropolitan Opera 1968 as the Trovatore Leonora, Tosca, Amelia in Un Ballo in Maschera, Santuzza, Aida, Turandot, Elisabeth de Valois and Violetta; Further engagements in Buenos Aires and at the Verona Arena. Address: c/o Metropolitan Opera, Lincoln Center, NY 10023, USA.

CURZI Cesare, b. 14 Oct 1926, San Francisco, USA. Singer (Tenor). Education: Studied privately. Debut: San Francisco 1947 as Pinkerton. Career: Sang in San Francisco and elsewhere in North America; Moved to Europe 1955 and appeared at opera houses in Kiel, Nuremberg and Frankfurt (Alfredo 1957); Salzburg Festival 1959, in Il Mondo della Luna by Haydn; Further engagements in Stuttgart, Hamburg, Berlin and Cologne; Maggio Musicale Florence, 1959 and 1973-74; Member of the Deutsche Oper am Rhein Dusseldorf from 1965; Other roles included Rodolfo, Ferrando in Così fan tutte, Ernesto and the Duke of Mantua. Recordings: Rigoletto (Electrola); Eine Nacht in Venedig; Die Fledermaus. Address: c/o Deutsche Oper am Rheim, Heinrich-Heine Allee 16, D-4000 Dusseldorf, Germany.

CVEJIC Biserka, b. 5 Nov 1923, Krilo-Jesenice, Split, Yugoslavia. Singer (Mezzo-soprano). Education: Studied at Belgrade Music Academy. Debut: Belgrade Opera 1950, as Maddalena in Rigoletto. Career: Sang at Belgrade 1954-60, notably as Charlotte in Werther and as Amneris on tour to Vienna 1959; Metropolitan Opera debut 1961, as Amneris; Vienna Staatsoper 1959-79, Zagreb Opera 1975-78; Further appearances at Covent Garden, Verona Arena, La Scala and Buenos Aires; Sang in Massenet's Marie-Magdalene at Paris, 1977; Other roles have included Eboli, Azucena, Carmen and Delilah; Retired 1990. Recordings: Eugene Onegin, The Queen of Spades, Prince Igor, Boris Godunov, The Snow Maiden; War and Peace; Zigeunerbaron. Address: c/o Vienna Staatsoper, Opernring 2, Vienna, Austria.

CYNAN JONES Eldrydd, b. 1965, Wales. Soprano. Career: Concerts and recitals throughout Europe, with opera in Wales and England; Repertory includes Handel's Giulio Cesare, Turandot and Adriana Lecouvreur; Also sings songs by Strauss and Duparc; Contestant at the 1995 Cardiff Singer of the World Competition. Address: 1 Hermon Street, Treorchy, Rhondda, Mid Glamorgan CF42 6PW, Wales.

CZAPO Eva, b. Nov 1944, Budapest, Hungary. Singer (Soprano); Teacher. Education:Studied at Bartok Conservatory, Budapest, in Basel and with Elsa Cavelti. Career: Sang with Trier Opera 1968-69; Guest appearances in concert and opera at Basel, Zurich, Lucca, 1981, Bologna and Spoleto 1981; Appearances at the Salzburg, Lausanne, Lucerne, Lugano, Schwetzingen, Helsinki and Granada festivals; Concert repertoire has included Bach's B minor Mass, Beethoven's Ninth, Messiah, Elijah and St Paul by Mendelssohn, Haydn's Schöpfung and Jahreszeiten, Mozart's Requiem and C minor Mass and works by Schoenberg, Nono, Dallapiccola, Stravinsky, Szymanowski, Messiaen and Hindemith; Further engagements at Berlin, Hamburg, Munich, Milan, Rome, Turin, Parma and Lisbon; Voice Teacher at Basel and Founder of the Divertimento Vocale, Basel, 1987. Recordings: Bach Cantatas and Cavalieri's Rappresentazione di anima e di corpo; Schoenberg's Moses und Aron, conducted by Gielen; Schubert Masses; Davidde Penitente by Mozart and Carissimi's Dives malus. Address: c/o Musik-Akademie der Stadt Basel, Leonhardsstrasse 6, CH-4501 Basel, Switzerland.

CZERWENKA Oscar, b. 5 July 1924, Vocklabruck, Linz, Austria. Singer (Bass). Education: Studied privately and with O Iro in Vienna. Debut: Graz 1947, as the Hermit in Der Freischütz. Career: Vienna Staatsoper from 1951, notably as Baron Ochs, Kecal in The Bartered Bride, Osmin, and parts in operas by Lortzing; Salzburg Festival from 1953, in the premieres of Einem's Der Prozess and Egk's Irische Legende and in Der Rosenkavalier, Ariadne auf Naxos, Haydn's Il Mondo della Luna and Le Nozze di Figaro; Glyndebourne Festival and Metropolitan Opera, 1959 and 1961, as Ochs; Hamburg Staatsoper 1965, in the premiere of Klebe's Jakobowsky und der Oberst; Guest appearances in Cologne, Berlin, Frankfurt, Munich, Lisbon and Stuttgart; Many concert engagements. Recordings: Abu Hassan in Der Barbier von Bagdad by Cornelius, conducted by Leinsdorf (Columbia); Tiefland, Salome, Le nozze di Figaro (Philips); Die Frau ohne Schatten (Decca). Publications: Lebenszeiten-Ungebetene Briefe, Vienna, 1987. Honour: Vienna Kammersanger, 1961. Address: c/o Vienna Staatsoper, Opernring 2, A-1010 Vienna, Austria.

CZYZ Henryk, b. 16 June 1923, Grudziadz, Poland. Conductor; Composer. m. Halina Buczacka. Education: Studied Law and Philosophy in Torun; Conducting & Composition at the Music High School, Poznan. Career: Conducting debut with Polish National Radio Orchestra, 1948; Art Director and Chief Conductor, Philharmonic Orchestra of Lodz, 1957-60 and 1974-80 and Krakow, 1964-68; Gave triple bill of works by Debussy, Honegger and Stravinsky at the Warsaw Opera in 1962; Conducted the premieres of Penderecki's St Luke Passion (Munster 1966) and The Devils of Loudun (Hamburg 1969); US debut 1973, with the Minnesota Orchestra; Conducted the Dusseldorf Orchestra, 1971-74; Professor at Warsaw Academy, 1980-95. Compositions: Etude for orchestra, 1949; Symphonic Variations, 1952; Comic Opera, The Dog Lover's Dilemma, 1967. Recordings include: St Luke Passion, Dies Irae and other works by Penderecki, Szymanowski's 2nd Symphony and excerpts from King Roger; Schumann's Das Paradies and die Peri, EMI. Publications: Writer, 7 books edited, 1973-85; Editor, 3 autobiographical books. Address: Moliera 2-21, Warsaw 00076, Poland.

D

D'ACCONE Frank A(nthony), b. 13 June 1931, Somerville, MA, USA. Musicologist; Professor. Education: BMus, 1952, MMus, 1953, Boston University; MA 1955, PhD 1960, Harvard University; Studied with Karl Geiringer, Gardner Read, Nino Pirrotta, A Tillman Merritt and Walter Piston. Career: Assistant, Associate, Professor of Music, State University of New York, Buffalo, 1960-68; Visiting Professor, 1965-66, Professor of Music, 1968-, University of California, Los Angeles; Editor, Music of the Florentine Renaissance, Corpus Mensurabilis Musicae series XXXII, 1966-. Publications: Alessandro Scarlatti's Gli equivoci nel sembiante: The History of a Baroque Opera, 1985; The Civic Muse: Music and Musicians in Siena during the Middle Ages and the Renaissance, 1997. Contributions to: Articles in many journals and publications including The New Grove Dictionary of Music and Musicians. Honours: Guggenheim Fellowship, 1980-81; International Galileo Galilei Prize of the Rotary Club of Italy, 1997. Memberships: American Musicological Society. Address: c/o Music Department, University of California, Los Angeles, CA 90024, USA.

D'ANGELO Gianna, b. 18 Nov 1929, Hartford, Conneticut, USA. Singer (Soprano). Education: Studied at the Juilliard School, New York, and in Italy with Toti dal Monte. Debut: Rome 1954, as Gilda. Career: Glyndebourne 1955-56 and 1962, as Rosina, Clorinda in La Cenerentola and Zerbinetta in Ariadne auf Naxos; Brussels Opera 1956; Metropolitan Opera from 1961, as Gilda, Amina in La Sonnambula, Lucia di Lammermoor, Rosina and Zerbinetta; 8 Seasons with 36 Performances in 7 roles; Guest appearances in Milan, Paris and London. Recordings: Rigoletto; La Bohème; Il Barbiere di Siviglia; Les Contes d'Hoffmann. Address: c/o Metropolitan Opera, Lincoln Center, New York, NY 10023, USA.

D'ANGELO James, b. 17 Mar 1939, Paterson, New Jersey, USA. Teacher; Composer; Pianist. m. Georgina Joysmith, 12 Dec 1970, 2 daughters. Education: Columbia University, 1956-57; New York University, 1957-68; BMus, 1961, MMus, 1966, Manhattan School of Music; Studies with Gunther Schuller, William Russo, John Lewis (MJQ) and Jan Gorbaty, 1969-75; PhD, New York University, 1983. Debut: Carnegie Recital Hall, New York, 1966. Career: Professor of Music, City University of New York, 1970-86; Lecturer, Goldsmiths' College, London, 1987-, and Huron University, 1994; Workshop Leader in the Psychology of Musical Performance Thereaputic Voice Work, 1992; Member of Advisory Board, Caduceus Journal, UK, 1993; As Composer, works performed at various colleges in USA, 1968-75, and at various London venues, 1985-; Song cycle debuted at Carnegie Recital Hall, 1971; Pianist, London concerts of own music, 1986-. Compositions: Tintinnabulations, song cycle for soprano; Toccata for solo percussionist; Songs on poems by E E Cummings; The Way of the Spiritual Warrior, 1989; The Elements, 1990; The Great Happiness, 1991. Contributions to: New International Dictionary of Opera; Hindemith Jahrbuch. Address: 14 Denmark Road, Ealing, London W13 8RG, England.

D'ARCANGELO Ildebrando, b. 1969, Pescara, Italy. Singer (Bass-baritone). Education: Studied with Maria Vittoria Romano and in Bologna. Career: Engagements in La Bohème at Chicago, I Capuleti by Bellini at the Berlin Staatsoper, Rossini's Armida and Guillaume Tell at Pesaro and as Mozart's Masetto at the New York Met, Figaro at Salzburg, 1996; Don Giovanni in Bonn and Leporello at the Bayerische Staatsoper; Banquo in Macbeth at Bologna and Colline in La Bohème at Covent Garden, 1996; Season 1997-98 as Figaro in Rome, Paris and New York, Enrico in Lucia di Lammermoor at the Edinburgh Festival and Leporello in Vienna. Recordings include: Rigoletto and I Lombardi under James Levine; Otello under Myung Wha Chung; Semiramidde; La nozze di Figaro; Don Giovanni (as Leporello, under John Eliot Gardiner); Don Carlos; Lucia di Lammermoor (with Mackerras); Don Giovanni (with Abbado). Honours include: Winner, Concorso Internazionale Toti dal Monte, Treviso. Address: c/o Lies Askonas Ltd, 6 Henrietta St, London WC2E 8LA, England.

D'ARES Ira, b. 29 May 1935, Brussels, Belgium. Singer (Mezzo-soprano). Education: Studied at the Brussels Conservatory. Career: Sang in concert from 1957, opera debut, 1958, as Hansel at the Théâtre de la Monnaie, Brussels; Member of the theatre from 1964 in such roles as Suzuki, the Princess in Suor Angelica, Wagner's Mary, the Nurse in Boris Godunov, Ortrud, Amneris and Azucena; Guest appearances elsewhere in Belgium. Address: c/o Théâtre Royale de la Monnaie, 4 Leopoldstrasse, B-1000 Brussels, Belgium.

D'ASCOLI Bernard, b. 18 November 1958, Aubagne, France. Education: Marseille Conservatoire, 1973-77; Private teachers. Career: Paris debut (Salle Cortot), 1981; London debut at QEH and RFH, 1982; Australian debut at Sydney Opera House, 1983; Amsterdam Concertgebouw, 1984; US debut in Houston,

1985; Vienna debut at Musikverein, 1986; Tokyo debut at Casals and Bunka Kaikan Halls, 1988; Orchestral engagements include appearances with Royal Philharmonic Orchestra, London Philharmonic, Philharmonia, BBC Symphony Orchestra, Chamber Orchestra of Europe, Amsterdam Philharmonic, Houston Symphony Orchestra, Orchestre National de Toulouse, Boston Symphony Orchestra, under such conductors as John Pritchard, Kurt Sanderling, Yehudi Menuhin, Sergiu Commissiona, Ivan Fischer, Michel Plasson, Tadaaki Otaka; Played Ravel and Gershwin at the Festival Hall, London, 1997. Recordings: 1st recording with EMI, 1982; Recent CD recordings include Schumann CD with Nimbus, 1989; Chopin CD; Regular television and radio broadcasts. Honours: Most talented French artist of the year, Megève, 1976; 1st Prize, Maria Canals Competition, Barcelona, Spain, 1978; 3rd Prize, Leeds International Piano Competition, England, 1981. Hobbies: Reading; Literature; Humane Sciences; Swimming. Current Management: c/o TransArt (mc) Limited, 8 Bristol Gardens, London W9 2JG, England. Address: c/o Van Walsum Management, 40 St Peter's Road, London W6 9BH, England.

D'AVALOS Francesco, b. 11 Apr 1930, Naples, Italy. Teacher; Composer; Conductor. Education: Studied Classics at college, Naples; Philosophy, Naples University; Started Piano study with Vicenzo Vitale at age 12, then Composition with Renato Parodi; Diploma in Composition, San Pietro a Majella Conservatory, Naples; Accademia Chigiana, Siena, with Franco Ferrara and Sergiu Celibidache. Debut: Concert as Conductor, RAI, Rome, 1964. Career: Conductor, Teatro Communale, Florence, San Carlo Opera, Naples, RAI Orchestra, Rome, Pomeriggi Musicali, Milan, major symphony orchestras and opera companies throughout Europe; Has appeared with Philharmonia Orchestra, London, 1987-; Has taught at several Italian conservatories; Currently holds Chair of Fugue and Advanced Composition and Chair of Conducting, San Pietro a Majella Conservatory, Naples. Compositions: Hymne am die Nacht, 1958, conducted by H W Henze, Hassischen Rundfunk; Studio Simfonica, 1982, conducted by d'Avalos, Lugano; Symphony for Orchestra and Soprano, premiered Norddeutscher Rundfunk, Hamburg; Qumran, study for orchestra, La Scala with Eliahu Inbal; Maria di Venosa-Gesualdo, musical drama in 2 acts, 1992; Die Stille Stadt for soprano and strings, 1994; Other orchestral works, works for voice, chamber music. Recordings: Over 30 including: Brahms, complete orchestral works, 4 CDs; Martucci, complete orchestral works, 4 CDs; Wagner, overtures, 4 CDs; Bruckner, Symphony No 7; Mendelssohn, complete orchestral works, 5 CDs; Maria di Venosa with Philharmonic Orchestra and Chorus, soloists, madrigalists, 2 CDs, 1994. Honours: Premio Marzotto for Composition; Grand Prix International du Disque for Martucci's Symphonies, Académie Charles Cros, 1990; MRA Award for Raff's Symphony No 3, Im Walde, 1993. Hobby: Collecting antiques. Address: 50 via dei Mille, Naples, Italy.

D'INTINO Luciana, b. 1959, San vito al Tagliamento, Pordenone, Italy. Singer (Mezzo-Soprano). Education: Studied at the Benedeto Marcello Conservatory, Venice. Debut: Sang Azucena in Il Trovatore, 1983. Career: Appearances as Rossini's Rosina in Macerata and Naples, 1984, 1986; Aida at Cagliari and Trieste; La Scala Milan from 1987 in Nabucco, Guillaume Tell; Jommelli's Fetonte, Adriana Lecouvreur and as Luggrezia in Pergolesi's Lo Frate 'nnamorato; Sang Frederica in Luisa Miller at Rome, 1990 and on Metropolitan Opera Debut, 1991. Turin 1990 as Eboli in Don Carlos and Savona 1991 as Arsace in Rossini's Auerliano in Palmira; Sang Preziosilla in Forza del Destino at Naples, Sara in Roberto Devereux at Bologna, 1992; Preziosilla at the 1992 Maggio Musicale, Florence; Amneris in Aida at Covent Garden, 1994; and at Buenos Aires, 1996. Recordings include: Lo Frate 'nnamorato, conducted by Riccardo Muti. Honours: include, Winner, Spoleto Singing Competition, 1993. Address: c/o Teatro alla Scala, Via Filodrammatici 2, 20121 Milan, Italy.

DA COSTA Noel (George), b. 24 December 1929, Lagos, Nigeria. Composer; Violinist; Conductor. Education: Studied at Queens College, Columbia University and with Luigi Dallapiccola in Italy. Career: Teacher at Queens and Hunter Colleges, New York, 1963-66; Rutgers State University of New Jersey from 1970; Has conducted College Orchestras in New York and the Accademia Chigiana; Music Director of the Triad Chorale, New York; Violinist with various New York theatre orchestras. Honours: include, Fulbright Fellowship, 1958-60. Compositions: include, Opera, The Cocktail Sip, 1958; Occurrence for Six, 1965; Verses with Vamps for Cello and Piano, 1968; The Confession Stone for Voices and Ensemble, 1969; In the Circle for Guitars, 1970; Counterpoint for Voices and Organ, 1970; November Song, Concert Scene, 1974; Magnolia Blue for Violin and Piano, 1975; A Ceremony of Spirituals, 1976; Sermon on the Warpland, 1980; Ukom Memory Songs for Organ and Percussion, 1981. Address: ASCAP, ASCAP Building, One Lincoln Plaza, New York, NY 10023, USA.

DA SILVA Miguel, b. 1960, France. Violist. Education: Studied at the Paris Conservatoire with Jean-Claude Pennetier

and with members of the Amadeus and Alban Berg Quartets. Career: Member of the Ysaye String Quartet from 1984; Many concert performances in France, Europe, America and the Far East; Festival engagements at Salzburg, Tivoli (Copenhagen), Bergen, Lockenhaus, Barcelona and Stresa; Many appearances in Italy, notably with the 'Haydn' Quartets of Mozart; Tours of Japan and the USA 1990 and 1992. Recordings: Mozart Quartet K421 and Quintet K516 (Harmonia Mundi); Ravel, Debussy and Mendelssohn Quartets (Decca). Honours: Grand Prix Evian International String Quartet Competition, May 1988, special prizes for best performances of a Mozart quartet, the Debussy quartet and a contemporary work; 2nd Prize, Portsmouth International String Quartet Competition, 1988. Address: c/o 12/13 Richmond Buildings, Dean Street, London W1V 5AF, England.

DABEK Stanislaw Franciszek, b. 3 Dec 1946, Ostrowiec Swietokrzyski, Poland. Musicologist. m. Teresa Kryza, 29 Dec 1973, 2 daughters. Education: Institute of Musicology, Catholic University of Lublin; Private Composition studies with Boguslaw Schaeffer, Music Academy, Krakow. Career: Teaching and research, Institute of Musicology, Catholic University of Lublin; PhD, 1984, Assistant Professor, 1997. Publications: Articles including: The songs of Karol Szymanowski to words by James Joyce, 1979; The music of Zbigniew Bargielski, 1979; The concept of form and sound in the Magnificat by Nicholas of Radom, 15th century, 1987; Research and cognitive categories in an analysis of the religious music of Twentieth Century Polish Composers, 1992; Books: Mass Oeuvre of Polish Composers in the Twentieth Century, 1900-1995, 1996; Polyphonic Repertoire of Handwritten Song-Books of the Benedictine Nuns Convent in Staniatki near Krakow, 16th-18th century, 1997. Honour: 3rd Prize, All-Polish Composers Competition, 1981. Memberships: Learned Society of Catholic University of Lublin; Polish Composers Union; International Musicological Society; International Fellowship for Research in Hymnology. Hobby: Swimming. Address: ul Wroclawska 24, PL 20730 Lublin, Poland.

DADAK Jaromir, b. 30 May 1930, Znojmo, Czechoslovakia. Composer; Conductor. m. 31 Oct 1981, 1 son, 3 daughters. Education: Janacek Academy of Art, Brno, 1956. Career: Conductor, Ostrava Radio Orchestra, 1960-63; Secretary, Czechoslovak Composer Federation, 1967-69; Director, Olomous State Symphony Orchestra, 1969-71; Political dissident, 1972-89. Compositions: Recorded: Orchestral: Never More, 1959, recorded, 1960; Concerto-Symphony for piano and symphony orchestra, 1959, 1964; Concertino for dulcimer and orchestra, 1965; Concerto for piano 4-hands and symphony orchestra, 1972, 1973; Sonata corta for string orchestra, 1977, 1990; Chamber music: 3 studies for piano 4-hands and percussions, 1965, 1969; Partita for violin, clarinet and piano, 1965, 1966; Music to delight for violin, clarinet, violoncello, 1989; Published: Perapera ad astra for organ, 1971, 1973; Viola Concerto, 1976, 1983; Recent compositions: Sonata for violin and piano, 1989; Ludi for string quartet and organ or symphony orchestra, 1991; 4 scautry Honours for bassoon and strings, 1991. Publications: Our Folk Song, 1991. Honours: National Prize, 1960, Prize, CMF, Prague, 1972. Memberships: Association of Music Artists and Scientists, Prague; Slovak Music Union,Bratislava; Founder Member, Contrast 91, Ostrava. Hobby: National and European folklore. Address: Cestmirova 27, 140 00 Prague 4, Czech Republic.

DAGGETT Philip, b. 1962, Chesterfield, England. Singer (Tenor). Education: Studied in Chesterfield and at Guildhall School of Music, 1985-. Career: Songman at York Minster, 1981-85; Concert appearances include Bach's Actus Tragicus in Paris and the St John Passion throughout Spain; Has sung in Mozart's C Minor Mass and Requiem; Mendelssohn's Lobgesang (Elizabeth Hall debut) and Elijah; Britten's Cantata Misericordium and St Nicolas; Operatic roles include Paris in La Belle Hélène, Beppe in Pagliacci and Mozart's Ferrando; Premiere of Birtwistle's Gawain at Covent Garden, May 1991; Also sings Count Almaviva in Il Barbiere di Siviglia; Sang Tamino with Opera Lirica at the Holland Park Theatre, 1992; Premiere of Maxwell Davies's The Doctor of Myddfai, 1996. Recordings include: The Fairy Queen with Harry Christophers and The Sixteen; A Festal Mass at the Imperial Court of Vienna and Charpentier's Vespers for the Feast of St Louis with the Yorkshire Baroque Soloists and Peter Seymour. Address: c/o Norman McCann International Artists Limited, The Coach House, 56 Lawrie Park Gardens, London SE26 6XJ, England.

DAHL Tracy, b. 1964, Winnipeg, Manitoba, Canada. Singer (Soprano). Education: Studied with the Merola Opera Program. Career: Sang in the USA from 1986, notably as Offenbach's Eurydice at Houston, Olympia at Chicago (1987), Serpetta in La Finta Giardiniera at St Louis (1988) and Oscar in Ballo in Maschera at San Francisco (1990); Also appeared as Oscar at the New York Metropolitan, 1990, returning 1991 in the premiere of The Ghosts of Versailles by Corigliano (repeated, 1995); Toronto Opera, 1992, as Nannetta, Sophie in Werther and Zerbinetta, 1995. Address: c/o Metropolitan Opera, Lincoln Center, New York, NY 10023, USA.

DAHLBERG Stefan, b. 3 May 1955, Sweden. Singer (Tenor). Education: Studied at the State Academy of Music and the State College of Musical Drama in Stockholm. Career: Concerts and Broadcasts throughout Scandinavia; Operatic roles include Rustighello in Lucrezia Borgia by Donizetti, Tamino, Beppo, Count Almaviva, King Charles in The Maid of Orleans by Tchaikovsky and Sextus in Giulio Cesare; Royal Opera Stockholm as Tamino, Sextus, Ferrando and Don Ottavio; Drottningholm 1987, as Titus in La Clemenza di Tito; visited Brighton with the Drottningholm Company, 1987; Season 1988-89 with concert performance of Haydn's Armida in Amsterdam; Grand Théâtre Geneva as Jacquino in Fidelio, conducted by Jeffrey Tate; Gounod's Faust at the Stockholm Opera; Concertgebouw Amsterdam, 1989, as Ubaldo in Rossini's Armida; Drottningholm, 1989, as Tamino; Sang Calaf in Busoni's Turandot at Lyons, 1992; Leading tenor role of Vicente Martin y Soler's Una Cosa Rara; Alfredo in Verdi's La Traviata, Stockholm Royal Opera, 1993; Haydn's Orlando at Drottningholm, 1994; Concert repertoire includes Suter's Der Abwesende Gott, Die Schöpfung by Haydn, Le Roi David by Honegger, Messiah, Puccini's Messa di Gloria and works by Thomas Jernefelt and Sven-David Sandström. Recordings: Videos of La Clemenza di Tito, Die Zauberflöte and Don Giovanni, from Drottningholm. Address: Nordk Artist AB, Sveavagen 76, S-11344 Stockholm, Sweden.

DAHLGREN Carl H P, b. 2 July 1929, New York City, USA. Professor; Arts Administrator. m. Ella Kate Bowes, 8 October 1961, 3 sons, 1 daughter. Education: BM, Westminster Choir College, Princeton, New Jersey, 1954. Career: Manager, Princeton Symphony Orchestra, 1956-50; Vice-President, Artistic Manager, Columbia Artists Management Incorporated; Partner, Division of Judd, Ries and Dahlgren, 1958-68; Vice-President, Artist Manager, Director of Sales, Sol Hurok Concerts Inc, 1968-70; Executive Director, Central City Opera House Association, General Manager, Central City Opera Company, 1970-72; Associate, Sol Hurok Concerts Inc, 1970-74; President, Dahlgren Arts Management Incorporated, Denver, Colorado, 1970-78; Executive Director-Secretary, Colorado Celebration of the Arts, Denver, 1974-76; Associate Professor, Director of Graduate Studies in Arts Administration, College-Conservatory of Music, University of Cincinnati, 1978-. Contributions to: Various magazines and journals. Hobbies: Travel; Reading; Family. Address: 2216 Bedford Terrace, Cincinnati, OH 45208, USA.

DAIKEN Melanie (Ruth), b. 27 Jul 1945, London, England. Composer. Education: Studied at the Royal Academy and at the Paris Conservatoire with Loriod and Messiaen. Career: Deputy Head of Composition at the Royal Academy from 1986. Compositions include: Operas: Eusebius, 1968, and Mayakovsky And The Sun, Edinburgh, 1971; Viola Sonata, 1978; Attica for Orchestra, 1980; Requiem for Piano, 1983; Der Gartner for 13 Solo Strings and Piano, 1988; Song settings of poems by Lorca, Beckett, Trakl and Baudelaire. Address: c/o PRS Ltd, 29-33 Berners Street, London, W1P 4AA, England.

DALAYMAN Katraina, b. 1968, Sweden. Singer (Soprano). Education: Studied at the Stockholm Royal College of Music. Debut: Stockholm Royal Opera 1991, as Amelia in Simon Boccanegra. Career: Stuttgart Opera from 1993, as Marie in Wozzeck, Desdemona, Eva in Die Meistersinger and Elisabeth in Tannhäuser (1997); Further appearances as Mimi and Marietta in Die tote Stadt at Stockholm, Strauss's Ariadne at the Brussels Opera (1997) and Marie at the Maggio Musicale, Florence (1998); Other repertory includes Mozart's Vitellia and Fiordiligi, and Elisabeth de Valois in Don Carlos; Concerts include Mahler's 8th Symphony with the LSO, Sibelius's Kullervo Symphony, under Colin Davis, and Penderecki's Requiem, conducted by the composer; Season 1998-99 with Parisian debut at the Opera National as Marie. Address: c/o Haydn Rawstron Ltd, 36 Station Road, London SE20 7BQ, England.

DALBERG Evelyn, b. 23 May 1939, Leipzig, Germany. Singer (Mezzo-Soprano). Education: Studied with Parry Jones at Guildhall School of Music, Annelies Kupper in Munich and with her father, Frederick Dalberg, at Cape Town and Mannheim. Debut: Koblenz 1964, as Venus in Tannhäuser. Career: Sang at various provincial German Opera Houses and in South Africa, notably Cape Town and Johannesburg; Other roles have included Verdi's Ulrica, Amneris, Eboli and Mistress Quickly, Nancy in Martha, Giulietta in Les Contes d'Hoffmann, Judith in Bluebeard's Castle, the Witch in Hansel and Gretel and Prince Orlofsky in Die Fledermaus. Address: c/o Johannesburg Operatic and Dramatic Society, PO Box 7010, Johannesburg 2000, Transvaal, South Africa.

DALBERTO Michel (Jean Jacques), b. 2 June 1955, Paris, France. Pianist. Education: Paris National Conservatory, 1972. Debut: Paris. Career: Appearances, major European Centres; Festivals: Edinburgh, Lucerne, Aix-en-Province, Montreux; Tours in Japan, Canada; Radio & television performances; Paris debut with the Orchestra de Paris, 1980; Partnerships with Henryk Szeryng, Augustin Dumay and Viktoria Mullova, Violin, and Nikita Magaloff, Piano. Recordings: Works of Schubert, Schumann, Brahms, Beethoven, Mozart. Honours: Clara Haskil Prize, 1975; First Prize, Leeds International Competition, 1978; Grand Prix Academie Charles Cros, 1980. Hobbies: Skiing; Tennis; Golf. Management: Opera Et Concert, Paris, France. Address: BD Plumhof 13, 1800 Vevey, Switzerland.

DALBY Martin, b. 25 April 1942, Aberdeen, Scotland. Composer. Education: Studied at the Royal College of Music from 1960, with Herbert Howells (composition) and Frederick Riddle (viola); Further study in Italy. Career: BBC Music Producer in London, 1965-71; Cramb Research Fellow in Composition at Glasgow University, 1972; Head of Music, BBC Scotland, 1972-. Compositions: include, Waltz Overture, 1965; Trio for Piano, Violin and Cello, 1967; Oboe Sonatina, 1969; Cantica for High Voice, Clarinet, Viola and Piano, 1969; Commedia for Clarinet, Violin, Cello and Piano, 1969; Symphony, 1970; Whisper Music, 1971; Concerto Martin Pescatore for Strings, 1971; The Keeper of the Pass for Soprano and Instruments, 1971; Cancionero Para Una Mariposa for 9 Instruments, 1971; String Quintet, 1972; Orpheus for Chorus, Narrator and 11 Instruments, 1972; Catigas del Cancionero for 5 Solo Voices, 1972; The Tower of Victory for Orchestra, 1973; Yet Still She is the Moon, Brass Septet, 1973; Viola Concerto, 1974; El Remanso del Pitido for 12 Solo Voices, 1974; Unicorn for Violin and Piano, 1975; Aleph for 8 Instruments, 1975; Ad Flumina Babiloniae, Motet, 1975; Almost a Madrigal for Wind and Percussion, 1977; El Ruisenor for Orchestra, 1979; Coll for the Hazel Tree for Chorus and Electronics, 1979; Man Walking, Octet for Wind and Strings, 1980; Antoinette Alone for Mezzo and Piano, 1980; Chamber Symphony, 1982; Nozze di Primavera for Orchestra, 1984; A Plain Man's Hammer for Symphonic Wind Ensemble, 1984; Piano Sonata No 1, 1985; De Patre ex Filio Octet for Wind and Strings, 1988; Piano Sonata No 2, 1989. Hobbies: Private Pilot's Licence; Railways; Hill Walking; Literature. Address: 23 Muirport Way, Drymen, Glasgow G63 0DX, Scotland.

DALE Clamma, b. 4 July 1948, Chester, Pennsylvania, USA. Soprano. Education: BMus 1970, MS 1975, Juilliard School, New York; Studied Voice, Philadelphia Settlement Music School. Debut: Operatic debut as Antonia, Les Contes d'Hoffman, New York City Opera, 1975. Career: Sang with numerous Opera Companies; Toured as Concert Singer; Roles include: Pamina, Countess Almaviva, Nedda, Musetta, Gershwin's Bess at the Theater des Westens, Berlin, 1988; Deutsche Oper Berlin, 1989, as Liù in Turandot. Recordings: For Deutsche Grammophon; RCA. Address: c/o New York City Opera, Lincoln Center, New York, NY 10023, USA.

DALE Laurence, b. 10 September 1957, Pyecombe, Sussex. Singer (Tenor). Education: Studied at the Guildhall School of Music, 1976-80 and at the Mozarteum, Salzburg. Debut: With English National Opera as Camille in The Merry Widow, 1981. Career: Covent Garden debut 1982, as Second Noble in Lohengrin; Sang Don José in Peter Brook's La Tragédie de Carmen in Paris, 1981 and on Broadway, 1983; in 1983 sang Gounod's Romeo at Basle and Ramiro at Glyndebourne; Visited Los Angeles with the Royal Opera, 1984, singing Pong in Turandot; English National Opera 1983, as Monteverdi's Orfeo; For Welsh National Opera has sung Mozart's Ottavio and Ferrando and Eisenstein in Die Fledermaus; With Opera North as Mozart's Tamino and Belmonte and Jenik in The Bartered Bride; Further appearances in Lyon, Paris, Hamburg, Amsterdam, Aix, Geneva, Brussels (Tamino and Idomeneo) and Zurich; Other roles include Tchaikovsky's Lensky, Jacquino in Fidelio, Méhul's Joseph and Gonzalve in L'Heure Espagnole; Concert engagements include Mozart's C Minor Mass and Haydn's St Cecilia Mass with the London Philharmonic; Bach's Christmas Oratorio with the Los Angeles Philharmonic; Britten's Spring Symphony at the Festival Hall; The Dream of Gerontius and Liszt's Faust Symphony at the Brighton Festival; Messiah in Vienna, Stravinsky's Pulcinella and Rossini's Stabat Mater; Appearances on television in Britain and Europe; On 27 January 1991 sang Tamino in Die Zauberflöte at the Landestheater Salzburg, to inaugurate the Mozart Bicentenary; Season 1991/92 as Ferrando at Stuttgart and Belfiore in La Finta Giardiniera at the Salzburg Festival; Sang Don Ottavio at Genoa, 1993; Pelléas at Brussels, 1996. Recordings: include, La Tragédie de Carmen; Videos of Princess Ida, Die Zauberflöte from Aix and Cenerentola from Glyndebourne; Mozart's C Minor Mass. Address: c/o Harrison Parrott Limited, 12 Penzance Place, London W11 4PA, England.

DALIS-LOINAZ Irene, b. 8 October 1925, San Jose, California, USA. Executive Director, Opera San Jose; Professor of Music. m. George Loinaz, 16 July 1957, 1 daughter. Education: AB, 1946, MS, Honours, 1957 San Jose State University; MA, Columbia University Teachers College, 1947; Studied Voice with Edyth Walker, New York City, 1947-50; Paul Althouse, 1950-51; Dr Otto Mueller, Milano, Italy, 1952. Debut: Berlin State Opera, 1955; Metropolitan Opera, New York City, 1957. Career: Leading Dramatic Mezzo-Soprano, Metropolitan Opera, 1957-77 as Eboli, Amneris, Santuzza, Azucena, Lady Macbeth and Dalila, 22 roles in 232 performances; 1st US born Kundry to open Bayreuth Festival, 1963; Opened the Met opera season as Amneris in Aida, 1963; Premiered Dello Joio's Opera, Blood Moon, 1961 and Henderson's Opera, Medea, 1972; In 1966 sang The Nurse in Die Frau ohne Schatten, at Sadler's Wells Theatre; Professor of Music, San Jose State University and Founder and Executive Director, Opera San Jose, from 1984; Hosted Symposium Redrawing the Man at San José, November 1989, on behalf of the Music Critics Association. Recording: Parsifal, Wagner. Honours: Fulbright Scholar, 1951; Distinguished Service Award, Columbia University, 1961; Wagner Medallion, 1963; Tower Award, San Jose State University, 1974; California Public Educators Hall of Fame, 1985; Award of Merit, People of the City of San Francisco, Honoured Citizen of San Jose, 1986; Honorary Doctor of Music, Santa Clara University, 1987. Address: 1731 Cherry Grove Drive, San Jose, California, CA 95125, USA.

DALLAPOZZA Adolf, b. 14 April 1940, Bozen, Austria. Singer (Tenor). Education: Studied with Elisabeth Rado in Vienna. Career: Sang in the chorus of the Vienna Volksoper while a student; Solo debut 1962, as Ernesto in Don Pasquale; Sang at the Volksoper until 1972, and guested in Munich, Hamburg, Milan, Brussels and Cologne; Bregenz Festival, 1972-84; Many roles in works by Mozart, Italian Opera and in Operas of the Baroque; Many appearances in Operettas; Wilheim Meister in Mignon at the Vienna Volksoper, 1988. Recordings: Die Fledermaus, Der Vogelhändler; Idomeneo; Intermezzo; Fidelio; Die Meistersinger; Königskinder by Humperdinck. Address: c/o Volksoper, Währingerstrasse 78, A-1090 Vienna, Austria.

DALLEY John, b. 1 June 1935, Madison, Wisconsin, USA. Violinist. Education: Studied at Curtis Institute, Philadelphia, with Ivan Galamian. Career: Member of the Oberlin Quartet, formerly teacher at Oberlin Conservatory, Performed in Chamber Music with Rudolf Serkin at the Marlboro Festival and prompted by Alexander Schneider to co-found the Guarneri String Quartet, 1984; Many tours in America and Europe, notably appearances at the Spoleto Festival, 1965, to Paris with Arthur Rubinstein and London 1970, in the complete quartets of Beethoven; Noted for performances of the Viennese Classics, and works by Walton, Bartok and Stravinsky; Season 1987-88 included tour of Japan and concerts at St John's Smith Square and the Elizabeth Hall, London; On faculty of the Curtis Institute, Philadelphia, and at the University of Maryland. Recordings: include, Mozart's Quartets dedicated to Haydn; Complete Quartets of Beethoven; With Arthur Rubinstein, Piano Quintets of Schumann, Dvorak and Brahms; Piano Quartets by Fauré and Brahms. Honours: include, Edison Award for Beethoven recordings 1971. Address: c/o Curtis Institute of Music, 1726 Locust Street, Philadelphia, PA 19103, USA.

DALTON Andrew, b. 29 September 1950, Melbourne, Australia. Singer (Countertenor). Education: Studied in Brisbane. Debut: Sang at Vadstena, Sweden in Provenzale's La Stellidaura vendicata. Career: Has sung in Baroque Opera at Venice, Innsbruck, Munich, Berne and Amsterdam; Appeared with Scottish Opera in Cavalli's Egisto and at the 1987 Buxton Festival as Fernando in Conti's Don Chisciotte in Sierra Morena; Season 1988-89 in Jommelli's Fetonte at La Scala, Milan, in Monteverdi's Ulisse with Opera de Lausanne at Mézières, and as Apollo in Death in Venice with Australian Opera at Sydney; Engagements in Germany and Switzerland as Britten's Oberon, and has sung in Monteverdi's Orfeo, Handel's Agrippina and Ariodante, and Jommelli's La Schiava Liberata; Sang in Purcell's Indian Queen at the Barossa Festival, Australia, 1995. Address: Australian Opera, Sydney Opera House, New South Wales, Australia.

DALTREY David Joseph, b. 30 Dec 1951, London, England. Session Musician; Composer; Tutor; Performer; Producer. m. Helen McIldowie, 20 July 1989. Education: Mid-Hertfordshire College; Guildhall School of Music and Drama, London; Studied with Rogers Covey-Crump. Debut: Central Hall, Westminister, 1968. Career: St Pauls Cathedral, 1968; Eammon Andrews TV Show, 1968; St Martins, 1971; Olympia, London, 1979; Indian Classical Group with Punita Gupta, 1980-81; Classical Jazz Group with Nigel Kennedy, 1981; Recording Artist, BBC. Compositions: The Pathway; Aurora; Morpheus; Planets. Recordings; Planets; Joseph and the Amazing Technicolour Dreamcoat. Memberships: Incorporated Society of Musicians; Musicians Union. Address: Pilgrims Rest 34, Guildhall Street, Bury St Edmunds IP33 1QF, Suffolk, England.

DAM-JENSEN Inger, b. 1961, Denmark. Soprano. Career: Many engagements in concert and opera throughout Scandinavia and elsewhere in Europe; Concerts with John Eliot Gardiner and Seiji Ozawa in Florence; Guest at Covent Garden London, with the Royal Danish Opera in Prokofiev's The Love for Three Oranges; Further appearances as Rossini's Elvira at Pesaro and the Fiakermilli in Arabella at Glyndebourne. Opera roles in Copenhagen include Zerbinetta, Norina, Sophie in Der Rosenkavalier, Blondchen and a Flowermaiden in Parsifal; Sang in the Danish premiere of Poulenc's Carmelites, 1997; Engaged as Sifare in Mozart's Mitridate at Geneva, 1997-98. Recordings include: Mahler Symphony No 4; Grieg's Peer Gynt. Honours include: Winner of the 1993 Cardiff Singer of the World Competition. Address: c/o Harrison Parrott Ltd, 12 Penzance Place, London, W11 4PA, England.

DAMARATI Luciano, b. 6 Feb 1942, Lucca, Italy. Musician. Education: Diplomas: Piano, 1965; Composition, 1970; Organ, 1971; Orchestral Conducting, 1975; Studies: Organ with Alessandro Esposito and Fernando Germani; Orchestral Conducting with Franco Ferrara; Choral Conducting with Nino Antonellini; Musicology at Chigiana Academy of Music, Siena. Career: Many concerts as Organist and Orchestral Conductor; Broadcasts as Composer, Orchestra Conductor and Choir Conductor on Italian Radio and Television. Compositions: Impressioni (viola and piano), 1968; Fuga (organ), 1970; Preludio (organ), 1978; Immagini (piano), 1980; Contrasti (piano), 1980; Preghiera semplice (voice, choir and orchestra), 1986; I due fanciulli (voice and piano), 1986; Inno di lode a Dio (voice, choir of mixed voices, violin and organ), 1988; Le Ciaramelle (voice, violin and piano), 1988; La voce (voice, violin and piano), 1989; A Silvia (voice and piano), 1991; Mottettone (choir of mixed voices, 2 trumpets, trombone, tam-tam, kettledrums and organ), 1995. Contributions to: La Provincia di Lucca, 1974; Actum Luce, 1980; Rivista di Archeologia Storia e Costume. Honour: 2nd Prize for Composition, Rodolfo del Corona, Leghorn. Membership: Italian Society of Musicology. Address: Piazza S Francesco 14, 55100 Lucca, Italy.

DAMASE Jean-Michel, b. 27 January 1928, Bordeaux, France. Composer; Pianist. Education: Conservatoire National Superieus de Paris. Career: United States debut 1954, as Pianist and Composer in a New York Concert. Compositions: Quintet for Flute, Harp and String Trio, 1947; Interludes for Orchestra, 1948; Rhapsody for Oboe and String Orchestra, 1948; Trio for Flute, Harp and Cello, 1949; Piano Concerto, 1950; Ballet La Croquese de Diamants, 1950; Violin Concerto, 1956; La Tendre Eleonore, Opera-Bouffe, Marseilles, 1962; Colombe, Comedie Lyrique, Bordeaux, 1961; Eugene Le Mysterieux, Feuillton Musical, Paris, 1964; Madame de Roman Musical, Monte Carlo, 1970; Eurydice, Comedie Lyrique, Bordeaux, 1972; L'heritiere, Opera in 4 Acts after Washington Square by Henry James, Nancy, 1974; Quartet for Flute, Clarinet and Piano, 1992; Concertos for Flute and Orchestra, 1993; Variations, Mozart: for Piano and Orchestra, 1994. Honour: Prix de Rome, 1947. Address: c/o PRS Limited, Member Registration, 29-33 Berners Street, London W1P 4AA, England.

DAMIANI Davide, b. 1966, Italy. Baritone. Career: Recital, concert and opera appearances throughout Italy and Europe; Contestant at the 1995 Cardiff Singer of the World Competition; Repertory includes Le Nozze di Figaro and Don Carlo, Lieder by Strauss and Schumann; Seasons 1995-99 will be House-Baritone at the Vienna State Opera. Address: c/o Miss Elin de Kat, Stage Door Management, Via Giardini 941/2, 41040 Saliceta San Giuliano (Modena), Italy.

DAMISCH-KUSTERER Sieglinde, b. 1951, Amsterdam, Netherlands. Singer (Soprano). Education: Studied at the Salzburg Mozarteum and in Vienna with Hilde Konetzni. Career: Sang at the Vienna Staatsoper from 1979, Salzburg Festival, 1981 (Das Buch mit sieben Siegeln by Schmidt); Further engagements at Augsburg and elsewhere in Germany as Fiordiligi, Elisabeth de Valois, Tatiana, Jenufa, Mimi and Pamina; Frequent concert appearances. Address: c/o Stadtische Buhnen Augsburg, Kasernstrasse 4-6, Pf 111949, W-8900 Augsburg, Germany.

DAMONTE Magali, b. 30 June 1960, Marseilles, France. Singer (Mezzo-Soprano). Education: Studied in Marseilles. Debut: Sang Zulma in L'Italiana in Algeri at Marseilles in 1978. Career: Many appearances in France with operas by Rossini, Cimarosa and Gounod; Paris Opera 1980, as Iphise in Rameau's Dardanus; Aix-en-Provence Festival from 1981, as Rosina, Cenerentola and Isaura in Tancredi; At the Opéra de Lyon has sung Aloès in L'Etoile (visit with the company to the Edinburgh Festival, 1985); Marseilles 1987, as Fidalma in Il Matrimonio Segreto, Théâtre des Champs Elysées, Paris 1989, as Hedwige in Guillaume Tell; Other Rossini roles include Isabella, Ragonde (Le Comte Ory) and Marie (Moise); Sang Carmen at Covent Garden, 1994 and at Vancouver, 1996. Recordings: include, L'Etoile, conducted by John Eliot Gardiner. Address: c/o Opera de Lyon, 9 Quai Jean Moulin, F-69001, France.

DAN Ikuma, b. 7 April 1924, Tokyo, Japan. Composer. Education: Studied at Tokyo Music School, graduation 1945 and with Moroi and Yamada. Career: Formed Group of Three Composers with Akutagawa and Mayuzumi, 1953; Film Music Director and Composer; Presenter of Popular Music Programmes on Television from 1967. Compositions: Operas: The Twilight Heron, 1952; The Listening Cap, 1955; Yang Kwei-fei, 1958; Luminous Moss, 1972; Chanchiki, 1975; 6 Symphonies, 1949-70; Sinfonia Burlesca, 1953; The Silken Road, dance suite for Orchestra, 1954; Japanese Poem for Orchestra, 1967; Hymn to the Sai-Kai for Chorus and Orchestra, 1969; A Letter from Japan for Orchestra, 1969; Rainbow Tower for Orchestra, 1970; Chamber: String Trio, 1947; String Quartet, 1948; Concerto Grosso for Harpsichord and Strings, 1965; Choruses. Address: JASRAC (Japan), Jasrac House 7-13, 1-Chome Nishishimbashi, Minato-ku, Tokyo 105, Japan.

DANCEANU Liviu, b. 19 July 1954, Romania. Composer. m. Rodica Danceanu, 27 August 1976. Education: Academy of Music C, Poroumbescu, Bucharest; University Studies, Musical composition with Stefan Niculescu. Debut: Academy of Music, C Porumbescu, 1978. Career: Concerts in Bucharest and other Musical Centres, London, Paris, Rotterdam, Torino, Warsaw, Prague, Moscow; Appearances on Romanian Radio and Television, BBC London, Radio France; Recordings with Electrecord Recording House, Bucharest; Leader and Conductor, The Workshop for Contemporary Music Archaeus. Compositions: include, Les Heros, Op 1, 1978; La Rocade De Janus, Op 2, 1978; Allegorie, Op 3, 1979; Sonate Pour Basson, Op 4, 1980; Archaeus, Op 5, 1981; Angulus Ridet, Op 7, 1981; Ossia, Op 9, 1982; Vers La Paix, Op 10, 1982; Quasifuga, Op 11, 1983; 3 Chansons Infantiles, Op 15, 1984; Florilege, Op 17, 1985; Protocantus, Op 18, 1985; Glass Music, Op 20, 1985; Quasitoccata, Op 21, 1985. Hobbies: Philosophy; Arts; Literature; Sport. Address: Calea Vacaresti No 276, B1, 63 Sc 2, Apt 44, Sector 4, 75176 Bucharest, Romania.

DANCO Suzanne, b. 22 January 1911, Brussels, Belgium. Singer (Soprano). Education: Studied at the Brussels Conservatory and with Fernando Carpi in Prague. Debut: Genoa Opera 1941, as Fiordiligi in Così fan tutte. Career: Sang at La Scala Milan, notably in the local premieres of Peter Grimes, 1947 and Oedipus Rex, 1948; Naples 1949, as Marie in Wozzeck; Glyndebourne Festival 1948-51, as Fiordiligi and Donna Anna; Covent Garden 1951, as Mimi in La Bohème; Broadcasts of Wozzeck and Pelléas et Mélisande; World-wide Concert Tours in the songs of Debussy, Berlioz and Ravel; Teacher at the Accademia Chigiana in Siena. Recordings: Pelléas et Mélisande, conducted by Ansermet; La Damnation de Faust; Le Roi David by Honegger; L'Heure Espagnole; Le nozze di Figaro; Don Giovanni.

DANCUO Mirjana, b. 16 January 1929, Karlovac, Croatia. Singer (Soprano). m. Zdenko Peharda. Education: Studied in Zagreb. Debut: National Opera, Zagreb 1945, as Giannetta in L'Elisir d'Amore. Career: Sang Belgrade, Sofia, Brno and elsewhere in Eastern Europe; Guest appearances at Teatro Liceo Barcelona, The Vienna Volksoper and Den Norske Opera, Oslo; Other roles have included Mozart's Countess and Donna Anna, Verdi's Amneris, Amelia, Ballo in Maschera and Trovatore Leonora, La Gioconda, Margherita in Mefistofele, Yaroslavna in Prince Igor, Leonore, Fidelio, Marina in Boris Godunov, Wagner's Sieglinde and Elisabeth, the Marschallin in Der Rosenkavalier, Tosca and Desdemona. Address: Jerikoveien 89B, 1052 Oslo, Norway.

DANEL Mark, b. 1965, England. Violinist. Education: Studied in London and with Feodor Droujinin, violist of Russia's Beethoven Quartet. Career: Many concerts throughout Britain, notably at the Aldeburgh Festival with Quartet in Residence, Huddersfield, Andover and Middle Temple; Repertoire includes quartets by Shostakovich and Fauré and English works. Honours: As member of Danel Quartet: Prizewinner in competitions at Florence, St Petersburg, Evian and London, 1991-94. Address: Manygate Management, 13 Cotswold Mews, 30 Battersea Square, London, SW11 3RA, England.

DANEMAN Sophie, b. 1968, England. Soprano. Education: Studied at the Guildhall School. Career: Appearances with Les Arts Florissants at Aix-en-Provence, Théâtre du Châtelet at Paris, Sydney, Buenos Aires, Rio de Janeiro and the Brooklyn Academy of Music; Has also sung with Philippe Herreweghe at the Sainte Festival and with the King's Consort in Dido and Aeneas on tour in spain; Handel's Rodelinda for Channel 4 TV. Recordings include: Rameau's Castor et Pollux; Monteclair Jephté; Dido and Aeneas; Rameau's Grand Motets; Charpentier's Médée. Address: Ron Gonsalves Management, 7 Old Town, Clapham, London, SW4 0JT, England.

DANG THAI SON, b. Hanoi, Veitman. Pianist. Education: Diploma, 1976; Moscow Tchaikovsky Conservatory, 1983. Career: Appearances at Several Major Festivals, including, Berlin, Geneva, Ravinia, Miami, Paris, Brescia, Bergamo, Cannes, Prague Spring, Dubrovnik, Bratislava, Russian Winter, December Nights, Chopin Festival of Nohant, Ruhr Piano Festival; Tour of North America, 1989; Played with World-Famous Orchestras including, Leningrad Philharmonic, Montreal Symphony, BBC Philharmonic, Dresden Philharmonic, Staatskapelle Berlin, Oslo Philharmonic, Warsaw National Philharmonic, Prague Symphony, NHK Symphony, Helsinki Philharmonic, Sydney Symphony, Hungarian Symphony, Moscow Philharmonic; Appearances with the Virtuosi of Moscow, the Polish, Moscow & Zurich Chamber Orchestras and with Sinfonia Varsovia; Honorary Professor, Kunitachi Music College, Tokyo. Honours: Gold Medal, 10th International Chopin Piano Competition, Warsaw, 1980. Address: c/o Latitude 45, Arts Promotion Inc, 109 St Joseph Blvd West, Montreal, Quebec H2T 2P7, Canada.

DANIEL Nicholas (Jeremy Gordon), b. 9 January 1962, Liss, Hampshire, England. Solo Oboist; Chamber Musician. m. Joy Farrall, 29 March 1986. Education: Chorister, Salisbury Cathedral School, 1972-74; Purcell School, London, 1974-80; Royal Academy of Music, 1980-83. Debut: South Bank, 1982. Career: Concerto and Recital appearances, at home and abroad; Professor, Guildhall School of Music and Drama; Proms Debut, 1990; Founder & Director, Haffner Wind Ensemble, 1990; Daniel-Drake Duo 12 years old; Regular broadcasts of wide repertoire; Tours include Hungary, Australia, Scandinavia, Netherlands, Italy, Bulgaria, Spain, France, Switzerland, Germany; Firm dedication to new music, many World & British premieres; Played Strauss Concerto at the 1993 Proms. Recordings: Virgin Classics, Hyperion, Chandos, Léman Classics; American Gramophone of Alwyn, Belgian music, Albinoni, Strauss, Martinu; Appearances with Lindsay, Brodsky, Allegri, Van Burgh & Brindisi String Quartets. Honours: BBC Young Musician of the Year, 1980; Gillet Young Artists Prize, Graz, 1984 and Munich, 1986; Associate, Royal Academy of Music, 1986; Honorary Fellow, Purcell School, 1988. Hobbies: Meditation; Reading; Theatre; Cinema; Walking; Cooking; Wine. Current Management: Neil Chaffrey; Patrick Garvey. Address: 26 Haddon Court, Milton Road, Harpenden, Herts AL5 5NA, England.

DANIEL Paul, b. 1 July 1958, Birmingham, England. Conductor. m. Joan Rodgers. Education: Sang in Choir of Coventry Cathedral and read music at King's College, Cambridge; Guildhall School, London, with Franco Ferrara in Italy and with Adrian Boult and Edward Downes. Career: Engagements with the Royal Philharmonic, City of Birmingham Symphony, Scottish National Orchestra, Rotterdam Philharmonic, London Symphony, London Philharmonic, Philharmonia, Minneapolis Orchestra, Rochester Philharmonic, New York, London Sinfonietta and Ensemble Inter Contemporain, Paris, and Munich Philharmonic, RSO Berlin, ORF Vienna, Hallé, Manchester; Principal conductor of the English Northern Philharmonica; US debut 1988 with the London Sinfonietta at the Pepsico Summer Fare; Music Director of Opera Factory, 1987-90; The Beggar's Opera, Cavalli's La Calisto, Birtwistle's Punch and Judy, Così fan tutte and a triple bill of works by Maxwell Davies, Ligeti and Weill; Productions for English National Opera include Ligeti's Le Grand Macabre, Glass's Akhnaten, Dargomizhsky's Stone Guest, Birtwistle's The Mask of Orpheus and the UK premiere of Reimann's Lear (1989); For Nancy Opera conducted the French premiere of Tippett's King Priam, 1988; Music Director, Opera North, 1990-96; Music Director, English National Opera, 1997-. Productions for Opera North include: British Stage Première of Jérusalem, Ariane et Barbe-bleue, Dukas; Verdi's Attila, Tippett's King Priam, 1991; British première of Schreker's Der ferne Klang, Rigoletto, Boris, Don Carlos, Wozzeck, Il Trovatore, Pelleas and Melisande, Luisa Miller, Medea, 1993, La Monnaie, Brussels, from 1994, with Così fan Tutte, Khovanshchina and Béatrice et Benédict, 1997; Premiere of Böse's Slaughterhouse Five at Munich, 1996. Address: c/o Harrison Parrott Limited, 12 Penzance Place, London W11 4PA, England.

DANIEL-LESUR Jean Yves, b. 19 Nov 1908, Paris, France. Composer. m. Simone Lauer, 1943, 1 s, 1 d. Education: Paris Conservatoire. Career: Musical Adviser, Radiodiffusion Television Francaise; Principal Inspector of Music, Ministry of Cultural Affairs; Administrator, Réunion des Theatres Lyriques Nationaux; Inspector-General of Music, Ministry of Cultural Affairs; President, Academy Charles Cros, 1979-84; Honorary President, 1984-; Writer of Film Music; Director Hon Schola Cantorum. Compositions include: French X Suite for Orchestra, 1935; Pastorale for Small Orchestra, 1938; Quatre Lieder for Voice and Orchestra, 1933-39; 3 Poems de Cecile Sauvage, 1939; L'enfance de l'Art, 1942; Clair Comme le Jour, 1945; Suite Medievale for Flute, Harp and Trio a Cordes, 1944; Berceuses a Tenir Éveillé, song, 1947; Ballade for Piano, 1948; 10 Popular Songs for 3 Voix Egales, 1950; Chansons Francaises for 4 Mixed Voices, 1951; L'Annonciation, cantata, 1952; Cantique des Colonnes for Female Vocal Ensemble and Orchestra, 1954; Le Bal du Destin, ballet; Symphonie de Danses, 1958; Fantasie for 2 Pianos, 1962; 2 Chansons de Marins for Male Choir, 1964; Andres del Sarto, 2 act opera, 1968; Le Voyage D'Automne for Voices and Orchestra, 1990; A La Lisière Du Temps for Voice and Orchestra, 1990; Duo Concertant for Flute, Harp and Orchestra; Fantasie Concertante for Cello and Orchestra, 1992; Quatre Nocturnes for Voices and String Quartet, 1993; Impromptu for Flute, Harp and Strings Orchestra, 1994; La Nuit Rêve for Voices and Strings Orchestra, 1994; Lamento for Harp and Strings Orchestra, 1995. Recording: Integrale Des Oeuvres pour Orgue. Honours include: Grand Officer, Legion of Honour; Commander, Ordre nat du Merite; Many prizes including Prix in International Maurice Ravel; Associate Member, l'Academie Royale de Belgium. Memberships: L'Academie Européenne des Sciences, des Arts es des Lettres; Honorary President, GFASMC. Address: 101 Rue Sadi Carnot, F-92800 Puteaux, France.

DANIELS Barbara, b. 7 May 1946, Grenville, Ohio, USA. Singer (Soprano). Education: Bachelors Degree, Ohio State University; Masters Degree, University of Cincinnati. Debut: West Palm Beach, Florida as Susanna, 1973. Career: Sang in Europe from 1974, notably in Innsbruck as Violetta and Cologne as Alice Ford, Rosalinda, Mozart's Countess and Manon Lescaut; Appeared in the Michael Hampe productions and films of Agrippina and Il Matrimonio Segreto; Covent Garden from 1978 as Musetta, Donna Elvira, Rosalinde and Alice Ford; Washington DC 1979, as Donizetti's Norina; San Francisco from 1980, as Zdenka in Arabella and as Violetta, Liu and Micaela; Zurich Opera as the Comtesse, in the Ponnelle production of Le Comte Ory; Metropolitan Opera from 1983, as Musetta, Violetta, Rosalinde, Marguerite and the title role in Les Mamelles de Tiresias; Musetta at Rome, 1987; Teatro Regio Turin, 1988, Violetta; Rosalinde in Fledermaus at the Metropolitan and Chicago, 1990; Jenufa at Innsbruck, 1990; Minnie in La Fanciulla del West at the Metropolitan, October 1991; Sang Sonta at Cincinnati, 1996; Concert appearances in Rossini's Mosè at Perugia; Boito's Mefistofele at the Zurich Tonhalle, Schumann's Scenes from Faust with the Berlin Philharmonic and the Missa Solemnis under Giulini at the Maggio Musicale Florence. Recordings include: Scenes from Faust; La Bohème conducted by Bernstein. Address: c/o Harrison Parrott Limited, 12 Penzance Place, London W11 4PA, England.

DANIELS Charles, b. 1960, Salisbury, England. Singer (Tenor). Education: Choral Scholar at King's College, Cambridge; Royal College of Music, with Edward Brooks. Career: Many appearances in the UK, Europe, Australia and Israel; Handel's Triumph of Time and Truth in Holland, Judas Maccabeus in San Sebastien and Solomon at the Halle Festival; Mendelssohn's Elijah and Puccini's Messa di Gloria, under Michel Corboz; Bach's St John Passion in St Gallen, the B Minor Mass with the Scottish Chamber Orchestra and the Christmas Oratorio in Dublin and Stavanger; Purcell's Dioclesian with the Academy of Ancient Music in London and Paris, the Fairy Queen with Les Arts Florissants and Rameau's La Guilande at the Flanders Festival; Lully's Atys in Paris and New York, Schubert's Mass in E Flat with the LPO and Handel's Acis and Galatea at Montpellier; Season 1996-97 with Messiah at Trondheim, Bach Cantatas and St John Passion in Newcastle, Monteverdi Vespers at Durham Cathedral and the Schütz Resurrection Story with Fretwork. Recordings include: Peachum in the Begger's Opera; Bach's Easter Oratorio with Andrew Parrott; The Fairy Queen, under William Christie; Hadyn's St Cecilia Mass; Vêpres aux Jesuites under Michel Corboz; Purcell albums with the King's Consort. Honours include: Hubert Parry Prize at the GKN English Songs Awards, 1986. Address: c/o Hazard Chase Ltd, Richmond House, 16-20 Regent Street, Cambridge CB2 1DB, England.

DANIELS Claire, b. 1963, England. Singer (Soprano). Education: Studied at the Royal Northern College of Music and in Paris with Janine Reiss. Career: Appearances include: Jennie Hildebrand, in Street Scene; A Nymph, in Rusalka; Niece, in Peter Grimes for English National Opera; Amor, in Orfeo ed Euridice for Opera North; Zerlina for Kent Opera; Purcell's King Arthur at the Buxton Festival; Rossini's L'Occasions fa il ladro and L'Italiana in Algeri and Grétry's Le Huron; Vespina, in Haydn's L'Infedeltà Delusa for Garsington Opera; Nanetta, in Falstaff for Opera Zuid in Holland; Mozart's Susanna, Servilia and Adina in L'Elisir D'Amore for Scottish Opera; The Girl, in Nigel Osborne's new commission, Sarajevo, for Opera Factory; Serpetta, in La finta giardiniera by Mozart for Klagenfurt Opera in Austria; Concert appearances throughout Germany and at Aix-en-Provence, Barcelona and Gothenberg; Mozart's Mass in C Minor with Charles Mackerras; Les Nuits d'Été at Perth Festival; Carmina Burana in Valencia; Sang in Peter Grimes with the London Symphony Orchestra under Rostropovitch; Sang Exultate Jubilate for concert tour of Great Britain with the Stuttgart Philharmonic Orchestra. Address: c/o Marks Management, 14 New Burlington Street, London, W1X 1FF, England.

DANIELS David, b. USA. Singer (Counter-tenor). Debut: Sang Nero in L'Incoronazione di Poppea at the Glimmerglass Opera Festival, 1994. Career: Handel's Tamerlano at Glimmerglass in 1995; Followed by Arsamenes in Xerxes with the Boston Lyric Opera Season 1995-96, in Israel in Egypt at the Vienna Musikverein, Messiah in Boston and Handel's Saul with the Philharmonia Baroque Orchestra; Salzburg Festival debut, as Hamor in Handel's Jeptha, 1996; Sang Didymus in Theodora at the Glyndebourne Festival, 1996; Opened the 1996-97 with English National Opera as Oberon in a Midsummer Night's Dream; London and New York recital debuts, at the Wigmore Hall and Lincoln Center, 1996; Engaged for Monteverdi's Ulise for Los Angeles Opera, as Sesto in Handel's Giulio Cesare for the London Royal Opera, 1997; The same role at the Metropolitan, 1999. Address: c/o Lies Askanas Ltd, 6 Henrietta St, London WC2E 8LA, England.

DANILEVSKI Alexander, b. 4 September 1957, Leningrad. Composer. m. Emilia, 9 September 1990, 3 sons, 2 daughters. Education: Composition, Leningrad Conservatoire, 1974-80; Lute, Scola Cantorum Basilensis, 1991-93. Debut: The I Sonato for Violin, St Petersburg Philharmony 1981 and Luth Recital. Career: 90 Solo Recitals and Concerts throughout Russia; Festivals, Recitals and Concerts in Europe (early music); Founder, "Syntagma" (ensemble of early music); Performances of Lauda, Antiphones, Sonata for Cello in Grand Festival des Musiques Slaves, Paris, 1996, 1997. Compositions: Sonatas for Violin, Violoncello and Piano; Missa for Choir and Orchestra; Seven Words of Christ on the Cross; Strophes enfilees (nai kai); Concerto for Organ, Harsichord and Piano; Quatuors 1-4, Chamber Music; Lauda, for voice and ensemble; Antiphones-I, for recorder quartet; Antiphones-II, for string quartet; Revelation, for cello, 1997; Sonatos 1-3 for piano; Concert and Night Music for 2 pianos; Seven Words for soprano and ensemble. Recordings: Guillaume Defay and Music of His time, with Ensemble Pro Anima, St Petersburg; Medieval and Renaissance Music with the same; Johannes Ciaconia and His Time; Solo; Francesco da Milano, Fancies and Ricercars, St Petersburg. Publication: Works for Piano, 1997-98. Membership: American Lute Society. Hobbies: Literature; Early Instruments. Address: 44 Grand Rue, 57050 Lorry-les-Metz, France.

DANKWORTH John Philip William, b. 20 Sept 1927, Walthamstow, England. Composer; Musician. m. Cleo Laine, 18 Mar 1958, 2 sons, 1 daughter. Education: Royal Academy of Music. Career: Involved with Post-War Development of Jazz, 1947-60; Founder, Large Jazz Orchestra, 1953; With Cleo Laine, Founded Performing Arts Centre, Wavendon Stables, 1970; Director, London Symphony Orchestra Summer Pops, 1985-90; Principal Guest Conductor, San Francisco Symphony Orchestra Pops, 1987-89; Numerous film scores and record albums. Compositions: Improvisations , 1959; Escapade, 1967; Tom Sawyer's Saturday, 1967; String Quartet, 1971; Piano Concerto, 1972; Grace Abounding, 1980; The Diamond And The Goose, 1981; Reconciliation, 1987; Dialogue and Songs for "Colette", 1980; Woolwich Concerto, 1995; Double Vision, for IBC Big Band (world premiere, BBC Proms), 1997; Dreams 42, string quartet, Kidderminster Festival, 1997. Publications: Sax From the Start, 1996; Jazz in Revolution, 1998. Honours: CBE, 1974; Honorary MA, Open University, 1975; Honorary DMus, Berklee School of Music, 1982; Honorary DMus, University of York, 1993. Memberships: Fellow, Royal Academy of Music. Hobbies: Driving; Household Maintenance. Current Management: Dankworth Management. Address: The Old Rectory, Wavendon, Milton Keynes MK17 8LT, England.

DANON Oskar, b. 7 February 1913, Sarajevo, Yugoslavia. Conductor; composer. Education: Studied at Prague Conservatory and University. Career: Conducted Opera and Concerts in Sarajevo from 1938; Director and Conductor of Belgrade Opera, 1945-60; Led performances of The Bartered Bride in Prague, then Prince Igor and Don Quichotte with the Belgrade Company on tour to Paris, 1958; Wiesbaden Festival, 1959; The Love for Three Oranges, Paris Opera 1960, with Boris Godunov; Edinburgh Festival, 1962 leading Don Quichotte, Prince Igor and the British premieres of Prokofiev's The Gambler and The Love for Three Oranges; Prince Igor at the Chicago Lyric Opera, 1962; Further engagements with Tristan und Isolde at Barcelona, 1969 and Arabella at Amsterdam, 1970; Opened the restored National Theatre Belgrade, 1990 with The Prince of Zeta by Konjovic. Recordings: Prince Igor and A Life for the Tsar with the Belgrade Company. Address: National Theatre, Belgrade, Croatia.

DANZ Ingeborg, b. Witten, Germany. Singer (Contralto). Education: Studied in Detmold. Career: Frequent appearances from 1987 as concert and oratorio singer; Tours of North and South America, USA, Japan, Russia and Europe, with Neville Marriner, Herreweghe, Harnoncourt and Helmuth Rilling; Season 1996 with Bach's St John Passion at the Amsterdam Concertgebouw and Handel's Jephtha with the Bamberg SO at the Salzburg Festival; Other festival engagements at Stuttgart, Oregon, Ludwigsburg, Schwetzingen and Tanglewood; Recital tour with Juliane Banse and Thomas Quasthoff, 1997. Recordings include: Mozart Masses with Nikolaus Harnoncourt, St Matthew Passion with Helmuth Rilling. Honours include: Scholarship from Richard Wagner Federation. Address: c/o Kunstler Sekretariat am Gasteig, Rosenheimerstrasse 52, D-81669 Munich, Germany.

DAO (Nguyen-Thien-Dao), b. 17 Dec 1940, Hanoi, Vietnam, Composer. m. Hélène Latapie, 11 May 1963. Education: Olivier Messiaen's class, Paris Conservatory. Debut: Festival de Royan, 1969. Compositions include: The 19, female voices, ensemble, 1969; Nho, soprano, cello, 5 double basses, 1970; Khoc To Nhu, mixed voices; Koskom, orchestra, 1971; Bai tap, ondes Martenot, piano, 1974; Camatithu, 6 percussions, 1974; Framic, bass flute, 1974; Mau va hoa, orchestra, 1974; Bao gio, 2 percussions, 2 pianos, 1975; Mua, harpsichord, 1976; A Mi K giao tranh, double bass, 1976; Giai phong, orchestra, electro-acoustics, 1977; Bay, percussions, 1977; Mai Sau, violin, strings, 1977; Phu Dong II, 4 (2) percussions, 1977; Noi Xa, 2 ondes Martenot, electric guitar, percussion, 1977; My-chau Trong-thuy, opera, 1978; Hoang Hon, soprano, orchestra, 1979; Ecouter/Mourir, opera, 1980; Concerto Ten Do Gu, percussion, orchestra, 1980; Chuong gam song, organ, 1981; Tuon Han, soprano, clarinet, 1982; Than Mong, cello concerto, 1982; Poussière d'empire, soprano, mixed voices, percussion, 1983; Tay-Son, percussion, 1984; L'Aube est une oeuvre, children's or female choir, string quartet, percussion, 1984; Piano concerto, 1984; Cimes murmerées, string trio, 1985; La mer pétrifiée, opera, 1986-87; Tim Lua, piano, 1987; Pli-ombre, bass clarinet, 1987; Temps songe, 7 percussionists (165 instruments), 1987; VV2, bassoon, 1987; Concerto, «Thien Thai», violin, orchestra, 1988; Concerto l'Envol, flute, strings, 1988; Symphonie pour pouvoir, symphony orchestra, soprano, 1989; Concerto 1989, string sextet, orchestra, 1989; 1789 l'aurore, string sextet; Voie-Concert, ensemble, 1990; Quatuor à Cordes No 1, 1991; Les Enfants d'Izieu, opera-oratorio, 1991-93; Les Perseides, 1992; Feuillets pour quatuor et perc, 1994; Hoa-Tau 1995, for string orchestra, 1995; Giao-Hoa Sinfonia, for orchestra, 1996; Khai-Nhac, for orchestra, 1997. Recording: Les Enfants d'Izieu, CD. Honours: Prix Gian Carlo Menotti, recording of Les Enfants d'Isieu. Address: 28 rue Madame, 75006 Paris, France.

DARA Enzo, b. 13 October 1938, Mantua, Italy. Singer (Bass). Education: Studied with Bruno Sutti in Mantua. Debut: Fano 1960, as Colline in La Bohème. Career: Reggio Emilia 1966, as Dulcamara in L'Elisir d'Amore; La Scala Milan debut 1970, as Bartolo in Il Barbiere di Siviglia; Sang Bartolo on his New York (1982) and Covent Garden (1985) debuts; Pesaro 1984, in a revival of Rossini's Il Viaggio a Reims; Guest appearances in Naples, Bologna, Moscow, Brussels, Venice, Palermo and Rome; Returned to Covent Garden 1987, as Dulcamara; Pesaro Festival, 1988, in Il Signor Bruschino; Don Pasquale at Venice, 1990; Teatro de la Zarzuela Madrid, 1990, in Il Turco in Italia; Sang Bartolo at the Verona Arena, 1996. Recordings: Il Barbiere di Siviglia and Il Viaggio a Reims; L'Italiana in Algeri; La Buona Figliuola by Piccinni; Donzetti's L'ajo nell' imbarazzo; Il Turco in Italia.

DARBELLAY Jean Luc, b. 2 July 1946, Berne, Switzerland. Composer; Conductor; Clarinettist. m. Elsbeth Darbellay-Fahrer, 21 Sept 1971, 1 s, 1 d. Education: Diploma as Physician, Berne University, 1971; Berne Conservatory, 1974-79; Studies in composition with Theo Hirsbrunner, Cristobal Halffter, Dimitri Terzakis; Lucern Conservatory with Edison Denisov and Klaus Huber; Foundation Ludus Ensemble Berne, 1978; Conducting studies with Pierre Dervaux and Franco Ferrara. Career: Concerts throughout Europe as Conductor of various orchestras including: Ludus Ensemble, Landesjugendchor Niedersachsen and Quaderni Perugini di Musica Contemporanea; Ensemble Contrechamps, MDR Kammerphilharmonie; John Cage Festival, Perugia. Compositions include: Glanum, 1981; Amphores, 1983; C'est un peu d'eau qui nous separe, 1989; Cello Concerto (Radio France recording) in Paris with Ensemble Denosjours, dedicated to Siegfried Palm, 1989; Interférences, 1991; Before Breakfast, film music, 1991; Pranam III, command of the Quaderni Perugini and Siegfried Palm, 1992; Cantus, command of the Altenburger Orgelkonzerte, 1993; Itinéraires, for St Petersburg Festival, 1994; Elégie, 1994; Incanto (Horn Concerto), Plauen, 1995; A la recherche, creation in Moscow; PRANAM IV (Cello Concerto for Siegfried Palm), in Halle. Recordings: Leading the Sächsisches Kammerorchester Leipzig: Mozart Divertimento, KV251, Violin Concerto, KV218, Haydn's Horn Concerto No 2 and Symphony No 1, Mozart's Serenade in C minor, KV 388, Darbellay's Espaces, Sept Poèmes Romands and Wind Octet; Aube Imaginaire with Choeur Novantiqua Sion; CD with pieces for violoncello and horn, with Olivier Darbellay, 1997. Honours: Order from CRPLF (Communauté des radios publiques de langue française); Order from MDR for Gin Garten for Orpheus; Order from Radio France. Memberships: Swiss Tonkünstler; SUISA; Alliance Française de Berne; President of the Swiss Section of the ISCM. Address: Editors Edition Modern, Amalienstrasse 40, D-76133, Karlsruhe, Germany.

DARLINGTON Stephen (Mark), 21 September 1952, Lapworth, Warwickshire, England. Organist; Fellow in Music. m. Moira Ellen Hill, 21 July 1975, 3 daughters. Education: FRCO; Christ Church, Oxford, 1971-74; MA (Oxon). Career: Assistant Organist, Canterbury Cathedral; Several TV and Radio appearances as accompanist, soloist and conductor; Organist, Enthronement of Archbishop Coggan, 1975; Concert Organist in most English cathedrals and in Netherlands, Belgium, France, Switzerland, Germany, Austria, Czechoslovakia; Master of the Music, St Alban's Abbey, Artistic Director, International Organ Festival, St Albans, Conductor, St Albans Bach Choir, until 1985; Fellow in Music, Christ Church and University Lecturer in Music, Oxford, 1985-. Recordings: Walton Church Music ZRG 725; Spirituals and Carols from Canterbury, GRS 1034; French Organ Music, Lammas 071; 20th Century English Church Music, Hyperion; Berkeley and Elgar, Priory; Organ Music by Saint-Saens and Vierne, Priory; In Honour of St Alban, Priory; Anthems by S S Wesley, Meridian; V Williams Mass NI 5083; Holst/Walton Christmas Music; Palestrina Mass for Pentecost, Weelkes Anthems and Lassus, Masses and Motets; Vaughan Wiliams, Oxford Elegy/Flos Campi; Frank Martin and Poulenc,

Masses; Byrd-Mass for 3 voices; Mass for 4 voices; Mass for 5 voices; Taverner Motets; Tippett choral music; Taverner to Tavener, N15328; Vivaldi Glorias (RV588 & RV589), N15278; Palestrina Missa O Sacrum Convivium, 4 Motets, N15394. Honour: Organ Scholar, Christ Church. Memberships: Council Member, Royal College of Organists. Current Management: Magenta. Address: Christ Church, Oxford OX1 1DP, England.

DARLOW Denys, b. 13 May 1921, London, England. Conductor; Composer; Organist; Professor. m. Sophy Margaret Guillaume. Career: Founder, Tilford Bach Festival, 1952, London Handel Festival, 1976, BBC Third Programme; Appearances in Sweden, Germany, Austria, Netherlands, Belgium, France, America, New Zealand; Concerts and radio; Professor at Royal College of Music; Conducted Handel's Alessanko Severo at the RCM, 1997. Compositions include: Te Deum; Stabat Mater; Requiem. Recordings: The Triumph of Time and Truth; Oratorio, Handel; Aminta e Fillide; Cantata, Handel. Honours: FRCO, 1946; FLCM, 1980; FRCM, 1984. Membership: Royal Society of Musicians; Hobbies: Gardening; Travel. Address: The Coach House, Drury Lane, Redmarley D'Abitot, Glos GL19 3JX, England.

DASZAK John, b. 24 February 1967, Ashton-under-Lyne, England. Singer (Tenor). Education: Guildhall School, London, and the Royal Northern College of Music, with Robert Alderson. Career: Opera roles have included Steva in Jenufa, Jack in Mahagonny and Pang in Turandot, for English National Opera; the Duke of Mantua and Mozart's Ferrando in Italy, Peter Grimes for English Touring Opera and Rustighello in Donizetti's Lucrezia Borgia at the Martina-Franca Festival; Concerts include Otumbo in Verdi's Alzira at Covent Garde, Don Ottavio for the Liverpool Mozart Orchestra, Britten's Serenade and Rossini's Petite Messe at the Buxton Festival; Verdi's Requiem at Chester Cathedral and the Manchester Free Trade Hall, Messiah in Blackburn Cathedral and St John's Smith Square, London; Season 1997-98 with Skuratov in From the House of the Dead and Dmitri in Boris Godunov for English National Opera; Peter Grimes and Dmitri for Welsh National Opera; Roles in Mahagonny at Lausanne. Address: c/o IMG Artists, Media House, 3 Burlington Lane, London W4 2TH, England.

DATYNER Harry, b. 4 February 1923, La Chaux-de-Fonds, Switzerland. Pianist. m. Bluette Blum, 14 June 1954, 1 son. Education: Etudes Conservatoire National a Paris with Marguerite Long and after with Edwin Fischer. Career: Concerts in Europe, Afrique du Nord et du Sud en Amerique du Nord et du Sud; Soloist with orchestras: Suisse Romande, Lausanne, Montreal, Bucarest, Montevideo, Baden-Baden, Madrid, Bruxelles National, London Philharmonic, Prague, Barcelona, Paris; Masterclass, Conservatoire de Musique de Genève; Festival appearances at Montreux, Lausanne, Montevideo, Salzburg, Ascona, Prague, Espagne and Portugal; Member of Jury at International Competitions at Genève, Cologne, Athens, Berlin, Mallorca, Lisbon; Conductors: Ansermet, Prêtre, Dutoit, Sawallisch, Stein, Jordan, Matacic, Carvalho, Dervaux, Groves; Cours d'Interpretation: Suisse, Television Suisse, Espagne, Canada. Honours: 1st Prize a l'unanimite Concours déxécution musicale, Geneva; Prix de l'institut Neuchatelois, 1973. Hobbies: Bridge, echecs. Address: 1245 Collonge-Bellerive, Switzerland.

DATZ Irene, b. 14 Apr 1963, Zhitomir, Ukraine. Soprano. Education: Studied at the Kiev State Conservatoire from 1980. Career: Sang with the Kiev State Radio Orchestra, 1985 and made her debut with Kiev National Opera in 1986, at first as Mezzo-Soprano; At Kiev and Bolshoi Operas has sung Donna Anna, Mimi, Tosca, Nedda, Cherubino, Marguerite, Marfa in The Tsar's Bride, and Iolanthe; Tours of North America from 1991 with appearances at the Metropolitan Opera as Tatiana; Solo recitals in Chicago, Philadelphia, Illinois and Washington; Sang Wagner's Elsa at the Kiev Opera in 1994. Address: Sonata Ltd, 11 North Park Street, Glasgow, G20 7AA, Scotland.

DAUGHERTY Michael, b. 28 Apr 1954, Cedar Rapids, Iowa, USA. Composer. Education: Studied at North Texas State (BM) and the Manhattan School of Music (MA, 1976); Jacob Druckman, Roger Reynolds, Bernard Rands and Gil Evans at Yale University, DMA, 1986; Further study at IRCAM, Paris, 1979-80, and with Ligeti at the Hamburg Musikhochschule, 1982-84.Career includes: Faculty of Oberlin Conservatory, 1986-91; Currently, Associate Professor of Composition, University of Michigan, Ann Arbor. Compositions include: Piano Plus, 1985; Snap - Blue Like an Orange for 16 players, 1987; Strut for string orchestra, 1989; Beat Boxer for string quartet and pre-recorded DAT tape, 1991; Firecracker for oboe and 6 players, 1991; Flamingo for chamber orchestra, 1991; Desi Bizarro and Niagara Falls for symphonic wind band, 1991-92; Sing Sing: J Edgar Hoover for string quartet and tape, 1992; Dead Elvis for bassoon and 6 players, 1993; Metropolis Symphony (premiered Carnegie Hall), 1988-93; Le Tombeau de Liberace, for piano and ensemble, 1994; Paul Robeson Told Me for string quartet and tape, 1994; Motown Metal for brass ensemble, 1994; Lounge Lizards for 2 pianos and 2 percussion, 1994; What's That Spell?

for 2 amplified sopranos and 16 players, 1995; Jackie's Song, for cello, 1996; Leap Day for orchestra, 1996; Concrete Jungle for orchestra, 1996; Jackie O, chamber opera in 2 acts (premiere Houston Opera), 1997. Recordings: Numerous for major labels. Address: c/o Faber Music, 3 Queen Square, London WC1N 3AU, England.

DAUSGAARD Thomas, b. 1964, Denmark. Conductor. Education: Studied in Scandinavia. Career: Assistant Conductor to Seiji Ozawa at the Boston Symphony Orchestra, 1993-96; Beethoven's Missa Solemnis with the Swedish Radio Symphony Orchestra and Chorus, 1993; Further concerts with the Danish National Radio SO; Season 1996-97 with the Oslo, St Petersburg and Royal Philharmonic Orchestras and the Montreal Symphony. Honours include: Music Critics' Circle Prize, Denmark, 1993; Prize winner at International Competitions. Address: c/o IMG Artists, Media House, 3 Burlington Lane, London W4 2TH, England.

DAVELUY Raymond, b. 1926, Victoriaville, Québec, Canada. Organ Virtuoso; Composer; Teacher. m. Hilda Metcalfe. Education: Began musical studies under father, Lucien Daveluy; Educated at Collège Jean-de-Brébeuf, Montréal; Studied harmony, counterpoint and composition with Gabriel Cusson; Studied organ and harmony under Conrad Letendre 1942, and Hugh Giles, New York. Career: Organist, St Jean-Baptiste Church, 1946-51; Immaculée-Conception Church, 1951-54, St Sixte Church, 1954-59; Principal Titular of Grand Organ at Oratoire Saint-Joseph, 1960-61; Concert tours in Canada, Europe, Far-East and USA, performing at various halls and churches including: Royal Festival Hall, London; Kaiser Wilhelm Gedächtnis Church, Berlin; St Germain-des-Prés Church, Paris; Sejong Cultural Centre Hall, Seoul; The Rockefeller Memorial Chapel, Chicago; has also sat on juries of several international competitions including: Munich, 1971; Philadelphia, 1977; St Albans, 1979-83; Frequent performer on CBC Radio; Also Soloist in Saint-Saëns Organ Symphony, with Orchestre Symphonique de Montréal; Played leading part in reform of organ building in Montréal since 1960; Teacher of organ and improvisation at Trois-Rivières and Montréal Conservatories; Director and Teacher of Organ and improvisation at Montréal Conservatoire; Visiting Lecturer, McGill University. Recordings: Recorded works of Bach, Marchand, Corrette, Franck, Liszt. Honours: Winner, Prix d'Europe, 1948; Laureate of Haarlem International Competition (The Netherlands), 1959; Member of The Order of Canada, 1980.

DAVENPORT Glyn, b. 3 May 1948, Halifax, Yorkshire, England. Singer (Bass/Baritone). m. Jane Keay, 1 Apr 1972, 2 sons. Education: Royal College of Music, London, 1966-70; ARCM, Viola, LRAM, Singing; Staatliche Musikhochschule, Hamburg, Germany, 1970-73. Debut: Wigmore Hall, London, England, 1973. Career: Opera appearances with English Opera Group, English Music Theatre, Scottish Opera, Royal Opera House, Kent Opera, Wexford Festival Opera; Recitals for BBC Radio 3, Songmakers' Almanac, British Council in Near and Middle East; Oratorio in major London venues and BBC, Switzerland, Germany and Iceland. Recordings: The English Cat, Hans Werner Henze. Hobbies: Cricket; Squash; Woodworking. Current Management; Concert Directory International; Musicmakers. Address: Wendover, Horsell Rise, Horsell, Woking, Surrey GU21 4BD, England.

DAVID Avram, b. 30 June 1930, Boston, Massachusetts, USA. Composer; Teacher; Pianist. m. Leslie, 3 December 1977. Education: BA Music, 1955; MA Music, 1956; DMA Musical Composition, 1964; Boston University; Berkshire Music Center, Tanglewood, Summer 1948; Kranichsteiner Musikinstitut, Darmstadt, West Germany, Summer 1961 and 1966; Private Study of Piano and Philosophy of Performance and Composition with Margaret Chaloff and Composition with Francis Cooke, Harold Shapero, Karlheinz Stockhausen, Pierre Boulez. Career: Private Teaching, 1960-64; Chairman, Composition Department, Composer-in-Residence, Boston Conservatory of Music, 1964-73; Director, Avram David Studio, 1973-77; Director, Margaret Chaloff Studio, 1977-; Lecturer, Harvard University and New England Conservatory of Music; Appearances as Solo Pianist in Concert and on TV and Radio. Compositions: Composer of 133 works including: 2 Orchestral Works including 1 Symphony; 21 works for Chamber Ensembles; 6 String Quartets; 2 Solo Violin Sonatas; 43 works for Solo Piano including 5 Sonatas; 24 works for Solo Winds; 8 Choral works. Recordings: Sonata for Horn Solo, Opus 101. Address: 249 Commonwealth Avenue, Boston, MA 02116, USA.

DAVID Thomas (Christian), b. 22 December 1925, Wels, Austria. Composer; Conductor. m. Mansoureh Ghassri. Education: Thomasschule, Leipzig Hochschule, Mozarteum, Salzburg. Career: Professor of the Hochschule für Musik in Vienna; Conductor of numerous orchestras including Riaorchester Berlin, the Munich Philharmonic, Niederoesterreichische Tonkunstlerorchester, Orchester des Osterreichischen Rundfunks. Compositions: Bagatellen and Sonata (Piano); Fantasie, Dux Michael, 3 Intermezzi; 3 Canzonen; Concert for 9

Solo Instruments; Songs based on Chinese Stories for Voice and Piano; Concerto for Violin and Orchestra, Piano and Orchestra, Oboe and Orchestra, 2 Violins and Orchestra, 3 Violins and Orchestra, Flute and Orchestra, Violin, Clarinet, Piano and Orchestra, 5 Winds and Orchestra, Orchestra, Violoncello and Orchestra; Prolog for Orchestra; Oratorio, The Song of Man; Church Opera, The Way to Emmaus; Choral Works. Honours: Prize of Vienna, 1973; Austrian State Prize, 1975; Prize of Niederosterreich, 1986. Memberships: The Austrian Composers Association. Address: Fugbachgasse 16/3, 1020 Vienna, Austria.

DAVIDOVICH Bella, b. 16 July 1928, Baku, USSR. Concert Pianist. m. Julian Sitkovetsky (dec), 1 son (Dmitri Sitkovetsky, q.v.). Education: Moscow Conservatory. Career: Recitalist, Orchestral Soloist, Chamber Musician, in all major music centres internationally; Duo recitals with son (violinist Dmitry Sitkovetsky); Professor of Piano: Moscow Conservatory, USSR, 16 years; Juilliard School of Music, New York, USA, 1983-; Engaged 1997-98 with the Rotterdam Philharmonic, Ulster Orchestra and Stuttgart Symphony Orchestra. Honours: 1st Prize, Chopin International Piano Competition, Warsaw, Poland, 1949. Hobbies: Opera; Literature; Film. Address: c/o Agnes Bruneau, 155 West 68th Street, No 1010, New York, NY 10023, USA.

DAVIDOVICI Robert, b. 1 Oct 1946, Sutu-Mare, Romania. Violinist; Professor of Violin. m. Tamara Golan, 8 Mar 1973, 2 sons, 2 daughters. Education: School of Music No 1, Bucharest, 1958-62; Conservatorium of Music High School, Sydney, Australia, 1962-63; Performers and Teacher Diploma, 1st Class Honours, 1966; Juilliard School, New York, USA, 1967-73; Post-graduate Diploma, 1970. Debut: Alice Tully Hall, New York, USA, 1972. Recordings: Recital with Steven DeGroote of works by Copland, Gunther Schuller, Walter Piston, Hugh Aitken and Paul Schonfield. Honours: 1st Prize, Carnegie Hall International American Music Competition, 1983; 1st Prize, Naumberg Competition, New York, 1972; Flaggler Award, 1973. Memberships: College Music Society; American String Teachers Association; Violing Society of America. Hobbies: Chess; Computers; Jogging; Reading Spy Novels. Current Management: Shaw Concerts Incorporated.

DAVIDOVSKY Mario, b. 4 Mar 1934, Buenos Aires, Argentina (American Citizen). Composer; Teacher. m. Elaine Davidovsky. Education: received violin lessons in childhood; Studied composition and theory with Guillermo Graetzer, Buenos Aires; Studied wuith Theodore Fuchs, Erwin Leuchter and Ernesto Epstein; Completed training with Aaron Copeland and Milton Babbitt, Berkshire Music Centre, Tanglewood, 1958. Career: Associated with Columbia-Princeton Electronic Music Centre, 1960-; Teacher, University of Michigan, 1964; Di Tella Institute, 1969-70; City College of the City University of New York, 1968-80; Columbia University, 1981-; Director, Columbia-Princeton Electronic Music centre, 1981-94' Professor of Music, Harvard University, 1994-. Compositions include: Synchronisms No 1 for flute and electronics, 1963, No 2 for flute, clarinet, violin, cello and electronics, 1964, No 3 for cello and electronics, 1965, No 4 for men's or mixed chorus and electronics, 1967, No 5 for percussion ensemble and electronics, 1969, No 6 for piano and electronics, 1970, No 7 for orchestra and electronics, 1973, No 8 for woodwind quintet and electronics, 1974; Orchestral: Concertino for percussion and strings, 1954; Pianos, 1961; Divertimento for cello and orchestra, 1984; Chamber: 4 String Quartets, 1954, 1958, 1976, 1980; Tape: Electronic Study No 1, 1961, No 2, 1962, No 3, 1965. Honours include: Guggenheim Fellowships, 1960, 1971; Rockefeller Felloships, 1963, 1964; American Academy of Arts and Letters Award, 1965; Pulitzer prize in Music, 1971; Naumberg Award, 1972; Guggenheim Award, 1982; Various commissions. Memberships: Elected to Institute of American Academy and Institute of Arts and Letters, 1982. Address: Music Department, Harvard University, Cambridge, MA, USA.

DAVIDSON Cheyne, b. 1965, USA. Singer (Baritone). Education: Studied at the Cleveland Institute of Music and the Manhattan School of Music. Career: Tour of Europe, Japan and Israel, as Escamillo in Peter Brook's Version of Carmen, La Tragédie de Carmen; Zurich Opera as the Speaker in Dir Zauberflöte, Massenet's Herode, Marcello, David in L'Amico Fritz, Sharpless, and Ramiro in L'Heure Espagnole; Guest appearances at Stuttgart as Sharpless and the Speaker, 1994; Escamillo at Hamburg; In Francesca da Rimini at the Bregenz Festival; Season 1996-97 as the Messenger in Robert Wilson's production of Oedipus Rex at the Paris Théâtre du Châtelet, and Schaunard in La Bohème at Zurich; Premieres include Ein Narrenparadies by Ofer Ben-Amot, at Vienna, and the song cycle with orchestra Vom Unvergänglichen by Franz Thurauer, at Bregenz. Address: c/o Opernhaus Zurich, Falkenstasse 1, CH-8008 Zurich, Switzerland.

DAVIDSON Joy, b. 18 August 1940, Fort Collins, Colorado, USA. Singer (Mezzo-Soprano). Education: Studied in Los Angeles, at Florida State University and with Daniel Harris. Debut: Miami, 1965 as Rossini's Cenerentola. Career: Sang at the opera houses of Dallas, Houston, New Orleans and San Francisco; Santa Fe 1969, in the US premiere of Penderecki's The Devils of

Loudun; Appearances with the Welsh National Opera and at Lisbon, Sofia, Vienna, Munich, Milan and Florence; Other roles include Carmen, Charlotte in Werther, Dalila, Verdi's Eboli and Preziosilla and Gluck's Orpheus; Also heard as concert Singer; Sang Baba the Turk in The Rake's Progress at the State Theatre, New York, 1984.

DAVIDSON Robert, b. 17 December 1965, Brisbane, Queensland, Australia. Composer. Education: BMus (Hons), University of Queensland, 1987; Further study with Terry Riley and LaMonte Young, 1995. Career: Freelance Composer; Performer in orchestra, including Queensland and Sydney SOs. Compositions include: Dodecahedron for string orchestra, 1985; Eight, for ensemble, 1986; Stained Glass for 2 violins, 2 cellos, 2 clarinets, 2 pianos, 1986; Zemar for piano, 1987; Sound Panels, for flute, string quartet and double bass, 1988; Triptych for orchestra, 1988; Tapestry, for viola, cello, clarinet and piano, 1989; Refrains, for double bass and piano, 1989; Adeney Cycle, for violin and viola, 1990; Strata for mixed ensemble, 1990; Variations and Episodes, for piano, 1990; Arch for 3 violins, 1992; Conversations, for viola, cello and clarinet, 1993; Mesh, for double bass and piano, 1993; Violin Concerto, 1994; Three Grounds, for ensemble, 1994; Chaconne for orchestra, 1994; Boombox Pieces for multiple cassette players, 1995. Address: c/o APRA, 1A Eden Street, Crows Nest, NSW 2065, Australia.

DAVIDSON Tina, b. 30 December 1952, Stockholm, Sweden. Composer; Pianist. m. 1 daughter. Education: BA, Piano and Composition, Bennington College, 1972-76; Composition Studies with Henry Brant, Vivian Fine, Louis Calabro. Career: Associate Director, RELACHE, The Ensemble for Contemporary Music, 1978-89; Piano Instructor, Drexel University, 1981-85; Residencies: Chamber Music Conference and Composers' Forum; Milay Colony for the Arts, October 1981; Yellow Springs Fellowship of the Arts, May 1982; Charles Ives Center, 1986; Composer-in-Residence, Orchestra Society of Philadelphia, 1992-94; Composer-in-Residence, Opera Delaware Symphony Orchestra & YWCA of Wilmington Delaware, 1994-97; Fleisher Art Memorial Composer in Residence, 1997-99. Compositions include: Inside And Out, piano and 2 players, 1974; Recollections of Darkness, string trio, 1975; Two Beasts From The Forest Of Imaginary Beings, narrator and orchestra, 1975, commissioned by Sage City Symphony, student commission, 1976; Five Songs from The Game of Silence, soprano and viola, 1976; Billy and Zelda, music theatre (8 singers, 1 actress, string quartet and percussion), 1977; Piano Concerto, piano and orchestra, 1981; Unicorn/Tapestry, mxxo-soprano, violoncello and tape, 1982; Other Echoes, 2 violins, 1982; Wait For The End Of Dreaming, 2 baritone saxophones, Double Bass, 1983-85; Shadow Grief, soprano (or alto saxophone), 1983; Day of Rage, and I Am The Last Witness, piano solo, 1984; Blood Memory: A Long Quiet After The Call, cello and orchestra, commissioned by Sage City Symphony, 1985; Bleached Thread Sister Thread, 1992; Fire on the Mountain, marimba, vibraphone and piano, 1993; They Come Dancing for full orchestra, 1994; Over Salt River, soprano, 1995; Star Fire, for youth orchestra, 1996; It Is My Heart Singing, string sextet, 1996; Of The Running Way, for clarinet (or alto saxophone) and piano, 1996; Lost Love Songs, for solo cello, 1997. Recordings: Cassatt, CD, 1994; I Hear the Mermaids Singing, 1996. Honours: Pennsylvania Council Fellowship, 1983-96; PEN Fellowship, 1992-94. Address: 508 Woodland Terrace, Philadelphia, PA 19104, USA.

DAVIES (Albert) Meredith, b. 30 July 1922, Birkenhead, England. Conductor. m. Betty Hazel Bates, 1949, 3 sons, 1 daughter. Education: Keble College, Oxford; Junior Exhibitioner, Royal College of Music, 1930; Accademia di S Cecilia, Rome, Italy. Career includes: Organist, Hurstpierpoint College, Sussex, 1939; Served World War II, 1939-45, Royal Artillery, 1942-45; Conductor, St Alban's Bach Choir, 1947; Organist and Master of Choristers, Cathedral Church of St Alban, 1947-49; Musical Director, St Alban's School, 1948-49; Organist and Choirmaster, Hereford Cathedral, and Conductor, 3 Choirs Festival, Hereford, 1949-56; Organist and Supernumerary Fellow, New College, Oxford, 1956; Associate Conductor, 1957-59, Deputy Music Director, 1959-60, City of Birmingham Symphony Orchestra; Conductor, City of Birmingham Choir, 1957-64; Musical Director, English Opera Group, 1963-65; Musical Director, Vancouver Symphony Orchestra, Canada, 1964-71; Chief Conductor, BBC Training Orchestra, 1969-72; Conductor, Royal Choral Society, 1972-85; Conductor, Leeds Philharmonic Society, 1975-84; Principal, Trinity College of Music, 1979-88; President, Incorporated Society of Musicians, 1985-86. Recordings: Delius: Violin Concerto, Double Concerto, Village Romeo and Juliet and Fennimore and Gerda; Vaughan Williams: Riders to the Sea and Sir John in Love. Honours: CBE, 1982. Address: 40 Monmouth Street, Bridgwater, Somerset TA6 5EJ, England.

DAVIES Arthur, b. 11 Apr 1941, Wrexham, Wales. Singer (Tenor). Education: Studied at the Royal Northern College of Music. Career: Has sung with Welsh National Opera as Nemorino, Albert Herring, Nadir in Les pêcheurs de Perles, Rodolfo, and Don José; Covent Garden debut 1976, in the world

premiere of We Come to the River by Henze: has returned in Lucia di Lammermoor, and as Alfredo, the Italian Tenor in Der Rosenkavalier, Steva in Jenůfa, and Pinkerton; Scottish Opera at the Edinburgh Festival as the Fox in The Cunning Little Vixen, and David in Die Meistersinger; Appearances with English National Opera as the Duke of Mantua, Alfredo, the Gounod Faust, and Werther; Opera North as Jenik in The Bartered Bride, Pinkerton, Don José and Nadir; Foreign engagements in Chicago, Cincinnati, Connecticut, Ghent, Leipzig, Lisbon, New Orleans, Moscow, Santiago and New York (Metropolitan House with the ENO company); Sang Faust with ENO, Jan 1990; Gaston, British stage premiere of Verdi's Jérusalem, Opera North; Cavaradossi and Pinkerton for Scottish Opera; Cincinnati Opera, July 1990 as Faust; Edinburgh Festival, 1990 as Yannakos in the Greek Passion by Martinů; Sang Cavardossi for Opera Pacific at Costa Mesa, 1992; Don José at San Diego and the Duke of Mantua for ENO; Sang Verdi's Foresto at Buenos Aires, 1993; Samson at Metz, 1996; Concerts include the Verdi Requiem at the Festival Hall, London, conducted by Giulini. Recordings: include, Rigoletto (EMI; also on video); The Dream of Gerontius, with the London Symphony Orchestra (Chandos); Elijah; Rossini's Stabat Mater; The Kingdom of Elgar. Address: c/o Stafford Law Associates, 6 Barham Close, Weybridge, Surrey KT13 9PR, England.

DAVIES David (Somerville), b. 13 June 1954, Dunfermline, Scotland. Conductor; Artistic Director. m. Virginia Henson, 15 September 1986. Education: Royal Scottish Academy of Music, University of Edinburgh; Salzburg Mozarteum; Conservatoire National De Marseille. Career: Assistant Principal Flute, Scottish National Orchestra, 1975-80; Principal Flute, Scottish Opera, 1980-85; Freelance Conductor, 1985-, working with BBC Scottish Symphony Orchestra, Scottish Chamber Orchestra, Royal Scottish National Orchestra, Royal Liverpool Philharmonic Orchestra in England; l'Orchestre Philharmonique de Radio France, l'Opéra de Marseille, l'Orchestre Philharmonique de Marseille in France; Ensemble Caput in Iceland and the Stadtorchester Winterhur in Switzerland; Conductor and Artistic Director, Paragon Ensemble, Scotland, Paragon Opera Projects, Scotland, 1985-; Lecturer, Royal Scottish Academy of Music and Drama, 1991-. Recordings: Two volumes of World premiere recordings of Scottish Contemporary music, 1991 and 1993, Continuum CDs. Address: c/o Paragon Ensemble Limited, 2 Port Dundas Place, Glasgow G2 3LB, Scotland.

DAVIES Dennis Russell, b. 16 Apr 1944, Toledo, OH, USA. Conductor; Pianist. Education: BMus, 1966, MS, 1968, DMA, 1972, Juilliard School of Music, New York; Studied piano with Berenice B MacNab, Lonny Epstein and Sascha Gorodnitzki; Conducting with Jean Morel and Jorge Mester. Career: Teacher, Juilliard School of Music, 1968-71; Co-founder with Luciano Berio, Conductor, Juilliard Ensemble, 1968-74; Music Director, Norwalk (Conn) Symphony Orchestra, 1968-73; St Paul (Minn) Chamber Orchestra, 1972-80; Cabrillo (Calif) Music Festival, 1974-92; American Composers Orchestra, NY, 1977-; Generalmusikdirektor, Wurttemberg State Theatre, Stuttgart, 1980-87; Principal Conductor and Director of Classical Music Programming, Saratoga, NY, Performing Arts Center, 1985-88; Generalmusikdirektor, City Theatre and Beethoven Hall Orchestra, Bonn, 1987-95; Guest Conductor with various opera companies and orchestras in North America and Europe; Champion of Contemporary Music; Conducted premieres by: Luciano Berio, John Cage, Hans Werner Henze, Philip Glass, Mauricio Kagel, William Bolcom, Joan Tower, Pauline Oliveros, Lou Harrison, Kurt Schwwentock; Conducted the premiere of William Bolcom's Songs of Innocence and Experience, Stuttgart, 1984; Music Director, Brooklyn Academy of Music, 1991-93; Principal Conductor, Brooklyn Philharmonic, 1991-95; Conducted the premiere of Manfred Trojhan's Enrico, Schwetzingen Festival, 1991; Chief Conductor: Stuttgart Chamber Orchestra, 1995-; Vienna Radio Symphony Orchestra from 1996; Led Thomson's Four Saints in Three Acts at the 1996 Llincoln Center Festival. Recordings: Many for various labels including Philip Glass, Heroes Symphony, 1997. Honour: Alice M Ditson Award for Conductors, 1987. Address: c/o Columbia Artists Management Inc, 165 West 57th Street, New York, NY 10019, USA.

DAVIES Eirian, b. 22 May 1954, Llangollen, Wales. Singer (Soprano). 1 son. Education: BA, Music, University College of Wales at Aberystwyth, Postgraduate course for performers, Royal Academy of Music, London. Debut: Vivaldi's Griselda, Buxton Festival, and Gounod's La Colombe, 1983. Career: Welsh National Opera: Rhinemaiden, in Das Rheingold and Götterdammerung; Gerhilde, in Die Walkyrie; Lisa in La Sonnambula; Aenchen in Der Freischütz; English National Opera: Pamina in The Magic Flute; Frasquita in Carmen; Orpheus in the Underworld; Opera North Mimi in La Boheme; Christine in Robert Saxton's Caritas (world premiere); Glyndebourne: World premiere of Nigel Osborne's Electrification of the Soviet Union and Rilke's Songs of Love and Death; Garsington: Rezia in L'Incontro Improviso; Music Theatre Wales: Dotty in world premiere of Hardy's Flowers; Edinburgh Festival: World premiere of Macmillan's Tourist Variations and Craig Armstrong's Anna; Semur en Auxois Festival; Mozart's Seraglio; Constanza; More

recent performances include: Princess Natalie in Der Prinz von Homburg, in Cologne; Gepopo in Le Grand Macabre and Aventures et Nouvelles Aventures, by Ligeti in Zurich; World premiere of Kubo's Rashomon in Graz; Salzburg Festival debut, 1997, in Feldman's Neither, also Wien Moderne Festival in rihm's Frau Stimme; Appearances on TV for BBC and HTV, and for BBC Radio 3. Recordings: include, Le Grand Macabre; Caritas by Robert Saxton. Honours: Catherine and Lady Grace James Award; Winner, Francisco Vinas International Competition, Barcelona, 1984. Current Management: Athole Still. Address: Forresters Hall, 25-27 Westow Street, London SE19 3RY, England.

DAVIES Hugh (Seymour), b. 23 Apr 1943, Exmouth, Devon, England. Composer; Peformer, invented instruments; Musicologist; Specialist in Electronic Music. m. Pamela Judith Bailey, 5 Sept 1981, 1 daughter. Education: BA Music, Oxford University, England, 1964. Career: Assistant to K Stockhausen, 1964-66; Director, Electronic Music Studio, University of London Goldsmiths' College, 1967-86; Consultant Researcher, 1986-91; Consultant, Music Department, Gemeentemuseum, The Hague, 1986-; Over 100 instruments and sound sculptures invented since 1967; performed and broadcast in most of Western Europe, USA, Canada, Argentina, Cuba, Uruguay, Poland, Hungary, Czechoslovakia, Iran, Japan; Exhibitions including many one-man shows in several Western European countries, Canada and USA; Compositions for traditional instruments, invented instruments and electronic music including several music theatre works; Member of now defunct performing groups, Gentle Fire, Music Improvisation Company, Naked Software, many solo performances, 1975-. Compositions include: Quintet, 1968; Shozyg I & II, 1968; Shozyg Sequence No 1, 1971, No 2 1977; No 3, 1990-91; Raisonnements, 1973; The Musical Educator, 1974; Natural Images, 1976; Meldoci Gestures, 1978; Ex Una Voce, 1979; Four Songs, 1979-81; I Have a Dream, 1984-85; Vision, 1987; Strata, 1987; Inventio, 1994. Recordings: Shozyg Music for Invented Instruments, solo performance of own compositions; Mikrophonie I, Sternklang; Gentle Fire; Music Improvisation Company. Companion to Contemporary Musical Thought, 1992. Publications: International Electronic Music Catalog (compiler), 1968; Chapters in Poesie Sonore Internationale, 1979; Electronic Music for Schools, 1981; Nuova Atlantide: il Continente della Musica Elettronica, 1900-86; Echo: the Images of Sound, 1987; Vitalite et Contradictions de l'Avant-Garde: Italie-France 1909-1924, 1988, Nordic Music Days/100 Years, 1988; Piano, 1988; Musiques Electroniques, 1999, also 300 entries in New Grove Dictionary of Musical Instruments, 1984. Contributions to: Numerous professional journals including Source Contact, Musics, EMAS Newsletter/Electro-Acoustic Music; Experimental Musical Instruments. Address: 25 Albert Road, London N4 3RR, England.

DAVIES Joan, b. 1940, Swansea, Wales. Singer (Mezzo-Soprano). Education: Royal College of Music, London. Career: Sang with the Glyndebourne Chorus, then with Sadler's Wells until 1969, notably as Offenbach's Hélène and in the premiere of Bennett's A Penny for a Song, 1965; Debut with Welsh National Opera as Meg Page in Falstaff; Sang Meg Page at Covent Garden and appeared in La Traviata and the premiere of Henze's We Come To the River, 1976; Other engagements in Munich and Berlin and with Scottish Opera, Opera North, Pheonix Opera, Basilica Opera and Dublin Grand Opera; New Sadler's Wells Opera from 1983 in The Mikado, The Count of Luxembourg, The Merry Widow and works by Gilbert and Sullivan (also in New York); Appearances at the Wexford Festival in The Devil and Kate, and Gazzaniga's Don Giovanni; Other roles include Mme Popova in Walton's The Bear (Lisbon), Auntie in Peter Grimes at the Royal Opera Ghent and Mozart's Marcellina in Bordeaux and Rouen; Television appearances as Meg Page, Marcellina and Mary in Der fliegende Holländer; Concert engagements with the Royal Liverpool Philharmonic and the Ulster Orchestra. Address: Music International, 13 Ardilaun Road, London N5 2QR, England.

DAVIES Menai, b. Wales. Singer (Mezzo-soprano). Education: Studied with Gwilyn Gwalchmai Jones and Valetta Jacopi. Career: Taught music for 14 years; Engaged with Welsh National Opera 1974-86, in repertory from Monteverdi to Britten, to the premiere of Metcalf's The Journey (1981); Mamma Lucia in Cavalleria Rusticana, 1995; Glyndebourne Touring Opera from 1987 (debut in L'Enfant et les Sortilèges) and Festival from 1989, as Grandmother in Jenufa, Auntie in Peter Grimes and Cleaner in The Makropoulos Case (1995); Other appearances with Scottish Opera, English National Opera and Opera North's Gloria, H K Gruber; Britten's Mrs Herring at Rome and Reggio Emilia, Mrs Grose in Peter Grimes at Cologne, Schwetzingen and Dresden; Theatre du Chatelet, Paris, in Jenufa and in premieres of operas by Fenelon and Philippe Manoury; The Makropoulos Case at Barcelona and New York; Ideally suited for older roles in modern works.

DAVIES Neal, b. Newport, Gwent, Wales. Singer (Baritone). Education: Studied at King's College, London, The Royal Academy of Music and the International Opera Studio, Zurich.

Career: Many roles at the Coburg Opera, Germany, including Papageno in a Brigitte Fassbaender production of Die Zauberflöte; Concerts at the Edinburgh Festival include Prokoviev's Hamlet, Janacek's Sarka, Schubert's Die Freunde von Salamanca, Leonore and Ninth Symphony by Beethoven, and the Scenes from Faust by Schumann, 1992-; Further opera includes Starveling in Midsummer Night's Dream with the LSO, Handel's Radamisto at Marseilles and Orlando at the City of London Festival, La Bohème with the Oslo PO and Maetto in Don Giovanni for Welsh National Opera; Season 1996-97 as Schaunard for WNO, in Stavinsky's Rosignol under Pierre Boulez for the BBC, Elijah with the Liverpool PO and Messiah with the Gabrieli Consort under Paul McCreesh; Debut with the Royal Opera in Rameau's Platee (also at Edinburgh), 1997; Many recital engagements. Recordings include: A Midsummer Night's Dream; Classics; Elijah; Messiah; Henri Dutilleux Songs with orchestra; Vivaldi Cantatas with Robert King. Honours include: Winner, Lieder Prize at the Cardiff Singer of the World Competition, 1991. Address: c/o Lies Askonas Ltd, 6 Henrietta St, London WC2E 8LA, England.

DAVIES Noel, b. 1945, London, England. Conductor. Education: Royal College of Music, with Richard Austin and Adrian Boult. Career: Conducting Staff, Sadler's Wells Opera, then Resident Conductor, English National Opera, 1974-; Many performances of the standard repertory, including operas by Mozart, Verdi and Puccini; Collaborations with Janet Baker, Ann Murray, Thomas Allen, Rosalind Plowright and Felicity Lott; Guest Conductor with Rigoletto for the Bergen Festival, Giulio Cesare at Houston and Gloriana at the Metropolitan, New York; Xerxes, Giulio Cesare and Don Giovanni, 1997, Bavarian State Opera, Il Trovatore at Dublin and Giulio Cesare for the Covent Garden company at the Barbican, season 1997-98; Performing editions with Charles Mackerras of operas by Handel, including Xerxes for English National Opera. Address: Athole Still Ltd, Foresters Hall, 25-27 Westow Street, London SE19 3RY, England.

DAVIES Penelope C B, b. 28 May 1955, Weymouth, England. m. Brian Davies, 26 June 1976. Education: BSc, London University; PGCE, Hull University; BMus, Hull University. Career: Piano Teacher; Piano Tutor, Junior Department, Welsh College of Music and Drama; Founder, Abertawe Festival for Young Musicians; Piano Mentor, Associated Board of the Royal Schools of Music; Regional Organiser for EPTA. Honour: High Sheriff's Award. Memberships: ISM; EPTA. Address: 16 Brynfield Road, Langland, Swansea, England.

DAVIES Peter Maxwell (Sir), b. 8 Sept 1934, Manchester, England. Composer. Education: Royal Manchester College of Music; Mus B (Hons), Manchester University, 1956. Musical Education: Studies with Goffredo Petrassi in Rome, 1957; Harkness Fellowship, Graduate School, Princeton University, studied with Roger Sessions, Milton Babbitt, Earl Kim. Career: Director of Music, Cirencester Grammar School, 1959-62; Founder and co-director (with Harrison Birtwistle) of the Pierrot Players, 1967-71; Founder, Artistic Director, Fires of London, 1971-87; Founder, Artistic Director, St. Magnus Festival, Orkney Islands, Scotland, 1977-86; Artistic Director, Dartington Summer School of Music, 1979-84; President, Schools Music Association, 1983-; President, North of England Education Conference, 1985; Visiting Fromm Professor of Composition, Harvard University, 1985; Associate Composer/Conductor, Scottish Chamber Orchestra, 1985-94; President, Composer's Guild of Great Britain, 1986-; President, St Magnus Festival, Orkney Islands, 1986-; President, National Federation of Music Societies, 1989-; Major retrospective festival as South Bank Centre, London, 1990; Conductor/Composer, BBC Philharmonic, 1992-; Associate Conductor/Composer, Royal Philharmonic Orchestra, 1992-; President, Cheltenham Arts Festival, 1994-; Composer Laureate of Scottish Chamber Orchestra, 1994-; President, Society for the Promotion of New Music, 1995-. Compositions: numerous including: Sonata for trumpet and piano, 1955; Fantasias on John Taverner's In nomine, for orchestra, 1962, 1964; Revelation and Fall, for soprano and ensemble, 1966; Eight Songs for a Mad King, music theatre work for ensemble, 1969; Salome, ballet in two acts, 1978; The Lighthouse, chamber opera, 1979; Piano Sonata, 1981; Sinfonia Concertante, for orchestra, 1983; Resurrection, opera, 1987; Turn of the Tide, orchestra and children's choir, 1992; A Spell for Green Corn: The MacDonald Dances, for orchestra, 1993; Strathclyde concerto no 9, for six woodwind instruments and string orchestra, 1994; The Three Kings, for chorus, orchestra and soloists, 1995; Concerto for piccolo, 1996; Job, oratorio for chorus, orchestra and soloists. Honours: many honours including: Fellow, Royal Northern College of Music, 1978; Honorary Member, Royal Academy of Music, 1979; Honorary Member, Guildhall School of Music and Drama, 1981; CBE, 1981; Knight Bachelor, for services to music, 1987; L'officier dans L'Ordre des Srts et des Lettres, France, 1988; First Award, Association of British Orchestras, outstanding contribution and promotion of orchestral life in UK; Gulliver Award for Performing Arts in Scotland, 1991; Fellowship, Royal Scottish Academy of Music and Drama, 1994; Charles Grove Award, outstanding contribution to British Music, 1995. Current Management: Judy Arnold. Address: c/o 50 Hogarth Road, London SW5 0PU, England.

DAVIES Ryland, b. 9 February 1943, Cwym, Ebbw Vale, Wales. Opera and Concert Singer (Tenor). m. (1) Anne Howells (divorced 1981); (2) Deborah Rees, 1983, 1 daughter. Education: FRMCM, Royal Manchester College of Music, 1971. Debut: Almaviva, Barber of Seville, Welsh National Opera, 1964. Career: Glyndebourne Chorus, 1964-66; Soloist and Freelance, Glyndebourne and Sadler's Wells, Royal Opera House, Covent Garden, Welsh National Opera, Scottish Opera, Opera North; Performances in Salzburg, San Francisco, Chicago, New York, Hollywood Bowl, Paris, Geneva, Brussels, Vienna, Lyon, Amsterdam, Mannheim, Rome, Israel, Buenos Aires, Stuttgart, Berlin, Hamburg, Nice, Nancy, Philadelphia; Sang Lysander in A Midsummer Night's Dream at Glyndebourne, 1989, Tichon in Katya Kabanova at the 1990 Festival; Other roles have included Mozart's Ferrando and Don Ottavio, Ernesto, Fenton, Nemorino, Pelléas, (Berlin 1984), Oberon, (Montpellier, 1987); Tamino, Lensky, Belmonte and Enéas in Esclarmonde; Sang Podestà in Mozart's Finta Giardiniera for Welsh National Opera, 1994; Arbace in Idomeneo at Garsington, 1996; Concert Appearances at home and abroad; Radio and TV Broadcasts; Appeared in films including: Capriccio, Entführung, A Midsummer Night's Dream; Trial by Jury, Don Pasquale. Recordings: include, Die Entführung; Les Troyens; Saul; Cosi fan Tutte; Monteverdi Madrigals, Messiah, Idomeneo, Il Matrimonio, L'Oracolo (Leoni), Lucia di Lammermoor, Thérèse, Judas Maccabeus, Mozart Requiem, Credo Mass, Mozart Coronation Mass and Vêspres Solenelle. Honours: Boise and Mendelssohn Foundation Scholarship, 1964; Ricordi Prize, 1964; Imperial League of Opera Prize, 1964; John Christie Award, 1965. Hobbies: Antique Art; Cinema; Sport. Address: 71 Fairmile Lane, Cobham, Surrey KT11 2WG, England.

DAVIES Wyn, b. 8 May 1952, Gowerton, Wales. Conductor. m. Jane Baxendale, 5 July 1975. Education: Christchurch, Oxford. Career: Conductor, Welsh National Opera; Appearances in concert with BBC National Orchestra of Wales, BBC Scottish Orchestra, Bournemouth Symphony Orchestra, English Chamber Orchestra, City of Birmingham Symphony Orchestra; English Northern Philharmonia; Guest Conductor, Opera North, English National Opera, Scottish Opera, New Sadler's Wells Opera, Welsh National Opera; Assistant Conductor, Metropolitan Opera, New York, USA, 1985-86. Hobbies: Italy; Food. Current Management: Performing Arts, 6 Windmill Street, London W1P 1HF, England. Address: Springbank Mill, Kerridge End, Rainow, Cheshire SK10 5TF, England.

DAVIS Andrew (Frank), b. 2 Feb 1944, Ashridge, Hertfordshire, England. Conductor. m. Gianna, 1 son. Education: DMusB (Organ Scholar), King's College, Cambridge; MA (Cantab), 1967; With Franco Ferrara, Rome, 1967-68; DLitt (Hons), York University, Toronto, 1984. Debut: BBC Symphony Orchestra, 1970. Career: Pianist, Harpsichordist, Organist, St Martin-in-the-Fields Academy, London, 1966-70; Assistant Conductor, BBC Scottish Symphony Orchestra, Glasgow, 1970-72; Appearances, major orchestras and festivals internationally including Berlin, Edinburgh, Flanders; Conductor, Glyndebourne Opera Festival, 1973-; Music Director, 1975-88, Conductor Laureate, 1988-, Toronto Symphony; Conductor, China, USA, Japan and Europe tours, 1983, 1986; Principal Guest Conductor, Royal Liverpool Philharmonic Orchestra, 1974-77; Associate Conductor, New Philharmonic Orchestra, London, 1973-77; Conducted: La Scala Milan, Metropolitan Opera, Covent Garden, Paris Opera; Music Director, Glyndebourne, 1988-; Chief Conductor, BBC Symphony Orchestra, 1989-; Conducted La Clemenza di Tito, Chicago, Oct 1989; Szymanowski King Roger, Festival Hall, London, 1990; Katya Kabanova and Tippett's New Year, (1990) Glyndebourne Festival; Opened 1991 Promenade Concerts, London, with Dream of Gerontius; Glyndebourne, 1992, Gala and The Queen of Spades; Conducted Elektra, at First Night, 1993 London Proms, Berg's Lulu, Festival Hall, 1994, returned 1997, for Stravinsky's Oedipus Rex, Persephone and The Rakes's Progress; Hansel and Gretel, 1996-97, and Capriccio, 1997-98, for the Met; forthcoming work planned with the Philadelphia, Chicago and Boston Orchestras, New York Philharmonic, and other leading American and European orchestras; Contracted to become Music Director and Principal Conductor of the Chicago Lyric Opera, 2000. Compositions: La Serenissima (Inventions on a Theme by Claudio Monteverdi); Chansons Innocentes. Recordings include: All Dvorák Symphonies, Mendelssohn Symphonies, Borodin Cycle; Enigma Variations, Falstaff, Elgar; Overtures: Coriolan, Leonore No 3, Egmont, Fidelio, Beethoven; Symphony No 10, Shostakovich, and violin concertos; Canon and other digital delights, Pachelbel; Cinderella excerpts; The Young Person's Guide to the Orchestra; Concerto No 2, Rachmaninoff; The Planets, Gustav Holst; Symphony No 5, Horn Concerto, Piano Concerto No 2, Hoddinott; Brahms piano concertos; Nielsen Symphonies nos 4 and 5; Currently working on The British Line series with the BBC SO including the Elgar Symphonies and Enigma Variations, Vaughan Williams, Delius, Britten and Tippett; Operatic releases including Glyndebourne productions of Katya Kabanova, Jenufa and Queen of Spades. Honours: 2 Grand Prix du Disque Awards, Duruflé's Requiem recording with Philharmonic Orchestra; Gramophone of Year Award, 1987, Grand Prix du Disque, 1988, Tippett's Mask of Time; Royal Philharmonic Society/Charles Heidsieck Award, 1991; CBE, 1992; Royal Phiharmonic Society Award, Best musical opera performance of 1994, Eugene Onegin, on behalf of Glyndebourne Festival Opera, 1995. Hobbies: Mediaeval stained glass; Mycology; Fishing. Address: c/o Harold Holt Ltd, 31 Sinclair Road, London W14 0NS, England.

DAVIS Anthony, b. 20 February 1951, Paterson, New Jersey, USA. Composer. Education: Studied at Yale University, BA 1975. Career: Appearances in United States of America and abroad in 1970's as Jazz Pianist and Director of Episteme, giving performances of improvised music; Co-Founder of Advent, 1973 and Trumpeter in Leo Smith's New Delta Ahkri Band, 1974-77; Played in New York with Violinist Leroy Jenkins, 1977-79 and other members of Advancement of Creative Musicians. Compositions: Opera X: The Life and Times of Malcolm X premiered at the New York City Opera, 1986 and Under the Double Moon, premiered at Opera Theatre of St Louis, 1989; Piano Concerto Wayand V, 1985; Notes from the Underground for Orchestra, 1988; Amistad, opera premiered by Chicago Lyric Opera, season 1997-98. Recordings: Of Blues and Dreams, 1978; Hidden Voices, 1979; Under the Double Moon, 1982. Address: ASCAP, ASCAP House, One Lincoln Plaza, NY10023, USA.

DAVIS Colin (Rex) (Sir), b. 25 Sept 1927, Weybridge, Surrey, England. Conductor. m. (1) April Cantelo, 1949, 1 son, 1 daughter, (2) Ashraf Naini, 1964, 3 sons, 2 daughters. Education: Royal College of Music. Career: Conductor Associate, Kalmar Orchestra and Chelsea Opera Group; Assistant Conductor, BBC Scottish Orchestra, 1957-59; Conductor, Sadler's Wells Opera House (ENO), 1959, Principal Conductor, 1960-65, Musical Director, 1961-65; Artistic Director, Bath Festival, 1969; Chief Conductor, BBC Symphony Orchestra, 1967-71, Chief Guest Conductor, 1971-75; Musical Director, Royal Opera House, Covent Garden, 1971-86; Guest Conductor, Metropol Opera, New York, 1969, 1970, 1972; Principal Guest Conductor, Boston Symphony Orchestra, 1972-84; Principal Guest Conductor, London Symphony Orchestra, 1975-; Bayreuth Festival, first British conductor, 1977; Vienna State Opera, debut, 1986; Music Director and Principal Conductor, Bavarian State Radio Orchestra, 1983-92; Honorary Conductor, Dresden Staatskapelle, 1990-; Principal Conductor, London Symphony Orchestra, 1995; Principal Guest Conductor, New York Philharmonic Orchestra, 1998-; Has worked regularly with many orchestras in Europe and America. Recordings: Extensive recording with Boston Symphony Orchestra, London Symphony Orchestra, Dresden Staatskapelle, Bavarian Radio Symphony Orchestra. Honours include: CBE, 1965; Commendate of Republic of Italy, 1976; Evening Standard Opera Award, 1976; Medal, Finland Sibelius Society, 1977; Grand Prix Awards, France, Belgium, 1977; Grosse Deutscher Schallplattenpreis, 1978; Knighthood, 1980; Grammy, Opera Recording of the Year, 1980; French Legion d'Honneur, 1982; Commander's Cross of the Order of Merit, Germany, 1987; Commander dans l'Ordre des Arts et Lettres, France, 1990; Freedon of City of London, 1992; Order of the Lion of Finland, Commander 1st Class, 1992; Bavarian Order of Merit, 1993; Royal Philharmonic Society Gold Medal, 1995; Grammy, Best Orchestral Recording, 1997. Hobbies: Reading; Knitting; Gardening; Cookery. Current Management: CAMI, New York. Address: c/o 39 Huntingdon Street, London N1 1BP, England.

DAVIS Howard, b. 9 Apr 1940, Wolverhampton. England. Musician. m. Virginia Black, 7 Aug 1965, 2 sons. Education: Royal Academy of Music. Career: Leader, Alberni String Quartet; Worldwide Tours with many broadcasts and television appearances; Professor, Royal Academy of Music, London. Recordings: Many including complete chamber music of Beethoven, Mozart, Schumann and complete quartets of Benjamin Britten. Honours: FRAM; FRSAMD; FRSA. Hobbies: Watercolour Painting; Photography. Current Management: Karen Durant, London. Address: Charlotte Cottage, 123 Sheering Road, Harlow, Essex CM17 0JP, England.

DAVIS Nathan (Joseph), b. 15 March 1955, Davis, California, USA. Assistant Professor of Cello. m. Elise Midelfort, 13 July 1979, 1 son, 1 daughter. Education: BA, Manhattan School of Music and New York University; MA, Montclair State College; PhD, New York University; Cello with Maurice Eisenberg, George Neikrug, David Wells; Ensemble studies with Raphael Bronstin, Juilliard Quartet and Lillian Fuchs. Career: Public Radio Broadcasts in New York and Minnesota; Cello Recording for original scoring; Faith Hubley Production, Cannes Award Winner in Animation; Currently Assistant Professor of Cello, Moorhead State University, Minnesota. Publication: Dissertation: The Baroque Violoncello and the Unaccompanied Cello Suites of J S Bach, 1986. Honours: Graduate Fellowship, Montclair State University; Awarded National and State Grants for String Outreach Projects. Memberships: Pi Kappa Lambda; ASTA; Music Educators National Conference; Chamber Music

America. Hobbies: Golf; Baseball. Address: Music Department, Moorhead State University, Moorhead, MN 56563, USA.

DAVISLIM Steve, b. 1967, Australia. Singer (Tenor). Education: Studied with Joan Hammond and John Modenos. Career: Engaged with the Zürich Opera, as Rossini's Almaviva, the Narrator in the Rape of Lucretia and Ferrando in Così fan tutte; Further appearances at Hamburg as Almaviva, at the Salzburg Festival in Concerts, First Prisoner under Solti, as Don Curzio (Figaro) and Athens as Don Ottavio, 1996, Ludwigsburg Festival as Tamino, 1998-; Concerts include Liszt's Faust Symphony, Beethoven's Missa Solemnis (with Roger Norrington, in London) and Matthew Passion (Bach), with Ricardo Chailly; Concerts with orchestras such as Chicago Symphony, Tonhalle Orchestra, Zürich, Cleveland Symphony, Wiener Philharmoniker, BBC Symphony, Camerata Bern. Recordings include: Beethoven's 9th, Schumann's Manfred, Broadway Songs; CD, Masses of Johann Zach; Bertoni's Orfeo. Honours include: Australia Arts Council Grant; Queen Elizabeth II Silver Jubilee Scholarship. Recordings include: Bertoni's Orfeo. Address: c/o Opernhaus Zurich, Falkenstrasse 1, CH-8008, Zürich, Switzerland.

DAVITASHVILI Mery, b. 13 March 1924, Tbilisi, Georgia. Composer. m. Dolidze Giv, 3 February 1947, 1 son. Education: Department of Composition, Tbilisi State Conservatoire, 1946. Debut: Piano Concerto N1 on radio, 1946; Festival of Soviet Music in Tbilisi, 1951. Appointments: Systematically cooperate with radio from 1946, and with TV frm 1957; General Secretary of organizing committee of the Annual Festival for Children, 1972-. Compositions: Two operas, Kadjana, Tbilisi State Opera, 1966; Natsarkekia, Tibilisi State Opera, 1981; Two Piano Concertos with orchestra; Fantasy for piano with orchestra; 12 suites for orchestral chamber music, vocal cycles, cycles for children, music for 30 cartoons, 3 movies and 50 plays. Recordings: Fanatsy for piano with orchestra, suite for orchestra from ballet, Wedding of the Sun; Two recording discs, Songs for Children. Contributions to: Cycle of articles regarding musical education of children and youth, in various Georgian and Russian magazines and newspapers, 1958-. Honours: People's Arts of Georgia, 1976; Laureate of Rustveli, 1981, and Gogebashvili, 1993; Professor of Conservatoire, 1994; Premier holder of Honour Order, 1997. Memberships: Georgian Society of Composers and Musicians, 1946; Secretary of the Society, 1968-90. Hobbies: Travelling; Art; History; Literature. Address: Griboedov st 29, Tbilisi 38008, Georgia.

DAVITASHVILI Shalva, b. 1 Jan 1934, Telavi, Georgia. Composer. m. Nino Zabukidze, 6 Nov 1959, 1 son, 1 daughter. Education: Tbilisi State Conservatoire. Debut: The tiger and the young man, symphonic poem, Tbilisi State Conservatoire, 1960. Career: Director, music school, Akhalnalexi. 1966-68; Georgian TV, 1968-70; Teacher at musical college, 1970-; Director, Polioshvili Museum, 1992-. Compositions: 2 symphonies; 3 symphonic poems; 2 ballets; 3 cantata; 5 concertos; 2 vocal-symphonic cycles; Choral works; Pieces for piano; Pieces for other instruments; Incidental music; Film scores; Songs. Recordings: 3 concertos for clarinet and orchestra; 9th April, symphonic poem; Vocal cycles; Parts of ballets; Sakartveloze, cantata; Songs. Publications: Concerto No 1, 1972; Concerto No 2, 1981; Concerto No 3, 1988; 9th April, 1990; Symphony No 2, 1992. Contribution to: Vladimir Kremen, Premier of Zviadauri in Kutaisi, Sovijetski balet, 1987. Honour: Merited Artist of Georgia, 1982. Membership: Georgian Union of Composers, 1980-96. Hobby: History of ballet. Address: Gorgasali str 39, app 21, 380014 Tbilisi, Georgia.

DAVY Gloria, b. 29 Mar 1937, Brooklyn, NY, USA. Singer (Soprano); Professor of Voice. Education: Studied at the Juilliard School with Belle Julie Soudant and in Milan with Victor de Sabata. Career: Sang the Countess in the US premiere of Strauss's Capriccio (Juilliard) 1954; World tour in Porgy and Bess; Recital and oratorio appearances before returning to NY in concert performance of Anna Bolena, at the Metropolitan as Pamina, Aida, Nedda and Leonora in Il Trovatore from 1958; Sang in Vienna in Aida, Covent Garden debut, 1959-60, as Aida, Deutsche Oper Berlin from 1961 with Wieland Wagner and Karl Böhm, as Aida, Amelia, Butterfly, Fiordiligi, Donna Anna, Donna Elvira and Salome; Guest engagements 1963-69 in Hamburg, Munich, Geneva, Paris, Madrid, Brussels and London; Sang in the premiere of Henze's Nachtstücke und Arien, 1957, Stockhausen's Momente, 1972, Vortrag uber Hu, 1974; Concert tours of Germany, Switzerland, Italy, and France, 1975-85; Debut recital at Wigmore Hall, London, 1983; Professor of Music in Voice at Indiana University School of Music, Bloomington, from 1985; Sang Berg's Sieben Frühe Lieder, Lulu and Der Wein, with the conductors Otmar Suitner and Kurt Masur, 1981-85; New Year's Eve in Milan, Dortmund, 1988-89; Other repertoire included Handel's Acis, Gluck's Iphigenie, Mozart's Countess and Pamina, Strauss's Daphne and Anaide in Mosé by Rossini, Bach St Matthew Passion, Beethoven Missa Solemnis, Handel's Deborah, Schoenberg Erwartung and Shostakovich 14th Symphony. Recordings include: Aida; Il Trovatore; Cavalleria Rusticana; Stockhausen's Momente; Zandonai's Conchita; Verdi's Requiem; Dido and Aeneas. Address: Indiana University, School of Music, Bloomington, IN 47405, USA.

DAWNEY Michael William, b. 10 Aug 1942, Romford, Essex, England. Music Journalist; Editor; Teacher; Lecturer; Pianist; Organist; Arranger. Education: Durham University; Lincoln College, Oxford, under Edmund Rubbra and Egon Wellesz; Institute of Dialect and Folk Life Studies, Leeds University; London International Film School, under Richard Arnell; Bournemouth University. Compositions: A Carolan Suite for harpsichord or strings; Five Irish Dances for orchestra; A Christmas Greeting for choir; Now Welcome Summer for choir; Christmas Morn for choir and orchestra; The Cattery, song cycle; Echoes for brass; Lions in Heraldry for brass; The Punk's Delight for brass; An Easter Improvisation, Fantasia, Finale, Veni Emmanuel, In Paradisum, Prelude and Fugue, Adeste Fidelis, Veni Creator Spiritus, Fuga Spirituale for organ; Many arrangements for organ of works by Saint-Saëns, Humperdinck, Purcell, Verdi, Fauré, Franck, others. Recordings: Hail Holy Queen, record; Hail Holy Queen in film The House of Mortal Sin; Reap Me the Earth, on record Hymns for Celebration. Publications: Folksong books for English Folk Dance and Song Society; Doon the Wagon Way, 1973; The Iron Man, 1974; The Ploughboy's Glory, 1976. Contributions to: Classical Music; Musical Opinion; Edmund Rubbra, book. Honours: Joint Winner, 1st Prize, Cork Choral Festival, 1976; Medal, Irish Folk Song Society, 1976; Queen Elizabeth II Silver Jubilee Prize, 1977. Memberships: Composers' Guild; Performing Right Society; Mechanical Copyright Protection Society; Musicians' Union. Address: 5 Queen's Road, Parkstone, Poole, Dorset BH14 9HF, England.

DAWSON Anne, b. 9 Feb 1959, Stoke, England. Singer (Soprano). Education: Studied at the Royal Northern College of Music. Career: Sang Angelica in Handel's Orlando at the Bath Festival, 1978, Grenoble Festival, 1979; Recital tours throughout UK; With Glyndebourne Touring Opera has sung Eurydice, Susanna and Micaela; Welsh National Opera as Gilda and Pamina; Marguerite, Gilda and the title role in The Cunning Little Vixen with English National Opera; Covent Garden debut in Don Carlos, 1988; Overseas engagements include Gilda in Frankfurt, the Vixen in Vancouver, and appearances with the Netherlands and Lausanne Operas; Sang Hero in Beatrice and Benedict, London Coliseum, 1990; Susanna for Welsh National Opera; Season 1992 as Ninetta in The Thieving Magpie for Opera North, Anne Trulove for Glyndebourne Touring Opera and Chloe in The Queen of Spades at the Festival; Concert repertoire includes Schubert's Fierrabras, at South Bank conducted by Jeffrey Tate, Carmina Burana, and Mozart's Exsultate Jubilate (Fishguard Festival). Recordings include: Songs by English composers. Honours: John Ireland Festival Centenary Competition and the Gerald Finzi Song Award Competition, 1981; Soprano prize at the 1981 International Singing Competition, s'Hertogenbosch; Kathleen Ferrier Memorial Scholarship, 1982. Current Management: Portland Wallis. Address: 50 Great Portland Street, London W1N 5AH, England.

DAWSON Lynne, b. 3 June 1956, York, England. Singer (Soprano). Education: Studied at the Guildhall School of Music, London. Career: Appearances from 1985 with Trevor Pinnock and the English Concert; John Eliot Gardiner, the Monteverdi Choir and English Baroque Soloists and Christopher Hogwood and the Academy of Ancient Music; Further concerts with Baremboim, Davis, Rattle, Mackerras, Ashkenazy, and Giulini; Tours of Europe and the USA; Opera debut as the Countess with Kent Opera, 1986; Monteverdi's Orfeo at Florence, 1988; Festival engagements at Aldeburgh, Edinburgh, Salzburg, Bruges, Aix-en-Provence, Paris, Vienna and Promenade Concerts; Opera career includes Zdenka in Arabella at the Châtelet, Pamina, Berlin Staatsoper; Appearances as Fiordiligi at Naples, Constanze Brussels, Teresa in Benvenuto Cellini for Netherlands Opera, 1991; Other roles include, Xiphares in Mitridate (Châtelet, Paris, 1991), Amenaide in Rossini's Tancredi, Berlin Staatsoper, 1994; Shéhérezade at the 1995 London Proms; Sang Nitocris in Belshazzar at the 1996 Handel Festival, Göttingen. Recordings: Over 50 including: Bach B Minor Mass, Monteverdi Orfeo, Purcell, Dido and Aeneas; Messiah; Mozart C Minor Mass; Purcell Timon of Athens and Dioclesian, Iphigénie en Aulide; Jephtha; Vespers by Mozart; Mozart's Requiem; Gluck's La Recontre Impréuve; Mozart's Elvira and Constanze, Beethoven 9, Midsummer Night's Dream, Acis and Galatea. Address: IMG Artists, Media House, 3 Burlington Lane, London W4 2TH, England.

DAWSON Ted, b. 28 April 1951, Victoria, British Columbia, Canada. Composer; Teacher. Education: Studied at Victoria School of Music, 1964-68; Composition with Brian Cherney and Rudolf Komorous at University of Victoria, BMus, 1972, followed by Composition and Electronic Music with Bengt Hambraeus and Alcides Lanza at McGill University, MMA, 1974; Music and Visual Arts Education at University of Toronto, BED, 1984; Composition, Computer Music, Performance, History and Theory with Charles Wuorinen, Peter Otto, Jan Williams, Jeremy Noble and Martha Hyde at State University of New York at Buffalo, PhD, 1994. Career: Lecturer at Concordia University, 1974-78 and Vanier College in Montreal, 1978-80; Assistant Professor at Queen's University, Kingston, Ontario, 1987-88; Assistant Professor at Brock University, St Catherines, Ontario, 1988-90; Founder of the ComPoster Project to promote Canadian music through education; Artistic Director of Canadian Music Days Festival of Contemporary Canadian Music, held in Estonia, 1993. Publication: Author of Teacher's Guide to Canadian Music, 1991. Compositions: Pentad for String Quartet, 1971; Concerto Grosso 1 for Tape with/without Amplified Viola, Bassoon, Trombone, and Percussion, 1972-74; Chameleon for Amplified Flute, 1975; The Land of Nurr, 1975; The Clouds of Magellan for Tape and Slides, 1976-77; Binaries for 4 Dancers, Amplified Piano and Percussion, 1978-80; Joint Actions for Solo Female Dancer and Male Double Bass Player, 1981; Phantasms for solo piano, 1986-87; Songs from the Late T'ang for Bass-Baritone and Piano, 1988; Portraits in a Landscape for Tape, 1988; Traces in Glass for Orchestra, 1986-92; China Beach for Amplified Piano and Tape, 1992; Symphony 1 for Orchestra, 1992-94. Address: SOCAN (Canada), c/o 41 Valleybrook Drive, Don Mills, Ontario M3B 2S6, Canada.

DAYMOND Karl Morgan, b. 1965, England. Singer (Baritone). Education: Studied at Guildhall School with Thomas Hemsley and at National Opera Studio. Career: Appeared at Glyndebourne Festival, 1992; Sang Valentin for Opera Northern Ireland; Season 1993 as Schaunard for Welsh National Opera and Mountjoy in Gloriana for Opera North; Has also sung in Rimsky's May Night, La Vida Breve, Angelique by Ibert, Margot-la-Rouge by Delius, Poulenc's Les Mamelles de Tiresias, A Midsummer Night's Dream (Demetrius) and the Henze-Paisiello Don Quixote as Sancho Panza; appeared as Purcell's Aeneas for BBC2 television, 1995; Marcello in La Bohème for Opera North, 1996. Honours: British Song Prize, 1987; Polonsky Foundation Award, 1989. Current Management: John Coast Limited. Address: 31 Sinclair Road, London W14 0NS, England.

DAZELEY William, b. 1966, England. Singer (Baritone). Education: Studied at Guildhall School, London. Career: Season 1990-91 as Onegin with British Youth Opera; Season 1991-92 as Schaunard with British Youth Opera and Don Giovanni for Opera North; British premiere of Schreker's Der Ferne Klang, 1992; Season 1992-93 with Opera North in Billy Budd and as Mozart's Count and Schaunard, also as Don Giovanni for English Touring Opera; Season 1993-94 as Mowgli in world premiere of Michael Berkeley's Baa Baa Black Sheep for Cheltenham Festival, also as Mowgli for Opera North, Harlekin for Broomhill and Papageno for Opera North; Season 1994-95 as Rossini's Figaro for Glyndebourne Touring Opera, as Demetrius for Teatro Regio, Turin, and as Pelléas for Opera North; Mozart's Count for GTO at Glyndebourne, 1996. Honours: Decca-Kathleen Ferrier Prize, 1989; Richard Tauber Prize; Winner, Walter Gruner International Lieder Competition, 1991. Address: c/o John Coast Ltd, 31 Sinclair Road, London W14 0NS, England.

DE BEENHOUWER Jozef, b. 26 Mar 1948, Brasschaat, Belgium. Concert Pianist. Education: Pharmacy, University of Louvain; Graduate, Chapelle Musicale Reine Elisabeth Argenteuil, 1974; Higher Diploma, Royal Flemish Conservatory, Antwerp, 1975. Career: Concert Pianist, with orchestras and solo recitals; Chamber Music: Vienna, (Musikverein, Konzerthaus with Vienna Symphony), Amsterdam, (Concertgebouw), Lisbon (Foundation Gulbenkian), London, Berlin, (Schauspielhaus), Dresden, (Semper-Oper), Rheinisches Musikfest, Flanders Festival, Estival de Paris and USA; Professor of Piano, Royal Flemish Conservatory, 1983-. Recordings include: Schumann Op 12; Ravel's Gaspard de la Nuit, 1982; Peter Benoit's Contes et Ballades and Sonata, 2 LPs, 1984; Joseph Ryelandt's Piano Works, 2 CDs, 1986; Clara Schumann's Complete Piano Works, 3 CDs, 1991; Robert Schumann's Op 16, 111 and 133, 1994; Robert Schumann's Dichterliebe with Robert Holl, 1994; Belgian Piano Music by P Benvit, L Mortelmans, J Jongen, M de Jong amd V Legley, 1997. Publications: Robert Schumann, Concertsatz 1839, 1987; Clara Schumann, Concertsatz 1847, 1994. Honours: Rutzky Prize, 1977; A De Vries Prize, 1984, Prix Caecilia, Prix Fuga, Sabam, 1986; Robert Schumann Preis der Stadt Zwickau, 1993. Memberships: Robert Schumann Gesellschaft Düsseldorf and Zwickau; Felix Mendelssohn Gesellschaft, Berlin; Kathleen Ferrier Society, England; Peter Benoitfonds, Antwerp. Address: Frilinglei 45, 2930 Brasschaat, Belgium.

DE BERNART Massimo, b. 1950, Rome Italy. Conductor. Education: Studied Piano, Composition and Conducting at Conservatories of Florence, Turin and Venice; Further study at Vienna Academy and Accademia Musicale Chigiana. Career: Has made many appearances in Italian opera houses, conducting 19th Century repertory and reviving neglected works; Conducted Ecuba by Nicola Manfroce and Caterina di Guisa by Carlo Coccia at Savona, 1991; Permanent Artistic Director of the Orchestra Giovanile Italiana, from 1977 and of the Orchestra Regionale Toscana 1980; Conducted Traviata at Savona, 1991, Leoncavallo's La Reginetta della Rose at Palermo, 1992; Adriane

Lecouvreur at Livorno, 1995. Recording: L'Ebreo by Guiseppe Appolini. Honours: Prizewinner, Vittorio Gui International Prize, 1979. Address: c/o Accademia Musicale Chigiana, Via di Citta 89, 1-53100 Siena, Italy.

DE CANDIA Roberto, b. 1960, Molfetta, Bari, Italy. Singer (Baritone). Education: Studied singing with Lajos Kosma and Sesto Bruscantini. Debut: Sang in Puccini's Messa di Gloria (concert) at the Santa Cecilia, Rome, and in Massenet's Manon at Parma. Career: Engagements as Gianni Schicchi at Turin, Rossini's Emilia; Marcello at the Verona Arena, Taddeo (L'Italiana in Algeri) and Masetto in Don Giovanni at the Salzburg Festival; Other roles include: Rossini's Figaro (Paris Opéra-Comique), Parmenione in L'Occasione fa il ladro (Pesaro) and Alcandro in Puccini's Saffo (Wexford Festival); La Scala, Milan, 1996-97, as Ubalde in Gluck's Armide and Poeta (Il Turco in Italia); Glyndebourne Festival 1997, as Lescaut in a new production of Manon Lescaut; Season 1997-98 as Massenet's Lescaut at the Metropolitan, Dandini, and Belcore (L'elisir d'amore). Address: c/o Metropolitan Opera, Lincoln Center, New York, NY 10023, USA.

DE CAROLIS Natale, b. 25 July 1957, Anagni, Italy. Opera Singer (Bass-Baritone). Education: Pont Institute of Vatican State, studied with Renato Guelfi and Maria Vittoria Romano. Debut: 1983. Career: La Scala, Milan; Metropolitan Opera, New York; La Fenice, Venice; Maggio Musicale, Florence; Salzburg Festpiele; La Zarzuela, Madrid; Sydney Opera House; Rossini Opera Festival; Pesaro Teatro Comunale; Bologna Opernhaus; Zurich Opera; Teatro Massimo, Palerno; Teatro Bellini, Catania; Colonia; Paris; Macerata; S Carlo, Napoli and Bonn; Sang Don Parmenione in a Rossini double bill at Cologne and Schwetzingen, 1992; Count Robinson in Il Matrimonio Segreto at the 1992 Ravenna Festival; Vienna, Musikverein, Staatsoper, Konzerthaus; Frankfurt, Don Giovanni, Figaro, Guglielmo, Belcore; Roma, Teatro Dell'Opera; Hamburg, Berlin, Lausanne, Montpellier, Aix-en-Province, Lisbon, Touloun, Oviedo; Sang Donizetti's Belcore at Covent Garden, 1997. Recordings: Signor Bruschino, Scala di Seta (Rossini); Don Giovanni (Mozart); Rinaldo (Handel); Mozart Recital; L'Occasione fa Il Ladro and L'Inganno Felice (Rossini); Le nozze di Figaro (Mozart); La Ninfa Pazza per Amore (Paisello); Mozart Recital; Don Giovanni, Così fan tutte, Le Nozze Di Figaro, Highlights. Honours: Spoleto; Baroque Festival Viterbo; Toti Dal Monte (Treviso); Lauri Volpi. Hobbies: Tennis; Football. Current Management: Luisa Petrov (Germany); Opera et Concert (France); Erich Seitter (Austria); Robert Lombardo Associates (USA). Address: c/o John Cost Ltd, 31 Sinclair Road, London W14 0NS, England.

DE CLARA Roberto, b. 30 July 1955, Hamilton, Ontario, Canada. Conductor. m. Anna Colangelo, 1 October 1983. Education: BMus, Summa Cum Laude, McMaster University, Canada; Wiener Meisterkurse; Vienna Mozarteum; Salzburg Sommerakademie; Accademia Chigiana, Siena; Aspen Music School; University of Toronto; Royal Conservatory, Toronto. Debut: Hamilton Philharmonic, 1981. Career: Assistant Conductor, Opera Hamilton, 1979-84; Assistant Conductor, Hamilton Philharmonic, 1981-82; Music Director, Prince George Symphony, 1984-87; Artistic Advisor, Symphony Hamilton, 1988-90; Music Director, York Symphony, 1990-. Honours: Heinz Unger Conducting Prize, Toronto, 1978; Canada Council Scholarships, 1979, 1980; Hans Haring Conducting Prize, Salzburg Mozarteum, 1984. Memberships: American Federation of Musicians; Opera America. Hobbies: Cookery; Soccer. Current Management: Ann Summers International. Address: 129 Sirente Drive, Hamilton, Ont L9A 5H5, Canada.

DE GIUSTO Pablo Alberto, b. 10 August 1962, Argentina. Musician. div, 1 son. Education: Guitar Formal Studies with Maria isabel Siewers; Professor of Composition, National University of Cordoba; Masterclasses with Eduardo Isaac, narciso Yepes, John W Duarte. Debut: San Martin Theatre, Cordoba, Argentina, 1981. Career: Concerts at Cordoba, Buenos Aires, Mendoza, Rosario, La Plata; Appearances on Television and Radio; Invitations to Guitar Festivals at Lublin, 1988 and La Habana, 1992. Recordings: Encuentro (Encounter), Guitar Duets with Gonzalo Bitarella, 1988; Musica de Camara Latinoamericana, 1996; Musica de Abel Fleury, 1998. Honours: National Competition 1st Prize, Rosario, Argentina, 1981; National Competition 2nd Prize, Argentina, 1983; Competition 1st Prize, Argentina, 1986; State Competition of Young Interpreters 1st Prize, 1986; Cordoba Town Hall Competition Music Edition Prize, 1995. Membership: Founder Member, Jeunesses Musicales of Cordoba. Hobbies: Reading; Movies. Address: Velez 157 Depto 17, 5003 Cordoba, Argentina.

DE GRANDIS Franco, b. 1958, Italy. Singer (Bass). Career: Prizewinner at the 1984 Maria Callas Competition and sang the same year in Donizetti's Sancia di Castiglia, at Bergamo; Further appearances at the Vienna Staatsoper (1986), in Barcelona (King in Aida, 1987) and at the Metropolitan New York (Ferrando in Trovatore, 1987); La Scala Milan, 1988, as Melcthal in Guillaume Tell; Other roles include the Grand Inquisitor and Mozart's Bartolo (at Turin), Sparafucile (Rome, 1990) and the Commendatore (Wuppertal, 1990); Verona Arena, 1992, as the Grand Inquisitor. Recordings include: Antonio in Le nozze di Figaro (EMI) and Don Giovanni (Chandos). Address: c/o Teatro alla Scala, Via Filodrammatici 2, 20121 Milan, Italy.

DE GRANDIS Renato, b. 24 October 1927, Venice, Italy. Composer. Education: Studied Musicology and Composition with Malipiero in Venice; Master Classes in Siena. Career: As Composer, has been concerned with dodecaphonic and aleatory techniques; Resident in Darmstadt, 1959-81, then Venice. Compositions: Unperformed Operas, La Fanciulla del Lago, Il Gave and Il Pastore, 1951-54; Il Cierco di Hyuga, 1959 (Staged Bonn, 1969), Gloria al Re, 1962 (Staged Kiel, 1967); Eduard und Kunigunde, Wiesbaden, 1971; Das Wahrhaftige ende des don Giovanni, Bonn, 1973; Die Schule Der Kahlen, Karlsruhe, 1976. Honours: Italian Radio Prize, 1945; National First Prize for Composition, 1953. Address: SIAE (Sezione Musica), Viale della Letteratura n.30, 00144 Roma (EUR), Italy.

DE GREY Michael (John), b. 6 Sept 1942, Hitchin, England. Music Administrator. m. Charlotte Ashe, 17 June 1989. Education: Eton College, 1955-60; Tours University, France, 1960; Pitman Business Course, 1961; Marketing Course, Ashridge Management Centre, 1968; Marketing Strategy Course, Coopers and Lybrand, 1987; Senior Managers Programme, Cranfield School of Management, 1988. Career: Concerts Manager, Victor Hochhauser Limited, 1970-72; General Manager, Administrator of Mozart Prize, London Mozart Players, 1972-81; General Manager, Royal Choral Society, 1976-79; Administrative Director, London Sinfonietta, 1981-88; Administrative Director, Opera Factory, 1984-88; Director, Association of British Orchestras, 1984-89; Member, Music Panel, South East Arts, 1987-91; Director, London Philharmonic Orchestra Limited, 1987-89; General Manager, London Academy of Music and Dramatic Art, 1989; Chief Executive, The National Youth Orchestra of Great Britain, 1991-. Hobbies: Travel; Photography; Wine; Reading; Gardening; Carpentry; Visual Arts; Theatre; Opera. Address: Crooked Cottage, The Hollow, Dunkerton, Bath BA2 8BG, England.

DE GROOTE Philip, b. 25 Dec 1949, South Africa. Cellist. Career: Co-Founder and Cellist of the Chilingirian Quartet, 1971; Resident Quartet of Liverpool University, 1973-76; Resident Quartet of Sussex University, 1978-; Resident Quartet of Royal College of Music, 1986-; Annual Series of Concerts at the Elizabeth Hall and Wigmore Hall; Performances at the Edinburgh, Bath, Aldeburgh Festivals; Munich Herkulessaal, Amsterdam Concertgebouw, Zurich Tonhalle, Vienna Konzerthaus, Stockholm Konserthuset; New York debut 1976; Annual coast-to-coast tours of the USA and Canada; Represented Britain at the New York International Festival quartet series; Tours of Australia, New Zealand, South America, the Far East; Television and Radio throughout Europe, National Public Radio in the USA, the BBC. Recordings: All Great Mozart Quartets; Late Schubert Quartets; Debussy and Ravel Quartets; Elgar Quartet and Piano Quintet; Schubert Cello Quintet and Octet; Mozart Clarinet Quintet; Complete Quartets of Bartók and Dvorak; Bartók Piano Quintet. Address: c/o Intermusica Artists Management, 16 Duncan Terrace, London N1 8BZ, England.

DE JONG Conrad (John), b. 13 January 1934, Hull, Iowa, USA. Composer; Professor. Education: BM, Music Education and Trumpet, North Texas State University, Denton, 1954; MM, Music Theory with B Heiden and Brass Instruments, Indiana University School of Music, 1959; T de Leeuw, Amsterdam, 1969. Career: Professor of Music, University of Wisconsin, River Falls, 1959-. Compositions: Prelude and Fugue for Brass Trio, 1958; 3 Studies for Brass Septet, 1960; Music for 2 Tubas, 1961; Essay for Brass Quintet, 1963; String Trio, 1964; Fun and Games for Any Woodwind, Brass or String Instrument(s) and Piano, 1966, revised 1970; Peace On Earth for Chorus and Organ, 1969; Aanraking (Contact) for Trombone, 1969; Hist Whist for Voice, Flute, Viola and Percussion, 1969; Grab Bag for Tuba Ensemble, 1970; The Silence of the Sky in My Eyes for 1/2 Track Stereo Tape, Musicians, Light and Optional Dance and Audience Participation, 1973; A Prayer for Chorus, Piano, Brass Wind Chimes and Optional Audience, 1975; Ring! My Chimes for Chimes, 1/2 Track Stereo Tape and Slides, 1977; 3 Short Variation Fanfares for Brass Quintet, 1980; La Dolorosa for English Horn, 1982. Address: c/o Music Department, University of Wisconsin at River Falls, River Falls, WI 54022, USA.

DE LA MORA Fernando, b. 1963, Mexico City. Singer (Tenor). Education: Studied in Mexico City, New York, Tel Aviv and at North Carolina University. Debut: Sang Borsa in Rigoletto at Mexico City. Career: Has appeared widely in Mexico as Pinkerton, Cavaradossi and Alfredo; San Francisco Opera, 1988-89, as Gounod's Romeo, and Rodolfo; Alfredo at Vienna Staatsoper and the Deutsche Oper Berlin 1989; Faust at Cologne and the Verdi Requiem on tour to Moscow with the ensemble of La Scala; Milan debut 1990, as Alfredo, which he sang also at the Santa Fe Festival, 1991; Barcelona 1992 as Nemorino. Address: c/o Teatro alla Scala, Via Filodrammatici 2, 20121 Milan, Italy.

DE LA VEGA Aurelio, b. 28 Nov 1925, La Habana, Cuba. Composer; Essayist on Music, Art, Literature; Educator. Education: BA, Humanities, De La Salle College, Havana, 1944; MA, Diplomacy, University of Havana, 1946; MA, Musicology, 1956, PhD, Music (Composition), 1958, Ada Iglesias Music Institute; Private studies in composition with Ernst Toch, Los Angeles, 1947-48. Career: Performances of works in the United States, Canada, Latin American countries, Europe, South Africa, Israel, Japan, India, Australia and New Zealand; Numerous commissions from orchestras, ensembles, patrons, institutions and music societies; Numerous appearances as lecturer on contemporary music subjects throughout the world; Also lectured on Latin American painting; Distinguished Professor of Music at California State University, Northridge, since 1959, and Director of Electronic Music Studio at the same institution. Compositions: Main works: Elegy for string orchestra, 1954; String Quartet in 5 Movements, In Memoriam Alban Berg, 1957; Structure for piano and string quartet, 1962; Intrata for orchestra, 1972; Septicilium for solo clarinet and chamber ensemble, 1975; Adios for orchestra, 1978; Testimonial for mezzo soprano and 5 instruments, 1990; Madrigales de Entonces for a cappella choir, 1991. Recordings include: Antinomies for piano, 1967; Tangents for violin and piano, 1974; Para-Tangents for trumpet and piano, 1974; Sound Clouds for guitar, 1975; Inflorescencia for soprano, bass clarinet and tape, 1976; Tropimapal for 9 instruments, 1983; Homenagem for piano, 1987. Hobbies: Painting; Art book collecting; Travel. Address: Music Department, California State University, Northridge, CA 91330, USA.

DE LAET Joris (Maurits), b. 12 Jul 1947, Antwerp, Belgium. Professor. m. Maria Vervoort, 11 Aug 1974, 1 d. Education: Basic music theory at Academies of Antwerp; Autodidact in electronic and computer music and recording techniques, computer information and composition, first performances in International Cultural Centre, Antwerp, 1974. Career: Tape music composition, Parametric; Live electronics, video-art at festivals in Europe, Canada and Brazil; Many radio appearances since 1973; International seminars and lectures; Concert Organiser of experimental and electronic music and video-art; Director of SEM; Manager of sound studio of the Antwerp Music Conservatory and Professor of Electronic Music Composition; Co-founder and Vice President of BeFEM/FeBeMe, Belgian Federation of Electroacoustic Music, 1994. Compositions include: Metrokunst, 1989; Installatie, 1989; Transparent Bodies, 1991; Commissioned works: Naderen, 1988, Blamis, 1990, Penetration, 1992, Irreversible, New Environment, 1992, Aural Silver, 1993, The Shift, 1994 and Fronts, 1995; Bauit Noir, 1995; Soleil Silencieux, 1996; Pigeon Piège, 1997. Recordings: All tape music and video-art on tapes/ cassettes including concerts of the SEM Ensemble. Publications: Editor, SEM magazine, 1975-79; Editor and part author, Documenta Belgicae II, 1985; Author of syllabus in use at Conservatory of Antwerp on Analogue Synthesis techniques, 1979; Various articles in newspapers and magazines. Honours: Sabam Price for electro-acoustic music, 1997. Memberships: SABAM, 1973-; Founder and Director, SEM (Studio for Experimental Music), in 1973; Vice President, co-founder, Belgian Federation of Electro-Acoustic Music. Hobbies: Sailing; Fencing. Address: Scheihagestraat 43, 2550 Kontich-Antwerp, Belgium.

DE LOS ANGELES Victoria, b. 1 November 1923, Barcelona, Spain. Soprano. m. Enrique Magrina Mir, 1948, 2 sons. Education: University and Conservatory of Barcelona. Debut: Barcelona, 1945. Career: Paris Opera and La Scala, Milan, 1949; Royal Opera House, Covent Garden, London, England, 1950; Metropolitan Opera House, New York, USA, 1951; Vienna State Opera, 1957; Numerous Appearances at other Opera Houses, Concert Tours; Roles included Mozart's Countess, Elisabeth in Tannhâuser, Marguerite, Ariadne, Mimi and Carmen (New York City Opera, 1979); Wigmore Hall Recitals, 1990. Recordings: Has made numerous recordings including Faust, Carmen, Butterfly, Pelléas Werther, Manon, Simon Boccanegra and La Bohème (EMI). Honours: Recipient of numerous Orders and Decorations including, 1st prize, Geneva International Competition, 1947; Cross of Lazo de Dama of the Order of Isabel the Catholic; Condecoracion Banda de la Orden Civil de Alfonso X (El Sabio), Spain. Address: c/o Wigmore Hall (Artists Contracts), Wigmore Street, London W1, England.

DE MAIN John (Lee), b. 11 January 1944, Youngstown, Ohio, USA. Conductor. Education: BM 1966, MS 1968, Juilliard School of Music, New York; Studied Piano with Adele Marcus; Conducting with Jorge Mester. Career: Associate Conductor, St Paul (Minn) Chamber Orchestra, 1972-74; Music Director, Texas Opera Theater, 1974-76; Houston Grand Opera, 1979-94; Opera/Omaha, 1983-; Conducted the local premiere of Britten's A Midsummer Night's Dream, Houston, 1993. Recordings: For Composers' Recordings Inc; RCA. Honours: Julius Rudel Award, 1971; Grammy Award, 1977; Grand Prix de Disque, 1977. Address: c/o Houston Grand Opera, 510 Preston Avenue, Houston, TX 77002, USA.

DE MEY Guy, b. 4 August 1955, Hamme, Belgium. Singer (Tenor). Education: Studied at Brussels Conservatory and at Amsterdam with Erna Spoorenburg; Further study with Peter Pears and Eric Tappy. Career: Has appeared in Baroque Opera at such centres as Berlin, Hamburg, Strasbourg and Spoleto; Lully's Atys under William Christie in Paris, Florence and New York; Alidoro in Cesti's Orontea at Innsbruck 1986, returning for Aegus in Cavalli's Giasone, 1988; Rameau's Hippolyte at Regio Emilia and Eurymachus in Il Ritorno di Ulisse at Mézières, 1989, conducted by Michel Corboz; London 1986 as Monteverdi's Orfeo; Brussels 1988, as the Painter in Lulu; Sang Don Polidoro in Mozart's La Finta Semplice at Innsbruck, 1991; Lully's Alceste at Opera Comique, Paris, 1992; Further engagements at Utrecht Early Music Festival, Zurich, Venice and Bologna; Sang in the French version of Don Carlos at Brussels (1996) and Orpheus by Monteverdi for the English National Opera; Concert Repertoire includes the Evangelist in Bach's Passions. Recordings: Le Cinesi by Gluck; A Scarlatti's La Giuditta; Lully's Atys; Der Geduldige Sokrates by Telemann, Monteverdi's Orfeo and Poppea; Cavalli's Xerse and Giasone, Alessandro by Handel, Orontea and Rameau's Platée. Address: Théâtre Royale de la Monnaie, 4 Leopoldstrasse, B-1000 Brussels, Belgium.

DE PALMA Sandro, b. 14 February 1957, Naples, Italy. Pianist. Education: Classical studies in Latin, Greek; Studied Piano privately with Vincenzo Vitales, Naples. Debut: Naples. Career: Appeared ORF, Vienna, 1977; Carnegie Hall, New York, 1978; Other appearances include: Dvorak Hall, Prague; Interforum, Budapest; Gewandhaus, Leipzig; Dresden; East Berlin; Performances with major Italian Orchestras: RAI, Rome; San Carlo; Fenice Venice; Milan; Tours, France; Italy, Switzerland, USSR. Recordings: include, 1st record at age 15: Liszt; 1st recording of Muzio Clementi's Gradus ad Parnassum, with Fonit Cetra. Honours: 1st Prize, Casella Competition, Naples, 1976; 1st Prize, Bruce Hungerford, New York, 1977. Hobbies: Computers; Archaeology; Chess. Current Management: Patrizia Garrasi, Via Manzoni 31, 20121 Milan, Italy. Address: Vid del Colosseo 23, Rome, Italy.

DE PEYER Gervase (Alan), b. 11 Apr 1926, London, England. Clarinettist; Conductor. m. (1) Sylvia Southcombe, 1950, divorced 1971, 1 s, 2 d. m. (2) Susan Rosalind Daniel, 1971, divorced 1979. m. (3) Katia Perret Aubry, 1980. Education: Studied with Frederick Thurston at the Royal College of Music and with Louis Cahuzac in Paris. Career: International Soloist, 1949-; Co-founded the Melos Ensemble, 1950; First clarinet with the London Symphony, 1955; Teacher at the Royal Academy of Music from 1959; As soloist has given the premieres of works by Arnold Cooke, Musgrave, Horovitz, Hoddinott and Sebastian Forbes; Joined the Chamber Music Society of the Lincoln Center, New York, 1969: performances with Barenboim, Rostropovitch, Menuhin, Perlman, and the Amadeus Quartet; Has conducted the English Chamber Orchestra, London Symphony and the Melos Sinfonia; Director, London Symphony Wind Ensemble; Associate Conductor, Haydn Orchestra of London; Conductor-in-Residence of the Collegium Musicum, in Assisi and Rome; Tour of the USA, 1988 with Quatuor pour le fin du Temps by Messiaen; Gives recitals and master classes throughout the world; Wigmore Hall concert with Gwenneth Pryor and the Allegri Quartet, 1989; Commissioned and premiered the Clarinet Quartet by Berthold Goldschmidt, 1994. Recordings: include, Many discs with the Melos Ensemble; French, English and German music for clarinet and piano, Brahms Sonatas, with Gwenneth Pryor (Chandos). Publications: include, Edition of Mendelssohn Sonata in E flat. Honours: include, Worshipful Company of Musicians Gold Medal, Royal College of Music, 1948; Charles Gros Grand Prix du Disque, 1961, 1962; Plaque of Honour from Academy of Arts and Sciences of America for recording of Mozart Concerto, 1962. Hobbies: Theatre; Good Food. Address: 16 Langford Place, St John's Wood, London NW8, England.

DE PONT DAVIES Rebecca, b. 3 July 1962, London, England. Singer (Mezzo-soprano). Musical Education: Performance and Opera courses, Guildhall School of Music and Drama. Debut: Death in Venice, Glyndebourne Touring Opera, 1989. Career: Gaea at Dartington, 1995; La Zia Principessa, Zita at Broomhill, 1995; Contemporary works by Judith Weir, Jonathan Dove, Henze, in Britain and Europe; Concert Appearances at major UK venues, Canada and Columbia; 3rd Lady in The Magic Flute, Opera Factory, 1996; Helene in Die Muschel at Garsington, 1997. Recordings: Antigone; Fleurs Jetées. Honours: Many educational prizes including award from Countess of Munster Musical Trust; AGSM; PDVT; Violet Openshaw Memorial Prize for Contraltos; Dorothy Openshaw Prize for Melodie. Hobbies: Running; Cinema; Theatre. Current Management: Robert Gilder & Co. Address: Ground Floor, Flat 13, Bedford Place, Brighton BN1 2PT, England.

DE SALAS Sergio, b. 1947, Spain. Singer (Bass-Baritone). Education: Studied in Madrid, Barcelona and Milan. Career: Sang at Opera Houses in Spain from 1971; Appeared as Rigoletto in Valencia and sang in Paris, Marseilles, Bologna and Seville; Liege 1987-88 as the four villians in Les Contes d'Hoffmann; Teatro Real Madrid, 1989, as Gerard in Andrea Chénier; Other roles include Wagner's Dutchman, Athanael in Thais, Mephistopheles in La Damnation de Faust and parts in operas by Verdi. Honours: Prizewinner at Beniamino Gigli Competition Macerata and the Voci Verdiane at Parma, 1974.

DE SARAM Rohan, b. 9 Mar 1939, Sheffield, Yorkshire, England. Cellist. Education: Studied in Ceylon, with Gaspar Cassado in Florence and with Casals in Puerto Rico; Further study with John Barbirolli. Career: Gave recitals and concerts in Europe; US debut with New York Philharmonic, Carnegie Hall, 1960; Further concerts in Canada, USSR, Australia and Asia; As a soloist in addition to standard repertoire has worked personally with Kodály, Walton, Shostakovich; Premieres of works by Pousseur and composers of the younger generation; Has taught at Trinity College of Music; Member, Arditti Quartet (repertoire includes works by Boulez, Carter, Ferneyhough, Henze, Ligeti and many other living composers); Has also premiered works by Böse, Britten, Bussotti, Cage, Davies, Glass, Gubaidulina, Hindemith, Kagel, Nancarrow, Rihm and Schnittke, with Arditti Quartet; As soloist has premiered Kottos for solo cello by Xenakis, Ligeti's Racine 19 and Berio's Il Ritorno degli Snovidenia for cello and orchestra; Played in the Russian Spring series at South Bank, May 1991, Quartets by Rozlavets, Schnittke and Firsova; Founder, de Saram Clarinet Trio and a duo with his brother Druvi; Interested in the music of his native Sri Lanka and plays the Kandyan drum. Address: 20 St Georges Avenue, London N7, England.

DE SICA Gennaro, b. 1938, Naples, Italy. Singer (Tenor). Education: Studied at Umberto Giordano Conservatory, Foggia, and with Carlo Tagliabue in Rome. Debut: Spoleto, 1963, as Ferrando in Così fan tutte. Career: Has sung in such Italian opera centres as Genoa, Milan, Florence and Naples; Guest appearances in Germany at Frankfurt, Karlsruhe, Darmstadt, Nuremberg, Bonn and Kiel; Has also sung at Royal Opera in Copenhagen; Other roles have included Mozart's Don Ottavio and Tamino, Donizetti's Ernesto and Nemorino, Lionel in Martha, Rossini's Almaviva, Comte Ory, Don Ramiro, Lindoro and Narciso, Il Turco in Italia, Verdi's Duke, Alfredo and Fenton, Lensky in Eugene Onegin and David in Die Meistersinger. Address: c/o Teatro alla Scala, 2 Via Filodrammatici, 20121, Milan, Italy.

DE SIMONE Bruno, b. 1957, Naples, Italy. Singer (Baritone). Education: Studied with Sesto Bruscantini. Debut: Spoleto, 1980, as Valentin in Faust and Albert in Werther. Career: La Scala Milan debut, 1990, in Pergolesi's Lo frate 'nnammurato; Teatro San Carlo, Naples, from 1991, in Pergolesi's Flaminio, Don Giovanni and Paisiello's L'Idolo cinese; Has also sung at Florence in Paisiello's Barbiere di Siviglia and Pergolesi's Livietta e Tracollo; Macerata, 1992, as Malatesta, Naples, 1994, in Haydn's Mondo della Luna; Other roles include Rossini's Figaro, Taddeo, Dandini, Magnifico, Rimbaud and Germano, Mozart's Figaro, Alfonso, Guglielmo, Count and Leporello, Donizetti's Dulcamara, Belcore and Sulpice; Sang Geronimo in Il Matrimonio Segreto at Rome, 1996. Address: Atholl Still Ltd, Foresters Hall, 25-27 Westow Street, London SE19 3RY, England.

DE SMET Raoul, b. 27 Oct 1936, Antwerp, Belgium. Professor of Linguistics; Composer. m. Marisa Seys, 26 May 1962, 1 son, 3 daughters. Education: MPhil, Catholic University of Louvain; Postgraduate Diploma in Spanish Literature, University of Salamanca, Spain; Music Academy, Deurne; Composition with A Verbesselt and Ton de Leeuw, electronic music with L Goethals, Ipem Gent. Debut: Darmstadt Ferienkurse Neue Musik. Career: Professor of Spanish Linguistics and Translation, Kath Vlaamse Hogeschool, Antwerp, 1969-97; Founder of Orphische Avonden playing concerts of new chamber music, 1974; Publisher, EM-Reeks, new music of Flemish Composers, 1981; Foundation of Orpheus-Prijs Contest for interpretation of new chamber music, 1987. Compositions: Chamber Opera: Ulrike 1979, 1988, Vincent, 1990; Concerto for Sax Alto, Strings, Accordion and Percussion, 1992; Concerto for Violin and Symphonic Orchestra, 1993; 2 String Quartets; Clarinet and String Quartet; Octopus for 8 Bass Clarinets; Track-Sack-Fantasy for 10 accordions; Logbook 1, cello suite; Gnomons 2 for 4 Trombones and Stereotape; Soledad Sonora for Sax Alto. Recordings: Numerous. Memberships: SABAM; Unie Belgische Componisten; Stichting Orpheus; CeBeDeM. Address: Ruytenburgstraat 58, B-2600 Berchem, Belgium.

DE VALOIS Ninette, Dame, b. 6 June 1898, Baltiboys, Blessington, County Wicklow, Ireland. Founder, Director, Royal Ballet; Founder, Royal Ballet School. m. Dr A.B. Connell, 1935. Career: Prima Ballerina, Royal Opera Season, Covent Garden (International), May to July 1919, again in 1928; Premiere Danseuse, British National Opera Company, 1918; Member, Diaghilev Russian Ballet, 1923-26; Choreographic Director to Old Vic, The Festival Theatre, Cambridge, and The Abbey Theatre, Dublin, 1926-30; Founder, The National School of Ballet, Turkey, 1947; Founder, Director, Royal Ballet (formerly the Sadler's Wells Ballet), Royal Opera House, Covent Garden and the Sadler's Wells Theatre Ballet, Sadler's Wells Theatre, 1931-63; Founder, Royal Ballet School (formerly the Sadler's Wells School of Ballet). Compositions: Principal Choreographic Works: Job; The Rake's Progress; Checkmate; Don Quixote. Publications: Invitation to the Ballet, 1937; Come Dance with Me, 1957; Step by Step, 1977. Honours: Hon DFA, Smith College, Massachusetts, USA, 1957; Hon LLD, Aberdeen, 1958, Sussex 1975; FRAD, 1963; Chevalier of the Legion of Honour, 1950; Gold Albert Medal, RSA, 1964; Jointly, Erasmus Prize Foundation Award (first woman to receive it), 1974; Irish Community Award, 1980; OM, 1992; CH, 1982; DBE, 1951; CBE, 1947; Hon DMus, Cambridge University, 1992. Address: c/o Royal Ballet School, 153 Talgarth Road, London W14, England.

DE VAUGHN Paulette, b. 8 August 1951, California, USA. Singer (Soprano). Education: Studied with Martial Singher at Santa Barbara, at Juilliard School and in Vienna. Debut: As Elisabeth de Valois at Paris Opera. Career: Appearances at National Theatre Prague from 1980, as Tosca, the Trovatore Leonora, Mimi, Amelia, Bello in Maschera, Lady Macbeth, Turandot, Violetta and Abigaille; Sang Tosca at Stockholm 1988 and in season 1989-90 appeared as Savonlinna, as Tosca at Graz, as Mozart's Electra at Mannheim, Manon Lescaut, Staatsoper Berlin, Elena in I Vespri Siciliani and Komische Oper Berlin, Dresden and Sofia; Saarbrucken as Aida, Salome, Senta, Elsa and Leonore in Fidelio; Sang Aida at Royal Opera Copenhagen, 1991 and at Palma and the Montpellier Festival 1992; Concerts and Lieder recitals in Austria, Germany and Sweden. Address: c/o Det Kongelige Teater, Box 2185, DK-1017, Copenhagen, Denmark.

DE VOL Luana, b. 30 November 1942, St Bruno, San Francisco, California, USA. Singer (Soprano). Education: San Diego University with Vera Rozsa in London and with Jess Thomas. Debut: San Francisco 1983, as Ariadne auf Naxos. Career: European debut Stuttgart 1983, as Leonore in Fidelio; Sang the Forza Leonora at Seattle 1983 and appeared at Aachen and Amsterdam; Member of Mannheim Opera from 1986; Appearances in Berlin, Staatsoper and Deutsche Oper from 1986 as Euryanthe, Agathe, Rezia in Oberon, Leonore and Senta; Staatsoper, Hamburg 1989, as Irene in Rienzi, Zurich and Vienna 1989 as Ellen Orford in Peter Grimes and Eva in Schreker's Irrelohe; Further engagements in Bologna, Dortmund, Gelsenkirchen and Frankfurt and at Bregenz and Orange Festivals; Sang Amelia in Ballo in Maschera at Stuttgart and Leonore in a concert performance at Festival Hall 1990; Gutrune in Götterdämmerung concert in Rome and Elsa in Lohengrin at Taormina, both conducted by Sinopoli 1991; Sang Marina in Dvorak's Dimitrij at Munich, Leonore at Zurich and Andromache in Reimann's Troades at Frankfurt, 1992; Sang Strauss's Empress at the Paris Châtelet, 1994; Other roles include Donna Anna, Isolde, Elisabeth de Valois and Elisabeth in Tannhäuser, Brünnhilde and the Marschallin; Concert repertoire includes the Britten War Requiem and Shostakovich's 14th Symphony. Recordings include: Eva in Schreker's Irrelohe (Sony). Address: c/o Nationaltheater, Am Goetheplatz, 6800 Mannheim, Germany.

DE WAAL Rian, b. 1958, The Netherlands. Concert Pianist. Education: Studied at Sweelinck Conservatory, Amsterdam; Master classes with Rudolf Serkin and Leon Fleisher. Career: Regular concert appearances with the Concertgebouw Orchestra, Rotterdam and Stuttgart Philharmonics, Polish and Radio Chamber Orchestra and the State Orchestra of Lithuania; Further concerts and recitals in Boston, Washington DC, Atlanta and Montreal and on tour to Poland; Performs works by Godowsky, Balakirev and Tausig, as well as contemporary Dutch composers, in addition to the standard repertoire. Recordings: Numerous. Honours: Prizewinner at Vianna da Motta Competition, Lisbon, 1979, and the Queen Elisabeth Competition in Brussels, 1983. Address: c/o Robert Gilder and Company, Enterprise House, 59-65 Upper Ground, London SE1 1PQ, England.

DE WAART Edo, b. 1 June 1941, Amsterdam, Netherlands. Conductor. Education: Studied oboe with Haakon Stotijn at the Amsterdam Conservatory; Conducting with Franco Ferrara at Hilversum, 1964; Assistant conductor, New York Philharmonic, 1965-66. Career: Co-principal oboe with Amsterdam Philharmonic, 1961, and Concertgebouw Orchestra, 1963; Conducted Stravinsky's The Soldier's Tale at the 1965 Spoleto Festival; Musical Director of the Netherlands Wind Ensemble and assistant conductor, Concertgebouw Orchestra, 1966; Co-conductor, Rotterdam Philharmonic, 1969; Musical Director, 1973-79; San Francisco Symphony, 1975-83; Minnesota Orchestra, 1988-95; UK debut, 1969, with Royal Philharmonic; Covent Garden debut, 1976, Ariadne auf Naxos; Bayreuth, 1985; Guest conductor with leading orchestras in the US and Europe; Recent engagements with the Berlin Philharmonic, Chicago Symphony and Boston Symphony Orchestras, Deutsches Sinfonie Orchester Berlin and the Royal Concertegebouw; Wagner's Ring cycle at San Francisco, 1985; Conducted John Adams's Nixon in China for Netherlands Opera, 1987-88; Artistic Director of the Dutch Radio Organization, Nederlandse Omroep Stichtung; Chief Conductor of the Netherlands Radio

Philharmonic from 1989; Recent Productions include Parsifal, The Trojans and Salome with the Netherlands Radio Philharmonic, and Boris Godunov for Geneva Opera; Further opera engagements include Der Rosenkavalier at the Opera de Bastille in Paris, and Die Zauberflöte at the Metropolitan Opera in New York; Conducted Chausson's Le Roi Arthus, at the 1994 Holland Festival; Chief Conductor and Artistic Director of the Sydney Symphony Orchestra, from 1993 (European Tour 1995). Recordings: Wide repertoire with the Concertgebouw, Rotterdam, San Francisco and London Philharmonic Orchestras; Mozart with the Netherlands Wind Ensemble and recent Mahler cycle with the Netherlands Radio Philharmonic for BMG. Address: c/o Harrison Parrott Ltd, 12 Penzance Place, London W11 4PA, England.

DEACON Nigel, b. 6 January 1957, Leicester, England. Chemistry Educator; Composer. m. Alison Glithero, 11 April 1995. Education: Natural Sciences, St Catharines College, Cambridge; Piano, 1967-82, Composition, 1982-88. Career: Energy Research, GEC Alsthom, 1978-; Chemistry Educator, Wyggeston and Queen Elizabeth I College, Leicester, 1979-; Composer, 1979-. Compositions: Five Fugues, 1986; Five French Nursery Tunes, 1986; Three Diversions, 1986; Six Folktune Settings, 1986; Six Miniatures, 1987; Twelve Folktune Settings, 1987; Three Chorals, 1987; Six More Minatures, 1988; Five Sonatas, 1989; Twenty Four Folktune Settings, 1995; Three Scottish Airs, 1995; Twelve Folktune Preludes, 1996; Six Preludes, 1996. Publications: Technical Publications, 1978-97; Scientific Articles, 1984-97. Contributions to: International Talking Machine Review. Membership: Association of Teachers and Lecturers. Hobbies: Collecting early keyboard music and complete works of minor composers. Address: 56 Arbor Road, Croft, Leicestershire LE9 3GD, England.

DEAK Csaba, b. 16 Apr 1932, Budapest, Hungary. Composer; Teacher. Education: Studied Clarinet and Composition, Bela Bartók Conservatory, Budapest, 1949-55; Composition with Ferenc Farkas, Budapest Academy of Music, 1955-56, with Hilding Rosenberg, Sweden; Composition, Clarinet, Conducting, Ingesund School of Music, Arvika; Teacher's Certificate Stockholm Musikhögskolan, 1969. Career: Teacher: Swedish State School of Dance, Stockholm, 1969-; University of Göteborg, 1971-74. Compositions: Jubilemus Salvatori, chamber cantata, 1958; 2 string quartets, 1959, 1967; Duo Suite for flute and clarinet, 1960; The Fathers, chamber opera, 1968; 121 for winds, percussion, double bass, 1969; Etude on Spring, 1970; Trio for flute, cello, piano, 1971; Andante och Rondo for wind quintet, 1973; Lucie's Ascent into Heaven, astrophonic minimelodrama, 1973; Verbunk for brass sextet, 1976; Bye-bye, Earth, A Play About Death, 1976-77; Hungarian Dances for Wind Quintet, 1977; Octet for wind quintet and string trio, 1977; Eden for symphonic band, 1978; The Piper's Wedding for wind quintet and symphonic band, 1979; Herykon for brass quintet, 1981; Vivax for orchestra, 1982; 5 Short Pieces for symphonic band, 1983; Farina Pagus for symphonic band, 1983; Massallians for trumpet, trombone, brass ensemble, percussion, 1985; Saxophone Quartet, 1986; Quintet for alto saxophone and string quartet, 1988; Concerto Maeutro for trumpet, euphonium, marimba, symphonic band, 1989; Quartet for tubas, 1990; Ad Nordiam Hungarica for chamber ensemble, 1991; Concerto for clarinet and wind orchestra, 1992; Anémones de Felix for symphonic band, 1993; Magie Noire for clarinet and string quartet, 1993; Novem for saxophone quartet and brass quintet, 1994; Piano pieces; Choruses; Songs. Recordings: Several compositions. Honour: Atterberg Music Prize, 1992. Memberships: Vice-Chairman, Samtida Musik chamber music society, Stockholm. Address: Döbelnsgatan 56, S-113 52 Stockholm, Sweden.

DEAN Robert, b. 4 September 1954, Surrey, England. Conductor; Vocal Coach. Education: Durham University, 1973-76; Royal College of Music; Royal Northern College of Music, 1976-78; National Opera Studio, 1978-80. Debut: As Baritone, Musica Nel Chiostro, Alidord, Crontea, 1979; As Conductor, Batgnano Festival, Leonora, 1987. Career: Appearances with Covent Garden, ENO, Glyndebourne Festival & Touring, Scottish Opera, Opera North, Welsh National Opera, 1979-86; Scottish Opera Music Staff, 1988-, Head of Music, 1990-; Conducted Over 100 Performances, 1993-; Freelance: Canadian Debut, Edmonton Opera, 1993; USA Debut, Kentucky Opera, 1995. Recordings: Coronation Anthems; Video, Rossini Barbierg Di Sniglia. Current Management: Robert Gilder & Co. Address: 51 Lyndhurst Drive, Leyton, London E10 6SB, England.

DEAN Roger Thornton, b. 6 September 1948, Manchester, England. Composer; Double Bass Player. Education: BA, Cambridge University, 1970, MA, PhD, 1973; DSc, Brunel University, 1984. Career: Professor, Brunel University, 1984-88; University of Sydney, 1988-. Compositions include: Destructures, for trumpet and large ensemble, 1979; Breaking Worlds, for violin, clarinet and double bass, 1980; Heteronomy 1-4 for ensemble, 1982; BA & BA for brass quintet, 1985; Timestrain, for clarinet and piano, 1989; Reel Choice for ensemble, 1989; Time Dance Peace, for dancers and 8 instruments, 1991; It Gets Complicated, for speaking pianist, 1992; Poet Without Language, for voices and electronics, 1992; Nuaghic Echoes, for voice and electronics, 1993. Honours include: Development Fellowships from the Arts Council of Great Britain. Address: c/o APRA, 1A Eden Street, Crows Nest, NSW 2065, Australia.

DEAN Stafford, b. 20 June 1937, Kingswood, Surrey, England. Singer (Bass). Education: Epsom College; Opera Scholar at Royal College of Music; Studied with Gordon Clinton and privately with Howell Glynne and Otakar Kraus. Career includes: Toured with Opera For All, 1962-63 and 1963-64; Glyndebourne debut as Lictor in L'Incoronazione di Poppea, 1964, also as Le Bailli in Werther and Rochefort in Anna Bolena; With Sadler's Wells Opera, ENO, 1964-70 with debut, Zuniga, also as Sarastro and Padre Guardiano; Covent Garden debut as Masetto, 1969-; also as Nightwatchman in Meistersinger, Narbal in Trojans and Alfonso d'Este in a new production of Lucrezia Borgia; Guest appearances at many international venues including: Metropolitan Opera, New York, Chicago Lyric Opera, Aix-en-Provence, San Francisco, Toronto, Stuttgart, Munich, West Berlin, Vienna, Paris, Barcelona, Madrid, Amsterdam, Geneva, Hamburg, Zurich, Cologne and Bonn; Concert appearances include: Beethoven's 9th Symphony, Missa Solemnis, Verdi Requiem; Bass Soloist in world premiere of Penderecki Requiem, Stuttgart 1984; TV appearances: Sparafucile in Rigoletto, Daland in The Flying Dutchman, BBC, Così fan tutte at Glyndebourne, Lucrezia Borgia, 300th performance as Leporello in Don Giovanni at Covent Garden; Other roles include: Arkel, Seneca, Kecal and Osmin; Sang Don Pedro in Beatrice and Benedict at London Coliseum, 1990, Gessler in Guillaume Tell at Covent Garden, 1990, 1992, Melisso in new production of Handel's Alcina, 1992-93; Sang Rocco in Fidelio for Scottish Opera at the 1994 Edinburgh Festival; Bishop of Cadiz in Pfnitzer's Palestrina at Covent Garden, 1997. Recordings: Idomeneo, I Lombardi; A Midsummer Marriage; Monteverdi Madrigals; Anna Bolena; Oedipus Rex; The Rake's Progress; The Beggar's Opera; Orfeo; Beethoven's 9th Symphony; L'Enfance du Christ; A Village Romeo and Juliet; Yeomen of the Guard; Mikado; Don Giovanni. Current Management: Allied Artists. Address: c/o Allied Artists, 42 Montpelier Square, London, SW7 1JZ, England.

DEAN Timothy, b. 1956, England. Conductor. Education: Studied at Reading University and at the Royal College of Music. Career: Has worked with Opera North, the Buxton Festival Opera and the Royal Opera House, Covent Garden; Kent Opera, 1983-90, conducting Cosi fan tutte, Agrippina, The Magic Flute, La Traviata, Carmen, Le Comte Ory and Don Giovanni on the company's visit to the Singapore Festival; Conducted Martin's Le Vin Herbé for the London Music Theatre Group and the British premiere of Legrenzi's Guistino for the Chichester Festival; Vivaldi's Juditha Triumphans at the Camden Festival; Acis and Galatea for the English Bach Festival in Italy; Music Director of British Youth Opera, conducting Don Giovanni and The Marriage of Figaro in London and on tour; Music Director of the London Bach Society from 1988, appearing with them at Chichester and City of London festivals and on the South Bank; Season 1990-91, Assistant Music Director of New D'Oyly Carte Opera Company (conducting in UK and USA); English National Opera debut, 1991, with Bluebeard's Castle and Oedipus Rex; Scottish Opera debut, 1991, with Barber of Seville; Music Director of The Opera Company, Tunbridge Wells, 1991-94; Also with British Youth Opera, conducting Così fan tutte, Eugene Onegin, La Bohème, Carmen and La Gazza Ladra; In 1994 conducted Kent Opera in The Prodigal Son at major UK festivals and for the BBC; Since Sept 1994 Head of Opera at the Royal Scottish Academy of Music and Drama, Glasgow; Conducted British Youth Opera in Albert Herring, 1996. Address: c/o RSAMD, School of Music, 100 Renfrew Street, Glasgow G2 3DB, Scotland.

DEAN Winton (Basil), b. 18 Mar 1916, Birkenhead, England. Author; Musicologist. m. Hon Thalia Mary Shaw, 4 Sep 1939, 1 s, 3 d (2 deceased, 1 adopted). Education: MA, Classics and English, King's College, Cambridge, 1940. Career includes: Translated Libretto of Weber's Opera Abu Hassan, Arts Theatre, Cambridge, 1938; War Service, Naval Intelligence, 1944-45; Music Panel, Arts Council, 1957-60; Ernest Bloch Professor of Music, University of CA, Berkeley, USA, 1964-65; Regent's Lecturer, 1977; Matthew Vassar Lecturer, Vassar College, 1979; Editor, with Sarah Fuller, Handel's Opera Julius Caesar, 1977; Trustee and Member Committee, The Handel Institute, 1987. Publications include: The Frogs of Aristophanes, 1937; Bizet, 1948, 3rd revised edition, 1975; Carmen, 1949; Introduction to The Music Of Bizet, 1950; Franck, 1950; Handel's Dramatic Oratorios and Masques, 1959; Shakespeare and Opera, 1964; Georges Bizet, His Life and Work, 1965; Beethoven and Opera, 1971; Editor, E J Dent, The Rise of Romantic Opera, 1976; The New Grove Handel, 1982; Handel's Operas 1704-1726 (with J M Knapp), 1987, revised edition, 1995; Essays on Opera, 1990. Contributions to: Grove's Dictionary of Music and Musicians; Music and Letters; Musical Times; Opera. Honours: Honorary Member, Royal Academy of Music, 1971; Fellow, British Academy, 1975; Corresponding Member, American Musicological Society, 1989. Memberships: Royal Musical Association, Council, 1965-, Vice President, 1970-; G F Handel Gesellschaft, Halle, Member of Vorstand, 1979-, Vice President, 1991-; Göttinger Handel Gesellschaft, Member of Curatorium, 1981-; International Musicological Society. Hobbies: Cricket; Shooting; Naval History. Address: Hambledon Hurst, Godalming, Surrey, GU8 4HF, England.

DEARNLEY Christopher (Hugh), b. 11 Feb 1930, Wolverhampton, England. Organist. m. Bridget Wateridge, 3 sons, 1 daughter. Education: MA, Worcester College, Oxford; DMus (Lambeth), 1987; DFA, Westminster College, 1989; FRCO. Career: Assistant Organist, 1954-57, Organist, Master of Choristers, 1957-68, Salisbury Cathedral; Organist, Director of Music, St Paul's Cathedral, London, 1968-90; Acting Director of Music, Christ Church St Laurence, Sydney, New South Wales, Australia, 1990-91; Organist locum tenens, St David's Cathedral, Hobart, Tasmania, 1991; Director of Music, Trinity College, University of Melbourne, Victoria, 1992-93; Master of Music, St George's Cathedral, Perth, Western Australia, 1993-94; Acting Organist and Master of the Choristers, St Andrew's Cathedral, Sydney, 1995; Acting Organist and Choirmaster, Christ Church Cathedral, Newcastle, 1996. Compositions: Various church music pieces; Arrangements and editions of early church music. Recordings: Great Cathedral Organ Series nos 112 and 117; Organ Music from Salisbury and St Paul's Cathedrals, St Nicholas' Harwich, and Churches of the Barossa Valley; Numerous choir discs. Publications: The Treasury of English Church Music, vol 3; English Church Music 1650-1750. Contributions to: Church music journals. Honours: LVO, 1990; FRSCM, 1996. Hobbies: Sketching; Gardening. Address: PO Box 102, Wilberforce, New South Wales 2756, Australia.

DEATHRIDGE John, b. 21 Oct 1944, Birmingham, England. Musicologist. Education: Studied at Oxford University with Egon Wellesz and Frederic Sternfeld. Career: Lived in Germany during 1970s working as Conductor, Organist and Broadcaster; Fellow of King's College, Cambridge, 1983; Visiting Professor, Princeton University, USA, 1990-91; University of Chicago, 1992. Publications: Study of Wagner's Sketches for Rienzi, 1977; New Grove Wagner, with Carl Dahlhaus, 1984; Verzeichnis der musikalischen Werke Richard Wagners und ihrer Quellen, with Martin Geck and Egon Voss, 1986; Editor, The Wagner Handbook; Essays on Wagner's Life and Work, 1992; Editor, Family Letters of Richard Wagner, 1991. Contributions to: Cambridge Opera Journal and programme notes (Logengrin, for Covent Garden, 1997). Memberships: International Musicological Society; Royal Musical Association; Gesellschaft der Musikforschung; American Musicological Society. Address: King's College, Music Department, Cambridge, England.

DECKER Franz-Paul, b. 22 June 1928, Cologne, Germany. Conductor. Education: Studied with P Jarnach and E Papst, Cologne Hochschule für Musik; Studied with E Bucken and K Fellerer, University of Cologne. Career: Music Director, Krefeld, 1946-50; 1st Conductor, State Opera Wiesbaden, 1953-56; Municipal Music Director, Wiesbaden, 1953-56; Generalmusikdirektor, Bochum, 1956-64; Chief Conductor, Rotterdam Philharmonic Orchestra, 1962-68; Music Director, Montreal Symphony Orchestra, 1967-75; Principal Guest Conductor and Music Adviser, Calgary (Alberta) Philharmonic Orchestra, 1975-77; Artistic Adviser, Winnipeg Symphony Orchestra, 1981-82; Principal Guest Conductor, New Zealand Symphony Orchestra, Wellington, 1980-89; Music Director, Barcelona Symphony, 1986-; Chief Conductor, New Zealand Symphony, 1990-; Principal Guest Conductor, National Arts Centre Orchestra, Ottawa, 1991-; Conducted Das Rheingold at Buenos Aires, 1995. Recordings: Various. Honours: Professor Dr honoris causa; Bundesverdienstkreuz 1st Class, Germany; Herscheppend Schep ik Roquette Pinto Medal, Brazil; Medal, Netherlands; Queen Elizabeth II Jubilee Medal, Canada. Addres: 486 B Mount Pleasant Avenue, Westmount, Quebec, Canada.

DECKER Richard, b. 1958, USA. Singer (Tenor). Education: Studied at the Manhattan School of Music (master classes with Judith Haskin and Nan Merriman); Further study at the Zurich Opera studio. Career: Sang with Zurich Opera from 1985 and made guest appearances in Saarbrucken, at the Aix and Macerata Festivals (Ferrando in Cosi fan Tutte) and at the Vienna Staatsoper (in Zimmermann's Soldaten); Other roles include Alwa in Lulu (at Aachen) and has made frequent concert appearances, in Germany and Switzerland. Address: c/o Opernhaus Zurich, Falkenstrasse 1, CH-8008 Zurich, Switzerland.

DECKER Willy, b. 1950, Cologne, Germany. Stage Director. Career: Produced the world premiere of Henze's Pollicino at Montepulciano, 1980; Wozzeck at Covent Garden and Arabella for the Lyric Opera of Chicago, 1984; Le Nozze di Figaro in Brussels and Cosi fan tutte at Drottningholm, 1985; Capriccio for the Maggio Musicale Fiorentino, 1987; Rigoletto, Turandot and Carmen for the Teatro Colon in Bogota; Cologne productions include a Midsummer Night's Dream, Faust, La Finta Giardiniera, Barbe Bleue (1990), Der fliegende Holländer (1991) and Billy Budd (1992); Figaro, Cosí fan tutte and the world premiere of

Macbeth by Antonio Bibalo for the Norwegian Opera; Bonn Opera, 1990-91, Il Barbiere di Siviglia and Orfeo ed Euridice; Giulio Cesare by Handel for Scottish Opera, 1992; Other productions (in Germany) include Don Giovanni, Der Freischütz, Cenerentola, Der Rosenkavalier and Ariadne auf Naxos; Also engaged for: Cosí fan tutte, Den Norske Opera, Oslo, 1991; Orfeo, Bonn State Theatre, 1992; Macbeth Revival, Den Norske Opera, Dresden, 1992; Das Schloss, Berlin, 1992; Eugene Onegin, Cologne, Wozzeck, Amsterdam, 1993; Barber of Seville, 1993; Peter Grimes, Brussels, 1994; Soldaten, Dresden and Das Schloss at Munich; Elektra at Amsterdam, 1996. Address: c/o Haydn Rawstron Limited, P O Box 654, London SE26 4DZ, England.

DECKERT Hans Erik, b. 11 Jan 1927, Hamburg, Germany. Cellist; Conductor. Education: Diploma in Cello, Conducting, Musical Theory, Royal Danish Conservatory of Music, Copenhagen; Further study under Pablo Casals, Maurice Gendron, Igor Markevitch and Sergiu Celibidache. Debut: Solo debut (cello), Royal Conservatory of Music, Copenhagen, 1952. Career: Cellist, Royal Chapel, Denmark; Docent, Cello, Conducting, Chamber Music, Ingesunds Academy of Music, Sweden; Docent, Cello, Chamber Music, Esbjerg Academy of Music, Denmark; Docent, Cello, Conducting, Jutland Academy of Music, Denmark; Initiator of the Cello Academy, a 12-part cello ensemble of young European musicians. Compositions: Canzona Per Dodici Violoncelli and numerous compositions for choir. Recordings: Frequent radio broadcasts as cellist and conductor in Germany and Denmark. Publications: Cello School, Wilhelm Hansen, 1964; Ed, Mogens Heimann String Quartet Studies, 1995. Honours: Much in demand throughout Europe as Lecturer, Masterclass Teacher and Chambermusic Animator. Memberships: Honorary President and Founder of ESTA (Danish section), 1981; Danish Soloists' Union. Address: Norsmindevej 170, DK-8340 Malling, Denmark.

DECOUST Michel, b. 19 Nov 1936, Paris, France. Composer. m. Irene Jarsky, 1969, 1 daughter. Education: Studied Paris Conservatory under Louis Fourestier, Olivier Messiaen, Darius Milhaud; Studies with Stockhausen & Pousseur, Cologne, 1964, 1965, conducting studies with Boulez, Basle, 1965. Career: Professor of Composition, Dartington College summer school, England, 1967-69; Set up regional French orchestra, Pays de la Loire, 1967-70; In charge of musical activities, Maisons de la Culture, Rennes & Nevers, 1970-72; Founder, Director, Pantin Conservatory, 1972-76; Head, Education Department IRCAM, 1976-79; Chief Inspector for Musical Research, Ministry of Culture & Communications, 1979-; His music performed at various festivals, Europe, Israel, New York, also broadcast on radio, Italy, Germany, Spain, England, Greece, Switzerland, Poland, USA. Compositions: Orchestral, small ensemble, wind band and vocal works; instrumental solos & duos, electroacoustic music, etc; Recent works include: Si et Si Seulement, orchestra, 1972; L'application des Lectrices aux Champs, Soprano & orchestra, 1977; Eole, flute quartet, 1985; Figures II, bassoon, double bass, 1986; Marbre, magnetic tape, 1986; Sept Chansons Erotiques, settings of poems for soprano & piano, 1986; Bleus, text Balise Cendrars, soprano & piano, 1986; De la Gravitation Suspendue des Memoires, orchestra, 1986; Je qui d'Autre, 3 voices & ensemble, 1987; Sonate a quatre, 1987; Sinfonietta, 1983, for 10 instruments; Sonnet, 1985 for 15 instruments; One plus One Equals Four, Piano Percussion, 1988; Spectre for Wind Band, 1978; Interphone, Magnetic Tape; Les Galeries de Pierre, Alto Soto, 1984; Onde, Five Blaser, 1982; Olos, Saxo Solo, 1983; le Cygne, flute Solo, 1982; Lierre, 12 Cordes, 1986; Cafe-theatre, Chant-piano, 1985. Recording: Releve d'Esquisse, le Cygne, sinfonietta, Harmonia Mundi France, HMC 5152-HM57. Publications: Cahiers Perspectives, 1987. Memberships: President, ISCM France. Hobbies: Nature; Architecture. Address: 35 Rue de Clichy, 75009 Paris, France.

DECSENYI Janos, b. 24 Mar 1927, Budapest, Hungary. Composer. Education: Studied composition with Rezsö Sugar, Budapest Conservatory, 1948-52; Endre Szervanszky, Budapest Academy of Music, 1952-56. Career: Hungarian Radio, Budapest, 1952-, latterly as Head, Department of Serious Music and Director, Electronic Music Studio. Compositions: Stage includes: An Absurd Story, ballet, 1962; Orchestral: Divertimento for Harpsichord and Chamber Orchestra, 1959; Csontvary Pictures, 1967; Melodiae Hominis for Chamber Orchestra, 1969; Thoughts by Day, by Night, 1971; Commentaries on Marcus Aurelius for 16 Solo Strings, 1973; Double for Chamber Orchestra, 1974; Variations for Piano and Orchestra, 1976; Concerto Boemo, 1976; Concerto Grosso for Chamber Orchestra, 1978; Who Understands the Speech of Crickets?, for Chamber Orchestra and Tape, 1983; Cello Concerto, 1984; The Third One for 15 Solo Strings, 1985; I Symphony, 1986; II Symphony, 1993; Vocal: Love for Soprano and Orchestra, 1957; Metamorfosi for Soprano and Piano, 1964; Shakespeare Monologues for Bass and Piano, 1968; The Plays of Thought, cantata for Soprano and Chamber Orchestra, 1972; Roads, etudes for Soprano and Piano, 1979; Twelfth Symphony of S.W. for Soprano and Percussion, 1980; Chamber: String Trio, 1955; Sonatina Pastorale for Flute and Piano, 1962; String Quartet, 1978; Old Hungarian Texts, for Soprano, Bass and Chamber Ensemble, 1992; Choral Music: Incidental music for theatre, films and radio; Electronic: Stones, 1987; Prospero's Island, 1989; Birds of the Cathedral, 1991; Pedagogical pieces. Recordings: Several compositions recorded. Honour: Merited Artist, Hungary. Address: Wesselenyi u.65, Budapest, Hungary.

DED Jan, b. 22 June 1936, Plzen, Czech Republic. Composer. Education: Plzen Conservatory. Compositions: Four songs on the words of folk poetry, chorus, op 1, 1962; Wistful Variations, small ballet for 5 dancers, 5 musicians and reciter, op 38; Short Czech Mass for combined chorus and symphonic orchestra, op 42; Sonatine for Solo Viola, op 43; Great Czech-Latin Mass to Our Lady for combined chorus, soloists, symphonic orchestra and organ, op 44, 1992; Concerto of a serenade in E flat for clarinet in B and piano, op 51, 1996; Chamber works; Instructive compositions for children and youth. Recordings: Sonatina for Soprano Recorder and Guitar, op 17, 1979; Sonatina for Alto Recorder, op 16a, 1974, recorded 1997; New compositions just recorded. Memberships: Music Centre of West Bohemia, Plzen; Czech Music Society, Prague. Hobby: Growing flowers. Address: Zelenhorska 2, 31704 Plzen, Czech Republic.

DEDEN Otto, b. 19 November 1925, Amsterdam, Netherlands. Composer; Conductor; Organist; Choirmaster. m. S.A.M van Dijk, 4 children. Education: Studied Composition with Henk Badings. Career: Appearances in Church Services on Radio and TV; Choral Concerts with various male, female and mixed choirs. Compositions: 29 Masses; 50 Motets; Te Deum; Hymns; Ballads; Oratorios; Arrangements of Folk Songs (commissions), Dirge, Soprano with Organ, 1993; 5 two ballads, 1992; Mysteria; Kain; 4 Cantates for mixed choir and orchestra and solo; Magnificat for mixed choir, organ, flute and alto solo; Several Cantatas for choir and orchestra preludes and fugas for great organ; Requiem for a Killed Soldier. Recordings: Ballade v.d. Bezemsteel (male voices), Maastricht, 1958; Raamconcerto, 1973; Requiem for a Killed Soldier. Honours: Royal Order of Knighthood of Oranje Nassau, 1982; Order of Knighthood of Gregorius Magnus, Vatican; Medal of Honour of the City of Dordrecht, Netherlands. Hobby: Painting. Address: Polluxhof 16, Dordrecht, Netherlands.

DEDIU Constantin, b. 25 Dec 1932, Dragusani, Bacau, Romania. Musicologist; Journalist; Editor; Artistic Director. m. Emilia Babii, 31 Jul 1966, 1 d. Education: Iasi Music High School; Cluj GH Dima Music Academy. Career: Founder and Chief Editor, Music, Iasi RTV Post, 1958-82; Artistic Director, Iasi Romanian Opera, 1982-91; Freelance Music Journalist. Compositions: About 50 musical pieces including Lieder, Mass Choruses, Romances and Light Music. Publications: Din Culisele Muzicii, 1980; Broadcasting Cycles at Iasi RTV, 1982; Romanian Composers of Yesterday and Today, 60 broadcasts; The Youth of Music, The Music of The Youth, 50 broadcasts. Broadcasting Cycles at Iasi Radio Post: Musical Itinerary Through The World, 12 broadcasts, 1993 and Music Lover Writers, 55 broadcasts, 1993-94. Contributions to: The Music; The Chronicle; Iasi Daily Flame; Columnist for various journals. Honours: The Workers Medal, 1966; Cultural Merit Award, 1971. Memberships: Romanian Society of Composers and Musicologists; Romanian Society of Journalists; Committee, Literature and Art Theory and History, Iasi Section, Romanian Academy; Member of Senate, Isai Music Academy, 1982-1990; President of Iasi Branch of Romanian Association of Musical Interpreters, Composers and Critics. Hobby: Chess. Address: Str Prof Tafrali Nr 4, Iasi 6600, Romania.

DEFLO Gilbert, b. 22 Sept 1944, Menen, Belgium. Stage Director. Education: Studied at Brussels and in Milan with Giorgio Strehler. Debut: Love of Three Oranges, Frankfurt, 1974. Career: Staged Boris Godunov at Frankfurt then Pelléas et Mélisande and Ligeti's Le Grand Macabre at Hamburg; Further productions of Zemlinsky's Der Traumgörge at Nuremberg, World Premiere, 1980, the premiere of Thijl by Gilse at Amsterdam and The Woman Without a Shadow for Welsh National Opera, 1981; At the Théâtre de la Monnaie, Brussels from 1981 has staged Idomeneo, Don Carlos, Tristan und Isolde, Der fliegende Holländer, The Cunning Little Vixen, Cendrillon, Der Rosenkavalier and Simon Boccanegra; Premiere of La Forêt by Liebermann at Geneva, 1987; Production of Aida for Scottish Opera seen also at the Royal Opera Copenhagen, 1991; Produced The Queen of Spades at Barcelona, 1992; L'Incororezione di Popea at Buenos Aires, 1996. Address: c/o Theatre Royale de la Monnaie, Leopoldstrasse 4, B-100 Brussels, Belgium.

DEGRADA Francesco, b. 23 May 1940, Milan, Italy. Musicologist; Professor; Writer; Music Editor. Education: Diploma, Piano, 1961, Composition Diploma, 1965, Conducting, Milan Conservatory; Arts Degree, University of Milan, 1964. Career: Teacher, Bolzano Conservatory, Brescia Conservatory; Lecturer, 1964-76, Professor of Music History, 1976-, Director of the Arts Department, 1983-, University of Milan; Teacher, Milan Conservatory, 1966-73; Founder-Director and Harpsichordist, Complesso Barocco di Milano, 1967-76; Consultant to the Publisher, G Ricordi, 1971-; Member, Editorial Boards of Critical Editions of Vivaldi, Pergolesi and Verdi. Publications: Al Gran Sole Carico d'Amore, Per Un Nuovo Teatro Musicale, 1974 2nd edition, 1977; Sylvano Bussotti e il Suo Teatro, 1976; Antonio Vivaldi da Venezia all'Europe, 1977; Il Palazzo Incantato, Studi Sulla Tradizione del Melodramma dal Barocco al Romanticismo, 2 volumes, 1979; Vivaldi Veneziano Europeo, 1980; Edited Studi Pergolesiani/Pergolesi Studies, 2 volumes, 1986, 1988; Andrea Gabrieli e il Suo Tempo, 1988. Contributions to: Many articles in scholarly journals. Membership: Societa Italiana di Musicologia. Address: Via de Amicis 33, 20123 Milan, Italy.

DEHNER Jan, b. 21 July 1945, Prostějov, Czech Republic. Musicologist; Critic. Education: Conservatoire, Ostrava, 1959-65; Charles University, Praha, 1965-70; PhD, 1972, Musicology, Academy of Music, Praha, 1970-. Career: Department for the Research of the Czech Theatre, Czechoslovak Academy of Sciences, Praha, 1987-93; Dramaturgist, National Theatre Opera, Praha, 1993-96; Senior Editor, Musica, 1997-. Contributions to: Enzyklopädie des Musiktheaters; New Grove Dictionary; Contemporary Composers; Divadelné Revue; Hudební Veda; Hudební Rozhledy; Lidové Noviny; Opus Musicum; Scéna. Hobby: Travel. Address: Vavrenova 6, 142 00 Praha 4, Czech Republic.

DEKANY Bela, b. 22 Apr 1928, Budapest, Hungary. Violinist. m. Dorothy Browning, 22 Jun 1961, 1 s, 1 d. Education: Franz Liszt Academy, Budapest with Professor Weiner; Academy for Music, Vienna, Austria, with Professor E Morawec, Debut: Budapest, 1947. Career: Has given recitals and broadcast performances; soloist with orchestras in Hungary, Austria, Switzerland, Australia and UK; Formed Dekany String Quartet, Netherlands, 1960-68; Leader, BBC Symphony Orchestra, London, England, 1969-92. Recordings: Haydn String Quartets with Dekany String Quartet. Hobbies: Reading; Table Tennis; Walking. Address: 68 Woodside Avenue, London, N6, England.

DEKLEVA Igor, b. 30 Dec 1933, Ljubljana, Slovenia. Professor; Concert Pianist. m. Alenka Dekleva, 2 sons. Education: Student, Postgraduate Student, Piano, Academy of Music, Ljubljana; Further studies, Siena, Salzburg and Musical Academy Munich; Doctorate in Philosophy of Music. Career: Concerts, recitals, performances with orchestras in Slovenia and abroad, with repertoire including baroque, romantic and contemporary works; Frequent appearances as Duo with Alenka Dekleva, including first appearance at Opatoja Theatre, 1967; Several concert tours and discs with world-famous violinist Michael Grube; Directed masterclasses in Piano in several countries; Author, Leader and Performer, 2 long TV series about piano masterpieces from the beginnings up to now and Slovene piano works; Professor of Piano and Piano Duet, Academy of Music, Ljubljana. Recordings: For radio and TV; Over 15 LPs. Publications: Many works for piano and choirs; 1st printed Slovene National Piano School, 8 volumes. Honours include: Betetto Prize; Highest Honorary Award of Cleveland City; Numerous honorary memberships and fellowships worldwide. Memberships: Vice-President, Association of Musical Artists; Kiwanis International. Address: Celovska 106, 61000 Ljubljana, Slovenia.

DEL BIANCO Tito, b. 3 Jul 1932, Trieste, Italy. Dramatic Tenor Opera Singer. 1 s, 1 d. Education: Studied with Augusta Rapetti Bassi in Trieste and with Renata Cotogni in Rome. Debut: New York, USA in Stabat Mater by Rossini, director Thomas Schippers, 1965; In Italy as Otello by Verdi, 8th Festival of Two World, S Poleto, 1965. Career: In Title role of Otello, Teatro Regio Parma, 1966-71; Bayerische Staatsoper Munchen, 1973; May Festival Wiesbaden, 1970; Festival Szeged, Hungary, 1971; Festival Varna Bulgaria, 1972; Maggio Musicale Florence, 1980; Sang Calaf in Turandot at Naples, 1965, Bologna, 1969, Parma Regio, 1970; Pollione in Norma, Genoa, 1967; Faone in Saffo, Naples, 1967; Radames in Aida at Naples, 1968; Ismaele in Nabucco, Trieste, 1969; Canio in Pagliacci, Parma Regio, 1969; Festival Torre del Lago Puccini, 1971; Director of Studies Centre A Rapetti Bassi, Trieste; Professor of Music Academy, Conservatorio in Trieste. Recordings: Numerous. Publications: A Festival for Giuseppe Verdi in Prima Pagina, Parma, Italy, 1981; La Voce Cantata: Tecnica Vocale ed Espressione dell' Anima, 1988; La Scuola di Canto di Augusta Rapetti Bassi, 1990; Il Canto e la Psiche: L'Approccio al canto come Terapia, 1991. Contributions to: L'Espressione del Canto Nella Lezione di Reynaldo Hahn, 1993; La Parabola di Tristan und Isolde, 1993; Misticismo in Musica: Bruckner, Schönberg e Brahms, 1994; Lo Strumento voce: Aspetti, Didattici e docimologici, in Capriccio di Strauss, 1996. Honour: Gold Medal, Giuseppe Verdi Prize, Parma, 1967. Hobbies: Reading; Swimming. Address: c/o G Freudlsperger, Eschenweg 8, Elsbethen, Salzburg A-5061, Austria.

DEL BOSCO Carlo, b. 1945, Italy. Singer (Bass). Career: Sang at Como and Treviso before appearances at La Scala,

Milan, in season 1970-71; Guest engagements at Barcelona (1972), Philadelphia (Colline in La Bohème) and Cincinnati (Geronte in Manon Lescaut, 1974); Verona Arena, 1980-85, notably as the King in Aida and Bizet's Zuniga; Covent Garden, London, 1986, as Ashby in La Fanciulla del West; Other roles have included Raimondo in Lucia di Lammermoor, Rochefort in Anna Bolena, Zurga in Les Pêcheurs de Perles and the Consul in La Vestale. Address: c/o Arena di Verona, Piazza Bra 28, 37121 Verona, Italy.

DEL CARLO John, b. 21 Sept 1951, USA. Singer (Bass-baritone). Career: Sang in The Love for Three Oranges at San Diego (1978) and appeared with Western Spring Opera, 1980-81; European career from 1980, in Donizetti's Olivo e Pasquale at Barga; member of the Cologne Opera from 1987, and Rossini's Cambiale di Matrimonio at the 1987 Schwetzingen Festival; San Francisco Opera from 1982, as Alidoro in Cenerentola and Wagner's Kothner; Sang Donner and Gunther in Ring cycles for Seattle Opera, 1984-92; Other roles include the Wanderer in Siegfried (Cologne, 1990), Mustafa, Don Alfonso, Dulcamara and Simon Boccanegra; Sang Dulcamara at Santiago, 1996. Recordings include: La Gioconda (Decca), La Cenerentola (Philips) and La Cambiale di Matrimonio (Warner video). Address: c/o Seattle Opera Association, PO Box 9248, Seattle, WA 98109, USA.

DEL MAR Jonathan (Rene), b. 7 Jan 1951, London, England. Conductor; Musicologist. m. Annabel Teh Gallop, 5 Sept 1992, 1 son. Education: MA, Music, Christ Church, Oxford, 1969-72. Musical Education: ARCM Diploma, Royal College of Music, 1976; Teatro La Fenice, Venice, 1976-77; Accademia S Cecilia, Rome, 1977. Debut: London Symphony Orchestra, Barbican, 1984. Career: Conductor, performed with London Symphony Orchestra and other UK orchestras; Recent concerts in Denmark, Switzerland, Spain, Portugal, Romania. Publications: Urtext editions of Beethoven, Schubert, Weber, Rossini, Spohr, for Hanover Band, Orchestre Révolutionnaire et Romantique and Orchestra of the Age of Enlightenment; New Bärenreiter Urtext Edition of Beethoven Symphonies, No 9, Nos 3,8, others forthcoming. Contributions to: Tempo; BBC Music Magazine; Beethoven Journal; Das Orchester. Honours: Prize, Imperial Tobacco International Conductors' Award, 1978; Prize, Nikolai Malko Competition, 1980; Prize, First Leeds Conductors' Competition, 1984. Memberships: Incorporated Society of Musicians; Dvorak Society. Hobbies: Numismatics; Autonumerology. Address: Oakwood, Crescent Lane, London SW4, England.

DEL MONACO Giancarlo, b. 27 Dec 1943, Treviso, Italy. Stage Director. Education: Studied music and languages at Lausanne. Debut: Siracusa, 1964, Samson and Dalila. Career: Assistant to Gunther Rennert, Wieland Wagner and Walter Felsenstein at Stuttgart, 1965-68; Personal assistant of the General Director of Vienna Staatsoper, 1968-70; Principal Stage Director at Ulm, 1970-73; Intendant at Kassel, 1980-82; Director, Macerata Festival, 1986-88; Staged Les Huguenots at Montpellier, 1990 and at Barcelona, Roberto Devereux, the first of a projected trilogy of Donizetti's Tudor Operas; L'Elisir d'Amore at Helsinki, 1991, followed by Metropolitan Opera debut with La Fanciulla del West; Intendant and Principal Producer at Bonn, 1992-97; Further guest engagements at Bayerische Staatsoper, Zurich Opera and Vienna Staatsoper; Staged Montemezzi's L'Amore dei tre re at Kassel, 1992 and Otello at Reggio Emilia; Staged at the Metropolitan Madame Butterfly and Simon Boccanegra, 1994-95; La Forza del Destino, 1995-96. Honours: Bundesverdienstkreuz, 1st Class, 1987; Cavaliere Ufficiale della Repubblica, 1987; Commendatore Dell' Ordine al Merito della Repubblica Italiana, 1993; Chevalier des arts et lettres, France, 1995; Cruzeiro del Sul, Brazil, 1995. Current Management: Zemsky/Green Division, Columbia Artists Management Inc, 165 West 57th Street, New York, NY 10019, USA. Address: c/o Oper der Stadt Bonn, Am Boselagerhof 1, 53111 Bonn, Germany.

DEL TREDICI David (Walter), b. 16 March 1937, Cloverdale, California, USA. Composer; Teacher. Education: Studied Piano as a youth; Took courses in composition with Seymour Shifrin, Andrew Imbrie and Arnold Elston, University of California, Berkeley, BA, 1959, and with Earl Kim and Roger Sessions, Princeton University, MFA, 1963. Career: Debut as Piano Soloist with the San Francisco Symphony Orchestra at age 16; Pianist, Aspen (Colorado) Music Festival, 1958, Berkshire Music Center, Tanglewood, 1964, 1965; Composer-in-Residence, Marlboro (Vermont) Music Festival, 1966, 1967; Teacher, Harvard University, 1966-72; State University of New York at Buffalo, 1973, Boston University, 1973-84, City College and Graduate School of the City University of New York, 1984-; Composer-in-Residence, New York Philharmonic Orchestra, 1988-. Compositions: String Trio, 1959; I Hear an Army for Soprano and String Quartet, after James Joyce, 1963-64; Night Conjure-Verse, after James Joyce, 1965; Syzygy for Soprano, Horn and Chamber Ensemble, after James Joyce, 1966; The Last Gospel for Soprano, Chorus, Rock Group and Orchestra, 1967, revised 1984; Pop-Pourri for Amplified Soprano, Mezzo-Soprano ad libitum, Chorus, Rock Group and Orchestra, 1968, revised 1973; An Alice Symphony, after Lewis Carroll, 1969-75; Adventures Underground, after Lewis Carroll, 1971, revised 1977; Vintage Alice: Fantascence on A Mad Tea Party for Amplified Soprano, Folk Group, and Orchestra, after Lewis Carroll, 1972; Final Alice for Amplified Soprano and Orchestra, after Lewis Carroll, 1977-81; March to Tonality for Orchestra, 1983-85; Haddock's Eyes for Soprano and Chamber Ensemble, 1985-86. Recordings: Various Compositions recorded. Honours: Guggenheim Fellowship, 1966; American Academy and Institute of Arts and Letters Award, 1968; Naumberg Award, 1972; National Endowment for the Arts Grants, 1973, 1974, 1984; Pulitzer Prize in Music, 1980; Friedheim Award, 1982; Various commissions. Memberships: Elected a member of the Institute of the American Academy and Institute of Arts and Letters, 1984. Address: ASCAP, ASCAP House, One Lincoln Plaza, New York, NY 10023, USA.

DEL VIVO Graziano, b. 1 Nov 1937, Florence, Italy. Singer (Bass). Education: Studied at Florence University and Conservatory. Debut: Spoleto, 1961, as Ramphis in Aida. Career: Teatro Regio Parma, as Onofrio in Galuppi's I tre amanti ridicoli, 1964, and as Achillas in Handel's Giulio Cesare and Sparafucile in Rigoletto; Florence, 1965, in Billy Budd and Katerina Ismailova, returning in Robert Le Diable by Meyerbeer, 1968, and Spontini's La Vestale, 1970; La Scala Milan as Pluto in Casella's Orfeo; Edinburgh Festival, 1969 and 1972; Sang in The Nose by Shostakovich at Rome and at Genoa and Naples in the Verdi Requiem; Pisa, 1973, in a centenary concert for Titta Ruffo.

DELACOTE Jacques, b. France. Conductor. m. Maria Lucia Alvarez Machado. Education: Paris Conservatory; Studied with Hans Swarowsky, Vienna Academy of Music. Debut: New York Philharmonic Orchestra. Career: Guest conductor with the Cleveland Orchestra, San Francisco Symphony, Orchestre de Paris, Orchestre National de France, London Symphony Orchestra, Scottish National Orchestra, Berlin Radio Symphony Orchestra, Bavarian Radio Orchestra, Cologne Radio Symphony Orchestra, Südfunk Stuttgart; Vienna Philharmonic Orchestra; Vienna Symphony Orchestra; BBC London, London Philharmonic, Vienna State Opera, Royal Opera House, Covent Garden London, Paris Opera, Hamburg State Opera; Deutsche Oper Berlin; National Orchestra of Belgium, Scottish Chamber Orchestra, English Chamber Orchestra, Danish Royal Orchestra, Copenhagen, Tokyo Philharmonic Orchestra, Bavarian State Opera, Munich, Pittsburgh Opera, Chicago Lyric Opera; Israel Philharmonic Orchestra, Teatro Liceo, Barcelona, Teatro Real, Madrid, Teatro Colon, Buenos Aires, Théâtre de La Monnaie, Brussels, Opera House, Zürich, Scottish Opera, Glasgow, Welsh National Opera, Cardiff, English National Opera, Coliseum and Yomiuri Nippon Symphony; Festivals at Flandres, Macerata, Blossom; Klangbogen in Vienna; Festival of Inverness. Recordings: With Royal Philharmonic, Royal Opera House, Covent Garden Orchestra, Bavarian Radio Orchestra, London Philharmonic, London. Honours: Gold Medal and 1st Prize, Dimitri Mitropoulos Competition, New York, 1971. Hobby: Chess. Current Management: Dr Germinal Hilbert, Mazimilianstr 22, D-80539 Munich, Germany. Address: Neutorgasse 9-9, 1010 Vienna, Austria.

DELAY Dorothy, b. 31 March 1917, Medicine Lodge, Kansas, USA. Teacher of Violin. Education: Studied at Oberlin College, 1933-34; Violin Studies with Michael Press, Michigan State University, Hans Letz and Louis Persinger, Juilliard Graduate School of Music, Diploma, 1941. Career: Teacher, Juilliard from 1947; Further posts at Sarah Lawrence College, 1948-87, Meadowmount School of Music, Westport, 1948-70, Aspen School of Music from 1971; Starling Professor of Violin, University of Cincinnati College-Conseratory of Music from 1974, New England Conservatory of Music, Boston 1978-87; Master Classes in USA and abroad; Students have included, Shlomo Mintz, Itzhak Perlman, Cho-Liang Lin, Midori, Nigel Kennedy, Kyoko Takezawa, Sarah Chang, Gil Shaham. Honours: Artist Teacher Award, American String Teachers Association, 1975; Honorary DMus, Oberlin College, 1981; DMus, Michigan State University, and University of Colorado; President's National Medal of Arts, 1994; Honorary DMus, Columbia University, 1994; Fellow, Royal College of Music; Sanford Fellow, Yale University, 1997; American Eagle Award of the National Music Council, 1995. Address: c/o Juilliard School of Music, Violin Faculty, 60 Lincoln Center Plaza, NY 10023, USA.

DELDEN Lex (Alex) Van, b. 21 June 1947, Amsterdam, Netherlands. Actor; Singer (Tenor). Education: Drama School, Amsterdam, 1966-67; Private singing lessons with Jan Keizer, Marianne Blok and Andrew Field. Debut: 1967. Career includes: Opera: Gianni Schicchi (G Puccini); Turandot (F Busoni); Die Fledermaus (Johann Strauss); Il Ritorno d'Ulisse (Claudio Monteverdi); Ariadne auf Naxos (Richard Strauss). Compositions include: Active as composer for theatre: Romeo and Juliet (W Shakespeare); Dance of Death (A Strindberg); The Spanish Brabantine (Bredero). Hobbies: Music; Painting; Sculpture; Architecture; Literature. Address: c/o The Spotlight, London, England.

DELLA CASA Lisa, b. 2 Feb 1919, Burgdorf, Switzerland. Singer (Soprano). m. Dragan Debeljevic. Education: Studied with Margarete Haeser in Zurich. Debut; Solothun-Biel, 1941, as Madama Butterfly. Career: City Theatre, Zurich, 1943-50, as Pamina, Gilda and Serena in Porgy and Bess, and in the premiere of Willy Burkhard's Die schwarze Spinne; Joined Vienna Staatsoper, 1947; Salzburg Festival from 1947, as Zdenka in Arabella, the Countess in Capriccio, Mozart's Donna Elvira, Countess and Pamina, Ariadne, Chrysothemis, Octavian, the Marschallin and in the premiere of Von Einem's Der Prozess, 1953; Glyndebourne Festival, 1951, as the Countess in Le nozze di Figaro; Bayreuth, 1952, as Eva in Die Meistersinger; Covent Garden and La Scala Milan from 1953; Metropolitan Opera, 1953-68, as Mozart's Countess, Donna Elvira, Arabella, Eva, the Marschallin and Octavian; Sang Arabella in a new production of Strauss's opera at Covent Garden, 1965; Guest appearances at Paris, Chicago, Buenos Aires, Munich and Rome; Retired, 1974. Recordings: Le nozze di Figaro; Don Giovanni; Cosi fan tutte; Arabella; Orfeo ed Euridice; La Vie Parisienne. Hobby: Collecting antiques and pictures. Address: c/o Staatsoper, Opernring 2, A-1010 Vienna, Austria.

DELLA PERGOLA Edith, b. 12 June 1918, Cluj, Rumania. Professor of Music. m. Luciano Della Pergola, 1935 (dec. 1991), 1 daughter. Education: Royal Conservatory of Music, Bucharest, with Luciano Della Pergola; Further study in Florence, 1939. Debut: December 1936. Career: Leading Soprano, roles in La Bohème, Il Trovatore, Aida, Cavalleria Rusticana, The Queen of Spades, Eugene Onegin, Pagliacci, The Consul, Von Heute auf Morgen, Fledermaus, Zigeunerbaron, Bartered Bride, others; Appearances at Royal Opera, Bucharest, Cluj, Staatsoper, Vienna, Stadttheater, Zurich, Teatro Verdi, Trieste, Teatro San Carlo, Naples, Théâtre Flamand, Brussels, elsewhere; Teaching, Alberto Della Pergola Conservatory, Bucharest, 1942-47; Came to Canada, 1955; Professor of Music, Director, McGill Opera Studio, McGill University, Montreal, 1956-; Recitals, CBC Radio. Recordings: Il Trovatore with Edith Della Pergola (Leonora) and Jon Vickers (Manrico), telecast 1956, included in video Jon Vickers sings Verdi and Puccini, released 1993. Publications: Opera at McGill: The Della Pergola Years 1956-1989 (with Luciano Della Pergola), 1991. Honours: Order of Cultural Merit, King Michael of Rumania, 1945; Société des Concerts des Ecoles Juives Populaires et des Ecoles Peretz, Montreal; Emeritus Professor, McGill University, 1989; Order of Canada, 1993. Address: 2 Westmount Square, Apt 207, Westmount, Quebec, Canada H£Z 2S4.

DELLER Mark (Damian), b. 27 Sept 1938, St Leonards-on-Sea, England. Singer (Counter-Tenor). m. Shelagh Elizabeth Benson, 3 sons. Education: Chorister, Canterbury Cathedral; Choral Scholar, St John's College, Cambridge. Career: Lay Vicar, Salisbury Cathedral, 1960-68; Founder and Director, Guildhall Winter Concerts, 1962; Artistic Director, First festival of the Arts, Salisbury, 1967; Vicar-Choral, St Paul's Cathedral, 1969-73; Choral Conductor; Began recording with father Alfred Deller, 1962; Joined Deller Consort in early 1960s; Has toured extensively in Europe, USA, Canada and South America, as member of Deller Consort and as a solo singer; Director, Deller Consort, 1979-; Director, Stour Music and Canterbury Festival. Recordings: As member of Deller Consort, the Vanguard, Argo and Nonesuch labels; Purcell's The Fairy Queen, King Arthur and The Indian Queen (Harmonia Mundi). Hobbies: Gardening; Watching cricket; Walking. Address: 2 Rural Terrace, Wye, Ashford, Kent, England.

DELLO JOIO (Justin) Norman, b. 18 Oct 1915, New York City, New York, USA. Composer. Education: BM, MM, Doctoral candidate, Juilliard School of Music, New York. Career: Currently Professor of Composition, New York University; His works performed by Detroit Symphony Orchestra, Juilliard Orchestra with Sixten Ehrling, members of the Mendelssohn String Quartet, and Primavera String Quartet; Piano Sonata premiered in National Gallery of Arts, Washington, District of Columbia (also broadcast); Collaborated with American novelist John Gardner on opera The Holy Sinner. Compositions: Works for orchestra, chamber orchestra, string quartet, vocal music and solo piano. Recording: String Quartet No 1, Primavera String Quartet. Publications: Sonata for Piano, 1986; Musica Humana, Symphonic Poem for Orchestra. Honours: Charles Ives Scholarship, National Institute and American Academy of the Arts; Grants: New York State Council on the Arts, 1983; National Endowment for the Arts, 1985; New York Foundation for the Arts, 1986. Address: c/o ASCAP, ASCAP House, One Lincoln Plaza, New York, NY 10023, USA.

DELOGU Gaetano, b. 14 Apr 1934, Messina, Italy. Conductor. Education: Studied music, University of Catania; Law degree, 1958; Studied conducting with Franco Ferrara, Rome and Venice. Career: Guest Conductor, Italian Radio, Rome, Milan, Turin and Naples; New York Philharmonic Orchestra and National

Symphony Orchestra, Washington DC, USA, 1968-69; Conductor, Teatro Massimo, Palermo, Italy, 1975-78; Music Director with various European and US orchestras and opera companies. Recordings include: Haydn's Symphonies Nos 83 and 101; Mahler's 1st Symphony; Hindemith's Symphonic Metamorphosis and Nobilissima Visione. Honours: 1st Prize, Young Conductors' Competition, Florence, 1964; Dimitri Mitropoulos Competition, New York, 1968. Address: c/o Harold Holt Ltd, 31 Sinclair Road, London W14 0NS, England.

DELVAUX Albert, b. 31 May 1913, Louvain, Belgium. Director; Music Professor. m. Fernande Tassignon, 4 Apr 1945, 2 sons, 1 daughter. Education: Royal Conservatory, Liège (Diploma of Virtuosity on Violincello); Higher Diploma, Chamber Music; 1st Prize, Harmony, Counterpoint and Fugue and History of Music. Career: Head, Counterpoint, Royal Conservtory, Liège, 1945; Professor, Conservatory of Louvain and Tirlemont Academy until 1945; Honorary Director, St Nicolas Academy, 1945-78; Honorary Professor, Brussels Royal Conservatory until 1978. Compositions include: Symphony orchestra: Scherzo; Poème; Symphonique Suite; Variations; Miniatures; Sinfonia II; Sinfonia Burlesca I; Mouvement Symphonique; Sinfonie III; Concerto I and II for violin; Sinfonia IV; Capriccio for Orchestra; Chamber orchestra: Esquisses; Concerto da Camera I and II; 5 Bagatelles; Introduttione e allegro; Sinfonia Concertante for Violin and Alto; Concerto for Violin and Violoncello; Concerto I and II for Violoncello; Prelude for Flute; Concerto for Viola. Recordings: Sinfonia Burlesca; Esquisses; Trio No 2; Sonata a quattro; Concerto for oboe, clarinet, bassoon and flute. Honours: 1sr Prize Queen Elizabeth Symphonisch Music; 3rd Prize, Queen Elizabeth Chamber Music. Hobbies: Reading; Gardening. Address: Kwadeplas 3, 9180 Belsele, Belgium.

DELZ Christoph, b. 3 Jan 1950, Basel, Switzerland. Pianist; Composer. Education: Teaching and Concert Diploma for Piano; Musical studies in Cologne, Piano with Alois Kontarsky, Composition with Karlheinz Stockhausen and Conducting with Volker Wangenheim; Studied Composition with Henri Pousseur in Liège. Career: Worked in Electronic Studio of Cologne Academy of Music, 1979-81; Studied German and Philosophy at University of Cologne at same time; Lived in Cologne until 1989, now living in Riehen, near Basel; As Pianist has taken part in many first performances of works by contemporary composers including Klarenz Barlow, Mauricio Kagel and Claude Vivier; His choral works and most of his orchestral pieces have been performed or have received their first performances by BBC Symphony Orchestra and BBC Singers, among others at the Almeida Festival, Donaueschingen Festival and at concerts by West German Radio in Cologne, at Venice Biennial Festival, in Paris with the Ensemble Inter-Contemporain, at Lucerne Music Festival, at Zurich June Festival and at World Music Festival of International Society of New Music, Graz and Zurich; Repertoire includes music by Bach, Schumann, Liszt, Mussorgsky, Debussy, Janacek, Schonberg and Stockhausen. Recordings: Most of Delz's compositions have been recorded. Address: Sonneggstrasse 9, CH-4125 Riehen-Basel, Switzerland.

DEMARINIS Paul, b. 8 Oct 1949, Cleveland, Ohio, USA. Composer. Education: Studied at Antioch College, Ohio, and with Robert Ashley at Mills College, Oakland. Career: Taught composition and computer at Mills College, 1973-78; Wesleyan University, 1979-81, San Francisco State University, 1987-89; Collaborations as a performer with Robert Ashley and David Tudor in New York and Paris and at New Music America Concerts, 1980-85; Computer audio-graphic systems installed at Museum of Contemporary Art, Chicago and the Wadsworth Atheneum; Audio installations at the Exploratorium San Francisco and the Children's Museum, Boston. Compositions: Computer-processed speech works Kokole, 1985, and I Want You, 1986; Installations Pygmy Gamelin, Paris, New York and Los Angeles, 1976-80; Music Room, Faultless Jamming, San Francisco and Boston, 1982-; Laser Disk, Eindhoven, Netherlands, 1989. Address: c/o San Francisco State University, Music Department, 1600 Holloway Avenue, San Francisco, CA 94132, USA.

DEMBSKI Stephen (Michael), b. 1949, Boston, Massachusetts, USA. Composer; Professor. Education: Diploma, Phillips Academy, Andover, 1967; Clifton College, Bristol, England, 1967-68; Ecole Normale de Musique, Paris, 1971; BA, Antioch College, 1973; MA, State University of New York, Stony Brook, 1975; MFA, 1977, PhD, 1980, Princeton University; Currently, Professor. Career: Currently Professor, Director of Advanced Composition Programme, School of Music, University of Wisconsin, Madison; Music presented by: UNESCO, Denmark, 1978; 5th International Festival of Electronic-Acoustic Music, Bourges, France, 1976; International Society for Contemporary Music, Bonn, 1976; New York New Music Ensemble; American Composers' Orchestra; Huddersfield Festival, England; Alan Feinberg; Ursula Oppens; Fred Sherry; Robert Black; Christopher Kendall. Compositions: Recorded: Pterodactyl for piano, 1974; Tender Buttons for piano, 1977; Trio, 1977; Digit for clarinet and computer synthesized tape, 1978; Stacked Deck for large chamber ensemble, 1979; Alba for chamber ensemble, 1980; Alta for piano, 1981; Spectra for orchestra, 1985; Sonata for violin and piano; Of Mere Being for soprano and large orchestra; Sonotropism, for saxophone, piano, electric guitar, 1996. Published music: Sunwood for guitar, 1976; Sonata for violin and piano, 1987-88; The Show, 1986; Fantasy for solo flute, 1988; On Ondine for piano, 1992; Three Scenes from Elsaveta, opera, 1992; Memory's Minefield, 1994; At Baia, 1994; Out of my System, 1995. Publications: International Musical Lexicon, 1980; Milton Babbitt - Words About Music (with Joseph N Straus), 1987. Contributions to: Articles: Misreading Martino, Perspectives of New Music, 1991; The Context of Composition, Theory and Practice, 1992. Honours: Goddard Lieberson Award, American Academy and Institute of Arts and Letters; Fellowships, National Endowment for the Arts, 1979, 1981, 1986; Segnalazione, Premio Musicale Città di Trieste, 1990. Memberships: ASCAP; AMC; SMT. Address: 96 Perry Street B-22, New York, NY 10014, USA.

DEMETEROVA Gabriela, b. 17 May 1971, Prague, Czech Republic. Violinist. Education: Prague Conservatory, The Academy of Music in Prague. Debut: In Prague, concert in the 100th season the Czech Philharmonic Orchestra. Career: Czech Radio, interviews, solo performances; Solo concerts in the Czech Republic, England, France, USA, Holland, Germany, Austria, TV; TV major programs of the Czech television; Video recorded. Recordings: CD, The Old Czech Masters, HIF Biber, Mysterly Sonatas I and II (2 CDs), Violin recital - Mozart, Beethoven, Brahms. Publication: The Strad, The Yehudi Menuhin, violin competition, 1993. Contributions: All major Czech magazines and journals. Honours: All major prizes, J Kocian Violin Competition, 1980-90; Prague Spring Violin Competition, 1992; All major prizes, Yehudi Menuhin International Violin Competition, 1993. Membership: Friends of the Prague Spring Festival. Hobbies: Horse-riding; Biking. Current Management: Ars/Koncert - Brno, Uvoz 39, 602 00 Brno, Czech Republic. Address: Bilkova 21, Prague 1, 110 00 Czech Republic.

DEMIDENKO Nikolai, b. 1 July 1955, Aniskino, Russia. Concert Pianist. m. (1), 1 son, (2) Julya Dougyallo, 15 Aug 1994. Education: Studied at Moscow Conservatoire with Dmitri Bashkirov. Debut: British debut with Moscow Radio Symphony Orchestra, 1985. Career: Has performed in Russia and abroad in concert and recital from 1976; Frequent tours of Japan and concerts with Bolshoi Symphony, Polish National Radio Orchestra, London Philharmonic, BBC Philharmonic and BBC Scottish Symphony, London Proms debut 1992 with Rachmaninov's 4th Concerto; Resident in Britain from 1990, teacher at Yehudi Menuhin School; Season, 1992-93 in concerts with the St Petersburg Philharmonic and the Philharmonia Orchestra; Recitals in Paris, Milan and the Concertgebouw, Amsterdam; Two-Piano recital with Dmitri Alexeev at Wigmore Hall, March 1993, to mark the 50th Anniversary of Rachmaninov's death; Six Piano Masterworks solo recitals at Wigmore Hall, January to June 1993 recreating concerts given by Alkan and Rubinstein in the 19th Century: The Classicists, The Age of Beethoven, The Early Romantics, The High Romantics, The Baroque Revival and Legacies and Prophecies, Liszt, Berg, Gubaidulina and Messiaen; Returned to London for German Romantic concerts, 1997. Recordings: Albums of Bach-Busoni, Chopin and Liszt; Medtner 2nd and 3rd Concertos with BBC Scottish Symphony Orchestra, Medtner and Chopin Concertos with Philharmonia; Live recordings at Wigmore Hall Masterworks series. Honours: Medallist, 1976 Concours International de Montreal and 1978 Tchaikovsky International Competition, Moscow. Address: c/o Georgina Ivor Associates, 66 Alderbrook Road, London SW12 8AB, England.

DEMPSEY Gregory, b. 20 July 1931, Melbourne, Victoria, Australia. Singer (Tenor). Education: Studied in Australia with Mavis Kruger and Annie and Heini Portnoj. Debut: National Opera of Victoria, 1954, as Don Ottavio. Career: Sang with Sadler's Wells/English National Opera from 1962, notably as Wagner's Mime and David, Don José, Peter Grimes, Tom Rakewell, and in the premiere of Bennett's The Mines of Sulphur (1965); Sang in the first local production of Janácek's The Makropoulos Case (1966) and The Excursions of Mr Broucek (1979); Other roles include the Drum Major in Wozzeck, Dionysius in The Bassarids by Henze (British stage premiere), Aeneas in Les Troyens and the Shepherd in Szymanowski's King Roger (New Opera Company); US debut, San Francisco, 1966, in The Makropoulos Case; Aldeburgh Festival, 1967, in the premiere of Musgrave's The Decision; Covent Garden debut, 1972, as Laca in Jenufa; Sang Bob Boles in Peter Grimes, Sydney, 1986; Prince Populescu in Countess Marita at Melbourne, 1986. Recordings include: Billy Budd; The Ring of the Nibelung, conducted by Reginald Goodall (EMI).

DEMPSTER Stuart (Ross), b. 7 July 1936, Berkeley, California, USA. Trombonist; Professor; Composer. m. Renko Ishida, 19 Dec 1964, 2 sons. Education: BA, Performance, 1958, MA, Composition, 1967, San Francisco State College; Private Trombone lessons with AB Moore, Orlando Giosi and John Klock. Career: Principal Trombonist, Oakland Symphony Orchestra, California, 1962-66; Member, Performing Group, Mills College, 1963-66; Tours as Soloist, 1962-; Teacher, San Francisco Conservatory of Music, 1961-66; California State College, Hayward, 1963-66; Assistant Professor 1968-78, Associate Professor 1978-85, Professor 1985-, University of Washington, Seattle; Master Classes, International Trombone Workshop, 1974-. Compositions: Sonata for Bass Trombone and Piano, 1961; Adagio and Canonic Variations for Brass Quintet, 1962; Chamber Music 13 for Voice and Trombones, 1964; The Road Not Taken for Voice, Chorus and Orchestra, 1967; Ten Grand Hosery, Mixed Media Ballet, 1971-72; Pipedream, Mixed Media Piece, 1972; Life Begins at 40, Concert Series and Musical Gallery Show, 1976; Standing Waves for Trombone, 1976; Didjeridervish for Didjeridu, 1976; Monty for Trombone, 1979; Fog Calling for Trombone and Didjeridu, 1981; Harmonic Tremers for Trombone and Tape, 1982; Hornfinder for Trombone and Audience, 1982; Roulette for Trombone and audience, 1983; Aix en Providence for Trombones, 1983; JDBBBDJ for Didjeridu and Audience, 1983; Don't Worry, It Will Come for Garden Hoses and Audience, 1983; Sound Massage Parlor for Didjeridu, Garden Hoses, Shell and Audience, 1986; SWAMI (State of Washington as a Musical Instrument), an Acoustic Guide to the State of Washington for the State's Centennial, 1987-89; Milanda Embracing for unspecified mixed ensemble, 1993-94; Underground Overlays for conches, chanters and trombone, 1994-95; Caprice for unicycle riding trombonist, 1995; Various co-composed compositions with Pauline Oliveros, others in the Deep Listening Band, 1988-. Recordings: Numerous for major labels. Publication: The Modern Trombone: A Definition of Its Idioms, 1979. Address: c/o School of Music 353450, University of Washington, Seattle, WA 98195, USA.

DEMUS Jörg (Wolfgang), b. 2 Dec 1928, St Pölten, Austria. Pianist. Education: Vienna State Academy of Music, Austria, 1939-45; Studied Piano with Walter Kerschbaumer, Organ with Karl Walter, Composition with Joseph Marx, Conducting with H Swarowsky and Joseph Krips; Diploma of the State Academy, Vienna; Studies with Yves Nat (Paris), W Gieseking, W Kempff, A Benedetti-Michelangeli, Edwin Fischer. Compositions: Franckiana, 6 Little Pieces for Piano. Recordings: Has made 350 records, notably of music by Bach, Beethoven and Schubert, often in partnership with pianist Paul Badura-Skoda, accompanist to leading musicians including Dietrich Fischer-Dieskau, Edith Peinemann and the late Antonio Janigro. Publications: Die Klaviersonaten L v Beethoven, 1974; Abenteuer der Interpretation, 1976. Honours: Premio Busoni, Bolzano, 1956; Honorary Professor of Austria, 1977; Edison Prize, Amsterdam; The Harriet Cohen Bach Medal, 1977; Beethoven Ring, Vienna, 1977; Mozart Medal, Vienna Mozartgemeinde, 1979. Hobbies: Antiquities; Photography; Natural history. Current Management: Mr Roland Sölder, Vienna, Austria. Address: c/o Mr Roland Sölder, Döblinger Haupstrasse 77a, A-1190, Vienna.

DEMUYNCK Charles Michael Jay, b. 2 Jan 1968, Leduc, Alberta, Canada. Conductor. Education: Bachelor of Music, University of Toronto, 1989; Master's and Graduate Performance Diploma, Peabody Conservatory, 1991, 1992; DMA ABD, Hartt School, student of Harold Farberman; All degrees in conducting. Debut: Knoxville Symphony Orchestra, 1995. Career: Conducting apprentice, Hartford, Connecticut; Formerly Assistant Conductor, Knoxville Symphony; Music Director, Oakville Chamber Orchestra, 1995-; Conducting appearances in Ontario: Mississauga Symphony, Oshawa-Durham Symphony; North York Concert Orchestra; Philharmonie des Jeunes d'Ottawa-Carleton; L'Ensemble du Jour Présent; Conducting Faculty, University of Toronto. Honours: Hartt School Award of Excellence; Major Canada Council Grant; Grants from Peabody Conservatory; Percy Faith Award, University of Toronto. Memberships: Association of Canadian Orchestras; American Symphony Orchestra League; Conductors' Guild. Hobbies: Reading, mainly humanities. Address: 157 Jones Ave, Toronto, ON M4M 3A2, Canada.

DENCH Chris, b. 10 Jun 1953, London, England. Composer. m. Diana Palmer, 1 d. Career: Commissioned by Elision resulting in Driftglass, 1990-91, which represented Australia at '92 International Rostrum of Composers in Paris; the French Ministry of Culture; The ABC; the BBC; the Arditti String Quartet; australYSIS; Synergy; and others. His works have been performed by Ensemble Accroche Note of Strasbourg, the Berlin Radio Symphony Orchestra, Ensemble Exposé, Ensemble InterContemporain, London Sinfonietta, Music Projects, London, the Xenakis Ensemble and such soloists as Andrew Ball, Laura Chislett, James Clapperton, Rolf Hind, Stephanie McCallum, and many others; He has had works presented at such events as the Brighton Festival, Darmstadt Ferienkurse für Neue Musik, the Hong Kong ISCM World Music Days, Insel Musik Berlin, many Festivals in France & Italy, the Sydney Spring Festival and the Venice Biennale. Compositions: Four large-scale solo flute works for Laura Chislett, including Sulle Scale della Fenice; Tilt for solo piano; several large ensemble pieces, including Enoncé and Afterimages, quattro frammenti and planetary allegiances; chamber music; atsiluth, heterotic strings; Propriocepts for four voices and orchestra; Current projects include Mentation for and orchestras; flesh and the mirror for Elision; beyond status geometry for Synergy. Recordings: Numerous recordings. Honour: Kranichsteiner Musikpreis, 1984. Hobby: Popular Musics, especially independents. address: c/o Australian Music Centre, PO Box N690, Grosvenor Place, Sydney 2000, Australia.

DENE Joszef, b. 31 Mar 1938, Budapest, Hungary. Singer (Bass). Education: Studied in Budapest; Sang at the Hungarian State Opera, notably as Alberich in Das Rheingold. Career: Many performances at the Zurich Opera, in works by Monteverdi, Berg, Verdi, Janácek and Wagner; Berlin Komische Oper, 1975, as Mozart's Figaro; Further engagements at La Scala, Bayreuth, San Francisco and the Metropolitan; Paris Opéra, 1982 and 1985, as Gloucester in Reimann's Lear and as Trithemius in the premiere of Boehmer's Docteur Faustus; Opéra du Rhin Strasbourg and Barcelona, 1985-96, as Des Grieux in Manon; Season 1987 at Graz as the Hangman in the premiere of Cerha's Rattenfänger and as Taddeo in L'Italiana in Algeri at the Schwetzingen Festival; Graz Opera, 1988-89, as Alberich in Siegfried and Götterdämmerung; Other roles include Mozart's Alfonso and Papageno, Don Pasquale, Pizarro, Kurwenal, Klingsor, Leporello and Handel's Claudius (Agrippina). Recordings: Don Giovanni, Boito's Nerone and Juditha Triumphans by Vivaldi; Il Ritorno di Ulisse, Zurich, 1982.

DENES Istvan, b. 1950, Budapest, Hungary. Conductor. Education: Piano, Conducting and Composition, Franz Liszt Academy, Budapest; Vienna Musikhochschule (Scholarship from Georg Solti). Career: Conductor, Budapest State Opera and Lecturer in Harmony, Franz Liszt Academy, 1980-84; Principal Conductor, Bremen Opera, 1987-95; Salieri's Axur, re d'Ormus at Verona and Salome at Montpellier; Further engagements at Prague, Essen, Stuttgart, Jena, Berlin, Darmstadt, Vienna Volksoper and Bregenz Festival; Conducted the first production this century of Zemlinsky's first opera, Sarema (Trier Opera, 1996). Compositions include: Logarithmische Rhythmen for percussion; Trio in Memoriam Bela Bartók for piano, cello and violin; Mohacs 1526, Hommage á Beethoven Funerailles for orchestra. Recordings include: Sarema (Koch International). Address: c/o Theater der Stadt Trier, Am Augustinherhof, D-5500 Trier, Germany.

DENISON John (Law), 21 January 1911, Reigate, England. Music Administrator. Widower, 1 daughter. Education: Chorister, St George's Chapel, Windsor Castle, 1921-25; Brighton College, 1925-28; Royal College of Music, 1930-32. Career: Professional Hornplayer, BBCSO/LPO, CBSO and others, 1932-39; War Service, 1939-46; Commissioned Somerset Light Infantry; DDA&QMG214 Infantry Brigade, 1945; Music and Theatre Control, Allied Control Commission, Germany; Assistant Music Director, British Council, 1946-48; Music Director, Arts Council of Great Britain, 1948-65; General Manager, Royal Festival Hall, 1965-67; Director, South Bank Concert Halls, 1967-76; Chairman, Cultural Committee, Queen's Silver Jubilee, 1977; Hon Member, Royal Philharmonic Society, 1989; Trustee, Prince Consort, FDN; Royal College of Music; Chairman, Governing Body, Arts Education Schools, 1976-91; Royal Concert in Aid of Musical Charities, 1976-89. Contributions to: Various magazines. Honours: CBE; FRCM; Hon RAM; Hon GSM; Cdr, Order of Lion, Finland; Chev Ordre des Arts et Letters, France; FRSA. Memberships: Royal Society of Musicians; Garrick Club. Address: 9 Hays Park, Shaftesbury, Dorset SP7 9JR, England.

DENIZ Clare (Frances), b. 7 Apr 1945, England. Concert Cellist; Teacher. Education: Private piano study from age 5; Private cello study with Madeleine Mackenzie from age 11; Won Junior Exhibition to Royal Academy of Music after only one years tuition; Teachers: Lilley Phillips and Derek Simpson, gaining LRAM; Further study with Christopher Bunting, Jacqueline du Pré and Antonia Butler; Master classes with Paul Tortelier then became a pupil. Debut: Purcell Room, London, 1983. Career includes: Former Principal Cellist with Royal Ballet Orchestra and sub-principal cellist with English National Opera; Many recitals specializing in British and French music as well as standard repertoire; Appeared at: Cambridge Festival, Cheltenham Lunchtime Concerts, Fairfield Hall Centenary Concert for Arnold Bax; Concertgebouw Amsterdam debut 1987, an unaccompanied Bach recital, returning in 1990; Recording for BBC Radio Oxford, 1987 and recorded a recital of French music in 1991; Invited to take part in Counterpoint II recital series by Incorporated Society of Musicians, 1990; 3 Concerts of first performances for the Wessex Composers Group, 1990, conceived by Incorporated Society of Musicians; Children's concerts and workshops; Played Haydn's C Major Concerto in 1990 and gave a Virtuoso Recital in 1992 for the Jacqueline du Pré Appeal Fund; Solo recitals given in Amsterdam, 1990 and 1992 and in Paris, 1993; Concert given for the EEC Brussels Commission, 1994. Honour: Elected Fellow of The Royal Society of Arts, 1990. Hobbies: Gardening; Badminton; Theology; CS Lewis Society at University of Oxford; Lesser Known Music; Heraldry. Address: 31 Friday Street, Henley-on-Thames, Oxfordshire, RG9 1AN, England.

DENIZE Nadine, b. 6 Nov 1943, Rouen, France. Singer (Mezzo-soprano). Education: Studied with Marie-Louise Christol and Germaine Lubin in Paris. Debut: Paris Opéra, 1967, as Marguerite in La Damnation de Faust. Career: Paris Opéra-Comique, as Charlotte in Werther; Appearances in Marseille, Lyons, Nice and Orange; Member of the Deutsche Oper am Rhein, Dusseldorf, from 1971; Strasbourg, 1974-77; Guest engagements at the Hamburg Staatsoper, Vienna Staatsoper and at La Scala Milan; Nancy Opera, 1981, as Carmen; Paris Opéra as Octavian and Jenufa; Other roles include Cassandre in Les Troyens, Eboli in Don Carlos, Wagner's Kundry and Honegger's Antigone; Opéra du Rhin, Strasbourg, 1986, as Ortrud; Teatro Colon, Buenos Aires, 1988, as Marguerite by Berlioz; Opéra-Comique, Paris, 1988, as Marina in Boris Godunov; Sang Brangaene at Nantes, 1989; Anna in Les Troyens, (1990), opening production of Opéra Bastille, Paris. Recordings: Carmen; Mireille; Les Pêcheurs de Perles; Manon; Il Barbiere di Siviglia. Address: c/o Opéra de Paris Bastille, 12 Rue de Lyon, 75012 Paris, France.

DENLEY Catherine, b. 1954, Northamptonshire, England. Singer (Mezzo-Soprano). m. Miles Golding, 3 sons. Education: Studied at Trinity College of Music, London. Career: Sang 2 years with the BBC Singers; Solo performances with major orchestras and conductors throughout Europe and as far afield as the USA, Canada, China, Japan and the Ukraine; US appearances at the Tanglewood Festival with the Boston Symphony Orchestra; San Francisco concerts with John Eliot Gardiner; Performances of Messiah with the Hallé Orchestra, City of Birmingham Symphony, the English Concert in Belgium and The Sixteen in Finland and Poland; Mozart's Requiem in Salzburg and Innsbruck; Elgar's The Music Makers and the Bliss Pastoral at South Bank; Bach B Minor Mass at Aldeburgh and York; Beethoven's Missa Solemnis at the Windsor Festival; Staged performances of L'Incoronazione di Poppea at Spitalfields; Operatic roles include: Olga in Eugene Onegin at the Aldeburgh Festival; Nutrice in Monteverdi's Poppea; Handel Operas: Guistino and Radamisto; Mrs Noah in Noye's Fludde; Radio and TV recordings in Britain and Europe; TV recordings include appearances in Channel 4's Maestro series and Mahler's 8th Symphony from Dublin; Sang Third Lady in Die Zauberflöte, 1990; Promenade Concerts; Sisera in Handel's Deborah at the 1993 Proms; Mahler 2 in Kiev and Odessa; Tucapsky Stabat Mater in the Czech Republic; Haydn Stabat Mater in Madrid and Handel Judas Maccabaeus in Berlin and Halle. Recordings: Monteverdi's L'Orfeo and L'Incoronazione di Poppea; Handel's Semele, Hercules, Il Duello Amorosa and Messiah; Vivaldi's Gloria; Requiem by Bruckner; In the Beginning by Copland; Die Zauberflöte. Honours: G.T.C.L.; F.T.C.L. Current Management & Address: Magenta Music International, 4 Highgate High Street, London N6, England.

DENMAN John (Anthony), b. 23 July 1933, London, England. Clarinettist. m. Paula Fan, 6 Oct 1982. Education: Clarke's College, London; Education: Royal Military School of Music, Kneller Hall. Career: Principal Clarinet, London Symphony Orchestra, English National Opera and other major British orchestras; BBC Soloist; Solo tours of Europe, USA, Far East and Australia as Recitalist, Symphony Soloist and Jazz Artist; Currently Principal Clarinet, Tucson Symphony, Arizona, USA. Compositions: Discovery of manuscripts of lost orchestral material to Spohr clarinet concerti; Discovery and editing of 3 Caprices by Mozart's clarinettist, Anton Stadler. Recordings: Concerti by Spohr, No 2, Stamitz, No 3, Finzi; Sonatas by Stanford, Hughes, Bax, Ireland, Benjamin, Alwyn, Brahms, Saint-Saëns, Reger, Mendelssohn, Hindemith, Bernstein, Tovey, Bowen. Publications: The Kinder-Klari Clarinet Learning System: Tutor and Instrument, a miniature clarinet for small children, 1990; Series of articles, Denmania, for International Clarinet Society. Hobbies: Golf; Model railroading. Current Management: Albert Kay Associates, New York City, USA. Address: 1542 E Lester, Tucson, AZ 85719, USA.

DENNER Bettina, b. 5 Jan 1960, Weimar, Germany. Singer (Mezzo-soprano). Education: Studied at the Leipzig Musikhochschule, notably with Hans Christian Polster. Career: Sang at the Leipzig Opera from 1983, as Zerlina, Carlotta in Die schweigsame Frau, and Nicklausse in Les Contes d'Hoffmann; Guest at the Berlin Staatsoper from 1987, as Cherubino and on tour to Japan; Other roles have included Dorabella, Idamante, Massenet's Charlotte, Hermia in A Midsummer Night's Dream and Orlovsky; Many concert engagements, notably at the Leipzig Thomasschule and the Gewandhaus. Address: c/o Deutsche Staatsoper Berlin, Unter den Linden 7, O-1060 Germany.

DENNING Angela, b. 1952, Sydney, New South Wales, Australia. Singer (Soprano). Education: Studied at the New South Wales Conservatory. Career: Sang with the State Opera of South Australia from 1976 and with the Australian Opera at Sydney from 1979; English National Opera, 1982-83, Deutsche Oper Berlin, 1984, and the Staatsoper, 1988; Sang Clorinda in La Cenerentola at Salzburg, 1988-89, and Dalila in Handel's Samson at the 1988 Göttingen Festival; Other roles include Donna Anna and Meyerbeer's Marguerite de Valois (both in Berlin), Lucia di Lammermoor, Gilda, Nannetta, the Queen of Night and Fiordiligi. Recordings include: Video of La Cenerentola (Virgin). Address: c/o Australian Opera, Sydney Opera House, Sydney, New South Wales, Australia.

DENNIS Elwyn, b. 10 August 1941, Los Angeles, USA. Composer. Education: BA, University of California, 1965. Career: Sculptor, Lecturer, Department of Architecture, University of Melbourne, 1974-75; Lecturer, Ballarat University, 1990-92; Manager of Clouds, a nature conservation area. Compositions include: Evidence of Origin, performance with sculpture, 1982; Particle Flow, 1983; Space of Concern, 1983; Clouds Are, 1984; Wimmera, 1986; A Mother's Day, 1987; Time Again, 1987; Invention for Guitar, 1988; Details of a Morning, 1988; Dry Country, 1992; Waiting Winter Out, tape with harpischord, 1994; Commissions Association of Australia and The Listening Room, ABC-FM. Honours include: Caulfield Arts Centre Purchase Prize, 1979. Address: c/o APRA, 1A Eden Street, Crows Nest, NSW 2065, Australia.

DENNISON Robert, b. 10 June 1960, Philadelphia, USA. Concert Pianist. Education: Studied in Philadelphia Music Academy, at temple University and the Peabody Conservatory; Further Study with Claude Frank and Horszowki. Debut: Philadelphia, with the Shostakovich Second Concerto, 1971. career: Concerts and recitals in Washington, Boston, Cleveland, Los Angeles, St Louis and Chicago; Russian Tours with concerts in Kiev, St Petersburg, Vilnius, Moscow and Novosibirsk, 1991-93; Further engagements at Chicago, New Jersey, Colorado, San Francisco, Boston, Essen, Berlin, Hamburg Music Festival, Lucerne Festival and in Hungary, Romania and Czechoslovakia, 1992-93; Repertoire includes contemporary works by American composers as well as the standard classics. Address: c/o Sonata, 11 Northgate Street, Glasgow G20 7AA, Scotland.

DENNISTON Patrick, b. 1965, New York, USA. Singer (Tenor). Education: Studied at Syracuse University and the Lyric Opera Center, Chicago. Career: Engagements with the San Francisco Opera, Houston Grand Opera, New York City Opera, Opera Pacific, Kentucky Opera, New Israeli Opera, Bonn Opera and at the Spoleto Festival; Further appearances throughout Canada; Roles have included Pinkerton, Don Carlos, Don José, Edgardo, Dmitri, Lensky and Alfredo; Glyndebourne Festival 1997, as Des Grieux in a new production of Manon Lescaut; Season 1997-98 with Pinkerton and Ismaele in Nabucco at Chicago, Erik in Der fliegende Holländer, and Radames at Houston; Cavaradossi at Madison. Address: c/o Lyric Opera Chicago, 20 North Wacker Drive, Chicago, IL 60606, USA.

DEPLUS Guy (Gaston Simon), b. 29 August 1924, Vieux Condé, France. Musician; Clarinettist. m. Yvette Vandekerkhove, 3 August 1946, 1 son. Education: Conservatoire National Superieur du Musique de Paris; 1st Prize, Clarinet and Chamber Music, 1945, 1946. Career: Guard Republican Band and Orchestra, 1947; Concerts Colonne, 1950; Domaine Musical, with Pierre Boulez, 1953; Ars Nova, with Marius Constant, 1963; Paris Octet, 1965; Opéra Comique, 1968; Opera, 1973; Professor, Chamber Music, Paris Conservatory, 1974; Concerts in Berlin, Salzburg, Vienna, 1977; Professor, Clarinet, Paris Conservatory, 1978; Judge, International Competitions; Professor Ecole Normale de Musique de Paris, 1991. Recordings: Mozart, Concerto, Trio, Quintet; Weber, 1st Clarinet Concerto, Concertino, Grand Duo; Rossini, Introduction, Theme and Variations; Beethoven Septet. Contributions to: The Clarinet, Chairman for France. Honours: Quoted by Stravinsky in Memories and Commentaries, 1959; 4 Prix de l'Academie du Disque Francais. Membership: International Clarinet Society; French Chairman. Hobbies: Reading; Walking. Address: 37 Square Saint Charles, 75012 Paris, France.

DEPOLTOVA Eva, b. 5 August 1945, Bratislava. Singer (Soprano). Education: University of Music Arts, Praha; Zdenka Zika; Elena Obraztsona. Debut: Prague National Theatre, 1974. Career: Sang in Conert with Czech Philharmonic Orchestra, European Tour at Prague, Vienna, Salzburg, Linz, Vienna, Lyon, Switzerland, Japan; Dvorak Requiem & Stabat Mater, Janacek Glagolitic Messe, Beethoven, The 9 Symphonies, 1976; Roles include: Lady Macbeth, Marenka, The Bartered Bride, Violetta, La Traviata; Sang Krasava, Libuse, Smetana at the National Theatre, Prague, 100 Anniversary Reopening, 1983. Recordings: Fibich-Sarka, Foerster, Eva Smetana, Dalibor, Libuse, The Kiss Mozart, Don Giovanni, The Miracle of Our Lady, Gilgamesh. Hobby: Nature. Address: NA Prikope 12, 110 01 Praha, Czech Republic.

DEPRAY Xavier, b. 22 Apr 1926, Albert, Somme, France. Singer (Bass). Education: Studied at the Paris Conservatoire, 1947-50. Career: Sang in opera at Mulhouse and Vichy from 1951, Rossini's Basilio at the Paris Opéra-Comique, 1952; Paris Palais Garnier from 1952, debut as Palemon in Massenet's Thais; Sang in the 1954 concert premiere of Profofiev's Fiery Angel and appeared at the Paris Opera as Sparafucile, Pogner and Ford;

Appearances at Lyon as Arkel and in Les Troyens, Bordeaux, Marseille (Commendatore) and Venice; Glyndebourne, 1958, as the Governor in Le Comte Ory; Professor at the Paris Conservatoire from 1973. Address: c/o Conservatoire National, 14 Rue de Madrid, F-75008 Paris, France.

DEPREIST James (Anderson), b. 21 November 1936, Philadelphia, Pennsylvania, USA. Conductor. m. (1) Betty Louise Childress, 10 August 1963, 2 daughters. m. (2) Ginette Grenier, 19 July 1980. Education: BS 1958, MA 1961, University of Pennsylvania; Studied with Vincent Persichetti, Philadelphia Conservatory of Music, 1959-61. Career: Conductor, Contemporary Music Guild, Philadelphia, 1959-62; Specialist in Music, US State Department, 1962-63; Conductor, Bangkok, Thailand, 1963-64; Assistant Conductor, New York Philharmonic Orchestra, 1965-66; Principal Guest Conductor, Symphony of the New World, 1968-70; European debut, Rotterdam Philharmonic Orchestra, 1969; Associate Conductor, 1971-75; Principal Guest Conductor, 1975-76; National Symphony Orchestra, Washington DC; Music Director, L'Orchestre Symphonique de Quebec, 1976-83; Oregon Symphony Orchestra, Portland, 1980-; Malmo Symphony Orchestra, 1991-94; Music director, Philharmonique De Monte-Carlo, 1994-; Guest Conductor with major orchestras in North America and Europe. Recordings: For Caprice: Delos; Records for KOCH, BIS, Ondine, Delos. Publications: Book of Poems, This Precipice Garden, 1987; Poetry Book, The Distant Siren, 1989. Honours: 1st prize, Dimitri Mitropoulos International Conducting Competition, New York, 1964; Merit Citation, City of Philadelphia, 1969; Medal, City of Quebec, 1983; Honorary MusD, Laval University, Quebec, 1980; Willamette University, 1987; Honorary DFA, University of Portland, 1983; Pacific University, 1985. Address: Oregon Symphony, 711 South West Alder, Ste 200, Portland, Oregon 97205, USA.

DERNESCH Helga, b. 3 Feb 1939, Vienna, Austria. Singer (Soprano and Mezzo-Soprano). Education: Studied at the Vienna Conservatory, 1957-61. Debut: Berne Opera 1961, as Marina in Boris Godunov. Career: Sang Antonia in Les Contes d'Hoffmann, Fiordiligi and Wagner roles; Wiesbaden, 1963-65; Cologne Opera, 1965-69; Bayreuth from 1965, as Freia, Gutrune and Eva; Scottish Opera from 1968, as Gutrune, Leonore, Brünnhilde, Isolde and the Marschallin; Salzburg Easter Festival from 1969, as Brünnhilde, Isolde and Fidelio; Covent Garden debut, 1970 as Sieglinde, followed by Chrysothemis in Elektra, the Dyer's Wife and the Nurse in Die Frau ohne Schatten, and Adelaide in Arabella, 1986; Debuts at Chicago, 1971 and Vienna, 1972 as Leonore in Fidelio; Created Fortner's Elisabeth Tudor, Berlin 1972, Goneril in Reimann's Lear, Munich 1978 and Hecuba in Reimann's Troades, Munich 1986; San Francisco from 1982, as Herodias in Salome, and Erda and Fricka in Der Ring des Nibelungen, 1984-85; Metropolitan Opera debut 1985, as Marfa in Khovanshchina; Tour of Japan with the Bayreuth ensemble, 1967 and with the Hamburg Staatsoper, 1984; Metropolitan 1989, as Fricka and Waltraute in the Ring and The Nurse in Die Frau ohne Schatten; Sang Mistress Quickly in Falstaff at Los Angeles, 1990; Fricka in the Ring at San Francisco; Covent Garden, in the Ring, 1991; Sang Clytemnestra in Elektra at San Francisco, 1991, and at the Opera Bastille, Paris, 1992; Eletress in Henze's Der Prinz Von Homburg at the 1992 Munich Festival; Frau von Luber in Weill's Silbersee at the 1996 London Proms. Recordings: Fidelio and Tristan und Isolde; Der Ring des Nibelungen; Elisabeth in Tannhäuser. Address: Salztorgasse 8/11, A-1013 Wien, Austria.

DEROUBAIX Jeanne, b. 16 Feb 1927, Brussels, Belgium. Singer (Mezzo-soprano). Education: Studied in Brussels. Career: Sang in ensemble Pro Musica, under the direction of Safford Cape (1947-53); Toured widely in Europe with repertoire specialising in music of 13th-16th centuries; Lieder recitals and programmes of French chansons; Often heard in contemporary music; Sang in the first performances of Stravinsky's Threni (Venice 1958) and A Sermon, a Narrative and a Prayer (Basle 1962); Also heard in Schoenberg's Pierrot Lunaire and works by Boulez; Professor at the Musikhochschule Detmold from 1957. Recordings: Lieder by Brahms; Beethoven's Missa Solemnis; Monteverdi's Orfeo; Le Marteau sans Maître by Boulez. Address: Staatliche Hochschule für Musik, Westfalen-Lippe Nordwestdeutsche Musikakademie, D-4930 Detmold, Allee 22, Germany.

DES MARAIS Paul (Emile), b. 23 Jun 1920, Menominee, Michigan, USA. Composer; Professor. Education: Studied with Leo Sowerby, Chicago, 1937-41; Nadia Boulanger, Cambridge, 1941-42 and Paris, 1949; BA, 1949, MA, 1953, Harvard University. Career: Teacher, Harvard University, 1953-56; University of California, Los Angeles, 1956-. Compositions: Stage: Epiphanies, chamber opera, 1968; Incidental music to Dryden's A Secular Masque, 1976; Shakespeare's A Midsummer Night's Dream, 1976; Sophocles's Oedipus, 1978; G B Shaw's St Joan, 1980; Dryden's Marriage à la Mode, 1981; Shakespeare's As You Like It, 1983; G Etherege's The Man of Mode, 1984. Dance: Triplum for Organ and Percussion, 1981; Touch for 2 Pianos, 1984. Chamber: 2 piano sonatas, 1947, 1952; Theme and Changes for Harpsichord, 1953; Capriccio for 2 Pianos and Percussion, 1962; 2 Movements for 2 Pianos and Percussion, 1972 revised and enlarged as 3 Movements, 1975; The Baroque Isles for 2 Keyboard Percussionists, 1986; Orpheus, theatre piece for Narrator and Instruments, 1987; The French Park, for two guitars, 1988. Choral: Six-part Mass for double chorus, 1947; Motet for Mixed Voices, Cellos and Double Basses, 1959; Psalm 121, 1959; Organum 1-6 for Chorus, Organ and Percussion, 1972, revised and enlarged, 1980; Brief Mass for Chorus, Organ and Percussion, 1973; Seasons of the Mind for Chorus, Piano 4-hands and Celesta, 1980-81. Vocal: Reflections on Faure for Voice and Paino, 1972; Late Songs for Voice and Piano, 1978; Slowsong for Voice and Piano, 1987; The French Park for two guitars, 1988. Publication: Harmony, 1962. Contributions to: Articles in Perspectives of New Music. Address: c/o Music Department, University of California at Los Angeles, Los Angeles, CA 90024, USA.

DESCHÊNES Bruno, b. 12 October 1955, Cap-Chat, Quebec, Canada. Composer. m. Shizuko Toguchi, 18 April 1981. Education: BMus, Composition, McGill University, Montréal, 1979; Master in Composition, University of Montréal, 1983; Currently doing research on Music Perception, Listening and Teaching. Career: Performing and Conducting on Radio and Concerts, 1980-; Compositions performed in France, USA, Venezuela, Brazil and Montréal, 1979-; Gives lectures, workshops and writes articles on Music Perception and Music Listening in Canada, USA and Europe. Compositions: Improvised Music: Expansion, Horizon, Pyramide, Chakras; Electronic Music: Murmures for Tape and Percussion; Different Chamber Groups: Dimension, Innerance, Prisme, Poemes Luminescence, Calme En Soi, Double Jeu; Choir: Ondes, Ondes et Particules. Contributions to: The Perceptions of Colour Through Music, Musicwork 26, 1984; Regularly publishes articles in the bulletin of the Centre Québécois de la Couleur. Hobbie: Computer Programming. Address: 5565 Rue Clark, Montréal, Québec, H2T 2V5, Canada.

DESDERI Claudio, b. 1945, Alessandria, Italy. Singer (Baritone); Conductor. Education: Studied at the Florence Conservatory. Career: Sang as first in concert; Opera debut as Guadenzio in Il Signor Bruschino at the 1969 Edinburgh Festival, with the Maggio Musicale; Has sung widely in Italy and in Munich, Salzburg, Paris, Amsterdam, Chicago, Philadelphia, and Vienna; Best known in opera by Verdi, Berlioz, Monteverdi, Nono, Rossini, Bellini, Mozart, Donzetti and Massenet; Regular appearances in Britain from 1981; Glyndebourne Festival (as Figaro and Alfonso), Promenade and Festival Hall concerts; Covent Garden debut as Mozart's Figaro, 1987; Alfonso in Cosi fan tutte, 1989; Conducts Chamber Orchestras in Italy; Master Classes at Musica di Fiesole; Conducted Cosi fan tutte and Le nozze di Figaro at Turin, 1989, Piacenza, 1990, Royal College of Music, London, 1990; Sang Don Magnifico in La Cenerentola at Covent Garden, 1990; Glyndebourne Festival as Falstaff, Maggio Musicale Florence as Leporello. Recordings: include, Cosi fan tutte and Le nozze di Figaro, conducted by Haitink. Address: c/o Royal Opera House, Covent Garden, London WC2, England.

DESIMONE Robert A, b. 1940, USA. Stage Director; Arts Administrator; Conductor. m. Angela Carol Bonica, 21 Jul 1974, 1 s, 1 d. Education: Performance Certificate, Music Academy of the West; BM, MA, University of Southern California; Diploma International Opera Centre, Zurich, Switzerland; DMA, University of Washington, USA. Debut: As Stage Director, Rome, Italy. Career: Director of Opera, University of Texas, Austin; Director of Opera, College Conservatory of Music, Cincinnati; Assistant Director, School of Music, University of Washington; Executive Director, Visual Arts Center, Anchorage, Alaska; Administrative Coordinator, Music Center Opera Association, Los Angeles; Director: City of the Angels Opera, Los Angeles; John F Kennedy Center for the Performing Arts, Washington DC; Lincoln Center for the Performing Arts, New York; Seattle Opera Association, Seattle, Washington; Stage Director: Teatro del' Opera, Rome; Teatro Goldini, Rome; Opernhaus, Zurich, Switzerland; Resident Stage Director, Seattle Opera Association, Seattle, Washington; Guest Director, theatres in Germany, Switzerland, Italy, USA. Memberships: National Opera Association; Metropolitan Opera Guild; College Music Society; Central Opera Association. Address: 3601 72nd Avenue SE, Mercer Island, WA 98040, USA.

DESSAY Natalie, b. 1964, Lyon, France. Singer (Soprano). Education: Studied at the Bordeaux Conservatory and in Paris. Career: After winning the 1990 Mozart Competition in Vienna sang in Bizet's Don Procopio at the Paris Opéra-Comique and at Montpellier in Ariadne auf Naxos; Liège and Nantes, 1990, in Si j'étais Roi by Adam and Le Roi l'a dit by Delius; Lyon Opéra from 1991, in Mozart's Schauspieldirektor and as Blondchen; Opéra Bastille, Paris, 1992, as Olympia in Les Contes d'Hoffmann; Mozart concert at the 1992 Aix-en-Provence Festival; Sang Lakmé at Nîmes, 1996. Address: c/o Opéra de Lyon, 9 Quai Jean Moulon, F-69001 Lyon, France.

DESSI Daniela, b. 1963, Genoa, Italy. Singer (Soprano). Education: Studied in Parma and Siena. Career: Sang at first in concert and made stage debut at Savona, in Pergolesi's Serva Padrona; Mozart roles have included the Countess and Fiordiligi (at La Scala and Genoa), Donna Elvira (at Florence) and Vitellia in Desdemona (to the Otello of Placido Domingo), Amelia Bocanegra (at Vienna, Venice, and Hamburg), and Elizabeth de Valois (notably with Pavarotti at La Scala, 1992); Sang Alice Ford at Boston and Amsterdam; Made debuts as the Trovotore Leonora and Violetta at Rome and Tokyo, 1993; Nedda in Pagliacci at Philadelphia and the New York Met, Mathilde (Guillaume Tell) at Pesaro and Mascagni's Iris in Rome; Zurich Opera as Aida (season 1996-97), Mimi, Donna Elvira, Desdemona and Ginerva in Giordino's La Lena della Beffe; Saog in Salieri's Danaides at Verona, 1996, Madama Butterfly in Florence and Tosca in Tokyo, 1997. Recordings include: Video of Don Carlos, from La Scala. Address: c/o Opernhaus Zürich, Falkenstrasse 1, CH-8008 Zürich, Switzerland.

DEUSSEN Nancy (Bloomer), b. 1 February 1931, New York City, New York, USA. Composer; Teacher. m. (1) Charles J Webster, 1952. m. (2) John H Bloomer, 1962. m. (3) Gary R Deussen, 1982, 1 son, 2 daughters. Education: Juilliard School of Music, 1949-51; Manhattan School of Music, 1951-53; BM, Composition, University of Southern California, School of Music, 1957-59; BM Music Education; Graduate Studies in Composition, University of California, Los Angeles, University of Southern California, Long Beach State University, San Jose State University. Career: Original ballet music The Little Hill performed New York City, 1952; Missa de Angelis premiere, Redlands, California, 1957; Suite for Clarinet and Piano premiere, 1959, Los Angeles, California; Woodwind Quintet premiere, 1985, TV premiere with interview, October 1988; Concert of original chamber music and orchestra premiere of Three Rustic Sketches, 1989. Compositions: Little Fugue and Harvest Suite, for Recorders, 1956; Missa de Angelis, 1957; Suite for Clarinet and Piano, 1959; The Serpent, Cantata, 1965; Woodwind Quintet, 1983; Three Rustic Sketches, for Orchestra, 1987; Prelude and Cascades for Piano, 1987; Fanfare and Andante for Winds, 1988; The Long Voyage, for Soprano and Recorders, 1988; Trio for Violin, Clarinet and Piano, 1988; (on commission) City Festival Overture, for Concert Band, 1989; Commission from Santa Clara Chorale Canticles of Our Land for SATB, Soli and Chamber Orchestra, World Premiere, 1991; Two Pieces for Violin and Piano, 1990; Trio for violin, cello and piano commissioned by The Brequan Trio, premiered 1993; Concerto for clarinet and small orchestra, commissioned by Richard Nanemaker, clarinettist, premiered 1995 by Consortium of 5 orchestras. Address: 3065 Greer Road, Palo Alto, CA 94303, USA.

DEUTEKOM Cristina, b. 28 Aug 1932, Amsterdam, Netherlands. Opera Singer (Soprano). 1 daughter. Debuts: Amsterdam, 1962, as the Queen of Night which she also sang on her Covent Garden debut; Appeared at Munich State Opera, 1966. Career: Vienna Festwochen, 1966; Sang at Metropolitan Opera, New York, 1967; Sang in all major opera houses in Europe, especially Italy and also in USA; Specialised in bel canto operas by Rossini, Bellini and Donizetti and the great Verdi operas; Among her roles were Mozart's Fiordiligi and Constanze, Bellini's Norma and Elvira, Rossini's Armida and Verdi's Odabella and Giselda. Recordings: Various. Honours: Grand Prix du Disque, 1969, 1972. Hobbies: Driving around the world; Singing; Shopping, especially for shoes. Address: c/o H R Rothenberg, Johannisthaler Chaussee 421, 1000 Berlin 47, Germany.

DEVIA Mariella, b. 1948, Imperia, Italy. Singer (Soprano). Education: Studied at the Accademia di Santa Cecilia, Rome. Debut: Spoleto 1972, as Despina in Cosi fan Tutte. Career: Rome Opera 1973, as Lucia di Lammermoor; Guest appearances in Italy and at Munich, Hamburg and Berlin; Has sung Donizetti's Adina in Dallas and Verdi's Oscar in Chicago; Metropolitan Opera from 1979, as Gilda, Constanze in Die Entführung, Nannetta in Falstaff, Despina and Constanze, 1990; Concert performace of Lakmé in New York; Sang title role in Donizetti's Elisabeth al Castello di Kenilworth at Bergamo, 1989; Elvira in I Puritani at Rome and Madrid, 1990; Maggio Musicale Florence, 1990 as Donizetti's Parisina; Rossini roles include Adele in Le Comte Ory, Amenaide in Tancredi and Semiramide; Pesaro Festival 1995, Zelmira; Sang Lucia di Lammermoor at Florence, 1996; at Teatro alla Scala: Capuleti e Montecchi, Lodorska (Cherubini), Lucia de Lammermoor, Die Entfuhrung, La fille du repiuvent, Turco du Stalia, 1990-97; Covent Garden: Die Zauberflöte, 1988; Rigoletto, 1990. Recordings: include, Rossini Adelaide di Borgogna, Donizetti Elisabetta al Castello di Kenilworth, Bellini La Sonnambula and I Puritani (Fonit Cetra); L'Elisir d'Aurore; Lucia de Lammermoor, with Zubin Mehta. Address: c/o R Lombardo Inc, One Harkness Plaza, 61 West 62nd Street, Suite 6F, New York, NY 10023, USA.

DEVICH Janos, b. 3 Apr 1938, Szeged, Hungary. Cellist; Professor. m. Sara Veslelszky, 12 Aug 1974, 3 sons. Education: Liszt Ferenc Academy for Music, Budapest. Career: Concerts regularly in almost all the countries in Europe, USA (five times), Australia, Japan (seven times), China, South Korea; Festivals in Besançon, Bath, Estoril, Prague, Warsaw, Babilin, Como,

Chamonix, Amiens, Devon. Recordings: Kodaly, Mozart, Dohnanyi, Contemporary composers string quartet; String Quartets (Debussy, Ravel, D'Indy); Piano Quintets (Brahms, Schumann, Schubert); Integrale (Schubert, Haydn). Honours: Franz Liszt Prize, 1970; Merited Artist of Hungary, 1990; Bartok - Pasztory Prize, 1996. Memberships: President, Magyar Zeneműveszeti Társaság; Vice President, Magyar Muzsikus Forum. Address: Budapest, Pusztaszeri-ut 30, Hungary 1025.

DEVINU Giusy, b. 1960, Cagliri, Italy. Singer (Soprano). Education: Studied at the Cagliari Conservatory. Debut: Sang in 1982. Career: Has sung Violetta at La Scala under Riccardo Muti and at other Italian centres; Further engagements in Rigoletto at Bologna, 1990, Rossini's L'Occasione fa il ladro at Pesaro, 1989, and in Don Pasquale and as the Countess in Le Nozze di Figaro at the Teatro La Fenice Venice, 1990-91; Sang in the Seven Stars concert at the Baths of Caracalla, 1991; Trieste 1991 as Lucieta in Wolf-Ferrari's Il Campielo, Rome 1992 as Marie in La Fille du Regiment; Macerata Festival 1992 as Traviata; Sang Bellini's Giulietta at Genoa, 1996. Address: c/o Teatro La Fenice, Campo S Fantin 1965, 30124 Venice, Italy.

DEVLIN Michael (Coles), b. 27 Nov 1942, Chicago, Illinois, USA. Singer, Bass-Baritone. Education: MusB, Louisiana State University, 1965; Vocal training with Treigle, Ferro, and Malas, New York. Debut: Operatic debut as Spalanzani, Les Contes d'Hoffmann, New Orleans, 1963. Career: First appearance with New York City Opera as the Hermit in US premiere of Ginastera's Don Rodrigo, 1966; On roster until 1978; British debut as Mozart's Almaviva, Glyndebourne Festival, 1974; Royal Opera Covent Garden, London, 1975, 1977, 1979; European debut, Holland Festival, 1977; Frankfurt Opera and Bavarian State Opera, Munich, 1977; Metropolitan Opera debut in New York as Escamillo, 1978; San Francisco Opera, 1979; Hamburg State Opera and Paris Opera, 1980; Miami Opera and Monte Carlo Opera, 1981; Dallas Opera, 1983; Chicago Lyric Opera, 1984; Los Angeles Opera, 1986; Other roles have been Don Giovanni, Eugene Onegin, Golaud, Don Alfonso, Ford, Wotan and the villains in Les Contes d' Hoffmann; At Santa Fe has sung Altair in Strauss's Die Aegyptische Helena and the Commandant in Friedenstag; Sang Pizarro in Fidelio at Los Angeles, 1990; Jochanaan in Salome at Covent Garden, 1992; Sang Escamillo at Los Angeles, 1992 followed by Boris Godunov, 1994; The Doctor in Wozzeck at the Metropolitan, 1997; Numerous appearances as soloist with major orchestras. Current Management: New Century Artist Management. Address: New Century Artist Management, PO Box 802, Tuxedo Park, NY 10987, USA.

DEVOS Louis, b. 15 Jun 1926, Brussels, Belgium. Singer (Tenor). Education: Vocul studies in Graz, Austria. Career: Founded Ensemble Musica Polyphonica 1950, for the performance of early music; Sang in the first performance of Stravinsky's Cantata, Brussels 1952, and in the premiere of the radio opera Orestes by Henk Badings, 1954; Concerts with the Munich Philharmonic from 1956, under the direction of Pierre Boulez and Hermann Scherchen; Sang in the premieres of Martin's Mystère de la Nativité (Geneva 1959) and Pilatus (Rome 1964); Cologne 1972, in Penderecki's Utrejna; Vienna Staatsoper 1974, as Aron in Schoenberg's Moses und Aron; Guest appearances in London, Milan, Amsterdam and Brussels. Recordings: Vocal music by Lully (Erato); Der Tod Jesu by Graun; Zelenka's Magnificat; Les Indes Galantes by Rameau; Lutoslawski's Paroles tissées; Moses und Aron (Philips); Rousseau's Le Devin du Village (CBS). Address: c/o Staatsoper, Opernring 2, A-1010 Vienna, Austria.

DEVOYON Pascal, b. 6 Apr 1953, Paris, France. Pianist. m. 29 Feb 1992, 2 sons. Education: French Baccalaureat Mathematics section; Ecole Normale de Musique Conservatoire de Paris. Career: Has played with major orchestras including Philharmonia, Leningrad Philharmonic, NHK Tokyo; Broadcasts over radio and television with Orchestre de la Suisse Romande, Orchestre National d'Espayne, Rotterdam, Stuttgart Philharmonic and RAI of Milan. Recordings: Ravel, Liszt, Tchaikovsky, Bach, Franck, Fauré, Schumann, Grieg, Saint-Saens. Honours: Second Prize, Viotti, 1973; Busoni, 1974; Third Prize, Leeds, 1975; Second Prize, Tchaikovsky, 1978. Hobbies: Video; Informatic. Current Management: Charles Finch, 11a Queens Road, Wimbledon, London SW19 8NG, England. Address: 50 Avenue de la Paix 93270 Sevran, France.

DEVREESE Frédéric, b. 2 Jun 1929, Amsterdam, The Netherlands. Composer; Conductor. Education: Malines conservatory with Father, studied composition with M Poot; Conducting with R Defossez, Brussels Conservatory; Composition with I Pizzetti, Accademia di Santa Cecilia, Rome, 1952-55; Conducting with H Swarowsky, Staatsakademie, Vienna, 1956. Career: Conductor Belgian TV, Composer of Symphonic Music, Opera, Ballet, Chamber Music and Film Music. Compositions: Orchestral: include,Symphony, 1953; Two Movements for String Orchestra, 1953-63; Mascarade, Ballet, 1955; L'Amour Don Juan, Ballet, 1973; Overture for Orchestra, 1976; Evocation, Suite, 1977; Prelude, 1983; l'Ouevre au Noir, Suite, 1988; Valse Sacrée, 1989; Thème et Danse dun Soir un Train, 1989. Soli and Orchestra: include, 4 Piano Concertos, 1949, 1952, 1956, 1983; Violin Concerto, 1951; Recitativo et Allegro for Trumpet and Orchestra, 1959; Chamber: includes, Suite No 1 for Brass Quintet, Hommage à J Ensor, 1970; Suite No 2 for Brass Quintet, 1981; Masque for Brass Band, 1989; 5 Divertimenti for 4 Sax, 1985; Valse Sacrée for Violin, Alto and Piano, 1989. Piano Solo: includes, Mascarade, 1953; Soundtrack, 1981-90; Black and White, 1983-90. Two Pianos: Gemini, 1980; Variations and theme for Strings, 1991; Piano Wiegelied voor Jesse, 1992. Address: c/o Gaillard Edition, Avenue Buysdelle 30, 1180 Brussels, Belgium.

DEW John, b. 1 June 1944, Santiago de Cuba, Cuba. Stage Director. Education: Studied in Germany with Walter Felsenstein and Wieland Wagner. Debut: The Rake's Progress, at Ulm, 1971. Career: Directed Mozart and Wagner cycles at Krefeld in the 1970's; Head of Production at Bielefeld from 1981, with Maschinist Hopkins by Brand, Schreker's Irrelohe and Der Singende Teufel, Hindemith's Neues vom Tage, Der Sprung über den Schatten and Zwingburg by Krenek; Bakchantinnen by Wellesz, Fennimore and Gerda, Nixon in China and Boito's Nerone; Season 1987-88 at the Deutsche Oper Berlin with Les Huguenots and the premiere of Los Alamos by Neikrug; Les Huguenots seen at Covent Garden, 1991; Other productions include La Juive at Bielefeld and Nuremburg, Clemenza di Tito at Zurich, Death in Venice at Nuremburg, 1992, Aida at Hamburg, 1993; Puritani, Vienna, 1994; Andrea Chenier, Berlin; Leipzig production of Le nozze di Figaro seen at the Israel Festival, 1992; Appointed Artistic Director of the Theatres of the City of Dortmund, 1995; Directed the premiere of Schnittke's Historia von D Johann Fausten, Hamburg, 1995; Floyd's Susannah at the Deutsch Oper, Berlin, 1997. Current Management: Athole Still International Management Ltd. Address: Foresters Hall, 25-27 Westow Street, London SE19 3RY, England.

DEXTER Harold, b. 7 Oct 1920, Leicester, England. Organist; Teacher; Conductor. m. Faith Grainger, 1 daughter. Education: MusB, MA, Cambridge University; Fellow, Royal College of Organists; Associate, Royal College of Music;, ADCM. Career: Organist, Southwark Cathedral, 1956-68; Professor, 1956-88, Head, General Music Department, 1963-85, Guildhall School of Music. Honours: Fellow, Guildhall School of Music; Fellow, Royal School of Church Music. Memberships: Past service on Royal College of Organists, Incorporated Society of Musicians and IAO Executives; Various associations with Royal School of Church Music. Address: 29 Allington Court, Outwood Common Road, Billericay, Essex CM11 2JB, England.

DEYOUNG Michelle, b. Colorado, USA. Singer (Mezzo-soprano). Education: Apprentice with the Santa Fe Opera and the Israel Arts Vocal Institute; Met Opera Young Artists' Program, appearing in Carmelites, Aida and Die Zauberföte, 1993-94. Career: Concert appearances with the San Francisco Symphony in Beethoven's Ninth, Mahler's Third and Das Klagende Lied, with the Boston Symphony in Mahler 2, the Houston Syphony in Schoenberg's Gurrelieder nd the New York Philharmonic (David Del Tredici premiere); Other Repertory includes the Verdi Requiem, Ravel's Sheherazade and Wagner's Wesendonck Lieder, in London, Amsterdam and Paris; Jocasta in Oedipus Rex, in Paris, season 1996; Engaged as Fricka at Seattle and Chicago, 1997-98. Honours include: Winner, Marilyn Horne Foundation Wings of Song; Marion Anderson Award. Address: c/o Lies Askonas Ltd, 6 Henrietta St, London WC2E 8LA, England.

DI BELLA Benito, b. 1942, Palermo, Sicily, Italy. Singer (Baritone). Education: Studied at the Palermo Conservatory and in Pesaro. Career: Sang at Spoleto and elsewhere in Italy before La Scala Milan debut, 1971, as Marcello in La Bohème; Sang further in Naples, Genoa, Venice and Palermo; Amonasro at the 1980 Verona Arena, Jack Rance at the 1985 Macerata Festival; Further appearances throughout North and South America as Verdi's Luna, Germont, Pietro (Simon Boccanegra) and Rigoletto, Gerard in Andrea Chenier, the Herald in Lohengrin and Escamillo. Address: c/o Arena di Verona, Piazza Bra 28, 37121 Verona, Italy.

DI BONAVENTURA Anthony, b. 12 Nov 1930, Follensbee, West Virginia, USA. Pianist. Education: Studied at the Curtis Institute with Vengerova. Debut: With the NY Philharmonic in 1943, playing Beethoven's C minor Concerto. Career: Beethoven cycle under Otto Klemperer with the London Philharmonic, 1959; Has performed widely in the US with major orchestras in the standard repertory and in works by contemporary composers; Vincent Persichetti, Luciano Berio, (Points on a Curve to Find), Alberto Ginastera and Milko Kelemen have written works for him; Teacher at the School of Music, Boston University, from 1973. Recordings: Works by Scarlatti, Chopin, Debussy and Prokofiev, Eighth Sonata.

DI BONAVENTURA Mario, b. 20 Feb 1924, Follensbee, West Virginia, USA. Conductor. Education: Studied conducting wth Igor Markevitch in Salzburg and Paris; Studied composition with Nadia Boulanger in Paris, 1947-53. Debut: With the Paris Conservatoire orchestra in the Prix de Paris, 1952. Career: Conducted the Fort Lauderdale Symphony, 1959-61, and has appeared as guest in the USA and Europe (Warsaw Philharmonic) and as leader of the Juilliard Contemporary Music Ensemble; Has led the premieres of Milhaud's 9th Symphony (1960), Walter Piston's Clarinet Concerto and Malipiero's Endecatode for chamber orchestra; Professor of Music at Dartmouth College, 1962-73; Vice-President of G Schirmer, New York, 1974-80; Director of the School of Music, Boston University, 1980-82. Honours include: Winner, Besançon International Conducting Competition, 1952; Lili Boulanger-Dinu Lipati Memorial Prize in Composition, 1953; Arnold Bax Memorial Award for Conducting, 1968.

DI CESARE Ezio, b. 1939, Rome, Italy. Singer (Tenor). Education: Studied in Rome. Career: Sang with a vocal sextet and made tours of Italy; Stage debut, 1975, in Bellini's Beatrice di Tenda; Many appearances in Italy and elsewhere in Europe as Alfredo, Rodolfo, and Tom Rakewell in The Rake's Progress; La Scala Milan, 1980, 1984, in Vivaldi's Tito Manlio and Idomeneo; Arvino, in Verdi's I Lombardi; Appearances in Holland and at the Verona Arena; Sang at Rome, 1986, in Spontini's Agnese di Hohenstaufen; Teatro Liceo, Barcelona, 1987, in the Spanish premiere of Mozart's Lucio Silla; Pesaro Festival, 1988, as Iago in Rossini's Otello; Sang Carlo in Pergolesi's Lo Frate Innamorato at La Scala, 1989; Gabriele Adorno at Cremona; Rome Opera, 1990, in Franco Mannino's Il Principe Felice; Season 1992 as Iarba in Jommelli's Didone Abbandonata at the Teatro Rossini, Lugo; Season 1994 as Ismaele in Nabucco at Verona; Sang the High Priest in Idomeneo at Florence, 1996. Recordings: Verdi's Stiffelio; La Finta Giardiniera; Alfano's Cyrano de Bergerac. Address: c/o Arena di Verona, Piazza Bra 28, 37121 Verona, Italy.

DI CREDICO Oslavio, b. 1942, Italy. Singer (Tenor). Career: Has sung at La Fenice, Venice, from 1969 (Pedrillo, 1971) and at Turin and Verona from 1970 and 1976; Piccola Scala Milan, 1979, in Albert Herring, and La Scala from 1984, in Il Viaggio a Reims, Tosca, Le nozze di Figaro and Adriana Lecouvreur; Premiere of Testi's Riccardo III, 1987; Turin, 1978, in Henze's Elegy for Young Lovers, Bologna, 1980, in Ligeti's Le Grand Macabre and Spoleto, 1989, in Rossini's Il Signor Bruschino; Other roles include parts in operas by Krenek, Berg, Busoni, Janacek, Dallapiccola and Prokofiev. Recordings include: Il Viaggio a Reims (DGG), La Donna del Lago (CBS), La Gazza Ladra (Sony) and Mascagni's Le Maschere (Fonti-Cetra). Address: c/o Teatro all Scala, Via Filodrammatici 2, 20121 Milan, Italy.

DI DOMENICA Robert (Anthony), b. 4 Mar 1927, New York City, USA. Flautist; Teacher; Composer. Education: Studied harmony, counterpoint, fugue and composition with Josef Schmid; BS in Music Education, New York University, 1951; Flute with Harold Bennett, 1949-55; Composition with Wallingford Riegger. Career: New York City Opera Orchestra; Freelance Flautist, New York Philharmonic Orchestra; Various engagements as solo artist; Faculty Member, 1969-, Associate Dean, 1973-76, Dean, 1976-78, New England Conservatory of Music, Boston. Compositions include: Operas: The Balcony, 1972, The Scarlet Letter, 1986; Beatrice Cenci, 1993; The Cenci, 1995; Francesco Cenci, 1996; Orchestral: Symphony, 1961, Concerto for Violin and Chamber Orchestra, 1962, Concerto for Wind Quintet, Strings and Timpani, 1964, Music for Flute and String Orchestra, 1967, Variations on a Theme by Gunther Schuller for 13 Instruments, 1983, Dream Journeys, 1984; Chamber: Sonata for Flute and Piano, 1957, Sextet for Woodwind Quintet and Piano, 1957, Quartet for Flute, Violin, Viola and Cello, 1960, Quintet for Clarinet and String Quartet, 1965, Sonata for Violin and Piano, 1966, Saeculum aureum for Flute, Piano and Tape, 1967, Sonata for Saxophone and Piano, 1968; Piano Pieces, Vocal: Wind Quintet for Soprano and Woodwind Quintet, 1963, Songs from Twelfth Night for Tenor, Flute, Viola da Gamba and Harpsichord, 1976, Hebrew Melodies for Soprano, Violin and Piano, 1983, Variations and Soliloquies for Orchestra, 1988. Recording: Leona Di Domenica in live first performance of the Solo Piano Music of Robert Di Domenica. Publication: Dream Journeys for Orchestra, 1984. Honours: Guggenheim Fellowship, 1972; Opera The Balcony premiered by the Opera Company of Boston, 1990 and Moscow's Bolshoi Theater, 1991. Address: 17 Paul Revere Road, Needham, MA 02194, USA.

DI DOMENICO Dino, b. 1957, Italy. Singer (Tenor). Education: Studied at the Accademia di Santa Cecilia in Rome, with Paolo Silveri, and with Carlo Bergonzi in Bussetto. Debut: Cremona, 1983, as Edgardo in Lucia di Lammermoor. Career: Sang in Der Rosenkavalier at Santiago (1987), Rodolfo in Luisa Miller at Rome (1990) and Pinkerton at the Staatsoper Berlin (1991); Further appearances at the Metropolitan, New York, and as Pinkerton at the Munich Staatsoper (1992). Recordings include: Nerone by Mascagni (Bongiovanni). Address: c/o Teatro dell'Opera, Piazza B Gigli 8, 00184 Rome, Italy.

DI FRANCO Loretta, b. 28 Oct 1942, New York City, New York, USA. Singer (Soprano). Education: Studied with Maud Webber and Walter Taussig in New York. Career: Sang in the chorus of the Metropolitan Opera until 1965; Solo appearances in New York in The Queen of Spades, Don Giovanni (Zerlina), Un Ballo in Maschera (Oscar), Gianni Schicchi (Lauretta), Le nozze di Figaro (Marcellina) and Lucia di Lammermoor (title role). Address: c/o Metropolitan Opera, Lincoln Center, New York, NY 10023, USA.

DI GIUSEPPE Enrico, b. 14 Oct 1932, Philadelphia, PA, USA. Tenor. Education: Studied with Richard Bonelli at Curtis Institute of Music, Philadelphia, with Hans Heinz at Juilliard School of Music, NY. Debut: Operatic debut as Massenet's Des Grieux, New Orleans, 1959. Career: Toured with Metropolitan Opera National Company; NY City Opera debut as Michele in The Saint of Bleecker Street, 1965; On roster, 1967-81; Metropolitan Opera debut in NY as Turiddu, 1970; Guest appearances with opera companies in Baltimore, Boston, Cincinnati, Dallas, Houston, Ottawa, Philadelphia, Pittsburgh, San Francisco, Toronto and other cities; Various engagements as concert artist. Recordings: Several recordings. Address: c/o Metropolitan Opera, Lincoln Center, New York, NY 10023, USA.

DI LOTTI Silvana, b. 29 Nov 1942, Aglie Canavese, Turin, Italy. Composer. Education: Studied in Turin and Salzburg, with courses at Siena notably with Berio and Boulez. Career: Teacher at the Turin Conservatory; Performances of her music in Italy and elsewhere. Compositions include: Contrasti for 2 Clarinets, 1981; Duo In Eco for Violin and Guitar, 1982; Conversari for Orchestra, 1982; Serenata for Chamber Orchestra, 1982; Piano Trio, 1986; A Solo for Clarinet and Ensemble, 1991. Address: c/o SIAE (Sezione Musicale), Viale della Letteratura n.30, 00144 Roma (EUR), Italy.

DI PIANDUNI Oslavio, b. 1939, Montevideo, Uruguay. Singer (Tenor). Education: Studied in Montevideo. Career: Appeared at Montevideo 1961-65 as Rinuccio in Gianni Schicchi and Lionel in Martha; Klagenfurt 1968-70 and Alfredo, Riccardo, Hoffmann, Don Jose, Pinkerton and Calaf at Bielefeld, 1970-75; Further engagements at the Theater am Gärtnerplatz, Munich, 1975-76, Vienna Volksoper, 1976-78 and Kiel 1979-82; Bremen 1982-84, Zurich 1988 as Edmund in Reimann's Lear; Hanover 1989, as Andrea Chenier; Other roles include Luigi in Il Tabarro, Hermann in The Queen of Spades and Otello, Oslo, 1999; Has also sung in operettas by Lehar, Johann Strauss and Offenbach; Many concert appearances and Lieder recitals. Address: c/o Niedersachische Staatstheater, Opernplatz 1, 3000 Hannover, Germany.

DI PIETRO Rocco, b. 15 September 1949, Buffalo, New York, USA. Composer. m. Juli Douglass, 28 May 1973, 1 son. Education: BPS, State University of New York, 1985; Studied with Hans Hagen, Lukas Foss and Bruno Maderna. Career: Lecturer on Modern Music; Performances of his compositions have been played in major cities of Europe and USA by such Musicians and Ensembles as Christiane Edinger, Christobal Halffter, Lukas Foss, Bruno Maderna, Bavarian Radio Orchestra, Brooklyn Philharmonic, St Paul Chamber Orchestra. Compositions: Overture to Combats for History, for Percussion Orchestra, 1980-81; Melodia Arcana for Percussion and Tarot Cards, 1980-83; Aria Grande for Violin and Orchestra, 1980; Tratto Bizzaro, Opera, 1984; Beauty and the Beast, Incidental Music for Theatre, 1986; Annales after Tasso for Madrigal Voices and Percussion, 1987. Publications: Melodia Nera for Timpani, AM Percussion Publications, 1985. Honours: ASCAP Fellowship to Berkshire Music Center, Tanglewood; Stipend to Darmstadt Ferienkurse für Neue Musik, Germany; Buffalo Foundation, 1986; Commission from the Kennedy Center for Imagination Celebration, 1986. Memberships: Composers' Forum of New York; Electro-Acoustic Society of Great Britain. Hobbie: Studies in Western History. Current Management: Sheldon Soffer, New York. Address: c/o American Percussion Publications, PO Box 436, Lancaster, NY 14086, USA.

DI STEFANO Giuseppe, b. 24 Jul 1921, Motta Santa Anastasia, Italy. Singer (Tenor). Education: Studied with Adriano Torchi and Luigi Montesanto in Italy. Career: Sang in broadcasts for Swiss Radio, 1944-45; Stage debut as Massenet's Des Grieux, Reggio Emilia, 1946; La Scala Milan from 1947; Metropolitan Opera, 1948-56, as the Duke of Mantua, Rodolfo, Faust, Rossini's Almaviva, Alfredo, Pinkerton, and Don José; Chicago Lyric Opera from 1954, as Edgardo, Arturo in I Puritani, Calaf, Riccardo in Un Ballo in Maschera and Loris in Fedora; Guest appearances in San Francisco, Vienna, Berlin, Paris, Mexico City and Sao Paulo; British debut, Edinburgh, 1957 as Nemorino; Covent Garden, 1961 as Cavaradossi; Other roles included Elvino in La Sonnambula, Fritz in L'Amico Fritz, Radames, Turiddu, Alvaro in La Forza del Destino and Nadir in Les pêcheurs de Perles; Sang with Callas on her farewell tour of 1973-74. Recordings: La Gioconda, La Forza del Destino, Lucia di Lammermoor, Manon Lescaut, Un Ballo in Maschera, La Bohème, Madama Butterfly, Rigoletto, Tosca, Werther, Carmen; Labels include HMV, Decca, RCA, Deutsche Grammophon and Cetra. Address: c/o Teatro alla Scala, Filodrammatici 2, Milan, Italy.

DI VIRGILIO Nicholas, b. 1937, New York, USA. Singer (Tenor). Education: Studied at the Eastman School and in New York. Debut: Sang Pinkerton with Chautauqua Opera, 1961. Career: Sang at Baltimore from 1956, San Francisco, 1966-67, Cincinnatti, New Orleans, 1969-70, San Diego, Pittsburgh and the New York City Opera, 1964-71; Metropolitan Opera from 1970, as Pinkerton and as Edgardo in Lucia di Lammermoor; European engagements at Brussels, Amsterdam and Lyon, 1968-70; London, 1978, in the Verdi Requiem; Other roles have included Mozart's Idomeneo, Don Ottavio and Ferrando, Verdi's Alfredo, Fento and Riccardo, Faust, Rodolfo, Hoffmann, Don José, Laca in Jenufa and Cavaradossi. Voice Teacher at the University of Illinois.

DIACONU Maria, b. 1959, Ballesti-Arges, Rumania. Singer (Soprano). Education: Studied in Bucharest and won prizes at competitions in Toulouse and Vienna. Career: Sang in Bucharest as Fiordiligi, Mozart's Countess, Musetta, and Lauretta in Gianni Schicchi; Guest at Geneva Opera as Marguerite (1986), at Bern as Offenbach's Antonia (also at the 1988 Bregenz festival) and at Liège as Amelia Grimaldi (1990); Other roles include Liu in Turandot (Limoges, 1992), Donizetti's Parisina d'Este and Micaela. Address: c/o Opéra Royal de Wallonie, 1 Rue des Dominicains, B-4000 Liège, Belgium.

DIAMAND Peter, b. 8 June 1913, Charlottenburg, Germany. Artistic Adviser. 1 son. Education: Berlin University, 1931-33. Career: Secretary to Pianist Artur Schnabel, 1934-39; Director, Holland Festival, 1948-65; Director, Edinburgh Festival, 1965-78; Artistic Adviser, Orchestre de Paris, 1977-; Artistic Adviser, Teatro alla Scala, Milan, 1977-78; Director, Mozart Festival, Paris, 1980-87. Contributor to: Various magazines. Honours: CBE; Officier Arts et Lettres, France; Commendatore della Repubblica, Italy; Offizier Verdienstkreuz, Austria; Knight, Order of Oranje Nassau, Netherlands; Honorary LLD, Edinburgh University, Scotland; Others. Memberships: Co-founder, European Association of Music Festivals, Geneva. Address: 28 Eton Court, Eton Avenue, London NW3 3HJ, England.

DIAMOND David (Leo), b. 9 July 1915, Rochester, New York, USA. Composer. Education: Cleveland Institute of Music, 1927-29; Eastman School of Music, University of Rochester, 1930-34; American Conservatory, Fontainebleau, France, summer 1937, 1938; New Music and Dalcroze Institute, New York City, 1934-36. Career: Teacher, composition, Metropolitan Music School, New York City, 1950; Lecturer, American music, Seminar in American Studies, Schloss Leopoldskron, Salzburg, Austria, 1949; Fulbright Professor, University of Rome, Italy, 1951-52; Slee Professor of Music, University of Buffalo, New York, 1961, 1963; Professor, Chairman, Department of Composition, Manhattan School of Music, New York City, 1965-67; Visiting Professor, University of Colorado, 1970; Composer-in-residence, American Academy in Rome, 1971-72; Lamont School, University of Denver, 1983; Juilliard School of Music, 1973-97. Compositions include: 11 Symphonies, concertos for violin, flute, piano and violoncello, string quartet with orchestra, 11 string quartets, chamber music, 52 preludes and fugues for piano, sonatas, choral music and songs, scores for motion pictures and other forms of instrumental music; Composer, Conductor, original score, Margaret Webster production, The Tempest, 1944-45; Incidental music, Tennessee Williams' Rose Tattoo, 1950; Ballets, Tom, Dream of Audubon; Opera, The Noblest Game. Recordings include: Music for albums, Romeo and Juliet, The Tempest Overture, 4th Symphony, 4th String Quartet; 5 volumes Symphonies. Memberships include: American Academy of Arts and Letters. Honours include: Edward MacDowell Gold Medal Award, 1991; Gold Medal, American Academy of Arts and Letters, 1993; Gold Medal, National Medal of the Arts. Address: 249 Edgerton Street, Rochester, NY 14607, USA.

DIANDA Hilda, b. 13 Apr 1925, Cordoba, Argentina. Composer. Education: Studied with Malipiero and Scherchen; Further study at Milan Electronic Music Studios and in Darmstadt. Career: Teacher at Cordoba until 1971; Performances of her music in Europe and North America; Educator and Lecturer. Compositions include: Requiem, 1984; Cantico, after St Francis of Assissi, 1985; Trio for Clarinet, Cello and Piano, 1985; Encantamientos for Tape, 1985; Viola Concerto, 1988; Paisaje for 4 Percussion, 1992; Mitos for Percusssion and Strings, 1993; Pitiales for Marimba, 1994. Honours include: Cultural Merit Medal, Italy. Address: c/o SADAIC, Lavalle 1547, Apartado Postal Number 11, Sucursal 44-B, 1048 Buenos Aires, Argentina.

DIAZ Justino, b. 29 Jan 1939, San Juan, Puerto Rico. Singer (Bass-Baritone). Education: Studied at the University of Puerto Rico, at the New England Conservatory and with Ralph Errolle and Frederick Jagel. Debut: Puerto Rico, 1957, in Menotti's The Telephone. Career: Metropolitan Opera from 1963, as Monterone and Sparafucile in Rigoletto, Figaro, Rossini's Maometto II and Colline; Festival Casals, Puerto Rico, 1964-65; Spoleto Festival, 1965; Salzburg Festival, 1966, as Escamillo; Created Antony in Barber's Antony and Cleopatra, New York Met, 1966; La Scala, Milan, 1969, in Rossini's L'Assedio do Corinto; New York City Opera, 1973, in Ginastera's Beatrix Cenci; Covent Garden, 1976, as Escamillo; Guest appearance in Hamburg, Vienna, Mexico City, Chicago and San Francisco; San Francisco and Milan, 1982, as Scarpia and Asdrubalo in La Pietra del Paragone; Sang Attila at Cincinnati, 1984, Iago at Covent Garden, 1990; Michelle in Il Tabarro at Miami, 1989, Iago and Scarpia at Los Angeles; Sang Escamillo at Rio de Janeiro, 1990; Debut as Amonasro at Cincinnati, 1990; Sang Iago in Zeffirelli's film, version of Otello, 1987; Greater Miami Opera, 1992 as Franchetti's Cristoforo Colombo; Sang Puccini's Jack Rance at Covent Garden, 1994, Scarpia in 1995. Recordings: Medea and La Wally (Decca); Thais by Massenet (RCA); L'Assedio di Corinto and Otello (EMI); Semele (Pye); Videos of Zeffirelli's Otello and Meyerbeer's L'Africaine, from San Francisco Opera. Address: c/o Stafford Law Associates, 6 Barham Close, Weybridge, Surrey KT13 9PR, England.

DIBAK Igor, b. 5 July 1947, Spisska Nova Ves, Czechoslovakia. Composer. m. Katarina Ormisova, 31 Jan 1970. Education: Piano study, Conservatorie Zilina, 1962-66; With Professor Jan Cikker, Department of Composition, University of Arts, Bratislava, 1966-71; Magister. Career: Editor, Musical Department, Czechoslovak TV, 1969-79; Editor-in-Chief, Musical Department, Czech Radio, Bratislava, 1979-87; Editor-in-Chief, Musical Department, Czech TV, Bratislava, 1987-90; Director of Music School, 1990. Compositions: Opera Candlestick; New Year's Eve Part; Ballet Portrait; Symphonic works; Chamber compositions; Compositions for children. Recordings: Moments musicaux 1, Fantasy for Viola and Orchestra, Divertimento for Strings, Opera Candlestick; Opera Candlestick, New Year's Eve Part, Ballet Portrait, Czech TV; Symphonic and Chamber works, Czech Radio Bratislava. Publication: Methodics of Piano Improvisation, 1981. Contributions to: Hudobny zivot (Music Live). Honours: Jan Levoslav Bella Award, 1979; Union of Slovak Music Composers Award, 1987. Memberships: Slovak Music Union, Bratislava; Slovak Protective Union of Authors, Bratislava. Current Management: Music Information Centre, Fucikova 29, 811 02 Bratislava, Slovakia. Address: Bajzova 10, 821 08 Bratislava, Slovakia.

DICHTER Misha, b. 27 Sept 1945, Shanghai, China. Concert Pianist. m. Cipa Dichter, 21 Jan 1968, 2 sons. Education: BSc, Juilliard School of Music, USA. Career: Performs in Recital and with major orchestras and in Chamber Music concerts world-wide; Performances with Chicago Symphony, Los Angeles Philharmonic, Philadelphia Orchestra, Israel Philharmonic Orchestra; Performs in duo-piano programmes with wife, Cipa Dichter. Recordings: include, Beethoven Sonatas No 14 in C Sharp Minor, Op 27 No 2, Moonlight; No 8 in C Minor, Op 13, Pathetique; No 28 in A Major, Op 101; Brahms Piano Concerto No 1 in D Minor; Brahms Piano Concerto No 2 in B Flat Major Op 83; Gershwin Rhapsody in Blue; Addinsell Warsaw Concerto; Litolff, Scherzo from Concerto Syphonique Op 102; Works by Liszt, including: Liszt complete Hungarian Rhapsodies; Fantasy on the Waltz from Gounod's Faust; Etudes de Concert; Schumann Symphonic Studies, Op 13 and Fantasie in C Major; Brahms: Variations and Fugue on a theme by Handel, Op. 24; Fantasius Op. 116; Waltzes, Op. 39. Contributions to: New York Times; Ovation; Contemporary Keyboard. Honours: Silver Medal, International Tchaikovsky Competition, Moscow, 1966. Hobbies: Tennis; Jogging; Drawing; Sketching. Address: Shuman Associates, 120 West 58 Street, New York, NY 10019, USA.

DICK James (Cordell), b. 29 June 1940, Hutchinson, Kansas, USA. Concert Pianist. Education: Bachelor of Music, University of Texas, Austin; Royal Academy of Music, London; Studied with Dalies Frantz, graduated with Special Honours in Piano, 1963; Certificate of Merit, Royal Academy of Music, London, 1963-65; Private study with Sir Clifford Curzon, London, 1964-65. Debut: Carnegie Hall, New York City, USA. Career: Performs professionally throughout the USA and abroad in orchestral, chamber and solo repertoire; Performed with conductors Kondrashin, Barbirolli, Ormandy, Maazel, Levine, Comissiona, Lombard, Schwarz, Fleisher, de Priest, Fiedler and Foster, among others; Has performed on radio in England, Germany, France, Netherlands, Switzerland, Mexico and US Commissions new music for piano and orchestra; Founder and Artistic Director of International Festival-Institute at Round Top, Texas. Compositions: Etudes for piano and orchestra, by Ben Lees, gave world premiere, 1975; Shiva's Drum, by Dan Welcher, gave world premiere in 1994; Krishna, from Malcolm Hawkins (England), world premiere in 1996. Recordings: Beethoven's Concerto No 4; Tchaikovsky Concerto No 1; Chopin Concerto No 1; Prokofiev Concerto No 3; Saint-Saens Concerto No 2; Welcher Concerto No 1; Rachmaninov Rhapsody. Contributions to: How to Teach Piano Successfully, by James W Bastien, 1973; Texas

Our Texas, by Bryan A Garner, 1984; Proceedings of The Philosophical Society of Texas, 1989; Remembering Horowitz, by David Dubal, 1993. Honours: Prize, Tchaikovsky Competition, Russia, 1965; Prize, Leventritt Competition, New York City, 1965; Prize, Busoni Competition, Italy, 1965; Fulbright Scholar, London, 1963-65; Associate, Royal Academy of Music, 1969; Honoured at White House by President Johnson, 1965; Pres Citation, National Federation of Music Clubs, USA; Chevalier des Arts et Lettres, French Ministry of Culture, 1995. Memberships: English Speaking Union; Philosophical Society of Texas; Texas Lyceum; Bohemians, New York City; Rotary International; Texas Federation of Music Clubs. Hobbies: Architecture; Landscaping; Poetry. Current Management: Alain Declert & Associates. Address: International Festival-Institute, PO Box 89, Round Top, TX 78954, USA.

DICKERSON Roger (Donald), b. 24 August 1934, New Orleans, Louisiana, USA. Composer. Education: Studied at Dillard University, New Orleans and with Bernard Heiden at Indiana University, Bloomington; Further study at the Akademie für Musik und Darstellende Kunst, Vienna. Career: Played double bass while in Military Service; Has taught and performed in the New Orleans area; Co-Founder of the Creative Arts Alliance, 1975; Subject of PBS programme, New Orleans Concert. Honours: include, Fulbright Scholarship, 1959-62; John Hay Whitney Fellowship, 1964; Louis Armstrong Memorial Award. Compositions: include, Perkussion, 1954; Variations for Woodwind Trio, 1955; Sonatina for Piano, 1956; String Quartet, 1956; Music I Hears for Soprano and Piano, 1956; Chorale Prelude for Organ, 1957; Music for String Trio, 1957; Concert Overture, 1957; Essay for Band, 1958; Fugue 'n' Blues for Band, 1959; Clarinet Sonata, 1960; Wind Quintet, 1961; A Musical Service for Louis, 1972; Orpheus as 'his Slide Trombone, 1975; New Orleans Concerto for Piano and Orchestra, 1976; Psalm XLIX, 1979. Address: c/o ASCAP, ASCAP Building, One Lincoln Plaza, New York, NY 10023, USA.

DICKIE Brian, b. 23 Jul 1941. m. (1) Victoria Teresa Sheldon, 1968, 2 s, 1 d. m. (2) Nancy Gustafson, 1989. Education: Haileybury; Trinity College, Dublin. Career: Administration Assistant, Glyndebourne Opera, 1962-66; Administrator, Glyndebourne Touring Opera, 1967-81; Glyndebourne Festival Opera: Opera Manager, 1970-81, General Administrator, 1981-89; Artistic Director, Wexford Festival, 1967-73; Artistic Advisor, Theatre Music de Paris, 1981-87; Chairman, London Choral Society, 1978-85; Vice-Chairman, TNC, 1980-85 (Chairman, TNCC Opera Committee, 1976-85); Vice President, Theatrical Management Association, 1983-85; General Director, Canadian Opera Company, 1989-93. Address: 405 Edgemere Way North, Naples, FL 33999, USA.

DICKIE John, b. 5 Sept 1953, London, England. Singer (Tenor). Education: Studied with Luise Scheidt and with Hilde Zadek at the Vienna Conservatory. Career: Sang at Wuppertal, 1979-82, Mannheim, 1982-85; Hamburg Staatsoper from 1985; Bregenz Festival, 1981-86, in L'Incontro Improvviso, Lucia di Lammermoor, Der Vogelhändler and Die Zauberflöte; Guest appearances in London, Geneva, Dusseldorf, Berlin and Vienna; Other roles include Mozart's Belmonte, Don Ottavio, Ferrando and Belfiore, Lionel in Martha, Nemorino in L'Elisir d'Amore, Berlioz's Benedict, Lensky in Eugene Onegin and Wagner's Steuermann and Froh; Also heard as concert singer. Address: c/o Hamburgsche Staatsoper, Grosse Theaterstrasse 34, D-2000 Hamburg, Germany.

DICKINSON Meriel, b. 8 Apr 1940, Lytham St Anne's, England. Singer (Mezzo-Soprano). Education: GRSM; ARMCM; Piano and Singing Performer's Diploma with Honours; Vienna Academy, Austria. Debut: London, 1964. Career: Frequent radio programmes; 2 BBC TV documentary films; Recital programmes with composer Peter Dickinson (brother) throughout Europe. Recordings: Contemporary British Composers (Crosse, Berkeley, Dickinson); Erik Satie Songs and Piano Music; Brecht-Weill series with London Sinfonietta. Honours: Countess of Munster Musical Trust Scholarship, 1964-66. Memberships: Society for Promotion of New Music; Park Lane Group; Incorporated Society of Musicians. Hobbies: Listening to jazz; Entertaining. Address: c/o Music International, 13 Ardilaun Road, London N5 2QR, England.

DICKINSON Peter, b. 15 Nov 1934, Lytham, Lancashire, England. Composer; Pianist; Emeritus Professor of Music. m. Bridget Jane Tomkinson, 2 sons. Education: Queens' College, Cambridge; MA, Music; LRAM; ARCM, Piano Performance; ARCO, Sawyer Prize; FRCO; DMus; Juilliard School of Music, New York, USA. Career: Various teaching posts in New York, London and Birmingham; First Professor of Music, 1974-84, Emeritus, 1984-, Keele University; Professor, Goldsmiths, University of London, 1991-; Regular performances as Pianist, mostly with sister Meriel Dickinson (mezzo), radio and television in UK and abroad. Compositions include: Orchestral works, concertos, chamber music, choral works, keyboard music, church music. Recordings: Piano Concerto; Organ Concerto; Outcry; A Mass of the Apocalypse; Winter Afternoons; Recorder Music; Extravaganzas; Surrealist Landscape; The Unicorns; Organ Music; Piano Music; Songs. Publications: Editor: 20 British Composers, 1975; The Complete Songs and Piano Music of Lord Berners, 1982; The Music of Lennox Berkeley, 1989. Contributions to: Various books and journals including book chapters and dictionaries. Honours: Recipient of various honours including: Fellowship of the Royal Society of Arts; Honorary FTCL. Memberships include: Performing Right Society; Association of Professional Composers; Sonneck Society; Royal Musical Association; Board, Trinity College of Music, 1985-; President, London Concert Choir, 1985-. Hobby: Books. Address: Goldsmiths, University of London, New Cross, London SE14 6NW, England.

DICKMAN Stephen (Allen), b. 2 Mar 1943, Chicago, Illinois, USA. Composer. Education: Studied composition with Jacob Druckman at Bard College, and theory and composition with Arthur Berger and Harold Shapero at Bandeis University; Further study with Ernst Krenek at the Berkshire Music Center and with Goffredo Petrassi in Rome. Career: Has travelled widely, in order to study the music of Asia and the Middle East. Compositions: include, 2 String Trios, 1965, 1971; The Snow Man for soprano and ensemble, 1966; Frei for tape, 1966; Lacerations for tape, 1966; 4 String Quartets, 1967-78; Damsel for 16 instruments, 1968; Violoncello, 1969; 2 Violins, 1969; Real Magic in New York, opera, 1971; Song Cycle, 1975-80; Musical Journeys 1-1V, 1972-76; 10 Not Long Songs, 1977; Magic Circle for chorus and ensemble, 1980; String Trio: Dance, 1980; Influence of India for ensemble, 1980; Everything and Everything for 3 trumpets and strings, 1982; Orchestra by the Sea for 4 sopranos and orchestra, 1983; Trees and other Inclinations for paino, 1983. Address: c/o BMI. 320 West 57th Street, New York, NY 10019, USA.

DICKSON Joan, b. 21 Dec 1921, Edinburgh, Scotland. Cellist; Teacher. Education: LRAM; ARCM; Studied in Paris and Rome. Career: Solo Cellist with major British Orchestras; Appearances at the London Promenade Concerts, Cheltenham Festival, Edinburgh Festival; Tours abroad; Regular Broadcaster; TV appearances; Professor of Cello, Royal College of Music, London; Teacher of Cello, Royal Scottish Academy of Music, Glasgow; Short Talks, BBC Radio. Recordings: Iain Hamilton Cello Sonata; Tam O'Bedlam's Song; Cesar Franck Sonata. Contributions to: Incorporated Society of Musicians Magazine. Honours: Fellow, Royal College of Music; Fellow, Royal Scottish Academy Music & Drama; Cobbett Gold Medal for services to Chamber Music. Hobbies: Gardening; Philately; Painting. Address: 4 Great Stuart Street, Edinburgh EH3 6AW, Scotland.

DICTEROW Glenn (Eugene), b. 23 December 1948, Los Angeles, California, USA. Violinist; Teacher. m. Georgeann Tobin, 27 June 1980, 2 daughters. Education: BMus, Juilliard School of Music, New York, 1970. Career: Associate Concertmaster then Concertmaster, Los Angeles Philharmonic Orchestra, 1972-79; Concertmaster, New York Philharmonic Orchestra, 1980-; Soloist with various USA Orchestras; Engaged in private teaching; Teacher, University of Southern California, Los Angeles and Manhattan School of Music, New York. Honours: 1st Prize, Young Musicians Foundation, 1962; 3rd Prize, Merriweather Post competition, 1963; Bronze Medal, Tchaikovsky International Competitions, 1970. Address: c/o New York Philharmonic Orchestra, Lincoln Center, New York, NY 10023, USA.

DIDONE Rosanna, b. 13 Feb 1952, Veneta, Italy. Singer (Soprano). Education: Studied at the Benedetto Marcello Conservatory Venice. Debut: Padua 1978, as Serpina in La Serva Padrona. Career: Appearances at Venice in Idomeneo, as Rosette in Manon and Bianca in La Rondine; Clarice in Il Mondo Della Luna at Turin and Frasquita in Carmen at Padau, 1982; At Trieste (from 1982) has sung Gnese in Il Campiello, Amor (Orpheus ed Euridice), Barbarina, and a Naiad in Ariadne auf Naxos; Rome Opera 1982 and 1988 in Don Carlos and as Mme Silberklang in Der Schauspieldirektor by Mozart; Other roles include Musetta, Marie-Louise in Kodály's Hary Janos, Biancofiore in Francesca da Rimini, Gilda, Susanna, Carolina (Il matrimonio segreto), Norina (Don Pasquale), Oscar, Nannetta, Laura and Despina; Guest appearances in Holland and Bulgaria. Recordings: include, Egloge in Mascagni's Nerone, and Francesca da Rimni (Bongiovanni).

DIEDERICH Cyril, b. 2 Oct 1945, Marseille, France. Conductor. Education: Studied in Toulouse and Rouen and at the Paris Conservatoire. Career: Founded his own chamber orchestra, 1969, and was assistant at the Lyon Orchestra, 1975-76; Associate Conductor of National Orchestra of Lille and Director of Montpellior Philharmonic, 1984; Music Director of the Montpellier Opera, 1985; Led the premiere of Noces de Sang by Charles Chaynes, 1988. Address: c/o Opéra de Montpellier, 11 Boulevard Victor Hugo, F-34000 Montpellier, France.

DIEMER Emma Lou, b. 24 Nov 1927, Kansas City, Missouri, USA. Composer; Musician; University Professor. Education: BM, 1949, MM, 1950, Yale School of Music; PhD, Eastman School of Music, 1960. Career: Pianist; Organist; Composer-in-Residence, Santa Barbara Symphony, 1990-; Professor of Composition, University of California, Santa Barbara, 1971-91; Organist, First Presbyterian Church, Santa Barbara, 1984-. Compositions: Over 100 published compositions; 10 listings in Schwann Catalogue, 17 works recorded; Concerto for Marimba, 1990; Concerto for Piano, 1991; Sextet, 1992; Four Biblical Settings for Organ, 1992; Kyrie, 1993; Fantasy for Piano, 1993; Kyrie and Gloria, 1996. Recordings: 10 including Declarations for Organ; Toccata and Fugue for Organ; Toccata for Piano; Summer of 82 for Cello and Piano; Quartet for Piano, Violin, Viola and Cello; Sextet for Woodwind Quintet and Piano; Youth Overture; Encore for Piano, 1991; Sextet, 1993; Concerto in One Movement for Piano, 1995; String Quartet No 1, 1995; Santa Barbara Overture, 1997. Publications: Over 100 including: Toccata for marimba, 1956; Sonata for Violin and Piano, 1968; Sextet for Woodwind Quintet and Piano, 1968; Anniversary Choruses for Chorus and Orchestra, 1970; Concerto for Flute, 1973; Symphony No 2, 1976; Toccata for Piano, 1979; Suite of Homages for Orchestra, 1985; String Quartet No 1, 1987; Choral - A Feast for Christmas, 1992; Marimba Concerto, 1994; Organ Works, 1957-95; Kyrie and Gloria, 1997. Honours: Kennedy Center Friedholm Award, for Concerto in One Movement for Piano, 1992; American Guild of Organists Composer of the Year, 1995. Address: 2249 Vista del Campo, Santa Barbara, CA 93101, USA.

DIENER Melanie, b. 1967, Germany. Singer (Soprano). Education: Studied with Sylvia Geszty in Stuttgart and with Rudolf Piernay in Mannheim; Further study at Indiana University. Career: Concerts include the Brahms Requiem in Paris and Zurich, Mendelssohn's St Paul under Philippe Herreweghe and Mahler's 2nd Symphony at Linz; Recitals in Stuttgart and Bonn; Opera debut as Mozart'sIlia at Garsington, England, 1996; Season 1996-97 with Elijah at the Berlin Philharmonie, Fiordiligi at Covent Garden and in Paris, First Lady in Die Zauberflöte at the Salzburg Festival; Asberta in Holzbauer's Gunther von Schwarzburg under Ton Koopman at the Amsterdam Concertgebouw under Claudio Abbado at Aix and in New York, the Strauss Four Last Songs at Turin and the Verdi Requiem at St Gallen. Honours include: Prize Winner, International Mozart Competition, Salzburg, 1995; Winner, Kirsten Flagsted Prize, Oslo, 1995. Address: Balmer & Dixon AG, 8006 Zurich, Grantiweg 2, Switzerland.

DIESSELHORST Jan, b. 1956, Marburg, Germany. Cellist. Education: Studied in Frankfurt and with Wolfgang Boettcher in Berlin. Career: Joined the Berlin Philharmonic Orchestra, 1979; Co-founded the Philharmonic Quartet Berlin, giving concerts throughout Europe, the USA and Japan; British debut, 1987, playing Haydn, Szymanowski and Beethoven at Wigmore Hall; Bath Festival, 1987, playing Mozart, Schumann and Beethoven (Op. 127); Other repertoire includes quartets by Bartok, Mendelssohn, Nicolai, Ravel and Schubert; Quintets by Brahms, Weber, Reger and Schumann. Address: c/o Berlin Pharhominc Orchestra, Philharmonie, Matthäuskirchstrasse 1, D-1000 Berlin 30, Germany.

DIETRICH Karl, b. 9 Jul 1927, Wachstedt, Eichsfeld, Germany. Composer; Teacher. m. Gerda Lins, 29 Apr 1952, 2 daughters. Education: Matriculation and Study, University Jena and High School of Music, Franz Liszt, Weimar, State Examination for Music Teachers. Career: Professor for Composition, High School of Music, Franz Liszt, Weimar. Compositions: Numerous including: 7 Symphonies; 2 Operas; Piano Concerto; Violoncello Concerto; Dramatic Szenes for 3 Flutes (1 soloist), Soloist and Orchestra; 2 Concertos for String Orchestra; Symphonic Choral Works; Chamber Music; Songs; O vos omnes, aus den Klageliedern des Jeremias, in memoriam G P Palestrina, for Soprano and String Quartet, 1991; Lobpreis und Bitte, for 4-6 voice mixed choir, Hymnus mit Orgelbegleitung, 1991, Kirchenmusik; Memorial for Streichorchester nach dem Bach-Choral, Vergiß mein nicht, 1993; Psalm 49, Die Vergänglichkeit des Menschen, 1994; Drei Chorstücke for gleiche Stimmen nach Texten von Johann Gottfried Herder, 1995; Was ist Gott?, für gemichten Chor a cappella, 1995; Barocke Version, für Streichorchester, 1995; Deutsche Messe für Männerchor a cappella, 1995; Rupert-Mayer-Reflexionen für Orgel-Solo, 1996; Klassische Variationen für Bläserquintett über das Eichsfeld-Lied, 1996; Schöndorfer Messe (lateinischer Text) für mittlere Singstimme und Orgelbegleitung, 1996; Konzertantes Präludium für Orchester, Neufassung, 1997; Des Nachts auf meinem Lager, aus dem salomonischen Hohelied, für 5 Blechbläser und gem chor, 1997; Doppelchöriger Zyklus Hoffnungen für 2 vierstimmige Männerchöre a cappella, 1997; Metoscopos oder Der Stirnschauer für Flöte, Oboe, Viola and Violoncello, forthcoming. Recordings include: Symphony No 4, contra bellum, Staatliches Sinfonieorchester Thüringen, Sitz Gotha, Conductor Lothar Seyfarth; Dramatische Szenen, Rundfunk Sinfonie Orchester Leipzig, Conductor, Herbert Kegel; CD, Sinfonie No 7. Publications include: Komische Oper, Pervonte, Berlin; Violoncello Concerto, Leipzig; Vision for Flute and Organ, Leipzig; Konzertsuite for String Orchestra, Berlin; Concertino giocoso for

String Orchestra, Leipzig; Three Cheerful Stories, cappella choir, Leipzig. Memberships: Mitglied; Deutscher Komponisten Interessenverband. Address: Auf dem Dürbache 10, D-99438 Weimar-Legefeld, Germany.

DIETSCH James (William), b. 21 Mar 1950, Kansas City, Missouri, USA. Opera Singer, Baritone. m. Susan Kay Schell, 23 Aug 1980, 1 s. Education: BME, 1972, MMus Voice, 1975, University of Missouri, Kansas City; Juilliard School of Music American Opera Center, 1979-82; Vienna Academy of Music, Austria. Debut: Fargo-Moorhead Civic Opera, 1975; New York Town Hall, 1981; Carnegie Hall, 1982. Career: Leading artist with numerous opera companies and concert appearances in USA and abroad, including: San Francisco Opera, New York City Opera, English Opera North, Karlsruhe Badisches Staatsheater; Saarbrucken Saarländiches Staatsheater; Michigan Opera, Milwaukee Opera, Dusseldorf Oper am Rhein, Minnesota Opera, Hawaii Opera, Staatsheater Essen, Santa Fe Opera, Spoleto Festival USA, New York Philharmonic, Mexico City Philharmonic; Season 1992 as Scarpia at Costa Mesa, (Opera Pacific) and Nabucco at Montreal. Recordings: Il Corsaro by Verdi, Historical Recording Incorporate, 1981. Hobbies: Golf; Skiing; Swimming; Basketball; Electric Trains; Coin Collections: Biking. Address: c/o Robert Lombardo Associates, 62 West 62nd Street, Suite 6F, New York, NY 10023, USA.

DIJKSTRA Hebe, b. 1952, Holland. Singer (Mezzo-Soprano). m. Jan Alofs. Education: Studied at the Hague Conservatory. Debut: Sang Gluck's Orpheus at Enschede, 1975. Career: Sang Mistress Quickly at Enschede, and appeared in Rimsky's Sadko at Bonn, 1976; Engaged at Detmold, 1976-79, Saarbrucken 1979-80, Freiburg, 1981-83; Krefeld, 1982-85, Wuppertal, 1987-89; Amsterdam, 1989, in Der Kreidekreis by Zemlinsky; Member of the Staatstheater am Gärtnerplatz, Munich from 1989; Sang Rossweise in Die Walküre at Bayreuth, 1988-91; Ulrica at Amsterdam 1992; Mary in Fliegande Holländer at the 1992 Bayreuth Festival; Other roles include Carmen, Fricka, Waltraute, the Nurse in Boris Godunov, and La Comandante in I Cavalieri di Ekebu by Zandonai. Address: c/o Staatstheater am Gärtnerplatz, Gärtnerplatz 3, 8000 Munich, Germany.

DILLON James, b. 29 Oct 1950, Glasgow, Scotland. Composer. Education: Glasgow School of Art, 1967-68; Polytechnic of Central London, 1972-73; Polytechnic of North London, 1973-76. Career: Works performed and featured at festivals throughout the world including: Antidogma (Turin), Bath, Darmstadt, Gulbenkian (Lisbon), ISCM (Toronto), La Rochelle, Musica Nel Nostro Tempo (Milan), Music of Eight Decades (London), Paris d'Automne, Warsaw, Zig-Zag (Paris), Châtelet (Paris), Donaueschingen (Germany); Guest Lecturer at the Universities of Keele, London, New York, Nottingham, Oxford also Universities of Central England and Gothenburg; Guest Composer at the 1982, 1984, 1986 Darmstadt Fierenkurse. Compositions: include, Spleen, 1980; Once Upon a Time, 1980; Come Live With Me, 1981; Parjanya-Vata, 1981; East 11th Street, 1982; String Quartet, 1983; Sgotham, 1984; La Coupure, 1986; Helle Nacht, 1987; Del Cuarto Elemento, 1988; L'Eclan Parfum, 1988; Shrouded Mirrors, 1988; La Femme Invisible, 1989; L'Oeuvrs Au Noir, 1990; Blitzschlag, 1991; String Quartet No 2, 1991; Nuée, 1991; Ignis Noster, 1991-92; Siorram, 1992; Vernal Showers, 1992; L'Evolution Du Vol, 1993; Viriditas, 1993. Recordings: Sgothan, AMI 861-862; Del Cuarto Elemento; La Femme Invisible; East 11th Street, NY 10003; Windows and Canopies; Dillug-Kefitsah; Evening Rain; Come Live With Me. Publications: Problemas Discursivos en La Muska Contemporanea, Valencia, 1989; Speculative Instruments: Timbre, Métaphore pour La Composition, 1991. Honour: Kranichsteiner Musikpreis, Federal Republic of Germany, 1982; Classical Music Personality of the Year, London Times, 1989. Current Management: c/o Peters Edition Ltd. Address: c/o Peters Edition Limited, 10-12 Baches Street, London M6DN, England.

DILWORTH-LESLIE Samuel, b. 17 Sept 1937, Savannah, Georgia, USA. Concert Pianist; Teacher. Education: Graduated, New York City High School of Music & Art, 1951; BMus, MMus, Manhattan School of Music, 1951-56; Studies with N Boulanger, M Munz, D Zaslavsky; MA, Columbia University, New York City, 1956; Master classes with A Rubinstein, C Curzon, R and G Casadesus, N Magaloff. Debut: Carnegie Recital Hall, New York City, 1954. Career: Performed throughout Europe and USA; Participated in TV film Finding True Freedom, 1971; 1st public performance of complete piano works of Gabriel Fauré, Paris, 1974, New Brunswick, New Jersey, 1973-74, London, 1984; Organiser, Participant, 1st Chopin Festival, Rutgers University, New Brunswick, 1977; Gave 1st performance outside USSR of Estonian Arthur Lemba's Concerto No 1 with Swedish National Orchestra of Gothenburg, 1982, also American premiere with same orchestra, conductor Neeme Järvi, 1983; Professor of Piano, Mason Gross School of the Arts, Rutgers University. Recording: Fauré, CRS, 1985. Address: Mason Gross School of the Arts, Department of Music, Rutgers University, New Brunswick, NJ 08903, USA.

DIMITROVA Anastasia, b. 16 Nov 1940, Pernik, Bulgaria. Singer (Soprano). Education: Studied at State Conservatory, Sofia and in Zagred. Debut: Sang in Nabucco at Skopje, 1965. Career: Many Appearances at Opera Houses in Bulgaria and Yugoslavia, notably, Belgrade, Sofia, Zagreb and Rijeka; Roles have included Verdi's Elizabetta and Leonora (Trovatore), Mimi, Yaroslavna (Prince Igor), Tatiana in Eugene Onegin, Marenka (Bartered Bride), Rusalka, Micaela, Euridice and Marguerite. Honours: Winner, Francisco Vinas (Barcelona 1969) and Bussetto Competitions. Address: c/o Sofia State Opera, Boulevard Dondoukov 58, 1000 Sofia, Bulgaria.

DIMITROVA Ghena, b. 6 May 195, Beglej, Bulgaria. Singer (Soprano). Education: Studied with Professor Christo Brumbarov in Sofia. Debut: Sofia, as Abigaille in Nabucco. Career: Sang widely in Bulgaria. From 1970 sang in Italy and at Strasbourg, Karlsruhe, Mannheim and Stuttgart; US debut, 1982, as Elvira in Ernani at Dallas; Verona Arena and La Scala Milan, 1982, 1983, as Turandot; Barcelona, 1984, as Verdi's Odabella; Salzburg Festival, 1984, as Lady Macbeth; Covent Garden debut, 1984, Turandot, returned, 1990; New York debut as Abigaille, 1984; Guest appearances in Buenos Aires, Vienna, Paris, Düsseldorf and Berlin; Other roles include Aida, Norma, Leonora in Il Trovatore and La Gioconda; Sang Norma at Houston, 1987, and Paris; Aida at Luxor, Egypt, 1987; Verona Arena, 1988, as Turandot; Sang Santuzza at Covent Garden and the Metropolitan, 1989; Season 1992 at the Festival of Caracalla and Tosca at Torre del Lago; Season 1993-94 included Aida and Cavalleria Rusticana at Arena di Verona and La Fanciulla del West at the Metropolitan Opera House, New York; Season 1994-95 as Turandot at Torre del Lago, Metropolitan Opera House, Caracas and Pasadena; Tosca with Rome Opera on tour to Nagoya, Japan and recitals in Teneriffe and Athens; Sang Lady Macbeth in Athens, 1997. Recordings: Nabucco; Aida; La Gioconda; I Lombardi and Oberto by Verdi; Video of Turandot. Address: c/o Marks Management Ltd, 14 New Burlington Street, London W1X 1FF, England (except for UK engagements).

DINESCU Violeta, b. 13 Jul 1953, Bucharest, Romania. Composer. Education: Bachelor's Degree, College Georghe Lazar, Bucharest, 1972; Master's Degree, 1977, Special Diploma and study year for composition, 1978, Conservatory Ciprian Porumbescu. Career: Instructor at George Enescu Music School, Bucharest, 1978-82; Instructor at Conservatory for Church Music, Heidelberg, Germany, 1986-90; Lecturer at various universities in Germany, RSA and USA, 1986; Instructor for Harmony and Counterpoint at Hochschule, Frankfurt, 1989-90; Instructor of Theory, Harmony and Counterpoint at the Academy of Church Music, Bayreuth, 1990-94; Professor of Composition, University of Oldenburg, 1996-. Compositions include: Orchestral and Vocal Compositions; Chamber Music; Solos, Duos, Trios, Quartets, Quintets, Sextets, and Septets; Works for Chamber Ensemble; 4 Operas; Children's Opera; Ballet Music; Film Music; Experimental Music. Recordings: Numerous radio and television recordings. Honours: Recipient of over 50 international prizes, distinctions and selections from several countries including: Romania, Germany, Canada, USA, Italy, England, Columbia, RSA, Hungary, Poland and Austria. Address: Presuhnstrasse 39, D-26133 Oldenburg, Germany.

DITTMER Luther Albert, b. 8 April 1927, New York, New York, USA. University Professor; Musicologist. m. Dr Ingeborg Dittmer, 29 December 1951, 2 sons. Education: AB, Columbia University, 1947; AM, Teachers College, Columbia University, 1947-49; PhD, University Basel, 1949-52. Publications include: Worcester Music Fragments, 1957; Eine Zentrale Quelle der Notre Dame-Musik, 1959; Firenze Pluteo 29, 1964. Honours: Numerous grants. Memberships: Music Society. Address: PO Box 295, Henryville, PA 18332-0295, USA.

DIVAKOVA Karla, b. 15 May 1939, Ostrava, Czechoslovakia. Secretary of Musical Comedy; Ensemble of Ostrava. Divorced, 1 daughter. Education: 11 Years of Private Studium of Music and Singing to Famous Opera Singers. Career includes: Part of Diana, Orpheus in Der Unterwelt, 1963; National Theatre, Modavian-Silesian in Ostrava City. Career: Part of Mariza, Gratin Mariza; Lisa in Lehar's, Das Land Des Lächelns. Honours: Honour of Literary Fund of Czechoslovak Republic, 1985; Honour for Excellent Performances in Classic and Musical Comedies, 1995. Hobbies: Cultivating the plants; Playing the piano; Knitting. Address: Cs Legil 14, 70104 Ostrava 1, Czechoslovakia.

DIVALL Richard (Sydney Benedict), b. 9 Sept 1945, Sydney, New South Wales, Australia. Conductor. Education: University of Melbourne. Musical Education: Conservatorium of Music, Sydney. Debut: Handel's Xerxes, Sydney, Australia. Career: Producer of Music, ABC, 1960-70; Musical Director, Queensland Opera, 1971-; Guest Conductor, ABC, 1972-; Music Director, Victoria State Opera, 1972-95, Principal Conductor, 1995-97; Associate Professor of Music, University of Melbourne, 1992-; Principal Resident Conductor, Opera Australia, 1997-; Edited 18th century symphonies, Series of volumes of Colonial

Australian repertoire music and 15 operas. Recordings: Numerous, including: 120 operas including Les Troyens, Elektra, Poppea, Don Carlos, Turandot. Honours: OBE, 1981; D Mus, Sao Paolo, 1989; Commendatore al Merito, 1989; Cavaliere di Grazia, Order of Malta, 1990; DLitt (Hons), Monash, 1992; Fellow, Queens College, University of Melbourne; Chairman, Marshall-Hall Trust, and Australian Catholic University Music Patron, 3MBS 1992-. Hobbies: Medical history; Health and charity work. Current Management: J Eddy Artists, Melbourne. Address: East Wing Flat, Queens College, University of Melbourne, Vic 3025, Australia.

DIVES Tamsin, b. 1968, England. Mezzo-Soprano. Education: Studied at the Guildhall School. Career: Opera appearances with Glyndebourne Festival, English National Opera, Opera North, Chelsea Opera and Edinburgh and Harrogate Festivals; Roles include Fidalma in Il Matrimonio Segreto and Mrs Grose in The Turn Of The Screw; Concerts with the Hallé Orchestra, Northern Sinfonia and The Nash Ensemble; Sang in the British Premiere of Korngold's Die tote Stadt, Queen Elizabeth Hall, 1996. Recordings include: Davies' The Martyrdom Of St Magnus; Macmillan's Visitatio Sepulchri. Address: Ron Gonsalves Management, 7 Old Town, Clapham, London, SW4 0JT, England.

DIVOKY Zdenek, b. 1954, Brno, Czechoslovakia. Horn Player. Education: Studied at the Janacek Academy in Brno with Frantisek Socl. Career: Wind Section of the State Philharmonic Orchestra in Brno; Czech Philharmonic, 1979; Solo peformer in concert and member of such chamber ensembles as the Prague Brass Trio, the Horn Quartet of the Czech Philharmonic, the Collegium Musicum Pragense and the Stamic Quartet; Solo engagements in Germany, Australia, England, Spain and Canada; Repertoire includes concertos by M and J Haydn, Telemann, Mozart, Punto, Rosetti, Schumann, Weber and Strauss; Recitalist in Beethoven, Mozart, Reicha, Brahms, Britten, Hindemith and Burghauser; Tours with the Czech Philharmonic and with various chamber ensembles to Europe, the USA and Japan. Honours: include, Prizewinner at Prague Spring International Festival and competitions in Munich and Markneukirchen. Address: c/o Anglo Swiss Limited, 3 Primrose Mews, 1a Sharpleshall Street, London NW1 8YW, England.

DIXON James, b. 26 Apr 1928, Estherville, Iowa, USA. Conductor. Education: Studied at the University of Iowa and with Dimitri Mitropoulos, 1949-60. Career: Conducted the US 7th Army Band in Germany; Led the University of Iowa Symphony, 1954-59; New England Conservatory Symphony in Boston, 1969-61; Conductor of the Tri-City Symphony in Davenport, Iowa, and Rock Island, Illinois; Associate Conductor of the Minneapolis Symphony, 1961-62; Guest Conductor with the National Orchestra of Greece in Athens, the Norddeutscher Rundfunk, Hamburg, the Westdeutscher Rundfunk, Cologne, the Tanglewood Orchestra, the Chicago Civic Symphony and the Chicago Symphony (1972); Conducted a student group at the International Society for Contemporary Music Festival in Boston, 1976; Has led the premieres of Charles Wuorinen's Piano Concerto and works by T J Anderson and William Matthews. Honours: include, Gustav Mahler Medal, 1963.

DJUPSJÖBACKA Gustav Mikael, b. 21 Dec 1950, Borgå, Finland. Pianist. m. Lena von Bonsdorff, 15 July 1977, 1 son, 1 daughter. Education: Sibelius Academy, 1969-73; Musical Academy, Prague, 1973-74; Hochschule für Musik, Vienna, 1975-77. Debut: Helsinki, 1978. Career: Keyboard Player, Radio Symphony Orchestra of Finland, 1977-87; Lecturer in Lied Music, Sibelius Academy, 1987-; Mainly lied recitals in Europe, USA and Mexico with Ritva Auvinen, Monica Groop, Tom Krause, Jorma Hynninen, others. Recordings: Winterreise and Sibelius Songs with Tom Krause; Sibelius Songs with Ritva Auvinen. Publications: Yrjö Kilpinen's Morgenstern Songs, 1992. Honour: Sylvi Kekkonen Scholarship, 1975, 1976. Memberships: Yrjö Kilpinen Society; Madetoja Foundation. Hobby: Etymology. Address: Töölöntorinkatu 3 A 2, 00260 Helsinki, Finland.

DLOUHY Dan, b. 26 Feb 1965, Brno, Czech Republic. Composer; Solo Percussionist. Education: Graduate, Department of Nuclear Equipment, Technical University of Brno, 1988; Percussion, Composition, Janacek Academy of Music and Dramatic Arts, Brno, 1992. Debut: Leipzig, 1985. Career: Over 800 Concert Performances; CD, Radio and TV Recordings in Prague, Berlin, Vienna, Warsaw, Bratislava; Leader, Dama Dama, Central European Percussion Ensemble, 1990-. Compositions: Over 30 Chamber, Orchestral and Electroacoustic Works. Recordings: Numerous. Publication: Development, Production and Exploitation of Untraditional Percussion Instruments, 1992. Honours: Czech Music Foundation Prize, 1991, 1992; Winner, European Percussion Ensemble Competition, Holland, 1991; Winner, Composition Competition, Generation, 1995. Membership: Czech Percussionists Association. Hobbies: Development of Musical Instruments; Physics. Current Management: ARS Koncert, Brno. Address: Berkova 35, 612 00 Brno, Czech Republic.

DLUGOSZEWSKI Lucia, b. 16 Jun 1934, Detroit, Michigan, USA. Composer. Education: Studied piano with Grete Sultan, music analysis at Mannes College and composition with Edgard Varese. Career: Devised the timbe piano, 1951; Association with Erik Hawkins Dance Company; Commissions from the New York Philharmonic, the Music Society of Lincoln Center, the American Composers Orchestra and the Louisville Orchestra. Compositions: include, Arithmetic Progressions for orchestra, 1954; Orchestral Radiant Ground, 1955; Here and Now with Watchers, dance, 1954-57; Naked Wabin for flute and ensemble, 1956; Suchness Concert for large percussion ensemble, 1958; Clear Places, ballet, 1958-60; Beauty Music, 1965; Naked Flight Nageire for chamber orchestra, 1966; Lords of Persia, ballet, 1966-68; Balance Naked Flung for clarinet and ensemble, 1966; Naked Quintet for brass, 1967; Blake Lake ballet, 1970; Space is a Diamond for trumpet, 1970; Angels of the Inmost Heaven, ballet, 1972; Strange Tenderness of Naked Leaping for orchestra, 1977; Amor now Titling Night for orchestra, 1978; Almost Elusive Empty August, woodwind quintet, 1979; Cicada Terrible Freedom for flute and ensemble, 1981; Startle Transparent Terrible Freedom for orchestra, 1981; Avanti, ballet, 1983; Duende Amor for orchestra, 1983; Quidditas Sorrow Terrible Freedom for orchestra, 1983; This Women Duende Amor, ballet, 1984; Quidditas, string quartet, 1984. Honours: include, Guggenheim Fellowship; Grant from the Martha Band Rockefeller Fund; Koussevitsky International Recording Award, 1977 for Fire Fragile Light. Address: c/o BMI, 320 West 57th Street, New York, NY 10019, USA.

DMITRIEV Alexsander, b. 1935, Leningrad, USSR. Conductor. Education: Leningrad Conservatory, under Kudriavtseva, Tiulin, Rabinovitch. Career: Conductor Karelian Radio and TV Symphony Orchestra, 1961, Principal Conductor, 1962-71; Principal Conductor, Maly Opera and Ballet Theatre, Leningrad, 1971-77, Symphony Orchestra, Leningrad Philharmoniya, 1977-. Recordings: include, Miaskovsky's Violin Concerto; Balakirev's Piano Concerto; Medtner's Piano Concerto No 1; Tchaikovsky Symphony Nos 4, 5, 6; Rachmaninov, Symphony No 2; Beethoven Symphony Nos 1-9; Handel Messiah, Haydn Schöpfung; Debussy Nocturnes, Ravel Valses nobles et sentimentales, Ma Mere l'Oye; Saeverud Peer Gynt, Symphony dolorosa. Honour: Prize, 2nd USSR Competition for Conductors, 1966. Current Management: Amdre Wider, Brussels. Address: Symphony orchestra St Petersburg Philharmonia, Mikhailovskaja str 2, St Petersburg 091011, Russia.

DOBBER Andrzej, b. 26 May 1961, Wiecbork, Poland. Singer (Baritone). Education: Studied in Warsaw (making his debut as Gremin while a student) and in Nuremburg. Career: Sang at Nuremberg Opera, 1987-91, debut as Tonio in Pagliacci; Frankfurt Opera from 1991, as Nardo in La finta giardiniera, Luna, the Herald in Lohengrin, Gremin and Marcello; Guest at the Vienna Staatsoper as Escamillo (1992) and frequent concert appearances; Sang Fyodor in The Invisible City of Kitezh at the Komische Oper, Berlin, 1996. Address: c/o Theater der Stadt Frankfurt, Untermeinanlage 11, W-6000 Frankfurt, Germany.

DOBBS Mattiwilda, b. 11 Jul 1925, Atlanta, Georgia, USA. Opera Singer (coloratura soprano); Professor. m. Bengt Janzon. Education: BA, Spelman College, USA; MA, Columbia University, USA; Studied voice, New York with Lotte Leonard, 1946-50; Special coaching in Paris with Peirre Bernac, 1950-52. Career: Appeared in Royal Dutch Opera, Holland Festival, 1952; Recitals, Sweden, Paris, Holland, 1952; Appeared in Opera, La Scala, Milan, 1953; Concerts in England and Continent, 1953; Glyndebourne Opera, 1953-54, 1956, 1961 as Zerbinetta, Constanze and the Queen of Night; Covent Garden Opera, 1953, 1954, 1956, 1958; Command Performance, Covent Garden, 1954; Annual Concert Tours, USA, 1954-; Australia and New Zealand, 1955, 1959, 1968; Australia, 1972, 1977; Israel, 1957 and 1959; USSR concerts and opera (Bolshoi Theatre), 1959; San Francisco Opera, 1955; Debut at Metropolitan Opera, 1956, there annually, 1956-; Appearances, Hamburg State Opera, 1961-63; Royal Swedish Opera, 1957 and then annually; Norwegian and Finnish Opera, 1957-64; Visiting Professor, University of Texas at Austin, 1973-74; Professor, University of Illinois, 1975-76; University of Georgia, 1976-77; Professor, Howard University, Washington, DC, 1977-91. Address: 1101 South Arlington Ridge Road, Arlington, VA 22202, USA.

DOBRÉE Georgina, b. 8 Jan 1930, London, England. Clarinet and Basset Horn Soloist; Teacher; Editor. Education: Royal Academy of Music, 1946-48; Studied with Gaston Hamelin, Paris, 1949. Career: Member of Chamber Music Ensembles; Recitals, broadcasts, lecture recitals and masterclasses in Europe and USA; Many premieres and recipient of numerous dedications; Professor, Royal Academy of Music, 1967-86; Director, Chantry Records, 1975-84, mainly of 19th and 20th Century works and own performances. Publications: Chantry Publications formed 1988, editions of mainly 19th century music for clarinet and/or basset horn; Editions of other works with clarinet for MR, OUP, Schott, Chester and Nova. Honours: French Government Scholarship, 1949; First Prize, Darmstadt, 1953; fellow, RAM, 1982. Memberships: RMA; International Clarinet Association; CASS; RAM Club; Royal Society of Musicians; Dvorák Society. Address: 6 The Grange, Grangewood Gardens, Leeds LS16 6EY, England.

DOBRONRAVOVA Svetlana, b. 1957, Taganrog, Russia. Soprano. Education: Studied at the Rostovondon Conservatoire. Debut: Lvov State Opera in 1982 as Tosca. Career: Sang with the Lvov Opera until 1989 notably as Santuzza, Yaroslavna and Gioconda; National Opera Kiev from 1989 as Abigaille, Elisabeth de Valois, Aida, Desdemona, Leonora in Forza del Destino, Elsa, Tatiana and Maria in Mazeppa; Guest engagements in Canada and throughout Europe, including concerts of the Mozart and Verdi Requiems; British debut in 1996 with the Perm Opera as Abigaille. Address: Sonata Ltd, 11 North Park Street, Glasgow, G20 7AA, Scotland.

DOBSON John, b. 1930, Derby, England. Singer (Tenor). Education: Guildhall School of Music, with Norman Walker; Study in Italy with Giovanni Inghilleri. Debut: Bergamo 1957, as Pinkerton. Career: New Opera Company 1958, in Sir John in Love and A Tale of Two Cities; Glyndebourne Festival 1959, in Der Rosenkavalier; Engagements with English National Opera, Welsh National Opera and Scottish Opera; Deutsche Oper am Rhein, Dusseldorf, Orange Festival and Maggio Musicale, Florence; Covent Garden, 1959-95, in 95 roles and 1900 performances: roles include Wagner's David, Mime, Loge and Melot, Beethoven's Jacquino and Mussorgsky's Shuisky; Sang Paris in the premiere of Tippett's King Priam, Coventry, 1962; Sang Luke in the 1977 premiere of Tippett's The Ice Break; With the Royal Opera at La Scala Milan, 1976 and the Far East, 1979, 1986 and 1992; Sang Mime in the first Japanese performances of Wagner's Ring with the Deutsche Oper, 1987; Sang in the British Premiere of Berio's Un Re in Ascolto, 1989; Borsa in Rigoletto; Inn Keeper in a new production of the Cunning Little Vixen, 1990, The Emperor in Turandot; Director of Young Singers Ensemble at Covent Garden; Sang Mime in Siegfried, 1991, Jakob Glock in a new production of Prokofiev's Fiery Angel, 1992; Sang Altoun in Turandot at Covent Garden, 1994; Freelance Singer from 1995. Recordings include: Videos of Peter Grimes, Otello, Samson et Dalila and La Fanciulla del West. Honour: OBE, 1985. Address: c/o Royal Opera House, Covent Garden, London WC2, England.

DODERER Gerhard, b. 25 March 1944, Kitzingen, Germany. Musicologist; Organist. m. C Rosado Fernandes, 11 September 1970. Education: PhD, University of Wüzburg; Bay. Staatskonservatorium of Würzburg. Career: Organ recitals, since 1970 in many European and Extraeuropean countries. Recordings: Longplays and CDs on historical Portuguese organs. Publications: Portuguese Clavichords of 18th Century, 1971; Organa Hispanica, 1971-84, 9 vols; Orgelmusik und Orgelbau in Portugal, 1976; Domenico Scarlatti: Libro di Tocate, 1991; The Organs at Braga Cathedral, 1992. Memberships: American, Spanish, Portuguese and German Musicological Societies. Hobbies: Travelling. Address: Alam D Afonso Henriques 48-5 Dt, P-1900 Lisboa, Portugal.

DODGE Charles, b. 5 Jun 1942, Ames, Iowa, USA. Composer. m. Katharine Schlefer, 1 Jul 1978, 1 s, 1 d. Education: BA, University of Iowa; MA, DMA, Columbia University; Studied composition with Richard Hervig, Darius Milhaud, Philip Bezanson, Gunther Schuller, Otto Luening, computer music with Godfrey Winheim. Career: Major performances: Tanglewood, 1965, 1973, 1986; Warsaw Autumn Festival, Poland, 1978, 1985, 1986; New Music, New York Festival, USA, 1979; Stockholm Festival of Electronic Music, Sweden, 1980, 1982; Venice Biennale, Italy, 1981; Calarts Festival, USA, 1983; Olympic Arts Festival, Los Angeles, 1984; New York Philharmonic, 1984; Los Angeles Philharmonic, 1984. Compositions: Folia; Changes: Earth's Magnetic Field; Speech Songs; Extensions; The Story of Our Lives; In Celebration; Cascando; Any Resemblance Is Purely Coincidental; The Waves. Recordings: Earth's Magnetic Field, Nonesuch; Charles Dodge-Synthetic Speech Music. Publication: Computer Music; Synthesis, Composition and Performing (with Thomas A Jerse), 1985. Contributions to: Musical Fractals, Byte Magazine, 1986. Honours: BMI Student Composers Awards, 1963, 1964, 1966, 1967; Joseph H Bearns Award, 1964, 1967; Margaret Lee Crofts Fellowship, 1964; Woodrow Wilson National Fellowship, 1964; Guggenheim Fellowships, 1972, 1975. Memberships: American Music Center (President 1979-82); American Composers Alliance (President 1971-75). Address: Conservatory of Music, Brooklyn College, City University of New York, NY 11210, USA.

DODGSON Stephen (Cuthbert Vivian), b. 17 March 1924, London, England. Composer. Education: Studied at the Royal College of Music with R O Morris and others. Career: Teacher at the Royal College of Music from 1964; Frequent broadcaster on BBC, Radio 3 (Record Review, Mainly for Pleasure). Compositions: A Bag of Winds for 5 String Quartets and Narrator; A Hymn to Harmony for Chorus and Strings; Bassoon Concerto; Cadilly for 4 Vocal Soloists and Wind Quintet; Concerto da Camera 1-3; Five Occasional Pieces for Cello and Piano; Four Fables for Chorus and Orchestra; 2 Guitar Concertos; 5 Operas for Children: Lammas Fair, The Miller's Secret, The Old Master; Strong Drink, and Threadneedle Street; Magnificat for Soloists, Chorus and Orchestra; Methought this Other Night, Piano Trio; The Old Cigarette Lighter for Flute, Oboe, Piano and Narrator; Quintet for Guitar and Strings; Quintet in C for Piano and Strings; Serenade for Oboe, Clarinet and Bassoon; 3 Sets of Six Inventions for Harpsichord; 2 String Trios; Sonata for Cello and Piano; 2 Suites for Clavichord; Suite for Wind Quintet; Te Deum for Soloists, Chorus and Orchestra; Three Winter Songs for Voice, Oboe, and Piano; Trio in One Movement, Piano Trio; Warbeck Dances for Recorder and Harpsichord; Wind Symphony for Symphonic Band; Music for Anthony Rooley and the Consort of Musicke. Address: c/o Chappell & Co, 129 Park Street, London W1, England.

DOESE Helena, b. 13 Aug 1946, Göteborg, Sweden. Singer (Soprano). Education: Studied in Göteborg, with Luigi Ricci in Rome and with Erik Werba and Gerald Moore in Vienna. Debut: Göteborg 1971, as Aida. Career: Bern Opera 1972-75, as Jenůfa, Micaela and Donna Anna; Royal Opera Stockholm from 1973 as Liu in Turandot, Mimi, Katya Kabanova and Eva in the Friedrich production of Die Meistersinger; Glyndebourne debut 1974, as Mozart's Countess: Fiordiligi 1975; Covent Garden from 1974 as Mimi, Gutrune in Götterdämmerung, Agathe in Der Freischütz and Amelia in Simon Boccanegra; Tatiana in Eugene Onegin for Scottish Opera; Guest appearances in Marseilles (Elisabeth de Valois), Sydney, (Aida), Paris Opéra, (Fiordiligi), Hamburg, (Agathe), San Francisco, (Countess) and Zürich (Sieglinde); Currently a member of Frankfurt Opera: has sung title roles in Ariadne auf Naxos, Jenůfa and Iphigénie en Tauride, Countess in Capriccio, the Marschallin, and Chrysothemis in Elektra; Deutsche Oper Berlin, 1987, as Agathe followed by the Marschallin at Copenhagen; Sydney, 1988, as Eva in Die Meistersinger; Sang Rosalinde at Oslo, 1988, Tosca 1989; Season 1991/92 as Fidelio at Toronto, Elsa at Frankfurt and Ariadne at Stuttgart; Sang Chrysothemis at Frankfurt, 1994. Recordings: include, Videos of Glyndebourne Così fan tutte and Covent Garden Bohème. Address: c/o Lies Askonas Limited, 6 Henrietta Street, London WC2, England.

DOGHAN Philip, b. 1949, England. Singer (Tenor). Education: BA, Durham University. Career: Sang as a boy in premiere of Tippett's King Priam, 1962; Sang in chorus at Glyndebourne and with the English Opera Group and English Music Theatre; English National Opera in Orfeo, the premiere of The Plumber's Gift and The Return of Ulysses; Has sung with Opera Factory in the premiere of Birtwistle's Yan Tan Tethera, 1986, La Calisto, The Knot Garden and Reimann's The Ghost Sonata; Appearances in Il Matrimomio Segreto and Les Pêcheurs de Perles in Rennes; Tom Rakewell at Cologne Opera, Alessandro in Il Re Pastore at the Théâtre des Champs Elysées; Mignon, La Straniera, La Cena delle Beffe, Elisa e Claudio and Gazzaniga's Don Giovanni at the Wexford Festival; Don Juan in The Stone Guest for the Berlin Kammeroper; Cosi fan tutte in Tours and Idomeneo in Metz; Concert engagements include Stravinsky's Threni for Italian Radio and appearances with Janowski, Hager, Rattle, Malgoire and Hogwood in Holland, Germany, Italy, Belgium and France; Sang several roles in the ENO revival of Busoni's Doctor Fraust, 1990; Regular broadcasts for the BBC, Radio France and RAI; Orphew in Lord's Masque by Castiglioni at La Fenice; Paris Opera Debut as Le Duc in Offenbach's, Les Brigands, 1993; Royal Opera House, Basilo in Figaro, 1994. Honour: Winner, Premier Grand Prix at Toulouse, 1980. Address: English National Opera, St Martin's Lane, London WC2N 4AP, England.

DOHMEN Albert, b. 1955, Krefeld, Germany. Singer (Bass-Baritone). Education: Studied in Cologne and with Gladys Kuchta, 1977-84. Career: Sang at the Deutsche Oper am Rhein Dusseldorf, 1983-85; Wiesbaden from 1986, Hamburg, 1986-87, Vienna Volksoper, 1987-90; Guest appearances at Stockholm (Assur in Semiramide, 1988), Catania (Kaspar in Der Freischütz) and Cairo, in Haydn's La Vera Costanza; Sang in the premiere of Bōse's Die Leiden des Jungen Werthers at Ludwigsburg, 1986 and in the German premiere of La Princesse de Cleve by Jean Francaix; Sang Don Giovanni in festivals at Prague and Macerata, 1991; Returned to Macerata 1992, as Don Parmenione in Rossini's L'Occasione fa il Ladro. Other roles include Mozart's Count and Alfonso, Don Magnifico, the Grand Inquisitor and Verdi's Procida and Paolo, Scarpia and Gianni Schicchi; Wagner's King Henry, Biterolf, Wotan, Donner, Gunther and Amfortas; Sang Simone in Zemlinsky's Eine Florentinische Tragödie at Florente, 1996; Concert repertoire includes the Verdi Requiem and Zemlinsky's Sieben Sinfonische Gesänge. Recordings: Spirit Messenger in Die Frau ohne Schatten, conducted by Solti. Address: c/o Volksoper, Wahringerstrasse 78, A-1090 Vienna, Austria.

DOHNANYI Christoph von, b. 8 Sept 1929, Berlin, Germany. Conductor. m. (1) Renate Zillessen, 2 children, (2) Anja Silja, 3 children. Education: Studied at the Munich Musikhochschule; Further study in USA with his grandfather, Erno von Dohnányi, and Leonard Bernstein. Career: Assistant to Solti at the Frankfurt Opera, 1952-56; Music Director at Lubeck, 1957-63; Kassel, 1963-66; London debut 1965, with the London Philharmonic; Chief Conductor Cologne Radio Symphony Orchestra, 1964-70; Conducted the premieres of Henze's Der junge Lord (Berlin 1965) and Die Bassariden (Salzburg 1966); Music Director Frankfurt Opera 1968-75; Hamburg Staatsoper 1977-84; Has conducted Schoenberg's Moses und Aron at Frankfurt, Vienna and elsewhere in Europe; Conducted Salome at Covent Garden 1974: later directed Wozzeck; returned for Die Meistersinger and Fidelio, 1990; Opera engagements at Metropolitan Falstaff and Der Rosenkavalier, La Scala Milan, Chicago (debut 1969, Der fliegende Holländer), Berlin, Paris, Munich, Salzburg and San Francisco (Die Frau ohne Schatten, 1990; Guest appearances with the BBC Symphony, New York Philharmonic, Zurich Tonhalle, Philadelphia Orchestra, Israel Philharmonic, Vienna Philharmonic and the Orchestre de Paris; Music Director of the Cleveland Orchestra from 1984: visited London, 1980, 1989, 1990, 1992; Far East tour, 1998; Conducted new production of Der Ring des Nibelungen at the Vienna Staatsoper, 1992-93; Salome at the 1992 and 1993 Salzburg Festival and Così fan tutte at 1993 Salzburg Festival; Principal Conductor of the Philharmonia Orchestra from 1997; Engaged to condict Robert Wilson's new Ring Cycle at Bayreuth, 2000. Recordings: include, with the Cleveland Orchestra: complete Symphonies of Brahms, Schumann and Beethoven; Works by Bartók, Schubert, Dvorak, Mahler, Busoni; Der Rheingold. Honours: include, Bartók prize of Hungary; Abraham Lincoln Award. Address: Harrison/Parrott Limited, 12 Penzance Place, London W11 4PA, England.

DOHNÁNYI Oliver von, b. 2 Mar 1955, Trencin, Slovakia. Conductor. m. Natalia Melnik, 23 Jan 1996, 1 daughter. Education: Konzervatorium in Bratislava (Violin, conducting and composition), Academy of Music Prague, Hochschüle Für Musik, Vienna (both conducting). Career: Conductor of the Radio Symphony Orchestra, Bratislava, 1979-86; Principal Conductor of the Slovak National Opera House in Bratislava, conducted new productions of Borodin's Prince Igor, Puccini's Tosca, Rossini's Il Barbiere di Seviglia, Smetana's The Bartered Bride, Verdi's Rigoletto, Gounod's Faust; Conductor, Slovak Philharmony Istropolitana Chamber Orchestra, concert tours of western Europe; Music Director of the National Theatre in Prague, 1993-96; Conducted Smetana's Libuse, Gounod's Romeo and Juliet, Puccini's La Bohéme, Verdi's Rigoletto, Prokoviev's Cinderella, and two Mozart operas; Don Giovanni and The Marriage of Figaro, which toured Japan, 1995, 1997; Regular guest conductor at Yomiuri Nippon Symphony Orchestra in Tokyo, Hungarian State Philharmony, Portugal State Symphony Orchestra, Northern Philharmony in Leeds, UK, Kosice State Philharmony and Slovak Symphonietta; Also conducted The Royal Liverpool Philharmonic, English National Opera, English Chamber Orchestra, London Mozart Players, Northern Philharmony in Leeds, BBC Belfast and Irish National Symphony Orchestra. Recordings: Smetana's Libuse and My Country (both with National Theatre of Prague); Famous Russian Masterpieces; Bach's Johannes Passion; Works by F Mendelssohn-Bartholdy. Current Management: Music International (UK). Address: Renoirova 2A, 152 00 Praha 5, Czech Republic.

DOIG Christopher, b. 4 Apr 1948, New Zealand. Singer (Tenor). Education: Studied in New Zealand and with Anton Dermota at the Vienna Music Academy. Career: Sang at the Vienna Staatsoper from 1976 as David, Jacquino, Steuermann, Dr Caius and Remendado in Carmen; Linz Opera from 1980 as Don Ottavio, Tamino, Lionel in Martha, Fenton, Nemorino and the Duke of Mantua; Guest engagements in Vienna and at La Scala and the Salzburg Festival; Debut with Australian Opera, 1988, as Nerone in L'Incoronazione di Poppea; Sang David in Meistersinger at Sydney, conducted by Charles Mackerras; Hamburg Opera 1991, as Elemer in Arabella; Director of the New Zealand International Festival of Arts; Also sang Jenufa at Sydney, 1992; Adriana Lecouvreur, Sydney, 1992; Carmen and Fliegende Holländer, Cologne, 1992; Wozzeck, Stuttgart; Salome, Melbourne and Don José in Barcelona; Walther von Stolzing at Sydney, 1994. Current Management: Haydn Rawstron Limited, London. Address: PO Box 654, London SE26 4DZ, England.

DOLEZAL Karel, b. 16 Jan 1948, Prague, Czechoslovakia. Musician; Viola Player. m. 18 June 1974, 2 s. Education: High School of Music, with absolutorium, 2 years; Postgraduate studies with professors Cerny and Maly. Debut: Knighthall of The Waldstein Palacve, Prague, 1973. Career: Solo Only: Prague Spring Festival, 1976; Bratislava Music Festival, 1977; Music Festivals: Brno, Karlovy Vary, T Teplice, Poland, GDR, Rumania; 1 Solo Concert, BBC, TV Prague and 12 Concerts for Radio Prague; With The Dolezal String Quartet Biographical film for Czech Film Corporation; Evening Programme for TV Prague, One hour-long programme for Radio NY 1981; Major Stage: Wigmore Hall, London; Birmingham; Dublin; Prague Spring Festival; Paris Festival; Bretagne; Tonhalle Zurich; Berlin; Halle; Concert Tours of Austria, Spain, Scandinavia, Hungary, Tunisia etc. Radio and TV Programmes for Hamburg, Bremen, Frankfurt, Wiesbaden, Saarbrucken; The Quartet was invited for a concert tour of USA 1980; Quartet: Concert tour of Japan, 1993; Concert tour of Spain, 1997; Kangasniemi Festival, Finland, 1997; Professor, Prague Conservatoire, 1993. Recordings: 2 String Quartets by Antonin Dvorak, 1983; 2 String Quartets by Leos Janacek, 1984; 5 LP records by Mozart, Dvorak, Janacek, Martinu, Shostakovich, Flosman and others; Solo: Viola and piano works by: Bloch, Rubinstein, Hindemith, Matousek, 1995, Mendelssohn, Bartholdy, Reger, Weber, 1997; Quartet: Quartets by Janacek, 1992; 2 Quartets by Dvorak, 1994; Quartets by Smetana, Fibich, 1996. Honours: Silver Medal, International Festival at Bordeaux 1977; Honorary Diploma of The Performing Arts Competition organized by The Czech Ministry of Culture, 1974; 3rd Prize of The Prague Spring International Competition (1st prize was not awarded), 1975. Memberships: The Union of Czech Composers and Musicians. Current Management: Andrew Dolezal, Milesovska Street 6, Prague 3, 130 00 Czech Republic. Address: Milesovska Street 6, Prague 3, 130 00 Czech Republic.

DOLIN Samuel, b. 22 August 1917, Montreal, Canada. Composer. Education: Studied under Tania and Vladimire Elgart, Stanley Gardiner and Vladimir Emenitov (piano and theory); Studied at Royal Conservatory of Music, Toronto; BMus, Doctor of Music Degree, University of Toronto, 1958; Studied Composition under John Weinzweig; Weldon Kilburn and E Robert Schmitz (piano) and Ernst Krenez (composition). Career: Teacher, Composition and Theory Department, Royal Conservatory of Music; Serves on the Board of Examiners; Founder, Electronic Music Studio, 1966; Revived and brought up-to-date ARCT Diploma Course in Composition and Theory; Artistic Director of Canadian Contemporary Music Workshop, 1984. Compositions: Opera: Casino, 1966-67, Orchestral Scherzo, 1950; Serenade for Strings, 1951; Sinfonietta, 1950; Sonata for String Orchestra, 1962; Symphony No 1 (Elk Falls), 1956; Symphony No 2, 1957; Symphony No 3, 1976; Soloists with Orchestra; Concerto for Accordion and Orchestra, 1984; Concerto for Piano and Orchestra, 1984; Drakkar, 1972; Fantasy for Piano and Chamber Orchestra, 1967; Golden Section: The Biography of A Woman, 1981; Hero of Our Time, 1985; Isometric Variables, 1957; Instrumental Ensemble: Adikia, 1975; Barcarolle, 1962; Blago's Trio, 1980; Concerto Grosso (Georgian Bay), 1970; Duo Concertante, 1977; Kinesis I and Kinesis II, 1981; Little Sombrero, 1964; Portrait, 1961; Quintet for Brass, 1981; Sonata, 1960; Sonata, 1978; Sonata Fantasia, 1980; Sonatina, 1954; Trio for Violin, Cello and Piano, 1980; Instrumental Solo: Little Toccata, 1959; Prelude, Interlude and Fantasy, 1976; Psalmody for Solo Oboe, 1982; Ricercar and Fantasy, 1975; Sonata, 1970; Three Sonatas, 1973; Stelcel, 1978; Voice: Bird of Time, 1979; Chloris, 1951; Deuteronomy XXXII, 1977; Julia, 1951; Ozymandias, 1951; Chorus: The Hills of Hebron, 1954; Marchbankantata, 1971; Mass, 1972; Piano Music. Address: c/o Canadian Music Center, Chalmers House, 20 St Joseph Street, Toronto, Ontario M4Z 1J9, Canada.

DOLLARHIDE Thomas, b. 30 August 1948, Sanya Rosa, USA. Composer; Musicologist. Education: MA and PhD, University of Michigan; Study with Leslie Bassett and William Bolcom. Career: Faculty of La Trobe University, 1981-89. Compositions include: Shadows, wind quintet, 1973; Theme and Variations, for 2 cellos, flute, clarinet and 2 speaking voices, 1976; Other Dreams, Other Dreamers, for orchestra, 1976; Shoestrings for flute and clarinet, 1977; Pluriels for orchestra, 1979; Punk for piano, 1980; By Thunder Mill Pond by trombone, 1981; Ragings of a One Pot Screamer, for piano, 1982; A Back Street for violin, 1983; Two Pieces, for piano, 1984; Madness in Paradise, for violin, viola, double bass, clarinet, guitar, mandolin and percussion, 1986. Honours include: Broadcast Music Award to Young Composers, USA, 1975-76. Address: c/o APRA, 1A Eden Street, Crows Nest, NSW 2065, Australia.

DOLMETSCH Jeanne-Marie, b. 15 Aug 1942, Hindhead, Surrey, England. Concert Artist (Recorder and Treble Viol). Education: Royal Academy of Music, Violin and Piano, 1961-64; LRAM (Piano Teacher). Debut: Elizabeth Hall, London, 1973. Career: Toured America, France, Ireland and Sweden with the Dolmetsch Ensemble; Recorder soloist and Assistant Director, Haslemere Festival; Appearances at Bath Festival, English Bach Festival; Numerous radio broadcasts and TV programmes. Recordings: Collections of early music with the Dolmetsch Ensemble. Hobbies: Painting; Gardening. Address: Jesses, Grayswood Road, Halsemere, Surrey, England.

DOLMETSCH Marguerite (Mabel), b. 15 Aug 1942, Hindhead, Surrey, England. Recorder and Viola da Gamba Player. m. Brian E Blood. Education: LRAM. Career: Travelled widely with the Dolmetsch Ensemble and the Dolmetsch Concertante, touring America, France, Germany, Sweden; Has performed at the Three Choirs Festival, Bath Festival and Haslemere Festival; Has also appeared at Elizabeth Hall, Purcell Room and Wigmore Hall; Radio broadcasts and TV programmes in Britain and Germany. Recitals: Various recitals with the Dolmetsch Ensemble; Director of the Dolmetsch Summer School and Partner in Dolmetsch Instruments Workshop. Recordings: CD, Cassette, Choice Consorts for Recorders; A Christmas Tapestry, in Words and Music; A Chest of Viols. Honour: LRAM. Memberships: National Federation of Decorative and Fine Arts Societies. Hobbies: Gardening; Dressmaking; Cooking. Address: Heartease, Grayswood Road, Haslemere, Surrey, England.

DOLTON Geoffrey, b. 1958, England. Singer (Baritone). Education: Studied at the Royal Academy of Music with Joy Mammen. Debut: With Opera North, as Guglielmo in Così fan tutte. Career: Further roles with Opera North as Mozart's Count, Lescaut in Massenet's Manon Lescaut and Henrik in the British premiere of Nielsen's Maskarade; With Opera Factory has sung Guglielmo (also television) and Orestes in Gluck's Iphigenia operas; Manoel Theatre Malta, Figaro in Il Barbiere di Siviglia; Season 1992 as Hector in Tippett's King Priam at Antwerp, Monteverdi's Otho for Opera Factory, in Krenek's What Price Confidence? at the Almeida Festival and as Alan in Birtwistle's Yan Tan Tethera; Other roles include Papageno for Welsh National Opera and Opera Northern Ireland; Schaunard in La Bohème for Scottish Opera; Hector in King Priam for Opera North, Malatesta in Don Pasquale for New Israeli Opera and the title role in Grétry's Le Huron at the Buxton Festival, 1990; Sang Guglielmo in Cosi fan tutte for ENO, 1990; Recitals with the pianist Nicholas Bosworth; Season 1994, ENO Eisenstein Die Fledermaus; Opera Northern Ireland, Figario in the Barber of Seville; Castleward Opera Dandini in La Cenerentola; Sang in La Traviata for GTO at Glyndebourne, 1996. Recordings: Donizetti's Emilia di Liverpool, with the Philharmonic Orchestra (Opera Rara). Honours include: Peter Pears Prize for Recital Singing at the RAM; Honorary ARAM, 1992. Address: Allied Artists Agency, 42 Montpelier Square, London SW7 1JZ, England.

DOMANINSKA Libuse, b. 4 Jul 1924, Brno, Czechoslovakia. Singer (Soprano). Education: Studied at the Prague Conservatory with Hana Pirkova and Bohuslav Sobesky. Debut: Brno 1946, as Vendulka in The Kiss by Smetana. Career: Sang at Brno in operas by Smetana and Janacek (Jenůfa, Katya Kababova and the Vixen); Prague National Opera, 1955-85; visited Edinburgh with the company in 1964, as Milada in Dalibor; Komische Oper Brelin 1956, Vienna Staatsoper, 1958-68; Holland Festival 1959, as Katya Kababova; Roles in Russian operas and in Mozart, Puccini and Verdi; Marenka in The Bartered Bride, Smetana's Libuse, Jenůfa, Aida, Elisabeth de Valois, Euridice and Foerster's Eva; Many concert appearances, notably in Janacek's Glagolitic Mass at La Scala. Recordings: Glagolitic Mass, The Cunning Little Vixen, The Devil's Wall by Smetana (Supraphon). Honours: Artist of Merit, 1966; National Artist, 1974. Address: c/o National Theatre, PO Box 865, 11230 Prague 1, Czech Republic.

DOMANSKY Hanus, b. 1 Mar 1944, Novy, Hrozenkov, Slovakia. Composer. Education: Studied piano with Jaroslav Shanel; Composition with Jan Duchan, Brno Conservatory; Composition with Dezider Kardos, graduated 1970, Bratislava Academy of Musical Arts. Career: Associated with Czech Radio; Bratislava. Compositions: Concerto piccolo for Orchestra, 1970; Symphony, 1980; Piano Concerto, 1984; Music for Trumpet, Flute and Bass Clarinet, 1966; Musica giocosa for Violin and Piano, 1971; Dianoia for Violin, 1976; Piano pieces; Organ music; About Winter, cantata for Narrator, Children's Choir and Orchestra, 1968; Fiat lux, oratorio for Narrator, Soprano, Chorus and Orchestra, 1970; Versifying for Chorus and Percussion, 1972; Recruiting Songs for Men's Chorus, 1978; Solo Songs. Honour: Slovak Composers Award, 1983. Address: c/o Czech Radio, Bratislava, Slovak Republic.

DOMINGO Placido, b. 21 Jan 1941, Madrid, Spain. Opera Singer (Tenor). m. Marta Ornelas, 3 sons. Education: National Conservatory of Music, Mexico City. Debut: Monterray, Mexico, 1961; Metropolitan Opera, New York, USA, 1968; British Debut, Verdi's Requiem, Festival Hall, 1969; Covent Garden, Tosca, 1971. Career: Aida, Carmen, 1973; Bohème, 1974; Un Ballo in Maschera, 1975; La Fanciulla del West; Has sung leading roles in approximately 50 operas; Recent engagements include: Tosca (conducting), Romeo and Juliet, Metropolitan Opera, New York, USA; Aida; Il Trovatore at Hamburg, Don Carlos, Salzburg; Vespri Siciliani and La forza del destino, Paris, France; Turandot, Barcelona; Otello in Paris, London, Hamburg; Carmen, Edinburgh; Film, Madama Butterfly with Von Karajan; La Traviata, 1982; Sang Luigi at the Met, 1989 in Puccini's Il Tabarro; Otello at Covent Garden, 1990, Lohengrin at the Vienna Staatsoper, Don José at Rio de Janeiro, Otello at the Met and Barcelona; Sang Don Carlos at Los Angeles, Dick Johnson at Chicago; Riccardo in Un Ballo in Maschera at the 1990 Salzburg Festival. Debut as Parsifal at the Met, 1991; Sang Otello at Covent Garden 1992, (also televised), Siegmund in Die Walküre at the Vienna Staatsoper, 1992; Metropolitan Opera, 1992, Hoffman; Season 1997 included Don José and Siegmund at the Met and Gabriele Adorno in the original version of Simon Boccamegra at Covent Garden. Recordings: Most recent include: Aida; Un Ballo in Maschera; Tosca; Tannhäuser, 1989; Video of Lohengrin, from Vienna, issued 1991, Die Frau ohne Schatten (1993), Gounod Roméo et Juliette, 1996. Publication: My First Forty Years, Autobiography, 1984. Honours: Doctor Honoris Causa, Royal

College of Music, 1982; Chevalier, Legion d'Honneur. Current Management: Metropolitan Opera Company, New York, USA. Address: c/o Metropolitan Opera Company, Lincoln Center Plaza, New York, NY 10023, USA.

DOMINGUEZ Guillermo, b. 1961, Caracas, Venezuela. Singer (Tenor). Education: Studied with Jose Castro in Caracas, then at Rome and Turin. Debut: Treviso, 1984, as Rodolfo. Career: Sang Rodolfo at Paris, Amiens and Munich; Zurich Opera as Don Ottavio and Ferrando and in Guillaume Tell; appearances at Monte Carlo as Edgardo in Lucia di Lammermoor and at Innsbruck as Cavaradossi and the Duke of Mantua, 1988; National Theatre Mannheim as Alfredo and Puccini's Edgar with the Dresden Staatskapelle; Engagements in Spain as the Duke; Many concert appearances. Address: c/o National Theater, Am Goetheplatz, 6800 Mannheim, Germany.

DOMINGUEZ Oralia, b. 15 Oct 1927, San Luis, Potosi, Mexico. Singer (Contralto). Education: Studied at the Mexican National Conservatory. Career: Sang in Debussy's La Demoiselle Elue while a student; Stage debut Mexico City 1950, appeared as Amneris in 1951; Sang in Europe from 1953, London debut at the Wigmore Hall; La Scala Milan 1953, in Adriana Lecouvreur; Covent Garden 1955, as Sosostris in the premiere of The Midsummer Marriage by Tippett; Glyndebourne Festival 1955-64, as Mistress Quickly, Isabella, and Arnalta in the Leppard-Monteverdi L'Incoronazione di Poppea; Venice 1960, in Alcina, with Joan Sutherland; Sang at the Deutsche Oper am Rhein Dusseldorf from 1960; Guest appearances in Buenos Aires, Vienna, Frankfurt, Paris, Rome, Naples, Florence, Chicago, Dallas and New Orleans. Recordings: Erda in The Ring, Mozart's Coronation Mass, Verdi Requiem (Deutsche Grammophon); Il Tabarro, La Gioconda (Decca). Address: c/o Deutsch Oper am Rhein, Heinrich-Heine Allee 16, D-4000 Dusseldorf, Germany.

DONADINI Giovanna, b. 1964, Italy. Singer (Soprano). Education: Studied in Venice and Ancona. Debut: Monteverdi's Selve Morale e Spirituale, at La Fenice Venice. Career: Mozart's Countess and Fiordiligi at Treviso, 1990-91; Season 1994 with Pamela Nubile by Farinelli at Treviso, and Camilla in Leo's Amor vuol Sofferanza at Martina Franca; Donna Elvira in Switzerland, and Galuppi's Le Nozze at Vicenza, 1996; Rossalane in Cimarosa's I Turchi Amanti Amanti at Citta di Castello, Fiordiligi in Tokyo and Mozart's Susanna at the Teatro Verdi, Sassari; Concerts include Pergolesi's Stabat Mater, Bach's Haydn's Stabat Mater, Beethoven's Ninth and the Four Last Songs at Treviso and Toulouse; 1994 Concorso Internazionale, Bilbao. Address: Athole Still Ltd, Foresters Hall, 25-27 Westow Street, London SE19 3RY, England.

DONAKOWSKI Conrad Louis, b. 13 Mar 1936, Detroit, Michigan, USA. Professor of Humanities and Music. m. Judith Wharton, 1 son, 1 daughter. Education: Diploma, First in Class, Palestrina Institute of Music, 1956; MA, Xavier University, Cincinnati, 1959; PhD (with distinction), Columbia University, New York, 1969. Appointments: Director of Music, St Hugo of the Hills Church, Bloomfield Hills, Michigan, 1960-66; Instructor, 1966-69, Assistant Professor, 1969-72, Associate Professor, 1973-75, Professor, 1975-, Associate Dean of Arts and Letters, 1979-86, Professor of Music, 1981-, Michigan State Univerity; Director of Music, St Thomas Aquinas Church, East Lansing, 1974-. Publications: A Muse for the Masses: Ritual in an Age of Democratic Revolution, 1977. Contributions to: American Historical Review, Church History, Choice, Germanic Studies Review, Selected Papers Consortium for the Study of Revolutionary Europe, Pastoral Music, Canadian Historical Review. Honours: NEH, 1973; Rockefller Foundation, 1975, 1976; DAAD, 1986; French National Social Science Research, 1987; MSU Foundation, 1995. Memberships: American Historicl Association; American Musicological Society; Jean-Jacques Rousseau Society; World History Association. Hobbies: Hiking; Gardening. Address: The School of Music, Michigan State University, East Lansing, MI 48824-1043, USA.

DONAT Zdislava, b. 4 July 1939, Poznan, Poland. Singer (Soprano Coloratura). Education: Studied with Zofia Bregy in Warsaw and Gino Bechi in Siena, Italy. Debut: Poznan 1964, as Gilda from 1971 in Teatr Wielki, Warsaw. career: Theater am Gärtnerplatz, Munich, as Queen of Night; Bayerische Staatsoper Munich, Hamburg; Vienna Staatsoper; London Covent Garden; La Scala, Milan; Met-Opera, New York; Teatro Colon Buenos Aires; Deutsche Oper, Berlin; San Francisco Opera; Opera in Moscow, Napoli, Zurich, Frankfurt and many others; Festivals in Salzburg, 1979-87; Bregenz, Orange, Munich, Tokyo, Athens, Wroclaw and others; Roles include: Lucia di Lammermoor, La Sonnambula, Giulia in Capuletti, Norina, Konstanze, Blonde, Zerlina, Olympia, Gilda, Violetta, Manon, (Massenet), Martha, (Flotow), Queen in Golden Cockerel, La Princess and Le Feu in l'Enfant at les Sortilèges by Ravel, Hanna (Moniuszko), Marzelline (Beethoven), Adele (Johann Strauss) and others; Television productions, recitals and appearances with symphony orchestras. recordings include: Die Zauberflöte, RCA, conductor J Levine; Operatic Arias, Polski Nagrania, conductor J Dobrzanski; Requiem by R

Maciejewski, conductor, T Strugala. Honours: Awards: Grand Prix in Toulouse; Kammersangerin, Munich, 1977. Address: Teatr Wiekli, Moliere 3, 00 076 Warsaw, Poland.

DONATH Helen, b. 10 Jul 1940, Corpus Christi, Texas, USA. Soprano. m. Klaus Donath, 10 Jul 1965, 1 s. Education: Del Mar College, Corpus Christi, Texas; Paolo Novikova; Maria Berini. Debut: Cologne Opera as Inez in Il Trovatore, 1960. Career: Hannover Opera; Bavarian State Opera, Munich; Salzburg Festival; Vienna State Opera; Deutsche Oper, Berlin; La Scala, Milan; Royal Opera, Covent Garden; Lisbon; Hamburg; Bayreuth Festival, San Francisco Opera; Paris Opéra; Sang Pamina at the 1970 Salzburg Festival; US debut as Sophie at San Francisco, 1971; Covent Garden debut as Anne Trulove in The Rake's Progress, 1979; Other roles include: Mozart's Zerlina, Ilia and Susanna, Micaela, Mélisande, Mimi, Oscar and Aennchen; Sang Eva in Die Meistersinger at Seattle, 1989; Season 1993-94 as Eva in Dresden and Agathe at the Berlin Staatsoper; Season 1996 as Mimi at Detroit and Mozart's Countess for Florida Grand Opera. Recordings: Beethoven, Fidelio (Angel); Britten, Turn of the Screw (Philips); Handel, Messiah (Deutsche Grammophon); Mozart, Requiem (Angel and Philips); Pfitzner, Palestrina (Deutsche Grammophon); Strauss, Arabella (Angel); Strauss, Der Rosenkavalier (London). Honours: Pope Paul Medal, 1967; Grand Prix du Disque, Deutsche Schallplatten Preis, 1990, Bavarian Kammersängerin; Culture Prize of Lower Saxony. Current Management: Shaw Concerts, 1900 Broadway, New York, NY 10023, USA. Address: Bergstrasse 5, D-3002 Wedemark 1, Germany.

DONATI Walter, b. 4 Sept 1938, Potsdam, Germanmy. Singer (Tenor). Career: Sang in Italy from 1983, notably at Treviso as Erik in Der fliegende Holländer, at La Scala in Tannhäuser, I Lombardi and Macbeth; Sang Don Carlos at Dublin (1985), Radames at Avignon (1986), and Dick Johnson at Buenos Aires; Further appearances at Venice as Foresto in Attila, at Florence as Dimitri in Boris Godunov, Paris Opéra as Raimaud in Robert le Diable (1985), returning as Pollione (1988); Manrico at Covent Garden (1990). Address: c/o Théâtre National de l'Opéra, 8 Rue Scribe, F-75009 Paris, France.

DONATONI Franco, b. 9 Jun 1927, Verona, Italy. Composer; Professor of Musical Composition. m. Susan Park, 1958, 2 s. Education: Bologna and Rome. Career: Professor of Composition, Bologna, 1953-55; Milan, 1969; Docente, Advanced course in Composition, Academy Chigiana di Siena, 1970. Compositions: include, Puppenspiel, 1951; 4 String Quartets, 1950-60; Serenata for soprano and 16 instruments; Sezioni, 1960; Per Ochestra, 1962; Asar, 1964; Puppenspiel (2), 1965; Souvenir, 1967; Etwas ruhiger im Ausdruck, 1967; Doubles II, 1969-70; Questo, 1970; Atem, theatre piece, 1984; Ecco for chamber orchestra, 1991. Honours: Marzotto Prize, 1966; Koussevitsky Prize, 1968; Many other prizes for composition. Address: Via Giovanni Milani, 1 Milano, Italy.

DONCEANU Felicia, b. 28 Jan 1931, Bacau, Rumania. Composer. Education: Studied at the Bucharest Conservatory, 1949-56. Career: Former Editor of Editura Musicala, Bucharest. Compositions include: Spinet Sonata, 1983; Moldavian Echoes, suite for Strings, 1985; Three Symphonic Sketches, 1982; The Clever Bell, chorus, 1986; Inscription On A Mast for Harp, 1989; The Music Lesson, song, 1992. Honours include: Composition Prize, Rumanian Composers' Union. Address: c/o PRS Ltd, Member Registration Rumania, 29-33 Berners Street, London, W1P 4AA, England.

DÖNCH Karl, b. 8 January 1915, Hagen, Westphalian, Germany. Singer (Bass-Baritone). Education: Studied at the Dresden Conservatory. Career: Sang in Gorlitz from 1936, followed by engagements in Reichenberg, Bonn and Salzburg; Vienna Staatsoper from 1947, notably in the 1956 premiere of Der Sturm by Frank Martin; Salzburg Festival until 1965, as Don Alfonso, the Doctor in Wozzeck, and Malatesta, and in the 1954 premiere of Penelope by Liebermann; Bregenz Festival 1955-84; Guest appearances in Milan, Dusseldorf and Berlin; Buenos Aires, 1952-53; Holland Festival, 1958; Metropolitan Opera, 1959-60, 1966-67, notable at the Witch in Hansel and Gretel; Director of the Vienna Volksoper from 1973-86: appeared as Jupiter in Orpheus in the Underworld, 1985. Recordings: Beckmesser in Die Meistersinger, Der Freischütz, Ariadne auf Naxos; Die Fledermaus, Wiener Blut, Eine Nacht in Venedig; Der Vogelhändler; Wozzeck; Die Zauberflöte; La Forza del Destino; Der Rosenkavalier. Address: c/o Volksoper, Währingerstrasse 78, A-1090 Vienna, Austria.

DONDI Dino, b. 10 July 1925, Casalecchio di Remo, Bologna, Italy. Singer (Baritone). Career: Sang at La Scala Milan from 1956, notably as Amonasro, Oreste in Iphigénie en Tauride, Don Carlo (Ernani), Scarpia, Escamillo, Valentin and Busoni's Faust; Guest appearances throughout Italy and at Monte Carlo (Rigoletto, 1961), Amsterdam (Nabucco, 1960) and Lisbon (Macbeth, 1958); Other roles included Riccardo in Puritani, Renato (Ballo in Maschera), Rolando in Verdi's Battaglia di

Legnano, and Teseo in Pizzetti's Fedra. Address: c/o Teatro alla Scala, Via Filodrammatici 2, 20121 Milan, Italy.

DONGEN Maria van, b. 23 Mar 1928, Holland. Singer (Soprano). Career: Sang Mozart's Countess and Pamina at Amsterdam; Member of the Zurich Opera, 1959-65, debut as the Forza Leonora; Guest appearances at Frankfurt, London, (Countess at the Albert Hall), Bologne, Parma (Elisabeth, 1963), and Pisa (Elsa); Amsterdam 1963-67, as Donna Elvira; Munich from 1964, Vienne from 1967 as Ariadne, Fiordiligi, Senta and Desdemona; Munich Opera 1967, as Strauss's Danae, and as Irene in Rienzi; Further engagements at Barcelona and Hamburg (as Leonora in Fidelio), Graz, the Deutsche Oper Berlin, Piccola Scala Milan and the Salzburg Festival (First lady in Die Zauberflöte, 1963-64); Sang Leonore at the Landestheater Salzburg, 1971; Frequent concert engagements. Address: c/o Tiroler Landestheater, Bennweg 2, A-6020 Innsbruck, Austria.

DONNELLY Malcolm (Douglas), b. 8 February 1943, Sydney, Australia. Opera Singer (Baritone). m. Dolores Ryles. Education: Sydney Conservatory and Opera School; London Opera Centre. Debut: Australian Opera, 1966. Career: Australian Opera, Scottish Opera, English National Opera, Opera North, Netherlands Opera, Victoria State Opera, State Opera South Australia, Welsh National Opera, Royal Opera House, Covent Garden, English National Opera Tour, Moscow Leningrad, 1991, Adelaide Festival 1991; Appearances at Edinburgh Festival, 1975, 1976; Wexford Festival, 1977, 1978; Glyndebourne, 1979, 1981, 1985; Hong Kong Festival, 1987; Brighton International Festival, 1988; Roles include, Macbeth, Simon Boccanegra, Rigoletto, Pizarro (Fidelio); Sang Kurewenal in Tristan und Isolde for Australian Opera, 1990, Macbeth with ENO on tour to Russia, Scarpia with Scottish Opera and Shishkov in From the House of the Dead for Welsh National Opera, 1990; Season 1992 in Ovations concert by ENO at the Barbican Hall, Don Carlos in Ernani for Welsh National Opera and Ford in Falstaff at the Coliseum; Boccanegra and Iago in Australia; Sharpless, Royal Opera House, Covent Garden; Kurwenal (Tristan und Isolde) Australian Opera, Macbeth and Telramund (Lohengrin) ENO, 1993; Di Luna (Il Trovatore) Victoria State Opera, Kurwenal (Tristan und Isolde) Scottish Opera; Verdi Requiem, Guildford Cathedral, 1994; Scarpia, Lyric Opera of Queensland; Nabucco, Australian Opera; Falstaff, State Opera South Australia, 1995; Sang Iago at Sydney, 1996. Honours: Sydney Sun Aria Competition, 1969; Australian Opera Auditions Scholarship, 1970. Hobbies: Philately; Gardening. Current Management: Ingpen & Williams Ltd, London. Address: 60 Nightingale Road, Carshalton, Surrey SM5 2EN, England.

DONNELLY Patrick, b. 1958, Sydney, Australia. Singer (Bass-Baritone). Education: Studied at the Conservatorium of Music, Sydney and at the Guildhall School of Music, London. Career: Concert debut at Sydney Opera House in Belshazzar's Feast by Walton; Also appeared at Tiresias (Oedipus Rex) and in the Monteverdi Vespers; Sang with Glyndebourne Chorus on the 1983 Tour, solo debut as Theseus in A Midsummer Night's Dream, 1985; Festival and Tour appearances in Idomeneo (Neptune), Don Giovanni (Masetto), La Traviata, Le nozze di Figaro (Bartolo) and L'Incoronzione di Poppea. Other roles include Mozart's Figaro for Opera 80, First Minister in Cendrillon at the Wexford Festival and Bartók's Bluebeard at the Barbican; Sang Polyphemus in Acis and Galatea on tour in France, Hayden in the premiere of 63 Dream Palace by Jurgen Böse in Berlin, 1990, and the Herald in Lohengrin for Australian Opera, October 1990; Licone and Caronte in Haydn's Orlando Paladino at Oxford; Concerts at most major London centres, including Stravinsky's Renard at the Elizabeth Hall. Recordings: include, Renard with the Matrix Ensemble; Pergolesi's La Serva Padrona (Meridan). Address: c/o Ron Gonsalves Management, 10 Dagnan Road, London SW12 9LQ, England.

DONOHOE Peter (Howard), b. 18 Jun 1953, Manchester, England. Pianist; Conductor. m. Elaine Margaret Burns, 23 Aug 1980, 1 d. Education: Chethams School of Music, Manchester, 1961-71; Leeds University, 1971-72; Royal Manchester College of Music, 1972-73; Royal Northern College of Music, 1973-76; Paris Conservatoire, 1976-77; Diplomas: ARCM; GRNCM; BMus. Career: Concert Appearances throughout the world as Recitalist, Soloist with Major Orchestras and Chamber Musician, including USA, Canada, Japan, Australia, USSR, Continental Europe, UK; Annual appearances at Henry Wood Promenade Concerts, 1979-; Regular appearances at South Bank, London, Broadcasts on TV and Radio; Appearances at several major festivals including Edinburgh, Cheltenham, Bath, Hollywood Bowl, La Roche d'Arraignon, Prague; Guest Conductor including Ulster Orchestra, City of Birmingham Symphony Orchestra, Royal Liverpool Philharmonic Orchestra, Hallé Orchestra, Moscow Chamber Orchestra; Played Tippett's Piano Concerto at the 1991 Promenade Concerts, London; Tchaikovsky's Second Concerto at the 1993 Proms; Played the Britten Concerto at the Barbican, 1997. Recordings: Numerous including: Stravinsky, Three Movements from Petrushka; Prokofiev, Sonata No 6; Tchaikovsky, Complete Works for Piano and Orchestra;

Messiaen, Turangalila Symphony; Rachmaninov Concerto No 3 and Etudes Tableaux and Preludes; Muldowney Concerto; Gershwin Rhapsody in Blue on The Jazz Album, with Simon Rattle. Honours: include, Dayas Gold Medal, Royal Manchester College of Music, 1977; Liszt-Bartók Competition, Budapest, 1976; Leeds International Piano Competition, 1981; Winner, 7th International Tchaikovsky Competition, Moscow, 1982; Honorary Fellow, Royal Northern College of Music, 1983.

DOOLEY Jeffrey Michael, b. 7 Oct 1945, Milwaukee, Wisconsin, USA. Singer (Counter-Tenor); Choral Conductor. Education: Milton College, Milton, Wisconsin; BA, Wisconsin Conservatory, 1968; Apprenticeship with Mark Deller, Deller Consort, Canterbury, England, 1974. Debut: Carnegie Hall, 1977. Career: Regular appearances in Early Music scene, New York: Basically Bach (Lincoln Center), Clarion Concerts, Amor Artis Ensemble, Waverly Consort, Boston Early Music Festival Orchestra, Milwaukee Symphony Orchestra, Connecticut Symphony; Recital-lecture presentations, The Art of the Counter-Tenor, duo with Richard Kolb, lutenist, founder of The Gotham Consort; Founder, Director, The Stuyvesant Singers, Toronto, Canada; Ongoing appearances with the following Baroque Orchestras: Tafel Musik, Toronto, Ars Musica, Michigan, Levin Baroque Ensemble, Amor Artis Ensemble, Concert Royal, ARTEC Ensemble, New York; European appearances, Madeira Bach Festival, 1981; Stour Music, England, 1985; Amor Artis tour, Switzerland and Italy, 1991; Specialist in the Handel Oratorio, frequently giving masterclasses in interpretation of the arias, and performing. Recordings: Henry Purcell: Airs and Duets, Nonesuch; J S Bach: Mass in B Minor, Nonesuch; Johannes Ockeghem: Masses, Nonesuch; G Dufay: Masses, Nonesuch; J S Bach: St John Passion, Newport Classic; G F Handel: Acis and Galatea, Newport; H Schütz: St Matthew Passion, Newport. Contributions to: The Counter-Tenor Voice Defined, 1977; The Counter-Tenor's Roles in Music, 1982. Memberships: Early Music, America; International Society of Early Music Singers. Hobbies: Reader; Gardening; Gourmet Cooking. Current Management: Melody Bunting International, 127 West 72nd Street, Suite 2-R, New York 10023, USA. Address: 229 East 11th Street, New York, NY 10003, USA.

DOOLEY William, b. 9 Sept 1932, Modesto, California, USA. Singer (Baritone). Education: Studied at the Eastman School of Music and in Munich with Viktoria Prestel and Hedwig Fichtmuller. Debut: Heidelberg 1957, as Posa in Don Carlos. Career: Sang at Bielefeld 1959-62; Member of the Deutsche Oper Berlin from 1962, notably in the premieres of Montezuma by Sessions (1964), Gespenstersonate by Reimann (1984) and Rihm's Oedipus, 1987; Salzburg Festival 1964, as Lucio Silla and 1966 in the premiere of The Bassarids by Henze; Metropolitan Opera from 1964, as Amonasro, Eugene Onegin, the villains in Les Contes d'Hoffmann, Telramund, Orestes (Elektra) and Mandryka; hamburg Staatsoper 1967, as Iago and 1979 in the premiere of Jakob Lenz by Wolfgang Rihm; Guest appearances at the Royal Opera Stockholm from 1967; Other roles include: Berg's Wozzeck and Dr Schön, Pizarro, Kothner, Macbeth, Escamillo, Nick Shadow, Captain Mary (Die Soldaten) and Goryanchikov in From the House of the Dead; Sang Eagle in the premiere of Los Alamos by Marc Neikrug at Berlin, 1989. Recordings include: Telramund in Lohengrin (RCA); Jakob Lenz (Harmonia Mundi). Address: c/o Deutsch Oper Berlin, Richard Wagnerstrasse 10, D-100 Berlin, Germany.

DOPP Bonnie Jo, b. 30 Mar 1942, Milwaukee, Wisconsin, USA. Music Librarian; Musicologist. Education: BA, American University, Washington, DC, 1963; MLS, 1971, MM, 1993, University of Maryland. Career: Public Librarian, 1968-95; Academic Music Librarian, 1996-. Publications: Numerology and Cryptography in the Music of Lili Boulanger: The Hidden Program in Clairieres dans le ciel, 1994. Contributions to: Library Journal. Honour: Pauline Alderman Prize, International Alliance for Women in Music, 1997. Memberships: Music Library Association; American Musicological Society; Sonneck Society; International Alliance for Women in Music; American Library Association. Hobbies: Giving Pre-Concert Talks; Writing Program Notes. Address: 804 Kennebec Avenue, Silver Spring, MD 20912, USA.

DORDI Patrizia, b. 1956, Italy. Singer (Soprano). Education: Studied at the Accademia di Santa Cecilia, Rome. Debut: Rome, 1979, in Schumann's Manfred. Career: Opera debut in Handel's Ariodante at La Scala, 1980; Guest at La Fenice, Venice, as Lisa in La Sonnambula and Mathilde in Guillaume Tell; Naples as Elmira in Jommelli's La schiava liberata and at Catania as Amor in Orfeo ed Euridice; Other repertory includes Micaela, Sabina in Cimarosa's Gli Orazi ed i Curiazi, Pamina (Ravenna Festival), Mimi and Musetta.

DORFMÜLLER Joachim, b. 13 Dec 1938, Wuppertal, Germany. Professor. m. Ursula Petschelt, 14 May 1976, 1 son, 2 daughters. Education: Universities of Cologne and Marburg; Studied piano and organ with father; Musikhochschule, Cologne. Career: Teacher, Music, Mathematics and Latin, Gymnasium, 1969-78; University of Duisberg, 1978-84; University of Münster and Music Academy, Cologne, 1984-; Founder, Artistic Director, Wuppertaler Orgeltage, 1973-; Over 2000 concerts on organ and piano in 21 countries including the USA and Japan. Recordings: Virtuoso organ music of the Romantic period; Famous Organ works by Saint-Saëns; Piano works by Grieg; Meditations: Bach, Bernstein and Messiaen; Transcriptions: Bach to Rachmanninoff. Publications include: Norweg, Klaviermusik 1900-1950, 1968; Zeitgenöss, Orgelmusik 1960-84, 1985; 300 Jahre Orgelbau im Wuppertal, 1988; Gesch des Sinfonieorchesters Wuppertal, 1991; Wuppertaler Musikgeschichte, 1995; Geistl Musik von Grieg, forthcoming; Geschichte der Orgelmusik, forthcoming. Contributions to: 120 articles for Herder-Musiklexikon, Rheinische Musikerbiographien und Musik in Geschichte und Gegenwart. Honours: Director of Church Music, 1990; Cultural Prize of the Rhineland, 1993. Memberships: Humboldt-Akademie der Wissenschaften, 1990; President, Deutsche Edvard Grieg-Gesellschaft, 1993; Research Group of the Norwegian Academy of Science and Letters, 1997. Hobbies: Family; Travelling; Good books. Address: Ringelstraße 22, D-42289 Wuppertal, Germany.

DORFMÜLLER Kurt, b. 28 Apr 1922, Munich, Germany. Musicologist; Librarian. m. Liselotte Laubmann, 2 sons. Education: Training and State Examination, Library Science; Musicology, University of Munich, 1946-52; Dr phil. Career: Bavarian State Library, 1954-84, including Head of Music Collection, 1963, Head of Acquisitions Division, 1969-, Vice-Director, 1972. Publications: Studien zur Lautenmusik in der ersten Hälfte des 16 Jahrhunderts, 1967; Beiträge zur Beethoven-Bibliographie, 1977; Bestandsaufbau an wissenschaftlichen Bibliotheken, 1989; Musik in Bibliotheken, 1997. Contributions to: Musicology and library science articles to journals, Festschriften and library exhibition catalogues. Honour: Ars Jocundissima, Festschrift für Kurt Dorfmüller, 1984. Memberships include: Honorary Member, International Association of Music Libraries; Board Member, International Inventory of Musical Sources. Hobby: Puns. Address: Gabriel-von-Seidl-Strasse 39, D-82031 Grünwald, Germany.

DORN Reinhard, b. 18 Feb 1957, Singer (Bass). Education: Cologne Musikhochschule. Career: Dr Bartolo in Il Barbiere di Siviglia, Städtische Bühnen Krefeld/Mönchengladbach, 1983; Offered permanent contract, Badisches Staatstheater, Karlsruhe; Sang Don Magnifico in Michael Hampe's production of La Cenerentola, 1986; Joined Cologne Opera, 1986; French debut as Leporello, Toulouse, 1990-91; Kezal in The Bartered Bride, Leporello in Don Giovanni, Semper Oper Dresden, 1992-93; Sang Dvorak's Requiem with Gewandhaus Orchestra, Leipzig, and La Finta Giardiniera, Festival de Radio France, Montpellier, 1994-95; Sang Figaro in new production of Le Nozze di Figaro, Dresden State Opera, 1995-96; Sang Papageno in Andreas Homoki's new production of Die Zauberflöte, Cologne Opera, and Frank in Die Fledermaus, Hamburg, 1995; Also performances in Die Verkaufte Braut, Der Wildschütz, in Cologne; Don Giovanni, Munich State Opera and Dresden State Opera; La Calisto by Cavalli, Staatsoper Berlin and Brussels Opera, all season 1995-96; North American debut, Taddeo in L'Italiana, 1997-98; Forthcoming engagements as Leporello for the Vienna State Opera, 1998, and also in San Diego for the season 2000. Current Management: Haydn Rawstron Limited, London. Address: PO Box 654, London SE26 4DZ, England.

DORNBUSCH Hans, b. 1946, Sweden. Singer (Tenor). Education: Studied at the Stockholm Academy and at the School of the Royal Opera. Debut: Stockholm, 1969, as Calaf. Career: Member of the Royal Opera Stockholm from 1970, notably as Manrico, Otello, Pinkerton, Turiddu, Andres in Wozzeck and the Steuermann in Fliegende Holländer: Sang Pope Alexander VII in the premiere of Christina, by Hans Gefors, 1986; Character roles in Albert Herring and Hansel und Gretel; Guest appearances in England and Germany; Frequent concert engagements. Address: c/o Kungliga Teatern, PO Box 10694, S-103 22 Stockholm, Sweden.

DOROW Dorothy, b. 1930, London, England. Singer (Soprano). Education: Studied at Trinity College, London. Career: Sang in London from 1958, notably in BBC Invitation Concerts (Webern conducted by John Carewe, and the British premier of Herzgewächse by Schoenberg, 1960); Has sung in the premieres of works by Birtwistle, Nono, Maderna, Dallapiccola, Bussotti, Ligetti, Boulez, Goehr and Bennett (The Ledge, Sadler's Wells, 1961); Sang Hilde Mack in the British premiere of Henze's Elegy for Young Lovers, Glyndebourne 1961; Lived in Sweden 1963-77, Holland from 1977: Professor of Voice at the Conservatoire of Amsterdam and The Hague; Master Classes in Europe and Scandinavia; Concerts and opera in Italy, at La Scala, Venice, Rome, Florence and Bologna (Le Grand Macabre by Ligeti); Repertoire from Monteverdi to the 20th Century; Covent Garden debut 1983, as Stravinsky's Nightingale.

DOUBEK Jiri, b. 22 September 1958, Chlumec nad Cidlinov. Composer; Music Director. m. Jana Kuplová Doubková, 4 December, 1992, 1 son, 1 daughter. Education: Guitar at Brno Conservatory, 1989; Composition and conducting at Prague Conservatory, 1991. Appointments: Teacher, Conservatory J Ferka in Prague, 1989; Music Director, 1991. Compositions: Wind Quintet, 1985; String Trio, for Czech Radio, 1986; Magic Universe (small musical), 1993; Carohdatky (cycle of songs for children), 1994; String Quartet, 1995; Scenic music for theatre and music for radio and CD. Recordings: String Trio, 1986; Duo for oboe and guitar, 1987; Carohre'tly, 1991. Membership: OSA Prague.

DOUBRAVOVA Jarmila, b. 23 June 1940, Chrudim. Musicologist; Aesthetician; Semiotician. m. Ing Bohumír Dubec, 30 Sept 1976, divorced 1984, 1 son. Education: Philosophical Faculty, Charles University, Aesthetics Musicology, 1957-62; PhD, 1967; Piano by Berta Kabelác, 1949-60. Publications: Music and Visual Ats, 1982; Semiotics and Musical Semiotics, 1992; Semantic Gesture, 1996; Dialogue and Imagination, 1997. Contributions to: Int Review for Aesthetics and Socio of Music; Semiotica; Muzikoloski zbornik. Honours: Member, Czech Artistic Forum, until 1990; Czech Linguistic Circle, until 1995; New York Academy of Sciences, until 1996. Memberships: Czech Musicological Society; Deutsche Gesell für Semiotik-Musik-Sek; Czech Aesthetic Society; Masaryk's Sociological Society. Hobbies: Gymnastics; Swimming; Gardening. Address: Pocernická 82, Prague 10, 10800 Czech Republic.

DOUFEXIS Stella, b. Frankfurt am Main, Germany. Singer (Mezzo-soprano). Education: Studied at the Hochschule für Musik, Berlin, and with Anna Reynolds; Master classes with Dietrich Fischer-Dieskau and Aribert Reimann. Debut: In Dido and Aeneas, Berlin, 1992. Career: Concert engagements in Schubert's Lazarus, under Fischer-Dieskau, Pergolesi's Stabat Mater (Konzerthaus, Berlin), Ravel's Sheherazade, under Ashkenazy, and Janacek's Glagolétic Mass; Season 1995-96 at the Heidelberg Opera, as Cherubino, Handel, Nicklausse, Gluck's Orfeo and in the German premiere of Birtwistle's Second Mrs Kong; UK debut at the Wigmore Hall in the International Songmakers series; Season 1996-97 in Provenzale's La Stelldaura Vendicata at Brussels and Rosina at Heidelberg; Schubert Lieder in Berlin and Lucerne, the Masses with the Deutsches SO. Recordings include: Webern and Fortner Lieder; Glagoloitic Mass. Address: c/o Lies Askonas Ltd, 6 Henrietta St, London WC2 8LA, England.

DOUGLAS Barry, b. 23 Apr 1960, Belfast, Northern Ireland. Pianist. m. Deirdre O'Hara, 1 son, 1 daughter. Education: Belfast School of Music; Royal College of Music, London, 1978-82; Diploma RCM (Performance); Private study with Maria Cureio in London. Debut: Berlin Philharmonic, 1987. Career: Wigmore Hall, London, 1981; New York recital debut Carnegie Hall, New York, 1988; Royal festival Hall with London Philharmonic, 1983; Subject of BBC documentary film Rhapsody in Belfast and film After the Gold; Appeared in John Schlesinger's film Madame Sousatska; Played Rachmaninov 2 with London Symphony Orchestra and Michael Tilson-Thomas in TV series Concerto; Broadcasts, BBC Radio 3, Radio Ulster, Radio London, BBC TV; Live performances with orchestras and recorded concerts; Performed for Thames TV; Concerts, USA, Japan, France, Germany, UK, Denmark, Sweden, Netherlands, Italy, Greece, Ireland, USSR, Australia, New Zealand; Performed with all major British orchestras; Played Beethoven's 4th Concerto at the Festival Hall, London, 1997. Recordings: Tchaikovsky Concerto No 1 with London Symphony Orchestra/Slatkin; Brahms Concerto No 2 with London Symphony Orchestra; Mussorgsky, Liszt and Beethoven solo works; Liszt Concertos 1 and 2 and Hungarian Fantasy with London Symphony Orchestra/Hirokami; Prokofiev Solo Sonatas 2, 7 and Cinderella; Berg and Liszt Sonatas; Brahms Quintet with Tokyo Quartet; Tchaikovsky 2, 3 and Concert Fantasy; Rachmaninov 2 coupled with some Rachmaninov Preludes; Corigliano Concerto with St Louis Symphony under Slatkin. Honours: Medal, Worshipful Company of Musicians; 1st Prize, classified, Paloma O'Shea Piano Competition, Spain, 1980; Concert Artists' Guild Award of New York, 1982; Silver Medal, Arthur Rubinstein Piano Master Competition, Israel; Gold Medal, Tchaikovsky Competition, Moscow, 1986; Honorary DMus, Queens University, Belfast, 1987; Honorary FRCM, Royal College of Music, London, 1988. Hobbies: Driving; Reading; Food; Wine. Current Management: IMG Artists, Media House, Media House, 3 Burlington Lane, London W4 2TH, England.

DOUGLAS James, b. 4 July 1932, Dumbarton, Scotland. Composer; Organist; Accompanist. m. Helen Torrance Fairweather, 16 Apr 1968, 2 sons, 1 daughter. Education: Heriot Watt College, Edinburgh. Musical Education: Conservatoire, Paris; Hochschule, Munich; Mozarteum, Salzburg; LRAM; ARCM. Debut: Wienersaal, Salzburg, 1951. Career: Director: Eschenbach Editions, Caritas Records, Caritas Voices and Caritas Ensemble; Professor, Académie des Sciences Humaines Universelles, Paris, 1992-. Compositions: 12 symphonies, 12 string quartets, 20 orchestral works, 200 songs, organ works, chamber and instrumental works, piano works; 3 operas: Mask, Molière, Cuthbert; choral works. Recordings: Visions of Glory, for voices; Symphony (A Cloud of Unknowing); A Vision, for organ. Publication: The Music of Hermann Reutter, 1966. Memberships:

MPA; PRS; MCPS; PPL. Hobbies: Literature; Art. Address: c/o Eschenbach Editions, 28 Dalrymple Crescent, Edinburgh EH9 2NX, Scotland.

DOUGLAS Nigel, b. 9 May 1929, Lenham, Kent, England. Singer (Tenor); Director; Writer; Broadcaster. m. Alexandra Roper, 21 July 1973, 1 son, 2 daughters. Education: Magdalen College, Oxford University; Musikakademie, Vienna, Austria. Debut: Rodolfo in La Bohème, Vienna Kammeroper, 1959. Career: Leading roles in opera houses and festivals, Aldeburgh, Antwerp, Barcelona, Basel, Berne, Brussels, Buenos Aires, Covent Garden, Dusseldorf, Duisburg, Edinburgh, English National Opera, Garsington, Glyndebourne, Sadler's Wells, Scottish Opera, Venice, Lisbon, Vienna Volksoper, Welsh National Opera, Wexford, Zurich, Tokyo, Catania, Paris-Bastille, Seoul and others; Repertoire of 80 roles including Peter Grimes, Captain Vere (Billy Budd), Aschenbach (Death in Venice), Eisenstein (Fledermaus), Danilo (Merry Widow), Loge (Rheingold), Herod (Salome), Captain (Wozzeck), Hauk-Sendorf (Makropoulos Case); Has written and presented over 300 programmes on opera and operetta for BBC Radio 2, 3, 4 and World Service; Regular television appearances in UK and Europe; Directed numerous productions for Sadler's Wells, Australian Opera, Royal Flemish Opera. Recordings: Owen Wingrave; Salome; Zigeunerbaron; Various recitals. Publications: English versions of Die Csardasfürstin (Kalman), 1982, Gräfin Mariza (Kalman), 1983, Merry Widow (Lehar), 1983; Legendary Voices, 1992; More Legendary voices, 1994; The Joy of Opera, 1997. Contributions to: Numerous articles to Times Literary Supplement; Opera Magazine; BBC Music Magazine. Honours: Nominated for Royal Philharmonic Society Book Prize, 1993. Hobbies: Gardening; Bee-keeping; Fishing. Current Management: Music International, UK. Address: Eythorne House, Eythorne, Dover, Kent CT15 4BE, England.

DOUSA Eduard, b. 31 Aug 1951, Prague, Czechoslovakia. Composer; Teacher. m. 21 Oct 1976, 2 sons. Education: Graduated, Gymnasium, 1969; Studied Musicology, Charles University, Prague, to 1972; Graduated in Composition, Theory of Music, Academy of Musical Arts, Prague, 1977. Career: Teacher, Theory of Music, Conservatoire, Prague, 1977-86; Teacher, Theory of Music, Philosophical Faculty, Prague, 1986-. Compositions: Published Compositions: Sonata for Organ; Variations on a Baroque Theme for Strings; Miniatures for Piano (for children); Sonatine for clarinet and piano (for children); Rhapsody for Clarinet and Piano; Three short suites for guitar (for children); Concerto for four saxophones and orchestra, 1993; Romantic Fantasy for two pianos, 1995; Fantasia for trumpet and organ, 1995; Uno per quattro per flaute, oboe, chittern ed violoncello, 1996; Imaginations for violin and guitar, 1997; Mosorico for violin solo, 1997. Recordings: Rhapsody for Clarinet and Piano, 1989; Variations on a Baroque Theme for Strings, 1988; Miniatures for Flute, Violin, Violoncello and harpsichord, 1990; Concerto for four saxophones, 1995; Many compositions were recorded for Czechoslovak Radio: Concertino for trumpet and orchestra, Sonata for piano, String-quartet, Romantic Phantasy for violin and piano, Rhapsody for clarinet and piano and many compositions for children, musical fairy tales, songs, choirs. Membership: Society of Czech Composers. Hobbies: History; Literature; Sport; Tennis; Swimming. Address: Tenisová 9, 102-00 Prague 10, Czech Republic.

DOW Dorothy, b. 8 Oct 1920, Houston, Texas, USA. Singer (Soprano). Education: Juilliard School, New York. Career: Sang in and directed various choirs in New York, 1938-44; Sang Santuzza in a Concert Performance of Cavalleria Rusticana, Buffalo, 1944; Columbia University, New York, in the premiere of the Mother of us All, by Thompson, 1947; Sang with the Zurich Opera, 1948-50; La Scala from 1950, as Elisabeth, Marie (Wozzeck), Danae by Strauss, Chrysothemis, Gioconda and Walton's Cressida; Sang Erwartung in the US premiere of Schoenberg's monodrama, with the New York Philharmonic, 1951; Glyndebourne Festival, 1952-53; Lady Macbeth and Ariadne; Carnegie Hall, New York, 1952, in the US premiere of Christophe Colombe by Milhaud; Florence 1953, Agnese di Hohenstaufen by Spontini; Sang Renata in the stage premiere of Prokofiev's Fiery Angel, Venice, 1955.

DOWLING Richard (William), b. 6 Sept 1962, Houston, Texas, USA. Concert Pianist. Education: BM, Summa Cum Laude, University of Houston, 1985; MM, Yale University, 1987; DMA, Piano Performance, University of Texas, Austin, 1990; Principal Teacher, Abbey Simon; Additional Studies: Le Conservatiore de Musique, Nice, France; Yale Norfolk Summer School and Music Festival, Connecticut, USA. Debut: With Fort Worth Symphony, Texas, 1981; Career: Solo Recitals throughout USA; PBS television solo recital programme debut aired nationally, 1986; Recital tour, France, 1991; Concerto appearances with Oklahoma Symphony, Houston Civic Symphony, Shreveport (Louisiana) Symphony, Midland-Odessa (Texas) Symphony, Brazos Valley (Texas) Symphony, Yale Trumbull Symphony, Arkansas Symphony; Concerto appearances with Jupiter Symphony, Tully Hall, Lincoln Center, New York City, 1992; 1st Holder of Walles Chair in the Performing Arts, Lamar University, 1989-90; Artist Faculty (Piano), The Harid Conservatory of Music, Boca Raton, Florida, USA; Recitals: Austria, Australia, South Africa, 1992; 2nd Tour of France, 1992; Gina Bachaeur Festival, Salt Lake City, Utah, 1993; Paris Recital Debut: Salle Cortot, 1994. Publication: New critical edition of Maurice Ravel's Trio for Piano, Violin and Cello, 1990. Current Management: LA Artist Managements, 21345 St Andrew's Blvd, Suite 260-207, Boca Raton, FL 33433, USA. Address: 261 West 71st Street, No 3, New York, NY 10023, USA.

DOWNES Andrew, b. 20 Aug 1950, Handsworth, Birmingham, England. Composer; Lecturer. m. Cynthia Cooper, 9 Aug 1975, 2 daughters. Education: Choral Scholar, 1969-72, BA Hons, 1972, St John's College, Cambridge; MA (Cantab), 1975; Royal College of Music, 1972-74; Singing with Gordon Clinton; Composition with Herbert Howells; Later study with Sir Lennox Berkeley. Debut: Wigmore Hall, 1969. Career includes: Established Faculty of Composition, 1975, Head of School, 1990, Professor, School of Composition and Creative Studies, 1992-, Birmingham Conservatoire; Chaired Symposium on Music Criticism, Indian Music Congress, University of Burdwan, 1994; Performances of own works include: Israel Philharmonic Guest House, Tel Aviv, 1989, Berlin Kaiser Willhelm Gedächtniskirche, 1990, Calcutta School of Music, 1994, Paris, 1995, University of New Mexico, 1995, 1997, Bombay, 1996, Barletta, Italy, 1996 New York, 1996; Caracas, Venezuela, 1997; Rudolphin, Prague, 1998. Compositions include: Sonata for Violin and Piano Opus 52, for concert in memory of Ernest Element, 1993; Sonata for 8 Horns Opus 54, University of New Mexico commission, 1994, performed by the horns of the Czech Philharmonic Orchestra, 1998; Fanfare for Madam Speaker Opus 55, for installation of Rt Hon Betty Boothroyd as Chancellor of Open University, 1995; Sonata for 8 Flutes; Sonata for Oboe and Piano Opus 56 composed for George Caird, oboist and Principal, Birmingham Conservatoire, 1995; Songs From Spoon River, performed at Tanglewood Festival and on Radio 3; Towards A New Age, performed by the Royal Philharmonic Orchestra in Birmingham, 1997. Recordings include: The Marshes of Glynn, cantata, commission for royal opening of Sir Adrian Boult Hall, Birmingham, 1966; O Vos Omnes, motet, Cantamus commission; Sonata for 2 Pianos; Fanfare for a Ceremony, commission for Open University; Centenary Firedances; Shepherd's Carol; The Soul of the Righteous, anthem, 1997; Sonata for Oboe and Piano, 1998. Publications: 68 works including 4 symphonies, 5 choral works, 2 double concertos, 3 string quartets, 2 brass quintets, flute octet, horn octet and horn quartet, 5 song cycles and 5 anthems. Honours include: Prizewinner, Stroud International Composers' Competition, 1980; Invited by Crane Concert Choir, University of New York, to conduct his choral work A St Luke Passion, 1993; Leather bound presentation copy of Fanfare for a Ceremony given to HRH Prince Edward on his visit to Birmingham Conservatoire, 1995; Bound presentation copy of Fanfare for Madam Speaker given to Rt Hon Betty Boothroyd MP at her installation as Chancellor of Open University, 1995. Memberships include: Representing Birmingham Conservatoire, Indian Music Congress; Leading Patron, Midland Chamber Players' Society; President, Central Composers' Alliance (Composers' Guild, Midland Region); PRS; MCPS; Fellow, Royal Society of Arts. Hobbies: Walking; Travel; Reading. Current Management: Publisher: Lynwood Music. Address: c/o Lynwood Music, 2 Church Street, West Hagley, West Midlands DY9 0NA, England.

DOWNES Edward (Olin Davenport), b. 12 Aug 1911, Boston, Massachusetts, USA. Music Critic; Musicologist; Broadcaster; Teacher; Writer. Education: Columbia University, 1929-30; University of Paris, 1932-33; University of Munich, 1934-36 and 1938; PhD, Harvard University, 1958. Career: Wrote music criticism for New York Post, 1935-38; Boston Transcript, 1939-41; New York Times, 1955-58; Program Annotator, New York Philharmonic Orchestra, 1960-74; Teacher, Wellesley College, 1948-49; Harvard University, 1949-50; University of Minnesota, 1950-55; Musicologist-in-Residence, Bayreuth Master Classes, 1959-65; Professor of Music, History, Queens College of the City University of New York, 1966-81, New York University, 1981-86; Professor of Music, Juilliard School of Music, 1986-; Quizmaster, Metropolitan Opera Saturday afternoon Radio Broadcast intermission feature, 1958-; Regular Music Critic Panellist, Syndicated Radio Programme, First Hearing. Publications: Translated Werfel and Stefan's Giuseppe Verdis Briefe as Verdi: The Man in his Letters, 1942; Adventures in Symphonic Music, 1943; Perspectives in Musicology, edited with Brook and Van Solkema, 1972; The New York Philharmonic Guide to the Symphony, 1976, 2nd edition, 1981 as Guide to Symphonic Music. Contributions to: Articles in various journals and other publications. Memberships: American Musicological Society. Address: 1 West 72nd Street, New York, NY 10023, USA.

DOWNES Edward (Thomas) (Sir), b. 17 Jun 1924, Birmingham, England. Conductor. Education: Studied at University of Birmingham & Royal College of Music (Composition and Horn); Further study with Hermann Scherchen. Career: Carl Rosa Opera, 1950-52; Covent Garden from 1952, notably Der Freischütz (1954), Les Contes d'Hoffmann, Katerina Ismailova (1963), Der Ring des Nibelungen (1967), Hamlet by Searle (1969), Victory (1970) and Taverner (1972); Many performances of operas by Verdi, British premiere of The Bassarids by Henze, BBC 1968; Conducted the premieres of Birtwistle's Chorales 1967, and Brian's Symphonies Nos 14 and 21, 1970; Musical Director of Australian Opera, 1972-76, conducting Prokofiev's War and Peace at opening of Sydney Opera House, 1973; Welsh National Opera 1975, Der fliegende Holländer; Conducted first performance of Prokofiev's opera Maddalena, BBC 1979; Conducted first modern performance of Tchaikovsky's Vakula the Smith, BBC 1989; Led Revivals of Otello and Il Trovatore at Covent Garden, 1990, new production of Attila; Principal Conductor, BBC Philharmonic from 1980; with the orchestra recorded a studio performance of Jerusalem by Verdi; Promenada Concerts 1989, with music by Bax, Walton, Strauss, John McCabe and Sibelius; Prokofiev's Symphonies in the Russian Spring series at the Festival Hall, 1991; Promenade Concerts, 1991, with the first Russian language performance of Prokofiev's Fiery Angel in Britain; Appointed Associate Music Director and Principal Conductor at Covent Garden, 1991; New Production of Verdi's Stiffelio, 1993; Season 1996-97 at Covent Garden with Tosca. Publications: Translations of Jenůfa, Katerina Ismailova and Khovanshchina. Honours: include, Commander of the British Empire, 1986. Address: Ingpen & Williams Ltd, 14 Kensington Court, London, W8 5DN, UK.

DOWNEY John (Wilham), b. 5 Oct 1927, Chicago, Illinois, USA. Composer. Professor. Education: BM, De Paul University, 1949; MM, Chicago Musical College, 1951; Paris Conservatoire, 1956; Doctor des lettres, Sorbonne, Paris, 1957. Career: Teacher, De Paul University, Chicago City College; Roosevelt University; Professor of Composition and Composer-in-Residence, University of Wisconsin, 1964-; Founder, Wisconsin Contemporary Music Forum. Compositions: Ageistics, ballet, 1967; Incidental music to Shakespeare's Twelfth Night, 1971; Orchestral: La Joie de la paix, 1956; Chant to Michelangelo, 1958; Concerto for Harp and Chamber Orchestra, 1964; Jingalodeon, 1968; Symphonic Modules, 1972; Tooter's Suite for Youth Orchestra, 1973; The Edge of Space for Bassoon and Orchestra, 1978, Discourse for Oboe, Harpischord and Strings, 1984; Double Bass Concerto, 1987; Declamations, 1985; Symphony No 1 (in two movements), 1992; Chamber: String Trio, 1953; For Those Who Suffered, for chamber orchestra, 1995; Violin Sonata, 1954; Wind Octet, 1954; 2 string quartets, 1964, 1976; Cello Sonata, 1966; Crescendo for 13 Percussionists, 1977; Agort for Woodwind Quintet, 1967; Almost 12 for Wind Quintet, String Quintet and Percussion, 1970; Ambivaliences I for Any Chamber Combination, 1972; High Clouds and Soft Rain for 24 Flutes, 1977; Duo for Oboe and Harpischord, 1981; Portrait No 2 for Clarinet and Bassoon, 1983 and No 3 for Flute and Piano, 1984; Piano Trio, 1984; Prayer for Violin, Viola and Cello, 1984; Recombinance for Double Bass and Piano, 1985; Solo Pieces: Tabu for Tabu, 1967; Lydian Suite for Cello, 1975; Silhouette for Double Bass, 1980; Call for Freedom (for Symphonic Winds), 1990; Ode to Freedom (Orchestral), 1991; Rough Road (flute and guitar), 1995; Angel Talk (eight cellos), 1995; Piano pieces: Adagio Lyrico (for two pianos), 1953; Eastlake Terrace (for solo piano), 1959; Edges (piano solo), 1960; Pyramids (piano solo), 1961; Portrait No 1 (piano solo), 1980; Yad Vashem - An Impression (solo piano), 1991; Memories (piano solo), 1991; Vocal music, including Tangents, jazz oratorio, 1981; Choral works: What If? for choir, brass octet and solo timpany, 1973; Suite of Psalms for a cappella choir, 1989; Ghosts, for twelve violins, 1996; Setting of Psalm 90 for choir, organ, brass octet, tympany and soprano soloist, 1997. Recordings: The Edge of Space; Cello Sonata on CRI; String Quartet No 2; John Downey Plays John Downey; A Dolphin Octet for Winds, What If?, Adagio Lyrica and Agort-a; John Downey played by the LSO: Declamations, Discourse, Jingalodeon, Concerto for Double Bass and Orchestra. Publication: Eastlake Terrace, 1959; Pyramids, 1960; Cello Sonata, Agort, Jingalodeon, Billaudot in Paris; Prayer, Silhouette, Portrait No 3, 1984; Theodore Presser; La musique populaire dans l'oeuvre de Bela Bartok, 1966; Lydian Suite, 1976; Discourse, 1984; Soliloquy, 1997. Address: 4413 North Prospect Avenue, Shorewood, WI 53211, USA.

DOYLE Gerard Anthony, b. 7 Oct 1944, Liverpool, England. Teacher and Lecturer in Music; Consultant; Conductor. m. 3 Jan 1974, 1 son, 1 daughter. Education: BA Mus, Music and Languages; BMus, postgraduate, 1st Class Honours; PhD; LRAM, Performing Diploma; LRAM, Teaching Diploma; Postgraduate Certificate in Education. Career: Recital, concerto and orchestral engagements and broadcasts in Britain and Europe; Conductor of regional choral and orchestral concerts; Specialist lecture recitals; Directs and coaches orchestras as leader and concertmaster; Teacher and Lecturer in Music Education; Individual violin and viola pupils; Consultant to professional players; Publishes in the field; Guest Lecturer and Tutor for universities of Liverpool, Lancaster and Open University, England; Currently Senior Lecturer in Music at University College of St Martin, Lancaster, responsible for undergraduate, postgraduate and in-service courses; Founding Conductor of Haffner Orchestra and of Classical Trust; Research interests include performance as conductor and violinist, the psychology of performance, especially stress and Alexander Technique, and historical performance styles. Publications include: Skill, Stress and the Alexander technique, PhD thesis, 1984; Computer Assessment of Musical Ability - ESRC, University of Lancaster, 1990; Editor, International Bulletin of European String Teachers' Association, 1992, 1993. Contributions to: 10 pedagogic papers in Journal of European String Teachers' Association, 1983-91. Memberships include: Music Education Council, Anglo-Austrian Society; Elected to Royal Society of Musicians, 1992. Address: Beck Bridge House, Moorside Road, Brookhouse, Lancaster LA2 9PJ, England.

DRABEK Vaclav, b. 29 August 1943, Litomysl, Bohemia. Musicologist. m. Miroslava Horackova, 19 March 1975. Education: PhD, 1974, CSc, 1983, Faculty of Arts, Masaryk University, Brno; Private Studies, Violin, Piano, Song, Conducting, Composition. Career: University Teacher, Department of Music, Faculty of Education; Artistic Director, Pardubice State Chamber Orchestra, 1978-85; Research Worker, Theatre Institute, Department of Music, Prague, 1985-87; University Teacher, Faculty of Education, Charles University; Cooperation with Czech Radio and Television, Prague. Publications: Popularizace hudby, 1992; Vilem Steinman a ceské sborové umeui, 1997. Contributions to: Journals and magazines. Honour: Memorial Medal, University of Music, Mozarteum, Salzburg, 1994. Memberships: International Musicological Society; European Association for Music in Schools; Czech Musicological Society. Hobbies: History; Literature; Tourism. Address: Sezimova 436/5, 14000 Praha 4, Czech Republic.

DRABOWICZ Wojciech, b. 1963, Poznán, Poland. Singer (Baritone). Education: Studied at the Poznán Academy, 1984-89. Career includes: Won prizes at the 1990 Tchaikowsky Competition, Moscow, and the Belvedere, Vienna; Member of the Poznán Opera from 1989 (debut as Eugene Onegin) and sang Morales at the 1991 Bregenz Festival; Other roles include Mozart's Guglielmo and Pagageno, Malatesta in Don Pasquale and other lyric repertory; Recitalist in songs by Schumann, Chopin and Schubert; La Monnaie, Brussels, 1992; European tour Theatre du Nord, Paris, 19992-93; Il Barbiere di Siviglia and Figaro, directed by Gerome Savari at Warsaw Opera House, 1993; Eugene Onegin at Glyndebourne Opera Festival including a BBC Prom, 1994; Cosi fan tutte at Monnaie, Brussels, 1994; Pelléas et Mélisande, Kiel State Opera, 1995; The Queen of Spades at Glyndebourne Opera Festival, 1995; Further engagements include King Roger by Szymanowski at Theatre des Champs Elysees, 1996, Eugene Onegin at Glyndebourne Opera Festival and Münchner Biennale in 1996 and Le nozze di Figaro at Glyndebourne Opera Festival in 1997. Address: c/o Poznán Grand Theatre, Fredry 9, 60-967 Poznán, Poland.

DRAGANOVA Dora, b. 29 Jan 1946, Sofia, Bulgaria. Composer. Education: Studied at the Sofia State Academy of Music. Career: Lecturer in Harmony at the Sofia State School of Music from 1972. Compositions include: Car Koshnichar, comic opera in one act, 1972; Children's musicals; 300 songs, chamber music, and popular music. Address: c/o SABAM, Rue d'Arlon 75-77, 1040 Brussels, Belgium.

DRAGONI Maria, b. 1958, Procida, Naples, Italy. Singer (Soprano). Education: Studied in Naples. Debut: Sang Imogene in Il Pirata at Naples, 1984 (Teatro di Jesi). Career: Appeared in the title role of Pergolesi's Il Flamino at the Teatro San Carlo Naples, 1984; Season 1988-89, as Fenena in Nabucco at La Scala, Turandot at Nancy and Revenna and Aida at Marcerata; Mathilde in Guillaume Tell and Bellini's Norma at the Théâtre des Champs Elysées and Mulhouse, 1989; Season, 1990-91, as Elisabeth de Valois at Turin and Donna Anna at the Teatro dell Opera at Rome; Sang Mimi at Naples and Elisabeth de Valois at the Verona Arena, 1992; Other roles include Paolina in Poluito by Donizetti, Donna Anna, and La Gioconda; Sang Aida at Florence, 1996.

DRAHEIM Joachim, b. 26 July 1950, Berlin-Schmargendorf, Germany. Musicologist; Pianist; Teacher of Latin and Music. Education: 1st State examination, 1974, 2nd State examination, 1978, promoted to PhD, Latin, Greek, Musicology, 1978, University of Heidelberg; Studied Piano with Ursula Draheim, 1955-68, Violoncello with Annlies Schmidt-de Neveu, 1963-68. Career: Concerts as solo, chamber music and lieder pianist in Germany and Switzerland; Freelance, many radio recordings of lieder and piano pieces, Süddeutscher Rundfunk Karlsruhe and Heidelberg, 1973-; Freelance, several German and foreign music publishers including Breitkopf and Härtel, Wiesbaden, and Wiener Urtext Edition, and recording companies, 1974-; Numerous editions including Brahms und seine Freunde-works for piano, works by Mozart, Beethoven, Loewe, Fanny Hensel, Liszt, Mendelssohn, Robert and Clara Schumann, Chopin, Ludwig Schuncke, Woldemar Bargiel, Brahms, Busoni, others; First editions: Mendelssohn: Albumblatt in A major, Sonata in D major and Sonata movement in G minor for two pianos; Brahms: Die Müllerin; Schumann: Der Korsar, Piano accompaniment to Bach's Suite in C major for solo cello, Violin setting of Schumann Cello Concerto in A minor op 129, Variations on a nocturne by Chopin for piano, others; Teaching at Lessing Gymnasium, Karlsruhe, 1978-; Works for the Neue Schumann-Gesamtausgabe, the Neue Weber-Gesamtausgabe and the new MGG. Hobbies: Music and playing the piano; Collecting autographs, scores and books. Address: Sophienstrasse 165, D-76185 Karlsruhe, Germany.

DRAHOS Béla, b. 1955, Kaposvar, Hungary. Flautist; Conductor. Education: Studied with Henrik Prohle at the Gyor Conservatory and with Lorant Kovacs at the Ferenc Liszt Academy, Budapest, graduated, 1978; From 1991 studied conducting with Professor Carl Osterreicher in Vienna. Career: Solo Flautist with the Budapest Symphony Orchestra from 1976, including many foreign tours; Solo Flautist with the Hungarian State Orchestra, 1990; Solo Career in Austria, Bulgaria, Belgium, Czechoslovakia, England, Finland, France, Soviet Union, Switzerland and Germany; Concerts with the New Zealand Symphony Orchestra, 1988; West Berlin Philharmonie, 1989; Leader and Founder Member, Hungarian Radio Wind Quintet; Music Director, Kaposvar Symphony Orchestra, 1990; Assistant Conductor, Hungarian State Symphony Orchestra, 1993; Guest Conductor of leading orchestras in Hungary; Conducts operas and concerts in Austria and Germany. Recordings: Mozart Concert K314; Paganini 24 Caprices; Bach 4th Brandenburg Concerto and Concerto for Two Flutes in F; Vivaldi Concertos (Hungaroton); 16 Haydn Symphonies for Naxos; Beethoven's Symphonies 1-9 and Overtures, Naxos. Honours: First Prize, Concertino Praha, 1971; Second Prize, Prague Spring International Competition, 1975; Grand Prize of UNESCO at the Bratislava Interpodium, 1979; Ferenc Liszt Prize, 1985; Artist of the Year, 1986; Bartok-Pastory Prize, 1988; Little Cross of Decoration (Order of Merit) given by the Hungarian Republic, 1994. Current Management: Co-Nexus Concert Limited, Budapest. Address: Budapest 1, Roham U 1 PO Box 437, H-1371 Budapest, Hungary.

DRAKE Bryan (Ernest Hare), b. 7 Oct 1925, Dunedin, New Zealand. Director of Opera; Baritone Singer. m. Jean Margaret Keen, 18 Apr 1949, 2 s, 1 d. Education: BA, University of Otago, New Zealand, 1946; Studied with Ernest Drake, New Zealand, Dawson Freer, London. Debut: Escamillo, Carmen, 1948, New Zealand. Career: Created roles in Benjamin Britten's Billy Budd, Curlew River, Burning Fiery Furnace, Prodigal Son; TV, Billy Budd, Peter Grimes; Royal Opera, English National Opera, Welsh National Opera; English Opera Group, English Music Theatre; Recitals, Curlew River, Burning Fiery Furnace, Prodigal Son, Billy Budd, Rape of Lucretia; Sang in the first modern revival of Verdi's Il Corsaro, St Pancras, 1966; Professor, Guildhall School of Music and Drama, 1971-81; Director of Opera, Royal College of Music, 1981-85; Voice Consultant, Britten-Pears School for Advanced Musical Studies at Snape, 1987-. Recordings: Numerous including, Curlew River, Burning Fiery Furnace, Prodigal Son, Billy Budd etc. Honours: Fellow, Royal College of Music, 1983. Hobbies: Gardening; Camping; Sailing. Address: 2 Fen Cottages, Aldringham, Leiston, Suffolk, IP16 4QR, England.

DRAKE George (Warren James), b. 4 Aug 1939, Auckland, New Zealand. Lecturer in Music; Musicologist. m. Carla Maria Driessen, 1 son, 1 daughter. Education: BA, 1961, MA, 1963, University of Auckland; PhD, University of Illinois, USA, 1972. Career: Senior Lecturer, University of Auckland; Dean, Faculty of Music, 1985-88; Head of the School of Music, 1988-91. Publications: The First Printed Books of Motets, Petrucci's Motetti a Numero Trentatre (Venice, 1502) and Motetti de Passione, de Cruce, de Sacramento, de Beata Virgine, de Huiusmodi (Venice, 1503): A Critical Study and Complete Edition, 1972; Liber Amicorum John Steele: A Musicologicl Tribute, editor, 1997. Memberships: President, New Zealand Musicological Society, 1982-85; American Musicological Society; Musicological Society of Australia; International Musicological Society. Address: c/o School of Music, University of Auckland, Auckland, New Zealand.

DRAKULICH Stephen, b. Iowa, USA. Singer (Tenor). Education: Studied at Southern Illinois University; Apprentice at the Lyric Opera of Chicago; Study with Norman Gulbranson at Northwestern University. Career: Sang in the Turn of the Screw, the Rake's Progress and Lucia di Lammermoor at Chicago; Wuppertal Opera as Mozart's Ferrando and Tamino, Rodolfo in Bohème and Britten's Albert Herring, Janacek's Fox, Ramiro (Cenerentola), Lensky, Steurmann in Fliegende Holländer and Jacquino, at Bremen Opera, 1982-89; Sergei in Lady Macbeth of the Mtensk District, Peter Grimes, Captain Vere (Billy Budd) and Jimmy in Mahagonny, Freiburg Opera, 1989-92; Guest appearancesas Arkenholz in Reimann's Gespenstersonate at Stuttgart and Hamburg; Sergei on tour to Japan with Cologne Opera; Tom Rakewell in Switzerland and Peter Grimes at the Glyndebourne Festival, 1992; Adam in the premiere of Der Garten by Josef Tal, 1988; Season 1996-97 in D'Albert's Tiefland and Wolf-Ferrari's Sly, in Germany. Honours include: Award winner at the Metropolitan Opera National Council Auditions. Address: c/o Magenta Music International, 4 Highgate High St, London N6 5JL, England.

DRAN Thierry, b. 1953, Bordeaux, France. Singer (Tenor). Education: Studied at the Bordeaux Conservatory and in Paris with Michel Senechal. Career: Appearances at the Paris Obera-Comique, the Berlioz Festival at Lyon (as Benedict), Rouen (Nadir and in Les Indes Galantes); Marseille (in Capuleti e i Montecchi) and Lyon, as Fenton in Falstaff; Grand Theatre Geneva, in Offenbach's Les Brigands and Barbe Bleue; Sang in the Ravel Double Bill at Glyndebourne, 1987-88; Paris Opera as Don Ottavio and as Mercure in Orphée aux Enfers; Guest appearances at Bordeaux, as Jean in Le Jongleur de Notre Dame, Liège (Ernesto, the Duke of Manuta and Rossini's Count Almaviva); Frequest concert engagements. Recordings: Messager's Fortunio and Duc de Mantoue in Les Brigands. Address: Ferme Commune, Villers sur Fere, 02130 La Fere en Tardenois, France.

DRATH Nina (Janina Irena Drath-Nowicka), b. 14 Oct 1954, Katowice, Poland. Solo Concert Pianist. m. Jerzy Bogdan Nowicki, 25 Oct 1981, 1 son. Education: Academy of Music, Warsaw; Artist's Diploma. Debut: With Silesian Philharmonic Orchestra, 1968; With WOSPRIT (Great Symphony Orchestra of Radio and TV), 1968. Career: 1st recital, Katowice, 1963; 1st recital abroad, Ostrava, Czechoslovakia, 1965; Regular concerts (solo and with orchestra) from age 14; Concert tours and performances, Poland, Spain, Italy, Germany, Belgium, France, USA, Czechoslovakia; Many radio and TV performances; Guest Artist, Annual Chopin Workshops, Texas A&M University, USA, 1981-94; Artist-in-Residence, Central State University, Oklahoma, 1985-87; Founder President: Fryderyk Chopin Society of Texas, 1990, International Chopin Piano Competition, Corpus Christi, 1993, Sonata and Sonatina International Youth Piano Competition, Corpus Christi, 1994; Artistic Director, Founder, Virtuoso Piano Performance Studies; Jury, international piano competitions. Recordings: With Vandor Music Group; Works of Haydn, Petrof, Chopin. Honours: 1st Prize, WOSPRIT Radio and TV Contest, Katowice, 1968; Bacewicz Sonata, Weimar, 1975; Bronze Medal and 4th Prize, Paloma O'Shea International Piano Competition, Santander, 1976; Beethoven Concerto No 4, Frankfurt, 1978; Finalist, Senigallia International Piano Competition, Italy, 1979; Prize, Slupsk National Piano Competition, Poland, 1979; International Order of Ambassadors, 1996. Memberships: Stowarzyszenie Polskich Artystow Muzykow; American Music Teachers Association; Regional Chairman, American Music Scholarship Association; President, Fryderyk Chopin Society of Texas; President, Ne Plus Ultra Club, 1991-. Hobby Antiques, especially Louis XV. Current Management: Sue Keenon Artist Management. Address: 4610 Abner Drive, Corpus Christi, TX 78411, USA.

DRESEN Adolf, b. 31 Mar 1935, Pomerania, Germany. Stage Director. Education: Studied at the Karl Marx University, Leipzig. Career: Emigrated to Vienna 1977 and produced Eugene Onegin at Hamburg, 1978; Zemlinsky's Der Zwerg and Eine Florentinische Tragödie staged 1981 and seen at Edinburgh 1983, Covent Garden, 1985 and the Vienna Volksoper 1990; Boris Godunov at Brussels 1986, followed by Fidelio 1988 (staged at Covent Garden 1990); Directed the three-act version of Lulu at the Châtelet, Paris, 1991. Address: c/o Royal Opera House (Contracts), Covent Garden, London, WC2, England.

DRESHER Paul (Joseph), b. 8 Jan 1951, Los Angeles, California, USA. Composer. m. 8 Mar 1986. Education: BA, Music, University of California, Berkeley, 1977; MA, Composition, University of California, San Diego, 1979; Private studies: North Indian Classical Music with Nikhil Banerjee, 1974-77; Ghanaian Drumming with C K and Kobla Ladzekpo, 1975-79: Javanese and Balinese Gamelan. Career: Composer, Performer throughout USA, Canada, Europe; Works performed at New York Philharmonic, San Francisco Symphony, Minnesota Opera, Brooklyn Academy of Music, Cal Arts Festival, New Music America, 1981, 1983, 1985, London International Festival of Theatre, Munich State Opera, Festival d'Automne, Paris; Commissions include Nonsuch Commission Award from American Music Center, and radio composition for Olympic Arts Festival; Founder, Artistic Director, Paul Dresher Ensemble (electro-acoustic chamber ensemble), 1993-, premiere on 6-city tour of Japan, and performing at Lincoln Center. Compositions: This Same Temple, 1977; Channels Passing, 1981; Night Songs, 1981; Liquid and Stellar Music, 1981; The Way of How, opera, 1981; Dark Blue Circumstance, electronic, 1982-84; Reaction, 1984; See Hear, opera, 1984; Other Fire, electronic, 1984; Slow Fire, opera, 1985-86; Water Dreams, electronic, 1986; Power Failure, opera, 1989; Double Ikat, trio, 1989; Cornucopia, chamber orchestra, 1990; Pioneer, opera, 1991; The Gates, 1993; Din of Iniquity, 6 instruments, 1994; Stretch, 6 instruments, 1995. Recordings: Liquid and Stellar Music, This Same Temple; Slow Fire, complete opera, 1992; Opposites Attract, 1992; Double Ikat, Channels Passing, Dark Blue Circumstance, Night Songs, 1993; Casa Vecchia, 1995. Contributions to: Sounding Eleven. Honours: Commissioned by Saint Paul Chamber Orchestra and Meet the

Composer. Memberships: BMI; American Music Center, Board of Directors. Current Management: Rena Shagan and Associates, New York, USA. Address: 51 Avenida Drive, Berkeley, CA 94708, USA.

DREW David, b. 1930, England. Writer on Music; Publisher, Producer and Editor. m. Judith Sutherland. Education: Cambridge University. Career: Publicity Consultant and Writer, The Decca Record Company, 1955-59; Producer, BBC Music Department, 1960; Music Critis, New Statesman, 1960-67; Musical Consultant to the Calouste Gulbenkian Foundation, UK Branch, and Artistic Director of the Foundation's recording series Music Today, EMI/Argo, 1961-75; European Representative and Advisor, The Kurt Weill Foundation for Music, 1971-76; Editor, later Advisory Editor, of Tempo, 1971-92; BBC Music Advisory Committee and Arts Council Music Panel, 1971-80; Advisor to the Holland Festival, 1971, Berlin Festival, 1974-75; Director of Contemporary Music, Boosey & Hawkes Music Publishers from 1975 until resignation in 1992; Programme Committee of Mürztal Music Workshop, Austria, 1983-91; Executive Committee of Les amis du compositeur Igor Markevitch, Lausanne and London, 1988-; Trustee, Britten-Pears Foundation, 1989-; Director of Recordings, Largo Records, Cologne, and Supervisory Editor, The Kurt Weill Edition, 1992-; Editions of many stage and concert works by Kurt Weill, notably Cry the Beloved Country, Carnegie Hall, 1988; Performing Edition of Roberto Gerhard's opera The Duenna, Madrid, Barcelona, Opera North, 1992. Publications: Über Kurt Weill, and Weill, Ausgewählte Schriften, 1975; Introduction to Ernst Bloch Essays on the Philosophy of Music, 1985; The Kurt Weill Handbook, 1987. Contributions to: Numerous Articles on 20th Century Composers such as Stravinsky, Messiaen, Gerhard, Spinner, Gorecki. Address: 12 Favart Road, London SW6 4AZ, England.

DREW James, b. 9 Feb 1929, St Paul, Minnesota, USA. Composer; Playwright; Pianist; Director. m. Gloria Kelly, 26 Mar 1960, 1 son, 1 daughter. Education: Certificate, New York School of Music, 1956; MA, Tulane University, 1964; Private study with Wallingford Riegger, 1956-69 and Edgard Varèse, 1956. Career: Composer for concert hall, theatre and film; Composer, Northwestern University, 1964-66, Yale University, 1966-73, Tanglewood, Lennox, MA, summer 1973, LSU, 1973-75; Director, Ghost Puppet Theatre, 1970-; Visiting Composer, California State University, 1976-77, University of California at Los Angeles, 1977-78; Director of American Music Theatre, 1978-, Mysterious Travelling Cabaret, 1980-, No Sleep Theatre, 1984-, and Greywolf International, 1993-; Director, Blast Operatheater, 1996-. Compositions include: Symphonies; Concerto for Small Percussion Orchestra; Mysterium, opera; Faustus - an Epilogue for 2 Pianos, Solo Viola and Chamber Ensemble; The Orangethorpe Aria; Five O'Clock Ladies, stage work; Last Dance, video work; Whisper, video; Cantobosolo for Contrabass Solo; Cantobosolo for Percussion and Orchestra; Live From the Black Eagle, video work; Cello Concerto; In This Place of Half Lights, Gloria..Sotto Voce, a monodrama; In Memoriam of Gloria Kelly Drew, 1990; Piano Concerto, Formingreforming, 1991; Easter Concerto for Violino Grand and Orchestra, 1992; Celestial Cabaret for Piano and Chamber Orchestra, 1993; Inaudible Answers for Orchestra, 1994; Book of Lights, 1994; Elephants Coming for String Quartet, 1994; Walden Songs for Chamber Orchestra, 1995; Sacred Dances of the Tunnel Saints, 1995; Hypothetical Structures, 1996; Survivors in Pale Light, 1996; Viola Concerto (Cellar-Lise's Alléluias). Recording: Sonata Appassionata for Cello and Piano (Cello America volume 2), 1994; Cantolobo Solo (monodnama). Honour: Guggenheim Fellow, 1973-74. Current Management: Cooke Associates, Nicolaistraat 17, 2517 SX Den Haag, Netherlands. Address: c/o Theodore Presser Co, Presser Place, Byrn Mawr, PA 19010, USA.

DREYFUS George, b. 22 July 1928, Wuppertal, Germany. Musician; Composer. m. Francis Kay Lucas, 4 Nov 1968. Education: Vienna Academy of Music, Austria, 1955-56. Career includes: Orchestral Musician, Australian Broadcasting Commission, 1953; Formed New Music Ensemble, Melbourne, 1958; Freelance Composer, 1965-; Foundation Member, Musical Director, International Society for Contemporary Music, Melbourne, 1965; Formed George Dreyfus Chamber Orchestra, Melbourne, 1970; Musica Viva Outback tour, 1974; 1-man show, Melbourne, Sydney and various country centres, 1977-78; Composer-in-residence: Rome, 1976, Jerusalem, 1980, Tianjin, 1983, Shanghai, 1986, and Nanjing, 1991. Compositions include: Galgenlieder, 1957; Songs, Comic and Curious, 1959; Music in the Air, 1961; The Seasons, 1963; Quintet for Wind Instruments, 1965; Garni Sands, 2-act opera by Frank Kellaway, 1965-66; Symphony No 1, 1967; Reflections in a Glasshouse, 1969; The Gilt-Edged Kid, 1-act opera by Lynne Strahan, 1970; Sextet for Didjeridu and Wind Instruments, 1971; The Lamentable Reign of Charles the Last, 1-act pantopera by Tim Robertson, 1975; Symphony No 2, 1976; Symphonie Concertante, 1978; An Australian Folk Mass, 1979; The Ballad of Charles Rasp; The Sentimental Bloke, 1985; Rathenau, 1-act opera by Volker Elis Pilgrim, 1993; Die Marx Sisters, 1-act opera by Volker Elis Pilgrim, 1995; Film and television scores. Recordings: Rush and the Adventures of Sebastian the Fox; Film Music of George Dreyfus; Serenade for Small Orchestra; Quintet, After the Notebook of J-G Noverre; The Marvellous World of George Dreyfus; Song of the Maypole; George Dreyfur Chamber and Orchestral Music, Symphonies 1 and 2, Sextet for Didgeridu and Wind Instruments; Larino, Safe Haven; Rush (Australian Fantasy). Publication: The Last Frivolous Book, autobiography. Honour: Order of Australia. Address: 3 Grace Street, Camberwell, Victoria 3124, Australia.

DREYFUS Huguette (Pauline), b. 30 Nov 1928, Mulhouse, France. Harpsichordist. Education: Diplomas, Piano, Harmony, Counterpoint, Ecole Normale de Musique, Paris; Conservatoire National Supérieur de Musique, Paris; Advanced studies, Harpsichord, Chigiana Academy, Siena. Career: Soloist, ORTF and various other radio and TV networks in France, South Africa, Germany, Belgium, Canada, UK, Switzerland, Austria, Brazil, Colombia, Denmark, Ecuador, Hungary, Italy, Luxembourg, Peru, Sweden, Czechoslovakia, Yugoslavia, Japan, USA; Harpsichord Teacher, Conservatoire National Supérieur de Musique de Lyon and Conservatoire National de Région de Rueil-Malmaison. Recordings: J S Bach: 6 English Suites, 6 French Suites; Rameau: Pièces de Clavecin; Couperin: Pièces de Clavecin; Scarlatti: Chronological Anthology of 70 Sonatas; Seixas: 14 Sonatas; Bartók: Pieces from Mikrokosmos; Chamber music by J S Bach, Leclair, Rameau, Haydn, Vivaldi, Corelli, C P E Bach, W A Mozart; J S Bach: Italian Concerto, Chromatic Fantasy and Fugue, Inventions and Sinfonias, 6 Partitas, French Overture, 4 Duetti, Praeludium, Fuga and Allegro in E flat major Goldberg variations; Wilhelm-Friedemann Bach: 9 Fantasien; J S Bach Harpsichord Transcriptions of 16 Concerti by various composers; J S Bach: The Well-Tempered Clavier, vol I; Henri Dutilleux: Les Citations, Diptyque for oboe, harpsichord, double bass, percussion; JS Bach: The Well-Tempered Clavier, Vol II. Honours: 1st Medal, Harpsichord, International Competition, Geneva, 1958; Prix du Président de la République, Académie Charles Cros, 1985; Officier, Ordre National du Mérite, 1987; Grosse Ehrenzeichen für Verdienste um die Republik Österreich, 1992; Chevalier dans l'Ordre de la Légion d'Honneur, 1995; Numerous Grand Prix for recordings. Address: 91 Quai d'Orsay, 75007 Paris, France.

DRISCOLL Loren, b. 14 Apr 1928, Midwest, Wyoming, USA. Singer (Tenor). Education: Studied at Syracuse and Boston University. Debut: As Caius in Falstaff, Boston, 1954; New York City Opera debut, 1957, as Timur in Turandot; Sang Tom Rakewell in The Rake's Progress at Santa Fe, 1957; Deutsche Oper Berlin from 1962, notably as Fenton, Pinkerton, Flamand (Capriccio), Don Otttavio and The Painter in Lulu; Sang in the premieres of Henze's Der junge Lord (1965) and Ulisse by Dallapiccola (1968); Glyndebourne Festival, 1962, Ferrando; Salzburg Festival, 1966, as Dionysos in the premiere of The Bassarids by Henze, repeating the role at La Scala and Santa Fe, 1968; Metropolitan Opera from 1966, as David, and Alfred in Die Fledermaus; Schwetzingen Festival, 1971, as the Architect in the premiere of Reimann's Melusine, repeated at Edinburgh; Brussels, 1973, in the premiere of Love's Labour Lost by Nabokov; Santa Fe, 1977, in the US premiere of Boulevard Solitude by Henze; Rome, 1982, with the company of the Deutsche Oper, in Undine by Lortzing; Further appearances in Hamburg, Cologne and Edinburgh. Recordings: Der junge Lord and Lulu; Oedipus Rex, Renard and The Nightingale, conducted by Stravinsky. Address: c/o Deutsche Oper Berlin, Richard Wagnerstrasse 10, 1000-Berlin, Germany.

DRIVALA Jenny, b. 1965. Soprano. Education: Studied at the Athens and Bremen Conservatories. Career: Appearances at the Vienna Staatsoper, La Scala Milan and in Naples, Rome, Melbourne, Paris Châtelet, Florence and Pretoria; Repertoire includes Donizetti's Lucia, Maria Stuarda and Lucrezia Borgia, Violetta, Thais and Mélisande; Sang title role in Gluck's Armide for ORF TV, Strauss's Daphne and Salome for Greek Radio and Glauce in Médée by Cherubini; Strauss concert with Charles Mackerras. Address: Ron Gonsalves Management, 7 Old Town, Clapham, London, SW4 0JT, England.

DROWER Meryl, b. 1949, Wales. Singer (Soprano). Education: Studied at the Royal College of Music and in Italy. Career: Joined English Music Theatre 1976 and sang Clorinda in La Cenerentola, Serpetta (La Finta Giardiniera), Miss Wordsworth (Albert Herring) and Papagena; Appearances with Kent Opera as Gilda, the Governess (Turn of the Screw), Susanna, Nannetta, Zerlina and Marzelline (Fidelio), Donna Elvira and Ellen Orford; Has sung Despina for English National Opera and Papagena at Glyndebourne; Scottish Opera as Tytania in A Midsummer Night's Dream and in a Rossini double bill; Covent Garden as Barbarina (Le Nozze di Figaro) and in Lulu and L'Enfant et les Sortilèges; Appeared with the Royal Opera in Los Angeles 1984, as Papagena and in Peter Grimes; European engagements as Poppea in Agrippina (La Fenice, Venice), Serpetta (Bordeaux), Susanna (Vienna) and Donna Elvira and Marzelline (Valencia); Concert repertoire includes African Sanctus by David Fanshawe (premiere, London, 1972), and works by Britten, Vaughan Williams, Brahms, Beethoven, Bach, Handel and Haydn. Recordings: include, Rossini double bill and A Night at the Chinese Opera (Kent Opera) for television. Address: c/o Korman International Management, Crunnells Green Cottage, Preston, Herts SG4 7UQ, England.

DROZDZEWSKI Piotr (Michal), b. 30 Nov 1948, Zbaszyn, Poland. Composer; Chemist. m. Marta Kurek, 18 Oct 1975, 2 daughters. Education: Diploma, Violin, Secondary Music School, Wroclaw, 1970; MA, Chemistry, 1971; PhD, Chemistry, 1976; MA, Composition, Academy of Music, Wroclaw, 1977; DSc, Chemistry, 1990. Compositions include: Symphonic works: Dance for Strings, 1979; Sinfonia da Camera, 1980; Expansion, 1980-86; Ballade for Clarinet and Strings, 1997; Choral work: Salve Regina; Chamber works: 3 String quartets, 1976, 1978, 1981; Sonata a due violini, 1983; Several solo selections for violin, piano (harpsichord) and organ. Recordings: For Polish Radio: Cadenza; Dance for Strings; Expansion. Honours: Polish Radio Composers' Competition, 1979; XXIII Young Composers' Competition, Polish Composers' Union, 1980; K Lipinski Composers' Competition, Wroclaw, 1990. Memberships: Polish Composers' Union; Polish Chemical Society, 1992. Hobbies: Electronics; Astronomy; All kinds of tinkering; Skiing. Address: Arctowskiego 24, 53211 Wroclaw, Poland.

DRUCKER Eugene, b. 17 May 1952, Coral Gables, Florida, USA. Violinist. Career: Co-leader of the Emerson String Quartet from its foundation in 1978; Public debut at Alice Tully Hall, New York in March 1979, playing works by Mozart and Bartók; Quartet-in-residence at the Smithsonian Institute, Washington, from 1980 and the Hartt School of Music and the Aspen Music Festival from 1983; European debut at the Spoleto Festival, 1981; Noted for performances of the quartets of Bartók, including all six works in a single evening; Has given the premieres of works by Mario Davidovsky, Gunther Schuller, Richard Wernick, John Harbison, Wolfgang Rihm and Maurice Wright; with Emerson Quartet 120 concerts annually in major musical capitals of Europe, US and Canada; Tours of Japan and Australia; Resident Quartet of Chamber Music Society of Lincoln Center, 1982-89. Recordings: include, Bartók complete Quartets, Mozart 6 Quartets dedicated to Haydn, Schubert Cello Quintet with Rostropovich, Ives and Barber Quartets, Prokofiev Quartets & Sonata for 2 violins; As soloist: Bach Sonatas and Partitas for violin and complete Duos and Sonatas by Bartok; Bartok: Two Sonatas for Violin and Piano and the Solo Sonata, forthcoming; With Emerson Quartet Complete Beethoven Cycle, 1997. Honours: include, Naumburg Award for Chamber Music, 1978; Gramophone Magazine: Best Chamber Music Record and Record of the Year for Bartók Quartets, 1989; Grammy for Best Chamber Music and Classical Record of the Year, also for Bartok, 1990. Current Management: IMG Artists. Address: c/o IMG Artists, 22 East 71 Street, New York, NY 10021, USA.

DRUIAN Rafael, b. 20 Jan 1922, Vologda, Russia. Violinist; Teacher. Education: Studied at Curtis Institute, Philadelphia, with Lee Luboshutz and Efrem Zimbalist. Career: Appointed leader of the Dallas Symphony, 1947; Later positions with the Minneapolis Symphony, the Cleveland Orchestra, 1960-69; New York Philharmonic, 1970-73; Has appeared widely as Concert Soloist and as Recitalist; Teacher at University of Minnesota, 1949-60; Teacher, Cleveland Institutes, University of California at San Diego and Boston University from 1982. Recordings: include, Sonatas by Bloch, Mozart, Bartok and Charles Ives. Address: Music Department, Boston University, Commonwealth Avenue, Boston, MA 02215, USA.

DRUIETT Michael, b. 1967. Singer (Bass). Education: Studied at the European Opera Centre in Belgium, the Scuola Superiore in Italy, and the National Opera Studio, London. Career: Appearances with English National Opera in The Love for Three Oranges, Wozzeck, Gianni Schicchi, Salome, Cunning Little Vixen, Rigoletto (Sparafucile), Ariodante (King), Don Carlos (Monk), A Masked Ball, Monteverdi's Orfeo and Lohengrin (Henry The Fowler); Sang in Wozzeck under Barenboim in Paris and appeared as Raimondo in Lucia di Lammermoor with Welsh National Opera; Principal Bass with the Royal Opera, Covent Garden, from 1993-94; Sang the Monk in Don Carlo, 1996; Concert repertoire includes Elijah, St John Passion, Puccini's Messa di Gloria, Haydn's Nelson Mass, Mozart's Requiem, Mahler's 8th with the CBSO/Elder, Messiah and Beethoven's Ninth, with the London Symphony Orchestra under Libor Pesek. Recordings: Floyd's Susannah, with the Opéra de Lyon. Address: c/o IMG Artists, Media House, 3 Burlington Lane, London W4 2TH, England.

DRUKH Igor E, b. 9 January 1966, Leningrad (St Petersburg), Russia. m. Alja Dzukh, 24 August 1986, 2 daughters. Education: Studied at Rimsky-Korsakov Musical College and Rimsky-Korskov Conservatory, St Petersburg. Debut: Pianist, Petersburg, Moscow, 1984; Wrozlaw Young Composers Festival, 1991. Career: Participator in festivals: Soundways, St Petersburg, 1990-97; Aspekte, Salzburg, 1992; Brandenburg Collegium,

1993-95; St Petersburg Musical Spring, 1995-97; Concerts in Aalen, Ulm, Heidenheim, 1993, 1995; Komposition Portarait on Radio St Petersburg. Compositions: Piano Sonata No 1, 1989, publication, 1998; String Quartet, 1990; Suite for Balalaika & Pianoforte (composer published), 1991; Scroveini Chapel Frescoes, 1992-95; Violin Concerto, 1995; Piano Sonata No 2, 1997; The Seven Sacraments for Chamber Ensemble, 1997. Publications: Suite for Balalaika & Pianoforte, 1997. Honours: 1st Prize, Vilnius Jazz Festival, 1989; UNESCO Young Composers Competition, 1996. Memberships: Composers Union of RF; Soundways Association (St Petersburg); Modern Music Association (St Petersburg); Brandenburg Collegium of Modern Music (Berlin). Hobby: Playing jazz. Address: Union of Composers, 45 Bolshaya Morskaya, 190000 St Petersburg, Russia.

DRUMM Imelda, b. 1969, Ireland. Singer (Mezzo-soprano). Education: Dublin City University; Leinster School of Music with Dr Veronica Dunne; National Opera Studio, London, 1996-97. Career: Roles with Glyndebourne Opera include Cherubino, 1994, Isolier in Le Comte Ory, 1997, Dorabella in Cosí Festival, 1995, Tisbe in La Cenerentola for Opera Ireland and Theodata in Handel's Flavio for OTC Dublin. Honours include: Richard Lewis/Jean Shanks Award and Esso Touring Award, Glyndebourne Opera. Address: c/o IMGArtists, Media House, 3 Burlington Lane, London W4 2HT, England.

DRUMMOND (Sir) John (Richard Gray), b. 25 Nov 1934, London, England. Arts Administrator. Education: Trinity College, Cambridge; MA, Cantab. Career: BBC Radio and TV, 1958-78, as Writer, Director, Producer and Editor; Member, Music Panel, Arts Council, 1970-78; Member, Dance Committee, Arts Council from 1974-80; Director, Edinburgh International Festival, 1978-83; Controller, BBC Music from 1985-92, BBC Radio 3, 1987-92; Director, Promenade Concerts, 1992-95. Honours include: KBE, 1995. Membership: Scottish Arts Club. Hobbies: Architecture; Conversation. Address: 61C Crompden Hill Court, London W8 7HL, England.

DU Ming Xin, b. 19 Aug 1928, Qian Jiang County, Hubei Province, China. Composer; Music Educator. m. 1 Sept 1966, 1 s, 1 d. Education: Yu Cai Music School, 1939; Tchaikovsky Music Conservatory, 1954-58. Debut: Piano Solo Concert, Shanghai, 1948. Career: Participated in the Asian Composer's Conference & Music Festival, Hong Kong, 1981; Two concerts, Hong Kong Philharmonic Orchestra of works by Du Mingxin, 1982, 1988, composed for the movie Wonderful China; Travelled to USA in 1986 for performance of Violin Concerto in John F Kennedy Center and gave lectures in some famous music institutes. Compositions: Ballet Suite, The Mermaid; The Red Detachment of Women; Symphonic Picture, The South Sea of My Mother Land; Symphonic Fantasia, The Goddess of the River Luo; Symphony, Youth; 2 Violin Concertos, 2 Piano Concertos, Great Wall Symphony; Flapping! the Flags of Army. Recordings: The Mermaid; The Red Detachment of Women; The South Sea of My Mother Land; The Goddess of the River Luo; Youth; Great Wall Symphony; 1st Violin Concerto; 1st Piano Concerto. Membership: Executive Director and General Secretary, Chinese Musicians Association. Hobbies: Watching Football and Sports Competitions. Address: Central Conservatory of Music, 43 Bao Jia Street, Beijing 100031, China.

DU PLESSIS Christian, b. 2 Jul 1944, Vryheid, South Africa. Singer (Baritone). Education: Studied with Teasdale Griffiths and Esme Webb in South Africa and Otakar Kraus in London. Debut: With the PACT Opera in Johannesburg, as Yamadori in Madame Butterfly, 1967. Career: Sang in a 1970 concert performance of Andrea Chenier in London and appeared as Valentin in Faust at Barcelona, 1971; Member of the Sadler's Wells/English National Opera, 1973-81, natably as Cecil in Maria Stuarda, and Verdi's Germont and Posa; Guest appearances in Barcelona, Johannesburg and elsewhere; Concert performances for London Opera Society and Opera Rara in L'Etoile du Nord by Meyerbeer, Gli Orazi ed i Curiazi by Mercadante, Donizetti's Torquato Tasso, Maria di Rudenz, Rosmonda d'Inghilterra and Maria Padilla, and Bellini's Il Pirata; Retired, 1988. Recordings: include, Germont in an English-Language Traviata conducted by Charles Mackerras; Maria Stuarda (Decca); Meyerbeer's Dinorah; L'Assedio di Calais by Donizetti (Opera Rara).

DUBAJ Mariusz Bernard, b. 12 March 1959, Krasnystaw, Poland. Composition; Theory of Music; Piano. Education: Piano, distinction, State School of Music, Lublin; Composition, Theory of Music, distinction, Academy of Music, Gdansk; Doctoral Disertation, Composition, Academy of Music, Krakow; Private Studies. Debut: Composition, Academy of Music, Gdansk, 1982. Compositions include: Piano: Structures, Sonata II, Reproductions, Book I, II, A World of Music, Book I, III, 24 Mini Preludes, 4 Poems, Ballad, 30 Impressions, Music For Beginners; Christmas Cards for Children; Chamber: String Quartet, Fragments, for Instruments and Percussion, A Tre, for Oboe and Piano, Spaces of Soul, for Flute, Alto Saxophone and Piano, Last Little Bear Story, for Flute and 3 Percussions, 5 Songs for Mezzo-Soprano and Piano; Choir: Colours of Sea, Sea Landscape, Santa Luizia, Prayers; Orchestra: Canti Movimenti, for Piano and Strings. Publications: George Crumb, 1985; Numerous articles. Honours include: 2 3rd Prizes, All-Polish Contest for Students of the Composition Forum, Gdansk, 1983; 1st Prize, All-Polish Contest, The Week of Talents, 1985; 1st Prize, All-Polish Contest Masters Thesis Academy of Music, 1987; Special Prize, Polish Composers Union, 1996. Membership: Polish Composers Union. Address: ul Szymonowicza 33s m 36, 22-300 Krasnystaw, Poland.

DUBAL David, b. Cleveland, Ohio, USA. Pianist; Teacher; Writer on Music. Education: Ohio State University; Juilliard School, New York; Piano studies with Arthur Loesser, Cleveland. Career: Concerts and Lecture Recitals in the US, Israel, Korea and Europe; Faculty of the Juilliard School, 1983-; Faculty of the Manhattan School of Music, 1994-; Lectures at The New School for Social Research and the Metropolitan Museum; Adjuciator of the Busoni, Cassagrande, Senagalia and other competitions.Recordings: Records of the Piano Music of Khachaturian; The Piano in America - Music of the Romantic Pianist-Composers-Invitation to the Dance.Publications: Reflections From the Keyboard, 1984; The Art of the Piano, 1995; Conversations with Menuhin, 1991; Evenings with Horowitz, 1991; Rembering Horowitz, with CD of Dubal's talks with Horowitz, 1991; Films: The Golden Age of Piano; American Piano Music from the Civil War Through World War I. Contributions to: Articles in various journals. Honours: Winner, The George Fisher Peabody Award' The Deems Taylor ASCAP Award for Innovative Broadcasting; Winner, Emmy Award, 1994. Address: The Juilliard School, 60 Lincoln Center Plaza, New York, NY 10023, USA.

DUBARRY Chantal, b. 1955, France. Singer (Mezzo-soprano). Education: Studied in Paris, notably with Jean Giraudeau and Jean-Christophe Benoit. Debut: Tourcoing, 1975, as Massenet's Dulcinée. Career: Appearances at Caen as Carmen and Olga, Avignon and Tourcoing; Strasbourg from 1983, in Die Walküre, as a Dryad in Ariadne, Dalila, Adalgisa, Mignon, and Marina in Boris Godunov; Guest engagements as Fenena in Nabucco at Besançon, Charlotte at Calais (1985) and at the Vienna Staatsoper (1990); Other roles include Dalila, and Marfa in Khovanshchina; Many concert outings. Address: c/o Opéra du Rhin, 19 Place Broglie, F-67008 Strasbourg, France.

DUBINBAUM Gail, b. 1958, New York, USA. Singer (Mezzo-Soprano). Education: Studied with Herta Glaz and with the Metropolitan Young Artists Program. Career: Sang at the Metropolitan from 1982, debut in L'Enfant et les Sortilèges; Appearances in New York and elsewhere in the USA as Rossini's Rosina and Isabella and as Mozart's Dorabella; Engagements at the Vienna Staatsoper 1986-88; Suzuki in Butterfly for Opera Pacific at Costa Mesa and again at Detroit, 1991; Sang in the Jeremiah Symphony with Leonard Bernstein conducting Boston Symphony, Los Angeles Philharmonic and the Pittsburgh Symphony (40th Anniversary of premiere), sang Suzuki and Bach Magnificat with Zubin Mehta and Israel Philharmonic. Address: 6614 W Kingston Lane, Glendale, AZ 85306, USA.

DUBOIS Jocelyne, b. 20 Feb 1965, Douai, France. Director of School of Music, Dance and Theatre; Dancer; Singer. Education: National Conservatory of Douai, 1976-84; Lille University, 1982-84; National High Conservatory of Paris, 1983-91; National Conservatory of Amiens, 1985-87; Maîtrise de musique, 1988, Agrégation, Musical Education, 1989, Paris-Sorbonne University; Career: Dancer, Compagnie Lyrique de France, 1979-82; Violinist, Jeune Orchestre Symphonique de Douai et des Hauts de France, 1979-82; Singer, Ensemble BWV, 1983-91 and as a soloist since 1992; Director, Municipal School of Music and Dance, Houilles, 1989-90; Director, National School of Music, Dance and Theatre, Marne-la-Vallée; Currently Director, Conservatory of the 16th arrondissement of Paris. Compositions: Cinq variations, for violins, 1991. Recordings include: Honegger's La Danse des morts, as Violinist, Jeune Orchestre Symphonique de Douai et des Hauts de France, 1981. Publication: Le Festin de l'Araignée, 1989. Contributions to: La Musique de Chambre avec piano et les oeuvres pour harmonica de verre, in new edition of Mozart, 1991. Hobby: Oriental philosophy. Address: 10 rue du Trésor, 75004 Paris, France.

DUBOSC Catherine, b. 12 Mar 1959, Lille, France. Singer (Soprano). Education: Studied at Strasbourg Conservatory, Ecole National in Paris from 1980 with Denise Dupleix and Hans Hotter; Further study with Eric Tappy at Lyons. Career: Sang at Lyon Opera, 1985-87, as Mozart's Despina, Pamina and Susanna, Nannetta, Blanche in Dialogues des Carmélites and Marzelline (Fidelio); Sang Gretel at Geneva, 1987 and Isipile in Cavalli's Giasone at Utrecht, 1988, and the Théâtre des Champs Elysées, Paris, 1990; Appearances at Montpellier (Pamina, 1991), Avignon, Nancy, Edinburgh and Strasbourg; Sang Mélisande at Lausanne, 1992 and at Frankfurt, 1994; Sang in the Danish premiere of Poulenc's Carmelites, Copenhagen, 1997. Recordings: include, Giasone, The Love for Three Oranges, Campra's Tancrède, Scylla et Glaucus by Leclair and Darande in Gluck's La Rencontre Imprevue (Erato).

DUBROVAY Laszio, b. 23 March 1943, Budapest, Hungary. Composer; Teacher. Education: Bartok Conservatory, Budapest; Graduated, Academy of Music, Budapest, 1966; Principal Teachers: Istvan Szelenyi, Ferenc Szabo, Imre Vincze; Completed training in Germany with Karlheinz Stockhausen, Composition and Electronic Music from Hans-Ulrich Rumpert, 1972-74. Career: Teacher of Music Theory, Budapest Academy of Music, 1976-; Residence in Berlin, 1985. Compositions: Orchestral Verificazione, 1970; Succession, 1974; Concerto for 11 Strings, 1979; Concerto for Flute and 45 Strings, 1981; Concerto for Trumpet and 15 Strings, 1981; Concerto for Piano, Orchestra and Synthesizer, 1982; Piano Concerto, 1984; Variations on an Oscillating Line, 1987; Concerts Romantico for Piano, 1990; Tripleconcert for Trumpet, Trombone, Tuba, 1989; Psychographic for Brass, 1989; March for Winds, 1990; Il Ricatto Opera, 1991; Chamber Stigmata for Tenor and Piano, 1969; 2 Brass Quintets, 1971, 1980; 2 Wind Quintets, 1972, 1983; Magic Squares for Violin and Cimbalom, 1975; Matuziada Nos 1 to 5 for 4 Flutes, 1975-76; Geometrum II: String Quartet No 2, 1976; Numberplay No 1 for 20 Players, 1976; Interferences No 1 for 2 Cimbalons, 1976; Music for 2 Cimbalons, 1977; Brass Septet for 3 Trumpets, Horn, 2 Trombones and Tuba, 1980; String Quartet No 3, 1983; Octet and Clarinet, Bassoon, Horn and String Quintet, 1985-87; Pieces for Solo Instrument; Choruses; Live Electronic Works; Tape Pieces; Computer Music; Deserts for Brass Orchestra, 1987; Recitativo and Aria for Soprano and Chamber Ensemble, 1988; The Sculptor Dance-Play in One Act, 1993. Address: H-1026 Budapest, Gardonyi G.u. 45/b, Hungary.

DUCLOUX Walter (Ernest), b. 17 Apr 1913, Kriens, Lucerne, Switzerland. Opera, Symphony and Ballet Conductor. m. Gina Rifino, 29 Nov 1943, 2 s, 1 d. Education: PhD, Philosophy, Music History, University of Munich, Federal Republic of Germany, 1935; Conducting Diploma, Academy of Vienna, Austria, 1937. Debut: Casino Lucerne, 1937. Career: Symphony and Opera Conductor, Lucerne, 1937-39; Assistant, Metropolitan Opera, New York, 1939, 1941; Guest Conductor, USA, France, Federal Republic of Germany, etc, 1945-49; Conductor, Prague National Opera and Radio, Czechoslovakia, 1945-48; Conductor, Ballet Russe, 1948; Musical Director, Voice of America, 1950, 1953; Professor of Opera and Conducting, University of Southern California, 1953-68; Professor of Opera and Conducting, University of Texas, Austin, 1968-; Artistic and Musical Director, Austin Lyric Opera, 1986-. Recordings: Sound track of Metro-Goldwyn-Mayer's Interrupted Melody. Publications: Opera translations into English including: All late works of Verdi; Many late works of Strauss, Hindemith, Prokofiev, Dvorak. Contributions to: Opera News; Other musical publications. Address: 2 Wildwind Point, Austin, Texas, TX 78746, USA.

DUDAROVA Veronika, b. 1916, Baku, Azerbaidjan. Conductor. Education: Studied in Baku and at the Leningrad and Moscow Conservatories. Career: Artistic Director and Chief Conductor, Moscow State Symphony Orchestra, 1960-, (first woman in Russia to hold such a post); Tours with the Orchestra to venues throughout Europe and South America; Left Moscow to conduct in Istanbul, 1989; Returned to Russia and established Symphony Orchestra of Russia, 1991; Repertoire has included music by Brahms, Beethoven, Schumann, Wagner, Scriabin, Tchaikovsky and contemporary Western and Russian works. Recordings incude: Music by Gershwin, Bizet, Myaskovsky and Strauss. Honours: Glinka Award and People's Artist of the USSR. Address: c/o Sonata, 11 Northpark Street, Glasgow G20 7AA, Scotland.

DUESING Dale, b. 26 Sept 1947, Milwaukee, USA. Singer (Baritone). Education: Began studies in Milwaukee as a pianist; Vocal studies at Lawrence University in Wisconsin. Career: San Francisco Opera as Britten's Billy Budd and Donizetti's Belcore; Seattle Opera as Wagner's Wolfram and Tchaikovsky's Eugene Onegin; Glyndebourne debut 1976, as Olivier in Capriccio; later sang Guglielmo in Così fan Tutte, conducted by Bernard Haitink; Ottone in L'Incoronazione di Poppea, Lysander in A Midsummer Night's Dream, 1989, and Figaro, 1989; Metropolitan Opera debut 1979, as Harlekin in Ariadne auf Naxos; Concert engagements with the New York Philharmonic, Berlin Philharmonic, Boston Symphony, Concertgebouw Orchestra, BBC Symphony and Santa Cecilia of Rome; Conductors include Giulini, Levine, Leppard, Ozawa, Sawallisch, Dohnányi and Previn; Recent opera engagements include Ariadne at La Scala, Billy Budd and Peter Grimes at the Metropolitan, Die Meistersinger in Brussels and Così fan Tutte at Santa Fe; Sang Figaro at Seattle, 1989; Goryanchikov in From the House of the Dead, at Brussels, 1990; Guglielmo at Barcelona and Olivier at the 1990 Glyndebourne Festival; Solo recitalist in the USA and Europe; World Premiere: Wade in Johnathan Wade by Carlisle Floyd, Houston Opera; Cosi at Liceo, Barcelona; Marriage of Figaro, Glyndebourne Opera under Rattle; Metropolitan Opera, New York, Pelléas and Papageno; Season 1991/92 as Mozart's Count at Brussels, 'I' in the premiere of Schnittke's Life with an Idiot at Amsterdam and

Nardo in La Finta Giardiniera at the Salzburg Festival; Prodocismo in Il Turo in Italia at Théâtre du Champs-Elysses, Paris, 1996; Brussels 1997, in Orphée aux Enfers. Recordings: include, Don Giovanni and Zemlinsky's Lyric Symphony; Così fan Tutte; Arias and Barcaroles, Leonard Bernstein. Address: c/o Lies Askonas Ltd, 6 Henrietta Street, London WC2, England.

DUFALLO Richard (John), b. 30 Jan 1933, East Chicago, Indiana, USA. Conductor. m. (1) Zaidee Parkinson, 15 Oct 1966, 2 sons, (2) Pamela Mia Paul, 19 June 1988. Education: BMus, American Conservatory of Music, Chicago, 1953; BA, 1956; MA, 1957, University of California; Studies with William Steinberg and Pierre Boulez. Debut: European debut with Paris Radio Orchestra, 1971. Career includes: Associate Conductor, Buffalo Philharmonic Orchestra, New York, 1962-67; Faculty, State University of New York, Buffalo, 1963-67; Conductor, Center of Creative and Performing Arts, Buffalo, 1964-67; Assistant Tour Conductor, New York Philharmonic tour of Japan and other Asian countries, 1967; Artistic Director, Aspen Music Festival's Conference on Contemporary Music, 1970-; Conductor, Mini-Met, adjunct to Metropolitan Opera, New York, 1972-74; Director and Conductor, 20th Century Music Series, Juilliard School of Music, New York, 1972-79; Artistic Adviser, Het Gelders Orkest, Arnhem, Netherlands, 1980-82; Guest appearances, including: Concertgebouw Orchestra of Amsterdam, London Symphony, Berlin Philharmonic, Chicago Symphony, Pittsburgh Symphony, Royal Philharmonic, BBC Symphony and Philadelphia Orchestra; Conductor at festivals in 10 countries; Television performances; Opera including Cincinnati Opera; Bath and Aldeburgh Festivals, Edinburgh, Saratoga, Casals and Holland Festivals. Recordings include: Mozart's Concerto for Two Pianos with National Philharmonic Orchestra; Escher's Symphony with Rotterdam Philharmonic; Peter Maxwell Davies' St Thomas Wake; Composers Voice Special 1987; Rotterdam Philharmonic; CD with Netherlands Wind Ensemble. Publications: Trackings - composers speak with Richard Dufallo. Current Management: Schofer/Gold, New York City; Interartists, Amsterdam.

DUGDALE Sandra, b. 1950, Pudsey, Yorkshire, England. Education: Studied in Leeds and at the Guildhall School, London. Debut: With Glynebourne Touring Opera as Despina in Cosi fan Tutte. Career: Has sung with English National Opera in operas by Mozart, Janacek and Strauss; Welsh National Opera in The Greek Passion by Martinu; Four principal roles with the Handel Opera Society; Handel roles with the English Bach Festival; Covent Garden debut 1983 as Fire and The Nightingale in the Ravel/Stravinsky double bill; returned 1985, as Adele in Die Fledermaus; Festival appearances include Hong Kong, Camden, Batignano, Wexford and Vienna; Frequent broadcasts with the BBC, including the Much Loved Music Show and Lo Speziale by Haydn (ITV); sang Adele for Opera Northern Ireland at the Grand Opera House, Belfast, 1990; Sullivan's Angelina for D'Oyly Carte at Bournemouth, 1990; Concert engagements with most major British orchestras, under the batons of Charles Mackerras, Roderick Brydon, Charles Groves, David Atherton, Philip Ledger, Mark Elder, John Eliot Gardiner and Vernon Handley; Regular visits to the USA. Recordings: include, Videos of operattas by Gilbert and Sullivan; Series, 100 Years of Italian Opera, with the Philharmonic Orchestra. Address: c/o Korman International Management, 24a Burnaby Gardens, London W4 3DP, England.

DUGGAN Mary Kay, b. 18 Nov 1938, Peru, Indiana, USA. Associate Professor. 2 daughters. Education: BMus, 1960, MA, 1962, Ohio State University; MLA, 1975, PhD, 1981, University of California, Berkeley. Career: Associate Professor, 1987-96, Professor, 1996-, School of Library and Information Studies, University of California, Berkeley; Associate Director, University of California Study Centre, London, 1991-93. Publications: Queen Joanna and her Musicians, Musica Disciplina, XXX, 1976; Early Music Printing in the Music Library of the University of California, Berkeley, 1977; Music Publishing and Printing in San Francisco, The Kemble Occasional No 24, 1980, and No 30, 1983; A System for Describing Fifteenth Century Music Type, Gutenberg-Jahrbuch, 1984; The Music Type of the Second Dated Printed Music Book, the 1477 Graduale Romanum, La Bibliofila, 1987; Italian Music Incunabula, 1992; Music in the Fifteenth-Century Printed Missal, in The Dissemination of Music, 1995. Contributions to: Fontes Artis Musicae; Electronic Information and Applications in Musicology and Music Theory, Library Trends, 1992. Honours: Fulbright Grant, Paris, 1962-63; Martha Baird Rockefeller Fund for Music, Venice, 1978-79. Address: 2229 Marin Avenue, Berkeley, CA 94707, USA.

DUHAMEL Antoine, b. 30 Jul 1925, Valmondois, France. Composer. Education: Studied with Messiaen and Liebowitz in Paris. Career: Wrote for the Club d'Essai, 1951-52 and later wrote film music for such directors as Truffaut and Godard; Staged performances of operas by Rameau (Pygmalion) and Scarlatti, (Il Triofo d'Amore). Compositions: Operas and other works for stage L'Ivrogne, 1952; Staged Tours, 1984; Gala de cirque, Strasbourg, 1965; Lundi, Monseir, vous serez riche, Paris 1969; L'Opera des Oiseaux, Lyons, 1971; Ubu a L'Opera, Avignon, 1974; Gambara, Lyons, 1978; Le Cirque Imperial, Avignon, 1979; Les Travaux d'Hercule, Vaise 1981; Le Transsiberien, Paris, 1983; Le Scieur de Long, Tours, 1984; Quatre-vingt-trieze, Fourvieres, 1989; Les Aventures de Sinbad le Marin, Colmar, 1991. Address: c/o SACEM, 225 avenue Charles de Gaulle, 92521 Neuilly sur Seine Cedex, France.

DUMAY Augustin, b. 17 Jan 1949, Paris, France. Concert Violinist. Education: Studied at the Paris Conservatoire from 1959 with Roland Charmy. Debut: Théâtre des Champs Elysées, Paris, 1963. Career: Studied further with Arthur Grumiaux, 1962-67, then played regularly in public; Partnerships with Jean-Philippe Collard and Michel Beroff; Concert with Karajan and the Berlin Philharmonic 1979 followed by Bartók's 2nd Concerto conducted by Colin Davis; Further engagements with L'Orchestre National de France, Suisse Romande Orchestra, London Symphony and English Chamber, and at the Montreux, Bath, Berlin, Lucerne, Monaco, Aix, Leipzig and Montpellier festivals; Other conductors include Ozawa, Dutoit, Sanderling, Sawallisch, Fruhbeck de Burgos and Skrowaczewski; Chamber music collaborations with Maria Joao Pires, Michel Dalberto, Lynn Harrell, Jean-Bernard Pommier, Yo Yo Ma and Richard Stoltzmann; Gave the premiere of Berio's Sequenza 9, for solo violin, and the premieres of the concertos by Marius Constant and Isang Yun; Director of the National Chamber Orchestra of Toulouse from 1988; Plays a 1721 Stradivarius, formerly belonging to Fritz Kreisler. Recordings: include, Lalo's Symphonie Espagnole, conducted by Michel Plasson, and Chausson's Concerto for piano, violin and string quartet, with Collard and the Muir Quartet; Mozart, Complete Violin Concertos; Tchaikovsky and Mendelsohn, Violin Concertos, London Symphony Orchestra; Mozart, Piano and Violin Sonatas; Brahms, Complete Violin and Piano Sonatas with Maria Joao Pires. Current Management: Transart, London; Valmalette, Paris; CAYI, New York City. Address: Granjinha Do Meio, Excalos De Baixo, 6005 Alcains, Portugal.

DUMINY Philippe, b. 1947, France. Singer (Baritone). Education: Studied at the Paris Conservatoire. Debut: Paris Opéra, 1973, as Antonio in Le nozze di Figaro. Career: Sang at the Opéra in Les Mamelles de Tiresias, as Rossini's Figaro, Oreste in Iphigénie en Tauride, Papageno, Masetto, and Achillas in Giulio Cesare; Guest appearances throughout France as Valentin in Faust, Sancho in Massenet's Don Quichotte and Count Luna; Paris Opéra Bastille from 1991, as Lescaut and as Frère Leon in St François d' Assise by Messiaen. Address: c/o Opéra de la Bastille, 120 Rue de Lyon, F-75012 Paris, France.

DUMITRESCU Iancu (Ioan), b, 15 July 1944, Sibiu, Romania. Composer; Music Critic; Conductor; Pianist. m. (1) Cristina Dumitrescu, 10 May 1979, (2) Ana-Maria Avram, Sept 1988. Education: High School of Music, Bucarest; Piano with Cici Manta; Composition with Alfred Mendelssoh, Stefan Niculescu, Aurel Stroe, and with Sergiu Celibidache, Trier, Germany. Career: Founder, Leader and Conductor, chamber music ensemble Hyperion; Pianist specialising in avant garde music; Compositions performed on TV and radio, Romania, Austria, Netherlands, France, Italy, 1970-; Commands: Radio France, Paris; Commande d'Etat, Minister of Culture, France; Kronos Quartet, San Francisco and G Enescu Philharmonic Orchestra; World premieres: Amsterdam, Berlin, Bremen, Bucharest, Cluj, Paris (Radio France), London (Royal Festival Hall), Royan, Warsaw, Vienna, Lisbon (Gulbenkian Foundation), Milan (Piccola Scala), Rome, Boston, New York, San Francisco; Head, Radio France, Paris Compositions include: Alternances, I, II, string quartet, 1968; Multiples, 3 groups of percussion, 1972; Apogeum for orchestra, 1973; Reliefs for two orchestras and piano, 1975; Orion I and II, for three groups of percussion, 1978; Perspectives au Movemur, string quartet 1979; Zenith, percussion, 1980; Nimbus, 3 trombones, percussion, tape, 1980; Cogito-Trompe L'oeil for ensemble, 1981; Grande Ourse for ensemble, 1982; Aulodie Mioritica, double bass, orchestra, 1984; Haryphonies (alpha, beta, gamma), double bass, percussion, harryphono, piano préparé, 1985; Holzwege, viola solo, 1986; Reliefs for orchestra; Harryphonies (epsilon), large orchestra, 1986; Monades (gamma and epsilon), for 6 monocords and harryphone, 1988; Gnosis, for double bass and string ensemble, 1988-97; L'Orbite D'Uranus; Astrée Lointaine, bass saxophone, orchestra, 1991; L'Empire des Signes, 1992; Au De La De Movemur; Clusterum, percussion, 1993; Galaxy, 3 harryphones, 3 percussions, micro-processor, 1993; 5 Impulsions, large orchestra, 1993; A Priori, chamber ensemble, 1994; Mythos, chamber ensemble, 1994; Kronos/Holzwege, string quartet; Impuls, bass flute, percussion, 1994; Mnemosyne, chamber ensemble, 1994; Pulsar Perdu for Kronos Quartet, string quartet, 1995; Fluxus, for tapes and large orchestra, 1996; Sirius Kronos Quartet, for string quartet and tape, 1996; Meteorites, electronic music, 1997; Ouranos, for distorted spectral sounds, string orchestra and electronic tape, 1997; La Chute dans le Temps, for six groups of instruments, new distorted spectral sounds and tape, 1997. Recordings: Opera Omnia, CDs; Edited by Edition Modern; Ed MN 1008, 1997; Ed MN 1009, forthcoming. Publications: Various interviews for music periodicals; In the Tome: Roumanie, terre du neuvième Ciel, by Ana Maria Avram and Harry Halbreich, 1992; Critical reviews for numerous music publications. Honours: Gaudeamus Prize, Amsterdam, 1978; Prize, Union of Composers of Romania, 1989. Memberships: SACEM, Paris; Union of Composers of Romania, Bucharest. Address: 16 Dr Draghiescu nr 16, sector 5, 76224 Bucharest, Romania.

DUNK Roderick, b. 1959, Birmingham, England. Conductor. Education: Studied at the Birmingham Conservatory. Career: Played double bass in the BBC Symphony Orchestra and Concert Orchestra, 1978-90; From 1990 regular guest conductor with the BBC Concert Orchestra, Birmingham Royal Ballet, London City Ballet, Royal Philharmonic Orchestra and London Symphony Orchestra; Arranger and Music Director with BBC TV, conductor of Carmen Jones at the Old Vic and music director for Travelling Opera in Carmen; Formed the London Palm Court Orchestra in 1986, giving performances of Edwardian and Victorian music. Address: Manygate Management, 13 Cotswold Mews, 30 Battersea Square, London, SW11 3RA, England.

DUNKI Jean-Jacques, b. 28 Feb 1948, Aarau, Switzerland. Pianist; Composer. m. Christine Baader, 6 Aug 1994. Education; Music Education, Aarau, Switzerland; Piano, Conducting, Musicology, Basel, Paris, London, Baltimore, New York. Debut: As Pianist, 1963; Composer, 1978. Career: Performing in most European Countries, 1988-, USA, 1993-, Japan, 1997-. Compositions: Lutezia, 1978; Tú...no tienes imaginación, 1979; Prokrustes, 1982; Tetrapteron O-IV, 1991; Pessoa, 1993; Nulla dies, 1994; Figures, 1997. Recordings: Piano Music of Berg and Webern; Chamber Music of Grieg, Schumann; Own music. Contributions to: Several articles in professional journals and magazines. Honour: 1st Prize, Arnold Schönberg Piano Contest, 1981. Hobbies: Theatre; Nature. Address: Vogesenstrasse 45, CH-4056 Basel, Switzerland.

DUNN Mignon, b. 17 June 1931, Memphis, Tennessee, USA. Singer (Mezzo-soprano). m. Kurt Klippstatter, 24 July 1972. Education: Southwestern University; University of Lausanne; Vocal studies with Karin Branzell and Beverly Johnson, New York. Debut: Operatic debut as Carmen, New Orleans, 1955. Career: New York City Opera debut, 1956, on roster until 1957, then 1972 and 1975; Metropolitan Opera debut, New York, as Nurse in Boris Godunov, 1958, regular appearances in over 50 major roles including Ortrud, Mother Marie (Carmélites), Amneris, Azucena, Marina, Fricka, Herodias and Anna (Les Troyens); Guest appearances with opera companies in Chicago, San Francisco, Boston, Miami, Berlin, Hamburg, Vienna, Florence and other cities; Sang the Kostelnicka in Jenufa at the 1988 Spoleto Festival; Season 1988-89 as the Witch in Rusalka at Philadelphia and Amneris in Chicago; Created Madame Irma in the premiere of The Balcony by Di Domenica, Boston, 1990; Clytemnestra in Nuria Espert's production of Elektra at Barcelona, 1990; Mistress Quickly in Falstaff for New York City Operqa, 1996; Soloist with orchestras in USA and Europe; Faculty, University of Illinois, 1990. Recordings: For several labels. Honours: Honorary DMus, Southwestern University, 1974.

DUNN Susan, b. 23 Jul 1954, Malvern, Arkansas, USA. Singer (Soprano). Education: Studied at Hendrix College, Arkansas and at Indiana University, Bloomington. Debut: Peoria Illinois, 1982, as Aida. Career: Sang Sieglinde in Act 1 of Die Walküre at Carnegie Hall, 1985; Appearances at the Lyric Opera, Chicago, 1986-88, and at San Francisco, Houston and Washington, notably in operas by Verdi; Teatro Communale Bologna 1986, 1988, as Elena in I Vespri Siciliani and Elisabeth de Valois in Don Carlo; Season 1988 as Leonora (La Forza del Destino) at Chicago, the Trovatore Leonora at San Diego and Amelia (Un Ballo in Maschera) at the Vienna Staatsoper; La Scala Milan, as Aida; Metropolitan Opera debut 1990, as Leonora in Il Trovatore. Recordings: include, Beethoven Mass in C and arias from Die Walküre, Tannhäuser, Un Ballo in Maschera, Vêpres Siciliennes, La Forza del Destino and Il Trovatore (Decca); Verdi Requiem (Telarc); Das klagende Lied; Gurrelieder. Current Management: Herbert H Breslin, Inc.

DUNSBY Jonathan Mark, b. 16 Mar 1953, Wakefield, Yorkshire, England. Musician; Professor of Music, University of Reading. m. (1) Anne Davis, 7 Sept 1974, 1 daughter. m. (2) Esther Cavett, 25 May 1983, 1 daughter. Education: ARCM, 1968; BA, Honours, New College, Oxford, 1973; PhD, Leeds University, 1976; Harkness Fellow, 1976. Debut: Piano, Wigmore Hall, 1972. Career: Bronze Medal, Geneva International Competition, 1970; Jury Prize, Munich International Competition, 1970; Winner, Commonwealth Competition, 1974; Regular appearances with Violinist, Vanya Milanova; Professor of Music, University of Reading. Publications: Structural Ambiguity in Brahms, 1981; Founding Editor of Journal of Music Analysis, 1981; Music Analysis in Theory and Practice (with Arnold Whittall: Faber, March 1987); Schoenberg, Pierrot Lunaire, 1992; Performing Music, 1995. Contributions to: Music and Letters; The Musical Quarterly; Journal of Music Theory; Perspectives of New Music; Journal of the Arnold Schoenberg Institute. Address: University of Reading, Department of Music, 35 Upper Redlands Road, Reading, Berkshire, RG1 5JE, England.

DUPHIL Monique, b. 24 Apr 1936. Pianist. m. Jay Humeston, 2 daughters. Education: Studied privately and at Conservatoire National Supérieur de Musique de Paris with Marguerite Long, Jean Doyen, Rose Lejour, Joseph Calvet and Pierre Pasquier. Debut: At Paris Théâtre des Champs Elysées with L'Orchestre de la Société des Concerts. Career: Regular concert appearances in chamber music and as soloist, in the USA with Cleveland and Philadelphia Orchestras, South America, Europe, Japan and Australia; Frequent partner of Pierre Fournier, R Ricci and Michel Debost; Member of the Amici and Villa Lobos Trios; Has performed with many conductors including Igor Markevich, E Ormandy, CH Dutoit and G Hurst; Pianist in Residence at Oberlin Music Conservatory, OH, USA. Recordings: JS Bach's French Suites; Piano Music by A Liadov; H Villa Lobos' Piano Trios Nos 1, 2 and 3 and Piano and Cello Sonata No 2. Hobbies: Nature; Animals. Current Management: Mariedi Anders, San Francisco. Address: Oberlin College, Music Conservatory, Oberlin, OH 44074, USA.

DUPONT Stephen, b. 1957, Texas, USA. Singer (Bass). Education: Studied at Memphis State University and the American Opera Center, New York. Career: Sang in La Bohème at New York and appeared in operas by Menotti at Spoleto and Palermo, 1984; Guest appearances at Venice in the Verdi Requiem and Don Carlos, in Paris and San Francisco; Mozart's Commendatore at La Scala, 1989, Colline and Ramphis at the Metropolitan, 1986-87; Sang Gremin at Strasbourg, 1990, Sparafucile at Bonn and Banquo for Miami Opera (1992). Address: c/o Metropolitan Opera, Lincoln Center, New York, NY 10023, USA.

DUPRÉ Heather, b. 30 Mar 1949, Channel Islands. Pianist. Education: Licenciate, Recital Diploma, Royal Academy of Music, 1967-72. Debut: Wigmore Hall, 1976. Career: Solo Pianist, Recitals in Britain including several appearances at Edinburgh Festival Fringe, Wigmore Hall and Purcell Room; Broadcast on Radio London, 1974; Junior Professor, Royal Academy of Music, 1973-76; Examiner, Associated Board of Royal Schools of Music, 1979-. Memberships: Solo Performers Section, Incorporated Society of Musicians. Hobbies: Reading; Walking. Address: 19c Abercorn Place, St Johns Wood, London NW8 9DX, England.

DUPUY Martine, b. 1952, France. Singer (Mezzo-Soprano). Debut: Aix-en-Province 1975, as Eurydice in Campra's Le Carnaval de Venise. Career: Has sung in the coloratura mezzo repertoire in Europe and North and South America; Marseilles Opera 1985, as Bellini's Romeo and as Isabella in L'Italiana in Algeri; Paris Opera 1985, as Neocles in Le Siège de Corinth; Other Rossini roles include Malcolm (La Donna del Lago) at Nice 1985 and Bonn 1990, Cenerentola (Lausanne) and Arsace in Semiramide at Valle d'Itria and Nice, 1985; Metropolitan Opera debut 1988, as Sextus in Giulio Cesare; Sang in the opening concert at the Bastille Opera, Paris, 13 July 1989; Season 1990-91 as Mère Marie in Les Dialogues des Carmélites for Lyon Opera, Jane Seymour (Anna Bolena) at Marseilles and Madrid and Armando in a concert performance of Meyerbeer's Il Crociato in Egitto at Montpellier; Other roles include Monteverdi's Nero and Penelope, Mozart's Cecilio (Lucio Silla) and Sextus (La Clemenza di Tito); Adalgisa in Norma dn Donizetti's Maffeo Orsini (Lucrezia Borgia) and Ada (Il Diluvio Universale); Has also sung in Buenos Aires, Salzburg and Lausanne; Brussels 1996, as Eboli in the French version of Don Carlos; The Prince in Cendrillon at Turin. Honours: include, Winner, International Singing Competition, Peschiera del Garda, 1975; Grand Prix 1985 from Opera International, France. Address: c/o Opéra de Lyon, 9 Quai Jean Moulin, F-69001 Lyon, France.

DURMELLER Jorg, b. 28 Aug 1959, Berne, Switzerland. Singer (Tenor). Education: Studied at Winther and Hamburg and with Christa Ludwig and Hermann Prey. Career: Appeared with the company of the Hamburg Staatsoper at the 1986 Schwetzingen Festival, in the premiere of Die Lieden des Jungen Werthers by Hans-Jurgen von Böse; Member of the Bielefeld opera from 1987, notably as Mozart's Ferrando and Tamino, Verdi's and Nicolai's Fenton, and Chateauneuf in Zar und Zimmermann; Sang Ramiro in Cenerentola, 1989; Tour of Russia and Spain, 1989, guest appearances in concert and opera in Brussels, Paris, Pesaro, Geneva and Mannheim; Innsbruck Early Music Festival, 1991, as Fracasso in Mozart's La Finta Semplice, conducted by René Jacobs. Recordings: Bruckner's Missa Solemnis in F. Address: Städtisches Buhnen, Brunnenstrasse 3, 4800 Bielefeld 1, Germany.

DÜRR Alfred, b. 3 Mar 1918, Charlottenburg, Germany. Musicologist; Writer on Music; Editor. Education: PhD, Musicology, University of Göttingen, 1950. Career: Member 1951-83, Assistant Director, 1962-81, Johann-Sebastian-Bach-Institute, Göttingen; Editor, Bach-Jahrbuch, 1953-74; Editor of works for Bach Neue Ausgabe sämtlicher Werke. Publications: Studien über die frühen Kantaten Johann Sebastian Bachs, 1951, 2nd Edition, revised 1977; Zur Chronolgie der Leipzigir Vokalwerke J Bachs (revised reprint from Bach-Jahrbuch 1957), 1976; Johann Sebastian Bach, Weihnachts Oratorium, 1967; Die Kantaten von Johann Sebastian Bach, 1971, 6th edition, revised, 1995; Johann Sebastian Bach: Seine Handschrift-Abbild seines Schaffens, 1984; Im Mittelpunkt Bach: Ausgewählte Aufsätze und Vorträge, 1988; Die Johannes-Passion von Johann Sebastian Bach: Entstehung, Überlieferung, Werkeinführung, 1988, 2nd edition, 1992; Bachs Werk vom Einfall bis zur Drucklegung, 1989. Contributions to: Articles in scholarly journals. Honours: Member, Akademie der Wissenschaften, Göttingen, 1976-; Festschrift published in honour of 65th birthday, 1983; Honorary doctorate, Baldwin-Wallace College, Berea, Ohio, 1982 and Oxford, 1995; Corresponding member, American Musicological Society, 1988-. Address: Leipziger Strasse 20, D-37120 Bovenden, Germany.

DÜRR Karl Friedrich, b. 1949, Stuttgart, Germany. Singer (Bass-baritone). Education: Studied German Literature and Political Science, receiving his PhD in 1978. Debut: Sang Antonio in Le nozze di Figaro at Ludwigsburg. Career: Studied further with Gunther Reich and sang with the Stuttgart Staatsoper from 1980, notable as Rihm's Jakob Lenz, Mozart's Figaro (production by Peter Zadek), Leporello, Don Alfonso, Klingsor (Parsifal) and Biterolf (Tannhäuser), Alfio (Cavalleria), Monterone, Zuniga in Carmen, Krishna in Satyagraha by Philip Glass, Faninal (Rosenkavalier); Tierbändiger and Atlet in Lulu by Berg; Kothner in Die Meistersinger; Appearances at the Ludwisburgh and Schwetzingen Festivals and with the ensemble of the Stuttgart Staatsoper on tour to Russia (Zimmermann's Die Soldaten); Further engagements as Kaspar in Der Freischütz, Kurwenal, and Wozzeck; Concerts in Kassel, Trieste, Berlin and New York, 1989; Vienna Festival 1990, as Krenek's Diktator and as the Boxer in Schwergewicht; Sang Don Alfonso at Stuttgart, 1991; Also in Paris, Bastille Opera (Die Soldaten) and Semper-Oper, Dresden (Leporello) and other German opera houses such as Düsseldorf and Bonn; Sang in Debussy's Chute de la Maison Usher at Stuttgart, 1996. Recordings: Eisenhardt in Die Soldaten. Address: c/o Staatstheater Stuttgart, Oberer Schlossgarten 6, 7000 Stuttgart, Germany.

DÜRR Walther, b. 27 Apr 1932, Berlin, Germany. Musicologist. m. Vittoria Bortolotti, 25 June 1960, 2 daughters. Education includes: PhD, Tübingen University, 1956. Career: Lecturer, Bologna University, Italy, 1957; Assistant, Tübingen University, Germany, 1962; General Editor, Neue Schubert-Ausgabe, 1965; Honorary Professor, Tübingen University; Broadcasts for radio stations Deutsche Welle, Cologne, Südwestfunk, Baden-Baden. Publications: Rhythmus und Metrum im italienischen Madrigal insbesondere bei Luca Marenzio, 1956; Serie IV (Lieder) of Neue Schubert Ausgabe, 1966; Franz Schuberts Werke in Abschriften; Liederalben und Sammlungen, 1975; Der Kleine Deutsch (with Werner Aderhold and Arnold Feil), 1983; Das Deutsche Sololied im 19 Jahrhundert, 1984; Franz Schubert (with Arnold Feil), 1991; Zeichen Setzung Aufsätze zur Musikalischen Poetik, 1992; Musik und Sprache, 1994; Schubert Handbook, editor with Andreas Krause, 1997. Contributions to: Die Musikforschung; Archiv für Musikwissenschaft; Österreichische Musikzeitschrift; 19th Century Music; MGG; New Grove Dictionary of Music and Musicians; Numerous honorary anniversary works and reviews. Memberships: Society for Musical Research; International Musicological Society. Address: Hausserstrasse 140, D-72076 Tübingen, Germany.

DUSSEK Michael, b. 1958, England. Concert Pianist. Career: Chamber musician throughout Europe, Japan and Australia, and Canada, notably with such soloists as Cho-Liang Lin, Anne Akiko Meyers, Kurt Nikkanen and Ofra Harnoy; Recent recitals in the Amsterdam Concertgebouw, Tokyo, Madrid, Milan and Vienna; Engagements throughout Britain with the cellist Alexander Baillie, oboist Douglas Boyd and violinist Lorraine McAslan; Concerto soloist with the London Mozart Players at the Festival Hall and work for BBC Radio 3 as chamber musician and accompanist; Purcell Room recital 1993 with Markus Stocker, featuring music by Schumann, Brahms, Liszt and Martinu. Recordings: include, Brahms Piano Trios and Horn Trio with the Dussek Trio, contemporary Finnish music with the Edoymion Ensemble, cello sonatas with Ofra Harnoy and cello sonatas by Reger; Professor, Royal Academy of Music.

DUTILLEUX Henri, b. 22 Jan 1916, Angers, France. Composer. m. Genevieve Joy, 1946. Education: Conservatoire National de Musique, Paris. Career: Devoted to Music, 1945-; Director, Service Creations Musicales Radiodiffusion Française, 1945-63; Professor of Composition, Ecole Normale de Musique, Paris, 1961-; President, 1969-, Associate Professor, 1970-71, Conservatoire National Superieur Musique, Paris; Former Member, UNESCO Music Council; Honorary Member, American Academy and Institute of Arts and Letters, NY, USA; Honorary Member, Accademia di Santa Ceceilia, Rome; Associate Member Royal Academy of Music, Belgium. Compositions: Sonata for Piano, 1948; Symphony No 1, 1951; Le Loup, ballet, 1953; Symphony No 2, Le Double, 1959; Metaboles for Orchestra, 1964; Cello Concerto, Tout un monde lointain, 1970; Figures de Resonances for 2 Pianos, 1971; Preludes for Piano, 1974; Ainsi la Nuit for String Quartet, 1976; Timbres Espace, movement for Orchestra, 1978; 2 Strophes sur le nom de Sacher for Cello, 1981; Violin Concerto, 1985; Mystère de L'instant for String Orchestra, 1988; Les Citations for Oboe, Harpsichord, Double Bass and Percussion, 1991. Honours: Grand Prix de Rome, 1938; Grand Prix du Disque, 1957, 1958, 1966, 1968, 1976, 1978, 1984; Grand Prix National de la Musique, 1967; Prix de la Ville de Paris, 1974; Koussevitzky International Recording Award, 1976; World Record Award, Montreux, 1983; Prix International Maurice Ravel, 1987; Prix UNESCO International Music Council, 1987; Grand Officier, Legion of Honour; Fraemium Imperiale Japan, 1994. Address: 12 rue St Louis en L'Isle, 75004 Paris, France.

DUTOIT Charles, b. 7 Oct 1936, Lausanne, Switzerland. Conductor. Education: Studied at the Lausanne Conservatory with Wachsmuth, Mermoud and Hans Haug; Further study at the Geneva Academy, the Accademia Musicale in Siena and at the Benedetto Marcello Conservatory in Venice; Courses with Charles Munch at Tanglewood. Career: Second Conductor of the Berne Symphony, 1964, Principal from 1967-78; Conductor and Artistic Director of the Zurich Radio Orchestra, 1967; Music Director of Mexico's National Symphony Orchestra, 1974-76; Conductor of the Gothenburg Symphony, 1975; Music Director of the Montreal Symphony Orchestra since 1977; Principal Guest Conductor, Minnesota Orchestra, 1983-85; Music Director of the Orchestre National de France, 1991-; Artistic Director and Principal Conductor of summer festivals with the Philadelphia Orchestra at Mann Centre for Performing Arts and Saratoga Performing Arts Centre; Principal Conductor at NHK Symphony Orchestra in Tokyo, 1996; Guest Conductor with all major orchestras in South America, Europe, Japan, Australia, United States and Israel. Recordings: Falla's Three Cornered Hat and El amor Brujo; The Planets by Holst; Tchaikovsky's 1st Piano Concerto, Argerich, Ravel, Daphnis et Chloe; Saint-Saëns 3rd Symphony; Bizet L'Arlesienne and Carmen Suites; Gubaidulina Offertorium, Boston Symphony; Symphonies by Honegger, 1, 2 and 4; Roussel's Symphonies, French National Orchestra; Saint-Saëns Piano Concertos, Pascal Rogé; Suppé Overtures; Berlioz Les Troyens, 1994. Address: Orchestre Symphonique de Montréal, Salle Winifred-Pelletier, Place des Arts, 200 West de Maisonneuve, Montréal, Province Québec, H2X 1Y9, Canada.

DUTT Hank, b. 4 Nov 1952, Muscatine, Iowa, USA. Violist. Career: Joined the Kronos String Quartet, 1977; Many performances of contemporary music, including the premieres of works of John Cage (30 Pieces for String Quartet), Pauline Oliveros (The Wheel of Time) and Terry Riley (G-Song, Sunrise of the Planetary Dream Collector and Cadenzas on the Night Plain); Formerly quartet-in-residence at Mills College, Oakland; From 1982 resident quartet at the University of Southern California; Appearances at the Monterrey Jazz Festival, Carnegie Recital Hall, San Quentin Prison and London's South Bank; New York debut 1984; Noted for 'cross-over' performances of jazz and popular music in arrangement. Address: c/o UCLA Music Department, University Park, Los Angeles, CA 90089, USA.

DUTTON Brenton (Price), b. 20 Mar 1950, Saskatoon, Canada. Composer; Tubist. 2 sons, 1 daughter. Education: BM, MM, Oberlin Conservatory of Music. Career: Tubist with Cleveland Orchestra, 1968-74; L'Orchestra Symphonique de Quebec, 1971-74, San Diego Symphony, 1980-; Solo Recital appearances throughout Canada, USA, Europe; Professor of Music, San Diego State University, 1980-, California Institute of the Arts, 1981-84; Brass Coach for the Jeunesses Musicales World Orchestra, in Europe, North and South America, 1986-. Compositions: Over 100 including Symphony No 2, 1972; Symphony No 3, 1974; Song of the Moon, solo flute; On Looking Back, Brass Quintet; December Set, Woodwind Quintet; Dialogues of the sybarites, 3 trumpets and organ; Circles; Chinese Reflections; A Rolling Silence; Songs of Love, all song cycles for baritone and chamber ensemble; Additional Works: Ecq theow Variants, Brass Quintet; On A Darkling Plain, Brass Quintet; Song of the Sun, solo viola; Hotel Europejski Suite, violin, piano; Gilgamesh, opera in 3 acts, 1977-78. Recordings: Symphony No 5 Dark Spirals, 1985; Character Dances and proud Music of the Storm, 1986; Carnival of Venice, brass Quintet, 1983; Olympic Entrance, Tuba Suite, 1984; many radio and TV broadcasts; Krakow, Summer; Quebec, Spring, both for string orchestra. Publications: Sonata in Fact for Trumpet, Piano; Resonances for Tuba Quarter. Hobbies: Woodwork; Long Distance Running. Address: Department of Music, San Diego State University, San Diego, CA 92182, USA.

DUTTON Lawrence, b. 9 May 1954, New York, USA. Violist. Career: Member, Emerson String Quartet, 1976-; Premiere concert at Alice Tully Hall, New York, 1977, with works by Mozart, Smetana and Bartók; European debut at Spoleto, Italy in 1981; Quartet-in-residence at Smithsonian Institute, Washington 1980-, at the Hartt School, 1981- and at Spoleto and Aspen Festivals, 1981-; First resident quartet at Chamber Music Society of Lincoln Center, season 1982-83; Tour of Japan and Australia 1987; Many performances of works by Bartók, including all six quartets in a single evening, and contemporary works; Premieres include Mario Davidovsky's 4th Quartet and works by

Maurice Wright and George Tsontakis. Recordings: include, Walter Piston's Concerto for string quartet, winds and percussion (CRI); Works by Andrew Imbrie, Henry Howell, Roy Harris and Gunther Schuller (New World); Bartók's Six Quartets (Deutsche Grammophon). Hobbies: Backpacking; Tennis. Address: 60 West 76th Street, Apartment 5E, New York, NY 10023, USA.

DUVAL Denise, b. 23 Oct 1921, Paris, France. Singer (Soprano). Education: Studied at the Bordeaux Conservatory. Debut: Bordeaux 1943, as Lola in Cavalleria Rusticana. Career: Sang at the Folies Bergères, Paris, 1944; Paris Opéra from 1947, notably as Salome in Herodiade by Massenet, and as Blanche in the French premiere of Dialogues des Carmelites, 1947; Sang at the Opéra-Comique Paris in the 1947 premiere of Poulenc's Les Mamelles de Tiresias: returned 1959 for the premiere of La Voix Humaine (repeated at La Scala 1960); Paris 1949, in the premiere of Le oui des jeunes Filles, by Hahn-Busser; Other roles were Thais, the Princess in Marouf by Rabaud, Concepcion, and Portia in La Marchande de Venise by Hahn; Edinburgh Festival with the Glyndebourne company in 1960, as Elle in La Voix Humaine; Glyndebourne Festival 1962-63, as Mélisande; Guest appearances in Milan, Vienna, Brussels, Amsterdam and Buenos Aires; Retired 1965 and became Professor at the Ecole Française de Musique in Paris. Recordings: L'Heure Espagnole, Les mamelles de Tiresias (Columbia); Dialogues des Carmélites (HMV).

DVORACEK Jiri, b. 8 June 1928, Vamberk, Czechoslovakia. Composer; Professor; Music Administrator. Education: Studied organ, Prague Conservatory, 1943-47; Studied composition with Ridky and Dobias, Prague Academy of Music, 1949-53. Career: Teacher 1953-67, Senior Lecturer 1967-78, Professor of Composition and Head, Composition Department 1979-90, Prague Academy of Music; President, Union of Czech Composers and Concert Artists, 1987-89. Compositions: Opera: Aphrodite's Island, 1967; Orchestral: 2 Symphonies, 1953, 1986; Symphonic Suite, 1958; Concertante Suite, 1962; Ex Post for Piano and Orchestra, 1963; Quattro Episodi, 1971; I am Living and Singing, cantata for Soloists, Choir, Reciter, Children's Choir and Orchestra, 1978; Giubilo, 1983; Concert for Violin and Orchestra, 1989; Chamber: Sonata Capricciosa for Violin and Piano, 1956; Invention for Trombone and Piano or Small Orchestra, 1961; Meditations for Clarinet and Percussion, 1964; Music for Harp, 1970; Due per duo for Horn and Piano, 1970; Dialogues for Flute and Piano, 1973; Brass Quintet, 1973; Music for Viola and Piano, 1976; Sonata for Trumpet and Piano, 1977; Organ Sonata, 1979; Accordian Sonata, 1979; Theme and Variations for Trombone and Piano, 1980; Prague Transformations for Wind Quintet, 1981; Clarinet and Piano Play, 1982; Violin and Organ Play, 1984; Partita for Oboe and Bassoon, 1986; Partita Piccola, for violin, guitar and harmonica, 1987; Trio for clarinet, violin and piano, 1994; Choral music; Songs. Recordings: Various compositions recorded. Address: Antala Staska 1015/43, 140 00 Prague 4, Czech Republic.

DVORAKOVA Ludmila, b. 11 July 1923, Kolin, Czechoslovakia. Soprano Singer. m. Rudolf Vasata, deceased 1982. Education: Studied with Jarmila Vavrdova at The Prague Conservatory. Debut: Ostrava 1949, as Katya Kabanova. Career: Sang in Ostrava as Rusalka, Elisabeth de Valois, Countess Almaviva and Aida; Sang in Bratislava and at the Smetana Theatre, Prague, from 1952; Member, Prague National Opera, 1954-57 as Milada in Dalibor, Elisabeth, Leonore, Senta, and in Czech operas; Sang Leonore at the Vienna Staatsoper, 1956; Sang at Berlin Staatsoper, 1960-84 as Brünnhilde, Venus, Elisabeth de Valois, Kundry, Isolde, Ortrud, Tosca and the Marschallin; Karlsruhe 1964 as Isolde; Bayreuth Festival, 1965-71 as Gutrune, Brünnhilde, Venus, Ortrud and Kundry; Covent Garden, 1966-71 as Brünnhilde, Isolde and Leonore; Metropolitan Opera, 1965-68; Paris Opera, 1966; Elektra, Graz 1973; Opera München, La Scala, Opera Roma, San Francisco, Buenos Aires, Deutsche Oper am Rhein Dusseldorf, 1973-74; Vienna Staatsoper, 1964-85; Salome, Herodias, Berlin, 1979-; Jenufa, Kusterin, 1980; Visited Japan, 1983, 1984, with the State Operas of Berlin and Hamburg; Jenufa, Vienna, 1984; Other roles included: Katerina Ismailova, (Vienna, 1965), Ariadne and The Dyer's Wife in Die Frau ohne Schatten; Recordings: Gutrune in Götterdämmerung, from Bayreuth; Wagner Recital. Address: 16200 Praha 6, Na Orechovce 14, Czech Republic.

DVORKIN Judith, b. 1926, New York, USA. Composer. Education: Studied with Otto Luening and Elliott Carter in New York; Further study with Roger Sessions at Berkeley. Compositions include: Chamber operas: Cyrano, 1964, Humpty Dumpty And Alice, 1988, and The Frog Prince, 1993; Four Women, song cycle, 1981; Perspectives for Flute, 1987. Address: c/o ASCAP, ASCAP Building, One Lincoln Plaza, New York, NY 10023, USA.

DVORSKY Peter, b. 25 Sept 1951, Partizanske, Slovakia. Opera Singer (Tenor). m. Marta Varsova, 19 July 1975, 2 daughters. Education: Basic Nine Year School; Graduated, Conservatory Bratislava, 1973. Debut: Slovak National Theatre, Bratislava in Onegin, 1973.Career: 5th Prize, Tchaikovsky Competition (Laureate), Moscow, 1974; 1st Prize, Geneva, 1975; La Boheme, La Scala, 1981; Manon, with Vienna State Opera, 1984; La Boheme, La Scala, 1985; Adriana Lecouvreur, 1989; Verdi Operatic Festival with Milnes and Sato, 1992; Puccini Operatic Festival, 1994; Regular appearances in: Bratislava, Prague, Budapest, Moscow, Vienna, Milan, London, New York, Munich, San Francisco, Chicago, Frankfurt, etc; Sang at Covent Garden from 1978, as Alfredo 1986, and Lensky and Riccardo 1988; Metropolitan New York and Barcelona, 1987, as Rodolfo and Edgardo; Salzburg Festival 1989, as Cavaradossi; Sang Massenet's Des Grieux at Modena and Barcelona, 1990; Maggio Musica Florence, 1992, as Don Alvaro in La Forza del Destino; Ballo in Maschera, Buenos Aires, 1994; Barcelona, with Milnes and Sato, 1995; Concerts with Caballe, Milnes and Sato, 1996; Tosca, La Boheme and concert, Japan, 1997. Recordings: Janacek: Makropulos Case, Jenufa, Kata Kabanova, all with Charles Mackerras; Verdi: Otello, Cassio with Georg Solti, La Bohème, Bartered Bride, Madame Butterfly, Elisir d'amore; Dvorak: Stabat Mater, Requiem; Recital 1,2,3; Folk Songs: Dusik: The Blue Rose, Operetta; Peter Dvorsky in Concert; G Puccini: La Bohème; Gounod: Faust; E Suchon: Katrena; Manon Lecsaut; P Mascagni: Cavalleria Rusticana; J Massenet: Werther; G Donizetti: Elisir d'amore; G Verdi: Requiem for OPUS, Supraphon, Ariola and Balcanton. Honours: People Artist, CSSR Music-Piano; Family. Current Management: Slovkoncert, Slovak Artistic Agency, Bratislava, Slovakia. Address: Slovak National Theatre/Slovenske narodne divadlo, Gorkeho 4, Bratislava, Slovakia.

DWORCHAK Harry, b. 1947, Hershey, Pennsylvania, USA. Singer (Bass-baritone). Education: AVA, Philadelphia, 1970. Career: Sang first at the Barcelona Opera (from 1970), then throughout North America, with a 1982 debut at the New York City Opera; Théâtre du Châtelet, Paris, 1982, as Banquo; Welsh National Opera, 1985, as Oroveso; Sang Ferrando in Trovatore at the Metropolitan in 1988, at the Munich Staatsoper, 1992; Der Holländer, Frankfurt, 1991, Washington DC, 1995; Scarpia, Covent Garden, 1996; Bayerische Staatsoper, 1997; Other roles include the Commendatore, Monteverdi's Seneca, Bellini's Capulet, Mephistopheles (Faust), Don Quichotte, Daland, Wagner's Dutchman, and Dosifey in Khovanshchina; Forthcoming engagements as Wotan, Rheingold, Augsburg; Wotan, Walküre, Augsburg; Der Wanderer; Pizarro in Fidelio, Buenos Aires; Entire Ring Cycle. Recordings: Das Schloss, Bayerische Staatsoper, Munich; Don Alfonso in Cosí fan Tutte, European Television Broadcast. Honours: Richard Tucker Award, 1987; Carnegie Hall Concert, 1987. Current Management: Lombardo; RAAB. Address: Metzstrasse 29a, D-81667 Munich, Germany.

DYACHKOV Yegor, b. 1974, Moscow, Russia. Cellist. Education: Studies with Alexander Fedorchenko, Moscow Conservatory, Radu Aldulescu, Rome, André Navarra, Vienna, Yuli Turovsky, Montreal, Boris Pergamenschikow, Cologne. Career: Numerous Recitals in the Former Soviet Union, Italy, Latin America, Taiwan, USA, Canada; Guest Soloist with Montreal Symphony Orchestra, Metropolitan Orchestra of Montreal, Orchestre Symphonique de Quebec, National Arts Centre Orchestra in Ottawa, I Musici de Montreal; Concert Performances in Quebec, Ontario, New Brunswick; Performances at the Lanaudiere International Music Festival, Domaine Forget International Music Festival, Chamber Music Festival in Ste-Pétronille, Orford International Music Festival, Scotia Festival of Music, Mozarteum in Caracas. Honours: Winner, 1st International Music Competition, Orford Arts Centre; 1st Prize, I Musici de Montreal Competition, 1st Prize, Monstreal Symphony Orchestra Competition; 1st Prize, International Stepping Stone Competition; 1st Prize, Orchestre Symphonique de Quebec Competition; Member, Millennium. Address: c/o Latitude 45, Arts Promotion Inc, 109 St Joseph Blvd West, Montreal, Quebec H2T 2P7, Canada.

DYSON (Barbara) Ruth, b. 28 Mar 1917, London, England. Pianist; Harpsichordist. m. Edward Eastaway Thomas, deceased. Education: Royal College of Music, 1935-39; Private ARCM, Piano, 1936; ARCM, Violin, 1939. Debut: Wigmore Hall, London, 1941. Debut: Wigmore Hall, 1993. Career: BBC; Solo recitals since 1951; Concertos with London Philharmonic, Royal Philharmonic, Mozart Players, London Studio Strings, Liverpool Philharmonic; Tours in Scandinavia for British Council, lectures and broadcasts, 1950-56; Professor of Harpsichord and Piano, Royal College of Music, 1964-87; Adjudicator, Bruges International Fortnight, 1972. Recordings: Howells and the Clavichord, 1982; For Two to Play, 1987; English Harpsichord Music, 1990. Publications: Articles on the Piano, in New Oxford Companion. Contributions to: Article on Wanda Landowska in CANOR, 1995. Honour: FRCM, 1980. Memberships: Galpin Society; NEMA; British Clavichord Society. Hobby: Ornithology. Address: 2 St Mary's Garden, Chichester, West Susex PO19 1NY, England.

DZEMJANOVA Emilia, b. 20 May 1959, Snina, Slovakia. Professor; Concert Organist. Education: Conservatory Kosice, Slovakia; Academy of Music, Bratislava, Slovakia; Masterclass Flor Peeters at Mechelen, Belgium. Career: Recitals, Concerts with Orchestra, Recordings for Radio and TV; Appearances in major European Cities, including Music Festivals, Organ Festivals; Professor at the Conservatory in Kosice, 1982-. Recordings: Contemporary Czechoslovak Composers, including Eben, Suchon and Burlas. Publications: Organ Works of Eugen Suchon (revised edition) HF Bratislava, 1989; Organ School, 1991; Collection of organ compositions, 1997. Honours: Prizes in National Competitions, 1983. Memberships: Neue Bachgesellschaft. Current Management: Slovkoncert, Bratislava, Slovakia. Address: Huskova 31, 040 11 Kosice, Slovakia.

DZIADEK Magdalena, b. 24 March 1961, Poland. Musicologist; Critic. m. Andrzej Dziadek, 30 June 1984, 1 daughter. Education: Diploma, Academy of Music, Katowice, 1984; Doctor Degree, Institute of Arts, Polish Academy of Science, Warsaw, 1991. Contributions to: Muzyka; Ruch Muzyczany; Canor; Opcje. Memberships: Polish Composers Union; International Musicological Society. Hobbies: Books; Gardening. Address: ul Sniezna 5, 43-400 Cieszyn, Poland.

DZODTSOEVA Agnesa Victorovna, b. 10 October 1944, Tbilisi, Georgia. Composer; Pianist; Music Teacher. m. Fikri Bashir, 27 August 1967, 2 sons. Education: Masters Degree, Gnesin's Academy, Moscow. Debut: Competition, Contemporary Music, Vladikavkaz. Career: Stage Appearances as Pianist with Orchestras and Solo in Bagdad, Beirut, Kuwait; Composer Appearance on Radio in Moscow and On Stage in Paris, USA, Italy, Bulgaria, Iraq, Jordan. Recordings: Triple for Orchestra; Arabic Suite; Two Movements for Orchestra; Fantasia, for Piano. Publications: Role of Women in the Middle East Culture; Study on Tone Poems of R Strauss and on Operas of Sergei Prokofieff. Contributions to: Journals and Magazines. Honours: 1st Prize, Composition, Ministry of Culture, Bagdad; Honour Committee, Foundation at Adkins, Chiti, Italy. Memberships: NACUSA, USA; SACEM, France; Corresponding Member, New York Women Composers Society. Hobbies: Archaeology; History; Visual Arts; Poetry. Address: PO Box 831096, Amman, Jordan.

E

EAGLE David (Malcolm), b. 21 Dec 1955, Montreal, Quebec, Canada. Composer; Flautist; Teacher. m. Hope Lee, 23 Aug 1980. Education: BMus, 1979, MMus, 1982, McGill University; Studied Flute with Cindy Shuter, Composition with Bengt Hamnbraeus and Donald Steven; Composition with Klaus Huber and Brian Ferneyhough, Hochschule für Musik, Freiburg, 1981-83; PhD, University of California at Berkeley, 1992. Career: Freelance Composer; Works played, Canada, Holland Festival, 1985, Germany, Switzerland; Broadcasts on CBC Radio Canada, BBC, Hessischer Rundfunk, Swiss Radio, KRO (Netherlands); Invited Guest Composer, Boswil Kunstlerhaus, Switzerland, 1985; Commissions from Montreal Chamber Orchestra, Array-Music, Toronto Consort, many individuals; Coordinator, Electroacoustic Music Studio, Assistant Professor, Composition, Theory, University of Calgary, 1990-. Compositions: include, Zhu Fong, string quartet, 1978; Strata-Vari for 14 strings, 1980; Within for solo cello, 1982; Strahlen for organ, 1983; Aura for septet, 1984; Renew'd at ev'ry glance for variable instruments, 1985; Toccare for harpsichord, 1986; Luminous Voices for early music ensemble and tape, 1987-88; Crossing Currents for orchestra, 1991; Hsuan for guzheng and tape, 1992; Nohocki for flute and cello, 1993; Music for AXIO, Open This Door, for AXIO (midi-controller), 1993; Sounding after Time for violin, cello, piano, computer, synthesizer, 1993. Address: 27 Stradwick Rise SW, Calgary, Alberta, Canada T3H 1G6.

EAGLEN Jane, b. 4 Apr 1960, Lincoln, England. Singer (Soprano). Education: Royal Northern College of Music; Study with Joseph Ward. Career: Engagements with English National Opera as Leonora in Il Trovatore and Elizabeth I in Mary Stuart; Western Australia Opera, Perth, as Tosca; Lyric Opera of Queensland, Brisbane, as Madama Butterfly; Scottish Opera, as Donna Anna; London Promenade Concert debut, 1989, as Sieglinde in Act III of Die Walküre; Sang Brünnhilde, 1991; Tosca for English National Opera, 1990; Donna Anna and Amelia (Ballo), Bologne, 1991; Sang Mathilde in Guillaume Tell at Covent Garden, Geneva, 1992; Scottish Opera as Norma in a new production of Bellini's Opera; Tosca, Buenos Aires. 1993, then Donna Anna in Don Giovanni, Vienna State Opera, and title role in Norma, Seattle Opera; Brünnhilde in Die Walküre, Opera Pacific, California, and Vienna State Opera, 1994; Norma with Riccardo Muti, Ravenna Festival, 1994; Title role in Ariadne, with English National Opera, 1994; Brünnhilde in Die Walküre, La Scala, Milan, 1994, and with Lyric Opera of Chicago, 1995; Amelia in Un Ballo in Maschera, Opéra de Paris Bastille, 1995; Engaged to open the Chicago Lyric, 1998-99 Season as La Gioconda; Isolde at Seattle, 1998; Concert appearances at the Wigmore Hall, Festival Hall and the Barbican Centre; Verdi Requiem and Mahler 8th Symphony; Recitals for the Wagner Societies of London, New York and Buenos Aires. Recordings: Die Flammen; Medea in Corintho; Norma, with Muti; Leonore in Fidelio, Elektra and Isolde, 1997-98. Honours include: Peter Moores Foundation Scholarship; Countess of Munster Award; Carl Rosa Trust Award. Address: c/o AOR Management Ltd, Westwood, Lorraine Park, Harrow Weald, Middlesex HA3 6BX, England.

EAGLESON Linda Louise, b. 29 Jan 1951, Suffern, New York, USA. Flautist. m. Douglas Miller Eagleson, 25 Aug 1984. Education: Westwood Regional Schools, New Jersey, 1956-69; Flute with Paige Brook, 1968-69; BM, Boston Conservatory of Music, 1973; Flute with James Pappoutsakis; MM, University of Maryland, College Park, 1992; Flute with William Montgomery, Julius Baker, Harold Bennett, Brenda-Jeanne Patterson, Thomas Perazzoli. Debut: Weill (Carnegie) Recital Hall, New York City, 1990. Appointments: Freelance Musician; Kirkwood Flute Ensemble; Guest Performer, Brandeis, 1992, and Strawbery Banke Music Festivals; Signature Theatre; Prince George's Philharmonic; Adelphi Chamber Orchestra. Recording: Intimate Thoughts: Just Us. Honours: Dean's Honour Award, Sigma Alpha Iota, 1972; Fulbright Scholarship, 1973; Finalist, Homer Ulrich Competition, University of Maryland, 1990; 2nd Prize, Flute Society of Washington Competition, 1991. Memberships: Washington DC Federation of Musicians; Pi Kappa Lambda; Sigma Alpha Iota. Hobbies: Aerobics; Hiking; Gardening; Nutrition. Address: 217 East Deer Park Drive, Gaithersburg, MD 20877, USA.

EARLE Roderick, b. 29 Jan 1952, Winchester, England. Singer (Bass-Baritone). Education: Chorister, Winchester Cathedral; St John's College, Cambridge; Royal College of Music, London; Further study with Otakar Kraus. Career: Has sung with English National Opera in Gianni Schicchi, Carmen, Aida, Force of Destiny, Tosca, Damnation of Faust; Principal Singer with Royal Opera Covent Garden, in Le nozze di Figaro, Un Ballo in Maschera, Don Giovanni, Siegfried, Götterdämmerung, Butterfly, Turandot, Elektra, Peter Grimes, Tosca, Carmen, Samson et Dalila, La Bohème; Cunning Little Vixen, Meistersinger, Fedora, Rigoletto, Hoffmann; Midsummer Marriage; Visited Japan and Korea with Royal Opera; Appearances with Opera North as Leporello and in I Puritani and Midsummer Marriage; Welsh National Opera as Fafner and Hunding in The Ring; Athens Festival as Jupiter in Castor et Pollux by Rameau; Israel Festival in Renard by Stravinsky; Buxton Festival from 1986, as Orestes in Giasone (Cavalli) and in Ariodante; Performances in Poland and Italy as Mephistopheles in Damnation de Faust; Concert engagements with Academy of St Martin in the Fields and Monteverdi Choir; Performances of Messiah in Stuttgart and Stravinsky's Les Noces in Tel Aviv; Edinburgh Festival with Scottish National Orchestra conducted by Neeme Järvi; Damnation of Faust with Orchestre de Lyon and RSNO; Beethoven, Philharmonia under Slatkin, Missa Solemnis with RAI under Bertini; Damnation of Faust with Philharmonia under Dutoit and Levine; Bach Christmas Oratorio in Denmark; Rossini Stabat Mater (Hickox), Liturgy of St John Chrysostom; Meistersinger, Boris Godunov and Samson et Dalila at Teatro Regeio; Ägyptische Helena at Garsington; Les Noces with Peter Eötvös at BBC Proms. Recordings: Dinorah (Meyerbeer); La Traviata; Il Trovatore; Maria Padilla (Donizetti); Videos of Covent Garden productions of La Fanciulla del West, Manon Lescaut, Der Rosenkavalier, Andrea Chenier, Salome, Carmen, Otello and La Traviata. Current Management: Musichall. Address: 6 Windmill Street, London W1P 1HF, England.

EARLS Paul, b. 9 June 1934, Springfield, MO, USA. Composer. m. Zeren Barutcuoglu, 13 Aug 1960, 1 son. Education: BMus, cum laude, Eastman School of Music, 1955; MM, 1956; PhD, University of Rochester, 1960. Career: Instructor, SW Missouri State, 1955-56, Duke University, 1959-60; Chairman, Music, Chabot College, 1961-62; Assistant Professor, University of Oregon, 1962-65; Associate Professor at Duke University, 1964-72, MIT, 1971-; Instructor at Massachusetts College of Art, 1972-78; Visiting Professor, University of California, 1972, University of Lowell, 1976-77, Industrial Arts, Helsinki, 1992-93. Compositions include: And On the Seventh Day, for orchestra, 1955; Flight, opera, 1964; Incidental music for The Love Suicide at Schofield Barracks, 1971; The Death of King Phillip, opera, 1975; Icarus/Ikarus, Sky opera, 1982-84; The Building of the Universe, 1983; Augenmusik, 1986; Eliotime, 1989; Mozart and Cosmology, 1991; Multi-media works (with lasers) throughout USA, Europe and Asia. Recordings: And On the Seventh Day; 2 Wedding Songs; Electronic Music of Paul Earls 1968-93, CD; Instrumental and Vocal Music of Paul Earls, CD, 1994. Contributions to: Groves Dictionary; Perspectives of New Music. Honours: Banjamin Award, 1955; Advanced Research Fulbright, 1965; Guggenheim, 1970; Two NEA Awards. Address: Senior Fellow, Centre for Advanced Visual Studies/MIT, 265 Massachusetts Avenue, Cambridge, MA 02139, USA.

EASTWOOD Thomas (Hugh), b. 12 Mar 1922, Hawley, Hampshire, England. Composer. m. Cristina Carneiro de Mendoncca Avelino, 4 Jun 1974, 2 s, 2 d. Education: Eton College, Windsor; Trinity College, Cambridge; Studied Composition with Necil Kazim Akses (Turkey), Boris Blacher (West Berlin), Erwin Stein (London). Career: Organiser, 4 Anglo-Turkish Music Festivals, British Council, Turkey, 1948-51; Director of British Council, West Berlin, 1951-54; Music Director of Save The Titian Gala Evening at London Coliseum, 1972; Artistic Director, Andover Festival, 1985, 1986; Music Director, Latin American Arts Association, organising Villa-Lobos Centenary 1986. Compositions: Operas: Christopher Sly (for English Opera Group); The Rebel (for BBC TV); The Beach of Aurora (for English National Opera); Love In A Village (new realizations for BBC Radio); Orchestral Works: Music To Celebrate; Hymm to Pan; Concerto for flute and strings; Chamber Works: Solitudes for tenor voice, guitar, flute, string quartet, Uirapura for flute or oboe and guitar; Ballade-Phantasy; Amphora; Romance for solo guitar; Song Cycles for voice and string orchestra, voice and piano; choral works; numerous other pieces for theatre, television and radio. Recordings: Ballade-Phantasy (solo guitar) 2 commercial recordings. Publications: Disasters In Concert, 1986. Contributions to: Musical Opinion; Music and Musicians; Composer; Musical times; Sleeve Notes for RCA; Virgin Classics and Decca; Twice nominated for Grammy Awards, 1972, 1973. Hobbies: Travel. Address: c/o Faber Music, 3 Queen Square, London WC1N 3AU, England.

EATHORNE Wendy, b. 25 Sept 1939, Four Lanes, Cornwall, England. Singer (Soprano); Teacher. 1 daughter. Education: Studied at the Royal Academy of Music, 1959-65; ARAM; LRAM; ARCM. Career: West End production, Robert and Elizabeth, 1965-67; Numerous concert appearances including Promenade Concerts, London; Engagements with the London Bach Choir, London Symphony Orchestra, Hallé Orchestra and other leading British orchestras; Repertoire includes works by Handel (Susanna and Belshazzar), Liszt (Missa Solemnis) and Haydn (The Creation); Appearances with Welsh National Opera, English National Opera and Royal Opera, Covent Garden; Glyndebourne, 1969-71, as Sophie in Werther, First Boy in Die Zauberflöte and Atalanta in The Rising of the Moon; Italian debut in Ariadne auf Naxos; Repertoire also includes Julia in La Vestale by Spontini and Marguerite in Faust; Festival Adjudicator; Many recitals with the pianist Geoffrey Pratley, programmes include groups of songs by Purcell to modern pieces; Head of Vocal Studies, Opera and Music Theatre at Trinity College of Music, 1989-94; Currently Senior Lecturer, Trinity College of Music. Recordings: Masses by Bach; A Village Romeo and Juliet; Monteverdi Madrigals Libro IV; A Scarlatti Clori e Zeffiro and St Cecilia Mass, Schubert Mass in A flat; Vaughan Williams The Pilgrim's Progress and Sir John in Love; Bridge, The Christmas Rose. Honours: Numerous prizes, Royal Academy of Music; Winner, Kathleen Ferrier Competition, 1965; Award, Gulbenkian Foundation, 1967; JP; Honorary FCSM; Fellow, Royal Society of Arts. Hobbies: Cooking; Dressmaking; Swimming; Gardening; Rambling. Address: 23 King Edward's Road, Ruislip, Middlesex HA4 7AQ, England.

EATON John C, b. 30 Mar 1935, Bryn Mawr, USA. Composer. m. Nelda Nelson, 31 May 1973, 1 s, 1 d. Education: AB, MFA, Princeton University. Career: Concerts: Columbia Artists in USA, Hamburg Opera, Maggio Musicale, Venice Festival, Los Angeles Philharmonic, Tanglewood, many more; Operas performed: The Tempest, 1985; The Cry of Clytaemnestra, 1980; Danton and Robespierre; The Lion and Androcles; Myshkin; Herakles. Compositions: The Tempest; The Cry of Clytaemnestra; Danton and Robespierre; The Lion and Androcles; Myshkin; Herakles; 2 Symphonies; Duo, mixed chorus; Mass; Blind Man's Cry; Concert Music for Solo Clarinet; Piano Variations; Microtonal Fantasy; Piano Trio; Concert Piece. Recordings: Danton and Robespierre; The Music of John Eaton; Microtonal Fantasy; Electro Vibrations. Publications: New Music Since 1950, 1974. His work was reviewed in, Time; New Yorker; London Financial Times; New York Times; High Fidelity; Opera News. Honours: include, Priz de Rome, 1959-61; Guggenheim, 1962, 1965; Fromm Commission, 1966; Koussevitzky Commission, 1970; Citation, NIAL, 1972; Composer in Residence, AAR, 1975; PBC Commission, 1970; Peabody Award, 1973; National Music Theater Award, 1988; MacArthur Fellow, 1990. Address: ASCAP, ASCAP House, One Lincoln Plaza, New York, USA.

EBBECKE Michael, b. 8 Dec 1955, Wiesbaden, Germany. Singer (Baritone). Education: Studied at the Richard Strauss Conservatory Munich and with Josef Metternich in Cologne. Debut: Stuttgart 1982, as Mozart's Figaro. Career: Member of the Stuttgart Staatsoper from 1982, notably as Belcore, Giulio Cesare, Eugene Onegin, Silvio, and Don Fernando in Fidelio; Guest appearances at the Berlin Komische Oper (Guglielmo, 1984) and Deutsche Oper (Orestes in Iphigénie en Tauride, 1988); Appearances at Karlsruhe, Paris, Lyon (Wolfram in Tannhäuser) and La Scala Milan (Scherasmin in Oberon, 1989); Sang Stolzius in Die Soldaten at Stuttgart, 1987, Papageno and Escamillo in Season, 1990-91, Guglielmo, 1991-92; Concert engagements include Bach's St John Passion at Amsterdam, 1987. Recordings: include, Die Soldaten. Address: c/o Stuttgart Staatsoper, Oberer Schlossgarten 6, 700 Stuttgart, Germany.

EBEL Gudrun, b. 1948, Hamburg, Germany. Singer (Soprano). Education: Studied with Fred Husler in Lugano and Erna Berger in Hamburg. Career: Sang at first in Coburg, Bielfeld and Nuremberg; Guest appearances in Dusseldorf, Berlin, Vienna, Munich and Hamburg; Cologne 1982, as Aennchen in Der Freischütz; Other roles include Mozart's Blondchen, Queen of Night and Zerlina; Zerbinetta and Sophie; Carlotta in Il Matrimonio Segreto; Lucia di Lammermoor and Gilda; Frau Fluth in Die Lustigen Weiber von Windsor; Many concert appearances. Recordings: include, Die Entführung aus dem Serail (Eurodisc). Address: c/o Oper der Stadt Köln, Offenbachplatz, D-5000 Cologne, Germany.

EBEN Petr, b. 22 Jan 1929, Zamberk, Czechoslovakia. Composer; Pianist; Lecturer. m. Sarka Hurnikova-Ebenova, 3 children. Education: Academy of Music, Prague. Debut: Pianist, Prague 1952; Composer, Concerto for organ and orchestra, Prague, 1954. Career: Music Director, TV, Prague, 1954; Lecturer, Institute for Musicology, Charles University, Prague, 1955-. Compositions: include, Sunday Music for Organ; Concerto, piano and orchestra; Apologia Sokratus, oratoria; Vox Clamantis, orchestra; Maidens and Swallows, female choir; Unkind Songs; Vespers, choir and organ; Pragensia; Greek Dictionary, cycle, female choir and harp; Nachtstunden (Night Hours), symphony, wind quintet and chamber orchestra; Faust, organ; Windows After Chagall, trumpet and organ; Mutationes, commissioned, Cardiff Festival; String Quartet; II Concerto, organ and Orchestra, commissioned, ORF, Vienna; Ballet, Curses and Blessings, commissioned, Nederlands Dans Theater; Prague Nocturne, orchestra; Tabulatura nova, guitar; Cantata, In Honorem Caroli, men's choir and orchestra. Recordings: Most compositions recorded, plus: Missa Adventus; Vespers. Publication: Cteni a hra partitur, co-author. Contributions to: Various journals. Honours: 1st prize, Gold Medal, 6 love songs, Moscow, 1957; 1st prize, The Lovers Magic Spell, cantata, Jihlava Vocal Festival, 1959; 1st prize, 10 children's duets, Jirkov, 1966; 2 prizes, Laudes, Kassel, 1965. Memberships: Union of Composers, Prague; Chairman,

Creative Section, Czechoslovakian Music Society. Current Management: Pragokoncert, Prague 1. Address: Union of Czech Composers, Prague 5, Czech Republic.

EBERHARDT Cornelius, b. 3 Jan 1932, Oberaudorf, Germany. Conductor. m. Ursula Schade, 7 Aug 1957, 1 daughter. Education: Universities of Munich and Hamburg, 1950-53; State Academy of Music, Munich, 1953-56; Accademia Chigiana, Siena, Italy, 1958. Career: Chorus Master of Municipal Opera, Ulm, Germany, 1956-60; Associate Conductor, Munich State Theatre, 1960-69; Music Director, Regensburg Symphony and Opera, 1969-77; Founder of Regensburg Music School; Co-Founder of Bavarian Festival of Modern Composers, 1973; Music Director of Corpus Christi Symphony, TX, USA, 1975-; Professor of Opera and Conductor, State Academy of Music, Munich, Germany, 1977-; Music Director of American Institute of Musical Studies, Dallas, TX, 1978-; Visiting Professor, 1979-80, Professor and Music Director, 1984-87, University of Texas, Austin; Visiting Professor, Corpus Christi State University, 1981-82; Guest Conductor in Europe and North and South America; Music Director, Mozart Festival International, 1991; President, State Academy of Music, 1991-95; Principal Guest Conductor, Munich Symphony, 1996-. Publications: Das Regensburger Orchester, 1972; Der Dirigent in Handbuch der Musikberufe, 1987; Volksmusik und Kunstmusik in Südosteuropa, 1988. Honour: Order of Merit, Federal Republic of Germany, 1996. Hobbies: Astronomy; History of Art. Address: Darmstaedterstrasse 11-7, D-80992 Munich, Germany.

EBERS Clara, b. 26 Dec 1902, Karlsruhe, Germany. Singer (Soprano). Education: Studied with Eduard Erhard in Karlsruhe. Career: Sang at Karlsruhe, Mönchengladbach, and Dusseldorf, 1924-28; Frankfurt Opera, 1928-44, notably as Olympia and Sophie and in the premieres of Carmina Burana, 1937 and Egk's Columbus, 1942; Guest appearances with the Frankfurt Company, 1938-41, in Bucharest, Sofia, Athens, Belgrade, Zagreb and Barcelona; Sang at Hamburg, 1945-65; Glyndebourne, 1950, as Mozart's Countess; Guest engagements in Milan, Berlin, Brussels and Munich; Other roles included Violetta, Rosina, Zerbinetta, Fiordiligi, the Marschallin and Elisabeth de Valois. Recordings include: Soprano solo in Ein Deutsches Requiem by Brahms.

EBERT Peter, b. 6 Apr 1918, Frankfurt, Germany. Director and Administrator. m. Silvia Ashmole, 10 Mar 1951, 5 s, 5 d. Education: Salem School, Germany; Gordonstoun School, Scotland. Career: Directed about 100 different operas in many countries and venues including international festivals; Taught at Academies of Music in Germany, Canada and Scotland; Directed many television opera from theatres and in studios; Administrator and Executive Director of theatres in Germany and Scotland, Director of Productions, Scottish Opera, 1965-75; General Administrator, 1977-80; University Lecturer. Contributions to: Numerous publications. Honour: Honorary Doctorate of Music, St Andrew's University, Scotland, 1979. Hobbies: Travel; Family. Address: c/o Scottish Opera, 39 Elmbank Crescent, Glasgow G2 APT, Scotland.

EBRAHIM Omar, b. 6 Sept 1956, England. Singer (Baritone). Education: Studied at the Guildhall School of Music, London. Career: Appearances with the Opera Factory in Punch and Judy, The Beggar's Opera, The Knot Garden, and La Calisto; Sang in the premieres of Birtwistle's Yan Tan Tethera, South Bank, 1986 and Nigel Osborne's The Electrification of the Soviet Union, Glyndebourne, 1986; Glyndebourne Touring Opera in Il Barbiere di Siviglia and La Bohème; Has sung Hector in King Priam for Kent Opera; With Scottish Opera has appeared in Mahoganny, Die Fledermaus and Iolanthe; Covent Garden, 1989, in the British premiere of Un Re in Ascolto by Berio; Sang Don Giovanni with Opera Factory at the Elizabeth Hall, 1990, Parkhearst in the premiere of Böse's 63: Dream Palace at the 1990 Munich Biennale; The Fool in the premiere of Birtwistle's Gawain, Covent Garden, May 1991; Sang the Voice of Goya in the premiere of Osborne's Terrible Mouth, Almeida Festival, 1992; Created Vermeer in Birtwistle's The Second Mrs Kong, Glyndebourne, 1994; Sang Horace Tabor in the British premiere of Moore's The Ballad of Baby Doe, Bloomsbury Theatre, 1996; Television appearances include Yan Tan Tethera, The Kiss of Michael Nyman and the title role in a BBC version of Marschner's Vampyr, 1992; Concert repertoire includes Morton Feldman/Beckett Words and Music, Aventures, Nouvelles Aventures (Ligeti), Enoch Arden (Strauss) and Ode to Napoleon Bonaparte (Schoenberg). Address: c/o Allied Artists, 42 Montpelier Square, London SW7 1JZ, England.

ECHOLS Paul (Clinton), b. 13 Feb 1944, Santa Monica, California, USA. Opera Director; Musicologist; Editor. Education: BA, Magna Cum Laude, Duke University, Durham, North Carolina, USA, 1966; MA, Musicology, New York University, 1968. Career: Deputy Chairman, 1971-75, Assistant Professor of Music, 1971-75, Department of Music, Brooklyn College, New York; Editorial Coordinator, The Charles Ives Society, 1976-82; International Director, Concert Music Division, Peer Southern Music Publishers, New York, 1982-85; Director, Historical Performance Programme, 1980-84; Director, Opera Program, 1988-, The Mannes College of Music, New York; Vice-President and Director of Publishing, G Schirmer/Associated Music Publishers Inc. New York, 1986-87; Editor, Historical Performance; The Journal of Early Music America, 1987-. Publications: Numerous Articles for scholarly journals and other publications including New Grove Dictionary of Music in America; Numerous editions of music including Renaissance and Baroque Choral Music and The Orchestral Works of Charles E Ives. Memberships: Board of Directors, The Charles Ives Society, Inc; Early Music America, Inc; American Musicological Society; Sonneck Society, and others. Address: The Mannes College of Music, 150 West 85th Street, New York, NY 10024, USA.

ECKHARDT Mária, b. 26 Sept 1943, Budapest, Hungary. Musicologist; Choral Conductor. Education: Diploma, Liszt Ferenc Academy of Music, Budapest, 1966. Career: Librarian and Research Worker, Music Department, National Széchényi Library, Budapest, 1966-73; Research Worker, Institute of Musicology, Hungarian Academy of Sciences, Budapest, 1973-87; Director, Liszt Ferenc Memorial Museum and Research Centre at Liszt Academy of Music, Budapest, 1986-. Publications: Franz Liszt und sein Kreis in Briefen und Dokumenten aus den Beständen des Burgenländischen Landesmuseums, with Cornelia Knotik, 1983; Liszt Ferenc Memorial Museum Catalogue, 1986; Franz Liszt's Estate at the Budapest Academy of Music, 1, Books, 1986; Franz Liszt's Music Manuscripts in the National Széchényi Library, 1986; Liszt Ferenc válogatott levelei 1824-1861, (selected letters 1824-1861), Budapest, 1989; Franz Liszt's Estate at the Budapest Academy of Music, II, Music, 1993. Contributions to: Studies on Liszt in: Studia Musicologica, Magyar Zene, The New Hungarian Quarterly, Journal of The American Liszt Society, Muzsika and others. Honours: Award of Excellence, American Liszt Society, 1985; Erkel Prize, 1987. Address: Ruszti ut 11, H-1022 Budapest, Hungary.

ECKHART Janis (Gail), b. 21 July 1953, CA, USA. Mezzo Soprano, Opera Singer. m. Harry Dworchak, 1990. Education: BA, magna cum laude, 1973, Sec Teaching Credential, 1974, University of California, Los Angeles; Academia Real de Musica, Madrid, Spain, 1974; Phi Beta Kappa. Debut: New York City Opera, 1981. Career includes: Numerous roles at New York City Opera including: Nabucco, 1981, Rigoletto, 1981, 1984, 1988 and 1989, Carmen, 1986 and 1988; In Rigoletto at Opera de Monte Carlo, 1983, and Aida, Opera Delaware, 1984; Sang in Il Trovatore, 1986, and in Un Ballo in Maschera, 1986, both at National Grand Opera; Carmen, Seattle Opera, 1982; Samson et Dalila, National Philharmonic of the Philippines, 1980; Les Contes D'Hoffmann at the Opera Metropolitana, Caracas, 1981; Nabucco, Teatro de Opera, Puerto Rico, 1988; Rigoletto, Opera Carolina, 1990; Carmen, Metro Lyric Opera, 1992; Carmen, Cairo Opera, Egypt, 1992; Concerts: Mahler's Kindertotenlieder and Songs of a Wayfarer, Nashville Symphony, Verdi's Requiem, Plymouth Church of the Pilgrims; Concert tour, Instituto Technológico de México, 1992; Kismet, Tapei Symphony, 1993; Ambassadors of Opera, Far East Concert Tour, 1993; Mid East Concert Tour, 1993; Cavalleria Rusticana, Hong Kong, 1994; Carmen, Madrid, Lisbon, 1995. Current Management: USA: Cameron Artists International; Europe: Albrecht Klora, International Concert Bureau Ariën, Belgium; Bontempi Music Management, Mark Holmes, Berlin, Germany. Address: 15 West 72nd Street, New York, NY 10023, USA.

ECKSTEIN Pavel, b. 27 Apr 1911. Opava, Czechoslovakia. Music Writer; Critic; Commentator; Organiser. m. Anna Gerberova, 1 daughter. Education: PhD, Prague University. Career: Music Critic; Lecturer, Germany, Holland, England, USSR, Australia, USA; General Secretary, International Musical Festival, Prague, Spring, 1948-52; Secretary, Czechoslovakian Composers Guild, 1952-71; Artistic Adviser, National Theatre, Prague, 1969-92; Chief Drama, State Opera, Prague, 1992-95; Member of the Board, Czech Music Council, 1993. Publications: David Oistrakh, 1959; Czechoslovak Opera, 1964; Czechoslovak Contemporary Opera, 1967. Contributions to: Encyclopaedias and Journals in Czechoslovakia, England, USA, Canada, Germany, Denmark, USSR. Hobbies: Reading; Theatre; Rambling. Address: Srobarova 23, 130 00 Prague, Czech Republic.

EDA-PIERRE Christiane, b. 24 Mar 1932, Fort de France, Martinique. Singer (Soprano). m. Pierre Lacaze. Education: Studied at the Paris Conservatoire. Debut: Nice 1958, as Leila in Les pêcheurs de Perles. Career: Aix-en-Provence, 1959, as Pamina in Die Zauberflöte; Opéra-Comique, Paris, 1961, as Lakmé; Paris Opéra from, 1962, as Lucia di Lammermoor, Constanze and in Milhaud's Médée and Rameau's Dardanus, 1980; Covent Garden, 1966, as Teresa in Benvenuto Cellini; Wexford Festival, 1976, as Imogene in Il Pirata; Metropolitan Opera with Paris Opéra Company, 1976, as Mozart's Countess; returned to New York from 1980 as Constanze, Antonio in Les Contes d'Hoffmann and Gilda; Guest appearances in Strasbourg, Lyons, Amsterdam, Barcelona, Chicago, Miami, Brussels (Vitellia in La Clemenza de Tito) and Moscow; Other roles include the Queen of Night and Zerbinetta; Sang in the premieres of D'Une Espace Deployé by Gilbert Amy (1973) and Erzsebet by Charles Chaynes (Paris Opéra 1983); Created the Angel in the premiere of Messiaen's François d'Assise, Palais Garnier Paris, 1983; Professor at the Paris Conservatiore from 1977. Recordings: include, Benvenuto Cellini, conducted by Colin Davis (Philips); Hero in Béatrice et Bénédict; Die Entführung; Arias by Grétry and Philidor; Dardanus (Erato). Address: c/o Conservatoire National, 14 Rue de Madrid, 75008 Paris, France.

EDDY Jenifer, b. 1933, Melbourne, Australia. Singer (Coloratura Soprano). Education: Studied in Melbourne with Henri Portnoj and in London with Bertha Nicklauss Kempner and Roy Henderson. Career: Frequent Guest Soloist with Australian Broadcasting Corporation in Concerts, Studio Broadcasts and on Television and Major Choral Groups, 1953-58; Elizabethan Opera Company, 1956-57 as Mozart's Susanna, Despina, Papagena and as Polly Peachum, Beggar's Opera; Covent Garden, 1959-69, roles including Xenia (Boris Godunov), Amor (Gluck's Orpheus), Fiakermilli (Arabella), Olympia (Tales of Hoffmann), Sophie (Der Rosenkavalier), Tytania (A Midsummer Night's Dream); Guest appearances with Sadler's Wells Opera, English National Opera, Welsh National Opera, Scottish Opera, English Opera Group, Bordeaux Opera, Maggio Musicale, Edinburgh, Leeds, Bath and Schwetzingen Festivals; Roles include, Despina, Rosina, Norina, Blondchen, Madame Herz (The Impressario), Musetta, Zerbinetta, Adele (Die Fledermaus); Appearances for BBC on radio, television and in concert; Managing Director, Jenifer Eddy Artists' Management, Melbourne, 1975-; Director, Lies Askonas Ltd, London, 1982-. Recordings include: Die Entführung, Gypsy Baron, Hansel and Gretel. Honour: Medal, Order of Australia, 1997. Address: Jenifer Eddy Artists' Management, Suite 11, The Clivedon, 596 St Kilda Road, Melbourne 3004, Victoria, Australia.

EDDY Timothy, b. USA. Violoncellist. Education: Studied with Bernard Greenhouse. Career: Duo recitals with pianist Gilbert Kalish and soloist with orchestras at Denver, Dallas, and the Maggio Musicale, Florence; Concerts with the Bach Aria Group and festival engagements at Santa Fe, Marlboro, Florida and at SUNY Stony Brook; Cellist with the Orion String Quartet, including appearances throughout the USA and at the Wigmore Hall, London; Further European appearances at the Lockenhaus and Turku (Finland) Festivals; Collaborations with Rudolf Serkin, Pablo Casals, and members of the Vegh, Budapest and Guarneri Quartets; Professor of Cello at SUNY, Stony Brook. Recordings: Albums with Columbia, Angel Vox, Vanguard, Nonesuch, New World and Delos. Address: Orion String Quartet, Ingpen & Williams Ltd, 14 Kensington Court, London W8 5DN, England.

EDELMANN Otto (Karl), b. 5 Feb 1917, Vienna, Austria. Opera Singer (Bass) m. Isle-Marie Straub, 1960, 2 s, 1 d. Education: Realgymnasium and State Academy of Music, Vienna. Debut: Opera Appearances, 1938. Career: POW in USSR for 2 years during 2nd World War; Member, Vienna State Opera, 1948-; with Saltburg Festival, 1948, sang Baron Ochs (Rosenkavalier) in first opera performance in the Festspielhaus 1960 (also filmed); Permanent Member, Metropolitan Opera, New York, 1954-; Took part in first post-war Bayreuth Festival, 1951; World famous as Sachs in Die Meistersinger; also well known as Mozart's Leporello, Beethoven's Rocco and Wagner's Amfortas and Gurnemanz. Honours: Knight, Order of Dannenbrog; Austrian Gold Cross of Honour for Sciences and Arts. Hobbies: Painting; Boxing. Address: Wien-Kalksburg 1238, Breitenfurterstrasse 547, Austria.

EDELMANN Peter, b. 1962, Vienna, Austria. Singer (Baritone). Education: Studied with his father (Otto) and at the Vienna Musikhochschule. Career: Sang Mozart's Figaro on tour in Europe; Member of the Koblenz Opera from 1985, notably in the title role at the premiere of Odysseus by Klaus Arp, 1989; Guest appearances in Mannheim, Dortmund, Wuppertal and Krefeld, as Mozart's Don Giovanni and Guglielmo, Marcello, the Forester in Cunning Little Vixen, Rossini's Figaro, Posa and Lord Tristan in Martha; Lieder recitals and concerts in Vienna, Budapest, Salzburg and Wexford; Member of the Deutsche Oper Berlin from 1990 (Papageno 1991); Sang in the premiere of Desdemona und ihre Schwestern by Siegfried Matthus, Schwetzingen 1991; Theseus in Enescu's Oedipe, Berlin, 1996. Honours: Winner, 1989 Belvedere Competitions, Vienna. Address: c/o Robert Gilder and Company, Enterprise House, 59-65 Upper Ground, London SE1 9PQ, England.

EDELMANN Sergei, b. 22 Jul 1960, Lvov, Russia. Pianist. Education: Studied with father, Head Piano Department, Lvov Conservatory; Studied with Rudolf Firkusny, Juilliard School, New York, 1979 with Claude Frank, Aspen (Colorado) Music School. Debut: First public appearance as soloist, Beethoven Piano Concerto No 1 with Lvov Philharmonic Orchestra, 1970. Career: More than 50 concerts throughout the Soviet Union; Toured widely in Europe and North America as soloist with leading orchestras and as a Recitalist. Recordings: For RCA. Honour: Gina Bachauer Memorial Scholarship Award, 1979. Address: c/o Shaw Concerts Inc, 1900 Broadway, New York, NY 10023, USA.

EDEN Danielle, b. 17 Sept 1964, Sydney, Australia. Piccoloist; Flautist. Education: BMus from the Sydney Conservatorium; Advanced Performers Course at the Royal Academy of Music; MMus from London University; Currently completing a Doctorate at London University; Studied flute with Sebastian Bell and piccolo with Francis Nolan. Career: Toured the USA with Sydney Conservatorium Symphony Orchestra; Past member of the Australian Youth Orchestra; Performances with the Australian Chamber Orchestra, BBC Welsh Symphony Orchestra, Glynbourne Touring Opera and D'Oyly Carte Opera; Presented the first solo piccolo recital at London's South Bank Center, 1993, including World premiere of Sarab by Malcolm Hill and UK premiere of Piccolo Play by Thea Musgrave; Tutor Piccolo!, Piccolo!, 1994; Repertoire includes compositions by Donatoni, Ferneyhough, Persichetti, Musgrave, Damaré, Harrington-Young and Vivaldi. Current Management: Morgenstern's UK.

EDER Helmut, b. 26 Dec 1916, Linz, Austria. Composer; Teacher. Education: Linz Conservatory; Training in composition from Hindemith in Salzburg, 1947, Orff in Munich, 1953-54, J N David in Stuttgart, 1954. Career: Teacher, Linz Conservatory, 1950-, co-founding its electronic music studio, 1959; Teacher, Salzburg Mozarteum, 1967, now Emeritus Professor Composer. Compositions: Operas: Oedipus, 1958; Der Kardinal, 1962; Die weisse Frau, 1968; Konjugationen 3, 1969; Der Aufstand, 1975; Georges Dandin oder Der betrogne Ehemann, 1978-79; Mozart in New York, 3-act opera, Salzburg Festival, 1991; Ballets: Moderner Traum, 1957; Anamorphose, 1963; Die Irrfahrten des Odysseus, 1964-65; Orchestral: Symphony No 1, 1950, No 2, 1962, No 3, 1969, No 4, Choral Symphony, 1973-75, No 5, Organ Symphony, 1979-80; Musica semplice, flute, harpsichord, strings, 1953; Music for 2 Trumpets and Strings, 1955; Concerto for piano, 15 wind instruments, double basses, percussion, 1956; Pezzo Sereno, 1958; Concerto semiserio, 2 pianos and orchestra, 1960; Oboe Concerto, 1962; 2 Violin Concertos, 1963, 1964; Danza a solatio, 1963; Concerto a dodici per archi, 1963; Nil admirari, 1966; Syntagma, 1967; Concerto for bassoon and chamber orchestra, 1968; L'Homme arme, concerto for organ and orchestra, 1968-69; Metamorphosen, flute, oboe, string quartet, orchestra, 1970; Melodia-ritmica, strings, 1973; Pastorale, strings, 1974; Divertimento, soprano, orchestral group, 1976; Jubilato, chamber orchestra , 1976; Serenade, 6 horns, 46 strings, 1977; Double Concerto, cello, double bass, orchestra, 1977-78; Cello Concerto, 1981; Concerto No 3, violin and orchestra, 1981-82; Concerto A B, chamber orchestra, 1982; Notturno, flute, oboe, strings, 1983, revised, 1984; Haffner Concerto, flute and orchestra, 1984; Concertino, classical orchestra, 1984; Pièce de concert, strings, 1984; Duetto-Concerto, 2 flutes and orchestra, op 95; Chamber: String Quartet, 1948; Szene for 6 horns, 1977; Suite with Intermezzo for 11 winds, 1979; Quintet, clarinet, 2 violins, viola, cello, 1982; Quartet, flute, string trio, 1983; String Quartet No 4, op 94; Piano pieces; Organ music; Choral works. Recordings: Numerous. Honours: Several prizes; Various commissions. Memberships: Programme Organiser, International Stiftung Mozarteum; Rotary Club, Salzburg-Nord. Address: c/o Hochschule für Musik und darstellende Kunst, Mozarteum, Schwarzstrasse 26, A-5020 Salzburg, Austria.

EDGAR-WILSON Richard, b. 1963, Ipswich, Suffolk, England. Singer (Tenor). Education: Studied at Christ's College, Cambridge (choral exhibition); The Royal College of Music with Edward Brooks. Career: Opera includes: Albert Herring, Tamino (Magic Flute), Quint (Turn of the Srew), Beauty (The Triumph of Beauty and Deceit, Gerald Barry, C4 TV); Concert repertoire includes Messiah, Bach's B minor Mass, the Monteverdi Vespers, Mozart's Coronation and C minor Masses and Carissimi's Jephtha; Works by Kodály, Stainer, Vaughan Williams, Berio and Britten; Solo appearances all over England and North America, France, Norway and Germany; Operatic roles include Handel's Acis and The Mad Woman in Britten's Curlew River; Work with conductors, Trevor Pinnock, Richard Hickox, Charles Mackerras, Robert King. Recordings: Purcell's Dioclesian, Pinnock; Stradella, San Giovanni Battista, Minkowski (winner Gramophone Award 1993); Schubert, Die Schöne Müllerin. Current Management: Ron Gonsalves Management. Address: 7 Old Town, Clapham, London SW4 0JT, England.

EDLUND Mikael, b. 19 Jan 1950, Tranås, Sweden. Composer. 1 daughter. Education: Musicology, University of Uppsala, 1970-72; Composition with I Lidholm and A Mallnäs, State College of Music, Stockholm, 1972-75. Career: Producer at Fylkingen, Stockholm, 1979; Teacher in Composition, State College of Music, Gothenburg, 1985-87. Compositions: The Lost Jugglery for mezzo-soprano, cello, piano and 2 percussionists, 1974-77; Trio Sun for clarinet, bassoon and piano, 1980; Leaves for 8 female voices, acoustic piano, electric piano, harp and 7 percussionists, 1977-81; Brains and Dancin' for string quartet, 1981; Fantasia on a City for piano, 1981-86; Jord for 5 percussionists, 1982; Små Fötter, a miniature for guitar, 1982; Music for double wind quintet, 1984; Orchids in the embers for piano, 1984; Ajar for orchestra, 1988-91; Blue Garden for piano trio; Dissolved Window for 21 strings, in progress. Recordings: Brains and Dancin'; Trio Sun; Orchids in the embers; Små Fötter; Leaves; Fantasia on a city. Honours: Christ Johnson, 1985. Memberships: Society of Swedish Composers; Swedish Performing Rights Society; International Society for Contemporary Music, Swedish Section; Fylkingen. Address: Backvägen 2, S-19145 Sollentuna, Sweden.

EDWARDS George (Harrison), b. 11 May 1943, Boston, Massachusetts, USA. Composer. m. Rachel Hadas, 22 July 1978. Education: BA, Oberlin College, 1965; MFA, Princeton University, 1967. Career: Theory Faculty, New England Conservatory of Music, 1968-76; Assistant Professor of Music, 1976-86, Associate Professor of Music, 1986-93, Professor, 1993, Columbia University. Compositions: String Quartet, 1967; Kreuz und Quer, 1971; Monopoly, 1972; Giro, 1974; Exchange-Misere, 1974; Draconian Measures, 1976; Gyromancy, 1977; Veined Variety, 1978; Northern Spy, 1980; String Quartet 2, 1982; Moneta's Mourn, 1983; Suave Mari Magno, 1984; A Mirth but Open'd, 1986. Recordings. Various. Hobbies: Tennis; Chess, Address: 838 West End Avenue, Apt 3A, New York, NY 10025, USA.

EDWARDS Joan, b. 1944, London, England. Singer (Mezzo-soprano). Education: Studied at the London Opera Centre. Debut: Schwertleite in Die Walküre at Covent Garden. Career: Sang with the English Opera Group in Britain and abroad, often with Benjamin Britten conducting; Opera North from 1978 as Marcellina in Le nozze di Figaro, Third Lady (Magic Flute), Mother in Hansel and Gretel, Juno and Minerva in Orpheus in the Underworld, Berta in Il Barbiere di Siviglia and Mary in The Flying Dutchman; Many concert performances; Appeared on BBC TV in La Traviata. Address: Norman McCann International Artists Ltd, The Coach House, Lawrie Park Gardens, London SE26 6XJ, England.

EDWARDS Owain Tudor, b. 10 Nov 1940, Ruabon, Wales. Musicologist. m. Grete Strand, 1965, 1 son, 2 daughters. Education: BMus, 1962, MMus, 1964, PhD, 1967, University of North Wales, Bangor. Career: Assistant Lecturer, 1965, Lecturer, 1967, Music Department, University College of Wales, Aberystwyth; Lecturer in Music, Open University, 1970; Lecturer in Music, Liverpool University, 1973; Reader and Head of Music History, 1974, Professor, 1985-, Norges Musikkhøgskole, Oslo, Norway; Organist, Kroer Church, 1980-. Compositions: Adventsgudstjeneste, 1986; 155 orgelsatser til gudstjeneste bruk, 1992; Processional Music for brass, 1995. Publications: Joseph Parry 1841-1903, 1970; Beethoven, 1972; People, Instruments and the Continuo, 1974; Suite, Sonata and Concerto, 1974; Matins, Lauds and Vespers for St David's Day, 1990; The Penpont Antiphonal, 1997. Contributions to: New Grove Dictionary of Music and Musicians; The Music Review; The Musical Quarterly; Proceedings of the Royal Musical Association; Revue Bénédictine; Cantus Planus; Studia Musicologica Norvegica. Membership: Norwegian Academy of Science and Letters, 1993. Hobbies: Fishing; Golf; Skiing. Address: Norges Musikkhogskole, Gydasv 6, Postboks 5190, Majorstua, 0302 Oslo 3, Norway.

EDWARDS Ross, b. 23 Dec 1943, Sydney, New South Wales, Australia. Composer. m. Helen Hopkins, 7 Aug 1974, 1 son, 1 daughter. Education: New South Wales State Conservatory of Music, University of Sydney; MMus, University of Adelaide, 1970. Career: International Society of Contemporary Music Festivals, Stockholm, 1966, Basel, 1970. Compositions: Sonata for 9 instruments; Quem Quaeritis, children's nativity play, 1967; Etude for Orchestra, 1969; Monos I, cello solo, II, piano solo, 1970; Mountain Village in a Clearing Mist for orchestra; Antifon for voices, brass ensemble, organ and percussion; 5 Little Piano Pieces; The Tower of Remoteness; Concerto for Piano and Orchestra; Christina's world, chamber opera; Shadow D-Zone, 1977;The Hermit of Green Light, 1979; Ab Estasis Foribus, 1980; Maninya I, 1981, II for string quartet, III, 1985, IV, 1985-86, V, 1986; Kumari, solo piano; Laikan I and II; Ten Little Duets, 1982; Marimba Dances, 1982; Etymalong, 1984; Reflections, 1985; Flower Songs, 1986; Maninyas for violin and orchestra, 1988; Varrageh for solo percussion and orchestra, 1989; Aria and Transcendental Dance for horn and string orchestra, 1990. Contributor to: Music Now; Australian Contemporary Music Quarterly. Memberships: Numerous professional organisations. Hobbies: Prospecting; Mountaineering. Address: 2 Diamond Road, Pearl Beach 2256, New South Wales, Australia.

EDWARDS Sian, b. 27 May 1959, West Chittington, Sussex, England. Conductor. Education: Studied at the Royal Northern College of Music and with Charles Groves, Norman Del Mar and Neeme Järvi; Further study with Ilya Alexandrovitch Musin at the Leningrad Conservatoire, 1983-85. Career: Concert engagements with the London Philharmonic, Royal Philharmonic, London Sinfonietta, Scottish National Orchestra, City of Birmingham Symphony, Hallé, BBC Philharmonic, BBC Scottish Symphony and the Royal Liverpool Philharmonic; Opera debut with Scottish Opera, 1986, Mahagonny by Weill; Glyndebourne Festival, 1987, La Traviata, L'Heure Espagnole and L'Enfant et les Sortilèges; Katya Kabanova with Glyndebourne Touring Opera, 1988; Covent Garden, 1988, as the first woman to conduct opera there (The Knot Garden by Tippett); Conducted the world premiere of Greek by Mark Anthony Turnage at the 1988 Munich Biennale (repeated at the Edinburgh Festival); Season 1989-90 included concerts with the London Philharmonic and the BBC Symphony at the Festival Hall; Rigoletto at Covent Garden; French debut with the Orchestre de Paris and US concerts with the San Francisco Symphony; The Gambler by Prokofiev for English National Opera; Conducted Il Trovatore at Covent Garden, 1990, Carmen, 1991; Music Director of English National Opera, 1993-95; Led the Docklands Sinfonietta in London Proms debut, 1993, with music by Britten, Dallapiccola and Mozart (K551). Honours include: British Council Scholarship, 1983; Winner, Leeds Conductors' Competition, 1984. Address: c/o Ingpen & Williams Ltd, 14 Kensington Court, London W8 5DN, England.

EDWARDS Terry, b. 1939, London, England. Choral Director. Career: Has formed and directed such groups as London Sinfonietta Voices, Electric Phoenix and London Voices; Concerts and recordings with radio choirs, choral societies and choruses the world over; Season 1988 with the BBC Singers and Choral Society at the Festival Hall, Bach's B minor Mass at Glasgow; Concerts with the London Sinfonietta in the Prom Concerts and festival appearances in Berlin, Geneva and Turin; Chorus Master for Georg Solti in three Verdi concerts in Chicago; Directed the chorus at the Michael Vyner Memorial at Covent Garden, 1990; Chorus Director at the Royal Opera House, Covent Garden, 1992-; Concerts with the Danish Radio Choir, 1991 and works by Erik Bergmann in Finland; Directed Sinfonietta Voices in Stockhausen's Stimmung at the Qiieen Elizabeth Hall, 1997. Recordings include: Messiaen Cinq Rechants, Rachmaninov and Tchaikovsky Vespers, A Boy was Born by Britten (Virgin Classics); Verdi Choruses and Otello (Decca). Address: c/o Royal Opera House, Covent Garden, London WC2, England.

EDWARDS Warwick (Anthony), b. 22 Apr 1944, Dewsbury, England. University Lecturer; Performer on Early Instruments. m. Jacqueline Freeman, 2 daughters. Education: King's College, University of Cambridge; MA; BMus; PhD. Career: Lecturer, 1971-, Senior Lecturer, 1986-, Glasgow University; Director, Scottish Early Music Consort, 1976-; Director, Glasgow International Early Music Festival, 1990-. Recordings: Mary's Music: Songs and Dances from the time of Mary Queen of Scots, Scottish Early Music Consort, W Edwards Director, 1984. Publications: Editor: Music for Mixed Consort (Musica Britannica 40), 1977; W Byrd: Latin Motets (from manuscript scores) (The Byrd Edition 8), 1984. Contributions to: Grove's Dictionary, 6th edition; Music and Letters; Proceedings of the Royal Music Association; Early Music; The Consort; British Book News. Hobby: Hill walking. Address: 22 Falkland Street, Glasgow G12 9PR, Scotland.

EENSALU Marika, b. 20 Sept 1947, Tallinn, Estonia. Singer (Mezzo-soprano). Education: Studied at Tallinn and with Irina Arkhipova in Moscow. Career: Sang at the Estonia Theatre, Tallinn, from 1980, as Rosina, Carmen, Dorabella, Bradamante in Alcina, Marfa and Ulrica; Savonlinna Festival, 1987, with guest appearances in Moscow and throughout Germany, Denmark and Hungary; Concert engagements in works by Estonian composers. Address: c/o Estonian State Opera, Estonian Boulevard, 200001 Tallinn, Estonia.

EEROLA Aulikki, b. 1947, Tuusula, Finland. Singer (Soprano). Education: Studied at the Sibelius Academy, Helsinki, and with Hilde Zadek and Erik Werba in Vienna. Debut: Sang in concert at Helsinki, 1975. Career: Savonlinna Festival, 1977, as Pamina in Die Zauberflöte, and has appeared widely in Germany, Austria, England, France and North America as concert soloist. Address: c/o Finnish National Opera, Bulevardi 23-27. SF-00180 Helsinki 18, Finland.

EEROLA Lasse Olavi, b. 24 September 1945, Kuusankoski, Finland. Composer; Music Teacher. m. Päivi Irmeli, 27 August 1983, 2 sons. Education: Sibelius Academy, Helsinki, Finland, 1970-77. Career: Clarinet and Saxophone Player, 1967-74; Teacher of Theory and Clarinet, 1969-; Composer, 1975-. Compositions: Variations for Wind Orchestra, 1975, recorded 1980 and 1992; Variations for Orchestra, 1977; Metamorphoses for Orchestra, 1979; Suite for Orchestra, 1980-81; Music for Clarinet and Piano, 1980-82; Miniature for Orchestra, 1982; Chamber Music, 1983-84; Aino, 1984-85; Ceremonial Fanfare for Kouvola, 1984, recorded 1988; Fantasy for Orchestra, 1985; Two Pieces for Orchestra, 1985-86; Syksyisia Kuvia, 1985; Fantasia for Clarinet and Wind Orchestra, 1986; Brass Quintet, 1987. Recordings include: Quintet for Brass, 1992; Scenes from Northern Carelia, 1990; Suite for Wind Orchestra, recorded 1995; Music for tuba and orchestra, 1991; Rose Red Music for brass and percussion instruments, 1994; Three Pieces for wind quintet, 1994; Amordus Play for tuba and piano, 1994-95; Three Pieces for tuba and piano, 1993-94. Honours: Province of North Karelia Art Prize, 1986 and 1995. Memberships: Society of Finnish Composers; The Finnish

Clarinet Society. Hobbies: Music; Reading. Address: Suutarinkatu 12, 80100 Joensuu, Finland.

EETVELT Francois van, b. 23 May 1946, Bornem, Belgium. Bass-Baritone. Education: Studied at the Brussels and Antwerp Conservatories and in Italy and Germany. Career: Sang Amfortas in Parsifal at Antwerp in 1976 and has sung there and in Brussels, Prague, Leipzig, Bratislava, Dresden and Helsinki as Don Giovanni, Wagner's Donner, Gunther, Wolfran and Kurwenal; Sang Appolo in Monteverdi's Orfeo, Jochanaan and Tarquinius in The Rape of Lucretia; Sang in the premiere of Das Schloss by Andre Laporte at Brussels in 1986; Festival engagements at Flanders and Aldeburgh; Television appearances include Monteverdi's Orfeo. Honours include: Winner, Belcanto Competition, Ostend in 1978. Address: Theatre Royal de la Monnaie, 4 Leopoldstrasse, B-1000 Brussels, Belgium.

EFRATY Anat, b. 1970, Israel. Singer (Soprano). Education: Studied at the Rubin Academy, Tel Aviv, and with Walther Berry in Vienna. Debut: Mahler's 2nd Symphony, with the Israel Symphony, 1993. Career: New Israeli Opera from 1993, as The Bird in Farber's The Journey to Polyphonia, Britten's Helena, Ninetta in The Love for Three Oranges and other roles; US debut, San Diego, 1995, in Vivaldi's Gloria; German debut, Stuttgart, 1995, as Flaminia in Haydn's Mondo della luna and Théâtre du Châtelet, Paris, 1995, as Tebaldo in Don Carlo; Other roles include Frasquita, Sophie in Werther, Nannetta and Despina. Address: Atholl Still Ltd, Foresters Wall, 25-27 Westow Street, London SE19 3RY, England.

EGEL Martin, b. 1949, Frieburg, Germany. Bass-Baritone. Education: Studied with his mother, Marga Höffgen, and in Frankfurt and Basle. Career: Sang at first in Basle; Sang at Salzburg Easter and Summer Fesivals from 1974, Bayreuth Festival, 1975-84 in Lohengrin, Die Meistersinger and Parsifal, and as Donner in Das Rheingold; Guest appearances in Hamburg, Berlin, Paris, Milan, Brussels, Paris and London; Barcelona in 1984 as Mozart's Figaro, Opéra du Rhin Strasbourg in 1985, sang in Dallapiccola's Ulisse at Turin in 1987, the Music Master in Ariadne at Trieste in 1988, and the Herald in Lohengrin at Nice in 1990; Sang Sempronio in Cimarosa's Il mercato di Malmantile, Colmar, 1996. Recordings: Lohengrin; Der Vampyr by Marschner; Armide by Gluck; Winterreise; Bach Cantatas. Address: c/o Théâtre de l'Opéra de Nice, 4&6 Rue St Françoise de Paule, F-06300 Nice, France.

EGERTON Francis, b. 14 Jul 1930, Limerick, Eire. Tenor. Career: Early appearances with Scottish Opera, the Glyndebourne Festival and at Sadler's Wells; Covent Garden from 1972 as Iopas in Les Troyens, Beppe, Flute, the Captain in Wozzeck and roles in Carmen, Les Contes d'Hoffmann and La Fanciulla del West; Has sung Mime in Siegfried for Scottish Opera and in San Francisco; Other roles include, Pedrillo, Strauss's Scaramuccio at Nice, Italian Tenor at Glasgow and Monsieur Taupe in Capriccio at Glyndebourne, Bardolfo in Falstaff at San Francisco, in concert at Chicago and at Los Angeles, conducted by Giulini; Sang Il Conte in Cimarosa's Il Fanatico Burlato at Drottningholm, the Captain in Wozzeck at Edinburgh and Los Angeles; Season 1990-91 with Mr Upfold in Albert Herring at San Diego, the four tenor roles in Hoffmann in Paris, Goro in Madame Butterfly and Eumaus in Il Ritorno di Ulisse in Los Angeles; Appearances in Prokofiev's The Fiery Angel at the Proms and Covent Garden, 1991-92, as the Doctor; Season 1995-96 as M le Comte in La Belle Vivette, after Offenbach for English National Opera. Address: c/o Athole Still Ltd, 113 Church Road, London, SE19 2PR, England.

EGMOND Max van, b. 1 Feb 1936, Semarang, Indonesia. Singer (Baritone). Education: Studied in Holland with Tine van Willigen-de Lorme. Career: After winning prizes in Holland, Brussels and Munich made many appearances as concert singer, notably in Baroque music, Holland, England, Brasil, Germany, Austria, Italy, Poland, Belgium, USA and Canada; Engagements at most leading music festivals and centres; Radio and TV broadcasts; Teacher of singing at the Amsterdam Musieklyceum from 1973. Recordings: St Matthew and St John Passions by Bach (Telefunken); Bach Cantatas conducted by Gustav Leonhardt and Nikolaus Harnoncourt; Der Tag des Gerichts by Telemann; Reger's Requiem; Il Ritorno d'Ulisse, Orfeo and Il Combattimento by Monteverdi; St Luke Passion by Schütz; Schubert's Schwanengesang; Lully's Alceste (CBS). Honours include: Winner, s-Hertogenbosch Competition, 1959; Edison Awards for Gramophone Recordings, 1969, 1971. Hobbies include: Theatre. Address: Willemsprakweg 150-1, Amsterdam 1007, Netherlands.

EHDE John (Martin), b. 25 Apr 1962, Stockholm, Sweden. Solo Cellist. Education: Royal Academy of Music, Aarhus, Denmark, 1979-85, 1986-87; Diploma, 1984; Soloist Diploma with debut, 1987; Hochschule fur Musik, Vienna, 1985-86, 1987-89. Debut: Recital, Royal Academy, Copenhagen, 1987. Career: First appeared on Swedish Radio aged 11; Recitals and concertos with orchestras in all Scandinavian countries, Iceland, England, Scotland, Austria, Canada and USSR; Radio and TV appearances in Scandinavia, Iceland, Italy; Solo Cellist, Helsingborg Symphony Orchestra, Sweden, 1989-; Speciality, Performing the music of Frederick Delius; Cello Concerto, sonata. Recordings: Numerous with The Lin Ensemble and with the pianist Carl-Axel Dominique (Sonatas by Alkan, Debussy and Delius). Honours: 1st Prize in many Swedish Youth Competitions; Cultural Grant, Malmo Lions Club, 1974; 1-year Grant for studies in Vienna, Swedish Institute for Science and Art, 1987; Awarded Scholarship from Foundation of Legendary Swedish Conductor Sten Frykberg, 1990. Membership: Leopold Stokowski Society, London. Hobbies: Performing Magic; Record Collecting. Address: Mandelpilsgatan 16, S-21231 Malmo, Sweden.

EHRLING Sixten, b. 3 Apr 1918, Malmo, Sweden. Conductor. m. Gunnel Lindgren, 2 daughters. Education: Studied at the Royal Academy of Music, Stockholm. Debut: Royal Opera Stockholm, 1940. Career: Assistant to Karl Böhm at Dresden, 1941; Music Director of the Royal Opera Stockholm, 1953-60; Visited Edinburgh and London with the premiere production of Blomdahl's Aniara, 1959; Director of Salzburg Mozarteum course for conductors, 1954; Music Director, Detroit Symphony Orchestra, 1963-73; Head of the conducting department at the Juilliard School, New York, from 1973; Metropolitan Opera, 1973-77, Peter Grimes, Der Ring des Nibelungen, Il Trittico, Simon Boccanegra, Bluebeard's Castle; Principal Guest Conductor, Denver Symphony Orchestra from 1979. Recordings include: Symphonies by Berwald with the London Symphony Orchestra; Music by Blomdahl with the Stockholm Philharmonic. Honours include: Knight Commander, Order of the White Rose, Finland (for championing the works of Sibelius). Address: c/o Juilliard School, Lincoln Plaza, NY 10023, USA.

EHRSTEDT Caj, b. 1941, Finland. Singer (Tenor). Education: Studied in Helsinki and Stockholm, with Anton Dermota in Vienna and in Milan. Debut: Helsinki, 1964, as Rodolfo in La Bohème. Career: Sang at the Royal Opera Stockholm from 1967, Oslo Opera from 1969; Repertory of more than 50 roles in Oslo and as guest throughout Scandinavia; Professor at the Norwegian State Theatre School, Oslo, from 1975. Address: Den Norske Opera, PO Box 8800, Youngstorget, N-0028 Oslo, Norway.

EIPPERLE Trude, b. 12 Aug 1910, Stuttgart, Germany. Singer (Soprano). Education: Studied at the Musikhochschule Stuttgart. Career: Sang at Wiesbaden from 1930, Brunswick, Nuremberg and Munich until 1944; Salzburg Festival 1942, Zdenka in Arabella, Cologne Opera, 1945-51, notably in the 1948 premiere of Die Verkundigung by Walter Braunfels, Bayreuth Festival 1952, as Eva in Die Meistersinger; Other roles included Desdemona, Elsa, Elisabeth, Pamina and Mozart's Countess, Madama Butterfly. Recordings include: Tannhäuser (Deutsche Grammophon); Die Schöpfung; Die Rose vom Liebesgarten by Pfitzner.

EIRIKSDOTTIR Karolina, b. 10 Jan 1951, Reykjavik, Iceland. Composer. m. Thorsteinn Hannesson, 1 Aug 1974, 1 daughter. Education: Graduated, Reykjavik College, 1971, Reykjavik College of Music, 1974; MMus Music History & Musicology, 1976, MMus Composition 1978, University of Michigan, USA. Career includes: Major performances of works: Iceland Symphony Orchestra (4 works), at Nordic Music Days in Helsinki 1980, Oslo 1982, Copenhagen 1984; At Scandinavia Today, Washington DC 1982; Opera, Nagon har jag sett in Vadstena in Sweden, 1988, Reykjavik, 1989; Sinfonietta performed by the BBC Scottish Symphony Orchestra during Breaking the Ice Festival in Glasgow, 1992; Six Movements for String Quartet performed by the Arditti String Quartet, London, 1992; Three Paragraphs for Orchestra performed by the Malmo Symphony Orchestra at Stockholm New Music Festival, Stockholm, 1993; Performances at Nordic Music Festival,Göteborg, 1991; Dark Music Days Festival in Reykjavik, 1993 and Kuhmo Festival in Finland, 1993; Commission, Icelandic State TV, work for symphony orchestra, 1985; Several performances, Iceland and abroad; Opera, I Have Seen Someone (1988) given British premiere by Lontaro, 1996. Compositions include: Notes, Sonans, Sinfonietta, for Orchestra; 5 pieces for chamber orchestra; 6 movements for string quartet; Rondo and Rhapsody for Piano; In Vultu Solis, violin; Trio, violin, cello, piano; 6 poems from the Japanese, & Some Days, voice & instruments; All pieces in manuscript at Iceland Music Information Centre, Reykjavic; Orcestral pieces, Notes, Sonans, Sinfonietta, Klifur, Three Paragraphs, Opera: Nagon har jag sett, chamber orchestra: Five pieces and Rhapsody in C; Land possessed by poems for baritone and piano, solo pieces for clarinet, harpsichord and guitar and chamber music; Concert for Clarinet and Orchestra, 1994; Solos for cello and violin. Recordings: Sinfonietta, Iceland Symphony Orchestra, conductor Paul Zukofsky; Other works recorded by Iceland State Broadcasting Service; Karolina Eiriksdottir - Portrait; Icelandic Chamber Music. Membership: Society of Icelandic composers. Address: Blatun 6, 225 Bessastadahreppur, Iceland.

EISENFELD Brigitte, b. 19 Sep 1945, Fralkenstein, Germany. Soprano. Education: Studied at the Berlin Musikhochschule. Debut: Chemnitz in 1970 as Papagena. Career: Engaged at Chemnitz, 1970-74, Staatsoper Berlin from 1974 notably in the premiere of Graf Mirabeau by Matthus and as Constanze in Die Entführung in 1989; Guest appearances with the Staatsoper ensemble in Tokyo, Moscow, Bologna and Lucerne; Schwetzingen Festival in 1989 as Zerbinetta in Ariadne auf Naxos; Other roles have included Blonchen, Zerlina, Aennchen in Der Freischütz, Rosina and Norina. Address: c/o Berlin Deutsche Staatsoper, Unter den Linden 7, 1086 Berlin, Germany.

EISMA Will Leendert, b. 13 May 1929, Sungailiat, Indonesia. Composer; Violinist. m. Wilhelmina A Reeser, 30 Nov 1960, 1 son, 1 daughter. Education: Conservatory of Rotterdam; Composition, Accademia di Santa Cecilia, Rome; Institute for Sonology, Utrecht. Career: Violinist: Rotterdam Philharmonic, 1953-59, Chamber Orchestra, Società Corelli, 1960-61, Chamber Orchestra, Radio Hilversum, 1961-89; Member of electro instrumental group ICE; Director, Studio for Electronic Music, Five Roses. Compositions: 3 Concerti for orchestra, 1 for 2 violins and orchestra; Taurus-A, Volumina for orchestra; Concerti for oboe, horn; Chamber and electronic music; Concerto for String Trio and Orchestra; Concerto for Percussion, 1979; Concerto for English Horn, 1981; Concerto for 5 Violas, 1982; Du dehors - Du dedans, 1983; Silver Plated Bronze, 1986; Te Deum, 1988; Passo del Diavolo, 1988; Mawar jiwa for gamelan, 1992. Hobby: Photography. Address: Oude Amersfoortsweg 206, Hilversum 1212 AL, Netherlands.

EK Harald, b. 1936, Jonkoping, Sweden. Tenor. Education: Studied in Gothenburg with G Kjellertz and R Jacobson. Debut: Gothenburg in 1966 in Die Lustige Witwe. Career: Sang at Drottningholm in 1967 as Almaviva in Paisiello's Il Barbiere di Siviglia, Stadtstheater Berne, 1969-72, and Bayreuth Festival in 1971 in Der fliegende Holländer and Das Rheingold; Member of the Staatsoper Hamburg, 1972-75, and Zurich Opera from 1975; Sang Don José at Gothenburg in 1988; Other roles include Don Ottavio, Tamino, Hoffmann, Comte Ory, Cavaradossi, Tom Rakewell and Alfred in Die Fledermaus. Recordings include: Der fliegende Holländer. Address: School of Theatre and Opera, University of Göteborg, Box 5439, S-40229 Göteborg, Sweden.

EKIZIAN Michelle, b. 21 Nov 1956, NY, USA. Composer. Education: Studied at the Manhattan School of Music and Columbia University. Compositions include: The Exiled Heart for Orchestra, 1982; Octoechos for Double String Quartet and Soprano, 1986; Saber Dances for Orchestra, 1992; David of Sassoun, chamber opera, 1992. Honours include: Prix de Rome, 1988; Guggenheim and NEA Fellowships. Address: c/o ASCAP, ASCAP Building, One Lincoln Plaza, New York, NY 10023, USA.

EKLUND Anna, b. 1964, Sweden. Soprano. Education: Studied at the Stockholm College of Music and the State Opera School. Debut: Stockholm Royal Opera as Papagena. Career: Sang in staged version of Carmina Burana at Stockholm in 1991; Roles have included Isamene in Haeffner's Elektra at Drottningholm, Novis Elisabeth in Forsell's Riket ar Ditt, the Queen of Night and Serpetta in La Finta Giardiniera; Season 1991-92 in the St Matthew Passion under Philippe Herreweghe in Sweden, Barcelona and Madrid, Betty in Salieri's Falstaff at Drottningholm; Season 1992-93 as Zemir in Gretry's Zemire et Azor at Drottningholm, and the leading female role in the premiere of Amorina by Lars Runsten at the Royal Opera Stockholm. Address: Nordic Artists Management, Sveavagen 76, S-11359 Stockholm, Sweden.

EKLUND Hans, b. 1 Jul 1927, Sandviken, Sweden. Composer; Professor. Education: Studied with Lars-Erik Larsson, Stockholm Musikhogskolan, 1949-52; Ernst Pepping, Berlin, 1954; Rome, 1957. Career: Professor of Harmony and Counterpoint, Stockholm Musikhogskolan, 1964-. Compositions include: Opera: Mother Svea, 1972; Orchestral: Symphonic Dances, 1954, Musica da Camera, No 1, 1955, No 2, 1956, No 3, 1957, No 4, 1959, No 5, 1970, No 6, 1970; Symphonies: No 1, Sinfonia Seria, 1958, No 2, Sinfonia Breve, 1964, No 3, Sinfonia Rustica, 1967-68, No 4, Hjalmar Branting in memoriam, 1973-74, No 5, Quadri, 1978, No 6, Sinfonia Senza Speranza, 1983, No 7, La Serenata, 1984, No 8, Sinfonia Grave, 1985, No 9, Sinfonia Introvertita, 1992; Other: Toccata, 1966, Concerto for Trombone, Winds and Percussion, 1972, Requiem Per Soli Coro Ed Orchestra, 1977-78, Horn Concerto, 1979, Concerto for Tuba and Brass Orchestra, 1980, Divertimento, 1986; Chamber: 2 Sonatas for Solo Violin, 1956, 1982, 3 Preludes for Piano, 1990, 2 Pastoral Songs for Choir, 1993; Various solo pieces, piano music and organ works and choruses. Honours: Member, Royal Swedish Academy of Music, 1975-; Awarded degree, Litteris et Artibus from the King of Sweden, 1985; Christ Johnson Fund Music Prize, 1989. Address: Bjornskogsgrand 63, 162 46 Vallingby, Sweden.

EL SISI Yousef Ibrahim, b. 19 Mar 1935, Shebin El Kom, Egypt. Conductor; Composer; Teacher. m. Nadia El Sisi, 12 Jul 1958, 2 sons. Education: Diploma, Piano, Higher Institute of

Music, Cairo, 1956; BA, English Literature, Faculty of Arts, Cairo University, 1959; Artistic Maturity degree in Conducting and Composition, Vienna Music Academy, 1965. Debut: Cairo, 1965. Career: Conductor, Artistic Director, Principal Conductor, Cairo Symphony Orchestra and Cairo Opera Troupe, 1965-; Guest Conductor for major orchestras in Albania, Austria, Bulgaria, Czechoslovakia, China, England, Germany, Italy, France, North and South Korea, Poland and USA; Visiting Professor for Postgraduates at most music institutions in Egypt; Managing Director, El Magalla El Mousikeya, monthly musical magazine, 1973-77; Egyptian Under Secretary for Music and Opera, Ministry of Culture. Compositions: 33 Radio drama music works; 170 Songs for children's choir; Suite for Brass Band; Variations on Sayed Darwish Theme for Soli Choir and Orchestra; 7 Compositions based on classical Arabic music forms. Recordings: Mozart: 3 complete operas in Arabic; Digital recording of Le Nozze di Figaro, Don Giovanni, Cosi fan Tutte with Polish National Radio Orchestra, OIA London; Over 200 recordings in films, TV and radio, live concerts in Cairo, Tirana, Peking and Pyong Yang; Carmina, Beethoven's Fantasia Burana and Adagio on documentary film. Publication: Invitation to Music, in Arabic, 1981. Current Management: Go Management, 1725 York Avenue Suite 27b, New York, NY 10128, USA. Address: 59 Medinet El-Alaam, Agouza, Cairo, Egypt.

EL-DABH Halim (Abdul Messieh), b. 4 Mar 1921, Cairo, Egypt. Composer; Teacher. Education: Studied piano and Western music at Sulcz Conservatory, Cairo, 1941-44; Graduated in Agricultural Engineering, University of Cairo, 1945; Studied composition with Aaron Copland and Irving Fine, Berkshire Music Center, Tanglewood; MM, New England Conservatory of Music, Boston; MFA, Brandeis University. Career: Teacher, Haile Selassie University, Addis Ababa, 1962-65, Howard University, 1966-69; Teacher, 1969-, Co-Director, 1979-, Center for the Study of World Musics, Kent State University. Compositions include: 3 Symphonies, 1950-56; String Quartet, 1951; Fantasia-Tahmeel for Darabukka or Timpani and Strings, 1954; Bacchanalia for Orchestra, 1958; Juxtaposition No 1 for Percussion Ensemble, 1959; Black Epic, opera-pageant, 1968; Opera Files, 1971; Drink Of Eternity, opera-pageant, 1981; Concerto for Darabukka, Clarinet and Strings, 1981; Tonography III for 5 Winds, 1984; Piano pieces and choruses. Publication: The Derabucca: Hand Techniques in The Art of Drumming, 1965. Honours: Fulbright Scholarship; 2 Guggenheim Fellowships; Commissions. Address: c/o Center for the Study of World Musics, Kent University, Kent, OH 44242, USA.

EL-KHOLY Samha, b. 27 July 1925, Cairo, Egypt. Musicologist; Educator. m. Gamal Abdel-Rahim, 8 December 1959, 1 daughter, (a son from previous marriage). Education: Diploma, Higher Institute for Music Education, Cairo, 1951; Licentiate, Royal Academy of Music, London (piano performance), 1954; PhD, Edinburg University, 1954. Career: Lecturer, Founding Committee Member, 1959-67, Professor, History of Music & Analysis, 1968-85, Dean 1972-81, Professor Emeritus, since 1985, Cairo Conservatoire; Presidnet, Academy of Arts (7 colleges including Cairo Conservatoire); Fulbright Professor, University of South Florida, Tampa, 1987-88; Presents weekly musical programme on TV, Egypt, 1975-; Founder, Present Chair, Egyptian Jeunesses Musicales, 1985. Publications: The Function of Music in Islamic Culture, up to 1100 a.d. (English); Music Education Teacher's Manual, co-author, 1958; Western Music in the 17th and 18th Centuries, in The Compendium of the Arts (Arabic), 1971; Traditions of Improvisation in Arab Music, Past and Present; Translations into Arabic, Our Musical Heritage (Curt Sachs), 1965, Musical Structure and Design (C T Davie), 1970, A History of Music (T Finney) with Gamal Abdel-Rahim, 1975, Improvisation in Arab Music, past and present, 1971, Nationalism, in Twentieth Century Music (Arabic), 1992. Address: 2/4 Lasilky Street, New Maadi, Cairo 11742, Egypt.

ELCHLEPP Isolde, b. 1958, Strasbourg, France. Singer (Mezzo-soprano). Education: Opera School of the Bavarian State Opera. Career: Sang first at Bremen, notable as The Woman in Schoenberg's Erwartung, 1985; Wiesbaden from 1986 as Wagner's Venus, Fricka and Waltraute, and Azucena in Il Trovatore; Hanover Opera as Carmen, Ortrud, Santuzza, Octavian, the Composer, Amneris and Kundry; Deutsche Oper Berlin, 1990, as Ortrud; Guest appearances in Dusseldorf, Mannheim, Brunswick, Karlsruhe, Basle (Herodias in Salome) and Brussels; Concert repertory includes Schoenberg's Pierrot Luniare, which she has sung in Paris and Nuremberg; Guest in Tokyo in Erwartung; Also sang Elektra with the Oslo Philharmonic; Troades, Frankfurt Opera; Fricka in Das Rheingold and Die Walküre at Hanover, 1992 as well as Hostess in the premiere of Reimann's Das Schloss, Deutsche Oper Berlin; Debut at Bayreuth Festival as Ortrud in 1993; Sang the Woman in Erwartung in a Pierre Audi production for Netherlands Opera. Current Management: Haydn Rawstron Limited, London. Address: PO Box 654, London SE26 4DZ, England.

ELDER Mark (Philip), b. 2 June 1947, Hexham, England. Conductor. m. Amanda Jane Stein, 1980. Education: BA, Honours, MA, Cambridge University. Career: Music Staff, Wexford Festival, 1969-70; Chorus Master. Assistant Conductor. Glyndebourne, 1970-71; Music Staff, Covent Garden Royal Opera House, London, 1970-72; Conducted Rigoletto, 1976; Staff Conductor, Australian Opera, 1972-74; English National Opera, 1974-77; Associate Conductor, 1977-79; Music Director, 1979-92, English National Opera; Conducted world premiere of Blake's Toussaint in 1977 and the British premiere of Busoni's Doktor Faust in 1986; Music Director, Rochester Philharmonic Orchestra, New York, 1989-94; Principal Guest Conductor, CBSO, 1992-95; Led ENO on tour of Russia, 1990; Conducted Reginald Goodall Memorial Concert, Festival Hall, June 1991; the British premiere of Rossini's Ermione with the Orchestra of the Age of Enlightenment at the Elizabeth Hall, 1992; Conducted Die Meistersinger at Bayreuth, 1981; Principal Guest Conductor, BBC Symphony Orchestra, London, 1982-85; London Mozart Players, 1980-83; Led new production of Tristan and Isolde for ENO, 1996; Original version of Simon Boccanegra at Covent Garden, 1997; Linda di Chamounix at South Bank, for the Donizetti bicentenary. Honours: Honorary degree, Royal Academy of Music, 1984; CBE, 1989. Address: 4 Ripplevale Grove, London N1, England.

ELIAS Brian (David), b. 30 August 1948, Bombay, India. Composer. Education: Royal College of Music, 1966; Private studies with Elisabeth Lutyens; Extra-mural composition workshop, New York, USA. Career: Freelance Editor, Arranger and Copyist; Clerk and Statistician Assistant, 1972-78; Composer, full-time with some Teaching Commitments. Compositions include: La Chevelure for soprano and chamber orchestra; Somnia for tenor and orchestra; L'Eylah for orchestra, commissioned by BBC for Promenade Concerts, 1984; Tzigane for solo violin; Peroration for solo soprano; Geranos for chamber ensemble, commissioned by The Fires of London, 1985; 5 songs to Poems by Irina Ratushinskaya for mezzo-soprano and orchestra commissioned by BBC for Winter Season, 1989-; The Judas Tree, ballet score commissioned by The Royal Ballet choreographed by Kennth MacMillan, 1992; Fanfare, Royal Ballet, choreographed by Matthew Hart, 1993. Honours: Joint 2nd Prize for Proverbs of Hell, Radcliffe Music Award, 1977. Memberships: Association of Professional Composers. Hobbies: Reading; Gardening. Address: c/o Chester Music, 8/9 Frith Street, London W1V 5TZ, England.

ELIAS Rosalind, b. 13 Mar 1929, Lowell, MA, USA. Singer; Opera Director. Education: Studied at the New England Conservatory, Boston and at the Accademia di Santa Cecilia, Rome; Further study with Daniel Ferro in New York. Career: Sang with New England Opera, 1948-52; Metropolitan Opera from 1954 as Cherubino, Dorabella, Rosina and Hansel, and in the premieres of Barber's Vanessa, and Antony and Cleopatra; Scottish Opera in 1970 as Rossini's La Cenerentola; Vienna Staatsoper in 1972 as Carmen; Glyndebourne Festival in 1975 as Baba The Turk in The Rake's Progress; Other appearances in Hamburg, Monte Carlo, Barcelona, Lisbon and Aix-en-Provence; Other roles include Verdi's Amneris and Azucena, Massenet's Charlotte and Giulietta in Les Contes d'Hoffmann; Sang Herodias in Salome at Houston in 1987; Produced Carmen at Cincinnati in 1988 and Il Barbiere di Siviglia for Opera Pacific, Costa Mesa in 1989; Sang Mistress Quickly in Falstaff at Boston, 1996. Recordings: La Gioconda; La Forza del Destino; Il Trovatore; Falstaff; Madama Butterfly; Rigoletto; Der fliegende Holländer. Address: c/o Opera Pacific, 3187 Red Hill Avenue, Costa Mesa, CA 92626, USA.

ELIASON Robert (Erwin), b. 28 March 1933, Flint, USA. Musician. m. Ellen Irene Easter, 30 August 1958, 2 sons, 1 daughter. Education: BM, University of Michigan, 1955; MM, Manhattan School of Music, 1959; DMA, University of Missouri, Kansas City, 1968. Career: 7th Army Symphony Orchestra, Principal Tuba, 1956-57; Public School Teacher, 1957-58, 1960, 1969-70; Principal Tuba, Kansas City Philharmonic, 1960-69; Research Associate, Smithsonian Institution, 1970-71; Curator, Musical Instruments, Henry Ford Museum, Greenfield Village, 1971-85; Technical Writer, New England Digital Corporation, 1985-90; Started Toad Hill Music, a computerized music engraving business, 1987; Technical Writer, Geographic Data Technology Inc, 1993-96. Recordings: Detroit Concert Band Recordings of Sousa Marches and Concert Band Repertoire, 1975-83; 19th Century Ballroom Music, 1976; Our Musical Past, 1976. Publications: Keyed Bugles in the United States, 1972; Graves & Co Musical Instrument Makers, 1975; Early American Brass Makers, 1979. Contributions to: 30 articles for Harvard Dictionary of Music, 1986; 19 articles, Grove Dictionary, 1980, American Grove, 1985; Over 25 articles for various journals and magazines. Hobbies: Flying; Commercial Pilots Licence with Multi Engine, Instrument, Flight Instructor and Instrument Instructor Ratings. Address: 43 Pico Road, Lyme, NH 03768, USA.

ELIASSON Sven Olaf, b. 4 Apr 1933, Sweden. Tenor. Education: Royal Music Academy, Stockholm. Career: Sang at Oslo from 1961, Stockholm from 1965; Guest appearances at the Hamburg Staatsoper, 1968-74; Further engagements at Zurich, Dusseldorf and Frankfurt; Glyndebourne in 1967 as Don Ottavio; Drottningholm Opera in 1967 as Belmonte in Die Entführung; Zurich Opera in 1968 and 1975 as Pfitzner's Palestrina and in the premiere of Klebe's Ein Wahrer Held; Stockholm Opera in 1970 in the premiere of Rosenberg's Hus Med Dubbel Ingang; Sang Schoenberg's Aron with the Hamburg Staatsoper in Israel in 1974; Other roles include Don José, Riccardo in Un Ballo in Maschera, Peter Grimes and Tom Rakewell in The Rake's Progress. Recordings include: Il Ritorno d'Ulisse in Patria by Monteverdi; Video of Swedish Opera production of Die Meistrsinger. Address: Kungliga Teatern, PO Box 16094, S-10322 Stockholm, Sweden.

ELKINS Margreta, b. 16 Oct 1932, Brisbane, Australia. Mezzo-Soprano. Education: Studied with Ruby Dent in Brisbane, with Pauline Bindley in Melbourne and Vera Rozsa in London; Further study with Campogalliani in Milan. Debut: Brisbane Opera Company in 1955 as Azucena. Career: Joined the Royal Opera, London in 1958 and sang Octavian, Adalgisa in Norma, Amneris and Marina in Boris Godunov; Sang Helen in the premiere of Tippett's King Priam, with the Royal Opera at Coventry in 1962; Sadler's Wells Theatre in 1963 in Giulio Cesare by Handel; Many appearances with Joan Sutherland; Guest engagements in Genoa, Naples, Barcelona, Boston, New Orleans and Philadelphia; Sang at Amsterdam in 1974 in Handel's Rodelinda; Sang with Australian Opera, Sydney from 1975, and sang Amneris at Brisbane in 1988 and Azucena in 1990; Repertoire ranges from Monteverdi to Wagner; Many concert appearances. Recordings include: Many opera sets; With Joan Sutherland: I Puritani, La Sonnambula, Faust, Shield's Rosina, Giulio Cesare and Griselda by Bononcini. Address: c/o Lyric Opera of Queensland, PO Box 677, South Brisbane, Queensland 4101, Australia.

ELKUS Jonathan (Britton), b. 8 Aug 1931, San Francisco, California, USA. Musician; Teacher. m. Marilyn McCormick, 30 July 1966, 1 son. Education: BA, University of California at Berkeley, 1953; MA, Stanford University, 1954; Career: Professor of Music, Lehigh University, 1957-73; Freelance Musical Editor and Consultant, 1973-; Director of Music, 1979-85, Chairman, Department of Humanities, 1985-89, Cape Cod Academy, Osterville; Chairman, Department of History, Stuart Hall School, Staunton, 1989-92; Director of Bands, University of California, Davis, 1992-; Proprietor, J B Elkus and Son, Music Publishers, Laureate Music Press, Overland Music Distributors and East Bay Books. Compositions: Tom Sawyer, musical play; Five Sketches for Two Clarinets; The Outcasts of Poker Flat, opera; Treasure Island, musical play; Three Medieval Pieces, organ; The Dorados, chorus; The Mandarin, opera (with Richard Franko Goldman); Of Players to Come, chorus; Act Your Age, musical play; Numerous compositions and transcriptions for concert band. Publications: Charles Ives and the American Band Tradition: A Centennial Tribute, 1975; The Charles Ives Society's critical edition of Thanksgiving and Forefathers's Day (orchestra), 1991. Contributions to: The Instrumentalist; Opera Journal; Yale Review; Nineteenth Century Music. Honours: Recipient of Ford Foundation Fellowship, 1962. Membership: American Society of Composers, Authors and Publishers. Address: PO Box 9526, Berkeley, CA 94709-0526, USA.

ELLA István, b. 1947, Veresegyház, Hungary. Organist. Education: Béla Bartók Conservatory; Ferenc Liszt Academy of Music; Graduate, Budapest Academy of Music, 1971; Studied organ and improvisation under Professor Ernst Köhler and conducting under Professor Olaf Koch, at Weimar and Leipzig; Conductor's Diploma, Wittenberg in 1974. Career: Artistic Director and Soloist, Corelli Chamber Orchestra. Honours: Prize Winner, Prague International Organ Competition, 1971; 2nd Prize, Bach International Organ Concours, Leipzig, 1972; 1st Prize, Anton Bruckner International Organ Competition, Linz, 1974; 1st Prize, JS Bach International Organ Concours, Brugge, 1976.

ELLERO D'ARTEGNA Francesco, b. 15 Dec 1948, Ravascletto, Italy. Bass Singer. Education: Studied at the Udine Conservatory and with Ettore Campogalliani. Debut: Verona Arena in 1981 as High Priest in Nabucco. Career: Appearances at such Italian opera centres as Trieste, Modena, Genoa, Carcalla as Timur in Turandot in 1986, Parma, Venice and Milan; Further engagements at Monte Carlo as Raimondo in 1987, Barcelona, Hamburg and Madrid as Leporello in 1989; Sang Ramphis in Aida at Verona, 1988-89 and Raimondo in Lucia di Lammermoor at the Lyric Opera Chicago in 1990; Other roles have included Bellini's Oroveso and Rodolfo, Verdi's Silva, Zaccaria, Sparafucile, Fiesco, Padre Guardiano and Fernando; Sang Mephistopheles in Faust and Haly in L'Italiana in Algeri; Sang Banquo at Reggio Emilia and Timur at the Festival of Caracalla in 1992; Sang in the Verdi Requiem at Wembley, London in 1994; Walter in Luisa Miller at Santiago, 1996. Recordings: La Bohème; Falstaff; Maria Stuarda; La Sonnambula. Address: c/o Arena di Verona, Piazza Bra 28, 37121 Verona, Italy.

ELLIOTT Alasdair, b. 1954, Hamilton, Scotland. Singer (Tenor). Education: Studied at the Royal Scottish Academy,

Glasgow, and with Laura Sarti at the Guildhall School of Music; Further study at Pears-Britten School of Advanced Musical Studies and National Opera Studio. Career: Opera: Has sung with Kent Opera; Curzio (Nozze di Figaro), Flich (Beggar's Opera); English Touring Opera: Ramiro (La Cenerentola), Belmonte (Entführung), also for Glyndebourne Touring Opera; Opera Northern Ireland: Leicester (Maria Stuarda), Pedrillio (Entführung); Scottish Opera: Squeak (Billy Budd), Basilio (Nozze di Figaro), Iopas (Les Troyens), Rector (Peter Grimes); Benda (The Jacobin); English National Opera: Jew (Salome), Priest (Christmas Eve), Andrés (Wozzeck), Servant (The Bachae, John Buller, world premiere); Brighella (Ariadne auf Naxos), Vova (Life with an Idiot); Royal Opera House: Fisherman (Guillaume Tell), Gelsomina (Il Viaggio a Reims), Vogelgesang (Die Meistersinger von Nürnberg), Priest (Die Zauberflöte), Junger Diener (Elektra); Pong (Turandot), Don Curzio (Nozze di Figaro); CBTO: Calasis (Les Boréades, Rameau); Covent Garden Festival Opera: Tamino (Die Zauberflöte); Edinburgh International Festival: Gerry (Tourist Variations, James Macmillan, world premiere); Netherlands Opera: Host (Benvenuto Cellini); Drottningholm Court Theatre: Armida (Haydn); Opéra Comique: Azeste (Ascanio in Alba); Concerts: Spain, Switzerland, Netherlands, Canada, Trevor Pinnock and the English Concert, London Mozart Players, Jane Glover (including the first performance of The Vessel, Stephen Oliver); Sang in Salome for ENO, 1996; Recitals: Queen's Hall, Edinburgh; Jubilee Hall, Aldeburgh; Purcell Room, Wigmore Hall, Royal Opera House, London. Recordings include: Arturo in La Straniera by Bellini. Current Management: Athole Still International Management Ltd. Address: 14 Ewing Court, Hamilton, Lanarkshire ML3 8UX, England.

ELLIOTT Anthony, b. 3 Sept 1948, Rome, New York, USA. Conductor; Concert Cellist. m. Paula Sokol, 9 June 1975, 4 daughters. Education: Rome Free Academy, Rome, New York, USA; Performers Certificate, 1969, School of Music, Indiana University; Bachelor of Music with Distinction, 1970, Indiana University. Debut: St Lawrence Centre of Performing Arts, Toronto, Ontario, Canada. Career: Soloist with Detroit Symphony, New York Philharmonic, CBC Toronto Orchestra, Minnesota Orchestra, Vancouver Symphony, Colorado Philharmonic; Recitals broadcast on NET, NPR and CBC, including premiere performances of 20th century compositions; Former Musical Director, University Symphony Orchestra, Western Michigan University; Former Assistant Music Director, Marrowstone Music Festival; Presently Professor of Music, University of Houston; Music Director of the Houston Youth Symphony and Ballet. Recordings: Solo cellist: Ravel, Mother Goose (complete ballet) Vox Records (2); Ravel, La Valse and Alborada del Gracioso, Vox Records; Ravel, Une Barque sur L'Ocean Vox; Rimsky-Korsakov, Russian Easter Overture, CBC Records; Holst, The Planets, CBC; Koch International Classics Series, Music by Slavic Composers. Hobbies: Reading; Outdoor Sports. Address: School of Music, University of Houston, Houston, TX 77204, USA.

ELLIOTT Paul, b. 19 Mar 1950, Macclesfield, Cheshire, England. Tenor; Teacher. m. Wendy Gillespie, 1982, 2 s. Education: Chorister at St Paul's Cathedral, London, 1959-62; The King's School, Canterbury, 1964-69; Choral Scholar, Magdalen College, Oxford, 1969-72; BA 1973, MA 1977, University of Oxford; Principal voice teachers: David Johnston and Peter Pears. Career includes: Vicar choral, St Paul's Cathedral, 1972-75; Member of John Alldis Choir, 1972-76, Cantores in Ecclesia, 1972-76, Schütz Choir of London, 1972-78, Monteverdi Choir, 1973-78; Founder member of Hilliard Ensemble, 1974-78; London Early Music Group, 1976-79; Vocal consort member of various consorts; Tours of Europe and USA as solo concert artist; Operatic engagements include: Handel's Acis in St Gall, 1984, Mozart's Belmonte, Indiana University, 1988, and Mozart's Arbace in Chicago, 1988; Artist-in-Residence at Washington University, St Louis, 1984-85; Visiting Lecturer, IN University School of Music, Bloomington, 1985-87; Associate Professor of Music, 1987-92, Professor of Music, 1992-, Early Music Institute, IN University School of Music; Member of Theatre of Voices, 1991-; Various workshops and seminars. Recordings: Numerous discs as member of various vocal ensembles; Many discs as soloist with works by Bach, Handel, Purcell. Memberships: National Early Music Association; Early Music America; National Association of Teachers of Singing, America. Address: 3702 Tamarron Drive, Bloomington, IN 47408, USA.

ELLIS Brent, b. 20 Jun 1944, Kansas City, MO, USA. Baritone. Education: Studied with Daniel Ferro in New York and with Luigi Ricci in Rome. Debut: Washington DC in 1967 in the premiere of Ginastera's Bomarzo. Career: Santa Fe Opera from 1972 notably as Mozart's Figaro, in the 1982 premiere of Rochberg's The Confidence Man and as Kunrad in Strauss's Feuersnot; New York City Opera debut in 1974 as Ottone in L'Incoronazione di Poppea; Glyndebourne from 1977 as Ford in Falstaff, Marcello, Don Giovanni and Germont in the Peter Hall production of La Traviata; Metropolitan Opera from 1979 as Silvio in Pagliacci, Rossini's Figaro and Donizetti's Belcore; Opera North, Leeds as Scarpia and Macbeth; Welsh National Opera as Zurga in Les Pêcheurs de Perles; Cologne Opera from 1984 in La Gazza Ladra, Wozzeck, Rigoletto and Eine Florentinische Tragödie by Zemlinsky; Appearances in the premieres of Pasatieri's Washington Square for Michigan Opera and The Seagull for Seattle Opera; Sang Germont at Glyndebourne, 1987, Santa Fe, 1989, also Kunrad in Feuersnot, 1988; San Francisco in 1989 as Iago, followed by Rigoletto at Covent Garden; Season 1992 as Amonasro at Seattle; Sang Dandini in Cenerentola at Toronto, 1996; Concert appearances in Mahler's 8th Symphony with the Chicago Symphony and with orchestras in San Francisco, Minnesota, Baltimore, Houston and Denver; Great Woods Festival with Michael Tilson Thomas. Address: c/o Harrison/Parrott Ltd, 12 Penzance Place, London, W11 4PA, England.

ELLIS David, b. 10 Mar 1933, Liverpool, England. Composer. Education: Royal Manchester College of Music, 1953-57; FRNCM; ARMCM. Career: Music Producer, 1964-77, Head of Music, 1977-86, BBC; Artistic Director, Northern Chamber Orchestra, 1986-94; Associate Director, Orquestra Sinfónica Portuguesa, 1994-. Compositions: Sinfonietta, 1953; String Trio, 1954; Dewpoint for soprano, clarinet and strings, 1955; Piano Sonata; Diversions on a theme of Purcell for strings, 1956; Violin Concerto, 1958; Piano Concerto, 1961; Opera Crito, 1963; Magnificat and Nunc Dimittis for choir and organ, 1964; Elegy for orchestra, 1966; Fanfares and Cadenzas for orchestra, 1968; Carols for an Island Christmas, 1971; Symphony No 1, 1973; Solus for strings, 1973; L for orchestra, 1977; Sonata for solo double bass, 1977; String Quartet No 1, 1980; Berceuse for clarinet and piano, 1981; Aubade for horn and piano, 1981; Suite Française for strings, 1987; Contraprovisations, 1994; Symphony No 2, 1995; String Quartet No 2, 1996. Honours: Royal Philharmonic Prize, 1956; Royal College of Music Patrons' Award, 1956; Theodore Holland Award, 1957; Silver Medal, Royal Manchester Institution, 1957; Ricordi Prize, 1957. Address: Vassaras, 14 Patch Lane, Bramhall, Cheshire, England.

ELLIS David, b. 1970, England. Baritone. Education: Studied at the Royal Northern College of Music. Debut: As Silvio in Pagliacci with Iceland Opera. Career: Appearances as Don Giovanni with English Touring Opera, and Marcello and Donizetti's Talbot for Scottish Opera; Member of Covent Garden Opera from 1994 in Carmen, Die Meistersinger, Un Ballo in Maschera, Peter Grimes, Fanciulla del West, Salome and Billy Budd; Other roles include Belcore, Guglielmo and Posa in Don Carlos. Address: c/o Harrison/Parrott Ltd, 12 Penzance Place, London, W11 4PA, England.

ELLIS Gregory (Charles), b. 3 Nov 1960, Preston, Lancashire, England. Violinist. m. Leslie Gail Toney, 22 Dec 1985, 1 son, 2 daughters. Education: Royal Academy of Music, London; DipRAM, 1983; ARAM, 1989; With Shmuel Ashkenasi at Northern Illinois University, USA; Also student of Carmel Kaine and Frederick Grinke. Debut: Wigmore Hall, London. Career: Violinist and Leader, Vanbrugh String Quartet, resident to Radio Telefis Eireann since 1986; Frequent tours, UK, Europe, Far East North and South America; Broadcasts on Radio 3, BBC World Service, Radio Telefis Eireann TV and Radio, Sky Channel (Arts), US and Canadian Radio, French TV, Brazilian and Mexican TV. Recordings: Several labels. Honours: Vanbrugh String Quartet 1st British string quartet to win the London/Portsmouth International String Quartet Competition, 1988. Hobbies: Aikido; Yoga; Gardening. Current Management: Neil Chaffey Concert Promotions. Address: Vanbrugh House, Castle Treasure, Douglas, Co Cork, Republic of Ireland.

ELLIS James (Antony), b. 5 Mar 1954, Ashton-under-Lyne, England. Composer; Conductor. m. Fiona Anne Johnson, 25 Feb 1978, 4 daughters. Education: Music Scholar, King's College, Cambridge, 1972-75; MA (Cantab); MMus, King's College, London, 1982. Career: Violinist Member of the Royal Philharmonic Orchestra, 1977-80, and Philharmonia, 1980-81; Assistant Tutor, King's College, London, 1982-84; Lecturer in Music, University of Keele, 1984-86; Composer-in-Residence, National Centre of Orchestral Studies, Goldsmith's College, London, 1986-87; Lecturer in Music, City University, 1989-; Conductor for Thames Chamber Players, Oxford Haydn Players and appearances with National Centre of Orchestral Studies, European Community Youth Orchestra, Capricorn. Compositions include: Chamber: String Quartet No 1, Summer Song; Works for Piano: Sonata No 1, Autumn Tale; Serenata; Variations for Orchestra, 1979; Festive Fanfare; Prelude, Dream Sequence and the Song Of The Washerwoman, from the opera Yerma; Appearances; The Name Of The Rose; Summer Cycle including Summer Night; Summer's Apotheose; String Quartet No2, L'Eveil Au Désir; Canti Cantici, Libro 1. Contributions to: Editorial Assistant, Music Analysis; Various reviews. Address: 2 Stanley Avenue, Chesham, Buckinghamshire, HP5 2JF, England.

ELLIS Osian (Gwynn), b. 8 Feb 1928, Fynnongroew, Flint, Wales. Harpist. m. Rene Ellis Jones, 1951, 2 sons. Education: Royal Academy of Music. Career: Numerous radio and television broadcasts; Recitals and concerts worldwide; Shared poetry and music recitals with Dame Peggy Ashcroft, Paul Robeson, Burton, C Day-Lewis among others; Member of Melos Ensemble; Solo harpist with London Symphony Orchestra; Professor of Harp at Royal Academy of Music, 1959-89; Works written for him include Harp Concertos by Hoddinott, 1957, Mathias, 1970, Jersild, 1972, Gian Carlo Menotti, 1977, and William Schuman, 1978; From 1960 worked with Benjamin Britten who wrote for him Harp Suite in C, Opus 83, and Canticle V for performance with Peter Pears, Birthday Hansel, and folk songs; With Peter Pears on recital tours to Europe and USA, 1974-. Recordings include: Concertos, recitals and folk songs. Publication: The Story of the Harp in Wales, 1991. Honours include: Paris Award for film, The Harp; Grand Prix du Disque; French Radio Critics Award; FRAM, 1960; Honorary DMus, University of Wales, 1970; CBE, 1971. Membership: Former Member, Music and Welsh Advisory Committees, British Council. Address: 90 Chandos Avenue, London, N20, England.

ELMING Poul, b. 1949, Aalborg, Denmark. Tenor. Education: Studied at the Conservatories in Aalborg and Aarhus, and with Paul Lohmann in Wiesbaden. Debut: Sang in recital from 1978. Career: Performed baritone roles with Jutland Opera, Aarhus from 1979; Royal Opera Copenhagen from 1984 in many roles including Mozart's Count, Eugene Onegin, Malatesta and Verdi's Germont and Posa; Further private studies with Susanna Eken of the Royal Danish Music Conservatory and Professor Oren Brown of the Juilliard School of Music in New York; Made his tenor debut as Parsifal at the Royal Opera, Copenhagen in 1989; Has sung Erik in Der fliegende Holländer and Spalanzani in Les Contes d'Hoffmann; Bayreuth Festival, Covent Garden, Deutsche Oper Berlin and the Vienna Staatsoper, Hannover and Mannheim from 1990 as Siegmund in Die Walküre and Parsifal; Many recitals and concerts including appearances with the Danish Radio Symphony Orchestra in Copenhagen; Sang Siegmund at Covent Garden, 1994; Parsifal at the 1996 Bayreuth Festival. Recordings include: Video of Parsifal from the Berlin Staatsoper, 1995. Address: c/o Ingpen and Williams Ltd, 26 Wadham Road, London SW15 2LR, England.

ELMS Lauris, b. 20 Oct 1931, Melbourne, Australia. Contralto. Education: Studied with Katherine Wielaert in Melbourne and Dominique Modesti in Paris. Career: Sang in concerts and oratorios, then made stage debut at Covent Garden in 1957 as Ulrica in Un Ballo in Maschera; Appeared with the Royal Opera on tour and in London as Mrs Sedley in Peter Grimes; Returned to Australia in 1959 and sang with local companies as Azucena, Lucretia, Olga and the Princess in Suor Angelica; Toured with J C Williamson's Company in 1965 as Arsace in Semiramide, with Joan Sutherland. Recordings: Peter Grimes; Highlights from Graun's Montezuma; Bononcini's Griselda; Video of Il Trovatore from Sydney Opera House. Address: c/o Australian Opera, Sydney Opera House, New South Wales, Australia.

ELMS Roderick (James Charles), b. 18 Oct 1951, Ilford, England. Pianist; Organist. Education: Licentiate, Guildhall School of Music, 1965; Licentiate, Royal Academy of Music, 1970; Fellow, Royal College of Organists, 1974. Debut: Wigmore Hall and Purcell Room, 1976. Career: Regular Recitalist on organ and piano; Participant in recordings and public concerts given by all major symphony orchestras, some broadcast on radio or television; Member of GNAFF Ensemble, which made successful television debut, Dec 1982. Compositions: Numerous arrangements and original compositions performed and broadcast by BBC; Several Christmas arrangements; Original Music to Love is a Gift. Recordings: Numerous works recorded with orchestras and choirs including numerous solo recordings with London Symphony, London Philharmonic and Royal Philharmonic Orchestras; Organ Music of Percy Whitlock, album; Solo piano album; Christmas arrangements recorded on Christmas Gift; Original Music to Love is a Gift recorded on Just For Today. Honours: Kate Steele Prize for Piano Playing, Royal Academy of Music, 1973; Fellow, Royal Society of Arts, 1979; Associate, Royal Academy of Music, 1994. Memberships: Royal Academy of Music Club; Royal College of Organists. Hobbies: Sound recording; Photography. Address: 23 Bethell Avenue, Cranbrook, Ilford, Esex IG1 4UX, England.

ELSNER Christian, b. 1965, Freiburg im Breisgau, Germany. Singer (Tenor). Education: Studied in Frankfurt. Debut: As Lensky in Eugene Onegin at Heidelberg. Career: Sang Tichon in Katya Kabanova, Mozart's Pedrillo at Darmstadt and Verdi's Macduff; Bavarian State Opera 1997-98 and Salzburg Festival 1997, as First Armed Man in Die Zauberflöte; Concerts include Lieder recitals at the Schubertiade Feldkirch and throughout Germany; Beethoven's Missa solemnis in Berlin, Haydn's Seasons under Armin Jordan, Das Lied von der Erde in Munich and Vienna, Bruckner's Te Deum at the 1997 Salzburg Festival and Beethoven's Ninth in London; Season 1997-98 with Mozart's Idomeneo in Oslo, Berlioz Requiem in Berlin and Missa Solemnis by Beethoven under Casto Maria Guilini. Recordings include: Schumann Dichterliebe and Liederkreis; Schubert's Songs; Mahler's Lieder eines Fahrenden Gesellen. Honours include: Winner, International Walter Gruner Lieder Competition, London,

1993; Second Prize, International competition ARD, Munich, 1994. Address: Kunstler Sekretariat am Gasteig, Rosenheimerstrasse 52, 81669 Munich, Germany.

ELSTE (Rudolf Otto) Martin, b. 11 Sept 1952. Bremen, Germany. Musicologist; Discologist; Music Critic. Education: University of Cologne; Rheinische Musikschule, Cologne; Certificate of Advanced Musical Studies, Music Faculty, King's College, London University, England; DPhil, Technische Universität, Berlin. Career: Curator, Staatliches Institut für Musikforschung Preussischer Kulturbesitz, 1982-; Review Editor, IASA Phonographic Bulletin, 1982-93; Panel member, German Record Critics Award, 1983-; Chairman, IASA Discography Committee, 1992-96; Vice President, IASA, 1996-; Consulting Musicologist, Bach-Tage Berlin, 1986-87; Advisory Board Member, CIMCIM, 1995-; Editorial Advisory Board Member, Music in Performance, 1997-. Publications: Internationale Heinrich Schütz Diskographie 1928-72, 1972; Verzeichnis deutschsprachiger Musiksoziologie, 1975; Bachs Kunst der Fuge auf Schallplatten, 1981; Co-contributor, Musikinstrumenten Museum Berlin, 1986; Co-contributor, Handwerk im Dienste der Musik, 1987; Co-contributor, 100 Jahre Berliner Musikinstrumenten Museum, 1988; Kleines Tonträger-Lexikon, 1989; Co-contributor, Kielklaviere, 1991; Co-contributor, Musikalische Interpretation, 1992; Modern Harpsichord Music: A Discography, 1995; Editor/Translator, Baines, Lexikon der Musikinstrumente, 1996. Contributions to: New Grove; Fono Forum; Fanfare; Die Musikforschung; Basler Jahrbuch für Historische Musikpraxis; Jahrbuch des Staatlichen Instituts für Musikforschung. Address: Regensburger Strasse 5A, D-10777 Berlin, Germany.

ELVIRA Pablo, b. 24 Sep 1938, San Juan, Puerto Rico. Baritone. Education: Studied at the Pablo Casals Conservtory, Puerto Rico. Debut: Indiana University, Bloomington, as Rigoletto in 1968. Career: Sang at opera houses in Santa Fe, San Diego and New Orleans; New York City Opera from 1974 with debut as Germont; Metropolitan Opera from 1978 as Rigoletto, Lescaut, Rossini's Figaro and Don Carlo in Ernani and La Forza del Destino; Chicago Lyric Opera in 1985 as Germont; Other roles include Berg's Wozzeck and Strauss's Mandryka; Sang Sharpless in Madam Butterfly at Pittsburgh in 1989; Also performs in concert; Sang in gala at opening of Detroit Opera House, 1996. Recordings include: Amore dei tre re; Cavalleria Rusticana; La Favorita. Address: c/o Pittsburgh Opera Inc, 711 Penn Avenue, 8th Floor, Pittsburgh, PA 15222, USA.

ELWES John, b. 1946, England. Tenor Singer. Education: Studied with George Malcolm at Westminster Cathedral; Further study at the Royal College of Music. Career: Chorister at Westminster Cathedral; Soloist in Britten's Missa Brevis and Abraham and Isaac; Frequent broadcaster for the BBC; Repertoire includes Baroque, Lieder and Contemporary Music on the concert platform and operas by Gluck, Handel, Mozart and Monteverdi on stage; Sang Orfeo in Monteverdi's opera with Phillipe Herreweghe and La Chapelle Royale at the Montpellier opera house and with Flanders Opera, Antwerp, 1989-90. Recordings include: Orfeo in the Death of Orpheus by Stefano Landi, with Tragicomedia directed by Stephen Stubbs.

ELYN Mark, b. 4 Feb 1932, Seattle, Washington, USA. Singer (Bass). Career: Sang from 1955 at the New York City Opera; San Francisco, 1958-59, as Ferrando, Colline, Monterone, and the King in Aida; Also appeared as the Spirit Messenger in the US premiere of Die Frau ohne Schatten, 1959; European engagements from 1960, notably at Basle, Cologne (1961-69), Monte Carlo, Munich and Barcelona; Other roles included Pimen in Boris Godunov, Daland, Sarastro, Zaccaria, King Philip in Don Carlos and Dosifey in Khovanshchina. Address: c/o Oper der Stadt Köln, Offenbachplatz, W-5000 Cologne 1, Germany.

EMMERLICH Gunther, b. 18 Sep 1944, Thuringia, Germany. Bass Singer. Education: Studied in Weimar and Dresden and with Pavel Lisitsian. Debut: Sang the Peasant in Die Kluge by Orff at the Dresden Staatsoper in 1978. Career: Appeared as Kuno in Der Freischütz at the re-opening of the Semper Oper, Dresden, and has sung with the Dresden Ensemble at the Vienna Volksoper and in Amsterdam as Don Alfonso in 1988; Other roles included Osmin in Die Entführung, Geronimo in Matrimonio Segreto, Rocco, Dulcamara and the Hermit in Der Freischütz; Many concert appearances. Recordings: Der Freischütz; Eugene Onegin. Address: c/o Staatsoper, 8012 Dresden, Germany.

ENCINAS Ignacio, b. 1958, Spain. Tenor. Education: Studied with Enzo Costantini and in Madrid; Masterclasses with Gianni Poggi and Gino Bechi. Career: Sang in Trovatore and La Favorita at the Santander Festival, Rigoletto at the Zaruela Theatre in Madrid and appeared further in Oviedo, Vallodilid and Malaga; At Dijon has sung as Pollione in Norma, Alfredo in Traviata, Rigoletto and Riccardo in Un Ballo in Maschera; Season 1989-90 as Maurizio in Adriana Lecouvreur at Liège, returning as Turiddu and Rodolfo in La Bohème; Sang in Verdi's Attila at the Theatro Romano of Benevento and as Macduff in a concert performance of Macbeth at the 1990 Gstaad Festival; Performances of Nabucco in Nimes and Puritani, and as Arturo at Marseille, 1990-91. Honours: Winner of numerous international competitions. Address: c/o Opéra de Marseille, 2 Rue Moliere, F-1321 Marseille Cedex 1, France.

ENDERLE Matthias, b. 16 Jun 1956, Switzerland. Violinist. Education: Studied at the Winterhur Conservatory, in Indiana, and at the University International Menuhin Academy in Gstaad. Career: Co-Founder and Leader of the Carmina Quartet, 1984; Appearances from 1987 in Europe, Israel, Japan and USA; Regular concerts at the Wigmore Hall from 1987; Concerts at the South Bank Centre, London, Amsterdam Concertgebouw, the Kleine Philharmonie in Berlin, and Konzertverein Vienna; Four engagements in Paris, 1990-91, and seven in London; Tours of Australasia, the USA and Japan; Concerts at the Hohenems, Graz, Hong Kong, Schleswig-Holstein, Montreux, Bath, Lucerne, and Prague Spring Festivals; Collaborations with Dietrich Fischer-Dieskau, Olaf Bär and Mitsuko Uchida. Recordings: Various. Honour: Joint Winner, with members of Carmina Quartet, Paolo Borciani String Quartet Competition in Reggio Emilia, Italy, 1987; Gramaphone Prize for Best Chamber Music Recording, 1992. Address: c/o Intermusica Artists' Management, 16 Duncan Terrace, London, N1 8BZ, England.

ENDO Akira, b. 16 Nov 1938, Shido, Japan. Conductor. Education: Studied violin with Vera Barstow, Eudice Shapiro, and Jascha Heifetz; BM, MM, 1962, University of Southern California, Los Angeles. Career: Violinist, Trojan String Quartet, 1960-62; 2nd Violinist, Pacific String Quartet, 1962-69; Conductor, Long Beach Symphony Orchestra, California, 1966-69, and West Side Symphony Orchestra, Los Angeles, 1968-69; Music Director, American Ballet Theatre, NY, 1969-79; Resident Conductor of Houston Symphony Orchestra, 1974-76; Music Director, Austin Symphony Orchestra, TX, 1975-82 and Louisville Orchestra, 1980-83.

ENGEL Karl, b. 1 June 1923, Basle, Switzerland. Concert Pianist. m. Barbara Wackernagel, 26 Oct 1976, 1 son, 1 daughter. Education: Humanistisches Gymnasium Basle; Basle Conservatory with Paul Baumgartner; Ecole Normale Paris with Alfred Cortot. Career: International career as concert pianist since 1948; Cycles of all Mozart piano concertos in Paris, Berlin, Munich, Salzburg, Vienna and Zurich; Cycles of all Beethoven piano sonatas in West Germany and Tel-Aviv; Series of all Mozart piano sonatas in Salzburg; Concert tours in Europe, USA and Japan; Guest of all major music festivals in Europe; Chamber music with Pablo Casals (Prades), Menuhin, Tortelier and Fournier; Lieder recitals with Dietrich, Fischer-Dieskau, Herman Prey and Peter Schreier; Professor of Piano at Hochschule für Musik Hanover, 1959-86; Masterclass at Berne Conservatory. Recordings: Complete piano works of Schumann; Complete Mozart piano concertos with the Mozarteum Orchestra conducted by Leopold Hager; Complete solo piano music by Mozart; Chamber music and Lieder. Honour: Prize, Queen Elisabeth Competition in Belgium, 1952. Membership: Schweizerischer Tonkunstlerverein. Hobbies: Chess; Walking. Address: 2 Chemin des Frenes, CH-1805 Jongny (VD), Switzerland.

ENGELMANN Hans Ulrich, b. 8 Sept 1921, Darmstadt, Germany. Composer; Professor. Education: Studied composition with Fortner, Heidelberg, 1945-49; With Leibowitz and Krenek, Darmstadt, 1948-50; Musicology with Gennrich and Osthoff, Philosophy with Adorno, University of Frankfurt am Main; PhD, 1952. Career: Music Advisor, Hessischen Landestheater, Darmstadt, 1954-61; Lecturer, 1969-73, Professor, 1973-, in composition, Hochschule fir Musik, Frankfurt am Main; Music Advisor, Theater Bonn, 1972-73. Compositions include: Stage Works: Doktor Fausts Hollenfahrt, 1949-59; Verlorener Schatten, 1960; Der Fall Van Damm, 1966-67; Magog, 1956-57; Orchestral Works: Musik for strings, brass and percussion, 1948; Impromptu, 1949; 5 Orchestra Pieces, 1956; Trias for Piano, orchestra and tape, 1962; Chamber: Cello Sonata, 1948; String Quartet, 1952; Integrate for saxophone and piano, 1954; Chamber Symphonie, 1984; Stele for chorus soloists, symphony orchestra, 1987; Duettini for piano and percussion, 1984; Piano pieces; Choral music including cantatas; New Works: Dialogue Piano Percussion, 1991; Clarinota, 1991, TastensÜck, 1991; Essay, 1992; Modus, 1992; Ciacona for chamber orchestra, 1993; Per Luigi, 1996. Recordings include: 99 Bars for Cembalo, HMV; Commedia Humana, Deutsche Grammophon; Ezra Pound Music, Harmonia Mundi; Harpsichord Pieces, Wergo-Mainz. Publications: Bela Bartok's Mikrokosmos, doctoral thesis. Contributions to: Melos; Neue Zeitschrift fÜr Musik; Musik und Bildung. Honours include: Scholarship, Harvard University, 1949; Goethe Medaille, 1986; Kreuz der BRD, 1992; Hessischer Verdienstorden, 1997. Memberships: President, Work-Commission, GEMA; President, German Composers' League. Address: Park Rosenhohe, Engelweg 15, 6100 Darmstadt, Germany.

ENGEN Keith, b. 5 Apr 1925, Irazee, Minnesota, USA. Bass Singer. Education: Studied at Berkeley, California and with Tino Pattiera and Pavel Ludikar in Vienna. Career: Appeared as a concert singer with stage debut at Graz in 1954; Sang with Bavarian State Opera Munich from 1955 in repertory operas and in the premieres of Hindemith's Harmonie der Welt in 1957 and David Kirchner's Belshazar in 1986; Bayreuth in 1958 as King Henry in Lohengrin; Guest appearances in Germany, Amsterdam, Turin, Florence, Buenos Aires and Edinburgh; Stuttgart in 1968 in the premiere of Orff's Prometheus; Concert engagements in oratorios by Bach and Handel and in lieder recitals. Recordings: Bach's B minor Mass and St Matthew Passion, Fidelio, Orff's Oedipus der Tyrann and Schoenberg's Gurrelieder, Verdi's Giovanna d'Arco, Idomeneo, Prometheus and Strauss's Feuersnot. Address: c/o Bavarian State Opera, Postfach 745, D-8000 Munich 1, Germany.

ENGERER Brigitte, b. 27 Oct 1952, Tunis, Algeria. French Pianist. Education: Commenced piano lessons with Lucette Descaves in Paris at age 5; 1st Prize, Paris Conservatory at age 15; Studied with Stanislav Neuhaus, Moscow Conservatory, 1970-75. Career: Major career since 1975; Soloist with many leading orchestras including Orchestre de Paris, Berlin Philharmonic Orchestra, London Symphony Orchestra, Vienna Symphony Orchestra, Chicago Symphony Orchestra with Daniel Baremboim, Czech Philharmonic Orchestra, Minnesota Orchestra, Los Angeles Philharmonic Orchestra and Toronto Symphony; Numerous recitals worldwide; Many festival and TV appearances; Video with Switzerland Orchestra with Strauss Burlesque. Recordings: Various. Honours: 6th Prize, Long-Thibaud Competition, 1969; 6th Prize, Tchaikovsky Competition, Moscow, 1974; 3rd Prize, Queen Elisabeth of Belgium Competition, 1978; Grand Prix du Disque with Schumann Carnaval. Address: c/o ICM Artists Ltd, 40 West 57th Street, New York, NY 10019, USA.

ENGERT Ruth, b. 9 Oct 1946, Frankfurt-am-Main, Germany. Mezzo-Soprano. Education: Studied at the Frankfurt Musikhochschule and with Josef Metternich in Cologne. Career: Sang at Koblenz, Freiburg and Hanover, 1969-79; Member of the Deutsche Oper Berlin from 1979 notably as Mozart's Cherubino and Dorabella, Verdi's Eboli and Meg Page, Wagner's Fricka, Brangaene and Waltraute, Octavian, Nicklausse in Les Contes d'Hoffmann and Charlotte in Die Soldaten; Guest appearances at Turin in Clytemnestra in 1987, Venice as The Composer in Ariadne auf Naxos and at Genoa, Madrid and Lisbon; Bayreuth Festival in 1989 as Venus in Tannhäuser; Sang Kundry at the Spoleto Festival in Italy and in Charleston, USA, 1986-90, and Octavian in Rosenkavalier at Catania in 1992; Sang Kundry for Flanders Opera, 1996. Recordings: Strauss's Feuersnot; Parsifal at Bayreuth, 1985; Die Walküre at Bayreuth, 1987; Eugene Onegin; Funeral Cantata by Cherubini. Address: c/o Festspielhaus, PO Box 100262, 8580 Bayreuth 2, Germany.

ENGLICHOVA Katerina, b. 13 June 1969, Prague, Czech Republic. Harpist. Education: Conservatoire, Prague; Curtis Institute of Music, Philadelphia; Hochschule fur Musik, Cologne-Aachen. Debut: Carnegie Hall, New York, 1998. Career: Modern Art Museum, Los Angeles, 1996; Villa Medici, Rome, Italy, 1998; T B A, Paris, France, 1998, Hong Kong, 1998; Festivals: Pacific Music Festival, Japan; Music by the Red Sea, Israel; Tanglewood Music Festival, USA; Rencontres Musicales d'Evian, France; Prague Autumn, Czech Republic; Bratislava Music Festival, Slovakia. Compositions: Ravel, Introduction and Allegro; Debussy, Danses Sacree et Profane, Triosonate; Britten, Voice and Harp; Hindemith, Sonate; Harmonia Mundi, A Roussel, with Czech Nonet; Panton, M Ravel, C Debussy, Solo and Chamber Recital; Koch, Discover, C Saint-Saens, L Spohr, P Hindemith, with Josef Suk, Violin. Honours: 2nd Prize, E Herbert Hobin Harp Competition, USA, 1993; European Broadcast Competition, 1997; 1st Prize, Pro Musicis International Award, New York, 1995. Membership: World Harp Society. Hobbies: Literature; Theatre; Travel. Address: Pod Klaudiankou 2, 14700 Praha 4, Czech Republic.

ENGLISH Gerald, b. 6 Nov 1925, England. Lyric Tenor; Educator; Administrator. m. (1) Jennifer Ryan, 1954, 2 sons, 2 daughters, (2) Linda Jacoby, 1974, 1 son. Education: Royal College of Music. Career: After war service began career as lyric tenor, subsequently travelling USA, and Europe; Appeared at Sadler's Wells, Covent Garden and Glyndebourne; Often heard in operas by Mozart and Monteverdi, and concert music by Bach, Stravinsky, Fauré and Dallapiccola; Professor, Royal College of Music, 1960-77; Director, Opera Studio, Victorian College for the Arts, Melbourne, Australia, 1977-89. Recordings: Schumann Song Cycles with Roger Smalley Piano; Whispers music by Andrew Ford and vocal music of Peggy anville Hicks. Honours: DMus honoris causa, Sydney University, 1989; Australian Creative Artist Fellowship, 1994. Address: PO Box 4177, Geelong, Victoria 3220, Australia.

ENGLISH Jon (Arthur), b. 22 Mar 1942, Kankakee, IL, USA. Composer; Trombonist; Percussionist; Double Bass Player.

m. Candace Natwig. Education: Studied at the University of Illinois with Kenneth Gaburo, BM, 1965. Career: Member of the Harry Partch Ensemble, 1961-62, the Illinois Contemporary Chamber Players, 1963-66 and the Savannah Symphony Orchestra, 1967; Associate Artist of the University of Iowa Center for New Music and New Performing Arts until 1974; Has worked from Cologne since 1976; Performances in Europe as soloist, with Candace Natwig, singer, and in new music groups. Compositions include: 404 1-2 East Green Street for Tape, 1965; Sequent Cycles for 6 players, 1968; ...Whose Circumference Is A Nowhere, 1970; Used Furniture Sale for Tape, 1971; Summerstalks for Performer and Tape, 1973; Shagbolt for Trombone, 1978; Electrotrombonics, 1979; Foursome, 1979; Dog Dreams, 1982; Harmonies For Charlie Mingus, 1983. Address: c/o ASCAP, ASCAP Building, One Lincoln Plaza, New York, NY 10023, USA.

ENGLUND Claës-W, b. 12 Apr 1938, Stockholm, Sweden. Director; Legal Advisor. m. Dorrit Englund, 4 Sept 1965, 1 son, 2 daughters. Education: Bachelor of Law, Stockholm University, 1966; Junior Judge, 1967-69. Appointments: Ministry of Finance and Ministry of Civil Service, 1962-71; Secretary and Assistant Director of Commercial Employer's Association, the Employer's Association for film and cinema and the Association of Swedish Theatres and Orchestras-TR, Teatrarnas Riksforbund, 1985-; Director and Legal Advisor at the music department of the Association of Swedish Theatres and Orchestras-TR, Teatrarnas Riksforbund; Secretary of IAOA, International Alliance of Orchestra Associations and the Nordic Orchestra Cooperation; Member of the Board of Swedish Section of ITI and Education Committee; Chairman of the Swedish committee for Occupational Theatre and Security within theatre and music; Chairman of Swedish Conductors Programme; Director of Music Department of Teatrarnas Riksforbund. Membership: ISPA. Hobbies: Theatre; Dance and classical music; Politics; Literature. Address: Teatranas Riksforbund, P O Box 1778, S-111 87 Stockholm, Sweden.

ENGLUND (Sven) Einar, b. 17 June 1916, Ljugarn, Gotland, Sweden. Composer; Pianist; Professor. m. (2) Maynie Sirén (Smolander), 3 Oct 1958, 2 sons, 2 daughters. Education: Sibelius Academy, Helsinki, 1933-41; Tanglewood Music Center, USA, 1949. Career: Composer and Professor hc; Music Critic, Helsinki's daily, Hufvudsbladet, 1956-76; Lecturer in Composition and Music Theory, Sibelius Academy, 1957-81. Compositions include: Symphony Nos 1,2,3,4,5,6,7, 1946-88; Sonata for Violin and Piano, 1979; Sonata for Cello and Piano, 1982; Trio, 1981; Quintet for Piano, 1991; Sonata for Violin and Sonata for Cello, 1982; Kanteletar-Sarja for Women's Choir, 1984; String Quartet, 1985; Concerto for Clarinet and Orchestra, 1991. Recordings: Concerto for Piano and Orchestra No 1, CD; The Complete Pianomusic; Concerto for Violin and Orchestra; Symphony No 1; Symphony No 2; Symphony No 4; Symphony 3 & 7; Sonata for Cello and Piano; Serenade for Strings; Symphony No 5, Fennica; Piano Trio; Sonata for Violin and Piano; Concerto for 12 Cellos; Concerto for Flute and Orchestra; Wind Quintet; Hymnus Sepulcralis; Concerto for clarinet and orchestra. Address: Lallukan Taiteilijakoti, Apollonkatu 13 A 48, SF-00100 Helsinki 10, Finland.

ENGSTRÖM Bengt Olof, b. 25 May 1926, Umeå, Sweden. Orchestra and Concert Hall Executive. m. Anne-Marie Lemner, 19 Apr 1954, 2 son, 1 daughter. Education: Graduated as Music Teacher, 1949, Higher Kantor, 1951 and Higher Organist, 1952, at Swedish Royal Academy of Music; Doctor of Musicology, University of Lund, 1997. Career: Organist, music teacher, Iggesund, Sweden, 1952-55; Music Teacher, Uppsala, 1955-58; Music Consultant, Stockholm, 1958-61; Manager, Norrköping Symphony Orchestra, 1961-64; Music Consultant, Royal Board of Education, 1964-69; Lecturer, Teachers Training College, Umeå, 1969-74; Secretary, Local Authorities Music Association, Stockholm, 1974-76; President, Stockholm Philharmonic Orchestra and Concert Hall, 1976-86. Publications: Form och stil i musiken, 1959; Brevkurs i musikhistoria, 1959-61; En bok om musik, 1966-69; Co-author, Vi Gör musik, 1970-81; Co-author, Lek med toner, 1971; Den Kommunala musikskolan, 1976; 75 år med Stockholms Konsertförening, 1977; Ny sång i fädernas kyrka, 1997. Memberships: Music Education Committee, 1964-68; Board, Stockholm Conservatory of Music, 1976-87; Central Music Committee, 1984-88; Board, Royal Academy of Music, Deputy Chairman, 1987-94; Board, Konstnarsnamnden, 1985-91; Board, Stockholm Opera College, 1988-91; Board, Swedish Singers Association, Chairman, 1988-94; Board, The Norrbotten Academy, Permanent Secretary, 1988-; Various clubs. Address: Johan Enbergs Väg 54A, S-17161 Solna, Sweden.

ENSTRÖM Rolf, b. 2 Nov 1951, Södertälje, Sweden. Composer. m. Karin Enström-Salomonsson, 3 May 1980, 2 sons, 1 daughter. Education: Engineer, studied Musicology and Philosophy at the universities in Stockholm and Gothenburg; Studied Music in Örebro, Musicology in Gothenburg; Composition self-taught. Debut: With multimedia piece Myr at the International Society for Contemporary Music Festival, Athens, 1979. Career: As multimedia artist has collaborated with artists in adjacent fields, including photographer Thomas Hellsing; His music performed worldwide; Directions played at International Society for Contemporary Music, Athens, 1979; Teaching at EMS, Stockholm; Summer courses at Nordens Biskops Arnö, near Stockholm; Participant, DAAD cultural exchange programme, 1991, then Composer-in-Residence, Berlin. Compositions: Tape music, music for instruments and electronics and multimedia works, including: Slutförbannelser, text by Elsa Grave, 1981; Fractal, multimedia piece (with Thomas Hellsing); Tjidtjag och Tjidtjaggaise, based on Lapp joik, 1987; Skizzen aus Berlin, 1991; Asylum, multimedia piece (with Thomas Hellsing); In Ice, Mirror, 1995. Recordings: Directions, Final Curses, Tjidtjag och Tjidtjaggaise; Fractal; Dagbrott, Sequence In Blue, Tonal Nagual, Tsentsaks; In Ice, Mirror. Honours: Honourable Mention for Sequence in Blue, Bourges, 1978; Prix Italia for Tjidtjag och Tjidtjaggaise, 1987; Honourable Mention for In Ice, Mirror, Ars Electronica, 1995. Memberships: ICEM, Swedish Section; International Society for Contemporary Music, Swedish Section; FST (Swedish Composers' Union); Fylkingen. Address: Helgestavägen 127, S-12541 Älvsjö, Sweden.

ENTREMONT Philippe, b. 7 Jun 1934, Rheims, France. Conductor; Pianist. Education: Studied under Jean Doyen at Paris Conservatoire. Debut: Barcelona at age 15. Career: US debut at National Gallery, Washington DC and with National Orchestral Association, NY, 1953; Appearances as recitalist and guest artist with major orchestras worldwide; Music Director, Conductor and Pianist with Vienna Chamber Orchestra; Has conducted many leading orchestras including Royal Philharmonic Orchestra, Ensemble Orchestral de Paris, Mostly Mozart, Dallas Orchestra, and Montreal Orchestra; Appeared in many major summer festivals including Schleswig-Holstein and Carinthian Festivals; World tour with Vienna Chamber Orchestra for Bicentennial of Mozart's death, 1991; Former President of Ravel Academy and Juror for international piano competitions; Permanent Conductor for Netherlands Chamber Orchestra, 1993. Recordings include: Works by Chopin, Mozart, Schubert, Stravinsky, Bernstein, Milhaud, and Debussy's Printemps, and Ravel's Bolero. Honours include: 1st Laureate, Grand Prize Winner, Marguerite Long, Jacques Thibaud Competition; Grand Prix du Disque; Edison Award, The Netherlands; Knight, Legion of Honour; 1st Class Cross of Honour for Arts and Sciences, Austria. Current Management: ICM Artists. Address: c/o ICM Artists, 40 West 57th Street, New York, NY 10010, USA.

EÖSZE László, b. 17 November 1923, Budapest, Hungary. Former Art Director. m. (1) 2 children, (2) 24 September 1983. Education: PhD, Aesthetics and Literature. Career: Music Teacher and Pianist; Concerts in Hungary and Europe, 1946-51. Publications: 16 books including, Zoltán Kodály élete és munkássága (Life and Work of ZK), 1956; Zoltán Kodály élete képekben (K's Life in Pictures), 1957; Az opera utja (History of Opera), 1960; Giuseppe Verdi, 1961, 2nd edition, 1966; Enlarged, 1975; Zoltán Kodály, His Life and Work, English, 1962, in German, 1965; Zoltán Kodály, 1967; Kodály, His Life in Pictures and Documents, 1971, English and German; Richard Wagner, 1969; Richard Wagner, Eine Chronik seines Lebens und Schaffens, 1969; Zoltán Kodály, életének krónikája, 1977; 119 római Liszt dokumentum, 1980; Essays and articles in various languages. Contributions to: The New Grove Dictionary of Music and Musicians; Brockhaus Riemann Musiklexikon; Numerous professional publications. Honours: Erkel Prize, 1977; Gramma Award, 1978. Memberships: Co-President, F Liszt Society; Executive Secretary, 1975-95, International Kodály Society. Address: Attila ut 133, 1012 Budapest, Hungary.

EÖTVÖS Peter, b. 2 Jan 1944, Hungary. Composer; Conductor. Education: Budapest Academy of Music, 1958-65; Cologne Musikhochschule, 1966-68. Career: Music Director, Ensemble Inter-Contemporain, Paris, 1979-91; Principal Guest Conductor, BBC Symphony Orchestra, 1985-88; First Guest Conductor, Budapest Festival Orchestra, 1992-95; Chief Conductor, Radio Kamerorkest Hilversum, 1994-; Conducted first performance of pieces by Birtwhistle, Boulez, Donatoni, Kurtag, Reich, Stockhausen and Xenakis; Operas include premiere of Stockhausen's Donnerstag and Montag aus Licht at Milan Scala and Covent Garden; Maderna, Hyperion in Paris; Stravinsky: Rake's Progress, Lille; Mozart: Don Giovanni, Lyon; Engaged by most major festivals in Europe as Conductor and Artistic Advisor; Professor, Hochschule für Musik, Karlsruhe, Bartók Seminar, Szombathely; Founder and President, International Eötvös Institute for Young Conductors; Conducted new production of Nono's Prometeo at Brussels, 1997. Compositions include: For orchestra: Chinese Opera, Shadows, Psychokosmos, Atlantis; For ensemble: Intervalles-Interieurs, Windsequenzen, Brass the Metalspace, Steine, Triangel; For string quartet: Korrespondenz; For music theatre and opera: Harakiri; Radames; Three Sisters; For vocal ensemble: 3 comedy madrigals; For solo: Psalm 151 for percussion. Recordings: Moro Lasso, 1963; Mese, 1968; Cricket-music, 1970; Intervalles-Interieurs, 1974-81; Sequences of the Wind, 1975; Chinese Opera, 1986. Honours: Officier de l'Ordre des Arts et des Lettres, France, 1986; Bartok Award, Budapest, Hungary, 1997. Address: Naarderweg 56, NL-1261 BV Blaricum, Netherlands.

EPPSTEIN Ury, b. 3 Feb 1925, Saarbrücken, Germany. Musicologist. m. Kikue Iguchi, 2 Jan 1965, 2 sons. Education: MA, Hebrew University of Jerusalem, 1945-49; Diploma in Music Theory, Jerusalem Academy of Music, 1950-53; Diploma in Japanese Language, Tokyo University of Foreign Studies, 1958-59; Diploma in Japanese Music, Tokyo University of Fine Arts and Music, Japan, 1959-63; PhD, Tel Aviv University, 1984. Career: Secretary, Music Research Centre, Hebrew University, Jerusalem, 1966-72; Lecturer, Tel Aviv University, Theatre and Musicology Departments, 1972-77; Hebrew University, Theatre and Musicology Departments, 1972-; Guest Lecturer, Copenhagen University, East Asian Institute, 1981, 1986; Lund University, Sweden, East Asian Institute and Musicology Department, 1986; Tokyo University of Fine Arts and Music, Dokkye University, Japan, 1997. Recordings: The Nuns of Gethsemane sing Russian-Orthodox Chants, 1972; Hassidic Tunes of Dancing and Rejoicing, 1976; Sephardic Songs of the Balkans, 1980; Jewish Yemenite Songs from the Diwan, 1982; Taqsim - Instrumental Improvisation in Near Eastern Traditions, 1991. Publications: Kanjinchō, The Subscription List, Kabuki Play translated from Japanese to Hebrew, 1993; The Beginnings of Western Music in Meiji Era Japan, 1994. Contributions to: Numerous, including: Transactions of the International Conference of Orientalists in Japan, 1961; Orient/West, 1967; Studies on Japanese Culture, 1973; China - Tradition Versus Changes, 1979; New Grove Dictionary of Music and Musicians, 1980; Maske und Kothurn; Israel Broadcasting Authority (radio programmes); Encyclopedia Judaica Yearbooks 1988-91; Monumenta Nipponica, 1985-1993; Proceedings of the XXXII (1986) International Congress for Asian and North-African Studies, Hamburg, 1992; Contact between Cultures, selected papers from the 33rd (1990) International Congress of Asian and North-African Studies, Toronto, 1992; Kyoto Conference on Japane4se Studies 1994, vol 3, 1996. Honours include: Order of the Rising Sun by the Emperor of Japan, 1989; Israel Minister of Education and Culture Prize for translation from Japanese, 1996. Memberships include: Israel Musicological Society; European Association of Japanese Studies. Address: 80 Tchernihovsky Street, Jerusalem, Israel.

EPSTEIN David M, b. 3 Oct 1930, New York City, USA. Composer; Conductor; Theorist; Professor. m. Anne Merrick, 21 June 1953, 2 daughters. Education: AB, Antioch College, 1952; MMus, New England Conservatory of Music, 1953; MFA, Brandeis University, 1954; PhD, Princeton University, 1968. Career includes: Guest conductor of well known orchestras, Germany, Austria, Czechoslovakia, Poland, Israel, France, Belgium, Mexico, USA and others; Member, Herbert von Karajan Musikgespräche, Salzburg, 1983-88. Compositions include: String Trio; Sonority - Variations for Orchestra; Fantasy Variations for Solo Viola or Violin; The Seasons; String Quartet, 1971; The Concord Psalter, 1978; Music for theatre, film and television. Recordings include: Bloch, Concerto Grosso No 2, Czech Radio Orchestra; Tillis, Festival Journey, The New Orchestra of Boston; Kurt Weill - Suite from Der Silbersee, MIT Symphony Orchestra; Copland - Dance Symphony, Piston - Incredible Flautist, MIT Symphony. Publications: Beyond Orpheus, Studies in Musical Structure, 1979; Shaping Time: Music, The Brain and Performance, 1995; Various articles and music arrangements. Honours: Ford Foundation Recording Award, 1972; Rockefeller Foundation Award, 1972; Alexander von Humboldt Award, 1987; Deutsche Forschungsgemeinschaft Award, 1981, 1992; ASCAP Deems Taylor Award, 1996. Memberships: Society for Music Theory; Society of Composers; American Brahms Society; ASCAP. Current Management: Thea Dispeker Inc, 59 East 57th Street, New York, NY 10222, USA. Address: Department of Music, Massachusetts Institute of Technology, Cambridge, MA 02139, USA.

EPSTEIN Matthew A, b. 23 Dec 1947, New York City, New York, USA. Opera Impressario; Consultant. Education: BA, European History, University of Pennsylvania, 1969. Career: Manager Representative with extensive list of operatic artists; Consultant to opera companies and symphony orchestras on production concepts and casting, USA and Europe; Formerly Artistic Director of BAM Opera at the Brooklyn Academy of Music and Artistic Consultant for a Concert Opera series at Carnegie Hall, SONY Classical, 1991-94; General Director, Welsh National Opera, 1993-94; Vice-President, Columbia Artists Management Incorporated; Artistic Advisor to Lyric Opera of Chicago and Artistic Consultant to Santa Fe Opera. Address: Columbia Artists, 165 W 57th Street, New York, NY 10019, USA.

EQUILUZ Kurt, b. 13 June 1929, Vienna, Austria. Singer (Tenor). Education: Studied in Vienna with Adolf Vogel. Career: Sang as chorister in Vienna from 1945; Solo career at the Vienna Staatsoper from 1957, notably as Mozart's Pedrillo, Beethoven's Jacquino and in operas by Strauss; Sang at the Salzburg Festival in the premieres of Liebermann's Penelope, 1954, Martin's Le Mystère de la Nativité, 1960 and Wagner-Regeny's Das Bergwerk zu Falun, 1961; Many concert appearances as Lieder singer and in religious music; Professor, Graz Musikhochschule, 1971-; Professor of Lieder and Oratorio, Academy for Music in Vienna, 1982-. recordings: Monteverdi's Orfeo and Il Ritorno di Ulisse; Cantatas by Bach and the St John and St Matthew Passions (Telefunken); Cavalieri's La Rappresentazione di Anima e di Corpo (Deutsche Grammophon). Address: Schwenkgasse 8/4, A-1120 Vienna, Austria.

ERB Donald (James), b. 17 Jan 1927, Youngstown, OH, USA. Composer; Music Educator. m. Lucille Hyman, 10 Jun 1950, 1 son, 3 daughters. Education: BS, Kent State University, 1950; MM, Cleveland Institute of Music, 1953; DMus, Indiana University School of Music, 1964; Studied with Harold Miles, Kenneth Gaburo, Marcel Dick, Bernhard Heiden in USA, and with Nadia Boulanger in Paris, 1953. Career: Teacher, 1953-61, Composer-in-Residence, 1966-81, Professor of Composition, 1987-, Cleveland Institute of Music; Composer-in-Residence, Dallas Symphony Orchestra, 1968-69; Staff Composer, Bennington Composers Conference, VT, 1969-74; Visiting Professor, 1975-76, Professor of Music, 1984-87, Indiana University School of Music; Meadows Professor of Composition, Southern Methodist University, 1981-84; Composer-in-Residence, St Louis Symphony Orchestra, 1988-90. Compositions include: Orchestral: Chamber Concerto for Piano and Strings, 1958, Symphony Of Overtures, 1964, Stargazing for Band and Tape, 1966, Christmasmusic, 1967, Autumnmusic for Orchestra and Electronic Sounds, 1973, Music For A Festive Occasion for Orchestra and Electronic Sounds, 1975, Trombone Concerto, 1976, Cenotaph (For EV) for Symphonic Band, 1979, Sonneries, 1981, Contrabassoon Concerto, 1984, The Dreamtime, 1985, Concerto for Brass and Orchestra, 1986; Chamber music, choral works and piano pieces. Recordings: Several. Contribution to: Article on orchestration in Encyclopaedia Britannica, 15th edition, 1974. Address: 4073 Bluestone Road, Cleveland Heights, OH 44121, USA.

ERBEN Valentin, b. 14 Mar 1945, Austria. Cellist. Education: Studied in Vienna, Munich and Paris. Career: Co-Founder and Cellist of the Alban Berg Quartet from 1971; Many concert engagements worldwide, including complete cycles of the Beethoven Quartets in 15 European cities, 1987-88 and 1988-89 seasons; Bartók/Mozart cycle in London, Vienna, Paris, Frankfurt, Munich, Geneva and Turin, 1990-91; Annual concert series at the Vienna Konzerthaus and festival engagements worldwide; Assocate Artist at the South Bank Centre in London; US appearances in Washington DC, San Francisco and at Carnegie Hall in New York. Recordings include: Complete Quartets of Beethoven, Brahms, Berg, Webern and Bartók; Late Quartets of Mozart, Schubert, Haydn and Dvorák; Quartets by Ravel, Debussy and Schumann; Live recordings from Carnegie Hall playing Mozart and Schumann, Konzerthaus in Vienna, and Opéra-Comique in Paris, playing Brahms. Honours include: Grand Prix du Disque; Deutsche Schallplatenpreis; Edison Prize; Japan Grand Prix; Gramophone Magazine Award. Address: Intermusica Artists' Management, 16 Duncan Terrace, London, N1 8BZ, England.

ERBSE Helmo, b. 27 Feb 1924, Rudolstadt, Germany. Composer. Education: Studied at the Musikhochschule of Weimar and Berlin, with Boris Blacher. Debut: Conducted in Berlin in 1951. Career: Freelance Composer; Has conducted and directed opera; Moved to Salzburg in 1957, with his opera, Julietta, being performed there in 1959. Compositions: Stage: Julietta, opera, 1957, Ruth, ballet, 1958, Der Herr In Grau, comic opera, 1966; Orchestral: Symphony in 4 Movements, 1964, Das Hohelied Salomons, 1969, for String and Wind Players, 1971, Symphony No 2, 1970, Triple Concerto, 1972; Chamber music and music for chorus. Honours include: Beethoven Prize, Bonn, 1961; Appreciation Award for Music, Austrian Ministry for Education and Art, 1973. Hobbies: Mountain Climbing; Skiing. Address: c/o GEMA, Postfach 80 07 67, D-81607 Munich, Germany.

ERCKENS Peter, b.1953, Hamburg, Germany. Conductor. Education: Hamburg Musikhochschule, with Horst Stein. Debut: Swan Lake at the Hamburg Staatsoper, 1976. Career: Assistant to Michael Gielen at Frankfurt Opera, 1977-80; Music Director at Bremen 1980-84, with tours to Tokyo, Graz and Budapest; Principal Conductor at Düsseldorf Opera am Rhein, 1984-88, and at Mainz 1990-96; Conducted productions of Parsifal, Otello, Macbeth, Ariadne, Peter Grimes, Rigoletto, Tristan und Isolde, The Greek Passion and Lady Macbeth of Mtsensk; Guest Conductor, Antwerp (Figaro, 1995), Sydney (Otello, 1996) and Hamburg (Il Trovatore, 1996); Season 1997-98 with La Bohème in Cologne, Hoffman in Gothenburg, Fidelio at Melbourne, Beatrice et Benedict in Sydney and Trovatore in Berlin; Concerts include Oslo Philharmonic, Orchestre National du Capitole (Toulouse) and the South Australia Radio SO in season 1997-98. Honours include: Wilhelm Oberdorffer Prize of the City of Hamburg, 1997. Address: c/o Haydn Rawstron Ltd, 36 Station Road, London SE20 7BQ, England.

ERDÉLYI Csaba, b. 15 May 1946, Budapest, Hungary. Viola Player; Conductor. m. Ju-Ping Chi, 8 Oct 1989, 3 s. Education: Artist and Teacher Diplomas, Franz Liszt Academy of Music, 1970; Influential teachers: Pál Lukács, Yehudi Menuhin, Bruno Giuranna. Career: Franz Liszt Chamber Orchestra, 1968-72; Eszterházy Baryton Trio, 1973-78; Principal Viola, Philharmonia Orchestra, London, 1974-78; Professor of Viola, Guildhall School of Music, London, 1980-87; Chilingirian String Quartet, 1981-87; Professor of Viola: Indiana University, Bloomington, 1987-91, Rice University, Houston, TX, 1991-95; Soloist in RFH, Promenade Concerts; Frequent Partner with Yehudi Menuhin; Master classes worldwide including: RAM London, Aldeburgh, Alaska, Beijing, Mexico, Budapest, USA; Annual summer classes in Gubbio Festival, Italy; Jury Member: BBC Young Musician of The Year and Lionel Tertis Viola Competition, Isle of Man; First US performance of Brahms/Berio Sonata for Viola and Orchestra; Opening recital at International World Viola Congress in Redlands, CA, 1989, and Vienna, 1992. Recordings: Hoddinott, Viola Concerto; Strauss Songs with Jessye Norman. Publications: Bartók: Viola Concerto; Bach: Suite Pour La Luth for Viola; Hummel: Fantasia; Mozart: Sinfonia Concertante KV 364 for String Sextet; Arrangement of Brahms's Sonata Op 78; Viola part to Schubert's Arpeggione Sonata. Contributions include: Music and The Fear of Violence in Classical Music. Honour: 1st Prize, Carl Flesch Competition, 1972. Memberships: Institute for the Development of Intercultural Relations through the Arts, Geneva. Hobbies: Rebirthing; Yoga; Massage; Cooking; Body-Mind Control; Mountain Walking. Address: 2420 Boston Road, Bloomington, IN 47401, USA.

ERDING-SWIRIDOFF Susanne, b. 16 Nov 1955, Schwabisch Hall, Germany. Composer. m. Paul Swiridoff, 11 Mar 1988. Education: Stuttgart University, 1975-77; Oxford and Cambridge, England in summers, 1976-80; Yale University, USA, 1976; Universite de Montreal, Canada, 1978; Studied music, piano and composition with Milko Kelemen, Stuttgart Academy of Music, 1974-79 and composition with Dieter Acker, Munich, 1980; Seminars on composition at Buenos Aires, 1981; International Summer School of Music with Peter Maxwell Davies, Dartington, England, 1985; Composition with Agosto Benjamin Rattenbach, Buenos Aires, 1985. Career: Many TV appearances, 1983-88. Compositions include: Orchestra: Yellan, 1981, Event, 1985, Il Visconte Dimezzato, 1994; Concertos: Konzert, 1983, Tierra Querida, 1986; Operas: Joy, chamber opera, 1983, Die Wundersame Geschichte Des Peter Schlemihl, marionette opera, 1991; Ballet: Yellan, 1981; Piano: Klaviersuite, 1982, Maske Und Kristall IV, 1992; Chamber Music: Grotesques Arabesques, 1980, Rotor, 1982, Homage To The City Of Dresden, 1985, Variations Serieuses, Fayence, 1986, Labirinto Del Sole, 1987, Gioielli Rubati, 1987, Blumen Und Blut, 1988, Zeitstimmen, 1993; Vocal: Okteondo, 1979, Initialen, 1986, Maske Und Kristall X, 1993, XII, 1994. Hobbies: Languages; Travel; Cooking; Literature; Art; Painting. Address: Am Postgutle 14, Post Box 620, D- 74506 Schwabisch Hall, Germany.

EREDE Alberto, b. 8 Nov 1908, Genoa, Italy. Conductor. Education: Studied in Genoa and at the Milan Conservatory; Conducting studies with Weingartner in Basle and Fritz Busch in Dresden. Debut: Accademia di Santa Cecilia, Rome, 1930. Career: Musical Director of the Salzburg Opera Guild, 1935-38; US debut with the NBC Symphony Orchestra in 1937; Glyndebourne Festival in 1939 conducting Le nozze di Figaro and Don Giovanni; Chief Conductor of the Turin Radio Symphony Orchestra, 1945-46; Musical Director of the New London Opera Company, 1946-48; Metropolitan Opera, 1950-55 and 1974-75, notably in La Traviata, Tosca and Turandot; Music Director of the Deutsche Oper am Rhein Dusseldorf, 1958-61; Chief Conductor of the Gothenburg Symphony Orchestra, 1961-; Conducted the San Carlo Opera, Naples at the Edinburgh Festival in 1963, and Lohengrin at the Bayreuth Festival in 1968; Artistic Director of the Paganini International Competition at Genoa from 1975. Recordings include: 14 Complete Opera Sets, mainly of works by Puccini and Verdi, also La Favorita, Cavalleria Rusticana, Roméo et Juliette and Il Barbiere di Siviglia. Address: c/o SA Gorlinsky Ltd, 33 Dover Street, London, W1X 4NJ, England.

ERICKSON Kaaren, b. 9 Feb 1953, Seattle, USA. Singer (Soprano). Education: Studied at Western Washington University, Bellingham, WA, 1970-74 and the Music Academy of the West with Martial Singher and Maurice Abravanel. Career: Sang Gilda in 1982 and won 1st prize 1982 Munich Competition; Sang at the Deutsche Oper Berlin and the Munich Staatsoper; Piccola Scala 1983, in Les Pélerins de la Mecque; US engagements at Seattle, San Francisco, Houston, Cincinnati and the City Opera New York; Metropolitan Opera from 1985 as Susanna in new production of Le nozze di Figaro; Appears in the Met videos of Wagner's Ring, Parsifal and Elektra; Blanche in Dialogues of the Carmelites, as Zerlina in Don Giovanni and a Flowermaiden in a new production of Parsifal (1991); Other roles have included Mozart's Pamina, Fiordiligi Micaela, Contessa, Ellen Orford and Marschallin in Der Freischütz; Sang in the premiere of The Voyage by Philip Glass, Metropolitan, 1992; Many Lieder recitals and concert appearances. Recordings: Le Cinesi by Gluck; The White Election by Gordon Getty; Messiah Handel Atlanta Symphony, Robert Shaw; Dvorak Stabat Mater with NJ Symphony, Zdenek Macal. Membership: National Association of Teachers of Singing. Current Management: Thea Dispeker Artist Management. Address: c/o Thea Dispeker Artists Management, 59 E 54th St, NY 10022, USA.

ERICSDOTTER Siw, b. 9 Feb 1919, Norrkoping, Sweden. Soprano. Education: Studied in Stockholm with Nanny Larsen-Todsen. Career: Member of the Royal Opera Stockholm, 1951-54; Sang with the Hamburg Staatsoper, 1954-59; Appeared in Berlin from 1959 notably as Wagner's Elsa, Eva and Sieglinde; Guest appearances in Vienna, Paris and in Italy; Stuttgart Opera, 1962-70; Other roles include Leonore, Amneris, Tosca and the title role in Judith by N Berg. Recordings include: Herodias in Salome and Der Evangelimann by Kienzl.

ERICSON Barbro, b. 2 Apr 1930, Halmstad, Sweden. Mezzo-Soprano. Education: Studied in Stockholm with Arne Sunnegard. Debut: Stockholm in 1956 as Eboli in Don Carlos. Career: Guest appearances in London, Berlin, Hamburg, Edinburgh, Helsinki, France, Holland and Italy; Sang at Paris Opera in 1964 as Venus in Tannhäuser, Bayreuth Festival from 1964 as Kundry and Venus, and Salzburg Easter Festival in 1967 in Die Walküre under Karajan; Metropolitan Opera debut in 1968 as Fricka, returning to New York in 1976 as Herodias in Salome. Recordings include: Die Walküre; Requiem and other works by Ligeti.

ERICSON Eric, b. 26 Oct 1918, Boras, Sweden. Professor; Conductor. m. Monica Spangenberg, 20 July 1976, 2 sons, 2 daughters. Education: Royal Academy of Music, 1938-43; Basel, 1948-49; Studies in Germany, England & USA. Career: Founder, Conductor, Eric Ericson Chamber Choir, 1945; Church Musician, St Jacobs Church, Stockholm, 1949-74; Conductor, Orphei Drangar, Uppsala, 1951-91; Choirmaster, Swedish Radio, 1952-83; Professor, Royal Academy of Music, 1953-90; Guest Conductor, Germany, England, Holland, France, USA and Denmark. Honours: Swedish Choral Conductors Prize, 1988; Danish Sonning Music Prize, 1991; Swedish Academy Royal Prize, Nordic Council Music Prize, 1995; Polar Music Prize, 1997. Memberships: Swedish Royal Academy of Music; Honorary Chairman, International Federation for Choral Music. Address: Armfeltsgatan 10, 11534 Stockholm, Sweden.

ERIKSEN Erling Ragnar, b. 21 December 1955, Kråkstad, Norway. Pianist; Associate Professor. 1 son. Education: Hochschule fur Musik, Hannover, 1975-79; Hochschule fur Musik, Munich, 1979-81; Diploma, 1981. Debut: Recital, Oslo, 1978. Career: Numerous Concert Appearances include performing the Whole of Bach's Well Tempered Clavier; Several International Music Festivals; Soloist with Various Orchestras; Worldwide concert appearances, several radio and TV performances. Recordings: Songs by Alnaes, 1994, Grieg, 1997, with soprano Bodil Arnesen. Hobby: Opera. Current Management: Pro Arte International Management. Address: Bjergsted Terrasse 8/854, N-4007 Stavanger, Norway.

ERLO Louis, b. 26 Apr 1929, Lyon, France. Stage Director. Education: Studied electrical engineering at Lyon, 1944-48. Career: Stage Manager, Lyon Opera, 1950, followed by production of Lohengrin and directorship in 1953; Head of Production, 1969, Administrator, 1973, Paris Opera-Studio; Directed Rabaud's Marouf at Venice in 1956 and worked further at San Francisco, Buenos Aires, Paris and many European centres; Director, Aix-en-Provence Festival from 1981, staging Don Giovanni and Pelléas et Mélisande, Les Contes d'Hoffmann in 1982 and Chabrier's L'Etoile; Other productions include Ohana's Auto da fe in 1973, The Love for Three Oranges and Martinu's Les Trois Souhaits at Lyon in 1973 and 1990, Don Giovanni at Nice in 1991 and Les Contes d'Hoffmann in 1993. Address: c/o Opéra de Lyon, 1 Place de la Comédie, F-69001 Lyon, France.

ERMEDAHL Mattias, b. 6 Mar 1971, Kävlinge, Sweden. Opera Singer. Education: Music School, Stockholm, 1981-90; Opera School, Stockholm, 1992-95. Debut: Gothenburg, 1994. Career: Concert with Ingvar Wixell, Stockholm, 1995; Ferrando, Gothenburg, 1996, Schloss Rheinsberg, 1996, Frankfurt, 1997; Belfiore, Gothenburg, 1997. Current Management: Nordic Artist AB. Address: Box 2001, S-103 11 Stockholm, Sweden.

ERMLER Mark, b. 5 May 1932, Leningrad, Russia. Conductor. Education: Studied at the Leningrad Conservatory with Khaikin and Rabinovich. Debut: Conducted the Leningrad Philharmonic in 1952. Career: Opera debut in 1953 with Die Entführung in Leningrad; Joined the staff of the Bolshoi Opera, Moscow in 1956: conducted Fidelio, Il Barbiere di Siviglia, Eugene Onegin and Le nozze di Figaro in his first season; Ballet debut 1964, with The Firebird and Petrushka; British debut with the Bolshoi Ballet at the London Coliseum, 1974; Opera tours with the Bolshoi Company to Montreal, 1967, Paris, 1970, Tokyo, 1970, 1989, Prague, 1973, Milan, 1974, New York and Washington,

1975, West Berlin 1980: Carmen, Faust, Werther, Cosi fan tutte, Tosca, Butterfly, Aida, Otello Rigoletto, Traviata, Trovatore and Don Carlos; Vienna Staatsoper with Boris Godunov, Don Carlos, Eugene Onegin, Cavalleria Rusticana and Pagliacci; Bayerische Oper Munchen new production Prince Igor, Vancouver Opera new production Eugene Onegin; New Productions of Eugene Onegin and The Bartered Bride for Welsh National Opera; Royal Ballet debut, 1985, Sleeping Beauty; Royal Opera debut, Carmen, 1986; Guest Conductor with USSR State Symphony Orchestra: tours to Italy, West and East Germany, USA, Canada, Japan, Holland, Hungary and Yugoslavia from 1976; Guest in Italy, USA, Bulgaria, Czechoslovakia and Hungary; Concerts with the Royal Liverpool Philharmonic Orchestra, London Symphony and the Orchestra of the Welsh National Opera; Khovanshchina, Sadko, Legend of Kitezh, Snowmaiden, Tzar's Bride and Mozart and Salieri by Rimsky-Korsakov, Rusalka by Dargomizksky, Ruslan and Ludmila by Glinka all at the Bolshoi Theatre; Seattle Opera, 1990, new production of War and Peace; Royal Opera House, Covent Garden: Butterfly, Onegin, Medea, Attila, Fanciulla del West; Guest in Germany, Japan, Sweden, Spain, Yugoslavia; Season 1992 with La Bohème and Samson et Dalila at Covent Garden; Tchaikovsky's The Oprichnik at the 1992 Edinburgh Festival; The Bartered Bride for New Israeli Opera, 1996. Recordings: Prince Igor, Francesca da Rimini by Rachmaninov, Iolanta, Eugene Onegin, The Queen of Spades, The Stone Guest (Dargomizhsky), Tosca, Butterfly, Norma, Così fan tutte, Boris Godunov, Khovanshchina and War and Peace by Prokofiev; Recording with Royal Opera House Orchestra, Swan Lake, The Nutcracker and Sleeping Beauty; Ivan Susanin by Glinka; The Story about a Real Man by Prokofiev; Vera Sheloga, Mozart and Salieri by Rimsky-Korsakov; Symphonic pieces of Prokofiev, Shostokovich, Liszt, Haydn and others. Honours include: Winner, Conducting Competition of Bolshoi Theatre, 1956; Glinka Prize, USSR, 1978. Address: c/o Allied Artists, 42 Montpellier Square, London SW7 1JZ, England.

EROD Ivan, b. 2 Jan 1936, Budapest, Hungary. Composer; Professor; Pianist. m. Marie-Luce Guy, 11 Apr 1969, 3 son, 2 daughter. Education: Academy of Music, Budapest, 1951-56; Academy of Music, Vienna, 1957-61. Debut: Budapest. Career: Coach for Vienna State Opera, 1962-64; Concert Pianist on 5 continents; Appearances include: Salzburg Festival, and Vienna Philharmonic with Karl Bohm; Full Professor for Composition and Music Theory at Hochschule für Musik und Darstellende Kunst, Graz, Austria, 1971-89, and Hochschule für Musik, Vienna, 1989-. Compositions: 2 Operas; Orchestral works, Concertos, Chamber Music, Cantatas, Lieder, Chorus works. Recordings: As pianist, 10 records with Rudolf Schock, tenor; Pierrot Lunaire (Die Reihe, Vienna), recordings in 10 countries; As composer, with various labels; Numerous radio recordings for BBC. Contributions to: Articles in Osterreichische Musikzeitschrift. Honours: Several Austrian State Prizes; Bartok Pasztory Prize, 1993. Hobbies: Literature; Theatre; Arts; Walking tours; Swimming; Travel; Games; Family. Current Management: Verlag Doblinger, Vienna, Austria. Address: Gumpendorfer Strasse 9-13, A-1060 Vienna, Austria.

ERÖS Peter, b. 22 Sept 1932, Budapest, Hungary. Symphony and Opera Conductor. m. (1) Georgia Weiser, 4 Dec 1956, 2 sons, (2) Jasmin Fay Roberts, 1985, divorced. Education: Franz Liszt Music Academy, Budapest; Studies with Zoltan Kodaly, Leo Weiner, Laszlo Somogyi. Career: Assistant to: George Szell (Cleveland Orchestra), Otto Klemperer (Holland Festival), Ferenc Fricsay, Assistant to Bayreuther Festival, 1957-60; Associate Conductor, Amsterdam Concertgebouw Orchestra, 1960-65; Music Director, Malmö Symphony Orchestra, Sweden, 1966-68; Principal Guest Conductor, Melbourne Symphony Orchestra, 1968-70; Music Director, San Diego Symphony Orchestra, Music Director, La Jolla Chamber Music Society, 1972-80; Principal Conductor, Western Australia Symphony Orchestra, Perth, 1975-79; Music Director, Peabody Symphony and Opera, Baltimore, USA, 1982-85; Music Director, Aalborg Symphony Orchestra, Denmark, 1983-89; Music Director, University of Washington Symphony Orchestra and Opera Department, 1989-; Numerous guest engagements with leading orchestras throughout the UK, Europe and the USA. Recordings: Siegfried Wagner, Orchestral Works; Gabriel von Wayditch, Jesus before Herod; Many recordings for Australian Broadcasting Commission and Swedish Radio. Contributions to: Various professional journals and newspapers. Hobbies: Reading; Theatre; Astronomy. Address: c/o University of Washington, Department of Music, Seattle, WA 98155, USA.

ESCHENBACH (Ringmann) Christoph, b. 20 Feb 1940, Breslau, Germany. Pianist; Conductor. Education: Piano studies with foster mother at age 8, with Eliza Hansen and studied conducting with Wilhelm Bruckner-Ruggeberg, Hamburg Conservatory. Career: London debut in 1966; Gave the premiere of Henze's 2nd Concerto at Bielefeld in 1968; USA debut as soloist with Cleveland Orchestra in 1969; Many world tours both as soloist with leading orchestras and as recitalist; Many duo piano appearances with Justus Frantz; Debut as opera conductor with La Traviata at Darmstadt in 1978; Generalmusikdirektor, Rheinland-Pflaz State Philharmonic Orchestra, 1979-81; 1st Permanent Guest Conductor, 1981-82, Chief Conductor, 1982-85, Tonhalle Orchestra, Zurich; Covent Garden debut in 1984 with Cosi fan tutte; Music Director of Houston Symphony Orchestra, 1988-; Barbican Hall, London, concert 1997 (Emperor Concerto and Bruckner's 4th Symphony); Conducted Robert Wilson's production of Parsifal in 1992; Guest Conductor with many major orchestras of the world. Recordings include: CD, Schumann's Violin Concerto and Fantasie in C, with Thomas Zehetmair and the Philharmonia. Honours: 1st Prize, Steinway Piano Competition in 1952; 2nd Prize, Munich International Competition in 1962; 1st Prize, Clara Haskil Competition, Montreux in 1965; Recording Prizes. Address: c/o Houston Symphony Orchestra, 615 Louisiana Street, Houston, TX 77002, USA.

ESCHKENAZY Vesko, b. 3 Dec 1970, Sofia, Bulgaria. Violinist. Education: Studied with Yfrah Neaman in London, Pierre Amoyal in Lausanne and at the Bulgarian Conservatory, leaving with an Honours degree. Career: Leader, Pioneer Youth Philharmonic Orchestra in Sofia, 1979, touring France, Italy, Germany and Brazil; Solo performances with the English Chamber Orchestra, Royal Philharmonic Orchestra, Sofia Philharmonic, Bulgarian Festival Symphony, Monte Carlo Symphony, City of London Sinfonia, Philharmonia and London Philharmonic (Beethoven Concerto, 1992); Festival engagements in Sofia, Varna, Cannes, Montpellier and Nantes, with tours to the former Soviet Union, throughout Europe, India, Brazil and China; Repertoire includes concertos by Bach, Brahms, Mozart, Prokofiev, Sibelius and Shostakovich; Sonatas by Tartini, Bach, Mozart, Beethoven, Franck and Schumann. Recordings include: Bruch and Mendelssohn Concertos, conducted by Emil Tchakarov; Brahms Violin Concerto with Sofia Philharmonic Orchestra and Emil Tabakov conducting. Honours: Winner of various competitions in Europe and China. Address: World Wide Artists Ltd, 6 Petersfield Crescent, Coulsdon, Surrey CR5 2JQ, England.

ESCHRIG Ralph, b. 2 Apr 1959, Dresden, Germany. Singer (Tenor). Education: Studied at the Musikhochschule Dresden. Career: Sang at the Dresden Staatsoper 1984-87, notably in the local premiere of The Nose by Shostakovich; Lyric Tenor at the Berlin Staatsoper from 1987, notably as Mozart's Ottavio, Belmonte, Tamino and Ferrando, Fenton by Nicolai and in the Singspiels Erwin und Elmire by Reichardt and Zar und Zimmerman by Lortzing; Concert appearances as the Evangelist in Bach's Passions, Lieder by Schubert and Schumann and The Diary of one who Disappeared by Janacek; Engagements with the Dresden Kreuz Choir and Chorus of St Thomas's Leipzig and broadcasting stations in Germany and Finland. Recordings include: Mendelssohn Motets and Bastien und Bastienne by Mozart. Honours: Prizewinner, 1984 International Bach Competition; 1987 Mozart Competition at Salzburg. Address: c/o Berlin Staatsoper, Unter den Linden 7, 1086 Berlin, Germany.

ESCOBAR Roberto B, b. 11 May 1926, Santiago, Chile. University Professor; Musician. m. Marte Cruchaga, 19 Mar 1950, 2 sons. Education: MA, Philosophy, Catholic University, Valparaiso; Conservatorio Nacional and Escuela Moderna de Musica, Santiago; Manhattan School of Music, New York. Career: Composer; Conductor, Chilean Modern Music Ensemble, 1973-78; Musicologist. Compositions: Over 60 works performed publicly, including: Symphonia de Fluminis, 1987, 1st performance, USA, 1992; Sinfonia Andres Bello, 1992, 1st performance, Chile, 1993. Recordings: Preludios Franceses; Homenaje a Amengual; Talagante; Cuarteto Estructural, Cuarteto Funcional, Macul, La Granja, Elegia, Quinteto La Paloma. Publications: Catalogue of Chilean Music, 1969; Chilean Musicians and Their Music, 1971; Chilean Composers, 1995. Contributions to: Various journals. Honours: Goethe Prize for Composition, 1982; Honorary Professor, University of Missouri, 1989; Claudio Arrau Prize, Chile, 1992. Memberships: President, Chilean Composers' Association, 1974-78; President, Sociedad Chilena de Filosofia, 1985-88. Hobby: Cooking. Address: PO Box 16360, Santiago 9, Chile.

ESCOT Pozzi, b. 1 Oct 1933, New York, New York, USA. Composer; Teacher; Writer on Music. Education: BS, 1956, MS course, 1957, Juilliard School of Music, New York; Studied with Philipp Jarnach at Hamburg Hochschule für Musik, 1957-61. Career: Teacher at New England Conservatory of Music, Boston, 1964-67, 1980-81, and Wheaton College, Norton, MA, 1972-; Professor, Graduate School, New England Conservatory, Boston, 1964-; Wheaton College, Norton, Massachusetts, 1972-; Editor, Sonus Journal, 1980-; Lecturer at University of Peking and University of Shanghai, 1984; Lecturer, Harvard, Princeton, Chicago, Stanford, Berkeley, Illinois, Northwestern Universities. Compositions: 5 Symphonies, 1952-57; 5 String Quartets; A Trilogy for chamber ensembles; Concerto for piano; Diverse chamber and solo works; 3 Poems Of Rilke for Narrator and String Quartet, 1959; 3 Movements for Violin and Piano, 1959-60; Lamentus, Trilogy No 1 for Soprano and 8 Players, 1962; Visione, Trilogy No 3 for Soprano, Speaker and 5 Players, 1964; Sands... for Orchestra, 1965; Neyrac Lux for 2 Guitars and Electric Guitar, 1978; Eure Pax for Violin, 1980; Concerto for Piano and Chamber Orchestra, 1982; Trio In Memoriam Solrac for Violin, Cello and Piano, 1984; Piano pieces and pieces for instrument and tape. Publications: Sonic Design: The Nature of Sound and Music, with Robert Cogan, 1976, 1981; Sonic Design: Practice and Problems, 1981. Contributions to: Mystics Quarterly; Interface; New York Theory Society Music and Practice; Edinburgh University Musical Praxis; Perspectives of New Music; Stanford University Humanities Review; University of Leuven, Belgium. Honours: MacDowell Colony Fellowships, 1962-65; Ford Foundation Grant, 1966; Harvard University Bunting Institute; Rockefeller Foundation Bellagio Center; Marshall Plan Fellowships; Retsma Foundation Grant; Radcliffe Institute Fellowships, 1968-70; Camargo Foundation Residence, Cassis, France, 1982. Memberships: President, 1993-, International Society of Hildegard von Bingen Studies. Address: 24 Avon Hill, Cambridge, MA 02140, USA.

ESCRIBANO Maria, b. 24 Jan 1954, Madrid, Spain. Composer; Pianist. Education: Studied with Kagel, Ligeti and Rodolfo Halffter. Career: Has participated in Darmstadt, Montepulciano and other festivals; Founded music theatre workshop in Spain, 1982; Duo partnership with flautist, Sputz Ronnenfeld. Compositions include: Music theatre pieces: Cantos De Lorca, 1977, Lady Macbeth, 1980, L'Histoire D'Un Son, 1981, and La Rosa Amarga, 1983; Jondo, 1989 and other chamber pieces; Quejio, 1989 and other piano music. Address: c/o SGAE, Fernando VI 4, Apartado 484, 28080 Madrid 4, Spain.

ESHAM Faith, b. 6 Aug 1948, Vanceburg, KY, USA. Soprano. Education: Studied at Juilliard School with Jennie Tourel and Beverly Johnson. Debut: New York City Opera in 1977 as Cherubino. Career: European debut as Nedda in Nancy; Sang Cherubino at Glyndebourne in 1981 and at La Scala in 1982; Vienna Staatsoper in 1984 as Micaela in Carmen; Geneva Opera in 1984 as Mélisande; New York City Opera as Pamina in Die Zauberflöte, Leila in Les Pecheurs de Perles, Marguerite in Faust and Massenet's Cendrillon; Washington DC as Zerlina in Don Giovanni; Pittsburgh Opera as Gilda; Las Palmas as Antonia in Les Contes d'Hoffmann; Metropolitan Opera debut in 1986 as Marzelline in Fidelio; Season 1990-91 as Musetta at Cologne, Pamina for Washington Opera and Susanna at Fort Lauderdale; Micaela for Cincinnati Opera, Butterfly at St Louis and Cherubino at the Dallas Opera, 1992; Concert appearances at the Mostly Mozart Festival, New York, Requiem and Schubert's A flat Mass, and Fauré's Requiem with the Pittsburgh Symphony under Charles Dutoit. Recordings include: La nozze di Figaro conducted by Haitink; Video of Carmen, with Domingo. Honours include: Young Artists Award from the National Opera Institute, 1978-79; Concours International de Chant de Paris Prize, 1981. Address: c/o Harrison Parrott Ltd, 12 Penzance Place, London, W11 4PA, England.

ESHPAI Andrey (Yakoulevitch), b. 15 May 1925, Kozmodemiansk, Russia. Composer; Pianist. m. Alexandra Stempnevski, 2 sons. Education: Studied with Miashoveky, Sofronitsky and Khachaturian at the Moscow Conservatory. Career: Regular TV and radio appearances. Compositions include: 4 Symphonies, 1959-82; 2 Violin Sonatas, 1966, 1970; Concerto for Orchestra, 1967; Festival Overture, 1970; The Circle, ballet, 1981; Oboe Concerto, 1982; Symphony No 5, 1985-86, No 6, (Liturgy) 1988-89, No 7, 1991; Concerto for Soprano Saxophone and Orchestra, 1986; Viola Concerto, 1988; Cello Concerto, 1989; Cello-Sonate, 1990; Violin Concerto No 3, 1990; Hungarian Tunes for viola and orchestra. 1953; Symphonic Dances, 1949; 2 Piano Concertos; Violin Concerto No 4, 1991; String Quartet (Concordia Discordans), 1992-95; Flute COncerto, 1994; Concerto for tromba and trombone wiwth symphony orchestra; Chamber Music includes: Rondeau-Etude for 4 saxophones; Music for over 60 films. Memberships: Secretary, Union of Russian Composers; First Secretary, Union of Composers of RSFSR. Address: Apartment No 121, Studentcheskaya st 44/28, 121 165 Moscow, Russia.

ESPERIAN Kallen, b. 8 Jun 1961, Waukegan, IL, USA. Soprano. Education: Studied at the University of Illinois. Career: Sang in various opera houses and concert halls in the USA then won the 1985 Pavarotti Competition and toured with the tenor to China, singing Mimi in La Bohème; Further appearances as Mimi at the Berlin and Vienna Staatsopers in 1986, the Lyric Opera of Chicago and the Metropolitan, NY, 1989; Returned to the Metropolitan as Elena in I Vespri Siciliani; Has sung Verdi's Luisa Miller in Vienna, 1986, Verona and Geneva, 1993; Sang Desdemona at the Opéra Bastille in Paris and Reggio Emilia, 1992, Mozart's Countess at St Louis, the Trovatore Leonora at Chicago and Nedda for Connecticut Grand Opera; San Francisco in 1991 as Donna Elvira in Don Giovanni; Sang Desdemona at Covent Garden, 1997 and Amelia in the original version of Simon Boccanegra. Address: c/o Grand Théâtre de Geneve, 11 Boulevard du Théâtre, CH-1211 Geneva 11, Switzerland.

ESPERT Nuria, b. 1935, Barcelona, Spain. Stage Director. m. Armando Moreno, 1954. Career: Performed as actress with Compania Titular Infantil del Teatro Romea, in Barcelona,

1947-52; Formed theatre company with husband and acted in performances in Spain, France, Germany, Iran and Britain (World Theatre season at the Aldwych); First production, The House of Bernarda Alba by Lorca at the Lyric, Hammersmith, 1986; Staged Madama Butterfly for Scottish Opera and at Covent garden; La Traviata for Scottish Opera in 1989, seen at the Teatro La'Zarzuela, Madrid, 1990 and Elektra at Barcelona in 1990; Returned to Covent Garden for Rigoletto in 1988 and Carmen in 1991 (also at the Seville Expo, 1992); Staged Elektra at Frankfurt, 1994. Address: c/o Royal Opera House, Covent Garden, London, WC2, England.

ESPINOSA Pedro, b. 13 Oct 1934, Galdar, Gran Canaria, Canary Islands. Pianist; Music Teacher. Education: Teachers: His mother (Juana Lorenzo), Luis Prieto, Javier Alfonso, Alfred Cortot, Marguerite Long, Margot Pinter, Edward Steuermann, Witold Malcuzynski, David Tudor. Debut: Teatro Perez-Galdos, Las Palmas de Gran Canaria, 16 Nov 1949. Career: Has played at Venice and Paris Biennials and Enescu Festival, Bucharest; Other festivals include Darmstadt, Granada, Santander and San Sebastian; Has appeared with the Orquesta Sinfónica de Bilbao, Orquesta de RTVE and Orquesta Sinfónica de Madrid; Spanish premiere of Messiaen's Les Oiseaux Exotiques, with the Orquesta Nacional, 1963; Other notable performances include Bartók's Sonata for 2 pianos and percussion (1955), complete works for piano of Schoenberg, Berg and Webern (1956), 2nd and 3rd Sonatas by Boulez (1961, 1967), Stockhausen's Klavierstück VI (1972) and first complete performance of Mompou's Música callada (1980); Lecture-concerts with Theodor Adorno; Professor at the Royal Conservatories of Madrid, Pamplona and Guadalajara; Classes at Lyon, Freiburg and Geneva Conservatories and various Spanish institutions; Piano works dedicated to him by many distinguished composers. Recordings: For many European broadcasting companies; Records in Germany and Spain, notably the complete Klavierstücke of Stockhausen. Honours: Kranichstein Prize, Kranichsteiner Musikinstitut, Darmstadt; 1st Prize, Real Conservatorio de Madrid; Fine Arts Award for interpretation of 20th century piano music, Fundación March, 1965; 1 of 3 Most Distinguished Interpreters of Ravel's Concerto for left hand, Ravel Academy, 1975; Annual Piano Competition in Galdar named after him, 1988. Memberships: Royal Academy of Fine Arts of the Canary Islands; Hijo Predilecto of City of Galdar. Hobby: Private life. Address: c/o Rafaela Bonilla 19, 28028 Madrid, Spain.

ESPOSITO Andrée, b. 7 Feb 1934, Algiers, Algeria. Singer (Soprano). Education: Studied at the Algiers and Paris Conservatoires. Debut: Suzel in Erlanger's La Juif Polonais. Career: Sang at the Paris Opéra from 1959, as Violetta, Juliette, Oscar, Gilda and Xenia in Boris Godunov; Paris Opéra-Comique, as Micalea, Mireille and Manon; Many appearances elsewhere in France, as Marguerite, Lucia and Thais and in the premieres of operas by Delerue, Daniel-Leseur (Andrea del Sarto) and Arrieu (Cymbeline). Address: c/o Théâtre National, 8 Rue Scribe, F-75009 Paris, France.

ESPOSITO Valeria, b. 10 Apr 1961, Naples, Italy. Soprano. Education: Studied at the Salerno Conservatoire. Debut: Teatro del Giglio in Lucca as Zerlina in Don Giovanni in 1986. Career: Appeared in concert productions at La Scala of Riccardo III by Flavio Testi and Berg's Lulu; Amsterdam in 1987 as Nausicca in Ulisse by Dallapiccola; Lucca in 1987 in Domenico Puccini's Il Ciarlatano; Teatro Lirico Milan as Sophie in Werther; US debut at Houston in 1988 in Werther; Teatro San Carlo Naples in 1988 as Amor in Orfeo e Euridice; La Scala in 1989 in Pergolesi's Lo Frate Innamorato; Radio France in 1989 in the title role of Linda di Chamounix by Donizetti; Welsh National Opera in 1989 as Amina in La Sonnambula; Sang Ippodamia in Paer's Achille at Lugo di Romagna in 1988; Sang Amina at the 1992 Macerata Festival and at Rome 1996; Featured Artist, Opera Now Magazine, Nov 1992. Honours: Winner, Aslico Competition, Milan, 1987; Winner, Cardiff Singer of the World Competition, 1987. Address: c/o Athole Still Management, 113 Church Road, Crystal Palace, London, SE19 2PR, England.

ESSER Hermin, b. 1 Apr 1928, Rheydt, Germany. Singer (Tenor). Education: Studied at the Schumann Conservatory Dusseldorf with Franziak Martiensen-Lohmann. Debut: Krefeld 1954. Career: Sang at Gelsenkirchen, the Komische Oper Berlin and Wiesbaden; member of the Deutsche Oper am Rhein, Dusseldorf, 1964-; Bayreuth Festival from 1966, as Froh, Erik, Tristan, Tannhäuser, Siegmund and Loge; Sang Tristan at Monte Carlo in 1973 and Parsifal at Rome in 1974; Sadler's Wells Opera 1973, with Scottish Opera as Tristan; Guest appearances in Paris, Moscow, Warsaw, Brussels, Zurich, Chicago, Geneva and Zurich; Sang Herod in Salome at the Staatsoper Berlin, 1988. Recordings: Das Rheingold; Der fliegende Holländer. Address: c/o Deutsche Staatsoper, Unter den Linden 7, D-1086 Berlin, Germany.

ESSWOOD Paul, b. 6 Jun 1942, Nottingham, England. Counter Tenor Singer. m. (1) Mary L Cantrill, 12 Feb 1966, (2) Aimee D Blattmann, 1990, 3 s, 1 d. Education: Royal College of Music, 1961-64. Debut: Operatic: Berkeley University of California, 1968; Concert: BBC Messiah, 1965. Career: Lay Vicar, Westminster Abbey, 1964-71; Professor: RCM, 1977-80; Baroque Vocal Interpretation, RAM, 1985-; European operatic debut, Basle in Title role of Il Tigrane, A Scarlatti; World premieres: Lyric Opera, Chicago, Paradise Lost by Penderecki, 1979, Stuttgart State Opera in Title role of Akhnaten by Philip Glass, 1984; Major performances in: Zurich, Cologne, Stuttgart, Milan, Covent Garden; Performed in major centres and festivals including: Edinburgh, Leeds Triennial, English Bach, Three Choirs, Vienna, Salzburg, Zurich, Naples, Israel, Holland, Wexford. Recordings: Most of Bach's Cantatas; Bach: Matthew Passion, Christmas Oratorio; Handel: Jephtha, Saul, Belshazzar, Messiah, Il Pastor Fido, Rinaldo, Xerxes; Chamber Duets; Monteverdi: Poppea, Ulisse (also on film), Vespers 1610; Solo recordings: Songs to My Lady, Lute songs, Music for a While, Purcell Songs, Schumann Liederkreis, Op 39 and Dichterliebe; Britten, Folksongs and Canticle II. Honours: ARCM, Teachers and Performers, 1964; Honorary RAM, 1990; German Handel Prize, 1992. Membership: Incorporated Society of Musicians. Hobbies: Organic Gardening; Apiculture. Current Management: Transart (UK) Ltd. Address: Jasmine Cottage, 42 Ferring Lane, Ferring, West Sussex, BN12 6QT, England.

ESTES Simon, b. 2 Mar 1938, Centreville, IA, USA. Bass-Baritone. Education: Studied with Charles Kellis at the University of Iowa and at the Juilliard School, NY. Career includes: Sang at various German opera houses from 1965 with debut at the Deutsche Oper Berlin as Ramfis in Aida; Member of Zurich Opera, 1976; Metropolitan Opera from 1976 in roles including Oroveso in Norma, La Scala in 1977 as Arkel in Pelléas et Mélisande, Hamburg Staatsoper in 1978 as King Philip in Don Carlos, Bayreuth Festival from 1978 as the Dutchman and Amfortas, Geneva Opera in 1984 as Jochanaan in Salome, and Covent Garden debut in 1986 as Wagner's Dutchman; Sang Wotan in new productions of Der Ring des Nibelungen at Berlin, 1984-85 and the Metropolitan, 1986-88; Appearances at San Francisco, Glyndebourne Festival, Paris Opera, Munich and Vienna; Other roles include the Villains in Les Contes d'Hoffmann, Escamillo, King Mark, Mephistopheles, the Pharoah in Rossini's Moses and Boris Godunov; Concert engagements include the US premiere of the 14th Symphony by Shostakovich with the Philadelphia Orchestra; Other concerts with the New York Philharmonic, Chicago Symphony, Boston Symphony and the Berlin Philharmonic; London Promenade concerts debut in 1989 in Act III, Die Walküre; Sang title role in the musical King, in London in 1990; Season 1992 included Macbeth for Greater Miami Opera and Wotan at Bonn; Sang Zaccaria in Nabucco at the 1994 Orange Festival, Porgy at Cape Town, 1996. Recordings include: Simon Boccanegra; Oberto by Verdi; Mahler's 8th Symphony; Fauré's Requiem. Address: c/o Harrison Parrott Ltd, 12 Penzance Place, London, W11 4PA, England.

ESTRIN Morton, b. 29 Dec 1923, Burlington, Vermont, USA. Concert Pianist; Teacher. m.(1) Eleanor Glassman, divorced 1944, 1 son, 1 daughter, (2) Roberta Green, 1986. Education: School of Education, New York University, 1942-44; Juilliard Graduate School, 1945; Studied piano privately with Vera Maurina-Press, 1941-49. Debut: Town Hall, NY, 1949. Career: Private piano teacher, 1942-; Professor of Piano and Theory, Hofstra University, 1958-; Numerous concerts and recitals at Town Hall, Carnegie Hall, Alice Tully Hall, Merkin Concert Hall, New York; Tours of the USA, London, Amsterdam and Berlin in 1982. Recordings: Works of Brahms, Rachmaninov, 1st ever recording of Scriabin's Etudes, Opus 8, Connoisseur Society records and tapes; Raff, Suite in D minor, Opus 91; Tchaikovsky's Sonata in G; Anton Rubinstein's Six Etudes. Contribution to: Article on Rachmaninov's Preludes in Clavier Magazine, 1972; Remembering Horowitz by David Dubal, 1993. Memberships: Pi Kappa Lambda, Hofstra University, 1975; Bohemian Club of New York, 1990. Hobbies: Gourmet Cooking; Cycling. Address: 9 Clotilde Court, Hicksville, NY 11801, USA.

ETHUIN Paul, b. 24 Sept 1924, Bruay-sur-Escaut, France. Conductor. Education: Studied at the Paris Conservatoire, 1943-46. Career: Professor of flute at the Rheims Conservatoire, 1944-51; Second Conductor at the Rheims Opera, 1948, Principal from 1955; Capital Théâtre, Toulouse, 1955-61; Opéra d'Avignon, 1962-66, Director of music at the Théâtre des Arts, Rouen, 1966, Paris Opéra and Opéra-Comique, 1968-71; Led the premiere of Bondeville's Antony and Cleopatra, 1974, and returned to Rouen, 1984-89.

ETZKORN K Peter, b. 18 Apr 1932, Karlsruhe, Germany. Sociologist; Anthropologist of Music; Ethnomusicologist. m. Hildegard Garve Etzkorn, 2 sons. Education: AB, Ohio University, Columbus, USA; AM, PhD, Princeton University; Studied Organ with Walter Schwan, Anton Boellinger, Carl Weinrich; Studied Musicology with August Herden and Arthur Mendel; Studied Ethnomusicology with George Herzog. Career: Assistant Professor, University of California, Santa Barbara, 1959-63; Associate Professor, University of Nevada, 1964-67; Professor, University of Western Florida, California University, Northridge, University of Missouri, St Louis, 1969-; Fulbright Professor, Hochschule fur Musik, Wien, 1987-89. Publications: Music and Society, 1973; Sociologists and Music, 1989; Editor, Journal of Ethnomusicology, 1985-88. Contributions to: Ethnomusicology; Koener Zeitschrift fur Soziologie and Sozialpsychologie; Social Forces; Journal for Research in Music Education; American Sociological Review; Sociology and Social Research; International Folk Music Council Yearbook. Honours: International Society for Music Education, Commission on Mass Media, Cultural Policies and Music Education, Commissioner, 1988-96, Chair of Commission, 1990-96; Organizer of Symposia, Chiba, Japan, 1992, Buffalo, New York, 1994, Cologne, Germany, 1996; Board Director, MEDIACULT, International Research Institute for Media, Communication and Cultural Development, President, 1995-; Princeton University Fellow; Haynes Foundation Fellow. Memberships: Society for Ethnomusicology, Council Member; Associate Current Anthropology; Fellow, American Anthropology Association, American Sociological Association; Board of Directors, President, St Louis New Music Circle; Chairman, University Symposia, Bicentennial Horizons of American Music, 1976. Hobbies: Tennis; Chamber Music. Address: 21 Ladue Ridge Road, St Louis, MO 63124, USA.

EVANGELATOS Daphne, b. 1952, Athens, Greece. Mezzo-Soprano. Education: Studied in Athens, Munich and Vienna. Career: Sang first at the Bayerische Staatsoper, Munich then in Vienna, Cologne, Frankfurt, Hamburg and Vienna; Théâtre de la Monnaie Brussels in 1982 in La Clemenza di Tito; Hamburg Staatsoper in 1984 in Cavall's L'Ormindo; Salzburg Festival in 1985 in Henze's version of Monteverdi's Il Ritorno d'Ulisse as Melanto; Cologne in 1986 as the Prince in Massenet's Cendrillon; Other roles include Octavian in Der Rosenkavalier, Mozart's Cherubino, Sextus and Annius, Preziosilla in La Forza del Destino, the Composer in Ariadne auf Naxos and Wagner's Waltraute; Sang Tisbe in La Cenerentola at the 1988 Salzburg Festival; Wolf-Ferrari's Le Donne Curiose at the 1990 Munich Festival; Has also appeared in Campra's Tancrède, at Aix, Ramiro in La Finta Giardiniera, Orpheus, Mozart's Annius and Sextus, Fricka, Waltraute and Varvara in Katya Kabanova. Address: c/o Music International, 13 Ardilaun Road, London, N5 2QR, England.

EVANGELIDES Petros, b. 1949, Limasol, Cyprus. Tenor. Education: Studied in Athens and Vienna. Career: Sang at Klagenfurt, 1973-74 and as Ernesto on tour in Switzerland, Germany and Holland, 1974; Stadttheater Berne, 1976-82, National Theatre Mannheim, 1982-84, Glyndebourne Festival in 1983 as Pedrillo in Die Entführung, Deutsche Oper Berlin as Monostatos and Pedrillo; Further appearances in Stuttgart, Amsterdam and Berlin, returned to Glyndebourne, 1984-88, in L'Incoronazione di Poppea, Falstaff, Die Entführung and Carmen; Vienna Staatsoper from 1984 notably in 1986 tour to Japan in Manon Lescaut and Tristan und Isolde; La Scala debut in 1986 as Monostatos; Sang Johannes in the premiere of Der Rattenfänger by Friedrich Cerha, Graz in 1987; Guest engagements at Hamburg as Brighella in Ariadne, Bonn, Zurich as Singer in Rosenkavalier, Strasbourg and Vichy. Recordings include: Video of L'Incoronazione di Poppea. Address: c/o Staatsoper, Opernring 2, A-1010 Vienna, Austria.

EVANS Anne, b. 20 Aug 1941, London, England. Soprano. Education: Royal College of Music, London; Conservatoire de Musique, Geneva. Career: Principal Soprano, English National Opera, 1968-78; Debut as Mimi in La Bohème, then Mozart's Fiordiligi, Verdi's Violetta, Strauss' Marschallin, Wagner's Elsa, Sieglinde and Kundry and Smetana's Mlada; Guest singer with Welsh National Opera; Has sung Strauss's Chrysothemis and Empress, Beethoven's Leonore, Mozart's Donna Anna, Dyer's Wife and Wagner's Brünnhilde and Isolde; Has sung extensively in Germany, Italy, France and America including Brünnhilde in Berlin, Nice, Paris, Turin, Zurich, Vienna and at the 1989-92 Bayreuth Festivals; Sang the title role in Ariadne auf Naxos for ENO in 1990; Made Metropolitan debut with Elisabeth in Tannhäuser in 1992; Recital at Edinburgh Festival in 1993, returning to ENO as the Marschallin in 1994; Sang Brünnhilde in Götterdämmerung at Covent Garden, 1996; Isolde at the Semperoper, Dresden, 1997. Recordings: Helmwige and Third Norn in ENO Ring under Goodall; Brünnhilde's Immolation scene; Brünnhilde in Der Ring des Nibelungen from Bayreuth, on CD, video and laserdisc. Current Management: Ingpen and Williams. Address: c/o Ingpen and Williams Ltd, 26 Wadham Road, London SW15 2LR, England.

EVANS Damon, b. 1960, Baltimore, MD, USA. Tenor. Education: Studied at the Interlochen Arts Academy on a Reader's Digest Foundation Scholarship. Career: Sang Amon in Akhnaten by Philip Glass at the New York City Opera in 1985; Virginia Opera Association in 1985 as Benji in the premiere of Musgrave's Harriet: The Woman Called Moses; Glyndebourne Festival in 1986 as Sportin' Life in Porgy and Bess; Has also sung Sportin' Life at Charleston, Boston, London with Philharmonic Orchestra and Moscow with the Finnish National Opera in 1988; Concert engagements include Beethoven's Ninth and Pulcinella, conducted by Simon Rattle; Bernstein's West Side Story at the Usher Hall in Edinburgh and a Bernstein Celebration at Alice Tully Hall in New York; Sang in the British premiere of Blitzstein's Airborne Symphony with the London Symphony, A Child of Our Time at the City of London Festival and Weill's 3 Concert Suites at the Almeida Festival; Carnegie Hall debut in 1989 in the premiere of a suite from Weill's Lost In The Stars; Has also sung Janácek's Diary of One Who Disappeared with Matrix at the Elizabeth Hall; Sang Don José in Carmen Jones in London, 1991; Sang in Porgy and Bess at Covent Garden in 1992 and in the Weill/Grosz concert at the 1993 London Proms; Sang Sporting Life at Costa Mesa, CA, 1996. Address: Harold Holt, 31 Sinclair Road, London, W14 0NS, England.

EVANS Edgar, b. 9 June 1912, Cardiganshire, Wales. Opera Singer (Tenor). m. Nan Walters, 1 son. Education: Private study with Dawson Freer, London, and Luigi Ricci, Rome Opera. Debut: London, 1947. Career: Professor of Singing, Royal College of Music; Founder Member and Principal Tenor, Royal Opera House, from 1946, as Don José, Alfredo, Mussorgsky's Dimitri, Calaf, Captain Vere, Tchaikovsky's Herman and Janacek's Laca; Numerous radio and television programmes. Recordings: Tristan und Isolde; Albert Herring. Honours: Honorary RCM, 1977. Membership: Incorporated Society of Musicians. Hobbies: Reading; Motoring; Gardening. Address: The White House, 110 Preston Hill, Harrow, Middlesex HA3 9SJ, England.

EVANS D John O, b. 17 Nov 1953, Morriston, South Wales. Head of Music, Radio 3; Musicologist; Broadcaster. Education: University College, Cardiff, 1972-78; ATCL Piano, 1974; BMus, 1975; MA, 1976; PhD, University of Wales, 1984. Career: First Research Scholar, Britten-Pears Library and Archive, Red House, Aldeburgh, England, 1980-85; Senior Music Producer, 1985-, Chief Producer, 1992, Head of Music Department, 1993-, BBC Radio 3; Postgraduate Music Tutor, University College, Cardiff, Wales, 1986-87; Artistic Director, Volte Face Opera Project, 1986-89; Executive Trustee of The Peter Pears Award, 1989-92; Artistic Director of Covent Garden Chamber Orchestra, 1990-93; Guest Lecturer for National Film Theatre, English National Opera, Fairfield Halls, Croydon, Britten-Pears School, Aldeburgh Festival, Royal College of Music, Goldsmith's College, University of London, Hull University, Camden Festival, Bath Festival, International Brown Symposium on Benjamin Britten at Southwestern University, Georgetown, TX, USA. Publications: Benjamin Britten: Pictures from a Life 1913-1976, with Donald Mitchell, 1978; A Britten Source Book, 1987; Benjamin Britten: His Life and Operas, Editor, revised 2nd edition, (Eric Walter White), 1983. Contributions include: The Britten Companion, 1984; Magazine articles; Death in Venice: The Apollonian Dionysian Conflict in Opera Quarterly, 1986. Honours: Prix Italia and Charles Heidsieck Award as Music Producer of BBC film of Bartók's opera Bluebeard's Castle; Royal Philharmonic Society Award as Music Producer of BBC 2 The Art of Conducting. Hobbies include: Musicals; Travel; Cooking; Contemporary Dance. Address: 114 Lauderdale Mansions, Lauderdale Road, Maida Vale, London, W9 1NF, England.

EVANS Joseph, b. 1950, USA. Tenor. Career: Sang with the New York City Opera, 1976-, in Les Pecheurs de Perles, Maria Stuarda, Don Giovanni, The Love of Three Oranges, Attila and La Traviata; Appearances with the Opera Company of Boston in Don Pasquale, Rigoletto, Benvenuto Cellini, War and Peace, I Capuleti e i Montecchi, Ruslan and Ludmilla, Die Soldaten by Zimmermann, Montezuma by Sessions and Orphée aux Enfers; Has also sung with Houston Grand Opera and with opera companies in San Diego, Palm Beach, Cincinnati, Cleveland, Hawaii, Fort Worth and Colorado; Sang in The Love of Three Oranges in Geneva, The Prodigal Son in Venice, Persephone by Stravinsky at Nancy, and Guidon in Rimsky's Tsar Saltan at La Scala; Season 1988-89 with The Devil and Kate and Marschner's Der Templar und Die Jüdin at Wexford; Sang Alwa in Lulu for the Opera de Nantes, and Max in Der Freischütz for Welsh National Opera; Concert engagements with Bernstein and the New York Philharmonic, Lukas Foss and the Brooklyn Philharmonic and with Julius Rudel and Michael Tilson Thomas; Has also sung with the Pittsburgh, Atlanta and Indianapolis Symphony Orchestras and appeared in concerts with the Orchestre de l'Isle de France; Sang Lucas Wardlaw in Floyd's Passion of Jonathan Wade, Santa Fe, 1996. Address: Music International, 13 Ardilaun Road, London, N5 2QR, England.

EVANS Nancy, b. 19 Mar 1915, Liverpool, England. Mezzo-Soprano. m. (1) Walter Legge, (2) Eric Crozier. Education: Studied with John Tobin in Liverpool, then Maggie Teyte and others. Debut: Liverpool in 1933 in recital. Career: Stage debut in Sullivan's The Rose Of Persia in 1938; Sang minor roles at Covent Garden and in Glyndebourne Chorus in 1930s; Associated with Benjamin Britten, who wrote A Charm of Lullabies for her; Glyndebourne, 1946-47 in the premieres of Britten's The Rape of Lucretia and Albert Herring; Sang with the English Opera Group in Britten's version of The Beggar's Opera; Created 8 roles in the premiere of Williamson's The Growing Castle, 1968; Also heard in recital, notably with French and British songs; Glyndebourne, 1957-60 in Die Zauberflöte and Der Rosenkavalier. Recordings include: Dido and Aeneas; The Rape of Lucretia.

EVANS Peter, b. England. Singer (Tenor). Education: Studied at the Royal Northern College of Music and the Royal Scottish Academy. Career: South Bank debut as Purcell's Aeneas with the English Chamber Orchestra, 1988; Further concerts with the Bournemouth Sinfonietta, London Bach Orchestra and Royal Liverpool Philharmoic; Repertory has included Elijah, Messiah (at Gdansk, Poland), Mozart's Requiem (Aix Festival), Purcell's King Arthur with the English Concert and Hindemith's Das Nusch-Nuschi with the BBC SO, 1995; Sang Monteverdi's Orfeo at the Aldeburgh festival, 1993; First Shepherd with ENO, 1996; Covent Garden Festival as Mozart's Schauspieldirektor and Lurcanio in Handel's Ariodante, 1996-97; Concert venues include the Queen Elizabeth Hall, St John's Smith Square and the Wigmore Hall. Honours include: NFMS Concert Artists Award, 1987. Address: c/o Magenta Music International, 4 Highgate High St, London N6 5JL, England.

EVANS Peter (Angus), b. 7 Nov 1929, West Hartlepool, England. Musicologist. Education: Studied with Arthur Hutchings and A E Dickinson at Durham University, 1947-51, BA in 1950; FRCO, 1952; BMus, Durham, 1953; MA, 1953; DMus, 1958. Career: Music Master, Bishop Wordsworth's School, Salisbury, 1951-52; Lecturer, Durham University, 1953-61; Professor of Music, Southampton University from 1961. Publications include: Articles on Britten and Jonathan Harvey in Tempo and The Musical Times; Chapter: The Vocal Works in Michael Tippett: A Symposium, 1965; The Music of Benjamin Britten, 1979; Articles on Britten and Rawsthorne in The New Grove Dictionary of Music and Musicians, 1980. Address: c/o New Grove Dictionary, 4 Little Essex Street, London WC2, England.

EVANS Peter (Geoffrey), b. 13 Jan 1950, Redhill, Surrey, England. Freelance Pianist; Teacher; Conductor. Education: Honours, ARCM Piano Performance Diploma at age 16, 1966; BMus, Honours, University of Edinburgh, 1972; Hochschule für Musik, Vienna, Austria, 1972-74. Career: Performances as solo pianist and in various duos and ensembles throughout UK, including Aldeburgh and Edinburgh Festivals, London's South Bank and Wigmore Halls, St John's Smith Square, also in Austria, Germany, France, Poland, Republic of Ireland, USA, USSR and Japan, 1974-; Appearances on Scottish, Tyne-Tees and BBC Television, including BBC 2 Beethoven cello/piano sonata series; Recordings for French and Swedish Radio and Radio 3; Soloist with all major orchestras in Scotland; Principal Conductor, Edinburgh's Meadows Chamber Orchestra, 1972-; Conducting debut in Spain at Festival of Torroella de Montgri, Catalonia, 1986; Close association with International Musicians Seminar, Cornwall, 1982-; Master classes, Oberlin College, Ohio, USA, 1980, Deal Summer Music Festival, 1985-; Membership of London-based Première Ensemble, 1990-; Artistic Co-Director of Hebrides Ensemble, 1991-. Recordings: Brahms and Martinu sonatas for cello and piano, with Steven Isserlis, cello; Cello and piano recital, with Alexander Baillie, cello, 1988; Solo piano in Britten's Young Apollo, with Scottish Chamber Orchestra, Serebrier, 1990; Recital of French music for cello and piano; Works by Webern, Lutoslawski and Rachmaninov for cello and piano, with William Conway; Over 70 for BBC, including large number for Radio 3. Address: 49 Spottiswoode Road, Edinburgh EH9 1DA, Scotland.

EVANS Rebecca (Ann), b. 19 Aug 1963, Neath, Wales. Soprano. Education: Guildhall School of Music and Drama, London. Debut: As Gretel in Hansel and Gretel, Welsh National Opera in 1990. Career: Has appeared in TV series, Encore and Rebecca Evans; Roles include Ilia in Ideomeneo, Oscar in Un Ballo in Maschera, Inez in La Favorita, the title role in Massenet's Cendrillon, and the Countess in Rossini's Count Ory; Season 1994 as Strauss's Sophie and Berlioz's Hero for Welsh National Opera, Marzelline in Leonore at the Edinburgh Festival; Janacek's Vixen with Scottish Opera, 1997. Recording: Mabel in The Pirates of Penzance; Belinda in Dido and Aenas. Honours: Prizewinner, BP Peter Pears, 1990; Young Welsh Singer of the Year, 1991. Hobbies: Cooking; Walking; Cinema. Current Management: Harlequin Agency Ltd. Address: 203 Fidlas Road, Llanishen, Cardiff, CF4 5NA, Wales.

EVERDING August, b. 31 Oct 1928, Bottrop, Germany. Head Manager; Producer. m. Gustava von Vogel, 30 Jul 1963, 4 sons. Education: Universities of Bonn and Munich, studied of Germanic studies, philosophy, theology and dramatic science. Career: Assistant Producer, Munich Chamber Players to Kortner, Schweikart; Producer in Munich and abroad; Stage Manager, 1959, Artistic Director, 1960, Manager, 1963, Münchner Kammerspiele, State Opera, Hamburg, 1973, and Bavarian Opera, 1977; Head Manager, Bavarian State Theatre, 1982; Lecturer, Ludwig-Maximillian University, Munich; Professor, College of Music, Munich; Productions include Die Zauberfl0te at the Savonlinna Festival, Der Fliegende Holländer at Bayreuth, 1969, Tristan und Isolde, 1971, Boris Godunov, 1974, Lohengrin, 1976, Khovanschchina, 1985 and Fliegende Holländer at the Metropolitan in 1990; Recent work includes Salome at Covent Garden, 1988 and Munich, Fidelio at Dusseldorf in 1990 and Mitridate, Re di Ponto at the 1990 Munich Festival; Engaged for The Ring cycle at the Lyric Opera, Chicago, 1992-95; Directed Triston und Isolde in Munich, 1996. Recordings include: Videos of Hansel and Gretel, 1981 and Die Zauberflöte. Memberships include: President, International Theatre Institute, Germany; Vice-President, German Stage Association; Chairman, Manager's Group, German Stage Association; Curatorium of Richard Strauss Foundation. Address: Generalintendanz der Bayerische Staattheater, Prinzregenstheater, Prinzregentenplatz, 8000 München 80, Germany.

EVERETT Paul (Joseph), b. 6 May 1955, London, England. Lecturer in Music. m. Margaret Mary Bernadette McLoughlin, 21 July 1979, 1 son. Education: BMus (Hons), Sheffield University, 1976; PhD, Liverpool University, 1984. Career: Lecturer in Music, Liverpool University, 1980-81; Lecturer in Music, University College, Cork, 1981-. Publications: Editor of various modern editions of music by D Purcell, J C Schickhardt, J B Loeillet and several works by Vivaldi for the Istituto Italiano Antonio Vivaldi; Scholarly articles on Italian sources, especially those of Vivaldi's music; The Manchester Concerto Partbooks, 2 vols, 1989. Contributions to: Music and Letters; Musical Times. Memberships: RMA. Address: Music Department, University College, Cork, Ireland.

EVROVA Katia (Ekaterina), b. 5 Oct 1947, Sofia, Bulgaria. Pianist (Chamber Music); Teacher of Piano. Divorced. Education: Diploma of Excellence in Piano and Musical Pedagogy classes, Bulgarian Superior Conservatoire of Music, Sofia, 1971; Diploma of Excellence in Professor Justus von Websky's Chamber Music class, Debussy Conservatoire, Paris, 1982. Career: First appearance with aunt Yova Kallova, teacher of piano, Sofia, 1952; Concerts as member of violin and piano duo and trio with piano, 1976-81; Concerts as violin and piano duo with Vladimir Lazov, 1983-89, performances including cycle of Schubert sonatas, 1987, cycle of 19 sonatas for piano and violin by Mozart, 1989; Concert tours, Europe and Asia; Piano Teacher, Chaumont, France, 1989; Founded the Mezzo-Forte Ensemble (piano, flute, classical guitar) with Franck Douvin and Gérard Montaudoin, 1989; Piano Teacher at School of Music, Pays de Langres, 1990; Concerts with the Mezzo-Forte Ensemble at Chaumont and 4th European Congress of Jewish Studies, Troyes, 1990; Debut, cycle of Mozart works for piano and violin as duo with Svetoslav Marinov, 1990; Cycle of Mozart works for piano and violin, Chaumont, Apr, June, Oct and Dec 1991; Tour of Brazil and Mexico, Aug 1991; Concerts, duo piano and violin with Svetoslav Marinov in France, 1992, 1993; Tour of Brazil, May 1993; Concerts in France in duo with Svetoslav Marinov, 1994, 1995-; Concerts, 1996, and the integral of Beethoven's sonatas for piano and violin, duo with S Marinov, 1997. Membership: Former Dramaturgist, Sofia Weeks of Music, Bulgarian International Festival; ABI. Address: 1 rue Bartholdi, 52000 Chaumont, France.

EVSTATIEVA Stefka, b. 7 May 1947, Rousse, Bulgaria. Singer (Soprano). Education: Sofia Conservatoire with Elena Kiselova. Career: Member of Rousse Opera, 1971-79; Roles have included Verdi's Amelia, Elisabeth de Valois, Aida and Desdemona, Margarita in Mefistofele, Yaroslavna in Prince Igor, Puccini's Mimi and Suor Angelica; Member of Bulgarian National Opera in Sofia from 1978; Guest appearances in Vienna, Frankfurt, Munich, Hamburg, New York, Berlin, Milan, Verona, Madrid and Paris; Roles include, Leonora in Il Trovatore, Elvira in Ernani, Madeleine de Coigny in Andrea Chénier, Donna Elvira in Don Goivanni and Lisa in Queen of Spades; Royal Opera debut in Manchester as Desdemona in Otello; London 1983 as Elisabeth de Valois; Metropolitan debut in 1983 as Elisabeth de Valois; San Francisco in 1984 and 1986 as Aida; Toronto, 1989-90 as Tosca, Mimi, Leonora in La Forzo del Destino and Desdemona; Appeared at Nimes in 1986 as Medora in the French premiere of Verdi's Il Corsaro; Sang at the Savonlinna Festival in 1990 as Aida; Season 1991-92 as Amelia in Ballo in Maschera at Antwerp, Tosca at Buenos Aires and the Forza Leonora at Florence; Sang Giordano's Maddalena at Buenos Aires, 1996; Many engagements as concert singer. Recordings: Rimsky-Korsakov's Boyartinya Vera Sheloga and The Maid of Pskov; 2 Recitals of Italian arias. Address: c/o San Francisco Opera, War Memorial Opera House, San Francisco, CA 94102, USA.

EWENS Craig R R, b. 26 Mar 1966, Wokingham, England. Piano Teacher; Pianist. Education: Royal College of Music Junior Department, 1979-84; Guildhall School of Music and Drama, 1984-90. Debut: St Johns Smith Square, London, 1988. Career: Many Recitals for National Music Societies in London; Solo Recitals at St John's Smith Square, Barbican Centre, St Martin in the Fields, St James's Piccadilly, St Bride's Fleet Street, Purcell Room. Recordings: Prokofiev 2nd Piano Concerto; Beethoven Sonatas op 57, 8la, 110; Chopin Ballades; Schubert's Wanderer Fantasy; Schumann's Fantasy op 17; Prokofiev Sonatas No 2, 3, & 6; Berg Sonata op 1. Honours: Concert Recital Diploma,

(Premier Prize), 1988; Teresa Carreno Memorial Piano Prize, 1984. Memberships: Incorporated Society of Musicians; European Piano Teachers Association; Fellow, Guild of Musicians and Singers. Hobbies: Cinema; Theatre; Reading. Address: 41a St Pauls Road, Islington, London N1 2LT, England.

EWING Alan, b. 1959, Northern Ireland. Bass Singer. Education: Read Music at University of East Anglia; Choral Scholar, Norwich Cathedral Choir; Guildhall School of Music with Rudolf Piernay, 1980-84. Career: Roles at the Guildhall School of Music include Sarastro, Colline, Bottom, Collatinus in The Rape of Lucretia, and Falstaff in The Merry Wives of Windsor; Has sung widely with Renaissance and Baroque groups, notably with the Consort of Musicke at major festivals in the USA, Australia, Japan, Israel and Europe; Has sung in oratorios throughout Europe and with the 1989 Young Songmakers' Almanac Concert; Appearances in The Rape of Lucretia at the Aldeburgh Festival and as the Voice of Neptune in Idomeneo with Rattle at the Elizabeth Hall; Sang Trulove in The Rake's Progress conducted by John Lubbock and in Kopernicus by Claude Vivier in a Pierre Audi production at the Almeida Festival; Sang Osmin in Die Entführung at the 1991 Buxton Festival; Sang Rocco in Fidelio for Opera Northern Ireland, 1996. Recordings: Various albums with the Consort of Musicke. Address: Kaye Artists Management, Barratt House, 7 Chertsey Road, Woking, GU21 5AB, England.

EWING Maria (Louise), b. 27 Mar 1950, Detroit, MI, USA. Soprano. m. Sir Peter Hall, 14 Feb 1982, 1 daughter, divorced 1990. Education: Piano studies with Mabel Barel and Gizo Santo; Studied singing with Marjorie Gordon, Eleanor Steber, Jennie Tourel and Otto Guth; Music Scholarship, Cleveland Institute of Music. Debut: Meadow Brook Festival, 1968. Career includes: Debut as Cherubino at the Metropolitan Opera in 1976 and at La Scala in Pelléas et Mélisande; Particularly known for her interpretations of Dorabella in Così fan tutte, Susanna and Cherubino in Figaro and the title roles in La Périchole and La Cenerentola; Roles at Glyndebourne include Carmen, Poppea and Ariadne; In 1988 gave Covent Garden debut as Salome; Season 1988-89 included Carmen at Earls Court in London; Sang Carmen in a new production at Covent Garden in 1991 and sang Salome there in 1992, filmed for TV; Sang Messiaen Poèmes Pour Mi with Philharmonia under Boulez in London and Paris in 1993, and sang the closing scene from Salome at 1993 London Proms; Season 1993-94 in premiere of new works by Michael Tilson Thomas, with LSO, Tosca and Madama Butterfly at the Vienna State Opera and The Trojans with Levine at the Metropolitan Opera; Season 1995 with Tosca at Covent Garden and Purcell's Dido for BBC Television; Marie in Wozzeck at the Met, 1997. Recordings: Andrea Chénier; Don Giovanni; Mozart's Requiem under Bernstein, 1988; Lady Macbeth of Mtzensk, title role, with Bastille Opera, 1993; Shéhérazade under Simon Rattle; Pelléas et Mélisande under Abbado. Hobby: Gardening. Current Management: Harold Holt Ltd. Address: c/o Harold Holt Ltd, 31 Sinclair Road, London, W14 0NS, England.

EYSER Eberhard, b. 1 Aug 1932, Marienwerder, Prussia, Germany. Composer; Violist. Education: Akademie für Musik und Theater, Hanover; Mozarteum, Salzburg; Accademia Chigiana, Siena, Italy. Career: Violist, Royal Swedish Opera Orchestra. Compositions: About 100 works including chamber and orchestral music, vocal and electronic music, computer music; Operas and chamber operas include Molonn, 1970, The Death of a Bird, 1971, A Dream of Man, 1972, Last Voyage, 1973, King of Hearts, 1973, Abu Said, 1976, Summer's Day, 1979, The Deep Water, 1980, Bermuda Triangle, 1981, Via Gravis, 1981, The Ravens, 1982, Roses and Ruins, 1982, The Last Day on Earth, 1982, The Red Book Mystery, 1984, Twilight in Granada, 1984, It Was Raining Yesterday, 1985, The Picture of Dorian Gray, 1986; The Aspern Papers, 1989; 5 saxophone quartets, orchestral works, Itabol, Metastrophy, Macbeth Overture; Charley McDeath, chamber opera, 1992. Recordings: King of Hearts, Last Voyage, The Deep Water, Overture, Circus Overture. Honours: Awarded 1st Carl Maria von Weber Prize for Chamber Operas, Dresden, Germany, 1978, 1986; 1st Prize, Florilège Vocal, Tours, France, 1990; 1990 Prize of Fundació pública de les Balears per la Música; Gregynog Award, Wales, 1994; Oare String Orchestra Award, Kent, 1995; Stockholm Culture Council Award, 1996. Memberships: FST; STIM; International Society for Contemporary Music. Address: Karlbergsv 71B, S-11335 Stockholm, Sweden.

F

FABBRI Franca, b. 28 May 1935, Milan, Italy. Soprano. Education: Studied in Milan with Adelina Fiori, Adelaide Saraceni and Giuseppe Pais. Debut: Spoleto in 1963 as Violetta. Career: Has sung widely in Italy and in Berlin, Hamburg, Cologne, Budapest, Warsaw, San Francisco and Aix-en-Provence; Sang in the premieres of L'Idiota and Riva delle Sirti by Chailly, Orfeo Vedevo by Savino and Al Gran Sole Carico d'Amore by Nono, 1975; Repertoire includes Lucia di Lammermoor, Musetta, Nedda, Fiordiligi, Gilda, Marguerite de Valois in Les Huguenots, the Queen of Night and Pamira in L'Assedio di Corinto by Rossini; Roles in operas by Britten, Shostakovich, Maderna and Malipiero. Address: c/o Opera La Scala, Via Filodrammatici 2, Milan, Italy.

FABBRICINI Tiziana, b. 1961, Asti, Piemont, Italy. Soprano. Education: Studied in Milan and other centres in Italy. Career: Won various singing competitions, 1982-85, and sang minor roles in provincial Italian opera houses; Made La Scala debut in 1990 as Violetta; Season 1991 in La Traviata at Naples and Elvire in a revival of La Muette di Portici by Auber at Ravenna; Sang Lucia di Lammermoor at La Scala in 1992 and at Houston, 1994, Fiorilla in Il Turco in Italia at the Théâtre des Champs-Elysées, 1996. Address: c/o Teatro alla Scala, Via Filodrammatici 2, 20121 Milan, Italy.

FABER Lothar, b. 7 Feb 1922, Cologne, Germany. Oboist. Education: Studied at the Cologne Musikhochschule and at the Paris Conservatoire. Career: Played with the WDR Orchestra, Cologne, from 1946, and has made many appearances at festivals throughout Europe: Berlin, Venice, Warsaw and Holland and Darmstadt; Has premiered works by Maderna, K Meyer, Baird, Fortner, Schuller and Zimmermann; Has given summer courses at Darmstadt and Siena, 1972-77. Address: c/o Kölner Rundfunk Sinfonie-Orchester, Appellhofplatz 1, W-5000 Cologne 1, Germany.

FABIAN Marta, b. 1946, Budapest, Hungary. Dulcimer Player. Education: Started playing the dulcimer at age 8; Studied at Beła Bartók Conservatory, 1960-64 and Ferenc Liszt Academy of Music, Budapest, 1967. Career: Soloist with Budapest Chamber Ensemble; Has made numerous guest performances in Austria, Belgium, Bulgaria, Czechoslovakia, Finland, France, Germany, UK, the Netherlands, Italy, Latin America, Mexico, Poland, Russia, Spain, Sweden, Switzerland, Turkey, USA and Yugoslavia and appeared at the Bratislava, Darmstadt, Holland, Lucerne, IGNM (SIMC) of Athens and Graz Festivals, Warsaw Autumn Festival of Modern Music, the Witten Festival and the Zagreb Biennial Festival of Modern Music. Recordings include: Cimbalom Recital. Honours: Grand Prize, French National Record Academy, 1977; Liszt Prize.

FAERBER Jorg, b. 18 June 1929, Stuttgart, Germany. Conductor; Composer. Education: Studied at the Hochschule für Musik, Stuttgart. Career: Theatre conductor and composer in Stuttgart and Heilbronn, 1952-60; Founded Württemberg Chamber Orchestra, 1960; Tours to Austria, Britain, France, Italy, USA and South Africa; Many performances in the Baroque repertory; Appearances with the European Community Chamber Orchestra, various BBC Orchestras, the Bournemouth Sinfonietta, the Thames Chamber Orchestra, and the Northern Sinfonia; Festival engagements at Swansea and with the English Bach Festival. Recordings: Bach Brandenburg Concertos; Boyce Symphonies; Vivaldi Four Seasons and other concertos; Bassoon Concertos by Weber, Graun, J C Bach, K Stamitz, Boismortier and Mozart; Concertos for cello, clarinet, viola and flute by Stamitz; Trumpet concertos by Torelli, Albinoni, Biber, Stölzel and Manfredini; Mozart piano concertos K413 and K450, violin concertos K218 and K219, flute concertos, Sinfonia Concertante, K297b and overtures. Address: Postfach 3730, D-7100 Heilbronn/Neckar, Germany.

FAGGIONI Piero, b. 12 Aug 1936, Carrara, Italy. Opera Producer. Education: Worked under Jean Vilar and Luchino Visconti in Italy. Debut: La Bohème at Venice in 1964. Career: Produced Alceste at La Scala in 1972, La Fanciulla del West in Turin in 1974 and at Covent Garden, Norma at Vienna in 1977, Carmen at Edinburgh in 1977, Macbeth at Salzburg in 1984, Francesca da Rimini at Metropolitan Opera in 1984 and production of Boris Godunov at Barcelona; Staging of Massenet's Don Quichotte seen at Paris Opéra in 1986, and Florence and Monte Carlo in 1992; Produced Il Trovatore at Covent Garden in 1989, first of a cancelled series to include all the Spanish operas of Verdi; Principal Guest Producer at Covent Garden until 1990; Don Quichotte at the Rome Opera, 1997. Address: c/o Teatro dell Opera, Piazza B Gigli 8, 00184 Rome, Italy.

FAHBERG Antonia, b. 19 May 1928, Vienna, Austria. Soprano. Education: Studied at the Vienna Music Academy. Career: Sang at Innsbruck from 1950, and Munich from 1952; Opera engagements in Hamburg, Vienna, Brussels and Amsterdam; Radio and TV engagements; Noted interpreter of works by Rossini (Stabat Mater), Beethoven (Christ at the Mount of Olives), Bruckner (Te Deum) and Bach. Recordings include: St Matthew Passion and Cantatas by Bach; Alexander Balus by Handel; Il Ritorno d'Ulisse and L'Incoronazione di Poppea; Diana in Gluck's Iphigénie en Tauride. Address: c/o Bayerische Staatsoper, Postfach 745, D-8000 Munich 1, Germany.

FÄHNDRICH Walter, b. 1 Apr 1944, Menzingen, Switzerland. Musician. 1 daughter. Education: Studied Music Theory and Viola at Lucerne, 1965-71. Career: International activities as a Viola Player, Composer and Improviser; Solo concerts; Music for Spaces; Improvisation; Professorship for Improvisation, Basel; Organisation of International Congresses. Compositions: Works for viola solo; Music for Spaces (sound installations); Musical landscape projects; Chamber music; Electroacoustical music. Recordings: Various radio and television recordings. Publications: Improvisation, 1992; Improvisation II, 1994; Improvisation III, 1998. Publications: Various publications on Music and Space. Memberships: Schweizerischer Tonkunstler-Verein; Intercommunication Center, Tokyo. Hobbies: Mountaineering; Pistol-shooting. Current Management: Katherin Fähndrich. Address: Piodina 20, CH-6614 Brissago, Switzerland.

FAIRBAIRN Clive (Stuart), b. 21 Apr 1946, London, England. Conductor. m. Nicola Swann, 18 Aug 1979, 1 daughter. Education: Royal Academy of Music, London. Debut: St Johns, Smith Square, London, 1977. Career: Principal Conductor, New Mozart Orchestra, 1977-; Principal Conductor, Lindstrom Philharmonic Orchestra, 1984-; Guest appearances include London Symphony Orchestra, London Philharmonic, Philharmonia, and Wren Orchestra; Has broadcast with New Mozart Orchestra, London Symphony Orchestra, and Wren Orchestra; Conducted in Germany, Switzerland, Turkey and Portugal. Membership: Incorporated Society of Musicians. Current Management: N McCann International Artists Ltd. Address: c/o N McCann International Artists Ltd, The Coach House, 56 Lawrie Park Gardens, London, SE26 6XJ, England.

FAIX-BROWN Winifred, b. 1954, USA. Singer (Soprano). Education: Studied in Illinois. Career: Sang in Europe from 1980, at Gelsenkirchen until 1984, Deutsche Oper Berlin, 1985-86; Guested as Lucia di Lammermoor at Mexico City, 1981, and at Chicago as Musetta (1987); Portland, 1983, as Fiordiligi, Miami, 1984 (Lucia), Milwaukee, 1989 (Donna Anna); Other roles include Elettra in Idomeneo (Miami, 1990), Leonora (Forza del destino), Desdemona and the Marschallin (Los Angeles, 1984). Current Management: Robert Lombardo Associates. Address: 61 West 62 Street, Suite 6F, New York, NY 10023, USA.

FALCON Ruth, b. 2 Nov 1946, Residence, LA, USA. Soprano. Education: After studies in New Orleans she moved to New York and was a semi-finalist in the Metropolitan Auditions on 1972; Further study in Italy with Tito Gobbi and Luigi Ricci. Debut: New York City Opera in 1974 as Micaela in Carmen. Career: Title role in Mayr's Medea in Corinto, Bern, 1975; Bayerische Staatsoper Munich, 1976-80 as Leonora in Trovatore and La Forza del Destino, and Mozart's Countess and Elettra; Guest artist in New York, Canada, Germany and France as Puccini's Manon Lescaut and Weber's Agathe; Paris Opera debut in 1981 as Mozart's Donna Anna; Covent Garden and Vienna Staatsoper in 1983 as the Trovatore Leonora; Sang Anna Bolena at Nice in 1985; Nancy Opera in 1986 as Norma; Aix-en-Provence Festival as Ariadne; Covent Garden in 1987 and Metropolitan in 1989 as the Empress in Die Frau ohne Schatten; Concert repertory includes Mahler's 8th Symphony, Beethoven's Missa Solemnis, Verdi's Requiem and works by Handel, Mozart, Brahms, Dvorák and Strauss. Recordings include: Die Walküre; Götterdämmerung. Address: c/o Robert Gilder and Co, Enterprise House, 59-65 Upper Ground, London SE1 9PQ, England.

FALEWICZ Magdalena, b. 11 Feb 1946, Lublin, Poland. Soprano. Education: Studied at the Warsaw Conservatory with Olga Olgina and Maria Kuninska-Opacka. Career: Member of the Warsaw Chamber Opera, 1971-72; Solo debut as Oscar in Un Ballo in Maschera at the Komische Opera Berlin in 1973; Sang Madame Butterfly with Welsh National Opera in 1978 and the London Coliseum in 1986; Member of the Staatsoper Berlin from 1984 with guest appearances in Frankfurt and Leipzig, and in the USA, Bulgaria, Finland and Holland; Dresden Staatsoper in 1985 as the Countess in the premiere of Siegfried Matthus' Weise von Liebe und Tod des Comten Christoph Rilke. Recordings include: Schubert's Alfonso und Estrella; Amor in Gluck's Orfeo ed Euridice; Die Kluge by Orff. Address: c/o Deutsche Staatsoper, Uner den Linden, 1086 Berlin, Germany.

FALIK Yuri, b. 30 July, 1936, Odessa, Russia. Composer; Conductor; Cellist. m. Valentina Papkova, 19 Mar 1957, 1 son, 1 daughter. Education: Central Special Music School, Odessa, 1945-55; Cello, Leningrad Conservatory of Music, 1955-60, Postgraduate, 1960-63, Composition, 1960-64; Teachers included Shtrimer (Cello), Rostropovich (Cello), Arapov (composition); Masterclasses with Shostakovich (composition) and Rabinovich (conducting). Career: Teacher, Leningrad Special Music School, 1960-71; Chief Conductor, Leningrad Conservatory Chamber Orchestra, 1964-68; Professor of Cello, 1965-81, Professor of Composition and Instrumentation, 1981-, Leningrad Conservatory; Visiting Profesor, Northwestern University, 1991-92; Guest Conducting Appearances: Tartu Chamber Orchestra, Estonia, 1984; St Petersburg Chamber Orchestra, Rostov Symphony, 1986-; Tallinn Chamber Orchestra, Estonia, 1987; Minsk Symphony, Byelorussia, 1988; Leningrad Chamber Orchestra, 1989; Lithuanian National Symphony, 1990; Leningrad Philharmonic Orchestra, 1990; Chicago Symphony Orchestra, 1990; Northwestern University Chamber Orchestra, 1991; Irkutsk Symphony, 1992-94; Odessa Philharmonic Orchestra, 1993-94; Volgograd Symphony, 1995-96. Compositions: Stage works: Till Euelenspiegel, Mystery Ballet, 1967; Oresteia, Choreographic Tragedy, 1968; Les Fourberries de Scapin, Opera, 1984; Polly and the Dinosaurs, Operas, performed in Concert in Chicago, 1990; Orchestral: Concertino, Oboe and Chamber Orchestra, 1961; Symphony, String Orchestra and Percussion, 1963; Concerto for Orchestra, 1967; Music for Strings, 1968; Easy Symphony, 1971; Concerto for Orchestra No 2, Symphonic Etudes, 1977; Chamber: 7 String Quartets, 1955-93; Trio for Oboe, Cello and Piano, 1959; Wind Quintet, 1964; Concerto for 6 Winds and Percussion (Bufoons), 1966; English Divertimento, Flute, Clarinet and Bassoon; Vocal Music including Solemn Song, Cantata, 1968; Winter Songs, 1975; Autumn Songs, 1970 for a Capella Chorus; Estonian Watercolours, Suite for Women's Chorus, 1976; 3 Concertos for Chorus a Capella, 1979, 1987, 1988; Russian Orthodox Liturgical Chants for Mixed Chorus and Soloists, 1990-92; Solo Songs; Concerto for Violin and Orchestra, 1971; Mourning Mass for Igor Stravinsky, for 16 Strings and 4 Trombones, 1975; Concerto della Passione for Cello and Orchestra, 1988; Vivat Chicago Symphony, Overture for Orchestra, 1991; Symphony N2 (Kaddish), 1993; Mass for soloists, mixed chorus and chamber orchestra, 1996. Publication: E Ruchievskaja, Yuri Falik, The Composer and His Works, 1981. Honours: Prize, Second Tchaikovsky International Competition, 1962; First Prize, Helsinki International Cello Competition, 1962. Address: St Petersburg N Rimsky Korsakov Conservatory, Teatralnaya Pl 3, 190001 St Petersburg, Russia.

FALLETTA JoAnn, b. 1960, New York City, New York, USA. Conductor. Education: Studied at Juilliard, Queens College and Mannes College. Career: Soloist with orchestras on classical guitar, lute, mandolin; Has conducted leading orchestras at Denver, Indianapolis, Phoenix, St Paul, Richmond, Toledo, Tucson and Columbus; European engagements in Italy, France, Switzerland and Denmark; Music Director of the Long Beach Symphony Orchestra, 1989; Music Director of the Virginia Symphony Orchestra, 1991, with guest appearances with the Symphony Orchestras of San Francisco, Savannah, Delaware, Hamilton and Antwerp; German debut with the Mannheim National Theatre Orchestra, in works by Barber, Gershwin and Brahms. Honours include: Winner of Stokowski, 1985, Toscanini, 1985, and Bruno Walter Awards, 1982-87. Current Management: ICM Artists. Address: 40 West 57th Street, New York, NY 10019, USA.

FALLOWS David, b. 20 December 1945, Buxton, England. Musicologist. m. Paulène Oliver, 1 son, 1 daughter. Education: BA, Jesus College, Cambridge; MMus, King's College, London; PhD, University of California, Berkeley, USA. Career: Lecturer, Music, University of Wisconsin, Madison, 1973-74; Lecturer, Music, 1976-82, Senior Lecturer, 1982-, Reader, 1992-, University of Manchester; Visiting Associate Professor, University of North Carolina, Chapel Hill, 1982-83. Publications: Dufay, 1982; Articles in Musicological Journals; Editions of Early Music. Contributions to: Gramophone; Times; Review Editor, Early Music; New Everyman Dictionary of Music, 1988. Honours: 1st Ingolf Dahl Prize in Musicology, 1971; Dent Medal, 1982; Chevalier de l'Ordre des Arts et des Lettres, 1994. Address: 10 Chatham Road, Manchester M16 0DR, England.

FALVAY Attila, b. 7 Sep 1958, Budapest, Hungary. Violinist. m. Maria Farnadi, 28 Jun 1983, 2 daughters. Education: Liszt Ferenc Academy of Music with Professor Semyon Snitkowsky and Vienna Music Academy with Professor Josef Sivo. Debut: Budapest at age 9. Career: 1st Violinist of Kodály Quartet, 1980-; First Concertmaster of Budapest Symphony Orchestra; Invited to Aspen, Colorado, USA by Miss Dorothy DeLay in 1981. Recordings include: Haydn String Quartets, Op 54, 55, 64, 71, 74, 76 and 103; Debussy String Quartet; Ravel String Quartet; The Last Seven Words of Jesus Christus; Piano Quintets by Schumann and Brahms with Jeno Jandó. Honours: Szigeti Competition, Budapest, 2nd Prize and the Jury Special Prize for the best Bartók solo sonata performance, 1978; Hubay Prize, 1980; 5th Prize, Carl Flesch Competition in London, 1986; Merited Artist of Hungary, 1990. Membership: Magyar Kodály Társaság. Hobbies: Collecting 17th and 18th Century Hungarian Maps and Prints. Current Management: Gergely Arts Budapest. Address: 1121 Budapest, Kázmér utca 40, H-1121, Budapest, Hungary.

FALVO Robert, b. 27 Aug 1963, New York City, USA. Percussionist. Education: BM, Music Education, Performer's Certificate, State University of New York, Fredonia, 1985; MM, Percussion Performance, 1987; DMA, Percussion Performance, Manhattan School of Music; Studied with Fred Hinger, Christopher Lamb, James Presiss, Claire Heldrich, Lynn Harbold, and Theodore Frazeur among others. Career: Performances with The New Music Consort, New York City, 1987-, NOA, Carnegie Hall, New York City, 1988-, English Chamber Orchestra with US tour in 1988, Pierre Boulez and the Scotia Festival Orchestra, Nova Scotia, Canada, 1991, Frick Hawkins Dance Company Orchestra with tour to Tokyo, Shanghai, Hong Kong and throughout USA, 1991-, and Tokyo Symphony with world tour in 1991; Has also appeared with Erie Chamber Orchestra, Hudson Valley Symphony Orchestra, and New Music Orchestral Project; Xylophone Soloist with Fredonia Symphony Orchestra; Many contemporary music recitals in New York area including Carnegie Hall, Merkin Hall, Miller Hall, Hubbard Hall and Town Hall; Has conducted the Manhattan School of Music Contemporary and Percussion Ensembles; Frequent lectures on contemporary composition techniques for percussion instruments; Assistant Professor of Music, teaching percussion at School of Music, Appalachian State University in North Carolina. Recordings: Various. Address: PO Box 368 DTS, Boone, NC 28607, USA.

FANDREY Birgit, b. 1963, Germany. Soprano. Education: Studied at the Carl Maria von Weber Musikhochschule in Dresden. Career: Associated with the Opera Studio of the Dresden Staatsoper, then appeared with the main company from 1987 notably as Mozart's Susanna, Papagena, Pamina and Zerlina, Euridice, Mimi, Gretel, Sophie Scholl in Udo Zimmermann's Die Weisse Rose and in parts in operas by Siegfried Matthus; Sang Handel's Galatea at the Halle Festival in 1987, Amor in Orfeo ed Euridice at the Leipzig Gewandhaus, Mozart's Constanze at Amsterdam and Pamina at St Gallen; Lieder recitals in works by Schubert, Schumann, Brahms and Strauss; Concert repertoire includes Beethoven's Mass in C at Amsterdam Concertgebouw, Bach's St John Passion, Messiah and Mozart's Exsultate Jubilate. Address: c/o Dresden Staatsoper, 8012 Dresden, Germany.

FANNING David (John), b. 5 Mar 1955, Reading, Berkshire, England. University Lecturer; Concert Pianist. m. (1) 26 July 1975, (div 1994), 1 son, (2) 4 August 1994. Education: MusB, Manchester University, 1973-77; PhD, 1984; GRNCM, Royal Northern College of Music, 1973-77. Career: Lecturer, Manchester University. Publications: The Breadth of the Symphonist: Shostakovich's Tenth. Contributions to: Gramophone; Music and Letters; The Independent; The Musical Times. Membership: Royal Musical Association. Hobbies: Languages. Address: c/o Department of Music, Denmark Road, Manchester M15 6FY, England.

FANSHAWE David (Arthur), b. 19 Apr 1942, Paignton, Devon, England. Composer; Explorer; Sound Recordist; Ethnomusicologist; Multi-Media Guest Speaker; Author; Photographer; Record Producer; Music Documentary Presenter. m. (1) Judith Grant, 8 May 1971, 1 son, 1 daughter, (2) Jane Bishop, 14 Dec 1986, 1 daughter. Education: St George's Choir School, Stowe; Foundation Scholar, Royal College of Music. Debut: Composer and Cantor Soloist, Queen Elizabeth Hall in London, 1970. Career: Composer for BBC, ITV, British Film Institute, documentaries, feature films and private commissions; Multi-Media Presenter on indigenous and traditional music and own compositions "One World One Music", active promoter and participant in concerts of own works worldwide, researcher and founder of The Fanshawe Collections, 1965-94, with 3000 tapes of traditional music from Arabia, Africa and the Pacific; Currently publishing, copying and cataloguing The Pacific Collections, establishing The World Music Foundation, completing major work, Pacific Odyssey for world premiere at Sydney Opera House; BBC Autobiographical codumentaris include: African Sanctus, Musical Mariner and Tropical Beat. Compositions include: African Sanctus; Fantasy on Dover Castle; Requiem For The Children Of Aberfan; The Clowns Concerto; Arabian Fantasy; The Awakening; Holy Jesus; Romanza Burlesque; Film music; Ethnic compilations include: Spirit of African Sanctus, Spirit of Polynesia, Micronesia and Melanesia, 1994. Recordings include: African Sanctus; Dona Nobis Pacem; Salaams. Address: PO Box 574, Marlborough, Wiltshire, SN8 2SP, England.

FARBACH Kent, b. 2 August 1961, Southport, Queensland, Australia. Composer. Education: BMus, 1989, MMus, 1995, Queensland Conservatory. Career: Senior Teacher, Forte Music School; Queensland Conservatory, 1992-. Compositions include: Mini Overture with Fanfares, for brass Septet and organ, 1989; Beneath the Forest Canopy, for ensemble, 1989; Life Stratum for orchestra, 1990; Tears for string orchestra, 1991; 1845: An Irish Elegy, for orchestra, 1992; From Quiet Places, for violin, cello, flute, clarinet, wind chimes, percussion and piano, 1993; Into the Landscape, for orchestra, 1994; Commissions from the Melbourne and Sydney SOs (1992), Queensland SO (1994) and Sydney Philharmonia Choir (1995). Honours include: Adelaide Chamber Orchestra Prize, 1992. Address: c/o APRA, 1A Eden Street, Crows Nest, NSW 2065, Australia.

FARBERMAN Harold, b. 2 Nov 1929, New York City, USA. Conductor; Composer. m. Corinne Curry, 22 Jun 1958, 1 son, 1 daughter. Education: Scholarship student, diploma, Juilliard School of Music, NY, 1951; BS, 1956, MS, 1957, New England Conservatory of Music, Boston. Career: Percussionist, Boston Symphony Orchestra, 1951-63; Conductor, New Arts Orchestra, Boston, 1955-63, Colorado Springs Philharmonic Orchestra, 1967-68, Oakland Symphony Orchestra, CA, 1971-79; Principal Guest Conductor, Bournemouth Sinfonietta, 1986-; Founder, First President, Conductors' Guild, 1975; Founder, Conductors' Institute, University of West Virginia, 1980, relocated to University of South Carolina in 1987. Compositions include: Opera: Medea, 1960-61; Mixed-Media, If Music Be, 1965; Ballets, film scores; Orchestral: Concerto for Bassoon and Strings, 1956, Timpani Concerto, 1958, Concerto for Alto Saxophone and Strings, 1965, Violin Concerto, 1976, Shapings for English Horn, Strings and Percussion, 1984; Chamber: Variations for Percussion and Piano, 1954, Music Inn Suite for 6 Percussion, 1958, Quintessence for Woodwind Quintet, 1962, Images for 5 Brass, 1964, Alea for 6 Percussion, 1976; Vocal works. Recordings include: Symphonies by Mozart, Schumann and Beethoven; Bartók's Divertimento and Sonata for Two Pianos and Percussion; Schoenberg/Handel Concerto; Bassoon Concertos by Weber and Hummel. Address: c/o ASCAP, ASCAP Building, One Lincoln Plaza, New York, NY 10023, USA.

FARKAS Andras, b. 14 Apr 1945, Budapest. Conductor. m. Francoise Viquerat, 23 Jun 1973, 1 son, 1 daughter. Education: Bela Bartók Academy, Budapest; Franz Liszt Academy, Budapest; Orchestra conducting with Hans Swarowsky, and horn at Akademie für Musik und Darstellende Kunst, Vienna. Debut: Budapest, 1973. Career: Settled in Switzerland in 1974 and performed in concerts throughout Europe; Invited Conductor, Orchestra of Hungarian Radio, Budapest Philharmonic, Orchestre de la Suisse Romande, Orchestre de Chamber de Lusanne, Orchestra of Slovakian Radio, Bratislava, Orchestra od Pilzn Radio, and Orchestre de Seville; Artistic Director and Founder, Nouvel Orchestre de Montreux, 1987. Recordings: Several for Hungarian and Swiss TV and Radio. Contributions to: Swiss Musical Review, 1975-77. Honour: Vermeil Medal, Arts, Sciences et Lettres, Paris, 1990. Memberships: Swiss Musicians Association; Centre Europeen de la Culture, Geneva. Address: Chemin des Bouvreuils 12. 1009 Pully, Switzerland.

FARKAS Andrew, b. 7 Apr 1936, Budapest, Hungary. Librarian; Educator. Divorced. Education: Eötvös Lóránd University of Law, Budapest, 1954-56; BA, Occidental College, Los Angeles, 1959; MLS, University of California, Berkeley, 1962. Career: Gift and Exchange Librarian, Chief Bibliographer and Assistant Head, Acquisitions Department, University of California, Davis, 1962-67 and Assistant Manager, Walter J Johnson Inc, New York City, 1967-70; Director of Libraries and Professor of Library Science, University of North Florida, Jacksonville, FL, 1970-. Publications: Music Editor to newspaper, Daily Democrat, Woodland, CA, 1965-67; Advisory Editor: 42 volume series, Opera Biographies, 1977; Titta Ruffo: An Anthology, 1984; Opera and Concert Singers: An Annotated International Bibliography, 1985; Editor: Lawrence Tibbett, Singing Actor, 1989; Enrico Caruso: My Father and My Family, joint author with Enrico Caruso Jr, 1990; Jussi, joint author with Anna-Lisa Björling, 1996; Series Editor, Opera Biographies, for Amadeus Press, 1989-; Librarians' Calendar and Pocket Reference, annual since 1984; Advisor and Contributor: International Dictionary of Opera, 1993. Address: Director of Libraries, University of North Florida, PO Box 17605, Jacksonville, FL 32216, USA.

FARKAS Ferenc, b. 15 Dec 1905, Nagykanizsa, Hungary. Composer; Professor of Composition. m. Margit Kummer, 1 son. Education: Graduate, Academy of Music, Budapest, 1928; Corso Superiore, Accademia St Cecilia, Rome; Study with Respighi, 1929-31. Debut: Concert of own works in Budapest, 1930. Career: Composer, Conductor of film music in Vienna, 1932, Copenhagen, 1934-36; Professor of Composition, Municipal Music School, Budapest, 1935-41, Conservatory in Kolozsvar, 1941-46; Director, Conservatory in Szekesfehervar, 1946-49; Professor, Academy of Music, Budapest, 1949-75, retired. Compositions include: Operas and ballets: The Magic Cupboard, The Sly Students, Panegyricus- A Gentleman From Venise; Cantatas and oratorios: Cantata Lirica, Cantus Pannonicus, Waiting For The Spring, Unfurled Flags, Apirationes Principis, Vita Poetae, Vivit Dominus, Omaggio a Pessoa, Requiem Pro Memoria M, 1992; Magnificat for female choir and ogue; Kölcsey Szózata, oratorio for tenor solo, mixed choir and orchestra; Orchestral works, concertos and chamber music, 4 masses and other choral works and songs, many recorded. Honours: Franz Joseph Prize, 1934; Klebelsberg Prize, 1942; Kossuth Prize, 1950, 1991; Erkel Prize, 1960; Merited Artist, 1965; Honoured Artist, 1970; Herder Prize, 1979; Cavaliere dell'ord Della Repubblica Italiana, 1984. Memberships: Hungarian Union of Musicians; National Choir Council; Chairman, Budapest Choir Council. Address: Nagyajai utca 12, H-1026 Budapest 11, Hungary.

FARKAS Katalin, b. 5 Jan 1954, Budapest, Hungary. Soprano. Education: Studied in Budapest. Career: Has sung at the Hungarian State Opera from 1982 as Rosina, Sophie (Werther), Sophie (Die Rosenkavalier), Mozart's Blondchen, Belinda, Nannetta (Falstaff), Oscar, Norina and Flotow's Martha; Glyndebourne Festival debut in 1985 as Zdenka in Arabella; Season 1986-87 in Liszt's Don Sanche at Naples and Amaryllis in Il Pastor Fido at the Göttingen Festival; Other roles include Beethoven's Marzelline, Donizetti's Gianetta (L'Elisir d'Amore) and Serafina (Il Campanello), Zerbinetta. Recordings include: World premiere recordings with Hungaroton; Handel: Terpsicore-Erato (conductor Nicholas McGegan, with Derek Lee Ragin); Handel: Atalanta, title role (conductor Nicholas McGegan); Telemann: Der geduldige Socrates-Erato (conductor Nicholas McGegan, with Paul Esswoood, Guy de Mey); Don Sanche (Liszt, under Tamás Pál); Other important recorded roles are Serpina (Pergolesi: La serva padrona); Amarilli (Handel: Il pastor fido, also with Esswood and McGegan). Address: Hungarian State Opera House, Andrassy ut 22, 1061 Budapest, Hungary.

FARLEY Carole, b. 29 Nov 1946, Le Mars, Iowa, USA. Singer(Soprano). m. José Serebrier, 29 Mar 1969, 1 daughter. Education: BMus, Indiana University, 1968; Fulbright Scholar, Hochschule für Musik, Munich, 1968-69. Debuts: Town Hall, New York, 1969; Paris, National Orchestra, 1975; London, Royal Philharmonic Society, 1975; South America, Teatro Colon Philharmonic Orchestra, Buenos Aires, 1975. Career: Soloist with major American and European symphonies, 1970-; Soloist, Linz Opera, 1969, Welsh National Opera, 1971 (Lulu in 1st production by British company of Berg's opera), 1972, Cologne Opera, 1972-75, Brussels Opera, 1972, Philadelphia Lyric Opera, 1974, Strasbourg Opera, 1975, Lyon Opera, 1976, 1977, New York City Opera, 1976, as Offenbach's Hélène, New Orleans Opera, 1977, Cincinnati Opera, 1977, Metropolitan Opera Company, 1977-, Zurich Opera, 1979, Canadian Opera, 1980, Dusseldorf Opera, 1980, 1981, 1984, Chicago Lyric Opera, 1981, Palm Beach Opera, 1982; Théâtre Municipale, Paris, 1983, Théâtre Royale de la Monnaie, Brussels, 1983, Teatro Regio, Turin, 1983, Nice Opera, 1984; Cologne Opera in Salome, conductor John Pritchard, 1985; Firenze Maggio Musicale, Teatro Comunale, 1985, as Lulu; La Voix Humaine, TV film, ABC Australia; Marie in Wozzeck at Buenos Aires, 1989; Metropolitan Opera premiere of Shostakovich Lady Macbeth of Mtzensk, 1994; Wozzeck at Opéra du Capitole de Toulouse, 1995. Recordings include: Final Scenes from Daphne and Capriccio by Strauss, Belgian Radio Orchestra, conductor José Serebrier; Songs, Prokofieff and Weill; Britten Les Illuminations; CD, Video, Poulenc, La Voix Humaine, Menotti The Telephone; Tchaikovsky Opera Arias; Milhaud Songs; Strauss Songs with Orchestra; Kurt Weill; Delius. Honours: Abbiati Prize, Best Opera Production (Lulu, Lyubimov, Turin Opera); Grand Prix du Disque, France, 1996; Diapason d'Or, France, 1997. Membership: American Guild of Musical Artists. Hobbies: Skiing; Jogging; Swimming; Dancing; Cooking; Entertaining; Reading. Current Management: Magenta Music International, London. Address: 270 Riverside Drive, New York, NY 10025, USA.

FARNCOMBE Charles (Frederick), b. 29 July 1919, London, England. Conductor. m. Sally Mae Felps, 23 May 1963, 1 daughter. Education: BSc in Engineering, London University, 1940; Royal School of Church Music, 1947-48; Royal Academy of Music, 1948-51; LRAM, 1952. Career: Musical Director, Handel Opera Society, 1955-85; Conducted first modern British performances of Rinaldo, Alcina and Deidamia, Rodelinda, Radamisto, Riccardo Primo, Scipione, Ottone, Atalanta, Ariodante, Ezio, Giustino and Rodrigo; Chief Conductor, Royal Court Theatre, Drottingholm, Sweden, 1972-79; Guest Conductor, London Chamber Opera, 1974-; Chief Guest Conductor of Badisches Staatstheater, Karlsruhe, 1979-95; Musical Director, London Chamber Opera, 1983-95; Musical Director, Malcolm Sargent Festival Choir, 1986-; Artistic Director, Llantilio Crossenny Festival; Conducted Cosi fan Tutte there, 1996. Recordings: Rameau's Castor and Pollux; Great Handel Choruses; Drottingholm Music; Handel's Rodrigo; CD of Handel Highlights, 1993. Honours include: Honorary Doctorates in Music, University of South Dakota, 1959, Columbus, Ohio, 1959, City University, London, 1988; Augustus Mann Prize, Royal Academy of Music, 1952; ARAM 1962; FRAM 1963; Royal Gold Medal of Drottingholm, 1971; Commander of the Order of the British Empire, 1977; Order of the Royal Northern Star, Sweden, 1982; Honorary DMus, City University, 1988; Gold Medal from the Handel Academy in Karlsruhe, 1992. Memberships: Fellow, Royal College of Music, 1963; Fellow, Royal Swedish Academy, 1972. Hobby: Smallholding in Wales. Current Management: Werner Kühnly, Wörthstrasse 31, 7000 Stuttgart, Germany. Address: 32 Trinity Court, 170A Gloucester Terrace, London W2 6HS, England.

FARNES Richard, b. 1964, England. Conductor. Education: King's College, Cambridge; National Opera Studio; Royal

Academy of Music; Guildhall School (Rossini's Journey to Rheims). Career: Music Staff, Glyndebourne and with Scottish Opera and Opera Factory; English Touring Opera, with Falstaff, La Bohème and The Barber of Seville; Gloriana, Figaro and The Secret Marriage for Opera North; Bastien und Bastienne and La Serva Padrona for European Chamber Opera; Macbeth for City of Birmingham Touring Opera; Season 1997-98 with The Makropoulos Case at Glyndebourne (Die Entführung on Tour) and Giovanna d'Arco for Opera North; Founded Equinox 1992, for the performance of modern chamber ensemble pieces. Honours include: Henry Wood and Philharmonia Chorus conducting scholarships at the RAM. Address: Ingpen & Williams Ltd, 26 Wadham Road, London SW15 7LR, England.

FARNON David (Graham), b. 12 Oct 1956, London, England. Composer; Conductor; Producer. m. Susie Best, 31 Aug 1989, 2 sons. Education: MA, Cambirdge University; Diplomas from Royal Academy of Music, Royal College of Music and Trinity College of Music, London. Career: Performances at The Barbican, Royal Festival Hall, London Paladium, The Queen Elizabeth Hall with orchestras including, London Symphony Orchestra and London Philharmonic Orchestra; Various TV and Radio Shows including Pebble Mill At One; The Royal Variety Show, 1981. Compositions: Approximately 300 for KPM, Chappell, Carlin, Destiny and Kanda Music Libraries; 2 Pieces for Orchestra, 1980; Overture: London By Day, 1981; Musical, Songs for Loving Swingers, 1991; Beyond The Furthest Star, for RCS, 1993; Pastourelle for violin and orchestra, 1993; 10 Pieces for wind band, 1989-94; 30 Pieces for woodwind ensemble, 1988-94; Various shows, TV and Radio Commissions. Recordings: Conducting with the Royal Philharmonic Orchestra, including Holst, Elgar, Strauss, Albinoni and various operatic arias; Music Producer on Albums with George Benson, Robert Farnon, Jose Carreras, Pia Zadora, Eileen Farrell and George Shearing. Membership: Musicians Union. Hobbies: Bridge; Tennis. Address: Les Villets Farm, Les Villets, Forest, Guernsey GY8 0HP.

FARNON Robert (Joseph), b. 24 Jul 1917, Toronto, Canada. Musician; Composer. m. Patricia Mary Smith, 13 Aug 1963, 4 sons, 1 daughter. Education: Broadus Farmer School of Music, 1930-32; Humberside College, 1932-34; Toronto Technical College, 1934-35. Career: Principal Trumpet, CBC Concert Orchestra, 1936-38; Musical Director, CBC, 1939-42; Conductor for BBC TV and Radio, 1946-; Served with the Canadian Army, 1943-46; Member, BBC Music Advisory Committee; Guest Conductor for various international orchestras. Compositions include: Symphony No 1, 1939, No 2, 1941; Film muisc in Britain, Canada and US from 1946; Canadian Impressions Suite, 1952; Rhapsody for Violin and Orchestra, 1956; Prelude And Dance for Harmonica and Orchestra, 1969; Saxophone Triparte, 1974. Address: c/o Warner Chappell Music Ltd, 129 Park Street, London, W1Y 3FA, England.

FARQUHAR David (Andross), b. 5 April 1928, Cambridge, New Zealand. Composer. m. Raydia d'Elsa, 2 June 1954, 1 son, 1 daughter. Education: BMus, University of New Zealand; MA, Cambridge University; Guildhall School of Music. Career: Lecturer, 1953-; Professor of Music, Victoria University of Wellington, New Zealand, 1976-93. Compositions: And One Makes Ten; Anniversary Duets, (2 sets); Concertino for Piano and Strings; Evocation; Suite for Guitar; Five Scenes for Guitar; On Your Own; Partita; Ring Round the Moon, dance suite; Three Pieces for Double Bass; Three Scots Ballads; Concerto for Wind Quintet; Three Pieces for Violin and Piano; Three Improvisations; Six Songs of Women; Three Songs of Cilla McQueen; Eight Blake Songs; Three Echoes, String Quartet, 1989; Waiata Maori; Ode for Piano; Five Canons for Two Clarinets; Symphony No 1; Symphony No 2; Scherzo for Orchestra; Folksong Trio (recorders); In Despite of Death. Recordings: Concerto for Wind Quintet; Symphony No 1; Three Improvisations; Three Pieces for Violin and Piano; Concertino for Piano and Strings; Evocation; Partita; Ring Round the Moon; Three Scots Ballads; In Despite of Death; Scherzo for Orchestra; Magpies and Other Birds, Echoes and Reflections; String Quartet, 1989; Suite for guitar. Memberships: Composers Association of New Zealand, Founding President; New Zealand Music Centre, Board Member. Address: 15 Nottingham Street, Wellington, New Zealand.

FARRELL Eibhlis, b. 27 Jul 1953, Rostrevor, County Down, Ireland. Composer. Education: Studied at Queen's University, Belfast and at Bristol University. Career: Deputy Principal at the College of Music, Dublin Institute of Technology, 1983. Compositions include: Concerto Grosso, 1988; Sinfon for Orchestra, 1990; Exultet, oratorio, 1991; Exaudi Voces and A Garland For The President for Solo Voices and Chorus, 1991; Soundshock for Concert Band, 1993; Solo vocal music including, The Silken Bed for Mezzo, Violin, Cello and Harpsichord, 1993; Chamber and instrumental pieces including, Earthshine for Harp, 1992. Address: c/o IMRO, Pembroke Row, Dublin 2, Ireland.

FARRELL Eileen, b. 13 Feb 1920, Williamantic, CT, USA. Opera Singer. m. Robert V Reagan, 1976, 1 son, 1 daughter. Career: Debut with Columbia Broadcasting Company in 1941 with her own programme for 6 years; Opera debut with San Francisco Opera in Il Trovatore; Sang at Carnegie Hall in 1951 as Marie in a concert performance of Wozzeck; Toured throughout the USA and abroad; Sang Berg's Marie and Cherubini's Medea in New York concert performances; Metropolitan Opera in 1960 as Gluck's Alceste followed by Santuzza, Gioconda, Maddalena and Leonora in La Forza del Destino; Sang Wagner's Brünnhilde and Isolde under Leonard Bernstein. Honours: Several honorary degrees; Grammy Award. Address: c/o Metropolitan Opera, Lincoln Center, New York, NY 10023, USA.

FARREN-PRICE Ronald (William), b. 2 Jul 1930, Brisbane, Australia. Pianist; University Academic. m. Margaret Lillian Cameron, 15 Jan 1982, 3 sons, 2 daughters. Education: Diploma in Music, University of Melbourne, 1951; Studies with Claudio Arrau on a personal scholarship donated by him, 1952-55, London and New York. Debut: Melbourne Symphony Orchestra, Concerto, 1947; Wigmore Hall, London, 1955. Career: Has played in over 30 countries including 7 concert tours of Russia and many performances at London's Wigmore Hall, Queen Elizabeth Hall, Purcell Room and St John's Smith Square; Performances at Carnegie Recital Hall, New York, National Gallery, Washington, and Tchaikovsky Hall, Moscow; Reader in Music, 1975-, Dean, Faculty of Music, 1986-, University of Melbourne; Has performed concertos with many leading conductors including Antal Dorati, Ferdinand Leitner, Eugene Goossens, Charles Groves, Willem van Otterloo, John Hopkins and Harry Blech; Has broadcast recitals in many countries and also appeared in TV recitals. Hobbies: Swimming; Walking; Travel. Address: Faculty of Music, University of Melbourne, Parkville, Victoria 3052, Australia.

FARRER John, b. 1950, USA. Conductor. Career: Many performances with leading orchestras in the USA, notably with the San Francisco Symphony Orchestra and as guest conductor elsewhere; Music Director of the Roswell Symphony Orchestra in New Mexico; Faculty Member of the Conducting Workshops of the American Symphony Orchestra League; London debut in 1986 with the London Philharmonic; Senior Guest Conductor with the English Sinfonia and further concerts with the Royal Philharmonic Orchestra and the Bournemouth Symphony Orchestra. Recordings include: Tchaikovsky album with the London Philharmonic, Dvorak with the RPO and Copland and Gershwin with the Bournemouth Symphony Orchestra. Address: Manygate Management, 13 Cotswold Mews, 30 Battersea Square, London, SW11 3RA, England.

FARULLI Piero, b. 13 Jan 1920, Florence, Italy. Professor of Viola. Education: Conservatorio di Stato Luigi Cherubini, Florence, under Gioacchino Maglioni. Career: Professor of Viola, 1957-77; For 30 years a member of Quartetto Italiano; Has also collaborated with Amadeus and Berg Quartets; Appeared with Trio di Trieste, 1978-; Has lectured at Accademia Chigiana di Siena, 1978-, and at Salzburg Mozarteum; Member of judging panel at several international competitions such as the Tchaikovsky Competition in Moscow and Tertis in London and has been active in many aspects of musical life and education in Italy, notably in Fiesole, where he founded the well-known Scuola di Musica di Fiesole in 1974 and is its Director. Recordings: With Quartetto Italiano: all String Quartets of Mozart, Beethoven, Schumann, Brahms and Webern; With Melos Quartet: Mozart Quintets K 593 and K 614. Honours: Medaglia della Cultura e dell'Arte; Premio Edison; Premio Viotti; Premio Abbiati, 1981; Premio Massimo Mila; Accademia Nazionalae di Santa Cecilia; Grand 'Ufficiale della Repubblica, 1994. Address: Via G d'Annunzio 153, Florence, Italy.

FASSBAENDER Brigitte, b. 3 Jul 1939, Berlin, Germany. Stage Producer; Mezzo-Soprano. Education: Studied in Nuremberg with her father, Willi Domgraf-Fassbaender. Debut: Munich in 1961 as Nicklausse in Les Contes d'Hoffmann. Career includes: Has sung in Germany and Milan as Eboli, Sextus, Hansel, Carlotta in Die schweigsame Frau, Clarice in La Pietra del Paragone, Marina and the Countess Geschwitz in Lulu; San Francisco in 1970 as Carmen, Covent Garden debut in 1971 as Octavian, Paris Opera in 1972 as Brangaene, Salzburg Festival, 1972-78 as Dorabella in Cosi fan tutte; Metropolitan Opera debut in 1974 as Octavian returning to New York in 1986 as Fricka; Vienna Staatsoper in 1976 in the premiere of Kabale und Liebe by Von Einem; Sang at Bayreuth Festival, 1983-84, La Scala Milan in 1986 in Die Frau ohne Schatten, Metropolitan Opera in 1986 as Fricka, Salzburg Festival in 1989 as Clytemnestra in Elektra; Produced Der Rosenkavalier at Munich in 1989, La Cenerentola at Coburg in 1990, Der Ferne Klang for Opera North in 1992, Hansel and Gretel in Augsburg in 1992, A Midsummer Night's Dream in Amsterdam in 1993 and Die Zauberflöte in Coburg in 1993; Sang Clairon in Capriccio at the 1990 Glyndebourne Festival; Concert artist in works by Bach and Mahler, and song recitalist; Masterclasses at the 1992 Brereton International Symposium. Recordings include: Over 100 since 1964 including Lulu, Die Fledermaus, Bach's St John Passion, Messiah, Mozart's La Finta Giardiniera, Bach's Christmas Oratorio; Video of Elektra (as Clytemnestra), under Abbado. Address: c/o Sekretariat, Haiming, 83119 Obing, Germany.

FASSLER Wolfgang, b. 1957, Vienna, Austria. Singer (Tenor). Education: Studied at the Vienna Hochschule. Career: Sang first with the Saarbrucken Opera, then with various theatres in Austria, Germany and Switzerland; Bremen Opera 1982-84, as Walther von Stolzing and Lohengrin; Debut as Parsifal at Naples, 1988, as Tristan at the Maggio Musicale Florence (1989 and as Siegfried at Mannheim; Other roles have included Cavaradossi, Pinkerton, Riccardo (Ballo in Maschera) Tannhäuser and Raoames; Appearances from 1985 at Hamburg, Munich, Berlin, Paris, Venice, Tokyo and Buenos Aires; USA debut at Baltimore 1995, as Samson; Wagner's Siegfried in The Ring at Seattle; Debut at Covent Garden as Siegfried in Götterdämmerung, under Bernard Haitink, 1996. Address: c/o Deutsche Oper Berlin, Bismarckstrasse, D-1000 Berlin, Germany.

FAST George (Allen), b. 27 Mar 1954, Leamington, Ontario, Canada. Countertenor Soloist; Voice Professor; Writer on Music. Education: BMusA, University of Western Ontario. Debut: With Waverly Consort, Kennedy Center, Washington DC, USA, 1979. Career: Soloist with Tafelmusik Baroque Orchestra, The Bach Ensemble, National Arts Centre Orchestra (Ottawa), CBC Vancouver Orchestra, Smithsonian Chamber Players, New York Oratorio Society, Oregon Symphony, Opera Atelier (Toronto), Casals Festival, Madeira Bach Festival, Wratislavia Cantans, Pacific Opera Victoria, Les Violons du Roy, Studio de Musique Ancienne de Montreal, L'Orchestre de la Nouvelle France, Edmonton Symphony, Louisville Bach Society and others; Assistant Professor of Early Music Voice, Director of Cappella Antica, McGill University. Recordings: The Christmas Story, The Waverly Consort, CBS Masterworks, 1983; Renaissance Favorites, The Waverly Consort, CBS Masterworks, 1985; Bach Cantatas 8, 78 and 99, Bach Ensemble, Joshua Rifkin, Decca, 1989; Complete Alto Cantatas of Buxtehude, McGill Records, 1989. Hobbies: Gardening; Painting. Current Management: Colwell Arts Management, RRNo 1, New Hamburg, Ontario, Canada. Address: 263 Bourchemin Ouest, St Hugues, Quebec, J0H 1N0, Canada.

FATH Karl, b. 1941, Germany. Bass Singer. Career: Sang at Giessen, 1963-67, Koblenz, 1968-72, Brunswick, 1972-74 and Saarbrucken, 1974-77; Engaged at Gesenkirchen from 1977 and has made guest appearances at Stuttgart, Karlsruhe, Frankfurt, 1984-86 and Cologne, 1987-88; Tour of Brazil in 1982 singing in Jakob Lenz by Wolfgang Rihm; Appeared as Don Magnifico in La Cenerentola at Bielefeld, 1989, Lunardo in I Quattro Rusteghi by Wolf-Ferrari at Hannover in 1991; Many lieder recitals and concert appearances. Recording: Petite Messe Solonnelle by Rossini. Address: c/o Niedersachsiche Staatstheater, Opernplatz 1, 3000 Hannover, Germany.

FAULCON Clarence A II, b. 8 Aug 1928. Professor of Music; Arts Consultant. m. Jacqueline Frances Beach, 1 son. Education: BS, Music Education and Supervision, MS, Music Education, University of Pennsylvania; MusD, Musicology, Philadelphia Conservatory of Music. Career includes: Chairperson, Sulzberger Junior High School, Philadelphia, Pennsylvania, 1951-63; Maryland Higher Education Representative, 1960-79; Chairperson, Cazenovia College, 1963-68; Chairperson, various orchestras and educational positions, 1968-79; Arts and Research Consultant, 1974-79; Evaluator, Conference of Music of India, sponsored by Governments of India and USA, University of Maryland, 1985; Arts Consultant, National Institute of Adolescent Pregnancy and Family Practices, 1986-. Honours include: Certificate with Recognition as Artiste. Address: PO Box 947, Runnymede, Hockessin, DE 19707, USA.

FAULCON Jacqueline Frances Beach, b. New York City, New York, USA. Concert Singer; Music Educator; Pianist; Choral Director; Teacher. m. Clarence A Faulcon II, 1 son. Education: BS, Music Supervision, Temple University; MS, Music Education, West Chester State College; Vocal studies, Academy of Vocal Arts, Philadelphia New School of Music; Piano, Philadelphia Musical Academy; Private coaching in Voice. Career: Teacher, Voice and Piano, schools in Wilmington, Delaware; Choir Director, schools and colleges; Soloist, Philadelphia, New York, Washington DC, Baltimore, New Jersey, Delaware; Many local and seaboard performances in lecture recitals and television appearances; Performances with Baltimore Symphony, Maryland Symphonette, Newark Delaware Symphony; Premiered music by contemporary Welsh and Uruguayan composers as result of President's People to People Exchange Programme; Participant, 1st Symposium of Symphonic by Black Composers, Johns Hopkins Univerfsity, Goucher College and Morgan College; Many operatic roles; Soprano Soloist in Verdi's Requiem. Honours: 1st Black Soloist to sing in Messiah and Brahm's Requiem with Historical Northern Delaware Oratorio Society; Several scholarships and awards. Memberships: Board of Directors, Grand Opera House, Wilmington; National Association for the Advancement of Colored People; Music Alumni, Temple University Association, 1st Black President; Alpha Kappa Alpha. Address: PO Box 947, Runnymede, Hockessin, DE 19707, USA.

FAULL Ellen, b. 14 Oct 1918, Pittsburgh, PA, USA. Soprano. Education: Studied in Pittsburgh then at the Curtis Institute and in New York. Career: Sang at the New York City Opera, 1947-70 as Donna Anna, Madama Butterfly, Eva and Mozart's Countess, and in the 1965 premiere of Lizzie Borden by Jack Beeson; Many appearances with regional companies in the USA; Concert appearances with orchestras in San Francisco, Boston, Chicago, Los Angeles, Cincinnati and Pittsburgh; Conductors include Solti, Serafin, Ormandy, Koussevitsky, Stokowski and De Sabata; Member of the voice department at the Juilliard School, and adjudicator for singing competitions including the Metropolitan Opera Auditions. Address: c/o The Juilliard School of Music, Lincoln Center Plaza, New York, NY 10023, USA.

FAUST Isabelle, b. Mar 1972, Esslingen, Germany. Violinist. Education: Colleges of Music in Saarbrücken, Detmold and Berlin. Career: Played with major orchestras: Hamburg Philharmonic, Yehudi Menuhin conducting, Württemberg Chamber Orchestra, Württemberg Philharmonic, Stuttgart Radio Symphony, Stuttgart Philharmonic, State Philharmonic of Rheinland-Pfalz, Bremen Philharmonic, Orchestra of Padua, West German Radio Symphony of Cologne, Stockholm Sinfonietta; US debut with Utah Symphony in 1995, Paganini Concerto No 1; Has toured: Germany, Israel, Spain, Italy, Japan; Chamber Music with: B Giuranna, B Pergamenschikow, N Brainin, J Goritzki, N Gutman, J Silverstein, L Hokanson, Ph Hirschorn; Played at festivals of: Schleswig-Holstein, Bad Kissingen, Colmar, Lyon, Berlin, Sarasota. Recordings: Radio: Bartók's Solo Sonata for Violin; Mozart's Violin Concerto in A Major; Prokofiev's Concerto No 1; Dvorak's Violin Concerto in A Minor; Mendelssohn's Violin Concerto in E Minor; Bruch's Violin Concerto in G Minor; Several recitals. Honours: 1st Prize, International Leopold Mozart Competition for Violinists, Augsburg, 1987; Premio Quadrivio Award in Rovigo, Italy for Outstanding Musical Achievement, 1990; 1st Prize in Paganini Competition in Genoa, Italy, 1993; Prize for Highly Talented Young Artists in Nordhein-Westfalen, 1994. Current Management: Shaw Concerts for America; Hazard Chase for Great Britain. Address: Lontelstrasse 19, D-70839 Gerlingen, Germany.

FAUST Michael, b. 16 Jan 1959, Cologne, Germany. Flautist. m. Debora Bendocchi Alves, 30 Dec 1985, 1 son, 1 daughter. Education: Hochschule fur Musik, Hamburg. Career: Principal Flautist, Santa Cecilia Orchestra, Rome, Hamburg Philharmonic, Stuttgart Opera, Munich Philharmonic, Cologne Radio Symphonie; Several Major Solo Concerts in Bonn, Munich, Cologne, Hamburg. Recordings: H W Henze El Cimarron; J S Bach to Mozart; 20th Century Flute Concertos, Ibert, Bernstein, Nielsen, E Carter, French Flute Music. Honours: Prizes and Awards at Competitions in Bonn, Rome, Prague, New York. Current Management: Rolf Sudbrack, Hamburg. Address: Worringer Strasse 21, 50668 Koln, Germany.

FECHNER Jerzy, b. 11 Jan 1945, Sobota, near Lowicz, Poland. Singer (Baritone). Education: Studied in Poznán. Debut: Poznán, 1977, as Miecznik in Moniusko's Haunted Castle. Career: Sang at Poznán as Janusz in Moniusko's Halka, as Rigoletto, Germont, Ford, Amonasro, Scarpia, Telramund and Escamillo; Sang in the first Polish performance of Britten's Curlew River, A Midsummer Night's Dream and Death in Venice; Jonson in the Polish premiere of Penderecki's Schwarze Maske, 1987; Guest engagements in Finland, Holland, France, Hungary and Russia; Many concert appearances. Address: c/o Poznán Grand Theatre, Fredry 9, 60-967 Poznán, Poland.

FEDDERLY Greg, b. California, USA. Singer (Tenor). Education: Studied at the University of Southern California. Career: Appearances with the Los Angeles Opera have included Britten's Albert Herring, Mozart's Monostatos, Pinkerton, Hylas in Les Troyens and Arturo in Lucia di Lammermoor, 1988-; European debut as Tom Rakewell at the Aldeburgh Festival, 1992; Engagements at the Théâtre du Châtelet, Paris, in Die Frau ohne Schatten and Moses und Aron; Philidor's Tom Jones at the Drottningholm Festival, 1995; Gluck's Orpheus, 1996; Further roles include Mozart's Ferrando, Alfredo in La Traviata, Washington, 1996, Rossini's Almaviva, Seattle, 1997, David in Die Meistersinger, Los Angeles, season 1997-98; Sang in the premiere of Florencia of the Amazons, at the Houston Opera, 1996. Recordings include: The Rake's Progress, for Swedish Television. Honours include: First recipient of the Marilyn Horne Scholarship at UCLA. Address: c/o Lies Askonas Ltd, 6 Henrietta St, London WC2E 8LA, England.

FEDER Donn-Alexandre, b. 23 Jun 1935, Philadelphia, PA, USA. Concert Pianist; Teacher. m. Janet Landis, 26 Aug 1960, 1 daughter. Education: BS, 1958, MS, 1959, DMA, 1973, Juilliard School of Music; Studies with Rosina Lhevinne, Kabos and Gorodnitzki; Study at Eastman and with Jorge Bolet. Debut: New York Town Hall in 1963. Career: Extensive concerting throughout Europe, Mexico, Canada and USA, and for NBC and ABC TV and BBC, England; Appearances with major European and American orchestras; Faculty, Philadelphia College of Performing Arts, 1971-81; Piano Faculty, Manhattan School of Music, 1978-; Member of 2-piano team, Feder and Gilgore; Co-director of Musicisti Americani Festival and Institute, Rome and Sulmona, Italy; Artist-Teacher, Taiwan International Festival, China, 1988 and 1989. Recordings: With the Netherlands Radio Philharmonic under Allers and Van Otterloo; Recordings include Szymanowski Piano Music, Excursions for Two Pianos, Music of Barber, Copland and Gershwin (with Elisha Gilgore), Bartók Sonata for 2 Pianos and Percussion, Stravinsky's Concerto for 2 Solo Pianos, with Elisha Gilgore. Current Management: Nicholas Choveaux Management, England. Address: 755 Palm Avenue, No 306, Sarasota, FL 34236, USA.

FEDER Susan (Elizabeth), b. 21 Feb 1955, New York City, USA. Writer; Music Editor. m. Todd I Gordon, 10 Apr 1983. Education: BA, Princeton University, 1976; MA, University of California, Berkeley, 1979. Career: Vice President and Director of Promotion, G Schirmer Inc, 1986-; Programme Editor, San Francisco Symphony, 1979-81; Freelance Writer. Publications: Editorial Co-Ordinator, New Grove Dictionary of American Music, 1981-86; Music Performance Trust Fund Orchestral Guide, 1982-83. Contributions to: Musical Times; Musical America; Stagebill; Programme Annotator for American Composers Orchestra, 1981-91, San Francisco Symphony, Boston Symphony and Dallas Opera; Grove's Dictionary articles. Honour: ASCAP Deems Taylor Award, 1986. Memberships: Board of Directors, MPA, 1988-; AMS; MCA; ASOL; Sonneck Society. Address: 53 Jaffray Court, Irvington, NY 10533, USA.

FEDIN Alexander, b. 11 Sept 1954, Russia. Singer (Tenor). Career: Sang at first in concert, then appeared at the Bolshoi, Moscow, from 1986, notably as Werther, Rossini's Almaviva and the Holy Fool in Boris Godunov; Guested with the Bolshoi at Glasgow, 1990, as the King in Tchaikovsky's Maid of Orleans, and at Rome, 1989, in a concert performance of Rachmaninov's Aleko; Berlin Staatsoper, 1991, as the Duke of Mantua; Further appearances at the Vienna Staatsoper, in Dortmund and at the Teatro Liceu, Barcelona. Address: c/o Bolshoi Opera, 103009 Moscow, Russia.

FEDOSEYEV Vladimir (Ivanovich), b. 5 Aug 1932, Leningrad, Russia. Conductor. m. Olga Ivanovna Dobrohotova. Education: Moscow Musical Institute; Moscow State Conservatory. Debut: With Mravinsky Orchestra at the Leningrad Philharmonic Concert Hall. Career: Principal Conductor for Academic Orchestra of Russian Folk Instruments, TV-Radio, Russia, 1957-74; Principal Conductor for Moscow Radio Symphony Orchestra, 1974-; Appeared regularly with RAI Milano Symphony Orchestra and French National Orchestra; Recent appearances with Munich Symphony Orchestra, Vienna Philharmonic Orchestra, Hamburg Radio Symphony, La Scala Opera, Istanbul and Ankara Symphony Orchestras, Antwerp Symphony Orchestra, Tokyo Philharmonic Orchestra, NHK Orchestra, and Osaka Symphony Orchestra, Japan; Conducted the Vienna Symphony Orchestra in La Damnation de Faust at the 1992 Bregenz Festival; Conducted Carmen at Vienna Staatsoper in 1993 and 3 performances of Verdi's Requiem with Luciano Pavarotti and World Festival Choir in Oslo, Stockholm in 1992 and Munich in 1993; Conducted Elektra at Rome, 1997. Recordings: About 100 with the Grand Moscow Radio Symphony Orchestra. Honours: 2nd Prize for Record of the Year, Tchaikovsky's 6th Symphony, Tokyo, 1983; Crystal Award, International Music Awards, Osaka, 1988; Silver Award for Best Concert of Season, Osaka, 1989; Golden Orpheus Award, French National Academy for recording of the opera, May Night. Hobby: Fishing. Current Management: Moscow Radio Symphony Orchestra. Address: Moscow Radio Symphony Orchestra, Piatnitskaia Str 25, 113326 Moscow, Russia.

FEGRAN Espen, b. 1960, Oslo, Norway. Singer (Baritone). Education: Studied at the Oslo Academy with Nicolai Gedda. Career: Sang at the Norwegian National Opera in Oslo as Papageno (1987), Marcello, Guglielmo, Mozart's Count amd similar repertory; Wiesbaden Opera from 1988, as Eugene Onegin, Belcore, Beckmesser, and in Henze's Verratene Meer; Bonn, 1992, in Jakob Lenz by Rihm. Address: c/o Hessisches Staatstheater, Christian Zais-Strasse 3-5, W-6200 Wiesbaden, Germany.

FEIGIN Joel, b. 23 May 1951, New York City, New York, USA. Composer. m. Severine Neff, 7 June 1986. Education: BA, Columbia University; DMA, The Juilliard School; Studied with Nadia Boulanger, Fontainebleau; Mellon Fellowship, Cornell University; Aaron Copland-American Society of Composers, Authors and Publishers Fellowship, Berkshire Music Center, Tanglewood. Career: Professor of Music, University of California at Santa Barbara. Compositions: Mysteries of Eleusis, opera; Echoes from the Holocaust for chamber ensemble; Transience for oboe and percussion; Nexus for flute and pianoforte; Four Poems of Linda Pastan for soprano and ensemble; Five Ecstatic Poems of Kabir for soprano. Recordings: 2-CD set entitled Transience includes 10 chamber works. Contributions to: Stil oder Gedanke? Die Schönberg-Nachfolge in Europa und Amerika; Roger Sessions Newsletter, Vol I; Perspectives of New Music, Vol 12. Honours: Dmitri Mitropoulis Prize, Tanglewood, 1981; Guggenheim Fellowship, 1986; Memberships: Broadcast Music Inc; American Composers Alliance; American Music Center. Hobby: Pianist. Address: c/o Rosalie Calabrese Management, Box 20580 Park West Station, New York, NY 10025-1521, USA.

FEIGIN Sarah, b. 1 Jul 1928, Riga, Latvia, (Israeli Citizen). Composer. Education: Studied at the Riga Music Academy. Career: Emigrated to Israel in 1972 and was director of the Music Conservatory at Holon from 1973. Compositions include: The Golden Tree, ballet, 1956; The House Of The Cat, children's opera, 1959, revised 1988; Violin Sonata, 1968; The Storm, ballet, 1969; Music for piano and organ, for educational use. Address: c/o ACUM Ltd, PO Box 14220, Acum House, Rothschild Boulevard 118, Tel-Aviv 61140, Israel.

FEINSTEIN Martin, b. 12 Apr 1921, NY, USA. Music Administrator. Education: Studied at Wayne State University and the City College of New York. Career: Director of Publicity, 1945-50, Vice-President, 1950-71, for Sol Hurok Concerts in New York; Visiting Professor at Yale University, 1971-73; Executive Director of the John F Kennedy Center for the Performing Arts, Washington DC, 1972-80; President and Chief Executive Officer of the National Symphony, 1979-80; General Director, Washington Opera, 1980-95; Consultant, Washington Opera, 1995-; Senior Consultant, University of Maryland Performing Arts Centre, 1995-. Address: 1120 Francis Scott Key Hall, University of Maryland, College Park, MD 20742, USA.

FEJER András, b. 1950, Hungary. Cellist. Education: Studied with András Mihaly at the Franz Liszt Academy, with the Amadeus Quartet and Zoltán Szekely. Career includes: Founder Member of the Takacs Quartet in 1975; Many concert appearances in all major European centres and the USA; Tours include New Zealand, Japan, England, Sweden, Belgium and Ireland; Bartók Cycle for festival at South Bank in 1990, and at the Théâtre des Champs-Elysées in 1991; Great Performers Series at Lincoln Center and Mostly Mozart Festival at Alice Tully Hall, NY; Visits to Japan in 1989 and 1992; Mozart Festivals at South Bank, Wigmore Hall and Barbican Centre in 1991; Beethoven cycles at the Zurich Tonhalle, in Dublin, at the Wigmore Hall and in Paris, 1991-92; Plays Amati cello made for the French Royal Family and loaned by the Corcoran Gallery, Washington DC. Recordings: Schumann Quartets, Opus 41, Mozart String Quintets with Denes Koromzay, 6 Bartók Quartets, Schubert's Trout Quintet with Zoltán Kocsis, Haydn, Opus 76, Brahms, Opus 51, Nos 1 and 2, Chausson Concerto with Joshua Bell and Jean-Yves Thibaudet; Works by Schubert, Mozart, Dvorák and Bartók. Honours: Winner, International Quartet Competition, Evian, 1977, and Portsmouth International Quartet Competition, 1979. Address: Artists Management International, 12-13 Richmond Buildings, Dean Street, London, W1V 5AF, England.

FELCIANO Richard (James), b. 7 Dec 1930, Santa Rosa, California, USA. Composer; Teacher. Education: Pupil of Milhaud, Mills College, Oakland, California, MA, 1955; Continued studies with Milhaud and Ple-Caussade, Paris Conservatory, 2 diplomas, 1955; Private studies with Dallapiccola, Florence, 1958-59, with Bezanson, University of Iowa, PhD, 1959. Career: Composer-in-Residence, National Center for Experiments in Television, San Francisco, 1967-71, City of Boston, 1971-73; Chairman of Music Department, Lone Mountain College, San Francisco, 1959-67; Professor, University of CA, Berkeley, 1967-; Founder, Center for New Music and Audio Technologies, University of CA, Berkeley, 1987. Compositions include: Chamber Opera: Sir Gawain and The Green Knight, 1964; Orchestral: Mutations, 1966, Galactic Rounds, 1972; Orchestra, 1980; Concerto for Organ and Orchestra, 1986; Symphony for Strings, 1993; Overture Concertante for clarinet and orchestra, 1995; Chamber: Evolutions for Clarinet and Piano, 1962, Glossolalia for Baritone, Organ, Percussion and Tape, 1967, Chod for Violin, Cello, Double Bass, Piano, Percussion and Live Electronics, 1972, Alleluia to The Heart of Stone for Reverberated Recorder, 1984, Shadows for Flute, Clarinet, Violin, Cello, Piano and Percussion, 1987, Palladio for violin, piano and percussion, 1989, Responsory for Solo Male Voice and Live Electronics, 1991, Camp Songs for Chamber Orchestra (15 Instruments), 1992, Cante Jondo for Bassoon, Clarinet and Piano, 1993, String Quartet, 1995; Piano pieces and various choral works. Recordings: Conducted own works on discs; In Celebration of Golden Rain, for Indonesian gamelan and organ, 1977; Concerto for organ and orchestra, 1986. Publications: Analysis and commentary on sketches for Edgard Varèse's Poème électronique in Space Calculated in Seconds (Treib), 1997. Honours: Fulbright Fellowship, 1958; Guggenheim Fellowship, 1969; American Academy of Arts and Letters Award, 1974; Various grants and commissions. Address: c/o Music Department, University of California, Berkeley, CA 94720, USA.

FELD Jindrich, b. 19 Feb 1925, Prague, Czechoslovakia. Composer; Music Teacher. m. Helena Feldova, 22 July 1955, 1 daughter. Education: Prague Conservatoire, 1945-48; Academy of Music, Prague. 1948-52; PhD, Charles University, Prague, 1952. Career: Composer; Music Teacher; Viz Composer-in-Residence, University of Adelaide, Australia, 1968-69; Professor, Conservatoire of Prague, 1972-86; Head, Department of Music, Czechoslovak Radio Prague, 1990-92; Guest lectures in Germany, Denmark, Norway, several Universities in the USA and Japan. Compositions include: Orchestral: Three Frescoes for symphony orchestra, 1963; Symphony No 1, for symphony orchestra, 1967; Dramatic Fantasy, the Days of August, for symphony orchestra, 1968-69; Symphony No 2, for symphony orchestra, 1983; Cosmae Chronica Boemorum, oratorio-cantata for Soloists, mixed chorus and symphony orchestra, 1988; Solo concertos: Flute concerto, 1954; Violoncello Concerto, 1958; Piano Concerto, 1973; Violin Concerto, 1977; Saxophone Concerto, 1980; Concertino for flute, piano and orchestra, 1991; Chamber solos: Sonatas for flute and piano, 1957; Piano, 1972; Violin and piano, 1985; Saxophone and piano, 1990; Concert Music for viola and piano, 1983; Partita concertante, for violoncello solo, 1991; Chamber Ensembles: 6 string quartets, 1949-93; Chamber Suite for nonet, 1960; Wind Quintet No 2, 1968; String Quintet, 1972; Saxophone Quartet, 1981; Concerto da camera, for two string quartets, 1987; Vocal music: Three Inventions for mixed chorus, 1966; Gloria cantus, mixed chorus on Latin text, 1984; Stage work: A Postman's Tale, children's opera, 1956. Publications: Numerous compositions published and recorded. Contributions to: Hudebni Rozhledy (Musical Review), Prague. Honours: Numerous prizes for compositions in Czechoslovakia and abroad; State Prize, for 4th string quartet, 1968. Memberships: Guild of Czechoslovak Composers, -1990; Association of Czech Musicians and Musicologists, 1990-; Prítomnust, Society of Contemporary Music; Society of B Martinu. Hobbies: History; Languages; Tennis; Skiing. Address: Peckova 17, 186 00 Prague 8 - Karlin, Czech Republic.

FELDBUSCH Eric, b. 2 Mar 1922, Grivegnee, Belgium. Composer; Cellist. Education: Studied at the Liege Conservatory, 1934-39. Career: Active as concert cellist and teacher; Professor de Violoncello, 1953-63, Director, 1963-73, Mons Conservatory; Director, Brussels Conservatory, 1974-87. Compositions include: Opera: Orestes, 1969, Ballet El Diablo Cojuelo, 1972; Orchestral: Contrastes, 1956, Les Moin Eaux De Baltimore, suite, 1958, Mosâique for Strings, 1961, Three Lorca Poems for Voice and Orchestra, 1964, Violin Concerto, 1967, Fentaisie - Divertissement, 1967, Cantique Des Cantiques for Soprano and Orchestra, 1970, Piccola Musica for Strings, 1971, Triade for Chamber Orchestra, 1977, Concertante for 2 Pianos and Orchestra, 1986, Cello Concerto, 1988; Chamber: Violin Sonata, 1957, 4 String Quartets, 1955-71, Duo for Flute and Piano, 1959, Trio for Flute, Cello and Violin, 1961, Septet for Soprano and Ensemble, 1969, Cheminement for Violin and Violin Ensemble, 1984; Piano music and incidental music for plays. Address: c/o SABM, Rue d'Arlon 75-77, 1040 Brussels, Belgium.

FELDERER Ingeborg, b. 28 Nov 1933, Innsbruck, Austria. Soprano. Education: Studied in Vienna and Milan. Career: Engaged at the Basle Stadttheater, 1955-59, notably in the premiere of Titus Feuerfuchs by Sutermeister and the local premiere of The Fiery Angel by Prokofiev, 1957, Wuppertal, 1959-62, Karlsruhe, 1962-65, and Basle, 1962-67; Sang minor roles at the Bayreuth Festival, 1961-63, and made guest appearances in Copenhagen, Frankfurt, Barcelona, Brussels, Zurich and Paris; Metropolitan Opera, NY, 1967-70 as Santuzza and the Trovatore Leonora; Vienna Staatsoper as Senta, Chyrsothemis in Elektra and Woglinde; Barcelona in 1969 as Elisabetta in Maria Stuarda; Other roles include Hecuba in King Priam with the German premiere at Karlsruhe in 1963, Tosca, Katya Kabanova and the Duchess of Parma in Doktor Faust by Busoni; Frequent concert appearances. Address: c/o Bayerische Staatsoper, Postfach 100148, 8000 Munich 1, Germany.

FELDHOF Gerd, b. 29 Oct 1931, Radevormwald, Cologne, Germany. Baritone. Education: Studied in Detmold. Debut: Essen in 1959 as Mozart's Figaro. Career: Guest engagements at Buenos Aires in 1960; Sang at Städtische Oper Berlin and Frankfurt Opera from 1961 and Metropolitan Opera from 1961 with debut as Kaspar in Der Freischütz; Further appearances in Helsinki, Hamburg, Copenhagen, Amsterdam, Montreal, Mexico City, Japan and Korea; Bayreuth Festival 1968-78, notably as Amfortas; Also sings Barak in Die Frau ohne Schatten. Recordings include: Lulu; Kothner in Die Meistersinger; Beethoven's 9th Symphony; Jonny Spielt Auf by Krenek; Hindemith's Mathis der Maler. Address: Festspielhaus, 85008 Bayreuth, Germany.

FELDHOFF Heinz, b. 1939, Radvormwald, Cologne, Germany. Singer (Bass). Career: Sang at Essen, 1964-66, Bremen, 1966-70, Mannheim, 1970-87; Bayreuth Festival, 1967-78, as Hans Ortel, Reinmar and Fafner; Other roles have included Leporello, Baculus in Lortzing's Wildschütz, Ochs, and Riedinger in Mathis der Maler; Guest at Lisbon (1981), Antwerp (1983) and Dublin (1984). Address: c/o Nationaltheater Mannheim, Am Goetheplatz, W-6800 Mannheim, Germany.

FELDMAN Barbara (Monk), b. 18 Jan 1953, Quebec, Canada. Composer; Theorist. m. Morton Feldman, 6 Jun 1987. Education: MMus, McGill University, 1983; PhD, Composition, SUNY, Buffalo, 1987. Career: Faculty, Internationale Ferienkurse für Neue Musik, Darmstadt, 1988, 1990. Compositions: Trio for Violin, Cello and Piano, 1983; Variations for Six String Instruments, 1986; Variations for String Quartet and Chorus, 1987; Duo for Piano and Percussion, 1988; The I and Thou for Solo Piano, 1988; Two Pianos, 1989; The Immutable Silence for Instrumental Ensemble, 1990; Pure Difference for Instrumental Ensemble, 1991; Infinite Other for Choir and Instruments, 1992. Publications: Article, All Things Being Unmeasured, in New Observations, 1989. Honour: Edgard Varese Fellowship, SUNY Buffalo, 1984-87. Address: 83 Oriole Road, Toronto, Ontario M4V 2G2, Canada.

FELDMAN Jill, b. 21 Apr 1952, Los Angeles, CA, USA. Soprano. Education: Studied at San Francisco, Basle and Paris; Studied Musicology at the University of California at Santa Barbara. Career: Has sung in Europe and the USA in many performances of early music; US opera debut in 1979 as Music in Monteverdi's Orfeo; Europe Opera debut in 1980 as Clerio in Cavalli's Erismena at Spoleto; Concerts with William Christie include Charpentier's Médée at the Salle Pleyel, Paris in 1984; Sang Vita in the first modern revival of Marco Marazzolli's La Vita Humana, at the Tramway, Glasgow, with the Scottish Early Music Consort, 1990. Recordings: Rameau's Anacreon; Cesti's Orontea; Cavalli's Xerse; Charpentier's Médée, Acteon and Les Arts Florissants; Incidental music for Molière's Le Malade Imaginaire, Purcell's Orpheus Britannicus and Harmonia Sacra. Address: 7 rue du Pot de Fer, 75005 Paris, France.

FELIX Václav, b. 29 March 1928,Prague, Czechoslovakia. Composer; Musicologist; Educator. m. Danuse Felixová, 1 son, 2 daughters. Education: Graduate, Musical Faculty, Academy of Musical Arts, Prague, 1953; PhD and Candidate of Science, Charles University, Prague. Career: Editor, Hudební Rozhledy, Prague, 1959-61; Assistant, Musical Faculty, 1951-54, Special Assistant, 1960-73, Docent in Music Theory, 1973-84, Professor, Composition and Music Theory, 1985-92, Dean of Musical Faculty, 1985-90. Compositions include: Sonata Capricciosa for flute and piano, 1981; Concerto for trumpet and orchestra, 1984; Symphony No 1 for female voice and orchestra, 1974; The Advertisement, chamber mini-opera, 1977; Sonata Lirica for oboe and piano, 1978; Double Concerto for violoncello, piano and string orchestra, 1978; Quartetto Amoroso for string quartet, 1979; Symphony No 2 for small orchestra, 1981; Mariana, Opera in 4 acts, 1982; Sonata Poetica for piano solo, 1988; Sonata Concertante for viola and piano, 1989; Sonata Melodiosa for English Horn and Piano, 1993; Concerto for violoncello and orchestra, 1990; Symphony No 3 for mixed choir and large orchestra, 1986; Symphony No 4 for large orchestra, 1987; Symphony No 5 for chamber orchestra, 1987; Symphony No 6 for large wind orchestra, 1990; Sententiae Nasonis for mixed choir, 1995; Numerous other published compositions. Publications: Janácek's Sonata Style, 1980; The Fundamental Problems of Musical Forms, 1983. Contributions to: Hudební Rozhledy; Zivá hudba. Memberships: Association of Musical Artists and Scientists, 1990. Hobbies: Entomology. Address: K Betáni 1099, 148 00 Praha 4-Kunratice, Czech Republic.

FELLE Amelie, b. 1961, Bari, Italy. Singer (Soprano). Education: Studied at the Bari Conservatory. Career: Sang at Spoleto from 1984, as Adina (debut) and other lyric roles; Sang Sofia in Rossini's Signor Bruschino at Naples (1987) and made debut at La Scala in 1988, as Jemmy in Guillaume Tell; Ravenna, 1988, as Colombine in Mascagni's Le Maschere; Rossini's Cambiale di Matrimonio at Cologne and Pesaro (1989, 1991); Other roles have included Mozart's Susanna and Donna Anna and parts in Jommelli's Fetonte and La Cecchina by Piccinni. Recordings include: Operas by Pergolesi and Mascagni. Address: c/o Teatro alla Scala, Via Filodrammatici 2, 20121 Milan, Italy.

FELLER Carlos, b. 30 July 1922, Buenos Aires, Argentina. Singer (Bass). Education: Opera Studio of Teatro Colon. Debut: Sang the Doctor in Pelléas et Mélisande, Buenos Aires, 1946. Career: Sang widely in South America and toured Europe with Argentinian Chamber Orchestra, 1958; Resident in West Germany from 1958, notably at Cologne Opera where he has sung Don Pasquale, Dulcamara, Dr Bartolo, Leporello and Don Alfonso; Glyndebourne Festival, 1959-60, as Don Alfonso, Figaro, the Speaker in Die Zauberflöte and Dr Bombasto in the British premiere of Busoni's Arlecchino; Appearances at the Salzburg, Edinburgh and Holland Festivals and in most major opera houses in Europe and the Americas; Metropolitan Opera debut, 1988 as Don Alfonso, followed by Dr Bartolo, 1990; Buenos Aires and Santiago, 1990-91; Other roles in Il Matrimonio Segreto, Venice and Washington; Wozzeck at Seattle; Zar und Zimmermann, Der Rosenkavalier, La Cambiale di Matrimonio and Il Signor Bruschino at Cologne; Season 1992 as Don Alfonso in performances of Cosi fan tutte in Paris and Lisbon conducted by John Eliot Gardiner; Season 1992-93, Nozze di Figaro on tour with John Eliot Gardiner to Lisbon, Paris, London; La Bohème, Opera Nationale, Paris, 1995; Season 1995-96, sang Alcindoro/Benoit in La Boheme, Opera Nationale in Paris, also for season, 1996-97; Season 1997-98 includes Nozze di Figaro, La Traviata and Lulu, Opera National, Paris, and from 1998-99 performances of Nozze di Figaro at the Brussels Opera. Recordings: Don Alfonso and Mozart's Bartolo with the Drottningholm Ensemble, conducted by Arnold Oestmann; Videos of Il Barbiere di Siviglia, Il Matrimonio Segreto, La Gazza Ladra and Agrippina. Current Management: Haydn Rawstron Limited, London. Address: PO Box 654, London SE26 4DZ, England.

FELLINGER Imogen, b. 9 Sept 1928, Munich, Germany. Musicologist. Education: University of Munich and Tübingen; PhD, University of Tübingen, 1956. Career: Research Collaborator, International Inventory of Musical Sources, RISM, Germany, 1957-62; Chairman, Research Department for Music Bibliography, 19th Century, Institute of Musicology, University of Cologne, 1963-70; Chairman, Music Archive of the 19th Century State Institute for Music Research, Prussian Culture Collection, Berlin, 1970-93; Head of Library, 1971-93; Scientific Councillor, 1974, Scientific Super Councillor, 1983. Publications: Uber die Dynamik in der Musik von Johannes Brahms, 1961; Verzeichnis der Musikzeitschriften des 19 Jahrhunderts, 1968; Periodica Musicalia 1789-1830, 1986; Editor, Klavierstücke op 118 and 119 von J Brahms, 1974; Richard Fellinger, Klänge um Brahms, Erinnerungen, new edition, 1997. Contributions to: MGG Edition 1-2; Riemann Musik Lexikon; Neue deutsche Biographie; Die Musikforschung; Studien zur Musikgeschichte des 19 Jahrhunderts; Beiträge zur rheinischen Musikgeschichte; The New Grove Dictionary of Music and Musicians; Fontes Artis Musicae; Mozart-Jahrbuch, 1978-79, 1980-83; Acta Musicologia, 1983-84; Bruckner-Symposium, Linz, 1983-85; Hamburger Jahrbuch für Musikwissenschaft, volume 7-8; Brahms-Studien, 1981, 1983, 1985; Brahms 1-2, Cambridge, 1983, 1987; Jahrbuch des Staatlichen Instituts für Musikforschung, 1971, 1987-88; The New Grove Dictionary of Opera; The New Grove Dictionary of American Music. Address: 10 St Anna-Platz, 80538 Munich, Germany.

FELLNER Till, b. 1972, Vienna, Austria. Concert Pianist. Education: Vienna Conservatory, 1981-; Further study with Alfred Brendel, Oleg Maisenberg and Meira Farkas. Career: Performances with a number of leading orchestras including Academy of St Martin in the Fields, Camerata Academica Salzburg, Chicago Symphony Orchestra, City of Birmingham Symphony Orchestra, Los Angeles Philharmonic, Orchestre de Paris, Vienna Philharmonic and Vienna Symphony, Philharmonia, London and has worked under many noted conductors including Claudio Abbado, Marek Janowski, Sir Neville Marriner and Kent Nagano; Chamber work with Thomas Zehetmair, Heinrich Schiff and the Virtuose Bläser Wien; Solo recitals and concerts in many cities including Amsterdam, Berlin, London, Moscow, Munich, New York, Paris, Salzburg and Vienna; Appearances at Schubertiade Feldkirch, Wiener Festwochen, Marlboro Festival, Mostly Mozart in New York, Tanglewood Festival, Edinburgh Festival, Salzburg Festival and others; Season 1997-98, solo cycle of three concerts with works by Schubert, Berg, Schönberg and Webern, with performances in London, Paris, Vienna and Vevey. Recordings include: Schubert, Vier Impromptus für Klavier; Schönberg, Suite für Klavier op 25; Beethoven, Sonate für Klavier, Appassionata in F minor; Mozart, Konzert für Klavier und Orchester, Rondo in A minor; Beethoven, Sonate für Klavier in C minor op 10; Schumann, Kreisleriana op 16; Reubke, Sonate in B minor; Schubert, Sonate in A minor op 143. Address: Ingpen & Williams Ltd, 26 Wadham Road, London SW15 2LR, England.

FELTSMAN Vladimir, b. 8 Jan 1952, Moscow, Russia. Pianist; Teacher. Education: Piano lessons from age 6 with mother; Studied at Central Music School Moscow and with Yakov Flier at Moscow Conservatory. Debut: Soloist with Moscow Philharmonic in 1963. Career: Toured Russia and Eastern Europe from 1971; Played in Japan in 1977 and France in 1978; Emigrated to USA in 1987; Performed at The White House in 1987; New York recital debut at Carnegie Hall in 1987; Professor, State University of New York, New Paltz, 1987-. Recordings: Various. Honours: 1st Prize, Prague Concertino Competition, 1967; Joint 1st Prize, Marguerite Long-Jacques Thibaud Competition, Paris, 1971. Address: c/o Music Department, State University of New York, New Paltz, NY 12561, USA.

FENNELL Frederick, b. 2 Jul 1914, Cleveland, OH, USA. Conductor; Teacher. Education: BM, 1937, MM, 1939, Eastman School of Music, Rochester, NY. Career: Conductor for National Music Camp, Interlochen, MI, summers 1931-33; Faculty, Eastman School of Music, conducting various ensembles, 1939-65; Founder, Conductor, Eastman Wind Ensemble, 1952; Conductor-in-Residence, University of Miami School of Music, Coral Gables, FL, 1965-80; Conductor of Kosei Wind Orchestra, Tokyo, 1984-; Guest Conductor with many USA ensembles. Recordings: Numerous discs recorded. Publications: Time And The Winds, 1954; The Drummers Heritage, 1956. Contributions to: Articles in The Instrumentalist. Honours: Many citations for championing the cause of wind ensembles.

FENNELLY Brian, b. 14 Aug 1937, Kingston, New York, USA. Composer; Theorist; Pianist; Professor of Music. m. (1) 1 son, (2) Jacqueline Burhans Baczynsky. Education: Bachelor of Mechanical Engineering, 1958, BA, 1963, Union College; MMus, Yale School of Music, 1965, PhD, Yale University Graduate School, 1968. Career: USAF, 1958-61; Teacher, Union College and Yale University Faculty, 1962-68; Professor, New York University, 1968-97; Editor, Contemporary Music Newsletter, 1969-77; Composers' Forum, 1968; Performances, USA and International Society for Contemporary Music International Festival, 1973, 1980, 1981, 1984. Compositions: Numerous including: SUNYATA, 1970; Tesserae I-IX, 1971-80; In Wildness is the Preservation of the World, 1976; Quintuplo, 1977-78; Tropes and Echoes, 1981; Canzona and Dance, 1982-83; Thoreau Fantasy No 2, 1985; Corollaries I-III, 1986-89; Brass Quintet, 1987; Keats on Love, 1988-89; Lunar Halos, 1990; A Sprig of Andromeda, 1991-92; On Civil Disobedience. 1993; Locking Horns, Brass Quintet No 2, 1993-94; Skyscapes, 1996; Chrysalis, 1997; Others recorded. Recordings: Wind Quintet; Evanescences; String Quartet in 2 Movements; In Wildness Is The Preservation Of The World; Sonata Seria; Scintilla Prisca; Prelude and Elegy; Empirical Rag; Tesserae VII; For Solo Flute; Concerto for Saxophone and String Orchestra; Tesserae II; Fantasy Variations; Two Poems of Shelley; On Civil Disobedience; A Spring of Andromeda; Paraphrasis. Contributions to: Dictionary of Contemporary Music, 1974; New Grove Dictionary of Music and Musicians; Perspectives of New Music; Journal of Music Theory. Honours: Guggenheim Fellowship, 1980; Koussevitsky Foundation Commission, 1983; 1st Prize, Louisville Orchestra New Music Competition, 1986; 1st Prize, International Trumpet Guild Composition Contest, 1990; 2nd Prize, Goffredo Petrassi Orchestral Competition, 1993; Lifetime Achievement Award, American Academy of Arts and Letters, 1997. Memberships: BMI; American Composers' Alliance; Society of Composers Inc; Society for Music Theory; Board of Directors, League of Composers, International Society for Contemporary Music, US Section. Address: 2 Schryver Court, Kingston, NY 12401, USA.

FERGUSON Barry (William Cammack), b. 18 Jul 1942, London, England. Cathedral Organist; Master of the Choristers. m. (1) Marjorie Kemp, 20 Oct 1971 (dec 1987), 1 d, (2) Sandra Wibrew, 30 Sep 1989. Education: MA, Cambridge University; FRCO; Exeter Cathedral Choristers School; Clifton College, Bristol; Organ Scholar, Peterhouse, Cambridge University; Honours degree in Music; Postgraduate, Royal College of Music. Career: Assistant Organist, Peterborough Cathedral, 1964-71; Organist, Wimborne Minster, 1971-77; Organist and Master of Choristers, Rochester Cathedral, 1977-94; Conductor, Rochester Choral Society; Directed courses for Royal School of Church Music in USA, Australia, New Zealand; Musical Advisor, Rochester Diocesan Church Music Committee; Organist, St Peter's, Shaftesbury, 1994-; Freelance Musician and Composer. Hobbies: Poetry; Art Galleries; Exploring the West Country. Address: 2 Hawkesdene, Shaftesbury, Dorset, SP7 8NT, England.

FERGUSON Howard, b. 21 Oct 1908, Belfast, Northern Ireland. Pianist; Musicologist; Composer. Education: Studied with Harold Samuel and with Morris and Sargent at the Royal College of Music in London. Career: Violin Sonata No 1 performed at the Wigmore Hall in 1932, and Two Ballads performed at the Three Choirs Festival in 1935; Assisted Myra Hess with wartime concerts at the National Gallery; Piano recitalist and duet partnerships with pianist, Denis Matthews and violinist, Yfrah Neaman; Editions of early keyboard music; Professor of Composition at the Royal Academy of Music, 1948-63. Compositions include: Two Ballads for Baritone, Chorus and Orchestra, 1928-32; Octet, 1933; Four Diversions On Ulster Airs for Orchestra, 1939-42; Piano Concerto, 1951; Amore Langueo for Tenor, Chorus and Orchestra, 1956. Recordings include: Partita, Opus 5b; Bagatelles; Violin Sonata No 2; Overture For An Occasion; Dream Of The Road. Publications: Editions of: Tisdall, Complete Keyboard Works, 1957, Purcell: Complete Harpsichord Works, 1964; Blow, Six Suites, 1965; Style And Interpretation, I-IV, 1963-69; Early French, Italian, German, English Keyboard Music, 2 volumes of each, 1966-69; Dagincourt, Pièces de Clavecin, 1969; Keyboard Interpretation, 1975; Croft, Complete Harpsichord Works, 1974; Schubert, Complete Piano Works, 1978; Pichi, Complete Keyboard Works, 1979; The Music of Howard Ferguson, 1989; Keyboard Interpretation, 1975; Entertaining Solo: A Cookbook, 1995; Keyboard Duets, 1995. Honours include: Honorary MusD, Queen's University, Belfast, 1959. Hobbies: Reading; Cooking. Address: 51 Barton Road, Cambridge, CB3 9LG, England.

FERGUSON Robert (Stanley), b. 6 May 1948, London, England. Pianist. Education: Studied piano with Cyril Smith, Royal College of Music; ARCM; LRAM; LGSM. Debut: Royal Festival Hall in 1973. Career: Piano duo with Christopher Kite with debut at Wigmore Hall in 1973, also giving regular Purcell Romm recitals, 1974-83, including use of original early pianos; Solo recital of 20th century music at Purcell Room in 1975; Appointed Examiner for Associated Board of Royal Schools of Music in 1982; Regular BBC Radio broadcasts with Christopher Kite, 1979, 1983 and tours of Ireland in 1983. Honours: Hopkinson Gold Medal, 1969; Dannereuther Prize, Royal College of Music, 1970. Membership: Incorporated Society of Musicians. Hobbies: Genealogy; Tropical Fish. Address: 98 Riverside, Cambridge, CB5 8HN, England.

FERKOVA Eva, b. 18 Dec 1956, Bratislava, Slovakia. Musicologist. m. Andrej Ferko, 14 July 1984, 2 sons. Education: Academy of Music Arts, 1981; Comenius University, 1984; PhD, Academy of Sciences, 1988. Career: Research Worker, Slovak Academy of Sciences; Teacher, Musicology, State Conservatory; Teacher, Computational Musicology, Academy of Music Arts. Publications: Computer Analysis of Classic Harmonic Structures, 1992; Systematics of Computational Musicology, 1992; Development of Slovak Musicology in Book Publications, 1993. Contributions to: Computing in Musicology; Opus Musicum, Brno. Memberships: Slovak Musicological Association; Study Group, Computer Aided Research, International Council for Traditional Music; Union of Teachers of Schools of Arts. Hobbies: Theatre; Literature; Computers. Address: Hummelova 1, 81103 Bratislava, Slovakia.

FERMAN Polly, b. 21 Oct 1944, Montevideo, Uruguay. Pianist. m. José R Sanchis Muñoz, 28 Aug 1987, 2 sons, 1 daughter. Education: Law School, undergraduate, Montevideo, English, Spanish, French, Italian, Portuguese, some Japanese; Studied piano and harmony with Santiago Reyes in J S Bach Conservatory; After graduation studied with Celia Bronstein in Buenos Aires; Further musical studies with Jeffrey Siegel, Eugene List and William Daghlian in New York. Debut: In recital at at age 7, Uruguay; Debut with SODRE Symphony Orchestra, Uruguay, at age 11. Career: Performances with the Indianapolis Symphony, the Jarkow Symphony Orchestra (Ukraine), the Manila Symphony Orchestra, the Sao Paulo State Symphony Orchestra, National Symphony Orchestra of Argentina, others. Recordings: Piano music by Ernesto Nazareth; Waltzes of the Americas;Habaneras, Tangos and Milonges. Honours: 1st Prize, Jeunesses Musicales, at age 9, Uruguay at age 9, 1954; 1st Prize, Musical Students' Competition, at age 10, Uruguay, 1955; 1st Prize, Artigas Washington Competition, sponsored by the US Government in Uruguay, 1955. Membership: Founder, President, Pan American Musical Research (non profit organisation promoting Classical music and performers of the Americas), New York City. Current Management: Mr Kiyoshi Tamamura, Music Office Sautille Co Ltd, Marukoshi Building 3F, 2-11-19 Jingumae, Shibuya-ku 150, Japan; Mrs Sara Tornay, Tornay Management, 127 W 72nd St, New York City, New York, USA. Address: 2-14-14 Moto-Azabu, Minato-ku, Tokyo 106, Japan.

FERMANI Simone, b. 1954, Italy. Conductor. Education: Studied at the Perugia Conservatory, Santa Cecilia Conservatory Rome and with Franco Ferrara; Assistant to Leonard Bernstein and the Vienna PO, 1986; Mozart repertory in Bologna, Padua, Venice and Milan; Artistic Director, 1991-, Orchestra Sinfonica Del Sacro Cuore, Milan; Further concerts in Rome, Wurzburg, Bangkok, Montreal, Canada, and Il Barbiere di Siviglia at Marseille; Other opera repertory includes works by Mozart, Wagner, Bizet, Rossini, Puccini and Verdi. Honours include: Perrenoud Prize, 1995 Conductor's Competition, Vienna. Address: Athole Still Ltd, Foresters Hall, 25-27 Westow Street, London SE19 3RY, England.

FERNANDEZ Nohema, b. 23 May 1944, Havana, Cuba. Pianist. 1 daughter. Education: Diploma, Conservatorio Internacional, Havana, 1960; BMus, DePaul University, USA, 1965; MMus, Northwestern University, 1966; DMA, Stanford University, 1983; Piano studies with Jorge Bolet, Adolph Baller, and duo-pianists Vronsky and Babin. Debut: Havana in 1960; New York debut at Carnegie Recital Hall in 1983. Career: Appearances at Festival de Musica Latino-Americana, Mexico City, Cabrillo Festival, and Sunriver Festival and recitals in Glasgow, Edinburgh, Vienna, Amsterdam, New York, Miami and San Francisco; Radio broadcasts in Mexico City, New York and San Francisco and TV appearances in Chicago and San Jose; Soloist with orchestras in US, Seoul; Recitals in Cuba, USA, Canada, Europe, South America; Member, Jaffe-Fernández Duo (cello and piano); Radio broadcasts in Mexico, US, Korea; TV appearances. Recordings: Various including Latin-American music for the Saarländisches Rundfunk. Contributions to: Articles in Piano Quarterly and Latin American Music Review. Honours: NEA Solo Recitalist Award, 1990-91; Distinction of Honour, La Rosa Blanca, Los Angeles, 1996. Current Management: Joanne Rile Artists Management. Address: c/o Joanne Rile Artists Management, 801 Old York Road, Noble Plaza, Suite 212, Jenkontown, PA 19046-1611, USA.

FERNANDEZ Wilhelmenia, b. 5 Jan 1949, Philadelphia, Pennsylvania, USA. Singer (Soprano). Education: Studied at Philadelphia, 1969-73, and at the Juilliard School. Debut: Houston Opera, 1977, as Gershwin's Bess. Career: Sang in Porgy and Bess on tour in the USA and Europe; Paris Opera, 1979, as Musetta in La Bohème; Appearances at the New York City Opera, in Boston and Michigan, and at Toulouse as Aida; Opéra du Rhin, Strasbourg, and Liège, 1987-88, as Marguerite; Theater des Westens, Berlin, 1988, as Bess; Bonn Opera, 1989, as Aida; Sang the title role in Carmen Jones, London, 1991; Winner of the Evening Standard Award for Best Actress in a Musical; National Indoor Arena, Birmingham, 1992; 1994-95, Aida at Deutsche Oper Berlin; Other roles include Mozart's Countess and Donna Anna, Purcell's Dido and the title role in Luisa Miller; Concert engagements include Beethoven's Ninth; Recital at Kensington Palace in the presence of HRH Princess of Wales; Regular recitalist throughout Europe and USA; Appeared in the film Diva. Address: c/o Marks Management Ltd, 14 New Burlington Street, London W1X 1FF, England.

FERNANDEZ-IZNAOLA Ricardo J, b. 21 Feb 1949, Havana, Cuba. Concert Artist; Pedagogue (Classical Guitar); Composer. m. Maria Victoria Santos Brandys, 22 Aug 1974, 2 sons. Education: Colegio Americano, Caracas, 1966; Diplomas: Manuel de Falla Courses, Granada, 1971, 1972, 1974; Escuela Lino Gallardo, Caracas, summa cum laude, 1968; Royal Conservatory, Madrid, 1978 (Postgraduate studies in composition). Debut: Madrid, May 1969. Career: Chair, Guitar Department, University of Denver's Lamont School of Music, 1983-; Director, International Guitar Week, Denver, 1984-; Over 1500 concerts, lectures, master classes in Europe, North and South America and Japan; Appearances include BBC (London), RTVE (Madrid), Bayerische Rundfunk (Munich), since 1970; Masterclasses since 1990, for Mannes College of Music, Manhattan School of Music, Yale University, the Cleveland Institute, the Royal Academy of Music, Trinity College of Music, the Guildhall of Music; Recent Concerts in new York City, Madrid. Compositions: 10 Concert Etudes; Death of Icarus (Etude No 11); Variations on a Theme of A Lauro; Monologue I; Monologue II; Musique de Salon; 5 Miniatures; Berceuse; Prelude and Valse; Chanson; Three Little Tales, 1996; Frank's Berries, choir and guitar, 1997; Tiempo Muerto, concerto for guitar and orchestra, 1997; Recordings: The Icarus Collection, 1995; Spanish guitar music from the time of Garcia Lorca, 1997. Publications: Kitharologus: The Path to Virtuosity, 1993; On Practising, 1994. Contributions to: Guitar and Lute Magazine; Ritmo; Cuadernos de Musica; Guitar International; EGTA Guitar Journal. Honours: 8 International Awards as Performer/Composer. Memberships: ASCAP; MTNA; CMS; Honorary Member, EGTA, UK; Pi Kappa Lambda. Hobbies: Reading; Haute Cuisine; Travelling. Current Management: Victoria Brandys Artists Management. Address: Lamont School of Music, 7111 Montview Blvd, Denver, CO 80220, USA.

FERNANDEZ-GUERRA Jorge, b. 17 Jul 1952, Madrid, Spain. Composer. Education: Studied at the Madrid Conservatory. Career: From 1970 has worked as musician, composer and actor in the Independent Theatre Movement; Opera, Sin Demonio No Hay Fortuna, based on the Faust legend and performed at Madrid's Sala Olimpia in 1987. Compositions include: Sin Demonio No Hay Fortuna, opera; Incidental music to plays by Aeschylus, Wilde, Beckett, Brecht and others; Chamber and orchestral music. Address: c/o SGAE, Fernando VI 4, Apartado 484, 28080 Madrid 4, Spain.

FERNEYHOUGH Brian (John Peter), b. 16 Jan 1943, Coventry, England. Composer. m. Stephany Jan. Education: Birmingham School of Music, 1961-63; Royal Academy of Music with Lennox Berkeley, 1966-67; Amsterdam Conservatory with Ton de Leeuw, 1968-69; Basle Academy with Klaus Huber, 1969-71. Career: Emigrated to Switzerland in 1969; Lecturer at Freiburg Musikhochschule, 1973-86; Lecturer, Darmstadt Summer Courses, 1976-96; Accademia Chigiana, 1980-81; Composition Masterclasses at Civica Scuola di Musica di Milano, 1983-86; Composition Teacher at Royal Conservatoire, The Hague, 1986-87; Professor of Music, University of California, San Diego, 1987-; Fondation Royanmont, 1990-; Terrain performed at the 1993 Prom Concerts in London. Compositions include: Sonatina for 3 Clarinets and Bassoon, 1963; Coloratura for Oboe and Piano, 1966; Sonata for 2 Pianos, 1966; Prometheus for Wind Sextet, 1967; Epicycle for 20 Strings, 1968; Firecycle Beta for Orchestra, 1969-71; Sieben Sterne for Organ, 1970; Time And Motion Study I for Bass Clarinet, II for Cello and Electronics, III for 16 Voices, Percussion and Electronics, 1971-77; Time and Motion Studies I-III, 1974-76; Transit, for 6 voices and large ensemble, 1975; La Terre Est Un Homme for Orchestra, 1976-79; Carceri d'Invenzione, 1980-86; Superscriptio for Piccolo, 1981; Adagissimo for String Quartet, 1983; Mnemosyne for Bass Flute and Tape, 1986; Quartet No 4, 1990; Tritticoper GS for Double Bass, 1989; Terrain for Solo Violin and Ensemble, 1992; On Stellar Magnitudes, 1995; Allgebrah, 1996; Flurries, 1997. Recordings include: Superscriptio; Intermedio Alla Ciaconna; Etudes Transcendantales; Mnemosyne; La Chute D'Icare; String Quartets played by the Arditti Quartet; Chamber Works, 1987; Terrain, Kurze Schatten II, 4th String Quartet, ASKO Ensemble, 1996; Carceri d'Invenzione III and other works, Ensemble Contrechamps, 1996. Publications: Collected writings, 1996. Contributions to: Darmstaedter Beitraege, Musiktexte,

Contemporary Music Review. Honours: Mendelssohn Scholarship, 1968; Koussevitsky Prize, 1977; Visiting Artist, Academic Exchange Service, Berlin, 1976-77; Chevalier dans l'Ordre des Arts et des Lettres, Paris, 1984; Royal Philharmonic Prize, 1995. Membership: Akademie der Künste, Berlin, 1996. Hobbies: Reading; Wine; Cats. Address: UCSD, La Jolla, CA 92093, USA.

FERRAND Emma, b. 1 Oct 1948, London, England. Cellist. m. Richard Deakin, 6 Sept 1969, 3 children. Education: International Cello Centre, London, 1965-66; Royal Academy of Music, London; Pupil of Pierre Fournier, Geneva. Debut: Wigmore Hall, 1974. Career: Solo concerts; BBC Recordings; BBC Television with Elgar Concerto, 1975; Chamber music concerts; Member, Deakin Piano Trio and Prelude Ensemble; Senior Lecturer, Royal Northern College of Music, 1983-; Artist in Residence, Stowe Summer School and Lake District Summer Music; Solo concerts; Member of the Prelude Ensemble; Visiting Professor, Eastman School of Music, NY, USA, 1994; Jury Member, South Africa International String Competition; Appearances on BBC 2, Radio 3. Recordings: C Hubert Parry, complete piano trios, piano quartet; Chamber Works with Piano, by Parry. Honours: Dip Perf Ram, 1972; Winner, Young Concert Artists Award, National Federation of Music Societies, 1974; ARAM, 1993. Membership: Incorporated Society of Musicians. Current Management: J Audrey Ellison International. Address: Ings Cottage, Berrier, Nr Penrith, Cumbria CA11 0XD, England.

FERRARI Elena, b. 1970, England. Singer (Soprano). Education: National Opera Studio, London. Career: Appearances with Opera North as Musetta (1996) and Bice in Korngold's Violanta (also at the 1997 London Proms); Mozart's Countess for English Touring Opera 1997 and Fiordiligi for Opera North, 1997-98; Other roles include Adina (L'Elisir d'Amore) Violetta, Donna Elvira, Marguerite, Mélisande, Cherubini's Medea and Polly Peachum in The Threepenny Opera; Jenny in Weill's Mahagonny Songspiel at the London Proms, 1997; Other concerts include the Verdi Requiem, Elijah, Italian Songs and French Melodies. Honours include: Gerald McDonald Award, National Opera Studio. Address: C&M Craig Services Ltd, 3 Kersley Street, London SW11 4PR, England.

FERRARINI Alida, b. 9 July 1946, Villafranca, Verona, Italy. Soprano. Education: Studied at the Verona Conservatory and in Venice. Debut: Trevisto in 1974 as Mimi. Career: Appearances at the Verona Arena from 1975 as Mercedes and Micaela in Carmen, Oscar and Gilda; Further performances in Rigoletto at Parma in 1987, Paris Opéra in 1988 and Bilbao in 1990; Sang Micaela and Adina at La Scala, Milan; Other roles have included Xenia in Boris Godunov and Liu in Turandot at Verona, Norina, Euridice, Ines in La Favorita at Bregenz, Nannette and Lauretta in Gianni Schicci; Season 1984 sang Gilda at Covent Garden, and made American debut as Adina at San Francisco; Appeared as Marie in La Fille du Regiment at the Paris Opéra and the Teatro Sao Carlos in Lisbon, 1988-89; Sang Pergolesi's Serpetta at Reggio Emilia, Micaela at Genoa and Liu at the Festival of Caracalla, 1992; Verona Arena 1996, as Micaela. Address: c/o Teatro alla Scala, Via Filodrammatici 2, 20121 Milan, Italy.

FERRÉ Susan (Ingrid), b. 5 Sept 1945, Boston, Massachusetts, USA. Concert Organist; Harpsichordist. m. Kenneth Charles Lang, 18 June 1980, 1 son. Education: BA, Philosophy and Music Literature, BMus, Texas Christian University, 1968; Diplome d'Orgue et Improvisation, Schola Cantorum, Paris, France, 1969; MMus, Eastman School of Music, New York, USA, 1971; DMA, North Texas State University, 1979; Studies with Jean Langlais, Marcel Dupré in France and David Craighead, USA. Career: Currently, Musical Director, Texas Baroque Ensemble and formerly Adjunct Faculty Member, North Texas State University, Denton and Southern Methodist University, Dallas; Organ and Harpsichord performances in North and South America, Europe and Scandinavia; Feature Artist, Lahti Organ Festival, Finland and at the World Council of Churches, Switzerland; Recitals at the Cathedral of Notre-Dame, Paris, France; Numerous radio broadcasts, USA; Musical Director, Texas Baroque Ensemble; Director, Early Music Festival Weekend, Round Top, Texas, 1986-. Compositions: Numerous compositions published and recorded by Avant Quart Company, France. Recordings: Works of Langlais on the Cavaillé organ at Ste Clotilde, Paris; Messe Solonelle by Louis Vierne (VQR Digital Recordings); Recordings for national radio and television, France, Hungary, Sweden, Finland, USA. Contributions to: The Diapason. Honour: Fulbright Scholar, 1968-69. Hobbies: Sailing; Hiking. Current Management: Independent Concert Artists, Garland, Texas, USA. Address: 2221 Royal Crest Drive, Garland, TX 75043, USA.

FERREIRA Paulo (Affonso de Moura), b. 11 Nov 1940, Araraquara, Brazil. Pianist; University Professor. m. (1) 1 son, 1 daughter, (2) Claudia Felícia Balduíno Ferreira, 1989. Education: Colégio Estadual Bento de Abreu Sampaio Vidal, Araraquara; Pianist, Conservatório Dramático e Musical de Sao Paulo, 1959; Music Teacher, Instituto de Educacao Caetano de Campos, 1961;

GRF, Piano Teacher, Hochschulinstitut für Musik, Trossingen, 1966. Career: Piano recitals, solo and chamber music, in Brazil, Uruguay, Argentina, Peru, Spain, Austria, Germany, Senegal, Costa Rica, Colombia, Mexico; Adjunct Professor, 1969-, Head of Music Department, 1969-71, University of Brasilia; Produced programmes about contemporary music for Brasilia Super Rádio FM, Mar 1987-89. Recordings: For Radio Bremen, Westdeutscher Rundfunk, Bayerischer Rundfunk, Norddeutscher Rundfunk, Radio Hilversum. Publications: Nova Música Brasileira para Piano, 1970; Catalogues of 43 Brazilian Composers, 1975-80; New Brazilian Piano Music, 1977. Honour: Medal, B Smetany, 1974. Membership: Sociedade Brasileira de Música Contemporanea, President 1974-82, 1985-87. Address: Superquadra Sul 105, Bloco B, Apto 506, CEP 70344-020 Brasilia (DF), Brazil.

FERRERO Lorenzo, b. 17 Nov 1951, Turin, Italy. Composer. Education: Studied with Massimo Bruni and Neore Zaffiri at Bourges (electronic resources) and Turin University. Career: Collaboration with the Musik Dia Licht Galarie in Munich from 1974, producing multi-media works; Artistic Consultant at the Puccini Festival at Torre del Lago, 1980-84; Artistic Director of the Arena di Verona from 1991; Works to attempt a reconcilliation between 19th century Italian opera and pop music. Works include: Theatre pieces, Rimbaud, Avignon, 1978; Marilyn, Rome, 1980; La Figlia del Mago, Montepulciano, 1981; Charlotte Corday, Rome, 1989; Le Bleu-blanc-rouge Et Le Noir, Paris, Centre George Pompidou, 1989. Address: c/o SAIE, Music Section, Viale della Letteratura n 30, 00144 Rome, Italy.

FERREYRA Beatriz (Mercedes), b. 21 June 1937, Cordoba, Argentina. Composer. Education: Piano study with C Bronstein, Buenos Aires, 1950-56; Harmony with Nadia Boulanger, 1962-63; Composition with György Ligeti and Earle Brown, Darmstadt, 1967; Electronic Techniques with Pierre Schaeffer, GRM Paris, 1963-64. Debut: GRM, Paris, 1964. Career: Professor Assistant: GRM, 1965-70, GMEB, 1973; B Baschet Musical Instrument Development, 1971; Music Therapy, 1973-76, 1989; Dartmouth College Computer System, 1975; Jury: 4th International Music Competition, GMEB, Bourges, 1976, 2nd International Radiophonic Competition Phonurgia Nova, Arles, 1987; Films: Antartide, 1971, Mutations, 1972; A la lueur de la lampe, ballet, 1973; Homo Sapiens, TV, 1975; La Baie St James, TV, 1980; Musiques en Feu, TV, 1981. Compositions: Demeures Aquatiques, 1967; Médisances, 1968; L'Orvietan, 1970; Etude aux Sons flegmatiques, 1971; Le Récit, 1971; Siesta Blanca, 1972; Canto del Loco, 1974; Tierra Quebrado, 1976; Echos, 1978; Jeux des Rondes, 1980-84; Cercles des Rondes, 1982; La Calesita, 1982; Boucles, rosettes et serpentines, 1982; Bruissements, 1983; Arabesque autour d'une corde raide, 1984; Passacaille déboîtée pour un lutin, 1984; Petit Poucet Magazine, 1985; The UFO Forest, 1986; L'Autre...ou le chant des marécages, 1987; Souffle d'un petite Dieu distrait, 1988, definitive version, 1997; Brise sur une fourmillère, 1988; Tata, tocame la toccata, 1990; Remolinos, 1990; Mirage Contemplatif?, 1991; Río de los pájaros, 1993. Recordings include: Pierre Schaefer, Solfège de l'Objet Sonore (assistant, co-author), 1967; Souffle d'un petit Dieu distrait, American Composers Forum, 1997. Contributions to forthcoming CDs. Honours: Diplome de meilleur disque, Medisances, 1971; Prix du Centre National du Cinéma Français, 1972; 3rd Prix de L'Electronic Music Competition, Sweden, 1975; Prix Rissolli Della Prima Opera, Italy, 1978; Prix Fance Culture (radio) de l'Innovation, Concours International de Création Radiophonique, France, 1986. Address: Bethleem, Nesle Hodeng, 76270 Neufchâtel-en-Bray, France.

FERRO Gabriele, b. 15 Nov 1937, Pescara, Italy. Conductor. Education: Studied Piano and Composition at the Accademia di Santa Cecilia in Rome with Franco Ferrara. Career: Has appeared at leading opera houses and concert halls in Italy from 1964; Founded the Symphony Orchestra of Bari, 1967; Regular concerts with the orchestras of Santa Cecilia, Suisse Romande, National de France, BBC London, Wiener Symphoniker, Bayerisches Staatsorchester, WDR Köln and the orchestras of RAI; Music Director of the Sicilian Symphony Orchestra at Palermo and Permanent Conductor of RAI Symphony Orchestra in Rome; Opera performances at La Scala, Milan, Covent Garden, London, San Francisco Opera, Lyric Opera Chicago, Opéra de Bastille, Paris, De Nederlandse Opera, Amsterdam, Bayerische Staatsoper München, Grand Théâtre de Genève and Maggio Musicale Firenze; General Music Director of the Stuttgart Staatsoper from 1992; Directed L'Italiana in Algeri there, 1996. Recordings: For various labels. Winner: RAI, Young Conductors' Competition, 1964. Address: c/o Staatstheater Stuttgart, Oberer Schlossgarten 6, 70173 Stuttgart, Germany.

FERWERDA John Diedrich, b. 1942, Holland, now Australian citizen. Violin Maker. Education: Adelaide Conservatorium, Australia under James Whitehead; Mittenwald School of Violin Making, Germany with Rudolf van Merrebach. Career includes: Cellist, New Zealand Symphony Orchestra, Brabants Orchestra, Holland, Concertgebouw Orchestra, Radio Philharmonic Orchestra of Holland, and Rheinische Philharmonic;

Established own business as violin and other stringed instrument maker in Adelaide, then moved to Melbourne in 1978; Orders for Ferwerda handcrafted instruments from Germany, UK, Austria, Holland, Israel, New Zealand, Australia and numerous well-known orchestras and players; Instruments usually based on traditional Stradivarius model, although can be made to personal requirements; Over 100 instruments completed including violins, violas, cellos, double bass, gambas and bowed guitar among others, since 1974; Exhibited in Australia, USA and Europe; Films and slides made demonstrating techniques of handcrafting; Early instruments commissioned from Victorian College of the Arts; Grants from Utah Foundation. Hobbies: Antiques; Painting; Books; Classical Music. Address: 291 Auburn Road, Hawthorn East, Melbourne, Victoria 3123, Australia.

FIALA George, b. 31 Mar 1922, Kiev, Ukraine. Composer; Pianist; Conductor. Education: Tchaikovsky State Conservatory, 1939-41; Studied composition with Hansmaria Dombrowski and conducting with Wilhelm Furtwängler, Akademische Hochschule für Musik, Berlin, 1942-45, and with Leon Jongen at Conservatoire Royal de Musique. Career: Active member of well-known Seminaire des Arts Brussels, participated in many musical events as composer, pianist and conductor; Settled in Montreal, Canada in 1949 and active as composer, pianist, organist and teacher; Currently Producer for Radio Canada International. Compositions include: Soloist with orchestra: Capriccio, 1962, Divertimento Concertante, 1965, Musique Concertante, 1968, Sinfonietta Concertata, 1971; Voices with orchestra: Canadian Credo, 1966; Orchestral: Autumn Music, 1949, Symphony No 4, 1973, Overtura Buffa, 1981, The Kurelek Suite, 1982; Chamber music: Cantilena and Rondo, 1963, Duo Sonata for Violin and Harp, 1971, Concertino Canadese, 1972, Partita Concertata, 1982, Quintet, 1982; Voice: Four Russian Poems, 1968, My Journey, 1982; Piano solos and duos. Recordings: Chamber Music for Five Wind Instruments; Montreal; Concertino; Suite Concertante; Three Movements; Sonata Breve; Sonata I for Two Pianos; Duo Sonata; The Kurelek Suite; Quartet No 2 for Saxophones; Sinfonietta Concertata. Address: PO Box 66, Station B, Montreal, Quebec, Canada, H3B 3J5.

FIALKOWSKA Janina, b. 1951, Canada. Pianist. Education: Studied at the Ecole de Musique, Vincent d'Indy in Montreal and in Paris with Yvonne Lefebure; Further study at the Juilliard School with Sasha Gorodnitzki. Career includes: Performed the world premiere of the alleged newly re-discovered 3rd Piano Concerto of Franz Liszt with the Chicago Symphony; Has appeared from 1974 with many American orchestras including the Pittsburgh Symphony and orchestras in Canada and Mexico; European engagements with leading orchestras including the Concertgebouw, Hallé, Philharmonia and French and Belgian National Radio Orchestras; To commemorate the 1986 centenary of Liszt's death, gave the Twelve Transcendental Studies in New York, Paris, Chicago, Los Angeles and London; Concert tour in 1989 of Britain including the Promenade Concerts and season 1989-90 included Bartók's Third Concerto at the Festival Hall; Played in concerts with the Cincinnati Symphony under Edo de Waart. Honours include: Prizewinner, First International Arthur Rubinstein Master Piano Competition, 1974. Address: c/o Ingpen and Williams, 26 Wadham Road, London SW15 2LR, England.

FIASCONARO Gregorio, b. 5 Mar 1915, Palermo, Sicily. Baritone; Stage Director. Education: Studied in Genoa and with Riccardo Stracciari in Rome. Debut: Genoa in 1937 as Germont in La Traviata. Career: Settled in Dublin after wartime internment; Director of the Opera School at the University of Cape Town, 1952-80; Produced and sang with the University of Cape Town Opera Company, including the title role in the British stage premiere of Duke Bluebeard's Castle at the Rudolf Steiner Theatre, London, 1957; Also sang Puccini's Scarpia and produced operas by Verdi and Puccini at many South African centres. Publications include: I'd Do It Again, Cape Town, 1982.

FICKLER Yehuda, b. 1925, Rumania. Symphony Orchestra Director. m. Erica Fickler, 3 Nov 1953, 2 children. Education: Student, Liceul Laurian, 1948; Conservatoire Ciprian Porumbescu, Bucharest, 1951; Jerusalem Music Academy, 1957; BA, Hebrew University, 1965. Career: Choir Conductor, Bucharest; Trumpet Player, Jerusalem's Radio Orchestra; Personnel Manager, Radio Orchestra, Jerusalem; Assistant Manager, Jerusalem Symphony Orchestra; General Manager of New Israeli Opera; Music Adviser and Producer of Concerts at Hebrew University; Producer, Israeli Festival; Founder of Jerusalem Chamber Orchestra; Music Adviser, Old Acre Concert Series.

FIDDES Ross Ashley, b. 20 Nov 1944, Newcastle, New South Wales, Australia. Composer; Conductor. Education: AMusA, 1971; Dip Law, 1968. Career: Solicitor, 1968-95; Musical Director, Novocastrian Arts Orchestra, 1991-95; Principal Conductor, Opera Hunter, 1992-95; Conductor and Musical Director, The Sound Construction Company, 1988-94. Compositions include: Four Ceremonies, for piano, 1982; Never Again, for male chorus, 1984; White Birds Flying, for female chorus, 1984; Children, for chorus, 1984; The Proposal, 1 act chamber opera, 1985; Combination Permutations, for piano duet, 1985; Suite for Brass Quintet, 1985; Trumpet Sonata, 1985; Ceremony, for symphonic wind band, 1987; Image and Refraction, for clarinet, bassoon, horn and string quintet, 1987; Bird Song, song cycle for soprano and clarinet, 1991; Abelard and Heloise, 2-act musical, 1997-. Honours include: Festival of Emerging Composers, USA, 1995; City of Newcastle Drama Award (CONDA), for outstanding achievement in Newcastle Theatre, for Abelard and Heloise, 1997. Address: P O Box 375, New Lambton, NSW 2305, Australia.

FIELD Helen, b. 14 May 1951, Awyn, North Wales. Soprano. Education: Royal Northern College of Music; Royal College of Music. Career: Has sung with Welsh National Opera as Poppea, Musetta, Mimi, Tatyana, Butterfly, Marenka, Jenufa, Marzellina, Vixen and Desdemona; Appeared with Opera North in first UK production of Strauss's Daphne in 1987 and Massenet's Manon; Appeared with English National Opera as Nedda, Pamina, Donna Anna, Violetta, Jenifer in Midsummer Marriage, and Gilda (also at Metropolitan, NY); Sang Jo-Ann in the premiere of Tippett's New Year at Houston in 1989, and Glyndebourne in 1990 as the Governess in The Turn of The Screw for Netherlands Festival and Cologne and Montpellier Operas, Butterfly at Deutsche Oper Berlin, Katya for Scottish Opera and Emma in Khovanshchina for Royal Opera, Covent Garden; Sang Pearl in the premiere of The Second Mrs Kong, Glyndebourne, 1994; Sang the title role in the premiere of MacMillan's Inès de Castro, Edinburgh, 1996; Concerts with all major UK orchestras; Butterfly and Liu sung in concert at Gewandhaus with Kurt Masur; Strauss's Vier Letzte Lieder with Gunther Wand, Norddeutscher Rundfunk and the BBC Symphony Orchestra at the Proms; Engaged as Salome at Los Angeles, 1998. Recordings: Gilda; Village Romeo and Juliet; Rossini's Stabat Mater, and Petite Messe Solonnelle; Hiawatha; Janácek's Osud. Address: c/o Lies Askonas Ltd, 6 Henrietta Street, London, England.

FIELD-HYDE Margaret, b. 4 May 1905, Musician. Education: Studied with father and in Germany; Studied performance of vocal music of 12th and 15th centuries. Debut: First stage revival of Purcell's King Arthur in 1928. Career: Numerous appearances in oratorio, opera and recitals singing in most cathedrals in Britain and at the Albert Hall, Queen's Hall and Festival Hall, most notably with works by Bach, Purcell and Fauré; Founder and Director of the quintet, The Golden Age Singers and touring in most European countries, North Africa, Canada and USA; Appeared at many festivals including Kings Lynn; TV and radio broadcasts and poetry readings for the BBC and British Council; Lecturer on Teaching of Solo Singing. Memberships: Royal Musical Association; Incorporated Society of Musicians. Hobbies: Gardening; Painting; Sewing. Address: Dulas Court, Dulas, Hereford, HR2 0HL, England.

FIELDSEND David, b. 1947, Yorkshire, England. Singer (Tenor). Education: Guildhall School of Music and Drama. Debut: Vanja in Katya Kabanova at the 1972 Wexford Festival. Career: Appearances with Scottish Opera as Jacquino in Fidelio, Arturo (Lucia di Lammermoor) and Rossini's Almaviva; Further engagements with the D'Oyly Carte Opera, Opera North, Travelling Opera, Chelsea Opera Group and Dorset Opera; Covent Garden debut, 1983, in Der Rosenkavalier, Bardolph (Falstaff) in Paris and Borsa (Rigoletto) at Jerusalem; Concerts and oratorios with orchestras and choral societies throughout Britain and Europe; Season 1996 included gala concert with the Royal Philharmonic and Gilbert and Sullivan evening at the Albert Hall. Recordings include: Five operetta albums with the D'Oyly Carte Opera. Honours include: Gold Medal at the GSMD, London. Address: Musicmakers, Tailor House, 63-65 High Street, Whitwell, Herts SG4 8AH, England.

FIERENS Guillermo, b. 1940, Argentina. Classical Guitarist. Education: Studied with Andres Segovia. Debut: Spain in 1963. Career: US debut in 1965 with concert tour of Mexico in 1967; Regular engagements in Britain with the LSO, Hallé Orchestra, English Chamber, Royal and London Philharmonics, Philharmonia and Orchestra of the Welsh National Opera; Played at Queen's Hall in Edinburgh in 1983 and festival appearances at Norwich, St Andrews, Harrogate, Lichfield, Newbury and Belfast; Further concerts in Holland, Switzerland, Spain, Hong Kong, Czechoslovakia, USA, Italy and Canada. Recordings: Music by Castlenuovo-Tedesco, Albeniz, Turina, Sor and Villa-Lobos. Honours include: Winner, 1967 Caracas International Guitar Competition; Citta d'Alessandria Competition in Italy; Gold Medal, Villa-Lobos Competition, Rio de Janeiro, 1971. Address: Anglo Swiss Ltd, Ste 35-37 Morley House, 320 Regent Street, London W1R 5AD, England.

FIFIELD Christopher, b. 1945, Croydon, Surrey, England. Conductor; Music Writer. Education: Manchester University; Royal Manchester College of Music; Guildhall School; Cologne Musikhochschule. Career: Assistant Director of Music, Capetown Opera followed by 12 years on music staff of Glyndebourne; Assisted Solti on 1977 recording of Otello; Former music Director, London Contemporary Dance Theatre; Currently Director, Lambeth Orchestra, Northampton Symphony Orchestra and Central Festival Opera; Frequent Conductor at Trinity College of Music; Director of Music, University College London, 1980-90, leading Massenet's Herodiade, Spohr's Faust (1852 version), Verdi's Il Corsaro, Giovanna d'Arco and Un Giorno di Regno, Puccini's Le Villi and Edgar; British premieres of Verdi's Oberto, Chabrier's Gwendoline, Bruch's Die Loreley and The Devil's Wall by Smetana; Music Director, Jubilate Choir and Reigate and Redhill Choral Society; Guest chorus master, Chelsea Opera Group; Conducted a revival of Max Bruch's Oratorio Odysseus at the Queen Elizabeth Hall, 1988; Figaro for Central Festival Opera, 1996. Publications: Contributions to Wagner in Performance, 1992; Max Bruch: His Life and Works, 1988; True Artist and True Friend: A Biography of Hans Richter, 1993. Contributions to: Viking Opera Guide; International Opera Guide; New Grove Dictionary of Opera, 1992; Reviews, BBC Music Magazine; Sleeve notes for Philips. Current Management: Music International. Address: Music International, 13 Ardilaun Road, London N6 2QR, England.

FIGUERAS Montserrat, b. 7 Mar 1940, Barcelona, Spain. Singer (Soprano). Education: Studied in Barcelona and Basle. Career: Performances with Ars Musicae and research into early singing techniques; Has worked with the Schola Cantorum Basiliensis and sung with members of the ensemble Hesperion XX and the Capella Reial; Sang in Martin y Soler's Una Cosa Rara at the 1997 Vienna Festival (Grosser Saal).

FIGUEROA Rafael, b. 27 Mar 1961, San Juan, Puerto Rico. Cellist. m. Irma I Justicia, 18 Apr 1987. Education: BM and Performer's Certificate, Indiana University School of Music; Violoncello studies with Janos Starker and Gary Hoffman. Debut: Recital debut at Terrace Theater, Kennedy Center for The Arts, Washington DC. Career: Recitals in major concert halls including Library of Congress, Kennedy Center, National Gallery of Art, Jordan Hall, Shriver Hall, Merkin Hall, Caslas Hall in Tokyo, Carnegie Recital Hall; Numerous radio broadcasts on National Public Radio. Recordings: F Mendelssohn's Concerto for Violina and Piano with Orpheus Chamber Orchestra, 1989; Schoenberg's Verklärte Nacht, 1990; Strauss's Le Bourgeois Gentilhomme and Divertimento Op 86, 1992; Weber's Clarinet Concertos and Rossini's Variations, 1992. Contributions to: Review; The Strad Magazine; Reviews, Strings Magazine. Hobbies: Gourmet Cooking; Wines; Reading. Current Management: Columbia Artists Management. Address: 16 Magaw Place 52C, New York, NY 10033, USA.

FIKEJZ Daniel, b. 21 Jun 1954, Prague, Czechoslovakia. Composer. m. 21 Jun 1979, 1 son, 1 daughter. Education: Technical University, Prague; Private lessons with Marta Oberthorova. Debut: Keyboard player and composer for group, Combo FH, 1974. Career: Continued with Combo FH, performing jazz and rock from 1974-88; Music for theatre plays, TV, film and ballet, 1983-. Compositions include: Laser Pilgrimage, audiovisual performance, 1979; Dried Strawberry's Dream, 1981; Music For Krizik Fountain, 1991; Shake-Up, ballet, 1993; New Testament, 1993. Recordings: Things, 1981; Situation On The Roof, 1986; Music For Kriziks Fountain, 1991; Don Juan, 1992. Publication: Article, Music and Technology, 1989. Honours: Musical Prize, Czech Critics, Cena Molodie, 1978. Memberships: OSA; SAI. Hobbies: Formula 1 Racing; Literature; Theatre. Address: 100 00 Praha 10, Kounicka 65, Czech Republic.

FILIP Ana Felicia, b. 1959, Romania. Singer. Education: Studied at the Bucharest Academy. Career: Sang at first at Brasov, then at the National Opera in Bucharest (debut, 1986, as Antonia in Les Contes d'Hoffmann); Guest appearances in Basle (as Violetta, 1991), Frankfurt and elsewhere; Many concert engagements. Address: c/o Stafford Law Associates, 6 Barham Close, Weybridge, Surrey KT13 9PR, England.

FILIPOVA Elena, b. 2 Dec 1957, Pasardjk, Bulgaria. Soprano. Education: Sofia Music High School; Piano and oboe at Sofia Music Conservatory. Debut: Marie in Bartered Bride, Bad Staatstheater Karlsruhe, 1981. Career: Badisches Staatstheater, 1981-86 with debut as Marenka in The Bartered Bride; Sang at Salzburg Festival in 1983; Guest performances at Hamburg, Frankfurt, Barcelona, Luxemburg, Hannover as Violetta in 1988, Bern, Vienna, and Nuremberg; Has also sung Donna Anna, Amelia Boccanegra and Tatiana, and sang Aida at Hannover in 1990; Concerts in Germany, Austria, France, Italy, and Switzerland, and TV appearances on ORF Salzburg Festival in 1983, ZDF, Berlin in 1983, SWF, Baden Baden in 1985 with Mozart and Handel Arias. Honour: 1st Prize, Karajan Foundation, Salzburg Festival, 1982. Hobbies: Cooking; Reading; Piano; Languages. Address: Staatstheater, Opernplatz 1, 3000 Hannover, Germany.

FILIPOVIC Igor, b. 18 Apr 1951, Ljublijana, Slovenia. Tenor. Education: Studied in Ljublijana and in Italy. Debut: Sang Ernesto in Don Pasquale, 1976. Career: Member of the Vienna Kammeroper, 1976-77, Lucerne Opera, 1977-78; Guest appearances in Europe, the USA and Canada as Rossini's Amenofi in Mosè in Egitto and Arnoldo in William Tell, Arturo in I Puritani, Edgardo in Lucia di Lammermoor, Enrico in Maria di Rudenz, Tonio in La Fille du Regiment, the Duke of Mantua in Rigoletto, Alfredo in La Traviata, Riccardo in Un Ballo in Maschera, Rodolfo in Luisa Miller, Cavaradossi in Tosca, and Don José at Bregenz Festival in 1992; Also sang at Prague, Venice, Milan, Rome, Turin, Palermo, Vienna Staatsoper and Volksoper, Stuttgart, Mannheim, Frankfurt, Brussels, Chicago and New York at the City Opera; Broadcasting engagements throughout Europe. Address: c/o Opernhaus Dortmund, Kuhstrasse 12, 44137 Dortmund, Germany.

FILSELL Jeremy (Daniell), b. 10 Apr 1964, Brentwood, Essex, England. Pianist; Organist. m. Elizabeth Overden, 1 son. Education: Keble College, Oxford, England, 1982-85; Royal College of Music, London, England, 1985-86. Career: Solo recitals in Festivals: London, Cambridge, Salisbury, Lichfield; Toured as Soloist: Germany 1985, 1993, USA 1995; Concertos: Beethoven, Shostakovich, Ireland BBC R3 Broadcasts as Soloist and Accompanist to BBC Singers; Organ Recitals in all major English cathedrals and town halls; Noted specialization as Pianist in English and as Organist in French Romantic. Recordings: Organ: Vierne 3rd Symphony Gramophone Critics Choice, 1992; Organ works of Marcel Dupré; Piano: Solo works of Herbert Howells and Bernard Stevens, 1993. Honours: Silver Medal of the Worshipful Co of Musicians, 1984; Critics Choice (Gramophone) for 1991 Recording of Vierne Symphony III. Hobbies: Cricket; Squash; Sculling. Current Management: Chameleon Arts Management. Address: 63 Thurpebank Road, Sherpherd's Bush, London W12 0PG, England.

FINCKEL David, b. 6 Dec 1951, Kutztown, PA, USA. Cellist. Career: Member of the Emerson String Quartet from 1977; Premiere concert at Alice Tully Hall in New York, 1977, with works by Mozart, Smetana and Bartók; European debut at Spoleto, Italy in 1981; Quartet-in-Residence at the Smithsonian Institute, WA, from 1980, at the Hartt School from 1981 and at the Spoleto and Aspen Festivals from 1981; First resident quartet at the Chamber Music Society of Lincoln Center, season 1982-83; Many performances of works by Bartók including all six quartets in a single evening, and contemporary works; Premieres include Mario Davidovsky's 4th Quartet and works by Maurice Wright and George Tsontakis, Beethoven series at South Bank, London, 1996. Recordings include: Walter Piston's Concerto for String Quartet, Winds and Percussion; Works by Andrew Imbrie, Henry Cowell, Roy Harris and Gunther Schuller; Bartók's Six Quartets.

FINDLAY Jane, b. 1960, England. Mezzo-Soprano. Education: Studied at the Royal Northern College of Music and with Peter Harrison and Paul Hamburger. Career: Sang with the Glyndebourne Festival Chorus, then as Hermia and Dorabella with the Touring Opera, and Third Boy in Die Zauberflöte at the Festival; Sung Dorabella with the Northern Ireland Opera Trust in Belfast and with Opera 80 in tour; Appearances at the Wexford Festival and with Opera Nancy; Sang in Margot-la-Rouge at the Camden Festival in 1984 and in Monteverdi's L'Orfeo at Florence under Roger Norrington; Tour of Germany with the Monteverdi Choir in 1985 including Irene in Handel's Tamerlano at the Göttingden Festival and concert performances in Cologne; Season 1987-88 in Opera 80's Cenerentola and appearances in The Gondoliers and La Belle Hélène for New Sadler's Wells Opera; Welsh National Opera debut in 1989 in La Traviata and Covent Garden debut in 1990 as Magdalena in Die Meistersinger; Concert repertoire includes The Dream of Gerontius, Shéhérazade by Ravel, Bach's Christmas Oratorio and Messiah. Honours include: South East Arts Award; Miriam Licette Award, 1985. Address: c/o Korman International Management, Crunnells Green Cottage, Preston, Hertfordshire, SG4 7UQ, England.

FINE Vivian, b. 28 Sep 1913, Chicago, IL, USA. Composer; Teacher. m. Benjamin Karp, 5 Apr 1935, 2 daughters. Education: Studied piano at Chicago Music College and with Djane Lavole-Herz; Studied harmony and composition with Ruth Crawford, Adolf Weidig and Henry Cowell and piano with Abby Whiteside, composition with Roger Sessions, and orchestration with George Szell. Career: Teacher at New York University, 1945-48, Juilliard School of Music, 1948, SUNY at Potsdam, 1951, Connecticut College School of Dance, 1963-64, and Bennington College, VT, 1964-87. Compositions: Chamber opera: The Women In The Garden, 1977; Theatre pieces; Orchestral: Elegiac Song for Strings, 1937, Concertante for Piano and Orchestra, 1944, Romantic Ode for solo Violin, Viola, Cello and Strings, 1976, Drama, 1982, Poetic Fires for Piano and Orchestra, 1984, After The Tradition for Chamber Orchestra, 1988; Chamber: String Trio, 1930, Violin Sonata, 1952, String Quartet, 1957, Dreamscape for 3 Flutes, Cello, Piano and Percussion Ensemble, 1964, Chamber Concerto for 7 Instruments, 1966, Quintet for String Trio, Trumpet and Harp, 1967, Brass Quintet, 1978, Piano Trio, 1980, Quintet for Oboe, Clarinet, Violin, Cello and Piano, 1984, Cello Sonata, 1986; Dancing Winds, 1987; Piano pieces, choral music, and works for voice and instruments. Honours:

Many grants and commissions; Guggenheim Fellowship, 1980. Memberships: American Society of Composers, Authors and Publishers; American Academy of Arts and Letters, 1980-. Address: 506 Beechwood Road, Hoosick Falls, NY 12090, USA.

FINE Wendy, b. 19 Dec 1943, Durban, South Africa. Soprano. Education: Studied with John van Zyl in Durban and with Christian Mueller, Erik Werba and Maria Hittorf at the Vienna Music Academy. Debut: Stadttheater Berne as Madame Butterfly. Career: Appearances at opera houses in London, Hamburg, Munich, Stuttgart, Berlin, Lisbon, Vienna and Geneva; Sang at Bayreuth Festival in 1971; Roles include Nedda, Micaela, Marguerite, Mimi, Sophie in Der Rosenkavalier, Desdemona, Fiordiligi, Donna Elvira, Pamina, Luise in Der Junge Lord (British premiere in 1965), Ophelia in Szokolay's Hamlet, and Maria in The Miracles of Our Lady by Martinu; Sang at Covent Garden, 1971-77 as Musetta, Gutrune, Donna Elvira, Fiordiligi and Jenufa, and at La Scala Milan in 1977 as Berg's Marie.

FINGERHUT Margaret, b. 30 March 1955, London, England. Pianist. Education: Royal College of Music, London; Peabody Conservatory, Baltimore. Career: Performed in the United Kingdom, America, Europe, Scandinavia, Africa, India, Turkey and Israel; Played with London Symphony, Royal Philharmonic, London Philharmonic and Philharmonia Orchestras; Broadcasts for BBC Radio and WFMT, Chicago; Appeared on film and television. Recordings: Chandos Records; Several with the London Philharmonic and London Symphony Orchestras, including world premiere recording of Arnold Bax's Winter Legends; Has also recorded music by Grieg, Dukas, Falla, Howells, Suk, Stanford and Moeran; Collections of Russian and French Composers. Honours: Hopkinson Gold Medal, 1977; Boise Foundation Scholarship, 1977; Greater London Arts Association, Young Musician of the Year, 1981. Current Management: Helen Houghton. Address: 9 Cromwell Road, Burgess Hill, Sussex RH15 8QH, England.

FINK Manfred, b. 15 Apr 1954, Frankfurt am Main, Germany. Singer. Education: Studied in Frankfurt. Career: Chorus of the Cologne Opera, 1979-81 then soloist with the Mainz Opera from 1981 with debut as Tamino; Deutsche Oper am Rhein Dusseldorf from 1982 as Mozart's Ferrando, Belmonte and Don Ottavio; Guest appearances from 1984 at Buenos Aires, Venice, Rome, Nice, Florence as David in Die Meistersinger in 1985, Frankfurt and Vienna; Other roles have included Edgardo in Lucia di Lammermoor, Des Grieux in Manon Lescaut, Rinuccio and Nemorino; Sang the Steuermann in Der fliegende Holländer for Cologne Opera in 1991, and Pedrillo in Die Entführung at the Schwetzingen Festival in 1991. Recording: Handel Dettingen Te Deum. Address: c/o Opera der Stadt Koln, Offenbachplatz, 5000 Cologne, Germany.

FINK Michael (Jon), b. 7 Dec 1954, Los Angeles, USA. Composer; Teacher. Education: Studied at the California Institute of the Arts with William Kraft, Harold Budd, Barney Childs and Mel Powell (MFA 1980). Career: Performances with the Negative Band and Stillife; Composer-in-Residence, North Michigan University, 1985; Teacher at California Institute of the Arts from 1982. Compositions include: Two pieces for piano, 1983; Work for chamber orchestra, 1986; Living to be Hunted by the Moon, for clarinet, bass clarinet, electronics, 1987; A Temperament for Angels, electronics and keyboards, 1989; Sound Shroud Garden, with Jim Fox, 1989; Epitaph, bass clarinet, 1990. Recordings include: Album vocalise. Publications include: Business Music in Contemporary Life, 1989. Address: c/o ASCAP, ASCAP Building, One Lincoln Plaza, NY 10023, USA.

FINK Myron S, b. 19 Apr 1932, Chicago, USA. Composer. Education: Juilliard School with Bernard Wagenaar and Castelnuovo-Tedesco, Burrill Phillips at the University of Illinois, Cornell University with Robert Palmer and in Vienna, 1955-56. Career: Former Teacher at Alma College, Hunter College New York, the Curtis Institute and the City University of New York; Opera, The Conquistador, premiered at San Diego, 1997. Compositions: Operas: The Boor, after Chekov, 1955, Susanna And The Elders, 1955, Jeremiah, 1962, Judith And Holofernes, 1978, Chinchilla, 1986, The Island Of Tomorrow, 1986; The Conquistadors, 1997. Honours include: Woodrow Wilson Memorial Fellowship, 1954. Address: c/o San Diego Opera, PO Box 988, San Diego, CA 92112, USA.

FINK Richard (Paul), b. 23 Mar 1955, USA. Baritone. Education: Kent State University; Oberlin College. Career: Worked and performed with the Houston Symphony, Pops, Houston Ballet, Houston Theatre Under The Stars; Other concerts include Youngstown Symphony, A Night At The Opera, as well as benefit concerts for churches and the homeless in Houston; Other productions include Falstaff, Boris Godunov, Eugene Onegin at Houston Opera, Tosca's Scarpia at Bremer Stadt Theater in Germany, 1988, Jokanaan in Salome, Enrico in Lucia di Lammermoor and Tchelio in The Love for Three Oranges at Bremen Opera, 1988-89, Kaspar in Der Freischütz, 1988-89, Escamillo in Carmen and as Rigoletto for Welsh National Opera, 1990-91, the Watergnome in Rusalka and Klingsor in Parsifal at Houston Grand Opera, 1991-92; 1992-93 season opened as Sid in Albert Herring with the Atlanta Opera, Kurwenal in Tristan, Count di Luna in Il Trovatore, Pizarro in Fidelio and Sebastiano at the Washington Opera Kennedy Center's staging of D'Albert's Tiefland; Sang Wagner's Dutchman at Sydney, 1996. Current Management: William Guerri, Trawick Artists Management, 129 West 72nd Street, NY 10023, USA. Address: 1310 Bridle Spur Lane, Houston, TX 77055, USA.

FINKE Martin, b. 1948, Rhede bei Bocholt, Germany. Tenor. Education: Studied with Hilde Wesselman at the Folkwang Hochschule Essen. Career: Sang first at opera houses in Augsburg, Cologne Stuttgart; Sang at Bayreuth Festival in 1975; Sang at Barcelona in 1983 as Jacquino in Fidelio and Bregenz Festival in 1984; Sang David in Die Meistersinger at the Théâtre de la Monnaie in Brussels, 1985 and at Salzburg Festival in 1986 in the premiere of Penderecki's Die schwarze Maske; Other roles include Mozart's Pedrillo and Monostatos and Mime in Der Ring des Nibelungen, Nice Opera, 1988; Concert singer in the Passions of Bach, Messiah and the Missa Solemnis. Recordings: Pagliacci, Intermezzo and Ariadne auf Naxos; Die Verschworenen by Schubert; Operettas by Lehar. Address: c/o Oper der Stadt Köln, Offenbachplatz, D-5000 Cologne, Germany.

FINKO David, b. 15 May 1936, Leningrad, Russia. Composer; Conductor. Education: Studied at the Leningrad School of Performing Arts, 1950-58 and Leningrad Conservatory, 1960-65. Career: Emigrated to the USA in 1979; Visiting Lecturer, University of Pennsylvania, 1979-81; Lecturer and Composer-in-Residence, University of Texas, El Paso, 1981. Compositions: Polinka, after Chekov, 1965; In A Torture Chamber Of The Gestapo, 1970; The Enchanted Tailor, 1983; Orchestral: 6 Tone Poems, 1965-78, Symphony No 1, 1969, Piano Concerto, 1971, Viola Concerto, 1971, Symphony No 2, 1972, Double Concerto for Violin, Viola and Orchestra, 1973, Double Concerto for Viola, Double Bass and Orchestra, 1975, Harp Concerto, 1976, Concerto for 3 Violins and Orchestra, 1981, Pilgrimage To Jerusalem, 1983; Chamber: Piano Sonata, 1964, Mass Without Words for Violin and Organ, 1968, Lamentations Of Jeremiah for Violin, 1969, Fromm Septet, 1983. Honours include: Grants and fellowships, ASCAP, The Fromm Foundation and the Memorial Foundation of Jewish Culture. Address: Music Department, University of Texas, El Paso, TX, USA.

FINLEY Gerald, b. 30 Jan 1960, Montreal, Canada. Baritone. m. Louise Winter. Education: Studied at King's College, Cambridge, the Royal College of Music and the National Opera Studio. Career: Glyndebourne Festival from 1986 as Sid in Albert Herring, Kuligin in Katya Kabanova, Count Dominik in Arabella and with the Touring Opera in Il Barbiere di Siviglia, Death in Venice and Die Zauberflöte; Sang Papageno as part of Roger Norrington's Mozart Experience; Covent Garden debut in Don Carlos; Other opera roles include Mozart's Figaro for Mecklenburgh Opera, Guglielmo for the British Pears School and Glyndebourne, and Britten's Demetrius at Aix-en-Provence; Salzburg Festival in 1991 in Der Schauspieldirektor; Concert appearances with the Northern Sinfonia, the City of London Sinfonia, the Orchestra of the Age of Enlightenment, the Hanover Band, The Sixteen and Monteverdi Choir and Orchestra; North American engagements in Messiah at St Louis, Ottawa and Montreal, Arvo Pärt's Passion in Chicago and at the Lincoln Center, NY; Has sung in works by Hadyn, Handel and Mozart in Utrecht, Vienna and elsewhere in Europe; Wigmore Hall, London debut in 1989 in a programme of Beethoven Lieder; BBC Radio 3 in the Mass by Amy Beach and Vivaldi's La Senna Festeggiante; BBC TV in Britten's Death in Venice; Sang in Haydn's The Seasons at the 1993 London Proms; Bach's St John Passion at the Festival Hall, 1997. Recordings include: L'Enfance du Christ by Berlioz; Albums of sacred music with the King's College Choir. Address: c/o Harrison Parrott Ltd, 12 Penzance Place, London, W11 4PA, England.

FINNIE Linda, b. 9 May 1952, Paisley, Scotland. Mezzo-Soprano. Education: Royal Scottish Academy of Music with Winifred Busfield. Debut: Scottish Opera, Glasgow in 1976. Career includes: After winning the Kathleen Ferrier Prize in 1977 sang widely in Europe including Paris Opéra and Madrid and Welsh National Opera from 1979; Roles with the English National Opera have included Eboli, Amneris and Ortrud in Lohengrin; Guest appearances in The Ring at Covent Garden; Sang in Mahler's 8th Symphony at the Promenade Concerts and under Claudio Abbado in Verdi's Requiem in Chicago, 1986; 1987 season included Prokofiev's Alexander Nevsky at the Proms, Messiah in San Francisco and Elgar's Sea Pictures; Frankfurt and Nice debuts in 1987 as Amneris and as Waltraute in Götterdämmerung, and Bayreuth debut in 1988 in a new production of The Ring under Daniel Barenboim; Sang Fricka, Siegrune and Second Norn at the 1990 Festival; Concert season 1992-93 with the New Japan Philharmonic, Orchestra National de France, Berlin Symphony, Czech Philharmonic and the Santa Cecilia Orchestra, Rome; Sang Ortrud in Lohengrin at Bayreuth, 1993-94. Recordings: Alexander Nevsky with the Choral Symphony; Elgar Sea Pictures with LPO under Thomson; Ravel's Sheherazade under P Tortelier; Respighi Il Tramonto under Vasary; La Rondine with LPO under Maazel; L'Enfant et Les Sortilèges with LSO under Previn; Eugene Onegin; Prokofiev's Ivan the Terrible with Philharmonia under Järvi. Address: c/o Christopher Tennant, Unit 2, 39 Tadema Road, London, SW10 0PY, England.

FINNILA Birgit, b. 20 Jan 1931, Falkenberg, Sweden. Contralto. m. Allan Finnila, 2 sons, 3 daughters. Education: Studied in Goteborg with Ingalli Linden and at Royal Academy of Music with Roy Henderson. Career: Concerts in Sweden from 1963; London debut in 1966 followed by concerts in Berlin, Hamburg, Hanover, Stuttgart and Dusseldorf; Tours of USA, Australia, Russia and Israel from 1968; Opera debut at Goteborg in 1967 as Gluck's Orpheus; Guest appearances at La Scala Milan and the Munich Staatsoper; Salzburg Easter Festival, 1973-74 as Erda in The Ring, under Karajan; Sang Brangaene in Tristan und Isolde at the Paris Opéra in 1976. Recordings: Cimarosa's Requiem; Mozart's Betulia Liberata; Bach's Magnificat; Bruckner's Te Deum; Dvorák's Requiem; Strauss's Aegyptische Helena; Bach's B minor Mass; Vivaldi's Tito Manlio. Honour: Grand Prix du Disque for Juditha Triumphans by Vivaldi. Address: c/o Svensk Konsertdirektion AB, Box 5076, 40222 Goteborg, Sweden.

FINNISSY Michael (Peter), b. 17 Mar 1946, London, England. Composer. Education: Royal College of Music, London. Career: Director of Music, London School of Contemporary Dance, 1969-74; Lecturer, Chelsea College, Chelsea School of Art, Dartington Summer School; Guest Artist, The Victorian College of The Arts, Melbourne, 1982-83; Composition Teacher, Winchester College, 1987-; Sussex University, 1989-; Royal Academy of Music, 1991-; Chairman, British Section ISCM, 1989-90; President, ISCM, 1991-96; Executive Councillor, ISCM, 1990-96. Compositions: World, 1968-74; Folk-Song Set, 1969-70; Tsuru Kame, 1971-73; Mysteries, 1972-79; Cipriano, 1974; 7 Piano Concetos, 1975-81; Offshore, 1975-76; Mr Punch, 1976-77; English Country-Tunes, 1977; Alongside, 1979; Sea and Sky, 1979-80; Kelir, 1981; Dilok, 1982; Whitman, 1981-83; Vaudeville, 1983; Ngano, 1983-84; String Quartet, 1984; Cabaret Vert, 1985; The Undivine Comedy, Stage Work, 1988; Red Earth, 1987-88; Gershwin Arrangements and More Gershwin, 1975-90; Obrecht Motetten, 1988-; Unknown Ground, 1989-90; Thérèse Raquin, Opera, 1992-93; Folklore, 1993-95; Shameful Vice, Stage Work, 1994; Liturgy of Saint Paul, 1995; Seventeen Immortal Homosexual Poets, for piano, 1997. Current Management: Oxford University Press, United Music Publishers, Universal Edition, London. Address: c/o Oxford University Press, Walton Street, Oxford OX2 6DP, England.

FINSCHER Ludwig, b. 14 Mar 1930, Kassel, Germany. Musicologist; Professor. Education: Pupil of Rudolf Gerber, PhD, University of Göttingen, 1954; Completed Habilitation, University of Saarbrücken, 1967. Career includes: Editor, 1961-68, Co-editor, 1968-74, Die Musikforschung; Professor of Musicology, University of Frankfurt am Main, 1968-81; University of Heidelberg, 1981-95, now retired. Publications include: Loyset Compère (c 1450-1518): Life and Works, 1964; Studien zur Geschichte des Streichquartetts: I, Die Entstehung des klassischen Streichquartetts: Von den Vorformen zur Grundlegung durch Joseph Haydn, 1974; Editor, Renaissance-Studien: Helmuth Osthoff zum 80 Geburtstag, 1979; Editor, Quellenstudien zur Musik der Renaissance: I, Formen und Probleme der Uberlieferung mehrstimmiger Musik im Zeitalter Josquin Desprez, 1981; Editor, Ludwig van Beethoven, 1983; Editor, Claudio Monteverdi: Festschrift Reinhold Hammerstein zum 70 Geburtstag, 1986; Editor, Die Musik des 15 und 16, Jahrhunderts, Neues Handbuch der Musikwissenschaft, volume 3/1-2, 1989-90; Editor, Die Musik in Geschichte und Gegenwart, 2nd edition, 1994-. Contributions to: Edited complete musical works of Gaffurius, 1955, 1960; The collected works of Compère, 1958-72; With, K von Fischer, the collected works of Hindemith, 1976-; Edited works for Neue Mozart-Ausgabe and the complete works of Gluck. Honours: Order Pour le Mérite, 1994; Great Order of Merit, Germany, 1997. Memberships: Honorary Member, International Musicological Society; Honorary Foreign Member, Royal Musical Association, London, 1978-; Mainz Academy of Sciences; Heidelberg Academy of Sciences; Academia Europaea. Address: Am Walde 1, D-38302 Wolfenbüttel, Germany.

FINSTERER Mary, b. 1962, Canberra, Australia. Composer. Education: Studied with Brenton Broadstock and Riccardo Formosa in Melbourne and Louis Andriessen in Amsterdam; BMus, MMus, Melbourne University, currently undertaking a PhD in composition. Career: Lecturer, various universities including Montreal, Dusquene in Pittsburgh, Wollongong, Melbourne and the Victorian College of Arts, Australia; Performances of her work at major national and international festivals including The Holland Festival, Pittsburgh Music Lives, Adelaide, Sydney Spring Festival; Many commissions and performances from leading ensembles in

Australia, Europe, Canada and the USA including Queensland Symphony Orchestra, Australian Chamber Orchestra, Pittsburgh New Music Ensemble and Ensemble Modern. Compositions include: Scat, for chromatic harmonica and orchestra, 1992; Catch, for soprano saxophone, bass clarinet and piano, 1992; Omaggio alla Pieta, for 6 voices, double bass (optional) and percussion, 1993; Scimmia, for string orchestra, 1994; Monkey, for string quintet, 1996; Magnet, for solo tuba, 1997; Ether, for solo flute, 1998; Pascal's Sphere, for chamber orchestra, 1998; Ruisselant, for chamber orchestra; Nyx, for chamber orchestra; Quicksilver, for chamber orchestra; Nextwave Fanfare, for orchestra. Honours: Le Nem Forum, 1991; ISCM Switzerland, 1991; Paris Rostrum, 1992; ISCM Germany, 1995; England, 1998; Has represented Australia in 3 ISCM World Music Day Festivals. Address: 157 Rankins Road, Kensington, Victoria, Australia.

FIORILLO Elisabetta, b. 1960, Naples, Italy. Singer (Mezzo-soprano). Career: Appeared as Ulrica at Naples, Musetta in Leoncavallo's Bohème at Venice and Azucena at Zürich, Macerata, Turin, Verna, and Parma, 1984-; Guest appearances in Berlin, Hamburg, Verona and Philadelphia as Amneris in Aida, 1993-96; Preziosilla in La Forza del destino at Barcelona, Azucena at Munich, Eboli in Turin and Fenena in Nabucco at Naples; Concert repertory includes the Verdi Requiem and song recitals; Further engagements at the Vienna Saatsoper and the Caracalla Festival, Rome. Honours include: Winner, Mattia Battistini Competition, 1983; Prizewinner, Voci Verdiane Competition Busseto and the Vincenzo Bellini Competition, 1984. Address: c/o Opernhaus Zürich, Falkenstrasse 1, CH-8008 Zürich, Switzerland.

FIORITO John, b. 1937, USA. Singer (Bass-baritone). Education: Studied at the New England Conservatory, Boston, with George London. Career: Sang at the New York City Opera from 1962 and at the Metropolitan Opera from 1965 until 1967 as Mozart's Count, Germont, Marcello and Escamillo; Bielefeld Opera, 1968-70, Von Einem's Der Prozess at the Vienna Staatsoper (1970); Further appearances in Philadelphia, Washington, Chicago and New Orleans, as Leporello, Alfonso, Mustafa, Dandini, Monterone and Escamillo.

FIRSOVA Elena, b. 21 Mar 1950, Leningrad, USSR. Composer. m. Dmitri Smirnov 1972. Education: Began music studies at college, Moscow, 1966; Moscow Conservatoire, 1970-75, with Alexander Pirumov (Composition) and Yury Kholopov (Analysis); Further study with Edison Denisov. Career: Her music featured outside USSR, 1979, in Cologne, Paris and Venice; UK debut with Petraca's Sonnets, 1980; BBC commissions: Earthly Life, 1986, Augury, 1991, Cassandra, 1993; Professor, Composer-in-Residence, Keele University, 1993-; Chamber opera The Nightingale and the Rose performed at Almeida Theatre, London, 1994. Compositions include: Earthly Life, cantata for soprano and ensemble, 1984; Fantasie, violin solo, 1985; Chamber Concerto No 3, piano, orchestra, 1985, No 4, horn, ensemble, 1987; Music for 12, 1986; Piano Sonata, 1986; Forest Walks, soprano, ensemble, 1987; Augury, orchestra, chorus, 1988; Autumn Music, 1988; Misterioso, String Quartet No 3, 1980; Amoroso, String Quartet No 4, 1989, No 5, Lagrimoso, 1992, No 6, 1994; No 7 Compassione, 1995; Monologue, bassoon, 1989; Nostalgia, orchestra, 1989; Stygian Song, soprano, ensemble, 1989; Odyssey, 7 performers, 1990; Verdehr-Terzett, violin, clarinet, piano, 1990; The Nightingale and the Rose, after Wilde, 1991; Seven Haiku, voice, lyre, 1991; Far Away, saxophone quartet; Sea Shell, voice, ensemble, 1991; Whirlpool, voice, flute, percussion, 1991; Silentium, voice, string quartet, 1991; Secret Way, orchestra, voice, 1992; Distance, voice, ensemble, 1992; Meditation in the Japanese Garden, flute, viola, piano, 1992; You and I, cello, piano, 1992; Starry Flute, flute, 1992; Vigilia, violin, piano, 1992; Otzvuki, flute, guitar, 1992; Cassandra, orchestra, 1992; Phantom, 4 viols, 1993; The Night Demons, cello, piano, 1993; Crucifixion, cello, bayan, 1993; Hymn to Spring, piano, 1993; Monologue, solo saxophone, 1993; The Enchanted Island, 1993; Album Leaf, cello, piano, 1993; Mad Vision, Piano Trio No 2, 1993; Insomnia, 4 singers, 1993; Before the Thunderstorm, soprano, ensemble, 1994; The Door is Closed (String Quartet no 9), 1997. Address: 32 Larchwood, Keele, Newcastle, Staffs ST5 5BB, England.

FIRTICH Georgy (Ivanovich), b. 20 Oct 1938, Russia. Composer. Divorced, 2 sons. Education: Leningrad Music College; Leningrad Conservatoire. Debut: Leningrad in 1953 as composer and musician. Career: Composer of symphonies, film scores, and music for radio and theatre; Currently Chairman of St Petersburg Association of Modern Music. Compositions include: 7 Sonatas for Piano and for Viola and Piano, 1960-90; Bug, 1961 and Return, 1964, ballets; About Motherland, symphony, 1963; Baths, opera, 1971; Concerto-Symphony, 1986; Vocal Cycle for Baritone, 1987; Vocal Cycle for Soprano and Piano, 1990; Choral works include: Leningrad, cantata in 6 movements, for Soprano, Baritone, Chorus and Symphony Orchestra, 1976. Recordings include: Adventures of Captain Vrungel, 1986; Edwards. Honours: Laureate of Leningrad Competitions; Honoured Worker of Arts,

Russia, 1993. Membership: Composers' Union of St Petersburg. Hobbies: Driving; Fishing; Mushrooms. Address: Novoalexandrovskaya St 11-29, St Petersburg 193012, Russia.

FISCHER Adam, b. 9 Sept 1949, Budapest, Hungary. Conductor. Education: Kodály School, Budapest; Conducting in Budapest, Vienna, Rome. Career: Won Milan Cantelli Competition, 1973; General Music Director, Graz Opera, Karlsruhe, Friburg; Conducted Fidelio at the Bavarian State Opera, followed ny Dvorak's Rusalka; US debut, San Francisco Opera with Don Giovanni, 1981; Conducted new production of Macbeth for Chicago Lyric Opera, 1981; US symphonic debut with Boston Symphony Orchestra, 1984; Paris Opera debut with Der Rosenkavalier, 1984; First Japanese tour, 1984; Led Hungarian State Symphony Orchestra's US Tour, 1985; La Scala, Milan, debut with Zauberflöte, 1986; Artistic Director, Austro-Hungarian Haydn Festival, 1987-; Musical Director, Kassel Opera, 1987-92; Royal Opera House debut with Die Fledermaus, 1989; Presenter and Conductor, first Gustav Mahler Festival, 1989; English National Opera debut, 1991; Conducted opening of Vienna Konzerthaus with Vienna Chamber Orchestra, 1991; Bluebeard's Castle, with ENO, 1992-93; Debut, Metropolitan Opera, New York, with Otello, 1992-93; Austro-Hungarian Haydn Orchestra debut, BBC Proms, London, 1993, and Lincoln Center, New York, 1994; Barber of Seville, 1995-96; Aida, 1996-97; Led Hungarian State Symphony Orchestra in Athens with Verdi's Macbeth, 1997; Mostly Mozart Festival, New York, 1997; Regular productions with the Vienna State and Zurich Operas. Recordings: Haydn's Complete Symphonies with Austro-Hungarian Haydn Orchestra; Queen of Sheba (1st recording), 1982; Hungarian repertoire (especially Bartók) with Hungarian State Symphony. Honours: BBC TV recording of Duke Bluebeard's Castle with London Philharmonic Orchestra won Italia Prize, 1989; Grand Prix du Disque for Queen of Sheba, 1982. Address: c/o Harold Holt Ltd, 31 Sinclair Road, London W14 0NS, England.

FISCHER György, b. 12 Aug 1935, Budapest, Hungary. Conductor; Pianist; Harpsichordist. Education: Franz Liszt Academy, Budapest; Salzburg Mozarteum. Career: Assistant to Karajan at the Vienna State Opera where he conducted Die Zauberflöte and Die Entführung; Currently Principal Conductor at the Cologne Opera, notably in a Mozart cycle produced by Jean Pierre Ponnelle; Bavarian State Opera with Don Giovanni, Ideomeneo and Die Zauberflöte in South America, and Cimarosa's Le Astuzie Femminili at Wexford; UK debut with the Welsh National Opera in 1973 returning for Cosi fan tutte and Le Nozze di Figaro; London debut in 1979 with the UK premiere of Mozart's Mitridate at the Camden Festival; English Chamber Orchestra from 1980; Debut with Australian Opera, 1987-88, conducting Cosi fan tutte in 1990; Don Giovanni for Vancouver Opera in 1988; Season 1992 with Le nozze di Figaro at Sydney; Accompanist to leading singers including his former wife the late Lucia Popp. Recordings include: Mozart Arias for Soprano Voice with Kiri Te Kanawa, Teresa Berganza and Cecilia Bartoli. Address: c/o Lies Askonas Ltd, 6 Henrietta Street, London, WC2, England.

FISCHER Hanne, b. 1968, Denmark. Singer (Mezzo-soprano). Education: Studied at the Royal Danish Conservatoire, Copenhagen. Debut: Royal Opera, Copenhagen, 1993, as Mozart's Cherubino and Third Boy (Die Zauberflöte); Sang Annius in La Clemenza di Tito for the Glyndebourne Tour (1995) and Isolier in Le Comte Ory at the 1997 Festival; Further roles at Copenhagen as Rosina, Dorabella and Zerlina; Kiel Opera 1993-97; Further engagements as Idamantes in Idomeneo at the Flanders Festival, and elsewhere in Europe as Siebel in Faust, Suzuki (Butterfly), Cenerentola, Hansel and Flosshilde in The Ring; Season 1997-98 as Annius at the Flanders Festival and appearances at the Royal Opera, Copenhagen. Address: c/o The Royal Opera House, Box 2185, DK-1017 Copenhagen, Denmark.

FISCHER Ivan, b. 20 Jan 1951, Budapest, Hungary. Conductor. 2 children. Education: Studied cello and composition in Budapest; Conducting studies with Hans Swarowsky, Vienna, and Nikolaus Harnoncourt, Salzburg. Career: Premio Firenze, 1974; Many engagements with British orchestras from 1976; Music Director of the Northern Sinfonia of England, 1979-82; Toured Britain with London Symphony Orchestra, 1980; Founded Budapest Festival Orchestra, 1983; Music Director of Kent Opera, 1984-89, conducting Agrippina, L'Incoronazione di Poppea, Die Entführung aus dem Serail, Le nozze di Figaro, Carmen, La Traviata, Die Zauberflöte, Il Re Pastore, Le Comte Ory, Fidelio, Don Giovanni and Peter Grimes; Season 1987-88 directed Die Zauberflöte for English National Opera and La Gazza Ladra at the Paris Opera; Season 1988-89 conducted Don Giovanni at the Vienna Staatsoper, returning for Le nozze di Figaro and Die Entführung; US engagements with orchestras in Pittsburgh, San Francisco, Los Angeles, Chicago and Cincinnati (Principal Guest Conductor of the Symphony Orchestra); Also conducts St Paul Chamber Orchestra and in Montreal and Toronto; Recent engagements with the Royal Concertgebouw, Amsterdam, and Berlin and Israel Philharmonics; Toured Switzerland, 1989, with Budapest Festival Orchestra and pianist Zoltan Kocsis, ending

with a visit to the Barbican Hall, London; First Guest Conductor, Cincinnati Symphonic Orchestra, 1990-95; Conducted the Orchestra of the Age of Enlightenment in Zaide at the Elizabeth Hall, 1991; Bluebeard's Castle at the 1992 Proms; Tour of Paris, Cologne, Vienna and New York with Bartók's Stage Works, 1996. Recordings include: Symphonies by Schubert, Mahler, Mozart and Mendelssohn, the Brahms Violin Concerto (with Boris Belkin and London Symphony Orchestra) and Don Pasquale, Bartók Concertos with Budapest Festival Orchestra and Zoltan Kocsis. Honours include: 1st Prize, Firenze International Concours, 1976; Winner, Rupert Foundation Competition, 1976; MUM Prize in USA and ERASMUS Prize in Holland for Bartók recordings. Address: c/o Budapest Festival Orchestra, Vorosmarty Tek 1, H-1062, Budapest, Hungary.

FISCHER Jan F, b. 15 Sept 1921, Louny, Czech Republic. Composer. m. 1969, 1 daughter. Education: Studied at the Prague Conservatory, 1940-45; Master Scholar for Composers, with Jaroslav Ridky, Prague University, 1945-48; Career: Committee member of the Pritomnost Association for Contemporary Music, 1945-49, and of the Union of Czechoslovak Composers, 1953-70. Compositions include: Operas: The Bridegrooms, Brno, 1957; Romeo, Juliet and Darkness, 1962; Oh, Mr Fogg (after Around the World in 80 Days), 1971; The Miracle Theatre, Radio Prague, 1973; Dekameron, 1977; Copernicus, 1983; Orchestral: Pastoral Sinfonietta, 1944; Violin concerto, 1946; Dance Suite, 1957; Fantasia for piano and orchestra, 1958; Symphony, 1959; Clarinet concerto, 1963; Harp concerto, 1973; Commemoration, 1973; Night Music for strings, 1973; Concerto for orchestra, 1980; Partita for string orchestra, 1983; Piano Quintet, 1949; Conversations with Harp for string trio, harp and flute, 1979; Brass Quintet, 1983; Sextet for harp and wind quintet, 1993; Concertos for two harps and string orchestra, 1997; Chamber operas: Excitement, 1996; Guard, 1996. Recordings: Prague Preludes for 5 harps; Suite for Flute and Harp; Etudes for harp solo; Monologues for harp solo; 130 works for Theatre, music for film and TV; Songs. Honours: State Award, Laterna Magica, Brussels, 1959; Prize, City of Prague, 1966; Prize, Guild of Composers, 1986. Memberships: Guild of Czech Composers, Presidium, 1959-67I VP FIAF, 1964-66; Society Present Time, 1991-97, current chairman. Address: 147 00 Prague 4, Jasna 18, Czech Republic.

FISCHER Klaus Peter, b. 16 Jan 1937, Breslau, Silesia, Germany. Musicologist. Education: Diploma in School Music, Franz-Liszt Hochschule, Weimar, 1958; PhD, Cologne University, 1970. Career: Scholarship Holder, German Historical Institute, Rome, Italy, 1970-72, German Research Association, 1972-76; Scientific Collaborator, Institute for Hymnological and Ethnological Studies, Cologne-Maria Laach, Germany, 1977-78; Lecturer, 1982-87, Associate Professor, 1988-, University of Pavia, Italy. Publication: Die Psalmkompositionen in Rom um 1600 (ca 1570-1630), 1979. Contributions to: Analecta Musicologica; Archiv für Musikwissenschaft; Studi Musicali; Die Musikforschung; Grove's Dictionary of Music and Musicians, 6th edition; Kirchenmusikalisches Jahrbuch; Die Music in Geschichte und Gegenwart (MGG), 2nd edition; Congress Reports. Memberships: Gesellschaft für Musikforschung; International Musicological Society; Società Italiana di Musicologia. Hobbies: Chess; Literature. Address: Via Villa Glori 5, I-26100 Cremona, Italy.

FISCHER Miroslav, b. 6 Dec 1932, Slovakia. Master of Stage; Opera Regisseur. m. (1) Olga Hanakova, 17 Oct 1977, (2) Jitka Saparova, 19 Oct 1977, 1 son, 1 daughter. Education: School of Musical Arts, Bratislava, 1955. Debut: Traviata, at Slovak National Theatre, Bratislava, 1955. Career: More than 130 operas and operettas performed in Bratislava, Banska, Bystrica, Kosice, Brno, Plzen, Ankara, Bilbao, Brussels, most notably: The Consul, 1956; Fliegende Holländer, 1957; Pelléas et Mélisande, 1958, Fidelio, 1960; Midsummer Night's Dream, 1963; La Forza del Destino, 1964; The Greek Passion, 1969; Salome, 1976; Lohengrin, 1976; Falstaff, 1978, Elektra, 1980; Don Carlos, 1981; Katarina Izmailova, 1984; Un Ballo in Maschera, 1985; Wozzeck, 1985. Hobbies: Dogs; Cooking; History; Gardening. Address: Dankovskeho 14, 811 03 Bratislava, Slovakia.

FISCHER Norman, b. 25 May 1949, Plymouth, MI, USA. Cellist. Education: Studied at the Interlochen Arts Academy and with Richard Kapuscinski at the Oberlin College Conservatory. Career: Member of the Concord String Quartet from 1971; Nationwide performances in a wide repertory, including many works by American composers; George Rochberg has written his Piano Quintet, String Quintet and String Quartets Nos 3-7 for the ensemble; Other composers who have been premiered include Lukas Foss (Third Quartet), Ben Johnston (Crossing) and Jacob Druckman (Third Quartet); Quartet in Residence at Dartmouth College, New Hampshire, from 1974. Recordings include: Fourth, Fifth and Sixth Quartets by George Rochberg. Honours include: Naumburg Award, 1971. Address: c/o Music Department, Dartmouth College, Hanover, NH 03755, USA.

FISCHER-DIESKAU Dietrich, b. 28 May 1925, Berlin, Germany.Baritone; Conductor. m. (1) Irmgard Poppen, 1949 (dec 1963), 3 sons, (2) Ruth Leuwerik, 1965, div. 1967, (3) Kristina Pugell, 1968, (4) Julia Varady, 1978. Education: High School, Berlin; Singing with Professors Georg Walter and Hermann Weissenborn. Career: Military service, 1943-45, POW in Italy until 1947; First Lyric and Character Baritone, Berlin State Opera, 1948-, debut as Posa in Don Carlos; Member, Vienna State Opera Company, 1957-; Professor, Hochschule der Kunste, Berlin, 1982-; Numerous concert tours of Europe, USA and Asia, in Lieder by Strauss, Schubert, Wolf and Schumann; Appeared at a number of festivals including Bayreuth, Salzburg, Lucerne, Montreux, Edinburgh, Vienna, Holland, Munich, Berlin, Coventry; Best-known roles in Falstaff, Don Giovanni, Le nozze di Figaro, Wozzeck and Die Frau ohne Schatten; First performances of contemporary composers such as Britten (War Requiem, 1962), Henze (Elegy for Young Lovers, 1961), König Hirsch, 1956, and Tippett (Vision of St Augustine, 1966); Premiered Von Einem's An die Nachgeborenen, 1975, Hartmann's Gesangsszene, 1964, Henze's Neapolitan Lieder, 1956, Lutoslawski's Les Espaces du Sommeil. 1978; Holofornes by Matthus, 1981, Reimann's Totentanz, Requiem Zyklus, Lear, 1978, and Three Poems of Michelangelo, 1986; Umsüngen by Wolfgang Rihm, 1986; Stravinsky's Abraham and Isaac, 1964, and 5th Symphony by Isang Yun, 1987; Retired as a singer 1992, but continues to conduct, eg Schubert concerts, 1997. Recordings include: Leading roles in Tosca, Macbeth, La Traviata, Götterdämmerung and Parsifal; Le nozze di Figaro; Tristan und Isolde; Genoveva; Les Contes d'Hoffmann; Lohengrin; Othello; Capriccio; Falstaff; Orfeo ed Euridice; Don Giovanni; Figaro; Così fan tutte; Die Zauberflöte; Fidelio; Salome; Elektra; Meistersinger; Tannhäuser; Lulu; La Damnation de Faust; Arabella; Wozzeck; Cardillac; Giulio Cesare, Doktor Faust; St Matthew Passion; Bach Cantatas; Complete male voice Lieder of Schubert, Mahler, Strauss, Brahms, Schumann, Beethoven, Mozart, Haydn, Wolf, over 1000 recordings in all. Publications: Texte deutscher Lieder, 1968; Aus den Spuren die Schubert-Lieder, 1971; Wagner und Nietzsche, der Mystagoge und sein Abtrunniger, 1974; Franz Schubert, ein Porträt, 1976; Robert Schumann-Wort und Musik, 1981; Nachklang, Echoes of a Lifetime, 1987; Wenn Musik der Liebe Nahrung ist, Künstlerschicksale im 19 Jahrhundert, 1990; Weil nicht alle Blütenrëume reiften, Johann Friedrich Reichardt, Hofkapellmeister dreier Preussenkönige, 1992; Claude Debussy und seine Welt, 1994; Many exhibitions of his paintings. Address: c/o Deutsche Verlanganstalt, Stuttgart, Germany.

FISER Lubos, b. 30 Sept 1935, Prague, Czecholsovakia. Composer. Education: Studied with Hlobil at the Prague Conservatory and with Borkovec at the Prague Academy of Music. Career: Worked with the Vit Nejedly Military Ensemble; First work publicly performed Four Pieces for violin and piano; Emigrated to the USA, 1971, and became composer-in-residence with the American Wind Symphony Orchestra in Pittsburgh; Fifteen Prints from the Apocalypse by Dürergiven at the Festival Hall, London, 1997. Compositions include: Four Pieces, chamber, 1954; String Quartet, 1955; 6 piano sonatas, 1955-78; Sextet for wind quintet and piano, 1956; 2 symphonies, 1956, 1960; Lancelot, chamber opera, 1961; The Good Soldier Schweik, 1962; Symphonic Fresco, 1963; Suite for orchestra, 1964; 15 Prints after Dürer's Apocalypse for orchestra, 1965; Caprichos for soloists and chorus, 1966; Pieta for Ochestra, 1967; Requiem, 1968; Lament over the Destruction of the City of Ur, vocal, 1969; Report for wind instruments, 1971; Changing Game, ballet, 1971; Kreutzer Etude for chamber orchestra, 1974; Cello Sonata, 1975; Ave Imperator, vocal, 1977; Labyrinth for orchestra, 1977; Piano Trio, 1978; Serenade for Salzburg for orchestra, 1978; Albert Einstein for organ and orchestra, 1979; Per Vittoria Colona for cello and female chorus, 1979; Sonata for 2 cellos and piano, 1979; Istannu, melodrama, 1980; Piano Concerto, 1980; Meridian for orchestra, 1980; Romance for violin and orchestra, 1980; Testris for string quartet, 1981; The Signe for soloists, chorus and orchestra, 1981; Sonata for solo violin, 1981; Address to Music, 1982, vocal; Centaurs for orchestra, 1983, Honours include: UNESCO Prize for 15 Prints after Dürer's Apocalypse, 1967. Address: c/o OSA Cs Armady 20, 160-56 Prague 6 Bubenec, Czech Republic.

FISHER Gillian, b. 1955, England. Singer (Soprano). m. Brian Kay. Education: Studied with John Carol Case at the Royal College of Music and with Jessica Cash. Career: Appearances in the world's leading concert halls, including Albert, Festival and Barbican Halls, London; Amsterdam Concertgebouw, Lincoln Center, New York and Suntory Hall, Tokyo; Handel Festivals in London and in Maryland, USA; Frequent broadcasts with repertoire ranging from Baroque music to the vocal symphonies of Milhaud; Featured in Central Television series Man and His Music; Sang in Theodora and other works by Handel for tercentenary year, 1985; Sang in Messiah with Ton Koopman and the Amsterdam Baroque Orchestra, Japan, 1987; Appearances in Italy, Japan and Australia with vocal group The Sixteen; Gluck's Euridice at Covent Garden, 1989. Recordings include: Purcell's King Arthur and Dioclesian with John Eliot Gardiner and the Monteverdi Choir; The Triumph of Time and Truth with Denys Darlow and the London Handel Orchestra; Great Baroque Arias and Pergolesi's Stabat Mater with the King's Consort and Michael Chance; Purcell's Fairy Queen and Bach cantatas with The Sixteen and Harry Christophers and Handel duets with the King's Consort and James Bowman. Current Management: Magenta Music. Address: c/o Brian Kay, Radio 3, BBC BRoadcasting House, Portland Place, London W1A 1AA, England.

FISHER Helen (Wynfreda McKee), b. 4 Feb 1942, Nelson, New Zealand. Composer. m. Peter Fisher, 14 May 1966, 3 d. Education: BA, English, Canterbury University, 1964; Diploma of Teaching, 1965; BM, Musicology, 1982, BM, Honours, Composition, 1991, Victoria University, Wellington. Career: Teaching Music and English, 1966-; Appointed by Arts Council to New Zealand Composer-in-Schools residency, 1990, 1991; Received New Zealand Japan Foundation Travel Award to attend performance of Pounamu at 1990 Asian Music Festival in Japan; Initiator, Artistic Coordinator for first New Zealand Composing Women's Festival, 1993. Compositions: Te Tangi A Te Matui, 1986; Woodwind Trio, 1987; Pounamu, 1989; Nga Taniwha, 1991; Nga Tapuwae o Kupe, 1992; Wahine Toa, 1992; Bone of Contention, 1993; String Quartet, 1994; Wings of The Wind, 1994. Honour: 1st Prize for Woodwind Trio, Composers Competition, Victoria University, 1987. Memberships: Composers Association of New Zealand; New Zealand Society of Music Education. Hobbies: Reading; Theatre. Address: 10 Winston Street, Crofton Downs, Wellington 6004, New Zealand.

FISHER John, b. 1950, Scotland. Conmductor. Education: Studied at the University of Glasgow and the Royal Academy of Music. Debut: Former member of the music staff at the Theatre La Monnaie, Brussels; Has conducted opera companies, including Netherlands Opera, Cologne Opera, the Maggio Musicale (Florence) and La Scala Milan; Artistic Director of Teatro La Fenice, Venice, from 1990; Has conducted Le nozze di Figaro, 1991, Semele, Rinaldo, 1989, and Così fan tutte (1990); Technical Consultant for Unitel films, including Jean-Pierre Ponnelle's Rigoletto; Former Artistic Director of the Rossini Opera Festival at Pesaro; Covent Garden debut, 1992, Alcina; Conducted Le Comte Ory at Toronto, 1994. Recordings include: Rinaldo, with Marilyn Horne; Plays harpsichord on video of Mozart's Mitridate, conducted by Harnoncourt. Address: c/o Teatro La Fenice, Campo S Fantin 1965, 30124 Venice, Italy.

FISHER Norma, b. 11 May 1940, London, England. Concert Pianist. m. Barrington Saipe, 3 Sep 1967, 2 s. Education: Guildhall School of Music with Sidney Harrison, 1951-57 and privately with Ilona Kabos, 1957-68 and Jacques Fevrier, Paris, 1962. Debut: Wigmore Hall, 1956; Proms, Royal Albert Hall, 1963. Career: Performances throughout Great Britain, Europe, USA, Canada and Israel in recitals, concertos and chamber music; Regular performer for BBC, London; Represented Great Britain twice at International Jeunesses Musicales Congress; Invited to give Masterclasses worldwide; Founded London Masterclasses in 1988. Honours: 2nd Prize, Busoni International Piano Competition, Italy, 1961; Piano Prize (Joint holder with Vladimir Ashkenazy), Harriet Cohen International Awards, 1963. Hobbies: Tennis; Theatre; Cooking. Current Management: J Audrey Ellison, International Artists Management, London, England. Address: 5 Lyndhurst Gardens, Finchley, London, N3 1TA, England.

FISHER Stephen (Carey), b. 18 May 1948, Norfolk, VA, USA. Musicologist. Education: BA, University of Virginia, 1969; PhD, University of Pennsylvania, 1985. Career: Assistant Professor, Widener University, 1985-87; Lecturer, University of Pennsylvania, 1989-. Publications: The Symphony 1720-1840, series B, volume IX, 1983; Joseph Haydn Werke, series 1, volumes 9-10, Sinfoniem um 1778-81, 1 and 2, Folge. Contributions to: Haydn-Studien; Mitteilungen der Internationalen Stiftung Mozarteum; Current Musicology; Haydn Studies, 1975; The Haydn Yearbook; The Eighteenth Century: A Current Bibliography; Eighteenth Century Studies; Journal of Musicology; New Grove Dictionary of Opera; Notes; Journal of the American Musicological Society; New Grove Dictionary of Music. Honours: Fulbright-Hays Grant, 1976-77. Memberships: American Musicological Society; International Musicological Society; Music Library Association. Hobby: Writing Science Fiction. Address: Department of Music, University of Pennsylvania, 201 South 34th Street, Philadelphia, PA 19104-6313, USA.

FISICHELLA Salvatore, b. 1948, Italy. Singer (Tenor). Studied in Catania and Rome. Debut: Spoleto Festival, as Werther. Career: Sang in Rigoletto and I Puritani at the Rome Opera and appeared widely in Europe and America as Arturo, Arnoldo (Guillaume Tell) and Gualtiero (Il Pirata); New York Met debut as Arturo, opposite Joan Sutherland; Engagements at the Zürich Opera under Nello Santi in I Puritani, Il Pirata and Guillaume Tell; Further leading roles in such operas as Traviata, Butterfly, La Favorita, Roberto Devereux, Faust, Mefistofole and Attila; Season 1996-97 as the Duke of Mantua at Zürich, Pinkerton and Alfredo at Palermo, Edgardo (Luci di Lammermoor) at La Scala and Fernando (La Favorita) at Catania; Further roles in Rossini's Mosè in Egitto and Otello, I Capuleti e i Montecchi, and The Two Widows. Honours include: Premio Bellini d'Oro in Catania; Premio Internazionale Giacomo Lauri Volpi, at Rome. Address: c/o Opernhaus Zürich, Falkenstrasse 1, CH-8008 Zürich, Switzerland.

FISK Eliot (Hamilton), b. 10 Aug 1854, Philadelphia, Pennsylvania, USA. Guitarist; Professor. Education: Pupil of Oscar Ghiglia, Aspen Music School, 1970-76; Andres Segovia, 1974-77; Ralph Kirkpatrick and Albert Fuller, BA, 1972, MMA, 1977, Yale University. Debut: Solo recital debut, Alice Tully Hall, New York, 1976. Career: Toured throughout the world as soloist with orchestras, as recitalist and chamber music performer; Teacher, Aspen Music School, 1973-82; Yale University, 1977-82; Mannes College of Music, 1978-82; Professor, Cologne Hochschule für Musik, 1982-89; Professor, Mozarteum, Salzburg, 1989-; Prepared transcriptions of works by Bach, Scarlatti, Mozart, Paganini for guitar; New works for guitar composed for him by Robert Beaser, Luciano Berio, Nicholas Maw, George Rochberg. Recordings: Various discs. Honours: Winner, International Classical Guitar Competition, Gargano, Italy, 1980. Address: c/o ICM Artists Ltd, 40 West 57th Street, New York, NY 10019, USA.

FISSORE Enrico, b. 23 January 1939, Piemonte, Italy. Singer (Bass-baritone). Education: Studied at the Milan and Turin Conservatories. Debut: Teatro Nuovo Milan 1964, as Don Giovanni. Career: Many appearances in Europe and North America in Italian operas of the 17th and 18th centuries; Glyndebourne debut 1967, as Schaunard in La Bohème; USA debut at San Francisco, as Rossini's Bartolo; La Scala Milan 1979, in Vivaldi's Tito Manlio; Further engagements as Verdi's Melitone and Dulcamara in L'Elisir d'Amore at the Metropolitan, Don Magnifico (La Cenerentola) with Florida Opera and Leporello at Portland (season 1997-98); Other appearances at the Chicago Lyric Opera, Vienna Staatsoper, Opera Bastille, Salzburg Festival and Munich; Glyndebourne 1997, as Bartolo in Le nozze di Figaro, followed by Puccini's Trittico in Brussels. Address: c/o Theatre de la Monnaie, 4 Leopoldstrasse, B-1000 Brussels, Belgium.

FITZGERALD Daire, b. 1966, Dublin, Ireland. Concert Cellist. Education: Studied with Rostropovitch, at the Menuhin School with William Pleeth and the Menuhin Academy with Radu Aldulescu. Career: Concerts throughout Western Europe, China, India, Israel and Czechoslovakia, while a student at the Society of Lincoln Center, New York, and concerts with such orchestras as the Royal Philharmonic, Warsaw Sinfonia, Central Philharmonic of Peking, Hallé and Berlin Radio Symphony; Soloist with the Camerata Lysy Gstaad on tour to Japan and Canada; Berlin debut with the Saint-Saens A minor concerto; New Year's Concert for Finnish TV, tour of USA playing chamber music with Menuhin and participation on Julian Lloyd Webber's Cellothon at South Bank, London. Address: c/o Anglo Swiss Ltd, Suite 35-37 Morley House, 320 Regent Street, London W1R 5AD, England.

FIZDALE Robert, b. 12 Apr 1920, Chicago, Illinois, USA. Pianist; Writer on Music. Education: Studied at the Juilliard School, New York. Career: Formed piano duo with Arthur Gold and debut recital at the New School for Social Research, with the premiere of two works by John Cage; New York Town Hall debut, 1946; First performances of works by Ned Rorem, Vittorio Rieti, Samnuel Barber and Virgil Thomson; French composers include Milhaud (Carnaval pour La Nouvelle-Orléans, 1947, Suite op 300 and Concertino d'automne), Auric (Partita), Poulenc (Sonata for Two Pianos), Tailleferre, Henri Sauguet; Premiere of Berio's Concerto for Two Pianos and Orchestra, with the New York Philharmonic, 1972; Further repertoire includes Mendelssohn's Concertos in E and A flat, Bartok's Concerto for Two Pianos and Percussion, Rorem's Four Dialogues and Mozart's Concerto K365; Worldwide tours until 1982. Publications include: Misia: The Life of Misoa Sert (with Arthur Gold), 1980.

FLAGELLO Ezio, b. 28 Jan 1931, New York City, New York, USA. Singer (Bass). Education: Studied with Friedrich Schorr and John Brownlee at the Manhattan School of Music; Further study with Luigi Ricci in Rome. Debut: Concert performance of Boris Godunov at Carnegie Hall, 1952. Career: Sang Dulcamara in Rome, 1956; After winning Metropolitan Auditions of the Air (1957) appeared in New York until 1987, as Leporello, Fiesco in Simon Boccanegra, Pogner, Philip II and Rossini's Basilio; Sang Enobarbus in the inaugural production of the Metropolitan Opera at Lincoln Center, Antony and Cleopatra by Barber (1966); Guest appearances in San Francisco, Dallas, Houston, Milan, Vienna, Berlin, Prague and Florence; Screen debut, Francis Ford Coppola's Godfather II; Sang Sarastro for Pennsylvania Opera Theater, 1991. Recordings include: Così fan tutte; Lucrezia Borgia; Lucia di Lammermoor; Un Ballo in Maschera;; Ernani; Luisa Miller; Rigoletto; La Forza del Destino; Alcina; I Puritani; Don Giovanni. Address: 2005 Samontee Road, Jacksonville, FL 32211, USA.

FLAKE Uta-Maria, b. 2 Feb 1951, Germany. Singer (Soprano). Education: Studied at the Hamburg Musikhochschule, at Bloomington and with Tito Gobbi and Mario del Monaco. Career: Sang in Offenbach's Orphée aux Enfers at the Hamburg Staatsoper, while still a student; Professional debut, Ulm, 1974, as the Forza Leonora; Dortmund Opera, 1976-80, notably as Eve in the German premiere of Penderecki's Paradise Lost; Stuttgart Staatsoper from 1980, as Leonore (Fidelio), Agathe, Elsa, Eva and Giuletta; Guest engagements at the Munich Staatsoper, Salzburg (in concert), Dusseldorf, Berlin Staatsoper (Lisa in The Queen of Spades) and Deutsche Oper (Leonore), Covent Garden (Elsa and Freia), Lisbon (Gutrune and Third Norn), Cologne, Trieste and Basle (Sieglinde). Recordings include: Daphne by Strauss. Address: c/o Stuttgart Staatsoper, Oberer Schlossgarten 6, 7000 Stuttgart, Germany.

FLAKSMAN Michael, b. 3 May 1946, Akron, Ohio, USA. Cellist. Education: BA, Harvard College, 1969; Teachers of Music: Nadia Boulanger, Pablo Casals, Ernst Silberstein, Maurice Eisenberg; Also Antonio Janigro, Stuttgart Musikhochschule (Künstlerische Abschlussprüfung), 1978. Debut: Cleveland Orchestra, 1963. Career: Marlboro Festival, 1964-65; Appearances at Salzburg, 1973, 1974; Prizewinner in International Competitions: Francesco Serato, Bologna, 1974; Pablo Casals, Barcelona, 1975; Rockefeller Fund Award, New York, 1981; Current positions held: Professor of Violoncello at Musikkonservatorium Schaffhausen, Switzerland (Violoncello-Meisterklasse), California State University, Northridge, California, and Stuttgart Musikhochschule. Recordings: Pergolesi Sinfonia; Works of Schumann and Mendelssohn.

FLECK William, b. 28 Aug 1937, Tyrone, Pennsylvania, USA. Singer (Bass). Education: Studied at the Eastman School and at the Manhattan School of Music. Career: Sang widely in the USA, at first as guest in Boston, Minneapolis and Hawaii; Metropolitan Opera from 1980, in Die Zauberflöte, Tannhäuser, Traviata, Bohème and Tosca; Sang Rocco at Mexico City, 1983; In the US premiere of Ruslan and Ludmilla at Boston and elsewhere as Leporello, Alfonso, Don Magnifico, and Morosus in Die schweigsame Frau; Baron Ochs in Der Rosenkavalier, directed by Jonathan Miller, New York City Opera debut, 1996. Current Management: Corbett Arts Management, San Francisco. Address: 24 Riverside Drive, Ridgefield, CT 06877, USA.

FLEET Marlene (Rose), b. 13 Feb 1942, Grimsby, South Humberside, England. Concert Pianist. m. Harry Terence Harvey Taylor, 5 June 1972. Education: LRAM, ARCM, Grimsby Technical College; Royal Academy of Music, 1960-65. Debut: Wigmore Hall, 1964. Career: Numerous concerts in Great Britain, Europe and America; Appearances at Wigmore Hall, Purcell Room, Queen Elizabeth Hall, Royal Festival Hall, London; Plays regularly for BBC and has performed on BBC TV; Played with most of the leading British orchestras and with many distinguished conductors. Recordings: Numerous recordings for BBC Radio 3. Honours: Winner of most of solo pianist prizes, Royal Academy of Music, 1960-65; Countess of Munster Scholarship; Martin Musical Scholarships. Address: 22 Fairefield Crescent, Glenfield, Leicester LE3 8EH, England.

FLEISCHER Randall (Craig), b. 14 Mar 1959, Ohio, USA. Conductor. m. Heidi Joyce, 18 Dec 1982. Education: BMus Oberlin Conservatory of Music; MMus, Conducting, Indiana University; Private study with Otto-Werner Mueller. Career: Associate Conductor: National Symphony; Music Director: Hudson Valley Phil; Adjunct Associate Professor, Catholic University of America; CBS National Broadcast: Kennedy Center Honours. Recordings: Dvorak Cello Concerto, Mstislav Rostropovich, Cellist. Live performance with NSO from St Petersburg. Honours: Fellowship, Aspen Choral Inst, 1982; Conducting Fellowship, 1989. Memberships: American Symphony Orchestra League. Hobbies: Weightlifting; Aerobics.

FLEISCHER Tsippi, b. 20 May 1946, Haifa, Israel. Composer. Education: Studied at the Tel Aviv and New York Universities and the Rubin Academy of Music. Career: Teacher at the Tel-Aviv and Bar-Ilan Universities. Compositions include: A Girl Named Limonad, music theatre, 1977; Girl-Butterfly-Girl, song cycle, for Soprano and Ensemble, 1977; Lamentations for Soprano, Women's Chorus, 2 Harps and Percussion, 1985; In The Mountains Of Armenia for Children's Chorus, 1988. Address: c/o ACUM Ltd, PO Box 14220, Acum House, Rothschild Boulevard 118, Tel-Aviv 61140, Israel.

FLEISCHMANN Ernest (Martin), b. 7 Dec 1924, Frankfurt, Germany. Music Administrator. Divorced, 1 son, 2 daughters. Education: Bachelor of Commerce, Chartered Accountant, University of the Witwatersrand, South Africa, 1950; Bachelor of Music, University of Cape Town, 1954; Postgraduate work, South African College of Music, 1954-56. Debut: Conductor with Johannesburg Symphony Orchestra, 1942. Career: Conductor of various symphony orchestras and operas, 1942-55; Music Organizer, Van Riebeeck Festival, Cape Town, 1952; Director of Music and Drama, Johannesburg Festival, 1956; General Manager, London Symphony Orchestra, 1959-67; Director for Europe, CBS Records, 1967-69; Managing Director, Los Angeles Philharmonic and General Director, Hollywood Bowl, 1969-98; Artistic Director, Osai Festival, 1998-; Consultant to orchestras, festivals and government bodies in USA and Europe. Publications: Commencement address, The Orchestra is Dead, Long Live the Community of Musicians, Cleveland Institute of Music, 1987; The Recession, Cultural Change, and a Glut of Orchestras, paper for Economics of The Arts seminar in Salzburg, 1993; Doctor of Music (honoris causa), Cleveland Institute of Music, 1987; Grand Cross of the Order of Merit, Germany, 1996. Address: c/o Los Angeles Philharmonic Association, 135 North Grand Avenue, Los Angeles, CA 90012, USA.

FLEISHER Leon, b. 23 July 1928, San Francisco, California, USA. Pianist; Conductor. Education: Studied piano with Artur Schnabel, 1938-48; Conducting with Pierre Monteux. Career: First public recital, 1934; Played Liszt's A Major Concerto with the San Francisco Symphony, 1942; Brahms D Minor Concerto in San Francisco and New York, 1943, 1944; International career from 1952; Gave concerts with George Szell and the Cleveland Orchestra; Joined faculty of the Peabody Conservatory of Music, Baltimore, 1959; Premiered Leon Kirchner's Concerto, Seattle, 1963; Lost use of right hand, 1965, and later played Piano Left Hand repertoire; Co-Director of the Theatre Chamber Players, Washington DC, 1968; Associate Conductor of the Baltimore Symphony Orchestra, 1973-78; Guest engagements as conductor with leading orchestras in the USA; Resumed bimanual solo pianist career, 1982; Artistic Director of the Tanglewood Music Center, 1985. Address: ICM Artists Ltd, Oxford House, 76 Oxford Street, London W1N 0AX, England.

FLEMING Amaryllis, b. 1920, London, England. Cellist. Education: Studied at the Royal College of Music, London, and with Pierre Fournier and Pablo Casals. Career: Has played at the Wigmore Hall, Albert Hall, and many other venues in Britain and abroad; Until 1987 played in Piano Trio with Manoug Parikian and Bernard Roberts; Professor of Cello at the Royal College of Music. Recordings include: Bach Suites for Solo Cello; Works for cello and piano. Honours include: Queen's Prize, Munich International Competition. Membership: Incorporated Society of Musicians. Hobby: Studying Bach. Address: 137 Old Church Street, London SW3, England.

FLEMING Renée, b. 14 Feb 1959, Rochester, New York, USA. Singer (Soprano). Education: Studied in New York. Career: First major role as Mozart's Countess at the Metropolitan, New York, returning as Pamina and Tatiana and as Rosina in the premiere of John Corogliano's The Ghosts of Versailles, 1991; Other appearances include Dvorák's Rusalka at Houston and Seattle, 1990, Donna Elvira at La Scala Milan, Massenet's Thais in Washington, Fiordiligi in Geneva and at Glyndebourne (1992) and the title role in Donizetti's Maria Padilla at Omaha, 1990; Further engagements as Mozart's Countess at Houston, San Francisco and Buenos Aires, 1991; Sang Dirce in Cherubini's Médée at Covent Garden, 1989, returning as Comtesse de Folleville in Rossini's Il Viaggio a Reims, 1992; Sang Anna in La Dame Blanche at Carnegie Hall and Mimi for Bath City Opera, 1992; Mozart's Countess at the 1994 Glyndebourne Festival; Sang Massenet's Thais at Nice and Gounod's Marguerite at the Met, 1997. Honours: Richard Tucker Award, 1990; Metropolitan Opera Auditions. Address: c/o IMG Artists, Media House, Burlington Lane, London W4 2TH, England.

FLETZBERGER Matthias, b. 24 Aug 1965, Vienna, Austria. Pianist. Education: Hochschule für Musik, Vienna. Career: Musikverein Wien; Mozarteum Salzburg Festival; Festivals, Puerto Rico, Lockenhaus, Athens, Naples; Soloist, Israel Philharmonic, Orchestre de Bordeaux, R Schumann Philarmonie, Hochschulorchester Vienna, Orquestra Sinfonica da Chile; Recitals in Europe, America, Australia; Musical Assistant to Elisabeth Schwarzkopf and Renata Tebaldi; Musical Director and Principal Conductor of the Superstiltheater in Vienna. Recordings: Production of video clips for ORF; Radio recordings; TV recordings; Conductor of the TV production of The Magic Flute at the Vienna Festival, 1991. Honours: Recipient, various prizes and awards. Hobbies: Musical Director, opera productions and staging assistance; Architecture; Mathematics. Address: Alban Bergweg 11, A 1130 Vienna, Austria.

FLEURY André, b. 1903, Neuilly-sur-Seine, France. Organist; Composer. Education: Conservatoire de Paris; Studied with Marcel Dupré. Career: Assistant to organist Eugene Gigout at St Augustin, at age 17; Assistant to Tournemire at Sainte Clothilde; Appointed Organist at Sainte Augustin in 1930; Jury Member, Conservatoire de Paris; Professor, Ecole Normale de Musique, Paris; Professor at Conservatory of Dijon, 1949-71; Organist, Dijon Cathedral, 1949-71; Co-Organist at St Eustache, Paris; Professor, Schola Cantorum, Paris; Numerous recitals in Paris and provinces, England, Germany, Switzerland, Belgium, Netherlands and Rome; Participated at Besançon, Vichy, Bordeaux, Toulon and York Festivals. Compositions include: Organ works: 2 Preludes and Fugues, Allegro Symphonique, 1 Triptych (Prelude, Andante and Toccata), 2 Symphonies, 1 Fantasia, 24 pieces for organ without pedals; Piano pieces and others. Honours: 1st Prize for Organ and Improvisation, Conservatoire de Paris, 1926; Various awards for composition. Address: 30 Rue Georges Chapelier, 78150 Le Chesnay, France.

FLIETHER Herbert, b. 29 Oct 1911, Velbert, Germany. Singer (Baritone). Education: Studied with Ivo H Gote in Berlin, 1949-53. Debut: Essen, 1953, as Orestes in Elektra. Career: Member of the Hamburg Staatsoper from 1957: Roles include Hans Sachs, Telramund, the Dutchman, Scarpia, Kaspar in Der Freischütz and Wotan in Der Ring des Nibelungen; Sang in the 1960 premiere of Henze's Der Prinz von Homburg; Glyndebourne Festival, 1961, 1963, as Pizarro in Fidelio; Metropolitan Opera, 1962-63; Sang The Wanderer in Siegfried at Covent Garden; Many concert appearances. Address: c/o Hamburgische Staatsoper, Grosse-Theaterstrasse 34, D-2000 Hamburg 36, Germany.

FLODIN Anders Bengt, b. 27 Mar 1961, Örebro, Sweden. Composer;Lecturer in Music Theory m. Ann-Kristin Olsson, 6 July 1996, 2 sons. Education: Kävesta Folkhögskola, 1982; MFA, Music Education, University of Örebro, 1987; Candidate Magister, The Norwegian State Academy of Music (Olav-Anton Thommessen), 1989; Dekanát Hudobnej Fakulty Vysorej Skoly Muzickych Umeni, Bratislava (Vladimir Bokes), 1990; Akademie Múzickych Faculty Umeni Hudebni Fakulta, Prague (Svátopluk Havelka), 1993; Summer course at Nordens Folkhögskola Biskops-Arnö (Rolf Enström, Jan W Mortenson). Debut: Oslo, 1989. Appointments: Radio appearances: Timat Ballet, Chamber Orchestra, Slovak Radio Broadcasting, 1990; Konsertant Music, Swedish Radio Broadcasting, 1994. Compositions: Intrig XX, for tape, 1988; Nocturne, for saxophone quartet, 1992; Preludium, for piano solo, 1995; Trakten Är Just Icke Leende, for computer, 1995; Sinfonia, for orchestra, 1996; Trio: Pl, VLN, VLC, 1997. Honours: Scholarship, Swedish Institute, Czechoslovakian Studies, 1989-90; Scholarship, Konstnärsnämnden (Board of Arts), Sweden, studies abroad, 1993, 1995; Scholarship, Royal Academy of Music, Sweden, studies abroad, 1995. Memberships: Föreningen Svenska Tonsättare (Society of Swedish Composers); STIM (Swedish Composers International Music Bureau). Hobbies: Literature; Completing fragments on Grieg's B-Minor Piano Concerto, 1997. Address: Tonsättare, Sandhamnsgatan 79, Box 27327, S-102 54 Stockholm, Sweden.

FLOR Claus Peter, b. 16 Mar 1953, Leipzig, Germany. Conductor. m. Sabine, 1985, 1 son. Education: Robert Schumann Conservatory, Zwickau, age 10; Franz Liszt Institute for Music, Weimar, 1966; Mendelssohn Bartholdy High School of Music, Leipzig, under Rolf Reuter and Felix Mendelssohn; Studied with Rafael Kubelik and Kurt Sanderling. Career: Principal Conductor, Suhler Philharmonic, 1981; Guest Conductor, Gewandhus Orchestra, Leipzig, Dresden Staatskapelle, Berlin Symphony Orchestra; Principal Conductor, Artistic Advisor, 1984, General Music Director, 1985, Berlin Symphony Orchestra, with world tour, 1988, at Edinburgh Festival, 1990; US debut, Los Angeles Philharmonic, 1985; Berlin Philharmonic debut, 1988, and concerts, Berlin Festival, 1993; Vienna Symphony Orchestra, 1991; New York Philharmonic debut, Principal Guest Conductor, Philharmonic, London, Principal Guest Conductor, Artistic Advisor, Tonhalle Orchestra, Zurich, 1991; Conducted Philharmonia at 1993 London Proms, Mendelssohn's 5th and Szymanowski's 3rd Symphonies, Bartók's 3rd Piano Concerto; Regularly with Munich Philharmonic, Bayerische Rundfunk Symphony, Radio Symphony Orchestras of Frankfurt, Hamburg, Cologne and Berlin, Orchestre de Paris (debut with Bruckner's 7th Symphony), Royal Concertgebouw Amsterdam, Rotterdam Philharmonic Orchestra; Recent guest engagements include Israel Philharmonic, NHK Symphony, Tokyo; Has worked with Boston, St Louis, Dallas, Montreal, Cincinnati and London Symphonies, Minnesota and Philadelphia Orchestras, Royal Philharmonic; Opera engagements, Deutsche Oper Berlin, Bayerische Staatsoper, Semper Oper Dresden; Regular visitor, Berlin Staatsoper, recently conducting La Traviata, Der Freischütz, Lohengrin; Conducted new Schaaf production of Entführung at Staatsoper Hamburg, 1992-93; Toured Japan with Vienna Symphony Orchestra, 1997; Appearances at major European festivals, 1997; Die Zauberflöte at Cologne Opera, 1997. Recordings include: Mendelssohn: A Midsummer Night's Dream; Martinu symphonies; Cherubini Requiem; New Year's Day concert of popular classics; Franck Symphony in D minor, Dvorák Symphony No 8, Royal Philharmonic; Mozart's Coronation Mass, Philharmonia; Shostakovich: 10th Symphony, Royal Concertgebouw. Honours include: Mendelssohn Scholar, 1979; 1st Prizes, competitions, Poland, Denmark. Address: c/o Intermusica Artists Management, 16 Duncan Terrace, London N1 8BZ, England.

FLOROS Constantin, b. 4 Jan 1930, Saloniki, Greece. Professor. Education: Diplomas in Composition and Conducting, Academy of Music, Vienna, 1953; DMus, University of Vienna, 1955; Habilitation, Hamburg University, 1961. Career: Professor of Science of Music, Hamburg University, 1967; Editor, Hamburger Beitrage zur Musikwissenschaft, 1971-; Editor, Hamburger Jahrbuch für Musikwissenschaft, 1975-. Compositions: Zwei Tricinien, 1958; Various lieder; Compositions for chorus, piano and organ. Publications: Das mittelbyzantinische Kontakienrepertoire, 3 volumes, 1961; Universale Neumenkunde, 3 volumes, 1970; Die geistige Welt Gustav Mahlers, 1977; Mahler und die Symphonik des 19 Jahrhunderts in neuer Deutung, 1977; Beethovens Eroica und Prometheus Musik, 1978; Mozart - Studien, 1979; Einfuehrung in die Neumenkunde, 1980; Brahms und Bruckner, 1980; Johannes Brahms: Sinfonie No 2, 1984; Gustav Mahler, Die Symphonien, 1985; Musik als Botschaft, 1989; Alban Berg, 1993; Gustav Mahler - The Symphonies, 1993; György Ligeti, 1995. Membership: President of the Gustav Mahler Vereinigung, Hamburg. Address: Schlangenkoppel 18, Germany.

FLOWERS Kate, b. 1950, Cheshire, England. Singer (Soprano). Education: Studied at the Northern School of Music and the Royal Northern College of Music; Further study in Paris. Career: Glyndebourne Festival from 1976, as Despina, Isotta in Die schweigsame Frau, Norina in La Fedeltà Premiata and the title role in The Cunning Little Vixen; Appearances with Opera North as Gretel, Despina, Susanna, Zerlina, Aennchen in Der Freischütz and Thérèse in Les mamelles de Tirésias; Polly Peachum in The Beggar's Opera for Scottish Opera; Micaela, Marenka and Jenufa for the Welsh National Opera; Concert engagements in Europe, and on London's South Bank with the Philharmonia, the English Chamber Orchestra, Royal Philharmonic, Hallé Orchestra, London Philharmonic and the Academy of St Martin in the Fields; Sang Jenny in The Threepenny Opera for Opera North, 1990; Sang Mrs Ford in Falstaff with City of Birmingham Touring Opera, 1995. Honours include: John Christie Award and Royal Society of Arts Scholarship, 1977. Address: c/o The Grand Theatre, 46 New Briggate, Leeds LS1 6NH, England.

FLOYD Carlisle, b. 11 June 1926, Latta, South Carolina, USA. Composer. Education: Studied at Converse College, Spartenberg, and with Ernest Bacon at Syracuse University (BA, 1946, MA, 1949); Piano with Rudolf Firkusny and Sidney Foster. Career: Teacher at Florida State University, 1947-76; M D Anderson Professor of Music at the University of Houston, 1976-. Compositions: Operas: Slow Dusk, 1949; Susannah, 1951; Wuthering Heights, 1958; The Passion of Jonathan Wade, 1962; The Sojourner and Mollie Sinclair, 1963; Markheim, 1966; Of Mice and Men, 1969; Bilby's Doll, 1976; Willie Stark, 1981; Other works: Pilgrimage, song cycle, 1956; Piano Sonata, 1957; The Mystery, song cycle, 1960; Flower and Hawk, monodrama for soprano and orchestra, 1972; Citizen of Paradise, song cycle, 1983. Address: c/o ASCAP, ASCASP Building, One Lincoln Plaza, New York, NY 10023, USA.

FLURY Urs Joseph, b. 25 Aug 1941, Bern, Switzerland. Composer; Violinist; Conductor. Education: Musicology, Art and Philosophy, Bern and Basel Universities; Conservatory Biel and Basel. Career: Stage, TV and Radio Appearances in Switzerland and other European Countries. Compositions: Chamber Music: Fantasia and Sonata for violin solo; 2 Suites for violin and Piano; Variations for Violin and Viola; Wind Quintet; Orchestral Works: 3 Suites, The Little Mermaid, Concerto di carnevale for rag band and Orchestra; Instrumental Concertos: Concertino Veneziano for violin and strings; Cello Concerto; Vocal Music: Christmas Oratorio, 3 masses, salve regina. Recordings: As Violinist and Conductor: Cello Concerto; Concertino Veneziano, Concerto for violin in D, Sonata for Violin Solo; Suite Nostalgique, Christmas Oratorio, The Little Mermaid. Publications: Pahlen Kurt: Oratorien der Welt, 1985; Pahlen Kurt, Neue Musikgeschichte der Welt, 1990; Hartnack Joachim: Grosse Geiger unserer Zeit, 1983. Contributions to: Several professional journals and magazines. Honours: Music Prize, Canton Solothurn, 1993. Hobby: Collecting Historical Recordings. Address: Zelglistrasse 5, CH-4562 Biberist, Switzerland.

FOCILE Nuccia, b. 1959, Catania, Sicily, Italy. Singer (Soprano). Education: Protegée of Pavarotti. Career: Season 1986-87, as Oscar in Ballo in Maschera at Turin and Philadelphia, Clarine, Thalia, in Rameau's Platée at Spoleto, Elvira (L'Italiana in Algeri) at Schwetzingen and Mistress Ford in Salieri's Falstaff at Peralade; Further engagements at Buenos Aires as Musetta, Valencienne in the Merry Widow at Venice and Nannetta at Covent Garden, 1988; Rio de Janeiro in 1989 as Rossini's Rosina, and Oscar at Naples, and Ascanio in Pergolesi's Lo frate 'nnamorato at La Scala; Returned to Milan in 1990 as Servilia in La Clemenza di Tito and appeared at Bergamo as Eleanora in Donizetti's L'Assedio di Calais; Pesaro Festival, 1990, as Giulia in La Scala di Seta, Teatro Valle Rome as Countess in Paisiello's Don Chisciotte; Returned to Philadelphia, 1991, as Norina, sang Mozart's Susanna at Houston and appeared at the Opéra Bastille, Paris, as Ilia in Idomeneo; Barcelona and Dallas, 1992, as Adina in L'Elisir d'Amore, Oscar at the Opéra Bastille, Paris, Tatiana at the Théâtre du Châtelet and Carolina (Matrimonio Segreto) at the 1992 Ravenna Festival; Sang Gounod's Juliette at the Paris Opéra-Comique, 1994; Season 1996-97 with Mozart's Ilia at Florence, Liù and Susanna for the Royal Opera, Mimi in Paris and Amelia Boccanegra and Butterfly for WNO. Recordings include: Lo frate 'nnamorato and L'Assedio di Calais. Honours: Turin International Competition, 1983; Pavarotti Competition, Philadelphia, 1986. Address: c/o Harold Holt Ltd, 31 Sinclair Road, London W14 oNS, England.

FODI John, b. 22 Mar 1944, Hungary. Composer; Music Librarian. m. 22 Oct 1971, 1 son, 1 daughter. Education: Studied composition with Lorne Betts; BMUS and MMus, University of Toronto, 1966-72; MLS, University of Toronto, 1987-90. Career: Supervisor, Sniderman Recordings Archive, University of Toronto, 1982-92; Head Cataloguer for recordings and supervisor of Sniderman Recordings Archive, 1992-; Technical Librarian, Music Library, University of Toronto, 1997-. Compositions: Pi, trombone and piano; Division IV, guitar; Concerto in four parts, accordion; bagatelles, tuba; Sonata: Cor Vigilans, bassoon and cello; Adagio, string orchestra; Kootenay, chamber orchestra; Rhapsody, bass clarinet and piano; Ballades, cello; The Green Roads, chamber orchestra, 1992; Against Black Woods, Long Streaks of Rain, viola solo, 1996; Distant Roads, chamber orchestra, 1997. Honours: Woodrow Wilson Fellow, 1970; Canadian League of Composers Prize, 1968, 1970; CAPAC St Clair Lowe Award, 1970; Premiere of Concerto a quattro (string quartet no 5), ISCM, Boston, 1976; Commissions from the CBC and various ensembles throughout Canada. Publications: Musical examples: Brian Cherney's Harry Somers, 1975; Stephen Adams' Murray Schafer, 1982-83; Tim McGee's Early Music Performance, 1984. Memberships: Canadian League of Composers; Canadian Association of Music Libraries; Canadian Music Centre. Hobbies: Reading science fiction; Cogitation. Address: 14 Times Road, Toronto, Ontario M6E 3B9, Canada.

FODOR Eugene (Nicholas Jr), b. 5 Mar 1950, Turkey Creek, Colorado, USA. Violinist. Education: Studied with Harold Wippler, Denver; Ivan Galamian, Juilliard School of Music, New York, 1966-68; Josef Gingold, Harry Farbiman and William Primrose, Indiana University School of Music, diploma 1970; Jascha Heifetz, University of Southern California at Los Angeles, 1970-71. Debut: Soloist at age 10 with Denver Symphony Orchestra. Career: Soloist with major orchestras, 1974-; Recitalist, Performed at the White House, Washington DC 1974, 1986. Recordings: For RCA. Honours: 1st Prize, Merriweather Post Competition, 1967; Paganini Competition, Genoa, 1972; Co-2nd Prize, Tchaikovsky Competition, Moscow, 1974. Address: c/o Hillyer International Inc, 888 Seventh Avenue Suite 300, New York, NY 10106, USA.

FOGELL Martin (Maurice), b. 3 Aug 1929, Glasgow, Scotland. Conductor; Teacher; Accompanist. m. Anne Goldwater, 20 Oct 1953, 1 son, 1 daughter. Education: BA; BMus; FTCL; ARCM; LTCL; Studying for PhD on music of Coleridge-Taylor. Career: Conductor: Fogell Ensemble, 1955-64; London Students Opera Society, 1956-65; Reading Symphony Orchestra, 1958-64; Southern Sinfonia Orchestra, 1964; Guest with Boyd Neel Orchestra, London Mozart Players, New London Orchestra, Nottingham Symphony Orchestra, Ostrava Symphony Orchestra; Broadcasts in Italy, Netherlands, Czechoslovakia. Compositions include: The Gravedigger, part-song; Orchestral and instrumental works; Kirsteen, 1-act opera. Recordings: 3 Highland Sketches; Toy Symphonies of Haydn and Romberg; Peter and the Wolf. Publications: Critical Appreciation and Analysis of the music of Coleridge-Taylor. Honours: Freeman of Ostrava, 1961; Barlow Cup for Composition, 1973, 1975, 1976, 1984-89. Memberships: Composers' Guild of Great Britain; Royal Musical Association. Hobbies: Walking; Reading; Research. Address: 63 Lachs Lane, Chester CH4 7LP, England.

FOLAND Nicolle, b. 1968, Des Moines, USA. Singer (Mezzo-soprano). Education: University of Northern Iowa. Career: Appearances with the Western Opera Theater on tour and in San Francisco as Adele and Rosalinda (1993), Donna Anna, and Tina in Argento's The Aspern Papers (Opera Center); San Francisco Opera, 1995-, as Kate Pinkerton, Clorinda (La Cenerentola), Gerhilde, Musetta, multiple roles in the premiere of Harvey Milk, and High Priestess in Aida; Guest with Indianapolis Opera as Adina in L'Elisir d'Amore; Season 1996-97 as Micaela with Cincinnati Opera, Musetta with Los Angeles Music Center Opera and Seattle Opera; Concerts include Placido Domingo special at San Francisco. Address: c/o San Francisco Opera, War Memorial Opera House, Van Ness Avenue, San Francisco, CA 94102, USA.

FÖLDES Imre, b. 8 Mar 1934, Budapest, Hungary. Musicologist; Professor of History. m. Dr Zsuzsa Vadász, 1 daughter. Education: Graduate in composition, Ferenc Liszt Academy of Music, Budapest. Career: Musicologist, Professor of Music History and Theory, Ferenc Liszt Academy of Music, Department of Teachers Training Institute; Educational Lecturer on Music for the general public and radio. Publications: Harmincasok, Beszélgetések magyar zeneszerzőkkel (Generation of The Thirties - Talks with Hungarian Composers), 1969; Life and Works of J S Bach, 1976; The Melody Dies Irae, 1977. Contributions to: Az ének-zene tanítása; Muzsika; Parlando. Honours: Art Prize for Socialist Culture, 1974; Art Prize, National Council of Trade Unions, 1975; Szabolcsi Prize, 1977; Ferenc Erkel Prize, 1986. Memberships: Hungarian Musicians Association; President, Music Department, Society for Propagating Sciences and Arts; Hungarian Ferenc Liszt Society; Hungarian Kodály Society; Lajos Bárdos Society; International Society for Music Education. Hobbies: Collecting CDs and Gramaphone Records; Hiking; Photography. Address: Kresz Géza utca 26, 1132 Budapest, Hungary.

FOLDI Andrew (Harry), b. 20 July 1926, Budapest, Hungary. Opera Director; Singer (Bass). m. Marta Justus, 19 May 1977, 1 son, 1 daughter. Education: MA, Musicology, 1948, PhB, Philosophy, 1945, University of Chicago. Debut: La Boheme, 1950. Career: Director of Music, Department of Adult Education, University of Chicago, 1949-61; Chairman of the Opera Department, DePaul University, 1951-57; Advisor, Netherlands Opera, 1977-80; Chairman and Artistic Director, Opera Department, Cleveland Institute of Music, 1981-91; Director, Chicago Lyric Opera Center for American Artists, 1991-95. Stage direction includes: The Barber of Seville (Atlanta Opera), 1989; The Merry Wives of Windsor, (Chicago Opera Theatre), 1990; La Tragédie de Carmen (Lyric Opera Center, Chicago), 1992. Television performances of Il Barbiere di Siviglia, 1967, The Merry Widow, 1977, Elixir of Love, 1978, and Lulu, 1980. Other performances include: Alberich in the Ring and Schigolch in Lulu at the Metropolitan Opera, Bartolo in Il Barbiere de Siviglia, Vienna Staatsoper and San Francisco, Cardillac at La Scala. Recordings include: Fiddler on the Roof, 1974; A Modern Psalm, 1975. Publications: Articles in Opera News, Alban Berg Society. Memberships: American Musicological Society. Address: Chicago Opera Theater, 20 East Jackson Boulevard, Suite 1400, Chicago, IL 60604, USA.

FOLWELL Nicholas, b. 1953, England. Singer (Baritone). Education: Studied with Raimund Herincx; Royal Academy of Music and London Opera Centre. Career: Sang with Welsh National Opera from 1978 as Mozart's Figaro and Leporello, Pizarro, Melitone, Escamillo, The Poacher in The Cunning Little Vixen, Alberich in The Ring of the Nibelung (also at Covent Garden with Welsh National Opera, 1986) and Wagner's Melot and Klingsor; As guest with other British companies has sung the Villians in The Tales of Hoffmann, Tonio, Beckmesser, Schaunard, Creon and The Messenger in Oedipus Rex, Alberich and Papageno (English National Opera 1990); Sang in Weill's Seven Deadly Sins with the London Sinfonia, 1988; Debuts in France, Italy, Austria and West Germany, 1987-90; Created Koroviev in York Höller's Master and Margarita in Paris, 1989; Covent Garden and Glyndebourne, 1990, as The Poacher (conducted by Simon Rattle) and Beethoven's Pizarro; Sang in The Weill Event at the 1990 Almeida Festival; Promenade Concerts, 1991, in Prokofiev's The Fiery Angel; Alberich in Rheingold (Opéra de Nantes), 1992; Mozart's Figaro for Glyndebourne Touring Opera at Sadler's Wells; Cecil, Maria Stuarda, Buxton Festival, 1993; Alberich in Siegfried at the Opéra de Nantes, 1993; Sang Sancho Panza in Don Quichotte for ENO, 1996. Recordings: Tristan and Isolde and Parsifal, conducted by Reginald Goodall; Poacher (Cunning Little Vixen); Pish-Tush (The Mikado). Honours: ARAM, 1990. Current Management: Robert Gilder & Co. Address: c/o Robert Gilder & Co, Enterprise House, 59-65 Upper Ground, London SE1 9PQ, England.

FONDA Jean (Pierre), b. 12 Dec 1937, Boulogne-sur-Seine, Paris, France. Concert Pianist. Education: Virtuosity Prize, Piano Instrumentation, Geneva Conservatory, Switzerland. Debut: Germany, 1958. Career: Concert tours in Europe, South America, USA, Japan, Middle East, Turkey, elsewhere; TV in Paris, Munich; Major European Summer Festivals including Lucerne, Montreux, Edinburgh and Monte Carlo. Compositions; Cadenzas for various piano concertos. Recordings: Numerous. Honours: Recipient, Harriet Cohen Medal, London, 1968; Chevalier des Arts et des Lettres, awarded by French Minister of Culture, 1980. Hobbies: Reading; Theatre; Films; Collecting and purchasing autographs. Current Management: Ingpen and Williams Limited, 26 Wadham Road, London SW15 2LR, England. Address: 20 Parc Château Benquet, Geneva, Switzerland.

FONDARY Alain, b. 1932, Bagnolet, France. Singer (Baritone). Education: Studied in Paris. Debut: Tonio in Pagliacci, Cherbourg, 1968. Career: Sang in many provincial French opera houses in 1970s; Appearances at the Paris Opera, 1985 and 1991, in Jerusalem by Verdi and as the High Priest in Samson et Delila; Royal Opera House, Covent Garden, in La Fanciulla del West, La Scala Milan as Amonasro, Metropolitan Opera in Cavalleria Rusticana; Sang Scarpia at San Francisco, returning in 1990 as Renato in Un Ballo in Maschera; Vienna Staatsoper and Barcelona, 1991, as the High Priest and Scarpia; Festival engagements include Orange, 1992, as Count Luna, and Bregenz, 1993, as Nabucco; Sang Massenet's Sancho Panza at Toulouse, 1992, and Count Luna at Orange; La Scala, 1993, as Scarpia; Sang in Massenet's Thais at Nice, 1997. Recordings include: Sancho Panza in Don Quichotte, conducted by Michel Plasson. Address: c/o Opéra de La Bastille, 120 Rue de Lyon, F-75012 Paris, France.

FONSECA Regina, b. 1932, Portugal. Singer (Mezzo-soprano). Career: Sang at Dusseldorf, 1958-59, Bremen, Saarbrucken, Mainz, Kiel and Kassel, 1959-69; Engaged at the Mannheim National Theatre, 1969-81, Gelsenkirchen, 1981-82, Dortmund, 1983-84; Guest appearances at Cologne and Nuremberg, Naples, Hamburg (Brangaene in Tristan und Isolde, 1967), Monte Carlo and the Deutsche Oper Berlin, 1975; Sang Kundry at the 1976 Bayreuth Festival and the Composer in Ariadne auf Naxos at the Vienna Staatsoper; Deutsche Oper am Rhein, Dusseldorf, 1983; Other roles have included Wagner's Venus, Ortrud, Waltraute and Fricka, Strauss's Clytemnestra and Nurse, Countess Geschwitz in Lulu, Verdi's Eboli, Lady Macbeth and Azucena, Zenobia in Handel's Radamisto and the Countess in Zimmermann's Die Soldaten.

FONTANA Bill, b. 25 Apr 1947, Cleveland, Ohio, USA. Composer; Radio Producer. Education: Studied at John Carroll University and at the New School for Social Research; BA, 1970; Private study with Louis Lane and Philip Corner. Career: Composer-in-residence and music director for the Toronto Free Theater, 1972-73; Compiled archive of natural sounds for the Australian Broadcasting Commission, 1975-78; Natural sound archive for the Oakland Museum in California, 1979; Assembled material for series of 365 programmes broadcast in San Francisco, 1983, as Soundscapes; Composer, sound sculptor and radio producer on various broadcasting stations. Compositions include: Phantom Clarinets, 1975; Handbell Sculptures, 1977; Wave Spiral, 1977; Music for a Resonant Space, 1977; Music for Carillon; Standing Wave Sculpture, 1978; Piano Sculpture, 1978; Ocarina Sculpture; Sound Sculpture for Brass Band; Space between Sounds, 1980; Flight Paths out to Sea; Grid Projections; Landscape Sculpture with Foghorns, 1981; Oscillating Steel Grids along the Brooklyn Bridge, 1983; Sound Recycling Sculpture, 1983; Soundscapes, 1983. Address: c/o ASCAP, ASCAP Building, One Lincoln Plaza, Lincoln Center, New York, NY 10023, USA.

FONTANA Gabriele, b. 1958, Innsbruck, Austria. Singer (Soprano). Education: Studied with Ilse Rapf at the Vienna Musikhochschule. Career: Sang Echo in Ariadne and Lauretta in Gianni Schicchi at the Opera Studio of the Vienna Staatsoper; Sang Pamina at Frankfurt; Hamburg Staatsoper from 1982, as Susanna, Servilia in La Clemenza di Tito and Sophie in Der Rosenkavalier; Sang in the premiere of Udo Zimmermann's Die Weisse Rose, revised version; Guest appearances in Bremen and Hanover; Glyndebourne, 1984, as the Countess in Le nozze di Figaro; Bregenz Festival, 1985, as Pamina; Vienna Staatsoper and Glyndebourne Festival, 1987, as Fiordiligi; Sang in Die weisse Rose at Innsbruck, 1989; Lieder recitals in London, Berlin, Brussels and Vienna; Season 1996-97 with First Lady in Die Zauberflöte at Amsterdam; Bruckner's Mass in F Minor, with Radio Symphony Orchestra of Leipzig, and with Dusseldorf Sinfoniker, 1997. Recordings include: Schubert Lieder and Bach Cantatas; Idomeneo, Arabella; Gluck's Paride ed Elena; Die grossmütige Tomyris by Reinhard Keiser; Rheintochter in Das Rheingold with Dohnanyi and the Cleveland Symphony Orchestra. Address: c/o Tiroler Landestheater, Rennweg 2, A-6020 Innsbruck, Austria.

FONTYN Jacqueline, b. 27 Dec 1930, Antwerp, Belgium. Composer. m. Camille Schmit, deceased, 2 children. Education: Studied theory and composition with Marcel Quinet; Studied in Paris and Vienna. Career: Professor of Composition, Conservatoire Royal de Bruxelles, 1971-90; Has given lectures and seminars in Egypt, France, Germany, Israel, Hungary, Korea, New Zealand, Poland, Singapore, Taiwan and USA; Participant in many international festivals. Compositions include: Orchestra: Mouvements Cocertants; Six Ebauches; Galaxie; Pour 11 Archets; Evoluon; Concerto fo violin and orchestra; Frises grand orchestre d'harmonie; Quatre Sites for symphony orchestra; Halo, harp and 16 instruments; Creneaux, for symphonic wind orchestra; In the Green Shade; Reverie and Turbulence, 1989; A l'Orée du Songe, 1990; Colinda for cello and orchestra, 1991; On a Landscape by Turner, 1992; Aratoro, 1992; Blake's Mirror for mezzo and symphonic band, 1993; Vocal Music: Deux Rondels de Charles d'Orleans; Alba, Pro and Antiverbs; Cheminement; Rosa; Rosae; Ku Soko; Rose des Sables; Sieben Galgenlieder; Instrumental and Chamber Music: Trio; Nonetto; Spirales; 2 Pianos; Six Climats; Shadows; Horizons; Zones; Le Gong; Rhumbs; Analecta. Honours include: Prix Arthur Honegger of the Fondation de France, 1988; Awarded title of Baroness by the King of Belgium in recognition of her artistic merits. Address: Rue leon Dekaise 6, B1342 Limelette, Belgium.

FORARE Sten Erik, b. 25 Jan 1955, Uppsala, Sweden. Composer; Musicologist. Education: Studied Violin, 1966-74, Composition, with Sune Smedeby, Piteå, 1972-74; Composition Class, with Professor Gunnar Bucht, Royal Academy of Music, Stockholm, 1975-79; Musicology, Stockholm University, 1979-83. Debut: UNM Stockholm, 1979. Career: Swedish Radio P2, 1980; Swedish Musical Spring Festival, 1984; Pejling Festival, Stockholm, 1987. Compositions include: Grand Caprice Vulgaire for Guitar Solo, 1981-82; Alphabetica I for treble recorder solo, 1982-84; Agnus Dei for 10-part mixed choir, 1991-92; String Quartet No 1 (In Memorium Ernst Krenek), 1992-96. Publications: To The Borders of the Extreme: A Treatise on the Chamber Music of Sven-David Sandström, 1990; Articles on Johan Helmich Roman, 1994, Henry Purcell, 1995, Anton Bruckner, 1996. Memberships: Society of Swedish Composers, 1981; ISCM, 1987. Hobbies: History; Literature.

FORBES Elizabeth, b. 3 Aug 1924, Camberley, Surrey, England. Critic; Writer on Music; Translator. Education: Autodidactic. Career: Freelance Music Critic, Financial Times, 1970-80. Publications: Opera from A to Z, 1977; Observer's Book of Opera, 1982; Mario and Grisi, 1985; Old Scores, detective story; Translations for Nottingham University of Spontini's La Vestale, Auber's La Muette de Portici, Meyerbeer's Robert le Diable and Berwald's Queen of Golconda; Translations for Radio 3: Schubert's Claudine von Villa Bella, Brand's Maschinist Hopkins and Wagner-Régeny's Die Bürger von Calais. Contributions to: Reviews and articles to Financial Times, Independent, Opera, Musical Times, Music and Musicians, Opera News, Opera International, Opera Canada, The Listener, About the House; Encyclopedia of Opera, 1976; New Grove Dictionary of Music and Musicians, 1980; The Performing Arts, 1980; New Grove Dictionary of American Music, 1986; New Grove Dictionary of Opera, 4 volumes, 1992; Viking Opera Guide, 1993. Address: Flat 3, 1 Bryanston Square, London W1H 7FE, England.

FORBES Elliot, b. 30 Aug 1917, Massachusetts, USA. Retired Professor. m. Kathleen Brooke Allen, 7 June 1941, 3 daughters. Education: MA, Harvard, 1947; Mozarteum, Salzburg, 1937; Westminster Choir College, 1946. Debut: Conductor, Harvard Glee Club and Radcliffe Choral Society, 1958. Career: Teacher at Cate School, California, 1941-43, Belmont Hill School, Massachusetts, 1943-45; Assistant Professor, 1947-54, Associate Professor, 1954-58, Princeton University; Professor of Music at Harvard University, 1958-84. Publications: Editor: Thayer's Life of Beethoven, 1964, Beethoven's Fifth, 1971, A History of Music at Harvard to 1972, 1988, A Report of Music at Harvard, 1972-90, 1993. Contributions to: Articles in American Choral Review and Music Quarterly. Honours: Phi Beta Kappa; Signet Society Medal, 1985; Harvard Medal, 1991; Hon MusD, New England Conservatory, 1996. Memberships: AAAS; American Musicological Society; College Music Association. Hobby: Nature Walks. Address: 975 Memorial Drive, Apt 210, Cambridge, MA 02138, USA.

FORBES (Rupert) Oliver, b. 27 Jan 1944, London, England. Singer (Tenor). m. Elisabeth Burnett, 10 July 1976, 2 sons. Education: St John's College, Cambridge University; With Pierre Bernac, Paris, and Luigi Ricci, Rome; Opera Studio, Zurich; Arturo Merlini, Milan. Career: Sang at the Zurich Opera 1970-75; Engaged at the Stadttheater Basel from 1975, singing Mozart's Monostatos and Pedrillo, Jacquino in Fidelio, Tybalt in Roméo et Juliette, Lindoro, (Haydn's La Fedeltà Premiata), the comic roles in Les contes d'Hoffmann, Wagner's Steuermann and Lord Barrat in Der Junge Lord; Guest appearances in Mannheim, Wiesbaden, Kassel, Bremen and Freiburg; Since 1990, freelance singer with Covent Garden, Scottish Opera, Glyndebourne, Rome, Wexford; Many engagements in concert and oratorio, notably in works by Bach. Recordings: Visitatio Sepulchri by James MacMillan; Salome by Strauss. Hobbies: Cookery; Gardening. Current Management: Music International. Address: 10 Mount Vernon Road, Edinburgh EH16 6BW, Scotland.

FORBES Sebastian, b. 22 May 1941, Amersham, Buckinghamshire, England. Composer; University Professor. m. (1) Hilary Spaight Taylor, 2 daughters, (2) Tessa Brady, 24 Sept 1983, 1 son, 1 daughter. Education: Royal Academy of Music, 1958-60; Kings College, Cambridge University, 1960-64; MA, Cantab; MusB, Cantab; MusD, Cantab; LRAM; ARCO; ARCM. Career: Treble Soloist, 1953-56; BBC Producer, 1964-67; Organist, Trinity College, Cambridge, 1968; Lecturer, Bangor University, 1968-72; Conductor, Aeolian Singers, 1965-69; Seiriol Singers, 1969-72; Horniman Singers, 1981-90; BBC Producer, 1964-67; University Lecturer, Bangor, 1968-72, Surrey, 1972-; Professor of Music, 1981-; Principal Commissions: Essay for Clarinet and Orchestra, Proms, 1970; Symphony, Edinburgh Festival, 1972; String Quartet No 3, BBC, 1982. Compositions: Essay for clarinet and orchestra, Proms, 1970; Symphony in Two Movements, 1972; Rondo for piano, 1996; Several works or ensemble (sonatas) and chamber music; Numerous works of church music. Recordings: String Quartet no 1, 1971; Capriccio for organ, 1980; Bristol Mass, 1992; Hymn to St Etheldreda, 1996. Publications: String Quartet No 1, 1970; Organ sancta, 1970; Violin Fantasy no 2, 1980; Seasonal Roundelay, 1985; Numerous choral pieces, Cathedral music. Contributions to: Articles for music journals. Honours: McEwen Memorial Prize, 1962; Clements Memorial Prize, 1963; Radcliffe Music Award, 1969; SPNM Prize, 1979; Carl Flesch Prize, 1980; ARAM, 1990; FRSA, 1997. Memberships: Executive Member, Composers' Guild of Great Britain; Performing Rights Society. Hobbies include: Haute cuisine; Table tennis. Current Management: STR Music Marketing. Address: Octave House, Boughton Hall Avenue, Send, Woking, Surrey GU23 7DF, England.

FORD Andrew, b. 1957, Liverpool, England. Composer; Conductor. Education: Graduated with honours, Composition, University of Lancaster, 1978; Composition study with Edward Cowie and John Buller; Doctor of Creative Arts, University of Wollongong, 1994. Career: Fellow in Music, University of Bradford, 1978-82; Founder, Music Director, Performer, Big Bird Music Theatre, 1982; Lecturer, Faculty of Creative Arts, University of Wollongong, New South Wales, Australia, 1983-95; Many world and Australian premieres with the Faculty's contemporary music ensemble SCAW, 1984-90, including Stockhausen's Stimmung, 1986; Conductor, Australia Ensemble, Seymour Group and Magpie Musicians; Composer in residence, Bennelong Programme, Sydney Opera House, 1985; Own works played Australia, Europe, American; Commissions; Writer and broadcaster on music; Featured composer, many festivals, including Aspekte, Salzburg, 1984, Ferrara 1985, Istanbul, Buffalo, Up-Beat to The Tate, Liverpool, Aspen, 1988; Composer in residence, Australian Chamber Orchestra, 1993-94, also Conductor. Compositions: Music theatre: Songs for the Lady Pan, 1981-83; From Hand to Mouth, 1984-85; Poe, opera, 1981-83; Whispers, 1990; Cassanova Confined, 1995; Children's opera: The Piper's Promise, 1986-87; The World Knot, 1987-88; Orchestral: Concerto for Orchestra, 1980; Prologue, Chorale and Melodrama, 1981; Epilogue to an Opera, 1982; Serenade for 20 Solo Strings and Percussion, 1984; The Big Parade, 1985-86; Imaginings, piano and orchestra, 1991; The Widening Gyre, chamber orchestra, 1993; The Great Memory, cello and orchestra, 1994; Chamber ensemble: Sonata for 4 Instruments, 1978; Chamber Concerto No 1, 1979, No 2: Cries in Summer, 1983; Bright Ringing Morning, 1981, Pit, 1981; Boatsong, 1982; Rant, 1984, Pea Soup, 1984; Four Winds, saxophone quartet, 1984; Foolish Fires, 1985; String Quartet, 1985; Deep Blue, 1986; On Canaan's Happier Shore, 1987; The Art of Puffing, 1989; Parabola, 1989; Ringing the Changes, 1990; Pastoral, 1991; Clarion, 1991; Solo instruments: Les débris d'un rêve, piccolo and reverb, 1992; Portraits, piano, 1981; Like Icarus Ascending, violin, 1984; A Kumquat for John Keats, piano, 1987; Swansong, viola; Several vocal works; Season Song, chorus and a cappella version, 1981-82; In somnia, chorus and ensemble; Vocal: Harbour, tenor and strings. Recordings: Boatsong; String Quartet; Ringing the Changes; Whispers; Pastoral; The Art of Puffing; Sacred Places. Publication: Composer to Composer: Conversations about contemporary music. Address: 3 Shepherd Lane, Chippendale, NSW 2008, Australia.

FORD Bruce (Edwin), b. 15 Aug 1956, Lubbock, Texas, USA. Singer (Lyric Tenor). m. Hetty Ypma, 18 Sept 1982, 1 son. Education: Studied at West Texas State University, Texas Tech University and the Houston Opera Studio. Debut: Houston Grand Opera, 1981. Career: Sang with Wuppertal Opera from 1983, as Belmonte, Rameau's Dardanus, Nureddin (Der Barbier von Bagdad) and Ramiro; Bordeaux 1985, as Almaviva; Minnesota Opera, 1985, as Tamino; Mannheim Opera from 1985, as Fenton, Tamino, Ferrando and Ramiro; Appeared at the 1986 Wexford Festival as Argirio in Rossini's Tancredi; Ferrando at the Salzburg Festival, 1993, and the Royal Opera House, Covent Garden, 1995; Sang Rinaldo in Armida by both Haydn and Rossini for VARA (Dutch Broadcasting), 1989; Berlioz's Lelio for the Dusseldorf Symphonic; Sang Agorante in Ricciardo e Zoraide at Pesaro, 1990; Also in Pesaro: Otello (Rossini), 1991; Almaviva, 1992; Antenore (Zelmira), 1995; Also heard as Uberto in La Donna del Lago at Dusseldorf and Rodrigo (Rossini Otello) for San Francisco Opera, 1994; Covent Garden debut 1991, Almaviva; La Donna del Lago (Uberto) at La Scala with Muti, 1992; Mitridate (title role) at Covent Garden, Amsterdam and Salzburg, 1991, 1993, 1997; Ernesto (Don Pasquale), Chicago Lyric Opera, 1995; Almarva, Met debut, 1997. Recordings include: Adriano in Crociato in Egitto by Meyerbeer; Giasone in Medea in Corinto by Mayr; Enrico in Rosmonda d'Inghilterra by Donizetti; Agorante in Ricciardo e Zoraide, rossini; Solo album, Romantic Heroes; Horace in Le Domino Noir, Auber; Edgardo in Lucia di Lammermoor; Messiah, Imene in Bertoni's Orfeo; Ghernando in Rossini's Armida; An English language recording of The Barber of Seville; Solo album of arias. Memberships: ISM; AGMA. Hobbies: Tennis; Sailing; Scuba Diving. Current Management: Athole Still International Management Limited. Address: c/o Athole Still International Management, 25-27 Westow Street, London SE19 3RY, England.

FORD Peter (John), b. 25 Sept 1946, Staffordshire, England. Repetiteur; Opera Coach; Chorus Master; Conductor. m. (1) Carol Henley, 1967, (2) Penelope Davis, 1971, (3) Seona Denholm, 1980, 1 son, 1 daughter. Education: Guildhall School of Music and Drama, 1971-72; London Opera Centre, 1972-73; GBSM; ABSM Teacher (Organ); ARCO. Debut: English National Opera, 1975. Career: Repetiteur, Assistant Chorus Master, Conductor, English National Opera, 1974-81; Visiting Professor,

Guildhall School of Music and Drama, 1981; Chef des Choeurs, Conductor, Opera of Nancy, France, 1982-84; Choral concerts in France; Private coaching, teaching, 1988-; Freelance work for Royal Opera House, Covent Garden. Membership: Incorporated Society of Musicians. Address: 104 Pirbright Road, Southfields, London SW18 5NA, England.

FORD Trevor, b. 28 Nov 1951, London, England. Music Administrator; Editor. m. Marianne Barton, 8 Dec 1979, 2 sons. Education: Recital Diploma, Royal Academy of Music, 1972-76. Career: Orchestral Flautist, 1976-; Personnel Manager, English Sinfonia, 1979-; Orchestral Manager: Philomusica of London, 1981-, Midland Philharmonic, 1982-, Ambache Chamber Orchestra, 1984-89; General Manager: English Festival Orchestra, 1984-; Board of Directors, 1985-88, Chairman, Negotiating Committee, 1994-, Association of British Orchestras; Director of Music, St John's Church, Palmers Green, 1992-; Chairman, Organists' Working Party, 1993-95; Treasurer, Incorporated Society of Musicians, 1996-; Member of Council and Executive, Managing Editor of Publications, Royal College of Organists, 1995-; Professor, Guildhall School of Music and Drama, 1996-. Publications: Editor: The Musician's Handbook, 1986, 2nd edition, 1991 3rd Edition, 1996; The Art of Auditioning, 1988; Church Music Quarterly, 1989-. Honours: ARAM, 1992. Memberships: Musicians' Union; Incorporated Society of Musicians; Association of British Choral Directors; Church Music Society. Hobbies: Architecture; Antiques; Antique maps. Address: 151 Mount View Road, London N4 4JT, England.

FORRAI Miklós, b. 19 Oct 1913, Magyarszék, Hungary. Professor. m. Mária Gyurkovics, 2 daughters. Education: Studied under Zoltán Kodály, Artúr Harmath, Lajos Bárdos; Chorus Master, 1934, Singing Master, 1935, Artist of Trumpet, 1937, Liszt Academy of Music, Budapest. Debut: As Chorus Master of the Forrai Chamber Choir, 1936. Career: Leader of concert series Kis Filharmónia, organised for children, 1936-44; Music programmes on Hungarian Radio, 1936-, on Hungarian Television, 1958-; Professor, Franz Liszt Academy of Music, 1941-83; Chorus Master of Budapesti Kórus, 1948-78. Recordings: Cantata Lyrica, 1960, and Cantus Pannonicus by F Farkas, 1961; Missa Choralis, 1963; Psalms, 1965; Christus, 1971; Prometheus by F Liszt, 1974; Requiem by R Schumann, 1976. Publications: A Karvezető, book for chorusmasters, 1936; Ezer év kórusa (Choral works of 1000 years), 1943; Ötévszázad kórusa (Choral works of 500 years), 1956; Deep River (Negro Spirituals), 1963; Singing Exercises, 1963. Contributor to: Musica Hungarica, 1965; Musica Mundana, 1974. Address: Budenz út 18, 1021 Budapest, Hungary.

FORREST Sidney, b. 21 August 1918, New York City, USA. Clarinettist; Educator; Arranger. m. Faith Levine Forrest, 16 November 1941, 1 daughter. Education: Juilliard School of Music; BA, University of Miami, 1939; MA, Columbia University, 1941; Studied clarinet with Simeon Bellison of New York Philharmonic, Otto Conrad, Berlin Philharmonic and Alexander Williams, NBC Symphony. Career: Principal Clarinet, National Symphony Orchestra, Washington, 1946-47, summers 1948-51; Professor, Peabody Conservatory of Johns Hopkins University, 1946-85; Director, Placement and Counselling, 1969-85; Adjunct Professor, Catholic University of America, 1954-; Professor of Clarinet and Chamber Ensembles, Interlochen Arts Camp, 1959-; American University, 1961-; Clincian, Chamber Music Coach; Member, National Woodwind and Brass Jury of Fulbright Commission, 1980-84; Member, Clarinet Jury, Quebec Conservatoire of Music, 1969-85; Students in major full Clarinet Recitals: Carnegie Recital, Brooklyn Museum, National Art Gallery, Philips Collection, Library of Congress and Europe. Compositions: Arrangements for Piano & Clarinet; Twelve Fantasias for Solo Clarinet by George Philip Telemann; Variations on a theme by Corelli, by G Tartini, for piano and clarinet. Recordings: Mozart Clarinet Quintet in A Major and Clarinet Trio in E Flat Major; Brahms Trio in A Minor; Weber Grand Duo Concertant and Variations; Berg Four Pieces; P Hindemith, Sonata for clarinet and piano. Publications: Articles on Clarinet Control and Technicalities in Clarinet Magazine, Bandwagon, Band Directors Guide. Memberships: National Music Teachers Association. Address: 9611 Kingston Road, Kensington, MD 20895, USA.

FORRESTER Maureen, b. 25 July 1930, Montreal, Quebec Province, Canada. Singer (Contralto). Education: Studied with Barnard Diamant in Montreal. Debut: Sang in concert at Montreal, 1953. Career: Alto solo in Mahler's 2nd Symphony at New York Town Hall, conducted by Bruno Walter, 1956; Many concert appearances with leading US orchestras in Boston, San Francisco, Philadelphia and elsewhere; Tours to Netherlands, Germany, France, Belgium, Spain and Scandinavia; Sang Gluck's Orpheus in Toronto, 1961, and appeared as Cornelia in Giulio Cesare to open New York City Opera's first season in Lincoln Center (1966); San Francisco debut, 1967, as La Cieca in La Gioconda, Metropolitan Opera, 1975, as Erda in Das Rheingold; Covent Garden, 1971, as Fricka in Der Ring des Nibelungen; Paris, 1981, in Massenet's Cendrillon; Has also sung at opera houses in Canada and South America; Other roles have included Mistress Quickly, Monteverdi's Arnalta, Brangaene (Tristan and Isolde), Ulrica, and the Witch in Hansel and Gretel; Sang with the Bach Aria Group, 1964-74, and toured the USA with the Montreal Symphony, 1982, with Les Nuits d'Eté by Berlioz; Pittsburgh Opera, 1989, as Clytemnestra in Elektra; Sang at San Diego and La Scala Milan, 1990, as Mme de Croissy in Dialogues des Carmélites and the Countess in The Queen of Spades. Recordings: Giulio Cesare; Beethoven's 9th and the Alto Rhapsody; Handel's Serse and Rodelinda; Elektra. Memberships: Chairman of the voice department at the Philadelphia Academy, 1966-71; Chairman of the Canada Council, 1984. Address: c/o Pittsburgh Opera Inc, 711 Penn Avenue, 8th Floor, Pittsburgh, PA 15222, USA.

FORSBERG Roland, b. 18 Sept 1939, Stockholm, Sweden. Director of Music; Organist. m. (1) Margaretha Widlund, 1967-91, (2) Lisbeth Carlborg, 1992, 2 sons, 1 daughter. Education: Professor of Music, Royal Academy of Music, Stockholm, 1961; Higher Organist Exam, 1963; Higher Cantor Exam, 1964; Diploma, Organist, 1968. Career: Director of Music: Norrmalm Church, Stockholm, 1964-89; Organists, Immanuel Church, Stockholm, 1989-; Musical Expert, Swedish State Psalm Committee, 1976-86. Compositions include: Liten Svit for organ, 1959; Passacaglia for organ, 1960; Verbum Christi, vocal, 1963; 12 Sacred Songs, 1964; Musica solenne for organ, 1965; Orgeljojk for 2 organs, 1975; Sicut Cervus Organ Symphony, 1977; Sonata lapponica for violin and piano, 1980; Sonatina da cappella for violin and organ, 1983; 3 piano sonatas; Concertos for flute and oboe; Sacred concertos for solo voices and organ; Songs; Hymns; Motets; Cantatas; Oratorios; Masses and other choral works; 8 organ suites; Psalm sonata for mixed chorus (English words), 1984; Credo Triptych for organ, 1988; Memoria for violin and piano or organ, 1988; Symphonic Pictures for Archipelago for organ and brass orchestra, 1995. Recordings: Kärlekens musik; Tre orglar i Västervik; En gång blir allting stilla; Sjögrens Legender; Autography, Swedish Composers play their own works; Orgelmusik i Sjövik; Skärgårdsorgel, Archipelago the Mod Eighteenth Century Organ of Utö, CD. Publications: Editions: Sjung svenska kanon, 1977; Fader wår (Gustaf Duben), 1980; Seven Sacred Songs (Anders Bond), 1981; Organ Fantasy (Otto Olsson), 1983; Two Organ Pieces (Anders Bond), 1985; 88 Preludes (Anders Bond); Organ Preludes I-III; Concerto grosso g-moll transkription for organ (Archangelo Corelli); Sinfonia IB26 transkription for organ solo (Johan Helmich Roman); Sinfonia in G Major, 1994. Honours: Numerous including Composers Scholarships, STIM, Stockholm, 1974, 1981, 1985; Foreningen Svenska Tousatlare, 1996. Memberships: Kammarmusikföreningen Samtida Musik; Föreningen Svenska Tonsåttare, Stockholm. Address: Dalarö Prästgård, 13054 Dalarö, Sweden.

FORSMAN John (Väinö William), b. 11 Aug 1924, Tavastehus (Savonlinna), Finland. Composer. m. Maria Luisa Chavez, 26 April 1958, 1 son, 3 daughters. Education: Royal Conservatory of Denmark, 1945-48; Studies with Paul Hindemith, Salzburg, 1948, A Honegger, Paris, 1949, Luigi Dallapiccola, Florence, Italy, 1954. Compositions include: 3 symphonic ballets; 1st Symphony, A Symphonic Song; 7 Piano Sonatas; Ein Lyrisches Märchen, chamber opera; Various piano works; Choral works; Christmas Oratorio for children; 150 songs for children, including English Through Music (didactic entertainment tool, teaching grammar and sound). Recordings: Romance for Violin and Piano; Christmas Oratorio for Children; 5 piano sonatas, 1997. Contributions to: Music Critic for Berlingske Aftenavis and Borsen; Articles to Musikrevyn, Verdens Gang, Dagbladet; Henry Bellamann's Award, 1963. Hobbies: Chess; Ping-pong; Reading. Address: Apartado Postal 4-004, Mexico 4 DF, CP 06400, Mexico.

FORST Judith, b. 7 Nov 1943, British Columbia, Canada. Singer (Mezzo-soprano). Education: Studied with Bliss Hebert in New York and with Robert Keyes in London. Debut: Vancouver, 1967, as Lola in Cavalliera Rusticana. Career: Sang at the Metropolitan Opera from 1968, as Hansel, Siebel and Lola; San Francisco debut, 1974, as Suzuki; Appearances at New Orleans, Santa Fe, Miami (Donna Elvira, 1988), Detroit and Toronto, 1987, as Preziosilla; Seattle, 1991, as Dorabella and Jane Seymour in Anna Bolena; Returned to the Met, 1991, as Donna Elvira; Other roles include Mozart's Cherubino, Olga (Eugene Onegin), Maddalena, Octavian, Carmen and Cenerentola; Sang Andromaca in the first British performance (concert) of Rossini's Ermione, Elizabeth Hall, 1992; Sang Gertrude in Thomas' Hamlet at San Francisco, 1996. Honours: Winner, Metropolitan Auditions, 1968. Address: c/o Metropolitan Opera, Lincoln Center, New York, NY 10023, USA.

FORSTER Andreas, b. 17 Sept 1949, Naumberg, Germany. Singer (Baritone). Education: Studied in Berlin and in Essen with Gladys Kuchta. Debut: Detmold, 1974, as Schaunard in La Bohème, Career: Sang at Kaiserslautern, 1975-76, Saarbrucken, 1976-78, Nuremberg, 1978-88; Staatstheater Hanover from 1988; Guest appearances at the Staatsoper Berlin, Dusseldorf, Cologne, Dortmund, Stuttgart, Munich, Wiesbaden and Orlando, Florida, USA; Roles have included Verdi's Nabucco, Rigoletto, Macbeth and Simon Boccanegra, Germont, Renato, Iago and Amonasro, Rodrigo, Luna, Donizetti's Enrico, Belcore and Dulcamara, Gerard, Escamillo, Eugene Onegin, Wolfram, Amfortas, Marcello, Olivier in Capriccio and Mozart's Don Giovanni and Count; Concert engagements in works by Bach, Handel, Beethoven, Brahms, Mahler and Penderecki; Lieder recitals and broadcast concerts in Germany, France and Italy. Address: Niedersachische Staatstheater, Opernplatz 1, 30159 Hannover, Germany.

FORSYTH Malcolm (Denis), b. 8 Dec 1936, Pietermaritzburg, South Africa. Composer; Conductor. m. (1) Lesley Eales, 1965, div 1984, (2) Constance Braun, 1992, 1 daughter. Education: BMus, 1963, MMus, 1966, DMus, 1972, University of Cape Town; Conductors class, Canford Summer School of Music, 1980-84. Career: Conductor: Chamber Choir and Orchestra, University of Cape Town, 1962-64; St Cecilia Orchestra, 1977-86; Edmonton Wind Sinfonia, 1978-79; West Wind Chamber Ensemble, 1980-83; Chamber Choir, University of Witwatersrand, 1983; Guest Conductor: Cape Town, CAPAB and Edmonton Symphony Orchestras, Alberta Ballet Orchestra, National Orchestra, SABC, Johannesburg; As Trombonist: Assistant Principal Cape Town Symphony Orchestra, 1961-67; Co-Principal, CAPAB Symphony Orchestra, 1971-72; Principal, Edmonton Symphony Orchestra, 1973-80; Junior Lecturer, College of Music, University of Cape Town, 1967; Assistant Professor, 1968-71, Associate Professor, 1971-77, Professor of Music, 1977-, Division Chairman, Concert Activity Chairman, 1984-86, Artistic Director, Music Department, 1987-89, McCalla Professor, 1990-91, University of Alberta, Edmonton, Canada; Visiting Professor, Cape Town and Witwatersrand Universities; Composer-in-Residence: Banff Centre, 1975-78; Festival of the Sound, 1991; Juror; Commissions include Canada Council, CBC and University of Cape Town; Fellow of the Camargo Foundation, Cassis, France, 1993; Composer-in-Residence, University of Alberta, 1996-; Saskatchewan New Music Festival, 1997. Compositions: Works for orchestra, band, ensembles, piano, vocal solos and choir. Recording: Electra Rising, 1997. Honours: Composer of the Year, Canada, 1989; JUNO Winner for Best Classical Composition, 1987, 1995. Current Management: BMG Ricordi, BMG Ariola. Address: 9259 Strathearn Drive, Edmonton, Alberta T6C 4E1, Canada.

FORTE Allen, b. 23 Dec 1926, Portland, Oregon, USA. Music Theorist. Education: Studied at Columbia University, MA, 1952. Career: Taught at Teachers' College of Columbia, 1953-59; Member of theory faculty at Mannes College, 1957-59; Yale University from 1959, Professor from 1968; Editor of the Journal of Music Theory, 1960-67; President of the Society for Music Theory, 1977. Publications include: Conception of Musical Structure, 1959; Bartók's 'Serial' Composition, 1960; The Compositional Matrix, 1961; Tonal Harmony in Concept and Practice, 1962; A Theory of Set-complexes for Music, 1964; A Program for the Analytical Reading of Scores, 1966; Computer-implemented Analysis of Musical Structure, 1966; Music and Computing the Present Situation, 1967; The Structure of Atonal Music, 1970; The Harmonic Organization of The Rite of Spring, 1978. Address: c/o Yale University, Music Department, New Haven, CT 06520, USA.

FORTUNATO D'Anna, b. 21 Feb 1945, Pittsburgh, Pennsylvania, USA. Singer (Mezzo-soprano). Education: Studied with Frederick Hagel and Gladys Miller at the New England Conservatory, 1965-72; Further study with Phyllis Curtin at the Berkshire Music Center. Career: Concert appearances in Pittsburgh, Detroit, Louisville, Atlanta and Minnesota; Recitals with the Chamber Music Society of Lincoln Center and with the Boston Musica Viva ensemble; Taught at Longy School of Music, Cambridge, 1974-82; Member of the Liederkreis Ensemble; European debut, Paris, 1980, as Purcell's Dido with the Boston Camerata; Sang in the premiere of John Harbison's opera Full Moon in March, New York, 1979; New York recital debut, 1981; New York City Opera debut, 1983, as Ruggiero in Handel's Alcina. Honours include: Co-winner, Naumburg Chamber Music Prize, 1980. Address: c/o New York City Opera, Lincoln Center, New York, NY 10023, USA.

FORTUNE George, b. 13 Dec 1935, Boston, Massachusetts, USA. Singer (Baritone). Education: Brown University, Providence; Boston University; Vocal studies with Todd Duncan. Debut: Ulm, 1960, as Fluth in Die Lustigen Weiber von Windsor. Career: Guest appearances in Bordeaux, Brussels, Strasbourg, Hamburg and Munich; Glyndebourne, 1964, as the Count in Le nozze di Figaro; Santa Fe, 1967, in the US premiere of Henze's Boulevard Solitude; Member of the Deutsche Oper Berlin from 1967; Roles include Mozart's Figaro and Guglielmo, Rigoletto, Giulio Cesare, Iago, Amonasro, Posa, Scarpia, Gerard and Wolfram; Further appearances in Dusseldorf, Frankfurt, Milan and Zurich; Debut at the Metropolitan Opera New York in 1985 with Tonio, further parts include Jack Rance, Scarpia, Amonasro and Alfio; Sang Scarpia at the Teatro San Carlos, Lisbon, 1988, the High Priest in Samson et Delilah at the Deutsche Oper Berlin,

1989; Many concert engagements. Recordings include: Thérèse by Massenet; Olympie by Spontini; Christus by Liszt. Address: c/o Deutsche Oper Berlin, Richard Wagnerstrasse 10, D-1000 Berlin, Germany.

FORTUNE Nigel (Cameron), b. 5 Dec 1924, Birmingham, England. Musicologist. Education: Studied music and Italian at Birmingham University (BA, 1950) and researched Italian monody at Cambridge under Thurston Dart (PhD, 1954). Career: Music Librarian at London University, 1956-59; Lecturer in music at Birmingham University, 1959-69, Reader in music from 1969; Secretary of the Royal Musical Association, 1957-71, Vice-President, 1991; Member of editorial committee, Musica Brittanica, 1975-77; Senior member, editorial committee, New Grove Dictionary of Music and Musicians, 1970-80; Editorial work for the New Oxford History of Music. Publications include: Continuo Instruments in Italian Monodies, 1953; Italian Secular Song from 1600 to 1635, 1954; Italian 17th Century Singing, 1954; Purcell's Autographs (with F B Zimmerman), 1959; A New Purcell Source, 1964; Philip Rosseter and his Songs, 1965; Editor, with Dennis Arnold, The Monteverdi Companion, 1968, and The Beethoven Companion, 1971; Opera and Church Music, 1630-1750 (editor with Anthony Lewis), 1975; Editions of John Dowland and sacred music by Purcell (with Thurston Dart and Anthony Lewis).

FOSS Lukas, b. 15 August 1922, Berlin, Germany. Composer; Conductor; Pianist. m. Cornelia Brendel, 1950, 1 son, 1 daughter. Education: Studies, Curtis Institute of Music (piano, composition, conducting), Yale University (composition), Berkshire Music Center (composing and conducting). Career includes: Pianist, Boston Symphony Orchestra, 1944-50, (premiered Hindemith's Four Temperaments, 1944), Professor of Conducting and Composition, University of California, 1953-62; Music Director, Ojai Festival, Buffalo Philharmonic Orchestra, 1963-70; Founder-Director, Center for Creative and Performing Arts, SUNY, Buffalo, 1963; Music Director, Brooklyn Philharmonic, 1971-90; Conductor, Jerusalem Symphony Orchestra, 1972-76; Music Director, Milwaukee Symphony Orchestra, 1981-86; Composer in Residence, Tanglewood, summers, 1989, 1990; Professor, Boston University, 1992-. Compositions: Over 120 including operas The Jumping Frog, 1949 and Griffelkin, 1955; Solo for piano, 1982; 4 Symphonies; Renaissance concerto for flute and orchestra, 1986; Chamber: 3 string quartets, 1947, 1973, 1975; Brass Quintet, 1978; Percussion Quartet, 1983; Tashi for clarinet, string quartet and piano, 1986; Piano pieces; Choral music. Recordings: Over 30 works recorded, some of which were also conducted by Foss. Publications: A Bio-bibliography, USA, 1991. Honours: New York Music Critics Circle Awards, 1944, 1954; Guggenheim Fellowships, 1945, 1960; Fellow, American Academy, Rome, 1950-51; Fulbright Grant, 1950-52; Brandeis University, Creative Arts Award, 1983; 9 Honorary Doctorates. Memberships: American Academy of Arts and Letters. Address: 1140 Fifth Avenue, New York, NY 10128, USA.

FOSTER Anthony, b. 11 Apr 1926, Gravesend, Kent, England. Musician. m. Barbara Humphreys, 26 July 1952, deceased 1991, 1 daughter. Education: LRAM, ARCO; Piano with Anne Collins, Arthur Tracy Robson; Organ with John Cook, John Webster; Orchestration with Gordon Jacob, Richard Arnell. Career: Teacher, Stratford-upon-Avon, Oxford and Brighton, 1952-77; Organist, Choirmaster, Churches of All Saints, Northfleet; All Souls, St Matthias, St Augustine of Canterbury, Brighton. Compositions: Jubilate Deo for Organ; Classical Suite for Organ; Prelude-Interlude-Postlude for Organ; Many Songs, Antuems and Service Settings for Choirs; Concertino for Piano & Strings. Recordings: Jubilate Deo; A Child is Born; Incidental Music for Various BBC Productions; Christ The Lord Is Risen Again (Easter Carol), The Choir of Christchurch Cathedral, directed by Alan Thurlow. Memberships: Composers Guild of Great Britain; Performing Right Society. Hobbies: Film, Video and Computer Animation. Address: 1 Cawley Road, Chichester, West Sussex PO19 1UZ, England.

FOSTER Beryl, b. 2 Sept 1944, London, England. Singer (Mezzo-soprano). m. Richard Watson, 5 Sept 1970. Education: Hatfield School, Hertfordshire, 1956-63; Colchester Institute, 1965-69; Royal College of Music, 1969-72; BMus (London), 1969: LRAM (Singing Teacher), 1967. Debut: Hexham Music Club, 1973. Career: Concert and Oratorio throughout UK; Lectures and Recitals on Norwegian Song, UK and Norway, from 1980; Music Festival Adjudicator, since 1980; Lecturer, International Grieg Symposium, Bergen, 1993. Compositions: Editions of Grieg's Songs: 3 volumes, 1990, 1992, 1997; Arrangement for Ladies' Choir of 'Three Norwegian Carols, 1993. Publication: The Songs of Edvard Grieg, 1990. Contributions: Studia Musicologica Norvegica, No 19, 1993; Grieg Companion, Vol 2, 1997. Memberships: Incorporated Society of Musicians; Association of Teachers of Singing; Secretary, Grieg Society of GB, 1992-97. Hobbies: Reading; Crosswords; Needlework. Address: 11 Burnham Road, St Albans, Hertfordshire, AL1 4QN, England.

FOSTER Donald H, b. 30 Apr 1934, Detroit, Michigan, USA. Professor. Education: BS, Wayne State University, 1956; MMus, 1960, PhD, 1967, University of Michigan. Career: Music Faculty, Olivet College, Michigan, 1960-67; Professor of Musicology, College-Conservatory of Music, University of Cincinnati, Ohio, 1967-. Publications: L'histoire de la femme adultère by Louis Nicolas Clérambault, 1974; Louis-Nicolas Clérambault 1676-1749: Two Cantatas for Soprano and Chamber Ensemble, 1979; Symphonies concertantes of Jean-Baptiste Davaux; Overtures of Franz Beck; Jean-Philippe Rameau: A Guide to Research, 1989; Sourcebook for Research in Music (co-author), 1993. Contributions to: Symphony Orchestras of the United States: Selected Profiles, 1986; Opera Quarterly; Recherches sur la musique française classique; The Diapason; Acta Musicologica; Current Musicology; L'orgue-cahiers et mémoires. Honours: Fulbright Grant, 1962. Memberships: American Musicological Society; Société française d'étude du XVIIIe siècle; American Association of University Professors. Hobbies: Travel; Hiking. Address: 393 Amazon Avenue, Cincinnati, OH 45220, USA.

FOSTER Jillian, b. 1970, England. Soprano. Education: Studied at the Royal Academy of Music. Career: Has sung with Kent Opera, Wexford Festival, Dublin Grand Opera and the Richard Strauss Society; Roles have included Tosca, Mimi, Donna Elvira, Violetta, Agathe and Arabella; Sang Garsenda in Francesca da Rimini with the Chelsea Opera Group and Messiah and Beethoven's Ninth with the Tokyo Philharmonic. Honours include: Winners' Concert at the 1992 Pavarotti Competition. Address: Helen Sykes Management, Fourth Floor, Parkway House, Sheen Lane, East Sheen, London, SW14 8LS, England.

FOSTER Lawrence (Thomas), b. 23 Oct 1941, Los Angeles, California, USA. Conductor. Education: Studied conducting with Fritz Zweig, Los Angeles; Attended the Bayreuth Master Classes and the Berkshire Music Center, Tanglewood, Massachusetts. Debut: Young Musicians' Foundation Debut Orchestra, Los Angeles, 1960. Career: Assistant Conductor, Los Angeles Philharmonic Orchestra, 1965-68; Chief Guest Conductor, Royal Philharmonic Orchestra, London, 1969-74; Conductor-in-Chief, Houston Symphony Orchestra, 1971-78; Chief Conductor, Opéra de Monte Carlo and Orchestre National (renamed Orchestre Philharmonique) de Monte Carlo, 1979-91; General Music Director, Duisberg, 1981-88; Music Director, Lausanne Chamber Orchestra, 1985-; Jerusalem Symphony Orchestre, 1988-; Conducted new production of Hamlet by Ambroise Thomas at Monte Carlo, 1993; Music Director, Aspen Music Festival, 1991-96; Music Director, City of Barcelona Symphony, 1996-. Recordings: For various labels. Honours: Koussevitzky Prize, 1966. Address: c/o Orchestre Philharmonique de Monte Carlo, Casino, Monte Carlo, Monaco.

FOSTER Martin, b. 17 June 1951, Rochdale, Lancashire, England. Violinist; Conductor; Teacher. 1 daughter. Education: Conservatoire de Montreal, 1970; Juilliard School, 1973. Debut: Carnegie Recital Hall, New York, 1973. Career: Recital Tours in Eastern and Western Europe, North America; Founding 1st Violin, American String Quartet; Faculty, Mannes College, New York, 1975-80, Conservatoire de Montreal, 1981-84, Université du Quebec à Montréal, 1982-. Recordings: Martin Foster: Brazilian Music; Martin Foster: Recital; Collection CD-Uquam: Greig, Sibelius, L'Orchestre de Chambre de l'UQAM. Honours: Coleman Chamber Music Competition, 1974; Naumburg Award, 1974; Villa-Lobos Medal, 1988. Hobby: Computers. Current Management: Les Concerts Davis Joachim. Address: 4418 Oxford Avenue, Montreal PQ, H4A 2Y6, Canada.

FOTEK Jan, b. 28 Nov 1928, Czerwinsk nad Wisla, Poland. Composer. Education: Studied with Stanislav Wiechowicz in Cracow and Szeligowski in Warsaw. Compositions: Operas: The Sea of Recovered Unity, Polish Radio, 1967; Galileo, 1969; The Spoons and the Moon, 1973-76; The Woodland Princess, opera-ballet, Warsaw, 1978; Man and Angels, misterium sacrum, 1982; Vir sapiens dominabitur astris, after Dante, Copernicus, St Francis and Michelangelo, Polish Radio, 1983; Other works: Opus Concertante for organ, piano and percussion, 1959; Gregorian Hymn for chorus and orchestra; A Cycle of Verses for children's chorus and orchestra, 1963; Epitasis for orchestra, 1967; The Last War for narrator, chorus and orchestra, 1971; Partita for 12 bassoons and 3 double bassoons, 1973; Musica Chromatica for strings, 1982; Sonata for tuba and piano, 1984; Czarnolas Suite for strings, 1986; Ecloga for counter-tenor and ensemble, 1987. Address: c/o ZAIKS, 2 rue Hipoteczna, 00 092 Warsaw, Poland.

FOU Ts'ong, b. 10 Mar 1934, Shanghai, China. Pianist. Education: Studied in China with Mario Paci and at the Warsaw Conservatory with Zbigniew Drzewiecki. Debut: With the Shanghai Municipal Orchestra, playing Beethoven's Emperor Concerto, 1951. Career: Gave 500 concerts in Eastern Europe while studying in Poland; Moved to London, 1958; Solo appearances in Europe, Scandinavia, the Far East, Australia and New Zealand, North and South America. Recordings include: Concertos by Beethoven, Haydn and Chopin; Solo recitals of Chopin, Debussy, Bach, Handel, Mozart, Beethoven and Schubert. Honours include: 3rd Prize, Bucharest Piano Competition, 1953; 3rd Prize, International Chopin Competition, Warsaw, 1955. Address: 62 Aberdeen Park, London N5 2BL, England.

FOUCHECOURT Jean-Paul, b. £0 Aug 1958, Blanzy, France. Singer (Counter Tenor). Education: Trained as conductor and saxophone player; Vocal studies under the influence of Cathy Berberian. Career: Many appearances with such early music groups as Les Arts Florissants, and Les Musiciens du Louvre; Rameau's Les Indes Galantes, Les Fêtes d'Héber, Zoroastre Lully's Atys and Charpentiers's David et Jonatas under the direction of William Christie, Concerts in France and on tour throughout Europe, America and Japan; Rameau's Hippolyte et Aricie and Lully's Phaeton under Marc Minkowski; Further engagements in Purcell's Fairy Queen at the Aix Festival, Monteverdi's Orfeo under René Jacobs at Salzburg, L'Incoronazione di Poppea with Christophe Rousset for Netherlands Opera and Monteverdi's Ulisse with Michel Corboz at Geneva; Other repertory includes the Berlioz Roméo et Juliette (with John Eliot Gardiner), Offenbach's Orphée aux Enfers, Mozart's Nozze di Figaro and Poulenc's Les Mamelles de Teresias with Seiji Ozawa, (on tour to Japan, 1996); Season 1997-98 in the title role of Rameau's Platée with the Royal Opera and at Edinburgh; L'Enfant et les Sortilèges at Florence, 1998; Debut at the Met in New York with Tales of Hoffmann. Recordings include; Lully's Atys and Phaeton; Mononville's Titon et L'Aurore and Les Fêtes de Paphos; Rameau's Les Indes Galantes, Pygmalion and Hippolyte et Aricie; Socrate by Satie; Les Nameelles du Tiresian. Address: c/o Lies Askonas Ltd, 6 Henrietta St, London WC2E 8LA, England.

FOUNTAIN Ian, b. 15 October 1969, Welwyn Garden City, England. Concert Pianist. Education: Chorister at New College, Oxford from 1976; Winchester College, 1982; Studied with Sulamita Aronovsky at the Royal Northern College of Music. Career: Has performed widely in Europe from 1986; Recital debuts in Frankfurt and Munich, season 1989-90; Further concerts in Madrid, Warsaw, Pasadena and Savannah (Georgia), the Sintra Festival (Portugal) and Montepellier Festival (France); Toured Germany with the Arthur Rubinstein Philharmonic, Lodz; Debut with the Royal Liverpool Philharmonic Feb 1990; Autumn 1991 with the Berlin Radio Symphony Orchestra (Rachmaninov 3) and London recital debut in the International Piano Series at South Bank. Honours include: Winner, Viotti-Valsesia International Piano Competition (Italy) 1986; Joint winner, Arthur Rubinstein International Piano Competition, 1989. Address: Current Management: Connaught Artists Management Limited. Address: c/o Connaught Artists Management Limited, 39 Cathcart Road, London SW10 9JG, England.

FOUNTAIN Primous III, b. 1 Aug 1949, St Petersburg, Florida, USA. Composer. Education: Studied at DePaul University in Chicago, 1968-69. Career: Freelance composer from 1968, including association with the Arthur Mitchell Dance Theatre of Harlem. Compositions include: Manifestations for orchestra, 1969; Grudges for orchestra, 1972; Ritual Dance of the Amaks for orchestra, 1973; Duet for flute and bassoon, 1974; Cello Concerto, 1976; Ricia for violin, cello and piano, 1980. Honours include: BMI Composition Award, 1968; Guggenheim Fellowships, 1974, 1977; Award, American Academy and Institute of Arts and Letters. Address: c/o ASCAP, ASCAP Building, One Lincoln Plaza, New York, NY 10023, USA.

FOURNET Jean, b. 14 Apr 1913, Rouen, France. Conductor. Education: Studied with PHilippe Gaubert at the Paris Conservatoire. Debut: Rouen, 1936. Career: Conducted in Rouen and Marseilles until 1944; Music Director of the Opéra-Comique, Paris, 1944-57; Conducting courses at Ecole Normale, Paris, 1944-62; Conducted Pelléas et Mélisande in Tokyo, 1958; Conductor of the Netherlands Radio Orchestra, 1961-68; Chicago Lyric Opera, 1965; Principal Conductor of the Rotterdam Philharmonic from 1968-73; Guest conductor in Europe, South America, USA and Israel; Metropolitan Opera debut, 1987, Samson et Dalila; Conducted Les Dialogues des Carmélites at Seattle, 1990. Recordings include: Berlioz Grande Messe des Morts, 1943; Louise by Charpentier, Pelléas et Mélisande and Les Pêcheurs de Perles; Mignon; d'Indy Symphonie; Saint-Saëns Piano Concertos; Fauré Requiem; Franck Symphonic Poems; Debussy La Damoiselle élue (Janine Micheau), Nocturnes, Ibéria and Prélude. Address: c/o Seattle Opera Association, PO Box 9248, Seattle, WA 98109, USA.

FOURNILLIER Patrick, b. 26 December 1954, Neuilly-sur-Seine, France. Conductor. Education: Studied with Louis Fourestier and Pierre Dervaux in Paris; Strasbourg Conservatoire with Jean-Sebastian Bereau, Salzburg Mozarteum with Leopold Hager, and with Franco Ferrara at the Accademiana Chigiana, Siena. Career: Assistant Conductor to Jean-Claude Casadesus at L'Orchestre National de Lille, 1983-85, Artistic Director, until 1986; Music Director, Nouvel Orchestre de St Etienne, 1988-, and Director, Sinfonietta d'Amiens, 1989-92;

Music Director, Massenet Festival, St Etienne, 1988-; Important revivals of such neglected Massenet operas as Amadis, Thérèse, Cléopatre, Esclarmonde and Grisélidis; Le Roi de Lahore by Massenet, 1997; Premieres have included Quatre-Vingt-Treize by Antoine Duhamel, 1989. Honours include: Hans Haring Prize, Salzburg, 1982; Second Prize, Besancon International Conductors Competition, 1984; Prize Winner, Vaclav Talich Competition Prague, 1985; Second Prize, Grzerorz Fitelberg Competition at Katowice, 1987.

FOWKE Philip (Francis), b. 28 June 1950, Gerrards Cross, England. Concert Pianist. Education: Scholarship to Royal Academy of Music, London, 1967-74; Piano studies with Marjorie Withers and Gordon Green; LRAM (Piano Performance); ARCM (Piano Performance); Recital Diploma. Debut: Wigmore Hall, 1974. Career: Professor of Pianoforte, Royal Academy of Music, London; Performs regularly with all major British orchestras including the four principal London orchestras; Frequent radio and TV broadcasts; Regular performer at the London Promenade Concerts since 1979; Made his US debut, 1982; Tours throughout Europe and Australia; Has played in Hong Kong and the Emirate of Oman; Invited to perform at the Serate Musicale de Milano; Appeared at Salzburg Mozart Week, 1984; Professor, Royal Academy of Music, 1984-91; Professor, Welsh College of Music and Drama, 1994; Director of Keyboard Studies, Trinity College of Music, 1995; Recitalist and piano tutor, Dartington International Summer School, 1996, 1997; Concerto appearances with the Hallé and in the USA, 1997. Recordings include: Carnival of the Animals; Bliss Piano Concerto; Virtuoso Piano Transcriptions; Britten's Scottish Ballad; Complete Chopin Waltzes; Chopin Sonatas Nos 2 and 3; Tchaikovsky's 1st and 3rd Piano Concertos; Rachmaninoff Concerto No 2; Paganini Rhapsody; Ravel Piano Concerto in G and Concerto for the left hand; Chopin Waltzes and Brahms Intermezzo; Delius Piano Concerto; Bliss Piano Recital; Hoddinott piano concerto and a CD of film scores, forthcoming. Contributions to: Times Educational Supplement, Review of Rubinstein Biography. Honours: Churchill Fellowship, 1976; Fellow, Royal Academy of Music. Memberships: Incorporated Society of Musicians; Savage Club. Hobby: Architecture. Current Management: Patrick Garvey Management. Address: c/o 59 Lansdowne Place, Hove, E Sussex BN3 1FL, England.

FOWLER Jennifer, b. 14 Apr 1939, Bunbury, Western Australia, Australia. Composer. Education: BA Hons, 1961, Dip Ed, 1962, BMus, 1967, University of Western Australia; Further study, Studio for Electronic Music, Utrecht, 1968-69. Career: Resident, London, 1969-; Music Teacher, schools, 1962-72; Freelance Composer. Compositions include: Hours of the Day, 4 mezzos, 2 oboes, 2 clarinets, 1968; Chimes, Fractured, ensemble, 1971; Look on this Oedipus, orchestra, 1973; Voice of the Shades, soprano, ensemble, 1977; Tell Out, my Soul: Magnificat, soprano, cello, piano, 1980; Music for Piano-Ascending and Descending, solo piano, 1980; Piece for EL, solo piano, 1981; The Arrows of St Sebastian, II, bass clarinet, cello, tape, 1981, I, ensemble, 1982; Invocation to the Veiled Mysteries, ensemble, 1982; Line Spun with stars, piano trio, 1983; When David Heard..., choir, piano, 1983; Echoes from an Antique Land, ensemble, 1983; Threaded Stars, solo harp, 1983; Blow Flute, solo flute, 1983; Letter from Haworth, mezzo, clarinet, cello, piano, 1984; Between Silence and the Word, wind quintet, 1987; Lament, baroque oboe, bass viol, 1987; We Call to You, Brother, ensemble, 1988; Restless Dust, cello, piano, 1988; And Ever Shall Be, mezzo, ensemble, 1989; Reeds, Reflections..., oboe, string trio, 1990; Remembering 1695, 4 wind instruments, 1994. Recordings: Chimes Fracture on Australian Festival of Music Vol 10; Blow Flute on The Flute Ascendant. Contributions: New Music Articles, Vol 4, 1985; Contemporary Music Review, 1995. Honours: Prize for Hours of the Day, Berlin Academy of the Arts; Radcliffe Award, UK, 1971; 1st Prize, Chamber Music, International Contest for Women Composers, Mannheim, 1974. Memberships: Fellowship of Australian Composers; Women in Music; International Alliance for Women in Music; Composers' Guild of Great Britain; Sonic Arts Network. Address: 21 Deodar Road, London SW15 2NP, England.

FOWLER John, b. 1956, USA. Singer (Tenor). Career: Sang in the USA as Edgardo in Lucia di Lammermoor, and in Norma; European engagements from 1983, including Rodolfo at Cologne and Hoffmann at Liège, 1985; Vienna Staatsoper, 1984-85, as Des Grieux, Leicester in Maria Stuarda and Arturo in I Puritani; Hamburg Staatsoper, 1984-85, in Rosenkavalier, Traviata and La Bohème; Welsh National Opera, 1986-87, as Edgardo and as Tonio in La Fille du Régiment; Further appearances in New Orleans, Houston (as Faust), Miami (Hoffmann, 1989), with Edmonton Opera (Duke of Mantua) and Liège (Gounod's Romeo, 1988); Concert showings in works by Respighi, Verdi (Requiem) and Mendelssohn (Elijah); Sang Percy in Anna Bolena at Barcelona and Donizetti's Edgardo at Dublin, 1991; Sang Hoffmann at Cincinnati, 1992. Honours: Winner, Metropolitan Opera Auditions, 1981. Address: c/o Herbert Barrett Management, 1776 Broadway, Suite 1610, New York, NY 10019, USA.

FOWLES Glenys, b. 4 Nov 1946, Perth, Western Australia, Australia. Singer (Soprano). Education: Studied with Margarita Mayer in Sydney, Kurt Adler in New York and Jani Strasser in London. Debut: Sang Oscar (Ballo in Maschera), Australian Opera in Sydney, 1969. Career: Sang in the USA, 1974-81, notably at the New York City Opera as Poppea, Susanna, Melisande, 1976, Mimi and Micaela; European engagements have included Ilia in Idomeneo at Glyndebourne (1974), Sophie and Titania for Scottish Opera (Midsummer Night's Dream); Other roles include Gounod's Juliette, Mozart's Zerlina and Pamina, Marzelline, Marguerite (Faust), Nannetta, Anne Trulove, Mimi and Lauretta; Sang Liu in Turandot for Australian Opera, 1991; Marschallin, 1992. Address: Australian Opera, Sydney Opera House, Sydney, New South Wales, Australia.

FOX Erika, b. 3 Oct 1936, Vienna, Austria. Composer. m. 3 Sept 1961 (now separated), 1 son, 1 daughter. Education: ARCM, Royal College of Music, London; Also private study with Jeremy Dale Roberts and Harrison Birtwistle. Career: Numerous commissions from leading contemporary music groups; Works performed at London's South Bank, Canada, Greece, Turkey, Czechoslovakia, festivals and broadcasts; Rehearsed orchestra at Menuhin School; Teaching includes Centre for Young Musicians, Pimlico; Junior Department, Guildhall School of Music and Drama; Composition workshops in various schools and privately; Sometime ballet pianist for Arts Educational Schools. Compositions include: Lamentations for Four, 1973; The Slaughterer, chamber opera, 1975; Paths Where the Mourners Tread, 1980; Litany for Strings, 1981; Movement for String Sextet, 1982; Shir, 1983; Kaleidoscope, 1983; Quasi Una Cadenza, 1983; Nick's Lament, 1984; Osen Shomaat, 1985; Silver Homage, 1986; Rivka's Fiddle, 1986; On Visiting Stravinsky's Grave at San Michele, 1988; Hungarian Rhapsody, 1989; The Bet, puppet music drama, 1990; The Dancer Hotoke, chamber opera, Garden Venture commission, 1992 (Olivier Award Nomination); The Moon of Moses, 1992; Currently writing piano concerto commissioned by Julian Jacobson, 1993; Tuned Spheres, 1995. Hobbies: Reading; Theatre. Current Management: Elinor Kelly, Westbrook Farm Cottage, Boxford, Nr Newbury, Berkshire RG16 8DL, England. Address: 78 Peterborough Road, London SW6 3EB, England.

FOX Fred(erick Alfred), b. 17 Jan 1931, Detroit, MI, USA. Composer. Education: Studied at Wayne State University, The University of Michigan, Indiana University, Bloomington with Bernhard Heiden. Career: Teacher at Franklin College, Indiana and Sam Houston University, Huntsville; Worked in Minneapolis; Assistant, Contemporary Music Project, Washington DC; Teacher, California State University, Hayward, 1964-74 and at Indiana University, 1974-, Chairman of Composition Department, 1980-. Compositions include: A Stone, A Leaf, an Unfound Door for Soprano and Ensemble, 1966; BEC for Chamber Ensemble, 1968; The Descent for Chorus and Percussion, 1969; Violin Concerto, 1971; Matrix for Cello, Strings and Percussion, 1972; Ternion for Oboe and Orchestra, 1973; Variables No 5 for Orchestra, 1974; Variables Nos 1-4 and 6 for Instruments, 1976; Time Excursions for Soprano, Speaker and Instruments, 1976; Beyond Winterlock for Orchestra, 1977; Ambient Shadows for 8 Instruments, 1978; Night Ceremonies for Orchestra, 1979; Sonaspheres Nos 1-5 for Chamber Ensemble, 1980-83; Nilrem's Odyssey for Baritone, Speaker and Chorus, 1980; Tracings for Orchestra, 1981; Bren for 13 Brass, 1982; Januaries for Orchestra, 1984; Shaking the Pumpkin for Saxaphone, Piano and Percussion, 1988; Auras for Chamber Ensemble, 1989; Nightscenes for Strings and Percussion, 1989; Devil's Tramping Ground for Chamber Ensemble, 1991; Echo Blues for Orchestra, 1992; Dreamcatcher for 13 Players, 1994; Impressions for Orchestra, 1995. Recordings: Music of Frederick Fox, CD; Shaking The Pumpkin, CD. Memberships: ASCAP; American Music Center; Composers' Forum. Address: 711 South Clifton Street, Bloomington, IN 47401, USA.

FOX Leland (Stanford), b. 25 Jan 1931, Worcester, MA, USA. University Music Professor and Administrator. m. Wanda R Nelson, 1 Mar 1955, 1 s, 1 d. Education: BM, 1956; MM, 1957, Baylor University; PhD, Florida State University, 1962. Career: Hearst Publications, NYC, 1948-51; Graduate Assistant, 1956-57, Instructor of Music, 1957-60, Baylor University; Graduate Assistant, Florida State University, 1960-62; Principal Tenor, Asolo Festival, 1962; Opera and oratorio performances; Instructor in Music, Pensacola Junior College, 1962-63; Associate Professor of Music, University of Oklahoma, 1963-66; Associate Professor to Professor, Director of Opera Theater, 1966; Associate Dean of Graduate School, University of Mississippi, 1986-. Publications include: Index of Italian Opera 1900-1970; Opéra Comique: A Vehicle for Classic Style, 1964; From Out of The Ashes: Santa Fe Opera's New Theater, 1968; La Belle Arsène 1773 by Pierre Alexandre Monsigny, 1969; The State of Opera: A Dialogue between Boris Goldovsky and Carlisle Floyd, 1971; Editor of numerous books. Contributions to: New Grove Dictionary of Music and Musicians; The Opera Quarterly; Editor, The Opera Journal, 1968-88. Hobbies: Golf; Smoking Pipes.

FOX Malcolm, b. 13 Oct 1946, Windsor, England. Composer. m. Pauline Elizabeth Scholz, 5 Apr 1980, 1 son. Education: Royal College of Music, University of Lndon; ARCM 1966; BMus(Hons), 1967; MMusRCM, 1968. Career: Music Director, Cockpit Theatre, London, 1972-74; Lecturer in Music, 1974-79, Senior Lectorer, 1980-, University of Adelaide, South Australia. Compositions: Sid the Serpent, opera, 1976; Six Miniatures, violin and piano, 1977; Violin Concerto, 1980; The Iron Man, opera, 1987; Pathways of Ancient Dreaming, string orchestra, 1990; Ten Thousand Years Goodbye, soprano, piano and clarinet, 1992. Publications: Music Education in South Education (1836-1986), chapter in From Colonel Light into the Footlights - The Performing Arts in South Australia from 1936 to the present, 1988. Contributions to: Siegfried's Death, 1989; The Swan Knight in Wagner's Lohengrin, 1989; Wotan's Spear, 1993. Memberships: Australasian Performing Right Association; Australia Music Centre; Fellowship of Australian Composers; Association of Professional Composers (UK). Address: 13 Whinham Street, Fitzroy, Adelaide, South Australia 5082, Australia.

FOX Tom, b. 1950, USA. Singer (Baritone). Education: Studied at the College Conservatory of Music in Cincinnati Opera Company. Career: Appeared with Texas Opera Theater, 1974, then with Houston Grand Opera; Resident member of Cincinnati Opera, 1976-80; Frankfurt Opera from 1981 as Orestes (Elektra), Amonasro, Don Pizarro, Escamillo, Klingsor, Ford, Figaro and Nick Shadow in The Rake's Progress; Wiesbaden, 1981, as Don Giovanni; Hamburg Staatsoper, 1983, as Arcalems in Amadis de Gaule by J C Bach; Has sung with Canadian Opera as Orestes, Jochanaan and Escamillo; Welsh National Opera, 1985, as Escamillo; Other roles include Iago (Teatro Colon, 1986), Claudius in Hamlet by Thomas (Pittsburgh), Alberich in The Ring for Nice Opera, at the Théâtre des Champs Elysées and in San Francisco; Gessler in Guillaume Tell in Nice; Dutchman, Amonasro, the villains in Hoffmann and Scarpia (Pittsburgh); Giovanni (Francesca di Rimini) in Turin; Barnaba in La Gioconda with Rome Opera; Invited to San Francisco for the US premiere of Henze's Das Verratene Meer; Season 1992/93 with debut in Washington as Iago, the role of Vesco di Blois in Massenet's Esclarmonde in Palermo, Telramund in Montpellier; Debut at the Metropolitan Opera, New York as Alberich, Jochanaan in San Francisco; 1993/94, Prus (Makropulos Case) in San Francisco and Bologna, his debut at the Lyric Opera of Chicago as Scarpia, his debut as Wotan at the Santiago Opera in Chile, Klingsor in a new production of Parsifal at the Munich Staatsoper and Kurwenal in a new production of Tristan at La Monnaie in Brussels; Sang Pizarro in Fidelio at the 1996 Salzburg Festival. Address: Kaye Artists Management Ltd, Barratt House, 7 Chertsey Road, Woking GU21 5AB, England.

FRACCARO Walter, b. 1968, Italy. Singer (Tenor). Career: Many appearances at leading opera houses from 1993; Season 1994-95 as Ismaele in Nabucco at Barcelona, Cavaradossi at Valencia and Lisbon, and Raffaele in Stiffelio at Madrid; Further engagements as Alfredo at Lisbon, Radames at Pittsburgh, Riccardo in Ballo in Maschera at Tenerife and Marseilles; Alfredo and the Verdi Requiem at the International Festival of Peralada in Spain; Season 1996-97 as Faust in Mefistofele at Pittsburgh, Radames at San Francisco, Pinkerton at the Metropolitan Opera and Verdi's Macduff in Hamburg. Honours include: Winner, 1993 Concorso di Vorallo Valesia (Jury Prize from Carlo Bergonzi); Placido Domingo Prize at the 1993 Concorso Internazionale di Canto Francisco Vinas, Barcelona. Address: c/o Metropolitan Opera, Lincoln Center, New York, NY 10023, USA.

FRACKENPOHL Arthur (Roland), b. 23 Apr 1924, Irvington, NJ, USA. Composer; Professor. Education: Studied with: Bernard Rogers, Eastman School of Music, BA, 1947, MA, 1949; Darius Milhaud, Berkshire Music Center, Tanglewood, summer 1948; Nadia Boulanger, Fontainebleau, 1950; DMus, McGill University, Montreal, 1957. Career: Teacher, 1949-61, Professor, 1961-85, Crane School of Music, State University of NY at Potsdam. Compositions: Chamber Opera: Domestic Relations (To Beat or Not to Beat), 1964; Orchestral: A Jubilant Overture, 1957; Largo and Allegro for Horn and Strings, 1962; Short Overture, 1965; Concertino for Tuba and Strings, 1967; Suite for Trumpet and Strings, 1970; Concerto for Brass Quintet and Strings, 1986; Band Music: Brass Quartet, 1950; 4 Brass Quintets, 1963, 1972, 1986, 1994; Trombone Quartet, 1967; Brass Trio, 1967; String Quartet, 1971; Breviates for Brass Ensemble, 1973; Suite for Brass Trio and Percussion, 1973; Trio for Oboe, Horn and Bassoon, 1982; Tuba Sonata, 1983; Piano Pieces; Choral Works: Te Deum, 1962; Gloria, 1968; Mass, 1990; Song Cycles; Solo Songs. Publications: Harmonization at the Piano, 1962, 6th edition, 1991. Membership: ASCAP. Address: c/o 13 Hillcrest Drive, Potsdam, NY 13676, USA.

FRANCAIX Jean, b. 23 May 1912, Le Mans, France. Composer; Pianist. Education: Studied at the Le Mans Conservatory and at the Paris Conservatoire, with Isidor Phillip and Nadia Boulanger. Career: Many tours of Europe and the USA as a piano virtuoso; Performances of his music at many music festivals including ISCM Festivals at Vienna, 1932, and Palermo, 1949. Compositions: Operas: Le Diable Boiteux, 1937; La Main de Gloire, 1945; Paris à nous deux, 1954; La Princesse de Cleves, 1961-65; Ballets: Les Malheurs de Sophie, 1935; Le Jeu Sentimental, 1936; Le Jugement du fou, 1938; Les Demoiselles de la nuit, 1948; La Dame dans la lune, 1958; L'Apocalypse selon St Jean, oratorio, 1942; Orchestral: Symphony, 1932; Concertino for piano and orchestra, 1932; Serenade for chamber orchestra, 1934; Fantasie for cello and orchestra, 1934; Quadruple Concerto, 1935; Piano Concerto, 1936; La Douce France, 1946; Symphony, 1953; Divertimento for horn and chamber orchestra, 1958; L'Horloge de Flore, suite for oboe and orchestra; 2-Piano Concerto, 1965; Flute Concerto, 1967; 2 Violin Concertos, 1970, 1979; Theme and Variations for orchestra, 1973; Concerto for double bass and orchestra, 1974; Theme and Variations for clarinet and strings, 1978; Concerto for 2 harps and strings, 1979; Bassoon Concerto, 1980; Chamber music: Piano Sonata, 1960; Clarinet Quintet, 1978; 6 Impromptus for flute and bassoon, 1979; Other chamber works. Address: SACEM, 225 Avenue Charles de Gaulle, 92521 Neuilly sur Seine Cedex, France.

FRANCESCH Homero, b. 6 Dec 1947, Montevideo, Uruguay. Concert Pianist. Education: Studied in South America and with Ludwig Hoffmann at the Munich Academy. Career: Many appearances as concert soloist throughout Europe, notably with the Ravel concertos and in the premiere of Henze's Tristan (London, 1974); Frequent radio and television appearances. Address: Anglo-Swiss Artists' Management Ltd, Suite 35-37 Morley House, 320 Regent Street, London W1R 5AD, England.

FRANCESCHETTO Romano, b. 1957, Italy. Singer (Bass-baritone). Education: Studied at the Parma Conservatory. Career: Has sung widely in Italy from 1981, notably at La Scala in Milan, Rome, Verona, Venice Turin, Palermo, Bologna, Trieste and Catania; Further engagements in Hamburg, Dresden, St Petersburg, Bordeaux, Tel Aviv, Rio de Janeiro, Seoul and elsewhere; Has performed all the major buffo roles such as Don Bartolo, Dulcamara, Don Magnifico; Leporello; Geronimo; Don Pasquale; Gianni Schicchi; Also leading roles in many baroque and classical operas. Recordings include: Morlacchi's Barbiere di Siviglia (Bongiovanni); Paisiello's Don Chisciotte; Rossini's Adina; Salieri's Falstaff, forthcoming. Current Management: Alberto Mirri, Rome. Address: Via Fornio 6/C, 43036 Fidenza, Italy.

FRANCI Carlo, b. 18 Jul 1927, Buenos Aires, Argentina. Composer; Conductor. Education: Studied at the Rome Conservatory and with Fernando Previtali at The Academy of St Cecilia. Career: Conducted symphonic music at first, then Hansel und Gretel at Spoleto in 1959; Appearances at many opera houses in Italy and abroad, including the Vienna Staatsoper; Led the Company of Rome Opera in Rossini's Otello at the NY Metropolitan, 1968, returning as guest, 1969-72; Other repertoire includes: Spontini's Fernand Cortez and Verdi's Nabucco, Berne, 1990; Conducted the Seven Stars concert at the Baths of Caracalla, 1991. Compositions include: L'Impertaore, Opera, produced at Bergamo, 1958. Address: c/o Teatro dell Opera di Roma, Piazza B Gigli 8, 00184 Rome, Italy.

FRANCI Francesca, b. 1962, Rome, Italy. Singer (Mezzo-soprano). Education: Studied with Rodolfo Celletti and Tito Gobbi. Debut: Sang Mahler's Lieder eines fahrenden Gesellen at Verona, 1984. Career: Appeared as Maddalena in Rigoletto at Genoa and Naples, Rosina at Bari and Suzuki in Bologna, 1988; Festival della Valle d'Itria 1988 in Donizetti's Maria di Rohan, as Armando; Edvige in Guillaume Tell at La Scala, Milan, returning as Fatima in Oberon; Sang Ernestina in Rossini's L'Occasione fa il Ladro at Pesaro; Further engagements at Rome and Naples (from 1987), Florence, Monteverdi's Otho, 1992, Paris and Wiesbaden; France 1992 as Stephano in Gounod's Roméo et Juliette; Season 1996 as Contessa d'Arco in Rossini's Matilde di Shabran at Pesaro and Fenena in Nabucco at the Verona Arena. Recordings include: Maria di Rohan. Address: c/o Teatro Alla Scala, Via Filodrammatici 2, 20121 Milan, Italy.

FRANCIS Alun, b. 1943, Kidderminster, England. Conductor. Education: Royal Manchester College of Music, 1960-63. Career: Played the horn in Hallé and Bournemouth Symphony Orchestras; From 1966 has conducted more than 60 orchestras in over 20 countries; Guest conductor at the Vienna Festival, Hong Kong Arts Festival with the BBC Scottish Symphony, Århus Festival in Denmark with the Philharmonia Hungarica, Promenade Concerts, London, with the Royal Philharmonic, and Festival Hall, 1983, in Henryk Szeryng Golden Jubilee concert; Chief Conductor and Artistic Director of the Ulster Orchestra, 1966-67, and the Northern Ireland Opera Trust, 1974-84; Director, Northwest Chamber Orchestra in Seattle, 1980-85; Director and Artistic Advisor, Overijssells Philharmonic in Holland, 1985-87; Currently Chief Conductor of the NordWestDeutsche Philharmonie and Principal Conductor of Berlin Symphony (from 1989); Repertoire includes Bel Canto opera (1978 revival of Donizetti Gabriella di Vergy, premiere of revised version, at Belfast) and 20th century music ranging from Berio to Stockhausen; Has composed music for the concert hall, films and theatre. Recordings: Donizetti's Ugo, Conte di Parigi, with the Philharmonia Orchestra; Offenbach's Christopher Columbus, with the London Mozart Players (Opera Rara); Other albums with the London Symphony, Royal Philharmonic, English Chamber and Northwest Chamber Orchestras. Address: Anglo-Swiss Management, Ste 35-37 Morley House, 320 Regent Street, London W1R 5AD, England.

FRANCIS Sarah (Janet), b. London, England. Oboist. m. Michael D C Johnson, 2 daughters. Education: ARCM, Scholar, Royal College of Music, London; French Government Scholarship, Paris; Boise Foundation Scholarship to study with Pierre Pierlot, Paris. Debut: BBC, 1959. Career: Principal Oboe BBC Welsh Orchestra; BBC Recitalist; Soloist, Chamber Music and Orchestral Player; Professor, Royal College of Music, London; Director, London Harpischord Ensemble, Dedicatee of many concert and chamber music works. Compositions: Seven Dedications: Gordon Jacob, Seven Bagatelles, 1971; Gordon Crosse, Ariadne, for solo oboe and 12 players, 1972; Phyllis Tate, The Rainbow and the Cuckoo, oboe quartet, 1975; Crosse, Little Epiphany Variations for oboe and cello, 1977; Anthony Payne, Concerto, 1980; William Mathias, Oboe Concerto, 1989; Stephen Dodgson, Oboe Quartet, 1994. Recordings: Britten Metamorphoses, Quartet, Crosse Ariadne; Boccherini Quintets,; Crusell, Reicha Quintets; Howells, Rubbra Sonatas; Rutland Boughton Oboe Concerto, RPO; Mozart and Krommer Concertos, LMP; Britten complete oboe music; Bax, Holst Quintets; Moeran, Jacob Quartets, Chandos; Complete Albinoni, Handel and Telemann Concertos LHE, Unicorn-Kanchana. Publications: Going Solo, Faber, 1995; Oboe Music to Enjoy, 1996. Contributions to: Joy Broughton: A Portrait; Double Reed News. Honour: Somerville Prize for Wind instruments, RCM, 1959. Memberships: British Music Society; Royal Society of Musicians; Incorporated Society of Musicians; Chairman, Double Reed Society. Hobbies: Theatre; Travel; Walking. Address: 10 Avenue Road, London N6 5DW, England.

FRANCK Mikko, b. 1980, Helsinki, Finland. Conductor. Education: Sibelius Academy (violin and conducting), 1992-; New York, Israel and Sweden. Career: Children's chorus member at the Finnish National Opera; Appeared as the young Sibelius at the Helsinki Swedish Theatre, 1992; Conductor with such Finnish orchestras as the Vaasa, Lappeenranta, Pori and the Chamber Orchestra of the Sibelius Academy, Helsinki; Season 1997-98 with the Turku Philharmonic, Tapiola Sinfonietta, Tampere Philharmonic and Netherlands Radio Philharmonic; Japanese tour with the Sibelius Academy Symphony Orchestra; Conductor, The Magic Flute, at the Finnish National Opera. Address: c/o Harrison/Parrott Ltd, 12 Penzance Lane, London W11 4PA, England.

FRANCKE Donald (Max), b. 26 October 1929, London, England. Singer. m. Margaret Rose Lindsay, 1 son 1 daughter. Education: Harrow; St Catharine's College, Cambridge University, England; The Royal College of Music. Debut: New Opera Company, Sadler's Wells Theatre. Career: Regular Broadcasts for BBC Sound OPera and TV; Recital with Gerald Moore at Wigmore Hall; Editor, Royal College of Music Magazine, 1969-74; Recital with John Ireland Society; Intimate Opera Company; Opera Players; Royal Opera, Covent Garden, London; Scottish National Opera; Phoenix Opera; New Opera Company; Park Lane Opera Company; Welsh National Opera; Opera North; Adjudicator, at all major Festivals in England, 1969-; Adjudicator in Canada, Trinidad and Tobago, Hong Kong, Bermuda. Compositions include: Mass; Lux et Origo; Anthem and Songs. Recordings: With Purcell Singers. Publications include: Editor, The Ways and Means of Vocal Expression - Dr Arnold Smith, 1974. Memberships: Fellow, Royal Musical Association; Fellow, Royal Astronomical Society. Current Management: June Epstein Associates, Flat 162 Compayne Gardens, London NW6 3RY, England. Address: Orama House, 263 Sheen Lane, London SW14 8RN, England.

FRANDSEN John, b. 13 Mar 1956, Aalborg, Denmark. Composer; Organist. m. Kirsten Grove, 5 Jan 1985, 1 d. Education: Aalborghus Statsgymnasium; MA in Music at Aarhus University; Composition and Organ at Royal Academy of Music, Aarhus. Career: Teacher at Aarhus University, 1979-83 and The Royal Academy of Music, Aarhus, 1980-; Organist at Ellevang Church, 1982-84 and Holy Ghost Church, Aarhus, 1984-; Conductor of Cantilena Choir, 1983-. Compositions: String Song for String Quartet, 1980; Wo Immer Wir Soielen for Mixed Choir, 1982; Songs of Innocence for Soprano and Guitar, 1984; Amalie Lever, opera, 1984; Avers/Revers for Wind Quintet, 1985; Deux Poèmes Sur Le Temps for Mixed Choir, 1985; Amalie Suite for Chamber Orchestra, 1985; Stabat Mater for Tenor and Organ, 1986; Petite Suite for Guitar, 1986; De/Cadences for Wind Quintet, 1987. Recording: Songs of Innocence with soprano Ellen Lunde and guitarist Erling Moldrup. Contributions to: Organistbladet; Dansk Mussiktidsskrift. Memberships: Chairman of Young Nordic Music, Danish Section, 1983-87; Chairman of Aarhus Unge Tonekunstnere, 1983-; Danisher Composers' Society. Address: Odinsvej 7, DK-8230 Aabyhoj, Denmark.

FRANK Claude, b. 2 Dec 1925, Numberg, Germany. Musician (Pianist). m. 29 Aug 1959, 1 daughter. Education: Studies, France and USA, with Artur Schnabel, K U Schnabel. Debut: New York Philharmonic, 1959. Career includes: Appearances with most major orchestras including New York Philharmonic, Boston Symphony, Chicago Symphony, Cleveland Orchestra, Philadelphia Orchestra, Berlin Philharmonic, Concertgebouw, London Symphony, Royal Philharmonic; Performed with conductors including Bernstein, Giulini, Leinsdorf, Mehta, Szell; Tours of Australia, Africa, Israel, Taiwan; Appearances at most major music festivals. Recordings: 32 Beethoven Piano Sonatas; Mozart Concertos; Beethoven Trios; Numerous other works. Contributions to: Piano Quarterly; Keynote Magazine. Honours: Emmy Award nomination, 1966; Beethoven Society Award, 1979. Hobbies: Languages; Sports; Bridge. Current Management: Columbia Artists Management Inc. Address: 825 West End Avenue, New York, NY 10025, USA.

FRANK Susanne, b. 2 Nov 1962, Switzerland. Violinist. Education:Studied at the Winterthur Conservatory in Paris and the International Menuhin Academy. Career: 2nd violin of the Carmina Quartet since 1987; Appearances from 1987 in Europe, Israel, Japan and the USA; Regular concerts at the Wigmore Hall from Oct 1987; Concerts at the South Bank Centre, London, Amsterdam Concertgebouw, the Kleine Philharmonie in Berlin, Konzertverein Vienna; Four engagements in Paris, 1990-91, seven in London; Tours to Australasia, USA, Japan, and concerts at the Hohenems, Graz, Hong Kong, Montreux, Schleswig-Holstein, Bath, Lucerne and Prague Spring Festivals; Collaborations with Dietrich Fischer-Dieskau, Olaf Bär and Mitsuko Uchida. Recordings: Albums for several labels (from 1991). Honours: Joint winner (with members of Carmina Quartet), Paolo Borciani String Quartet Competition in Reggio Emilia, Italy, 1987; Gramophone prize for best recording of chamber music, 1992. Address: c/o Intermusica Artists' Management, 16 Duncan Terrace, London N1 8BZ, England.

FRANKE-BLOM Lars-Åke (Harry), b. 4 Apr 1941, Norrköping, Sweden. Composer. m. Gunilla Marie-Louise Dalin, 2 Jan 1965, 1 son, 2 daughters. Education: Master's degree, Romance Languages, University of Uppsala, 1965; Logopede, Karolinska Institute, Stockholm, 1967; Composition largely self-taught, but also with Nils Eriksson and Daniel Börtz. Debut: With orchestral work Motions, 1975. Career: Active in Norrköping, collaborating with the local symphony orchestra on several occasions; The troll battle commissioned and performed by the Folkopera, Stockholm, 1979; The well of the virgins, ballet, commissioned by Swedish Television, 1982; The web of yearning commissioned by Norrköping Symphony Orchestra, 1984, presented on Swedish Television, 1988; HP commissioned by the Royal Theatre, Stockholm, 1990. Compositions: Motions for orchestra, 1973; Music for mobile for orchestra, 1975-77; Concertos for violoncello, 1977, viola, 1980, contrabasso, 1983; The troll battle, opera for children, 1979; 3 symphonies, 1982, 1993, 1994; Web of yearning, symphonic poem, 1984; Impossible reality, chamber music, 1986; HP, opera in 2 acts, 1990-95; Music for art, chamber music, 1991. Recordings: Music for mobile, CD; Web of yearning, cassette and TV film; Music for art, CD; Several radio recordings. Honours: Prize Winner, International New Music Composers' Competition, 1989-90. Memberships: Association of Swedish Composers, 1978. Address: Mastgatan 15, 60365 Norrköping, Sweden.

FRANKL Peter, b. 2 Oct 1935, Budapest, Hungary. Pianist. m,. Annie Feiner, 1958, 1 son, 1 daughter. Education: Franz Liszt Academy of Music, Budapest, 1943-56. Debut: London, 1962. Career: New York debut with Cleveland Orchestra under George Szell in 1967; Has performed with major international orchestras including: Berlin Philharmonic, Amsterdam Concertgebouw, Israel Philharmonic, Leipzig Gewandhaus, all the London and the major American orchestras; Has worked with such eminent conductors as Abbado, Boulez, Colin Davis, Dorati, Haitink, Herbig, Leinsdorf, Maazel, Masur, Muti, Rozhdestvensky, Salonen, Sanderling and Solti; Visiting Professor of Piano at Yale University School of Music; 25th Anniversary Concerts with the Pauk-Frankl-Kirshbaum Trio, 1997. Recordings include: Complete works for piano by Schumann and Debussy; A solo Bartók and Chopin album; Hungarian Anthology; Mozart Concerti with members of the English Chamber Orchestra; The Complete 4-Hand Works by Mozart with Tamás Vásáry; The 3 Brahms Violin Sonatas with Kyung Wha Chung; Brahms, Schumann, Dvorák and Martinu Quintets with the Lindsay Quartet. Honours: First Prize in international competitions, Paris, Munich, 1957, Rio de Janeiro, 1959; Order of Merit, Hungarian Republic, 1995. Current Management: Transart Ltd. Address: 5 Gresham Gardens, London, NW11 8NX, England.

FRANKLIN James (Jim), b. 14 Feb 1959, Sydney, New South Wales, Australia. Education: BMus (Hons), 1982, MMus, 1989, University of Sydney; Shihan (Master performer), International Shakuhachi Research Centre, Japan, 1996; Study with Peter Sculthorpe, 1978-81, Milko Kelema, 1982-85, Ton de Leeuw 1985-86. Career: University of Sydney, 1987-93; Lecturer in Music Technology, University of Western Sydney, Nepean, 1994-; Founder Member, OHM, Electronic Music Group. Compositions include: Corno Inglese, for choir, 1979; Talisman, for piano, 1980; Three Glimpses of Aquilon, for piano, 1980; Across the Swan's Riding, for piano and orchestra, 1981; The Unliving Seed, chamber opera, 1983; Boundaries for the Child of Flame, for string quartet, 1984; Fragments of a Broken Land, for orchestra, 1984; Triptych, for 8 voices and ensemble, 1984; Dream Within a Dream, for tape, 1988; Raising Dust, for synthesizer, 1988; The Hours of the Sea-Bird, for voices, keyboard, synthesizer, sampler and sequencer, 1988; Fountain of Light, for Shakuhachi and electronics, with Riley Lee, 1991; Middle Dance, for voices and ensemble, 1992; Naratic Visions, dance theatre, 1993; Heart, for Shakuhachi, voice and live electronics, 1994; Three Treasures: Columns and Webs, for koto quartet, percussion, Shakuhachi and electronics, 1996; Water Spirits, for koto, shakuhachi and electronics, with Satsuki Odamura, 1994-96. Honours include: Munich International Multi-Media Festival, Best Original Sound Track, 1990. Address: Department of Music, University of Western Sydney, Nepean, P O Box 10, Kingswood, NSW 2747, Australia.

FRANKLIN Peter (Robert), b. 19 Dec 1947, London, England. University Teacher. Education: BA, DPhil, University of York, 1966-72. Career: Teacher of Music and German, Harlaxton College, Lincolnshire, 1974-79, and at William Jewell College, Liberty, Missouri, USA, 1979; Lecturer, Department of Music, University of Leeds, 1980-. Publications: Natalie Bauer-Lechner Recollections of Gustav Mahler (editor, annotator), 1980; The Idea of Music, Schoenberg and Others, 1985. Contributor to: Many journals including The Music Review, Music and Letters, Opera (1992), The Musical Quarterly and The Musical Times, on Mahler and Schreker; Programme Notes (eg Pfitzner's Palestrina at Covent Garden, 1997). Address: Department of Music, University of Leeds, 14 Cromer Terrace, Leeds, West Yorkshire LS2 9JR, England.

FRANKS WILLIAMS Joan, b. 1 Apr 1930, New York, USA, Israeli Citizen. Composer. Education: Studied at the Eastman and Manhattan Schools, notably with Wayne Barlow and Vladimir Ussachevsky, Career: Directed the concert series, New Dimension in Music, at Seattle, 1962-71; Gave concerts in Israel from 1971 including series, Israeli Composers Plus One, and returned to Seattle in 1989. Compositions include: String Quartet, 1964; Cassandra, monodrama for Soprano and Ensemble, 1969; Frogs for Soprano, Strings, Piano and Tape, 1975; If Stones Send Up Their Witness, musique concrete, 1978; Song Of Songs for Mezzo, Flute and Guitar, 1983; Hilda-Ness for Viola Da Gamba, 1991; Frogs Revisited, 1992. Address: c/o ACUM Ltd, PO Box 14220, Acum House, Rothschild Boulevard 118, Tel-Aviv 61140, Israel.

FRANOVA Tatiana, b. 3 Aug 1945, Czechoslovakia. Pianist. m. Eduard Ihring, 20 Aug 1966, 1 daughter. Education: Bratislava Conservatoire, 1959-64; Academy of Music and Dramatic Arts, Bratislava, 1964-69; Music Academy, Vienna, 1969-73; Postgraduate studies in Bratislava, 1980-83. Career: Concert tours in Austria, Brazil, Cuba, Egypt, France, Germany, Hungary, India, Italy, Luxembourg, Poland, Rumania, Spain, Gran Canaria, Switzerland, Sweden, USSR; Professor, Academy of Arts, Cairo, Egypt, 1983-87; Professor of Piano, Academy of Music Arts, Bratislava, 1987-. Recordings: Brahms: Sonata in F sharp minor Op 2, 1975; Rachmaninov: Sonata in B minor Op 36, 1975; Etudes - Chopin, Liszt, Scriabin, Rachmaninov, 1978; Rachmaninov: Concerto No 1 in F sharp minor, 1982; De Falla: Nights in the Gardens of Spain, 1982; Complete works of Glazunov, 1991. Honours: 1st Prize in Radio Competition, Young People's Studio, 1964; Silver Medal at International Festival, Bordeaux, 1974; F Kafenda Prize, 1980. Membership: Slovak Music Union. Hobbies: Painting; Reading; Travel. Current Management: Slovkoncert. Address: Gorkeho 7, 81101 Bratislava, Slovakia.

FRANTZ Justus, b. 18 May 1944, Hohensalza, Germany. Pianist. Education: Hamburg Hochschule für Musik, with Eliza Hansen; Wilhelm Kempff in Positano. Career: European concerts from 1960; Mozart concerto series with Karajan and the Berlin Philharmonic; US debut, 1975, with the New York Philharmonic under Bernstein; Later performances in New York and Washington with Kempe, Giulini and Haitink; 1983 tour of USA, Japan and Europe with pianist Christoff Eschenbach; Professor, Hamburg Musikhochschule, 1985-; Founded Schleswig-Holstein Music Festival, 1986 and directed until 1994; Performed the Beethoven concerti, 1988; Performed complete cycle of Mozart concerti in several European cities, season 1987-88. Recordings: Concerti by Dvorák and Schumann under Bernstein; Duos by Mozart and Schubert with Eschenbach; Bach concerti, 1985; Mozart concerti for 2 and 3 pianos with Eschenbach, Helmut Schmidt and the London Philharmonic. Address: c/o Anglo-Swiss Artists Management, Suite 35-37, Morley House, 320 Regent Street, London W1R 5AD, England.

FRANZEN Olov (Alfred), b. 22 Jan 1946, Umeå, Sweden. Composer; Cellist. m. Ingeborg Axner, 12 Nov 1977. Education: Stockholm Music Academy, 1966-73; Music Teacher Examination, 1970; Cello with Gunnar Norrby, 1966-72; Composition with Ingvar Lidholm, 1969-73. Debut: As composer, A Wind Quintet in Lund, 1963; As Cellist, Nyström, 1971. Career: Cellist in Norrkoping Symphony Orchestra, 1971-72; Harpans Kraft, Stockholm, 1971-77; Swedish TV Film, Sundcreme with Harpans Kraft, 1976; Freelance in Härnösand and Founder, HND Ensemble, 1977-92; Cellist, Sundsvall Chamber Orchestra, 1983-90; Teacher of Composition, Kapellsberg Music School, Härnösand, 1983-92; In 1986 started Faimo Edition for publishing music scores and recordings; Freelance in Skokloster, 1992-; Has played with Harpans Kraft and HND in Sweden, Finland, Austria on radio; Composition played in all Nordic countries and abroad; Cellist, Skokloster Chamber Soloists, 1994-. Compositions include: Cytoplasma for song and Piano, 1968; Fiesta for Percussion Ensemble, 1982; Har for Soprano and Harp, 1983; From The Junction Point for Bassoon and Live Electronics, 1985; Suite for 3 Flutes, 1986; Agnim for Symphony Orchestra, 1987; It's Getting Sunny for Brass Band, 1988; Gaps for Violin and Piano, 1990; Apmel for Flute, Clarinet, Percussion, Piano and String Quartet, 1992; The Unseen Present for Cello and Reciter, 1993; Opus NN for Mezzo Soprano, Guitar and Cello, 1994; Clouds on Blue Sky for Symphony Orchestra, 1995; Organic music No 2 for cello solo, 1995; String Quartet, 1996; Lamentode, for soprano, bass clarinet and piano, 1997. Recording: Beyond, CD, with 6 Pieces for Winds and Piano, 1991. Address: Abbotvägen 18, S-74695 Skokloster, Sweden.

FRASER Malcolm (Henry), b. 1 Aug 1939, Kingston-upon-Thames, England. Opera Director. m. 25 Apr 1964, 4 sons. Career: Associate Director, Lincoln Repertory, 1966-68; Resident Director, Welsh National Opera Company, 1968-76; Senior Lecturer, Royal Northern College of Music, 1976-87; Founder, Artistic Director, Buxton International Festival, 1979-87; J Ralph Corbett Distinguished Professor of Opera, University of Cincinnati, 1987-; Guest Director, London Opera Centre, New Sadler's Wells Opera, Portland Opera, Seattle Opera, Calgary Opera, Edmonton Opera, Virginia Opera, Arkansas Opera, until 1990; Permanent Guest Director, Arkansas Opera, 1988-; Associate Artistic Director, Buxton International Festival, 1988-; Florentine Opera of Milwaukee; Artistic Director, Opera Theatre of Lucca, 1996-. Honours: Churchill Fellow, 1969; Prize for Mise-en-Scène, Prague International TV Festival, 1975; Kodály Medal, Hungarian Government, 1982; 14 times winner, National Opera Association Prize for best college production in USA. Address: College Conservatory of Music, University of Cincinnati, Cincinnati, OH 45221, USA.

FRECCIA Massimo, b. 19 Sept 1906, Florence, Italy. (American). Conductor. Education: Cherubini Royal Conservatoire, Florence. Career: Guest Conductor, New York Philharmonic Orchestra, 1938, 1939, 1940; Musical Director, Conductor, Havana Philharmonic Orchestra, 1939-43, New Orleans Symphony Orchestra, 1944-52, Baltimore Symphony Orchestra, 1952-59; Chief Conductor, Rome (RAI) Orchestra, 1959-65; Frequent appearances as guest conductor of famous orchestras in Europe and USA; Tours in Australia, 1963, Japan, 1967, South Africa, 1969; Appearances at various international festivals including Vienna, Prague, Berlin, Lisbon, Montreux. Honours: Honorary DMus, Tulane University, New Orleans; Order of the Star of Italian Solidarity. Recordings include: Symphonies by Haydn, Mozart and Mendelssohn, with the Santa Cecilia Orchestra; Shostakovich 5th Symphony and Symphonie Fantastique, Royal Philharmonic.

FREDMAN Myer, b. 29 Jan 1932, Plymouth, Devon, England. Conductor. m. Jeanne Winfield, 26 Aug 1954, 2 s. Education: Dartington Hall; The Opera School, London. Debut. Cork. Career: Glyndebourne Festival with operas by Mozart. Verdi, Maw and Von Einem; Glyndebourne Touring Opera, 1968-74; State Opera of South Australia; Seymour Group; Guest Conductor throughout Europe, America and Australia; BBC TV; Wexford, Perth and Adelaide Festivals also at Hong Kong Fest; Conductor in Poland, Belgium, Romania and Germany; Conducted Cavalli's L'Ormindo at Brussels in 1972, Bizet's Carmen in Hamburg, 1973 and Il Barbiere di Siviglia in Sydney, 1974; Season 1992 with La Bohème for the Canadian Opera Company at Toronto and Le nozze di Figaro in Sydney; Head of Opera at the New South Wales Conservatorium, 1981-92 including the premiere of Lawrence Hargrave by Nigel Butterfly in 1988; Associate Artist of The Australian Opera, 1991-; Concert debut of South America in 1992 at Montevideo and Buenos Aires; Conducted Australian premieres of Midsummer Marriage, Death in Venice and One Man Show. Recordings: Bax Symphonies 1 and 2, LPO, No 3 with Sydney Symphony; H Brian Symphonies 16 and 22 with LPO; Delius Paradise Garden with LPO; Benjamin Overture to An Italian Comedy; Respighi Sinfonia Drammatica, Piano Concerto with Sydney Symphony; Puccini Le Villi with Adelaide Symphony; CDs of Britten and Delius recordings. Honour: Bronze Medal by Italian Government, 1965. Hobbies: Walking; Theatre; Scrabble. Current Management: Jenifer Eddy, Australia. Address: 7 Macquarie, Philips Landing, 247 Burwood Road, Concord, NSW 2137, Australia.

FREDERIKSSON Karl-Magnus, b. 6 February 1968, Stockholm, Sweden. Singer (Baritone). Education: Music High School; Opera High School,1989-91; Masterclass for D Fischer-Diskau, 1991. Debut: Stockholm Royal Opera, 1996. Career: Recital at Wigmore Hall, 1994, 1995; Recital at Helsinki Opera Stage, 1996; And in Stockholm Opera stage, 1997; Die lnstige Weiber von Windsor, O Nicolai in Stockholm Opera, 1997; Radio Opera in Swedish Radio, 997; Several tours with Eric Ericson in Europe. Recordings: Kullerro (Sibelius) with Sir Colin Davis; Die Lustige Native (Lehar) with J-E Gardiner; Nordic Romances (solo recording). Honours: Major soloist prize from the Swedish Royal Music Academy, 1993; Miriam Helin Competition in Helsinki. Membership: The Swedish Theatre Order. Current Management: Kristina Hennel-Lee, Nordic Artist AB. Address: Vastmannag 76, S-113 26 Stockholm, Sweden.

FREEDMAN Gertrud, b. 1933, Germany. Singer (Soprano). Education: Studied at the Augsburg Conservatory. Career: Sang at Passau and Mainz, 1957-60, Munich Staatsoper, 1960-80; Guest appearances at Lisbon and Barcelona as Sophie and Blondchen, Komische Oper Berlin as Rosina in Paisiello's Barbiere di Siviglia; Other roles include Mozart's Papagena and Despina, Anna in Intermezzo, Zdenka, Oscar, Musetta, and Adele in Die Fledermaus. Address: c/o Bayerische Staatsoper, Max-Joseph-Platz, W-8000 Munich 1, Germany.

FREEDMAN Harry, b. 5 Apr 1922, Lodz, Poland. Composer. m. Mary Louise Freedman, 15 Sept 1951, 3 daughters. Education: Winnipeg School of Art, 1936-40; Royal Conservatory of Music, Toronto, 1945-50; Tanglewood Music Centre, 1949. Career: English Horn for Toronto Symphony Orchestra, 1946-70; Host of Junior Round-Up, Music Segment CBC TV, 1958-60; Host, CBC Thursday Music, 1967-69; Many guest appearances on Television and Radio. Compositions: Tableau; Images; 3 Symphonies; 9 Ballets; 2 String Quartets; Numerous orchestral works, chamber works, choral works, song cycles; Scores for films, television, theatrical and radio; 1 act opera, Abracadabra; Sonata for Winds, 1990; Spirit Song, soprano and string quartet, 1993; Indigo, string orchestra, 1994; Viola Concerto, 1996; Borealis, orchestra and 4 choirs, 1997. Recordings: Images with Toronto Symphony, Ozawa; Tangents with Vancouver Symphony; The Flame Within with Festival Singers; Poems of Young People, Maureen Forrester; Town, Esprit Orchestra; Touchings, Nexus (percussion) with Esprit Orchestra. Hobbies: Golf; Painting. Address: 35 St Andrew's Gardens, Toronto, Ontario M4W 2C9, Canada.

FREEMAN David, b. 1 May 1952, Sydney, New South Wales, Australia. Stage Director. m. Marie Angel. Career: Founded Opera Factory in Sydney, 1973, and in Zurich, 1976, with 20 Swiss productions; Productions for Opera Factory in London (founded 1981) have included The Knot Garden, Punch and Judy, The Beggar's Opera, Cavalli's La Calisto, Birtwistle's Yan Tan Tethera (world premiere 1986); Eight Songs for a Mad King by Peter Maxwell Davies, Ligeti's Adventures/Nouvelles Aventures and Reimann's The Ghost Sonata; Mozart's 3 Da Ponte operas presented at the Elizabeth Hall as part of the bicentenary celebrations; Has also produced Osborne's Hells Angels; Founded Opera Factory Films in 1991; Directed Prokofiev's The Fiery Angel for Marinsky Theatre, St Petersburg, Covent Garden and Metropolitan, New York; Operas by Birtwistle, Maxwell Davies, Ligeti and Mozart have been shown on BBC and Channel 4 television; For English National Opera has produced Orfeo, Akhnaten by Glass (British premiere), The Mask of Orpheus (world premiere) and The Return of Ulysses; Productions elsewhere have included: La Bohème for Opera North, Manon Lescaut at the Opéra-Comique, Paris, and work in Germany, Houston and New York; The Magic Flute, for Opera Factory, 1996. Honours: Chevalier, l'Ordre des Arts et Lettres, 1985. Current Management: Allied Artists. Address: c/o Opera Factory, 9 The Leather Market, Weston Street, London SE1 3ER, England.

FREEMAN Paul (Douglas), b. 2 Jan 1936, Richmond, Virginia, USA. Conductor. m. Cornelia Perry, 1 son. Education: Received lessons in piano, clarinet and cello; BMus 1956, MMus 1957, PhD 1963, Eastman School of Music, Berlin Hochschule für Musik, 1957-59; Studied conducting with Richard Lert and Pierre Monteux. Career: Director, Hochstein Music School, Rochester, New York, 1960-66; Music Director, Opera Theater, Rochester, 1961-66; Director, San Francisco Community Music Center, 1966-68; Conductor, San Francisco Conservatory Orchestra, 1966-67; Music Director, San Francisco Little Symphony Orchestra, 1967-68; Associate Conductor, Dallas Symphony Orchestra, 1968-70; Resident Conductor, Detroit Symphony Orchestra, 1970-79; Principal Guest Conductor, Helsinki Philharmonic Orchestra, 1974-76; Music Director, Victoria (BC) Symphony Orchestra, 1979-; Chicago Sinfonietta, 1987-; Guest Conductor, North America and Europe. Recordings: For Columbia, Fanfare, Finlandia, Laurel, Orion, Seraphin, Spectrum and Vox.

FREEMAN Roland, b. 7 May 1927, London, England. Composer; Arranger. m. Marian Freeman, 18 Dec 1976. Education: Wiltshire College of St Mark and St John, Chelsea, 1945-47; London School of Economics, 1953-56; BA, Music, honours, Southampton University, 1994-97; MMus, in progress, Exeter University, 1997-. Appointments: Schoolmaster, 1947-53; NUS President, 1956-58; Roland Freeman Ltd, 1958-89; Director, London Broadcasting Ltd, 1972-75; London Weekend Television Ltd, 1981-90; Composer, Arranger, 1994-. Compositions: Requiem in B Minor for Soloists, Chorus and Orchestra; Clarinet Rhapsody; Piano Quartet, Quest; Piano Suite; Organ Fugue; Evening Canticles. Memberships: Incorporated Society of Musicians; Composers Guild of Great Britain; Fellow, Institute of Chartered Secretaries and Administrators; Institute of Public Relations; Reform Club. Hobbies: Mountain Walking; Gardening; Piano and Organ Playing. Address: Brockswood, Canal Lane, Alderbury, Salisbury, Wilts SP5 3NY, England.

FREI Andrea, b. 14 Dec 1967, Marktoberdorf, Bavaria, Germany. Singer (Soprano). Education: Studied at the Augsburg Conservatory with Leonore Kirchstein. Career: As concert artist toured South East Asia with Orff's Carmina Burana; Studied further in Munich and made opera debut, 1990, as the Queen of Night at Essen; Guest appearances at Leipzig, Frankfurt, Hamburg, Dusseldorf and Barcelona; Ulm Opera from 1991. Address: c/o Ulm Theater, Olgastrasse 73, W-7900 Ulm, Germany.

FREIRE Nelson, b. 18 Oct 1944, Minas Gerais, Brazil. Pianist. Education: Studied in Brazil and Vienna. Career: Many performances in South America and Europe as concert soloist and chamber musician, notably with Martha Argerich and Mischa Maisky. Recordings include: Chopin 24 Preludes. Honours include: Prize winner at Rio de Janeiro Competition, 1957, and Vianna da Motta, Lisbon, 1972; Edison Prize for Chopin recording.

FREITAG Erik, b. 1 Feb 1940, Vienna, Austria. Composer; Violin Teacher. Education: Diploma, Academy of Music, Vienna. Career: With Radio Sweden, 1964-66; Violinist, Philharmonic Orchestra, Stockholm, 1967-70; Teacher, Conservatory of Vienna, 1970-. Compositions: Suite for Orchestra; Overture Danoise; 2 Pieces for Strings; Music in memory of a great artist; Quintet; Cello Sonata; Helle Nacht for strings; Reflections in Air for violin, viola and violoncello; Symphony Nocturnes. Recordings: 3 Pieces for String Quartet, radio; Divertimento for Wind Quintet; Limericks, 5 songs for medium voice and 6 instruments; Elegie und Tanz for oboe and string quartet; Quasi una Marcia for 15 players; Nachtstücke for violin and viola, radio; Passages in the Wind; Helle Nacht for strings, CD; Sonata for cello and piano, CD. Address: Schippergasse 20, A-1210 Vienna, Austria.

FRÉMAUX Louis (Joseph Félix), b. 13 Aug 1921, Aire-sur-Lys, France. Orchestral Conductor. Education: Conservatoire National Supérieur de Musique, Paris. Career: Musical Director and Permanent Conductor of Orchestre National de l'Opéra de Monte Carlo, Monaco, 1955-66; Principal Conductor, Rhônes-Alpes Philharmonic Orchestra, Lyons, 1968-71; Principal Conductor and Musical Director, City of Birmingham Symphony Orchestra, 1969-78; Particularly known for performances of Berlioz; Chief Conductor, Sydney Symphony Orchestra, 1979-81, Principal Guest Conductor, 1982-85; Guest appearances in Austria, Belgium, Holland, France, Italy, New Zealand, Norway, Switzerland, South America and Germany; Has premiered Panufnik's Sinfonia Sacra, 1964, McCabe's 2nd Symphony, 1971, and Columbia Falls by Nicola le Fanu, 1975. Recordings include: French Baroque music by Gilles, De La Lande, Rameau, Campra, Mouret and Charpentier; Poulenc Stabat Mater and La Bal Masqué; Berlioz Grande Messe des Morts and overtures, Bizet Symphony, Saint-Saëns 3rd Symphony; Poulenc Les Biches, Piano Concerto and Gloria; Symphonie Fantastique; Rimsky's Scheherazade. Honours: 8 Grand Prix du Disque Awards; Koussevitsky Award. Address: Christopher Tennant Management, Unit 2, 39 Tadema Road, London SW10 0PY, England.

FRENI Mirella, b. 27 Feb 1935, Modena, Italy. Opera Singer (Soprano). m. (1) Leone Magiera, 1955, 1 daughter, (2) Nicola Ghiarouv. Debut: 1955 at Modena, as Micaela. Career: Glyndebourne Festival, 1961; Royal Opera House, Covent Garden, 1961; Metropolitan Opera House, New York, 1965; Appearances at Vienna State Opera and Salzburg Festival and in leading opera houses throughout the world; Major roles include Nannetta in Falstaff, Mimi in La Bohème, Zerlina in Don Giovanni, Susanna, Adina in L'elisir d'amore, Violetta in La Traviata, Desdemona in Otello, centenary performance at La Scala, 1987; Grand Opera, Houston, 1987, as Aida; Marked 35th anniversary of debut in 1990 at Modena, as Manon Lescaut; Gala concert with the Boston Opera/Boston Symphony, 1990; Gran Teatro del Liceo, Barcelona, 1989, as Tatyana and Adriana Lecouvreur, Manon Lescaut, 1990; La Scala Milan, 1990, as Lisa in The Queen of Spades; Sang Alice Ford at the Metropolitan, 1992; Rome Opera and Barcelona, 1992, as Mimi; Sang Giordano's Fedora at Covent Garden, 1994 and at the New York Met, 1997. Recordings include: Carmen; Falstaff; La Bohème; Madama Butterfly including video; Alcina; Tosca; Guillaume Tell; Verdi Requiem; Simon Boccanegra; Don Carlos; Aida; Faust; Turandot; L'Amico Fritz; Don Giovanni; L'Elisir d'Amore; Le nozze di Figaro. Address: c/o Harold Holt Ltd, 31 Sinclair Road, London WC14 0NS, England.

FRENKLOVA Jana, b. 17 Sept 1947, Prague, Czechoslovakia. Pianist. 1 daughter. Education: Prague Conservatoire, 1962-67, Honours Graduate; Leningrad Conservatoire, 1967-68 (studies curtailed after Russian invasion of Czechoslovakia). Debut: Prague, 1956. Career: Pianist in Residence, Lancaster University, 1975-79; Pianist in Residence, University College of North Wales, 1979-; Recording Artist for BBC Radio 3, 1977-. Honours: Numerous first prizes in Czechoslovakia up to 1968; Finalist, Alfredo Casella Competition, Naples, 1970; Winner, Dudley Competition, 1971. Hobby: Enjoying rural peace. Current Management: Encore Concerts. Address: Maen Hir Bach, Dwyran, Anglesey, Gwynedd LL61 6UU, North Wales.

FRETWELL Elizabeth, b. 13 Aug 1920, Melbourne, Australia. Operatic Soprano; Adjudicator; Vocal Consultant. m. Robert Simmons, 1 s, 1 d. Career: Joined National Theatre, Melbourne, 1950; Came to Britain in 1955; Joined Sadler's Wells, 1956 and Elizabethan Opera Company, Australia, 1963; Tours: West Germany, 1963; USA, Canada and Covent Garden, 1964; Europe, 1965; Guest Soprano with Cape Town and Durban Opera Companies, South Africa, 1970; Joined Australian Opera, 1970; Roles included Violetta, in La Traviata, Leonore in Fidelio, Ariadne in Ariadne auf Naxos, Senta in Flying Dutchman, Minnie in Girl of the Golden West, Leonora in Il Trovatore, Aida, Ellen Orford in Peter Grimes, Leonora in Forza del Destino, Alice Ford in Falstaff, Amelia in Masked Ball, Giorgetta in Il Tabarro, opening season, Sydney Opera House, 1973; Has sung in BBC Promenade Concerts and on television. Recordings: Il Trovatore; Land of Smiles, by Lehar. Honour: Order of British Empire, 1977. Membership: Music Board, Austalian Opera Foundation, 1982-. Address: 47 Kananook Avenue Bayview, New South Wales 2104, Australia.

FREUDENTHAL Otto, b. 29 July 1934, Gothenburg, Sweden. Composer; Pianist; Violist. 1 son. Education: TCL, England; Studied piano with Ilona Kabos. Debut: (as pianist) Wigmore Hall, London. Career: Recitals and Concerts in England, Germany, Switzerland, Netherlands, Scandinavia, Japan; Broadcasts; Teacher, Royal College of Music, Manchester; Assistant to Dr Otto Klemperer to 1973. Compositions: Chamber music, viola concerto, concert piece for trombone and orchestra; In Highgate Cemetery for strings; Chamber opera; A BankoMat cantata; The Song About Our Town; A cantata to Linkopings 700 year jubilee; Symphony, 1989; String Quartet, 1991; Saxophone Quartet, 1992. Recordings: Coliseum records, BBC, Swedish Radio; CD Wir Wandelten, with Cheryl Jonsson, soprano, WANDA CD. Publications: (essay) Music and Equity (with Irene Lotz); Chamber Music with Wollenweber Edition, Munich. Honours include: Harriet Cohen Memorial Medal for interpretation of Beethoven; Swedish State Cultural Stipend, 1977, 1987. Memberships: Swedish Society of Composers, STIM. Address: Vastanagatan 25, 58235 Linkoping, Sweden.

FREY Alexander (James), b. 5 Oct 1961, Chicago, Illinois, USA. Organist; Pianist; Music Director; Conductor. Education: BMus (honours), organ, piano, conducting, 1984, MMus (honours), organ, conducting, 1986, University of Michigan, Ann Arbor; Teachers include Gavin Williamson (piano), Robert Glasgow (organ), Gustav Meier (conducting); Dietrich Fischer-Dieskau (opera and lieder accompanying), Berlin. Career: Appeared as Pianist and Organist with Berlin Philharmonic Orchestra, Hollywood Bowl Orchestra, Deutsches Sinfonie Orchester, Rundfunk-Sinfonie Orchester Berlin, Brandenburg Chamber Orchestra (also Guest Conductor, 1993-94), Ars Longa Chamber Orchestra of Germany (also Principal Guest Conductor, 1991-94), Ensemble Europa (also Conductor, 1995), members of Chicago Symphony Orchestra, (under Mauceri, Abbado and others); Annual worldwide recital tours; Music Director, Hamburg Kammerspiele Theater, 1992-93, Berliner Ensemble, 1992-95, collaborating with Peter Zadek; Music Director, Antony and Cleopatra at Edinburgh Festival, Vienna Festwochen, Holland Festival, Berlin, 1994, Das Wunder von Mailand, Venice Festival, 5th European Festival, Berlin, 1995, Ich bin das Volk, Heidelberg Festival, Berlin, 1995; Conducted Ensemble Europa, Israel, Berlin, to commemorate end of WW II, 1995; Chamber music with Ruggiero Ricci, Vermeer Quartet and Donald McInnes; Featured pianist or organist in 3 films; TV and radio, USA, Canada, Europe including Germany. Recording: Piano Soloist, Korngold's Between Two Worlds, John Mauceri conducting Rundfunk Sinfonie Orchester Berlin, 1995; Principal Conductor, Philharmonia Orchestra of Berlin, 1995-; Principal Conductor, Artist-in-Residence and Aristic Advisor, Festival Ruidoso, 1995-. Honours include: Mortar Board, 1984; 2nd Prize, Organ Improvisation International Competition, San Anselmo Festival, 1985; Phi Kappa Epsilon, 1986; 2nd Prize, Organ Competition, American Guild of Organists, 1988; Critics' Prize, Edinburgh International Festival, 1994. Memberships: American Guild of Organists. Current Management: Artist Recitals, 3427 Fernwood Avenue, Los Angeles, CA 90030, USA.

FREY Paul, b. 1942, Heidelberg, Toronto, Canada. Singer (Tenor). Education: Studied at Toronto Conservatory with Louis Quilico. Career: Played professional ice hockey until retirement through injury; San at first concert then appeared in Toronto as Werther; Member of the Basle Opera from 1978, notably in operas by Strauss and Wagner; Sang Lohengrin at Karlsruhe, 1985, Florestan at Heidelberg, 1984-85; Guest appearances at Mannheim and Lyon; Bayreuth Festival, 1987-89, as Lohengrin; Munich Festival, 1986 and 1988, as Apollo in Daphne and Midas in Die Liebe der Danae; Metropolitan Opera debut, 1987, as Bacchus in Ariadne auf Naxos; Karlsruhe and Santiago, 1988, as Lohengrin and Walther von Stolzing; La Scala Milan, 1989, as Huon in Oberon; Has also sung in Tel-Aviv and Sydney (Walther, 1988); Cologne Opera, 1990-91, as Siegmund in Die Walküre; Other roles include Parsifal, Peter Grimes, Flamand in Capriccio, the Emperor in Die Frau ohne Schatten and Mozart's Don Ottavio and Titus; Sang Siegmund at Bonn, 1992; Sang the title role in the premiere of Dreyfus by Jost Meier, Deutsche Oper Berlin, 1994; Engaged for Schoeck's Venus, Geneva, 1997. Recordings include: Die Frau ohne Schatten, EMI; Ariadne auf Naxos, conducted by Kurt Masur. Current Management: Theateragentur Dr Germinal Hilbert. Address: Maximilianstrasse 22, D-8000 Munich, Germany.

FREY-RABINE Lia, b. 12 Aug 1950, Crosby, Minnesota, USA. Opera Singer; Dramatic Soprano. m. Eugene Rabine, 27 June 1976, 1 son. Education: BMus, MMus, Indiana University, Bloomington; Private vocal studies with Eugene Rabine (Founder and Director of the Rabine Institute for Functional Voice Pedagogy, Bonstadt, Germany). Debut: Municipal Theatre, Bern, Switzerland, 1973. Career: Principal Singer, Bern, 1973-75, Flensburg, Germany, 1975-77, Nürnberg, 1977-79, Hagen, 1979-84, Frankfurt, 1984-; Guest appearances in numerous other German, Austrian and Swiss theatres and in Barcelona, Ghent, Rome, Naples, Vienna State Opera and other European cities; Sang the Siegfried Brünnhilde at Dortmund, 1991; and Elektra there, 1996. Honours: Metropolitan Opera Auditions National Finalist, 1971; Outstanding Musician of 1983, State of Nordrhein-Westfalen. Hobbies: Baking; Cooking; Children's activities. Current Management: Kühnly Agency, Stuttgart, Germany. Address: Kleinstrasse 6, 61194 Niddatal-2, Germany.

FREYER Achim, b. 30 Mar 1934, Berlin, Germany. Stage Director; Theatre Designer. Education: Studied at the Akademie der Kunste, East Berlin. Debut: Designed sets and costumes for the Ruth Berghaus production of Il Barbiere di Siviglia at the Berlin Staatsoper, 1967. Career: Emigrated to the West, 1973, and created designs for Cardillac and Pelléas et Mélisande at the Cologne Opera 1973-75; Directed and designed Iphigénie en Tauride at the Munich Staatsoper 1979 (seen at Amsterdam and Basle, 1990); Philip Glass's Satyagraha and the premiere of Akhnaten at the Stuttgart Staatsoper (1981, 1984); Orfeo ed Euridice at the Deutsche Oper Berlin, 1982, Die Zauberflöte at Hamburg (seen at the Vienna Festival 1991); Iphigénie en Tauride at the Deutsche Staatsoper, 1994; Die Zauberflöte for Salzburg, 1997. Address: c/o Deutsche Staatsoper, Unter den Linden 7, 1086 Berlin, Germany.

FRIED Joel (Ethan), b. 22 Apr 1954, California, USA. Conductor. m. Mary Anne Massad, 9 Dec 1990, 1 stepdaughter. Education: BMus, 1973; MMus, Piano Performance, DMA, University of Southern California, 1979. Debut: Hidden Valley Opera, 1978; European debut, Heidelberg Castle Festival, 1981. Career: Assistant Conductor, New York City Opera, 1980-82; Resident Conductor, Heidelberg Castle Festival, 1981-; Studienleiter, Saarland State Theatre, 1983-86; Chorus Master, Cleveland Opera, 1990-92; Chorus Master and Music Administrator, Pittsburgh Opera, 1992-; Conducting appearances with Zurich Opera, Fort Worth Opera and Cleveland Opera. Honours: 2nd Prize, American Conductors Competition, 1978; Special Prize for Contemporary Music, Hans Swarowsky International Conducting Competition, Vienna, 1984. Address: c/o Pittsburgh Opera, 711 Penn Avenue, Pittsburgh, PA 15222, USA.

FRIED Miriam, b. 9 September 1946, Satu-Mare, Rumania. Violinist. Education: Rubin Academy of Music, Tel-Aviv; Graduate Studies, Europe & USA (Juilliard School, Ivan Galamian). Debut: Carnegie Hall, New York, 1969; Royal Festival Hall, England. Career: Appearances, orchestras worldwide incldluing, Los Angeles Philharmonic; Philadelphia, Cleveland, Chicago, Boston Symphonies; New York Philharmonic; Berlin and Munich Philharmonics; Vienna Symphony; Zurich Tonhalle; Orchestre Nationale de France; Recent appearances include Stuttgart Radio Orchestra (conducted Neville Marriner); Danish Radio (Kurt

Sanderling); Jerusalem Symphony at Berlin Festival; Orchestre Nationale, Belgium; Philharmonic Orchestras, Monte Carlo, Stuttgart, Nuremburg; Nouvel Orchestre Philharmonique, Paris; Opened Helsinki Festival (with Helsinki Philharmonic conducted Gennadi Rozhdestvensky), 1988; Hollywood Bowl (Yuri Temirkanov), 1988; Cleveland Orchestra (Mariss Jansons), 1989; Santa Cecilia (Temirkanov), 1989; Orchestre de Paris (Kurt Sanderling), 1989; American engagements for 1994-95, Chicago Symphony Orchestra, Cleveland Orchestra, Boston Symphony Orchestra, Philadelphia Orchestra; Frequent engagements, Royal Philharmonic Orchestra;BBC TV & Promenade Concerts; Edinburgh Festival; Scottish National Orchestra; Bournemouth Symphony; Numerous recitals. Recordings: Recital LP, Deutsche Grammophon; Solo Violin Works, Bach; Sibelius Violin Concerto, Helsinki Philharmonic (Okko Kamu), 1988. Honours include: Scholarship, overseas studies, American Israel Cultural Foundation; 1st Prizes, Paganini International Competition, Genoa Italy, 1968, Queen Elisabeth Competition, Belgium, 1971. Current Management: Agence de Concerts et Spectacles Caecilia. Address: c/o Agence de Concerts et Spectacles Caecilia, 5 Place de la Fusteri, 1204 Geneve, Switzerland.

FRIEDE Stephanie, b. 1959, New York City, New York, USA. Singer (Soprano). Education: Studied at the Juilliard School and the Oberlin Conservatory. Debut: Houston Opera, 1985, as Siebel in Faust. Career: Sang further at Houston as Zerlina, Micaela and Manon; European debut at Stuttgart, 1987, as Adina; Amsterdam, 1987, as Massenet's Cendrillon; Season 1991 as Donna Anna at Munich and Elettra in Idomeneo at Glyndebourne; Liège, 1992, as Salome in Herodiade by Massenet; Further engagements at the Buxton Festival as Eleanore d'Este in Torquato Tasso by Donizetti, at Cologne as Violetta and elsewhere in Europe as Gounod's Juliette, Anne Trulove, and Mimi. Address: c/o Bayerische Staatsoper, Max-Joseph-Platz, W-8000 Munich 1, Germany.

FRIEDEL Martin (Kurt), b. 3 August 1945, Warwateil, Germany. Composer. Education: BSc (Hons), 1967, PhD, 1972, University of Melbourne. Career: Fellowships and Residences in Australia and Germany, 1976-95; Commissions from theatres in Australia, and the Adelaide Festival of the Arts, 1992. Compositions include: Sin, 7 act opera for 4 voices and orchestra, 1978; Two Songs, for soprano and ensemble, 1982; South of North, 1 act chamber opera, 1985; Conversations Before the Silence, cantata, 1989; Foxy, 1 act chamber opera, 1991; The Heaven Machine and Seduction of a General, 1 act operas for soprano and electronics, 1991; Four Choral Fragments for Walter Benjamin, 1992; Songs from the Astronauts, for soprano, baritone and ensemble, 1994; The Third Planet, oratorio, 1995; Three Night Pieces, string quartet, 1995. Honours includes: Best Score, Chicago International Film Festival, 1994. Address: c/o APRA, 1A Eden Street, Crows Nest, NSW 2065, Australia.

FRIEDERICH (Albert) Matthias, b. 16 June 1954, Heidelberg, Germany. Oboist; Recorder Player; Composer. m. Margaret Joy Stone, 30 Aug 1980, 1 son. Education: Studied at Cologne Music College with G Hoeller, H Hucke and A Meidhof. Debut: Recorder Soloist, Vivaldi's Sopranini Recorder Concerto in C major, Heidelberg, 1966. Career: Concerts with George Malcolm, Amadeus Quartet, Mozarteum Quartet, Munich String Trio, and Sinfonia Varsovia, Poland; Since 1988, member of Pifferari di Santo Spirito Trio, Heidelberg (with Margaret Friederich and Peter Schumann); Concerts, Berlin, Paris, Dallas and Tokyo. Compositions: Happy Birthday Variations, 1989; Highstreet Dixie, 1990; Enigma Blues for FGB, 1991; Jubilee Stomp, 1992; Amusement, 1994. Recordings: CD, Music for Fun, 1991; CD, Pifferari Safari, 1993. Contributions to: Article, Jazz on the oboe and the cor anglais, to Rohrblatt. Membership: International Double Reed Society. Hobbies: Table-tennis; Swimming; Painting; Drawing. Address: Floringasse 2, 69117 Heidelberg, Germany.

FRIEDLI Irene, b. 1965, Rauchlisberg, Switzerland. Singer (Mezzo-soprano). Education: Studied with Kurt Widmer at the Basle Music Academy and attended master classes with Dietrich Fischer-Dieskau and Brigitte Fassbaender. Career: Shepherd and Hope in Montevedi's Orfeo and Dryad in Ariadne auf Naxos, Lucerne Opera, 1993-94; Zurich Opera as Gertrude in Roméo et Juliette, Suzuki, Third Lady in Die Zauberflöte, Mercédès (Carmen) and the title role in L'Enfant et les Sortilèges, 1994; Opera and concert engagements with such conductors as Helmuth Rilling, Horst Stein, Michel Corboz and Neeme Järvi; Has appeared widely as guest in Switzerland and abroad, notably in contemporary concert music. Honours include: Prize winner at the Hugo Wolf (Stuttgart), Schubert (Graz) and Othmar Schoeck (Lucerne) Competitions. Address: c/o Opernhaus Zürich, Falkenstrasse 1, CH-8008 Zürich, Switzerland.

FRIEDMAN Erick, b. 16 Aug 1939, Newark, NJ, USA. Violinist; Professor. Education: Pupil of Samuel Applebaum; Studied with Ivan Galamian, Juilliard School of Music and with Nathan Milstein; Private study with Jascha Heifetz, 1956-58. Career: Professional debut as Soloist, Little Orchestra Society, NY, 1953; Carnegie Hall recital debut, NY, 1956; Soloist with leading orchestras, as Recitalist and Chamber Music player; Mischa Elman Professor at Eastman School of Music, Rochester, NY, 1975-. Recordings: Several. Honour: Winner, Music Education League Competition, 1953. Address: c/o Friedman School of Music, University of Rochester, Rochester, NY 14627, USA.

FRIEDMAN Gérard, b. 3 Apr 1926, Paris, France. Singer (Tenor). Education: Studied at the Paris Conservatoire with Roger Bourdin and Charles Panzera. Career: Sang Don Curzio in Don Giovanni at the 1955 Aix Festival, Théâtre des Champs Elysées, Paris, 1954, in the premiere (concert) of Prokofiev's Fiery Angel; Sang widely in France until 1988 as Spalanzani in Les Contes d'Hoffmann, a Brahmin in Padmavatî by Roussel and Torquemada in L'Heure Espagnole by Ravel; Professor at the Metz Conservatory from 1970. Recordings include: Auber's Manon Lescaut (HMV), Samson et Dalila (DGG), Fauré's Pénélope and Chausson's Le Roi Arthus (Erato), Te Deum by Lully, Masses by M A Charpentier and songs by Fauré. Address: c/o Conservatoire National de Région Metz, 2 Rue Paradis, F-57036 Metz, France.

FRIEDMAN Leonard (Matthew), b. 11 Dec 1930, London, England. Violinist. m. twice, 2 sons, 3 daughters. Education: Guildhall School of Music and Drama. Debut: Central Hall, 1938; Conway Hall, 1949. Career: Joint Founder, Haydn Orchestra and Cremona Quartet; Member, Adolph Busch Chamber Orchestra, English Chamber Orchestra, Rostal, Hurwitz, Bath Festival; Founder Leader, Northern Symphony; Deputy Leader, Royal Philharmonic Orchestra and Leader, Bremen Philharmonic; Leader, Westphalia Symphony; Founder, Scottish Ensemble; Guest Leader, Scottish Chamber; London Festival; Member, Melos of London; Duo with Allan Schiller, and with son Richard Friedman; Director, Friedman Ensemble. Recordings: Director, Music at Hopetoun; Director, Music at Drumlanrig; Scandinavian Serenade; String Orchestra Music by Mozart; Baroque Cello Concertos; English Serenade; Schubert String Quintet; Bach Concertos; Tribute to Kreisler. Honours: Gold Medal, Guildhall School of Music, 1953; Royal Patronage of Duke of Edinburgh, 1975; Citizenship Prize of Edinburgh, 1980-81; Founder/Director, Camerata of St Andrew, 1988. Memberships: Honorary Member, Royal Overseas; Scottish Arts; New Club. Hobbies: Cricket; Comparative religion; Global politics; History of art. Address: 17a Dublin Street, Edinburgh EH1 3PG, Scotland.

FRIEDMANN Susana, b. 24 Apr 1945, Colombia. Musicologist. 1 son. Education: BA, Mills College, 1967; MA, New York University, 1972; PhD, Kings College, London, 1997. Publications: 2 books and numerous articles in professional journals. Contributions to: New Grove Dictionary; Grove's Dictionary of Women Composers. Honours: Biggerstaff Award, 1963-67; Central Research Fund, 1985; Visiting Scholar, Stanford University, 1997-98. Memberships: RILM; ICTM; IAML. Address: Instituto de Investigaciones, Apartado Aereo 54933, Bogotá, Colombia.

FRIEDRICH Götz, b. 4 Aug 1930, Naumburg, Germany. Opera Producer. m. Karan Armstrong. Education: Studied at the German Theatre Institute in Weimar. Career: Worked at the Komische Oper Berlin, 1953-72 (Director of Productions from 1968); Stagings included Jenufa, Tosca, Così fan tutte and Porgy and Bess; Principal Producer, Hamburg Staatsoper, 1973-81; Staged Schoenberg's Moses und Aron at Vienna, 1973, and La Scala, 1975; Principal Producer, Royal Opera House, Covent Garden, 1976-81; Lulu and Der Ring des Nibelungen; Other productions include Tannhäuser, 1972, Lohengrin, 1978, and Parsifal, 1982, at Bayreuth; Die Meistersinger in Stockholm, 1977; Fidelio in Munich, 1977; Tristan und Isolde in Berlin, 1980; World premiere of Un Re in Ascolto by Berio (Salzburg 1984); Der Ring des Nibelungen at the Deutsche Oper Berlin, 1984-85; Schoenberg's Erwartung and Duke Bluebeard's Castle by Bartók (Vienna 1985); Oedipus by Wolfgang Rihm in Berlin, 1988; US productions include Wozzeck in Houston, 1982, Otello and Katya Kabanova in Los Angeles, 1986, 1988; Production of The Ring at Covent Garden, 1989-91; From 1981 Director of the Deutsche Oper Berlin, where he staged Tannhäuser in 1992; Faust for Zurich Opera, 1997; Engaged for Samson et Dalila with New Israeli Opera, 1998; TV films of many productions including Die Meistersinger and Elektra. Publications include: Walter Felsenstein - Weg und Werk, 1961. Address: c/o Deutsche Oper Berlin, Richard Wagner Strasse 10, 1000 Berlin 10, Germany.

FRIEDRICH Reinhold, b. 14 July 1958, Weingarten, Baden, Germany. Trumpet Player. m. Annette Friedrich, 2 sons. Education: Studies with Edward Tarr, Pierre Thibaud, Paris, 1979-83. Debut: Berlin Philharmony. Career: Swiss TV in Zurich, 1995; TV & Live Broadcasting of the EBU Opening Concerto with B A Zimmermann's Nobody Knows De Trouble I See, Biennale Berlin 1997 Trumpet Concerto by Benedict Mason. Compositions: BA Zimmermann, Nobody Knows De Trouble I See, 1994; Hummel, First Recordings of the Concerto in E Major with the Historical Keyed Trumpet, 1996. Recordings: B A Zimmermann, Nobody Knows De Trouble I See; Hummel & Puccini, Recordings with the Historical Keyed Trumpet; Orchestra, Wiener Akademic. Contributions to: Frankfurter All-Germeine Zeitung. Honours: 1st Prize, German Music Competition, 1981; Winner, ARD Competition, Munich, 1986. Memberships: International Trumpet Guild. Current Management: Astrid Schoerke, Hannover. Address: Badener Str 49a, D-76229 Karlsruhe, Germany.

FRIEND Caroline, b. 1950, England. Singer (Soprano). Career: Concert appearances in Britain, Switzerland, Belgium, France, Germany and the Netherlands; Repertoire includes Handel's Oratorios, Bach's Oratorios and Cantatas, Schubert's A flat Masses, Mozart's Oratorio, Britten's War Requiem under Stephen Cleobury in King's College, Vaughan Williams' Sea Symphony, Howells' Hymnus Paradisi, Rossini's Stabat Mater, Dvořák's Stabat Mater; Mahler's 4th Symphony and Les Nuits d'Eté with the Netherlands Philharmonic under Franz-Paul Decker; Appearances with the Songmakers' Almanac in England and Ireland, performing Robin Holloway's Women in War; Sang Diane in Rameau's Hippolyte et Aricie for the English Bach Festival under Jean-Claude Malgoire in Athens and Versailles and at Covent Garden; Other roles include Mozart's Donna Anna, Susanna, Pamina, Countess and Fiordiligi (Pavilion Opera), Rosalinde (Die Fledermaus), Norina (Don Pasquale), Hannah in The Merry Widow, Tosca and Mimi, (Puccini), Berta in The Barber of Seville and performances of Balfe's The Siege of Rochelle; Engagements in all the major London concert halls and with many choral societies; Conductors include Adrian Boult, John Eliot Gardner and Charles Mackerras. Address: 33 Wetherby Mansions, Earls Court Square, London SW5 9BH, England.

FRIEND Lionel, b. 13 Mar 1945, London, England. Conductor. m. Jane Hyland, 2 Aug 1969, 1 son, 2 daughters. Education: Royal College of Music, London, 1963-67; London Opera Centre, 1967-68. Debut: Welsh National Opera, 1969. Career: Welsh National Opera, 1968-72; Glyndebourne Festival Opera, 1969-72; Staatstheater, Kassel, Germany, 1972-75; Staff Conductor, English National Opera, 1976-89; Musical Director, Nexus Opera, 1981-; Musical Director, New Sussex Opera, 1989-96; Guest Conductor: BBC Symphony; Philharmonia; Swedish Radio; Orchestre National de France; Hungarian Radio; Opera National, Brussels; Many internation festivals. Recordings: Works by Anthony Milner, Havergal Brian (BBC Symphony Orchestra), Alan Rawsthorne (BBC Scottish Symphony Orchestra), Nicholas Maw, Anthony Payne, Bliss, Poulenc, Colin Matthews, Debussy, Simon Holt, Schoenberg (Nash Ensemble), Stravinsky (Scottish Chamber Orchestra); Has conducted over 100 world premiere performances. Hobbies: Theatre; Reading. Current Management: Allied Artists, London SW7 1JZ, England. Address: 136 Rosendale Road, London SE21 8LG, England.

FRIGERIO Ezio, b. 16 July 1930, Como, Italy. Stage Designer. Education: Studied architecture at Milan Polytechnic. Career: Costume Designer, Giorgio Strehler's Piccolo Teatro d'Arte from 1955; Collaborations with Strehler, Eduardo de Filippo and other directors in Italy and elsewhere; Designed Don Pasquale at the Edinburgh Festival, 1962, Tosca at Cologne, 1976, and Carmen at Hamburg, 1988; Collaborations with Nuria Espert for Madame Butterfly and Traviata at Scottish Opera (1987 and 1989), Rigoletto at Covent Garden, 1988, and Elektra at Barcelona, 1990; La Scala Milan, 1990, with Fidelio and The Queen of Spades; Designs for Il Turco in Italia and Anna Bolena at Madrid, season 1990-91; Andrea Chenier for Buenos Aires, 1996; Frequent associations with costume designer Franca Squarciapino. Address: c/o Royal Opera House (Contracts), Covent Garden, London WC2, England.

FRISCH Walter M, b. 26 Feb 1951, New York City, New York, USA. Professor of Music. m. Anne-Marie Bouché, 27 Aug 1981, 2 sons. Education: BA, Yale University, 1973; MA, 1977, PhD, 1981, University of California, Berkeley. Career: Assistant Professor of Music, 1982-88, Associate Professor, 1988-94, Professor, 1994-, Columbia University; Research in music of 19th and 20th centuries, especially the Austrian tradition (Schubert, Brahms, Schoenberg). Publications: Brahms's Alto Rhapsody (editor, facsimile edition), 1983; Brahms and the Principle of Developing Variation, 1984; Schubert: Critical and Analytical Studies (editor), 1986; The Early Works of Arnold Schoenberg, 1993. Contributions to: Co-editor, 19th Century Music, 1984-92. Honours: Winner, American Society of Composers, Authors and Publishers-Deems Taylor Award for outstanding book on music, 1985, 1995. Memberships: American Musicological Society; American Brahms Society. Address: Department of Music, Columbia University, New York, NY 10027, USA.

FRISELL Sonja, b. 5 Aug 1937, Richmond, Surrey, England. Stage Director. Education: Studied piano and acting at the Guildhall School. Career: Associated with Carl Ebert at the Städtische Oper Berlin and at Glyndebourne; Staff Producer, La Scala, solo producer in North and South America; Directed La Favorite at the 1977 Bregenz Festival, Vivaldi's Tito Manlio at La Scala, 1979 and Handel's Agrippina at Venice, 1985; Directed Carmen at Buenos Aires, 1985, Aida at the Metropolitan, 1988;

Lyric Opera of Chicago, 1989-90; Don Carlos: Khovanshchina at San Francisco, 1990; Directed: Die Zauberflöte for Washington Opera at Kennedy Center, 1991; Forza del Destino at San Francisco, 1992; Otello at Washington, 1992; Ballo at Chicago, 1992; Rigoletto at Gothenburg, 1993; Trovatore at Chicago, 1993; Lucia at Calgary, 1994; Eugene Onegin, Calgary, 1996; La Gioconda, La Scala, 1997; Elena da Feltre, Wexford, 1997. Current Management: CAMI New York, USA. Address: c/o Drosslweg 45, 85687 Oberpframmern, Germany.

FRITH Benjamin, b. 11 Oct 1957, Sheffield, England. Concert Pianist. m. Donna Sansom, Apr 1989, 3 daughters. Education: Private study with Fanny Waterman, OBE, since childhood; BA (Hons) 1st Class, Music, Leeds University, 1979. Debut: Official London debut in recital at Wigmore Hall, 1981, sponsored by Countess of Munster Trust. Career: Performing career of recitals, concertos and participation in chamber music ensembles in London and the Provinces including South Bank, Wigmore Hall, Usher Hall Edinburgh, Aldeburgh, Harrogate and many major festivals; TV and radio appearances; Concerts in Italy, Spain, Germany, Poland, Israel and America. Recordings: CDs: Diabelli and 32 variations by Beethoven; Chamber music; CD: Schumann piano music, Davidsbündlertänze (opus 6), Fantasiestücke (opus 12); Martin Ellerby, piano and chamber works, and Collage, French and English, clarinet and piano music with Linda Merrick; Mendelssohn, complete solo piano works and complete works for piano and orchestra; Messiaen, Visions de l'Amen, with Peter Hill, Malcolm Arnold, complete piano works. Honours: Joint Top Prize Winner, Busoni International Pianoforte Competition, 1986-; Gold Medallist and joint 1st Prize Winner, Arthur Rubenstein International Piano Masters Competition, 1989. Membership: Incorporated Society of Musicians. Current Management: Modena International Music, Italy; Rosalia Heifetz, Israel. Address: 6 Carisbrook Road, Carlton in Lindrick, Nottinghamshire S81 9NJ.

FRITTOLI Barbara, b. 1970, Milan, Italy. Singer (Soprano). Education: Studied at the Giuseppe Verdi Conservatory, Milan. Career: Sang first at the Teatro Comunale, Florence and has appeared as Mozart's Countess under Abbado, Fiordiligi in Vienna and Ravenna, 1996; Donna Elvira at Naples; Desdemona with Antonio Pappano at Brussels and with Abbado at the Salzburg Easter Festival, 1996. New York Met and Covent Garden debuts as Mimi and Micaela; Medora in Verdi's Il Corsaro, Turin, 1996; Engaged for Glyndebourne Festival, 1998; Concerts include Strauss's Vier Letzte Lieder in Milan, Rome and London, Rossini's Stabat Mater, Ein Deutsches Requiem and the Verdi Requiem. Recordings include: Il Trittico, with Mirella Freni; Il Barbiere di Siviglia; Pergolesi's Stabat Mater, with Riccardo Muti. Honours include: Winner of several international competitions. Address: c/o Harold Holt Ltd, 31 Sinclair Road, London W14 ONS, England.

FRITZSCH Johannes, b. 1960, Meissen, Germany. Conductor. Education: Studied with his father and at Dresden Hochschule für Musik from 1975. Career: Second Kapellmeister, Rostock Opera, 1982-87; Conducted Il Barbiere di Siviglia and Il Matrimonio Segreto at the Semper Opera Dresden, 1987; Nearly 200 performances at the Dresden Staatsoper with the Dresdener Staatskapelle; Guest Conductor, Royal Swedish Opera in Stockholm; Regular orchestra concerts in former East Germany; West German debut October 1990 with Beethoven's Fifth Piano Concerto and the New World Symphony with the National Theatre Orchestra, Mannheim; Danish debut, October 1991 with the Orchestra of Danish Radio at COpenhagen; Also engaged for Don Giovani, Royal Opera, Stockholm, 1991; Rialto Theatre, Copenhagen, 1991; Entführung, Nozze di Figaro and Don Giovanni, Royal Opera Stockholm, 1991; La Traviata, Hanover, 1991; Hansel and Gretel at Sydney, with Australian Opera, 1992; Die Bassariden at Freiburg, 1993; Music Director, 1993-. Current Management: Haydn Rawstron Management, England. Address: PO Box 654, London SE26 4DZ, England.

FROBENIUS Wolf, b. 1 June 1940, Speyer/Rhein, Germany. Musicologist. Education: Studies in Musicology, History of Art and History, Freiburg i/Br, Germany and Paris, France; PhD, Freiburg i/Br, 1968; Habilitation, Freiburg i/Br, 1988. Career: Staff Member, Handwörterbuch der musikalischen Terminologie, Akademie der Wissenschaften und der Literatur, Mainz, 1968-88; Teacher, University of Freiburg i/Br, 1971-88; Professor, University of Saarbrücken. Publications: Hohannes Boens Musica und seine Konsonanzenlehre, 1971. Contributions to: Handwörterbuch der Musikwissenschaft; The New Grove; Die Musik in Geschichte und Gegenwart. Address: Akazienweg 56, D-66121 Saarbücken, Schafbrücke, Germany.

FROUNDBERG Ivar, b. 12 Apr 1950, Copenhagen, Denmark. Composer. m. Inge Sønderskov Madsen, 1 son. Education: Organist and Choirleader, 1976; MA, Composition, State University of New York, USA, 1981; Royal Danish Academy of Music, 1986. Career: Gave courses in electro-acoustic music at the Royal Danish Academy of Music, 1986-92, Assistant Professor and Musical Coordinator of the 1994 ICMC. Compositions: Peripeti; Phantasia Dekadenz; Five echoes of a sonata; Thrice-told tunes; Faust Variations II; En vue de Roesnaes; Drei-Klang; Frescobaldi - epitaph; Pro pacem pugnandum est; Haliksa'i; Henri Michaux preludes; Embryo; D; Multiple Forms; And the fire and the rose are one; At the stillpoint of the Turning World; Other echoes inhabit the garden; What did the Sirens sing as Ulysses sailed by?; A Pattern of Timeless Motion, 1989; Time and the Bell, 1990; Kreppvaar, 1991. Recordings: Henri Michaux preludes; Phantasie Dekadenz; Five echoes of a Sonata; Haliksa'i; Drei-Klang; A Pattern of Timeless Motion. Publications: Theory and Praxis in the compositional methods of Iannis Xenakis - an exemplification; Komponisten Pierre Boulez, 1985. Contributions to: Dansk Musiktidskrift; Nutida Musik. Address: Melchiorsvej 1, DK 3450 Allerød, Denmark.

FRUGONI Orazio, b. 28 Jan 1921, Davos, Switzerland. Pianist. Education: Graduated Milan Conservatory, 1939; Attended master classes of Alfredo Casella at the Accademia Chigiana, Siena, and Dinu Lipatti at the Geneva Conservatory. Career: Played in concerts in Italy from 1939 and in the USA from 1947; Piano professor at the Eastman School, Rochester, until 1967; Director, 1967-72; Teacher of piano at the Luigi Cherubini Conservatory at Florence from 1972. Recordings include: Beethoven's E flat concerto of 1784 (premiere recording); Mendelssohn's Piano Concerto. Honours include: Prix de Virtuosité, Geneva Conservatory, 1945. Address: Conservatorio di Musica L Cherubini, Piazzetta delle Belle Arti, Florence, Italy.

FRÜHBECK DE BURGOS Raphael, b. 15 Sept 1933, Burgos, Spain. Conductor. m. Maria Carmen Martinez, 1959, 1 son, 1 daughter. Education: Music Academies in Bilbao, Madrid and Munich and University of Madrid. Career: Chief Conductor, Municipal Orchestra, Bilbao, 1958-62; Music Director and Chief Conductor, Spanish National Orchestra. Madrid, 1962-78; Music Director of Dusseldorf and Chief Conductor, Dusseldorf Symphoniker, 1966-71; Musical Director, Montreal Symphony Orchestra, 1974-76; Principal Guest Conductor, National Symphony Orchestra, Washington, USA, 1980-90; Principal Guest Condcutor, Yomiuri Nippon Symphony Orchestra, Tokyo, 1980-90; Honorary Conductor, Yomiuri Nippon Symphony Orchestra, Tokyo, 1991; Conducted opening concert of 1989 Edinburgh Festival, Falla's Atlantida and La Vida Breve; Cheif Conductor of the Vienna Symphony Orchestra, 1991-96; Music Director, Deutsche Oper, Berlin, 1992-97; Conducted Carmen at Genoa, 1992; Don Carlos in Berlin; Chief Conductor, Rundfunk Sinfonieorchester Berlin, Germany, 1994; Led new production of Faust at Zurich, 1997; Der fliegende Holländer in Berlin. Recordings include: Falla El amor brujo; La vida breve, Nights in the Gardens of Spain and L'Atlantida; Mozart Requiem and Schumann 3rd Symphony; Mendelssohn Elijah and St Paul; Orff, Carmina Burana, Le Sacre du Printemps, Prokofiev Violin Concertos, Mendelssohn Violin Concerto; Beethoven's Symphonies and the complete works of Falla, with ballets by Stravinsky and Bartók with the LSO, for Collins Classics. Honours: Gran Cruz de la Orden del Mérito Civil Orden de Alfonso X, El Sahio, 1966; Orden de Isabel la Catolica, 1966; Member, Real Academia de Bellas Artes de San Fernando, Madrid, 1975-; Doctor Honoris Causa, University of Navarra, 1994; Grossen Silbernen Ehrenzeichen, Austria, 1996; Jacinto-Guerrero Prize, Spain, 1996; Gold Medal to Civil Merit of Austrian Republic, Vienna, 1996; Gold Medal, International Gustav Mahler Society, Vienna, 1996. Hobbies: Reading; Swimming. Current Management: Vitoria, Madrid. Address: Boulevard d Italie 44, Monte Carlo, Monaco.

FRUSONO Maurizio, b. 22 Sept 1945, Rome, Italy. Singer (Tenor). Education: Studied in Rome. Career: Sang at Siena from 1971, Florence from 1973 (as Andrei in Khovanshchina); Appeared at the Piccola Scala, 1974, Schwetzingen Festival, 1976, in Paer's Leonora; Florence, 1975, as Lensky; US debut at the Spoleto Festival, Charleston, 1978; Sang with the Welsh National Opera, 1980, 1982, Radames at Buenos Aires and Verona, 1983-84; Appearances at Livorno, 1990, as Nanni in La Lupa by Marco Tutino, and as Manrico at the Teatro Colon, Buenos Aires, 1991; Has also sung at the Paris Opera, Pittsburgh, Toronto, Zurich, Bologna, Strasbourg, Macerata and Parma; Other roles include the Duke of Mantua, Alfredo, Pollione (Norma), Licinio in La Vestale, the Rodolfo of Puccini and Leoncavallo, Pinkerton, Cavaradossi, Gregor in The Makropoulos Case and Tom Rakewell; Sang Mascagni's Guglielmo Ratcliff at Livorno, 1996. Address: c/o Teatro Colon, Cerrito 618, 1010 Buenos Aires, Argentina.

FRYKBERG Susan, b. 10 Oct 1954, Hastings, New Zealand. Composer. Education: Studied at the University of Canterbury. Career: Teacher in Vancouver and at the University of Auckland. Compositions include: Electro-acoustic music theatre pieces: Saxarba, 1985, Caroline Herschel Is Minding The Heavens, 1988, Woman And House, 1990, Mother Too, 1991, and Diaries for Low Voice and Tape, 1993. Address: c/o New Zealand Music Centre, PO Box 10042, Level 13, Brandon Street, Wellington, New Zealand.

FU Haijing, b. 1960, China. Singer (Baritone). Education: Studied in London and New York. Career: Concert engagements include Mozart's Requiem with the Montreal Symphony Orchestra, Zemlinsky's Lyric Symphony, Beethoven's Ninth, Carmina Burana with the Pacific Symphony and the Cleveland Orchestra, Verdi's Requiem in Geneva; Mendelssohn's Erste Walpurgisnacht with the Boston Symphony and Mozart's C minor Mass with the Cincinnati Orchestra; Metropolitan Opera debut 1990, as Germont, followed by Sir Richard Forth in I Puritani; Renato with Atlanta Opera, Enrico and Verdi's Miller at Philadelphia and Filippo in Bellini's Bianca e Fernando at Catania, Italy, 1992; Appearances as Rigoletto with the San Diego and Edmonton Opera companies; Other roles include Marcello in La Bohème, and Posa in Don Carlos; Sang Germont at Philadelphia, 1992. Honours include: Second Prize, Benson and Hedges Gold Award International Competition, London, 1987; Winner, Metropolitan Opera National Council Competition, 1988. Address: IMG Artists, Media House, 3 Burlington, London W4 2TH, England.

FUCHS Barbara, b. 1959, Zurich, Switzerland. Singer (Soprano). Education: Studied at Frankfurt and Zurich, with masterclasses by Erik Werba, Sena Jurinac and Elisabeth Schwarzkopf. Career: Sang at the Ulm Opera, 1983-85, as Blondchen, Adele, Olympia, Rosina and Susanna; Gelsenkirchen, 1985-87, as Sophie, the Queen of Night and Annina in Eine Nacht in Venedig; Frankfurt from 1990, as Zerbinetta, Helena in Reimann's Troades and other coloratura roles; Guest appearances throughout Germany and frequent concert engagements. Address: c/o Theater der Stadt Frankfurt, Untermainanlage 11, W-6000 Frankfurt-am-Main, Germany.

FUGELLE Jacquelyn, b. London, England. Soprano Singer. m. George Johnston, 1975, 1 d. Education: Studied at Guildhall School of Music; Vienna Academy and in Rome. Debut: Wigmore Hall, London, 1975. Career: Extensive repertoire in oratorio, recital and opera; Appearances in England, Canada and Europe; Television and radio appearances in the Netherlands, Sweden and for the BBC; Debut at Royal Opera House, Covent Garden, 1991 as Arbate in Mozart's Mitridate; Other roles at Royal Opera House include Falcon, in Die Frau ohne Schatten; Debut with Scottish Opera, 1993; Major oratorio performances include Elijah with LPO, conducted by Kurt Masur; Broadcasts include Messiah in Norway, Mendelssohn's 2nd Symphony in Paris and B Minor Mass in Iceland. Recordings: Operatic Favourites with Joan Sutherland, Luciano Pavarotti; Music by Bottesini with Tomás Martin on double bass and Anthony Halstead on piano. Honours: Silver Medal, Worshipful Company of Musicians; Countess of Munster; Royal Society of Arts Scholarships; 2nd Prize, Kathleen Ferrier Competition. Memberships: ISM; Equity. Hobbies: Geology; Gardening. Address: 38 Wadham Road, Portsmouth, Hants, PO2 9EE, England.

FUJIKAWA Mayumi, b. 27 July 1946, Asahigawa City, Japan. Solo Violinist. Education: Toho Conservatoire, Tokyo; Antwerp Conservatory, Belgium; Further study with Leonid Kogan in Nice. Career: Concerts with leading orchestras in South America, Australia, Israel, Asia, Japan and Europe; American orchestras in Philadelphia, Boston, Chicago, Pittsburgh and Cleveland; Festival engagements at Aldeburgh with Previn, Edinburgh with the Concertgebouw Orchestra and Kondrashin; Other conductors include Barenboim, Dutoit, Foster, Haitink, Levine, Ormandy, Sanderling and Rattle; TV appearances playing the Mozart Concertos with the Scottish Chamber Orchestra; Promenade Concerts, London, 1991, in Mozart's Sinfonia Concertante. Recordings: Mozart Concertos with the Royal Philharmonic conducted by Walter Weller; Beethoven's Kreutzer and Franck's Sonata with Michael Roll; Tchaikovsky and Bruch Concertos with the Rotterdam Philharmonic; Sonatas by Prokofiev and Fauré. Honours: 2nd Prize, Tchaikovsky International Competition, Moscow, 1970; 1st Prize, Henri Vieuxtemps Competition, Verviers, Belgium, 1970. Hobbies include: Chamber music; Reading; Plays; Movies; Concerts; Being with friends; Drawing. Current Management: Terry Harrison Artists Management. Address: The Orchard, Market Street, Charlbury, Oxon OX7 3PJ, England.

FUJIOKA Sachio, b. 1962, Tokyo, Japan. Conductor. Education: Studied in Japan with Kenichiro Kobayshi and Akeo Watanabe; Royal Northern College of Music, 1990-. Career: Assistant Conductor of the BBC Philharmonic, 1994; Season 1995-96 as Conductor of the Japan Philharmonic and Principal Conductor of the Manchester Camerata; Season 1996-97 with Royal Philharmonic Bournemouth, Norwegian Radio, Stavanger and Singapore SOs; Royal Liverpool and Guildford Philharmonics, the Ulster Orchestra and the Orchestra National du Capitole de Toulouse. Recordings include: Album with the BBC Philharmonic, 1996. Honours include: Sir Charles Grove Conducting Fellowship, 1993. Address: c/o IMG Artists, Media House, 3 Burlington Lane, Londom W4 2TH, England.

FUKAI Hirofumi, b. 10 Feb 1942, Saitama, Japan. Violist. Education: Studied with Ivan Galamian at Juilliard, at the Toho School, Tokyo, and the Basle Conservatory. Career: Soloist with the Berne Symphony and the Hamburg Philharmonic, 1970-87; NDR Symphony from 1988; Concert performances throughout Europe, notably in the premieres of works by Zimmermann, Rihm and Henze (Compases para preguntas ensimismadas); Professor at the Hamburg Musikhochschule from 1974. Address: Hochschule für Musik, Harvesthuderweg 12, 2000 Hamburg 12, Germany.

FULGONI Sarah, b. 1970, London, England. Mezzo-Soprano. Education: Studied at the Royal Northern College of Music. Career: Has sung with the Welsh National Opera from 1994 as Prince Charming in Cendrillon and Beatrice in Beatrice and Benedict; Season 1995 as Dorabella with English National Opera, Strauss's Composer at Broomhill Opera, Celia in Haydn's Fedelta Premiata at Garsington and Hyppolita in A Midsummer Night's Dream at the Ravenna Festival; Further engagements at the Harrogate and Schleswig-Holstein Festivals, at La Scala in Elektra and in Berlin in Mahler's Third Symphony; Sang Carmen with Welsh National Opera, 1997; Other roles include Charlotte in Werther (at Tel-Aviv), Monteverdi's Penelope (Geneva) and Leonora in La Favorita (Nice). Honours include: Frederic Cox Award, Curtis Gold Medal, Runner-up in 1993 Kathleen Ferrier Awards. Address: c/o Harrison Parrott Ltd, 12 Penzance Place, London, W11 4PA, England.

FULKERSON James (Orville), b. 2 July 1945, Manville, Illinois, USA. Composer; Trombonist. Education: Studied trombone and composition at Illinois Wesleyan University, composition at the University of Illinois, MM, 1966. Career: Fellow at the Center for Creative Performing Arts, State University of New York at Buffalo, 1969-72; Residencies at the Deutscher Akademischer Austauschdienst in Berlin, 1973, and the Victorian College of the Arts, Melbourne, 1977-79; From 1981 resident at Dartington College, South Devon. Compositions include: Guitar Concerto, 1972; To See a Thing Clearly for orchestra, 1972; Co-ordinative systems nos 1-10, 1972-76; Orchestral Piece, 1974; Music for Brass Instruments nos 1-6, 1975-78; Raucasity and the Cisco Kid or, I Skate in the Sun, theatre piece, 1978; Concerto for amplified cello and chamber orchestra, 1978; Vicarious Thrills for amplified trombone and pornographic film, 1979; Symphony, 1980; Force Fields and Spaces for trombone, tape and dancers, 1981; Cheap Imitations IV for soloist, tape and films, 1982; Put Your Foot Down Charlie for 3 dancers, speaker and ensemble, 1982; Rats Tale for 6 dancers, trombone and ensemble, 1983; Mixed-media works, television and film music; Various instrumental pieces under the titles Space Music, Patterns, Metamorphosis and Chamber Musics. Address: c/o ASCAP, ASCAP Building, One Lincoln Plaza, New York, NY 10023, USA.

FULLER Albert, b. 21 July 1926, Washington DC, USA. Harpsichordist; Conductor. Education: Studied organ with Paul Callaway at the national Cathedral in Washington; Peabody Conservatory; Georgetown, Johns Hopkins and Yale Universities (Ralph Kirkpatrick and Paul Hindemith); Studied French Baroque Keyboard Music in Paris. Career: Performer on the harpsichord in New York from 1957, Europe from 1959; Repertoire includes French music and the sonatas of Scarlatti; Professor of Harpsichord at the Juilliard School from 1964; President and Artistic Director of the Aston Magna Foundation (for the study of Baroque music), 1972-83; Summer Acadmies at Great Barrington, Massachusetts; Conductor of Rameau's Dardanus and Les Sauvages (Les Indes Galantes); Handel's Acis and Galatea and Xerxes, 1978, 1985; Teacher at Yale University, 1976-79. Publications include: Edition of the harpsichord music of Gaspard Le Roux. Address: c/o Juilliard School of Music, Lincoln Plaza, NY 10023, USA.

FULLER David (Randall), b. 1 May 1927, Newton, Massachusetts, USA. Musicologist; Organist; Harpsichordist. Education: Studied at Harvard University, MA 1951, PhD 1965; Organ with E Power Biggs, William Self and André Marchal; Harpsichord with Albert Fuller. Career: Instructor, Robert College, Istanbul, 1950-53; Assistant Professor, Dartmouth College, 1954-57; Professor of Music, State University of New York, Buffalo, from 1963. Publications: Editions of keyboard works by Armand-Louis Couperin and Handel; Numerous articles in The New Grove Dictionary of Music and Musicians, 1980; The New Harvard Dictionary of Music, 1986; Early Music and others; A Catalogue of French Harpsichord Music, 1699-1780, 1990. Recordings include: Music by Armand-Louis Couperin (with William Christie). Memberships: American Musicological Society; American Guild of Organists. Address: c/o State University of New York, Buffalo, NY, USA.

FULLER Louisa, b. 1964, England. Violinist. Education: Studied at the Royal Academy of Music with Emanuel Hurwitz; Further study with David Takeno. Career: Extensive tours of Europe as Principal second Violin of the Kreisler String Orchestra, winner in 1984 of Jeunesses Musicales Competition in Belgrade; Co-founder and Leader of the Duke String Quartet, 1985-, performing throughout Britain, with tours of Germany, Italy, Austria and Baltic States and South Bank series, 1991 with Mozart's early quartets, made the soundtrack for Ingmar Bergman documentary, The Magic Lantern, for Channel 4 TV, 1988, BBC debut feature, features for French TV, 1990-91 playing Mozart, Mendelssohn, Britten and Tippett works, Brahms Clarinet Quintet for Dutch radio with Janet Hilton, Live Music Now series with concerts for disadvantaged people, The Duke Quartet invites... at the Derngate Northampton, 1991 with Duncan Prescott and Rohan O'Hora, Resident Quartet of the Rydale Festival in 1991, Residency at Trinity College, Oxford, with tours to Scotland and Northern Ireland and a concert at Elizabeth Hall in 1991, appeared on Top of the Pops and Radio 1, Number 1 album in 1993 with, Little Angels, featured on BBC Def II and in German TV documentary, String parts for Lloyd Cole, Blur, the Cranberries and Pretenders, 1994-95 and extensive work with choreographers, Bunty Mathias, Union Dance and Rosas, 1994-95. Recordings include: With Duke Quartet: Quartets by Tippett, Shostakovich and Britten, Dvorák (American) Barber Quartet and Kevin Volans Works, 1995. Honours include: Poulet Award from RAM; Top 3 Newcomers Cannes Classical Music Award, for Duke's American disc, 1994. Current Management: Scott Mitchell. Address: 81B Sarsfeld Road, London, SW12 8HT, England.

FULTON Thomas, b. 18 Sept 1949, Memphis, Tennessee, USA. Conductor. Education: Studied with Eugene Ormandy at the Curtis Institute, Philadelphia. Career: Has conducted at the Hamburg Staatsoper and the San Francisco Opera: Metropolitan Opera on tour; New York performances from 1981, including Manon Lescaut, Madama Butterfly and works by Verdi; Paris Opéra, 1979, Robert le Diable by Meyerbeer; Deutsche Oper Berlin, 1986, Macbeth; Conducted La Voix Humaine and Il Tabarro for Miami Greater Opera, 1989, Billy Budd at the Metropolitan and Nabucco at the Orange Festival, France; Don Carlos, 1990. Address: c/o Greater Miami Opera Association, 1200 Coral Way, Miami, FL 33145, USA.

FURGERI Biancamaria, b. 6 Oct 1935, Rovigo, Italy. Composer; Organist. Education: Studied in Milan, Venice and Padua. Career: Teacher at Bologna Conservatory from 1969. Compositions include: Organ Sonata, 1964; Mass for Low Voice, Chorus and Organ, 1973; Antifonie for Piano and Orchestra, 1975; Moods for Orchestra, 1983; Duplum for Violin and Piano, 1981; Cantico for Soprano, Flute and Harp, 1983; Levia for Strings, 1987; Farben for Flute, Violin and Piano, 1990; Erzählung for Violin and Strings, 1990. Honours include: Prizewinner at competitions in Mannheim in 1985, Warsaw, and Zurich in 1987. Address: c/o SIAE, Music Section, Viale della Letteratura n 30, 00144 Rome, Italy.

FURLANETTO Ferruccio, b. 16 May 1949, Sacile, Italy. Singer (Bass). Education: Studied with Campogaliani and Casagrande. Career: Sang at Vicenza in 1974 as Sparafucile in Rigoletto; Trieste, 1974, as Colline in La Bohème, with José Carreras and Katia Ricciarelli; Appearances at La Scala, Banquo, Turin, Leporello, and San Francisco as Alvise in La Gioconda; Metropolitan Opera, 1980; Salzburg Festival from 1986, as Philip II and Leporello, 1990, conducted by Riccardo Muti; San Diego and Covent Garden, 1988, as Mephistopheles and Leporello; In 1989 sang Mozart's Figaro at Geneva and Fernando in La Gazza Ladra at the Pesaro Festival; Season 1991-92 included Le nozze di Figaro in Paris, London, Salzburg and New York; Sang in Semiramide and Don Giovanni at the Metropolitan; Concert performances of Mozart's Da Ponte operas with the Chicago Symphony; Other roles include Philippe II, Don Giovanni, Leporello with Karajan, Figaro (Salzburg), Figaro, Bastille, Procida in Vespri Siciliani, Scala; Festival appearances 1996 at Salzburg (Don Giovanni) and Florence (Orestes). Recordings include: Don Alfonso in Così fan tutte, conducted by James Levine; Roles in Mozart's Da Ponte operas, conducted by Daniel Barenboim; Videos of Don Carlos, Metropolitan and Salzburg, Rigoletto, Metropolitan, Vespri Siciliani, La Scala, and Don Giovanni, Metropolitan and Salzburg; Innumerable CDs, also many films and videos. Membership: Ambassador of Honour of the United Nations. Hobbies: Golf; Porsches. Address: Musicaglotz, 11 Rue de Verrier, 75006 Paris, France.

FURRER-MÜNCH Franz, b. 2 Mar 1924, Winterthur, Switzerland. Composer. m. Cécile Brosy. Education: 1st artistic training, Zürich and Basel; Studied Flute, Piano, Harmony, Counterpoint and Composition, Basel Konservatorium; Scientific studies, ETH, Zürich; Musicology with K von Fischer and P Müller, Zürich University; Study visits: Federal Republic of Germany including Studio für elektronische Musik, Freiburg i Br, and USA including State University of New York at Stony Brook and University of Bennington, Vermont. Recordings include: Dialogue for oboe and clarinet, 1972; Timbral Variations, 1973; Images sans cadres, for voice and clarinet quartet, 1982, 1990; Souvenir mis en scène, for 2 cellos, Thomas and Patrick Demenga, 1988-89. Publications: Zur Semiotik graphischer Notation (Walter Gieseler), 1978; Instrumentation in der Musik des 20 Jahrhunderts (W Gieseler. L Lombardi and R D Weyer), 1985; Franz Furrer-Münch: Das geistige Ameublement in Eugen Gomringers Konstellation, betrachtet vom Standpunkt eines Musikers, in Deine Träume - mein Gedicht, 1989. Contributions to: Thomas Meter: Aus dem Notenbuch eines Träumers: der Komponist Franz Furrer-Münch, 1993. Honours: Composition commissions: City of Zürich, 1989; Stiftung proArte, 1989; Canton of Zürich, 1990. Memberships: Schweizerischer Tonkunstlerverein; SUISA; Musikforschende Gesellschaft der Schweiz, Zürich. Hobby: Guest recitals. Address: Hohfurristrasse 4, CH-8172 Niederglatt, Switzerland.

FÜRST Janos, b. 1935, Budapest, Hungary. Conductor. Education: Studied at the Liszt Academy, Budapest, and in Brussels. Career: Formed Irish Chamber Orchestra, 1963; London debut, 1972, with the Royal Philharmonic Orchestra; Appearances with all major London orchestras; Engagements in Finland, Sweden, Denmark, Germany, Spain, Italy and Israel; Tours of Australia and New Zealand; Chief Conductor of Orchestra of Malmö, Sweden, 1974-78; Music Director of the Aalborg Symphony Orchestra, Denmark, 1980-83; Music Director of the Opera and Philharmonic Orchestra in Marseille; Former Conductor of the Irish Radio Orchestra in Dublin; Currently Music Director of the Stadtorchester Winterthur, Switzerland; Has conducted opera in Stuttgart, Gothenburg and Copenhagen and for English National Opera and Scottish Opera; Elektra at Marseille, 1989; Creator and leader of the International Conductors' Course for the Dublin Master Classes, 1982-89; Mahler series with the RTE Orchestra, 1988-89; US debut, 1990, with the Indianapolis Symphony Orchestra. Recordings include: Salome by Peter Maxwell Davies; Numerous with Swedish companies; Mahler's Lieder eines fahrenden Gesellen and Kindertotenlieder, with the RTE Orchestra. Honours include: Premier Prix at the Brussels Conservatory; Swedish Gramophone Prize, 1980. Address: c/o EMI Classics, 30 Gloucester Place, London W1A ES, England.

FUSCO Laura de, b. 1950, Catellammare di Stabia, Italy. Concert Pianist. Education: Studied at the Conservatorium San Pietro a Maiella in Naples. Career: Many concert appearances from 1966, notably in Europe, USA, South America and Japan; Orchestras have included the Detroit Symphony, Philadelphia, Orchestra National de Paris, Budapest Philharmonic, Santa Cecilia Rome, Moscow Symphony, Residentie Den Haag and the Yomiuri Nippon Symphony; Conductors have featured Muti, Mehta, Ceccato, Chailly, Inbal, Maag, De Burgos and Fedoseyev; Marlboro Festival concerts at the invitation of the late Rudolf Serkin; Debut with the BBC Philharmonic, Feb 1991. Recordings: Several albums. Address: c/o Anglo-Swiss Management, 4-5 Primrose Mews, Sharpeshall Street, London NW1 8YW, England.

FUSSELL Charles C(lement), b. 14 Feb 1938, Winston-Salem, North Carolina, USA. Composer; Conductor; Teacher. Education: Piano with Clemens Sandresky, Winston-Salem; BM, Composition, 1960, with Thomas Canning, Wayne Barlow and Bernard Rogers; Piano with José Echaniz; Conducting with Herman Genhart, Eastman School of Music, Rochester, New York; Pupil of Boris Blacher, Berlin Hochschule für Musik, 1962; MM, Eastman School, 1964. Career: Teacher, Theory, Composition, University of Massachusetts, 1966, Founder-Director of its Group for New Music, 1974, later renamed Pro Musica Moderna; Teacher, Composition, North Carolina School of the Arts, Winston-Salem, 1976-77; Boston University, 1981; Conductor, Longy School Chamber Orchestra, Cambridge, Massachusetts, 1981-82; Artistic Director, New Music Harvet/Boston, Boston's first city-wide contemporary music festival, 1989. Compositions: Caligula, opera, 1962; Orchestral: Symphony No 1, 1963, No 2, 1964-67, No 3, Landscapes, 1978-81; 3 Processionals, 1972-73; Northern Lights, chamber orchestra, 1977-79; 4 Fairy Tales, 1980-81; 3 Portraits, chamber orchestra, 1986; Chamber: Trio, violin, cello, piano, 1962; Dance Suite, 5 players, 1963; Ballades, cello and piano, 1968, revised, 1976; Greenwood Sketches: Music for String Quartet, 1976; Free-fall, 7 players, 1988; Vocal: Saint Stephen and Herod, drama, 1964; Julian, drama, 1969-71; Voyages, soprano, tenor, women's chorus, piano, winds, recorded speaker, 1970; Eurydice, soprano and chamber ensemble, 1973-75; Resume, song cycle, soprano and 3 instruments, 1975-76; A Prophecy, chorus and piano, 1976; Song of Return, chorus and piano, 1983; Cymbeline, drama, soprano, tenor, narrator, chamber ensemble, 1984; The Gift, soprano and chorus, 1986; 5 Goethe Lieder, soprano or tenor and piano, 1987, for soprano or tenor and orchestra, 1991; A Song of Return, chorus and orchestra, 1989; Wilde, symphony No IV, baritone and orchestra; Last Trombones, 5 percussionists, 2 pianos, 6 trombones, 1990; Symphony No V, for large orchestra, 1994-95; Night Song, for piano solo, 1995; Specimen Days, a cantata, for baritonr solo, chorus and orchestra, 1993-94; Being Music (Whitman) for baritone solo and string quartet, 1993. Recordings: Goethe Lieder; Specimen Days; Being Music. Honours: Ford, Fulbright, Copland Grants and commissions. Address: ASCAP, ASCAP House, One Lincoln Plaza, New York, NY 10023, USA.

G

GABEL Gerald R, b. 5 Apr 1950, Dodge City, Kansas, USA. Composer; Theorist; Conductor; Educator. m. Jeraldine Kotani, 9 Oct 1977, 1 daughter. Education: BM, University of Northern Iowa, 1974; MA, 1977, PhD, 1984, University of California at San Diego. Career: Choral Director, University of California at San Diego, 1977-81; Director, La Jolla Civic/University Chorus, 1980-81; Assistant Professor, Music and Arts Institute, San Francisco, 1982; Instructor, San Diego Mesa College, 1983-84; Visiting Professor, Dartmouth College, 1984-87; Assistant Professor, Texas Christian University, Fort Worth, 1987-; Co-editor, ex tempore, 1983-; Composer in Residence, New Hampshire Music Festival, 1985-; Director, New Hampshire Music Festival Composers Conference, 1986-; Founder and Director, Upchurch Studio for Electro-Acoustic Music, 1989-. Compositions: Three Songs; Nocturnes for Piano; Statics for Bass Clarinet Solo; The Wicked Walk on Every Side; The Labyrinth; Saraph for Three Bassoons; Songs and Epitaphs of the Golden Sun; Flight; Fantasy for Woodwind Quintet; The Garden of Forking Paths I; The Garden of Forking Paths Ib; Cantos de Lorca; Una Bofetada para la Luna Naciente; A Dream!. Address: Department of Music, Texas Christian University, Fort Worth, TX 76129, USA.

GABOS Gábor, b. 4 Jan 1930, Budapest, Hungary. Pianist. m. Ingeborg Sandor, 20 Oct 1951, 1 son, 1 daughter. Education: Performer's Diploma, Ferenc Liszt Academy of Music, Budapest. Debut: Budapest, 1952. Career: Festival Hall, London; Musikverein, Vienna; Châtelet, Paris; Palais des Beaux-Arts, Brussels; Further appearances in Italy, USSR, Japan, Federal Republic of Germany, Sweden, Greece, Switzerland, Peru, South America and throughout Europe. Recordings: Various. Honours: Liszt Ferenc Award of Hungarian Government, 1959; Lauréat du Concours International Reine Elisabeth, Brussels, 1960; 1st Prize, International Liszt-Bartók Competition, 1961; Top Award for the Japan Record Academy, 1968; Merited Artist of the Hungarian People's Republic, 1976. Hobby: Bridge. Current Management: Interkoncert, Budapest, Hungary. Address: Nyul utca 10, 1026 Budapest, Hungary.

GABUNIA Nodar, b. 9 July 1933, Tbilisi, Georgia. Composer; Pianist; Teacher. m. Zizi Apkhazava, 21 June 1967, 2 daughters. Education: Graduated, Special Music College in Tbilisi, 1951; Graduated, Moscow State Conservatory, Pianist 1957, Composer 1962; Postgraduate Pianist, 1960. Debut: Recital at the Conservatory Concert Hall, where beside classical music, performed his compositions. Career: Appeared on the Stage as a Pianist in different cities of USSR up to late 70's; Thirty two piano sonatas of Beethoven; Apart from classical, romantic and postromantic repertoire and modern music. Compositions: Three Sonatas for piano; Three Concertos for piano and orchestra; Concerto for violin and orchestra; Three Symphonies; Two String Quartets; Sonata for piano, trumpet and percussions; Stanzas for piano and voice; Fable for three soloist vocalists, instrumental septet and narrator. Recordings: Beethoven: Sonatas: op 13 in C Minor, op 27 in C Sharp Minor, op 81a in E flat Major, op 111 in C Minor; Fifth Concerto and Orchestra; Grieg Concerto for piano and orchestra; Mozart Rondo in A Minor; J S Bach Aria and 30 variations. Publications: Of Motive Commentary of Musical Texture, 1971. Contributions to: An essay on Bela Bartók; Many articles dealing with the problems in our musical life. Current Management: Rector of Tbilisi State Conservatory. Address: State Conservatory, Griboedov str 8, Tbilisi 380008, Georgia.

GADD Stephen, b. 1964, England. Singer (Baritone). Education: St John's College, Cambridge; Royal Northern College of Music. Career: Appearances with: Scottish Opera as Colline, in La Bohème; Opera North as Le Herault, in the British stage premiere of Verdi's Jerusalem, 1991; Royal Opera Covent Garden as Angelotti, in Tosca, 1992; Purcell's Fairy Queen, in Lisbon; Die Zauberflöte in Geneva; Sang Pisander in Dallapiccola's Ulisse for the BBC, 1993; Poacher in Cunning Little Vixen for English National Opera; Rangoni in Boris Godunov at Tel Aviv; Count in The Marriage of Figaro for Scottish Opera; Ping in Turandot, 1996; Concert repertoire includes Verdi Requiem, Messiah in Singapore, Handel's Samson under Ivor Bolton, A Child of Our Time, Belshazzar's Feast and the Missa Solemnis in Seville; Recordings include: Mozart's Coronation Mass; Purcell's Dioclesian for DGG with Trevor Pinnock and the English Concert. Honours include: Kathleen Ferrier Memorial Scholarship. Address: c/o IMG Artists Europe, Media House, 3 Burlington Lane, London, W4 2TH, England.

GADDARN James, b. 12 Mar 1924, Pembrokeshire, Wales. Conductor. Education: Trinity College of Music, London. Debut: St Peter's, Eaton Square, 1951. Career: Conductor, London Orpheus Choir, 1952-; Founder and Conductor, London Orpheus Orchestra, 1960-; Conductor, Ealing Choral Society, 1968-; Music Director, Croydon Philharmonic Society, 1973-; Director, Opera Seria, 1962-67; BBC Broadcasts; Royal Albert Hall, Festival Hall, Queen Elizabeth Hall, Wigmore Hall; Professor, Trinity College of Music, 1957-92; First Conductor performances in England of Donizetti Requiem Mass and Messi di Gloria e Credo with Ealing Choral Society; Elizabeth Maconchy's Heloise and Abelard and Antonin Tucapskys Stabat Mater with Croydon Philharmonic Society; Kennedy Scott's Everyman with the BBC. Honours: Hon FTCL, 1963; GTCL; LRAM; ARCM. Memberships: Royal Philharmonic Society; Incorporated Society of Musicians; Royal Society of Musicians of Great Britain. Hobbies: Reading; Travel; Classic Cars. Address: 2 Tenby Mansions, Nottingham Street, London W1M 3RD, England.

GADDES Richard, b. 23 May 1942, Wallsend, Newcastle-upon-Tyne, England. Opera Administrator. Education: Studied at Trinity College of Music, London. Career: Founded Wigmore Hall Lunchtime Concerts, 1965; Emigrated to USA, 1969; Artistic Administrator of Santa Fe Opera, 1969-78; Founded Opera Theater of St Louis, 1975;Production of Britten's Albert Herring for WNET and BBC TV, 1978 Visited Edinburgh Festival with St Louis Company in 1983, bringing the first production of Margot-la-Rouge by Delius. Honours include: Honorary Doctor of Musical Arts, St Louis Conservatory, 1983; Honorary DFA, University of Missouri, St Louis, 1984; Honorary DA, Webster University, 1986. Memberships: Boards of Directors, William Matheus Sullivan Foundation and Opera America Inc. Address: Santa Fe Opera, PO Box 2408, Santa Fe, NM 97504-2408, USA.

GAEDE Daniel, b. 25 April 1966, Hamburg, Germany. Leader, Vienna Philharmonic Orchestra. m. Xuesu Liu, 4 August 1992. Education: Studies with Thomas Brandis, Berlin, Max Rostal, Switzerland, Josef Gingold, USA; Scholar, Studienstiftung des Deutschen Volkes & Abbado European Musicians Trust. Career: Regular Performances as Soloist and Chamber Musician in European Countries, Asia, North & South America; Soloist with Philharmonia Orchestra London, City of London Sinfonia, Vienna Philharmonic Orchestra; Leader, Vienna Philharmonic Orchestra, 1994-. Recordings: Several CD's & TV Performances. Honours: 1st Prize, German National Competition, Jugend musiziert, 1983; Prize Winner, Carl Flesh Competition, London & Artist International Competition, New York; Eduard Söring Prize, 1987; Joseph Joachim Prize, 1989. Address: Mariahilferstrasse 49-1-14, 1060 Vienna, Austria.

GAGE Irwin, b. 4 Sept 1939, Cleveland, Ohio, USA. Pianist. Education: Studied with Eugene Bossart at the University of Michigan; Yale University with Ward Davenny; Vienna Akademie with Erik Werba, Klaus Vokurka and Hilde Langer-Rühl. Career: Accompanist to leading singers, including Hermann Prey, Dietrich Fischer-Dieskau, Christa Ludwig, Gundula Janowitz, Jessye Norman, Elly Ameling, Lucia Popp, Brigitte Fassbaender, Tom Krause, Arleen Auger, Anna Reynolds, René Kollo, Peter Schreier and Edita Gruberova plus younger singers François Le Roux, Cheryl Studer, Thomas Hampson, Siegfried Lorenz and Francisco Araiza; Festival appearances at every major festival in the world; Professor at the Zurich Conservatory and master classes throughout the world; Anniversary concerts of Brahms, Ravel, Schubert and Mendelssohn, 1997. Recordings: Over 50 recordings, some of which have won prizes such as the Gramophone Award (3 times), Grand Prix du Disque, Deutsche Schallplatten Preis (5 times), Edison Prize, recording prizes from Spain, Belgium, Finland and Japan and the Ovation-MUMM Awards in USA. Address: Künster Sekretanat am Gasteig, Rosenheimer Strasse 52, 81669 Munich, Germany.

GAGNE Marc, b. 16 Dec 1939, Saint Joseph de Beauce, Quebec, Canada. Professor; Composer. m. Monique Poulin, 27 Dec 1969, 1 s, 2 d. Education: Doctor of Letters, University Laval, Quebec, 1970; 3 years at School of Music, University Laval with Jacques Hétu, José Evangélista and Roger Matton. Career: Symphonie de chants paysans created at Moncton Choralies Internationals, 1979; His Symphonie-itineraire was principal work by Quebec Symphony Orchestra at Festival marking 375th anniversary of the discovery of Canada; L'opéra Menaud was given on television in the form of a scenic Cantata, May 1992. Compositions: Les Chansons de la tourelle, in the folklore mode, 1975; Jeu a deux faces, Piano Sonata No 1; Ceremonial d'orgue pour la fete du Tres Saint-Sacrement, 1976; Deux chorals pour la temps de la Passion for Organ, 1976; Les Jeunes Filles a marier, suite for a Capella Choir on folklore themes, 1977; Short Mass, Du Peuple de Dieu, 1981; Messe "Des enfants de Dieu", 1993; Sonate du roi Renaud for Alto Saxophone and Piano, 1983; Vari-anes et moulin-ations for Solo Marimba, 1983; Symphonie-itineraire, 1983-84; Menaud, opera in 3 acts and a prologue, 1984-86; Évangéline et Gabriel, opera in 2 acts, 1987-90; Le Père Noël, la sorcière et l'enfant conte de Noël for Chamber Orchestra, Choir and Soloists, 1993. Hobbies: Walking; Physical activities generally; Reading. Address: 677 Avenue du Chateau, Sainte-Foy, Quebec G1X 3N8, Canada.

GAGNON Alain, b. 1938, Trois-Pistoles, Québec, Canada. Composer. Education: Ecole de Musique, Laval University; Graduate degree in Composition studying under Jeanne Landry, Jocelyne Binet and Roger Matton; Studied with Henri Dutilleux, Ecole Normale de Musique, Paris; Studied with Olivier Alain, Ecole César-Franck, Paris; Studied composition and orchestration with André-François Marescotti, Geneva Conservatory; Initiated into electro-acoustic music at University of Utrecht. Career: His works have been performed in France, Switzerland, Germany, Latin America and Canada and several have been recorded or published; Sat on several juries including Competition for Young Composers, 1980, with Murray Schafer, Barbara Pentland and Toru Takemitsu; Teacher, Techniques of Composition, Ecole de Musique, Laval University, 1967-; Director of Composition Programme, Laval University, 1977-. Compositions include: Works for orchestra, chamber music, string quartets and piano; Trio pour flûte, violon et violoncello; Septuor; Les oies sauvages; Prélude pour orchestra, 1969; Ballet score, 1983. Honours: Received Prix d'Europe, 1961; Association de musique actuelle de Québec honoured him by performing 3 of his works including Incandescence. 1982.

GAHL Dankwart (Arnold), b. 18 Dec 1939, Korbach, Germany. Cellist; Professor. m. Irmgard Schuster, 23 May 1964, 1 son, 1 daughter. Education: Private cello and viola da gamba instruction (with Johannes Koch/Kassell); Summer class with Casals, 1959; Entry to the Akademie für Musik und darstellende Kunst, Vienna, Oct 1959; Student of Wilfried Boettcher; Theory with Erwin Ratz; Pedagogics Diploma, 1963; Final Concert Diploma with 1st class honours. Career: Foundation member of the Vienna Soloists, 1959, touring with this formation all over the world, participating in many famous festivals, for example playing with Casals at Prades Festival; Originating from this same ensemble is the Alban Berg Quartet and the Austrian String Quartet, of which he has been a member since 1972; Quartet in residence at Mozarteum, Salzburg, 1972-, holder of the cello class, 1972-; Foundation member of the piano trio Trio Amade, Salzburg, 1979; Ordinary Professor at the Hochschule, 1984-; Concerts in the USA and several tours to the Far East; Guest classes in South Korea on many occasions; Has given classes with the Quartet at Salzburg Summer Academy, Mozarteum for many years; Invited jurist of international chamber music competitions on many occasions. Honours: Scholarship, Studienstiftung des deutschen Volkes. Membership: Vienna Symphony Orchestra. Hobbies: Books; Jogging; Mountain biking; Hiking. Address: Carl Storch-Strasse 10, Salzburg, Austria.

GÄHMLICH Wilfried, b. 14 July 1939, Halle, Germany. Singer (Tenor). Education: Studied at the Musikhochschule Freiburg and with Alfred Pfeifle in Stuttgart. Debut: Giessen, 1968, as Pedrillo in Die Entführung. Career: Sang at Wuppertal, 1973, in the premiere of Blacher's Yvonne, Prinzessen von Burgund; Appearances in Dusseldorf, Zurich, Vienna, Stuttgart, Wiesbaden and London; Salzburg, 1983, in Dantons Tod by Von Einem; Other roles include Florestan, the Drum Major in Wozzeck, Tamino, Andrea Chénier, Don José and Max in Der Freischütz; Bregenz Festival, 1987-88, in Les Contes d' Hoffmann; Sang Pedrillo in Die Entführung at the Theater an der Wien, Vienna, 1989; The Sailor in Krenek's Orpheus und Eurydike for the Austrian Radio; Salzburg Festival, 1992, as The Hunchback in Die Frau ohne Schatten. Recordings: Dantons Tod; Die Entführung; Video of Elektra conducted by Abbado (as the Young Servant). Address: c/o Staatsoper, Ringstrasse, Vienna, Austria.

GAILLARD Paul (André), b. 26 Apr 1922, Veytaux-Montreux, Switzerland. Chorus Master; Composer; Musicologist. Education: Studied at Montreux and the Lausanne Conservatory, the Winterthur School of Music and the Geneva Conservatory; Conducting with Franz von Hoesslin and violin at the Zurich Conservatory; Study with Hindemith, Willy Burkhard and Willy Schuh. Career: Played viola in various Swiss chamber orchestras; Conducted choirs in Luxembourg, Germany, Britain, Belgium, Spain and Poland; Directed the Wagner Seminar at the Bayreuth Festival, 1951-59; Professor of Musical History at the Lausanne Conservatory, 1956; Conductor of the Chor des Festspieltreffens, 1957, Musical Assistant, 1961; President of the Swiss Society of Professional Music Directors, 1962; Founded International Choir Festival at Montreux, 1964; Chorus Master at the Geneva Opera, 1969-87; Professor of Musicology at Zurich, 1973-79. Compositions include: Choral, vocal, piano and chamber music. Recordings include: Handel's Belshazzar (Collegium Academicum de Génève). Publications include: Die Formen des Troubadours-Melodien, 1945; Zeitgenössische Schweizer Musik, 1950; Adolphe Appia, 1955; Il coro nell' opera di Wagner, 1961; Les Compositeurs Suisses et l'opéra, 1974. Contributions to: Articles to Musik in Geschichte und Gegenwart.

GAJEWSKI Jaromir (Zbigniew), b. 2 Apr 1961, Pryzyce, Poland, Musician; Composer; Conductor. Education: MA, Academy of Music, Poznan. Debut: Poznan, 1986. Career: Teacher of Conducting, Composition and Harmony, 1988-; Founder of Academy Orchestra, 1991-. Compositions: Altana - Songs for voice and piano, 1986; 2 String Quartets, 1986, 1988; Penetration for symphony orchestra, 1989; From Dawn to Dusk for orchestra, 1989; To Cage, opera, 1990. Recordings: Altana - Songs; 2 String Quartets. Memberships: Polish Composers'

Society; Polish Society for Contemporary Music. Hobbies: Physics; Swimming. Address: ul Boguslawa 24/3, 79-200 Pyrzyce, Poland.

GAL Zahava, b. 29 Aug 1948, Haifa, Israel. Singer (Mezzo-soprano). Education: Piano, Rubin Academy, Jerusalem; Voice, Opera, Juilliard School with Jennie Tourel and Daniel Fero. Career: Feodor in Boris Godunov, La Scala, 1979; Salzburg Easter Festival production of Parsifal, 1980; Angelina in La Cenerentola, Netherlands Opera, Amsterdam, 1980; Feodor, Carmen, Paris Opera, 1981; Sang Carmen in Peter Brook's Carmen, Hamburg, Zurich; Rosina in Barber of Seville, Washington DC (2 seasons), Glyndebourne Festival Opera, at Santiago de Chile, Scottish Opera in Lyon, Avignon, Nantes, Dario Fo's Amsterdam production, Frankfurt Opera (2 seasons); Isolier in Le Comte d'Ory, Pesaro, Italy; Cherubino in Marriage of Figaro at Monte Carlo, Vienna Staatsoper and Santa Fe Festival; Ariodante in Nancy, Paris, Lausanne, Dejanira in Hercules, title role in Teseo, Covent Garden, Siena, Athens Summer Festival, Handel Year, 1985; Nicklausse, Rosina, Carmen with New Israeli Opera, 1988-89; Rinaldo, Paris; Elmira in Floridante with Tafel Baroque Orchestra in Toronto, San Francisco; Zerlina in Don Giovanni, Nancy; Concert repertoire includes Scheherazade, L'Enfant et les Sortilèges (Ravel), Songs of a Wayfarer, 3rd and 4th Symphonies (Mahler), Romeo and Juliet (Berlioz), Requiem, C-minor Mass (Mozart), Bruckner's Te Deum, Beethoven's 9th, Pergolesi's Stabat Mater; Has sung with Mehta and Israel Philharmonic, Barenboim and New York Philharmonic, Abbado with La Scala Orchestra and Chicago Symphony, Armin Jordan and Orchestre de la Suisse Romande, Mata with Pittsburgh and Dallas Symphonies; TV, Switzerland, Italy, France, Israel. Recordings include: Mussorgsky's choral works with Abbado; Amaltea in Moses in Egypt; L'Incoronazione di Poppea (disc, video); Duet selection; Donizetti cantata. Honours: Grand Prix, 1st Prize, Mélodie Française Concours International de Chant, Paris; Top Prize, Lieder, Munich International Competition; 1st Place, Kathleen Ferrier Young Artists Award. Current Management: Robert Lombardo. Address: c/o Robert Lombardo, 61 West 62nd Street 6F, New York, NY 10023, USA.

GAL Zoltan, b. 1960, Hungary. Violist. Education: Studied at the Franz Liszt Academy, Budapest, and with Sandor Devich, György Kurtag and András Mihaly. Career: Member of the Keller String Quartet from 1986, debut concert at Budapest, Mar 1987; Played Beethoven's Grosse Fuge and Schubert's Death and the Maiden Quartet at Interforum 87; Series of concerts in Budapest with Zoltán Kocsis and Deszo Ranki (piano) and Kalman Berkes (clarinet); Further appearances in Nuremberg, at the Chamber Music Festival La Baule and tours of Bulgaria, Austria, Switzerland, Italy (Ateforum 88, Ferrara), Belgium and Ireland; Concerts for Hungarian Radio and Television. Recordings: Albums (from 1989). Honours: 2nd Prize, Evian International String Quartet Competition, May 1988. Address: c/o Artist Management International, 12/13 Richmond Buildings, Dean Street, London W1V 5AF, England.

GALAS Diamanda, b. 29 Aug 1955, San Diego, California, USA. Vocalist; Composer. Education: BA, MA Music, University of California, San Diego. Career: Lead role in Globokar's Un Jour Comme Une Autre, Avignon Festival, 1979; Sang her solo works at Théâtre Gérard Philippe St Denis, Paris, also festivals throughout Europe; US and Central America premieres of works by Iannis Xenakis and Vinko Globokar with L'Ensemble Intercontemporaire, Musique Vivante and Brooklyn Philharmonic; Solo performances, New York Philharmonic's Horizons Festival, Pepsico Festival, Brooklyn Philharmonic's Meet the Moderns, 1982, 1983, 1984, San Francisco Symphony's New and Unusual Music, 1984, Creative Time's Arts in the Anchorage, many others; Appeared in film Positive Positive; Solo tours, Australia, Sweden, Yugoslavia, Netherlands, Italy, Spain, Bavaria, 1988; UK premiere of Masque of the Red Death, Queen Elizabeth Hall, London, 1989, then Lincoln Center, New York; Plague Mass performed, 1990, Berlin, Basel, Barcelona, Olympic Festival, Helsinki Festival, world premiere of newest section at St John the Divine Cathedral, New York, then 1991 Athens Festival; World premiere of Vena Cava, the Kitchen, New York City, 1992; Opened 1993 Serious Fun! Festival, Lincoln Center, with electroacoustic work Insekt; 1993 world tour included USA, Spain, Netherlands, Austria, Slovenia, Switzerland, Belgium, Norway; Director, Intravenal Sound Operations, New York. Compositions include: Published: Tragouthia ap to Aima Exoun Iona, 1981; The Litanies of Satan, 1981; Panoptikon, 1982; Wild Women with Steak Knives, 1982; Eyes without Blood, 1984; Free among the Dead, 1985; Deliver Me from Mine Enemies, 1986; Recorded: The Litanies of Satan, 1982; Diamanda Galas, 1984; The Divine Punishment, 1986; Saint of the Pit, 1987; You Must Be Certain Of The Devil, 1988; The Masque of the Red Death, 1985, trilogy, 1989; The Singer, 1992; Vena Cava, 1993; Film music; The Sporting Life, 1994; Schrei X, 1996; Malediction and Prayer, 1998. Honours: Research Fellow, Center for Music Experiments, 1981-82; Grants: Meet the Composer; Ford Foundation. Memberships: American Society of Composers, Authors and Publishers. Current Management: International Production Associates. Address: 584 Broadway, Suite 1008, New York, NY 10012, USA.

GALE Elizabeth, b. 8 Nov 1948, Sheffield, Yorkshire, England. Singer (Soprano). Education: Studied at the Guildhall School of Music, London, with Winifred Radford. Debut: With the English Opera Group, in Purcell's King Arthur. Career includes: Appeared in The Turn of the Screw with the EOG; Scottish Opera (Glasgow) as the Queen of Shemakha in The Golden Cockerel; Welsh National Opera (Cardiff) as Blondchen in Die Entführung; Glyndebourne, 1973-86, as Barbarina, Papagena, Susanna, Nannetta, Zerlina, Marzelline in Fidelio, Drusilla in L'Incoronazione di Poppea, Titania (A Midsummer Night's Dream, 1984) and Miss Wordsworth (Albert Herring, 1985); Covent Garden as Zerlina and as Adele in Die Fledermaus; Zurich Opera as Susanna, Ilia (Idomeneo), Ismene (Mitridate), Nannetta and Drusilla; Frankfurt, 1980, in Castor et Pollux by Rameau; Guest appearances in Amsterdam, Geneva and Cologne; Sang at San Diego, in La Voix Humaine by Poulenc, 1986, US debut; Appeared with Chelsea Opera Group at the Elizabeth Hall, 1989, as Massenet's Thais; Glyndebourne Festival, 1990, as Miss Wordsworth, repeated at Los Angeles, 1992; Sang ion Owen Wingrave at Glyndebourne, 1997; Many concert engagements, in particular in works by Handel; Guest, Opera Houses, Vienna and Paris. Recordings include: Le nozze di Figaro and Don Giovanni; Amor in Orfeo ed Euridice; Israel in Egypt; Messiah; Handel's Saul; Dido and Aeneas; Semele in Die Liebe der Danae, in a BBC recording of Strauss's opera. Address: Harrison/Parrott Ltd, 12 Penzance Place, London W11 4PA, England.

GALIMIR Felix, b. 20 May 1910, Vienna, Austria. Violinist. m. Suzanne Hirsch, 18 Feb 1945. Education: Pupil of Adolf Bak, Vienna Conservatory, Diploma, 1928; Carl Flesch, Berlin and Baden-Baden, 1929-30. Career: Founder, Galimir String Quartet, Vienna, 1929; US debut, Town Hall, New York, 1938; Founder, reconstituted Galimir String Quartet, New York, 1938; First Violinist, NBC Symphony Orchestra, New York, 1939-54; Concertmaster, Symphony of the Air, New York, 1954-56; Teacher-Performer, Marlboro (VT Festival and Music School, 1954-); Teacher, Juilliard School of Music, New York, 1962; Head, Chamber Music Department, Curtis Institute of Music, Philadelphia, 1972-; Teacher, Mannes College of Music, New York, 1977-. Recordings: Various. Honours: Grand Prix du Disque, 1937, 1938; Honorary DMus, New School of Music, Philadelphia, 1984 and Mannes College of Music, 1987. Address: 225 East 74th Street, New York, NY 10021, USA.

GALINDO Juan, b. 1947, San Sebastian, Spain. Singer (Baritone). Education: Studied at the San Sebastian Conservatory and at La Scala Milan with Giuseppe di Stefano. Debut: Barcelona, 1973, as Enrico in Lucia di Lammermoor, with Pavarotti. Career: Has sung widely in Italy as Carlos in Forza del Destino, Rigoletto, Macbeth and Iago; Guest appearances in Liège, Berne, Zurich, Graz, Copenhagen and Munich, notably as Marcel in Puccini's Il Tabarro. Address: c/o Teatro alla Scala, Via Filodrammatici 2, 20121 Milan, Italy.

GALL Hugues R, b. 1940, Honfleur, France. Opera Director. Education: Studied at the Sorbonne. Career: Worked in French Education and Cultural Ministries; Secrétaire Général de la Réunion des Théâtre Lyriques Nationaux, 1969; Deputy Director of the Paris Opéra, 1973-1980; Directeur Général of the Grand Théâtre de Genève 1980-95; Was responsible for over 100 opera productions in Geneva; Director of the Opéra National de Paris from Aug 1995. Address: Directeur Général, Opéra de la Bastille, 120 Rue de Lyon, F-75012 Paris, France.

GALL Jeffrey (Charles), b. 19 Sep 1950, Cleveland, OH, USA. Singer (Counter Tenor). m. Karen Rosenberg, 24 Jun 1978. Education: BA, Princeton University, 1968-72; MPhil, Yale University, 1972-76; Private study with Blake Stern at Yale School of Music, 1972-75, and Arthur Burrows, 1976-80. Career includes: Member, Waverly Consort, 1974-78; Debuts: Brooklyn Academy of Music in Cavalli's Erismena, Spoleto Festival, Italy, 1980, La Scala, 1981, Edinburgh Festival, 1982, San Francisco Opera, 1982, La Fenice, 1984, Teatro di San Carlo Naples, 1984, Canadian Opera, 1984, Handel Festival at Carnegie Hall, 1984, Chicago Lyric Opera, 1986, Sante Fe Opera, 1986, and Metropolitan Opera, 1988; Has sung in operas by Jommelli, Lully, Pergolesi, Cesti, Purcell, Scarlatti and Mozart; Television appearances include the title role in Handel's Giulio Cesare; Season 1992 included Britten's Oberon at Los Angeles and in Conti's Don Chisciotte at the Innsbruck Festival of Early Music; Performed Oberon in Britten's Midsummer Night's Dream with the Frankfurt Opera, Ottone in Monteverdi's Poppea for the Cologne Opera, David in Handel's Saul with the Boston Caecelia Society, 1993; Returned to Metropolitan Opera in Britten's Death in Venice in 1994; Sang Medieval Carmina Burana for Clemencic Consort, Oberon in for the New Israeli Opera and Ottone for the Dallas Opera, repeated at Amsterdam, 1996. Recordings include: Flavio conducted by René Jacobs. Honours: First Prize, Bodky Award for Performance of Early Music, 1977. Current Management: William Knight. Address: c/o William Knight, 309 Wood Street, Burlington, NJ 08016, USA.

GALLA Jan, b. 21 dec 1955, Nova Zahky, Czechoslovakia. Singer (Bass). Education: Studied at the Bratislava Conservatory. Career: Member of the National Theatre Bratislava, in the Italian and Slavonic opera repertory; Guest appearances in Rio de Janeiro (as Ramphis in Aida, 1986), the Paris Opéra and Opéra-Comique, and Opera North, Leeds; Sang Verdi's Attila with the Bratislava company at Edinburgh, 1990. Address: c/o Slovak National Theatre Opera, Gorkého 4, 815 06 Bratislava, Slovakia.

GALLAGHER Jack B, b. 27 June 1947, Forest Hills, New York, USA. Composer; Conductor; Trumpeter; Educator. m. April Lorenz, 19 Aug 1977, 1 son, 1 daughter. Education: BA, cum laude, Hofstra University, 1969; MFA, Composition, 1975, DMA, Composition, 1982, Cornell University. Debut: Carnegie Recital Hall, New York City, 1978. Career: Trumpet, National Orchestra Association, NY, 1968-70; Graduate Teaching Assistant, Cornell University, 1971-75; Professor of Composition, Music Theory and Trumpet, The College of Wooster, OH, 1977-; Associate Music Director, Wooster Symphony Orchestra, 1984-85, Music Director, 1985-86, Acting Chair, Department of Music, 1992-93. Compositions include: Orchestral: Berceuse, 1977; Diversions, 1986; Two Pieces for String Orchestra, 1990, Symphony in 1 movement: Threnody, 1991; The Persistence of Memory, (in memoriam Brian Israel), 1995; A Quiet Musicke, 1996; Symphonic Band: Mist-Covered Mountain, 1983, Proteus Rising from the Sea, 1994; A Psalm of Life, 1997; Vocal and Choral: Three Songs of Love, Joy and the Beauty of The Night, 1975, Three Wordsworth Poems, 1982, Darest Thou Now, O Soul, 1983; Chamber Music: Heritage Music for Piano, Violin, Cello and Horn, 1988, Sonatas for Cello, trumpet, and tuba; Exotic Dances for violin and piano, 1996; Piano music. Recordings: Recordings with various orchestras, ensembles and performers. Publications include: Ancient Evenings and Distant Music for Woodwind Quintet, 1995. Honours include: Fellow, Yaddo Corp, 1984; Ohio Arts Council Individual Artist Fellowships, 1992, 1996; Ohio Music Teachers Association Composer of the Year, 1996. Memberships include: Society of Composers; American Music Center; Broadcast Music Inc (BMI); Cleveland Composers Guild. Hobbies: Reading; Films; Sport. Address: Scheide Music Center, The College of Wooster, Wooster, OH 44691, USA.

GALLI Dorothea, b. 11 Nov 1951, Zurich, Switzerland. Singer (Soprano). m. Rudolf Bamert. Education: Studied with Elsa Cavelli and Elisabeth Schwarzkopf and at the Salzburg Mozarteum. Career: Sang at the Zurich Opera, 1976-78, Kaiserlautern, 1978-79, Gelsenkirchen, 1979-82; Guest appearances at the Deutsche Oper am Rhein Dusseldorf, Karlsruhe, Mannheim, Dortmund, Heidelberg and Amsterdam; Roles have included Mozart's Donna Elvira, Fiordiligi and Ramiro (La Finta Giardiniera), Leonore, Marguerite, Mimi, Tatiana, the Marschallin, Arabella, Emilia Marty and Giorgietta in Gianni Schicchi; Many Lieder recitals and performances of oratorio. Address: c/o Opernhaus Zurich, Falkenstrasse 1, CH-8008 Zurich, Switzerland.

GALLO Denise Patricia, b. 21 Apr 1948, Rockville Centre, New York, USA. Lecturer; Musicologist. m. Albert M Gallo Jr, 24 Aug 1990, 2 sons. Education: BA, Merrimack College, 1970; MA, Southern Illinois University, 1972; BA, 1984, BA, 1986, University of Maryland; MA, Antioch University, 1992; PhD, Catholic University of America, 1997. Appointments: Lecturer, Music History, Catholic University of America, Johns Hopkins University, 1995-; Visiting Faculty, Peabody Conservatory, 1996-97; Program Lecturer, The Phillips Collection, Baltimore Opera and Washington Opera, 1997-. Publications include: Giovanni Pacini's Giuditta: The Dramatic Possibilities of the Oratorio, 1997; Pacini's Carmelita and Don Diego: A Case of Recycling, 1997. Contributions to: Moldenhauer Catalogue. Honour: Lowens Award, Student Research, 1993. Memberships: American Musicological Society; College Music Society; Societa Italiana di Musicologia. Address: 8100 Ashford Blvd, Laurel, MD 20707, USA.

GALLO F Alberto, b. 17 Oct 1932, Verona, Italy. Professor of History of Music. Education includes: LLD; PhD. Publications include: Antonii Romani Opera, 1965; Mensurabilis Musicae Tractatuli, 1966; Il Codice Musicale 2216 della Biblioteca Universitaria di Bologna, 1968-70; Franchini Gafurii Extractus Parvus Musicae, 1969; Petrus Picardus Ars Motettorium Compilata Breviter, 1971; Johannes Boen Ars Musicae, 1972; La Prima Rappresentazione al Teatro Olimpico, 1973; Italian Sacred Music, 1976; Storia della Musica: Il Medioevo, 1977; Il Codice Musicale Panciatichi 26 della Biblioteca Nazionale di Firenze, 1981; Geschichte der Musiktheorie, 1984; Music of the Middle Ages, 1985; Musica e Storia tra Medio Evo e Età Moderna, 1986; Italian Sacred and Ceremonial Music, 1987; Musica nel castello Bologna, 1992; Il Codice Squarcialupi, Firenze, 1992. Contributions to: Acta Musicologica; Annales Musicologiques; Archiv für Musikwissenschaft; Die Musik in Geschichte und Gegenwart; Grove's Dictionary; Handwörterbuch der

Musikalischen Terminologie; Musica Disciplina; Quadrivium. Honours: Dent Medal, 1966; Premio Iglesias, 1992; Accademia Olimpica, 1994. Memberships: International Musicological Society; Italian Musicological Society; American Musicological Society; Gesellschaft für Musikforschung. Address: L Alberti 34, 40137 Bologna, Italy.

GALLO Lucio, b. 1958, Taranto, Italy. Singer (Bass-baritone). Education: Studied in Turin. Career: Sang Marcello to Pavarotti's Rodolfo in Peking, China; Escamillo in Turin and Leporello at the Vienna Staatsoper, 1989; Returned to Vienna as Valentin in Faust, Marcello, and Paolo in Simon Boccanegra; Further appearances at the Hamburg Staatsoper as Mozart's Count (also at Covent Garden), Dandini in Cenerentola at Bologna and Don Alvaro in Il Viaggio a Reims at Pesaro; Metropolitan Opera New York debut, 1991, as Guglielmo; Mozart's Figaro, 1992, with the Covent Garden company on tour to Japan; Sang Dallapiccola's Prigioniero at Florence, 1996; Concert repertory includes Les Béatitudes by Franck, Winterreise, and Lieder by Wolf. Recordings include: Bartolo in Il Barbiere di Siviglia (DGG). Address: c/o Staatsoper, Opernring 2, A-1010 Vienna, Austria.

GALOS Andrew (John), b. 18 Feb 1918, Hungary. Violinist; Conductor; Educator. m. Ruth Fishberg, 2 Nov 1945, 1 son. Education: City College of New York; Teachers College, Columbia University; BS, 1942; MD, 1952; MA, Music Education and Conducting, 1952; EdD, 1958; Scholarship in Violin. Juilliard School of Music; Fellowship in Conducting. Debut: Brahms Violin Concerto A, Abravanel conducting the Utah Symphony, Utah, 1956. Career: 1st Violinist, NBC Symphony under Toscanini; Assistant Concert Master, Baltimore Symphony, Maryland, 1946-48; Member of Mischakoff and Galimir String Quartets, 1950; Concert Master, Assistant Conductor, Portland Symphony, Maine, 1969-74; Savannah Symphony, Georgia; Soloist with Boston Pops, 1973, 1974; New Orleans Symphony; Columbus Symphony, Georgia; Assistant Conductor, Co-Concert Master, Fort Meyers Symphony, Florida, 1986-; Violin Professor, Peabody Conservatory of Music, Baltimore; Violin Professor, Chamber Music Professor and Director of Orchestra, Utah State University, 1956-60; University of Akron, Ohio; University of Tulsa, Oklahoma; Chairman of the Music Department, Columbus College, 1969-80; Wilkes University, 1988; Pacific University, 1990; University of Tampa. Recordings: Symphonies 1-9 by Beethoven and Brahms Symphonies 1-4, all as 1st Violinist with NBC Symphony under Toscanini. Hobbies: Swimming; Photography. Address: 4214 Golf Club Lane, Tampa, FL 33624, USA.

GALOUZINE Vladimir, b. 1961, Russia. Singer (Tenor). Education: Studied at Novosibirsk Conservatoire. Career: Sang at the Novosibirsk Opera, 1988-90, Kirov Theatre St Petersburg, 1990-; Tours with the Kirov to Spain, Italy, France and the Edinburgh Festival; Appearances as Otello in St Petersburg and as Guest in Stuttgart, Dresden, Amsterdam, Brussels and Japan; Grishko in the Kupfer production of Rimsky's Invisible City of Kitezh (Bregenz, 1995), and Sergei in the Graham Vick Production of Lady Macbeth of the Mtsensk District, at the Metropolitan, 1996; Season 1996-97 as Pinkerton at Cologne and Alexei in The Gambler by Prokofiev at La Scala; Many engagements at the Vienna Staatsoper (debut as Hermann in The Queen of Spades); Season 1997-98 with Otello at Brussels and for the New Israeli Opera, Lensky in Eugene Onegin at Buenos Aires; Other roles include Radames, Don Carlos, Calaf, Cavaradossi, Chevalier des Grieux, Andrei in Tchaikovsky's Mazeppa and Vladimir in Prince Igor. Recordings include: Title role in Rimsky's Sadko (CD and video; Philips). Address: Bureau de Concert Maurice Werner, 7 Rue Richerance, 75008 Paris, France.

GALSTIAN Juliette, b. 1970, Armenia. Singer (Soprano). Education: Graduated, Piano and Voice, Yerevan Conservatoire, 1995. Career: Appearances in Armenia as piano recitalist and concert soloist; From season 1996 engagements at leading opera houses, including Mimi in the centenary production of La Bohème at Turin; Zerlina in Don Giovanni at La Fenice, Susanna in Le Nozze di Figaro and Xenia in Boris Godunov at Turin, Flowermaiden in Parsifal at the Opéra Bastille, Paris, Valencienne in The Merry Widow at Covent Garden. Honours include: Laureate, Maria Callas Grand Prix, Athens; Winner, Viotti International Competition; Prize Winner, Jose Carreras Competition at Pamplona. Address: Athole Still Ltd, Foresters Hall, 25-27 Westow Street, London SE19 3RY, England.

GALTERIO Lou, b. 29 Nov 1942, New York City, New York, USA. Opera Director and Administrator. Education: Studied at Marquette University, Milwaukee (BA 1964). Career: Worked as an actor and theatre director; Opera productions for the Opera Theater of St Louis include Così fan tutte, Le nozze di Figaro, Albert Herring, Ariadne auf Naxos and the US premiere of Prokofiev's Maddalena, 1982; Director of opera production at the Manhattan School from 1977; Santa Fe Opera, Il Barbiere di Siviglia and Hindemith's Neues vom Tage, 1981; Kennedy Center, Washington, Argento's Postcard from Morocco, 1979; New York City Opera, 1980, La Cenerentola; Chicago Opera Theater, 1984, Don Giovanni; Staged Don Giovanni at Santa Fe, 1992. Address: Manhattan School of Music, 120 Claremont Avenue, New York, NY 10027, USA.

GALVANY Marisa, b. 19 June 1936, Paterson, New Jersey, USA. Singer (Soprano). Education: Studied with Armen Boyajian. Debut: Seattle Opera, 1968, as Tosca. Career: New York City Opera from 1972, as Elizabeth I in Maria Stuarda, Anna Bolena, Medée, Santuzza and Violette; Mexico City and San Francisco, 1972-73, Aida; New Orleans, 1974, as Rachel in La Juive; Guest appearances in Philadelphia, Warsaw, Prague, Belgrade and Rouen; Metropolitan Opera from 1979, as Norma, Ortrud, and the Kostelnicka in Jenufa; Other roles include Verdi's Hélène, Abigaille and Elvira, Turandot, Mozart's Countess, Massenet's Salomé and Tchaikovsky's Iolanta. Recordings include: Title role in Medea in Corinto by Giovanni Simone Mayr. Address: c/o Metropolitan Opera, Lincoln Center, New York, NY 10023, USA.

GALWAY James, b. 8 Dec 1939, Belfast, Northern Ireland. Flute Player. m. (1) 1965, 1 son, (2) 1972, 1 son, 2 daughters, (3) Jeanne Cinnante, 1984. Education: Royal Academy of Music; Guildhall School of Music; Conservatoire National Supérieur de Musique, Paris. Career: Wind Band, Royal Shakespeare Theatre, Stratford-upon-Avon, then Sadler's Wells Orchestra, Royal Opera House Orchestra, BBC Symphony Orchestra; Principal Flute, London Symphony, 1966; Royal Philharmonic, 1967-69; Principal Solo Flute, Berlin Philharmonic, 1969-75; International Soloist, 1975-, appearing widely in recitals, with world's leading orchestras, at chamber music engagements and popular music concerts; Plays classical and contemporary music; Premiered David Heath Concerto with Philharmonia at Royal Festival Hall and Lowell Liebermann Flute Concerto with St Louis Symphony Orchestra, 1993; Premiered, George Nicholson's Concerto and Jindrich Feld Concerto for Flute, Piano and Orchestra with Tonhalle Orchestra, Zurich, 1994; Regular visits, USA, Japan, Hong Kong; Major European festivals; Master classes. Recordings include: Wind Beneath My Wings; I Will Always Love You; Mozart Flute and Harp Concerto, with Marisa Robles; Masterpieces: The Essential Flute of James Galway; Mozart Flute Quartets with Tokyo String Quartets; James Galway at the Movies. Publications: James Galway: An autobiography, 1978; Flute, Menuhin Music Guide, 1982; James Galway's Music in Time, 1983; Masterclass, performance editions of great flute literature, 1987. Honours: OBE, 1977; Hon MA, Open University, 1979; Hon DMus: Queen's University and New England Conservatory of Music, 1980; FRCM, 1983; Officier des Arts et des Lettres, 1987; Grand Prix du Disque, 1976; Other prizes, recordings. Membership: Fellow, Birmingham Schools of Music. Hobbies: Music; Walking; Swimming; Films; Theatre; TV; Chess; Backgammon; Computing; Talking to people. Current Management: IMG Artists (Europe). Address: c/o Kathryn Enticott, IMG Artists, Media House, 3 Burlington Lane, Chiswick, London W4 2TH, England.

GAMBA Piero, b. 16 Sep 1936, Rome, Italy. Conductor. Education: Studied piano and score reading with his father. Career: Conducted Beethoven's 1st Symphony at the Rome Opera House, aged 8; Tours of Europe and North and South America whilst a child; British debut 1948, conducting Beethoven and Dvorák in London; Moved to Madrid in 1952; Guest engagements in London, 1959-63 often with the London Symphony Orchestra; Musical Director of Winnipeg Symphony Orchestra, Canada, 1970-81; Principal Conductor, Adelaide Symphony Orchestra from 1982-88. Recordings include: Rossini's Overtures with the London Symphony Orchestra; Beethoven's Piano Concertos with Julius Katchen as soloist.

GAMBARYAN Maria, b. 1 October 1925, Erevan, Armenia. Pianist. widow. Education: Graduate, Moscow Tchaikovsky Conservatoire. Debut: Moscow Tchaikovsky Conservatoire. Career: Grand hall, Moscow Conservatoire, Tchaikovsky Concert Hall, Moscow, Concert Hall of Tokyo Conservatoire, Cazals Hall, Japan, Superior le Musica Liceu de Barcelona, Spain, 1940-97. Recordings: Melodia, 1978, 1990; Several CD's. Publications: Komitai and His Piano Pieces, 1965; To The Memory of My Teacher, 1974; Professor Tgumnov and His Methods, 1996. Contributions to: Soviet Music; Musical Life; American Culture. Honours: Honourable Artist of Armenia, 1963; Doctor, 1975, Professor, 1996, Russian Academy of Music. Memberships: All-Russian Scrialin Society; International Musicians Society. Hobby: Travel. Address: Skatertnyj pereulok d 22 kv 40, 121 069 Moscow, Russia.

GAMBERINI Leopoldo, b. 12 Mar 1922, Como, Italy. Composer; Musicologist. m. Graziella Benini, 27 Dec 1961, 2 children. Education: Graduate, Conservatory of Genoa; Student of Markevich (Salzburg, Austria); Accademia Chigiana (Siena, Italy). Career includes: Founder and Conductor, I Madrigalisti, Genoa; Numerous conducting tours, Europe; Lecturer in History of Music Theory, Professor of Music History, Faculty of Arts, University of Genoa; Music Critic, Il Nuovo Cittadino. Genoa. Compositions include: Sonata for flute and harpsichord, 1974; Various piano works, symphonic suites and symphonies, chamber music. Recordings: Numerous recordings of ancient and Renaissance music. Contributions to: Various scholarly journals. Honours: Decoration, Belgian Government; Award, International Music Festival, Belgium. Memberships: Honorary Member, Royaume de la Musique; Founder, Associazione I Madrigalisti de Genova. Address: Via Trieste 8/13, Genova, Italy.

GAMBERONI Kathryn, b. 11 Jun 1955, Pennsylvania, USA. Soprano. Education: Studied at the Curtis Institute. Debut: St Louis in 1981 as Gerda in the US premiere of Fennimore and Gerda by Delius. Career: Sang with the St Louis Company at the Edinburgh Festival in 1983 as Margot la Rouge by Delius; Seattle Opera from 1985 as Adina, Despina, Adele, Juliette, Zerbinetta and Marzelline, 1991; Santa Fe in 1985 in the US premiere of The English Cat by Henze, returning in 1989 in Judith Weir's A Night At The Chinese Opera and as Satirino in La Calisto; Guest appearances in Paris, Dallas, Cologne, Chicago and Melbourne; Other roles include Mozart's Blondchen, Susanna and Papagena, and Fanny in Rossini's La Cambiale di Matrimonio; Sang Rosina in Paisiello's Il Barbiere di Siviglia for Long Beach Opera in 1989 and the title role in The Cunning Little Vixen at the New York City Opera in 1991. Address: c/o New York City Opera, Lincoln Center, New York, NY 10023, USA.

GAMBILL Robert, b. 1955, Indianapolis, IN, USA. Tenor. Education: Studied at the Hamburg Musikhochschule with Hans Kagel. Debut: Milan 1981 as Michael in the premiere of Stockhausen's Donnerstag aus Licht. Career: Sang at Frankfurt from 1981 notably in Die Gezeichneten by Schreker; Sang at Wiesbaden as Ernesto, Tamino, Don Ottavio and Nicolai's Fenton; Glyndebourne in 1982-85 as Almaviva in Il Barbiere di Siviglia and Don Ramiro in La Cenerentola, La Scala Milan in 1982, Teatro La Fenice, Venice as Ferrando in Cosi fan tutte in 1983; Sang David in Die Meistersinger at the renovated Zurich Opera in 1984; Geneva and Aix-en-Provence in 1984 as Rossini's Lindoro and Almaviva; Season 1987-88 as Belmonte at Buenos Aires and the Steersman in Fliegende Holländer at La Scala, also at the Metropolitan in 1989; Schwetzingen Festival in 1987 as Rossini's Almaviva, Theater au der Wien Vienna in 1988 in Schubert's Fierrabras, sang Almaviva at Munich in 1990 and Wagner's David at Covent Garden; Other roles include Mozart's Ferrando, Renaud in Armide, Verdi's Fenton and Iopas in Les Troyens; Sang in Rossini double bill at Cologne and Schwetzingen in 1992; Sang Offenbach's Barbe-bleue at Stuttgart, 1996. Recordings include: Rossini's Stabat Mater; Evander in Gluck's Orfeo ed Euridice; Tenor Solo in Messiah. Address: c/o Staatstheater Stuttgart, Oberer Schlossgarten 6, D-7000 Stuttgart 1, Germany.

GAMMON Philip (Greenway), b. 17 May 1940, Chippenham, Wiltshire, England. Pianist; Conductor. m. Floretta Volovini, 1963, 2 sons. Education: Royal Academy of Music, 1956-61; Pupil of Harold Craxton; Badische Musikhochschule, 1961-64; Pupil of Yvonne Loriod. Career: Joined Royal Ballet, Covent Garden, 1964; Ballet for All Principal Pianist, 1968-71; Teaching appointments at Watford School of Music and Trinity College; Returned to Royal Ballet, 1972; Solo Pianist for many ballets including Elite Syncopations, A Month in the Country and Return to the Strange Land; Conducting debut with Ballet for All at Richmond Theatre, 1970; At Covent Garden, 1978, Sleeping Beauty; Radio 3 broadcasts in recitals as soloist and accompanist; Debut Festival Hall and Barbican Hall in 1984 as Piano Soloist. Recordings: Elite Syncopations, with musicians from the Covent Garden Orchestra; A Month in the Country, Chopin/Lanchbery. Publications: First orchestral arrangement of La Chatte Metamorphosée en femme, premiered in 1985 at the Royal Opera House. Honours: Recital Diploma, 1960; MacFarren Gold Medal, 1961; Karlsruhe Culture Prize, 1962; Badische Musikhochschule Diplom, 1963; ARCM (Performers), 1969; ARAM, 1991. Hobbies: Walking; Yoga; Reading. Address: 19 Downes Avenue, Pinner, Middlesex HA5 5AQ, England.

GANTER Martin, b. 15 May 1965, Feiburg, Germany. Singer (Baritone). Education: Studied in Berlin, Germany. Debut: Mozart's Count at Coblenz, 1989. Career: Sang in the premiere of Henze's Das verratene Meer, Berlin, 1990; Appearances at the Bavarian State Opera, Munich from 1991, as Ned Keene in Peter Grimes, Schaunard (La Bohème), Papageno, Silvio and Malatesta; Guglielmo (Cosí fan tutte) in Basle, Barcelona and Dresden (1997); Don Giovanni at Hof and Rossini's Figaro at Baden-Baden (1985), Dandini in La Cenerentola at the Dresden Staatsoper, 1996. Honours include: Winner, VDMK Competition, Berlin, 1988. Address: c/o Haydn Rawstron Ltd, 38 Station Road, London SE20 7BQ, England.

GANZAROLLI Wladimiro, b. 9 Jan 1932, Venice, Italy. Bass Singer. Education: Studied at the Bendetto Marcello Conservatory in Venice. Debut: Teatro Nuovo in Milan in 1958 as Mephistopheles in Faust. Career: Sang at La Scala Milan from 1959, notably as Falstaff and as Bottom in the local premiere of Britten's A Midsummer Night's Dream, Spoleto in 1959 in a revival of Il Duca d'Alba by Donizetti, Monte Carlo in 1960, Vienna Staatsoper from 1964, Teatro Colón Buenos Aires in 1966 as Leporello in Don Giovanni and as a guest in the USA, notably in San Francisco, Chicago, Dallas and at the Metropolitan Opera in 1968. Recordings: Le nozze di Figaro; Così fan tutte; Don Giovanni, conducted by Colin Davis; La Vera Costanza by Haydn under Antal Dorati; Un Giorno di Regno and Stiffelio by Verdi; Les Huguenots by Meyerbeer; Luisa Miller. Address: c/o Teatra alla Scala, Via Filodrammatici 2, Milan, Italy.

GARAVANTA Ottavio, b. 26 Jan 1934, Genoa, Italy. Tenor. Education: Studied with Rosetta Noli and Vladimiro Badiali. Debut: Milan in 1954 as Don Ottavio. Career: Sang major roles in Italy at La Scala and in Rome, Florence and Verona; Guest engagements in Vienna, Buenos Aires, Berlin, Marseilles, Brussels, Chicago, San Francisco, Lisbon and Belgrade; Glyndebourne Festival in 1967 as Rodolfo in La Bohème; Has often appeared in revivals of neglected Italian operas; Sang at Théâtre de la Monnaie, Brussels in 1980 in Donizetti's Il Duca d'Alba, Genoa in 1985 as Cadmo in Donizetti's Il Diluvio Universale and sang Carlo in a concert performance of Verdi's Giovanna d'Arco with Margaret Price at Festival Hall in London, 1989; Sang at Teatro Regio Turin in 1990 as Radames. Recordings: Scenes from Rossini's Otello with Virginia Zeani; Mosè in Egitto by Rossini; Admeti in Dejanice by Catalani. Honours: Winner of the Verdi Competition at Bussetto and competitions at Genoa and Modena. Address: c/o Teatro di Torino, Piazza Castello 215, I-10124 Turin, Italy.

GARAZZI Peyo, b. 31 Mar 1937, St Jean Pied de Port, Basses Pyrenees, France. Tenor. Education: Studied in Bordeaux and Paris. Career: Sang first at the Théâtre de la Monnaie in Brussels; Sang at Royal Opera Ghent in 1962 as Nadir in Les Pêcheurs de Perles, Paris, 1977 in Gwendoline by Chabrier and guest appearances in Bordeaux, Munich and Berlin; Covent Garden Opera in 1983 as Don Carlos in a French language revival of Verdi's opera; Other roles include Florestan, Aron in Moses und Aron by Schoenberg and parts in operas by Delibes, Donizetti, Offenbach and Puccini. Recordings include: Don Quichotte by Massenet.

GARBATO Maria Luisa, b. 1952, Sardinia, Italy. Singer (Soprano). Career: Won the 1975 singing competition at Spoleto and sang at the Teatro Nuovo there from the same year; Has appeared throughout Italy as Mimi, Violetta and Lucia di Lammermoor; Madrid, 1981, in L'Arbore di Diana by Martin y Soler; Opéra du Rhin Strasbourg, 1987, as Nedda in Pagliacci; Further engagements at the Teatro del Giglio at Lucca. Recordings include: Catalani's Dejanice and Loreley (Bongiovanni). Address: c/o Opéra du Rhin, 19 Place Broglie, F-67008 Strasbourg, France.

GARCIA José, b. 1959, USA. Singer (Bass). Career: Sang with the Wolf Trap Opera Company, 1986, Sarastro with the Pennsylvania Company, 1987, and Masetto and the Commendatore in a production of Don Giovanni in New York by Peter Sellars; Sang the Grand Inquisitor at Bologna, 1988, Polidore in Rossini's Zelmira at Venice, 1988, and Frère Laurent in Roméo et Juliette at Seattle; Opera North at Leeds, 1990, in Showboat and as Roger in the British stage premiere of Verdi's Jerusalem; Glyndebourne Touring Opera, 1990, as Sarastro. Recordings include: Zelmira (Erato). Address: c/o Opera North, The Grand Theatre, 46 New Briggate, Leeds, Yorkshire LS1 6NU, England.

GARCIA BANEGAS Cristina, b. 1 Mar 1954, Montevideo, Uruguay. Organist; Professor; Choir Conductor. Education: Renee Bonnet's Conservatory; Montevideo National Conservatory of Music; Conservatoire de Geneve; Conservatoire de Rueil-Malmaison, Paris. Debut: Montevideo, 1970. Career: Organ Concerts, Buenos Aires, Sao Paulo, Mexico City, Cuzco, Lima, Morelia, Pasadena, Cleveland Museum of Arts, New York, Tokyo, Israel, St Pauls Cathedral, London, Lahti Festival, Finland, Stockholm, Frankfurt, Munich, Geneva, Paris, Vienna, Bratislavia, Madrid; Complete Bach Organ Works, Uruguay, 1985; Conductor, St Matthew Passion, Uruguay, 1995; Professor, University School of Music; Conductor, De Profundis choir. Publications: Cataloguing and Restoring South American Organs. Contributions to: Magazines and reviews, South America. Honours: 1st Prize, Conservatory, Geneva, 1981, Conservatory Rueil-Malmaison, Paris, 1982; Echevarria Organ Prize, Spain, 1981; Rolex Award for Enterprise, 1990; Fraternity Prize, B'Nai B'rith, Uruguay, 1993. Memberships: Uruguayan Society of Interpretors. Hobby: Languages. Address: Juan Paullier 1126, Montevideo 11200, Uruguay.

GARCIA Navarro Luis, b. 30 Apr 1941, Chiva, Valencia, Spain. Conductor. Education: Studied at Valencia and Madrid Conservatories and in Italy with Franco Ferrara and at Vienna Academy with Hans Swarowsky. Career includes: Founded the Spanish University Orchestra in 1963; Permanent Conductor of the Valencia Symphony, 1970-74; Musical Director of San Carlos Theatre at Lisbon, 1980-82; Principal Guest Conductor of the Radio Symphony Orchestra, Stuttgart, 1984-87, the Vienna State Opera, 1987-91, and the Tokyo Philharmonic Orchestra, 1992-; Generalmusikdirektor of the Stuttgart State Opera, 1987-91; Musical and Artistic Conductor of the Barcelona Symphony Orchestra, 1991-93; Permanent Guest Conductor at Deutsche Oper Berlin, 1992-; Appearances in most major international opera theatres including Covent Garden in La Bohème in 1979 and Tosca in 1983, La Scala Milan in Madame Butterfly in 1987 and Vienna State Opera in Falstaff, La Bohème, Tosca, La Forza del Destino and Andrea Chénier; Has also conducted many leading orchestras including the Vienna Philharmonic, London Symphony and Philharmonia, Leningrad Philharmonic, Chicago Symphony, Pittsburgh Symphony, and Los Angeles Philharmonic. Recordings: Several. Honours: 1st Prize, Madrid Conservatory, 1963; Prizewinner, International Competition Besançon, 1967; Gold Medal, Paris City, 1983. Membership: Royal Academy of San Carlos, Spain. Address: Conciertos Vitoria, Amaniel 5-50-2, 28015 Madrid, Spain.

GARCIA-ASENSIO Enrique, b, 22 Aug 1937, Valencia, Spain. Conductor. Education: Master's degree, Violin, Harmony, Counterpoint, Fugue, Chamber Music, Composition, Royal Conservatory of Music, Madrid; Orchestra Conducting, Munich Higher School of Music, with Professors Lessing, Eichhorn and Mennerich; Further study, Accademia Chigiana, with Sergiu Celibidache. Career: Has conducted all leading Spanish orchestras; Music Director, Conductor: Las Palmas Philharmonic, Canary Islands, 1962-64, Valencia Municipal Orchestra, 1964-65, Spanish Radio and TV Orchestra, Madrid, 1966-84; Assistant Conductor, National Symphony Orchestra, Washington DC, season 1967-68; Currently: Principal Guest Conductor, Valencia Orchestra, Music Director, Conductor, Madrid Symphonic Municipal Band; Led orchestras in Canada, USA, Mexico, Dominican Republic, Brazil, Uruguay, Argentina, Portugal, France, Italy, England, Belgium, Russia, Japan, Northern Ireland, Israel, Netherlands, Greece, Denmark, Rumania, Puerto Rico, Czechoslovakia, Austria, Germany, Bulgaria, Switzerland, Iceland; Symphonic and operatic repertory; Assistant to Celibadache at master classes, Bologna, Munich; Professor of Conducting, Royal Conservatory of Music, Madrid, 1970-; International master classes, Netherlands, Dominican Republic; Presenter, The World of Music educational TV programme, 4 years. Recordings: Numerous including: Zarzuela, Teresa Berganza and English Chamber Orchestra, 1976; Ernesto Halffter, English Chamber Orchestra, 1991. Honours: RAI Prize, 1962; Chigian Academy Prize, 1963; 1st Prize, Gold Medal, Dimitri Mitropoulos International Competition for Conductors, 1967; Prize, Best Conductor in Madrid Opera Season, 1967; Charles Cros Academy Prize, 1976; Ministry of Culture Prize, 1991; National Music Prize, Cultura Viva, 1992. Memberships: San Carlos Royal Royal Academy of Fine Arts, Valencia; Cultural Council, Government of Valencia. Address: Gavilan 8, 28230 Las Rozas, Madrid, Spain.

GARCISANZ Isabel, b. 29 Jun 1934, Madrid, Spain. Soprano. Education: Studied with Angeles Ottein in Spain and with Erik Werba in Vienna. Debut: Vienna Volksoper in 1964 as Adèle in Le Comte Ory. Career: Sang in Paris at the Opéra and the Opéra-Comique; Guest appearances in Bordeaux, Marseille, Nancy, Nice, Cologne, Barcelona and Miami; Glyndebourne, 1966-68, 1970 as Concepcion in L'Heure Espagnole, Nerillo in L'Ormindo and Zaida in Il Turco in Italia; Toulouse, 1972-73 in the premieres of operas by Casanova and Nikiprowetsky; Strasbourg in 1974 in the premiere of Delereue's Medis et Alissio; Engagements with French Radio, Paris, in the first performances of works by Mihalovici; Was the first singer of Hahn's Sybille. Recordings: L'Ormindo; Le Mâitre de Chapelle by Paer; Le Roi Malgré Lui by Chabrier; Cantigas; Sybille; Mass by Ohana; 3 Centuries of Spanish Melodies; Spanish Songs by Rodrigo, Falla, and Garcia. Memberships: Acanthes; Union des Femmes Artists Musiciennes. Current Management: Agence Therèse Cedelle, 78 Boulevard Makesherres, 75008 Paris, France. Address: c/o Opéra du Rhin, 19 Place Broglie, F-67008 Strasbourg Cédex, France.

GARD Robert, b. 7 Mar 1927, Cornwall, England. Singer (Tenor). Education: Studied with Dino Borgoli, Walter Hyde at The Guildhall School of Music and Professor Kaiser Breme in Bayreuth. Debut: English Opera Group in Lennox Berkeley's Ruth, 1957. Career: Sang for Welsh Opera then at Aldeburgh and in Australia as Britten's Peter Quint in the Turn of The Screw, Albert Herring, Male Chorus and Aschenbach; Sang Anatol in War and Peace at the opening of the Sydney Opera House in 1973, appearing on television in this production, and Charpentier's Louise and Manon; Sang Aschenbach in a film version of Britten's Death in Venice in 1981, commissioned by the Britten Foundation; Other roles have included Aegisthus, Herod, Loge, Siegmund, Tamino, Steva in Jenufa, Peter Grimes, Tom Rakewell and Le Mesurier in the premiere of Meale's Voss, 1986; Sang Mr Upfold in Albert Herring at Sydney, 1996. Honours: Awarded the OBE in 1981. Address: c/o Australian Opera, Sydney Opera House, Sydney, NSW, Australia.

GARDELLI Lamberto, b. 8 Nov 1914, Venice, Italy. Conductor. Education: Studied at the Licio Musicale Rossini in Pesaro and in Rome. Career: Assistant to Serafin in Rome; Opera debut at Teatro Reale Rome in 1944 with La Traviata; Conducted the Royal Opera Stockholm, 1946-55; Conductor of the Danish Radio Symphony Orchestra, 1955-61; Guest appearances in Berlin and Helsinki; Music Director of Budapest Opera from 1961; US debut at Carnegie Hall, New York, in 1964 in Bellini's I Capuleti e i Montecchi, Glyndebourne, 1964 and 1968 in Macbeth and Anna Bolena, Metropolitan Opera from 1966 with Andrea Chénier, Rigoletto and Madama Butterfly, Royal Opera Covent Garden in 1969 in Otello and Royal Opera Copenhagen from 1973; Conducted La Forza del Destino at Budapest in 1990, and Rossini's Moise et Pharaon in 1992. Recordings include: Guillaume Tell by Rossini; Verdi's La Forza del Destino; Macbeth; I Lombardi; Nabucco; Respighi's La Fiamma; Belfagor; Maria Egiziaca. Address: c/o Hungarian State Opera, Nepoztarsasag utca 22, 1061 Budapest, Hungary.

GARDINER John Eliot, b. 20 Apr 1943, Fontmell Magna, Dorset, England. Conductor; Musical Director. m. Elizabeth Suzanne Wilcock, 1981, 3 daughters. Education: Bryanston School; MA History, King's College, Cambridge University; Certificate, Advanced Studies in Music, King's College, London, 1966; Study with Nadia Boulanger, Paris and Fontainebleau, 1966-68; Doctorate Honorours Causa Univerité Lumière de Lyon, 1987. Debut: Sadler's Wells Opera, Coliseum, 1969; Royal Opera House, Covent Garden, 1973; Royal Festival Hall, 1972. Career: Founded Monteverdi Choir, following performance of Monteverdi's Vespers of 1610, King's College Chapel, Cambridge, 1964; Monteverdi Orchestra, 1968, English Baroque Soloists (period instruments) 1978; Orchestre de l'Opera de Lyon, 1982; Orchestre Révolutionaire et romantique, 1990; Youngest Conductor, Henry Wood Promenade Concert, Royal Albert Hall, 1968; Guest engagements conducting major European orchestras in Paris, Brussels, Frankfurt, Dresden, Leipzig, London and in North America in Boston, Cleveland, San Francisco, Detroit, Montreal and Toronto; European music festivals in Aix-en-Provence, Aldeburgh, Bath, Berlin, Edinburgh, Flanders, City of London etc; Concert revivals, major dramatic works of Purcell, Handel, Rameau (London), culminating in world premiere (staged) of Rameau's opera, Les Boréades, Aix-en-Provence, France, 1982; Principal Conductor, CBC Vancouver Orchestra, 1980-83; Musical Director, Lyons Opera, 1983-88; Artistic Director, Göttingen Handel Festival, 1981-90; Conducted Idomeneo at the Elizabeth Hall, June 1990, followed by La Clemenza di Tito, Dido and Aeneas at Salerno Cathedral; Orfeo et Euridice at the Prom Concerts and on South Bank, 1990 and 1991; La Damnation de Faust at the Châtelet, Paris; Principal Conductor of the North German Radio Orchestra, Hamburg, 1991-94; Founded the Orchestra Révolutionnaire et Romantique, 1990; Returned to Covent Garden, 1997 (Massenet's Chérubin) and conducted Manon Lescaut at the 1997 Glyndebourne Festival. Recordings: Over 100 ranging from Monteverdi and Mozart to Massenet, Rodrigo and Central American percussion music; Les Brigands by Offenbach; Gluck's La Rencontre Imprévue, Iphigénie en Aulide and Orphée et Eurydice; La Damnation de Faust; Handel's Agrippina. Publications: Editor: Monteverdi/1'Orfeo; Gay/Beggar's Opera; Vlaude le Jeune/Helas! Mon Dieu, 1971. Contributor to: Opera Handbook, Gluck/Orfeo, 1980. Honours: French Government Scholarship, 1966-68; Awards, Grand Prix du Disque, 1978, 1979, 1982; International Critics Award, 1983; Prix Caecilia, 1982, 1983, 1984, 1985, 1986; Edison Award, 1982, 1986, 11987, 1988, 1989; Deutscher Schallplatten Preis, 1986; Gramophone Award, 1978, 1988, 1989, 1990, 1991 (Missa Solemnis); CBE, New Years Honours List, 1990. Hobbies: Forestry and organic farming. Address: Gore Farm, Ashmore, Salisbury, Wilshire, England.

GARDNER Jake, b. 14 Nov 1947, Oneonta, New York, USA. Singer (Baritone). m. Cynthia Clarey, 17 June 1978, 1 son. Education: State University of New York, Potsdam;; Syracuse University. Career: Spent first 10 years of career studying and performing with the tri-Cities Opera, Binghamton, New York; Sang Valentin in Faust at Houston, 1975; Carnegie Hall, 1976, in a concert performance of Le Cid by Massenet; Sang James Stewart in premiere of Thea Musgrave's Mary, Queen of Scots at 1977 Edinburgh Festival, and repeated the role at Norfolk, Virginia, 1978 and elsewhere; Appeared with Boston Opera in 1979 US premiere of Tippett's The Ice Break and has sung at opera houses in Washington, Detroit, San Diego, San Francisco, New Orleans and St Louis; Has sung Mozart's Guglielmo and Figaro with Netherlands Opera, Escamillo in Peter Brook's version of Carmen throughout Europe and at Lincoln Center; Wexford Festival debut 1987 as Valdeburgo in La Straniera; Has also sung the title role of Il Ritorno di Ulisse conducted by Nicholas McGegan for Long Beach Opera and in the premiere of Musgrave's Incident at Owl Creek Bridge, for BBC Radio 3; Principal baritone at Cologne Opera from 1989, as Valentin, Nardo in La Finta Giardiniera, Mozart's Count, Puccini's Lescaut and Marcello, Belcore in L'Elisir d'Amore; Concert performances of Figaro and the Glagolitic Mass, conducted by Simon Rattle; Glyndebourne Festival debut 1991, as Guglielmo; Other roles in Shostakovich The Nose for

Cologne Opera and title role in Don Giovanni for Dresden Opera, 1994; Ned Keene in Peter Grimes, Châtelet, 1995. Recordings include: El Cid, CBS; Mary, Queen of Scots. Current Management: Harold Holt Limited. Address: 31 Sinclair Road, London WC14 0NS, England.

GARDNER John (Linton), b. 2 March 1917, Manchester, England. Composer. m. Jane Margaret Mary Abercrombie, 19 February 1955, 1 son, 2 daughters. Education: BMus, Exeter College, Oxford. Career includes: Music Staff, Royal Opera House, 1946-52; Tutor, Morley College, 1952-76 (Director of Music 1965-69); Professor, Royal Academy of Music, 1956-86. Compositions: 5 operas, including The Moon & Sixpence; 3 symphonies; 3 string quartets; 3 piano sonatas, concertos for piano, trumpet, organ, oboe and flute; Brass Chamber Music; 12 major Cantatas for chorus & orchestra, including, The Ballad of the White Horse; Music for smaller groups, Much unaccompanied choral music. Recordings: A Latter-Day Athenian Speaks; Theme & Variations for Brass; Quartet for Saxes; Tomorrow Shall Be My Dancing Day; Ecossaises. Contributions to: Schumann, A Symposium; Musical Companion; Journals including Listner, Musical Times, RAM Magazine, Tempo, Dublin Review. Honours: Gold Medal, Bax Society, 1958; CBE, 1976. Memberships: Deputy Chairman, PRS, 1983-88; Chairman, 1963, Composers' Guild. Hobbies: Tesseraphily; Egrephily. Address: 20 Firswood Avenue, Epsom, Surrey KT19 0PR, England.

GARDNER Kay L, b. 8 Feb 1941, Freeport, NY, USA. Composer; Performer; Teacher of Healing Properties of Music. Divorced, 2 children. Education: MMus, State University of New York, Stony Brook; Private study with Samuel Baron and Antonia Brico; Masterclasses with Jean Pierre Rampal; Workshops with Charlotte Selver in sensory awareness; Seminars with Elizabeth Green in orchestral conducting. Career: Appearances in concert and recital in 40 US states and in Canada, Mexico, United Kingdom and the Netherlands; TV interviews on local stations in USA and regular playing of compositions on national radio series and on England, Finland, Japan, Denmark and Austrian Radio; Music used in national public TV science series, Nova, USA. Compositions: Mooncircles, 1975; Rainforest, 1978; Winter Night, Gibbous Moon, 1980; The Rising Sun, 1981; Ladies Voices, 1981; The Seasons, 1982; The Rootwomen, 1982; Golden City, 1983; A Rainbow Path, 1984; Vocalise; A River Sings, 1985; Samba For Sunwomyn; The Elusive White Roebuck; Dancing, 1988; Viritidas, 1989; North Coast Nights for String Quartet, 1990; Ouroboros - Seasons of Life, 1994. Recordings include: Women's Orchestral Works, 1981; Moods And Rituals, 1981; Fishersdaughter, 1986; Troubadour Songs, 1986; Avalon, 1989; Garden Of Ectasy, 1989; Sounding The Inner Landscape, 1990; Ocean Moon, 1991; Amazon, 1992; Ouroboros, 1994. Publication: Author, Sounding The Inner Landscape: Music As Medicine, book, 1990. Hobbies: Swimming; Hiking; Kayaking. Address: Box 33, Stonington, ME 04681, USA.

GARDOW Helrun, b. 8 Jan 1944, Eisenach, Germany. Mezzo-Soprano. Education: Studied in Berlin and Milan and with Josef Metternich in Cologne. Career: Sang at the Bonn Opera, 1969-76, and Zurich Opera, 1976-87 in various roles including Orpheus and Dorabella; Appeared in the premieres of Kelterborn's Ein Engel Kommt nach Babyon, 1977 and Der Kirschgarten in 1984; Guest appearances at Copenhagen, Dusseldorf, Edinburgh, Berlin, Dresden, Munich, Milan and Vienna; Concert engagements at Frankfurt, Madrid, Amsterdam, Cologne and Naples; Active in Seoul, Korea from 1987 as singer and director of Art-Com, in computer visual art and music. Recordings: Minerva in Il Ritorno di Ulisse; L'Incoronazione di Poppea; Dido and Aeneas; Bach Cantatas and Magnificat; Haydn's Theresia Mass; Mozart's Missa Brevis in D. Address: c/o Opernhaus Zurich, Falkenstrasse 1, CH-8008 Zurich, Switzerland.

GARETTI Helene, b. 1943, France. Soprano. Education: Studied at the Paris Conservatoire and with Regine Crespin. Career: Sang first at Nice then Paris Opéra from 1968 as Marguerite, Iphigenie en Tauride, Médée, Chrysothemis in 1987 and Desdemona in 1988; Sang Massenet's Grisélidis at Strasbourg in 1986; Appearances at the Paris Opéra-Comique as Mimi, Butterfly, Katya Kabanova and Donna Elvira in 1988; Sang Sieglinde at Rouen and elsewhere in France; Other roles have included Leonore, Ariadne and Marguerite in Damnation de Faust.

GARIBOVA Karine, b. 1965, Moscow, Russia. Violinist. Education: Studied at the Central Music School, Moscow. Career: Co-Founder, Quartet Veronique, 1989; Many concerts in the former Soviet Union and Russia, notably in the Russian Chamber Music Series and the 150th birthday celebrations for Tchaikovsky, 1990; Masterclasses at the Aldeburgh Festival, 1991; Concert tour of Britain in season 1992-93; Repertoire includes works by Beethoven, Brahms, Tchaikovsky, Bartók, Shostakovich and Schnittke. Recordings include: Schnittke's 3rd Quartet. Honours include: Winner, All-Union String Quartet Competition, St Petersburg, 1990-91; Third Place, International Shostakovich Competition at St Petersburg, 1991, both with the Quartet Veronique. Address: c/o Sonata (Quartet Veronique), 11 Northpark Street, Glasgow G20 7AA, Scotland.

GARILLI Fabrizio, b. 29 Jul 1941, Monticelli d'Ongina, Placenza, Italy. Pianist; Composer. m. Anna Paola Rossi, 8 Sep 1968, 1 son. Education: Diploma in Piano, Composition and Choral Music; Teaching qualification. Debut: Piano Soloist with orchestra, Beethoven's 3rd Concerto, Teatro Municipale, Piacenza. Career: Concerts as solo pianist with orchestra and chamber music; Conservatory Director. Compositions: Fantasie for Piano; Cantico delle Creature for Soloists, Choir and Organ; Contrappunti Su Temi Gregoriani for Organ and Orchestra; Metamorfosi for 2 Pianos and Percussion; Laude for Female Choir, Narrator and Orchestra. Recordings: Music of 17th Century Italians, Ciampi, Galuppi and Scarlatti, and JS Bach Well-Tempered Clavier, 2 records. Publications: Studi per Pianoforte; La Cartellina; Pezzi Per Cordo di Voci Bianche; Pezzi per Organo. Honours: 1st Prize, FM Neapolitano Composition Competition, Naples; 2nd Prize, Pedrollo, Milan; 1st Place, Assisi Prize; Various compositions commended in other composition competitions. Hobby: Music. Address: Via A da Sangallo 22, 29100 Piacenza, Italy.

GARINO Gerard, b. 1 June 1949, Lancon, Provence, France. Singer (Tenor). Education: Studied at the Bordeaux Conservatoire and in Italy. Debut: Bordeaux, 1977 as Rossini's Almaviva. Career: Appearances at Bordeaux as Gerald in Lakmé and in La Dame Blanche and Gounod's Mireille; Further engagements as Mozart's Ferrando at Toulouse and Nadir in Les Pêcheurs de Perles at Aix; Paris Opera and Liège 1981, in Il Matrimonio Segreto and Don Pasquale (Ernesto); Returned to Liège 1982 and 1987, as Idomeneo and in Grétry's Zemire; Portrait de Manon, Monte Carlo 1989; Season 1991, as Nadir at the Opéra-Comique, Paris, Pylades in Iphigénie en Tauride by Piccinni at Rome and Masaniello in La Muette de Portici at Marseille; Other roles include Tonio (La Fille du Regiment), Macduff, Ismaele (Nabucco) and Nicias (Thais); Traviata and Romeo and Juliette at Liège, Bohème at Toulouse, Thérèse (Massenet) at Monte Carlo, 1989; Manon (Massenet) at Bordeaux, Anna Bolena at Marseille, 1990; Werther at Festival Massenet and Festival de La Coruna, Spain, 1993. Recordings: L'Abandon d'Arianne by Milhaud; Don Sanche by Liszt; Messiaen's St François d'Assise; Il Pitor Parigino by Cimarosa; Video of Carmen (as Remendado); La Mort d'Orphée, Berlioz. Honours Include: Winner, 1973 Enrico Caruso Competition. Address: Teatro dell 'Opera, Piazza B Gigli, 00184 Rome, Italy.

GARNER Françoise, b. 17 Oct 1933, Nerac, Lot-et-Garonne, France. Soprano. Education: Studied at the Paris Conservatoire, the Accademia di Santa Cecilia, Rome and in Vienna. Debut: Paris Opéra-Comique in 1963 in the premiere of Menotti's Le Dernier Sauvage. Career: Sang in Paris as Rosina, Leila, Lakmé and Olympia; Paris Opéra as Gilda and Lucia di Lammermoor, and Aix-en-Provence Festival in 1971 as the Queen of Night in Die Zauberflöte; Sang Marguerite in Faust at La Scala Milan in 1977, and at Verona Arena as Butterfly and Gounod's Juliette, 1977-79; Many performances in France and Italy in operas by Bellini. Address: c/o Teatro alla Scala, Via Filodrammatici 2, 20121 Milan, Italy.

GARO Edouard, b. 6 July 1935, Nyon, Switzerland. Chorus Master; Composer. m. Verena Rellstab, 2 Apr 1963, 1 son, 1 daughter. Education: Arts, History, Philology, University of Lausanne; Composition, Singing, Academy of Lausanne; Studies, Pierre Mollet and Maroussia Le Mar Hadour, Geneva and Sylvia Gähwiller, Zürich. Career: Founder, Conductor, Ensemble Choral de la Côte; Music Master, Gymnase Cantonal de Nyon; Professor, Séminaire Pédagogique de l'enseignement secondaire, Lausanne. Compositions: Prospectrum, piano and tape, 1971; Les Sept contre Thèbes, 8 female voices and percussion, 1978; Incantation a 3, clarinet solo and tape, 1980; Agamemnon, opera, 1982; Le Masque blanc sur fond rouge, opera-ballet, 1984; Un Instant seul, 1989; Petra cantat, 1994; Joutes, 1996; La Grande Eclipse, 1996; String Quartet No 1, 1993-97, No 2, 1995-97, No 3, 1998. Publication: Invention for Music Teaching: SOLMIPLOT. Honours: Grand Prix UFAM, with Medal from Ville de Paris, 1972; Silver Medal, International Exhibition of Inventions and New Techniques, Geneva, 1974. Memberships: ASM; SUISA; SSA. Address: 16 rue de la Porcelaine, 1260 Nyon, Switzerland.

GARRARD Don, b. 31 July 1929, Vancouver, Canada. Bass Singer. Education: Studied at the Toronto and Vancouver Conservatories; Music Academy of the West at Santa Barbara with Lotte Lehmann. Debut: Toronto in 1952 as the Speaker in Die Zauberflöte. Career: Sang Don Giovanni for Canadian TV; Sadler's Wells Opera London from 1961 as Attila, Sarastro, Rocco, Raleigh in Gloriana, Trulove in The Rake's Progress and in the British premiere of Pizzetti's L'Assassinio nella Cattedrale in 1962; Scottish Opera in 1963 in the British premiere of Dallapiccola's Volo di Notte; Aldeburgh Festival in 1964 in the world premiere of Curlew River by Britten; Glyndebourne Festival, 1965-76 as Rochefort in Anna Bolena, Gremin, Pastor in the local premiere of Von Einem's The Visit of The Old Lady, Trulove and Arkel in Pelléas et Mélisande; Hamburg Staatsoper debut in 1968 and Covent Garden debut in 1970 as Ferrando in Il Trovatore followed by Prince Gremin in E Onegin, 1971-72; English National Opera as Sarastro; Mephisto (Faust); Rocco (Fidelio); Beckett in Murder in the Cathedral; Attila; Guardiano (Forza); Daland in Flying Dutchman; The Wanderer in Siegfried; Guest appearances in Santa Fe, Johannesburg, Toronto, Ottawa, Washington and Edinburgh; Sang the Grand Inquisitor in Don Carlos at Toronto in 1988, Daland in Der fliegende Holländer for Pacific Opera at Victoria BC, in 1989; Sang King Mark in Tristan und Isolde for Capab Opera at Cape Town in 1992; Many concert appearances. Recordings include: The Rake's Progress. Honours: 1st Prize Singing, Stars of Tomorrow and NOS Futures Etoiles, Canada, 1953, 1954; Vercelli Concours, 1961; Queen's Jubilee Medal, 1977. Address: The Villa, 18 Van Der Poll Avenue, Tokai 7945, Cape Town 8000, South Africa.

GARRETT David, b. 1981, USA. Concert Violinist. Career: Appearances with the Chamber Orchestra of Europe under Abbado and the Munich Philharmonic under Mehta; UK debut at the 1993 Brighton Festival with the Bournemouth Symphony, returned in 1994 with the London Philharmonic under Matthias Bamert and in 1995 with City of Birmingham Symphony Orchestra under Stefan Sanderling; US debut with the Los Angeles Philharmonic in 1994 under Zubin Mehta. Recordings include: Exclusively for Deutsche Grammophon, Recital and Concerto albums. Address: c/o Harold Holt Ltd, 31 Sinclair Road, London, W14 0NS, England.

GARRETT Eric, b. 1935, Yorkshire, England. Bass-Baritone. Education: Studied at the Royal College of Music in London and with Eva Turner and Tito Gobbi. Debut: Covent Garden in 1962 in La Bohème. Career: Many character roles at Covent Garden from 1962; Appearances with Scottish Opera and the Welsh National Opera, Brussels and Ghent, 1978-79 as Bartolo in Il Barbiere di Siviglia, Dulcamara in L'Elisir d'Amore and in Adriana Lecouvreur; Antwerp, 1981 as Baron Ochs in Der Rosenkavalier; Sang Mustafà in L'Italiana in Algeri at Covent Garden in 1988, Ceprano in Rigoletto in 1989, Skula in a new production of Prince Igor in 1990, followed by Don Pasquale and Alcindoro; Other roles at Covent Garden include Gianni Schnicci, Don Fernando, Sacristan, Swallow, Varlaam and Frank; Has also sung Falstaff, Melitone, Scarpia, Ochs, Kecal Schigolch in Lulu and Rocco; Guest appearances include San Francisco, Los Angeles, Marseilles, Montpellier and Munich; Flemish Deputy in Don Carlos at Covent Garden, 1996. Recordings include: La Fanciulla del West; Billy Budd. Address: Stafford Law Associates, 6 Barham Close, Weybridge, Surrey KT13 9PR, England.

GARRETT Lesley, b. 10 Apr 1955, Thorne, Doncaster, England. Soprano. Education: Studied at the Royal Academy of Music and with Joy Mammen. Career: Has sung Dorinda in Handel's Orlando, the title role in Mozart's Zaide at the Wexford Festival and Hysiphile in Cavalli's Giasone at the Buxton Festival; Further appearances with the Glyndebourne Festival and Touring Company as Zerlina and Despina, and with Opera North as Sophie in Werther; European engagements include Servilla in La Clemenza di Tito in Geneva, The Fairy Queen at Maggio Musicale, Florence and a Schoenberg cabaret song recital at the Pompidou Centre in Paris; English National Opera from 1984 as Bella in The Midsummer Marriage, Valencienne in The Merry Widow, Atalanta in Xerxes, also televised, and Yum-Yum in Jonathan Miller's production of The Mikado for Thames TV; Further appearances as Eurydice in Orpheus in The Underworld, Papagena, Zerlina, Alsi in the European premiere of Philip Glass's The Making of The Representative for Planet 8 in 1988, Oscar in a new production of A Masked Ball and Princess Ninetta in The Love For Three Oranges, 1989, Susanna at ENO in 1990, Atalanta on tour to Russia and Brazil, Papagena in a revival of The Magic Flute and sang in a concert performance of Nabucco at the Festival Hall in 1991; Season 1991-92 as Adele in Die Fledermaus, Rose in Weill's Street Scene and Zerlina at the Coliseum; Sang Euridice in a new production of Gluck's Orpheus for ENO, 1997. Recordings include: Diva and Primadonna. Honours include: Winner, Kathleen Ferrier Memorial Competition, 1979. Address: c/o Allied Artists, 42 Montpelier Street, London, SW7 1JZ, England.

GARRISON Jon, b. 11 Dec 1944, Higginsville, MO, USA. Tenor. Career: Has sung widely in North America notably at opera houses in Houston, Montreal, Santa Fe and San Diego; Metropolitan Opera from 1974 in Death in Venice, Manon Lescaut, Cosi fan Tutte as Ferrando and Die Zauberflöte as Tamino; New York City Opera from 1982 as Admete in Alceste, Don Ottavio, Rodolfo, Nadir, the Duke of Mantua, Tom Rakewell, Tamino and Nicholas in the premiere of Reise's Rasputin in 1988; Sang Prince Edmund in the premiere of Stewart Copeland's Holy Blood and Crescent Moon at Cleveland, 1989, and sang Shuratov in the US stage premiere of From The House of The Dead, in New York, 1990; Sang the title role in Oedipus Rex at the Festival Hall, London, 1997; Idomeneo at the 1996 Garsington Festival. Address: c/o New York City Opera, Lincoln Center, New York, NY 10023, USA.

GARRISON Kenneth, b. 6 Dec 1948, West Monroe, Louisiana, USA. Singer (Tenor). Education: Studied at the Salzburg Mozarteum and with Hans Hopf in Munich. Debut: Regensburg, 1977, as Mozart's Basilio. Career: Sang at Regensburg until 1980, Oldenburg, 1980-82, Karlsruhe, 1982-84 (Wagner's Mime and Steersman); Munich Staatsoper from 1984, as Luzio in Wagner's Das Liebesverbot, Dvorak's Dimitri, the Prince in Love for Three Oranges, Max and Narraboth; Guest engagements as Strauss's Emperor at Karlsruhe, Radames at Saarbrucken and Parsifal at Brunswick and Essen; Mainz, 1990, as Otello; Many concert appearances, notably in Beethoven's Ninth and Rossini's Stabat Mater. Address: c/o Bayerische Staatsoper, Max-Joseph-Platz, Pf 100148, W-8000 Munich 1, Germany.

GARWOOD (Miriam) Margaret, b. 22 Mar 1927, New Jersey, USA. Composer; Pianist; Teacher. m. Donald Chittum, 18 July 1981. Education: Private study, Piano, 1938-69; MA, Music Composition, Philadelphia Colleges of the Arts, 1975; Self-taught in Composition. Debut: Carnegie Recital Hall, 1965. Career: Teacher, Philadelphia Musical Academy and Muhlenberg College, 1953-84; Concert Pianist; Vocal Coach and Accompanist; Composer, 1965-. Compositions: Operas: The Trojan Women, 1967; The Nightingale and the Rose, 1973; Roppaccini's Daughter, 1983; Joringel and the Songflower, 1986; Other works: Aesop's Fables, short ballet, 1968; The Cliff's Edge, song cycle, 1968; Springsongs, 1969; Lovesongs, 1970; Haiku, 1978; A Joyous Lament for a Gilly Flower, 1982; Autumn Soliloquy, 1985; Six Japanese Songs, 1985; Tombsongs, chorus and orchestra, 1989; Rainsongs, chorus and orchestra, 1991; Homages, piano, violin, cello, 1992. Honours: National Education Grants, 1976, 1980, 1982; MacDowell Fellow, 1978, 1979, 1980, 1981, 1988. Hobbies: Reading; Gardening; Tropical fish. Address: 6056 N 10th Street, Philadelphia, PA 19141, USA.

GASDIA Cecilia, b. 14 Aug 1960, Verona, Italy. Soprano. Education: Studied classics and piano in Verona. Debut: Florence in 1982 as Giulietta in I Capuleti e i Montecchi by Bellini. Career: La Scala in 1982 as Anna Bolena in the opera by Donizetti; Perugia and Naples in 1982 in Demophoon by Cherubini and as Amina in La Sonnambula; Paris Opéra debut in 1983 as Anais in Moise by Rossini; Pesaro in 1984 in a revival of Il Viaggio a Reims by Rossini; US debut in Philadelphia in 1985 as Gilda in a concert performance of Rigoletto; Chicago Lyric Opera and Metropolitan Opera in 1986 as Giulietta and as Gounod's Juliette; Other roles include Violetta, Liu in Turandot, Hélène in Verdi's Jérusalem and Mrs Ford in Salieri's Falstaff; Sang Rosa in Fioravanti's Le Cantatrici Villane, Naples, 1990; Season 1991-92 as Adina at Chicago, Mimi at Bonn, Nedda at Rome, Elena in La Donna del Lago at La Scala and Rosina at the Festival of Caracalla; Pesaro Festival 1994, as Semiramide; Zurich 1997, as Gounod's Marguerite. Recordings include: Catone in Utica; Motets by Vivaldi; Il Viaggio a Reims; Video of Turandot; Rossini's Armida and Ermione. Address: c/o Teatro San Carlo, Via San Carlo 98F, I-80132 Naples, Italy.

GASPARIK Robert, b. 25 July 1961, Slovakia. Composer. Education: Conservatory of Bratislava, 1985-97; University of Musical Arts, Bratislava, 1996-. Debut: The Another Inside of Me, Symphonic Poem, Concert Hall, Conservatory of Bratislava, 1990. Career: Performances with Ensemble Societa Rigata; Festival of The New Slovak Music, 1992, 1994, 1996; Music Recordings for Czech TV, 1994; Slovak Broadcasts, 1994-97. Compositions: Memory, for Mixed Choir, 1990; Ant Hill, for String Quartet, 1993; In The Lonely House, for Accordion, 1994; Dark Blue, 1997. Memberships: Slovak Musical Union; Committee, Association of Slovak Composers. Hobbies: Eastern Philosophies; Pop Music; Sport. Address: Studenohorska 16, 841 03 Bratislava, Slovakia.

GASTEEN Lisa, b. 1957, Queensland, Australia. Soprano. Education: Studied at the Queensland Conservatorium with Margaret Nickson and in San Francisco and at the London Opera Studio. Debut: Lyric Opera of Queensland in 1985 as the High Priestess in Aida and Diana in Orpheus in The Underworld. Career: Appearances with Australian Opera as Miss Jessel in Turn of The Screw, Frasquita, Madame Lidoine in Carmelites, both Leonoras, Elsa, Donna Elvira and Leonore in Fidelio; Victorian State Opera as Elisabeth in Tannhäuser, Elisabeth de Valois and Desdemona, Leonora Trovatore, 1993; Season 1991-92 as the Trovatore and Forza Leonoras for Scottish Opera, Amelia in Un Ballo in Maschera for Welsh National Opera and Washington Opera, Donna Anna in Prague and Fidelio Leonore in Stuttgart; Concert repertoire includes Rossini's Stabat Mater and Elijah for the Sydney Philharmonia, Beethoven's Ninth in Sydney, Melbourne and Tasmania, Tokyo Philharmonic; Sang Verdi's Requiem for Hungarian Radio in 1993, Maddelena in Andrea Chénier for Deutsche Oper Berlin in 1994 and Aida for Australian Opera in 1995; Sang the Trovatore Leonora at Sydney, 1996. Honours: Winner, Metropolitan Opera, NY, Competition, Australian Regional Finals, 1982; Covent Garden Scholarship, 1984; First Australian Recipient of Metropolitan Opera Educational Fund Grant; Received Advance Australia Award, 1991; Winner, Cardiff Singer of The World Competition in 1991. Address: c/o IMG Artists, Media House, 3 Burlington Lane, Chiswick, London, W4 2TH, England.

GASZTECKI Marek, b. 1953, Poland. Singer (Bass). Debut: Poznan, 1977, as Theseus in A Midsummer Night's Dream. Career: Sang at Poznan until 1980, then with Darmstadt Opera as Don Magnifico in Cenerentola, the Water Spirit in Rusalka and many other roles; Many guest appearances elsewhere in Germany, notably at Bonn as Cecil in Donizetti's Maria Stuarda and in The Lighthouse by Maxwell Davies; Has also sung in contemporary works by Klebe and Cerha and has sung in concert in works by Bach, Handel and Haydn. Address: c/o Oper der Stadt Bonn, Am Boeselagerhof 1, Pf 2440, W-5300 Bonn, Germany.

GASZTOWT-ADAMS Helen (Catriona), b. 29 Sep 1956, Geelong, Victoria, Australia. Soprano. Education: Victorian College of The Arts, Melbourne; National Opera Studio, London, 1989; Studied with Audrey Langford and Janice Chapman. Debut: Pamina in Die Zauberflöte, State Opera of South Australia, 1983. Career: Sang in Don Giovanni, Manon, Countess Maritza, and Figaro for State Opera of South Australia, 1985-86; Debut with Australian Opera as Nanetta in 1986 then in Suor Angelica, Il Tabarro, Médée, Poppea, and Carmen; London debut, Anna Bolena at National Opera Studio Showcase, Queen Elizabeth Hall in 1989; BBC Cardiff Singer of the World finals in 1989; European concert debut, Grusse aus Wien, Robert Stolz Club, recorded for Belgian Radio and TV, 1990; Sang Gilda in Rigoletto, Australian Opera in 1990; English National Opera debut as Donna Elvira in 1991; Other appearances include Rossini's Petite Messe Solennelle, Netherlands and Belgian tour, Strauss's Vier Letzte Lieder, Koninklijk Ballet van Vlaanderen, Antwerp, Belgium, Mozart's Requiem, English String Orchestra, Bath Mozart Festival, and as Pamina in Die Zauberflöte, Victoria State Opera, Melbourne; Extensive radio and TV recital and concert work including Handel's Messiah, Mendelssohn's Elijah, A Midsummer Night's Dream, Orff's Carmina Burana, and Vier Letzte Leider; Performed with Melbourne and Sydney Symphony Orchestras, Australian Chamber Orchestra, and opera and concert performances in Britain, Barbados, Australia, France and Spain. Address: c/o English National Opera, St Martin's Lane, London WC2, England.

GATENS William John, b. 15 Sept 1950, Upland, Pennsylvania, USA. Church Musician; Writer; Critic; Broadcaster. Education: BA, Swarthmore College; MA, DPhil, Oxford University; Private Piano Study, Dorothea Persichetti; Private Organ Study, Robert Smart; American Guild of Organists Certification, FAGO, CHM. Career: Organist, Choirmaster, Church of the Good Shepherd, Rosemont, Pennsylvania; Organist, Beth David Reform Congregation, Gladwyne, Pennsylvania; Announcer, Classical Radio WFLN-FM, Philadelphia, 1986-97; Reviewer, American Record Guide, 1990-; Part-time Private Instructor, Swarthmore College; Organist; Recitalist; Accompanist. Compositions: The Lord Is My Shepherd. Publications: Victorian Cathedral Music in Theory and Practice, 1986; John Ruskin and Music, 1989. Contributions to: New Grove; New Dictionary of National Biography; Music and Letters. Memberships: American Guild of Organists. Hobby: Scottish and English Country Dancing. Address: 2622 Sandelands Street, Chester, PA 19013-4711, USA.

GATES Crawford, b. 28 Dec 1921, San Francisco, California, USA. Conductor; Composer. m. Georgia Lauper, 19 Dec 1952, 2 sons, 2 daughters. Education: BA, San Jose State College; MA, Brigham Young University; PhD, Music, Eastman School of Music, University of Rochester; Conducting studies with Eleazar de Carvalho and Hans Swarowsky. Debut: Stanford University, as composer, 1938; Utah Symphony, as conductor. Career: Chairman, Music Department, and Conductor, Symphony Orchestra and Opera, Brigham Young University, 1960-66; Artist-in-Resident, Professor, Chair of Music Department, Beloit College, Beloit, Wisconsin, 1966-89; Music Director: Beloit Janesville Symphony, 1966-; Quincy Symphony, 1969-70; Rockford Symphony Orchestra, 1970-86. Compositions include: 5 stage works, 5 symphonies, numerous choral arrangements, 4 major choral works, trumpet concertino and horn sonata; Pentameron for piano and orchestra (commissioned by Grant Johannesen); Over 100 titles published including Suite for String Orchestra. Recordings: Symphony No 2, Orchestral Setting of Beloved Mormon Hymns on Philadelphia Orchestra Album; The Lord's Prayer and A Jubilant Song; Music to the New Hill Cumorah Pageant, 1988; Promised Valley. Publications: Catalogue of published American choral works. Hobbies: Tennis; Running; Swimming; Reading; Travel. Address: 911 Park Avenue, Beloit, WI 53511, USA.

GATI Istvan, b. 1947, Budapest, Hungary. Tenor. Education: Studied at the Franz Liszt Academy, Budapest. Career: Member of the Hungarian State Opera from 1972 notably in the premieres of Csongor and Tunde by Attila Bozay in 1985 and Ecce Homo by Sandor Szokolay, 1987; Appearances at the Vienna Staatsoper from 1986; Sang Don Giovanni at Liège in 1988, Nick Shadow at the Deutsche Oper Berlin in 1989 and Antonio in Le nozze di Figaro at the 1991 Vienna Festival; Guest appearances in Italy, France, Poland, Spain, Holland and Austria and concert engagements in works by Bach, Handel, Mozart, Beethoven and Liszt. Recordings include: Cantatas by Bach, Don Sanche and The Legend of St Elisabeth by Liszt; Salieri's Falstaff; Paisiello's Barbiere di Siviglia; Don Pasquale; Simon Boccanegra; Telemann's Der Geduldige Sokrates; Balthazar and Jonas by Carissimi; Ein Deutsches Requiem; Mahler's Lieder eines Fahrenden Gesellen; Oronte in Handel's Floridante. Honours: Competition Winner at Salzburg, Vienna, Trevisto and Moscow at Tchaikovsky International in 1974. Address: c/o Hungarian State Opera, Nepoztarsasag utja 22, 1061 Budapest, Hungary.

GATTI Daniele, b. 1962, Milan, Italy. Conductor. Education: Studied at the Giuseppe Verdi Conservatory, Milan. Career includes: Conducted Verdi's Giovanna d'Arco in 1982; Concerts with the Maggio Musicale Fiorentino Orchestra, the Milan Angelicum and the Bologna Municipal Orchestra; Appearances with the regional orchestras of Italian Radio; Conducted Gianni Schicchi at the Osimo Festival in 1987, the premiere of Rabarbaro by Pedini, and Werther in Milan, Bergamo and Brescia; Season 1988-89 with Il Barbiere di Siviglia in Bari, Linda di Chamounix in Milan and Cremona; La Scala debut in 1988 with Rossini's L'Occasione fa Il Ladro; Rossini Festival Pesaro in 1989 in Bianca e Falliero; Led Bellini's I Capuleti e i Montecchi and Rigoletto at Bologna; US debut in Chicago in 1991 in Madama Butterfly; Led new production of I Puritani at Covent Garden in 1992, engaged for Toronto Symphony Orchestra in 1991 and conducted Rigoletto at Bologna in 1992; Other repertory includes Rossini's Mosè in Egitto and Verdi's Un Ballo in Maschera and Simon Boccanegra; Conducted Turandot at Covent Garden 1994, currently Guest Conductor; Concerts with the Bavarian Radio Symphony, London Philharmonic, Cleveland Orchestra, Boston and Chicago Symphonies and the Accademia Santa Cecilia, Rome; Music Director of the Royal Philharmonic Orchestra from 1995; Season 1997 with Rigoletto at Covent Garden and Strauss/Ravel concert with the RPO ast the Barbican Hall. Address: Via Scaglia Est 134, 41100 Modena, Italy.

GATTI Gabriella, b. 5 Jul 1908, Rome, Italy. Soprano. Education: Studied piano at the Accademia di Santa Cecilia in Rome. Debut: Rome in 1933 as Anna in Verdi's Nabucco. Career: Rome in 1934 in a concert performance of Monteverdi's Orfeo, Verona, 1937-38 as Elena in Mefistofele and Elisabeth in Tannhäuser, Maggio Musicale Florence, 1939-40 as Rossini's Semitamide in the premiere of Frazzi's Re Lear and in the title role of Gluck's Iphigénie en Aulide, La Scala debut in 1940 as Reiza in Oberon, and Rome in 1942 as Marie in the Italian premiere of Berg's Wozzeck with Tito Gobbi; Concert performances in London; Other roles included Abigaille in Nabucco, Mozart's Countess, Desdemona and Mathilde in Rossini's Guillaume Tell; Retired as singer in 1952 and taught at the Accademia di Santa Cecilia. Recordings include: Le nozze di Figaro and Nabucco.

GAUCI Miriam, b. 1962, Malta. Singer (Soprano). Education: Studied in Italy. Career: Made US debut as Butterfly at Santa Fe, 1987; Has sung Mimi at Santa Fe and Los Angeles, 1987-88, and Ginerva in Giordano's La cene delle beffe at the Wexford Festival; Essen, 1988, as Elisabeth de Valois and Earl's Court, 1989, Micaela; Has also appeared in Geneva (Violetta, 1989), Madrid, Lisbon and the Berlin Staatsoper; Sang in Falstaff at the Hamburg Staatsoper, 1997. Recordings include: Madama Butterfly, Manon Lescaut and Pagliacci (Naxos). Address: c/o Grand Théâtre de Genève, 11 Boulevard du Théâtre, CH-1211 Geneva, Switzerland.

GAUTIER Georges, b. 1951, France. Singer (Tenor). Education: Studied at the Paris Conservatoire and the studio of the Paris Opéra. Career: Member of the Lyon Opéra from 1976, with guest appearances in Paris and elsewhere in France; Member of the Paris Opera, 1980-83; Roles have included Tamino, Nemorino, the Painter in Lulu and the character parts in Les Contes d'Hoffmann; Sang in the 1983 Paris premiere of Messiaen's St François d'Assise; At Edinburgh, 1985, in Chabrier's L' Etoile and Aix-en-Provence, 1989, in The Love for Three Oranges; regular appearances at the Opera de Paris. Recordings: The Love for Three Oranges and Rameau's Dardanus; Les contes d'Hoffmann; L'enfant et les Sortilèges; Ravel's L'Heure espagnole. Honour: Grammy Award, 1993. Current Management: Musicaglotz. Address: 11 rue le Kernier, F-75006 Paris, France.

GAVANELLI Paolo, b. 1959, Padua, Italy. Baritone. Debut: Sang Leporello at the Teatro Donizetti, Bergamo in 1985. Career: Season 1988-89 as Mephistopheles at Barcelona and Marcello in La Bohème in Madrid; Further engagements as Marcello at Venice, Bologna and the State Operas of Munich and Vienna in 1991; Sang Luna in Trovatore at the Metropolitan in 1990 returning in Puritani and as Germont in 1992; Sang Gerard in Andrea Chénier at San Francisco and Stuttgart, Renato in Un Ballo in Maschera at Chicago and Verdi's Falstaff at the Rome

Opera; Festival appearances at Pesaro as Germano in La Scala di Seta, 1990 and the Arena Verona; Has also appeared at La Scala from 1991 and Genoa as Renato; Other roles include Rossini's Figaro and Verdi's Iago, Rigoletto and Amonasro; Festival appearances 1996 at Ravenna (as Alfio) and Rome (Gerard). Recording: Marcello in La Bohème. Address: c/o Metropolitan Opera House, Lincoln Center, New York, NY 10023, USA.

GAVAZZI Ernesto, b. 7 May 1941, Seregno, Monza, Italy. Tenor. Education: Studied at the Milan Conservatoire with Bruno Carmassi and at the Scuola della Scala with Vladimiro Badiali. Debut: Treviso in 1971 as Nemorino in L'Elisir d'Amore. Career: Many appearances in Italy and elsewhere in Europe as Elvino in La Sonnambula, Paolina in Il Matrimonio Segreto and Rossini's Almaviva, Don Ramiro, Giocondo in La Pietra del Paragone, Edward Milfort in Il Cambiale di Matrimonio, Rodolphe in Guillaume Tell and Don Eusebio in L'Occasione fa il Ladro; Has sung at Pesaro and La Scala in several Rossini revivals including Zefirio in Il Viaggio a Reims, 1984-85; Sang Goro in Madama Butterfly and Chekalinsky in The Queen of Spades at La Scala, 1990-97. Recordings include: Il Viaggio a Reims; Captain in Simon Boaccanegra; Borsa in Rigoletto; Uldino in Attila; Guillaume Tell under Riccardo Muti. Address: c/o Teatro alla Scala, Via Fildrammatici 2, I-20121 Milan, Italy.

GAVIN Julian, b. 1965, Melbourne, Victoria, Australia. Singer (Tenor). Education: Studied in Melbourne and at the National Opera Studio, London. Career: Has appeared widely in Britain and Ireland as Alfredo, Des Grieux, Nemorino, Rodolfo, Tamino, Don José and the Duke of Mantua; Further appearances in Franck's Hulda, Alvaro in La Forza del Destino, Ismaele in Nabucco, Arrigo in Verdi's Battaglia di Legnano, Pinkerton, and Laca in Jenufa (Opera North, 1995); Pollione in Norma in Lucerne, 1996; Steersman in The Flying Dutchman for the Australian Opera, 1996; Concert repertoire includes Messiah, Rossini's Stabat Mater, The Dream of Gerontius, the Verdi Requiem with David Willcocks and Mahler's 8th Symphony at the Festival Hall; Sang Beaumont in Maw's The Rising of the Moon for the BBC; Season 1996-97 as the Duke of Mantua, Alfredo and Pinkerton for ENO; Engaged as Hoffmann, 1998. Current Management: c/o Mary Craig, C&M Services Ltd. Address: 3 Kersley Street, London SW11 4PR, England.

GAVRILOV Andrei, b. 21 Sept 1955, Moscow, Russia. Pianist. Debut: Recital Festival, Salzburg, 1974. Career: Appeared with all major London Orchestras; Recitals, Queen Elizabeth Hall, Barbican, Royal Festival Hall, London; Also in Austria, Belgium, France, Germany, Holland, Spain, Switzerland, Italy, Japan, Canada, New Zealand; Festivals in Salzburg, Roque d'Antheron, Schleswig Holstein, New Zealand, 1986; Regular visits to USA include concerts with Philharmonic Orchestra, with Muti and Frühbeck de Burgos; Other conductor's include, Abbado, Haitink, Muti, Ozawa, Svetlanov and Tennstedt. Recordings include: EMI, Scriabin, Chopin; Rachmaninov, Concerto No 2 and 3, Paganini Variations; One record specially negotiated, Stravinsky, Concerto, Rite for Spring, with Vladimir Ashkenazy; Chamber recordings, Shostakovich; Violin Sonata; Gavrilov/Kremer; Britten, The Golden Vanity, Friday Afternoons, with Vienna Knabenchor, solo pieces; Romeo and Juliet, Goldberg Variations. Honours: 1st Prize, Tchaikovsky Piano Competition, 1974; Contract with EMI, 1976-90; Musical Prize, Gramophone, for Prokofiev's Piano Concerto No 1 with Simon Rattle and London Symphony Orchestra, 1978; Musical Prize, Deutscher Schallplattenpreis for Prokofiev recording, Sonata No 8, 1981; Grand Priz International du Disque de l'Acadèmie Charles Crois, for Scriabin recording, 1985; High Fidelity International Record Critics Award, for EMI Scriabin, 1985; Grand Prix International du Disque de l'Academie Charles Crois, for Rachmaninov solo recording, 1986; Siena, Premio Internationale Academie Musicale Chigiana, best pianist of the world, 1989; Man of the Year, Board of International Research, ABI, 1995; Gold Record of Achievement; World Lifetime Achievement Award. Address: Am Walberstück 7, 65520 Bad Camberg, Germany.

GAWRILOFF Saschko, b. 20 Oct 1929, Leipzig, Germany. Violinist. Education: Early studies with his father; Leipzig Conservatory, 1942-44 with Gustav Havemann and Martin Kovacz in Berlin, 1945-47. Career: Leader of the Dresden Philharmonic, 1947-48, Berlin Philharmonic, 1948-49, Berlin Radio Symphony, 1949-53, Museum Orchestra of Frankfurt am Main, 1953-57, and Hamburg Radio Symphony, 1961-66; Teacher at the Nuremberg Conservatory, 1957-61; Professor at the North-West German Music Academy, 1966-69, at the Folkwanghochschule in Essen from 1969; Currently Head of masterclasses for violin at the Cologne Musikhochscule; Appearances with leading orchestras include Germany and Britain and concerts in Vienna, Milan, Madrid, Rome, Paris, India and Japan; Conductors include Boulez in Berg Concerto, Solti, Dohnányi, Gielen and Inbal; Has given the premieres of works by Maderna, Dieter Kaufmann and Schnittke; Formed a trio with Alfons Kontarsky and Klaus Storck in 1971; Currently Member of the Robert Schumann Trio with Johannes Goritzki and David Levine; Contemporary music with Siegfried Palm and Bruno Canino. Recordings: Various. Honours: Winner, International Competitions at Berlin and Munich in 1953; Genoa Paganini Competition and City of Nuremberg Prize, 1959. Address: c/o Ingpen and Williams Ltd, 14 Kensington Court, London, W8 5DN, England.

GAY (George) Errol, b. 8 February 1941, Canada. Conductor. m. R Ann Cooper Gay, 22 April 1975, 2 daughters. Education: BMus, Univ of BC, 1962; MA, University of North Carolina, Chapel Hill; DMA, Stanford University, 1969. Debut: Canadian Opera Company, Toronto, 1972. Career: Professional Organist, 1966-95; Professional Opera Singer, 1972-86; Major Roles: Despina, Susanna, Gulda, Violetta, Anne Trulove, Mimi, Cio-Cio-San; University Teacher, 1988-96; Vocal Pedagogy, Womens Chorus, Opera Stage Director, Private Voice & Music Education; Conductor, Choral & Orchestral Ensembles; Founder, Artistic Director, High Park Girls Choir of Toronto, 1986-; Founder, Youth Orchestra of Toronto, 1994. Recording: Louis Riel - Harry Somers. Honours: 2nd Prize, Canadian Broadcasting Corporation Talent Festival, 1972; Scholarship to Study German, Institute of International Education; Distinguished Alumni Award, Austin College, Texas. Memberships: National Association of Teachers of Singing; American Choral Directors Association; Association of Canadian Orchestras; Ontario Choral Federation; Association of Canada Choral Conductors. Hobbies: Genealogy; Travel. Address: 276 MacPherson Avenue, Toronto, Ontario M4V 1A3, Canada.

GAYER Catherine, b. 11 Feb 1937, Los Angeles, CA, USA. Soprano. Education: Studied in Los Angeles. Career: Sang in the premiere of Nono's Intolleranza in 1960, at Venice in 1961, Covent Garden in 1962 as the Queen of Night, Deutsche Oper Berlin from 1963 notably as Hilde Mack in Henze's Elegie für Junge Liebende, Berg's Lulu and Marie in Zimmermann's Die Soldaten and Nausicca in the 1968 premiere of Dallapiccola's Ulisse, and Scottish Opera from 1968 as Susanna, Hilde Mack, the Queen of Shemakha in The Golden Cockerel and in the 1975 premiere of Orr's Hermiston; Sang at Schwetzingen Festival in 1971 in the premiere of Reimann's Melusine, at Edinburgh Festival in 1972 with the company of the Deutsche Oper Berlin in Die Soldaten; Sang the leading role in the premiere of Joseph Tal's Der Versuchung at Munich in 1976; Other roles include Ulisse at La Scala, Zerbinetta, Gilda and Mélisande, sang the Woman in Schoenberg's Erwartung at the Komische Opera Berlin in 1988, songs by Reimann and Szymanowski at the 1990 Aldeburgh Festival, Berlin Kammeroper in 1991 with Berio's Sequenza III, Tal's Die Hand, The Medium by Maxwell Davies and Weisgall's The Stronger; Sang at Stuttgart in 1992 as the Grand-Mother in Dinescu's Eréndira and in Rag Time, an arrangement of Joplin's Treemonisha at the 1992 Schwetzingen Festival and in 2 productions of Schoenberg's Pierrot Lunaire. Recordings: Woodbird in Siegfried; Elegie für Junge Liebende; Die Israeliten in Der Wüste by CPE Bach; Il Giardino d'Amore by Scarlatti. Honours: Winner, San Francisco Opera Auditions, 1960 and Berlin Kammersängerin in 1970. Address: c/o Deutsche Oper, Richard Wagnerstrasse 10, Berlin, Germany.

GAYFORD Christopher, b. 1963, Wilmslow, England. Conductor. Education: Studied at the Royal Coollege of Music with Christopher Adey, John Forster and Norman del Mar. Career: Repetiteur at Graz Opera, 1987; Junior Fellow in Conducting at the Royal Northern College of Music, 1988; Conducted Don Carlos and A Midsummer Night's Dream at the RNCM in 1990; Debut with the London Mozart Players at the Barbican Hall in 1990, in L'Elisir d'Amore for RNCM and Don Giovanni for Opera North; Assistant Conductor to Royal Liverpool Philharmonic Orchestra, 1992-93; Conducted Cosi fan Tutte for British Youth Opera at Sadler's Wells in 1992. Honour: Winner, 39th Besançon International Competition for Young Conductors in 1989. Address: c/o Christopher Tennant Management, Unit 2, 39 Tadema Road, London, SW10 0PY, England.

GEBHARDT Horst, b. 17 Jun 1940, Silberhausen, Germany. Tenor. Education: Studied in Weimar and Berlin. Debut: Schwerin in 1972 as Chateauneuf in Lortzing's Zar und Zimmermann. Career: Sang at Leipzig, the Staatsoper Dresden and Berlin; Member of the Leipzig Opera from 1985 including role as Erik in Fliegende Holländer in 1989, and has made guest appearances in France, Italy, Spain, England, Yugoslavia, Russia, Poland, Japan and Cuba; Other roles have included Max, Mozart's Belmonte, Ottavio, Titus, Tamino and Ferrando, Lensky, Fenton, Strauss's Narraboth and Flamand, Jacquino in Fidelio, David in Die Meistersinger, Alfredo and Sextus in Giulio Cesare. Recordings: Idomeneo; Parsifal; Palestrina; Alfonso und Estrella. Honours include: Prizewinner, International Bach Competition, Leipzig and National Opera Competition, East Germany, 1972. Address: Stadtische Theatre, 7010 Leipzig, Germany.

GEDDA Nicolai, b. 11 Jul 1925, Stockholm, Sweden. Operatic Tenor. Education: Musical Academy Stockholm. Debut: Stockholm in 1952. Career: Concert appearances in Rome, 1952, Paris, 1953 and 1955, Vienna, 1955, Aix-en-Provence and Rome, 1953, Paris, London and Vienna, 1954, Salzburg Festival, 1957-59, and Edinburgh Festival, 1958-59; With Metropolitan Opera, NY from 1957, created role of Anatol in Barber's Vanessa in 1958; Worldwide appearances in opera, concerts and recitals; First London recital in 1986 and in concert performances of Bernstein's Candide at the Barbican Hall in London, 1989; Sang Christian II in the first modern performance of Naumann's Gustaf Wasa at Stockholm in 1991; Sang in Pfitzner's Palestrina at Covent Garden, 1997. Recordings include: Les Contes d'Hoffman; Boris Godunov; Il Barbiere di Siviglia; Il Turco in Italia; I Capuleti e i Montecchi; La Damnation de Faust; Carmen; Les Pêcheurs de Perles; Faust; A Life for The Tsar; Louise; Fra Diavolo; Lady Macbeth of Mtensk; Manon; Thais; Cosi fan tutte; Die Zauberflöte; Don Giovanni; Roussel's Padmâvati; Bach's St Matthew Passion; Rossini's Petite Messe Solonnelle; La Bohème; Carmen with Callas; Werther; Der Barbier von Bagdad; Der Rosenkavalier; Capriccio; Die Fledermaus; Rigoletto; Vanessa; Benvenuto Cellini; War and Peace; Pfitzner's Palestrina; Schubert's Die Zwillingsbrüder; Weber's Abu Hassan; Der Freischütz; Gluck's Le Cadi Dupé; Die Entführung; Lortzing's Undine. Current Agent: Lies Askonas, 6 Henrietta Street, London, WC2, England. Address: Valhallavagen 110, 114 41 Stockholm, Sweden.

GEDGE Nicholas Paul Johnson, b. 12 Mar 1968, Brecon, Wales. Bass-Baritone. m. Kate Robinson, 16 Sept 1995, 1 daughter. Education: St John's College, Cambridge, 1987-90; MA, Law, University of Cambridge; Royal Academy of Music, 1990-94. Debut: Theseus in Midsummer Night's Dream, Covent Garden Festival, 1994. Career includes: Sang Leporello at Royal Academy of Music, Charon at Batignano, Narumov at Glyndebourne Festival, Dr Bartolo and Don Magnifico with English Touring Opera; Concerts with London Philharmonic Orchestra, Ulster Orchestra, CLS; Recitals, Buxton Festival and Wigmore Hall. Honour: Queen's Commendation for Excellence, Royal Academy of Music. Hobbies: Tennis; Squash; Golf; Swansea City Football Club. Address: 28 Vestry Road, London SE5 8NX, England.

GEERTENS Gerda, b. 11 Aug 1955, Wildervank, Netherlands. Composer. Education: Studied with Klaas de Vries, 1981-85. Career: Performances of works at the Concertgebouw in Amsterdam, and at Darmstadt. Compositions include: Mexitli for Solo Voices and Ensemble, 1982; Trope for Cello, 1987; As En Seringen for Ensemble with Percussion, 1988; String Trio, 1990; Contrast for Saxophone Quartet, 1990. Address: c/o Vereniging Buma, PO Box 725, 1180 AS Amstelveen, The Netherlands.

GEFORS Hans, b. 8 Dec 1952, Stockholm, Sweden. Composer. Education: Studied composition with Per-Gunnar Alldahl and Maurice Karkoff; Pupil of Ingvar Lidholm at Stockholm Academy of Music, 1972; Per Norgård at Jutland Conservatory of Music, Diploma in 1977. Career: Active as composer, music critic and editor; Professor of Composition at Malmö College of Music, 1988; Der Park premiere at the 1992 Wiesbaden Festival; Clara, premiere at the 100th anniversary of the Opera Comique, Paris, 1998. Compositions: Operas: The Poet And The Glazier, 1979, Christina, 1986, Der Park, 1991; Vargen Kommer, 1997; Clara, 1998; Music Theatre: Me Morire En Paris, 1979, The Creation No 2, 1988; Orchestral: Slits, 1981, Christina Scenes, 1987, Twine, 1988, Die Erscheinung Im Park, 1990; Chamber: Aprahishtita, 1970-71, La Boîte Chinoise, 1976, L'Invitation Au Voyage for Voice, Guitar and Violin, 1981, Krigets Eko for Percussionist, 1982, Tjurens Död, 1982, Flickan Och Den Gamle, 1983, Galjonsfiguren, 1983, One Two, 1983; Vocal: Singer On Förtröstan for Voice and Guitar, 1970, Whales Weep Not! for 16 Part Choir, 1987, En Obol, sonnets, for Voice, Clarinet, Cornet, Cello and Piano, 1989; Song cycle: Lydias Sånger, 1997. Recording: Scenes from Christina. Honour: Christ Johnson Fund Prize, 1993. Memberships: STIM; Royal Academy of Music. Address: STIM, Sandhamnsgatan 79, PO Box 27327, S-102 54 Stockholm, Sweden.

GEHANN Ada Beate, b. 3 December 1957, Hunedoara, Romania. Musicologist; Teacher. Education: Universita di Bologna, Italy, 1980-81; MA, Musicology, Italian, Tuebingen University, Germany, 1985; PhD, Heidelberg University, 1993. Career: Teacher, Music School, Tuebingen, 1982-; Text Writer, Radio Station, Süd-deutscher Rundfunk, Stuttgart, 1985-86; Improver, Publishing House, G Henle, Munich, 1995. Publication: G.B. Sammartini: Die Konzerte, 1995. Address: Jakob-Degen Str 46, D-73614 Schorndorf, Germany.

GEIGER Ruth, b. 30 Jan 1923, Vienna, Austria. Pianist. Education: Studied in Vienna with Hans Gal and Julius Isserlis, Juilliard School, New York, with Josef Lhevinne. Debut: Town Hall, New York, 1944. Career: Recitals and appearances with orchestras in USA; Radio and TV Broadcasts in New York; Annual concert tours of Europe from 1957; Orchestras include Suisse Romande, New Philharmonia, English Chamber Orchestra; BBC Series, My Favourite Concertos; Appearances on BBC solo recital series at St Johns Smith Square, London; Live broadcasts, Pebble Mill, Birmingham, Concert Hall, Broadcasting

House London; Live concerto broadcasts with Glasgow BBC Orchestra; Complete Schubert Sonatas for Basle Radio; Toured Sweden, Holland, Belgium, Switzerland, Austria, England; Master Classes at University of Sussex, 1971; Chamber Music with the Allegri Quartet; Concert and teaching week's residency at Yale University, USA; Most recent appearances on Live BBC Concert series; Lunchtime Recital at St David's Hall, Cardiff, 1992; Live Broadcast of Lunchtime Recital at St John's Smith Square, London, 1992; 1995 includes recital on Sunday Morning Coffee Concerts, Wigmore Hall, London; Master Class and Recital, Newton Park College, Bath; Recital in Tours, France; Solo recitals in Tours, France, 1995, 1997, also collaboration in Tours with French mezzo-soprano in Lieder by Schubert and Brahms. Recordings include: Schubert Sonatas for Critics Choice Records. Honours: Naumburg Award, New York, 1943; Finalist, Leventritt Competition, 1944 and Rachmaninov Competition, 1948. Hobbies: Photography; Literature; Nature. Address: 160 W 73 Street, New York, NY 10023, USA.

GEIRINGER Bernice, b. 24 Apr 1918, Minnesota, USA. Pianist. m. Karl Geiringer, 1987, 2 sons, 1 daughter. Education: University of California, Los Angeles; Studied with Arnold Schoenberg, Alfred Mirovitch, Victor Aller and Dusi Mura. Debut: Beaux Arts Theatre, Los Angeles, 1940. Career: Guest Artist with La Mirada Symphony, University of California at Santa Barbara, Santa Barbara Symphony and West Coast Symphony. Publication: This I Remember (co-author), 1993. Honour: National Federation of Music Clubs. Membership: American Musicological Society. Hobby: Writing. Address: 161 Rametto Road, Santa Barbara, CA 93108, USA.

GELIOT Michael, b. 27 Sep 1933, London, England. Opera and Theatre Director. m. Diana Geliot, 2 children. Education: BA, Cambridge University. Career: Staged first UK production of Liebermann's School For Wives, while at Cambridge in 1958; Sadler's Wells from 1960; Burt's Volpone for the New Opera Company in 1961 and Weill's Mahagonny in 1963; Resident Producer then Director of Productions with Welsh National Opera, 1965-78; Productions for Scottish Opera, Kassel, Zurich, Barcelona, Wexford, Amsterdam, Ottawa, Lausanne, Netherlands Opera with Wozzeck in 1973, and Munich Opera with Fidelio in 1974; Staged the premiere of Maxwell Davies's Taverner at Covent Garden in 1972; Translations of Mozart's Zauberflöte and Nozze di Figaro; Stagings at Kassel Opera include Le nozze di Figaro in 1980; Collaborations with the designer, Ralph Koltai. Honours include: Critics' Prize, Barcelona, 1974. Hobbies: Cricket; Sailing; Walking; Chess.

GELLHORN Peter, b. 24 Oct 1912. Conductor; Pianist; Composer. 2 sons, 2 daughters. Education: University of Berlin; Music Academy, Berlin. Career: Musical Director, Toynbee Hall, 1935-39; Assistant Conductor, Sadler's Wells Opera, 1941-43; Conductor, Royal Carl Rosa Opera, 1945-46; Conductor and Head of Staff, Royal Opera House, Covent Garden, 1947-53; Conductor and Chorus Master, Glyndebourne Festival Opera, 1954-61; Director, BBC Chorus, 1961-72; Co-Founder, Director, Opera Barga, Italy, 1967-69; Musical Director, Barnes Choir, The Opera Players Limited; Visiting Coach, Opera School of the Royal College of Music, 1980-88; Professor, Guildhall School of Music and Drama, 1981-92. Contributions to: Music journals. Honours: FGSM, 1989. Memberships: Incorporated Society of Musicians; Musicians' Union; RPS; BBC Club; President, Twickenham Choral Society. Hobbies: Walking; Swimming; Theatre. Address: 33 Leinster Avenue, London SW14 7JW, England.

GELLMAN Steven D, b. 16 Sep 1947, Toronto, Canada. Composer; Pianist; Professor of Music. m. Cheryl Gellman, 18 Oct 1970, 1 s, 1 d. Education: Juilliard School of Music, NY, USA; Conservatoire de Paris. Career: Soloist with CBC Symphony Orchestra in own Concerto for Piano and Orchestra, aged 16; Compositions performed in USA, Canada, France, Europe, South America and Japan; European tour with Toronto Symphony, 1983; Gellman's Awakening performed 10 times throughout Europe; Universe Symphony, Inaugurated the International Year of Canadian Music, 1986; From 1994 appointed Full Professor of Composition and Theory, Faculty of Music, University of Ottawa. Compositions include: Orchestral: Odyssey, 1971, Symphony No 2, 1972, Chori, 1976, The Bride's Reception, 1983; Chamber Music: Mythos II for Flute and String Quartet, recorded, 1968, Wind Music for Brass Quintet, recorded, 1978, Dialogue for Solo Horn, 1978, Transformation, 1980, Chiaroscuro, 1988, Concertino for Guitar and String Quartet, 1988, Red Shoes, 1990, Musica Eterna for String Quartet, 1991, Child-Play for Chamber Orchestra, 1992, Sonata for Cello and Piano, 1995; Piano: Melodic Suite, 1972, Poeme, recorded, 1976, Waves and Ripples, 1979, Keyboard Triptych for Piano-Synthesizer, 1986; Orchestra: Love's Garden for Soprano and Orchestra, 1987, Piano Concerto, 1988-89; Canticles of St Francis for choir and orchestra, 1989. Publication: Album for Piano, 1994. Honour: Named Composer of The Year, 1987. Memberships: Associate of Canadian Music Centre; Canadian League of Composers. Address: c/o Music Department, Stewart Street, University of Ottawa, Ottawa, Ontario, K1N 6N5, Canada.

GELMETTI Gianluigi, b. 11 Sep 1945, Rome, Italy. Conductor. Education: Studied at the Accdemia di Santa Cecilia in Rome with Franco Ferrera, with Sergiu Celibidache and in Vienna with Hans Swarowsky. Career: Musical Director of Pomeriggi Musicale of Milan, and teacher at the Conservatory until 1980; Artistic Director of RAI Symphony Orchestra at Rome, 1980-84; Musical Director of Rome Opera, 1984-85; Chief Conductor of the South German Radio Symphonie Orchestra, 1989; Musical Director, Orchestre Philharmonique of Monte Carlo in 1990; Has conducted the first performances of Castiglioni's Sacro Concerto in 1982, Donatoni's In Cauda in 1983 and Henze's 7th Symphony in 1984; Conducted Tosca at La Fenice in Venice, 1989 and a double bill of Rossini's La Cambiale di Matrimonio and Il Signor Bruschino at the 1989 Schwetzingen Festival, Rossini's La Gazza Ladra with Katia Ricciarelli at Pesaro in 1989 and Salieri's Les Danaides at the 1990 Ravenna Festival; Season 1992 with Tancredi at Bologna, Rossini double bill at Schwetzingen and Il Matrimonio Segreto at the Ravenna Festival; Conducted Mascagni's Iris at Rome, 1996. Recordings include: Telerecording of Rossini Double Bill. Address: Symphonie Orchester des Suddeutsche Rundfunk, Neckarstrasse 230, Postfach 837, D-7000 Stuttgart, Germany.

GELT Andrew (Lloyd), b. 2 Feb 1951, Albuquerque, New Mexico, USA. Composer; Conductor; Performer. Education: BM, cum laude with distinction, Music Theory, University of New Mexico, 1973; MM, Clarinet Performance, University of Southern California, 1975; DMA, Theory and Composition, University of Miami, 1978; Studied at University of Denver; Clarinet Student of Mitchell Lurie; Studied with Stanley Drucker. Career: Professor of several Universities and Colleges including University of Miami, University of North Carolina, Richmond Technical College, Temple University, Princeton University; Specialises in the analysis of Microprocessor Devices as applied to Music; Main Expertise in the Theory and Composition of Music in the Ecletic Vein. Compositions: Symphony No 1, Op 34, The Art of Eclecticism, premiered by Frederick Fennell, second performance by the Orchestra Society of Philadelphia; Lamento for Strings, Op 22; Homage to Gesualdo, Op 33; Suite Eclectique, Op 35; Concerto-Quintet for Five Clarinets Assorted, Op 19; Sonatina Veehemente, Op 26; Armageddon; Works housed at the American Music Center in New York. Current Management: The American Music Center, 30 West 26th Street, Suite 1001, New York, NY 10010-2011, USA. Address: PO Box 922, Hollywood, FL 33022, USA.

GEMERT Theo Van, b. 20 Oct 1940, Kerkrade, Holland. Baritone. Education: Studied at the Maastricht Conservatory. Career: Professional Footballer, including Dutch National Team, before career as a singer; Sang at Aachen, 1970-71 as Germont and Jochanaan, and at Wuppertal from 1973 as Wotan and Gunther in The Ring, Creonte in Médée, Rigoletto, Iago, Nabucco, Count Luna, Simon Boccanegra, Telramund, Amfortas and Orestes; Guest appearances in Germany, France, Holland and Barcelona. Address: c/o Stadtische Buhnen, Spinnstrasse 4, 5600 Wuppertal, Germany.

GEMROT Jiri, b. 15 Apr 1957, Prague, Czechoslovakia. Composer. m. 16 Oct 1982. Education: Prague Conservatorium, 1972-76; Graduated in Composition, Academy of Musical Arts, Prague, 1981; Master Composers Course with Franco Donatoni, Accademia Chigiana, Siena, Italy, 1981. Career: Producer of Radio Prague, 1982-86, 1990-; Editor, Panton Publishing House, 1986-90. Compositions: Published: Sonata for Piano No 1, 1981, Tributes for Orchestra, 1983, 5 Lyrical Songs To Poems by Ingeborg Bachmann for Soprano and Piano, 1984, Inventions for Violin and Viola, 1984, Sonata for Piano No 2, 1985, Maxims for 15 Strings, 1986, Rhapsody for Bassoon and Piano, 1986; Preludium and Toccata for harpsichord, Rhapsody for Oboe and Piano, 1988; Sonatina for violin and piano; Sonata for Piano, 1990; Inventions for Cello and Double Bass, 1991; Concerto for Flute and Orchestra, 1992; Psalmus 146 for mixed chorus and orchestra, 1992;' Lauda, Sion, for baritone and wind orchestra, 1994; Schalmeiane fpor 6 oboes, 1996; IV Sonata for piano, 1996; Concertino for orchestra, 1997. Recordings: Tributes; Dances And Reflections; Cello Concerto; Sonata for Harp; Bucolic for String Quartet; Meditation for Viola and Organ; Invocation for Violin and Organ; Sonatina for Flute and Piano; Maxims for 15 Strings; Piano Sonatas. Hobbies: Gardening; Cycling. Address: Na Valech 32, Prague 6, Czech Republic.

GENCER Leyla, b. 10 Oct 1928, Ankara, Turkey. Singer (Soprano). Education: Studied at the Ankara Conservatory; Further study with Giannina Arangi Lombardi and Apollo Granforte. Debut: Ankara, 1950 as Santuzza. Career: Teatro San Carlo Naples, 1953 as Madame Butterfly; La Scala Milan from 1956, notably in the premieres of Poulenc's Dialogues des Carmélites, 1957 and Pizzetti's L'Assassinio nella Cattedrale, 1958; San Francisco from 1956; Spleto Festival in 1959 as Renata in The Fiery Angel by Prokofiev; Salzburg Festival in 1961 as Amelia in Simon Boccanegra; Covent Garden in 1962 as Elisabeth de Valois and Donna Anna; Sang Norma at the Verona Arena, 1965, Mozart's Countess, 1962-63 and Anna Bolena, 1965

at Glyndebourne, Rome Opera in 1971 as Giulia in La Vestale by Spontini, Naples in a revival of Caterina Cornaro by Donizetti and Edinburgh Festival in 1969 and 1972; Further appearances in Vienna, Munich, Moscow, Warsaw, Oslo, Buenos Aires and Rio de Janeiro. Recordings include: Don Giovanni; Mozart's Figaro; Anna Bolena; Maria Stuarda, Roberto Devereux; Jérusalem; Belisario; Caterina Cornaro; Il Trovatore; Attila; Pacini's Saffo; La Vestale; I Puritani; Spontini's La Vestale; Verdi's Macbeth, Forza del Destino, Rigoletto, Aida and Un Ballo in Maschera; Massenet's Werther. Honours include: Numerous including: Ambrogino d'Oro of Milan, 1988, Artista di Stato della Turce, 1989 and Dottore honoris causa, University of Istanbul, 1990. Address: c/o Viale Majno 17A, 92122 Milan, Italy.

GENS Veronique, b. 1966, Orleans, France. Singer (Soprano). Education: Studied at the Paris Conservatoire. Career: Has sung with Les Arts Florissants from 1986; Solo engagements include Mozart's Cherubino and Vitellia, under Jean-Claude Malgoire, the Countess with Opéra de Lyon, 1994, and Donna Elvira at Tourcoing; Sang Venus in King Arthur with Les Arts Florissants in Paris and at Covent Garden, 1995; Mozart's Idamante in Lisbon, 1995; Has also worked with such conductors as William Christie, Marc Minkowski and René Jacobs; Season 1996 with Les Talens Lyriques at the Versailles Baroque Days as Venus in Les Festes de Paphos by Mondonville, Beaune Festival with Les Musiciens du Louvre as Lully's Galatée; Solo engagements include Fiordiligi with Vlaamse Opera, Belgium, 1997. Recordings: Dido and Aeneas; Les Arts; W Christie; Hippolyte et Aricie by Rameau; Les Musiciens du Louvre; M Minkowski. Honour: Revelation Musciale de l'année, 1995. Current Management: Opéra et Concert, Paris, France. Address: 1 rue Volney, 75002 Paris, France.

GENTILE Ada, b. 26 Jul 1947, Avezzano, Italy. Composer. m. Franco Mastroviti, 2 Jul 1972. Education: Diploma in Piano, 1972 and Composition in 1974, S Cecilia Conservatoire, Rome; Advanced course with Goffredo Petrassi, Accademia di Santa Cecilia, 1975-76. Career: Participant in international composition competitions; Her works performed throughout Europe, Canada, USA and Australia; Invited to festivals of contemporary music including Huddersfield, Aarhus, Zagreb, Warsaw, Alicante, Bacau and Kassel; Commissions from RAI, French Ministry of Culture and Accademia di Santa Cecilia; Artistic Director, G Petrassi Chamber Orchestra, 1986-88, and Nuovi Spazi Musicali Festival, Rome; Currently teacher at S Cecilia Conservatoire and presenter of contemporary music festivals for RAI-Radiotre. Compositions: 34 published works and several recorded works. Recordings: Monographic record with 4 works; Records with 2 works and with 1 work and a CD with 1 work. Hobbies: Books; Cuisine; Cats. Address: Via Divisione Torino 139, 00149 Rome, Italy.

GENTILE Louis, b. 2 Sept 1957, Connecticut, USA. Singer (Tenor). Education: Studied in New York. Career: Guest appearances in opera and broadcasting houses in Europe and the USA; Sang at Darmstadt, 1983-86; Krefeld, 1986-88 as Alfredo, among other roles; Netherlands Opera at Amsterdam, 1988, in Fidelio, Berlin Staatsoper, 1986, in Judith by Siegfried Matthus; Appeared at the Deutsche Oper Berlin 1990, as Schwalb in Mathis der Maler; Pedro in Tiefland at the Theater am Gärtnerplatz, Munich, 1991; Sang Don José at Oslo, 1991; Other roles include Tamino, Rossini's Almaviva, Boris in Katya Kabanova, Cavalli's Ormindo, Rodolfo and Erik in Der fliegende Holländer; Sang Bibalo's Macbeth for Norwegian Opera at Oslo, 1992. Honours: Winner Young Talent Presents, Competition, 1981. Address: c/o Deutsche Oper Berlin, Richard Wagnerstrasse 10, D-1000 Berlin, Germany.

GENTILESCA Franco J, b. 30 May 1943, New York City, USA. Stage Director; Producer. Education: Sacred Heart, Chicago, 1960; St Johns University New York, 1964; Pace University, New York, 1967; Private studies in piano and voice. Debut: With Andrea Chenier, Richard Tucker at Philadelphia Grand Opera, 1973. Career: Assistant to Luchino Visconti, Roman Polanski, Spoleto, 1974; Assistant Artistic Director, Artists International, 1975; Resident Stage Director, Connecticut Grand Opera, 1983-92; Stage Director, New Jersey State Opera, Philadelphia Grand Opera, New York Grand Opera, Florentine Opera, Milwaukee, Connecticut Opera Association, Tulsa Opera, Oklahoma, Opera Metropolitana, Caracas, Venezuela; Teaching: New York School of Opera, IIVA; MCA, Franklin Institute; AIMS, Graz, Austria; Escuela de Opera, Caracas, Venezuela. Memberships: Member, American Guild of Musical Artists; Actor's Equity. Address: 2109 Broadway, Apartment 14-10, New York, NY 10023, USA.

GENZMER Harald, b. 9 Feb 1909, Bremen, Germany. Composer. m. 1949. Education: Abitur, Marburg; Berlin College of Music. Career: Director of Studies and Choral Reptitor, Opera House, Breslau, 1934-37 and Berlin, 1938-; Professor, Freiburg, 1946-57 and National College of Music, Munich, 1957-. Compositions: 3 Symphonies, concertos for piano, flute, trautonium, violins, violas, cello and orchestra; Zauberspiegel Suite for Orchestra; Numerous works for chamber orchestra, also organ, choral and electronic works. Recordings: 2 Concertos for Trautonium and Orchestra; Organ Works; Harp Music; Irische Harfe (Irish Harp); Concerto for Trumpet and Orchestra; Concerto for 2 Clarinets. Publication: Harald Genzmer. Honour: Arts Prize, Bavarian Academy of Fine Arts, 1961. Memberships: Academy of Fine Arts, Munich; Academy of Fine Arts, Berlin; Medaille: München Lenchtet, 1989. Hobbies: Astronomy; Natural Sciences. Address: 8 München 80, Eisensteinstrasse 10, Germany.

GEORG Mechthild, b. 1956, Germany. Singer (Mezzo-soprano). Education: Studied in Dusseldorf with Ingeborg Reichelt and at the Cologne opera studio. Career: Sang at first in concert, then at the Essen Opera from 1989; Guest engagements throughout Germany as Monteverdi's Octavia and Penelope, Cherubino, the Composer in Ariadne auf Naxos, Flosshilde (Hamburg, 1992), and Henrietta in Graf Mirabeau by Matthus; Concerts in Belgium, Austria and Switzerland; Sang Atalanta in Handel's Serse at Copenhagen, 1996. Recordings: Suor Angelica and Gianni Schicchi (RCA); Messiah and Schumann Requiem (EMI). Address: c/o Theater Essen, Rolandstrasse 10, W-4300 Essen 1, Germany.

GEORGE Alan (Norman), b. 23 Dec 1949, Newquay, Cornwall, England. Violist. m. Lesley Schatzberger, 2 daughters. Education: MA, King's College, Cambridge University. Debut: As member of Fitzwilliam Quartet, Purcell Room, London, 1973. Career: Member, Fitzwilliam Quartet, 1969-, Quartet in Residence, University of York, 1971-74, 1977-86, University of Warwick, 1974-77; Lecturer, University of York, 1986-88, Finchcocks Quartet, 1992-; Participant, 1st performance of Quartets, No 2 by Sebastian Forbes, Edward Cowie, David Blake, Cuaderna by Bernard Rands, Clarinet Quintet by David Blake; Michael Blake Clarinet Quintet, 1st British performances, Shostakovich Quartets 13, 14, 15; Alfred Schnittke, Canon in Memory of I F Stravinsky; Fitzwilliam Quartet, affiliate artists at Bucknell University, Pennsylvania, USA, 1978-86; Principal Viola, English Baroque Soloists, Orchestre Révolutionnaire et Romantique; Member, New London Consort, Lumina contemporary music group; 1st performances, ...et Quart by John Paynter, Clarinet Trio by William Sweeney; Concerts and recordings, London Classical Players, Age of Enlightenment, Academy of Ancient Music, English Baroque Soloists, New London Consort, Hanover Band, Yorkshire Baroque Soloists. Recordings: Shostakovich Quartets Nos 1-15; Franck Quartet in D; Borodin Quartets Nos 1 and 2; Delius Quartet; Sibelius Voces Intimae; Brahms Clarinet Quintet; Wolf Italian Serenade; Schubert String Quintet; Beethoven Quartets ops 127, 130, 132, 133, 135; Shostakovich Piano Quintet with V Ashkenazy; Mozart Clarinet Trio with A Hacker and K Evans; Schumann Piano Quintet and Piano Quartet with R Burnett; Mozart Clarinet Quintet with L Schatzberger. Publication: Shostakovich Chamber Music. Address: 10 Bootham Terrace, York YO3 7DH, England.

GEORGE Donald, b. 13 Sept 1955, San Francisco, USA. Singer (Tenor). Education: Studied at Louisiana State University in Berlin and with Josef Metternich in Munich. Career: Sang lyric tenor roles at the Theater am Gärtnerplatz, Munich, Brussels and the Vienna Staatsoper, 1986, in the premiere of Das Schloss by Andre Laporte and as Belmonte; Deutsche Oper Berlin, 1988-89, as Bernstein's Candide and as Fenton in Die Lustigen Weiber von Windsor; Guest appearances at Madrid in the local premiere of Lulu, Wurzburg (as Belmonte), Komische Oper Berlin (Tamino); Leopold in La Juive (Bielefeld 1989); Giessen (Mozart's Titus) and Bregenz (Steuermann in Der fliegende Holländer); Other roles include Faust, Ferrando, Leukippos (Daphne), Jason in Médée and Jenik in The Bartered Bride; Sang Antonio in Prokofiev's The Duenna at the 1989 Wexford Festival; Title role in Rossini's Aureliano in Palmira at Bad Wildbad, 1996; Concerts at the Barbican Hall, London; Other repertoire includes works by Bach, Handel, Orff and Vaughan Williams. Recordings include: Alzira by Verdi. Address: c/o Deutsche Oper Berlin, Richard Wagnerstrasse 10, D-1000 Berlin, Germany.

GEORGE Lila-Gene, b. 25 September 1918, Sioux City, Iowa, USA. Composer; Pianist; Teacher. m. Richard Painter George, 11 September 1944, 1 son, 1 daughter. Education: BA, BMus, University of Oklahoma, 1940; Postgraduate, Northwestern University, 1950, Columbia University, 1962-65; Private Piano Study, Lila Plowe Kennedy, Herbert Ricker, Egon Petri, Silvio Scionti, Edward Steuermann; Private Composition Study, Nadia Boulanger, 1971-78. Career: Piano Soloist, Oklahoma City Little Symphony, Houston Symphony. Composition: Madrigals. Honours: Composers Award, Sigma Alpha Iota, 1984; Guild of Piano Teachers Hall of Fame, 1994. Memberships: American Music Center; American Musicological Society; International Alliance for Women in Music; Past President, Tuesday Music Club. Hobbies: Genealogy; Swimming. Address: 2301 Reba Drive, Houston, TX 77019, USA.

GEORGE Michael, b. 1950, England. Baritone. Education: Chorister at King's College Cambridge; Royal College of Music, London. Career: Solo engagements and as member of leading early music ensembles in Britain and Europe; Sang in Handel's L'Allegro at the 1988 Promenade Concerts, Brahms Requiem with the London Symphony Orchestra and Kurt Sanderling, Haydn's Creation in Madrid, Beethoven's Missa Solemnis and Choral Symphony with the Hanover Band, Purcell's Dioclesian with John Eliot Gardiner, and performances of Messiah with The Sixteen in London, Italy, Spain, Poland and France; Engagements at the Three Choirs Festival, Royal Festival Hall, Oslo, Brussels and tour of Austria, Germany and Yugoslavia with the Orchestra of St John's; Twentieth century repertoire includes Threni by Stravinsky for the BBC, A Child of Our Time with the Bournemouth Symphony Orchestra, the premiere of John Metcalf's The Boundaries of Time for the BBC at the Swansea Festival and Christus in the St John Passion by Arvo Pärt during a tour of Britain with the Contemporary Music Network; Sang in 3 Promenade Concerts in 1990, and in Bach's Cantata Herz und Mund und Tat und Leben, Bonfire of the Vanities and Janácek's Glagolitic Mass; Sang Abinoam in Handel's Deborah at the 1993 Proms; Grimbald in Purcell's King Arthur at Rome, 1996; Sang in Oswald von Wolkenstein concert at the Purcell Room, London, 1997. Recordings include: Medieval Carmina Burana; Monteverdi's Vespers of 1610; At The Boar's Head by Holst; Purcell's St Cecilia Ode; Complete Purcell Odes with the King's Consort. Current Management: IMG Artists. Address: IMG Artists Europe, Media House, 3 Burlington Lane, Chiswick, London, W4 2TH, England.

GEORGIADIS John (Alexander), b. Rochford, Essex, England. Conductor. Education: Royal Liberty; RAM, London. Career: Concertmaster, CBSO, 1962-65; Concertmaster, LSO, 1965-79; Music Director, London Virtuosi, 1972-; Gabrieli Quartet, 1987-90; Music Director, Bangkok Symphony Orchestra, 1994-. Recordings: London Symphony Orchestra, Chandos and Pickwick; Gabrieli Quartet, Chandos; Various Naxos. Honours: FRAM, 1968; FGSM, 1969; Honorary Doc, Essex University, 1990. Memberships: RAM Guild. Hobby: Golf. Address: Purton Corner, Purton Lane, Farnham Royal, Bucks SL2 3LY, England.

GEORGIADIS Nicholas, b. 14 Sep 1925, Athens, Greece. Stage Designer. Education: Studied architecture in Athens and New York, and painting and theatre design at the Slade School in London, 1953-54. Career: Collaborations with the late Kenneth Macmillan at Sadler's Wells, the Royal Ballet, the Stuttgart Ballet and the Deutsche Opera Berlin; Teacher at the Slade School, 1960-86; Designed productions of Aida and Les Troyens at Covent Garden, 1968-69, Cherubini's Médée at Frankfurt in 1971, Anna Bolena in 1976, Don Giovanni in Athens, and La Clemenza di Tito at Aix-en-Provence in 1988. Honours include: CBE, 1984. Address: c/o Théâtre d'Opera du Festival, Aix-en-Provence, France.

GEORGIAN Karine, b. 5 Jan 1944, Moscow, Russia. Cellist. m. Anthony Philips, 15 Dec 1990, 1 son. Education: Gnessin School, Moscow, 1950-61; Private studies with Armen Georgian, father, 1949-61; Moscow Conservatory with Mstislav Rostropovich, 1961-68. Career: Regular appearances with leading Soviet, European and American orchestras and festivals; Debut tour in 1969 at Carnegie Hall with Chicago Symphony, returning in 1970 in a performance of Khatchaturian Cello Rhapsody; Recital at Prague in 1970; Played with Berlin Philharmonic Orchestra in 1970, Leningrad Philharmonic Orchestra in 1973, and Royal Philharmonic Orchestra in 1982; Professor of Cello at Staatliche Hochschule für Musik since 1984; Played at BBC Proms, Henry Wood Promenade Concerts in 1985 and 1990, and with Philadelphia Orchestra in 1990. Recordings: Brahms Trio in B with Dmitri Alexeyev and Liane Isakadze; Denisov Concerto in C with Moscow Philharmonic and Dmitri Kitayenko; Khatchaturian Cello Rhapsody with Bolshoi Radio Symphony and Aram Khatchaturian; Sonatas by Shostakovich and Locatelli, Aza Amintayeva; Couperin Music for 2 Cellos with Natalia Gutman; Brahms Trio in A minor with Thea King and Clifford Benson. Honours: 1st Prize, All Union Music Competition, 1966; 1st Prize and Gold Medal, Tchaikovsky International Competition, Moscow, 1966. Address: c/o Olivia Ma Artists Management, 28 Sheffield Terrace, London, W8 7MA, England.

GERAETS Theodora, b. 13 Oct 1961, Bosch en Duin, Netherlands. Concert Violinist. Education: Studied in Amsterdam, with Dorothy Delay in New York and with Kyung Wha-Chung in London. Career: American debut, 1980, with the St Louis Symphony under Leonard Slatkin; British debut at the Wigmore Hall, 1979; Regular appearances on radio and TV and in concert throughout Europe, and in USA, Central and South America; Repertoire includes the Mendelssohn Concerto; Mozart's Sonata K380, Ravel's Sonata and Ysaÿe's Extase; Teacher at the Hague Conservatory. Honours include: Second Prize, National Youth Violin Competition, Amsterdam, 1971; Finalist, International Conservatory at Glasgow, 1976; Winner, National Oskar Back Concours in Amsterdam, 1979; Winner, International Bartók Competition in Aspen, Colorado, 1980; Netherlandse Musiekprijs, 1989. Address: Meenkselaan 21, 3972 JP Dreibergen, Germany.

GERBER Steven (Roy), b. 28 Sep 1948, Washington, USA. Composer; Pianist. Education: BA, Haverford College, 1969; MFA, Princeton University, 1971; Composition with Robert Parris, Milton Babbitt, JK Randall, Earl Kim. Piano with Robert Parris, Agi Jambor, Irwin Gelber. Career includes: Many recitals with Christine Schadeberg and concerts of his music with her and with violinist Rolf Schulte among others; Received 3 commissions; World premiere of his compositions Symphony No 1 and Serenade for String Orchestra during tour of Russia in 1990, returning in 1991 to perform several more concerts of his orchestral and chamber works including a concert at Tchaikovsky Hall in Moscow, since then has returned numerous times. Compositions include: Dirge and Awakening for Orchestra premiered by the Russian National Orchestra under Mikhail Pletnev; Violin Concerto written for the American violinist Kurt Nikkanen who premiered it in Moscow and Novosibirsk in 1994 and playing it again at Kennedy Center in Washington with National Chamber Orchestra, 1995. Recordings: Many of his nearly 50 compositions have been recorded including Une Saison en Enfer. Honours include: Fellowship, Princeton University; Winner of competitions held by The New Music Consort with String Quartet No 2 and Musicians' Accord with Concertino; Duo in 3 Movements for Violin and Piano won The American Composers' Alliance 50th anniversary recording award. Memberships: Several professional organizations. Address: 639 West End Avenue 10D, New York, NY 10025, USA.

GERELLO Vassily, b. Chernovitsky District, Ukraine. Singer (Baritone). Education: Studied at the St Petersburg Conservatory. Career: Sang as professional while a student, and with the Kirov Opera as Verdi's Germont and Posa, Valentin (Faust), Napoleon in War and Peace, Balearalz in Mussorgsky's Salambo and the Venetian Guest in Rimsky's Sadko; On tour to Edinburgh Festival, 1991; Season 1993-94 as Papageno and Mozart's Figaro in St Petersburg, Rossini's Figaro with Netherlands Opera; Season 1994-95 as Paolo in Simon Boccanegra at the Bastille Opéra and Covent Garden; Eugene Onegin for Toronto Opera and the Vienna Staatsoper, 1998; Yeletsky in the Queen of Spades at Buenos Aires and Posa at the Sao Paulo Opera; Season 1995-96 with Bohème, Giulio Cesare and Boccanegra at the Bastille Opera; New York Met debut, as Alfio in Cavalleria Rusticana, 1997. Recordings include: Dr Pustrpalk in Salatán by Pavel Haas; Tchaikovsky's Moscow Canatata. Address: c/o Lies Askonas Ltd, 6 Henrietta St, London WC2E 8LA, England.

GERGIEV Valery, b. 2 May 1953, Moscow, Russia. Conductor. Education: Studied piano and conducting in Ordzhonikidze, later at Leningrad Conservatory; Whilst a student won the All Union Conductors Competition Prize in Moscow and the Karajan Competition in Berlin. Career: Conductor at Kirov Opera, 1977- and chief conductor of the Armenian State Orchestra; Appeared with the Russian State Symphony Orchestra in France in 1987; Guest engagements with the Berlin Philharmonic, L'Orchestre de France and Dresden Philharmonic; London debut in 1988 with the London Symphony Orchestra at the Barbican, with later engagements with the City of Birmingham Symphony Orchestra, Royal Liverpool Philharmonic, Bournemouth Symphony and BBC Philharmonic; Succeeded Yuri Temirkanov as music director of Kirov Opera and Ballet Theatre in 1988; Conducted Welcome Back St Petersburg at the Kirov Gala at Covent Garden in 1992 with debut in opera there in Eugene Onegin in 1993; Conducted Boris Godunov at the Helsinki Fair Centre, Khovanschina at Rome in 1992, Kirov Opera at the Metropolitan in 1992 in The Fiery Angel, The Queen of Spades and Boris Godunov; Prince Igor at Caesarea in Israel and Otello at the Metropolitan in 1994; Season 1994/95 with Rimsky's Invisible City of Kitezh in London and Edinburgh; Conducted Lohengrin at Covent Garden (1997) and Parsifal at the 1997 Savonlinna Festival. Address: c/o Harold Holt Ltd, 31 Sinclair Road, London, W14 0NS, England.

GERGIEVA Larissa, b. Beltsy, Moldova. Pianist. Education: Studied at Vladikavkas with Zarama Lolaeva. Career: Repetituer at the Vladikavkas Opera, then at the Tchaikovsky Opera House Perm, 1987-; Russian recitals at Moscow and St Petersburg and partnerships with leading singers in Italy, Germany, United States and Britain (Edinburgh, Wigmore Hall and Queen Elizabeth Hall); Season 1994-95 included recitals at the Edinburgh Festival with Olga Borodina and Galina Gorchakova, and at the Wigmore Hall in the Wigmore/Kirov series; Coaching engagements have included The Fiery Angel and Ruslan and Ludmila with the San Francisco Opera, 1994-95; Accompanied Kirov artists in Shostakovich Songs for the BBC, 1995; Master classes for singers at Perm, and general director of Rimsky-Korsakov Competition for singers at St Petersburg. Recordings include: Tchaikovsky Songs, and the Mighty Handful, with Olga Borodina. Honours include: First prize at the Kazan and Tallin National Competitions. Address: c/o Lies Askonas Ltd. 6 Henrietta St, London WC2E 8LA, England.

GERINGAS David, b. 29 Jul 1946, Vilna, Russia. Concert Cellist. m. Tatiana Schatz. Education: Studied with Rostropovitch at the Moscow Conservatoire, 1963-71. Career: Concert tours of Germany in 1970 and Hungary in 1973; Resident in Germany from 1976; Many recitals with pianist, Tatiana Schatz, and Professor at Hamburg Conservatoire; Played in the orchestra of the North German Radio and has given solo performances of works by Honegger, Milhaud, Hindemith and Kabalevsky; Premiered the Sonata for Solo Cello by Gottfried von Einem in 1987; Piano trio performances with Gerhard Oppitz and Dmitri Sitkovetsky; Also plays the baryton and has formed the Trio Geringas with the violinist, Vladimir Mendelssohn and the cellist, Emil Klein. Recordings include: Gubaidulina Offertorium with the Boston Symphony under Dutoit. Honours include: 1st Prize, Baku Competition, 1969; Winner, Tchaikovsky International Competition, 1970. Address: c/o DGG (Contracts), 1 Sussex Place, London, W6 5AX, England.

GERLE Robert, b. 1 Apr 1924, Abbazia, Italy. Violinist; Teacher; Conductor. Education: Franz Liszt Academy of Music, Budapest; National Conservatory, Budapest. Career: Soloist with many European Orchestras, and toured as recitalist in Europe; Head of String Department at University of Oklahoma, 1950-54; Teacher at Peabody Conservatory of Music, 1955-68, Mannes College of Music, 1959-70, Manhattan School of Music, 1967-70 and Ohio State University, 1968-72; Head of Instrumental Program at University of Maryland, 1972-. Recordings: Several discs. Publication: The Art of Practising the Violin, 1983. Honour: Hubay Prize, 1942. Address: c/o Siegel Artist Management, 3003 Van Ness Street North West, Suite 205, Washington, DC 20008, USA.

GERSTENENGST Iosif, b. 3 Jul 1920, Ciacova, Romania. Organist. Education: Graduate of Normal High School, Timisoara, 1939 and Theological Academy, Timisoara, 1944; 8 Years of piano and musical theory with Professor Elizabeth Andrée and 4 summer mastercourses in Organ with Professor Franz Xaver Dressler, Sibiu. Debut: Timisoara in 1945. Career: Performed concerts and recitals in all main Cathedrals in Romania such as Bucharest, Timisoara, Arad, Alba Iulia, Jassy, Oradea, Satu-Mare, Sibiu and abroad in Vienna, Salzburg, East and West Berlin, Hamburg, Cologne, Munich, Paris, Rome, Brussels, Stockholm, Warsaw, Belgrade, Sofia, Leipzig, Riga, Odessa, Prague and New York. Recordings: Works by Frescobaldi and Pachelbel; Organ collaborations in the issue of other recordings on disc. Hobby: Reading Classics in Music and Literature. Current Management: Romanian Agency of Artists Management, Bucharest, Romania. Address: Str Nuferilor 19, 70749 Bucharest, Romania.

GERTIG Suzanne L, b. 26 February 1950, Exeter, New Hampshire, USA. Musicologist; Harpist; Music Librarian. m. John K Gertig, 13 October 1990, 1 daughter. Education: BMEd, magna cum laude, James Madison University, 1974; MLS, 1979, MA, 1982, Kent State University. Publications: A Choice or a Bitter Fruit: Contemporary Criticism; A Musical Anachronism: Reynaldo Hahn and His Music. Contributions to: American Harp Journal; ARS Musica Denver. Memberships: American Musicological Society; American Harp Society; Music Library Association; American Federation of Musicians; Reznicek Society; Pi Kappa Lambda; Beta Phi Mu. Hobbies: American Civil War; Egyptology. Address: 11658 West 84th Lane, Arvada, CO 80005, USA.

GESSENDORF Mechthild, b. 1937, Munich, Germany. Soprano. m. Ernő Weil. Education: Studied at the Munich Musikhochschule and with Joseph Metternich in Cologne. Career: Sang with the Vienna Kammeroper from 1961 then at Bremen and Bonn, Staatsoper Munich from 1981 as Aida, the Empress in Die Frau ohne Schatten, Rosenkavalier, Don Carlos and in The Turn of The Screw, at Salzburg Festival in 1981 as Amelia Boccanegra and Bregenz Festival in 1983 as Agathe; US debut in 1983 as the Marschallin in Rosenkavalier at Tulsa, at Philadelphia in 1985 as Ariadne, Metropolitan Opera debut in 1986 as the Marschallin returning in 1989 as the Empress in Die Frau ohne Schatten, and Senta in 1990; Sang at Vienna State Opera, Oper Köln, Dusseldorf, Deutsche Opera Berlin, Staatsoper Hamburg, Grand Opera Paris, at Covent Garden in 1987 in Tannhäuser and Lohengrin in 1988, Scala Milano as Senta in 1988, at the Savonlinna Festival, Edinburgh Festival, Aix-en-Provence, Lyric Chicago, Toronto, Montreal and Detroit; Sang Sieglinde in Die Walküre for Greater Miami Opera in 1989, Ariadne at Lyon and Barcelona, the Marschallin in Paris and Agathe in Der Freischütz at Monte Carlo; Sang in Beethoven's Choral Symphony at the 1989 Promenade Concerts, as Elsa in Lohengrin at Lisbon in 1990, and the Marschallin at the Metropolitan in 1991. Recordings include: Die Lustige Witwe; Penthesilea by Schoeck. Address: c/o Kaye Artists, Barratt House, 7 Chertsey Road, Woking, GU21 5AB, England.

GESZTY Sylvia, b. 28 Feb 1934, Budapest, Hungary. Soprano. Education: Studied at the Budapest Conservatory and the Budapest Music Academy with Erszebeth Hoor-Tempis. Career: Sang at the Berlin Staatsoper from 1961 with debut as Amor in Orfeo ed Euridice, Komische Oper Berlin, 1963-70, and Hamburg Staatsoper, 1966-72; Covent Garden and Salzburg Festival debuts in 1966 and 1967 as the Queen of Night; Sang at Stuttgart Opera from 1971, Glyndebourne Festival, 1971-72 as Zerbinetta and Constanze, Los Angeles in 1973 with the company of the New York City Opera as Sophie in Der Rosenkavalier and Schwetzingen Festival in 1976 as Gismonda in Cimarosa's Il Marito Desparato; Sang Rosina in Haydn's La Vera Costanza at Vienna in 1984, also televised; Guest appearances in Buenos Aires, Vienna, Paris, Brussels, Amsterdam and Moscow; Many concert appearances. Recordings include: Ariadne auf Naxos; Die Israeliten in der Wüste by CPE Bach; Cantatas by JS Bach; La Rappresentazione di Anima e di Corpo by Cavalieri; Die Zauberflöte; Così fan tutte; Barbier von Bagdad by Cornelius; Mozart's Die Schuldigkeit des Ersten Gebotes; Sixth International Coloratura Competition held in her name, 1998. Address: c/o Secretary ICSC, Postbox 1163, D-75390, Gechingen, Germany.

GHAZARIAN Sona, b. 2 Sep 1945, Beirut, Lebanon. Soprano. Education: Studied at the Armenian College in Beirut, at the Accademia Chigiana, Siena and at the Accademia Santa Cecilia in Rome. Career: Member of the Vienna Staatsoper from 1972 notably as Oscar in Un Ballo in Maschera and as Violetta; Bregenz Festival in 1983 as Aennchen in Der Freischütz; Guest appearances in Hamburg, Paris, Brussels, Geneva and Salzburg; Sang at Verona Arena in 1985, Barcelona in 1988, and Metropolitan Opera in 1989 as Musetta in La Bohème; Sang in JC Bach's Adriano in Siria for Austrian Radio, conducted by Charles Mackerras. Recordings: Il Re Pastore by Mozart; Marzelline in Fidelio; Un Ballo in Maschera. Address: c/o Metropolitan Opera, Lincoln Center, New York, NY 10023, USA.

GHENT Emmanuel, b. 15 May 1925, Montreal, Quebec, Canada. Composer. Education: Studied at McGill University and with Ralph Shapey in the US. Career: Freelance Composer of instrumental, electronic and computer music; Composed computer music at Bell Telephone Laboratories, 1968-78; Practiced Psychoanalysis in New York; Inventor of the Polynome and Coordinome for the performance of multiple tempo music. Compositions include: Movement for Wind Quintet, 1944; 3 Duos for Flutes, 1944; Lament for String Quartet, 1958; Quartet for Winds, 1960; Dance Movement for Trumpet and String Quartet, 1962; Trialty I and II for Violin, Trumpet and Bassoon, 1964; Dithyrambos for Brass Quintet, 1965; Hex, an Ellipsis for Trumpet, Ensemble and Tape, 1966; Helices for Violin, Piano and Tape, 1969; Lady Chatterly's Lover, L'Après midi d'un Summit Meeting, Our Daily Bread and 12 Electronic Highlights, all for tape, 1969-70; Phosphones, 1971; Lustrum, 1974; Program Music 1-29, 1977-79; Baobab, 1979. Recordings: Helices; Entelechy; Five Brass Voices; Phosphones. Contributions to: Perspectives of New Music; Electronic Music Review. Honours include: MacDowell Fellowship, 1964-65; Guggenheim Fellowship, 1967; NEA Grants, 1974, 1975. Address: 131 Prince Street, New York, NY 10012, USA.

GHEORGHIU Angela, b. 7 Sept 1965, Adjud, Rumania. Singer (Soprano). m. Roberto Alagna, 1997. Education: Studied at the Budapest Academy. Career: Appearances from 1992 at Covent Garden as Zerlina, Mimi, Nina in Massenet's Chérubin and Violetta; further engagements as Adina in Vienna, Liu at the Metropolitan and Gounod's Juliette at Washington; Sang Donizetti's Adina at Covent Garden, 1997. Recordings include: Videos of La Traviata from Covent Garden and L'Elisir d'amore from Lyon. Address: c/o Stafford Law Associates, 6 Barham Close, Weybridge, Surrey, KT13 9PR.

GHEORGHIU Stefan, b. 13 Aug 1951, Constanta, Romania. Artist Instrumentalist. m. Cornelia Gheorghiu, 5 Oct 1975, 2 sons. Education: Music High School, Bucharest, 1963-70; Music Academy, Bucharest, 1970-74. Debut: Recital, 1973; First Concert as Soloist (Arad), 1975; Soloist with George Enescu, Philharmonic Orchestra, 1976. Career: Since 1974, Member of George Enescu Philharmonic Orchestra, First Viola since 1985; Soloistic Career in Romania and Italy; Founder Member of Romantica String Trio, one of the best Romanian Chamber Music Ensemble; Since 1986, Professor at Darmstadt Summer Courses for Contemporary Music; Since 1993, Professor at the Music Academy, teaching Viola. Recordings: 1975-95 recordings as Soloist and Chamber Music at Romanian Radio and TV Broadcasting System; 1984, LP at Electrecord with Mozart-Symphonia Concertante for violine and viola; 1986, LP at Electrecord with Miriam Marbe. Honours: Medal, Markneukirchen (DDR), 1977; Special Prize for Interpretation of a French Piece, Evian, France, 1979; Prize, Darmstadt, Germany, 1984. Memberships: President, Romanian Federation on the Musicians Union; President, Union of Interpretative Creation of Romanian Musicians. Hobby: Football. Address: Str Frumoasa 52, et 4, ap 18, 78116 Bucharest, Romania.

GHEZZO Dinu, b. 2 Jul 1941, Tuzla, Romania. Composer; Conductor. m. Marta Ghezzo, 3 Oct 1961, 1 daughter. Education: State Diploma in Education, 1964, in Composition, 1966, Romanian Conservatory; PhD, University of California, Los Angeles, 1973. Career: Program Director, Composition, Director, Professor of Composition, New York University; Director, George Enescu International Composition Competition; Co-Director, New Repertory Ensemble of New York. Compositions include: Aphorisms; Structures; Sketches, recorded; Breezes Of Yesteryear; Sound Shapes I and II; From Here To There; Two Prayers for Soprano and Tape; A Book Of Songs; Ostrom; Doina. Recordings: Several. Publications: Most works published. Contributions to: Tomis; Living Musician. Hobbies: Photography; Computers; Travel. Address: New York University, Music Department, 35 West 4th Street, New York, NY 10003, USA.

GHIAUROV Nicolai, b. 13 Sep 1929, Velingrad, Bulgaria. Bass Singer. m. Mirella Freni. Education: Sofia Music Academy, Moscow Conservatoire. Debut: Played violin, piano and clarinet from an early age; Sang at Sofia Opera House as Don Basilio in Barber of Seville in 1955. Career: Appeared in Bologna in 1958, La Scala Milan and as Varlaam in Boris Godunov in 1959; Regular appearances at La Scala, and Covent Garden from 1962; Sang at Metropolitan Opera from 1965 with debut as Mephistopheles, later as King Philip, Padre Guardiano and Fiesco in Simon Boccanegra, and at Vienna State Opera; Major roles include the title role in Boris Godunov, Don Giovanni and Massenet's Don Quixote; Sang Ramphis at the opening of Houston Grand Opera in 1987, and Ivan Khovansky in Khovanschina at the Vienna Staatsoper in 1989; Gran Teatre del Liceu Barcelona, 1989-90 as Gremin in Eugene Onegin and Boris; Season 1992 as Colline in La Bohème at Rome and Goryanshikov in From The House of The Dead at the Salzburg Festival; Returned to Covent Garden in 1993 as Gremin; Season 1996-97 in Don Carlos and La Bohème at Vienna Staatsoper, La Gioconda at La Scala, Eugene Onegin in Zurich and Pelléas in Turin. Address: c/o Harold Holt Ltd, 31 Sinclair Road, London W14 0NS, England.

GHIGLIA Lorenzo, b. 26 Nov 1936, Florence, Italy. Stage Designer. Education: Studied in Florence. Career: Worked at the Bergamo Festival in 1958 then designed the premiere of Pizzetti's Il Calzare d'Argento at La Scala in 1961 for director Margherita Wallmann; Has also collaborated with Franco Enriquez, Mario Missiroli and Filippo Crivelli; Designed La Bohème at Palermo in 1961, Attila at Florence in 1962 and Petrassi's Il Cordovano at Turin in 1966; US commissions include Pagliacci and Rigoletto for Houston Opera and Samson et Delilah at Dallas; Glyndebourne, 1965-66 with Anna Bolena and Dido and Aeneas; Further designs at Florence with Le Villi and Busoni's Arlecchino in 1972 and 1975, La Scala and Suor Angelica in 1973 and Catania with Médée in 1977. Address: c/o Teatro alla Scala, Via Filodrammatici 2, I-20121 Milan, Italy.

GHIGLIA Oscar, b. 13 Aug 1938, Livorno, Italy. Concert Artist; Guitarist. m. Anne-Marie d'Hauteserre, 6 Dec 1966, 1 daughter. Education: Honours Graduate, Conservatory Santa Cecilia, Rome, 1962. Career: Concert tours in North America, 1965-; Performed with Juilliard, Tokyo, and Emerson String Quartets, Julius Baker, Victoria de Los Angeles, and Jean Pierre Rampal; Performances worldwide include Turkey, Israel, Japan, Australia and New Zealand; Artist in Residence at Hartt School of Music, University of Hartford, USA, and Musik Akademie de Stadt, Basel; Summer Instructor at Aspen, Colorado Music Festival, 1969, Academia Musicale Chigiano, Siena, Italy, 1976 and Banff Centre for The Arts, Canada, 1978-. Recordings include: Paganini Sonata; The Guitar In Spain; The Spanish Guitar of Oscar Ghiglia. Current Management: 197 South Quaker Lane, West Hartford, CT 06119, USA. Address: Helfenberg Strasse 14, Basel, CH-4059, Switzerland.

GHIUSELEV Nicola, b. 14 Aug 1936, Pavlikeni, Bulgaria. Bass Singer. Education: Studied with Khristo Nrambarov at the Sofia National Opera School. Debut: Sofia in 1961 as Timur in Turandot. Career: Metropolitan Opera from 1965 with debut as Ramphis in Aida; Holland Festival in 1966 as King Philip; Guest appearances in Vienna, Paris, Moscow and Milan; Stockholm in 1974 as Rossini's Moses; Covent Garden debut in 1976 as Pagano in I Lombardi returning in 1984 as Boris Godunov; Further engagements in Bucharest, Budapest, Monte Carlo, Naples, Leipzig and Berlin; Sang the title role in Czech TV film of Don Giovanni; Sang Rossini's Basilio at Chicago in 1989 and Ramphis in Aida at Caracalla, Rome in 1990, Prince Galitzky in a new production of Prince Igor at Covent Garden in 1990, Silva in Ernani at Parma and Verdi's Attila at the Vienna Staatsoper; Season 1992 as Colline in La Bohème at Bonn and Mustafa in L'Italiana in Algeri at the Deutsche Opera Berlin. Recordings include: Khovanschina; Aleko by Rachmaninov; La Gioconda; Les Huguenots; Les Contes d'Hoffmann; La Bohème; Turandot; La Battaglia di Legnano by Verdi. Honours include: Prizewinner at competitions in Sofia, Prague and Helsinki. Address: c/o Kaye Artists Management, Barratt House, 7 Chertsey Road, Woking, Surrey, GU21 5AB, England.

GIACALONE Nicolino, b. 28 November 1956, Montreal, Canada. Classical Opera Singer; Voice Teacher; Artistic and Musical Director. m. Sophia Pinelli, 22 March 1997. Education: Marianopolis College, 1974-76; McGill University, 1976-78; Conservatoire de Musique, Quebec, 1977-79; BFA, Concordia University, 1980-82; Studied singing with Benjamin Luxon, Vera Rosza, James Bowman, Rita Streich, Max van Egmond, Daniel

Ferro. Debut: Director, Dido and Aeneas, Waltham Abbey, 1995; Singing, St John's Smith Square, London, 1997; BBC Radio debut, Glenn Gould, Tobacco, Bach. Career: Teacher, Singing, Privately, Masterclasses in Canada, Ireland, England, 1974-; Singing, Modern World Premiere Singing Title Role of Full Staged Complete Performance of H Purcell's Dioclesian, Dartington and Croatia with Paul Goodwin Conducting, 1995, 19th and 20th Century Austrian Lieder to Mark Austria's Thousand Years, 1996; Artistic Director, Founding Member, Handel Opera Company, 1995. Recordings: Music of the Second Generation, 1995; Dioclesian by H Purcell, 1995; Baroque Opera Arias for Bass, 1997. Publication: A Scarlatti Cantatas and Serenatas, 1997. Honours: Pauline Donalda Memorial Scholarship, Montreal Opera, 1981; CBC National Competition Winner, 1985; Dartington International Scholarship, 1995. Membership: National Association of Singing Teachers. Hobby: Building Harpsichords. Current Management: Angelmuse Enterprises, and J Audrey Ellison International Artists Management. Address: 17 Cascade Road, Buckhurst Hill, London 1G9 6DX, England.

GIACOMINI Giuseppe, b. 7 Sep 1940, Veggiano, Padua, Italy. Tenor. Education: Studied with Elena Fava Ceriati in Padua, Marcello del Monaco in Treviso and Vladimiro Badiali in Milan. Debut: In 1966 as Pinkerton in Madame Butterfly. Career: Sang in Berlin and Vienna from 1972, Hamburg from 1973, La Scala debut in 1974, Paris Opera debut in 1975, and US debut at Cincinnati Opera from 1976 as Alvaro in La Forza del Destino, Verdi's Macduff, Don Carlos and Manrico, Puccini's Cavaradossi and Canio in Pagliacci; Further appearances in Barcelona, Boston, Budapest, London, Munich and Tokyo; Sang Verdi's Otello at San Diego in 1986; Season 1992 as Alvaro at Naples, Canio at Rome and Radames at the festival of Caracalla; Other roles include Puccini's Calaf, Luigi, Rodolfo and Des Grieux, Pollione in Norma, Turiddu in Cavalleria Rusticana, Giordano's Andrea Chénier, Verdi's Radames in Aida, and Ernani; Sang Radames at the Verona Arena, 1996. Recordings include: Norma; Fausta by Donizetti; Manon Lescaut; Cavalleria Rusticana; Tabarro and Tosca, both new editions, recorded in Philadelphia under Riccardo Mutio. Honours include: Prizewinner in competitions at Naples, Vercelli and Milan. Address: c/o Patricia Greenan, 196 Belsize Lane, London NW3 4DU, England.

GIAIOTTO Bonaldo, b. 25 Dec 1932, Ziracco, Udine, Italy. Bass Singer. Education: Studied in Udine and with Alfredo Starno in Milan. Debut: Teatro Nuovo Milan in 1957. Career: Sang widely in Italy then appeared as Rossini's Bartolo at Cincinnati in 1959; Metropolitan Opera debut in 1960 as Zaccaria in Nabucco and has sung in New York for 25 years in 300 performances, notably as Ramphis, Raimondo and Timur; Further engagements in Paris, London, Bordeaux, Rome, Geneva, Vienna, Hamburg and Madrid; Concert tour of South America in 1970; Season 1985 as Banquo in Zurich, Attila at the Verona Arena and in a revival of Donizetti's Il Diluvio Universale at Geneva, as Noah; La Scala Milan debut in 1986 as Rodolfo in La Sonnambula; Season 1988-89 as Ramphis in Aida at Chicago, Fiesco in Simon Boccanegra at Piacenza and Padre Guardiano in Miami and Verona; Sang Timur in Turandot at Turin in 1990; Season 1992 as Alvise in La Gioconda at Rome and Philip II and Ramphis at the Verona Arena; Sang in the French version of Don Carlos at Brussels, 1996. Recordings: Ferrando in Il Trovatore; Brogni in La Juive; Luisa Miller; Aida; La Traviata; Turandot; La Cieco in Massenet's Iris conducted by Patanè. Address: c/o Arena di Verona, Piazza Bra 28, I-37121 Verona, Italy.

GIBAULT Claire, b. 1955, Le Mans, France. Conductor. Education: Studied at the Le Mans Conservatory and in Paris. Career: Staff Conductor and Assistant to John Eliot Gardiner at the Lyons Opera, 1983-89, leading Pelléas et Mélisande, La Finta Giardiniera, Il Barbiere di Siviglia and Iphigénie en Tauride; For Nice Opera has conducted Mitridate, Rossini's Donna del Lago, La Traviata and Die Zauberflöte, and Idomeneo at Liège; Assistant to Claudio Abbado at the Vienna Staatsoper in 1986 and engaged there in 1988; Debut with the Royal Opera at Covent Garden in 1993 in Pelléas et Mélisande; Le Comte Ory at Glyndebourne, 1997. Address: c/o OWM, 14 Nightingale Lane, London N8 7QU, England.

GIBB James, b. 7 Mar 1918, Monkseaton, Northumberland. Pianist; Teacher; Professor Emeritus. Education: Merchiston Castle School, Edinburgh, Scotland; Taught piano by Mabel Lander, a pupil of Leschetizky. Debut: Promenade Concert 1949 in Royal Albert Hall. Career includes: Concerto Soloist, Berlin Philharmonic Orchestra and North-West German Radio Orchestra under Hans Schmidt-Isserstedt; Extensive tours in Central America and the Caribbean; Concert with BRNO State Radio Symphony Orchestra, conducted by Carlo Maria Giulini, Prague Spring Festival. Schubert Piano Sonatas for Meridan. Publications: Article in Penguin's Keyboard Music edited by Denis Matthews (later issued by David & Charles). Honours: Professor Emeritus, Guildhall School of Music & Drama, 1995; Fellow, Guildhall School of Music & Drama, 1967. Membership: Incorporated Society of Musicians. Hobbies: Theatre; Literature; Photography. Current Management: Anthony Purkiss. Address: 35 Fonthill Road, Hove, E Sussex BN 3 6HB, England.

GIBBONS Jack, b. 2 Mar 1962, England. Pianist. Debut: London Solo Debut, 1979. Career: Numerous solo and concert appearances from the age of 10; Annual solo concert at the Queen Elizabeth Hall, London, since 1990; Performances at the Barbican, London; Symphony Hall, Birmingham; New York and Washington DC Debuts, 1994; Debut, Lincoln Centre, New York, 1997; Many appearances on BBC radio, television and Classic FM radio, and with various orchestras. Compositions: Solo piano arrangements of Gershwin's Concert Works and Overtures, and transcriptions of Gershwin's original piano improvisations from recordings and piano-rolls. Recordings: For series of solo piano albums; The Authentic George Gershwin Vols 1, 2, 3 and 4; Alkan's Complete Opus 39 Etudes, Vols 1 and 2; Lambert's Rio Grande with the English Northern Philharmonia Orchestra, Opera North, conductor David Lloyd-Jones. Honours: First Prize, Newport International Pianoforte Competition, 1982; MRA Award for best solo instrumental recording for The Authentic George Gershwin, 1993. Current Management: Norman McCann International Artists Limited, London; Carolyn Sachs, Trillium Productions Inc, New York, USA. Address: c/o Carolyn Sachs, Trilium Productions Inc, 345 Rivrside Drive, Suite 6A, New York, NY 10025, USA.

GIBBS Alan Trevor, b. 21 Apr 1932, Chipping Norton, England. Composer. m. Vivienne Whysall, 21 Apr 1963, 1 son. Education: Durham University, 1950-53; Private Study with Edwin Rose, Matyas Seiber, John Webster, Norman J Barnes, Joan McKinnell, Conrad Eden. Career: Head of Music, Archbishop Tenison School, London, 1957-86; Musical Advisory Board, RSCM, 1965-69. Compositions: Reflections on a Life, for Violin and Orchestra; Festival Concertino, for Chamber Orchestra; Tenison Psalms; Over 50 Choral Pieces; 20 Organ Works and arrangements; Piano and Chamber Music; Songs. Recordings: Sonata 2, Conrad Eden; Celebration, Martin Weyer; Goodbye To Love, Grainger Arrangement. Publication: Editor, Holst's Music: A Guide by A E F Dickinson, 1995. Contributions to: Various magazines. Honours: Pears Scholarship in Music, Durham University, 1950; Best Sound Nomination, Radio Drama, International Radio Festival, New York, 1991. Membership: FRCO. Hobby: Grandchildren. Address: 8 St Margarets Drive, Twickenham, Middlesex TW1 1QN, England.

GIBBS Christopher (Howard), b. 20 Feb 1958, New York, New York, USA. Musicologist. m. Helena Sedlackova, 1993. Education: BA, hons, Music, Haverford College, 1980; MA, 1986, MPhil, 1987, PhD, 1992, Historical Musicology, Columbia University. Appointments: Faculty, Friends Seminary, New York City, 1980-83; Instructor, 1985-90, Columbia University; Music Auditor, New York State Council for the Arts, 1989-; Visiting Assistant Professor, Music, Haverford College, 1992-93; Visiting Assistant Professor, Music, 1993-97, Assistant Professor, Music, 1997-, State University of New York, Buffalo; Musicological Director, The Schubertiade, 1994-97; Music Critic, Chautauquan Daily, 1994-. Publications include: Komm geh' mit mir': Schubert's Uncanny Erlkönig, 1995; Editor, Cambridge Companion to Schubert, 1997. Honours: University Fellowship, Columbia University, 1983-84; Research Grant, Vienna, 1988-89; President's Fellowship, Columbia University, 1989-92; Lane Cooper Fellowship, New York Community Trust, 1990-91; Dissertation Prize, Austrian Cultural Institute, 1992. Memberships: Music Critics Association; American Musicological Society; College Music Society. Address: Department of Music, State University of New York at Buffalo, 222 Baird Hall, Buffalo, NY 14260, USA.

GIBIN Joao, b. 1929, Lima, Peru. Singer (Tenor). Education: Studied in Lima and at the Scuola della Scala, Milan, Italy. Career: Sang first in Italy then guested with the Netherlands Opera in Amsterdam as Andrea Chenier and Calaf; Vienna Staatsoper from 1958; Covent Garden 1959, as Edgardo opposite Joan Sutherland's Lucia; leading roles at La Scala from 1960; New York City Opera and Maggio Musicale, Florence, 1961, as Radames and Don Carlos. Recordings: Fanciulla del West, with Birgit Nilsson (Columbia); Lucia di Lammermoor, with Sutherland. Honour: Winner, MGM South American Caruso Competition, 1954. Address: c/o Teatro alla Scala, Via Filodrammatici 2, I-20121 Milan, Italy.

GIBSON Jon (Charles), b. 11 Mar 1940, Los Angeles, CA, USA. Flautist; Saxophonist; Composer. Education: Studied at Sacramento and San Francisco State Universities. Career: Co-founded the New Music Ensemble in 1961; Associated with minimalist group of composers including participation in the premiere of Terry Riley's In C, 1964, and membership from 1968 of the Philip Glass Ensemble; Visual arts involved in compositions, some of which written for dancers; Solo appearances as instrumentalist in the USA and Europe. Compositions include: Opera: Voyage Of The Beagle, 1985; Who Are You, Vocal and Tape Delay; Visitations: An Environment Soundscape And Radioland for Tape, 1966-72; Instrumental: Multiples, 1972, Song I-IV, 1972-79, Melody I-IV, 1973-75, Cycles for Organ, 1973, Recycle I and II, 1977, Call, 1978, Return, and Variations both for Small Ensemble, 1979-80, Extensions, dance score, 1980, Relative Calm, dance score, for Small Ensemble and Tape, 1981, Interval for Video Tape, 1985. Recordings include: Einstein On The Beach, with the Philip Glass Ensemble. Honours include: Grantee, Creative Artist Public Service Program, 1974, 1981 and Rockefeller Foundation, 1982. Address: c/o ASCAP, ASCAP Building, One Lincoln Plaza, New York, NY 10023, USA.

GIBSON Rodney, b. 1960, Winchester, England. Baritone. Education: Studied at the Royal College of Music and with Paolo Silveri and Raimund Herincx. Career: Sang first at the Teatro Ghione in Rome; Early roles were The Forester in The Cunning Little Vixen, Falstaff, Pistol in At The Boar's Head by Holst and Don Alfonso; Season 1985-86 with Mecklenburgh Opera and Abbey Opera, at the Camden Festival in The Tsar has his Photograph Taken by Weill, and with the Modern Music Theatre Troupe; Further appearances as Dapertutto with Beaufort Opera and concerts with Baroque Music; Has sung Ping in Turandot for Regency Opera and at the Royal Albert Hall; Concert repertoire includes Puccini's Gloria and Mozart's Coronation Mass, Moses und Aron by Schoenberg and Carmina Burana by Orff. Address: c/o Korman International Management, Crunnells Green Cottage, Preston, Hertfordshire, SG4 7UQ, England.

GIBSON Stephen (Brodie), b. 27 Mar 1957, Barnet, Herfordshire, England. Composer. Education: BMus, Honours, Composition, Birmingham University, 1978; Studied with John Casken, John Joubert and GW Hopkins. Career: Composer, Banff Centre Music Theatre Studio Ensmble, Alberta, Canada, 1982-84; Music performed extensively in the Netherlands, Belgium, Canada, Spain, USA and in Britain at Huddersfield Festival, 1982-83; Commissions from Banff Centre, Birmingham University and various ensembles and performers including Copas Ensemble, and oboists Catherine Pluygers and David Wilson. Compositions include: Meridian for Violins, Violas and Oboe, for video piece OLAM, 1982; From The Seed There Weeps A Willow..., published by The Premiere Magazine, 1983-85; Self-published major works: Extensions II-IV for various combinations, 1979-82, Mystery-Bouffe, one-act music theatre work, 1979-84, Baby On A Leash, opera, 1982-83, Stomp for Piano, 1982, also recorded, Ghost Town, 2-act music theatre work, 1983, Sub-Class Four Million, 1-act music theatre work, 1983-84, There Once Was A Time for Baritone and Ensemble, 1984, Symphony, Urban Street Songs for Large Orchestra, 1985-86. Honours: Bursaries: Vaughan Williams Trust, Hinrichsen Foundation, The Banff Centre. Memberships: Performing Rights Society; The Composers' Guild; Society for The Promotion of New Music. Address: 40 Campbell Close, London, SE16 6NG, England.

GIEBEL Agnes, b. 10 Aug 1921, Heerlen, Netherlands. Soprano. m. Herbert Kanders, 1 son, 2 daughters. Education: Studied at the Folkwang-Schule Essen with Hilde Wesselmann. Career: Gave first public concert in 1933 with Lieder by Strauss and Reger; Adult career from 1947 giving many concerts and recitals in Europe and North America; Bach Cantatas series with Karl Ristenpart for Berlin Radio, 1950-51; Repertoire includes 20th century works, Mozart arias and much Baroque music. Recordings include: Bach's Christmas Oratorio; St Matthew Passion; St John Passion; Beethoven's Missa Solemnis; Die Schöpfung; Bach Cantatas; Ein Deutsches Requiem; Song recitals, and CD with Hermann Prey and Celibidache. Address: EMI Records, Publicity (Classical), 20 Manchester Square, London, W1A 1ES, England.

GIELEN Michael (Andreas), b. 20 Jul 1927, Dresden, Germany. Conductor. m. Helga Augusten, 20 May 1957, 1 s, 1 d. Education: Dresden, 1936; Berlin, 1937; Vienna, 1940; After emigration in 1940 studied music in Buenos Aires with Dr Erwin Leuchter. Career: Coach, Teatro Colon, Buenos Aires, 1947-50; Conductor, Vienna State Opera, 1950-60; Chief Conductor with Stockholm Royal Opera, 1960-65; Freelance Conductor, Cologne, Germany, 1965-68; Conducted the premiere of Zimmermann's Die Soldaten, 1965; Music Director, Belgian National Orchestra, Brussels, 1969-73; Chief Conductor of Netherlands Opera, 1973-75; Music Director and General Manager of Frankfurt Opera House, 1977-87; Music Director, Cincinnati Symphony Orchestra, USA, 1980-86; Chief Conductor of SWF Radio Orchestra, Baden-Baden, Germany, 1986-; Professor of Conducting at Mozarteum in Salzburg, 1987-; Television Series in 6 parts with SWF Orchestra, Orchester-Farben, 1993; Conducted Lulu at the Berlin Staatsoper, 1997. Compositions: 4 Gedichte von Stefan George, 1958; Variations for 40 Instruments, 1959; Un dia sobresale, 1963; Die glocken sind auf falscher spur, 1969; Mitbestimmungs Modell, 1974; String Quartet, 1983; Pflicht und Neieune for Ensemble, 1988; Rückblick, trio for 3 Cellos, 1989; Weitblick, sonata for Solo Cello, 1991. Recordings include: Schoenberg's Moses und Aron and Piano and Violin Concertos; Alfred Brendel, Wolfgang Marschner; Zimmermann's Die Soldaten; Ligeti's Requiem and Cello Concerto (Siegfried Palm); Stockhausen's Carré; Werle's Dreaming of Thérèse, with the

Royal Stockholm Orchestra; Recordings with Cincinnati CSO, a series of 25 CDs, Gielen Edition with SWF Orchestra. Address: c/o South West German Radio, D-76530 Baden-Baden, Germany.

GIERSTER Hans, b. 12 Jan 1925, Germany. Musical Director. Education: Musikhochschule, Munich; Mozarteum, Salzburg. Career: Formerly Musical Director of Freiburg-im-Breisgau Municipal Theatres; General Musical Director, Nuremberg, 1965; Director, Musiktheater Nuremberg, 1971; Currently, Conductor at Munich Staatsoper; Guest Conductor at State Operas of Hamburg, Munich and Vienna; Guest appearances at festivals in Munich, 1964, Edinburgh with Bavarian State Opera in Così fan Tutte in 1965, Glyndebourne with Magic Flute in 1966, Zurich in 1971 and Vienna in 1972; Concerts with Philharmonic Orchestras of Bamberg, Berlin, Munich, Vienna, London, and Mexico City. Address: Musiktheater Nürnberg, 8500 Nuremberg, Hallerweisse 4, Germany.

GIERZOD Kazimierz, b. 6 Aug 1936, Warsaw, Poland. Pianist. m. Jolanta Zegadlo, 14 Jul 1974. Education: Graduated, Warsaw Frederic Chopin Academy of Music, 1962 under Professor Margerita Trombini-Kazuro; Diploma of Merit, Accademia Chigiana, Siena, Italy under Professor Guido Agosti. Career: Regular recitals and concerts in Europe, Japan, USA amd South America from 1964; Pedagogical career: Tutor, 1969-73, Assistant Professor, 1973-86, Professor, 1986-, Dean of the Piano Department, 1975-87, F Chopin Academy of Music in Warsaw, Elected as Rector of F Chopin Academy of Music in 1987 and again, 1990-93. Recordings: Archival recordings for Polish Radio of Polish music, recordings for American and Cypriot Radio and TV recordings for Polish and Japanese TV; Creative Works: Lectures on musical interpretation, masterclasses in Poland, Japan, USA, Venezuela and Cyprus; Radio and TV commentator during International F Chopin Piano Competition in Warsaw, 1985, 1990; Radio and TV interviews and interviews for local and foreign press; Visiting Professor, Soai University, Osaka, Japan, 1988-. Memberships: Jury's Member of the Piano Competititon, Europe, Japan and Venezuela; President, F Chopin International Foundation, Warsaw, Poland, 1992-. Address: ul Sygietynskiego 36, 05-805 Otrebusy, Poland.

GIETZ Gordon, b. 1968, Canada. Singer (Tenor). Education: Studied in Montreal. Career: Opera de Montreal, as Ferrando, Paris in La Belle Hélène, Tebaldo in I Capuleti, Tamino and Hoffmann; Other engagements as Agenore in Il Re Pastore for the Canadian Opera Company, Albert Herring for Calgary Opera and Rossini's Almaviva at St Louis; Concerts include: L'Enfance du Christ under Charles Dutoit, Verdi Requiem with the Winnipeg SO, Stabat Maters of Schubert and Rossini and Messiah at Montreal; Berlioz Huits Scenes de Faust with the Toronto SO, Houston SO and at the London Proms under John Eliot Gardiner; Season 1997-98 with Berlioz's Benedict at Alice Tully Hall, New York, the Duke of Mantua at Peking Alfredo with Philadelphia Orchestra. Recordings include: L'Enfance du Christ and Berlioz's Lelio (Decca); Les Mamelles de Teresias (Philips). Address: IMG Artists, Media House, 3 Burlington Lane, London W4 2TH, England.

GIFFORD Anthea, b. 17 Feb 1949, Bristol, England. Classical Guitarist. m. John Trusler, 18 Jul 1970, 1 son, 1 daughter. Education: Accademia Musicale Chigiana, Siena, Italy; Royal College of Music, London. Debut: Purcell Room, London. Career: Many solo recitals and over 30 programmes on BBC Radio 3 with violinist, Jean-Jacques Kantorow; Recitals at the Purcell Room, Wigmore Hall, Fairfield Hall, Barbican Centre, Queen Elizabeth and Festival Halls; TV appearances on Channel 4, BBC 2 TV, and TSW among others, frequent chamber music recitals with Delmé String Quartet and adjudicator for Overseas League; Performances in Italy, France, Spain and Germany; Director of Droffig Recordings. Recordings: Paganini and his Contemporaries by Kantorow-Gifford Duo, 1991; Solo Recital, 1991; Paganini Ensemble, 1991; Kantorow-Gifford Violin and Guitar Duos, 1993; Dodgson Duo Concerto with Northern Sinfonia, 1994. Contributions to: Guitar International. Honours: Recipient, Young Musician of the Year, Greater London Arts Association Award. Memberships: Incorporated Society of Musicians; Overseas League. Address: 24 Donovan Avenue, London, N10 2JX, England.

GIFFORD Helen, b. 5 Sep 1935, Melbourne, Australia. Composer. Education: MusB, Melbourne University Conservatorium of Music, 1958. Career: Composer in Residence, Melbourne Theatre Company, 1970-; Commissions from Melbourne Chorale, Astra Chamber Music Society, Australian Broadcasting Commission, Australian Percussion Ensemble. Compositions include: Chamber Music: Fantasy for Flute and Piano, 1958, Skiagram for Flute, Viola and Vibraphone, 1963, String Quartet, 1965, Canzone for Chamber Orchestra, recorded, 1968, Sonnet for Flute, Guitar and Harpsichord, 1969, Overture for Chamber Orchestra, 1970, Images For Christmas for Speaker, Electric Guitar, Small Organ with Percussion, Celesta and Effects for 5 Players, 1973; Piano: Piano Sonata, 1960, Waltz, 1966, Cantillation, 1966; Orchestral: Phantasma for String Orchestra, recorded, 1963, Imperium, 1969; Vocal, Choral: As Dew In Aprille, Christmas carol for Boy or Female Soprano, Piano or Harp or Guitar, 1955, Vigil, a cappella, 1966, Bird Calls From An Old Land for 5 Soprano Soloists, a Cappella Female Choir, 1971; Brass: Company Of Brass for Ensemble, 1972; Theatre: Incidental music and songs, Jo Being, 1-act opera, 1974. Address: c/o J Albert and Son, 139 King Street, Sydney, New South Wales 2000, Australia.

GIGAURI Nodar, b. 30 July 1930, Gori, Georgia. Composer; Producer; Stage Manager. m. Natela Kortava, 10 Apr 1968, 1 son, 1 daughter. Education: Central Musical School, Tbilisi, 1948-52; Department of Composition with Professor Andria Balanchivadze, Tbilisi State Conservatoire, 1955-60. Debut: Tele-opera Preceptor on Moscow Central Television, 1961. Career: Producer, Stage Manager, Tele-Radio Department, Tbilisi, 1961-88. Compositions: Preceptor, opera; Spring Tales, opera for children; Psalms of Remorse - King David IV, the Builder, opera; Concertos, for piano and large symphony orchestra, for violin and chamber orchestra, for bassoon and string orchestra. Recordings; Variety songs: I'm a guy from Tbilisi, Here comes April, Tell me silently, Tbilisi and Pirosmani, Alluring Spring, I was waiting for a spring; Many songs for children. Publications: Chorale Ristaveli, 1970; A cycle of songs for children, 1977; Spiritual songs, 1995. Contributions to: Article about opera Preceptor, Ekran magazine, Poland, 1962. Honours: 1st Grade Diploma for Preceptor, 1961; Honoured Art Worker. Membership: Union of Composers of Georgia. Hobbies: Painting; Restored and now supervisor of a church. Address: Rcheulishvili str, corp 7, apt 29, Tbilisi, Georgia.

GILBERT Alan, b. 1965, Switzerland. Conductor. Career: Regular concerts with the Orchestre de la Suisse Romande, 1994-; Further engagements with Suddeutsches Rundfunk Orchestra, Stuttgart, Museum Gesellschaft (Frankfurt) and in Japan with Tokyo Philharmonic, Tokyo Symphony and NHK Symphony; Season 1996-97 with the Orchestre de Chambre de Lausanne, Orchestre Philharmonique de Radio France, Cincinnati Symphony and the Cleveland Orchestra (assistant to Christoph von Dohnányi). Honours include: First Prize in the International Competition for Musical Performance, Geneva, 1994. Address: c/o IMG Artists, Media House, 3 Burlington Lane, London W4 2TH, England.

GILBERT Anthony (John), b. 26 July 1934, London, England. Composer; Teacher of Composition. Education: MA, DMus, Leeds; Fellow, Royal Northern College of Music; Composition with Anthony Milner, Mátyás Seiber, Alexander Goehr and Gunther Schuller; Conducting with Lawrence Leonard, Morley College, London. Career: Lecturer in Composition, Goldsmiths' College, 1968-73; Composer-in-Residence, University of Lancaster, 1970-71; Lecturer in Composition, Morley College, London, 1972-75; Senior Lecturer in Composition, Sydney Conservatorium, Australia, 1978-79; Composer-in-Residence, City of Bendigo, Victoria, 1981; Currently Director of Composition Studies, Royal Northern College of Music, England. Compositions include: Orchestral: Symphony; Sinfonia; Ghost and Dream Dancing; Crow Cry; Towards Asavari; Tree of Singing Names; Operas: The Scene Machine (with George MacBeth), The Chakravaka-Bird (with Mahadevi and A K Ramanujan); Chamber: 3 String Quartets; Saxophone Quartet; Quartet of Beasts; Nine or Ten Osannas; Vasanta with Dancing; Instrumental: Moonfaring; Dawnfaring; Igorochki; 2 Piano Sonatas; Spell Respell; Ziggurat; The Incredible Flute Music; Treatment of Silence; Vocal: Certain Lights Reflecting; Love Poems; Inscapes; Long White Moonlight; Beastly Jingles. Recordings: Nine or Ten Osannas (Music projects, London); Beastly Jingles (Jane's Minstrels). Memberships include: Composers Guild; Association of Professional Composers; Performing Right Society. Hobbies: Walking; Running; Conservation; Art Galleries; Photography. Address: c/o Royal Northern College of Music, 124 Oxford Road, Manchester M13 9RD, England.

GILBERT Jane, b. 1969, New York City, New York, USA. Singer (Mezzo-soprano). m. John Hancock. Education: Studied at the Juilliard Opera Center. Career: Season 1993-94 at Cenerentola at Kansas City, Varvara in Katya Kabanova for Canadian Opera, Britten's Lucretia at the Brooklyn Academy and Ragonde in Comte Ory at Spoleto Festival, USA; Season 1994-95 as Bartók's Judith at Melbourne (also at Edinburgh), Olga in Eugene Onegin at Toronto, Cuniza in Oberto for Opéra de Nice and Federica in Luisa Miller for Washington Opera; Concert repertoire includes the Berlioz Mort de Cléopâtre. Address: Atholl Still Ltd, Foresters Hall, 25-27 Westow Street, London SE19 3RY, England.

GILBERT Kenneth, b. 16 Dec 1931, Montreal, Canada. Harpsichordist; Organist. Education: Honorary, MusD, McGill University. Career: Professor of Harpsichord, Hochschule für Musik, Stuttgart and the Mozateum, Salzburg; Summer courses at Accademia Chigiana, Siena. Recordings include: Complete Harpsichord Works of François Couperin, and Rameau; Bach's English and French Suites and Well-Tempered Clavier; Goldberg Variations, 1987; Music by Lully, 1988, Bach English Suites, 1988, Couperin's Four Books for Harpsichord, 1989; Music by Frescobaldi, Byrd, Froberger, Purcell, Handel, Rameau, Bach, Couperin and Scarlatti, 1988. Publications: Complete Harpsichord Works of Rameau, François Couperin, D'Anglebert, Bach's Goldberg Variations, Frescobaldi Toccatas; Complete Keyboard Sonatas of Scarlatti in 11 volumes. Honours: Canada Council Arts Fellowship, 1968, 1974; International Calouste Gulbenkian Foundation Award, 1970; Artist of The Year, Canada, 1978; Officer, Order of Canada, 1986; Professor of Harpsichord, Paris Conservatoire, 1988. Current Management: Basil Douglas Artists' Management, 8 St George's Terrace, London, NW1 8XJ, England. Address: 11 Rue Ernest-Psichari, F-75007 Paris, France.

GILBOA Jacob, b. 2 May 1920, Kosice, Czechoslovakia. Composer. m. Shoshana Bregman, 22 Mar 1961, 1 daughter. Education: Academy of Music, Jersualem; Music Teacher's Seminary, Jerusalem. Compositions: Orchestra: The Twelve Chagall Windows, Cedars, From The Dead Sea Scrolls, Kathros Upsanterin, 7 Ornaments To A Theme By Paul Haim, The Beth Alpha Mosaic, Safiah, The Lament Of Kalonymos; Chamber Music: Dew, Steps Of Spring, Toccata In Black, White And Grey, Sonata for Cello, C'Est Q'ua Vu Le Vent D'Est, Reflections On Three Chords By Alban Berg, Crystals, Three Lyric Pieces In Mediterranean Style, Irith Flowers, Melancholy-Triptychon, Bedu, String Quartet, 7 Little Insects, The Grey Colours Of Kaethe Kollwitz, 1990, Blossoms In The Desert, 1991, Three-Coloured Melancholy, 1992. Recordings: The Twelve Chagall Windows; The Beth Alpha Mosaic; Three Lyric Pieces In Mediterranean Style. Honours: Acum Prize, 1968, 1970, 1973, 1989; Engel Prize, 1972, 1979; Prize, Prime Minister of Israel, 1982. Membership: Israeli Composers' Association. Hobby: Painting. Address: Israeli Music Publication (IMP), 25 Keren Hayessod Street, Jerusalem 94188, Israel.

GILCHRIST Diana, b. 1970, Canada. Soprano. Education: Studied at Banff School of Fine Arts and in Los Angeles and London. Career: Founded Opera Lyra at Ottawa and sang at Koblenz Opera from 1989, notably as Susanna, Janácek's Vixen and Gilda; Sang Mozart's Blondchen with Mainz Opera, followed by Zerbinetta; Bielefeld in 1991 as Grétry's Zemire, Vienna Volksoper in 1992 as the Queen of Night, returning as Offenbach's Olympia; Concerts in Canada and Germany have included Orff's Carmina Burana. Address: Helen Sykes Management, Fourth Floor, Parkway House, Sheen Lane, East Sheen, London, SW14 8LS, England.

GILDER Eric, b. 25 Dec 1911, London, England. Lecturer; Author; Composer. m. 23 Dec 1939, 2 daughters. Education: Royal College of Music. Career: About 1000 radio and television appearances as Pianist, Conductor, Actor, Playwright, Singer, Story and Script Writer. Compositions: Symphonic works; 200 songs; 13 stage musicals. Publications: Dictionary of Composers and Their works, 1978, 1985; Catterels; Sharing Music with Eric Gilder; Many Parts. Address: 21 Fieldend, Twickenham, Middlesex TW1 4TF, England.

GILES Alice, b. 1961, Australia. Concert Harpist. Education: Studied in Australia with June Loney and with Alice Chalifoux in Cleveland. Career: Has concertised extensively in Australia, the USA, Israel and Germany; Festival engagements at Schleswig-Holstein, Bayreuth (International Youth Festival) and Dusseldorf New Music Festivals, Adelaide (Britten's Canticles with Barry Tuckwell and Gerald English), Sydney, Marlboro Music Festival (USA), and Bath Mozartfest; New York Merkin Hall debut, 1983, 92nd Street 'Y' Concert, 1988; Wigmore Hall debut, June 1989, and tour with Luciano Berio; Featured Soloist at festivals including Salzedo Centennial, Austin, Texas, World Harp Congress, Copenhagen, and World Harp Festival, Cardiff, Wales; Concertos with Collegium Musicum Zurich, Badische Staatskapelle Karlsruhe, English Symphony Orchestra, all major symphony orchestras in Australia and tour of North and South America with Australian Youth Orchestra; Chamber concerts with violinist Thomas Zehetmair and pianist Arnan Wiesel. Recordings include: CD, recital, Fauré's Impromptu in D flat major, 2 Preludes of Debussy, Tournier's 2nd Sonatine, 5 Preludes of Salzedo; CD, recital of works for solo harp by Carlos Salzedo; Chamber music for flute and harp with Geoffrey Collins, flute. Honours include: Churchill International Fellowship, 1980; Winner, International Harp Competition, Israel, 1982. Membership: Co-Founder, Director, EOLUS - International Salzedo Society. Address: Robert Gilder & Co, Enterprise House, 59-65 Upper Ground, London SE1 9PQ, England.

GILFEDDER John Francis, b. 27 Jan 1925, Melbourne, Victoria, Australia. Composer. Education: BMus, 1958, BEd (Hons), 1962, University of Melbourne. Career includes: Faculty Member, Queensland Conservatorium, 1970-; Concert Presenter and Producer. Compositions include: The Trojan Doom for speaking voice, string quartet, flute, cor anglais and horn, 1972; Orbits About a Theme for piano, 1981; Colours of the Cosmos, for percussion ensemble, 1985; The Legend of Tibrogargan, for orchestra, 1986; Raga of the Morning for cello, 1989; Reedy

Rivers, for woodwind, 1992; Transparencies in Violet, for viola and string orchestra, 1994; Conversazione Pastorale, for saxophone quartet, 1994; Te Deum in Montage, for choir, 1995; Commissions from the Queensland Philharmonic (1994) and others. Address: c/o APRA, 1A Eden Street, Crows Nest, NSW 2065, Australia.

GILFRY Rodney, b. 11 Mar 1959, California, USA. Singer (Baritone). Career: Sang in opera at Los Angeles as Guglielmo, Mozart's Figaro, the Villains in Contes d'Hoffmann and Ford in Falstaff, 1990; European engagements as Figaro at Hamburg, Tel Aviv and Zurich; Frankfurt Opera from 1989, as Gounod's Mercutio, Ernesto (Il Pirata) and Massenet's Herod; Geneva, 1988, as Lescaut in Manon, Santa Fe, 1991, in the US premiere of Oedipus by Rihm; Concert engagements include Bach's B minor Mass in Paris and at La Scala, Milan; Season 1992 as Guglielmo in Barcelona and at the Holland Festival, Don Giovanni at the Opéra de Lyon; Sang Sharpless in Butterfly at Los Angeles, 1996; Guglielmo at Covent Garden, 1997; Met debut as Demetrius in A Midsummer Night's Dream, 1997. Recordings: Ein Deutsches Requiem (Philips); Così fan tutte (DGG). Address: c/o Opéra de Lyon, 9 Quai Jean Moulin, F-69001 Lyon, France.

GILL Timothy, b. 1960, England. Cellist. Career: Co-founded the Chagall Piano Trio at the Banff Centre for the Arts in Canada, currently resident artist; Debut concert at the Blackheath Concert Halls in London in 1991; Further appearances at the Barbican's Prokofiev Centenary Festival, the Warwick Festival and the South Place Sunday Concerts at the Conway Hall in London; Purcell Room London recitals in 1993 with the London premiere of piano trios by Tristan Keuris, Nicholas Maw and Dame Ethel Smyth (composed in 1880); Premiere of Piano Trio No 2 by David Matthews at the Norfolk and Norwich Festival in 1993; Engaged for the Malvern Festival in 1994. Address: Chagall Trio, South Bank Centre, Press Office (Pamela Chowham Management), London, SE1, England.

GILLARD David (Owen), b. 8 Feb 1947, Croydon, Surrey, England. Critic; Writer. Education: Tavistock; Croydon. Career: Scriptwriter, Associated British Pathé, 1967-69; Film and Theatre Critic, Daily Sketch, 1969-70; Ballet Critic, 1971-89, Opera Critic, 1971-, Daily Mail; Founder Editor, ENO and Friends, 1982-92; Radio Correspondent, Radio Times, 1983-91. Publication: Beryl Grey: A Biography, 1977. Contributions to: Daily Mail; Radio Times; BBC Music Magazine; Music and Musicians. Memberships: The Critics' Circle; The Green Room Club. Hobbies: Hill walking; Collecting children's books. Address: 16 Grasmere Road, Bromley, Kent BR1 4BA, England.

GILLES Marie-Louise, b. 1937, Duren, Germany. Mezzo-Soprano. Education: Studied at the Folkwang-Hochschule Essen with Hilde Wesselmann. Career: Wiesbaden Opera from 1962 as Octavian, Dorabella and the Composer in Ariadne auf Naxos; Staatsoper Munich, 1964-66, Bremen, 1966-68 and from 1968 at Hannover notably as Azucena, Brangaene, Eboli, Waltraute, Fricka, Ortrud, Berg's Marie and Countess Geschwitz and Santuzza; Bayreuth Festival, 1968-69, appearances at the Dubrovnik and Salzburg Easter Festivals and concert engagements in Washington, New York, Vienna, Paris and Lisbon; Professor at the Hannover Musikhochschule from 1982. Recordings: Petite Messe Solennelle by Rossini; Bach Cantatas; Hans Heiling by Marschner. Address: Hochscule für Musik und Theater, Emmichplatz 1, 3 Hannover, Germany.

GILLESPIE Rhondda (Marie), b. 3 Aug 1941, Sydney, New South Wales, Australia. Concert Pianist. m. Denby Richards, 1973. Education: New South Wales Conservatory, Sydney, with Alexander Svergensky; UK with Denis Matthews and Louis Kentner. Career: Recitals and concerto appearances throughout the world, including UK, USA, Australia, Far and Near East, Europe and Scandinavia; BBC TV series on Liszt's Christmas Tree; From 1984 many tours with Robert Weatherburn as Duo, Two's Company. Recordings: Duets (with Robert Weatherburn); Sonatas by Bliss and Lambert; Concertos by Usko Meriläinen; Sonata, 2 Ballads and Christmas Tree Suite by Liszt; Works by Camilleri. Honours: New South Wales Concerto Prize, 1959; Harriet Cohen Commonwealth Medal, 1966. Membership: Lansdowne Club. Hobbies: Exotic cooking; Golf. Address: 2 Princes Road, St Leonards-on-Sea, East Sussex TN37 6EL, England.

GILLESPIE Wendy, b. 1950, New York, USA. Viol Player. Career: Member of Fretwork with first London concert at the Wigmore Hall in 1986; Appearances in the Renaissance and Baroque repertoire in Sweden, France, Belgium, Holland, Germany, Austria, Switzerland and Italy; Radio broadcasts in Sweden, Holland, Germany and Austria and a televised concert on ZDF, Mainz; Tour of Russia in 1989 and Japan in 1991; Festival engagements in Britain; Repertory includes In Nomines and Fantasias by Tallis, Parsons and Byrd, dance music by Holborne and Dowland including Lachrimae, six-part consorts by Gibbons and William Lawes, songs and instrumental works by Purcell; Collaborations with vocal group, Red Byrd in verse anthems by Byrd and Tomkins, London Cries by Gibbons and Dering, Resurrection Story and Seven Last Words by Schütz; Gave George Benjamin's Upon Silence at the Elizabeth Hall in 1990; Wigmore Hall concerts, 1990-91 with music by Lawes, Purcell, Locke, Dowland and Byrd. Recordings: Heart's Ease, late Tudor and early Stuart; Armada, courts of Philip II and Elizabeth II; Night's Black Bird by Dowland and Byrd; Cries And Fancies (fantasias, In Nomines and The Cries Of London by Gibbons); Go Nightly Cares, consort songs, dances and In Nomines. Address: c/o OWM, 14 Nightingale Lane, London N8 7QU, England.

GILLETT Christopher, b. 1958, London, England. Singer (Tenor). Education: Studied at the Royal College of Music with Robert Tear and Edgar Evans; National Opera Studio, London. Debut: Sadler's Wells as Edwin in The Gypsy Princess, 1981. Career: sang with New Sadler's Wells Opera in Gilbert and Sullivan; Has appeared with Glyndebourne Touring Opera as Ferrando and Albert Herring; Hermes in King Priam for Kent Opera; Royal Opera House Covent Garden from 1984 as Flute in Midsummer Night's Dream, Rodrigo in Otello, Dov in Knot Garden, Pang and Hermes and in Parsifal, Un Re in Ascolto and Idomeneo; Sang Nooni in The Making of the Representative for Planet 8 at the London Coliseum and in Amsterdam; Season 1990-91 with the Martyrdom of St Magnus by Maxwell Davies in London and Glasgow; Mozart's Ferrando at Garsington Manor and Arbace with the English Bach Festival at Covent Garden and in the Vichy Festival, France; Pysander in Netherlands Opera Ulisses; Sang Musil in the premiere of Broken Strings by Param Vir, Amsterdam, 1992; Tichon in Katya Kabonova for Glyndebourne Touring Opera and Britten's Flute at the 1992 Aix-en-Provence Festival; Concert engagements include Elgar's The Kingdom with the London Philharmonic, Tippett's Mask of Time with the Hallé; Bach's St John Passion in Hong Kong, Cambridge and Greenwich and Elijah with the Bach Choir; Season 1997 with Britten's Flute and Pirzel in Die Soldaten for English Natioonal Opera and M Triquet for Netherlands Opera. Honours include: Winner, Grimsby Singing Competition, 1980; Countess of Munster Award, 1981. Address: Harrison/Parrott Ltd, 12 Penzance Place, London W11 4PA, England.

GILLINGHAM Bryan (Reginald), b. 12 Apr 1944, Vancouver, Canada. Professor. m. Susanna, nee Burton, 29 Oct 1983, 2 sons, 3 daughters. Education: BA, Maths and English, 1966, BMus, 1968, University of British Columbia; ARCT, Piano Performance, Toronto Conservatory, 1969; MMus, Musicology, King's College, London, England, 1971; PhD, Musicology, University of Washington, 1976. Appointments: Teacher, Music, Herdman Collegiate High School, Corner Brook, Newfoundland, 1970-72; Instructor, Extension, Memorial University, 1970-72; Lecturer, Music, Mount Allison University, 1975-76; Lecturer, Music, University of Alberta, 1975-76; Guest Lecturer, Music, University of Ottawa, 1977-79; Assistant Professor, 1976-80, Associate Chair, 1980-84, Chairman, 1984-91, Professor, 1986-, Music, Carleton University. Publications: Books include: Beyond the Moon: Festschrift Luther Dittmer, 1990; Secular Medieval Latin Song: An Anthology, 1993; Indices to the Notre-Dame Facsimiles, 1994; A Critical Study of Secular Medieval Latin Song, 1995; Articles include: Modal Rhythm and the Medieval Sequence, 1977; The Proemium to Notker's Liber ymnorum, 1978; Four Pre-Transitional Polyphonic Sequences, 1979. Honours: Award for Musicology, Graduating Class, 1968; Foreign Exchange Tuition Scholarship, University of Washington, 1974; Scholarly Achievement Award, 1984, 1988, Carleton University; Research Achievement Award, Carleton University, 1991; Faculty Teaching Award, Carleton University, 1997. Address: 1270 Lampman Crescent, Ottawa, ON K2C 1P8, Canada.

GILMORE Gail, b. 21 Sept 1950, Washington, District of Columbia, USA. Singer (Mezzo-soprano). Education: Xavier University, New Orleans; MMus, Indiana University, Bloomington. Career: Sang at Krefeld, Germany, 1975-79; Appearances at Giessen, Enschede (Netherlands) and the Vienna Staatsoper; Staatsoper Wiesbaden, 1979-82; Deutsche Oper am Rhein Duesseldorf, 1981-82, returning in 1986 (Penthesilea by Schoeck); New York City Opera, 1981-82; Teatro La Fenice, Venice, 1983-84, as Kundry in Parsifal; Sang at the Verona Arena, 1983-86, as Carmen and as Ulrica (Un Ballo in Maschera); Further engagements in Frankfurt, Nice, Cologne, Nuremberg, Barcelona and Hannover; Other roles include Cassandre (Les Troyens), Octavian, the Composer, Eboli, Gluck's Orpheus, Fricka, Brangaene, Cenerentola, Begonia (Der junge Lord) and Venus; Teatro Fenice Venice, 1987, as Ortrud; Metropolitan Opera debut, 1987, as Fricka in Das Rheingold; Zurich Opera, 1990, as Azucena; Season 1992-93 as Amneris at San Juan and the Festival of Caracalla, and premieres in Prague as Salome, in Buenos Aires as the Countess in Lulu, and in Bergen (Norway) and Tel-Aviv as Dalila in Samson and Dalila; Concert performances of Schoenberg's Gurrelieder, Passions by Bach, Brahms Alto Rhapsody, Les nuits d'été (Berlioz), La voix humaine (Poulenc) and works by US composers such as Barber, Joplin, Arlen, Bernstein and Gershwin. Recordings: CD of famous opera arias, 1992; CD of Gershwin songs with Royal Philharmonic Orchestra, London, 1993. Address: c/o Gilmore Music Productions, Apollolaan 125, 1077 AP Amsterdam, Netherlands.

GILMOUR Russell (Scott), b. 21 May 1956, Penrith, New South Wales, Australia. Composer. Education: BA, University of New England, 1986; Australian Chamber Orchestra's Composer Workshop, 1987, 1993. Career: Faculty Member, All Saints College, Bathurst, 1987-90; Canterbury College, Queensland, 1990-; Commissions from Bathurst City and Chamber Orchestras, 1987, 1989. Compositions include: A Peaceable Kingdom, for chamber orchestra, 1987; Mud, for tuba, 1989; Songlines, for orchestra, 1989; Edge, for flute, 1990; Wood Dance, for Marimba, 1991; Point II, for recorder, 1991; Blowpipes, for flute quartet, 1993; Cantate Domino, for choir, 1993; String Quartet: The Art of Reckoning, 1993; A Way Along, for choir and marimba, 1994. Contributions include: Sounds Australian (Spring 1992). Address: c/o APRA, 1A Eden Street, Crows Nest, NSW 2065, Australia.

GILVAN Raimund, b. 1938, Manchester, England. Singer (Tenor). Education: Studied at the Cologne Musikhochschule. Career: Sang at the Mainz Opera from 1961, Mannheim, 1963-74; Among his best roles have been Capito in Mathis der Maler, Lensky, Henze's Junge Lord, Adrasto in Traetta's Antigone, David in Die Meistersinger and Pfitzner's Palestrina; Many concert appearances. Recordings: Beethoven Missa solemnis, Bach B minor Mass, Lieder by Wolf.

GIMENEZ Eduardo, b. 2 Jun 1940, Mataro, Barcelona. Tenor. Education: Studied with Carmen Bracons de Clomer and Juan Sabater in Barcelona and Vladimiro Badiali in Rome. Debut: Reggio Emilia in 1967 as Nemorino in L'Elisir d'Amore. Career: Has sung widely in Italy and at the Teatro Liceo, Barcelona; Holland Festival in 1970 in La Fedeltà Premiata by Haydn; Guest appearances in Brussels, Nice, Monte Carlo, Venice, Budapest, Bordeaux, Tel Aviv, Seattle and Washington; Sang at Pesaro and La Scala Milan, 1984-85 in a revival of Rossini's Il Viaggio a Reims; Well known in operas by Cimarosa, Bellini, Paisiello, Galuppi, Mozart, Verdi and Puccini; Has sung in Paisiello's Il Barbiere di Siviglia at Leningrad, and at Barcelona in 1988 in the premiere of Libre Vermell by Xavier Benguere returning as Ferrando in Così fan tutte in 1990; Season 1992 as Rossini's Don Ramiro at the Semper Oper Dresden and in Barcelona. Recordings include: Elvino in La Sonnambula; Don Pasquale; L'Atlantida by Falla; Rossini's Armida. Address: John Coast, 31 Sinclair Road, London, W14 0NS, England.

GIMENEZ Raul, b. 14 Sep 1950, Argentina. Tenor. Education: Studied in Buenos Aires. Debut: Teatro Colon Buenos Aires in 1980 as Ernesto in Don Pasquale. Career: Sang in concert and opera throughout South America before his European debut as Filandro in Cimarosa's Le Astuzie Femminili at the 1984 Wexford Festival; Sang in Paris and Venice as Roderigo in Rossini's Otello and appeared as Elvino in La Sonnambula in 1989 at the Théâtre des Champs-Elysées; Season 1987 sang at the Pesaro Festival in Rossini's L'Occasione fa Il Ladro, at Amsterdam as Ernesto and as Alessandro in Il Re Pastore at Rome; Aix-en-Provence in 1988 as Gernando and Carlo in Rossini's Armida; Toronto and Zurich in 1989 as Almaviva; US debut at Dallas as Ernesto, Lisbon in 1989 as Tonio in La Fille du Régiment and Covent Garden 1990-93 as Almaviva, Ernesto and Ramiro; Season 1990 with appearances as Argirio in Tancredi at Geneva, Cosí fan tutte at Buenos Aires and Salieri's Les Danaides at the Ravenna Festival as Lyncée; Debuts at Vienna State Opera in 1990 as Almaviva , La Scala in 1993 in Tancredi, and at Florence in 1993 in La Cenerentola; Further guest appearances in Naples, Bologna, Verona, Turin, Frankfurt, Toulouse, Monte Carlo, Lausanne, Schwetzingen Festival and Brussels; Season 1996 sang Appio in Pacini's L'Ultimo giorno di Pompei, Martina Franca. Recordings include: Arias by Mozart, Rossini, Bellini and Donizetti; Les Danaides; L'Occasione fa il Ladro conducted by Michelangelo Veltri; Il Turco in Italia; Rossini's Messa di Gloria, 1992; Il Barbiere di Siviglia; Viaggio a Reims. Address: c/o Patricia Greenan, 19b Belsize Park, London, NW3 4DU, England.

GIMSE Havard, b. 15 Sept 1966, Kongsvinger, Norway. Pianist. Education: Norway State Academy of Music; Bergen Music Conservatory; Mozarteum, Salzburg; Musikhochschule, Berlin. Debut: Trondheim Symphony Orchestra, 1981. Career: Soloist with Major Scandinavan orchestras, such as Oslo Philharmonic, Bergen Philharmonic, Helsinki Radio, since 1981; Concerts in Europe and North and South America; Played with conductors including Kitajenko, Talmi, Schonwandt, Iona Brown; Several chamber music appearances; Oslo Philharmonic Tour of Great Britain, 1995-96; Schleswig-Holstein Festival, 1997; Valdemossa Chopin Festival, 1997. Recordings: Liszt: Piano Sonata; Chopin: Piano Music; Grieg: Piano and chamber music; Tveitt: Piano Music. Honours: Princess Astrid's Music Prize, 1985; Robert Levin Festival Prize, 1986; Jugend Musiziert Frankfurt, 1987; Steinway prize, Berlin, 1995; Grieg Prize, Norway, 1996. Current Management: Pro Arte International Management. Address: Fosswinchelsrt 9, N5007 Bergen, Norway.

GINKEL Peter van, b. 10 Mar 1933, Eindhoven, The Netherlands. Bass-Baritone. Education: Studied at the Quebec Conservatory and with Kurt Herbert Adler in San Francisco. Debut: Woodstock, NY, as Colonel Ibbetson in Peter Ibbetson by Deems Taylor. Career: Has appeared at most Canadian opera houses and in Chicago in the premiere of Penderecki's Paradise Lost in 1978; German engagement at Cologne, Dortmund, Stuttgart, Mannheim, Dusseldorf and Nuremberg; Roles have included Mozart's Figaro and Alfonso, Verdi's Iago and Rigoletto, Caspar, Wagner's Dutchman, Wotan and Alberich, Escamillo, Wozzeck and Jochanaan; Many concert appearances. Recordings include: Lieder by Beethoven and Wolf. Address: c/o Stadtische Buhnen, Richard Wagner-Platz 2-10, 8500 Nuremberg, Germany.

GINZER Frances, b. 19 Sept 1955, Calgary, Alberta, Canada. Singer (Soprano). Education: Studied at Calgary, North Texas State and Toronto Universities. Debut: Canadian Opera Toronto, as Clothilde in Norma. Career: Sang Antonia in Les Contes d'Hoffmann at Toronto, followed by the Verdi Requiem, Messiah, Beethoven's Ninth and Die Schöpfung; European opera debut Karlsruhe, 1983 as Antonia; Engaged at Dusseldorf from 1987 and has made guest appearances at Hamburg, Stuttgart, Cologne, Bonn, London (English National Opera), Munich State Opera, Frankfurt, Zurich, Warsaw, Maastricht, Vancouver, Calgary, Edmonton, Winnipeg and USA debut in Dallas, Texas; Welsh National Opera 1991, as Violetta; Duisburg 1991, as Frau Fluth in Die Lustige Weiber von Windsor; Early roles included Micaela, Constanze, Donna Anna and Mozart Countess; Lucia, Cleopatra, Sophie in Der Rosenkavalier, Aminta (Die schweigsame Frau), Jenufa, Leila (Les Pêcheurs des perles) and Mimi; Present Repertoire includes Turandot, Ariadne, Senta and Tosca. Recordings include: Handel's Rodrigo; Adriana Lecouvreur. Address: c/o Welsh National Opera, John Street, Cardiff CF1 4SP, Wales.

GIORDANI Marcello, b. 1963, Sicily. Singer (Tenor). Debut: Spoleto Festival 1986, as Duke of Mantua. Career: La Scala debut 1988, as Rodolfo, and US debut at Portland, as Nadir; Season 1991 in Live from Lincoln Center (New York) concert and debut at the Verona Arena, as the Duke; Recent engagements as Nemorino, Rodolfo and Alfredo at the Metropolitan (season 1996-97), Pinkerton, Edgardo and Gounod's Roméo at Houston, Alfredo at Covent Garden under Georg Solti, Tonio (La Fille du Régiment) and Hoffmann at Portland and Faust at the Opera Bastille, Paris; Further engagements at San Francisco Seattle, Chicago, Vienna (in Rosenkavalier and I Puritani), Hamburg, Munich and Berlin; Season 1997-98 as Werther at the Metropolitan, in Lucrezia Borgia at La Scala, L'Elisir d'Amore in Dallas and as Pinkerton at San Francisco. Address: Kantor Concerts Ltd, 67 Teignmouth Road, London NW2 4EA, England.

GIOVANINETTI Christoph, b. 1960, France. Violinist. Education: Studied at the Paris Conservatoire with Jean-Claude Pennetier and with members of the Amadeus and Alban Berg Quartets. Career: Member of the Ysaye String Quartet from 1984; Many concert performances in France, Europe, America and the Far East; Festival engagements at Salzburg, Tivoli in Copenhagen, Bergen, Lockenhaus, Barcelona and Stresa; Many appearances in Italy notably with the Haydn Quartets of Mozart; Tours of Japan and the USA in 1990 and 1992. Recordings: Mozart Quartet K421 and Quintet K516; Ravel, Debussy and Mendelssohn Quartets. Honours: Grand Prix Evian International String Quartet Competition, 1988; Special prizes for best performances of a Mozart quartet, the Debussy quartet and a contemporary work; 2nd Prize, Portsmouth International String Quartet Competition, 1988. Address: c/o Artist Management International, 12-13 Richmond Buildings, Dean Street, London, W1V 5AF, England.

GIPPS Ruth (Dorothy Louisa), b. 20 Feb 1921, Bexhill, Sussex, England. Musician; Composer; Conductor; Organist. m. Robert Baker, 19 Mar 1942, 1 son. Education: Bexhill School of Music; Private tuition; ARCM, Piano Performers, 1936; Royal College of Music, 1937-42, Caird Scholarship, 5 prizes; BMus (Dunelm) by examination, 1941; Matthay Piano School, 1942-43; DMus (Dunelm) by examination, 1948. Debut: Wigmore Hall, 1940. Career: Concert Pianist and Orchestral Oboist until 1952; Chorus Master, City of Birmingham Choir, 1948-50; Lecturer in Music, Oxford Extra-Mural Delegacy, 1948-59; Conductor, London Repertoire Orchestra, 1955-86; Professor, Trinity College, London, 1959-66; Conductor, London Chanticleer Orchestra, 1961-; Professor, Royal College of Music, 1967-77; Principal Lecturer in Music, Kingston Polytechnic, 1977-79; Organist, High Hurstwood Parish Church, 1986-90; Organist, Ripe with Chalvington, 1990-93; Conductor, Heathfield Choral Society, 1990-92; Conductor, Chalvington Singers, 1992-94. Compositions: 5 symphonies; 6 concertos; Choral works: The Cat: Goblin Market; Seascape for 10 wind instruments; Wind Octet; Sinfonietta for 10 wind and tam-tam; Numerous songs; Chamber music. Recordings: Numerous. Contributions to: Musical Times; Musical Opinion; Composer. Honours: FRCM; Honorary RAM; FRSA; Cobbett Prize; MBE, 1981. Memberships: Composers' Guild, Chairman 1967, Council Member 1991-; President, Hastings Festival, 1957-88; President, John Bate Choir; Vice-President, London Repertoire Orchestra. Hobby: Photography. Address: Tickerage Castle, Pound Lane, Framfield, Uckfield, East Sussex TN22 5RT, England.

GIRAUD Suzanne, b, 31 Jul 1958, Metz, France. Composer. Education: Studied at the Strasbourg and Paris Conservatoires; Further study with Tristan Murail and Brian Ferneyhough. Compositions include: Tentaive-Univers for percussion, 1983; String Quartet, 1983; Terre Essor for Orchestra, 1984; Ergo Sum for 15 Instruments, 1985; Le Rouge Des Profondeurs for 6 Instruments, 1990; L'Oeil Et Le Jour for Percussion, 1990; String Trio, 1991. Address: c/o SACEM, 225 avenue Charles de Gaulle, 92521 Neuilly sur Seine Cedex, France.

GIRAUDEAU Jean, b. 1 Jul 1916, Toulon, France. Tenor. Education: Studied in Toulon and Paris. Debut: Montpelier in 1942 in Mignon by Thomas. Career: Strasbourg in 1947 in the premiere of Rabaud's Martine, and Paris Opéra-Comique in 1947 as Nadir in Les Pêcheurs de Perles; Later appeared in the premieres of operas by Wisser and Tailleferre and in a revival of Philidor's Blaise Le Savetier; Sang at Paris Opéra as Tamino and in the premiere of Milhaud's Bolivar in 1950; Guest appearances in Nice, Monte Carlo, Marseilles and Brussels; BBC, London in 1952 as Aeneas in Les Troyens; Director of the Paris Opéra-Comique, 1968-71. Recordings: Thaïs by Massenet; L'Heure Espagnole; Les Mamelles de Tiresias by Poulenc; The Nightingale by Stravinsky; The Fiery Angel by Prokofiev; Les Troyens.

GIROLANI Renato, b. 1959, Amelia, Torino, Italy. Baritone. Education: Studied in Germany with Ernst Haefliger and Dietrich Fischer-Dieskau and in Italy with Sesto Bruscantini. Career: Sang Mozart's Figaro and Leporello at Passau, Germany, St Gallen, Switzerland and at Salzburg Landestheater, 1987-89; From 1989 with ensemble at Vienna Volksoper singing Figaro, Leporello and Guglielmo in Così fan tutte; From 1991 member of Vienna Staatsoper where he added Bartolo in Barber of Seville, also in Stuttgart, 1992-94, Belcore in L'Elisir d'Amore, Sharpless in Madame Butterfly and Taddeo in L'Italiana in Algeri; Other roles include Somarone with Neville Marriner in London, 1990, Papageno at Barcelona in 1991, the Count in Le nozze di Figaro at Bari, 1991, Schaunard in La Bohème at Naples in 1992 and at Tokyo in 1993, and Enrico in Lucia di Lammermoor at Marseilles in 1994. Address: Friedgasse 57-2, A-1190 Vienna, Austria.

GISCA Nicolae, b. 30 Sept 1942, Tibirica, Romania. Conductor; Professor of Conducting and Orchestration. m. Elena Gisca, 28 Jan 1965, 1 daughter. Education: Music Conservatory George Enescu, Iasi, Romania, 1960-65. Debut: Conductor with Conservatory Choir, 1962. Career: Conductor of over 750 choral, chamber and symphony concerts with Conservatory Symphony and Chamber Orchestras, Conservatory Choir and Chamber Choir, Bacau and Botosani Philharmonic Orchestras; Performances and tours of concerts in Romania, Austria, Germany, Belgium, Luxembourg, Switzerland, Wales, France and Spain with Chamber Choir, Cantores Amicitae; TV and Radio appearances; Professor of Conducting at George Enescu Arts Academy. Compositions: Arrangements and choral processing of European, American, African and Asian Folksongs for Choir; 145 Musical pieces. Recordings: 3 LPs: The Tour of The World in 16 Melodies; Winter Songs From Everywhere; The Festival of Political Song; 6 CDs: Christmas Carols from Romania and From the World; Romanian Choral Music; Cantores Amicitae Sings the World; Christmas Carols from Everywhere; Kripenspiel; P Constantinescu: The Byzantine Oratorio for Christmas. Publications: The Conductor's Art, 1982; The Treaty of Instruments Theory, 1987; The Chorus Conductor's, 1992. Contributions to: Romanian magazines, reviews and journals. Honours: 1st prize Youth and Music, Vienna, 1980; 1st prize, Singing of Romania, 1981, 1983, 1985, 1987, 1989; 3rd Prize, Llangollen International Muscial Eisteddfod, 1991; Excellent Mention, Montreux, 1995; Special Prize, Caantonigros, Spain, 1995; Second Prize, Llangollen International Musical Eisteddfod, 1995. Hobby: Travel. Current Management: Rector of Arts University, George Enescu, Iasi, Romania. Address: Str Gr Ureche, No 1, B1 Maracineanu et 9, ap 33, 6600 Iasi, Romania.

GITECK Janice, b. 27 Jun 1946, NY, USA. Composer; Pianist. Education: Studied at Mills College with Darius Milhaud and Morton Subotnick; Paris Conservatoire with Olivier Messiaen, 1969-70; Aspen School with Milhaud and Charles Jones; Has also studied electronic music, Javanese gamelan and West African percussion. Career: Teacher at Hayward State University, the University of California at Berkeley, 1974-76, and Cornish Institute, Seattle from 1979; Co- Director of the Port Costa Players, 1972-79. Compositions include: Piano Quintet, 1965; 2 String Quartets; How To Invoke A Garden, cantata, 1968; Traffic Acts for 4-Track Tape, 1969; Sun Of The Center, cantata, 1970; Magic Words, 1973; Messalina, 1973; Helixes for Ensemble, 1974; A'gita, opera, 1976; Sandbars On The Takano River, 1976; Thunder Like A White Bear Dancing, 1977; Callin' Home Coyote, burlesque, 1978; Far North Beast Ghosts The Clearing, 1978; Peter And The Wolves for Trombone with Actor and Tape, 1978; Breathing Songs From A Turning Sky, 1980; When The Crones Stop Counting for 60 Flutes, 1980; Tree, chamber symphony, 1981; Hopi: Songs Of The Fourth World, 1983; Loo-Wit for Viola and Orchestra, 1983. Honours include: Grants from The California Arts Council, 1978 and The National Endowment For The Arts, 1979 and 1983; Commissions from soloists and ensembles. Address: c/o ASCAP, ASCAP Building, One Lincoln Plaza, New York, NY 10023, USA.

GITLIS Ivry, b. 22 Aug 1922, Haifa, Israel. Concert Violinist. m.Paule Deglon. Education: Studied at the Ecole Normale de Musique, Paris and with Flesch, Enescu and Thibaud. Career: First played in public at age 8 in Israel; Worked in British Troop entertainment during the War; Debuts with the London Philharmonic, BBC Symphony and other British orchestras during the 1940s; Paris debut in 1951, Israel debut in 1952 and US debut in 1955; Many recitals and concert appearances with leading orchestras; Often heard in works by 20th century composers. Recordings include: Concertos by Berg, Stravinsky, Bartók and Tchaikovsky. Honour: Winner, Thibaud Prize, 1951.

GIULIANI Roberto, b. 14 Oct 1961, Rome, Italy. Professor. m. Paola Besutti, 16 July 1992. Education: Musicological Studies, Pavia University; Pianoforte and Composition, Conservatory of Music. Career: Professor, Storia della musica per didattica, Roma Conservatory S. Cecilia; Professor, Storia della teoria e della didattica compositiva e Pedagogia Musicale, Macerata University; Professor, Storia della musica contemporanea e riprodotta, Lecce University; Council Member, Società Italiana di Musicologia e Associazione Italiana Archivi Sonori e Audiovisivi; Collaborator, Rai-Radiotelevisione Italiana; Ricordi; IRTEM: Istituto di Ricerca per il Teatro Musicale; Member, International Commission of Discoteca di Stato for Project Jukebox of European Communities. Publications include: Luca Marenzio. Discografia, 1988; Dal preesistente alla spazialità nella musica di Sciarrino, 1991; Le fonti audiovisive e gli archivi dei teatri italiani (Mozart e Rossini), 1993; Te madrigale nel XX secolo; Musicologia, discografia, prassi, 1995; La comunicazione, formante della storia della musica per didattica, 1998. Contributions to: Amadeus, Bequadro, Le Fonti Musicali in Italia, Maggio Musicale Fiorentino, Mozart-Jahrbuch, Musica domani, Nuova Rivista Musicale Italiana, Rivista Italiana di Musicologia. Memberships: AMS; AIASA; GATM; IAML; IASA; IMS; SEdEM; SIEM; SIdM. Address: Via Orvieto 24, 00182 Rome, Italy.

GIULINI Carlo Maria, b. 9 May 1914, Barletta, Italy. Conductor; Former Music Director. m. 3 sons. Education: Accademia di Santa Cecilia, Rome. Debut: As conductor, Rome 1944. Career: Formed the Orchestra of Milan Radio, 1950; Principal Conductor at La Scala, 1953-55; Associated with Callas and conducted her in La Traviata and Gluck's Alceste; Debut in Britain conducting Verdi's Falstaff and at Edinburgh Festival in 1955; Closely associated with Philharmonia Orchestra from 1955; Debut at Royal Opera House Covent Garden in Don Carlos, 1958; Principal Guest Conductor of Chicago Symphony Orchestra, 1969-78; Music Director, Vienna Symphony Orchestra, 1973-76, and Los Angeles Philharmonic Orchestra, 1978-84, often heard in music by Verdi, Bach, Mozart and Beethoven; Conducted new production of Falstaff in Los Angeles and at Covent Garden in 1982, after 14 years absence from opera (co-production by Los Angeles Philharmonic, Covent Garden and Teatro Communale); Conducted Schumann's Third Symphony and Brahms's Fourth at the 1996 Rhineland Festival. Recordings include: CD, Brahms's Violin Concerto with Chicago Symphony, Perlman; Le nozze di Figaro and Don Giovanni with Philharmonia; Mozart Arias; Schubert's 8th Symphony with Philharmonia; Schumann's 3rd with Los Angeles Philharmonic; Don Carlos with Covent Garden Orchestra. Honours: Honorary Member, Gesellschaft der Musikfreunde, Vienna, 1978; Honorary DHL DePaul University, Chicago, 1979; Gold Medal, Bruckner Society; Una Vita Nella Musica. Hobby: Sailing. Address: c/o Robert Leslie, 53 Bedford Road, London, SW4, England.

GIUNTA Joseph, b. 8 May 1951, Atlantic City, NJ, USA. Music Director; Conductor. m. Cynthia Reid, 5 Jun 1982. Education: BMus, Theory, 1973, MMus, Conducting, 1974, Northwestern University School of Music. Career: Music Director, Conductor, Waterloo Cedar Falls Symphony Orchestra and Chamber Orchestra of Iowa, 1974-; Numerous guest conducting including Chicago Symphony, Philharmonia, London, Minnesota Orchestra, Indianapolis Symphony, Phoenix Symphony, Florida Symphony, Akron Symphony, Syracuse Symphony, and Rhode Island Philharmonic. Honours: Helen M Thompson Award for Outstanding Young Conductor in USA, 1984; Honorary DFA, Simpson College, 1986. Memberships: Pi Kappa Lambda; Phi Mu Alpha; Iowa Arts Council. Hobbies: Tennis; Golf. Address: 1630 Aspen Drive, Waterloo, IA 50701, USA.

GIURANNA Bruno, b. 6 Apr 1933, Milan, Italy. Violist. Education: Studied at the Santa Cecilia Conservatory in Rome. Career: Founder Member of the ensemble, I Musici, with tours of

Europe, North and Central America; Solo career from 1954 with the premiere of Ghedini's Concerto; Appearances with the Berlin Philharmonic, Concertgebouw Orchestra and Orchestra of La Scala; Artistic Director of the Padova Chamber Orchestra, 1983-92 and Professor at the Berlin Hochschule. Recordings include: Mozart's Sinfonia Concertante with Henryk Szeryng and Anne-Sophie Mutter, Vivaldi Concerti, Mozart Piano Quartets and complete Beethoven String Trios. Address: c/o Hazard Chase, Richmond House, 16-20 Regent Street, Cambridge, CB2 1DB, England.

GIZBERT STUDNICKA Bogumila, b. 16 Mar 1949, Cracow, Poland. Harpsichordist. 1 son. Education: MMus with honours, Academy of Music, Cracow, 1973; Study with Jos Van Immersel, Conservatoire Royal, Antwerp, Belgium; Diploma with special honours, Conservatoire Royal, 1979; Masterclasses with Zuzana Ruzickova, Kenneth Gilbert, and Ton Koopman. Career: Numerous concert appearances including with Polish Orchestra of Wojciech Rajski, Poland and other European countries; Active participant in many chamber music ensembles; Currently Assistant Professor, Department of Harpsichord and Early Instruments and Department of Chamber Music, Academy of Music, Cracow. Recordings: Concertos of Antonio Vivaldi, JS Bach's transcriptions, Polskie Nagrania Musa; Recordings for Polish and Belgian Radio and TV and Dutch Radio. Honours include: Prize, Polish Piano Festival, Slupsk, 1974; Prize with Distinction, International Harpsichord Competition, Bruges, Belgium, 1977. Membership: Polish Society of Musicians. Hobbies: Riding; Skiing. Address: ul Meissnera 4 m 66, 31462 Cracow, Poland.

GJEVANG Anne, b. 1948, Norway. Contralto Mezzo-Soprano. Education: Studied in Oslo, the Accademia di Santa Cecilia in Rome and with Erik Werba, Music Academy in Vienna. Debut: Klagenfurt in 1972 as Baba the Turk in The Rake's Progress. Career: Sang in Ulm from 1973, and Bremerhaven, 1977-79; Staatstheater Karlsruhe, 1979-80 as Carmen, Ulrica and Orpheus, Bayreuth, 1983-86 as Erda in Der Ring des Nibelungen and again for a new production of Der Ring in 1988, 1989 and Erda and First Norn in 1990; Zurich Opera, 1985-90 as Maddelena in Die Meistersinger, Carmen, L'Italiana in Algeri, Ulrica and Erda; Many concert appearances notably in Messiah in Chicago in 1984 and the Missa Solemnis, Lied von der Erde; Lieder recitals in Germany and Austria; La Scala in 1987 in Beethoven's Missa Solemnis and Salome; Metropolitan Opera in a new production of Der Ring des Nibelungen in 1988 and 1990; Sang Lady Macbeth in the premiere of Bibalo's Macbeth at Oslo in 1990 repeated in 1992; Covent Garden in 1991 as Erda in the Ring; Sang Clytemnestra in Elektra at Amsterdam, 1996. Recordings: Tiefland; Norn in Götterdämmerung; Messiah; Schumann's Das Paradies und die Peri; Ponchielli's La Gioconda; Solo Recitals in works by Wolf, Sibelius, Liszt, Grieg and de Falla; Video of Mitridate by Mozart as Farnace. Address: c/o Den Norske Opera, Storgarten 23, N-0184 Oslo 1, Norway.

GLANVILLE Mark, b. 24 May 1959, London, England. Singer (Bass). Education: Studied at Oxford University and the Royal Northern College of Music. Debut: Sang the 2nd Soldier in Les Troyens and the Doctor in Macbeth for Opera North, 1987. Career: Has sung Nourabad (Les Pêcheurs de Perles), the King (Aida), the King of Clubs in The Love for Three Oranges, Hobson in Peter Grimes and Betto di Signa in Gianni Schicchi for Opera North; Scottish Opera debut, 1988, as the Commendatore in Don Giovanni; Radio Vara, Amsterdam, as Lord Rochefort in Anna Bolena; Omaha Opera as Ferrando in Il Trovatore; Sang Iago at Haddo House, 1996; Concert engagements include Bruckner's Te Deum for the Hallé Orchestra and Messiah with the Royal Liverpool Philharmonic; Opera: King (Oranges) in Lisbon, 1991; Father (Jewel Box) for Opera North, 1991; New Israeli Opera, 1992; Concerts: Beethoven 9 (Ulster Orchestra conducted by Tortelier and Netherlands Philharmonic, conducted by Menuhin); Mozart Requiem, Bournemouth Sinfonietta conducted by Menuhin, City of London Orchestra conducted by Judd, Stravinsky's Oedipus (RAI Milano conducted by Gatti). Recordings include: Donizetti's L'Assedio di Calais (Opera Rara); Schubert's Mass in G. Honours include: Scholarships from the Peter Moores Foundation and the Countess of Munster and Ian Fleming Trusts; Ricordi Opera Prize and Elsie Sykes Fellowship, Royal Northern College of Music. Current Management: Athole Still International Management Ltd. Address: Foresters Hall, 25-27 Westow Street, London SE19 3RY, England.

GLANVILLE Susannah, b. 1964, England. Soprano. Education: Studied with Margaret Field at the Birmingham Conservatoire and with Margaret Kingsley at the Royal College of Music; Further study at the National Opera Studio. Career: With Glyndebourne Touring Opera has sung Mozart's Vitellia; Mimi for English Touring Opera; Appearances as Musetta with GTO, 1995; Luisa Miller at Opera North; Other roles include Lisa in The Queen of Spades, Tatiana and Donna Elvira; Sang in the BBC Symphony Orchestra Hindemith Festival, 1995 (Nusch-Nuschi and Mörder, Hoffnung der Frauen) European debut as Mozart's Countess at Nice, 1996; Season 1997-98 as Pamina for ENO and Giovanna d'Arco for Opera North. Address: c/o Harold Holt Ltd, 31 Sinclair Road, London, W14 0NS, England.

GLASER Werner (Wolf), b. 14 Apr 1910, Cologne, Germany. Composer; Pianist; Conductor. m. Renée Glaser, 4 children. Education: University; Pupil of: Abendroth; Dahmen; Jarnach; Hindemith. Debut: Pianist, 1918. Career: Conductor, Opera of Chemnitz, 1929-31; Teacher in Denmark; Teacher, Västerås, Sweden, 1945-; Composer; Critic; Soloist; Various programmes at the Swedish Broadcasting Service; Series of recitals; Conferences; Vice Director, Town Music School, Västerås. Compositions: 13 Symphonies; 5 Operas; 14 String Quartets; Col Legno, German Recital; Chamber Music; 2 Ballets; Cantatas; Work for Solo Instruments; Concertos; Stage Work Performances at: Stockholm; Gothenberg; Västerås. Recordings: Phono Suecia, Linnea rezza for Solo; Opus III: for duo; Fermat, for duo; Coronet, for Sax Quartet; Caprice, for Trio. Publications: Trumma och triangel, 1946; Den sköna leken, 1947; Poems 1-7, 1969-77; Poems, 1981; Poems, 1992. Address: Djäknegatan 16, 722 15 Västerås, Sweden.

GLASGOW Glenn (Loren), b. 24 Jul 1924, Pine City, MN, USA. Composer; Educator. Education: Studied with Ernst Krenek at Hamline University, MA 1948 and at the University of Illinois; Further study with Wolfgang Fortner at Detmold. Career: Member of Music Faculty at California State University, Hayward from 1961; Wrote on variation technique in Schoenberg's String Quartet Op 30, dissertation. Compositions include: Piano Sonata, 1948; Requiem, 1954; Grass Harp, incidental music, 1957; Two Egrets for Chorus, 1957; Piano Trio, 1958; Canto Kechwa for Alto and Ensemble; Fantasy Variations for Orchestra, 1967; Rakka for Violin and Tape, 1970. Address: c/o ASCAP, ASCAP Building, One Lincoln Plaza, New York, NY 10023, USA.

GLASS Beaumont, b. 25 Oct 1925, New York, New York, USA. Opera Coach; Stage Director; Recital Accompanist; Author; Lecturer; University Professor. m. Evangeline Noël Young, 7 June 1958, 1 daughter. Education: BS, US Naval Academy, Annapolis, 1949; Graduate studies, San Francisco State College and University of California at Berkeley, 1955; Private music study in Piano, Violin and Theory. Debut: As Stage Director, Northwest Grand Opera, Seattle, 1956. Career: Northwest Grand Opera, 1956-57; Assistant to Lotte Lehmann, Music Academy of the West, 1957-59, 1961; Coach, New York City Opera, 1959; Coach, Studienleiter, Zurich Opera, 1961-80; Accompanist, Grace Bumbry Recital Holland Festival, 1965; Accompanist, Grace Bumbry Brahms Lieder Recital, Salzburg Festival, 1965; Coach, Harpsichordist, Recital Accompanist, Festival of Aix-en-Provence, 1974, 1976-78; Director of Opera, University of Iowa, 1980-; Stage Director, Utah Opera Company, autumn 1988; Stage Director, Cedar Rapids Symphony, 1987, 1989, 1991, 1993, 1995, 1997. Publications: Biography of Lotte Lehmann, 1988; Schubert's Complete Song Texts, Volume I, 1996, Volume II, 1997. Contributions to: Contributing and consulting editor, The Opera Quarterly, 1983-89. Honours: University of Iowa Presidential Lecturer, 1988. Hobbies: Translating operas and art songs; History; Art; Travel; Nature; Shakespeare; Theatre. Address: 301 Richards Street, Iowa City, IA 52246-3521, USA.

GLASS Paul Eugène, b. 19 Nov 1934, Los Angeles, California, USA. Composer. m. Penelope Margaret Mackworth-Praed, 12 July 1977. Education: Piano, Trombone, Composition, Theory, from early age; University of Southern California, 1952-56, BMus, 1956; Composition with Boris Blacher, Ingolf Dahl, Hugo Friedhofer, 1952-56, Goffredo Petrassi, Accademia di Santa Cecilia, 1957-59, Roger Sessions, Princeton University, 1959-60, Witold Lutoslawski, Warsaw, 1960-62. Debut: 1st public performance of compositions, 1956. Career: Composer, concert music, film and TV music; Professor, Conservatorio di Musica della Svizzera Italiana and Franklin College, Switzerland. Compositions: All works published; Orchestral includes: Sinfonia No 3, 1986, No 4, 1992; Lamento dell'acqua, 1990; Quan Shi-qu, 1994; Corale per Margaret, 1995; How to begin, 1995; Chamber includes: Quartet for flute, clarinet, viola, violoncello, 1966; Wie ein Naturlaut for 10 instruments, 1977; Saxophone Quartet, 1980; String Quartet No 1, 1988; Vocal includes: 3 Songs for Baritone and Piano, 1954; 5 chansons pour une Princesse errante for baritone and piano, 1968, baritone, orchestra, 1992; Sahassavagga, children's chorus, text Gantama Buddha, 1976; Un sogno, children's chorus, text Alberto Nessi, 1981; Deh, spiriti miei, quando mi vedete for chorus, text Guido Cavalcanti, 1987; Pianto de la Madonna for soprano, baritone, chorus, orchestra, text Jacopone da Todi, 1988; Film scores include: The Abductors, 1957; Lady in a Cage, 1962; Bunny Lake is Missing, 1965; Catch My Soul, 1972; Overlord, 1974; The Late Nancy Irving, 1983. Recordings: Portrait Paul Glass; Sinfonia No 3, Quartetto I, 5 pezzi per pianoforte, Lamento dell'acqua; Jan Fryderyk, 2 concerts, Cologne; Concerto per pianoforte estemporaneo e orchestra; I Cantori della Turrita, Guilys; Sahassavagga; Many for Swiss Radio. Honours: Los Angeles Chamber Symphony Award, 1957; BMI Award, 1957; Fulbright, 1957, renewed, 1958; Franklin Murphy Award, 1960; Minister of Higher Education, 1961, Minister of Culture Award, 1962, Warsaw; Musica Ticinensis, 1988; Edition Musicale Suisse, 1988; Pro Helvetia, 1991; ASCAP awards. Memberships: ASCAP; Association des Musiciens Suisses; Société Suisse de Pédagogie Musicale. Hobby: Studying languages, presently Chinese. Address: Presso Conservatorio della Svizzera Italiana, Via Tasso 8, CH-6900 Lugano, Switerland.

GLASS Philip, b. 31 Jan 1937, Baltimore, Maryland, USA. Composer; Musician. m. (1) Jo Anne Akalatis, 1 son, 1 daughter, (2) Luba Burtyk. Education: Studied Flute, Peabody Conservatory, Baltimore, Piano, Mathematics, Philosophy, University of Chicago, 1952-56, Composition with Persichetti, Juilliard School, New York, Mississippi, 1962, Counterpoint with Boulangerin Paris, 1964. Appointments: Founder-Director, Philip Glass Ensemble, 1968 with numerous tours in North America and abroad; Trilogy of Satyagraha, Akhnaten and Einstein On The Beach perfd in Stuttgart, 1990; Piano recital at the Festival Hall in London, 1992; The White Raven premiered at Lisbon, 1998. Compositions: Dramatic: Einstein On The Beach, 1976; Madrigal Opera: The Panther, 1980, Satyagraha, 1980, The Photographer, 1983, Akhnaten, 1983, The Civil Wars: A Tree Is Best Measured When It Is Down, 1983, The Juniper Tree, 1985, A Descent Into The Maelstrom, 1986, In The Upper Room, 1986, Violin Concerto, 1987, The Light for Orchestra, 1987, The Making Of The Representative For Planet 8, 1988, The Fall Of The House Of Usher, 1988, 1000 Airplanes On The Roof, 1988, Hydrogen Jukebox, 1989, The Voyage, 1992, The White Raven, 1998; Incidental music, film scores, chamber music, choral works and songs; Collaboration with David Bowie on Heroes Symphony, 1997; Recordings: Various discs with Philip Glass Ensemble. Honours: BMI Award, 1960; Lado Prize, 1961; Benjamin Award, 1961-62; Ford Foundation Young Composer's Award, 1964-66; Fulbright Scholarship, 1966-67; Musician of the Year, Musical America Magazine, 1985. Memberships: ASCAP; SACEM, France. Address: c/o ASCAP, ASCAP Building, One Lincoln Plaza, New York, NY 10023, USA.

GLASSMAN Allan, b. 1950, Brooklyn, NY, USA. Tenor; Baritone. Education: Studied at Hartt College of Music and Juilliard School. Career: Sang as a baritone at Michigan Opera from 1975, then at Philadelphia, Washington and the City Opera, NY; Roles have included Dandini in La Cenerentola, Rossini's Figaro, Belcore, Enrico in Lucia di Lammermoor, Ford and Schaunard; Studied further in New York and sang tenor roles at the Metropolitan from 1985 with debut as Edmondo in Manon Lescaut; Further appearances in USA and at Frankfurt as Tybalt in Romeo et Juliette, Cassio, Bacchus, Alfredo, Hoffman, Faust and Eisenstein; Sang Tichon in Katya Kabanova at the Metropolitan in 1991, Marcello in Leoncavallo's La Bohème at St Louis, Dimitri in Boris Godunov at Pittsburgh in 1991, and Arrigo in I Vespri Sicilani at Nice in 1992. Address: 1704 Garnet Lane #3002, Ft Worth, TX 76112, USA.

GLAUSER Elisabeth, b. 1 Jun 1943, Interlaken, Switzerland. Mezzo-Soprano. Education: Studied in Berne, Stockholm and Italy. Career: Sang in Pforzheim, 1971-73, Freiburg, 1973-75, Dortmund, 1975-82, and Staatsoper Stuttgart, 1982-88; Sang Rossweise at Bayreuth Festival, 1976-80, Adelaide in Arabella at Glyndebourne Festival in 1989; Guest appearances at Rome Opera as Herodias in Salome in 1988 and Komische Oper Berlin in Dusseldorf, Zurich, Bologna, Venice, Cologne, Lisbon, Hanover and Schwetzingen Festival; Other roles have been Marcellina, Maddalena, Kundry, Fricka, Waltraute, Octavian, Clytemnestra and the Countess Geschwitz in Lulu; Concert soloist in works by Bach, Handel, Mozart, Brahms, Beethoven and Liszt; Teacher, Berne Conservatory, 1988-. Address: c/o Konservatorium für Musik und Theater, Kramgasse 36, CH-3011, Switzerland.

GLAZ Herta, b. 16 Sep 1908, Vienna, Austria. Mezzo-Soprano. m. Josef Rosenstock, deceased, 1985. Education: Studied in Vienna. Debut: Breslau in 1931 as Erda in Der Ring des Nibelungen. Career: Left Germany in 1933 and gave concerts in Austria and Scandinavia; German Theatre Prague, 1935-36; Toured North America in 1936 with the Salzburg Opera Guild; Los Angeles in 1937 in Das Lied von der Erde and the St Matthew Passion, conducted by Klemperer; Chicago Lyric Opera, 1940-42, and Metropolitan Opera, 1942-56 as Annina in Der Rosenkavalier, Mary in Der fliegende Holländer, Berta in Il Barbiere di Siviglia, Nicklausse, Mozart's Marcellina and Wagner's Magdalena; Taught at the Manhattan School of Music from 1956. Recordings include: Brangaene in Tristan Love Duet with Helen Traubel and Torsten Ralf. Address: c/o Manhattan School of Music, 120 Claremont Avenue, New York, NY 10027, USA.

GLAZER David, b. 7 May 1913, Milwaukee, WI, USA. Clarinettist; Teacher. m. Mia Helen Deutsch, 16 Feb 1959. Education: BE, Milwaukee State Teachers College, 1935; Berkshire Music Center, Tanglewood, MA, summers 1940-42. Career: Bandleader, Plymouth High School, WI, 1935-37; Teacher, Longy School of Music, Cambridge, MA, 1937-42; Member of Cleveland Orchestra, 1946-51, New York Woodwind Quintet, 1951-85; Soloist with various orchestras; Numerous recitals; Teacher at Mannes School of Music, New York College of Music, New York University, State University of New York at Stony Brook and Hebrew Arts School; Masterclasses around the world; Served on juries of various competitions. Recordings: Various. Address: 25 Central Park West, New York, NY 10023, USA.

GLAZER Gilda, b. 1949, New York, New York, USA. Pianist. m. Robert Glazer. Education: BA, Music, Queens College, City University of New York; MA, Music, Columbia University; Piano student of Nadia Reisenberg. Debut: Kaufman Concert Hall, New York. Career: Resident Keyboardist, Chicago Symphony; Resident Keyboardist, St Louis Symphony; Guest Soloist, Chicago, St Louis, North Carolina Symphonies; Resident Soloist, New York String Symphony; Pianist, Glazer Duo, 1970-; Pianist, New York Piano Quartet; Guest Pianist with Mendelssohn Quartet; World premieres of works by Leo Ornstein, David Ott; Piano Faculties: Hartt College of Music; Chicago Musical College; Extensive solo tours; Appearances in Lincoln Center, Carnegie Hall and Ravinia Festival; Pianist, New Friends of Chamber Music, New York. Recordings: Piano solos and chamber music of Leo Ornstein, Joaquin Turina, Easley Blackwood and David Amram. Publications: Album of works for Piano and Viola, edited, 1980; Schubert Arpeggione Sonata, edited 1993. Contributions to: American Piano Magazine. Current Management: Robert M Gewald Management, Address: Prestige Concerts International, 14 Summit, Englewood, NJ 07632, USA.

GLAZER Robert, b. 1945, Anderson, Indiana, USA. Violist; Conductor. m. Gilda Glazer. Education: BMus, MMus, Chicago Musical College; Studied Viola with William Primrose, Conducting with Franco Ferrara. Career: String Faculty, Columbia University; Member, Chicago Symphony; Co-Principal Viola, St Louis Symphony; Violist, Hartt String Quartet; Music Director, New York String Symphony; Violist of Glazer Duo, 1970-; Guest Soloist: St Louis Symphony, Louisville Orchestra, Hartford Symphony; Guest Violist with Lenox Quartet, Manhattan and Mendelssohn Quartets; Extensive solo tours; World premieres of works by David Epstein and Leo Ornstein; Conductor, American Chamber Orchestra, Brevard Music Festival. Recordings: Soloist, Morton Gould Viola Concerto with Louisville Orchestra; Violist, Lyric by George Walker; Works by Joaquin Turina and Easley Blackwood. Publications: Editor: Album for Viola and Piano, 1980; Schubert Arpeggione Sonata, 1993. Contributions to: Conductors Guild Journal; Instrumentalist. Current Management: Robert M Gewald Management. Address: Prestige Concerts International, 14 Summit, Englewood, NJ 07632, USA.

GLENN Bonita, b. 1960, Washington, USA. Soprano. Education: Studied at the Philadelphia Academy of Music. Career: Sang with the Vereingen State Orchestra under Eugene Ormandy, the Oakland Symphony, Toronto Symphony and Rochester Orchestra; Recitals at Carnegie Hall, Avery Fisher Hall, Tully Hall, and Kennedy Hall and in Canada and Costa Rica; Sang in La Bohème with Philadelphia Grand Opera and in Turandot at the Salzburg Landestheater under Leopold Hager; Sang Manon in Houston and Pamina with Santa Fe Opera; Appeared as Musetta, Suppé's Galatea and Corilla in Viva La Mamma at Berne and St Gallen in Switzerland; Concert engagements in Europe, Canada and the USA, in Germany with the Nuremberg Symphony Orchestra, the Stuttgart Symphony in Four Last Songs under Neville Marriner, and the Bavarian Radio Symphony Orchestra; Sang Clara in Porgy and Bess with the Royal Liverpool Philharmonic conducted by Libor Pesek and with the Scottish Chamber Orchestra under Carl Davis, 1989-90. Honour: Winner, Philadelphia Orchestra Vocal Competition. Address: c/o Norman McCann Ltd, The Coach House, 56 Lawrie Park Gardens, London, SE26 6XJ, England.

GLENNIE Evelyn, b. 19 July 1965, Aberdeen, Scotland. Professional Musician (Timpani and Percussion). m. Greg Malcangi, 1993. Education: Studied from age 12; Ellon Academy, Aberdeenshire; Royal Academy of Music; Further studies in Japan on Munster Trust Scholarship, 1986. Debut: Wigmore Hall, 1986. Career: Concerts with major orchestras worldwide; Tours in UK, Europe, USA, Canada, Australia, New Zealand, Far East, Japan, Middle East, South America, China; Performs work specially written for her including Bennett, Bourgeois, Heath, Macmillan, McLeod, Muldowney and Musgrave; First solo percussionist to perform at the Proms, London, 1989, with subsequent appearances in 1992, 1994, 1996 and 1997. Recordings include: Rebounds; Light in Darkness; Dancin'; Rhythm Song; Veni, Veni, Emmanuel; Wind in the Bamboo Grove; Drumming, Her Greatest Hits; The Music of Joseph Schwantner; Sonata for Two Pianos and Percussion, Bela Bartok; Last Night of the Proms. 100th Season. Honours: GRSM; FRAM; FRCM; Honorary Doctorates in Music, Aberdeen, 1991, Bristol, 1995, Portsmouth, 1995, Leicester, 1997; Honorary Doctorate in Letters, Warwick, 1993, Loughborough, 1995; Numerous prizes including Queen's Commendation Prize; Gold Medal, Shell/LSO Music Scholarship, 1984; Charles Heidsieck Soloist of the Year Award, Royal Philharmonic Society, 1991; Outstanding Individual Award, Alexander Graham Bell Association, 1997. Hobbies:

Walking; Cycling; Reading. Current Management: IMG Artists. Address: PO Box 6, Sawtry, Huntingdon, Cambridgeshire PE17 5WE, England.

GLENNON Jean, b. 1960, USA. Soprano. Career: Professional career from 1983 when she was a winner of the Metropolitan Opera Auditions; Many appearances with opera companies in Miami, Virginia and New York; Season 1993 gave her British concert debut with the Academy of St Martin in the Fields and further concerts at Dusseldorf, Brescia and Montreux; Season 1994 with Musetta at Antwerp, Aida at Wurzburg, and Mimi in Dortmund; Concerts of the Verdi Requiem at Bordeaux and Beethoven's Ninth in Strasbourg; Season 1995-96 as Tosca at St Gallen, Butterfly at Malmo and Donna Anna for New Zealand Opera. Recordings include: Floyd's Susannah, with Opéra de Lyon. Address: Helen Sykes Management, Fourth Floor, Parkway House, Sheen Lane, East Sheen, London, SW14 8LS, England.

GLESS Dominique, b. 1957, Strasbourg, France. Singer (Soprano). Education: Studied at the Strasbourg Conservatory. Career: Sang in concert at Paris and Berlin; Opera career from 1982 at Nantes, Vienna Staatsoper, 1983; Basle, 1986-87, as the Queen of Night; Sang Donna Anna at Strasbourg, 1990, Ophelia in Hamlet by Thomas at Turin, 1990, and Lucia di Lammermoor at Munich, 1991; Other roles include Lakmé by Delibes. Address: c/o Opéra du Rhin, 19 Place Broglie, F-67008 Strasbourg Cédex, France.

GLICK Srul (Irving), b. 8 Sep 1934, Toronto, Canada. Composer. m. 18 Sep 1957, 1 s, 2 d. Education: BMus, 1955, MMus, 1958, University of Toronto; Continued studies with Darius Milhaud, Louis Saguer and Max Deutch. Career: Teacher of Theory and Composition, Royal Conservatory of Music and York University; Composer-in-Residence at Beth Tikvah Synagogue, Toronto, 1969-. Compositions include: Chamber music, orchestral, works for solo instruments with orchestra, vocal, choir with instruments, and piano. Recordings: 4 Preludes for Piano; Petite Suite for Solo Flute; Suite Hebraique No 1; Songs from The Sabbath Festivals and High Holy Days; I Never Saw Another Butterfly; Gathering In, a symphonic concept for Strings; Suite Hebraique No 2; 2 Landscapes for Tenor and Piano; Music for Passover; Suite Hebraique No 4; Prayer and Dance for Cello and Piano; String Quartet No 1; Violin Concerto; 4 CD anthology released by CBC including 17 works including Northern Sketches and Fantasy for Violin and Orchestra (Vision of Ezekiel).

GLOBOKAR Vinko, b. 7 Jul 1934, Anderny, Meurthe et Moselle, France. Composer; Trombonist. m. Tatjana Kristan, 27 Jun 1963, 2 s. Education: Diploma, Ljubljana Conservatory, 1954; Trombone at Conservatoire National de Musique, Paris, 1954-59; Composition and Conducting with René Leibowitz, 1959-63; Composition with Berio, 1965; University Physics, 2 years. Career: Trombone Soloist; Conductor; Played with group for new music, Buffalo University, 1966; Teacher of Trombone, Staatliche Hochschule für Musik, Cologne, 1968-76, and Composition, New Music Courses, Cologne; Founder, New Phonic Art Quartet, 1969; Director of Department for Instrumental and Vocal Research, IRCAM, Paris, 1973-79; Professor, Scuola di Musica, Fiesole-Florenna, 1983-; Solo performer of works written for him by Stockhausen, Berio, Kagel and others; UK premiere with Heinz Holliger of Gemeaux by Toru Takemitsu, Edinburgh, 1989; Played his Kolo at Dartington Summer School, 1992. Compositions include: Accord for Soprano and Ensemble, 1966; Concerto Grosso for 5 Instruments, Chorus and Orchestra, 1970; Laboratorium for Ensemble, 1973; Les Emigres, 1982-86; Labour, 1992; Blinde Zeit for Ensemble, 1993; Dialog Über Feuer, 1994; Dialog Über Erde, 1994; Dialog Über Wasser, 1994; Dialog Über Luft, 1994; Masse, Macht und Individuum, 1995. Recordings include: Les Emigrées; Vinko Globokar; Globokar by Aulos. Publications: Vzdih-Izdih; Einatmen-Ausatmen Komposition und Improvisation by Vinko Globokar. Contributions to: About 30 articles in musical magazines. Honours: 1st Prize: Trombone, Paris, 1959, Gaudeamus, Composition, 1968 and Radio Yugoslavia, 1973. Hobbies: Tennis; Skiing; Jogging. Address: 2 Rue Pierre et Marie Curie, 75005 Paris, France.

GLOCK William (Frederick) (Sir), b. 3 May 1908, London, England. Musician; Pianist; Music Critic; Administrator. m. (1) Clement Davenport Hale, 1944, 1 daughter, (2) Anne Balfour Geoffroy-Dechaume, 1952. Education: Christ's Hospital, 1919-26; Gonville & Caius College, Cambridge University, 1926-30 Honours Degree; Pupil of Artur Schnabel, Berlin, 1930-33. Career: Music Critic, Daily Telegraph, 1934; The Observer, 1934-45; New Statesman, 1958-59; Service with RAF World War II, 1941-46; Director, Summer School of Music, Bryanston, 1948-52; Dartington Hall, Devon, 1953-79; Founder & Editor, The Score, 1949-61; Controller of Music, British Broadcasting Corporation, 1959-72; Director, Bath Festival, 1975-84; Chairman, London Orchestra Concert Board, 1975-86; Chairman, British Section, ISCM, 1954-58. Publications: Editor, Eulenburg books on Music, 1973-86; Autobiography, 1991. Honours: Knight; Commander of the Order of the British Empire; DMus, Nottingham University; Doctor of University of York; Albert Medal, Royal

Society of Arts, 1971; Fellowship, Royal Northern College of Music, 1981; DLitt, Bath University, 1984; DMus, Plymouth University, 1993. Memberships: Board of Directors, Royal Opera House, Covent Garden, 1968-72; Honorary Royal Philharmonic Society, 1971; Arts Council of Great Britain, 1971-75; Member of the South Bank Board, 1986-91. Address: Vine House, Brightwell-cum-Sotwell, Wallingford, Oxon OX10 0RT, England.

GLONTI Felix (Phillip), b. 8 Nov 1927, Batumi, Russia. Composer; Professor. m. Eteri Ahvlediani, 1 son. Education: Conservatory of St Petersburg. Debut; World premiere of Dawn, a ballet in 2 acts, libretto and staging by V Chabukiani, in Tbilisi, 29 Oct 1967. Career: World premiere in Brussels Symphony No 1 Romantic (Horizons du Monde), 1966; Symphony No 6 Vita Nova, World Premiere, Tbilisi, 1979. Compositions: Symphonies: No 6, Vita Nova, 1979, No 7, Fiat Lux, 1981, No 8, Symphonic Groups, 1982, No 10, Pax Humana, 1984, No 1, Romantic, 1986. No 11, The Open World, 1987. Recordings: Romantic Symphony No 1; Vita Nova, Symphony No 6; Symphonic Meditations on a theme by Francesco Petrach; Marienbadische Elegie (Symphonic Concerts); Wanderjahre (Symphony concertante). Contributions to: Georgian Literature, 1981; Soviet Music, 1983. Honours: Merited Honour of Arts, 1979; People's Artist of Georgia, 1988; Laureate of Georgian State Prize, 1989; Membership: Government of Georgian Composer's Union. Hobbies: Metaphysical implications of science. Address: Republic of Georgia, Cirti Tbilisi 380077, Alexander Kazbegi str No 20/9.

GLOSSOP Peter, b. 6 Jul 1928, Sheffield, England. Baritone. m. (1) Joyce Blackham, 1955, divorced 1976, (2) Michele Yvonne Amos, 1977, 1 daughter. Career: Joined Sadler's Wells Opera in 1952, and Covent Garden Opera Company, 1962-66 as Renato, Amonasro, Iago, Rigoletto, Nabucco, Escamillo, Britten's Demetrius, Verdi's Posa and Boccanegra; Sang Verdi's Iago at Salzburg; Freelance singer from 1966; Sang at Metropolitan Opera from 1971 as Scarpia, Don Carlo in La Forza del Destino, Britten's Mr Redburn and Balstrode, Falstaff and Wozzeck, and English National Opera in 1980 as Mandryka. Honours: 1st Prize, Bulgarian First Competition for Young Opera Singers, 1961; Honorary DMus, Sheffield, 1970. Hobby: Golf. Address: Elmcroft, 91 Cambridge Road, Teddington, Middlesex, England.

GLOVER Jane (Alison), b. 13 May 1949, Helmsley, Yorkshire, England. Conductor. Education: BA, MA, DPhil, St Hugh's College, Oxford University. Debut: Oxford University Opera Club in 1971 with Le Nozze di Figaro; As professional conductor at Wexford Festival in 1975 with Cavalli's Eritrea. Career includes: Lecturer in Music at St Hugh's College, 1976-84, St Anne's College, 1976-80, and Pembroke College, 1979-84; Musical Director, London Choral Society, 1983-, and Huddersfield Choral Society, 1989-96; Artistic Director, London Mozart Players, 1984-91; Senior Research Fellow, 1982-91, Honorary Fellow, St Hugh's College, 1991-; Operas and concerts for BBC, Musica Nel Chiostro, English Bach Festival, Glyndebourne Festival Opera (Musical Director, Touring Opera, 1982-85), Covent Garden (debut in 1988), English National Opera (debut in 1989), Royal Danish Opera, Glimmerglass Opera, New York and Australia Opera; Conductor with many orchestras including London and Royal Philharmonic Orchestras, English Chamber Orchestra, Royal Scottish National Orchestra, Bournemouth Symphony City of Birmingham Symphony, BBC Symphony and Philharmonic Orchestras, and many orchestras in Europe, USA, Australia and New Zealand; Appearances in documentaries and presentation for BBC and LWT, especially the Orchestra and Mozart series; Conducted Mozart's Requiem at St Paul's Cathedral in 1991 and Britten's War Requiem at the 1995 Proms; Gluck's Iphigenie en Tauride at the 1997 Glimmerglass Festival (La Calisto there, 1996); Orpheus for ENO, 1997. Recordings: Series of Haydn and Mozart Symphonies. Publication: Cavalli, 1978. Contributions include: Music and Letters; Musical Times. Honours include: Several honorary degrees; Fellow, Royal College of Music; ABSA/Daily Telegraph Arts Award, 1990. Hobbies: Times Crosswords; Theatre. Address: c/o Lies Askonas Ltd, 6 Henrietta Street, London, WC2E 6LA, England.

GLUBOKY Pyotr, b. 1947, Gordiyenki, near Volgograd, Russia. Singer (Bass). Education: Studied at the Moscow Conservatoire and the Bolshoi Theatre. Career: Appearances at the Moscow Bolshoi from 1975, as Rossini's Bartolo and Basilio, Leporello and Alfonso, Pimen, King Philip, Mendoza in Prokofiev's Betrothal in a Monastery and parts in his War and Peace; Guested with the Bolshoi at the 1991 Edinburgh Festival as Panas in Rimsky-Korsakov's Christmas Eve; Concert appearances in Greece, England, Canada, USA, Australia, France, Italy and Japan. Address: c/o Bolshoi Theatre, 10309 Moscow, Russia, CIS.

GLUSHCHENKO Fedor, b. 1944, Rostov-on-Don, Russia. Conductor. Education: Studied at the Rostov Musical Academy and the Moscow and Leningrad Conservatories. Career: Chief Conductor of the Karelian Radio and TV Symphony Orchestra, Finland, 1971; Formerly Chief Conductor of the Ukranian State

Symphony Orchestra; Regular Guest Conductor with the Moscow Philharmonic, the Russian State Symphony Orchestra, the Moscow Symphony and the Ministry of Culture Orchestra, and orchestras in Riga, Vilnius, Sverdlovsky, Tbilisi and Tashkent; Season 1989-90 with appearances at the Soviet Contemporary Music Festival, Cheliabinsk and at the Athens Festival with the Athens Broadcasting Orchestra; Concerts with the Prague Symphony Orchestra and visits to Belgium, Greece and Istanbul; British debut in 1989 with the BBC Scottish Symphony returning to appear with Royal Liverpool Philharmonic and the Scottish Chamber Orchestra. Honours: Diploma of Distinction at the Soviet Concourse of Conductors; People's Artist of the Ukranian SSR. Address: c/o Norman McCann International Artists Ltd, The Coach House, 56 Lawrie Park Gardens, London, SE26 6XJ, England.

GLYNN Gerald, b. 3 Sept 1943, Brisbane, Queensland, Australia. Composer. Education: BA (Hons), University of Queensland, 1965; MA, University of Sydney, 1967; Electronic studios of French Radio, 1968-70; Study with Peter Maxwell Davies, Olivier Messiaen, and Larry Sitsky; Compositions seminars with Iannis Xenakis and Henri Pousseur, 1968-69. Career includes: NSW Conservatory, 1981; Commissions from Seymour Group (1982) and Symeron (1992). Compositions include: Masses, for organ, 1972; Chanson de Ronsard, for soprano, counter tenor and percussion, 1974; Changes, for cello, 1975; Syntheses, for string quartet, 1977; Interplay for cello and piano, 1980; William Blake Triptych for chorus, 1981; Chamber Concerto, 1982; Love's Coming, song cycle for medium voice and piano, 1986; Toccata-Sonata, for piano, 1989; Filigrees 1, 2 and 3, for piano, 1981-91; The Rose of Amherst, song cycle for medium voice and piano, 1991; Strata for violin and piano, 1994; Filigrees 4 for piano, 1997. Address: 13 Rue Chaligny, 75012 Paris, France.

GNAM Adrian, b. 4 Sept 1940, New York, New York, USA. Conductor; Music Director; Oboist. m. Catharine Dee Morningstar, 16 Aug 1983, 1 son, 1 daughter. Education: BMus, 1961, MMus, 1962, College Conservatory of Music, Cincinnati; BS, DMus, ABD, University of Cincinnati, 1962. Debut: Carnegie Recital Hall and Town Hall, New York, 1962. Career: Principal Oboe: American Symphony Orchestra under Stokowski, Cleveland Orchestra under Szell; Member: Heritage Chamber Quartet, Carnegie Wind Quintet, Chamber Arts Ensemble; Faculty: University of Cincinnati College-Conservatory of Music, 1967-76, Ohio University, 1969-76; Guest Conductor throughout the USA; Orchestras in Romania, Yugoslavia, Venezuela, Mexico City, Italy, Brazil, Spain; Congress of Strings, Temple and Georgetown Universities, Peabody Conservatory, Universities of Michigan, Georgia and Houston, Colorado Philharmonic; Assistant Music Director, 1976-82, Music Director, 1982-84, National Endowment for the Arts; Principal Guest Conductor, Philadelphia Concerto Soloists Chamber Orchestra, 1977-88; Music Director: Midland Symphony, Michigan, 1982-86, Macon Symphony, Georgia, 1983-, Eugene Symphony, Oregon, 1985-89, Tuscaloosa Symphony, Alabama, 1993-96. Recordings: For several labels. Memberships include: President, Conductors' Guild; AFM; American Symphony Orchestra League. Hobbies: Golf; Tennis; Skiing; Photography. Address: 85440 Appletree Court, Eugene, OR 97405, USA.

GOBBATO Angelo (Mario Giulio), b. 5 July 1943, Milan, Italy. Opera Producer; Baritone; Artistic Director Opera, Cape Town. Education: BSc, Honours, University of Cape Town; LTCL, Piano; Studied singing with Albina Bini, Carlo Tagliabue and Fred Dalberg. Debut: Cape Town. Career: Sang in opera, oratorio and concerts throughout South Africa as well as broadcasting and TV appearances; Roles include Mozart's and Rossini's Figaro, Papageno, Guglielmo, Sharpless, Ford in Falstaff, Enrico in Lucia; Produced Aida, La Forza del Destino, Il Trovatore, Tosca, Figaro, Così fan tutte, and Magic Flute for PACT, CAPAB, NAPAC and PACOFS; Resident Producer of opera for CAPAB for 5 years; Head of Opera School at University of Cape Town, 1982-88; Artistic Director for CAPAB Opera and Director of the University of Cape Town Opera School from 1993. Hobby: Bridge. Address: Cape Performing Arts Board, PO Box 4107, Cape Town 8000, South Africa.

GOBLE Theresa, b. 1970, England. Singer (Mezzo-soprano). Education: Studied at the Guildhall School, National Opera Studio, Britten-Pears School and European Opera Centre, with Vera Rozsa and Nicolai Gedda. Career: Concert repertoire includes the Verdi Requiem, Rossini Stabat Mater and Petite Messe, Messiah, Dvorák Stabat Mater and Tippett's Child of Our Time; Created the Aunt in Param Vir's Snatched by the Gods, for ENO Contemporary Opera Studio; Sang Flosshilde in Das Rheingold for Scottish Opera, and appeared as Baba the Turk in The Rake's Progress at the Elizabeth Hall (1997); Ulrica (Ballo in Mashera) for Opera Holland Park; Other roles include Dorabella, Verdi's Amneris, Eboli and Mistress Quickly, Charlotte (Werther), Carmen, Adalgisa, Leonora (La Favorita) and Laura in La Gioconda. Address: C&M Craig Services Ltd, 3 Kersley Street, London SW11 4PR, England.

GOCKLEY David, b. 13 Jul 1943, Philadelphia, PA, USA. Administrator. Education: Studied at Brown and Columbia Universitites and New England Conservatory, Boston. Career: Sang at first in opera and became House Manager at Santa Fe Opera, 1968; Assistant Managing Director at Lincoln Center, NY, 1970; General Director, Houston Opera, 1972 presiding over premieres of Pasatieri's The Seagull, 1974, Floyd's Bilby's Doll, 1976, Willie Stark, 1981 and revised version of The Passion of Jonathan Wade, 1991 and Harvey Milk by Stewart Wallace and Michael Korie; Also Glass's Akhnaten, 1984, and The Making of The Representative for Planet 8, (1988), Nixon in China by John Adams, (1987), Tippett's New Year, (1989), Meredith Monk's Atlas, (1991) and Robert Moran's Desert of Roses, 1992; Has introduced surtitles and educational programmes and initiated the touring Texas Opera Theatre. Honours include: Honorary Doctorate of Humane Letters, University of Houston, 1992; Honorary Doctorate of Fine Arts at Brown University, 1993; Opera Magazine feature, People: 222, July 1996. Address: c/o Houston Grand Opera Association, 510 Preston Avenue, Houston, TX 77002, USA.

GODAR Vladimir, b. 1956, Czechoslovakia. Composer. Education: Bratislava Conservatory; Academy of Music and Drama, 1980. Career: Editor, OPUS Publishing House. Compositions include: Trio for Oboe, Violin and Piano, 1973; Fugue for String Orchestra, 1975; Three Songs, 1977; Overture for Symphony Orchestra, 1978; Symphony, 1980; Wind Quintet, 1980; Trio for Violin, Clarinet and Piano, 1980; Ricercar, 1980; Melodarium, 20 dances, 1980; Melodarium, 72 duets, 1981; Lyrical Cantata, 1981; Partita, 1983; Talisman, 1983; Grave Passacaglia for Piano, 1983; Four Serious Songs, 1984; Orbis Sensualium Pictus, oratorio, 1984; Concerto Grosso Per Archi e Cembalo, 1985; Sonata In Memoriam Viktor Shklovski, 1985. Honours: Jan Levoslav Bella Prize, Slovak Music Fund. Address: SOZA, Kollarova nam 20, 813 27 Bratislava, Slovakia.

GODFREY Daniel (Strong), b. 20 Nov 1949, Bryn Mawr, Pennsylvania, USA. Composer; Music Professor. m. Diana Carol Bottum, 13 Mar 1976, 1 son. Education: BA magna cum laude, Yale University; MMus, Composition, Yale School of Music, 1975; PhD, Composition, University of Iowa, 1982. Career: Director, Yale Russian Chorus, including tours of USA and USSR, 1969-72; Visiting Assistant Professor, Music Composition and Theory, University of Pittsburgh, Pennsylvania, 1981-93; Assistant Professor, 1983-88, Associate Professor, 1988-93, Professor, 1993-, Director, 1997-, Syracuse University School of Music, Syracuse, New York. Compositions: String Quartet, 1974; Progression, 1975; Trio, 1976; Five Character Pieces for viola and piano, 1976; Celebration, 1977; Music for Marimba and Vibraphone, 1981; Scrimshaw for flute and violin, 1985; Concentus for small orchestra, 1985; Dickinson Triptych for soprano and piano, 1986; Three Marian Eulogies for high voice, viola and piano, 1987; Mestengo for orchestra, 1988; Numina for 6 instruments, 1991; Clarion Sky for orchestra, 1992; String Quartet No 2, 1993; Two Scenes in Chiaroscuro for 10 performers, 1994; Serenata Ariosa for clarinet, viola and piano, 1995; From a Dream of Russia, for clarinet, violin and piano, 1996; Jig, for wind ensemble/concert band, 1996; Sinfonietta for string orchestra, 1996; Lightscape for orchestra, 1997. Recordings: Scrimshaw; Trio; Five Character Pieces; Celebration; String Quartet; Progression; Music for Marimba and Vibraphone; Intermedio for string quartet. Publications: Music since 1945, Elliott Schwartz (co-author), Contributions to: Elliott Carter's String Quartet No 3: A Unique Vision of Musical Time, to Sonus, Volume 8, No 1. Membership: Founder and Co-Director, Seal Bay Festival. Current Management: Gayle Davidge, 990 Glenhill Road, St Paul, MN 55126-8104, USA. Address: 222 Kensington Place, Syracuse, NY 13210, USA.

GODFREY Peter (David Hensman), b. 3 Apr 1922, Bluntisham, Huntingdon, England. Musician. m. (1) Sheila Margarette McNeile, 1945, 4 daughters, (2) Jane Barnett, 1994. Education: King's College, Cambridge, 1941-42, 1945-46; Royal College of Music, 1946-47. Career: Assistant Music Master, Felsted School, 1946-47; Assistant Music Master, Uppingham School, 1947-49; Assistant Music Master then Director of Music, Marlborough College, 1949-58; Lecturer, 1958-70, Associate Professor, 1971-73, Dean and Head of Department, 1974-82, Professor Emeritus, 1983-, Auckland University, New Zealand; Director of Music, Auckland Cathedral, 1958-74; Conductor, Auckland Dorian Choir, 1961-83; Conductor, Symphonia of Auckland, 1959-68; Conductor, Director, National Youth Choir of New Zealand, 1979-88; Director of Music, Wellington Cathedral, 1983-89; Conductor of Wellington Orpheus Choir, 1984-91; Founder and President, New Zealand Choral Federation, 1985-; Tour of England and Europe, 1988; Director of Music, Trinity College, Melbourne, 1989-91; Advisor to the Board of the International Federation of Choral Music, 1990-; Conductor, Kapiti Chamber Choir, 1992; Conductor Cantoris, Wellington, 1993; Conductor, Kapiti Chorale, 1994-. Recordings: Music of the Church's year; The Way of the Cross; The Dorian Singers, 1969; Five Centuries of Sacred Music, 1975; Visions I, 1977; The Blue Bird; Motets of Peter Philips, 1981; The Dorians Sing, 1982; Hail Gladdening Light, 1989; Wellington Cathedral Choir, 1991; Carols, Anthems, Psalms, Trinity College Chapel Choir, Melbourne. Honours: MBE, 1978; CBE, 1988. Hobby: Gardening. Address: 11 Karaka Grove, Waikanae, New Zealand 6454.

GODFREY Victor, b. 10 Sep 1934, Deloraine, Canada. Bass-Baritone. Education: Studied with Gladys Whitehead in Winnipeg and Joan Cross in London; Further study with Hans Hotter in Munich and with Giovanni Inghilleri. Debut: Covent Garden in 1960 as the Doctor in Macbeth. Career: Appeared with the Covent Garden Company at Coventry in 1962 in the premiere of King Priam by Tippett, and Aldeburgh Festival in 1966 in the premiere of The Burning Fiery Furnace by Britten; Guest appearances at Drottningholm and at opera houses in Glasgow with Scottish Opera, Edinburgh, Florence, Naples, Berlin, Dusseldorf, Montreal, Nice and Amsterdam; Other roles included Scarpia, Amonasro, Zaccaria in Nabucco, Wotan, Wolfram, Orestes and Jochanaan; Also sang in operas by Busoni, Dallapiccola and Hindemith; Many concert engagements.

GODSON Daphne, b. 16 Mar 1932, Edinburgh, Scotland. Violinist. Education: LRAM; ARAM; Royal Academy of Music, London; Brussels Conservatoire. Career: Principal Soloist for Scottish Baroque Ensemble, 1969-87; Principal for Scottish Chamber Orchestra, 1974-76; Member of Bernicia Ensemble, Scottish Early Music Consort; Leader, Edinburgh Bach Players; Soloist with BBC Scottish, Scottish National Orchestra and the Bournemouth Symphony Orchestra; Teacher, RSAMD, Broughton High School Special Music Unit. Recordings: Various. Honours: Premiere Prize, Brussels Conservatoire, 1956; ARAM, 1988. Memberships: Incorporated Society of Musicians; Soroptimist International. Address: 48-11 Learmonth Avenue, Edinburgh, EH4 1HT, Scotland.

GODZISZEWSKI Jerzy, b. 24 April 1935, Wilno, Poland. Artist Musician; Pianist. Education: Diploma with distinction, 1960, MA, Superior Music School, Warsaw; Summer Master Clases in Piano with Benedetti Michelangeli, Arezzo, Italy, 1960, 1961. Career: Regular appearances as Soloist and with Orchestras, Poland and abroad; Performed, Complete PianoWorks of Maurice Ravel, 1975; Complete Piano Works of Karol Szymanowski, 1982; Chamber Music Appearances; Piano Classes, Superior Music School, Wroclaw, 1967-77; Piano Classes, 1978-, Professor, 1988-, Academy of Music, Bydgoszcz; Appearances in International Music Festivals (among others, Warsaw Autumn, Chopin Festivals). Recordings: Piano Works of Chopin, Szymanowski, Debussy, Ravel, Prokofiev and others for Polish Radio and TV, also Polish Record Companies, Muza and Wifon. Honours: Distinction, 6th F Chopin International Piano Competition, Warsaw, 1960. Memberships: Polish Artists Musicians Association, 1961-. Current Management: Elite, ul Piekna 15, 85-303 Bydgoszcz, Poland. Address: ul Zamojskiego 17 m 4, 85-063 Bydgoszcz, Poland.

GOEBEL Reinhard, b. 31 Jul 1952, Siegen, Westphalia, Germany. Violinist. Education: Studied in Cologne and Amsterdam; Teachers include Maier, Gawriloff and Leonhardt. Career: Founder of Musica Antiqua Köln in 1973 for the performance of early music, touring in Europe, North and South America, the Far East and Australia; Played in a concert at the 1989 York Festival in England with music by Legrenzi, Schmelzer and Biber; Season 1996 with Gluck's Orpée et Eurydice at Drottingholm and Handel's Serse at Copenhagen. Recordings include: CDs of Bach's Art of Fugue and Musical Offering; Biber's Mensa Sonora and Solo Violin Sonata in A; Orchestral Suites by Telemann. Address: Hochstadenstrasse 10, 5 Cologne 1, Germany.

GOEBELS Franzpeter, b. 5 Mar 1920, Mülheim-Rhur, Germany. Pianist; Harpsichordist; Professor. m. Gertraud Kockler, 1 son, 1 daughter. Education: Universities of Cologne and Berlin. Debut: 1940. Career: Solo Pianist, Deutschanlandsenderm, Berlin; Docent, Robert Schumann Konservatorium, Dusseldorf; Professor, Hochschule für Musik, Detmold. Compositions: (Pseudonym Angfied Traudger) Dependances for Harpsichord and Strings, 1970; Byrd-Boogy, 1971; Bach: Goldberg Variations for Harpsichordist and Strings. Recordings include: 6 Sonatas by Bach and Bach Concertos for Harpsichord, Publications: Das Sammelsurium, 1968; Handbuch der Pianistik, 1973. Contributions to: Melos; Musica; Musik und Bildung. Honours: Honourable Professor, University of Barcelona; IAM; Ruhr Preis für Kunst und Wissenschaft, 1969. Membership: VDMK. Hobbies: MSS; Sculpture; Modern Graphics. Address: An Der Pyramideneiche, (Privatzufahrt: Clara Schumann Weg), Postfach 4023, D-493 Detmold 14, Germany.

GOEHR Alexander, b. 10 Aug 1932, Berlin, Germany. Composer; Professor of Music. Education: Royal Manchester College of Music; Paris Conservatoire. Career: Lecturer, Morley College, 1955-57; Music Assistant, BBC, 1960-67; Winston Churchill Trust Fellowship, 1968; Composer-in-Residence, New England Conservatory, Boston, USA, 1968-69; Associate Professor of Music, Yale University, 1969-70; West Riding

Professor of Music, Leeds University, England, 1971-76; Artistic Director, Leeds Festival; Fellow, Trinity Hall, University of Cambridge, 1976-; Visiting Professor, Peking Conservatoire of Music, 1980; Board of Directors, Royal Opera House, London, 1982-87; Opera Arianna premiered at Covent Garden, 1995. Compositions include: 4 string quartets, 1957-90; Fantasia, Op 4; Violin Concerto; Little Symphony; Pastorals; Romanza for cello; Symphony in 1 Movement, Op 29; Sutter's Gold, cantata; The Deluge, cantata; Arden Must Die, opera, 1967; Piano Concerto, 1970; Concerto for Eleven, 1972; Metamorphosis/Dance, 1973; Lyric Pieces, 1974; Konzertstuck, 1974; Kafka Fragments, 1979; Sinfonia, 1980; Deux Etudes, 1981; Behold the Sun, opera, 1985; Symphony with Chaconne, 1986; Eve Dreams in Paradise, mezzo, tenor and orchestra, 1988; Carol for St Steven, 1989; Sing, Ariel, mezzo, 2 sopranos and 5 instruments, 1989-90; Still Lands, 3 pieces for small orchestra, 1990; Variations on Bach's Sarabande from the English Suite in E minor for wind instruments and timpani, 1990; Death of Moses, 1992; Colossus or Panic for orchestra, 1993-95; Arianna, opera, 1995; Schlussgesang for viola and orchestra, 1997. Recordings: Cello Romanza, Symphony in 1 Movement, 1993; Sing Ariel, 1993; The Death of Moses, 1994; Piano Concerto, Symphony in 1 Movement, 1995. Honours: Honorary FRMCM; Honorary FRAM, 1975; Honorary FRNCM, 1980; Honorary FRCM, 1981; Honorary Vice-President, SPNM, 1983-; Honorary DMus: Southampton, 1973, Manchester, 1989, Nottingham, 1994; Foreign Member, American Academy of Arts and Letters, 1992. Address: Faculty of Music, 11 West Road, Cambridge CB3 9DP.

GOEKE Leo, b. 6 Nov 1936, Kirksville, MO, USA. Tenor. Education: Studied at Louisiana State University, State University of Iowa with David Lloyd and New York with Hans Heinz and Margaret Harshaw. Debut: Metropolitan Opera in 1971 as Gaston in La Traviata. Career: Sang Tamino, Edgardo, Alfredo, the Duke of Mantua, Ferrando and Don Ottavio in New York; Glyndebourne Festival, 1973-78 as Flamand in Capriccio, Idamante, Tom Rakewell, Don Ottavio and Tamino; Stuttgart in 1981 in the German premiere of Satyagraha by Philip Glass, repeated in 1990; Other roles include Ernesto in Don Pasquale, Almaviva, Rodolfo, Belmonte, Pinkerton and Massenet's Des Grieux; Guest engagements at the New York City Opera and in Seattle, Strasbourg, Baltimore and Amsterdam; Television appearances include Gandhi in the Stuttgart production of Satyagraha in 1983. Address: Staatstheater Stuttgart, Oberer Schlossgarten 6, D-7000 Stuttgart 1, Germany.

GOENNENWEIN Wolfgang, b. 29 Jan 1933, Schwabisch-Hall, Germany. Conductor; Educator. Education: Studied music in Stuttgart, and philosophy at Heidelberg and Tubingen Universities. Career: Director of the South German Madrigal Choir at Stuttgart, 1959; Tours throughout Europe from 1964 and to South America in 1971; Director of the Cologne Bach Choir, 1969-73; Repertoire has included Palestrina, Bach, Schütz and Stravinsky; Chair of Choirmastership at Stuttgart Musikhochschule, 1968; Artistic Director at the Ludwisburg Castle Festivals from 1972 conducting Die Zauberflöte, Fidelio and Der Freischütz, 1972-89; Principal of the Hochschule für Musik und Darstellende Kunst at Stuttgart, 1973; Has also conducted the Bach Passions and Christmas Oratorio, Haydn Oratorios and Masses by Mozart and Bruckner; General Director, Staatstheater Stuttgart in opera, ballet and theatre, 1985, and at Ludwigsburg Festival in 1990 with Die Entführung. Recordings include: Bach Cantatas, St Matthew Passion and Magnificat; Mozart's Requiem, with the Consortium Musicum; Handel's Dettinger Te Deum; Haydn's Creation and Seasons, with the Ludwigsburg Festival Orchestra; Mozart's Mass in C minor; Beethoven's Missa Solemnis, with the Collegium Aureum; Brahms's Ein Deutsches Requiem; Bruckner's E minor Mass. Address: Staatstheater Stuttgart, Oberer Schlossgarten 6, D-7000 Stuttgart 1, Germany.

GOERGEN Eva Maria, b. 1928, Germany. Singer (Mezzo-soprano). Career: Sang at Krefeld Opera from 1951, Wiesbaden from 1953, then Frankfurt and Mannheim until 1958; Member of the Theater am Gärtnerplatz, Munich, 1958-92, as Nicklausse, the Ice Queen in Svanda the Bagpiper, the Spring Fairy in Rimsky's Snow Maiden, Mignon and Cenerentola; Also many operetta roles, including Orlofsky in Die Fledermaus. Address: c/o Theater am Gärtnerplatz, Gärtnerplatz 3, W-8000 Munich 5, Germany.

GOERGEN Viviane, b. 17 Jun 1948, Paris, France. Pianist. Education: Studied French and German, Nancy University; Graduated, Conservatoire de la Ville de Luxembourg, 1965; Graduated, Conservatory of Nancy, France, 1967; Licence de Piano, Paris Conservatory and Ecole Nationale de Musique, Paris. Debut: Luxembourg. Career: First appeared, Paris, 1971; London, 1973; Zurich, 1974; Bonn, 1975; Brussels, 1976; Prague, 1978; Vienna, 1979; Frankfurt, 1982; Madrid, 1983; Berlin, 1991; Since 1978 has taken part in regular foreign tours to Czechoslovakia with Prague Philharmony, and Austria; Numerous radio appearances; Several first performances of works, partly especially composed for her; Currently devotes her attention to the music of Robert Schumann and Claude Debussy. Recordings: Schumann: Davidsbündlertänze, Drei Romanzen Op 28; Johannes Brahms: Sonata Op 5 and Sonata Op 38; Cesar Franck: Sonata in A Major; Ludwig van Beethoven: Sonatas Op 5; Dimitri Shostakovich: Sonata Op 40. Honour: Order of Merit, for artistic achievements, Luxembourg, 1993. Membership: Founded the Institute for the Mental Training of Musical Performers, 1994. Hobby: Psychology. Address: Nelkenstr 1, D-63322 Rödermark 2, Germany.

GOERNER Stephan, b. 23 Oct 1957, Switzerland. Cellist. Education: Studied at the Winterhur Conservatory, at Juilliard and the International Menuhin Academy in Gstaad. Career: Co-Founder and Cellist of the Carmina Quartet, 1984 with appearances from 1987 in Europe, Israel, Japan and USA; Regular concerts at the Wigmore Hall from 1987 and at the South Bank Centre in London, Amsterdam Concertgebouw, the Kleine Philharmonie in Berlin, and Konzertverein Wien in Vienna; Four engagements in Paris, 1990-91, seven in London and tours to Australasia, USA, and Japan with concerts at the Hohenems, Graz, Hong Kong, Montreux, Schleswig-Holstein, Bath, Lucerne, and Prague Spring Festivals; Collaborations with Dietrich Fischer-Dieskau, Olaf Bär and Mitsuko Uchida. Recordings: Various. Honour: Joint winner with members of Carmina Quartet, Paolo Borciani String Quartet Competition in Reggio Emilia, Italy, 1987. Address: c/o Intermusica Artists' Management, 16 Duncan Terrace, London, N1 8BZ, England.

GOERTZ Harald, b. 31 Oct 1924, Vienna, Austria. Conductor; Musicologist; Pianist; Manager. m. Carola Renner, 1 son, 1 daughter. Education: PhD, University of Vienna, 1947; Advanced studies of piano with Wührer and conducting with Reichwein, Krips and Swarowsky, Academy of Music, Vienna. Career: Assistant to von Karajan, Scala di Milano, Lucerne and others; Music Director, opera and concerts, Ulm, Germany, 1955-63; Guest Conductor, Stuttgart, Vienna, Berlin and others; Teacher, Academy of Music, Stuttgart and Salzburg Mozarteum; Professor, Leader of Conductor's Class, Opera Section, Hochschule für Musik, Vienna and seminars for interpretation; Chorus Director, Vienna Opera to 1991; President, Austrian Society of Music, 1963-; Writer and Commentator, Austrian Television. Publications: Editor, Osterreichisches Musikhandbuch, Dictionary of Contemporary Austrian Composers, Vienna, 1989, new edition, 1993; Author, Mozart's Dichter Lorenzo da Ponte, 1988; Gerhard Wimberger, monography, 1990; Österreichische Komponisten der Gegenwart, Editor, 1994. Contributions to: Grove Dictionary of Music and Musicians. Honours: Officer of the British Empire; Bundesverdienst-Kreuz, Germany. Hobbies: Literature; Archaeology; Architecture. Address: Wiedner Hauptstrasse 40, A-1040 Vienna, Austria.

GOETHALS Lucien (Gustave Georges), b. 26 June 1931, Ghent, Belgium. Composer. m. Maria De Wandelaer, 12 July 1958, 1 son. Education: Royal Conservatory of Ghent; Studied composition with Norbert Rosseau and modern technics with Godfried Michael Koenig. Career: Organist, 1958-62; Producer, IPEM, 1962; Professor, Analysis, Royal Conservatory, Ghent; Producer, BRT 3, 1964. Compositions: Cellotape for cello, piano and electronic music, 1969; Endomorfie for violin, piano and electronic music, 1969; Contrapuntos, electronic music, 1974; Llanto por Salvador Allende for trombone solo; Klankstrukturen organ solo; Triptiek, violin and harpsichord; Sinfonia en Grismayor, 2 orchestras and electronic music; Many electronic compositions, chamber music and compositions for orchestra. Publications: Lucien Goethals, Le Constructivisne Bifuntionel by Dr H Sabbe; Lucien Goethals, Composer, by H Sabbe. Contributions to: Professional journals. Honours: Mathieu Prize, 1956; Provincial Composition Prize, 1960; Koopal Prize, 1977; Culture Prize, City of Ghent, 1981. Hobby: Literature. Address: Verschansingsstraat 32, B-9030 Ghent, Mariakerke, Belgium.

GOJKOVIC Andrijana, b. 3 October 1926, Lazarevac Beograd, Serbia, Yugoslavia. Ethnomusicologist. m. Blasko Grce, 7 July 1970. Education: Music Academy, Belgrade, 1948; Ethnology, Anthropology, University School of Philosophy, Belgrade, 1952. Publications: African Musical Instruments, 1987; Musical Instruments of Yugoslavia, Belgrade, 1989; Study of Folk Musical Instruments in Serbia, Belgrade, 1990; Musical Instruments: Myth and Legend, Symbolism and Function, Belgrade, 1994. Contributions to: Journals and magazines. Memberships: Founder Member, Directoryof the Union of Folklorists of Yugoslavia, 1951-91; Association of Folklorists of Serbia, 1951-; UNESCO International Council for Traditional Music, 1962-; Editorial Board, Secretary, Journal, Revue d Ethnologie, 1965-68; Association of Composers of Serbia, 1968-; President, Association of Folklorists of Serbia, 1985-88; Editorial Board, Journal, The Folklorist, 1985-. Address: Proleterskih Brigada 79, 11000 Belgrade, Serbia, Yugoslavia.

GOLAN Itamar, b. 1970, Vilnius, Lithuania. Pianist. Education: Studied in Israel with Lara Vodovoz and Emmanuel Krasovsky; Further study in Boston, 1985-88. Career: Recitals and chamber music performances in Israel and the USA 1977-; Collaborations with Mischa Maisky, Ivry Gitlis and the Aurora Piano Quartet; Appearnaces at the Ravinia, Edinburgh, Besançon, Ludwigsburg and Wyoming Festivals; Concert partners have included Maxim Vengerov, Shlomo Mintz and Tabea Zimmerman; Trio formation with Mintz and Mat Haimovitz (violin and cello); Solo engagements with the Israel Philharmonica under Zubin Mehta and the Jerusalem SO with David Shallon; Faculty member of the Manhattan School of Music, 1991-; Paris Conservatoire, 1994-. Recordings include: Albums with Teldec and DGG. Address: Lies Askonas Ltd, 6 Henrietta St, London WC2E 8LA, England.

GOLANI Rivka, b. 22 Mar 1946, Tel Aviv, Israel. Viola Virtuoso Soloist. Education: University of Tel Aviv, with Professor Oedon Partos. Career: One of the world's most highly acclaimed soloists, giving concerts throughout the world in both traditional and contemporary repertoire; Inspired close to 200 works to date of which 25 are concerti; Examples, Viola concerti by Holloway (UK); Hummel (Germany); Fontajn (Belgium); Colgrass (USA); Vagn Holmboe (Denmark); Yuasa (Japan); Turner (Canada) and others; Solo works by Holliger (Switzerland); Holmboe (Denmark); Many others. Recordings include: Rubbra Viola Concerto and Elgar Cello Concerto (arr Tertis) and Bax Phantasy with Vernon Handley and The Royal Philharmonic Orchestra; Bartók Viola Concerto in Hungary with Andras Ligeti and the Budapest Symphony Orchestra; Martinu Rhapsody Concerto with Peter Maag and the Bern Symphony; Arnold Viola Concerto; Viola and Piano, Brahms Sonatas, Joachim (Conifer Records); Contemporary recordings include Colgrass Chaconne (CBS), Viola Nouveau and Prouesse (Centrediscs) and others. Publications: A book of drawings entitled Birds of Another Feather. Honour: Grand Priz du Disque for Viola Nouveau, 1985. Current Management: Fox Jones and Associates, Canada. Address: c/o Margaret Barkman, Fox Jones and Associates, 50 Prince Arthur Avenue, Suite 107, Toronto, Ontario M5R 1B5, Canada.

GOLD Catherine A, b. 19 May 1924, South Hadley, Massachusetts, USA. Professor of Music History; Writer. m. Arthur Gold, 24 Mar 1994, 2 stepdaughters. Education: BA, Music, Hamline University, 1945; MA, Musicology, Smith College, 1948; Solesnes Abbey and University of Innsbruck, 1950; Berkshire Music Center, Tanglewood, 1954; PhD, Musicology, Catholic University of America, 1968. Career: NE Representative, Gregorian Institute of America, 1948-49; Organist, School Music Teacher, St Rose School and Church, Connecticut, 1949-53; Supervisor, Elementary School Music, Holyoke, 1953-55; Instructor, University of Massachusetts at Amherst, 1955-56; Professor of Music History, Westfield State College, 1956-90; Columnist, Holyoke Transcript Telegram, 1991-93; Writer, 1993-. Publications: Books: Puerto Rican Music following the Spanish American War, 1983; Einstein on Music, 1991; Yella Pessl, First Lady of the Harpsichord, 1992; Editor: Palestrina Haec Dies; Regina Coelia 4, SATB. Contributions to: MGG; Notes; Sacred Music. Honours include: Professor of the Year, 1975, Distinguished Service Awards, 1979, 1980, 1982, 1983, Westfield State College; Installed as Member of the Academy of Arts and Sciences, Puerto Rico; Plaque, Springfield Massachusetts Symphony Orchestra Association, 1982; Pride in Performance from Governor Michael Dukakis, 1988; Professor Emeritus, 1993. Memberships: American Musicological Society; College Music Society; Church Music Association of America; International Sacred Music Society. Hobbies: Golf; Swimming. Address: 8559 Casa Del Lago #41A, Boca Raton, FL 33433, USA.

GOLDBERG Reiner, b. 17 Oct 1939, Crostau, Germany. Tenor. Education: Carl Maria von Weber Hochschule für Musik, Dresden with Arno Schellenberg. Debut: As Luigi in Il Tabarro at Dresden in 1966. Career: Dresden State Opera, 1973-77 and Deutsche Staatsoper East Berlin from 1977; Roles include Florestan, Turiddu, Cavaradossi, Hermann in The Queen of Spades, Aron in Schoenberg's Moses und Aron, and Sergei in Katerina Ismailova; Guest appearances in Leipzig, Leningrad, Vienna, Prague and Italy; Toured Japan with Dresden Company in 1980; Covent Garden debut in 1982 as Walther in Die Meistersinger; Paris 1982 in a concert performance of Strauss's Die Liebe der Danae, Bayreuth Festival in 1988 in a new production of The Ring produced by Harry Kupfer, New York debut in 1983 in a concert performance of Strauss's Guntram, La Scala Milan in 1984 as Tannhäuser, and Teatro Liceo, Barcelona in 1985 as Siegfried; Sang Walther at Covent Garden in 1990, Erik in Der fliegende Holländer at Bayreuth in 1990 and Bayreuth Festival in 1992, Florestan and Tannhäuser at the Metropolitan in 1992; Aegisthus in Elektra at Florence, 1996. Recordings: Drum Major in Wozzeck; Parsifal in the film version of Wagner's opera by Syberberg, with role mimed by a woman; Max in Der Freischütz; Guntram; Siegmund in Haitink's recording of Die Walküre. Address: c/o Allied Artists Ltd, 42 Montpelier Square, London, SW7 1JZ, England.

GOLDENZWEIG Hugo de la Paz, b. 21 Aug 1943, Rosario, Argentina. Concert Pianist; Artist Teacher. m. Virginia Strazziuso, 8 May 1969. Education: Undergraduate degree, University of

Rosario; Postgraduate Diploma, Mannes College of Music, NYC; MMus, Manhattan School of Music; PhD, Piano Performance, New York University. Debut: Carnegie Recital Hall, NY, 1976; Wigmore Hall London, 1981. Career: Recitals and concerto appearances in the Netherlands, Spain, Italy, England, USA, and Argentina; TV and radio as well as concert stage in major halls; Appeared in world premieres of Lanza's Concerto for Piano and Chamber Orchestra, National Symphony of Argentina, 1993 and Camarero's Finale, dedicated to him, in Palma de Mallorca in 1993. Recordings include: Live recording of public performances in New York City; Works by William Mathias, New York premiere, Mario Davidovsky and Ginastera on Melopea CD; 2 Videos; Complete Chopin Etudes; Argentine Piano Music of the Last 50 Years, a lecture and demonstration. Publication: Selected Piano Etudes of Frederic Chopin: A Performance Guide, microfilm, 1987. Honours: Jóvenes Concertistas Prize, Buenos Aires, 1966; Jóvenes Solistas Prize, Santa Fe, 1967. Memberships: College Music Society, USA; Faculty, Piano and Piano Pedagogy, Mannes College of Music, NYC, 1989-. Hobbies: Reading; Cycling; Visiting Art Galleries and Museums. Current Management: PAMAR. Address: 116 East 57th Street, 3rd Floor, New York, NY 10022, USA.

GOLDING Robin (Mavesyn), b. 4 June 1928, London, England. Administrator; Freelance Writer; Editor. m. (1) Claire Simpson, 18 August 1956, div, 1 daughter, (2) Felicity Lott, 22 Dec 1973, div. Education: Westminister School; MA, Christ Church, Oxford. Career: Freelance Writer on musical subjects; Experience of local journalism (The Kensington News), the record industry (Vox), music and general publishing (George Rainbird); Librarian, Boyd Neel Orchestra, 1953-56; Administrative Assistant, 1961-65, Registrar, 1966-87, Royal Academy of Music. Publications: Editor, Royal Academy of Music Magazine, 1963-87; Innumerable Programme Notes, 1953-. Contributions to: Gramophone; Musical Times; Music and Musicians; Records and Recording; The Strad; Arts Review. Honours: Hon ARAM, 1965; Hon RCM, 1971; Hon RAM, 1976. Memberships: Savage Club; Travellers Club; Chelsea Arts Club; Royal Musical Association; Royal Society of Musicians; Critics' Circle. Hobbies: People; Buildings; Pictures; Travel; Early Keyboards. Address: 33 Prentice Street, Lavenham, Sudbury, Suffolk CO10 9RD, England.

GOLDOVSKY Boris, b. 7 June 1908, Moscow, Russia. Pianist; Conductor; Opera Producer; Lecturer; Broadcaster. m. Margaret Codd, 1933, 1 son, 1 daughter. Education: Studied piano with uncle, Pierre Luboshutz; Moscow Conservatory, 1918-21 and with Schnabel and Kreutzer, Berlin Academy of Music, 1921-23; Dohnányi's Masterclass at Budapest Academy of Music, graduating in 1930; Studied conducting with Reiner at the Curtis Institute of Music, Philadelphia, 1932. Debut: Soloist, Berlin Philharmonic Orchestra, 1921. Career: Head, Opera Department, New England Conservatory, Boston, 1942-64, Berkshire Music Center, Tanglewood, 1946-61, and Curtis Institute of Music, 1977-; Founder-Director, New England Opera Theater, Boston, 1946 becoming Goldovsky Opera Institute in 1963; Toured with own opera company until 1984; Commentator, Metropolitan Opera Radio broadcasts from 1946; Lecturer; Translator of opera librettos into English. Publications: Accents on Opera, 1953; Bringing Opera to Life, 1968; Bringing Soprano Arias to Life, with A Schoep, 1973; Manual of Operatic Touring, with T Wolf, 1975; My Road to Opera, with C Cate, 1979; Good Afternoon, Ladies and Gentlemen!; Intermission scripts from the Met broadcasts, 1984; Studies in Opera, 4 volumes, 1991-93; The Adult Mozart: A Personal Perspective. Honours: Honorary MusD, Bates College, 1956, Cleveland Institute of Music, 1969, and Southeastern Massachusetts University, 1981; Honorary DFA, Northwestern University, 1972; Fellow, American Academy of Arts and Sciences. Address: 183 Clinton Road, Brookline, MA 02146, USA.

GOLDRING Malcolm (David), b. 12 July 1949, Croydon, England. Lecturer; Conductor. m. Susan Elizabeth Austin, 11 Sept 1971, 3 sons. Education: GRSM, ARCM. Royal College of Music, London, 1971; PGCE, Durham University, 1972; MEd, Nottingham University, 1982. Career: Assistant Teacher of Music, Southmoor School, Sunderland, 1972-74; Head of Music, Shepshed High School, Leicestershire, 1974-81; Head of Music, Charles Keene College of Further Education, Leicester; Lecturer, Leicestershire School of Music, 1981-86; Inspector of Schools (Music), Metropolitan Borough of Solihull, West Midlands, 1986-95; Director of Music, Welsh College of Music and Drama, Cardiff, 1995-; Guest Conductor, including Leicester Philharmonic Choir, Cecilian Singers, Cambridge Youth Orchestra, Guernsey Symphony Orchestra, Guernsey Youth Orchestra; Conductor of Choral Workshop, Cavendish Singers, Royal Leamington Spa Bach Choir, Solihull Youth Orchestra, Solihull Youth Chamber Orchestra. Honours: Winston Churchill Fellow, 1990; Fellow of Royal Society of Arts, 1991. Hobbies: Food; Photography; Gardens. Address: 145 Widney Lane, Solihull, West Midlands, England.

GOLDSMITH Barry, b. 4 June 1959, New York, USA. Concert Pianist. Education: Peabody Conservatory of Music; Johns Hopkins University, BM, DMA, Piano Scholarship; MM, Piano, Indiana University School of Music; Piano Scholarship, Manhattan School of Music. Debut: Carnegie Recital Hall, New York City, 1982. Career: Solo Recitals in USA, Canada and Europe; Cities include, New York, Philadelphia, Washington DC, Baltimore, San Francisco, Vancouver, London, Oslo, The Hague, Brussels, Milan; Performed in Major Concert Halls: Carnegie Recital Hall, New York City; Wigmore Hall, London; Diligentia Hall, The Hague; University Hall, Oslo; Solo Recitals at Interlochen Arts Academy; Guest Appearances at Universities on the East Coast and Midwest, USA; Soloist with Peabody Symphony, The Queensborough Symphony and Orchestras in New York; Live Performances on WNYC FM Radio in New York City; Taped Performances on National Public Radio, USA. Compositions: Works for Piano, Voice or Violin and Piano; The Heritage, Suites for Violin and Piano. Honours: Winner, Peabody Concerto Competition, Baltimore, 1973; Austin Conradi Memorial Piano Award, Baltimore, 1974; Pauline Favin Memorial Award, Outstanding Pianistic Achievement, 1975; Winner, Mieczyslaw Münz Piano Competition, Baltimore, 1981; Winner, International Piano Tape Recording Competition, Beethoven Event, 1984; Winner, Distinguished Artist Award, Artists International, New York, 1991. Membership: College Music Society, USA. Hobbies: Writing; Ping Pong; Photography; Hiking. Current Management: International Artists Alliance. Address: 75-07 171 Street, Flushing, NY 11366, USA.

GOLDSTEIN Malcolm, b. 27 Mar 1936, Brooklyn, NY, USA. Composer; Violinist. Education: Studied at Columbia University with Otto Luening. Career: Has taught at Columbia-Princeton Electronic Music Center, 1959-60, Columbia University, 1961-65, New England Conservatory, 1965-67, Goddard College, VT, 1972-74, and Bowden College, Brunswick, ME, 1978-82; Co-Director of the concert series, Tone Roads, 1967-69, giving performances of works by Ives, Varèse and Cage; Director of the New Music Ensemble and Collegium at Dartmouth College, 1975-78; Has toured Europe and North America as violinist. Compositions include: Emanations for Violin and Cello, 1962; Ludlow Blues for Wind and Tape, 1963; Overture To Fantastic Gardens, 1964; Majority for String Trio, 1964; Sirens For Edgard Varèse, 1965; Sheep Meadow for Tape Collage, 1967; Frog Pond At Dusk, 1972; Upon The Seashore Of Endless Worlds, 1974; Yosha's Morning Song Extended, 1974; Hues Of The Golden Ascending for Flute and Ensemble, 1979; On The First Day Of Spring There Were 40 Pianos, 1981; A Breaking Of Vessels, Becoming Song, flute concerto, 1981; The Seasons, Vermont, 1980-82; Of Bright Mushrooms Bursting In My Head for Ensemble, 1984; Cascades Of The Brook (Bachwasserfall) for Orchestra, 1984. Publications include: Edition of the 2nd Symphony by Ives; From Wheelock Mountain, scores and writings, 1977. Address: c/o ASCAP, ASCAP Building, One Lincoln Plaza, New York, NY 10023, USA.

GOLDSTONE Anthony (Keith), b. 25 July 1944, Liverpool, England. Concert Pianist. m. Caroline Clemmow, 26 July 1989. Education: Royal Manchester College of Music. Debut: Wigmore Hall, London, 1969. Career: Appearances throughout England with all major symphony orchestras and in recital; Many festivals; Several London Promenade Concerts including the Last Night in 1976; Very frequent broadcaster; Tours, North and South America, Africa, Asia, Europe, Australasia; Flourishing piano duo with wife Caroline Clemmow and numerous chamber activities including founding Musicians of the Royal Exchange in 1978. Recordings: Solo piano: Parry, Elgar, Holst, Lambert, Moussorgsky, Britten, Bridge, A Moyzes, others; Chamber: Beethoven, Sibelius, Mendelssohn, Holst, others; Piano Duo: Two-piano works by Holst (Planets), Brahms (Sonata), George Lloyd, Soler, others; Piano duets by Rimsky-Korsakov, Stravinsky, Elgar, virtuoso variations, romantic sonatas, others; Concertos: Beethoven (from London Promenade Concerts), Alkan, Saint-Saëns. Honours: International Piano Competitions, Munich, Vienna, 1967; BBC Piano Competition, 1968; Gulbenkian Fellowship, 1968-71; Fellow, Royal Manchester College of Music, 1973. Membership: Incorporated Society of Musicians. Hobbies: Antique Maps; Birdwatching. Address: Walcot Old Hall, Alkborough, N Lincolnshire DN15 9JT, England.

GOLDTHORPE (John) Michael, b. 7 Feb 1942, York, England. Singer (Tenor). Education: MA, Trinity College, Cambridge, 1964; Certificate of Education, King's College, London, 1965; Guildhall School of Music & Drama, London, 1966-67. Debut: Purcell Room, London, January 1970. Career includes: Paris debut, 1972; Opera Royal, Versailles, 1977; Royal Opera, Covent Garden and BBC Television, 1980; Regular Broadcaster, BBC Radio; US debut, Miami Festival, 1986; Appearances in Singapore, Iceland, most countries Western Europe; Concertgebouw, Amsterdam, 1986, Directed Medieval Concert in Rome, 1987; Noted Bach Evangelist and exponent of French Baroque, Lecturer; Lucerne Festival's performance of Frank Martin's Golgotha, 1990; Series of concerts for the Sorbonne, Paris, 1992; Recent London performances Verdi Requiem, Janácek's Glagolitic Mass, Britten's Cantata Misericordium Beethoven's Missa Solemnis; Teacher, Trinity College of Music, London. Recordings include: Rameau: Hippolyte et Aricie, La Princesse de Navarre and Pygmalion; Charpentier Missa Assumpta est Maria; Mondonville Motets; Cavalli Ercole Amante; 100 Years of Italian Opera; Delius Irmelin; L'Incoronazione di Poppea; Monteverdi Madrigali Libri Primo, Secondo, Sesto; Blanchard Cantats; The Snowy Pearl (Victorian & Edwardian Ballads). Honours: Lieder Prize GSM, 1967; Choral Exhibition, Cambridge, 1961; GLAA Young Musicians Award, ISM Young Musicians Award, Park Lane Group's Young Musician Award, early 1970's; Wingate Scholarship, 1994. Memberships: Hon Fellow, Cambridge Society of Musicians, 1993. Hobbies: Languages; Reading; Brewing; Gardening; Computing. Address: 23 King Edward's Road, Ruislip, Middlesex HA4 7AQ, England.

GOLIANEK Ryszard Daniel, b. 22 Mar 1963, Ukta, Poland. Musicologist; Music Critic. Education: MA, Musicology, 1988, PhD, Musicology, 1993, Adam Mickiewicz University, Poznan; MA, Cello, Musical Academy, Poznan, 1989. Publication: Book, Dramaturgia Kwartetow Smyczkowych Dymitra Szostakowicza, with abstract in English, Dramaturgy of Dmitri Shostakovich's String Quartets, 1995. Contributions to: Articles in Muzyka, Studio, Ruch Muzyczny and Proceedings of some international conferences including Trento, 1992. Memberships: Society of Polish Composers; The Poznan Society for the Advancement of the Arts and Sciences. Address: Os Boleslawa Smialego 36/122, 60-682 Poznan, Poland.

GOLIGHTLY David (Frederick), b. 17 Nov 1948, England. Freelance Composer. Education: BA, Honours 2:1, Huddersfield University; Postgraduate Certificate of: Advance Studies Composition, Guildhall School of Music and Drama; Education Certificate, Leeds University; A MusM, Nottingham University. Career: Composer. Compositions include: The Eye, a Chamber Opera premiered 1992; Rites of Passage and The St Petersburg Mass premiered 1994 in the State Capella Hall, St Petersburg, Russia by the Roussland Soglasie Choir; Frontiers (Five arrangements of American folk songs for male voice choir); Songs of the Cliff Top for Baritone and Piano; Star Flight and Northumbrian Fantasy (Brass Band) Septet for Brass; Little Suite for Brass Quintet; Three Pieces for Tombone Quartet (Vol 1 & 2) Concert Fanfare for Brass and Percussion; Four Preludes for Flute and Guitar; Moods for Solo Clarinet: Serenade for Solo Tuba. Recordings: Septet for Brass; Three Pieces for Trombone Quartet (Vol 1 & 2); Rites of Passage: Frontiers: & The St Petersburg Mass; Music for the Theatre and Film, The Railway Children, Suddenly Last Summer, Snow Queen, Disorderly Women, The Glass Menagerie, Hans Witch and the Goblin, On the Razzle, Blood Wedding, The Voyage of the Dawn Treader, and Under Milkwood. Memberships: Performing Rights Society; Composers' Guild of Great Britain; Chairman, North West Composer's Association, Cheshire. Current Management: Modrana Music Promotions Ltd. Address: c/o Modrana Music Publishers, 41 Parklands Way, Poynton, Cheshire SK12 1AL, England.

GÖLLNER Theodor, b. 25 Nov 1929, Bielefeld, Germany. Musicologist; Administrator. m. Marie Louise Martinez, 1 son, 1 daughter. Education: PhD, University of Heidelberg, 1957; Phil habil, University of Munich, 1967. Career: Lecturer, 1958-62, Assistant, 1962-67, Associate Professor, 1967, Professor, 1973-, Chair in Musicology and Director, Institute of Musicology, 1973-, Dean, Division of History and Fine Arts, 1975-77, University of Munich; Associate Professor, 1967-71, Professor, 1971-73, University of California, Santa Barbara, USA; Member, Bavarian Academy of Sciences, 1982-. Publications: Formen früher Mehrstimmigkeit, 1961; Die mehrstimmigen liturgischen Lesungen, 2 volumes, 1969; Die Sieben Worte am Kreuz bei Schütz und Haydn, 1986; Editor: Münchener Veröffentlichungen zur Musikgeschichte, 1977-; Münchener Editionen zur Musikgeschichte, 1979-. Contributions to: Various publications. Memberships: International Musicological Society; Gesellschaft für Musikforschung; Gesellschaft für Bayerische Musikgeschichte, President 1981-. Address: Musikwissenschaft Institut, University of Munich, Geschw Scholl Platz 1, 80539 Munich, Germany.

GOLOVIN Andrei, b. 11 Aug 1950, Moscow, Russia. Composer. Education: Moscow Conservatoire, 1971-76; Postgraduate Course, 1977-79. Career: Teacher of Composition at Gnesins' State Musical College, 1975-, and Gnesins' Russian Academy of Music, 1989-. Compositions: Published: Cadence and Ostinato for 5 Timpani, Bells, Tam-tam and Piano, 1979, Concerto Symphony for Viola, Cello and Symphony Orchestra, 1980, Sonata for Oboe and Cembalo, 1980, Sonata for Piano, 1981, Duet for Violin and Piano, 1981, Duet for Viola and Cello, 1981, Sonata Breve for Viola and Piano, 1982, Japanese edition, 1992, 2 Pieces for Piano, 1982, Sonata for Cello Solo, 1983, 2 Pieces for Flute and Piano: Portrait, and, Landscape, 1983, Prelude for Vibraphone, 1984, Legend for Piano, 1984, 3 Easy Pieces for Piano, 1985, 1st Quartet for 2 Violins, Viola and Cello, 1986, Music for String Quartet, 1986, Sonatina for Piano, 1986, Japanese edition, 1991, Fairy-Tale for Horn and Piano, 1987,

Concert Symphony for Viola, Piano and Orchestra, 1988, Symphony for Full Symphony Orchestra, 1990, Elegy for Cello Solo, 1990, Poeme Nocturne for Viola and Piano, 1991, Plain Songs: Canata to Verses by N Rubtsov for Mezzo-Soprano, Bass, Piano and Chamber Orchestra, 1991, Remote Past for Piano, 1991. Recordings: Simple Songs: Cantata, Elegy for Cello Solo; Sonata Breve for Viola and Piano; Elegy for Cello Solo; Concert Symphony for Viola, Piano and Orchestra; Quartet for 2 Violins, Viola and Cello; 2 Pieces for Flute and Piano; Music for Strings. Membership: Russian Composers' Union. Address: Shumkin St 3, k2, Ap 45, Moscow 107113, Russia.

GOLOVINSKY Grigory, b. 18 Feb 1923, Gitomir, Russia. Musicologist. m. Margarita Kapnist, 30 Jul 1946, 1 daughter. Education: Postgraduate of the Moscow Conservatory. Career: Teacher, Musical School, 1945-55, and Musical College, 1954-60; Chief Assistant of the Musicology Commission of the Union of Soviet Composers, 1957-67; Senior Researcher, Institute of Art Studies, 1967. Publications: Borodin's Chamber Ensembles, 1972; Sergei Balasanian, with B Schachnasarova, 1972; Co-author and Editor, Book of Music, 1975; Composer and Folklore, 1981; Co-Author and Editor, M P Mussorgsky and Twentieth-Century Music, 1990; Mussorgsky and Folklore, 1991. Contributions to: Articles in History of Music of the Soviet Peoples, 1973, 1974; Questions of Art Sociology; Social Function of Art and Its Forms; Perception of Music; Come Into Existence A Sound Image; Sovjetskaja Muzika Magazine. Honour: Doctor of Science, 1985, Musicology, Doctor of Art Studies. Memberships: Union of Soviet Composers; Institute Mediacult, Vienna. Address: Uralska Street No 8 Ap 97, 107207 Moscow, Russia.

GOLTZ Christel, b. 8 Jul 1912, Dortmund, Germany. Soprano. m. Theodor Schenk. Education: Studied with Ornelli-Leeb in Munich and with Theodor Schenk. Career: Sang first at Plauen as Eva, Santuzza and Octavian; Sang at the Dresden Staatsoper from 1936 notably as Reiza in Oberon, in the premiere of Sutermeister's Romeo und Julia in 1941 and in the local premiere of Orff's Antigonae in 1950; Sang in Berlin from 1947, then in Munich and Vienna as Salome, Elektra, the Countess in Capriccio, Tosca and Leonore; Covent Garden, 1951-52 as Salome and as Marie in the local stage premiere of Wozzeck; Salzburg Festival from 1954 in the premiere of Liebermann's Penelope and as Elektra and Leonore, and as Salome at the Metropolitan Opera in 1954; Guest engagements in Paris, Brussels and Milan; Sang at the State Operas of Munich and Vienna until 1970. Recordings: Salome; Die Frau ohne Schatten. Address: c/o Vienna State Opera, Ring Strasse, Vienna, Austria.

GOLUB David, b. 22 Mar 1950, Chicago, USA. Pianist. Education: Studied with Alexander Uninsky in Dallas and with Beveridge Webster at the Juilliard School, New York; Graduated, 1974. Debut: With Dallas Symphony Orchestra, 1964. Career: Appeared with orchestras in Philadelphia, Cleveland, Dallas, St Louis, Pittsburgh, Cincinnati, Chicago, Minnesota, Washington and Atlanta; Solo appearances also with orchestras of Toronto, Ottawa, Edmonton, Montreal, Calgary and Vancouver; Has performed at all major North American music festivals; International appearances with such conductors as Maazel, Mata, Horst Stein, Zinman, Conlon, Chailly, Levine, Dutoit, Bychkov, DeWaart, Foster, Skrowaczewski and Albrecht; European engagements with orchestras in London, Rome, Paris, Milan, Geneva, Florence, Rotterdam, Amsterdam and Prague; Appeared in film From Mao to Mozart, which documented tour to China in 1979 with Isaac Stern and formed a piano trio with Colin Carr and Mark Kaplan. Recordings: Gershwin and Rachmaninov with London Symphony Orchestra and complete piano trios of Schubert, Mendelssohn and Brahms. Current Management: Harold Holt Limited. Address: 31 Sinclair Road, London W14 0NS, England.

GOMEZ Jill, b. 21 Sep 1942, New Amsterdam, British Guyana. Soprano. Education: Royal Academy of Music; Guildhall School of Music. Debut: Operatic: As Adina in L'Elisir d'Amore, Glyndebourne Touring Opera in 1968, and Glyndebourne Festival Opera in 1969 as Mélisande. Career includes: Sang with Royal Opera, English Opera and Scottish Opera in roles including Pamina, Ilia, Lauretta in Gianni Schicchi and Governess in Turn of The Screw; Created the role Flora in Tippett's Knot Garden in 1970 and the Countess in Thea Musgrave's The Voice of Ariande in 1974, also the title role in William Alwyn's Miss Julie in 1977; Sang in the premiere of Eighth Book of Madrigals at Zurich Monteverdi Festival in 1979, sang Cleopatra at Frankfurt in 1981, Donna Anna at Kent Opera in 1988 and Rosario in Granados' Goyescas in 1988; Regular engagements in France, Austria, Belgium, Netherlands, Germany, Scandinavia, Italy, Switzerland, Spain and USA and at various festivals including Spoleto, Edinburgh, and the BBC Promenade Concerts; Sang in the world premiere of The Song of Inês de Castro, commissioned by her from David Matthews, at the Proms in 1988; Sang songs by Berlioz and Canteloube with the RPO at the Festival Hall in 1992. Recordings include: Handel's Acis and Galatea; Tippett's The Knot Garden; Three recital discs of French, Spanish and Mozart songs; Ravel's Trois Poèmes de Mallarmé; Villa Lobos' Bachianas Brasileiras No 5; Cabaret Classics with John Constable; Cabaret Songs by Britten and Cole Porter; Premiere recordings include Seven Early Songs by Mahler. Honour: FRAM, 1986. Address: 16 Milton Park, London, N6 5QA, England.

GOMEZ-MARTINEZ Miguel-Angel, b. 17 Sept 1949, Granada, Spain. Conductor; Composer. Education: Studied at the Granada and Madrid Conservatories, in USA and Vienna with Hans Swarowsky. Career includes: Conducted opera in Lucerne, Berlin, Frankfurt, Munich and Hamburg, at Covent Garden in London, Paris, Geneva, Berne, Houston, Chicago, Florence, Rome, Venice and Palermo; Resident Conductor for Berlin Deutsche Oper, 1973-77, and Vienna Staatsoper, 1977-82; Festivals in Berlin, Vienna, Munich, Macerata in Italy, Granada, Santander, San Sebastián, Savonlinna in Finland and Helsinki; Repertoire of over 50 operas including works by Mozart, Puccini, Rossini, Verdi and Wagner; Conductor for Radiotelevision Española Orchestra, 1984-87; Artistic Director and Chief Conductor, Teatro Lirico Nacional Madrid, 1985-91; General Musikdirektor, Nationaltheater Mannheim and Chief Conductor of the Nationaltheater Orchestra, 1990-93; Chief Conductor of Hamburg Symphony, 1992-, and General Music Director of the Finnish National Opera, Helsinki, 1993-; Concerts with most major orchestras in Europe, Far East and America; Chief Conductor, Orchestra of Valencia. Compositions include: Suite Burlesca; Sinfonia del Descubrimiento, first performed in 1992, at Mozart Saal, Rosengarten, Mannheim; Five Canciones sobre poemas de Alonso Gamo, for soprano and orchestra, first performed Grosse Musikhalle, Hamburg, 1996. Honours: Several decorations and nominations; Gold Medal, City of Granada, 1984; Encomienda du Número de la Order del Mérito Civil. Current Management: Balmer and Dixon Management AG, Zürich, Switzerland. Address: c/o Hamburg Symphony Orchestra, Dammtorwall 46, Hamburg, Germany.

GONDA-NIGG Anna, b. Jan 1950, Miskole, Hungary. Mezzo-Soprano. Education: Studied at Franz Liszt Academy in Budapest and in Berlin. Debut: Sang Gluck's Orpheus in Berlin, 1976. Career: Sang at Rostock, 1976-78, Vienna Staatsoper from 1981 notably on tour to Japan in 1986 and at Salzburg Festival in 1984 in the premiere of Un Re in Ascolto by Berio; Appeared in Zigeunerbaron at Zurich Opera conducted by Nikolaus Harnoncourt in 1990; Lieder recitals and concerts in Austria, France and Switzerland; Other roles include Verdi's Azucena, Ulrica, Mistress Quickly, Amneris, Maddalena and Preziosilla, Wagner's Erda and Brangaene, Marina in Boris Godunov, Clytemnestra and Penelope in Il Ritorno di Ulisse. Recordings include: Zulma in L'Italiana in Algeri; Margaret in Wozzeck. Address: c/o Opernhaus Zurich, Falkenstrasse 1, CH-8008 Zurich, Switzerland.

GONDEK Juliana (Kathleen), b. 20 May 1953, Pasadena, CA, USA. Soprano. 1 daughter. Education: Violin study; BM, 1975, MM, 1977, University of Southern California School of Music; Britten-Pears School of Advanced Musical Studies, Aldeburgh, England. Debut: San Diego Opera. Career includes: Sang Contessa in Le nozze di Figaro with Netherlands Opera in 1986, Heroines in The Tales of Hoffmann in 1986, Alcina in 1987 at Opera Theatre of St Louis, title role in Bianca e Falliero at Greater Miami Opera in 1987, Fiordiligi in Così fan tutte at Hawaii Opera in 1989, Vitelia in La Clemenza di Tito for Scottish Opera in 1991, title role in Beatrice di Tenda in 1991, Elvira at Seattle Opera in 1991 and Gismonda in Othone, 1992; Zenobia in Radamisto, 1993; Title role in Esther, 1994; Gineva in Ariodante at the Handel Festival, Göttingen, 1995; Aspasia in Mozart's Mitridate, 1993; Leyla in Bright Sheng's The Song of Majnun with San Francisco Symphony, 1992; Triple role of Diane Feinstein/Harvey's Mama/The Hooker in world premiere of Harvey Milk with Houston Grand Opera, New York City Opera and San Francisco Opera, 1995-96; Appeared in concert in Canada, USA and in Europe; Appeared as soloist at Edinburgh, Caramoor, Marlboro, Mostly Mozart, Newport, Lincoln Center, Bard, Bowdoin, Göttingen and Avignon Festivals and as recitalist in USA and Europe; Sang as soloist with New York Philharmonic, Minnesota Orchestra, symphonies of St Louis, San Francisco, Montreal, Toronto, Detroit, Dallas, Seattle, Indianapolis and Baltimore; Philharmonia Baroque and Freiburger Barock Orchestras;. Recordings: As Gismonda in Handel's Ottone, 1992; Video, Live From The Met, as 1st Lady in Die Zauberflöte with Metropolitan Opera, 1992; As Zenobia in Handel's Radamisto, 1993; Fortuna in Handel's Giustino, 1994; Ginevra in Handel's Ariodante, 1995; With the Yoav Chamber Ensemble; BBC Documentary, The Making of West Side Story; Sang Ela in the premiere of Carlson's Dreamkeepers, Salt Lake city, 1996. Current Management: Colbert Artists Management Inc. Address: c/o Colbert Artists Management Inc, 111 West 57th Street, New York, NY 10019, USA.

GONLEY Stephanie, b. 1966, England. Violinist. Education: Studied at Chetham's School of Music, at Guildhall School of Music, with Dorothy DeLay at Juilliard School and in Berlin. Career: Mozart Concertos with Manchester Camerata, Mendelssohn, Walton, Brahms and Bruch with Royal Philharmonic, Walton with the London Philharmonic Orchestra and Beethoven in the Netherlands with Adrian Leaper; Further engagements with English Chamber Orchestra in 1990, Philharmonia and Halle, at Montpellier Festival and in Hong Kong, Belgium and Canada, played Vivaldi's Four Seasons with English Chamber Orchestra at Festival Hall in 1993; Prom Debut in 1995 with BBC Scottish Symphony Orchestra; Leader, English Chamber Orchestra; (Masterclasses at Banff, Canada, Aspen, USA and Prussia Cove, Cornwall, England); Co-Founded the Vellinger String Quartet in 1990; (Particpated in master classes with the Borodin Quartet, Pears-Britten School in 1991); Concerts at Ferrara Musica Festival in Italy and debut on South Bank with the London premiere of Roberts Simpson's 13th Quartet; BBC Radio 3 debut in 1991; Season 1994-95 with concerts in London, Germany, Spain, USA, Italy at Sweden, Paris, at Davos Festival, Switzerland; Played at Wigmore Hall several times (with Haydn Op 54 No 2, Gubaidulina and Beethoven Op 59 No 2), and at the Purcell Room with Haydn's Last Seven Words. Recordings include: Elgar's Quartet and Quintet with Piers Lane. Honour: winners of 1994 London International String Quartet Competition. Address: c/o Robert Gilder and Company, Enterprise House, 59-65 Upper Ground, London SE1 9PQ, England.

GONNEVILLE Michel, b. 1950, Montreal, Canada. Lecturer; Composer. Education: Studied piano at an early age; Studied at Ecole de Musique Vincent-d'Indy, 1968-72; BMus, 1972. Career: Composer, studying analysis and composition with Giles Tremblay at Conservatoire de Musique de Montreal, 1973, obtaining first prizes in Analysis and Composition in 1974 and 1975; Attended Stockhausen's seminars in Darmstadt in 1974 and his composition classes in Cologne for three semesters, also working in the Electronic Studio at Cologne Musikhochschule; Student and Personal Assistant to Henri Pousseur at Liège; His professors included Frederic Rzewski and Joh Fritsch; Returning to Canada in 1978 he lectured on analysis and composition at Montreal and Rimouski Conservatories and at the Universities of Montreal and Ottawa. Compositions: Composed works for Louis-Philippe Pelletier, Michael Laucke, Robert Leroux, Gropus 7, L'Ensemble d'Ondes de Montreal, the SMCQ and a recent work premiered by the Orchestre des Jeunes du Quebec; His works have been performed in Montreal, Quebec, Toronto, Metz, Cologne, Bonn, Liège and Paris and several have been recorded and broadcast by CBC and WDR in Cologne. Membership: Board of Directors, Societe de Musique Contemporaine du Quebec. Address: c/o SOCAN, 41 Valleybrook Drive, Don Mills, Ontario M3B 2S6, Canada.

GONZAGA Otoniel, b. 1944, Philippines. Singer (Tenor). Career: Has appeared at opera houses in Europe and North America, 1967-; Engaged at Trier, 1973-77, Frankfurt-am-Main, 1977-88; Member of Cologne Opera, 1988-; Guest engagements at Stuttgart, Munich (Theater am Gärtnerplatz), Vienna (Volksoper), Barcelona, Berne and Genoa; Sang Otello at Aachen, Edgardo in Lucia di Lammermoor at Cincinnati, 1990; Other roles have included Ferrando, Faust, Almaviva and Luigi in Il Tabarro; Many concert appearances. Address: c/o Stadttheater, Theaterstrasse 1-3, 5100 Aachen, Germany.

GONZALES Dalmacio, b. 12 May 1945, Olot, Spain. Tenor. Education: Studied in Barcelona and at the Salzburg Mozarteum with Arleen Auger and Paul Schilharsky; Further study with the late Anton Dermota in Vienna. Debut: Teatro Liceo Barcelona in 1978 as Ugo in Parisina by Donizetti. Career: New York City Opera and San Francisco in 1979 as Alfredo and in Rossini's Semiramide and Tancredi; Metropolitan Opera from 1980 as Ernesto in Don Pasquale and later as Almaviva, Fenton and Nemorino; Sang at La Scala Milan and Aix-en-Provence in 1981 in Ariodante and Tancredi, at Pesaro and La Scala, 1984-85 in a revival of Rossini's Il Viaggio a Reims and further appearances in Rome, Los Angeles, Chicago, Berlin, Zurich, Trieste and London; Sang Ford in Salieri's Falstaff at Parma in 1987 and at Munich Festival in 1990 as Catullus in Catulli Carmina by Orff; Sang Ugo at the 1990 Maggio Musicale, Florence; Other roles include Rossini's Argiro in Tancredi, Idreno in Semiramide, Lindoro, James V in La Donna del lago and Rénaldo in Armida; Season 1992 as Nemorino at Barcelona and Demetrio in Rossini's Demetrio e Polibio at Martina Franca. Recordings: Verdi's Requiem, Falstaff and Il Viaggio a Reims; La Donna del Lago by Rossini. Address: c/o Teatre alla Scala, Via Filodrammatici 2, I-20121 Milan, Italy.

GONZALEZ Carmen, b. 16 Apr 1939, Vallodid, Spain. Mezzo-Soprano. Career: Studied at the Madrid Conservatory and with Magda Piccarolo and Rodolfo Celetti in Milan. Debut: Madrid Chamber Opera in 1968 as Isolier in Le Comte Ory. Career: Sang in Rome, Bologna, Trieste and Venice; Turin in 1974 in the local premiere of Die drei Pintos by Weber/Mahler, returning in 1986 as Ulrica in Un Ballo in Maschera; La Scala Milan in 1979 in a revival of Tito Manlio by Vivaldi; Further appearances in Washington, Florence, Rome, Paris, Brussels, Mexico City, Belgrade and New York at City Opera; Sang Mistress Quickly in Falstaff at Rome in

1989, at Holland Festival in 1990 as Fortune-Teller and Mother Superior in The Fiery Angel by Prokofiev. Recordings: Orlando Furioso by Vivaldi; Anacreon by Cherubini. Address: c/o Netherlands Opera, Waterlooplein 22, 1011 PG, Amsterdam, Netherlands.

GONZALEZ Manuel, b. 30 April 1944, Madrid, Spain. Singer (Baritone). Education: Studied at the Madrid Conservatoire. Debut: Théâtre de la Monnaie Brussels in the lyric baritone repertoire at opera houses in Brussels, Antwerp, Ghent and Liège; Guest engagements in Dortmund, Esen, Frankfurt, Hamburg, Stuttgart and Mannheim; Barcelona, Lisbon, Paris, Nice, Marseilles and Geneva, and at the Vienna Volksoper; Sang roles in operas by Donizetti, Bizet, Mozart, Puccini, Rossini, Massenet and Verdi; Wagner's Wolfram von Eschenbach and Tarquinius in Britten's The Rape of Lucretia; Wexford Festival 1973, in Donizetti's L'Ajo nell'imbarazzo (The Tutor in a Fix); Many concert appearances. Address: c/o Théâtre de la Monaie, 4 Leopoldstrasse, B-1000 Brussels, Belgium.

GOOD Timothy (Charles), b. 7 Aug 1942, London, England. Violinist; Author. Education: Dulwich College Preparatory School, 1953-56; The King's School Canterbury, 1956-59; Royal Academy of Music, London, 1959-63; Teachers include, Ronald Good (father), David Martin, Frederick Grinke, Sacha Lasserson, Maxim Jacobsen. Career: As Freelancer: Royal Philharmonic Orchestra, Philharmonia Orchestra, English Chamber Orchestra, Mantovani Orchestra, London Philharmonic Orchestra, London Sinfonietta, 1963-78; Associate Member, London Symphony Orchestra, 1964-78; Since 1978, Session Player for Films, Television; Leader, Oxford Pro Musica, 1979-83. Publications: Above Top Secret, 1987; Alien Liaison, 1991; Beyond Top Secret, 1996. Contributions to: Record Sleeve Photos for CBS and RCA. Honours: Gwynne Kimpton Scholarship, 1959; Sir Edward Cooper Prize, 1962; Rowsby Woof Prize, 1962; Roth Prize, 1962; F Vivian Dunn Prize, 1963. Membership: Royal Society of Musicians. Hobbies: Photography; Travel; Swimming; Aerospace. Address: c/o 247 High Street, Beckenham, Kent, BR3 1AB, England.

GOODALL Howard (Lindsay), b. 26 May 1958, London, England. Composer; Arranger. Education: ARCO, 1975; Chorister, New College, Oxford; Music Scholar, Christ Church, Oxford. Career: Composer, TV Scores & Songs of: Not the Nine O'Clock News; The Black Adder; Composer & Performer in: Rowan Atkinson in Revue, UK Tours 1977-87, World Tour 1982, West End, 1981, 1986, Broadway, 1986. Compositions: Musicals: The Hired Man, with Melvyn Bragg, 1984; Girlfriends, 1987; Days of Hope, 1991; Operas: Der Glöchner von Notre-Dame, 1983; Silas Marner, 1993; Choral: Psalm 122, 1992; Let Us Be True to One Another, 1990; Christ Church Mass, 1993; Orchestral: Land of the Lakes Suite, 1986; Voces Redentes, 1988; The Borrowers, 1992. Recordings: The Hired Man; Rowan Atkinson Live in Belfast; Not Just a Pretty Face; Not the Nine O'Clock News; Hedgehog Sandwich; The Memory Lingers; Days of Hope, 1991; The Hired Man, at the Palace Theatre, 1992. Honours: MA, Oxon; Ivor Novello Award, Best Musical, 1984. Memberships: BASCA; Liberal Club; PRS; MU; European Movement; Liberal Club. Hobbies: Gardening; Cricket; Reading. Current Management: PBJ Management. Address: 5 Soho Square, London W1V 5HL, England.

GOODALL Valorie, b. 23 Sept 1936, Waco, Texas, USA. Soprano; Voice Teacher; Opera Director. m. William P Mooney, 21 Jan 1962, 2 sons. Education: BM cum laude, Baylor University, 1958; MM, University of Colorado, 1959; Advanced study with Paola Novikova, Berton Coffin and Werner Singer. Debut: Graz Opera House, Austria. Career: Leading Lyric Soprano, roles of Mimi, Micaela, Mélisande, Zdenka, Composer, Fiordiligi, Cherubino, Graz Opera; Performances at opera houses of Graz, Geneva, Bern, Theater an der Wien in Vienna, Prague; Star/producer, State museum tour of Venus and Adonis with early instruments, New Jersey, USA, 1981; Founder/director of Opera at Rutgers; Performer in oratorio, song recital and musical theatre; Resident Stage Director: New England Lyric Operetta, Stamford, Conn. Recordings: Land des Lächelns by Lehar, opposite Giuseppe di Stefano, London Records. Address: Voice Department, Mason Gross School of the Arts, Rutgers University, New Brunswick, NJ 08903, USA.

GOODE Richard (Stephen), b. 1 Jun 1943, New York City, USA. Pianist. m. Marcia Weinfeld, 10 Apr 1987. Education: Diploma, Curtis Institute of Music, 1961-64; BSc, Mannes College of Music, 1967-69; Marlboro School of Music. Debut: New York Young Concert Artists, 1962. Career: Concerts in USA, England, Europe, South America, Australia, Far East with various orchestras including: New York Philharmonic, Los Angeles Philharmonic, Baltimore, Orpheus, Philadelphia, ECO and Royal Philharmonic; Founding Member, Chamber Music Society of Lincoln Center; European tours with Orpheus; Played Bach, Chopin and Schubert at the Wigmore Hall, London, 1997. Recordings: Complete cycle of 32 Beethoven Sonatas; Schumann, Fantasy, Humoresque; Schubert, 3 Posthumous Sonatas; Brahms, Late Piano Music; Mozart, Piano Concerti; Various chamber music recordings. Honours: Clara Haskil 1st Prize, 1973; Avery Fisher Prize, 1980. Hobbies: Book Collecting; Museums. Current Management: Frank Salomon Association, New York City. Address: 12 East 87th Street Apt 5A, New York, NY 10128, USA.

GOODING Julia, b. 1965, England. Soprano. Education: Studied at the Guildhall School. Career: Opera appearances at the Innsbruck Festival and the Opéra-Comique, Paris; Dido and Aeneas in Mexico; Concerts with such conductors as Malgoire, Minkowski, Leonhardt, Bruggen and Mackerras in Europe, North America and the Far East. Recordings include: King Arthur; Handel's Belshazzar; Handel's Teseo; Purcell Odes; Monteverdi's Orfeo; Blow Venus and Adonis. Address: c/o Ron Gonsalves Management, 7 Old Town, Clapham, London, SW4 0JT, England.

GOODLOE Robert, b. 5 Oct 1936, St Petersburg, Florida, USA. Singer (Baritone). Education: Studied at Simpson College Indianola (Iowa) and with Harvey Brown and Armen Boyajian. Debut: Des Moines, Iowa, 1963, as Mozart's Figaro. Career: Has sung principally at the Metropolitan Opera, also in Hartford, Baltimore, Philadelphia and San Francisco; Roles include Puccini's Scarpia, Michele and Marcello; Enrico (Lucia di Lammermoor); Mercutio in Roméo et Juliette; Germont in La Traviata and Paolo in Simon Boccanegra. Address: c/o Metropolitan Opera, Lincoln Center, NY 10023, USA.

GOODMAN Alfred, b. 1 Mar 1920, Berlin, Germany. Composer; Musicologist. m. Renate Roessig, 14 July 1966, 1 son. Education: BS, Columbia College, New York; MA, Composition, Musicology, Columbia University; PhD, Technische Universität, Berlin. Career: Editor, Westminster Records, New York City; Composer, Movietone, New York City; Music Editor, Bavarian Broadcasting Commission; Lecturer, Academy of Music, Munich Service, 1971-; Lecturer, Academy of Music, College of Music, Munich, 1976-. Gave lecture at Arnold Schoenberg Symposium, Duisburg, Germany, 1993. Compositions: Psalm XII; The Audition, opera in 1 act; Pro Memoria for orchestra; Individuation, symphonic work; Chamber works, songs, choral compositions, television and film scores, orchestral works; The Lady and the Maid, opera in 1 scene; Across the Board for brass ensemble (for Locke Brass Consort, London); Brassology for Eleven (for Brunn Brass Ensemble, Czechoslovakia); Works for organ and brass; Timpani; Works for organ and saxophone, organ and flute or trumpet; Universe of Freedom-Orchestrology, 1991; Orchestrette in 7 parts, 1992. Publications: Musik im Blut; Lexikon: Musik von A-Z; Die Amerikanischen Schuler Franz Liszts; Dictionary of Musical Terms, 1982. Hobbies: Walking; Reading. Address: Bodenstedt Strasse 31, 81241 Munich, Germany.

GOODMAN Craig (Stephen), b. 6 July 1957, Pittsburgh, Pennsylvania, USA. Flautist; Conductor; Educator. Education: BA, Yale University, 1978; MM, Yale School of Music, 1979; Private study with Marcel Moyse and theory with Narcis Bonet. Debut: Konzerthus, Vienna, Austria, 1975. Career: Solo Flutist, Opera Company, Philadelphia, 1978-79; Freelance, American Symphony, New York City Ballet, St Luke's Chamber Orchestra, Musica Aeterna, 1979-86; Solo engagements, Australia, Europe, USA; Musical Director, The Players of the New World, New York; Chamber Music performances with L'Ensemble, New York City, Bach Aria Group, New York City and Ensemble i, Vienna, Austria; Solo videos of Bach and Gossec, WYNC Television, New York; Featured artist on Sunday Morning with Charles Kuratt, CBS TV. Recordings: Bach Aria Group, Bach Brandenburg Concerto No 4 with James Buswell, Samuel Baron and Festival Strings, Ensemble I recording, Bach Trio Sonata in G for 2 flutes and continuo; Musical Heritage Society recording, Morton Gould's Concerto for wind quartet, piano and violin. Hobbies: Wilderness and outdoor activities; Art.

GOODMAN Erica, b. 19 Jan 1948, Toronto, Canada. Harpist. m. Morris Jacobs. Education: Royal Conservatory of Music, Toronto; National Music Camp, Interlochen, Michigan; University of Southern California, Los Angeles; Curtis Institute of Music, Philadelphia. Debut: Alice Tully Hall-Lincoln Centre, New York, 1972. Career: Child prodigy, accompanied opera singer Teresa Stratas on national TV at the age of 13, 1961; Played for President Kennedy at the White House, 1962; Youngest musician ever to join the Toronto Musicians Association, 1962; Member of Toronto and CBC Symphony Orchestras, 1962-66; Conducted by Igor Stravinsky, 1964; Soloist, Philadelphia Orchestra, 1968; Toured Japan with flautist Robert Aitkin at invitation of Toru Takemitsu to perform his work, 1995; Performed at the Royal Palace in Stockholm with horn player Sören Hermansson, 1996; One of the most active studio harpists on the continent and played on numerous scores of films, TV and radio productions. Recordings include: Erica Goodman In Concert; Erica Goodman And Friends; The Virtuoso Harp; Flute And Harp; Erica Goodman Plays Canadian Harp Music; Horn And Harp Odyssey. Honours: Grande Prix de Disque, Canada, 1980; Juno Award Best Solo Recording, 1995; Best Classical Musician, NOW Magazine reader's poll for Best of Toronto, 1996. Memberships: Toronto Musicians Association; World Harp Congress; American Harp Society; Recording Musicians Association. Address: 51 Blyth Hill Road, Toronto, Ontario, Canada, M4N 3L6.

GOODMAN Richard (Edwin), b. 25 Dec 1935, New York City, New York, USA. Baritone; Artistic Director. 3 daughters. Education: BA, 1955, MS, 1958, Cornell University; PhD, University of California, Berkeley, 1964; Studied Piano and Musicianship with Hedy Spielter, as a child; Piano coaching with Alexander Aronowsky; Voice studies with Janet Parlova, Frederick Sharp, Lenoir Hosack and others; Attended AIMS, Graz, Austria. Career: Founder, Artistic Director, Berkeley Opera Company; Over 50 opera roles in Berkeley Opera, West Bay Opera, Lamplighters, Pocket Opera; Recitals and appearances, London and Austria; Main roles include Falstaff (Verdi and Vaughan Williams), Don Pasquale, Figaro (Mozart), Rigoletto, Rocco, George (Of Mice and Men) and Bartolo (Rossini and Paisiello); Founder and Co-Director, Opera da Camera, 1995 Address: 715 Arlington, Berkeley, CA 94707, USA.

GOODMAN Roy, b. 26 Jan 1951, Guildford, Surrey, England. Conductor; Director; Violinist. Education: Chorister, King's College, Cambridge, 1959-64; Royal College of Music, 1968-70; Berkshire College of Education, 1970-71. Career: From 1971 successively: Head of Music at two comprehensive schools, Senior String Tutor for Berkshire, Director of Music at University of Kent and Director of Early Music at Royal Academy of Music; Founded the Brandenburg Consort in 1975; Co-Director of the Parley of Instruments, 1979-86; Principal Conductor of the Hanover Band, 1986-94; Seven tours of USA, 1988-94; Musical Director of the European Union Baroque Orchestra, 1988-; Guest Conductor with Finnish and Swedish Radio, Lahti, Tampere, Ulster and Norrkoping Symphony Orchestras, Scottish Chamber Orchestra, City of London Sinfonia, German Handel Soloists and the New Orlean's Hall Orchestra; Conducted complete Beethoven Symphonies in Hannover, Handel's Tamerlano in Paris and with Opera North in Leeds, Scipione, Tamerlano and Ezio and Amadigi in Karlsruhe, Mozart's Bastien and Bastienne in Portugal and Don Giovanni in Belfast; Revival of Arne's Artaxerxes, London 1995; Appointed Principal Conductor of Umea Symphony Orchestra from July 1996; Conducted the New Queen's Hall Orchestra at the Barbican Hall, 1997. Recordings: As conductor, violinist and keyboard player, has directed some 100 CD recordings for various labels of repertoire ranging from Monteverdi to Rossini, including major orchestral works by Purcell, Corelli, Bach and Handel, and the symphonies of Haydn, Beethoven, Schubert, Weber, Berwald and Schumann. Hobbies: Squash; Windsurfing; Skiing. Address: 97 Mill Lane, Lower Earley, Reading, Berkshire, RG6 3UH, England.

GOODWIN Andrew, b. 11 November 1947, Hillingdon, Middlesex, England. Education: Wolverhampton Grammar School, 1959-66; BA, Honours, Music, University of Liverpool, 1967-70; MA, University College of North Wales, Bangor, 1970-72. Career: Organist and Master of the Choristers at Bangor Cathedral, 1972-; Organ Recitalist, Choral Conductor, Music Examiner, Teacher. Memberships: Fellow, Royal College of Organists, 1970; Incorporated Society of Musicians. Hobbies: Theatre; Wildlife conservation; Railways (Member, Railway Users' Consultative Committee for Wales). Address: 34 Ffordd Gwenllian, Llanfairpwll, Isle of Anglesey, LL61 5QD.

GOODWIN Paul, b. 2 Sept 1956, England. Conductor; Oboist. Education: City of London School, Temple Church Choir, Nottingham University; Guildhall School of Music; Vienna Hochschule für Musik. Career: Associate Director of the Academy of Ancient Music; Director, Dartington Festival Baroque Orchestra and the Royal College of Music Baroque Orchestra; Guest engagements with Ulter Orchestra, RTE Dublin, CBSO, English Chamber Orchestra, Swedish Chamber Orchestra, Orchestra National de Lille, European Baroque Orchestra, and in the USA with the Portland Baroque Orchestra and St Pauls Chamber Orchestra; Conducted staged production of the Bach St Matthew Passion in collaboration with Jonathan Miller; 1998 performances wityh Karlsruhe Opera, Openhaus Halle and Opera North. Recordings: Solo recordings on the oboe: (Bach, Telemann, Albinoni, Vivaldi, Haydn, Mozart); As a Conductor with the AAM (Mozart, Handel, Schutz and Tavener). Address: c/o Harold Holt Ltd, 31 Sinclair Road, London W14 0NS, England.

GOODWIN (Trevor) Noël, b. 25 Dec 1927, Fowey, Cornwall, England. Writer and Critic (Music, Dance). m. Anne Mason Myers, 23 Nov 1963, 1 stepson. Education: BA (London). Career: Assistant Music Critic: News Chronicle, 1952-54, Manchester Guardian, 1954-55; Music and Dance Critic, Daily Express, 1956-78; Associate Editor, Dance and Dancers, 1958-; Executive Editor, Music and Musicians, 1963-71; London Dance Critic, International Herald Tribune, Paris, 1978-83; London Correspondent, Opera News, New York, 1980-91; Overseas News Editor, 1985-91, Editorial Board, 1991-, Opera; Planned and presented numerous radio programmes of music and records for BBC Home and World Services during past 35 years; Frequent contributor to music and arts programmes on Radios 3 and 4. Publications: London Symphony, portrait of an orchestra, 1954; A Ballet for Scotland, 1979; A Knight at the Opera (with Geraint Evans), 1984; Royal Opera and Royal Ballet Yearbooks (editor), 1978, 1979, 1980; New Grove Dictionary of Music and Musicians (area editor, writer), 1980; A Portrait of the Royal Ballet (editor), 1988. Contributions to: Numerous journals and magazines; Encyclopaedica Britannica, 15th edition, 1974; Encyclopaedia of Opera, 1976; Britannica Books of the Year, annually, 1980-93; Cambridge Encyclopaedia of Russia and the Soviet Union, 1982, and revised edition, Cambridge Encyclopaedia of Russia and the former Soviet Union, 1994; New Oxford Companion to Music, 1983; Pipers Enzyklopädie des Musiktheaters, 1986-91; New Grove Dictionary of Opera, 1992; Viking Opera Guide, 1993; International Dictionary of Ballet, 1993; Metropolitan Opera Guide to Recorded Opera, 1993. Memberships include: Trustee-Director, International Dance Course for Professional Choreographers and Composers; Formerly: Arts Council of Great Britain, Dance and Music Advisory Panels; HRH The Duke of Kent's UK Committee for European Music Year. Address: 76 Skeena Hill, London, SW18 5PN, England.

GOOSSENS Sidonie, b. 19 Oct 1899, Liscard, Cheshire, England. Harpist. m. (1) Hyam Greenbaum, 1924, (2) Norman K Millar, 19 Dec 1945. Education: Studied at the Royal College of Music. Debut: Played with orchestra, 1921. Career: Played at Savoy Hill, 1924, with the British Broadcasting Company and the 2LO Wireless Orchestra; Appeared on television, 1936; Founder member of the BBC Symphony Orchestra, 1930; Played with BBC Symphony Orchestra until 1980, notably in modern scores conducted by Boulez; Subsequent guest appearances; Participation in many first performances; Professor of Harp at the Guildhall School of Music from 1960. Honours: Order of the British Empire; FGSM; FRCM; Honorary RAM. Address: Woodslock Farm, Gadbrook, Betchworth, Surrey RH3 7AH, England.

GORBENKO Pavel, b. 1956, Moscow, Russia. Violinist. Education: Studied at Gnessin Music Institute with Dr Kiselyev. Career: Co-founder, Amistad Quartet, 1973, now Tchaikovsky Quartet; Many concerts in Russia with repertoire including works by Hadyn, Mozart, Beethoven, Schubert, Brahms, Tchaikovsky, Borodin, Prokofeiv, Shostakovich, Bartók, Barber, Bucci, Golovin and Tikhomirov; Recent concert tours to: Mexico; Italy; Germany. Recordings include: Recitals for a US-Russian company. Honours include: Winner with Amistad Quartet: Bela Bartók Festival, 1976; Bucchi Competition, Rome, 1990. Address: c/o Sonata (Tchaikovsky Quartet), 11 Northpark Street, Glasgow, G 20 7AA, Scotland.

GORCHAKOVA Galina, b. 1 Mar 1962, Novokuznetsk, Rusia. Singer (Soprano). Education: Studied at Novosibirsk Academy and Conservatory. Career: Appearances with Sverdlovsk Opera, 1988-, as Tatyana, Butterfly, Yaroslavna in Prince Igor, Santuzza, Katerina (Lady Macbeth of Mtsensk), Liu, Militrissa (The Legend of Tsar Saltan), Tamara (The Demon by Rubinstein), and Clara in Prokofiev's The Duenna; Guest appearances elsewhere in Russia, notably as the Trovatore Leonora, Yaroslavna and Lisa in The Queen of Spades at Maryinsky Theatre; Sang Renata in The Fiery Angel by Prokofiev at 1991 Promenade Concerts (UK debut), at St Petersburg, and at Covent Garden (UK stage premiere of the opera in the original Russian), 1992; Sang Natalya in concert performance of Tchaikovsky's The Oprichnik Edinburgh, 1992, Renata at the Metropolitan, New York; Season 1995 as Tosca at Covent Garden and Butterfly in New York, returned to London as Tosca, 1997. Honours include: Prizewinner, Mussorgsky and Glinka Competitions. Address: c/o IMG Artists, Media House, 3 Burlington Lane, London W4 2TH, England.

GORDIEJUK Marian (Stanislaw Wlodzimierz), b. 9 Feb 1954, Bydgoszcz, Poland. Composer; Music Theory Lecturer; Music Journalist; Musicologist. m. 2 July 1977, 1 son, 2 daughters. Education: State College of Music, Lodz, Pedagogic studies with Assistant Professor Antoni Kedra, 1976; Studies in Music Theory under Professor Franciszek Wesolowski, 1977; Studies in conducting vocal-instrumental groups with Professor Zygmunt Gzella, 1978; Studies in Composition, with Professor Jerzy Bauer, 1979. Compositions include: Suite, Birds, for two transverse flutes (Lodz) 1976, published: Edition Agencja Autorska Warszawa, 1986, Contemporary Polish Music, Series of Chamber Music Compositions; Games for flute and harp (Gdansk) 1987, recorded: Polskie Radio, Gdansk, 1987; Children's Quart Miniature for Oboe or Flute and Piano (Lodz) 1987, recorded: Telewizja Polska, Lodz, 1987; String Quartet (with amplifier) Gdansk, 1991. Contributions to: Reviews of Concerts at Filharmonia Pomorska im T J Paderewskiego in Bydgoszcz published in Ilustrowany Kurier Polski, 1977-78; Discussions of Compositions for Programme Leaflets of Concerts in Filharmonia Pomorska in T J Paderewskiego in Bydgoszcz during 1978-88. Publication: Edition Agencia Antorsko, Promocja, Warsaw, 1993. Hobbies: Artistic Photography; Numismatics; History of Art. Address: ul Tczewska 12, 85-382 Bydgoszcz, Poland.

GORDON Alexandra, b. 1945, Dannevirke, New Zealand. Singer (Soprano). Education: Studied at London Opera Centre and with Walter Midgley. Debut: Sang First Boy in Die Zauberflöte and Despina in Cosi fan tutte for New Zealand Opera, aged 19. Career: Sang with Opera for All at Glyndebourne and with Scottish Opera, notably as the Queen of Night and Flotow's Martha, and in The Nightingale by Stravinsky; Many concert appearances and radio broadcasts; Sang Delia in new production of Rossini's Il Viaggio a Reims, Covent Garden, 1992. Honours include: Friends of Covent Garden Scholarship, at London Opera Centre. Address: c/o Royal Opera House, Covent Garden, London WC2, England.

GORDON David (Jamieson), b. 7 Dec 1947, Philadelphia, USA. Concert/Opera Singer (Tenor). m. Barbara Bixby, 14 June 1969. Education: College of Wooster; McGill University; Conservatoire de Quebec. Debut: Lyric Opera of Chicago, 1973. Career: Frequent appearances with North American and European orchestras and opera companies, including Metropolitan Opera, Lyric Opera of Chicago, San Francisco Opera, Hamburg Staatsoper, Boston Symphony, Philadelphia Orchestra, Cleveland Orchestra, Los Angeles Philharmonic; Specialist in music by J S Bach; Also appears regularly as master class teacher and lecturer; Bach Festivals of Bethlehem, Carmel, Oregon and Winter Park (USA) Stuttgart, Tokyo. Recordings: Bach Magnificat - R Shaw/Atlantic Symphony; Acis and Galatea, Seattle Symphony; Pulcinella, St Paul Chamber Orchestra; other recordings on Telarc, London Decca, Delos, RCA Red Seal and Nonesuch/Electra. Current Management: Thea Dispeker, Inc, 59 East 54 Street, New York, NY 10022, USA. Address: 84 South Clinton Street, Doylestown, PA 18901, USA.

GORDON Peter, b. 20 June 1951, New York, USA. Composer; Saxophonist. Education: Studied at the University of California, San Diego, and Mills College; Teachers included Robert Ashley, Kenneth Gaburo, Terry Riley and Pauline Oliveros. Career: Co-founded the art-rock group Love of Life Orchestra 1977; Performances and recordings in the USA, Europe and Canada; Collaborations with the Italian group Falso Movimento; Co-founded video and music production company Antartica 1982. Honours include: Obie award for music to Otello, 1985. Recordings: Albums of his own music; Albums as saxophonist and clarinettist playing music by various groups. Compositions include: The Birth of a Poet, text by Kathy Acker; The Return of the Native, after Hardy; Shoptalk, collage based on talk by eight composers; Frozen Moments of Passion for saxophone, speech fragments and tape; Otello, mixed media work based on Shakespeare; Collaboration with Robert Ashley on Perfect Lives (Private Parts). Address: c/o ASCAP, ASCAP Building, One Lincoln Plaza, New York, NY 10023, USA.

GORDON Priscilla (Ann), b. 2 Jan 1938, Martinsville, VA, USA. Singer (Soprano). m. Alberto Figols, 12 Sep 1962, 1 s, 2 d. Education: Madison College, Harrisonburg, VA; BM, New England Conservatory of Music, Boston, MA, 1960; Scuola Basiola, Milan, Italy; Nadia Boulanger, Paris, France. Debut: At age 5. Career: Performances at Metropolitan Opera, State Theatre, Gran Teatro del Liceo, Barcelona, Opera houses of Toulouse, France, Geneva, Switzerland, San Jose, Costa Rica, Amsterdam, The Netherlands; Toured internationally with Touring Concert Opera Company and Boston Symphony Orchestra. Recordings include: Numerous recordings sung at live performances, including opera, operetta, popular, oratorio and sacred music as well as French, German and English concert songs; Recuerdos de Navidad, arias and duets from Spanish opera and Zarzuela; Beethoven's Ninth Symphony with Boston Symphony Orchestra. Contributions to: Numerous newspapers and magazines. Hobbies: Travel; Taking care of 15 acre estate. Address: c/o Ramon Alsina, 228 East 80th Street, New York, NY 10021, USA.

GORECKI Henryk (Mikolaj), b. 6 Dec 1933, Czernica, near Rybnik, Poland. Composer. m. Jadwiga Gorecki, 1959, 2 children. Education: Composition, Katowice State Higher School of Music, under B Szabelski. Career: Docent, Faculty of Composition, Rector 1975-79, Extraordinary Professor 1977-, State Higher School of Music, Katowice. Compositions: Symphony No 1, for strings and percussion, 1959; Scontri for orchestra, 1960; Concerto for 5 Instruments and String Quartet, 1957; Genesis for instrumental ensemble and soprano, 1963; Cantata for organ, 1968; Canticum Graduum for orchestra, 1989; Ad matrem for soprano, chorus and orchestra, 1971; Symphony No 2 Copernican, 1972, No 3 Lamentation Songs, 1976; Beatus Vir for baritone, chorus and orchestra, 1979; Harpischord Concerto , 1980; Lullabies and Dances for violin and piano, 1982; O Domina Noztra for soprano and organ, 1985/90; Already it is Dusk, String Quartet, 1988; Good Night, for soprano and ensemble, 1990. Honours: 1st Prize, Young Composers' Competition, Warsaw for Monologhi, 1960; 1st Prize, Parish Youth Biennale, for 1st symphony, 1961; Prize, UNESCO International Tribune for Composers for Refrain, 1967; for Ad Matrem, 1973; 1st prize, Composers Competition, Szczecin for Kantata, 1968; Prize, Union of Polish Composers, 1970; prize, Committee for Polish Radio & TV, 1974; Prize, Minister of Culture & Arts, 1965, 1969, 1973; State Prize 1st Class for Ad Matrem & Nicolaus Copernicus Symphony, 1978. Membership: Council of Higher Artistic Education, Ministry of Culture & Arts. Address: U1 Feliksa kona 4 m 1, 40-133 Katowice, Poland.

GOREN Eli, b. 23 Jan 1923, Vienna, Austria. Violinist; College Professor. m. Doreen Stanfield. Education: Studied in Vienna and at the Jerusalem Conservatory; Further study with Max Rostal in London. Career: Leader of the Jerusalem Symphony Orchestra 1947-50; London Mozart Players 1953-59; Melos Ensemble 1952-57; Leader of the Allegri String Quartet 1953-68, co-leader of the BBC Symphony Orchestra 1968-77; Has given early performances of music by Tal, Maconchy and Seiber; Professor of Violin and Chamber Music at the Guildhall School of Music and Drama from 1961; Member of jury on international competitions. Address: c/o Guildhall School of Music and Drama, Barbican, London EC2, England.

GORMLEY Clare, b. 1969, Australia. Soprano. Career: Frequent concert and recital appearances throughout Australia and in Europe; Repertory includes Lieder by Mozart and Schumann, Bach's St Matthew Passion and Goyescas by Granados; Contestant at the 1995 Cardiff Singer of the World Competition; Season 1995-96 as Alexandra in the premiere of The Eighth Wonder, at Sydney and Gretel at Brisbane (also at the Met). Address: c/o 711 West End Avenue, A[partment 7FS, New York, NY 10025-6887, USA.

GORNE Annette Vande, b. 6 Jan 1946, Charleroi, Belgium. Composer. Education: Studied at the Mons, Brussels and Paris Conservatories; Teachers have included Jean Absil, Pierre Henry and Pierre Schaeffer. Career: Teacher of electroacoustic music at Liège and Brussels. Compositions include: Lamento Ou La Deliverance Du Cerce, 1982; Exil: Chant II, 1983; Faisceaux for Tape, 1985; Noces Noirs, 1986; Terre for 8-track Tape, 1991. Address: c/o SABAM, Rue d'Arlon 75-77, 1040 Brussels, Belgium.

GÖRNE Matthias, b. 1966, Weimar, Germany. Singer, Baritone. Education: Studied in Liepzig from 1985, then with Fischer -Dieskau and Elisabeth Schwarzkopf. Career: Performed with the children's choir at Chemnitz Opera; Sang in Bach's St Matthew Passion under Kurt Masur, Leipzig, 1990; Appearances with Hanns Martin Schneidt and Munich Bach Choir and with NDR Symphony Orchestra Hamburg; Further engagements under Horst Stein, with Bamberg Symphony and in Hindemith's Requiem under Wolfgang Sawallisch; Concerts at Leipzig Gewandhaus under Helmuth Rilling and in Amsterdam and Paris; Lieder recitals with pianist Eric Schneider; Sang title role in Henze's Prinz von Homburg, Cologne, 1992, Marcello in La Bohème at Komische Oper Berlin, 1993; Engaged for Die Zauberflöte at the 1997 Salzburg Festival. Recordings include: Winterreise, 1997; Entarte Musik. Address: c/o IMG Artists, Media House, 3 Burlington Lane, Chiswick, London W4 2TH, England.

GOROKHOVSKAYA Yevgena, b. 1944, Baku, Russia. Singer (Mezzo-soprano). Education: Studied at Leningrad Conservatory. Debut: Maly Theatre, Leningrad, as Lehl in The Snow Maiden by Rimsky-Korsakov, 1969. Career: Member, Maryinsky Opera Leningrad (now St Petersburg), 1976-; Roles have included Lubasha in The Tsar's Bride by Rimsky, Eboli (Don Carlos) and Azucena; Guest appearances, Germany, Rumania, Spain, France, Greece, USA, Switzerland, Czechoslovakia; On Tour to UK, 1991, sang Mme Larina in Eugene Onegin at Birmingham and Marfa in Khovanshchina at Edinburgh Festival. Recordings: Several albums. Address: c/o Maryinsky Opera and Ballet Theatre, St Petersburg, Russia, CIS.

GORR Rita, b. 18 Feb 1926, Zelzaete, Belgium. Singer (Mezzo-soprano). Education: Studied in Ghent and at the Brussels Conservatory. Debut: Antwerp 1949, as Fricka in Die Walküre, Strasbourg Opera 1949-52, as Orpheus, Amneris and Carmen; Paris Opéra-Comique and Opéra debuts 1952, as Charlotte (Werther) and as Magdalene in Die Meistersinger; Bayreuth Festival 1958, as Ortrud and Fricka; La Scala Milan 1960, as Kundry; Covent Garden 1959-71, debut as Amneris; Edinburgh Festival 1961 in Iphigénie en Tauride, with the Covent Garden company; Metropolitan Opera from 1962, as Amneris, Eboli, Santuzza, Azucena and Dalila; London Coliseum 1969, in a concert performance of Roussel's Padmavati (British premiere); Other roles have included Margared (Le Roi d'Ys), Massenet's Herodiade, the title role in Médée by Cherubini and Didon in Les Troyens by Berlioz; Sang the Mother in Louise by Charpentier at Brussels, 1990; First Prioress in Dialogues des Carmélites at Lyon, 1990 followed by Herodias in Salome; Toronto 1997, in The Carmelites. Recordings: Pelléas et Mélisande; Dialogues des Carmélites, Iphigénie en Tauride; Aida, Lohengrin; Louise by Charpentier. Honours include: Winner, Competition at Verviers, 1946; Winner, Lausanne International Singing Competition, 1952.

21. Address: c/o Opéra de Lyon, 9 Quai Jen Moulin, F-69001 Lyon, France.

GORRARA Riccardo (Richard), b. 29 May 1964, Metz, France. Classical Guitarist; Lutenist; Conductor. Education: Studied sciece, general art, Italy and England; Graduated, science diploma, London; studied music, major colleges, London including Guildhall School of Music; Diploma, Royal Academy of Music; Studied, Paris Music College. Debut: Genoa Cathedral, Italy. Career: Appeared in most European halls and festivals, Milan, Rome, Turin, London, Paris, Madrid; Paris Festival, Edinburgh Festival. Compositions: Varied; Music for guitar and lute from 15th Centuryto present, including Dowland, Frescobaldi, Ferrbasco, Couperin, Weiss, Bach, Sor, etc. Recordings: Various major recordings for guitar and lute, particularly works from 15th Century to 20th Century rarely played; 7 Gramophone recordings, also for radio broadcasting; Various national radio stations in Italy, Denmark, Switzerland. Contributions to: Various reviews for Guitar and lute method, technique, interpretation for Italian guitar and music magazines. Honours: 2 certificates with merit, guitar, Royal Academy of Music, 1984. Memberships: Royal Philharmonic Society; National Early Music Association; Lute Society; Dutch Lute Society; Brussels Philharmonique Society. Address: PO Box 195, London WC1H 8NA, England.

GORTON Susan, b. 1946, Cheshire, England. Singer (Mezzo-soprano). Education: Studied at the Royal Manchester College of Music. Debut: Feklusha in Katya Kabanova for the Glyndebourne Tour, 1992. Career: Further appearances with GTO, as Filippyevna in Eugene Onegin and Marcellina in Le nozze di Figaro; Glyndebourne Festival 1995-97, as the Chambermaid in The Makropoulos Case; Further engagements as Mistress Quickly and Mrs Sedley in Peter Grimes, for English National Opera; Florence Pike in Albert Herring for English Touring Opera, Martha in Faust and Mamma Lucia in Cavalleria Rusticana for Welsh National Opera; Premieres include Julian Grant's A Family Affair for the Almeida Festival and The House of Crossed Desires by John Woolrich for Music Theatre Wales, 1996; Season 1997-98 as the Hostess in Boris Godunov for WNO, and Mrs Sedley for the Lyric Opera, Chicago. Address: c/o Harlequin Agency Ltd, 203 Fidlas Road, Cardiff CF4 5NA, Wales.

GORZYNSKA Barbara, b. 4 December 1953, Cmielow, Poland. Violinist. m. Ryszard Rasinski, 5 June 1982, 1 son. Education: MA (honours), Lodz Academy of Music, 1977. Debut: Played the Mendelssohn Concerto with the Great Symphony Orchestra of Polish Radio, 1969. Career: Solo appearances with London Philharmonic Orchestra, Royal Philharmonic Orchestra, Dresden Staatskapelle, Warsaw Philharmonic Orchestra; London debut at the Festival Hall, 1981, with the London Philharmonic followed by concerts with the Royal Philharmonic and the English Chamber Orchestra; Tour of England with the Warsaw Philharmonic, 1987; Further engagements in France, Mexico, Russia and Czechoslovakia; Professor of Violin, Lodz Academy of Music. Recordings: Studio recordings for Polish Radio & TV, Westdeutscher Rundfunk and the BBC; Gramophone recordings for Le Chant Du Monde and Wifon Labels. Honours: First Prize, Carl Flesch International Violin Competition, London, 1980; First Prize and the Henryk Szeryng Special Prize, Zagreb International Competition, 1977. Hobbies: Film; Theatre. Current Management: Christopher Tennant Artists'. Address: Sienkiewicza, 101-109 m 48, 90-301 Lodz, Poland.

GOSMAN Lazar, b. 27 May 1926, Kiev, USSR. Violinist; Conductor. m. Eugenia Gosman, 16 Apr 1950, 1 son. Education: Central Music School, Moscow, 1934-44; Diploma, Honours, Tchaikovsky Conservatory of Music, Moscow, 1945-49. Career: Violinist, Leningrad Philharmonic Orchestra; Music Director, Leningrad Chamber Orchestra, 1962-77; Associate Concertmaster, St Louis Symphony, USA, 1977-82; Music Director, Tchaikovsky Chamber Orchestra, formerly Soviet Emigré Orchestra; Professor, Violin, State University of New York, Stonybrook. Recordings: Over 40 with Leningrad Chamber Orchestra; Two records with Tchaikovsky Chamber Orchestra. Current Management: Herbert Barrett Management, New York. Address: 3 East Gate Street, Setauket, NY 11733, USA.

GOSSETT Philip, b. 27 Sep 1941. Music Professor. m. 2 children. Education: BA, Amherst College, 1958-61, 1962-63; Columbia University, 1961-62; MFA, Princeton University, 1963-65; Research in France and Italy, 1965-67; PhD (1970) Princeton University, 1967-68. Career includes: Teacher, University of Chicago, 1968-, currently Robert W Reneker Distinguished Service Professor; Radio Programmes for Metropolitan Opera, NY and for WFMT, Chicago; Lectures for Metropolitan Opera, Opera of Chicago, Chicago Symphony Orchestra, Philadelphia Orchestra, Chicago Chamber Choir, Houston Grand Opera, Teatro la Fenice, Venice, Teatro Communale in Florence, Rossini Opera Festival in Pesaro, colleges and universities; Consultant for National Endowment for Humanities, IL Humanities Council, Social Sciences and Humanities Research Council of Canada and various University Presses; Board of Directors, Chicago Symphony Orchestra;

Dean, Division of the Humanities, University of Chicago, 1989-; Gauss Seminars, Princeton University, 1991; Vocal ornamentation and stylistic advisor for various opera houses and recording companies including: Metropolitan Opera, Teatro dell'Opera in Rome, Rossini Opera Festival in Pesaro, Miami Opera; Fellow, American Academy of Arts and Sciences, 1989-. Publications include: Many books and articles, programme notes for various organisations; General Editor of Edizione critica delle opere di Gioachino Rossini and Works of Giuseppe Verdi and various editorial boards; Critical Edition Rossini Tancredi, 1983 and Rossini Ermione with P Brauner, 1995. Honours: Honorary member, Academia Filarmonica di Bologna, 1992; DHL, Amherst College, 1993; Grand ufficiale della Repub Italy, 1997. Memberships include: President, American Musicological Society, 1994-96; President, Society for Textual Scholarship, 1993-95. Address: Dept of Music, University of Chicago, 5845 S Ellis Ave, Chicago, IL 60637, USA.

GOTHONI Ralf, b. 2 May 1946, Rauma, Finland. Pianist; Conductor; Composer. 2 sons. Education: Sibelius Academy, Helsinki. Debut: Jyvaskyla Summer Festival, 1967. Career: Concert Tours as Pianist and Chamber Musician, Worldwide; Principal Guest Conductor, Turku Philharmonic. Compositions: Chamber Operas. Recordings: Britton Piano Concerto; 2 Concerts by Rautavaara; Piano Quartets by Brahms, Strauss. Honours: Medal, Austrian Ministry of Culture, 1979; Prize of Honour, Cultural Foundation of Finland, 1988; Order of Pro Finland, 1991; Gilmore Award, 1994. Address: Hortnagel GmbH, Postfach 86 05 20, 81632 Munchen, Germany.

GOTSINDER Mikhail, b. 1950, Moscow, Russia. Violinist. Education: Studied at Moscow Conservatoire with David Oistrakh. Career: Co-founder, Amistad Quartet, 1973, now Tchaikovsky Quartet; Many concerts in Russia with repertoire including works by Haydn, Mozart, Beethoven, Schubert, Brahms, Tchaikovsky, Borodin, Prokofiev, Shostakovich, Bartók, Barber, Bucci, Golovin and Tikhomirov; Recent concert tours to: Mexico; Italy; Germany. Recordings include: Recitals for a US-Russian company; All Tchaikovsky's quartet works on CD. Honours include: Winner with Amistad Quartet: Bela Bartók Festival, 1976; Bucchi Competition, Rome, 1990. Address: c/o Sonata (Tchaikovsky Quartet), 11 Northpark Street, Glasgow, G20 7AA, Scotland.

GOTTLIEB Gordon, b. 23 Oct 1948, Brooklyn, New York, USA. Percussionist; Conductor; Composer. Education: Total Musicianship with James Wimer, 1961-71; Graduate, High School of Performing Arts, 1966; Timpani and Percussion with Saul Goodman, 1966-71; BM, 1970, MM, 1971, Juilliard School of Music. Career: Extensive performing with New York Philharmonic, including solo appearances in 1974 and 1986; Commissioning and performing new works for piano and percussion with brother Jay, active in contemporary music and has played with Contemporary Chamber Ensemble, Speculum Musicae, The Juilliard Ensemble, the Group for Contemporary Music and others; As Conductor performed the New York premiere of Vesalii Icones by Peter Maxwell Davies and made his Carnegie Hall debut conducting William Walton's Facade with Anna Russell narrating, 1981; In 1986 conducted Histoire du Soldât of Stravinsky with L'Ensemble and Shaker Loops of John Adams at the Santa Fe Chamber Musical Festival. Compositions: Graines gemellaires, improvisation 1; Traversées, improvisation 2, Saudades do Brasil. Recordings: Bartók, Sonata for 2 Pianos; Histoire du Soldât, I Stravinsky. Membership: Percussive Arts Society. Hobbies: Scuba diving; Underwater photography. Address: 29 W 17th Street, 8th Floor, New York, NY 10011, USA.

GOTTLIEB Jack S, b. 12 Oct 1930, New Rochelle, New York, USA. Composer. Education: Studied at Queens College, Brandeis University, the University of Illinois and the Berkshire Music Center; Teachers included Karol Rathaus, Irving Fine, Aaron Copland and Boris Blacher. Career: Assistant to Bernstein at the New York Philharmonic, 1958-66; Music Director at Temple Israel, St Louis, 1970-73; Composer-in-residence then Assistant Professor, Hebrew Union College, New York, 1973; Publications Director, Amberson Enterprises from 1977. Compositions include: String Quartet 1954; Tea Party, opera, 1955; Kids' Calls for chorus and piano 1957; Piano Sonata 1960; In Memory of .... for chorus and organ, 1960; Wind Quintet 1961; Love Songs for Sabbath 1965; Articles of Faith for orchestra and tape 1965; Shout for Joy 1967; The Silent Flickers for piano four hands 1968; New Year's Service for Young People 1970; Sharing the Prophets for solo voices, chorus and ensemble 1975; The Song of Songs, which is Solomon's opera 1976; Four Affirmations for baritone, chorus and brass sextet or organ 1976; Psalmistry 1979; The Movie Opera: a Music Drama for Torch Singer and a Chorus of People in her Life. Honours include: Awards from Brown and Ohio Universities; National Federation of Music Clubs and NEA awards. Address: c/o ASCAP, ASCAP Building, One Lincoln Plaza, New York, NY 10023, USA.

GOTTLIEB Jay (Mitchell), b. 23 Oct 1954, New York, USA. Pianist; Composer. Education: BA, Hunter College, 1970; MA, Harvard University, 1972; Chatham Square Music School, NY;

Conservatoire Americain de Fontainbleau, France with Nadia Boulanger; Festivals of Tanglewood and Darmstadt with Messiaen, Loriod, Ligeti, Kontarsky. Career: Recitals in New York: Alice Tully Hall, Merkin Hall, Carnegie Recital Hall, Third Street Settlement, Cooper Union, Radios WQXR, WNYC, New York University, Theatre des Champs-Elysées, Centre Pompidou, Paris, Alte Oper, Frankfurt; Soloist with Boston Symphony, Orchestra Della Radiotelevisione in Italy, Nouvel Orchestre Philharmonique, Paris, L'Orchestre Philharmonique d'Europe, Paris, L'Orchestre du Rhin, Geneva and Radio and TV in New York, Boston, Washington, Paris, Switzerland, Frankfurt, Cologne, Rome; Festivals of Berlin, Rome, Milan, Venice, Paris, Almeida, Aldeburgh, Autumn in Warsaw, Musica in Strassburg, Avignon, Toulouse, Frankfurt, Amsterdam. Compositions: Synchronisms for Two Percussionists and Tape; Sonata for Violin and Piano; Improvisations for Piano & Percussion; Essay for Orchestra; Soundtrack for film, La Discrète. Recordings: Trois Contes de L'Honorable Fleur; Lys de Madrigaux; Piano & Percussion-Jay and Gordon Gottlieb; Appello of Barbara Kolb; Harawi of Messiaen; Figure of Michèle Reverdy; La Discrète, soundtrack; Arcane of Allain Gaussin. Contributions to: Professional journals including Piano magazine; Jury member for advanced piano examinations at Paris Conservatory; Piano Faculty at Flaine Summer Music Academy, conservatoire Américain in Fontainebleau; Master Classes at Schola Cantorum, Paris. Hobbies: Travel; Theatre; Cinema; Museums; Reading. Address: 29-31 Rue des Boulets, 75011 Paris, France.

GOTTLIEB Peter, b. 18 Sept 1930, Brno, Czechoslovakia. Singer (Baritone). Education: Studied in Rio de Janeiro and in Florence with Raoul Frazzi. Career: Sang at first in Italy, Belgium and North America; Paris Opera in 1962 premiere of L'Opéra d'Aran by Becaud and as Don Giovanni, Figaro, Papageno, Scarpia and Wozzeck, 1985; Glyndebourne Festival 1966-79 as Albert in Werther, Barber in Die schweigsame Frau, Mercurio in the first modern performance of Cavalli's Calisto, (1970) and Zastrow in the premiere of The Rising of the Moon by Nicholas Maw; Théâtre de la Monnaie Brussels 1983, in the premiere of La Passion de Gilles by Boesmans; Opéra du Rhin Strasbourg in 1984 premiere of H H Ulysses by Jean Prodromides; Other roles include Iago, Don Carlos in La Forza del Destino and the Count in Capriccio; Professor, Paris Conservatoire from 1982. Recordings include: La Calisto (Decca); Opera D'Aran (Pathe); La Passion de Gilles (Ricercare); H H Ulysses (Harmonia Mundi); La Cocarde de Mimi Pinson (Decca); La Traviata (Sofca). Address: 361 rue Lecourbe, 75015 Paris, France.

GÖTZ Cornelia, b. 1960, Stuttgart, Germany. Singer (Soprano). Education: Studied in Karlsruhe, Vienna and Munich. Career: First major role as Mozart's Zaide, at the Munich Stattsoper; Appearances as the Queen of Night in Die Zauberflöte throughout Germany and at the Wiener Festwochen; Nuremberg Opera 1992-94, as Mozart's Serpetta and Zerlina, Suppe's Galathée, and Rosina; Further roles include Mozart's Papagena, Blondchen and Constanze; Adele in Die Fledermaus and Olympia; First Flower Maiden in Parsifal at Covent Garden; Concerts include Bach Passions, Messiah, Haydn Creation and Seasons, Mozart's C Minor Mass, and Carmina Burana; Schoenberg's Herzgewäcsche and Second String Quartet with Bavarian Radio. Address: Athole Still Ltd, Foresters Hall, 25-27 Westow Street, London SE19 3RY, England.

GÖTZ Werner, b. 7 Dec 1934, Berlin, Germany. Singer (Tenor). Education: Studied with Friedrick Wilcke and W Kelch in Berlin. Debut: Oldenburg 1967, as Alvaro in La Forza del Destino. Career: Sang in Dusseldorf, Karlsruhe, Munich, Stuttgart and Hamburg; Roles include Wagner's Erik, Lohengrin and Parsifal, Mozart's Tamino, Lionel in Martha by Flotow and parts in operas by Puccini, Janácek and Verdi; Further engagements in London, Zurich, Lodz, Barcelona, Amsterdam and Frankfurt; Munich Opera 1978, in the premiere of Lear by Reimann. Recordings include: Lear (Deutsche Grammophon); Melot in Tristan und Isolde; Eine Florentinische Tragödie by Zemlinsky (Fonit-Cetra). Address: c/o Bayerische Staatsoper, Postfach 745, D-8000 Munich 1, Germany.

GÖTZEN Guido, b. 1959, Dusseldorf, Germany. Singer (Bass). Education: Studied in Cologne with Joseph Metternich. Career: Sang first at the Cologne Opera Studio and at Berne, as Angelotti in Tosca, the Major Domo in Capriccio, Hobson in Peter Grimes, and Sarastro, 1988-89; Bayerische Staatsoper Munich, as the King in Aida, Colline, Masetto and roles in Palestrina, Meistersinger, Mathis der Maler, Parsifal, Orff's Trionfi, Dvork's Dimitri and the Love for Three Oranges, 1989-94; Zürich Opera as Sparafucile in Rigoletto (under Nello Santi), Mozart's Commendatore and Sarastro, and the Bonze in Madama Butterfly, from 1994. Recordings include: Die Meistersinger, conducted by Sawallisch. Honours include: Prizewinner at the Belvedere Competition, 1987. Address: c/o Opernhaus Zürich, Falkenstasse 1, CH-8008 Zürich, Switzerland.

GOWLAND David, b. 1958, England. Senior Coach, Glyndebourne Festival Opera. Education: Studied at the Royal

College of Music and National Opera Studio, London. Career: Member of Glyndebourne Music Staff from 1987, as pianist, repetiteur and assistant conductor in a wide repertory; Paris Opéra with La Clemenza di Tito and La Bohème, pianist in Porgy and Bess; Head of Music Staff at the Geneva Opera 1989-96, and appointments with Royal Danish Opera, Netherlands Opera, Covent Garden and Dublin Grand Opera; Festivals of Aix, Orange and Wexford; Weill's Threepenny Opera at RADA, London; Concerts include Edinburgh and Aldeburgh Festivals, London Proms and BBC orchestras; Season 1997-98 with The Ring in Australia, and Tristan, Idomeneo and Lohengrin in Copenhagen; Lucia di Lammermoor Turandot and Porgy and Bess at Orange; La Traviata for the Opéra Bastille, Paris. Honours include: Jani Strassi Award, Glyndebourne, 1988. Address: c/o Glyndebourne Festival Opera, Lewes, Sussex B8 5UU, England.

GOY Pierre, b. 29 Nov 1961, Lausanne, Switzerland. Pianist. Conservatoire Lausanne, 1979-82; Ecole Internationale, Piano Lausanne, 1982-85. Debut: Montreux 1983. Career: Radio Suisse Romande, 1976; Concerto with Orchestra TV Romanian, 1982; Recital Trento, 1984; Recital Roma, 1985; Chamber Music Karlsruhe, Germany, 1986; Solisten Audition, 1987; Festival Piano Roque-d'Antheron, 1987; Bern Concerto 1988; Professor, Lausanne Conservatoire, 1990-. Honours: Swiss Competition for Young Musicians, 1976, 1979; Vercilli International Pino Competition, Gold Medal, 1985; University of Maryland USA, William Kapell International Piano Competition, Boucher Memorial Prize, 1988. Memberships: European Piano Teachers Association; Swiss Society of Musical Pedagogy; Frank Martin Society. Hobbies: Bonzai; Pianoforte. Address: Ricercare Case Postale 56, 1820 Montreux 2, Switzerland.

GRADENWITZ Peter (Werner Emanuel), b. 24 Jan 1910, Berlin, Germany. Musicologist. m. (1) Rosi Wolfsohn, 1933 (dec. 1965), 1 son (dec. 1963), 1 daughter, (2) Ursula Mayer-Reinach, 1967. Education: Studied at Universities of Berlin, Freiburg/Br and Prague, and London Polytechnic; PhD, Musicology, German University of Prague; Composition studies with Julius Weismann and Joseph Rufer. Career: Founder, Editor-Director, Israeli Music Publications Ltd, 1949-82; Lecturer, Musicology, Tel Aviv University, 1968-76; Lecturer, Musicology, Honorary Professor, University of Freiburg/Br, 1980-; Lecturer at other European and American universities. Compositions: Editor of newly-discovered works by Salomone Rossi, Stamitz family and Franz Schubert; Symphony and chamber music. Publications include: Johann Stamitz, Das Leben, 1936; The Music of Israel, 1949, new enlarged edition, 1995; Music and Musicians in Israel, 3, 1978; Johann Stamitz, Life and Works, 2 vols, 1984; Leonard Bernstein, Infinite Variety of a Musician, 1984, published in 5 languages including 4th edition in German, 1995, new English edition, 1995; Arnold Schoenberg's 4th String Quartet, 1986; Kleine Kulturgeschichte der Klaviermusik, 1986; Yiddish Love Songs (editor), 1988; Literatur und Musik in geselligem Kreise, 1991. Honours: International Critics' Prize, Salzburg, 1971; Golden Insignia of Salzburg, 1978; Frank Pelleg Memorial Prize, Haifa, 1988. Memberships: International Musicological Society; Israeli Section, International Music Council. Hobby: Mountain tours. Address: PO Box 6011, Tel Aviv 61060, Israel.

GRAEBNER Eric (Hans), b. 8 Jan 1943, Berrington, England. 1 son. Composer; Pianist; Lecturer; Conductor. Education: MA, Cambridge University; PhD, York University; ARCO. Career: Lecturer in Music, University of Southampton, 1968-; Visiting Fellow, Princeton, New Jersey, USA, 1973, 1981-82, 1983; Assistant Professor, William Paterson College, New Jersey, 1981-82. Compositions: Thalia, 1975; Between Words, 1976; String Quartet No 1, 1979; String Quartet, No 2, 1984; 4 Songs and an Aria, 1980; Aspects of 3 Tetrachords, 1973 Quintet, 1981; The Winter Palace, 1982; La mer retrouvée, 1985-86; 3rd Quartet, 1985; Dollbreaker, 1987; Trapeze Act, 1988; Berenice, 1990-91; Introduction and Passucaglia, 1993; Venus in Landscape, 1995; Resurge, 1997. Publications: New Berlioz Edition, 1971-72. Contributions to: Soundings; Perspectives of New Music; In Theory Only; Music Analysis. Honours: Fulbright-Hayes Fellowship, 1973; Dio Award, 1977; Fellow, Salzburg Seminar of American Studies, 1976. Membership: EMAS (Sonic Arts Network), PRS. Current Management: Metier Sound & Vision, P O Box 270, Preston, Lancashire PR2 3LZ, England. Address: Music Department, University of Southampton, Highfield, Southampton, Hampshire, England.

GRAEME Peter, b. 17 Apr 1921, Petersfield, England. Oboist. m. Inge Anderl, 14 Jule 1952, 1 son, 3 daughters. Education: Royal College of Music. Career: LPO, 1942-46; Freelance Oboist; First Oboe in various orchestras including Kalmar Orchestra; Haydn Orchestra; Boyd Neel Orchestra; Philomusica; Goldsborough Orchestra; English Chamber Orchestra; Melos Ensemble of London; Oboe Professor, Royal College of Music, 1949-71, 1991; Royal Northern College of Music, 1974-90; Teaching and Adjudicating with occasional freelance playing, currently. Recordings: Various with Kalmar Orchestra, Melos Ensemble of London, English Chamber Orchestra. Honours: Hon ARCM, 1959; FRCM, 1979; FRNCM, 1989. Memberships: Musicians Union. Address: Grenovic, 4 French Mill Lane, Shaftesbury, Dorset SP7 8EU, England.

GRAF Hans, b. 15 Feb 1949, Linz, Austria. Conductor. Education: Studied at the Bruckner Conservatory of Linz and the Academy of Music at Graz; Further study with Franco Ferrara, Sergiu Celibidache and Arvid Yansons. Career: Director of the Iraqi National Symphony Orchestra, 1975; Vienna Staatsoper debut 1977, conducted new production of Petrushka, 1981; Munich and Vienna Festivals, 1980; In 1984 conducted Rigoletto at the Maggio Musicale Florence and appeared at the Prague Spring, Bregenz, Helsinki and Salzburg Festivals; Paris Opera 1984, with Die Entführung and Il Barbiere di Siviglia; Music Director of the Mozarteum Orchestra of Salzburg, 1984; Guest appearances with the Vienna Symphony; Vienna, Leningrad, Dresden, Helsinki and Liverpool Philharmonic Orchestras; Leipzig Gewandhaus, RAI Symphony of Milan and the ORF (Austria) Symphony; Bournemouth Symphony Orchestra; Has led productions of Der Ring des Nibelungen and Fidelio at La Fenice, Venice; Cosi fan tutte at the Deutsche Oper Berlin; Otello at the Salzburger Kulturtage; Conducted Die Zauberflöte at the 1986 Orange Festival at Tokyo with the Vienna Staatsoper 1989 and the 1992 Savonlinna Festival; Production of Ariadne auf Naxos with John Cox for TV, 1994; Conducted Wozzeck at Catania, 1996. Honours include: First Prize, Karl Böhm Conductors Competition, Salzburg, 1979. Recordings include: Songs with Brigitte Fassbaender; Zemlinsky's Es war Einmal; Complete Symphonies of Mozart, with the Mozarteum Orchestra of Salzburg. Address: Unit 2, 39 Tadema Road, London SW10 0PY, England.

GRAF Maria, b. 1929, Germany. Singer (Mezzo-soprano). Education: Studied at the Vienna Academy with Anny Konetzni. Career: Sang in the chorus of the Vienna Staatsoper, 1950-55, solo debut at Innsbruck, 1955; Sang at Munster and Frankfurt, then Karlsruhe Opera, 1969-69; Guested at Bayreuth, 1955 (as Flosshilde and Rossweise) and Italy in operas by Wagner (Die Walküre at La Scala, 1963); Sang Helen in the German premiere of Tippett's King Priam, 1963; Other roles included Mozart's Marcellina, Herodias in Salome, Marie (Wozzeck) and Mistress Quickly (Falstaff).

GRAF Peter-Lukas, b. 5 Jan 1929, Zurich, Switzerland. Flautist; Conductor. Education: Studied at the Paris Conservatoire with Marcel Moyse (flute) and Eugene Bigot (conducting). Career: First flautist with the Winterthur Orchestra, 1951-57; Conductor at the Lucerne State Theatre 1961-66; Played in the Lucerne Festival Orchestra 1957- and toured as soloist with the Edwin Fischer and Gunther Ramin; Performances with the English Chamber Orchestra, the Academy of St Martin in the Fields and the Lucerne Festival Strings; As Soloist and Conductor, tours of Europe, South America, Australia, Japan and Israel; Teacher at the Basle Conservatory 1973-. Recordings include: Spohr Concertante for violin, harp and orchestra; Bach A minor Triple Concerto and Saint-Saëns A minor Concerto (English Chamber Orchestra); Mozart Flute Concertos and Concerto K299 (Lausanne Chamber Orchestra); Swiss music with Orchestra della Radio Svizzera, and the Zurich Tonhalle. Honours include: First prizes in flute and conducting, Paris Conservatoire, 1950, 1951; Winner, International ARD Competition, 1953; Bablock Prize, Harriet Cohen International Music Award, London, 1958.

GRAF Uta, b. 5 Jan 1915, Karlsruhe, Germany. Singer (Soprano). Education: Studied with Heinrich Schlusnusand Anna Bahr-Mildenburg. Career: From 1940 sang in Dortmund, Dresden, Stuttgart, Aachen and Cologne; US debut San Antonio 1948, as Sophie in Der Rosenkavalier; sang in opera at San Francisco and Toronto and made concert tour of South America; US concerts with Leopold Stokowski; Covent Garden 1950-51, as Sophie and Pamina, conducted by Kleiber, and Marcellina in Fidelio; Munich Staatsoper 1954; Holland Festival 1955-58, notably in the 1956 premiere of Sampiero Corso by Tomasi; Teacher at the Peabody Conservatory 1958-66, Manhattan School of Music from 1964. Recordings: Don Giovanni; Les Contes d'Hoffmann; Bach B Minor Mass; Soprano Solo in Schoenberg's 2nd String Quartet, with the Juilliard Quartet.

GRAF-ADNET Carmen, b. 23 July 1929, Vitoria, Brazil. Pianist; Professor. m. Hans Graf, 27 Jan 1953, 2 daughters. Education: University of Rio de Janeiro; Music Academy, Vienna; Studied with Profs Josef Turczynsky and Bruno Seidhofer; Master courses with Edwin Fisher and Alfred Cortot; Language studies, English, French, German, Spanish, Italian. Debut: Vitoria, Brazil, age 11. Career: Concerts in Europe, North and South America; Master courses, Salzburg, Austria and Indiana University, USA; Radio appearances; Soloist with major orchestras; Professor, Hochschule für Musik, Vienna. Recordings: With Vienna Symphony Orchestra under Hans Swarowsky. Honours: Prizes at piano competitions, Warsaw and Munich; Officer, Cruzeiro do Sul, Brazilian Government; Villa-Lobos Medal. Membership: Piano Teachers Association. Hobbies: Bridge; Movies; Crossword puzzles; Travel by car. Address: Laudongasse 44/6, 1080 Vienna, Austria.

GRAFFMAN Gary, b. 14 Oct 1928, New York, USA. Pianist. m. Naomi Helfman, 1952. Education: Curtis Institute of Music under Mme Isabelle Vengerova. Debut: with Philadelphia Orchestra, 1947. Career includes: Concert tours worldwide; Annual appearances with major orchestras, USA; Teacher, Curtis Institute, Manhattan School of Music, 1980-. Recordings: For Columbia, Masterworks, RCA Victor, including concertos of Tchaikovsky, Rachmaninoff, Brahms, Beethoven, Chopin, Prokofiev; Also plays piano left hand repertory. Publication: I Really Should Be Practising, autobiography, 1981. Honour: Leventritt Award, 1949.

GRAHAM Alasdair, b. 19 Apr 1934, Glasgow, Scotland. Pianist; Professor. Education: BMus, Edinburgh University; Performers Diploma, Vienna Hochschule fur Musik; Royal Academy of Music with Peter Katin. Debut: Bishopsgate Hall, 1958. Career: Soloist with Scottish National Orchestra, London Philharmonic Orchestra, BBC Symphony Orchestra (Proms, 1963), Royal Liverpool Philharmonic, Hallé Orchestra, Sydney Symphony Orchestra, Melbourne Symphony Orchestra (Australian tour), 1967; Recitals, BBC, TV, Britain, Turkey, India; As Accompanist with Elisabeth Söderström, Josef Suk, John Shirley-Quirk; Professor, Royal College of Music, London. Recordings: Schubert: Sonata in B flat, 8 Ecossaises. Honours: Harriet Cohen Commonwealth Medal, 1963; Honorary RCM, 1973. Membership: Royal Society of Musicians of Great Britain. Address: 184 Can Hall Road, London E11 3NH, England.

GRAHAM Colin, b. 22 Sep 1931, Hove, Sussex, England. Stage Director; Librettist; Artistic Director. Education: New Covenant School of Ministry, St Louis, 1985-87, ordained Minister in 1988; Diploma, Royal Academy of Dramatic Art; Private study. Debut: Playhouse Theatre, Nottingham, England. Career: Artistic Director, Aldeburgh Festival, 1969-82, English Music Theatre, 1976-, Opera Theater of St Louis, 1982-; Director of Productions, English National Opera, Sadler's Wells Opera, 1976-82; Over 350 productions in opera, TV and theatre; Staged the premiere of Corigliano's The Ghosts of Versailles at the Metropolitan, 1991, A Midsummer Night's Dream at St Louis, 1992, production of Britten's Death in Venice at Covent Garden, 1992, and world premiere of Susa's The Dangerous Liaisons at San Francisco, 1994; The Barber of Seville at St Louis, 1996. Publications: Opera Libretti: The Golden Vanity by Britten, 1970, Penny for a Song by Bennett, 1970, King Arthur by Purcell, 1972, The Postman Always Rings Twice by Paulus, 1983, Joruri by Miki, 1985, The Woodlanders by Paulus, 1985. Contributions to: Opera Magazine; Musical Times; Opera News, 1992. Honours: Winston Churchill Fellowship, 1975; Prize for Opera Production for Orpheus, Germany, 1977; Honorary Doctor of Arts, Webster University, 1985 and University of Missouri, 1992. Memberships: Equity; Canadian Equity; American Guild of Musical Artists; Arts and Educational Council, 1993; Award of Personal Achievement in the Arts. Hobbies: Weightlifting; Motorcycles; The Bible. Address: PO Box 19190, St Louis, MO 63119, USA.

GRAHAM Janet, b. 4 Jun 1948, Consett, County Durham. Composer; Music Therapist. Education: Studied at the Royal Academy and with Elisabeth Lutyens, 1972-74. Compositions include: Piano Sonata, 1973; String Quartet No 3, 1975; The Journey Of Everyman, music drama, 1977; String Quartet No 4, 1982; Until The Sunset Hour for Mezzo and Ensemble, 1985; The Sons Of Cronos for Orchestra, 1984; Two Winter Songs for Female Chorus, 1988; Earth Cry for Oboe, Trumpet and Piano, 1990. Address: c/o British Music Information Centre, 10 Stratford Place, London W1N 9AE, England.

GRAHAM Susan, b. 23 July 1960, Roswell, New Mexico, USA. Singer (Mezzo-soprano). Education: Studied at Manhattan School of Music; Texas Tech University. Career: Sang Masseenet's Cherubin while a student; Engagements with St Louis Opera as Erika in Vanessa, Charlotte and at Seattle as Stephano in Roméo et Juliette; Season 1989-90 included Chicago Lyric Opera debut as Annius in La Clemenza di Tito, Sonia in Argento's Aspern Papers at Washington, Dorabella and the Composer at Santa Fe; Carnegie Hall debut in Des Knaben Wunderhorn and Bernstein concert in New York; Season 1990-91 as Octavian with San Francisco Symphony, Minerva in Monteverdi's Ulisse with San Francisco Opera, Berlioz's Beatrice at Lyon, Cherubino at Santa Fe; Mozart's C minor Mass under Edo de Waart and with Philadelphia Orchestra under Neville Marriner; Season 1991-92 at Metropolitan as Second Lady, Cherubino, and Tebaldo in Don Carlos; L'Opera de Nice as Cherubino and Les Nuits d'Été in Lyon; Beethoven's 9th in Spain conducted by Marriner; Salzburg Mozart Week, 1993, as Cecilio in Lucio Silla, Easter and Summer Festivals as Meg Page in Falstaff; Season 1993-94 as Massenet's Chérubin and Dorabella at Covent Garden, Ascanio in Les Troyens at the Met, Annius in Tito at San Francisco and 1994 Salzburg Festival; Octavian for Welsh National Opera, and Vienna State Opera and Marguerite in La Damnation de Faust for L'Opera de Lyon; Season 1995 as

Dorabella and as Arianna in the premiere of the opera by Goehr at Covent Garden; Season 1997 with Chérubin at Covent Garden and in Lucio Silla at Salzburg. Recordings include: Falstaff conducted by Solti; La Damnation de Faust conducted by Kent Nagano; Beatrice et Benedict conducted by John Nelson; Stravinsky's Pulcinella. Honours include: Winner, Metropolitan Opera National Council Auditions. Address: c/o IMG Artists, Media House, 3 Burlington Lane, London W4 2TH, England.

GRAHAM-HALL John, b. 1955, Middlesex, England. Singer (Tenor). Education: Studied at King's College, Cambridge and Royal College of Music. Debut: Opera North, as Ferrando in Cosi fan Tutte, 1983. Career: Has sung Albert Herring at Covent Garden and Glyndebourne, Pedrillo for Kent Opera, Cassio for Welsh National Opera and Don Ottavio for Opera Northern Ireland; Glyndebourne Touring Opera as Britten's Aschenbach, Lysander, Basilio and Ferrando; English National Opera debut as Cyril in Princess Ida, 1992, returning as Basilio, Tanzmeister in Ariadne and Schoolmaster in Cunning Little Vixen; Engagements at Lyon as Lensky and Frère Massée in Messiaen's St François d'Assise, Vancouver as Ferrando, Brussels and Lisbon as Cassio and Antwerp as Achilles in King Priam; Glyndebourne Festival as Kudrjas in Katya Kabanova and Flute in Midsummer Night's Dream; Scottish Opera as Eisenstein, and Schoolmaster in Cunning Little Vixen; Aix-en-Provence as Lysander and Bordeaux as Tanzmeister in Ariadne; Amsterdam as Basilio and Curzio; Conductors have included Haitink, Janowski, Tate, Rattle and Abbado; Concert career with all major British orchestras including Pulcinella with BBC Symphony, 1993; Recent appearances included Moses and Aron in Amsterdam, La Belle Hélène with English National Opera, and Shapkin in House of the Dead in Nice; Season 1996 with Narciso in Il Turco in Italia at Garsington and in Moses and Aron at Salzburg. Recordings include: Carmina Burana; L'Incoronazione di Poppea; A Midsummer Night's Dream; As Bob Boles in Peter Grimes. Address: c/o IMG Artists, Media House, 3 Burlington Lane, London W4 2TH, England.

GRAHN Ulf (Ake Wilhelm), b. 17 Jan 1942, Solna, Sweden. Composer. m. Barbro Dahlman, 15 Aug 1969, 1 son. Education: Degree in Violin Pedagogy, SMI, Stockholm, 1968; MM, Catholic University, Washington DC, USA, 1973; Business Administration, Development Studies, Uppsala University, Sweden, 1986. Career: Music Instructor, Stockholm and Lidingo Schools, 1964-72; Teaching Assistant, Instructor, Catholic University, Washington, 1972-76; Founder, Music Director, Contemporary Music Forum, 1973-85; Lecturer, Northern VA Community College, 1975-79; Lecturer, Associate Professor, George Washington University, 1983-87; Founder, Artistic Director, The Aurora Players, 1983-; Artistic and Managing Director, Lake Siljan Festival Sweden, 1988-90; Composer-in-Residence, Charles Ives Center, USA, 1988; Publisher and Owner, Edition NGLANI, 1985-. Compositions: Major orchestral works including Symphonies Nos 1 and 2; Concertos for piano, guitar and double bass; Chamber and Choral Music; Solo works for Guitar, Piano, Violin; Three Dances with Interludes, premiered in Stockholm, 1990; Blå Dunster, 1990, an instrumental opera premiered in Örebro, Sweden, 1991. Recordings: Cinq Preludes; Snapshots; Sonata for Piano with Flute and Percussion; In The Shade, Caprice; Sonata for Piano. Contributions to: Many articles, and reviews in Europe; Tonfallet; Musik Revy and Ord och Ton. Honours: Stockholm International Organ Days, 1973; League International Society for Contemporary Music Piano Competition, 1976; First Prize in Music for, Toccata for Carillon, Dalarna Composition Contest, 1990. Memberships: STIM Sweden; Society of Swedish Composers. Hobby: Photography. Address: PO Box 5684, Takoma Park, MD 20913-5684, USA.

GRANAT Juan (Wolfgang), b. 29 Nov 1918, Karlsruhe, Baden, Germany. Violist. Education: Gisela High School, Munich; High School of Education, Munich; Studied under Rudolf Zwinkel, grandfather; Sevcik-Marteau Master School, Munich, with Herma Studeny; With Alexander Petschnikoff, Buenos Aires. Career: Member, Jewish Kulturbund Orchestra, Frankfurt-am-Main and Violist, Kleinberg Quartet, 1937-38; Solo Violist, Swiss-Italian Broadcasting Symphony, Monteceneri and Violist, Monteceneri String Quartet, Lugano, 1939-40; Came to Argentina, 1940; Soloist, 1st Latin-American performance of William Walton's Viola Concerto with Cordoba Symphony, Teodoro Fuchs conductor, 1945; Solo Violist, Havana Philharmonic, 1945-53, invited by Erich Kleiber, numerous recitals and performances, also played with Cuban Chamber Music Society; Violist, Minneapolis Symphony, 1954-56; Violist, Philadelphia Orchestra, 1956; Solo recitals, 1956; 1st New York City performance of I Handoshkin's Viola Concerto, 1962; 1st Washington DC performance of Elizabeth Gould's Viola Sonata, 1970; Debut with Liberty Bell String Trio, 1984; Inaugurated New Philadelphia Orchestra Chamber Music Series, 1985; Instrumental in abolishment of compulsory retirement for musicians, 1986-87; Retired, Philadelphia, 1991-. Compositions: For piano and violin: Some pieces, 1941-45; Suite Judaica, 1945; Arrangement of Paganini Caprices Nos 13 and 14, 1947; Adaptation of 3 Spanish Suites by Joaquin Nin, 1947. Recordings: With Philadelphia Orchestra, several labels; Non-commercial recordings of viola recitals. Honours: New York Annual Madrigal Society's Town Hall Debut Award, 1957. Memberships: American Federation of Musicians, New York City and Philadelphia locals; American Viola Society, affiliated to International Viola Society. Hobbies: Listening to records, CDs, tapes; Reading; Hiking; Swimming. Address: 4738 Osage Avenue, Philadelphia, PA 19143-1815, USA.

GRANDISON Mark, b. 9 December 1965, Adelaide, South Australia. Composer. Education: BMus (Hons) 1987, MMus 1990, University of Adelaide; Study with Richard Meale, 1983-87. Career includes: Teacher and Acting Co-ordinator, Marryatville Special Interest Music Centre, Adelaide, 1992-93; Kambala School, Sydney, 1994-. Compositions include: Four Poems of Wilfrid Owen for contralto and ensemble, 1985; Contrasts for orchestra, 1987; Night Interiors for orchestra, 1988; Los Caprichos for chamber orchestra, 1989; Five Blake Songs for soprano and piano, 1990; Toccata for chamber ensemble, 1992; Three Dances for string orchestra, 1993; Surface Tension for string quartet, 1996; Kinetica for youth orchestra, 1997; Tarantella for Orchestra, 1998; Commissions from the Adelaide Chamber Orchestra, Vrizen and Australian Broadcasting Association. Honours include: South Australia Young Composer's Award, 1993. Address: c/o APRA, 1A Eden Street, Crows Nest, NSW 2065, Australia.

GRANGE Philip (Roy), b. 17 Nov 1956, London, England. Composer. m. Elizabeth Caroline Hemming, 1986. Education: York University, 1976-82; BA, 1979; Doctorate in Composition, 1984; Dartington Summer School of Music, Composition class with Peter Maxwell Davies, 1975-81. Career: Promenade Concert debut, 1983; Fellow in the Creative Arts, Trinity College, Cambridge, 1985-87; Northern Arts Fellow in Composition, Durham University, 1988-89; Appointed Lecturer in Composition at Exeter University, 1989; Reader in Composition, Exeter University, 1995; Performances of music at most major festivals in UK, and in Europe and USA. Compositions: Cimmerian Nocturne, 1979; Sextet, 1980; The Kingdom of Bones, 1983; La Ville Entière, 1984; Variations, 1986; Out in the Dark, 1986; In Memorian HK, 1986; The Dark Labyrinth, 1987; Concerto for Orchestra; Labyrinthine Images, 1988; In A Dark Time, 1989; Changing Landscapes, 1990; Focus and Fade, 1992; Lowry Dreamscape, 1992; Piano Polyptich, 1993; Bacchus Bagatelles, 1993; Des fins sont des commencements, 1994. Recording: La Ville Entière for clarinet and piano. Publications: In Memoriam HK; Others. Hobbies: Languages; Linguistics; Literature; Classics. Current Management: Maecenas Music, 5 Bushey Close, Old Barn Lane, Kenley, Surrey CR8 5AU, England. Address: Department of Music, University of Exeter, Knightley, Streatham Drive, Exeter EX4 4PD, England.

GRANT Clifford (Scantlebury), b. 11 Sept 1930, Randwick, New South Wales, Australia. Singer (Bass). m. (1) Jeanette Earle, 1 son, 2 daughters, (2) Ruth Anders, 1992. Education: Studied at Sydney Conservatorium with Isolde Hill; Melbourne with Annie Portnoj; London with Otakar Kraus. Debut: New South Wales Opera Company, as Raimondo in Lucia di Lammermoor, 1952. Career: Sang with Sadler's Wells/English National Opera from 1966, debut as Silva in Ernani; Leading roles in Oedipus Rex, The Mastersingers, Peter Grimes, The Magic Flute, Madama Butterfly, The Barber of Seville, The Ring of the Nibelung, Don Giovanni, The Coronation of Poppea, and Don Carlos; Sang in San Francisco, 1966-78; Glyndebourne Festival as Nettuno in Il Ritorno d'Ulisse, 1972; Further engagements with Covent Garden Opera, Welsh National Opera and in Europe; Sang in Sydney from 1976, as Nilakantha (Lakmé), 1986; Retired 1990, after singing in Les Huguenots with Australian Opera; Returned to UK, 1992; Returned to stage, May 1993, as Alvise in new production of La Gioconda, Opera North; Many concert appearances. Recordings: Don Giovanni; Rigoletto; Esclarmonde; L'Oracolo; Fafner in The Rhinegold and Hunding in The Valkyrie, conducted by Reginald Goodall; Bartolo in Le nozze di Figaro; Il Corsaro; The Apostles by Elgar; Tosca; Les Huguenots. Hobbies: Gallery owner; Oil painting; Making scones. Address: c/o Australian Opera, Sydney Opera House, Sydney, NSW, Australia.

GRANT Robin, b. 17 November 1955, Bilston, West Midlands, England. Composer. Education: Composition with Anthony Gilbert, Royal Northern College of Music, 1982-86; GMus, RNCM, PG Dip, Birmingham Conservatoire, 1995. Debut: Dumb Show (Sextet) Circle, Southampton International New Music Festival, 1985. Compositions: I Am...In Search of John Clare, Chamber Opera; A Dot On The Sun, Chamber Opera; A Pretty Wench, Song Cycle, Mezzo; The Nailmakers, Song Cycle, for Tenor; Mirror Mirror, Song Cycle, Soprano and Guitar; Out Of The Dark, Chamber Concerto; To Dance Upon Nothing, Oboe and Piano; Iron Mad Wilkinson, Young Voices and Orchestra. Publication: Instrumental Pieces For Young Players. Honours: John Clementi Collard Fellowship, Worshipful Company of Musicians, 1996. Membership: Performing Right Society. Address: 46 Austin Street, Whitmore Reans, Wolverhampton WV6 0NW, England.

GRAUBART Michael, b. 26 November 1930, Vienna, Austria. Composer; Conductor; Lecturer. m. (1) Ellen Barbour, 1962, 1 son, 2 daughters, (2) Valerie Coumont, 1996. Education: BSc, Physics, University of Manchester, England, 1952; Studied Composition privately with Matyas Seiber, 1953-57; Flute with Geoffrey Gilbert, 1953-56. Career includes: Conductor, Ars Nova Chamber Orchestra, 1960; Conductor, Hampstead Chamber Orchestra, 1962-66; Music Director, Focus Opera Group, 1967-71; Director of Music, Morley College, 1966-91; Adjunct Professor of Music, Syracuse University London Centre, 1989-91; Senior Lecturer, School of Academic Studies, Royal Northern College of Music, Manchester, 1991-96. Compositions include: Sonata for cello and piano; Sinfonia a 10 for 10 winds; Quintet for flute, clarinet, viola, cello and vibraphone; Canzonetta for triple chamber orchestra; Declensions for 10 instruments; To a Dead Lover for soprano and 7 instruments; Untergang for baritone, chorus and 11 instruments; Quasi una Sonata for piano; Three Bagatelles for cello and piano; Sure I am only of uncertain things for a cappella chorus; Two songs for mezzo-soprano and piano; Concertino da Camera for viola and for woodwinds; Diptych (The Seed and the Harvest, Broken Mirror) for 4 winds; Scena and Capriccio for piano; Variants and Cadenzas for orchestra; Nightfall for chorus and piano; Elegy for orchestra; Speculum Noctuinum for 9 winds, cello and bass; Scena II and Finale for euphonium, 2 flutes, viola and cello, 1992 and 1995; Ricordanze for recorders and piano, 1995, 1997; Editions: Music by Pergolesi, Dufay and Josquin. Publications: 4 articles on Leopold Spinner, including one for the revision of New Grove's Dictionary of Music; Articles, reviews and translations in Tempo and Encounter; A chapter in the Musical Companion, 1977. Memberships: Composers' Guild of Great Britain; Society for the Promotion of New Music. Hobbies: Hill Walking; Philosophy and Aesthetics; Modern Art and Architecture. Address: 18 Laitwood Road, Balham, London SW12 9QL, England.

GRAUNKE Kurt, b. 30 Sept 1915, Stettin, Germany. Violinist; Conductor; Composer. Education: Pupil in violin of Gustav Havemann, Berlin Hochschule für Musik; Received training in composition from Adolf Lessle and Hermann Grabner, in violin from Hanns Weiss and Hans Dunschede, and in conducting from Feliz Husadel; Completed violin studies with Wolfgang Schneiderhan. Career: Played violin in the Vienna Radio Orchestra; Founder-Conductor, Graunke Symphony Orchestra, Munich, 1945-. Compositions: 8 symphonies: 1969, 1972, 1975, 1981, 1982, 1983, 1985; Violin Concerto, 1959; Other orchestral works. Recordings: Numerous discs as well as movie and television sound tracks. Address: c/o Symphonie Orchester Graunke, Schornstrasse 13, D-8000 Munich 30, Germany.

GRAVES Denyce, b. 1963, Washington DC, USA. Singer (Mezzo-soprano). Education: Studied at the Oberlin College and New England Conservatories. Career: Early roles included Maddalena at Washington and Giuletta in Les Contes d'Hoffman at the Spoleto Festival; Further engagements as Dalila in Philadelphia and Montreal, Honegger's Antigone, the High Priestess in La Vestale at La Scala, Adalgisa in Zürich and Donizetti's Leonora (La Favorita) at Catania; Appearances as Carmen at San Francisco, Vienna, the Bergen Festival, Covent Garden, Berlin, Zurich, Houston, Los Angeles, Buenos Aires and Munich; Concert repertory includes Messiah, the Verdi Requiem, Rossini's Stabat Mater, Ravel's Sheherazade and Mahler's Kindertotenlieder. Recordings include: Gertrude in Hamlet by Amboise Thomas; Emilia in Otello. Honours include: Met Opera National Finalist; Grand Prix du Concours International du Chant de Paris; Marian Anderson Award. Address: c/o Opernhaus Zürich, Falkenstrasse 1, CH-8008 Zürich, Switzerland.

GRAY George, b. 26 May 1947, USA. Singer (Tenor). Career: Sang Cavaradossi at Colorado Springs, 1984, Canio and Radames with North Carolina Opera, 1986, 1988; New Jersey Festival, 1987, as Bacchus, Seattle, 1987, as Otello, Tristan at Columbus, Ohio; Season 1988 in Schoenberg's Gurrelieder at Frankfurt, and Pollione in Norma; Tristan at Nancy, 1990, with Aeneas at the opening of the Bastille Opera, Paris; Sang Parsifal at Chicago, 1990, Siegfried at Zurich, 1988; Further appearances as Bacchus at Kassel in Schreker's Schatzgräber at the Holland Festival and Meyerbeer's Vasco da Gama at the Berlin Staatsoper, 1992; Lohengrin at Leipzig. Address: c/o Berlin Staatsoper, Unter den Linden 7, O-1060 Berlin, Germany.

GRAY James, b. 1 Jan 1956, London, England. Singer (Counter-Tenor); Keyboard Player; Conductor. Education: Royal Academy of Music, London; Private study with Maria Curcio, London; Academy of Fine Arts, Prague; Centro Studi Musicali Rinascimento, Florence. Debut: Prague, 1976, Czech Philharmonic Society. Career: Guest Director of Prague Madrigalists, 1980-81 (Berlin TV debut 1981); Repétiteur Nationaltheater, Mannheim, 1981-82; La Chaise-Dieu Festival, 1984 (French TV); Domenico Scarlatti Tercentenary Celebrations, 1985 (Radio Madrid, Spanish TV); Many subsequent appearances as singer, conductor and accompanist throughout mid and Eastern Europe. Recordings: Domenico Scarlatti Unpublished Cantatas, 1985; Monteverdi Lamento d'Arianna (awarded Grand Prix Academie du Disque Français), 1986; Benedetto Marcello Unpublished Vocal Works, 1990. Hobbies: Composing; Skiing; Walking. Address: Via Romana 34, 50125 Firenze, Italy.

GRAY Linda Esther, b. 29 May 1948, Greenock, Scotland. Opera Singer (Soprano). m. Peter McCrorie, 1 daughter. Education: Royal Scottish Academy of Music and Drama, Cinzano Scholarship, 1969; Goldsmith School, 1970; James Caird School, 1971. Career: London Opera Centre, 1969-71; Glyndebourne Festival Opera, as Mimi and Mozart's Electra, 1972-75; Scottish Opera, 1974-79; Welsh Opera, 1980-; English National Opera, as Donna Anna, Wagner's Eva, Strauss's Ariadne and Verdi's Amelia, 1979-; American Debut, 1981; Royal Opera House, Sieglinde, 1982; Fidelio, 1983; Record of Tristan and Isolde, 1981; Principal Roles: Isolde, Sieglinde, Kundry (Wagner); Tosca (Puccini); Fidelio (Beethoven). Honours: Kathleen Ferrier Award, 1972; Christie Award, 1972. Hobbies: Cooking; Swimming. Address: 171 Queens Road, London SW19, England.

GRAY-FOW Bette Jane, b. 11 July 1950, Madison, Wisconsin, USA. Music Educator; Conductor; Singer. Divorced, 1 daughter. Education: BA, 1st class honours, Medieval and Modern History, Nottingham University, 1972; PGCE, distinction, Nottingham College of Education, 1975; Singing Studies with Pamela Cook at Birmingham School of Music; Oratorio Lieder and Opera Work at Britten-Pears School and University of Michigan; Postgraduate work in musicology at University of Illinois with Nicholas Temperley. Career: Teacher, Nottingham High School, Arnold Hill School, Wilford Meadows School; Director of Music, King's School, Grantham, 1992-95; Conductor, Kings School Chamber Singers, 1992-95, Ruddington and District Choral Society, Nottingham, 1995-98, Northampton High School Gospel choir and chamber orchestra, 1996-; Head of Music, Northampton High School, 1996-. Contributions to: The Times Educational Supplement; Schools Music Association Bulletin. Honours: Phi Kappa Phi; University Exhibition and A C Wood Prize in History, Nottingham University. Memberships: Incorporated Society of Musicians; Schools Music Association; Association of British Choral Directors; British Federation of Young Choirs. Hobbies: Walking; Reading; Computers. Address: 10 Claremont Drive, West Bridgford, Nottingham NG2 7LW, England.

GREAGER Richard, b. 5 November 1946, Christchurch, New Zealand. Singer (Tenor). Education: Studied in Australia. Career: Junior Principal at Covent Garden until 1975; Lyric Tenor at Scottish Opera from 1975, then sang widely in Germany, notably at Hanover, Dortmund, Wiesbaden, Karlsruhe and Bonn; Roles included Don Ottavio, Ferrando, Tamino, Rodolfo, the Duke of Mantua, Fenton and Ernesto; Australian Opera from 1980, as The Painter in Lulu, Edgardo (opposite Sutherland's Lucia), Peter Grimes, Lensky, Don José and Peter Quint (The Turn of the Screw); Guest appearances at the Grand Théâtre Geneva as Peter Quint, the Painter and the Negro in Lulu (Jeffrey Tate conducting) and Edgardo; Opéra de Lyon as Huon in Oberon; Season 1988-89 as Rodolfo at Melbourne and Covent Garden; Eisenstein in Die Fledermaus for Scottish Opera; Peter Quint in Schwetzingen and Cologne; Covent Garden 1991 as Arthur in the world premiere of Gawain by Harrison Birtwistle; Other roles include Tonio (La Fille du Régiment) and Werther; Season 1991-92 as Arbace in Idomeneo at Helsinki, Herod in Salome at Wellington and Mozart's Basilio with the Royal Opera in Japan; Sang Don José and Don Ottavio for Wellington. City Opera, 1997. Honours include: Winner, Sun Aria Competition, Australia. Current Management: Cameron's Management Pty Ltd. Address: Suite 5 Edgecliff Court, 2 New McLean Street, Edgecliff, New South Wales 2027, Australia.

GREEN Anna, b. 27 Jan 1933, Southampton, England. Singer (Soprano). m. Howard Vandenburg. Education: Studied at the Royal College of Music 1951-54, and with Rodolfo Mele in London. Debut: Deutsche Oper am Rhein Dusseldorf 1961, as Amelia (Un Ballo in Maschera). Career: Has sung in Hamburg, Nuremberg, London, Cologne, Barcelona, Graz, Ottawa, Toronto, San Diego, Barcelona and Washington; Roles included Brünnhilde, Leonore, Donna Anna, Aida, Amelia Boccanegra, Ariadne, Tosca, Desdemona, Isolde, Marie (Wozzeck), and the Mother in IL Prigioniero by Dallapiccola; Teatro Liceo Barcelona, 1986 as Brünnhilde in Götterdämmerung. Address: Ingpen and Williams Ltd, 14 Kensington Court, London W8 5DN, England.

GREEN Anna, b. 27 Jan 1939, Southampton, England. Opera Singer. m. Howard Vanderburg, 13 May 1965. Education: ARCM, Royal College of Music, London, 1954. Debut: Amelia in Verdi's Un Ballo in Maschera, Deutsche Oper am Rhein, Dusseldorf, 1961. Career: Sang Aida, Tosca and Abigaille; Later sang German roles including Fidelio and Marschallin, followed by Isolde, Brünnhilde and Elektra; Appeared as Hecuba in King Priam at Royal Opera House, Covent Garden, London, Brünnhilde for English National Opera and Welsh National Opera, Elektra for Vienna State Opera and in Karslruhe and Mannheim, Brünnhilde in Barcelona, Florence, Naples, Nice, Warsaw, Lisbon, Hamburg, Stuttgart and Cologne, Isolde in Berlin, Mannheim, Karlsruhe and Wiesbaden, Kostelnicka in Jenufa in Stuttgart; Also sang in Canada and USA, as Brünnhilde at founding of Pacific Northwest Wagner Festival and in subsequent 4 seasons; Concert appearances include Stravinsky's Les Noces at Albert Hall, London, under Pierre Boulez, Schönberg's Erwartung in Scotland, under Gari Bertini, Altenberg Lieder for RAI, Rome, Wagner concert with Los Angeles Philharmonic conducted by Zubin Mehta. Recordings: Aus dem Essener Musikleben; Betulia Liberata KV 118 Mozart. Membership: Genossenschaft Deutscher Bühnen. Current Management: Wolfgang Stoll, Munich, Germany. Address: Theateragentur, Martiusstrasse 3, 80802 Munich, Germany.

GREEN Barry, b. 10 Apr 1945, Newark, New Jersey, USA. Symphony Bassist; Professor; Author; Soloist. m. Mary Tarbell Green, 7 Oct 1984, 2 sons, 1 stepson. Education: BMus, Indiana University School of Music; Performers Certificate; MMus, University of Cincinnati. Career: Principal Bassist, Nashville Symphony, 1965-66; Principal Bassist, Cincinnati Symphony, 1967-; Faculty, University of Cincinnati, 1967-; Cassals Festival Orchestra, 1979-87; International Workshops, 1982-86. Recordings: (Solos) Baroque Bass; Romantic Music for Double Bass; New Music for Double Bass; Bass Evolution; Sound of Bass, Volume 1 (Chamber Music Recordings) Heritage Chamber Quartet; Music Now; What of My Music Opus One. Publications: Fundamentals of Double Bass Playing; Advanced Techniques of Double Bass Playing, 1976; Inner Game of Music, 1986. Contributions to: Founder-Executive Director, International Society of Bassists, Suzuki Journal; American Music Teacher; Instrumentalist; Bass World. Memberships: International Society of Bassists, Founder Director, Life Member; ASTA. Hobbies: Skiing; Tennis; Golf; Running. Address: 3449 Lyleburn Place, Cincinnati, OH 45220, USA.

GREENAN Andrew, b. 5 Feb 1960, Birmingham, England. Singer (Bass). m. Susannah Davies, 30 Sept 1989, 2 sons, 1 daughter. Education: St Marys College, Liverpool; St Johns College, Cambridge; MA, Modern Languages; Royal Northern College of Music with John Cameron. Debut: La Scala, Milan, 1983. Career: Bayreuther Festspielchor, 1985-87; UK Opera debut, Mozart's Bartolo Opera 80, 1989; Principal Bass, English National Opera, 1992-97; Roles include: King Henry, Sarastro, Rocco, Commendatore, Timur Sparafucile, Swallow; Other engagements include: Bottom in Midsummer Night's Dream at Teatro Regio, Turin, 1995; Landgraf in Tännhauser at Queen Elizabeth Hall; For Royal Opera Covent Garden: Swallow with Mackerras, Ataliba in Alzira with Elder, 1st Nazarene in Salome with Dohnanyi, Pietro in Simon Boccanegra with Solti, Rocco for Welsh National Opera, Abimélech in Samson et Dalila for New Israeli Opera, Swallow for Hamburg State Opera and Welsh National Opera; Recent concert work includes Verdi Requiem with Belgian National Orchestra and appearances with the English Chamber and BBC Symphony Orchestras. Recordings: The Nightingale by Stravinsky, with the Philharmonia and Robert Craft; Video recordings of Peter Grimes with ENO and Salome with the Royal Opera; Appears as Raymond/Larimondo in the film Lucia based on Donizetti's opera. Hobbies: Food; Wine; Cats. Current Management: Robert Gilder & Company. Address: 3 Wheatsheaf Gardens, Lewes, East Sussex BN7 2UQ, England.

GREENAN Andrew John, b. 5 February 1960, Birmingham, England. Singer. m. Susannah Ruth Davies, 30 September 1989, 1 son, 1 daughter. Education: St Marys College, Liverpool; St Johns College Cambridge; MA, Modern Languages; Royal Northern College of Music with John Cameron. Debut: La Scala, Milan, 1983. Career: Bayreuther Festspielchor, 1985-87; UK Opera Debut, Mozart's Bartolo Opera 80, 1989; Principal Bass, English National Opera, 1992-97; Roles include, King Henry, Sarastro, Rocco, Commendatore, Sparafucile, Swallo; Other Engagements include, Bottom (Midsummer Nights Dream) at Teatro Regio, Turin, 1995. Recordings: Video Recordings of Swallow (Peter Grimes); Salome Dohany. Hobbies: Food; Wine; Cats. Current Management: Robert Gilder & Company. Address: 3 Wheatsheaf Gardens, Lewes, East Sussex BN7 2UQ, England.

GREENAWALD Sheri (Kay), b. 12 Nov 1947, Iowa City, Iowa, USA. Soprano. Education: Studied with Charles Matheson at the University of Northern Iowa and with Hans Heinz, Daniel Ferro and Maria DeVarady in New York; Further studies with Audrey Langford in London. Debut: Manhattan Theater Club 1974, in Les mamelles de Tiresias by Poulenc. Career: Sang in the premieres of Bilby's Doll by Carlisle Floyd and Washington Square by Thomas Pastieri (Houston and Detroit, 1976); European debut with Netherlands Opera as Susanna in Le nozze di Figaro, 1980; Regular concert appearances with the St Louis and San Francisco Symphony Orchestras and the Rotterdam Philharmonic; Sang in the premiere of Bernstein's A Quiet Place, Houston 1983; Other roles include Violetta, Ellen Orford (Peter Grimes), Mozart's Despina and Zerlina, Sophie in Werther and Norina in Don Pasquale; Season 1991/92 at Chicago as Pauline in the US Stage premiere of Prokofiev's The Gambler and Mozart's Donna Anna, Fiordiligi at Seattle; Sang the Marschallin with Welsh National Opera, 1994; Susa's Transformations at St Louis, 1997. Address: c/o Houston Grand Opera Association, 510 Preston Avenue, Houston, TX 77002, USA.

GREENBAUM Stuart (Geoffrey Andrew), b. 25 Dec 1966, Melbourne, Australia. Composer. Education: Studied at the University of Melbourne; BMus, hons, MMus, PhD (pending), Teachers include Brenton Broadstock and Barry Conyngham. Debut: Upon the Dark Water (text by Ross Baglin), premiered at Sydney Opera House, 1990, by the Song Company. Career: Works performed by groups including: The Modern Wind Quintet, I Cantori di New York, The Song Company, Melbourne Symphony, The Oxford University Philharmonia, The Arcadian Singers, Ormond College Choir, The Pacific Ocean Symphony Orchestra. Compositions: Ice Man, solo piano, 1993; The Killing Floors, orchestra, 1995; Four Minutes in a Nuclear Bunker, orchestra, 1995; Nelson, soprano, baritone, string quartet, 1997; The Foundling, choir, string quartet, vibraphone, 1997. Recordings: CDs: Upon the Dark Water, song company; Greenbaum, Hindson, Peterson, anthology; Music for Theatre, playbox; Portrait and Blues Hymn; Polar Wandering, Fairfield Days. Honours: ANA Composition Award, 1991; Dorian Le Galliene Composition Award, 1993. Memberships: AMC; FAC; CPCF. Hobbies: Playing pool; Red Wine; League football. Address: 4/111 Rushall Crescent, North Fitzroy, Vic 3068, Australia.

GREENBERG Sylvia, b. 1955, Rumania. Singer (Soprano). Education: Studied at the Tel Aviv Academy of Music and with Marc Belfort in Zurich. Debut: Tel Aviv concert, conducted by Zubin Mehta. Career: Stage debut Zurich 1977, as the Queen of Night: later sang Zerbinetta, Olympia in Les Contes d'Hoffmann, and in operas by Monteverdi; Guest appearances in Hamburg, Berlin, Vienna, Munich and Cologne; Glyndebourne Festival 1978, Die Zauberflöte; US debut Chicago 1981, in Die Schöpfung, conducted by Solti; Bayreuth Festival 1983, as Waldvogel in Siegfried; Salzburg Festival 1984, premiere of Un Re in Ascolto by Berio; At La Scala in 1985 sang the Queen of Night; Aix-en-Provence as Ilia in Idomeneo, 1986; Sang in Doktor Faustus by Giacomo Manzoni at La Scala, 1989; Olga in Fedora at Bologna, 1996. Recordings include: Die Schöpfung; Te Deum by Bizet; Poulenc's Gloria; Carmina Burana. Address: c/o Teatro all Scala, Via Filodrammatici 2, 1-20121 Milan, Italy.

GREENFIELD Edward (Harry). b. 30 July 1928. Music Critic. Education: Trinity Hall, University of Cambridge (MA). Career: Joined Staff of Manchester Guardian, 1953; Record Critic, 1955; Music Critic, 1964; Succeeded Sir Neville Cardus as Chief Music Critic, 1977 until 1993; Broadcaster on Music and Records for BBC Radio, 1957-; Member, Critics Panel, Gramophone, 1960-; Goldener Verdienstzeichen, Salzburg, 1980. Publications: Puccini: Keeper of the Seal, 1958; Monographs on Joan Sutherland, 1972, André Previn, 1973; With Robert Layton, Ivan March and initally Denis Stevens, Stereo Record Guide, 9 volumes, 1960-74; Penguin Stereo Record Guide, 1st Edition, 1975, 4th edition 1984; Penguin Guide to Compact Discs, 1st edition, 1986, 9th edition, 1995. Honours: Gramophone Special Award, 1993; OBE, 1994. Hobbies: Work; Living in Spitalfields. Address: 16 Folgate Street, London E1, England.

GREENHOUSE Bernard, b. 3 Jan 1916, Newark, New Jersey, USA. Cellist; Teacher. m. Aurora Greenhouse, 2 daughters. Education: Diploma, Juilliard Graduate School of Music, New York, 1938; Studied with William Berce, Felix Salmond, Emanuel Feuermann, Diran Alexanian, Pablo Casals. Career: Principal Cellist, CBS Symphony Orchestra, New York, 1938-42; Member, Dorian String Quartet, 1939-42; Solo Cellist, US Navy Symphony Orchestra; Member, Navy String Quartet, 1942-45; Annual recitals, Town Hall, New York, 1946-57; Member, Harpischord Quartet, 1947-51; Bach Aria Group, 1948-76; Founder-member, Beaux Arts Trio, 1955-87; Guest artist, Juilliard, Guarneri and Cleveland String Quartets; Numerous appearances on major concert series and with festivals worldwide; Professor, Manhattan School of Music, New York, 1950-82; Juilliard School of Music, New York, 1951-61; Indiana University School of Music, Bloomington, summers 1956-65; State University of New York, Stony Brook, 1960-85; New England Conservatory of Music, Boston, 1986-92; Rutgers, the State University of New Jersey, 1987-92; Master classes around the globe. Recordings: Numerous. Honours: Many recording awards including Prix Mondial du Disque; Union de la Presse Musicale Belge; Gramophone Record of the Year; Stereo Review Record of the Year; 3 Grand Prix du Disques; American String Teachers Association Teacher of the Year Award, 1982; US Presidential Citation, 1982; US Presidential Medallion, 1985; Honorary Doctorate, State University of New York, Stony Brook, 1988. Memberships: Cello Society, president, 1955-59, 1987-; Honorary Member, American String Teachers Association. Address: 12 East 86th Street, New York, NY 10028, USA.

GREENSMITH John Brian, b. 12 Apr 1929, Bournemouth, England. Cellist; Orchestra Manager and Administrator. m. Magdalen Aurelia Green, 3 sons. Education: Birmingham School of Music; Guildhall School of Music; Licentiate, Trinity College of London; Associate, Royal College of Music. Career: Bournemouth Municipal Orchestra, 1952-53; Principal, British Broadcasting Corporation, Glasgow, 1956-63; Instrumental Teacher, West Riding County Council, 1963-74; Visiting Tutor, Bretton Hall, 1965-82; Orchestral Manager, Yorkshire Concert Orchestra, 1965-72; Teacher in charge, Batley Music Centre, 1967-74; Member, Advisory Committee, 1968-73, Governor, 1988-, City of Leeds College of Music; Orchestral Manager, Yorkshire Sinfonia, 1972-75; Coordinator for Instrumental Music, Barnsley Metropolitan Borough Council, 1974-90; General Manager, Yorkshire Philharmonic Orchestras, 1975-; Director, Company Secretary, Wakefield Metropolitan Festival Co Ltd, 1975-, Wakefield Opera House, 1981-; Visiting Tutor, Wakefield Tertiary College, 1982-90; Arts and Financial Marketing Consultant, 1982-; Managing Director, Music for All Occasions, 1988-; Adviser for Yorkshire and Humberside Arts, 1993-. Recordings: Various. Address: Torridon House, 104 Bradford Road, Wrenthorpe, Wakefield WF1 2AH, England.

GREENWOOD Andrew, b. 1954, Todmorden, Yorkshire, England. Conductor. Education: Studied at Clare College, Cambridge and at the London Opera Centre. Career: Opera For All, 1976; Member of the music staff of Covent Garden 1977-84, studying with Edward Downes and conducting the Dutch Radio and Television Orchestra; Principal Guest Chorus Master of the Philharmonia Chorus from 1981: concerts with Previn, Davis, Giulini, Sinopoli and Solti; Conducted Rossini's Petite Messe Solennelle at the Istanbul Festival 1985; Chorus master at Welsh National Opera from 1984, and has conducted performances of operas by Mozart, Bizet, Puccini, Verdi, Berlioz (The Trojans), Beethoven, Strauss and Smetana; Many concerts on BBC Radio 2 and 3, notably with the BBC Welsh Symphony Orchestra; Debut with the Rotterdam Philharmonic 1990, Cologne Opera 1990, The Bartered Bride and Die Fledermaus; English National Opera 1990-92, The Magic Flute and Madame Butterfly; Conducted Manon Lescaut for the Chelsea Opera Group, 1992, Don Giovanni for ENO; The Pearl Fishers for English Touring Opera, 1996. Address: Kaye Artists Management, Barratt House, 7 Chertsey Road, Woking, GU21 5AB, England.

GREER David (Clive), b. 8 May 1937, London, England. Professor of Music. m. Patricia Regan, 25 August 1961, 2 sons, 1 daughter. Education: Dulwich College, 1952-55; Oxford University, 1957-60; BA, 1960; MA, 1964; MusD, Dublin, 1991. Career: Lecturer in Music, Birmingham University, 1963-72; Hamilton Harty Professor of Music, Queen's University, Belfast, 1972-84; Professor of Music, Newcastle University, 1984-86; Professor of Music, Durham University, 1986-; Mellon Visiting Fellow, 1989, Mayers Visiting Fellow, 1991, at Huntington Library, California; Folger Visiting Fellow, Folger Shakespeare Library, Washington DC, 1994; Chairman, Accreditation Panel, Hong Kong Baptist University, 1994. Publications: Editor with F W Sternfeld, English Madrigal Verse, 3rd edition, 1967; English Lute Songs, facsimile series, 1967-71; Hamilton Harty, His Life and Music, 1979; Songs from Manuscript Sources, 1979; Collected English Lutenist Partsongs (Musica Britannica, vols 53-4), 1987-89; A Numerous and Fashionable Audience: The Story of Elsie Swinton, 1997; Editor, Journal (formerly Proceedings) of the Royal Musical Association, vols 103-115. Contributions to: Music and Letters; Proceedings of the Royal Musical Association; Lute Society Journal; Musical Times; Shakespeare Quarterly; English Studies, Notes and Queries; Early Music; Music Review. Honour: Fellow, Royal Society of Arts, 1986. Address: Department of Music, University of Durham, Palace Green, Durham DH1 3RL, England.

GREEVE Gilbert-Jean de, b. 11 Nov 1944, St Truiden, Belgium. Concert Pianist. Education: Studied Piano with Eugene Traey, Royal Conservatory of Antwerp, Belgium, 1958-69; Performing major, with First Prizes in Piano and Chamber Music and a Diplome superieur for Chamber music; Composition major, with First Prizes in Music Theory, Harmony, Analysis, Counterpoint and Fugue; 1970 Peabody Institute of Music, Baltimore, Maryland, USA; Private studies with Rudolph Serkin, Eugene Ormandy and Leonard Pearlmann; 1972, Franz Liszt Academy of Budapest, Hungary. Career: Active world-wide as pianist 1970-; Director of the State Music Academy of Antwerp and Professor of the Royal Conservatory of Antwerp, 1970-; Working in a permanent duo with the Belgian soprano Martine De Craene, 1988-, repertoire of more than 14 hours music from Baroque until today, including 3 books of melodies by Gabriel Fauré; Lieder cycles by composers from Hungary and Canada have been dedicated to and world-created by the Duo. Concerts and Master Classes in 5 continents; Major foreign tours: Canada, Australia, New Zealand, Africa, Finland, Netherlands, Antilles, Greece. Compositions: Chamber Music, a Lieder cycle of 36 Lieder on poems by James Joyce. Recordings: Belgian Radio and Television; CBC Canada; Hungarian Radio Budapest. Address: Anselmostraat 38, 2018 Antwerpen, Belgium.

GREEVY Bernadette, b. 3 July 1940, Dublin, Ireland. Singer (Mezzo-soprano). Career: Concert appearances with many of the world's great orchestras and numerous recitals in all the major capitals of the world; Operatic repertoire includes Eboli, Charlotte, Dalila, Herodiade in the opera by Massenet and Gluck's Orfeo; Tour of the People's Republic of China 1985, giving recitals and holding Master Classes; Recital series at the National Concert Hall in Dublin and on RTE Radio and Televiion; Has sung Mahler's Rückert Lieder and the Choral Symphony with the Oslo Philharmonic; the Brahms Alto Rhapsody and Elgar's Sea Pictures in Ottawa; Recent concerts in Denmark, Italy, Spain, USA, France, Finland and Norway; Mahler series in London with the Royal Philharmonic under Charles Dutoit, 1989. Recordings: Handel Arias, Orlando, Ariodante; Brahms Lieder; Nuits d'Eté by Berlioz and songs by Duparc, with the Ulster Orchestra (Chandos); Bach Arias; Sea Pictures; Mahler's Lieder eines fahrenden Gesellen and Kindertotenlieder, with the RTE Orchestra. Honours: Harriet Cohen International Music Award; Order of Merit of the Order of Malta; Honorary DMus, National University of Ireland; DMus, Trinity College Dublin, 1988; Pro Ecclesia et Pontifice, 1988. Address: c/o Trinity College, Dublin, Eire.

GREGOR Bohumil, b. 14 July 1926, Prague, Czechoslovakia. Conductor. Education: Studied with Alois Klima at the Prague Conservatory. Career: Worked at the Prague 5th May (Smetana) Theatre from 1947; Conducted at the Brno Opera 1949-51; Musical Director Ostrava Opera 1958-62; Performances of Janácek's Katya Kabanova and The Excursions of Mr Broucek and premieres of works by Pauer, Kaslik and Trojan; Conductor at the Prague National Theatre from 1962: led the company in the first British productions of Janácek's From the House of the Dead (Edinburgh 1964 and 1970); Royal Opera Stockholm 1966-69, Hamburg Staatsoper 1969-72: premiere of Kelemen's Belagerunqzustand (after The Plague by Camus, 1970) and operas by Verdi, Smetana and Janácek; Performances of The Cunning Little Vixen in Vienna, Edinburgh, Brussels and Amsterdam; San Francisco Opera from 1969, Jenufa, Otello and Salome; Conducted The Cunning Little Vixen at Zurich, 1989 and at the Bayreuth Youth Festival, 1990; New production of Dvorák's The Devil and Kate at Prague, 1990; Season 1993 with Katya Kabanova and a new production of The Bartered Bride; Principal Guest Conductor, National Theatre, Prague. Recordings: Several sets of Czech opera: The Makropoulos Case, The Cunning Little Vixen, Jenufa and From the House of the Dead; Dvorak Symphonic Poems; Concert overtures; Slavonic rhapsodies. Address: Janackovo Nabrezi 7. 150 00 Prague 5, Czech Republic.

GREGOR Joszef, b. 8 Aug 1940, Rakosliget, Hungary. Singer (Bass). Education: Studied in Budapest with Endreh Poessler and sang in choir of Hungarian army. Career: Appearances at the Szeged Opera from 1964; Sang Sarastro at the Hungarian State Opera, Budapest, 1966; Played title role in Hungarian premiere of Attila, 1972 and appeared in operas by Goldmark, Rossini, Donizetti, Puccini and Bartók (title role in Duke Bluebeard's Castle); Visited the Wiesbaden Festival 1970 and sang elsewhere in Germany as guest; Houston Grand Opera 1986 as Varlaam in Boris Godunov, Monte Carlo Opera 1988, in Cimarosa's Il Pittore Parigino; Sang Dulcamara at the Erkel Theatre, Budapest, 1995; Many radio and television performances from 1975; Frequent concert engagements. Recordings: Goldmark's die Königin von Saba; Haydn's L'Infedeltà delusa and La Fedeltà Premiata; Paisiello's Barbiere di Siviglia; Guntram (Strauss), Nerone (Boito) and Mosè in Egitto (Rossini); Don Pasquale, Gianni Schicchi and La Fiamma by Respighi; Duke Bluebeard's Castle; Liszt's Missa solemnis and Legend of St Elisabeth; Beethoven's Missa solemnis and 9th Symphony; Salieri's Falstaff; La Serva Padrona; Il Pittore Parigino; Andrea Chénier and Fedora; Der Geduldige Sokrates by Telemann (Hungaroton). Address: Hungarian State Opera House, Nepoztarsasag utja 22, 1061 Budapest, Hungary.

GREGSON Edward, b. 23 July 1945, Sunderland, England. Composer; Conductor. m. Susan Carole Smith, 30 Sept 1967, 2 sons. Education: Royal Academy of Music, 1963-67; LRAM, 1966; GRSM, 1967; BMus, University of London, 1977; ARAM, 1983; FRAM, 1990. Career: Lecturer, 1976, Reader in Music, 1989, Professor of Music, 1996, Goldsmiths College, University of London; Principal, Royal Northern College of Music, 1996-; Active as Conductor, particularly contemporary music; As Composer commissioned by numerous orchestras, organisations, ensembles, UK and abroad, 1970-, including English Chamber Orchestra, 1968, York Festival, 1976, Royal Shakespeare Company, 1988, 1990, Bournemouth Festival, 1991, also National Centre for Orchestral Studies, Wren Orchestra of London, BBC, Royal Liverpool Philharmonic; Extensive judging panel work includes BBC Young Musician of the Year and Royal Philharmonic Society, amongst others. Compositions include: Orchestral: Music for Chamber Orchestra, 1968; Tuba Concerto, 1976; Trombone Concerto, 1979; Metamorphoses, 1979; Contrasts, 1983; Trumpet Concerto, 1983; Celebration, 1991; Blazon, 1992; Clarinet Concerto, 1994; Concerto, piano and wind, 1995-97; Choral, vocal: In the Beginning, 1966; 5 Songs of Innocence and Experience, 1979; Missa Brevis Pacem, 1988; Make a Joyful Noise, anthem, 1988; A Welcome Ode, 1997; Instrumental, chamber: Divertimento, 1967; 6 Little Piano Pieces, 1982; Piano Sonata in one movement, 1986; Alarum, 1993; Three Matisse Impressions, 1993; Brass Band: Connotations, 1977; Dances and Arias, 1984; Of Men and Mountains, 1990; Symphonic Wind Band: Festivo, 1988; The Sword and the Crown, 1991; The Kings Go Forth, 1997; Educational music. Recordings include: Tuba Concerto; Horn Concerto; Intrada; Connotations; Brass and music composed and conducted the composer; Dances and Arias; Of Men and Mountains; Make a Joyful Noise; The Sword and the Crown; The Kings Go Forth. Publications include: The Contemporary Repertoire of Brass Bands in the 20th Century, 1979. Contributions to: Articles and reviews in journals. Honours: Honorary DMus, Sunderland University, 1996; FDCA, 1997. Current Management: Novello and Company, 8/9 Frith Street, London, England. Address: c/o The Royal Northern College of Music, 124 Oxford Road, Manchester M13 9RD, England.

GRELA-MOZEJKO Piotr, b. 15 Mar 1961, Bytom, Poland. Composer; Music Critic. m. Kasia Zoledziowski 30 June 1990. Education: MA, University of Silesia, Katowice; Studied Composition with Dr Edward Boguslawski, Katowice, Dr Boguslaw Schaeffer, Cracow, Dr Alfred Fisher, University of Alberta. Debut: The Silesian Tribune of Composers, 1982. Career: 1st performance of work, 1977; Works performed at major festivals such as Warsaw Autumn Festival, Poznan Music Spring Festival, Gdansk Meetings of Young Composers; Founder, Fascinating Music Festival, Katowice, 1983-86; Co-Founder, J S Bach Festival, Cracow-Katowice, 1985; Took part in many exhibitions of musical scores, Institut Polonais, Paris, Royal Academy of Music, London, Warsaw, Salzburg, Katowice; Numerous interviews, Polish TV and Radio, also CBC; Polish TV documentary on activities and the Fascinating Music Festival, 1992; Completed MMus Degree in Composition at the University of Alberta, Edmonton, 1992. Compositions: Archival radio recordings, Poland, Canada, USA: Ravenna, harpischord; minimum-optimum-maximum, chamber ensemble; en attendant Bergson, string quartet; The Dreams of Odysseus, tape (performed in Warsaw, Poland, as part of the first exhibition of Polish artists in exile, Jestesmy); Epitaph for Jerzy, for tape included in A BEAMS Compilation; Other works: Xylotet Concerto, saxophone, orchestra; Horror Vacui, strings; Ordines, saxophone, organ, cello; Melodramas I-VI, solo instruments; Festivals: Canada, Pacific Market, Fringe, The Edmonton Music Festival, Warsaw. Hobbies: No 8 8807 101st Street, Edmonton, Alberta, T6E 3Z9, Canada.

GRICE Garry (Bruce), b. 25 Jan 1942, Dayton, Ohio, USA. Opera Singer (Tenor). m. Patricia A Michael, 9 July 1983, 1 son, 2 daughters. Education: BA, History, University of Daytn, 1964; Musical studies with Hubert Kockritz, Cincinnati and Adelaide Saraceni, Milan. Debut: National Opera, USA, 1970-71. Career: 8 seasons in German and Swiss opera houses including: Debut, Stadttheater, St Gallen, Switzerland, 1974, Debut, Bavarian State Opera, 1974; Debut as Don José in Carmen, Florentine Opera, Milwaukee, 1980; Bacchus in Ariadne auf Naxos, Des Moines Metro Opera, 1980; Debut, New York City Opera, 1981; Bermuda Festival, 1981; Debut, Chicago as Don José in Carmen, 1983; Debut, Calgary Opera Association, 1985; Debut, Cairo, 1990; Has sung with conductors Kleiber, Prêtre, Guadagno, Keene and Rescigno; Has appeared in over 50 roles including Otello, Florestan, Bacchus, Canio, Max and Radames; Has sung throughout USA, also Canada, Bermuda and Europe mainly Germany, Austria, Switzerland; Faculty Voice and Opera, University of Notre Dame, 1991; Artistic Director, Indian Opera North since 1990; Performance: New Orleans Debut, Verdi Requiem, 1992. Recordings: Title role in Otello, TV Public Broadcasting, 1984; Turiddu in Cavalleria Rusticana, Canadian Public Radio, 1985. Publications: Translations into English of Otello, Il Trovatore and Tales of Hoffmann. Current Management: Warden Associated INc, 127 W 72nd Street, Suite 2-R, New York, NY 10023, USA.

GRIER Francis, b. 1955, England. Organist; Pianist; Composer. Education: Chorister at St George's Chapel, Windsor Castle; Eton College; Organ Scholar at King's College, Cambridge; Piano Studies with Joseph Cooper, Fanny Waterman and Bernard Roberts; Organ with Gillian Weir. Career: Assistant Organist to Simon Preston, at Christ Church Cathedral, Oxford; Organist and Director of Music, 1981; Organ recitals throughout Britain; First Organ recital at the BBC Promenade Concerts, 1985; Sudied in India from 1985; Then worked with mentally handicapped in London and Bangladore; Resident in England from 1989; Works as psychodynamic counsellor. Compositions: Advent Responsories for King's College Chapel, 1990; Mass with motets for Westminster Abbey; Sequences of Readings and Music for Ascension, for the 550th anniversary of Eton College, 1990; The Cry of Mary, for BBC2, 1992; St Francis, opera, for Eton College and National Youth Music Theatre, 1993; Mass in Time of Persecution, for Soloists, Chorus and Orchestra, including poems of Ratushinskaya, 1994; My Heart Dances, settings of Tagore, for Soloists, Chorus and Orchestra, commissioned by 3 Choirs Festival, 1995. Recordings: Bach; Mendelssohn; Couperin, Franck; Messiaen: Messe de la Pentecôte and L'Ascension, all on the Rieger organ at Christ Church Cathedral. Membership: FRCO. Address: 65 Tynemouth Road, London, N15 4AU, England.

GRIER (Hugh) Christopher, b. 4 Dec 1922, Derby, England. Music critic; Lecturer. m. Mary Elisabeth Martin, 1 son. Education: MA, MusB, King's College, Cambridge. Career: Music Officer, Scandinavia, British Council, 1947-49; Music Critic, The Scotsman, 1949-63; Music Critic, The Standard, 1970-93; Freelance, 1970-; Professor, Royal College of Music, 1971-84; Professor, Royal Academy of Music, 1976-83. Honours: Honorary RCM, 1975; Honorary RAM, 1979. Memberships: Incorporated Society of Musicians; Institute of Journalists; Critics Circle; Scottish Arts Club. Hobbies: Skiing; Tennis; Reading.

GRIESBACH Karl-Rudi, b. 14 June 1916, Breckerfeld, Westphalia, Germany, Composer. Education: Studied Composition with Philipp Jarnach at Cologne Hochschule fur Musik (graduated 1941). Career: Worked in Hamburg as Composer and Pianist, then moved to Dresden, 1950; Music Critic, Lecturer, Artistic Adviser to Dresden Staatsoper; Professor of composition at the Carl Maria von Weber Academy of Music. Compositions include: Kolumbus, opera, first performed Erfurt and Neustrelitz, 1958; Die Weibermuhle, opera, first performed Weimar, 1960; Marike Weiden, opera, first performed Weimar, Görlitz and Neustrelitz, 1960; Der Schwarze, der Weibe und die Frau, opera, first performed Dresden, 1963; Aulus und sein Papagei, opera, first performed Dresden, 1982; Florian, opera, 1984; Noah, opera, 1987; Belle und Armand, opera, 1988; Ballets: Kleider machen Leute, first performed Berlin, 1954; Schneewittchen, first performed, Berlin, 1956; Reineke Fuchs, first performed Dresden, 1985, Samson, 1982; Works for Orchestra: Afrikanische Sinfonie, first performed Berlin, 1962; Konzertante Musik für Klavier und Kammerorchester, first performed Berlin, 1964; Sinfonie 1967, first performed Dresden, 1986; Chamber Music: Blues-Impressions, Klavierstücke im Jazzstil, first performed Dresden, 1962; Streichquartet, first performed Berlin, 1977; Vocal Music: Nacht der Faeben, Lieder für Streichquintett und Harf, first performed Berlin, 1967; Und Va kamst Du, sieben Lieberlieder für mittlere Stimme und Klavier, first performed Berlin, 1967. Address: c/o GEMA, Postfach 80 07 67, D-81607 Munich, Germany.

GRIFFEL Kay, b. 26 Dec 1940, Eldora, Iowa, USA. Singer (Soprano). m. Eckhard Sellheim. Education: Studied at Northwestern University, Illinois, in Berlin and with Lotte Lehmann at Santa Barbara. Debut: Chicago 1960, as Mercédès in Carmen. Career: Sang at the Deutsche Oper Berlin and in Bremen, Mainz, Karlsruhe, Hamburg and Dusseldorf; Salzburg 1973 in the premiere of De Temporum fine Comoedia by Orff; Glyndebourne Festival 1976-77, as Alice Ford in Falstaff; Tour of Japan with the Staatsoper Berlin 1977, as the Marschallin, Donna Elvira and Mozart's Countess; Lisbon 1978, Eva in Die Meistersinger; Metropolitan Opera from 1982, as Electra in Idomeneo, Rosalinde, Arabella, Tatiana and the Countess; Further appearances in Brussels, Moscow, Cologne and at the Orange Festival; Sang Eva in Die Meistersinger at Wellington, New Zealand, 1990. Recordings: Janácek Diary of one who Disappeared (Deutsche Grammophon); De Temporum fine Comoedia; Italian Arias. Honour: Doctorate of Fine Arts, Simpson College, Indianola, Iowa 1982. Current Management: Robert Lombardo, New York, USA; Stoll and Hilbert in Germany. Address: c/o Wellington City Opera (contracts), PO Box 6588, New Zealand.

GRIFFIN Judson, b. 7 Sept 1951, Lewes, Delaware, USA. Violist; Violinist. m. Mara Paske, 7 May 1988. Education: DMA 1977, MM 1975, Juilliard School of Music; BM, Eastman School of Music, 1973. Debut: Carnegie Recital Hall, New York City, January 1981. Career: Violist, Rochester Philharmonic Orchestra, 1970-73; Freelance Violist, New York City, 1973-77; Assistant Professor, University of North Carolina at Greensboro, 1977-79; Principal Viola, Aspen Chamber Symphony, 1977-80; Freelance Violinist and Violist, New York City, 1979-; Current activities, Violist of Smithson String Quartet and Smithsonian Chamber Players (Smithsonian Institution, Washington DC); Atlantis Ensemble (Europe); Violinist of Four Nations and Sonata a quattro (New York); Regular appearances with almost all period-instrument organisations in USA. Recordings: Chamber music on labels, Nonesuch, Harmonia Mundi (France, USA), L'Oiseau-Lyre, Reference, Harmonia Mundi (Germany), Columbia, CRI, CP2, Pro Arte, Newport; Many radio recordings. Address: 170 Claremont Avenue No 7, New York, NY 10027, USA.

GRIFFITH Lisa, b. USA. Singer (Soprano). Education: Studied at the Indiana University of Pennsylvania and the Cincinnati Conservatory. Debut: Seattle Opera, 1984. Career: Sang at Wiesbaden Opera, 1984-89, Hannover, 1989-91, notably as Zerbinetta; Deutsche Oper am Rhein Dusseldorf, from 1991, as Susanna in The Marriage of Figaro and Sophie in Rosenkavalier; Other roles include Gilda and Pamina; Guest at the Munich Staatsoper, the Komische Oper Berlin and Staatsoper Stuttgart; Frequent concert appearances. Address: c/o Deutsche Oper am Rhein, Heinrich-Heine-Allee 16a, W-40213 Dusseldorf, Germany.

GRIFFITH-SMITH Bella, b. 1920, USA. President, Coral Gables Civic Opera and Orchestra, Inc; Opera Singer; Coach; Conductor. Education: Private Tutors; Howard Thain, Franco Iglesias, Dr Paul Csonka. Debut: Civic Opera of the Palm Beaches. Career: Appeared with Louis Quilico, Metropolitan Artist; Robert Merill, Guiseppe Campora, a Television Concet Version-Spanish Translation, Channel 2, Miami; Madam Butterfly; Radio-La Traviata; Leading Roles in Madam Butterfly; La Bohème, Tosca, Cavalleria Rusticana, Pagliacci, Suor Angelica, Il Tabarro, Faust, Carmen (Micaela), Cosi Fan tutte (Fiordiligi), Tales of Hoffmann (Antonia), Don Pasquale-Norina, L'Oca del Cairo (Celidora), La Traviata, Oratorio-Elijah, L'Enfant Prodigue, Messiah, Vivaldi's Gloria, Stabat Mater, Rossini; Concerts-Salome, Otello, Turandot, with Alain Lombard/Greater Miami Philharmonic; Guest Soloist. Hobbies: Writing; Painting; Reading-research; History; Literature. Address: 700 Santander Avenue, Coral Gables, FL 33134, USA.

GRIFFITHS Graham (Charles Thomas), b. 13 May 1954, Tiverton, England. Conductor; Pianist; Lecturer. m. Miriam Regina Zillo, 18 Jan 1985, 2 sons. Education: Bryanston School 1967-72; BMus (hons) Edinburgh University, 1976; PGCE (Cantab) Cambridge University, 1977. Career: Founder-Member, Edinburgh Experimental Arts Society, 1972-76; Founder-member, Grand Toxic Opera Company, Edinburgh, 1974-76; Member, Cambridge Contemporary Music Ensemble, 1976-78; Marketing/Education Officer, Scottish National Orchestra, 1978-81; Co-Administrator, International Musica Nova Festival, Glasgow, 1978-81; Arts Journalist, Scottish Television, 1981-86; Principal Conductor, Glasgow Chamber Orchestra, 1985-86; Lecturer in Twentieth Century Music, Sao Paulo State University, Brazil, 1987-89; Founder-Director, Jardim Musical Arts Centre, 1987-; Founder-Conductor, Ensemble Grupo Novo Horizonte, 1988-; Director of Education, Mozarteum Brasileiro, 1987-; Conductor, Choir of Cultura Inglesa, Sao Paulo, 1988-90; Choral Director, 1st National Festival of Brazilian Colonial Music (Juiz de Fora) 1990; Guest Conductor, Campos do Jordao Festival, 1990; Guest Conductor, Orquestra Sinfonica e Madrigal da Universidade Federal da Bahia, Salvador, 1990-; Director of Conducting Course, Festival Seminarios Internacionais Salvador, 1991; Lecture-Recital piano tours: 1990 Bridges Across Time, Brazil, Denmark, United Kingdom; 1991 New World Experience, Brazil, Denmark (25 concerts); Co-Founder-Director, Mostra de Musica Contemporanea, Ouro Preto, 1991; Regular broadcasts on Radio e Televisao Cultura, Sao Paulo, 1988-; Visiting Lecturer, Federal Universities of Rio de Janeiro, 1990, Bahia 1990/91, Uberlandia 1992; Guest Conductor, Camerata Antigua de Curitiba, 1993. Compositions: Sacred Choral Works include: Anglican Hymn Collection, 1988-; The Lords Prayer, 1990; Ta Voix, 1991; Cançao de Quatá for Trombone Quartet, 1993. Current Management: Jardim Musical, Sao Paulo. Address: Rua Angatuba 97, Pacaembu, 01247-000 Sao Paulo, SP, Brazil.

GRIFFITHS Hilary, b. 1950, Leamington Spa, England. Conductor. m. Andrea Andonian, 28 June 1978, 2 sons. Education: Studied at the Royal Academy of Music, London Opera Centre and in Siena and Milan. Career: Former principal staff conductor at the Cologne Opera, with appearances also in Dresden, Dusseldorf, Nuremberg and Basle; Former music director of Oberhausen Opera with further engagements in Oslo, Antwerp, Leeds (Opera North) and at the Edinburgh, Prague and Schwetzingen Festivals; Conductor at the State Opera Prague from 1992 (operas by Zemlinsky and Strauss), music director at Regensburg from 1993 and at the Eutin opera festival (Die Zauberflöte, Il Trovatore, Der Freischütz and Turandot); Season 1997 with Don Giovanni and Intermezzo at Regensburg, Die Zauberflöte and Aida in Cologne and Otello and Butterfly in Prague; Don Giovanni at the Perth Festival, Australia and Der Prinz von Homburg to open the Wiesbaden May Festival; Concerts with the Rotterdam Philharmonic, the BBC Welsh Symphony and the West German Radio Orchestra. Recording: CD, Jommelli, Mass in D and Te Deum. Publications: World Premieres: Das Gauklermärchen and Lulu (Rota); German Premieres, A Christmas Carol and Simon Bolivar both by Thea Musgrave. Contributions to: TV and Video: Il matrimonio segreto, from the Schwetzingen Festival, Lulu from Cologne. Address: Graf-Adolf-Strasse 28, 51065 Cologne, Germany.

GRIFFITHS Howard (Laurence), b. 24 Feb 1950, Hastings, England. Conductor. m. Semra Griffiths, 24 July 1971, 1 son, 1 daughter. Education: Viola with Cecil Aronowitz, Royal College of Music, London; ARCM; Conducting with Leon Barzin, Paris, Erich Schmid, Zurich. Debut: Queen Elizabeth Hall, English Chamber Orchestra, 1989; Royal Festival Hall, Royal Philharmonic Orchestra, 1991. Career: Principal Viola, Ankara State Opera until 1979; Member, Lucern String Quartet; Principal Guest Conductor, Oxford Orchestra da Camera, 1994; Director and Principal Conductor, Zurich Chamber Orchestra, 1996-; Has conducted many prominent orchestras including Royal Philharmonic Orchestra, English Chamber Orchestra, Warsaw Philharmonic Orchestra, Basel Radio Symphony Orchestra, Istanbul State Symphony Orchestra, Northern Sinfonia of England, Stadtorchester Winterthur, Polish Chamber Orchestra, Tonhalle Orchestra Zurich, National Orchestra of Spain, London Mozart Players, Slovak Radio-Symphony Orchestra, Moscow Symphony Orchestra; Artistic Director, Allensbach Chamber Music Festival, Germany, 1992-. Recordings: Over 30 CDs include 18th Century Swiss Composers Stalder and Reindl, English Chamber Orchestra; Instrumental Works of Othmar Schoeck, English Chamber Orchestra; Mozart Horn Concertos, Kalinski and Polish Chamber Orchestra; Works of Max Bruch, Royal Philharmonic Orchestra; 3 CDs of music by Turkish composers Saygun, Erkin, Rey, with Northern Sinfonia of England; Baroque Oboe Concertos and Mozart Sinfonia Concertante; Caspar Fritz Violin Concerto, English Chamber Orchestra. Membership: Schweizerischer Tonkünstlerischeverein. Hobbies: Tennis; Reading. Current Management: Zürcher Kammerorchester, Mühlebach Str 86, 8032 Zürich, Switzerland. Address: Laubholzstrasse 46, 8703 Erlenbach, Switzerland.

GRIFFITHS Paul, b. 24 Nov 1947, Bridgend, Glamorgan, Wales. Critic; Writer on Music. m. Rachel Griffiths. Education: BA, MSc, Lincoln College, Oxford. Career: Music critic for various journals from 1971; Area Editor, 20th Century Music, New Grove Dictionary of Music (1980); Chief Music Critic, The Times, 1982-92; New Yorker from 1992; Author of 2 novels; Compiled Mozart pasticcio The Jewel Box for Opera North, 1991. Publications: Modern Music 1978; The String Quartet 1983; New Sounds, New Personalities: British Composers of the 1980s, 1985; An Encyclopedia of 20th Century Music 1986; Modern Music and After, 1995; Studies of Boulez, Cage, Stravinsky's The Rake's Progress, Ligeti, Davies, Bartók and Messiaen. Contributions to: The Grove Concise Dictionary of Music and Musicians 1988; Numerous professional journals. Address: Darville Cottage, Lower Heyford, Oxford, England.

GRIFFITHS Paul (Wayne), b. 1958, England. Conductor. Education: Studied at Royal Northern College of Music and London Opera Centre. Career: Conducted The Judgement of Paris by John Woolrich in Royal Opera House Garden Venture Series, Orchestra of Royal Opera at Windsor Festival and Symphony Hall, Birmingham; Paris debut at Théâtre du Champs Elysées, with Orchestre du Conservatoire National; Further concerts with Royal Philharmonic, English Chamber Orchestra and Tokyo Philharmonic; Season 1992-93 with Il Trovatore for Scottish Opera, L'Elisir d'Amore at Gothenburg, concert in Athens with Grace Bumbry and London with Josephine Bartsow and Montserrat Caballé; Covent Garden debut with Rigoletto (1994), returning for La Bohème and Turandot; Artistic Director and Accompanist of Luciano Pavarotti Master Class; Recital Accompanist with Geraint Evans, José Carreras, Katia Ricciarelli, James King, Thomas Allen and Yevgeny Nesterenko; Staff Conductor, Royal Opera House, Covent Garden. Address: c/o Harold Holt Ltd, 31 Sinclair Road, London W14 0NS, England.

GRIGORIU Theodor, b. 25 July 1926, Galatzi, Romania. Composer. m. 28 Mar 1951. Education: Studied with Mihail Jora, Conservatory of Bucharest, Romania, and Aram Khachaturian, P I Tchaikovsky, Moscow, USSR; Faculty of Architecture, Bucharest. Career: Secretary-General, Union of Romanian Composers; Freelance Composer; His works performed worldwide. Compositions: Orchestral works include: Sinfonia Cantabile, Op 1, 1950, revised 1966; Variations Symphoniques sur une Chanson d'Anton Pann, (Six Tableaux d'Epoque), 1955; Concerto pour Double Orchestre de Chamber et Hautbois, 1957; Rêve Cosmique-poéme orchestral, 1959;Hommage à Enesco, 8(16) violons, 1960; Orchestral version of Sept Chansons (works Clement Marot), 1964; Tristia, in memoriam Ionel Perlea, Melodie Infinie, 1972; Suite Carpatine, string orchestra, 1980; Pastorale si Idylles de Transylvanie, 1984; Concerto pour violon et orchestre "Byzance aprés Byzance, 1994; Chopin Orchestral, 25 Pieces pour un ballet imaginaire, 1995; Choral Music: Elegia Pontica, (vers d'Ovide), choir, baritone-bass, 1969; Canti per Europa (oratorio), mixed choir and orchestra, 1976; Les Vocalises de la Mer (choral symphony), mixed choir, organ and orchestra, 1984; Chamber music: Columna Modala (Cahiers I, II), investigations dans l'ethos roumain, piano, 1984; Quatuor à cordes "A la recherche de l'echo", 1983; Film Music: Codine, 1963; La Foret des Pendus, 1965; Theatre music. Recordings: Various works, Electrocord. Publication: Muzica si Numbul Poeziei. Hobbies: Painting; Design; Graphics. Address: Str Pictor Rosenthal 2, Bucharest 71288, Rumania.

GRIGSBY Beverly, b. 11 Jan 1928, Chicago, IL, USA. Composer. Education: Studied in California with Ernst Krenek and Ingolf Dahl and at Stanford University and the Royal College, London. Career: Teacher at California State University, Northridge, 1963-92. Compositions include: Stage works: Augustine The Saint, 1975, Moses, 1978, The Vision Of St Joan, 1987; Trio for Violin, Clarinet and Piano, 1984; Wind Quintet,

1990; Keyboard Concerto, 1993; Concerto for Orchestra, 1994; Computer music. Address: c/o ASCAP, ASCAP Building, One Lincoln Plaza, New York, NY 10023, USA.

GRILLO Joann, b. 14 May 1939, New York, USA. Singer (Mezzo-Soprano). m. Richard Kness, 1 son. Education: BS, Hunter College, New York; Private study with Loretta Corelli, Franco Iglesias and Daniel Ferro. Debut: New York City Opera 1962, as Gertrude in Louise; Metropolitan Opera, as Carmen, Meg Page in Falstaff, Preziosilla in La Forza del Destino, Santuzza, Laura in La Gioconda, Neocle in The Siege of Corinth and Suzuki (226 performances); Sang Massenet's Charlotte at Barcelona in 1963; Amneris at Frankfurt (1967); Carmen at the Vienna Staatsoper and in Paris (1978, 1981); Guest appearances in Essen, Hamburg, Zurich, Dallas, Philadelphia, Lisbon and Marseille; Other roles include Marguerite in The Damnation of Faust, Saint-Saëns's Dalila, Olga in Eugene Onegin, Fricka in The Ring and Verdi's Eboli, Ulrica and Azucena; Sang Amneris at Rio de Janeiro, 1988; Concert appearances as Jocasta in Oedipus Rex. Hobbies: Egyptology; Cooking; Travel. Current Management: Eric Semon Associates, 111 W 57th Street, New York City, NY 10019, USA. Address: 1550-75 Street, Brooklyn, NY 11228, USA.

GRIMM Hans-Gunther, b. 1925, Germany. Singer (Baritone); Professor. Education: Studied in East Berlin. Career: Sang at Berlin Staatsoper, 1950-52, Bremen, 1952-54, Mannheim, 1954-60; Engaged at Cologne, 1960-64, Theater am Gartnerplatz, Munich, 1964-66, Dortmund, 1966-70; Sang in Cologne, 1961, in German premiere of Nono's Intolleranza 60; Guest appearances as concert and opera singer, Frankfurt, Japan, North America, France and Barcelona; Roles included Mozart's Count, Don Giovanni, Guglielmo and Papageno, Malatesta, Marcello, Wolfram, Escamillo, Don Fernando in Fidelio and Carlos in Forza del Destino; Professor at Maastrich Conservatory, Netherlands, 1973-82. Recordings include: Undine by Lortzing; Eine Nacht in Venedig; Rossini's Petite Messe solennelle; Beethoven's Ninth.

GRIMSLEY Greer, b. 1962, New Orleans, Louisiana, USA. Singer (Baritone). Career: Sang Jochanaan in Salome with Scottish Opera, 1988; Saratoga Opera, 1988, as Alfonso in Così fan tutte and Wexford Festival in Der Templer und die Jüdin by Marschner; Tour of Australia, Canada and Europe in Peter Brook's La Tragédie de Carmen; Bregenz Festival, 1991, as Escamillo; Santa Fe in the US premiere of Henze's English Cat and appearances with the Lake George Festival as Pizarro and Don Giovanni; Italian debut, Bologna, 1995, as Escamillo; Metropolitan Opera, 1995-96, as Balstrode (Peter Grimes) and Jochanaan; Escamillo at Vancouver, 1996. Address: c/o Atholl Still Ltd, Foresters Hall, 25-27 Westow St, London SE19 3RY, England.

GRINDE Nils, b. 8 Jan 1927, Enebakk, Norway. Musicologist; Organist. m. Kirsti Wilhelmsen. Education: Candidate Mag, Musicology, University of Oslo, 1953; Higher Examination in Organ, Oslo Music Conservatory, 1959. Career: Docent in Musicology; Currently Professor of Musicology, University of Oslo. Publications include: the Halfdan Kjerulf Bibliography, 1956; Halfdan Kjerulf's Piano Music, 1961; Textbook in Counterpoint in the Style of Bach, 1966; History of Norwegian Music, 1971; Norwegian Music: An Anthology, 1974; Contemporary Norwegian Music 1920-80, 1981; History of Norwegian Music, Russian Ed, 1982; A History of Norwegian Music, English Ed, 1991; Editor, Studia Musicologica Norvegica Volumes 2-4, 1976-78; Editor, Halfdan Kjerult: Collected Works, volumes 1-5, 1978-97; History of Norwegian Music 3rd edition, 1993; Editor, Edvard Grieg Piano Duet, dramatic music, 1982; Editor with Dan Fog, Edvard Grieg Songs, 1990-91. Contributions to: Grove's Dictionary, 6th edition; Sohlmans Musiklexikon, 2nd edition. Address: Slemdalsvn 91, B 0373 Oslo 3, Norway.

GRINDENKO Tatyana, b. 1946, Kharkov, Ukraine. Concert Violinist. Education: Studied at: Central Music School, Kharkov; Moscow Conservatoire. Debut: Kharkov, playing works by Bach, Wieniawski and Paganini, with orchestra, 1954, aged 8. Career: Gave concerts throughout Russia and Europe as soloist and with major ensembles and in chamber concerts; Appeared with New York Philharmonic, London Symphony Orchestra, Leipzig Gewandhaus, Berlin Radio Symphony, Vienna Symphony, Chamber Orchestra of Europe; Conductors have included Mravinsky, Kondrashin, Kurt Masur and Nikolaus Harnoncourt; Formed with Alexei Lyubimov, Academy of Ancient Music, Moscow, 1982 the only ensemble in Russia performing on authentic instruments; Tours 1988-: USA, Germany, France, Italy, Netherlands, India, Austria, Belgium, Czechoslovakia, Hungary and Finland; Festival engagements: Namur, Schleswig-Holstein, Passau, Lockenhaus, Brno and Bratislava; London debut, playing the Roslavetz Violin Concerto with Royal Philharmonic under Ashkenazy, 1991. Recordings: Many for various companies. Honours include: 1st Prize, World Youth Festival, Sofia, Bulgaria, 1968; Prizewinner, Tchaikovsky Competition, Moscow, 1970. Address: c/o Sonata, 11 Northpark Street, Glasgow, G20 7AA, Scotland.

GRIST Reri, b. 29 Feb 1932, New York, USA. Coloratura Soprano. Education: Music and Art High School, New York; Queens College. Debut: Consuelo, West Side Story, 1957. Career: Appeared at: Metropolitan Opera, New York, 1966-77; Vienna State Opera Austria, 1963-88; Munich State Opera, Germany, 1965-83; San Francisco Opera Association, 1963-76, 1983, 1990; Royal Opera House, Covent Garden, London, 1962-1974; La Scala, Milan, 1963, 1977-78; Opernhaus Zurich, Switzerland, 1960-66; Netherlands Opera, Amsterdam, 1990-91; Chicago Lyric Opera, 1964; Deutsche Oper, Berlin; Washington Opera Society; European Debut, Cologne, Germany, 1960; New York City Opera, 1959; Santa Fe Opera, New Mexico, 1959; Festival Appearances include: Salzburg, Austria, 1964-77; Munich Festival, 1967-83; Vienna Festival, 1963-80; Holland Festival, 1963; Glyndebourne Festival, 1962; Spoleto Festival, Italy, 1961; The most important new productions were with the stage directors Guenther Rennert, Giorgio Strehler, Pierre Audi, Lofti Mansouri, Otto Schenk, Carl Ebert, Josef Gielen, Joshua Logan and Jerome Robbins; Repertoire: Mozart: Susana, Queen of Night, Despina, Zerlina, Blondchen, Madame Herz; R Strauss: Zerbinetta, Sophie, Aminta, Italian Singer; Verdi: Gilda, Oscar, Nannetta; Donizetti: Adina, Norina, Marie; Rossini: Rosina, Fanny, Elvira; J Strauss: Adele; Offenbach: Olympia; Delibes: Lakmé; Poulenc: Constance; D Moore: Baby Doe; Britten: Titania; Morton Feldman: The Woman (Neither); Stravinsky: Le Rossignol; Concert appearances with NY Philharmonic, Wiener Philharmoniker, Boston Symphony, Munich Philharmonic, Die Reihe, etc and others with conductors: Bernstein, Ozawa, Boulez, Sawallisch, Paumgarnter, Cerha, etc; Song recitals in Austria, France, Germany and USA; Pedalogical activities: Professor of Voice, IN Univ, Bloomington, IN, 1981-83, Hochschule für Musik, Munich, Germany, 1984-95; Steans Institute, Ravinia, IL, Song interpretation 1992-; Tanglewood Festival, London Opera Centre, Hochschule der Kuenste: Basel, Switzerland. Recordings: Marriage of Figaro, Don Giovanni, Die Entführung, Così fan tutte, The Impressario, Il Re Pastore; Ariadne auf Naxos; Ballo in Maschera, Rigoletto; Scarlatti's Endimione e Cintia; Le Rossignol. Honour: Bayerische Kammersaengerin. Address: c/o Columbia Artists Management, 165 West 57th Street, New York, NY 10019, USA.

GRITTON Susan, b. England. Singer (Soprano). Education: Studied Botany at London and Oxford Universities, before a career in music. Career: Many engagements in such repertory as Mozart's Requiem, Schumann's Faust (at the Edinburgh Festival), Handel's Deborah (with the King's Consort at the Proms) and Schubert's Der Hirt auf dem Felsen; Orchestras include the Gothenburg Symphony, the LSO under Colin Davis, and the Orchestra of the Age of Enlightenment; Concerts at the London Proms under Richard Hickox, René Jacobs and Trevor Pinnock, 1996; Opera roles include Mozart's Susanna and Barbarina at Glyndebourne, Belinda in Dido and Aeneas at the Berlin Staatsoper, Fulvia in Handel's Ezio at the Théâtre des Champs-Elysées. Beethoven's Marzelline with the Rome Opera and Mozart's Blonde at the Istanbul Festival; Season 1997-98 with the Royal Opera in Rameau's Platée, Pilgrim's Progress by Vaughan Williams and Britten's Paul Bunyan; Atalanta in Xerxes, Caroline in the Fairy Queen and Handel's L'Allegro with English National Opera. Recordings include: Haydn's Schöpfungsmesse and Vivaldi's Ottone in Villa; Purcell/Britten arrangement; Handel's Deborah and Occasional Oratorio; Messiah and Vestas Feuer by Beethoven, Honours include: Winner, Kathleen Ferrier Memorial Prize, 1994. Address: c/o Lies Askonas Ltd, 6 Henrietta St, London WC2E 8LA, England.

GRINOV Vsevolod, b. 1968, Russia. Singer (Tenor). Education: Studied at the Russian Chorus Academy and the Russian Music Academy. Career: Soloist with the New Opera company of the Moscow Municipal Theatre, from 1990; Roles have included Bayan in Ruslan and Ludmilla, Lensky (Eugene Onegin) and Leicester in Maria Stuarda; Concerts with the Toscanini Orchestra, Italy, under Rudolf Barshai, with Beethoven's Missa solemnis and Bach's B minor Mass, 1991-92, Ghent 1992, as Don José in Peter Brook's Tragédie de Carmen. Recordings include: Filmed version of Eugene Onegin, 1993. Address: Lies Askonas Ltd, 8 Henrietta Street, London WC2E 8LA, England.

GROBEN Françoise, b. 4 Dec 1965, Luxembourg. Cellist. Education: Köln Musikhochschule with Boris Perganenshikov, Amadeus (also William Pleeth, Daniel Shafran). Debut: Musikverein, Vienna, Festspielhaus, Salzburg. Career: Major concert halls in Europe, Russia, Japan and Israel including Suntory Hall, Tokyo, St Petersburg Philharmonic Hall, Hamburg Musikhalle, Brussels Palais des Beaux Arts, Berlin Philharmonie; Soloist of St Petersburg Philharmonic Orchestra, Moscow Radio-TV Orchestra, Russian State Orchestra, NHK Orchestra, Tokyo; Jerusalem Philharmonic Orchestra, Conductor, Svetlanov, Kitajenko, Rostropovitch; Bavarian Radio Sinfonia; Festivals: Berliner Festwochen, Schleswig-Holstein Festival, Radio France Montpellier, Kuhno, St Petersburg Spring, Wallonie, MDR, Bratislava; Member of Zehetnair String Quartet. Recordings: many radio and television recordings, CDs of Busoni and Pulenc cello music. Honours: 2nd Prize (Silver Medal) Interntional Tchaikovsky Competition, Moscow, 1990; Several special prizes. Current Management: Cecilia, Weinstadt, Tokyo Artists. Address: Miolkestr 31, D 50674 Köln, Germany.

GRONER Earl, b. 23 Oct 1935, Stroudsburg, Pennsylvania, USA. Conductor; Teacher. Education: BMus, University of Michigan, Ann Arbor; MMus, New England Conservatory of Music; Scholarship Fellow, Tanglewood Music Center, 1956-57; Scholarship Student, National Orchestral Association, New York City, 1961-62. Career: Teacher, Lakeland Schools, Shrub Oak, New York, 1962-72; Scarsdale Public Schools, New York, 1972-; Music Director, Conductor, Empire State Symphony Orchestra, Empire State Pops Orchestra, Empire State Chamber Orchestra, 1987-. Honours: Phi Mu Alpha Sinfonia, 1956; Pi Kappa Lambda, 1958. Memberships include: President Elect (1997), New York State School Music Association; Chair, Council of Music Education Associations, New York State; Former Member, 7th US Army Symphony Orchestra, Stuttgart, Germany; Past President, Westchester County (NY) School Music Association; Vice Chair, University of Michigan School of Music Alumni Board of Governors; President, University of Michigan Club of Westchester; American Symphony Orchestra League; Conductors Guild; Music Educators National Conference; American String Teachers Association; National School Orchestra Association. Current Management: Empire State Concert Productions, 130 Garth Road, Suite 123, Scarsdale, NY 10583, USA. Address: 142 Garth Road, Scarsdale, NY 10583, USA.

GRONROOS Walton, b. 1939, Aland Islands, Finland. Singer (Baritone); Administrator. Education: Graduated as organist, Sibelius Academy, Helsinki 1966. Career: Served as cantor and organist at Lapinjarvi, 1964-71; Studied voice in Vienna and gave first concert 1971; Helsinki concert debut 1971, Stockholm 1973; Deutsche Oper Berlin from 1975, as Antonio in Le nozze di Figaro (debut), Mozart's Count, Luna; Sharpless and Dandini; Posa in Don Carlos, Cardinal Morone in Palestrina and Wolfram in Tannhäuser; Finnish National Opera from 1974, and Posa at the Savonlinna Festival; Maggio Musicale, Florence, 1983-87, all over the world; US debut, 1984, Chicago, Boston, Cleveland, New York; As concert artist has sung in Bach's St Matthew Passion in London and Paris (1979, 1981); Artistic Director, Savonlinna Festival 1987-91; Finnish National Opera from 1992. Recordings: Lieder by Schumann, Tannhäuser (EMI); Songs by Brahms, Sibelius and Rangström (BIS); Iphigénie en Tauride (Orfeo); Tchaikovsky Iolanta (Erato). Address: c/o Helsing katu 58, 00250 Helsinki, Finland.

GROOP Monica, b. 1958, Finland. Singer (Mezzo-soprano). Education: Studied at the Conservatory and Sibelius Academy in Helsinki; Masterclasses with Kim Borg, Hartmut Holl, Mitsuko Shirai and Erik Werba. Career: Has appeared with the Savonlinna Opera Festival from 1986 and the Finnish National Opera in Helsinki from 1987; Sang Dorabella in a production of Così fan tutte conducted by Salvatore Accardo at Naples, 1989; Concert performance of Cosi fan tutte in Rome, 1991; Concert engagements with leading Finnish and other Scandinvian orchestras under Erich Bergel, Jukka-Pekka Saraste, Leif Segerstam and Walter Weller; Tour of West Germany 1989 with the Drottningholm Baroque Orchestra in Bach's St John Passion (Bachwoche Ansbach Festival); Season 1989-90 with the Bach B minor Mass and St John Passion in Stockholm, Berlin and Edmonton, Canada; Mozart's Betulia Liberata with the Bachakademie in Stuttgart under Helmuth Rilling, 1991; Mahler/Schoenberg project with Philippe Herreweghe and the Ensemble Musique Oblique; Season 1991/92 with Cherubino at Aix-en-Provence, Wellgunde and the Walküre Waltraute at Covent Garden (debut), the Missa Solemnis at Aix, 1992; Tour of Così fan tutte with Sigiswald Kuijken to Spain, France and Portugal and appearances with the Drottningholm Theatre at the Barbican; Season 1993 with Cherubino at Toulouse, the Composer at the Paris Opéra Comique and Bach's St John Passion in Spain, Lucerne and Stockholm; Sang Mélisande for Netherlands Opera, 1996. Recordings include: Bach B minor Mass; Così fan tutte for television. Current Management: IMG Artists Europe (GM); Nordic Artists Management (Nordic Countries). Address: c/o IMG Artists Europe, Media House, 3 Burlington Lane, London W4 2TH, England.

GROSCHEL Werner, b. 18 Sept 1940, Nuremberg, Germany. Singer (Bass). Education: Studied at the Richard Strauss Conservatory Munich with Marcel Cordes and Josef Metternich. Debut: Flensburg 1967, as Fiesco in Simon Boccanegra. Career: Member of the Zurich Opera from 1972, as Rocco, Mephistopheles, Falstaff (Nicolai) and Dikoy in Katya Kabanova; Mozart's Osmin, Don Giovanni and Sarastro; Verdi's King Philip, Silva (Ernani) and Zaccaria (Nabucco); Wagner's Daland, Landgrave, King Henry and Pogner; Sang in the 1975 premiere of Klebe's Ein Wahrer Held and the premiere of Kelterborn's Ein Engel kommt nach Babylon, 1977; Guest appearances elsewhere in Switzerland and in Germany; Many concert engagements, notably in music by Bach and Monteverdi.

Recordings include: Plutone in Monteverdi's Orfeo, L'Incoronazione di Poppea and Il Ritorno di Ulisse. Address: c/o Opernhaus Zurich, Falkenstrasse 1, CH-8008 Zurich, Switzerland.

GROSGURIN Daniel, b. 13 Jul 1949, Geneva, Switzerland. Cellist. m. Ferhan Güraydin, 21 Jun 1990. Education: Classical Baccalaureat, Geneva, 1967; Conservatoire Geneva, 1st Prize, 1968; Master of Music, Indiana University, 1972. Debut: London, 1976. Career: Lucerne Festival, 1975; Festival Strings, Lucerne, 1975, 1978; Regular appearances with Orchestre de la Suisse Romande, 1978-; Chamber music with Martha Argerich, Professor, State Music College, Heidelberg, Mannheim, Germany, 1978-90; Tours with Stuttgart Philharmonic, 1987; Professor, Geneva Conservatory of Music, 1990; Salzburg Festival, 1990; London Festival Hall with LSCO, 1991; Tibor Varga Festival, 1991; Eastern Music Festival, USA, 1992; Founder of Les Solistes de Genève, piano trio with Jean-Pierre Wallez and Dominique Merlet, 1995. Recordings: Swiss and German Radio Recordings; TV Programme with Pierre Fournier. Hobbies: Literature; Swimming; Hiking. Current Management: Wissmer, Geneva, Switzerland. Address: 15 Route de Florissant, 1206 Geneva, Switzerland.

GROSS Eric, b. 16 Sept 1926, Vienna, Austria. Composer; Lecturer. m. Pamela Margaret Mary Davies. Education: MA, MLitt, DMus, University of Aberdeen, Scotland; FTCL, LMusTCL, Trinity College of Music, London. Career: Freelance Pianist, Arranger, Conductor, Composer, 1941-58; Lecturer, New South Wales, Australia, 1959-60; Lecturer, Senior Lecturer, Associate Professor, Department of Music, Sydney University, New South Wales, 1960-91, retired 1991; Visiting Professor of Music, University of Guyana, Georgetown, 1989; Now Freelance Composer. Compositions: Symphonies Nos 1 and 2; Violin Concerto; Piano Concerto; Oboe Concerto; 2 Mandolin Concertos; The Amorous Judge, opera; Pacem in Terris, cantata; The Shepherd, cantata; 5 Burns Songs, 6 Henry Lawson Settings. Recordings: Symphony No 1, 1975; Quintet for Alto Saxophone and String Quartet; Klavierstücke I, II, III, 1990; Concerto No I for Mandolin and Chamber Orchestra; Concerto No II for Mandolin and Chamber Orchestra; 6 Henry Lawson Settings and 5 Burns Songs. Publications: Background and Problems for an Historical and Critical Edition of the String Quartets of F X Dusek, 1972; Music Manuscripts in the Library of St Bonifaz, Munich - a Preliminary Catalogue, 1975. Contribution to: The Contemporary Australian Composer and Society, 1971. Honours: DAAD Scholarship, Germany, 1974, 1981; Albert H Maggs Composition Award, Melbourne University, 1976. Memberships: Fellowship of Australian Composers; Musicological Society of Australia; MAGA. Hobby: Soccer. Current Management: Inquiries to Australian Music Centre, Sydney, New South Wales. Address: 54/84 St George's Crescent, Drummoyne, NSW 2047, Australia.

GROSS Ruth, b. 1959, Kleve, Germany. Singer (Soprano). Education: Studied Viola at Essen, Voice with Edda Moser, Cologne. Debut: Regensburg, as Leonore in Fidelio, 1987. Career: Sang at Ulm, 1988-89, notably in Golem by d'Albert and in operetta; Bayreuth Festival, 1989-90, as Ortlinde in Die Walküre; Sang Leonore at Basle, 1989; Has appeared at Staatsoper Stuttgart, 1989-, as Iphigénie (in Aulide), Arabella and Elsa in production of Lohengrin conducted by Silvio Varviso. Address: Staatsoper Stuttgart, Oberer Schlossgarten 6, 7000 Stuttgart, Germany.

GROVES Paul, b. 24 November 1964, Lake Charles, Los Angeles, USA. Singer (Tenor). m. Charlotte Hellekant. Education: Louisiana State University; Juillian Opera. Debut: Steuermann in Der fliegende Holländer, Metropolitan Opera, 1992. Career: Appearances in New York as Mozart's Ferrando and Verdi's Fenton, and roles in Ariadne, Death in Venice, Les Troyans, Parsifal, Die Zauberflöte and The Ghosts of Versailles; European debut as Belfiore in La Finta Giardiniera, for Welsh National Opera; Mozart's Don Ottavio at Salzburg, Idamante at Geneva and Tamino at Munich; Season 1995-96 with Tamino at La Scala, Tom Rakewell for WNO and New York recital debut at Alice Tully Hall; Season 1996-97 with Tom Rakewell at the Paris Châtelet, Nemorino, Flamand in Capriccio and Rossini's Almaviva at the Vienna Staatsoper; Recitals throughout the USA; Further roles include Nadir for Vancouver Opera, Lensky at St Louis and Arturo in I Puritani for Boston Lyric Opera. Recordings include: Rigoletto Parsifal and Idomeneo (DGG); Der fliegende Holländer (Sony); Manon Lescaut (Decca). Address: c/o IMG Artists, Media House, 3 Burlington Lane, London W4 2TH, England.

GRUBE Michael, b. 12 May 1954, Uberlingen. Violin-Virtuoso; Violin Professor. Education: Privately with his violinist father, Professor Max-Ludwig Grube; Further violinistic studies with Professor Henryk Szeryng, Professor Ivan Galamin, Professor Eugene Effenberger; Conservatory Diploma, 1975; Studies of Musicology and Composition (Professor Gunther Becker). Debut: West Berlin, 1964. Career: Concert Soloist in 110 countries of all continents, performances before His Majesty King Tupou IV of Tonga and Queen of Tonga; Concerts and Festival Performances in Vienna, Copenhagen, Prague, Warsaw, Leningrad, Moscow, New York, Washington DC, Jerusalem, Caracas, Buenos Aires, Canberra, Singapore, Osaka, Bangkok, Bogota, Sao Paulo, Delhi, Panama City, Madrid, Istanbul; Pro Musica International USA. Compositions: Souvenir de Senegal for Solo Violin (Radio Dakar); Hommage a Colville Young an Olanchito (Landestonkunstler Festival 1986-87). Recordings: Garnet Records, Dusseldorf; Violin Concertos by Bruch, Mendelssohn, Mozart; Violin Music by Dvorak; Smetana, Suk, Handel, Paganini, Reger, Haas, also with Max Ludwig Grube (violin) and Helen Grube (Piano). Hobbies: Philosophy; Indian Classical music; Austrian bakery of the old tradition. Current Management: Konzertdirektion Olga Altmann. Current Management: Konzertdirektion Olga Altmann, Jaquingasse 37/55, -1030 Wien, Austria.

GRUBER Andrea, b. 1965, New York City, New York, USA. Singer (Soprano). Debut: Scottish Opera, 1990, as Leonore in Forza. Career: Sang Third Norn in Götterdämmerung at the Metropolitan, 1990, followed by Elisabeth de Valois and Aida at the Met; Amelia (Ballo), Amelia (Simon Boccanegra); Opera debut as Leonora in Forza with Scottish Opera; Professional debut as Soprano Soloist in Verdi's Requiem with James Levine, Chicago Symphony, Ravinna Festival, 1989; Seattle Opera, 1992, as Aida, Cologne, 1993, as Amelia (Ballo in maschera); Further guest appearances in Toronto, at the Vienna Staatsoper and in Italy; Covent Garden debut 1996, Arabella; Sang Chrysothemis in Elektra at Seattle, 1996. Recording: Götterdämmerung. Address: c/o Metropolitan Opera, Lincoln Center, New York, NY 10023, USA.

GRUBER H(einz) K(arl), b. 3 Jan 1943, Vienna, Austria. Composer. Education: Studied at the Vienna Hochschule für Musik 1957-63 and with Gottfried von Einem 1963-64. Career: Sang in Vienna Boys' Choir 1953-57; Double Bass player in ensemble Die Reihe from 1961; Principal Double Bass Tonkünstler Orchestra 1963-69; Co-Founder of MOB Art and Tone ART ensemble 1968-71; Has worked with Austrian Radio, Vienna, from 1969; conducted the premiere of his opera Gomorra at the Vienna Volksoper, 1993. Compositions: 4 pieces for solo violin 1963; Manhattan Broadcasts 1962-64; 5 Kinderlieder for female voices 1965, revised 1980; The Expulsion from Paradise for speakers and 6 solo instruments 1966, revised 1979; 3 MOB Pieces for 7 instruments and percussion 1968, revised 1977; 6 Episodes from a Discontinued Chronicle for piano 1967; Frankenstein !! for baritone, chansonnier and orchestra 1976-77, ensemble version, 1979; Phantom-Bilder for small orchestra 1977; Violin Concerto 1977-78; Demilitarized Zones for brass band 1979; Charivari for orchestra 1981; Castles in the Air for piano 1981; Rough Music, concerto for percussion and orchestra 1982; Anagram for 6 cellos 1987; Nebelsteinmusik (2nd Violin Concerto) 1988; Cello Concerto 1989; Gomorra (opera), 1992; Gloria von Jaxtberg, music theatre, 1992-94; Television appearances include Nekrophilius the Pawnbroker in Bring Me the Head of Amadeus (for the Mozart Bicentenary, 1991). Address: c/o Boosey & Hawkes Ltd, 295 Regent Street, London W1, England.

GRUBEROVA Edita, b. 23 Dec 1946, Bratislava, Czechoslovakia. Singer (Soprano). Education: Studied with Maria Medvecká in Prague and with Ruthilde Boesch in Vienna. Debut: Bratislava 1968, as Rosina. Career: Sang at the Vienna Staatsoper 1970, as the Queen of Night: sang Zerbinetta in Vienna 1976; Glyndebourne Festival 1973; Salzburg Festival from 1974, as the Queen of Night, conducted by Herbert von Karajan; Metropolitan Opera debut 1977, as the Queen of Night; Covent Garden 1984, as Giulietta in a new production of I Capuleti e i Montecchi by Bellini; Guest appearances at the Bregenz Festival and at La Scala, the Munich Staatsoper (Massenet's Manon) and the Hamburg Staatsoper; Other roles include Gilda, Lucia, Constanze and Violetta; Sang Lucia at La Scala, 1984, Chicago 1986 and Barcelona 1987; La Scala 1987, Donna Anna, Zurich Opera 1988, as Marie in La Fille du Régiment; Metropolitan Opera 1989, as Violetta; Sang Rossini's Rosina and Semiramide (concert) at Munich 1990; Barcelona 1990, as Ariadne; Vienna Staatsoper Oct 1990, as Elizabeth I in Donizetti's Roberto Devereux, Season 1992 as Lucia at Munich and Semiramide at Zurich; Linda di Chamounix, 1995; Anna Bolena at the 1997 Munich Festival. Recordings: Video of Rigoletto, with Luciano Pavarotti; Lucia di Lammermoor; La Traviata; I Puritani; Roberto Devereux; Linda di Chamounix; La Fille du Régiment; Don Giovanni; Die Zauberflöte. Address: Harold Holt Ltd, 31 Sinclair Road, London W14 0NS, England.

GRUBERT Naum, b. 1951, Riga, USSR. Pianist. Education: Studied at the Riga Conservatory and with Professor Gutman in Moscow. Career: Performed first in Russia, Eastern Europe, Italy and Finland; Emigrated from USSR 1983 and has performed with the London Symphony, the Hague Philharmonic, Netherlands Philharmonic Orchestre de la Suisse Romande, Helsinki Philharmonic and orchestras in Germany and Spain; Conductors include Paavo Berglund, Sergiu Commisiona, Franz-Paul Decker, Valeri Gergiev, Hartmut Haenchen, Vernon Handley, Thomas Sanderling, Horst Stein and Christopher Seaman; Further engagements with the Rotterdam Philharmonic, the Tonkunstler Orchestra Vienna and the Scottish National Orchestra. Honours include: 2nd Prize, International Piano Competition, Montreal, 1977; Prize winner at the 1978 Tchaikovsky Competition, Moscow. Address: c/o Ingpen and Williams Ltd, 14 Kensington Court, London W8 5DN, England.

GRUENBERG Erich, b. 12 Oct 1924, Vienna, Austria. Violinist. Education: Studied in Vienna and at the Jerusalem Conservatory. Debut: Jerusalem 1938. Career: Leader of the Palestine Broadcasting Corporation Orchestra 1938-45; Solo career from 1947; Leader of the Stockholm Philharmonic orchestra 1956-58, the London Symphony 1962-65, Royal Philharmonic 1972-76; Appearances as soloist throughout Europe, the USA and Canada, Australia, Holland, Germany, Switzerland and Scandinavia; Gave the first Russian performance of Britten's Concerto, in Moscow; Engagements with the Hungarian State Symphony Orchestra in Budapest and visits to the Far East; Associated with contemporary works by Goehr, Gerhard and david Morgan; Formerly leader of the London String Quartet and chamber music player with William Glock, Franz Reizenstein, Edmund Rubbra and William Pleeth; Professor at the Royal Academy of Music; Master Classes and Competition Jury appearances around the world. Recordings: Beethoven's Concerto conducted by Horenstein and the complete Violin Sonatas with David Wilde; Works by Bach, Stravinsky, Messiaen (Quatuor pour la fin du Temps), Durko, Parry and Vaughan Williams; Labels include EMI, Decca, Argo, Chandos, Hyperion, Hungaroton and Lyrita. Honours include: Winner, Carl Flesch Competition, London, 1947. Address: c/o Intermusica, 16 Duncan Terrace, London N1 8BZ, England.

GRUENBERG Joanna, b. 1957, Stockholm, Sweden. Concert Pianist. Education: Studied with Fanny Waterman, Louis Kentner and Peter Frankl; Guildhall School of Music with James Gibb. Career: Appearances at the Aldeburgh and Harrogate Festivals, at the Fairfields Hall, Croydon and for the City Music Society, London; Festival Hall debut 1978, with the Royal Philharmonic Orchestra; Recital tours with her father, Erich Gruenberg; Concerts with the GLC series at Ranger House and visits to Ireland and Spain; Played with the Bournemouth Symphony and Sinfonietta 1983-85; Barbican Centre with Tchaikovsky's 1st Concerto and the Grieg Concerto with the Royal Liverpool Philharmonic, 1984-85; Further engagements with the Hallé Orchestra (Mendelssohn's 1st Concerto, 1988) the Philharmonia at the Barbican. Recordings include: Album for Unicorn. Records include: RAOS, Silver Medal 1980. Address: Intermusica Artists' Management, 16 Duncan Terrace, London N1 8BZ, England.

GRUESSER Eva, b. 1965, Black Forest, Germany. Violinist. Education: Studied at: Freiburg Hochschule; Rubin Academy in Jerusalem; Juilliard School, USA. Career: Leader of Lark Quartet, USA; Recent concert tours to: Australia; Taiwan; Hong Kong; China; Germany; Netherlands; US appearances at: Lincoln Center, NY; Kennedy Center, Washington DC; Boston; Los Angeles; Philadelphia, St Louis; San Francisco; Repertoire includes quartets by Haydn, Mozart, Beethoven, Schubert, Dvořák, Brahms, Borodin, Bartók, Debussy and Shostakovich. Honours include: With Lark Quartet: Gold Medals at 1990 Naumberg and 1991 Shostakovich Competitions; Prizewinner: Premio Paulio Borciani, Reggio Emilia, 1990; Karl Klinger Competition, Munich, 1990; London International String Quartet, 1991; Melbourne Chamber Music, 1991. Address: c/o Sonata (Lark Quartet), 11 Northpark Street, Glasgow, G20 7AA, Scotland.

GRUHN Nora, b. 6 Mar 1905, London, England. Singer (Soprano). Education: Studied with her father, Hermann Grunebaum, and with Hermine Bosetti in Munich. Debut: Kaiserslautern 1928. Career: Sang at the Cologne Opera 1929-30; Covent Garden 1929-32 and 1936, as Adele in Die Fledermaus and as Gretel; Sang at Sadler's Wells from 1945, notably in the 1946 British premiere of I Quattro Rusteghi, by Wolf-Ferrari. Recordings include: Woodbird in Siegfried with Lauritz Melchoir (HMV). Contributions to: Opera Magazine (Articles, Not Quite a Prima Donna).

GRUMBACH Raimund, b. 20 Jan 1934, Eibelstadt, Wurzburg, Germany. Singer (Baritone). Education: Studied in Wurzburg. Career: Sang at the Stadttheater Wurzburg 1956-59; Nuremberg Opera 1959-62; Bayerische Staatsoper Munich from 1962, as Mozart's Sharples and Marcello; Wolfram in Tannhäuser; Guest appearances in Edinburgh (1965, with the Munich company), Paris, Vienna, Madrid and Tokio; Many concert appearances; Teacher at the Munich Hochschule from 1972. Recordings: Il Barbiere di Siviglia (Deutsche Grammophon); Der Mond by Orff (Eurodisc); Leoncavallo's La Bohème (Orfeo); Feuersnot by Strauss (Acanta); Sutermeister's Romeo und Julia; Der Freischütz (Decca); Tristan und Isolde (Philips); Intermezzo (EMI). Address: c/o Staatliche Hochschule für Musik, Arcisstrasse 12, Munich 12, Germany.

GRUMMET Adey, b. 1960, Adelaide, South Australia. Singer (Soprano). Education: BMus Elder Conservatorium, Adelaide. Career: Concerts include Messiah, Elijah, Rossini's Stabat Mater and Petite Messe, Haydn's Nelson Mass, Poulenc's Gloria and Orff's Carmina Burana; Solo recitals include New College, Oxford, and St John's Smith Square; Founded Women's Vocal Group The Curate's Egg, 1992; Education projects include ENO Baylis Programme; Opera includes premiere productions of Playing Away by Mason and In The House of Crossed Desires by Woolrich (1994-95); Roles include Mozart's Donna Elvira and First Boy with English Touring Opera, Adele in Fledermaus for D'Oyly Carte, Grilletta in Haydn's Apothecary and Oscar (Ballo in Maschera); Further appearances on South Bank, London, and with Sinfonia 21. Recordings include: Die Fledermaus (Sony); Mozart's Blondchen (Die Entführung) with Opera d'Autome, France. Address: C&M Craig Services Ltd, 3 Kersley Street, London SW11 4PR, England.

GRUNDHEBER Franz, b. 27 Sept 1937, Trier, Germany. Singer (Baritone). Education: After service in the Luftwaffe studied in Trier and Hamburg; Further study at Indiana University and the Music Academy of the West, San Diego. Career: Has sung at the Hamburg Staatsoper from 1966; Tours of the USA and many appearances in European opera houses; Vienna Staatsoper 1983, as Mandryka in Arabella; Salzburg Festival 1985, as Olivier in Capriccio; Other roles include Mozart's Masetto and Guglielmo, Faninal in Der Rosenkavalier, and Escamillo; Salzburg and Savonnlina Festivals 1989, as Orestes and Amonasro; Sang Barak in Die Frau ohne Schatten at the Holland Festival, 1990; Season 1992 as Germont at Barcelona; Wozzeck at the Châtelet, Paris, and Macbeth at Cologne; Sang Wozzeck at Chicago, 1994; Rigoletto at Covent Garden, 1997. Recordings include: Video of Elektra (as Orestes) conducted by Abbado, Don Giovanni; Video of Wozzeck conducted by Barenboim, 1997; Doktor Faust by Busoni; Die drei Pintos by Weber/Mahler. Address: Kaye Artists Management, 7 Chertsey Road, Woking GU21 5AB, England.

GRUNEWALD Eugenie, b. 1962, USA. Singer (Mezzo-soprano). Career: Appearances as Amneris in Aida at Michigan, Orlando, Austin, Miami and for the San Francisco Opera (1997); European debut as Giovanna Seymour in Anna Bolena at Barcelona; Dido in Les Troyens at Toulouse and Athens, Tchaikovsky's Joan of Arc and Lyubov (Mazeppa) with the Opera Orchestra of New York; Azucena and Wagner's Venus with Austin Lyric Opera, the mezzo roles in Puccini's Trittico with the Chicago Lyric Opera and Santuzza with Tulsa Opera; Fenena in Nabucco with Connecticut Opera, Preziosilla at Barcelona and the Nurse in Dukas' Ariane et Barbe-bleue at Hamburg (1997); Concerts with the New World Symphony under Michael Tilson Thomas, the Boston Philharmonic, Little Orchestra Society and the Pacific Symphony at the Aspen Festival. Address: c/o Austin Lyric Opera, PO Box 984, Austin, TX 78767, USA.

GRUSKIN Shelley, b. 20 July 1936, New York, USA. Flautist; Recorder Player. Education: Studied at Eastman School, Rochester, graduated 1956. Career: Member, New York Pro Musica, 1961-74, playing recorder and other early wind instruments; Associated with such singers as Charles Bressler, Bethany Beardslee, Jan De Gaetani, Russel Oberlin; Premiere of liturgical drama The Play of Herod at the Cloisters, New York 1963; Tour of Europe, 1963, USSR 1964; Final performances with group in Marco da Gagliano's La Dafne, 1974; Formed Philidor Trio 1965, with soprano Elizabeth Humes and harpischordist Edward Smith; Performances with group until 1980; Teacher of music history and early music performance practice at various institutions; artist-in-residence, College of St Scholastica, Duluth, Minnesota 1978-; President of the American Recorder Society, 1980-88. Recordings include: Albums with New York Pro Musica and Philidor Trio. Address: College of St Scholastica, Duluth, Minnesota 55811, USA.

GUADAGNO Anton, b. 2 May 1925, Castellammare de Golfo, Trapani, Italy. Conductor. m. Dolores Guidone, 1 son. Education: Graduate, Conservatory of Vincenzo Bellini; Degree in Conducting, Degree Composition, Conservatory Santa Cecilia, Rome; Postgraduate Conducting, Academia Mozarteum. Career: Conducted Opera in Mexico City then made Carnegie Hall Debut, 1952; Also conducted Philadelphia Lyric Opera and the Vienna Staatsoper; London debut 1970 at Drury Lane, Andrea Chenier; Covent Garden debut 1971, Un Ballo in Maschera; Conducted La Fanciulla del West at the Deutsche Oper Berlin 1989, Luisa Miller at the Shubert Theatre Philadelphia and Andrea Chenier at Versailles. Compositions: Hymn for Holy Infancy, Vatican, Holy Year, 1950. Recordings: On Angel Records, RCA Victor, London Decca and EMI. Honours: 1st Prize, conducting, Academia Mozarteum 1948; Silver Medal, Lima, Peru, 1953; Gold Medal, Mexico, 1957; Order of Cavalier, Italian Government, 1965; Gold Medal, Chile, 1970, Spain, 1971; Critic's Award, Chile, 1970; Grand Prix du Disque, Paris, 1973. Current Management: Columbia Artists Management Inc, 165 W 57th Street, New York, NY 10019, USA.

GUARNERA Piero, b. 1962, Italy. Singer (Baritone). Debut: Spoleto, 1987, as Belcore. Career: Has sung at Spoleto as Malatesta, Enrico (Lucia di Lammermoor) and Ned in Treemonisha; Rome Opera debut, 1989, as Masetto, followed by Gluck's Oreste and Verdi's Ford; Other roles include Rossini's Figaro (at Naples), Mozart's Figaro (Florence), Fabrizio in Salieri's La locandiera at Lugo, Dandini in Malaga, Marcello on tour to Holland (1994), and Tarquinius in The Rape of Lucretia; La Scala Milan from 1990, in Idomeneo, Henze's Das verratene Meer and Arabella. Address: Atholl Still Ltd, Foresters Hall, 25-27 Westow Street, London SE19 3RY, England.

GUARRERA Frank, b. 3 Dec 1923, Philadelphia, Pennsylvania, USA. Singer (Baritone). Education: Studied with Richard Bonelli at the Curtis Institute, Philadelphia. Debut: New York City Opera 1947, as Silvio in Pagliacci. Career: Metropolitan Opera from 1948, as Escamillo, Amonasro, Don Alfonso, Eugene Onegin, Gianni Schicchi, Germont and Ford, 34 roles in 427 performances; La Scala Milan 1958, as Zurga in Les Pecheurs de Perles; Other appearances in London, San Francisco, Paris, Chicago, and Los Angeles. Recordings include: Faust (Philips); Cavalleria Rusticana, Così fan tutte and Lucia di Lammermoor (CBS); Falstaff conducted by Toscanini (RCA). Address: 423 Second Avenue, Bellmawr, NJ 08031, USA.

GUBAIDULINA Sofia, b. 24 Oct 1931, Chistopol, USSR. Composer. Education: Graduated from Kazan Conservatory, 1954; Moscow Conservatory, 1954-59, with Nikolai Peiko; Postgraduate work under Vissarion Shebalin. Career: Has lived in Moscow as freelance composer, 1963-91, since 1991 in Germany; Regarded as a leading representative of New Music in Russia; Offertorium performed at the 1991 Promenade Concerts, London. Compositions: Orchestral: Fairytale Poem, 1971; Stufen (Steps), 1972-92; Detto II for cello and ensemble, 1972; Concerto for bassoon and low strings, 1975; Concerto for orchestra and jazz band, 1976; Te Salutant, Capriccio for large light orchestra, 1978; Introitus, concerto for piano and chamber orchestra, 1978; Offertorim, concerto for violin and orchestra, 1980-86; Seven Words for cello, bayan and strings, 1982; Stimmen...vetummen..., symphony in 12 movements, 1986; Answer without Question, collage for 3 orchestras, 1988; Pro et Contra for large orchestra, 1989; And: The Festivities at Their Height, for cello and orchestra, 1993; Vocal: Phacelia, vocal cycle for soprano and orchestra, 1956; Night in Memphis, cantata for mezzo-soprano, male chorus and chamber orchestra, 1968-92; Roses, 5 romances for soprano and piano, 1972; Counting Rhymes, 5 children's songs, 1973; Hour of the Soul for mezzo-soprano and large orchestra, 1976; Perception for soprano, baritone and 7 string instruments, 1981-86; Hommage à Marina Tsvetava, suite in 5 movements for chours a cappella,1984; Hommage à T S Eliot for soprano and octet, 1987-91; Witty Waltzing in the style of Johann Strauss for soprano and octet, 1987, for piano and string quartet, 1989; Jauchzt vor Gott for chorus and organ, 1989; Alleluja for chorus, boys soprano, organ and large orchestra, 1990; Aus dem Stundenbuch for cello, orchestra, male chorus and female speaker, 1991; Chamber: Now Always Snow for chamber ensemble and chamber choir on poems of Gennady Aigi, 1993; Piano Quintet, 1957; Allegro rustico for flute and piano, 1963; Five Etudes for harp, double bass and percussion, 1965; Vivente non vivente for synthesizer, 1970; Concordanza for chamber ensemble, 1971; String Quartet No 1, 1971; Music for harpsichord and percussion, 1971-93; Rumore e Silenzio for percussion and harpsichord, 1974; Ten Preludes for solo cello, 1974; Quattro for 2 trumpets and 2 trombones, 1974; Sonata for double bass and piano, 1975; Light and Darkness for solo organ, 1976; Dots, Lines and Zigzag for bass clarinet and piano, 1976; Trio for 3 trumpets, 1976; Duo-Sonata for 2 bassoons, 1977; Quartet for 4 flutes, 1977; Misterioso for 7 percussionists, 1977; Detto I sonata for organ and percussion, 1978; De profundis for solo bayan, 1978; Sounds of the Forest for flute and piano, 1978; In Croce for cello and organ, 1979; Jubilatio for 4 percussionists, 1979; Garten von Freuden und Traurigkeiten for flute, harp and viola (speaker ad lib), 1980; Rejoice, sonata for violin and cello, 1981; Descensio for ensemble, 1981; In the Beginning there was Rhythm for 7 percussionists, 1984; Et exspecto, sonata for solo bayan, 1985; Quasi Hoquetus for viola, bassoon, cello and piano, 1985; String Quartet No 2, 1987, String Quartet No 3, 1987; Two Songs on German Folk Poetry for soprano, flute, harpsichord and cello, 1988; String Trio, 1988; Silenzio, 5 pieces for bayan, violin and cello, 1991; Even and Uneven for 7 percussionists, 1991; Tatar dance for 2 double basses and bayan, 1992; Dancer on a Tightrope, for violin and piano, 1993; Meditation on the Bach-Choral Vor deinen Thron tret ich hiermit, for harpsichord, 2 violins, viola, cello and double bass, 1993; String quartet No 4, 1993; Piano Music. Address: Internationale Musikverlage Hans Sikorski, Johnsallee 23, 20139 Hamburg, Germany.

GUBRUD Irene (Ann), b. 4 Jan 1947, Canby, Minnesota, USA. Singer (Soprano). Education: Studied at St Olaf College, Northfield, Minnesota, and at Juilliard, New York. Career: Concert engagements with leading US orchestras; Tour of East Germany with the Baltimore Symphony; Premiere of Star-Child by George Crumb with the New York Philharmonic conducted by Pierre Boulez, 1977; European engagements with the Stuttgart and Bavarian Radio Orchestras; Opera debut 1981, as Mimi with the Minnesota Opera, St Paul; Recitals at Lincoln and Kennedy Centers 1981; Appearances at the Aspen, Blossom and Meadowbrook Festivals; Teacher at Washington University, St Louis, 1976-81. Honours include: First Prize, Concert Artists Guild competition 1970; Ford Foundation performance competition 1971; Rockefeller and Minna Kaufmann Ruud competitions, 1972; Winner, Naumburg International Voice Competition, 1980.

GUDBJORNSSON Gunnar, b. 1965, Reykjavik, Iceland. Singer (Tenor). Education: Studied at New Music School, Reykjavik, with Hannelore Kuhse in Berlin, and with Nicolai Gedda in London. Debut: Icelandic Opera, as Don Ottavio, 1988; Sang Clotarco in Haydn's Armida at Buxton Festival, 1988; Appearances with Opera North and Welsh National Opera; Opera galas at St David's Hall, Cardiff, and with Royal Philharmonic; Sang the Lawyer in Punch and Judy at Aldeburgh Festival and engaged with Wiesbaden Opera as Almaviva, Ottavio and Tamino; Concert repertoire includes St Matthew Passion (Queen's Hall, Edinburgh), Britten's Serenade, Die schöne Müllerin; Recitals at Covent Garden and Wigmore Hall, 1993; Further appearances at the BBC Proms (Les Noces, 1996), the Opéra Bastille, Bregenz Festival, Aix-en-Provence, Geneva and Lisbon. Recordings include: Die schöne Müllerin; Albums in Mozart complete edition; Radio recordings for BBC, Radio France and Hessische with broadcasts in most of Europe. Honours: Gunnar Thoroddson Scholarship, 1987; Leoni Sonnering Prize, 1988. Address: Harold Holt Ltd, 31 Sinclair Road, London W14 0NS, England. Address: 5 rue Mazenod, 69003 Lyon, France.

GUDIASHVILI Nikoloz, b. 19 May 1913, Tbilisi, Georgia. Composer. m. Elene Pataraia, 6 June 1947, 2 daughters. Education: Tbilisi Conservatoire. Debut: Concerto for Piano & Orchestra, Tbilisi Theatre. Career: Assistant Professor, 1966, Professor, 1981-, Tbilisi Conservatorie. Compositions: Concerto for Violin, Cello, Piano & Symphony Orchestra, 1957; Symphony No 3, The The Heros of Tbilisi; 5 String Quartets. Recordings: 1st Concerto for Piano & Orchestra; Georgian Fantasy; IVth Quartet; String Quintet. Honours: Merited Artist of Georgia, 1961; Georgia's Peoples Artist, 1989; Georgia's State Prize, 1990. Memberships: Georgias Union of Composers; Soviet Union of Composers. Hobby: Chess. Address: Mosashvili St 8, 380062 Tbilisi, Georgia.

GUDMUNDSEN-HOLMGREEN Pelle, b. 21 Nov 1932, Copenhagen, Denmark. Composer. m. Gunvor Kaarsberg, 21 Nov 1959, 1 s, 1 d. Education: Studied Theory and History of Music at The Royal Danish Conservatory of Music, 1953-58. Career: Teacher, Royal Danish Academy of Music in Aarhus, 1967-73; Works have been played at Scandinavian Music Days, Royal Danish Ballet and Music Festival, ISCM, on Danish Television and on Radio worldwide; Music for plays and films. Compositions include: Terr Stages ace in 5 Stages for Woodwind Quintet, 1970; Plateaux pour Deux for Cello and Percussion, 1970; Mirror II for Orchestra, 1973; Songs Without for Mezzo Soprano and Piano, 1976; Symphony, Antiphony for Orchestra, 1977; String Quartet V Step by Step, 1982; VI Parting, 1983; VII Parted, 1984; VIII Ground, commissioned by the Kronos Quartet, 1986; Concord, Sinfonietta, 1987; Octopus for Organ and 2 Players, 1989; Concerto Grosso for String Quartet and Symphonic Ensemble, 1990, For Piano, 1992; Turn for Guitar, Bass Flute, Harp and Soprano, 1993; Traffic, Sinfonietta, 1994. Recordings: Solo for Electric Guitar, 1972; Symphony, Antiphony for Orchestra, 1977; Prelude to Your Silence, octet, 1978; Your Silence, septet for Soprano, 1978; Mirror Pieces for Clarinet Trio, 1980; Triptych, concerto for Percussion, 1985. Contributions to: Dansk Musiktidsskrift; Nutida Musik. Honour: Antiphony, Symphony was awarded the 1980 Music Prize of the Nordic Council. Membership: The Society for the Publication of Danish Music. Address: Eggersvej 29, 2900 Hellerup, Denmark.

GUELFI Giangiacomo, b. 21 Dec 1924, Rome, Italy. Singer (Baritone). Education: Studied in Florence and with Titta Ruffo. Debut: Spoleto 1950, as Rigoletto. Career: Sang at the Teatro Fenice Venice and in Catania; La Scala Milan from 1952; Chicago Lyric Opera from 1954; Appearances in Rome, Paris, Cairo, Naples, Berlin and Dallas; Covent Garden 1975, as Scarpia, Chénier; Verona Arena 1960, 1970, 1972; Rio de Janeiro 1964, as Macbeth and Scarpia; Lisbon 1965, as Guillaume Tell; Metropolitan Opera 1970, as Scarpia, and Jack Rance in La Fanciulla del West; Appeared at the Maggio Musicale Florence in revivals of L'Africaine by Meyerbeer 1971 and Agnese di Hohenstaufen by Spontini; Sang in Giordano's La Cene delle Beffe at La Scale 1977. Recordings include: Tosca and Aida (Cetra); Cavalleria Rusticana (Deutsche Grammophon); Verdi's I Due Foscari, I Lombardi, Nabucco and Attila. Address: c/o Teatro alla Scala, Via Filodrammatici 2, 1-20120 Milan, Italy.

GUEST George (Hywel), b. 9 Feb 1924, Bangor, Wales. Choral Director; Organist. m. Nancy Mary Talbot, 31 Oct 1959, 1 s, 1 d. Education: Chester Cathedral Choir School, 1935-39; King's School, Chester, 1939-42; MA, MusB (Cantab); Organ

Student at St John's College, Cambridge, 1947-51; FRCO, 1942. Career: Served in RAF, 1942-46; John Stewart of Rannoch Scholar in Scared Music, 1948; Organist and Choirmaster, St John's College, Cambridge, 1951-91; University Assistant Lecturer in Music, Cambridge, 1953-56, University Lecturer, 1956-82; Professor of Harmony and Counterpoint, RAM, London, 1960-61; Director of Berkshire Boys Choir in USA, 1967, 1970; University Organist, Cambridge University, 1974-91; Special Commissioner, Royal School of Church Music, 1953-; Examiner to Associated Board of Royal Schools of Music, 1959-92; Director, Côr Cenedlaethol Ieuenctid Cymru, 1984-86; Artistic Director, Llandaf Festival, 1985; Concerts with St John's College Choir in USA, Canada, Japan, Australia, Hong Kong, Brazil and most countries in West Europe; Concerts and Choral Seminars in the Philippines and South Africa; Concerts with Community of Jesus Choir, USA in Hungary, Yugoslavia and Russia. Compositions: Arrangements of church music. Recordings include: About 100 with St John's College Choir including: Haydn Masses, Purcell Funeral Music, Liszt Missa Choralis, Beethoven Mass in C, Fauré Requiem and works by Britten. Publication: A Guest at Cambridge, 1994 Contributions to: Various magazines. Honour: CBE, 1987. Hobby: Welsh Language. Address: St John's College, Cambridge, CB2 1TP, England.

GUHL Helmut, b. 1945, Hamburg, Germany. Singer (Baritone). Education: Studied in Hamburg. Debut: Eutin Festival, 1973, as the Count in Lortzing's Wildschütz. Career: Sang with Oldenburg Opera, 1974-78, notably as Sharpless, Papageno, Germont and Wolfram; Eutin Festival as Guglielmo, Rossini's Figaro and Belcore; Hanover Opera from 1978, as Don Giovanni, Orpheus, Rossini's Mosè, and Beckmesser; Guest appearances at the Deutsche Oper am Rhein, Dusseldorf, and in Hamburg, Mannheim and Stuttgart. Address: c/o Staatstheater Hanover, Opernhaus, Opernplatz 1, W-3000 Hanover 1, Germany.

GUI Henry, b. 1926, Bordeaux, France. Singer (Baritone). Education: Studied in Paris. Career: Sang in operetta at The Theâtre du Chatelet, Paris; Sang Debussy's Pelléas at the Vienna Staatsoper and at the Glyndebourne Festival, 1962; Wexford Festival 1967-68, as Mercutio in Roméo et Juliette and as Pelléas; Strasbourg 1967, in Der junge Lord by Henze; Brussels 1973, in The Mines of Sulphur by Bennett; Appearances at the Aix-en-Provence Festival, the Paris Opéra-Comique, La Scala Milan and the Teatro Liceo Barcelona.

GUIDARINI Marco, b. 1952, Genoa, Italy. Conductor. Education: Studied conducting with Mario Gusella at Pescara, cello in Vienna with Andre Navarra; Masterclasses with Franco Ferrara in Verona and Assisi. Career: Conducting career began in Italy; Conducted Falstaff with the Opéra de Lyon 1986; Le Comte Ory in Lyon, Annecy and St Etienne; Wexford Festival and Queen Elizabeth Hall, London 1988-89, with Mercadante's Elisa e Claudio and Mozart's Mitridate; Season 1989-90 with IL Barbiere di Siviglia for Opera North, Madame Butterfly in Dublin, 1990-91 included Tosca with English National Opera, La Bohème for Scottish Opera; Concerts with the RAI in Rome; Season 1991-92, Die Fledermaus and The Magic Flute for WNO, Carmen with Scottish Opera and debut with Australian Opera at Sydney, Tosca; 1993 and 1994: Orphée in the opera by Gluck; Barbiere di Siviglia at Deutsche Staatsoper, Berlin. Address: Allied Artists Ltd, 42 Montpellier Square, London SW7 1JZ, England.

GUIDARINI Marco, b. 1956, Genoa, Italy. Conductor. Education: Studied conducting with Franco Ferrara, and at the Academy of Pescara. Career: Led regional orchestras in Italy, then assisted John Eliot Gardiner at the Lyon Opera, making debut 1986 with Falstaff; Wexford Festival and London 1988-89, with the local premieres of Mercadante's Elisa e Claudio and Mozart's Mitridate; Season 1990-91 with Tosca at English National Opera, Figaro for Welsh National Opera, La Bohème for Scottish Opera and Manon Lescaut in Dublin; Vancouver and Sydney debuts with Don Pasquale and Tosca; Season 1993-94 with La Traviata at Stockholm, I Lombardi at Bologna and Il Barbiere di Siviglia at the Berlin Staatsoper; Season 1997 with Don Giovanni at Copenhagen, Rigoletto in Geneva, Barbiere at Los Angeles (US debut) and Don Carlos in Marseilles; Other repertory includes Cosí fan tutte (Australian Opera), Die Zauberflöte, Un Ballo in Maschera and Nabucco (Nice Opera). Address: Allied Artists, 42 Montpelier Square, London SW7 1JZ, England.

GUILLAUME Edith, b. 14 June 1943, Bergerac, France. Opera and Concert Singer; Lyric Mezzo; Resident Member, Royal Danish Opera, Copenhagen. m. Niels Hvass, 2 children. Education: Soloist Diploma, Royal Danish College of Music, Copenhagen; Private study, Copenhagen and Paris. Debut: (Opera) Thérèse, Dreaming of Therese, Jutland Opera. Career includes: Sang with opera in Copenhagen, Aarhus, Hamburg, Mannheim, Geneva, Montpelier, Nancy, Metz, Lille, Liège, Le Havre; Roles with these companies include Bartók, Judith (Bluebeard's Castle); Bibalo, Julie (Miss Julie); Bizet, Carmen (Carmen); Campra, Clorinde (Tancrède); Davies, Miss Donnithorne's Maggott; Gluck, Orfeo; Gounod, Siebel (Faust); Mascagni, Santuzza (Cavalleria Rusticana); Massenet, Charlotte (Werther); Monteverdi, Ottavia and Poppea (L'Incoronazione di Poppea), Penelope (Ritorno d'Ulisse); Mozart, Cherubino (Le nozze di Figaro), Dorabella (Così fan tutte), Idamante (Idomeneo); Offenbach, La perichole (La Perichole); Penderecki, Jeanne (The Devils of Loudun); Poulenc (Voix Humaine); Ravel, Concepcion (L'Heure Espagnole); Rossini, Zaida (Turco in Italia), Angelina (Cenerentola); Strauss, Octavian (Der Rosenkavalier); Verdi, Maddalena (Rigoletto), Meg (Falstaff). Recordings: Various Danish songs. Honours include: Critics Prize of Honour, 1970; Tagea Brandt Memorial Fund, 1977. Address: Ellebakken 2, 2900 Hellerup, Copenhagen, Denmark.

GUILLOU Jean, b. 18 Apr 1930, Angers, France. Organist; Composer; Pianist. Education: Paris Conservatoire from 1945 with Dupré, Durufle and Messiaen. Career: Professor, Instituto de Alta Cultura, Lisbon, 1953-57; recitalist in residence in West Berlin. 1958-62; Organist, St Eustache, Paris, 1963; Professor, International Master Class, Zurich, 1970-. Compositions: Organ: Sinfonietta, 18 Variations, Fantasie, 1958; Pour le Tombeau de Colbert, Toccata, 1966; Sagas, Symphonie Iniatique, La Chapelle des abimes, 1970; Scénes d'Enfants, Sonate en Trio, 1985; 5 Concertos for Organ and Orchestra, Hyperion, 1987; Chamber works: Colloques no 1 to 6 Concertos no 1 and 2 for piano and orchestra; Judith-Symphonie for mezzo-soprano and orchestra; Peace and Aube for 12 voices and organ, 1991; Missa Interrupta, 1994; Eloge, for organ; Alice au Pays de l'Orgue, 1995; Fete for clarinet and organ, 1995. Recordings: Many by Philips and Dorian including J S Bach, Goldberg Variations, Complete Organ Works; C Franck, complete organ works; Vivaldi, 5 concertos; J Reubke, piano and organ sonatas; Mussorgsky, Pictures at an Exhibition; Stravinsky, Petrushka; The Art of Improvisation; Joseph Jongen, Symphonic Concertante; Guillou Plays Guillou, 3 CDs. Publications: Author of the book about organ, history and design, L'Orgue, Souvenir et Avenir, Ed Buchet, Chastel. Honours: Gramophon Critics Prize, 1980; International Performer of the Year, USA, 1980; Prize of the Liszt Academy, Budapest, 1982; Diapason d'Or and Prix Choc of Le Monde, 1991. Address: 179 rue Saint-Jacques, 75005 Paris, France.

GUIOT Andrea, b. 11 Jan 1928, Garon-Saint-Gilles, Nimes, France. Singer (Soprano). Education: Studied in Nimes and with Janine Micheau in Paris. Debut: Nancy Opera 1955, in Faust. Career: Sang at the Opéra-Comique Paris as Antonia in Les Contes d'Hoffmann, Micaela, Mireille, Mimi and Manon; Paris Opéra debut as Marguerite; Wexford Festival 1961, Chicago Lyric Opera 1963; Carnegie Hall New York 1964 in Dialogues des Carmélites by Poulenc; Retired as Singer 1973; Professor at the Paris Conservatoire from 1977.

GULDA Friedrich, b. 16 May 1930, Vienna, Austria. Pianist; Composer. Education: Grossmann Conservatory; High School of Music and Dramatic Art, Vienna with Bruno Seidhofer and Joseph Marx. Debut: 1944. Career: Numerous concert tours with leading orchestras; Carnegie Hall debut 1950; Often heard in Bach, Beethoven, Mozart and Schubert; Founded Classical Gulda Orchestra of the Vienna Symphony; Founded small jazz band; Jazz club engagements from 1956; Founded Eurojazz Orchestra; Modern Jazz Competition in Vienna 1966; Has performed flute and baritone saxophone with various partners; Founded International Musikforum at Ossiach, Carinthia, 1968; TV series playing Mozart Sonatas; Played Mozart's Concerto K488 with the Vienna Philharmonic at gala concert conducted by Claudio Abbado. Compositions include: 2 Piano Concertos; Cadenzas for repertory works; Galgenlieder for baritone and orchestra 1951; Numerous jazz compositions. Recordings: Classical Sonatas and Concertos for Decca. Publication: Wrote zur Musik 1971. Contribution to: Osiach müssteerfunden werden 1971. Honours include: First Prize, Geneva International Competition 1946; Beethoven Ring from the Vienna Academy of Music 1970. Hobbies: Chess; Record Collecting. Address: c/o Wiener Philharmoniker, Bösondorfstrasse 12, A-1030 Vienna, Austria.

GULEGHINA Maria, b. 1964, Odessa, Russia. Singer (Soprano Absoluta). Education: Studied in Odessa. Career: Sang at the Minsk Opera from 1984 at first in small roles but after winning the Glinka Competition as Tatiana, Elisabeth de Valois, Aida and Rosina; La Scala, Milan, 1987, as Amelia (Ballo in maschera), Tosca, Lisa (Queen of Spades) and Elisabeth; Sang Tosca at Hamburg, 1990, and made Metropolitan Opera debut as Maddalena in Andrea Chenier; Further guest appearances at the Vienna Staatsoper (as Tosca), the Deutsche Oper Berlin, Bastille, Paris, Rome Opera (Macbeth), Florence Opera, Covent Garden, Chicago and San Francisco, sang Verdi's Elvira at London's Barbican Hall, 1994; Verdi's Odabella as Macerata and Abigaille at Verona Arena, 1996; Sang Tosca at the Metropolitan and Lady Macbeth at La Scala, 1997. Address: c/o Lies Askonas Ltd, 6 Henrietta St, London WC2E 8LA, England.

GULIN Angeles, b. 18 Feb 1943, Ribadavia, Orense, Spain. Singer (Soprano). m. Antonio Blancas-La Plaza. Education: Studied with her father. Debut: Montevideo 1963, as the Queen of Night. Career: Appearances in Barcelona, London, San Francisco, Dusseldorf, Amsterdam, Naples, Turin, Monte Carlo and Mexico City; Festivals of Edinburgh, Aix-en-Provence, Rome, Florence and Verona; Hamburg Staatsoper 1973-77; Other roles include: Abigaille, Aida, Norma, Valentine in Les Huguenots, Donna Anna, Senta, Turandot and La Gioconda; Many concert appearances. Recordings include: Oberto, Il Corsaro and Stiffelio by Verdi, Fernand Cortez by Spontini; Andrea Chénier. Honours: Winner, Verdi Competition at Busseto, 1968; International Competition Madrid 1970. Address: c/o Hamburg Staatsoper, Grosse-Theaterstrasse 34, D-2000 Hamburg, Germany.

GULKE Peter, b. 29 Apr 1934, Weimar, Germany. Conductor. Education: Studied at the Franz Liszt Hochschule Weimar, the Friedrich Schiller University Jena and the Karl Marx University, Leipzig (PhD 1958). Career: Repetiteur at the Rudolstadt Theatre 1959; Music Director at Stendal 1964 and Potsdam 1966; Stralsund 1972-76; Kapellmeister at the Dresden Opera 1976; Musical Director at Weimar 1981; as Musicologist Technical University, Berlin 1984; Musical Director, Wuppertal Opera, 1986; Work as musicologist includes edition of a 10th Symphony by Schubert, from sketches, broadcast at the Schubert Congress in Detroit, 1978; Lecturer at the Hochschule für musik in Dresden; Conducted Poulenc's Dialogues des Carmélites at Wuppertal 1989, to commemorate the bicentenary of the French Revolution and numerous other operas including the Ring et Wuppertal, Graz, Kassel. Publications: Bruckner, Brahms, zwei Studien (Kassel), 1989); Schubert und seine Zeit, 1991. Recordings include: Beethoven Piano Concerto of 1784 and Udo Zimmermann's Der Schuhu und der fliegende Prinzessin (Eterna), works by Berg, Webern, Baird, Schubert. Address: Wuppertaler Bruhnen, Spinnstrasse 4, D-5600 Wuppertal, Germany.

GULLI Franco, b. 1 Sept 1926, Trieste, Italy. Concert Violinist. m. Enrica Cavallo. Education: Studied with father and at Trieste Conservatory; Accademia Chigiana, Siena. Debut: 1932. Career: Worldwide appearances with leading orchestras, including Cleveland, Pittsburgh, Ottawa; Chamber music activity with wife and with Trio Italiano d'Archi; Former member, Pomeriggi Musical Orchestra of Milan and of I Virtuosi di Roma; Gave premieres of concertos by Malipiero and Viozzi and of Paganini's 5th Concerto (1959); Master classes, Accademia Chigiana, Siena, 1964-72; Professor of Music, Lucerne Conservatory, 1971-72; Professor of Music, Indiana University from 1972, currently Distinguished Professor of Music. Recordings include: Duos with Bruno Giuranna; String Trios by Beethoven with the Italian Trio; Paganini's Concerto No 5; Beethoven Sonatas, with Enrica Cavallo; Mendelssohn Sonata in F; Mozart Violin Concerti (complete). Honours include: Premio dell'Accademia Chigiana, Siena. Memberships include: Accademia Nazionale Santa Cecilia, Rome. Current Management: Columbia Artists New York, 165 West 57th Street, NY 10019, USA.

GULYAS Dénes, b. 31 Mar 1954, Budapest, Hungary. Singer (Tenor); Producer. Education: Studied at the Liszt Academy and the Budapest Conservatory. Debut: Budapest 1978, as Alfredo. Career: Vienna Staatsoper debut 1978; Sang in the Verdi Requiem at Budapest and La Scala Milan 1981; US debut Philadelphia 1981; Royal Opera House Covent Garden 1984-85; Metropolitan Opera from 1985, as the Singer in Der Rosenkavalier, Romeo, Rodolfo, Massenet's Des Grieux and Andrei in Khovanshchina; Appearances in Belgium, France, Germany and Italy; Other roles include Don Ottavio, Ferrando, the Duke of Mantua, Almaviva and Ernani; Performances in La Bohème, Rigoletto, Massenet's Manon, Khovanshchina, Gounod's Romeo and Juliet; San Francisco, Così fan tutte, 1986; Florence - Elisir d'amore, Genoa; Staged and sang leading role in Roméo et Juliette at Budapest, 1988-89; Sang Faust with the Florentine Opera at Milwaukee, 1989 (recreated at Montreal); San Diego, 1990 as Tamino; Debut as Barcelona, 1989, as Lensky in Eugene Onegon; Sang Lensky at Tel Aviv, 1992. Recordings: Gianni Schicchi, Salieri's Falstaff, Hunyadi Laszlo by Erkel, Paisiello's Il Barbiere di Siviglia, Liszt's Hungarian Coronation Mass (Hungaroton). Honours: Winner, Pavarotti Competition, Philadelphia 1981. Address: c/o Hungarian State Opera House, Népoztársaság utja 22, 1061 Budapest, Hungary.

GULYAS György, b. 11 Apr 1916, Korostarca, Hungary. Conductor. m. Eva Manya, 6 Nov 1958, 3 daughters. Education: Composition and Conducting, Academy of Music, Budapest, 1942. Career: Teacher, Music Teachers' Training College, Debrecen, 1942-46; Founder-Director, Music High School, Bekestarhos, also conductor, Tarhosi Korus, 1946-54; Director, Music High School, Debrecen, 1954-66; Debrecen Academy of Music, Budapest, 1966-76; Founder, Chief Conductor, Kodály Choir, Debrecen, 1955-83; Békéstarhosi Zenei Napok, music director 1976-. Publications: Author, Bekestarhos Zenei tanulsagai, 1968; Az enekkari intonacio kerdesei, 1972; Articles in various professional journals; Büneim...Büneim?, biography, 1988. Address: 8 Blaháné, Debrecen 4024, Hungary.

GUNDE Peter, b. 1942, Budapest, Hungary. Conductor. Education: Studied Oboe at the Budapest Conservatory;

Composition, Coducting, Franz Liszt Academy, Budapest; Seminars in Weimar and Petersburg with Arvid Jansons, 1965-75. Career: Oboist, National Orchestra, Budapest, 1961-63; Kapellmeister in Miskolc, Hungary, 1972-73; Opera Kappellmeister, Hungarian State Opera, 1973-75; Founder, Director, Corelli Chamber Orchestra, Budapest, 1975-77; Conductor, Artistic Director, Chorus and Orchestra, Kapisztran and Palestrina Choir, Budapest, 1973-77; Director of the Chamber Orchestra and Lecturer at the International Youth Festival, Bayreuth, 1975-77; Assistant to Peter Maag, Christoph von Dohnanyi, Herbert von Karajan, Salzburg Festival, 1977-78; Lecturer, University of Bielefeld and University of Osnabrück; Guest Conductor, Stavanger, Oslo and Hungary, 1981-83; Concerts with the Sudwesteutschen Kammerorchester in Pforzheim and Reutlingen; Concerts in Hungary and USA, 1984; Guest Conductor in Tokyo and Israel; Broadcasts with the Westdeutschen Rundfunk Cologne, 1985-89; Concert Tour with the Hungarian Virtuosi Orchestra, 1990-93, 1993-. Address: Heeperstrasse 52a, 33607 Bielefeld 1, Germany.

GUNDRY Inglis, b. 8 May 1905, Wimbledon, England. Composer; Lecturer on Music. m. Nina Peggy Maggs, 22 Aug 1957, 2 daughters. Education: Mill Hill School, 1918-23; MA, Balliol College, Oxford 1923-27; Middle Temple, 1927-29; Barrister-at-Law; ARCM, Royal College of Music 1935-38; Founder: The Sacred Music-Drama Society - Music Director, 1960-86. Compositions include: Unpublished: Operas: Naaman, The Return of Odysseus, Avon, The Tinners of Cornwall, The Horses of The Drawn, The Logan Rock, The Three Wise Men, The Prisoner Paul, The Prince of Coxcombs (Morley College Prize 1964); A Will of Her Own, The Rubicon, Lindisfarne, Claudia's Dream, 2 Symphonies, Harp Concerto, orchestral suite The Logan Rock; 5 Song-Cycles; Cantata, The Daytime of Christ. Published: Opera: The Partisans (WMA); Orchestral Suite: Heyday Freedom (Hinrichsen); Choral Suite with Orchestra: Five Bells (Hinrichsen); The Shepherds (Ed Medieval Music Drama), OUP; Male Voice Choir: Sing From The Chamber To the Grave, OUP; First Will and Testament, OUP; Cornish Carols: Now Carol We, OUP; Harp Variations (Thames); Orchestral Suite: Lindisfarne, 1992; Galileo, opera in 5 Acts and 5 Choral Episodes, 1993. Recordings: Discs: Excerpts From the Three Wise Men; Excerpts From The Prisoner Paul; Song Cycles; The Black Mountains, Woman's Heart and Songs of Experience; Harp Variations and Two Songs from A Will of Her Own; Medieval Music Dramas for Christmas and Easter; Tape Recordings: A Will of Her Own, A Fountain of Gardens; Songs of Friendship; Song Cycle: Songs of Friendship, 1994; Opera, Galileo, 1995. Publications: The Nature of Opera as A Composite Art (Royal Music Association) 1947; Canow Kernow - Songs and Dances from Cornwall 1966, 3rd edition 1984; Composers by the Grace of God, a study of Music and Religion, 1989; Libretto of Galileo, 1993; Canow Kernow Songs and Dances of Cornwall, Editor. Contributions to: The Composer 1964; Composition in More Than Twelve Tones. Honours: Cobbett Prize at RCM 1936; Won Morley College Opera Competition 1964; The Horses of The Dawn was one of the winning librettos in a Competition for School Operas sponsored by The Council for Social Services 1951; 90th birthday celebration concert of own works at St John's, Smith Square, London, May 1995. Memberships: Composers' Guild Performing Right Society; Federation of OLd Cornwall Societies; Vice President, Cornish Music Guild. Hobbies: Pastel Painting; Gardening. Address: 11 Winterstoke Gardens, Mill Hill, London NW7 2RA, England.

GUNN Jacqueline, b. 1959, Scotland. Stage Designer. Career: Opera designs have included The Rake's Progress for Opera Integra, La Voix Humaine at the Bloomsbury Festival, La Pietra del Paragone at Wuppertal, Tannhäuser for New Sussex Opera, Henze's Labirinto at the Munich Biennale, Otello, L'Elisir d'Amore and Trovatore for Lucerne Opera and Così fan tutte for English National Opera in 1994. Address: Performing Arts, 6 Windmill Street, London, W1B 1HF, England.

GUNS Jan, b. 22 Nov 1951, Antwerp, Belgium. Bass Clarinet Player; Soloist, 1 son, 2 daughters. Education: Royal Flemish Conservatorium, Antwerp; Summer courses, Nice, France. Debut: Royal Flemish Opera, Antwerp, 1971. Career: Assistant Professor of Clarinet, Royal Conservatorium, Gent, 1979; Played with Opera of Flanders, 1980; BRT Philharmonic Orchestra, 1983; Associate Professor, 1984, Professor of Bass Clarinet, 1991-, Royal Flemish Conservatorium, Antwerp; Bass Clarinet Player and Percussionist with Gemini Ensemble, 1990-. Recordings: Introduction and Concertante for Bass Clarinet and Clarinet Choir, opus 58 (Norman Heim), with Walter Boeykens Clarinet Choir, 1986; Harry's Wonderland for Bass Clarinet and 2 Tapes (Andre Laporte), 1987; Mladi sextet (Leos Janacek), with Walter Boeykens Ensemble, 1992; Spotlights on the Bass Clarinet, Concerto for Bass Clarinet and Concert Band (Jan Hadermann), with Concert Band of the Belgian Guides, conducted by N Nozy, 1993; With Gemini Ensemble, 1993; Sonata (Frits Celis); Van Heinde en Verre (Wilfrid Westerlinck); Due Concertante (Ivana Loudova); Giuco per Due (Dietrich Erdmann); Exercises (Jean Segers); Tango (Frederic Devreese). Address: Hagelandstraat 48, B-2660 Hoboken (Antwerp), Belgium.

GUNSON Ameral, b. 1960, England. Singer (Mezzo-soprano). Career: Many concerts and broadcasts in Britain and Europe; Frequent appearances at the Promenade Concerts London; Season 1985-86 with Walton's Gloria at the Last Night of the Proms and Hecuba and Anna in a concert performance of Les Troyens by Berlioz at Portsmouth, conducted by Roger Norrington; Sang Lady Toodle in a Frankfurt Opera production of The English Cat by Henze; L'Enfant et les Sortilèges in Rotterdam, conducted by Simon Rattle; Verdi's Aida in Glasgow and Requiem at the Albert Hall, conducted by David Willcocks; Elgar's Sea Pictures and Mozart's Mass in C Minor, conducted by Richard Hickox; Bach's Mass in B Minor and the Choral Symphony with the Bournemouth Symphony orchestra; Haydn Masses televised by Austrian TV, with Roger Norrington; Tour of France with the Bach B Minor Mass; Many recitals with the pianist Paul Hamburger; Premiere recording of Britten's The Rescue for the BBC; Sang in the premiere of Goehr's Eve Dreams of Paradise, 1989 (Prom Concerts 1990), Season 1990-91 in Texeira's Mass, with the Sixteen, Berg's Altenberg Lieder with the Rotterdam Philharmonic Hindemith's Requiem in Geneva and Mozart's Requiem conducted by Jane Glover; Covent Garden 1992 as a Young Nun in Prokofiev's The Fiery Angel. Recordings include: Maw's Scenes and Arias (EMI); Copland's In the Beginning, with the choir of King's College, Cambridge; Auntie in Peter Grimes, 1996. Address: Magenta Music International, 64 Highgate High Street, London N6 5HX, England.

GUNSON Emily Jill, b. 28 Jan 1956, Melbourne, Australia. Flautist; Musicologist. Education: BMus, hons, University of Western Australia, 1980; Postgraduate Study with William Bennett, 1981-82; Performance Diplomas, LMusA, 1978, LRAM, LGSM, ARCM, 1980. Career: Concerto Debut, 1973; Principal Flute, West Australia Arts Orchestra, 1982-83; Performances with West Australian and Sydney Symphony Orchestras; Artistic Director, Leader, Australian Chamber Ensembles, Wendling Quartet, Cambini Quintet, Emanuel Ensemble, Music'Autentica, performing on both modern and historical flutes; Musicological Research in field of 18th century flute history, performance and repertoire, as Doctoral Scholar, University of Western Australia, 1993-; International authority on Wendling family of musicians and singers in 18th century Mannheim and Munich. Publications: Johann Baptist Wendling (1723-1797): A Thematic Catalogue. Contributions to: 7 articles to New Grove Dictionary (7th ed); RISM errata; Editor, 18th and 19th Century Flute Music. Memberships: Musicological Society of Australia. Hobbies: Rare Historical Memoirs; Alsatian Wine. Current Management: Flutissimo, PO Clackline 6564, Western Australia. Address: Emanuel Farm, 14 Boondine Road, Clackline 6564, Western Australia.

GÜNTER Horst, b. 23 May 1913, Leipzig, Germany. Voice Teacher; Professor of Voice; Singer (Baritone). m. 4 May 1938, 2 sons, 2 daughters. Education: Choirboy, St Thomas, Leipzig; Musicology and Philosophy, Universities of Leipzig and Bologna; Voice, Leipzig Conservatory; Most influential teachers: Karl Straube, Fritz Polster, Emmi Leisner. Debut: Matthäus-Passion, St Thomas, Leipzig, 1939; Count in Marriage of Figaro, Schwerin State Opera, 1941. Career: Leading Lyric Baritone, Hamburg State Opera, 1950-68; Knappertsbusch and Böhm, Munich State Opera, 1958-63; Edinburgh Festival, 1952, 1956; Holland Festival, 1961; Guest Singer: Vienna State Opera, Frankfurt, with Solti; Ansbach Bach Festival, 1951-58; Numerous radio recordings: TV: 12 operas; First performance of Moses and Aaron in Hamburg; Teaching: Nordwest-deutsche Musikakademie, Detmold, 1959-65; Staatliche Musikhochschule, Freiburg, 1965-68; University of Southern California, Los Angeles, 1978-80; University of California, Los Angeles, 1981; Visiting Professor: Many US universities including Southern Methodist University, Dallas, North Texas State University, Denton, Oberlin Conservatory of Music, University of Minneapolis, University of Alaska; Musashino Academia Musicae, Tokyo, 1984, 1986, 1987, 1990, 1991, 1992; Frequent Judge, international voice competitions such as Munich, Budapest, Leipzig, s'Hertogenbosch, Los Angeles, Dallas, Osaka. Recordings include: Lohengrin; Schüchter, Moses und Aron; Zillich, Così fan Tutte, Jochum, Don Giovanni, Klemperer, Zauberflöte, Rother, La Traviata, Wagner, Die Fledermaus; Schüchter, Weihnachts Oratorium; Karl Richter, Matthäus Passion; Kurt Redel, Zar und Zimmermann; La Bohème, Erede. Hobbies: Scientific work about the history of singing; Books about the human voice; Gardening. Address: Unterer Heimbach 5, D-79280 Au bei Freiburg, Germany.

GUNTER John, b. 1950, England. Stage Designer. Education: Central School of Art and Design, London. Career: Head of Theatre Department at the Central School, then Head of Design at the National Theatre, London; Opera designs for the Glyndebourne Festival include Albert Herring, Simon Boccanegra, Porgy and Bess (British company premiere, 1986), La Traviata and Falstaff; Le nozze di Figaro 1994, revived 1997; Further engagements with English National Opera, Welsh National Opera, Scottish Opera, Opera North and the Salzburg Festival; La Scala, Milan, and opera houses at Munich, Cologne, Hamburg, Buenos Aires, Sydney and Los Angeles; Original 1857 version of Simon Boccanegra for Covent Garden, 1997; Season 1996-97 with Samson et Dalila for Queensland Opera; Simon Boccanegra for Glyndebourne, 1998 season. Address: c/o Peter Murphy, Curtis Brown, Haymarket House, 28-29 Haymarket, London SW1Y 4SP, England.

GUNZENHAUSER Stephen (Charles), b. 8 April 1942, New York City, USA. Conductor. m. Rochelle E Davis, 14 June 1970, 2 daughters. Education: BMus, Oberlin College, 1963; Diploma, Salzburg Mozarteum, 1962; MMus, New England Conservatory of Music, 1965; Artist diploma, Cologne Hochschule für Musik, 1968. Career: Assistant Conductor, Monte Carlo National Orchestra, 1968-69; American Symphony Orchestra, New York, 1969-70; Music Director, Brooklyn Center Chamber Orchestra, 1970-72; Kennett (Pennsylvania) Symphony Orchestra, 1974-78; Wilmington (Delaware) Chamber Orchestra, 1976-79; Delaware Symphony Orchestra, Wilmington, 1978-; Principal Conductor 1978-81, Music Director 1981-, Lancaster (Pennsylvania) Symphony Orchestra; Artistic director, 1974-82, Artistic Administrator 1982-87, Wilmington Music School; Guest Conductor with various North American and European orchestras; Recording Contract, HNH International, 1985; Named as Cultural Ambassador for the State of Delaware, 1990. Recordings: Several discs; Over 35 CDs recorded. Address: c/o Delaware Symphony Orchestra, PO Box 1870, Wilmington, DE 19899, USA.

GUSCHLBAUER Theodor, b. 14 Apr 1939, Vienna, Austria. Conductor. Education: Studied at the Vienna Academy of Music. Career: Conducted the Vienna Baroque Ensemble, 1961-69; Assistant at the Vienna Volksoper 1964-66; Chief Conductor of the Salzburg Landestheater 1966-68; Lyon Opera 1969-75; General Musik-Direktor, Linz-Bruckner Symphony Orchestra and the Landestheater Linz 1975-83; Chief Conductor of the Strasbourg Philharmonic, 1983-97; Rhineland-Palatinate Philharmonic, 1997-; Guest appearances at many festivals including those at Salzburg, Aix-en-Provence, Prague, Bregenz, Flanders, Oxford, Luzern, Montreux, Ascona, Maggio Musicale Fiorentino, Regular Guest conductor with the Vienna and Hamburg Operas, Geneva, Paris (Bastille), Munich, Cologne and Lisbon. Recordings: Symphonies by Mozart, Haydn, Schubert and Beethoven; Concertos by Strauss, Mozart, Haydn, Mendelssohn and Weber; Mozart's Divertimento K287, Cassation K99, Masses K194 and K220, Vesperae Solennes, Sinfonia Concertante K297b, Bassoon Concerto, Flute Concertos (Rampal), and Piano Concertos K271, K453 and K467 (Maria Joao Pires); K415; K488; Strauss Burleske, Horn Concerto No 2 and Oboe Concerto; Beethoven's 6th Symphony and Schubert's Ninth, with the New Philharmonia; Bruckner 7, D'Indy, Hindemith, Grieg, Rachmaninoff, Waldteufel, Dvorak, Scriabine. Honours: Received Grand Prix du Disque, for seven of his numerous recordings; Awarded Mozart Prize, Goethe Foundation, Basel, 1988; Légion d'Honneur, 1997. Address: c/o Staatsphilharmonie Rheinlandpfalz, Heinigstrasse 40, D-67059 Ludwigshafen, Germany.

GUSLITSER Boris, b. 28 June 1952, Baku, Russia. Pianist. m. Victoria Guslitser, 18 April 1979, 1 daughter. Education: Special Music School of Azerbaijan State Conservatory, Baku; PhD, Rimsky-Korjakov Conservatorium, St Petersburg. Career: Performances with the Israel Philharmonic Orchestra, 1979-80; Recital in Japan, 1980, Melbourne, Brisbane, Perth, Adelaide, 1987-91, Melbourne Concert Hall, 1988, Boston, USA, 1992; Founder, Artistic Director, Lima Sonfonia Orchestra. Honours: 2nd Prize, 4th Zakavkazic State Competition, 1972; Prize, Liszt-Bartok International Piano Competition, Budapest, 1976. Hobbies: International History; Politics; Soccer. Address: Music Department, Geelong Grammar School, Corio 3214, Australia.

GUSSMANN Wolfgang, b. 1953, Germany. Stage and Costume Designer. Career: Collaborations from 1985 with Willy Decker at Cologne, including designs for La Finta Giardiniera, Billy Budd, Der fliegende Holländer, Eugene Onegin and Il Trittico; Capriccio at Florence, Bibalo's Macbeth (premiere) and Così fan tutte at Oslo; Partnership with Johannes Schaaf on Boris Godunov at Munich and Die Entführung aus dem Serail at Hamburg; Season 1996-97 with Freischutz and Don Giovanni at Dresden, the premiere of Das Schloss by Reimann in Berlin, Die Frau ohne Schatten in Geneva and at the Paris Châtelet, Eugene Onegin at the Paris Opéra Bastille, Idomeneo in Munich and Tristan at Leipzig; Season 1997-98 with La Bohème at Cologne, Tosca at Stuttgart, Lulu at the Bastille, Katya Kabanova in Amsterdam, Lohengrin at Bayreuther Festspiele, Pelleas et Melisande at Hamburg, Billy Budd and Lulu at the Vienna Staatsoper and The Ring in Brussels. Address: c/o Haydn Rawstron Ltd, 36 Station Road, London SE20 7BQ, England.

GUSTAFSON Nancy, b. 27 June 1956, Evanston, Illinois, USA. Singer (Soprano). m. Brian Dickie. Education: Studied in

San Francisco on the Adler Fellowship Program. Career: San Francisco Opera debut as Freia in Das Rheingold: returned as Musetta in La Bohème and Antonia in Les Contes d'Hoffmann and Elettra in Idomeneo; Opera Colorado as Donna Elvira; Minnesota Opera as Leila in Les Pêcheurs de Perles; Canadian debut as Violetta for Edmonton Opera; Festival performances as Rosalinda in Sante Fe and Britten's Helena for Chataugua Opera; European debut as Rosalinde in Paris, season 1984-85; Glyndebourne debut as Donna Elvira, while tour to Hong Kong: Festival appearances as Katya Kabanova, in a new production of Janácek's opera, 1988, returned 1990; Chicago Lyric Opera debut as Marguerite in Faust; Covent Garden debut 1988, as Freia; Scottish Opera 1989, as Violetta; Metropolitan Opera debut 1989, as Musetta; Sang Freia in Rheingold at Munich, 1990; Seattle Opera 1989, as Elettra in Idomeneo, Antonia in Les Contes d'Hoffmann 1990; Sang Eva at La Scala and Amelia in a new production of Simon Boccanegra at Brussels 1990; Sang Lisa in The Queen of Spades at Glyndebourne 1992; Season 1991-92 as Violetta and Alice Ford at Toronto; Sang the Letter Scene from Eugene Onegin at the 1993 London Proms; Eva in a new production of Die Meistersinger at Covent Garden , 1993; Concert engagements in Mahler's 8th Symphony, with the San Francisco Symphony, and at the Carmel Bach Festival, California; Engaged as Floyd's Susannah, Houston, 1996; Returned to Covent Garden as Eva, 1997. Address: c/o IMG Artists, Media House, 3 Burlington Lane, Chiswick, London W4 2TH, England.

GUSTAVSSON Jan, b. 8 Dec 1959, Vadstena, Sweden. Musician. m. Jessica Gustavsson, 13 July 1996, 1 son. Education: Studied at Gothenburg Music Conservatory; Trumpet Soloist. Debut: Lisbon, Portugal, 1989. Career: Principal Trumpet, Norrköping, 1982-92; Principal Trumpet, Royal Stockholm Philharmonic Orchestra, 1992-; Trumpet Soloist appearances in Sweden, Portugal, Austria and Switzerland. Recordings: Leopold Mozart, Giuseppe Tartini, Trumpet Concertos as Soloist with Winterthur Stadtorchester, conductor Franz Welser Möst, 1989. Honour: 2nd Prize, Budapest International Trumpet Solo Competition, 1984. Address: Kungliga Filharmoniska Orkestern, Box 7083, SE-103 87 Stockholm, Sweden.

GUSTIN Denis-Pierre, b. 25 Jan 1971, Brussels, Belgium. Flautist. Education: General Certificate of Education, St Michael College, Brussels, 1988; First Prizes in flute and chamber music at Brussels and Paris High Conservatories - 1991, teachers A Marion and M Bourgue. Debut: Soloist of the Ensemble Jeunes Solistes RTBF, 1988. Career: Foreign tours: Czechoslovakia 1989; Germany, Spain 1990; France 1991; Italy 1992; Debut with BRT Philharmonic Orchestra, 1990; TV and Radio appearances: RTBF, BRT, NHK, BBC, TVE, Radio-France; Collaboration with main Belgian orchestras: National Orchestra, New Belgian Chamber Orchestra, RTBF Symphonic Orchestra. Honours: First Prizes of: Pro Civitate Competition, 1988; National for Musicians, 1989; Tenuto Competition, 1990; Second Prize of the Brussels Mozart International Competition, First Flautist nominated, 1991; Laureated of the Yehudi Menuhin Foundation and of the Vocation Foundation. Address: 236 Avenue Albert, 1180 Brussels, Belgian.

GUTHRIE Frederick, b. 31 Mar 1924, Pocatello, ID, USA. Bass Singer. Education: Studied with Glynn Ross and Hugo Strelitzer in Los Angeles; Later study with Elisabeth Rado, Ludwig Weber and Josef Witt in Vienna. Career: Sang in a concert performance of Oedipus Rex conducted by Karajan in Vienna in 1953; Vienna Staatsoper, 1954-74; Glyndebourne Festival in 1956 as Sarastro in Die Zauberflöte; Frankfurt from 1958 and made guest appearances in Trieste, Munich and Rome; Salzburg Festival in 1960 in the premiere of Le Mysteré de la Nativité by Frank Martin. Recordings include: Die Schöpfung by Haydn; Das Buch mit Sieben Siegeln by Franz Schmidt; Bruckner's F minor Mass.

GUTIERREZ Horacio, b. 28 Aug 1948, Havana, Cuba. Pianist. m. Patricia Asher. Education: Juilliard School of Music, New York City, USA, 1967-70. Debut: At age 11 with havana Symphony Orchestra. Career: Performed most major symphony orchestras as soloist in recitals throughout the world; Appearances on BBC-TV and also in France and USA; Tours in USA, Canada, Europe, South America, Israel, USSR, Japan. Recordings: Numerous. Honours: Recipient, 2nd Prize, Tchaikowsky Competition, 1970; Avery Fisher Prize, 1982. Current Management: ICM Artists Ltd. Address: 40 West 57th Street, New York, NY 10019, USA.

GUTMAN Natalia, b. 14 Jun 1942, Moscow, Russia. Cellist. Education: Began cello studies aged 5 at Gnessin Music School, Moscow under R Saposhnikov, later at Moscow Conservatory with Rostropovich. Career: After winning awards at competitions in Moscow, Prague, Munich and Vienna she made many tours of Europe, American and Japan, appearing with the Vienna Philharmonic Orchestra, Orchestre National de France, Berlin Philharmonic Orchestra, the Philharmonia and the Concertgebouw Orchestra; Conductors include Abbado, Sawallisch, Muti, Rozhdestvensky, Stokowski, Svetlanov and Sinopoli; Tours of the USA with the Russian State Symphony Orchestra and of Russia with the BBC Symphony Orchestra and John Pritchard; Plays chamber music in Russia and Europe with Eliso Virsaladze and Oleg Kagan and chamber concerts with Sviatoslav Richter; Has performed works by various Russian composers including Gubaidulina, Denisov and Schnittke. Recordings include: Both Shostakovich Concertos. Addres: c/o Harold Holt Ltd, 31 Sinclair Road, London, W14 0NS, England.

GUTSTEIN Ernst, b. 15 May 1924, Vienna, Austria. Baritone. Education: Studied at the Vienna Music Academy. Debut: Inssbruck in 1948 as Fernando in Fidelio. Career: Sang at Innsbruck, 1949-52, Heidelberg, 1953-54, Kassel, 1954-56, Deutsche Opera am Rhein Dusseldorf, 1958-59, Frankfurt am Main, 1956-57, and Vienna, 1967-89; Further appearances in London, Cologne, Florence, Moscow, Paris, Chicago, Rome and Brussels; Salzburg Festival in 1959 in Il Mondo della Luna by Haydn; Zurich Opera in 1975 in the premiere of Ein Wahrer Held by Klebe; Many engagements in operas by Verdi and Wagner; Sang in Berg's Lulu at the Festival Hall London, 1994. Recordings: Jochanaan in Salome; Rigoletto; La Rappresentazione di Anima e di Corpo by Cavalieri; Notre Dame by Schmidt. Address: Puchheimerg 23, A-2851 Krumbach, Austria.

GUTTLER Ludwig, b. 13 Jun 1943, Sosa, Germany. Trumpeter; Conductor; Professor. Education: Degree in Architecture; Studied trumpet with Armin Mennel, Leipzig Hochschule für Musik, 1961-65. Debut: Soloist with orchestra in 1958. Career: Solo Trumpeter, Handel Festival Orchestra, Halle, 1965-, and Dresden Philharmonic, 1969-81; Founder, Director, Leipziger Bach-Collegium, 1976-, Blechbläserensemble Ludwig Guttler, 1978-; Virtuosi Saxoniae, 1985-; Solo tours throughout the world; Lecturer, 1972-80, Professor, 1980-, Head of masterclasses in wind playing, 1982-, Dresden Hochschule für Musik; Guest Teacher at Weimar International Music Seminar, 1977-, also in Austria, Japan and the USA. Recordings: Over 21 discs. Honours: National Prize, German Democratic Republic, 1978; German Phonoakademie Recording Prize, 1983; Music Prize, City of Frankfurt, 1989. Address: c/o Gotthart Wilke, Edinger Konzer-und Kunstleragentur, Lindenstrasse 26, D-8011 Zorneding, Germany.

GUTTMAN Albert, b. 12 Oct 1937, Galati, Romania. Pianist. Education: Conservatoire of Music, Bucharest; Graduate in Piano, Florica Musicescu; Studied Piano Accompaniment under Dagobert Buchholz; Graduate, Biennial Master Classes, magna cum laude, Santa Cecilia Conservatoire, Rome with teacher Guido Agosti. Career includes: Professor of Piano, Chamber Music and Piano Accompaniment, Bucharest Conservatoire of Music, 1960-76; Official Assistant for Chamber Music, Santa Cecilia National Academy in Rome, 1972; Invited by Yehudi Menuhin to teach chamber music at International Menuhin Academy of Music, Gstaad, Switzerland, 1982-84; Taught summer courses in Italy and Switzerland between 1969 and 1983; Professor of Piano, Musikschule Saanenland, Gstaad and Professor of Piano Accompaniment, including permanent Masterclass for Graduate Pianists specializing in Piano Accompaniment, Musik Akademie der Stadt Basel, 1983-; Worldwide tours and participant in numerous festivals; Recitals with Radu Aldulescu and Silvia Marcovici, and often performed with Yehudi Menuhin, Pierre Fournier, Ruggiero Ricci, Enrico Mainardi, Jean Pierre Rampal, Christian Ferras, Lola Bobesco, Pina Carmirelli, Ivry Gitlis, Raphael Sommer. Recordings include: Radio and Television recordings worldwide; Discopgraphy: Beethoven, Integral Edition Five Sonatas for Piano and Cello, Radu Aldulescu on cello; Schumann, Frauen Liebe und Leben; De Falla, Siete Canciones Populares Espanolas, Elena Cernei, mezzo; Shostakovich Sonata Op 40 for Cello and Piano; Hindemith Sonata Op 11 No 3 for Cello and Piano, Radu Aldulescu on Cello; Bach Sonata No 4 for Violin and Piano BWV 1017; Beethoven Sonata Op 30 No 3 for Piano and Violin, Lola Bobesco on Violin; Brahms Sonata No 2 Op 100 in A major and No 3 Op 108 in D minor for Piano and Violin, Angela Gavrila Dieterle on Violin; Beethoven Seven Variations in E flat-dur WoO46 for Piano and Cello, Mirel Iancovici on Cello. Honours include: The Hephzibah Menuhin International Prize for Pianists, 1981. Address: Chalet Bel Air, App 216, 3780 Gstaad, Switzerland.

GUY Barry (John), b. 22 Apr 1947, Lewisham, London, England. Musician (Double Bass; Violone); Composer. Education: AGSM. Career includes: Freelance Bassist; principal, City of London Sinfonia; Solo recitalist; Artistic Director, London Jazz Composers Orchestra; Plays with improvisation groups, Evan Parker Trio; Marilyn Crispell; Gerry Hemingway; Barry Guy Trio; Cecil Taylor; Room; Mats Gustafsson and Iskra 1903; Bill Dixon Quartet; Guy-Homburger Duo. Compositions include: Statements II, 1972; String Quartet III, 1973; Anna, 1974; Play, 1976; EOS for Double Bass and Orchestra, 1977; Details, 1978; Hold Hands and Sing, 1978; Waiata, 1980; Pfiff, 1981; Flagwalk, 1974; Voyages of the Moon, 1983; RondOH!, 1985; Circular for solo oboe, 1985; The Road to Ruin, 1986; Harmos, 1987; The Eye of Silence, 1988; UM 1788, 1989; Look Up!, 1990; Theoria, 1991; After the Rain, 1992; Bird Gong Game, 1992; Mobile Herbarium, 1992; Portraits, 1993; Witch Gong Game, 1993; Witch Gong Game II, 1994; Un Coupe Dés, 1994; Buzz, 1994; Celebration, 1995; Ceremony, 1995. Recordings include: Over 40 albums including: Ode, 1972; Endgame, 1979; Incision, 1981; Tracks, 1983; Zurich Concerts, 1988; Double Trouble, 1990; Elsie jo Live, 1992; Theoria, 1992; After the Rain, 1993; Fizzles, 1993; Portraits, 1994; Vade Mecum, 1994; Imaginary Values, 1994; Witch Gong Game II, 1994; Cascades, 1995; Obliquities, 1995; Iskva 1903, 1995. Honours: Radcliffe Award 1st Prize, 1973; Royal Philharmonic Prize for Chamber Scale Composition, 1991. Memberships include: Musicians Union; PRS; MCPS' APC; RPS; ISM. Hobbies: Squash; Sailing; Painting. Address: Bramley's House, Shudy Camps, Cambridge CB1 6RA, England.

GUY (Ruth) Maureen, b. 10 Jul 1932, Penclawdd, Glamorgan, South Wales. Mezzo-Soprano. Education: Guildhall School of Music and Drama. Debut: As Dryad in Ariadne auf Naxos, Sadler's Wells. Career: Principal Mezzo-Soprano at Sadler's Wells, Royal Opera House Covent Garden and Frankfurt Opera; Recitals, oratorio and orchestral concerts worldwide; Tours of New Zealand, Australia and Europe; Performed in opera in New Zealand, Spain, Portugal, France and Budapest; Her roles include Delilah, Eboli, Amneris, Azucena, Fricka, Erda, Orpheus, Mrs Sedley and Adriano in Rienzi; Performed Oedipus Rex in Herodus Atticus in Athens, conducted by Stravinsky; Currently Vocal Tutor at the Welsh College of Music and Drama. Recordings: Solti, Götterdämmerung; Leinsdorf, Die Walküre; Sadler's Wells, Rigoletto as Maddalena. Honour: Glamorgan County Scholarship to Guildhall School. Hobby: Interior Decoration. Address: The Verzons Granary, Munsley, Ledbury, Hertfordshire, England.

GWIZDALANKA Danuta, b. 22 Jun 1955, Poznan, Poland. Musicologist. Education: MA, 1979, Doctorate, 1989, Mickiewicz University, Poznan. Publications: Brzymienie Kwartetow Smyczkowych Beethovena (Sonority in String Quartets of Beethoven), Poznan, 1990; Slowniczek Skrotow i Oznaczen Muzycznych (Little Dictionary of Musical Terminology), Poznan, 1995; Co-author: Tadeusz Szeligowski, Bydgoszcz, 1987, Konstanty Regamey, Warsaw, Grosse Chorwerke, 1988, Kassel, 1994; Editor: Chopin Studies I, 1985, II 1987. Contributions to: Various journals in Poland and Sweden; Papers issued by Music Academies and Musical encyclopaedia, Cracow, 1978-. Membership: Union of Polish Composers. Address: Kurt Schumacher 10 W 51, 51427 Bergisch Gladbach, Germany.

GYLDENFELDT Graciela Von, b. 22 Jun 1958, Buenos Aires, Argentina. Singer (Soprano). Education: Studied in Buenos Aires. Debut: Sang Norina in Don Pasquale at Buenos Aires in 1979. Career: Sang at Bern Opera from 1980, debut as Gilda, then as Zerlina, Martha, Pamina, Echo in Ariadne auf Naxos and Corilla in Donizetti's Convenzione Teatrali; Sang at Vienna Staatsoper, 1982-86, Salzburg Festival, 1984-86, as Frasquita and Tebaldo in productions of Carmen and Don Carlos conducted by Karajan; Sang at Enschede Netherlands from 1988 as Suor Angelica, Mimi and Donna Elvira; Member of Kiel Opera as Chrysothemis, Katya Kabanova and Ellen Orford, 1989-94; Sang the Princess in Zemlinsky's Es War Einmal in 1991, Marietta in Die Tote Stadt; Cincinnati, 1991 as Carmen; Appearances at Teatro Comunale, Florence, as Elena in Mefistofele and concert engagements in Beethoven's 9th and Janácek's Glagolitic Mass, Salud in La Vida Breve of Manuel de Falla at Dallas Opera, 1993; Teatro Colon, Buenos Aires debut as Donna Elvira in Don Giovanni; Appearances throughout Germany as Amelia in Simon Boccanegra and Madama Butterfly. Recordings: CD, Mefistofele as Elena, with Samuel Ramey, 1990. Honour: Nomination for the Callas Award for her appearance as Salud in La Vida Breve at the Dallas Opera, 1993. Address: Muhliusstrasse 70, 24103, Kiel, Germany.

GYSELYNCK Jean-Baptiste, b. 22 Mar 1946, Ghent, Belgium. Professor. m. Bruyneel Arlette, 1 Jun 1946, 1 son, 1 daughter. Education: Royal Atheneum of Ghent; Royal Music Conservatory of Ghent, 1962-66; Conservatory of Brussels, 1966-78. Career includes: Teacher of Counterpoint, Royal Flemish Music Conservatory of Antwerp, 1970; Professor of Harmony, Counterpoint and Composition at Lemmens Institute of Louvain, 1970-79; Professor Written Harmony, 1970-, Professor of Harmony, Art Humanities Department, 1974-75, Royal Music Conservatory of Brussels. Compositions include: Recorded: Simfonia Da Camera, radio and TV, 1975, Intermezzi for Wood Instruments, LP and radio, 1977, Trio for Strings, radio, 1979, Adagio En Allegro for Alto Saxophone, radio, 1979, Adagio En Allegro for Alto Saxophone, Diptyque for Violin and Piano, radio, 1980, Diptyque for Violin and Piano, radio, 1982; Published: Intermezzi, Illuminatio, Diptyque, Music for 6 poems written by Johan Daisne. Honours include: International Music Competition Queen Elisabeth Laureat of Composition, 1980; Silver Prize of Her Majesty Queen Fabiola Composition Competition Sabam, 1980; 6 Poems of Johan Daisne given at the Albertine, Brussels, 1985. Address: Kortrijksesteenweg 934, 9000 Ghent, Belgium.

H

HAAR James, b. 4 Jul 1929, St Louis, MO, USA. Musicologist. Education: BA, 1950, PhD, 1961, Harvard University; MA, 1954, University of North Carolina. Career: Faculty, Harvard University, 1960-67, University of Pennsylvania, 1967-69, New York University, 1969-78, University of North Carolina, 1978-; General Editor, Journal of The American Musicological Society, 1966-69. Publications: The Tugendsterne of Harsdorffer and Staden, 1965; Essays on Italian Poetry and Music in The Renaissance 1350-1600, 1986. Contributions to: Articles in many journals. Membership: President, 1976-78, American Musicological Society. Address: c/o Department of Music, University of North Carolina, Chapel Hill, NC 27599, USA.

HAAS Kenneth, b. 8 Jul 1943, Washington DC, USA. Symphony Orchestra Executive. m. (1) Barbara Dooneief, 14 Feb 1964, divorced 1990, 2 d, (2) Signe Johnson, 23 Mar 1990, 1 s. Education: BA, Columbia College, 1964. Career: Assistant to Managing Director, New York Philharmonic, 1966-70; Assistant General Manager, 1970-75, General Manager, 1976-87, Cleveland Orchestra; General Manager of Cincinnati Symphony Orchestra, 1975-76; Managing Director of Boston Symphony Orchestra, 1987-; Chairman of Orchestra Panel, National Endowment for The Arts, 1982-85; Co-Chairman of Music Overview Panel, National Endowment for The Arts, 1983-85; Chairman of Challenge Grant Panel, Ohio Arts Council, 1985-86. Memberships: American Symphony Orchestra League, Executive Committee, 1980-82, Board of Directors, 1993-94; Managers of Major Orchestras, US, Chairman, 1980-82. Hobby: Bicycling. Address: Symphony Hall, 301 Massachusetts Avenue, Boston, MA 02115, USA.

HAASS Erich Walter, b. 25 Sep 1936, Cologne, Germany. Music Publisher. m. 17 Jul 1965, 1 s, 1 d. Education: Piano instruction with Professor Hans Haass, Kläre Bormann and Lia Kipper, 1943; Academy of Music, Cologne, 1956-59; Examination as Teacher of Music and Literature; Doctor of Musicology, Universities of Cologne and Marburg, 1983. Debut: Competitor in Youth Makes Music, Düsseldorf, 1948. Career: Organ concert, WDR Cologne, 1958; Piano and Choir concerts, Cologne and Leverkusen; Co-Partner, Hans Gerig Music Publishers, Cologne, 1978; Owner of Music Publishing House. Publications: Cantata for Soli, Choir and Orchestra, 1955; Compositions for Choir; Compositions for Piano. Recordings: Tapes of works by Bach, Handel, Debussy and Haass for Flute, played by Hans-Jürgen Horn, for Piano played by Walter Haass, and Piano Solo. Publications: Studies about the L'Homme Arme Masses of the 15th and 16th centuries, 1984; Poems, in progress. Contributions to: The song, L'Homme arme, in publication in honour of Professor Dr Heinrich Hueschen. Honours: Oberstudienrat, 1974; Dr phil, 1983; Man of The Year, American Biographical Institute, USA, 1993. Memberships: GEMA, Berlin; Committee, Youth Makes Music, Cologne. Hobbies: Hiking; Photography. Address: Kermeterstrasse 24, D-50935 Koeln, Germany.

HABBESTAD Kjell (Helge), b. 13 Apr 1955, Bomlo, Hordaland, Norway. Teacher; Composer. m. Inger Elisabeth Brammer, 30 Dec 1976, 1 son, 2 daughters. Education: Studies of Church Music (organ), 1975-79; Studied Composition, Norwegian State Academy of Music, 1979-81. Career: Organist, Snaroya Church, Baerum 1977-81, Langhus Church, Ski 1986-87; Teacher of Harmony, Counterpoint, Composition, Bergen Conservatory of Music 1981-86, Ostlandets Conservatory of Music, Oslo, 1986-96; Norwegian State Academy of Music, 1996-. Compositions: 3 Cantica (Magnificat, Nunc Dimittis, Benedictus Dominus), 1978-83; Lament, soprano and orchestra, 1981; Mostraspelet, baritone solo, choir, orchestra and mediaeval instruments, 1983; Ave Maria, concerto for organ and string orchestra, 1984; Something New - Below Ground, concerto for tuba and brass band, 1985; Mostrasuite for baritone solo, unison choir and orchestra, 1986; Introduction and Passacaglia, over a theme by Fartein Valen, organ solo, 1987; Hammerklavier, piano solo, 1989; Orpheus, flute, piano and ballet dancer, 1993; One Night on Earth, oratorio, 1993; Hans Egedes Natt, opera, 1995; Ibsen Songs, song and piano, 1996; Liturgic dramas/church plays, choral works, chamber music, cantatas, organ chorals, motets. Publications: Cantate - Handbook of Norwegian Sacred Choral Works, 1989; Themes, Trends and Talents, 25 Years of Contemporary Norwegian Music, co-editor, 1992; Arrangements, Arenas and Actors in Contemporary Norwegian Music, editor and writer, 1992; Yearbook of Contemporary Norwegian Music, 1977, editor and writer, 1997. Honours: 1st Prize, TONO Competition for Choral Works, 1978; 1st Prize Jubal in competition for a new organ, Borgund Church, 1981; The Oslo City Cultural Stipendium, 1994; FestivalComposer, Festival of Northern Norway, 1995. Memberships: Norwegian Society of Composers, 1981-, Board Member, 1987-96, Vice Chairman, 1990-96, Chairman of the Advisory Board, 1996-. Address: Wesselsvei 5, N-1412 Sofimyr, Norway.

HABERMANN Michael (Robert), b. 23 Feb 1950, Paris, France. Pianist; Piano Instructor; Composer. Education: AAS, Nassau Community College, Garden City, NY, 1976; BA 1978, MA 1979, Long Island University, Greenvale, NY; DMA, Peabody Conservatory, Baltimore, MD, 1985. Debut: Carnegie Recital Hall, 1977. Career: American Liszt Festival appearances in 1978, 1982, 1993; International Piano Festival, University of Maryland in 1979; Grand Piano Programme, National Public radio recital in 1981; McMaster University, Hamilton, Ontario, Canada, 1983; Rocky River Chamber Music Society, OH, 1984. Recordings: Sorabji: A Legend in His Own Time; Sorabji: Le Jardin Parfumé; Sorabji: Piano Music, volume 3; Piano Music of Alexandre Rey Colaço Educo. Publications: Kaikhosru Shapurji Sorabji, The Piano Quarterly, 1983; The Exotic Piano Masterpieces of Sorabji, Soundpage and Score, Keyboard Magazine, 1986; A Style Analysis of The Nocturnes for Solo Piano by Kaikhosru Shapurji Sorabji with special emphasis on Le Jardin Parfumé, University Microfilms International; Author of Sorabji's Piano Music, in Sorabji: A Critical Celebration, 1993; Author, Essay for Remembering Horowitz: 125 Pianists recall a legend, 1993. Hobbies: Computers; Jogging; Films; Swimming; Cycling. Address: 4208 Harford Terrace, Baltimore, MD 21214, USA.

HACKER Alan (Ray), b. 30 Sept 1938, Dorking, Surrey. Clarinettist; Conductor; Lecturer. m. (1) Anna Maria Sroka, 1959, 2 daughters, (2) Karen Evans, 1977, div, 1 son, (3) Margaret Shelley Lee, 1995. Education: Royal Academy of Music; FRAM. Career: Joined London Philharmonic Orchestra, 1958; Professor, Royal Academy of Music, 1960-76; Co-Founder, Pierrot Players, 1965; Founded Matric, 1971, Music Party for authentic performance of classical music, 1972, Classical Orchestra, 1977; Member, Fires of London, 1970-76; Guest Conductor, Orchestra La Fenice, Venice, 1981; Revived basset clarinet, restored original text to Mozart's concerto and quintet, 1967; Revived baroque clarinet, 1975; 1st modern authentic performances, 1977-, including: Mozart Symphonies 39, 40; Beethoven Symphonies 2, 3, 7, 9 and Egmont; Haydn Harmonie and Creation Masses, Symphony 104, Trumpet Concerto; Premieres, music by Birtwistle, Boulez, Feldman, Goehr, Maxwell Davies, Stockhausen, Blake, Mellers, Sciarrino; Conductor, 5 staged performances of Bach St John Passion, European Music Year, 1984; Directed Hallström's Den Bergtagna revival, Swedish National Opera (for Norrlands Operan), 1986-87, and 1st production of complete La Finta Giardiniera; Conducted Kaiser's Claudius, Vadstena Academy, Sweden, 1989; Premiered Judith Weir's The Vanishing Bridegroom, Scottish Opera, 1990; Cosi fan tutte, La Finta Giardiniera, Opera North, 1990-91; Stuttgart Opera, 1990-96, Don Giovanni and Monteverdi's Ulisse; Cosi fan tutte, La Cenerentola, Barcelona, 1992, Giulio Cesare, Halle Handel Festival; Le Clemenza di Tito, Vienna, 1994; Opera de Paris Bastille, Magic Flute; Stuttgart Opera, Purcell's King Arthur, 1996-97; Handel's Xerxes, Cologne, 1996-97; Sir Robert Mayer Lecturer, Leeds University, 1972-73; Senior Lecturer, Music, York University, 1976-85; Orchestral work with major orchestras worldwide. Recordings: Many including Brahms Clarinet Sonatas, 1989. Publications: Mozart Concerto and Quintet scores, 1972; Reconstructed Mozart Concerto, 1st edition, 1973; Schumann's Soirestücke, 1985. Honours: OBE, 1988; Patron, Artlink, 1993; Hobby: Cookery. Address: Hindlea, Broughton, Malton, North Yorkshire YO17 0QJ, England.

HADARI Omri, b. 10 Sep 1941, Israel. Conductor. m. Osnat Hadari, 29 Jun 1965, 1 son, 1 daughter. Education: Tel-Aviv Music College; Guildhall School of Music and Drama, London. Debut: London in 1974. Career: Conductor, London Lyric Orchestra; Principal Guest Conductor, Adelaide Symphony Orchestra; Conducted Shostakovich's New Babylon in London in 1982, New York and Helsinki and at the Flanders Festival; Debut with Australian Opera in 1988 in La Bohème; Music Director and Principal Conductor, Cape Town Symphony Orchestra, South Africa, 1989-; Guest Conductor for Royal Philharmonic Orchestra, London Symphony Orchestra, City of Birmingham Symphony Orchestra, The Australian Opera, Sydney Symphony Orchestra, Melbourne Symphony Orchestra, South Australia Symphony Orchestra, Queensland Symphony Orchestra, Israel Chamber Orchestra, Jerusalem Symphony Orchestra, Beer-Sheva Sinfonietta, Het Brabant Symphony Orchestra, Dutch National Ballet, Victorian State Opera, Ulster Orchestra, National Symphony Orchestra of South Africa, Natal Philharmonic, Columbus Symphony Orchestra, Ohio, San Francisco Chamber Orchestra, Orchestra of Radio City New York, Lahti Symphony Orchestra, Avanti Orchestra, and Tasmania Symphony Orchestra. Honours: Winner, Dr Leo Kestenberg Prize, Israel, 1969; Conducting Prize, Guildhall School of Music, 1974; Capsalic Cup for Conducting, 1974; Fellow, Guildhall School of Music, 1983. Membership: Incorporated Society of Musicians. Current Management: Christopher Tennant Artists' Management. Address: 7 Hurstwood Road, London, NW11 0AS, England.

HADDOCK Marcus, b. 19 June 1957,Fort Worth, Texas, USA. Singer (Tenor). Career: Appearances at opera houses of Fort Worth and Dallas, Baton Rouge, Boston, Miami, Atlanta and Pennsylvania, 1984-; Roles have included Lindoro (L'Italiana in Algeri), Almaviva, Ramiro (Cenerentola) and Pinkerton; Washington Opera, 1987-88 as Gounod's Romeo, Lindoro and Jacquino; European engagements include Ford in Salieri's Falstaff and Nemorino for Hungarian National Opera at Bordeaux, Ernesto, Tamino, Rodolfo and Edgardo at Aachen, 1988-90; Karlsruhe 1990-, as Edgardo, Rudolfo, Alfredo and Tamino; Guest appearances at Cologne as Pinkerton and Nemorino, Vienna, Zurich, Hamburg (Wilhelm Meister in Mignon) and Opera Bastille, Paris (Idomeneo 1991); La Scala Milan debut, 1992 as Matteo in Arabella; Season 1992-93 at Bonn (Hoffmann, Werther) Reggio Emilia (Cassio), Cologne, Munich (Mitridate) and Essen; Sang Rodolfo in La Bohème for Bath City Opera, 1992; Gounod's Roméo at Geneva, 1996; Concert appearances with Leonard Slatkin and Simon Rattle in USA in works by Britten, Janacek, Berlioz and Mozart; Further showings with Dusseldorf and Aachen Symphonies, Philharmonica Hungarica and Berlin Concert Choir. Address: Atholl Still Ltd, Foresters Hall, 25-27 Westow Street, London SE19 3RY, England.

HADJINIKOS George, b. 3 May 1923, Volos, Greece. Conductor; Concert Pianist; Lecturer; Teacher. m. Matina Crithary, dec, 1 s. Education: Athens University; Diploma, Athens Conservatoire; Soloist and Conducting degrees with Distinction, Special Award of the Lilly Lehmann Golden Medal, Mozarteum at Salzburg; Postgraduate studies with Carl Orff, Munich, Ed Erdmann, Hamburg and G Chavchavadze, Paris. Career: Concert soloist, Conductor, Lecturer in Europe, USA, South Africa, India and Brazil; World premieres of works by Nikos Skalkottas; Soloist with many international orchestras including: BBC Orchestra with Antal Dorati, Hallé Orchestra with Sir John Barbirolli, NDR with Herman Scherchen, Suisse Romande, Zurich and Copenhagen Radio; Conductor of many orchestras worldwide including: London Bach Festival Ensemble, RAI Milan Orchestra (Athens Festival opening concert), Rio de Janeiro Radio Orchestra, Sinfonie Orchester Berlin and numerous international youth orchestras; Concert tour of US universities; Prepared and Conducted 1st Greek performance of Brahms's German Requiem, 1992; Nexus Opera Workshop; Lectured, Wuerzburg European Council Symposium; Developed fresh approach, Logic and Foundations of Musical Interpretation presented at open seminars and articles; Musical Director of the Hortos International Seminars, where Greek musical youth meets musical youth from Europe, Russia, America and other countries, 1983-; Teacher, Royal Manchester and Royal Northern Colleges of Music, 1961-88. Recordings: Album with works by Bach, Bartók, Skalkottas, Konstantinidis and Poniridis. Publications: Monographs on Skalkottas, 1981 and Mozart's Recitative, 1991; Co-editor, The Complete works by Nikos Skalkottas. Current Management: PIA Agency. Address: PIA Aency, Amerikis 15, Athens 10672, Greece.

HADLEY Jerry, b. 16 Jun 1952, Peoria, Illinois, USA. Tenor. m. Cheryll Drake Hadley. Education: Studied at Univeresity of Illinois and with Thomas LoMonaco. Debut: Sarasota, FL in 1978 as Lionel in Martha. Career includes: New York City Opera debut in 1979 as Arturo in Lucia di Lammermoor, returning as Werther, Tom Rakewell, Rodolfo, Pinkerton and Nadir; Vienna Staatsoper debut in 1982 as Nemorino in L'Elisir d'Amore; Glyndebourne debut in 1984 as Idamante in Trevor Nunn's production of Idomeneo; Covent Garden in 1984 as Fenton in Falstaff; Metropolitan Opera debut in 1987 as Des Grieux in Manon; Guest engagements in Chicago, Hamburg, Berlin, Munich and Geneva; Other roles include Gounod's Faust, the Duke of Mantua and the tenor leads in Anna Bolena and Maria Stuarda; Hamburg in 1987 as Tamino and sang Edgardo at the Deutsche Oper Berlin and Washington, 1988-89; Candide in a concert performance of Bernstein's work in London in 1989; Sang Hoffmann in London in 1992; Sang Tom Rakewell at the 1994 Salzburg Festival; Created the title role in Myron Fink's The Conquistador, San Diego, 1997; Concert engagements with the Pittsburgh Symphony, Boston Symphony, Chicago Symphony, Philadelphia Orchestra, Vienna Philharmonic and Los Angeles Philharmonic; Recitals with pianist, Cheryll Drake Hadley. Recordings include: Schubert Mass in E flat; La Bohème; Beethoven's Choral Symphony; Requiems of Mozart and Verdi with the Robert Shaw Chorale; Britten's Serenade, Nocturne and Les Illuminations; Il Re Pastore conducted by Neville Marriner. Address: c/o IMG Artists, Media House, 3 Burlington Lane, Chiswick, London W4 2TH, England.

HAEBLER Ingrid, b. 20 Jun 1926, Vienna, Austria. Concert Pianist. Education: Studied at the Salzburg Mozarteum, the Vienna Academy and the Geneva Conservatory; Further study in Paris with Marguerite Long. Debut: Salzburg in 1937. Career: Many concert tours of Europe, Australia, USA, Canada, South Africa and Japan; Festival appearances at Salzburg, Bath, Edinburgh, Wiesbaden, Amsterdam and Prague; Concerts with the Concertgebouw Orchestra, London Symphony, Royal Philharmonic, Vienna and Berlin Philharmonics, Boston Symphony, Lamoureux Orchestra, Stockholm and Warsaw Philharmonics, and London Mozart Players; Teacher at the Salzburg Mozarteum from 1969. Recordings include: Two Cycles of the Complete Piano Concertos of Mozart; Complete Sonatas of

Mozart and Schubert; Beethoven's 2nd and 4th Concertos; Schumann Piano Concerto; Symphonic Variations by Franck; Works by JC Bach on the Fortepiano. Honours: Winner, International Competition Munich and Schubert Competition Geneva, 1954; Beethoven Medal, Harriet Cohen Foundation, 1957; Grand Prix du Disque, Paris, 1958; Puthon Prize, Salzburg Festival; Mozart Medal, Vienna, 1971. Address: 5412 St Jakob am Thurn, Post Buch Bei Hallein, Land Salzburg, Austria.

HAEFELI Anton, b. 3 February 1946, Brugg, Switzerland. Musicologist; Professor. 1 son, 1 daughter. Education: University of Zurich, 1966-71; Conservatory, Zurich, 1966-71; Musicology under Kurt Van Fischer; Music Theory under Rudolf Velterborn. Career: Director, Music School Spreitenbach, Switzerland, 1977-87; Professor, Board Member, Musikhochschule Basel, 1987-. Publications: Die Geschrichte der TGNM, 1982; Jacques Wildberger Oder Die, 1996; Vom Musik Padagogischen Eros, 1998. Contributions to: Music of the 20th Century. Memberships: ISM; ISCM. Hobbies: Flying; Climbing. Address: Stapferstr 14, 5000 Aarau, Switzerland.

HAEFLIGER Ernst, b. 6 July 1919, Davos, Switzerland. Tenor. Education: Studied in Zurich and with Fernando Carpi in Geneva; Further study with Julius Patzak in Vienna. Debut: In 1942 as the Evangelist in Bach's St John Passion. Career: Sang with Zurich Opera, 1943-52; Many concert appearances in Switzerland, Germany, Austria, France and Holland, notably in the St Matthew Passion and Lieder cycles by Schubert; Salzburg Festival in 1949 as Tiresias in the premiere of Antigonae by Orff, returning for Ideomeneo and the Choral Symphony; Glyndebourne Festival, 1956-57 as Tamino in Die Zauberflöte and as Belmonte in Die Entführung; Guest appearances in Munich, Hamburg, Florence, Aix-en-Provence, Brussels and Berlin at the Deutsche Oper, 1952-74; Sang in the first performances of the oratorios Le Vin Herbé, Golgotha and in Terra Pax, by Frank Martin; Visited Moscow and Leningrad with the Munich Bach Choir in 1968; Professor at the Musikhochschule Munich from 1971; Sang the Shepherd in Tristan und Isolde at Munich, 1996. Recordings: St Matthew Passion; Missa Solemnis; Oedipus Rex; Pelléas et Mélisande; Die Entführung; Fidelio; Don Giovanni; Die Zauberflöte; Der fliegende Holländer; Brockes Passion by Handel; Die Israeliten in der Wuste by CPE Bach. Publication: Die Singstimme, 1984. Address: c/o Ingpen and Williams Ltd, 14 Kensington Court, London, W8 5DN, England.

HAENCHEN Hartmut, b. 21 Mar 1943, Dresden, Germany. Conductor. Education: Member of the Dresden Kreuzchor, 1953-60, under Rudolf Mauersbergee and at the Dresden Musikhochschule, 1960-66. Career includes: Directed the Robert-Franz-Singakademie and the Halle Symphony, 1966-72; Music Director at the Zwickau Opera, 1972-73; Permanent Conductor of the Dresden Philharmonic, 1973-76, Philharmonic Chorus of Dresden, 1974-76 and permanent guest conductor of the Staatsoper Dresden; Musical Director of the Schwerin Staatstheater and conductor of the Mecklenburg Staatskapelle, 1976-79; Professor of Conducting, Dresden Musikhochschule, 1980-86; Permanent Guest Conductor at Komische Oper Berlin and Berlin Staatsoper; Guest appearances in Europe, USA, Canada and Japan, at leading opera houses in Europe and at Kirishima Festival in Japan; From 1980 Director of the CPE Bach Chamber Orchestra, Berlin; From 1986 Musical Director of the Netherlands Opera and Principal Conductor of the Netherlands Philharmonic Orchestra founded in 1985, and the Netherlands Chamber Orchestra; Conducted Bluebeard's Castle, La Damnation de Faust, Elektra, Salome, Rosenkavalier, Le nozze di Figaro, Entführung, Don Carlos, Tristan, Parsifal, Boris Godunov, Orphée et Euridice; Conducted Gluck's Orfeo ed Euridice at Covent Garden in 1991 followed by Mozart's Mitridate; Die Frau ohne Schatten, Mitridate, La Damnation de Faust and Samson et Dalila at Amsterdam in 1992; Opened the 1994 season for Netherlands Opera with Lady Macbeth of the Mtsensk District; Elektra at Amsterdam, 1996. Recordings: Numerous including Gluck's Orfeo ed Euridice earning the Preis der Deutschen Schallplatten and Gramophone Award Nomination. Address: De Nederlandse Opera, Waterlooplein 22, 1011 PG Amsterdam, Netherlands.

HAENDEL Ida, b. 15 Dec 1923, Chelm, Poland. Concert Violinist. Education: Gold Medal at age 7, Warsaw Conservatorium; Private teachers, Carl Flesch and Georges Enesco. Debut: British Queen's Hall London with Brahms Concerto under Henry Wood. Career: Concerts for British and US Troops and in factories, World War II; Then career developed to take in North and South America, Russia, Far East, Europe; Has played with conductors such as Beecham, Klemperer, Szell, Barenboim, Mata, Pritchard and Rattle; Has accompanied British orchestras on tours to China, Hong Kong and Australia; Performances with major orchestras worldwide include, Boston Symphony, New York Philharmonic, Berlin Philharmonic, City of Birmingham Symphony Orchestra, London Philharmonic, Philharmonia and Royal Philharmonic Orchestra; Major festival appearances including regular performances at BBC Promenade Concerts, London; Played the Britten Concerto at the 1994 Proms. Recordings: Numerous records including Bach Solo Partitas, 1996. Publication: Woman with Violin, autobiography, 1970. Honours: Huberman Prize, 1935; Sibelius Medal, Sibelius Society of Finland, 1982; New Years Honours List Awarded CBE for Outstanding Services to Music, 1991. Current Management and Address: c/o Harold Holt Ltd, 31 Sinclair Road, London, W14 0NS, England.

HAENEN Tom, b. Amsterdam, Netherlands. Singer (Bass). Education: Studied at Amsterdam Conservatoire. Debut: As Don Alfonso in Cosi fan Tutte for Netherlands Opera. Career: Appearances in the Netherlands and elsewhere as the General in Prokofiev's The Gambler, Arkel in Pelléas et Mélisande and Ferrando in Il Trovatore, Osmin in Die Entführung for Opera North and Leporello and Geronte in Manon Lescaut in Dublin; Further engagements as Sparafucile in Rigoletto at Barcelona, Don Cassandro in La Finta Semplice and Tom in Un Ballo in Maschera for Flanders Opera in 1992; Guest appearances at Spoleto, Israel and Las Palmas Festivals. Honours include: Prizewinner at the International s'Hertogenbosch and Rio de Janeiro Competitions. Address: c/o Anglo Swiss Management, Suite 35-37 Morley House, 320 Regent Street, London W1R 5AD, England.

HAGEGARD Erland, b. 27 Feb 1944, Brunskog, Sweden. Baritone. m. Anne Terelius. Education: Studied in Sweden with Arne Sunnegaard, Erik Werba in Vienna and Gerald Moore in Vienna. Debut: Vienna Volksoper in 1968 in Trois Opéras Minutes by Milhaud. Career: Sang with Frankfurt Opera, 1971-74; Member of the Hamburg Staatsoper from 1974; Guest with the Vienna Staatsoper from 1976; Appearances at the Drottningholm Court Opera in Sweden; Danish TV in Xerxes by Handel; Roles include Escamillo, Valentin, Don Giovanni, Eugene Onegin, Albert in Werther and Germont in La Traviata; Lieder singer in works by Schubert; TV appearances include Suppé's Boccaccio.

HAGEGARD Håkan, b. 25 Nov 1945, Karlstad, Sweden. Baritone. m. Barbara Bonney, 2 children. Education: Music Academy of Stockholm; Student of Tito Gobbi, Rome, Gerald Moore, London, and Erik Werba, Vienna. Debut: As Papageno in The Magic Flute, Royal Opera, Sweden, 1968. Career: Metropolitan Opera debut in 1978 as Donizetti's Malatesta; Member of Royal Opera Stockholm; Appeared with major opera companies throughout Europe, in film of The Magic Flute in 1975 and at Glyndebourne from 1973 as the Count in Figaro and Capriccio and as Mozart's Guglielmo; Created role of Crispin in Tintomara, Royal Opera Stockholm in 1973; Covent Garden debut in 1987 as Wolfram in Tannhäuser, also at Chicago in 1988; Metropolitan Opera in 1988 as Guglielmo; Sang Eisenstein in Die Fledermaus at Chicago in 1989; Created Beaumarchais in The Ghosts of Versailles by Corigliano at the Metropolitan in 1991; Deutsche Oper Berlin in 1992 as Wolfram; Season 1996 at the Met as Prus in The Makropoulos Case and in April Gala; Recitalist. Recordings include: Die Zauberflöte under Armin Jordan; Don Giovanni, in title role, from Drottningholm. Current Management: Thea Dispeker. Address: c/o Thea Dispeker Artists' Management, 59 East 54th Street, New York, NY 10022, USA.

HAGEN Christina, b. 1956, Hamburg, Germany. Mezzo-Soprano. Education: Studied singing with Naan Pold and Hilde Nadolowitsch; Concert Diploma, Exam as Private Music Instructor, Opera Diploma with Distinction, Hochschule für Musik und Darstellende Kunst, Hamburg; Masterclasses including with Sena Jurinac and at International Studio for Singing, Herbert von Karajan Stiftung, with Christa Ludwig. Career: Engaged at Staatstheater Oldenburg, 1983-84, then Deutsche Oper am Rhein, Dusseldorf-Duisburg, 1984-; Guest appearances in Germany at Berlin, Hamburg and Köln, at Bolshoi Theatre in Moscow, Antwerp, Amsterdam and Staatsoper Berlin, National Theater Munich; Participant at Bayreuth Festival in 1989, 1990, 1991; Has sung Rosina in Barber of Seville, Micha in Samson by Handel, Judith in Bluebeard's Castle by Bartók and Jocasta in Oedipus Rex at Oldenburg, Olga in Eugene Onegin and Second Woman in Die Zauberflöte at Oldenburg and Dusseldorf, the Composer in Ariadne auf Naxos, Dorabella in Così fan tutte, Nicklausse in Tales of Hoffmann, Orlowsky in Die Fledermaus, Maddalena in Rigoletto, Fatima in Weber's Oberon, Sextus in Julius Caesar by Handel, Flosshilde, Erda and Fricka in Rheingold and in Walküre, Second Norn and Waltraute, Fenena in Nabucco, Britten's Lucretia, Olga in Das Schloss, Ottavia in Monteverdi's L'Incoronazione di Poppea, Eboli at Dusseldorf, Clytemnestra (Gluck) at Dusseldorf and Berlin, Fricka in Walküre at Munich, Santuzza in Cavalleria Rusticana at Eutiner Festival; Many lieder recitals and concert appearances. Honours: Nominated Chamber Singer of Deutsche Oper am Rhein at Dusseldorf, 1992. Address: c/o Deutsche Oper am Rhein, Heinrich-Heine Allee 16, 40213 Dusseldorf, Germany.

HAGEN-GROLL Walter, b. 15 Apr 1927, Chemnitz, Germany. Choral Conductor. Education: Studied at the Stuttgart Musikhochschule, 1947-52. Career: Assistant Conductor at the Stuttgart Opera, 1952; Chorus Master at the Heidelberg Opera, 1957, and Deutsche Oper Berlin, 1961; Directed the chorus of the Berlin Philharmonic from 1961; Assisted Wilhelm Pitz at Bayreuth, 1960-62; Chorus Master at Salzburg Festival from 1965, Philharmonia Chorus, London, 1971-74; Chorus Master at the Vienna Staatsoper 1984, Vienna Singakademie 1987; Choral Director at the Salzburg Mozarteum from 1986.

HAGENAH Elizabeth (Artman), b. USA. Concert Pianist; Conductor; Pedagogue. m. Henry H Hagenah, 20th June 1953, 2 sons, 1 daughter. Education: Valedictorian, Le Roy High School; BM; MM; Performer's Certificate; Graduate with distinction, Eastman School of Music, Rochester, NY, USA; Advanced Study with Isabella Vengerova, Chairman of Piano Department of Curtis School of Music; Fulbright Scholar to Germany: Hochschule fur Musik, Freiburg im Breisgau; Hochschule fur Musik, Hamburg; Doctoral study nearly completed at School of Music, Boston University. Debut: Manhattan's Town Hall, NYC, USA; Orchestral debut, Eastman Theatre, Rochester, NY, USA. Career: Faculty Member, Eastman School of Music, 1953-55; Fulbright Scholar to Germany, 1955-57; 3 Solo Concerts, Town Hall, NY, 1968; Teaching Fellow, Doctoral Candidate and Professor of Piano, Boston University, 1965-84; Performer on New York's Radio WNYC, Keyboard Masters Series, 1968-69; Founder and Artistic Director, Stockbridge Concerts International Inc, 1975-; Organized Summer Konzerte Mulkenkur, Heidelberg, 1983; Collaborator with Principals and Members of Boston Symphony Orchestra; Frequent recitalist and soloist with orchestral and chamber ensemble in major cities in USA, Canada and Europe. Address: 68 Kenilworth Street, Pittsfield, MA 01201, USA.

HAGER Leopold, b. 6 Oct 1935, Salzburg, Austria. Conductor. m. Gertrude Entleitner, 2 Jul 1960, 1 d. Education: Graduated in organ, piano, conducting, harpsichord, High School for Music (Mozarteum), Salzburg. Career: Assistant Conductor, Staedtische Buhnen, Mainz, Germany, 1957-62; Principal Conductor: Landestheater, Linz, Austria, 1962-64; Opernhaus, Cologne, Germany, 1964-65; General Music Director: Staedtische Buhnen, Freiburg, Germany, 1965-69; Principal Conductor, Mozarteum Orchestra, Salzburg, 1969-81; Has conducted many performances of early operas by Mozart; Led the first modern performance of Mitridate, Salzburg, 1971; Symphony Orchestra, Radio Luxembourg, 1981-; Guest Conductor: Vienna Opera; Munich Opera; Metropolitan Opera; Covent Garden; Teatro Colón, Buenos Aires; Berlin and Vienna Philharmonics; Conducted Cosi fan tutte at the Metropolitan, 1991; Figaro, 1997. Recordings: Mozart Piano Concertos, with Karl Engel; Bastien und Bastienne, Lucio Silla, Il re Pastore, Ascanio in Alba, Mitridate Re di Ponto; CD of La Finta Semplice released 1990. Honour: Decorated, Ehrenkreuz 1 klasse fur Kunst und Wissenschaft, Austria. Address: Morzgerstr 102, A-5034 Salzburg, Austria.

HÅGGANDER Mari Anne, b. 23 Oct 1951, Trokorna, Sweden. Soprano. Education: Opera School, Gothenburg. Debut: As Micaela in Carmen, Ponelle production, Royal Opera, Stockholm. Career: Has sung Cherubino, Elisabetta in Don Carlo at Savonlinna in Finland, Pamina and the Countess in Figaro at Bonn and Buxton Festival, Eva in Meistersinger at Bayreuth in 1981, Mimi at Stockholm and Hamburg, Eva at the Metropolitan in 1985, and Elsa in Lohengrin at San Francisco; Guest appearances include Berlin, Munich, Paris, Brussels, Vienna, New York, Seattle and Toronto; Other roles include Butterfly, Amelia in Un Ballo in Maschera and Simon Boccanegra, Marschallin, Titiania in Eugene Onegin, Lisa in The Queen of Spades, Sieglinde, Arabella, and Donna Anna. Recordings: Das Rheingold with Levine; Peer Gynt with Blomstedt; Several lieder and sacred music recordings. Honour: Court Singer to His Majesty the King of Sweden. Current Management: Ulf Tornqvist. Address: c/o Artistsekretariat Ulf Tornqvist, Sankt Eriksgatan 100 2 tr, S-113 31 Stockholm, Sweden.

HAGLEY Alison, b. 9 May 1961, London, England. Soprano. Education: Studied at the Guildhall School of Music and the National Opera Studio. Career: Sang in Handel's Rodelinda at the Aldeburgh Festival and Handel's Flavio with Musica nel Chiostro at the 1985 Batignano Festival in Italy; Camden Festival in 1986 in La Finta Giardiniera by Mozart; Sang Clorinda in Opera 80's 1987 production of La Cenerentola; Glyndebourne debut in 1988 as the Little Owl in L'Enfant et Les Sortilèges, returning in Jenufa and as Susanna, Nannetta, Papagena and Zerlina; Glyndebourne Tour as Varvara in Katya Kabanova, Despina and Papagena; Covent Garden as a Flowermaiden in Parsifal and in Peter Grimes; English National Opera in 1991 as Lauretta in a new production of Gianni Schicchi and Gretel in Hansel and Gretel; Scottish Opera appearances as Musetta in La Bohème and Adele in Die Fledermaus; Sang Mélisande in 1992 with Boulez and Peter Stein, WNO; Sang Nannetta for ENO in 1992; Glyndebourne 1994, as Susanna; Covent Garden 1997, in Massenet's Chérubin. Honours include: FPC Opera Singer of the Year, National Opera Studio. Address: c/o Harrison Parrott Ltd, 12 Penzance Place, London, W11 4PA, England.

HAGLUND J T Tommie, b. 15 Jan 1959, Kalmar, Sweden. Composer. 2 daughters. Education: Royal Academy of Music, Århus, Denmark. Debut: Konserthuset, Stockholm, 1987. Career:

Concerts performed in chamber music festivals in Sweden and Denmark, and a musical portrait on Swedish Radio Berwaldhallen; Appearances on TV and radio in Sweden, Canada, Denmark; World premiere in London's Wigmore Hall, 1997; Concerts in several European countries; Commission for the celebration of King Carl Gustav XVI 50th birthday, 1996. Compositions: Intensio Animi; Voces; L'Infinito; Speglingar; Inim-Inim; Other chamber music and choral works; To the Sunset Breeze, 1997. Recording: CD of chamber music. Publications: Känsloresan, Children's emotional and imaginative development through musical experience, 1996. Contributions to: Articles on the music of Delius to magazines and journals. Honours: Anniversary Scholarship, County of Halland; Scholarship, Society of Swedish Composers; Hallandsposten's Cultural Prize. Membership: Society of Swedish Composers. Hobbies: Cooking; Contemplation; Absurd comedy. Current Management: Res Medica AB (Ltd). Address: Långeby Paradisäppelhuset, 31031 Eldsberga, Sweden.

HAHN Barbara, b. 1965, Stuttgart, Germany. (Mezzo-Soprano) Singer. Education: Studied in Stuttgart and at Salzburg Mozarteum. Career: Sang at Bielefeld from 1987 as Dorabella, Cherubino and Orlofsky; Nicklausse in Les contes d'Hoffmann at Bregenz Festival, 1987; Appeared as Dorabella and Nicklausse at Hanover, 1988; Sang Grimgerde in Die Walküre at Bologna; Angelina, in La Cenerentola at Passau; Freiburg Opera, 1989-91, as Octavian, Idamantes, Hansel and Sonja in Der Zarewitsch; Concert performance of Schreker's Der ferne Klang in Berlin, 1990; Frankfurt Opera, 1992-, debut as Dorabella. Recordings: Der ferne Klang, conducted by Gerd Albrecht. Address: c/o Athole Still International Management Ltd, Foresters Hall, 25-27 Westow Street, London, SE19 3RY, England.

HAHN Hilary, b. 27 November 1979, Lexington, Virginia, USA. Violinist. Education: BMus, Curtis Institute of Music, Philadelphia. Debut: Age 6 years, Baltimore, 1986. Career: First Full Recital, Age 10 years, 1990; Major Orchestra Debut with Baltimore Symphony Orchestra, 1991; Utah & Florida Symphonies, 1992; Philadelphia Orchestra, 1993; New York Philharmonic Orchestra and Cleveland Orchestra, 1994; European concerto debut in Budapest, with Budapest Festival Orchestra, and European Recital Debut at Festival de Sully et d'Orleans, France, 1994; German Debut at 15 Playing Beethoven Violin Concerto with Bavarian Radio Symphony Orchestra and Lorin Maazel, Munich, 1995; Carnegie Hall Debut at 16 with Philadelphia Orchestra and Christoph Eschenbach, 1996; Concerto Debuts in Berlin, Frankfurt, Hannover and Rotterdam, 1996; Recital Debuts in Kennedy Center (DC), Alice Tully Hall, New York, Munich, Rotterdam and Paris, 1997; Concerto Debuts in London, Glasgow, Birmingham, Zurich & Vienna with Bavarian Radio Symphony, and in Paris with French Radio Symphony Orchestra, 1998; As Chamber Musician Appears Regularly at Marlboro Music Festival, Skaneateles Festival and with the Chamber Music Society of Lincoln Center, New York. Recordings include: Solo Sonatas and Partitas of J S Bach. Honour: Avery Fisher Career Grant, 1995. Current Management: IMG Artists. Address: c/o IMG Artists, 450 West 45th Street, New York, NY 10036, USA.

HAIGH Andrew (Wilfred), b. 26 Apr 1954, Lagos, Nigeria. Pianist. Education: Student, 1969-74; Associate, Royal College of Music, London, 1975; Studied with the late Cyril Smith, Phyllis Sellick, Albert Ferber, 1974; Licenciate, Royal Academy of Music, 1975. Debut: London Philharmonic Orchestra, Royal Festival Hall, 1965; Wigmore Hall, 1971. Career: Soloist with all major British orchestras including: London Symphony; London Philharmonic; Philharmonia; Royal Philharmonic; BBC Philharmonic Orchestra; Soloist, Herbert von Karajan Festival, Berlin, 1970; Recitals in Europe; Head of Piano, Kent Centre for Young Instrumentalists; Examiner, Trinity College of Music, and Adjudicator. Honours: Gold Medallist, 1969; Winner, BBC Mozart Competition, 1969; Winner, Royal Overseas Competition; National Piano Competition; Hopkinson Silver Medal, 1973; Dannreuther Concerto Prize, Royal College of Music. Membership: Incorporated Society of Musicians. Hobbies: Swimming; Hill Walking; Classic Cars. Address: 15 Dornden Drive, Langton Green, Tunbridge Wells, Kent, TN3 0AA, England.

HAILSTORK Adolphus (Cunningham), b. 17 Apr 1941, Rochester, NY, USA. Composer. Education: Studied at Howard University, Washington DC, with Nadia Boulanger in France and at the Manhattan School, MMus, 1966; Further study at Michigan State University, PhD, 1971. Career: Teacher at Michigan State, 1969-91, Youngstown State University, 1971-76, Norfolk Virginia State College, 1977-. Compositions include: The Race For Space, theatre piece, 1963; Phaedra, tone poem, 1966; Horn Sonata, 1966; Statement, Variation And Fugue for Orchestra, 1966; Sextet for Strings, 1971; Violin Sonata, 1972; Bagatelles for Brass Quintet, 1973; Pulse for Percussion Ensemble, 1974; Bellevue and Celebration, both for Orchestra, 1974; Concerto for Violin, Horn and Orchestra, 1975; Spiritual for Brass Octet, 1975; American Landscape, Nos 1, 3 and 4 for Orchestra, 1977-84; American Landscape for Violin and Cello, 1978; Piano Sonata, 1981; Sport of Strings, 1981; Unaccompanied choral music, and with brass and percussion accompaniment. Honours include: Ernest Bloch Award, 1971; Commissions from the Edward Tarr Brass Ensemble and the Virginia Symphony. Address: c/o ASCAP, ASCAP Building, One Lincoln Plaza, New York, NY 10023, USA.

HAIMOVITZ Matt, b. 3 Dec 1970, Tel Aviv, Israel. Solo Concert Cellist. Education: Juilliard School, NY, 1982-87; Graduated, Collegiate School, NY, 1989; Princeton University, 1989- and Harvard University, 1993-; Studied cello with Gabor Rejto and Leonard Rose, music analysis with Carl Schahter. Career includes: Appeared with Israel Philharmonic Orchestra under Mehta at Mann Auditorium, Tel Aviv, broadcast on Israel National TV, 1985; London debut with English Chamber Orchestra under Barenboim at the Barbican, 1985; Appearances with many conductors and orchestras and regular recitals throughout USA and Europe since 1985; Debut with Philharmonia Orchestra and Giuseppe Sinopoli at Royal Festival Hall in London, 1987; Debut with Chicago Symphony Orchestra under James Levine at Ravinia Festival, 1988; First tour to Japan in 1988, to Europe in 1989, and to Australia with Sydney and Melbourne Symphony Orchestras in 1991; Live concert appearance, The Performing Arts Pay Tribute to Public Television, PBS TV, 1988; Documentary on early life, CBS TV, 1989; First American recital tour in 1990; Debut with Berlin Philharmonic under James Levine in Berlin, 1990; Lucerne Festival debut with solo recital programme in 1990; Recital debuts with solo cello repertoire at Montreux Festival, Washington DC, New York and Paris in 1991; Debut with Dallas Symphony in 1992. Recordings include: Lalo and Saint-Saëns Concerti with Chicago Symphony under Levine, 1989; Solo Cello in works by Reger, Britten, Crumb and Ligeti, 1991. Honour: Avery Fisher Career Grant Award, 1985. Hobbies: Hiking; Tennis; Writing; Reading. Current Management: Harold Holt Ltd. Address: c/o Harold Holt Ltd, 31 Sinclair Road, London, W14 0NS, England.

HAITINK Bernard (John Herman), b. 4 Mar 1929, Amsterdam, Netherlands. Conductor. Education: Studied Conducting with Felix Hupke, Amsterdam Conservatory. Debut: Holland, 1956. Career: First conducted Concertgebouw, 1956; US debut 1958 with Los Angeles Philharmonic; Appointed, with Jochum, Concertgebouw's Permanent Conductor, 1961 and became Chief Conductor, 1964-88; Principal Conductor, London Philharmonic, 1967-79; Music Director, Glyndebourne Opera, 1978-88, with debut in 1972; Music Director, Royal Opera House, 1988-97; Leading new productions of The Ring (1989-91, 1994-95), Prince Igor (1990) and Katya Kabanova (1994); President, London Philharmonic, 1990-; Music Director of the European Union Youth Orchestra, 1994-; Principal Guest Conductor, Boston Symphony Orchestra, 1995-, and Guest Conductor for many major international orchestras. Recordings include: With London Philharmonic: Shostakovich, Liszt, Elgar, Holst and Vaughan Williams; With Concertgebouw: Complete symphonies of Mahler, Bruckner and Beethoven; With Vienna Philharmonic: Brahms and Bruckner; Opera includes: Don Giovanni, Cosi fan tutte and Figaro with Glyndebourne and the LPO; The Ring Cycle with Bayerische Rundfunk; Peter Grimes with Royal Opera House. Honours include: Recipient of many awards in recognition of his services to music including: Honorary KBE in 1977 and Honorary Doctorate of Music by University of Oxford, 1988; Erasmus Prize in Holland, 1991. Current Management: Harold Holt Ltd. Address: c/o Harold Holt Ltd, 31 Sinclair Road, London, W14 0NS, England.

HAJOSSYOVA Magdalena, b. 25 July 1946, Bratislava, Czechoslovakia. Singer (Soprano). Education: Studied at the Bratislava Music Academy. Debut: Slovak National Theatre Bratislava, 1971, as Marenka in The Bartered Bride. Career: Sang at the National Theatre Prague and elsewhere in Czechoslovakia; Berlin Staatsoper from 1975, as Mozart's Pamina, Fiordilgi, Contessa, Donna Anna, Handel's Alcina, Wagner's Eva, Elsa, Strauss's Arabella, Marschallin, Capriccio, Dvorak's Rusalka; Has also sung in the operas of Jan Cikker; Guest appearances as opera and concert singer in England, Belgium, Spain, Holland, Greece, Italy, France, USA, Japan, Russia, Austria, Persia and German Capitals. Recordings include: The Cunning Little Vixen, Don Giovanni and Mahler's 4th Symphony; Erindo by Sigismund Kusser; Beethoven's 9th Symphony; Mozart's Requiem; Dvorak's Requiem, Stabat Mater; Britten: Illuminations; Janacek: Missa Glagolitica; Dvorak: Dimitri; Mahler-II Symphony; Schumann: Paradies und der Peri; Gounod: Margarethe; Wagner: Wesendonk-Lieder; Strauss: Brentano-Lieder, 4 Letzte Lieder; Bruckner: Te Deum, and F minor Mass; Schubert: G major Mass and Stabat Mater; H Wolf, Italienisches Liederbuch; Mahler G and Alma: Lieder J Brahms, Lieder. Current Management: Deutsche Staatsoper Berlin, Unter den Linden 7, Germany. Address: Kopenicker Str 104, O-Berlin 19179, Germany.

HAKOLA Riika, b. 1961, Finland. Singer (Soprano). Education: Studied at the Sibelius Academy, Helsinki, in Italy and Berlin and with Vera Rozsa in London. Career: Sang in the 1989 premiere of The Knife by Paavo Heininen, at the Savonlinna Festival; National Opera, Helsinki, 1990, as Lucia di Lammermoor; Guested in London in Haydn's opera Orfeo; Sang Marzelline in Fidelio at Savonlinna, 1992, and other roles have included Rosina, Gilda, Susanna, the Queen of Night and Violetta; Frequent concert engagements in Finland and abroad. Address: c/o Finnish National Opera, Bulevardi 23-27, SF-00180 Helsinki 18, Finland.

HALA Tomás, b. 6 Sept 1963, Prague, Czechoslovakia. Conductor; Composer. Education: Prague Conservatory, Piano, Composition, 1978-84; Prague Academy of Music, Piano, Conducting, 1984-90. Career: Conductor of Opera House, České Budějovice, 1990-91; Conductor, Prague National Theatre Opera, Mozart: Don Giovanni (Assistant to Sir Charles H Mackerras), Die Zauberlöte, since 1991, Le Nozze di Figaro; Verdi: La Forza Del Destino. Compositions: Chamber Opera: Vejstupný Syn (Disobedient son); Composition with Baritone Solo - Rough Sea; Variations for Cello; Piano Concerto. Recording: Chamber Opera, Vejsstupny Syn, Czech Radio and TV, 1985. Publication: Score of Opera Vejstupný syn, 1986. Membership: Czech Musical Fund. Hobbies: Nature; Hiking; History. Address: Zavadilova 13, 160 00 Prague 6, Czechoslovakia.

HALASZ Laszlo, b. 6 Jun 1905. Debrecen, Austria-Hungary, US citizen in 1943. Conductor; Teacher. m. Suzette F Forgues, 1 son, 1 daughter. Education: Studied piano and conducting at Budapest Conservatory, graduating in 1929. Career: Toured Europe as a pianist and conductor, 1929-36; Music Director, St Louis Grand Opera, 1937-42; General Director, New York City Opera, 1944-51; Conductor, Chicago Opera Company, 1949-52; Music Director, Remington Records Inc, 1953-55; Conductor of German repertory at Gran Teatro del Liceo, Barcelona, 1955-59; Artistic Director, Empire State Music Festival, NY, 1957-65 and National Grand Opera, NY, 1983-; Head, Conducting Department, Eastman School of Music, Rochester, NY, 1965-67; Faculty, State University of New York College, Old Westbury, 1968-71, State University of New York, Stony Brook, 1971-75. Recordings: Several discs. Address: 3 Leeds Drive, Port Washington, NY 11050, USA.

HALBREICH Harry (Leopold), b. 9 Feb 1931, Berlin, Germany. Belgian Musicologist. m. Helène Chait, 11 Apr 1961, separated, 1 son, 2 daughters. Education: Geneva Conservatory, 1949-52; Studies with Arthur Honegger at Ecole Normale de Musique, Paris, 1952-54, and at Paris Conservatoire, 1955-58. Career: Teacher of Musical Analysis at Royal Conservatory, Mons, Belgium, 1970-; General Musical Adviser to the Brussels Philharmonic Society with about 180 concerts annually; Numerous lectures and seminars in Italy including Turin, Cagliari and Venice, in Spain at Madrid and Granada, in Japan at the Akiyoshidai Festival of Contemporary Music, and elswhere; Artistic Board (programme adviser), at the Venice Biennale for Contemporary Music; International jury member for International Record Critics Award, High Fidelity, New York, Academie Charles-Cros, Paris, Prix Cecilia, Brussels, and for several composition competitions at Parma, Turin and Cagliari; Regular Producer of radio programmes for RTB, Brussels and RSR in Geneva. Publications include: Edgard Varèse, in French, 1970; Olivier Messiaen, in French, 1980, revised edition, 1996; Claude Debussy, in French, 1980; Arthur Honegger, Un Musicien dans la Cité des Hommes, 1992; L'Oeuvre d'Arthur Honegger, 1993; Arthur Honegger, in the series, Les Grands Suisses, 1995; Founding Member and Co-Editor of the music magazine, Crescendo, Brussels; Large participation to the Fayard Music Guides, Paris: Piano Music, 1987, Chamber Music, 1989 and Choral Music, 1993, also several titles in the series, L'Avant-Scène Opéra, including Moses und Aron. Contributions include: Harmonie, Paris, 1965-84; Le Monde de la Musique, Paris, 1982-89; Encyclopaedia Universalis; Crescendo. Address: Avenue Brugmann 513, 1180 Bruxelles, Belgium.

HALDAS Beatrice, b. 1952, Switzerland. Soprano. Education: Studied in Berne and Milan. Debut: Stadttheater Berne in 1976 as Mozart's Countess. Career: Sang at Basle, 1977-79, Opéra du Rhin Strasbourg in 1979 as Gluck's Euridice, and Vienna Staatsoper in 1980 as Micaela; Has been based at the Hamburg Staatsoper from 1980; Other roles include Mozart's Fiordiligi and Ilia, Handel's Cleopatra, Liu in Turandot and Antonia in Les Contes d'Hoffmann; Has sung Mimi at Lucerne and appeared widely in opera and concert. Recordings include: Die Sieben Letzten Worte Unseres Erlösers am Kreuz by Haydn; Zemlinsky's Der Zwerg.

HALE Robert, b. 22 Aug 1943, Kerrville, Texas, USA. Singer (Bass-Baritone). m. Inga Nielsen, 3 sons. Education: Studied at the New England Conservatory with Gladys Miller; Boston University with Ludwig Bergman; Oklahoma University; With Boris Goldovsky in New York. Debut: Denver 1965, as Mozart's Figaro. Career: Sang with New York City Opera from 1967, debut in La Bohème; Guest appearances in Philadelphia, Pittsburgh, San Diego, Frankfurt, Paris, Munich, Berlin, London, San Francisco, Tokyo, Buenos Aires, Vienna, Zurich; Cologne

Opera 1983, as Escamillo; Metropolitan debut 1990, Dutchman; Concert appearances with the Orchestras of Chicago, Boston and Montreal; Festival engagements at Wolf Trap, Tanglewood, Lausanne and Bordeaux; Repertoire includes roles in operas by Handel, Mozart, Gounod, Bizet and Wagner; has sung Wagner's Wotan at Wiesbaden and withDeutsche Oper Berlin tour to Japan 1987, and Washighton DC, 1989; Berlin 1987, as Scarpia, Covent Garden debut 1988, as Jochanaan in Salome, returned 1990, as Orestes in Elektra; Sang the Dutchman at the 1989 Bregenz Festival; San Francisco Opera 1990, as Wotan; Pizarro in Fidelio at the 1990 Salzburg Festival; Sang Wotan in a new production Der Ring des Nibelungen at the Vienna Staatsoper, 1992-93, and at the Met, 1996; Salzburg Festival 1992, as Barak in Die Frau ohne Schatten. Recordings include: Bellini Requiem; Messiah; Das Rheingold and Die Walküre, conducted by Christoph von Dohnányi; Fliegende Holländer, Verdi Requiem; Video of Die Frau ohne Schatten. Honours include: Singer of the Year. Hobbies: Photography; Antique Cars. Address: Pflugstevistrasse 20, CH-8703 Erleubech, Switzerland.

HALE Una, b. 1922, Adelaide, South Australia. Singer (Soprano). m. Martin Carr, 1960. Education: Studied in Adelaide and at Royal College of Music, London. Career: Sang with Carl Rosa Opera Company in many roles, notably as Marguerite in Faust; Royal Opera House, Covent Garden from 1953, as Micaela, Mimi, Musetta, Mozart's Countess, Eva, Ellen Orford, Liu (Turandot), Freia, Marschallin and Walton's Cressida; Sang with Sadler's Wells from 1964, Tosca, Ellen Orford, tour of Australia with the Elizabethan Opera Company, 1962, Théâtre de la Monnaie, Brussels, 1963; Further appearances at Aldeburgh Festival and Gulbenkian Festival in Portugal; Further study with Tiana Lemnitz in Berlin and Hilde Konetzni in Vienna; Sang Ariadne, Donna Anna and Alice Ford on tour in Australia. Address: Madron, Ostlings Lane, Bathford, Bath BA1 7RW, Avon, England.

HALEM Victor Von, b. 26 Mar 1940, Berlin, Germany. Singer (Bass). Education: Studied at the Musikhochschule Munich with Else Domberger. Career: Has sung at the Deutsche Oper Berlin, 1966-; Guest appearances in Hamburg, Munich, Stuttgart, Cologne, Rome, Geneva, Montreal, Athens and London; Roles include: Wagner's Daland, Pogner, King Henry, Fafner, Fasolt and Hans Sachs, Verdi's Padre Guardiano, The Grand Inquisitor, Mozart's Sarastro and Osmin, Puccini's Colline; Mephistopheles at Strasbourg, St Bris in Les Huguenots at Berlin and at the Spoleto Festival in Parsifal as Gurnemanz; Sang King Heinrich in Lohengrin at Nice, and in Meistersinger as Hans Sachs at Spoleto, Charleston; La Scala debut 1994, Walküre, Hunding; Dallas Opera debut 1994 in Der fliegende Holländer; San Francisco 1994, Tannhäuser, Landgraf; Many concert appearances. Address: c/o Deutsche Oper Berlin, Richard Wagnerstrasse 10, D-10585 Berlin, Germany.

HALEVI Hadar, b. 1966, Israel. Mezzo-Soprano. Career: Appearances in Israel and throughout Europe in concerts and opera; Repertory includes Carmen, Bizet, Werther, Massenet, Il Barbiere, Rossini, Mozart operas, Ravel; Contestant at the 1995 Cardiff Singer of the World Competition. Address: 10 rue St Bernard, Toulouse, 31000 France.

HALFFTER Cristobal, b. 24 March 1930, Madrid, Spain. Composer; Conductor. m. Maria Manuela Caro, 2 sons, 1 daughter. Education: Madrid Conservatory 1947-51, with Del Campo; Private studies with Alexander Tansman. Career: Studied harmony and composition with Conrado del Campo and at the Real Conservatorio de Musica in Madrid, graduated in 1951; 1961-1966 teacher of composition and musical forms at the Real Conservatorio de Musica-in Madrid and director of this institute 1964-66; scholarships for the United States (Ford Foundation) and Berlin (DAAD); 1970-1978 Lecturer at the University of Navarra; Lecturer at the Internationale Ferienkurse für Neue Musik at Darmstadt; 1976-1978 president of the Spanish section of the ISCM; 1979: Artistic Director, Studio for electronic music at the Heinrich Strobel-Stiftung in Freiburg, 1980; Member, European Academy of Science, Arts and Humanities, Paris; 1981: was awarded the Gold Medal for Fine Arts by King Juan Carlos of Spain, 1983; Member, Royal Academy of the Fine Arts San Fernando, Madrid; Since 1989 Principal Guest Conductor of the National Orchestra, Madrid, since 1970 conductor of the chief orchestras in Europe and America; lives in Madrid. Compositions: Stage: Ballet Saeta 1955; Orchestral: Piano Concerto 1955; 5 Microformas 1960; Rhapsodia espanola de Albeniz for piano and orchestra 1960; Sinfonia for 3 instrumental groups 1963; Sequencies 1964; Lineas y Puntos for 20 winds and tape 1967; Anillos 1968; Fibonaciana for flute and strings 1970; Plaint for the Victims of Violence 1971; Requiem por la libertad imaginada 1971; Pinturas negras 1972; Processional 1974; Tiempo para espacios for harpischord and strings 1974; Cello Concerto 1975; Elegias a la muerte de tres poetas espanoles, 1975; Officium defunctorum 1979; Violin Concerto; Tiento 1980; Handel Fantasia 1981; Sinfonia Ricercata 1982; Versus 1983; Parafrasis 1984; 2nd Cello Concerto 1985; Double Concerto for violin, viola and orchestra 1984; tiento del Primer tono y Batalla Imperial 1986; Concert for Cello and Orchestra, No 2 (first performed by Rostropvitch), 1986; Dortmund Variations 1987; Piano Concerto 1988; Preludio and Nemesis 1989; Concerto for saxophone quartet and orchestra 1989; Vocal: Regina Coeli 1951; Misa Ducal 1956; In exspectatione resurrectionis Domini 1962; Brecht-Lieder 1967; Symposium 1968; Yes Speak Out 1968; Noche pasiva del sentido 1971; Gaudium et Spes for 32 voices and tapes 1972; Oracion a Platero 1975; Officium Defunitorum 1978; Noche Pasiva del Sentido 1979; Leyendo a Jorge Guillen 1982; Dona Nobis Pacem 1984; Tres Poemes de la Lirica Espanola 1984-86; Dos Motetes para Caro a Cappella, 1988; Muerte, Mudanza y Locura, for tape and voices, 1989 (text by Cervantes); Chamber: 2 String Quartets 1955, 1970; Solo Violin Sonata 1959; Codex for guitar 1963; Antiphonismoi for 7 players 1967; Noche activa del espiritu 1973; Mizar for 2 flutes and electronic ensemble 1980; Piano Music. Recordings: For Soprano, Baritone and Orchestra: 2nd Cello Concerto Rostropovitch and Orchestra National De France, Erato. Publications: Universal Edition. Memberships: Real Academia De Bellas Artes, Spain; Akademie Der Künste, Berlin; Kungl Musikaliska Akademien, Sweden, Stockholm. Current Management: Jürgen Erlebach, Konzertdirektion, Erlebach. Address: Universal Edition, Bösel Dorfer Strasse 12, A1015 Wien, Austria.

HALFVARSON Eric, b. 1953, Texas, USA. Singer (Bass). Education: Studied at Houston Opera Studio. Career: Sang at Houston from 1977, notably as Sarastro, 1980; Carnegie Hall, New York, in Hamlet by Amboise Thomas, 1981; San Francisco, 1982-, notably as Hagen in The Ring, 1990; Spoleto 1983, in European premiere of Barber's Antony and Cleopatra; Further appearances at Chicago, Toronto, Miami, St Louis (US premiere of Il Viaggio as Reims, 1986) and Dallas (premiere of The Aspern Papers by Dominick Argento, 1988); Sang Raimondo in Lucia di Lammermoor at Washington, 1989, Wagner's King Henry at Dallas and the Landgrave in Tannhäuser at Montpellier, 1991; Engagements at Santa Fe as Baron Ochs, 1989, 1992, and Morosus in Die schweigsame Frau, 1991; Other roles include Ramphis (Dallas 1991), Banquo, Rocco, Sparafucile, the Commendatore in Don Giovanni, Puccini's Colline, Alvise in La Gioconda and Gremin in Eugene Onegin; Sang the King in Schreker's Der Schatzgräber at the 1992 Holland Festival; Pogner in Die Meistersinger at the 1996 Bayreuth Festival. Recordings include: Enobarbus in Antony and Cleopatra. Address: c/o Santa Fe Opera, PO Box 2408, Santa Fe, NM 87504, USA.

HALGRIMSON Amanda, b. 28 Nov 1956, Fargo, North Dakota, USA. Singer (Soprano). Education: Studied at Northern Illinois University. Career: Appearances at opera houses in 32 American States, notably as Fiordiligi, Norina, Clarice in Il Mondo della Luna and Rosalinde; Sang with Texas Opera on tour, 1987-88, as Lucia di Lammermoor; European debut 1988, as the Queen of Night with Netherlands Opera; Further engagements in Vienna (Volksoper and Staatsoper), St Gallen and Dusseldorf; Concert performances include Mozart's Schauspieldirektor and Salieri's Prima la musica, poi le parole with Houston Symphony; Sang the Queen of Night in a new production of Die Zauberflöte at the Deutsche Oper Berlin, 1991; Member of the ensemble of the Deutsche Oper Berlin, 1992-93; Sang Beethoven's Missa Solemnis with the Boston Symphony Orchestra under Roger Norrington, 1993; Sang Beethoven's 9th Symphony at the re-opening of the Liederhalle in Stuttgart under G Gelmetti, 1993; Schumann's Faust/Gretchen with the Minnesota Orchestra as well as Beethoven's Missa Solemnis with the Boston Symphony Orchestra at the Tanglewood Festival; Sang Donna Anna with the Birmingham Symphony Orchestra under Simon Rattle, 1993; Concerts of Mozart's Requiem in London, Berlin and Paris with the Chamber Orchestra of Europe, 1993; Queen of Night at the Grand Théâtre de Genève, 1994; Sang the Trovatore Leonora at the Deutsche Oper Berlin, 1996. Honours include: Prize winner at Voci Verdiana (Bussetto) Competition, 1985 and the Metropolitan Auditions, 1987. Address: c/o Deutsche Oper Berlin, Richard Wagnerstrasse 10, D-1000 Berlin, Germany.

HALL Janice, b. 28 Sept 1953, San Francisco, USA. Singer (Soprano). Education: Studied in Boston with Grace Hunter. Career: Sang in Cavalli's Egisto for the Wolf Trap Opera Company, 1977; New York City Opera 1978-81, as Ann in Die Lustigen Weiber von Windsor and Mozart's Servillia; European debut with the Hamburg Opera, 1982; Further appearances in Tel Aviv, Venice and Drottningholm; Salzburg Festival 1985, as Fortuna in the premiere of Henze's version of Il Ritorno di Ulisse; Cologne 1985, as Poppea in Handel's Agrippina; Has returned to the USA to sing at Houston, Washington DC, Santa Fe (Cavalli's Calisto 1989); Sang La Cambiale di Matrimonio at the 1989 Schwetzingen Festival; Other roles include Verdi's Oscar, Gilda and Violetta, Rosina, Pamina and Lauretta.

HALL John, b. 1956, Brecon Wales. Singer (Bass). m. Julie Crocker, 1 son, 2 daughters. Education: Studied at the Birmingham School of Music and at the Royal College of Music with Frederick Sharp. Career: Sang Rossini's Basilio and Mozart's Bartolo for Opera 80; Appearances with the English Bach Festival at Covent Garden and the Athens Festival; Glyndebourne Festival from 1981; Glyndebourne Touring Opera as Masetto in Don Giovanni (Hong Kong 1986), Mozart's Figaro and Quince in A Midsummer Night's Dream; Théâtre du Châtelet, Paris, 1985, in The Golden Cockerel; Opera North, 1986, in The Trojans and Madama Butterfly, and returned in Carmen, Tosca, Nielsen's Maskarade and Don Giovanni (as Leporello); Kent Opera, 1989, in The Return of Ulysses; Almeida Festival, 1989, in the premiere of Golem by John Casken; Glyndebourne Touring Opera, 1989-90, as Basilio and Rocco in Fidelio; Covent Garden, 1991, in Boris Godunov, as Mitiukha; English National Opera, 1992, in Return of Ulysses, as Time, Antinous; Throughout France in Midsummer Night's Dream, 1993-94; Premiere of Gruber's Gloria at Huddersfield Contemporary Music Festival, 1994; Midsummer Night's Dream at Torino and Ravenna, 1995; Sang Mozart's Antonio for GTO at Glyndebourne, 1996; Concert repertory includes Vaughan Williams's Serenade to Music (Last Night of the Proms, 1987), Messiah and Elijah. Recording: Title role in Casken's Golem. Current Management: Self-managed. Address: Ivydene, Vicarage Way, Ringmer. East Sussex BN8 5LA, England.

HALL Peter (John), b. 7 Apr 1940, Surbiton, England. Tenor. Education: BA 1964, MA 1968, King's College, Cambridge; Choral Scholarship, Private vocal study with Arthur Reckless, John Carol Case. Career includes: Lay-Vicar, Chichester Cathedral, 1965-66; Vicar-Choral, St Paul's Cathedral, London, 1972-; Member, various professional choral groups including John Alldis Choir, Schütz Choir of London, London Sinfonietta Voices; Sang Ugo and Il Prete in La Vera Storia (Berio), Florence 1986, at composer's personal request. Recordings: Carmina Burana (Orff), with Hallé Orchestra; Transit (Ferneyhough), with London Sinfonietta; At the Boar's Head (Holst), with Royal Liverpool Philharmonic Orchestra; Christmas Vespers (Monteverdi) with Denis Stevens; Prometeo (Nono) and The Flood (Stravinsky) with the London Sinfonietta. Honour: Choral Scholarship, Cambridge. Memberships: Incorporated Society of Musicians. Hobbies: Good Food and Wine; Travel; Motoring; Languages. Address: 51 Treachers Close, Chesham, Bucks HP5 2HD, England.

HALL Peter (Reginald Frederick) (Sir), b. 22 Nov 1930, Bury St Edmunds, Suffolk, England. Theatre Director. m. (1) Leslie Caron (diss 1965), (2) Jacqueline Taylor (diss 1982), (3) Maria Ewing (diss 1989), 2 sons, 3 daughters. Education: Perse School and St Catharine's College Cambridge; MA (Hons) Cantab. Career: Director, Oxford Playhouse, 1954-55; Founder, International Playwrights Theatre, 1957; Managing Director, Royal Shakespeare Company, 1960-68; Created RSC as permanent ensemble and opened its home at Aldwych Theatre; Succeeded Sir Laurence Olivier as Director of National Theatre of Great Britain (1973), which transferred from Old Vic to London's South Bank, 1976; Artistic Director, Glyndebourne Festival Opera, 1984-90; Opera Productions include The Moon and Sixpence by John Gardner, Sadler's Wells, 1957; Covent Garden, Moses and Aaron 1965, The Magic Flute 1966, the Knot Garden 1970, Eugene Onegin 1971, Tristan und Iolde 1971; Glyndebourne, La Calisto 1970, IL Ritorno d'Ulisse in Patria 1972, Le nozze di Figaro 1973, Don Giovanni 1977, Così fan tutte 1978, Fidelio 1979, A Midsummer Night's Dream 1981, Orfeo ed Euridice 1982, L'Incoronazione di Poppea 1984, Albert Herring 1985, Carmen 1985, Simon Boccanegra 1986, La Traviata 1987, Falstaff 1988, Le nozze di Figaro 1989; Metropolitan Opera New York 1982, Macbeth; Bayreuth Festival 1983, Der Ring des Nibelungen, Salome in Los Angeles, 1986; Production of Albert Herring seen at Covent Garden 1989; New Year 1989, Houston Grand Opera (Glyndebourne 1990). Publications include: Peter Hall's Diaries. Honours include: Sidney Edwards Award, 1982; Honorary Doctorates, York, Reading, Liverpool, Leicester and Cornell Universities; CBE, 1963; KBE, 1977. Memberships: Garrick; Athenaeum; RAC. Hobbies: Music; Literature. Address: The Peter Hall Company, 18 Exeter Street, London WC2E 7DU, England.

HALL Vicki, b. 13 Nov 1943, Jefferson, Texas, USA. Singer (Soprano). Education: Studied in New York and with Josef Metterson in Cologne. Career: Sang at New York City Opera, 1970-; Made guest appearances in Vienna (Volksoper), Munich (Theater am Gärtnerplatz), Cologne, Wuppertal and Bregenz; Roles have included mozart's Susanna and Blondchen, Carolina in Matrimonio Segreto, Frau Fluth in Die Lustige Weiber von Winsor, Olympia, Strauss's Sophie, Adele in Fledermaus, Gretel, and Janacek's Vixen; Many concert appearances.

HALLDORSSON Skúli (Kristján), b. 28 Apr 1914, Flateyri, Önundarfjödur, Iceland. Composer. m. Steinunn Gudny Magnusdottir, 14 May 1937, 1 son, 1 daughter. Education: Degree from the Commercial School of Iceland, Reykjavik, 1932; Diplomas as a Pianist and Composer, Reykjavik Conservatory, 1947 and 1948. Career: Performed with many soloists and choirs as an accompanist and also as a solo pianist. Compositions: More than 140 songs (Lieder), 20 piano works and 16 orchestral works including a symphony, ballet suites, a cantata and overtures; Chamber Music, Flautosolo, Duo, Trios, Quintet, Sextet and Nonett. Recordings: LP Record, Sounds From Iceland,

Saunamusiikki, Helsinki and many recordings for the Icelandic Radio and Television. Honours: Prize from the Icelandic Radio Love Songs by Jonas Hallgrimsson, 1960. Memberships: Board Member, The Icelandic Composers Society and STEF (PRS), 1950-87, President of STEF (PRS), 1968-87. Address: Bakkastigur 1, 101 Reykjavik, Iceland.

HALLGRIMSSON Hafldi, b. 18 September 1941, Akureyri, Iceland. Composer; Cellist. m. 31 August 1975, 3 sons. Education: The Music School, Reykjavik, Iceland; Academia Sancta Cecilia, Rome; Royal Academy of Music, London; Private studies in composition with Dr Alan Bush and Sir Peter Maxwell Davies. Career: Member, Haydn String Trio, 1967-70; English Chamber Orchestra, 1971-76; Principal Cellist, Scottish Chamber Orchestra, 1977-83; Mondrian Trio, 1984-88; Many recitals, appeared as Soloist with Symphony Orchestras and performed on BBC Radio 3. Compositions: Poemi; Verse I; Five Pieces for Piano; Seven Folksongs from Iceland; Scenes from Poland. Recordings: Strond; Poemi; Vers I; Daydreams in Numbers; Tristia; Jacob's Ladder. Honours: Suggia Prize for Cello playing, 1967; Viotti Prize, Italy, 1975; Nordic Council Prize, 1986. Memberships: Society of Promotion for New Music; Society of Scottish Composers; Performing Right Society. Hobbies: Reading; Drawing; Walking. Current Management: Chester Music. Address: 5 Merchiston Bank Gardens, Edinburgh EH10 5EB, Scotland.

HALLIN Margareta, b. 22 Feb 1931, Karlskoga, Sweden. Singer (Soprano); Composer. Education: Studied at the Royal Stockholm Conservatory with Ragnar Hulten. Career: Sang at the Royal Opera, Stockholm, 1954-84, in the premieres of Blomdahl's Aniara 1959 and Drommen om Therese 1964 and Tintomora 1973, by Werle; Also heard as Constanze, Blondchen, Lucia di Lammermoor, Gilda and Leonora in Il Trovatore; Sang Anne Trulove in the Swedish premiere of The Rake's Progress, 1961; Glyndebourne Festival 1957, 1960, as the Queen of Night; Covent Garden 1960, with the Stockholm Company in Alcina by Handel; Drottningholm Court Opera from 1962, notably in the Abbé Vogler's Gustaf Adolf och Ebba Brahe, 1973; Appearances in Florence, Edinburgh, Hamburg, Zurich, Rome and Munich; Later in career sang Elsa, Elisabeth de Valois, Mathilde in Guillaume Tell, the heroines in Les Contes d'Hoffmann, Violetta, Donna Anna, Senta, Butterfly and the Marschallin; Sang Cherubini's Médée, 1984. Compositions include: Miss Julie, opera after Strindberg. Honours: Swedish Court Singer 1966; Order Litteris et artibus, 1976. Address: c/o Kungliga Teatera, PO Box 16094, S-10322 Stockholm, Sweden.

HALLSTEIN Ingeborg, b. 23 May 1937, Munich, Germany. Singer (Soprano). Education: Studied with her mother. Debut: Stadtheatre Passau 1956, as Musetta in La Bohème. Career: Sang at Basle 1958-59, Munich from 1959; Salzburg Festival from 1960, as Rosina in La Finta Semplice and in the premiere of The Bassarids by Henze (1966); Theater an der Wien 1962, as the Queen of Night in Die Zauberflöte, conducted by Karajan; Sang in the first performance of Henze's Cantata Being Beauteous, Berlin, 1964; Guest appearances in Hamburg, Stuttgart, Dresden, Karlsruhe, Kassel, Venice, Paris, Montreal, Ottawa, Stockholm and Amsterdam, Royal Opera House Covent Garden, as the Queen of Night; Other roles include Mozart's Constanze, Fiordiligi and Susanna; Sophie in Der Rosenkavalier and Zerbinetta; Norina (Don Pasquale) and Aennchen in Der Freischütz; Professor at the Wurzburg Musikhochschule from 1981. Recordings: Die Frau ohne Schatten (Deutsche Grammophon); Marzelline in Fidelio, conducted by Klemperer; Operettas by Lortzing and Benatzky. Address: c/o Hochschule für Musik, Holfstallstrasse 6-8, D-8700 Würzburg, Germany.

HALMEN Pet(re), b. 14 Nov 1943, Talmaciu, Rumania. Stage and Costume Designer; Director; Light Designer. Education: Studied in Berlin. Career: Worked at Kiel and Dusseldorf, then collaborated with director Jean-Pierre Ponnelle at Zurich from 1975 in cycles of operas by Monteverdi and Mozart; Munich 1978-, with premiere of Reimann's Lear and Troades, 1986, Das Liebesverbot by Wagner and Berg's Lulu, 1985; Designs for Aida at Berlin; Chicago and Covent Garden 1982-84; Parsifal at San Francisco 1988 and 2 Ring Cycles; Designed and Directed Lohengrin at Dusseldorf 1987, Paer's Achille at Bologna 1988, La Straniera at Spoleto Festival, Charleston 1989, and Nabucco for Munich Festival, 1990; Designs for Parsifal seen at Mainz 1991, Mozart's Lucio Silla at Vienna Staatsoper; Directed The Golden Cockerel at Duisburg, 1991, La Clemenza di Tito at Toulouse, 1992; Directed and designed Turandot at Deutsche Oper am Rhein, Dusseldorf, 1993; Directed and designed: Aïda at Staatsoper Berlin, 1995, Turandot at Opera de Nice, France, 1995, Don Giovanni at Staatsoper Hamburg, 1996, Rosenkavalier at Staatstheater Darmstadt, 1997, Orfeo by Gluck at Opernhaus Halle, 1997, Ariadne auf Naxos at Toulouse, France, 1988, Idomeneo at Salzburg Festspielhaus, 1998, Ezio by Handel at Festspiele Halle, 1998 and Goethe's play Der Grosskophta for the Festival Kulturhauptstadt Weimar, 1999. Address: Tengstrasse 26, D-80798 Munich, Germany. Address: Tengstrasse 26, D-80798 Munich, Germany.

HALMRAST Tor, b. 26 Apr 1951, Sarpsborg, Norway. Composer. Education: MSc, Engineering (Acoustics), 1976; BMus, University of Trondheim, 1984; Private studies in Composition, State Scholarship, Sweelinck Conservatory, Amsterdam, 1988. Career: Composer-in-Residence, Music Conservatory, Tromsoe, 1988-90; Festival Composer, Northern Norwegian Festival, 1990; In charge of acoustic design of several buildings for music, concerts and theatre, and studios. Compositions: Works for symphony orchestra, chamber works, solo works, music for television, films and records and sound installation, including the prize-winning music for the Norwegian Pavillion at the World's Fair, Expo92 in Seville, Spain, and for ice/music sculpture for the Olympics in Lillehammer, 1994; Alfa and Romeo, radiopera for Norwegian Radio, 1997. Recordings: Hemera 2901; Music for EXPO92 and other electroacoustic works: Aquaduct, Icille, Oppbrudd, Varang, Motgift. Publications: Several papers on room acoustics. Honours: European Broadcasting Union, Rostrum for Electro-Acoustic Music, 1990; AMI for Norwegian Pavillion at EXPO92; Winner, Norwegian Cassette Tax Foundation's competition for Music-Dramatic Works, 1995. Memberships: Co-Founder, Norwegian Section, International Confederation of Electro-acoustic Music; Board Member of several societies including: Norwegian Network for Technology, Acoustics and Music. Address: Spaangberg v 28a, N-0853 Oslo, Norway.

HALSEY Simon (Patrick), b. 8 Mar 1958, Kingston, Surrey, England. Conductor. m. Lucy Lunt, 14 June 1986. Education: Winchester College, 1971-75; King's College, Cambridge, 1976-79; MA (Cantab); Conducting Scholar, Royal College of Music, 1979-80. Career: Conductor, Scottish Opera-Go-Round, 1980, 1981; Director of Music, University of Warwick, 1980-88; Chorus Director, City of Birmingham Symphony Orchestra, 1982-; Associate Director, Philharmonia Chorus, 1986-; Music Director, City of Birmingham Touring Opera, 1987-, Wagner's Ring, 1990-91; Britten's Church Parables in London and elsewhere, 1997; Director, Academy of Ancient Music Chorus, 1988-92; Director, Salisbury Festival, 1989-93; Chorus Director, Flanders Opera, Antwerp, 1991-95; Guest Conductor, Chicago Symphony Chorus, 1993-94. Recordings: Over 20 including Rossini's Petite Messe Solennelle and Bruckner's Mass in E Minor, 1990. Publications: Editor, Choral Music, Faber Music. Honours: Gramophone Record of the Year, 1989; Deutsche Schallplatten Prize, 1993. Current Management: Magenta Music International, 4 Highgate Street, Highgate Village, N6 5JL. Address: 279 High Street, Henley in Arden, B95 5BG, England.

HALSTEAD Anthony (George), b. 18 June 1945, Manchester, England. Conductor; Horn Player; Harpsichordist; Composer. m. Ellen O'Dell, 6 Sept 1985, 2 sons, 1 daughter. Education: Chetham's School, 1956-62; Royal Manchester College of Music, 1962-66; Private study with Dr Horace Fitzpatrick, 1966 and 1978, Myron Bloom 1979-80, George Malcolm, 1979. Career: Bournemouth Symphony Orchestra, 1966; BBC Scottish Symphony Orchestra, 1966-70; London Symphony Orchestra, 1970-73; English Chamber Orchestra, 1972-86; Professor, Guildhall School of Music, 1971-; Directed the Hanover Band at the Wigmire Hall, London, 1997. Compositions: Divertimento Serioso, 1973; Prologue and Passus, 1976; Serenade for oboe and strings, 1978; Concertino Elegiaco, 1983; Suite for solo horn and trumpet. Recordings: Weber-Horn Concertino, World Premiere Recording on Original Instruments, 1986 (Nimbus); Mozart Horn Concertos, (Nimbus), 1987; L'Oiseau-Lyre, 1993; Haydn Horn Concertos (Nimbus), 1989; Britten-Serenade (Nimbus), 1989. Honours: FRMCM, 1975; FGSM, 1979. Memberships: Musicians Union; British Horn Society; International Horn Society. Hobbies: Poetry; Religion. Current Management: Patrick Garvey Management. Address: 2 Clovelly Road, London N8 7RH, England.

HALTON Richard, b. 1963, Devon, England. Singer (Baritone). Education: Studied at the University of Kent and the Guildhall School of Music with Johanna Peters. Career includes: Has sung with most leading British opera companies including: Capriccio and Romeo and Juliette with the Royal Opera, Novice's Friend (Billy Budd) and Harry Easter (Street Scene) with English National Opera, Schaunard with Glyndebourne Touring Opera, Ravenal in Showboat at the London Palladium and on 2 national tours with Opera North/RSC, Glyndebourne Festival Opera, 1989, Opera 80, as Danilo in The Merry Widow; Other operatic appearances include: Capriccio at Covent Garden, 1991, in Billy Budd (ENO) and La Bohème (GTO); Holofernes in the world premiere of Ian McQueen's Line of Terror at the Almeida Festival, Harlequin (Ariadne auf Naxos) and Perrucchetto (La Fedeltà Premiata) for Garsington Opera; Repertoire also includes Mozart's Count in Figaro, Tarquinius in The Rape of Lucretia; Street Scene, by Kurt Weill, ENO, 1992; Italian Girl in Algiers by Rossini, Buxton Festival, 1992; Dancairo, Carmen, Dorset Opera, 1992; Janko in Petrified by Juraj Benes for Mecklenburg Opera, 1992-93; Papageno, The Magic Flute, Scottish Opera, 1993; Sang Sid in Albert Herring at Garsington, 1996; Concert engagements include: A Child of Our Timee, St John Passion and Messiah with the City of London Sinfonia conducted by Richard Hickox and Carmina Burana in Perugia and the Royal Albert Hall; Recital works includes Schumann's Dichterliebe with Stephen Barlow at St John's Smith Square; Further engagements include Jason in Gavin Bryars' Medea (Glasgow and BBC Radio 3), Valentin in Faust and Dandini in La Cenerentola. Honours include: Walter Hyde Memorial Prize; Schubert Prize; Lawrence Classical Singing Bursary. Address: Portland Wallis, 50 Gt Portland Street, London W1N 5AH, England.

HALTON Rosalind, b. 4 Oct 1951, Dunedin, New Zealand. Harpsichordist; Musicologist. m. David Halton, 24 Mar 1979. Education: New Zealand Junior Scholarship, Otago University 1969-72, BA (Honours); Commonwealth Scholarship to Oxford University 1973-80, St Hilda's College, DPhil (Oxon). Career: Research and Editing of Classical Symphonies (Beck-Holzbauer) and Cantatas of Alessandro Scarlatti; Concerts of 17th and 18th Century Chamber Music using period instruments; Solo performances on Harpsichord and Pianos of 18th and early 19th century; Lecturer, Performance, University of New England, Armidale, Australia, 1986-; Senior Lecturer, Performance, UNE, 1991. Publications: Various reviews. Contributions to: Music and Letters. Hobbies: Cricket; Musical Instruments. Address: 72 Dangar Street, Armidale, NSW 2350, Australia.

HAMARI Julia, b. 21 Nov 1942, Budapest, Hungary. Singer (Mezzo-soprano). Education: Studied piano at first, then singing with Fatima Martin and at the Music Academy Budapest. Debut: Vienna 1966, in the St Matthew Passion, conducted by Karl Richter. Career: Rome 1966, in the Brahms Alto Rhapsody, conducted by Vittorio Gui; Concert appearances with Karajan, Kubelik, Solti, Böhm, Boulez and Celibidache, most often heard in works by Mahler, Monteverdi, Handel, Bach, Beethoven, Mozart and Verdi; Stage debut Salzburg, 1967; Stuttgart 1968, as Carmen; US debut with Chicago Symphony Orchestra, 1972; Sang Celia in Haydn's La Fedeltà Premiata at Glyndebourne, 1979; Metropolitan Opera from 1984, as Rosina and Despina; Stuttgart and Philadelphia 1984, as Sinaide in Mosè and as Cenerentola in the opera by Rossini; Sang Vivald's Griselda at Ludwigshaven, 1989. Recordings: St Matthew Passion (Electrola); Oberon, Il Matrimonio Segreto, Giulio Cesare, Beethoven Mass in C, Mozart Requiem (Deutsche Grammophon); Ernani (RCA); Tito Manlio by Vivaldi (Philips); Cavalleria Rusticana, I Puritani (EMI); Bach B minor Mass (CBS); Pergolesi Stabat Mater (Hungaroton); Hansel und Gretel, Die Meistersinger, Eugene Onegin (Decca). Address: c/o Staatsheater Stuttgart, Oberer Schlossgarten 6, D-7000 Stuttgart 1, Germany.

HAMBLIN Pamela, b. 14 June 1954, Cookeville, Tennessee, USA. Singer (Soprano). Education: Studied at North Texas State University and Salzburg Mozarteum. Debut: Karlsruhe, as Euridice in Orphée aux Enfers by Offenbach, 1980. Career: Has sung at Karlsruhe in such roles as Handel's Florinda (Rodrigo), Almirena (Rinaldo) and Romilda (Serse); Micaela, Mozart's Susanna, Pamina, Constance and Sandrina, Verdi's Gilda and Oscar, Constance in Cherubini's Les Deux Journées, Strauss's Sophie and Aminta (Die schweigsame Frau) and Titania in A Midsummer Night's Dream; Guest appearances at Dresden, Stuttgart, Zurich, Essen, Heidelberg, Strasbourg, Madrid, Barcelona and Athens. Recordings include: Rodrigo. Address: Kriegsstrasse 71, 76133 Karlsruhe, Germany.

HAMBRAEUS Bengt, b. 29 Jan 1928, Stockholm, Sweden. Composer; Organist; Musicologist. Education: Studied organ with Alf Linder, 1944-48; Uppsala University, PhD, 1956; Summer Courses at Darmstadt 1951-55, with Krenek, Messiaen and Fortner; Worked for Swedish Broadcasting Corporation from 1957, Director of Chamber Music 1965-68, Production Director 1968-72; Composed at Electronic Studios of Cologne, Munich, Montreal and Milan; Professor at McGill University, Montreal from 1972, Professor Emeritus, 1995-. Compositions: Chamber Operas Experiment X, 1971; Se Människan, 1972; Sagan, 1979; L'oui-dire, 1986; Concerto for organ and harpsichord, 1951; Antiphones en rondes for soprano and 24 instruments, 1953; Crystal Sequence for soprano choir and ensemble, 1954; Rota for 3 orchestras and tape, 1956-62; Transfiguration for orchestra, 1962-63; Constellations I-V, 1958-83; Segnali for 7 instruments, 1960; Mikrogram for ensemble, 1961; Interferences for organ, 1962; Klassiskt spel, electronic ballet, 1965; Fresque Sonore for soprano and ensemble, 1967; Rencontres for orchestra, 1971; Pianissimo in due tempi for 20 string instruments, 1972; Ricercare for organ, 1974; Advent for organ 10 brass instruments and percussion, 1975; Ricordanza for orchestra, 1976; Continuo for organ and orchestra, 1975; Livre d'orgue, 1980-81; Symphonia Sacra for 5 soloists, choir, wind instruments and percussion, 1985-86; Apocalypsis cum figuris for bass solo, choir and organ, 1987; Five Psalms for choir, 1987; Litanies for orchestra, 1988-89; Nocturnals for chamber orchestra, 1989; Piano Concerto, 1992; St Michael's Liturgy, 1992; Missa pro Organo, 1992; Organum Sancti Jacobi, 1993; Meteoros, 1993; Songs of the Mountain, The Moon and Television, 1993; Eco dalla montagna lontana, 1993;

Triptyque pour orgue avec MIDI, 1994; Due Rapsodie, 1994; Concentio, 1995; Quatre tableaux, 1995; Horn Concerto, 1995-96. Publications: Codex Carminum Gallicorum, 1961; Om Notskifter (On Notation) 1970; Numerous articles and essays published since 1948. Address: RR1, Apple Hill, Ontario, K0C 1B0, Canada.

HAMBURGER Paul, b. 3 September 1920, Vienna, Austria. Pianist; Writer; Educator. m. Clare Walmesley, dec, 1 son, 1 daughter. Education: Vienna State Academy; ARCM, London. Career: Freelance Accompanist and Chamber Music Player; Member, Coach, English Opera Group, 1953-56; Member, Coach, Glyndebourne Opera, 1956-62; Staff Accompanist, 1962-75, Radio Producer, 1976-81, BBC; Currently Professor, Guildhall School of Music and Royal College of Music, London; Seminars for Singers and Accompanists in England, Germany, Austria. Recordings: With various singers including April Cantelo, Bernadette Greevy, Janet Baker, Heather harper, Laura Surti, Clare Walmesley, Benvenuto Duo. Publications: Mozart Songs, annotated edition, 1991; Translations: Music and Music Making (Bruno Walter), 1961; Leos Janácek (Hans Hollander), 1963. Contributions to: A Britten Symposium, 1954; A Mozart Companion, 1956; A Chopin Symposium, 1966; Music Survey; Music Review; Tempo; Music and Musicians. Honours: FGSM, 1982; Honorary RAM, 1992; Austrian Order of Science and Art, 1992. Memberships: Incorporated Society of Musicians; Society for the Promotion of New Music. Address: The Bakery, East Stoke House, Stoke sub Hamdon, Somerset TA14 6UF, England.

HAMEENNIEMI Eero Olavi, b. 29 Apr 1951, Valkeakoski, Finalnd. Composer. m. Leena Peltola, 7 Oct 1977, (div Oct 1989), 1 daughter. Education: Diploma, Sibelius Academy, 1977; State Higher School of Music, Cracow, 1979; Eastman School of Music, Rochester, New York, USA, 1980-81. Career: Commissions for the Finnish Radio SO, Swedish RSO, Helsinki Festival, Finnish National Ballet; Works performed by (the above) and Scottish National Orchestra, Malmo Symphony Orchestra, Gothenburg Symphony Orchestra; Senior Lecturer, Sibelius Academy, 1982-. Compositions: Symphony, 1982-83, 1984; Dialogue for Piano and Orchestra, 1987; Sonata for Clarinet and Piano; Loviisa, a ballet in two acts, premier 19 Mar 1987, Finnish National Ballet; Second Symphony, 1988; 2 String Quartets, 1989, 1994; Leonardo, ballet in 2 acts; The Bird and the Wind for strings, soprano and two Indian classical dancers (choreography by Shobana Jeyasingh), 1994. Recordings: Duo I, for Flute and Cello; Pianosonata, 1979; sonata for Clarinet and Piano, 1987. Publications: ABO - johdatus uuden musiikin teoriaan, Sibelius Academy Publictions, 1982 (An Introduction to the Theory of Contemporary Music); Tekopalmun alla (Under an Artificial Palm Tree), essays on the interaction of cultures. Honours: Nattuvanar for male voice choir won the UNESCO Rostrum of Composers in 1994. Hobbies: Cooking; Oriental Literature; Squash. Address: Lapilantie 8B7, 04200 Kerava, Finland.

HAMELIN Marc-Andre, b. 1961, Verdun, Canada. Concert Pianist. m. Judy Karin Applebaum. Education: Studied, Vincent d'Indy School of Music and Temple University, Philadelphia. Career: Recitals in Montreal, Toronto, New York and Philadelphia; Concerto appearances in Toronto, Quebec, Ottawa, Albany, Detroit, Indianapolis, Minneapolis, New York (Manhattan Philharmonic and Riverside Symphony) and Philadelphia; Toured with the Montreal Symphony to Spain, Portugal and East Germany, 1987; Duo partnership with cellist Sophie Rolland from 1988; Beethoven cycles in New York, Washington, Montreal and London (Wigmore Hall, Mar 1991); Soloist, Turangalila Symphony with the Philadelphia Orchestra and Andrew Davis, 1996-97. Recordings include: Works by Leopold Godowsky (CBS Enterprises); William Bolcom Twelve New Etudes, Stefan Wolpe Battle Piece and Ives Concord Sonata (New World Records); Sorabji Sonata No 1, Rzewski The People Will Never Be Defeated (Altarus). Honours: 1st Prize, Carnegie Hall International American Music Competition, 1985; Virginia P Moore Prize, Canada, 1989. Address: c/o Norman McCann International Artists Ltd, The Coach House, 56 Lawrie Park Gardens, London SE26 6XJ, England.

HAMILTON David, b. 1960, USA. Singer (Tenor). Career: Appearances with opera companies at Philadelphia, San Diego, Tulsa, Sarasota, Hawaii, New York (City Opera), Milwaukee and St Louis; Metropolitan Opera debut, season 1986-87; Season 1991-92, as Tamino for Opera de Nice, Lensky with Manitoba Opera, and Pinkerton with Chattanooga Opera; Season 1992-93, as Tamino with Vancouver Opera, Peter Quint in Turn of the Screw for Edmonton Opera and Lensky with Scottish Opera; Concert repertoire includes Messiah, Rinaldo by Brahms, Mozart's Requiem, Dvorak's Stabat Mater, the Berlioz Roméo et Juliette and Schumann's Scenes from Faust; Soloist with Israel Philharmonic, Baltimore Symphony, Mostly Mozart Festival Orchestra and Indianapolis Symphony under Raymond Leppard; As recitalist gave premiere of Hugo Weisgall's cycle Lyric Interval; Sang Belmonte in Die Entführung with the Metropolitan Opera. Honours include: Winner, Paris International Voice Competition, 1984. Address: c/o IMG Artists, Media House, 3 Burlington Lane, London W4 2TH, England.

HAMILTON David (Peter), b. 18 Jan 1935, New York, USA. Music Critic; Writer on Music. Education: Princeton University; AB 1956, MFA in Music History, 1960. Career: Music and Record Librarian, Princeton University, 1961-65; Assistant Music Editor 1965-68, Music Editor 1968-74, W W Norton & Company, New York; Music Critic, The Nation, 1968-; Music Correspondent, Financial Times, London, 1969-74; Associate Editor, Musical Newsletter, 1971-77. Publications: The Listener's Guide to Great Instrumentalists, 1981; The Music Game: An Autobiography, 1986; Editor, Metropolitan Opera Encyclopedia: A Guide to the World of Opera, 1987. Contributions to: Many articles and reviews in periodicals. Address: c/o The Nation, 72 Fifth Avenue, New York, NY 10011, USA.

HAMILTON Iain (Ellis), b. 6 June 1922, Glasgow, Scotland. Composer. Education: BMus, University of London, 1950; USA, 1961; DMus, Honours, University of Glasgow, 1970. Career: Engineer, 1939-47; Lecturer: Morley College, London, 1951-60; London University, 1952-60; Chairman, Composer's Guild of Great Britain, 1958; Chairman, Secretary, Institute of Contemporary Arts, London, 1958-60; Mary Duke Biddle Professor of Music, Duke University, USA, 1961-78; Composer in Residence, Tanglewood, MA, 1962; Chairman of Department, 1966-67. Compositions: Operas: Agamemnon, 1961, 1968; Royal Hunt of the Sun, 1968; The Catiline Conspiracy, 1973; Tamburlaine, 1976; Anna Karenina, 1978; Lancelot, 1983; Raleigh's Dream, 1984; The Tragedy of Macbeth, 1990; London's Fair, 1992; 4 Symphonies, (1950-81); Chamber Works and Vocal Works. Recordings: Le Jardin de Monet: Palinodes, solo piano; String Quartet No 3. Honours: Recipient of Koussevitsky Foundation Award, 1951; Royal Philharmonic Prize, 1951; Arnold Bax Gold Award, 1957; Vaughan Williams Award, 1974. Memberships: Fellow, Royal Academy of Music; Founding Member, International Webern Society; Founding Member, American Society of University Composers. Address: 85 Cornwall Gardens, Flat 4, London, SW7 4XY, England.

HAMILTON Robert, b. 1 Apr 1937, South Bend, Indiana, USA. Pianist; Educator. m. Beverley Daube, 23 Aug 1958, 1 son, 3 daughters. Education: Indiana University School of Music. Debut: Town Hall, New York City, 1963; With Orchestra, Chicago, 1965. Career: Major appearances in New York Town Hall; Orchestra Hall, Chicago; Kennedy Center, Washington; Wigmore Hall, London; Concertgebouw, Amsterdam; Tchaikovsky Hall, Moscow; Mozarteum, Salzburg; Teatro San Carlo, Naples; With Major Orchestras, Chicago, National, Milwaukee; SODRE, Chautaguqua Festival, St Louis Symphony, Indianapolis, Grant Park, Phoenix, Seattle and National gallery; Carnegie Hall; Symphony Hall, Taipei; Hoam Hall, Seoul; Offical Pianist, US Army, 1959-62; Faculty, Indiana University, 1967-75; Wichita State University, 1975-80; Arizona State University, 1980-89; Appeared on BBC Radio, London, Radio Zurich; ABC Network (USA); National Public Radio (USA); Voice of America; Radio Warsaw, Polish National Television; Russian National Television; 20 tours of Europe; Annual tours of the Far East; Artistic Director of London Piano Festival (annual/summer); Recordings: Numerous for major labels. Honours: Major international prizes: Busoni, Casella, Rudolph Ganz and Montevideo Competitions. Address: School of Music, Arizona State University, Tempe, AZ 85287, USA.

HAMILTON Stuart, b. 28 Sept 1929, Regina, Saskatchewan, Canada. Pianist. Education: ARCT, Royal Conservatory, Canada; Studied privately with Alberto Guerrero. Debut: New York Town Hall, 1967. Career: Solo concerts across Canada, New York, London, Paris; Accompanist for Maureen Forrester, Lois Marshall, José Carreras, Louis Quilico, Jon Vickers; Producer and Musical Director, Opera in Concert, 1974-94; Broadcaster for CBC since 1982 and at Metropolitan Opera New York, 1991-; Many radio and TV appearances on CBC. Recording: With Lois Marshall, CBC recording. Contributions to: Reviews on Opera Magazine, 1962-72. Honours: Order of Canada, 1984; Toronto Arts Award, 1989; Governor-General of Canada's Medal, 1993. Address: 424 Yonge Street, Apt 612, Toronto, Ontario, M5B 2H3, Canada.

HAMMES Lieselotte, b. 1932, Siegburg, Germany. Singer (Soprano); Professor. Education: Studied in Cologne. Debut: Cologne, as Amor in Orfeo ed Euridice, 1957. Career: Guest appearances at Stuttgart, Hamburg, Berlin (Deutsche Oper), Naples, Rome, Lisbon and Paris (1971); Glyndebourne Festival 1965, as Sophie in Der Rosenkavalier; Sang at Cologne until 1975 as Mozart's Pamina, Susanna and Papagena, Marzelline, Mimi, Manon Lescaut, Nedda, Marenka in The Bartered Bride and Anne Trulove in The Rake's Progress; Teacher at Bonn then Siegburg from 1973; Professor at Cologne Musikhochschule, 1985-. Address: Staatliche Hochschule für Musik, Dagobertstrasse 38, 5000 Cologne 1, Germany.

HAMMOND-STROUD Derek, b. 10 Jan 1926, London, England. Concert and Operatic Baritone. Education: Studied with: Elena Gerhardt, Gerhard Hüsch, Trinity College of Music, London. Debut: London 1955, in the British Premiere of Haydn's Orfeo et Euridice. Career: Guest Artist with numerous opera companies; Principal Baritone, English National Opera, 1961-71, as Rossini's Bartolo, Verdi's Melitone and Rigoletto, Wagner's Alberich and Beckmesser; Royal Opera, Covent Garden, 1971-; Glyndebourne, 1973-; Broadcasts on BBC and European radio; Opera and Recital appearances: Netherlands; Denmark; Iceland; Germany; Austria; Spain; USA; Opera appearances: Metropolitan Opera, New York, 1977-89; Teatro Colón, Buenos Aires, 1981; National Theatre, Munich, 1983; Other roles include: Publio, in La Clemenza di Tito; Don Magnifico; Roles in the British premieres of La Pietra del Paragone and Der Besuch der Alten Dame; Also, Faninal in Der Rosenkavalier. Recordings: Many recordings for various companies including the ENO Ring of the Nibelung. Honours: OBE, 1987; Honorary Member, Royal Academy of Music; Honorary Fellow, Trinity College of Music, London; Sir Charles Santley Memorial Award by Worshipful Company of Musicians. Membership: Incorporated Society of Musicians. Hobbies: Chess; Study of Philosophy. Address: 18 Sutton Road, Muswell Hill, London N10 1HE, England.

HAMON Deryck, b. 1965, Guernsey. Singer (Bass). Education: Royal Northern College of Music. Career: Concert performances throughout Britain of Messiah, Elijah, Samson, Haydn's Nelson Mass, Five Elizabethan Songs by Vaughan Williams and the Mozart and Fauré Requiems; Member of the D'Oyly Carte Opera, notably as The Mikado; Rossini's Basilio and Escamillo for Travelling Opera, Dikoy in Katya Kabanova at the Opera Theatre, Dublin, and Banquo in Macbeth for City of Birmingham Touring Opera; Other roles include Mozart's Sarastro, Commendatore and Alfonso, Rossini's Bartolo, Puccini's Angelotti (Tosca) and Colline (La Bohème). Address: C&M Craig Services Ltd, 3 Kersley Street, London SW11 4PR, England.

HAMPE Christiane, b. 1948, Heidelberg, Germany. Singer (Soprano). Education: Studied in Heidelberg and in Munich with Annelies Kupper. Career: Sang at the Hagen Opera, 1971-73, Basle, 1974-76, Wuppertal, 1976-78, and Karlsruhe, 1979-80; Bregenz Festival, 1974, as Clarice in Haydn's Il mondo della luna, Vienna Staatsoper as Susanna and further guest appearances in Hamburg, throughout Europe and in the USA; Professor at the Karlsruhe Musikhochschule from 1988. Recordings include: Lortzing's Undine (Capriccio). Address: c/o Badisches Staatstheater, Baumeisterstrasse 11, Pf 1449, W-7500 Karlsruhe, Germany.

HAMPE Michael, b. 3 Jun 1935, Heidelberg, Germany. Actor; Director in International Opera Houses and Theatres. Education: Study of Music (cello), Syracuse University, USA; Study of Literature, Musicology and Philosophy at Munich and Vienna Universities; PhD. Career: Vice-Director, Schauspielhaus, Zürich, 1965-70; Intendant, National Theatre, Mannheim, 1972-75; Member of Salzburg Festival Board of Directors, 1985-89; Intendant, Cologne Opera, 1975-95; Director of Opera: La Scala Milan, Covent Garden London (Andrea Chénier 1984, Il Barbiere di Siviglia 1985, Cenerentola, 1990), Paris Opéra, Salzburg and Edinburgh Festivals, Munich, Stockholm, Cologne, Geneva, Sydney, San Francisco, Buenos Aires, Tokyo and Zurich Operas, German, Austrian and Swedish TV; Director of Drama: Munich, Bavarian State Theatre, Zurich Schauspielhaus, Schwetzingen Festival (double-bills of Rossini seen at Cologne, Schwetzingen and the Paris Opéra-Comique; Directed Handel's Serse at Cologne, 1996); Teaching: Professor at State Music Academy, Cologne and Cologne University, Kunitachi College of Music, Tokyo; Consulting: Consultant for Theatre Building, 1977-82; Vice President, Deutsche Bühnentechnische Gesellschaft, Jury Opéra Bastille, Paris; Actor and Director in German Theatres; About 160 productions in opera, plays and TV; Intendant, Dresden Music Festival, 1993-. Address: Dresdner Musikfestspiele, Tiergartenstrasse 36, D 01219 Dresden, Germany.

HAMPSON Thomas, b. 28 June 1955, Elkhart, Indiana, USA. Singer (Baritone). Education: BA, Government, Eastern Washington University, Cheney; BFA, Voice with Marietta Coyle, Fort Wright College; Studied with Gwendolyn Koldowsky and Martial Singher, Music Academy of the West, summers 1978-79, with Elisabeth Schwarzkopf (Merola), and Horst Günther, 1980. Debut: Hansel and Gretel, 1974. Career includes: Sang first Marcello in La Bohème, 1981; Dusseldorf Ensemble, 1981-84; Guglielmo in Cosi fan tutte, St Louis Opera, sang title role in Henze's Der Prinz von Homburg, Darmstadt, 1982; Debuts, Cologne, Hamburg, Munich, Santa Fe, 1982-84; Debut, Edinburgh Festival, Schumann's Dichterliebe and German songs to Robert Burns texts, 1993; North American tour which featured solo recital debuts in St Paul, Ann Arbor, Omaha, Kansas City and Toronto, 1993; Solo Recital, Barber and Mahler songs, Salzburg Festival, 1994; Leading role of Vicomte de Valmont in world premiere of Conrad Susa/Philip Littell opera, The Dangerous Liaisons, San Francisco Opera, 1994; Sang first Das Lied von der Erde at Carnegie Hall under James Levine, 1995; Sang in Schubert's Alfonso und Estrella, Vienna Festival, 1997; Marquis de Posa in Verdi's Don Carlos, Chatelet Paris and Covent Garden, London,

1996; Riccardo in Bellini's I Puritani (Met, New York) and title role in Eugene Onegin (Vienna Staatsoper), 1997. Recordings: La Bohème, Mahler songs, with Bernstein; Des Knaben Wunderhorn solo album; Hamlet; Mahler songs with Geoffrey Parsons, critical edition; Voices from the Heart, 1996; I Hear America Singing, 1997; Schubert's Winterreise. Publications: Co-editor, Mahler songs critical edition, 1993. Honours include: Cannes Classical Award, Male Singer of Year, 1994; Toblacher Komitte Award (Mahler songs), 1994; Echo Preis, 1994; Six Grammy Nominations; Citation of Merit for Lifetime Contribution to Music and Education, National Arts Club of America; Artist of the Year, EMI. Membership: Honorary Member, Academy of Music, London. Current Management: IMG Artists. Address: Media House, 3 Burlington Lane, Chiswick, London W4 2TH, England.

HAMVASI Sylvia, b. 1972, Budapest, Hungary. Singer (Soprano). Education: Franz Liszt Academy and Leo Weiner Conservatory, Budapest. Career: Roles with Budapest Youth Opera have included Mozart's Blonde and Mme Herz, Serpina in La Serva Padrona and Olympia; Concert tour with the Youth Opera Studio to Kuwait; Repertory includes Bach's St John Passion, Christmas Oratorio and Masses, Mozart, Liszt and Kodály Masses, Carmina Burana and Handel's Messiah, Dixit Dominus and Solomon. Recordings include: Album with the Hungarian Radio Youth Orchestra, conducted by Tamas Vasary. Honours include: European Mozart Foundation Award, at the 1996 Hommage a Lucia Popp Competition, Bratislava. Address: Ingpen & Williams Ltd, 26 Wadham Road, London SW15 2LR, England.

HAN Wan-Zhai, b. 20 June 1941, Jiaocheng, China. Professor; Composer; Conductor; Musicologist. m. 16 Aug 1975, 1 daughter. Education: Composing Class, Middle School of Xian Conservatory; Composing Department, Xian Music University. Debut: F ditty, cello concerto, Xian, June 1962. Career: Conductor of 200 operas and 20 symphonies in Sichuan, such as The Moon Down and the Cock Crowing, 1980-90; Professor of Conservatory, 1983-93; Conductor, Opera and Dance, Thailand, 1994. Compositions: Lantern Festival Sketch, picture symphony; Lady Meng Jiang, fiddle concerto; Song without Words, violin solo; Overture, piano solo; Oh, What a Beautiful Spring, song. Recordings: Beijing Melody, opera; Tracing a Black Fox, telefilm; 50 cassettes and discs, including: Oh, What a Beautiful Spring. Publications: 1 in Chinese, published in USA, 1993; Chinese World, published in England, 1995. Contributions to: 200 articles to People's Music (China), 90's Monthly (Hong Kong), Chinese World (England). Honours: 1st Award for Composition, for cantata, 1985; 1st Award for Composition, for opera The Moon Down and the Cock Crowing, 1990. Memberships: Director, Music Association of Sichuan; Vice-Chairman, Zigong Music Association. Hobbies: Art; Writing; Reviewing. Address: Music Department, Sichuan Teachers' University, Chengdu, Sichuan 610066, China.

HANAK Bohus, b. 8 Jan 1925, Banovce, Czechoslovakia. Singer (Bass- Baritone). Education: Studied in Bratislava. Career: Sang at Bratislava from 1950 and made guest appearances with the company at Prague, Sofia and Wiesbaden; Engaged at Linz, 1958-60 and at Stadttheater Basle, 1968-88; Further performances at the Komische Opera Berlin, Bolshoi Moscow, Leningrad, State Operas of Dresden and Munich, Naples, Geneva, Innsbruck, Berne and Paris at Théâtre des Champs Elysées; Roles have included Mozart's Figaro and Don Giovanni, Pizarro, Rigoletto, Renato, Amonasro, Count Luna, Macbeth, Simon Boccanegra, Wolfram, Telramund, the Dutchman, Alberich, Prince Igor, Eugene Onegin, Scarpia, Cardillac, Nabucco and Mandryka. Address: c/o Theater Basel, Theaterstrasse 7, CH-4010 Basel, Switzerland.

HANANI Yehuda, b. 19 Dec 1943, Jerusalem, Israel. Cellist. m. Hannah Glatstein, 21 Mar 1971, 1 son. Education: Rubin Academy of Music, Israel; Juilliard School, USA. Career: Guest Performer with Chicago Symphony, Philadelphia Orchestra, Baltimore Symphony, St Paul Chamber Orchestra, Berlin Radio Symphony, Israel Philharmonic, BBC Welsh Symphony etc; Aspen Music Festival; Chautauqua; Marlboro; Artistic Director, Chamber Music Series, Miami Center for the Fine Arts; Cello Faculty, The Peabody Conservatory and Cincinnati College-Conservatory. Recordings: Miaskovsky Cello Sonatas; Alkan Cello Sonata; Vivaldi Cello Sonatas; Aleksander Obradovic Cello Concerto; Leo Ornstein Sonata; Samuel Barber Sonata; Lukas Foss Capricio. Honours: Nomination for Grand Prix du Disque; Recipient of 3 Martha Baird Rockefeller Grants for Music; America Israel Cultural Foundation Award.

HANCOCK John, b. 1968, New York City, New York, USA. Singer (Baritone). m. Jane Gilbert. Education: Studied at the Juilliard Opera Center, New York. Career: Sang Oreste in Iphigénie en Tauride at Strasbourg, 1993, Rossini's Dandini in Kansas City and Raimbaud for the Spoleto Festival, USA; La Haine in Lully's Armide in Paris and Antwerp, Marcello in La Bohème at Glyndebourne and with the Canadian Opera Company, 1995, Rossini's Barber for the New Israeli Opera and Valentin in Philadelphia; Other roles include Silvio in Pagliacci, Malatesta and Tarquinius; Sang Lord Henry Wootton in the premiere of Lowell Liebermann's The Picture of Dorian Gray, Monaco, 1996; Concert repertoire includes Mahler's Kindertotenlieder at Alice Tully Hall and Des Knaben Wunderhorn. Address: Atholl Still Ltd, Foresters Hall, 25-27 Westow Street, London SE19 3RY, England.

HANCOCK Paul, b. 6 May 1952, Plymouth, Devon, England. Composer. m. Joan Baigent, 11 Oct 1986, sep, 3 stepsons, 1 stepdaughter. Education: Sherborne School, 1965-71; MA, MusB, Trinity Hall, Cambirdge, 1971-76. Career: Composing and Private Music Teaching in Plymouth 1976-79, York 1979-83, Oxford 1983-85, Cambridge 1985-87; First London Recital at BMIC, Jan 1986. Compositions: Main Compositions: 24 Preludes (Piano Solo), 1979-81; String Quartet, 1982; Who? (Songs for Children), 1981; With The Mermaids (Wind Quartet), 1983; The Gift Of A Lamb (Children's Opera), 1985; Maen Tans-Boskednan (Piano Solo), 1984; Silent Love (Song Cycle), 1985; Zennor (Clarinet and Viola), 1986; Little Gidding Variations (Orchestra), 1985-86; Viola Concerto, 1986; (All Published by Trewhella Music); The Mermaid of Zennor (Opera), 1986-88; ...O Very Most The Hidden Love...(Song Cycle), 1986; The Voice of the Hidden Waterfall (Ensemble), 1987; Nocturne for Ragnhild (Soprano & Piano Duet), 1988; Dancing On A Point Of Light (Ensemble), 1988; Round 12 O'Clock Rock (Baritone and Piano); Sea Change, percussion ensemble, 1989; Vespers of St Mary Magdalene, soprano and organ, 1990, piano sonatas 1,2 and 3, 1990-91; Ogo Pour, percussion solo, 1991; Matrice, piano duet, 1991; The Ring of Fire, piano solo, 1992; Journey Out of Essex, baritone and ensemble, 1993. Recordings: Two Cassetts of Piano Music, produced by Trewhella Music. Membership: Composers Guild of Great Britain. Address: Brunnion Farmhouse, Lelant Downs,Hayle, Cornwall TR27 6NT, England.

HANCORN John, b. 1954, Inverness, Scotland. Singer (Baritone). Education: Studied at Trinity College of Music and The National Opera Studio; Further studies with Hans Hotter in Munich and London. Debut: Edinburgh 1981, as Masetto in Don Giovanni. Career: Aldeburgh from 1981 in Albert Herring, The Rape of Lucretia and Eugene Onegin; Glyndebourne Touring Opera from 1983 in The Love of Three Oranges, Kent Opera as Masetto in Don Giovanni and Fidelio; Debut at Covent Garden as Hermann in Les Contes d'Hoffmann; Tour of Italy 1986 with Monteverdi's L'Orfeo conducted by Roger Norrington; Concert performance of Charpentier's Médée with the Orchestra of the Age of Enlightenment, 1987; Season 1989-90 with Welsh National Opera as Kilian in Der Freischütz, Hector in King Priam with Musica nel Chiostro in Batignano, Italy, Handel's Israel in Egypt with the Royal Choral Society, 1990; Concert repertory also includes the Brahms Requiem; Appearances with the Royal Philharmonic Orchestra, Scottish Chamber Orchestra, Bournemouth Sinfonietta and at the festivals of Camden, Greenwich, Brighton, Aldeburgh, Flanders and Frankfurt; Sang in Weber's Oberon at the Edinburgh and Tanglewood Festivals and at the Alte Oper, Frankfurt conducted by Ozawa; Season 1992-94 worked with Welsh National Opera and English National Opera in many major roles; Sang Jove in Semele by John Eccles, for Mayfield Chamber Opera, 1996; The Devil in Ordo Virtuum by Hildegard of Bingen for Vox Animae at the 1996 York Early Music Festival. Recordings: Recording with Consort of Musicke and Anthony Rooley, 1994. Current Management: Robert Gilder and Co. Address: c/o Robert Gilder and Co, Enterprise House, 59-65 Upper Ground, London, SE1 9PQ, England.

HANDLEY Vernon (George), b. 11 Nov 1930, Enfield, England. Conductor. m. Barbara Black 1954, divorced, 1 son, 1 daughter (1 son deceased), (2) Victoria Parry-Jones (divorced) 1 son, 1 daughter, (2) Catherine Margaret Newby, 1 son. Education: Balliol College, Oxford; Guildhall School of Music. Career: Conductor, Oxford University Musical Club and Union, 1953-54; Oxford University Dramatic Society, 1953-54, Tonbridge Philharmonic Society 1958-61, Hatfield School of Music and Drama 1959-61; Proteus Choir, 1962-81; Musical Director, Conductor, Guildford Corporation, Conductor, Guildford Philharmonic Orchestra & Choir, 1962-83; (Guest Conductor 1961-83); Professor, Orchestra & Conducting, Royal College of Music 1966-72, for Choral Class, 1969-72; Guest Conductor, 1961-; Bournemouth Symphony Orchestra, City of Birmingham Symphony Orchestra, Royal Philharmonic Orchestra, BBC Welsh Orchestra, BBC Northern Symphony (now BBC Philharmonic) Orchestra, London Philharmonic Orchestra, New Philharmonia (now Philharmonia) Orchestra; Conducted London Symphony Orchestra in International Series, London, 1971; Tours of Germany 1966, 1980, South Africa 1974, Holland 1980, Sweden 1980, 1981, Germany, Sweden, Holland and France, 1982-83; Conducted the BBC Concert Orchestra at the 1993 London Proms (Delius Cello Concerto, Vaughan Williams On Wenlock Edge and Bliss Colour Symphony); Chief Guest Conductor, Royal Liverpool Philharmonic Orchestra and Melbourne Symphony Orchestra; Chief Conductor, West Australian Orchestra; Associate Conductor, Royal Philharmonic Orchestra; Conducted Holst's Perfect Fool for the BBC, 1995. Recordings include: CDs of Elgar Violin Concerto (Kennedy), Wand of Youth and 2nd Symphony (London Philharmonic); Vaughan Williams 5th Symphony and Flos Campi (Liverpool Philharmonic); Bridge The Sea and Britten Sea Interludes (Ulster Orchestra); Bax Enchanted Summer, Walsingham and Fatherland (Royal Philharmonic); Delius Florida Suite, North Country Sketches, Violin Concerto, Suite and Legende (Ralph Holmes) Dvorak Overtures and Scherzo Capriccioso; Finzi Cello Concerto (Rafael Wallfisch); Moeran Symphony; Simpson 2nd, 4th, 6th, 7th, 9th and 10th Symphonies, all Stanford Symphonies; all Vaughan Williams Symphonies, Elgar Dream of Gerontius. Address: Hen Gerrig, Pen-y-Fan, Nr Monmouth, Gwent, Wales.

HANDT Herbert, b. 26 May 1926, Philadelphia, Pennsylvania, USA. Tenor; Conductor; Musicologist. Education: Juilliard School New York; Vienna Academy. Debut: Vienna Staatsoper, 1949. Career: Sang in the premieres of Venere Prigioniera by Malipiero (Florence 1957) and Maria Golovin by Menotti (Brussels 1958); Appeared in the Italian and French premieres of works by Henze, Berg, Busoni and Britten; Debut as Conductor, Rome, 1960; Founded own opera group and gave revivals of works by Boccherini, Rossini and Geminiani; Also heard in Haydn's Orfeo ed Euridice (L'Anima del Filosofo); Settled in Lucca, Italy and founded the Associazione Musicale Lucchese and the Lucca Chamber Orchestra. Recordings: Maria Golovin (RCA); Don Giovanni, Haydn's Orfeo, Idomeneo (Nixa); Giuseppe, Figlio di Giacobbe by Luigi Rossi; Rossini's Otello; Temistocle by JC Bach; Sesto in Giulio Cesare by Handel (Vox). Publications include: Performing editions of early Italian vocal music.

HANGEN Bruce (Boyer), b. 2 Feb 1947, Pottstown, Pennsylvania, USA. Conductor. Education: MusB, Eastman School of Music, 1970; Postgraduate studies, summers 1972, 1973, Berkshire Music Center. Career: Conducting Assistant, Buffalo Philharmonic Orchestra, 1972-73; Assistant Conductor, Syracuse (NY) Symphony Orchestra, 1972-73; Assistant Conductor 1973-76, Associate Conductor 1976-79, Denver Symphony Orchestra; Music Director, Portland (Maine) Symphony Orchestra, 1976-86, Omaha Symphony Orchestra, 1984-95; Conductor Laureate, Omaha Symphony Orchestra, 1995-96; Artistic and General Director, Portland (Maine) Opera Repertory Theatre, 1995-. Honours: Eleanor Crane Prize, Berkshire Music Center, 1972; Honorary DFA, University of New England, Biddeford, Maine, 1982; Bruce Hangen Day observed by City of Portland, Maine, 1986. Hobby: Bicycling. Address: 5524 Pine Street, maha, NE 68106, USA.

HANKIN Marion, b. 25 October 1920, Doncaster, England. Private Teacher of Music. m. K A Mowbray Robinson, 22 February 1951, 1 son 1 daughter. Education: Private Tuition, Pianoforte, Singing, Organ, 1927-50; St Gabriels Training College, London, 1939-41; Choir Training, 1939-42; Pianoforte Performance Wakefield Cathedral, 1941-50. Career: Teenage Concert Pianist, including Chamber Music, Recitals and Professional Accompaniment; Lifelong Assistant in Church and Choral Music; Concerts, Solo Recitals, Lectures in Musical Appreciation; Adjudication and School Teaching, 1935-. Honours: Licenciate, Royal Academy of Music, 1945-; Associate, Royal College of Music. Memberships: Incorporated Society of Musicians. Hobby: Reading. Address: c/o 40 St Marys Road, Doncaster, South Yorkshire DN1 2NP, England.

HANLON Kevin (Francis), b. 1 Jan 1953, South Bend, Indiana, USA. Composer. Education: Studied at Indiana University, the Eastman School of Music and the University of Texas, DMA 1983; Further study with Mario Davidovsky at the Berkshire Music Center. Career: Taught at the University of Kentucky, 1982-83; Composition and electronic music faculty at the University of Arizona, Tucson; Director of the Arizona Contemporary Music Ensemble; Appearances as Singer and Conductor. Compositions include: Through to the End of the Tunnel for low voice and tape delay 1976, revised 1980; Second Childhood for soprano and ensemble, 1976; Cumulus numbus for orchestra, 1977; Variations for alto saxophone and tape delay, 1977; Toccata for piano, 1980; String Trio, 1981; An die ferne Geliebte for low voice and piano, 1980; Lullaby for my Sorrows for chamber orchestra, 1982; Ostinato Suite for harpsichord, 1982; Centered for chamber ensemble and tape, 1983; A E Housman Song Cycle for low voice and chamber ensemble, 1982; Choral Introits for chorus and ensemble, 1982; Trumpet Sonata, 1983; Sratae for orchestra, 1983; Relentless Time for small orchestra, 1984. Honours include: Joseph H Bearns Prize, 1978; Koussevitzky Prize, 1981. Address: c/o ASCAP, ASCAP Building, One Lincoln Plaza, NY 10023, USA.

HANLY Brian (Vaughan), b. 3 Sept 1940, Perth, Australia. Concert Violinist; Music Professor. m. Jeri Ryan Hanly, 25 Aug 1968, 2 sons. Education: Performers Diploma 1960, Teachers Diploma 1961, Australian Music Examinations Board. Career: Violinst, Arts Trio, in residence at University of Wyoming and University of Houston, Texas, USA; Numerous tours with Western Arts Trio, Europe, USA, Mexico, also concerts throughout South

America and Australia; Soloist with orchestras throughout Australia, Mexico, USA, with particular success with Beethoven and Prokofiev Concertos. Recordings: 1st recording of Claude Debussy's recently discovered piano trio; 7 LPs with Western Arts Trio. Honour: Winner, Australian Broadcasting Commission Concerto Competition. Hobby: Swimming. Address: Music Department, University of Wyoming, Laramie, WY 82071, USA.

HANNAH Ron, b. 14 Dec 1945, Moose Jaw, Saskatchewan, Canada. Composer; Teacher. Education: BSc, Chemistry, 1969, BMus, Theory, Composition, 1973, MMus, Composition, 1975, EdDip, 1980, University of Alberta, Edmonton; Student of Violet Archer, Manus Sasonkin, Malcolm Forsyth. Career: Member, Da Camera Singers, 1973-; Instructor, Department of Extension, University of Alberta, 1975-76; Instructor, Harmony, Ear Training, Red Deer College, 1977-78; Music Instructor, Edmonton Public Schools, 1980-; Founder, Owner, Composer Publications, Edmonton, 1989; Commissions include: 1 from Edmonton Symphony Orchestra and 2 from Canadian Broadcasting Corporation; Founding Editor, The Alberta New Music Review, magazine of Edmonton Composers' Concert Society. Compositions include: From Song of Solomon, SATB, piano, 1972; An Immorality, SATB, piano, 1972; The Dinner Party, song cycle, soprano, clarinet, piano, 1973; String Quartet No 1, 1973; Sonata for Violoncello and Piano, 1973; Three African Songs, tenor, piano, 1974; The Shrine of Kotje, chorus and orchestra, 1975; Variations on a Theme of Violet Archer, piano, 1975; Concert Piece, flute, piano, 1975; Visions of Nothingness, piano sonata in 2 movements, 1975; Sonata for French Horn and Piano, 1976; Prelude and Meditation on Coventry Cathedral, trumpet, organ, 1978; Five Preludes, organ, 1978; Songs of Myself, song cycle, soprano, violin, piano, French horn, 1979; The Lonely Princess, flute, guitar, 1981; Suite for Elan, piano, 1982; Piano Trio No 1, 1982; Four Canons for three Voices, mixed chorus, piano, 1983; Mademoiselle Fifi, chamber opera, 1983; Three Songs on Poems of Robert Graves, voice, electronic tape, 1984; Fantasia on Ein Feste Burg, organ, 1984; Hypatia, a play with songs, 1984; Three Romantic Madrigals, 1985; Concerto for Piano and Tape, 1986; Morning's Minion: 4 songs after G M Hopkins, soprano, piano, 1987; Alleluia, SATB, 1989; Credo, mezzo-soprano, viola, piano, 1990; Divertimento for Strings, 1991; Pastoral Suite for solo guitar, 1992-93; Suite of Orchestral Dances, 1992; Toccatissimo! for 2 pianos and 2 percussionists, 1993-94. Recordings: 5 Preludes for Organ; Concert pieces for flute and piano; Meditation for cello and piano. Membership: Co-founder and Co-ordinator, Edmonton New Music Festival. Address: 11627-46 Avenue, Edmonton, Alberta, T6H 0A6, Canada.

HANNAN Eilene, b. 4 Nov 1946, Melbourne, Australia. Singer (Soprano). Education: Studied in Australia and London. Debut: Australian Opera 1971, as Barbarina in Le nozze di Figaro. Career: Sang Natasha in Prokofiev's War and Peace at the opening of the Sydney Opera House, 1973; Other Australian roles have been Janacek's Vixen, Santuzza, Mozart's Zerlina and Cherubino and Leila in Les pêcheurs de Perles, Glyndebourne and Wexford 1977, as the Vixen and as Salomé in Herodiade by Massenet; English National Opera from 1978, as Janacek's Mila (Osud) and Katya Kabanova, the Dutchess of Parma in Busoni's Doctor Faust, Mozart's Pamina and Susanna, Mélisande, Poppea (Monteverdi) and Natasha; Covent Garden debut 1978, in the British premiere of The King Goes Forth to France, by Sallinen; Sang in Britten's The Turn of the Screw at Brisbane in 1988; Season 1992, as Jenufa at Sydney, Pat Nixon for the State Opera of South Australia and at Dusseldorf. Address: c/o Ingpen & Williams, 26 Wadham Road, London SW15 2LR, England.

HANNAN Michael (Francis), b. 19 Nov 1949, Newcastle, New South Wales, Australia. Composer; Writer; Educator; Keyboard Performer. Education: BA 1972, PhD 1979, University of Sydney; Graduate Diploma of Musical Composition, University of Sydney, 1982. Career: Teacher, University of New South Wales 1975-76, University of Sydney 1977-83; Lecturer in Composition, Queensland Conservatorium of Music, 1985-86; Head of Music, Northern Rivers College of Advanced Education, 1986-; Research, Post-doctoral Scholar, University of California, Los Angeles, 1983-84; Research Affiliate, University of Sydney, 1985-. Compositions: Voices in the Sky for piano, 1980; Rajas for solo cello, 1982; Zen Variations for piano, 1982; Island Song for recorders, percussion and organ, 1983; In the Utter Darkness, for solo flute, 1983; Callisto for piano, 1986. Recordings: The Piano Music of Peter Sculthorpe, Move Records, 1982. Publications: Peter Sculthorpe: His Music and Ideas, 1929-79, 1982. Contributions to: Various publications. Hobbies: Surfing; Cooking; Wine; Ornithology. Address: c/o School of the Arts, Northern Rivers College of Advanced Education, Lismore, NSW 2480, Australia.

HANNAY Roger (Durham), b. 22 Sept 1930, Plattsburg, New York, USA. Composer; Conductor; Teacher. m. Janet Roberts, 1 daughter. Education: BMus, Syracuse University, 1948-52; MMus, Boston University, 1952-53; PhD, Eastman School of Music, 1954-56; Berkshire Music School, 1959; Princeton Seminar for Advanced Studies, 1960; Bennington Composers Conference, 1964-65. Debut: Music in Our Time, New York City, 1964. Career: Teacher on the faculities of SUNY, Hamilton College, University of Wyoming, Concordia College; Teacher, University of North Carolina, where founded and directed Electronic Studio and the New Music Ensemble, 1967-82; Conducted the North Carolina Symphony Orchestra in his Symphony No 4, American Classic, 1983, Greensboro Symphony Orchestra premiere of his orchestral suite, The Age of Innocence, 1985, Peter Fuchs Conductor; Winston-Salem Symphony Orchestra premiere of Symphony No 6, 1990; Residencies, Charles Ives Center for American Music, MacDowell Colony, Yaddo, Ives Center for American Music. Compositions include: 7 symphonies, 5 chamber operas, 4 string quartets; Sphinx, trumpet and tape; Pied Piper, clarinet and tape; Clarinet Voltaire, saxophone, percussion and speaker; The Journey of Edith Wharton, opera in 2 acts for 5 voices and chamber orchestra, 1982; Rhapsody, flute and piano; Sic Transit Spiritus, 1984; Souvenir and Souvenir II, 1984 and 1986; Ye Musick for the Globe Theatre, 1985; The Nightingale and the Rose, 1986; Prologue to Chaucer's Canterbury Tales, commissioned. Recordings: Symphony for Band; Architecture in Sound, 1997. Publications: Transcribed and edited, Sonate for viola and piano by Mrs H H Beach, 1984; My Book of Life, collection of autobiographical essays, 1997. Hobbies: Literature; Travel. Address: 609 Morgan Creek Road, Chapel Hill, NC 27514, USA.

HANNIKAINEN Ann-Elise, b. 14 Jan 1946, Hangö, Finland. Composer; Pianist. Education: Academia Moderna de Musica, Peru, 1964-66; Diploma, Sibelius Academy, Finland, 1967-72; Studies with composer, Ernesto Halffter, Spain, 1972-. Debut: As Composer, orchestral piece, Anerfálicas, Valencia, Spain, 1973. Career includes: Tournée as pianist, Andalucia, 1975; Performance, world premiere, Piano Concerto, Helsinki, 1976; Anerfálicas, Teatro Real, Madrid, Spain, 1977; Finnish Radio broadcasts, Spanish Radio; Piano recitals; Festival Kuhmoinen, Andalucia, Madrid and others. Compositions include: Anerfálicas, orchestral, 1973; Pensamientos for Piano, 1974; Toccata Fantasia for Piano, 1975; Concierto for Piano and Orchestra, in memoriam Manuel de Falla's 100th Anniversary, 1976; Cosmos for Orchestra, 1977; Trio, Sextetto, 1979; Chachara for Flute and Piano, 1980; Solemne for Solo Piano, 1982; Zafra for Violin and Piano, 1986. Recordings: Tape recordings; Finnish Radio. Publications: Pensamiemtos, 1974; Toccato Fantasia; Chachara; Some works included in, Centre de Documentation de la Musique Contemporaire, Paris, France. Honours: 1st Prize, Second Contest for Young Composers, JJMM Barcelona, 1980. Memberships: Société des Auteurs; Compositeurs et Editeurs de Musique, Paris; Society of Finnish Composers. Hobby: Oil Painting. Address: Mannerheimintie 21-23B, 00250 Helsinki 25, Finland.

HANNULA Kaisa, b. 1959, Finland. Singer (Soprano). Education: Studied at the Sibelius Academy, Helsinki, and in London and Vienna. Career: Sang at first in concert and appeared at the 1989 Savonlinna Festival, in the premiere of The Knife by Paavo Heininen; Savonlinna, 1991, as Marenka in The Bartered Bride and Helsinki, 1992, in Pohjalaisia by Madetoja; Other roles include Marguerite and Violetta. Address: c/o Finnish National Opera, Bulevardi 23-27, SF 00180 Helsinki 18, Finland.

HANNULA Tero, b. 1950, Vehmaa, Finland. Singer (Baritone). Education: Studied in Finland with P Salomaa, in Rome with Luigi Ricci and at Musikhochschule Vienna. Career: Sang Escamillo and Posa in Don Carlos at Kaiserslautern, 1976; Nationaltheater Mannheim from 1977, as Wolfram, Enrico, Counts Luna and Almaviva, Eugene Onegin, Marcello, Rossini's Figaro and Lortzing's Tsar; Sang Almaviva at Ludwigsburg 1980-81, Savonlinna Festival 1981-89, as Papageno and in the 1984 premiere of Sallinen's The King Goes Forth to France; Stuttgart Staatsoper 1982-, notably in the 1984 premiere of Akhnaten by Philip Glass; Guest appearances at Hamburg, Hanover, Karlsruhe, Aachen, Vienna, Moscow, Leningrad and Munich; Finnish National Opera, Helsinki, as Rigoletto, Deutsche Oper Berlin as Thoas in Iphigénie en Aulide; Sang Blancsac in La Scala di Seta at Stuttgart Staatsoper, 1991; Forester in The Cunning Little Vixen at Karlsruhe, 1996. Recordings include: Akhnaten. Address: c/o Stuttgart Staatsoper, Oberer Schlossgarten 6, 7000 Stuttgart, Germany.

HANSELL Kathleen (Amy Kuzmick), b. 21 Sept 1941, Bridgeport, Connecticut, USA. Musicologist; Organist; Harpsichordist. 1 son, 1 daughter. Education: BA, Wellesley College, Massachusetts, 1963; MMus, University of Illinois at Urbana, 1969; PhD, University of California at Berkeley, 1980; Studied piano organ and harpsichord with private teachers. Career: Instrucot in Music History, by correspondence, University of Illinois, 1967-68; Organist, Lutheran Church of the Good Shepherd, Sacramento, California, 1969-71; Gloria Dei Lutheran Church, Iowa City, 1973-74; Instructor in Musicology and Harpsichord, Grinnell College, Iowa, 1976; Instructor in Music History, Cornell College, Mt Vernon, Iowa, 1979; Archivist, Swedish Music History Archive, Stockholm, Sweden, 1982-. Publications: Editor, Mozart: Lucio Silla for Neue Mozart Ausgabe, 1986; Franz Berwald Complete Works, Volume 14, Duos (Barenreiter), 1987, Hindemith, Organ Concerto, 1962 for Hindemith-Ausgabe; Il Balletto e l'Opera Italiana, in Storia dell'opera Italiana (Turin), 1988; Editor, Rossini: Zelmira, for Tutte le opere di Gioachino Rossini. Contributions to: Numerous professional magazines and publications including Grove's Dictionary, 6th edition. Memberships: American, International, Italian and Swedish Musicology Societies; International Association of Music Libraries; College Music Society; Chairman, Editorial Board, Monumenta Musicae Svecicae. Address: c/o New Grove Dictionary, 4 Little Essex Street, London WC2.

HANSEN Flemming (Christian), b. 1 Jan 1968, Copenhagen, Denmark. Organist (Composer). Education: Recorder, Clarinet, Saxophone, Piano, in childhood; Preliminary Organ Studies to 1988; Organ at Royal Danish Academy of Music, 1992-; Composition studies with Professor Ib Norholm, Andy Pape and Bent Sorensen. Career: As composer: Performances in Denmark, Norway, Finland, Germany, USSR, Hungary, France, Belgium; Attended festivals in Russia 1989, 1990, 1992, and Moldavia 1991. Compositions: November-Music for clarinet, vibraphone and viola, 1986; Andre Naetter for orchestra, 1988; Kantele for tape, 1988; A la Memoire de Dali for saxophone quartet, 1989; De Profundis for organ, 1990. Recordings: CD: A la Memoire de Dali with New Danish Saxophone Quartet. Honours: Several scholarships, Art Foundation of the Danish State; Participant in Rostrum 91. Membership: Danish Composers Society. Hobby: Travel. Address: H C Andersensgade 9 1, 4800 Nykobing F, Denmark.

HANSON Robert (Frederic), b. 24 Oct 1948, Birmingham, England. Composer; Musicologist; Teacher. m. (1) Anthea Judith Carter, 11 Jul 1970, 1 d, (2) Rosalind Thurston, 1 Nov 1980, 2 s. Education: ARCO, 1967, BA, 1970, PhD, 1976, Southampton University. Career: Founder, Conductor, Southampton University Chamber Orchestra, 1970-72; Analytical research into the music of Webern, 1970-73; Freelance Teacher and Composer, 1973-74; Lecturer in Music, Dartington College of Arts, 1974-91; Degree Course Leader, 1983-91; Acting Head of Music, 1990-91; Director of Studies, Morley College, 1991-. Compositions: Numerous unpublished compositions; Metaphysical Verses for Soprano and Orchestra, 1980; Changes for String Orchestra, 1982; Chamber Concerto, 1986; Song Cycles: Auguries of Innocence, 1988; Clarinet Concerto, 1991; Thanksgiving Music, 1994. Contributions to: Tempo; Lutoslawski's Mi-Parti; Music Analysis; Webern's Chromatic Organisation. Memberships: Society for the Promotion of New Music; Performing Rights Society. Hobby: Architecture. Address: Morley College, 61 Westminster Bridge Road, London, England.

HANUS Jan, b. 2 May 1915, Prague, Czechoslovakia. Composer. Education: Studied composition with O Jeremias, 1932-40. Career: Has worked for music publishers, 1934-, (critical editions of Dvorák and Fibich) notably Panton, 1963-70. Compositions include: Operas: Flames, 1956, The Servant of Two Masters, 1959, Prometheus's Torch, 1965, The Story of One Night, 1961-68, A Dispute over The Goddess, Czech Television, 1986; Ballets: Othello, Prague, 1959, Salt Above Gold, Olomouc, 1953, Labyrinth, Prague, 1983; 7 Symphonies, 1942-90; Concertante Symphony for Organ, Harp, Timpani and Strings, 1954; Double Concerto for Oboe, Harp and Orchestra, 1965; Three Essays for Orchestra, 1975-76; Chamber: Serenade for Nonet, 1953, Viola sonatina, 1958, Frescoes for Piano Trio, 1961, Suite Domestica for Wind Quintet, 1964, Concertino for Timpani and Tape, 1970, Tower Music for Brass Quintet, 1976, The Praise of Chamber Music for Flute, Oboe, String Trio and Harpsichord, 1979, Ecce Homo, oratorio, 1980; Glagolitic Mass for Bass, Chorus, Organ and Bells, 1985; Requiem for Soli, Chorus, Children's Choir, String, Brass and Percussion Orchestras and Organ, 1990-94. Address: 169 00 Prague 6, Tomanova 38, Czech Republic.

HANUSZEWSKA-SCHAEFFER Mieczyslawa, b. 1 Oct 1929, Borszow, near Tarnopol, Poland. Musicologist; Philosopher; Journalist. m. Boguslaw Schaeffer, 23 Nov 1953, 1 son. Education: Languages, Philosophy, Musicology, Jagiellonian University, Cracow; Music Theory, State Higher School of Music. Debut: 1953. Publications: Collaborated in Lexicon of 20th Century Composers, 1965 and New Grove Dictionary; Editor, Almanach kompozytorow polskich (Lexicon of Polish Contemporary Composers), 3rd edtion, 1981; Tysiac kompoztorow (Lexicon of 1000 Composers), 4th edition, 1985; Musical Editor, Zycle Literackie. Contributions to: Some 400 articles in magazines such as Zycie Literackie, Ruch Muzyczny. Honour: Music Prize for Music Journalism, 1989. Membership: Grupa Karkowska. Hobbies: Philosophy; Reading. Address: Osiedle Kolorowa 4, Cracow 31 938, Poland.

HAQUE Asadul, b. 1 March 1930, Pabna, Bangladesh. Retired. m. Firoza Asad, 3 June 1955, 1 son, 1 daughter. Education: Studies of Classical, Sami Classical and Folk Songs. Career: Researcher, National Poet Kazi Nazrul Islam and

Classical Music of the Sub-Continent; Music Producer, Radio Pakistan, Karachi, 1963-65, Rawalpindi, 1969-71; Performer, Vocal Songs on Radio and Television. Publications include: Nazrul Sangiter Rupaker, 1990; Nazrul Saralipi, vol 4, 1990; Antaranga Aloke Nazrul O Pramila, 1994; Chalachitrey Nazrul, 1994. Contributions to: Leading Newspapers of Bangladesh and Calcutta. Honours: Sanad E Khidmat, 1st Class, Pakistan Government, 1970; Nazrul award, Churulia Nazrul Academy, West Bengal, 1997. Memberships: Bangla Academy, Dhaka. Hobbies: Research; Writing. Address: 12/D Eastern Housing, Sidheswari, Dhaka 1217, Bangladesh.

HARA Kazuko, b. 10 Feb 1935, Tokyo, Japan. Composer. Education: Studied in Japan, with Dutilleux in Paris and with Techerepinn, 1962; Singing at Venice Conservatory, 1963, Gregorian Chant in Tokyo. Career: Her operas have been successfully performed in Tokyo. Compositions include: Operas, The Casebook of Sherlock Holmes, the Confession, 1981; On the Merry Night, 1984; A Selection for Chieko, 1985; Sute-Hime: The Woman who Bit off a Man's Tongue, 1986; A Love Suicide at Sonezaki, 1987; Beyond Brain Death, 1988; Yosakoi-bushi: Junshin and Omma, 1990; Princess Iwanaga, 1990; Pedtro Kibe: recanted not, 1992; Nasuno-Yoichi, 1992; Tonnerre's miraculous tree, 1993. Address: JASRAC, Jasrac House 7-13, 1-Chome Nishishimbashi, Minato-ku, Tokyo 105, Japan.

HARADA Hiroshi, b. 23 Feb 1939, Hiroshima, Japan. Professor. m. Hideko Takahashi, 20 Mar 1972, 1 son. Education: Tokyo University of Arts. Appointment: Professor, Hiroshima University. Publications: Domenico Scarlatti, 1974; Black and White, 1978; Brahms/Chamber Music, 1981; Childrens Song in Hiroshima, 1984. Contributions to: Printed and manuscript copies of Keyboard Sonatas of D Scarlatti. Memberships: Japanese Musicological Society; International Musicological Society; American Musicological Society. Hobbies: Sports; Gardening. Address: 2169-3 Jike, Saijo, Higashi, Hiroshima 739-0041, Japan.

HARADA Sadao, b. 4 Jan 1944, Tokyo, Japan. Cellist. Education: Studied at the Juilliard School with members of the Juilliard Quartet. Career: Cellist of the Tokyo Quartet, 1969-; Regular concerts in the USA and abroad; First cycle of the complete quartets of Beethoven at the Yale at Norfolk Chamber Music Festival, 1986; Repeated cycles at the 92nd Street Y (NY), Ravinia and Israel Festivals and Yale and Princeton Universities; Season 1990-91 at Alice Tully Hall, the Metropolitan Museum of Art, New York and in Boston, Washington DC, Los Angeles, Cleveland, Detroit, Chicago, Miami, Seattle, San Francisco, Toronto; Tour of South America, two tours of Europe including Paris, Amsterdam, Bonn, Milan, Munich, Dublin, London, Berlin; Quartet-in-Residence at Yale University, the University of Cincinnati College-Conservatory of Music. Recordings: Schubert's Major Quartets; Mozart Flute Quartets with James Galway and Clarinet Quintet with Richard Stolzman; Quartets by Bartok, Brahms, Debussy, Haydn, Mozart and Ravel; Beethoven Middle Period Quartets (RCA). Honours: Grand Prix du Disque du Montreux; Best Chamber Music Recording of the Year from Stereo Review and the Gramophone; Four Grammy Nominations. Address: Intermusica Artists Management, 16 Duncan Terrace, London N1 8BZ, England.

HARBISON John (Harris), b. 20 Dec 1938, Orange, New Jersey, USA. Composer; Conductor. Education: Pupil of Walter Piston, Harvard College, BA 1960, Boris Blacher, Berlin Hochschule für Musik 1961, and Roger Sessions and Earl Kim, Princeton University, MFA 1963; Studied conducting with Eleazer de Carvalho, Berkshire Music Center, Tanglewood, Massachusetts and with Dean Dixon, Salzburg. Career: Teacher, Massachusetts Institute of Technology, 1969-82; Conductor, Cantata Singers and Ensemble, 1969-73, 1980-82; Composer-in-Residence, Reed College, 1968-69, Pittsburgh Symphony Orchestra 1982-84, Berkshire Music Center, 1984; New Music Adviser 1985-86, Composer-in-Residence 1986-88, Los Angeles Philharmonic Orchestra. Compositions: Operas: The Winter's Tale, 1974; Full Moon in March, 1977; Ballets: Ulysses' Bow, 1984; Ulysses Raft, 1983; Orchestral: Sinfonia for violin and double orchestra, 1963; Confinement for chamber ensemble, 1965; Elegiac Songs for mezzo-soprano and chamber orchestra, 1973; Descant-Nocturne, 1976; Diotima, 1976; Piano Concerto, 1978; Snow Country for oboe and strings, 1979; Violin Concerto, 1980; Symphony No 1, 1981; Deep Potomac Bells for 250 tubas, 1983; Remembering Gatsby, 1986; Viola Concerto, 1989; Chamber: Serenade for 6 instruments, 1968; Piano Trio, 1969; Bermuda Triangle for amplified cello, tenor Saxophone and electric organ, 1970; Die Kurze for 5 instruments, 1970; Woodwind Quintet, 1979; Organum for Paul Fromm for chamber group, 1981; Piano Quintet, 1981; Exequien for Carlo Simmons for 7 instruments, 1982; Overture, Michael Kohlhass for brass ensemble, 1982; Variations for clarinet, violin and piano, 1982; String Quartet, 1985; Choral Pieces; Songs. Recordings: Several compositions recorded. Honours: Guggenheim Fellowship, 1978; Pulitzer Prize in Music, 1986; Many commissions including opera The Great Gatsby, for performance at the Metropolitan on January 1 2000. Address: 4037 Highway 19, De Forest, WI 53532, USA.

HARDENBERGER Hakan, b. 27 Oct 1961, Malmo, Sweden. Trumpeter. Education: Trumpet with Bo Nilsson in Malmo aged 8; Royal College of Music, Malmo; Paris Conservatoire with Pierre Thibaud. Career: Prizewinner at competitions in Paris, Munich, Toulon and Geneva; Extensive tours of Europe and North and South America; UK debut Aug 1984, playing the Howarth Trumpet Concerto at Crystal Palace; Tour of Germany 1984 with the Dresdner Baroque Soloists; 1985 Bournemouth Sinfonietta with Andrew Parrott playing Hummel and Bach; Harrogate and Warwick Festivals 1985, and South American tour with the Munich Bach Collegium; London Promenade Concert debut 1986, with the premiere of Array by Gordon Crosse conducted by James Loughran; May 1987 premiere of Harrison Birtwistle's Endless Parade with the Collegium Musicum Zurich conducted by Paul Sacher; Aug 1987 premiere of John McCabe's Rainforest II at the Harrogate Festival; Concerts with the Scottish National Orchestra and Neeme Jarvi and the Northern Sinfonia with George Malcolm; Other conductors with whom he has worked include Peter Eövtös, Charles Mackerras, John Pritchard, Seiji Ozawa and Rostropovitch; Edinburgh Festival debut 1989, playing the Haydn Concerto with Esa-Pekka Salonen conducting the Swedish Radio Symphony; Premiered Henze's Concerto 1992 (Japan); Season 1993-94 with South America tour, appearances at Salzburg and the London Proms, tour of Europe with the London Sinfonietta; Played Michael Haydn's Concerto at St John's, London, 1997. Recordings: Concertos by Haydn, Hummel, Hertel, Stamitz and Telemann with the Academy of St Martin in the Fields under Neville Marriner (Philips); Birtwistle Endless Parade, Concertos by Davies and Watkins; Mysteries of the Macabre, Baroque Trumpet Recital, At the Beach. Honours: RPO Charles Heidseele Music Award for best instrumentalist in 1988, 1989. Current Management: Svenek Konsertdirektion AB. Address: c/o Svensk Konsertdirektion AB, Henrik F Lodding, Box 5076, 402 22 Göteborg, Sweden.

HARDING Daniel, b. 1975, England. Conductor. Education: Student at Cambridge University. Career: Season 1993-94 conducted the Miraculous Mandarin Suite with the City of Birmingham Symphony, followed by Schnittke's Viola Concerto with Yuri Bashmet; Other CBSO repertory includes Das Lied von der Erde, The Rite of Spring and Stockhausen's Gruppen; Season 1994-95 with the Rotterdam Philharmonic, London Symphony, Scottish Chamber Orchestra and BBC Philharmonic Orchestra; Tour of Britain in 1995 with the Birmingham Contemporary Music Group in The Soldier's Tale; Further engagements with the Netherlands Wind Ensemble and the Jeunesse Musicales World Orchestra; London Proms debut 1996 (as youngest ever conductor), Principal Conductor of the Trondheim Symphony Orchestra (1997) and Principal Guest of the Norköpping Symphony Orchestra; Engaged 1998 for Don Giovanni at Aix and Jenufa for Welsh National Opera. Address: c/o Harold Holt Ltd, 31 Sinclair Road, London, W14 0NS, England.

HARDY Janet, b. 1940, Atlanta, Georgia, USA. Singer (Dramatic Soprano). Education: Studied at the Mississippi Southern and Louisiana Colleges; BM in Music Education, Louisiana College; Further study with Dorothy Hulse, Dominique Modesti, Gladys Kuchta and Hilde Zadek. Career: Has sung in Gelsenkirchen, Kassel and Augsburg as Elektra, Ortrud, Leonore in Fidelio, the Kostelnicka in Jenufa, Kundry, Isolde, Senta and Turandot; Guest appearances in Frankfurt, Salzburg, Copenhagen, the Berlin Staatsoper, Trieste, Leipzig, Berne, Mannheim, Toulon and Dusseldorf; Season 1988-89 with the title role in new productions of Mona Lisa by Schillings in Augsburg and Elektra in Innsbruck; Sang Elektra at the Vienna Staatsoper, June 1991; Brünnhilde in Die Walküre at Liège, the Dyer's Wife in Die Frau ohne Schatten at Augsburg, Nov 1991; Sang Elektra with Welsh National Opera, 1992. Address: Music International, 13 Ardilaun Road, London N5 2QR, England.

HARDY Rosemary, b. 1949, England. Singer (Soprano). Education: Studied at the Royal College of Music and at the Franz Liszt Academy, Budapest. Career: Performances with Roger Norrington, Micel Corboz and John Eliot Gardiner in The Baroque repertoire; Solo cantatas with the Drottingholm Baroque Ensemble, Sweden, at the Berlin Staatsoper and the Wigmore Hall; Sang in Jonathan Miller's production of Orfeo by Monteverdi; Modern repertoire includes Webern's music for voice at the Venice Biennale 1983 and the Cheltenham Festival; Webern recital at the Vienna Konzerthaus 1983; Schoenberg's 2nd Quartet (Arditti) for the Maggio Musicale, in Geneva and in London (BBC); Premieres of Jonathon Harvey's Passion and Resurrection and Song Offerings; Tours of France with Ensemble Intercontemporain, performing Boulez, Ravel, Varèse and Kurtag (Scenes from a Novel): has also given Kurtag's Sayings of R V Troussova; Appearances at the Glyndebourne Festival in Knussen's Where the Wild Things Are and Higgelty Piggelty Pop: concert showings with the Hallé, City of Birmingham, San Diego, Danish Radio, BBC Symphony and London Symphony Orchestras; Has sung in Henze's The English Cat for the BBC and in Frankfurt and Italy; Concert with the Schoenberg Ensemble and the Nieuw Ensemble at the Holland Festival; Pierrot Lunaire in Milan, 1991; Tour with Capricorn on the Contemporary Music Network; Has also sung in Schubert Masses with the London Philharmonic, Mozart and Handel concert for the Cambridge Festival and concerts at the Aldeburgh Festival. Recordings: Cavalli's Ercole Amante (Erato); Monteverdi's Combattimento, Il Ballo delle Ingrate and Scherzi Musicale. Honours include: Artijus Prize, Hungary, 1983. Address: Magenta Music International, 4 Highgate Street, London N6 5JL, England.

HARE Ian (Christopher), b. 26 Dec 1949, Kingston upon Hull, England. Organist; Conductor; Composer. m. (1) Carol Russell, 23 Apr 1973, (2) Pauline Crosland, 21 Mar 1985, 2 daughters. Education: Organ Scholar, MA, Mus B, King's College, Cambridge, 1968-72; Associate, Royal College of Music, 1973-74; Fellow, Royal College of Organists (CHM); ADCM. Career: Lecturer in Music, University of Lancaster, 1974-; Musical Director, Lancaster Singers, 1975-; Organist and Master of the Choristers, Cartmel Priory, 1981-89; Sub-Organist, Carlisle Cathedral, 1989-; University Organist, Lancaster, 1983-. Compositions: Thou, O God, Art Praised in Sion, anthem, 1973; Beethoven's Hymn to Joy, organ arrangement, 1974; A Child is Born, anthem, 1987; Triptych, for organ, 1993. Recordings: Handel's Messiah, Bach Cantata 147 and motets, Britten's Missa Brevis, St Nicolas, Once in Royal David's City, Hymns for All Seasons, King's College Choir, Cambridge, 1968-72; The Organ of Carmel Priory, 1985; Cassette: English Organ Music, 1987; Haydn & Schubert CD, 1989 (Haydn Society of Great Britain). Contributions to: The Organ. Honour: John Stewart of Rannoch Scholarship in Sacred Music, 1969-72. Memberships: Fellow, Royal College of Organists; Incorporated Association of Organists; Incorporated Society of Musicians. Hobbies: Reading; Walking; Gardening. Address: Prior Slee Gatehouse, The Abbey, Carlisle, Cumbria CA3 8TZ, England.

HAREWOOD The Earl of (George Henry Hubert Lascelles), b. 7 Feb 1923, London, England. Musical Administrator. m. (1) Maria Donata Stein, 1949 (divorced 1967), (2) Patricia Tuckwell, 1967, 4 s. Education: King's College, Cambridge University. Career includes: Board Directors, 1951-53, 1969-72, Administrative Executive, 1953-60, Royal Opera House, Covent Garden, London; Chairman, British Council Music Advisory Committee, 1956-66; Director General, 1958-74, Chairman, 1988-90, Leeds Musical Festival; Artistic Director, Edinburgh International Festival, 1961-65; Arts Council Music Panel, 1966-72; Artistic Advisor, New Philharmonic Orchestra, 1966-76; General Advisory Council, BBC, 1969-77; Managing Director, Sadler's Wells Opera, 1972; Managing Director, 1974-85, Chairman, 1986-95, English National Opera; Governor of BBC, 1985-87; President, British Board of Film Classification, 1985-; Artistic Director, Adelaide Festival, 1988; Artistic Advisor, Buxton Festival, 1993-. Publications: Editor, Opera, 1950-53; Editor, Kobbé's Complete Opera Book, 1954, 1973, 1987, 1989; Autobiography, The Tongs and The Bones, 1982; Kobbé's Illustrated Opera Books, 1989. Honours include: KBE, 1987. Hobbies: Opera; Theatre; Association Football. Current Management: Ingpen and Williams. Address: Harewood House, Leeds, LS17 9LG, England.

HARGAN Alison, b. 1943, Yorkshire, England. Singer (Soprano). Education: Studied piano and singing at the Royal Northern College of Music. Debut: With Welsh National Opera, as Pamina in Die Zauberflöte. Career: Concert performances of music by Strauss and Mahler, Four Last Songs and Resurrection Symphony, and Verdi (Requiem); Appearances include Tippett's A Child of our Time with Neville Marriner, the Fauré Requiem with the Royal Philharmonic Orchestra and Bach's B Minor Mass in Lisbon; Britten's War Requiem with the Boston Symphony Orchestra and Mahler's 8th Symphony at La Fenice, Venice, conducted by Eliahu Inbal; Has also worked with Andrew Davis, Eugen Jochum, Erich Leinsdorf, Leppard, Ozawa, Pritchard, Colin Davis, Lorin Maazel, Simon Rattle, Richard Hickox and Rozhdestvensky; Orchestras include the Vienna Philharmonic, Munich Philharmonic and Los Angeles Philharmonic, as well as leading orchestras in Britain. Address: c/o IMG Artists Europe, Media House, 3 Burlington Lane, Chiswick, London W4 2TH, England.

HARGITAI Geza, b. 1940, Hungary, Violinist. Education: Studied at the Franz Liszt Academy, Budapest. Career: Second Violinist of the Bartók Quartet from 1985; Performances in nearly every European country and tours of Australia, Canada, Japan, New Zealand and the USA; Festival appearances at Adelaide, Ascona, Aix, Venice, Dubrovnik, Edinburgh, Helsinki, Lucerne, Menton, Prague, Vienn, Spoleto and Schwetzingen; Tour of Britain 1986 including concerts at Cheltenham, Dartington, Philharmonic Hall Liverpool, RNCM Manchester and the Wigmore Hall; Tours of Britain 1988 and 1990, featuring visits to the Sheldonian Theatre, Oxford, Wigmore Hall, Harewood House and Birmingham; Repertoire includes standard classics and Hungarian works by Bartók, Durko, Bozay, Kadosa, Soproni,

Farkas, Szabo and Lang. Recordings include: Complete quartets of Mozart, Beethoven and Brahms; Major works of Haydn and Schubert (Hungarton); Complete quartets of Bartók (Erato). Address: c/o Ingpen and Williams Ltd, 12 Wadham Road, London SW15 2LR, England.

HARGREAVES Glenville, b. 1950, Bradford, England. Singer (Baritone). Education: Studied at St John's College, York, Royal Northern College of Music and London Opera Centre. Debut: Title role in Il Barbiere di Siviglia, 1981. Career: Covent Garden debut, 1982, in Les Contes d'Hoffmann; English National Opera from 1982, notably in Magic Flute, War and Peace, Salome; Modern repertory includes The Old Man, in Purgatory by Gordon Crosse; Walworth in Wat Tyler by Alan Bush; Longinus in The Catiline Conspiracy by Iain Hamilton (creation); Ullmann's Emperor of Atlantis; Mittenhofer in Henze's Elegy for Young Lovers (Queen Elizabeth Hall, London); Sir Charles Keighley in John Metcalf's Tornrak (creation, 1990); Appeared with Opera North as The Dark Fiddler in A Village Romeo and Juliet, Kothner in Meistersinger and roles in Tosca and The Bartered Bride; Welsh National Opera debut as Marcello in La Bohème; Has sung Rossini's Figaro in Netherlands and Belgium, and Falstaff with City of Birmingham Touring Opera; Season 1992 with Don Magnifico for Pimlico Opera and the Guardian in Elektra and title role in Don Pasquale for Welsh National Opera; Ankarstroem in Un Ballo in Maschera, WNO, 1993, also Don Alfonso for English Touring Opera; Other roles include Zurga (Les Pêcheurs de Perles), Nick Shadow, Germont, Don Giovanni, Mandryka, Paolo (Simon Boccanegra), Tonio, Scarpia, Demetrius (A Midsummer Night's Dream), Mozart's Count; Concert repertory includes Elijah, Judas Maccabeus, The Kingdom, Messiah, Bruch's Odysseus, Puccini's Messa di Gloria, Sea Drift by Delius, Lieder eines fahrenden Gesellen by Mahler; Has sung with Hallé Choir, National Orchestra of Spain, Royal Choral Society and Royal Philharmonic Orchestra; Also sings in Bach's Passions and Carmina Burana; Appearances at Garsington Opera: Musiklehrer in Ariadne, 1993 and Count in Capriccio, 1994; Rigoletto for English Touring Opera, 1996 (Germont 1997). Recording: Old Man, in Purgatory. Current Management: IMG Artists Europe. Address: c/o IMG Artists Europe, 3 Burlington Lane, London W4 2TH, England.

HARLAN Christoph, b. 30 Mar 1952, Dreilingen, Germany, Classical Guitarist; Educator. m. Iris Mallet, 27 July 1975, 2 sons. Education: Abitur, Gymnasium, West Germany, 1970; Teaching Certificate 1972, Academy of Music, Austria. Career: Numerous radio broadcasts, WCLV Cleveland, CIM Concert Hall, Kent in Concert, USA; Television broadcasts, Continental Cable, 1983; Concert tours, 18 recitals, Essen, Hannover, Osnabruck, other venues, Germany; Concert appearances, New York, Buffalo, Pittsburgh, Cleveland, Cincinnati, Lubbock, Toronto, Quebec (USA and Canada); Has held various masterclasses; Appearances, most major concert series, solo/chamber music, Ohio; Many world & American premieres, various works including own compositions; Appearances, several American Festivals, Guitar Symposia (USA/Canada). Compositions: Anthologia Judaica, Vol I, II; Romanesca; Fantasy and Ecstasy; Trilogy; Tsigayner Doyna; Choral Variations; Britten's Ayre. Recordings: With members of Cleveland Orchestra, 2 records, works by Vivaldi, Bach, Boccherini, Haydn, Handel. Publications: Editions of chamber music, 1982; 3 suites by JJ Froberger, transcribed & fingered, 1983. Address: c/o Iris Rozanski, 1215 Driftwood Drive, Pittsburgh, PA 5243, USA.

HARLE John (Crofton), b. 20 Sept 1956, Saxophonist; Composer; Arranger; Conductor. m. 1985, Julia Jane Eisner, 2 sons. Education: Royal College of Music, Foundation School; ARCM, Hons 1978; Private study in Paris, 1981-82; FGSM 1990. Career: Leader of Myrha Saxophone Quartet, 1977-82; Formed duo with Pianist John Lenehan, 1979; Saxophone soloist, 1980-, with major international orchestras including, LSO, English Chamber Orchestra; Basel Chamber Orchestra; San Diego Symphony Orchestra; Principal Saxophone, London Sinfonietta, 1987-; Professor of Saxophone, GSMD, 1988-; Formed Berliner Band, 1983, John Harle Band, 1988; Premiered Birtwistle's Panic at the Last Night of the London Proms, 1995. Compositions: Several Ensembles, 1983-, including London Brass and LSO; Frequent composer and soloist on TV and feature films; Regular broadcaster on BBC Radio; Featured in One Man and his Sax, BBC2 TV, 1988; Recordings: Has made many recordings; Major works written for him by Dominic Muldowney, Ned Rorem, Richard Rodney Bennett, Luciano Berio, Michael Nyman, Gavin Bryars, Mike Westbrook and Stanley Myers. Publication: John Harle's Saxophone Album, 1986. Honours: Dannreuther Concerto Prize, Royal College of Music, 1980; GLAA Young Musician, 1979, 1980. Hobbies: Family Life; Cooking; Becoming a nicer person. Address: c/o The Bauhaus Production Company, 10 Haslemere Road, London N8 9QX, England.

HARLING Stuart, b. 1955, Bournemouth, England. Singer (Baritone). Education: Studied at St John's College Cambridge and at the London Opera Centre. Career: Has appeared with the Royal Opera, Covent Garden, in Le Rossignol, Don Carlos, The King goes Forth to France, La Fanciulla del West and Lohengrin; English National Opera in The Merry Widow, Romeo and Juliet and Les Mamelles de Tiresias; Mozart's Count and Eugene Onegin for Welsh National Opera; Has sung Papageno, The Dark Fiddler (A Village Romeo and Juliet), Albert (Werther) and Ned Keene (Peter Grimes) with Opera North; Netherlands Opera as Sandini in La Cenerentola and Don Giovanni for Northern Ireland Opera Trust; Sang Nardo in La Finta Giardiniera for English Music Theatre; Took the title role in Ullmann's The Emperor of Atlantis at the Imperial War Museum, 1985; Toured Japan as Morales in Carmen, 1989; Concert engagements with the London Symphony under Claudio Abbado and Gennadi Rozhdestvensky. Address: c/o Korman International Management, Crunnells Green Cottage, Preston, Herts SG4 7UQ, England.

HARMAN David (Rex), b. 9 Nov 1948, Redding, California, USA. Conductor; Clarinettist. m. 15 May 1981, 2 daughters. Education: BA 1970, MA 1971, California State University, Sacramento; Boursier de l'Etat Francais, Paris, 1971-72; Advanced study, Paris Conservatory; DMA, Eastman School of Music, University of Rochester, 1974. Career: Conductor, orchestra, opera, University of Louisville, Kentucky; Visiting Professor and Director of Orchestral Activities; The University of Rochester (NY) and Conductor of the Rochester Philharmonic Youth Orchestra, assistant conductor, The Louisville Orchestra, 1986-87; Guest Conductor, Cincinnati Symphony, Kentucky Opera, Opera Theater of Rochester, Rochester Philharmonic National Opera Orchestra of Slovenia, Tucson Symphony; Clarinet Debut: Carnegie Recital Hall, New York City, 1981; Clarinet recitals: BBC Radio 3, Wigmore Hall, Purcell Room, London, UK; National Public Radio, WGBH, WQXR; ORTF, Paris. Recordings: Crystal Records; Garparo Records; Musical Heritage Society. Publications: Editor, Quartet for Clarinet & String Trio, Jean Lefèvre, Musica Rara. Honours: Yamaha performance award, 1973; French Govt Scholar, 1971; Executive Secretary, Grawemeyer Award for Music Composition. Memberships: ASOL; Conductors' Guild; ASTA. Hobbies: Languages; Hiking; Fishing. Address: 1000 Park Avenue, Rochester, NY 14610, USA.

HARNESS William, b. 26 Nov 1940, Pendleton, Oregon, USA. Singer (Tenor). Education: Studied in San Francisco. Career: Sang at first in concert, then with Seattle Opera, 1974; New York City Opera, 1976, Metropolitan, 1977; Further appearances in Houston, Boston, Toronto and Hamburg; Among his best roles have been Mozart's Belmonte and Ferrando, Rinuccio (Gianni Schicchi), Elvino (La Sonnambula), Pinkerton and Faust. Address: c/o Metropolitan Opera, Lincoln Center, New York, NY 10023, USA.

HARNONCOURT Nikolaus, b. 6 Dec 1929, Berlin, Germany. Musician (Conductor and Cellist). m. Alice Hoffelner 1953, 3 sons, 1 daughter. Education: Studied in Graz, then with Paul Grummer and Emanuel Brabec at the Vienna Academy. Career: Cellist with the Vienna Symphony Orchestra 1952-69; Gave concerts as solo performer on the viola da gamba; Formed Vienna Concentus Musicus 1953, tours from 1957 in early and Baroque repertory; UK debut 1966, Handel's Messiah; Debut in US and Canada 1966; Professor, Mozarteum and Institute of Musicology, University of Salzburg, 1972-; Conductor, Zurich Opera, notably in works by Monteverdi, and the Amsterdam Concertgebouw Orchestra; Conducted Monteverdi's Il Ritorno d'Ulisse (Vienna 1971) and Orfeo (Amsterdam 1972); Tours in Europe, Australia and the USA; Conducted the Chamber Orchestra of Europe at the 1989 Promenade Concerts, London; Conducted La Clemenza di Tito at Zurich, 1989, Così fan tutte for Netherlands Opera, 1990; Beethoven's Ninth at the Barbican Centre, London, 1991; Beethoven series with the Philharmonia, London, 1994; Conducted Schubert's Alfonso und Estrella and Des Teufels Lustschloss at the 1997 Vienna Festival. Recordings: Many works with the Concentus Musicus, notably Messiah, the Brandenburg Concertos and Cantatas by Bach, operas by Monteverdi and Rameau (Castor et Pollux) and Bach's B Minor Mass; Don Giovanni (Teldec, 1990); Die Schöpfung (Vienna Symphony Orchestra); Idomeneo (Zurich Opera); Telemann Tafelmusik. Publications: Musik als Klangrede, Wege zu einem neuen Musikverständnis, 1982; Der Musikalische Dialog, 1984. Honours: Shared Erasmus Prize, 1980; HG Nägeli Medal, Zurich, 1983; Awards for recordings include Prix Mondiale du Disque, Grand Prix du Disque, Deutscher Schallplattenpreis; University of Edinburgh Honorary Degree, DMus, 1987. Hobbies: Cultural History; Woodwork. Address: 38 Piaristengasse, A-1080 Vienna, Austria.

HARNOY Ofra, b. 31 Jan 1965, Hadera, Israel. Cellist. Education: Studied with father, Vladimir Orloff, William Pleeth; Master Classes with Mistislav Rostropovich, Pierre Fournier, Jacqueline du Pre. Debut: Aged 10, as Soloist with Dr Boyd Neel and his Orchestra. Career: Soloist with numerous major orchestras, and solo recitals, USA, Canada, Japan, France, Austria, Hong Kong, Italy, Turkey, Germany, England, Israel, Australia, Holland, Belgium, Spain, Luxembourg, Venezuela; Featured in over 500 nationally televised solo-concerts or documentaries in Canada, England, Japan, Australia, Holland, Belgium, Italy, France; Radio broadcasts throughout the world; Regular Soloist, world premiere of Jacques Offenbach Cello Concerto, North American premiere, Sir Arthur Bliss Cello Concerto. Recordings: 38 solo albums RCA Victor; London; Pro Arte, including Vivaldi Cello Concertos. Honours: 1st Prize, Montreal Symphony Competition, 1978; Canadian Music Competition Winner, 1979; Concert Artists Guild Award, New York, 1982; Grand Prix du Disque, 1988; Juno Award (as Best Classical Soloist, Canada), 1988, 1989, 1990, 1992. Address: Suite 1000, 121 Richmond Street West, Toronto, Ontario M5H 2K1, Canada.

HARPER Edward (James), b. 17 Mar 1941, Taunton, Somerset, England. Composer; Teacher. m. Dorothy Shanks, 22 Oct 1984, 1 son, 1 daughter. Education: Studied music at Christ Church, Oxford, 1959-63, composition with Gordon Jacob at Royal College of Music; Further study with Franco Donatoni in Milan, 1968. Career: Lecturer, 1964-, currently Reader, Faculty of Music, Edinburgh University; Director of New Music Group of Scotland, 1973-91. Compositions include: Piano Concerto, 1969; Sonata for Chamber Orchestra, 1971; Bartók Games for Orchestra, 1972; Quintet for Piano, Flute, Clarinet, Violin and Cello, 1974; Ricecari in Memoriam Luigi Dallapiccola for 11 Instruments, 1975; Fanny Robin, chamber opera, 1975; Fantasia 1 for Chamber Orchestra, 1976; Fantasia II for 11 Strings, 1976; Fantasia III for Brass Quintet, 1977; Fern Hill for Chamber Orchestra, 1977; Poems, to text by E E Cummings for Soprano and Orchestra, 1977; Chester Mass for Chorus and Orchestra, 1979; Symphony, 1979; Clarinet Concerto, 1982; Intrada after Monteverdi for Chamber Orchestra, 1982; Hedda Gabler, full length opera, 1985; Mass, Qui Creavit Coelum, 1986; In Memoriam Kenneth Leighton for Cello and Piano, 1989; Homage to Thomas Hardy for Baritone and Orchestra, 1990; The Lamb for Soprano, Chorus and Orchestra, 1990. Recordings: Bartók Games; Fanny Robin; Fantasia III; Ricercari. Address: 7 Morningside Park, Edinburgh, EH10 5HD, Scotland.

HARPER Heather, b. 8 May 1930, Belfast, N Ireland. Soprano. m. 2nd Eduardo J Benarroch, 1973. Education: Trinity College of Music, London. Career: Created Soprano Role in Britten's War Requiem, Coventry Cathedral, 1962; Toured USA with BBC Symphony Orchestra, 1965, USSR 1967; Soloist, Opening Concerts, Maltings, Snape, 1967, Queen Elizabeth Hall, principal Soloist, BBC Symphony Orchestra on 1982 tour of Hong Kong and Australia; Principal Soloist, Royal Opera House, La Scala, Milan, 1976, Japan and Korea, 1979, USA Visit 1984; Professor and Consultant, Royal College of Music, London, 1985-; Director of Singing Studies, Britten-Pears School, Snape, 1986-; First Visiting Lecturer in Residence, Royal Scottish Academy, Glasgow, 1987-; Concerts in Asia, Middle East, Australia, European Music Festivals, South America; Principal Roles at Covent Garden, Bayreuth Festivals, La Scala (Milan), Teatro Colon (Buenos Aires), Edinburgh Festival, Glyndebourne, Sadler's Wells, Metropolitan Opera House (New York), San Francisco, Frankfurt, Deutsche Oper (Berlin), Japan (with Royal Opera House Covent Garden Co), Netherlands Opera House, New York City Opera; Renowned performances of Arabella, Ariadne, Chrysothemis, Empress, Marschallin; TV Roles include Ellen Orford; Mrs Coyle (Owen Wingrave); Ilia; Donna Elvira; La Traviata, La Bohème; Principal Soloist, Promenade Concerts, 25 consecutive years; Sang in the first performance of Britten's War Requiem 1962 and Tippett's 3rd Symphony 1972; Last solo appearance in the Four Last Songs of Strauss, Belfast March 1989; Nadia in The Ice Break at the 1990 Promenade Concerts. Recordings include: Les Illuminations (Britten); Symphony No 8 (Mahler); Don Giovanni (Mozart); Requiem (Verdi) and Missa Solemnis (Beethoven); Seven Early Songs (Berg); Marriage of Figaro; Peter Grimes; Strauss's Four Last Songs (First British soprano recording). Honours: CBE; Honorary Fellow, Trinity College of Music; Honorary Member, RAM; Hon DMus, Queen's University; Edison Award, 1971; Grammy Award, 1979; Grand Prix Du Disque, 1979; Grammy Award (Best Solo Recording), 1984. Hobbies: Gardening; Cooking.

HARPER Thomas, b. 1950, Oklahoma, USA. Singer (Tenor). Education: Studied in Los Angeles, Kansas City, Paris and Italy. Career: Sang in opera at Coburg, 1982-85, Kaiserslautern, 1985-87, in buffo and character roles; Stadttheater Hagen, 1987-, as the Duke of Mantua, Radames, Almaviva, Don Ottavio, Alwa in Lulu and Daniel in Belshazar by David Kirchner; Sang Fritz in Der Ferne Klang by Schreker, 1989; Seattle Opera, 1991, as Mime in Der Ring des Nibelungen; Dortmund Opera, 1991-92, as Mime and in premiere of Sekunden und Jahre des Caspar Hauser, by Reinhard Febel. Recordings include: Der Ferne Klang (Marco Polo). Address: c/o Seattle Opera Association, PO Box 9248, Seattle, WA 98109, USA.

HARRELL Lynn, b. 30 Jan 1944, New York City, USA. Solo Cellist. m. Linda Blandford, 7 Sept 1976, 1 s, 1 d. Education: Studies with Lev Aronson, Dallas, Leonard Rose, Juilliard School and Orlando Cole, Curtis Institute; Masterclasses with Gregor Piatigorsky, Casals. Debut: Dallas Symphony Orchestra, 1957. Career: Solo Principal Cellist with Cleveland Orchestra, conductor

George Szell, 1963-71; Numerous appearances with major orchestras in USA, Europe and Japan and worldwide recitals, 1971-; Piatigorsky Chair of Cello at University of Southern CA, Los Angeles, 1986-92; International Chair of Cello Studies, Royal Academy of Music, London, UK, 1986-92; Artistic Director of Los Angeles Philharmonic Institute, 1988-91; Music Adviser, San Diego Symphony, 1988 and 1989; Principal, Royal Academy of Music, 1993-95. Recordings: Dvorák Concerto with Ashkenazy, Cleveland; Lalo, Chailly, RSO; Shostakovich No 1 and Bloch Schelomo, Haitink, Concertgebouw; Schumann Concerto, Marriner, Cleveland; Brahms and Beethoven Sonatas, Ashkenazy; Beethoven Trios, Ashkenazy, Perlman; Solo Bach Suites. Honours: Merriweather Post Contest, 1960; Piatigorsky Award, 1962; 1st Winner, with Murray Perahia, Avery Fisher Prize, 1974. Hobbies: Chess; Opera; Fishing. Current Management: IMG. Address: c/o IMG, Media House, 3 Burlington Lane, Chiswick, London W4 2TH, England.

HARRHY Eiddwen, b. 14 Apr 1949, Trowbridge, Wiltshire, England. Singer (Soprano). m. Gregory Strange, 22 Jan 1988, 1 daughter. Education: Studied at the Royal Manchester College of Music and in London and Paris. Career: Sang in concert at Welsh Eisteddfods and with the Royal Liverpool Philharmonic; Queen Elizabeth Hall 1974, in Rinaldo; Alcina with the Handel Opera Society at Sadler's Wells; Covent Garden debut 1974; English National Opera from 1977, debut as Adele in Le Comte Ory; Kent Opera as Pamina and the title role in Iphigénie en Tauride; Glyndebourne Touring Opera as Donna Anna; Glyndebourne debut 1979, as Diana in La Fedeltà Premiata; Sang Madama Butterfly at the London Coliseum 1984 and Berg's Marie with Welsh National Opera 1986; Other roles include Dido in Les Troyens (concert performance conducted by Roger Norrington); Sang Mercian in the premiere of David Blake's The Plumber's Gift, ENO, 1989; Hecuba in a new production of King Priam for Opera North, 1991; Sang Kabanicha in Katya Kabanova for Glyndebourne Tour, 1992; Owen Wingrave at the Festival, 1997. Concert appearances include Promenade Concerts London 1989, in Vivaldi's Gloria and Bach's Magnificat, conducted by Richard Hickox. Recordings include: Isabelle in Rossini's L'Assedio di Corinto and A Hundred Years of Italian Opera, 1810-20, (Opera Rara). Address: Gonsalves Artists' Management, 5-7 Old Town, Clapham, London SW4 0JT, England.

HARRHY Paul, b. 6 Sept 1957, Port Talbot, Wales. Singer (Tenor). Education: Studied at Guildhall School of Music and Drama. Debut: Sang Alfredo with Opera 80, returning as Tom Rakewell. Career includes: English National Opera, 1986-, as High Priest and in Akhnaten, Valzacchi and in Der Rosenkavalier, Truffaldino in Love for Three Oranges and Jenik, in The Makropoulos Case; Appearances with Scottish Opera as Pedrillo, Mime, The Novice, in Billy Budd and Remendado, in Carmen; Opera North as Tom Rakewell and Truffaldino, also televised; Engagements with: Glyndebourne Festival; Touring Opera; The Chelsea Opera Group; Opera Factory; Musica nel Chiostro, in Batignano; Almeida Festival, 1988, 1989, 1990; Wolpe's Anna Blume and Street Music; Premieres of John Casken's Golem and Gerald Barry's Intelligence Park; Other festivals include: Strasbourg; Venice; Bath; Florence; Royal Albert Hall; Sang Mime and Loge with City of Birmingham Touring Opera, 1990-91; Pedrillo in Die Entfürung for Opera 80, 1991; Nencio, in Haydn's L'Infeltà, 1993; Appeared with New Israeli Opera as Truffaldino, 1992, returning to sing the role in 1995; Appeared as Pong, in Turandot with Royal Opera House at Wembley Arena; Appeared in European premiere of Sondheim's Assassins at Donmar Warehouse as Giuseppe Zangara; Opera Factory appearances have included: Pylades, in Iphigenias; Lurcano, in Poppea; Opera Forum, Netherlands, 1993, as Goro, in Madame Butterfly. Recordings: Casken's Golem; Stravinsky's Renard; Milhaud's Les Malheurs d'Orphée with Matrix Ensemble. Honours include: BP Opera and Boise Foundation Scholarships to Guildhall School. Address: c/o Athole Still International Management Ltd, Foresters Hall, 25-27 Westow Street, London, SE19 3RY, England.

HARRIES Clive, b. 5 June 1951, Clivedon, England. Conductor; Harpsichordist; Organist; Counter-Tenor. m. Catherine Tyzack, 22 Oct 1982, 4 sons. Education: MA, Open Choral Scholar, King's College, Cambridge University, 1973; Fellow, Royal College of Organists; Church Music/Choir Training Diploma; LRAM; ARCM. Career: Conductor, Kings Consort of Voices (Choir and Orchestra), Conductor, Choral Scholars from Kings, 1970-73; Assistant Director, Music, Millfield, 1973-77; Conductor, Clive Harries Singers and Orchestra, 1974-77; Director of Music, Ipswich School, 1977-78; Director of Music, Cranborne Chase, 1978-82; Organist, Master of Choristers, Christchurch Priory, 1980-83; Artistic Director, Finance Director, Christchurch International Summer Festival, 1981-83; Conductor, Christchurch Festival Orchestra, 1981-83; Examiner, Associated Board, Royal Schools of Music, 1981-; Director, Musica Reservata Singers, 1982-; Director of Music, Polam Hall, 1983-85; Conductor, York Early Music Choir and English Renaissance Orchestra, 1986-; Harpischordist, The Heritage Orchestra, 1987-; Adjudicator-member, British Federation of Music Festivals, 1971-; Musical Director of English Renaissance Orchestra & York Early Music Choir. Recordings: 35 with Kings College, Cambridge, for record, radio and TV, with Bach Choir, Vienna Concentus Musicus, Britten, Solo Organ Recordng from Christchurch. Honours: Freedom of the City of London, 1989. Membership: Fellowship of Royal Society of Arts, 1991-. Hobbies: Rotary; Squash; Golf; Country Pursuits. Current Management: Direct Booking. Address: Hill Top House, Birkby, Northallerton, North Yorkshire DL7 0EF, England.

HARRIES Kathryn, b. 15 Feb 1951, Hampton Court, Middlesex, England. Singer (Soprano). Education: Studied at the Royal Academy of Music with Constance Shacklock. Career: Presented BBC Television series Music Time; Festival Hall, London, debut 1977: concert repertoire ranges from Monteverdi to the 20th Century; Operatic debut with the Welsh National Opera 1982, as Leonore: returned as Sieglinde and Gutrune (also at Covent Garden, 1986), Adalgisa, and the Composer in Ariadne auf Naxos; English National Opera as Eva, Female Chorus in The Rape of Lucretia, Irene (Rienzi) and Donna Anna in The Stone Guest by Darghomyzhsky; Appearances with Scottish Opera as Leonore, the tile role in the premiere of Hedda Gabler by Edward Harper, and Senta; Metropolitan Opera 1986, as Kundry in Parsifal: returned 1989, as Gutrune in a new production of Götterdämmerung; Sang Dido in the first complete performance of Les Troyens in France, Lyon 1987, Senta for Paris Opéra, Sieglinde in Nice and Paris and Leonore in Buenos Aires; Covent Garden debut 1989, in the British premiere of Un Re in Ascolto by Berio; returned 1991 as Gutrune in a new production of Götterdämmerung; Dido in Les Troyens for Scottish Opera, 1990, also at Covent Garden; season 1990-91 with Katya Kabanova at ENO, Bartók's Judith for Scottish Opera, Dukas' Ariane, Netherlands Opera, Massenet's Cléopatre in St Etienne and Giulietta in Les Contes d'Hoffmann at the Châtelet in Paris; Season 1992 with the Berlioz Dido in Brussels and Carmen at Orange; Sang Brangaene for Scottish Opera, 1994; Kundry in Parsifal at the Opera Bastille, Paris, 1997. Address: c/o Ingpen & Williams Ltd, 14 Kensington Court, London W8 5DN, England.

HARRIS Alice (Eaton), b. 5 Aug 1924, Milwaukee, Wisconsin, USA. Pianist; Harpsichordist; Clavichordist; Forte Pianist; Educator. m. David H Harris, 18 June 1947, 1 daughter. Education: Vassar College 1940-41; BA Barnard College (Columbia University) 1944; As student of Mikhail Sheyne received Professional Artists' Diploma from Westchester Conservatory of Music; Graduate Studies at SUNY, Purchase, New York with Anthony Newman; Also studied with Malcolm Bilson. Debut: Solo Piano Recital, New York Times Hall, 1945. Career: Solo Piano Recitals, Carnegie Recital Hall and Town Hall, New York City; Solo Harpischordist with Westchester Chamber Music Society; and Westchester Symphony Orchestra; Founder/Director of Scarsdale Baroque Ensemble; Inaugural Recital Fortepiano, University of California, Riverside; Fortepiano Recitals, White Plains, New York, 1979 and 1983; Many lecture-recitals and workshops on early keyboard instruments in New York State and California; Faculty Member, Westchester Conservatory of Music 1944-. Address: 58 Brite Avenue, Scarsdale, NY 10583, USA.

HARRIS Donald, b. 7 Apr 1931, St Paul, Minnesota, USA. Composer; Administrator; Musicologist; Dean. m. Marilyn Hackett, 29 Jan 1983, 2 sons from previous marriage. Education: BMus 1952, MMus 1954, University of Michigan; Studied with Paul Wilkinson, St Paul, Minnesota, Ross Lee Finney, University of Michigan, Nadia Boulanger, Max Deutsch and André Jolivet in Paris, France. Career: Dean, Hartt School of Music, University of Hartford; Incidental Music, Poet with the Blue Guitar, Connecticut Public Radio, 1979; Incidental Music, Fires, Connecticut Public Radio, 1983. Compositions: Numerous, including: Piano Sonata; Violin Fantasy; Symphony in Two Movements; On Variations; For the Night to Wear; Balladen; Little Mermaid, opera; String Quartet; Ludus I; Ludus II; Of Hartford in a Purple Light (Wallace Stevens); Les Mains (Marguerite Yourcenar). Recordings: CRI, Delos Records, Golden Crest. Publications: Co-Editor, Correspondence between Alban Berg and Arnold Schoenberg, New York; Music: Editions Jobert, Paris, France; Theodore Presser, Bryn Mawr, Pennsylvania. Contributor to: Journal of the Arnold Schoenberg Institute; Perspective of New Music; Newsletter, International Alban Berg Society; Music Journal; Alban Berg Studien, Universal Edition. Address: c/o ASCAP, ASCAP Building, One Lincoln Plaza, New York, NY 10023, USA.

HARRIS Hilda, b. 1930, Warrenton, North Carolina, USA. Singer (Mezzo-soprano). Education: Studied at North Carolina State University and in New York. Career: Sang in musicals on Broadway; Made opera debut at St Gallen, Switzerland, 1971, as Carmen; Returned to New York, 1973, as Nicklausse in Les Contes d'Hoffmann at City Opera and in Virgil Thomson's Four Saints in Three Acts (as St Theresa) at the Metropolitan; Further roles at the Met have included the Child in L'Enfant et les Sortilèges, Cherubino, Hansel, Stephano in Roméo et Juliette and parts in Lulu; Sang Nicklausse at Seattle, 1990, Cherubino at the 1990 Spoleto Festival; Frequent concert appearances. Address: c/o Metropolitan Opera, Lincoln Center, New York, NY 10023, USA.

HARRIS John, b. 1949, England. Tenor. Education: Studied at the Birmingham School of Music. Career: Appearances with the Welsh National Opera, English National Opera, Scottish Opera and Opera North; Concert work inludes Messiah and Verdi's Requiem at the Royal Albert Hall; Roles have included: Mime, Wagner's Ring Cycle; Don José, Carmen; Peter Grimes; Lensky, Eugene Onegin; Skuratov, From the House of the Dead; Tichon in Katya Kabanova; Bardolfo, Falstaff; Goro, Madame Butterfly. Recordings include: Martinu's Greek Passion; Verdi's I Masnadieri; Tristan und Isolde; Parsifal. Address: c/o Ron Gonsalves Management, 7 Old Town, Clapham, London, SW4 0JT, England.

HARRIS Matthew, b. 18 Feb 1956, North Tarrytown, New York, USA. Composer. m. 4 Dec 1988. Education: New England Conservatory, with Donald Martino, 1974-75; Fontainbleau School, with Nadia Boulanger, France, 1976; BM, 1978, MM, 1979, DMA, 1982, Juilliard School of Music; Harvard Graduate School, 1985-86. Career: Major performances: New York New Music Ensemble, 1983; Houston Symphony, 1986; Minnesota Orchestra, 1987; League/ISCM, New York, 1987; Florida Symphony Orchestra, 1988; Alea III, Boston, 1988; Assistant Professor, Fordham University, 1982-84; Instructor, Kingsborough College, City University of New York, 1985; Music Editor, Carl Fischer Inc, 1987-. Compositions: Music After Rimbaud; Songs of the Night, soprano, orchestra; Ancient Greek Melodies, orchestra; As You Choose, monodrama; Starry Night, piano trio; Invitation of the Waltz, string quartet; string Quartet No 7. Recording: Music After Rimbaud, Opus One Commissions: Casa Verde Trio, 1984; Haydn-Mozart Orchestra, 1985; Scott Stevens: Leigh Howard Stevens, marimbist, 1986; Minnesota Composers Forum: Omega String Quartet, 1988; The Schubert Club; Anthony Ross, cellist, 1988. Memberships: Broadcast Music Inc; Composers Forum; American Music Center; Board Member, League-International Society for Contemporary Music. Address: American Composers Edition, 170 W 74th Street, New York, NY 10023, USA.

HARRIS Richard (Leigh), b. 4 Jan 1956, Bristol, England. Harpsichordist; Composer; Lecturer; Critic; Writer. Education: Birmingham School of Music, 1975-78; GBSM, University of Reading, 1978-79; PG Cert Ed, 1986-89; MMus, 1989; Studied Harpsichord with Robert Woolley and Virginia Black; Masterclasses with George Malcolm, Kenneth Gilbert, Jill Severs and Davitt Moroney. Career: Head of Music, Bicester School, Oxon, 1979-80; Associate Lecturer in Music, Oxford Polytechnic, 1984-88; Radio includes, Satie's Vexations on Today Programme, 1977; BBC R4 John Wain's Oxford, Pride of Place, 1984; BBC Radio Oxford: Contemporary British Harpsichord Music, 1987, 1990; Lecturer in Composition, Birmingham Conservatoire, 1991-. Compositions include: Baroque Flickers, piccolo, oboe and clarinet; Still Life, solo guitar; Cantata: The Return of Spring; O Magnum Misterium, SSA Chorus; Aria for Orpheus, oboe and tape; Magnificat and Nunc Dimittis, SATB and organ; Three Celtic Folksongs, ensemble; Epiphany Preludes, 1992, for bass clarinet, marimba and cello; String Quartet No2 (Parakeelya I), 1993; Dark Comes Down, Let Mine Eyes See Thee, for soprano, alto and 3 clarinets, 1993-94; Returning Elegies, for guitar and string quartet, 1994. Recordings: Richard Leigh Harris plays Bach, Couperin, Scarlatti and Soler; At Home, with George Haslam, sax. Contributions to: Articles for The Musical Times, Tempo, Music Teacher, Classical Guitar, on 20th Century Composers. Address: 1 Ferry Road, New Marston, Oxford OX3 0ET, England.

HARRISON Jonty, b. 27 Apr 1952, Scunthorpe, England. Composer; Lecturer. m. Alison Warne, 28 May 1985. Education: BA, DPhil, University of York, 1970-76; British Youth Symphony Orchestra, National Youth Orchestra of Great Britain; Studied composition with Bernard Rands. Career: National Theatre, London; Visiting Composer, University of East Anglia Recording and Electronic Music Studio, 1978; Visiting Lecturer, The City University, London, 1978-80; Senior Lecturer in Music, Director of Electroacoustic Music Studio, The University of Birmingham, 1980-; Hungarian Radio, 1982; IRCAM, 1985; Groupe de Recherches Musicales, Paris, 1986; Groupe de Musique Expérimentale de Bourges, 1987. Compositions: Q, 1976; Lunga, 1977; Pair/Impair, 1978; SQ, 1979; Rosaces 3, 1980; EQ, 1980; Monodies, 1981; Rosaces 4, 1982; Klang, 1982; Sons tranmutants/sans transmutant, 1983; Hammer and Tongs, 1984; Paroles héritiques, 1986; Tremulous Couplings, 1986; Farben, 1987; Aria, 1988; Concerto Caldo, 1991; ...et ainsi de suite..., 1992; Ottone, 1992; Hot Air, 1995; Unsound Objects, 1995. Recordings: Sons transmutants/Sans transmutant (Fine Arts Brass Ensemble); Ottone (Fine Arts Brass Ensemble); Klang; EQ (Daniel Kientzy); ...et ainsi de suite...; EQ (Stephen Cottrell). Contributions to: Electro-Acoustic Music; Music and Letters; The Musical Times; Lien (Musiques et Recherches-Belgium); Upbeat to the Tate 88 - Liverpool (Programme Book). Hobbies: Travel; Reading; Food and Drink; Conducting. Address: 9 Prospect Road, Moseley, Birmingham B13 9TB, England.

HARRISON Lou, b. 14 May 1917, Portland, Oregon, USA. Composer. Education: Studied with Henry Cowell, San Francisco, 1934-35, Arnold Schoenberg, Los Angeles, 1941, 1942; Grant, American Academy and Institute of Arts and Letters, 1947. Career: Positions as: Florist; Record Clerk; Poet; Dancer; Dance Critic; Music Copyist; Playright; Instrument Builder; Teacher, Portland, Oregon, Black Mountain College; Animal Hospital Worker, 1957-60; Senior Scholar, East-West Centre, University of Hawaii, 1963; Teacher, various Universities Including: Stanford, 1974, San Jose State, 1974-82, Centre for World Music, Berkeley, 1975, Southern California, 1977, Mills College, 1980-82; Milhaud Chair, Mills College, until his retirement, 1985. Compositions: Works include: Javanese Gamelan; American Gamelan; Cirebon Gamelan; European Orchestral; Sudanese Gamelan Degung; Ensemble; Solo Instrumental Works; Solo Vocal Works; Orchestrations; Choral; Stage Works; Film Scores; Co-Designer with William Colvig of 2 Javanese Gamelan Orchestras. Recordings: Numerous including: Double Concerto; Gending Pak Cokro; Fugue for Percussion; Concerto for Violin and Percussion Orchestra; Concerto for Organ and Percussion Orchestra; String Trio; Serenade for Guitar. Publications include: About Carl Ruggles, 1946; Lou Harrison's Music Primer, 1969; 19 Items, 1970; Articles in professional journals. Honours include: Fromm Award, 1955; Rockefeller Grant, Recipient, numerous other honours and awards. Memberships: American Institute of Arts & Letters. Address: 7121 Viewpoint Road, Aptos, CA 95003, USA.

HARRISON Sally, b. 1965, England. Singer (Soprano). Education: studied at Oxford and Royal Northern College of Music; Further study with Ava June. Career: Sang Manon and Gilda with Royal Northern College of Music, 1987-88; Season 1988-89 as Musetta in Singapore, Handel's Morgana at Royal Northern College of Music and Amour in Rameau's Pygmalion for the English Bach Festival at Elizabeth Hall; Season 1989-90 with Scottish Opera as Polly in The Threepenny Opera, Minette in Henze's English Cat at Guttersloh and Berlin, repeated at Montepulciano Festival and for BBC, and Messiah with Bournemouth Sinfonietta; English National Opera debut, 1991, as Barbarina in Le nozze di Figaro; Sang Handel's Galatea with the English Bach Festival at Elizabeth Hall, 1992; Despina, at the 1992 Buxton Festival; Other concert repertoire includes Elgar's The Kingdom, Henze's Being Beauteous (Barbican Hall debut, 1990) and works with the Hague Philharmonic and Ensemble Modern of Frankfurt; Sang Gilda at Bristol, 1994; Pamina, for English National Opera, 1996; Television appearance in The English Cat, for German TV. Honours include: Peter Moores Foundation Scholarship. Address: c/o English National Opera, St Martin's Lane, London WC2, England.

HARSHAW Margaret, b. 12 May 1909, Philadelphia, Pennsylvania, USA. Singer (Soprano); Teacher. Education: Studied at the Curtis Institute, then the Juilliard School New York with Anna Schoen-Rene. Career: Sang first with various opera companies in Philadelphia; Steel Pier Grand Opera in New York, 1934; Metropolitan Opera from 1942-64 as Second Norn in Götterdämmerung (debut), Azucena, Mistress Quickly, Amneris, Isolde, Kundry, Santuzza, Ortrud, Senta and Brünnhilde; Paris Opéra 1948, as Dalila, Amneris and Brangaene; Covent Garden 1953-56, as Brünnhilde; Glyndebourne Festival 1954, Donna Anna; Teacher at Indiana University School of Music, Bloomington, from 1962: sang Brünnhilde there 1970. Recordings: Duets with Zinka Milanov and Eleanor Steber; Private recordings from the Metropolitan Opera.

HART William (Sebastian), b. 30 Oct 1920, Baltimore, Maryland, USA. Symphony Orchestra Conductor. m. Regina Margaret Litsch, 10 Apr 1950. Education: Graduate cum laude, Peabody Conservatory of Music, Baltimore, 1939; BA Political Science, Johns Hopkins University, 1940; PhD Psychology, Golden State University, 1956; Advanced studie in conducting with Franz Bornschein, Stanley Chapple, Felix Robert Mendelssohn. Career: Timpanist, Baltimore Symphony Orchestra, 20 years; Teacher, Peabody Conservatory of Music; Radio, then TV Conductor, Commentator, Concert Hall, Maryland and 13 other states, 1939-69; Founder, Conductor, Gettysburg Symphony Orchestra, 1958-; Appeared as Conductor, Royal Philharmonic Orchestra, 1965, 1969, 1977, 1983; Conductor, National Symphony Orchestra, Washington, 1969, London Philharmonic Orchestra, England, 1983, London Mozart Players, 1983. Compositions: Timpani duet. Recordings: Dominion Records: Gettysburg Symphony Orchestra; 1st Piano Concerto, F Chopin; 1st Piano Concerto, Mendelssohn; Rienzi Overture, Wagner; Operatic Arias. Contributor to: Baltimore newspapers; Musical journals. Current Management: John Higham International Artists Ltd, 16 Lauriston Road, London SW19 4TQ, England.

HARTE Ruth, b. Bristol, England. m. Vivian Langrish, deceased, 1 son. Education: Eizabeth Stokes Scholarship at Royal Academy of Music. Career: Professor, Royal Academy of Music, London, 1968-90; Adjudicator, UK, Far East, New Zealand; Examiner, Mentor, Associated Board Royal Schools of Music. Debut: Cowdray Hall, London, 1948; Wigmore Hall, 1950. Career: Solo Pianist, Ensemble Player, Henry Wood Birthday and Promenade Concerts; Wigmore Hall, Purcell Room Broadcasts BBC; Radio Cyprus; Recital Tours, Master Classes, Lectures in Canada, Far East, New Zealand, Europe. Recordings: 2 piano works with Vivian Langrish for Arnold Bax Society. Honours: LRAM, 1946; ARAM, 1954; FRAM, 1971. Memberships: Warden, Private Teachers Section Incorporated Society Musicians, 1992-93; Royal Society Musicians. Hobbies: Travel; Photography; Reading. Address: 50 The Avenue, Beckenham, Kent, BR3 5ER, England.

HARTELIUS Malin, b. 1961, Vaxjo, Sweden. Singer (Soprano). Education: Studied at the Vienna Conservatory with Margaret Bence. Debut: Vienna (Raimund-Theater) as Christel in Der Vogelhändler, 1986. Career: Sang at Baden and St Gallen, then Ludwigsburg Festival, 1990, as Blondchen; Vienna Staatsoper from 1990, notably as Esmerelda in The Bartered Bride; Member of the Zurich Opera, 1991-92, as Papagena, Sophie and Adele; Salzburg Festival, 1992, as Barbarina in Le nozze di Figaro; Many appearances in operetta and on the concert platform. Address: c/o Zurich Opera, Falkenstrasse 1, CH-8008 Zurich, Switzerland.

HARTH Sidney, b. 5 Oct 1929, Cleveland, Ohion, USA. Violinist; Conductor; Professor. m. Teresa Testa Harth. Education: Cleveland Institute of Music, MB, 1947; Pupil of Joseph Fuchs and Georges Enesco. Career: Debut, Carnegie Hall, New York, 1949; Concertmaster and Assistant Conductor, Louisville Orchestra, 1953-58; Faculty Member, University of Louisville; Concertmaster, Chicago Symphony Orchestra, 1959-62; Faculty Member, De Paul University; Concertmaster, Casals Festival Orchestra, San Juan, 1959-65, 1972; Professor of Music and Chairman of the Music Department, Carnegie-Mellon University, Pittsburgh, 1963-73; Concertmaster and Associate Conductor, Los Angeles Philharmonic Orchestra, 1973-79; Music Director, Puerto Rico Symphony Orchestr, 1977-79; Interim Conductor, New York Philharmonic Orchestra, 1980; Orchestral Director, Mannes College of Music, New York, 1981-. Recordings: Various discs. Address: c/o Mannes College of Music, 150 West 85th Street, New York, NY 10024, USA.

HARTKE Stephen (Paul), b. 6 July 1952, New Jersey, USA. Composer. m. Lisa Stidham, 12 Sept 1981, 1 son. Education: BA, magna cum laude, Yale University, 1973; MA, University of Pennsylvania, 1976; PhD, University of California, Santa Barbara, 1982; Composition study with James Drew, George Rochberg and Edward Applebaum. Career: Fulbright Professor of Composition, University of Sao Paulo, Brazil, 1984-85; Professor of Composition, University of Southern California, 1987-; Composer-in-Residence, Los Angeles Chamber Orchestra, 1988-92. Compositions: Alvorada; Iglesia Abandonada; The King of The Sun; Maltese Cat Blues; Oh Them Rats is Mean in My Kitchen; Pacific Rim; Sonata Variations; Songs for an Uncertain Age; Caoine; Night Rubrics; Post-Modern Homages; Symphony No 2; Four Madrigals on Old Portuguese Texts; Wir Küssen Ihnen Tausendmal die Hände; Violin Concerto; Wulfstan at The Millennium, 1995; The Ascent of the Equestrian in a Balloon, 1995; Sons of Noah, 1996; The Horse with the Lavender Eye, 1997. Recordings: Caoine; Iglesia Abandonada; Oh Them Rats is Mean in My Kitchen; Wir Küssen Ihnen Tausendmal die Hände; The King of The Sun; Sonata-Variations; Night Rubrics. Contributions to: Caderno de Musica, 1985; Minnesota Composers Forum Newsletter, 1988. Honours: Rome Prize, 1992; Academy Award, American Academy of Arts and Letters, 1993; Chamber Music Society of Lincoln Center Stoeger Award, 1997; Guggenheim Fellowship, 1997-98. Membership: American Music Center. Hobbies: Walking; Reading. Address: School of Music, University of Southern California, Los Angeles, CA 90089, USA.

HARTMAN Vernon, b. 12 July 1952, Dallas, Texas, USA. Singer (Baritone). Education: Studied at West Texas State University and in Philadelphia. Debut: Philadelphia, as Masetto, 1977. Career: Sang with New York City Opera from 1977 and made guest appearances at Cincinnati, San Antonio and Seattle; Spoleto Festival, 1977-78, as Guglielmo; Metropolitan Opera, 1983-, as Rossini's Figaro, Count Almaviva, Schaunard and Guglielmo; Other roles have included Rigoletto, Malatesta, Silvio, Marcello, Frank in Die Tote Stadt and Falke in Fledermaus; Sang Almaviva and Marcello at Milwaukee, 1991. Address: c/o Metropolitan Opera, Lincoln Center, New York, NY 10023, USA.

HARTMANN Rudolf A, b. 1946, Germany. Singer (Baritone). Education: Studied at the Munich Musikhochschule. Career: Sang at first as a bass, at Augsburg, then at Nuremberg in the baritone repertory; Member of the Zürich Opera from 1972, as Fluth in Die Lustige Weiber von Windsor, Faninal, Sharpless, Schaunard Frank in Die Fledermaus (season 1996-97) and in the Swiss premiere of Jakob Lenz by Wolfgang Rihn; Guest engagements as Beckmesser at the Vienna and Hamburg State Operas and the Dresden Semperoper; Concert and recital engagements at Bayreuth, Florence, Salzburg, Munich and Vienna; Radio and CD recordings as Papageno, in the Solti Meistersinger, and the Eighth Book of Madrigals by Monteverdi,

under Niklaus Harnoncourt; Teacher of Voice at Munich Conservatory and Musikhochschule. Address: c/o Opernhaus Zürich, Falkenstrasse 1, CH-8008, Switzerland.

HARTWIG Hildegard, b. 1951, Munich, Germany. Singer (Mezzo-soprano). m. Diether Jacob. Education: Studied in Munich and at Cologne Opera Studio. Career: Sang minor roles at Cologne, then engaged at Bonn, 1976-81, Deutsche Oper am Rhein, 1980-86, notably in the 1985 premiere of Goehr's Behold the Sun; Schwetzingen Festival, 1986, as Lotte in premiere of Bose's Die Leiden des Jungen Werthers; Guest engagements at Hamburg, 1982, and Copenhagen, 1989, as Bartók's Judith; Other roles include Dorabella, Magdelena, Octavian, Lola, the Countess Geschwitz in Lulu and Meroe in Schoeck's Penthesilea; Many concert appearances. Recordings include: Beethoven's Ninth, conducted by Gunter Wand.

HARUTUNIAN John Martin, b. 29 August 1948, Watertown, MA, USA. Musicologist. Education: BM, Composition, Wheaton College, IL, USA; Graduate Study, Music, Harvard University; MA, Musicology, University of Pennsylvania; PhD, Musicology, UCLA; Piano with Gladys Ondricek, Boston, 1956; Reginald Gerig, Wheaton College, 1965-69; Composition with David Del Tredici, Ralph Shapey George Crumb, George Rochberg. Debut: Piano Soloist with Boston Pops Orchestra, June 1965. Career: Performed original composition (Fantasy-Gavotte) at Youth Concerts with Boston Symphony Orchestra, March, April, 1966; Performed at Radcliffe College, 1970; Worms Opera House, Germany, 1973; Chamber recitals at New England Conservatory with Musicians from Boston Symphony Orchestra, 1983, 1984, 1985, and at Park Street Church, Boston, with Musicians from Boston Pops Esplanade Orchestra, 1986, 1988; Composition, Nocturne, Westwind: UCLA's Journal of the Arts, 1980). Publications: Hadyn and Mozart: Tonic-Dominant Polarity in Mature Sonata-Style Works, The Journal of Musicological Research IX/4, 1990. Honours: Paderewski: Medal, National Guild of Piano Teachers Auditions, 1966; Adjudicator, National Guild of Piano Teachers Auditions, 1986. Membership: American Musicological Society, 1988. Hobby: Reading Christian literature. Address: 355 Newtonville Avenue, Newtonville, MA 02160, USA.

HARVEY Jean, b. 2 January 1932, Glasgow, Scotland. Professor of Music; Concert Pianist; Violinist. Education: Studied at Royal Academy of Music, London with Frederick Grinke and Harold Craxton; Child Prodigy with Moisewitsch, Myra Hess and Albert Sammons. Debut: 7 years old with Scottish National Orchestra. Career: Broadcasts regularly as violinist and pianist after giving a Promenade Concert with a Piano and Violin Concerto; Chief Examiner to Associate Board of the Royal Schools of Music, London; Head of String Faculty and Chamber Music, 1991, at RAM. Honours: Fellow, Royal Academy of Music; Silver Medal, Worshipful Company of Musicians. Memberships: Incorporated Society of Musicians; European String Teachers' Association; IPTEC. Address: Kittswood, Three Gates Lane, Haslemere, Surrey, England.

HARVEY Jonathan (Dean), b. 3 May 1939, Sutton Coldfield, England. Composer; Professor of Music. m. Rosaleen Marie Barry, 1960. 1 son, 1 daughter. Education: St Michael's College, Tenbury; Repton; MA, DMus, St John's College, Cambridge; PhD, Glasgow University. Career: Lecturer, Southampton University, 1964-77; Harkness Fellow, Princeton University, 1969-70; Reader 1977-80, Professor of Music 1980-95, Sussex University; Professor of Music, Stanford University, 1995-; Works performed at many festivals and international centres. Compositions include: Persephone Dream for orchestra, 1972; Inner Light (trilogy) for performers and tape, 1973-77; Smiling Immortal for chamber orchestra, 1977; Gong-Ring for ensemble with electronics, 1984; Madonna of Winter and Spring for orchestra, 1986; Lightness and Weight for tuba and orchestra, 1986; 3 String Quartets; One Evening for voices, instruments and electronics, 1994; Lotuses for flute quartet; Inquest of Love opera, 1992; Adraya, for cello and electronics, 1994; Percussion Concerto, 1997; Wheel of Emptiness, for ensemble, 1997; Numerous choral and church pieces. Recordings: Bhakti NMCD001, Mortuos Plango, Vivos Voco, Song Offerings, Valley of Aosta; Cello Concerto; From Silence; String Quartets. Publications: The Music of Stockhausen, 1975; Numerous Articles. Honours: Hon Doctor of Music, Southampton, 1991, Bristol, 1994; The Britten Award for Composition, 1993. Memberships: Academia Europaea, 1989; Fellow, Royal College of Music, 1994. Hobbies: Tennis; Walking; Meditation. Address: 35 Houndean Rise, Lewes, Sussex BN7 1EQ, England.

HARVEY Keith, b. 1950, England. Cellist. Education: Studied with Douglas Cameron at Royal Academy of Music and with Gregor Piatigorsky in Los Angeles. Career: Formerly youngest ever principal cellist of London Philharmonic Orchestra, then principal of English Chamber Orchestra; Plays cello by Montagnana of 1733, formerly belonging to Bernard Romberg; Founder member of Gabrieli Ensemble, with chamber music performances in UK and abroad; Co-founded the Gabrieli Quartet, 1967, and toured with them to Europe, North America, Far East and Australia; Festival engagements in UK, including Aldeburgh, City of London and Cheltenham; Concerts every season in London, participation in Barbican Centre's Mostly Mozart Festival; Resident Artist at University of Essex, 1971-; Has co-premiered by William Alwyn, Britten, Alan Bush, Daniel Jones and Gordon Crosse, 2nd Quartets of Nicholas Maw and Panufnik (1983, 1980) and 3rd Quartet of John McCabe (1979); UK premiere of the Piano Quintet by Sibelius, 1990. Recordings include: 50 CDs including early pieces by Britten, Dohnányi's Piano Quintet with Wolfgang Manz, Walton's Quartets and the Sibelius Quartet and Quintet, with Anthony Goldstone. Honours include: Emmy Award for solo playing in films. Address: c/o Anglo Swiss Management, Suite 35-37 Morley House, 320 Regent Street, London W1R 5AD, England.

HARVEY Peter, b. 1958, England. Singer (Baritone). Education: Choral Scholar at Magdalen College Oxford, Guildhall School of Music. Career: Concert appearances with the St James Baroque Players in Telemann's St Matthew Passion at Aldeburgh and London; Visit to Lisbon with The Sixteen; Concerts of Monteverdi and Purcell in Poland and the Flanders Festival with London Baroque; Sang with Joshua Rifkin and the Bach Ensemble at St James Piccadilly, 1990; Engagements with La Chapelle Royale and Collegium Vocale in Belgium, France and Spain; Bach Cantatas for French television and tour of Messiah with Le Concert Spirituel; Other repertoire includes the War Requiem, Elijah and the Five Mystical Songs of Vaughan Williams; St John in The Cry of the Ikon by John Tavener (also televised); Bach's St John Passion (Westminster Abbey) and Christmas Oratorio; Schubert's E flat Mass; Visited Brazil 1989 with The Sixteen for Messiah; Belgium 1991 in Teixeira's Te Deum, conducted by Harry Christophers; Sang with Les Talens Lyriques at Versailles Baroque Days in Mondonville's Les Fêtes de Paphos, 1996. Recordings: Dido and Aeneas; Sacred music by CPE Bach with La Chapelle Royale (Virgin Classics); Gilles Requiem with Le Concert Spirituel. Honours include: Walther Gruner International Lieder Competition, 2nd Prize winner; Nonie Morton Award (leading to Wigmore Hall debut). Address: c/o Hazard Chase Ltd, Richmond House, 16-20 Regent Street, Cambridge CB2 1DB, England.

HARVEY Richard (Allen), b. 25 Sept 1953, London, England. Composer/Performer. Education: Associate, Royal College of Music, 1971. Debut: Conductor, London Symphony Orchestra, Barbican Centre, 1985. Career: Recorder/Woodwind Player; Conductor and Composer; Founder, London Vivaldi Orchestra; Guest Conductor, Royal Philharmonic and London Symphony Orchestras; Toured with guitarist John Williams, 1984-; Conductor and Performer with English Chamber Orchestra, Barbican Centre, London, 1987. Compositions: Concerto Antico for guitar and orchestra; Reflections on A Changing Landscape, viola concerto; Plague and the Moonflower, eco-oratorio; A Time of Miracles, children's opera; Compositions for films and television include Game, Set and Match, G.B.H, Jake's Progress and Defence of the Realm. Recordings: Italian Recorder Concertos; The Genteel Companion; Brass at La Sauve-Majeure; Four Concertos for Violins and Recorder; GBH soundtrack; Jake's Progress soundtrack. Membership: Founder member, ARC. Hobbies: Cricket, Alvis cars; Travel. Current Management: Iam Amos, ICM, 76 Oxford Street, London W1R 1RB, England.

HASHIMOTO Eiji, b. 7 Aug 1931, Tokyo, Japan. Harpsichordist. m. Ruth Anne Laves, 8 Jun 1963, 1 s, 2 d. Education: BM in Organ, 1954, Graduate Diploma in Organ, 1955, Tokyo University of Fine Arts; MA in Composition, University of Chicago, 1959; MM, Harpsichord, Yale University School of Music, 1962. Career: Harpsichord Instructor at Toho Gakuen School of Music, Tokyo, 1966; Assistant Professor of Harpsichord and Artist-in-Residence, 1968-72, Associate Professor of Harpsichord and Artist in Residence, 1972-77, Professor of Harpsichord and Artist in Residence, 1977-, University of Cincinnati College Conservatory of Music; Concerts, recitals and or solo appearances in Australia, Austria, Belgium, Brazil, Canada, Chile, England, Finland, France, Germany, Holland, Hong Kong, Iran, Italy, Japan, Luxembourg, Mexico, New Zealand, Philippines, Spain, Switzerland, USA and Venezuela. Recordings: 17 recordings (including 5 CDs) of solo, solo with orchestra, conducting and ensemble performances. Publications: Editions: D Scarlatti, 100 Sonatas, in 3 volumes, G Schirmer, 1985 and 1988, Zen-On, 1975, 1984 and 1990, J B Loeillet, Pièces pour Clavecin, 1985, C P E Bach, Sonatas, in 3 volumes, Vivaldi-Hashimoto, Concerto for four harpsichords and strings in E minor; Various Keyboard Collections including the works of D Scarlatti, 1985; J B Loeillet, 1985; C P E Bach, 1988. Current Management: ICA Management for USA and Europe; Camerata Tokyo Inc for Japan. Address: 4579 English Creek Drive, Cincinnati, OH 45245, USA.

HASNAS Irina, b. 15 Jul 1954, Bucharest, Rumania. Composer. Education: Studied at the Bucharest Music High School and Conservatory. Career: Editor at Rumanian Broadcasting, Bucharest from 1987. Compositions include: Metamorphose for 8 Voices and Wind Instruments, 1978; Concerto for Orchestra, 1978; Evocation for Orchestra, 1980; Polychromie I for Ensemble, 1982; Monodie for Bassoon, 1989; Games for Cello, 1991; Symphony No 1, 1991. Address: c/o Radio Budapest, Budapest, Hungary.

HASS Sabine, b. 8 Apr 1949, Brunswick, Germany. Singer (Soprano). m. Artur Korn, 1979. Education: Studied with Karl-Heinz Lohmann in Berlin; Munich with Esther Muhlbauer; Richard Strauss Conservatory Munich. Career: Sang at the Stuttgart Staatsoper from 1970; State Operas of Munich and Vienna 1976, as Senta and Ariadne; Bregenz Festival 1977, as Reiza in Oberon; Guest appearances in Paris, London, Lisbon, Trieste, Venice, Turin, Rome, Barcelona and Buenos Aires; Munich Staatsoper and La Scala Milan 1983, as Isabella in Das Liebesverbot and as Elsa in Lohengrin; Metropolitan Opera 1985-86, as Elsa and Senta; Sang the title role in a new production of Die Liebe der Danae by Strauss at the 1988 Munich Festival; Season 1987/88 as Senta at Philadelphia and Leonore at Frankfurt and with the company of the Cologne Opera at Tel-Aviv; Deutsche Oper Berlin 1988, as Sieglinde; Seattle and Théâtre du Châtelet Paris 1989, as Leonore; Sang Isolde at Basle, Feb 1990; Season 1992 with Wagner's Elisabeth at the Deutsche Oper Berlin and Senta at the Bayreuth Festival; Many concert appearances. Recordings include: Der Wein by Berg (Deutsche Grammophon). Address: c/o Bayersiche Staatsoper, Postfach 745, D-8000 Munich 1, Germany.

HASSON Maurice, b. 6 July 1934, Berck-Plage, France. Concert Violinist. Education: Studied at Paris Conservatoire and with Henryk Szeryng. Career: Played the Mendelssohn Concerto in Paris, aged 16; Resident in London, 1973-; Has appeared with orchestras and given recitals in Europe, Israel, USA, South America, Australia, New Zealand and Hong Kong; Conductors have included Masur, Mata, Rattle and Alexander Gibson, Colin Davis, Rafael Fruebeck De Burgos; US debut with Cleveland Orchestra under Lorin Maazel, 1978; Guest concerts with European broadcasting stations; Professor of Royal Academy of Music, 1986; Plays the Benvenuti violin by Stradivarius, 1727. Recordings include: Paganini Concerto No 1, Prokofiev No 1, Brahms and Bruch; Bach Double Concerto, with Szeryng and the Academy of St Martin in the Fields; Brilliant showpieces for the Violin, Virtuoso Violin and Concerto by Gonzalo Castellanos Yumar; recently recorded French Sonatas (Franck - Debussy - Fauré) with Ian Brown. Honours include: Grand Prix and Prix d'Honneur at Paris Conservatoire; Honorary member of the Royal Academy. Address: 18 West Heath Court, North End Road, London NW11 7RE, England.

HASTINGS Baird, b. 14 May 1919, New York City, USA. Musician; Writer; Educator. m. Louise (Lily) Laurent, 22 Dec 1945. Education: AB, Harvard College, 1939; Diploma, Paris Conservatory, 1946; Diploma, Tanglewood, 1957; Diploma, Mozarteum, Salzburg, 1961; MA, Queens College, 1966; PhD, Sussex College, 1976. Career: Conductor, Mozart Chamber Players, 1957-60; Conductor, Mozart Festival Orchestra, 1960-; Music Advisor, Eglevsky Ballet, 1961-78; Lecturer in Music, Conductor of Band and Orchestra, Trinity College, 1965-70; Administrator, Juilliard School of Music, New York City, 1972-85; Music Advisor, School of American Ballet, New York City, 1973-85; Music Director, Westport Point, Massachusetts, Summer Episcopal Church, 1974-92; Guest Conductor, American Symphony; Consultant, Royal Academy of Music, London; Panelist, Hofstra Mozart Conference, New York. Recordings: Music for Strings; Mozart Concerto for Piano and Orchestra, with Beveridge Webster; Michael Haydn Symphony; Other Mozart works. Publications: Berard, 1960; Sonata Form in Classic Orchestra, 1966; Treasury of Librettos, 1969; Don Quixote by Minkus, 1975; Choreographers and Composers, 1983; Mozart Research Guide, 1989. Contributions to: American Record Guide; Carnegie Hall programmes; Alice Tully Hall programmes; Prose of Distinction to Ballet Review; Juilliard Journal; Guide to Thamos by Mozart, Conductor's Journal. Honours: Fulbright Fellowship, 1949-50, Tanglewood, 1957. Memberships: The Bohemians; Musicians Union; American Musicological Society. Hobbies: Collecting Art; Tennis. Address: 33 Greenwich Avenue, New York, NY 10014, USA.

HATHCOCK John Edward, b. 6 September 1955, Memphis, Tennessee, USA. Vocal Performer. Divorced, 1 daughter. Education: BA, University of Memphis, 1986; Studied Sacred and Opera Vocal Performance with Ethel Maxwell, 15 years; Studied Music Theory and Composition with Dr David Williams, University of Memphis, 1992-97; Studied Piano with Sam Viviano and Genaro Santoro. Career: Vocal Performer, Composer of Sacred and Opera Music, 1981-; President, Positron Productions, 1988-90; Product Script Writing and Video Co-Editing; Performer, Producer, Music Video, 1988; Director of Public Relations, The Beethoven Club, 1993; President, Founder, Soaring Spirit Music, 1996-. Compositions: Chamber Music: Sacred Art Songs and Instrumentals, 1988-; Incomplete Sacred Opera, 1995; Seasons of Wonder, 1995; A Day of Grace, 5 Piece Musical Work of Instrumentals and Sacred Art Songs, 1996. Recording: Grace: The Eternal Song, vocalist and executive producer, 1997. Contributions to: Journal of Psychology; Crisis Intervention Strategies; Poetry in publications. Honours include: Wheelchair Mr America Award, 1990; Man of the Year Special Achievement Award, HAPPI International Talent, 1990; Trailblazer Award, City of Memphis, 1990. Memberships: Beethoven Club, 1989-; Vocal Arts Ensemble, 1993; International Platform Association, 1995-; Life Fellow, International Biographical Association, 1995-; Heritage Foundation, 1996-; Gospel Music Association, 1996-; Christian Coalition, 1996-; International Society of Poets, 1997. Hobbies: Weightlifting; Painting. Address: P O Box 382220, Memphis, TN 38183-2220, USA.

HATINA Zdenek, b. 6 April 1941, Brno, Czech Republic. Musician; Organist; Educationalist; Composer; Conductor; Choir Master. m. Jitka Vanurova-Hatinova, 11 July 1964, 2 daughters. Education: Academy of Music, Brno, 1965-71. Career: Regular Organ Concerts, 1965-; Several Solo Organ Concerts of Czech and World Organ Music Corporation with Brno-Zabrodovice Choir and its Soloists, 1971-. Compositions: Missa Dominicalis, opus 3, for Solos, Mixed Choir, Organs and Orchestra; Requiem, opus 5, for Solos, Choir, Strings and Organ. Recording: Missa Dominicalis. Contributions to: Singende Kirche; Musica Sacra. Honour: 1st Prize, Organ Competition, Krnov, 1961. Memberships: Musica Sacra; Organ Society, Moravian Museum; Diocesan Committee for Catholic Liturgy, Interest in Sacral Architecture. Address: Mathonova 68, 613 00 Brno, Czech Republic.

HATRIK Juraj, b. 1 May 1941, Orkucany, Presov, Czechoslovakia. Composer. m. 17 Apr 1965, 2 s. Education: Academy of Music and Dramatic Arts, Bratislava. Debut: Sinfonietta, 1963. Career: Musical Education, Aestheitcs and Psychology of Music, Academy of Music. Compositions include: Double Portrait for Orchestra, 1971; Da Capo al Fine for Orchestra, 1976; Diary of Tanja Savitchova for Brass Quintet and Soprano, 1976, TV version 1983; Happy Prince, opera after Oscar Wilde, 1978; Sans Souci, symphony, 1979; Vox Memoriae, cycle for 4 instruments, 1983; Canzona for Organ, Alto and Viola, after John Roberts, R Tagora, 1984; Submerged Music for Soprano and Strings, 1985; Moment Music avec J S Bach for Soprano and Chamber Group, 1985; Victor, 2nd symphony, 1988; Compositions for children, choirs and 4 monologues for Accordion; Adam's Children, chamber opera after Slovak national proverbs and bywords, 1991; Diptych for Vino, Vlello, Pft, 1989; The Lost Children for String Quartet with Basso Solo after Gregory Orr, 1993; The Brave Tin Soldier, musical by Hans Andersen, 1994. Contributions to: Slovak Music; Musical Life. Honour: Premio di città Castelfidardo (Composition for Accordion Solo), 1993. Membership: Slovak Roma Club. Hobbies: Educational projects for children; Moderation of music programmes; Creative Art; Literature; Nature. Current Management: Academy of Music and Dramatic Arts, Bratislava, music analysis and composition. Address: Dubnická 2, 85102 Bratislava, Slovakia.

HATTORI Joji, b. 1969, Japan. Concert Violinist. Education: Studied in Vienna with Rainer Küchl; Further lessons with Lord Menuhin and Vladimir Spivakov. Career: Concert engagements throughout Europe and USA; UK debut with the Royal Philharmonic Orchestra; Concerts with Yehudi Menuhin at the Festival Hall and with Vienna Kammerorchester at the Vienna Konzerthaus; Appearances with the English Chamber Orchestra, the Radio Symphony of Netherlands and The European Community Chamber Orchestra; Israel and Zurich Chamber Orchestras, Orchestre de la Suisse Romande, Bavarian Radio Symphony and most major Japanese orchestras including New Japan Philharmonic under Seiji Ozawa; Wigmore Hall, London, debut 1996, with pianist Bruno Canino; Plays a Guarneri del Gesu violin (Hämmerle 1733). Honours include: Winner, Young Musician of the Year in Japan, 1992; Menuhin International Violin Competition, Folkestone. Address: c/o Harold Holt Ltd, 31 Sinclair Road, London W14 0NS, England.

HATZIANO Markella, b. 1960, Athens, Greece. Singer (Mezzo-soprano). Education: Studied with Gogo Georgilopoulu at the Athens National Conservatory and Tito Gobbi in Rome. Career: Sang Eboli in Don Carlos with the National Opera of Greece and made her US debut, as Azucena at Boston, in 1987; Returned to Boston as Suzuki, Amneris, Neris in Cherubini's Médée and in Verdi's Requiem; French repertory includes Carmen (Mexico 1992, under Enrique Batiz), Massenet's Charlotte (Malaga, 1993) and Marguerite in La Damnation de Faust (Trieste, 1993); Sang Dido in Les Troyens with the London Symphony Orchestra at the Barbican Hall, under Colin Davis, 1993; Further appearances as Judith in Bluebeard's Castle at the Salzburg Festival, Dido at La Scala, 1996, Amneris at Florence, under Zubin Mehta; Sang Dalila and Amneris at Covent Garden, 1996; Concert repertory includes Mahler's Das Lied von der Erde, Kindertotenlieder and 2nd and 3rd Symphonies; Season 1996-97 concerts with the New York Philharmonic, Chicago Syphony Orchestra, Los Angeles Philharmonic and the Orchestre de la Suise Romande; Debut with the London Symphony in Schoenberg's Erwartung, 1997. Recordings include: Verdi Requiem, with the LSO under Richard Hickox. Honours include: Winner, Tito Gobbi International Competition, 1983; American-Israel Competition, 1987. Address: c/o Lies Askonas Ltd, 6 Henrietta St, London WC2E 8LA, England.

HAUBOLD Ingrid, b. 1943, Berlin. Singer (Soprano). m. Heikki Toivannen. Education: Studied in Detmold and at the Munich Musikhochschule with Annelies Kupper. Career: Sang at the Munich Theater am Gärtnerplatz, 1965-66; Detmold Landestheater 1970-72, Bielefeld 1972, Lubeck from 1979; Guest engagements at Hanover (from 1981) and Karlsruhe (1981-84); Sang Isolde at Madrid 1986, Turin and Berlin 1988, Lucerne Festival 1989; Has also appeared at the Teatro Massimo Palermo, Teatro Comunale Bolgna, the Vienna Staatsoper, Schwetzingen Festival (Ariadne, 1989) and the Metropolitan Opera, 1990-91; Other roles include Senta (Savonlinna Festival 1990), Pamina, Wagner's Elsa, Elisabeth, Brünnhilde, Gutrune, Eva, Freia, Sieglinde, Irene (Rienzi) and Ada (Die Feen); Leonore, Strauss's Chrysothemis and Marschallin, Janacek's Jenufa and Katya Kabanova; Many concert appearances. Address: c/o Deutsche Oper Berlin, Richard Wagnerstrasse 10, Berlin, Germany.

HAUDEBOURG Brigitte, b. 5 Dec 1942, Paris, France. Harpsichordist; Pianofortist; Concertist; Teacher. m. Paul Cousseran, 1 son, 1 daughter. Education: Studied Piano with Marguerite Long and Jean Doyen; Master Class with R Veyron-Lacroix. Debut: Paris. Career: Many TV and Radio appearances in France, USA, Canada, Europe, Russia, Tunisia, Hong Kong, Bangkok, Tahiti. Recordings: 70 Albums and CD's, including, Daquin, Dandrieu, 2 albums of suites; Devienne, for flute and harpsichord; Chevalier de St Georges, for violin and harpsichord; Jean Pierre Baur, for harp and harpsichord; W F Bach, 2 albums, No 1,3,4,5; CD's include, Louis Couperin, for harpsichord; Josse Boutmy for harpsichord, world premiere; Padre Antonio Soler; J Schobert for pianoforte; J A Benda for pianoforte. Publications include: 2nd book of Josse Boutmy, (harpsichord). Honours: First Prize (harpsichord class) of the Conservatoire National Supérieur de Musique de Paris; Gold Medal from Viotti; Soloist of French Broadcasting; Grand Prix du disque. Memberships: Artistic Directors of Baroque Summer Festival; Vice President of the Association of Wanda Landowska's Friends. Hobbies: Books; Travel; Photography. Current Management: Musilyre (Europe), Paris, France; A Declert (North America), Texas, USA. Address: 10 Avenue F Roosevelt, 92150 Suresnes, France.

HAUG Halvor, b. 20 Feb 1952, Trondheim, Norway. Composer. Education: Degree, School Music Teacher, Conservatory of Music, Veitvet, Oslo, 1970-73, Sibelius Academy, Helsinki, 1973-74; Studies with Kolbjörn Ofstad, Oslo, 1974-75, London, 1978. Career: Performances in Norway and abroad with major musicians and orchestras; numerous radio and TV performances in Norway and overseas. Compositions include: Orchestra: Symphonic Picture, 1976; 3 Symphonies, 1981-82, 1984, 1991-93; Silence for Strings, 1977; Poema Patetica and Poema Sonora, 1980; Song of the Pines, 1987; Insignia, 1993; Glem aldri henne, song cycle for mezzosoprano and orchestra, 1997; Chamber: Brass Quintet, 1981; 2 String Quartets, 1985, 1996; Piano Trio, 1995. Recordings include: Symphony No 1; Silence for Strings; Sinfonietta with the LSO and Dreier; Symphonic Picture and Poema Patetica, with the LPO and Dreier; Symphony No 2; Symphony No 3; Insignia; Song of the Pines; Silence for Strings, with Norrköping Symphony Orchestra, English Chamber Orchestra and Ruud. Membership: Society of Norwegian Composers. Hobbies: Bird Watching; Fishing. Current Management: Warner Chappell Music Norway A/S. Address: c/o Postbox 4523, Torshov 0404, Oslo, Norway.

HAUGLAND Aage, b. 1 Feb 1944, Copenhagen, Denmark. Singer (Bass). Education: Studied medicine at first, then music with Moegens Wöldike and Kristian Riis in Denmark. Career: Sang in Oslo from 1968, then Bremen; Member of the Royal Opera Copenhagen from 1973; Covent Garden debut 1975 as Hunding in the Friedrich production of Die Walkure; Hagen in Götterdämmerung with English National Opera; returned to London for new productions of Boris Godunov and Der Rosenkavalier, 1984; Appearances in Venice as Mussorgsky's Varlaam, Geneva, (Ochs in Der Rosenkavalier), Paris and Vienna; Netherlands Opera as Banquo in Macbeth; US debut 1979, as Boris Godunov in St Louis; Metropolitan Opera in works by Wagner, Mussorgsky and Tchaikovsky; Salzburg debut 1982, as Rocco in Fidelio; Bayreuth Festival from 1983, as Hagen and Fafner in the Ring; Edinburgh Festival 1990 as Marke in Tristan and Isolde (Concert); Sang at the Metropolitan 1990-91 as Baron Ochs and in Katya Kabanova and Parsifal; Season 1992 with Boris in Lady Macbeth of Mtsensk at La Scala and King Mark at Aarhus; Sang Varlaam in Boris Godunov at the 1994 Salzburg Easter Festival; Season 1996-97 as Schoenberg's Moses at the Festival Hall and as Varlaam at Salzburg; Concert appearances with the London Symphony, London Philharmonic, Philharmonia, Vienna Philharmonic and the Philadelphia, Boston and Chicago Symphony Orchestras. Recordings: Roles in Götterdämmerung, Boris Godunov, Katerina Ismailova, Parsifal and Moses und Aron; Video of Wozzeck, as the Doctor, conducted by Abbado (Virgin). Address: c/o Lies Askonas Ltd, 6 Henrietta Street, London WC2, England.

HAUNSTEIN Rolf, b. 1940, Dresden, Germany. Singer (Baritone). Education: Studied with Johannes Kemter in Dresden and Kurt Rehm in Berlin. Career: Sang in Bautzen, Freiberg and Cottbus, before engagement at the Dresden Staatsoper, 1971; Roles have included Germont, Posa, Ford, Scarpia, Beckmesser, Rigoletto, Pizarro, Klingsor, Telramund, Onegin and Wagner's Dutchman; Guest engagements at Leipzig, the Komische Oper Berlin, Kiel, Wiesbaden and Stasbourg; Member of the Zürich Opera from 1991;season 1996-97, Telramund, the Minister in Fidelio and Dikoj in Katya Kabanova; Conductors have included Harnoncourt, Dohnanyi, Masur and Suitner and opera producers such as Ruth Berghaus, Robert Wilson, Joachim Herz and Harry Kupfer, 1976. Address: c/o Opernhaus Zürich, Falkenstrasse 1, CH-8008 Zürich, Switzerland.

HAUPTMANN Cornelius, b. 1951, Stuttgart, Germany. Singer (Bass). Education: Graduated Stuttgart Musikhochschule 1982; Berne Conservatoire with Jakob Stampfli; Further study with Dietrich Fischer-Dieskau in Berlin and masterclasses in Salzburg with Eric Tappy and Elisabeth Schwarzkopf. Career: Sang at Stuttgart from 1981, notably as Masetto; Heidelberg Opera 1985-87, as King Philip in Don Carlos and Osmin; Stadttheater Karlsruhe from 1987, as Sparafucile (Rigoletto), Plutone (Orfeo), Sarastro and Mozart's Figaro; Festival appearances at Lucerne, Salzburg, Singapore, Sapporo, Schwetzingen (1983 premiere of Henze's The English Cat) and Ludwigsburg (recital 1991); Further engagements in Munich, Paris, Berlin, Leipzig, Orleans, London, Lyon and Amsterdam (Publio and Sarastro in concert performances of La Clemenza di Tito and Die Zauberflöte, 1990); Sang Sarastro at Ludwigsburg, 1992; Conductors include John Eliot Gardiner, Hogwood, Janowski, Tilson Thomas, Masur, Barenboim, Hogwood, Maazel, Lothar Zagrosek, Roger Norrington, Neville Marriner, Pierre Boulez, Philippe Herreweghe; Concert performances include the St Matthew Passion (Gardiner) and Mozart's Requiem (Bernstein) in 1988; Frequent Lieder recitals, and other concerts under Nikolaus Harnoncourt, Trevor Pinnock, Helmut Rilling and Gary Bertini; Sang Rocco in a concert performance of Fidelio at Lyon, 1996. Recordings: Bach St John and St Matthew Passion, Mozart C minor Mass, Idomeneo, La Clemenza di Tito, and Die Entführung, with Gardiner and Mozart Requiem and C minor Mass (Bernstein) for Deutsche Grammophon; Beethoven: Missa Solemnis (Herreweghe); Schoenberg's Jakobsleiter (Inbal); Haydn Stabat Mater, with Pinnock (DG) and Die Zauberflöte with Norrington; Enescu Oedipe with Foster (EMI); Akhnaten by Philip Glass (CBS). Current Management: Bureau de Concerts Maurice Werner, 7 Rue Richepance, 7-75008 Paris, France. Address: Waldburgstr 121, D-70563 Stuttgart, Germany.

HAUSCHILD Wolf-Dieter, b. 6 Sept 1937, Greiz, Germany. Conductor. Education: Studied at Franz Liszt Musikhochschule, Weimar, with Ottmar Gerster and Hermann Abendroth; Further study with Hermann Scherchen and Sergiu Celibidache. Career: Conductor of the Deutsche National theater Weiners and from 1963 Chief Conductor of the Kleist Theatre at Frankfurt Oder (also of Frankfurt Philharmonic); Chorus Master for RDA Radio, 1971-74, joint conductor of Berlin Radio Symphony Orchestra, 1974-78; Chief Conductor of the Symphony Orchestra of Radio Leipzig, 1978-85; Professor of Conducting at the Musikhochschule of Berlin and Leipzig from 1981; Guest Conductor of Berlin Symphony Orchestra; Chief Conductor of Stuttgart Philharmonic Orchestra, 1985-91; Professor of Conducting at Karlsruhe Musikhochschule, 1988; Artistic Director and Chief Conductor at Essen Opera, 1991; Guest appearances at Berlin Staatsoper and Komische Opera and the Semper-Oper Dresden; Conducted a new production of Tristan und Isolde at Essen, 1992. Address: c/o Theater und Philharmonie, Rolandstrasse 10, 45128 Essen, Germany.

HAUSER Alexis, b. 1947, Vienna, Austria. Music Director. Education: Student at the Conservatory and the Academy of Music and Performing Arts in Vienna; Graduated summa cum laude in the masterclass of Professor Hans Swarowsky; Also studied with Franco Ferrara in Italy and Herbert von Karajan, Salzburg, Mozarteum. Debut: With Vienna Symphony, 1973. Career: Several concerts and broadcasts with Vienna Symphony; Invitations to conduct many other European orchestras including the Berlin RIAS Symphony, Belgrade Philharmonic and the Vienna Chamber Orchestra; Invited by Seiji Ozawa to spend summer of 1974 in Tanglewood; USA Debut with New York City Opera, 1975; Conducted Atlanta Symphony with Itzhak Perlman as soloist, 1975; Subsequently conducted with Symphonies of San Francisco, Minnesota, Seattle, Kansas City (with Maureen Forrester as soloist) and the Rochester Philharmonic; Music Director, Orchestra London Canada, 1981-; Led orchestra on its first European tour to the Festival Internationale dell Aquila in Italy; Directed Conductors' Seminar at the Royal Conservatory of Music in Toronto; Conducted the Toronto, Winnipeg and Kansas City Symphonies; Appeared at Chicago's Grant Park Festival. Honours: Winner of several conducting awards in Austria including 1st International Hans Swarowsky Conducting Competition in Vienna; Awarded Koussevitzky Conducting Prize at Tanglewood, 1974; In 1984 Orchestra London Canada received the Award of Merit presented by the Canadian Performing Rights Organization.

HAUTZIG Walter, b. 28 Sept 1921, Vienna, Austria. Concert Pianist. m. Esther Rudomin, 10 Sept 1950, 1 son, 1 daughter. Education: State Academy of Vienna; Jerusalem Conservatory; Curtis Institute, Philadelphia; Principal Teacher, Mieczyslaw Munz; Private Study with Artur Schnabel. Debut: Town Hall, New York, 31 Oct 1943. Career: Recitals and Orchestral Appearances in over 50 Countries; Soloist with Berlin Philharmonic, Orchestra National Belgique, Oslo, Stockholm, Copenhagen, Helsinki, Zurich, New York, Baltimore, St Louis, Buffalo, Vancouver, Honolulu, Tokyo, Sydney, Melbourne, Auckland, Wellington, Mexico, Bogota, Jerusalem and Tel Aviv; Played for BBC, Australian, New Zealand, Japanese, USA and Canadian Radio; Professor of Piano, Peabody Conservatory of the Johns Hopkins University, Baltimore, USA, 1960-87. Recordings: Numerous for labels including, RCA, Monitor, Vox, Turnabout, Musical Heritage Society. Contributions to: Musical America; American Record Guide. Hobbies: Ping Pong; Photography; Swimming.

HAVENSTEIN Birgit, b. 4 Jan 1954, Berlin, Germany. Composer; Flautist. Education: Studied at the Berlin Hochschule and in Zurich. Compositions include: Jeu for Flute, 1982; Four Poems for Flute and Voice, 1984; Szene for Orchestra, 1985; Lament for String Quartet, 1985; Graffiti for Flute, Cello and Harp, 1987; Im Jasmin for Cello, 1989. Honours include: Prizes for Szene, performed by the Berlin Philharmonic Orchestra in 1985, and Graffiti. Address: c/o GEMA, Postfach 80 07 67, D-81607 München, Germany.

HAVERINEN Margareta, b. 1951, Finland. Singer (Soprano). Education: Studied with Pierre Bernac in Paris, Anita Välkki in Helsinki, Gladys Kuchta in Dusseldorf and Vera Rozsa in London. Career: After winning the 1978 Geneva International Competition sang in opera at Helsinki and Oslo as Gilda, Violetta, Tosca and Donna Anna; Welsh National Opera, 1988, and Dublin, 1992, as Tosca; London, 1992, in the British premiere of Sibelius's opera The Maiden in the Tower; Many concerts and Lieder recitals in Europe and the USA (Carnegie Hall, New York, and the Westminster Artsong Festival in Princeton). Address: c/o Dublin Grand Opera Society, John Player Theatre, 276-288 Circular Road, Dublin 8, Eire.

HAVLAK Lubomir, b. 27 Feb 1958, Prague, Czech Republic. Jarmila Havlakova, 26 Aug 1983, 1 son, 1 daughter. Education: Violinist, Conservatoire in Prague; Academy of Music in Prague; Master Classes: Nathan Milstein in Zürich; Masterclasses with leading ensembles: Tel Aviv, Amadeus, Guarneri, Juilliard and Alban Berg Quartets. Debut: Prague Spring Festival, 1980; Member, (Martinu) Quartet. Career: Leader of Havlak and Martinu Quartet: Prague Spring Festival; UNESCO Hall in Paris, Kuhmo Festival (Finland), Wigmore Hall, London, Bath Festival, Festivals in Dartington, in Evian (France), Arjeplog (Sweden), Bratislava (Slovakia), Orlando Festival (Holland), Frankfurter Sonoptikum; Film: Meeting with Segerstam; Concerts in Europe, USA and Japan; TV, Radio. Recordings: Leader of Martinu-Quartet; Martinu Quartets (Naxos); Debussy, Martinu (Panton); Old Czech Composers - Krommer, Richter; Dvorak, Smetana-String Quartets; Antonin Wranitsky - Concertante Quartets; Honegger, Feld S G; Ullmann S G (Romantic Robot). Honours: With Havlak Quartet: Prague Spring Competition, 2nd Prize, 1979; Evian: Contemporary Music, 1st Prize, 1978; Portsmouth, 2nd Prize, 1982; München, 2nd Prize, 1982; Florence, 2nd Prize, 1984. Hobbies: Travel; Sports; Photography; Films; Cycling. Current Management: Pragoart Concerts. Address: Pod Vlastnim Krovem 27, 182 00 Praha 8, Czech Republic.

HAVLIK Jiri, b. 20 July 1956, Tabor, Czech Republic. Musician. m. Helena Havlikova, 18 March 1978, 2 daughters. Education: French Horn, Composition, Conservatoire, Prague, 1971-77; Composition, 1977-78, Horn, 1978-81, Academy of the Musical Arts. Career: Member, Czech Philharmonic, 1979-, Horn Trio Prague, 1985-; Chamber and Solo Performances in Czech Republic, Switzerland, Holland, Japan, Canada; Founder, Horn Music Agency, Prague, 1991. Compositions: Concerto for Horn and Orchestra, 1976; The Cycle of the Piano Compositions, 1978; Three Fugues for Three Horns and Piano, 1997. Recordings: Czech Philharmonic Horn Section, 1989; Old Czech Concertos for 2 and 3 Horns, 1992. Honours: 2nd Prize, Concertino Prague International Competition, 1970; Special Prize, Czech Ministry of Culture, 1978; 3rd Prize, Prague Spring International Competition, 1978. Hobbies: Flying Models; House and Garden. Current

Management: Pragoart Prague. Address: Na Spravedlnosti 1152, 27101 Nove Straseci, Czech Republic.

HAUSSWOLFF Carl Michal von, b. 13 October 1956, Linkoping, Sweden. Composer. 2 daughters. Education: Literature, Musicology, Goteborg University. Debut: Royal Academy for Fine Arts, Stockholm, 1988. Career: Composing Electroacoustic Music, 1977-97; Performance Artist, 1977-97. Compositions: Conductor, Radium, 1983; Godtphauss, 1994; Sub Rosa, 1995; Mingling, 1997; As Quiet as a Campfire, 1997. Contributions to: Index; ND; Nutida Music; Siks. Membership: Swedish Composers Association. Address: c/o Rahm, Rolsgasgatan 58, 113 54 Stockholm, Sweden.

HAWALTA Franz, b. 26 December 1963, Eichstatt, Germany. Singer (Bass). Education: Munich Musikhochschule, with Ernst Haefliger, Hans Hotter and Erik Werba. Debut: Gartnerplatztheater, Munich, 1986. Career: Engagements at the Komische Oper Berlin and in Munich, with guest appearances as Altoum in Busoni's Bartolo in Dortmund; Baron Ochs in Der Rosenkavalier at Wurzburg, for Welsh National Opera, New York Metropolitan (1995) and the Paris Opéra Bastille (1998); Peneios at Hamburg, Wozzeck at Bad Urach, Rocco in Beethoven's Leonore, on tour with John Eliot Gardiner, Leporello at Covent Garden and Osmin in Die Entführung at Salzburg (1996); Vienna State Opera 1994-95 as Nicolai's Falstaff, Kaspar, Don Pasquale, Sarastro and Baron Ochs. Recordings include: Mephisto in Spohr's Faust, from the Bad Urach Festival. Honours include: Prize Winner, 1987 Belvedere International Singing Competition, Vienna. Address: IMG Artists, Media House, 3 Burlington Lane, London W4 2TH, England.

HAWKES Tom, b. 21 June 1938, England. Stage Director. Education: Trained at the Royal Academy of Music. Career: Resident Staff Producer at Sadler's Wells 1965-69; For English National Opera has produced Un Ballo in Maschera, Madama Butterfly, La Vie Parisienne, La Gazza Ladra and Die Fledermaus; English Bach Festivals (seen at Covent Garden and in France, Greece, Italy and Spain) include Rameau's Castor et Pollux and Platée, Handel's Teseo and Gluck's Alceste and Orphée et Eurydice; Dido and Aenea in London and at the Athens Festival; Artistic Director for Phoenix Opera and Director of Productions for the Handel Opera Society; La Finta Giardiniera for the English Music Theatre; Wat Tyler by Alan Bush, Hansel and Gretel and operettas at the Sadler's Wells Theatre; Season 1990-91 with The Maid of Orleans for Northern Opera, La Bohème in Hong Kong, Mitridate in Monte Carlo and Handel's Riccardo Primo at the Royal Opera House and in Limasol for the English Bach Festival; Has also conducted in Dublin, Nottingham, Oxford, Belgium and Guelph and St Louis, USA; Season 1993/94 with Rigoletto and Die Fledermaus at Singapore, L'Orfeo, for EBF at Royal Opera House, Covent Garden and in Spain; Director of Productions for the Singapore Lyric Theatre and for Crystal Clear Productions UK. Address: c/o Music International, 13 Ardilaun Road, London N5 2QR, England.

HAWKINS Brian, b. 13 Oct 1936, York, England. Viola Player; Teacher. m. Mavis Spreadborough, 30 Dec 1960, 1 s, 1 d. Education: National Youth Orchestra, 1951-54; Royal College of Music, 1954-60. Career: Chamber Music, Edinburgh Quartet; Martin Quartet; Vesuvius Ensemble; Nash Ensemble; London Oboe Quartet; Gagliano String Trio; Member, English Chamber Orchestra, Academy of St Martin-in-the-Fields, London Sinfonietta, London Virtuosi; Professor, Viola and Chamber Music, Royal College of Music, 1967-; String Faculty Adviser, Royal College of Music, 1989; Head of String Faculty, Royal College of Music, 1992. Recordings: With the Nash Ensemble, London Virtuosi, London Oboe Quartet and Gagliano Trio. Honours: Silver Medal, Worshipful Company of Musicians, 1960; Fellowship of The Royal College of Music, 1991. Memberships: Royal Society of Musicians; European String Teachers' Association; Incorporated Society of Musicians. Hobbies: Food; Wine; Travel; Photography. Address: The Old Vicarage, 129 Arthur Road, London, SW19 7DR, England.

HAWKINS Deborah Anne, b. 6 Nov 1956, Alton, Illinois, USA. Musicologist. Education: BA, Music, Millkin University; MA, Doctoral Study, University of Iowa. Career: Faculty, St Louis Symphony Community Music School. Publications: Essays on Margaret Bonds, in Dictionary of Black Composers. Memberships: Sonneck Society; American Musicological Society; Music Teachers National Association. Hobbies: Travel; Gardening. Address: 136 South Clearview Drive, East Alton, IL 62024, USA.

HAWKINS John, b. 26 July 1944, Montreal, Canada. Composer; Pianist. Education: Studied under Istvan Anhalt and received Master's degree in Composition, McGill University. Career: Joined Faculty of Music, University of Toronto, teaches theory and composition, 1970-; Remained active as pianist and performed frequently in the concerts of Societe de Musique Contemporaine du Quebec as well as Toronto's New Music Concerts, of which he is a member of Board of Directors; Conductor, Pierre Boulez' conducting seminar, Switzerland 1969. Compositions: Composed over 70 new works which include pieces for harpsichord and organ. Honours: Won several major awards including first John Adaskin Memorial Fund Award, 1968 and BMI Student Composers' Award, 1969. Address: CAPAC, 1240 Bay Street, Toronto, Ontario M5R 2C2, Canada.

HAWKINS Malcolm, b. 8 Mar 1944, Oporto, Portugal. Composer; Teacher. m. 2 Aug 1987. Education: Rugby School; Royal Academy of Music; BMus (London), 1966; LRAM; Mozarteum, Salzburg; Diploma in Composition, 1970; MMus (London), 1976. Career: Freelance Double Bass Player and Pianist; Assistant Director of Music, Cranleigh School, 1971-76; Professor, Royal Academy of Music, 1979-88; Wells Cathedral School, 1988-90. Compositions: A Day in Town (suite for orchestra), UMP; This Endris Night (carol), UMP; On Stage (suite for Piano Duet), Stainer and Bell; (version for orchestra) Basil Ramsey; Animal City (8 songs for school choirs) S and B; Glimpses of a Garden (flute or recorder and keyboard) Bardie edition; The Riders (Carol) Stainer and Bell; Stepping Out for Flute and Jazz Trio (BBC) commission RVW Trust 1987; Cantata, Sancta Sophia, Litchfield Festival, 1991. Recordings: On Stage (suite for orchestra) BBC Radio 3; Diversions for Oboe Quartet (Berlin); Dancing Partners for Wind Quartet (Berlin); Four Songs for Baritone, Saxophone and Piano (DRF Salzburg); Festival Fanfare La Marseillaise Round Top, Texas, 1989; Ghost Games for Piano, 1991; Oboe Concerto, 1991. Honour: First Prize in International Song Competition, Das Neue Lied, Salzburg, 1975. Memberships: Composers' Guild; Savile Club. Address: Old Forge, Old Frome Road, East Horrington, Wells, Somerset, BA5 3DP, England.

HAWKINS Osie, b. 16 Aug 1913, Phenix City, Alabama, USA. Singer (Baritone). Education: Studied in Atlanta and with Friedrich Schorr in New York; Sang at the Metropolitan Opera from 1942, as Wagner's Telramund, Kurwenal, Bitterolf, Wotan, Amfortas, Donner and Gunther; Zuniga in Carmen and Monterone in Rigoletto; Also sang with Central City Opera, Colorado and the Cincinnati Summer Opera; Many concert appearances; Executive Stage Manager at the Metropolitan 1963-78; 926 performances with the Metropolitan Opera, played 54 roles in 39 different operas in German, Italian, French and English. Honours: Awarded Metropolitan Opera National Council Verdi Memorial Award of Achievement, 1978; Inducted into Philadelphia Academy of Vocal Arts Hall of Fame, 1987. Address: c/o Metropolitan Opera, Lincoln Center, New York, NY 10023, USA.

HAY Diana (Pereira), b. 20 Feb 1932, Sri Lanka. Composer. Education: Studied at the Copenhagen Royal Conservatory. Career: Founded the Women in Music Association in 1980; Composer of computer music from 1990. Compositions include: Exercises In Metamorphosis for Piano, 1966, and for String Quartet, 1967; Sonata In Three Phases for Piano, 1978; I'm Still Alive for Piano, 1983. Address: c/o SLPRS, 5th Floor, 267 Union Place, Colombo 2, Sri Lanka.

HAYASHI Yasuko, b. 19 Jul 1948, Kanagawa, Japan. Soprano Singer. m. Giannicola Pigliucci. Education: Studied in Tokyo with Shibata and Rucci; Studied with Lia Gurani and Campogalliani in Milan. Debut: La Scala 1972, as Madama Butterfly. Career: Appearances in Florence, Rome, London, Venice, Turin, Barcelona, Chicago and Aix-en-Provence; Other roles include Donna Anna, Fiordiligi, Carolina in Il Matrimonio Segreto, Luisa Miller, Anne Trulove and Liu, in Turandot; Turin 1976, in Bianca e Fernando by Bellini; Sang Donna Anna at reopening of Stuttgart Staatsoper, 1984; Genoa 1985, in a revival of Il Diluvio Universale by Donizetti; Season 1987-88 as, Butterfly at Verona and Leonora, in La Forza del Destino in Tokyo; Appearances on TV and in concert. Recordings: I Lituani by Ponchielli; Rachel in La Juive; Requiem by Bottesini, Fonit-Cetra; Video of Madama Butterfly from La Scala. Address: c/o Marks Management Ltd, 14 New Burlington Street, London, W1X 1FF, England.

HAYES Jamie, b. 1959, England. Stage Director. Career: Productions of The Gonmdaliers, The Magic Flute and Midsummer Night's Dream at Freemason's Hall; Aïda, Opera Northern Ireland; Il Barbiere di Siviglia and La Cenerentola for Garsington Opera, Thieving Magpie, Figaro, Così fan tutte and Albert Herring for British Youth Opera at Sadler's Wells and Edinburgh; Director of productions for Clonter Opera For All, with La Traviata and La Bohème; Buxton Festival with L'Italiana in Algeri, Le Huron and L'Italiana in Londra; Wexford Festival with Zaza and Le Rencontre Imprévue; Other productions include Alcina for Royal Northern College of Music and The Pearl Fishers for Victorian State Theatre, Robinson Crusoe, British Youth Opera; Appointed Director of Productions, British Youth Opera, in 1996. Address: Helen Sykes Management, First Floor, Parkway House, Sheen Lane, East Sheen, London, SW14 8LS, England.

HAYES Malcolm (Lionel Fitzroy), b. 22 Aug 1951, Overton, Marlborough, Wiltshire, England. Music Journalist; Writer; Composer. Education: St Andrews University; BMus Honours, Edinburgh University, 1974. Career: Music Critic, The Times, 1985-86; Music Critic, The Sunday Telegraph, 1986-89; Music Critic, The Daily Telegraph, 1989-95; Frequent broadcasts (talks) for BBC Radio 3, 1985-, and Radio 4, 1986-; Music performed at Bath Festival, 1985, ICA, London, 1985, BBC, London, 1986, Viitasaari Festival, Finland, 1987. Publications: New Music 88 (co-editor), 1988; Anton von Webern, 1995. Contributions to: Numerous articles for Tempo, 1982-92; The Listener, 1985-89; Musical Times, 1985-86; International and Opera Guide, 1987; New Music 87, 1987; Opera Now, 1991-; Classic FM Magazine, 1995-. Honours: Tovey Prize for Composition, Edinburgh University, 1974. Address: Sunday Telegraph, 1 Canada Square, Canary Wharf, London E14 5DT, England.

HAYES Quentin, b. England. Singer (Baritone). Education: Studied at Dartington College, the Guildhall School with Arthur Reckless and Rudolph Pernay, and at the National Opera Studio. Career: Created Eddy in Mark-Anthony Turnage's Greek, Munich, 1988, repeated it at Edinburgh and the London Coliseum; Rossini's Figaro with Glyndebourne Touring Opera, Verdi's Ford for CBTO, Morales in Carmen for Welsh National Opera, and Angelotti for Scottish Opera; Ford, Papageno and Marcel Proust in Schnittke's Life with an Idiot for English National Opera, 1995; Concerts include Les Troyens at the Amsterdam Concertgebouw, St Matthew Passion with Scottish Chamber Orchestra, Elijah in Wells Cathedral, L'Enfance du Christ in Spain and music by Purcell with Collegium Vocale; Season 1997 with The Dream of Gerontius at Bath, Handel's Semele at the Berlin Staatsoper, Britten's Church Parables for CBTO and Henze's Elegy for Young Lovers with the London Sinfonietta. Recordings include: Pepusch Death of Dido for the BBC; Greek; Britten, Rejoice in the Lamb. Honours include: Winner VARA Dutch Radio Prize at the Belvedere Singing Competition, Vienna, 1992. Address: Portland Wallis Artists' Management, 50 Great Portland Street, London W1N 5AH, England.

HAYMON Cynthia, b. 6 Sept 1958, Jacksonville, Florida, USA. Singer (Soprano). m. Barrington Coleman. Education: Graduate, Northwestern University. Debut: Santa Fe Opera, as Diana in Orpheus in the Underworld, 1985. Career: Sang Xanthe in US premiere of Die Liebe der Danae, Santa Fe, 1985; Has sung Micaela for Seattle Opera and Liu in Boston; Created Harriet, A Woman Called Moses, Virginia, 1985; European debut, 1986, as Gershwin's Bess at Glyndebourne; With Covent Garden has sung Liu on tour to Far East and Mimi in London; State Operas, Hamburg, Munich, as Liu, Theatre de la Monnaie, Brussels, as Gluck's Amor; Israel Philharmonic as Micaela, conducted by Zubin Mehta; Season 1988-89 with Eurydice at Glyndebourne, Mimi for Baltimore Opera, Marguerite with Opera Grand Rapids; Season 1989-90 includes Susanna for Seattle Opera, Canadian Opera debut as Micaela; Coretta King opposite Simon Estes, West End; 1990-91 highlights: Lauretta in Gianni Schicchi at Seattle, Liu in Miami, and Mozart's Pamina at Bastille Opera, Paris; 1991-92 highlights: San Francisco Opera debut as Micaela in Carmen, premiere of Rorem's Swords and Plowshares with Boston Symphony, Pamina at Opera Bastille, Liu at Royal Opera House, Covent Garden, Gershwin in concert at Teatro La Fenice, Venice, recital at Northwestern University, Carmina Burana with Detroit Symphony Orchestra, Mendelssohn's Symphony No 2 for RAI, Rome, Gershwin and Tippett concert with London Symphony Orchestra, Gala concert, Glyndebourne Festival, 1992-93 highlights: Bess in Porgy and Bess, Royal Opera House, Pamina at Opera Bastille, Micaela in Birmingham and Dortmund, Marguerite at Deutsche Oper Berlin, Mimi at Santa Fe Opera; Sang Musetta at Amsterdam, 1996; Concert engagements in Brahms Requiem conducted by Kurt Masur, Rossini's Stabat Mater (London debut) with London Symphony Orchestra conducted by Michael Tilson Thomas; Other conductors: Seiji Ozawa, Bernard Haitink, Isaiah Jackson. Recordings include: Tippett's A Child of Our Time, London Symphony Orchestra, Richard Hickox, conductor; Bess in Porgy and Bess, Glyndebourne Festival Opera, Simon Rattle, conductor. Honour: Grammy Award, 1990. Address: c/o Columbia Artists Management Inc, 165 West 57th Street, New York, NY 10019, USA.

HAYS Sorrel (Doris), b. 6 Aug 1941, Memphis, Tennessee, USA. Composer; Keyboard Musician; Media Artist in Audio and Film/Video. Education: Artist Diploma, Hochschule für Musik, Munich, Germany, 1966; MMus, University of Wisconsin, 1968; Studies with Hilda Somer, Paul Badura-Skoda, Harold Cadek, Hedwig Bilgram. Career: Recently in 80s added film and video to media art; Commissions from West German Broadcasting Cologne; Film, music video production shown at Museum of Modern Art, New York and Stedelijk Museum, Amsterdam; Commissions from Westdeutscher Rundfunk, Cologne, 1988; Echo, Whatchasay Wie Bitte, 1989; The Hub, Megopolis Atlanta and Sound Shadows, commissioned as opening work for Whitney Museum Acoustica Festival, April 1990; Bits, NY City premiere, 1993, Merkin Hall; Performances of Opera, The Glass Woman, NYC, Interart Theater, 1993; Premiere, The Clearing Way, Chattanooga Symphony, 1992. Compositions: Southern Voices for Orchestra and Soprano, 1982, 21 minutes; Celebration of No, tape, Soprano, Violin, Piano, Cello, 1983; Sunday Nights, Piano, 1979; HUSH, Soprano, 2 Percussion, 1986; The Clearing Way, for full orchestra, contralto, SATB chorus; 3 act opera, 11 soloists and chorus, The Glass Woman, 1993. Honours: Opera America, production award for opera, The Glass Woman, 1989 and National Endowment for the Arts, 1992. Memberships: ASCAP International League of Women Composers Frau und Musik. Hobby: Herb and Flower Gardening. Address: 697 West End Avenue, PHB, New York, NY 10025, USA.

HAYWARD Robert, b. 1956, England. Singer (Bass-baritone). Education: Studied at the Guildhall School of Music and the National Opera Studio, Career: Sang Falstaff and Mozart's Figaro while at college; Glyndebourne Touring Opera, 1986, as Don Giovanni; Has sung Figaro, Don Giovanni, Marcello, Count and Sharpless for Welsh National Opera; Theseus and Haushofmeister (Capricco) for Glyndebourne Festival; English National Opera appearances as Tomsky in The Queen of Spades and Escamillo; US debut as Figaro for Houston Grand Opera, 1988; German debut, 1990, as Don Giovanni for the Bayerische Staatsoper on tour to Teatro Liceo Barcelona; For Opera North Guglielmo, Figaro, Count, Escamillo, Don Giovanni, Malatesta, Marcello, Robert in Iolanta, Debussy's Golaud; For Royal Opera House, Spirit Messenger (Frau); For Glyndebourne Tour Count and Onegin; Sang Germont for GTO at Glyndebourne, 1996; Concert engagements include Messiah with the Royal Liverpool Philharmonic, Hallé and London Philharmonic Orchestras; The Mask of Time, Elijah, Beethoven's Ninth and the Brahms Requiem with the Hallé; Das klagende Lied and Gurrelieder with the English Northern Philharmonia; The Dream of Gerontius with the Scottish National Orchestra; Haydn's Creation with the Bournemouth Sinfonietta and the Philharmonia conducted by Claus Peter Flor; Mozart Requiem with Georg Solti; New Israeli Opera as: Malastesta, Guglielmo. Recordings: Beethoven's 9th Symphony; Das klagende Lied. Current Management: Ingpen & Williams. Address: Ingpen & Williams, 26 Wadham Road, London SW15 2LR, England.

HAYWARD SEGAL Marie (Pauline). Opera Singer; Teacher. m. Michael Segal, deceased, 1 son. Education: Royal Academy of Music; London Opera Centre; Tito Gobbi, Italy; MA; ARAM; LRAM; RAMDipl. Debut: Royal Opera House. Career: Numerous Worldwide Appearaces, including Royal Albert Hall, Festival Hall, Musikverein, Vienna, London Colisseum, Kiel Opera House, Germany, under Klavs Tennstedt; Verdi and Wagner roles; BBC broadcasts, Melodies for You, Friday Night is Music Night. Recordings: Serenade to Music; Pilgrim's Progress; Sir Adrian Boult, Ave Maria. Honours: ARAM, 1993; 2nd Prize, Shertogenbosch International Competition Medal of Distinction, Geneva. Membership: ISM Committee. Hobbies: Writing; Theatre. Address: 27 Cyprus Avenue, Finchley N3 1SS, England.

HAYWOOD Lorna (Marie), b. 29 Jan 1939, Birmingham, England. Singer (Soprano). m. Paul Crook. Education: Royal College of Music, with Mary Parsons and Gordon Cinton; Juilliard School with Sergius Kagen and Beverly Johnson. Debut: Juilliard 1964, as Katya Kabanova. Career: Covent Garden debut 1966, in Die Zauberflöte: sang Jenufa in 1972; English National Opera from 1970, notably Janacek's The Makropoulos Case and Katya Kabanova; Appearances with Welsh National Opera and at the Glyndebourne Festival; Guest engagements in Prague, Brussels, New York, Chicago, Dallas, Washington and Seattle: roles include Marenka in The Bartered Bride, Mimi, Micaela in Carmen, Sieglinde, Elizabeth Zimmer in Elegy for Young Lovers, Mozart's Countess, Madama Butterfly, Ariadne, the Marschallin and Lady Billows in Albert Herring; Masterclass for Ohio Light Opera, 1996. Address: J Audrey Ellison International Artists Management, 135 Stevenage Road, London SW6 6PB, England.

HAZELL Andrea, b. 1965, Southampton, England. Singer (Mezzo-soprano). Education: Studied at Royal Academy of Music. Career: Many appearances throughout UK in oratorio; Sang Second Witch in Dido and Aeneas for Amersham Festival, Offenbach's Perichole in Reading and Dorabella at the 1990 Cheltenham Festival; Sang in Carmen at Earl's Court, 1989, and on tour to Japan; Royal Opera, Covent Garden, 1990-, in Les Huguenots and Die Frau ohne Schatten and as Tefka in Jenufa, 1993; Other roles include Marcellina in Le nozze di Figaro. Address: c/o Royal Opera House, Covent Garden, London WC2, England.

HAZUCHOVA Nina, b. 24 May 1926, Slovakia, Opera Singer (Mezzo-soprano). Education: Conservatory, Bratislava. Career: Appeared with Slovak National Theatre; Roles include: Carmen, Amneris in Aida; Azucena in Il Trovatore; Eboli in Don Carlos; Maddalena in Rigoletto; Suzuki in Madame Butterfly; Rosina, in the Barber of Seville; Marina in Boris Godunov; Cherubino in The Marriage of Figaro; Nancy in Martha; Isabella in The Italian Girl in Algiers; Catherine in The Taming of the Shrew; Appears as a Concert Singer performing with the best Czech orchestras; Has toured many countries including USSR, Germany, Austria, Belgium, Italy, Yugoslavia, Arabia, China, Mongolia; Vocal-Teacher, Academy of Music Arts (Vysoka skola muzickych umeni) Bratislava. Recordings: Has made numerous records. Honours: Meritorious Artist, 1968. Membership: Slovak Music Foundation, Bratislava. Address: Grösslingova 6, 811 08 Bratislava, Slovakia.

HEADLEY Erin, b. 1948, Texas, USA. Lirone and Viola da Gamba Player. Career: Member of Tragicomedia, three musicians performing in the Renaissance and Baroque repertory; Concerts in Britain and at leading European early music festivals; Gave Stefano Landi's La Morte d'Orfeo at the 1987 Flanders Festival; Francesca Caccini's La liberazione di Ruggiero dall'isola d'Alcina at the 1989 Swedish Baroque Festival, Malmo. Recordings (on Hyperion and Virgin) include: Proensa (troubadour songs), My Mind to me a Kingdom is (Elizabethan ballads, with David Cordier); A Musicall Dreame (duets from Robert Jones's 1609 collection); Biber's Mystery Sonatas; Concert programmes include The Lyre of Timotheus (incidental music by Handel, Bach, Vivaldi and Abel); Orpheus I Am (music based on the Orpheus myth by Landi, Monteverdi, Lawes and Johnson); Il Basso Virtuso (songs by Landi, Monteverdi, Strozzi, Huygens and Purcell, with Harry van der Kamp); Three Singing Ladies of Rome; Monteverdi Madrigals from Book VIII and L'Orfeo; Early Opera: Peri's Euridice, Landi's La Morte d'Orfeo and Rossi's Orfeo. Address: c/o 14 Nightingale Lane, London N8 7QU, England.

HEADRICK Samuel (Philip), b. 14 Sept 1952, St Louis, Missouri, USA. Composer; Conductor; Professor. m. Kathryn Ann Marshall, 16 Aug 1974, 3 sons, 1 daughter. Education: BM 1975, MM 1977, North Texas State University; PhD Music Composition, Eastman School of Music, 1981; Courses in Computer Music, Massachusetts Institute of Technology, 1983; Composition study with Samuel Adler, Warren Bensen, Martin Mailman, Joseph Schwanter and James Sellers. Career: Visiting Instructor of Music, Crane School of Music, State University of New York, 1980-81; Assistant Professor of Composition and Theory, Boston University, 1981-; Director of Electronic Music, Boston University, 1981-89; Co-Director, Boston University Contemporary Collegium, 1983-84; Guest Conductor, 2nd Annual Festival of Contemporary Chamber Music at the State University of New York, Potsdam, 1984; Music Director, Huntington Theater Company, 1984; Guest Conductor, St Louis Symphony Chamber Players, 1988. Compositions: Commissions and performances include ALEA III, St Louis Symphony Chamber Players, Dinosaur Annex, Boston Conservatory Wind Ensemble, Boston University Contemporary Collegium, NUMA New Music; Boston University Symphony, Lukas Foss conductor; Atlantic Brass Quintet; Sanford Sylvan; Opera Laboratory, Theatre Company, Craig Wich director; The Fall of Communism, for orchestra, 1992; Hostage - an opera, 1995; Numerous chamber compositions. Honours: National Endowment for the Arts Grants, 1989, 1992; Massachusetts Artist Fellowship, 1984. Address: 11 Hagar Lane, Waltham, MA 02154, USA.

HEALD-SMITH Geoffrey, b. 30 Mar 1930, Mexborough, South Yorkshire, England. Conductor. Divorced, 1 son, 1 daughter. Education: Mexborough Grammar School; Royal College of Music. Career: Music Adviser, Hull; Pianist; Conductor; Artistic Director from age 22 years; Orchestras conducted include: Sadler's Wells, English Northern Philharmonic, Stavanger Symphony, Siegerland Orchestra, Radio and TV Eirean, Sao Paulo Municipal, Chamber Orchestra of Brazil. Compositions: Film Score: Eve Island; Local radio music. Recordings: Edward German, Norwich Symphony; Granville Bantock Hebridean Symphony; Overture Macbeth; Overture Little Minister, Mackenzie, Holbrooke; Piano Concerto, 3 discs Havergal Brian World Premiere recordings; Bantock, Scenes from the Scottish Highlands; Arensky, Variations on a Theme of Tchaikovsky; Nepomuceno Serenata, Brasil Camerata. Publications: Group of Songs to be published by Da Capo. Hobbies: Model Railways; Boating; Gardening; Travel. Address: Tir Nan Og 7, Ganavan Road, Ganavan By Oban, Argyll PA34 5TU, Scotland.

HEALEY Derek, b. 2 May 1936, England. Composer. Education: Studied organ with Harol Darke and composition with Herbert Howells at Durham University; Further study at the Royal College of Music and with Petrassi and Celibidache in Italy. Career: Tutor: University of Victoria, BC, Australia, 1969-71, College of Arts, University of Guelph, 1972-78; Professor of Composition and Theory, University of Oregon, 1979, returning to Britain in 1988. Compositions include: Opera Seabird Island, 1977, and children's opera, Mr Punch, 1969; Ballets Il Carcerato 1965 and The Three Thieves, 1967; Orchestral: The Willow Pattern Plate, 1957; Concerto for organ, strings and timpani, 1960; Butterflies for mezzo and chamber orchestra, 1970; Artic Images, 1971; Tribulation, 1977; Music for a Small Planet, 1984; Mountain Music, 1985; Chamber: String Quartet, 1961; Cello sonata, 1961; Mobile for flute and ensemble, 1963; Laudes for flute and ensemble, 1966; Maschere for violin and piano, 1967; Wood II for soprano and string quartet, 1982; Piano music including Lieber Robert, 1974; Organ music and songs. Address: 29 Stafford Road, Ruislip Gardens, Middlesex HA4 6PB, England.

HEARTZ Daniel (Leonard), b. 5 Oct 1928, Exeter, NH, USA. Educator. Education: AB, University of NH, 1950; MA, 1951; PhD, 1957, Harvard University. Career: Assistant Professor, Music, University of Chicago, 1957-60; Assistant Professor, 1960-64, Associate Professor, 1964-66, Professor, 1966-, Chairman, 1968-72, Music, University of CA, Berkeley. Publications: Pierre Attaingnant, Royal Printer of Music, 1969; Edition of Mozart's Idomeneo, Neue Mozart Ausgabe, 1972; Mozart's Operas, 1990; Haydn, Mozart and The Viennese School 1740-1780 (800 page book), 1995. Contributions to: Professional Journals. Honours: Dent Medal, RMA, 1970; Kinkeldey Prize, American Musicological Society, 1970; Guggenheim Fellowship, 1967-68, 1978-79; Elected Fellow of American Academy of Arts and Sciences, 1988. Memberships: American Musicological Society, Vice President, 1974-76; IMS; RMA; Societe Française de Musicologie; Gesellschaft fur Musikforschung. Address: 1098 Keith Avenue, Berkeley, CA 94708, USA.

HEATER Claude, b. 1930, Oakland, California, USA. Singer (Tenor). Education: Studied in Los Angeles; Further study in Europe with Mario del Monaco and Max Lorenz. Career: Sang at first as baritone, on radio and tv and in Broadway Musicals; Bayerische Staatsoper 1964, in König Hirsch by Henze; Sang Wagner roles in Amsterdam, Brussels, Hamburg, Berlin and Milan; Bayreuth Festival 1966, as Siegmund and Melot; Other roles included Turiddu, Otello, Florestan and Samson; Guest appearances in South America; Sang Tristan at Spoleto, 1968 and appeared at Dresden, 1968, Barcelona, Bordeaux and Geneva, 1968-69; Budapest and Venice, 1970. Recording: Tristan und Isolde, conducted by Karl Böhm (Deutsche Grammophon).

HEATH Edward (Richard George) (Sir), b. 9 July 1916, St Peters-in-Thanet, Kent, England. Conductor; Writer on Music. Education: Chatham House School, Ramsgate, Kent, 1926-35; Balliol College, Oxford, 1935-39; MA (Organ Scholar). Career: Has conducted the London Symphony Orchestra, Royal Philharmonic, Philharmonia, Liverpool Philharmonic, Birmingham and Bournemouth Symphony Orchestras, Northern Sinfonia, English Chamber Orchestra, New Queen's Hall Orchestra; Zurich Chamber Orchestra, Leningrad Conservatoire Symphony Orchestra, Georgian TV Orchestra Tbilisi, Prague Opera Chamber Orchestra, Calgary Symphony Orchestra, Berlin Philharmonic, Barcelona Symphony Orchestra, European Community Youth Orchestra, Chicago, Cleveland and Philadelphia Symphony Orchestras, Shanghai Symphony Orchestra and Central Philharmonic Orchestra of China, Peking. Recordings: Elgar Cockaigne Overture with the London Symphony Orchestra; Robert Mayer Christmas Concert 1973 with the Academy of the BBC Orchestra and BBC Singers; Carols, The Joy of Christmas with the English Chamber Orchestra and the George Mitchell Singers; Black Dyke Mills Band, 1977; Carols, The Joy of Christmas, 1980; Beethoven Triple Concerto with the English Chamber Orchestra and Trio Zingara; Boccherini Cello Concerto in G with Felix Schmidt and the English Chamber Orchestra, 1989. Publications: Music-A Joy for Life; Carols-the Joy of Christmas. Memberships: Trustee, London Symphony Orchestra; Vice-President, London Bach Choir; Vice-President, Oxford Bach Choir; Governor, Royal College of Music, 1960-70; President, European Community Youth Orchestra, 1977-83; Chairman, London Symphony Orchestra Trust, 1963-70. Hobbies: Sailing; Travel. Address: House of Commons, Westminster, London SW1 0AA, England.

HEBERT Bliss, b. 30 November 1930, Faust, New York, USA. Stage Director; Eduation: Studied Piano at Syracuse University with Robert Goldsand, Simone Barrere, Lelia Gousseau. Career: Debut at Stage Director, Santa Fe, 1957; General Manager, Washington Opera Society, 1960-63; Stage Director, New York City Opera, 1963-75, Metropolitan Opera, New York City, 1973-75 (debut with Les Contest d'Hoffmann); Guest Director, Juilliard School, 1975-76; Director of Opera Companies of San Francisco, 1963; Washington 1959; Houston, 1964; Fort Worth, 1966; Caramoor Festival, Katonah, New York, 1966; Seattle Opera, 1967; Cincinnati, 1968; La Gune Festival, 1968-; Portland, Oregan, 1969; Vancouver, 1969; San Diego, 1970; New Orleans, 1970; Toronto, 1972; Baltimore, 1972; Tulsa, 1975; Miami, Florida, 1975; Charlotte, North Carolina, 1975; Dallas, 1977; Shreveport, Los Angeles, 1977; Chicago, 1983; Montreal, 1984; Boston, 1984; Cleveland, 1988; Opera Northern Ireland, 1988; Virginia Opera, 1991; Opera Mexico City, 1993; Austin Opera, 1993; Florentine Opera, Milwaukee, 1994; Don Giovanni, 1996. Address: c/o Florentine Opera Company, 735 North Water Street, Suite 1315, Milwaukee, WI 53202, USA.

HEBERT Pamela, b. 31 Aug 1946, Los Angeles, California, USA. Singer (Soprano). Education: Studied at the Juilliard School with Maria Callas, Tito Capobianco, Margaret Hoswell and Boris Goldovsky. Debut: New York City Opera 1972, as Donn Anna. Career: Appearances in New York as Mimi, title role in L'Incoronazione di Poppea, Vespina in Haydn's L'Infedeltà delusa and the Composer in Ariadne auf Naxos; Frequent concert engagements. Address: c/o New York City Opera, Lincoln Center, New York, NY 10023, USA.

HECHT Joshua, b. 1929, New York City, USA. Singer (Baritone). Education: Studied with Lili Wexberg and Eva Hecht in New York and with Walter Tassoni in Rome. Debut: Baltimore 1953, as Des Grieux in Manon. Career: Sang in Boston, Chicago, Miami, Pittsburgh, San Francisco, Seattle and New Orleans; Metropolitan Opera from 1964; Further appearances at the New York City Opera and in Graz, Johannesburg, Barcelona, Bucharest, Dublin and Vancouver; Roles include the Wanderer in Siegfried, Amfortas, Rigoletto, Iago, Scarpia and the title role in Einstein by Dessau (Gelsenkirchen 1980); Sang Prospero in Martin's Der Sturm (The Tempest), Bremen, 1992.

HECKMANN Harald, b. 6 December 1924, Dortmund, Germany. Director, Deutsches Rundfunkarchiv (German Broadcast Archives). m. Elisabeth Dohrn, 25 August 1953, 1 son. Education: Gymnasium, Dortmund, 1934-43; Musicology, Freiburg/Breisgau, 1944-52; Assistant to Wilibald Gurlitt, Freiburg/Breisgau, 1952-54. Career: Teacher of Church Music History, College of Music, Freiburg/Breisgau, 1950-54; Director, German History of Music Archives, Kassel, 1955-71; Director, German Broadcasting Archives, Frankfurt am Main, 1971-91. Publications: Deutsches Musikgeschichtlichs Archiv, Katalog der Filmsammlung, 1955-72; W A Mozart, Thamos, Koenig in Aegypten, Choere und Zwischenaktmusiken, 1956; W A Mozart, Musik zu Pantomimen und Balletten, 1963; Ch W Gluck, La Rencontre imprévue, Editor and Critic, 1964; Elektronische Datenverarbeitung in der Musikwissenschaft, 1967; Das Tenorlied, 3 volumes, co-editor, 1979-86; Musikalische Ikonographie, co-editor, 1994; Various essays on musicology. Memberships: Honorary President, International Association of Music Libraries; President, International Inventory of Musical Sources; Board Member, Robert-Schumann Society; Co-President, International Repertoire of Music Iconography; History of Music Commission, FRG; President, International Schubert Society; Rotary. Address: Im Vogelshaag 3, D65779 Ruppertshain/Ts, Germany.

HEDGES Anthony (John), b. 5 March 1931, Bicester, England. Reader in Composition; Composer. m. Delia Joy Marsden, 1957, 2 sons, 2 daughters. Education: Keble College, Oxford, MA, BMus, LRAM. Career: Teacher, Lecturer, Royal Scottish Academy of Music, 1957-63; Lecturer in Music, University of Hull, 1963, Senior Lecturer 1968; Reader in Composition, 1978-95; Founder-conductor, The Humberside Sinfonia, 1978-81. Compositions include: Orchestral: Comedy Overture, 1962; Sinfonia Semplice, 1963; Expressions, 1964; Concertante Music, 1965; Variations on a theme of Rameau, 1969; An Ayrshire Serenade, 1969; Celebrations, 1973; Symphony, 1972-73; Sinfonia Concertante, 1980; Scenes from the Humber, 1981; Showpiece, 1985; Symphony No 2, 1997; Divertimenti for String Orchestra, 1997; Choral: Gloria, unaccompanied, 1965; Epithalamium for chorus and orchestra, to text by Spenser, 1969; Bridge for the Living, for chorus and orchestra, to text by Philip Larkin, 1976; I Sing The Birth, for chorus and chamber orchestra, 1985; I'll Make Me a World, chorus and orchestra, 1990; Chamber: Five preludes for piano, 1959; Sonatinas for flute, viola and trombone, 1982; Flute Trios, 1985, 1989; Piano Quartet, 1992; Many anthems, partsongs, albums of music for children; Music for television, film and stage. Recordings: Scenes from the Humber; Kingston Sketches; Bridge for the Living. Publications: Basic Tonal Harmony, 1987, Comprehensive Archive in Hall Central Music Library. Contributions to: regular contributor to The Guardian, The Scotsman, The Glasgow Herald, The Musical Times, 1957-63; The Yorkshire Post, 1963-73. Honour: Honorary DMus, University of Hull, 1997. Memberships: Chairman, Composers' Guild of Great Britain, 1972, Joint Chairman 1973; Executive Committee of Composers' Guild 1969-73, 1977-81, 1982-87; Council Member, Composers' Guild. Address: 76 Walkergate, Beverly, East Yorkshire, HU17 9ER, England.

HEDWALL Lennart, b. 16 Sept 1932, Gothenburg, Sweden. Composer; Conductor; Musicologist. m. Ingegerd Henrietta Bergman, 13 Apr 1957, 4 s. Education: Royal College of Music, Stockholm, 1951-59; Composing and Conducting at Darmstadt, Vienna, Hilversum and Paris. Debut: As composer, 1950; As professional conductor, Messiah, 1954. Career: Conductor: Riksteatern, 1958-60, Great Theatre Gothenburg, 1962-65, Drottningholmteatern, 1966-70, Royal Theatre, 1967-68, Örebro Orchestra Society, 1968-74; Teacher, Dramatic School in Gothenburg, 1963-67, State Opera School, 1968-70, 1974-80, 1985-97; Director of Swedish National Music Museum, 1981-83; Mermber of the Royal Swedish Academy of Music and the Accademia Filarmonica of Bologna. Compositions: 2 Operas: Herr Sleeman Kommer and America, America; Sagan, symphonic phantasy; Jul igen, a Christmas Rhapsody; Several works for String Orchestra; Concertos for Flute, Oboe, Violoncello; Chamber Music: 2 String Quartets and 2 String Trios and others; Organ and Piano works; Several Song Cycles; Choir pieces and cantatas; Stage and television works. Recordings: As conductor with Orebro Chamber Orchestra, Värmland Sinfonietta, Musica Vitae and Östersunds Serenade Ensemble; As accompanist, several song recitals; Also others as Organist and Pianist. Publications: Hugo Alfvén, monography, 1973; Operettas and Musicals, 1976; The Swedish Symphony, 1983; Wilhelm Peterson-Berger, a biography in pictures, 1983; The Concert Life in Åbo 1872-76, 1989; Hugo Alfvén, a biography in pictures, 1990; The Musical Life in the Manors of Vermland 1770-1830, 1992; Form Structures in Roman's Sinfonias, 1995; A Survey of The Music in Vermland, 1995; Swedish Music History, 1996. Contributions to: Dagen Nyheter, 1957-85; Musikrevy and others. Hobbies: Literature; Theatre. Address: Mårdvägen 37, 16756 Bromma, Sweden.

HEELEY Desmond, b. 1 June 1931, West Bromwich, England. Stage Designer. Education: Trained at the Shakespeare Memorial Theatre, Stratford, 1947-52. Debut: La Traviata for Sadler's Wells 1960. Career: Productions for Glyndebourne (I Puritani, 1960) and English National Opera (Maria Stuarda, 1973); Work for the Metropolitan Opera includes Norma 1970, Pelléas et Mélisande 1972, Don Pasquale 1978 and Manon Lescaut 1980; Chicago designs for La Traviata seen at Detroit and Seattle, 1996. Address: c/o Lyric Opera of Chicago, 20 North Wacker Drive, Chicago, IL 60606, USA.

HEENAN Ashley (David Joseph), b. 11 Sept 1925, Wellington, New Zealand. Composer; Conductor; Lecturer; Broadcaster. m. (1) Jean Margaret Ross, 30 Mar 1951, 2 sons, 2 daughters, (2) Maureen Elizabeth Roberts. Education: Diploma, Music, MusB, Victoria University of Wellington; Royal College of Music, London, England. Career: Musical Director, Schola Musica and New Zealand Symphony Orchestra, 1961-84; Musical Advisor, Orchestra Coordinator, QE II Arts Council, 1964; New Zealand Youth Orchestra, 1965-75; Musical Director, New Zealand Ballet Trust, 1966-68. Compositions: Film scores: Moana Roa; Rotorua Symphony; Jack Winter's Dream, radio drama; War and Peace, incidental music; Scottish Dances; A College Overture; Maori Suite; Cindy; Sea Songs; Orchestral works; Various vocal and instrumental works, arrangements and transcriptions of traditional Maori music. Recordings: Numerous with Schola Musica and New Zealand Symphony Orchestra. Publications: The New Zealand Symphony Orchestra, 1971; Schola Musica, 1974. Contributions to: Challenges in Music Education; Indiana Musicator; Journal of the Polynesian Society. Hobbies: Croquet; Private aviation; New Zealand history; Commemorative Collectables. Address: 11 Kiwi Street, Alicetown, Wellington, New Zealand.

HEGAARD Lars, b. 13 Mar 1950, Svendborg, Denmark. Composer. m. Susanne Taub, 10 Oct 1984, 4 sons. Education: High School, 1966-69; Diploma in Guitar, 1973; BA, Music, 1975; Examination of Teaching, 1977; Diploma in Composition, 1980. Career: Has played at all major festivals in Denmark and Scandinavia including on Radio; Has several commissions through The Danish Arts Foundation and 3 year Stipendium, 1983. Compositions include: Orchestra: Symphone No 1 and 2, Letter To My Son; Chamber Orchestra: Decet, Intersections; The Rolling Force, cello concerto; The Seasons According to I Ching; Chamber Works: Five Fragments for String Quartet: the Four Winds, clarinet, cello, piano; Music For Chameleons, wind quintet; Configurations, alto flute, guitar; Six Studies for Two Guitars, Song-lines, guitar trio; 13 short pieces for flute, viola, harp; Dreamtracks, flute, clarinet, horn, percussion, guitar, cello; Four Square Dances for Saxophone Quartet; partials' Play, flute, guitar, cello; Solo works: Variations, guitar; The Conditions of a Solitary Bird, guitar; Canto, cello; The Great Beam..., piano; Worldes Bliss, organ; Labyrinthus, electric guitar; Vocal: Hymns, baryton, sinfonietta; Haiku, soprano, violin, piano; Far Calls, Coming Far, mezzo soprano, electric guitar, percussion, Text: James Joyce; The Dimension of Stillness, soprano, flute, guitar, cello, Text: Ezra Pound; Orchestra: Symphony No 3; Chamber Orchestra: Twine for 9 instruments; Chamber works: Four visions for String Quartet; Invocations for Organ and 2 saxophones; Vocal: Night Flower; Four Poems by Sylvia Plath for mezzo-soprano, percussion, piano, viola, double-bass; Nogle Lykkelige Sekunder: 4 Poems by Poul Borum for organ and basso. Recordings include: The Great Beam of the Milky Way, piano. Contributions to: Interviews in Dansk Musiktidskrift. Current Management: Publishers: The Society for Publication of Danish Music, Gråbrodrestraede 18,1, 1156 Copenhagen, Denmark. Address: c/o Danish Composers' Society, Gråbrodre Torv 16, 1154 Copenhagen K, Denmark.

HEGARTY Mary, b. 1960, Cork, Eire. Singer (Soprano). Education: Studied at the Cork School of Music, at Aldeburgh and the National Opera Studio in London; Further study with Josephine Veasey. Career includes: Has sung for Radio Telefis Eireann in Britten's Quatres chansons Françaises and the Brahms Requiem; Bach's Christmas Oratorio with Harry Christophers; Recitals in Ireland, the USA and at the Aix-en-Provence Festival (Une Heure avec Mary Hegarty); Covent Garden debut as a Flowermaiden in Parsifal, followed by Pousette in Manon; English National Opera as Nannetta and Naiad (Ariadne); Appearances with Opera Factory in La Calisto; With Opera North as Leonora in the British premiere of Nielsen's Maskarade (1989) in Ariane et Barbe-Bleue, the Mozart pasticcio The Jewel Box (1991) and as Frasquita; Buxton Festival 1991, in Mozart's Il Sogno di Scipione; Requiem for RTE; Princess Laula in Chabrier's Etoile, (Opera North); Papagena in Magic Flute (ENO); Eurydice in Orpheus in The Underworld, (D'Oyly Carte); Adele in Die Fledermaus, (Dublin Grand Opera Society); Eurydice in Orpheus In the Underworld; Cherubino in The Marriage of Figaro, Elisa in Mozart's Il Re Pastore, The Italian Soprano in Strauss's Capriccio and Gloria in world premiere of Gloria-A Pigtale, Nerina in La Fedeltà Premiata, Tanterabogus in The Fairy Queen; 1996-97 with the English National Opera included Norina in Don Pasquale, Blonde in Die Entführung aus dem Serail and Elvira in L'Italiana in Algeri; Fiorilla in Il Turco In Italia for Garsington in 1996. Recordings: Debut solo album, A Voice is Calling; Title role in Gilbert and Sullivan's Patience; Eurydice in Offenbach's Orpheus in the Underworld; Mendelssohn Lobgesang with Naxos. Honours include: Winner, Golden Voice of Ireland, 1984; Bursary for study at Aldeburgh; Irish Life, Sunday Independent Classical Music Award, 1988; Allied Irish Bank, RTE Natioal Entertainments Award for Classical Section, 1987. Address: c/o Harold Holt, 31 Sinclair Road, London W14 0NS, England.

HEGEDUS Olga, b. 18 Oct 1920, London, England. Cellist. Education: London Violoncello School; Private Study, Pierre Fournier. Debut: Recital, Wigmore Hall, London. Career: Solo recitals; Many BBC and television appearances with trios, chamber ensembles and others; Member, Davey String Quartet. Recordings: Art of Fugue, Bach and Musical Offering, with Tilford Festival Ensemble; The Curlew, Warlock, with Haffner Ensemble; Vivaldi Motets with Teresa Berganza and English Chamber Orchestra; Dvorák Serenade, with English Chamber Orchestra Wind Ensemble; Schubert Quintet in C, with Gabrieli Quartet. Contributions to: A Pictorial Review, English Chamber Orchestra, 1983. Memberships: Incorporated Society of Musicians; Musicians Union. Hobbies: Reading; Art Galleries; Swimming. Address: 8 Kensington Place, London, W8 7PT, England.

HEGGEN Almar, b. 25 May 1933, Valldal, Norway. Bass Singer. Education: Studied at Oslo Conservatory, with Paul Lohmann in Wiesbaden and with Clemens Kaiser-Breme in Essen. Debut: Oslo, 1957, as Masetto, in Don Giovanni. Career: Sang in: Wuppertal, Berlin, Frieburg, Wiesbaden, Nuremburg, Munich; Guest performances in Sweden and Yugoslavia and others; Nuremburg 1969, in premiere of The Dream of Liu-Tung by Isang Yun; Roles include: Rocco, (also filmed), King Philip, Padre Guardiano, Sarastro, Don Alfonso, Tiresias, (in Oedipus Rex), Daland, Pogner, Fafner, Hagen, Baron Ochs, Ptolomeo, in Giulio Cesare; Wagner: Landgraf, King Henry, Marke, Hunding; Verdi: Zacharias, Ramphis; Mozart: Osmin; Rossini, Don Basilio; Smetana, Kezal; Many oratorios including: Creation and Seasons of Haydn, Verdi's Requiem, Mozart's Requiem; Teacher of singing. Memberships: Norsk Operasangerforbund, Norsk Musikerforening; Norsk Tonekunstnersamfunn, Kunsterforeningen. Address: Hareveien 40A, N-1413 Tårnasen, Norway.

HEICHELE Hildegard, b. Sept 1947, Obernburg am Main, Germany. Singer (Soprano). m. Ulrich Schwalb. Education: Studied at the Munich Musichochschule. Debut: Klagenfurt, as Jennie in Aufstieg und fall der Stadt Mahagonny. Career: Munich Staatsoper from 1971, notably as Mozart's Zerlina, Despina, Susanna and Ilia; Appearances in Vienna, Cologne (as Gretel), Karlsruhe (as Adina), Berlin, Zurich and Barcelona; Covent Garden 1977, 1983, as Adele in Die Fledermaus; Frankfurt 1981, in the Symphony of a Thousand, by Mahler; Monte Carlo 1982, Brussels 1984, as Susanna; Bayreuth Festival 1984, as the Woodbird in Siegfried; Sang at Kassel and Hanover 1988, as Elsa and Elisabeth; Concert engagements in Vienna, Graz and Venice (1985). Recordings include: Mahler's 8th Symphony; Egisto by Cavalli (Eurodisc); Bach Magnificat, Handel Dettinger Te Deum (Telefunken); Video of Die Fledermaus (Covent Garden 1983). Address: c/o Lies Askonas Ltd, 6 Henrietta Street, London WC2, England.

HEIDEN Bernhard, b. 24 Aug 1910, Frankfurt am Main, Germany. Composer; Pianist; Harpsichordist; Conductor; Professor Emeritus. Education: Training in piano, clarinet, violin, theory and harmony; Student of Paul Hinemith, Berlin Hochschule für Musik, 1929-33, of Donald Grout, AM, Cornell University, 1946. Career: Teacher, Detroit Art Center Music School; Conductor, Detroit Chamber Orchestra; Faculty member, Indiana University School of Music, Bloomington, 1946-81. Compositions include: Opera: The Darkened City, 1962; Incidental music for plays; Orchestral: 2 Symphonies, 1938 and 1954; Euphorion: Scene, 1949, Memorial, 1955, Philharmonic Fanfare, 1958, Envoy, 1963, Cello Concerto, 1967, Concerto for Strings, 1967, Horn Concerto, 1969, Tuba Concerto, 1976, Concerto for Trumpet and Winds, 1981, Fantasia Concertante for Alto Sax, Winds and Percussion, 1987, Recorder Concerto for Recorders and Chamber Orchestra, 1987, Salute for Orchestra, 1989, Bassoon Concerto for Bassoon and Chamber Orchestra, 1990, Preludes for Flute, Bass and Harp, 1988; Chamber: Sonata for Alto Saxaphone and Piano, 1937, 2 String Quartets, 1947, 1951, Quintet for Horn and String Quartet, 1952, Quintet for Clarinet and

Strings, 1955, Sonata for Cello and Piano, 1958, Woodwind Quintet, 1965, Quintet for Flute, Violin, Viola, Bassoon and Contrabass, 1975, Quartet for Horns, 1981; Piano Music, Choral works, Songs; Voyage for Symphonic Wind Ensemble, 1991; Trio for oboe, Bassoon and Piano, 1992; Divertimento for Tuba and 8 Solo Instruments, 1992; Serenata for 4 Celli, 1993. Recording: Trio for Oboe, Bassoon and Piano, 1992. Honours: Mendelssohn Prize, 1933; Guggenheim, 1966. Address: c/o School of Music, Indiana University, Bloomington, IN 47405, USA.

HEIFETZ Daniel (Alan), b. 20 Nov 1948, Kansas City, Missouri, USA. Violinist; Teacher. Education: Pupil of Theodore Norman; Studied with Sascha Jacobson, Israel Baker, and Heimann Weinstine, Los Angeles Conservatory, 1962-65, and with Efrem Zimbalist, Ivan Galamian, and Jascha Brodsky, Curtis Institute of Music, Philadelphia, 1966-71. Career: Debut as soloist in the Tchaikovsky Violin Concerto with the National Symphony Orchestra of Washington DC, on tour in New York; Thereafter regular tours of North America and the world; Appointed to the faculty of the Peabody Conservatory of Music, Baltimore, 1980. Recordings: For Leonarda. Honours: 1st prize, Merriweather-Post Competition, Washington DC, 1969; 4th prize, Tchaikovsky Competition, Moscow, 1978. Address: c/o Shaw Concerts Inc, ASCAP Building, 1900 Broadway, New York, NY 10023, USA.

HEIFETZ Robin (Julian), b. 1 Aug 1951, Los Angeles, California, USA. Composer. Education: Studied at UCLA with Paul Chihara and Roy Travis; University of Illinois with Salvatore Martirano and Ben Johnston, DMA 1978. Career: Composer-in-residence at Shiftelsen Electronic Studio, Stockholm, 1978-79; Worked at various music departments in Canada and the USA; Director of the Centre for Experimental Music at the Hebrew University of Jerusalem, 1980. Honours: Awards at the Concours International de Musique Electro-Acoustique, Bouges, France, 1979, 1981; International Computer Music Competition at Boston, 1983. Compositions include: 2 Pieces for Piano 1972; Leviathan for piano 1975; Chirp for euphonium and piano 1976; Susurrus for computer and tape 1978; Child of the Water for piano 1978; For Anders Lundberg Mardrom 29 30 10 for tape 1979; A Clear and Present Danger for tape 1980; Spectre for tape 1980; Wanderer for synthesizer 1980; The Unforgiving Minute for 9 instruments 1981; In the Last, Frightened Moment for tape 1980; The Vengeance for Synthesizer 1980; The Arc of Crisis for tape 1982; A Bird in Hand is Safer than one Overheard for 2 or more performers 1983; At Daggers Drawn for tape 1983. Address: c/o ASCAP, ASCAP Building, One Lincoln Plaza, New York, NY 10023, USA.

HEILGENDORFF Simone, b. 4 Apr 1961, Opladen, West Germany. Violist; Musicologist. Education: Graduated. Final Artistic Examination in Viola Performance, Staatliche Hochschule fuer Musik im Rheinland, Cologne, Germany, 1987; Magister Artium in Musicology, Albert-Ludwigs-University in Freiburg, Germany, 1989; Master of Music in Viola Performance, University of Michigan, 1991. Career: Member of symphonic orchestras: Junge Deutsche Philharmonie 1985-87, German training orchestra; Sinfonietta Basel, Philharmonische Werkstatt Switzerland, Serenata Basel (chamber orchestra) and the Freiburger Bachorchester; Conductors; Gerd Albrecht, Rudolf Barschai, David Shallon, Mario Venzago, Laurence Foster; Performances: Contemporary Music: Ensemble Modern (ISCM-Ens), Aventure Freiburg, Contemporary Ensemble (Aspen Music Festival 1991); Opera: Opera Factory Zurich 1990 with Figaros Hochzeit; Early Music: Akademie für AlteMusik Berlin, Concerto Köln; Tours of Germany, France, Italy, Poland, Spain and the United States; Management and performance of her own concert programmes; Currently on Faculty, Hochschule für Musik Hanns Eisler Berlin; Member of chamber ensemble Canzonetta Berlin and the Contemporary Music Ensemble. Publications: Various musicological publications; Glossolalie von Dieter Schnebel - Anmerkungen zur Konstruktion in Schnebel 60 edited by W Gruenzweig, G Schroeder und M Supper. Recordings: Numerous CD productions. Address: Reusratherstrasse 26, 5090 Leverkusen 3, Germany.

HEILMANN Uwe, b. 7 Sept 1960, Darmstadt, German. Singer (Tenor). m. Tomoko Nakamura. Education: Studied in Detmold with Helmut Kretschmar. Career: Sang at Detmold from 1981 as Tamino, Don Ottavio and the Italian Singer in Rosenkavalier; Stuttgart Staatsoper from 1985, notably as Tamino, Belmonte, Don Ottavio, Cassio in Otello and Max in Der Freischütz; Munich Staatsoper as Don Ottavio, Vienna as Tamino; Sang Pylades in Iphigénie en Tauride at the Deutsche Oper Berlin; Appearances at the Salzburg and Ludwigsburg Festivals, 1988-89, including Max; Concert engagements and Lieder recitals, notably in works by Schubert and Wolf; Sang Cassio in Metropolitan Opera Gala, 1991. Recordings include: Tamino in Die Zauberflöte, conducted by Solti; Belmonte in Die Entführung conducted by Hogwood; Die schöne Mullerin, with James Levine; Haydn's Orfeo ed Euridice, with Cecilia Bartoli (L'Oiseau Lyre, 1997). Address: Harold Holt Ltd, 31 Sinclair Road, London W1A 0NS, England.

HEININEN Paavo, b. 18 Jan 1938, Järvenpää, Finland. Composer. Education: Studied Theory and Composition, Sibelius Academy, Helsinki, Finland, College of Music, Cologne, Germany and at Juilliard School of Music, NY, USA, 1956-62; Training as Pianist, Conductor and Musicologist. Career: Teacher of Theory and Composition, Turku Institute of Music, Turku, Finland, and at Sibelius Academy, Helsinki, 1966-. Compositions include: Orchestral Works: Symphony No 1, 1958, revised 1960, Piano Sonata, Symphony No 3, 1969, revised 1977, Dia, 1979; Works for Solo Instrument and Orchestra: Concerto for Piano and Orchestra No 3, 1981; Chamber Music: Jeu I and II, 1980; Works for Solo Instrument: Gymel for Bassoon and Tape, 1978; Vocal and Choral Works: The Silken Drum, opera, 1980-83, Floral View with Maidens Singing, folk melody, 1980-83, Dicta, computer music, 1980-83. Recordings include: Adagio with Royal Philharmonic Orchestra under Walter Süsskind; Da Camera Magna; Sonatine, 1957; Sonatina Della Primavera; The Autumns, Finnish Radio Chamber Choir under Harald Andersén; Maiandros, tape composition; Discantus I; Touching; Concerto III with Paavo Heininen on Piano, the Sibelius Symphony Orchestra under Ulf Söderblom. Address: TEOSTO, Lauttassarentie 1, 00200 Helsinki 20, Finland.

HEINIÖ Mikko, b. 18 May 1948, Tampere, Finland. Composer; Professor of Musicology. m. Riitta Pylvänäinen, 2 Apr 1977, 1 son, 1 daughter. Education: MA, 1972, PhD, 1984, University of Helsinki; Hochschule der Kunste, West Berlin, 1975-77; Diploma in Composition, Sibelius Academy. Career: Composer, 1972-; Teacher, University of Helsinki, 1977-85; Professor, Musicology, University of Turku, 1985-. Compositions include: Orchestral: 6 piano concertos; Concerto for French horn and orchestra; Concerto for Orchestra; Possible Worlds, Sumphony No 1; Dall'ombra all'ombra Trias; Symphony No 2 (Songs of Night and Love); Chamber music: Duo for Violin and Piano; Brass Mass; Piano Trio; In G, violoncello and piano; Wintertime, harp and marimba/vibraphone; Piano Quintet; Vocal: Landet som icke är, children's choir and piano; Vuelo de alambre, soprano and orchestra; The Shadow of the Future, soprano and brass instruments; La, piano and 4 voices; Wind Pictures, choir and orchestra; Hermes, piano, soprano, string orchestra and dance theatre, 1994. Recordings include: Notturno di fiordo for flute and harp; Champignons à l'hermeneutique; Genom kvällen; Vuelo de alambre; Possible Worlds; Wind Pictures; Duo for Violin and Piano; Piano Quintet; Hermes piano trio; In G. Publications: Contemporary Finnish Composers and their background, 1981; Contemporary Finnish Music, 1982; The Idea of Innovation and Tradition, 1984; The Reception of New Classicism in Finnish Music, 1985; The Twelve Tone Age in Finnish Music, 1986; Postmodern Features in New Finnish Music, 1988; Contextualisation in the research of art music, 1992; Finnish Composers (co-author), 1994; Finnish Music History 4: Music of Our Time, 1995. Memberships: Preisdnet, Finnish Composers' Society, 1992-; Board Member, Copyright Organisation TEOSTO, 1984-. Address: University of Turku, Department of Musicology, 20500 Turku 50, Finland.

HEINRICH Adel (Verna), b. 20 July 1926, Cleveland, Ohio, USA. Professor of Music Emeritus. Education: BA, Magna Cum Laude, Flora Stone Mather College, Case Western Reserve University, Cleveland, Ohio; MSM, Union Theological Seminary, New York City; A Mus D, The University of Wisconsin-Madison; Studied organ with Hugh Porter and John Harvey, and in master classes with E Power Biggs, André Marchal and Jean Langlais; Studied conducting with Robert Shaw and Robert Fountain. Career: Held several full-time Church positions before 1964; Assistant Orchestra Conductor of the Colby Community Symphony Orchestra, preparing and conducting several concerts, 1964-74; Served on the Faculty each summer of the Colby Church Music Institute, 1964-87; Full-time Faculty Member, Colby College, Waterville, Maine, 1964-88; Numerous recitals or lecture/recitals. Compositions: Over 55 Works include Carol Dramas, Choric-Dances, Choral Works on American Poet Texts, Solo Works for Instruments or Voice, Chamber Ensembles, an Oratorio, Chamber Dance-Drama, and Nature Portraits. Publications: Bach's Die Kunst der Fuge: A Living Compendium of Fugal Procedures, Washington DC, 1982; Organ and Harpsichord Music by Women Composers, Westport, Connecticut, 1991. Contributions to: Articles, A Collation of the Expositions in Die Kunst der Fuge of J S Bach, Significance of the Original Subject and Its Variants in Bach's Die Kunst der Fuge, Heretofore Unpublished Conclusions for the Incomplete Quadruple Fugue (Die Kunst Der Fuge), includes her own original conclusion. Hobbies: Oil Painting; Writing Poetry. Address: Hemlock Hills, 14903 Hook Hollow Road, Russell, OH 44072, USA.

HEINRICH Siegfried, b. 10 Jan 1935, Dresden, Germany. Conductor; Künstlerischer Direktor für Oper und Festspielkonzerte Bad Hersfeld. Education: Studied in Dresden and Frankfurt-on-Main, 1954-61. Debut: Sänger im Dresdner Kreuzchor, 1948. Career: Conductor, Frankfurt Chamber Orchestra, 1957; Since 1961, Artistic Director, Hersfeld Festival Operas and Concerts; Lecturer, Music Academy of Kassel; Conductor, Radio Symphony Orchestras, Prague, Frankfurt-on-Main, Hanover, Luxemburg, ORTF, France, Budapest, Warsaw, Katowice, Krakow, Venice, Stuttgart; Concert Tours throughout Europe; New Interpretations of Bach's The Art of the Fugue, Beethoven's opera Fidelio with parts of Leonore I, Handel's Messiah, Monteverdi's Marian Vespers, Orfeo, Poppea, Il ritorno d'Ulisse. Recordings: Bach, Beethoven, Bizet, Brahms, Britten, Bruckner, Carissimi, Dvorak, Honegger, Liszt, Mahler, Mozart, Monteverdi, Ockeghem, Spohr, Telemann, Weber. Publications: Prospectusses and press reviews from Jubilate Schallplatten; Bärenreiter, Koch International. Honours: Bundesverdienstmedaille, 1976; Goethe-Medaille, 1983; Bundesverdienstkreuz, 1988. Current Management: Rainer Zagovec, Rathausstr 42, 65428 Rüsselsheim. Address: Sekretariat Nachtigallenstr 7, D-36251 Bad Hersfeld, Germany.

HEISINGER Harold (Brent), b. 27 Jan 1937, Stockton, California, USA. Professor of Music. m. Barbara Anne Dale, 15 June 1958, 3 sons. Education: BA 1958, MA 1962, Music, San Jose State University; DMA, Stanford University, 1968; Student of Stanley, Hollingsworth, Leland Smith, Leonard Ratner and Humphrey Searle. Career: Public School Music Teacher, 1958-62; Professor of Music, San Jose State University, 1962-; Composer-in-Residence, Montalvo Centre for the Arts, 1982-84; Planner - Writer, Hawaii Curriculum and Research Group, 1970-72; Pianist/Trombonist, Hawaii New Music Ensemble, 1971-72; Project Director, SJSU Programmes, Contemporary Music Project, 1969-70. Compositions: Minim for piano, 1985; Concerto for Piano, Winds and Percussion, 1984; Fanfare and Prayer for band, 1981; Fantasy on a B Flat Blues for piano, 1979; Ekelktikos in Five Pieces, piano, 1973; Statement, band, 1971; A Cycle of Thoughts, sopranoa and piano, 1971; Hymn for Band, 1970; Soliloquy for Band, 1968; O Praise the Lord, choir and brass, 1967; Fantasia for Band, 1966; Essay for Band, 1965; March for Timpani and Brass, 1964. Recordings: Eklektikos, In Five Pieces, CRS Aiko Onishi piano; Essay for Band, Vorstelijke Melodieen, Basart Records; March for Timpani and Brass, Pembroke Records Inc. Publications: Comprehensive Musicianship through Band Performance, Zone 5 Book A, 1972, Zone 4 Book A, 1973, Zone 4 Book B, 1976. Contributions to: Living Music, 1987; Music Educators' Journal, 1965. Address: 1315 Avalon Drive, San Jose, CA 95125, USA.

HELD Alan, b. 1962, Washburn, USA. Singer (Bass-baritone). Education: Studied at Millikin and Wichita State Universities. Career: Appearances with the Met Opera New York, in Billy Budd, Boris Godunov, Rigoletto, Tannhäuser and Tosca, from 1989; European debut at the Spoleto Festival, as the Villains in Les Contes d'Hoffman, 1989; Frankfurt Opera, as Siskov in From the House of the Dead, the Rheingold Wotan and Leporello, from 1993; Royal Opera Covent Garden, as Gunther in Götterdämmerung, Borromeo in Palestrina and Orestes in Elektra, from 1996; Season 1997-98 with San Francisco Opera as Orestes and in Wagner's Ring, Gunther at Munich and Kurwenal for Chicago Lyric Opera; Further appearances with Washington Opera (ten roles), Seattle Opera and the Théâtre de la Monnaie, Brussels. Honours include: Richard Tucker Music Foundation Career Grants; Winner Birgit Nilsson Competition. Address: Lies Askonas Ltd, 6 Henrietta St, London WC2E 8LA, England.

HELESFAY Andrea, b. 18 Nov 1948, Budapest, Hungary. Violinist. Education: Bela Bartók Conservatoire, 1968-73; Franz Liszt University of Music; Study with Vilmos Tatrai, Andras Mihaly. Debut: Aged 11, Budapest. Career: Member, Hungarian Chamber Orchestra, Budapest Chamber Ensemble, often as Soloist; Zurich Chamber Orchestra, Tonhalle Orchestra, Zurich, 1973-; Many appearances as soloist in Germany, Switzerland; frequent appearances on Radio & TV; Founder, Trio Turicum. Honours: Award Winner, International Mozart Violin Competition, Salzburg. Memberships: various professional organisations. Hobbies: Hiking; Travel; Cooking; Photography; Children. Address: Hadlaubstrasse 148, CH 8006 Zurich, Switzerland.

HELEY John, b. 1950, England. Cellist. Education: Studied at the Guildhall School of Music. Career: Sub-Principal Cellist of the Royal Philharmonic Orchestra, 1970-80; Freelance career from 1981 with chamber recitals and orchestral work with the Academy of Ancient Music, London Sinfonietta and other ensembles; Associate Principal Cellist of the Academy of St Martin-in-the-Fields from 1986 including solo appearances; Member of the Instrumental Quintet of London, with repertoire including works by Jongen, Villa-Lobos, Debussy and Mozart. Address: Upbeat Management, Sutton Business Centre, Restmor Way, Wallington, Surrey, SM6 7AH, England.

HELFFER Claude, b. 18 June 1922, Paris, France. Pianist. m. Mireille de Nervo, 3 June 1946, 2 sons, 2 daughters. Education: Ecole Polytechnique, 1942. Career: Numerous recital tours and concert tours with orchestra, Europe, USA, North and South America, Australia, Japan. Recordings: Various including music by Boulez, Xenakis, Debussy and Schoenberg. Honours: Chevaler de la Legion d'Honneur; Croix de guerre, 1939-45; Officier des arts et lettres; Numerous prizes for records including

President of the Republic's Prizes for record of contemporary music, 1986, 1993. Hobby: Religious problems. Address: 6 rue Mignet, 75016 Paris, France.

HELFRICH Paul M, b. 5 May 1955, Philadelphia, USA. Composer. Education: BMus, Pennsylvania State University, 1978; MMus, Composition, Temple University, 1980; DMA, Composition, Temple University, 1986, studied with Clifford Taylor and Maurice Wright. Career includes: Owner, Nu Trax Recording Studio, Upper Darby, PA, 1981-; Senior Project Manager, 1987-91, Assistant Director, Exhibit Development, 1991-, Franklin Institute Science Museum, PA. Compositions include: Sine Nomine for brass chorale, 1974; Metamorphosis 1 for string orchestra, 1976; Theme and Five Variations for string orchestra and percussion, 1977; Five Short pieces for piano, 1977; Sonata Allegro in G for symphonic wind ensemble, 1978; Winds from a longer Distance, for tape and seven dancers, 1989; Song for healing, tape and solo dancer, 1990; The Robot Game Show, for tape, 1990; Movie soundtracks: Spirits in the Valley II, 1991, The Alchemist's Cookbook, 1991. Address: 130 Cunningham Avenue, Upper Darby, PA 19082, USA.

HELIN Jacquelyn, b. 24 Sept 1951, Chicago, Illinois, USA. Concert Pianist. Education: BM, University of Oregon, 1973; Graduate Studies, Yale University School of Music, 1973-74; MA, Stanford University, 1976; DMA, University of Texas, 1982. Career: Performances at Wigmore Hall, London, The Chagall Museum, Nice, American Embassy, Paris, Merkin Hall and Town Hall, New York, Dumbarton, Oaks, The Corcoran Gallery, Hirshhorn Museum, Washington DC and The Brooklyn College Conservatory of Music; The Dame Myra Hess Series; The Beethoven Discovery Series, The Aspen Music Festival; Featured Artist, PBS TV programme honouring Virgil Thomson's 90th birthday; Premiered Joan Tower's Piano Concerto with Hudson Valley Philharmonic, 1986; Numerous radio appearances; WFMT Chicago, WNCN New York, WGMS Washington and throughout USA on National Public Radio. Recordings: For Musical Heritage, Virgil Thomson Ballet and Film Scores for Piano.

HELLAWELL Piers, b. 14 July 1956, Chinley, Derbyshire, England. Composer; University Lecturer. Education: New College, Oxford, 1975-78; BA (Hons 1st Class), 1978; MA, 1984. Career: Composer-in-Residence, 1981-85, Lecturer in Music, 1986-, Queens University of Belfast; Northern Ireland Coordinator, European Music Year, 1985; Regular broadcasts, BBC, Radio 3. Compositions: Xenophon, commissioned, performed Belfast, elsewhere, Radio 3, by Ulster Orchestra, 1985; How Should I Your True Love Know, 1st performed by The Fires of London, Elizabeth Hall, Peter Maxwell Davies conducting, 1986; Sound Carvings From Rano Raraku, commission (ACNI), 1st performed Northern Ireland tour and BBC, Martin Feinstein Quartet, 1988; Das Leonora Notenbuch, commissioned North West Arts, 1st performed Buxton Festival by William Howard, 1989, 1st broadcast BBC Radio 3, 1990; The Erratic Aviator's Dance, commissioned, performed at the Dance Place, Washington DC and elsewhere by Alvin Mayes Dance and Collaborations Ensemble, 1989; Memorial Cairns, commission, premiere, Ulster Orchestra, 1992, BBC Radio 3, 1993; River and Shadow, commission, premiere, Hilliard Ensemble, Antwerp, 1993, CBC Radio Canada, 1994; Victory Boogie-Woogie, commission, premiere, Riga Piano Duo, Riga, 1993; High Citadels, commission, premiere, Jorg Vögel, Meerbusch Kunst Expo (Germany), 1994; Truth or Consequences, BBC broadcast, 1994; Camera Obscura, commission, premiere, Philip Mead, Rainbow Over Bath, 1994; Sound Carvings from the Ice Wall, BBC commission, premiered by Psappha, Manchester, 1995, BBC, 1995; Takla Makan, commission, premiere, Evelyn Glennie at Cheltenham Festival, 1995, BBC, 1995. Current Management: Maecenas Music, London. Address: Department of Music, Queens University of Belfast, Belfast BT7 1NN, Northern Ireland.

HELLEKANT Charlotte, b. 15 January 1962, Hogalid, Sweden. Singer (Mezzo-soprano). Education: Eastman School of Music, with Jean DeGaetani, and Curtis Institute. Career: Opera engagements include Cherubino for Portland and Washington Operas, Dorabella for the Canadian Opera Company, Charlotte and the Composer in Ariadne for Glimmerglass Opera and Musetta in Leoncavallo's Bohème at St Louis; Season 1995-96 as Bartók's Judith with the Orchestre de Paris, Charlotte at Washington, the Page in Salome for the Metropolitan Opera (debut role) and Ino in Semele at Aix-en-Provence; Contemporary roles include Lotte in Böse's Werther at Santa Fe, Erika in Barber's Vanessa, Cherubino in Corigliano's Chosts of Versailles, at Chicago, the leading role in Bergman's The Singing Tree, for Finnish National Opera and Nastassja in Krasa's Verlobung in Traum; Concerts include Marguerite in La Damnation de Faust (Stockholm PO), Mahler's 2nd Symphony (San Francisco SO), Les Nuits d'Eté (Cleveland) Mahler's Rückert Lieder and Das Lied von der Erde (Netherlands Radio PO); Berlioz L'Enfance du Christ with John Nelson and Mozart's Requiem under Neeme Järvi; Berio's Epiphanies with the composer conducting, Des Knaben Wunderhorn with the Swedish Radio SO and Le Martyre de Saint Cherubino at the Opéra Bastille, Salzburg debut as Amando in

Ligeti's Le Grand Macabre, and Charlotte for New Israeli Opera. Recordings include: Krasa's Verlobung in Traum (Decca); Mahler's 2nd Symphony (Decca); Ligeti's Le Grand Macabre (Sony). Address: IMG Artists, Media House, 3 Burlington Lane, London W4 2TH, England.

HELLER Alfred, b. 8 Dec 1931, New York City, USA. Composer; Conductor; Pianist. m. 1) Alice Ewing Jones, 31 Mar 1965, 1 son, 2) Karen S Cottrell, 28 Nov 1981. Education: High School of Music and Art, New York City, 1949; BM, Composition, Syracuse University, 1952; MM, Piano, Manhattan School of Music, 1954; Fulbright Scholar, Italy, Opera Conducting, 1954-55; DMus, Instrumental Conducting, Indiana University, 1974. Debut: Opera, La Vacanze Musicali, Venice, 1955; Symphony, Adzerbaijan, USSR, 1971; Composer, High School of M & A, 1949. Career: Protege of Heitor Villa-Lobos, 1956-59; Assistant Conductor, Chicago Lyric Opera, New York City Opera, 1958-63; Coach/Accompanist for Frank Guarrera, Jan Peerce, Giuseppe di Stefano, John Brownlee, 1954-80; Guest Conductor: Hungarian State Symphony, Adzerbaijan State Symphony, Georgian State Symphony, Brasov Philharmonic, Tatar State Symphony, Latvian Radio and Television Symphony, Baton Rouge Symphony. Compositions: Compositions performed in West Germany, Austria, Mexico, USSR, UK and USA; Songs on Emily Dickinson Poems sung by Arleen Auger. Recordings include: Villa-Lobos Violin Sonatas and Piano Suites, KTC 1101; Villa-Lobos Piano Works, KTC 1123; Villa-Lobos Vocal Music, Vol II, 1994. Address: 153 East 92nd Street, 4R, New York, NY 10128-2479, USA.

HELLER Barbara, b. 6 Nov 1936, Ludwigshafen, Germany. Composer; Pianist. Education: Studied at the Mannheim and Munich Hochschule and at Chigiana and Darmstadt. Career: Has worked with women artists and created sound-installations, influenced by the environment. Compositions include: Solovioline, 1982; Eins Für Zwei for Violin and Cello, 1985; Bohmisches Lied for Piano, 1989; Auf der Suche Nach dem Frühling for Flute, 1993. Address: c/o Postfach 80 07 67, D-81607 München, Germany.

HELLER Jack (Joseph), b. 30 Nov 1932, New Orleans, LA, USA. College Professor; Conductor. m. Judith A Krawetz, 9 Jun 1957, 2 s, 1 d. Education: Diploma, Violin, Juilliard School of Music, 1952; MMus, University of MI, 1958; PhD, University of IA, 1962. Debut: Violin Soloist, New Orleans Symphony, 1947. Career: Assistant Concert Master, New Orleans Opera, 1947-49; Freelance Violinist, NYC, Radio, TV, Chamber Groups, 1950-55; Concertmaster, Toledo Symphony, 1955-58; Professor, University of CT, 1960-85; Conductor and Music Director, Manchester (CT) Symphony and Chorale, 1968-85; Founder and Conductor, Nutmeg Chamber Orchestra, 1984-; Conductor and Music Director, Tampa Bay Symphony, 1986-; Conductor and Music Director, Spanish Lyric Theatre, 1992-; Professor, 1985-, and Director, 1985-95, Music School, University of South Florida, Tampa, 1985-. Contributions to: Numerous on research in the psychology of music in professional journals, 1968-. Address: Music School, FAH 110, University of South Florida, Tampa, FL 33620, USA.

HELLER Richard (Rainer), b. 19 Apr 1954, Vienna, Austria. Composer. m. Shihomi Inoue, 26 Aug 1980. Education: Diploma in Composition, 1979; Final Examination in Composition for Audio-Visual Media, 1978, Final Examination for Cultural Management, 1979, Hochschule für Musik und Darstellende Kunst, Vienna. Career: Numerous performances of own works in Argentina, Austria, Belgium, Bulgaria, Czechoslovakia, Denmark, Egypt, France, Germany, Greece, Hungary, Italy, Japan, Kazakhstan, Netherlands, Rumania, Russia, Switzerland, Spain, Saudi Arabia, South Africa, Turkey, Uruguay, Yugoslavia; Teaching Composition and Music Theory, Music Academy, Augsburg, Germany, 1979-. Compositions include: Concerto for violin; Concerto for 2 pianos and orchestra; Sinfonietta for wind orchestra; Concerto for bass clarinet; Concerto for marimba; Concertino for orchestra; Concerto per fiati; Toccata for wind orchestra; Novelette, piano trio; 3 moments musicaux, guitar quartet; string quartet; Cellophonie, 8 violoncellos; Statement, string trio; Elegy on texts out of Duineser Elegien by R M Rilke; Ballade, piano 4 hands; Various pieces for chamber ensembles; Songs; Solo pieces for piano, organ, bass clarinet; Numerous commissions. Recordings: LP, Augsburger Gitarrenquartett; CD, organ-piano; MC, live documentations; Numerous radio recordings. Address: Reichenberger Strasse 24, D-86161 Augsburg, Germany.

HELLERMANN William, b. 15 July 1939, Wisconsin, USA. Composer. m. 17 Sept 1985, 1 son, 1 daughter. Education: MA Composition, 1969, DMA, 1976, Columbia University School of Arts; Private Study with Stefan Wolpe. Compositions: Time and Again, for orchestra, 1967; Anyway..., for orchestra, 1976; But the Moon..., for guitar and orchestra, 1975; Tremble, for solo guitar; Squebek for desk chair, 1978; Post/Pone for guitar and 5 instruments, 1990; Hoist by Your Own Ritard, 1993. Recordings: Ariel, for electronic tape, 1967; At Sea; Ek-Stasis I; Passages 13-The Fire. Publications: Articles published; Beyond Categories,

1981; Experimental Music, 1985; Scores: Tip of the Iceberg, Time and Again for symphony orchestra; Long Island Sound; Distances/Embraces; Circle Music 2 and 3; Passages 13 - The Fire; To the Last Drop; Ek-Stasis I. Honours: Prix de Rome, American Academy, 1972; NEA Fellowship, 1976-79; Composer in Residence, Center for Culture and Performing Arts, State University of New York at Buffalo. Memberships: BMI; ACA. Address: Box 850, Philmont, NY 12565, USA.

HELLMAN Claudia, b. 1931, Berlin, Germany. Singer (Mezzo-soprano). Education: Studied in Berlin. Debut: Oper, Munster, 1958-60. Career: Stuttgart Staatsoper, 1960-66, Nuremberg, 1966-75; Appearances at Bayreuth Festival, 1958-61, as Wellgunde and a Flower Maiden; La Scala Milan, 1963, as Flosshilde; Sang in concerta at the Salzburg Festival, 1961-85; Hamburg Staatsoper from 1960, Théâtre de la Monnaie Brussels, 1963-67; Other roles have included Marcellina, Magdalena in Die Meistersinger, Mistress Quickly, Fidalma in Matrimonio Segreto and Frau von Hufnagel in Henze's Der Junge Lord; Many concert and oratorio appearances. Recordings: Ismene in Orff's Antigonae, Bruckner's F minor Mass; Die Walküre; Bach's Easter Oratorio; Bach Church Cantatas. Address: c/o Stuttgart Staatsoper, Ober Schlossgaten 6, 7000 Stuttgart, Germany.

HELLWIG Klaus, b. 3 Aug 1941, Essen, Germany. Pianist; Educator. m. Mi-Joo Lee. Education: Folkwang Hochschule Essen with Detlek Kraus, in Paris with Pierre Sancan; Summer Courses with Guido Agosti and Wilhelm Kempff. Career: Concerts throughout Europe, USA and Canada, Far and Middle East, all German radio stations, BBC London, NHK Tokyo; Professor, Hochschule der Künste, Berlin. Recordings: FX Mozart Concerti in C and E Flat, Cologne Radio Orchestra, conductor Roland Bader (Schwann); Haydn Concerto in D, Mozart Concerto KV 537; Bach Inventions (RSM); Recordings of 20 other records; Carl Reinecke: The Four Piano Concerti, (CPO). Honours: Prize at the Concours Internationale M Long-J Thibaud, Paris, 1965; First Prize, Concorso Internazionale G B Viotti, Vercelli, Italy, 1966. Current Management: Raymond Weiss Artist Management, New York. Address: Regensburgerstrasse 27, 10777 Berlin, Germany.

HELM E(rnest) Eugene, b. 23 Jan 1928, New Orleans, Louisiana, USA. Musicologist; Professor. Education: Southeastern Louisiana College, BME, 1950; Louisiana State University, MME, 1955; North Texas State University, PhD, 1958. Career: Faculty Member, Louisiana College 1953-55, Wayne (Neb) State College 1958-59, University of Iowa 1960-68; Associate Professor 1968-69, Professor 1969-, of Music, Chairman, Musicology Division 1971-87, University of Maryland; Coordinating Editor, Carl Philipp Emanuel Bach Edition, 1982-. Publications: Music at the Court of Frederick the Great, 1960; With A Luper, Words and Music, 1971, 2nd edition 1982; A Thematic Catalogue of the Works of Carl Philipp Emanuel Bach, 1987. Contributions to: Articles in numerous periodicals and other publications. Address: c/o Department of Music, University of Maryland, College Park, MD 20742, USA.

HELM Everett (Burton), b. 17 July 1913, Minneapolis, Minnesota, USA. Composer; Writer on Music. Education: Studied at Harvard University, PhD 1939; Studies in Europe with Malipiero and Vaughan Williams. Career: Head of music department of Western College, Oxford, Ohio, 1944-46; Music Oficer with the US Military in Germany 1948-50; Resident in Asolo, near Venice, from 1963; Guest lecturer at the University of Ljubljana, 1966-68; Editor, Musical America, New York, 1961-63; Compositions have been performed by the New York Philharmonic, Berlin Philharmonic and BBC Symphony Orchestras. Publications: The Beginnings of the Italian Madrigal and the Works of Arcadelt, 1939; The Chansons of Arcadelt, 1942; Bela Bartók in Selbsteugnissen und Bilddokumenten Hamburg, 1965; Composer, Performer, Public, Florence, 1970; Bartók, London, 1971; Franz Liszt, Hamburg, 1971; Music and Tomorrow's Public, Wilmeshaven, 1981. Compositions include: Two Piano Concertos, 1951, 1956; Adam and Eve, adaptation of a medieval mystery play, 1951; Concerto for 5 instruments, percussion and strings, 1953; The Siege of Tottenburg, radio opera, 1956; Le Roy fait battre tambour, ballet, 1956; 500 Dragon-Thalers, singspiel 1956; Divertimento for flutes, 1957; Sinfonia d Camera, 1961; Concerto for double bass and string orchestra, 1968; 2 String Quartets; Woodwind Quintet, 1967; Songs and piano music. Address: c/o ASCAP, ASCAP Building, One Lincon Plaza, New York, NY 10023, USA.

HELM Hans, b. 12 Apr 1934, Passau, Germany. Singer (Baritone). Education: Studied with Else Zeidler and Franz Reuter-Wolf in Munich, Emmi Muller in Krefeld. Debut: Graz 1957, in Boris Godunov. Career: Sang in Vienna, Cologne, Frankfurt, Munich, Dusseldorf and Hanover; Salzburg Festival 1973, in the premiere of De Temporum fine Comoedia by Orff; Glyndebourne Festival 1976, as the Count in Le nozze di Figaro; Vienna Staatsoper, 1987 and 1990, as Agamemnon in Iphigénie en Aulide, and in Die Soldaten; Munich 1989, as Faninal in Der Rosenkavalier; Sang The Forester in The Cunning Little Vixen at the Vienna Volksoper, 1992; Many concert appearances.

Recordings: Otello (EMI); De Temporum fie Comoedia and Die Frau ohne Schatten (Deutsche Grammophon). Address: c/o Staatsoper, Opernring 2, A-1010 Vienna, Austria.

HELM Karl, b. 3 Oct 1938, Passau, Germany. Singer (Bass). Education: Studied with Else Zeidler in Dresden and with Franz Reuter-Wolf in Munich. Debut: Berne 1968, as Don Alfonso in Così fan tutte. Career: Member of the Bayersiche Staatsoper, Munich; Guest appearances in Geneva, Paris, Dusseldorf, Hamburg and Stuttgart; Other roles include Arkel in Pelléas et Mélisande, Rocco, King Philip, Zaccaria, Varlaam, Fasolt, Falstaff in Die Lustigen Weiber von Windsor, Dulcamara, and Melitone in La Forza del Destino; Berlin Staatsoper 1987, in La Cenerentola; Munich 1990, as First Nazarene in Salome; Sang Swallow in Peter Grimes at Munich, 1991; Many concert appearances. Recordings include: Die Feen by Wagner. Address: Bayerische Staatsoper, Postfach 745, D-8000 Munich 1, Germany.

HELMS Joachim, b. 24 June 1943, Rostock, Germany. Singer (Tenor). Education: Studied at the Franz Liszt Musikhochschule Weimar and in Dresden. Debut: Erfurt, 1974, as Ernesto in Don Pasquale. Career: Sant at Erfurt, 1974-83, as Mozart's Ferrando and Tamino, the Duke of Mantua, Nemorino, Don Carlos, Max in Der Freischütz and Sergei in Katerina Ismailova; Dresden Staatsoper from 1984, as Rodolfo, Alfredo and Don Ottavio; Guest appearances in the former Soviet Union, Poland, Bulgaria, Austria and Switzerland; Sang Ernesto at Leipzig, 1989; Many concert appearances and broadcasting engagements. Address: c/o Staatsoper, 8012 Dresden, Germany.

HELPS Robert, b. 23 Sept 1928, New Jersey, USA. Composer; Pianist; Professor. Education: Juilliard Preparatory Department and Institute of Musical Arts, 1936-43; Private study with Abby Whiteside, piano; and Roger Sessions, composition, 1943-60. Debut: Recital, New York, 1990. Career: Active piano and chamber music performances including many premieres with leading contemporary music groups in New York, Boston, Chicago, San Francisco, Los Angeles; Tours with Bethany Beardslee, Soprano, Rudolf Kolisch, Isidore Cohen, Jorja Freezanis, Violin. Compositions: Symphony, Two Piano Concertos, various chamber music and songs; Many solo piano pieces, voice and orchestra. Recordings include: Nocturne, 3 Hommages; Hommage a Faure; 3 Hommages, Nocturne for string quartet. Publications include: Nocturne, 1975; Valse Mirage, 1978; Eventually the Carousel Begins, 1991; The Running Sun, 1976; Symphony No 1; Piano Concerto No 1. Address: 4202 E Fowler Avenue, USF 30838, Tampa, FL 33620-9951, USA.

HELTAY Laszlo (Istvan), b. 5 Jan 1930, Budapest, Hungary. Conductor. Education: MA, Franz Liszt Academy of Music, Budapest, with Kodály and Bardos; BLitt, Oxford. Career: Director of Music, Merton College, Oxford, 1960-64; Associate Conductor, New Zealand Broadcasting Corporation Symphony Orchestra 1964-65; Musical Director, New Zealand Opera Company, 1964-66; Conductor, Phoenix Opera Company, London, 1967-69, 1973; Conductor, Collegium Musicum of London, 1970-89; Director of Music, Gardner Centre, Sussex University from 1968-78; Founded Brighton Festival Chorus of the Academy of St Martin in the Fields, 1975-; Director of Royal Choral Society, 1985-; Has conducted leading orchestras in Britain and Abroad including the Philharmonia, the Royal Philharmonic, the London Philharmonic and the Dallas Symphony Orchestras. Recordings: Choral works of Kodály, Respighi, Rossini and Haydn on Argos and Decca Labels; Paco Pena, Misa Flamenca for Virgin. Honours: International Kodaly Medal, 1982. Hobbies: Chess; Skiing; Tennis. Current Management: Influence. Address: c/o International House, Wendell Road, W12 9RT, England.

HEMBERG (Bengt Sven) Eskil, b. 19 Jan 1938, Stockholm, Sweden. General Director of Opera. m. Birgit Sofia Ohlsson, 8 July 1962, 2 sons, 1 daughter. Education: Music Teacher's degree; Higher Organist's degree; Higher Cantor's degree; Orchestra Conducting Class. Debut: Conductor, Uppsala, 1961. Career: Executive Producer, Swedish Radio, 1963-70; Planning Manager, Head, Foreign Relations, National Institute of Concerts, 1970-83; General Director, Stora Teatern, Gothenburg, 1983-87; General Director, Royal Opera, Stockholm, 1987-96. Compositions: Operas: Love, Love, Love; Pirates of the Deep Green Sea; Saint Erik's Crown; Herr Apfelstadt wird Künstler, chamber opera, 1989; Utopia, 1997. Recordings: Various compositions. Publication: Dr Stanley R Wold: Eskil Hemberg - Swedish Composer, Choral Conductor and Administrator: A Survey of His Works, 1987. Honours: HM the King's Medal, 1993; Commander, Portuguese Order of Merit, 1991; Commaner, Grosses Bundesverdienstkreuz, 1995; Royal Opera Gold Medal, 1996. Memberships: Union of Swedish Composers, President, 1971-83; STIM, Vice President, 1974-83; Royal Academy of Music, 1974; International Music Council of UNESCO, President, 1991-93. Address: Floravagen 3, S-131 41 Nacka, Sweden.

HEMM Manfred, b. 1961, Modlin, Austria. Singer (Baritone). Education: Studied at the Vienna Conservatory with Waldemar Kmentt. Debut: Klagenfurt 1984, as Mozart's Figaro. Career: Sang at Augsburg 1984-86, Graz, 1986-88, notably as Papageno, Leporello and Polyphemus in Acis and Galatea; Vienna Staatsoper from 1988 (title role in the premiere of Von Einem's Tuliphant, 1990); Guest appearances as Bayreuth, Basel, Berne, Zurich, Salzburg (Figaro, 1989-91) and Orange; Sang Figaro at the Deutsche Oper Berlin, 1990, Aix-en-Provence Festival, 1991; Metropolitan Opera debut 1991, as Papageno; Salzburg Festival, 1992 as the One Eyed Brother in Die Frau ohne Schatten; Frequent Lieder recitals and concert appearances. Recordings include: Video of Die Zauberflote, from the Met. Address: c/o Metropolitan Opera, Lincoln Center, New York, NY 10023, USA.

HEMMINGS Peter (William), b. 10 Apr 1934, London, England. Opera Company Administrator. m. Jane Frances Kearnes, 19 May 1962, 2 sons, 3 daughters. Education: Gonville and Caius College, Cambridge, 1954-57; Choral Exhibitioner, Cambridge. Career: Harold Holt Limited, London, 1958; Repertory and Planning Manager, Sadler's Wells Opera, 1959-65; General Manager, New Opera Company, 1957-65; General Administrator, Scottish Opera, 1962-77; General Manager, Australian Opera, 1977-79; Managing Director, London Symphony, 1980-84; General Director, Los Angeles Music Center Opera, 1984-. Honours: fellow of the Royal Scottish Academy of Music; Honorary LLD, University of Strathclyde; Honorary Fellow of the Royal Academy of Music. Memberships: Governor, Royal Academy of Music; President, Sadler's Wells Association; Board Member, Opera America; Garrick Club; Vice Chairman, Opera America. Address: 775 South Madison Avenue, Pasadena, CA 91106, USA.

HEMSLEY Thomas, b. 12 Apr 1927, Coalville, Leicestershire, England. Opera and Concert Singer; Producer; Teacher; Lecturer. m. Gwenllian James, 9 Nov 1960, 3 sons. Education: Brasenose College, Oxford; Private music studies. Debut: Opera, Mermaid Theatre, London, 1951. Career: St Paul's Cathedral, London, 1950-51; Stadttheater, Aachen, Federal Republic of Germany, 1953-56; Deutsche Oper am Rhein, 1957-63; Opernhaus Zurich, Switzerland, 1963-67; Performed at Glyndebourne, 1953-83, as Hercule (Alceste), Masetto (Don Giovanni), Sprecher (Zauberflöte), Minister (Fidelio), Dr Reischmann (Elegy for Young Lovers), Musiklehrer (Ariadne), Aeneas (Dido), Arbace (Idomeneo); Edinburgh and Bayreuth Festivals, (1968-70, as Beckmesser), Covent Garden, Scottish Opera, Welsh Opera, English National Opera, English Opera Group, Kent Opera (Falstaff, 1980); Created Demetrius in A Midsummer Night's Dream (Aldeburgh 1960), Mangus in The Knot Garden at Covent Garden, 1970, and Caesar in Iain Hamilton's Catiline Conspiracy, 1974; Produced The Return of Ulysses for Kent Opera, 1989; Soloist with many major orchestras; Frequent broadcast on radio and TV; Repertoire includes more than 150 Operatic Roles; Masterclasses, BBC TV, Danish TV, Music colleges in Britain, Denmark, Sweden, Norway; Visiting Professor, Royal College of Music, London and Royal Northern College of Music; Guest Professor, Royal Danish Academy of Music. Recordings: Operas: Dido and Aeneas; The Fairy Queen; Saul; Xerxes; Alcina; Alceste; Midsummer Night's Dream; Savitri; The Knot Garden; Meistersinger; Cantatas: Bach; Handel; Schütz; Songs: Schubert; Schumann; Wolf; Berkeley; Choral: Delius Requiem. Honour: Honorary RAM, 1974; Hon FTCL, 1988; FGSM, 1996. Memberships: Equity; ISM; Garrick Club; Member, Royal Philharmonic Society; Fellow Royal Society of Arts. Hobbies: Gardening; Mountain Walking. Address: 10 Denewood Road, London N6 4AJ, England.

HENAHAN Donal, b. 28 Feb 1921, Cleveland, Ohio, USA. Music Critic. Education: Ohio University; Northwestern Univerity, BA, 1948. Career: Staff Writer, 1947-57, Music Critic, 1957-67, Chicago Daily News; Staff Writer, 1967-80, Chief Music Critic, 1980-, New York Times. Honour: Pulitzer Prize in music criticism, 1986. Address: 229 West 43rd Street, New York, NY 10036, USA.

HENDERSON Gavin (Douglas), b. 3 Feb 1948, Brighton, England. College Principal. m. Mary Jane Walsh, 1992, 2 sons. Education: Brighton College of Art; Kingston Art College; Slade School of Fine Art; University College, London; Trumpet, privately then Goldsmith's Travelling Scholarship to USA. Debut: as Soloist, Wigmore Hall, 1972. Career: Performer, Frequent BBC Radio and TV, Festivals - City of London, Brighton; Artistic Director, festivals, Brighton, York, Portsmouth, Crawley, Bracknell (Jazz, Folk and Early Music), Bournemouth; Chief Executive, the New Philharmonia and Philharmonia Orchestra, 1975-79; Chairman, Music Panel, Arts Council of England; Chairman British Arts Festivals Association; Vice President, The European Festivals Association; Principal, Trinity College of Music, London. Publications: Picasso and the Theatre, 1982; Festivals UK - Arts Council, 1986; National Arts and Media Strategy (Festivals Section), 1991. Contributions to: Musical Times; Classical Music; Tempo; The Listener. Honours: Hon MA, Sussex; Hon Fellow, Sussex University; Hon Fellow, University of Brighton. Memberships: Royal Society of Arts; ISM; Musicians Union; Worshipful Company of Musicians; Royal Society of Musicians. Hobbies: Seaside piers and seafood cooking. Address: Trinity College of Music, Mandeville Place, London W1M 6AQ, England.

HENDERSON Moya, b. 2 Aug 1941, Quirindi, New South Wales, Australia. Composer. Education: Studied at the University of Queensland and with Maurice Kagel in Cologne. Compositions include: Sacred Site for Organ and Tape, 1983; The Dreaming for Strings, 1985; Celebration 40,000, piano concerto, 1987; Currawong: A Symphony Of Bird Sounds, 1988; Waking Up The Flies, piano trio, 1990; Wild card for Soprano, Cello and Piano, 1991; Music theatre pieces, chamber and vocal music. Address: c/o 1A Eden Street, P O Box 567, Crows Nest, NSW 2065, Australia.

HENDERSON Roy (Galbraith), b. 4 July 1899, Edinburgh, Scotland. Retired Baritone and Teacher of Singing (private); Professor of Singing. m. Bertha Collin Smyth, 1926, dec 1985, 1 son, 2 daughters. Education: Royal Academy of Music, London (Worshipful Company of Musicians Medal). Debut: As Baritone Singer, Queen's Hall, London, 1925. Career: Has sung at all leading Festivals in England; International Festival for Contemporary Music, Amsterdam, 1933; Principal parts in all Glyndebourne Opera Festivals, 1934-40, as Mozart's Count, Guglielmo, Papageno and Masetto; Recitals at first two Edinburgh Festivals, 1947, 1948; Associated chiefly with works of Delius, Elgar and Vaughan Williams, and sang many first performances of contemporary music; Retired from concert platform, 1952, to devote his whole time to teaching (among his pupils was the late Kathleen Ferrier); Conductor, Huddersfield Glee and Madrigal Society, 1932-39; Founder, Conductor, Nottingham Oriana Choir, 1937-52; Conductor, Bournemouth Municipal Choir, 1942-53; Adjudicator, International Concours, Geneva, 1952, and triennially, 1956-65; Member, Jury of International Muziekstad s'Hertogenbosch, Netherlands, 1955-62, 1965, and Barcelona, 1965; Professor of Singing, Royal Academy of Music, London, 1940-74; Master Classes in Singing: Royal Conservatory of Music, Toronto, 1956; Toonkunst Conservatorium, Rotterdam, 1957, 1958; s'Hertogenbosch, 1967. Recordings: Decca's first classical artist. Publications: Contributed to: Kathleen Ferrier (editor Neville Cardus), 1954; Opera Annual, 1958; The Voice (editor Sir Keith Falkner), 1983. Honours: FRAM, 1932; CBE, 1970. Membership: Incorporated Society of Musicians. Address: Ivor Newton House, Edward Road, Bromley, Kent BR1 3NQ, England.

HENDL Walter, b. 12 Jan 1917, West New York, New Jersey, USA. Conductor; Pianist; Composer. m. Barbara Helsley, 1 daughter by previous marriage. Education: Studied piano with Clarence Adler; Piano scholarship student of David Saperton and conducting scholarship student of Fritz Reiner, Curtis Institute of Music, Philadelphia; Conducting student of Serge Koussevtizky, Berkshire Music Center, Tanglewood, Massachusetts, summers 1941-42. Career: Assistant Conductor, New York Philharmonic Orchestra, 1945-49; Music Director, Dallas Symphony Orchestra, 1953-72; Associate Conductor, Chicago Symphony Orchestra, 1958-64; Music Director, Ravinia Festival, 1959-63; Director, Eastman School of Music, Rochester, New York, 1964-72; Music Director, Eire (Pa) Philharmonic Orchestra, 1976-. Recordings: For Desto and RCA. Address: c/o Erie Philharmonic Orchestra, 409 G Daniel Baldwin Building, Erie, PA 16501, USA.

HENDRICKS Barbara, b. 20 Nov 1948, Stephens, Arkanas, USA. Singer (Soprano). Education: Juilliard School of Music with Jennie Tourel. Debut: Mini-Met, New York, 1973 in Four Saints in Three Acts. Career: Glyndebourne 1974, in La Calisto; San Francisco, 1976, as Monteverdi's Poppea; Berlin Deutsche Oper, 1978, as Susanna in Le Nozze di Figaro; Orange Festival, 1980, as Gilda; Paris Opera, 1982, as Gounod's Juliette; Los Angeles and Covent Garden, 1982, as Nannetta in a new production of Falstaff conducted by Giulini; Metropolitan Opera debut 1986, as Sophie in Der Rosenkavalier (returned 1987, as Susanna); Song recitals in the US, Europe and Russian with Dimitri Alexeev, Daniel Barenboim, Michel Béroff and Radu Lupu as accompanists; Concert appearances with Barenboim, Bernstein, Dorati, Giulini, Karajan, Maazel, Mehta and Solti; Tours of Japan with Karajan, Bernstein and the Vienna State Opera; Festival engagements at Aix, Edinburgh, Montreux, Orange, Prague, Salzburg and Vienna; Debut at La Scala 1987, Susanna; Sang at the opening concert of the Opéra Bastille Paris, 1989; Norina in Don Pasquale at Lyons, 1989 (also at Venice 1990); Debut as Manon at Parma, 1991; Sang Micaela at Orange, 1992. Recordings include: Mahler 2nd Symphony and Mozart Masses (Deutsche Grammophon); Haydn Nelson Mass (EMI); Handel's Solomon, Les Pêcheurs de Perles (Philips); La Bohème, Don Pasquale and Le Roi d'Ys (Erato); Orphée et Eurydice and Hänsel und Gretel (EMI). Honours include: Commandeur des Arts et des Lettres, 1986; Goodwill Ambassador of the High Commissioner for Refugees at the United Nations, 1987. Address: IMG, Media House, 3 Burlington Lane, London W4, England.

HENDRICKS Marijke, b. 18 Apr 1956, Schinveld, Holland. Singer (Mezzo-soprano). Education: Studied in Maastricht and Cologne. Career: Sang at the Cologne Opera 1981-85, notably as

Nancy in Martha, Cherubino, Hansel, Meg Page and Olga in Eugene Onegin; Sang the Marchesa in Musgrave's The Voice of Ariande at the 1982 Edinburgh Festival; Guest appearances at Geneva 1985, as Cherubino, Salzburg, 1986 as Second Lady in Die Zauberflöte and Innsbruck, 1986 in the title role of Cesti's Orontea; Bordeaux and Lyon 1987, as Ramiro in La Finta Giardiniera; Amsterdam 1987, in a concert performance of Tancredi, as Isaura; Visits to the Orange Festival and to Israel with the company of Cologne Opera, 1984; Antwerp 1988, as Dulcinée in Massenet's Don Quichotte; Maastricht 1989 in La Belle Hélène; Television appearances in Austria and Switzerland. Address: Oper der Stadt Köln, Offenbachplatz, 5000 Cologne, Germany.

HENDRIE Gerald (Mills), b. 28 Oct 1935. Professor of Music. m. (1) Dinah Florence Barsham, 1962, deceased 1985, 2 s, (2) Lynette Anne Maddern, 1986. Education: Royal College of Music; MA, MusB, PhD, Selwyn College, Cambridge; FRCO; ARCM. Career includes: Professor and Chairman of Department of Music, University of Victoria, BC, Canada, 1967-69; Professor, Open University, 1969-90 (retired); Supervisor, 1977-85, Director of Studies, 1981-85, Music, St John's College, Cambridge; Visiting Fellow in Music, University of Western University, 1985. Publications: Musica Britannica XX, Orlando Gibbons: Keyboard Music, 1962, 2nd revised edition 1967; Anthems für Cannons in 3 volumes, 1985, 1987, 1991; Anthems für die Chapel Royal in 1992, Utrecht Te Deum and Jubilate, in press, all for Halle Handel Society's Collected edition of Handel's Works; Iolanthe, Critical edition in full score for the new Collected Edition of the Gilbert and Sullivan operas, in press, NY; Various articles for professional journals; Own works published include: Quintet for Brass, 1988, Magnificat and Nunc Dimittis for Boys' Voices for St Paul's Cathedral, 1988, Te Deum and Jubilate for Men's Voices for St Paul's Cathedral, 1988, Other services for St John's College, Cambridge, New College at Oxford and Canterbury Cathedral, Organ music includes Choral: Hommage à César Franck, 1990, Le Tombeau de Marcel Dupré, 1991-93 comprising Toccata and Fugue, Prelude and Fugue, Prelude and Fugue on BACH, Two Sketches on BACH, In Praise of St Asaph, commissioned by the Arts Council of Great Britain/Welsh Arts Council for the North Wales Music Festival, ST Asaph, 1994; Sonata: In Praise of Reconciliation, private American commission, 1995. Address: The Garth, 17 The Avenue, Dallington, Northampton, NN5 7AJ, England.

HENDRIKX Louis, b. 13 Mar 1927, Antwerp, Belgium. Singer (Bass). Education: Studied at the Antwerp Conservatory and with Willem Ravelli. Debut: Antwerp 1963, as Samuel in Un Ballo in Maschera. Career: Sang in Antwerp and Kassel; Further appearances in Hannover, Cologne; Dortmund; Munich; Hamburg, Nuernberg, Lyon, Bordeaux, Toulose, Venice, Palermo, Milan, Monte Carlo, Stockholm, Glasgow and London (Gurnemanz at Covent Garden); Promenade Concerts 1972; Théâtre de la Monnaie and Rome Opera 1973, as Boris Godunov and as King Mark in Tristan und Isolde; Also Salzburg, Fafner in Rheingold and Pogner in Mastersinger for the Easter Festivals. Recordings include: Gessler in Guillaume Tell (EMI); Rheingold with Herbert von Karajan. Address: c/o Théatre de la Monnaie, 4 Léopoldstrasse, B-1000 Brussels, Belgium.

HENKEL Kathy, b. 20 Nov 1942, Los Angeles, California, USA. Composer; Writer; Lecturer. Education: BA, History, University of California, Los Angeles, 1965; BM, Composition, California State University at North Ridge, 1976; MA, Music Composition, 1982. Career: Music Reviewer, Los Angeles Times, 1979; Program Annotator, Education Coordinator, Chamber Music, Los Angeles Festival, 1987-95; Program Annotator, Los Angeles Chamber Orchestra, 1988-; Works Premiered and Performed at Gubbio Music Festival, Italy, Montevarchi Festival, Italy, Alaska Women Festival, Fairbanks, Dana Festival, Ohio, Toronto Guitar Society, Live Broadcasts, KFAC, Los Angeles, London, England, Greenwich Village, New York. Compositions: Pioneer Song Cycle, 1968; Trumpet Sonata, 1979; Lost Calendar Pages, 1984; Moorland Sketches, 1985; Piano Sonata, 1986; Bass Clarinet Sonata, 1987; River Sky for Solo Guitar, 1988; Book of Hours for Solo Harp, 1990; Sonata for Flute and Piano, 1992; Alaskan Fantasy and Fanfare, 1993; Sea Songs, 1997. Contributions to: Performing Arts Magazine. Memberships: Phi Beta Kappa; Chamber Music America; Phi Beta Women's Professional Arts Fraternity. Hobby: Cornwall Coastal Path Walking. Address: 2367 Creston Drive, Los Angeles, CA 90068, USA.

HENN Brigitte, b. 21 Oct 1939, Freudenthal, Czechslovakia. Singer (Soprano). m. Raymond Henn, Education: Studied in Frankfurt, in Wiesbaden with Helena Braun and in Basle. Career: Sang at the Basle Opera, 1968-75, Deutsche Oper Berlin, 1976-80; Guest appearances at Basle from 1982, and in Dusseldorf, Frankfurt, Zurich and Hanover; Roles have included Mozart's Countess, Donna Anna and Fiordiligi, Agathe, Euridice, Marenka in The Bartered Bride, Wagner's Senta, Elsa and Sieglinde, Elisabeth de Valois, Alice Ford and Amelia in Un Ballo in Maschera; Operetta engagements in works by Lehar and Zeller; Many concert appearances.

HENNING Sven, b, 18 Sept 1940, Trondheim, Norway. Director. Education: BA, English Langauge and Literature, Russian Language and Literature, BA, Musicology, Oslo University; Piano studies in Olso and Copenhagen. Debut: As stage director, 1967. Career: Main music theatre productions in Norway including: Die Fledermaus; Hair; Fiddler On The Roof; The Threepenny Opera; A Little Night Music; Candide; Concert version of Peer Gynt; Professional appointments include: Stage director, Trondelag Theatre, Trondheim, and Den Nationale Scene, Bergen; Artistic Director, 1972-76, currently Artistic Advisor, Bergen International Festival; Artistic Director, Den Nationale Scene, Bergen, 1976-82; Head of Stage Directors' Department at the State Drama Academy, Oslo, 1982-1988; Chairman, Nordic Competition for Conductors, 1994; Advisor, Norwegian Foreign Ministry; Director of Concerts, 1988-97, Director of International Projects, 1997-, Norwegian Concert Institute (Rikskonsertene). Memberships: Chairman, Nordic Music Committee; Committee Member, Ultima Festival of Contemporary Music, Oslo; Board member, International Society for the Performing Arts, 1998-. Publications: Articles on music and theatre. Address: Brinken 16D, N-0654 Olso, Norway.

HENRY Didier, b. 1953, France. Singer (Baritone). Education: Studied at the Paris Conservatoire and the studio of the Grand Opéra. Career: Sang at St Etienne, 1988, in a revival of Massenet's Amadis; Aix-en-Provence, 1989, in The Love for Three Oranges and in Belfast as Valentin the same year; Season 1990 as Marc-Antoine in Massenet's Cléopâtre at St Etienne, followed by Blondel in Gretry's Richard Coeur de Lion; Has sung in Moscow in Pelléas et Mélisande, in Marseille as Pietro in La Muette de Portici by Auber and at the Paris Théâtre du Châtelet in L'Enfant et les Sortilèges. Recordings include: Pelléas et Mélisande (Decca), The Love for Three Oranges (Virgin) and Massenet's Amadis and Cléopatre, Mélodies de Ravel, Massenet, Poulenc and Saint-Saëns (REM). Address: BP 27 - 28290 Arrou, France.

HENSCHEL Jane, b. 1950, California. Singer (Mezzo Soprano). Education: Studied at the University of Southern California. Career: Sang Gilbert and Sullivan with Opera a la Carte in Los Angeles; Aspen Music Festival, 1977, with Haydn's Berenice, Respighi's Il Tramonto with the Cleveland Quartet and Ottavia in L'Incorohazione di Poppea; Aachen Opera 1977-80; Sang at Wuppertal from 1980, notably as Schoeck's Penthesilea; Dortmund Opera as Eboli, Nancy (Martha), Amneris, Brangaene and the Witch in Rusalka; Concert engagements with the Frankfurt Radio Orchestra in Mahler's 8th Symphony and Beethoven's 9th, conducted by Eliahu Inbal; Baroque repertoire includes Vivaldi's oratorio Juditha Triumphans (Radio France); Sang the Nurse in Die Frau ohne Schatten at Covent Garden 1992, Judy in Birtwistle's Punch and Judy for Netherlands Opera, 1993; Season 1996 as Fricka at Covent Garden and Baba the Turk at Salzburg; The Rake's Progress at the Festival Hall, London, 1997. Address: c/o Music International, 13 Ardilaun Road, London N5 2QR, England.

HENSHALL Dalwyn (James), b. 20 Feb 1957, Liverpool, England. Composer. Education: BMus, MMus, PhD, UCNW, Bangor; Sibelius Academy, Helsinki. Compositions: Variations & Fugue, 1982; Oboe Concerto, 1979; Harp Concerto, 1980; The Silent Land, 1982; Cello Concerto, 1982; Et in terra pax, 1983; Sinfonietta No 1, 1980; Sinfonietta No 2, 1982; Sinfonietta No 3, 1987; Dic Penderyn, 1986; Twin Sion Cati, 1988. Contributions to: Welsh Music; Western Mail. Memberships: Chairman, Young Welsh Composers' Guild; Gorsedd of Bards, Royal National Eisteddfod; Performing Rights Society. Hobbies: Conducting; Adjudicating. Address: 10 Lon-y-Tresglen, Caerfilli, Wales CF8 2QP.

HENZE Hans Werner, b. 1 July 1926, Gutersloh, Germany. Composer; Conductor. Education: Studied at the Staatsmusikhochschule Brunswick; Kirchenmusikalisches Institut, Heidelberg. Career: Musical Director at the Deutsches Theatre Constanze 1948; Artistic Director, Ballet of the Hessian State Theatre, Wiesbaden, 1950; Has lived in Italy as independent artist from 1953; Professor of Composition, Mozarteum, Salzburg 1962-67 and Hochscule für Musik, Cologne, 1980-91; Artistic Director, Accademia Filarmonia Romana, 1982; Founder and Artistic Director of the Munich Biennale for Contemporary Music Theatre since, 1988; BBC Henze Festival at the Barbican, 1991; First Composer-in-Residence, Berlin Philharmonic Orchestra, 1990; British premiere of Requiem at the 1993 London Proms; Venus and Adonis premiered at Munich, 1997. Compositions: Operas and Music Theatre: Das Wundertheater 1948; Boulevard Solitude 1951; Ein Landarzt 1951; Das Ende einer Welt 1953; König Hirsch 1955, rev as Il Re Cervo 1962; Der Prinz von Homburg 1958; Elegy for Young Lovers 1961; Der junge Lord 1964; The Bassarids 1965; Moralties, scenic cantatas 1967; Der langwierige Weg in die Wohnung der Natascha Ungeheuer 1971; La Cubana 1973; We Come to the River 1976; Don Chisciotte della Mancia, after Paisiello 1976; Pollicino, for children 1979; Il Ritorno d'Ulisse in Patria, after Monteverdi 1982; The English Cat 1983; Das Verratene Meer, 1990; Venus and Adonis, 1997; Ballets: Jack Pudding 1949; Ballet-Variationen 1949; Rosa Silber 1950; Die Schlafende Prinzessin 1951; Labyrinth 1951; Der Idiot 1952; Maratona 1956; Des Kaisers Nachtigall 1959; Undine 1956-71; Tancredi 1964; Orpheus 1978; Tanzstunden, Ballet Triptych, 1997; Orchestral: 8 symphonies 1947-93; Quattro Poemi 1955; Antifone 1960; Los Caprichos 1963; Telemanniana 1967; Heliogabalus Imperator 1972; Tristan, preludes for piano, orchestra and tape 1973; Ragtimes and Habaneras for brass band 1975; Barcarola 1983; Chamber Orchestra: Sinfonie 1947; Symphonic Variation 1950; Sonata for Strings 1958; 3 Dithyrambs 1958; In Memoriam: Amicizia 1976; Aria de la folia espanola 1977; Apollo Trionfante 1979; Canzona 1982; I Sentimenti di Carl P E Bach 1982; Sonata for 6 1984; Concertos: 2 for Violin, 1947, 1971; 2 for piano, 1950, 1967; Jeux des Tritons 1957; Ode to the West Wind for cello and orchestra 1953; Concerto per il Marigny 1956; Double Concerto, with oboe and harp 1966; Double Bass Concerto 1966; Compases para preguntas ensimisadas 1970; Il Vitalino raddoppiato 1977; Le Miracle de la Rose for clarinet and 13 players 1981; Guitar Concerto 1986; Sieben liebeslieder for cello and orchestra, 1986; Allegro brillante, 1989; Requiem for instruments, 1990-91, Trumpet Concerto, 1992; Vocal: Whispers from Heavenly Death 1948; Der Vorwurf 1948; Apollo and Hyacinth 1949; 5 Neapolitan Songs 1956; Nocturnes and Arias 1957; Chamber Music 1958; Novae de Infinito Laudes 1962; Ariosi 1963; Being Beateous 1963; Choral Fantasia 1964; Muses of Sicily 1966; Essay on Pigs 1968; Das Floss der Medusa 1968; El Cimarron 1970; Voices 1973; Jephte, after Carissimi 1976; The King of Harlem 1979; Canzoni for Orpheus 1980; Chamber music includes 5 String Quartets, 1947-76, 2 Wind Quintets, 1952, 1977, Royal Winter Music for guitar, 1976, 1979 and Capriccio for cello 1983; Serenade for solo violin, 1986; Keyboard music. Honours: Siemens Prize, Munich, 1990; Apollo d'Oro, Bilbao, 1990. Address: c/o Schott & Co Ltd, 48 Great Marlborough Street, London W1, England.

HEPPNER Ben, b. 14 Jan 1956, Murrayville, British Columbia, Canada. Singer (Tenor). Career: Many oratorio and concert performances in Canada; Opera Bacchus in Ariadne auf Naxos; Canadian Opera Company as Zinovy in Lady Macbeth of Mtsensk; American debut in Tannhäuser at the Chicago Lyric Opera, 1988; Has sung the Prince in Rusalka with the Philadelphia Opera Company, Seattle Opera (1990) and at the Vienna State Opera (1991); European debut at the Royal Opera Stockholm 1989, as Lohengrin; Sang Walther von Stolzing on his La Scala and Covent Garden debuts (1990) and in Seattle and Toronto; San Francisco Opera debut 1989, as Lohengrin; Season 1991-92 with Janacek's Laca at Brussels, the Emperor in Die Frau ohne Schatten at Amsterdam and the premiere of William Bolcom's McTeague in Chicago; Season 1992 with Dvorak's Dimitrij at Munich, Mozart's Titus at Salzburg; Sang Lohengrin at Seattle, 1994; Walther at the Met, New York, 1995; Engaged to sing Tristan under Abbado at Salzburg, 1999. Recordings: Two of Die Meistersinger, conducted by Wolfgang Sawallisch and by Solti (1997); Andrey in Tchaikovsky's Mazeppa (DGG). Address: c/o Columbia Artists Management, 165 West 57th Street, New York, NY 10019, USA.

HERBERT Jocelyn, b. 23 Feb 1917, London, England. Stage Designer. Career: Designed in London for productions of avant-garde plays at the Royal Court Theatre and the National Theatre; Designed Monteverdi's Orfeo for Sadler's Wells, 1967; La Forza del Destino at the Paris Opéra, 1975; La Forza del Destino at the Paris Opera, 1975; For the Metropolitan Opera has designed productions of Lulu (local premiere, 1977), Die Entführung, and Aufstieg und Fall der Stadt Mahagonny (both 1979). Address: c/o Metropolitan Opera, Lincoln Center, New York, NY 10023, USA.

HERBIG Gunther, b. 30 Nov 1931, Usti-nad-Labem, Czechoslovakia. Conductor. Education: Studied with Hermann Abendroth at the Franz Liszt Academy, Weimar, and with Hermann Scherchen; Further study with Herbert von Karajan. Career: Held posts in Erfurt, Weimar, Potsdam and East Berlin; General Music Director, Dresden Philharmonic Orchestra, 1972-77; London debut with the New Philharmonia Orchestra, 1973; Music Director, Berlin Symphony Orchestra, 1977-83; Guest Conductor, Dallas Symphony Orchestra, 1979-81; Principal Guest Conductor, BBC Philharmonic Orchestra, 1982-86; Music Director, Detroit Symphony, 1984-90; Debut with London Symphony Orchestra, 1986; Orchestre de Paris, 1986; Appearances with the New York Philharmonic, Boston Symphony, Philadelphia Orchestra and Los Angeles Philharmonic from 1984; Music Director, Toronto Symphony, 1989-94; Toured Europe, 1989 with the Detroit Symphony Orchestra and Gidon Kremer as soloist. Recordings include: Haydn's London Symphonies; Reger's Piano Concerto; Beethoven's ballet Die Geschöpfe des Prometheus; Brahms 4 Symphonies and Nielsen's 5th. Address: Terry Harrison Artists Management, The Orchard, Market Street, Charlbury, Oxon OX7 3PJ, England.

HERFORD (Richard) Henry, b. 24 Feb 1947, Edinburgh, Scotland. Singer (Baritone). m. Lindsay John, 14 Feb 1982, 2 s, 1 d. Education: Classics and English at King's College, Cambridge, 1965-68; MA Honours; Royal Northern College of Music, 1971-76; ARNCM, Performers and Teachers, with Distinction; GRNCM. Career: Glyndebourne Chorus, 1977-78; Forester in Janácek's Cunning Little Vixen; Roles with Royal Opera House, Covent Garden, Scottish Opera, Handel Opera, Chelsea Opera Group, Batignano, Nancy, English Bach Festival; Frequent concerts with leading orchestras in Britian, Europe and North and South America; Appearances with many ensembles and on radio and television (Maxwell Davies: The Lighthouse, BBC2); Numerous recitals. Recordings: Recital of American Songs; As High Priest in Rameau's, Castor and Pollux; Handel's Messiah, excerpts with Scottish Chamber Orchestra and George Malcolm; Biggin, The Gates of Greenham; Dickinson, A Dylan Thomas Song Cycle; Handel's Dixit Dominus with King's College Cambridge Choir; Joubert, The Instant Moment with English String Orchestra, Albany; Vaughan Williams's Five Tudor Portraits, Five Mystical Songs, Hyperion; Britten's A Midsummer Night's Dream; Charles Ives: Songs, 2 volumes; Songs with Instruments with Ensemble Modern; Maxwell Davies, Resurrection; Bridge, The Christmas Pearl, Michael Berkeley, Prière du doux repos, ASV; George Lloyd, Albany; Stravinsky, Pulcinella, Naxos; Edward Gregson, Missa Brevis Pacem. Honours: Curtis Gold Medal, RNCM, 1977; Benson and Hedges Gold Award, Aldeburgh, 1980; 1st prize, American Music Competition at Carnegie Hall, 1982; Record of the Year, MRA. Hobbies: Family; House Renovation; Reading; Hill Walking. Current Management: Ron Gonsalves, London. Address: Pencots, Northmoor, Oxford, OX8 1AX, England.

HERINCX Raimund, b. 23 Aug 1927, London, England. Singer (Bass-Baritone). Education: Studied with Van Dyck in Belgium and with Valli in Milan. Career: Concerts in Belgium and France, 1950; Stage debut Welsh National Opera 1950, as Mozart's Figaro; Sang Mephistopheles in Faust 1956; Sadler's Wells Opera from 1956, as Count Almaviva, Rigoletto, Germont, Pizarro, Nick Shadow, Creon in Oedipus Rex, and in the premiere of Our Man in Havana by Malcolm Williamson, 1963; Sang in the 1964 British premiere of The Makropoulos Case; Philharmonic Hall New York 1966, in A Mass of Llfe by Delius; Boston Opera 1967; BBC 1967, in L'Erismena by Cavalli; Covent Garden from 1968, as King Fisher in The Midsummer Marriage and in the premieres of The Knot Garden 1970 and Taverner 1972; Other Covent Garden roles include Escamillo, Macbeth and Alfio; Salzburg Easter Festival 1973-74, as Pogner in Die Meistersinger and Fafner in Siegfried, conducted by Karajan; English National Opera 1974-76, in the British stage premiere of The Bassarids by Henze and as Wotan and Hagen in The Ring; Seattle Opera 1977-81; Metropolitan Opera debut 1977, as Matthisen in Le Prophète; San Francisco 1983 in The Midsummer Marriage; Les Contes d'Hoffmann for Opera North 1983; Sang in the US premiere of Taverner at Boston, 1986; Sang Dalua in Boughton's The Immortal Hour, Glastonbury, 1996; Has reviewed opera for Music and Musicians magazine. Recordings include: Dido and Aeneas (Decca); Les Contes d'Hoffmann (Electrola); Hansel and Gretel, Koanga, A Village Romeo and Juliet, I Capuleti e i Montecchi, The Pilgrim's Progress, Aronte in Armide by Gluck, Oedipus Rex (EMI); The Midsummer Marriage (Philips); Das Liebesverbot by Wagner. Address: c/o English National Opera, St Martins Lane, London WC2, England.

HERING Karl-Josef, b. 14 Feb 1929, Westonnen, Germany. Singer (Tenor). Education: Studied with Fred Husler, Max Lorenz and Franz Volker. Debut: Hanover 1958, as Max in Der Freischütz. Career: Engagements at the Deutsche Oper Berlin and in Cologne, Karlsruhe, Stuttgart, Vienna and Hamburg; Royal Opera House Covent Garden, as Siegfried in Der Ring des Nibelungen, 1966; Further appearances in Trieste, Toronto, Barcelona, Marseille and Buenos Aires; Other roles include Florestan, Canio, Aegisthus, Hermann in The Queen of Spades and Erik in Der fliegende Holländer; Many concert performances. Address: c/o Deutsche Oper Berlin, Richard Wagnerstrasse 10, D-1000 Berlin, Germany.

HERLEA Nicolae, b. 28 Aug 1927, Bucharest, Rumania. Singer (Baritone). Education: Studied at the Bucharest Conservatory with Aurelius Costescu-Duca and at the Accademia di Santa Cecilia, Rome. Debut: Bucharest 1951, as Silvio in Pagliacci; Guest appearances at Covent Garden (Rossini's Figaro, 1960), Milan, Prague, Brussels, Moscow, Boston, Cleveland and Vienna; Metropolitan Opera debut 1964; Other roles include Verdi's Germont, Luna and Rigoletto. Recordings include: Il barbiere di Siviglia, La Traviata, Rigoletto and Pagliacci (Electrocord); Opera arias (Deutsche Grammophon).

HERMAN Mark Norman, b. 9 Dec 1942, Brooklyn, New York, USA. Translator. m. Ronnie Susan Apter, 18 June 1967, 2 sons. Education: Columbia University; University of California at Berkeley; Private vocal and instrumental training. Debut: First production of a translation, Mozart's Die Entführung aus dem Serail, New York City, 1979. Career: Translations for major publishers include Donizetti's Maria Stuarda (new critical edition), Puccini's La Bohème (new revised edition), Ferrero's La figlia del mago, Verdi's Ernani (new critical edition), Luisa Miller (new critical edition) and Il trovatore (new critical edition); Additional translations of 12 operas and operettas, 2 choral works. Publication: Alessandro Scarlatti, Eraclea, first performing edition, 1994. Contributions to: Translation Review; Opera Journal; Translation: Theory and Practice, Tension and Interdependence, article, 1991. Memberships: Opera America; American Translators Association. Address: 5748 West Brooks Road, Shepherd, MI 48883-9202, USA.

HERMAN Silvia, b. 1954, Vienna, Austria. Singer (Soprano). Education: Studied in Vienna with Anton Dermota: worked at the Opera Studio of the Vienna Staatsoper, 1976-79. Career: Appearances in Vienna 1979-82, Hamburg 1983-85; Guest engagements in Stuttgart, Geneva, Barcelona, Madrid and Cologne, 1989-90; Salzburg Festival, 1978-81; Bayreuth Festival 1978 as a Flowermaiden, 1985-88 as Wellgunde and Waltraute in Die Walküre; Bruckner Festival in Linz, 1982-88, and elsewhere, in Lieder recitals and concert showings. Recordings: Das Rheingold and Die Walküre, conducted by Haitink; Schumann's Das Paradies und der Peri. Address: Oper der Stadt Koln, Offenbachplatz, 5000 Cologne, Germany.

HERMAN Vasile, b. 10 Jun 1929, Satu Mare, Rumania. Composer. m. Titina Herman, 2 children. Education: Diploma of Composition, 1957, Doctor of Musicology, 1974, High School; Diploma of Teacher of Music, 1960. Career: TV and Radio appearances. Compositions: Double Concerto; Poliphony; Concert of Strings; Chamber works: Melopee, Variante, Epsodi, 5 Symphonies, Concerto for Strings and Percussion. Recordings: Cantilations; Rimes Nostalgique; Symphony No 2, Variante. Publication: Form and Style in the Contemporary Rumanian Music, 1977. Contributions to: Muzica; Steaua; Tribuna; Utunk, Rumania. Honours: Prize, Composers' Union, Rumania; Prize, Rumanian Academy. Membership: Composers' Union of Rumania. Hobbies: Numismatics; National History. Address: Str Jozsa Bela 33 Apt 4, 3400 Cluj-Napoca, Rumania.

HERMAN Witold (Walenty), b. 14 Feb 1932, Torun, Poland. Solo Cellist; Professor of Music. m. Catherine Bromboszcz, 1 June 1970, 1 son, 1 daughter. Education: Diploma with distinction, Szymanowski Conservatory, Torun, 1950; MA, Academy of Music, Cracow, 1956; Diploma, Ecole Normale de Musique, Paris, France, 1960; Cultural Doctorate in Philosophy of Music, World University, Tucson, Arizona, USA, 1984. Debut: State Philharmonie, Cracow, May 1954. Career: Cello concerts with orchestras and cello recitals in Poland and other European countries; Professor, Music Acdemy, Cracow; Visiting Professor of the Franz Liszt Musik Akademie in Weimar, 1972; Jury of the International Pablo Casals Cello Competition in Budapest, 1968. Recordings: For radio and television in Poland and the rest of Europe including Radio Luxembourg; As a solo cellist with major symphony orchestras. Publications: Notes for Cello, edited in Poland, Polish Music Edition. Hobbies: Sociology; Theatre; Tennis. Current Management: Academy of Music, ul Starowislna 3, Cracow, Poland. Address: ul Friedleina 49 m 5, 30-009 Cracow, Poland.

HERMANN Roland, b. 17 Sept 1936, Bochum, Germany. Singer (Baritone). Education: Vocal studies with Pau Lohmann, Margarethe von Wintrefeldt and Falmino Contini. Debut: Trier 1967 as Count Almaviva. Career: Member of the Zurich Opera from 1968; Guest appearances in Munich, Paris, Berlin and Cologne; Buenos Aires 1974, as Jochanaan in Salome and Wolfram in Tannhäuser; US debut 1983, with the New York Philharmonic; La Scala Milan debut 1986, with Claudio Abbado; Roles include Don Giovanni, Amfortas, Germont, Gunther in Götterdämmerung and the title roles in Karl V by Krenek and Doktor Faust by Busoni; Apollo (L'Orfeo), Cinna (Lucio Silla), Morald (Die Feen), Forester (The Cunning Little Vixen); Mauregato (Alfonso und Estrella); Beckmesser, Achille (Penthesilea); Vendramin (Massimila Doni), Orff's Prometheus; Took part in the European stage premiere of Die Jakobsleiter by Schoenberg (Hamburg 1983) and the world premiere of Kelterborn's Der Kirschgarten (Zurich 1984); Sang in the premiere of Krenek's Oratorio Symeon der Stylites at the 1988 Salzburg Festival, conducted by Lothar Zagrosek; BBC London 1989, in the title role of Der Prinz von Homburg by Henze; sang the Forester in The Cunning Little Vixen at Zurich 1989, The Master in the premiere of York Höllier's Der Meister und Margarita (Paris 1989) and Gunther at a concert performance of Götterdämmerung at the Holland Festival; Season 1992 as Nekrotzar in Le Grand Macabre at Zurich, followed by the Count in Capriccio; Sang Paolo in Simon Boccanegra at Zurich, 1996; Many Lieder recitals and concert appearances. Recordings include: Penthesilea by Schoeck (BASF); Prometheus and Trionfi by Orff, Die Meistersinger, CPE Bach's Magnificat (Deutsche Grammophon); Moses und Aron by Schoenberg (CBS); Zemlinsky's Der Kreidekreis; Mathis der Maler by Hindemith; Peer Gynt by Werner Egk; Der Vampyr by Marschner; Schumann's Genoveva. Address: c/o Ingpen & Williams Ltd, 26 Wadham Road, London SW15 2LR, England.

HERMANOVA Vera, b. 9 Sept 1951, Brno, Czech Republic. Organist. m. Zdenek Spatka, 8 July 1977. Education: Conservatoire in Brno, 1967-73; Master's degree, Janacek Academy of Performing Arts in Brno, 1973-77; Postgraduate study at the Janacek Acdemy, 1978-81; Conservatoire National de Saint-Maur, Paris (with Professor Gaston Litaize), 1980-81; Postgraduate study of musical science, Doctor's degree, Masaryk University in Brno Faculty of Philosophy, 1991-97. Career: Special attention to French and Czech organ music of all periods; Master course with prominent European organists (Gaston Litaize, Piet Kee, Guy Bovet, Ewald Kooiman, Lionel Rogg); Radio and TV recordings in Czech Republic, Denmark, Germany, Austria, Slovenia; Organ recitals in a number of European culture centres including Prague, Paris, Vienna, Linz, Berlin, Munich, Hamburg, Dresden, Copenhagen, Oslo, Lublana, Haarlem, Utrecht, and in festivals at home and abroad (Great Britain, Germany, Denmark, The Netherlands, Austria). Recordings: French Organ Works (Messiaen, Dupré, Alain); Les Grandes Orgues de Notre Dame de Chatres (French Organ Music); Musica Nova Bohemica (Eben, Kohoutek); Musik der Gegenwart (Bodorová); Old Czech Organ Music of the 18th Century; Czech Organ Music of the 20th Century. Honours: Finalist, International Organ Competition, Bologna, 1975; Premier Prix à l'Unanamité, Saint-Maur, 1981; Czech Music Fund Prize for CD recordings, Prague, 1992. Membership: Association Jehan Alain, Romainmôtier, Switzerland. Hobby: History. Address: Udolní 13, 602 00 Brno, Czech Republic.

HERMANSON Åke (Oscar Werner), b. 16 Jun 1923, Mollösund, Sweden. Composer. m. Britt Anderson, 10 Apr 1948, 1 daughter. Education: Studies in Composition, Counter Point, Instrumentation with Hilding Rosenberg; Piano with Knut Back; Organ with Alf Linder. Career: Chairman and Board Member, Swedish Society of Composers, 1967-71; Royal Swedish Academy of Music, 1973-; Composer for Whole Times. Compositions: 4 Symphonies for Orchestra; Utopia for Orchestra; Ultima for Orchestra; In Voco for String Orchestra; 2 String Quartets; Vocal music for choirs; Solo works for French Horn, Flute and Oboe; Rockall, op 29 for Winds Vision; Hymn To Salto, op 31; Recordings: All works recorded. Publications: Konsertnytt, 1983; Nutida Musik. Hobby: Sailing. Address: Villa Vindila Sma, S-13054 Dalaro, Sweden.

HERNANDEZ IZNAGA Jorge, b. 1950, Havana, Cuba. Musician. m. Lozano Carola, 1972, 1 son, 1 daughter. Education: National School of Art, Havana, 1964-72; Conservatory Tchaikovsky, Moscow, 1976-79, 1981-83. Debut: Havana, 1972. Career: Professor, Viola, Conservatory Roldan, Havana, 1972-76, Superior Institute of Arts, Havana, 1983-92; Principal Viola, National Symphonic Orchestra of Cuba; Founder, The Havana String Quartet; TV and Radio Appearances in Cuba, 1972-92, Moscow, 1977, 1979, Hungary, 1979, Argentina, 1987, 1988, Uruguay, 1988, Korea, 1988, Bulgaria, 1990, Mexico, 1990, Spain, 1992-97; Co-Principal, Orchestra of Cordova, Spain. Recordings: Havana String Quartet, L Brouwer's Quartets and M Ravel-H Villa Lobos No 1. Honours: Prize, Interpretive Mastery, Chamber Music Festival of Havana, 1987. Memberships: Writers and Artists Union of Cuba; Individual Member, Chamber Music of America. Current Management: KH Productions SL. Address: Basilica No 18, Madrid 28020, Spain.

HERNANDEZ-LARGUIA Cristian, b. 6 Oct 1921, Buenos Aires, Argentina. Choir Conductor. m. Eugenia Barbarich, 29 Dec 1953. Education: Studied with T Fuchs, E Leuchter, R Shaw, N Greenberg and G Graetzer. Debut: Madrigal Group, Asoc Ros de Cultura Inglesa 1941. Career: Conductor, Coro Estable de Rosario, since 1946; Founder and Conductor, Pro Musica de Rosario, 1962; Appearances in concert tours to North, Central and South America and Europe, 1967-92, Hunter College, NY, Coolidge Auditorium, Washington DC and St Martin in the Fields, London; Professor of Choir Conducting, Musical Morphology and Acoustics, University of Litoral, University Rosario. Recordings: 35 titles including LP, Cassettes and CD's. Publications: Performances: Mass in B Minor, Bach's first version with Argentine cast, 1985; St John Passion, Bach, 1977; First Argentine audition of complete and original version Messiah, 1973, Brocke's Passion, 1980, Handel. Honours include: Numerous personal and joint awards (with Pro Musica and CER) as well as National Culture Glory, 1984, Illustrious citizen, 1985, Concorso Internazionale Guido D'Arezzo, Italy, 1967-81. Hobbies: Model Railroads; Electronics; Handcraft; Repairing musical instruments. Address: San Luis 860, 4J 2000 Rosairo, Argentina.

HERNON Paul, b. 1947, Northumberland, England. Director; Designer. Career: Co-founded the London Music Theatre Group, 1982, and directed the British stage premieres of Martin's Le Vin Herbé and Vivaldi's Juditha Triumphans at the Camden Festival, London; British premieres of Salieri's Prima la Musica and Ward's The Crucible; Directed a tercentenary production of Handel's Acis and Galatea for the English Bach Festival in Reggio Emilia, Seville and Madrid; In Northern Ireland has directed Don

Giovanni, Così fan tutte, Le nozze di Figaro, Die Zauberflöte and Der Schauspieldirektor and works by Haydn, Donizetti, Puccini and Purcell; Has designed productions of Hansel and Gretel at Sadler's Wells, La Favorita in Dublin, Offenbach operas in Belfast and Crispino e la Comare at the Camden Festival; Designed the Yuri Lyubomov productions of Jenufa (first in Zurich, 1986) and Das Rheingold at Covent Garden, 1986, 1988; Eugene Onegin for Bonn, 1987, and Tannhäuser for Stuttgart, 1988. Address: Music International, 13 Ardilaun Road, London N5 2QR, England.

HERR Karlheinz, b. 27 Dec 1933, Zellhausen, Germany. Singer (Bass). Education: Studied with Paul Lohmann in Frankfurt. Career: Sang first in opera at Mainz, 1959, then appeared at Darmstadt, 1960-63, Mannheim from 1963 until 1988; Among his best roles have been Klingsor, Osmin, Mozart's Bartolo, Leporello, Rocco, Daland, and Varlaam in Boris Godunov; Guest appearances at the Paris Opéra, 1974, Bayreuth Festival, 1974, and in The Ring at Warsaw, 1988-90; Concert engagements in Haydn's Seasons and Creation, Messiah, Rossini's Stabat Mater and the Verdi and Fauré Requiems. Address: c/o Nationaltheater Mannheim, Am Goetheplatz, W-6800 Mannheim, Germany.

HERREWEGHE Phillippe, b. 2 May 1947, Ghent, Belgium. Conductor; Choral Director. Education: Studied piano at Ghent Conservatory; Studied medicine and psychiatry, graduated 1975. Career: Founder, Collegium Vocale of Ghent, 1975; Founder, La Chapelle Royale, 1977; Orchestre des Champs Elysées, 1991; Ensemble Vocal Européen; Collaborator with Ensemble Musique Oblique on 20th century music; Performances include: St Matthew's Passion, Bach, with La Chapelle Royale; C Minor Mass and Requiem, Mozart; Elias, Paulus, A Midsummer Night's Dream, Mendelssohn; Missa Solemnis, Beethoven; German Requiem, Brahms; Les Nuits d'Eté, L'Enfance du Christ, Berlioz; Guest conductor with many orchestras including: Concertgebouw Orchestra, Rotterdam Philharmonic, Orchestra of Lyon Opera and Vienna Philharmonic; Artistic Director, Saintes Festival, 1982-; Cultural Ambassador for Flanders, 1993-; Musical Director, Royal Flanders Philharmonic Orchestra, 1998. Recordings: Over 40 with the above ensembles. Honours: Officier des Arts et Lettres, Doctor Honoris Causa, Leuven University, 1997-. Address: c/o Stephane Maciejewski, 10 rue Coquillere, 75001 Paris, France.

HERRMANN Anita, b. 1947, Karlsruhe, Germany. Singer (Mezzo-soprano). Education: Studied in Strasbourg and with Joseph Metternich in Cologne. Career: Sang with the Bonn Opera, 1971-79, Karlsruhe, 1980-86, with further engagements at the Staatsoper Stuttgart, the Berlin Deutsche Oper and the Vienna Volksoper; Bregenz Festival, 1987-90, in Contes d'Hoffmann and Fliegender Holländer; Roles have included Mozart's Marcellina, Ino in Semele, Mistress Quickly in Falstaff, Lubasha in Sadko, Carolina in Elegy for Young Lovers and Mirza in Judith by Matthus (Berne, 1992). Address: c/o Stadttheater Bern, Nägelistrasse 1, CH-3011 Bern, Switzerland.

HERRMANN Karl Ernst, b. 1936, Neukirch, Upper Lusatia, Germany. Stage Director and Designer. Education: Studied at the Hochschule für Bildende Kunst at Berlin. Career: Designed for the theatre at Ulm from 1961 and associated with Peter Stein at Bremen and Berlin, 1969-78; Designed Das Rheingold and Die Walküre at the Paris Opéra, 1976; Théâtre de la Monnaie, Brussels, from 1978, with a cycle of seven operas by Mozart, La Traviata and Orfeo ed Euridice; Eugene Onegin at Hamburg, 1979; Die Zauberflöte at the Salzburg Landestheater, to inaugurate the Mozart Bicentenary, 1991; Die Entführung at the Vienna Staatsoper, 1991; Brussels productions of La Clemenza di Tito and La finta Giardiniera seen at Salzburg Festival, 1992; Designed sets for the Peter Stein production of Pelléas et Mélisande at Welsh National Opera, 1992. Address: Théâtre Royale de la Monnaie, 4 Leopoldstrasse, B-1000 Brussels, Belgium.

HERZ Gerhard, b. 24 Sept 1911, Düsseldorf, Germany. Musicologist. m. Mary Jo Fink, 2 June 1943. Education: University of Freiburg/Br, 1930; University of Vienna, 1931; Berlin University, 1931-33; Zurich University, 1933-34; PhD magna cum laude. Career: University of Louisville, USA, 1938; Indiana University, 1945-46; Professor, 1946-78, Chairman, Department of Music History, 1956-78, Emeritus Professor, 1978-, University of Louisville; Visiting Professor, Chicago University, 1965. Publications: Joh Seb Bach im Zeitalter des Rationalismus und der Frühromantik, 1935, 1936, reprint, 1985; Bach, Cantata No 4, 1967; Bach, Cantata No 140, 1972; Bach-Quellen in Amerika/Bach Sources in America, 1984; Essays on J S Bach, 1985; Essays on the Music of J S Bach and Other Divers Subjects: A Tribute to Gerhard Herz, 1981. Contributions to: The Musical Quarterly, 1938-77; Bach, Riemenschneider Bach Institute quarterly, 1970-; Bach-Jahrbuch, 1974, 1978, 1986; American Choral Review, 1970s, 1980s; Orbis Musicae, 1986; Bach Studies, 1989; Wm H Scheide Festschrift, 1993. Honours: 1st Chairman of American Chapter, 1972-74, Honorary Member, 1992, Neue Bachgesellschaft; Distinguished Lecturer, University of Louisville, 1978. Address: 729 Middle Way, Louisville, KY 40206, USA.

HERZ Joachim, b. 15 June 1924, Dresden, Germany. Professor; Director of Production. m. Charlotte Kitze, 17 July 1954, 1 son. Education: Colleges of Music, Leipzig/Dresden, 1942, 1945-49; State Exams, Musicology, Humboldt University, Berlin, 1949-51. Debut: Dresden National Opera: Die Bremer Stadtmusikanten, 1950. Career: Producer: Dresden Touring Opera, 1951-53, Berlin Komische Oper, 1956, Cologne, 1957, Director, Leipzig Opera, 1976; Managing Director, Berlin Komische Oper, 1981; Dresden National Opera, 1981-; Chief, 1991, Freelance, Music Theatre Department, College of Music, Dresden; Music Coach, Dresden, 1946-49; Assistant, 1949-51, Teacher, 1951-53, Dresden Drama Studio; Teacher: Berlin, 1953-56, Cologne, 1957; Lecturer, Berlin University, 1956; Professor, Leipzig University, 1976-; Visiting Lecturer, Leipzig Drama College, Universities of Munich, Salzburg, Eichstatt, Paris VIII, London, California, Göttingen, Lisbon, Heidelberg. Cincinnati, British Columbia, New York City, Banff Centre; Guest Producer, Buenos Aires, London, Cardiff, Moscow, Stockholm, Belgrade, Bern, Munich, Glasgow, Essen, Hamburg, Frankfurt, Vienna, Vancouver, Zurich, Salzburg, Helsinki; Film: The Flying Dutchman (DEFA); TV: Xerxes, Copenhagen; Radio Producer; Produced Lohengrin at Vienna, 1975, Così fan tutte, Helsinki, 1989, The Love for Three Oranges at Dresden Music Festival; Director of Productions at the Dresden National Opera, 1981-1991; Tours with Salzburg Così fan tutte to Japan and with Leipzig Xerxes through 13 countries; Guest Lecturer, Europe and the former Soviet Union; Staged Peter Grimes for Scottish Opera, 1994. Recordings: Freischütz, Carlos Kleiber; Zauberflöte, Colin Davis; Meistersinger, Dresden Semperoper; Freischütz; Rosenkavalier. Publications: Musiktheater - Felsenstein/Herz; Joachim Herz - Regisseur im Musiktheater - Irmer/Stein; Oper als idee und Interpretation-Herz; Joachim Herz über Musiktheater; Gesammelte Schriften. Contributor to: Magazines, newspapers, programmes, congresses, others. Memberships: Academy of Arts, Berlin; Honorary Board, Music Theatre Committee; Honorary Member, Bolshoi Theatre. Hobbies: Early music; Travel; Museums. Current Management: Freelance. Address: Altmarkt 17, Dresden, D 010654, Germany.

HESS Andrea, b. 7 May 1954, London, England. Cellist. m. John Leonard, 20 Jan 1985. Education: Recital Diploma, Royal Academy of Music, 1974; Nordwestdeutschemusikakademie, Detmold, Germany. Debut: Wigmore Hall, London, 1979. Career: Numerous performances as a soloist throughout United Kingdom, Europe, Canada and the Far East; Performed as a member of several chamber ensembles notably the Kreisler Trio of Germany and the Raphael Ensemble; Appeared on stage as solo cellist in National Theatre production of The Elephant Man, 1980-81; Solo Cellist for Royal Shakespeare Company, 1982-87; Appearances in drama productions for BBC and major independent television companies; Several broadcasts for BBC Radio 3; Composer and Onstage Solo Cellist in the National Theatre and West End for Arthur Miller's Broken Glass, 1994-95. Recordings: Volker David Kirchner Trio, Wergo; Chopin cello works and Chamber Music with the Kreisler Trio, Pantheon; Hyperion recordings of both Brahms sextets, Dvorak, Quintet and Sextet, Korngold Sextet and Schoenberg's Verklärte Nacht, Martinu and Schulhoff Sextets, Arensky Quartet, and Tchaikovsky's Souvenir de Florence Sextet, Strauss Sextet from Capriccio, Bruckner quintet, Schubert string trio and double cello quintet and both Brahms quintets with the Raphael Ensemble. Hobbies: Sculpture; Cooking; Large plants. Address: 10 Belsize Park, London NW3 4ES, England.

HESS Robert W, b. 17 May 1930, Brooklyn, New York, USA. Vocal Coach; Translator. Education: BMus, Piano, Carnegie Mellon University, 1952; MMus, Opera, New England Conservatory, 1954. Career: Musical Assistant, New England Opera Theater; Faculty, American Musical and Dramatic Academy, 1968-79; Visiting Lecturer, Hartt School of Music, University of Hartford, 1971-92; Recital Accompanist for Singers; Musical Director, Musicals-New York, Hyannis, Massachusetts & Beverly, Massachusetts; Master Classes in Musical Theatre; 92nd St "Y", 1993-94; Master Class in Opera Performance, 92nd St "Y". Publications: Translations, Puccini La Rondine, 1969; Haydn: Die Reisende Ceres, 1977; Offenbach-Les Bavards, 1982; Rimsky Korsakov-Complete Songs 7 volumes, 1980; Sadko, Snegurochka, 1985. Honours: National Endowment for the Arts; Grant for Translation of Haydn's La Vera Costanza, 1974, performed at Caramoor Festival, 1980. Memberships: ASCAP; American Federation of Musicians. Hobbies: Travel; Architecture. Address: 115 W 73rd Street, Apt 9D, New York, NY 10023, USA.

HESSE Axel (Ernst), b. 16 July 1935, Berlin, Germany. Musicologist; Educator. m. Flora Perez Diaz, 29 Feb 1964, 1 son, 1 daughter. Education: Musicologist, Latin American Music History, German Folk Song, Musical Transculturation Theory, Humboldt University, Berlin; Karl Marx University, Leipzig; Cuban Biblioteca Nacional, Havana, 1963-65; Diploma of Philosophy, 1961; PhD, 1971. Career: Oberassistent Musicologist, Humboldt University, 1970; Visiting Professor of Ethnomusicology, Lima, Peru, 1978; Academy of Sciences, East Germany, 1987-89; Co-Founder, Ciplice Folk Sound Archives, Freyburg, 1989; Lecturer, Humboldt University, 1990; Visiting Professor of Musicology, Cátedra Francisco Salinas, University of Salamanca, Spain, 1990-93, founding the multidisciplinary Salinas Coloquium on Rhythm. Recordings: Cuban Folk Music, in field, 1965; Afro-Peruvian music, 1978; German folk song, Hungary and German Democratic Republic, 1975-82; Childrens holiday camp songs, East Germany, 1975-87; Approximately 10,000 items, Folk Sound Archive, Hesse. Publications: Cancionero Violeta Parra, Translator and Editor, 1977; Chapters on Aztec, Mayan and Inca music in Geschichte der Musik volume 1, 1977; Ungarndeutscher Rosengarten, German Songs from Hungary. Address: Apartado 29, E-370080 Salamanca, Spain.

HESSE Ruth, b. 18 Sept 1936, Wuppertal, Germany. Singer (Mezzo-soprano). Education: Studied with Peter Offermans in Wuppertal and with Hildegard Scharf in Hamburg. Career: Sang in Lubeck from 1958; Hamburg Staatsoper from 1960; Operas by Wagner, Verdi and Strauss at the Deutsche Oper Berlin from 1962; Bayreuth Festival as Mary, Magdalene and Ortrud; Berlin, 1965, in the premiere of Der junge Lord by Henze; Vienna Staatsoper, 1966, Ortrud, Brangaene and Eboli; Paris Opéra, 1966, 1972, as Kundry and as The Nurse in Die Frau ohne Schatten; Salzburg Festival, 1974-75, as The Nurse; Sang Clytemnestra in Elektra at the Deutsche Oper Berlin, 1988; Concert and oratorio appearances. Recordings: Die Meistersinger; Die Frau ohne Schatten; Der junge Lord; Fricka in Der Ring des Nibelungen; Violanta by Korngold. Address: c/o Deutsche Oper Berlin, Richad Wagnerstrasse 10, D-1000 Berlin, Germany.

HESSE Ursula, b. 1970, Cologne, Germany. Singer (Mezzo-soprano). Education: Studied at the Berlin Musikhochschule with Ingrid Figur and Gundula Hintz-Lukas; Master classes with Hilde Rossl-Majdan and Brigitte Fassbaender; Lieder study with Aribert Reimann. Career: Komische Oper Berlin, in the song cycle Love, Life and Death by Siegfried Matthus, 1995; Toured Brussels, London, Dresden and Copenhagen in Mozart concert arias for the ballet Un Moto di Gioa, 1995; Concerts at the Berlin Festival with the Berlin Singakademie and with the New Bach Collegium in Brussels and Amsterdam; Season 1996-97 as Carmen at Lubeck and in Die Zauberflöte at Brussels; Alcina, Handel, Amsterdam. Recordings include: Webern Lieder, with Aribert Reimann. Honours include: Prizewinner, Paula-Saloman-Lindberg Lieder Competition, 1993; Deutscher Musikweitbewer, 1995. Address: c/o Harrison/Parrott Ltd, 12 Penzance Place, London W11 4PA, England.

HETHERINGTON Hugh, b. 1958, England. Singer (Tenor). Education: Studied at the Guildhall School of Music, at St John's College, Cambridge, and with Frederick Cox in Manchester; Further studies with Audrey Langford. Career: With Glyndebourne Festival and Touring Companies has sung Dr Caius (Falstaff), Truffaldino (Love of Three Oranges), Where the Wild Things Are and Idomeneo; Appearances with Scottish Opera as Dema in Cavalli's L'Egisto, Pang in Turandot, The Devil in The Soldier's Tale, Basilio in Le nozze di Figaro and roles in Iolanthe, Lulu, La Vie Parisienne and Eugene Onegin; With English National Opera as Piet in Ligeti's Le Grand Macabre and in The Return of Ulysses and L'Orfeo (1992); Covent Garden from 1985 in King Priam and Samson et Dalila; Further engagements with University Opera, New Sussex Opera, Opera Factory, Zurich and London Sinfoniettas, the Singers' Company, Channel 4 TV and the Endymion Ensemble double bill of Monteverdi and Michael Nyman (1987); New York debut, 1989, in HMS Pinafore with New Sadler's Wells Opera at the City Center Theater; Concerts with the City of Birmingham Symphony and the Matrix Ensemble. Address: c/o Oper Factory, 8a The Leather Market, Weston Street, London SE1 3ER, England.

HETTRICK Jane (Schatkin), b. New York, New York, USA. Organist; Musicologist. m. William E Hettrick III. Education: AB, Queens College, CUNY; MM, DMA, University of Michigan; Study at Hochschule für Musik und darstellende Kunst, Vienna. Career: Professor of Music, Rider University, Lawrenceville, New Jersey, 1974-; Solo Concert Organist with numerous recitals; Musicologist. Publications: Antonio Salieri, Concerto per l'Organo, 1981; Antonio Salieri, Italians in Vienna, 1983; Antonio Salieri, Messe in B-Dur, 1988; Antonio Salieri, Missa stylo a cappella, 1993; Antonio Salieri, Mass in D Major, 1994; Pietro Sales, Concerto in G Major, 1996; Anna Bon, Six Sonatas for Keyboard Op II, 1997; Arnolt Schlick, Spiegel der Orgelmacher und Organisten: Study and Translation, forthcoming. Contributions to: The American Organist; The Diapason; Journal of Church Music; Fontes Artis Musicae; Studien zur Musikwissenschaft; Learned music journals; Over 80 reviews of books and music in journals. Honours: Rider University, Summer Research Fellowship, 1976, Grant-in-Aid, 1987; Fulbright-Hays Scholarship, Hochschule für Musik und darstellende Kunst, Vienna, 1964-65; NEH Fellowship, 1983-84; NEH Summer Institute, University of Maryland, 1985; District of Columbia American Guild of Organists Foundation Grant, 1986; Gesellschaft zur Herausgabe von Denkmälern de

Tonkunst in Österreich, election only, 1988; San Francisco Chapter, American Guild of Organists, Projects Fund, 1991. Address: 48-21 Glenwood Street, Little Neck, NY 11362, USA.

HETTRICK William (Eugene), b. 15 Nov 1939, Toledo, Ohio, USA. Musicologist; University Professor. m. Jane Schatkin Hettrick, 5 June 1966. Education: BMus, 1962, MA, 1964, PhD, 1968, University of Michigan; University of Munich, Germany, 1966-67. Career: Professor of Music, Hofstra University; Board of Governors, 1988-94, President, 1995-99, American Musical Instrument Society. Publications: Editor: Gregor Aichinger, Cantiones ecclesiasticae (1607), 1972; Bernhard Klingenstein, Rosetum Marianum (1604), 1977; Gregor Aichinger, The Vocal Concertos, 1986; Translator and editor: The Musica instrumentalis deutsch of Martin Agricola: A Treatise on Musical Instruments (1529 and 1545), 1994; Editor, Journal of the American Musical Instrument Society, 1979-85, 1992 (Editorial Board Member, 1986-95). Contributions to: Notes; The New Grove; Journal of the American Musical Instrument Society; American Recorder; Journal of the American Musicological Society; Recorder and Music Magazine; Studien zur Musikwissenschaft; The Sixteenth Century Journal. Honours: Pi Kappa Lambda, 1960; Phi Beta Kappa, 1961; Stanley Medal, University of Michigan School of Music, 1962. Address: 48-21 Glenwood Street, Little Neck, NY 11362, USA.

HEUCKE Stefan, b. 24 May 1959, Gaildorf, Germany. Composer. Education: Studied Piano with Professor Renate Werner, Stuttgart, 1978-82; Piano with Professor A von Arnim, Composition with Professor G Schafer, Musikhochschule, Dortmund, 1982-86. Debut: Premiere of Vier Orchesterstücke, op 5, performed by Saarland State Orchestra, Saarbrucken, 1985. Career: Dozent (University Lecturer) in Theory of Music, Musikhochschule, Dortmund, 1989-; Production and editing live for WDR, SDR and Saarlandischer Rundfunk broadcasting stations; Numerous performances in Germany, Russia, Netherlands, France and Chile. Compositions: Self-published: Vier Orchesterstücke, op 5, 1983; Variations on a theme of Webern for orchestra, op 10, 1988; Piano trio, op 11, 1989; Symphony No 1, op 12, 1990; Symphony No 2, op 19, 1993; The Selfish Giant for narrator and orchestra, op 20, 1994; Sonata for bass clarinet and piano op 23, 1995; Quintet for violin, viola, violoncello, double bass and piano op 25, 1995; The Happy Prince, 21 Easy Piano Pieces op 28. Recording: CD, Abendgebete, op 14, with Berthold Schmid, tenor, and Sinfonietta Tubingen. Honours: Prize, Forum of Young German Composers Competition, 1985; Grant, City of Dortmund, 1990. Memberships: GEMA; Interessenverband deutscher Komponisten. Hobbies: Reading; Cooking; Hiking. Address: Markt 10a, D-59174 Kamen, Germany.

HEUERMANN Patricia (Calhoun), b. 4 Aug 1936, Atlanta, Georgia, USA. Stage Director; Designation, Set Designer. m. (1) Eric Heuermann Jr, 12 June 1956, (2) Vete Nowik, 29 Mar 1985, 1 son, 3 daughters. Education: Westminster School, Atlanta, Georgia; Voice Performance, Curtis Institute of Music, 1956; Private study, Stage Direction, Frank Corsare, Wesley Balk; Voice, Ludwig Fabri, Eufemia Giannini, Gregory Wilfred Pelletier, New York. Career: Director, Emory Opera Theatre, Emory University, 1967-73; Director, Opera Theater, Clark College, 1971-73; Founder, Artistic Director, Georgia Opera, 1974-78; Artistic Director, Atlanta Civic Opera, 1978-80; Managing Director, North Carolina Opera, 1980-82; Artistic Director, Theater of New York, 1982-; Director, Performance Workshop for Young Professional Singers, Manhattan School of Music, 1986-; Artistic Director, Reimann Opera Theatre of New York University, 1989-; Guest Director with regional opera companies throughout USA. Current Management: Association of Artistic Enterprises. Address: 481 Ft Washington Avenue No 68, New York, NY 10033, USA.

HEWITT Angela, b. 26 July 1958, Ottawa, Canada. Pianist. Education: Began studies with parents aged 3; Royal Conservatory of Music, Toronto, 1964-73; BMus, University of Ottawa, 1973-77. Debut: First recital aged 9, Toronto. Career: Appeared around the world as soloist with orchestra (Canada, USA, UK, Japan, Australia) and in recitals (in China, Mexico and throughout Europe); New York debut, Alice Tully Hall, 1984; Wigmore Hall debut in 1985; Proms debut in 1990. Recordings: First Bach recording in 1986; Cycle of Bach on CD: Inventions, 1994, French Suites, 1995, Partitas, 1997; Granados' Spanish Dances. Honours: International Bach Piano Competition, 1985; Prizewinner in Washington DC (Bach, 1975; Leipzig, 1976; Zwickau, 1977; Cleveland, 1979; Milan, 1980; First Prize in Viotti Competition, Italy, 1978; First Prize in Toronto International Bach Piano Competition, 1985; Honorary Doctorate, University of Ottawa, 1995; Key to the City of Ottawa, 1997. Current Management: Seldy Cramer Artists. Address: 3436 Springhill Road, Lafayette, CA 94549, USA.

HEWITT Harry (Donald), b. 4 Mar 1921, Detroit, Michigan, USA. Composer. m. Elizabeth Rolfe, 15 May 1943. Education: Studies with Homer LaGassey, Edward Murray and Joseph Barone. Career includes: Composer, over 60 years; Over 400 pieces publicly performed; Works played throughout USA by orchestras including New York Little Symphony, Pennsylvania Philharmonic, Egerinsky Sinfonia, Concerto Soloists of Philadelphia and Orchestra Society, Philadelphia; Chamber works performed at many colleges and numerous broadcasts; Former Music Director, Main Line Playhouse; Currently: President and Chief Executive Officer, Composer Services Inc; Director of CSI Publications, 1990-. Compositions include: Major works: 29 symphonies, 23 string quartets, operas, concerti; Most recent: 24 preludes for 2 Euphoniums, published 1989. Contributions to: Numerous journals and other publications; Editor, Penn Sounds, 1989-. Memberships: Founder, Delaware Valley Composers, President 1976-88; Writer Member, American Society of Composers, Authors and Publishers; Past Secretary, Guild for Contemporary Music. Address: 345 South 19th Street, Philadelphia, PA 19103, USA.

HEYER John (Hajdu) (formerly HAJDU, John H), b. 4 Jan 1945, Altoona, Pennsylvania, USA. Musicologist; Conductor. m. Sandra Lee Heyer, 1 Sept 1973, 2 sons. Education: BMus, Composition, DePauw University, 1966; MA, PhD, Musicology, University of Colorado, 1971-73; Studied with Nadia Boulanger, 1967-70. Career: Teacher, University of Colorado, 1971-73; Teacher, 1973-87, Chairman, Music Department, 1980, University of California, Santa Cruz; Lecturer, Programme Annotator, Carmel Bach Festival, 1979-; Dean, College of Fine Arts, Indiana University of Pennsylvania, Indiana, Pennsylvania, 1987-; Member of International Committee preparing the New Collected Works of Jean-Baptiste Lully for publication; President, Rocky Ridge Music Center Foundation, 1989-. Recording: Conducted J Gilles, Messe des Morts, Musical Heritage Society, 1981. Publications: Critical Edition: Jean Gilles, Messe des Morts, 1983; Lully and the Music of the French Baroque, 1989. Contributions to: Notes; The New Grove. Address: College of Fine Arts, 110 Sprowles Hall, Indiana University of Pennsylvania, Indiana, PA 15705, USA.

HEYNIS Aafje, b. 2 May 1924, Krommenie, Netherlands. Singer (Contralto). Education: Studied with Aaltje Noordewier-Reddingius, Laurens Bogtman and Bodi Rapp; Further study with Roy Henderson in England. Career: Sang at first in oratorio and other sacred music; Amsterdam, 1956, in Der Wildschütz by Lortzing; Concertgebouw Amsterdam, 1958, in the Alto Rhapsody Mahler, Bach (St Matthew Passion, B Minor Mass), Monteverdi, Schubert, Handel, Beethoven and Frank Martin. Recordings: Orfeo ed Euridice by Gluck; Madrigals by Monteverdi; Music by Bach. Honours include: Harriet Cohen Medal, 1961. Address: c/o Concertgebouworkest, Jacob Obredhstrasse 51, 1017 Amsterdam, Netherlands.

HICKEY Angela, b. 1949, England. Singer (Mezzo-soprano). Education: Guildhall School of Music. Career: Appearances with Royal Opera House, English National Opera, Scottish Opera, Opera North, Glyndebourne, City of Birmingham Touring Opera, Opera Northern Ireland, Monte Carlo Opera, Teatro Carlo Felice, Genoa; Roles include: Verdi's Preziosilla; Mistress Quickly and Azucena Kabanicha in Katya Kabanova; Jocasta in Oedipus Rex; Carmen; Helene in War and Peace with ENO; Annina in Der Rosenkavalier with Monte Carlo Opera; Mrs Sedley in Peter Grimes; Madame Larina in Eugene Onegin; Marcellina in Figaro with Opera Northern Ireland, 1991, Glyndebourne, 1992, Opera North, 1996; Mother Goose at Glyndebourne, 1994; Concerts include: Stabat Mater, Rossini; Requiem, Verdi; The Dream of Gerontius and Sea Pictures, Elgar; Ninth Symphony and Missa Solemnis, Beethoven; 2nd Symphony, Mahler; Nuits d'Eté; Appearances throughout Spain, France, Germany, Italy, Brazil, Czech Republic and Denmark. Recordings include: Hippolyte et Aricie, Rameau; Street Scene, Weill; Arianna, Alexander Goehr; Sea Pictures, Elgar. Address: Athole Still Ltd, Foresters Hall, 25-27 Westow Street, London SE19 3RY, England.

HICKOX Richard (Sidney), b. 5 Mar 1948, Stokenchurch, Buckinghamshire, England. Conductor; Music Director. m. Frances Ina Sheldon-Williams, 1976, 1 son. Education: Royal Academy of Music (LRAM); Organ Scholar, Queens' College, Cambridge (MA). Debut: As Professional Conductor, St John's Smith Square, 1971. Career: Prom debut, 1973; Artistic Director, Woburn Festival, 1967-, St Endellion, 1974-, Christ Church Spitalfields Festival, 1974-, Truro Festival, 1981-, Summer Music Festival, 1989; Appeared at other festivals including Flanders, Edinburgh, Bath and Cheltenham; Conductor, Music Director, City of London Sinfonia and Richard Hickox Singers, 1971-, London Symphony Chorus, 1976-, Bradford Festival Choral Society, 1978-; Principal Guest Conductor, Dutch Radio Operator, 1980-85; Artistic Director, Northern Sinfonia, 1982-; Associate Conductor, San Diego Symphony Orchestra, 1983-84; Regularly conducts LSO, RPO, Bournemouth Symphony Orchestra and Sinfonietta, Royal Liverpool Philharmonic Orchestra, BBC Symphony, Concert, Scottish and Welsh Orchestras, BBC Singers, Hallé Orchestra, Aarhus and Odense Orchestras; Conducted ENO, 1979; Opera North, 1982, 1986, Scottish Opera, 1985, 1987; Royal Opera, 1985, Los Angeles Opera, 1986; Conducted Rimsky's Mozart and Salieri at the Festival Hall, 1990, A Midsummer Night's Dream at Sadler's Wells; Season 1992/93 with Rossini Birthday Gala at the Barbican Hall and Giulio Cesare at Schwetzingen; Conducted the City of London Sinfonia at the 1993 Prom Concerts (Strauss's Oboe Concerto, Saxton's Viola Concerto and Mendelssohn's 4th Symphony); Conducted Rusalka at Rome, 1994; New production of Fidelio for English National Opera, 1996; Ariadne auf Naxos for Australian Opera, 1997. Recordings include: Belshazzar's Feast, with David Wilson-Johnson; Britten's Frank Bridge Variations; Elgar's Cello Concerto and Bloch's Schelomo (Steven Isserlis); Moeran's Sinfonietta and Serenade in G; Finzi Dies Natalis and Clarinet Concerto (Martyn Hill, Michael Collins); Rossini Stabat Mater (Field, D Jones, A Davies, Earle); L'Incoronazione di Poppea (Auger, Jones); Alcina (Auger); A Midsummer Night's Dream. Address: 35 Ellington Street, London N7, England.

HIDAS Frigyes, b. 25 May 1928, Budapest, Hungary. Composer. m. Erzsebet Zombori, 5 July 1966, 1 daughter. Education: Degree in Composing, Academy of Music, Budapest, 1946-51. Career: Music Director, Budapest National Theatre, 1951-66; Music Director, Budapest Operetta Theatre, 1974-79; Freelance Composer. Compositions include: Cedar, ballet in 2 acts, 1975; Three Movements for orchestra, 1987; The Undanced, ballet, 1989; Chamber music: Three Sketches, 1982; Divertimento, 1982; Hungarian Folksongs, 1985; Pian-Org, 1985; Musique pour six, 1985; Alteba Trio, 1986; String Quartets Nos 1, 2, 3; Brass chamber music: Trio, 1980; Six Etudes, 1980; Play, 1981; Three Little Scherzos, 1982; Movement, 1982; Septet, 1982; Training Patterns, 1982; 5 x 5, 1983; Trumpet Fantasy, 1983; Little Suite, 1983; Academic Quintet, 1983; Musik für Bläser, 1983; Four-in-Hand, 1985; Sextets Nos 1 and 5 for bass trombone and wind quintet; Tuba Quartet, 1990; Saxophone Quartet, 1990; Works for concert band: Ballet Music, 1980; Merry Music, 1980; Concertino, 1981; Suite, 1981; Fantasy and Fugue, 1984; Folksong Suites Nos 1 and 2, 1985; Circus Suite, 1985; Festive Music, 1985; 17 concertos including: Ballad, 1982; Rhapsody, 1982; Flute Concerto No 2, 1983; Trumpet Concerto No 2, 1983; Baroque Concerto, 1984; Széchenyi Concerto, 1984; Quintetto concertante, 1985; Oratorios; Music for films, TV and theatre. Recordings: Wind Concerto No 2; Flute Concerto No 2; Toccata, Movement No 3 of Organ Sonata; Violin Concertino; Oboe Concerto; Rhapsody for Brass Trombone; Training Patterns, excerpts; Four-in-Hand. Honours: Erkel Prize, 1958, 1982; Merited Artist of the Hungarian Republic, 1987. Address: Attila ut 133, 1012 Budapest, Hungary.

HIELSCHER Ulrich, b. 29 Apr 1943, Schwarzengrund, Germany. Singer (Bass). Education: Studied in Dusseldorf and with Paul Lohmann in Wiesbaden. Career: Sang at Essen from 1967, member of the Cologne Opera from 1974; Guest appearances at Hamburg, Hanover, Wuppertal, Frankfurt, Dusseldorf, Stuttgart and the Vienna Staatsoper, Ghent Opera, 1984-85, and further appearances as concert singer in Netherlands, Belgium, France, Switzerland and Colombia; Further guest appearances, Stadtstheater Schwerin, Staatsoper Berlin, Staatsoper Dresden, Theatre in Kiel and Freiburg; Opera roles have included Mozart's Osmin, Figaro, Leoporello, Alfonso, Sarastro and Speaker, Verdi's Falstaff and Padre Guardiano, Kecal in The Bartered Bride, Mephistopheles in Faust, Plunket in Martha; Wagner's Daland, Hagen and Gurnemanz, Baron Ochs, the Doktor in Wozzeck, Don Pasquale, Rodrigo in Lulu, Rocco in Fidelio, Pogner in Die Meistersinger and Massenet's Don Quichotte; Concert showings in works by Bach, Handel, Haydn, Mozart, Beethoven and Bruckner; Lied repertoire includes Schubert, Schumann, Beethoven, Richard Strauss, Wolf, Brahms, P Cornelius, Dvorák, F Martin, C Loewe, Paul Gräner, Hans Pfitzner, Moussorgsky, Mendelssohn and Robert Franz. Recordings include: Messa di Gloria by Puccini. Address: Oper der Stadt Köln, Offenbachplatz, 50667 Cologne, Germany.

HIERHOLZER Babette, b. 27 March 1957, Freiburg, Breigau. Pianist. m. D Michael Simpler, 31 August 1990. Musical Education: Studied with Elisabeth Dounias-Sindermann, Berlin, 1964-73; With Herbert Stessin, pre-college of Juilliard School of Music, New York, 1973-74; With Lili Kraus, Texas Christian University, Fort Worth, 1973-74; With Wolfgang Saschowa, Berlin, 1974-76; With Maria Tipo, Florence, Italy, 1975; With Paul Badura-Skoda, Folkwang-Hochschule Essen (Kunstlerische Reieprüfung Diploma, 1981), and Vienna, 1976-; With Bruno Leonardo Gelber, Buenos Aires, Argentina, 1979. Debut: With orchestra at age 11 at Philharmonic Hall, Berlin. Career: Regular appearances with orchestra and solo recitals in Berlin, Hamburg, Bonn, Frankfurt, Munich, Salzburg, Lausanne, Torino, Bordeaux, Caracas, Santiago, New York, Chicago, St Louis, Pittsburgh, Washington DC; Numerous engagements with the Berlin Philharmonic Orchestra with conductors: Sir Colin Davis, Klaus Tennstedt, Leopold Hager, Semyon Bychkov, Lothar Zagrosek, Gerd Albrecht, Sixten Ehrling, Paavo Berglund; USA debut with Pittsburgh Symphony Orchestra, 1984; Recital-debut at Carnegie Hall, New York, 1991; Canada -debut with Saskatoon Symphony Orchestra, 1994; Several Performances of the Clara Schumann

Piano Concerto (on the occasion of the 100th anniversary of Clara Schumann's death) in Berlin, Winnipeg, Ottawa, Festivals at Merida and Maracaibo, Venezuela; Solo recitals with an original recital program of Clara Schumann at Schumann Houses at Bonn and Zwickau. Recordings: CDs: Music by Couperin, Debussy, Schumann, Mozart, Schubert, Scarlatti Piano Sonatas Vol 1 and Vol 2; Played Soundtrack and Double for Clara Wieck (played by Natassja Kinski)in the Schumann Movie: Spring Symphony (by Peter Scahmoni). Address: 46 Aspinwall Road, Red Hook, New York 12571, USA.

HIESTERMANN Horst, b. 14 Aug 1934, Ballenstadt, Harz, Germany. Singer (Tenor). Career: Stadttheater Brandenburg from 1957, debut as Pedrillo in Die Entführung; Sang in Leipzig, Weimar, Berlin and Dresden; Deutsche Oper am Rhein Dusseldorf, 1976-84; Salzburg Festival from 1978, as Monostatos, as the Dancing Master in Ariadne auf Naxos, and as Robespierre in Dantons Tod, 1983; Dallas Opera, 1982, as Loge in Das Rheingold; Tokyo, 1983, as Mime in Siegfried; Other appearances in Geneva, Rouen, Amsterdam, Houston and New York (Metropolitan Opera); Barcelona, 1984, as Aegisthus in Elektra; Member of the Zurich Opera from 1984; Deutsche Oper Berlin, 1984, in the premiere of Reimann's Gespenstersonate; Vienna Staatsoper, 1987, as Herod in Salome; Sang Mime in a new production of The Ring at the Metropolitan, 1988-90; Shuisky in Boris Godunov at Barcelona, 1990; Herod in Berlin; Sang Aegisthus at Athens, 1992; Other roles include the Captain in Wozzeck (Catania, 1996) and David in Die Meistersinger. Recordings: Wozzeck; The Duenna by Prokofiev; Puntila by Dessau; Carmina Burana; Trionfi by Orff; Die Zauberflöte; Karl V by Krenek; Die Meistersinger conducted by Karajan. Address: c/o Deutsche Oper Berlin, Richard Wagnerstrasse 10, D-1000 Berlin, Germany.

HIETIKKO Jaakko, b. 16 May 1950, Kurikka, Finland. Singer (Bass). Education: Studied at the Helsinki Sibelius Academy. Career: Sang in the chorus of the Finnish National Opera from 1975 and was appointed as a soloist in 1980; Has appeared in most of the classical bass roles; Has specialised in such modern repertory as The Red Line by Sallinen (premiere, 1978), Vincent by Rautavaara (premiere, 1990); Sang in the premiere of The Book of Jonah by Olli Kortekanges, Helsinki, 1995 and The Last Temptations by Kokkonen; Many appearances at the Savonlinna Festival and as a concert singer. Address: c/o Finnish National Opera, PO Box 176, 00251 Helsinki Finland.

HIGGINBOTTOM Edward, b. 16 Nov 1946, Kendal, Cumbria, England. University Lecturer; Director of Music, New College, Oxford. m. Caroline M F Barrowcliff, 30 Oct 1971, 3 s, 4 d. Education: FRCO; John Stewart of Rannoch Scholar in Sacred Music; MA; PhD; BMus; Corpus Christi College, Cambridge, 1966-73; Organ Scholar, 1966-69. Career: Research Fellow, Corpus Christi College, Cambridge, 1973-76; Director of Music and Fellow of New College, Oxford, 1976-; Conseiller, French Ministry of Culture. Recordings: Organ Music and over 50 issues as Director of New College Choir, Oxford. Publications: Various editions of music and contributions to Grove 6. Contributions to: Musical Times; Organists Review; Music and Letters. Honours: Harding and Read Prizes, Royal College of Organists; Officier de l'Ordre des Arts et des Lettres. Address: New College, Oxford, England.

HILEY David, b. 9 May 1947, Littleborough, England. University Professor. m. Ann Fahrni, 28 Feb 1975, 2 daughters. Education: BA (Oxon), 1973; PhD, London, 1981. Career: Assistant Music Master, Eton College, 1968-73; Lecturer, Royal Holloway College, London, 1976-86; Professor, Regensburg University, Germany, 1986-. Publications: New Oxford History of Music II (co-editor), 1990; Western Plainchant: A Handbook, 1993. Memberships: Royal Musical Association; Plainsong and Mediaeval Music Society; Gesellschaft für Musikforschung; International Musicological Society; Henry Bradshaw Society. Address: Sonnenstrasse 10, 93152 Nittendorf, Germany.

HILL David (Neil), b. 13 May 1957. Master of Music; Organist. m. (1) Hilary Llystn Jones, 1979, 1 s, 1 d, (2) Alice Mary Wills, Dec 1994. Education: Chetham's School of Music, Manchester; MA, St John's College, Cambridge (organ scholar - toured Australia 1977, USA and Canada, 1978, Japan, 1979). Career: Conductor, Alexandra Choir, 1979-; Musical Director, Alexandra Choir, London, 1980-87; Sub Organist, Durham Cathedral, 1980-82; Organist, Master of Music, Westminster Cathedral, 1982-88; Organist and Master of Choristers at Winchester Cathedral from 1988 and Artistic Director, Philharmonia Chorus, the first British conductor to hold the post; Concerts in 1993 included performances with the Bournemouth Sinfonietta, Bournemouth Symphony and the Philharmonia Orchestra and Chorus; Also conducted the Bournemouth Symphony Orchestra, The Waynflete Singers and the Cathedral Choir in a concert televised for ITV at Christmas; In 1994 conducted in South Africa, Singapore, Denmark and Spain; Frequently invited to direct choral workshops and summer schools, particularly in Britain, USA and Australasia. Contributions

to: Has written several articles on choir training. Recordings: With Westminster Cathedral Choir. Honour: Gramophone Award, 1985. Hobbies: Wine; Beer; Cricket; Reading; Snooker. Address: 5 The Close, Winchester Cathedral, Winchester, Hampshire, England.

HILL George R, b. 12 July 1943, Denver, Colorado, USA. Musicologist; Music Bibliographer. Education: AB, Music, with Dpeartment Honours, Stanford University, 1965; AM, Library Science, University of Chicago, 1966; PhD, Historical Musicology, New York University, 1975. Career: Librarian, Music Division, New York Public Library, 1966-70; Assistant Music Librarian, New York University, 1971-72; Fine Arts Librarian, University of California, Irvine, 1972-73; Associate Professor of Music, Baruch College, City University of New York, 1973-. Publications: A Thematic Locator for Mozart's Works as Listed in Kochel's Chronologisch-Thematisches Verzeichnis - 6th Edition (principal author), 1970; A Preliminary Checklist of Research on the Classic Symphony and Concerto to the Time of Beethoven (excluding Haydn and Mozart), 1970; A Thematic Catalogue of the Instrumental Music of Florian Leopold Gassmann, 1976; Florian Leopold Gassmann, Seven Symphonies, 1981; Joseph Haydn Werke, Floetenuhrstuecke, 1984; A Handbook of Basic Tonal Practice, 1985. Contributions to: Articles and Reviews to various professional journals, including The New Grove Dictionary of Music and Musicians. Address: 84 Highgate Terrace, Bergenfield, NJ 07621-3922, USA.

HILL Jackson, b. 23 May 1941, Birmingham, Alabama, USA. Composer; University Professor of Music. m. Martha Gibbs, 5 June 1966, 1 son. Education: AB, 1963, MA, 1966, PhD, Musicology, 1970, University of North Carolina; Composition with Iain Hamilton, 1964-66, and Roger Hannay, 1967-68. Career: Assistant/Associate Professor of Music, 1968-80, Head of Department of Music, 1980-90, Associate Dean of Faculty, 1990-, Bucknell University, Lewisburg, Pennsylvania; Conductor, Bucknell Symphony Orchestra, 1969-79; Member, Research Unit, Manchester College, Oxford, England, 1975; Choral Conductor Assistant, Exeter College, Oxford; Hays/Fulbright Fellow, Japan, 1977; Visiting Fellow, Clare Hall, Cambridge, England, 1982-83. Compositions: More than 100 works including: Serenade, 1970; Three Mysteries, 1973; Paganini Set, 1973; Missa Brevis, 1974; English Mass, 1975; By the Waters of Babylon, sonata, 1976; Whispers of the Dead, 1976; Streams of Love, 1979; Enigma Elegy, 1987; Symphony No 1, 1990. Recordings: Sonata: By the Waters of Babylon; Ecce vidimus eum. Publications: The Music of Kees van Baaren, 1970; The Harold E Cook Collection of Musical Instruments; Numerous articles on music and mysticism, Japanese music and Buddhist liturgical music. Contributions to: Ethnomusicology; Studio Mystica; Notes. Hobbies: Travel; History; Book collecting. Address: Bucknell University, Lewisburg, PA 17837, USA.

HILL Jenny, b. 20 June 1944. Opera and Concert Singer (Soprano). div., 2 daughters. Education: National School of Opera, London Opera Centre. Debut: Sandman, Hansel and Gretel, Sadler's Wells Opera Company (now known as English National Opera). Career: English Opera Group with Benjamin Britten performing in London, Russia and Canada; Created role of Pretty Polly in Punch and Judy premiere, Aldeburgh and Edinburgh Festivals, and Mrs Green in Birtwistle's Down by the Greenwood Side premiere at the London and Brighton Festivals, 1968; Repertory operas performed include Traviata, Lucia, La Sonnambula, Rigoletto, Marriage of Figaro, Magic Flute, A Midsummer Night's Dream; Concert appearances include: A Mother Goose Primer, with the Pierrot Players, and Petrassi's Magnificat, with Giulini, both British premieres at the Royal Festival Hall, 1972; City of London Opening Concert, Bach's B minor Mass with Giulini at St Paul's Cathedral; Opening Concert, English Bach Festival, Blenheim Palace; Performances on radio and television as well as numerous song recitals of classical and avant-garde music. Recordings include: The Rape of Lucretia, as Lucia; Schumann's Faust; Bach's St John's Passion. Honours: Leverhulme Scholarship, 1960-63; Gulbenkian Fellowship for Most Outstanding Young Performer, 1969-72. Memberships: Equity; Incorporated Society of Musicians; Association of Singing Teachers. Hobbies: Swimming; Reading; Travel. Current Management: Direct booking only. Address: 5 Oaklands Grove, London W12 0JD, England.

HILL John Walter, b. 7 Dec 1942, Chicago, Illinois, USA. Professor of Music. m., 4 sons, 2 daughters. Education: AB, University of Chicago, 1963; MA, 1966, PhD, 1972, Harvard University, Cambridge, Massachusetts. Career: Assistant Professor, University of Pennsylvania, 1971-78; Associate Professor, 1978-84, Professor of Music, 1984-, University of Illinois, Urbana; Editor-in-Chief, Journal of the American Musicological Society, 1983-85. Publications: The Life and Works of F M Veracini, 1979; Studies in Musicology in Honor of Otto E Albrecht, 1980; Vivaldi's Ottone in Villa: A Study in Musical Drama, 1983. Contributions to: The Journal of the American Musicological Society; Music and Letters; Acta Musicologica. Memberships: American Musicological Society; International Musicological Society; Società Italiana di Musicologia. Address:

2136 Music Building, University of Illinois, 1114 West Nevada, Urbana, IL 61801, USA.

HILL Martyn, b. 14 Sept 1944, England. Singer (Tenor). m. Marleen De Maesschalck, 1974, 3 sons, 1 daughter. Education: Royal College of Music; ARCM; Vocal Studies with Audrey Langford. Career: Established a reputation as one of the most distinguished international tenors of his generation; He is known throughout the world as a concert and oratorio soloist and recitalist; Repertoire includes Elgar's Dream of Gerontius, Berlioz's, Damnation of Faust, Brucker's Te Deum, Verdi's Requiem and Mahler's Das Lied von der Erde; Performs regularly the works of Benjamin Britten; Recently sang War Requiem with the Sydney Symphony and Edo de Waart, Spring Symphony with the Hallé Orchestra and Kent Nagano, and Serenade with the Czech Philharmonic and Christopher Seaman; Evangelist in Bach's St John Passion, Festival Hall, 1997. Recordings include: Britten's Serenade with the RPO and Vladimir Ashkenazy; Herbert Howells' Missa Sabrinensis with the London Symphony Orchestra and Rozhdestvensky for Chandos and Bach's St Matthew Passion with the choir of King's College, Cambridge for Columns Classics. Address: Owen/White Management, 14 Nightingale Lane, London N8 7QU, England.

HILL Peter, b. 14 June 1948, Lyndhurst, England. Pianist; University Lecturer. m. Charlotte Huggins, 21 Apr 1981, 2 daughters. Education: MA, Oxford University; Royal College of Music. Debut: Wigmore Hall, London, 1974. Career: Regular broadcasts, BBC; International festival appearances include: Harrogate, Bath, English Bach, Dublin, Stuttgart; Founder Member, Ensemble Dreamtiger; Professor, University of Sheffield. Recordings: Complete Piano Music of Havergal Brian; Dreamtiger; East-West Encounters; Nigel Osborne: Remembering Esenin; Piano Works by Nigel Osborne, Douglas Young, Howard Skempton; Messiaen: the Complete Piano Music; Beethoven: Diabelli Variations. Publication: The Messiaen Companion (editor). Contributions to: Tempo. Honours: Chappell Gold Medal, Royal College of Music, 1971; 1st Prize, Darmstadt Ferienkurs, 1974. Address: c/o Department of Music, University of Sheffield, Sheffield S10 2TN, England.

HILL Richard George, b. 3 November 1972, Scotland. Conductor; Composer; Teacher; Arranger. Education: Loudoun Academy, Galston, 1984-90; BEd, Northern College of Education, Aberdeen, 1990-94. Career: Principal Euphonium, Loudon School Band, 1985-90; Conductor, The Morven Singers, 1992-94; Orchestrated Musical Score for The Sleeping Beauty, 1991, Boomtown, 1992; Teacher of Music, Nicolson Institute, Stornoway, 1994-97; Assistant Musical Director/Orchestrator, Pantomania, 1993; Founder, Stornoway Chamber Orchestra, 1995; Musical Director, Arranger. Conductor, Solas Dhé, MNE Television, 1997, broadcast December 1997. Compositions: Gloria; Ora Pro Nobis; Recorder Concerto; Papillons; Little One Sweet; Recent commissions include Portrona, 1996 and Conductor, MD Conductor, orchestration and recording of Dorabella, ballet, 1997. Recordings: Several. Honours: Winner of Classical Section, Livingstone Music Festival, 1996; Winner, Cambridge Contemporary Music Festival, 1996. Memberships: Scottish Society of Composers; British Music Writers Council; Musicians Union. Hobbies: Walking; Reading; Writing. Current Management, Vanderbeek & Imrie Ltd. Address: c/o Vanderbeek & Imrie Ltd, 15 Marvig, Lochs, Isle of Lewis HS2 9QP, England.

HILL Robert (Stephen), b. 6 Nov 1953, Philippines. Harpsichordist; Fortepianist; Musicologist. Education: Solo Diploma, Amsterdam Conservatory, 1974; Licentiate, Trinity College of Music, London, 1974; MA, 1982, PhD, 1987, Harvard University, USA. Career: Tours with Musica Antiqua Köln; Radio and TV broadcasts for West German, British, Dutch, Belgian and French networks, and National Public Radio and CBC, USA. Recordings: J S Bach. Sonatas for Violin and Harpsichord with Reinhard Goebel; J S Bach, Art of Fugue, early version; Solo Harpsichord. Contributions to: Early Music; Bach Jahrbuch. Honours: Erwin Bodky Award, 1982; Solo Recitalist Award, National Endowment for the Arts, 1983; Noah Greenberg Award, American Musicological Society, 1988. Hobby: Early 20th century recordings. Current Management: Andreas Braun, Cologne, Germany. Address: Staatliche Hochschule für Musik Freiburg, Freiburg, Germany.

HILL SMITH Marilyn, b. 9 Feb 1952, Carshalton, Surrey, England. Soprano Singer. Education: Guildhall School of Music. Career: Toured in: USA; Canada; Australia; New Zealand; Appearances at: Syney Opera House; Hollywood Bowl; English National Opera from 1978 as: Adele, in Fledermaus, Susanna, in Le nozze di Figaro, Olympia in Les Contes d'Hoffmann, Zerbinetta and Mozart's Despina, Papagena and Blonde; Covent Garden debut, 1981 in Peter Grimes; New Sadler's Wells Opera in works by Lehar, Kalman and Sullivan; Principal roles with Canadian Opera, Welsh National, Scottish Opera and Lyric Opera, Singapore; Other engagements include, Camden Festival, English Bach Festival, London Promenade Concerts; Regular concerts and broadcasts; Foreign appearances in Hong Kong,

Coburg, Versailles, Granada, Siena, Cologne, Athens, Rome, Madrid, Seville, Oman and Cannes; Sang Mozart's Countess for Central Festival Opera, 1996. Recordings: Several works for Chandos, That's Entertainment, Opera Rara, including A Hundred Years of Italian Opera, and award winning operetta series. Address: c/o Music International, 13 Ardilaun Road, Highbury, London, N5 2QR, England.

HILLEBRAND Nikolaus, b. 1948, Oberschlesien, Germany. Singer (Bass). Education: Studied with Rolf Dieter Knoll in Cologne and Hanno Blaschke in Munich. Debut: Lubeck, 1972. Career: Israel, 1972, as Mosè in the opera by Rossini; Salzburg Easter Festival, 1974, in Die Meistersinger; Vienna Staatsoper, 1974; Bayreuth Festival, 1974-75, in Parsifal and Die Meistersinger; Further engagements in Munich (Lohengrin), Karlsruhe, London, Paris, Rome and Brussels; Many concert appearances, notably in music by Bach; Conductors include Abbado, Böhm, Kleiber, Karajan and Muti. Recordings include: Stefano Colonna in Rienzi; Johannes Passion by Bach; Egisto by Cavalli; Romeo und Julia by Sutermeister; Reger's Requiem. Address: c/o Ingpen & Williams Ltd, 14 Kensington Court, London W8 5DN, England.

HILLEBRANDT Oskar, b. 15 Mar 1943, Schopfheim, Baden, Germany. Singer (Baritone). Education: Studied at Cologne Musikhochschule with Josef Matternich. Career: Sang at the Stuttgart Staatsoper from 1969; Appearances at Saarbrucken, Kiel and Brunswick from 1971; Member of the Dortmund Opera from 1985; Guest appearances at Hamburg, Munich, Dusseldorf, Mannheim and Zurich; La Scala Milan as Telramund and the Teatro Zarzuela Madrid as Achillas in Giulio Cesare by Handel; Seattle Opera as Alberich in the Ring; Further engagements in Antwerp, Copenhagen and at the Santander Festival, Marseilles and Turin, 1986, as Kaspar and Donner; British debut, 1989, as Mandryka at the Glyndebourne Festival; Other roles include Pizarro, Scarpia, Count Luna, Amonasro, Simon Boccanegra and Jochanaan in Salome, Wagner's Dutchman, Amfortas and Klingsor; Sang Alberich at Santiago, 1996; Concert showings in Paris, London, New York, Barcelona and Rome. Address: Opernhaus, Kuhstrasse 12, D-4600 Dortmund, Germany.

HILLEBRECHT Hildegard, b. 26 Nov 1927, Hanover, Germany. Singer (Soprano). Education: Studied with Margarethe von Winterfeld, Franziska Martianssen Lohmann and Paul Lohmann. Debut: Freiburg, 1951, as Leonora in Il Trovatore. Career: Sang at Zurich, 1952-54, notably in the premiere of the revised version of Hindemith's Cardillac (1952); Dusseldorf, 1954-59, Cologne, 1956-61; Sang Maria in Strauss's Friedenstag at Munich, 1961; Many appearances at the State Operas of Vienna, Hamburg and Munich; Salzburg Festival, 1946, 1964, as Ilia, Chrysothemis and Ariadne; Deutsche Oper Berlin, 1968, in the premiere of Ulisse by Dallapiccola; Covent Garden, 1967, as the Empress in Die Frau ohne Schatten; Metropolitan Opera, 1968-69; Sang with the Zurich Opera from 1972; Appearances in Rio de Janeiro, Paris, Rome, San Francisco, Edinburgh, Copenhagen, Barcelona, Dresden, Brussels and Prague; Repertoire includes works by Wagner, Puccini (Tosca), Verdi and Strauss, Elena in I Vespri Siciliani, Elisabeth de Valois, Desdemona, Sieglinde, Jenufa and Ursula in Mathis der Maler. Recordings: Excerpts from Don Giovanni and Tannhäuser; Cavalleria Rusticana; Der Rosenkavalier; Ariadne auf Naxos; Don Giovanni; Duchess of Parma in Doktor Faust by Busoni; Die Zauberflöte.

HILLIER Paul (Douglas), b. 9 Feb 1949, Dorchester, England. Singer; Conductor; Writer. m. Lena-Liis Kiesel, 19 Mar 1977, 2 d. Education: AGSM, 1970; Guildhall School of Music. Debut: Purcell Room, London, 1974. Career: Vicar-Choral, St Paul's Cathedral, 1973-74; Director, Hilliard Ensemble, 1974-90; Early Music Masterclasses, York, London, Vancouver, Canada; Visiting Lecturer, University of California, Santa Cruz, 1980-81; TV debut, Music in Time, 1983; Copland Fellow, Amherst College, MA, 1984; Director, Theatre of Voices, 1989-; Professor of Music, University of California, Davis, 1990-; Directed the Theatre of Voices at the Wigmore Hall, London, 1997. Recordings: Many for various labels. Publications: 300 Years of English Partsongs, 1983; Romantic English Partsongs, 1986; The Catch Book, 1987; The Music of Arvo Pärt, 1996. Honour: Edison Klassik, 1986. Hobbies: Books; Looking at Islands; Composing. Address: 4625 Inverness Wood, Bllomington, IN 47401, USA.

HILLIS Margaret (Eleanor), b. 1 Oct 1921, Kokomo, Indiana, USA. Conductor; Professor. Education: BA, Indiana University, 1947; Graduate student in choral conducting, Juilliard School of Music, New York, 1947-49; Studies with Robert Shaw. Career: Music Director, American Concert Choir and Orchestra, New York, from 1950; Assistant Conductor, Collegiate Chorale, New York, 1952-53; Conductor, American Opera Society Chorus, New York, 1952-68; Choral Director, New York City Opera, 1955-56; Music Director, New York Chamber Soloists, 1956-60; Founder-Conductor, Chicago Symphony Orchestra Chorus, 1957-; Choral Director, Santa Fe (New Mexico) Opera, 1958-59; Music Director, Kenosha (Wisconsin) Symphony Orchestra, 1961-68; Resident Conductor, Chicago Civic Orchestra, 1967-; Conductor, Cleveland Orchestra Chorus, 1969-71; Music Director, Elgin (Illinois) Symphony Orchestra, 1971-85; Conductor, San Francisco Symphony Orchestra Chorus, 1982-83; Guest Conductor with various US orchestras; Teacher, Juilliard School of Music, 1951-53; Director of Choral Activities, Northwestern University, 1970-77; Visiting Professor of Conducting, Indiana University School of Music, Bloomington, 1978-; Master classes in choral conducting. Recordings: Prepared choruses for many award-winning discs by the Chicago Symphony Orchestra. Address: c/o Chicago Symphony Orchestra, Orchestra Hall, 220 S Michigan Avenue, Chicago, IL 60604, USA.

HILLMAN David, b. 1936, England. Singer (Tenor). Education: Studied at the National School of Opera. Career: Sang at Sadler's Wells, London, from 1962 as Tamino, Ferrando, Hoffmann, Rodolfo and Essex in Gloriana; Sang also in the premieres of Benjamin's Tartuffe, 1964, Bennett's The Mines of Sulphur, 1965, Williamson's The Violins of St Jacques, 1966, and Musgrave's Mary Queen of Scots (Edinburgh, 1977); English premiere of Nielsen's Saul and David, 1977, as David, and in Szymanowski's King Roger with the New Opera Company, 1975; Guest appearances as Macduff at Covent Garden, at Stuttgart, Bonn, with Netherlands Opera (as Tom Rakewell, 1972), Santa Fe (Oliver's Duchess of Malfi, 1978) and at Glyndebourne (Elemer in Arabella, 1985); Also appeared in operettas by Gilbert and Sullivan.

HILTON Janet (Lesley), b. 1 Jan 1945, Liverpool, England. Clarinettist. m. David Richardson, 6 July 1968, 2 sons, 1 deceased, 1 daughter. Education: Music, Royal Manchester College of Music, 1961-65; ARMCM; Vienna Konservatorium, 1966. Career: Soloist with BBC Philharmonic, concert tours with Margaret Price; Festival appearances include Bath, Cheltenham, Aldeburgh, Henry Wood Proms, 1979; Edinburgh; BBC2 TV with Lindsay Quartet; Principal Clarinettist, Welsh National Opera, 1970-73; Scottish Chamber Orchestra, 1973-80; Kent Opera, 1984; Teacher, Royal Scottish Academy of Music and Drama, 1974-80; Royal Northern College of Music, 1982-86; Head of Woodwind, Birmingham Conservatoire, 1992; Principal Clarinet of Manchester Camerata and Director of Camerata Wind Soloists; Professor, University of Central England, Birmingham. Recordings include: Weber clarinet concertos with CBSO; Chamber Music of Brahms and Weber; Concertos of Malcolm Arnold, Nielsen, Copland, Stanford. Honour: Boise Foundation Scholarship; Prize, National Federation of Music Societies. Hobbies: Cooking; Reading; Walking. Current Management: Robert Gilder & Company. Address: Holly House, 2 East Downs Road, Bowdon, Altrincham, Cheshire WA14 2LH, England.

HIMMELBEBER Liat, b. 27 Apr 1956, Stuttgart, Germany. Singer (Mezzo-soprano). Education: Studied in Berlin, and in Hamburg with Judith Beckmann; Master classes with Aribert Reimann and Dietrich Fischer-Dieskau. Career: Sang at the Eutin Festival, 1982-83, Oldenburg, 1984-85, and from 1985 as member of the Theater am Gärtnerplatz, Munich; Among her best roles have been Rosina, Mozart's Dorabella and Cherubino, and Hansel; Guest with the Hamburg Staatsoper and appearances with the Augsburg Opera from 1992; Concerts include premieres of works by Reimann, Von Böse and Manfred Trojahn; Sang also in the Munich 1987 premiere of Miss Julie by A Bibalo. Address: c/o Städische Buhnen Augsburg, Kasernstrasse 4-6, Pf 111949, 86159 Augsburg, Germany.

HIND Rolf, b. 1964, England. Concert Pianist. Education: Studied at Royal College of Music with John Constable and Kendall Taylor; Los Angeles with Johanna Harris-Heggie. Career: Played piano solo in Des Canyons aux Etoiles and Sept Haikai by Messiaen; Has premiered works by Ligeti, Xenakis, David Sawer and Tristan Murail; Concerts at the main London venues and at the Bath, Canterbury, Cheltenham, Brighton, King's Lynn and Avignon Festivals; Has appeared with London Brass, Spectrum, the London Sinfonietta and the Ulster Orchestra (Szymanowski conducted by Jan Latham Koenig); Played in St Lucia, 1990, and was soloist in Eight Ligeti Piano Studies for a Belgian dance company; Seasons 1990-92 in Grenoble, Rotterdam, Metz, Brussels, Antwerp, Paris, Essen, Salzburg, Utrecht and New York. Recordings include: Solo works by Ligeti, Carter and Martland; Xenakis Econta and Ruders Breakdance, with London Brass; Messiaen Trois Petites Liturgies de la Présence Divine, with the London Sinfonietta. Address: c/o Norman McCann International Artists Ltd, The Coach House, 56 Lawrie Park Gardens, London SE26 6XJ, England.

HIND O'MALLEY Pamela, b. 27 February 1923, London, England. Composer; Cellist and Pianist. m. Raymond O'Malley, deceased 1996, 2 sons, 1 daughter. Education: ARCM (performance); Studied Cello with Ivor James, Piet Lentz and Pablo Casals; Piano with Dorothea Aspinall and Imogen Holst; Composition with Herbert Howells. Debut: Wigmore Hall, 1963. Career: Cello Soloist and Ensemble Player; As One Pair of Hands, gives recitals for solo cello and solo piano in programmes that always include one contemporary work; Solo recitals playing Cello and Piano from 1967; Wigmore Hall 1969 and 1970; Teacher of Cello and Piano, Cambridge; Part time Cello Teacher, Kings College School; Part time Ensemble Coach, Cambridge University Music Society. Compositions: Keyboard Music, Songs, Duo for Violin and Cello, Trio for Flute, Violin and Cello; Suite for String Orchestra. Publications: Cycle of Four Rounds for Four Violins; Arrangements of two Fauré songs for either Viola or Cello with Piano. Contributions to: Royal College of Music Magazine; Casals as Teacher (Royal College of Music Magazine, 1950); Casals and Intonation (ESTA News and Views, 1981, and re-printed in the STRAD, 1983). Memberships: Incorporated Society of Musicians; European String Teachers Association; International Cello Centre; Herbert Howells Society; Cambridge University Music Society. Hobbies: Walking; Reading; Gardening. Address: 23 Nightingale Avenue, Cambridge CB1 4SG, England.

HINDERAS Natalie (Henderson), b. 16 June 1927, Oberlin, Ohio, USA. Pianist; Teacher. Education: Studied at the Juilliard School and with Eduard Steuermann at the Philadelphia Conservatory. Debut: Played the Grieg Concerto with the Cleveland Women's Symphony Orchestra, 1939. Career: Gave concerts in Europe after completing studies and made New York debut in 1854; Toured for the US State Department in Africa, Poland, Sweden and Yugoslavia in the 1960s; Toured black colleges of the southern United States, 1968, presenting classical music of black composers; Solo appearances with the Chicago Symphony Orchestra, the Cleveland Orchestra and the New York Philharmonic; Teacher at Temple University. Honours include: Honorary doctorate, Swarthmore College, 1976.

HINDS Esther, b. 3 Jan 1943, Barbados, West Indies. Singer (Soprano). Education: Studied with Clyde Burrows in New York, and at Hartt College, Hartford, with Helen Hubbard. Debut: New York City Opera, 1970, as First Lady in Die Zauberflöte. Career: Has sung in New York as Donna Elvira, Madama Butterfly and Gershwin's Bess (on Broadway); Engagements at opera houses in Houston, Cincinnati and San Diego; Other roles include Liu (Turandot) and Micaela; Spoleto Festival, 1983, as Cleopatra in Antony and Cleopatra by Samuel Barber; Many concert performnces. Address: c/o New York City Opera, Lincoln Center, New York, NY 10023, USA.

HINDS Geoffrey (William John), b. 2 April 1950, Auckland, New Zealand. Composer; Piano Teacher. Education: BA, Auckland, 1974; MPhil (Mus) Auckland, 1976; BDiv, Melbourne College of Divinity, 1980; LRSM (Piano Teachers), 1983. Compositions: Held in New Zealand Music Archive Canterbury University - Sonata for Viola and Pianoforte, 1975; Suite for String Quintet, 1975; String Quartet, 1976; Cantata Upon This Rock, 1982; Held in Music Library, Radio New Zealand, Wellington Motet for the Lord has Purposed, 1980-81; Overture into a Broad Place, 1981; String Quartet, 1981; Symphonic Moments of Our Time, 1982; And His Name Shall Be Called, 1981; Through The Grapevine, 1982; Anthems written for St Barnabas Choir; Song Cycle, Water Water Everywhere, 1985; Song Cycle, Pieces of Peace, 1986; Colyton Overture, 1986-87, written for Manawatu Youth Orchestra; String Quartet 1983-84; Song cycle, Innocence and Experience, 1987; Blowing in the Wind for wind quintet, 1987; Song Cycle, Nine Mystical Songs, 1988-89; Godzone Re-evaluated for Youth Orchestra, 1989; Great Outdoors Suite for Piano, 1989; String Quartet, 1989; Symphony, St Barnabas Ballads (Tenor and piano), Creation Cantata, The Good Life (Musical), 1990; Piano Sonata, Two Edged Sword (Song Cycle for Soprano and piano), Sonata for Trombone, Organ, 1991-; Flights of Fancy, for Clarinet & String Quartet, Gardens (SATB), Suite for Viola, Our Good Keen Men (Song cycle for Tenor and piano), 1992; A Tree For All Seasons (Soprano, cello and piano); City of ... (Song cycle for Tenor, Piano), 1993; String Quartet No 2, 1995; The Mind, canticle (Soprano, Piano), 1995; Reflections, 1995; From the Rising of the Sun, 1996; Solitude: A Pilgrim's Progress; Creation in Reverse, 1997; Spiritual, suite for guitar, 1997. Honour: Recorder Week Composition Competition, 1996. Memberships: Composers Association of New Zealand; Institute of Registered Music Teachers of New Zealand. Hobbies: Political Science; Crossword Puzzles; Nature walks. Address: 72 Valley Road, Mount Eden, Auckland 1003, New Zealand.

HINES Jerome, b. 8 Nov 1921, Hollywood, California, USA. Singer (Bass); Composer; Organic Chemist, Mathematician, BA's UCLA, 1943. Education: Studied with Gennaro Curci in Los Angeles and with Samuel Margolis & Rocco Pandiscio in New York. Debut: San Franciso, 1941, as Monterone in Rigoletto. Career: Metropolitan Opera from 1946, as Mephistopheles, Philip II in Don Carlo and the Grand Inquisitor, Gurnemanz, Sarastro, Boris Godunov and Don Basilio; Over 50 broadcasts and 830 performances in 41 years; Engagements in La Scala, Torino, Rome, Naples, Palermo, Budapest, Mexico City and Buenós Aires; Concerts with Toscanini; Glyndebourne Festival in Edinburgh, 1953, as Nick Shadow in the British premiere of The Rake's Progress; Munich, 1954, as Don Giovanni; Further European appearances in Turin, Rome, Naples, Palermo, Florence and Milan; Bayreuth, 1958-61, as Gurnemanz, King Marke and Wotan; Moscow, 1962, as Boris; Sang Filippo in Don

Carlo, Mefistotele, Silva in Ernani, Attila in Teatro Colon, Buenos Aires, 1951-1965, 1992. Compositions include: I am the Way, opera on the life of Christ. Recordings: Beethoven Missa Solemnis, conducted by Toscanini; Macbeth; Lohengrin; La Favorite; Messiah; Le Prophète; Duke Bluebeard's Castle; Don Carlos. Publications include: This is my Story, this is my Song, 1968; Tim Whosalver, 1970; Theory of Extranumencal Information, 1980; Great Singers on Great Singing, 1982. Honours include: Caruso Award, 1946; Cornelius Bliss Award, 1950. Address: Spira Music Theatre International, 1024 Broad St, Newark, NJ 07102, USA.

HINTERMEIER Margareta, b. 11 Sept 1954, St Polten, Austria. Singer (Mezzo-soprano). Education: Studied in Vienna with Hilde Konetzi. Career: Has sung at the Vienna Staatsoper from 1982 as Dorabella, Cherubino, Octavian, the Composer in Ariadne auf Naxos and Federica (Luisa Miller); Tour of Japan with the Staatsoper Company as Cherubino; Guest appearances at Geneva, Lisbon (as Orlofsky), Liege (Idamante in Idomeneo) and Dresden; Salzburg Festival, 1978-83, as Idamante; Concert appearances include Beethoven's Ninth at the 1989 Vienna Festival and Wagner's Wesendonck Lieder; Schubert Festival Hohenems, Carinthia Summer and Flanders Festivals; Further concert engagements in Istanbul, Nice and Bologna; Sang in Mahler's 3rd Symphony with the Vienna Symphony Orchestra at the Festival Hall, London, 1993. Recordings include: Maidservant in video of Elektra, conducted by Abbado; Die Walküre; Beethoven's Ninth. Address: c/o Staatsoper, Opernring 2, A-1010 Vienna, Austria.

HINTON Alistair, b. Dunfermline, Scotland. Composer; Archivist. m. Terry Piers-Smith. Education: Royal College of Music, London; Composition with Humphrey Searle, Piano with Stephen Savage. Career: Numerous Appearances Worldwide; Founder and Curator of The Sorabji Archive. Compositions include: String Quintet, 1969-77; Violin Concerto, 1980; Pansophiæ for John Ogdon, 1990; Sequentia Claviensis, 1993-94; 5 Piano Sonatas, 1962-95; Variations for Piano and Orchestra, 1996; Szymanowski-Etude, 1992-96; Sinfonietta, 1997. Recordings: Variations and Fugue on a Theme of Grieg, 1970-78; Pansophiæ for John Ogdon, 1990. Publications: Sorabji: A Critical Celebration, 1992, reprinted, 1994. Contributions to: Grove's Dictionary of Music and Musicians; Tempo; The Organ; Godowsky Society Newsletter; Notes, USA. Hobbies: Hill Walking; Reading; Travel; Good Food and Fine Wine. Address: The Sorabji Archive, Easton Dene, Bailbrook Lane, Bath BA1 7AA, England.

HIROKAMI Jun'ichi, b. 5 May 1958, Tokyo, Japan. Conductor. Education: Studies, Tokyo Music University. Debut: Israel Philharmonic Orchestra, 1988, London Debut, London Symphony Orchestra, 1989. Career: Assistant Conductor, Nagoya Philharmonic Orchestra, 1983; International career from 1984; Conducted the NHK Symphony Orchestra, 1985, Orchestre National de France, 1986; Royal Philharmonic Orchestra, 1990; Further engagements with the Stockholm Philharmonic, Norrkoeping Symphony Orchestra (Principal Conductor from 1991), Malmo and Gothenburg Symphony Orchestras and radio orchestras in Holland and Italy; Operatic debut (July 1989), Un Ballo in Maschera followed by Rigoletto and La Forza del Destino all with the Australian Opera; International concert activities spread to other countries: Spanish National Orchestra, Berlin Radio Symphony, Royal Concertgebouw Amsterdam, Montreal Symphony and with many European Orchestras; Conducted all major Japanese orchestras and appointed Principal Guest Conductor of the Japanese Philharmonic Orchestra. Recordings: Debut with the London Symphony Orchestra (BMG) and subsequent recordings with BIS Records of Sweden and Fun House Records, Japan mainly made with his own Norrkoping Symphony Orchestra. Honours: Winner, 1st International Kondrashin Conducting Competition, Amsterdam, 1984. Address: c/o Terry Harrison Artists Management, The Orchard, Market Street, Charlbury, Oxon OX7 3PJ, England.

HIRSBRUNNER Theo, b. 2 Apr 1931, Thun, Switzerland. Writer. Education: Pupil of Pierre Boulez. Career: Teacher, Berne Conservatory until 1987. Publications: Books on Debussy, 1981, Stravinsky, 1982, Boulez 1985, Messiaen, 1988, Ravel, 1989. Contributions to: Many articles to periodicals. Honours: Janácek Medal, 1978; Medal, Year of Czech Music, 1984; Honorary Member, Accademia Musicale Ottorino Respighi. 1988. Address: Optingenstr 53, CH-3013 Bern, Switzerland.

HIRSCH Leonard, b. 19 Dec 1902, Dublin, Ireland. Violinist; Music Educator; Conductor. m. 2 d. Education: Royal Manchester College of Music with Adolph Brodsky; FRCM, London; FRNCM, Manchester. Debut: Dublin. Career includes: Hallé Orchestra, 1921-37; Toured America with RAF Symphony Orchestra during World War II; Leader of Philharmonia Orchestra, 1941-49; Hirsch String Quartet, re-established, 1944-62 and Harry Isaacs Trio, 1944-52; Played in front of Churchill, Truman and Stalin at the Potsdam Conference, after the War; Associated with the National Youth Orchestra, 1948-66; Conductor of Hirsch Chamber Players, 1961-67; 1st Musical Director, BBC Training Orchestra, 1966-69; Chief Music Consultant, County of Hertfordshire, 1964-84; Professor, Royal College of Music. Recordings include: Bartók Quartet No 1; Bloch No 2 String Quartet; Hugo Wolf Serenade. Contributions to: Book, Sir Hamilton Harty, 1978. Honours: Fellow, Royal Manchester College of Music; Fellow, Royal College of Music. Hobbies: Walking; Gardening; Travel. Address: Keenlyside, 24 Eighth Avenue, Bristol, BS7 OQT, England.

HIRSCH Peter, b. 1956, Cologne, Germany. Conductor. Education: Studied at the Hochschule, Cologne. Career: Assistant to Michael Gielen at the Frankfurt Opera, 1979; Guest conductor at theatres in Hamburg, Dusseldorf, Karlsruhe and Wiesbaden; Debut at La Scala, 1985, with Prometo by Luigi Nono; Has conducted Die Fledermaus and Rigoletto for Vancouver Opera; La Bohème and Der Freischütz for Welsh National Opera and Così fan tutte with Scottish Opera; Benvenuto Cellini for Netherlands Opera; Concert engagements with the radio orchestras of Stuttgart, Hanover and Berlin, the Residentie Orkest and the Radio Chamber Orchestra of Hilversum, Netherlands, and L'orchestre National de Belgique; Regular engagements with the Bournemouth Sinfonietta and the Bournemouth Symphony; Regular Guest Conductor at Staatsoper unter den Linden and Komische Oper, Berlin. Address: Konzertdirektion Jürgen Erlebach, Grillparzerstrasse 24, 22085 Hamburg, Germany.

HIRST Grayson, b. 27 Dec 1939, Ojai, California, USA. Singer (Tenor). Education: Studied at the Music Academy of the West with Martial Singher and at the Juilliard School with Jennie Tourel. Debut: Sang Cavalli's Ormindo with the Opera Society of Washington, 1969. Career: Sang Tonio in La fille du régiment at Carnegie Hall, 1970; New York City Opera debut, 1970, in Britten's The Turn of the Screw; Kennedy Center, Washington, in the premiere of Ginastera's Beatrix Cenci; Other premieres include works by Robert Aitken, Ned Rorem, Robert Starer, Virgil Thomson (Lord Byron) and Jack Beeson; Further appearances in France, Brazil, England and Switzerland; Other roles include Don José, Pelléas, Faust and Mozart's Tamino, Ferrando and Belmonte. Recordings include: Schubert's Die schöne Müllerin.

HIRST Linda, b. 1950, Yorkshire, England. Singer (Mezzo-soprano). Education: Flute and singing at the Guildhall School of Music, London. Career: Joined Swingle Singers and often appeared with Cathy Berberian; Concerts with the London Sinfonietta with Berio, Ligeti and Henze conducting their works; Premiere performances of Muldowney's Duration of Exile, Osborne's Alba, Simon Holt's Canciones and Judith Weir's The Consolations of Scholarship; Performances of Schoenberg's Pierrot Lunaire in Paris and Florence and for Channel 4 TV; Glyndebourne Festival debut, 1985, Knussen's Where the Wild Things Are; 1986 world premiere of Osborne's The Electrification of the Soviet Union; Appearances at Bath and Almeida Festivals; Frankfurt Opera, Henze's Elegy for Young Lovers; Arts Council Network Tour with the London Sinfonietta; Also performs earlier music such as Incoronazione di Poppea in Spitalfields for Opera London; Sang in the premiere of Vic Hoyland's La Madre (written for her), London, 1990. Recordings: Songs Cathy Sang; Ottavia in L'Incoronazione di Poppea. Address: c/o Norman McCann International Artists Ltd, The Coach House, 56 Lawrie Park Gardens, London SE26 6XJ, England.

HIRSTI Marianne, b. 1958, Oslo, Norway. Singer (Soprano). Education: Studied in Oslo and Lubeck. Career: Sang at Kiel, 1980-81; Staatsoper Hamburg, 1981-85; Cologne, 1985-87; Staatsoper Stuttgart from 1987; San Meroe in Reinhard Keiser's Die grossmütige Tomyris at Ludwigshafen, followed by Constanza in Bononcini's Griselda and Blondchen in Die Entführung; Cologne Opera as Maire in Zar und Zimmermann; Ludwigsburg Festival as Susanna in Le Nozze di Figaro; Théâtre de la Monnaie, Brussels, as Berta in Il Barbiere di Siviglia, 1992; Other roles have included Despina, Marzelline, Gretel, Sophie in Werther and Tytania in A Midsummer Night's Dream; Many Lieder recitals and concert appearances, including Wigmore Hall, London, 1988. Recordings include: Beethoven Missa Solemnis; Die Grossmütige Tomyris; Der Zwerg by Zemlinsky; Blondchen in Die Entführung, conducted by Hogwood. Address: c/o Staatsoper Stuttgart, Oberer Schlossgarten 6, 7000 Stuttgart, Germany.

HIRTE Klaus, b. 28 Dec 1937, Berlin, Germany. Singer (Baritone). Education: Studied at the Stuttgart Musikhochschule with Hans Hager. Career: Sang at the Stuttgart Staatsoper from 1964; Bayreuth Festival, 1973-75, as Beckmesser in Die Meistersinger; Salzburg Festival as Antonio in Le Nozze di Figaro; Ludwigsburg Festival, 1972, as Papageno; Further appearances in Nuremberg, Munich, Dusseldorf, Mannheim, Venice, Chicago and San Antonio; Other roles include Don Pasquale and Dulcamara by Donizetti; Wagner's Kurwenal and Klingsor and parts in operas by Strauss, Gluck, Mascagni and Weber; Sang Oberon in the premiere of Der Park by Hans Gefors, Wiesbaden, 1992. Recordings include: Tannhäuser; Die Meistersinger; Le Cadi Dupé by Gluck; Der Schauspieldirektor; Cavalleria Rusticana; Intermezzo; Die schweigsame Frau. Address: c/o Staatstheater Stuttgart, Oberer Schlossgarten 6, D-7000 Stuttgart 1, Germany.

HIRVONEN Anssi, b. 1948, Finland. Singer (Tenor). Education: Studied at the Sibelius Academy, Helsinki and at the Conservatoire of Tampere, Helsinki; Private studies with Jolanda di Maria Petris; Further studies in Berlin and Wien. Career: Appearances as Oratorio and Concert Soloist in Finland, Sweden, Germany, Hungary, USA, Estonia, Russia and Latvia; Opera Debut at Tampere Opera, 1975; Solo engagements at the Heidelberg Opera, 1979-80, the Savonlinna Opera Festival 1978-, the Finnish National Opera 1980-, and provincial operas in Finland; Sang in the 1990 premiere of Rantavaara's Vincent; Guest Soloist at the operas of Stockholm and Tallinn; Numerous TV and Radio appearances and recordings; Professor and Lecturer of Singing, Sibelius Academy; Guest Soloist, Finnish National Opera; Sang Beppo in Pagliacci for Tampere Opera, 1996. Recordings include: Contemporary Finnish Choir Music; Sacred Songs of C Franck, T Kuusisto, Y Karanko, E Linnala, A Maasalo and L Madetoja; Christmas Songs of O Kotilainen, A Maasalo, S Palmgren and S Ranta; Musica Humana, Sacred Songs of P Kostiainen and J Sibelius. Address: c/o Finnish National Opera, Bulevardi 23-27, SF-00180 Helsinki 18, Finland.

HIRZEL Franziska, b. 28 Nov 1952, Zurich, Switzerland. Singer (Soprano). Education: Studied in Basel, Fribourg, Frankfurt am Main and Zurich. Career: Sang at Darmstadt Opera from 1980, notably in the 1983 premiere of Klebe's Die Fastnachtsbeichte and as Mozart's Blondchen, Donna Elvira, Fiordiligi and Pamina, Micaela, Martha, Euridice, Gilda, Musetta and Gretel; Concert repertoire has included sacred works by Bach, Beethoven, Mozart, Haydn and Schoenberg; Many Lieder recitals and broadcasting engagements; Guest appearances at concert halls and opera houses throughout Germany. Address: Staatstheater, Postfach 111432, 6100 Darmstadt, Germany.

HITCHCOCK Hugh Wiley, b. 28 Sept 1923, Detroit, Michigan, USA. Musicologist; Writer on Music. Education: BA, Dartmouth College, 1944; PhD, University of Michigan, 1954; Additional study with Nadia Boulanger in Paris. Career: Taught at Michigan, 1947-61; Professor of Music, Hunter College, 1961-71; Professor of Music at Brooklyn College from 1971 (Distinguished Professor, 1980-93); Founder-Director, Institute for Studies in American Music, Brooklyn College, 1971; Getty Scholar, J Paul Getty Center for Art History and the Humanities, 1985-86; Editor, Prentice-Hall History of Music Series, 1965-; Member of the executive committee and area editor for the Americas, The New Grove Dictionary of Music and Musicians, 1980; Co-editor, The New Grove Dictionary of American Music, 1984; Research interests include French and Italian Baroque, as well as American music. Publications: The Latin Oratorios of M A Charpentier, PhD dissertation, 1954; Music in the United States: A Historical Introduction, 1969, 1975, 1988; Earlier American Music (editor), 1972; Charles Ives Centennial Festival-Conference, 1974; Recent Researches in American Music (editor), 1976-93; Ives, 1977, revised 1983; The Phonograph and our Musical Life, 1980; The Music of Ainsworth's Psalter 1612 (co-author), 1981; The Works of M A Charpentier: A Catalogue Raisonné, 1982; Editions of music by Caccini (Le nuove musiche, 1970), Leonardo Leo, Charpentier and Lully. Honours: Fulbright Grants, 1954-55, 1968-69; Guggenheim Grant, 1968-69; Grant, National Endowment for the Humanities, 1982-83; President-Elect, American Musicological Society, 1989-90 (President 1990-92). Memberships: Music Library Association, 1954-; American Musicological Society, 1954-; President, Charles Ives Society 1973-93. Address: 1192 Park Avenue, New York, NY 10128, USA.

HLAVAC Jiri, b. 12 October 1948, Czech Republic. Clarinetist. 1 son. Education: Graduate, Conservatory, Bruno; Graduate, Music Academy of Art, Prague. Career: Participant of Competitions in Belgrade and Budapest; Solo Appearances in Italy, France, Austria, Poland; Professor of Clarinet, Conservatory in Pilsen, 1974-84; Professor of Clarinet, Music Academy, Prague, 1990; Member, Czech Wind Trio; Artistic Director, Baroque Jazz Quintet. Compositions: Largo For EB; King's Journey; Blue for An Old Lady; Sonate for Saxophone and Piano; Shadows. Recordings: Genus; Direct Journey; F V Krommer - Concerts for Clarinet and Orchestra; Bertramka Live; The Music From the Heart of Europe; Clarinettisimo. Honours include: Grammy Classic; Golden Shield, Panton Production, 1992. Memberships: Academy of Contemporary Music. Hobbies: Sport; Literature. Address: Hlavni 8, 25090 Nove Jirny, Czech Republic.

HLAVAC Miroslav, b. 23 Oct 1923, Protivin, South Bohemia. Composer. m. Kvetoslava Zdarkova, 25 Sept 1970, 1 daughter. Education: Music School, Pilsen, studying composition under B Mikoda, J Ridky and K Slavicky. Debut: Pilsen, Prague. Career includes: Civil Engineering College, Prague, 1945-50; Bridge Designer, Civil Engineering College, Prague, 1950-67; Professional Composer since 1967; Symphony, Festival of the Czechoslovakia Symphony Orchestras, Prague, 1961; Ballet, The Sorcerer's Apprentice, Pilsen, 1963, Prague TV, 1973, Opava,

1987; Ballet, Electroacoustic, Nocturne at the Fountain, Halle, 1977, Pilsen, 1980; Gorlitz, 1981; Opera, Inultus, suite, 1970, Prague. Compositions: Sinfonietta Epitaffica, for Symphonic Orchestra, 1974; Sinfonietta, for String Orchestra, 1982; Hero and Leandros, 1987; Symphonic Poem - ballet after Musaios, Concerto for Violina and Symphonic Orchestra, 1978. Recordings: Discs: include, Sterograms, Postludium, Impulsioni, Serenata, Episodio, Sinfonietta Elegikon, Concerto for Violin and Symphonic Orchestra. Publications: Printed Works: Sinfonietta Elegibou, Musica Dialogica; Getting Up Songs and Lullabies; YearRings, Wind Quintet, Serenata Impulsioni, Postludium, Poetic Etudes (2 Parts). Honours: Czechoslovak Electronic Contest, 1969, awarded Biochronos; World Contest of the Italian Society for Contemporary Music in Rome, 1972, awarded, Fontana Cantans. Memberships: Association of Musical Artists and Scientists; Society of the Electro-acoustic Music. Hobbies: Tourism; Swimming; Reading; Mushroom Picking. Address: Zelenecska 26, 194 00 Praha 9, Czech Republic.

HLAVSA Jan, b. 10 Dec 1922, Vrbno Nad Lesy, Czech Republic. Opera Singer. m. Olga Olbrichova, 11 July 1960, 1 daughter. Education: Prague Music Conservatoire and Music Science. Debut: Usti Nad Labem, 1949. Career: 170 Operas. Recordings: Leos Janacek, Prihody Lisky Bystrousky; Zdenek Fibich, Nevesta Messinska; W A Mozart, Cosi Fan Tutte. Honour: Member, Prague National Theatre. Hobby: Education of Young Opera Singers. Current Management: Prague Private Opera School. Address: Velvarska 5, 16000 Praha 6, Czech Republic.

HLINKA Jiri, b. 21 Mar 1944, Prague, Czech Republic. Professor. m. Kamila, 22 July 1972, 2 sons, 1 daughter. Education: Music Academy, Prague. Debut: Dvorak Hall, Prague, 1964. Career: Many Concerts on TV and radio in Czech Republic and Norway; Appearances in Prague, Vienna, Gracz, Dresden, Moscow, Weimar. Composition: Martin's Sunday, Suite for Young Pianists. Recordings: Prokofiev, Piano Sonatas no 2 and no 6; Liszt Sonate in B Minor; Haydn Sonates; Tchaikowski Dumka and The Seizons. Honours: Tchaikovski Final, Moscow, 1966; In Norway: Lindeman Award, 1992; Bergen Forum of Arts and Culture Award, 1992; Grieg Prize, 1995. Hobby: Fishing. Address: Stativ 24b, N-5300 Kleppesto Norsko, Norway.

HO Allan (Benedict), b. 30 Mar 1955, Honolulu, Hawaii, USA. Musicologist. Education: BA, Music History, 1978, MA, Musicology, 1980, University of Hawaii; PhD, Musicology, University of Kentucky, 1985. Career: Discovered a copy of the lost full score of Wilhelm Stenhammar's First Piano Concerto, the manuscript of which was believed destroyed during WWII, and which was the most widely performed Swedish composition at the turn of the century. Publications: A Biographical Dictionary of Russian/Soviet Composers, 1989; Music for Piano and Orchestra: The Recorded Repertory; Critical editions of the 2-piano score and full score of Wilhelm Stenhammar's First Piano Concerto; Shostakovich's Testimony: Reply to an Unjust Criticism, 1995-96; Shostakovich Reconsidered, 1998. Contributions to: Journal of the American Liszt Society, 1984-; Notes; The New Grove Dictionary of American Music; New Grove Dictionary of Opera; New Grove Dictionary of Women Composers. Memberships: American Musicological Society; American Liszt Society; Pi Kappa Lambda. Hobbies: Record collecting; Sports. Address: Box 1771, Music Department, Southern Illinois University, Edwardsville, IL 62026, USA.

HO Wai-On, b. 26 May 1946, Hong Kong. Composer. Education: Chinese and English Literature, Chinese University of Hong Kong; Royal Academy of Music; Film and Television Direction and Production, London; First International Dance Course for Professional Choreographers and Composers; Computer Music Workshop, Stanford University; Contemporary and Electronic Music, Cardiff University. Career: Composer and Creator/Director of Cross-Cultural Combined-Arts Projects; Her works have been performed in England, Hong Kong, USA, Denmark and Taiwan; Festival performances include Greenwich, Edinburgh Fringe, Asian Arts, Newcastle, Huddersfield and Contemporary Chinese Composers; Founder and Artistic Director of Inter Artes and has staged many cross-cultural combined-arts projects in England and abroad. Compositions: Various combinations,vocal, instrumental, orchestral, electronic, computer, multi-media and the scores for three short films; Spring River Flower Moon Night for Flute, Guitar and Harp, 1979; Impression Of An Opera for Clarinet, 1982; Interwind for Wind Orchestra, 1990; The Story So Far, music theatre, 1991; Germination for Vocal Soloists and Ensemble, 1992; Wiseman, Fool And Slave, music theatre, 1993; Multi-media and computer pieces. Address: 25 Wellington Road, Wanstead, London E11 2AS, England.

HOBBS Allen (Alain), b. 10 May 1937, Denver, Colorado, USA. Retired Organist and Teacher; Active Composer and Musicologist. Education: Studies with Simone Plé-Caussade, C-A Estyle, André Marchal, Jean Langlais and Marcel Dupré, Paris, France; Diploma in Virtuosity, Organ and Improvisation, Schola Cantorum, Paris, 1964. Career: Organist of the Cathedral,

Denver, 1953-70; Organist/Director of Music, Church of the Holy Ghost, Denver, 1988; Retired and Disabled, November 1994; Co-founder with Daniel-Lesur of the International Charles Tournemire Association, 1987; Concert Appearances in USA, France, Italy, Switzerland, Japan and China. Compositions: Stabat Mater, 1964; Xristus, 1965; Way of the Cross, 1973; Trilogy of Psalms, 1991. Publications: Organ Method, 1980; Manual for Score Reading, 1981; The Essentials of Harmony Explained in Common Language, 1986; Treatise on the Fugue, 1990; Treatise on Strict Counterpoint (in collaboration with Yvonne Desportes, 1991); Charles-Marie Widor: Studies for the 50th Anniversary of his Death, 1986; Charles Tournemire (I) 1989, (II) 1992. Honour: Chevalier de la Légion d'Honneur, France, 1997. Memberships: Life Member, Société Française de Musicologie, 1968; Les Amis de l'Orgue, Paris. Address: Barclay Towers, No 503, 1625 Larimer Street, Denver, Colorado 80202-1527, USA.

HOBKIRK Christopher, b. 1965, Henley-on-Thames, England. Singer (Tenor). Education: Studied at the Royal Scottish Academy and at Royal College of Music with Neil Mackie. Career: Concert engagements in Finland and Norway with Britten's St Nicolas and Bach's St John Passion; Bach's Magnificat with the Las Palmas Philharmonic, the B minor Mass at Edinburgh and Telemann's Luke Passion at St John's Smith Square; Created Eochd in Edward McGuire's opera The Loving of Etain, 1990, at Glasgow; Season 1991 with Britten's Serenade at Palma, Bach's St Matthew Passion at Darmstadt and Bergen, Mozart's Requiem with the Manchester Camerata and the B minor Mass conducted by William Boughton; Sang Misael in The Burning Fiery Furnace for St James's Opera, 1991. Address: c/o Anglo Swiss Management, Suite 35-37, Morley House, 320 Regent Street, London W1R 5AD, England.

HOBSON Ian, b. 1953, Wolverhampton, England. Pianist; Conductor, m., 4 sons, 1 daughter. Education: Began private piano studies aged 5; BA, Magdalene College, Cambridge; MA, DMus, Yale University. Career: Finalist in 1978 Baltimore Symphony Conducting Competition; Silver Medals at Artur Rubinstein and Vienna-Beethoven Competitions; 1st Prize, Leeds International Piano Competition, 1981; Soloist with Royal Philharmonic Orchestra, Philharmonia and Scottish National Orchestra; USA with Orchestras of Chicago, Philadelphia, Pittsburgh, St Louis, Baltimore, Indianapolis and Houston; Complete cycles of Beethoven's Sonatas; Founded Sinfonia da Camera, 1984; The Age of Anxiety for Bernstein's 70th birthday, 1988; As conductor led Mozart's Concertos from the keyboard with English National Orchestra on its Far Eastern tour; Illinois Opera Theatre in Cosi fan tutte and Die Fledermaus; 1988-89 season engagements with San Diego Chamber Orchestra and in Israel; Professor, University of Illinois, 1983-. Recordings: Chopin/Godowsky Etudes and the complete piano sonatas of Hummel; Strauss's Burlesque and the Paregon on the Symphonia Domestica, with the Philharmonia; Concertos by Françaix, Saint-Saëns and Milhaud, with the Sinfonia da Camera; 24 Chopin Etudes, Rachmaninov Transcriptions and Mozart's Concertos Nos 23 and 24. Address: c/o Norman McCann International Artists Ltd, The Coach House, 56 Lawrie Park Gardens, London SE26 6XJ, England.

HOCH Beverly, b. 1956, Kansas City, Kansas, USA. Singer (Soprano). Education: Studied in New York. Career: Concert performances from 1980, notably at Carnegie Hall, New York, and the Kennedy Center, Washington; European concerts in Madrid, Gothenburg and Brussels; Opera appearances at Spoleto, the Wexford Festival (Philine in Mignon), and Santa Fe; Her best known role is Mozart's Queen of Night, which she sang at the 1991 Glyndebourne Festival. Recordings include: Die Zauberflöte (EMI). Address: c/o Glyndebourne Festival Opera, Lewes, Sussex, England.

HOCH Francesco, b. 14 Feb 1943, Lugano, Switzerland. Composer; Professor of Music. m. 1 May 1971, 2 sons. Education: G Verdi Conservatory, Milan; Composition, Padua, Darmstadt. Career: Professor of Music, Lugano; Assistant, Composition Course, Chigiana Academy, Siena Italy, 1974; Invited, International Laboratory, Venice Biennial, 1975; Founder Oggimusica Association of Contemporary Music, 1977; Regular radio broadcasts of compositions, all Europe, Israel, Canada, Australia, TV(TSI) recordings. Compositions: 63 published works including: Dune, 3 instruments, 2 percussion, 2 voices, 1972; L'Oggetto Disincantato, 13 instruments, 1974; Trittico, clarinet, viola; Leonardo e/und Gantenbein, opera-ballet, 1980-82; Ostinato variabile, I, bass clarinet, 1981, II, bass clarinet, piano, III, 2 guitars, IV, piano, violin, 1982; Sans, oboe, orchestra, 1985; Un Mattino, 2 flutes, 1986; Der Tod ohne des Mädchen, string quartet, 1990; Memorie da Requiem, choir, orchestra, 1989-91; Postludio degli Spettatori, choir, 1991; Péché d'outre-tombe, for clarinet and string quartet, 1993; La Passerelle des Fous, opera, for 3 sopranos, 5 actors and 8 instruments, 1994-95. Publications: Enc Musica; Francesco Hoch, Swiss Composer, by Pro Helvetia, 1994. Contributions to: Schweizer Komponisten Unserere Zeit; Swiss Musica Review; Enc Musica Garzanti; Milano Prospettive Musicali, Pescara; Encyclopedia UTET, Torino, 1988; Musikrevy;

Swiss Composer. Honours include: Premio Angelicum, Milan, 1975; Sans, chosen 20 years of Union European Radiodiffusion, 1987; Foundation Pro Arte, Bern, 1976; First Jubileumspreis, UBS, 1991. Memberships include: Association of Swiss Musicians; Swiss Society of Learning. Address: Campo dei fiori 9, 6942 Savosa, Switzerland.

HOCHMANN Klaus, b. 29 Dec 1932, Angerbürg, Ostpreußen, Poland. Composer (German citizen). Education: Studied Composition and Conducting at Stuttgart and Salzburg. Career: Piano Teacher in Music School of Herrenberg. Compositions include: Der Findling, opera, 1970; Midsummer Night, 5 choirs ac, 1963; Requiem für einen Unbekannten, 3 songs for bass and organ, 1965; Concertino I for percussion, 1969; Concertino III for percussion solo and tutti, 1974; Bilder des Todes for recorder and percussion, 1991; -one to four- for string quartet, 1991; Mary, poem with music, text by Dorothea Spears, 1992. Recordings: Requiem für einen Unbekannten, 1968; Tenebrae factae sunt for mixed choir ac, 4 speaker, percussion, 1992; In Memoriam, song cycle for baritone and piano, 1980; Und suche Gott, for mixed choir ac and speaker, 1991; Mein Bruder Tod for mixed choir a cappella, after Agnes Miegel, 1985; Intrada for organ, 1993; Selbst die Steine umarmen wir-; Strophen for 5 solo voices a cappella, after Nelly Sachs, 1994. Honours: Composition Prizes, Kassel, 1965, Bern, 1975, Bonn, 1984; Promotion Prizes, 1971, 1977. Memberships: Society for Promotion of Radio Symphony Orchestra Stuttgart; Leos Janácek Society, Bern. Hobbies: Literature; Art; Travel. Address: Beethovenstrasse 62, D-71083 Herrenberg, Germany.

HOCHREITHER Karl, b. 27 Oct 1933, Speyer, Germany. Church Musician (Organist and Choirmaster); Professor. m. Gertrud Wien, 23 June 1959, 1 son, 2 daughters. Education: Studies in German Philology, History and Philosophy, University of Freiburg, 1953-54; Church Music, Organ with M Schneider, Staatliches A-Exam; Continuing studies, Conducting and Chamber Music, Nordwestdeutsche Musikakademie, Detmold, 1954-58; Musicology, Heidelberg University, 1962-63. Career: Organist and Choirmaster, Protestant Palatine Church Council, Speyer; Member of Faculty, Berliner Kirchenmusikschule, 1963; Director, Bach-Chor and Bach-Collegium, Kaiser-Wilhelm-Gedächtniskirche, Berlin, 1964; Guest Professor, Wittenberg University, Springfield, Ohio, USA, 1968; Artist-in-Residence, Music Department, University of Western Ontario, London, Ontario, Canada, 1975, 1977; Artist-in-Residence, Asian Institute for Liturgy and Music, Manila, Philippines, 1984; Artist-in-Residence, Tainan Theological Seminary, Tainan, Taiwan, 1989; Concert tours as organist and conductor, teaching and lecturing, worldwide. Recordings: S Scheidt, Motets and Concertos (harpsichord), 1964; H W Zimmermann, Vesper, harpsichord and organ, 1967; J S Bach, Cantatas 56 and 82, conductor, 1972; Franz Liszt, Organ Works, 1974. Publications: Ernst Peppings Toccata und Fuge, Mitten wir im Leben sind, 1971; O Messiaen, La Nativité du Seigneur (co-editor), 1974; Zur Aufführungspraxis der Vokal-Instrumentalwerke J S Bachs, 1983. Honours: Winner, Berlin Organ Competition, 1961; Awarded Grand Prix de Disque by the International Liszt Society, 1975; Professor hc for his cultural engagement for the City of Berlin by the Governing Major of Berlin, 1993. Address: Ev Johannesstift, Franckehaus, 13587 Berlin, Germany.

HOCKNEY David, b. 9 July 1937, Bradford, Yorkshire, England. Painter; Photographer; Stage Designer. Debut: First stage designer Brecht's Ubu Roi for the Royal Court Theatre, London, 1966. Career: Designed The Rake's Progress and Die Zauberflöte for Glyndebourne, 1975, 1978; Metropolitan Opera, 1981, with two triple bills; Parade (Les Mamelles de Teresias, L'Enfant et les Sortilèges, Parade) and Stravinsky (Oedipus Rex, Le Sacre du Printemps, Le Rossignol); Turandot in Los Angeles; Die Frau ohne Schatten for Covent Garden, 1992. Address: c/o 7508 Santa Monica Boulevard, Los Angeles, CA 90046, USA.

HODDINOTT Alun, b. 11 Aug 1929, Bargoed, South Wales. Composer. m. Beti Rhiannon Huws, 1953, 1 son. Education: University College, Cardiff. Career: Lecturer, Cardiff College of Music and Drama, 1951-59; Lecturer, 1959-65, Reader, 1965-67, Professor, Music, 1967-87, University College, Cardiff; Artistic Director, Cardiff Festival of 20th Century Music, 1966-89. Compositions include: 12 piano sonatas, 1959-93; Welsh Dances; Investiture Dances; Black Bart; Dives and Lazarus, 1965; Variants, 1966; Fioriture, 1968; Sonatas, harp, clarinet, horn; The Tree of Life, 1971; Ritornelli; The Beach at Falesa, opera, 1974; 2 sonatas, cello, piano, 1977; The Magician, opera; Ancestor Worship, 5 Landscapes, song cycles; A Contemplation Upon Flowers, songs, soprano, orchestra; What the Old Man Does Is Always Right, opera; Sonatina, guitar; Sonatina, 2 pianos; The Rajah's Diamond, opera; The Trumpet Major, 3-act opera; Nocturnes and Cadenzas, solo flute; Doubles, oboe, harpsichord, strings; 5 Studies, orchestra; 4 Scenes from The Trumpet Major, orchestra; Quodlibet, orchestra, 1982, brass quintet, 1983; Masks, oboe, bassoon, piano, 1983; Lady and Unicorn, cantata; Piano Trio No 2; Bagatelles, oboe, harp; String Quartet No 2, 1984, No

3, 1988; Scenes and Interludes, trumpet, harpsichord, strings; Bells of Paradise, cantata, 1984; Scena, string orchestra; Sonata, 2 pianos; The Silver Hound, song cycle; Fanfare with variants for brass band; Sonata, 4 clarinets, 1985; Triple Concerto, Divisions for Horn, Harpsichord, Strings; Concerto, orchestra, 1986; Concerto, clarinet and orchestra; Welsh Dances, brass band; The Legend of St Julian, 1987; Lines from Marlowe's Dr Faustus, mixed voices, brass, percussion; Noctus Equi, cello, orchestra, 1989; Songs of Exile, tenor, orchestra; Star Children, orchestra; Symphony for organ and orchestra; Advent Carol, SATB, organ; Emynan Pantycelyn, baritone solo, chorus, orchestra, 1990; Novelette, flute, oboe, piano; Sonata, flute, piano, 1991; Sonata No 5, violin, piano, 1992; Chorales Variants and Fanfare, organ, brass, 1992; Symphony No 8, brass, percussion, 1992, No 9, A Vision of Eternity, brass, orchestra, 1993; Gloria, chorus, organ; 3 Motets, chorus, organ; Wind Quintet, 1993. Recordings include: Symphony No 6 and Star Children, BBC WSO; Passagio, Otaka; Piano Sonatas 1-10, Martin Jones; Noctis Equi; 3 Advent Cards, St John's College Choir. Honours: Walford Davis Prize, 1954; Bax Medal, 1957; Fellow: University College, Cardiff, 1981; Welsh College of Music and Drama, 1991; Honorary DMus (Sheffield), 1993; CBE; Hopkins Medal, St David's Society, New York. Address: Maesawelon, Mill Road, Lisvane, Cardiff, Wales.

HODGES Nicolas, b. 4 June 1970, London, England. Composer; Pianist. Education: Studied composition at Dartington and Winchester with Morto Feldman and Michael Finnissy; Piano with Robert Bottone and privately with Susan Bradshaw; Music at Cambridge University. Career: As pianist, premieres including music by Finnissy, Weir, Skempton, Toovey, Powell, Holloway, Bill Hopkins, some as part of the Bach project, broadcast on Radio 3. Compositions: Piano Studies, solo piano, 1988-92; Small Shadows, 1990; Toothreefourfive, violin and piano, 1991-92; Do I detect a silver thread between you and this young lady, solo viola, 1993; Concertino, 1993; Scripture for soprano, oboe d'amore and 2 percussion, 1994. Recordings: Bach Project released on CD. Contributions to: Various articles and reviews to Tempo, Musical Times, including The Music of Bill Hopkins, 1993, The Music of Luigi Nono 1950-58 - Analytical investigations. Hobbies: Reading; Cooking; Wine; The countryside. Address: Flat 3, 68 Norwood Road, Herne Hill, London SE24 9BB, England.

HODGSON Julia, b. 1960, England. Viol Player. Career: Member of Fretwork, first London concert at the Wigmore Hall, London, July 1986; Appearances in the Renaissance and Baroque repertoire in Sweden, France, Belgium, Netherlands, Germany, Austria, Switzerland and Italy; Radio broadcasts in Sweden, Netherlands, Germany and Austria; Televised concert on ZDF, Mainz; Tour of Soviet Union, Sept 1989, and Japan, June 1991; Festival engagements in Britain; Repertory includes In Nomines and Fantasias by Tallis, Parsons and Byrd; Dance music by Holborne and Dowland (including Lachrimae); Six-part consorts by Gibbons and William Lawes; Songs and instrumental works by Purcell; Collaborations with vocal group Red Byrd in verse anthems by Byrd and Tomkins, London Cries by Gibbons and Dering, Resurrection Story and Seven Last Words by Schütz; Gave George Benjamin's Upon Silence at the Elizabeth Hall, Oct 1990; Wigmore Hall concerts, 1990-91, with music by Lawes, Purcell, Locke, Dowland and Byrd. Recordings: Heart's Ease (late Tudor and early Stuart); Armada (Courts of Philip II and Elizabeth I); Night's Black Bird (Dowland and Byrd); Cries and Fancies (Fantasias, In Nomines and The Cries of London by Gibbons); Go Nightly Care (consort songs, dances and In Nomines by Byrd and Dowland). Address: Fretwork, c/o Wigmore Hall, Wigmore Street, London W1, England.

HODKINSON Juliana, b. 17 Mar 1971, Exeter, England. Composer. Education: King's College, Cambridge, 1990-93; MA Double Honours, Music and Philosophy, University of Cambridge, 1993; Diploma in German; Private studies under Hans Abrahamsen and Per Nørgård, Jutland Academy of Music, Denmark; MA, Japanese Studies, Sheffield University, 1997. Debut: 1st professional performance of composition Recalling Voices of the Child, Capricorn ensemble, ICA, London, 3 Mar 1994. Career: Works performed at ICA, London, Den Anden Opera, Copenhagen, Musikhalle, Hamburg, Paul Gerhardt Kirche, Berlin, Tokyo University of Fine Arts, elsewhere; Presently Artistic Director, Ensemble 2000, Denmark and Affiliated Composer of Orchestra of Mons, Belgium. Compositions: In Slow Movement, 1994; Die Wurzelkirche for 12 cellos, 1995; Water like a Stone, 1996; Korrektur, 1997; Chopiniana for flute, clarinet, cello and piano, 1997. Recordings: Die Wurzelkirche, for NHK Japan broadcast, 1995; Water like a stone, for P2 Denmark broadcast, 1996, and European broadcast, 1997; Korrektur, P2 broadcast, 1997. Contributions to: Dansk Musik Tidsskrift, 1994, 1997; Japanese Society Proceedings, 1996. Honours: Danish Arts Council Commission for In Slow Movement, 1994; Scholarship, Daiwa Anglo-Japanese Foundation, 1995-97; Akiyoshidai Festival Scholarship, Japan, 1996; Pépinières Européens Jeunes Artistes residency, 1997-98. Memberships: Dansk Komponist Forening; Koda-NCB, Denmark. Hobby: Languages. Address: Olof Palmes Gade 1, 4.sal, DK-2100 Copenhagen Ø, Denmark.

HOEKMAN Guus, b. 16 Oct 1913, The Hague, Netherlands. Singer (Bass). Education: Studied with Aaltje Noordewier-Reddingius, N de Haan-Liégeois and Lucie Frateur (singing) and Lothar Wallerstein and Felix Hupka (opera). Career: Concert debut, 1938; Opera debut, 1951, as Osmin with the Flemish Opera at Antwerp; Netherlands Opera from 1953, notably in Don Carlo by Verdi and Don Pasquale by Donizetti; Netherlands Opera from 1956, notably in Die Kluge by Orff and Der Wildschütz by Lortzing; Salzburg Festival, 1960, in the stage premiere of Martin's Mystère de la Nativité; Glyndebourne, 1962-63, 1969, as Arkel in Pélléas et Mélisande; Deutsche Oper am Rhein Dusseldorf from 1960; Appearances in Boston and at the New York City Opera; Taught in the USA, 1972-79; Amsterdam, 1981-85, as Lumey (in Thijl by van Gilse), Sarastro, Titurel and Trulove in The Rake's Progress. Recordings: Sarastro in Die Zauberflöte; Basilio in Il Barbiere di Siviglia; Bach Matthäus Passion conducted by Anthon van der Horst; Pélléas et Mélisande conducted by Ansermet; Bruckner Te Deum.

HOELSCHER Ulf. Musician (Violinist). Education: Privately with father and Bruno Masurat; Studied with Max Rostal in Cologne; Studied 3 years in USA with Josef Gingold, Indiana University, and with Ivan Galamian, Curtis Institute, Philadelphia, USA. Career: Member, International Geiger Elite; Violin Concertos of Kirchner with Berlin Philharmonic, 1984; Franz Hummel's Violin Concerto, Baden-Baden, 1987; Performed Double Concerto by Aribert Reimann, with Wolfgang Reimann, Hannover, 1989; Performances and recordings from a wide repertoire featuring Frankel, Tchaikovsky, Schumann, Mendelssohn, Richard Strauss, Brahms and Beethoven, and the chamber music of Bartok, Cèsar Franck,and Szymanowski. Recording: Hummel's Violin Concerto, with USSR State Symphony Orchestra. Current Management: Astrid Schoerke. Address: c/o Monckebergallee 41, 30453 Hannover, Germany.

HOENDERDOS Margriet, b. 6 May 1952, Santpoort, Holland. Composer. Education: Studied at the Zwolle and Sweelinck Conservatories, notably with Ton de Leeuw. Compositions include: Blue Time for 2 Pianos, 1981; Het Nieuwe Verlaat for Orchestra, 1985; Borrowed Flesh for Organ, 1987; Hunker Schor and Hasselar for Orchestra, 1987; De Lussen Van Faverey for Wind Quintet, 1990. Address: c/o Vereniging Buma, PO Box 725, 1180 AS Amstelveen, The Netherlands.

HOEPRICH Thomas (Eric), b. 5 September 1955, Baltimore, Maryland, USA. Clarinettist. Education: AB cum laude, Harvard University, 1976; Solo Diploma, Royal Conservatory of Music, Netherlands, 1982. Career: Principal Clarinet, Orchestra of the 18th Century, 1983-; Founding Member of Amadeus Winds, Stadler Trio (basset horns), Nachtmusique and Trio d'Amsterdam; Regular appearances with London Classical Players, Tafelmusik and The Orchestra of the Handel and Haydn Society; Professor, Royal Conservatory of Music, Netherlands. Recordings: Mozart Clarinet Concerto and Quintet with Orchestra of the 18th Century, Philips; Other recordings as soloist: Taverner Players, EMI; Musica Antiqua Cologne, DGG-Archiv; Other recordings for Decca, Harmonia Mundi, Accent, Erato and SONY Classical. Contributions to: Early Music; Tibia; Galpin Society Journal; NOTES. Honours: Mozart Clarinet Concerto and Quintet recording named one of the best 15 CDs of 1988, Le Monde de la Musique. Hobbies: Squash; Instrument-making. Address: Bredeweg 39-2, 1098 BN Amsterdam, Netherlands.

HOFFMAN Donald (Stuart), b. 11 June 1931, San Francisco, California, USA. Independent TV Producer. Education: BA, Dartmouth College; MA, Harvard University; ATCL (Trinity College London); ALCM (London College of Music); 2 years advanced study at Oxford University. Career: Instructor of Music, American College for Girls, Istanbul, Turkey, 1957-63; Assistant Professor of Music, Robert College, 1965-78; Solo singer, producer of chamber operas, part-time patron of the arts, play producer and record producer. Compositions: Fantasia on Black is the Colour; Clarinet Sonata; Trio for clarinet, violin and piano; Madrigal, Fantasia, Prelude and Fancy, for recorders. Recording: CD, Songs of the Earth. Publications: Since All Things Love (Walter Porter), 1961; Three Early English Motets, 1968; A tree to climb, stories for children, 1971. Contributions to: An Introduction to Music in Modern Turkey, to The Consort; Some Shakespearean Music, to Shakespeare Survey; The Chromatic Fourth, to The Consort. Hobbies: Reading; Horses. Address: 416 West Broadway, Bismarck, ND 58501, USA.

HOFFMAN Grace, b. 14 Nov 1926, Cleveland, Ohio, USA. Singer (Mezzo-soprano). Education: Studied with Friedrich Schorr in New York, Mario Basiola in Milan, and with Maria Wetzelsberger in Stuttgart. Debut: With the US Touring Company as Lola, 1951. Career: Sang at Florence from 1951; Zurich, 1952, as Azucena; Wurttemberg Staatsoper Stuttgart from 1955; La Scala Milan, 1955, as Fricka in Die Walküre; Bayreuth Festival, 1957-70, as Brangaene, Fricka and Waltraute; Metropolitan Opera, 1958, Brangaene; Covent Garden debut, 1959, as Eboli in Don Carlos; Florence, 1961, as Ortrud in Lohengrin; Carnegie Hall, New York, 1964, as Elisabetta in Donizetti's Maria Stuarda; Appearances in Paris, Vienna, Munich and Dusseldorf; Teacher of singing at the Stuttgart Musikhochschule from 1978; Sang Mary in Der fliegende Holländer at Stuttgart, 1989; Other roles include Mother Wesener in Die Soldaten by Zimmermann (Strasbourg, 1988). Recordings: Das Lied von der Erde; Salome;Der Barbier von Bagdad; Tristan und Isolde. Address: c/o Staatstheater Stuttgart, Oberer Schlossgarten 6, D-7000 Stuttgart 1, Germany.

HOFFMAN Irwin, b. 26 Nov 1924, New York City, USA. Symphony Conductor; Violinist. m. Esther Glazer Hoffman, 3 s, 1 d. Education: Juilliard School of Music. Career: Conductor of Vancouver Symphony, BC, Canada, 1952-64; Associate Conductor and Acting Music Director, Chicago Symphony, IL, USA, 1964-70; Music Director of The Florida Orchestra, 1968-87; Chief permanent conductor of Belgian Radio and Television Symphony, 1972, 1976; Guest Conductor for various leading orchestras in Europe, North America, Israel and South America. Recordings: Several. Address: c/o Everett Wright, 3876 Oak Grove Drive, Sarasota, Florida, USA.

HOFFMAN Joel (Harvey), b, 27 Sept 1953, Vancouver, British Columbia, Canada. Composer; Pianist; Teacher. m. 30 Dec 1988. Education: BM, University of Wales, Cardiff, Wales, 1974; MM, 1976, DMA, 1978, Juilliard School, New York, USA. Career: Graduate Teaching Assistant, Juilliard School, New York, 1976-78; Professor of Composition, College-Conservatory of Music, University of Concinnati, Ohio, 1978-; Commissions: Cincinnati Symphony Orchestra, 1993; Shanghai String Quartet, 1993; National Chamaber Orchestra, 1993; Golub-Kaplan-Carr Trio, 1991; Artistic Director, Music Ninety-eight Festival. Compositions: Variations for violin, cello and harp, 1978; September Music for double bass and harp, 1981; Music from Chartres for 10 brass instruments, 1984; Double Concerto, 1984; Sonata for harp, 1985; Chamber Symphony, 1986; 5 pieces for 2 pianos, 1986; Violin Concerto, 1986; Fantasia Fiorentina, for violin and piano, 1988; Hands Down, for piano, 1986; Crossing Points for string orchestra, 1990; Partenze, for solo violin, 1990; Each for Himself/90, for piano solo, 1991; Cubist Blues for violin, cello and piano, 1991; Music in Blue and Green, for orchestra, 1991; Metasmo for percussion trio, 1992; self-Portrait with Mozart, violin, piano and orchestra, 1994; Music for Chamber Orchestra, 1994; ChiaSsO for orchestra, 1995; L'Immensitá dell'Attimo, song cycle for mezzo and piano, 1995; The Music Within the Words, 1996; Portogruaro Sextet, 1996; Millennium Dances, for orchestra, 1997. Recordings: Duo for viola and piano, 1991; Partenze, 1992; Music for Two Oboes, 1995; Fantasy Pieces, 1997. Honours: National Endowment for the Arts Commissions, 1985, 1991; BMI Award, 1972; Bearns Prize, Columbia University, 1978. Address: College-Conservatory of Music, University of Cincinnati, Cincinnati, OH 45221, USA.

HOFFMAN Stanley, b. 8 Dec 1929, Baltimore, Maryland, USA. Violinist; Violist. Education: Private study with Arthur Grumaux, Belgium; BSc, Juilliard School of Music; Study with Mischa Mischakoff, Raphael Bronstein and Oscar Shumsky. Debut: Carnegie Recital hall, New York City. Career: Regular Member, New York Philharmonic Orchestra under Leonard Bernstein, 1961-64, Jerusalem Radio Symphony Orchestra, Israel, 1981-83. Recordings: Vocal Chamber Music, Volume I with Susan Reid-Parsons as soprano, 1971, Volume II with Elinor Amlen & Rose Macdonald, sopranos, 1973; Taping session for Radio Kol Israel, 1984, 1986; Solo violin sonatas, Bela Bartok, Honegger, Hindemith, Ralph Shapey, Paul Ben-Haim, Bach C Major, Roger Sessions. Memberships: Bohemians, New York; Local 802 Association Federation of Musicians. Hobbies: Jogging; Reading; Travel. Address: Poste-Restante, Tel Aviv, Israel.

HOFFMANN Horst, b. 13 June 1935, Oppelen, Germany. Singer (Tenor). Education: Studied with Thilde Amelung in Hildesheim and Otto Kohler in Hanover. Debut: Hanover, 1961, in Zar und Zimmermann. Career: Has sung at the Stuttgart and Munich State Operas and the Deutsche Oper am Rhein, Dusseldorf; Komische Oper Berlin and the Opéra du Rhin, Strasbourg; Bayreuth Festival, 1967-68; Further appearances in Cologne, Lisbon, Zurich, Vienna (Volksoper) and Sydney, 1984 (Lohengrin and Siegmund, 1987 and 1989); Teatro Regio, Turin, 1987, as Don Ottavio; Otello, Sydney and Melbourne, 1988, and in Sydney, 1992; From the House of the Dead, Cologne, Germany, 1992; Sang Florestan at Sydney, 1992; Tristan and Isolde, Sydney and Melbourne, 1993, and Essen, Germany, 1993; Die Meistersinger, Sydney, 1993; Roles include Tamino, Belmonte, Nemorino, Edgardo, Pinkerton, Alfredo in La Traviata and Alfred in Die Fledermaus; Sang Otello at Sydney, 1996. Recordings include: Bruckner Te Deum. Address: c/o Australian Opera, Sydney Opera House, Sydney, New South Wales, Australia.

HOFFMANN Manfred, b. 10 Oct 1940, Kahl am Main, Germany. Singer (Bass). Education: Studied at the Frankfurt Musikhochschule. Career: Sang at Saarbrucken, 1970-71, Lucerne, 1972-74, Mainz, 1974-77, St Gallen, 1977-80; Engaged at Berne, 1980-84, Graz from 1984, notably in the 1987 premiere of Der Rattenfänger by Friedrich Cerha; Guest appearances in

Germany and Switzerland; Roles have included Rossini's Bartolo, Mozart's Alfonso and Sarastro, Rocco, Raimondo, Geronimo in Matrimonio Segreto, Pietro in Simon Boccanegra, the Landgrave (Tannhäuser), Dulcamara, the Grand Inquisitor (Don Carlos) and Count Waldner in Arabella; Further engagements in operetta. Address: c/o Vereinigte Buhnen, Kaiser Josef Platz 10, A-8010 Graz, Austria.

HOFFMANN Richard, b. 20 Apr 1925, Vienna, Austria. Composer; Musicologist. Education: Studied at the University of New Zealand and the University of California at Los Angeles; Composition studies with Arnold Schoenberg. Career: Secretary and assistant to Schoenberg, 1948-51; Teacher of University of California at Los Angeles, 1951-52, Oberlin College from 1954; Visiting Professor at the University of California, Berkeley, 1965-66; Co-editor of the complete works of Schoenberg, 1961, edited the score of Von Heute auf Morgen. Compositions include: Prelude and Double Fugue for strings, 1944; Piano Sonata, 1946; Violin Concerto, 1948; 4 String Quartets, 1947, 1950, 1974, 1977; 3 Songs, 1948; Duo for violin and cello, 1949; 3 Songs, 1950; Piano Quartet, 1950; Fantasy and Fugue for organ, 1951; Piano Sonatina, 1952; Piano Concerto, 1954; Cello Concerto, 1956-59; String Trio, 1963; Memento Mori for male voices and orchestra, 1966-69; Music for strings, 1971; Decadanse for 10 players, 1972; Changes for 2 chimes, 4 performers, 1974; Souffler for orchestra, 1976; In memorium patris for computer-generated tape, 1976; Intavolatura for strings and percussion, 1980. Honours include: Guggenheim Fellowships, 1970, 1977. Address: c/o ASCAP, ASCAP Building, One Lincoln Plaza, New York, NY 10023, USA.

HOFFMANN-ERBRECHT Lothar, b. 2 March 1925, Strehlen Schlesien, Germany. Professor. m. Margarete Fischer, 2 daughters. Education: Graduate, Academy of Music, Weimar, 1949; PhD, University of Jena, 1951; Habilitation, Department of Musicology, University of Frankfurt, 1961. Career: Professor of Musicology, University of Frankfurt am Main. Publications include: Deutsche und italienische Klaviermusik zur Bachzeit, 1954; Thomas Stoltzer, Leben und Schaffen, 1964; Thomas Stoltzer, Ausgewaehlte Werke II-III; Heinrich Finck, Ausgewaehlte Werke, I-II; Beethoven Klaviersonaten (with Claudio Arrau); Henricus Finck-musicus excellentissimus, 1445-1527, 1982; Musikgeschichte Schlesiens, 1986. Contributions to: Various professional journals. Memberships: Society for Music Research; International Musicological Society. Address: 9 Amselweg, D-63225 Langen, Germany.

HOFMANN Peter, b. 12 Aug 1944, Marienbad, Germany. Singer (Tenor). m. Deborah Sasson, 1983, div. 1990. Education: Karlsruhe Hochschule. Debut: Lubeck, 1972, as Tamino in Die Zauberflöte. Career: Early engagements at Wuppertal and Stuttgart; Bayreuth Festival from 1976, as Siegmund, Lohengrin and Parsifal; Vienna State Opera, 1976; as Loge, then Siegmund and Lohengrin; Covent Garden debut, 1976, as Siegmund; Returned to London as Max in a new production of Der Freischütz and as Alfred in Die Fledermaus; Metropolitan Opera debut, 1980, as Lohengrin; Returned to New York as Parsifal, Siegmund and Walther; Sang Tristan at Bayreuth in 1986, and Siegmund in Harry Kupfer's new production of The Ring, 1988; Guest appearances in Moscow, Lisbon, San Francisco, Los Angeles, Munich and Chicago. Recordings: Parsifal; Die Zauberflöte; Die Walküre; Tristan und Isolde; Lohengrin; Orfeo ed Euridice. Address: PO Box 100262, Bayreuther Festspiele, 8580 Bayreuth 1, Germany.

HOFMANN Rosmarie, b. 1 July 1937, Lucerne, Switzerland. Singer (Soprano). Career: Concerts, throughout Europe, overseas; Appeared, many regular international festivals; Many recent world premieres, including works composed for her; Extensive repertoire includes: J S Bach: Johannes, Matthäus and Markus Passions, Mass in B minor, Mass No 2 A major, Weihnachts-Oratorium, Magnificat plus Einlagesätze, 6 solo soprano and some 60 other cantatas; Beethoven: 9th Symphony, Christus am Oelberge, Chorphantasie, Missa solemnis, Mass C major, lieder; Brahms: Ein Deutsches Requiem, lieder, duets, quartets; Bruckner: Requiem D minor, Te Deum, Grosse Messe No 3 F minor, Grosse Messe D minor; Carissimi: Historia de Jephther; Charpentier: Te Deum, Messe de Minuit; Durufle: Requiem; Dvorák: Te Deum, Stabat Mater, Mass in D, Zigeunerlieder; Fauré: Requiem; Franck: Messe solenne A major, Die sieben Wörte Christi am Kreuz, Magnificat; Handel: Israel in Egypt, Dettinger and Utrechter Te Deums, Brockes and Johannes Passions, Messias, Joshua, Saul, Jephtha, Judas Maccabeus, Das Alexanderfest, Belsazar, Psalms 96, 109, 112, 51, German arias, duets, cantatas Cäcilien Ode, Ode for Queen Anne, Salve Regina; J Haydn: L'incontro improvviso (1st soprano), L'anima del Filosofo (Genio, Euridice), Die Schöpfung, Die Jahreszeiten, Die sieben Wörte des Erlösers am Kreuz, Stabat Mater, 6 Grosse Messen, many other Masses; Honegger: Le Roi David, Jeanne d'Arc au bucher, La Vierge, La danse des morts; Frank Martin: In Terra Pax, Golgotha; Mendelssohn: Paulus, Elias, 2nd Symphony Lobgesang, Hochzeit des Camacho (main role), lieder, duets; Monteverdi: Vespreae della Maria Vergine, Magnificat, Psalm 111, solo motet, duets; Mozart: Solo motets Exsultate jubilate, Venti, Fulgura, Procellae, Litanien, Vespreaes, Konzertarien, oratorio La Betulia liberata, Die Schuldigkeit des ersten Gebots, cantatas, funeral music, Requiem, Regina Coeli KV 108, KV 127, many small works, C minor Mass, Davidde penitente, many masses, lieder; Pergolesi: Stabat Mater, Salve Regina, Psalm 112; Poulenc: Gloria, Stabat Mater; Schubert: Magnificat, Salve Regina, Masses Der Hirt auf dem Felsen, Auf dem Strom; Saint-Saëns: Christmas Oratorio, Requiem Mass, oratorio Le Déluge; Schütz: Die Weihnachts-Historie, Die Auferstehungs-Historie, sacred concertos and duets; Telemann: Matthaus-Passion 1746, Lukas-Passion 1744, Magnificat, Grosse Kantate, many solo cantatas; Vivaldi: Gloria, Magnificat, Psalm Laudate pueri, cantatas, solo motets; Wide repertoire of ancient music, lieder; Leading roles, 8 operettas; Classes, Musikakademie Basel, Schola Cantorum Basiliensis, Lehr- und Forschungs Institut für Alte Musik, over 10 years. Recordings: Phyllis und Thirsis, C P E Bach; Canzonette amorose, Rossi; Stabat Mater, Dvorák; Sacred music, J and M Haydn; Bach cantatas; Mozart motets, Scholar Cantorum Basiliensis Orchestra, conductor Peter Sigrist; Quiteria (main role), Die Hochzeit des Camacho, 1993; Many more. Address: Mozartstrasse 46, 6006 Lucerne, Switzerland.

HOGMAN Christina, b. 18 February 1956, Danderyd, Sweden. Singer. m. Nils-Erik Sparf, 17 May 1991, 2 sons. Education: Musicology, History of Art, University of Uppsala, Sweden, 1974-78; Royal Music Academy, Stockholm, 1978-83; State Opera School, Stockholm, 1984-86; Masterclasses: Elisabeth Schwarzkopf, Nicolai Gedda, Geoffrey Parsons, Vera Rosza. Debut: Drottningholm Court Theatre, 1985. Career: Hamburg State Opera, Germany, 1986-88; Guest Contracts, 1988-97; Basel Opera, Innsbruck Opera, Opera du Rhin, Strasbourg, Monte Carlo Opera, Montpellier Opera, Royal Opera in Stockholm; Major Roles: Donna Elvira, Countess Almaviva, Cherubino, Annio, Erste Dame (Mozart; Soloist with Academy of Ancient Music, Mozart Tour, Japan, 1991). Recordings: Donna Elvira in Don Giovanni; Vitige in Flavio (Handel); Telemacho in Ilritorno di Ulisse in Patria & Valelto in L'Incoronazione di Poppea (Monteverdi); English Lute Songs with Jakob Lindberg; Lieder by Clara Schumann; Les Illuminations by B Britten; 2nd String Quartet by A Schoenberg; Matthew Passion & John Passion (Bach). Hobbies: Reading; Drawing; Needlework. Current Management: Kristina Hennel-Lee, Nordic Artist AB. Address: Box 12881, S-11298 Stockholm, Sweden

HOGWOOD Christopher (Jarvis Haley), b. 10 Sept 1941, Nottingham, England. Harpsichordist; Conductor; Musicologist; Author. Education: Cambridge University; Charles University, Prague; MA; FRSA. Career: Founder Member of Early Music Consort of London, 1967-76; Founder and Director of The Academy of Ancient Music, 1973-; Faculty, Cambridge University, 1975-; Artistic Director, Handel & Haydn Society, Boston, USA, 1986-; Honorary Professor of Music at Keele University, 1986-89; Director of Music, 1987-92, Principal Guest Conductor, St Paul Chamber Orchestra, Minnesota, USA, 1992; International Professor of Early Music Performance at Royal Academy of Music, London, 1992-; Visiting Professor, Department of Music, King's College London, 1992-; Artistic Director, Summer Mozart Festival National Symphony Orchestra, USA, 1993-; Conducted Handel & Haydn Society in Gluck's Orfeo, Edinburgh, 1996; Associate Director, Beethoven Academie, Antwerp, 1998-. Recordings include: Many recordings of Baroque and classical music including: 6 volumes of Symphonies by Haydn, La Clemenza di Tito, Pergolesi Stabat Mater, and Purcell's Dido and Aeneas (The Academy of Ancient Music). Publications: Music at Court, 1977; The Trio Sonata, 1979; Haydn's Visits To England, 1980; Co-author, Music in Eighteenth-Century England, 1983; Handel, 1984; Editor, Holmes' Life of Mozart, 1991; Many editions of musical scores. Contributions to: New Grove Dictionary of Music and Musicians. Honours: Walter Willson Cobbett Medal, 1986; CBE, 1989; Honorary Fellow, Jesus College, Cambridge, 1989; Freeman, Worshipful Company of Musicians, 1989; Honorary Fellow, Pembroke College, Cambridge. Address: 10 Brookside, Cambridge, CB2 1JE, England.

HOHEISEL Tobias, b. 1956, Frankfurt, Germany. Stage Designer. Education: Studied in Berlin. Career: Collaborations with director Nikolaus Lehnoff include Janácek Trilogy (Katya, Jenufa and Makropoulos Case) at Glyndebourne and Pfitzner's Palestrina at Covent Garden (season 1996-97, also seen at the Metropolitan, New York); Debut as set and costume designer with Salome at Rio de Janeiro; Britten's Death in Venice for the Glyndebourne Tour, La Boheme, and the Tales of Hoffmann for English National Opera (1997-98); Further engagements at Berlin (Deutsche and Staats-Oper), Vienna, La Scala Milan, San Francisco, Chicago, Amsterdam, Antwerp, Zürich and Cologne; Lohengrin at Theatre de la Monnaie Brussels, for Anja Silja's debut as producer; Season 1997 with Der Freischütz in Berlin, Ariadne at Brussels, Macbeth in Hamburg and Don Carlos at the Opéra Bastille, Paris. Address: c/o English National Opera, St Martin's Lane, London WC2, England.

HOHN Carola, b. 3 Mar 1961, Erfurt, Germany. Singer (Soprano). Education: Studied at the Franz Liszt Musikhochschule, Weimar. Career: Sang at Eisenach, 1984-87, Altenburg, 1987-88; Berlin Staatsoper from 1988, notably as Marie Antionette in the 1989 premiere of Graf Mirabeau by Siegfried Matthus; Other roles have included Antonia, Mozart's Fiordiligi and Pamina, Gretel, Marie in Zar and Zimmermann and Sophie in Der Rosenkavalier; Concert repertoire includes Carmina Burana by Orff; Guest engagements elsewhere in Germany and broadcasting commitments; Pamina in Die Zauberflöte at Bordeaux, 1992. Address: Deutsche Staatsoper Berlin, Unter den Linten 7, 1086 Berlin, Germany.

HOIBY Lee, b. 17 Feb 1926, Madison, WI, USA. Composer; Pianist. Education: BA, University of WI, 1947; MA, Mills College, 1952; Diploma, Curtis Institute, 1952; Private study with Egon Petri and Gunnar Johansen. Debut: As Pianist at Alice Tully Hall, New York City, 1978. Career: Commissions from Ford Foundation, Curtis Institute, St Paul Opera, Des Moines Metro Opera, USIA, Dorian Wind Quintet, G Schirmer, Library of Congress. Compositions: Operas: The Scarf, 1954, A Month in the Country, 1964, Summer and Smoke, 1971, Something New for the Zoo, 1980, The Tempest, 1986, This is the Rill Speaking, 1993; Sonata for Violin and Piano; Serenade for Violin and Orchestra; The Italian Lesson, musical monologue; Galilo Galilei, oratorio; For You O Democracy; A Hymn of the Nativity, Cantatas; The Tides of Sleep, symphonic song; Various solo piano works, songs and choral pieces. Recordings: After Eden, ballet; Piano Concerto; Choral Music of Lee Hoiby. Honours: Fulbright Fellow, 1952; Arts and Letters Award, 1957; Guggenheim Fellow, 1958; Honorary Member, American Guild of Organists; Honorary DFA, Simpson College, 1983. Membership: American Society of Composers, Authors and Publishers. Address: 800 Rock Valley, Long Eddy, NY 12760, USA.

HOINIC Bujor, b. 17 Feb 1950, Timisoara, Rumania. Conductor. m. Ayse Bilal, 7 Jjly 1984, 1 son. Education: Licentiate in Piano, Timisoara Music School; Licentiate in Composition and Conducting, Bucharest Conservatory. Debut: Concerto with Iasi Symphony Orchestra, 1973. Career: Conductor, Rumanian Opera, 1973-81; Conductor, Ankara State Opera, 1981-; Concerts and performances in Rumania, Yugoslavia and Turkey; Collaborator for musical broadcasts, Rumanian Radio, 1975-76, 1982-84; Professor, Ankara Conservatory, Ankara, Turkey, 1986-. Compositions: String Quartet, 1970; Pavane for orchestra, 1972; Concerto for cello and string orchestra, 1973; Prelude, Choral and Fugue for orchestra, recorded Radio Bucharest), 1976; Dacia Felix, ballet (recorded and filmed Rumanian TV), 1980; Angora for orchestra and women's choir (recorded Rumanian Radio), 1982; Balade and Deniz lirikleri for choir and chamber orchestra (recorded Turkish Radio-Television), 1985. Recordings: Cornel Trailescu's opera Balcescu, Rumanian Radio and TV, 1979. Honours: 1st Prize for performance with ballet Dacia Felix, Cantarea Romaniei National Festival, 1981. Membership: Rumanian Composers' Union. Hobby: Skiing. Address: Atac Sok 73/17 Yenisehir, Ankara, Turkey.

HOISETH Kolbjorn, b. 29 Dec 1932, Borsa, Norway. Singer (Tenor). Education: Studied with Egil Nordsjo in Oslo and with Ragnar Hulten and Set Svanholm in Stockholm. Debut: Stockholm, 1959, as Siegmund in Die Walküre. Career: Sang Wagner roles in Stockholm: Siegfried, Tristan, Tannhäuser, Walther, Parsifal, Erik and Loge; British debut, Covent Garden, 1963, as Lohengrin; Guest appearances in Berlin, Dusseldorf, Bordeaux, Lyon and Drottningholm; Edinburgh Festival with the Stockholm Company, 1974, as Laca in Jenufa; Metropolitan Opera, 1975, as Froh, Loge and Siegmund, in Der Ring des Nibelungen; Other roles include Florestan, Don Carlos, Gregor in The Makropoulos Case, Radames, Otello, Aegisthus, Herod and Don José. Honours include: Set Svanholm Memorial Prize, 1974. Address: c/o Kungliga Teatern, PO Box 16044, S-10322 Stockholm, Sweden.

HOJSGAARD Erik, b. 3 Oct 1954, Århus, Denmark. Composer. Education: Studied Composition with Per Norgård, Royal Academy of Music, Århus; Diploma, 1978; Student of Composition, Cantiere Internazionale d'Arte, 1976; Royal Academy of Music, Copenhagen, 1982-84. Career: Manager, Århus Young Composers' Society, 1974-76; Member of Organising Committee, Young Nordic Music Festival, 1974-81; Music Committee, Århus Regional Council, 1977-78; Music Copyist, 1977-82; Teacher, Royal Academy of Music, Copenhagen, 1982-; Member of Governing Body, Society for the Publication of Danish Music, 1982-92; His works performed at various music festivals in the Nordic countries, also at International Society for Contemporary Music festivals (1980, 1983). Compositions: Orchestral: Untitled symphony, 1974; Cello Concerto, 1975; Refleksion, 1977; Scherzo e notturno, 1982; Piano Concerto, 1984-85; Four Sketches, 1990; Chamber music: Dialogues, 1972; Solprismer, 1974; The Sunflower, 1978; Intrada, 1981; Fantasy Pieces, 1982-84; Watercolours, 1983; Intermezzi, 1983; Carillon, 1986; Two Mobiles, 1990; Paysage blême, 1991; Solo instruments: Cendrée, 1976; Sonata in C major, 1980; C'est la mer mêlée au soleil, 1981; Epreuve, 1993; Solo voice with instruments: Landet som icke är, 1974; Tuan's Songs, 1976; Variations: 6 Songs of Autumn, 1976; Vise, ballad, 1977; Täglich kommt die gelbe Sonne, 1977; Joyous, 1979; Fragments, 1979; The Lost Forest, 1980; Summer Songs, 1981; The Rose, 1981; Two Songs, 1985; Le città continue, 1986; Two songs for mixed choir, 1985-86; Don Juan kommt aus dem Krieg, opera, 1991. Recordings: Numerous. Address: Esbern Snaresvej 16, 4180 Soro, Denmark.

HOKANSON Leonard (Ray), b. 13 Aug 1931, Vinalhaven, Maine, USA. Concert Pianist; Professor of Piano. m. Rona Wolk, 17 Apr 1976. Education: BA, Clark College, 1952; MA, Bennington College, 1954; Studied piano with Hedwig Rosenthal, 1947-48, Artur Schnabel, 1948-51, Karl Ulrich Schnabel, 1951-53 and Claude Frank, 1952-55. Debut: Philadelphia Orchestra. 1949. Career: Played at festivals of Aldeburgh, Berlin, Lucerne, Prague, Salzburg, and Vienna; Played with Philadelphia Orchestra, Halle Orchestra, Vienna Symphony, Berlin Philharmonic, Bavarian Radio Symphony Orchestra and Rotterdam Philharmonic; Radio and TV appearances throughout Europe; Extensive touring in North and South America, Europe, Russia and Southeast Asia; Recognised also as a chamber music player and song accompanist; Professor of Piano, University of Frankfurt School of Music, 1976-86 and Indiana University School of Music, 1986-. Recordings: Solo, chamber music and song recital recordings. Publications: Beethoven Piano Sonatas Op 49/1 and 2 Fingerings and Notes on Interpretation, 1986. Current Management: Konzertdirektion Dr, Goette, Hamburg, Germany. Address: 839 Sheridan Road, Bloomington, IN 47401, USA.

HOLAB William (Joshua), b. 6 May 1958, Chicago, Illinois, USA. Composer. Education: BA, Music Composition, University of Michigan, 1980; The Juilliard School, 1980-82; Private study with William Albright, William Bolcom, and David Diamond in Composition; Solfege with Marianne Ploger and Rebecca Scott; Conducting with Vincent La Selva. Career: Music Engraver and Editor, Music Publishing Services, 1980-86; Orchestrator, Theater-by-the-Sea, Rhode Island, 1982; Music Editor, C F Peters Corporation, 1983-; Resident Orchestrator, The Candlewood Playhouse, New Fairfield, Connecticut, 1983-; Associate Director, Composers Concordance. Compositions include: Violin Sonata for violin and piano, 1977; Duo for 2 flutes, 1977; Gin and Tonic for vocal quartet, 1977; 2 Love Songs for bass-baritone and piano, 1977; 3 Airs for solo guitar, 1978; Arioso for solo piano, 1980; In The Twilight for 5 trombones, 1980; Thoughts While Driving Home for medium voice and piano, 1980; Ode to a Nightingale for tenor and orchestra, 1981; Twilight for violin, viola and cello, 1982; The Bells for chorus and chamber ensemble, 1982; Soliloquy for solo horn, 1983; To Sleep for soprano and harp, 1983; The Tracks of Angels for baritone and string quartet, 1985; To My Dear and Loving Husband for soprano and organ, 1985; Diana in New York for woodwind quintet, 1986; The Mikado, modern updated arrangement of Gilbert and Sullivan work, 1986; Confidence Game, musical based in The Alchemist by Ben Jonson, 1986. Hobby: Gourmet cooking. Address: 804 West 180th Street, Apartment 43, New York, NY 10033, USA.

HOLBROOK Elizabeth, b. 16 Dec 1937, Altrincham, Cheshire, England. Solo Violist. m. William Redgrave, 4 Jan 1973 (dec. 1986), 1 son, 2 daughters. Education: ARMCM, distinction, Royal Manchester College of Music; Eastman School of Music, USA; University of California, Institute for Special Music Studies with William Primrose. Debut: Manchester, 1960; London, Wigmore Hall, 1966. Career: Turner String Quartet, 1959-63; Teacher, Royal Manchester College, 1958-72, Royal Northern College of Music, 1973; Solo programmes in Switzerland, Hungary, Netherlands, Spain, USA; Viola and piano duo with Peter Pettinger; Viola and organ recitals with Keith Bond; Many first performances given; Solo, duo and with orchestra. Recordings: Reger, Suites for Hilversum. Publications: Concert Fantasy - Reizenstein, 1967; The Swan, for viola; Kol Nidrei, 1972. Hobby: Languages. Address: 23 Hungate Street, Aylsham, Norwich, Norfolk NR11 6AA, England.

HOLD Trevor (James), b. 21 Sep 1939, Northampton, England. University Lecturer. m. Susan Turner, 21 Jul 1962, 2 d. Education: Northampton Grammar School, 1950-57; University of Nottingham, 1957-62; BMus, First Class Honours, 1961; MA, 1963; PhD, 1989. Career: Head of Music, Market Harborough Grammar School, 1962-63; Assistant Lecturer, Music, UCW, Aberystwyth, 1963-65; Lecturer in Music, University of Liverpool, 1965-70; Lecturer and Staff Tutor, Music, Department of Adult Education, 1970-89; Senior Lecturer, Department of Adult Education, 1980-; Freelance Composer, Writer and Lecturer, 1989-. Compositions: The Unreturning Spring, song cycle, 1963; Kemp's Nine Daies Wonder, piano suite, 1970; Cello Sonata, 1973; The Lilford Owl, piano folktune arrangements, 1977; Symphony, 1977; The Second Death, opera, 1987; Concerto for String Orchestra, 1991; Piano Concerto, 1992; Many song cycles. Publications: The Walled-In Garden, A Study of the Songs of Roger Quilter, 1978; A Northamptonshire Garland, 1989; Three Volumes of Poetry: Time and the Bell, 1971; Caught in Amber, 1981; Mermaids and Nightingales, 1991. Contributions to: Various contributions and reviews to Music and Letters and Music Review; Musical Times; Choir and Organ. Honours: Clements Memorial Prize, 1965; Royal Amateur Orchestral Society Prize, 1968. Hobbies: Walking; Ornithology; Gardening; English Literature. Address: Dovecote House, Wadenhoe, Northamptonshire, via Peterborough, PE8 5SU, England.

HOLEK Vlastimil, b. 1950, Czechoslovakia. Violinist. Education: Studied at the Prague Conservatory. Career: Founder member of the Prazak String Quartet, 1972; Tour of Finland, 1973, followed by appearances at competitions in Prague and Evian; Concerts in Salzburg, Munich, Paris, Rome, Berlin, Cologne and Amsterdam; Tour of Britain, 1985, including Wigmore Hall debut; Tours of Japan, the United States, Australia and New Zealand; Tour of UK, 1988, and concert at the Huddersfield Contemporary Music Festival, 1989; Recitals for the BBC, Radio France, Dutch Radio, the WDR in Cologne and Radio Prague; Appearances with the Smetana and LaSalle Quartets in Mendelssohn's Octet. Recordings: Several albums. Honours: 1st Prize, Chamber Music Competition of the Prague Conservatory, 1974; Grand Prix, International String Quartet Competition, Evian Music Festival, 1978; 1st Prize, National Competition of String Quartets in Czechoslovakia, 1978; Winner, String Quartet Competition of the Prague Spring Festival, 1978. Address: c/o Ingpen and Williams Ltd, 14 Kensington Court, London W8 5DN, England.

HOLICKOVA Elena, b. 1950, Czechoslovakia. Singer (Soprano). Education: Conservatory of Music, Bratislava; Academy of Music and Drama, Bratislava. Career: Slovak National Theatre; Musetta in La Bohème, Lisa in the Queen of Spades, Rusalka in Rusalka, Jenufa, Julietta, Adriana in Adriana Lecouvreur, Marina in Dimitriy; Verdi's Gilda; Feodor in Mussorgsky's Boris Godunov; Small Shepherd in Suchon's The Whirlpool; Nuri in The Lowlands; Queen in Dance over the Crying; Swallow in The Happy Prince; A Servant in Electra; Marenka in The Bartered Bride; Orphan in The Siege of Bystrica; Amelia Grimaldi in Simon Boccanegra, 1984-85. Recordings: Songs by Mikulus Schneider-Trnavsky; Cycles by Alexander Moyzes; Glimpse into the Unknown; Mutations by Ilja Zeljenka, 1980; Ode to Joy, 1983; Submerged Music. Honours: Slovak Music Fund Prize, 1984. Address: c/o Slovak National Theatre, Gorkého 2, 815 06 Bratislava, Slovakia.

HOLL Robert, b. 1947, Rotterdam, Netherlands. Singer (Bass). Education: Studied with Jan Veth and David Hollestelle. Career: Sang with the Bayerische Staatsoper Munich from 1973; Has concentrated on concert career from 1975; Appearances at the Vienna, Holland and Salzburg Festivals, the Schubertiade at Hohenems; Salzburg Mozartwochen, 1981-83, as the Priest in Thamos, König in Ägypten, as the Voice of Neptune in Idomeneo and Cassandro in La Finta Giardiniera; Many engagements as a singer of Lieder, in music by Schubert, Brahms and Wolf; Concert appearances with Bernstein, Giulini, Harnoncourt, Jochum, Karajan, Sawallisch, Stein and De Waart; Promenade Concerts, London, 1987, in the Choral Symphony; Judge, Walter Gruener International Lieder Competition, London, 1989; Sang in Schubert's Fierrabras at the Theater an der Wien, Vienna, 1988; Season 1992 at Zurich, as Assur in Semiramide and La Roche in Capriccio; Sang Hans Sachs at the 1996 Bayreuth Festival; Vienna Festival, 1997, Schubert's Das Teufels Lustschloss. Recordings include: Mozart's Requiem; Mozart and Salieri by Rimsky-Korsakov; Lieder by Pfitzner; Requiems by Bellini and Donizetti; Mozart's Zaide and La Finta Semplice; St Matthew Passion by Bach; Die Schöpfung; Utrecht Te Deum by Handel; Mozart's Mass in C Minor; Bach Mass in B Minor. Honours include: Winner, Munich International Competition, 1972. Address: c/o Ingpen & Williams Ltd, 26 Wadham Road, London SW15 2LR, England.

HOLLAND Ashley, b. 1969, England. Baritone. Career: Many concert and opera engagements throughout the United Kingdom; Opera repertory includes Handel's Giulio Cesare and Walton's The Bear; Also sings Mahler's Rückert Lieder; Contestant at the 1995 Cardiff Singer of the World Competition. Address: Flat 10, 169 Upper Chorlton Road, Whalley Range, Manchester M21 9RA, England.

HOLLAND Mark, b. 1960, England. Singer (Baritone). Education: Studied with John Cameron at the Royal Northern College of Music and with Roberto Benaglio in Italy. Career: Joined Welsh National Opera in 1984 and has appeared as Rossini's Figaro, Mozart's Count, Eugene Onegin, Schaunard in La Bohème, Don Carlo in Ernani and Enrico in Lucia di Lammermoor; Sonora in La Fanciulla del West, 1991; Festival engagements include Piccinni's La Buona Figliola at Buxton; Season 1989-90 as Falke in Fledermaus for Opera Northern Ireland and Masetto for Dublin Grand Opera; Season 1990-91 as Ford in Falstaff at the Théâtre des Champs Elysées, tour to Japan with La Bohème and Carmina Burana with the Royal Philharmonic; Sang Puccini's Marcello and Mozart's Allazim (Zaide) with the City of Birmingham Touring Opera, 1991-92; Bregenz Festival, 1992, as Morales in Carmen. Address: Robert Gilder and Company, Enterprise House, 59-65 Upper Ground, London SE1 9PQ, England.

HOLLANDER Julia, b. 1965, Bristol, England. Stage Director. Education: St Catherine's College, Cambridge, and also in Paris. Career: Opera productions have included Orfeo ed Euridice for The Cambridge Arts Theatre, Les Mamelles de Tiresias at The Edinburgh Festival, Giovanna d'Arco at the Bloomsbury Theatre in London, Samson and Delilah for Northern Opera in Newcastle, The Rake's Progress for Aldeburgh, Acis and Galatea for Gregynog and Manchester Festivals, Turn of The Screw at the Britten Theatre in London, La Bohème for Mid Wales Opera, La Wally at the Bloomsbury Theatre and Love of Three Oranges in London; Staff Producer at ENO, 1988-91 working on numerous productions and reviving Xerxes, Lear and Macbeth in London and abroad; Solo production debut for ENO with Fennimore and Gerda, 1990, returning for the premiere of John Buller's Bakxai, 1992 and Eugene Onegin in 1994; Directed Margareta Hallin's Miss Julie for Operate at Hammersmith, 1996. Address: c/o Ingpen and Williams Ltd, 14 Kensington Court, London, W8 5DN, England.

HOLLANDER Lorin (D), b. 19 July 1944, New York City, New York, USA. Pianist. Education: Studied with Eduard Steuermann at the Juilliard School and with Leon Fleisher and Max Rudolf. Debut: Carnegie Hall, 1955. Career: Has performed with leading orchestras in the USA including the New York Philharmonic, Philadelphia Orchestra, Washington National and Chicago Symphony Orchestra; European engagements with the Warsaw Philharmonic, Orchestre de la Suisse Romande, London Philharmonic and Concertgebouw; Has performed in prisons, hospitals and other institutions; Series of programmes on television; Adviser to the Office of the Gifted and Talented for the US Government; Lecturer on psychological aspects of musical performance.

HÖLLE Matthias, b. 8 July 1951, Rottweil am Nekkar, Germany. Singer (Bass). Education: Studied in Stuttgart with Georg Jelden and in Cologne with Josef Metternich. Career: Sang first in concerts and oratorios; Sang in opera at Cologne from 1976; Ludwigsburg Festival, 1978, as the Commendatore in Don Giovanni; Has appeared at the Bayreuth Festival from 1981 as the Nightwatchman, Titurel, Fasolt and Hunding (1988 in Der Ring des Nibelungen, conducted by Daniel Barenboim); King Marke in Tristan und Isolde at Bologna (1983), Florence (1989) and Cologne (1990); Sang in the premiere of Stockhausen's Donnerstag (1981) and created Lucifer in Stockhausen's Samstag aus Licht at the Palazzo dello Sport with the company of La Scala Milan, 1984; Guest appearances in Hanover, Geneva, Tel Aviv and New York (Fidelio at the Metropolitan, 1986); Season 1989 as Don Fernando in Fidelio at Brussels, Daland in Stuttgart and the Commendatore at Parma; Sang Hunding at Bonn and the Bayreuth Festival, 1992; Fafner in The Ring at Covent Garden, 1996; Television appearances in Die Schöpfung and Beethoven's Christus am Olberge. Recordings include: Don Giovanni; Haydn's Seven Last Words on the Cross; Handel's Saul; Lieder by Schumann; Fourth Shepherd in Daphne, conducted by Haitink; Samstag aus Licht; Gurnemanz in Parsifal, conducted by Barenboim. Address: Vischerweg 11, D-7290 Freudenstadt, Germany.

HÖLLER York (Georg), b. 11 Jan 1944, Leverkusen, Germany. Composer. Education: Studied at the Cologne Musikhochschule, 1963-70, with B A Zimmermann and Herbert Eimert; Ferienkurse Darmstadt, 1965, with Boulez; Worked at the Electronic Music Studios, Cologne, with Stockhausen. Career: Freelance composer from 1965; First orchestral work, Topic, performed at Darmstadt, 1970; Invited by Boulez to work at the studios of IRCAM, 1978; Piano Concerto given French premiere by Daniel Barenboim, Paris, 1988; Der Meister und Margarita last new production at the Paris Opéra, Salle Garnier, before the opening of the Opéra de la Bastille; Professor for analysis and music theory at the College Musikhochschule, 1975-89; Director of the Electronic Studio at WDR Cologne, 1990-. Compositions: 5 Pieces, piano, 1964; Diaphonie, 2 pianos, 1965; Topic, orchestra, 1967; Sonate Informelle, 1968; Cello Sonata, 1969; Epitaph, violin, piano, 1969; Piano Concerto, 1970, No 2, 1983-84; Chroma, orchestra, 1972-74; Horizont, electronics, 1972; Tangent, electronics, 1973; Klanggitter, electronics, 1976; Antiphon for string quartet, 1977; Arcus, orchestra, 1978; Moments Musicaux, flute, piano, 1979; Umbra, orchestra, 1979-80; Mythos, orchestra, 1979-80; Résonance, orchestra, tape, 1981-82; Schwarze Halbinselu, orchestra, tape, 1982; Traumspiel, soprano, orchestra, tape, 1983; Magische Klanggestalt, orchestra, 1984; Improvisation sur le nom de Pierre Boulez, 1985; Der Meister und Margarita, opera, 1985-89; Piano Sonata No 2, Hommage à Franz Liszt, 1987; Fanal, trumpet, orchestra, 1990; Pensée, piano, orchestra, electronics, 1991; Aùna, large orchestra, 1992; Caligùla, opera after A Camus, 1992. Recordings: Schwarze Halbinselu; Résonance; Arcùs. Publications: Composition of the Gestalt on the making of an organism, 1984; B A Zimmermann Moine et Dionysos, 1985; Auf der süche nach den Klang von Morgan, 1990. Honours: Chevalier, Ordre des Arts et des Lettres, Paris; Rolf-Liebermann Preis für Opera Komponisten. Address: c/o Boosey & Hawkes Ltd, 295 Regent Street, London W1R 8JH, England.

HOLLEY William, b. 4 Dec 1930, Bristol, Florida, USA. Singer (Tenor). Debut: Landestheater Salzburg, 1961, as Faust. Career: Sang at Gelsenkirchen Opera, 1962-63, Essen, 1965-67, and later at the State Operas of Berlin, Munich and Stuttgart; Member of the Deutsche Oper am Rhein at Dusseldorf from 1966 to 1984; Further guest appearances in San Francisco (Don Ottavio, 1968), Vienna, Houston, Amsterdam and Hamburg; Salzburg Festival, 1969-71, in Cavalieri's La Rappresentazione di anima e di corpo; Other roles have include Tamino, Ferrando and Belmonte (Mozart), Alfredo, Hoffmann, Fenton, Ismaele, Don Carlos, Calaf, Don José, Andrea Chenier and Laca in Jenufa. Address: c/o Deutsche Oper am Rhein, Heinrich-Heine-Allee 16a, W-4000 Dusseldorf 1, Germany.

HOLLIDAY Melanie, b. 12 Aug 1951, Houston, Texas, USA. Singer (Soprano). Education: Studied at Indiana University School and at the Graz Academy of Music. Career: Sang at Hamburg and Klagenfurt from 1973; Basle Opera as Zerbinetta in Ariadne auf Naxos; Vienna Volksoper from 1976, as Olympia in Les Contes d'Hoffmann, Frau Fluth, Constanze, Philine in Mignon, Adele (Die Fledermaus), Valencienne (Die Lustige Witwe) and in Die Schöne Galatea by Suppé; Tours of Japan with the Volksoper, 1979, 1982, 1985; Guest appearances in Germany, Italy, Netherlands, Spain and Switzerland; Vienna Staatsoper; Houston Opera, 1983; Operetta tour of West Germany with René Kollo, 1984; Theater am Gärtnerplatz, Munich, 1986, as Musetta in La Bohème. Recordings include: Die Fledermaus; Film of L'Elisir d'Amore. Address: c/o Volksoper, Währingerstrasse 78, A-1090 Vienna, Austria.

HOLLIGER Heinz, b. 21 May 1939, Langenthal, Switzerland. Oboist; Composer; Conductor. Education: Berne, Paris and Basle under Emile Cassagnaud (oboe) and Pierre Boulez (composition). Career: Professor of oboe, Freiburg Music Academy, 1965-; Has appeared at all the major European music festivals and in Japan, USA, Australia, Israel; British premiere of Scardanelli Cycle at the Elizabeth Hall, 1988; Has recorded over 200 works, mainly for two labels; Berio, Krenek, Henze, Stockhausen and Penderecki have written works for him; Played in the British premiere of Gemeux by Takemitsu, Edinburgh, 1989; Premiered Henze's Doppio Concerto, 1966, Eucalypts I and II by Takemitsu, 1970-71, Ferneyhough's Coloratura and Ligeti's Double Concerto, 1972, Lutoslawski's Double Concerto, 1980, and Carter's Oboe Concerto, 1988; Conducted the Chamber Orchestra of Europe in Beethoven's 7th Symphony and Schnittke's 3rd Violin Concerto, London, 1992; Conducted the London Sinfonietta in his own music at the Elizabeth Hall, London, 1997. Compositions include: Der magische Tanzer; Trio; Siebengesang; Wind Quintet; Dona nobis pacem; Pneuma; Psalm; Cardiophonie; Kreis; String Quartet; Atembogen; Die Jahreszeiten; Come and Go; Not I; Trema; Turm-Mask, Tonscherben, Scardanelli-Cycle; 2 Liszt Transcriptions; Gesänge der Frühe; What Where. Honours: Recipient of several international prizes. Address: c/o Ingpen and Williams, 26 Wadham Road, London SW15 2LR, England.

HOLLIGER Ursula, b. 8 June 1937, Basle, Switzerland. Harpist. m. Heinz Holliger. Education: Studied in Basle and at the Brussels Conservatoire. Career: Worldwide appearances with leading orchestras, including the Philharmonics of Berlin, Vienna and Los Angeles, the Orchestre de Paris, English Chamber Orchestra, Orchestra of South German Radio and the Schweizerisches Festspielorchester Luzern; Conductors have included Pierre Boulez, Michael Gielen, Simon Rattle, André Prévin and Neville Marriner; Composers who have written for her and her husband include Edison Denisov, Henze (Doppio Concerto, 1966), André Jolivet, Ernst Krenek, György Ligeti (Double Concerto, 1972), Witold Lutoslawski (Double Concerto, 1977); Several works written for her by her husband; Professor at the Basle Music Academy. Recordings include: Spohr Concertos for Harp and Concertos for Violin and Harp. Address: c/o Ingpen and Williams Ltd, 26 Wadham Road, London SW15 2LR, England.

HOLLOP Markus, b. 1968, Berlin, Germany. Singer (Bass). Education: Studied at the Munich Musikhochschule. Career: Major roles with the opera studio of the Bayerische Staatsoper, from 1991; Sarastro in Die Zauberflöte and Rossini's Basilio in Gorlitz; Ulm Opera as the King in the Love for Three Oranges, Offenbach's Crespel at Wiesbaden and engagements with the Bayerische Staatsoper, from 1993; Further appearances in Schumann's Genoveva (Zurich), Hamlet and Wozzeck (Geneva) and Salome (Paris Châtelet, under Semyon Bychkov, 1997); Concerts include Weill's Ozeanflug in Munich and Solo Voice in Schoenberg's Moses und Aron with the Philharmonia Orchestra under Christoph von Dohnányi at the Festival Hall, London, 1996. Honours include: Winner, Carl Maria von Weber Competition, Munich, 1993. Address: c/o Bayerische Staatsoper, Max-Joseph Platz, Pf 100148, D-8000 Munich 1, Germany.

HOLLOS Mate, b. 18 July 1954, Budapest, Hungary. Composer. Education: F Liszt Academy of Music, Budapest. Career: Managing Director, Hungaroton Classic; Artistic Director, Akkord Music Publishers. Compositions include: Cantatas: Kajetan Tyl, Voyelles de Rimbaud, Songs of Love; Chamber Music: Looking Up on a Star; Duli Duli; Promenade; O Songs Float from my Lips; Arparmonia; New song without Words; Toccata Lirica; Hommage a Szeged, for string orchestra; L'EAR-A, sextet; Six and a Half Flute Duets; Rhapsodic Monologue, clarinet solo. Recordings: On the Edge of Non-Existence; Impromptu; O Songs Float from my Lips. Publications: Scores published by Editio Musica Budapest; Works in Kritika, Muzsika, Parlando, Magyar Nemzet. Honours: Creative Youth, 1980; Public Prize, Rostrom of the Hungarian Radio, 1992. Memberships: Vice President, Hungarian Composers Union; Hungarian Kodaly Society; Jeunesses Musicales (Board). Address: Bimbo ut 5, H-1022 Budapest, Hungary.

HOLLOWAY David, b. 12 Nov 1942, Grandview, Missouri, USA. Singer (Baritone). m. Deborah Seabury. Education: Studied at University of Kansas and with Luigi Ricci in Rome. Debut: Kansas City Lyric Opera, 1968, as Belcore in L'Elisir d'Amore. Career: Sang Britten's Billy Budd in Chicago, 1970; New York City Opera, 1972, as Guglielmo in Così fan tutte; Metropolitan Opera debut, 1973, in Madama Butterfly, returning as Puccini's Schaunard, Sharpless and Lescaut; Guglielmo, 1984; European appearances, in particular at the Deutsche Oper am Rhein, Dusseldorf; Glyndebourne, 1985, as Escamillo; Other roles include Mozart's Papageno, Count and Nardo (La Finta Giardiniera), Rossini's Figaro and Dandini, Donizetti's Malatesta, and Nick Shadow in The Rake's Progress. Recordings include: The Taming of the Shrew by Goetz. Honours include: Hi Fidelity Award, 1971. Hobbies: Camping; Fishing; Sailing; Motorcycling; Piano. Address: c/o Columbia Artists Management, 165 W 57th Street, New York, NY 10019, USA.

HOLLOWAY Robin (Greville), b. 19 Oct 1943, Leamington Spa, England. University Teacher; Critic; Composer. Education: St Paul's Cathedral Choir School; King's College School, Wimbledon; King's College, Cambridge; New College, Oxford; MA; PhD; DMus. Compositions include: Numerous compositions in all genres; First Concerto for Orchestra, 1969; Scenes from Schumann for orchestra, 1970; Domination of Black for orchestra, 1974; Clarissa, opera, 1976, premiered, 1990; 2nd Concerto for Orchestra, 1979; Brand, dramatic ballad, 1981; Seascape and Harvest for orchestra, 1984; Peer Gynt, dramatic ballad, 1985; The Spacious Firmament for chorus and orchestra, 1990; Hymn to the Senses for chorus, 1990; Serenade for strings, 1990; Winter Music for sextet, 1993; 3rd Concerto for Orchestra, 1993. Recordings: Sea Surface Full of Clouds, chamber cantata, Opus 28; Romanza for violin and small orchestra, Opus 31; 2nd Concerto for Orchestra, Opus 40; Horn Concerto Op 43; Violin Concerto Op 70. Publications: Debussy and Wagner, 1978. Contributions to: Numerous articles to periodicals and contributions to anthologies. Address: Finella, Queens' Road, Cambridge CB3 9AH, England.

HOLLOWAY Stephen, b. 1951, England. Bass. Education: Studied at the Guildhall School and with Vera Rozsa; Christ's College, Cambridge. Career: Appearances with Scottish Opera as Don Fernando in Fidelio, Private Willis in Iolanthe, Doctor Grenvil in La Traviata and Thanatos/The Oracle in Alceste; Sparafucile and Mozart's Bartolo for European Chamber Opera; The Speaker in The Magic Flute under Jane Glover at the Covent Garden Festival; Chub in Tchaikovsky's Cherevichki and The Chamberlain in Stravinsky's Nightingale for Chelsea Opera Group. Current Management: Musikmakers. Address: Little Easthall, St Paul's Walden, Hertfordshire SG4 8DH, England.

HOLLREISER Heinrich, b. 24 June 1913, Munich, Germany. Conductor. Education: Akademie der Tonkunst Munich. Career: Conducted at opera houses in Wiesbaden, Mannheim, Darmstadt and Duisburg; Munich Opera from 1942, notably with operas by Strauss, then Musical Director in Dusseldorf; Hamburg Opera, 1947, with the local premiere of Peter Grimes by Britten; Vienna Staatsoper from 1952; Principal Conductor at the Deutsche Oper Berlin, 1961-64; Blacher's Zweihundertausend Thaler, 1969; Modern repertory includes operas by Bartók, Hindemith and Berg; Bayreuth Festival, 1973-75, Tannhäuser and Die Meistersinger; Wagner's Ring at the Vienna Staatsoper, 1976; Guest Conductor with the Cleveland Orchestra, 1978. Recordings include: Mozart Piano Concertos; Tchaikovsky and Mendelssohn Violin Concertos; Bartók Cantata Profana and Concerto for Orchestra; Symphonies by Schubert, Brahms, Dvorák, Tchaikovsky, Bruckner, Stravinsky's Apollo, Pulcinella and Jeu de Cartes. Address: c/o PO Box 100262, Bayreuther Festspiele, 8580 Bayreuth 1, Germany.

HOLLWEG Werner, b. 13 Sept 1936, Solingen, Germany. Singer (Tenor). m. Constance Daucha, 2 children. Education: Studied in Detmold, Munich and Legano. Debut: Vienna Kammeroper, 1962. Career: Bonn, 1963-67; Gelsenkirchen, 1967-68; Maggio Musicale, Florence, 1969, as Belmonte in Die Entführung; Guest appearances in Hamburg, Munich, Berlin, Rome, Paris, New York and Los Angeles; Salzburg Festival as Mozart's Tamino, Ottavio, Ferrando and Belmonte; Osaka, Japan, 1970, in Beethoven's 9th Symphony; Covent Garden debut, 1976, as Mozart's Titus; Paris Opera, 1986, as Jason in Cherubini's Médée; Promendade Concerts, London, 1989, in Psalmus Hungaricus by Kodály; Created Matthew Levi in Höller's Der Meister und Margarita, Paris, 1989; Sang the High Priest in Idomeneo at Salzburg, 1990; Acted in Henze's Il Re Cervo at Wuppertal, 1996. Recordings: Haydn, Die Jahreszeiten; Mozart, Le nozze di Figaro; Mahler, Das klagende Lied; Mozart, La Finta Giardiniera and Zaide; Lehar, Die lustige Witwe; Mozart, Mitridate and Idomeneo; Monteverdi, Il Combattimento; Ballads by Schubert, Schumann and Loewe. Address: c/o Ingpen and Williams Ltd, 26 Wadham Road, London SW15 2LR, England.

HOLM Mogens (Winkel), b. Oct 1936, Copenhagen, Denmark. Composer. Education: Studied Oboe and Composition, Royal Danish Academy of Music, Copenhagen. Career: Oboe player in various Copenhagen orchestras including the Danish Radio Light Orchestra, 1964-65; Choreographer to his own ballet scores, 1975-. Compositions include: Opera: Aslak, 1961; Sonata for Four Opera Singers, 1967-68; Ballet: Tropisms, 1963; Chronicle, 1968; Galgarien, 1970; Report, 1972; Tarantel, 1975; Eurydice Hesitates, 1977; Whitethroat under an Artificial Firmament, 1979-80; To Bluebeard, 1982; Orchestra: Kammerkoncertante, 1959; Concerto piccolo, 1961; Cumulus, 1965; Ricercare, 1966; The Glass Forest, 1974; Aiolos, symphony in 1 movement, 1972-77; Cries, 1983-84;Chamber Music: Abracadabra, 1960; Tropismer, 1960; Sonata, 1965; Transitions, 1972; Seven Letters to Silence, 1976; Adieu, 1982; Note-book, 1983; Vocal: October Morning, 1964; Transitions, 1971; Nightmare, 1973; For Children, 1984. Recordings: Has made numerous recordings. Address: KODA, Rosenvaengets Hovedvej 14, 2100 Copenhagen, Denmark.

HOLM Peder, b. 30 Sept 1926, Copenhagen, Denmark. Composer; Educator. Education: Graduate in Violin and Theory, Royal Danish Conservatorium, 1947; Teacher's Examination in Piano and Violin. Career includes: Director, Western Jutland Conservatorium; Director, West Jutland Symphony Orchestrs. Compositions include: Pezzo Concertante for orchestra, 1964; VYL for orchestra, 1967; Khebeb for 2 pianos and orchestra, 1968; 2 pieces for wind quintet, 1968; Music for brass band, 1969; Ole Wivel, children's song for children's choir, 1970; Concertino for clarinet and chamber orchestra, 1970; Legend, Erik Knudsen, for children's choir, 1971; Ene Mene, Inscription, Mobile, September Evening, Regards to Borge, 5 choral songs for mixed choir; Pikkutikka for children's choir and orchestra, 1973; Arrangements: Works by Schumann, Grieg, Couperin and Mozart; Pieces for the Musica Ensemble Series; Works for solo voice, orchestra, symphonic works, concertos and chamber music. Publications include: The String Method; Wind Method; Violin 1 and 2 (editor); All part of Wilhelm Hansen's MUSICA-Methods series. Memberships: Programme Committee, Danish Radio, 1963-67; Music Committee, State Cultural Foundation, 1965-68. Address: Skolegyden 37, Nr Soby, 5792 Årslev, Denmark.

HOLM Renate, b. 10 Aug 1931, Berlin, Germany. Singer (Soprano). Education: Studied with Marie Ivogun in Vienna. Career: Sang in films and entertainment programmes from 1953; Vienna Volksoper from 1957, debut as Gretchen in Der Wildschütz by Lortzing; Appearances at the Vienna Staatsoper, Bolshoi Theatre, Moscow, Covent Garden, London, and the Teatro Colon, Buenos Aires in the soubrette repertory, including Despina, Norina, Sophie, Zerlina and Marzelline; Salzburg Festival from 1961, as Blondchen in Die Entführung, Papagena and Musetta. Recordings: Die Fledermaus, Der Vogelhändler, Das Land des Lächelns; Die Zauberflöte; Die Entführung. Address: c/o Staatsoper, 1010 Vienna, Austria.

HOLMAN Peter, b. 1946, London, England. Harpsichordist; Chamber Organist. Education: King's College, London with Thurston Dart. Career: As student, directed the pioneering early music group Ars Nova; Founded, The Parley of Instruments, with Roy Goodman, 1979, The Parley now recognised as one of the leading exponents of Renaissance and Baroque string consort music; Musical Director, 1985, newly formed Opera Restor'd which specialises in authentic productions of eighteenth century English operas and masques; Past Professor, Royal Academy of Music in London for 10 years and has taught at many conservatories, universities and summer schools in England; Artistic Director of the annual Suffolk Village Festival; Joint Artistic Director, with Paul O'Dette, of the 1995 Boston Early Music Festival; Presently, Senior Associate Lecturer at Colchester Institute School of Music; Regular Broadcaster on BBC Radio 3; He spends much of his time in writing and research; Special interests in the early history of the violin family, in European instrumental ensemble music of the renaissance and Baroque and in English seventeenth and eighteenth century music; Edition of Arne's Artaxerxes performed London, 1995; Directed Opera Restor'd in Lampe's The Dragon of Wantley, 1996. Publications: Many editions of early music; Four and Twenty Fiddlers; The Violin at the English Court 1540-1690, 1993; Ed, London: Commonwealth and Restoration in The Early Baroque Era, C A Price in the Man and Music (Music and Society in the USA) series (London), 1993; Paper on Monteverdi's string writing in the Nov 1993 issue of Early Music; Henry Purcell, A General Survey of Purcell's Music, 1st edition, 1994. Contributions to: Various articles and reviews to a range of newspapers and journals. Address: 119 Maldon Road, Colchester, Essex CO3 3AX, England.

HOLMES Eugene, b. 7 Mar 1932, Brownsville, Tennessee, USA. Singer (Baritone); Kammersänger. m. Katja L Holmes. Education: AM&N College; BS, Music Education, Indiana University, Bloomington; Special award, Performer's Certificate; Studied with W D Walton in St Louis, Frank St Leger at the Indiana University in Bloomington, and with Dorothy Ziegler in Miami. Debut: Goldovsky Opera, New York, 1963, in The Crucible by Ward. Career: Kammersänger, Deutsche Oper am Rhein, Düsseldorf; Sang in San Diego, San Francisco, Seattle and New York (City Opera, 1971, in the premiere of The Most Important Man by Menotti); Washington, 1970, in the US premiere of Koanga by Delius; Dusseldorf, 1983, as Don Carlos in La Forza del Destino, Nabucco, and Enrico in Lucia di Lammermoor; Munich, 1983, in a concert performance of Porgy and Bess; Other roles include Amonasro, Macbeth, Iago, Rigoletto, Boccanegra, Jochanaan and parts in operas by Mozart, Wagner and Puccini; Verdi's La Traviata, Germont, Puccini's La Bohème, Marcello, Madama Butterfly, Sharpless, Manon Lescaut, Verdi's Il Trovatore, Count di Luna; Performed with the Deutsche Oper am Rhein in the USSR, Magic Flute; Concert tours in Japan and Israel. Recordings include: Porgy and Bess; Koanga. Address: c/o Deutsche Opera am Rhein, Heinrich Heine Allee 16, D-4000 Dusseldorf, Germany.

HOLMQUIST Ake, b. 2 Aug 1943, Stockholm, Sweden. President; Musical Director. m. Britt Ingrid Kullberg, 3 Nov 1967, 1 son, 2 daughter. Education: BA, 1967; MA, 1970; PhD, 1972; Music Theoretical and Pianistic Studies, Stockholm and Vienna. Career: Planning Manager, 1973-74, Regional Director, 1975-80, Head, Uppsala Music Authorities, 1978-82; Programme Director, 1980-86, Institute for National Concerts, Sweden; President, European Music Year, Sweden, 1983-85; Executive and Artistic Director, Stockholm Concert Hall Foundation, Royal Stockholm Philharmonic Orchestra, 1986-; Board, Swedish-Greek Cultural Exchange Foundation, 1992-96; Director, Stockholm Composer Festival, 1986-; Chairman of Board, Swedish Festival, 1993-; Chairman of Board, Hugo Alfvén Society, 1993-; Board, Renewal and Restoration of the City of Stockholm, 1993-95; Commissioner, Stockholm Exposition, 1993-95; Chairman, Royal Swedish Festival, 1994-; Board Member, International Society for the Performing Arts, 1995-; Chairman, Edsberg's Music Institute, 1994-; Member, European Concert Hall Organization, 1992-; Chairman, Board, Royal University College of Music, 1998-; Chairman, Committee, International Society for the Performing Arts, Stockholm Conference (1998), 1996-. Publications: Fran signalgivning till regionmusik, 1974; The Music in Stockholm 1719-1976, 1976; Arnold Schoenberg - A Small Biography, 1976; To Commission Music for the Regional Music, 1976. Contributions to: Musikrevy, 1970-. Memberships: IMC; Royal Swedish Academy of Music, 1994. Address: Stockholm Concert Hall Foundation, Box 7083, S-103 87 Stockholm, Sweden.

HOLOMAN D(allas) Kern, b. 8 Sept 1947, Raleigh, North Carolina, USA. Musicologist; Conductor; Music Educator. m. Elizabeth R Holoman, 1 son, 1 daughter. Education: Studied bassoon and conducting, North Caroline School of the Arts; Accademia Musicale Chigiana, Siena, Italy, 1967, 1968; BA, Duke University, 1969; MFA, 1971, PhD, 1974, Princeton University. Career: Founding Director, Early Music Ensemble, 1973-77, 1979, Conductor, Symphony Orchestra, 1978-, Chairman, Music Department, 1980-88, University of California at Davis; Founding Co-Editor, 19th Century Music Journal, 1977; General Editor, Recent Researches in the Music of the Nineteenth and Early Twentieth Centuries, 1989; Guest Lecturer, various professional organisations. Publications: The Creative Process in the Autograph Musical Documents of Hector Berlioz, c 1818-1840, 1980; Musicology in the 1980s (edited with C Palisca), 1982; Dr Holoman's Handy Guide to Concert-Going, 1983; Catalogue of the Works of Hector Berlioz, 1987; Writing About Music: A Style-Sheet from the Editors of the 19th Century Music, 1988; Berlioz, 1989; Berlioz's Roméo et Juliette, New Berlioz Edition (editor). Contributions to: Numerous articles and reviews to journals and other publications. Memberships: American Musicological Society; Music Library Association; Association National Hector Berlioz. Address: c/o Department of Music, University of California at Davis, Davis, CA 95616, USA.

HOLOUBEK Ladislav, b. 13 Aug 1913, Prague, Czechoslovakia. Composer; Conductor. Education: Academy of Music and Dramatic Arts, Bratislava, with Viterzslav Novak,

Prague. Career: Conductor, National Theatre, Bratislava, 1933-52 and 1958-66; Conductor, State Theatre, Kozice, 1955-58 and 1966-. Compositions: Stella, opera in 3 acts, 1937-38; Dawn, opera 3 acts, 1940; Yearning, opera 3 acts, 1943; The Family, opera 3 acts, 1958; Professor Mamlock, opera 2 acts, 1964; Many chamber and orchestra music and song cycles. Publications: Translated a number of Russian, Italian and German opera librettos. Honours: Recipient of many honours including Excellent Labour, 1960; Order of Labour, 1984. Membership: Union of Slovak Composers. Address: Rustaveliho 16, 83106 Bratislava, Slovakia.

HOLST Per, b. 23 June 1949, Copenhagen, Denmark. General Manager. m. Anne Holst, divorced, 1987. Appointments: Trainee, Edition Wilhelm Hansen, 1982-85; Founder, Tivoli Festival Agency, 1987-95; General Manager, Odense Symphony Orchestra, 1995-. Address: Odense Symfoniorkester, Odense Koncerthus, Claus Berg Gade 9, 5000 Odense C, Denmark.

HOLSZKY Adriana, b. 30 Jun 1953, Bucharest, Rumania. Composer. Education: Studied at the Bucharest Conservatory with Milko Kelemen, in Germany and with Franco Donatoni in Italy. Career: Teacher at the Stuttgart Hochschule, 1980-89. Compositions include: Space for 4 Orchestras, 1980; Erewhon for 14 Instruments, 1984; Bremer Freiheit, opera, 1987; Lichtflug for Violin, Flute and Orchestra, 1990; Gemalde Eines Erschlagenen for 74 Voices, 1993; and other vocal and chamber music. Honours include: Prizewinner in competitions in Rome, Paris, Mannheim and Heidelberg.

HOLT Simon, b. 21 Feb 1958, Bolton, Lancashire, England. Composer. Education: Bolton College of Art, 1977-78; Composition, Piano and Harpsichord at Royal Northern College of Music, 1978-82. Career: Featured composer at Bath Festival, 1985; Commissions from London Sinfonietta: Kites, Ballad of the Black Sorrow and Nash Ensemble: Shadow Realm, Era Madrugada, Canciones, Sparrow Night, All Fall Down, Banshee in The House, 1994 and Nigredo, 1994, and Proms for 1987 and 1992; Also featured at Music in London now Festival in Japan, 1986. Compositions include: Lunas Zauberschein; Palace at 4am; Mirrormaze; Maiastra; Burlesca Oscura; Tauromaquia; Syrensong; Duendecitos; Capriccio Spettrale; String Quartet: Danger of The Disappearance of Things; Lilith; Walking With the River's Roar; Tanagra; Figurine; Icarus Lamentations; A Knot of Time; Some Distant Chimes; A Shapeless Flame; Minotaur Games; The Thing That Makes Ashes; Daedalus Remembers for Cheltenham Festival, 1995. Recordings: CD, Era Madrugada, Canciones, Shadow Realm, Sparrow Night with Nash Ensemble. Honour: Fellow of RNCM, 1993. Address: c/o Chester Music Ltd, 8/9 Frith Street, London W1V 5TZ, England.

HOLTEN Bo, b. 1948, Denmark. Composer. Compositions include: Works for symphony orchestras, with/without chorus; Works for large/small chamber ensembles; Vocal and instrumental music; Choral works with/without instruments; Opera, The Bond, 19378-79; Tape, film scores; Symphonic works include: Mahler-Impromptu, 1972-73; Caccia, 1979;Symphony, 1981, 1982; Imperia, 1983; Tertia Die, 1985; Conducts vocal group, Ars Nova, performances of rare works; Music critic and editor, Dansk Musiktidsskrift; Pioneer, many unusual concerts combining classical music/jazz. Hobby: Football. Address: KODA, Rosenvaengets Hovedvej 14, 2100 Copenhagen, Denmark.

HOLTENAU Rudolf, b. 1937, Salzburg, Austria. Singer (Baritone). Education: Studied in Linz and in Vienna with Alfred Jerger. Career: Sang in concert, 1959-61; Opera engagements at Klagenfurt, 1961-62; Regensburg, 1962-65; Bielefeld, 1965-67; Essen, 1967-75; Further appearances at Cologne, 1972-73; Vienna Staatsoper, 1973-75, Graz, 1977-79; Guest throughout the 1970s at Stockholm, Lyon, Brussels, Barcelona, Monte Carlo, Lisbon, Marseille and Bologna; Performances of Der Ring des Nibelungen at Seattle, 1978-79; Sang such roles as Wagner's Dutchman, Sachs, Wotan, Gunther, Kurwenal and Amfortas, Strauss's Mandryka and Verdi's Amonasro at Hamburg, Berlin (Deutsche Oper), Buenos Aires, Venice, San Francisco and Rio de Janeiro; Sang at Cape Town, 1982, 1985. Recordings: Ballads by Carle Loewe.

HOLTHAM Ian, b. 1 Feb 1955, Melbourne, Victoria, Australia. Concert Pianist; Educationalist. Education: BA, PhD, DipEd, Melbourne University; BMus, Durham University; Studied with Peter Feuchtwanger, Geza Anda and Geoffrey Parsons. Debut: Purcell Room and Wigmore Hall, both 1977. Career: Appearances in UK, Switzerland, France, Austria, Italy, Thailand, Hong Kong and Australia; Concerto soloist and recitalist; Numerous radio and TV appearances including frequently for Australian Broadcasting Corporation. Recordings: Chopin: 24 Etudes, Op 10 and Op 25; Godowsky: Selection of transcriptions of Chopin Etudes; Imo pectore-music by Beethoven, Schubert, Schumann and Rachmaninov. Publication: The Essentials of Piano Technique, 1992. Hobby: Golf. Current Management: Alan Watkinson Management. Address: Heavitree, PO Box 412, Canterbury, Victoria 3126, Australia.

HOLTMANN Heidrun, b. 18 Oct 1961, Munster, Westphalia, Germany. Pianist. Education: Study with Eleonore Jäger, Münster, 1966-70; Professor Renate Kretschmar-Fischer, Musikhochschule Detmold/Westphalia, 1970-83; Nikata Magaloff, Geneva, Switzerland, 1978; Vladimir Ashkenazy, Lucerne, Switzerland, 1981. Career: Concerts in England, France, Germany, Israel, Italy, Japan, Yugoslavia, North Africa, Austria, Poland, Hungary, Switzerland, USA; Concerts at Festivals in Bordeaux, France; Brescia & Bergamo, Italy; Salzburg; Lockenhaus, Austria; Lucerne, Switzerland; Berlin, West Germany; Concerts with Detroit Symphony Orchestra (Ivan Fischer), Royal Philharmonic Orchestra, London (Antal Dorati) Mozarteum Orchestra/Salzburg, Tonhalle Orchestra/Zurich (Gerd Albrecht, Ferdinand Leitner, David Zinman), ARD/NDR-ZDF, West Germany; DRS-TV, Zurich, Switzerland; RTV Skopje, Yugoslavia; TV Recordings at ARD & ZDF, West Germany; Radio Recordings several times with all Radio stations in West Germany. Recordings: Gidon Kremer Chamber Music Festival, 1983; Anneliese Rothenberger Presents, 1984; Bach, Goldberg Variations, 1986; Schumann, Carnaval and Kreisleriana, 1987. Hobbies: Music; Literature; Modern Arts. Current Management: Konzertagentur Fahrenholtz, Oberweg 51, D-6000 Frankfurt/Main 1. Address: Büsingstrasse 1, D-1000 Berlin 41, Germany.

HOLTON Ruth, b. 1961, England. Singer (Soprano). Education: Choral exhibitioner at Clare College, Cambridge; Further study with Elizabeth Lane, Nancy Long and Julie Kennard. Career: Appearances from 1985 in Baroque music at Bruges, Turku (Finland), Berlin, Amsterdam, Rome, Vienna, Paris; Recitals in Cambridge, Oxford, London, Glasgow and at the Three Choirs Festival in Gloucester; Fauré's Requiem at the Théâtre du Châtelet, Paris, and Ilia in Idomeneo, 1991; Radio broadcasts, BBC Recital, Radio 3, 1992, 1994, 1995, 1996, 1997; WDR Recital, 1992; Worldwide broadcast of Bach's St John Passion with choir of St Thomas', Leipzig, 1997; Concert work with Fretwork, Orchestra of the Age of Enlightenment, Ton Koopman, John Eliot Gardiner, Gustav Leonhardt, Tavener Consort. Recordings: Bach's St John Passion and Cantatas, Jephtha by Handel and Carissimi, Dido and Aeneas, Handel's Messiah, Mozart's Salzburg Masses, works by Schütz and Buxtehude; Angel in Schütz's Christmas Story with the King's Consort; Grand Pianola Music by John Adams, also music by Steve Reich. Address: 27 Casewick Road, London SE27 0TB, England.

HOLZAPFEL Helmut, b. 4 Dec 1941, Robertson, South Africa. Singer (Tenor). Education: Studied at the Vienna Academy with Erik Werba. Debut: Cape Town, 1963, as Don Ottavio. Career: Sang in opera at Innsbruck, 1972-77, and was member of the Staatsoper Stuttgart from 1977 (premiere of Akhnaten by Philip Glass, 1984); Has also sung in modern repertory by Henze, Penderecki, Rihm, Kagel and Zimmermann; Guest appearances throughout Germany and in South America and Switzerland; Concerts as the Evangelist in Bach's Passions and Lieder recitals at the Salzburg Mozartwoche; Sang Lescaut in Henze's Boulevard Solitude at Bonn, 1996. Publication: Doctorate on South African Song Composer S le Roux, 1992. Recordings include: Akhnaten (CBS); Die Soldaten by Zimmermann (Teldec). Address: c/o Staatstheater Stuttgart, Oberer Schlossgarten 6, W-7000 Stuttgart 1, Germany.

HOLZMAIR Wolfgang, b. 1952, Austria. Singer (Baritone). Education: Studied in Vienna. Career: Appearances in opera and concert halls throughout Germany, Austria and Switzerland; British Lieder recitals from 1990, including Schubert's Schwanengesang, with Imogen Cooper at the Wigmore Hall, 1993; Engagements with Berne Opera from 1985, including Rossini's Figaro, Valentin and Papageno, 1985-86; Gluck's Orpheus and Eugene Onegin, 1991; Season 1987-88 in Udo Zimmermann's Die Weisse Rose at the Vienna Konzerthaus, as Ireo in Cesti's Semiramide at Innsbruck and as Serezha in The Electrification of the Soviet Union by Nigel Osborne at Wuppertal; Season 1989-90 as Peri's Orfeo at Wuppertal, in Die Weisse Rose at Innsbruck and as Pelléas at Essen; Covent Garden debut, 1993, as Papageno, Wigmore Hall, recital, 1997. Recordings: Lieder albums. Address: c/o AMI Ltd, 22 Tower Street, Covent Garden, London WC2H 9NS, England.

HOMOKI Andreas, b. 16 Feb 1960, Marl, Germany. Director. Education: Studied at Bremen Hochschule and Academy of Fine Arts in Berlin. Career: Assistant at Deutsche Oper Berlin, Theater des Westens and Komische Oper, Berlin; Assistant to Harry Kupfer at Salzburg Festival, Stuttgart State Opera and Cologne Opera, 1986-87; From 1987, has assisted Michael Hampe, Willy Decker and Harry Kupfer, at Cologne Opera; Assistant to Michael Hampe at Salzburg Festival; Opera productions have included: Mozart's Bastien und Bastienne in Oslo; Le nozze di Figaro for Kammeroper Herdecke, 1988; Fidelio and Jakob Lenz by Wolfgang Rihm for the Cologne Music Academy, 1989-90; Directed the Michael Hampe Australian Opera production of Die Meistersinger, 1990, for New Zealand International Festival of the Arts; Il Trovatore for Wellington City Opera, 1991; Instructor of Drama at Opera Department, Cologne

Music Academy, 1988-93; Since 1993, Freelance Director; Opera productions have included: L'Enfant et les Sortilèges, 1992 for Cologne Music Academy; Die Frau ohne Schatten, Geneva Grand Opera, 1992; Cav and Pag in State Theatre, Mainz, 1993; Madame Butterfly, Essen, 1993; Das Schloss, Hannover, 1994; Frau Ohne Schatten, Paris, 1994; Wildschütz, Cologne, 1994; Rigoletto, Hamburg, 1994; Tristan und Isolde, Wiesbaden, 1994; Idomeneo at the Nationaltheater, Munich, 1996. Honour: French Theatre Critics Award for Best Opera, 1994. Address: c/o Haydn Rawstron Ltd, PO Box 654, London, SE26 4DZ, England.

HONECK Manfred, b. 1963, Vienna, Austria. Career: Assistant Conductor to Claudio Abbado in the Gustav Mahler Youth Orchestra, from 1987; Principal Conductor of the Jeunesse Orchestra, Vienna, and regular concerts with the NDR Orchestra Hanover and the Radio Symphony Orchestras of Berlin, Leipzig, Munich, Frankfurt, Cologne, Saarbrucken and Stuttgart; Kapellmeister at the Zürich Opera from 1991; Opera productions include Die Fledermaus, Figaro and Il Barbiere di Siviglia at the Vienna Volksoper, 1989-90; Giodano's Fedora and Andre Chenier, Massenet's Herodiade at Zürich; Così fan Tutte at Hamburg, 1993; The premiere of Herbert Willi's opera Sclafes Bruder, 1996; Ballet includes Pulcinella at the Vienna Staatsoper, 1990; Debut with the Vienna Philharmonic Orchestra and Houston Symphony, 1994; Season 1995 with the Chicago Symphony Orchestra and the BBC Symphony at the Festival Hall, London; Season 1996-97 with the Dresden Staatsapelle, Oslo Philharmonic, Danish Radio Symphony and Royal Danish Orchestras; Music Director of Norwegian Opera from 1997; Further concerts with the BBC SO, 1997-98. Honours include: European Prize for Conducting, 1993. Address: c/o IMG Artists, Media House, 3 Burlington Lane, London W4 2TH, England.

HONEGGER Henri (Charles), b. 10 June 1904, Geneva, Switzerland. Cellist. m. Claire Pallard, 1 son, 1 daughter. Education: Cello studies in Geneva; Leipzig, Germany (with Julius Klengell); Ecole Normale, Paris, France, with Diran Alexanian and Pablo Casals. Career: Soloist with major European orchestras, North and South American and Japanese orchestras; Gave first performance of entire set of Bach's Suites in New York, 1950, Leipzig, 1952, China (1st Western musician invited to give concerts in Peking, Shanghai and other Chinese venues); Television appearances, Tokyo, Hong Kong, Singapore and so on; Numerous festival appearances; Numerous recordings. Hobbies: Mountaineering; Skiing. Address: 21 Chemin de Conches, CH 1231 Conches, Switzerland.

HONEYMAN Louise (Mary), b. 23 Feb 1933, Shrewsbury, Shropshire, England. Orchestra Management. Divorced, 1 s, 2 d. Education: Ludlow Girls High School. Career: Orchestra Management: London Mozart Players, English Bach Festival, London Bach Society, Steinitz Bach Players, London Bach Orchestra and Fires of London; Until 1995 Executive Director of The London Mozart Players. Memberships: Director of the ABO; Board, Trinity College of Music; The Arts Club. Address: 92 Chatsworth Road, Croydon, CR0 1HB, England.

HONG Hei-Kyung, b. 1958, Seoul, South Korea. Singer (Soprano). Education: Studied at the Juilliard School, New York, until 1983. Debut: Houston, 1983, as Gilda in Rigoletto. Career: Sang Musetta at Chicago, 1983, and at the Metropolitan Opera from 1985 (debut as Servilia in La Clemenza di Tito), followed by Mimi, Despina, Susanna, Lauretta (Gianni Schicchi), Ilia and Pamina; Toronto, 1992, as Gounod's Juliette; Other roles include Leila (Les Pêcheurs de Perles), Manon, Butterfly, Bellini's Giulietta and Woglinde in Das Rheingold; Sang Zerlina at Dallas, 1996. Recordings include: Rheingold and Götterdämmerung (DGG). Address: c/o Metropolitan Opera, Lincoln Center, New York, NY 10023, USA.

HOOPER Adrian (John), b. 6 May 1953, Sydney, New South Wales, Australia. Conductor; Mandolinist. m. Barbara Michele Jackson, 9 Jan 1975, 2 sons, 1 daughter. Education: Studied at New South Wales Conservatorium of Music. Career: Founder and Conductor of Australia's foremost mandolin orchestra, The Sydney Mandolins; Regular player with the Australian Opera and Ballet Orchestra which accompanies the Australian Opera, and performed in such works as Otello and the Merry Widow; Worked with Sydney Symphony Orchestra in such works as Agon by Stravinsky; Regularly takes part in radio and concert performances as a Mandolin Soloist and Conductor for the Australian Broadcasting Commission; Soloist, Australian Chamber Orchestra; Mandolin Teacher, New South Wales State Conservatorium of Music, 1983; Teacher in Performance, Sydney University, 1996-. Recordings: Have released 57 CDs of music by Australian composers; 3 LP records. Publications: Published and edited a number of Ancient Mandolin works; Currently editing all Mandolin Concertos. Address: 24 Kitchener Street, Oatley, NSW 2223, Australia.

HOOPER-ROE Janice, b. Buxton, Derbyshire, England. Singer (Mezzo-soprano). Education: Studied at the Birmingham School of Music and London Opera Centre. Career: Sang with the English Opera Group and English Music Theatre in operas by Mozart, Henze, Oliver, Britten, Tchaikovsky and Weill; Appearances in London, Venice and Brussels and at the Edinburgh, Florence and Schwetzingen Festivals; Sang at the Aldeburgh Festival in the premiere of Death in Venice (1973) and in the British premiere of Paul Bunyan; Covent Garden debut, 1979, as Olga in Eugene Onegin, returning in Parsifal, Lohengrin and Alceste; Concert engagements at the Barbican Hall and South Bank; Appearances in musicals and Gilbert and Sullivan in Europe and America. Address: c/o Korman International Management, Crunnells Green Cottage, Preston, Herts SG4 7UQ, England.

HOOVER Katherine, b. 2 Dec 1937, Elkins, WV, USA. Composer; Flautist. Education: Studied at the Eastman and Manhattan Schools of Music. Career: Teacher and Flautist in New York City. Compositions include: Homage To Bartók for Ensemble, 1975; Divertimento, 1975; Medieval Suite for Flute and Piano, 1980; Lyric Trio for flute, cello and piano, 1982; Summer Night for Flute, Horn and Strings, 1986; Clarinet Concerto, 1987; Da Pacem, piano quintet, 1988; Two Sketches for Orchestra, 1989; Double Concerto for 2 Violins and Strings, 1989; Oboe Sonata, 1991; Night Skies for Orchestra, 1992; Piano, choral and other vocal music. Honours: Recipient, National Endowment Composer's Fellowship, 1979; American Academy of Arts and Letters, 1994; Academy Award in Composition. Address: 160 W 95th Street (5B), New York, NY 10025, USA.

HOPE Daniel, b. 1974, South Africa. Concert Violinist. Education: Studied at the Menuhin School of Music and with Felix Andrievsky at the Royal College of Music Junior Department. Career: Played duos with double-bassist Garry Karr, 1983, Bartók duos with Yehudi Menuhin for German TV, 1984; International debut with the Jyväskylä Symphony Orchestra of Finland, playing the Mendelssohn Concerto; Brighton Festival in Bach's Fifth Brandenburg Concerto, recitals at the Purcell Room, London, the Bach Violin Concertos with the Milton Keynes Chamber Orchestra and concert with the Hallé Orchestra under Menuhin; Vivaldi's Four Seasons with the Aachen City Orchestra, Prokofiev's First Concerto in Finland and London, and the Beethoven Concerto on tour in Europe; Appearances at the Schleswig-Holstein Festival, Germany. Honours: Winner: Hugh Bean Violin Competition, 1986; Peter Morrison Concerto Competition, 1989. Address: c/o Anglo Swiss Management, Suite 35-37 Morley House, 320 Regent Street, London W1R 5AD, England.

HOPFERWEISER Josef, b. 25 May 1938, Graz, Austria. Singer (Tenor). Education: Musikhochschule Graz. Career: Frequent appearances at the Vienna Volksoper, notably in Notre Dame by Schmidt; State Operas of Hamburg, Munich and Stuttgart; Further engagements in Nancy, Frankfurt, Graz, Milan, Rome and San Francisco; Sang in the premiere of Troades by Aribert Reimann, Munich, 1986; Sang Froh in Das Rheingold at Munich, 1987, Alwa in Lulu at Madrid, 1988; Vienna Staatsoper, 1990, as Walther in Die Meistersinger; Many concert appearances. Recordings include: Alwa in Berg's Lulu, conducted by Christoph von Dohnányi.

HOPKIN John (Arden), b. 11 Feb 1947, Laramie, Wyoming, USA. Opera Director; Singer; Music Educator. m. D Lorraine Rudd, 11 Aug 1969, 5 sons. Education: BMus, Brigham Young University, 1971; MMus, North Texas State University, 1974; DMA, Eastman School of Music, 1978. Debut: Fort Worth Opera Company. Career: Appeared as Baritone in 30 opera/musical theatre roles with Fort Worth Opera, Boris Goldovsky Opera Company, Chautauqua Opera Company, Syracuse Opera, Beaumont Opera; Recitalist and Concert Artist, North and Central America; Specialist in Latin American vocal music; Opera Director and Studio Voice Teacher, 1977-, Head of Vocal Studies, 1977-87, Texas Christian University; Opera Director, Bay View Music Festival, 1981-88; Guest Director: Fort Worth Opera, Arkansas Opera, Southwestern Opera Institute. Recording: Andrew Barton's The Disappointment (1st American Opera). Publication: The Influence of the Commedia dell'Arte on Opera Buffa of the Eighteenth Century, 1974.

HOPKINS Antony, b. 21 Mar 1921, London, England. Musician; Author. m. Alison Purves, 1947 (dec 1991). Education: Royal College of Music with Cyril Smith and Gordon Jacob. Career: Lecturer, Royal College of Music, 15 years; Director, Intimate Opera Company, 1952-64; Series of radio broadcasts, Talking About Music, 1954-92. Compositions include: Operas: Lady Rohesia; Three's Company; Hands Across the Sky; Dr Musikus; Ten o'clock Call; The Man from Tuscany; Ballets: Etude; Cafe des Sports; 3 Piano Sonatas; Numerous scores of incidental music including: Oedipus; The Love of Four Colonels; Cast a Dark Shadow; Pickwick Papers; Billy Budd; Decameron Nights. Publications include: Understanding Music, 1979; The Nine Symphonies of Beethoven, 1980; The Concertgoer's Companion, 2 volumes, 1984, 1986. Honours: Gold Medal, Royal College of Music, 1943; Italia Prize for Radio Programme, 1951, 1957; Medal, City of Tokyo for Services to Music, 1973; Commander of the British Empire, 1976. Address: Woodyard, Ashridge, Berkhamsted, Hertfordshire, HP4 1PS, England.

HOPKINS John (Raymond), b. 19 July 1927, Preston, England. Conductor; Director. m. (1) Ann Rosemary Blamey (dec.), 5 daughters, (2) Geraldene Catherine Scott, 1 July 1987. Education: Cello student, Associate Fellow, Royal Manchester College of Music. Career: Assistant Conductor, BBC Glasgow, 1949-52; Conductor, BBC Northern Orchestra, 1952-57; National Orchestra, New Zealand; Musical Director, New Zealand Opera Company, 1957-63; Director of Music, ABC, 1963-73; Dean, School of Music, Victoria College of Arts, Melbourne, Australia, 1973-86; Principal Conductor, Auckland Philharmonic Orchestra, 1983-; Director of New South Wales State Conservatorium of Music, 1986-93; Artistic Adviser, Sydney Symphony Orchestra, 1986-88; Education Consultant, Sydney Symphony Orchestra. Recordings: Various with Melbourne, New Zealand and Moscow Symphony Orchestras. Honours: OBE, 1970; Queen's Silver Jubilee Medal, 1977; Title of Professor, Sydney University, 1991. Hobbies: Gardening; Walking. Address: 1290 Mountain Lagoon Road, Bilpin, NSW 2758, Australia.

HOPKINS Sarah, b. 1958, Lower Hutt, New Zealand. Composer; Performer. Education: New South Wales Conservatorium of Music High School; Victorian College of the Arts Music School. Career: Toured extensively throughout Australia, Britain, Europe and the USA; Musician in Residence, GIAE, Gippsland, Victoria, Australia, 1978; Musician in Residence, CIT, Caulfield, Victoria, 1979; Composer in Residence, Arts Victoria Music '81, 1981; Musician in Residence, 1981, Guest Artist in Residence, 1983, Brown's Mart Community Art Project; Let's Make Music, Northern Territory, 1982; New Music ACTION Residency, Victorian College of the Arts, Melbourne, 1982; Composer-Performer in Residence, Darwin Theatre Group, 1984; Artist in Schools, 1985, 1986; Composer-Performer, Sky Song Project, Brown's Mart, Darwin, and major tour, 1987 and 1988; Performer in Residence, The Exploration San Francisco, 1988; Composer in Residence, Northern Territory Arts Council, Darwin, 1989. Compositions: Ensemble works: Cello Timbre, 1976; Seasons II, 1978; Cellovoice, 1982; Whirlies, 1983; Sunrise/Sunset, 1983; Interweave, 1984; Deep Whirly Duo, 1984; Aura Swirl, 1986; Eclipse, 1986; Bougainvillea Bells, 1986; Cello Chi, 1986; Flight of the Wild Goose, 1987; Ring, 1987; Songs of the Wind, 1989; Circle Bell Mantra, 1989; Spiral Bells, 1989; Soul Song, 1989; Transformation, 1989; Heart Songs, 1989. Recordings: Soundworks 1: Collaborative Works; Soundworks 2: Solo and Duo Works; Soundworks 3: Whirliworks Performance; Interweave; Soundworks Performance.

HOPKINS Tim, b. 1963, London, England. Stage Director. Education: Graduated from Queen's College, Cambridge in 1986. Career: Worked at the Edinburgh Festival in the mid 1980s and assisted at Scottish Opera from 1987; Productions at Musica nel Chiostro, Battignano, 1989-91; The Gondoliers for New Doyle Carte in 1991, Falstaff for English Touring Opera in 1992, Mario and the Magician for Almeida Opera, 1992, Cosi fan tutte for Welsh National Opera and Zampa at the 1993 Wexford Festival; Staged the premiere of Judith Weir's Blond Eckbert for English National Opera in 1994 and Berio's Vera Storia at the Festival Hall; Yeoman of the Guard for Welsh National Opera in 1995 (also seen at Covent Garden) and Rimsky's Golden Cockerel for Rome Opera and Covent Garden, 1995-96; Season 1996 with Die Entführung for English National Opera, Il Trovatore for Graz Opera in 1997. Address: c/o English National Opera, St Martin's Lane, London WC2, England.

HOPPE Heinz, b. 26 Jan 1924, Saerbeck, Germany. Singer (Tenor). Education: Studied with Fred Husler in Detmold. Debut: Munster, 1953, as Xerxes in the opera by Handel. Career: Bremen, 1955-57; First Lyric Tenor at the Hamburg Staatsoper, 1957-70; Glyndebourne Festival, 1961, as Belmonte in Die Entführung; Concert tours of North America, Spain, Belgium and France; Successful in operetta and on German television; Teacher at the Musikhochschule Mannheim from 1977. Recordings include: Operettas; Narraboth in Salome.

HORACEK Jaroslav, b. 29 Apr 1924, Dehylov, Czechoslovakia. Singer (Bass); Teacher. Education: Studied with Rudol Vasek, Karel Kugler and Peter Burja in Ostrava, Apollo Granforte in Prague. Debut: Opava, 1945, as Kecal in The Bartered Bride. Career: Sang in Ostrava, 1951-53, then at the National Theatre, Prague; Sang in the standard bass repertory, and in operas by Smetana, Janácek and Dvorák; Took part in the 1959 premiere of Mirandolina by Martinu; Guest appearances in Warsaw, Sofia, Amsterdam, Boston, Edinburgh (1964, with the Prague Company), Naples, Barcelona and Boston; Sang Debussy's Arkel at Prague, 1986; Don Giovanni at the bicentenary performance of the opera, 1987; Many concert appearances; Producer of Czech operas at La Scala Milan; Teacher at the Prague Conservatory. Address: c/o National Theatre, PO Box 865, 112 30 Prague 1, Czech Republic.

HORAK Josef, b. 24 Mar 1931, Znojmo, Czechoslovakia. Bass Clarinettist; Music Educator. Education: State High School of Musical and Dramatic Arts. Career: Clarinettist, Czech Radio Symphony Orchestra and State Philharmonic, Brno; Concert Soloist; Professor, State Music High School, Prague; Chamber Music Lecturer, Biberach, West Germany; Member, chamber music ensemble Due Boemi di Praga, with Emma Kovarnova, Prague, 1963-; Concerts in Europe, USA, Asia and Africa; TV programmes in Czechoslovakia, Germany and Rumania; Radio programmes, many European countries and USA; Discovered the bass clarinet as a solo instrument, giving the first bass clarinet recital in the world (1955); Chamber soloist of the Czech Philharmonic Orchestra. Recordings: Due Boemi di Praga; At the New Ways; Bass Clarinet, the New Solo Instrument; The Paganini of the Bass Clarinet; The Singing Bass Clarinet; CD: Horák-New Age of Bass Clarinet, Horák and his Bass Clarinet-New Sound, The Singing Bass Clarinet; Also about 85 single recordings on various records. Honours: Gold Medal, 1958; Prize, L Janácek Competition, 1959; Hi-Fi Festival, Paris, 1965; Pick of the Year, London, 1974; Clarinet Super Record, Tokyo, 1986. Memberships: Union of Czech Interpreters; Honorary member, Jeunesses Musicales de Suisse. Address: Bubenska 39, 170 21 Prague 7, Czech Republic.

HORIGOME Yuzuko, b. 1960, Tokyo, Japan. Violinist. Education: Studied at Toho Gakuen School of Music, Tokyo, with Toshiya Eto; Graduated, 1980. Career: Won Queen Elisabeth of the Belgians International Competition, 1980; London debut, 1983, concerts with London Symphony Orchestra under Claudio Abbado and André Prévin; US debut, 1982, at Tanglewood, with Boston Symphony; Later appearances in Pittsburgh, Chicago, Los Angeles and Montreal; 1988/89 season included concerts in Europe and Japan with the Salzburg Camerata, Royal Liverpool Philharmonic and Scottish National Orchestras, and at the Prague Spring Festival; USA tour with the Chamber Music Players of Marlboro, 1995; Featured in film Testimony on the life of Shostakovich. Recordings: Bach Concerti with the English Chamber Orchestra; Bach's Solo Violin Sonatas; Sibelius and Mendelssohn Concertos with the Concertgebouw Orchestra and Ivan Fischer, music by Bruch (Tring, 1996). Address: c/o Harrison/Parrott Ltd, 12 Penzance Place, London W11 4PA, England.

HORN Heiner, b. 20 June 1920, Darmstadt, Germany. Singer (Bass-baritone). Education: Studied in Darmstadt and Berlin. Career: Sang at first in Darmstadt, then at the Cologne Opera; Retired, 1985; Sang Jochanaan, Kaspar in Der Freischütz and Wozzeck at the Paris Opera, Amsterdam, Brussels, Luxembourg, Zurich, Bern, Venice, Bologna, Trieste, Lisbon, Barcelona; Der fliegende Holländer; Bett in Zar und Zimmermann, Plunkett in Martha and Kothner in Die Meistersinger; Other roles: Pizarro, Mephisto (Gounod, Berlioz), Ramphis, Sarastro, Nick Shadow, Dapertutto, King Henry, Gunther, Klingsor, Fasolt, Fafner, Daland, Zar Saltan, Varlaam, Tomsky, Scarpia, Alfio, Escamillo, Basilio, Father Guardian, Inquisitor, and many more; 15 years in WDR Opera and about 20 Germany opera houses; Sang in the 1965 premiere of Die Soldaten by Zimmermann; Concert appearances, and guest engagements elsewhere in Germany. Recordings: Sparafucile in Rigoletto; Die Soldaten. Address: c/o Oper der Stadt Köln, Offenbachplatz, D-5000 Cologne, Germany.

HORN Volker, b. 1945, Klagenfurt, Germany. Tenor. Education: Studied at the Vienna Musikhochschule. Career: Sang as boy soprano in the Bayreuth production of Tannhäuser directed by Wieland Wagner, 1954-55; Has sung at the Deutsche Oper Berlin from 1976; Guest appearances in Lyon, Karlsruhe, Munich and Strasbourg as Max in Der Freischütz and Loge in Das Rheingold, and at Bayreuth and Salzburg Easter Festivals in 1980; Deustche Oper Berlin in 1987 as Galba in Die Toten Augen by d'Albert; Sang Hans Kraft in Der Kobold by Siegfried Wagner, Rudolstadt, 1992; Concert and oratorio appearances in Germany, Austria and Switzerland. Recordings: Die Zauberflöte; Nabucco. Address: c/o Deutsche Oper Berlin, Richard Wagnerstrasse 10, D-1000 Berlin, Germany.

HORNE David, b. 1970, Stirling, Scotland. Concert Pianist; Composer. Education: Studied at St Mary's Music School in Edinburgh, the Curtis Institute, Philadelphia and Harvard University. Career: Soloist with BBC Philharmonic and Symphony, Welsh and Scottish Orchestras, CBSO, the Scottish National and London Sinfonietta; Festival engagements at Edinburgh, Aldeburgh, Almeda and London; BBC Promenade Concert debut in 1990 with Prokofiev's Third Concerto; Other repertory includes Ravel G major, Gershwin Concerto, Brahms Concerto in D minor, Beethoven 1st Concerto and Choral Fantasia, Iain Hamilton 2nd Concerto (world premiere), Mozart K271, Frank Symphonic Variations, and Tchaikovsky 1st Concerto. Compositions: String Quartet, 1988; Splintered Unisons for Clarinet, Violin, Cello and Piano, 1988; Towards Dharma for 6 Instruments, 1989; Light Emerging for Symphony Orchestra, 1989; Out Of The Air, 1990; Contraries And Progressions for Ensemble, 1991; Northscape for Chamber Orchestra, 1992; Piano Concerto, 1992. Honours: 1st Prize, National Mozart Competition, 1987; 1st Place for Piano, BBC Young Musician of The Year, 1988; Winner, Huddersfield Contemporary Music Festival Composers Competition, 1988. Address: c/o Boosey and Hawkes, 295 Regent Street, London, W1R 8JH, England.

HORNE Marilyn, b. 16 Jan 1934, Bradford, PA, USA. Mezzo-Soprano. Divorced, 1 daughter. Education: University of Southern California under William Vennard. Debut: Gelsenkirchen, 1957; San Francisco Opera in 1960 as Berg's Marie. Career: Performed with several German Opera Companies in Europe in 1956 then appeared at Covent Garden, the Chicago Lyric Opera, La Scala Milan, and Metropolitan Opera; Repertoire includes Eboli, Marie in Wozzeck, Adalgisa in Norma, Jane Seymour in Anna Bolena, Amneris, Carmen, Rosina, Fides in La Prophète, Mignon, Isabella in L'Italiana in Algeri, Romeo, Tancredi, Orlando in Orlando Furioso, and Dalila; Returned to Covent Garden in 1989 as Isabella; Other Rossini roles include Malcolm in La Donna del Lago at Covent Garden in 1985, Falliero and Andromache in Ermoine at Pesaro in 1986 and 1987 and Calbo in Maometto II at San Francisco in 1988; Sang Rosina at the Metropolitan in 1989, Vivaldi's Orlando at San Francisco and Gluck's Orpheus at Santa Fe in 1990; Season 1992 in a Rossini 200th birthday gala at Fisher Hall, NY and as Isabella at San Francisco; Last appearance in Rossini as Isabella in L'Italiana in Algeri at Covent Garden in 1993. Recordings include: Semiramide; Orfeo ed Euridice; Anna Bolena; Don Giovanni; Il Trovatore; Le Prophète; Mignon; Tancredi; Il Barbiere du Siviglia; Suor Angelica; Carmen; Norma; Falstaff; Orlando Furioso; La Navarraise; L'Italiana in Algeri; La Damnationa de Faust. Honours: 5 Honorary Doctorates. Hobbies: Needlepoint; Swimming; Reading; Sightseeing. Address: c/o Columbia Artists Management Inc, 165 West 57th Street, New York, NY 10019, USA.

HORNIK Gottfried, b. 5 Aug 1940, Vienna, Austria. Baritone. Education: Studied in Vienna. Career: Sang at Klagenfurt as Papageno and as Silvio in Pagliacci; Graz Opera as Mozart's Figaro, Don Giovanni and Alberich; Deutsche Oper Berlin and San Francisco as Beckmesser in Die Meistersinger; Salzburg Easter Festival as Kurwenal in Tristan und Isolde, under Karajan; Sang Alberich and other Wagner roles at the Vienna Staatsoper; Sang at Leipzig Opera as the Villains in Les Contes d'Hoffmann, Cologne Opera in 1983 as Klingsor in Parsifal, Covent Garden in 1987 as Faninal in Der Rosenkavalier, Deutsche Oper Berlin in 1988 as Alberich in The Ring and sang Wozzeck at the Metropolitan in 1990; Sang Orestes in Elektra at Athens in 1992. Recordings: Die Zauberflöte, Tosca, and Die Meistersinger conducted by Karajan; Der Wildschütz by Lortzing.

HOROVITZ Joseph, b. 26 May 1926, Vienna, Austria. Composer. Education: New College Oxford; Royal College of Music, London; Nadia Boulanger, Paris. Career: Music Director, Bristol Old Vic, 1949-51; Conductor, Festival Gardens Orchestra, London, 1951; Co-conductor, Ballets Russes English Season, 1952; Associate Director, Intimate Opera Company, 1952-63; Assistant Conductor, Glyndebourne Opera, 1956; Professor of Composition, Royal College of Music, 1961-. Compositions: 16 Ballets, including Alice in Wonderland, Les femmes d'Alger, Concerto for Dancers; Two one-act Operas, The Dumb Wife and Gentleman's Island; Orchestral: Concertos for violin, trumpet, jazz-harpsichord, 2 for clarinet, tuba, oboe, percussion; Horizon Overture; Jubilee Serenade; Sinfonietta; Fantasia on a Theme of Couperin; Toy Symphony for 17 instruments and piano quintet; Choral: Samson, oratorio; Captain Noah and his Floating Zoo; Summer Sunday; Endymion; Brass Band Music includes a Euphonium Concerto, Ballet for Band and Concertino Classico; For Wind Band, Ad Astra, Windharp, Dance Suite, Bacchus on Blue Ridge; Chamber, 5 String Quartets, Oboe Sonatina; Oboe Quartet, Clarinet sonatina; Two pieces for Hoffnung Concerts, Metamorphoses on a Bed-Time Theme and Horroratorio; Numerous scores for theatre productions, films and TV series. Honour: Gold Order of Merit, City of Vienna, 1996. Memberships: Council of Composers' Guild, 1970; Board of Performing Rights Society, 1971-96; Fellow, Royal College of Music, 1981; President, CIAM of the International Federation of Societies of Authors and Composers, 1981-89. Address: 7 Dawson Place, London W2 4TD, England.

HORSLEY Colin, b. 23 April 1920, Wanganui, New Zealand. Pianist; Professor. Education: Royal College of Music. Debut: At Invitation of Sir John Barbirolli at Hallé Concerts, Manchester, 1943. Career: Soloist with all leading orchestras of Great Britain, the Royal Philharmonic Society, 1953, 1959, Promenade Concerts; Toured Belgium, Hollad, Spain, France, Scandinavia, Malta, Ceylon, Malaya, Australia and New Zealand; Festival appearances include Aix-en-Provence, International Contemporary Music Festival, Palermo, British Music Festivals in Belgium, Holland and Finland; Broadcasts frequently. Recordings: EMI Meridian; Symposium Records; CDs of John Ireland Piano Concerto and Mozart Quintet for Piano and Wind. Honours: OBE, 1963; FRCM, 1973; Hon RAM. Hobbies: Gardening. Address: Belmont, Dreemskerry, Maughold, Isle of Man.

HORVAT Milan, b. 28 Jul 1919, Pakrac, Yugoslavia. Conductor. Education: Studied at the Zagreb Music Academy, 1939-46. Career: Began as pianist and choral conductor; Conductor of the Zagreb Philharmonic, 1946-53 and 1958-59; Chief Conductor of the Radio Telefis Eireann Symphony, 1953-58; Principal Conductor of the Zagreb Opera, 1958-65 with many premieres of Yugoslav music; Guest Conductor with many major orchestras in Europe and the USA; Musical Director of the Dubrovnik Festival, 1965; Principal Conductor of the Austrian Radio Symphony, 1969-75; Professor of Conducting at the Graz Academy, 1975; Conductor of the Zagreb Symphony Orchestra, 1975-. Recordings: Haydn Harpsichord Concertos, with Robert Veryon-Lacroix; Mozart Violin and Piano Concertos, with Jean Fournier and Jörg Demus; Hindemith Mathis der Maler Symphony; Shostakovich Symphonies Nos 1 and 9, and 1st Piano Concerto with the Zagreb Philharmonic; Beethoven Violin Concerto, with Igor Ozim. Address: c/o Zagreb Philharmonic Orchestra, Trjanska 66, 4100 Zagreb, Croatia.

HORVATH László, b. 14 Jul 1945, Koszeg, Hungary. Clarinettist. Divorced, 1 son, 1 daughter. Education: Music Gymnasium, Gyor, 1960-64; Studied with Professor Gyorgy Balassa, 1964-69, MMus with distinction, 1969, Liszt Ference Academy of Music, Budapest; Bursary student, Conservatoire de Musique, Paris, 1969-70; Studied with Professor Ulysse Delecluse. Debut: Competition in Budapest in 1965. Career: Clarinettist, 1965-68, Soloist and Leading Clarinettist, 1968-, Hungarian State Symphony Orchestra, Budapest; Professor at Conservatory of Music Debrecen, 1974-79, and at Bela Bartók Conservatory of Music, Budapest, 1980-; Toured as soloist, Buffet-Crampon Company, Japan, 1981, 1986; Many solo recitals worldwide and appearances as clarinet duo with Klara Kormendi, and chamber music with Philharmonic Wind Quintet in Europe, USA, Canada, Australia and Japan, 1983-; Recitals at Claude Champagne Hall, Montreal, 1991 and 1993; Radio broadcasts in Budapest, Paris, London and Tokyo and TV appearances in Hungary; Masterclasses at Montreal, 1991, 1993 and Jury Member for International Competition for Musical Performers, Geneva, 1990. Recordings: Works by Leo Weiner, 1970, Attila Bozay, 1976, 1979, Carl and Johann Stamitz, 1979, Johann Molter, 1979, 1991, Mozart, 1981; 20th Century Clarinet Music, 1991; Clarinetto all'Ungherese, 1992. Current Management: Interkoncert, Vorosmarty ter 1m, H-1368 Budapest, Hungary. Address: 6 Jászai Mari Tér V-44, H-1137 Budapest, Hungary.

HORVAY Erzsebet, b. 14 Dec 1916, Szeged. Violinist. m. István Hajdu, 21 June 1946, 1 daughter. Education: Business School; Music Academy of Budapest (with Ferenc Rados, Ede Zathurecky and Leo Weiner). Debut: Beethoven's Romance F Dur, Szeged, 1923. Career: Played in Orchestra under Willem Mengelberg in Szeged, 1926; Appointed Concertmaster in Szeged Philharmonic Orchestra under Mengelberg, 1932; Concertmaster of Budapest State Symphony Orchestra under Fricsay, 1933; Concertmaster of Rotterdam Philharmonic Orchestra, 1957-83. Hobby: Playing chamber and orchestral music. Address: Chabotlaan 83, 3055 AC Rotterdam, Netherlands.

HORWOOD Michael (Stephen), b. 24 May 1947, Buffalo, NY, USA. Composer. m. 16 Aug 1974, 2 sons. Education: BA, Music, 1969, MA, Composition, 1971, State University of New York, Buffalo. Debut: Performance of his works at Baird Hall, SUNY, Buffalo in 1966. Career: Instructor in Music at Humber College of Applied Arts and Technology, Ontario, Canada, 1972-. Compositions include: Durations for 1-4 Keyboards, 1965; Piece Percussionique No 1 for 6 percussionists and piano, 1965, revised 1979; Women Of Trachis, incidental music for Chamber Orchestra, 1966; Piece Percussionique No 3 for 3 percussionists, 1966; Piece Percussionique No 4 for 4 percussionists, 1967, revised 1981; Concerto for Double Bass and String Orchestra, 1967, revised, 1988; Double Quintet for 2 Wind Quintets, 1968; Asteroids for Brass Quartet, 1969; 9 Microduets, 1969-83; Sextet for Chamber Ensemble, 1971; 5,3,4 for Jazz Orchestra and Percussion Ensemble, 1973; Facets for Augmented Chamber Group, 1974; Talos IV for Solo Accordion, 1975; Interphase for Chamber Sextet, 1975; Andromeda for wind ensemble, 1976, revised 1980; Bipolarity for Accordion and String Trio, 1979; Birds, 1979; Io for double bass and violin, 1979; Psalm 121 for Soprano and Piano, 1980; 1, 1982; Exit To Your Left for Wind Quintet, 1982; String Quartet No 1, 1982; Sonata for Cello and Piano, 1983; Brass-Fast for Brass Quintet, 1984; Symphony No 1, 1984; Three Landscapes for solo piano, 1984; Suite for Accordion and Percussion, 1985; Amusement Park Suite, for orchestra, 1986; Nervous Disorder, chamber, 1988; Broken Chords for Solo Piano, 1990; National Park Suite for Orchestra, 1991; Symphony No 2, Visions of a Wounded Earth, for chorus and orchestra, 1995; Do You Live For Weekends? for chamber orchestra, 1996; Symphony No 3 for tenor saxophone and orchestra, 1996; Intravariations for piano and orchestra, 1997. Recordings: Overture for Piano Player and 2 Assistants; Piece Percussionique No 5, 1982; Birds, 1982; Dynamite, 1983; Six Pieces for Piano; Motility, 1986. Publications: Birds, 1982;

Brass-Fast, 1992. Address: 8 Grovetree Place, Bramalea, Ontario L6S 1S8, Canada.

HORYSA Inghild, b. 2 Jan 1944, Bielitz, Germany. Mezzo-Soprano. Education: Studied with Helena Braun in Munich. Debut: Munich Staatsoper in 1966 in Hansel and Gretel. Career: Munich in 1969 in the premiere of The Play of Love and Death by Cikker; Sang at Nuremberg, the Vienna Volksoper, Dusseldorf, Frankfurt, Mannheim, Hamburg and Stuttgart; Other roles include Dorabella, Amneris, Eboli, Venus, Brangaene, Marina in Boris Godunov, Orsini in Lucrezia Borgia, Fricka in Walküre, Clytemnestra in Elektra, Baba the Turk in The Rake's Progress and Octavian; Frequent concert appearances. Address: c/o Nuremberg Opera House, Nuremberg, Germany.

HOSE Anthony (Paul), b. 24 May 1944, London, England. Musician; Conductor. m. Moira Griffiths, 8 July 1977, 2 daughters. Education: Junior Exhibitioner, 1955-62, Student, 1962-66, Royal College of Music, London; ARCM. Career: Glyndebourne Festival, 1966-68; Bremen Opera, Federal Republic of Germany, 1968-69; Welsh National Opera, 1969-83; Music Director, Buxton Festival, 1979-87; Artistic Director, Welsh Chamber Orchestra, 1986-; Artistic Director, Beaumaris Festival, 1986-; Realisation of Cavalli's Giasone; Artistic Director, Buxton Festival, 1988-91; Professor, Royal College of Music, 1991-; Professor, Royal Academy of Music, 1992-; Artistic Director, Rhyl Easter Festival, 1994-; Artistic Director, Llandudno October Festival, 1994-. Publications: English translation: Grétry: Le Huron; Elektra (Strauss); Ariodante (Handel); Don Quixote (Conti). Hobbies: Good food and wine; Football. Address: Fairfield House, Aberdare, Mid-Glamorgan CF44 7PL, Wales.

HOSEK Jiri, b. 20 Aug 1955, Prague, Czechoslovakia. Solo Concert Violoncellist. m. Marie Kaplanova, 2 Apr 1977, 2 daughters. Education: Prague, Conservatory; Academy of Music Prague; Conservatory National Paris; International courses at Nice and Szombately. Debut: Tchaikovsky's Rococco Variations, 1974. Career: Tours to Russia, Germany, France, Italy and Poland; Many TV and radio appearances including Anton Kraft Concertos. Recordings: Elgar Concerto, 1985; Anton Kraft Concertos; Radio recordings: Vivaldi Concerto, D Popper Konzertstücke, Dvorák's Rondo, Tchaikovsky's Rococco Variations, Prokofiev Symphony Concerto and Elgar Concerto. Current Management: Radio Symphony Orchestra, Prague, Czechoslovakia. Address: Sudomerska 29, 13000 Prague 3, Czech Republic.

HOSIER John, b. 18 Nov 1928, England. College Principal. Education: MA, St John's College, Cambridge, 1954. Career: Lecturer in Ankara, Turkey, 1951-53; Music Producer, BBC Radio for Schools, 1953-59 then seconded to ABC, Sydney to advise on educational music programmes, 1959-60; Music Producer and subsequently Senior and Executive Producer for BBC TV, pioneering the first regular music boradcasts to schools, 1960-73; ILEA Staff Inspector for Music, Director of Centre for Young Musicians, 1973-76; Principal at Guildhall School of Music and Drama, 1978-88; Director, Hong Kong Academy for Performing Arts, 1989-93. Compositions: Music for Cambridge revivals of Parnassus, 1949 and Humourous Lovers, 1951; Something's Burning, Mermaid, 1974; Many Radio and TV productions. Publications: The Orchestra, 1961, revised edition, 1977; Various books, songs and arrangements for children. Contributions to: Professional journals. Honours: FGSM, 1978; Honorary RAM, 1980; FRCM, 1989; CBE, 1984; FRNCM, 1985; Honorary DMus, The City University, 1986; Honorary FTCL, 1986. Memberships: Founder Member, Vice Chairman, UK Council for Music Education and Training, 1975-81; Gulbenkian Enquiry into Training Musicians, 1978; Trustee, Hirnichsen Foundation, 1981-88; Music Panel, British Council, 1984-88; GLAA, 1984-86; Vice Chairman, Kent Opera, 1985-88; Council of Management, Royal Philharmonic Society, 1982-89; Governing Body, Chetham's School; Governing Body, NYO FRSA, 1976; Hong Kong Council for the Performing Arts; General Committee, Hong Kong Philharmonic Orchestra. Address: 1 Hartham Close, London, N7 9JH, England.

HOTEEV Andrei, b. 2 December 1946, St Petersburg, Russia. Pianist. m. Olga Hoteeva, 4 June 1982, 3 sons. Education: St Petersburg Conservatoire; Moscow Conservatoire. Debut: Moscow, 1983, Rotterdam, 1990. Career: Recitals: Shostakovitch in Concertgebouw, Amsterdam, 1990; Prokoffiev in Musikhalle, Hamburg, 1991; Hommage a Sohnittke, hamburg, 1992; Manuscript Version of Mussorgsky's Pictures at an Exhibition, 1st UK Performance in Purcell Room, London, 1993; VARA TV Holland, TV St Petersburg, 1995; Interpreter, Manuscript, Tchaikovsky's 3rd Piano Concerto. Recordings: Tchaikovsky Piano Concerto No 3; All the Works of Tchaikovsky for Piano & Orchestra. Contributions to: Creschendo, Brussels, 1993; Zurichsee-Zeitung, 1996; No 1 Fono Forum, 1997. Current Management: Interartists. Address: Kastanienallee 13, 21521 Wohltorf, Germany.

HOTTER Hans, b. 19 Jan 1909, Offenbach, Germany. Bass-Baritone. m. Helga Fischer, 1936, 1 son, 1 daughter. Education: Studied with Matthaus Remer in Munich. Career: Stage debut at Troppau in 1930 then sang in Prague, 1932-34, at Staatsoper Hamburg, 1934-37, and Munich Staatsoper from 1937 notably in the premieres of Strauss's Friedenstag in 1938 and Capriccio in 1942; Sang at Salzburg from 1942 as Mozart's Count, Sarastro, Don Giovanni, Mandryka in Arabella and Morosus in Die schweigsame Frau; Sang Jupiter in the premiere of Die Liebe der Danae in 1944 and at Bayreuth Festival from 1952 notably as Hans Sachs, Wotan, Gurnemanz, Pogner, Kurwenal, Gunther and as The Dutchman; Sang with the company of the Vienna Staatsoper at Covent Garden in 1947 as Mozart's Count and Don Giovanni returning as Sachs and Wotan and as producer of The Ring, 1962-64; Metropolitan Opera debut in 1950 as The Dutchman and sang in the premiere of Von Einem's Besuch der Alten Dame at Vienna in 1971; Sang Wotan for the last time at Paris Opéra in 1972, but continued to appear at Munich as Schigolch in Lulu and as the Speaker in Die Zauberflöte at Milan in 1985; Returned to London in 1989 as the Speaker in Schoenberg's Gurrelieder at the Festival Hall; Noted concert singer in the lieder of Schubert and in the Choral Symphony. Recordings: Die Zauberflöte; Die Frau ohne Schatten; Die Walküre; Siegfried; Lulu; Parsifal; Der fliegende Holländer; Wagner's Ring, Bayreuth, 1953. Address: Emil-Dittler-Str 26, D-81479 München, Germany.

HOU Runyu, b. 6 Jan 1945, Kunming, China. Orchestral Conductor. m. Su Jia Hou, 15 Sep 1971, 1 son, 1 daughter. Education: Musical study at Middle School of Shanghai Conservatory and conducting at Shanghai Conservatory; Further study at Musikhochschule, Cologne, Germany and at the Mozarteum, Salzburg, Austria, 1981-85. Debut: Kunming in 1954. Career: Orchestral Conductor, 1977, Vice Music Director, 1986, Shanghai Symphony Orchestra; Guest Conductor for Rheinische Philharmonic, 1985, China Broadcasting Symphony Orchestra, 1988, China Central Philharmonic, 1988, and Hong Kong Philharmonic, 1988; Principal Conductor for Shanghai Symphony Orchestra, 1990, with debut at Carnegie Hall in New York in 1990 for the 100 years celebration of Carnegie Hall. Honour: Honorary Member, Richard Wagner-Verband, Cologne. Membership: Chinese Musicians Association. Hobbies: Sport; Literature. Current Management: Konzertdirektion Drissen, International Artists' Management, Postfach 1666, D-6500 Mainz, Germany. Address: 105 Hunan Road, Shanghai, China.

HOUGH Stephen, b. 22 Nov 1961, Heswall, Cheshire, England. Pianist. Career: Performances with many leading orchestras including: Chicago, Detroit, Toronto, Philadelphia and Baltimore Symphonies, Cleveland and Los Angeles Philharmonics, all major British orchestras including London Symphony, Philharmonia, Royal and London Philharmonics, BBC Symphony, English Chamber; Numerous radio broadcasts, UK and USA; Recitals and orchestral appearances throughout UK, USA, Canada, Germany, France, Scandinavia, Spain, Italy, Holland, Australia and Far East; London Proms debut, 1985 and appeared annually until 1997; Appeared annually, Ravinia Festival, 1984-90, Blossom Festival, Mostly Mozart Festival, 1988, 1989, and 1996, Hollywood Bowl, annually; Mendelssohn Anniversary concerts at the 1997 Salzburg Festival; Recordings: 2 Hummel Piano concertos; 2 Mozart piano concertos; Music by Liszt and Schumann; Piano Albums 1 and 2; Brahms 1st and 2nd Piano Concertos; Britten Piano Music; Scharwenka and Sauer piano concertos; Solo piano music, Franck, York Bowen, Mompou; Complete Mendelssohn music for piano and orchestra with the CBSO (1997). Honours: Dayas Gold Medal, Royal Northern College of Music; Winner, Naumburg International Piano Competition; Best Concerto Record Award, Gramophone magazine, 1987, 1996; Fellow, Royal Northern College of Music, 1993; Gramophone Record of the Year, 1996; Deutsche Schallplatteupreis; Diapason d'Or. Current Management: Harrison Parrott Ltd, London, England. Address: c/o Harrison Parrott Ltd, 12 Penzance Place, London W11 4PA, England.

HOULIHAN Phillip, b. 17 Apr 1956, Jersey, Channel Islands. Pianist; Teacher; Composer of Educational Music. Education: Piano Scholar, Downside, 1970-71; Clifton College, 1971-74; ARCM, Piano Performance, 1974; Royal College of Music, 1974-79. Debut: Purcell Room, London, 1981. Career: Recitals in the UK. Compositions: Two. Publication: Tales With Scales, 1998. Honours: Royal College of Music Exhibition, 1975; Hopkinson Silver Medal, 1979; Maisie Lewis Award; Worshipful Company of Musicians, 1980; Memberships: Incorporated Society of Musicians; RCM Union. Hobbies: Reading; Walking; Psephology. Address: 118 Kenilworth Avenue, Wimbledon Park, London SW19 7LR, England.

HOULIHAN Timothy (de Quetteville), b. 3 October 1954, Jersey, Channel Islands. Concert Pianist; Private Tutor. Education: Royal Academy of Music, 1972-79; ARCM, 1972; LRAM, 1975; Recital Diploma, 1977. Debut: Jersey Opera House, 1980; Wigmore Hall, London, 1987. Career: Recital and Concert Engagements in England, Major London Venues: St Martin-in-the-Fields, Purcell Room, Southbank. Recordings: Television and Radio. Honours: Hodgeson Memorial Scholarship, 1975; Martin Musical Scholarship, 1976. Memberships: Incorporated Society of Musicians; Royal Academy of Music Club; Royal Society of Musicians of Great Britain. Hobbies: Gardening; Crossword Puzzles. Address: 7 Elizabeth Place, St Helier, Jersey JE2 3PN, Channel Islands.

HOUSEWRIGHT Wiley Lee, b. 17 Oct 1913, Wylie, Texas, USA. Professor of Music. m. Lucilla Gumm, 27 Dec 1939. Education: BS, University of North Texas; MA, Columbia University; EdD, New York University. Career: Retired Professor and Dean, School of Music, Florida University, Tallahassee. Publication: A History of Music and Dance in Florida 1565-1865, 1991; Music of 16th Century French Settlement in Florida. Honours: Distinguished Professor, Florida State University; Distinguished Alumni, University of North Texas. Memberships: President, Music Educators National Conference, 1958-60; American Musicology Society. Hobbies: Travel; Swimming. Address: 515 South Ride Road, Tallahassee, FL 32303, USA.

HOVHANESS Alan, b. 8 Mar 1911, Somerville, MA, USA. Composer. Education: Studied at Tufts University and New England Conservatory with Frederick Converse. Career: Freelance composer of over 400 works, influenced by Armenian and Far Eastern music; Travelled to India and Japan on Fulbright Fellowship; Composer-in-Residence at University of Hawaii, 1962. Compositions: Operas: Etchmiadzin, 1946, Blue Flame, 1959, The Burning House, 1960, Spirit Of The Avalanche, 1962, Pilate, 1963, Travellers, 1965, Lady Of The Light, 1969, Pericles, 1975, Tale Of The Sun Goddess Going Into The Stone House, 1978; Orchestral: Cello Concerto, 1936; 61 Symphonies, 1937-84 including: Arjuna, 1947, St Vartan, 1950, Mysterious Mountain, 1955, All Men Are Brothers, 1960, Odysseus, 1973, Consolation, 1975, The Broken Wings, 1977, To The Green Mountains, 1981, Mount St Helens, 1982 and Journey To Vega, 1982, Artik, Horn Concerto, 1948, Zertik Parkim, concerto for Piano and Chamber Orchestra, 1948, Talin, concerto for Viola and Strings, 1952, Accordion Concerto, 1959, Concerto for Harp and Strings, 1973, Concerto for Soprano, Saxophone and Orchestra, 1980, And God Created Great Whales for Orchestra with Tape of Humped Back Whales; Chamber Music: 5 String Quartets, 1936-76, Sonata for 2 Bassoons, 1973, Fantasy for Double Bass and Piano, 1974, Suite for 4 Trumpets and Trombone, 1976, Sonata for Clarinet and Harpsichord, 1978, Saxophone Trio, 1979, 2 Sonatas for 3 Trumpets and 2 Trombones, 1979; Psalm for Brass Quintet, 1981, Organ Sonata, 1981; Choral music, solo vocal music and piano music. Membership: Institute of the American Academy and Institute of Arts and Letters, 1977. Address: c/o ASCAP, ASCAP Building, One Lincoln Plaza, New York, NY 10023, USA.

HOVHANISIAN Edgar (Sergey), b. 14 Jan 1930, Armenia, Russia. Composer. Education: Studied at the Erevan Conservatory and in Moscow with Khachaturian, graduating in 1957; Career: Director of the Alexander Spendiaryan Theatre of Opera and Ballet in Erevan, 1962-68; Artistic Director for Armenian radio and television, principal of the Erevan Competition, 1986. Compositions include: David of Sasun, opera ballet, 1976; Journey to Erzrum, 1987; Ballets and instrumental music.

HOVLAND Egil, b. 18 Oct 1924, Mysen, Norway. Composer; Organist. Education: Studied at Oslo Conservatory, 1946-49, with Holmboe in Copenhagen, Cupland at Tanglewood and Dallapiccola in Florence. Career: Music critic and organist in Frederiksrad. Compositions: Church opera the Well, 1982; Ballets Dona Nobis Pacem, 1982; Den Heliga Dansen, 1982; Veni Creator Spiritus, 1984; Danses de la Mort, 1983; 3 Symphonies, 1953, 1955, 1970; Concertino for 3 trumpets and strings, 1955; Music for 10 instruments, 1957; Suite for flute and strings, 1959; Missa Vigilate, 1967; Mass to the Risen Christ, 1968; All Saints' Mass, 1970; The Most Beautiful Rose, after Hans Christian Andersen, 1972; Trombone Concerto, 1972; Missa Verbi, 1973; Violin Concerto, 1974; Piano Concerto, 1977; Tombeau de Bach for Orchestra, 1978; Pilgrim's Mass, 1982; Concerto for piccolo and strings, 1986; Chamber music including Piano Trio, 1965, 2 Wind Quintets, 1965, 1980, and String Quartet, 1981; Opera Captive and Free, 1993. Honours include: Knight of the Royal Order of St Olva, 1983. Address: c/o 4 Galleri Oslo, Toyenbekken 21, Postboks 9171, Gronland, 0134 Oslo 1, Norway.

HOWARD Ann, b. 22 July 1936, Norwood, London, England. Opera Singer (Mezzo Soprano), m. Keith Giles, 1 daughter. Education: Studied with Topliss Green and Rodolfo Lhombino; Special Grant, Royal Opera House Covent Garden, to study with Modesti, Paris, France. Debut: As Czipra in Gypsy Baron at Sadler's Wells Opera, 1964. Career: In various shows, chorus, Royal Opera House, Covent Garden; Principal, Sadler's Wells; Freelance appearances with English National Opera, National Opera, Scottish Opera, Welsh National Opera, Royal Opera House, Santa Fe Festival Opera, Canadian Opera Company, Metropolitan Opera New York, New York City Opera, Baltimore Opera, New Orleans Opera, Fort Worth Opera, Vienna

State Opera, Performing Arts Center, New York State University; Many leading roles including Carmen, Amneris, Fricka, Brangaene, Dalila, Azucena, Cassandra, Grande Duchess, Helene, Gingerbread Witch; Appearances in Mexico, Italy, Chile, Belgium, Portugal, France, Canada and USA; Regular broadcasts BBC, radio and television, Scottish Television; Marzellina, Marriage of Figaro, 1989; Step-mother, Into the Woods, Sondheim, 1990; Auntie, Peter Grimes; Prince Orlofsky, Die Fledermaus, ENO, 1992; Sang the Hostess in Boris Godunov for Opera North, 1992; Strauss Concerts at the 1993 London Proms; 2nd Official, The Doctor of Myddfai, Peter Maxwell Davies world premiere, Welsh National Opera, 1996; Emma Jones, Street Scene (Weill); Forthcoming roles include: Auntie in Peter Grimes, WNO, 1998-99; Performances in Aix-en-Provence Festival, and performances with Nederlands Opera. Recordings: Has made many recordings including the Witch in Hansel and Gretel; Old Lady in Candide, Scottish Opera. Hobbies: Gardening; Cooking. Current Management: Stafford Law Associates, Surrey. Address: 6 Barham Close, Weybridge, Surrey KT13 9PR, England.

HOWARD Brian Robert, b. 3 January 1951, Sydney, NSW, Australia. Composer; Conductor. Education: BMus (Hons), University of Sydney, 1972; DMus, University of Melbourne, 1985; Composition studies with Peter Sculthorpe, Bernard Rands, Richard Meale and Maxwell Davies; Conducting with Nevilale Marriner and Michael Gielen, 1974-76. Career includes: Resident, Royal Danish Ballet 1980-81, State Opera of South Australia, 1989; Musical Director, Western Australia Ballet, 1983-85; Dean, WA Conservatory, 1992-95; Commissions from Festivals of Sydney and Perth, and from Opera Factory Zurich (1991), among others. Compositions include: A Fringe of Leaves, for chorus and orchestra, 1982; Metamorphosis, opera for 6 voices and chamber ensemble, 1983; The Rainbow Serpent, for ensemble, 1984; Fly Away Peter, for wind quintet, 1984; Sun and Steel, for string orchestra, 1986; The Celestial Mirror, for orchestra, 1987; Whitsunday, opera for 10 voices and chamber ensemble, 1988; Wildbird Dreaming for orchestra, 1988; The Enchanted Rainforest, musical, 1989; Masquerade for orchestra, 1994. Recordings include: Sun and Steel, Chandos. Address: c/o APRA, 1A Eden Street, Crows Nest, NSW 2065, Australia.

HOWARD Jason, b. 1960, Merthyr Tydfil, Wales. Baritone. Education: Studied at Trinity College of Music and with Norman Bailey at the Royal College of Music (performances of the Ballad Singer in Paul Bunyan, 1988). Career: Gained early experience as Alfio, Blow's Adonis, Zurga, Don Giovanni and Sharpless; With Scottish Opera has sung Guglielmo, Don Giovanni, Germont and Figaro; Further engagements as Ned Keene for English National Opera, Billy Budd and Ezio in Attila for Opera North, and Ramiro in L'Heure Espagnole for Scottish Opera; Concert appearances in Carmina Burana, L'Enfance du Christ, Messiah, Fauré's Requiem, The Kingdom, Elijah and Haydn's Lord Nelson Mass; Other engagements include Rossini's Figaro and Eugene Onegin for Seattle Opera, 1992-93; Television showings in Scotland and Wales; Sang Marcello at Covent Garden, 1996. Recordings include: Student Prince; Song of Norway; A Little Night Music. Honours: Ricordi Prize, Rowland Jones Award and Singing Faculty Award, TCM. Address: Harold Holt, 31 Sinclair Road, London, W14 0NS, England.

HOWARD Jeffrey (John), b. 19 Mar 1969, Cardiff, Wales. Vocal Coach; Freelance Organist, Pianist and Arranger. Education: Piano studies, Welsh College of Music and Drama, 1983; BMus, Cardiff University, 1987; Advanced Organ studies, Royal Academy of Music, London, 1990. Career: Accompanist to many male voice and mixed choirs; Solo Organist and Pianist in recital and concert; Appeared as Accompanist on several recordings and TV and radio work; Foreign tours; Currently Voice Coach at Welsh College of Music and Drama and Musical Director for several amateur dramatic societies; Has worked extensively with the Swansea Bach Choir, BBC Welsh Chorus, South Glamorgan Youth Choir and early music performances including the Orchestra of the Age of Enlightenment; Performer on the Live Music Now scheme. Recordings: Several Christian recordings with Cambrensis (South Wales Baptist Choir) including Hymns CD, 1995; Recording as Organist with Cor Meibion de Cymru, 1995. Honours: Glynne Jones Prize for Organ, 1990; Michael Head Accompaniment Prize, 1991. Membership: Musicians' Union. Hobbies: Tap dancing; Going to Shows. Address: 72 Penarth Road, Grangetown, Cardiff CF1 7NH, South Glamorgan, Wales.

HOWARD John (Stuart), b. 22 Dec 1950, Glasgow, Scotland. Composer; Lecturer; Writer; Conductor. m. Ellen Jane Howard, 15 Apr 1974, 1 son, 1 daughter. Education: Ilford County High School; Junior Exhibitioner, Royal College of Music, 1965-69; BA, 1st Class Honours, University of Durham, 1969-72; PhD in Composition awarded, 1979. Career: School teaching, various posts; Senior Lecturer and Principal Lecturer, Kingston Polytechnic/University, 1979-92; Associate Professor and Head of Music, Nanyang Technological University, Singapore, 1993-; Honorary Senior Research Fellow, Kingston University, 1993-95. Compositions: Dunstable Cantus for Piano, 1974; The Two Regions for Brass Band, 1976; Bubbles for Ever? for Flute, Clarinet, Violin and Cello, 1981; Games/End Game for Chinese Orchestra, 1983; Sonata for Brass Quintet, 1983; Fantasia and Dance, for Chinese Orchestra, 1985. Publications: Learning to Compose, Cambridge, 1990; Performing and Responding, Cambridge, 1995. Contributions to: Various; Schools Council Magazine; Pears Encyclopedia; Music File, four articles, 1991-93; IJME, Reviewer; Proceedings of British-Swedish Ethnomusicology Conference, 1991. Memberships: PRS; ISME. Hobbies: Sport; Reading. Address: Division of Music, National Institute of Education, Nanyang Technological University, 469 Bukit Timah Road, Singapore 259756.

HOWARD Leslie (John), b. 29 April 1948, Melbourne, Australia. Pianist; Composer. Education: AMusA, 1962; LMus, 1966;BA, 1969; MA, Monash University, 1973; Piano Studies with June McLean, Donald Britton and Michael Brimer (Australia), Guido Agosti (Italy) and Noretta Conci (London). Debut: Melbourne 1967. Career: Staff, Monash University, 1970-73; Guildhall School of Music and Drama, London, 1987-92; Concertos with various orchestras in Australia, England, Europe, America, South America, Asia; Regular broadcasts as Pianist, Chamber Musician and Musicologist for BBC, ABC, RAI, and various American networks; Telecasts in the Americas, Australia and Southeast Asia. Compositions: Fruits of the Earth, ballet; Hreidar the Fool, opera; Prague Spring, opera; Sonatas for violin, clarinet, percussion, double bass horn, cello and piano; Piano Solo; Canzona for brass ensemble; Missi Sancti Petri, 1993; Songs; Motets; Trios, String Quartets. Recordings: Complete keyboard works of Grainger; Works by Franck, Rakhmaninov, Glazunov, Rubinstein, Granados, Mozart, Beethoven, Tchaikovsky, Stravinsky; 80 CDs of the works and transcriptions of Liszt. Publications: Edition of complete works of Liszt for cello and piano, 1992, and Piano Trio, 1993; A Liszt Catalogue, with Michael Short, 1993. Contributions to: Liszt Society Journal, on Liszt; Music and Musicians, on Grainger; Musical Opinion, on Liszt; Viking Opera Guide, on Liszt and Rakhmaninov; Dubal's Hovowitz Symposium. Honours: Diploma d'Onore, Siena, 1972, Naples, 1976; Ferenc Liszt Medal of Honour, 1986; Liszt Grand Prix du Disque, Liszt Academy Budapest, 5 times; Ferenc Liszt Medal of Honour, Hungarian Republic, 1989. Memberships: Council, Royal Philharmonic Society; Trustee, Geoffrey Parsons and Erich Vietheer Memorial Trusts; President, Liszt Society; Grainger Society. Hobbies: Literature; Languages; Bridge; Snooker; Swimming. Current Management: Robin Anderton. Address: 128 Norbury Crescent, Norbury, London SW16 4JZ, England.

HOWARD Michael (Stockwin), b. 14 Sep 1922, London, England. Conductor; Organ Recitalist; Composer. Education: Ellesmere College; Organ and composition scholar at Royal Academy of Music; Studied with GD Cunningham, 1939-43 and privately with Marcel Dupré. Career: Organist at Tewkesbury Abbey, 1943-44; Director, The Renaissance Singers and Renaissance Society, 1944-64; Broadcaster and subsequent TV appearances, 1946-; Organist, Master of Choristers at Ely Cathedral, 1952-59; Conductor for Cantores in Ecclesia, 1964-; International travel as broadcaster for radio and TV; Artistic Director, Rye Spring Music, 1976-79; Various festival appearances at home and abroad. Compositions include: Prayer Book Canticles, 1946-49; Seven Songs for Counter-Tenor, 1949; Mass, 1961; Sequentia de Insomnia, 1981; Carillon Des Larmes for Organ, 1982; Cantique D'Un Oiseau Matinal for Organ, 1983; Cantiones Iduithae, 1983. Recordings include: Three Mass Settings; Byrd; Lamentations Of Jeremiah-Tallis; Missa Aeternae Christi Munera-Palestrina; Music for the Fest of Christmas - Dufay to Messiaen; Commemoration of Charles-Marie Widor and Louis Vierne, 1987. Publication: A Tribute to Aristide Cavaille-Coll, 1986. Address: 40 Chapel Park Road, St Leonards On Sea, Sussex, England.

HOWARD Patricia, b. 18 Oct 1937, Birmingham, England. Writer. m. David Louis Howard, 29 Jul 1960, 2 d. Education: BA, 1959, MA, 1963, Lady Margaret Hall, Oxford University; PhD, University of Surrey, 1974. Career: Lecturer, Tutor, Music, Open University, 1976-; Many broadcasts both on network and for Open University. Publications: Gluck and the Birth of Modern Opera, 1963; The Operas of Benjamin Britten: An Introduction, 1969; Haydn in London, 1980; Mozart's Marriage of Figaro, 1980; C W Gluck: Orfeo, 1981; Haydn's String Quartets, 1984; Beethoven's Eroica Symphony, 1984; Benjamin Britten: The Turn of The Screw, 1985; Christoph Willibald Gluck: A Guide to Research, 1987; Music in Vienna, 1790-1800, 1988; Beethoven's Fidelio, 1988; Music and the Enlightenment, 1992. Contributions to: Musical Times; Music and Letters; The Consort; The Listener; The Gramophone; Opera; ENO and Friends; Programme books for Covent Garden Opera, Glyndebourne Opera. Honours: Susette Taylor Travelling Fellowship, 1971; Leverhulme Research Award, 1976; British Academy Research Award, 1988. Membership: Royal Musical Association. Address: Stepping Stones, Gomshall, Surrey, GU5 9NZ, England.

HOWARD Yvonne, b. 1960, Staffordshire, England. Mezzo-Soprano. Education: Studied at the Royal Northern College of Music. Career: Operatic appearances as Mozart's Marcellina with Glyndebourne Touring Opera, Cenerentola for English Touring Opera and Suzuki for Birmingham Music Theatre; Sang Fricka and Waltraute in The Ring of the Nibelungen, City of Birmingham Touring Opera; Season 1990-91 sang Mercedes at Covent Garden, and Meg Page in Falstaff for ENO; Sang Amastris in Xerxes, Meg Page and Maddalena in Rigoletto for ENO in 1992; Concert engagements include Mozart's Requiem under Menuhin at Gstaad, Messiah with the Tokyo Philharmonic, Vivaldi's Gloria with the English Chamber Orchestra, Messiah with the Hallé Orchestra and Liverpool Philharmonic, De Falla's Three Cornered Hat at Festival Hall and with Ulster Orchestra; Song recitals include Wigmore Hall debut in 1989. Honour: Curtis Gold Medal, RNCM. Address: c/o Anglo Swiss Management, Suite 35-37 Morley House, 320 Regent Street, London W1R 5AD, England.

HOWARTH Elgar, b. 4 Nov 1935, Cannock, Staffordshire, England. Freelance Musician (Conductor, Composer, Trumpeter). m. Bridget Neary, 1 son, 1 daughter. Education: MusB, Manchester University; ARMCM, 1956, FRMCM, 1970, Royal Manchester College of Music. Career: Played in the orchestra of the Royal Opera House, Covent Garden, 1958-63; Royal Philharmonic Orchestra, 1963-69; Member, London Sinfonietta, 1968-71; Philip Jones Brass Ensemble, 1965-76; Freelance Conductor, 1970-; Conducted the premieres of Ligeti's Le Grand Macabre (Stockholm 1978) and Birtwistle's The Mask of Orpheus (London Coliseum 1986); Musical Advisor, Grimethorpe Colliery Brass Band, 1972-; Principal Guest Conductor, Opera North, 1985-88; Conducted the BBC Symphony Orchestra at the 1989 Promendade Concerts, in a programme of Bartók, Birtwistle and Stravinsky; Conducted Le Grand Macabre at the Festival Hall, 1989; British professional premiere of Nielsen's Maskarade for Opera North, 1990; Premiere of Birtwistle's Gawain at Covent Garden, 1991; Premiere of Birtwistle's The Second Mrs Kong at Glyndebourne, 1994; Conducted Zimmermann's Die Soldaten for English National Opera, 1996; British premiere of Strauss's Die Aegyptische Helena at Garsington, 1997. Recordings: Maxwell Davies's Trumpet Concerto and Birtwistle's Endless Parade, 1991. Publications: Various compositions for brass instruments and an arrangement of Mussorgsky's Pictures at an Exhibition for Brass Band. Honours: Doctor's degree, University of Central England, 1993; Fellow of the Royal Northern College of Music, 1994. Current Management: Allied Artists, 42 Montpellier Square, London, England. Address: 27 Cromwell Avenue, London N6, England.

HOWARTH Judith, b. 11 Sept 1962, Ipswich, Suffolk. Soprano. m. 1 daughter. Education: Studied at the Royal Scottish Academy and at the Opera School; Further studies with Patricia Macmahon. Debut: Mozart arias with the English Chamber Orchestra, 1984. Career: Student roles included Donna Anna, Countess Almaviva, Pamina, Fiordiligi and Mimi; Covent Garden debut in 1985 as First Maid in Zemlinsky's Der Zwerg; Salzburg and Aix debuts in 1991 in Der Schauspieldirektor and as Susanna; US debut in Seattle in 1989 in a concert with Domingo and further collaborations with Domingo in Brussels and Amsterdam, televised; Promenade Concerts in 1991 in Dvorák's The Spectre's Bride; Appearances in Tony Palmer's films of Handel and Puccini and concerts in 1992 with Domingo at Hong Kong, Adelaide and Auckland; Sang Morgana in a new production of Handel's Alcina, at Covent Garden 1992-93, Beethoven's 9th at 1993 London Proms and Gilda in Rigoletto at Covent Garden; Has sung for Royal Opera, Opera North, Scottish Opera, with BBC Symphony and London Philharmonic Orchestras, City of Birmingham Symphony, and Huddersfield Choral Society among others; Other roles include Siebel, Barbarina (televised), Iris in Semele, Adele, Norina, the Woodbird in Siegfried and Marguerite de Valois; Sang Sophia in Philidor's Tom Jones at Drottningholm, 1995; Engaged as Donizetti's Marie, Geneva, 1998. Recordings include: Menotti's The Boy Who Grew Too Fast; Madame Butterfly under Sinopoli; Caractacus, 1992; Elgar's Light of Life, 1993. Honours include: Lieder Prize, Governor's Recital Prize and the Margaret Dick Award at Royal Scottish Academy; John Noble Prize, 1984; Kathleen Ferrier Prize, 1985; Heinz Bursary for Young Singers at Covent Garden, 1985-87. Address: c/o Lies Askonas Ltd, 6 Henrietta Street, London WC2, England.

HOWELL Gwynne (Richard), b. 13 Jun 1938, Gorseinon, Wales. Principal Bass. m. Mary Edwina Morris, 1968, 2 sons. Education: BSc, University of Wales; DipTP, Manchester University; MRTPI, 1966; Studied singing with Redevers Llewellyn while at University; Part-time student, Manchester Royal College of Music with Gwilym Jones; Studied with Otakar Kraus, 1968-72. Career includes: Principal Bass at Sadler's Wells singing roles including Monterone and the Commendatore; Sang at Glyndebourne and Covent Garden in debut as First Nazarene in Salome, 1969-70; Metropolitan House debut in 1985 as Lodovico in Otello and Pogner in Die Meistersinger; Sang Gurnemanz in a new production of Parsifal at London Coliseum in 1986; Sang the Parson and the Badger in a new production of The Cunning Little

Vixen in 1990 and sang the Fliedermonolog at the Reginald Goodall Memorial Concert in London, 1991; Sang at London Coliseum in 1992 as King Philip in a new production of Don Carlos, Daland at Covent Garden and Mozart's Bartolo on tour with the company to Japan; Sang Dikoy in Katya Kabanova at Covent Garden, 1997; Seneca in Poppea for WNO; Repertory includes Verdi and Mozart Requiems, and Missa Solemnis; Sings in Europe and USA and records for BBC and major recording companies; Other roles include the King in Aida, Mephisto in Damnation of Faust, High Priest in Nabucco, Hobson in Peter Grimes, and Sparafucile in Rigoletto. Address: 197 Fox lane, London, N13 4BB, England.

HOWELLS Anne, b. 12 Jan 1941, Southport, Lancashire, England. Mezzo-Soprano. m. (1) Ryland Davies, (2) Stafford Dean, 1 son, 1 daughter. Education: Royal Manchester College of Music with Frederik Cox; Later study with Vera Rosza. Debut: Manchester College in 1963 in the British premiere of Gluck's Paride ed Helena. Career includes: Sang at Covent Garden from 1967 in roles including Rosina, Siebel in Faust, Ascanio in Benvenuto Cellini and Mélisande; Sang Ophelia in the London premiere of Searle's Hamlet and Lena in the world premiere of Bennett's Victory; Glyndebourne Festival from 1967 as Erisbe in L'Ormindo, Dorabella, Minerva in Il Ritorno d'Ulisse, the Composer in Ariadne auf Naxos and as Cathleen in the 1970 premiere of The Rising of The Moon, by Maw; US debut in 1972 as Dorabella at Chicago; Appearances with Scottish Opera, at the Metropolitan Opera and with the Covent Garden Company at La Scala in 1976; Geneva Opera in 1987 as Régine in the premiere of La Fôret by Liebermann, Chicago Lyric Opera in 1989 as Orlofsky in Die Fledermaus and sang Magdalene in Die Meistersinger at Covent Garden in 1990; Sang Adelaide in Arabella and Meg Page in Falstaff at the 1990 Glyndebourne Festival; Covent Garden in 1992 as Giulietta in Les Contes d'Hoffmann; Season 1992 with Despina at Covent Garden, and Weill's Begbick at Geneva; Prince Orlofsky in Die Fledermaus for Scottish Opera, 1997. Recordings include: L'Ormindo; Der Rosenkavalier; Les Troyens. Current Management: IMG Artists Europe. Address: c/o IMG Artists Europe, Media House, 3 Burlington Lane, Chiswick, London, W4 2TH, England.

HOWELLS David, b. 26 Jan 1954, Bedfordshire, England. Piano Recitalist. m. Clare Lange, 22 Oct 1977, 1 son, 1 daughter. Education: Guildhall School of Music and Drama; London Opera Centre; Private Study with Yonty Solomon. Debut: Edinburgh Festival, 1985. Career: Repetiteur, Cologne Opera House, Germany, 1978-79; Solo Recitals, 1979-; Edinburgh Festival Fringe Recitals, 1985-95, Purcell Room, 1986, St Johns Smith Square, 1989; Extensive Recitals for Children, 1991-; Piano Professor, Welsh College of Music and Drama, 1991-94; Performed Etudes of Henselt at Schwabach, Bavaria at Centenary Celebration, Complete Transcendental Etudes of Lyapunov, Complete Impromptus Faure, 12 Etudes Saint-Saens, Richard Rodney Bennett 5 Studies, Peter and the Wolf, Story of Babar with music and narration: Premiere of Piano Version, Little Red Riding Hood, Paul Patterson, 1993; Premiere, Twentieth Century Sidelights, Paul Pelley, 1995; Premiere, Moon Dances, Morris Pert, 1996; Premiere, Piano Tuner, Roxanna Panufnik, 1995. Memberships: ISM; RSM. Hobbies: Cycling; Travel; Calligraphy. Current Management: Helen Sykes Artists Management. Address: 67 Belsize Lane, Hampstead, London NW3 5AX, England.

HOWES Andrew, b. 29 Jan 1951, Isle of Wight. Musician; Composer; Teacher. Divorced, 2 sons. Education: Postgraduate Certificate, Secondary Music; BA, Music, honours, Southampton University and Reading University; External Student, Trinity College. Debut: Singer, Florilegium Vocace Tours, 1990; Classical Guitarist, Turner Sims Concert Hall, 1991. Appointments: Teacher, Classical Guitar and Strings, Head of Music, Mullion Comprehensive School, Cornwall. Compositions: Ariel - Aria for Counter Tenor and Wind Ensemble, 1992; Symphonic Work for Strings. Recordings: Two Recordings of Sacred Choral Music with Romsey Singers; Bass Soloist in Vaughn Williams Major Works. Publication: Amanuensis For Folk Songs of Old Hampshire, 1987. Membership: Incorporated Society of Musicians. Hobbies: Golf; All things Celtic; Long distance sailing. Address: Whitegates, Old Romsey Road, Cadnam. Hampshire SO40 2NP, England.

HOWLETT Neil (Baillie), b. 24 July 1934, Mitcham, Surrey, England. Baritone. m. Elizabeth Robson, 2 daughters. Education: MA (Cantab); St Paul's Cathedral Choir School; King's College, Cambridge; Hochschule für Musik, Stuttgart. Debut: In the world premiere of Britten's Curlew River at Aldeburgh in 1964. Career: Major roles with Sadler's Wells, English Opera Group, Royal Opera House, Covent Garden, Hamburg, Bremen, Nantes, Bordeaux, Toulouse, Nice, and Marseille; Principal Baritone for English National Opera, London; Has sung most major baritone roles; Sang title roles in the premieres of Blake's Toussaint and Crosse's The Story of Vasco; Appearances at most major festivals; Sang Hector in King Priam with the Royal Opera at Athens in 1985 and Amfortas in Buenos Aires in 1986; Sang Scarpia in Tosca with English National Opera, 1987-90; Holland Festival in 1990 as Ruprecht in Prokofiev's The Fiery Angel; Other roles include Goland in Pelléas, King Fisher in The Midsummer Marriage and Wagner's Dutchman; Recitalist, teacher and regular broadcaster; Professor at Guildhall School of Music. Honour: Kathleen Ferrier Memorial Prize. Hobbies: Sports; Jogging; Cycling; Languages; Reading; Host; Theatre. Current Management: Ingpen and Williams Ltd. Address: c/o English National Opera, London Coliseum, St Martin's Lane, London, WC2, England.

HOYLAND Vic, b. 11 Dec 1945, Wombwell, Yorkshire, England. Composer. Education: Studied Fine Arts, Music and Drama at the University of Hull; DPhil in Music at York University with Robert Sherlaw Johnson and Bernard Rands. Career: Hayward Fellow in Music, University of Birmingham, 1980-83; Visiting Lecturer at York University, 1984 and Lecturer at the Barber Institute for Fine Arts, University of Birmingham, 1985-; Senior Lecturer, 1993-. Founder Member and Co-Director of the Northern Music Theatre; Compositions have been featured at the Aldeburgh, Bath, Holland and California Contemporary Music Festivals; Survey of works at the 1985 Musica Concert Series in London; Commissions from the Northern Music Theatre, the Essex Youth Orchestra, New MacNaghten Concerts, Musica, the Barber Institute, BBC Promenade series, BCMG, Southbank Summerscope, Huddersfield Festival, Almedia Festival and the York Festival. Compositions include: Em for 24 Voices, 1970; Jeux-Theme for Mezzo and Ensemble, 1972; Esem for Double-Bass and Ensemble, 1975; Xingu, music theatre, 1979; Reel for Double-Reed Instruments, 1980; Michelagniolo for male voices and large ensemble, 1980; Quartet Movement, 1982; Head And Two Tails, 3 pieces for Voice(s) and Ensemble, 1984; String Quartet, 1985; Seneca/Medea for Voices and Ensemble, 1985; In Transit for Orchestra, 1987; Work-Out for Trombone, 1987; Work-Out for Marimba, 1988; Trio, 1990; The Other Side Of The Air for Rolf Hind, piano solo, 1991; In Memoriam P.P.P., 1992; Piano Quintet, 1992; Concerto for Pianoforte Ensemble, 1993; String Quartet No III, Bagatelles, 1994; In preparation: New work for full orchestra for first performance at the Cheltenham Festival, 1997. Address: Universal Edition Ltd, 48 Great Marlborough Street, London, W1V 2BN, England.

HOYLE Ted, b. 17 Aug 1942, Huntsville, Alabama, USA. Cellist. Education: BMus, Eastman School of Music; MMus, Yale University; DMA, Manhattan School of Music, 1981; Studied with André Navarra, Ecole Normale de Musique, Paris, France. Career: Cellist, Kohon Quartet; Professor of Music, Kean College, New Jersey; Cellist, Performing Arts Trio, New Jersey; Co-Director, Hear America First, Manhattan concert series, 1978-81. Compositions: Edited works by Bach, Schumann, Scriabin for Belwin Mills. recordings: A number with the Kohon Quartet including: String quartets by Walter Piston, Peter Mennin, Charles Ives, William Schuman, Aaron Copland, Julia Smith, Roger Sessions and Penderecki; Quartet of Joseph Fennimore; Quintet of Robert Baksa; Trio Sonatas of J S Bach, G F Handel, G Telemann. Memberships: Violoncello Society; American String Teachers' Association; Phi Kappa Phi. Hobbies: Swimming; Reading. Address: 276 Riverside Drive, New York, NY 10025, USA.

HRADIL Peter, b. 29 Apr 1940, Brno, Czech Republic. Choir Conductor. m. Margite Hambálek-Hradil, 3 July 1974, 1 son, 1 daughter. Education: Conservatoire, organ; Music and Dance Faculty of the University of Arts Bratislava, choral and orchestral conducting. Debut: Bratislava, 1968. Career: Pedagogic of choral conducting in University of Muses Arts in Bratislava, from 1965, Choirmaster, Opera Slovak National Theatre; Assistant Chiefmaster, Slovak Philharmonic Choir, 1971-76; Conducted many amateur choirs; Lucnica Choir; Slovak Teachers' Choir; Performed in almost all European Countries, Prague, Brno, Bratislava, Brussel, Strasbourg, Barcelona, Sofia, Budapest, Stockholm, Vienna, Salzburg, Copenhagen, Parma, San Marino, Novi Sad, in Asia: Pchojgang, 1989, Seoul, Taipei, 1991, in South America: Buenos Aires, Mar del Plata, 1992, Mexico City, 1995, Jerash, 1995, Vancouver, Victoria, Seattle, 1996; Conductor, many choir compositions for Slovak Radio, for recording companies, for Slovak Television and also for other television companies abroad/Yugoslavia, Taiwan, Malta; Frequent Jury Member of international choral competitions. Honours: Awarded many prizes (first prizes and others) at the world's international competitions. Memberships: IFCM; Chairman, Artistic Council of Slovak Choirs Association. Hobby: Sport. Address: Heyrovského 14, 841 03 Bratislava, Slovakia.

HSIEH Li-Ping (Liu Chere), b. 7 Jan 1941, Nanjing, China. Soprano. m. Hsien-Tung Liu, 5 Jun 1964, 1 son, 1 daughter. Education: Conservatorio di Musica Giuseppe Verdi, Milan; Juilliard School, NY; BM, 1977, MM, 1979, Duquesne University, Pittsburgh; Pupil of Licia Albanese, Eleanor Steber and Martin Rich, NY, Luigi Ricci in Rome and Ettore Campogalliani in Milan; Attended Aspen and Tanglewood. Career: Sang with San Francisco and Merola Operas, 1966, and Pittsburgh Opera, 1969; Recital tours of USA from 1966; Tour of Italy and Germany, 1969 and Taiwan from 1985; Appeared in Vienna in 1986 and tour of Korea, 1989-; Many appearances as soloist with symphony orchestras and choirs including Juilliard, Knoxville, Tennessee, San Francisco Opera, and Bach Choir of Pittsburgh; Lecturer of music at La Roche College, 1978-80 and Point Park College, 1983-86. Recordings: Mozart Coronation Mass and Mass in C minor, and Schubert's Mass in G major with St Paul, Pittsburgh; Chinese Art Songs, Bel Canto Arias, Sacred Songs with AirCraft, Pittsburgh, in progress. Current Management: Albert Kay Associates Inc, 58 West 58th Street, NY, NY 10019, USA. Address: 2205 Bentley Drive, Bloomsburg, PA 17815, USA.

HSU John T, b. 21 April 1931, Swatow, China. Professor of Music; Performer on Cello, Viola da gamba, and Baryton. m. Martha Russell, 31 July 1968. Education: BMus 1953, MMus 1955, New England Conservatory of Music. Career: Teacher, 1955-; Fellow, Cornell Society for the Humanities, 1971-72; Instructor, 1955-58; Professorial Staff, 1958-76; Chairman, Department of Music, 1966-71; Artist-Faculty, Aston Magna Foundation, 1973-90; Old Dominion Professor of Music and Humanities, Cornell University, Ithaca, New York, 1976-; Barytonist, Haydn Baryton Trio, 1982-; Artist-in-Residence, University of California, Davis, 1983; Regents Lecturer in Music, University of California, Santa Cruz, 1985; Viola da gamba Recitalist, including radio broadcast, in North America and Europe; Director, Aston Magna Performance Practice Institute, 1986-90; Artistic Director, Aston Magna Foundation for Music and the Humanities, 1987-90; Music Director and Conductor, Appollo Ensemble, 1991-; John Hsu in a course in French Baroqua Viol Playing, presented by The Viola da gamba Society of America. Rcordings include: Pièces de Viole, by Louis de Caix d'Hervelois and Antoine Forqueray, Belgium, 1966; 3 Gamba Sonatas, by J S Bach, Da Camera, Germany, 1971; First complete recording of the 5 suites for viola da gamba by Antoine Forqueray, Musical Heritage Society, 1972; Series of 5 discs of Pièces de viole by Maria Marais, MHS, 1973-76' Pièces de viole, by Charles Dollé and Jacques Morel, MHS, 1978; 2 CDs of Baryton Trios by Joseph Haydn, Gaudeamus, London, 1988-89; Apollo Ensemble and John Hsu, Conductor; 2 CDs of Symphonies by Joseph Haydn, Dorian Recordings, USA, 1993-95 Publications: Editor, The Instrumental Works, by Marin Marais (1656-1728), volume I, 1980, volume II 1987, volume III, 1995; A Handbook of French Baroque Viol Technique, 1981. Contributions to: Early Music, 1978. Honours: Doctor of Music, New England Conservatory of Music, 1971; Doctor of Arts, Ramapo College of New Jersey, 1986. Current Management: Rohr Artists Management (New York and Copenhagen). Address: 402 Hanshaw Road, Ithaca, NY 14850, USA.

HUA Lin, b. 8 Aug 1942, Shanghai, China. Composer; Associate Professor. Education: Graduated with honours, Shanghai Conservatory of Music, 1966; Piano and Composition with Sang Tong, Wang Jianzhong, Chen Mingzhi. Career: Composer, Shanghai Wind Band, 1967-76, Shanghai Opera and Ballet House, 1976-79; Associate Professor, Counterpoint, Fugue, Shanghai Conservatory of Music, 1979-; Consultant, Shanghai Philharmonic Association, 1982-. Compositions include: Bright Mountain Flowers in Full Bloom, ballet, 1976; Fantasy, piano, accordion, 1978; Love of the Great Wall, piano, accordion, 1978; Farewell Refrains at Yang Gate Pass, piano quartet, 1978; Beauty of Peking Opera, string quartet, 1979; Album of Woodcuts, piano quintet, 1979; Amid Flowers Besides a River Under the Spring Moon for four harps, 1979; Flower and Song, concertino for soprano and orchestra, 1980; Suite, Tragedy, chamber symphony, 1988; 24 Preludes and fugues on Reading Sikong Tu's Shipin (Personalities of Poetry in Tang Dynasty), 1990; Album of Chinese Folk Songs, piano, 1991; Stage, film, TV music. Publications: Guide the Teaching of Polyphony by Using Creative Psychology, 1980; Stravinsky Techniques in Polyphonic Writing, 1987; The Sense of Ugliness and its Application in Western Music, 1988; Abstraction of Art and Abstractionism, 1989. Address: 20 Fenyang Road, Shanghai, China.

HUANG An-Lun, b. 15 Mar 1949, Canton, China. Composer. m. Ruili Ouyang, 15 Sept 1974, 1 son. Education: Conservatory of Music, Beijing; Fellowship in Composition, Trinity College, London, 1983; MMus, Yale University, 1986. Career: Composer-in-Residence, Central Opera House of China, Beijing, 1976-; Freelance Composer since 1980; President, Canadian Chinese Music Society of Ontario, 1987-. Major stage, film, TV and radio appearances. Compositions: Two Grand Operas, 6 grand opera scores, 1 musical, 3 ballets, 4 films and over 20 orchestral works, 2 oratorios as well as chamber, electronic, incidental, choral and vocal music. Recordings include: Piano Concerto in G, 1988; Selections from the ballet, Dream Of Dunhuang for Orchestra, 1990; Poem For Dance for Piano Solo, 1992; Chinese Rhapsody No 2 for Piano Solo, 1992; The Special Orchestra Album, 1997. Publications: Numerous music scores. Honours: Numerous; Dream of Dunhuang selected one of the Masterpieces of Chinese Music in the 20th Century, 1993. Hobbies: Reading; Travel. Address: 15 Carlton Road, Markham, Ontario L3R 1Z3, Canada.

HUANG Yijun, b. 4 May 1915, Suzhou, China. Conductor. m. Zhang Han-Zhen, 27 Feb 1939, 3 sons. Education: National Conservatory of Music, Shanghai. Career: Conductor and Composer for Chinese films and stage productions, Shanghai, 1936-56; Trumpet Player with Shanghai Municipal Symphony Orchestra, 1938-42 and French Horn Player, 1946-50; Associate Professor, Trumpet and French Horn at Shanghai Conservatory of Music, 1948-56; Conductor and Director, 1950-, Honorary Director, 1985-, for Shanghai Symphony Orchestra, 1950-; Guest Conductor for Helsinki Symphony Orchestra, 1956, Central Philharmonic Orchestra, Peking, 1957 and 1962, National Symphony Orchestra, Russia, 1958, Berlin Philharmonic Orchestra, 1981, Singapore Symphony Orchestra, 1984, and Yomiuri Nippon Symphony Orchestra, 1986. Compositions: Fair Flowers Under Full Moon for Folk Ensemble; Selections From Folk Tunes; The Jiangnan Suite for Orchestra. Memberships: Standing Committee, 1979-, Vice Chairman of Shanghai Branch, 1962-, Chinese Musicians Association; National Committee of Chinese People's Political Consultative Conference, 1978-. Address: 105 Hunan Lu, Shanghai, China.

HUANG Zhuan, b. 25 Jun 1926, Huang Yan County, Zhe Jang Province, China. Composer. Education: Studied with Xie Xinhai and others. Career: Composer at the Peking Film Studio, 1949 and Resident at the Shanghai Studio, 1951. Compositions include: Film scores: Old Man And Nymph, 1956, Red Women Soldiers, 1960, Sisters On Stage, 1964 and Horsekeeper, 1982; Television music and songs. Address: c/o Music Copyright Society of China, 85 Dongsi Nan Jajie, Beijing 100703, China.

HUBARENKO Vitaly, b. 13 Jun 1934, Kharkov, Ukraine. Composer. Education: Studied at the Kharkov Conservatory. Career: Teacher of Theory and Composition, Kharkov Conservatory, 1961-72; Freelance Composer of stage music and other works. Compositions include: The Destruction of The Squadron, musical drama, 1967; The Story Host (Don Juan), ballet, 1968; Mamay, musical drama, 1970; Letter to Love, monodrama, 1972; Reborn May, lyric drama, 1974; Through Flames, opera in 3 acts, 1976; Viy, opera-ballet, 1984; The Reluctant Matchmaker, lyric comedy, 1985; Al'piyskaya Ballada, lyric scenes, 1985; In The Steppes of Ukraine, lyric comedy, 1986-87; Remember, My Brotherhood, opera-oratorio, 1990-91; The Loneliness, monodrama, 1993. Address: c/o Nikolaeva Str, 3B op 151 Kyiv 253225, CIS.

HUBER Klaus, b. 30 Nov 1924, Berne, Switzerland. Composer. Education: Studied at the Zurich Conservatory 1947-49 with Stefi Geyer and Willy Burkhard; Further study with Boris Blacher in Berlin. Career: Taught violin at the Zurich Conservatory from 1950; Lucerne Conservatory 1960-63; Basle Music Academy from 1961. Compositions: Orchestral: Invention und Choral, 1956; Litania instrumentalis, 1957; Terzen-Studie, 1958; Alveare vernat, 1967; James Joyce Chamber Music, 1967; Tenebrae, 1967; Tempora for violin and orchestra, 1970; Turna, 1974; Choral: Quem terra, 1955; Das Te Deum Laudamus Deutsch, 1956; Antiphonische Kantate, 1956; Soliloquia, 1959-64; Cuius legibus rotantur poli, 1960; Musik zu eines Johannes-der-Taufer Gottesdienst, 1965; Kleine Deutsche Messe, 1969; ...inwendig voller figur... after the Apocalypse and Durer, 1971; Hiob xix, 1971; Vocal: Abendkantate, 1952; Kleine Tauf Kantate fur Christof, 1952; 6 Kleine Vokalisen, 1955; Der Abend ist mein Buch, 1955; Oratorio Mechtildis, 1957; Des Engls Anredung an der Seele, 1957; Auf die ruhige Nacht-Zeit, 1958; Askese, 1966; Psalm of Christ, 1967; Grabschrift, 1967; Der Mensch, 1968; Traumgesicht, 1968; ...ausgespant..., 1972; Jot oder Wann kommt der Herr zuruck, opera, 1973; Instrumental: Ciacona for organ, 1954; Concerto per la camerata, 1955; In Memoriam Willy Burkhard for organ, 1955; Partita, 1955; Noctes intelligibis lucis for oboe and harpsichord, 1961; Moteti-Cantiones for string quartet, 1963; 6 Miniaturen, 1963; In te Domine spervai for organ, 1964; Sabeth, 1967; Ascensus for flute, cello and piano, 1969; 3 kleine Meditationen for string trio and harp, 1969; Ein Hauch von Unzeit (-III, 1972. Honours: First Prize at the 1959 ISCM Competition, Rome (for Die Engels Anredung an die Seele); Arnold Bax Society Medal, 1962; Beethoven Prize of Bonn, 1970 (for Tenebrae). Address: Salzgasse 5, D-W-7801, Ehrenkirchen, Germany.

HUBERMAN Lina, b. 1955, Moscow, Russia. Violinist. Education: Studied at Moscow Conservatoire with Yanketevich. Career: Member of the Prokofiev Quartet, founded at the Moscow Festival of World Youth and the International Quartet Competition at Budapest; Many concerts in the former Soviet Union and on tour to Czechoslovakia, Germany, Australia, the USA, Canada, Spain, Japan and Italy; Repertoire includes works by Haydn, Mozart, Beethoven, Schubert, Debussy, Ravel, Tchaikovsky, Bartók and Shostakovich. Current Management: Sonata, Glasgow, Scotland. Address: C/O Prokofiev Quartet, 11 Northgate Street, Glasgow G20 7AA, Scotland.

HUBNER Fritz, b. 25 Apr 1933, Sachsengrun, Czechoslovakia. Bass Singer. Education: Studied at the Dessau Conservatory with J Stieler. Debut: Landestheater Bernburg as Sparafucile in Rigoletto. Career: Sang at Cothen, 1953-55 and Dessau, 1955-56; Sang in chorus of Leipzig Opera house, for Dresden-Radebeul, 1960-62, Berlin Komische Opera, 1962-74 and Staatsoper Berlin from 1974 as Hagen and Fafner in The Ring, Daland in Der fliegende Holländer, Landgrave in Tannhäuser, Osmin in Die Entführung and Sarastro in Die Zauberflöte; Guest appearances in Hamburg and Prague in Wagner roles; Bayreuth Festival, 1979-85 as Hagen and Fafner, and Las Palmas Festival in 1985 as Sarastro; Engagements at Covent Garden in Ring Cycles directed by Götz Friedrich; Sang Ramfis in Aida with the Deutsche Oper am Rhein in 1989, Galitzky in Prince Igor at the Berlin Staatsoper and Osmin on tour to Japan in 1987. Recordings include: Der Ring des Nibelungen, Bayreuth Festival, 1980. Address: c/o Ingpen and Williams Ltd, 26 Wadham Road, London SW15 2LR, England.

HUDECEK Vaclav, b. 7 Jun 1952, Rozmital, Czechoslovakia. Violinist. m. Eva Trejtnarova, 8 Feb 1977. Education: Academy of Music Prague and private lessons for 4 years with David Oistrakh in Moscow. Debut: With Royal Philharmonic Orchestra in London, 1967. Career: Concert tours in Europe, Japan and USA since London debut, and tours in Europe, USA, Japan and Australia; Soloist with Czech Philharmonic Orchestra, 1983. Recordings: Most of the world violin repertoire. Honours: Artist of Merit of Czechoslovakia, 1980; Record of the Year in 1992 for Vivaldi's Four Seasons and Best Selling Record of Czechoslovakia. Memberships: Central Committee, Union of Czech Composers and Concert Artists; Association of Czech Musicians. Hobbies: Films; Paintings; Sculpture. Current Management: Euroconcert Bellebern 10a, 78234 Engen, Germany. Address: 120 00 Praha 2, Londynská 25, Czech Republic.

HUDSON Barton, b. 20 July 1936, Tennessee, USA. Professor. m. Elizabeth Kesselring, 1 June 1959, 1 daughter. Education: BMus, Midwestern University, 1956; MMus, distinction, 1957, PhD, 1961, Indiana University; Staatliche Hochschule fur Musik, Freiburg, 1960. Publications: Contributor to Collected Works of Jacob Obrecht, Josquin des Prez; Editor, Collected Works of Thomas Crecquillon, Ninot le Petit, Antoine Brumel; Articles to Journal of the American Musicological Society; Computer and Music; Musica Disciplina; The Musical Quarterly; Revue Belge de Musicologie; Acta Musicologica; Tijdschrift van de Vereniging voor Nederlandse Muziekgeschiedenis; New Grove Dictionary of Music and Musicians. Honours: Pi Kappa Lambda; Fulbright Scholarship, 1959-60, Research Fellowship, 1992; Benedum Distinguished Scholar, West Virginia University, 1987; NEH Grants. Memberships include: American and Dutch Musicological Societies; Southeastern and Midwestern Historical Keyboard Societies. Address: 473 Devon Road, Morgantown, WV 26505, USA.

HUDSON Benjamin, b. 14 Jun 1950, Decatur, IL, USA. Violinist. Education: Studied in New York. Career: Co-founded the Schoenberg String Quartet in 1977 becoming Columbia String Quartet in 1978; Has performed many modern works including the premieres of Charles Wuorinen's Archangel in 1978 with trombonist, David Taylor, and 2nd String Quartet in 1980, Berg's Lyric Suite in its version with soprano, Bethany Beardslee, NY, 1979, and Roussakis' Ephemeris in 1979; Further premieres include quartets by Morton Feldman in 1980, Wayne Peterson in 1984 and Larry Bell in 1985. Recordings include: String Quartet No 3 by Lukas Foss and Ned Rorem's Mourning Song with baritone, William Parker. Honours include: National Endowment of The Arts Grants, 1979-81.

HUDSON John, b. Barnsley, Yorkshire, England. Singer (Tenor). Education: Studied at the Guildhall School with Laura Sarti; Further study with Josephine Veasey. Debut: English National Opera, as Verdi's MacDuff, 1993. Career: Seasom 1993-94 with ENO as Rodolfo, Nadir in the Pearl Fishers and Don Orravio; Alfredo in La Traviata for Welsh National Opera and for Auckland Opera, New Zealand; Concerts include Beethoven's Ninth at the Barbican and in Paris, Messiah in Ottawa with Trevor Pinnock and Mozart's Requiem with the English Chamber Orchestra; 50th Anniversary Concert with ENO and TV appearance with Lesley Garrett in Viva la Diva, on BBC2; Season 1996-97 as Alfredo and Nadir with ENO. Address: c/o Jane Livingston, Head of Press, English National Opera, St Martin's Lane, London WC2N 4ES, England.

HUDSON Richard, b. 1960, Rhodesia (now Zimbabwe). Stage Designer. Education: Wimbledon School of Art. Career: Designs for English National Opera include The Force of Destiny and Figaro's Wedding; Premieres of Judith Weir's A Night at the Chinese Opera (Kent Opera) and The Vanishing Bridegroom (Scottish Opera); Glyndebourne debut 1992, The Queen of Spades, followed by Eugene Onegin, The British stage premiere of Rossini's Ermione, and Maon Lescaut (1997); Die Meistersinger von Numberg at Covent Garden, 1993; Further engagements with I Puritani at La Fenice, Venice, The Rake's Progress for the Lyric Opera Chicago, Lucia di Lammermoor at Zurich and Munich, Rossini's L'Inganno felice at the Pesaro Festival; The Rake's Progress at the Saito Kinen Festival, Japan; Ernani and Guillaume Tell at the Vienna Staatsoper, season 1997-98; Other designs for Manon (Opera North), Mary Stuart (Scottish Opera) and Les Contes d'Hoffmann (Staatsoper, Vienna). Address: c/o English National Opera, St Martin's Lane, London WC2, England.

HUEBER Kurt (Anton), b. 9 July 1928, Salzburg, Austria. Composer; University Lecturer. Education: Diploma, Piano and Conducting, Musik Hochschule Mozarteum, Salzburg, 1948. Career: Section Leader, Konservatorium der Stadt Wien; Works performed in concerts and on radio; Teacher, Musical Acoustics, Hochschule für Musik, Vienna, 1980-93. Compositions: Scenic Music for Stage, Linz, 1958-60; Schwarz auf Weiss, 1st opera composed for Austrian TV, 1968; Symchromie I, 1970; Symchromie II, 1972; Formant spectrale for string orchestra, 1974; Sonata for viola solo; Sonata for trumpet and piano; Opera, The Canterville Ghost (O Wilde), 1990-91; Dankos Herz, string quartet, 1992-93; Völuspa, 3 mythological scenes for violin and string orchestra. Recordings: Glockenspektren for pipe-bells and piano; Iris for piano and percussion; Horn und Tuba, Requiem for 4 Wagner-Tubas and Contrabass Tuba, 1977; Osiris Hymnus; Schein und Sein; 22 songs for Baritone and Piano; CD: Musik for Violoncello and Piano, 1994; CD: Trondheim Bläserquintett Hören über Grenzen, Wind Quintet op 10, 1995. Publications: Mathematisch-physikalische Grundlagen einer ekmelischen Intervallehre, Mikrotone II, 1988; Ekmelische Harmonik, Mikrotone III, 1990. Contributions to: Pseudoharmonische Partialtonreihen, Ihre ekmelischen Intervallstrukturen, Ein Neuer Klangraum der Musiktheorie, Acustica, vol 26, 1972; Instrumentenbau Musik International, 1975; Mikrotone, 1986; Various other professional publications. Honours: Honorary Prize for Music from Lower Austria, 1992. Membership: President, International Society of Ekmelische Musik, 1991-. Hobbies: Mathematics; Physics; Swimming; Travel. Address: Paradisgasse 14, A 1190 Vienna, Austria.

HUFFSTODT Karen, b. 31 Dec 1954, IL, USA. Soprano. Education: Studied at the Illinois Wesleyan and Northwestern Universities. Career: Sang with the New York City Opera from 1982 as Lehar's Merry Widow, Micaela, Violetta and Donna Anna; Santa Fe Opera in 1984 as the Soldier's Wife in the US premiere of Henze's We Come to The River, returning in 1989 as L'Ensoleillad in Massenet's Chérubin; Other engagements with Chicago Opera as Magda in La Rondine and Fiordiligi, Illinois Opera in title role in Mary, Queen of Scots by Thea Musgrave, Washington Opera in the premiere of Menotti's Goya in 1986, Cologne Opera as Constanze, Agrippina, Donna Anna and Mozart's Countess, and Metropolitan Opera as Violetta and Rosalinda in season 1989-90; Other roles include Musetta at Los Angeles and Hamburg, Thais at Paris Opéra, Nancy and Toulouse, Amalia in I Masnadieri by Verdi for Australian Opera, Salome at Lyon, Agathe and Arabella at Catania, and Odabella in Attila for Opera North in 1990 and Covent Garden in 1991; Season 1992 as Tosca at Antwerp, Turandot at Lyons, and Chrysothemis at the Opera Bastille Paris; Opened season at La Scala in 1993 as Spontini's Vestale; Sang Strauss's Ariadne at the Opera Comique, Salome at the Bastille Opera and Alice Ford at Antwerp in 1994; Season 1996-97 as Sieglinde at Covent Garden and Salome at San Francisco. Recordings include: Salome in a French language version of Strauss's opera. Address: c/o Athole Still Ltd, 113 Church Road, London, SE19 2PR, England.

HUGGETT Monica, b. 16 May 1953, London, England. Violinist. Education: Studied at the Royal Academy of Music with Manoug Parikian; Early performance practice with Sigiswald Kuijken, Gustav Leonhardt and Ton Koopman. Career: Co-founded the Amsterdam Baroque Orchestra with Koopman, 1980, and was its leader until 1987; Many performances on authentic gut-string violins with such ensembles as the Hanover Band, Academy of Ancient Music, Raglan Baroque Players and Hausmusik; Worldwide tours as soloist, director and chamber musician in a repertoire extending from the late Renaissance to the Romantic with performances and recordings of Mozart, Beethoven, Schubert, Mendelssohn and the concertos of Vivaldi and Bach; Played the Beethoven concerto with the Orchestra of the Age of Enlightenment under Ivan Fischer at the Elizabeth Hall, Apr 1991; the Mendelssohn concerto under Charles Mackerras, 1992; Professor of Baroque and Classical Violin at the Hochschule für Kunste in Bremen and Artistic Director of the Portland Baroque Orchestra, USA. Recordings include: Symphonies by Beethoven with the Hanover Band (as director); Vivaldi La Stravaganza and Schubert Octet with the Academy of Ancient Music; Vivaldi La Cetra and Schubert Trout Quintet with the Raglan Baroque Players and Hausmusik; Rameau Pièces de Clavécin en Concerts and Corelli Violin Sonatas Op 5 with Trio Sonnerie and Vivaldi Four Seasons, Mozart Violin Concertos; Bach Violin Concertos with the Amsterdam Baroque Orchestra; Beethoven Concerto and Mendelssohn Concerto with the Orchestra of the Age of Enlightenment. Address: c/o Francesca McManus, 71 Priory Road, Kew Gardens, Surrey TW9 3DH, England.

HUGH Tim, b. 1965, England. Concert Cellist. Education: Studied at Yale and with William Pleeth and Jacqueline Du Pré. Career: Former solo cellist with the BBC Symphony Orchestra and currently joint principal with the London Symphony Orchestra; Many concerts with the Liverpool Philharmonic Orchestra, the Royal and BBC Philharmonics, Bournemouth Symphony Orchestra and Sinfonietta, and London Mozart Players; Appearances at the Leipzig Gewandhaus, La Scala Milan and Amsterdam Concertgebouw; Solo cello suites by Bach and Britten at 1994 Glasgow Mayfest, tour of Britain with the Polish State Philharmonic and engagements at Aldeburgh and the London Proms; Chamber music by Fauré and others with Domus and the Solomon Trio. Recordings include: Britten's Suites; Sonatas by Beethoven and Grieg with Yonty Solomon; CP Bach and Boccherini Concertos. Honours include: Prizewinner at 1990 Tchaikovsky International Competition, Moscow. Address: c/o Andrew Jamieson, Baron's Gate, 33-35 Rothschild Road, London, W5 5HT, England.

HUGH-JONES Elaine, b. 14 Jun 1927, London, England. Composer. Education: Studied with Harold Craxton and Lennox Berkeley. Career: Former teacher at Malvern Girls' College and BBC accompanist. Compositions include: Song Cycles Walter De La Mere Songs, 1966-88, A Cornford Cycle, 1972-74, Four American Songs, 1978 and Six Songs Of RS Thomas, 1991; The Dragon Fear, operetta, 1978. Address: c/o New Zealand Music Centre, PO Box 10042, Level 13, Brandon Street, Wellington, New Zealand.

HUGHES Martin (Glyn), b. 23 Mar 1950, Hemel Hempstead, England. Pianist. 1 son, 1 daughter. Education: Salisbury Cathedral Choir School, 1960-63; Music Scholar, Bryanston School, 1963-66; Paris Conservatoire, France, 1966-67; Private study with Yvonne Lefebure, 1967-70; Moscow Conservatory, Russia, 1970-71. Debut: Wigmore Hall, London, England, 1972. Career: Proms, 1972; French radio and television, 1972; Cheltenham Festival, 1973; Making a Name, BBC Television, 1974; Tour of USSR, 1974; RPO and LSO debuts, 1975; Chichester and Llandaff Festivals, 1975; Recital and Concerto debut, Queen Elizabeth Hall, 1977; Tours and radio recitals, Portugal and Germany, 1977; Beethoven Sonata Cycle, 1979; regular Radio 3 broadcasts, solo appearances including: Royal Festival Hall, European tours, 1980-; Founder, 1984, Artistic Director of Music, Fens Festival and summer school, 1984, 1986; Fengate Music trust; Director, Annual Summer School, Val de Saire, France, 1988, 1989; Bath Festival, 1983, 1985, 1986; Member, Kreutzer Piano trio, 1985; Tours of USA, Israel, 1987-88; Study with Wilhelm Kempff, 1980; Professor, Hochschule fur der Kunste, Berlin, Germany, 1991-; Tour of Japan, 1993; Guest teacher, Academy of Music, Bucharest, 1993, 1994, 1995. Publications: Russian School of Piano Playing, translation and editing, 1976. Contributions to: Chapter in Performing Beethoven, 1994. Honours include: Bronze Medal, Marguerite Long Competition, 1969; British Council Scholar, 1970-71; Arts Council of Great britain Award, 1975; Honorary MMus, University of Surrey, 1991. Address: Leibnizstrasse 58, 10629 Berlin, Germany.

HUGHES Owain Arwel, b. 21 Mar 1942, Cardiff, Wales. Conductor. m. Jean Bowen Lewis, 23 Jul 1966, 1 son, 1 daughter. Education: University College Cardiff, Royal College of Music with Adrian Boult and Harvey Philips, 1964-66, and with Kempe in London and Haitink in Amsterdam. Career: Professional career from 1968; Music Director, Royal National Eisteddfod of Wales, 1977, and Huddersfield Choral Society, 1980-86; Associate Conductor for BBC Welsh Symphony Orchestra, 1980-, and Philharmonia Orchestra; Guest Conductor with Welsh and English National Operas, in Europe and with the BBC Welsh Symphony and Hallé Orchestras (Mahler's Resurrection Symphony and Tippett's 4th Symphony in Manchester); Concerts in the UK and abroad including Shostakovich' 10th and Leningrad Symphonies, the Verdi Requiem and Elgar's Violin Concerto with Itzhak Perlman; Founded and became Artistic Director of the Welsh Proms in 1986; Series of programmes for BBC TV in 1987 featuring settings of the Requiem Mass; Rossini's Stabat Mater in TV for Holy Week in 1988 and conducted Mahler's 8th Symphony on Channel 4 TV in 1990. Honours: Honorary DMus, University of Wales and from Council for National Academic Awards in London; Fellowship, University College, Cardiff and from Polytechnic of Wales; Honorary Bard of Royal National Eisteddfod of Wales. Recordings include: Music by Paul Patterson with London Philharmonic, and by Delius and 2nd Symphony by Vaughan Williams; Works with Hallé Orchestra and Huddersfield Choral Society. Hobbies: Rugby; Cricket; Driving; Swimming; Soccer. Address: c/o 0181-874 3900.

HUGO Robert, b. 15 Jun 1962, Prague, Czechoslovakia. Organist; Conductor. Education: Charles University, Faculty of Life Sciences; Academy of Music, Prague, 1988-. Debut: Dafne by M da Gagliano, Summer School of Ancient Music, Czechoslovakia. Career: Organist: Church of Saint Salvator, 1990, Monastery of Saint Franciscus, 1992; Founder of Capella Regia Musicalis, ensemble, 1992; Guest Conductor at Janácek's

Opera House, Brno, Rappresentatione di Anima et di Corpo by Cavalieri, 1992-93. Recordings: Adam Michna CD, Czech Baroque Music, 1992; J D Zelenka, Penitential sepolchro del Redeutore, oratorio, and Michua, MissaSaint Nicolas, both for Czech Radio. Honour: Czech Grammy Classic for CD Michua Requiem, 1993. Hobby: Repairing ancient key instruments. Address: Jeremenkova 60, 147 00 Prague, Czech Republic.

HULA Pavel, b. 23 Jan 1952, Prague, Czechoslovakia. Violinist. m. Helena Sirlova, 29 June 1976, 1 daughter. Education: Violin, 1970-74, and Chamber Music, 1980-82, Academy of Music Arts, Prague. Debut: Prague Festival, Spring 1976. Career: First Violin, Kocian Quartet, 1975-, with performances at over 2000 concerts in 28 countries; Appearances on Radio and TV; Wigmore Hall debut, 1992. Recordings: Virtuoso Violin Duetts; Mozart's String Quartets; Dvorák's String Quartets; Haydn Quartets; Hindemith's String Quartets. Honours: 1st Prize, Kocian Violin Competition, 1963, 1964; 2nd Prize, Concertino Praga, Radio Competition, 1969; Prize, Society of Chamber Music of Czech Philharmonic, 1981; Grand Prix du Disque de l'Académie Charles Cross, Paris, 1997. Hobbies: Photography; Sport. Address: Vyzlovska 2251, 100 00 Prague 10, Czech Republic.

HULMANOVA Stefania, b. 20 Jan 1920, Dolné Dubové. Singer (Soprano). m. Cyril Hulman, 23 Feb 1943, 2 sons. Education: State Conservatory, Bratislava. Debut: Sang Rusalka in Dvorak's Rusalka, State Theatre, Kosice, 1948. Career: Soloist, Opera of the State Theatre, Kosice, 1948-51; Soloist, Opera of the Slovak National Theatre, Bratislava, 1952-79; Core repertoire: Julia in Jakobin by A Dvorak, Marienka in Bartered Bride by B Smetana, Vendulka in The Kiss by B Smetana, Halka in Halka by Moniuszko, Santuzza in Cavalleria Rusticana by Mascagni, Countess in The Marriage of Figaro by W A Mozart, Aida in Aida by G Verdi, Nella in Gianni Schichi by G Puccini; Soloist, Opera of the Slovak National Theatre, Bratislava, 1952; Numerous other roles performed include Leonora in Troubadour, Alzbeta in Don Carlos, Desdemona in Othello, all by Verdi; Tosca in Tosca by Puccini; Guest Performances include The Whirlpool, Dresden, East Germany; Tosca, Moscow; Svatopluk, Perugia, Italy; Concert, Peking, China; Concert, Hanoi, Vietnam; The Whirlpool, Budapest, Hungary. Recordings: Operas, Milka (Juro Janosik), 1954; Katka (Beg Bajazid), 1959; Helena (The Family), 1960. Memberships: Honorary Member, Opera of the Slovak National Theatre. Hobbies: Travel; Gardening; Crafts. Address: Ostravska 7, 811 04 Bratislava, Slovakia.

HUMBLET Ans, b. 17 Sep 1957, Maastricht, Netherlands. Soprano. Education: Studied with Elisabeth Ksoll and at Amsterdam. Career: Appearances with Netherlands Opera from 1983 and Wuppertal Opera, 1986-90 in such roles as the Queen of Night, Blondchen, Marie in Zar und Zimmermann, Woglinde, Despina and Musetta; Sang Kunigunde in the German premiere of Bernstein's Canide at Wuppertal in 1990; Enschede Holland in 1990 as Ninetta in Mozart's La Finta Giardiniera; Guest appearances at Dusseldorf and Aachen as the Queen of Night, and at Monchengladbach as Frasquita in Carmen; Concert engagements in Beethoven's 9th, Mendelssohn's St Paul, Bruckner's Te Deum, Carmina Burana and Masses by Haydn and Mozart; Broadcasts in Holland, Germany and Belgium; Engaged at Maastricht from 1990. Address: De Nederlandse Opera, Waterlooplein 22, 1011 PG Amsterdam, Netherlands.

HUMPHREYS Garry (Paul), b. 22 Feb 1946, Nottingham, England. Singer (Baritone); Lecturer; Writer; Chartered Librarian. m. (1) Janet Zimmermann, 30 July 1977, divorced, (2) Linda Fullick, 11 Dec 1997. Education: University of North London School of Information Studies; ALA, 1970; Studied singing with Norman Platt, Nigel Rogers and, principally, John Carol Case; Conducting with Bryan Fairfax. Career: Professional chorister and soloist in concerts, recitals and broadcasts; Song recitals with Patricia Williams; Anthology entertainments with Hardwick Players, Voice and Verse; Lectures and Lecture-recitals for music clubs and recorded music societies; Committee Member, English Song Award, 1982-89; Chairman, 1986-89; Secretary of Association of English Singers and Speakers, 1988-95; Presenter, Talking Notes, 1995-; Occasional Conductor. Publications: Member of Editorial Committee, A Century of English Song, 1993-; Record sleeve and concert programme notes; Periodical articles and book reviews including The Year in Reference, 1993-. Honour: FRSA. Memberships: Association of English Singers and Speakers; Elgar Society; Incorporated Society of Musicians; Library Association. Hobbies: Listening to music; Books; Theatre; Walking; Watching cricket. Address: 69 Park Avenue, Palmers Green, London N13 5PH, England.

HUNKA Pavlo, b. 7 Apr 1959, England. Bass Singer. Education: Studied with Joseph Ward at the Royal Northern College of Music. Career: Has performed in concerts throughout Britain as soloist and conductor; Royal Albert Hall in London, 1988 in a concert celebrating 1000 years of Christianity in the Ukraine; Opera debut as Melisso in a 1989 production of Handel's Alcina at the RNCM; Has also sung Theseus in A Midsummer Night's Dream and Philip II in Don Carlos with the RNCM;

Professional opera debut as Basilio in Il Barbiere di Siviglia with Welsh National Opera, 1990; Recent engagements as Rangoni in Boris Godunov for Basle Opera and Dulcamara in L'Elisir d'Amore; Other roles include Colline in La Bohème and Prince Gremin in Eugene Onegin; Now on contract to Basel Stadttheater, Switzerland. Honours include: Diploma with Distinction in Performance, RNCM, 1990; Ricordi Opera Prize; Peter Moores Foundation and Wolfson Foundation Scholarships. Address: c/o Harrison Parrott Ltd, 12 Penzance Place, London, W11 4PA, England.

HUNT Alexandra, b. 1940, USA. Opera and Concert Singer (Soprano); Librettist and Libretto Translator. Education: BA, Vassar College; BS, Juilliard School of Music; Sorbonne University, Paris, France. Debut: As Marie in La Scala's first production of Wozzeck in German, 1971, conducted by Claudio Abbado. Career: Sang title role of Lulu at Metropolitan Opera, Katya Kabanova sung in Czech, Janacek Festival, Brno; Jenufa at Lincoln Center, NY; Soprano Soloist in Penderecki Passion According to St Luke, Philadelphia Orchestra; Amelia in Ballo in Maschera, Providence, RI, and Bucharest; Title role of Tosca in Bulgaria, Romania and Czechoslovakia; Sang Marie in Wozzeck at Hamburg Staatsoper; Lady Macbeth in Macbeth at Florentine Opera and Kentucky Opera; Soprano Soloist in Mahler's Fourth Symphony, Bogota Filarmonica; In Beethoven's Ninth Symphony, Omaha and Des Moines Symphonies; Many other roles. Recordings: Songs of John Alden Carpenter, Charles T Griffes and Edward MacDowell. Publications: Author, New English Translation of Mozart's Don Giovanni and Cosi fan tutte; Book Reviewer for Best Sellers Magazine. Address: 170 West 74th Street, Apt 1106, New York, NY 10023, USA.

HUNT Donald, b. 26 July 1930, Gloucester, England. Director of Music. m. Josephine Benbow, 24 July 1954, 2 sons, 2 daughters. Education: Private study with Herbert Sumsion; FRCO; ARCHM. Career: Assistant Organist, Gloucester Cathedral, 1947-54; Director of Music, King's School, Gloucester; Master of the Music, St John's, Torquay, 1954-57; Director of Music, Leeds Parish Church, 1957-74; Organist and Master of the Choristers, Worcester Cathedral, 1974-; Conductor, Halifax Choral Society, 1957-88; Conductor, Worcester Three Choirs Festival and Worcester Festival Choral Society, 1975-. Compositions: Suite for Organ; Hymnus Paschalis; Missa Brevis; Missa Nova; The Worcester Service Song Cycle Strings in the Earth and Air; Magnificat and Nunc Dimittis; Christmas Night; Te Deum; Several short choral works: Recordings: 8 with Leeds Parish Church Choir; 30 with Worcester Cathedral Choir and Festival Choral Society; 6 organ recitals; 1 with Halifax Choral Society. Publication: SS Wesley: Cathedral Musician. Honours: Honorary DMus, Leeds University; OBE, 1993. Hobbies: Sport; Reading; Poetry. Address: 13 College Green, Worcester WR1 2LH, England.

HUNT Fionnuala, b. 1960, Belfast, Northern Ireland. Concert Violinist. Education: Studied at Ulster College of Music, Royal College of Music and The Vienna Hochschule für Musik with Wolfgang Schneiderhan. Career: Leader and Soloist with the Vienna Chamber; Former member of the Bavarian State Opera Orchestra in Munich; Co-Leader of the RTE Symphony Orchestra in Dublin; Guest Leader of the Ulster Orchestra; Duo recitals with pianist sister, Una Hunt, performing throughout: Ireland; Austria; Germany; Czechoslovakia; Italy; Britain; Member of the Dublin Piano Trio; Solo appearances with: The National Symphony Orchestra of Ireland; The RTE Concert Orchestra; The Ulster Orchestra; Played Lutoslawski's Partita at the Maltings Concert Hall, Snape; Artistic Director and Leader of the Irish Chamber Orchestra. Address: c/o Owen and White Management, 14 Nightingale Lane, London, N8 7QU, England.

HUNT Gordon, b. 1950, London, England. Oboist. Education: Studied with Terence MacDonagh at the Royal College of Music. Career: Principal Oboist with the Philharmonia Orchestra, formerly principal with the BBC Welsh and London Philharmonic Orchestras; Guest Oboist with the Berlin Philharmonic Orchestra and solo and chamber music appearances throughout Europe, USA and the Far East and in New Zealand; Played Bach's Double Concerto on 1994 world tour with Pinchas Zukerman and the ECO, 1994; Music Director of various ensembles including The Swedish Chamber Winds; Consultant Professor at the Royal Academy of Music. Recordings include: Works by Mozart, Malcolm Arnold, Vivaldi, Strauss and Haydn with English CO, London Philharmonic and Berlin Radio Orchestra. Address: c/o Hazard Chase, Richmond House, 16-20 Regent Street, Cambridge, CB2 1DB, England.

HUNT Lorraine, b. 1954, San Francisco, USA. Singer (Mezzo-soprano). Education: Studied in San Francisco and began career as a violist. Career: Concert appearances include Krasa's Chamber Symphony with the Boston SO, tour of Australia with the Australian CO, Dido and Aeneas with the Philharmonia Baroque, San Francisco, and L'Enfance du Christ under Roger Norrington, at the Paris Théâtre des Champs Elysées; Further concerts with the San Francisco, Houston, Boston and St Louis Symphonies;

Mark Morris Dance Group, as singer, at the Adelaide, Edinburgh and Brooklyn Academy Festivals; Season 1995-96 with Haydn's Scena di Berenice at Tanglewood, Charpentier's Médée with Les Arts Florissants in Europe and New York; Handel's Ariodante at the Göttingen Festival and Xerxes at the Los Angeles Music Center; Season 1996 with Irene in Handel's Theodora at Glyndebourne, the Berlioz Nuits d'Ete under Nicholas McGeegan, recitals with Dawn Upshaw in New York and tour of Europe with the Australian CO; Season 1996-97 with Sesto in Handel's Giulio Cesare and the title role in Carmen at the Paris Opéra Bastille, Massenet's Charlotte with the Opéra de Lyon; Further opera enagements in Vienna, Brussels, Lausanne, Aix, Amsterdam, Tokyo and Boston. Recordings include: Britten's Phaedra and Charpentier's Médée (Erato); Handel's Susanna, Theodora, Clori, Tirsi e Fileno, and Messiah, Purcell's Fairy Queen, Monteverdi's Ulisse (Harmonia Mundi); Videos of Peter Sellars productions of Don Giovanni (as Donna Elvira), Giulio Cesare (Sesto) and Theodora (Glyndebourne 1996). Address: c/o IMG Artists, 420 West 45th Street, New York, NY 10036-3503, USA.

HUNT Michael, b. 1957, London, England. Stage Director. Education: Studied at Liverpool University. Debut: Gounod's Mireille for Liverpool Grand Opera. Career: Artistic Director of the Cheltenham Arts Centre from 1980, staging a number of plays and Cosi fan Tutte; Directed the British premiere of Berwald's Queen of Golconda at Nottingham and The Rake's Progress at Cambridge; Staff Director at English National Opera, directing Aida and Orpheus in the Underworld, also Madama Butterfly for the Education Unit; Oedipus Rex for Opera North; Rossini's Tancredi at Las Palmas; Der Freischütz in an outdoor touring production; Oedipus Rex and Iolanthe for Scottish Opera; La Traviata for Dublin; Figaro and British Youth Opera; World Premieres of Giles Swayne's Le nozze di Cherubino and Harmonies of Hell; Artistic Director, Bloomsbury Festival; Director of Performing Arts, Riverside Studios in London; Teacher at The Royal Academy, Birmingham School of Music and various Drama Schools; In 1996 directed Puccini's La Bohème at the Royal Albert Hall. Address: Performing Arts, 6 Windmill Street, London, W1P 1HF, England.

HUNTER Francis John, b. 2 Sept 1946, Horsham, England. Musician. m. Pamela Mary Johnson, Apr 1972, 2 sons. Education: Magdalen College, Oxford; BA, MA, Oxon; BBC Training Orchestra; Freiburg High School for Music. Career: Solo Oboe, Zurich Opera House; Manager, AMG Music Society, Basel, Switzerland; Intendant, Bamberg Symphony Orchestra, Germany, 1996-97.

HUNTER Rita, b. 15 Aug 1933, Wallasey, Cheshire, England. Prima Donna; Leading Soprano. m. John Darnley Thomas, 1960, deceased 1994, 1 daughter. Education: Wallasey then joined Carl Rosa, 1950. Debut: Berlin in 1970, Covent Garden in 1972, Metropolitan Opera in 1972 as Brünnhilde in Die Walküre, Munich in 1973, Australia in 1978 returning in 1980 and 1981, and Seattle Wagner Festival in 1980. Career: Sang Brünnhilde in first complete Ring Cycle with Sadler's Wells in 1973, and Norma at New York Metropolitan in 1975; Leading roles in Aida, Trovatore, Masked Ball, Cavalleria Rusticana, Lohengrin, Flying Dutchman, Idomeneo, Don Carlos, Turandot, Nabucco, Macbeth, Tristan and Isolde and Elektra; Leading Soprano at Sadler's Wells, 1958- and Australian Opera, 1981-; Lecturer in Voice at UCLA, USA; Sang in Act III of Die Walküre at the Festival Hall in 1990 and title role in concert performances of Turandot at the Albert Hall in 1990; Runs JDT Singing Academy, Sydney and the JDT Scholarship Australia. Recordings include: The Ring; Complete Euryanthe; Several recital discs. Publication: Wait Till The Sunshines Nellie, autobiography, 1986. Honours: RAM, 1978; DLitt Warwick, 1978; CBE, 1980; Honorary DMus, Liverpool, 1983. Hobbies: Sewing; Oil Painting; Reading; Gardening; Caravanning; Swimming. Address: 305 Bobbin Head Road, North Turramurra, New South Wales 2074, Australia.

HURD Michael (John), b. 19 Dec 1928, Gloucester, England. Composer; Author. Education: Pembroke College, Oxford University, 1950-53. Career: Professor of Theory, Royal Marines School of Music, 1953-59; Freelance Composer and Author, 1959-. Compositions include: Opera: Widow of Ephesus, 1971; The Aspern Papers, 1993; Choral: Missa Brevis, 1966; Music's Praise, 1968; This Day to Man, 1974; Shepherd's Calendar, 1975; Phoenix and Turtle, 1975; Genesis, 1987; Night Songs of Edward Thomas, 1990; Orchestral: Dance Diversions, 1972; Concerto da Camera, 1987; Overture to Unwritten Comedy, 1987; Chamber Music: Flute Sonatina, 1964; Violin Sonata, 1987; Various other works. Publications include: Immortal Hour: Life and Times of Rutland Boughton, 1962; Outline History of European Music, 1968; Ordeal of Ivor Gurney, 1978; Vincent Novello and Company, 1981; Rutland Boughton and the Glastonbury Festivals, 1993. Contributions to: New Grove Dictionary of Music and Musicians; New Oxford Companion to Music; Athlone History of British Music; Musik in Geschichte und Gegenwart. Address: 4 Church Street, West Liss, Hampshire GU33 6JX, England.

HURFORD Peter, b. 22 Nov 1930, Somerset, England. Organist. m. Patricia Matthews, 6 Aug 1955, 2 s, 1 d. Education: Royal College of Music, 1948-49; ARCM; Organ Scholar, Jesus College, Cambridge, 1949-53; MA, Music and Law; MusB; FRCO. Debut: Royal Festival Hall, London, 1957. Career: Master of the Music, St Albans Cathedral, 1958-78; Concert tours of Europe, America, Australasia and Japan, 1958-; Founder, International Organ Festival, 1963; Visiting Professor, Universities of Cincinnati, 1967-68 and Western Ontario, 1976-77; Visiting Artist in Residence, Sydney Opera House, 1980-82; Betts Fellow, University of Oxford, 1992-93; Radio and television appearances. Recordings: Over 65 including: Complete Organ Works of J S Bach, F Couperin, Handel and Hindemith. Publications: Making Music on the Organ, 1988; Articles in Musical Times. Honours: FRSCM, 1977; Gramophone Award, 1979; DMus, Baldwin-Wallace College, Ohio, 1981; Honorary Member, RAM, 1982; OBE, 1984; FRCM, 1987; DMus, Bristol University, 1992. Memberships: Council, 1964-, President, 1980-82, Royal College of Organists; Incorporated Society of Musicians. Hobbies: Walking; Wine. Current Management: North America only: Karen McFarlane Artists Inc, 12429 Cedar Road, Suite 29, Cleveland, OH 44106, USA. Address: Broom House, St Bernard's Road, St Albans, Hertfordshire, AL3 5RA, England.

HURLEY Laurel, b. 14 Feb 1927, Allentown, PA, USA. Soprano. Education: Studied with her mother. Debut: Sang in the Student Prince at New York in 1943. Career: New York City Opera debut as Zerlina in 1952; Sang at the Metropolitan Opera from 1955 as Oscar, Musetta, Mimi, Adele, Susanna, Olympia, Papagena, Zerlina and Perichole; Also sang in I Capuleti e i Montecchi by Bellini; Many concert appearances in North America.

HURNEY Kate, b. 14 Sep 1941, Quincy, MA, USA. Lyric Coloratura Soprano. m. Robert J Braverman, 1 s, 1 d. Education: BA, Tufts University; Columbia University; New England Conservatory; Juilliard School; Manhattan School; Accademia Chigiana; International Opernstudio, Zurich; Dalcroze School. Debut: With American Opera Society at Carnegie Hall. Career includes: Appearances with Houston, Miami and Buffalo Symphonies, National Orchestra, Santo Domingo, Sudwest Funk; Extensive chamber music and recital work particularly in salon and American 19th century repertoire, with American Opera Society, Houston Grand Opera, Opera Company of Boston, Dallas Civic Opera, Opera Rara, London, Théâtre Monnaie, Brussels, Zurich Opera, Freiburg Opera, Germany, New Opera Theatre, Brooklyn Academy, San Juan, Guggenheim Museum (Virgil Thomson), Kennedy Center, Wolf Trap Festival; Co-founder of Public Opera Theater, 1972; Concerts of Irish-related material at St Patrick's Cathedral, New York City, 1986 and 1987, Opéra de Nice, Théâtre Champs Elysées, France, Belfast and Wexford Festivals. Recording: Poseidon and Ardee, Rubini Society, 1992. Honours: Recipient of various musical honours. Memberships: AGMA; Equity. Hobbies: Travel; Gardening; Cooking; Antiques. Current Management: Tornay Management, 127 West 72nd Street, New York, NY 10023, USA. Address: Apt 10B, 235 West 76th Street, New York, NY 10023, USA.

HURNIK Ilja, b. 25 Nov 1922, Ostrava, Czechoslovakia. Composer; Pianist; Writer. m. Jana Hurnikova, 26 Mar 1966, 1 son. Education: Academy of Musical Arts, Prague. Debut: As Composer, Piano Piece, 1933; As Pianist, Concert, Prague, 1942. Career: Professor, Prague Conservatorium; As Pianist gave concerts in Europe and USA, including piano duo with wife Jana; Regular guest appearances on radio and TV as composer, pianist and music commentator. Compositions: Lady Killers, opera; Diogenes, opera; Ezop, cantata; Sonata da camera; Variations on qa theme of Pergolesi. Recordings: Compositions: Oboe Concerto; Sulamith; Esercizi for wind quartet; Maryka, cantata; Musica da camera for strings; Ezop; As Pianist: Debussy, Preludes, Images, Estampes, Arabesques. Publications: Beletrie: Trumpeter of Jericho, 1965; The Geese of the Capitol, 1969; En Route with the Aviator; 2 radio plays. Honours: Grand Prix for Variations on a Theme of Pergolesi, Piano Duo Association of Japan, 1990; 1st Prize for Innocenza, International Competition, Piano Duo Association of Japan, 1992; DSc honoris causa, 1992. Memberships: Association of Composers, Prague. Hobby: Natural Science (Botany). Address: 11000 Prague, Varodni tr 35, Czech Republic.

HURSHELL Edmund, b. 1921, USA. Singer (Bass-baritone). Education: Studied in the USA and Germany. Career: Engaged at the Stadtische Oper Berlin, 1952-53, Kiel 1953-55, Vienna Staatsoper 1955-60, as Amonasro, Scarpia, Alfio, Pizarro Hans Sachs, Orestes and Mandryka; Théâtre de la Monnaie Brussels, 1961, as the villains in Les Contes d'Hoffmann, Bologna and Amsterdam 1963, as Wolfram and Wotan; Sang Handel's Giulio Cesare at Barcelona 1964, the Dutchman and the Wanderer at Buenos Aires and Lille, 1965; Further engagements at Nuremberg, Rome, Tel Aviv, Athens and Philadelphia; Metropolitan Opera 1967, as Kurwenal in Tristan; Appearances at Graz 1967-69; Other roles included Kaspar, the Grand Inquisitor and Falstaff. Address: c/o Vereinigte Buhnen, Kaiser Josef Platz 10, A-8010 Graz, Austria.

HURST George, b. 20 May 1926, Edinburgh, Scotland. Conductor. Education: Various preparatory and public schools in England and Canada; Royal Conservatory, Toronto. Career: Assistant Conductor, Opera, Royal Conservatory of Music, Toronto, 1946; Lecturer, Harmony and Counterpoint, Composition etc, Peabody Conservatory of Music, Baltimore, USA, 1947; Conductor, York Pennsylvania Symphony Orchestra, 1950-55, concurrently of Peabody Conservatory Orchestra, 1952-55; Assistant Conductor, LPO 1955-57 with tour of Russia, 1956; Associate Conductor, BBC Northern Symphony Orchestra, 1957; Principal Conductor, BBC Northern Symphony Orchestra (previously BBC Northern Orchestra), 1958-68; Artistic Adviser, Western Orchestral Society, 1968-73; Staff Conductor, Western Orchestral Society (Bournemouth Symphony Orchestra and Bournemouth Sinfonietta), 1973-; Principal Guest Conductor, BBC Scottish Symphony Orchestra, 1986-89; Principal Conductor, National Symphony Orchestra of Ireland, 1990-93; Frequent Guest Conductor, Europe, Israel, Canada, 1956-. Address: 21 Oslo Court, London NW8, England.

HURTEAU Jean-Pierre, b. 5 Dec 1924, Montreal, Canada. Singer (Bass). Education: Studied in Montreal and with Marital Singher, 1950-52. Debut: Sang in concert at Montreal, 1949. Career: Opera debut Montreal 1950, as Frère Laurent in Roméo et Juliette; Studied further in Europe and sang in Toulouse from 1957; Paris Opéra and Opéra-Comique 1958-70, as Mozart's Commendatore, Alfonso and Figaro, La Roche in Capriccio and Mephistopheles; Guest appearances in Lyon, Marseilles and Monte Carlo; Rome 1974, Toronto 1976, festival engagements at Orange; Sang in concert from 1970 after returning to Canada. Address: c/o Canadian Opera Company, 227 Front Street East, Toronto, Ontario M5A 1EB, Canada.

HURWITZ Emanuel, b. 7 May 1919, London, England. Violinist. Education: Royal Academy of Music and with Bronislav Huberman. Career: Led the Hurwitz String Quartet, 1946-51, and the Goldsborough (later English Chamber) Orchestra, 1946-68; Leader of the Melos Ensemble, 1956-72, and the New Philharmonia Orchestra, 1969-71; Leader of the Aeolian Quartet from 1970; Visiting Professor, Michigan University, Music Department, East Lansing, Michigan, USA, 1995-. Recordings include: Brandenburg Concertos; Handel's Concerti Grossi with the English Chamber Orchestra; Schubert's Octet and Trout Quintet, Mozart and Brahms Clarinet Quintets with the Melos Ensemble; Complete Haydn Quartets edited by H C Robbins Landon; Ravel, Debussy and Late Beethoven Quartets. Membership: President, 1995-96, Incorporated Society of Musicians. Honours: Gold Medal, Worshipful Company of Musicians, 1967; CBE, 1978. Hobbies: Collecting books and antique bows for string instruments; Photography. Address: 25 Dollis Avenue, London N3 1DA, England.

HUS Walter, b. 2 July 1959, Mol, Belgium. Composer; Pianist. Education: Diploma supérieur, Brussels Royal Conservatory, 1984. Career includes: Recitals as classical pianist since early childhood, Italy, Germany, Poland; Performances as improviser/interpreter of own compositions, 1982-; Concerts throughout Europe with group Maximalist, own compositions, 1984-; Member, Belgisch Pianokwartet, Simpletones, etc; Various radio and television appearances; Video film with Marie André and Walter Verdin; Currently active as composer, several works for ballet, full-sized opera. Compositions include: 8 etudes on improvisation, piano solo; Music for fashion show, Yamamoto, Brussels; Muurwerk, music for choreography, Roxane Huilmand; Die Nacht, opera, 2 acts, libretto by Wolfgang Klob (unfinished); Compositie, video film by Marie André about W Hus; Hus/Verdin, video tape by Walter Verdin; Liefde, composition for 4 pianists at 2 pianos; La Theorie, idem, both written for Belgisch Pianokwartet. Recordings: 8 etudes on improvisation, 1984; Maximalist, LP, 1985; Muurwerk, 1986; Die Nacht, radio recording, 1987. Honours: 1st Prize, Piano 1981, Harmony 1981, Practical Harmony 1983, Brussels Royal Conservatory. Current Management: Lucifer Productions.

HUSA Karel, b. 7 Aug 1921, Prague, Czechoslovakia. Composer; Conductor; Professor Emeritus. m. Simone Perault, 2 Feb 1952, 4 daughters. Education: Conservatory of Music, 1941-45; Academy of Music, 1945-47; Ecole Normale de Musique de Paris with Arthur Honegger, 1946-48; Conservatoire de Musique de Paris, 1948-49; Private study with Nadia Boulanger (composition), Andre Cluytens, (conducting). Career includes: Assistant Professor, 1954, Associate Professor, 1957, Full Professor, 1961, Kappa Alpha Professorship, 1972, Teaching composition, theory, conducting and orchestration, Cornell University; Conductor, Cornell University Orchestra, 1956-75, Ithaca Chamber Orchestra, 1955-61; Guest Conductor with national orchestras throughout Europe, USA, Hong Kong, Puerto Rico, Asia and Japan. Compositions include: Symphony No 1, for orchestra, 1953; String Quartet No 3, 1968; Music for Prague, 1968; Apotheosis of this Earth, 1972; An American Te Deum, for baritone chorus and orchestra, 1977; Fanfare for brass and timpani, 1980; Pastoral for string orchestra, 1980; Three Dance Sketches, 1980; Intradas and Interludes, 1980; The Trojan Women, 1981; Concertino for piano, 1983; Concerto for orchestra, 1984; Symphonic Suite, 1986; Concerto for organ, 1987;Concerto for trumpet, 1987; Frammenti for organ, 1987; Concerto for violoncello, 1988; String Quartet No 4, 1990; Concerto for violin, 1993. Recordings include: Conducted recordings with Cento Soli Orchestra in Paris (Bartok and Brahms), Stockholm and Prague Symphonies (Husa); Orchestre des Solistes (Husa Fantasies); CD Discs; Music for Prague, 1968; String Quartets No 2 and 3 and Evocations of Slovakia; Symphony No 1 Serenade, Mosaiques, Landscapes; Apotheosis of this Earth, Monodrama; Concerto for percussion. Publications include: Variations for Piano Quartet, 1984; Sudler Award, for Concerto for Winds, 1985; Concerto for Orchestra, 1986; Concerto for Violoncello, 1989, among others. Honours: Pulitzer Prize, for String Quartet No 3, 1969; Honorary music degrees from Coe College, 1976, Cleveland Institute of Music, 1985, Ithaca College, 1986, Baldwin College, 1991, St Vincent College, 1995, Hartwick College, 1997; Sudler International Prize, 1987; Grawemeyer Award, for Violoncello Concerto, 1993; Czech Gold Medal, President Havel, 1st Order, 1995; Memberships: Belgian Royal Academy of Arts & Sciences; American Academy of Arts and Literature. Address: 1030 Hanshaw Road, Ithaca, NY 12850, USA.

HUSS Hugo (Jan), b. 26 Jan 1934, Timisoara, Romania. Symphony Orchestra Conductor. m, Mirella Regis, 1 Aug 1970, 1 daughter. Education: Bucharest Conservatory of Music and Roosevelt University of Chicago. Debut: Concert, Romanian Athenaeum, Bucharest. Career: TV appearance, performance of Tosca with Placido Domingo; Radio broadcasts with La Crosse Symphony, Wisconsin; Radio Louisville with Louisville Symphony, Kentucky; Radio Birmingham with Alabama Symphony; Guest Conductor, Cape Town Symphony, South Africa; Tbilisi, Russia; Cracow, Poland; Brno, Czechoslovakia; Sarajevo, Yugoslavia; Veracruz, Mexico; Grand Rapids, Michigan and Huntsville, Alabama, USA; Music Director and Conductor of Arad Symphony, Romania; Principal Guest Conductor of Gunthe Symphony, Munich, Germany; Titular Director and Principal Conductor of Guadalajara Symphony, Mexico; Music Director of the La Crosse Symphony, Wisconsin, USA; Currently accepting Guest Conducting engagements around the world. Hobbies: Philately; Computers; Nature. Address: N1972 Hickory Lane, La Crosse, WI 54601, USA.

HUSSON Suzanne, 4 Apr 1943, Buenos Aires, Argentina. Pianist. Education: Began musical studies at age 5 with Mrs E Westerkamp; Later attended Conservatoire M de Falla, Buenos Aires; Conservatory of Geneva (Prof Hilbrandt); Staatliche Hochschule fur Musik, Köln (Prof B Seidhofer); Special Courses given by Maestro Arturo Benedietti Michelangeli (Italy and Switzerland). Debut: 1st Public Recital at age 8, Buenos Aires. Career: Various International Performances in Recitals and as Soloist with Conductors such as J Guyonnet, Marc Andreae, W Sawallisch, C Dutoit, and Orchestra Philarmonique de Lyon, Stuttgart Philharmonic, Orchestra de la Radio Suisse Italienne and Orchestra of Swiss Romande; TV and Radio Appearances in Germany and Switzerland; Radio Appearances in Argentina, Poland and France. Recordings: Stravinsky, Les Noces, directed by Charles Dutoit, Erato Label, 1973; R Vuataz, Concert for Piano and Orchestra, Opus 112, Orchestra of Swiss Romande, directed by Wolfgang Sawallisch, CBS Label, 1981; Scarlatti-Ginastera-Debussy-Ravel, Fono Label, 1987. Hobbies: Swimming; TV; Reading. Current Management: Wismer-Casetti, Rue Merle-d'Aubigné 26, 1207 Geneva, Switzerland. Address: 8 Rue Daubin, 1203 Geneva, Switzerland.

HUSZAR Lajos, b. 26 Sept 1948, Szeged, Hungary. Composer. Education: Secondary Music School, Szeged, with Istvan Vantus, 1963-67; Academy of Music, Budapest, with Endre Szervanszky and Zsolt Durko, 1967-73; Academy of St Cecilia, Rome, Italy, with Goffredo Petrassi, 1975. Compositions include: 5 Monologues to poems by Janos Parancs for mezzosoprano and orchestra; Csommorkany for 10 players, 1973; Hold-lepte uton, cantata for children's or female choir and orchestra; Musica concertante for 13 players, 1975; 69th Psalm for tenor and piano, 1976; 5 Pieces for piano, 1977; 2 Songs to poems by Endre Ady for bass and piano, 1977-83; Scherzo and Adagio for chamber orchestra, 1979; Sonata for harpsichord, 1979-85; 5 Variations for cello solo; Brass Quintet, 1980; 3 Songs to poems by Else Lasker-Schüler for soprano and viola, 1981-89; Serenata Concertante for flute and string orchestra; Songs of Solitude for soprano and percussion, 1983; Notturno for piano, 1984; Concerto rustico for chamber orchestra, 1985; Chamber Concerto for cello and 17 strings, 1987; String Quartet, 1991; Libera me for organ, 1993; The Silence, opera in 2 acts, 1994-95; Caligaverunt, Dies Sanctificatus, Ave Maria and Song of Fate, for female choir; Under the Silver Rose for male choir; 2 Madrigals to poems by Sándor Weöres and The Flower of Silence, for mixed voices; Pedagogic pieces for choirs. Recordings: Musica concertante; Ave Maria and Dies Sanctificatus, female choirs; Chamber Concerto. Memberships: Association of Hungarian Composers;

Hungarian Society of Music. Address: Postás u 12, 6729 Szeged, Hungary.

HUTCHESON Jere (Trent), b. 16 Sept 1938, Marietta, Georgia, USA. Composer; Professor of Music. m. (1) Virginia Bagby, 1 daughter, (2) Mary Ellen Gayley Cleland, 21 June 1982, 1 son, 1 daughter. Education: BMus, Stetson University; MMus, Louisiana State University; PhD, Michigan State University; Berkshire Music Center. Compositions include: Passacaglia for band; 3 Things for Dr Seuss; Shadows of Floating Life; Wonder Music I, II, III, IV, V; Sensations; Transitions; Construction Set; Colossus; 3 Pictures of Satan; Electrons; Fantaisie-Impromptu; Nocturnes of the Inferno; Passing, Passing, Passing; Patterns; Cosmic Suite; Earth Gods Symphony; Chromophonic Images for symphonic band; Will-O-The-Wisps for solo violin; The Song Book for Tenor and Flute; Duo Sonata for clarinet and percussion; Concerto for Piano and Wind Orchestra; Metaphors for orchestra; Interplay for alto saxophone and mallet percussion; Ritual and Dance for female chorus; Five French Portraits for wind orchestra; Duo Concertante in memoria di Margot Evans for violin and piano; Concerto for Violin and Small Orchestra; Long Live the Composer, chamber opera; Dance of Time Symphony, 1995; Caricatures for Wind Symphony, 1997; Portfolio for cello and chamber ensemble, 1997. Publication: Musical Form and Analysis, text, 1995. Hobbies: Chess; French; Travel; Gardening. Address: 6064 Abbott Road, East Lansing, MI 48823, USA.

HUTCHINSON Nigel, b. 1963, England. Concert Pianist. Education: University of Glasgow, Guildhall School with Craig Sheppard and Juilliard with Earl Wild. Debut: Wigmore Hall, 1988; Career: Concerts in France, Germany, Italy, Czechoslovakia and elsewhere in Europe; Concerto debut with the London Mozart Players under Jane Glover; Festival engagements at Harrogate and Glasgow, and recitals at the Salle Pleyel Paris, Barbican Centre and Festival Hall, London and Symphony Hall Birmingham; Broadcasts for BBC and Italian Radio; Purcell Room recital 1993, with Schubert (D664), Liszt and Debussy. Recordings: Rachmaninov music for six hands, with John Ogdon and Brenda Lucas, and Carnival of the Animals with the London Symphony Orchestra under Barry Wordsworth. Address: c/o South Bank Centre, Press Office, Opian Productions, London SE1, England.

HUTCHINSON Stuart, b. 3 Mar 1956, London, England. Conductor; Concert Accompanist. Education: Royal Academy of Music, London; Cambridge University; BMus (Honours), 1977; LRAM, 1979; Studied with Bernstein and Pritchard. Career: Opera, Ballet and Music-Theatre Conductor: Productions for English National Opera, Scottish Opera, Theater des Westens Berlin, New Sadler's Wells Opera Company, Sadler's Wells Theatre/ROH, London International Opera Festival, Royal Academy of Music; Conductor, Scottish Ballet, 1991; Chorus Master, Dublin Grand Opera and Wexford Festival Opera; Music Staff, English National Opera, Opera North; Director of Music, Organist, University of London Chaplaincy, 1976-89; Music Director, Northcott Theatre, Exeter, 1982-84; Music Director, Artistic Director, Morley Opera, London, 1986-90; Music Director, Jonathan Miller's Company/Old Vic Theatre, 1988-89; World premiere, Alice in Wonderland (Carl Davis), Lyric Theatre, Hammersmith, 1986; British premiere, Postcard From Morocco, (Dominick Argento) LIOF, 1988; World premiere, Tables Meet, (Stephen Oliver), Royal Festival Hall, 1990; Also productions for the Royal Shakespeare Company, (London), On Your Toes, with Makarova, West End, 1984. Compositions: Many scores for BBC plays, including When We Are Married and the serialisations of Little Women and Good Wives; Incidental theatre music including King Lear (Miller/Old Vic); Frequent arranger and orchestrator. Recordings: National Philharmonic Orchestra with James Galway, RCA; Several recordings for BBC Radio 3 and 4; Many for BBC Radio Drama; BBC and Independent Television. Publications: Prepared/Edited the 1995 (Opera North) Version of William Walton's Troilus and Cressida. Contributions to: Opera magazine; (Troilus and Cressida: Forty Years On), 1995. Memberships: Performing Right Society; Musicians Union. Current Management: Music International, 13 Ardilaun Road, London N5 2QR, England. Address: 149 De Beauvoir Road, London N1 4DL, England.

HUTCHISON D Warner, b. 15 Dec 1930, Denver, Colorado, USA. Composer; French Horn Player; Author; Educator. m. Merilyn Etheridge Hutchison, 27 Jan 1967, 1 son, 1 daughter. Education: Bachelor of Sacred Music, SW Baptist Theological Seminary, Fort Worth, TX, 1954; MMus, 1956, PhD, 1971, University of North TX School of Music; Studies in composition with Samuel Adler, University of North TX, Wayne Barlow and Kent Kennan, Eastman School of Music, Roy Harris, Indiana University. Debut: Premieres at Lincoln Center for Performing Arts, Tully Hall, New York: Hornpiece 1 - Horn and Tape, 1971 (nominated for Pulitzer Prize); Narnian Suite - Chorus, Percussion, Horn, 1977. Career includes: University Lecturer; Professor of Music, Composition and Director of Experimental Music Laboratory, New Mexico State University; Visiting Lecturer, London University (American Institute of Foreign Studies), 1986; Macdowell Colony Fellowships, 1973, 1974. Compositions

include: Numerous including: The Sacrilege of Alan Kent, for Orchestra, Baritone and Tape; Dirge and Hosanna, Fantasy Variations for Band; Narnian Suite, for Chorus, Percussion and Horn; Homage to Jackson Pollock, for Percussion, Tape, Slides, Speaker; Ceremonies Ballet, for Oboe, Interior Piano; Tape; Three Love Songs, for Soprano and Orchestra; Apocalypse I, for Brass Quintet; Tam-Tam Bells; Varied Carols and The Desert Shall Bloom As The Rose, for Orchestra; Mass, 5 movements, for Chorus, Soloists, Wind Ensemble. Recordings: Apocalypse I, Apocalypse V, for Brass Quintet, Poe-Songs for soprano, horn, vibraphone, CD; Numerous publications. Publications: User Manual for Electronic Music, 1973, 1975, 3rd edition 1982; Editor, Proceedings, Journal of American Society of University Composers, 1971-76; Over 50 music scores. Honours: 25 ASCAP Awards, 1972-95; Ernest Bloch Composers Symposium, 1994. Address: 3025 Broadmoor, Las Cruces, NM 88001, USA.

HUTTENLOCHER Philippe, b. 29 Nov 1942, Neuchatel, Switzerland. Singer (Baritone). Education: Studied with Julette Bise in Fribourg. Career: Sang with the Ensemble Vocal de Lausanne and with the Choeurs de la Foundation Gulbenkian, Lisbon; Festival appearances in Montreux, Lausanne, Strasbourg and Ansbach in the Baroque repertory; Tour of Japan 1974; Zurich Opera 1975, as the title role in Monteverdi's Orfeo, produced by the late Jean-Pierre Ponnelle; London Bach Festival, 1978; Guest appearances in Vienna, Berlin, Hamburg, Milan and Edinburgh. Recordings include: Bach Cantatas and operas by Monteverdi including Il Ritorno di Ulisse, (Telefunken); St Matthew Passion (CBS); Le Devin du Village by Rousseau; Die Jahreszeiten by Haden, Bach B Minor Mass (RCA); Les Indes Galantes by Rameau, Cosi fan tutte, Il Maestro di Capella, Pénélope, St John Pasion, Handel Dettingen Te Deum and works by Carissimi, MA Charpentier and Gabrieli (Erato).

HUYBRECHTS Francois, b. 15 June 1946, Antwerp, Belgium. Conductor. Education: Studied Cello and Clarinet at the Antwerp Conservatory; Conducting studies with Daniel Sternefeld, Bruno Maderna and Hans Swarowsky. Deubt: As Cellist, 1960; Conducting, 1963 The Fairy Queen by Purcell, Royal Flemish Opera. Career: Conducted the Netherlands Chamber Opera, 1966-67; Concerts at the Salzburg Mozarteum 1967; Assisted Bernstein at the New York Philharmonic and conducted the Los Angeles Philharmonic and the Berlin Philharmonic; Musical Director of the Wichita Symphony 1972-79, San Antonio Symphony 1979-80; Recordings include: Janacek's Taras Bulba and Lachian Dances (London Philharmonic); Nielsen's 3rd Symphony (LSO/Decca). Honours: Winner, Dimitri Mitropoulos Competition, New York, 1968; Prizewinner, Herbert von Karajan Foundation Competition, 1969. Address: c/o Polygram Classics, PO Box 1420, 1 Sussex Place, Hammersmith, London W6 9XS, England.

HVOROSTOVSKY Dmitri, b. 16 Oct 1962, Krasnoyarsk, Siberia, Russia. Singer (Baritone). Education: Studied at the Krasnoyarsk High School of Arts with Jekatherina Yofel, 1982-86. Career: Soloist with the Krasnoyarsk Opera, 1986-; Appeared on BBC Television as winner of the Cardiff Singer of the World Competition, 1989; Sang songs by Tchaikovsky and Rachmaninov at the Wigmore Hall, Dec 1989; Recitals at New York Alice Tully and at Washington Kennedy Center, Mar 1990; Opera engagements include Yeletsky in The Queen of Spades at Nice 1989 (western operatic debut), Eugene Onegin in Venice, 1991; I Puritani at Covent Garden, 1992; Sang Onegin at the Paris Châtelet, 1992, Germont at the Chicago Lyric Opera, season 1993-94; Promenade Concert debut 1993, Mussorgsky's Songs and Dances of Death; Concert showings in Boston, Paris, Moscow and St Petersburg; Recital of Russian songs at the Barbican Hall, London, 1997. Recordings include: Arias by Tchaikovsky and Verdi with the Rotterdam Philharmonic conducted by Valery Gergiev; Arias from Cavalleria Rusticana, Eugene Onegin and Don Carlos (Philips Classics). Honours: First Prize, USSR National Competition, 1987; Toulouse Singing Competition, 1988; BBC Cardiff Singer of the World Competition, 1989. Address: Philips/Polygram Artists, PO Box 1420, 1 Sussex Place, London W6 9XS, England.

HYDE-SMITH Christopher, b. 11 Mar 1935, Cairo, Egypt. Flautist; Teacher. 1 son, 1 daughter. Education: Eton College, England; Royal College of Music, London. Debut: Royal Festival Hall, 1962. Career: Member, Camden Wind Quintet, London Mozart Players; Many flute and piano and/or harpsichord concerts with Jane Dodd; Appearances in Holland, Switzerland, Italy, France, Germany, Spain, Portugal, Scandinavia, Russia, North and South America; Professor, Royal College of Music; Dedicatee of works by Alwyn, Dodgson, Horovitz, Mathias and Rawsthorne; Judge at Leeds, Mozart and Tunbridge Wells Competitions. Recordings: Numerous recordings. Memberships: Haydn Mozart Society; Chairman, British Flute Society. Current Management: Lotte Nicholls, 16 Upper Wimpole Street, London WC1, England. Address: 94 Dorien Road, London SW20 8EJ, England.

HYKES David (Bond), b. 2 Mar 1953, Taos, New Mexico, USA. Composer. Education: Studied Classical Azerbaijani and

Armenian Music with Zevulon Avshalomov, 1975-77; North Indian Raga Singing with S Dhar from 1982. Career: Founded the Harmonic Choir, 1975; Resident at the Cathedral of St John the Divine, New York from 1979; Tours of the USA and Europe from 1980. Compositions: Harmonic Tissues for electronics, 1971; Shadow Frequencies for piano and electronics, 1975; Looking for Gold/Life in the Sun for children's voices and ensemble, 1975; Well-struck Strings for dulcimer, 1975-83; Special Delivery/Rainbow Voice for low voice, 1975-84; Test Studies for Harmonica Orchestra for ensemble, 1975-85; Hearing Solar Winds for voices, 1977-83; Outside of Being There for voices, 1981; Turkestan for synthesizer, 1979; Current Circulation for voices, 1984; Subject to Change for low voice and drones, 1983; Desert Hymns, 1984. Honours: Grants from the National Endowment for the Arts, 1978, 1983, The Rockefeller Foundation 1980-83, and UNESCO, 1983. Address: c/o ASCAP, ASCAP Building, One Lincoln Plaza, NY 10023, USA.

HYNNINEN Jorma, b. 3 Apr 1941, Leppävirta, Finland. Opera Singer (Baritone). m. Reetta Salo, 6 Aug 1961, 1 son, 1 daughter. Education: Sibelius Academy, Helsinki, 1969. Debut: As Silvio in Pagliacci, Finnish National Opera. 1969. Career: Staatsoper Vienna, 1977; La Scala, Milan, 1977; Paris Opera, 1978; Bavarian State Opera, Munich, 1979; Metropolitan Opera, New York, 1984; San Francisco Opera, 1988; Lyric Opera of Chicago, 1989; Deutsche Oper Berlin, 1991; Lied recitals, New York, London, Europe and Beijing; Soloist with Vienna Symphony, Boston Symphony and Israel Philharmonic; Sang Anfortas in Parsifal at Antwerp, 1996. Recordings: Le nozze di Figaro with Riccardo Muti; Orestes in Elektra with Seiji Ozawa; Brahms's Requiem and Mahler's Eighth with Klaus Tennstedt; Winterreise, Die schöne Müllerin, Dichterliebe; Songs of Sibelius; Die schöne Magelone; Lieder eines Fahrenden Gesellen; Evergreen Love Songs. Honours: Professor of Arts, Finland, 1990. Hobbies: Painting; Cross country skiing; Jogging. Current Management: Allied Artists, London Opera et Concert Paris. Address: Ruskokuja 3 B, 01620 Vantaa, Finland.

HYTNER Nicholas, b. 7 May 1956, Manchester, England. Opera Producer. Education: Trinity Hall, Cambridge, graduated 1977. Debut: Dreigroschenoper at Cambridge. Career: The Turn of the Screw for Kent Opera, 1979; Tippett's King Priam in season 1984-85; Wagner's Rienzi for English National Opera, 1983; Xerxes, 1985; Covent Garden debut 1987, with the British premiere of Sallinen's The King Goes Forth to France; The Knot Garden, 1988; The Magic Flute for English National Opera and Netherlands Opera; Debut with Geneva Opera 1989, Le nozze di Figaro; Glyndebourne debut 1991, La Clemenza di Tito; La Forza del Destino, for ENO, 1992; Staged The Cunning Little Vixen at the Théâtre du Châtelet, Paris, 1996; Film work includes The Crucible, 1997. Recordings include: Videos of Xerxes and King Priam. Address: c/o Lies Askonas Ltd, 6 Henrietta Street, London WC2, England.

I

IANNACCONE Anthony, b. 14 October 1943, New York, USA. Composer; Conductor; Teacher. m. Judith Trostle, 1 son, 1 daughter. Education: BMus, MMus, Manhattan School of Music; PhD, Eastman School of Music. Career: Conducted Orchestras, Choruses, Wind Ensembles and Chamber Groups throughout the USA including: Lincoln Centre, New York; Many University appearances as Guest Conductor and Composer; Teacher, Manhattan School of Music, 1967-68; Composition Professor, 1971, Director of Collegium Musicum, 1973; Record Debut as Conductor of Cornell Wind Ensemble, 1983. Compositions include: Approximately 40 published works, 14 commercially recorded for orchestra, chorus, Wind Ensemble and Chamber Ensembles. Recordings include: Partita, for Piano, 1967; Hades, for Brass Quartet, 1968; Bicinia, for Flute and Alto Saxophone, 1974; Sonatina, for Trumpet and Tuba, 1975; After a Gentle Rain, for Concert Band, 1979; Walt Whitman Song, for Chorus, Soloists and Winds, 1981; No 2 Terpsichore, 1981; Images of Song and Dance, No 1 Orpheus, 1982; Divertimento, for Orchestra, 1983; Two Piano Inventions, 1985; Night Rivers, Symphony No 3, 1992. Address: PO Box 1525, Ypsilanti, MI 48197, USA.

IBBOTT Daphne, b. 29 Apr 1918, London, England. Pianist. m. (1) Rev John Frost (deceased), (2) Wilfred Smith, 2 d. Education: Royal Academy of Music; LRAM; FRAM. Career: Specialist in chamber music and accompaniment in particular in association with violinist Nona Liddell; Conducts master classes for accompanists; Adjudicator. Recordings: Vaughan Williams music with Jean Stewart, Viola; Songs by Elgar, Warlock, Gurney, Britten and Quilter with various artists; Voice of the Violin with Derek Collier; Somervell's Maud and Butterworth's Shropshire Lad with John Carol Case; Spanish Dances by Sarasate and Wieniawski with Campoli. Address: 8 Riverview Gardens, Barnes, London, SW13, England.

IDANE Yasuhiko, b. 1962, Japan. Singer (Tenor). Career: Frequent appearances in the Far East and Europe, in operas by Puccini (Il Tabarro), Leoncavallo (La Bohème) and Mascagni (Cavalleria Rusticana); Also songs by Japanese composers, including Kobayashi; Contestant at the 1995 Cardiff Singer of the World Competition. Address: 6-23-3 Akatsuka, Itabashi-ku, Tokyo, Japan.

IHLE Andrea, b. 17 Apr 1953, Dresden, Germany. Singer (Soprano). Education: Studied at Musikhochschule Dresden. Debut: Dresden Staatsoper, 1976, as Giannetta in L'Elisir d'Amore. Career: Appearances in Dresden have included Aennchen and Marianne, in the productions of Freischütz and Rosenkavalier which opened the rebuilt Semperoper, 1985; Other roles in Dresden and elsewhere in Germany, have included Mozart's Papagena and Despina, Euridice, Gretel, Sophie (Der Rosenkavalier), Carolina (Il Matrimonio Segreto) and Marie in La Fille du Regiment; Concert and oratorio engagements. Recordings: Freischütz and Rosenkavalier; Bach's Christmas Oratorio; Missa Brevis by Carl Friedrich Fasch. Address: Semper Oper Dresden, 8012 Dresden, Germany.

IHLOFF Jutta-Renate, b. 1 Nov 1944, Winteberg, Germany. Singer, Soprano. Education: Studied with Marja Stein in Hamburg and with Giorgio Favaretto in Rome and Siena. Debut: Staatsoper Hamburg 1973, as Zerlina in Don Giovanni. Career: Has sung in Munich, Berlin, Vienna and Salzburg; Frequent guest appearances elsewhere in Europe; Other roles include Mozart's Despina, Susanna, Blondchen and Pamina; Marzelline in Fidelio; Monteverdi's Poppea; Sophie and Zdenka; Mimi; Marie in Die Soldaten by Zimmermann; Adele, Die Fledermaus; Nannetta, Falstaff. Recordings: Serpetta in La Finta Giardiniera by Mozart.

IKAIA-PURDY Keith, b. 1956, Hawaii, USA. Singer (Tenor). Education: Studied with Tito Gobbi, and with Carlo Bergonzi in Busetto. Career: Sang in opera throughout the USA from 1983, notably as Turiddu, the Duke of Mantua, Riccardo (Ballo in maschera), Cavaradossi, and Don José; Florestan in the original version of Fidelio at Berkeley, 1987; European debut at Bussetto, 1988, as Corado in Il Corsaro; Guested at Wiesbaden, 1989, as Alfredo, returning as Tebalo in Bellini's Capuleti; Vienna Staatsoper, 1993, Alfredo; Concert repertory includes Schubert's Die schöne Müllerin. Address: c/o Staatsoper, Opernring 2, A-1010 Vienna, Austria.

IKEDA Kikuei, b. 31 Aug 1947, Yokosuka, Japan. Violinist. Studied at the Juilliard School with Dorothy DeLay and members of the Juilliard Quartet. Career: Second violin, Tokyo Quartet from 1974; Regular concerts in the USA and abroad; First cycle of the complete quartets of Beethoven at the Yale at Norfolk Chamber Music Festival, 1986; Repeated cycles at the 92nd Street Y NY, Ravinia and Israel Festivals, Yale, Princeton Universitites; Season 1990-91 at Alice Tully Hall, the Metropolitan Museum of Art, New York, Boston, Washington DC, Los Angeles, Cleveland,

Detroit, Chicago, Miami, Seattle, San Francisco, Toronto; Tour of South America, two tours of Europe including Paris, Amsterdam, Bonn, Milan, Munich, Dublin, London, Berlin; Quartet-in-residence at Yale University and at the University of Cincinnati College-Conservatory of Music. Recordings: Schubert's Major Quartets; Mozart Flute Quartets with James Galway and Clarinet Quintet with Richard Stolzman; Quartets by Bartok, Brahms, Debussy, Haydn, Mozart and Ravel; Beethoven Middle Period Quartets. Honours: Grand Prix du Disque du Montreux; Best Chamber Music Recording of the Year from Stereo Review and the Gramophone; Four Grammy nominations. Address: Intermusica Artists' Management, 16 Duncan Terrace, London N1 8BZ, England.

IKONOMOU Katharina, b. 1957, Tashkent, Usbekistan, Russia. Singer (Soprano). Education: Studied in Tashkent and at the Cologne Musikhochschule with Joseph Metternich. Debut: Wurzburg, 1984, as Salome. Career: After further study in Italy sang Salome at Zurich, 1986, and Jenufa at the 1988 Spoleto Festival (Chrysothemis, 1990); Sang Beethoven's Leonore at Trieste, 1990, and Fevronia in Rimsky's Invisible City of Kitezh (Florence, 1990); Rome, 1991, as Ariadne, Amelia in Ballo in maschera at Genoa and Wagner's Senta at Catania, 1992. Recordings include: Songs by Russian composers. Address: c/o Theater Massimo Bellini, Via Perrotta 12, 95131 Catania. Italy.

ILLES Eva, b. 1939, Hungary. Singer (Soprano). Education: Studied in Hungary. Career: Sang at the Regensburg Opera, 1967-69, Freiburg, 1969-71, Zurich, 1971-75, and Hanover, 1974-81; Guested at Covent Garden as Senta, 1972, at Barcelona and the Vienna Staatsoper; Other roles included Wagner's Elsa and Elisabeth, Ariadne, Amelia Grimaldi, Maddalena (Andrea Chenier), the Forza Leonora, and Turandot. Address: c/o Staatstheater Hanover, Opernhaus, Opernplatz 1, W-3000 Hanover 1, Germany.

ILOSVALVY Robert, b. 18 June 1927, Hodmezovasarhely, Hungary. Singer, Tenor. Education: Studied with Andor Lendvai at the Budapest Academy. Career: Soloist with the Artistic Ensemble of the People's Army from 1949; Budapest Opera from 1954, debut in the title role of Erkel's Hunyadi Laszlo; Sang widely in eastern Europe; San Francisco Opera 1964-68, New York Metropolitan Opera 1966; Member of Cologne Opera from 1966; Covent Garden, 1968, as Des grieux in Manon Lescaut; Concerts with the Berlin Philharmonic and the Orchestra of the Accademia di Santa Cecilia; Career has centred on the Budapest Opera from 1981; Theatre de la Monnaie Brussels 1985, as Walther in Die Meistersinger; Sang Walther von Stolzing at the 1986 Maggio Musicale, Florence; Other roles include Rodolfo, Tamino, Dick Johnson, Don Jose, Alfredo, Manrico and the Duke of Mantua. Recordings: Madama Butterfly and Manon Lescaut, Hungaroton; Roberto Devereux, with Beverly Sills; Requiem by Dvorak, conducted by Kertesz. Address: c/o Hungarian State Opera House, Nepoztarsasag utja 22, 1061 Budapest, Hungary.

IMAI Nobuko, b. 18 March 1943, Tokyo, Japan. Violist. m. Aart von Bochove, 1981, 1 son, 1 daughter. Education: Toho School of Music, Tokyo; Yale University; Juilliard School of Music, New York. Career: Member of Vermeer Quartet, 1974-79; Soloist with the London Symphony Orchestra, Royal Philharmonic, Chicago Symphony, Concertgebouw Orchestra, Montreal Symphony, Boston Symphony, Vienna Symphony, Stockholm Philharmonic; Festivals include: Marlboro, Casals, South Bank Summer Music, Bath, Cheltenham, Aldeburgh, London Promenade Concerts, International Viola Congress, Houston. Recordings: Tippett Triple Concerto and Berlioz Harold in Italy with the London Symphony Orchestra conducted by Colin Davis; Mozart, Haydn Duos with Mark Lubotsky (Philips); Brahms Sonatas, Schumann Märchenbilder; Schubert Arpeggione, Beethoven Notturno Op 42 with Roger Vignoles (Chandos); Shostakovich Sonata, Glinka Sonata, Schnittke Viola Concerto and Mozart Quintets with the Orlando Quartet (BIS); Mozart Sinfonia Concertante with Iona Brown; Hindemith Sonatas for solo viola, Denisov Concertos (BIS); Walton Concerto, Franck and Vieuxtemps Sonatas (Chandos). Honours: 1st Prize, Munich International Viola Competition; 1st Prize, Geneva International Viola Competition. Hobbies: Golf; Cooking. Address: Terry Harrison Management, The Orchard, Market Street, Charlbury, Oxfordshire OX7 3PJ, England.

IMBRIE Andrew W, b. 6 Apr 1921, New York, USA. Composer; Professor. m. Barbara Cushing, 31 Jan 1953, 2 sons, 1 deceased. Education: Studied Piano with Leo Ornstein and Robert Casadesus; Composition with Roger Sessions. Career: Professor, University of California, Berkeley, 1949-91; Vising Professor at various universities and institutions. Compositions include: Orchestral: Violin Concerto, 1954; Three Symphonies, 1965, 1970; Cello Concerto, 1972; 3 Piano Concertos, 1973, 1974, 1992; Flute Concerto, 1977; Chamber: 5 String Quartets, 1942-87; 2 Piano Trios, 1946, 1989; Impromptu, for violin and pianoforte, 1960; To A Traveller for Clarinet, Violin and Piano, 1971; Pilgrimage for Flute, Clarinet, Violin, Cello, Piano and Percussion, 1983; Dream Sequence for Flute, Oboe, Clarinet,

Violin, Viola, Cello, Piano and Percussion, 1986; Spring Fever, for flute, oboe, clarinet, 2 violins, viola, violoncello, pianoforte, percussion, 1996; Vocal: Opera, Angle of Repose, (Stegner-Hall), 1975, commissioned by San Francisco Opera; Requiem for Soprano, Chorus and Orchestra, 1984; Adam, cantata for Mixed Chorus, Soprano Solo, Chamber Orchestra, 1994. Recordings: Pilgrimage; Collage Ensemble, Gunther Schuller; Trio No 2, Francesco Trio; Quartet No 4, Emerson Quartet; Quartets No 4 and No 5, Pro Arte Quartet; Impromptu for violin and pianoforte; Parnassus Ensemble: Dream Sequence, Five Roethke Songs, Three Piece Suite, Campion Songs, To a Traveller, Symphony No 3, London Symphony; Serenade; Piano Sonata. Publication: Extra Measures and Metrical Ambiguity in Beethoven, 1973. Honours: Guggenheim Fellowship, 1953-54, 1959-60; Naumberg Award, 1960; Holder, Jerry and Evelyn Hemmings Chambers Chair in Music, University of California, Berkeley, 1989-91; Various grants and commissions. Memberships: American Academy of Arts and Letters; American Academy of Arts and Sciences; Phi Beta Kappa. Address: 2625 Rose Street, Berkeley, CA 94708, USA.

IMDAHL Heinz, b. 9 Aug 1924, Dusseldorf, Germany. Singer, Baritone. Education: Studied with Berthold Putz in Krefeld and at the Cologne Musikhochschule. Debut: Detmold 1948, as Morales in Carmen. Career: Sang in Bremen, Berlin and Dusseldorf, the became a member of the Bayerische Staatsoper Munich; Guest appearances in Florence 1953, Rio de Janeiro, Turin 1972 and Oslo 1973; Repertoire included leading roles in operas by Wagner, Verdi, Strauss and Verdi. Recordings: Das Liebesverbot by Wagner.

IMRIE Martyn, b. 4 Mar 1947, Bangor, County Down, Northern Ireland. Music Publisher. m. 1976, divorced, 1 s, 1 d. Education: BA Honours, Queen's University, Belfast, 1969; BA Honours, Music, Bristol University, 1977. Career: Co-founder with Bruno Turner of Mapa Mundi series of Renaissance Performing Scores; Editor of numerous editions published and unpublished of Renaissance Church Music, principally late 15th and early 16th century Spanish, including editions of Guerrero, Penalosa, La Rue's Requiem, Morales, Wert and others; Publisher of 20th century music by Bourgeois, Victory, Moody, Beaumont, Butterworth, Painter and Ward, as Founder of Vanderbeek and Imrie Ltd. Recordings: Editions recorded by Westminster Choir, Pro Cantione Antiqua and Hilliard Ensemble. Publications: Major contributor to Mapa Mundi series of Renaissance Performing Scores, including 20 works by Guerrero, also 17 complete motets for 4 and 5 voices by Penalosa, 1990. Hobbies: Sailing; Golf; Cycling; Running; Reading (astronomy, biology, palaeontology). Address: 15 Marvig, Lochs, Isle of Lewis, Scotland, HS2 9QP.

INBAL Eliahu, b. 16 Feb 1936, Jerusalem. Conductor. m. Helga Fritzsche, 19 July 1968, 2 sons, 1 daughter. Education: Diploma in Violin & Music Theory, Academy of Music, Jerusalem, 1956; Study of Conducting, Conservatoire National Superieur, Paris, 1960-62; Courses with Franco Ferrara, Hilversum. Career: Opera debut at the Verona Arena 1969, Don Carlos; Chief Conductor, Frankfurt Radio Symphony Orchestra, 1974-90; Guest Conductor of major orchestras in Milan, Rome, Florence, Venice, Berlin, Munich, Hamburg, Vienna, London, Paris, Tel-Aviv, New York, Chicago and Tokyo; Appearances at festivals in Salzburg, Lucerne, Berlin, Holland; Chief Conductor, Teatro La Fenice, 1984-; Maria di Rudenz at Venice, 1981; Conducted La Forza del Destino at Zurich, 1992; Principal Conductor of the Orchestra Nazionale d'Italia from 1996; Cycle of Mahler Symphonies with the Tokyo Metropolitan Orchestra by 1998. Recordings: Schumann; Complete works for Orchestra with NPO, London; Debussy's, La Mer and Trois Nocturnes with Concertgebouw, Amsterdam; Chopin, Complete works for Piano and Orchestra, with Arrau, LPO; Scriabin complete works for orchestra with RSO, Frankfurt; Donizetti, Maria di Rudenz with La Fenice Venice; Bruckner, Symphonies Nos 3, 4 and 8 in their first edition, with RSO Frankfurt; Puccini, Messa da Gloria with RSO, Frankfurt; Gustav Mahler, all Symphonies which received the German critic prize, 1988; Bruckner all symphonies. Honours: 1st Prize, Guido Cantelli International Competition for Conductors, Novara, Italy, 1963; Premio Decennale, Palermo, 1975; Israel Prize for Interpretation, 1980. Current Management: Harold Holt Ltd, 31 Sinclair Road, London, W14 ONS, England. Hobbies: Hi-Fi; Photography. Address: 3 Av Gounod, 78290 Croissu sur Seine, France.

INCIHARA Taro, b. 2 Jan 1950, Yamagata, Japan. Singer, Tenor. Education: Studied in Japan and at the Juilliard School, New York. Debut: Tokyo, 1980, as Gounod's Faust. Career: European debut, 1982, as Calaf at the Teatro San Carlo, Naples; Paris Oper from 1983 as Macduff, Riccardo, Don Carlos and the Duke of Mantua; Guest appearances at Nice, Turin, Naples, Santiago and Buenos Aires, Verdi's Requiem, 1987; Macerata Festival, 1987, Orange, 1989, as Isamale in Nabucco; Metropolitan Opera, 1987-89, as the Italian Singer and the Duke of Mantua; Further European engagements at Turin and Genoa; Sang Riccardo in Un Ballo in Maschera for Opera Pacific at Costa California, 1991; Other roles include Gabriele Adorno, La Scala, 1989; Verdi's Rodolfo and Alfredo, Enzo in La Gioconda and

Edgardo in Lucia di Lammermoor. Address: c/o Opera Pacific, 3187 Red Hill Avenue, Suite 230, Costa Mesa, CA 92626, USA.

INGLE William, b. 17 Dec 1934, Texhoma, Texas, USA. Singer, Tenor. Education: Studied at the Academy of Vocal Arts in Philadelphia with Dorothy di Scala; With Sidney Dietsch in New York and Luigi Ricci in Rome. Debut: Flensburg 1965, as Tamino. Career: Sang at the Linz Opera, Dusseldorf, Kassel, Frankfurt, Graz, Leipzig, Montreal, Hanover, Wellington and Vienna; Other roles include Ernesto, Don Ottavio, Manrico, Lohengrin, Parsifal, Walther, Canio, Erik, Radames, Ferrando, Rodolfo, Almaviva, Flamand in Capriccio, the Duke of Mantua and Alfredo; Sang at Linz, 1976, in the premiere of Der Aufstand by Nikolaus Eder; Masaniello in La Muette de Portici by Auber, 1989; TV appearances as Herod, (Salome), in Canada and Tom Rakewell, (The Rake's Progress), in Austria.

INGOLFSSON Atli, b. 21 Aug 1962, Keflavik, Iceland. Composer. m. Thuridur Jonsdottir, 18 Aug 1990. Education: Diploma in Classical Guitar, 1983, BM, Theory and Composition, 1984, Reykjavik School of Music; BA, Philosophy, University of Iceland, 1986; Study with D Anzaghi, Milan Conservatory, 1985-88; Private study with G Grisey and Auditor at CNSMP, Paris, 1988-90. Career: Performances at Young Nordic music festivals, other Nordic music festivals and various occasions in Iceland, 1981-; His Due Bagattelle for Clarinet premiered in Milan, 1986 and widely performed; Various performances in Europe, 1990-, including Montreuil, May 1991, Varese, July 1991; Amsterdam, Sept 1991, Milan, Nov and Dec 1991; Commissioned by IRCAM, Paris to write for computer piano and ensemble, 1993. Compositions: Recorded on CD, ITM6-03 ITM Reykjavik; Due Bagettelle for Clarinet; CD ENMD 03 Paris: Et Toi Pale Soleil, for 4 voices and instruments; A Verso for piano, and O Versa for piano and 12 instruments, OPNA for bassclarinet and marimba; Le Pas Les Pentes for 8 instruments. Address: Borgarvegur 28, 260 Njardvik, Iceland.

INGRAM Jaime (Ricardo Jean), b. 13 Feb 1928, Panama City, Panama. Concert Pianist; Diplomat. m. Nelly Hirsch, 29 Jan 1950, 2 sons, 1 daughter. Education: Piano Diploma, Juilliard Institute of Music, New York, USA, 1949, studied with Olga Samarof and Joseph Bloch; Piano Diploma, Conservatoire Nationale de Paris, France, 1950, studied with Yves Nat; Additional studies with Alberto Sciarretti, Panama, and Bruno Seidlhofer, Vienna. Career: Professor of Piano, National Conservatory of Music, Panama, 1952-56; Escuela Paulista de Musica, Sao Paulo, Brazil, 1958-60; Escuela Profesional, Panama, 1962-64, Conservatorio Jaime Ingram, 1964-69, University of Panama, 1972-74; Director of Culture, 1969-73; General Director of Culture, 1974-78, Panamanian Ambassador to Spain, 1978-82; Panamanian Ambassador to the Holy Sea, 1982-; Concert tours as soloist and piano duo with Nelly Hirsch; South and Central America, Cuba, Spain, Italy, Federal Republic of Germany; Bulgaria, Poland, Zurich and Geneva, switzerland, London, England, Amsterdam, Netherlands, USSR, Israel. Publications: Hector Villa Lobas; Muzio Clementi, the Father of the Pianoforte, Antonio de Cabezon, Tientos y Diferencias; Orientacion Musical 1974, Historia, Compositores y Repertorio del Piano 1978. Hobbies: Chess; Philately; Books; Painting.

INOUE Michiyoshi, b. 23 December 1946, Tokyo, Japan. Conductor. Education: Studies, Toho Gakuen Academy of Music with Professor Saitoh. Career: Associate Conductor of the Tokyo Metropolitan Symphony Orchestra, 1970; Conducted at La Scala, 1971; Conducted Orchestras in Paris, Vienna, Geneva, Berlin, Brussels, Hamburg, Munich, Stuttgart, Madrid, Naples, Turin, Florence, Lisbon, London, Helsinki, Leipzig, Copenhagen; Tours of Israel, Eastern Europe, Russia; Conducted the East Berlin Orchestra on tour to Japan; Concerts in Australia, New Zealand and with the Washington National Symphony in the USA; Conducted Opera in Vienna and at Cluj, Rumania; Music Director, New Japan Philharmonic Orchestra, 1983-88; Music Director of the Kyoto Symphony Orchestra, 1990. Recordings include: Mahler's 6th, 5th and 4th Symphonies with the Royal Philharmonic; Albums with the Netherlands Chamber Orchestra (Nippon Columbia). Honours include: First Prize, Guido Cantelli Competition, Milan, 1971. Address: c/o Terry Harrison Artists Management, The Orchard, Market Street, Charlbury, Oxon OX7 3PJ, England.

INWOOD Mary (Ruth Brink), b. 27 July 1928, Boston, MA, USA. Composer. m. (1) The Rev Charles P Berger, 18 June 1946, deceased 1955, (2) The Rev Jay M Inwood, May 1957, divorced 1968. Education: Yale School of Music, 1946-48; BA, Music, Piano, magna cum laude, 1975, MA, Composition, 1979, Queen's College; PhD composition, with Leo Kraft and Hugo Weisgall, New York University, 1997. Career: Performances of own music at Brooklyn Academy of Music, Queens College, Brooklyn College, The Graduate School and University Center; Performances at New York University and Merkin Hall, NY, South America, Asia and various churches in the Brooklyn Heights area; Ensemble Librarian at Brooklyn College for several years; Teacher, The Roosa School of Music, 1980-86; Currently Teacher in Composition Program, NYU Sehnap, Department of Music and Music Profession, NY; Theory and Composition Faculty Member, NYU. Compositions include: 3 Movements for Brass Sextet; String Quartet No 3; Suite for Clarinet Bb and Bassoon; Verses from the Song of Songs for Flute and Soprano; Cheerful and Tender Songs; Brass Quintet No 2 recently performed at Weill Hall, NY (Carnegie Recital Hall); Parody for Flute Quartet, 1994; Summer Music, 7 short organ preludes, 1994; String Quartet No IV, 1997, all published. Recordings: Sonata for Trumpet and Piano on New Sounds From the Village; Songs recorded in China by Hong-Yo Chen. Publications: Editor, Sinfonia turchesca in C Major by Franz Xavier Süssmayr in volume XIV of The Symphony 1720-1840. Memberships: ASCAP; New York Women Composers. Address: 166 Congress Street, Brooklyn, NY 11201, USA.

IOACHIMESCU Calin, b. 29 Mar 1949, Bucharest, Romania. Composer. m. Anca Vartolomei-Ioachimescu, 1 s, 1 d. Education: Graduate, Bucharest Music College, 1968; Graduate, 1st Place, Bucharest High School, Academy of Music, Composition with Stefan Niculescu, 1975; Computer music courses, IRCAM, Paris, 1985; International New Music Holiday Courses, Darmstadt, 1980, 1984. Debut: In concert, Bucharest Radio Symphonic Orchestra, 1978. Career includes: Symphonic, chamber and electronic works played throughout Romania and 7 other countries; Compositions broadcast: Bucharest, France and Brussels; Sound Engineer, Romanian Broadcasting; Head, Computer Music Studio, Bucharest. Compositions include: Magic Spell for Female Voices, Strings and Percussion, 1974; String Quartet No 1, 1974; Tempo 80, 1979; Oratorio II, 1981; Hierophonies, 1984; String Quartet No 2, 1984; Spectral Music for Saxophones and Tape, 1985; Concerto for Trombone, Double Bass and Orchestra, 1986; Celliphonia for Cello and Tape, 1988; Palindrom 7, 1992; Concerto for Saxophones and Orchestra, Ministry of Culture, France, 1994; Les Eclats de l'Abîme for Double Bass, Saxaphone and Tape, Radio France, 1995; Film music. Recordings: Various labels. Publications: Oratorio II, Paris; Bucharest: Tempo 80; String Quartet No 2; Celliphonia. Honours: Prize, Romanian Composers Union, 1974, 1979, 1982, 1988, 1992; Kranich Steiner Musik Award, Internationales Musikinstitut, Darmstadt, 1984; Prize, Romanian Academy, 1993. Memberships: Romanian Composers and Musicologists Union; SACEM, France. Address: Str Ardeleni 28, Sect 2, 72164-Bucharest, Romania.

IONESCO-VOVU Constantin, b. 27 May 1932, Floresti, Romania. Pianist; Professor. m. Margareta Gabriel, 7 September 1961, deceased 1983. Education: Bucharest Superior Music Conservatory Hochschule, (University of Music), 1955. Career: Concerts as Soloist with Symphony Orchestras, Piano Recitals and Chamber Music in Romania, France, Germany, Poland, Russia, Sweden, Denmark, Netherlands, Hungary, Czechoslovakia, Switzerland, Austria, Portugal, USA, Warsaw Autumn Festival, Evian Festival; Professor, (concert class, piano) Head of Piano Section, University of Music, Bucharest; Masterclasses, Member of International Juries for Piano Competitions in Romania, Europe, France, Germany, Italy, Portugal. Recordings: Radio Recordings and discs in Romania, Germany, the Netherlands, Austria. Publications: Editor, Romanian Piano Music, C Silvestri Piano Works, 1st Volume 1973, II Volume, 1979. Contributions to: Music Critics And Studies about Technique and Aesthetics of Pianistic Interpretation in several Romanian Reviews. Memberships: European Piano Teachers Association (EPTA). Hobbies: Books; Mountains; Nature; Travel. Address: Str Vasile Lascar 35, 70211 Bucharest, Romania.

IRANYI Gabriel, b. 6 June 1946, Cluj, Romania. Composer; Pianist; Lecturer. m. Elena Nistor, 20 Aug 1969, 1 son. Education: Special School of Music, Cluj, 1955-65; George Dima High School of Music, Cluj, Composition and Musicology Department, Student of Prof D Sigismund Todutza. Career: Teaching Assistant, George Enesco High School of Music, Jassy, Romania, 1971-76; Lecturer, Clar Saba Conservatoire, 1982-86; Since 1988 Professor of the Leo - Borchara - Musikschule in Berlin. Composition: Segments, De Profundis; Bird of Wonder; Until the Day Breaks; Portraits of JS Bach; For solo piano; Laudae for 2 pianos; Song of Degrees for Chamber Ensemble; Altermances for percussion; Alef for soprano voice, clarinet, cello and piano; Realm for solo cello and electric amplification; Solstice for violin, cello and clarinet; Electric Amplication; Shir Hamaalot for organ; Tempora for string quartet, Meditation and Prayer, for violin and 15 strings; Laudae, for 2 pianos, or with chamber orchestra. Hobbies: Chess; Swimming; Excursions. Address: Gierkeplatz 10, Berlin 10585, Germany.

IRELAND (William) Patrick, b. 20 Nov 1923, Helston, Cornwall, England. Viola Player. m. Peggy Gray, 4 children. Education: Wellington College; Worcester College, Oxford; ARCM; MMus, Honoris Causa, Hull University. Career: Viola, Allegri String Quartet, 1953-77, 1988-; Has taken part in the premieres of quartets by Martin Dalby, 1972, Nicola LeFanu, Peter Sculthorpe, Elizabeth Maconchy; Robert Sherlaw-Johnson and Sebastian Forbes; Two Clarinet Quintets by Jennifer Fowler and Nicola LeFanu, 1971; 4 Quartets by Barry Guy, Jonathan Harvey, Alison Bauld, Edward Cowie, 1973; Complete Beethoven Quartets at the 1974 Cheltenham Festival. Recordings: With Allegri String Quartet; Bach Brandenburg Concertos with Menuhin and Bath Festival Orchestra; 2 CDs with Lindsay Quartet, as 2nd viola: Dvorak and Mozart Quintets. Honour: Doctor of Music, honoris causa, Southampton University. Hobbies: Bird Watching; Antique Clocks and Musical Boxes; Carpentry. Address: Hillgrove House, Dunkerton, Bath, Avon BA2 8AS, England.

IRMAN Regina, b. 22 March 1957, Winterthur, Switzerland. Composer. Education: Studied guitar and percussion at Winterthur Conservatory Compositions include: In Darkness Let me Dwell for mezzo and ensemble, 1982; Speclum for 4 clarinets and 2 percussion, 1984; Zahlen for prepared piano, 1986; Passacaglia for clarinet 1990; Requiem for unaccompanied chorus, 1992. Address: c/o SUISA, Bellariastrasse 82, 8038 Zurich, Switzerland.

IROSCH Mirjana, b. 24 Oct 1939, Zagreb, Yugoslavia. Singer, (Soprano). Education: Studied at the Zagreb Conservatory with Fritz Lunzer. Debut: Linz 1962, as Mercedes in Carmen. Career: Sang for many years at the Vienna Volksoper: Took part in the 1968 premiere of the revised version of Der Zerrissene by Von Einem; Tour of Japan 1982; Guest appearances in Graz, Frankfurt, Basle, Brussels and Munich; Other roles include Micaela, Marenka in The Bartered Bride, Fiordiligi, Donna Elvira, Judith in Duke Bluebeard's Castle, Concepcion in L'Heure Espagnole, Rosina and Rosalinde. Recordings: Die Lustige Witwe. Address: Volksoper, Wahringerstrasse 78, A-1090 Vienna, Austria.

IRVINE Robert, b. 11 May 1963, Glasgow, Scotland. Cellist. Education: Royal College of Music, London; Studied with Christopher Bunting, Amaryllis Fleming. Career: Member, Brindisi String Quartet, 1984-; Philharmonia Orchestra, 1986-; Appeared on Channel 4 TV, and BBC TV and Radio; Principal Cello, London Soloists Chamber Orchestra, Britten-Pears Orchestra, 1985-86. Recordings: Britten 2nd Quartet; Berg Op 3 Quartet, Merlin Records. Honours: Foundation Scholar, Royal College of Music; Ivor James Cello Prize; Stern Award for Diploma Recital; Dip.RCM; ARCM. Memberships: Musicians Union. Hobbies: Fly Fishing; Hang-Gliding; Cooking; Travel; Eating Out; Wine Connoisseur. Address: 8 Berwyn Road, London SE24 9BD, England.

IRVING David (Gerow), b. 23 May 1935, Kankakee, Illinois, USA. Composer; Conductor; French Horn Player. Education: BA, MA, Columbia University; New England Conservatory of Music; Vienna Academy of Music, Austria. Career: Director and Founder of Phoenix, a New York City new music organization; Compositions performed in Europe and USA including Concerts at Caecelia Society, Columbia Composers and Composers Concordance; The Witch, an opera in one act premiered by the Concert Society of Putnam and Northern Westchester, New York; Featured Guest at Museum of the American Piano in New York for series Contemporary Trends in Piano Music. Contributions to: The Horn Call, Journal of the International Horn Society, Fresno, California, 1978. Honours: Magna cum laude, Columbia University. Memberships: Phi Beta Kappa. Address: 100 W 67th Street, Apt 5NW, New York, NY 10023, USA.

IRWIN Jane, b. 1968, England. Singer (Mezzo-soprano). Education: Lancaster University and Royal Northern College of Music. Career: Early appearances in Mahler's 3rd Symphony, under Kent Nagano, and Des Knaben Wunderhorn; Tchaikovsky's Maid of Orleans at the RNCM, 1994; Recitals at the Paris Châtelet, Bienne, Poland, Japan and Geneva; Elgar's Sea Pictures in Scotland, Beethoven's Ninth and Missa Solemnis at the Edinburgh Festival, 1996-97; Rossini's Stabat Mater under Semyon Bychkov, Penderecki's Te Deum with the composer and The Dream of Gerontius conducted by David Willcocks; Covent Garden 1995-96, in Götterdämmerung and Die Walküre; Season 1997 in Die Zauberflöte and Ariadne auf Naxos at Aux, concert tour with the English Concert to Italy and Vienna and Hallé Orchestre concert. Honours incude: Decca Kathleen Ferrier Prize, 1991; Frederic Cox Award, 1992; Winner, 1993 Singers' Competition at the Geneva International Competition; Richard Tauber Prize, 1995. Address: Ingpen & Williams Ltd, 14 Kensington Court, London W8 5DN, England.

ISAACS Jeremy, b. 28 Sept 1932, Glasgow, Scotland, England. General Director. m. 1. Tamara Weinreich, 1958, dec 1986, 2. Gillian Widdicombe, 1988. Education: Glasgow Academy; MA, Merton College, Oxford. Career: Television Producer, Granada TV, 1958; BBC TV, Panorama, 1965; Controller of Features, Thames Television, 1968-74; Director of Programmes 1974-78; Chief Executive, Channel Four TV Company 1981-87; Member, Board of Directors, Royal Opera House Covent Garden, 1985-97, General Director, 1988-97. Publication: Storm over Four: A Personal Account, 1989. Honours: Desmond David Award for outstanding creative contribution to television, 1972; Cyril Bennett Award for outstanding contribution to television programming, RTS, 1982; Lord Willis Award for Distinguished Services to Television, 1985; Lifetime Achievement Award, Banff, 1988; Commandeur de l'Ordre des Arts et des Lettres, France, 1988. Hobbies: Reading; Walking. Address: Royal Opera House, 45 Floral Street, London WC2E 9DD, England.

ISAACS Mark, b. 22 June 1958, London, England (Australian Citizen). Composer; Pianist. Education: BMus, University of Sydney, 1976; MMus, Eastman School of Music, 1986; Study with Peter Sculthorpe, Josef Tal and Samuel Adler, among others. Career: Freelance composer and pianist; Member of Mark Isaacs Jazz Trio; Commissions from Musica Viva, Australia Ensemble, Sydney String Quartet and Seymour Group, among others; Conductor and producer of various theatrical projects. Compositions include: Moving Pictures for piano and orchestra, 1982; Four Lyric Pieces, for string trio, 1982; Diversion for Six Players, 1983; So It Does, for six instruments, 1985; Ballade for Orchestra, 1985; Memoirs, for vibraphone, marimba, percussion and piano, 1986; Elegy, for cello and piano, 1987; Burlesque Miniatures for string quartet, 1988; Debekuth for violin and orchestra, 1988; Piece for Flute and Strings, 1988; Variations, for flute, clarinet and cello, 1989; Beach Dreaming, music theatre in 1 act, 1990; Songs of the Universal, for clarinet, viola, cello and piano, 1994. Address: c/o APRA, 1A Eden Street, Crows Nest, NSW 2065, Australia.

ISAKOVIC Smiljka, b. 23 Mar 1953, Belgrade, Yugoslavia. Harpsichordist; Pianist. Education: Music secondary school, with honours, Belgrade 1965-69; American Community Schools, Athens, National Honour Society, 1969-71; Graduated, Belgrade Music Academy, 1974; Master's degree, Faculty of Music, Belgrade, 1979; Postgraduate piano studies, Tchaikovsky Conservatory, Moscow, USSR, 1978-79; Graduate, harpsichord, Royal Conservatory of Music, Madrid, Spain, 1984. Debut: Belgrade, 1972. Career: Performances throughout the former Yugoslavia, including festivals at Dubrovnik, Ljubljana, Ohrid, Belgrade, East and West Europe, UK, USSR, USA, Cuba, Columbia; Master classes, harpsichord, international Centre des Jeunesses Musicales, Groznjan, Yugoslavia; Lectures, harpsichord; Music reviews, Evening News and Student newspapers, and Radio Belgrade. Recordings: LP records and CD; Radio and TV appearances, Yugoslavia, Spain, Columbia. Honours: First Lady of the Harpsichord; Masaryk's Prize, artistic activities, Masaryk Academy of Arts, Prague, 1997. Memberships: President, Association of Serbian Musicians. Hobbies: Music. Current Management: Direccion artisitca Daniel, Los Madrazo, 16, 28014 Madrid, Spain. Address: Admirala Geprata 10, 11000 Belgrade, Serbia.

ISEPP Martin (Johannes Sebastian), b. 30 Sept 1930, Vienna, Austria. Pianist; Harpsichordist; Conductor. m. Rose Henrietta Harris, 1966, 2 sons. Education: Lincoln College, Oxford; Education: Private study with Professor Leonie Gombrich, Oxford; Associate, Royal College of Music, London. Career: English Opera Group, 1950s; Music Staff, 1957, Chief Coach, 1973, Head of Music Staff, Glyndebourne Festival Opera, 1978-93; Head of Opera Training, Juilliard School of Music, New York City, USA, 1973-77; Head of Music Studies, National Opera Studio, London, 1978-95; Head of Academy of Singing, Banff Centre School of Fine Arts, Banff, Alberta, Canada, 1981-93; Accompanist to leading singers including: Ilse Wolf, Janet Baker, John Shirley-Quirk, Elisabeth Schwarzkopf, Elisabeth Söderström, Jessye Norman, Anne Howells, Sheila Armstrong and Hugues Cuenod; As Conductor: Le nozze di Figaro, 1984; Don Giovanni, 1986; Glyndebourne Touring Company, Entführung, Washington Opera, 1986-87 season; Music Director for The Actor in Opera courses at William Walton Foundation on Ischia, 1992-; Various Opera productions at Fondation, Royaumont, Centre de la Voix, annually, 1998-. Recordings: As accompanist and continuo player for various record labels. Honours: Carroll Donner Stuchell Medal for Accompanying, Harriet Cohen International Musical Foundation, 1965. Hobbies: Swimming; Walking; Photography. Address: 37A Steeles Road, London NW3 4RG, England.

ISHII Kan, b. 30 Mar 1921, Tokyo, Japan. Composer. Education: Studied at the Mmasashino School of Music, 1939-43 and with Carl Orff in Munich, 1952-54. Career: Taught at the Toho Gakuen School of Music, 1954-56, the Aichi Prefectural Arts University at Nagoya, 1966-86, and 1939-43 and with Carl Orff in Munich, 1952-54. Compositions: The Mermaid and the Red Candle, 1 act opera, 1961; Princess Kaguya, 1 act opera, 1963; En no Gyoja, 3 act opera, 1965; Kesa and Morito, 3 act opera, 1968; Women are Wonderful, comic opera in 1 act, 1978; Kantomi, 3 act opera, 1981; Blue Lion, operetta, 1989. Address: c/o JASRAC, Jasrac House 7-13, 1-Chome Nishishimbashi, Minato-ku, Tokyo 105, Japan.

ISHIKAWA Shizuka, b. 2 Oct 1954. Tokyo, Japan. Violinist. m. Jiri Schultz, 26 May 1978. Education: Diploma, Prague Music Academy, 1978; Studied with Professor Shin-ichi Suzuki and Saburo Sumi. Career: Performances at The Prague Spring Festival; Belgrade Music Festival; Warsaw Autumn Festival; Hungarian Music Week; Helsinki Music Festival; Czechoslovak Music Festival in Japan; Performances in Tokyo, Copenhagen, Prague, Vienna, Brussels, Bonn; Numerous Radio and Television broadcasts; Soloist with many major orchestras. Recordings: Concertos by Bartok, Bruch, Mozart, Myslivecek and Paganini. Honours: 2nd Prize, Wieniawski International Violin Competition, 1972; Silver Medal, Queen Elisabeth in Brussels, 1976; 3rd Prize, International Violin Competition of F Kreisler, 1979. Current Management: Konzerburo Andreas Braun, Koln 41, Lindenthal; Japan Arts Corp, Tokyo, Japan.

ISHIKAWA Yoshiyuki (Yoshi), b. 26 Jan 1953, Tokyo, Japan. Bassoonist; Artistic Director. m. Brenda F Ishikawa. Education: BMusEd, MMus, Northwestern University; DMA in Bassoon Performance, University of Michigan; Studied Bassoon with L Hugh Cooper, Alan Goodman, Wilbur Simpson, Bernard Garfield and Norman Herzburg. Career: Active as Soloist and Clinician; Performance credits include tour of Japan, and solo and chamber music performances throughout the USA; Performances with Chicago Opera Studio Orchestra, Chicago Civic Orchestra, Ann Arbor Symphony Orchestra; Currently, Artistic Director and Founder of Sierra Wind Quintet; Principal Bassoon with Las Vegas Symphony Orchestra and Reno Philharmonic; Solo Bassoon and Personnel Manager, Las Vegas Chamber Players; Faculty, University of Nevada, Las Vegas and Nevada School of Arts. Honour: Director and Host in 1987 at Conference of the International Double Reed Society. Address: 3023 East Chapala, Las Vegas, NV 89120, USA.

ISOKOSKI Soile, b. 1960, Finland. Singer, Soprano. Education: Studied at the Sibelius Academy, Kuopio and with Dorothy Irving in Sweden. Debut: Formerly church organist, then gave concert debut as singer at Helsinki, 1986; Guest appearances at concert halls in Europe and Japan; Sibelius's Kullervo Symphony with the LSO under Colin Davis, 1991, also televised; Les Illuminations by Britten with the English String Orchestra; Engagements with the Finnish National Opera at Helsinki as Mimi, Liu and Mozart's Countess and Fiordiligi; Guest appearances as Donna Elvira in Cologne, Gluck's Alceste at Ludwigshafen, Firodiligi in Stuttgart and Micaela in Holland; Season 1993 with Salzburg Festival debut, as First Lady in Die Zauberflöte, and Mozart's Countess at Hamburg; Covent Garden debut 1997 as Fiordiligi in Così fan tutte. Honours: Winner, Lappeenranta Singing Competition, 1987; 2nd prize, Cardiff Singer of the World Competition, 1987; Winner, Elly Ameling and Tokyo International Competitions. Address: IMG Artists, Media House, 3 Burlington Lane, London W4 2TH, England.

ISOMURA Kazuhide, b. 27 Dec 1945, Tokyohashi, Japan. Violinist. Education: Studied at the Juilliard School with members of the Juilliard Quartet. Career: Violist of the Tokyo Quartet from 1969; Regular concerts in the USA and abroad; First cycle of the complete quartets of Beethoven at the Yale at Norfolk Chamber Music Festival, 1986; Repeated cycles at the 92nd Street Y, NY, Ravinia and Israel Festivals, Yale, Princeton Universities; Season 1990-91 at Alice Tully Hall, Metropolitan Museum of Art, NY, Boston, Washington DC, Los Angeles, Cleveland, Detroit, Chicago, Miami, Seattle, San Francisco, Toronto; Tour of South America and two tours of Europe including Paris, Amsterdam, Bonn, Milan, Munich, Dublin, London, Berlin; Quartet-in-residence at Yale University; The University of Cincinnati College-Conservatory of Music. Recordings: Schubert's major Quartets; Mozart Flute Quartets with James Galway and Clarinet Quintet with Richard Stolzman; Quartets by Bartok, Brahms, Debussy, Haydn, Mozart and Ravel; Beethoven Middle Period Quartets. Honours: Grand Prix du Disque du Montreux; Best Chamber Music Recording of the Year from Stero Review and the Gramophone; Four Grammy nominations. Address: Intermusica Artists' Management, 16 Duncan Terrace, London N1 8BZ, England.

ISRAEL Robert, b. 12 June 1918, Berlin, Germany. Violist; Teacher; Composer. m. Tamar Amrami, 20 December 1951, 1 son, 1 daughter. Education: Studied violin with Rudolph Bergmann, Viola with Oedeon Partos; Theory, Harmony Counterpoint Composition with Yitshak Edel, Rosowsky and Mordecai Seter; Teaching Diploma, 1942; Viola Diploma, Rubin Academy, Jerusalem and Tel Aviv. Debut: Elegie for Viola with string orchestra by Mordecai Seter, 1969. Career: Violist and Tubist, Opera Orchestra, Tel Aviv; Violin Teacher at various Kibbuzine, 1946-48; Teacher of Violin and Viola and Theory at Conservatory Hadera, 1952-; Member, Bass, Rinat Choir, 1957-58; Principal Violist, Haifa Symphony Orchestra, 1962-83; Performed with many chamber music groups. Compositions include: Five verses from Song of Songs for 2 voice choir, 1955; 3 pieces for violin and piano, 1988; Arrangement of rosamunde, the Trout, Marche militaire (Schubert), 3 violins or 2 violins and viola, 1989; 14 songs, arrangement for popular orchestra, 1990; 27 pieces for violin or any melody instrument and guitar, 1991; Saraband, Bourée, Polonais (J S Bach), Sonatine (Beethoven), arranged for two violas or viola and violoncello, 1993; 3 easy pieces for violin and piano; 3 less easy pieces for violin and piano. Recordings: Baroque music with recorder and harpsichord, 1973. Honours: Rinat Choir, awarded Premier Prix, Paris, 1957. Memberships: Amateur Chamberni Music Players; ASTA Hobbies: Drawing Landscapes, People, and Animals in Motion; Reading; Walking; Swimming. Address: Ytsiat-Europa st 11, Beth Eliezer POB 10772, Hadera 38484, Israel.

ISSERLIS Steven, b. 19 Dec 1958, London, England. Cellist. Education: International Cello Centre, 1969-76; Oberlin College, Ohio, 1976-78. Debut: Wigmore Hall, London, 1977. Career: Concerto, recital and chamber music appearances worldwide; Artistic Advisor to Cricklade Music Festival, Wiltshire; Played the Elgar Concertos with the Philharmonia, London, 1997; Chamber music by Mendelssohn at the 1997 Salzburg Festival. Compositions: Various arrangements for cello including Beethoven's Mandolin Variations. Recordings include: Britten Cello Symphony with City of London Sinfonia; Elgar Concerto, Bloch Schelomo with London Symphony Orchestra, Hickox; Tchaikovsky: Rococo Variations with Chamber Orchestra of Europe, Gardiner; Boccherini Concertos and Sonatas; John Tavener: The Protecting Veil with London Symphony Orchestra, Rozhdestvensky; Saint-Saëns: Concerto No 1, Sonata No 1, The Swan with London Symphony Orchestra, Tilson Thomas, Dudley Moore, CD and video; Tavener, Eternal Memory, Bloch, From Jewish Life with Moscow Virtuosi, Spivakov; Mendelssohn: Cello works with Melvyn Tan; Fauré: Cello works with Pascal Devoyon. Memberships include: Liszt Society, London; Dvorák Society. Hobbies include: Reading: Eating; Sleeping; Talking on the phone; Worrying about doing too many concerts; Worrying about doing too few concerts. Current Management: Harrison & Parrott Ltd. Address: c/o Harrison & Parrott Ltd, 12 Penzance Place, London W11 4PA, England.

ISTOMIN Eugene (George), b. 26 Nov 1925, NY, USA. Pianist. m. Marta Montanez Casals, 1975. Education: Curtis Institute, Philadelphia; Studied under Kyriena Silote, Rudolf Serkin. Debut: As Concert Pianist, 1943. Career: Toured with Adolf Busch Chamber Players, 1944-45; First European Appearance, 1950; Several World tours; Founded Trio with Isaac Stern and Leonard Rose, 1961. Recordings: Numerous recordings of solo, chamber works and orchestral music. Honours: Leventritt Award, 1943. Memberships: Charter Member, Casals, Prades and Puerto Rico Festivals, 1950-. Hobbies: Archaeology; History; Painting; Baseball.

ITIN Ilya, b. 1970, Russia. Concert Pianist. Education: Studied with Natalia Litvinova at the Sverdlovsk Music School for Gifted Children; Tchaikovsky State Conservatoire, Moscow; New York with Yin Cheng Zong, from 1990. Career: Appearances with leading orchestras including the Cleveland under Dohnanyi, and National Symphony under Skrowaczewski, from 1991; Recitals at Washington Kennedy Center and Lincoln Center, New York; Further concerts with European orchestras; Season 1997-98 debut at the London Proms with the BBC Philharmonic under Sinaisky, engagements associated with the Leeds Piano Competition, and European tour with the City of Birmingham Symphony under Simon Rattle. Honours include: First Prize and Chopin Prize in the Ninth Robert Casadesus Competition, Cleveland; First Prize and Contemporary Music Prize in the Leeds International Piano Competition, 1996. Address: c/o Harold Holt Ltd, 31 Sinclair Road, London W14 ONS, England.

IVALDI Jean-Marc, b. 6 May 1953, Toulon, France. Singer (Baritone). Education: Studied in Paris at the Conservatoire National and The School of the Grand Opera. Debut: Paris Opera in 1983 as Yamadori in Butterfly. Career: Sang Rossini's Figaro at Liege, 1983, and appeared at Bordeaux, Toulouse, Nancy, Metz, Dijon, and Tours; As Bretigny in Manon and Ramiro in L'Heure Espagnole at Paris; Philadelphia in 1986 as Morales in Carmen, and Heidenheim 1989 as Escamillo; Other roles include Alfonso in La Favorite, Belcore, Albert in Werther, Ourrias in Mireille, Manuel in La Vida Breve, Germont, Paquiro in Goyescas, Frederic in Lakmé and Jarno in Mignon; Sang Valentin in Faust at St Etienne in 1990; Concert engagements include Carmina Burana at St Etienne and Joseph in L'Enfance du Christ at Nancy; Sang Escamillo at St Etienne, 1995. Recordings: La Favorite; Sonora in La Fanciulla del West, conducted by Leonard Slatkin. Address: Saison Lyrique de Saint Etienne, 8 Place de l'Hotel de Ville, F-42000 St Etienne, France.

IVANOV Emil, b. 1960, Rome, Italy. Singer (Tenor). Education: Studied in Sofia, Bulgaria. Career includes: Sang first at the National Opera, Sofia, then appeared as Don Carlos at Essen, 1987; St Gallen, 1988-89, as Ernani and Pollione in Norma; Macerata Festival as Manrico; Guest engagements as Cavaradossi and Radames at Frankfurt, Zamoro in Verdi's Alzira at Fidenza, as the Prince in Rusalka at Houston and Don José at the Bregenz Festival, 1991; Vienna Staatsoper, 1992, as Dvorak's Dimitri; Aida, La Traviata, Madama Butterfly, Carmen at Wien-Staatsoper, 1993-94; Il Tabarro at Volksoper; Attila at Nice; Tosca at Metropolitan New York, 1993-94; 1994-95 Season: Carmen, La Traviata, Hérodiade, Madama Butterfly at

Wien-Staatsoper; in Carmen at Cologne; Il Tabarro at Birmingham and Don José at Pretoria; I Lombardi at St Gallen; Otello at Varna. Address: Karl Schweighofer 8/1/1. 1070 Vienna, Austria.

IVEY Jean (Eichelberger), b. 3 July 1923, Washington, DC, USA. Composer. Education: MM in piano Peabody Conservatory 1946; MM in composition Eastman School 1956; DMus University of Toronto, 1972. Career: Founded electronic music studio at Peabody Conservatory, 1969; Co-ordinator of the composition Department, 1982; Tours of Europe, the USA and Mexico as piano soloist. Compositions: The Birthmark, opera, 1982; Little Symphony, 1948; Passacaglia for chamber orchestra, 1954; Festive Symphony, 1955; Piano Sonata, 1957; String Quartet, 1960; Woman's Love song cycle, 1962; Terminus for mezzo and tape, 1970; Forms in Motion Symphony, 1972; 3 Songs of Night for soprano, instruments and tape, 1972; Aldebaran for viola and tape, 1972; Hera, Hung from the Sky for mezzo and ensemble, 1973; Testament of Eve, monodrama for mezzo, tape and orchestra, 1976; Solstice for soprano and ensemble, 1977; Prospero, scena, 1978; Cortege for Charles Kent, electronics 1979; Sea-Change for orchestra and tape, 1979; Ariel in Flight for violin and tape, 1983; Notes toward Time, 3 songs for mezzo and ensemble, 1984; Voyager, a Cello Concerto, 1985. Contributions: Musical Quarterly; Music Educators Journal. Honours: Grant from National Endowment for the Arts; Awards from Martha Baird Rockefeller Fund, Guggenheim Fellowship. Memberships: Board of Directors, League of Composers, ISCM, 1972-75, 1979. Address: 320 W 90 St, Apt 3 A, New York, NY 10024, USA.

IWAKI Hiroyuki, b. 6 Sept 1932, Tokyo, Japan. Conductor. Education: Studied percussion at the Tokyo Music Academy and conducting with Akeo Watanabe. Career: Assistant Conductor of the NHK, Japanese Broadcasting Symphony Orchestra, 1954; Conducted many premieres between 1957 and 1960; Conducted the Philharmonic Choir of Tokyo and was Musical Director of the Fujiwara Opera Company, 1965-67; Guest conductor of orchestras in Hamburg, Vienna and Berlin, 1966-69; Musical Director of the NHK Symphony from 1969, the Melbourne Symphony Orchestra from 1974; Director of the Orchestra-Ensemble Kanazawa, 1988; Conducted the first performances of works by Dallapiccola, (Concerto per la notte di natale de l'anno, 1956); Takemitsu (Marginilia, 1976), Dreamtime, 1982, A Way to Love, 1982 and Star-Isle, 1982; Isang Yun, (Symphony No 4, 1986). Recordings include: Beethoven's 9th Symphony, with the NHK Orchestra; Bartók Concerto for Orchestra (Melbourne Symphony); Hungarian Rhapsodies by Liszt (Vienna State Opera Orchestra); Messiaen Couleurs de la cité céleste, Oiseaux Exotiques, Reveil des Oiseaux and Sept Hai-Kai (Decca); Dutch music with the Hague Philharmonic. Address: c/o Melbourne Symphony, PO Box 443, East Caulfield, Vic 3145, Australia.

IWASAKI Ko, b. 16 Aug 1944, Tokyo, Japan. Cellist. m. Yurie Ishio, 21 Dec 1979, 2 sons. Education: Toho Conservatoire; Juilliard School of Music, USA, 1964-66; Studied with: Leonard Rose, Harvey Shapiro, 1964-66; Pablo Casals, Puerto Rico, 1966. Debut: Recital at Carnegie Recital Hall, New York, 1966. Career: Recital at Wigmore Hall, London, England, 1968; Performed with: London Symphony, 1972; Participant, Summer Festivals: Marlboro; Portland, Oregon; Kuhmo, Finland; Lockenhaus, Austria; Performances in USA, Europe, Russia and the Orient; Director, Moonbeach Music Camp, Okinawa, Japan, 1979-; Director, Cello Master Class, Southern Methodist University, USA. Recordings: Ko Iwasaki Plays Schubert Arpeggione Sonata; Beethoven Sonatas; Shostakovich Sonata; Japanese Contemporary Works for Cello; Ko Iwasaki and Staffan Scheja Play Sonata, Rachmaninoff and Grieg; Iwasaki, Requibros; 19 Short Pieces, Compact Disc; Beethoven: 2 Trios; Dvorak, Tchaikovsky with Polish National Radio Symphony; Haydn Cello Concerto No 1 & No 2, with Polish Chamber Orchestra. Honours: 3rd Prizes: Vienna International Cello Competition, 1967; Munich International Competition, 1967, Budapest International Cello Competition, 1968, Tchaikovsky International Competition; 2nd Prize, Cadao International Cello Competition. Hobby: Driving. Address: 5732 Still Forest Drive, Dallas, TX 75252, USA.

IZZO D'AMICO Fiamma, b. 1964, Rome, Italy. Singer, Soprano. Education: Studied at Santa Cecilia Conservatory, Rome, 1981-84. Debut: Sang Mimi in La Boheme at the Teatro Regio, Turin, 1984. Career: Sang Violetta at Treviso 1985, was discovered by Herbert von Karajan, Sang Elisabeth de Valois at the 1986 Salzburg Festival followed by Micaela in Carmen; US debut Philadelphia 1986 in La Boheme, with Luciano Pavarotti, celebrated his 15th anniversary with him at Modena, 1986; Bologna 1986 in La Traviata, conducted by Riccardo Chailly; Season 1987-88 with appearances in Bohème at Vienna, Metropolitan, New York; Manon in Genoa, Tosca and the Verdi Requiem at Salzburg; Further engagements at the Paris Opera, London, Chicago, Monte Carlo, Monaco and Hamburg. Address: Metropolitan Opera, Lincoln Center, NY 10023, USA.

J

JABLONSKI Krzysztof, b. 2 Mar 1965, Wroclaw, Poland. Musician, Pianist. Education: Karol Szymanowski Academy of Music in Katowice, 1986 with Professor Andrzej Jasinki. Career: Numerous concert engagements in Poland and abroad, including Austria, Belgium, Bulgaria, Canada, Czechoslovakia, Denmark, Germany, Finland, Great Britain, Holland, Israel, Italy, Japan, Norway, Soviet Union, Spain and USA. Many recordings for radio and TV in Poland and abroad. Recordings: Chopin: 24 Preludes Op 28; Haydn: Sonata in C Minor No 33, Beethoven: Sonata in C Minor Op 13, Pathetique; Mozart: Piano Concerto in F Major K 459, Orchester der Ludwigsburger Festspiele, W Goennenwein, Bayer Records; Chopin: 24 Preludes Op 28, Polonaise in A flat Major, Op 43, Heroique, Study in G flat Major Op 10-5 Black Keys, Study in C Minor Op 10-12, Revolutionary, Yamaha Piano Player; Chopin: Sonata in B Minor Op 58, Barcarolle in F sharp Major Op 60, Polonaises in A flat Major Op 53, Heroique in G Minor in B flat Major, in A flat Major, Nocturnes, in B flat Major Op 9-3 in F sharp Major Op 15,2; More recently: Mussorgsky: Piano solo, Pictures at an Exhibition; Schumann: Kinderszenen Op. 15; Debussy: Children's Corner, Kos Records, Kos CD 10 CD, 1993. Address: Ul Kwiska 43-9, 54-210 Wroclaw, Poland.

JABLONSKI Peter, b. 1971, Lyckeby, Sweden. Concert Pianist. Education: Studied at the Malmo Music College and the Royal College of Music, London. Career: Has appeared with such orchestras as the Royal and Moscow Philharmonics, Philharmonica, Philadelphi and the Los Angeles and Japan Philharmonics in Berlin and Milan, the Harrogate Festival and the Elizabeth Hall, London; Tour of Japan from 1992, with visits to Australia and New Zealand; Season 1997 with Far East tour and concerts with the Detroit, Gothenburg and Montreal Symphonies. Recordings include: Concertos by Gershwin, Rakhmaninov, Lutoslawski and Tchaikovsky; Chopin Waltzes and solo music by Liszt; Grieg recital, 1997. Address: c/o Harrison/Parrott Ltd, 12 Penzance Place, London W11 4PA, England.

JACKSON Francis (Alan), b. 2 October 1917, Yorkshire, England. Organist; Composer. m. Priscilla Procter, 1 November 1950, 2 sons, 1 daughter. Education: Sir Edward Bairstow; DMus, Durham, 1957. Career: Chorister, York Minster, 1929-33; Master of the Music, York Minster, 1946-82; Conductor, York Musical Society, 1947-82 and York Symphony Orchestra, 1947-80; Patron, Percy Whitlock Trust. Compositions: Symphony in D minor; Concerto for organ, strings, timpani and celesta; Ecologue for piano and organ; Missa Matris Dei; Services in G Major, D, E flat, G minor, F sharp; St Bride's and Temple Services; Several Athems and Organ Pieces; 4 Organ Sonatas; 3 Duets for Organ. Recordings: Complete Bairstow Organ Works, (Mirabilis); The Composer (Amphion) Plays His Own Works; Stanford at Sledmere, 1994; Own Works (Priory), 1994; Whitlock Sonata, Royal Albert Hall, 1994. Honours: OBE; FRCO Limpus Prize, 1937; Doctor of York University, 1982; Fellow, Westminster Choir College, 1970. Memberships: Royal College of Organists; ISM. Hobbies: Gardening; Art; Architecture. Address: Nether Garth, East Acklam, Malton, North Yorkshire YO17 9RG, England.

JACKSON Garfield, b. 1955, England. Violist. Career: Founder-member and Violist of the Endellion Quartet, from 1979; Many concerts in Munich, Frankfurt, Amsterdam, Paris, Salzburg and Rome; South Bank Haydn Festival 1990 and Quartet Plus series 1994; Wigmore Hall Beethoven series 1991; Quartet in Residence at the University of Cambridge from 1992; Residency at MIT, United States, 1995. Recordings include: Works by Haydn, Barber, Bartók, Dvorak, Smetana and Walton (Virgin Classics). Address: Hazard Chase, Richmond House, 16-20 Regent Street, Cambridge CB2 1DB, England.

JACKSON Isaiah, b. 22 Jan 1945, Virginia, USA. Conductor. m. Helen Tuntland, 6 Aug 1977, 1 son, 2 daughters. Education: MS, Juilliard School of Music, 1969; DMA, 1973. Career: Assistant Director, American Symphony, 1970-71; Associate Conductor, Rochester Philharmonic, 1973-87; Music Director, Royal Ballet, Covent Garden, 1987-90; Music Director, Dayton Philharmonic, 1987-95; Principal Guest Conductor, Queensland Symphony, 1993-; Music Director, Youngstown Symphony, 1996-; Guest conducting, New York Philharmonic, Cleveland Orchestra, Boston Pops, San Francisco Symphony, Orchestre de la Suisse Romande, BBC Concert Orchestra, Berlin Symphony, Royal Liverpool Philharmonic, Houston Symphony. Recordings: String orchestra compositions of Herrmann, Waxman, Rozsa, Berlin Symphony; Dance music of William Grant Still, Berlin Symphony; Gospel at the Symphony, Louisville Orchestra; Harp concerti of Ginastera and Mathias, English Chamber Orchestra. Honours: 1st Governor's Award for Arts, Virginia, 1979; Signet Society Medal for the Arts, Harvard University, 1991. Address: c/o United Arts, 3906 Sunbeam Drive, Los Angeles, CA 90065, USA.

JACKSON Larisa Petrushkevich, b. 20 July 1960, Novgorod, Russia. Musicologist. 1 son. Education: BA, Musorgsky Music College, Leningrad, Russia, 1981; MA, 1989, MPhil, 1992, PhD, 1996, Columbia University. Appointments: Instructor, Columbia University, 1989-95; Lecturer, Conservatory of Music, Purchase College, 1996. Publication: Recent Trends in Soviet Musicology, 1993. Honours: 1st Prize, Harmony, 2nd Prize, Solfége, Leningrad Conservatory of Music Theory Competition, 1979; Columbia University Presidents Fellowship, 1988; Mellon Fellowship, 1988-95. Membership: American Musicological Society. Address: 258 Brookside Avenue, Creskill, NJ 07626, USA.

JACKSON Laurence, b. 1967, Lancashire, England. Concert Violinist. Education: Studied at Chethams School of Music and at the Royal Academy with Maurice Hasson and Anne-Sophie Mutter. Career: Concerto repertoire includes works by Bruch, Mendelssohn, Vaughan Williams and Tchaikovsky; Aldeburgh Festival, 1988, in the Concerto Grosso by Schnittke; Soloist at the Casals Festival Hall, 1990, in The Four Seasons; Recitals at the Fairfields Halls, Queens Hall, Edinburgh, Brangwyn Hall and Turner Sims Hall; Member of Britten-Pears Ensemble tour of USA, 1991; As member of Borante Piano Trio has performed from 1982 at the Purcell Room and Wigmore Hall, in Dublin and Paris, and at the 1989 Festival Wiener Klassik (Beethoven's Triple Concerto); Season 1990 at the Bath and Perth Festivals, tour of Scandinavia, Russia and the Baltic States and master classes with Andras Schiff at Prussia Cove, Cornwall; Duo partnership with pianist Scott Mitchell; Solo concert tour of Chile, Colombia and Venezuela, 1991; Concerto and recital performances in Spain, 1992. Recordings: Solo recording with the ensemble Laureate, 1991. Honours include: David Martin Concerto Prize, 1987, and Principal's Prize, 1988; The Royal English Heritage Award, 1983, 1985, 1986; 1st Prize at Vina del Mar, Chile, 1990; 3rd Prize, First Pablo Sarasate International Violin Competition, 1991. Current Management: Scott Mitchell Management, 26 Childebert Road, London SW17 8EX, England. Address: 23 Fulwell Park Avenue, Twickenham, Middlesex TW2 5HF, England.

JACKSON Nicholas (Fane St George) (Bart) (Sir), b. 4 Sep 1934, London, England. Organist; Harpsichordist; Composer. m. Nadia Michard, 1971, 1 s. Education: Radley College; Wadham College, Oxford; Royal Academy of Music with C H Trevor, George Malcolm, Gustav Leonhardt; LRAM, ARCM. Debut: Wigmore Hall, 1964. Career: Organist at St James's, London, 1971-74; St Lawrence Jewry next Guildhall, 1974-77; Organist and Master of the Choristers of St David's Cathedral, 1977-84; Organ recital at Royal Festival Hall, 1984; Director of Concertante of London, 1987-; Masterclasses at Segovia, Spain, 1989; Director of Festival Bach, Santes Creus, Spain; Solo performances at South Bank, London and at Nôtre Dame Paris, Teatro Real Madrid and New York; World premiere of his opera The Relunctant Highwayman at Broomhill, 1995. Compositions: Mass for a Saint's Day; 4 Images for Organ; 20th Century Merbecke; Divertissement for Organ; Anthems and Choral Settings; Mass for Organ, 1984; Opera: The Reluctant Highwayman, 1992; Organ Sonata, 1995. Recordings include: The Organ of St David's Cathedral; Bach's Christmas Organ Music for Trumpet and Organ; 2 LPs with Maurice Murphy; Complete Organ Works of Richard Arnell; Bach's 2 and 3 Part Inventions; François Couperin; Harpsichord Concertos; Mass for a Saint's Day. Honour: Honorary Fellowship, Hertford College, Oxford, 1995. Memberships: Master of the Worshipful Company of Drapers, 1994-95; Liveryman of the Worshipful Company of Musicans. Current Management: Nuria Corts de Vila, Reus, Spain. Address: 42a Hereford Road, London, W2 5AJ, England.

JACKSON Rhonda, b. 20 Jan 1968. Singer; Songwriter. Education: New York University; Ophelia DeVere New York Acting Academy; Alain Ailey Dance Studio; Bernice Johnson Dance Studio; Studied under Ann Bernstein, Tom Butler, Bob Giraldi and Ben Gooding. Career: Singing: Performances at Waldorf Astoria hotel, New York City, 1989, Martin Luther King Centre, 1989, Bryant Park Music Event, 1996, Cami Hall, 1996, Peppers Restaurant, 1997, The Dave Gold Show, 1998; Featured singer: IBIS Nightclub, 1997, Manhattan Neighbours Network, 1998. Compositions: Promises, 1997; Passion, 1997; Quiet Moments; Fool; Remember Me. Recordings: Let Me Rest; Destiny Served; Walk Away; Promises; Fool; One Nation; Passion. Publications: Melodies of Life, Vol 1, 1997; Daybreak on the Land, 1997; Of Sunlight and Shadows, 1997; Treasure the Moment, 1997; The Best New Songwriters, 1997. Honours: Editor's Choice Award, National Library of Poetry, 1997; Amherst Society Award, 1997; Inducted, International Poetry Hall of Fame. Memberships: International Society of Poets; Songwriters Guild of America; BMI; Gospel Music Association; International Women's Writing Guild; Songwriters Club of America; National Association of Composers. Hobbies: Writing poetry; Acting; Swimming; Bowling. Address: P O Box 650136, Fresh Meadows, NY 11365, USA.

JACKSON Richard, b. 1960, Cornwall, England. Singer (Baritone). Education: Study with Pierre Bernac and Audrey Langford. Career: Widely known as a concert singer, in song and oratorio; Founder member of the Songmakers' Almanac, with appearances in the USA, at the Saintes Festival, Three Choirs Festival and the Wigmore and Elizabeth Halls; Solo recital with songs by Poulenc at the Wigmore Hall, 1989; Concerts with David Willcocks, Neville Marriner, Bertini, Rostropovitch, Mackerras and Gardiner; Has sung Bach and Handel in Spain and Portugal; Monteverdi's Vespers in Venice; The Starlight Express by Elgar; Opera engagements at the Glyndebourne and Aldeburgh Festivals and with Kent Opera, New Sadler's Wells Opera and with the Handel Opera Society; Sang Aeneas to the Dido of Janet Baker; Almeida Festival, London, 1987-88, in the British premiere of Jakob Lenz by Wolfgang Rihm and the world premiere of The Undivine Comedy by Michael Finnissy. Address: c/o Ron Gonsalves, 10 Dagnan Road, London SW12 9LQ, England.

JACOBS René, b. 30 Oct 1946, Ghent, Belgium. Singer (Countertenor); Editor; Conductor. m. Suzy Depporter. Education: Licentiaat, Klassieke Filologie, University of Ghent; Solo singing with Louis Devos (Brussels) and Lucie Frateur (The Hague). Career: Recitals in Europe, Canada, USA, Mexico and the Philippines; Performances with madrigal ensembles and with such early music groups as the Leonhardt Consort, Il Complesso Barocco, La Petite Bande and groups led by Alan Curtis and Nikolaus Harnoncourt; Sings Baroque music and directs his own ensemble Collegium Vocale; Best known in operas by Monteverdi, Cesti, Handel, Gluck and Cavalli; Sacred music by Charpentier and Couperin; Teacher of performing practice in Baroque singing, Schola Cantorum, Basle; Appointments at the International Summer School for Early Music, Innsbruck, and the Aston Magna Academy for Baroque Music, USA; Conducted Cavalli's Giasone in his own edition at the 1988 Innsbruck Festival; Flavio, 1989; L'Incoronazione de Poppea with the ensemble I Febi Armonici, 1989; Conducted Graun's Cleopatra e Cesare at the 1992 Baroque Festival, Versailles; Conti's Don Chisciotte at the 1992 Innsbruck Festival of Early Music; Led Poppea at the Teatro Colon, Buenos Aires, 1996. Recordings: Cesti's L'Orontea, from the 1982 Holland Festival; Arias by Monteverdi and Benedetto Ferrari; Motets by Charpentier; Bach's St Matthew Passion; Handel's Admeto and Partenope; Lully's Bourgeois Gentilhomme; Gluck's Orfeo ed Euridice and Echo et Narcisse; Giasone and La Calisto by Cavalli; Handel's Alessandro and Tamerlano; Charpentier's David et Jonathas; Handel's Giulio Cesare. Address: Langenakkerlaan 34, 9130 Lochristi, Belgium.

JACOBSON Bernard (Isaac), b. 2 Mar 1936, London, England. Writer on Music. m. (1) Bonnie Brodsky, 11 Aug 1968 (marriage dissolved 1982), 1 s, 1 d, (2) Dr Laura Dale Belcove, 3 Jan 1983. Education: City of London School, 1947-54; Corpus Christi College, Oxford as Open Scholar, 1956-60; Classical Honour Moderations, 1958; Lit Hum - BA 1960; MA 1962. Career includes: Music Critic, Chicago Daily News, 1967-73; Director, Southern Arts Association, Winchester, England, 1973-76; Deputy Director of Publications, 1979-81, Director of Promotion, Boosey and Hawkes Music Publishers Ltd, London, 1982-84; Manager, Publications and Educational Programmes, 1984-88, Programme Annotater and Musicologist, 1988-91, Philadelphia Orchestra; Artistic Director, Residentie Orkest, Hague Philharmonic, 1992-94; Independent Associate, Joy Mebus Artists' Management, 1993-94; Artistic Adviser, North Netherlands Orchestra, 1994-. Compositions: Libretto, 16 poems, for Death of a Young Man, song cycle by Wilfred Josephs commissioned and performed by 1971 Harrogate Festival; Poems for Songs and other works by Richard Wernick. Recordings: Schoenberg Ode to Napoleon, 1968; Stravinsky, The Flood, 1995. Publications include: The Music of Johannes Brahms, USA and London, 1977; Conductors on Conducting, USA and London, 1979; A Polish Renaissance, in press; Many translations including Holofernes, Judith and Die Weise von Liebe und Tod des Cornets Christoph Rilke for Schott. Contributions to: Dictionary of 20th Century Music, 1974; The New Grove, 1980. Hobbies: Food and Wine; Travel; Photography; Watching Cricket and Baseball. Address: Buys Ballotstraat 89, 2563 ZK Den Haag, The Netherlands.

JACOBSON Daniel C, b. 27 July 1955, California, USA. Musicologist; Music Theorist. m. Grace Eugenia Mannion, 20 Dec 1986, 1 son, 1 daughter. Education: BA, Voice, Westminster College, Utah; MA, Music History, California State University; PhD, Musicology and Music Theory, University of California, 1986. Career: Faculty, University of California, Santa Barbara, 1986-89; Coordinator, Lehmann Centennial, 1988; Faculty, University of North Dakota, Grand Forks, 1989-. Recordings: The Lotte Lehmann Centennial Album, LP, 1988, CD, 1994. Publications: A Listener's Introduction to Music, 1991; Co-Editor, The Norton CD-Rom Masterworks Series; The Norton CD-Rom Listening Guides, for The Enjoyment of Music, 7th edition, 1995. Contributions to: NATS Journal, 1991; The Opera Quarterly, 1991; Dvorák in America, 1993; Mozart-Jahrbuch, 1994; The Journal of Musicology, 1995; Schubert: durch die Brille, 1995. Honours: Stanley Krebs Prize in Musicology, 1983, 1984, 1986; National Endowment for the Humanities Fellowship Grant, 1991; Faculty Award, 1993, Service Award, 1994, University of North Dakota College of Fine Arts; Outstanding Faculty Scholar, for

Research, Creativity, Teaching and Service, University of North Dakota, 1995. Memberships: American Musicological Society; Society for Music Theory; College Music Society; Music Theory Mid-West, Secretary 1995; International Franz Schubert Society; Lotte Lehmann League. Hobbies: Midi composition; Computer programming; Baseball; Travel. Address: 12 Vail Circle, Grand Forks, North Dakota, USA.

JACOBSON Julian, b. 1947, Scotland. Pianist. Education: Studied piano with Lamar Crowson and Louis Kentner; Composition with Arthur Benjamin and Humphrey Searle; Graduate, Royal College of Music and Oxford University. Debut: London, Purcell Room, 1974. Career: Appearances in 28 countries including concerto engagements with London Symphony, BBC Symphony, City of Birmingham Orchestra, English Chamber Orchestra, London Mozart Players, Bournemouth Sinfonietta; Chamber music recitals with: Nigel Kennedy, Lydia Mordkovitch, Zara Nelsova, Steven Isserlis, Colin Carr, Emma Johnson, Christian Lindberg, Brodsky and Arditti Quartets; Artistic Director, Paxos Festival, Greece; Teacher and Performer, Dartington International Summer School; Head of Keyboard Studies, Welsh College of Music and Drama; Solo recitals include Two cycles of the 32 Beethoven Sonatas; Concerts; Masterclasses in France, Malta, Hungary and China, 1994-95; Partnership with violinist Susanne Stanzeleit, including Purcell Room Recitals, 1993, 1994 and Complete Beethoven Sonata Cycle, Bracknell, 1994. Compositions: Songs; Piano Works; Chamber Music; 6 Film Scores. Recordings include: Albums on various labels; CD recordings of Complete piano sonatas of Weber. Address: 34 St Margaret's Road, London, SE4 1YU, England.

JACOBSON Rut, b. 1927, Jokkmokk, Lapaland, Sweden. Singer (Soprano). m. Per Stokholm. Education: Studied at the Stockholm Academy of Music and in Vienna. Career: Sang first at Graz and at the Vienna Volksoper (1954-58) then at the Stora Theatre Gothenburg; Sang at the Royal Opera Stockholm, 1964-65 and Malmo 1970-71; Also sang in Reykjavik; Roles include Constanze, Pamina, Fiordiligi, Gilda, Violetta and Butterfly; From 1971 Professor at the Gothenburg Academy of Music. Address: c/o Malmo Stadttheater, Box 17520, S-200 10 Malmo, Sweden.

JACOBSSON John-Eric, b. 6 Oct 1931, Hogran, Sweden. Singer (Tenor). Education: Studied in Stockholm with Toivo Ek, Arne Sunnegaard and Sonny Peterson. Debut: Royal Opera, Stockholm, 1964, as Turiddu in Cavalleria Rusticana. Career: Sang at Stockholm in the premiere of Kalifens Son by Eiyser (1976) and as Alwa in the local premiere of Berg's Lulu; Other roles include Pedrillo in Die Entführung, Jacquino in Fidelio, Cavaradossi, Albert Herring, Eisenstein in Die Fledermaus and Ismaele in Nabucco, Steva in Jenufa and title role in Xerxes and more than 100 different roles; Guest appearances in Oslo, Copenhagen, Hamburg, Munich, Edinburgh, Moscow, Hong Kong and at the Drottningholm Festival; Many concert appearances. Address: c/o Kungliga Teatern, PO Box 16094, S-10322 Stockholm, Sweden.

JACOBY Robert, b. 8 Apr 1940, Sussex, England. Violinist; Conductor; Teacher. m. Elisabeth Duddridge, 3 Sept 1963, 1 son, 1 daughter. Education: Guildhall School of Music; Royal College of Music, London; University of Wales; MA; PhD; FLCM; LRAM; ARCM. Debut: Wigmore Hall, London. Career: First concert, aged 7; Radio and TV appearances as concerto soloist and in chamber music; Sibelius concerto under Sir Adrian Boult; Solo Violinist and First Konzertmeister with Westphalian Symphony Orchestra; Leader, resident professional String Quartet, University College of Wales; Founder and Conductor, Oakwood Symphony Orchestra, Philomusica of Aberystwyth; Currently Musical Director, Dorset Chamber Orchestra. Publications: Violin Technique, a Practical Analysis for Performers, 1985; Reviews for The Library, British Journal for 18th Century Studies. Hobbies: Walking; Antiquarian studies. Current Management: Direct booking only. Address: Burton House, West Bexington, Dorchester DT2 9DD, England.

JAFFE Monte, b. 5 June 1940, USA. Singer (Baritone). Education: Studied at the Curtis Institute and with Giorgio Tozzi. Career: Appearances with Krefeld Opera as Wotan, Kaspar (Der Freischütz), Dr Schön (Lulu), Reimann's Lear, the Dutchman, and in Cerhaa's Baal and the premiere of Judith by Matthus. Further engagements at the Metropolitan in Death of Venice, Lear with English National Opera, the Hoffmann villains for Israel Opera and Bluebeard (Bartók) for Scottish Opera; Returned to English National Opera for the title role in the premiere of Timon of Athens by Stephen Oliver, 1991, and has also sung at Karlsruhe (Graf Mirabeau by Matthus), Berne (Nekrotaz in Le Grand Macabre), Tel Aviv (Mephistopheles in Faust), Bonn (Gianni Schicchi), 1993, Turin (Walkure Wotan), Antwerp (Klingsor) and Bielefeld (Barak in Die Frau ohne Schatten); Other roles include Scarpia, Konchak (Prince Igor), Zaccaria (Nabucco) and Old Sam in Bernstein's A Quiet Place. Address: Ingpen & Williams Ltd, 26 Wadham Road, London SW15 2LR, England.

JAFFE Stephen, b. 30 Dec 1954, Washington DC, USA. Composer. m. Mindy Oshrain, 29 May 1988, 2 daughters. Education: AM, AB summa cum laude, University of Pennsylvania, with George Crumb, George Rochberg and Richard Wernick, 1973-78; Also at University of Massachusetts and Conservatoire de Musique, Geneva. Career: Director, Encounters with the Music of Our Time, Duke University, 1981-; Performances with San Francisco, New Jersey, New Hampshire Symphonies, Rome Radio Orchestra, New York New Music Ensembe, Spectrum concerts, Berlin, Aurora and Ciompi Quartets. Compositions: First Quartet, 1991; Double Sonata, two pianos, 1989; Four Songs with Ensemble, for mezzo soprano and ensemble, 1988; Four Images, 1983-87; The Rhythm of the Running Plough, 1988; Triptych, for piano and wind quintet, 1993; Pedal Point, baritone, low strings, harp and timpani, 1992; Pedal Point, baritone and consort of low instruments, 1994. Recordings: First Quartet; Centering for two violins; Three Figures and a Ground; The Rhythm of the Running Plough; Double Sonata; Four Songs with Ensemble; Fort Juniper Songs. Publications: First Quartet, 1991; Double Sonata, 1992; Three Figures and a Grand, 1993; Four Images for Orchestra, 1988. Contributions to: Contemporary Music Review; Conversation between JS and SJ on the New Tonality, article, 1992. Honours: American Academy of Arts and Letters Prize, 1993; Brandeis University Creative Arts Citation, 1989. Current Management: Theodore Presser Co, Bryn Mawr, PA 19010, USA. Address: Box 90656, Durham, NC 27708, USA.

JAFFEE Kay, b. 31 Dec 1937, MI, USA. Musician; Musicologist. m. Michael Jaffee, 24 Jul 1961. Education: BA, University of Michigan, 1959; MA, New York University, 1965. Debut: Carnegie Recital Hall, 1966. Career: Founding Member and Associate Director, The Waverly Consort, 1964-; Performer on Renaissance wind and keyboard instruments, harps, psalteries and percussion; Annual tours of North America since 1967; Also tours to Great Britain and Latin America; Festival appearances include: Casals Festival, 1981 and 1983, Madeira Bach Festival, 1981, Hong Kong Festival, 1988 and Caramoor Festival; Television appearances in USA. Recordings: 10 with the Waverly Consort. Publications: Articles and reviews to the Journal of Musicology, The American Recorder and The Brass Quarterly. Memberships: American Musicological Society; Society for 17th Century Music; Renaissance Society of America. Current Management: Musicians Corporate Management Ltd, PO Box 589, Millbrook, NY 12545, USA. Address: PO Box 386, Patterson, NY 12563, USA.

JAHN Gertrude, b. 13 Aug 1940, Zagreb, Croatia. Singer (Mezzo-soprano).; Education: Studied at the Vienna Music Academy with Elisabeth Rado and Lily Kolar; Further study with Erik Werba and Josef Witt. Debut: Basle, 1963, as Gluck's Orpheus. Career: Appearances at the State Operas of Vienna, Hamburg, Munich and Stuttgart; Glyndebourne, 1968, as Olga in Eugene Onegin; Salzburg Festivals from 1967, as Feodor in Boris Godunov, Mozart's Ascanio, Margret in Wozzeck and Countess Laura in the premiere of Penderecki's Die schwarze Maske, 1986; Munich and Madrid, 1988, as Adelaide in Arabella and the Countess Geschwitz in Lulu; Further engagements in Dusseldorf, Salzburg, Moscow, Trieste and Montreal; Other roles include Carmen, Giulietta in Les Contes d'Hoffmann, Octavian, Eboli, Preziosilla (La Forza del Destino), Fatima in Oberon and Magdalene in Die Meistersinger; Frequent concert appearances. Recordings include: Masses by Haydn and Schubert; Missa Choralis by Liszt; Wozzeck.

JAHNS Annette, b. 1958, Dresden, Germany. Singer (Mezzo-soprano). Education: Studied at the Dresden Musikhochschule and with Judith Beckmann in Hamburg and Ute Niss in Berlin. Career: Sang with the Dresden Opera, 1982-, as Mozart's Ramiro (Finta giardiniera), Dorabella and Cherubino, Nicklausse, Mistress Quickly, and Maddalena in Rigoletto; Carmen, Orpheus, Hansel and Olga; Has also performed in the Brecht/Weill Sieben Todsunden. Address: c/o Staatsoper Dresden, Theaterplatz 2, O1067 Dresden, Germany.

JAHREN Helen (Mai Aase), b. 2 May 1959, Malmö, Sweden. Solo Concert Oboist. Education: MFA, 1977, Postgraduate Diploma, Oboe, 1978, Malmö College of Music; Hochschulabschlussprüfung, Staatliche Hochschule für Musik, Freiburg, 1980; Solistendiplom, Konservatorium für Musik, Berne, 1983. Debut: 1st solo appearance with orchestra, age 17. Career: Tours, France, Italy, Spain, Germany, Switzerland, Poland, Denmark, Norway, Finland, Iceland, Japan, 1980-; Belgian tour with Orchestre National de Belgique, 1982; Vienna debut, Grosses Konzerthaus, 1983; Toured Colombia, Ecuador, Peru, Argentina, Uruguay, Brazil, Venezuela, Costa Rica, Mexico, 1984; Debut with Stockholm Philharmonic Orchestra, 1987; Invited to Louisville Symphony Orchestra's 50th Anniversary, USA, 1987; Pan Music Festival, Seoul, 1988; Gala Opening Concert, with Hong Kong Philharmonic Orchestra, World Music Days, Hong Kong, 1988; Debut with Swedish Orchestra, 1988; Many TV and radio appearances worldwide; Artist Portrait by Swedish Television, 1991-93; Teaching: Malmö College of Music, 1984-87; Ingesund College of Music, 1991-93; Stockholm Royal College of Music, 1993-; Masterclasses; Initiator and Artistic Director of Båstad Chamber Music Festival. Recordings include: Swedish music for oboe and organ with Hans-Ola Ericsson, 1986; Schnittke Double Concerto for oboe and harp, with Stockholm Chamber Orchestra, 1987; J H Roman, Oboe Concerto, 1988; L-E Larsson, Oboe Concertino, 1990; J Kaipainen, Oboe Concerto, 1995. Current Management: Svensk Konsertdirektion AB, Gothenburg, Sweden. Address: c/o Svensk Konsertdirektionen AB, Box 5076, S-40222 Gothenburg, Sweden.

JAKOBSSON Claes, b. 1924, Uddevalla, Sweden. Singer (Baritone). m. Suzanna Brenning, 1964. Education: Studied at the Stockholm Music High School with Gjurja Leppee. Career: Sang at Stora Teatern, Gothenburg, 1948-78, as Mozart's Count and Don Giovanni, Rigoletto, Germont, Iago, Ford, Escamillo and Eugene Onegin; Guest appearances at the Vienna Volksoper (as Danilo in Die Lustige Witwe), Oslo and Milwaukee; Concert tours of Scandinavia, Austria and the USA (1974); Teacher at the Gothenburg Opera School from 1973. Recordings include: Tintomara by Werle. Address: c/o Stora Teatern, Box 53116, S-400 15 Gothenburg, Sweden.

JAKSIC Djura, b. 30 Apr 1924, Karlovac, Yugoslavia. Conductor; Writer on Music. m. Slobondanka Ilic, 21 July 1962, 2 sons. Education: School of Music, Belgrade, 1939-45; Music Science, Charles University, Prague and Prague Conservatoire, 1945-48; Diploma, Academic Musician-Conductor, Academy of Music, Zagreb, 1948-50. Debut: Symphonic concert, Radio Belgrade Symphony, 1950. Career: Conductor, Radio Symnphony, Radio Chamber and Radio Studio Orchestras, 1950-53; Associate Conductor, Belgrade Philharmonic Orchestra, 1953-66; Art Director, Principal Conductor, Chamber Orchestra Pro Musica, 1967-; Art Director, National Opera/Ballet, Belgrade, 1977-80; Concerts and tours in Yugoslavia, Austria, Belgium, Bulgaria, Czechoslovakia, Denmark, France, UK, Hungary, Italy, Netherlands, Norway, Rumania, Spain, Switzerland, Turkey and USSR; Autobiography broadcast on Belgrade Radio and TV, 1987, 1988. Recordings: Vivaldi, The Seasons, and J Slavenski, Suite of Dances, both with Chamber Orchestra Pro Musica; Pro Musica Plays Vivaldi, 1991; Over 300 radio recordings. Publications: On the Symphony Orchestra, 1954; State of Music in Serbia, 1969; Two Symphonies of Amando Ivancic; Revisions, editions and orchestrations of Yugoslav composers from the 15th to 19th century; Essays on Vivaldi, Telemann, on conducting performers' rights, Britten's War Requiem, Berg's Wozzeck, Finnish music, Bulgarian music; Amando Ivancic and Slovakia, 1986; G B Shaw on Music: Selection of music criticisms, Serbocroat translation, selection and comment, 1989; Over 200 other articles. Contributions to: Editor in chief, Pro Musica magazine, 1964-90; Yugoslav Music Encyclopaedia, 1958-. Hobbies: National history; Collecting icons and old prints on Serbia. Address: Pozeska 92, YU-11031 Belgrade, Serbia.

JAMES David, b. England. Singer (Countertenor). Education: Choral scholar at Magdalen College, Oxford. Career: From 1978 has sung with the Hilliard Ensemble and other early music groups; Tours of Russia and Mexico, Schütz's Psalms of David and Cesti's Orontea in Innsbruck and at the Holland Festival; Handel's Orlando in Spain and Portugal with the Amsterdam Baroque Orchestra; Messiah in Finland and with The Sixteen (tours include visit to Utrecht 1990); Concerts with the Collegium Vocale Gent and La Chapelle Royale; Bach's St John Passion in London and Salzburg, the B minor Mass at Bruges and Cantatas in Finland (1991); Promenade Concerts 1990, in the cantata Herz und Mund und Tat und Leben; Contemporary Music Network tour with the Hilliard Ensemble in Pärt's St John Passion; Has sung at the Aldeburgh Festival, for Handel Opera in London, English National Opera and at Covent Garden. Recordings: Orlando; Messiah; Pärt St John Passion (ECM) Bach St John Passion. Honour: Winner, 1978's Hertogenbosch Competition, Holland. Address: c/o Hazard Chase Ltd, Richmond House, 16-20 Regent Street, Cambridge CB2 1DB, England.

JAMES Eirian, b. 1952, Cardigan, Wales. Singer (Mezzo-Soprano). Education: Royal College of Music with Ruth Packer. debut: Kent Opera, 1977, as Olga in Eugene Onegin, returned as Cherubino, Poppea, Rosina and Meg Page in Falstaff. Career: English National Opera in The Makropoulos Case, War and Peace, Rigoletto and Rusalka; Buxton Festival in Handel's Ariodante; Lyon Opera as Fatima (Oberon) and Rossini's Isolier; Genera Opera as Hansel; Houston Opera as Siebel in Faust and Sesto in Handel's Guilio Cesare; Aix-en-Provence as Dorabella (Così fan tutte); Covent Garden debut 1987 as Annina in Der Rosenkavalier, returned as Smeton in Anna Bolena, 1988 and Nancy in Albert Herring, 1989; Sang Dorabella at Aix-en-Provence, 1989, second Lady in Die Zauberflöte at the 1990 Prom Concerts; Ascanio in Benvenuto Cellini for Netherlands Opera, Cherubino at Houston; Concert Appearances at the BBC Promenades, Aldeburgh Festival, the Barbican and with the BBC Welsh Symphony; repertoire includes the Lieder eines fahrenden Gesellen (Lyon), Beethoven's Mass in C (London), Mozart's C Minor Mass (Edinburgh and Paris); Haydn's

Harmoniemesse; Mendelssohn's Elijah; Gluck's La Corona (City of London Festival); Hermia, Midsummer Night's Dream, Aix-en-Provence, 1991; Orlofsky, Fledermaus, 1991, English National Opera; Rosina (Barber of Seville), 1992; Scottish Opera, Sextus (Julius Caesar), 1992; Sang Cyrus in Handel's Belshazzar at the 1996 Göttingen Festival. Recordings include: Zerlina in Don Giovanni, conducted by John Eliot Gardiner, (Deutsche Grammophon); Sextus (Julius Caesar by Handel) conducted by Jean-Claude Malgoire. Current Management: IMG Artists Europe. Address: Media House, 3 Burlington Lane, Chiswick, London W4 2TH, England.

JAMES Ifor, b. 30 Aug 1931, Carlisle, England. Horn Players; Conductor. m. Helen Hames. Education: Royal Academy of Music. Career: Radio and TV performances in Britain and abroad; Orchestral concerts; Chamber music recitals. Recordings: Brahms Trio op 40: Mozart Quintet K407 and Sinfonia Concertante K297b; Solo recital records; Philip Jones Brass Ensemble records. Publication: Practice Method, 1976. Contributions to: Various journals. Hobby: Pen drawing. Address: Pinnacles, Thaxted, Cutlers Green, Thaxted, Essex, England.

JAMES Kevin (Geoffrey Gordon), b. 30 July 1961, Toronto, Canada. Violist; Violinist; Researcher; Writer. Education: Carleton University, University of Ottawa, 1982-88; Summer sessions in historical performance at University of Toronto, 1979-80; Oberlin College, 1990; McGill University, 1994. Career: Baroque Violinist, Passamezzo Players 1980-83 (Toronto) and (Baroque Group), Amsel 1989-91 (Ottawa); Principal Violinist, Nepean Symphony Orchestra 1988-91 and Ottawa Valley Festival Orchestra, 1994-; Member, Orpheus Operatic Society Orchestra, Ottawa 1985-, and Savoy Society Orchestra, Ottawa 1988-91; Founder and Concertmaster, CAMMAC Messiah Chamber Orchestra, Ottawa, 1991-95; Performer in television and radio music chamber broadcasts; Staff Writer, Researcher for Encyclopedia of Music in Canada, 1989-91 (2nd edition, University of Toronto Press, 1991-; Articles on Canadian topics for The Strad, Early Music, Musick, Performing Arts in Canada, Continuo, Newsletter of the American Musical Instrument Society, Canadian Viola Society Newsletter; Bibliographic research on Canadian instrument makers for Opus, Canadian Museum of Civilization, 1992; Co-Editor, Canadian Viola Society Newsletter, 1992-; Premieres, Jan Jarvlepp, Encounter (1992, viola and conga drums) and Moonscape (1995, transcription for viola and electric guitar); Alyssa Ryvers, Two Songs for Viola and Voice, 1990 and Synergy 1994, nine violas (commissioned). Address: #5-171 MacLaren Street, Ottawa, Ontario K2P 0K8, Canada.

JAMES Peter (Haydn), b. 17 Oct 1940, Melbourne, Australia. Vice-Principal. m. Angela Heather Lewiws, 5 Sept 1967, 1 son, 1 daughter. Education: BMus; PhD. Career: Lecturer, 1970-74, Director of Studies, 1974-83, Birmingham School of Music; Lay-Clerk, Lichfield Cathedral, 1969-74; Warden, 1983-, Vice Principal, Royal Academy of Music, London. Recordings: Various editions of music by Byrd, East, Alcock, Tomkins and Weelkes; Editions: Know You Not by Tomkins, 1972; Exalt Thyself, O God, by Byrd, 1982. Contributions to: Music and Letters; Johnson Society; Soundings. Honours: Hnorary RAM; RCM; FBSM, 1984. Memberships: Royal Music Association. Hobbies: Wine; Sport. Address: c/o Royal Academy of Music, Marylebone Road, London NW1 5HT, England.

JAMES Verona, b. 1963, Cardigan, Wales. Singer (Mezzo-soprano). Education: Studied at the Guildhall School of Music and Drama. Career: Sang Giacinta in La Finta giardiniera at the Camden Festival and Meg Page in Falstaff at the Brighton Festival; Appearances in the UK premieres of Smetana's The Devil's Wall and Rihm's Jakob Lenz; Other roles include Vitige in Handel's Flavio, Fyodor in Boris Godunov (Opera North), Rosina, Proserpina in Peri's Euridice and Hansel; Concet Repertoire includes the St Matthew Passion, Alto Rhapsody, Beethoven's Mass in C, Elijah (National Eisteddfod) and Messiah (Singapore SO); European debut as Britten's Hermia for Netherlands Opera, 1994. Address: Helen Sykes Management, Fourth Floor, Parkway House, Sheen Lane, East Shane, London SW14 8LS, England.

JANACEK Bedrich, b. 18 May 1920, Prague, Czechoslovakia. Organist. m. Elisabet Wentz, 1 Jan 1951, 1 son. Education: Soloist in Organ, 1942, Master Class in Organ, 1945-46, Diploma, 1946, State Conservatory of Music, Prague; Choir Master Degree, Royal High Music School, Stockholm, Sweden, 1961. Career: Organist, various concerts in Europe and USA, including Royal Festival Hall, London, England, 1942-; Soloist with orchestras; Teacher of Organ, State Conservatory of Music, Prague, 1946-48; Parish Musician, Cathedral Parish, Lund, Sweden, 1965-85. Compositions: Organ compositions; Choral works including 2 cantatas with orchestra; Works for brass and organ. Recordings: Various. Honours: City of Lund Cultural Prize, 1980, 1988; Commander of Merit, Ordo Militaris et Hospitalaris Sancti Lasari Hierosolymitani, 1992; Litteris et Artibus, Sweden, 1993. Address: Kyrkogatan 17, 222 22 Lund, Sweden.

JANARCEKOVA Viera, b. 23 Sept 1944, Svit, Czechoslovakia. Composer. Education: Studied at the Bratislava Conservatory and the Prague Academy. Career: Keyboard performer and composer in Germany from 1981. Compositions include: Radio drama Biomasse, 1984; 4 string quartets, 1983-89; Pausenfabrik for 2 clarinets and ensemble, 1987; Beschattungtheater for 4 cellos, 1990; Piano concerto, 1991; Vocal music including Donna Laura for mezzo and 15 instruments, 1989; Der Gehemnisvolle Nachen for mezzo cello, 1989. Address: c/o OSA. Cs armady 20, 160-56 Prague 6 - Bubenec, Czech Republic.

JANDÖ Jenö, b. 1952, Pecs, Hungary. Pianist. Education: Piano Department, Ferenc Liszt Academy, Budapest, under Professors Katalin Nemes and Pal Kadosa; Graduated, 1974. Career: Assistant to Professor Pal Kadosa, Piano Department, Budapest Academy of Music; Soloist with top Hungarian symphony orchestra, giving concerts in concert halls and studios of Hungarian Radio and Television; Guest performances in most European countries including Austria, UK, Federal Republic of Germany, Finland, France, Netherlands, Italy and Turkey, also in Australia, Canada and Japan. Address: Budapest Academy of Music, Budapest, Hungary.

JANDER Owen (Hughes), b. 4 June 1930, Mount Kisco, New York, USA. Musicologist; Music Educator. Education: BA, University of Virginia, 1951; MA, 1952, PhD, 1962, Harvard University. Career: Faculty Member, 1960-1992, Chairman, 3 terms, Department of Music, Wellesley College; Founder Collegium Musicum, originated and oversaw project to build the Fisk Organ, Wellesley College; Editor, The Wellesley Edition and The Wellesley Edition Cantata Index Series, 1962-74. Publication: Charles Brenton Fisk, Organ Builder (co-editor), 1986. Contributions to: Articles on 17th century Italian music and on Beethoven to various journals; 78 articles, The New Grove Dictionary of Music and Musicians, 1980. Honours: Guggenheim Fellowship, 1966-67; National Endowment for the Humanities Fellowship for Senior Scholars, 1985; Catherine Mills Davies Professorship in Music History, Wellesley College. Membership: American Musicological Society. Address: 72 Denton Road, Wellesley, MA 02181, USA.

JANES Fiona, b. 1961, Sydney, NSW, Australia. Singer (Mezzo-soprano). Education: Studied at the New South Wales Conservatory and in Munich with Sena Jurinac. Career: Member of the Australian Opera 1988-91, notably as Mozart's Annio, Cherubino, Dorabella and Zerlina; Siebel in Faust for Victoria State Opera and Rosina for the Lyric Opera of Queensland; Buxton Festival 1992 as Nero in Handel's Agrippina and sang Rosina with English National Opera; Season 1993-94 at the Edinburgh Festival, as Sesto in La Clemenza di Tito for the Glyndebourne Tour, and Australian Opera as Cenerentola; Season 1995-96 at the Semperoper Dresden, Mozart's Idamantes with the Flanders PO and Rossini's Isabella in Australia under Richard Bonynge; Concerts include Mozart's Requiem, Beethoven's Missa Solemnis (under Walter Weller), and Ninth Symphony under Charles Mackerras; Berlioz Faust with the Scottish National Orchestra. Address: Lies Askonas Ltd, 6 Henrietta St, London WC2E 8LA, England.

JANEVA-IVELIC Veneta, b. 1950, Bulgaria. Singer (Soprano). Education: Studied at Sofia Conservatory. Career: Sang at the Sofia Opera from 1973, National Opera Zagreb, from 1980; Guest appearances in Salzburg (with Zagreb company as Norma, 1985), Berlin Staatsoper, Paris Opéra (Abigaille in Nabucco), Luxembourg and Karlsruhe; Other roles have included Maddalena (Andrea Chénier), the Forza and Trovatore Leonoras, Violetta, Desdemona, Lady Macbeth, Butterfly and Elvira in I Puritani. Honours: Prize Winner, Rio International Competition, 1980. Address: Slovensko Narodno Gledaslisce, Zupancicava 1, 61000 Ljubljana, Serbia.

JANICKE Heike, b. 20 Dec 1962, Dresden. Education: Diploma of Violin, Musikhochschule, Dresden, 1987; Soloist Degree, Musikhochschule Freiburg, 1990. Career: Violin Soloist with Philharmonic Dresden, Berliner Sinfonie Orchestra, Rundfumksinfonie Orchestra Berlin, Radio Sinfonieorchestra Stuttgart, Gewandhaus Orchestra, Leipzig, Odense Sinfonie Orchestra, Bucharest Philharmonic; Solo and Chamber Music Concerts throughout Europe, Middle East, Japan, Middle and South America; TV and Radio Productions; Member of Berlin Philharmonic Orchestra, 1991-93; Member, London Symphony Orchestra, 1993-; Concertmaster of Dresden Philharmonic Orchestra, 1995-. Honours: Scholarship, Mendelssohn, 1988; International Violin Competitions, Music Competition, Geneva, 1985; Fritz Kreisler, France, 1987; Georg Kulenkampff, Cologne, 1988; Carl Nielsen, Odense, 1988; Zino Francescatti, Marseille, 1989. Address: Flat 7, Linden Gardens, London W2 4HA, England.

JANIS Byron, b. 24 Mar 1924, McKeesport, Pennsylvania, USA. Pianist. m. (1) June Dickson-Wright, 1 son, (2) Maria Veronica Cooper. Education: Studied with Josef and Rosina Lhevinne in New York and with Adele Marcus and Horowitz. Debut: With Pittsburgh Symphony Orchestra, 1944, in Rachmaninov's 2nd Concerto. Career: Carnegie Hall debut, 1948; European debut with Concertgebouw Orchestra, 1952; Toured Russian, 1960, 1962, appearing with Moscow Philharmonic Orchestra; Further engagements with Boston Symphony, Philadelphia Orchestra and Indianapolis Symphony; Liszt concerts in Boston and New York, 1962; Repertoire also includes Chopin, Prokofiev and Gottschalk; Career interrupted by illness in 1960s but resumed in 1972; White House concert, 1985; Discovered manuscripts of two Chopin waltzes in France, 1967. Honours: Harriet Cohen Award; First American to receive Grand Prix du Disque; Chevalier of the Order des Arts et Lettres, 1965; Ambassador for the Arts of the National Arthritis Foundation, 1985. Recordings include: Concertos by Liszt and Rachmaninov.

JANK Helena, b. 1955, Salvador, Bahia, Brazil. Concert Harpsichordist. m. Eduardo Ostergren, 11 July 1992, 1 daughter. Education: Studied at Staatliche Hochschule für Musik, Germany. Debut: Munich, 1967. Career: Professor at Campinas State University, Brazil; Harpsichordist with Münchener Bach-Orchester; Performances as soloist and in chamber music ensembles in Germany, USA and Brazil. Recordings: Helena Jank Plays Bach, Scarlatti, Ligeti; The Finest Baroque Sonatas, Erich; Mozart Sonatas; J S Bach Goldberg Variations: A Guide for the Complete Person. Publications: Goldberg Variations. Honours: Academic Recognition for Excellence in Teaching. Membership: International Bach Society. Hobbies: Sport; Theatre; Travel. Address: Rua Alvaro Muller 150, Ap 32, 13023 180 Campinas, Sao Paulo, Brazil.

JANKOVIC Eleonora, b. 18 Feb 1941, Trieste, Italy. Singer (Mezzo-soprano). Education: Studied in Trieste and Milan. Career: Member of the Opera at Zagreb, then made Italian debut at Trieste, 1972, in Smareglia's Nozze Istriane; Appearances at La Scala from 1974, Bologna, 1975, Florence, 1976, Teatro Lirico Milan, 1975, in the premiere of Al gran sole carico d'Amore by Luigi Nono; Guest engagements at Turin, Venice, Naples and Catania; Verona Arena, 1975-78, 1983, 1987; Rio de Janeiro and Buenos Aires, 1982-83; Sang Enrichetta in I Puritani at Rome, 1990, and appeared in Luisa Miller at Trieste, 1990; Sang in Wolf-Ferrari's I Quattro Rusteghi, for Geneva Opera, 1992; Has also sung the Countess in The Queen of Spades, Ulrica, Amneris, Leonora in La Favorita, Carmen, Charlotte, Marina in Boris Godunov and Mother Goose in The Rake's Progress; Many concert appearances. Address: Teatro dell'Opera di Roma, Piazza B Gigli 8, 00184 Rome, Italy.

JANOSIK Tomas, b. 2 August 1970, Bratislava, Slovakia. Flutist. Education: State Conservatory, Bratislava; Academy of Music & Dramatic Arts, Bratislava; Ecole Normale de Musique Conservatoire M Dupré, Paris; Masterclasses with V Brunner, M Kofler, A Nicolet, A Adorjan, R de Reede. Career: First Solo Flute, Slovak Radio Symphony Orchestra, 1987; Member, Slovak Philharmonic, 1991; Member, Chamber Soloists Bratislava, 1991; Member, Solistes Europeens Luxembourg, 1996; Performed all Mozart Flute Concertos with Slovak Philharmonic and Chamber Soloists Bratislava, 1994-96; Recitals and Chamber Music Performances in France, Germany, Austria, USA, Czech Republic, Slovakia; Many Recordings for Slovak Broadcasting Corporation and Slovak Television; Teacher, Flute, Academy of Music & Dramatic Arts, Bratislava. Recordings: C.PH.E.Bach: Sonata A Minor; J S Bach: Partita A Minor; S Prokofjev: Sonata F; Poulenc: Sonata; G Fauré: Fantasy with H Gafforova, Piano; C.PH.E. Bach: Concerto for Flute and Orchestra in D Minor. Honour: 1st Prize, National Flute Competition, 1988. Memberships: Deutsche Flöten Gesselschaft, Germany; National Flute Association, USA. Hobbies: Tennis; Skiing. Address: Medzilaborecka 19, 821 01 Bratislava, Slovakia.

JANOVICKY Karel, b. 18 February 1930, Plzen, Czechoslovakia. Composer; Pianist; Broadcaster. m. Sylva Simsova, 22 May 1950, 1 son, 1 daughter. Education: Realne Gymnasium; Surrey College of Music, England; Private Studies with Jan Sedivka (chamber music) and Matyas Seiber (composition). Debut: Wigmore Hall, London, 1956. Career: Many scores in MS; Recent performances at British Music Information Centre; Sonata for Bass Clarinet and Piano, Three Cambridge Songs. Contributions to: New Edition of Leos Janacek: A Biography by Jaroslav Vogel, for Orbis Publishing, London, 1981; Introducing Mr Broucek, English National Opera, 1978; Jaroslav Seifert's Nobel Prize, The Listener, 1984. Honours: First Prize, Shakespeare Competition, Bournemouth Symphony Orchestra, 1957 for Variations on a Theme of Robert Johnson Op 17; Sonata for 2 Violins and Piano on SPNM Recommended List, London. Memberships: Composers Guild of Great Britain. Hobbies: Outdoor Pursuits; Gardening; Photography. Address: 18 Muswell Avenue, London N10 2EG, England.

JANOWITZ Gundula, b. 2 Aug 1937, Berlin, Germany. Opera Singer (Soprano). m. 1 daughter. Education: Academy of Music and Performing Arts, Graz; Administrator. Debut: With Vienna State Opera. Career: Sang with Deutsche Oper Berlin,

1966; Metropolitan Opera, New York, 1967, as Sieglinde in Die Walküre, conducted by Karajan; Salzburg Festival, 1968-81, as Mozart's Donna Anna, Fiordiligi and Countess, Strauss's Marschallin and Ariadne; Teatro Colon, Buenos Aires, 1970, Munich State Opera, 1971, Grand Opera, Paris, 1973, Covent Garden Opera, 1976, La Scala, 1978; Concerts in major cities throughout the world; Appearances at Bayreuth, Aix-en-Provence, Glyndebourne (as Ilia in Idomeneo), Spoleto, Salzburg and Munich festivals; Member, Vienna State Opera and Deutsch Oper Berlin; Among her roles were Mozart's Pamina, Wagner's Eva and Elisabeth, Strauss's Empress, and Arabella and Puccini's Mimi; Returned to Covent Garden, 1987, as Ariadne; Opera Director at Graz, 1990-91; Recent concert engagements in Four Last Songs by Stausss; Schubert Bicentenary concert at St John's, London, 1997. Recordings: For three labels. Hobbies: Modern literature. Address: Vereinigte Bühnen, Kaiser Josef Platz 10, A-8010 Graz, Austria.

JANOWSKI Marek, b. 18 Feb 1939, Warsaw, Poland. Conductor. Education: Studied at Cologne Musikhochschule and in Siena. Career: Assistant Conductor in Aachen, Cologne and Dusseldorf opera houses; London debut, 1969, leading the Cologne Opera in the British premiere of Henze's Der junge Lord; Musical Director, Freiburg and Dortmund Operas, 1973-79; Guest Conductor at opera houses in Hamburg, Paris, Munich and Berlin; American opera debut, San Francisco, 1983; Metropolitan Opera, 1984, Strauss's Arabella; Artistic Adviser and Conductor, Royal Liverpool Philharmonic Orchestra, 1983-86; Currently Chief Conductor of the Nouvel Philharmonique de Radio France and the Gurzenich Orchester, Cologne; Conducted the company of the Cologne Opera in Fidelio at Hong Kong, 1989; Die Meistersinger at the Théâtre du Châtelet, Paris, 1990; Conducted Elektra at Orange, 1991. Recordings: Opera sets including the first compact disc Ring, with the Dresden Staatskapelle, Weber's Euryanthe, Strauss's Die schweigsame Frau and Penderecki's The Devils of Loudun; Weber's Oberon, 1997. Address: IMG Artists (Europe), Media House, 3 Burlington Lane, Chiswick, London W4 2TH, England.

JANSEN Jacques, b. 22 Nov 1913, Paris, France. Singer (Baritone). Education: Studied with Charles Panzera and Claire Croiza in Paris. Debut: Opéra-Comique, Paris, 1941, as Debussy's Pelleas. Career: Sang Pelléas at the Holland Festival, 1948, and at Covent Garden in 1949; Further appearances in Vienna (Theater an der Wien, 1946), the Metropolitan Opera and the Opéra-Comique (Valerian in Hahn's Malvina, 1945, and Pierne's Fragonard, 1946); Paris Opera, 1952, as Ali in Les Indes galantes by Rameau and Aix-en-Provence, 1956, as Citheron in Rameau's Platée; Other roles were Rabaud's Marouf, and Danilo in Die lustige Witwe, which he sang 1500 times, principally at the Théâtre Mogador in Paris. Recordings include: Pelléas et Mélisande; Platée.

JANSEN Rudolf, b. 19 Jan 1940, Arnhem, Netherlands. Pianist. m. (1) Margreet Honig, 2 children, (2) Christa Pfeiler, 2 children. Education: Prix d'Excellence, Amsterdam Conservatory. Career: Soloist; Accompanist for numerous leading singers and other artists throughout the world. Recordings: More than 80 recordings as Lieder Accompanist or Chamber Music Player. Current Management: Nederlands Impresariaat, Amsterdam, Netherlands. Address: Schepenenlaan 2, 1181 BB Amstelveen, Netherlands.

JANSONS Arturs Edmund, b. 27 May 1952, Toronto, Canada. Violist. Education: BMus, University of Toronto, 1977; BM, 1980, MM, 1981, Juilliard School. Debut: Carnegie Recital Hall, New York, 1981. Career: Recitals, Toronto, Ottawa, Montreal, Vancouver, Seattle, Cleveland, Rochester, London, 1972-77; Founding Member, Canadian String Quartet, 1977-79; New York recitals and chamber music performances, 1978, 1980, 1981, 1983, 1990; Canadian Opera Company Orchestra, 1978-79; Faculty Member, Royal Conservatory of Music, 1983-90; Principal Viola, Stratford Festival, Canada, 1985-93; Extensive Tours to Hawaii, 1993, 1994, Alaska, 1994, Singapore, 1995, Hong Kong, 1995, with Livent of Canada; Independent recording of chamber music by Latvian composers, 1988; Numerous broadcasts. Membership: Toronto Latvian Concert Association. Hobbies: Sailing; Scuba diving. Address: 744 Glengrove Avenue West, Toronto, Ontario M6B 2J6, Canada.

JANSONS Mariss, b. 14 January 1943, Latvia. Conductor. Education: Studied at Leningrad Conservatory and in Vienna and Salzburg with Swarowsky and Karajan; Winner, Herbert von Karajan Competition, 1971. Career: Associate Conductor of Leningrad Philharmonic Orchestra and from 1979 Music Director of the Oslo Philharmonic; Successful tours to Italy, Spain, France, the Edinburgh Festival, America and Japan; Regularly Conducts Leading Orchestras of North America and Europe, including the Baltimore, Boston, Chicago and Pittsburgh Symphony Orchestras, the Cleveland and Philadelphia Orchestras, the Berlin Philharmonic, Vienna Philharmonic, Royal Concertgebouw, London Symphony, the London Philharmonic and New York Philharmonic. Recordings: With the Oslo Philharmonic, St

Petersburg Philharmonic, Berlin Philharmonic, Royal Concertgebouw, The London Philharmonic and the Philharmonia Orchestras; Professor of Conducting at the St Petersburg Conservatorie. Honours: Norwegian Cultural Prize of Anders Jahre; Norwegian Order of Merit; Commander with Star of The Royal Norwegian Order of Merit for his work and achievements with the Oslo Philharmonic Orchestra. Address: IMG Artists, Media House, 3 Burlington Lane, Chiswick, London W4 2TH, England.

JANSSENS Robert, b. 27 July 1939, Brussels, Belgium. Composer; Director. m. Dominique van der Moere, 29 Aug 1962, 2 daughters. Education: Advanced Diplomas, Conservatoires of Brussels and Liège. Career: Director, Brussels Music Academy; Professor, Royal Conservatory, Brussels; Director, Brussels Festival Orchestra; Freelance Director. Compositions: Symphonies; 2 piano concertos; 2 violin concertos; 2 horn concertos; Yerma, ballet; Messe des Artistes; Noëls da Capo. Recordings: Messe des Artistes; Noëls da Capo; 3 CDs. Honours: Fuerison Prize, Royal Academy for Arts, Belgium; Chevalier de l'Ordre de la Couronne. Memberships: SABAM; Cercle Royal Gaulois; Lions Club; Cinquantenaire. Address: Rue Albert I 63 B, 1330 Rixensart, Belgium.

JANULAKO Vassilio, b. 14 Sept 1933, Athens, Greece. Singer (Baritone). Education: Studied at the Athens Conservatory. Debut: Athens, 1961, as the High Priest in Alceste. Career: Engagements at opera houses in Stuttgart, Berlin, Dusseldorf, Hamburg, Munich, Vienna, Frankfurt, Nuremberg, Zurich, Toulouse and San Francisco; Roles include Pizarro, the Dutchman, Telramund, Amfortas, Don Giovanni, Mozart's Count, Gerard, Scarpia, Escamillo, Mandryka, Milhaud's Christopher Columbus and parts in operas by Verdi; Cologne, 1986, as Pandolfe in Cendrillon by Massenet; Spoleto and Philadelphia, 1988, in Jenufa and Rusalka; Sang Paolo in Simon Boccanegra at Cologne, 1990. Address: c/o Oper der Stadt Köln, Offenbachplatz, D-5000 Cologne, Germany.

JAPE Mijndert, b. 11 July 1932, Geleen, Limburg, Netherlands. Lutenist; Guitarist; Writer; Music Historian. m. Marie-Hélène Habets, 2 Aug 1960 (dec. 20 Sept 1987). Education: Guitar: Muzieklyceum Heerlen, 1956, 1957; Conservatory of Maastricht, 1958; Higher Diploma cum laude, Schola Cantorum, Paris, 1960; Studied with Hans-Lutz Niessen, Ida Presti, Alexandre Lagoya; Lute: Royal Conservatory of the Hague and summer schools, England, France, Netherlands, Belgium, Germany, 1972-77; Studied with Toyohiki Satoh, Eugen Dombois, Thomas Binkley, Anthony Bailes; Musicological and Pedagogical study. Career: Soloist, Accompanist on lute instruments, baroque operas, vocal groups, Belgium, Netherlands, France; Director, Delitiae Musicae, specialising in 1550-1650 music and poetry concerts, Netherlands, Belgium, France; Plays 1820 Moitessier guitar and 8 lute instruments; Guest Lecturer; Teacher of Lute and Guitar, 1955-92, Musical director, 1986-92, Sittard Musical School, 1955-92; Teaching Lute and Guitar, Music Academy, Maasmechelen and Tongeren, Belgium. Recordings: 4 (solo, ensemble), Belgium, Netherlands. Publications: Fernando Sor - Opera Omnia for the Guitar; On Lute Tuition, 1987; Classical Guitar Music in Print, bibliography, 12 vols (with Marie-Hélène Habets), volumes 5,8 and 9, 1980-1989; Louys de Moy - le Petit Boucquet, 1990; Elementa Pro Arte, lute tutor, in progress; The "Wilhelmus van Nassouwe", Dutch National Anthem, development and relationship to the lute music, 1994. Address: POB 81, NL-6190 Beek, Limburg, Netherlands.

JARDA Tudor, b. 11 Feb 1922, Cluj, Rumania. Composer. Education: Studied in Cluj and Timosoara, 1941-48. Career: Played the trumpet at the Rumanian Opera in Cluj, 1945-48; Teacher of harmony, Cluj Conservatory, 1949-88. Compositions: Operas: The Soimaru Kin, 1956; The Forest with Vultures, 1961; The Power of Life, 1984; Angel and Demon, 1989; 3 symphonies; Symphonic Suite; Concerto for flute and orchestra; Ballets: Morning Star of the Day; Rounds of the World: the Carol; Instrumental and chamber music. Address: Str Galati 16, 3400 Cluj-Napoca, Rumania.

JARMAN Douglas, b. 21 Nov 1942, Dewsbury, Yorkshire, England. Lecturer; Writer. m. Angela Elizabeth Brown, 26 Sept 1970, 2 daughters. Education: BS Honours, Music, Hull University, 1964; PhD, Durham University, 1968; Research Fellow, Liverpool University, 1968-70. Career: Lecturer in Music, University of Leeds, 1970-71; Lecturer, 1974-86, Principal Lecturer, 1986, Academic Studies, Royal Northern College of Music, Manchester. Recordings: Talk, Lulu; The Historical Background, recording of The Complete Lulu. Publications: The Music of Alban Berg, 1979, 1983; Kurt Weill, 1982; Wozzeck, 1989; The Berg Companion, 1989; Alban Berg, Lulu, 1991; Expressionism Reassessed, 1993. Contributions to: Perspectives of New Music; Musical Quarterly; Musical Times; Music Review; Journal of Royal Musical Association; Newsletter of International Alban Berg Society; Alban Berg Studien, volume 2. Honours: Honorary Fellow, Royal Northern College of Music, 1986. Memberships: Director, Alban Berg Society; Director, Square

Chapel Building and Arts Trusts; Advisory Board, Music Analysis. Address: 1 Birch Villas, Birchcliffe Road, Hebden Bridge HX7 8DA, England.

JARRETT Keith, b. 8 May 1945, Allentown, Pennsylvania, USA. Pianist; Composer. Career: First solo concert, aged 7, followed by professional appearances; 2-hour solo concert of own compositions, 1962; Led own trio in Boston; Worked with Roland Kirk, Tony Scott and others in New York; Joined Art Blakely, 1965; Toured Europe with Charles Lloyd, 1966, with Miles Davis, 1970-71; Soloist and Leader of own groups, 1969-. Recordings include: Bach's Well-Tempered Clavier. Address: c/o Vincent Ryan, 135 West 16th Street, New York, NY 10011, USA.

JÄRVI Neeme, b. 7 June 1937, Tallinn, Estonia. Conductor (Symphony and Opera). m. 2 Sept 1961, 2 sons, 1 daughter. Education: Tallinn Music School; Percussion, Choral Conducting; Under Professor Nicolai Rabinovich and Yevgeni Mravinski, Leningrad State Conservatory, 1955-60; Postgraduate studies, 1968. Career: Music Director, Estonian State Symphony Orchestra, 1960-80; Music Director, Principal Conductor, Theatre Estonia, Tallinn, 1964-77; Guest Conductor with Leningrad Philharmonic, Moscow Philharmonic, USSR Radio Philharmonic Moscow, USSR State Symphony Orchestra, USSR and abroad; New York Philharmonic, Philadelphia, Boston, Chicago and Los Angeles Philharmonic Orchestras; San Francisco, Washington, Toronto, Cincinnati, Atlanta, Montreal and Ottawa, 1980-; Metropolitan Opera, Eugene Onegin, 1979, 1984; Samson and Delila, 1982; New production of Mussorgsky's Kovanshchina, 1985/1986 season; Music Director, Principal Conductor, Göteborg Symphony, 1982-; Musical Director, Principal Conductor, Scottish National Orchestra, 1984-88; Music Director, Detroit Symphony Orchestra, 1989-; Guest Conductor, Paris, Cologne Radio, Amsterdam Concertgebouw, Bavarian Radio, Berlin Philharmonic, Hamburg Radio, Bamberg Symphony; Scandinavian orchestras. Recordings: Complete symphonies by Berwald, Niels Gade, Prokofiev, Tubin, Dvořák, Brahms, Rimsky-Korsakov, Stravinsky, Tchaikovsky, Shostakovich, Glazunov, Scriabin and Rachmaninov; Rachmaninov's Aleko and Zandonai's Francesca da Rimini, 1997. Honours: 1st Prize, Conductor Competition, Academy di Santa Cecilia, Rome; Toblach Prize, 1993, for best Mahler Symphony, new recording (Mahler 3 with Royal Scottish National). Current Management: Columbia Artists Management, New York, USA. Address: Göteborgs Konserthus, Stenhammarsgatan 1, 41256 Gothenburg, Sweden.

JÄRVI Paavo, b. 1962, Tallinn, Estonia. Conductor. Education: Studied in Tallinn, at the Juilliard School, with Bernstein in Los Angeles and Max Rudolf at the Curtis Institute. Career: Has conducted all the major Scandinavian Orchestras, notably as chief conductor of the Malmo Symphony (from 1994) and Principal guest of the Stockholm PO (from 1995); Further engagements with the BBC, Royal and Rotterdam Philharmonics, Dallas SO, Orchestra of the Age of Enlightenment and the Russian National Orchestra; Productions of Puccini's Trittico in Gothenburg, Tosca in Stockholm and I Vespri Siciliani for Norwegian National Opera; Conducted the OAE at South Bank, London, in concert of French music, 1997. Recordings: Sibelius album with the Royal Stockholm PO; Sibelius Kullervo Symphony, 1997. Address: Harrison/Parrott Ltd, 12 Penzance Place, London W11 4PA, England.

JARVLEPP Jan Eric, b. 3 Jan 1953, Ottawa, Ontario, Canada. Composer; Teacher; Freelance Cellist. Education: BMus, University of Ottawa, 1976; MMus, McGill University, Montreal, Canada, 1978; PhD, University of CA, San Diego, USA, 1981. Career: CBC Chamber Music Broadcasts; Member, Ottawa Symphony Orchestra, 1981-; Nepean Symphony Orchestra, 1981-91; Electronic compositions performed on several different Canadian and US University campuses and Radio stations; Music Director of Espace Musique New Music Concert Society, 1993-. Compositions: Lento, 1975; Ice, 1976; Aurora Borealis, 1976; Buoyancy, 1977; Flotation, 1978; Transparency and Density, 1978; Trumpet Piece, 1979; Cello Concerto, 1980; Time Zones, 1981; Night Music, 1982; Harpsichord Piece, 1984; Evening Music for Carillon, 1984; Cadenza for Solo Cello, 1985; Guitar Piece, 1985; Morning Music for Carillon, 1986; Afternoon Music for Carillon, 1986; Sunrise, 1987; Sunset, 1987; Trio, 1987; Liquid Crystals, 1988; Camerata Music, 1989; Dream, 1990; Life in The Fast Lane, 1990; Encounter, 1991; Underwater, 1992; Music from Mars, 1993; Moonscape, 1993; Robot Dance, 1994; Pierrot Solaire, 1994; Transformations, 1995; Tarantella, 1996; Bassoon Quartet, 1996; Saxophone Quartet, 1996; Trio No 2, 1997. Recordings: Chronogrammes; Soundtracks of The Imagination. Publications: Compositional Aspects of Berio's Tempi Concertati, Interface, volume II, No 4, 1982; Pitch and Texture Analysis of Ligeti's Lux Aeterna, ex tempore, volume 2-1, 1982; Alchemy in the Nineties, 1997. Address: 2-424 Lisgar Street, Ottawa, Ontario, Canada, K1R 5H1.

JASINSKA Danuta, b. 14 June 1947, Chrzanów, Poland. Musicologist. Education: Institute of Musicology, Warsaw

University, 1966-71; Editing of Music, Academy of Music, Cracow, 1971-73; Doctor of Liberal Arts in Musicology, Adam Mickiewicz University, Poznan, 1983. Career: Assistant Editor, PWM-Edition, Cracow, 1971-73; University Teacher, Jagellonian University, Cracow, 1973-76; University Teacher, Adam Mickiewicz University, Poznan, 1976-. Publications: Technique and Musical style of Michal Spisak; Style Brillante and Music of Chopin, 1995. Contributions to: Articles to Muzyka Periodical on XXth Century Music; Encyclopedia of Music, Cracow, 1979-; Dictionnaire de la Musique, Bordas, 1986. Memberships: Musicological Section, Polish Composers Union. Hobbies: Mountain Trips. Address: ul Chociszewskiego 54 a 6, 60-261 Poznan, Poland.

JASINKA-JEDROSZ Elzbieta, b. 11 Jan 1949, Katowice, Poland. Musicologist. m. Janusz Jedrosz, 25 July 1970, 1 son. Education: Musicological studies, Warsaw University, 1968-73. Career: Engaged in bibliographic documentation of Polish musical works and in other tasks at Archive of 20th Century Polish Composers, Warsaw University Library Music Collections, 1973-. Publications: The Manuscripts of Karol Szymanowski's Musical Works, catalogue, 1983; Co-author, Karol Szymanowski in the Polish Collections, guide-book, 1989; The Manuscripts of the Young Poland's Composers, catalogue, 1997. Contributions to: Ruch Muzyczny, 1980, 1981, 1983. Memberships: Polish Composers Union; Karol Szymanowski Music Association, Zakopane; Polish Librarians Association; Association of Polish Musicians. Hobby: Poetry. Address: ul Janinówka 11 m 122, 03562 Warsaw, Poland.

JEDLICKA Dalibor, b. 23 May 1929, Svoyanov, Czechoslovakia. Singer (Bass-baritone). Education: Studied in Ostrava with Rudolf Vasek. Debut: Opava, 1953, as Mumlala in The Two Widows by Smetana. Career: Sang at the National Theatre, Prague, 1957-77, also guest appearances with the company in Brno, Amsterdam, Zurich and Edinburgh (1970 in the British premiere of The Excursions of Mr Broucek by Janácek); Engagements at Belgrade, Zagreb, Warsaw, Venice and Bologna; Repertoire included buffo roles and German, French and Czech operas; Mozart's Figaro and Papageno, Don Pasquale and Kaspar in Der Freischütz; Opéra Comique, Paris, 1988, in From the House of the Dead. Recordings include: Janácek's Katya Kabanova, The Cunning Little Vixen and From the House of the Dead, conducted by Charles Mackerras; Pauer's Suzanna Vojirva and Don Giovanni; Another recording of Cunning Little Vixen.

JEDLICKA Rudolf, b. 22 Jan 1920, Skalice, Czechoslovakia. Singer (Baritone). Education: Studied with Tino Pattieri, Pavel Ludikar and Fernando Carpi in Vienna and Prague. Debut: Dresden Staatsoper, 1944, as Marcel in La Bohème. Career: Sang in Prague from 1945; Produced opera at Usti nad Labem, 1946-49; Guest with the Staatsoper Berlin from 1958; Appearances at the Vienna Staatsoper and in Russia, German and Polish opera houses as Mozart's Figaro and Don Giovanni, Posa in Don Carlos and Rossini's Figaro; Sang with the Prague National Opera at the Edinburgh Festival, 1964, 1970, in the British premieres of Janácek's From the House of the Dead and The Excursions of Mr Broucek; Professor at the Prague Conservatory, 1973-75; Director of the National Theatre, Prague, 1989; Sang Grigoris in Martinu's Greek Passion at Wiesbaden, 1990. Recordings: Jenufa. Address: National Theatre, PO Box 865, 112 30 Prague 1, Czech Republic.

JEFFERS Ronald (Harrison), b. 25 Mar 1942, Springfield, Illinois, USA. Composer; Conductor. Education: Studied composition with Ross Lee Finney at University of Michigan; University of California at San Diego, 1970-72, with Pauline Oliveros, Kenneth Gaburo and Robert Erickson; Choral conducting at Occidental College, Los Angeles, 1968-72. Career: Director of choral activities at Stony Brook, New York, and at Oregon State University; Tours of Europe, 1978 and 1982. Compositions include: Missa concrete for 3 choruses, 1969, revised, 1973; In Memoriam for chamber ensemble, 1973; Time Passes for mezzo, tape and ensemble, 1974-81; Transitory for chorus and tape, 1980; Arise My Love for 12 voices, chimes and gongs, 1981; Crabs for tape, 1981. Address: c/o ASCAP, ASCAP Building, One Lincoln Plaza, New York, NY 10023, USA.

JEFFERSON Alan (Rigby), b. 20 Mar 1921, Ashtead, Surrey, England. Author. m. Antonia Dora Raeburn, 24 Sept 1976, 2 sons, 3 sons, 1 daughter from previous marriages. Education: Rydal School, Colwyn Bay, 1935-37; Old Vic Theatre School, 1947-48. Career: Theatre Stage Manager/Director; Administrator, London Symphony Orchestra, 1968-69; Manager, BBC Concert Orchestra, 1969-73; Visiting Professor in Vocal Interpretation, Guildhall School of Music and Drama, London, 1968-74; Editor, The Monthly Guide to Recorded Music, 1980-82. Publications: The Operas of Richard Strauss in Great Britain 1910-1963, 1964; The Lieder of Richard Strauss, 1971; Delius (Master Musicians), 1972; The Life of Richard Strauss, 1973; Inside the Orchestra, 1974; Strauss (Music Masters), 1975; The Glory of Opera, 1976, Norwegian version, 1980, 2nd edition, 1983; Discography of Richard Strauss's Operas, 1977; Strauss (Short Biographies), 1978; Sir Thomas Beecham, 1979; The Complete Gilbert &

Sullivan Opera Guide, 1984; Der Rosenkavalier, 1986; Lotte Lehmann, A Centenary Biography, 1988, German language edition, 1991; Elisabeth Schwarzkopf (biography), 1996. Contributions to: Blätter Internationale Richard Strauss Gesellschaft, Vienna; Classical Express. Memberships: Royal Society of Musicians of Great Britain; Savile Club. Hobbies: Listening to chamber music; Paternal enjoyment. Current Management: Watson, Little Ltd., London. Address: c/o Watson, Little Ltd., 12 Egbert Street, London, NW1 8LJ, England.

JEFFERY Peter, b. 19 Oct 1953, New York City, New York, USA. Professor of Music. m. Margot Fassler, 1983, 2 sons. Education: MFA, 1977, PhD, 1980, Princeton University. Career: Hill Monastic Manuscript Library, 1980-82; Mellon Faculty Fellow, Harvard University, 1982-83; University of Delaware, 1984-92; Boston College, 1992-93; Princeton University, 1993-. Publications: A Bibliography for Medieval and Renaissance Musical Manuscript Research, 1980; Re-Envisioning Past Musical Cultures. Contributions to: Journal of the American Musicological Society; Studia Liturgica; Archiv für Liturgiewissenschaft; Created Gregorian Chant Home Page on the World Wide Web. Honours: Alfred Einstein Award, 1985; National Endowment for the Humanities Grant, 1986-88; John D MacArthur Fellowship, 1987-82. Memberships: American Musicological Society; Medieval Academy of America; North American Academy of Liturgy; Societas Liturgica. Address: Music Department, Princeton University, NJ 08544, USA.

JEFFES Peter, b. 1951, London, England. Singer (Tenor). Education: Royal College of Music, London; Rome with Paolo Silveri. Career: Italian debut in Rome Opera in Spontini's Agnese di Hohenstaufen; Paris Opéra in Doktor Faust; With English Bach Festival at Covent Garden in Rameau's Castor et Pollux; Nero in L'Incoronazione di Poppea for Swiss TV; European engagements as Lohengrin, Tamino and Lensky; Sang Mozart in Rimsky's Mozart and Salieri at Barcelona in 1987; Festival appearances at Aix-en-Provence, Orange, Monte Carlo, Athens and in the USA; Engagement with British companies in Roméo et Juliette, Les Contes d'Hoffmann, Die Zauberflöte, The Rake's Progress and A Midsummer Night's Dream; Opera North in the British premiere of Strauss's Daphne, 1987; Season 1988-89 in The Love for Three Oranges for Opera North; Since 1988, repertoire, roles in Cavalleria Rusticana, Pagliacci, Idomeneo, Faust, Werther, Salome, Fliegende Holländer, Macbeth, Attila and Eisenstein in Die Fledermaus; Now sings extensively in Europe and regularly in Israel; The Prince in the Love for Three Oranges, 1992. Address: c/o Music International, 13 Ardilaun Road, Highbury, London N5 2QR, England.

JEFFREYS Celia, b. 20 Jan 1948, Southampton, England. Singer (Soprano). Education: Studied music at the Royal College of Music, ARCM. Debut: Welsh National Opera, 1970, as Adele in Die Fledermaus. Career: Sang at various regional opera houses in Britain; Appeared on BBC and Southern TV, Britain; Sang at: Kassel and Darmstadt, Germany, Theater am Gärtnerplatz, Munich from 1976, Stadtheater Basel, 1978-81; From 1981-88 appeared as guest artist in: Bern, Berlin Koblenz, Salzburg, Theater an der Wien, Schlosspiele Heidelberg, Festspiele, Bregenz; From 1988-91 engagements in Linz, Austria; Appearing regularly in Salzburg and Linz, 1997-; Opera roles include Donna Elvira, in Don Giovanni; Mimi, in La Bohème, the Marschallin in Rosenkavalier; Agathe in Der Freischütz; Nedda, in Pagliacci, Leonore, in Fidelio; Operetta roles include: Hanna Glawari, in The Merry Widow and Rosalinde in Die Fledermaus; Teacher, Bayerische Theaterakademie, Munich. Recordings: Student Prince; Brahms, German Requiem. Current Management: ASM, Obergütschrain 3, CH 6003 Lucerne, Switzerland. Address: Grasmeierstrasse 12 B, D-80805 Munich, Germany.

JELEZNOV Irina, b. 4 Oct 1958, Astrakhan, Russia. Duo Pianist; Docent of Chamber Music. m. 29 Aug 1980, 1 son. Education: Piano Faculty, 1981, Piano Duo postgraduate course, 1987, Tchaikovsky Conservatoire, Moscow. Debut: Tashkent Conservatoire Hall, 1984. Career includes: Recitals and orchestra performances, Tashkent, yearly 1984-93; Appearances in Moscow: The Maly Hall, Moscow Conservatoire, 1986, 1987, Rachmaninov Hall and Shuvalova's Home, 1991; Piano Duo Festivals: Sverdlovsk, 1989, Leningrad, 1990, Nizny Novgorod, 1991, Novosibirsk, 1992; International Piano Duo competitions: Belgrade Yugoslavia, 1989, Caltanissetta, Italy, and Hartford, Connecticut, USA, 1990, Miami, Florida, 1991; TV and radio appearances, Docent, Chair of Chamber Music, Tashkent Conservatoire. Membership: International Piano Duo Association, Tokyo, Japan. Address: Prospekt Kosmonavtov d 12-106, 700015 Tashkent, Uzbekistan.

JELEZOV Maxim, b. 19 May 1958, Moscow, Russia. Duo Pianist. m. 29 Aug 1980, 1 son. Education: Piano Faculty, 1981, Postgraduate course as Piano Duo, 1987, Tchaikovsky Conservatoire, Moscow. Debut: Tashkent Conservatoire Hall, 1984. Career includes: Performances: Tashkent, yearly 1984-93; Maly Hall, Moscow Conservatoire, 1986, 1987; Sverdlovsk Piano

Duo Festival, 1989; Belgrade, Yugoslavia, 1989; International Piano Duo Festival Leningrad, 1990; Hartford, USA, 1990; Caltanissetta, Italy, 1990; Rachmaninoff Hall, Moscow, 1991; Shuvalova's Home, Moscow, 1991; Nizny Novgorod Piano Duo Festival, 1991; International Piano Duo Festival, Ekaterinburg, 1991-93; Piano Duo Festival, The Masters of Piano Duo, Novosibirsk, 1992; TV and radio appearances. Hobbies: Football; Table tennis. Address: Prospekt Kosmonavtov d 12-106, 700015 Tashkent, Uzbekistan.

JELINEK Ladislav, b. 21 Feb 1944, Brno, Czechoslovakia. Concert Pianist. m., 2 sons. Education: State Conservatory in Brno, 1958-62; Janácek University of Musical Arts, Brno, majoring in solo piano under Professor Frantisek Schäfer. Debut: Besedni Dum, Brno, 1966. Career: Appearances as soloist of Janácek Philharmonic Orchestra, solo pianist and chamber musician in Czechoslovakia and majority of Eastern European countries; Radio and television appearances in Eastern Europe, 1968-81; Numerous appearances in Western Europe, 1981-; University Teacher at the Frankfurter Hochschule für Musik and Darstellende Kunst, 1984-. Recordings: Numerous solo recordings at Bayerischer Rundfunk (radio), Munich, with compositions by Liszt, Prokofiev, Jan Novak, V Novak, Smetana, Haydn, Chopin and Dvorák. Honours: Piano competitions: Academy of Music, Czechoslovakia, 1961; Hradec Kralove, 1963. Membership: Artistic Advisory Board, Janácek University of Musical Arts, Brno. Hobbies: Travel; History; Cooking; Reading. Current Management: Conzertmanager Edith Roschlau. Address: Lerchenweg 2, 61350 Bad Homburg, Germany.

JELINEK Miloslav, b. 25 May 1965, Brno, Czech Republic. Musician. m. Marcela Braunerova, 11 July 1992, 2 daughters. Education: Conservatoire in Kromeriz; Janacek Academy of Music Arts, Brno. Debut: Brno Chamber Orchestra, 1990. Career: Kusevickj with Philharmonie of B Martinu, 1986; Bottesini with Moravia Philharmonie Olomouc, 1987; Recordings for TV Eccles Sonata, 1988; Member, Double Bass Group in Brno, Philharmonie, 1989; Pedagogue of Janacek Academy, Brno, 1990; Vanhal with Brno Philharmonie, 1991; Principal, Solo Player, Double Bass Group, Philharmonie, 1994; Over 70 Solo Recitals in Czech Republic, Austria, Germany, Switzerland. Recordings: CD, J B Vanhal: Concert, for Double Bass & Orchestra, with Brno State Philharmonic Orchestra, 1991; K D Von Dittersdorf: Concert, for Double Bass and Orchestra, Concertant Sinfonie, for Viola and Double Bass with Orchestra, with Czech Chamber Soloists, 1992. Honours: 3rd Prize, Competition of Conservatories, Czech Republic, 1980; 2nd Prize, International Competition of Double Bass, Kromeriz, 1982; 1st Prize, International Competition, Kromeriz, 1984; 1st Prize, Competition of String Instruments, Janacek Academy, 1985. Membership: Bass Club, Kromeriz. Address: Brezinova 38, 61600 Brno, Czech Republic.

JENCKOVA Eva, b. 11 March 1949, Novy Bydzov, Czech Republic. Professor. m. Jaroslav Jencek, 24 June 1988, 2 sons. Education: Pedagogical Faculty, Teachers Training College, Hradec Kralove, 1971; Philosophy Faculty, Charles University, Prague, 1982, PhD, 1983; Musicology, Charles University. Debut: Concert with Pardubice Chamber Orchestra, Prague Spring Festival, 1972. Publications: Music for Children, 1992; Select Piano Works for Music Teachers, 1992; Music and Movement, 1997; Working With A Song, 1997. Contributions to: Magazines, Reviews and Journals. Honours: Charles University Rectors Award, Best University Textbook, 1992. Memberships: Czech Musical Society; European Association for Music in Schools. Hobbies: Dancing; Literature; Hiking. Address: Kamenicna 90, 564 01 Zamberk, Czech Republic.

JENISOVA Eva, b. 1963, Presov, Slovakia. Singer (Soprano). Education: Studied at the Bratislava Conservatory. Career: Soloist with the National Theatre Bratislava from 1986; Further appearances (from 1988) with the Deutsche Oper Berlin, Bolshoi Moscow, Budapest State Opera, National Theatre Prague and the Israel and Edinburgh Festivals; Vienna Staatsoper from 1990, as Marguerite in Faust, Donna Elvira, Katya Kabanova and Rusalka; Elvira under Harnoncourt at Amsterdam, Pamina and Violetta at Trieste, and Janacek's Vixen at the Paris Châtelet; Covent Garden debut 1997, as Katya Kabanova; Season 1997-98 as the Duchess of Parma in Busoni's Faust at Lyons, the Vixen in Madrid, and Mozart's Vitellia at Nancy; Concerts include Mareiken in Martinu's Legends of Mary, with the Vienna SO, the Missa Solemnis at Madrid, the German Requiem in Bologna, Carmina Burana in Munich, and Dvorák's Stabat Mater at Salzburg; Mahler's Second Symphony in Graz, and Rusalka at the Salle Pleyel, Paris; Teatro Regio Turin 1997, as Mélisande. Address: c/o 13 Ardilaun Road, London N5 2QR, England.

JENKINS Carol, b. 1965, Toronto, Canada. Violinist. Education: Studied at University of Toronto with Rodney Friend and Victor Danchenki. Career: Associate Leader, Denver Symphony Orchestra and other orchestras; Second Violinist, Da Vinci Quartet from 1988, founded in 1980 under the sponsorship of the Fine Arts Quartet; Many concerts in USA and elsewhere in a repertoire including works by Mozart, Beethoven, Brahms, Dvorak, Shostakovich and Bartók. Honours: (With the Da Vinci Quartet), Awards and Grants from the NEA, the Western States Arts Foundation and the Colorado Council for the Humanities; Artist in Residence, University of Colorado. Current Management: Sonata, Glasgow, Scotland. Address: C/O Da Vinci Quartet, 11 Northpark Street, Glasgow G20 7AA, Scotland.

JENKINS Graeme (James Ewers), b. 1958, England. Conductor. m. Joanna, 2 daughters. Education: Studied at Dulwich College and Cambridge University; Royal College of Music with Norman Del Mar and David Willcocks; Adrian Boult Conducting Scholar. Debut: Conducted Albert Herring and the Turn of the Screw at college. Career: The Beggar's Opera, Die Entführung and Le nozze di Figaro for Kent Opera; Andrea Chénier, Brighton Festival; Cesti's La Dori (Spitalfields); Il Trovatore, Le nozze di Figaro and Così fan tutte with Scottish Opera; Così fan tutte with English National Opera (ENO debut), 1988; European debut, 1987, Hansel and Gretel and Ravel Double Bill with Geneva Opera; Simon Boccanegra, Netherlands Opera, 1989; As Music Director of Glyndebourne Touring Opera has conducted A Midsummer Night's Dream, Albert Herring, Simon Boccanegra and Così fan tutte; La Traviata and Death in Venice (on BBC TV), 1989; Glyndebourne Festival debut, 1987, with Carmen and Capriccio; Returned for Ravel Double Bill and Falstaff; Arabella, 1989; Oedipus Rex and Petrushka with Scottish Opera, 1989; Further engagements include Carmen and La Rondine with Canadian Opera in Toronto, La Bohème with Australian Opera, 1990; Concert appearances with the Hallé Orchestra, BBC Scottish, BBC Philharmonic, BBC Symphony, Royal Philharmonic, Krakow Radio Symphony and Scottish Chamber Orchestras; Fidelio (Glyndebourne Tour); Iphigénie en Tauride (Netherlands Opera); La Bohème (Australian Opera), 1990; Idomeneo (Glyndebourne Festival), 1991; Appearance at Hong Kong Festival, 1991; Conducted the world premiere of Stephen Oliver's Timon of Athens, London Coliseum, 1991; Residente Orkest The Hague, Netherlands Chamber Orchestra, 1991; Così fan tutte, US Opera debut, Dallas; Death in Venice at the 1992 Glyndebourne Festival, Cologne Opera, 1996, Handel's Serse; Meistersinger, Australian Opera; Music Director, Dallas Opera, 1994; Principal Guest Conductor, Cologne Opera, 1997; Season 1997-98, numerous opera performances including Billy Budd, Katya Kabanova (with David Alden), Dallas; Macbeth (with Robert Carsen), Cologne; Appearances with Finnish Radio Symphony Orchestra; Debut with Utah and Dallas Symphony Orchestras; Engaged to conduct London Philharmonic at Royal Festival Hall; Work as orchestral conductor with major orchestras in Britain and with broadcasts on radio; Music Director, Arundel Festival, Sussex; Conducted LPO at Royal Festival Hall, 1998; Director, Arundel Festival, 1992-; Has strong reputation in Holland and has worked with many other leading European orchestras. Address: c/o Harold Holt Ltd, 31 Sinclair Road, London W14 0NS, England.

JENKINS Neil, b. 9 Apr 1945, Sussex, England. Opera and Concert Singer (Tenor). m. Penelope Anne, 26 Apr 1982, 4 sons, 1 daughter. Education: Choral Scholar, King's College Cambridge, 1963-66; MA, Royal College of Music, 1966-68. Debut: Purcell Room, London, Song Recital with Roger Vignoles, 1967. Career: Guest Soloist, Israel Chamber Orchestra, 1968-69; London Bach Society, 1971, 1973; Member of Deller Consort, 1967-76; Appearances at festivals in Israel, Paris, London and Spain; Performances with Welsh National Opera, Scottish Opera, Opera North, Glyndebourne, Edinburgh and Frankfurt, Kent Opera; New productions of Le nozze di Figaro and the Ravel double bill in Geneva; Wexford 1989 in Prokofiev's The Duenna; Sang in Bernstein's Candide, 1989; Also heard in oratorio and concert, in the orchestral version of Tippett's The Heart's Assurance at Canterbury, 1990; Debut at the ENO in Monteverdi's Orfeo and Il Ritorno d'Ulisse, 1992; Sang the Marquis in Lulu at the 1996 Glyndebourne Festival. Compositions include: Christmas Carols for unaccompanied SATB singers in Christmas is Coming, 1993. Recordings include: Bernstein Candide; Britten, Peter Grimes; Tippett, King Priam; Mozart, Le nozze di Figaro; Henze Kammermusik, 1958; Britten, Serenade for tenor, horn and strings, with Oriol Ensemble. Publications: Editor, The Carol Singer's Handbook, 1993; Editor, Bach: St Matthew Passion; Sing Solo Sacred. Hobbies: Visiting ancient monuments; 18th Century Music Research. Current Management: Music International. Address: 10 Hartington Villas, Hove, Sussex BN3 6HF, England.

JENKINS Speight, b. 31 Jan 1937, Dallas, Texas, USA. Administrator. Education: Studied at the University of Texas and Columbia University Law School, graduating in 1961. Career: Editor, Opera News, 1967-73; Music Critic for the New York Post, 1973-81; Host for the Live from the Met broadcasts, 1981-83; General Director of Seattle Opera, 1983-; Has presided over such productions as The Ring Cycle, 1986-87, 1991, War and Peace, Die Meistersinger, and Werther in the version for baritone, 1989, the US premiere of Gluck's Orphée et Eurydice and the West Coast premiere of Glass's Satyagraha, 1988; Les Dialogues des Carmelites, 1990, Glass Artist Dale Chihuly's scenic debut in Pelléas et Mélisande, 1993, Norma, 1994; Der Rosenkavalier, 1997. Honours: Honorary Doctorates: Seattle University, 1992; University of Puget Sound, 1992. Address: Seattle Opera Association, PO Box 9248, SEattle, WA 98109, USA.

JENKINS Terry, b. 9 Oct 1941, Hertford, England. Operatic Tenor. m. Pamela Ann Jenkins, 14 Sept 1965, 1 son, 1 daughter. Education: BSc (Eng), University College, London, 1964; Guildhall School of Music, 1964-66; London Opera Centre, 1967-68. Debut: Opera for All, 1966-67, Nemorino (L'Elisir d'Amore). Career: Basilic Opera, 1968-71; Glyndebourne Touring Opera, 1969-71; Malcolm (Macbeth), M Triquet (Eugene Onegin), Schmidt (Werther), Scarramuccio (Ariadne auf Naxos); Glyndebourne Festival Opera, 1971, Major Domo (Queen of Spades), Officer (Ariadne auf Naxos); Glyndebourne Festival Opera, 1972, Scarramuccio; Sadler's Wells Opera, 1972-74; English National Opera, 1974-, roles include Basilio (Marriage of Figaro), Pedrillo (Entführung), Remendado (Carmen), Goro (Madam Butterfly), Gaston (La Traviata), Vanya (Katya Kabanova), Spoletta (Tosca), Schmidt (Werther), Fenney (Mines of Sulphur), Tchekalinsky (Queen of Spades), Loge (Rheingold), Borsa (Rigoletto), Duke (Patience), Orpheus (Orpheus in the Underworld); Various roles, Pacific Overtures, Hauk Sendorf (Makropoulos Case), Schoolmaster (Cunning Little Vixen), Dr Caius (Falstaff); English National Opera tour, USA, 1984; New Opera Company, 1976, 1979, 1980; Royal Opera, Covent Garden, 1976, 1977, 1981; English Bach Festival, 1983, Versailles and Sadler's Wells; City of London Festival, 1978; Barbican Hall, 1984-88; Seattle Opera, 1983, Loge-Rheingold; Vienna Festival with English National Opera, 1985; Chelsea Opera Group, 1986; Boston Concert Opera, USA, 1986, Guillot-Manon; Aix-en-Provence Festival, 1991, 1992, Snout, A Midsummer Night's Dream, Britten. Recordings: Justice Shallow in Sir John in Love, Vaughan Williams; Borsa in Rigoletto; Pacific Overtures, Street Scene; Several video recordings. Contributions to: Musicians' Handbook. Hobbies: DIY; Crosswords. Current Management: Music International, Ardilaun Road, London N7, England. Address: 9 West End Avenue, Pinner, Middlesex, England.

JENKINS Timothy, b. 21 Nov 1951, Oklahoma City, Oklahoma, USA. Singer (Tenor). Education: Studied at Texas State University. Debut: Sang Baron Douphol in La Traviata with Fort Worth Opera, 1974. Career: Metropolitan Opera debut, 1979, as Schmidt, in Aufsteig and Fall der Stadt Mahagonny; Returned to the Met as Parsifal, 1983, Laca (Jenufa), High Priest in Idomeneo, Macduff, Wagner's Siegmund and Froh and Stravinsky's Oedipus; Bayreuth Festival, 1985, as Froh in Das Rheingold; Guest appearances in concert and opera in the USA. Recordings: Idomeneo. Address: 6712 Elmhurst, Amarillo, TX 79106, USA.

JENNER Alexander, b. 4 Apr 1929, Vienna, Austria. Concert Pianist; Professor of Piano. m. Marytza Rangel, 31 Oct 1957, 1 son, 2 daughters. Education: Realgymnasium, Matura, 1947; Reifeprufung with Bosendorfer award, 1948; Akademie für Musik, Vienna. Debut: Beethoven's 5th Piano Concerto, Badgastein, Austria, 1948. Career: Recitals and concerts with orchestra and chamber music concerts in most European countries, North and South America, Far and Middle East including live radio and television performances and studio recordings. Recordings: Mostly classical and romantic piano music for various record companies and radio and television stations. Memberships: Vice President, International Chopin Society of Vienna; Vienna Beethoven Society. Address: Grosse Sperlgasse 16, A-1020 Vienna, Austria.

JENNI Donald (Martin), b. 4 Oct 1937, Milwaukee, Wisconsin, USA. Composer; Professor of Music; Head of Composition and Theory. Education: AM, University of Chicago, 1962; BMus, DePaul University, 1958; DMA, Stanford University, 1966. Career: Ford Foundation Composer-in-Residence, Ann Arbor, Michigan, 1960; Director of Music, La Compagnie de Danse Jo Lechay, Montreal, Canada, 1975-82; Professor of Music Theory and Composition, University of Iowa, Iowa City, USA, 1974-; Figura Circulorum premiered at Center for New Music, Iowa City, 1993. Compositions: Axis, 1968; R-Music, Asphodel, 1969; Eulalia's Rounds, 1972; Musica dell'autunno, 1975; Long Hill May, 1976; Crux Christi Ave!, 1977; Canticum Beatae Virginis, 1979; Pharos, 1980; Ballfall, 1981; The Opalion, 1984; Sam mbira, 1985; Figura Circulorum for strings and metallophones, 1993. Recordings: Musique Printaniere, 1967; Cucumber Music, 1969. Publication: Cum novo cantico: A Primer of Biblical and Medieval Latin, 1983. Hobby: Linguistics. Address: 1026 MB, The University of Iowa, Iowa City, IA 52242, USA.

JENNINGS Diane, b. 1959, California, USA. Singer (Soprano). Education: Studied at the San Diego Opera School. Career: Sang small roles in opera at San Diego, then studied further in Munich, 1984-86; Sang at the Landestheater Salzburg, 1986-87, as Marzelline in Fidelio, Susanna, Pamina and Marenka in The Bartered Bride; Aachen Opera, 1988-91, as Mimi; Mainz, 1990, as Donna Anna; Concert engagements in Vienna, Graz, Munich and Verona. Recordings include: Suor Angelica and Brixi's Missa pastoralis (Eurodisc). Address: c/o Stadtheater Aachen, Theaterplatz, W-5100 Aachen, Germany.

JENSON Dylana (Ruth Lockington), b. 14 May 1961, Los Angeles, CA, USA. Violinist. Education: Began violin training with mother; Pupil of Manuel Compinsky, Jascha Heifetz and Josef Gingold; Master classes with Nathan Milstein in Zurich, 1973-76. Career: First public appearance as soloist in the Bach A Minor Concerto at age 7; Professional debut as soloist in the Mendelssohn Concerto with the New York Philharmonic Orchestra, 1973; European debut as soloist with the Zurich Tonhalle Orchestra, 1974; Thereafter regular tours worldwide as a soloist with leading orchestras, as a recitalist, and as a chamber music player. Recordings: Several. Honour: 2nd Prize in Tchaikovsky International Competition in Moscow, 1978. Address: c/o Konzertdirektion Jurgen Erlebach, Beim Schlump, D-2000 Hamburg 13, Germany.

JEPPSSON Kerstin (Maria), b. 29 Oct 1948, Nyköping, Sweden. Composer. Education: BA, Musicology, Pedagogy, Social University of Stockholm, 1977; Studies, 1968-73, Music Teacher's Diploma, 1973, Stockholm Conservatory of Music; Composition with Maurice Karkoff, Stockholm, 1968-73, with Krzysztof Meyer and Krzysztof Penderecki, Cracow Conservatory of Music, Poland, 1974, 1977; Composition with Melvin Powell, 1978-79, MFA, 1979, California Institute of the Arts. Compositions include: Orchestral, chamber, solo instrumental, piano, vocal and choral works and songs, including: 3 Sentenzi for orchestra, 1970; Tre visor, choral, 1972; Blomstret i Saron, choral, 1972; Tre ryska poem for soprano and clarinet, 1973; 5 Japanese Images, choral, 1973; Hindemith in memoriam for clarinet and piano, 1974; Crisis for string orchestra and percussion, 1976-77; Vocazione, guitar solo, 1982; Prometheus for percussion, 1983; Tendenze for strings and piano, 1986; Kvinnosånger (female songs), published. Recordings: Various pieces. Address: Föreningen Svenska Tonsättare, Sandhamnsgatan 79, Box 27 327, S-1002 54 Stockholm, Sweden.

JERIE Marek Jan, b. 15 Dec 1947, Prague, Czechoslovakia. Musician (Cellist). m. Beatrix Elisabeth Schneider, 31 Oct 1974, 1 son, 2 daughters. Education: Prague and Basle Conservatories; Prague Music Academy; Concert and solo diplomas; Master classes with Casals, Rostropovich and Navarra. Career: Soloist, Chamber Musician with K Ragossnig, I Klansky, I Straus, Smetana Quarter and others, 1975-; Professor, Luzern Conservatory, 1979-; TV performances in Prague; Radio recordings throughout Europe; Discovered Czech cello concertos of 18th century (Reicha, Fiala); Performances of compositions by Reicha and Tchaikowsky (Valse-sentimentaler for cello and guitar); Fisher's Solo-Sonate dedicated to him. Recordings: Reicha Cello Concerto; Cello Miniatures with I Klansky, Attaca; Brahms Cello Sonatas. Publications: Reicha Cello Concerto, 1980; Tchaikovsky, Valse Sentimental, 1987. Hobbies: Skiing; Swimming. Address: Engelgasse 104, CH 4052 Basel, Switzerland.

JEROME Marcus, b. 19 Jun 1957, Fort Worth, TX, USA. Singer (Tenor). Career: Appearances at opera houses of Fort Worth and Dallas, Baton Rouge, Boston, Miami, Atlanta, Pennsylvania, 1984-; Roles have included Lindoro in L'Italiana in Algeri, Almaviva, Ramiro in Cenerentola and Pinkerton; Washington Opera, 1987-88, as Gounod's Roméo, Lindoro and Jacquino; European engagements include: Ford, in Salieri's Falstaff and Nemorino for Hungarian National Opera at Bordeaux; Ernesto, Tamino, Rodolfo and Edgardo at Aachen, 1988-90; Karlsruhe, 1990-, as Edgardo, Rudolfo, Alfredo and Tamino; Guest appearances at Cologne as Pinkerton and Nemorino; Vienna; Zurich; Hamburg as Wilhelm Meister in Mignon; Opera Bastille, Paris, as Idomeneo, 1991; La Scala, Milan debut, 1992, as Matteo in Arabella; Season 1992-93 at Bonn as Hoffmann and Werther; Cassio at Cologne; Munich (Mitridate) and Essen; Sang Rodolfo in La Bohème for Bath City Opera, 1992; Concert appearances with Leonard Slatkin and Simon Rattle in USA in works by Britten, Janácek, Berlioz and Mozart; Further showings with Dusseldorf and Aachen Symphonies, Philharmonica Hungarica and Berlin Concert Choir. Current Management and Address: c/o Athole Still International Ltd, Foresters Hall, 25-27 Westow Street, London, SE19 3RY, England.

JERSILD Jörgen, b. 1913, Copenhagen, Denmark. Composer. Education: Studied Composition and Music Theory with Poul Schierbeck and Piano with Alexander Stoffregen; Studied under Albert Roussel, Paris, France; Further studies in USA and Italy; MA, University of Copenhagen, 1940. Career: Danish Radio Music Department, 1939; Professor of Theory, Royal Academy of Music, Copenhagen, 1943-75. Compositions: Orchestral: Pastorale, 1946; Little Suite, 1950; The Birthday Concert, 1945; Ballet, Kings Theatre, 1954; Capricious Luicinda; Chamber Music; Music Making in the Forest, 1947; Fantasia e Canto Affetuoso, 1969; String Quartet, 1980; Für Gefühlvolle Spieler for Two Harps, 1982; Solo Instruments: Trois Pieces en Concert, for Piano, 1945; Pezzo Elegiaco, for Harp, 1968; Fantasia, for Harp, 1977; Fantasia, for Piano, 1987; 15 Piano

Pieces for Julie, 1985; Jeu Polyrythmique for Piano, 1990; Fantasia per Organo, 1985; Vocal Music: 3 Songs, 1944; 3 Danish Madrigals, 1958; 3 Danish Love Songs; 3 Romantiske Korsange, 1984; 3 Latin Madrigals, 1987; Il Cantico delle Creature, 1992; Music for Children: Quaretti Piccolo, 1950; Duo Concertante, 1956, 30 Polyrythmic Etudes, 1975. Publications: Laerebog i Rytmelaesning, 2nd edition, 1961; Laerbog i Melodilaesning, 2nd edition, 1963; Ear Training I-II, 1966; Elementary Rhythm Exercises; Advanced Rhythmic Studies, 1975; Romantic Harmony, 1970; Analytical Harmony I-II, 1989. Honours: Recipient of several honorary appointments. Address: Söllerödvej 38, 2840 Holte, Denmark.

JERUSALEM Siegfried, b. 17 Apr 1940, Oberhausen, Germany. Singer (Tenor). Education: Studied violin, piano and bassoon in Essen; Voice with Hertha Kalcher in Stuttgart. Career: Played bassoon in various orchestras and made debut as singer at Stuttgart in 1975; Appeared widely in Germany as Lohengrin; Bayreuth Festival from 1977, as Parsifal, Lohengrin, Walther, Siegmund and Siegfried (1988); Deutsche Oper Berlin, 1977-80, as Mozart's Tamino and Idomeneo, Weber's Max, Tchaikovsky's Lensky and Beethoven's Florestan; Metropolitan debut, 1980, as Lohengrin; Guest appearances in Munich, Milan, Hamburg, San Francisco and Geneva; In 1986 sang Parsifal at the London Coliseum and Erik in Der fliegende Holländer at Covent Garden; Sang Loge and Siegfried in The Ring at the Metropolitan, 1990 (also televised); Siegfried at the 1990 Bayreuth Festival; Season 1992 with Parsifal at the Met and Siegfried at Bayreuth; Featured Artist (People No 182), Opera Magazine, Aug 1992, pp 904-909; Sang Tristan in a new production at Bayreuth, 1993, returned 1996. Recordings: Martha, Les Contes d'Hoffmann, Violanta, Leonore, Die Zauberflöte, Die Walküre, Tannhäuser; Videos of Parsifal and Die Meistersinger from Bayreuth, The Ring from the Metropolitan, Der Ring des Nibelungen, conducted by Haitink. Address: c/o Theateragentur Dr G Hilbert, Maximilianstr 22, D-80538 München, Germany.

JEURISSEN Herman G A, b. 27 Dec 1952, Wijchen, Netherlands. Horn Player; Arranger. Education: Soloist Diploma, Brabants Conservatorium, Tilburg, 1976. Career: Co-1st Horn, Utrecht Symphony Orchestra, 1975-78; Solo Horn, The Hague Philharmonic Orchestra, 1978-; Solo and concerto, radio and TV appearances with orchestras in Netherlands, Austria, Germany, France and USA. Recordings: Mozart's Complete Horn Concertos; Complete Horn Music, by Leopold Mozart; Chamber Music, Franz and Richard Strauss; Compositions for horn and organ; Compositions for brass and carillon. Publications: Reconstruction and completion of Mozart's unfinished Horn Concertos K370b and K371, K 494A; Compositions and arrangements for horns; Mozart and the Horn, 1978; Basic Principles of Horn Playing, 3 volumes, 1997. Contributor to: Mens en Melodie; Praeludium; Horn Call Brass Bulletin; Historic Brass Society Journal. Honours: Prix d'excellence, 1978; Silver Laurel of the Concertgebouw Friends, 1979. Address: Jacob Mosselstraat 58, 2595 RJ The Hague, Netherlands.

JEWELL Ian, b. 1950, England. Violinist. Education: Studied at the Royal College of Music with Cecil Aronowitz and in Italy with Bruno Giuranna. Career: Solo performances of the Walton and Rubbra Concertos, Harold in Italy by Berlioz and the Mozart Concertante; Philharmonic at the Royal Academy of Music and Head of Strings, Purcell School; Co-founder, Gabrieli Quartet, 1967, and toured with them to Europe, North America, the Far East and Australia; Festival engagements in Britain, including the Aldeburgh, City of London and Cheltenham; Concerts every season in London in the Barbican's Mostly Mozart Festival; Resident Artist, University of Essex, from 1971; Co-premiered works by William Alwyn, Britten, Alan Bush, Daniel Jones and Gordon Crosse, 2 Quartets of Nicholas Maw and Panufnik, 1980, 1983, and the 3rd Quartet of John MacCabe, 1979; British premiere of the Piano Quintet by Sibelius, 1990. Recordings include: 50 CDs, including early pieces by Britten, Dohnányi's Piano Quintet with Wolfgang Manz, Walton's Quartets and the Sibelius Quartet and Quintet, with Anthony Goldstone. Address: Gabrieli Quartet, 3 Primrose Mews, 1a Sharpleshall Street, London NW1 8YW, England.

JIA Lü, b. 1964, Shanghai, China. Conductor. Career: Chief Conductor of the National Youth Orchestra of China, 1987; Further engagements with the Leipzig Gewandhaus, Berlin Symphony nd NDR Hamburg Symphony Orchestras; Chief Conductor and Music Director of the Trieste Opera, 1991-95; Principal Conductor of the Orchestra della Toscana, Principal Conductor of Opera of Genova, Carlo Felice, Florence, appearances with the Santa Cecilia Orchestra, Rome, and at the Bologna Opera; Season 1995-96 included debuts with the Bamberg and Chicago Symphonies, English Chamber Orchestra, Deutsch Oper Berlin, Orchestre National de Lyon and Chamber Orchestra of Europe; Season 1996-97 with the Oslo and St Petersburg Philharmonic Orchestras. Honours include: Winner, National Chinese Conducting Competition, 1986; First Prize, Pedrotti Competition in Trento, 1990. Address: c/o IMG Artists, Media House, 3 Burlington Lane, London W4 2TH, England.

JILEK Frantisek, b. 22 May 1913, Brno, Czechoslovakia. Conductor. Education: Studied with Kvapil and Chalabala at Brno, with Vitezslav Novak in Prague. Career: Repetiteur with the Brno Opera, 1937-39; Conductor of the Ostrava Opera, 1939-48; Returned to Brno, 1948, and was Artistic Director at the Opera, 1952-78; Gave the complete operas of Janácek in 1958, and conducted Martinu's Greek Passion and Prokofiev's Fiery Angel and War and Peace; Guest appearances in Czechoslovakia and abroad, notably in works by Janácek; Chief Conductor, Brno State Philharmonic Orchestra from 1978. Recordings include: Janácek's The Beginning of a Romance, Osud, Jenufa and The Excursions of Mr Broucek, 1976-80; Martinu's Comedy on the Bridge and Alexandre Bis, 1985-86. Address: c/o Brno State Philharmonic Orchestra, Moravske Namesti 1a, 60200 Brno, Czech Republic.

JIRA Milan, b. 7 Apr 1935, Prague, Czech Republic. Composer; Pianist; Pedagogue. m. Milena Strunecká, 27 April 1953, 1 son. Education: Prague Conservatoire, Piano; Academy of Performing Arts, Composition. Career: Voice-coach; Opera; Radio-editor; Professor of Prague Conservatoire; Deputy Director, Prague Conservatoire. Compositions: Unhappy Wedding; 3rd and 7th Symphony; Fantasia Concertante per Pianoforte e Orchestra; 8 String Quartets; 7 Piano Sonatas. Memberships: Association of Musical Artists and Musicologists. Hobbies: Literature; Theatre; Gardening. Address: Verdiho 670, Praha 4, 149 00 Czech Republic.

JIRACKOVA Marta, b. 22 Mar 1932, Kladno, Czechoslovakia. Composer. m. 1964, 2 daughters. Education: Composition with Emil Hlobil, Conservatoire of Music, Prague; Modern Harmony and Composition with Alois Haba; Janacek Academy of Performing Arts, Brno, with Alois Pinos. Career: Music for orchestra, chamber music, vocal music, scene music, electro-acoustic music, including music for stage, film, radio and TV. Compositions: The Children's World, piano cycle of etudes, 1977; Three Songs Without Words for Soprano and Instrumental Ensemble, 1982; Nanda Devi, 1st Symphony, 1984; Ave Seikilos, for String Orchestra and Percussion, 1985; Silbo, 2nd Symphony, 1987; Eight Wonders of The World for Human Voices, Harp and Percussion, 1988; Dodekaria I, sonata for Violin and Piano, 1993; Dodekaria II for Flute and Cymbal; Dodekaria Tristis III for Baset, Horn and Piano; Electro-acoustic Music: Lullabye; The Outlook from My Balcony; Five Times a Woman; The Ship of Fools by Hieronymus Bosch; Bees and the Sunflower. Honours: Czech Music Fund Annual Prize, 1992. Hobbies: Music; Literature; Painting and sculpture; Family. Address: Ve Stresovickach 45, Brevnon, 16900 Prague 6, Czech Republic.

JIRASEK Ivo, b. 16 Jul 1920, Prague, Czechoslovakia. Composer. Education: Studied at the Prague High School of Music, Conservatoire, 1940-45. Career: Conductor of Opera in Opava, 1946-56; Teacher and later Freelance Composer from 1956. Compositions include: Operas: Mr Johanes, 1956, Dawn over the Waters, 1961, The Bear, 1964, Danse Macabre, 1971, Master Jeronym, 1980, The Miracle, 1981, Ballet Faust, 1985. Address: u Háje 39a, 147 00 Prague 4, Braník, Czech Republic.

JIRIKOVSKY Petr, b. 24 June 1971, Prague, Czech Republic. Pianist. Education: Conservatory in Prague (Emil Leichner); Academy of Performing Arts in Prague (Ivan Klansky); Conservatoire De Paris (Solo Piano - Theodor Paraschivesco, Chamber Music - Itamar Golan); Hochschule für Musik in Vienna (Chamber Music - Michael Schnitzler); Masterclasses and private lessons - Eugen Indjic. Career: Concerts at major festivals in Czech Republic, in subscription of cycles of Czech Philharmony, Germany, France, London, Holland, Italy, Spain, Japan, Yugoslavia, Macedonia; More than 30 recordings in Czech radio; Solo performances with Hradec Symphony Orchestra, Moravian Philharmony, Prague Chamber Orchestra, Talich Chamber Orchestra; Member, Academia Trio. Recordings: B Smetana, CD, Czech Dances, 1994; B Smetana, CD, My Country (Piano Four Hands), 1995; B Smetana, Polkas (complete), 1997; A Dvorák, CD, Piano Trios (Academia Trio), 1997; Dvorák, Brahms, CD, Gypsy Songs (with Bernarda Fink - Mezzo Soprano), 1997; B Martinu, CD, Concerto Grosso for 2 Pianos and Chamber Orchestra (with Josef Hala, Prague Chamber Orchestra), 1997. Honours: 1st Prize, Beethoven Piano Competition, Czech Republic, 1986; 1st Prize, Chopin Competition, 1987; 3rd Prize, Smetana Piano Competition, 1988; 1st Prize, North London Festival, 1992; 1st Prize, Heerlen (Holland), with Academia Trio, 1995. Address: Konevova 189, 13000, Prague 3, Czech Republic.

JO Sumi, b. 22 Nov 1962, Seoul, South Korea. Singer (Soprano). Education: Studied in Seoul and at the Accademia di Santa Cecilia, Rome, 1983-86. Debut: Teatro Verdi, Trieste, 1986, as Gilda. Career: Sang at Lyon, Nice and Marseille, 1987-88; Discovered by Karajan and sang Barbarina at the 1988 Salzburg Festival; Oscar in Un Ballo in Maschera, 1989-90, conducted by Solti; Guest appearances at Munich from 1988, Vienna from 1989, and Paris; La Scala Milan in Ravel's L'Enfant et les Sortilèges, conducted by Lorin Maazel, and as Zerlina in Auber's Fra Diavolo, 1992; Metropolitan Opera as Gilda, 1988 and 1990; Royal Opera, Covent Garden, as Olympia in Tales of Hoffmann and as Elvira in I Puritani in 1991 and 1991; Chicago Lyric Opera as Queen of Night in 1990 and as Queen of Night with Danish Philharmonic conducted by Zubin Mehta in 1991; Season 1992 as Matilde in Rossini's Elisabetta at Naples, Olympia at Covent Garden (followed by Adina); Sang Zerbinetta at Lisbon, 1996; Season 1997-98 with L'Enfant et les Sortilèges at Boston, Zerbinetta at Lisbon and in Mozart's Lucio Silla at Mozart Festival, New York. Recordings: Arias; Adèle in Le Comte Ory; Un Ballo in Maschera; Queen of Night in Die Zauberflöte, conducted by Armin Jordan; Queen of Night in Die Zauberflöte, conducted by Solti; Fiorilla in Rossini's Il Turco in Italia, conducted by Neville Marriner; Soprano soloist in Mahler Symphony No 8, conducted by Sinopoli; Soprano soloist in Rossini's Messa di Gloria, conducted by Neville Marriner. Angèle d'Olivarès in Auber's Le Domino Noir. Address: Columbia Artists Management, 165 West 57th Street, New York, NY 10019, USA.

JOACHIM Otto, b. 13 Oct 1919, Düsseldorf, Germany. Composer; Violist; Violinist; Gambist. separated, 1 son. Education: Concordia School, Düsseldorf; Buths-Neitzel Conservatory, Düsseldorf; Rheinische Musikschule, Cologne. Career: CBC Soloist, Montreal String Quartet, L'Ensemble des Instruments Anciens de Montreal, Canada; 1st Violist, Montreal Symphony. Compositions include: Nonet, 1960; Psalm for Choir, 1960; Concertante No 2 for string quartet and string orchestra, 1961; Fantasia for organ, 1961; 12 Twelve-tone Pieces for Children, 1961; Contrastes for orchestra, 1967; Kinderspiel for violin, cello, piano and speaker, 1969; 5,9 for 4-channel tape, 1971; Night Music for alto flute and guitar, 1978; 4 Intermezzi for flute and guitar, 1978; Requiem for violin or viola or cello, 1969. Honours: Prix Calixa Lavallée Société St Jean Baptiste, 1990; Ordre National du Québec, 1993; Grand Prix Paul Gilson, 1969; LL.D h.c Concordia University, 1994. Hobbies: Musical electronics; Constructing replicas of ancient instruments; Painting. Address: 7910 Wavell Road, Côte St-Luc, Montreal, Quebec Province, Canada H4W 1L7.

JOBIN André, b. 20 Jan 1933, Quebec, Canada. Singer (Tenor). Education: Studied as an actor in Paris and worked with Jean-Louis Barrault. Career: Sang at first as a baritone in Parisian musicals; Operatic roles as tenor from 1962, notably Pélleas at Marseilles, Nice, Paris, Madrid and San Francisco, 1965; Glyndebourne Festival, 1976, New York City Opera from 1970; Other roles have been Romeo, Don José, Massenet's Des Grieux, Rodrigo and John the Baptist, Julien (Louise) and Hoffmann; Many appearances at Quebec, Lyon, Brussels, Berlin and Madrid; Liège Opera, 1982-87, as Rodrigo in Le Cid, John the Baptist (Herodiade) and Des Grieux; Cologne Opera, 1987, as Werther; Engaged in musical sand operettas in Chicago, London and Detroit. Recordings: Albums under several record labels.

JOCHUM Veronica, b. 1930, Berlin, Germany. Pianist. m. Wilhelm Viggo von Moltke, 15 Nov 1961. Education: MA, 1955, Concert Diploma, 1957, Staatliche Musikhochschule, Munich, Germany; Private study with Edwin Fischer, Josef Benvenuti, 1958-59 and Rudolf Serkin, 1959-61. Debut: Germany, 1954. Career: Numerous appearances as soloist with orchestras in Europe North and South America, 1961-; Appeared with Boston Symphony, London Symphony Orchestra, London Philharmonic Orchestra, Berlin, Hamburg and Munich Philharmonics, Vienna Symphony and Concertgebouw Orchestra among others; Radio and TV appearances; Recitals in over 50 countries in Europe, North and South America, Africa and Asia; Featured in a German film, Self-Attempt, on a novel by Christa Wolf. Recordings: Tudor, GM, CRI, Laurel, others. Honour: Cross of Order of Merit by German President (Bundesverdienstureuz), 1994; Address: New England Conservatory of Music, 290 Huntington Avenue, Boston, MA 02115, USA.

JOEL Emmanuel, b. 1958, Paris, France. Conductor. Education: Studied with at the Paris Conservatoire. Career: Early engagements with Opêra de Lyon and at the Aix-en-Provence Festival; Paris Opéra debut with Offenbach's Les Brigands, 1993; Semele and Les Pecheurs de Perles in Melbourne and regular appearances with the Opera de Nantes; Boildieu's La Dame Blanche at the Wexford Festival and Don Quichotte for English National Opera, 1996; La Belle Hélène for Scottish Opera, Carmen and Werther in Israel; Season 1996-97 with Chausson's Le Roi Arthus in Montpellier, Samson et Dalila in Sydney and Israel, Butterfly in Rouen, La Bohème for ENO and Eugene Onegin in Toulouse. Address: c/o Allied Artists, 42 Montpellier Square, London SW7 1JZ, England.

JOHANNESEN Grant, b. 30 July 1921, Salt Lake City, Utah, USA. Concert Pianist. m. Zara Nelsova, 1963-73. Education: Studied with Robert Casadesus at Princeton University and with Egon Petri at Cornell University. Debut: Times Hall, New York, 1944. Career: First international tour, 1949; Tour of Europe with New York Philharmonic and Mitropoulos, 1956-57; Tour of USSR and Europe with Cleveland Orchestra and George Szell, 1968; Solo tours of the USSR, 1962, 1970; Appearances at all major music festivals; Aspen Festival for 6 seasons; On faculty of Aspen Music School, 1960-66; Music Director of the Cleveland Institute of Music, 1974-84. Recordings: Fauré's complete piano music; Works by Dukas, Roussel and De Sévrac; Sonatas for cello and piano with Zara Nelsova.

JOHANNSEN Kay, b. 1 Oct 1961, Giengen, Germany. Organist; Church Musician. m. Andrea Ermer, 29 Apr 1987, 1 son, 1 daughter. Education: Studies at Freiburg in organ and conducting; Organ studies at NEC, Boston, with William Porter. Career: Concerts in major German cities and in foreign countries, broadcast concerts with almost all German stations, several concerts with orchestras such as the Nurnberg Symphonic, Radio Symphony Orchestra Prague, Radio Symphony Orchestra Hannover, Staatsphilharmonic Rheinland-Pfalz, Philharmonic Orchestra Gelsenkirchen, Berlin Philharmonic Orchestra and Stuttgart Philharmonic Orchestra; Teacher, Karlsruhe Conservatory, 1991-; Guest Teacher, Freiburg Conservatory, 1992-93; Organist of the Siftskirche Stuttgart, 1994-. Recordings: CDs: Bach, Reger, Fortig, 1990; Christian Hommel, Bach, Mozart, Huber ars musici; 1993; French organ music from the 19th century, 1993; Brahms, Complete Organ Works, 1996; Bach, trio Sonatas, 1997. Honours: Various prizes in music competitions; German National Foundation Scholarship. Hobbies: Windsurfing; Spending time with the family. Address: c/o Evang Bezirkskantorat, Altes Schloss, Schillerplatz 6, 70173 Stuttgart, Germany.

JOHANNSSON Kristjan, b. 1950, Akureyi Du, Iceland. Tenor. Education: Studied at Nicolini Conservatory, Piacenza and with Campogalliani and Tagliavini. Debut: National Theatre of Iceland, Reykjavik, as Rodolfo in 1961. Career: Sang Pinkerton in a production of Madam Butterfly, by Ken Russell, at Spoleto, 1983; Engagements as guest artist at the Chicago Lyric Opera in Faust, 1991, Metropolitan New York, Vienna, Staatsoper and La Scala Milan; Roles have included Radames, Alvaro in La Forza del Destino, Cavaradossi and Dick Johnson; Sang Turiddu in Cavalleria Rusticana at Naples and Florence, season 1990-91; Calaf at the Verona Arean, 1991; Sang Manrico in the opening production at the New Teatro, Carol Felice, Genoa, 1991; Andrea Chenier at Florence, Calaf at Chicago, Cavaradossi at Rome and Manrico at Turin, 1992; Calaf at Torre del Lago, 1996.

JOHANOS Donald, b. 10 Feb 1928, Cedar Rapids, Iowa, USA. Conmductor. m. (1) Thelma Trimble, 27 Aug 1950, 2 sons, 3 daughters, (2) Corinne Rutledge, 28 Sept 1985. Career: MusB, 1950, MusM, 1952; Eastman School of Music, Rochester, New York; Advanced conducting studies with Eugene Ormandy, George Szell, Sir Thomas Beecham, Eduard van Beinum, Herbert von Karajan, Otto Klemperer, 1955-58. Career: Teacher, Pennsylvania State University, 1953-55; Music Director, Altoona (Pennsylvania) Symphony Orchestra, 1953-56; Johnstown (Pennsylvania) Symphony Orchestra, 1955-56; Associate Conductor, 1957-61, Resident Conductor, 1961-62, Music Director, 1962-70, Dallas Symphony Orchestra; Teacher, Southern Methodist University, 1958-62; Hockady School, 1962-65; Associate Conductor and Director, Pittsburgh Symphony Orchestra, 1970-80; Music Director, Honolulu Symphony Orchestra, 1979-; Artistic Director, Hawaii Opera Theater, 1979-83; Guest conducting engagements with various orchestras at home and abroad. Recordings: For various labels. Honours: American Symphony Orchestra League and Rockefeller Foundation advanced study grants, 1955-58; Winner, Netherlands Radio Union conducting competition, 1957. Membership: American Federation of Musicians. Address: c/o Honolulu Symphony Orchestra, 1441 Kapiolani Boulevard, Suite 1515, Honolulu, HI 96814, USA.

JOHANSSON Eva, b. 25 Feb 1958, Copenhagen, Denmark. Singer (Soprano). Education: Studied at the Copenhagen Conservatory, 1977-81; Opera School of the Royal Opera, Copenhagen, 1981-84; New York, with Oren Brown. Career: Sang at the Royal Opera, Copenhagen, 1982-88, as the Countess in Figaro (debut), Tatiana, Pamina, Marie in Wozzeck and Chrysothemis (Elektra); Guest appearances in Oslo as Marie and Donna Anna (1985, 1987); Marie at the Paris Opera, 1986; Sang in productions of Der Ring des Nibelungen at Berlin and Bayreuth, 1988, as Gutrune and as Freia and Gerhilde; Sang Freia in a concert performance of Das Rheingold at Paris, 1988, conducted by Daniel Baremboim; Vienna Staatsoper, 1989, as Fiordiligi; Tel Aviv, 1990, as Donna Anna in Don Giovanni, conducted by Claudio Abbado; Since 1990: Elsa in Lohengrin at Bayreuth; Guest appearances in Barcelona, Munich, Dresden, Japan, Paris, Seville, Nizza, Madrid, Stuttgart, Cologne and Hamburg; Debut as Donna Anna, at Covent Garden, 1992; Sang Elsa at the Accademia di Santa Cecilia, Rome, 1996. Recordings: Das Rheingold conducted by Bernard Haitink; Es War Einmal, by Zemlinsky. Address: Bühnenagentur Marianne Bottger, Dahlmannstrasse 9, D-1000 Berlin 12, Germany.

JOHNS William, b. 2 Oct 1936, Tusla, Oklahoma, USA. Singer (Tenor). Education: Studied in New York. Debut: Lake George, 1967, as Rodolfo in La Bohème. Career: Sang with the Bremen Opera as the Prince in The Love of Three Oranges and

the Duke of Mantua; Welsh National Opera, 1970-72, as Radames and Calaf; Further appearances in Cologne, Dusseldorf, Dallas, Hamburg, Bregenz, Houston, Vienna, Aix-en-Provence, Rome and New York (Metropolitan Opera); Covent Garden debut, 1987, as Bacchus in Ariadne auf Naxos; Philadelphia Opera, 1988, as Florestan in Fidelio; Holland Festival, 1989, as Siegfried in a concert performance of Götterdämmerung; Other roles include Wagner's Lohengrin, Tannhäuser, Siegmund and Tristan, Huon (Oberon), the Emperor in Die Frau ohne Schatten, Jason in Medea in Corinto by Mayr, Hoffmann and Verdi's Otello; Sang Tristan at San Francisco, 1991. Address: c/o San Francisco Opera, War Memorial Opera House, San Francisco, CA 94102, USA.

JOHNSON Camellia, b. 1960, Delaware, USA. Singer (Soprano). Education: Studied at Daytona Beach, Florida, and the Manhattan School of Music, New York. Debut: Strawberry Woman, in Porgy and Bess at the Metropolitan, 1985. Career: Sang in Porgy and Bess at Glyndebourne, 1986, and Helsinki, 1989, 1992; Season 1992-93, in Don Carlos at San Francisco and as Aida at Michigan; Beethoven's Ninth in Indianapolis and Montreal; Verdi's Requiem with the Saint Louis Symphony and the Long Island Philharmonic; Metropolitan Opera as Serena in Porgy and Bess, High Priestess in Aida and Madelon in Andrea Chenier; Mozart's Solemn Vespers and Requiem with the Cincinnati Symphony; Other repertoire includes the Four Last Songs of Strauss, Les Nuits d'Eté, Schubert's Rosamunde, Rossini's Stabat Mater and Beethoven's Missa Solemnis. Recordings: Porgy and Bess. Address: c/o Metropolitan Opera, Lincoln Center, New York, NY 10023, USA.

JOHNSON David (Carl), b. 30 Jan 1940, Batavia, New York, USA. Composer; Flautist. Education: Studied composition with Donald Keats and David Epstein at Antioch College; Leon Kirchner at Harvard University and Nadia Boulanger in Paris, 1964-65; Further study in Cologne. Career: Teacher at the Rheinische Musikschule Cologne, 1966-67; Worked with Stockhausen in the creation of Hymnen at the studios of West German Radio; Member of the Stockhausen ensemble at the Osaka World Fair, 1970; Co-founded Feedback Studio at Cologne, 1970; Director of the electronic music studio at the Basle Music Academy, 1975. Compositions: Five movements for flute, 1962; Bells for flute, guitar and cello, 1964; Thesis for string quartet, 1964; 3 Pieces for string quartet, 1964; 3 Pieces for string quartet, 1966; Tonantiton for tape, 1968; Process of Music for tape and instruments, 1970; Sound-environment pieces Music Makers, Gyromes mit und für Elise, Cybernet, Gehlhaar, Organica I'IV and Klangkoffer, 1969-74; Proganica for speaker and 2 electric organs, 1973; Audioliven for flute and electronics, 1976; In Memoriam Uschi for tape and 3 instruments, 1977; Jadermann incidental music to play by Hoffmansthal, 1980; Bach: Encounter of the Third Kind, stage piece, 1981; Calls in Search, for tape, 1981. Address: c/o ASCAP, ASCAP Building, One Lincoln Plaza, New York, NY 10023, USA.

JOHNSON David (Charles), b. 27 Oct 1942, Edinburgh, Scotland. Composer; Musical Historian; Writer; Music Publisher; Cellist. 1 s. Education: MA, Aberdeen; BA, PhD, Cambridge. Career: Organised recitals for Edinburgh Festival, 1975, 1985, 1986, 1988; Cellist, McGibbon Ensemble, 1980-95; Tutor, Musical History, Edinburgh University, 1988-94; Founded self-publishing company, 1990; Research Fellow, Music, Napier University, 1995-. Compositions: 4 Operas; Church Music; Piobaireached for Solo Recorder; God, Man and The Animals for Soprano and Instruments; Guess Who I Met Last Night?, 2 School Ensembles and Symphony Orchestra; Piano Trio; Sonatas for Violin, Trumpet and Cello all with Piano; Seven MacDiarmid Songs for Soprano, Trumpet, Piano; Other songs, chamber and orchestral music; 12 Preludes and Fugues for Piano. Publication: Music and Society in Lowland Scotland, 1972; Various editions of 18th Century Scottish Instrumental Music; Editor, Ten Georgian Glees for Four Voices, 1981; Scottish Fiddle Music in the 18th Century, 1984; The Scots Cello Book, 1990; Stepping Northward, 1990; Scots on the Fiddle, 1991. Contributions to: The New Grove Dictionary, 1981. Membership: Music Publishers' Association; PRS; MCPS. Address: 1 Hill Square, Edinburgh, EH8 9DR, Scotland.

JOHNSON Douglas, b. 1958, CA, USA. Singer (Tenor). Education: Studied at the University of Los Angeles. Career: Appearances in Les Dialogues des Carmelites, La Fille du Régiment and La Clemenza di Tito while a student; Sang at Aachen, 1984-87, notably as Don Ottavio, Handel's Serse, Jacquino, Count Almaviva, Rinuccio in Gianni Schicchi, Belmonte and the Steuermann; Hanover, 1988-89, Frankfurt am Mainz, from 1989 notably as Tamino, 1991; Salzburg Festival, 1987, 1991 in Moses und Aron and as Arbace in Idomeneo; Guest appearances at Hamburg, Chateauneuf in Zar und Zimmermann, Deutsche Oper Berlin, Nicolai's Fenton, Vienna Staatsoper, Tamino, Cologne, Nemorino, 1987 and Ludwigshafen, Gualterio in Vivaldi's Griselda, 1989; Sang Rossini's Almaviva at Seattle, 1992. Recordings include: L'Oca del Cairo by Mozart.

JOHNSON Emma, b. 20 May 1966, Barnet, Hertfordshire, England. Clarinettist. Education: Pembroke College, Cambridge University; Studied with John Brightwell, Sidney Fell. Debut: Barbican, London, 1985. Career: Appearances with ECO, London Symphony Orchestra, Ulster Orchestra, Royal Liverpool Philharmonic Orchestra, Hallé Orchestra, City of London Sinfonia and Royal Philharmonic Orchestra; Debut in Vienna at the Musikverein, 1985; French Debut, with Polish Chamber Orchestra, 1986; Performances in Holland, Finland and Monte Carlo; TV and Radio appearances in United Kingdom; Japanese debut, Tokyo, 1990; New York debut, 1992; Schumann Weekend concerts at Blackheath, 1997. Recordings: Mozart Clarinet Concerto, 1984; Crusell Clarinet Concerto No 2, 1985; Bottesini Duo for Clarinet and Double Bass with Tom Martin, 1986; Weber Clarinet Concerto No 1, 1987; Recital Disc La Clarinette Française with Gordon Back, 1988; The Romantic Clarinet (concertos by Weber, Spohr and Crusell); Finzi and Stanford Concertos with Royal Philharmonic Orchestra, 1992; Recital of Encores, 1992; Michael Berkeley Concerto, 1993. Honours: BBC TV Young Musician of the Year, 1984; Bronze Award European Young Musician of the Year Competition, Geneva, 1984; Voted Young Professional All Music Musician, Wavendon All Music Awards, 1986. Hobbies: Literature; Theatre; Cinema. Address: Lies Askonsas Limited, 6 Henrietta Street, London WC2E 8LA, England.

JOHNSON Gordon (James), b. 25 Oct 1949, St Paul, Minnesota, USA. Music Director; Conductor. 2 sons. Education: BS, Bemidji State University, 1971; MS, Northwestern University, 1977; DMA, University of Oregon. Career: Associate Professor of Music, University of Great Falls, Montana, 1981-; Conductor, University of Oregon Sinfoniette, 1981-82; Music Director and Conductor, Great Falls Symphony Association, Montana, 1981-; Music Director and Conductor, Glacier Orchestra, Kalispell, Montana, 1984-97; Music Director and Conductor, Arizona Mesa Symphony, 1997-; Guest Conductor of Spokane Symphony Orchestra, 1984, Dubuque Symphony Orchestra, 1985, Cheyenne Symphony Orchestra, Charlotte Symphony Orchestra and Lethbridge Symphony Orchestra, Alberta, Canada, 1986, West Shore Symphony, Michigan 1988, Kumamoto Symphony, Japan 1991, Kankakee Symphony, Illinois 1993 and Toulon Symphony, France 1994; Guam Symphony, 1995; Wilmslow Symphony, England, 1996; Music Director of Amy Grant's Coming Home for Christmas, NBC Television special; Artistic Director of Flathead Festival, Montana, 1988-97. Address: 205 Glenwood Court, Great Falls, MT 59405, USA.

JOHNSON Graham (Rhodes), b. 19 July 1950, Rhodesia. Concert Accompanist. Education: Royal Academy of Music, London; FRAM, 1984; FGSM, Guildhall School, 1988. Debut: Wigmore Hall, 1972. Career: Accompanist to Brigitte Fassbaender, Elisabeth Schwarzkopf, Jessye Norman, Victoria de los Angeles (US tour, 1977), Janet Baker, Peter Pears, Felicity Lott, Margaret Price (US tour, 1985), Peter Schreier, John Shirley Quirk, Tom Krause; Work with contemporaries led to formation of The Songmakers' Almanac (Artistic Director); Has devised and accompanied more than 150 London recitals for this group since Oct 1976; Tours of USA with Sarah Walker, Richard Jackson and of Australia and New Zealand with The Songmakers' Almanac, 1981; Writer and Presenter, major BBC Radio 3 series on Poulenc songs, and BBC TV series on Schubert songs; Lecturer, song courses, Savonlinna (Finland), USA and at Pears-Britten School, Snape; Artistic Advisor and Accompanist, Alte Oper Festival, Frankfurt, 1981-82; Appearances at Salzburg, Hohenems and Munich Festivals. Recordings: Recitals for several labels, including recitals with Felicity Lott and Ann Murray; Complete cycle of Schubert Lieder; Gramophone solo vocal award, 1989, for recital with Janet Baker; Has recorded with Elly Ameling, Peter Schreier, Arleen Auger, Thomas Hampson, Margaret Price and Lucia Popp. Publication: The Spanish Song Companion, 1992. Contributions to: The Britten Companion (editor Christopher Palmer), 1984; Gerald Moore, The Unashamed Accompanist, revised edition, 1984; Reviews to the Times Literary supplement. Honour: OBE, 1994. Hobby: Eating in good restaurants with friends and fine wine. Current Management: Lies Askonas Ltd. Address: 83 Fordwych Road, London NW2 3TK, England.

JOHNSON James (David), b. 7 Aug 1948, Greenville, South Carolina, USA. Concert Pianist; Professor of Music; Organist and Choirmaster. m. Karen Elizabeth Jacobson, 1 Feb 1975. Education: BMus, 1970, MMus, 1972, DMA, 1976, University of Arizona; Master of Church Music, Westminster Choir College, 1986. Debut: Soloist with the Greenville (South Carolina), Symphony, aged 13. Career: Performances with the Royal Philharmonic, London, England, Boston Pops, Victoria Symphony (British Columbia), Yugoslavian National Radio Orchestra, St Petersburg Philharmonic, Anchorage and Fairbanks Symphonies; Chamber musician with the Alaska Trio, the Cambridge String Quartet and North Star Consort. Recordings: Chaminade; Dohnányi: Five Piano Pieces, 1977 (chosen for inclusion on Clavier Magazine's Ten Best List); Mendelssohn: Concerto in D Minor, Concerto in G Ninor, 1978; Beethoven: Concerto No 1 in

C Major; Concerto No 3 in C Minor; Kabalevsky Third Concerto; Muczynski Concerto. Contributions to: Various professional journals. Address: Music Department, University of Nebraska at Omaha, Omaha, NE 68182, USA.

JOHNSON Laurie, b. 1927, London, England. Composer. m., 1 daughter. Education: Royal College of Music. Career: Taught at Royal College of Music; Orchestral pieces broadcast by age 20; Composer and arranger for the Ted Heath Band and all major bands and orchestras of the 1950's; Entered film industry, 1955; Co-owner, film production companies including Gainsborough Pictures, 1979-; Founder, The London Big Band (25 British jazz and orchestral musicians), for concerts and recordings with international star guests, 1994. Compositions include: Lock Up Your Daughters, musical; Pieces of Eight, revue; The Four Musketeers, musical; Scores for over 400 cinema and television films including: Dr Strangelove; First Men In The Moon; The Avengers; The Professionals; The New Avengers; Television themes include: This Is Your Life; World In Action; Whicker's World. Recordings: Synthesis, symphony; The Wind In The Willows, tone poem; Suite for symphonic band (RAF commission for 50th anniversary of the Battle of Britain); The Conquistadors, music for Royal occasions; Numerous albums with own studio orchestra. Honours: Various awards and nominations for music scores and record or film productions. Address: The Laurie Johnson Organisation Ltd, 10 College Road, Harrow, Middlesex HA1 1DA, England.

JOHNSON Marc, b. 1945, USA. Cellist. Education: Studied at the Eastman School of Music and Indiana University. Career: Played with the Rochester Philharmonic while a student; Solo appearances in Rochester and with the Denver Philharmonic; Recital and chamber concerts in Washington DC, St Louis and Baltimore; Founder member of the Vermeer Quartet at the Marlboro Festival, 1970; Performances in all major US centres, Europe, Israel and Australia; Festival engagements at Tanglewood, Aspen, Spoleto, Edinburgh, Mostly Mozart (New York), Aldeburgh, South Bank, Santa Fe, Chamber Music West, and the Casals Festival; Resident quartet for Chamber Music Chicago; Annual master classes at the Royal Northern College of Music, Manchester; Member of the Resident Artists' Faculty of Northern Illinois University. Recordings: Quartets by Beethoven, Dvorak, Verdi and Schubert; Brahms Clarinet Quintet with Karl Leister. Honours: Denver Symphony and Washington International Competitions; Received title of Kämmersängen during the 1960s. Address: Allied Artists, 42 Montpelier Square, London SW7 1JZ, England.

JOHNSON Mary Jane, b. 22 Mar 1950, Pampa, Texas, USA. Singer (Soprano). Education: Studied at West Texas University, and elsewhere in USA. Debut: New York Lyric Opera as Agathe in Der Freischütz, 1981. Career: Philadelphia and Santa Fe, 1982, as Musetta and Rosalinde; Sang at the San Francisco Opera from 1983, as Freia in Das Rheingold, Jenifer in the US premiere of The Midsummer Marriage, 1983, Marguerite, and the Empress in Die Frau ohne Schatten, Washington Opera from 1984, Boston and Cincinnati from 1986; European engagements with Opera North at Leeds, Torre del Lago (Puccini Festival), Bologna, Geneva and the Baths of Caraccala at Rome (Minnie in La Fanciulla del West); Sang Salome at Santiago, 1990, Desdemona at Pittsburgh and Minnie at the 1991 Santa Fe Festival; Helen of Troy in Mefistofele at Chicago, 1991; La Scala and Opera Bastille, Paris, 1992, in the title role of Lady Macbeth of Mtsensk; Teatro Municipal Santiago as Senta in Der fliegende Holländer, 1992; Other roles include Mozart's Countess, Leonore, Alice in Falstaff, Tosca, Giulietta, the Duchess of Parma in Busoni's Faust, and Mrs Jessel in The Turn of the Screw; Sang Janácek's Emilia Marty at Vancouver, 1996. Address: c/o Santa Fe Opera, PO Box 2408, Santa Fe, NM 87504, USA.

JOHNSON Nancy, b. 1954, California, USA. Singer (Soprano). Education: Studied at California State University, Hayward. Career: Sang at the Landestheater Detmold, 1980-81, Wiesbaden, 1981-82, Mannheim, 1982-87; Engaged at the Stuttgart Staatsoper from 1987 and has made guest appearances at Dusseldorf, the Vienna Staatsoper, San Francisco (Eva in Die Meistersinger, 1988); Other roles have included Manon Lescaut, and the Empress in Die Frau ohne Schatten (Mannheim, 1984). Address: c/o Stuttgart Staatsoper, Oberer Schlossgarten 6, 7000 Stuttgart, Germany.

JOHNSON Patricia, b. 1934, London, England. Mezzo-Soprano. Education: Vocal studies with Maria Linker in London. Career: Sang at Sadler's Wells Opera as Carmen, Dalila and Azucena; Basle Opera from 1957 notably in the title role of La Cenerentola; Deutsche Oper Berlin from 1961 as Azucena, Eboli and Fricka; Sang in the premiere of Der Junge Lord by Henze in 1965 and in Lulu as Countess Geschwitz and La Calisto in 1975; Salzburg Festival, 1962-63 as Marcellina in Le Nozze di Figaro, Glyndebourne Festival, 1965-68 as Jane Seymour in Anna Bolena, the Sorceress in Dido and Aeneas and Storge in Jeptha; Sang the Countess de Coigny in Andrea Chénier at Covent Garden in 1985; Deustche Oper Berlin in 1989 as Kabanichka in Katya Kabanova; Sang Dorabella at Salzburg and Lady Billows at Glyndebourne, with video; BBC's Lady Macbeth and many appearances in concerts and oratorios. Recordings: Lulu; Der Junge Lord; Le nozze di Figaro; Dido and Aeneas; Video of Andrea Chénier. Address: c/o Deutsche Oper Berlin, Richard Wagnerstrasse 10, D-1000 Berlin, Germany.

JOHNSON Robert, b. 10 Dec 1940, Moline, Illinois, USA. Singer (Tenor). Education: Studied at Northwestern University in Evanston and at New York. Debut: New York City Opera, 1971, as Count Almaviva. Career: Sang in New York, Chicago, Baltimore, Houston, New Orleans and Washington as Mozart's Ferrando, Belmonte and Tamino; Ernesto, Beppo in Donizetti's Rita, Alfredo, Fenton in Falstaff, Hoffmann, Rodolfo, Sali in A Village Romeo and Juliet, and Tom Rakewell; Frequent concerto appearances. Address: c/o New York City Opera, Lincoln Center, New York, NY 10023, USA.

JOHNSON Theodore, b. 9 Oct 1929, Elkhart, Indiana, USA. Professor of Music. m. Carol A Jolliff, 22 June 1968, 2 sons, 2 daughters. Education: BMus, 1951, MMus, 1952, DMA, 1959, University of Michigan. Career: Music Faculty, University of Kansas; Professor of Music, Michigan State University; Beaumont String Quartet, 1964-80; Concertmaster, Lansing Symphony Orchestra, 1967-69; Concertmaster, Grand Rapids Symphony, 1972-73; Principal Violist, Lansing Symphony, 1982-86; Recitalist and Chamber Musician; Chair of Music Theory, Michigan State University, 1984-88. Compositions: Here on the Cross He Lies; Trust in the Lord with All Your Heart. Publications: An analytical survey of the fifteen two-part inventions by J S Bach, 1982; An analytical survey of the fifteen Sinfonies (three-part inventions) by J S Bach, 1986. Honours: Stanley Medal, University of Michigan, 1951; Fulbright Scholarship, 1956-57; Rackham Fellowship, 1957-58. Memberships: Phi Kappa Lambda; Phi Mu Alpha; Phi Kappa Phi; Phi Eta Sigma. Address: 651 Hillcrest Avenue, East Lansing, MI 48823, USA.

JOHNSON Tom, b. 18 Nov 1939, Greeley, Colorado, USA. Composer. Education: BA, 1961, MMus, 1967, Yale University; Private study with Morton Feldman. Career: Music Critic, Village Voice, New York, 1971-82; Freelance Composer, 1982-. Compositions include: Spaces, 1969; An Hour for Piano, 1971; The Four Note Opera, 1972; Septapede, 1973; Verses for alto flute, horn and harp, 1974; The Masque of Clouds, opera, 1975; Verses for viola, 1976; Trinity for SATB, 1978; Dragons in A, 1979; Movements for wind quintet, 1980; Harpiano,, 1982; Predictables, 1984; Voicings for 4 pianos, 1984; Tango, 1984; Choral Catalogue, 1985; Pascal's Triangle, 1987; Riemannoper, 1988. Publications: Imaginary Music, 1974; Private Pieces, 1976; Symmetries, 1981; Rational Melodies, 1982. Address: c/o ASCAP, ASCAP Building, One Lincoln Plaza, New York, NY 10023, USA.

JOHNSSON Bengt (Gustaf), b. 17 July 1921, Copenhagen, Denmark. Professor; Pianist; Organist. m. Esther Paustian, 1 daughter. Education: MA, Musicology, University of Copenhagen, 1947; Studies with Georg Vasarhelyl and Walter Gieseking; Degree as Organist and Church Musician, Royal Academy of Music, Copenhagen, 1945. Debut: Copenhagen, 1944. Career: Concert tours, broadcasts, Scandinavia, German Federal Republic, Switzerland, France, Netherlands; Recitals in many European countries; US tour, 1964; Organist, Danish Broadcasting, 1949-70; Teacher, Royal Academy, Copenhagen, 1958-61; Professor, Royal Academy of Music, Aarhus, Jutland; Numerous master classes; Studied at Vatican Library, Rome, 1977, Benedictine Monastery, Montserrat, Spain, 1978, 1980-83; Spanish Cultural Department invitation to study in libraries in Barcelona and Montserrat, 1979, 1983. Recordings include: N W Gade Piano Music; Rissager, Complete Piano Works; Chamber Music of Beethoven, Brahms, Busoni; Roman Organ and Harpsichord Music from the 17th Century, 1982; Rued Langgaard: Piano Music, 1985; Catalan Organ Music, 1988. Publications include: History of the Danish School of Music until 1739, 1973; Roman Organ Music for the 17th Century; Roman Harpsichord Music from the 17th Century; Piano Music of Manuel Blasco de Nebra, 1984; 23 Piano Sonatas for Josep Galles, 1984; Editor: Heptachordum Danicum 1646 (translation, historical comments, source studies), 1977; Hans Mikkelsen Ravn: The Vatican Manuscript, 1981; Selected Sonatas of D Scarlatti including 1st edition of 4 new editions, 1985; Selected Piano Music of N W Gade, 1986; Catalan Organ Music of the 18th Century, 1986; Scarlatti Vol II, 1988, vol II, 1992; Niels W Gade: Klavierwerke, 1989; Piano Music for Franz Liszt, 1989; Selected Piano Works of Rued Langgaard, 1994. Honours: Bronze Medal Winner, Piano Music of Manuel Blasco de Nebra, International Book Messe, Leipzig, 1986. Address: Porsevænget 18, Kongens Lyngby, DK-2800 Copenhagen, Denmark.

JOHNSTON Ben(jamin) Burwell, b. 15 Mar 1926, Macon, Georgia, USA. Composer; Teacher. Education: AB, College of William and Mary, 1949; MM, Cincinnati Conservatory of Music, 1950; MA, Mills College, 1953. Career: Faculty member, University of Illinois, 1951-83. Compositions: Concerto for brass, 1951; St Joan, ballet, 1955; Passacaglia and Epilogue for orchestra, 1955-60; Septet for wind quintet, cello and bass, 1956-58; Gambit, ballet, 1959; Knocking Piece for 2 percussionists and piano, 1962; Gertrude, or Would She Be Pleased to Receive It?, opera, 1965; Quintet for groups, 1966; Carmilla, opera, 1970; Trio for clarinet, violin and cello, 1982; The Demon Lover's Doubles for trumpet and microtonal piano, 1985; Symphony, 1988; 9 string quartets; Piano pieces; Choruses; Songs. Honours: Guggenheim Fellowship, 1959-60. Address: c/o Music Department, University of Illinois, Urbana-Champaign, Urbana, IL 61801, USA.

JOHNSTONE Harry (Diack), b. 29 April 1935, Vancouver, Canada. University Lecturer. m. Jill Margaret Saunders, 5 August 1960, deceased 8 April 1989, 1 son, 1 daughter. Education: Royal College of Music, London, 1954-57; Balliol College, Oxford, 1957-63; MA, DPhil (Oxon), 1968; BMus (TCD); FRCO; FTCL; ARCM. Career: Assistant Organist, New College, Oxford, 1960-61; Assistant Lecturer, Music, University of Reading, 1963; Lecurer, 1965, Senior Lecturer, 1970, Tutorial Fellow, Music, St Anne's College, Oxford; Lecturer, Music, St John's, 1980; Visiting Professor, Music, Memorial University, St John's, Newfoundland, 1983. Publications: Editor and part Author of the Blackwell History of Music in Britain IV; The Eighteenth Century, 1990; Editor, Maurice Greene: Cambridge Ode and Anthem, Musica Britannica 58, 1991; Numerous editions of 18th century music, mainly English; Articles and Reviews in The Musical Times, Music and Letters, Proceedings of the Royal Musical Association, Organists' Review, The New Grove. Address: Faculty of Music, University of Oxford, St Aldate's, Oxford OX1 1DB, England.

JOLAS Betsy, b. 5 Aug 1926, Paris, France. Composer; Professor of Composition and Advanced Analysis. m. Gabriel Illouz, 27 Aug 1949, 2 sons, 1 daughter. Education: French Baccalaureat; Studied composition with Paul Boepple, piano with Helen Schnabel and organ with Carl Weinrich and graduated from Bennington College, USA, 1940-46; Studied with Darius Milhaud, Simone Ple-Caussade and Olivier Messiaen at Paris Conservatory, 1946. Career: Replaced Olivier Messiaen at his course at Paris Conservatory, 1971-74, Appointed to Faculty, 1975; Also taught at: Tanglewood, Yale, Harvard, Darius Milhaud Chair at Mills College, Berkeley, University of Southern California and San Diego University, USA. Compositions include: 9 Episodes for Solo Instruments, 1964-90; Motet II for Chorus and Ensemble, 1965; Quatuor II, 1964; Points d'aube, 1968; Quatuor III, 1973; Le Pavillon au bord de la Rivière for Chamber Opera, 1975; 4 Duos for Alto and Piano, 1979; Living Ballade, baritone and orchestra, 1980; Points d'or, saxophone and ensemble, 1982; Trio for Piano, Viola and Violoncello; Schliemann, opera in 3 acts, 1988; Quatuor IV, 1989; Trio Les Heures for String Trio, 1990; Frauenleben for Viola and Orchestra, 1991; Perriault le Deluné for 12 Voices, 1993; Quatuor V, 1994; Sigrancia Ballade, 1995; Petite symphonie concertante, violin and orchestra, 1996; Lumor Flieder, 1996. Recordings include: Stances; Points d'Aube: D'un opéra de voyage. Honours include: Prizewinner, International Conducting Competition, Besançon, 1953; Copley Foundation of Chicago, 1954; ORTF, 1961; Grand Prix National de la Musique, 1974; Grand Prix de la Ville de Paris, 1981; Grand Prix De La SACEM, 1982; Prix International Maurice Ravel, 1992; Personnalité de l'année, 1992; Chevalier de la Légion d'Honneur, 1997. Memberships: American Academy of Arts and Letters, 1983; American Academy of Arts and Sciences, 1995. Current Management: Leduc, Salabert, Billaudot Publishers. Address: 12 Rue Meynadier, 75019 Paris, France.

JOLL Philip, b. 14 Mar 1954, Merthyr Tydfil, Wales. Singer (Baritone). Education: Studied at the Royal Northern College of Music with Nicholas Powell and Frederick Cox; Further study at the National Opera Studio in London. Career: Sang with English National Opera from 1979, as Donner and The Dutchman; Welsh National opera as Wotan (also with the company at Covent Garden, 1986), Kurwenal, Amfortas, Chorebus in The Trojans, The Forester (Cunning Little Vixen), Onegin, Orestes, Don Fernando in Fidelio, Jochanaan in Salome and Barak in Die Frau ohne Schatten; Covent Garden debut, 1982, in Salome, returning in Der Freischütz, Das Rheingold and Die Frau ohne Schatten; German debut, Frankfurt, 1983, as Amfortas, returning for The Dutchman; Guest appearances in Dusseldorf, 1985-86, Berlin and Wiesbaden (with the Welsh National Company in The Midsummer Marriage, 1986); Metropolitan Opera debut, 1988, as Donner in Das Rheingold; Australian debut as Jochanaan, for the Lyric Opera of Queensland, 1988; Bregenz Festival, 1989, in Der fliegende Holländer; Lyric Opera of Queensland, 1989-90, as Jochanaan in Salome and Marcello; Sang Orestes in Elektra and Rigoletto for Welsh National Opera, 1992-97. Recordings include: The Greek Passion by Martinu; Amfortas in Parsifal; Kurwenal in Tristan und Isolde, conducted by Reginald Goodall. Address: IMG Artists, Media House, 3 Burlington Lane, Chiswick, London W4 2TH, England.

JOLY Simon, b. 14 Oct 1952, Exmouth, Devon, England. Conductor; Repetiteur. Education: Corpus Christi College, Cambridge; BA, MA; ARCO; FRCO. Career: Music staff, Welsh

National Opera, 1974-78; Conducted The Barber of Seville, 1978; Assistant Chorus Master, 1978-79, Associate Chorus Master, 1979-80, English National Opera; Currently Conductor of the BBC Singers, notably in contemporary music; Concerts with BBC Singers: Proms, 1990; Helsinki Biennale, 1991; Peter Grimes, Dublin, 1990; Nicholas Maw's The Rising of the Moon, 1990 Wexford Festival; Guest conductor of the BBC Symphony Orchestra in works by Hindemith, Bax, Rubbra, Howells and Bedford, Koechlin, Franck, Walton, Debussy and Ives; BBC Philharmonic on 1986 German tour; BBC Welsh Symphony in Swiss music; Concerts with the English Chamber Orchestra and London and Bournemouth Sinfoniettas; Endymion Ensemble in Les Noces at the 1987 Proms and Birtwistle's ...agm...at the Barbican 1988; Opera performances for the BBC; The Bartered Bride for English National Opera, Gazzaniga's Don Giovanni and Busoni's Turandot at 1988 Wexford Festival; Broadcast premieres of works by Jonathan Lloyd, James Ellis and many others. Hobbies: Food; Cinema. Address: c/o Musikmakers, Little Easthall Farm House, St Paul's Walden, Herts SG4 8DH, England.

JONAS Hilda (Klestadt), b. 21 Jan 1913, Düsseldorf, Germany. Concert Harpsichordist and Pianist; Teacher of Harpsichord and Piano. m. Gerald Jonas, 30 Jan 1938, 2 daughters. Education: Hochschule für Musik, Cologne, 1932-33; Honour Diploma, Gumpert Conservatory, 1934; Studies with Professor Michael Wittels, Cologne, Rudolf Serkin, Switzerland and Wanda Landowska, Paris, France. Career: Concert soloist and recitalist worldwide with recitals in France, Germany, Spain, Italy, Austria, Belgium, Australia, New Zealand, Hawaii, USA; Colleges, Universities, museums and art centres, Harvard, Carnegie-Mellon, Cincinnati Taft Museum, Haifa Music Museum, Milano Centro Culturale San Fedele, Empire Saal of Schloss Esterházy, Eisenstadt, Brussel's Musée Instrumental, Castello Buonconsiglio, Trento, Palais Wittgenstein, Düsseldorf, Stanford University, California, Palace of the Legion of Honour San Francisco, San Francisco State University, Goethe Institute, Californaia West Coast from Olympia Evergreen State College to Santa Barbara, Westmont, Ventura, Monterey Peninsula Colleges, Sacramento Crocker Art Museum, Ojai Valley Art Center and other cultural centres in Marin County and San Francisco; Soloist with major symphony orchestras including: Cleveland, Cincinnati; Regular series and May festivals under Max Rudolf and Josef Krips, Honolulu, Oxford, Jerusalem, Strasbourg and elsewhere; Owner of private piano studio, Honolulu, 1938-42 and Cincinnati, 1942-75; Founder, 1965, Director, 1965-75, Harpsichord Festival Put-in-Bay, Ohio. Recordings include: Listen Rebecca, The Harpsichord Sounds, for children of all ages; Johann Kuhnau: Six Biblical Sonatas, with text based on authentic edition; Hilda Plays Bach: Italian Concerto, Chromatic Fantasia and Fugue, Partita 1, Capriccio on the departure of his beloved brother, and others; Johann Sebastian Bach: Goldberg Variations. Contributions to: Various music magazines. Memberships: Life Member, Hadassah; Life Member, Brandeis University. Address: 50 Chumasero Drive 1-L, San Francisco, CA 94132, USA.

JONAS Peter, b. 14 Oct 1946, London, England. General Director, Bavarian State Opera. m. Lucy Hull, Nov 1989. Education: University of Sussex; Northern College of Music; Royal College of Music, London; Eastman School of Music, University of Rochester, USA; BA, Honours; LRAM. Career: Assistant to Music Director, 1974-76, Artistic Administrator, 1976-85, Chicago Symphony Orchestra; Director of Artistic Administration, Orchestral Association, Chicago, 1977-85; General Director, English National Opera, 1985-93; General Director (Staatsintendant), Bavarian State Opera, Munich, 1993-; Board of Management, National Opera Studio, 1985-93; Member of Council, Royal College of Music, 1988-95; Fellow of The Royal College of Music, FRCM, 1989; Member of Council, London Lighthouse, 1990-93; Member, Deutsche Opernkonferenz, 1993-; Member, Deutsche Buhnverein, 1994-. Honours: CBE, 1993; Honorary DMus, University of Sussex, 1994. Memberships: Athenaeum; Reg's Club; Fellow, Royal Society of Arts; Advisory Board, Bayerische Vereinsbank, 1994-. Hobbies: Cinema; 20th Century Architecture; Theatre; Mountain Hiking. Address: c/o Bayerische Staatsoper, Nationaltheater, Max-Joseph-Platz 2, D-80539 Munich, Germany.

JONES Della, b. 13 Apr 1946, Neath, Wales. Singer (Mezzo-soprano). Education: Royal College of Music, London, and Centre Lyrique Music School, Geneva. Career: Sang first at Grand Théâtre, Geneva; Member of English National Opera, 1977-82, in La Gazza Ladra, Il Barbiere di Siviglia, La Cenerentola, Le Comte Ory, Figaro, Giulio Cesare, Orfeo, Carmen, L'Incoronazione di Poppea and La Forza del Destino; Appearances with Welsh National Opera in Les Troyens, Salome, Barbiere di Siviglia and Tristan und Isolde; Scottish Opera in L'Egisto, Hansel and Gretel and Don Giovanni; Opera North as Rosina and in La Cenerentola, Le Comte Ory, Die Meistersinger, Oedipus Rex and Salome; Other engagements with English Music Theatre (world premiere of Tom Jones by Stephen Oliver and the Threepenny Opera), Dublin Opera and Handel Opera Society; Baba the Turk in Rake's Progress in Geneva and Venice; Ruggiero in Alcina for Los Angeles Opera; Sang Cecilio in Lucio Silla, also La Finta Giardiniera for Mostly Mozart Festival, New York; Other festivals in London (English Bach), Cheltenham, Aldeburgh, Chester, Salisbury, Athens, Orange, throughout France, Switzerland and Edinburgh; Sang Preziosilla in Forza del Destino for Scottish Opera, 1990; Ruggiero in Alcina at Geneva and Théâtre du Châtelet, Paris; Mrs Noye in Noyes Fludde at 1990 Promenade Concerts, Hermia in Midsummer Night's Dream at Sadler's Wells, many other Prom appearances including Last Night, 1993; Marchesa Melibea at Covent Garden, 1992 (Il Viaggio a Reims); Sang Gluck's Armide at the Baroque Festival Versailles, 1992 and Clytemnestra in Iphigénie en Aulide for Opera North, 1996; Welsh National Opera, 1994, as Ariodante; Sang Rossini's Isabella for English National Opera, 1997; Concerts and recitals in USSR, USA, Europe and Japan. Recordings include: Haydn L'Incontro Improvviso and Il Ritorno di Tobia, conductor Dorati; Alcina, conductor Hickox; Marcellina in Figaro and Elvira in Don Giovanni, conductor Arnold Östmann; Donizetti L'Assedio di Calais; L'Incoronazione di Poppea; Rossini Stabat Mater and Arias, Bliss Pastoral, conductor Hickox; Recital of French Songs with Malcolm Martineau; The Bear by Walton; Dido in Dido and Aeneas; Video of ENO production of Giulio Cesare.

JONES Geraint (Iwan), b. 16 May 1917, Porth, Glamorgan, Wales. Conductor; Organist; Harpsichordist. m. (1) M A Kemp, 1940, (2) Winifred Roberts, 1949, 1 daughter. Education: Royal Academy of Music. Career: Concert Organist, National Gallery Concerts, 1940-44; Conductor, Purcell's Dido and Aeneas, Mermaid Theatre, London, 1950-53; Founder, Geraint Jones Singers and Orchestra, 1951; Musical Director, Lake District Festival, 1960-78, Kirckman Concert Society, 1963-; Artistic Director, Salisbury Festival of the Arts, 1972-77, Manchester International Organ Festival, 1977-87; Professor and Fellow, Royal Academy of Music; Frequent violin and harpsichord recitals with wife Winifred Roberts; Many frequent tours of Europe and America, 1948-; As Consultant has designed many organs, notable for the RNCM, RAM at Marylebone Parish Church, University of St Andrews, Tsin Sha Tsui Concert Hall, Hong Kong and the Academy for Performing Arts, Hong Kong. Recordings: Has recorded on most historic organs in Europe; Numerous recordings with his singers and orchestra; Complete organ works of Bach in London, 1945-46 and 1955. Publications: Translations: Théorie-Pratique de la Facture de l'Orgue by Clicquot; Robert Davy's Les Grandes Orgues de l'Abbatiale St Etienne de Caen, both 1985. Honours: Grand Prix du Disque, 1959 and 1966. Hobbies: Photography; Antiques; Architecture. Address: The Long House, Arkley Lane, Barnet Road, Arkley, Hertfordshire, England.

JONES Gordon, b. 1960, Northampton, England. Singer (Bass-baritone). Education: Studied at York University; Choral Scholarship to York Minster. Career: Concert engagements include visits to the Lincoln Center in New York, the Royal Palace in The Hague, Hallé Orchestra, Martin's Le Vin Herbé at the Siena Festival and The Fairy Queen on tour in Italy; Performances of Berio's Sinfonia conducted by the composer, Simon Rattle and Esa-Pekka Salonen; Bach's St John and St Matthew Passions with the Choir of King's College, Cambridge; Sang in Arvo Pärt's St John Passion at the 1986 Almeida Festival and on tour of Britain, 1988; Further engagements in Bristol and Aberdeen and at the Malvern and Aix-en-Provence Festivals; Bach's St John Passion with The Sixteen on tour in Spain. Recordings: Vierne's Les Angelus; Lully's Idylle pour la Paix, BBC; Schütz Schwanengesang and Bach Motets with the Hilliard Ensemble; Pärt St John Passion.

JONES Gwyneth (Dame), b. 7 Nov 1936, Pontenywynydd, Wales. Singer (Soprano). m. Till Haberfeld, 1 daughter. Education: Royal College of Music, London; Accademia Chigiana, Siena; Zurich International Opera Centre. Career: With Zurich Opera House, 1962-63; Royal Opera House, Covent Garden, 1963-; Vienna State Opera House, 1966-; Bavarian State Opera, 1967-; Guest performances, numerous opera houses world wide including La Scala Milan, Rome Opera, Berlin State Opera, Munich State Opera, Hamburg, Paris, Metropolitan Opera (New York), San Francisco, Los Angeles, Zurich, Geneva, Dallas, Barcelona, Chicago, Teatro Colon (Buenos Aires), Tokyo, Bayreuth Festival (debut 1966), Salzburg Festival, Arena di Verona, Edinburgh Festival, Welsh National Opera; Known for many opera roles including: Brünnhilde, Ring des Nibelungen; Marschallin, Rosenkavalier; Leonora, Il Trovatore; Desdemona, Otello; Aida and Turandot (Covent Garden 1990); Leonore, Fidelio (Beethoven); Senta, The Flying Dutchman; Medea; Elisabeth, Don Carlos; Madama Butterfly; Tosca; Donna Anna, Don Giovanni; Salome; Kundry, Parsifal; Helena, Ägyptische Helena; Dyer's Wife, Frau ohne Schatten (San Francisco 1989); Elektra (Geneva 1990); Elisabeth/Venus, Tannhäuser; Sang Brünnhilde at San Francisco, 1990, Covent Garden, 1990-91; Sang the Dyer's Wife at Covent Garden, 1992, Los Angeles, 1993; Wagner's Liebestod at the 1993 Prom Concerts, London; Sang Ortrud in Lohengrin at Covent Garden, 1997. Recordings: Various labels and TV films, including: Fidelio; Aida; Flying Dutchman; Beethoven 9th Symphony; Tannhäuser; Poppea (Monteverdi); Rosenkavalier; Die Walküre, Siegfried; Götterdämmerung; Die Lustige Witwe; Turandot. Honours: CBE, 1976; DBE, 1986; Dr hc, University of Wales; Bundes Verdienstkreuz 1 Klasse; Honorary Member, Vienna State Opera. Address: PO Box, 8037 Zürich, Switzerland.

JONES Ieuan, b. 1955, Wales. Harpist. Education: Royal College of Music, with Marisa Robles. Career includes: Appearances, UK, Dutch and Italian TV; Soloist, London Rodrigo Festival, 1986; Soloist, Mozart Concerto for Flute and Harp, Bournemouth Sinfonietta, 1986; Invited performer, World Harp Congress, Vienna, 1987; Recitals, Spain, North America; Featured, premiere of Alan Hoddinott's Tarantella for Harp and Orchestra, St David's Day Concert, Cardiff, 1988; Mozart and Daniel Jones Concertos, Flute and Harp, Swansea, Aberystwyth, 1988; Replaced Marisa Robles, Mozart Flute and Harp Concerto, Debussy's Danses Sacrées et Profanes, Margam Festival, Swansea, 1988; Radio 2 Billy Butler Show, Croydon, 1989; USA Miami recital, North Wales tour; Promotional video, Welsh Development Board, 1990; Brussels, Mozart Concert Recordings release, 1990; Premiere, Rodrigo Concerto, Wales, 1991; Guest soloist of Enrique Batiz and the State Orchestra of Mexico, 1992; Soloist, Rodrigo Homage Concert, Seville EXPO celebrations, 1992; Welsh premiere of Sonata for Harp by William Mathias (dedicated to Ieuan Jones), at 1993 Machynlleth Festival. Recordings: The Uncommon Harp, selection of light classics and ballads, 1987; 2 Sides of Ieuan Jones, 1988; ...In The French Style, 1990; Mozart in Paris, 1990; All Through The Night, with Huw Rhys-Evans (tenor). Honours: All major prizes including Tagore Gold Medal and 1st-time award from HM the Queen Mother, Royal College of Music; All honours including overall Gold Medal, Royal Overseas League Music Competition; Joint winner, Israel International Harp Contest. Current Management: Neil Chaffey Concert Promotions, 8 Laxton Gardens, Baldock, Herts SG7 5DA, England.

JONES Isola, b. 27 Dec 1949, Chicago, Illinois, USA. Musician; Singer (Mezzo-soprano). m. Russell Thomas Cormier, 31 Mar 1984. Education: Bachelor's degree in Musical Education, Northwestern University, 1971. Debut: Olga in Eugene Onegin, Metropolitan Opera, 15 Oct 1977. Career: Live From the Met television series; Maddalena in Rigoletto, 1977, 1981; Lola in Cavalleria Rusticana, 1978; Girl in Mahagonny, 1979; Madrigal in Manon Lescaut, 1980; Recital with Placido Domingo, 1982; The Met Centennial Gala, 1983; Preziosilla in La Forza del Destino, 1984; Smaragdi in Francesca da Rimini; Spoleto Festival, 1989, as Giulietta in Les Contes d'Hoffmann. Recordings: Porgy and Bess, with Cleveland Orchestra conducted by Lorin Maazel; Flying Dutchman, with Chicago Symphony conducted by Georg Solti; Les Noces, with Chicago Symphony conducted by James Levine; Cavalleria Rusticana, with New Philharmonic Orchestra conducted by James Levine. Honours: Merit Award, Northwestern University, 1984. Hobby: Tennis (husband teaching tennis professional). Current Management: Robert Lombardo Associates.

JONES Karen, b. 8 Jul 1965, Hampton, Middlesex, England. Concert Flautist. Education: Studied at the Guildhall School, in Vienna with Wolfgang Schulz and in New York. Career: Played the Ibert Concerto with the LSO, 1985; Concerto performances with Neville Marriner at the Queen Elizabeth Hall, Andrew Litton at the Festival Hall and George Malcolm at the Snape Concert Hall; Further engagements with the Ulster Orchestra, the Philharmonia, the Wren Orchestra and London Musici; Solo recitals at the Purcell Room and Wigmore Hall; Member of the Pears-Britten Ensemble with performances in Britain and the USA; Guest Principal with the Australian Chamber Orchestra at the 1992 Promenade Concerts. Recordings include: Arnold's Concerto No 1 and Panufnik's Hommage a Chopin; Malcolm Arnold Flute Concerto No 2; The Flute Album - Karen Jones. Honours include: Winner, Woodwind Section, BBC TV Young Musician of the Year, 1982; Gold Medal of The Shell, LSO Scholarship, 1985. Current Management: Owen/White Management. Address: c/o Owen/White Management, 14 Nightingale Lane, London, N8 7QU, England.

JONES Kenneth (Victor), b. 14 May 1924, Bletchley, England. Composer; Conductor; Professor. m. Anne Marie Heine, 20 Mar 1945, 1 s, 1 d. Education: King's School, Canterbury; Queen's College, Oxford; Royal College of Music. Debut: Royal Festival Hall. Career: Assistant Organist, Choirmaster, St Michael's College, Tanbury, 1941; RAF, 1942-47; Assistant Conductor: London Symphonic Players, 1952, Redhill and Reigate Choral Society, 1956-64, Hill Singers, Wimbledon, 1954-60; Professor, Royal College of Music, 1958-91; Conductor, 1961-70, Founder and President, 1970-, Wimbledon Symphony; Conductor, Sinfonia of London, 1966-70; Founder Member and Governor, Rokeby Educational Trust, 1966-; Visiting Tutor, University of Sussex, 1971-73. Compositions include: Paean for Organ; Sussex Suite for Junior Orchestra; 2 Sinfoniettas; 4 Sonatas; 2 Wind Quintets; String Quartet; 4 Works for Orchestra; 6 Song Cycles; Collections; 2 Brass Works; 3 Concerti; 2

Cantatas; 44 Piano Works; 24 Works for Violin, Viola, Cello and Piano; 85 Film, Play and TV Scores; Various Church Music; Dialysis; Rembrancer of an Inward Eye; The Rites Mysterious for Trumpet and Organ. Recordings include: Dialysis; Chorale; Ceremony and Toccata; Organ Sonata No 1; A Gay Psaltery; Serpentine Dances; Sonata for Solo Violin. Publications: Numerous books including: A Musical Progress for Piano, 43 pieces, Dialysis for Violin and Harpsichord. Honour: FRCM. Memberships: Royal Philharmonic Society; Composers' Guild; Royal Air Force Club. Current Management: CCA. Address: Cleavers, Bishopstone Village, Seaford, East Sussex, BN25 2UD, England.

JONES Leah-Marian, b. 1964, Wales. Singer (Mezzo-soprano). Education: Studied at the Royal Northern College of Music and the National Opera Studio. Career: Appearances with the Royal Opera at Covent Garden as Mercedes (Carmen), Zulma (L'Italiana in Algeri), Flosshilde (Rheingold), Second Lady (Die Zauberflöte), Emilia (Otello), Rosette (Manon), Flora (La Traviata), Annina (Der Rosenkavalier), Dorotea (Stiffelio), Elena (Aroldo), Flosshilde (Götterdämmerung); Season 1995/96 with Welsh National Opera as Lola in Cavalleria Rusticana; Other roles include Maddalena, Carmen, Siebel, Isolier (Comte Ory) Adalgisa (Norma); Season 1996 with Royal Opera as Fenena (Nabucco) and Dorabella and Carmen for English National Opera. Address: c/o Harold Holt Ltd, 31 Sinclair Road, London W14 0NS, England.

JONES Martin, b. 4 Feb 1940, England. Concert Pianist. Education: Studied in London. Debut: Played at the Elizabeth Hall, London, and Carnegie Hall, 1968. Career: Regular appearances with major British orchestras at the Festival Hall, the Barbican and other venues; Tour of Canada with the BBC Welsh Symphony Orchestra and recitals in Florida, Tennessee and California; Broadcasts in Britain, Ireland and the USA; Pianist-in-Residence at University College, Cardiff, 1971-88; Brahms recital at the Wigmore Hall, 1993; Repertoire includes many standard concertos and also those by Busoni, Benjamin, Barber, Mathias, McCabe, Lambert and Scharwenka; Played Grainger's Bridal Lullaby and Mock Morris on the soundtrack of the film Howard's End. Recordings: Extensively for Nimbus Records. Address: c/o Owen/White Management, 14 Nightingale Lane, London N8 7QU, England.

JONES Maureen, b. 1940, Australia. Pianist. Education: Studied at the New South Wales Conservatorium, Sydney. Career: Formed Trio with Breton Langbein and Barry Tuckwell and gave the premiere of the Horn Trio by Don Banks at the 1962 Edinburgh Festival; Regular tours of Australia and Europe, including recent appearances in Dublin, Siena, Innsbruck, Paris, Sydney and Melbourne; Duo recitals with Barry Tuckwell; Concert debut playing Beethoven's 1st Concerto with the Sydney Symphony; Appearances at the Edinburgh Festival include concerts with the Berlin Philharmonic. Address: c/o Harold Holt Ltd, 31 Sinclair Road, London W14 0NS, England.

JONES Nerys, b. Wales. Singer (Soprano). Education: Studied with Patricia MacMahon at the Royal Scottish Academy and at the Guildhall School with Jessica Cash; Further study with Janice Chapman. Dabut: Karolka in Jenufa for Scottish Opera. Career: Appearances with Scottish Opera as Marzelline in Fidelio and Welsh National as Norina in Don Pasquale; English National Opera debut as Melissa in Ken Russell's production of Princess Ida, 1992; Further roles with ENO (Principal from 1994) include Babarina, Atalanta in Xerxes, Garcias in Don Quixote, Cherubino and Zerlina; Sang in the premiere of Blond Eckbert by Judith Weir, 1994; Many concert engagements. Honours include: Peter Morrison Prize at the Royal Scottish Academy. Address: c/o ENO Press Office, English National Opera, St Martin's Lane. London WC2N 4ES, England.

JONES Philip (Burnell Rees), b. 16 Mar 1951, Stourport-on-Severn, England. Lecturer in Music; Conductor; Writer; Arranger. m. Jane Rosamond Hewitt, 8 Sep 1984. Education: Birmingham School of Music, 1969-70; University of York, 1970-74; Eastman School of Music, NY, USA, 1974-75; University of Birmingham, 1975-76. Debut: City of Birmingham Symphony Orchestra, 1977. Career: Fellow in Music, University of Bradford, 1976-78; Lecturer in Music, University of Keele, 1978-89; Head of Faculty of Art and Music, Bath College of Higher Education, 1989-92; Music career: Principal Conductor of English Philharmonic Orchestra, 1976-79, Guest Conductor of Orchestra da Camera, English String Orchestra, BBC Northern Symphony Orchestra and Royal Liverpool Philharmonic Orchestra, Artistic Director of the Fourth Delius Festival 1982, the First British Music Week, 1984, and Keele Concerts Society, 1983-89. Publication: The American Sources of Delius's Style, 1990. Contributions to: Musical Times; Delius Society Journal; Music Quarterly. Honours: BA, York, 1973; BPhil, York, 1974; PhD, Birmingham, 1981. Memberships: Royal Musical Association. Address: Department of Music, University of Keele, Staffordshire, ST5 5BG, England.

JONES Philip (Mark), b. 12 March 1928, Bath, England. Musician; Pioneer of Chamber Music for Brass Ensembles; Principal, Trinity College of Music, London, 1988-94. m. Ursula Strebi, 1 August 1956. Education: Royal College of Music, London. Career: Principal Trumpet, all major London Orchestras, 1948-72; Founder, Director, Philip Jones Brass Ensemble, 1951-86; Head, Wind and Percussion, Royal Northern College of Music, Manchester, 1975-77; Editor, Just Brass Music Series, Chester Music, London, 1975-89; Head, Wind and Percussion, Guildhall School of Music and Drama, London, 1983-88; Member, Arts Council of Great Britain, 1984-88; Governor, Chetham's School, Manchester, 1988-94; Vice Chairman, Executive Committee, Musicians Benevolent Fund, 1993-. Recordings: Over 50 records with Philip Jones Brass Ensemble. Honours: OBE, 1977; CBE, 1986. Hobbies: History; Mountain Walking; Skiing. Address: 14 Hamilton Terrace, London NW8 9UG, England.

JONES Richard, b. 7 June 1953, Lambeth, London, England. Producer. Education: Studied at the Universities of Hull and London. Debut: A Water Bird Talk by Dominick Argento for Scottish Opera, 1982. Career: Has directed for the theatre and for the following opera companies: Musica nel Chiostro, Battingano (Mozart's Apollo et Hyacinthus 1984); Salieri's La Grotta di Trofonio and Paisiello's Il re Teodoro in Venezia, 1985; Opera Northern Ireland (Don Pasquale, 1985); Wexford Festival (Mignon 1986); Cambridge University Opera (The Magic Flute, 1986); Opera 80 (The Rake's Progress, 1986, Rigoletto, 1987); Opera North (Manon, 1987, Carmen and The Love for Three Oranges, 1987); Scottish Opera-Go-Round (Macbeth and Die Entführung, 1987); Scottish Opera (Das Rheingold, 1989); Kent Opera (Le Comte Cry and A Night at the Chinese Opera, 1988); The Love for Three Oranges and David Blake's The Plumber's Gift, world premiere, for English National Opera, 1989; Bregenz Festival, Austria (Mazeppa, 1991); Netherlands Opera (The Flying Dutchman, 1993); Bavarian State Opera (Julius Caesar), 1994; Royal Opera House (Das Rheingold and Die Walküre, 1994, Siegfried and Götterdämmerung, 1995); Netherlands Opera (Mazeppa, 1991); English National Opera (Die Fledermaus, 1991); Scottish Opera (Die Walküre, 1991); Engaged for The Midsummer Marriage at Munich, 1998. Honours include: Laurence Olivier Award as Best Newcomer in Theatre in 1988; Best Director at the 1990 Evening Standard Drama awards. Current Management: Judy Daish Associates, London.

JONES Roland (Leo), b. 16 Dec 1932, Ann Arbor, Michigan, USA. Performer and Teacher of Violin and Viola. Education: BMus, University of Michigan; 5 years study in New York City at Columbia University and privately; 3 years with National Orchestra Association Training Orchestra; Summers at Interlochen Music Camp, Meadowmount Music School and Tanglewood Music School. Career: Soloist with Ann Arbor Civic Symphony, 1951, 1953; Violinist, Denver Symphony Orchestra, 1960-75; Jackson Hole, Wyoming Fine Arts Festival, 1964-65; Tours throughout USA and Canada; Founder, 1st Violinist, Highland Chamber Players, 1978-79; 1st Violinist, Highland String Quartet, 1979-; Tour with Denver Chamber Orchestra and San Francisco Opera, Western Opera Theater, 1987. Compositions: New Cadenzas for all the Mozart Violin Concertos, 1991. Recordings: With orchestra, Milena by Alberto Ginastera and Concertos No 2 of Chopin. Publications: New Cadenzas for all the Mozart Violin Concertos, 1992. Address: 3004 S Kearney, Denver, CO 80222, USA.

JONES Samuel, b. 2 June 1935, Inverness, Mississippi, USA. Composer; Conductor; Educator. m. (1) 2 daughters, (2) Kristin Barbara Schutte, 22 December 1975. Education: BA, Millsaps College, 1957; MA, PhD, Eastman School of Music, University of Rochester, 1958-60. Career: Director of Instrumental Music, Alma College, Michigan, 1960-62; Music Director, Saginaw Symphony, 1962-65; Conductor, Rochester Philharmonic, 1965-73; Founding Dean, Shepherd School of Music, 1973-79; Professor of Conducting and Composition, Rice University, 1973-; Guest Conductor, Buffalo Philharmonic Symphonies of Detroit, Pittsburgh, Houston, Prague and Iceland. Compositions: In Retrospect; Symphony No 1 (recorded); Elegy for String Orchestra (recorded); Overture for a City; Let Us Now Praise Famous Men (recorded); Spaces; Contours of Time; Fanfare and Celebration; A Christmas Memory; A Symphonic Requiem; Variations on a Theme of Howard Hanson; The Trumpet of the Swan; Listen Now, My Children (recorded); Two Movements for Harpsichord; Canticles of Time, Symphony No 2; Symphony No 3 (Palo Duro Canyon), 1992; The Seas of God, 1992; The Temptation of Jesus (oratorio), 1995. Recordings: Symphony No 3 recorded by Amarillo Symphony. Current Management: Carl Fischer Inc. Address: Shepherd School of Music, Rice University, PO Box 1892, Houston, TX 77251, USA.

JONES Warren, b. 11 Dec 1951, Washington, District of Columbia, USA. Vocal Coach; Accompanist. Education: BM, New England Conservatory of Music, 1973; MM, San Francisco Conservatory of Music, 1977. Career: Accompanist to Luciano Pavarotti, Marilyn Horne, Frederica von Stade, Judith Blegen, Håkan Hagegård, Elisabeth Söderström, Martti Talvela, Carol

Vaness, Lynn Harrell, Thomas Allen, Roberta Peters, Robert Alexander and Samuel Ramey; Appearances at Tanglewood, Ravinia, Caramoor and Salzburg Festivals; Assistant Conductor, Metropolitan Opera, San Francisco Opera; Classes at Harvard, San Francisco Conservatory of Music, Hartt School of Music, California State University. Membership: Lifetime Member, Pi Kappa Lambda. Hobbies: Running; Cooking; Reading. Address: 711 West End Avenue, Apartment 6JN, New York, NY 10025, USA.

JONES Wynford (Lyn), b. 11 Oct 1948, Merthyr Tydfil, Wales. Teacher. m. Julie Avril Fellingham, 2 sons. Education: BA, Music, Leeds University; Graduate Certificate of Education; Associate, Royal College of Music. Career: Began teaching in Wakefield, Yorkshire; Conductor, small group singers, Radio Leeds, 1973; Deputy Conductor, Dowlais Male Voice Choir, 1975, making conducting debut with this choir at Luxembourg Cathedral during tour, May 1975, becoming its Musical Director, 1977-87, and conducting over 200 concerts with it; Several concerts and appeared on BBC TV, Wales, 1975; 3 appearances at the Royal Albert Hall; Concert tours of Bulgaria, 1980, USA, 1982, Netherlands, 1984; Conductor, Wales first Royal Gala Concert; Musical Director, Pontypridd Choral Society, 1988-90; Appearances on French TV; Musical Director, Cwmbach Male Choir, 1991, with which he became the first to conduct a choir at a Five Nations Rugby International at Cardiff Arms Park, 1992, also touring Netherlands and Germany with it, 1993. Address: 3 Sycamore Close, Landare Park, Aberdare, Glamorganshire, Wales.

JORDAN Armin (Georg), b. 9 Apr 1932, Lucerne, Switzerland. Conductor. m. Kate Herkner, 1 son, 1 daughter. Education: University of Fribourg; Conservatoire of Lausanne (degrees in piano teaching and conducting). Debut: Bienne Opera, 1957. Career: Chief Conductor in Biene, 1961-63; First Conductor, Zurich Opera, 1963-71; Music Director, Basle Opera from 1971; Music Director, Orchestre de Chambre de Lausanne, 1973-85; Music Director, Orchestre de la Suisse Romande from 1985; Principal Guest Conductor, Ensemble Orchestral de Paris from 1986; Conducted Massenet's Manon at the Geneva Opera, 1989; Numerous appearances on TV and radio in various countries; International career from 1963; Guest conductor at the Lyon, Vienna, Munich, Hamburg, Geneva, Brussels and Seattle Operas; Paris, Orchestre National de France and Nouvel Orchestre Philharmonique; Season 1991/92 with Die Fledermaus at Geneva and Don Giovanni at Aix-en-Provence; Engaged for Tristan und Isolde at Seaattle, 1998; Led Parsifal at the Opéra Bastille, Paris, 1997; Engaged for the Ring at Seattle, 2001. Recordings: Actor and Conductor in Syberberg's film of Parsifal; Orchestral works by Dukas, Mozart, Dvorák, Ravel, Chausson, Schubert, Chopin and Franck; Mozart Violin Concertos, with Franco Gulli. Honours: Grand Prix, Académie Charles Cros, 1985; Cecilia Award, Belgium, 1985; Académie du Disque Lyrique, Paris, 1987; Prix de la Critique Internationale, 1987; Prix Académie du Disque Françcais, 1988. Address: 234 Bunishoferstrasse, CH-8706 Feldmeilen (ZH), Switzerland.

JORDAN Irene, b. 25 Apr 1919, Birmingham, Alabama, USA. Singer (Soprano). Education: Studied at Judson College, Alabama, and with Clyrie Mundy in New York. Career: Sang first as mezzo-soprano (Mallika in Lakmé at the Metropolitan, 1946), and after further study sang Donna Anna and Micaela at the Chicago Lyric Theatre, 1954; Appeared at the New York City Opera and the Metropolitan (the Queen of Night) in 1957; Elsewhere in America she sang Verdi's Aida and Lady Macbeth, Madame Butterfly, Weber's Euryanthe, Mozart's Vitellia (La Clemenza di Tito) and Leonore in Fidelio. Recordings include: Stravinsky's Pulcinella, conducted by the composer, and songs by Schoenberg.

JORDAN John, b. 13 Aug 1927, Stockleigh Pomeroy, Devon, England. Composer. m. 1958, 1 son, 1 adopted daughter. Education: Secondary School Teacher Training College, 1968-71; BMus, Goldsmiths College, London, 1978; MMus, Leeds University, 1988. Debut: Sherman Theatre, Cardiff; British Music Information Centre, London. Career: Composer, 1945-; Teacher, 1971-90; Summer Music School Tutor; Lecturer. Compositions: Symphony in F; Piano Music; 3 String Quartets; Opera, Die Penderyn; Rondo, for Orchestra; Songs; Song Cycles; Choral Works. Publications: Eight Greenpeace Rounds for Piano Solo and Duet, 1990; Song Cycle (5 songs), 1995; Reflection for Flute and Piano, 1996. Memberships: Composers Guild of Great Britain; Society for the Promotion of New Music; English Dance and Folk Song Society. Hobby: Reading. Address: 3 Famet Close, Purley, Surrey CR8 2DX, England.

JORDAN Paul, b. 12 Mar 1939, New York, New York, USA. Conductor; Composer; Organist; Recorder Player; Educator. Education: Studied at Harvard and Columbia Universities; Private Studies with Tui St George Tucker, Emil Platen, Hanns Eppink, Grete Sultan, Helmut Walcha, Irwin Fischer, Jerome Laszloffy; Degrees: Yale School of Music, Frankfurt Staatliche Hochschule für Musik; Doctor of Musical Arts, Conducting, American

Conservatory of Music, Chicago, ongoing. Debut: Performances in New York beginning at age 12; Carnegie Recital Hall and Tully Hall debuts, 1969, 1971. Career: Director of Music, United Church on the Green, New Haven, Connecticut, 1964-74; Teacher, Sarah Lawrence College, Yale University, 1967-69; Member, Faculty, Binghamton University (SUNY), 1973-95; Guest Conductor, California Institute of the Arts, 1984; Concerts in over 100 cities on 4 continents, 1967-; Recordings for the Radio in Berlin, Frankfurt, Hannover, 1973- (including the complete Art of the Fugue by J S Bach, Berlin, 1986). Recordings: Bach: Complete Orgelbüchlein (Double Album), 1976, 1980; From Amsterdam to Leipzig, Spectrum 1981; Viva Vivaldi, Nonesuch 1984; Buxtehude, Moondog & Co, Spectrum (CD) 1989. Publications: Author of An Organ City in Connecticut, The American Organist, 1973; Organ Playing, Epic Poem by Hermann Hesse (Translation), 1973; Helmut Walcha: Artist Teacher, The American Organist, 1984. Contributions to: Bachstunden: Festschrift für Helmut Walcha, 1977. Hobbies: Travel (Europe and Asia); Reading (Philosophy and Psychiatry). Address: 16 Hughes Place, New Haven, CT 06511-4904, USA.

JORDAN Robert, b. 2 May 1940, Chattanooga, Tennessee, USA. Concert Pianist; Professor of Piano. Education: BMus, Eastman School of Music, 1962; MMus, Juilliard School, 1965. Career: Tours of Europe, North and South America and West Africa; Appeared as soloist with orchestras of Prague, Munich, Baltimore and Buffalo; Annual appearances at the Fête Musicale du Touquet, France, 1984-. Recordings: Music of Franz Liszt and Dean C Taylor, David Borden and Talib Rasul Hakim; Schubert, Six Moments Musicaux and Schumann Sonata No 2 in G Minor, Opus 22. Honours: One of 13 pianists chosen to commission a work from an American composer and give a world premiere at Kennedy Center; Chancellor's Award for Excellence in Teaching; Named Martin Luther King Professor at University of Michigan, Mar 1991. Hobbies: Languages; Reading. Address: Department of Music, State University College, Fredonia, NY 14063, USA.

JORGENSEN Jerilyn, b. 1960, New York, USA. Violinist. Education: Studied at the Juilliard School with Joseph Fuchs. Career: Soloist with several orchestras in the Brahms and Tchaikovsky Concertos; Further study with members of the Juilliard Quartet and Co-founded the Da Vinci Quartet, 1980, under the sponsorship of the Fine Arts Quartet; Many concerts in the USA and elsewhere in the repertoire including works by Mozart, Beethoven, Brahms, Dvorak, Shostakovich and Bartók. Honours include: With the Da Vinci Quartet: Awards and grants from the NEA, the Western States Arts Foundation and the Colorado Council for the Humanities; Artist in Residence at the University of Colorado. Address: 11 Northpark Street, Glasgow G20 7AA, Scotland.

JOSEFOWICZ Leila, b. 1978, USA. Concert Violinist. Career: Engagements with the Chicago Symphony Orchestra (Tchaikovsky Concerto, Philadelphia Orchestra under Sawallisch, Los Angeles Philharmonic and London Philharmonic with Franz Welser-Möst; Carnegie Hall debut with the Academy of St Martin in the Fields under Neville Marriner, 1994; Returned to New York, with the Boston Symphony and Seiji Ozawa, 1996; Season 1996-97 with the Bamberg Symphony, the Rotterdam Philharmonic under Gergiev, the Danish Radio SO, Monte Carlo Orchestra, Dallas SO; Tour of USA with Neville Marriner and Mendelssohn's Concerto at the London Proms, 1997; 1997-98 Season with Sydney SO, Swedish RSO,tour of Germany with Neville Marriner and ASMF, Orchestre National de France/Dutoit, Budapest Festival Orchestra, Finnish RSO. Recordings include: Tchaikovsky and Sibelius Concertos with the Academy of St Martin in the Fields; Bartok's Solo Sonata and pieces by Pagnanini, Ysaye, Kriesler and Ernst; Bohemian Rhapsodies with Marriner/ASMF. Honours include: Cover Feature, BBC Music Magazine, 1997. Address: c/o IMG Artists, Media House, 3 Burlington Lane, London W4 2TH, England.

JOSEPH David (Robin), b. 27 January 1954, Melbourne, Victoria, Australia. Composer; Music Tutor. Education: BMus (Hons), University of Melbourne, 1979. Career: Adelaide Chamber Orchestra, 1986-87; Tutor, University of Melbourne, 1993-95; Commissions from Kammermusiker Zurich, Adelaide CO, Queensland Ballet and others. Compositions include: Images for orchestra, 1983; The Dream, for orchestra, 1986; Clarinet Concerto, 1987; Horn Concerto, 1988; 2 String Trios, 1988, 1990; Symphony, 1989; The Haunting for orchestra, 1990; Chamber Concerto for strings, 1992; Dialogues for violin and strings, 1992; Pelleas and Melisande, ballet, 1994; The Memory, for orchestra, 1994; From Endymion for 2 sopranos, alto, tenor, baritone, and bass, 1995. Honours include: Alex Burnard Scholarship, 1980; AC International and AC Composers Fellowships, 1982, 1992. Address: c/o APRA, 1A Eden Street, Crows Nest, NSW 2065, Australia.

JOSEPHS Wilfred, b. 24 July 1927, Newcastle-on-Tyne, England. Composer. m. Valerie Wisbey, 1956, 2 daughters. Education: BDS, University of Durham, Newcastle (now Newcastle University), 1951; Guildhall School of Music, 1954; Musical composition with Maître Max Deutsch, Paris, 1958-59. Career: Composer, many concert works and film and TV scores; Visiting Professor of Composition, Composer-in-residence: University of Wisconsin, Milwaukee, 1970; Roosevelt University, Chicago, 1972. Compositions include: The Appointment, TV opera; Pathelin, 1-act opera; Through the Looking-Glass and What Alice Found There, children's opera; Alice in Wonderland, children's opera; King of the Coast, children's musical; Equus, ballet; Rebecca, 3-act opera; Cyrano de Bergerac, ballet for Covent Garden Royal Ballet; Music for: The Great War; I, Claudius etc. Publications include: Requiem; Symphonies 1-10; Concertos; Sonatas; Quartets; Honours: Hon DMus, Newcastle; Many others. Memberships: Incorporated Society of Musicians; British Association of Film and Television Artists; Council, Composers' Guild of Great Britain; Association of Professional Composers; Council, Performing Right Society; Hobbies: Writing music; Swimming; Reading; Opera; Theatre; Videos; Films. Address: 15 Douglas Court, Quex Road, London NW6 4PT, England.

JOSHUA Rosemary, b. 1964, Wales. Singer (Soprano). Education: Studied in London; Master classes with Thomas Allen, Graziella Sciutti and Claudio Desderi. Career: Engagements with Opera Northern Ireland as Pamini, and at the 1992 Buxton Festival as Blondchen in Die Entführung; English National Opera as Adele in Die Fledermaus, Yum-Yum in The Mikado, Princess Ida, Norina, Sophie in Der Rosenkavalier and Susanna; Covent Garden Festival, 1993, as Pamina; Royal Opera debut, 1994, as Pousette in Manon; Angelica in Orlando at Aix-en-Provence Festival, Poppea in Agrippina and Susanna, Cologne Opera, 1994; Sang Sophie with ENO, 1997. Honours include: Royal Philharmonic Award in debut category. Address: IMG Artists, Media House, 3 Burlington Lane, London W4 2TH, England.

JOSIPOVIC Ivo, b. 28 Aug 1957, Zagreb, Croatia. Composer; Lawyer. Education: PhD, Law, University of Zagreb; Graduate, Music Academy, Zagreb. Debut: 2 children's songs, 1978. Career: Compositions performed in nearly all European countries, USA, Canada and Japan (EBU concert transmitted over 30 stations worldwide); Recordings for several radio and TV stations; Performances at several European music festivals; Director of Music, Zagreb Biennale, 1981-; Docent, Music Academy, University of Zagreb, 1992-. Compositions include: Variations for piano; Play of the Golden Pearls for piano; Enypion for harp solo; Quartetto rusticano for string quartet; Per fiati for wind quintet; Passacaglia for string orchestra; Samba da camera for 13 strings; Dyptich for large orchestra; Epicurus' Garden for symphony orchestra; Man and Death for soloists, choir and orchestra; Pro musica for accordenon orchestra; The Most Beautiful Flower for voice and instrumental ensemble; Mrmesh for Mr Penderecki for folk orchestra; Thousands of Lotuses for choir and instrumental ensemble; Jubilus for piano solo; Elegaic Song for violin and piano; Dreams for voice and string orchestra. Recordings: Several compositions on CDs. Honours: Prize, University of Zagreb, 1980; Youth Prize for Art, 1981; 1st Prize at Jeunesses Musicales Competition for Composition and EBU Prize (Samba da camera, 1985); Several Croatian prizes for compositions. Memberships: Vice-President, International Federation of Jeunesses Musicales, 1987-89; Secretary-General, Croatian Composers' Society, 1987-. Address: Palmoticeva 26, 10000 Zagreb, Croatia.

JOUBERT John (Pierre Herman), b. 20 Mar 1927, Cape Town, South Africa. Composer; University Lecturer. m. Florence Mary Litherland, 1951, 1 son, 1 daughter. Education: Diocesan College, Cape Town; Royal Academy of Music, London. Career: Lecturer in Music, University of Hull, England, 1950-62; Lecturer (later Reader) in Music, University of Birmingham, 1962-86. Compositions: 4 String Quartets, 1950, 1977, 1987, 1988; Concertos, for violin, 1954, piano, 1957, bassoon, 1973; 2 Symphonies, 1955, 1969; 2 Sonatas for piano, 1957, 1972; Pro Pace Motets for unaccompanied choir, 1959; String Trio, 1960; Octet, 1961; Silas Marner, opera, 1961; Under Western Eyes, Opera, 1969; 6 Poems of Emily Brontë for solo voice, 1969; Déploration for orchestra, 1978; The Turning Wheel for solo voice, 1979; Herefordshire Canticles for choir and orchestra, 1979; Gong-Tormented Sea for choir and orchestra, 1981; Temps Perdu for orchestra, 1984; Rorate Coeli for unaccompanied choir, 1985; Piano Trio, 1987. Honours: Royal Philharmonic Society Prize, 1949; Fellow, Royal Academy of Music, 1957; Honorary DMus, University of Durham, 1991. Memberships: Composers' Guild of Great Britain; Association of Professional Composers. Hobby: Reading. Address: 63 School Road, Moseley, Birmingham B13 9TF, England.

JOULAIN Jeanne, b. 22 Jul 1920, Paris, France. Musician. Education: Conservatory of Amiens, 1934-43 winning 5 first prizes in solège, piano, violoncello, organ and harmony; Ecole César Franck of Paris, 1941-45 gaining 5 diplomas in piano, violoncello, organ, composition and chamber music; Conservatory of Paris, 1947-52 winning first prize in organ and improvisation. Debut: With mother. Career: Professor of Organ, Improvisation, Harmony and Counterpoint at the Conservatoire Régional de Lille, 1951-82; Organist Titular at St Maurice's Church in Lille, 1954-86; Numerous recitals in Europe, USA and at St Paul's Cathedral in London. Compositions: 15 Pieces for Organ; Patchwork for Two Organs; Mass for Counter-Tenor and Organ; Cortege for Trumpet and Organ; 15 Songs for Voice and Piano; Booz, oratorio for 4 Soloists, Choir and Orchestra. Recordings: CD of music played on the historical organs at St Ouen at Rouen, St Severin at Paris and St Maurice at Lille; Transcription of Pierre Cochereau's Improvisations of 9 Pieces forming the Suite Françoise. Publications: 7 Pieces for Organ in L'Organiste; 6 Pieces for Organ in Orgue et Liturgie; Editor, 3 Pieces for Organ, Chantraine at Tournai. Contributions to: Several articles in L'Orgue, Paris. Honours: Médaille d'Argent, Society of Arts, Sciences and Letters, Paris; Chevalier des Arts et Lettres, Paris; Médaille, Pro Eclesia et Pontifice. Memberships: Society of Sciences, Agriculture and Arts, Lille; Founder and President, Orgue Vivant, Lille, 1974. Address: 7 Rue Georges Maertens, 59800 Lille, France.

JOVANOVIC Zoran, b. 6 April 1936, Skopje, Macedonia. Piano and Chamber Music Professor; Composer. m. Sophia, 4 June 1978, 1 son. Education: Postgraduate Studies, Academy of Music, belgrade, 1967-69; Juilliard School of Music, New York, USA. Debut: Pianist, 1961; Composer, 1973. Career: Recitals in Yugoslavia, USA, France; Recordings for Radio and Television in Belgrade, Skopje and Novi Sad; Authors Evening Concerts. Compositions: 3 Piano Concertinos; Piano Concerto No 1; 40 Piano Miniatures; 2 Sonatinas, 1 on White Keys, Another on Black Keys Only; Concertos for All String Instruments, Separately, Violin, Viola, V-Cello, K-Bass; Concertos for Wind Instruments, Flute, Clarinet, Trumpet; Virtuoso Pieces for Violin, Viola, V-Cello, Flute; The Obscure Scherzo for Violin or Clarinet, V-Cello and Piano; Elegy for 2 V-Cellos and Piano. String Quartet Pastorales, based on Folk Style. Recordings: Concert Solo Songs; Piano concertinos; Violin, V-Cello and Flute Concerto; 2 Sonatinas. Honours: 2 1st Prizes, Concert Songs, 1973. Memberships: Union of Composers of Serbia & Voyvodina. Hobbies: Water Colour Paintings; Long Walks. Address: King Alexanders Boulevard 98/II-4, Belgrade, Yugoslavia.

JUDD James, b. 30 Oct 1949, Hertford, England. Conductor. Education: Trinity College of Music, London. Career: Assistant Conductor, Cleveland Orchestra, 1973-75; Associate Conductor, European Community Youth Orchestra, 1978-; Founder/Director, Chamber Orchestra of Europe; Music Director, Florida Philharmonic Orchestra; Artistic Director, European Communities Youth Orchestra, 1990; Artistic Director of Greater Miami Opera, 1993-; Guest Conductor with the Vienna and Prague Symphonies, Berlin Philharmonic, Orchestre National de France, Zurich Tonhalle and Suisse Romande Orchestra; Conducted La Cenerentola at Glyndebourne, 1985; Traviata, Il Trovatore, Il Barbiere di Siviglia, Rigoletto and Figaro for English National Opera; US Opera debut, 1988, with Don Giovanni in Miami; Season 1992/93 included tours with the Hallé and English Chamber Orchestras, London Symphony Orchestra, Royal Philharmonic and the Chamber Orchestra of Europe and Salzburg Festival; Conducted the Michael Nyman Band and the Philharmonia in the premiere of Nyman's Concerto for Saxophone and Orchestra, 1997. Recordings: With Chamber Orchestra of Europe; With English Chamber Orchestra; With Philharmonia Orchestra. Current Management: Christopher Tennant Artist Management. Address: Unit 2, 30 Tadema Road, London SW10 0PY, England.

JUDD Wilfred, b. 1952, Hertford, Hertfordshire, England. Opera Director. Education: Studied at Oxford and London Opera Centre. Career: Began as freelance director, 1979; Has been producer with Royal Opera, 1984-, for which has staged Die Zauberflöte, Tosca, and La Fanciulla del West; Notable recent production Finnissy's Thérèse Raquin for The Garden Venture; Artistic Director, Royal Opera House Garden Venture, 1988-93; Director of Productions, Opera 80, 1988-91. Address: c/o Roberta Kanal, 82 Constance Road, Whitton, Twickenham, Middlesex, England.

JUDGE Ian, b. 21 July 1946, Southport, England. Education: King George Grammar School, Southport; Guildhall School of Music & Drama, London. Career: Director, joined the RSC in 1975, productions there include: The Wizard of Oz, The Comedy of Errors, Love's Labours Lost, The Relapse, Twelfth Night, A Christmas Carol, Troilus and Cressida; Opera productions include: Faust, The Merry Widow, Cavalleria Rusticana, Pagliacci, Don Quixote La Belle Vivette for the ENO: Macbeth, Tosca, Acis and Galatea, Boris Godunov, Attila; The Flying Dutchman (Royal Opera House); He has staged operas regularly in Europe, Australia and the USA; Macbeth (Cologne), Tales of Hoffman (Houston), Tosca and Madama Butterfly (Los Angeles); Directed the original version of Verdi's Simon Boccanegra at Covent Garden, 1997; His credits include many plays and musicals, A Little Night Music (Piccadilly Theatre), Show Boat (London Palladium) and currently West Side Story in Australia. Current Management: Simpson Fox Association. Address: 52 Shaftesbury Avenue, London W1V 7DE, England.

JUDSON Colin, b. 1968, England. Singer (Tenor). Education: Graduated Guildhall School of Music, 1992. Career: Engagements with touring opera companies, British Youth Opera, De Vlaamse Opera, Antwerp and at the Covent Garden Festival; Roles have included Remendado (Carmen), Isaac in La Gazza Ladra, Rossini's Almaviva, Purcell's Aeneas and Mozart's Monostatos, Tamino and Ferrando; Season 1996 with Werther for English Touring Opera, season 1997 as Coryphée in Le Comte Ory at Glyndebourne and in the Verdi Requiem at Hereford; Haydn's Nelson Mass for the Brightion Festival; Concerts include Schumann's Dichterliebe, Bach's Christmas Oratorio, The Dream of Gerontius, Puccini's Messa di Gloria and Stravinsky's Pulcinella. Address: C&M Craig Services Ltd, 3 Kersley Street, London SW11 4PR, England.

JUHANI Matti, b. 26 Feb 1937, Helsinki, Finland. Singer (Tenor). Education: Studied at the Sibelius Academy, Helsinki. Career: Member of the Deutsche Oper am Rhein at Dusseldorf, 1964-74; Conductor and Teacher of Singing at Helsinki from 1973; Sang with Netherlands Opera, 1974-81 and with the Frankfurt Opera, 1977-84; Guest appearances at the Vienna Staatsoper, Brussels, Savonlinna Festival, 1975 and Marseilles, 1980; Roles have included Pedrillo and Painter in Lulu and The Fox in The Cunning Little Vixen; Concert engagements include the Finnish premiere of Schoenberg's Gurrelieder, 1983. Recordings: Evangelist in Bach's St Matthew Passion. Address: c/o Städtische Buhnen, Untermainanlage 11, 6000 Frankfurt am Main, Germany.

JUNE Ava, b. 23 July 1934, London, England. Singer (Soprano). Education: Studied with Kate Opperman, Clive Carey and Joan Cross in London. Career: Joined Sadler's Wells Chorus, 1953; Sang solo roles from 1957, Leila in The Pearl Fishers, 1959; Covent Garden debut, 1958, as the Heavenly Voice in Don Carlos; Sang Mrs Schomberg in the 1970 premiere of Victory by Richard Rodney Bennett; Appearances with the Welsh National Opera, Phoenix Opera, Scottish Opera and in Sofia, Vienna, Dusseldorf, Paris, Zagreb and Johannesburg; English National Opera, 1973, as Sieglinde in The Ring, conducted by Reginald Goodall; US debut, San Francisco, 1974, as Ellen Orford; Sang Countess Vrouskaya in the premiere of Iain Hamilton's Anna Karenina, English National Opera, 1981; Other roles have included Countess Almaviva, Pamina, Agathe, Musetta, Butterfly, Violetta, Eva, the Marschallin, Elizabeth in Gloriana and in Maria Stuarda, Donna Anna, Marzelline, Micaela, Norina, Marguerite, Tosca, Aida and Santuzza; Currently Teacher of Singing. Recordings include: Mrs Grosse in The Turn of the Screw; The Ring of the Nibelung, from the London Coliseum. Address: c/o English National Opera, St Martin's Lane, London WC2, England.

JUNG Doris, b. 5 Jan 1924, Centralia, Illinois, USA. Dramatic Soprano. m. Felix Popper, 3 Nov 1951, 1 son. Education: University of Illinois; Mannes College of Music; Vienna Academy of Performing Arts; Student of Julius Cohen, Emma Zador, Luise Hellesgruber and Winifred Cecil. Debut: As Vitellia in Clemenza di Tito, Zurich Opera, Switzerland, 1955. Career: Appearances with Hamburg State Opera, Munich State Opera, Vienna State Opera, Royal Opera Copenhagen, Royal Opera Stockholm, Marseille and Strasbourg, Naples Opera Company, Catania Opera Company, Italy, New York City Opera, Metropolitan Opera, and in Minneapolis, Portland, Oregon, Washington, and Aspen, Colorado; Soloist, Wagner concert conducted by Leopold Stokowski, 1971; Soloist, Syracuse Symphony, New York, 1981; Voice Teacher, New York City, 1970-. Address: 40 W 84th Street, New York, NY 10024, USA.

JUNG Manfred, b. 9 July 1940, Oberhausen, Germany. Singer (Tenor). Education: Studied in Essen with Hilde Wesselmann. Career: Bayreuth Youth Festival, 1967, as Arindal in Die Feen by Wagner; Sang in the Bayreuth Festival Chorus, 1970-73; Sang in Dortmund and Kaiserslautern from 1971; Member of the Deutsche Oper am Rhein Dusseldorf from 1977; Bayreuth Festival from 1977, as Tristan, Parsifal and Siegfried (production of Der Ring des Nibelungen, 1983, by John Bury and Peter Hall); Sang in Wagner operas at the Salzburg Easter Festival, under Karajan (Tristan and Parsifal, 1980); Metropolitan Opera debut, 1981; Guest appearances in Zurich, Chicago, Toronto, Vienna; Hamburg, Munich, Barcelona, Cologne, Frankfurt, Lisbon, Rome and Montreal; Other roles include Walther, Florestan, Loge and Siegmund; Sang Herod in Salome at Munich, 1990, Aegisthus in Elektra at the Spoleto Festival; Season 1991/92 as Herod at Barcelona and Valzacchi in Rosenkavalier at Catania; Season 1997-98 as Mime in The Ring, at Kassel. Recordings include: Siegfried in The Ring from Bayreuth. Address: c/o Hilbert Agentur, Maximilianstr 22, 8000 Munich 22, Germany.

JUNGHANEL Konrad, b. 1960, Germany. Lutenist; Musical Director. Career: Appearances as soloist and member of early music ensembles throughout Europe, in the USA, Japan, South America and Africa; Collaborations with René Jacobs as soloist and continuo player in opera performances from the Baroque era and concerts with La Petite Bande, Musica Antiqua Koln, Les Arts Florissants and Tafelmusik; Founded Cantus Cölln 1987, with festival performances at Berne, Stuttgart, Utrecht, Innsbruck and Breslau; Repertory centres on Italian and German Renaissance and Baroque music. Recordings include Lute solos by Silvius Leopold Weiss; Schein's Diletti Pastorali; Rosenmuller's Vespro della beata Vergine (Harmonia Mundi). Honours include: German Critics' Prize, for Weiss lute solos. Address: c/o Harmonia Mundi (Artists), 19-21 Nile Street, London N1 7LL, England.

JUNGWIRTH Manfred, b. 4 June 1919, St Polten, Germany. Singer (Bass). Education: Studied with Alice Goldberg in St Polten; Further study in Vienna, Bucharest, Berlin and Munich. Debut: Bucharest, 1942, as Mephistopheles. Career: Sang at the Salzburg Festival from 1946; Sang at Innsbruck and after winning the 1948 International Singing Competition appeared at Zurich, the Komische Oper Berlin, Dusseldorf and Frankfurt; Further appearances at Hamburg, Cologne, Stuttgart, Paris, Athens, Lisbon and London; Glyndebourne debut, 1965, as Baron Ochs in Der Rosenkavalier; Vienna Staatsoper from 1967; Member of the Bayerische Staatsoper Munich; Covent Garden debut, 1981, as Waldner in Arabella; Dallas, 1982, as Baron Ochs; Other roles have included Osmin, Rocco, La Scala, 1978; Pietro in Simon Boccanegro and Severolus in Pfitzner's Palestrina; Salzburg Festival, 1985, and Florence, 1987, as La Roche in Capriccio. Recordings include: Mozart Arias; Der Rosenkavalier, Biterolf in Tannhäuser.

JUON Julia, b. 28 Nov 1943, St Gallen, Switzerland. Mezzo-Soprano. Education: Studied in the Zurich Conservatory. Career: Sang in opera at St Gallen, 1975-80, Karlsruhe, 1980-83, and Kassel from 1984 notably as Ortrud and as Tina in the European premiere of The Aspern Papers by Dominick Argento; Guest appearances as Fricks at Amsterdam and at the Hamburg Staatsoper as the Nurse in Die Frau ohne Schatten, 1989; Other roles include Waltraute, Carmen, Agrippina, Donizetti's Leonora, Verdi's Ulrica, Eboli, Amneris and Azucena, Wagner's Kundry, Venus and Brangaene; Modern repertoire includes Bartok's Judith, the Priestess in Schoeck's Penthesilea and Catherine in Jeanne d'Arc au Bucher by Honegger; Sang Kabanicha in Katya Kabanova at Basel in 1991 and Kundry at Essen in 1992; Concert engagements in Switzerland and Germany, at the Bregenz Festival and in Vienna. Address: Staatstheater, Friedrichplatz 15, 3500 Kassel, Germany.

JUPP Bridget Mary, b. 18 Nov 1946, Jersey, Channel Islands. Classical Church Organist; Live Musical Entertainer. m. David Jupp, 10 Apr 1975, 1 son, 3 daughters. Education: BA Honours, Music, University of London, 1968; Piano Grade 8; Music and Drama; Classical Music; Music Theory. Debut: Classical Organ Recital, Hull City Hall, 1972-74. Career: Classical Church Organist, Recitalist and Light Musical Entertainer; Klavarskribo Musician and Choral Accompanist; Plays 17th century and classical music; Recitals of Mendelssohn, Händel and Bach; Recordings for BBC Southwest, Bristol, and BBC South, Southampton; Private electronic organ, church organ and music theory tuition to beginners. Compositions: Classical music midi arrangements; Klavar transcriptions; General music. Publications: Klavar 21st Century Music Notation, 1986; Toon en Teken Netherlands, 1993. Contributions to: Organist; Keyboard Player; Readers Digest. Memberships: Musicians Union; Former Member, Incorporated Society of Musicians; Musicians Union. Hobby: Musical Internet correspondence courses. Current Management: KMSIL. Address: 30 Milbury Crescent, Bitterne, Southampton, Hampshire SO18 5EH, England.

JUREK Jan, b. 1950, Bratislava, Slovakia. Singer (Tenor). Education: Studied in Bratislava and Frankfurt. Career: Won prizes at the Mario del Monaco and Munich competitions and appeared in Frankfurt, 1984, as Armed Man in Die Zauberflöte; Sang Boris in Katya Kabanova at Mainz, the Duke of Mantua at Oberhausen and Cavaradossi with a touring Italian company; Regensburg Opera, 1986-90, as Andrea Chenier, Turiddu, Pollione, Alfredo, Riccardo, Hoffmann, Dimitri (Boris Godunov) and Radames; Nuremberg Opera from 1990. Address: c/o Städtische Buhnen, Richard Wagner-Platz 2-10, W-8500 Nüremberg 80, Germany.

JURGUTIS Vytautas, b. 10 July 1930, Silale, Lithuania. Composer. m. Virginja Joana Jurgutiene, 23 May 1975, 3 sons. Education: Graduate, Lithuanian Academy of Music, 1960. Career: Teacher of Music Theory, Vilnius Pedagogical Institute, 1960; Assistant Professor, Lithuanian Academy of Music, 1973-;, Professor, Lithuanian Music Academy, 1990-. Compositions: Symphonic Poems: Cicinskas, 1959; Forty of Death, 1962; Concerto for Violin and Symphony Orchestra; 2 Quintets for Winds; Sonata for Oboe and Piano; Sonata for Piano. Recordings: Concerto for Violin and Orchestra; Oratarios: Donelaitis, Soldiers Letters; Sonata for Oboe and Piano; Piano Cyde, The Child and the Birds. Publications: Vocal Cycles: Visions, 1970; Girl In the Shadows; Analysis of Music Compositions, 2 vols, 1978-83. Memberships: Lithuanian Composers Union, 1961-. Hobbies: Travel; Reading. Address: Birutes 11/40, Apt 3, Vilnius 2004, Lithuania.

JURICA Leon, b. 2 May 1935, Orlova, Czech Republic. Composer; Conservatory Teacher of Music. m. Helena Moldrzykova, 9 Nov 1963, 2 sons. Education: Unfinished study of Medicine, 1953-57; Studied Musicology, J E Purkyne University, 1966-72, BA 1969, MA 1972, PhD 1991. Career: Archivist, Czechoslovak Radio, 1963-75; Musical Director, Czechoslovak TV as an external worker. Compositions include: The Musicians, play, songs for soprano and piano, 1980; The Stones, songs for soprano and piano, 1980; Only useless Memories are Left to Me, songs for bass and piano; Three songs to K H Macha, songs for soprano and violoncello; Three songs of Renaissance, songs for soprano and piano, 1989; Music for choirs: Lullaby of a Fisher (for women's choir); Folk Printer (for Children's choir); Instrumental compositions include: Sonata for violin and piano; Sonata for violoncello and piano; Roznov Romance; Romance for trumpet and Brass Orchestra, 1978; Musica familiaris-variations (for violin, piano and drums) 1990; The third brass Quintet, 1993; King Jecminek, an opera for children, 1993; The lion, fox and deer, miniopera, 1993; Captivating with a charm, miniopera, 1993; The egg-wanderer, a ballet for children, 1993; Characters: 1. Sanguinic, 2. Melancholic, 3. Flegmatic, 4. Choleric, for the bassoon and piano; Sweet Scoundrel, opera, one act, 1995; The Prayers, 3 songs for soprano, 1995; St Adalbertus, cantata, 1997; Two Psalms No 61 aand 150 for alto, French horn and organ, 1997; Sundial, song cycle for soprano and piano, 1997; Ardour of Love-Sorrow of Love, song cycle for soprano and piano, 1997. Recordings: Wail Over Dead Arthur, 1970; Orlova (cantata) 1925; Three Choirs for Children, 1986; Let's Play the Opera, 1986; The Most Beautiful Path, 1989; The Fairy-tale End (ballet) 1989; Sweet Scoundrel, in Czech television Ostrava. Publication: Harmony of O Hostinsky (Brno 1972). Membership: Chairman, Ostrava Centre of the Association of Musical Artists and Scientists. Address: 943 V Zimnem Dole Street, 735 41 Petrvald, Czech Republic.

JURINAC Sena, b. 24 Oct 1921, Travnik, Yugoslavia. Opera Singer (Soprano). m. Dr Josef Lederle. Education: Studied with Maria Kostrencic. Career: First appearance as Mimi, Zagreb, 1942; Member, Vienna State Opera Company, 1944-83 (last performance as the Marschallin); Now works as voice teacher; Sang at Salzburg Festival from 1947, as Dorabella, Cherubino, Amor in Orpheus, Marzelline in Fidelio, Octavian, the Composer in Ariadne, Mozart's Countess and Elisabeth in Don Carlo; Glyndebourne Festival, 1949-56, as Dorabella, Fiordiligi, Ilia, Cherubino, Donna Elvira, Donna Anna and Leonora in La Forza del Destino; Also sang Strauss's Octavian and Tatiana in Eugene Onegin; Sang in Der Rosenkavalier, Tosca, Iphigénie en Tauride; Numerous tours and recordings. Honours: Austrian State Kammersängerin, 1951; Ehrenkreuz dienste um die Republik Österreich, 1967; Ehrenring der Wiener Staatsoper, 1968; Ehrenmitglied der Wiener Staatsoper, 1971. Address: c/o State Opera House, Vienna 1, Austria.

JURTH (Attila) Ferenc, b. 15 May 1945, Budapest, Hungary. Composer; Music Teacher. m. Reka Kocsardi, 30 Apr 1975, 2 sons, 2 daughters. Debut: Leningrad, 1963. Career: Conductor, 1956-; Piano Recitalist, Leningrad, USSR, 1963-65; Chief Organist, Hungarian Roman Catholic Diocese, Vienna, Austria, 1967-82; Music Director, Organist, Hungarian Pax Romana Congresses, 1971-79; Teacher in Piano, Solfeggio, Theory, Musicianship, 1972-; Artistic Director, LKGT Quartet, 1989-. Compositions: Educational piano and string music; Grand Sonata for Piano; The Tale of a Ninth Chord for harp; Spleen for cello and piano; Consonant Music for strings; Lieder; Hungarian folk song arrangements and fantasies: Run, Goat, Run, The Four Mosquitos, Hurdy Birdy for string quartet; A Long Way Off for piano quintet. Publication: Orsegi daloskonyv, collection of Hungarian folksongs in East Austria, 1971. Address: 17 Shannon Street, Redbank Plains, Brisbane 4301, Queensland, Australia.

JURTH Levente Attila, b. 1965, Vienna, Austria. Cellist; Composer. Education: AMusA; Studied cello with Magdalena Kerekes, 1983-86, Richard Dedecius, 1986-87, Gary Williams, 1988-; Piano with Yefim Stesin, 1984-88, Attila Jurth, 1988-90, Gwenyth Sitcheff, 1990-; Percussion with Paul Freer, 1990-91; Cello masterclasses with Kato Havas, Christopher Bunting, Gwyn Roberts; In 1991 at the age of 11 was youngest ever candidate to graduate with the Associate Diploma in Music, Australia. Debut: Brisbane, 1987. Career: Speaker, Cellist, LKGT Quartet, 1987-; Performed World Expo '88, Fiesta '89, 1990; Stage: Kolya in A Month in the Country, Royal Queensland Theatre Company, 1990; Oliver in Oliver, Ipswich Orpheus Chorale, 1990. Compositions: Chamber music: Melody No 7 for Flute and Cello, 1985; Melody No 18 for String Quartet, 1985; Pieces for Piano. Current Management: LKGT (music); Quadran (theatre, film, TV). Address: 17 Shannon Street, Redbank Plains, Brisbane 4301, Queensland, Australia.

JUVARRA Antonio, b. 1959, Italy. Singer (Baritone). Education: Studied at the Padua and Verona Conservatories. Career: Sang in Verdi's I Lombardi at Bussetto, then appeared in opera at Venice, Bergamo and Rovigo; Milan, La Scala, debut, 1987, as Mozart's Bartolo, Palermo, 1989, as Schaunard in La

Bohème, Verona, 1990, in Carmen; Other roles include the Duke in Rossini's Torvaldo e Dorliska; Concert appearances in Como and Montepulciano and with the chamber orchestras of Padua and Veneto; Guest at the Bonn Opera, 1991-92. Address: c/o La Scala Milan, 2 Via Filodrammatici, 20121 Milan, Italy.

K

KAASCH Donald, b. 1960, Denver, CO, USA. Tenor. Education: Studied at Colorado and Northwestern Universities. Career: Sang at the Chicago Lyric Opera, 1985-88; European engagements at Florence in 1989 in Idomeneo and at Geneva; Metropolitan Opera in 1989 in the character roles of Les Contes d'Hoffmann and returned for Jacquino in Fidelio and Mozart's Titus; Opéra Bastille in 1991 as Idamante in Idomeneo, Salzburg, 1992 as Argirio in Rossini's Tancredi; Other roles include Mozart's Tamino, Ferrando and Don Ottavio, Count Almaviva, the Prince in Lulu, Rinuccio and Argento's Edgar Allan Poe; Frequent concert performances; Sang the Priest in Stravinsky's Persephone at the Festival Hall, London, 1997; Royal Opera debut 1998, in The Golden Cockerel. Address: c/o Metropolitan Opera, Lincoln Center, New York, NY 10023, USA.

KABAIVANSKA Raina, b. 15 Dec 1934, Burgas, Bulgaria. Singer (Soprano). Education: Studied in Bulgaria and in Italy with Zita Fumagalli. Debut: Sofia, 1957, as Titania in Eugene Onegin. Career: Italian debut, 1959, as Nedda; La Scala, 1961, in Beatrice di Tenda by Bellini, with Sutherland; Covent Garden, 1962-64, as Desdemona and Liu; Metropolitan Opera from 1962, Nedda, Mimi, Elisabeth de Valois, Alice Ford, Lisa in The Queen of Spades, and Butterfly; Guest appearances at the Hamburg Staatsoper from 1971; Genoa and Trieste, 1973, as Tosca and Gioconda, Turin, 1973-74, Elena in I Vespri Siciliani and Francesca da Rimini; Paris Opéra debut, 1975, as Leonora in La Forza del Destino; Further engagements in Dallas, Chicago, New Orleans, San Francisco, Buenos Aires and Vienna; Verona Arena, 1978-82, Butterfly and Mimi; Sang Adriana Lecouvreur at Rome, 1989; Returned 1990, as Butterfly and Hanna Glawari in The Merry Widow; Sang the Trovatore Leonora at Parma, 1990; Season 1991/92 as Leonora at the restored Carlo Felice Theatre, Genoa, and Hanna Galwari at Rome; The Governess in The Turn of the Screw at Bologna, 1997. Recordings include: Il Trovatore, Francesca da Rimini, Madama Butterfly, Fausta by Donizetti; Wagner's Rienzi; Video of Tosca.

KACZANOWSKI Andrzej, b. 22 Apr 1955, Bialystok, Poland. Double Bass Player. m. 14 Dec 1974, 2 s, 1 d. Education: Chopin Academy of Music, Warsaw, diploma with Honour, 1980, MA, Double Bass Player. Debut: Dragonetti Concerto with Bilalystok Philharmonic Orchestra, 1975. Career: Regular appearances as soloist or chamber player with famous orchestras; Warsaw Chamber Orchestra, 1978-84; Salle Pleyel, under K Teutsch, 1980; Chamber Filharmonic, Karol Teutsch conducting, 1980-84; Santa Cecilia, under J Kasprzyk, 1981; Carnegie Hall, under K Teutsch, 1982; Polish Chamber Orchestra with Jerzy Maksymiuk, 1984-85; Camerata Vistula Chamber soloist, 1986; Teatro alla Scala under Delmann; Barbican Centre under Maksymiuk; Teatro alla Scala under Abbado; Akademie der Künste, Berlin, 1992; Warsaw Autumn, Warsaw, 1992; Teacher, Josef Elsner First Music School in Warsaw, 1991-; Played in Spain and Germany in 1994. Recordings: Polish Chamber Orchestra, Warsaw; Chamber Philharmonic Orchestra, Bach Keyboard Concerts, 1980; Lutoslawski, Prokofiev and Gorecki, 1990; Schubert's Quintet, op 114, Trout; Dvorak, op 77 for Polish Radio SA. Honours: Festivals: Lille 1979, Bordeaux 1980, Bergen, Tivoli, 1981, Cheltenham, 1982, Brighton 1984, Glasgow 1988, Warsaw Autumn, 1985, 1986, 1988 and 1989. Hobbies: Yachting; Cycling; Walking. Address: Pradzynskistr 20a-109, 05-200 Wotomin, Poland.

KAGEL Mauricio, b. 24 Dec 1931, Buenos Aires, Argentina. Composer; Film Maker; Dramatist. Education: Piano, theory, cello, organ, singing and conducting privately; Composition self-taught. Career: Conductor, Colon Chamber Orchestra and Teatro Colon, Buenos Aires, 1955; Settled in Cologne, 1957; Professor, Cologne Musikhochschule's new music-theatre, 1974; Sle Professor of Composition, Buffalo, 1964-65; Lecturer at Berlin Film and Television Academy, 1967; Music Director, Institute of New Music, Rheinische Musikschule, Cologne, 1969. Compositions include: String Sextet, 1953; Journal de théâtre, 1960; Heterophonie, 42 instruments, 1959-61; Metapiece, keyboard, 1961; Antithese, electronic and public sounds, 1962; Die Frauen, 2 solo female voices, other ladies, 1962-64; Diaphonie, chorus, orchestra, 2 slide projectors, 1962-64; Phonophonie, 4 melodramas, 1963-64; Match, 2 cellos, percussion, 1965; Tremens, Szenisches Montage, 1963-65; Camera Obscura, Chromatisches Spiel, 1965; Die Himmelsmechanik, 1965; Musik für Renaissanceinstrumente, 1965-66; String Quartet, 1965-67, No 3, 1988; Variaktionen, voices, actors, tape, 1967; Kommentar Extempore, 1967; Montage, 1967; Phantasie, organ with obbligato tape, 1967; Hallelujah, chorus (from film), 1968; Der Schall, 1968; Acustica, tape, 1968-70; Unter Strom, 5 players, 1969; Ludwig Van (from film). 1969; Staatstheater, Ballet for non-dancers with instrumentation and chamber pot, 1969-70; Klangwehr, military band, 1970; Zwei-Mann-Orchester, 1971-73; Programm, Gasprache mit Kammermusik, 1972; Exotica, 1972; Variationen ohne Fuge, orchestra, 1973; 1898, children's chorus, instruments, 1973; Kantrimusik, Pastoral for voices, instruments, 1975; Mare Nostrum, 1975; Bestiarium, 1975; Die Umkehrung Amerikas, radio play, 1976; Variete, concert spectacle, 1977; Die Erschöpfung der Welt, opera, 1979; Aus Deutschland, Liederopera, 1981; Nach einer Lektüre von Orwell, stage work, 1984; La trahison orale, orchestra, 1984; Two Ballads of Guillaume de Machaut, 1984; Sankt Bach Passion, 1985; Piano Trio, 1985; A Letter, concert scene for mezzo and orchestra, 1986; Dance School, ballet, 1988; Quodlibet, women's voices, orchestra, 1988; Osten, salon orchestra, 1989; Fragende Ode, chorus, wind, percussion, 1989. Honours include: Koussevitzky Prize, 1966; Karl Sczuka Prize for play Ein Aufnahmezustand, 1969; Scotoni Prize for film Hallelujah, City of Zurich, 1969. Address: c/o Universal Edition, Bösendorfestrasse 12, Postfach 3, A-1015 Vienna, Austria.

KAHANE Jeffrey (Alan), b. 12 Sept 1956, Los Angeles, California, USA. Pianist. m. Martha Philips, 9 Sept 1979, 1 son. Education: BMus, San Francisco Conservatory of Music, 1977. Debut: San Francisco, California, 1973. Career: Soloist, New York and Los Angeles Philharmonics, Pittsburgh, San Francisco and Atlanta Symphonies; Frequent performances with Tokyo String Quartet; Has worked with Conductors such as M Tilson Thomas, Zubin Mehta, Edo de Waart, Semyon Bychkov and John Nelson; Soloist in Bernstein's Age of Anxiety at the 1991 Promenade Concerts, London. Recordings: Bach D Major Partita; 15 Sinfonias, on Nonesuch Records. Honours: Grand Prize, Arthuir Rubinstein International Piano Competition, Tel Aviv, Israel, 1983; 4th Prize, Van Cliburn International Piano Competition, 1981. Membership: Piano Faculty, New England Conservatory of Music, Boston. Current Management: IMG Artists. Address: c/o IMG Artists, 22 E 71st Street, NY 10021, USA.

KAHLER Lia, b. 1952, USA. Singer (Mezzso-soprano). Education: Studied in Los Angeles, New York and Milan. Career: Sang at the Holland Festival, 1982, Detmold, 1983-85, notably as Eboli and Brangaene; Sang at Gelsenkirchen 1985-89, as Laura in La Gioconda, Monteverdi's Ottavia, the Witch and Mother in Hansel und Gretel, and in the premiere of Deinen Kopf, Holofernes by Blumenthaler, 1989; Other roles at Gelsenkirchen and elsewhere in Germany have included Ortrud, Maddalena, Marina in Boris Godunov, Dalila and Baba the Turk in The Rake's Progress; Many concert appearances. Address: Musiktheater im Revier, Kennedyplatz, 4650 Gelsenkirchen, Germany.

KAHMANN Sieglinde, b. 28 Nov 1937, Dresden, Germany. Singer (Soprano). m. Sigurdur Bjornsson. Education: Studied in Stuttgart. Debut: Stuttgart Staatsoper 1959, as Aennchen in Der Freischütz. Career: Engaged at the Theater am Gärtnerplatz Munich and sang at Hamburg, Vienna, Stuttgart, Leipzig, Karlsruhe and Kassel; Roles have included Mozart's Pamina, Donna Elvira, Countess and Cherubino, Lortzing's Gretchen and Mair, Martha and Musetta; Guest appearances at Lisbon, Strasbourg, Bucharest, Salzburg and Edinburgh, as Micaela, Lisa (Queen of Spades), Marenka (Bartered Bride) and Adele in Fledermaus. Address: c/o Stuttgart Staatsoper, Oberere Schlossgarten 6, 7000 Stuttgart, Germany.

KAIPAINEN Jouni (Ilari), b. 24 Nov 1956, Helsinki, Finland. Composer. m. Sari-Anne Liljendahl, 9 Sept 1977, 1 son. Education: Sibelius Academy of Helsinki, 1975-81. Career: Freelance Composer, 1981-. Compositions: The Miracle of Konstanz, TV Opera, 1985-87; Symphony, Opus 20, 1980-85; String Quartets, I 1973; II, 1974; III, 1984; Ladders To Fire (A Concerto for 2 pianos), 1979; Trios, I, 1983; II, 1986; III, 1987; Cinq poemes de René Char, Opus 12a, for soprano and orchestra, 1978-80. Chamber Music; Vocal Music; Incidental Music. Publications: Contribution to the book, Ammatti: säveltäjä (Profession: Composer), edited by R Nieminen and P Hako, Helsinki, 1981. Contributions to: Numerous essays and articles in different Finnish magazines including Finnish Music Quarterly (in English). Honours: UNESCO International Rostrum, The Chosen Work of the Year Prize, 1981; Spurs of Criticism (The most eminent debut of the year) by The Union of Finnish Critics, 1982. Hobbies: Literature; Cinema; Cooking (especially oriental). Address: Martinkyläntie 64, G 35 01660 Vantaa, Finland.

KAISER Barbara, b. 1 June 1947, Bremen, Germany. Conductor. Education: Abitur; Studied in Schulmusik, Violin and Singing, Hochschule fur Musik, Freiburg/Breisgau, 1967-73; Studies in Conducting, Hochschule der Künste, Berlin, 1979-85. Debut: Guest Conductor, Philharmonisches Staatsorchester, Bremen, 1986. Career: Founding Member, Musikfrauen Berlin, 1978; Manager, several projects with contemporary music of women composers; Manager of series of concerts with contemporary music at Hochschule der Künste Berlin, 1984-; Neue Musik Berlin in cooperation, 1986; Lecturer at Hochschule der Künste Berlin, 1986-; Guest Conductor, Philharmonisches Staatsorchester Bremen, Filharmonia Pomorska, Poland and Orchester der Stadt Heidelberg. Recordings: Instrumental and Vocal, Musik von Komponistinnen, 1985; Komponistinnen in Berlin, 1987. Contributions to: Some interviews on radio, magaznes and journals. Membership: International Arbeitskreis Frau und Musik; Kulturinstitut Komponistinnen gestern-heute, Heidleburg. Address: Gneisenaustrasse 94, 1000 Berlin 61, Germany.

KAKUSKA Thomas, b. 25 Aug 1940, Austria. Violist. Education: Studied in Vienna. Career: Violist of the Alban Berg Quartet from 1981; Many concert engagements including complete cycles of the Beethoven Quartets in 15 European cities, 1987-88, 1988-89 seasons; Bartók/Mozart cycle in London, Vienna, Paris, Frankfurt, Munich, Geneva, Turin, 1990-91; Annual concert series at the Vienna Konzerthaus and festival engagements worldwide; Associate Artist at the South Bank Centre, London; US appearances San Francisco and New York (Carnegie Hall). Recordings include: Complete quartets of Beethoven, Brahms, Berg, and Bartók; Late quartets of Mozart and Schubert; Ravel, Debussy and Schumann quintet; Live recordings from Carnegie Hall (Mozart, Schumann); Konzerthaus in Vienna (Brahms); Opéra-Comique Paris (Brahms); South Bank concerts for the Schubert bicentenary, 1997. Honours include: Grand Prix du Disque; Deutsche Scallplatenpreis; Edison Prize; Japan grand Prix; Gramophone Magaxine Award. Address: Intermusica Artists Management, 16 Duncan Terrace, London N1 8BZ, England.

KALABIS Viktor, b. 27 Feb 1923, Cerveny Kostelec, Czech Republic. Composer. m. Zuzana Rusickova, 8 Dec 1952. Education: Composition, Prague Conservatory and Academy of Arts and Music, 1945-48; Philosophy and Musical Science, Charles University, Prague. Career: Editor, Musical Producer, Czech Radio, 1953-72; Full-time Composer, 1972-. Compositions include: Orchestral works: 5 symphonies, 1957, 1961, 1971, 1972, 1976; Concerto for large orchestra, 1966; 9 instrumental concertos; 3 compositions for chamber orchestra; Chamber works include: 2 nonets; Spring Whistles, octet for wind, 1979; 2 wind quintets; 7 string quartets; Sonatas for violin and harpsichord, violoncello and piano, clarinet and piano, trombone and piano, violin and piano, 1967-82; 6 string quartet, 1988; Solo works include: 3 piano sonatas; 3 pieces for flute; Reminiscences for Guitar, 1979; Four Enigmas for Graham, piano solo, 1989; Several choral works; Five romantic love songs for higher voice and strings, 1977; Two Worlds (Alice in Wonderland), ballet, 1980; Incantations for 13 wind instruments, 1988; Carosal of live songs for bass and piano, 1989. Recordings: Diptych for strings, CD; Chant du Monde. Honours: Musical Critics Portrait Prize, 1967; State Prize, 1969; Artist of Merit, 1983; President, Bohuslav Martinu Foundation, 1991. Membership: Czech Musical Society. Address: Slezska 107, 13000 Prague 3, Czech Republic.

KALE Stuart, b. 27 Oct 1944, Neath, Glamorgan, Wales. Singer (Tenor). Education: Studied at the Guildhall School of Music and Drama and at the London Opera Centre. Debut: With Welsh National Opera in 1971, as the Prince in the first production by a British company of Berg's Lulu. Career: Sang with English National Opera notably as Don Ottavio and in Jonathan Miller's production of The Mikado; Sang Wagner's Siegfried at Bucharest in 1983 and appeared in the local premiere of Prokofiev's The Fiery Angel for South Australian Opera in 1988; Covent Garden debut 1988, in Manon, returning in 1989 as Bob Boles in Peter Grimes; has sung the Captain in Wozzeck at Strasbourg, 1987, Reggio Emilia, 1989 and Toronto 1990; In 1989 sang in L'incoronazione di Poppea at the Théâtre du Châtelet, Paris, the Drum Major in Wozzeck at Turin and Zinovy Ismailov in Lady Macbeth of the Mstensk District at Nancy, France; Sang Don Eusebio in Rossini's L'Occasione fa il ladro at the 1992 Schwetzingen festival; Sang Shuisky at Montpellier, 1996. Recordings: Video of Idomeneo (title role) from Drottningholm (Virgin Classics). Address: c/o Athole Still International Management Ltd, Foresters Hall, 25-27 Westow Street, London SE19, England.

KALICHSTEIN Joseph, b. 15 Jan 1946, Tel-Aviv, Israel. Pianist. Education: Studied at the Juilliard School with Eduard Steuermann and Ilona Kabos. Debut: New York Recital, 1967. Career: Appeared with the New York Philharmonic in a televised performance of Beethoven's 4th Piano Concerto, 1968; European debut with Previn and the London Symphony, 1970; Appearances with the London Philharmonic, Israel Philharmonic, Cleveland Orchestra, Chicago Symphony, Boston Symphony and Berlin Philharmonic; Tours to Australia, Japan and South America; Performances in Piano Trio with Jaime Laredo and Sharon Robinson from 1976; Brahms series with the Guarneri Quartet in New York, 1983; Season 1996-97 included concerts with the Royal Scottish Orchestra and Singapore and Oregon Symphonies. Honours: Young Concert Artist Award, 1967; Winner, Leventritt Competition, 1969. Address: c/o Harrison/Parrott Ltd, 12 Penzance Place, London W11 4PA, England.

KALININA Galina, b. 1951, Russia. Singer (Soprano). Education: Studied in Moscow. Career: Member of the Bolshoi Opera, Moscow from 1977, notably as Donna Anna, Verdi's

Trovatore Leonora, Elisabetta, Desdemona and Amelia (Ballo in Maschera); Tchaikovsky's Tatiana and Lisa and Madame Butterfly; Guest appearances in the West from 1982, notably as Tosca at Stuttgart 1988, and with Scottish Opera, Yaroslavna in Prince Igor at Wiesbaden and Zemfira in a Concert Performance of Rachmaninov's Aleko at Rome; Season 1987-88, as Tatiana at Buenos Aires, Butterfly in Oslo and Yaroslavna at Verona; Covent Garden 1991, as Tosca; Aida at Buenos Aires, 1996. Recordings: Fevronia in The Legend of the Invisible City of Kitezh by Rimsky Korsakov.

KALISH Gilbert, b. 2 July 1935, New York, USA. Pianist; Teacher. Education: BA, Columbia College, 1956; Columbia University Graduate School of Arts and Sciences, 1956-58; Pupil of Isabelle Vengerova, Leonard Schure and Julius Herford. Career: New York Recital debut, 1962; European debut, London, 1962; Subsequent tours of the US, Europe and Australia; Pianist with the Contemporary Chamber Ensemble and the Boston Symphony Chamber Players; Regular accompanist to Jan DeGaetani until 1989; Artist-in-Residence, Rutgers, The State University of New Jersey, 1965-67, Swarthmore College, 1966-72; Head of Keyboard Activities, Chairman of Faculty, 1985-, Tanglewood Music Center, Tanglewood, Massachusetts; Faculty Member, Head of Performance Faculty, State University of New York at Stony Brook, 1970-. Recordings: Numerous discs as a soloist chamber player, and accompanist. Honours: Recipient, Paul Fromm Award, University of Chiacgo for Distinguished Service to the music of our time, 1995. Address: c/o Music Department, State University of New York, Stony Brook, NY 11794, USA.

KALJUSTE Tonu, b. 1953, Tallinn, Estonia. Choral Director; Conductor. Education: Studied at the Tallinn and Leningrad Conservatories. Career: Conducted works by Mozart, Britten and Weber with Estonian Opera; Founded the Estonian Philharmonic Chamber Choir, 1981; Artistic Director of choral festivals Tallinn '88 and Tallinn '91; Founded the Tallinn Chamber Choir, 1992; Principal Conductor of the Swedish Radio Choir, from 1994; Guest conductor with choir and orchestras in Europe, Australia and North America; Has featured contemporary Estonian composers and concert series of Bach and other Baroque composers; Lecturer at the Tallinn Conservatory. Recordings include: Pårt Te Deum. Honours include: Nomination at 1995 Grammy Awards, for Best Choral Performance. Address: c/o Harrison Parrott Ltd, 12 Penzance Place, London W11 4PA, England.

KALLIR Lilian, b. 6 May 1931, Prague, Czechoslovakia. Pianist; Teacher. m. Claude Frank, 1959. Education: Pupil of Isabelle Vengerova; Studied with Herman de Grab, Mannes College of Music, New York, 1946-49. Career: Debut as solost with the New York Philharmonic Orchestra at age 17; New York recital debut at Town Hall at age 18; Subsequent tours of the US, South America, Europe and Israel; Many appearances as a soloist with orchestras and as a recitalist, including concerts in season 1990-91 at the Tanglewood, Marlboro, Norfolk, Grant Park and Mostly Mozart (Seattle) Festivals; Also duo appearances with husband; Chamber recitals with the Cleveland, Emerson, Guarneri, Juilliard and Tokyo Quartets; European engagements at the Festival Hall, London, the Vienna Musikverein, the Berlin Philharmonic and in Salzburg, Stuttgart, Munich, Luxembourg and Brussels; Orchestras have included the Chicago Symphony, London Symphony, Royal Concertgebouw, Berlin Philharmonic, Leipzig Gewandhaus, Salzburg Mozarteum and English Chamber; Faculty Member, Mannes College of Music, New York, 1975-. Honours: Winner, National Music League Award and of the American Artists Award of the Brooklyn Institute of Arts and Sciences. Address: c/o Mannes College of Music, 150 West 85th Street, NY 10024, USA.

KALLISCH Cornelia, b. 1955, Marbach am Neckar, Germany. Singer (Mezzo-soprano). Education: Studied in Stuttgart and Munich with Jose Metternich in Cologne and with Elisabeth Schwarzkopf. Career: Sang at first as Lieder recitalist, then sang in opera at Gelsenkirchen and elsewhere from 1984; Roles have included Orpheus, Octavian, the Composer in Ariande auf Naxos, Monteverdi's Nero, Sesto in La Clemenza di Tito, (Ludwigsburg 1983-84), and Dorabella; Sang Cornelia in a concert performance of Tito at the Grosses Festspielhaus Salzburg, 1991; Arsace in Semiramide and Clairon in Capriccio at Zurich, 1992; Lieder recitals and concerts at Berlin, Vienna, Stuttgart and Frankfurt and in France and Italy; Performances of Wagner's Brangaene in concert with the Pittsburgh Symphony Orchestra and Kundry at Brussels, 1998; Bartók's Judith at Zurich, 1996. Recordings: Le Roi David by Honegger; Bach's Christmas Oratorio. Address: Kunstler Sekretanat am Gasteig, Rosenheimer strasse 52, 81669 Munich, Germany.

KALMAR Magda, b. 4 Mar 1944, Budapest, Hungary. Soprano. Education: Department of Singing, Bela Bartok Conservatory, Budapest. Career: Budapest State Opera, 1969-; Frequent performer in Hungary's concert halls and on Hungarian radio and television; Guest Performer at numerous operas including Austria, Belgium, Cuba, Czechoslovakia, Teatro la Fenice, Italy, Berlin, Leningrad, Stockholm and Paris; Roles include Mozart's Blondchen, Despina and Cherubino, Verdi's Oscar, Adele in Die Fledermaus, Don Pasquale and Norina by Donizetti, Adina in L'Elisir d'Amore, Mozart's Pamina, Rossini's Rosina, Alban Berg's Lulu, Sophie in Der Rosenkavalier and Gilda in Rigoletto; Sang at Budapest 1987, in the premiere of Szokolay's Ecce Homo. Recordings: Has made numerous recordings including Haydn's Il Ritorno di Tobia, Rossini's Mosè in Egitto and Dittersdorf's oratorio Esther; Motets. Honours: Grand Prix du Disque, 1975, 1977; 1st Prize, International Rostrum for Young Performing Artists, Bratislava, 1972; Scholarship, Budapest State Opera, 1967. Address: c/o Hungarian State Opera House, Népöztarsasag utja 22, 1061 Budapest, Hungary.

KALUDOV Kaludy, b. 1953, Varna, Bulgaria. Singer (Tenor). Education: Studied at Sofia Conservatory with Jablenska, graduating in 1976. Career: Member of the Sofia Opera from 1978; Guest engagements in Europe and North America, including Dimitri in Boris Godunov at Houston and Chicago, conducted by Abbado; Sang Faust in Mefistofele at Lisbon 1990, Alvaro in La Forza del Destino at Poznan, 1991; Riccardo (Ballo in Maschera) at Genoa 1991, Puccini's Des Grieux at Trieste and Radames at Tel Aviv, 1992; Manrico in Trovatore at Festivals of Salzburg 1992, Deutsche Oper Berlin 1992 and 1993, Wiener Staatsoper, 1994; Puccini's Des Grieux at La Scala, Milan, 1992 and at Palermo, 1993; Foresto in Attila at Wiener Staatsoper, 1984 and at La Scala 1991 (conducted by Riccardo Muti) and RAI Video; Singer in Rosenkavalier at Wiener Staatsoper, 1990 and at Deutsche Oper Berlin 1993, Staatsoper Berlin, 1992; Don Carlo in Don Carlo at Bayerische Staatsoper, Munich 1993, National Opera, Sofia 1988, Madrid 1986; Requiem, G Verdi at London 1983 at Festival Hall, Houston 1992, Tel Aviv with Israel Philharmonic Orchestra conducted by Zubin Mehta; Radames in Aida at Staatsoper Berlin 1993, Finland 1994 and Philadelphia, 1996. Recordings: Goltsin in Khovanschchina and Vladimir in Prince Igor, with forces of the Sofia Opera conducted by Emil Tchakarov; Janacek's Glagolitic Mass with Charles Dutoit, Montreal, Decca, 1991; Rachmaninov's The Bells with Charles Dutoit, Philadelphia, Decca, 1992; Puccini's Des Grieux (Manon Lescaut) with BRT Philharmonic Orchestra, Brussels (conducted by Alexander Rahbari), Naxos, 1992. Address: Sreniawitow 7 m 59, 03-188 Warsaw, Poland.

KALUZA Stefania, b. 1950, Katowice, Poland. Singer (Mezzo-soprano). Education: Studies in Wroclaw and Vienna with Hans Hotter and Anton Dermota. Debut: Opera, Wroclaw. Career: Sang in Warsaw and Poznan; Also at the Landestheater Salzburg from 1984, and made guest appearances at the Vienna Staatsoper, Bregenz Festival and Brussels (in The Cunning Little Vixen); Versailles Festival, 1989, as Bersi in Andrea Chenier, Dusseldorf 1989, as Amneris; Appearances with the Zurich Opera from 1988, as Marcellina in Figaro, Martha in Mefistofele, Pamela in Fra Diavalo and Larina in Eugene Onegin, 1991; Sang Preziosilla at Zurich, 1992; Other roles include Dorabella, Frau Fluth, Ulrica and Rosina; Concert engagements in Poland, Hungary, Italy and Russia; Sang Amneris at San Diego, 1996. Recordings include: Frau Litumlei in Zemlinsky's Kleider Machen Leute. Honours include: Winner, Belvedere International Competition, Vienna, 1983. Address: c/o Opernhaus Zurich, Falkenstrasse 1, CH-8008 Zurich, Switzerland.

KAMBASKOVIC Rastislav, b. 20 June 1939, Prokuplje, Yugoslavia. Professor. div, 1 son, 1 daughter. Education: Academy of Music, Belgrade, 1961; Diploma, Theory of Music, 1961; Diploma, Composition, 1967; MA, 1969. Debut: Serious Variation for Violins, Belgrade, 1965. Career: Teacher, Music High School, 1962-64; Editor, Editor-in-Chief, Chamber and Vocal, Symphonic Music, 1964-88; Chief Administrator, Belgrade Radio-Television Symphony Orchestra, 1970-76; Professor, Theory and Music Analysis, Theory Department, Faculty of Music, Belgrade, 1988-, Head, Theory Department, 1992-. Compositions: Solo Instrumental Music: Violin and Piano Sonata in G, 1964; Sonata for Two Violins, 1975; Six Piano Preludes, 1991; Chamber Music: Serious Variations for Flute and String Orchestra, 1966; Wood Wind Quintet, 1967; Piano Trio, 1975; Kumb Brass Wind Quintet, 1980; Pester Sketches for 14 Flutes, 1988; Four Harp Sonata, 1991; Jefimia Lamentoso for Cello and String Orchestra, 1993. Publications: Interaction - Diatonic and Chromatic in Prochofiev Symphonies, 1992. Honours: Belgrade Music Festival Award, 1974; Serbian Association of Composers Award, 1974, 1975, 1982, 1983; Belgrade Radio-Television Award, 1982. Hobbies: Hunting; Ecologic Fruit Growing. Address: 109 Nova 22, 11060 Belgrade, Yugoslavia.

KAMENIKOVA Valentina (Jurijevna), b. 20 Dec 1930, Odessa, Russia. Pianist. m. Jaroslav Kamenik, 1954, 2 sons. Education: Odessa Music High School; Prague Academy of Arts. Career: Prague Spring Festival; Salzburg Festival; Concerts in West Berlin, London, Madrid, Vienna, Palma de Mallorca; Chopin Festival in Polensa; Concert Tour, Europe; Professor, Prague Academy of Arts. Recordings: Tchaikovsky, Great Sonata and Dumka; Rachmaninov, Piano Concerto No 1; Rhapsody on Paganini Theme; Chopin, Ballades; Mazurkas; Beethoven, Piano Sonatas No 4 and No 32; Tchaikovsky, Piano Concerto No 1; Mozart, Sonatas No 11 and 12; Haydn, 4 Piano Concertos; Liszt, Sonata in B Minor; Mephisto Waltz; Brahms, Sonata No 1; Rhapsodies; Liszt, Piano Concertos No 1 and 2; Prokofiev, Sonatas No 1 and 3. Honours: Prize Supraphon for Recording of Tchaikovsky Piano Concerto No 1, 1973; Wiener Flotenhhr, Preis der Mozartgeminde, Wien. Membership: Jury Member, International Piano Competitions. Hobby: Cars. Address: Cechovo nam 9, 101 00 Prague, Czech Republic.

KAMINKOVSKY Rimma, b. 1940, Russia. Violinist. Education: Studied in Odessa and Warsaw, at Tel Aviv from 1969 and in the USA with Samuel Ashkenazi. Career: Teacher at the Rubin Academy of Music in Jerusalem, former co-leader of the Jerusalem Symphony Orchestra; Member of the Israel Philharmonic, with appearances as soloist; Co-Founder, Jerusalem String Trio, 1977, performing in Israel and Europe from 1981; Repertoire includes String Trios by Beethoven, Dohnányi, Mozart, Reger, Schubert and Tanyev, Piano Quartets by Beethoven, Brahms, Dvorak, Mozart and Schumann; Concerts with Radu Lupu and Daniel Adni. Recordings: Albums under several record labels. Address: Anglo Swiss Ltd, Ste 35-37 Morley House, 320 Regent Street, London W1R 5AD, England.

KAMINSKI Pawel (Witold), b. 9 Mar 1958, Warsaw, Poland. Pianist; Teacher; Editor of Music. m. Ewa Kaminska, 22 Jan 1991. Education: MA with distinction, Academy of Music, Warsaw, 1983. Career: Assistant Professor, Academy of Music, Warsaw, 1984-; Co-Editor in the National Edition of F Chopin's works, Polish Music Publications, 1985-; Chopin recitals in Poland and abroad (Austria, France, Arab Emirates), 1980-; Appearances as soloist with Polish orchestras, 1983-; Interview on editing Chopin on Polish Radio, 1990. Publications: F Chopin: Studies 1990; Various Pieces 1990; Preludes 1991; Various Works, 1991; Nocturnes, Polonaises, Sonatas, 1995. Honours: Ministry of Culture and Arts Prize for outstanding achievements in studies, 1983. Hobbies: Swimming; Wind-surfing; Trying to understand scientific magazines. Address: ul Chocimska 33 m 6, 00-791 Warsaw, Poland.

KAMINSKY Laura, b. 28 Sept 1956, New York, USA. Composer. Education: Studied at Oberlin College and City College of New York. Career: Co-founder in 1980 of the ensemble, Musicians' Accord; Artistic Director of New York Town Hall, 1988-92. Compositions include: String Quartet, 1977; Duo for Flute and Percussion, 1982; Steepletop Dances for Oboe and Percussion, 1984; Proverbs Of Hell for Soprano, Marimba and Piano, 1989; Triftmusik for Piano, 1991; Whitman Songs for Baritone and Piano, 1992. Address: c/o ASCAP, ASCAP Building, One Lincoln Plaza, New York, NY 10023, USA.

KAMNITZER Peter, b. 27 Nov 1922, Berlin, Germany. Violist; College Professor. Education: Studied at the Juilliard and Manhattan Schools, New York. Career: Co-founded the La Salle String Quartet at the Juilliard School, 1949; Many concerts featuring modern composers and the quartets of Beethoven; European debut 1954; Composers who have written for the ensemble include, Hans Erich Apostel, Earle Brown, Henri Pousseur, Mauricio Kagel, György Ligeti, Penderecki and Witold Lutoslawski; Quartet-in-Residence, Colorado College 1949-53, the Quartet-in-Residence and Professor, Cincinnati College-Conservatory of Music; Quartet disbanded 1988. Reordings include: Works by Berg, Schoenberg, Webern and Zemlinsky; Beethoven's Late Quartets. Address: c/o Cincinnati College-Conservatory of Music, Cincinnati, OH 45221, USA.

KAMP Harry van der, b. 1947, Kampen, Holland. Singer (Bass). Education: Studied with Alfred Deller, Pierre Bernac, Max von Egmond and Herman Woltman. Career: Appearances in solo recitals and in oratorios; Conductors include Nikolaus Harnoncourt, Gustav Leonhardt and Ton Koopman; Leading parts in operas by Monteverdi, Handel, Mozart, Pergolesi and Rossini in Milan, Venice and elsewhere in Europe; Engagements at the Berlin, Carinthian, Flanders, Spoleto and Holland Festivals; Founder and Director of the Dutch vocal ensemble Gesualdo Consort Amsterdam; Member and Artistic Adviser of The Netherlands Chamber Choir; Guest Teacher at the Early Music Academy in Bremen and Antwerp; Sang in the Towards Bach concert series on London's South Bank, Aug 1989; Sang in Cesti's L'Orontea at the 1990 Innsbruck Festival of Ancient Music. Recordings include: Le Testament de Francois Villon, by Ezra Pound. Honours include: Edison Prize, for Ezra Pound Recording. Address: c/o De Netherlandse Opera, Waterlooplein 22, 1011 PG Amsterdam, Holland.

KAMPE Anja, b. 1968, Germany. Soprano. Career: Many appearances in opera throughout Germany and elsewhere in Europe, notably in Rossini's Il Turco in Italia and as Fiordiligi in Così fan tutte; Also sings songs by Bizet and Wolf (Spanisches Liederbuch); Contestant in the 1995 Cardiff Singer of the World Competition. Address: c/o Via Alfieri no 9, Cento (Fe) 44042, Italy.

KAMPEN Bernhardt (Anthony) van, b. 4 Mar 1943, Bushey, Hertfordshire, England. Double Bass Player. Education: Hornsey College of Art; Guildhall School of Music. Career: Art Editor, Aldus Books, 1964-66; Founder Member, New British Broadcasting Corporation Orchestra (later Academy of the British Broadcasting Corporation), 1966; Principal Bass, New British Broadcasting Corporation Orchestra, 1967-68; Freelance in London with London Symphony Orchestra, Royal Philharmonic Orchestra, and others; British Broadcasting Corporation Symphony Orchestra, 1972-78; Freelance Musician and Artist, Composer and Conductor, viols, violone, and Baroque and Classical double-bass with various early music groups; Teacher; Pianist; Harpsichordist. Recordings: With British Broadcasting Corporation Symphony Orchestra, Academy of Ancient Music, London Classical Players, City of London Sinfonia, Hanover Band, London Sinfonietta and many others; Founder and Director, "Harmonie Universelle". Hobbies: Astronomy; Travel; Reading; History; Natural History; Conservation. Address: Schwarzenberger Strasse 15, D-51647 Gummersbach/Hülsenbusch, Germany.

KAMU Okko, b. 7 Mar 1946, Helsinki, Finland. Conductor. Education: Violin studies with Väinö Arjava at the Sibelius Academy, Helsinki. Career: Leader of the Suhonen Quartet, 1964; Leader of the Finnish National Opera Orchestra, 1966-69; Conducted Britten's The Turn of the Screw in Helsinki, 1968; Guest Conductor, Swedish Royal Opera, 1969; Chief Conductor, Finnish Radio Symphony Orchestra, 1971-77; Music Director, Oslo Philharmonic, 1975-79; Music Director, Helsinki Philharmonic, 1981-; Principal Conductor, Dutch Radio Symphony, 1983-86; Principal Guest Conductor, City of Birmingham Symphony Orchestra, 1985-88; Principal Conductor, Sjaelland Symphony Orchestra, Copenhagen, 1988-; Guest engagements with the Berlin Philharmonic, Suisse Romande Orchestra, Vienna Philharmonic and orchestras in Mexico, South America, Australia and Europe; Conducted the premieres of Sallinen's operas The Red Line and The King Goes Forth to France; Metropolitan Opera, 1983, US premiere of The Red Line; Covent Garden, 1987, in the British premiere of The King Goes Forth to France; Opera Conductor at the Savonlinna Festival, Finland; Gothenburg Opera, Don Giovanni, and Il Barbiere di Siviglia; Premiere of The Palace, by Sallinen, 1995. Recordings: Various for several labels; Sallinen's Shadows, Cello Concerto and 5th Symphony. Honours: Winner, 1st Herbert von Karajan Conductors' Competition, Berlin, 1969. Address: Terry Harrison Artists Management, The Orchard, Market Street, Charlbury, Oxon OX7 3PJ, England.

KANAZAWA Masakata, b. 6 Jan 1934, Tokyo, Japan. Musicologist; University Professor. m. Chizuko Yasukawa, 1 son. Education: BA, International Christian University, Tokyo, 1957; AM 1961, PhD 1966, Harvard University. Career: Teacher, Fellow, Tutor in Music, Harvard University, 1963-66; Lecturer in Music 1966-82, Professor in Musicology 1982-, International Christian University, Tokyo; Fellow in Music, Harvard University Centre for Italian Renaissance Studies, Florence, 1970-71; Visiting Professor, various colleges in the USA. Publications: The Complete Works of Anthony Holborne 1967, 1973; Antonii Janue opera omnia, 1974; The Musical MS Montecassino 871, 1978 (co-author); Contributor to New Grove Dictionary; Musicology Reference Books and Journals. Honours: John K Paine Fellowship, 1962; Deems Taylor Award, American Society of Composers, Authors and Publishers, 1980. Memberships: Japanese, American and International Musicological Societies. Hobbies: Theatre; Travel. Address: 2-2-7 Nishikata, Bunkyo, Tokyo 113-0024, Japan.

KANG Dong-Suk, b. 28 Apr 1954, Seoul, Korea. Violinist. m. Martine Schittenhelm, 7 Oct 1983, 1 son, 1 daughter. Education: Juilliard School, 1967-71; The Curtis Institute of Music, Diploma, 1975. Career: Solo appearances with orchestras of Philadelphia, Cleveland, St Louis, San Francisco, National Symphony, Montreal, Stuttgart Philharmonic, Munich Philharmonic, Orcestre national de France, Royal Philharmonic, Philharmonia, BBC Orchestras, Birmingham, Hallé, Scottish National, Bournemouth, Northern Sinfonia, London Mozart Players; Promenade Concerts London 1987 (Glazunov Concerto), 1990 (Sibelius) and 1991 (Tchaikovsky); Season 1992-93 included tour to Japan and concerts throughout England. Recordings: Sibelius Violin Concerto with Orchestre National de Belgique, G Octors Conducting; J Fontyn Violin Concerto (DG); Franck and Lekeu Violin Sonatas with Pascal Devoyon Piano, (RGIP); Nielsen Violin Concerto, Göteborg Orchestra, M W Chung Conducting, (BIS), 1987; Elgar Concerto (Polish National Radio Symphony/Leaper). Honours: San Francisco Symphony Foundation Competition, 1971; Merriweather Post Competition, 1971; Carl Flesch Competition, 1974; Montreal Competition, 1975; Queen Elizabeth Competition, 1976. Address: 23 rue Daumesnil, 9430 Vincennes, France.

KANG Philip, b. 10 Apr 1948, Seoul, South Korea. Singer (Bass). Education: Studied in Seoul and Berlin. Career: Sang small roles at the Deutsche Oper Berlin from 1976; Engagements at Wuppertal, Kiel and Nuremberg, Nationaltheater Mannheim from 1986; Roles have included Sarastro, Rocco, Kaspar, Verdi's Sparafucile, Ramphis, Philip II, Ferrando and Padre Guardiano, Wagner's Daland, Pogner, Mark, King Henry and Gurnemanz; Sang in Italy from 1982, Rodolfo in Sonnambula at Toulouse 1983, Lisbon 1984, as Attila, Sarastro at the Théâtre des Champs Elysées, 1987; American engagements at New York and Philadelphia, European at Madrid, Rome, Frankfurt (as Rocco) and Cologne, as Rossini's Basilio; Théâtre de la Monnaie Brussels as Pimen in Boris Godunov and as Antonios in Stephen Climax by Hans Zender, 1990; Bayreuth Festival 1987-92, as Fafner, Hagen and Hunding. Honours: Winner, Mario del Monaco Competition, 1979. Address: c/o Théâtre Royale de la Monnaie, 4 Leopoldstrasse, B-1000 Brussels, Belgium.

KANGA Skaila, b. 8 Jan 1946, Bombay, India. Harpist. Divorced, 2 sons, 2 daughters. Education: Royal Academy of Music, Junior Exhibitioner, 1959-64; Full-time Student, 1964-66; Studied Piano with Professor Vivian Langrish and Harp with Professor Tina Bonifacio. Career: BBC Concert Orchestra and Freelance with regional and major London orchestras; Solo career includes concertos and broadcasts as well as numerous commercial recordings with such artists as Sutherland, Domingo, Pavarotti, Kiri te Kanawa and composers John Williams, Richard Rodney Bennett, Michel Legrand; Performed the Ravel Introduction and Allegro at the Proms, 4th time, 1994; Michael Tippett's 90th Birthday Celebrations, Barbican Hall, 1994; Fauré and the French Connection, festival in Manchester, 1995; Professor of Harp, Royal Academy of Music. Recordings include: 3 Chamber works of Arnold Bax for Hyperion the Elegiac Trio, The Harp Quintet and the Nonet; French Chamber Music with Academy of St Martins; 2 Solo Albums with Tommy Reilly; Mozart Flute and Harp Concerto, City of London Sinfonia; Bax Chamber Music, Nash Ensemble. Honours: LRAM, 1966; ARAM, 1990; FRAM, 1994. Memberships: PRS; BASCA; MCPS. Hobbies: Cooking; Sewing; Gardening. Address: Harewood Lower Road, Chorley Wood, Herts WD3 5LQ, England.

KANKA Michal, b. 23 May 1960, Prague, Czechoslovakia. Musician; Violincello. m. 11 Sep 1982, 2 d. Education: Prague Conservatory and Academy of Performing Arts, University of Southern California, 1983-84. Debut: Dvorak Concerto with Czech Philharmonic Orchestra, 1983. Career: Regular appearances with Czech Orchestras, 1982-; Foreign tours to Europe, America, Japan and Australasia, 1982-; Member of the Prazak Quartet, 1986-; Berlin debut with RIAS, 1987; Regular concerts in Salzburg, Munich, London, Amsterdam, Milan, Tokyo and Sydney. Recordings: Chopin, Sonata; Stravinsky's Italian Suite, 1984; Schubert's Sonata in C, 1989; Franck, Sonata, 1989; Mozart's Concertone with S Accardo, 1990; Martinu, 3 Sonatas, 1991; Beethoven, Mozart and Janácek works with Prazak Quartet, 1989-91; Vivaldi, 7 Cello Concertos, 1993; Complete works for cello and orchestra by B Martinu, 2 CDs, 1995. Honours: Laureate, Tchaikovsky Competition in Moscow, 1982; 1st Prize, Prague Spring Competition, 1983; Winner, Cello International Competition, ARD Munich, 1986; Soloist of the State Philharmony Brno, 1995. Hobbies: Skiing; Tourism. Address: Peckova 17, Karlin, 18600 Prague 8, Czech Republic.

KANN Hans, b. 14 Feb 1927, Vienna, Austria. Concert Pianist; Composer; Professr of Piano. m. Kue Hee Ha, 17 Jan 1953, 1 son, 1 daughter. Education: Vienna Music Academy, Piano Professors, Bloch, Göllner, Wührer, Schulhof; Composition Professors, Lechthaler, Polnauer. Debut: Brahmssaal, Vienna, 1946. Career: Concerts in whole of Europe, Russia, Asia, China (3 concert tours), South America and USA, 1946-; Professor at Ueno University of Arts, 1955-58; Big concerts in Japan, 1955-58, 1960, 1972, 1974, 1976, 1980-86; Professor at the Hochschule für Musik, 1977-. Compositions: Sonatina for piano; Abschnitt; 10 Stücke ohne Bass-schlüssel; Fingerübungen; Concertino; Chamber Music; Music for Television; Experimental Music. Recordings: 120 records for RCA; Musical Heritage Society; Vox; Toshiba-EMI; Amadeo; Phonogram; Supraphon; Muza; Preiser-Records; Toshiba-EMI, popular piano music. Publications include: Sonatina; Abschnitt 37; Tägliche Fingerübungen für Pianisten; Models; 4 Stücke für Blockflöte und Klavier; Piano enso oboegaki, 1987; Pianists Memories. Contributions to: Osterrech Musikzeitung; Gendai Ongaku (Tokyo). Honours include: Körnerpreis, 1961, 1963; nestroy, Ring der Stadt Wien, 1983; Ehrenkreuz für Wissenschaft und Kunst 1st Class, 1987; Enrenmedaille der Stadt Wien in Gold, 1992; Grosses Silbernes Ehrenzeichen, 1992; Orden vom Heiligen Schatz am Halsband mit den Goldenen Strahlen, Japan, 1994. Memberships: AKM; Austro-Mechana, IGNM, OGZM; Vorstandsmitglied der Austro-Mechana, 1987; Vorsitzender des Fonds der Austro-Mechana, 1988. Hobbies: Collecting Antiques, Instruments, Early Music Prints. Address: Wien 1010, Sonnenfelsgasse 11/7, Vienna 1010, Austria.

KANNEN Günter von, b. 22 Mar 1940, Rheydt, Germany. Singer (Bass-Baritone). Education: Studied Philology and History and then Voice and Music with Paul Lohmann and Franziska Martienssen. Career: Sang first at the Pfalztheater Kaiserslautern; subsequently member of the troupe in Bonn and Karlsruhe, and from 1979-90 Principal Bass at the Zurich Opera; since 1992, at the Staatsoper in Berlin; Guest appearances in Cologne, Hamburg, Deutsche Oper Berlin, Washington DC, Vienna, Brussels, Dresden, Amsterdam, Paris Châtelet, with NHK Symphony Tokyo (Pizarro under Ferdinand Leitner), Israel Philharmonic (Doktor in Wozzeck under Daniel Barenboim), Chicago Symphony Orchestra (Klingsor in Parsifal); Sang at the Festivals of Santa Fe, Salzburg, Drottningholm, Schwetzingen, Aix-en-Provance, Lucerne; From 1988-92, Alberich in the Bayreuth Festival's Ring cycle, conducted by Daniel Barenboim and produced by Harry Kupfer; Sang also Klingsor at Bayreuth, (conductor James Levine); Alberich at both Berlin Opera Houses and at Hamburg State Opera; Other important roles are Hans Sachs (Meistersinger); Ochs Von Lerchenau (Rosenkavalier), La Roche (Capriccio); Cardillac. Recordings include: Lebendig Begraben by Schoeck (Atlantis); Bartolo in Nozze di Figaro (Barenboim); Klingsor in Parsifal (Barenboim/Berlin Philharmonic); Osmin in Entführung aus dem Serail; Tiresias in Oedipus Rex by Stravinsky (Neeme Järvi); Manasse in Brautwahl by Busoni (Barenboim); Commendatore in Gazzaniga's Don Giovanni; Alberich in the Bayreuth Ring (Barenboim); Doktor in Wozzeck and Pizarro in Fidelio (Colin Davis); Sang Alberich in Harry Kupfer's production of The Ring at the Berlin Staatsoper, 1996. Current Management and Address: Bulmer & Dixon, Granitweg 2, 8006 Zurich, Switzerland.

KANO Misako, b. 16 March 1964, Yamaguchi, Japan. Pianist; Composer. m. Yoshihara Yoshroka, 25 October 1992. Education: BMus, Shimane University; Study, Music, Kent State University, Ohio, USA, 1985-86; MMus, Manhattan School of Music, New York; Private Study with Rochre Berrach. Career: Blue Note, USA; Sweet Basil, USA; NHK, Japan; FM Tokyo, Japan; Short Circuit Radio, Japan. Compositions: Breakthrew; Mao; Freezing Drizzle; Bath Talk; Waltz For Rachel; Before the Dawn; Cat; Scramble. Recordings: Breakthrew; Watch Out; Traveling On. Contributions to: Downbeat; Jazz Life; Japan Tribune. Honours: Missionary Scholarship, Educational Ministry of Japan, 1985-86. Memberships: JASRAC; Japanese Musicians Union. Hobby: Movies. Address: 2-6-36 Kawanishi, Iwakani, Yamaguchi 741, Japan.

KANSKI Józef (Celestyn), b. 21 Oct 1928, Warsaw, Poland. Pianist; Musicologist; Music Critic. m. Teresa Grabowska, 1 d. Education: MA, University of Warsaw; Piano Diploma, Academy of Music, Warsaw. Debut: Bydgoszcz, Poland, 1961. Career: Numerous performances including with National Philharmonic, Warsaw; Co-Editor, Ruch Muzyczny; Head of Opera Department, Polish Radio until 1979; Numerous radio and television appearances. Publications: Ludomir Rózycki, 1955, 3rd edition, 1983; Editor, The Stars of the Polish Opera, historical series of LP recordings, 1960; Przewodnik operowy, 1963, 6th edition, 1995; Golden Pages of Polish Pianistic Art, historical series of LP recordings, 1968; Mistrzowie sceny operowej, 1974; Ludomir Rózycki's Symphonic Poems, 1971; A Chopin Discography, historical catalogue of recordings, 1986. Memberships: Union of Polish Composers; Board, Fréderic Chopin Society, Warsaw. Hobbies: Collecting Records; Swimming; Tennis; Skiing; Driving. Current Management: Edition, Ruch Muzyczny, Warsaw, Poland. Address: ul Perzyriskiego 8 m 14, 01-872 Warsaw, Poland.

KANTA Ludovit, b. 9 July 1957, Bratislava, Czechoslovakia. Solo Cellist. m. 9 July 1977, 2 sons. Education: Bratislava Conservatorium with Professor G Vecerny; Academy of Music, Prague, with Professor A Vectomov. Debut: Strauss-Don Quijote, with Slovak Philharmonic, International Music Festival, Bratislava, Oct 1982. Career: 1st Solo Cello, Slovak Philharmonic, Bratislava, 1983; Concert tours and international festivals as Soloist with Slovak Philharmonic, Bulgaria, 1984, USSR and Poland, 1985, Japan, 1987, Spain, 1988; Other foreign tours, Germany, 1980, 1983, 1986, Italy, 1981, Bulgaria, 1983, 1985, Yugoslavia, 1985, Romania, 1985, 1987, Sweden, 1985; Solo Cellist, Orchestra Ensemble, Kanazawa, Japan, 1990-; Associate Professor, Aichi Prefectural University of Arts, Nagoya, 1995-. Recordings: Dvorák-Cello Concerto, Haydn-Concerto in D Major, with Large Orchestra of Bratislava Radio, conducted by Kurt Hortnagel and Ondrej Lenárd; Igor Dibak-premiere recording of Cello Concerto, with Slovak Philharmonic, conductor Bystrik Rezucha; Haydn-Boccherini Concertos, Capella Istropolitana, conductor Peter Breiner; Cello Recital, 1997. Honours: 1st Prize, Beethoven Competition, OPAVA, 1977; 2nd Prize, Prague Spring International Competition, 1980; Concert Imagine; Concert Service Co. Hobbies: Photography; Walking in the mountains. Address: Midorigaoka 1-2, 929-03 Tsubata-machi, Ishikawa, Japan.

KAPELLMANN Franz-Josef, b. 23 Sept 1945, Cologne, Germany. Education: Studied in Cologne. Career: Sang at the Deutsche Oper Berlin, 1973-75, Dortmund from 1975, notably as Verdi's Luna, Posa, Germont, Iago and Amonasro, Scarpia, Gianni Schicchi, Wolfram, Beckmesser and Kurwenal; Alberich in a new production of Das Rheingold, 1990; Guest appearances at Dusseldorf, Wiesbaden, Karlsruhe, Klagenfurt, Lubeck and Paris (Alberich in Götterdämmerung); Other roles have included Riccardo in Puritani, Guglielmo, Papageno, Toby in The Red Line by Sallinen, Escamillo (at Regensburg), Mozart's Figaro (Gelsenkirchen) and Don Fernando in Fidelio (Granada Festival); Gala concert at the Alte Oper Frankfurt, 1989; Sang Alberich in Siegfried at Brussels, 1991, Beckmesser at Trieste, 1992; Pizarro in a concert of Fidelio, Edinburgh, 1996. Recordings: Handel's L'Allegro, il Pensieroso ed il Moderato. Address: c/o Operhaus, Ruhstrasse 12, 4600 Dortmund, Germany.

KAPETANOVIC Goran, b. 31 May 1969, Sisak, Croatia. Composer. Education: Graduated High School of Mathematics, Belgrade, 1987; Dr V Vuckovic Music School, Belgrade; Graduated, Department of Composition and Orchestration, Faculty of Music, Belgrade, 1996. Career: Assistant Professor, Faculty of Music, Belgrade. Compositions: A Brief Account of the Inexorable and Tragic Course of Destiny Which Led the Little Mermaid's Fragile Being into Disaster for chamber ensemble and tape; Speed for symphony orchestra; Alcune le Stesse Cose for 2 pianos. Recording: CD, A Brief Account of the Inexorable and Tragic Course of Destiny Which Led the Little Mermaid's Fragile Being into Disaster. Honours: 2nd Prize, International Review of Composers, Belgrade, 1994; October Prize, City of Belgrade, 1994; 1st Student Prize, International Review of Composers, Belgrade, 1997. Membership: Association of Composers of Serbia. Hobby: Bridge. Address: Nana Milutinovica 72/27, 11000 Belgrade, Yugoslavia.

KAPLAN Abraham, b. 5 May 1931, Tel Aviv, Israel. Conductor. Education: Studied at the Israel Academy in Jerusalem and at the Juilliard School, 1954-57; Conducting studies with William Steinberg and Frederick Prausnitz, composition with Darius Milhaud. Career: Directed the Kol Israel Chorus, 1953-54 and 1958-59; Conductor of the Haifa Oratorio Society, 1958-59; Founded the Camerata Singers, USA, 1960; Director of Choral Music at Juilliard, 1961-77 and the Symphonic Choral Society of New York, 1968-77; Founded the Camerata Symphony Orchestra 1968 and appeared as Guest Conductor with leading orchestras in the US and Israel; Teacher at the Berkshire Music Center and at Union Theological Seminary New York, 1961-73; Director of Choral Studies at Chautauqua, New York, 1976; Professor of Music at University of Washington, Seattle, 1977; Many choral engagements and recordings with the New York Philharmonic. Address: University of Washington, Department of Music, Washington State, USA.

KAPLAN Lewis, b. 10 Nov 1933, Passaic, New Jersey, USA, Concert Violinist. m. Adria Goodkin, 6 Aug 1961, 1 son, 1 daughter. Education: Bachelor's degree, 1958, Master's degree, 1960, Juilliard School. Debut: Town Hall, New York, 1961. Career: Solo concerts, USA, Europe and Far East, 1953-; Violinist-Founder, Aeolian Chamber Players, 1961-; Violin and Chamber Music Faculties, the Juilliard School, 1964-; Artistic Director and Co-Founder, Bowdoin Summer Music Festival, 1964-; Violin Faculty, Summer Academy Mozarteum, Salzburg, Austria, 1987; Violin Faculty, Mannes College of Music, 1987-; Numerous conducting appearances in USA and Europe. Recordings: Numerous. Publication: Caprice Variations for Unaccompanied Violin by George Rochberg (editor), 1973. Honours: Numerous grants from Rockefeller Foundation; National Endowment for the Arts; New York State Council on the Arts. Memberships: Board of Directors, Béla Bartók Society; Aeolian Chamber Players, President; Bowdoin Summer Music Festival. Current Management: Joanne Rile Artists Management. Address: 173 Riverside Drive, New York, NY 10024, USA.

KAPLAN Mark, b. 30 December 1953, Boston, Massachusetts, USA. Violinist. Education: Studied with Dorothy DeLay at Juilliard School, New York; Fritz Kreisler Memorial Award. Career: US engagements from 1973, after gaining the Award of Special Distinction in the Leventritt Competition; Performances with the Cleveland, Philadelphia, Los Angeles, Pittsburg and Baltimore Orchestras; Summer Festivals of Aspen, Blossom, Ambler, Grant Park and Santa Fe; European career from 1980; Concerts with the Berlin Philharmonic and Klaus Tennstedt; Engagements in England and Israel with Rudolf Barshai, and thereafter with all major European Orchestras gave the European premiere of Marc Neikrug's Violin Concerto with the Hallé Orchestra; BBC Promenade Concerts and Concerts with the Royal Philharmonic in London and Italy; Associations with the Conductors Marek Janowski, Michael Gielen and Charles Dutoit; Piano Recitals in Europe and America; Recitals with the Golub/Kaplan/Carr Trio playing each season in the USA and Europe; In 1994-95 the Trio toured Italy and the UK appearing at St John's Smith Square. Recordings: Paganini and Wieniawski concertos repertoire; Mendelsohn and Brahms Schubert Piano Trios; Sarasate Solo Violin Works. Address: c/o Harold Holt Ltd, 31 Sinclair Road, London W14 0NS, England.

KAPLAN Robert (Barnett), b. 26 July 1924, Brookline, Massachusetts, USA. Professor. Education: New England Conservatory, 1935-39; Scholarship, Jules Wolffers, 1945-46; Scholarship, Settlement Music School, 1946; Boston University, 1965-67. Debut: Vendome, 1939; Composition, Wilson Osborne. Career: Concert Pianist, WMEX; Composer, WBUR; Many local recitals, concerts as Director of Music and Composition, Salon of Allied Arts; Many Concerts as President, American Composers Society for Propagation, Publication and Performance of 20th Century Masterpieces; Many Concerts, Harvard Musical Association; Professor, Pianoforte and Composition. Compositions: Opus 1 - Temp di Ballo, 1939; Opus 2 - Intermezzo for String Quartet, 1940; Opus 31 - Sonatina, Piano, 1953; Sonata, Piano, 1954; Opus 32, Andante con Variazioni - Opus 33, 1972; Trio Concertante Opus 34, 1973; Notturno, Flute, 1974; Opus 35, Duo da Camera, 1975; Opus 36, String Quartet, 1976; Opus 37, Conceto for Violin and Orchestra, 1980; Opus 38, Impromptu, Piano, Opus 39, 1980; Fantasy Variations, 1981; Opus 40, Sonata, Violin, 1981; Opus 41, Sonata, Cello, 1982; Opus 42, Rhapsody, 1983; Opus 43, Concerto, Piano, 1984; Opus 44, Capriccio, Piano, 1985; Opus 45, Sonata, Clarinet, 1986, Opus 46; Concerto for Violoncello and Orchestra (1987-88) Opus 47. Recordings: Many including early piano and chamber recordings (in the archives of Ventress Library, Marshfield). Publications: A Compendium of Orchestral Matters, 1982; Notes in the Life of an Artist, 1968. Hobbies: Astronomy. Address: 196 Old Ocean Street, Marshfield, MA 02050, USA.

KARAI József, b. 8 Nov 1927, Budapest, Hungary. Composer; Pianist; Conductor. m. Katalin Kertész. Education: Studied composition and 3 years conducting training, Academy of Music, Budapest, 1947-54. Debut: 1950. Compositions: About 300 works for chorus based on 20th Century Hungarian Poets' poems and poems of Goethe, Shelley, C Sandburg, Christina Rossetti, Petrarca, Edward Lear, Rilke, Trakl, J R Jimenez, G Strom, Christian Morgenstern, G Carducci; Works for wind instruments, strings, piano, organ and orchestra; 88 works published by Edition Musica and 49 by other publishers. Recordings: 58 Works. Publications: Children and Female Choruses, 1970; Mixed Choruses, 1977; Twelve Spirituals, 1978; Easy Children's Choruses, 1978; Tenders of The Fire, 14 mixed choruses, 1968-69; Selected Female Choruses, Zen-on, Tokyo, 1992; Hungarian Christmas Songs, suite, 1993; St Paul Cantata, 1994. Honours: Erkel Prize, 1972; SZOT Prize, 1980. Memberships: Association of Hungarian Composers; Hungarian Art Foundation; Hungarian Kodály Society. Hobbies: Drawing; Collecting Car and Train Models; Sport. Address: 1151 Budapest, Gyóztes u 19, Hungary.

KARAKAS Branko, b. 2 May 1930, Laki, Macedonia. Composer; Poet; Translator; Librettist; Musicologist; Critic; Director. div, 2 sons, 1 daughter. Education: Military Music School, Zagreb; Music Department, Pedagogy Academy. Career: Chorister, Zagreb Opera House; Musician, Military Orchestra; Several Appearances with the Philharmonic Orchestra and Opera in Skopje; Composer, Music Illustrator for Performances of the Dramatic Theatre, Skopje; Permanent Music Critic, Nova Makedonija; Chief of Music Propaganda and Publishing, Music Department, Ministry of Defense; Editor-in-Chief, Yugoslav Composers Union Bulletin; Director, Festival of Popular Military Songs and Marches, International Festival of Military Brass Bands, Susreti na Miljacki. Compositions include: Galeb, 1982; Ljubav na pesku, 1985; Impresije-Baletska svita, 1989. Publications: Antologija poslijeratnih makedonskih pjesnika, 1960; Makedonski muzicki stvaraoci, 1970; Muzicki zivot u JNA 1945-1985, 1987; Antologija makedonskih narodnih pesama, 1995. Contributions to: Professional Journals and Magazines. Honours: Winner, Number of Domestic and Foreign Awards and Acknowledgements. Memberships: Yugoslav Writers Union; Yugoslav Composers Union; Yugoslav Translators Union. Address: Knez Danilova 12/XIV/112, 11000 Beograd, Yugoslavia.

KARAS Joza, b. 3 May 1926, Warsaw, Poland (Czech Citizen). Violinist; Musicologist. m. Anne Killackey, 14 Feb 1976, 5 sons, 1 daughter. Education: Academic Gymnasium, Prague, 1945; State Conservatory of Music, Prague, 1949; Hartt College of Music, University of Hartford, USA, 1957. Career: Violin Soloist, Recitalist, USA and Canada; Founder, Karas String Quartet. Compositions: Violin Method. Recordings: Hans Krása's "Brundibár", 1993. Publication: Music in Terezín 1941-1945, 1985. Contributions to: STTH; Jewish Digest; Journal of Synagogue Music. Membership: Czechoslovak Society of Arts and Sciences in America. Hobbies: Travel; Photography. Address: 212 Duncaster Road, Bloomfield, CT 06002, USA.

KARASIK Gita, b. 14 Dec 1952, San Francisco, California, USA. Concert Pianist. m. Lee Caplin, 25 June 1975. Education: Private study with Mme, Rosina Lhevinne, Juilliard; Karl Ulrich Schnabel; Lev Schorr; San Francisco Conservatory of Music. Debut: San Francisco/SF Symphony, 1958; NYC/Carnegie Hall, 1969. Career: First American Pianist to make official concert tour of People's Republic of China; Guest Soloist, National Television Debut, The Bell Telephone Hour, NBC, 1963; Guest Soloist, San Francisco Symphony, 1958, 1969, 1972, 1974; Los Angeles Philharmonic, 1971; St Louis Symphony, 1974-75; Boston Pops Orchestra with Arthur Fiedler, 1975; Indianapolis Symphony, 1972, 1976; Atlanta Symphony, 1972; Singapore Symphony, 1980-81; Hong Kong Philharmonic, 1980-82; Tours of Latin America, Far East, Europe, USA; Film Scores, Andy Warhol: Made in China, 1986; The Serpent and the Rainbow, 1988; To Die For, 1989; Son of Darkness, 1992. Compositions: Concerto for Gita Karasik No 2 by Andrew Imbrie, as first prize Ford Foundation Artists Award, World Premiere with Indianapolis Symphony for Bicentennial, 1976. Address: 8332 Melrose Avenue, Hollywood, CA 90069, USA.

KARASTOYANOVA Elena, b. 1 Oct 1933, Sofia, Bulgaria. Composer. Education: Studied at the Sofia Academy of Music. Career: Lecturer at Sofia State School of Music and Director of School of Choreography, 1979-82. Compositions include: Violin Sonata, 1967; Symfonietta for Strings, 1969; Song Cycle for Solo Voices, 1977; Summer for Piano, 1982. Address: c/o Musicautor, 63 Tzar Assen Street, 1463 Sofia, Bulgaria.

KARAYANIS Plato, b. 26 Dec 1928, Pittsburgh, USA. Opera Administrator. Education: Voice at Carnegie Mellon University, and at Curtis Institute; Administration and Stage Technology at Hamburg. Career: Six years as a leading baritone in major European houses; Director of Rehearsal Department, San Francisco Opera; Assistant Stage Director and Administrator for Metropolitan Opera National Company, 1965-67; Executive Vice President of Affiliate Artists Incorporated until 1977; General Director, the Dallas Opera, 1977-; President of Board of Directors, OPERA America, 1993-97; Currently presides over sustained financial and artistic growth of the Dallas Opera, including a complete Ring cycle, the world premier of Argento's The Aspern Papers in 1988; US Premieres of operatic works by Vivaldi and deFalla, and institutional stabilization of this major American opera company; Under his direction the company has committed to innovative productions of traditional repertoire, regular inclusion of major 20th century opera and new American works. Honour: 1993 Award for Excellence in the Creative Arts, Dallas Historical Society. Address: c/o Dallas Opera, 3102 Oak Lawn Avenue, Suite 450, Dallas, TX 75219, USA.

KARCHIN Louis, b. 9 Aug 1951, Pennsylvania, USA. Composer. m. Julie Sirota, 6 Jul 1987, 2 daughters. Education: BMus, Eastman School of Music, 1973; PhD, Harvard University, 1978. Compositions: Capriccio for Violin and Seven Instruments, 1979; Duo for Violin and Cello, 1981; Viola Variations, 1982; Songs of John Keats, 1984; Songs of Distance and Light, 1988; Sonata for Cello and Piano, 1989; String Quartet, 1990; Galactic Folds for Chamber Ensemble, 1992; CascaDES, 1997; Also, Romulus, an Opera in One Act, 1990. Recordings: Duo for Violin and Cello; Songs of John Keats; Capriccio for Violin and Seven Instruments; Galactic Folds, Songs of Distance and Light. Honours: Hinrichsen Award, American Academy of Arts and Letters, 1985; Koussevitsky-Tanglewood Award, 1971. Address: 24 Waverly Place, Rm 268, New York, NY 10003, USA.

KARCZYKOWSKI Ryszard, b. 6 Apr 1942, Tczew, Poland. Singer (Tenor). Education: Studied in Gdansk with Halina Mickiewiczowna. Career: Sang in Gdansk and Stettin, then at the Landestheater Dessau (debut as Beppo in Pagliacci 1969); Other roles included Tamino, Ferrando, Fenton and Rodolfo; Sang in Leipzig from 1974, then in Berlin, Dresden (Tamino and Lensky), Moscow, Zurich, Vienna, New York, Rome, Prague and Aix-en-Provence; Covent Garden debut 1977, as Alfred in Die Fledermaus, returned as the Duke of Mantua, Ferrando and Alwa in the first local production of Berg's Lulu, 1981; Sang in the 1981 stage premiere of Prokofev's Maddalena (Graz) and the same year sang in Haydn's Orlando Paladino, at the Vienna Festival; Other roles include Ernesto, Nemorino, Rinuccio, Lionel (Martha), Jenik (Bartered Bride), Belmonte, Macduff and Elemer in Arabella; Further appearances in Boston (Duke of Mantua, 1981), Washington, Leningrad, Los Angeles, Zagreb and Lisbon; Sang in Rigoletto with the company of the Deutsche Oper Berlin at the Wiesbaden Festival, 1989. Recordings include: Szymanowski's 3rd Symphony, The Bells by Rachmaninov, Shostakovich 13th Symphony (Decca); Die Lustige Witwe and Die Fledermaus (Denon). Address: c/o Allied Artists Agency, 42 Montpelier Square, London SW17 1JZ, England.

KARIS Aleck, b. 21 Jan 1945, Washington DC, USA. Pianist. Education: BM, Manhattan School 1976, with Charles Wuorinen; Juilliard School with Beveridge Webster; Private study with Artur Balsam and William Daghlian. Career: Latin American debut 1981 at Sao Paulo; New York debut 1984, playing Chopin, Schumann, Stravinsky and Elliott Carter; Has premiered works by Mario Davidovsky, Milton Babbitt and Morton Subotnick; Member of Speculum Musicae from 1983 and has performed with the Contemporary Chamber Ensemble, New York, St Luke's Chamber Ensemble and the Group Contemporary Music; Associate in Music Performances at Columbia University from 1983. Honours include: Prize Winner, Rockefeller Foundation International Competition, 1978; fromm Foundation Grant, 1983. Address: Music Department, Columbia University, City University of New York, USA.

KARKOFF Maurice (Ingvar), b. 17 Mar 1927, Stockholm, Sweden. Composer. 2 sons, 1 daughter. Education: Music Theory with Karl Birger Blomdahl, 1944-46; Studied Composition with Lars-Erik Larsson, Royal Conservatory of Music, Stockholm, 1948-53; Piano, 1945-46; Counterpoint, 1949-53; Conducting, 1950-52; Teacher's Degree, 1951; Additional composition studies with Erland von Koch, Hans Holewa, Wladimir Vogel, André Jolivet. Debut: Duo for Clarinet and Bassoon, Fylkingen, 1951. Career: Assistant Music Critic, Stockholmstidningen, 1962-66; Teacher, Stockholm Municipal Institute of Music, 1965-96. Compositions include: Lyric Suite for Chamber Orchestra; Nine Aphoristic Variants; 12 Symphonies and 5 Small Symphonies; 14 Solo Concertos; Dolorous Symphony for String Orchestra No 9; Symphonic Reflections; Voices from the Past for Soprano and Strings; Quartet; 2 Tr Horn and Trombone; Characters for Flute, Oboe, Clarinet, Bassoon, French Horn, Trombone, Euphonium, percussions; 4 Momenti for Violin and Piano; Aspects for Guitar; Spring in Hanger; Poem for Flute (or Alto Flute); Ballata, intermezzo e leggenda per Pianoforte; 15 Album leaves for piano; Glühende Rätsel Fünf Lieder, Middle Voice and Piano; Early Summer, Songs for Middle Voice and Pianoforte: Scenes in the Desert, for low voice and pianoforte; When The Day Waned for High Voice and Pianoforte; 2 Fantasies for left hand; Kleine Music, English Horn; Chamber opera, The Frontier Kibbutz op 115. Recordings include: Six Chinese Impressions; 7 Pezzi per Grande Orchestra; Swedish Radio Symphony Orchestra; Vision Swedish Radio Orchestra, Serious Songs with Filharmonic Orchestra Kemstin Merzer; Symphony No 4; Glühende Rätsel, soprano and piano; Dolorous Symphony (ninth) for strings; Symphony No 11 (Symphony of Life); 9 Chinese Songs, soprano, piano;Oriental Pictures for piano, (composer plays); Ernst und Spass for Saxophone Quartet; Sonatin for Alto Saxophone and Piano, new CD. Memberships: Royal Swedish Academy of Music; Swedish Society of Composers. Hobby: Photography. Address: Tackjärnsvägen 18, 16868 Bromma, Sweden.

KARKOSCHKA Erhard, b. 6 Mar 1923, Mor Ostrava, Czechoslovakia. Composer; Composition Teacher. m. Rothraut Leiter, 27 July 1950, 3 sons, 1 daughter. Education includes: DPhil. Career: Conductor, University Hohenheim, 1948-68; Professor, Musikhochschule Stuttgart, 1958-; Executive Board, Institut für Neue Musik und Musikerziehung, Darmstadt, 1964-72; President, IGNM, Section West Germany, 1974-80; Lectures worldwide. Compositions: About 100 including music for orchestra, chamber music, chorus scenic works, opera, electronic music, organ music and multimedia projects; Recordings: Ad Hoc 1; Bläsergedichte (Wind Poems) for woodwind quintet, 1988; Desideratio Dei for Organ, 1963; Quattrologe for string quartet, 1966; Antimony for wind quintet, 1968; Dialog for Bassoon and Electronics, 1982; Doch Fülle Zwei und Werde Vier, 1982; Entfalten for 4 soloists and big orchestra, 1983. Publications: Das Schriftbild Der Neuen Musik, 1965; Notation in New Music, 1972, Japanese translation 1977, Chinese translation, 1996; Analyse Neuer Musik, 1976; Hörerziehung Mit Neuer Musik, Ear Education With New Music, 1981. Contributions to: Melos; Musik und Bildung; Musica; Musik und Kirche; Die Musikforschung. Memberships: President, 1974-80, Gesellschaft für Neue Musik. Hobby: Astronomy. Current Management: Musikhochschule Stuttgart, Urbanplatz, 7000 Stuttgart 1, Germany. Address: Nellingerstrasse 45, 7000 Stuttgart 75, Germany.

KARLINS M(artin) William, b. 25 Feb 1932, New York City, USA. Composer; Educator. m. Mickey Cutler, 6 Apr 1952, 1 son, 1 daughter. Education: Manhattan School of Music, New York, 1958-61; BM, Composition; MM, Composition; PhD, Composition, University of Iowa, 1965. Career: Assistant Professor of Music, Western Illinois University, 1965-67; Associate Professor 1967-73, Director, Contemporary Music Ensemble 1967-81; Professor of Theory and Composition 1973-, Northwestern University, Evanston, Illinois; His music performed worldwide, 1959-; Guest, Visiting Composer in USA and England, France and Germany, Netherlands and Hungary. Compositions include: Concert Music No 1, orchestra, II, chorus and orchestra III, woodwinds, brass, piano, percussion, IV and V, orchestra, Symphony No 1 for orchestra; Chamber music includes, Infinity, oboe d'amore, clarinet, viola, female voice; 2 woodwind quintets; 3 saxophone quartets; Quintet, alto saxophone and string quartet; Catena I for clarinet and little orchestra, II for soprano, saxophone and brass quintet and III concerto for horn and orchestra; Various choral works a cappella; 3 piano sonatas; Solo piece with passacaglia, clarinet; Relfux, concerto for amplified double bass, solo wind ensemble, piano percussion; Concerto for alto saxophone and orchestra; Chameleon, harpsichord; Drei kleiner Cembalostücke, 1994; Impromptu, alto saxophone and organ; Suite of Preludes for piano, 1988; Saxtuper, saxophone, tuba and percussion; Introduction and Passacaglia, 2 saxophones and piano; Looking out of My Window, treble chorus and viola; Quartet For Strings with soprano in the last movement, 1959-60; Nostalgie for ensemble of 12 saxophones, 1991; Elegy for orchestra, 1992; Nightlight; Quartet for Saxophones No 3, 1992-93; Lamentations-In Memoriam, 3 flutes (piccolos), 3 trumpets, 3 trombones, tuba, harp, percussion, organ and narrator; Under and Over, for flute (alto flute) and contrabass; Graphic Mobile, for any 3 or multiples of 3 instruments (with or without dancers). Hobbies: Collecting Records; Literature; Art; Cinema; Theatre. Current Management: c/o American Composers Alliance, 170 West 74th Street, New York, NY 10023, USA. Address: School of Music, Northwestern University, Evanston, IL 60208, USA.

KARLSEN Turid, b. 1961, Oslo, Norway. Soprano. Education: Studied at the Maastricht Conservatory, Holland. Career: Prizewinner at the 1984 Francisco Vinas Competition, Barcelona and sang at the Weikersheim Festival in 1985 as Romilda in Xerxes and Gluck's Euridice; Karlsruhe Opera from 1986 in Wiener Blut and as Donna Elvira, which she has also sung in Stuttgart, Wiesbaden and Dusseldorf; Sang in the premiere of Graf Mirabeau by Matthus at Stuttgart in 1989; Guest at Dresden in 1989 as Isotta in Schweigsame Frau and Luxembourg in 1991 as Butterfly; Other roles include Mozart's Countess and Pamina, Mimi, Natasha in War and Peace and Violetta; Concert engagements include Bach's St Matthew Passion at Bogota. Address: c/o Badisches Staatstheater, Baumeisterstrasse 11, Pf 1449, W-7500 Karlsruhe, Germany.

KARLSSON Erik (Mikael), b. 10 Dec 1967, Nynäshamn, Sweden. Composer. Education: Studied composition and computer music with Tamas Ungvary, Anders Blomquist and others. Career: Composer at EMS, Stockholm, Swedish Broadcasting Corporation, Danish Institute for Electroacoustic Music, Aarhus, also in Berlin and France; Appearances at festivals and concerts for electroacoustic music in Europe and elsewhere and many international radio appearances. Compositions: Threads and Cords, 1990; Anchorings, Arrows, 1992; La Disparition de L'Azur, 1993; Interiors and Interplays, 1994; Épitaphe pour Iqbal Masih, 1995, all recorded. Publications: Author, Circle Almost Closing, and Fylkingen - 60 Years of Experimental Art, 1994. Contributions to: Various articles on contemporary music in Nutida Musik. Honours: EBU/UNESCO Rostrum Prize, 1992, and 1994; 2 First prizes, Grand Prix Internationaux in Bourges and France; 1st Prize in Radio France/NDR's Radiophonic Competition, 1995; Honourable mentions, Prix Ars Electronica, Linz, Austria, 1993 and 1995; Grants from Deutscher Akademischer Austuachdienst Berliner Künstlerprogramm, Royal Swedish Academy of Music. Memberships: Fylkingen in Stockholm; Society of Swedish Composers; Swedish Section of ISCM and ICEM. Current Management: Swedish Music Information Center, Box 27327, S-115 28 Stockholm, Sweden. Address: Junkergatan 16/II, S-126 53 Hägersten, Sweden.

KARLSSON Lars Olof, b. 24 Jan 1953, Jomala, Åland, Finland. Composer. m. Helena Hartikainen, 31 Dec 1994, 1 son, 1 daughters. Education: Studies at the Sibelius Academy, 1972-82; Cantor Organist, 1976; Higher Degree in Piano, 1979; Composition Studies at the Hochschule der Künste, West Berlin, 1982-83; Diploma in Composition, 1983. Career: Lecturer at the Sibelius Academy, 1983-; Co-founder of the Åland Culture Festival, 1983. Compositions: Five Aphorisms for Piano, 1973; Med Havet, song cycle for Baritone and Piano, 1976; Canto Drammatico, for Solo Violin, 1980; Concerto for Violin and Orchestra, 1993; Suite for Helena, for Wind Quintet, 1994; Toccata, Variations and Fugue on the Chorale Den Blomstertid Nu Kommer, for Organ, 1994; Ludus Latrunculorum, Oratorio, 1996; String Quartet, 1997; Two Love Scenes and a Daydream, for Voice, Soprano Saxophone and Big Band, 1997. Recordings: Arioso; Canto Drammatico; Composition for Organ; Passacaglia et Fuga B+A-C-H. Contributions to: Critic for Hufvudstadsbladet, 1982-89; The Isle Is Full Of Noises, Nordic Sounds No. 3, 1996. Honours: 3-year grant from the Svenska Kulturfonden, 1986; 5-year State artists grant, 1995. Memberships: Society of Finnish Composers; Board Member, Scandinavian Guitar Festival, 1986-. Hobbies: History; Cooking; Fishing. Address: Tilkgränden 8C 26, 00300 Helsinki, Finland.

KARMINSKI Mark, b. 30 Jan 1930, Kharkov, Ukraine. Composer. m. Irini Smichcovitch, 30 Aug 1955, 1 son. Education: Department of Philology and Literature, Kharkov State University; Composition, Kharkov State Conservatory. Career: 1st orchestral works and instrumental music performed in USSR cities; Opera Bukovinians premiered at Kharkov Opera House, 1957, Moscow, 1960; Other opera stagings: Ten days that shook the world, Donetsk, 1970, Prague National Theatre, 1972, Lvov, 1977, 1984; Irkutsk story, Kiev, Kharkov, Chelabinsk, Saratov, 1977-78; Only one day, Odessa, Lvov, 1987; Musical Robin Hood, Moscow, 1968, then 25 cities, USSR; Author, Philharmonic Concertos (radio, TV). Compositions include: 4 operas; Rembrandt, ballet; Symphony; Oratorio; 5 Suites for string orchestra including Baroque faces and Play music in ancient style; 6 partitas for piano; Concertina for violin and piano, for flute and piano; Instrumental pieces; Vocal and choral works; Music for over 100 plays. Recordings include: The soldier forgot nothing, TV film; Robin Hood; Songs from Robin Hood; O K Musketry, disco musical; Merri pencil, children's songs; M Karminsky's 9 songs; Symphony with Gorky Symphony Orchestra, conductor I Husman. Publications: Collected songs, 1970-85; Ten days that shook the world, 1973; Robin Hood songs, 1981; Irkutsk story, 1985; Choral music books, 15 choruses a cappella, 1988; Music for children, piano pieces, 1990; Kharkov Selected Works, 1995; 27 Pieces in Three-Part Rhythm, music for piano, 1996-. Contributions to: Various newspapers and magazines, including literature essay (Kultura), 1993, and essays about Schubert, Mendelssohn, Schumann, 1993, 1994, 1995. Honours: Laureate: All-Union and Republican Competitions, operas (twice), All-Union Competitions, youth songs, war songs, best music for plays; Honoured Arts Worker of Ukraine. Memberships: Union of Composers, USSR and Ukraine, 1953-; Founding Member, creative society Kruge. Hobbies: Books; Poetry; Theatre; History; Museums; Painting albums; Chess. Address: Klotchkovskaja str 150-a, ap 40, Kharkov 310145, Ukraine.

KARNEUS Katarina, b. 1966, Stockholm, Sweden. Singer (Mezzo-Soprano). Education: Trinity College of Music, London; National Opera Studio. Career: Varied concert repertoire including Beethoven's Ninth with Frans Brüggen and the Hallé Orchestra, C Minor Mass in the Salzburg Festival with Roger Norrington, Les Nuits d'Eté and a Sylvester Concert with the Filharmonisch Orkest and Grant Llewellyn, Rossini-Mozart programme with Nicholas McGegan and the Hanover Band, Pergolesi Stabat Mater with the Netherlands Chamber Orchestra and Hartmut Haenchen and a concert at Buckingham Palace with Franz Welser Möst; Prom debut with Rafael Frühbeck de Burgos and Edinburgh Festival debut with Sir Charles Mackerras; Appearances at the Albert Hall with Sir David Willcocks and at the Royal Festival Hall with the Bach Choir; Broadcast Die Lieder eines fahrenden Gesellen with Grant Llewellyn and the Ulster Orchestra; Two concerts with Scottish Chamber Orchestra; South Bank debut in Purcell Room with a programme of Spanish and Scandinavian songs; Wigmore Hall recital as part of the Voices series; For Welsh National Opera: Angelina in La Cenerentola, Cherubino in Le Nozze di Figaro and Rosina in Il Barbiere di Siviglia; Mercédès in Carmen for ENO abd Opéra de Paris; Rosina and the title role in Carmen for Opéra Comiquie, Paris; The Page in Salome for Lyric Opera of Chicago; Tamiri in Il Re Pastore for Netherlands Opera; Future engagements include Sesto in La Clemensa di Tito for WNO; Debut with Glyndebourne Festival Opera as Dorabella; Cherubina at La Monnaie; Varvara in Katya Kabanova for Metropolitan Opera; Returns to the Bastille in 1999 to sing Dorabella, to the Opéra Comique for Carmen and as Annio in La Clemenza di Tito at the Bayerische Staatsoper; Returns to WNO as Octavian in Der Rosenkavalier in 2000. Recording: First CD plans underway. Honours: Christine Nielson Award, 1994; Winner, Cardiff Singer of the World Competition, 1995. Address: c/o Musicmakers, Tailor House, 63-65 High Street, Whitwell, Hertfordshire SG4 8AH, England.

KARNI Gilad, b. 5 July 1968, Israel. Violist. m. Jill, 22 December 1994, 1 son. Education: Samuel Rubin Academy, Tel Aviv; Telma Yulin School of the Arts, Israel. Career includes: Principal Violist, Bamberger Symphoniker, Germany; Soloist with Orchestras in Israel, France, Germany, Austria, South Africa and USA; Participation in Several Chamber Festivals. Honours: 1st Prize, Lionel Tertis International Viola Competition, 1994, 3rd Prize, ARD Munich International Music Competition; 3rd Prize, Bryan International String Competition, USA; 1st Prize, Israeli Broadcasting Authority Competition for Best Performance; Peter Schidlof Prize, Most Beautiful Tone; Lionel Tertis Viola Competition, Best Interpretation Prize. Address: Sonnenleite No 12, Bischberg Trosdorf 96120, Germany.

KAROLYI Sandor, b. 24 Sept 1931, Budapest, Hungary. Professor. m. Suzanne Godefroid, 3 July 1954, 2 sons, 1 daughter. Education: Virtuosity Diploma, Franz Liszt Music Academy, Budapest, 1948; Virtuosity Diploma with distinction, Music Conservatory of Brussels, 1954; Teachers include Ede Zathureczky, Leo Weiner, Antal Molnar, André Gertler. Debut: Franz Liszt Academy, 1941. Career: Violin solo, Opera House in Frankfurt, 1956; Professor, Musikhochschule, Frankfurt am Main and at the Akademie Tonkunst Darmstadt; Concerts for the BBC and broadcasting companies in Europe; TV appearances in Germany, Japan, Philippines and Australia. Recordings: Paul Hindemith: 4 Violin Sonatas with Werner Hoppstock, piano, and Károlyi String Quartet recorded Quartets Nos 2 and 6 plus the Clarinet-Quartet of Paul Hindemith; Max Reger: Violin Sonatas A and C major with Suzanne Godefroid, piano; Prelude and Fugas for violin solo; Giuseppe Tartini Devil's Trill. Publication: Gustav Mahler Orchestra studies for the 10 symphonies, 1989. Honours: Awards: Diploma Contests in Geneva, 1947, Budapest, 1948, London, 1953; Contemporary Contest, Darmstadt, 1952; Vieuxtemps Prize, Belgium, 1959; Medaille Eugene Ysaye, Brussels, 1967. Membership: Deutsche Bachsolisten. Hobbies: Gardening; Computer games. Address: Dehnhardtstrasse 30, 60433 Frankfurt am Main, Germany.

KARPATI Janos, b. 11 July 1932, Budapest, Hungary. Musicologist; Professor; Librarian. Education: PhD, Eotvos Lorand University, Budapest; Diploma, Faculty of Musicology, Ferenc Liszt Acdemy, Budapest; DSc, Musicology, Hungarian Academy of Sciences. Career: Folk Music Research in Morocco, 1957-58; Recording production, Hungaroton, 1959-61; Head

Librarian and Lecturer, Ferenc Liszt Academy of Music, Budapest, 1961-; Professor, 1983-; Folk Music Research in Japan, 1988. Recording: Kagura: Japanese Shinto Ritual Music. Publications: D Scarlatti, 1959; A Schoenberg, 1963; Muzsikalo zenetortenet, volumes II, IV, 1965, 1973; Bartók String Quartets, 1975; Bartók kamarezeneje, 1976; Kelet zeneje, Music of the East, 1981; Bartók's Chamber Music, 1994. Contributions to: Muzsika; Magyar Zene; Studia Musicologica; Fontes Artis Musicae; The World of Music; Orbis Musicae (Tel Aviv). Honour: Erkel Prize, 1971; Grand Prix of Hungarian Creative Artist's Association, 1994. Memberships: Chairman, Huungarian National Committee, International Association of Music Librarians; Board Member, Hungarian Music Council; Hungarian Musicological Society. Address: Mester u 77, 1095 Budapest IX, Hungary.

KARR Gary, b. 20 Nov 1941, Los Angeles, California, USA. Double Bass Player. Education: Studied with Herman Reinshagen, Warren Benfield and Stuart Sankey. Debut: New York 1962 in concert with Leonard Bernstein, ad at New York Town Hall. Career: European tour 1964, playing at Wigmore Hall London; Founded the International Institute for the String Bass, 1967; Teaching appointments at Juilliard School, Yale School of Music, Indiana University, New England Conservatory and Hartt School of Music, Hartford (1976); Formed duo with keyboard player Harmon Lewis in 1972, tours of Europe, the Far East, USA and Canada; Appearances as Soloist with the Chicago Symphony, New York Philharmonic, English Chamber Orchestra, London Symphony and Toronto Symphony; Composers who have written for him include Vittorio Giannini, Henze, Wilfred Josephs, Lalo Schifrin, John Downey and Gunther Schuller; Debut tour of Australia 1987-88; Television appearances include series Gary Karr and Friends on CBC in Canada and Bass is Beautiful for Channel 4, England; Further TV engagements in France, Belgium, Japan, Norway, Switzerland and USA; Karr Doublebass Foundation Inc formed 1983 to provide valuable instruments for talented players. Recordings: Transcriptions of Paganini's Moses Fantasy and Dvorak Cello Concerto; Concerto by Lalo Schifrin. Address: Kaye Artists Management, 7 Chertsey Road, Woking, Surrey GU21 5AB, England.

KARR-BERTOLI Julius, b. 11 June 1920, Munich, Germany. Conductor. m. Charlotte Langesee, 1957, 1 daughter. Education: Graduate, Akademie der Tonkunst, Munich, 1939, Career includes: Conductor, Bavarian State Theatres, age 18; Conductor, Dortmund Opera, 1942-45; Freelance, Bavarian Radio, 1945-60; Concerts, Festival House, Salzburg, Pergolesi Festival, Zurich, 1959; 1st German to conduct George Enescu Philharmonic, Bucharest, 1966; Permanent Guest Conducting, Romania, 1966-71; Vienna, Rio de Janeiro, 1967; Paris, 1969; Cimarosa's The Secret Marriage, Augsburg, 1971; Professor, Richard Strauss Conservatory, Munich, 1972-85; Permanent Guest Conductor, USSR and Russia, incited by Shostakovich, concerts in Baku, Tbilisi, Vilnius, and many other towns, 1976-; Musica Bayreuth, Bayreuth, 1984, 1987; Concert, Yehudi Menuhin's 70th Birthday, Munich, 1986; Festivals, Austria, with Moravian Chamber Philharmonic, 1988; 1st German Conductor, Tirana, 1991; 1st Guest Conductor, Suk Chamber Orchestra, Prague, 1992; 1st International Festival for Classical Music, Almaty, Kazakhstan, 1994, with Symphony Orchestra and Kazakhstan State Chamber Orchestra, then Latvian Philharmonic Orchestra, Riga; Kazakhstan, 1995, and festive concert, Munich, for his 75th birthday, 1st performances of Beethoven Symphony No 10 1st Movement and Piano Concerto No 4 (version as played by the composer himself); Earlier 1st performances include Shostakovich Symphony No 8 (1st German) and Dvorák Symphony No 7, Wladimir Vogel's work in memory of Pergolesi, Shostakovich Symphony No 9 (1st Swiss); Has conducted Orchestra del Teatro la Fenice, Venice, Munich-Berlin-and St Petersburg Philharmonics, Janácek Philharmonic (Bronó), Scarlatti Orchestra, Suk Chamber Orchestra; Concerts in Argentina, Uruguay, Panama, Indonesia, Taiwan, Cuba, Malta, Palma de Mallorca (Spain), China. Recordings: Pergolesi, Rumanian composers, 1967; Music by Pergolesi and with Josef Suk, violin, 1993. Climbing; Hiking; Reading; Music. Address: Sommerstraße 9, D-81543 Munich, Germany.

KARRASCH Ingrid, b. 1942, Hagen, Germany. Mezzo-Soprano. Education: Studied with Max Lorenz, among others. Career: Sang at Gelsenkirchen from 1967, and Deutsche Oper am Rhein, Dusseldorf, 1972-91; Guest appearances at the State Opera of Hamburg, Munich and Stuttgart and in Rome, Paris, Monte Carlo and Stockholm; Bayreuth Festival, 1983-86 as Waltraute in Die Walküre; Other roles have included Mozart's Marcellina, Mary in Der fliegende Holländer, Carlotta in Schweigsame Frau, and Ragonde in Comte Ory. Address: c/o Deutsche Opera am Rhein, Heinrich Heine Allee 16a, W-4000 Dusseldorf 1, Germany.

KARSON Burton Lewis, b. 10 November 1934, Los Angeles, USA. Professor; Pianist; Harpsichordist; Organist; Conductor; Musicologist. Education: BA, 1956, MA, Musicology, 1958, DMA, 1964; Piano Study with Paul Stoye, John Crown, Gwendolyn Williams Koldofsky; Harpsichord with Alice Ehlers; Conducting with Charles Hirt, Ingolf Dahl; Musicology with Pauline Alderman, Raymond Kendall. Career: Boy Soprano, Los Angeles; Many Appearances in Western America as Pianist with Singers; Anglican Church Musician; Founder, Artistic Director, Conductor, Baroque Music Festival Corona del Mar, 1981-; Lecturer, Philharmonic Society, Orange County, Carmel Bach Festival, Pacific Symphony, San Diego Opera & Symphony, Los Angeles Philharmonic. Contributions to: Musical Quarterly; Los Angeles Times. Honours: Distinguished Professor, School of the Arts, California University, Fullerton, 1997; Twice Honoured with Professional Promise Awards, CSUF. Memberships: American Musicological Society; American Guild of Organists; Pi Kappa Lambda; Phi Mu Alpha. Hobbies: Foreign Travel; Food & Wines. Address: 404 De Sola Terrace, Corona del Mar, CA 92625, USA.

KARTTUNEN Aussi (Ville), b. 30 Sept 1960, Helsinki. Cellist; Artistic Director. m. Muriel Von Braun, 16 Aug 1985. 1 son, 1 daughter. Education: Musical, Sibelius Acadamy, Helsinki, 1969-78; Teachers Vili Pullinen, Erkki Rautio, Private studies in London with William Pleeth, 1978-81; Jacqueline du Pré, 1980-86; In Holland with Tibor de Mackula, 1981-83. Career: Soloist with all major Scandanavian Orchestras; London Sinfonietta, Philharmonia Orchestra, Los Angeles Philharmonia, Tokyo Metropolitan, Tokyo Symphony, Ensemble modern and The Residentie Orchestra; Recitals in most European countries, the Americas, and Japan. Appearances in major festivals including: Edinburgh, Lockenhaus, Berlin, Helsinki, Vienna and Venice. Performed many works by a variety of artists. Major recordings including the complete Beethoven Sonatas; 20th Century Solo Cello; Zimmermann and Hindemith; Concertos with London Sinfonietta; Saarihaó Concerto with the Los Angeles Philharmonia. Honours: First prize in Young Concert Artist Competition, Tunbridge Wells, England, 1981. First Prize and Gold Medal at the Festival Des Jeunes Solistes, in Bordeaux, 1982. Memberships: Artistic Director, AVANTI! Chamber orchestra, 1994-; Artistic Director, Helsinki Biennale, 1995. Address: Kanneltie 14 B 8, 00420 Helsinki, Finland.

KASAROVA Vesselina, b. 1963, Stara Zagora, Bulgaria. Mezzo-Soprano. Education: Studied at the Sofia Conservatory. Career: Appearances at the Sofia National Opera as Fenena, Rosina, Preziosilla and Dorabella; Member of the Zurich Opera, 1988-91 as Annio in Clemenza di Tito, Stephano in Roméo et Juliette, and Anna in Les Troyens; Salzburg Festival 1991-92 as Annio and Rossini's Tancredi; Further appearances as Rosina at the Vienna Staatsoper in 1991 and the Geneva Opera, and as Pippo in La Gazza Ladra at Barcelona in 1992; Season 1996 with Mozart's Zerlina at the Salzburg Festival and Idamonte at Florence; Concert repertory includes Mozart's Requiem in Milan, and Agnese in Bellini's Beatrice di Tenda in Vienna. Address: c/o Staatsoper, Opernring 2, A-1010 Vienna, Austria.

KASHKASHIAN Kim, b. 31 Aug 1952, Detroit, Michigan, USA. Violist; Teacher. Education: Studied with Walter Trampler, 1969-79 and Karen Tuttle, 1970-75, Peabody Conservatory of Music, Baltimore. Career: Various engagements as a soloist with leading orchestras in North America and Europe; Retials; Chamber Music appearances; Faculty Member, New School of Music, Philadelphia, 1981-86, Mannes College of Music, New York, 1983-86, Indiana University School of Music, Bloomington, 1985-87; Staatliche Hochschule für Musik, Freiburg, 1989-; Has prepared transcriptions and has commissioned various works for viola. Recordings: Many discs as a soloist and chamber music artist. Address: Hartliebstr 2, 8000 Munchen 19, Germany.

KASPRZYK Jacek, b. 10 Aug 1952, Biala, Poland. Conductor. Education: Studied at Warsaw Conservatory. Debut: Warsaw Opera, 1975. Career: Principal Conductor and Music Director of the Polish National Radio Symphony until leaving for England 1982; Guest Conductor with Berlin Philharmonic, Orchestre National de France, the Stockholm and Oslo Philharmonic Orchestras, the Bavarian Radio Symphony and the Rotterdam Philharmonic; 1982 debuts with the Philharmonia and Detroit Opera and the San Diego Symphony; British orchestras include the Hallé, Northern Sinfonia, Scottish National Orchestra and regional BBC Orchestras; London Prom Concert Debut 1984, with the BBC Welsh Symphony; Return visits to Frankfurt, Vienna, Hamburg and Scandinavia and to the Cincinnati and San Diego Orchestras; Guest at Lyon Opera for A Midsummer Night's Dream, at Bordeaux for Eugene Onegin and at the Stockholm Royal Opera for Die Zauberflöte; Season 1988-89 Fledermaus for Scottish Opera and Der fliegende Holländer for Opera North; English National Opera debut 1992, The Barber of Seville. Recordings: For EMI and Cirrus, as well as Polish and Czech companies. Address: c/o Harold Holt Ltd, 31 Sinclair Road, London W14 0NS, England.

KASRASHVILI Makvala, b. 13 Mar 1942, Kutaisi, Georgia, Russia. Singer (Soprano). Education: Studied with Mdme Davidova in Tblisi. Debut: Bolshoi Theatre Moscow 1968, as Countess Almaviva. Career: Member of the Bolshoi ensemble, with guest appearances in Warsaw, Sofia and Brno; Savonlinna Festival Finland 1983, as Elisabeth de Valois; Covent Garden debut 1984, as Donna Anna; Many appearances in operas by Tchaikovsky, Verdi and Puccini; Verona Arena 1985, as Aida; Wiesbaden Festival 1987, as Tosca; Sang Voislava in Rimsky's Mlada at the Bolshoi, 1988 (also at Pittsburgh 1989); Sang in Mlada at the Barbican Hall, 1989 (first British performance). Recordings include: Francesca da Rimini by Rachmaninov (Melodyia). Honours: Prizewinner, Sofia International Competition, 1968; Winner, Montreal Competition, 1973. Address: c/o Bolshoi Theatre, Pr Marxa 8/2, 103009 Moscow, Russia.

KASSEL Wolfgang, b. 1930, Germany. Singer (Tenor). Career: Sang at the Flensburg Opera, 1954-57; Engagements at Mainz, 1957-58, Wuppertal 1958-60, Krefeld 1960-66, Bielefeld 1967-74;Sang at Nuremberg, 1974-80 and made guest appearances at Munich 1973-76; Appeared as Tannhäuser at Covent Garden, 1973, Siegmund at Rouen, 1975; Other roles have included Lohengrin, Walther, Siegfried, Florestan, Max, Herod in Salome and Bacchus (Ariadne auf Naxos); Further engagements at Toulouse, Oslo, Wurzburg and elsewhere in Europe. Address: c/o Stadtische Buhnen, Richard Wagnerplatz 2-10, 8500 Nuremberg, Germany.

KASTU Matti, b. 3 Feb 1943, Turku, Finland. Tenor. Education: School of Royal Opera, Stockholm. Career: Principal Tenor at Stockholm Opera from 1973 with debut as Laca in Jenufa at Edinburgh in 1974; Roles include Rodolfo in La Bohème, Bacchus in Ariadne auf Naxos, Walter in Die Meistersinger, Parsifal, and Florestan in Fidelio; Guest appearances in Vienna, San Francisco, Munich, Dusseldorf, Frankfurt and Berlin; Tour of USA in 1979 appearing in Detroit, Washington and New York; Welsh National Opera in 1981 as the Emperor in Die Frau ohne Schatten, Milan in 1983 in Mahler's Das klagende Lied; Created the Guide in Sallinen's The King Goes Forth To France, Savonlinna, 1984; Sang at Edinburgh Festival in 1990 as Tristan in a concert performance of Wagner's opera with the Jutland Opera; Sang Tristan at Aarhus in 1992. Recordings include: Menelaos in Aegyptische Helena.

KASZA Katalin, b. 1942, Szeged, Hungary. Soprano. Education: Graduate, Ferenc Liszt Academy, Budapest, 1967. Debut: Abigail in Nabucco, Budapest State Opera, 1967. Career includes: Judith in film of Duke Bluebeard's Castle and guest performer as Judith in the Edinburgh Festval, 1973 and at many other international venues; Brünnhilde in Wagner's Ring at Covent Garden Opera House, London, 1974-76 and at Geneva and several German cities, 1977-78; US debut in Duke Bluebeard's Castle, Los Angeles, CA, 1980; Sang Eudossia in Respighi's La Fiamma at Erkel Theatre, Budapest, 1989; Other roles include: Octavia in L'Incoronazione di Poppea, Leonore in Fidelio, Lady Macbeth, Title roles of Salome and Elektra, Senta in Der fliegende Holländer, Ortrud in Lohengrin, Fricka in Rheingold, Isolde in Tristan und Isolde and Kundry in Parsifal. Recordings: Radio and TV film recording of Fidelio, 1969; As Judith in Duke Bluebeard's Castle, 1970, in TV film and the same role for the complete Bartók edition; Kundry in Parsifal, 1983. Honours: The Best Dramatic Performer's Diploma, Sofia International Singing Concours, 1968; Liszt Prize 1, 1974; Bela Bartók - Ditta Pasztory Prize, 1992. Address: c/o Hungarian State Opera House, Andrássy ut 22, 1061 Budapest, Hungary.

KATAGIRI Hitomo, b. 24 Jan 1958, Wakayama, Japan. Mezzo-Soprano. Education: Studied in Osaka and Vienna. Career: Sang at the Vienna Staatsoper in 1985 and has appeared widely in Europe and the USA; Bayreuth Festival, 1988-92 in Walküre and Parsifal, Geneva, 1989-90 in L'Enfant et Les Sortilèges and Ariane et Barbe-Bleue; Rome in 1991 as Second Norn and Flosshilde in a concert performance of Götterdämmerung; Opera repertory in works by Strauss, Verdi and Puccini and concerts with works by Mahler, Mozart, Bach and Schoenberg. Address: c/o Bayreuth Festival, PO Box 100262, 8580 Bayreuth 2, Germany.

KATES Stephen (Edward), b. 7 May 1943, NY, USA. Cellist; Teacher. Education: Attended Josef Gingold's chamber music classes, Meadowmount School of Music, 1961-62 and Gregor Piatigorsky's master classes, University of Southern CA, Los Angeles, 1964-67; Studied with Leonard Rose, Claus Adam, Robert Mann and Walter Trampler, Juilliard School of Music, NY, diploma, 1968. Career: New York debut, 1963; Soloist with major US orchestras; Many recitals and chamber music engagements; Faculty, Ohio State University, Columbus, 1969-72; Member, Cello and Chamber Music Departments, Peabody Institute, 1974-; Various Masterclasses; Commissioned and played premiere of Claus Adam's Cello Concerto; Solo Tour of Russia, 1987 with guest appearance at Leningrad Philharmonic, Shostakovich' Cello Concerto No 1; Soloist with Baltimore Symphony, 1989; Member, Faculty, Music Academy of the West, Santa Barbara, CA, 1984-91; Major tour of Russia, 1988, Leningrad Philharmonic, Kiev, Riga, Leningrad recital. Publications: Articles in Strad, Strings and Musical America. Recordings: Various labels. Honours: 2nd Prize, Tchaikovsky Competition, Moscow, 1966. Memberships: Violoncello Society, President, 1983-87; Member Jury VIII International Tchaikovsky Cello Competition Moscow,

1986. Address: c/o Peabody Institute, John Hopkins University, 1 East Mount Vernon Place, Baltimore, MD 21202, USA.

KATIMS Milton, b. 24 Jun 1909, New York, New York, USA. Conductor; Violist. m. Virginia Peterson (Cellist), 7 Nov 1940, 1 son, 1 daughter. Education: BA, Columbia University; Private violin study from age 8; Conducting at National Orchestra Association with Leon Barzin, 1931-35. Debut: NBC Symphony, 1947. Career: Solo Violist and Assistant Conductor, WOR, Mutual Broadcasting Company, 1935-43; Faculty, Juilliard, 1947-64; NBC New York, First Desk Violist with Toscanini, Staff Conductor, 1943-54; Principal Guest Conductor with NBC Symphony, 1947-54 (52 broadcasts); Music Director, Seattle Symphony, 1954-76; Guest Conductor of orchestras on five continents; Solo viola appearances, chamber music with Budapest String Quartet, Pablo Casals and Isaac Stern; Artistic Director, University of Houston School of Music, 1976-84. Compositions: Editions for Viola for International Music Company include 6 Solo Suites of Bach, 3 Gamba Sonatas of Bach, 2 Brahms Sonatas, Schubert Arpeggione Sonata and 18 other compositions. Recordings: Numerous as Conductor and Violist including: Bach Solo Viola Suites, Bach Gamba Sonatas, with Milton Katims and colleagues. Contributions to: Various journals. Honours include: Alice M Ditson Award, 1964; Chair named after him, National Orchestral Association, 1982; Arturo Toscanini Artistic Achievement, 1986; Honorary Doctorates; Milton Katims Scholarship, UH School of Music, 1984; Distinguished Service Award, American String Teachers, 1988; Nominated for Kennedy Center Honor in 1989 and National Medal in The Arts, 1995. Memberships: American Viola Society; American String Teachers Association. Hobbies: Tennis; Chess. Address: Fairway Estates, 8001 Sand Point Way NE, Seattle, WA 98115, USA.

KATIN Peter, b. 14 Nov 1930, London, England. Concert Pianist. m. Eva Zweig, 20 Feb 1954, div, 2 sons. Education: Westminster Abbey Choir; Royal Academy of Music. Debut: Wigmore Hall, 1948. Career: International concert career involving appearances in major concert halls and collaboration with the best known orchestras and conductors; Teaching achievements include professorships at Royal Academy of Music, University of Western Ontario, Royal College of Music. Recordings: Approximately 35 recordings for several major companies; Complete sets include Grieg's Lyric Pieces, Mozart's Sonatas, Chopin's complete Polonaises and Waltzes, Chopin's Nocturnes and Impromptus, Rachmaninov's Preludes. Publications: Autobiography currently in preparation; Various contributions notably to Classical Music (UK) and Clavier (USA). Hobbies: Reading; Writing; Theatre; Photography; Record Collecting; Recording Techniques. Current Management: Maureen Lunn. Address: NB Management. Address: c/o Ashlea, Oakwood Drive, East Horseley, Surrey KT24 6QF, England.

KATS-CHERNIN Elena, b. 4 November 1957, Tashkent, Uzbekistan (Resident in Australia from 1975). Composer; Lecturer. Education: Diploma of the State Conservatorium of Music, NSW, 1979; Hanover Musikhochschule 1980-84, with Helmut Lachenmann. Career: Composer of incidental music for dance theatre in Germany, 1985-93; Lecturer, New South Wales Conservatory, 1995; Commissions from ZKM Karlsruhe (1993), Munchener Biennale (1994) and Sydney Alpha Ensemble (1995), among others; Sehrayahn Resident, Ministry for the Arts Lower Saxony, 1984-85. Compositions include: Piano Concerto, 1979; Bienie for orchestra, 1979; In Tension, for 6 instruments, 1982; Reductions, for 2 pianos, 1983; Duo I for violin and piano, 1984; Stairs, for orchestra, 1984; Transfer, for orchestra, 1990; Tast-en, for piano, 1991; Totschki: Dots, for oboe and clarinet, 1992; Clocks, for 20 musicians and tape, 1993; Retonica for orchestra, 1993; Clip for percussion, 1994; Concertino for violin and 11 players, 1994; Coco's Last Collection, dance theatre, for 2 pianos, 1994; Cadences, Deviations and Scarlatti for 14 instruments, 1995; Portrait CD, Clocks, 1997. Honours include: Sounds Australian, 1996. Address: c/o APRA, 1A Eden Street, Crows Nest, NSW 2065, Australia.

KATZ Arnold, b. 18 Sept 1924, Baku, Russia. Conductor. Education: Studied Violin at the Central Music School and the Moscow State Conservatoire; Conducting at the Leningrad State Conservatoire. Career: Conducting career in Russia from 1956; Founded the USSR Philharmonic of Novosibirsk and brought the orchestra on tour of England 1988; German tour, 1989; Guest appearances with the Stockholm Philharmonic, BBC Welsh Symphony Orchestra, Tivoli Orchestra (Copenhagen), Residentie Orchestra (Netherlands) and RT Luxembourg in season 1990-91. Recordings include: Music by Shostakovich and Siberian composers with the USSR Philharmonic of Novosibirsk; Russian music with the Leningrad Philharmonic. Address: c/o Residentie Orkest, PO Box 11543, 2502 AM The Hague, Netherlands.

KATZ Martin, b. 27 Nov 1945, Los Angeles, California, USA. Pianist; University Professor. Education: Studied at the University of Southern California at Los Angeles, accompaniment with Gwendolyn Koldovsky. Career: Pianist for the US Army chorus in Washington, 1966-69; Accompanist to such leading singers as José Carreras, Kiri Te Kanawa, Teresa Berganza, Katia Ricciarelli and Nicolai Gedda; Concert tours of North and South America, Australia, Europe and Asia, notably with Marilyn Horne; Editions of Rossini operas performed by Houston Grand Opera and at the Rossini Festival, New York, 1982-83; Edition of Handel's Rinaldo performed at the Ottawa Festival 1982, Metropolitan Opera 1984; Associate Professor at Westminster Choir College, 1976; Professor at the University of Michigan, 1983. Address: Music Department, University of Michigan, Ann Arbor, MI 48109, USA.

KATZ Paul, b. 1941, USA. Cellist. Career: Member of the Cleveland Quartet, 1969-94; Regular tours of the USA, Canada, Europe, Japan, Russia, South America, Australia, New Zealand and the Middle East; On Faculty of the Eastman School, Rochester and in residence at the Aspen Music Festival, co-founding the Center for Advanced Quartet Studies; Tour of the Soviet Union and five European countries, 1988; Season 1988-89 with appearances at the Metropolitan Museum and Alice Tully Hall, New York; Concerts in Paris, London, Bonn, Prague, Lisbon and Brussels; Festivals of Salzburg, Edinburgh and Lucerne; Many complete Beethoven cycles and annual appearances at Lincoln Center's Mostly Mozart Festival; In addistion to standard repertory, has commissioned works by John Harbison, Sergei Slonimsky, Samuel Adler, George Perle, Christopher Rouse, Toru Takemitsu, Stephen Paulus, Libby Larsen, John Corigliano and Oswaldo Golyov. Recordings: Repertoire from Mozart to Ravel; Collaborations with Alfred Brendel (Schubert Trout Quintet), Pinchas Zukerman and Bernard Greenhouse (Brahms Sextets), Emanuel Ax, Yo Yo Ma and Richard Stoltzman; Complete Beethoven Quartets, 1982. Publications: Interpretation problems of the Beethoven Quartets, RCA, 1982. Contributions to: Numerous articles in Chamber Music Magazine and Editor of Chamber Music Forum for American String Teacher Magazine. Memberships: President, Chamber Music America, 1987-93. Current Management: ICM Artists, New York. Address: Eastman School of Music, 26 Gibbs Street, Rochester, NY 14604, USA.

KATZ Shelley, b. 1960, Montreal, Canada. Concert Pianist; Accompanist. Education: Studied at the Montreal Conservatoire and the Juilliard School in New York. Career: Concert performances under such conductors as Solti and Bernstein, with appearances in London, New York, Tokyo and Munich; Solo repetiteur at the Deutsche Oper am Rhein from 1987, Koblenz from 1989 and assistant to the music director at Mainz Opera; Accompanist to such singers as Nicolai Gedda, Gwyneth Jones and Jochen Kowalski. Address: Helen Sykes Management, Fourth Floor, Parkway House, Sheen Lane, East Sheen, London, SW14 8LS, England.

KATZER Georg, b. 10 Jan 1935, Habelschwerdt, Germany. Composer. m. Angelika Szostak, 13 May 1975, 3 sons. Education: Hochschule für Musik, Berlin; AMU, Prague; Akademie der Kunste, Democratic Republic of Germany. Career: Freelance Composer, 1960; Professor of Composition, Academy of Fine Arts, Berlin. Compositions: Mainly published; Chamber music; More than 10 symphonic works; Solo concertos (with orchestra), for flute, oboe, piano, cello, harp and cello; Electro-acoustic works; Multi-media works; 2 ballets; 3 operas; Offene Landschaft for orchestra; Landschaft mit steigender Flut for orchestra. Recordings: Sound House, after F Bacon's The New Atlantis, for 3 orchestras, organ and tape; Kommen und Gehen, woodwind quintet and piano; Aide-Memoirem, tape composition; Harpsichord Concerto; Konzert für Orchester No 1; Baukasten for orchestra; Empfindsame Musik; Streichermusik 1; Wergo 6274-2. Hobbies: Skiing; Hiking; Literature; Theatre; Arts; Cooking. Address: Weserstrasse 5, 15738 Zeuthen, Germany.

KAUFMAN Frederick, b. 24 Mar 1936, Brooklyn, New York, USA. Composer. Education: Studied Composition with Vittorio Giannini at the Manhattan School, MMus, 1960; Juilliard School with Vencent Persichetti. Career: Played trumpet in the New York City Ballet Orchestra and for various New York bands; Composer-in-Residence at the University of Wisconsin, 1969; Director of Music for the city of Haifa, Israel, 1971-72; Music performed by major Israeli orchestras and dance companies; Chairman of the Music Department at Eastern Montane College, 1977-82; Professor of Composition at the Philadelphia College of the Performing Arts, 1982. Compositions: A Children's Opera, 1967; The Nothing Ballet, 1975; 3 Symphonies, 1966, 1971, 1978; Concerto for violin and strings, 1967; Interiors for violin and piano, 1970; Violin Sonata, 1970; And the World Goes On for percussion and ensemble, 1971; 3 Cantatas for chorus and organ, 1975; Triple Concerto, 1975; 5 Moods for obe, 1975; Percussion Trio, 1977; Echoes for chorus, clarinet and percussion, 1978; 5 Fragrances for clarinet, harp and percussion, 1980; When the Twain Meet for orchestra, 1981; Metamorphosis for piano, 1981; Southeast Fantasy for wind ensemble, 1982; Mobile for string quartet, 1982; Stars and Distances, spoken sounds and chorus, 1981; Meditation for a Lonely Flute, 1983; Kiddish Concerto for cello and strings, 1984; A/V Slide Show for trombone, 1984; Masada for chorus, clarinet and percussion, 1985. Publications include: The African Roots of Jazz, 1979. Address: c/o ASCAP, ASCAP Building, One Lincoln Plaza, NY 10023, USA.

KAUFMANN Julie, b. 25 May 1955, Iowa, USA. Singer (Soprano). Education: Studied at Iowa University, at the Zurich Opera Studio and at the Musikhochschule in Hamburg. Career: Sang at Hagen, then at Frankfurt as Oscar in Un Ballo in Maschera, Blondchen, and Norina; Appearances in Hamburg, Bonn, Stuttgart, Berlin, Salzburg and Dusseldorf; Bayerische Staatsoper Munich, 1983, as Despina, Sophie and Zdenka; Aminta in Schweigsame Frau; Covent Garden debut, 1984, as Zerlina in Don Giovanni; Gave the premiere of Udo Zimmermann's Gib Licht meiner Augen, 1986; Sang at the Salzburg and Wiesbaden Festivals, 1987, as Blondchen and Despina; Aminta in Die schweigsame Frau at the Munich Opera, 1988 (tour of Japan, 1988), Woglinde in the Ring, 1989 (also televised); Ludwigsburg Festival, 1989, as Susanna, and Carmina Burana at the 1990 Munich Festival; Sang Zdenka in Arabella at La Scala, 1992; Woglinde in Wagner's Ring at Paris Châtelet, 1994; World premiere of Manfred Trojahn's Frammenti di Michelangelo, 1995; Sang Atalanta in Handel's Serse at the 1996 Munich Festival. Recordings: Despina in Così fan tutte; Amor in Orfeo ed Euridice; Walther in La Wally; Woglinde in Das Rheingold, conducted by Haitink; Echo in Ariadne and Naxos, Schumann's Mignon Requiem and Mendelssohn's Lobgesang; Solo Recital CD with Schoenberg, Debussy, Strauss, 1993, with Irwin Gage; Rezia in Pilgrims from Mecca; Nannetta in Falstaff, with Colin Davis; Brahms Duette and Lieder with Marilyn Schmiege and Donald Sulzen; Beethoven Welsh, Scottish, Irish Songs with Neues Münchener Klavietrio. Honours: Bayrische Kammersängerin, 1991. Address: c/o Impresariat Sonia Simmenauer, Isestr 65, 20149 Hamburg, Germany.

KAVAFIAN Ani, b. 10 May 1948, Istanbul, Turkey. Voilinist; Teacher. Education: Pupil of Ara Zerounian, 1957-62, and Mischa Mischakoff, 1962-66, Detroit; Studied with Ivan Galamian and Felix Galimir, Juilliard School of Music, New York, MA, 1972. Debut: Carnegie Recital Hall, New York, 1969; European debut, Salle Gaveau, Paris, 1973. Career: Soloist with many major orchestras; Recitalist; Duo recitals with sister, Ida Kavafian; Artist-Member, Chamber Music Society of Lincoln Center, New York, 1980-; Teacher, Mannes College of Music, New York, 1982-, Manhattan School of Music, New York 1983, Queens College of the City University of New York, 1983-. Recordings: Discs as a recitalist and chamber music artist. Honours: Avery Fisher Prize, 1976. Address: c/o Herbert Barrett Management, 1776 Broadway, NY 10019, USA.

KAVAFIAN Ida, b. 29 Oct 1952, Istanbul, Turkey. Violinist. Education: Studied with Ara Zerounian and Mischa Mischakoff, Detroit and with Oscar Shumsky and Ivan Galamian, Juilliard School, New York, MA, 1975. Career: Founding Member of the chamber group Tashi, 1973; New York recital debut, 1978; European debut, London, 1982; Appearances in duo recitals with sister, Ani Kavafian; Violinist of the Beaux Arts Trio, appointed 1992. Recordings: Discs as a chamber music artist; RCA and Nonesuch. Honours: Winner, Vienna da Motta International Violin Competition, Lisbon, 1973; Silver Medal, International Violin Competition of Indianapolis, 1982; Avery Fisher Career Grant, 1988; Artistic Director of 2 Festivals, Music from Angel Fire, N M and Bravo! Colorado, Vail; Artist Member of Chamber Music Society of Lincoln Center. Current Management: Harry Bell. Address: c/i Beall Management, PO Box 30, Teneafly, NJ 07670, USA.

KAVAKOS Leonidas, b. 1967, Athens, Greece. Violinist. Education: Studied at the Greek Conservatory with Stelios Kafantaris; Further studies with Joseph Gingold at the University of Indiana. Debut: Athens Festival, 1984. Career: Cannes Festival, 1985; US debut with the Santa Barbara Symphony, 1986; Athens Festival 1988, conducted by Rostropovitch, leading to concerts with the National Symphony Orchestra in Washington DC; Concerts at the Helsinki Festival and with the Swedish Radio Symphony conducted by Esa-Pekka Salonen; European tour with the Helsinki Philharmonic conducted by Okku Kamu, 1989; Further appearances in Italy, Spain, France, Cyprus, Turkey, Hungary and Japan; TV and radio recordings in greece, France, Germany, Spain and England. Honours include: Winner, 1985 Sibelius Violin Competition, Indianapolis; 1986 International Competition; 1988 Winner, Naumburg Competition, New York; Winner 1988 Paganini Competition, Genoa. Address: c/o Ingpen & Williams Ltd, 26 Wadham Road, London SW15 2LR, England.

KAVRAKOS Dimitri, b. 26 Feb 1946, Athens, Greece. Singer (Bass). Education: Athens Conservatory of Music. Debut: Athens Opera 1970, as Zaccaria in Nabucco. Career: Athens Opera until 1978; US debut at Carnegie Hall, in Refice's Cecilia; Metropolitan Opera debut 1979, as the Grand Inquisitor in Don Carlos, returned to New York as Silva (Ernani), Walter (Luisa Miller), Ferrando (IL Trovatore), Capulet (Roméo et Juliette) and in I Vespri Siciliani; Chicago Lyric Opera in Aida, Lakmé, Les Contes d'Hoffmann and Fidelio; San Francisco Opera in La Gioconda; Guest engagements at La Scala, Paris Opera,

Aix-en-Provence, Spoleto, Lyons and Avignon; British debut Glyndebourne 1982, as the Commendatore in Don Giovanni; London debut at the Barbican Hall in Cherubini's Medée; Covent Garden debut 1984, as Pimen in Boris Godunov, returned in new productions of La Donna del Lago (Douglas 1985), Le nozze di Figaro (Bartolo) and Anna Bolena (Enrico VIII 1988); Rome Opera 1989, as Silva in Ernani, Bellini's Giorgio in Florence; Sang Fiesco in Simon Boccanegra at Cologne, 1990 and Prince Gremin in Eugene Onegin in Chicago; Maggio Musicale Florence, 1990 as Ernesto in Donizetti's Parisina; Season 1992-93 as Timur in Turandot at Chicago, Rossini's Mosè with the Israel Philharmonic, Banquo at Cologne and the Commendatore at Aix-en-Provence; Don Giovanni (Commendatore) and nozze di Figaro (Bartolo, Salzburg); I Puritani, Bregenz, 1985; Il barbiere di Siviglia, Florence, 1994; Paris Opera: Don Carlos and Puritani, 1987; Lucia, 1995; Lucrezia Borgia, Teatro San Carlo Napoli, 1992; La Vestale, La scala, 1993; Sang Banquo at Florence, 1995. Recordings include: Don Giovanni; La Vestale, La Scala, 1993; Rigoletto, La Scala, 1994; Ravenna Norma, 1994; Sonnambula by Nightingale. Address: c/o Patricia Greenan, 19B Belsize Park, London NW3 4DU, England.

KAWAHARA Yoko, b. 3 Sept 1939, Tokyo, Japan. Singer (Soprano). Education: Studied with Toishiko Toda in Tokyo and with Ellen Bosenius at the Cologne Musikhochschule. Debut: Niki Kai Opera Tokyo 1958, as Fiordilgi. Career: Sang in Bonn as Pamina, 1969; Bayreuth Festival 1972-77, as the Woodbird in Siegfried; Member of the Cologne Opera from 1975; Guest appearances in Frankfurt, Hamburg and Tokyo; Staatsoper Hamburg 1986, in La Clemenza di Tito; Other roles include Euridice, Sophie in Der Rosenkavalier, Desdemona, Freia and Liu; Many concert appearances. Recordings includ: Reger's Requiem (Schwann). Address: c/o Oper der Stadt Köln, Offenbachplatz, D-5000 Cologne, Germany.

KAWAHITO Makiko, b. 6 Sept 1956, Tokyo, Japan. Viola Player. m. Hideo Etani, 26 Oct 1986. Education: Master, Tokyo University of Arts, 1981; Master, Staatliche Musikhochschule, Freiburg, West Germany, 1983. Debut: Tokyo 1985. Career: String Quartet with Florin Paul in West Germany and Les Arc, France, 1982-84; Viola Concerto with Orchestra conducted by Yoko Matsuo in Besancon, France, 1984; Recital in Tokyo, 1985; String Chamber Ensemble with Tokyo Vivaldi Ensemble, 1980-; Radio Appearances on Japan and German Radio. Honours: 4th Prize,William Primrose International Viola Competition, USA, 1979. Memberships: Tokyo Vivaldi Ensemble. Hobby: Appreciation For Arts. Address: c/o KAWAHITO, 4-6-6 Fujimicho, Higashimurayama-shi, Tokyo, Japan.

KAWALLA Szymon (Piotr), b. 2 June 1949, Cracow, Poland. Conductor; Composer. m. Hanna Kiepuszewska, 28 Apr 1973, 1 daughter. Education: Studies as Solo Concert Violinist 1972, as Conductor 1973, as Composer 1974, Chopin Academy of Music, Warsaw. Debut: Philharmonic, Cracow, 1964. Career: Conductor, Philharmonic Poherien, 1974-78; Conductor-Director, Torun Chamber Orchestra, 1978-80; Conductor-Director, Philharmonic and Opera Zielona Gora, 1980-86; Symphonic Orchestra and Chorus, RTV Cracow, 1985-; Concerts in Austria, Bulgaria, Canada, Cuba, England, Germany, Holland, France, Italy, Poland, Romania, Spain, Czechoslovakia, Russia, Vatican, Radio, TV and Films; Professor, Chopin Academy of Music, Warsaw. Compositions: Divertimento, Capriccio for violin solo, Oratorio, Pater Kolbe, Cantata, Wit Stwosz, Stabat Mater, Quartet for Strings. Hobbies: Car Driving; Walking in the Mountains; Cooking. Address: Lazurowa 6/100, 01-315 Warsaw, Poland.

KAWASAKI Masaru, b. 19 Apr 1924, Tokyo, Japan. University Professor; Composer. m. Taeko Koide, 11 June 1953, 2 sons. Education: Diploma 1947, Postgraduate Diploma 1949, Tokyo Academy of Music. Career: 1st performance of Compos at Festliche Musiktage Uster, Switzerland, 1971, 1974, 1977, 1981; Director, International Youth Musicale, Shizuoka, Japan, 1979, 1982 and 1985. Compositions: March Ray of Hope, 1963; March Forward for Peace, 1966; Essay on a Day for flute and piano, 1969; March Progress and Harmony, 1969; Warabe-Uta for symphony band, 1970; Prayer Music Number 1, Dirge, commissioned by Hiroshima City, 1975; Poem for symphony band, 1976; Prayer Music Number 2, Elegy, 1977; Romantic Episode, 1979; Romance for trumpet and symphony band, 1982; March Dedicated to Cupid, 1983; In the Depth of Night for flute and cello, 1993. Publications: Instrumentation and Arrangement for Wind Ensemble, 1972; New Band Method, 1979. Contributions to: Band Journal, Tokyo. Honours: Composition Prize, Ministry of Education and President of NHK, 1956; Creative Artists Fellow, UNESCO, 1966-67. Memberships: International Society Contemporary Music; Japanese Society Rights Authors and Composers; National Band Association. Hbby: Gardening. Address: 4-2-38 Hamatake, Chigasaki-shi, Kanagawa-Ken 253, Japan.

KAY Donald (Henry), b. 25 Jan 1933, Smithton, Tasmania. Composer. Education: BMus, University of Melbourne, 1955; Study with Malcolm Williamson, 1959-64. Career: Faculty member, Tasmanian Conservatorium, 1967-; Commissions from APRA, Lyrian String Quartet, Tasmanian Symphony Chamber Players, and others. Compositions include: Dance Movement for small orchestra, 1968; Four Australian Folk Songs, for women's or young voices, 1971; The Quest, for string quartet, 1971; There is an Island, for children's choir and orchestra, 1977; The Golden Crane, opera for children and adults, 1984; Dance Cameos, for ensemble, 1986; Hastings Triptych, for flute and piano, 1986; Northward the Strait, for chorus, soprano, baritone and wind band, 1988; Tasmania Symphony: The Legend of Moinee, for cello and orchestra, 1988; Haiku, for women's voices, piano and string quartet, 1990; Night Spaces, for flute, string trio and piano, 1990; Piano Concerto, 1992. Honours include: Sounds Australian Awards, 1989, 1990. Address: c/o APRA, 1A Eden Street, Crows Nest, NSW 2065, Australia.

KAY Norman (Forber), b. 5 Jan 1929, Bolton, England. Composer; Music Director. m. 22 Jan 1951, 3 sons, 1 daughter. Education: Bolton School, 1940-45; ARMCM, Organ, Composition, 1947; ARCO, 1947; Royal Manchester College of Music; Royal College of Music, London. Career: Composer-Critic, London, 1950-76; Music Director, HTV, 1976-85; Music critic, Daily Telegraph, 1964-81; Music Consultant to numerous independent television companies, 1989-91. |Compositions: Miniature Quartet for Woodwind, 1950; String Quartets 1 and 2; Passacaglia for Orchestra, Cheltenham Festival, 1966; Variations for Strings, Harrogate Festival, 1968; King Herod, Cantata, Soloists, CHorus, Orchestra, Llandaff Festival, 1966; 3 Choirs Festival, 1967; Song Without Words, BBC Television; Rose Affair, Opera, BBC television, 1968; Xmas Carol, television opera; Robin Hood, Opera for Young People, Buxton Festival, 1986; Daniel, full-scale cantata, St David's Hall, Cardiff starring Sir Geraint Evans, 1988; Piano trio, Howard Shelley, BBC Radio 3. Publications: Shostakovich, 1971. Contributions to: Articles and reviews to Musical Times, Music and Musicians, Tempo, Times LIterary and Educational Reviews. Honours: Italia Prize, 1967; Salzburg Television Opera Prize, 1980. Membership: Savile Club, London. Current Management: Polygram Limited. Address: Summerhouse, St DOnats, Llantwit Major, South Glamorgan CF61 1ZB, Wales.

KAZARAS Peter, b. 1956, New York, USA. Tenor Singer. Debut: New York in 1981 in a concert performance of Khovanshchina. Career: Houston in 1983 as Francois in the premiere of Bernstein's A Quiet Place; Santa Fe and Seattle in 1985 in Henze's English Cat and as Steva in Jenufa; Returned to Seattle as Wagner's Froh and Erik, Hoffmann, Lensky and Pierre in War and Peace; New York City Opera debut in 1988 as Quint in The Turn of The Screw; Sang with Metropolitan Opera from 1990 as Narraboth in Salome, Shuisky in Boris Godunov and Almaviva in the premiere of Corigliano's The Ghosts of Versailles; Other modern repertory includes Udo Zimmermann's Die Weisse Rose, at Omaha in 1986, Pelegrin in the premiere of Tippett's New Year, at Houston in 1989, and Busoni's Die Brautwahl at Berlin Staatsoper in 1991; Sang Boris in the New Zealand premiere of Katya Kabanova, 1996. Address: c/o Metropolitan Opera, Lincoln Center, New York, NY 10023, USA.

KAZARNOVSKAYA Lyubov, b. 1956, Moscow, Russia. Singer (Soprano). Education: Studied at the Moscow Conservatory 1976-81, with Irina Arkhipova and Elena Shumilova. Debut: Stanislavsky Theatre Moscow 1981, as Tatiana in Eugene Onegin. Career: Has sung at the Bolshoi, Moscow, as Nedda Mimi and Lida in La Battaglia di Legnano; Tour of Italy with the Maily Theatre, Leningrad, 1984; Kirov Theatre, Leningrad from 1986 as Leonora (La Forza del Destino and Trovatore), Marina, Violetta, Marguerite, Donna Anna and Tchaikovsky's Iolanta; Paris Opera and Covent Garden 1987, as Tatiana with the Kirov Company; Salzburg Festival 1989, in the Verdi Requiem, conducted by Karajan; Zurich Opera 1989-90, as Amelia Boccanegra and the Trovatore Leonora; Cologne Opera 1989-90, as Manon Lescaut and Amelia; Covent Garden 1990, as Desdemona; Concert and oratorio appearances, song recitals with works by Brahms, Wolf, de Falla, Dvorak and Rachmaninov; Sang Pauline in The Gambler by Prokofiev with the Kirov Company in Paris and at La Scala, 1996.

KEATING Roderic (Maurice), b. 14 Dec 1941, Maidenhead, Berkshire, England. Opera and Concert Singer (Tenor). m. Martha Kathryn Post, 31 Aug 1968, 1 d. Education: Classics Exhibition, Gonville and Caius College, Cambridge, 1960; BA, Music Tripos, 1963, MA, 1967, Cambridge University; MMus, Yale University, USA, 1965; Doctor of Musical Arts, University of TX, USA, 1970. Debut: Houston Grand Opera, Tales of Hoffmann, 1970. Career: Glyndebourne Touring and Festival Opera, 1971-73; Theater an der Wien, Freddy, My Fair Lady, 1971; Permanent contracts in: Lübeck, 1972-74, Saarbrücken, 1974-80, Wuppertal, 1980-86, Bonn, 1986-89, Stuttgart, 1989-; Over 80 roles as lyric and buffo tenor; Guest throughout Germany; Guest appearances: Tbilisi, Russia, 1976, Interlaken Festspiel, 1975, Wiesbaden, 1977, Paris Opera, 1981, London Coliseum, 1982, Warsaw, 1983, Cologne, 1985, Salzburg Festival, 1986, Covent Garden, 1988, Moscow, 1989, Vienna and

Schwetzingen Festivals, 1990; Sang Tiresias in Henze's The Bassarids at Stuttgart, 1989; Der Rosenkavalier, Théâtre Châtelet, Paris, 1993 and Bologna, 1995; Weill's Seven Deadly Sins, Tel Aviv, 1997; Concerts and radio recordings for BBC, Bavarian Radio, and SWF, WDR, SDR in Germany; Oratorio and church concerts in: Italy, France, Spain, Belgium, Holland, Germany. Publications: The Songs of Frank Bridge, 1970. Contributions to: Musical Times; Musical Opinion. Hobbies: Tennis; Photography; Cross Country Skiing. Current Management: Werner Kühnly, Wörthstr 31, 70563 Stuttgart, Germany. Address: Lehenbühlstrasse 36, 71272 Renningen, Germany.

KEATS Donald (Howard), b. 27 May 1929, New York City, New York, USA. Composer; Professor. m. Eleanor Steinholz, 13 Dec 1953, 2 sons, 2 daughters. Education: MusB primi honoris, Yale University School of Music, 1949; MA, Columbia University, 1952; Staatliche Hochschule für Musik, Hamburg, 1954-56; PhD, University of Minnesota. Career includes: Professor of Music, Antioch College, Ohio; Visiting Professor of Music, University of Washington, Seattle; Professor of Music, University of Denver, Colorado, 1975-; Composer, Pianist, at concerts in USA, England and Israel. Compositions include: Symphonies No 1 and No 2 (An Elegiac Symphony); String Quartets No 1 and No 2; Piano Sonata The Hollow Men (T S Eliot), for chorus and instruments; Anyone Lived in a Pretty How Town (Cummings), for a cappella chorus; The Naming of Cats (T S Eliot), for chorus and piano; Tierras del Alma (Poemas de amor), song cycle for soprano, flute and guitar; Theme and Variations for Piano; Concerto for Piano and Orchestra; Diptych for cello and piano; Polarities for violin and piano; A Love Triptych (W B Yeats), song cycle; Musica instrumentalis for 9 instruments; Elegy for full or chamber orchestra; Branchings for orchestra; Revisitations for violin, cello and piano, 1992. Recordings: String Quartets No 1 and No 2; Piano Sonata; Elegy for Orchestra; The Hollow Men; Anyone Lived in a Pretty How Town. Address: School of Music, University of Denver, 7111 Montview, Denver, CO 80220, USA.

KEBERLE David (Scott), b. 6 June 1952, Wausau, Wisconsin, USA. Composer; Clarinettist; College Professor. Education: BM, Composition, with distinction, Indiana University, 1975; BM, Education, with distinction, Indiana University, 1975; MMus, Composition, New England Conservatory of Music, Boston, 1977; Accademia di S Cecilia, Rome, 1980; Studied composition with Bernhard Heiden and Donald Martino, clarinet with Earl Bates, Joe Allard and W O Smith. Career: Instructor of Music, University of Wisconsin, Baraboo, 1977-81; Co-Founder of Electravox Ensemble, Rome, 1983; Instructor of Music, Loyola University, Chicago, Rome Centre, 1984-88; As Clarinet Soloist, performed in Brazil, Uruguay, Argentina, France, Italy, Israel, Austria and USA; Performed on National Italian Radio, 1987, 1988; Instructor of Music, St Mary's College, Rome Program, 1991-. Compositions: Incantation for clarinet and live electronics, published by EDI-PAN Rome, 1986; Galoppando Attraverso il Vuoto for solo clarinet 1986, published by EDI-PAN Rome; Concerto for Trumpet and Chamber Ensemble, 1980, published by EDI-PAN Rome; Murmurs for solo flute, published by EDI-PAN Rome, 1989. Recordings: ElectraVox Ensemble Incantation for Clarinet and Live Electronics 1986, EDI-PAN Rome; Musicisti Contemporanei Clarinet and Piano EDI-PAN, 1989. Honour: Fulbirght Scholarship in Composition, 1979. Memberships: American Music Center, New York. Address: Via del Pellegrino 75, Int 18, 00186 Rome, Italy.

KECHABIAN Rafael, b. 14 Feb 1949, Yerevan, Armenia. Violinist; Concert Performer; Professor of Violin. m. Irene Kechabian, 25 Mar 1978, 2 sons. Education: Special Musical School and Musical Secondary School, Sukhumi, 1957; State Yerevan Conservatory, Armenia, 1969; Postgraduate Course, State Yerevan Conservatory, Armenia, 1989-92; Diploma Violinist, Concert Performer, Professor of Violin and Chamber Music. Career: Professor of Violin, Yerevan Music School, Armenia, 1970-83; Concertino, National Symphony Orchestra, Nicaragua, 1983-87; Professor of Violin, National Conservatory, Nicaragua, 1983-87; Soloist, State Chamber Ensemble of Armenia, 1987-93; Professor of Chamber Music, State Yerevan Conservatory, Armenia, 1987-93; Principal of the second violins, Symphony Orchestra of the Murcian Region, Spain, 1993-94; Professor of Violin, Musical Academy, Murcia, Spain, 1995; Violin Maker, Murcia, Spain, 1995. Recordings: Violinist, over 30 titles including: first recording of classical music in history of Nicaragua with National Symphony Orchestra, Miami, USA, 1984; Violinist, joint recordings with Orchestra Moscow Virtuosos of Spivakov, Moscow, 1983. Honour: Diploma, Ministry of Culture of the Republic of Nicaragua, 1987. Hobbies: Painting; Chess. Address: c/o Mariano Aroca, 7-4 1zq, 30011 Murcia, Spain.

KECSKEMÉTI István, b. 21 Dec 1920, Budapest, Hungary. Musicologist. Education: Doctor in Economics, Budapest University, 1945; Graduate, Pianist, 1943, Musicologist, 1957, Academy of Music, Budapest. Career: Dissertation on Mozart's Salzburg Piano Concertos, 1957; Librarian, Head of Music Division, National Széchényi Library, Budapest, 1957-81;

Arranger of exhibitions in Hungary and Austria on Haydn and minor classical masters, Dohnányi and Kodály, 1970-80; Analysing the music autographs of Z Kodály, Kodály Archives, Budapest, 1981-. Publications: Kodály, The Composer, Budapest, 1986; Images of Handwriting in Kodály's early music autographs in Bulletin of The International Kodály Society, 1988-89; Discoverer and Editor of Autographs by J J Fux, Süssmayr, Schubert, Liszt and has prepared thematic catalogues of the Süssmayr and Dittersdorf manuscripts of the Hungarian National Library; Stylistic studies on the music of Mozart, Chopin, Liszt, Goldmark and Kodály; Z Kodály's Compositions, Pecularities of a Thematic Catalogue, 1992. Honour: Erkel Prize, 1976. Address: PF14, H-1400 Budapest, Hungary.

KEE Piet, b. 30 August 1927, Zaandam, Netherlands. Organist; Composer. 2 children. Education: Studied with father, Cor Kee; Organ with Anthon van de Horst, Final Certificate cum laude, 1948, Conservatoire of Amsterdam. Debut: Zaandam, 1941. Career: Organist of Schnitgerorgan, St Laurens Church, Alkmaar, 1952-87; Municipal Organist, St Bavo Church, Haarlem, 1956-89; Professor of Organ, Conservatoire of the Society Muzieklyceum, Sweelinck Conservatoire, Amsterdam, until 1987; Professor, International Summer Academy, Haarlem; Many concert tours worldwide; TV films of compositions Confrontation and Integration. Compositions: Variations on a Carol, 1954; Triptych on Psalm 86, 1960; Two Organ Works, 1962; Four Manual Pieces, 1966; Music and Space for 2 Organs and 5 Brasswinds, 1969; Intrada for 2 Organs; Chamber Music; Valerius Gedencklanck, 1976; Confrontation for 3 street organs and church organ, 1979; Integration for mixed choir, flageolet, mechanical birds, barrel organs and church organ, 1980; Frans Hals Suite for Carillon, 1990; Flight for flute solo, 1992; Bios for organ, 1994; Network for 2 organs, electronic keyboard, alto saxophone and descant recorder, 1996; Op-streek, for violin and piano, 1997. Recordings include: Baroque music, romantic and modern music; New series of CDs including Bach organ works (4 volumes); Franck organworks (San Sabastian); Piet Kee at Weingarten; Piet Kee at the Concertgebouw; Piet Kee plays Sweelinck; Piet Kee plays Brahms. Publications: The Secrets of Bach's Passacaglia, Musik und Kirche, 1982; The Diapason, 1983; Astronomy in Buxtehude's Passacaglia, The Diapason, Ars Organi, Het Orgel, 1984; Numbers and Symbolism in the Passacaglia and theCiacona, Het Orgel, 1986; Musik und Kirche, 1987; Loosemore Papers. Honours: Prix d'Excellence and Jubilee Prize, Maatschappij Toonkunst; 1st Prize, International Improvisation Concours, Haarlem, 1953, 1954. 1955; Awarded Bach Medal of the Harriet Cohen Foundation, London, for English Bach concerts, 1958; Honorary Fellow, Royal College of Organists, 1988; Knight in the Order of Oranje-Nassau. Hobbies: Ornithology; History. Address: Nieuwe Gracht 41, 2011 ND Haarlem, Netherlands.

KEEFFE Bernard, b. 1 Apr 1925, London, England. Conductor; Broadcaster. m. Denise Walker, 10 Sept 1954, 1 son, 1 daughter. Education: BA Honours, Clare College, Cambridge, 1951; Private studies: Cello with Di Marco, Voice with Roy Henderson and Lucie Manen, Conducting with Berthold Goldschmidt. Career includes: Appearances as solo baritone in opera, concerts, musical plays (London, Edinburgh Festival); Producer and Conductor, 1955-60, Head of Radio Opera, 1959, BBC Music Department; Controller of Opera Planning, Royal Opera House, London, 1960-62; Conductor, BBC Scottish Orchestra, 1962-64; Many appearances on BBC TV as Commentator and Conductor; Concerts and broadcasts with major orchestras; Chief Conductor, Bournemouth Municipal Choir, 1972-81; Professor, Trinity College of Music, 1966-89; Many engagements as international jurist for various competitions including Italia Prize for Broadcasting, Anvers, Liège, Sofia, London. Recordings: L'Oiseau-Lyre, as conductor with Melos Ensemble and Janet Baker; Music of Ravel and Delage. Publications: English National Opera Guide to Tosca; Harraps Dictionary of Music and Musicians (editor); Authorised translations: Janácek, Diary of One Who Disappeared; Petrassi, Death in the Air. Contributions to: BBC Music Magazine, World Service; Hi-Fi News; Music Teacher; Classical Music Fortnightly. Honours: Honorary Fellow, Trinity College, London, 1968. Memberships: Former Warden, Solo Performers Section, Incorporated Society of Musicians; Executive Committee, Anglo-Austrian Music Society. Hobbies: Photography; Languages. Address: 153 Honor Oak Road, London SE23 3RN, England.

KEEGAN Liane, b. 1968, Australia. Singer (Mezzo-soprano). Education: National Opera Studio, London, Graz Summer School and Bayreuth. Career: Appearances as Suzuki in Butterfly for Opera North (1996) Barbara in Korngold's Violanta at the 1997 London Proms and Waltraute in Act III of Die Walküre at the 1997 Edinburgh Festival; Other roles include Charlotte, Dalila, Ulrica, Mistress Quickly, Dorabella and Rosina; Recitals throughout Britain and in France and Austria; Concerts include Mahler's Lieder eines fahren den Gesellen, Das Lied von der Erde, Symphonies 2 and 3; Elijah, The Dream of Gerontius, Verdi Requiem, the Wesendoncklieder and Elgar's Sea Pictures; Schubert documentary on German TV, 1995 Engaged as Erda and First Norn in Der Ring des Nibelungen for the State Opera of South Australia, 1998. Address: C&M Craig Services Ltd, 3 Kersley Street, London SW11 4PR, England.

KEENLYSIDE Raymond, b. 9 May 1928, Southsea, Hampshire, England. Musician; Violinist. m. Cynthia J Page, 2 sons, 1 daughter. Education: Trinity College of Music, London. Career: Principal of Chamber Orchestras including: Boyd Neel; Philomusica; English Chamber Orchestra; Academy of St Martin-in-the-Fields; member of London Harpsichord Ensemble, 1959-62; David Martin String Quartet; Aeolian String Quartet, 1962-81; Professor of Violin, Royal College of Music; Senior Tutor, Royal College of Music Junior Department; Numerous radio appearances; Series on BBC Television of late Beethoven String Quartets; Other television appearances. recordings: Complete Haydn String Quartets, reissued, 1997; Works by Schubert, Mozart, Elgar, Vaughan Williams, Ravel, Debussy, all with the Aeolian Quartet; Others with other groups. Contributions to: Daily Telegraph Magazine. Honours: LTCL (TTD); Honorary MA, Newcastle University, 1970; Honorary FTCL, 1983; Honorary FRCM. Hobbies: Fly Fishing; Watercolour painting; Reading; Beekeeping; Gardening; Birdwatching. Address: Bailiwick, Upper Woodford, Salisbury, Wiltshire SP4 6PF, England.

KEENLYSIDE Simon, b. 3 Aug 1959, London, England. Singer (Baritone). Education: Studied at the Royal Northern College of Music. Career: Gave concert performances, then engaged with Scottish Opera as Papageno and Billy Budd; Season 1994-95 as Mozart's Count and Guglielmo at Covent Garden, Hamlet in the opera by Thomas at Geneva; Sang Guglielmo at the reopened Palais Garnier, Paris, 1996 and Thomas's Hamlet in Geneva; also sings lieder by Schubert; Concerts include Britten's War Requiem at the Festival Hall (CBSO, 1997); Engaged as Marcello and Figaro at the Vienna State Opera, 1999. Honours include: Winner, Richard Tauber Competition, 1986. Address: c/o Askonas Ltd, 6 Henrietta Street, London, WC2.

KEHL Sigrid, b. 23 Nov 1932, Berlin, Germany. Singer (Soprano and Mezzo-Soprano). Education: Studied in Erfurt, at the Berlin Musikhochschule and with Dagmar Freiwald-Lange. Debut: Berlin Staatsoper 1956, in Prince Igor. Career: Member of the Leipzig Opera from 1957, notably as Brünnhilde in Der Ring des Nibelungen, 1974; Engagements at the Berlin Staatsoper from 1971, Vienna Staatsoper from 1975; Further appearances at the Komische Oper Berlin and in Prague, Bucharest, Rome, Bologna, Geneva, Warsaw and Basle; Lausanne Festival 1983, as Isolde.

KEKULA Josef, b. 1952, Czechoslovakia. Violinist. Education: Studied with Václav Snítil and members of Smetana Quartet, Kostecky and Kohout. Career: Co-founder and 2nd Violinist, Stamic Quartet of Prague, 1977; Performances at Prague Young Artists and Bratislava Music Festivals; Tours to: Spain, Austria, France, Switzerland, Germany, Eastern Europe; USA tour, 1980; Debut concerts in Britain at London and Birmingham, 1983; British tours, 1985, 1987, 1988 at Warwick Arts Festival, 20 concerts in 1989; Season 1991-92: Channel Islands, Holland, Finland, Austria, France, Edinburgh Festival, Debut tours of Canada, Japan and Indonesia; In 1994 visited Korea and Japan; In 1995 visited USA. Recordings: Shostakovich No 13; Schnittke No 4 Panton; Mozart K589 and K370, Lyrinx; Dvorák; Martinu; Janácek complete quartets, Cadenza; Complete Dvorák String Quartets; Complete Martinu String Quartets; 1 CD, Clarinet Quintets by Mozart and Krommer. Publications: Complete Works of Smetana and Janácek String Quartet. Honours: With members of Stamic Quartet: Winner, International Festival of Young Soloists, Bordeaux, 1977, Winner, EBU International String Quartet Competition, 1986, Academie Charles Cros Grand Prix du Disque, 1989 for Dvorák Quartets, 1991 for Martinu Quartets; Diapason d'Or, 1994 for Dvorák Quintets. Current Management: Robert Gilder and Co. Address: c/o Robert Gilder and Co, Enterprise House, 59-65 Upper Ground, London, SE1 9PQ, England.

KELEMEN Milko, b. 30 Mar 1924, Slatina, Croatia. Composer. Education: Studies, Zagreb Academy of Music and with Messiaen and Aubin, Paris; Further study with Wolfgang Fortner, Freiburg, also Siemens Electronic Music Studio, Munich. Career: Taught Composition, Zagreb Conservatory, 1955-58, 1960-65; Founder, Zagreb Biennial Festival, President, 1961; Taught, Schumann Conservatory, Düsseldorf, 1972; Professor of Composition, Hochschule für Musik, Stuttgart, 1973. Compositions include: The Abandoned, ballet, 1964; O Primavera, tenor, strings, 1965; Words, cantata, 1966; Composé, 2 pianos, orchestra, 1967; Changeant, cello, orchestra, 1968; Motion, string quartet, 1969; The Siege, opera after Camus, 1970; Floreal, orchestra, 1970; Varia Melodia, string quartet, 1972; Gasho, 4 choir groups, 1974; Seven Agonies, mezzo, 1975; Mageia, orchestra, 1978; Apocalypse, ballet opera, 1979; Grand Jeu Classique, violin, orchestra, 1982; Love Song, strings, 1984; Dramatico, cello, orchestra, 1985; Fantasmus, viola, orchestra, 1986; Archetypon, orchestra, 1986; Landscapes, mezzo, string quartet, 1986; Memories, string trio, 1987; Sonnets, string quartet, 1987; Nonet, 1988; Requiem, speaker, ensemble, 1994; Salut au Monde, oratorio, soloists, 2 choruses, orchestra, projections, light actions, text Walt Whitman, 1995; To You, for big orchestra; Concerto for Oboe, English Horn, Oboe D'Amore and chamber orchestra; Good Bye My Fancy for violin and piano. Recordings: Various labels. Publications: Klanglabyrinthe, 1981, French, 1985, Croatian, 1994; Poruka Pateru Kolbu, 1995; Klangwelten, 1995, English, 1995. Contributions to: Over 120 articles to German, French, Italian, Croatian, US, Hungarian and other publications. Honours include: Beethoven Prize, Germany, 1961; Simc Prize, Italy, 1965; Federal Service Cross, Germany; Chevalier des Arts et des Lettres, France; Bernhard Sprengel-Preis, 1969; Vladimir Nazor Prize, 1986; Lisinski Prize, Croatia, 1994; Marko Marulic, Croatian (Service) Cross, 1996. Memberships: GEMA; Drustvo Skladatelia Hrvatske; Academy of Science and Arts, Zagreb; Heinrich Schütz Gesellschaft. Hobbies: Philosphy; Travel; Photography. Address: Bergstrasse 62/II, 70186 Stuttgart, Germany.

KELLER Andras, b. 1960, Hungary. Violinist. Education: Studied at the Franz Liszt Academy, Budapest and with Sandor Devich, György Kurtag and Andras Mihaly. Career: Member of the Keller String Quartet from 1986, debut concert at Budapest March 1987; Played Beethoven's Grosse Fuge and Schubert's Death and the Maiden Quartet at Interforum 87; Series of concerts in Budapest with Zoltan Kocsis and Deszõ Ranki (Piano) and Kalman Berkes (Clarinet); Further appearances in Nuremberg, at the Chamber Music Festival La Baule and tours of Bulgaria, Austria, Switzerland, Italy (Ateforum 88 Ferrara), Belgium and Ireland; Concerts for Hungarian Radio and Television. Recordings: Albums for Hungaroton (from 1989). Honour: 2nd Prize, Evian International String Quartet Competition, May 1988. Address: c/o Artist Management International, 12/13 Richmond Buildings, Dean Street, London W1V 5AF, England.

KELLER Heinrich, b. 14 Nov 1940, Winterhur, Switzerland. Flautist; Composer. m. 14 June 1968, 3 sons. Education: Conservatory, Zurich, 1961-65. Debut: 1965. Career: Philharmony, Bremen, 1965-66; Orchestra of St Gallen, 1967-72; Musikkollegium Winterthur, solo Flautist, 1972-. Compositions: Aleph, 1966; Blaserquintett, 1972; Puzzle, 1973; Streichquartett, 1973-74; Reduktion, 1974; Refrains, 1975; Ritual, 1979; Rencontre, flute and harpsichord, 1985. Recordings: Flotenmusik aus Frankreich & Italien; Schubert, ihr Blumlein; Baroque & Rokoko, Flute music. Honour: Prize for composing String Quartet, Tonhalle, Zurich, 1974. Membership: Schweizerischer Tonkunstlerverein. Hobby: Private Concerts, Musica riservata. Address: Gruzenstrasse 14, CH-8400 Winterthur, Switzerland.

KELLER Helen, b. 5 Mar 1945, Horgen, Zurich, Switzerland. Singer (Soprano). Education: Studied in Zurich and with Agnes Giebel in Cologne. Career: Concert performances in Switzerland and elsewhere from 1971 with a repertoire including Rossini's Stabat Mater, L'Enfance du Christ, Schöpfung and Jahreszeiten, Elijah and St Paul, works by Bach and Handel and Honegger's Roi David; Appearances at Amsterdam, Antwerp, Paris, Milan, Annsbach, Karlsruhe and the USA in Britten, Brahms, Schubert, Monteverdi, Pergolesi, Vivaldi and Schumann; Stage engagements as Salome in San Giovanni Battista by Stradella at St Gallen and in Le Convenzione Teatrali by Donizetti at Zurich. Recordings: Messiah, Schubert's Mass in G and San Giovanni Battista. Address: c/o Peter Keller, Opernhaus Zurich, Falkenstrasse 1, CH-8008 Zurich, Switzerland.

KELLER Kjell, b. 25 May 1942, Wilderswil, Switzerland. Musician; Musicologist; Composer. m. 25 Mar 1977, 2 s, 1 d. Education: DPhil, Musicology, University of Berne, 1974; Konservatorium Berne. Career: Assistant, Musikwissenschaftliches Seminar at University of Berne, 1972-76; Producer of New Music and Ethnomusicology, Swiss Broadcasting Corporation, radio and television, 1976-; University Teacher at Berne, 1991. Compositions: Numerous Lieder, 1981-; Worte und Klänge zu Bruder Klaus, 1987; Wie den Menschen Flügel Wachsen, 1989; Unter dem Schwarzen Regenbogen, 1990-92. Recordings: Worte und Klänge zu Bruder Klaus, 1988; Numerous lieder. Publications: Aspekte der Musik von Klaus Huber, 1976; Musik Dossier Urs Peter Schneider, 1988. Contributions to: Neue Musik und ihre Vermittlung, 1986; Numerous articles, various reviews in Switzerland and Germany. Honour: Zurcher Radiopreis, 1981. Membership: Arts Council of Switzerland Pro Helvetia.

KELLER Peter, b. 16 Mar 1945, Thurgau, Switzerland. Singer (Tenor). m. Helen Keller. Education: Studied in Zurich, with Ernst Haefliger in Berlin and Agne Giebel in Cologne. Career: Has sung at the Zurich Opera from 1973, notably in the Monteverdi series and as Pedrillo, Monostatos, Jacquino, Wagner's David and Steuermann, Valzacchi in Rosenkavalier and M Triquet in Eugene Onegin (1991); Guest engagements at Munich, Hamburg, Dusseldorf (Edgar in Reimann's Lear), Milan, Edinburgh, Berlin and Vienna; Concert singer in Europe and on tour with Helen Keller in the USA; Sang in Puccini's Trittico at Zurich, 1996. Recordings include: Die Zauberflöte, Il Ritorno di Ulisse and

Monteverdi's Orfeo; Diary of One who Disappeared by Janacek; Handel's Israel in Egypt and Mendelssohn's Christus; Zemlinsky's Kleider Machen Leute. Address: c/o Peter Keller, Opernhaus Zurich, Falkenstrasse 1, CH-8008 Zurich, Switzerland.

KELLER Verena, b. 8 Sept 1942, Schwerin, Germany. Singer (Mezzo-soprano). Education: Studied in Vienna with Hans Hotter and in Berlin; Leider with Erik Werba. Career: Engaged at Hanover 1963-66, Bonn 1979-88, Mainz 1983-86; Guest appearances at Cologne, Geneva, Naples, Herrenhausen and Gottingen; Roles have included Mozart's Ramiro, Carmen, Santuzza, Ortrud, Brangaene, Kundry, Venus, Fricka; Verdi's Amneris, Azucena and Ulrica, Strauss's Clytemnestra and Herodias, Janacek's Kabanicha and the Witch in Hansel and Gretel; Concert engagements in Baroque music throughout Germany and in Paris, Rome, Los Angles and Vancouver. Recordings include: Dvorak's Mass in D. Address: Staatstheater, Gutenbergplatz 7, 6500 Mainz, Germany.

KELLOGG Cal (Stewart), b. 26 July 1947, Long Beach, CA, USA. Conductor; Composer. Education: Conservatorio di Musica Santa Cecilia, Rome, Diplomas in Basson, Composition and Conducting. Debut: Symphonic: Monte Carlo, 1975; Opera: Rome Opera, 1976. Career: As Bassoonist, Toured with Renato Fasano's Piccola Teatro Musicale di Roma, 1967-72; Soloist with RAI Orchestra of Rome, 1972; Conductor of Symphonic Concerts with Baltimore Symphony, New World Symphony, Monte Carlo, Accademia Nazionale di Santa Cecilia, Maggio Fiorentino, La Fenice, San Carlo, RAI Orchestras of Rome, Torino and Naples, Antwerp Philharmonic, Spoleto Festival Orchestra, Orchestra of Illinois, Seattle Symphony, Israel Sinfonietta of Beersheva; Director of Opera at Rome Opera, Teatro Communale di Firenze, San Francisco Opera, San Carlo, Teatro Reggio di Parma, NYC Opera, Santa Fe, Washington Opera, St Louis, Houston Grand Opera, Canadian Opera Company, Opera Montreal, Seattle Opera, Edinburgh Opera Festival, Israel Festival, Spoleto Festival, Chautauqua Festival PBS TV live from Lincoln Center, New York City Opera production of Menotti's The Saint of Bleecker Street; Radio broadcasts of Tosca, 1978, Houston Grand Opera, Ballo in Maschera, 1981, Canadian Opera Company, Il Trovatore, 1984 and Macbeth, 1986. Compositions: Sullivan Ballou's Letter to his Wife for Bass Baritone and Orchestra, a setting of a Civil War letter, 1990. Recordings: Thomas Pasatieri: Three Sisters, opera in 2 acts, 1986. Current Management: Trawick Artists Management. Address: 129 West 72nd Street, New York, NY 19924, USA.

KELLY Bryan, b. 3 Jan 1934, Oxford, England. Composer; Pianist; Conductor. Education: Royal College of Music 1951-55, with Gordon Jacob and Herbert Howells; Paris with Boulanger. Career: Has taught at the Royal Scottish Academy of Music; Professor of Composition, Royal College of Music, 1962-84; Resident at Castiglione del Lago, Italy, 1984-. Compositions: Orchestral: The Tempest Suite, for strings, 1964; Cookham Concertino, 1969; Divertimento for brass band, 1969; Oboe Concerto, 1972; Edinburgh Dances for Brass Band, 1973; Guitar Concerto, 1978; Andalucia and Concertante Music or Brass, 1976, 1979; 2 Symphonies, 1983, 1986; Vocal: Tenebrare Nocturnes for tenor, chorus and orchestra, 1965; Magnificat and Nunc Dimittis for chorus and organ, 1965; The Shield of Achilles for tenor and orchestra, 1966; Sleep little Baby, carol, 1968; Stabat Mater, 1970; At the Round Earth's Imagin'd Corners for tenor, chorus and strings, 1972; Abingdon Carols, 1973; Let There Be Light for soprano, narrator, chorus and orchestra, 1973; Latin Magnificat, 1979; Te Deum and Jubilate for chorus and organ, 1979; Piano Sonata, 1971; Prelude and fugue for organ, 1960; Pastorale and Paen for organ, 1973; Chamber music; Children's Pieces: Herod to your Worst, nativity opera, 1968; On Christmas Eve, suite of carols, 1968; The Spider Monkey Uncle King, opera pantomime, 1971. Recordings: The Choral Music of Bryan Kelly, Abbey Records. Hobby: Cookig. Address: c/o Novello & Co, 8 Lower James Street, London WC1, England.

KELLY Denise, b. 24 Apr 1954, Belfast, Northern Ireland. Composer. Education: Studied at the Royal Irish Academy and studied harp in London with Sidonie Goossens. Compositions include: Helas Mon Dieu for Mezzo, Flute and Harp, 1974; Journey Of A Soul, settings of Joyce for Voice and Harp, 1977; Dialogue To Unity for Flute, Harp and String Quartet, 1978; Idle Dreams for Mezzo, Flute and Harp, 1980; Soundings for Cello and Harp, 1984. Address: c/o British Music Information Centre, 10 Stratford Place, London W1N 9AE, England.

KELLY Frances, b. 1955, England. Harpist. Career: Regular performances with the New London Consort in medieval and renaissance music; Has toured in Europe and the Far East; Early Music Network tours in Britain 1986 and 1988; Freelance engagements with the Consort of Musicke, and the Gabrieli Consort and Players Recitals with soprano Evelyn Tubb; On modern harp was member of the Ondine Ensemble, giving performances in Britain and the USA; Partnership with the flautist Ingrid Culliford from 1977; BBC Recital with tenor Ian Partridge; Concerto soloist in the premieres of Edward Cowie's Concerto in

Newcastle and London and for Tyne Tees Television; Season 1988 included Debussy and Ravel with the Lindsay Quartet, chamber music by Bruch for the BBC and concerts in London, Denmark, Bruges and Utrecht as continuo player with the Consort of Musicke; South Bank Summer Music Festival with the New London Consort; Played in Oswald von Wolkenstein concert, 1997. Recordings include: Debussy's Trio Sonata with the Athena Ensemble: Debussy's Trio Sonata with the Athena Ensemble; Britten's A Ceremony of Carols with the Choir of Christ Church Cathedral, Oxford; Mozart's Concerto K299 with the Academy of Ancient Music; Solo, Harp collection, (Amon Ra). Address: South Bank Centre, Press Ofice, London, SE1, England.

KELLY Janis, b. 1955, Glasgow, Scotland. Singer (Soprano). Education: Studied at Royal Scottish Academy of Music, the Royal College of Music and in Paris. Career: Represented Britain at the UNESCO Young Musicians' Rostrum at Bratislava, 1981; Operatic roles include Mimi, Serpetta in La Finta Giardiniera (Camden Festival and Glyndebourne, 1991); Flora in The Knot Garden and Mozart's Despina, Zerlina and Susanna, 1991, for Opera Factory; English National Opera as Amor (L'Incoronazione di Poppea), Flora (The Turn of the Screw), Kitty (Anna Karenina by Iain Hamilton), Barbarina, Bekhetaten in Akhnaten, Woman/Fury in The Mask of Orpheus, Papagena, Yum-Yum, and Rose in Street Scene; Polly in The Beggar's Opera for Scottish Opera and Magnolia in Show Boat for Opera North; Concert appearances in the USA, Canada, Paris and Czechoslovakia; Season 1992 as Ottavia in The Coronation of Poppea, and Countess in Marriage of Figaro for Opera Factory, Governess in Turn of the Season, Bath City Opera, Tatyana in Eugene Onegin for Kentish Opera; In 1995 sang the Countess in Figaro (English National Opera), Amaranta in La fedeltà Premiata (Garsington), and Fairy in Purcell's Fairy Queen, for English National Opera; Rosalinda in Die Fledermaus for Scottish Opera, 1997. Recordings: Magnolia, Showboat; Rose, Street Scene; Mozart, Gluck, Puccini, Massenet Arias on Inspector Morse soundtrack albums. Honours include: Anna Instone Award, Royal College of Music; Countess of Munster, Caird and Royal Society of Arts Scholarships. Current Management: Ron Gonsalves, London. Address: c/o Ron Gonsalves Management, 7 Old Town, Clapham, London SW4 0JT, England.

KELLY Robert, b. 26 Sept 1916, Clarksburg, WV, USA. Composer. m. Mary Kelly, 25 Dec 1942, 3 sons. Education: BM, Composition, Curtis Institute of Music, 1942; MM, Composition, Eastman School of Music, 1952. Career: Professor of Composition, 1946-76, Professor Emeritus of Composition, 1976-, University of Illinois. Compositions: Chamber music, songs, symphonies, concerti, for large ensembles, operas, ballet, choral works, all published. Recordings: Symphony No 2 with Japan Philharmonic under Akeo Watanabe; Cello Music by Robert Kelly featuring Roger Drinkall, cellist; Suite for Solo Cello; 3 Expressions for Violin and Cello; Sonata for Cello and Piano; Sonata for Oboe and Harp, with oboist Joseph Robinson and harpist, Deborah Hoffman; Sunset Reflections from Adirondack Suite for orchestra, Leopold Stokowski and the NBC Symphony, CD. Publications: Theme and Variations, A Study of 12-Tone Composition; Audio and Visual Recognition, ear-training series, ibid, both 1985. Current Management: Broadcast Music Inc. Address: 101 W Windsor Road #314, Urbana, IL 61801, USA.

KELLY Valeria, b. 20 Mar 1944, Bardejov, Slovakia. Pianist. Divorced, 2 daughters. Education: Konzervatorium Kosice, 1959-63; Janacek Music Academy, Brno, 1963-64; Postgraduate, Bratislava, 1990-92. Debut: Brno, 1967. Appointments: Professor, Konzervatorium Zilina, 1967-70; Professor, Konzervatorium Bratislava, 1970-77; Assistant, VSMU Bratislava, 1977-93; Docent, VSMU Bratislava, 1993-. Compositions: Solo Concerts in Slovakia with Orchestras Radio Bratislava, Philharmonie Kosice, SKO Zilina; Chamber Concerts in Prague, Yugoslavia, Russia, Hungary, Germany, Poland, Cuba, Austria, Switzerland; Solo and Chamber Music on Radio Bratislava. Honour: Magister, Docent. Memberships: Association of Concert Artists, Bratislava. Hobbies: Literature; Art; Travelling. Address: Narodne Hudobne Centrum, Michaiska 10, 81536 Bratislava, Slovakia.

KELM Linda, b. 11 Dec 1944, Utah, USA. Singer (Soprano). Education: Studied with Jennie Tourel at the Aspen Schoolof Music and in New York. Debut: Seattle 1977, as Helmwige and Third Norn in the Ring. Career: Sang Turandot with Wilmington, 1979, followed by performances at Seattle, New York City Opera, 1983; Chicago, San Francisco and Amsterdam; Sang Salome at St Louis and Princess in Rusalka at Carnegie Hall; Perugia 1983, as Dirce in Cherubini's Demofoonte; Seattle Opera, 1985; as Brünnhilde; Further guest appearances include: Helmwige in the Ring.

KELTERBORN Rudolf, b. 3 Sept 1931, Basel, Switzerland. Composer; Conductor; Professor. m. Erika Kelterborn Salathe, 6 July 1957, 1 son. Education: Diplomas in Theory and Conducting, Music Academy, Basel, 1953; Studied composition with Blacher and Fortner, Salzburg and Detmold, and conducting with

Markewitch. Career: Teacher, Conductor, Basel, 1956-60; Professor of Composition: NW German Music Academy, Detmold, 1960-68, HS Zurich, Swiss Music Review, 1968-75; Head of Music Department, Swiss Radio, 1975-80; Professor of Composition, HS Karlsruhe, 1980-83; Director of Music Academy, Basel, 1983-94. Compositions include: Four Symphonies and five Operas Kaiser Jovian, 1967; Ein Engel Kommt nach Babylon, 1977; Der Kirschgarten, 1984; Ophelia, 1984; Julia, 1990; A ballet; Various works for Orchestra; Concertos for various solo instruments; Chamber music including 5 string quartets, 1954-89; Cantatas; Piano and organ works. Recordings: Several under various labels. Publication: Komponist, Musikdenker, Vermittler (various authors), Zurich, Bern, 1993. Honours include: Conrad Ferdinand Meyer Prize, 1971; Zurcher Radio Prize, 1973; Kunstpreis der Stadt, Basel, 1984; Komponistenpreis des Schwerizerisches Tonkünstlervereins, 1984. Memberships: Honorary, Association of Swiss Composers and Interpreters; Akademie der Freieu Künste, Mannheim. Hobbies: Contemporary Arts and Literature; Mountain Climbing. Address: Pilgerstrasse 31, CH-4055 Basel, Switzerland.

KELZ Mahalia (Astrid Linda), b. 12 Feb 1972, Bonn, Germany. Harpist. Education: Abitur, Gymnasium, Bonn, 1991; Conservatory of Lausanne with Chantal Mathieu, 1991-95; Russian Academy of Music with Natalia Shameyeva, Moscow, 1995-96; Studies in Literature, Linguistics and Didactics, University of Lausanne, 1995-. Career: Solo recitals with several appearances at Radio Suisse Romande, 1995-; Soloist with Capella Istropolitana, Chamber Orchestra of St Petersburg and Orchestre de la Suisse Romande; Recitals throughout Switzerland and Germany; Appearances at music festivals in Italy (Musica Riva), Belgium (Megève) and France (Molines). Contributions to: Regular contributions to the international magazine Harpa. Honours: 1st Prize of virtuosity and distinction, 1994, Concert Diploma, 1995, Conservatory of Lausanne; 1st Prize, international competition ASTH, France, 1993; 1st Prize, of all instruments, COOP competition, Lausanne, 1995; Louis Spohr medal of city of Seesen, 1995; 2nd Prize, international competition, Arpista Ludovico, Spain, 1996; 2nd Prize and Swiss Prize, international music competition, Geneva, 1997; 1st Prize, international Felix Codefroid Competition, Belgium, 1997. Memberships: World Harp Congress; 1998 Harp Almanac; Swiss Harp Association; Association Suisse de Musiciens. Hobbies: Horseback riding; Literature. Current Management: Rudolf Frick, Dorneckstr 105, CH-4143 Dornach, Switzerland. Address: Chemin du Capelard 1, CH-1007 Lausanne, Switzerland.

KEMENY Alexander, b. 22 Apr 1943, Solna, Sweden. Violinist. Divorced, 1 d. Education: Bratislava Conservatory, Czechslovakia, 1960-66; Music Academy in Prague with Professor A Plocek, 1966-70. Debut: 1970. Career: Concertmaster, Innsbruck Symphonic Orchestra, 1973-75; Violinist, Prague Symphonic Orchestra, also Norrkoping Symphony Orchestra, Sweden; Freelance Concert Violinist, 1978-; Soloist with orchestra playing works by Myslivecek, Mozart, Beethoven, Brixi, Mendelssohn, Wieniawski, Eklund, and chamber music player of both classical and modern music, concerts in Czechoslovakia, Sweden, Denmark and Poland; Performed in Piano Trio and in Duo with guitarist Vladimir Vectomov; Radio performances, Czechoslovakia, Sweden and Austria; Performed at Bornholm Music Festival, Denmark, 1987. Recordings: Paganini, Giuliani, and Kowalski, Radio Prague and Bratislava; Smetana, Johansson and Telemann, Radio Sweden; Suk, Smetana, Foerster, and Suchon, Radio Austria. Hobbies: Sport; Reading Books; Foreign Languages.

KEMMER Mariette, b. 1960, Luxembourg. Singer (Soprano). Education: Studied at the Luxembourg Conservatoire and at the Rheinland National College of Music in Düsseldorf. Career: Sang at the Théâtre de la Monnaie Brussels as Mélisande, Sophie, Pamina, Micaela and Mozart's Countess; Guest appearances at the Vienna Staatsoper, Munich, Berlin, Hamburg, Frankfurt, Dresden, Stuttgart, Zurich, Geneva, Basle, Berne, Lausanne, Verona, Karlsruhe, Mannheim, Nürnberg, Strasbourg, Nancy, Montpellier, Nantes, Avignon, Metz and Liège; Has appeared at the festivals of Aix-en-Provence, Wexford and Bregenz; Other roles include Mozart's Ilia, Fiordiligi and Donna Elvira, Marguerite, Antonia, Tatiana and the Countess in Capriccio. Address: Music International, 13 Ardilaun Road, London N5 2QR, England.

KEMP Brian (George), b. 29 June 1940, Aberdeen, Scotland. Opera Singer (Baritone). m. Helen Robertson, 27 July 1964, 2 sons. Education: London Opera Centre, 1965-67; Private Study with E Herbet-Caesari, Tito Gobbi, Lorenzo Malfatti. Debut: Théâtre Royal De La Monnaie, Brussels as Count, Le nozze di Figaro, 1967. Career: Principal Baritone, Scottish Opera, 1967-72; Freelance, Europe, USA; Debut, Royal Opera House, world premiere of We Come to the River, by Hans Werner Henze, 1976; Formerly Principal Baritone, Stadttheater, Aachen, 1984-88, roles include: Posa, Don Carlos, Don Carlos (Forza del Destino), etc; Appearances at Wexford Festival, Ledlanet Festival, Edinburgh Festival; Guest Artist, Netherlands Opera, English National

Opera, Royal Opera House, Scottish Opera, Brussels, Trieste. Honour: Peter Stuyvesant Foundation Scholarship, 1965. Membership: Incorporated Society of Musicians. Current Management: Athole Still International Management, London. Hobbies: Golf; Squash; Horse Riding; History. Address: Brüsseler Ring 32, 52074 Aachen, Germany.

KEMPF Frederick, b. 1977, England. Concert Pianist. Education: Studied at the Royal Academy of Music, with Ronld Smith; Further study with Christopher Elton. Debut: Mozart's Concerto K414, with the Royal Philharmonic, 1985. Career: Concerto engagements with the Royal Liverpool PO, London Mozart Players, European Community CO, Netherlands Radio SO, BBC National Orchestra of Wales and the Hallé Orchestra; Conductors have included Libor Pesek, Ashkenazy, Tadaki Otaka and Fedor Gluschenko; Solo recitalsat the Chichester, Canterbury, Bath, Guidlford and Exeter Fetsivals; Season 1996 with debut appearance at Berlin (Deutsches Symphonie Orchester), Munich and Prague recitals and debut with the Philharmonia Orchestra; Season 1996-97 with tour of Japan, recitals in Washington and New York and concerts with American orchestras. Honours include: Joint winner, National Mozart Competition, 1987; Winner, BBC Young Musician of the Year, 1992. Address: c/o Harrison/Parrott Ltd, 12 Penzance Place, London W11 4PA, England.

KENDALL Christopher (Wolff), b. 9 Sept 1949, Zanesville, Ohio, USA. Conductor; Lutenist; Artistic Director. Education: BA, Antioch College, 1972; MM, Conducting, University of Cincinnati Conservatory, 1974; Dalcroze School of Music, NY, 1969-70. Career: Director of 20th Century Consort in residence at the Smithsonian Institution, Washington, 1976-, Associate Conductor of the Seattle Symphony, 1987-; Founder and Lutenist of Folger Consort, Ensemble-In-Residence at Folger Shakespeare Library in Washington DC 1977-; Artistic Director of Millennium Inc, 1980-; Guest Conductor: Seattle Symphony, Chamber Music Society of Lincoln Center, Eastman Musica Nova, Da Capo Chamber Players, Washington Sinfonia. Recordings: 20th Century Consort Volume I and II (4 discs), Smithsonian Collection; Into Eclipse (Stephen Albert) 20th Century Consort, Nonesuch; Shakespeare's Music, Folger Consort, Delos; A Distant Mirror, Carmina Burana, Folger Consort, Delos. Honours: Gold Award, Houston Film Festival for Millennium: 10 Centuries of Music 1986; Emmy Award for 20th Century Consort PBS Programme on Aaron Copland 1984.

KENDALL William, b. 1960, London, England. Singer (Tenor). Education: King's School Canterbury; Choral Scholar, Cambridge University; Further study with Robert Tear and Peter Pears. Career: Concert appearances under such conductors as Hogwood, Harnoncourt, Gardiner, Mackerras and Boulez; Works by Tippett and Tavener conducted by the composers; Sang in the world premiere of Penderecki's Polish Requiem; Tour of Germany, 1989 with the Monteverdi Choir and Orchestra in the Missa Solemnis and Beethoven's Mass in C; Further appearances in season 1990-91 as the Evangelist in the St John Passion, in The Dream of Gerontius and Britten's Serenade in Australia; Mozart Requiems in Oxford and Cambridge and Bach's B Minor Mass with The Sixteen at St John's Smith Square; London Promanade concert appearances and showings at the Holland Festival, Festival Berlin, 1987, and the 1989 Salzburg Festival. Recordngs: Beethoven Missa Solemnis and Mass in C; Bach and Schütz with the Stuttgart Kammerchor; Sacred music by Haydn. Address: 4 Highgate High Street, London N6 5JL, England.

KENGEN Knud-Erik, b. 17 July 1947, Copenhagen, Denmark. Organist; Pianist; Composer. m. Gerlinde Maria Pagel, 6 Dec 1969, 1 son, 1 daughter. Education: Studies in Musicology, University of Copenhagen, 1972-76; Final Diploma, Royal Danish Academy of Music, 1974; Studied under Professor Aksel Andersen; Consultations in Composition with Leif Kayser. Career: Assistant Organist, Dome of Copenhagen, 1974; Organist, Gladsaxe Church, Copenhagen, 1979-; Performances: Concert Organist at numerous concerts, mainly in Denmark but also in Germany, England and Sweden; also played as Soloist at first performance of Musica Autumnalis by Axel Borup Jorgensen in The Danish Broadcasting Corporation; as Pianist, Rehearser and Chorus Master; Accompanist at Lieder-Recitals. Compositions: Organ and Choir-Music in style somewhat indebted to modern French church-music since Langlais, Duruflé and early Messiaen; For Organ: Toccata, Opus 5; Choral Preludes, Opus 14 and 26; Rhapsody, Surrexit Dominus, Opus 22; Organ Fantasy, Victimae Paschali, Opus 24; Missa Fons Bonitatis, Opus 26; Proprium for Hallo-Mass, Opus 28; Choral Fantasy, Veni Creator Spiritus, Opus 40; For Choir: Psalm 12, Opus 21; Cantatas with Instruments, Opus 35. Publications: Contributed to the lexical part of the History of Music in Denmark, 1978. Address: Tranegardsvej 69, 1 TV, DK 2900 Hellerup, Denmark.

KENNEDY Michael, b. 19 Feb 1926, Chorlton-cum-Hardy, Manchester, England. Critic; Journalist; Author. m. Eslyn Durdle, 16 May 1947. Education: Berkhamsted School. Career: Joined editorial staff of The Daily Telegraph in Manchester, 1941, Northern editor, 1960-86; Staff music critic, Sunday Telegraph, 1989-. Publications: The Hallé Tradition, 1960; The Works of Ralph Vaughan Williams, 1964; Portrait of Elgar, 1968; Portrait of Manchester, 1970; Barbirolli, 1971; History of Royal Manchester College of Music, 1971; Mahler, 1974, revised 1990; Strauss, 1976, revised 1995; Britten, 1980, revised 1993; Concise Oxford Dictionary of Music, 1980, revised 1996; The Hallé 1858-1983, 1983; Oxford Dictionary of Music, 1985, 2nd edition 1994; Adrian Boult, 1988; Portrait of Walton, 1989; Music Enriches All: the First 21 Years of the RNCM, Manchester, 1994. Contributions to: Gramophone, Listener, Musical Times, Music and Letters. Honours: Fellow, Institute of Journalists, 1967; Fellow, Royal Northern College of Music, 1981; Order of the British Empire, 1981; Commander of the Order of the British Empire, 1997. Hobby: Cricket. Address: 3 Moorwood Drive, Sale, Cheshire M33 4QA, England.

KENNEDY (Nigel Paul), b. 28 Dec 1956, Brighton, England. Solo Concert Violinist. Education: Yehudi Menuhin School; Juilliard School of Performing Arts, New York; ARCM. Debut: Royal Festival Hall with the London Philharmonic Orchestra, 1977. Career: Regular appearances with London and Provincial orchestras, 1978-; Berlin debut with Berlin Philharmonic, 1980; Henry Wood Promenade debut, 1981; Tour of Hong Kong and Australia with the Hallé Orchestra, 1981; Debut with the BBC Symphony Orchestra, 1987; Foreign tours, 1978-; India, Japan, South Korea, Turkey, USA; many appearances as Jazz Violinist with Stephane Grappelli, including Edinburgh Festival, 1974 and Carnegie Hall, 1976; many TV and Radio appearances including Coming Along Nicely, BBC TV documentary on early life, 1973-78; Played the Berg Concerto at the Festival Hall, 1991, dressed in a Dracula outfit; It's about death innit? says Nige; Informal Music Making from 1993; Returned to public concerts at South Bank, London, 1997 (works by Bach, Bartok and Jimi Hendrix, arranged). Recordings: Exclusive Recording Contract with EMI: Strad Jazz (Oct 1984); Elgar Sonata with Peter Pettinger (Jan 1985); Elgar Concerto, London Philharmonic Orchestra, conducted by V Handley; Tchaikovsky, Chausson Poème, London Philharmonic Orchestra (Oct 1988); Bartók Sonata, Ellington Black, Brown & Beige Suite; Vivaldi - Four Seasons, Sibelius, Bruch, Mendelssohn, Walton Concertos, Walton's Viola Concerto, Brahms Violin Concerto, 1991; Elgar Concerto conducted by Simon rattle, 1997. Honours: Best Classical Record 1985, British Record Industry Awards, for Elgar Concerto; Guiness Book of Records, for Vivaldi Four Seasons at No 1 in UK Classical Chart over one year, 1990; Winner, Golden Rose of Montreux 1990 (TV Special); Variety Club Showbusiness Personality of the Year, 1991. Hobbies: Boxing; Football; Cricket; Golf; Driving. Address: c/o Harold Holt Ltd, 31 Sinclair Road, London W14 0NS, England.

KENNEDY Roderick, b. 7 May 1951, Birmingham, England. Bass Baritone. Education: Studied at Guildhall School and with Otakar Kraus. Debut: Covent Garden, 1975. Career: Over 30 roles with the Royal Opera; Created Lt of Police in The Ice Break of Tippett, 1977; Appeared with Royal Opera on visits to La Scala, 1976, Korea and Japan in 1979 and 1986; Sang The Doctor in Wozzeck at Edinburgh and San Francisco, 1980-81, with further engagements at opera houses throughout Europe; Glyndebourne debut, 1981 as Don Fernando in Fidelio, followed by Alidoro, Rocco, Seneca in Poppea, and Britten's Theseus; Further festival appearances at Aldeburgh, Aix-en-Provence, Montpellier, Starasbourg and Florence; Regular performances with English National, Welsh National and Scottish Operas; Repertoire includes: the Coloratura Works of Handel and Rossini; Roles include: Don Alfonso, King Philip, Pogner, Bottom as well as many 20th century works; Regular Promenade and Concert appearances in UK and abroad; Has worked with such conductors as Muti, Kleiber, Colin Davis, Ozawa, Harnoncourt, Solti, Haitink, Mehta, Prêtre and Mackerras; Sang Britten's Bottom for ENO, 1996. Recordings include: Messiah; La Traviata; Herodiade; La Forza del Destino; Maria Padilla; Die Sieben Todessunden; Offenbach's Robinson Crusoe, The Immortal Hour and Le Comte Ory; TV Films and videos of Lucrezia Borgia, Giulio Cesare, Idomeneo, L'Egisto, Herodiade, L'Incoronazione di Poppea, La Cenerentola and A Midsummer Night's Dream. Membership: Director of Winter Gardens, Bournemouth, England, Charitable Trust. Current Management: IMG Artists, Media House, 3 Burlington Lane, London, W4 2TH. Address: Talbot Haven, Nairn Road, Talbot Woods, Bournemouth, BH3 7BD, England.

KENNER Kevin, b. 19 May 1963, California, USA. Concert Pianist. Education: Peabody Conservatory, Baltimore; Hochschule für Musik in Hannover; Studied with Leon Fleisher. Career: Has appeared in Europe, North and Central America, the Orient and former Soviet Union, since 1989 performing with St Paul Chamber Orchestra, Rochester Philharmonic and ensembles in San Diego, San Francisco, Kansas City and Baltimore; Recitals at the Salle Pleyel in Paris, the Châtelet, Elizabeth Hall London (International Piano Series) and at the Kennedy Center, Washington DC; Broadcasts in Japan, Australia, Poland, Germany and Costa Rica. Honours include: Winner: Gina Bachauer Competition, Utah, 1988; Van Cliburn Competition, Fort Worth, 1989; International Tchaikovsky Competition, Moscow, 1989; International Terence Judd Award, Manchester, 1990; International Chopin Piano Competition, 1990. Current Management: Connaught Artists Management Ltd, 39 Cathcart Road, Fulham, London SW10, England. Address: c/o Joan Parry, 14 Nursery Road, Sunbury-on-Thames, Middlesex TW16 6LB, England.

KENNY Courtney (Arthur Lloyd), b. 8 Nov 1933, Dublin, Eire. Pianist; Repetiteur; Accompanist. m. Caroline Anne Florence Arthur, 15 Jan 1972, 1 son. Education: Wellington College, Berkshire, 1947-51; Royal College of Music, London, 1951-54. Career: Musical Director, Bristol Old Vic, 1954-57; Solo Pianist, Royal Ballet, 1957; Member, Glyndebourne Festival Opera Music Staff; Founder, Western Opera, Ireland, 1963; Wexford Festival Opera Staff since 1963; Head of Music Staff, 1974; Senior Repetiteur, 1982; New Sadler's Wells Opera Head of Music Staff, 1983-89; Associate Music Director, Ohio Light Opera, 1983; Member of various ensembles including, Bureau Piano Trio, Barbican Ensemble, Peter Lloyd Baroque Trio; Faculty, Blossom Festival School of Cleveland Orchestra and Kent State University, 1972-80; Many concert appearances as soloist and accompanist in Europe, USA, Middle East; One-Man show of songs at the piano called Let Me See You Smile; Conducting Debut, John Curry Theatre of Skating, then Ohio Light Opera, New Sadler's Wells Opera. Recordings: With Glyndebourne Festival Opera; Recitals with Ian Wallace. Contributions to: Opera. Memberships: Incorporated Society of Musicians. Hobbies: Musical Theatre; Gardening. Address: 14 Grange Grove, London N1 2NP, England.

KENNY Jonathan (Peter), b. 1960, England. Countertenor. Education: Studied at Exeter University and the Guildhall School. Career: Appearances with English National Opera, Opera Theatre Company, Dublin, Opera Factory Zurich, Musica nel Chiostro and at Karlsruhe; Roles have included Bertarido in Rodelinda, Arsamenes in Xerxes, Guido in Flavio, Medoro in Orlando and Britten's Oberon; Other engagements as Andronico in Tamerlano for Glimmerglass Opera, US debut 1995, Amadigi at Prague and Monteverdi's Ottone at the Brooklyn Academy; Concerts throughout Europe including St Matthew Passion, in Jonathan Miller's dramatisation and Handel's Theodora in Berlin. Address: c/o Ron Gonsalves Management, 7 Old Town, Clapham, London, SW4 0JT, England.

KENNY Yvonne, b. 25 Nov 1950, Sydney, Australia. Singer (Soprano). Education: BSc, Biochemistry, Sydney University; Sydney Conservatory of Music; Opera School of La Scala Milan, 1973-74. Debut: London 1975 as Donizetti's Rosamunda d'Inghilterra (concert performance); Covent Garden 1976, in the world premiere of Henze's We Come to the River; Later appeared as Mozart's Susanna, Ilia (Idomeneo) and Pamina, Verdi's Oscar, Bizet's Micaela and Handel's Semele 1988, Liu in Turandot; English National Opera debut 1977, as Sophie, in Der Rosenkavalier, returned as Romilda in Handel's Xerxes; (Also on USSR Tour) Semele at La Fenice, Venice; Guest appearances at La Scala, Paris, Lyon, Vienna, Cologne, Hamburg, Sydney and Munich; Festivals of Salzburg, Aix, Strasbourg, Edinburgh and Glyndebourne (Ilia 1985); Sang Alcina in a new production of Handel's opera at Covent Garden, 1992-93; Deborah in Handel's oratorio in the 1993 Proms; Strauss, Capriccio, at Berlin Staatsoper in 1993; Sang in Purcell's Fairy Queen at the London Coliseum 1995 (also televised); Concert engagements under Pritchard, Colin Davis, Leppard, Harnoncourt, Solti, Abbado, Mackerras and Tennstedt; Featured artist (People, no 185) Opera Magazine, Dec 1992; Debut as the Marschallin 1997, English National Opera; Sang in a revival of Cavalli's La Didone at the 1997 Schwetzingen Festival. Recordings: Britten folk songs, Etcetera; Barbarina in Figaro, Solti; Constanze in Die Entführung and Aspasia in Mitridate with Harnoncourt; Donizetti's Ugo Conte di Parigi and Il Castello di Kenilworth; Bach's Cantata Der zufriedengestellte Aeolus, Telefunken; Elgar's The Kingdom; Mozart's Requiem; Sings Aspasia in Unitel film of Mitridate directed by Jean-Pierre Ponnelle; Vaughan Williams, Sea Symphony; Mendelssohn's Elijah; Stravinsky, Pulcinella; Mozart's Coronation Mass. Honours: Member of Order of Australia (AM) for services to music in 1989. Current Management: IMG Artists Europe, Media House, 3 Burlington Lane, Chiswick, London W4 2TH, England.

KENT Christopher, b. 12 August 1949, London, England. Musicologist; Organist; Teacher. m. Angela Thomas, 21 July 1973. Education: BMus, University of Manchester; MMus, PhD, King's College, London; FRCO; ARMCM. Career: Assistant Music Master, City of London School for Girls, 1975-80; Editorial Board, Elgar Complete Edition, 1979-. Publications: Co-Editor, 5 volumes of Elgar Complete Edition: Symphony No 1, 1981; The Dream of Gerontius, 1982; The Apsotles, 1983; The Kingdom, 1984; Music for Organ, 1987; The Music of Edward Elgar: A Guide to Research, 1993. Contributions to: Musical Times; The Listener, Journal of British Institute of Organ Studies; The Organ Year Book; Music and Letters, Journal of the Royal College of

Organists; Proceedings of the Royal Music Association. Hobbies: Flying; Railways; Natural History. Address: Department of Music, University of Reading, 35 Upper Redlands Road, Berks RG1 5JE, England.

KENYON Nicholas, b. 23 Feb 1951, Altrincham, Cheshire, England. Writer; Administrator. m. Marie Ghislaine Latham-Koenig. Education: BA, Modern History, Balliol College, Oxford. Career includes: Music critic, The New Yorker, 1979-82; Music critic, The Times, 1982-85; Music Editor, The Listener, 1982-87; Music critic, The Observer, 1986-92; Programme Advisor, Mozart Now Festival at South Bank, London, 1991; Controller, BBC Radio 3, 1992-; Director, BBC Proms, 1996-. Publications include: The BBC Symphony Orchestra 1930-80; Simon Rattle, the making of a Conductor; Authenticity and Early Music, Editor; Co-Editor, Viking Opera Guide, 1993. Address: BBC, Broadcasting House, London W1A 1AA, England.

KERMAN Joseph (Wilfred), b. 3 Apr 1924, London. Music Educator; Author. m. Vivian Shaviro, 1945, 2 sons, 1 daughter. Education: AB, New York University; PhD, Princeton University. Career: Director, Graduate Studies, Westminster Choir Coillege, Princeton, 1949-51; Music Faculty, x 1951-; Chairman, 1960-63, Professor of Music, 1974-94; J and E H Chambers Professor, 1986-88, University of California, Berkeley; Heather Professor of Music, Oxford University, Fellow of Wadham College, Oxford, 1972-74; Co-editor 19th Century Music, 1977-89; Editor, California Studies in 19th Century Music, 1980-; Fellow American Academy of Arts & Sciences; etc; Chairman, 1991-93. Publications: Opera as Drama, 1956, new edition, 1988; The Elizabethan Madrigal, 1962; Beethoven Quartets, 1967; History of Art & Music, with HW Janson, 1968; Ludwig van Beethoven: Autograph Miscellany 1786-99, Kafka Sketchbook, editor, 2 volumes, 1970; Listen, 1972; Masses and Motets of William Byrd, 1981; New Grove Beethoven, with A Tyson, 1983; Musicology, 1985; Write All These Down, 1994; Music at Turn of Century, 1990, Editor, 1994. Contributions: Hudson Review; New York Review; San Francisco Chronicle, etc. Honours: Guggenheim, Fulbright, NEH Fellowships; Visiting Fellow, All Souls College, Oxford, UK, 1966; Society for the Humanitites, Cornell University, 1970; Clare Hall, Cambridge, UK, 1971; Honorary degrees, Kinkeldey Award x 2; ASCAP; Deems Taylor Award x 2; Corresponding Member, British Academy. Memberships: Honorary Foreign Member, Royal Musical Association; Honorary Member, American Musicological Society. Address: Music Department, University of California, Berkeley, CA 94720, USA.

KERN Johannes, b. 5 Dec 1965, Fürstenfeld, Austria. Composer. m. Inge Kern-Stöger, 13 Nov 1987, 2 sons, 1 daughter. Education: Musikhochschule Graz. Career: Teacher, Musikhochschule Graz; Performances Internationally, 1992-93; Director, Deutschlandsberger Komponistenwerkstatt. Compositions: Symphonie No 1; Several Songs for Voice and Piano; Die Schlacht an der Beresina, Micro Opera for Puppet Theatre; Als Eva einen Schnupfen hatte; In memoriam Ernst Happel; Happy Birthday to Me; Sonderbarer Traum; Several Works for Theatre. Honours: Musik förderungspreis der Stadt Graz, 1982, Gleisdorf, 1983; Several Scholarships. Hobbies: Cooking; Art. Address: Schubertstrasse 66/3, A-8010 Graz, Austria.

KERN Patricia, b. 14 July 1927, Swansea, Wales. Singer (Mezzo-soprano). Education: Guildhall School, London, with Parry Jones (1949-52). Career: Sang with Opera for All 1952-55; Sadler's Wells/English National Opera from 1959, debut in Rusalka; appearances as Rossini's Isloier, Rosina, Cinderella and Isabella; Mozart's Cherubino, Monteverdi's Messenger; Sang in the 1966 premiere of Malcolm Williamson's Violins of St Jacques; Covent Garden debut 1967, as Zerlina in Don Giovanni: returned as Cherubino and as Mrs Herring (1989); US debut 1969, Washington Opera; Scottish Opera in A Midsummer Night's Dream, L'Incoronazione di Poppea, Cenerentola and The Rape of Lucretia; Premiere of Iain Hamilton's Catiline Conspiracy, 1974; Foreign engagements include Cherubino at the New York City Center and Dallas Civic Opera; Rossini's Cenerentola in Stratford Ontario and Isolier in Washington; Isabella in Spoleto; Monteverdi's Ottone at Drottningholm; Concerts in Paris, Turin and Hong Kong; Chicago Lyric Opera, 1987, as Marcellina in Le nozze di Figaro, Repeated for Vancouver Opera, 1992. Recordings: Stravinsky, Cantata; Berlioz, Roméo et Juliette conducted by Colin Davis; Anna Bolena, Manon and Les Contes d'Hoffmann with Beverly Sills; Monteverdi Madrigals conducted by Raymond Leppard; Video of L'Incoronazione di Poppea, Glyndebourne, 1984. Address: c/o Music International, 13 Ardilaun Road, Highbury, London N5 2QR, England.

KERR Virginia, b. 1964, Ireland. Singer (Soprano). Education: Royal Irish Academy and the Guildhall School, London. Career: Appearances with Dublin Grand Opera as Leila, Liu (Turandot), Musetta, Micaela and Elvira in L'Italiana in Algeri (1996); Other roles include Fiordiligi for City of Birmingham Touring Opera, Anita in Krenek's Jonny Spielt Auf (at Leipzig), Mozart's Countess (Malta), and Grete in Schreker's Der ferne Klang (Opera North); Appearances with Scottish Opera as Jenufa, Salome, Julia in Dvorák's Jacobin and the soprano lead in Judith Weir's The Vanishing Bridgegroom; Ariadne for Castleward Opera, Tchaikovsky's Enchantress for New Sussex Opera and Donna Elvira at Leipzig (season 1996-97); Ortlinde in Die Walküre and Jenifer in The Midsummer Marriage at Covent Garden; Concerts include Stravinsky's Pulcinella, Schreker's Von Ewigen Leben (BBC PO), Missa solemnis and Verdi Requiem (Mississippi SO) and Carmina Burana at the Festival Hall; Beethoven's Ninth and Mahler's 2nd Symphony in Mexico. Address: c/o Robert Gilder & Co, Enterprise House, 59-65 Upper Ground, London SE1 9PQ, England.

KERRY Gordon, b. 1961, Melbourne, Victoria, Australia. Composer; Writer and Critic. Education: BA (Hons), University of Melbourne, 1983; Study with Barry Conyngham. Career: Freelance composer; Music Critic for the Sydney Morning Herald, from 1996; Commissions from Musica Viva, ABC, Adelaide Chamber Orchestra, and others. Compositions include: Winter Through Glass, for piano, 1980; Canticles for Evening Prayer, for choir, 1983; Siderius Nuncius for Oragn, 1985; Obsessions, for mezzo and piano, 1985; Phaselus, for ensemble, 1986; Ongaku, for mandolin, 1987; Paradi, for viola and piano, 1988; Cantata for chorus and chamber orchestra, 1989; Cipangu for choir and orchestra, 1990; Torquing Points, for string quartet, 1991; Viola Concerto, 1992; Medea, chamber opera in 3 scenes, 1992; Quadrivial Pursuits, for clarinet, piano, viola and cello, 1993. Honours include: Sounds Australian Award, 1990. Address: c/o APRA Ltd, 1A Eden Street, Crows Nest, NSW 2065, Australia.

KERSJES Anton (Frans Jan), b. 17 Aug 1923, Arnhem, Netherlands. Conductor. m. Margaretha van de Groenekan, 8 Aug 1946. Career: 1st Violinist, Arnhem Symphony Orchestra, 194...41; Choir Conductor, 1945-46 and 1949; Co-founder, Kunstamaand Chamber Orchestra, 1953; Conductor, Netherlands Ballet Sonia Gaskell, 1953-61; 1st Conductor 1953-83, Principal Guest Conductor 1983-, Amsterdam Philharmonic Orchestra; Conductor, Netherlands Opera Company, 1955-60; Conductor, Amsterdam Ballet, 1960-62; Conductor of all Dutch symphony orchestras including Concertgebouw Orchestra, Orchestra Radio Hilversum; Guest Conductor, Netherlands Opera Company; Permanent Guest Conductor, Netherlands Philharmonic Orchestra, Amsterdam; Leader of conductors' class, Amsterdam Muzieklyceum, Sweelinck Conservatory, 1969-79; Leader conductors' and opera class, Deputy Director, Maastricht Conservatory; Tours in Europe, Scandinavia, UK and USSR; Conductor of over 125 concerts, 5 operas on television. Recordings: For EMI and HMV. Honours: Decorated Officer, Order of Orange Nassau; Silver Medal, City of Amsterdam; Silver Medal, Concertgebouw. Address: 6 Honthorst Straat, 1071 Amsterdam, Netherlands.

KERSTERS Willem, b. 9 Feb 1929, Antwerp, Belgium. Composer. Education: Studied at the Brussels Conservatoire with Jean Absil, Marcel Quinet and Marcel Poot. Career: Teacher until 1961 then Programme Director of Belgian Radio and TV until 1968; Lecturer, Maastricht Conservatory, 1967-94; Teacher of Composition at the Antwerp Conservatory, 1970-94. Compositions include: Tragicomic Opera, Gansendonk, 1984; Ballets: Parwati, 1956, Triomf van de Geest, 1959 and Ulenspiegel de Geus, 1976; Orchestral: Sinfonietta, 1955, Sinfonia Concertante for Wind Instruments, 1957, Divertimento for Strings, 1958, 5 Symphonies, 1962-87, Sinfonietta for Wind Orchestra, 1967, Contrasts for Percussion and Orchestra, 1968, Capriccio, 1972, Laudes for Brass and Percussion, 1973, Serenade for Chamber Orchestra, 1976, Piano Concerto, 1977, Ballade for Alto Saxophone and Strings, 1987; Chamber: Wind Quintet, 1954, Partita for Violin and Piano, 1956, 2 String Quartets, 1962 and 1964, Solo Violin Sonata, 1965, Piano Quartet, 1970, Nonetto, 1985; Vocal: A Gospel Song for Soloists, Chorus and Orchestra, A Hymn of Praise, oratorio, 1966, Canticum Solis Fratris, cantata, 1986, Kinderwereld for Trumpet Chorus, 2 Pianos and Timpani, 1988; Songs; Most recent works: Concerto for Violin and Orchestra, 1989, L'enamorat li deia for Mixed Capella Choir, 1992; De feesten van Angst en Pijn for Soloists, Chorus, Harp, Piano, Percussion and Strings, 1995. Membership: Royal Academy of Sciences, Arts and Letters of Belgium, 1990-. Address: Vijverlaan 37, 2610 Wilrijk-Antwerp, Belgium.

KERTESI Ingrid, b. 1961, Budapest, Hungary. Soprano. Education: Studied at the Franz Liszt Academy in Budapest and in Bayreuth. Debut: Budapest in 1985 as Oscar in Un Ballo in Maschera. Career: Sang Olympia at the Vienna Volksoper in 1987, Sophie in Budapest and Frasquita in Carmen at the 1991 Bregenz Festival; Other roles include Blondchen, Despina, Susanna and Mozart's Zerlina, Donizetti's Norina, Lucia and Adina, Amina in La Sonnambula, Gilda, Nannetta and Aennchen in Der Freischütz; Sang Adina at Budapest, 1996; Concert repertory includes works by Handel, Haydn, Mozart, Bach and Vivaldi. Address: c/o Bregenz Festival, Postfach 311, A-6901 Bregenz, Austria.

KERTESZ Otto, b. 1960, Hungary. Cellist. Education: Studied at the Franz Liszt Academy, Budapest and with Sandor Devich, György Kurtag and András Mihaly. Career: Member of the Keller String Quartet from 1986, debut concert at Budapest March 1987; Played Beethoven's Grosse Fuge and Schubert's Death and the Maiden Quartet at Interforum 87; Series of concerts in Budapest with Zoltán Kocsis and Deszö Ranki (piano) and Kalman Berkes (clarinet); Further appearances in Nuremberg, at the Chamber Music Festival La Baule and tours of Bulgaria, Austria, Switzerland, Italy (Ateforum 88 Ferrara), Belgium and Ireland; Concerts for Hungarian Radio and Television. Recordings: Albums for Hungaroton (from 1989). Honour: 2nd Prize Evian International String Quartet Competitin, May 1988. Address: c/o Artist Management International, 12/13 Richmond Buildings, Dean Street, London W1V 5AF, England.

KESSLER Minuetta (Shumiatcher), b. 5 Sept 1914, Gomel, Russia. Composer; Pianist; Teacher. m. Dr Myer M Kessler, 14 Sep 1952, 1 s, 1 d. Education: Full Scholarship with Ernst Hutcheson, Juilliard School of Music; Graduate Diploma; Piano and Postgraduate Diploma as Artist and Teacher with Distinction; Studied with Ania Dorfman in Piano and Ivan Langstroth in Composition. Career: Teacher of Piano at Juilliard School of Music; Concerts throughout Canada and US; Solo Pianist and Composer including: Boston Pops with Arthur Fielder, Montreal CBC Orchestra; Radio and TV appearances; Performed own compositions including, Alberta Concerto for Piano and Orchestra; Also appeared in Boston at Jordan Hall, Boston Lyric Opera, Morning Pro Musica on WGBH Radio; Private teaching studio from 1952-; Creator, Minuetta Kessler Music Kindergarten Method from 1965; Director and Founder of Concerts in the Home, 1965-79; Recordings: CD, MMC Bratislava Series, volume II; CD, Minuetta Kessler's composition, Alberta Concerto performed by Slovak Radio Symphony Orchestra, Robert Black conducting, Helena Vesterman, solo piano. Honours include: 2 CAPAC Awards for Serious Composition; Brookline Library Composition Award; 1st Prize for Left Hand Piano Composition; Nocturne in Purple Commission. Memberships include: ASCAP New England Jewish Music Forum; Founder, American Women Composers; Boston Juilliard Alumni Association; Founder, National League of American Pen Women, Music Chairman. Hobby: Hiking in Canadian Rockies. Address: 30 Hurley Street, Belmont, MA 02178, USA.

KESSNER Daniel (Aaron), b. 3 June 1946, Los Angeles, California, USA. Composer; Conductor; Educator. m. Dolly Eugenio, 29 June 1968, 2 sons. Education: AB cum laude, 1967; MA, 1968; PhD with Distinction, 1971; University of California, Los Angeles. Career: Founder and Director of CSUN New Music Ensemble, 1970-; Guest Conductor, Los Angeles Philharmonic New Music Group, conducting 5 concerts, 1984-91; Frequent Guest Lecturer for Los Angeles Philharmonic Orchestra with 65 appearances to date; Guest Conductor with Black Sea Philharmonic, Constanta, Romania. Compositions include: 72 compositions including 8 orchestral works, 7 choral/stage works, 4 pieces for symphonic band, 28 works for various chamber ensembles and 25 solo and duo works. Hobby: Skiing. Address: 10955 Cozycroft Avenue, Chatsworth, CA 91311, USA.

KESSNER Dolly Eugenio, b. 7 Nov 1946, Hanapepe, Kauai, Hawaii, USA. Professor; Pianist; Theorist; Composer. m. Daniel Aaron Kessner, 29 June 1968, 2 sons. Education: BA, cum laude, Music Education; MA, Composition, University of California, Los Angeles; PhD, Music Theory, University of Southern California; Studied Piano with Aube Tzerko, Composition, Henri Lazarof, Leon Kirchner, Robert Linn, Music Theory, Robert Moore, William Thomson. Appointments: Professor, Moorpark College; Concert Pianist, European, US and West Coast Premieres; Soloist, Orquesta Sinfonica de El Salvador, San Salvador, Filarmonica Marea Neagra, Constanza, Romania, Moorpark Masterworks Orchestra, California. Compositions: Five Piano Pieces, 1980; Toccata for Piano, 1992. Recordings: Lyric Piece for Piano and Orchestra; Equali II, for Piano Celeste and Three Percussionists. Publication: Article, Structural Coherence in Twentieth Century Music: The Linear-Extrapolation Paradigm, 1993. Honours: Grant, The Fund for US Artists; University of Southern California Graduate Merit Fellowship in Music; Meritorious Performance and Professional Promise Award, California University, Northridge. Memberships: College Music Society; Association for Technology in Music Instruction. Hobby: Skiing. Address: 10955 Cozycroft Avenue, Chatsworth, CA 91311, USA.

KESTEREN John Van, b. 4 May 1921, The Hague, Holland. Singer (Tenor). Education: Studied in The Hague with Lothar Wallerstein and with Nadia Boulanger in Paris; Further study with Vera Schwarz in Salzburg. Debut: Scheveningen 1947, as the Italian Singer in Der Rosenkavalier. Career: Sang operetta in Holland, on Dutch Radio and in Utrecht; Sang at the Komische Oper Berlin from 1951, Städtische Oper Berlin from 1953; Salzburg Festival from 1957, as Basilio in Le nozze di Figaro and in concert; Guest appearances in Vienna (from 1954), Dusseldorf, Munich, Stuttgart, Frankfurt, Ghent, Milan, the Drottningholm

Festival (Stockholm), New York City Opera, Boston, Cincinnati, Dallas and Buenos Aires; Many concert appearances. Recordings: Belmonte in Die Entführung; Le Postillon de Lonjumeau by Adam; Pfitzner's Palestrina, Ariadne auf Naxos, Die Kluge by Orff (Deutsche Grammophon); Leonore by Paer (Decca); Carmina Burana (Eurodisc).

KETELSEN Hans-Joachim, b. 17 Feb 1945, Thüringen, Germany. Singer (Baritone). Education: Studied in Dresden with Arno Schellenberg. Debut: Freiberg, as Count Eberbach in Lortzing's Wildschutz, 1973. Career: Sang at Freiberg, 1973-76, Chemnitz, 1976-82 and Dresden Staatsoper, 1982-90; Notably in the reopening of the Semper-Oper, 1985 as Ottokar in Der Freischütz; Deutsche Staatsoper Berlin, 1990-93 and Sächsische Staatsoper Dresden; Regular starring performances in Berlin, Chemnitz; Solo and ensemble starring performances in Japan, Spain, Greece, Sweden, Italy, Cuba, Switzerland, Hungary, Germany, and Las Palmas, 1993-; 1994 Debut in the Met New York as Mandryka in Arabella; 1996 Debut in Bayreuth as Kothner in Meistersinger; Participation in radio and TV broadcasts and concerts; Specialisation in German Opera (Wagner and Strauss); Major roles include Telramund in Lohengrin, Jochanaan in Salome by Strauss, Faninal in Rosenkavalier, Kurwenal in Tristan and Isolde, Wolfram in Tannhäuser, lago in Otello, Mandryka in Arabella, Amfortas in Parsifal by Wagner and Carmina Burana by Carl Orff. Recordings include: Pfitzner's Palestrina, (1995) as Morone, Götterdämmerung, Der Freischütz as Ottokar, Kothner in Meistersinger by Wagner.

KETTING Otto, b. 3 Sept 1935, Amsterdam, Netherlands. Composer. Education: Studied at the Hague Conservatory, 1952-58. Career: Trumpeter in The Hague Philharmonic Orchestra 1965-60; Teacher of composition, Rotterdam Conservatory 1967-71 and at the Royal Conservatory in The Hague 1971-74; Artistic Adviser to the Utrecht Symphony Orchestra 1983; Opera Ithaka was premiered at the opening of the Muziektheater Amsterdam, 1989. Compositions include: Operas: Dummies 1974 and O, Thou Rhinoceros 1977; Ballets The Last Message 1962; Interieur 1963; Barriers 1963; The Golden Key 1964; Choreo-struction 1963; Theatre Pice 1973; Concerto for solo organ 1953; Sinfonietta 1954; Sonata for brass quartet 1955; Piano Sonatia 195 ; Passcagalia for orchestra 1957; Serenade for cello and piano 1957; Concertino 1958; Symphony 1959; Concertino for jazz quintet and orchestra 1960; Variations for wind, hrp and percussion 1960; Series of works entitled Collage; Minimal Music for 29 toy instruments 1970; In Memoriam Igor Stravinsky for orchestra 1971; Time Machine for wind and percussion 1972; For Moonlight Nights for flute and 26 players 1973; Adagio for chamber orchestra 1977; Symphony for saxophones and orchestra 1978; Opera Thaka 1989. Honours include: Guadeamus Prize 1958; Warsaw Autumn Festival Award 1963. Address: c/o BUMA/STERMA huis, Postbus 725, 1180 AS Amstelveen, The Netherlands.

KEYES John, b. 1964, Illinois, USA. Singer (Tenor). Education: Studied in Chicago. Career: Based with the Chicago Lyric Opera until 1991; Season 1991-92 with Siegmund in Die Walküre for Scottish Opera, Radames at Mexico City and Parsifal in Robert Wilson's production of Wagner's opera for Houston Grand Opera; Concert performances of Otello (as Rodrigo) in Chicago an New York under Solti, 1991; Season 1992-93 as Siegmund at Hamburg and Nantes, Erik in Fliegende Holländer at Toulouse and Parsifal at Antwerp and Hamburg; Other roles include Walther von der Vogelweide and Eisenstein (Houston), Samson, Don Carlos, Don José and Dick Johnson; Sang Lohengrin in a new production of Wagner's opera for English National Opera, 1993; Season 1996-97 with Parsifal at Munich; Jean in Massenet's Herodiade at San Francisco and Turiddu and Canio for Israel Opera; Florestan at Buenos Aires and Siegmund in Amsterdam. Recordings include: Otello. Honours include: Winner, 1990, San Antonio Competition; Ruth Richards Grant in 1990 Richard Tucker Competition; Concert repertoire includes Beethoven's Ninth. Address: c/o Harold Holt Ltd, 31 Sinclair Road, London W14 0NS, England.

KEYLIN Misha, b. 5 March 1970, St Petersburg, Russia. Violinist. Education: The Juillard School. Debut: Carnegie Hall in New York (aged 11), 1981. Career: Performed both in recital and as soloist in major concert halls in over 30 countries. Recordings: The complete cycle of the Henry Vieuxtemps' Violin Concertos for Naxos. Honurs: Winner of Hannover Paganini Sarasate and Sigall International Violin Competitions. Hobbies: Computers; Fishing; Travel. Current Management: MGAM in Philadelphia and Toronto. Address: PO Box 705, New York, NY 10023, USA.

KEYS Ivor, b. 8 Mar 1919, Littlehampton, Sussex, England. Musician. m. Margaret Anne Layzell, 1944, 2 sons, 2 daughters. Education: Christ's Hospital, 1931-38; Christ Church Oxford, 1938-40, 1946-47, as music scholar and assistant organist; MA, BA, BMus 1940, DMus 1947. Career: Lecturer at Queens University Belfast, 1947-54; Reader 1950, Sir Hamilton Harty Professor 1951; Professor, Nottingham University, 1954-68; Professor, Birmingham University, 1968-86; Emeritus Professor, 1986; Visiting Professor, University of Western Australia (Perth); President, Royal College of Organists, 1968-70; Currently Council Member, Trinity College of Music and of National Federation of Music Societies; Examiner and Adviser in Music, Kenyatta University, Kenya, 1987-; Active as player of keyboard instruments in particular the organ. Compositions: Clarinet Concerto, 1960; Cello Sonata, 1960; Miscellaneous Church Music and Editions. Publications: The Texture of Music, 1964; Mozart, 1980; Brahms Chamber Music, 1981; Johannes Brahms, 1989. Contributions to: Music and Letters; Musical Times. Honour: Commander of the British Empire, 1976. Hobbies: Bridge; Watching Cricket; Railways. Address: 6 Eastern Road, Birmingham B29 7JP, England.

KEYTE Christopher (Charles), b. 11 Sept 1935, Shorne, Kent, England. Singer (Bass-Baritone). m. June Margaret. Education: Choral Scholar, King's College, Cambridge. Career: Oratorio, concert and recital appearances; Founder Member, Purcell Consort of Voices, 1963-75; Opera with The Fires of London; Professor of Singing, Royal Academy of Music, 1982-87; Royal Opera House, Covent Garden, 1989-. Recordings: Monteverdi Songs, Sacred Concertos; Purcell Anthems, Indian Queen; Haydn and Schubert Masses; Vaughan Williams Serenade to Music and Pilgrim's Progress; Songs by Quilter, Gurney and Glazunov; Mass of the Sea by Paul Patterson; The Lighthouse by Peter Maxwell Davies. Honours: Honorary RAM, 1983. Hobbies: Opera; Athletics; Theatre. Address: 20 Brycedale Crescent, Southgate, London N14 7EY, England.

KHADEM-MISSAGH Bijan, b. 26 Oct 1948, Tehran, Iran. Violinist; Conductor; Composer. Education: University of Vienna, Austria; Diploma with distinction, Academy of Music, Vienna, 1971. Debut: As soloist with orchestra aged 13. Career: Concert tours, including radio and TV appearances and festivals throughout Europe, Asia, Latin America,Australia; Founder, Eurasia Quartet, 1969-75; Founder, The Dawnbreakers, Austrian Baha'i Singing group, 1970; Founder, Conductor, and Soloist, Tonkuenstler Chamber Orchestra, Vienna, 1974-; Artistic Director, International Chamber Music Festival, Austria, 1979-; Midsummer Music Festival, Sweden, 1981-90; Badener Beethoventage, 1983-86; Musical Director, Music Forum Landegg, Switzerland, 1991-. Compositions: Instrumental and Vocal Works. Recordings: LPs, MCs and CDs; Works by: Beethoven, Schubert, Schönburg, Weigl, Mendelssohn, Vitali, Paganini, Debussy, Szymanowski, Bach, Tchaikovsky, Haydn, Handel, Dvorák, Respighi, Bartók, Strauss, Kreisler; Dawnbreakers LP, 1976; The Child LP, 1979; LP To A Friend, 1982; LP Vision, 1986; Cassettes: Call of the Beloved; Phoenix; Glad Tidings; Wie Sterne. Publications: Lieder - Book of Songs, 1976. Membership: AKM Vienna. Honours: Grand Prize, 1st Prize, International Chamber Music Competition, Colmar, France, 1971; Culture Award of Baden, Austria, 1988, 1994; Silver Medal of the State of Lower Austria, 1993. Memberships: AKM Vienna; Austrian Association of Composers; Club of Budapest; President, GlobArt. Address: Secretariat Dr Margaret Ley, Germerg 16, A-2500 Baden/Wien, Austria.

KHANZADIAN Vahan (Avedis), b. 23 Jan 1939, Syracuse, NY, USA. Operatic Tenor; Teacher. Education: BEd, University of Buffalo, 1961; Curtis Institute of Music, 1963. Debut: San Francisco Spring Opera as Ruggero in Puccini's La Rondine, 1968. Career: Many roles in numerous productions including: Wozzeck, Fra Diavolo, Madam Butterfly, Lucia di Lammermoor; Appearances with major opera companies throughout USA and Canada including: NY City Center, Baltimore, Houston, Memphis, New Orleans, St Paul, Providence, Birmingham, Kentucky, Kansas City, Dayton, Toledo, Portland, Honolulu, Montreal, Edmonton, Vancouver; Guest soloist with major orchestras including: Boston, Chicago, Philadelphia, Baltimore, Boston Pops; Numerous recital tours; Master Classes; TV and Radio Broadcasts; Tenor soloist in world premiere of Menotti's Lanscapes and Remembrances at Milwaukee, 1976; European debuts: Cavaradossi in Tosca at Aachen, 1992, Title role in Don Carlo at Basel, 1992, Metropolitan Opera debut as Gustavus in Ballo in Maschera, 1993, Lyric Opera, Chicago debut as Gustavus, 1993; Bavarian State Opera, Munich as Calaf in Turandot, 1995; Cincinnati Opera, USA as Radames in Aida, 1995. Hobbies: All major sports; Tennis. Current Management: Thea Dispeker Inc, 59 East 54th Street, New York, NY 10022, USA. Address: 3604 Broadway, Apt 2N, New York, NY 10031, USA.

KHARITONOV Dimitri, b. 18 Oct 1958, Kuibyshev, Russia. Singer (Baritone). Education: Rimsky-Korsakov College of Music, Leningrad from 1976; Vocal studies, piano, with honours, Nezhdanova State Conservatory, Odessa, 1978-84. Career: Recital Singer, Odessa Philharmonic Society; Principal Baritone, Odessa State Opera, 1984; Sang 55 times at the Bolshoi Opera, Kremlin Hall, roles included: Prince Yeletsky, Queen of Spades, Duke Robert, Iolanta (Tchaikovsky), Duenna (Prokofiev); Also sang in Moussorgsky's Khovanshchina and Boris Godunov, Rimsky-Korsakov's Tzar Saltan, Germont (La Traviata) and Conte di Luna, Il Trovatore (Verdi), Figaro, Il Barbiere di Siviglia (Rossini), Silvio in Pagliacci; Sang in main opera houses and concert halls, Moscow, Leningrad, Kiev, Minsk; Appeared regularly on Russian television, settled in England, 1989; UK debut as Jokanaan in Salome, Edinburgh Festival, 1989, returning for Tchaikovsky's Cantata Moskow; Season 1989-90 as Germont in Liège Opera de Wallonie; In America sang at the Chicago Lyric Opera with Placido Domingo in La Fanciulla del West (Puccini) amongst others; In 1992 gave recital in Brussels at the Palais des Beaux Arts; In 1994 sang title role of Nabucco in Genova at the Teatro Communale Carlo Felice; Also sang Oslo and Lillehammer in Rachmaninoff lieder recitals; Sang in Buenos Aires at the Teatro Colon Sharpless in Madama Butterfly; In 1993 was Prince Yeletsky (The Queen of Spades) in the Glyndebourne Festival Opera and gave 3 recitals at the Risor Festival in Norway. Recordings include: CD of Shostakovich's romances on Pushkin's poems with the City of Birmingham Symphony Orchestra; CD of Tchaikovsky's Ode to Joy; Eugene Onegin; Khovanshchina; Prince Yeletsky in Queen of Spades, Glyndebourne production video. Honours include: Winner All-Ukranian Lysenko Competition for Opera Singers, Kiel, 1983, Odessa, 1984; All-USSR M I Glinka Competition with special prize for best interpretation of Rimsky-Korsakov works, 1984; Grand Prix, Verviers International Opera Competition, Belgium, 1987; Gold Medal, Bastianini International Competition, Siena, 1988; Voci Verdiane Competition, Brusseto, 1988;; Carlo Alberto Cappelli Competition, Arena di Verona, for International Competition Winners. Address: Allied Artists, 42 Montpelier Square, London SW7 4JZ, England.

KHARITONOVA Yelena, b. 1960, Moscow, Russia. Violinist. Education: Studied at the Moscow Conservatoire with Andrei Shislov. Career: Co-Founder, Glazunov Quartet, 1985; Many concerts in the former Soviet Union and recent appearances in Greece, Poland, Belgium, Germany and Italy; Works by Beethoven and Schumann at the Beethoven Haus in Bonn; Further engagements in Canada and Holland; Teacher at the Moscow State Conservatoire and resident at the Tchaikovsky Conservatoire; Repertoire includes works by Borodin, Shostakovich and Tchaikovsky, in addition to the standard works. Recordings include: CDs of the six quartets of Glazunov. Honours include: Prizewinner of the Borodin Quartet and Shostakovich Chamber Music Competitions with the Glazunov Quartet. Address: c/o Sonata (Glazunov Quartet), 11 Northgate Street, Glasgow G20 7AA, England.

KHERSONSKAJA Natalya (Mikhailovna), b. 1 Nov 1961, Poltava, Ukraine. Musicologist; Pianist; Organist. m. Sergei Zagny, 26 Jul 1986, 1 son. Education: Piano and Musicology at Poltava Music College, 1981; Preparatory Section of Philosophical Faculty of Moscow State M Lomonosov University, 1982-83; Studied organ with Professor L I Roizman at Moscow State Conservatory, 1984-89; Musicologist, 1990 and Postgraduate, 1993, Moscow State Conservatory. Career: Editor of the chief edition of Ostankino, TV-Radio company musical broadcasting, Moscow, 1990-; Chief Scientific Collaborator of Database Section (electronic musical encyclopaedia) of the Computer Centre of Moscow State Conservatory, 1995-. Recordings include: Many broadcasts as author and interviewer including cycles, Music of 20th Century including Webern, Berg, Schoenberg, Scriabin, Mosolov and Boulez, Sviatoslav Richter plays Franz Schubert, Rondo, Masters of Antique Music including English virginalists and S Scheidt and Schütz, 9 Hours of French Music from Perotin to Messiaen. Publications include: Author of musicologic works including separate studies of the music of Samuel Scheidt (first in Russia) entitled, Word and Number as a Structural Idea of Organ Composition of S Scheidt, 1987, Tabulatura Nova of S Scheidt, new concept, 1990, Word For Windows As Possible Cover for Database, 1995. Contributions to: Author for Kultura (formerly Sovetskaja Kultura), Musikant, and Musical Review. Memberships: Society of the Friends of Organ, Moscow, 1991; Russian Schubert Society, Moscow, 1994. Address: Ul Vagonoremontnaja 5 korpus 1, kv 23, Moscow 127411, Russia.

KHOLMINOV Alexander, b. 8 Sept 1925, Moscow, Russia. Composer. Education: Studied with Golubev at the Moscow conservatory, graduated 1950. Career: Stage works have been widely performed in Moscow and Elsewhere in Russia. Compositions: Operas An Optimistic Tragedy Frunze, 1965; Anna Snegina, Gorky, 1967; The Overcoat, after Gogol, 1975; The Carriage, after Gogol, Moscow, 1975; Chapayev, Moscow Radio, 1977; The Twelfth Series, Moscow, 1977; The Wedding, after Chekhov, Moscow, 1984; Vanka, Monodrama after Chekhov, Moscow, 1984; The Brothers Karamazov, after Dostoyevsky, Moscow, 1985; Hot Snow, 1985. Honours: USSR State Prize, 1978; People's Artist of the URSSR, 1984. Address: c/o RAO, Bolchaia Bronnai 6-a, Moscow 103670, Russia.

KHOMA Natalia, b. 5 Dec 1963, Lviv, Ukraine. Cellist. m. Suren Bagratuni, 5 July 1986, 1 daughter. Education: BM, Lviv Music School; MM, DMA, Tchaikovsky Moscow Conservatory; Diploma, Boston University. Debut: Soloist with Lviv Philharmonia Orchestra, 1975. Career: Performances and Recitals at: Weill Recital Hall, Carnegie Hall, New York, Merkin Hall, New York, Jordan Hall, Boston, Rachmaninoff Hall, Moscow, Moscow

Conservatory Small Hall, Academy of Music Big Hall, Oslo, Norway, Palais des Beaux Arts, Brussels, Belgium, Schauspielhaus, Berlin, Germany, Grand Hall of Academy of Music, Budapest; Performed Throughout the Soviet Union, East Europe, Spain, Germany, Belgium, Italy, Norway, Canada, USA. Recordings: Numerous. Honours: 1st Prize, All Ukrainian Competition, 1981; Max Reger Special Prize, 1985; 2nd Prize, Markneukirchen International Competition, Germany, 1987; 1st Prize, Belgrade International Competition, 1990; 4th Prize, Tchaikowsky Competition, Moscow, 1990. Address: 4106 Englewood Drive, Champaign, IL 61821, USA.

KHOPINSKI Erik, b. Warwick, England. Pianist. Education: Private Studies with Kathleen Arnold, London; D Josefovicz, Vienna; Franz Reizenstein & Solomon, London. Debut: Promenade Concerts, Royal Albert Hall, London, 1945. Career: Numerous Radio & TV Appearances in England, France, Italy, Spain, Germany, Sweden, Holland, Yugoslavia. Recordings: Beethoven Sonatas. Publication: A Handbook of Piano Playing, 1954. Honours: ARCM, 1934; Hon FLCM, 1962; Hon ARAM, 1974; Hon RAM, 1978; Knight Templar, 1983. Hobby: Reading Philosophy. Current Management: Norman McCann Concert Agency Ltd. Address: 6 East Heath Road, London NW3 1BN, England.

KHRENNIKOV Tikhon (Nikolayevich), b. 10 June 1913, Elets, Liptsk Region, Russia. Composer. m. Klara Arnoldovna Vax 1936, 1 daughter. Education: Moscow Conservatoire; Gnesing School and College, Moscow, 1929-32; Moscow Conservatoire, 1932-36. Career: Director of Music, Central Theatre of Soviet Army, 1941-54; General Secretary 1957-; Deputy to USSR Supreme Soviet, 1962-; Committee Member, USSR Parliamentary Group; Member, Central auditing Committee, CPSU, 1961-; Prinicpal Compositions: 3 Piano Concertos, 1933, 1971, 1983; 5 Pieces for Piano, 1933; First Symphony, 1935; 3 Pieces for Piano, 1935; Suite for Orchestra from Music for Much Ado About Nothing, 1936; In the Storm (Opera), 1939; Second Symphony 1940-43; Incidental Music for Play, Long Ago, 1942; Frol Skobeyev (Opera), 1950; Mother (Opera) 1956; Concerto for Violin and Orchestra, 1959; A Hundred Devils and One Girl (Operetta), 1961; Concerto for Cello and Orchestra, 1964; White Nights (Operetta), 1967; Boy Giant (opera for children), 1969; Our Courtyard (ballet for children), 1970; Much Ado About Hearts (Chamber Opera), 1976; Concert No 2 for Violin and Orchestra, 1975; The Hussar's Ballard (Ballet), 1979-80; Dorotea - comic opera, 1983; Golden Calf - comic opera, 1985; String Quartette - 1967. Publications: Sovetskij Kompozitor; Several Recorded Works. Memberships: Member of Santa Cecilia Academy, 1983; Tibara Academy, 1985; Prize of UNESCO International Music Council (IMC), 1977; Chairman of Tchaikovsky Contest Organising Committee, of International Music Festival in the CIS. Address: Composers' Union, 103009, Ulitsa Nezhdanovoi str 8/10, Moscow, Russia.

KIBERG Tina, b. 30 Dec 1958, Copenhagen, Denmark. Singer (Soprano). Education: Studied in Copenhagen. Debut: Royal Opera Copenhagen, 1983, as Leonora in Nielsen's Maskarade. Career: Sang Elsa in Lohengrin at Copenhagen, 1984, the Marschallin 1988, Mozart's Countess and Purcell's Dido, 1990, Helene in Les Vepres Siciliennes, 1991; Guest appearances at Geneva and Frankfurt, 1988, as Agathe and the Countess, at Aarhus as Mimi, Vienna Staatsoper 1990, as Elsa and Opera Bastille Paris, 1991 as Lisa in The Queen of Spades; Lieder recitals in England, Germany and Italy from 1984; Sang Strauss's Ariande at Copenhagen and Elisabeth in Tannhäuser at Bayreuth, 1992; Sang Wagner's Eva with the Royal Danish Opera, 1996; Other roles in opera have included Donna Elvira, Pamina, Desdemona, and Tatiana in Eugene Onegin; Concert repertoire includes Schmidt's Das buch mit Sieben Siegeln (Copenhagen), Beethoven's Mass in C (Lausanne), Haydn's Lord Nelson Mass (Vienna) and Elijah in Berlin; Tour of Moscow, Dresden, Berlin and London with Missa Solemnis conducted by Antal Dorati. Recordings include: Lulu by Kuhlau. Address: c/o Det Kongelie Teater, Box 2185, DK 1017 Copenhagen, Denmark.

KIELISCH Melody (Aristo), b. Milwaukee, Wisconson, USA. Singer (Soprano). m. Giorgio Aristo. Education: BFA, Judson College, Elgin, Illinois; MMus, University of Wisconsin, Milwaukee. Career: Resident Soprano in Passau and in Essen; Freelance Singer, 1991-; Engagements in Hanover, Berlin, Hamburg, Frankfurt, Kassel, Mannheim, Dortmund, Bremen and others; Japan tour as Susanna in Le nozze di Figaro; Carnegie Hall debut, Mozart's Requiem and Lord Nelson Mass; repertoire includes Oratorio works of Bach, Handel, Haydn, Schubert and Mozart; Opera roles include: Martha, Frau Fluth, Norina, Gilda, Musetta, Adele, Olympia; Concerts in New York, Zurich, Edinburgh, Tampere, Barcelona, Grenoble and Sunderland; television appearances as Rosina in The Barber of Seville, Susanna in The Marriage of Figaro, Hanna in The Merry Widow and Kathy in The Student Prince. Recordings: Live Opera Concert as Gilda, LP; Impresario as Madame Herz with the Seattle Symphony conducted by Klaus Donath, CD. Address: c/o Frau Erbeck, Hanover Opera House, Hanover, Germany.

KIEMER Hans, b. 9 Feb 1932, Munich, Germany. Singer (Bass-Baritone). Education: Studied in Munich. Career: Engaged at Innsbruck, 1968-70, Augsburg, 1970-76, Wiesbaden, 1976-79; Appearances at Karlsruhe from 1979, notably at the Dutchman and Wagner's Kurwenal, Wotan and Amfortas, Verdi's Falstaff and Amonasro, in the 1986 premiere of Kunaud's Der Meister und Margarita and as Waldner in Arabella, 1989; Guest engagements at Amsterdam, Barcelona, Brussels, (the Wanderer in Siegfried, 1981), Bordeaux (as Jochanaan), Trieste (Pizarro), Vienna, Lisbon and Warsaw (Wanderer, 1989); Other roles include Strauss's Mandryka and Barak, Borromeo in Palestrina, Baron Ochs, Don Alfonso and Scarpia; Noted interpreter of the Ballades of Carl Loewe; Sang Mefistofele at Innsbruck, 1990. Address: Rebisches Staatstheater, Baumeisterstrasse 11, 7500 Karlsruhe, Germany.

KIERNAN Patrick, b. 1962, England. Violinist. Debut: Wigmore Hall, 1984 with Peter Pears. Career: Co-Founder, Brindisi String Quartet, Aldeburgh, 1984; Concerts in a wide repertory throughout Britain and in France, Germany, Spain, Italy and Switzerland; Festival engagements at Aldeburgh (residency, 1990), Arundel, Bath, Brighton, Huddersfield, Norwich, Warwick and Prague Spring Festival; First London performace of Colin Matthews' 2nd Quartet, 1990, premiere of David Matthews' 6th Quartet, 1991; Quartet by Mark Anthony Turnage, 1992; World premiere of Colin Matthews' 3rd Quartet, Aldeburgh, 1994; Many BBC recitals and resident artist with the University of Ulster. Recordings include: Quartets by Britten, Bridge and Imogen Holst; Works by Pierné, Lekeu, Schoenberg, Berg and Webern. Honours include: Prize Winner, Third Banff International String Quartet Competition in Canada, 1989, with Brindisi Quartet. Address: c/o Owen/White Management, 14 Nightingale Lane, London N8 7QU, England.

KIEVMAN Carson, b. 27 Dec 1949, Los Angeles, CA, USA. Composer; Stage Director. m. Carrie Manfrino, 5 Sep 1987. Education: BFA, 1975, MFA, 1977, California Institute of The Arts. Career: The Public Theater, New York City, New York Shakespeare Festival J Papp; Tanglewood, 1978, Boston Symphony; The Pennsylvania Ballet, Schubert Theater, 1983, Darmstadt, 1976, Rotenfabrick, Zurich, 1976, Basel State Theatre, 1977, Kyoto, 1980, Hong Kong, Philippines, Australia, New Zealand and Singapore; Major commission from New York Shakespeare Festival for Hamlet Opera. Compositions: Intelligent Systems; Piano Concerto; California Mystery Park; Wake Up, It's Time To Go To Bed; Multinationals And The Heavens; The Temporary And Tentative Extended Piano; Aspen Symphony; Hamlet-Opera; Tesla, opera. Recordings: Belgium Radio, Sudwestfunk Radio, Japan Radio, National Public Broadcasting.

KIKUCHI Yoshinori, b. 16 Sept 1938, Yawatahama, Japan. Conductor. Education: Studied at Tokyo National University of Fine Arts and Music. Career: Chief Assistant at the Nikikai Opera, Tokyo, 1961-64; Studied further with Kasei Yamada in Japan, with Peter Maag at the Accademia Chigiana at Siena and with Franco Ferrara in Rome; Engagements at Palermo (Teatro Lirico and Teatro Massimo), 1973-77; Hessisches Staatstheater Wiesbaden, 1978-84; Guest Conductor in Japan, Italy, Germany, France, Spain and Belgium; La Scala, Milan, 1985-86; Verona Arena, 1987. Address: c/o Theateragentur Luisa Petrov, Glauburgstrasse 95, D-60318 Frankfurt am Main, Germany.

KILDUFF Barbara (Jane), b. 31 May 1959, Huntington, New York, USA. Opera Singer (Soprano). Education: BM, State University College, New York at Fredonia, 1981; MM, University of Connecticut, Storrs, 1983; MM, Vale University, 1984. Debut: Washington Opera, Blonde. Career: Performances include: Sang Blonde with Metropolitan Opera, conductor James Levine, 1990; With Baltimore Symphony, David Zinman, July 1990; With Zurich Opera, April-May 1990, Barenreiter - Carlos Kalmar; Sang Zerbinetta in Munich 1987 and 1988; Conductors Bender, Sawallisch, Köhler in Vienna, 1987, 1991; Conductor Theodor Guschlbauer, Metropolitan Opera, 1987; James Levine, Hamburg, 1988; Julius Rudel, Basel, 1988; Vancouver, January 1989 (Martin André); In Vienna, April 1991 with Horst Stein; Olympia, Bregenz, Summer 1987 and 1988; Marc Soustrot, in Geneva, June 1990; Sang Adele at Metropolitan Opera, 1987, 1988, 1990, 1991; E Rosenthal, Julius Rudel, in Bonn December 1988; Guschlbauer in San Francisco, November 1990; Julius Rudel; Cleopatra, Metropolitan, October 1988; Trevor Pinnock; Sophie, Munich October 1989, 1990, 1991; Director: Brigitte Fassbaender, Heinrich Hollreiser; Metropolitan Opera, March 1991, Jiri Kout; Queen of the Night, Oviedo, Spain, September 1991; Many concert appearances and TV and Radio performances; Season 1993 as the Countess in Capriccio at Vienna; Appears as Papagena in Met video of Die Zauberflöte. Address: c/o CAMI, Crittenden Division, 165 West 57 Street, New York, NY 10019, USA.

KILLEBREW Gwendolyn, b. 26 Aug 1939, Philadelphia, USA. Singer (Mezzo-Soprano). Education: Templeton University; Juilliard School; Metropolitan Opera Studio. Debut: Metropolitan Opera 1967, in Die Walküre. Career: 1968-69 sang Carmen in Munich and at the New York City Opera; 1970 Copenhagen, Geneva and Prague in Handel's Tamerlano; 1972-73 Salzburg Festival, as Amneris and in the premiere of Orff's De Temporum fine Comedia; 1973 Washington Opera as Baba the Turk (The Rake's Progress) and San Francosco as Marina (Boris Godunov); Deutsche Oper am Rhein, Dusseldorf, from 1976, as Gluck's Orfeo, Verdi's Preziosilla and Azucena and Rossini's Isabella; Bayreuth debut 1978, as Waltraute in Götterdämmerung; Zurich 1981, as Mistress Quickly in Falstaff; Sang Frau Leimgruber in Klebe's Der Jüngste Tag, Duisburg, 1989; Season 1991-92 as the Nurse in Rimsky's Golden Cockerel and Strauss's Herodias at Duisburg; Also sings in concert. Recordings: Tamerlano; Orlando Paladino by Haydn; Edgar (Puccini), Schvanda the Bagpiper; De Temporum fine Comedia (Orff); Mahler's 3rd Symphony. Honours: Outstanding Musician, Temple University, 1971. Hobbies include: Creative Cooking; Walking; Modern Dance. Address: c/o Ingpen and Williams Limited, 14 Kensington Court, London W8 5DN, England.

KIM Earl, b. 6 Jan 1920, Dinuba, California, USA. Composer; Professor; Pianist; Conductor. m. (1) Nora Philipsborn, 1947, 1 daughter. m. (2) Miriam Odza, 1958. m. (3) Martha Potter, 1977, 1 daughter. Education: Studied Piano with Homer Grun; Compositions and Theory with Schoenberg, University of California, Los Angeles, 1939; MM 1952, studied Composition with Bloch and Sessions, University of California, Berkeley. Career: Professor, Princeton University, 1952-67; James Edward Ditson Professor of Music, Harvard University, 1967-90; Pianist and Conductor; Emeritus, 1990-; Composer-in-Residence, Princeton Seminar in Advanced Musical Studies; Marlboro, Dartmouth, Tanglewood and Cape and Islands Festivals; Aspen Center for Compositional Studies. Compositions: Opera: Footfalls, 1981; Orchestral: Dialogues for Piano and Orchestra, 1959; Violin Concerto, 1979; Chamber: 2 Bagatelles for Piano, 1952; 12 Caprices for Violin, 1980; Scenes from Childhood for Brass Quintet, 1984; Vocal: Letters Found Near a Suicide, Song Cycle, 1954; Exercises En Route for Soprano and 8 Instruments, 1961-71; Narratives for High Soprano, Women's Voice, Actor, 7 Instruments, Television and Lights, 1973-76; Now and Then for Soprano, Flute, Harp and Viola, 1981; Where Grief Slumbers for Soprano, Harp and String Orchestra, 1982; Cornet for Narrator and Orchestra, 1983; The 7th Dream for Soprano, Baritone, Violin, Cello and Piano, 1986; The 11th Dream for Soprano, Baritone, Violin, Cello and Piano, 1989; 4 Lines from Mallarmé for Voice, Flute, Vibes, and 4 Percussion, 1989; Some Thoughts on Keats and Coleridge for Unaccompanied Voices, SATB, 1990. Recordings: Two Bagatelles for Piano (Robert Helps); Earthlight (Merja Sargon, Martha Potter, Earl Kim); Violin Concerco (Itzhak Perlman, Seiji Ozawa, Boston Symphony); Where Grief Slumbers, Chamber Version (Dawn Upshaw); Dear Linda, Womens Voice, Flute/Piccolo, Piano Marimba, Percussion, Cello. Publications: Lawson-Gould, EB Marks, Mobart. Address: 57 Francis Avenue, Cambridge, MA 02138, USA.

KIM Ettore, b. 14 November 1965, Korea. Singer (Baritone). Education: Studied in South Korea and Italy. Debut: Theatro Delle Erbe, Milan in Salieri's Arlecchinata, 1990. Career: Sang in Henze's We Come to the River at La Scala and in the premiere of Ferroro's La Figlia del Mago at the Teatro San Carlo, 1992; Concert performances of Otello, as lago, at Bordeaux, 1992; Engaged as Germont at Covent Garden, 1993, Chorebus in concerts of Les Troyens with the London Symphony Orchestra and on stage at La Scala, 1993-94, Belcore at Strasbourg, Antonio in Linda di Chamounix at Stockholm and Riccardo in Puritani for Bavarian Radio; Other roles include Scarpia, and Gerard in Andrea Chenier. Recordings include: Linda di Chamounix and I Puritani, both with Edita Gruberova. Honours include: Gold Medal, International Giuseppe Verdi Competition at Bussetto, 1989. Current Management: Atholl Still International Management Limited. Address: c/o Athole Still International Management Limited, Foresters Hall, 25-27 Westow Street, London SE19 3RY, England.

KIM Michael Injae, b. 13 Feb 1968, Quebec, Canada. Professor of Piano; Concert Pianist. Education: BMus, University of Calgary; MM, DMA, Juilliard School New York. Debut: Calgary Philharmonic Orchestra, Canada, 15 years old. Career: Performances with major orchestras of Canada and US, including Boston, Cincinnati, Oklahoma City, Toronto, Vancouver, National Arts Centre, Calgary, Edmonton, Regina, Saskatoon, Winnipeg, London, toured Scotland with the Royal Scottish National Orchestra; Appearances in Glasgow, Edinburgh, Dundee, Aberdeen (1994); BBC Scottish Symphony, Glasgow (1992); Recitals throughout Canada and US, including appearances in virtually every series in Canada; Recital tour, Scotland, 1994; Recitals broadcast regularly by CBC, BBC, National Public Radio; As Chamber Musician, appeared throughout Canada and US with sister violinist Helen Hwaya Kim (The Kim Duo), including appearances at Carnegie Hall, New York, 1992. Recordings: Chamber Works of Saint-Saens; Ballades of Chopin & Grieg; Works of Stravinsky, Rachmaninoff, Mussorgsky. Honours: Laureate of 1992 Scottish (Glasgow), 1993 Leeds, 1993 Ivo Pogorelich (Pasadena, California) International Piano

Competitions; Grand Prize Winner, 1988 Canadian Music Competitions (Montreal, Quebec) and 1989 Canadian Broadcasting Corporation Competition for Young Performers, Toronto; Government of Alberta Achievement Award; Commendation, Government of South Korea; Commendation, Government of Canada. Hobbies: Chess; Hiking; Badminton; Video Games. Current Management: Andrew Kwan Artists Management Inc, 1315 Lawrence Avenue East, Suite 515, Toronto, Canada. Address: c/o Conservatory of Music, Lawrence University, 420 East College Avenue, Appleton, WI 54911, USA.

KIM Sun-Joo, b. 5 Oct 1929, Sun Cheh Pyung an Buk-Do, Korea. Conductor; Educator. m. Hye Sook Lee, 5 May 1955, 1 child. Education: BMus, Kyung Hee University, 1961. Career: Principal Associate Conductor, Korean Broadcasting Symphony, Seoul, 1963-; Instructor, Yung-Hee University, Seoul, 1965; Principal Associate Conductor, Seoul Philharmonic, 1965-69; Principal Conductor, National Symphony Korea, 1969-70; Professor, Kyung Hee University; Currently Conductor, Korean Symphony Orchestra, Seoul. Membership: Board of Executives, 1975-82, Korean Musicians Union. Address: Kyung-Hee University, School of Music, Whoe Ki Dong, Seoul, Korea.

KIM Young Uck, b. 1 Sept 1947, Seoul, Korea. Concert Violinist. Education: Studied with Ivan Galamian at the Curtis Institute, Philadelphia from 1958. Debut: Philadelphia Orchestra conducted by Ormandy, 1963. Career: Tours of Aouth America and Europe: appearances with the Berlin Philharmonic, Concertgebouw Orchestra, Vienna Philharmonic and London Symphony; Season 1987-88 in USA with the St Paul Chamber Orchestra, St Louis Symphony, Cleveland Orchestra, Pittsburgh Symphony and the New York Philharmonic; Concerts in Sweden, Italy and the UK; Season 1988-89, with the Hallé and BBC Welsh Orchestras; Tours to Eire, Sweden, Norway and Germany; USA recitals with Peter Serkin playing Beethoven sonatas; Piano Trio recitals with Emanuel Ax and Yo-Yo Ma: 1989 concerts in Switzerland, Germany and Italy; Concerto repertoire includes works by Bach, Berg, Mozart, Prokofiev, Sibelius, Stravinsky and Vivaldi; Concerts and Recitals American and Europe: New York Philharmonic, Los Angeles Philharmonic, London Symphony Orchestra, Hong Kong Philharmonic, Rotterdam Philharmonic; Tours, America and Far East; Season 1992 with World and European Premieres of newly commissioned concerto by Gunther Schuller (New York and Rotterdam). Recordings include: 5 Mozart Concertos with the London Philharmonic under Christoph Eschenbach; Ax/Kim/Ma Trio recording of Dvorak Trios (Sony Classical-Record of the Year Award, 1988); Mozart Piano Quartets with Previn, Heichiro and Gary Hoffman. Address: c/o Harold Holt Limited, 31 Sinclair Road, London W14)NS, England.

KIM Young-Mi, b. 6 November 1954, Seoul, Korea. Opera and Concert Singer (Soprano). m. Sung-Ha Kim, 21 July 1984. Education: Seoul Art School, 1973; BA, Conservatory of San Cecilia, Rome, 1979; MA, Academy of Santa Cecilia, Rome, 1980. Debut: Alice Tully Hall, New York Lincoln Center, 1980. Career: Appearanceswith New York City Opera, Los Angeles Music Center Opera, Houston Grand Opera, Opera Company of Philadelphia, Opera de Paris, Bastille Orchestra, National Symphony, Seattle Symphony, San Diego Symphony, Minnesota Orchestra, Colorado Symphony. Recordings: Sung-Eum Gramophone. Honours: Verona International Contest, 1977; Giacomo Contest, 1979; Maria Callas International Voice Competition, 1980; Luciano Pavarotti International Voice Competition, 1981. Address: c/o Athole Still International Management Limited, Foresters Hall, 25-27 Westow Street, London SE19 3RY, England.

KIMBERLIN Cynthia Tse, b. 11 Apr 1940, Ganado, Arizona, USA. Ethnomusicologist. m. Jerome Kimberlin, 1 daughter. Education: BA Music, University of California at Berkeley; MA, Musicology, PhD, Musicology, University of California at Los Angeles. Publications: The Music of Ethiopia, 1980, 1983; Ethiopia III: Three Chordophone Traditions, 1986; What Am I to Be?: Female, Male, Neuter, Invisible...Gender Roles and Ethnomusicological Fieldwork in Africa, 1991; Co-editor, International Music, volume 1, 1995, volume 2, 1998. Honours: Fulbright Dissertation Award, 1972; Recipient, Beyond War Award, 1987; Grant, American Council of Learned Societies, 1988; Fulbright Lecturer and Research Award, 1996. Memberships: Society for Ethnomusicology; International Council for Traditional Music; National Peace Corps Association. Address: POB 70333, Point Richmond, CA 94807, USA.

KIMBROUGH Steven, b. 17 Dec 1936, Athens, Alabama, USA. Singer (Baritone). education: Studied at Birmingham Southern College, Duke University, Princeton Theological seminary; Further study in Italy. Debut: Mantua, 1968, as Marcel in La Bohème. Career: Appearances in Mannheim, Frankfurt, London, San Francisco, New York and Philadelphia; Member of the Bonn Opera, 1971-; Sang in the premiere of Christophorus by Schreker, Freiburg, 1978; Essen 1989 as Mirabeau by Siegfried Matthus; Concert tours of the USA, Germany, Italy and Austria; Guest appearances at the opera houses of Vancouver, Cincinnati, Rio de Janeiro, Barcelona; Repertoire includes roles in operettas and musicals; German premiere Op 2 Zemlinsky, 1994. Recordings include: Lieder by Schreker, Korngold, Zemlinsky, Weill, Kienzl, Schreker, Schoenberg for EMI and Koch. Memberships: American Guild of Musical Artists; Actors Equity. Address: 128 Bridge Avenue, Bay Head, NJ 08742, USA.

KIMM Fiona, b. 24 May 1952, Ipswich, Suffolk, England. Singer (Mezzo-Soprano). Education: Studied at the Royal College of Music, London. Career: Has sung at the Glyndebourne Festival in Die Zauberflöte, The Love for Three Oranges, Titus L'Enfant et les Sortilèges; Appearances with Opera North as Hansel, Mercedes, Rosalind in The Mines of Sulphur, Hermia (A Midsummer Night's Dream) and Baba the Turk; Sang in the premiere of Edward Cowie's Kate Kelly's Road Show, Chester, 1983; With English National Opera has sung Orlofsky, Lola and Fyodor (Boris Godunov), and in Orpheus in the Underworld and Rusalka; Covent Garden debut in Boris Godunov; Berlioz Festival at Lyon in Dido and Aeneas; Sang in the premiere of Greek by Mark Anthony Turnage (Munich 1988) and again at the Edinburgh Festival; Scottish Opera in Lulu, Die Zauberflöte, Eugene Onegin and Das Rheingold; Bath Festival in El Rey de Harlem by Henze, with Ensemble Modern; Sang Smeraldina in The Love for Three Oranges, ENO 1989, Siebel in Faust, 1990; Opera North/RSC at Stratford as Julie in Showboat; Glyndebourne Festival 1990, as Third Lady in Die Zauberflöte; Michael Berkeley, Baa Baa Black Sheep, world premier, 1993; Concert performaces with the London Symphony, English Chamber Orchestra, City of Birmingham Symphony and London Sinfonietta; Conductors include Abbado, Haitink, Elder, Hickox, Andrew Davis, and Roger Norrington; Sang in Param Vir's Snatched by the Gods, for Almeida Opera, 1996; Television appearances in The Gondoliers, L'Enfance du Christ and Man and Music series on Channel 4. Address: c/o Ron Gonsalves Management, 10 Dagnan Road, London SW12 9LQ, England.

KINCES Veronica, b. 1949, Hungary. Singer (Soprano). Education: Studied at the Budapest Academy and the Accademia di Santa Cecilia Rome. Career: Member of the Hungarian State Opera from 1973: roles include Susanna, Fiordiligi, Sulamith in Die Königin von Saba by Goldmark, Euridice, Mimi and Madama Butterfly; Teatro Liceo Barcelona and Montreal, 1986, as Donna Elvira and as Suor Angelica; 3 Concerts in Chicago, 1981; Budapest 1986, as Eva in Die Meistersinger; Frequent concert appearances; Has appeared in several Hungarian TV programmes; Guest performer in Austria, Belgium, Czechoslovakia, Germany, France, Holland, Italy and Russia; Teatro Colon, Buenos Aires, Caracas, 1987; Deutsche Oper West-Berlin, 1985, 1986; Sang Madama Butterfly at Chicago, 1989. Recordings: Die Königin von Saba, Haydn's Der Apotheker and La Fedeltà Premiata; Songs by Bellini; Liszt's Hungarian Coronation Mass; Madama Butterfly; Orfeo ed Euridice; La Bohème. Honours: Winner, Dvorak International Singing Concours, Prague, 1971; Prix de l'Academie du Disque, Paris, 4 times; Kossuth Prize, Hungarian People's Republic. Address: Hungarian State Opera House, Népöztarsasag utja 22, 1061 Budapest, Hungary.

KING Alexander Hyatt, b. 18 Jul 1911, Beckenham, Kent, England. Musicial Scholar. m. Evelyn Mary Davies, 1943, 2 sons. Education: MA, King's College, Cambridge. Career: Entered Department of Printed Books, British Museum, 1934; Deputy Keeper, 1959-76; Superintendent, Music Room, 1944-73; Music Librarian, Reference Division, British Library, 1973-76; Honorary Secretary, British Union Catalogue of Early Music, 1948-57; Council Mamber, Royal Musical Association, 1949-; President, International Association of Music Libraries, 1955-59; Vice Chairman, joint committee, International Musicological Society/AIML, for International Inventory of Musical Sources, 1961-76; Trustee, Hinrichsen Foundation, 1976-82; President, Royal Musical Association, 1974-78. Publications include: Mozart in Retrospect, 1955, 3rd edition, 1976; Mozart in the British Museum, 1956, 1975; Some British Collectors of Music, 1963; 400 Years of Music Printing, 1964, 1968; Handel and His Autographs, 1967; Mozart Chamber Music, 1968, 1986; Mozart Wind and String Concertos, 1978, 1986; Printed Music in the British Museum (account of collections, catalogues and their formation, up to 1920), 1979; A Mozart Legacy: Aspects of British Library Collections, 1984; Musical Pursuits, Selected Essays, 1987; Various exhibition catalogues, Editor, co-editor, further scholarly works on music. Contributions to: Year's Work in Music, 1947-51; Schubert, a Symposium, 1947; Music, Libraries and Instruments, 1961; Deutsch Festschrift, 1963; Essays in honour of Victor Scholderer, 1970; Grasberger Festschrift, 1975; Essays in honour of Sir Jack Westrup, 1976; The New Grove, 1980; Rosenthal Festschrift, 1984; Various articles. Honours include: Scholarship, King's College, Cambridge; Honorary member, International Association of Music Libraries, 1968; Honorary degrees, Universitites of York and St Andrews; Book, Music and Bibliography: Essays in honour of Alec Hyatt King, ed Oliver Neighbour, 1980. Hobbies: Watching Cricket; Opera; Exploring Suffolk. Address: 37 Pier Avenue, Southwold, Suffolk IP18 6BU, England.

KING Andrew (Graham), b. 8 May 1953, Bury St. Edmunds, England. Singer (Tenor). Education: Early lessons of Piano and Flute; Read Music at St John's College, Durham, BA Hons, Dunelm, 1975; Postgraduate, King's College, Cambridge, PGCE Cantab, 1976; ARCM, 1974; Durham Cathedral Choir, 1972-75; King's College Choir, 1975-76; Vocal Studies with Graham Watts, Ivor Davies, David Johnston, Eric Vietheer, Iris dell' Acqua. Debut: Wigmore Hall, 1977; Proms, Baroque Cantatas, BBC Singers, 1978. Career: Lay Clerk, Guildford Cathedral, 1976-77; BBC Singers, 1977-80; Sang with many emerging early music groups, including Tallis Scholars, Clerkes of Oxenford, The Sixteen, Medieval Ensemble of London, Landini Consort, Gothic Voices, Taverner Consort, King's Consort, New London Consort: Member of Consort of Musicke since 1978; Performed contemporary works with the song group English Echoes and Singcircle; Noted as an Interpreter of Renaissance and Baroque Music and is in particular demand as Evangelist in the Bach Passions; Performances throughout Europe, also USA, Canada, Middle East, Japan and Australia; Festival appearances include Bruges, Edinburgh, Prague, Salzburg, Utrecht, York and many appearances at the Proms; He has given a number of world premieres, most notably Leaving by Mark-Anthony Turnage with City of Birmingham Symphony Orchestra. Recordings: Over 80 including Monteverdi Vespers (New London Consort/Decca, also Taverner Consort/EMI), Apollo and other roles in Monteverdi's Orfeo (NLC/Decca), many Monteverdi Madrigal recordings (Consort of Musicke/Decca/Harmonia Mundi/Musica Oscura/Virgin Classics) Handel's Esther (Academy of Ancient Music/Decca), Purcell's Ode on St Cecilia's Day (Taverner Consort/EMI), Purcell late songs (Mantle of Orpheus-Consort of Musicke/Musica Oscura); Many other recordings of Medieval and Renaissance Music; Frequent radio broadcasts BBC Radio 3 and WDR; Video of Monteverdi Madrigals Banquet of the Senses with Consort of Musicke; Several TV appearances including Proms and a series of Music in Venice with King's Consort (Channel 4). Honours: Choral Scholarship, Durham Cathedral, 1972-75. Hobbies: Piano; Tennis; Church Activities. Current Management: Magenta Music International, 4 Highgate High Street, London N6 5JL. Address: 49 Dalmeny Avenue, London SW16 4RS, England.

KING James, b. 22 May 1925, Dodge City, Kansas, USA. Singer (Tenor). Education: Studied at Louisina University, University of Kansas City and with Martial Singher in New York. Debut: San Francisco 1961, as Don José. Career: Moved to Europe 1961 and sang Cavaradossi in Florence; Deutsche Oper Berlin from 1962; Salzburg Festival 1962-64, as Achilles in Iphigénie en Aulide and Aegisthus in Elektra; Vienna Staatsoper from 1963, debut as Bacchus in Ariadne auf Naxos; Bayreuth Festival 1965, as Siegmund; Covent Garden 1967, as the Emperor in Die Frau ohne Schatten, returned 1985, as Bacchus; Metropolitan Opera from 1966, Florestan, the Emperor, Siegmund, Walther and Don José; La Scala 1983, in Cherubini's Anacreon; Sang Jove in Il Ritorno di Ulisse (arranged Henze) at Salzburg 1985 (also televised); Returned to Salzburg 1989, as Aegisthus in Elektra; Sang the Drum Major in Wozzeck at the Metropolitan 1990; Lohengrin at Nice; Holland Festival 1990, as the Emperor in Die Frau ohne Schatten; Sang Aegisthus at the Met, 1992; Other roles include Parsifal, Otello (San Francisco 1974); Pfitzner's Palestrina, Manrico and Calaf. Recordings: Die Frau ohne Schatten, Daphne, Die Meistersinger, Lohengrin, Parsifal (Deutsche Grammophon); Salome, Die Walküre, Fidelio (Decca); Die Walküre (Philips); Mathis der Maler by Hindemith and Ariadne auf Naxos (EMI); Samson et Dalila (RCA); Video of Elektra conducted by Abbado (Virgin). Address: c/o Metropolitan Opera, Lincoln Center, NY 10023, USA.

KING Mary, b. 16 June 1952, Tonbridge Wells, England. Mezzo-Soprano Singer. Education: BA, English, Birmingham University; PGCE, St Anne's College, Oxford; Postgraduate Diploma, Guildhall School of Music. Career: Sang in opera at Glyndebourne, 1980, US debut, 1985, Covent Garden, 1990; Regular appearances with major British orchestras; Spanish tour with BBC Symphony Orchestra, 1991; Proms, 1991; New music a speciality with many first performances including: The Undivine Comedy by Finnissy in Paris and London, Valis, by Machover in Paris, Boston, and Tokyo; Teacher, Guildhall School of Music, London, 1990-; Artistic Director of Live Culture, a youth group of English National Opera, Baylis Programme; Formed Green Light Music Theatre, 1990; Has sung Marcellina and Baba the Turk at Glyndebourne, The Cockerel in The Cunning Little Vixen at Covent Garden; Sang Florence Pike in Albert Herring at Garsington, 1996. Recordings: Where the Wild Things Are, by Knussen; The Cunning Little Vixen; Britten's Praise We Great Men; Machover's Valis; Birtwistle's Meridian; Stilgoe's Brilliant the Dinosaur. Memberships: Equity; Association of Teachers of Singing. Hobbies: Gardening; Tapestry; Cats; Books. Current Management: Mary Craig. Address: 34a Garthone Road, Honor Oak, London, SE23 1EW, England.

KING Robert (John Stephen), b. 27 June 1960, Wombourne, England. Conductor; Harpsichordist; Editor. Education: MA, St John's College, Cambridge. Career: Director, The King's Consort, 1980-; Guest Conductor: Netherlands

Chamber Orchestra, Orquesta Sinfonica Euskadi, Atlanta Symphony Orchestra, English Chamber Orchestra, Madrid Symphony Orchestra, Netherlands Chamber Choir, Filharmonisch Orkest van Vlaanderen; Editor. Recordings: 65 CDs with The King's Consort. Publication: Henry Purcell, 1994. Hobbies: Cricket; Skiing; Cultivating lupins. Address: 34 St Mary's Grove, London W4 3LN, England.

KING Stephen Paul, b. 1958. Organist. Education: Studied under Gladys Puttick as Junior Exhibitioner at Trinity College of Music, 1969-76; LTCL (Performer's Diploma) for piano and organ; Organ Scholar, studying under John Birch, Sussex University, 1976-79; ARCO, 1976; FRCO, 1977. Career: Accompanist, Hutton and Shenfield Choral Society, 1980-; Organist, Brentwood Cathedral, 1992-; Has made many appearances as organist and continuo player with Collegium Musicum of London, at St John's, Smith Square and elsewhere, including playing at Herbert Howells Centenary Concert, Queen Elizabeth Hall, 1992. Publications: Three Carols. Honours: Sawyer Prize; Lord St Audries Prize; Harding Prize; Turpin Prize; Dr F J Read Prize; Silver Medallist, Worshipful Company of Musicians. Address: 82 Lodge Avenue, Gidea Park, Romford RM2 5AL, England.

KING Terry B, b. 20 Aug 1947, Santa Monica, California, USA. Cellist; Conductor; Teacher. m. Leslie Morgan, 18 dec 1976. Education: BM, Mt St Mary's College, Los Angeles, 1970; Postgraduate, Claremont Graduate School, 1974; University of Northern Iowa, 1989-91; Assistant Professor, University of Northern Iowa, 1990-. Debut: Carnegie Recital Hall, New York, 1975. Career: Assistant to Piatigorsky, University of Southern California, 1971-72; Instructor, San Francisco Conservatory, 1972; Lecturer, California University, Fullerton, 1972-75; Artist-in-Residence, Grinnell College, 1975-; Vienna Chamber Orchestra, 1978; St Paul Sunday Morning, 1984-87; Voice of America, America in Concert, Music from the Frick Museum, New York, Austrian Radio, NPR, PBS, several documentaries; Piatigorsky, McPhee, Harrison. Compositions: Arrangements, Trio music by Anderson, Enesco, de Falla, Fauré, Glinka; Voice and Instruments, Mozart, Bachelet, Godard; Cello Ensembles, Sibelius, Prokofiev, Shostakovich. Recordings: 17 recordings, Cello Music by Cowell, Barber, Cooper, Harris; Concertos by Harrison, Reale, Beethoven, Haydn; Trios with Mirecourt Trio, Beethoven to present day composers.

KING Thea, b. 26 Dec 1925, Hitchin, Hertfordshire, England. Clarinettist; Professor of Clarinet. m. Frederick Thurston (deceased). Education: ARCM, 1944, 1947, Royal College of Music, London. Career: Frequent appearances as soloist, broadcaster, recitalist and principal clarinet with English Chamber Orchestra; Member of Melos Ensemble of London and Robles Ensemble; Purcell Room recital 1997 (Finzi, Brahms and Stravinsky). Recordings include: Mozart, Brahms, Spohr, Finzi, Bruch, Mendelssohn, Stanford and Crusell; 20th Century Music. Publications: Editor and Arranger of Clarinet Solos; Chester Woodwind Series; Arrangements of J S Bach Duets for 2 Clarinets, Schumann for The Clarinet, 1991, and Mendelssohn for The Clarinet, 1993; The Romantic Clarinet, Mendelssohn, 1994 and Tchaikovsky, 1995. Honours: FRCM, 1975; OBE, 1985; FGSM, 1992. Hobbies: Skiing; Painting; Lacemaking; Cows. Address: 16 Milverton Road, London, NW6 7AS, England.

KINGDOM Elizabeth, b. 1932, USA. Singer (Soprano). Career: Sang in opera at Bielefeld, 1958-63, notably in the 1962 German premiere of Scarlatti's Griselda, Nuremberg, 1962-68, (Hostess in the 1980 premiere of Zemlinsky's Der Traumgörge); Guest appearances at Cologne 1964, Oslo 1970, Graz 1982, and London 1988; Other roles have included Mozart's Donna Anna and Fiordiligi, Verdi's Elisabetta, Forza Leonora and Aida, Elisabeth in Tannhäuser, Giulietta and Myrtocle in Die Toten Augen by d'Albert. Recordings include: Don Giovanni. Address: Stadtische Buhnen, Richard-Wagnerplatz 2-10, 8500 Nuremberg, Germany.

KINGSLEY Colin, b. 15 Apr 1925, London, England. Lecturer; Pianist. m. 16 Apr 1955, 2 s, 2 d. Education: King's Scholar, Westminster School, 1938-43; BMus, Gonville and Caius College, Cambridge, 1946; DMus, Edinburgh, 1968; RCM, 1943-44, 1946-47; Leverhulme Scholar, ARCM, 1945. Debut: 1947. Career: Freelance Keyboard Playing, Broadcasting, 1948-; Solo Pianist, Royal Ballet, 1957-59; Several performances of contemporary music, mainly in London and Paris; Member of Macnaghten Committee, 1957-63; Associated Board Examiner, 1959-93; Pianist, University College of Wales, Aberystwyth, 1963-64; Principal Radio: Concertos, 1955-; University of Edinburgh Lecturer, 1964; Senior Lecturer, 1968, retired 1992; Series, Piano Music of P R Fricker, 1974 followed by Premiere of his Anniversary for Piano, Cheltenham International Festival, 1978; Series, The English Musical Renaissance, Piano Music, 1977. Recordings: Lyrita Sonatas for Piano by John White; Various BBC Recordings for broadcasting purposes. Hobbies: Gardening; Languages. Address: 236 Milton Road East, Edinburgh, EH15 2PF, Scotland.

KINGSLEY Margaret, b. 20 Feb 1939, Poole, Cornwall, England. Singer (Soprano and Mezzo-Soprano). m. W A Newcombe. Education: Royal College of Music; ARCM; LRAM. Debut: With Opera for All. Career: Glyndebourne debut 1966, in Die Zauberflöte; Appearances with Covent Garden Opera, English National Opera, Scottish Opera, Opera North, State Operas of Hamburg, Munich, Stuttgart and Vienna; Stockholm Royal Opera; Paris Opera; Naples, Miami, Washington, Roles include Wagner's Gutrune; Beethoven's Leonore; Waltraute, Eboli, Elvira, Verdi's Amelia and Lady Macbeth; Mozart's Fiordiligi, Donna Anna and Electra; Cassandre in Les Troyens; Reiza in Oberon; Gluck's Euridice; ENO as Brünnhilde; Title role in Ariadne auf Naxos; Azucena; English National Opera 1983-84, as Amneris, Marina (Boris Godunov), Akhrosimova (War and Peace) and Mrs Grose (The Turn of the Screw); Concert appearances with leading British orchestras and on TV; Professor of Singing, Royal College of Music. Honour: FRCM, December 1994. Hobbies: Gardening; Cooking; Walking. Address: Bryher Cottage, Lynx Hill, East Horsley, Surrey KT24 5AX, England.

KIPNIS Igor, b. 27 September 1930, Berlin, Germany. Harpsichordist; Fortepianist. m. Judith Robison, divorced. 1 son. Education: Diploma, Westport School of Music, Connecticut, 1948; Harvard University, 1952. Debut: Harpsichordist, New York, 1959; Fortepianist, Festival Music Society, Indianapolis, 1981; Debut as pianist, New York, 1995. Career: Concerts and recitals throughout USA and Canada, 1962-; Extensive tours abroad, 1967-; Faculties, Berkshire Music Centre, Tanglewood, 1964-67; Chairman, Baroque Dept, Berkshire Music Centre, Tanglewood, 1965-67; Visiting Tutor in Harpsichord and Baroque Music Studies, Royal Northern College of Music, Manchester, 1982-; Associate Professor of Fine Arts, 1971-75, Artist in Residence, 1976-78, Fairfield University, Connecticut; Harpsichord Workshop, Indianapolis, summers 1974-84; Host of weekly radio programme, Age of Baroque WQXR, New York, 1966-68; Host of syndicated radio series, WGBH, Boston, The Classical Organ, 1992-93. Recordings: 81 albums, of which 55 are solo. Publications include: A First Harpsichord Book, 1970; Dussek, the Sufferings of the Queen of France, 1975; Telemann, Overture in E Flat, 1977; Krebs, 6 Preludes, 1985; Vivaldi, Harpsichord Concerto in A (Rv 780) (reconstruction), 1987. Contributions to: Contributions and Record Reviewer, International Piano Quarterly, International Classical Record Collector, Goldberg, Fl, Stereophile, Musical America, Stereo Review, the American Record Guide, Schwann/Opus Clavier, Yale Review. Honours: 6 Grammy Nominations, 3 Record of the Year Awards from Stereo Review; Deutsche Schallplatten Prize, 1969; Best Harpsichordist, Keyboard Magazine, 1978, 1979, 1980; Best Classical Keyboardist, 1982, 1986; Gold Star Award, Musica, 1988; Hon Dr of Humane Letters, Illinois Wesleyan Unviersity, 1993; Honorary Phi Beta Kappa, Harvard, 1977. Memberships include: Grainger, Stokowski, Barbirolli, Dolmetsch, Galpin Societies; ASCAP; Local 802 AF of M; Bohemians; Co-artistic Director and VP, Connecticut Early Musical Festival, 1983-95; President, Friends of Music (CT), 1995-. Hobbies: Photography; Record Collecting. Current Management: John Gingrich Management, PO Box 1515, New York, NY 10023, USA. Address: 20 Drummer Lane, West Redding, CT 06896, USA.

KIRCHNER Leon, b. 24 Jan 1919, Brooklyn, New York, USA. Composer; Pianist; Conductor. Education: Studies with Schoenberg at University of California, Berkeley (BA 1940) and in New York with Sessions; Further study at Berkeley (MA). Career: Lecturer at Berkeley from 1949; Lecturer, then Professor at the University of Southern California, 1950-54; Luther Brusie Marchant Professor at Mills College in Oakland, 1954-61; Appointed to Harvard Faculty, 1961, Walter Bigelow Rosen Professor of Music from 1966; Director of the Harvard Chamber Players, 1973; Director of the Harvard Chamber Orchestra and Friends, 1975; Pianist and Conductor of his own music and the Viennese Classics; Composer-in-Residence and Performer at the Santa Fe Chamber Music Festival, 1983; Tanglewood Music Center, 1985; Soloist and Conductor, Boston Symphony, New York Philharmonic, Philadelphia Orchestra, S F Symphony, St Paul Chamber Orchestra, Sudwest Funk Baden Baden, Tonhalle Zurich, London Sinfonietta, Buffalo Philharmonic. Compositions: Opera, Lily 1973-76; Orchestral, Sinfonia 1951; 2 Piano Concertos 1953, 1963; Toccata for strings, wind and percussion; Concerto for violin, cello, 10 wind instruments and percussion 1960; Music for Orchestra, 1969; Music for Flute and Orchestra; Vocal, Words from Wordsworth for chorus, 1968; The Twilight Stood, song cycle after Emily Dickinson, 1983; Instrumental, Duo for violin and piano, 1947; Piano Sonata, 1948; Little Suite for piano, 1949; 3 String Quartets, 1949, 1958, 1966; Sonata Concertante for violin and piano, 1952; Trio for violin, cello and piano, 1954; A Moment for Roger for piano; Five Pieces for piano, 1987; Interlude for piano, 1989; For Solo Violin II, 1987; For Solo Violin II, 1988; Triptych, Violin, Cello, 1988; Five Pieces for piano; Music for Twelve, 1985. Honours: George Ladd Paris Prize, University of California; Two Awards from New York Music Critics' Circle (First tow string quartets); Naumburg Award for 1st Piano Concerto; Pulitzer Prize for 3rd String Quartet; Commissions from the Ford Foundation and the New York Philharmonic. Memberships: National Institute of Arts and Letters; American Academy of Arts and Sciences. Address: c/o ASCAP, ASCAP Building, One Lincoln Plaza, NY 10023, USA.

KIRCHSTEIN Leonore, b. 29 Mar 1933, Stettin, Germany. Singer (Soprano). Education: Studied at the Robert Schumann Conservatory, Dusseldorf, with Franziska Martiensen-Lohman. Career: Sang first with the Städtische Opera Berlin, from 1958; Kiel 1960-63, Augsburg 1963-65, Cologne 1965-68; Has sung with the Bayerische Staatsoper Munich from 1968; Salzburg Festival 1961 and 1970, Edinburgh Festival 1965 and 1971; Montreux Festival, 1965; Guest appearances in Hamburg, Stuttgart, Zurich and Vienna; Concert tours of USA, Argentina, England, Italy and Turkey. Recordings include: Die Zauberflöte and Cardillac (Electrola); Bach Cantatas; Beethoven's Missa solemnis (RCA).

KIRK Elise (Kuhl), b. 14 Feb 1932, Chicago, Illinois, USA. Musicologist; Pianist; Lecturer. m. Robert L Kirk, 3 children. Education: BMus 1953, MMus 1954, University of Michigan; PhD, Catholic University of America, 1977; Studies in Musicology with Kurt von Fischer, University of Zurich, 1961-63; Studies in Piano with Claudio Arrau Aspen Institute of Music, 1953. Career: Adjunct Lecturer, Baruch College, City University of New York, 1972-77; Visiting Professor, Catholic University of America, summers, 1976, 1977; Adjunct Professor of Music, University of Dallas, 1978-. Publications: Editor, Dallas Civic Opera Magazine, 1978-; Co-Editor, Opera and Vivaldi, 1984; Music at the White House: A History of the American Spirit, 1986. Contributions to: American Music Teacher; Notes; Musical Quarterly; Current Musicology; Symposium; Grove's Dictionary, 6th edition; Opera News; Dallas Civic Opera Magazine; Bulletin for Research in the Humanities; Miscellanea Musicologica; Library of Congress Performing Arts Annual. Address: c/o Lyric Opera of Dallas, 2733 Oak Lawn, Suite 201, Dallas, TX 75219, USA.

KIRK Vernon, b. 1966, England. Singer (Tenor). Education: Royal Academy of Music and Actors Centre, London; Britten-Pears School, Aldeburgh. Career: Concerts include tour of Germany and Holland in Monteverdi's Christmas Vespers with the Academy of Ancient Music; Bach St Matthew Passion with the London Baroque Soloists, St John Passion in Norway; Messiah and The Creation under David Willcocks; Berlioz L'Enfance du Christ and Brahms Lieder at the London Proms; Schumann's Manfred at the Festival Hall, Die schöne Müllerin at St Martin in the Fields; Lutoslawski Paroles Tissées at the Barbican Hall; Opera roles include Mozart's Tamino, Ferrando and Don Ottavio, Donizetti's Ernesto and Nemorino; Lensky, and Gonslave in L'Heure Espagnole (season 1996-97). Address: C&M Craig Services Ltd, 3 Kersley Street, London SW11 4PR, England.

KIRKBRIDE Simon Alexander, b. 5 May 1971, Newcastle upon Tyne, England. Singer (Baritone). Education: Royal College of Music, London, 1990-96; QEQM Scholar, 1994-96. Debut: Figaro, Glyndebourne Touring Opera, 1996; Publio, Welsh National Opera, 1997. Career: Concert works include: Requiems of Mozart, Faure, Durufle, Saint-Saëns and Brahms; Elgar's Dream of Gerontius; Handel's Messiah; Appearances with many leading orchestras and choirs in the UK and Canada. Recording: Saint-Saëns Requiem, 1993. Honour: President's Rose Bowl, 1996. Hobbies: Walking; Cinema; Golf. Current Management: Colwell Arts Management, Canada. Address: 67 Furnace Lane, Nether Heyford, Northant NN7 3JS, England.

KIRKBY Emma, b. 26 Feb 1949, Camberley, Surrey, England. Singer (Soprano). Education: Studied Classics at Oxford; Vocal studies with Jessica Cash. Debut: London Concert, 1974. Career: Many concert appearances with the Consort of Musicke directed by Anthony Rooley, Andrew Parrott's Taverner Players and the Academy of Ancient Music with Christopher Hogwood; Later repertoire with London Baroque; Tour of USA, 1978; Tours to Middle East with Anthony Rooley, 1980-83; Appearances with Andrew Parrott at the Promenade Concerts in Monteverdi's Vespers and the Bach B Minor Mass; Sang Dorinda in Handel's Orlando, 1989; TV appearances in Messiah and the Central TV series Man and his Music; Repertoire ranges from 15th Century Italian songs to arias by Haydn and Mozart; London Prom Concerts 1993, in Charpentier's Messe pour les Trépassés and Monteverdi Madrigals Book VI; Sang in Behind the Masque, a Purcell Celebration, at the London Barbican, 1996. Recordings include: Monteverdi's Orfeo and German arias by Handel: Handel and Italian cantatas, Mozart Motets; Dido and Aeneas; Venus and Adonis by Blow and Locke's Cupid and Death with the Consort of Musicke; Arne Cantatas (The Parley of Instruments); Bach Cantatas 211 and 212 (Academy of Ancient Music); Handel Aci, Galatea e Polifemo (London Baroque) and Athalia; Monteverdi Sacred Vocal Music; Pergolesi Stabat Mater; Songs by Maurice Greene, Arie Autiche; Songs by Arie and Handel; Vivaldi opera arias. Address: c/o Hazard Chase Ltd, Richmond House, 16-20 Regent Street, Cambridge CB2 1DB, England.

KIRKENDALE Ursula, b. 6 Sept 1932, Dortmund, Germany. Music Historian. m. Warren Kirkendale, 16 June 1959,

3 daughters. Education: Dr phil, Bonn, 1961. Career: Taught at University of Southern California, University of California, Duke University, Columbia University, USA, as Visiting Professor. Publications: Antonio Caldara: Sein Leben und seine venezianisch-römischen Oratorien, 1966. Contributions to: Acta Musicologica; Journal American Musicological Society; Chigiana; Music and Letters; Dizionario Biografico degli Italiani. Honours: fellow, Deutscher Akademischer Austauschdienst; American Council of Learned Societies; Alfred Einstein Award; Deems Taylor Award; Elected Wirkendes Mitglied der Gesellschaft zur Herausgabe von Denkmälen der Tonkunst in Österreich; Festschrift: Musicologia Humana (with bibliography), 1994. Address: Via dei Riari 86, 00165 Rome, Italy.

KIRKENDALE Warren, b. 14 Aug 1932, Toronto, Canada. Music historian. m. Ursula Schöttier, 1959, 3 daughters. Education: BA, University of Toronto, 1955; PhD, University of Vienna, Austria, 1961. Career: Assistant Professor, University of Southern California, 1963-67; Associate Professor, Duke University, 1967-75; Professor, 1975-82; Professor Ordinarius, University Regensburg, Germany, 1983-92. Publications: Fuge and Fugato in der Kammermusik des Rokoko und der Klassik, 1967, English, 1979; L'Aria di Fiorenza, 1972; Madrigali a diversi Linguaggi, 1975; The Court Musicians in Florence during the Principate of the Medici, 1993. Contributions to: Journal of American Musicological Society; Acta Musicologica; Music Quarterly; Mozart-Jahrbuch; Quadrivium; Dizionario Biografico degli Italiani. Honours: Fellow, Deutscher Akademischer Austauschdienst; NEH; American Council of Learned Societies; Volkswagen-Stiftung Visiting Scholar, Harvard University Centre for Italian Renaissance Studies in Florence; Elected Wirkendes Mitglied der Gesellschaft zur Herausgabe von Denmälern der Tonkunst in Österreich; Doctor honoris causa, University of Pavia, 1986; Accademico Filarmonico honoris causa, Bologna, 1987; Medal, Collège de France, 1994; Festschrift: Musicologia Humana (with bibliography), 1994. Memberships: International, Italian and American Musicological Societies. Hobby: Mountain climbing. Address: Via dei Riari 86, 1-00165 Rome, Italy.

KIRKOP Oreste, b. 26 July 1923, Hamrun, Malta. Singer (Tenor). Education: Studied with Nicolo Baldacchino and Giuseppina Ravaglia in Malta and with Emilio Ghirardini in Milan. Debut: Malta 1945, as Turiddu. Career: Sang with visiting Italian companies and with Tito Gobbi and Maria Caniglia; Joined the Carl Rosa Company, England, 1950; Sadler's Wells from 1952, as Turiddu, Cavaradossi and Rodolfo in Luisa Miller; Appeared as Canio in Pagliacci on BBC TV; Covent Garden debut 1954, as the Duke of Mantua; Contract with Paramount films led to a leading role in The Vagabond King, 1956; Sang at Las Vagas and the Hollywood Bowl and appeared on NBC TV in pioneering presentations of Madame Butterfly, La Traviata and Rigoletto; Covent Garden 1958-59 in La Bohème and Rigoletto; Retired 1960.

KIRSHBAUM Ralph, b. 4 Mar 1946, Denton, TX, USA. Cellist. Education: Studied with his father Joseph Kirshbaum, with Lev Aronson in Dallas and with Aldo Parisot at Yale University. Debut: With the Dallas Symphony, 1959. Career includes: From 1970 has performed with most leading orchestras including those in: London, Berlin, Amsterdam and Paris; USA engagements with many American orchestras including the Boston Symphony, Chicago Symphony and the Los Angeles Philharmonic; Tours of Germany, Hungary, Switzerland, Israel, Scandinavia, New Zealand, Australia and Japan; Debut with the Orchestre de Paris in 1990; Festival appearances include: Edinburgh, London's South Bank and the Mostly Mozart Festival in NY; Promenade Concerts in London include premiere of Tippett's Triple Concerto in 1980; Premiered the Cello Concerto by Peter Maxwell Davies with Cleveland Orchestra under Christoph von Dohnanyi in 1989; Has appeared with many renowned conductors including: Georg Solti, Yuri Temirkanov, Simon Rattle, André Previn and Colin Davis; Founder and Artistic Director of the RNCM Manchester International Cello Festival; Fellow and Tutor at The RNCM; Regular concerts with violinist György Pauk and pianist Peter Frankl; Frequent guest of the violinist and conductor Pinchas Zukerman, playing Brahms's Double Concerto in London, Edinburgh, Tokyo and Chicago; Played the Schumann Concerto at St John's, London, 1997. Recordings include: Barber Concerto; Elgar Concerto; Tippett Triple Concerto; Bach Suites; Haydn Concertos. Honours include: Winner, International Tchaikovsky Competition in Moscow, 1970. Current Management: Ingpen and Williams Ltd. Address: c/o Ingpen and Williams Ltd, 14 Kensington Court, London, W8 5DN.

KIRYU Yoshihide, b. 15 Aug 1940, Tokyo, Japan.Bassoon Player. m. Masae, 13 Dec 1973, 2 sons. Education: Studied with Professor Kazutsugu Nakata, Professor Heihachirou Mita, Professor Harold Golshire at Juilliard, Professor Leonard Sharow in Aspen and Professor Sherman Walt. Debut: 1959 Recital TWIS Woodwind Quintet. Career: Member Yomiuri Nippon Symphony Orchestra; Soloist in Mozart bassoon concerto; Member NHK Symphony Orchestra, Principal Player; Soloist of Mozart and Haydn Concertante and Richard Strauss Double Concerto. Honours: Japan Music Competition 1st Prize; 10th Arim Prize. Memberships: Tokyo Fagottiade; TWIS Woodwind Quintet. Address: 6-21-3 Shimo-Shakujii, Tokyo 177, Japan.

KISCH Alistair (Royalton), b. 20 Jan 1919, London, England. Conductor; Artistic Director. m. Aline Stewart, 1940, 1 son, 2 daughters. Education: Clare College, Cambridge. Career: Conductor: Royal Festival Hall concerts with London Philharmonic Orchestra; Royal Philharmonic Orchestra. Guest conductor: Halle Orchestra, City of Birmingham Symphony Orchestra, Palestine Symphony Orchestra, Florence Philharmonic Orchestra, Athens State Symphony Orchestra, Pasdeloup Orchestra of Paris, Royal Opera House, Orchestra of Rome, San Carlo Symphony Orchestra of Naples, Vienna Symphony Orchestra, etc. Broadcasts, BBC, with London Symphony Orchestra, Royal Philharmonic Orchestra, Philharmonia Orchestra. Currently Artistic Director, Cork Street Art Gallery, Specialist, English & French paintings, 20th Century; Freelance conductor of symphony concerts. Recordings: Decca. Memberships: Friends of Tate Gallery. Hobbies: Good Food & Wine. Address: 2 Edwardes Square, Kensington, London W8, England.

KISER Wieslaw (Maria), b. 20 July 1937, Poznan, Poland. Conductor; Critic; Composer. Education: High School of Music, Poznan. Debut: As composer, Poznan, 1965; As Conductor, Poznan, 1963. Career: Over 750 concerts in Poland, Bulgaria, Finland, France, Germany, USSR and Czechoslovakia; Artistic Manager, The Boys Choir of Gniezno, Poland, 1989; Music Lecturer and Promotor of Music Life, 1990-; The Thrushes; Television and Radio broadcasts in Poland, Finland, France, USSR and Germany. Compositions: From the Years 1989-1990; Scherzo for the violin and string orchestra; Aria to J S Bach's chorale for the violin and string orchestra; Trio for the viola, violoncello and contrabass; Impromptu for the viola, violoncello and contrabass; Six Children compositions for the piano Sonata for the piano; Over 70 choral compositions. Recordings: Radio & TV Poland, Finland, USSR, Germany and France. Publications: Organisation and Education of Children's Choirs, 1971; Aerials of Poznan, 1975; The Selected Problems of Music History, 1969; Watchword, The Music, in Encykloeadia Wielkopolska, The Great Poland Encyclopaedie; Watchword, The Music, in Dzieje Poznania, The Aets of Poznan, 1989-90. Hobbies: Working with Youth. Address: u Szelagowska 12, 61-626 Poznan, Poland.

KISSIN Evgeny, b. 10 Oct 1971, Moscow, Russia. Concert Pianist. Education: Studied with Anna Cantor at Gnessin Institute of Music from 1977. Debut: Played Beethoven sonatas and a Mozart concerto aged 7. Career: Appearances with the USSR State Symphony Orchestra under Svetlanov and the Moscow Philharmonic; Tour of Japan with the Moscow Virtuosi under Vladimir Spivakov; Played with the Berlin Radio orchestra, November 1986; British debut at the 1987 Lichfield Festival with the BBC Philharmonic; London Symphony Orchestra concert May 1988 conducted by Valery Gergiev; Concerts with the Royal Philharmonic and Yuri Temirkanov, March 1990; Promenade concert debut with the BBC Symphony under David Atherton, playing Tchaikovsky's 1st Concerto, 1990; US Debut September 1990 with the New York Philharmonic conducted by Zubin Mehta; Carnegie Hall recital playing Schumann, Prokofiev, Liszt and Chopin; Tour of America, 1991, performing at Tanglewood, Mann Music Center, Ravnia and the Hollywood Bowl; Season 1992-93 at Grammy Award Ceremonies, performances with the Chicago Symphony, Philadelphia Orchestra and Boston Symphony; London recital debut and concert with the Philharmonia; Prokofiev Concertos with the Berlin Philharmonic under Abbado; Played Chopin and Schumann at the Festival Hall, London, 1997. Recordings include: Rachmaninov 2nd Concerto and Etudes Tableaux with the London Symphony conducted by Gergiev; Rachmaninov Concerto No 3; Chopin Volumes I and II, live recital from Carnegie Hall; Prokofiev Piano Concertos 1 and 3 with Berlin Philharmonic conducted by Claudio Abbado. Current Management: Harold Holt Ltd, 31 Sinclair Road, London W14 0NS, England.

KISSOCZY Marc, b. 5 July 1961, Montreal, Quebec, Canada. Conductor. m. Barbara Kissoczy, 5 July 1991, 1 son, 1 daughter. Education: Studied Violin at Conservatories of Zurich and Berne; Conducting in Zurich and at Pierre Monteux School, USA; Masterclasses with Celibidache, Boulez and others. Debut: With Tonhalle Orchestra, Zurich, 1992. Career: Conducted major orchestras in Europe including Paris, Zurich, Lyon, Geneva, Cologne and Saarbrücken, in Asia including Taipei and Hanoi, in Sao Paulo, Brazil; Currently Music Director, Vietnam National Symphony Orchestra. Honours: Award, Swiss Association of Musical Artists, 1989; Award, City of Zurich, 1990; 3rd Prize, International Conductor Competition, Geneva, 1994; Prix du Rayonnement Français. Memberships: Swiss Association of Musical Artists; Conductors Guild of America; ASOL. Hobbies: Skiing; Carpentry. Current Management: Melos, CH-6900 Lugano, Switzerland. Address: Limmattalstrasse 74, CH-8049 Zurich, Switzerland.

KISTETENYI Melinda, b. 25 July 1926, Budapest, Hungary. Composer. Education: Studied at the Budapest Academy of Music, 1945-53. Career: Professor of Music Theory at the Budapest Academy, 1956-89; Organist in Hungary and throughout Europe. Compositions include: Ballets: Ballad Of The Girl Dancing To Death, 1958, and Serenade, 1958; Organ Concerto, 1962; British Folk Song Setting; Looking On The Water for Baritone, Flute, Guitar and Cello, 1973; Choruses. Address: c/o ARTISJUS, PO Box 593, H-1538 Budapest, Hungary.

KIT Mikhail, b. 1950, Russia. Singer (Bass). Education: Studied at the Odessa Conservatoire. Career: Sang first with the Perm Opera, then joined the Kirov Opera, 1966, singing Pimen, Boris, Prince Igor, Dosifei, Ivan Susanin, Gremin, Basilio, Leporello, Mephistopheles, Iago and Sarastro; Visited Edinburgh and the Metropolitan with the Kirov, 1991-92, Japan, 1993; Sang Dosifei in Khovanshchina with the Kirov Opera at Tel Aviv, 1996; Engaged as Gremin at the Opéra Bastille, Paris, 1997. Recordings include: The Fiery Angel and the title role in Prince Igor (Philips); Shostakovich songs with Larissa Gergieva for the BBC. Address: Lies Askonas Ltd, 6 Henrietta Street, London WC2E 8LA, England.

KITCHEN Linda, b. 1960, Morecambe, Lancashire, England. Soprano. Education: Studied at Royal Northern College of Music with Nicholas Powell; National Opera Studio, 1983; Later study with David Keren. Career: Sang Blonde in Mozart's Die Entführung 1983 and Monteverdi's Amor at the 1984 Glyndebourne Festival; Later sang Flora in The Knot Garden at Covent Garden and Barbarina in The Marriage of Figaro at the London Coliseum; Other roles include Mozart's Susanna, Papagena and Zerlina; Concert repertory includes Rossini's Stabat Mater, Mozart's Requiem, Poulenc's Gloria and Schoenberg's Pierrot Lunaire; In 1988 sang Iris in Handel's Semele, at Covent Garden; Later Studied with David Ceren and Audrey Langford; Sang Oscar in Ballo in Maschera, Flora in The Knot Garden, Sophie in Werther, Jemmy in Guillaume Tell; In Dublin, Pamina, Magic Flute; Opera North, Cherubino, Zerlina, Serpetta in Finta Gardiniera and Magnolia in Showboat; Other Roles include Adele; Sang Eurydice in a new production of Orpheus in the Underworld for Opera North, 1992, followed by Susanna in The Marriage of Figaro; Season 1997-98 with Despina and Martinu's Julietta for Opera North and Drusilla in Poppea for Welsh National Opera. Recordings: A Serenade to Music, for Hyperion. Honours: Heinz Bursary. Current Management and Address: c/o Harrison/Parrott Ltd, 12 Penzance Place, London W11 4PA, England.

KITCHINER John, b. 2 Dec 1933, England. Singer (Tenor). Education: Studied at the London Opera Centre with Joan Cross. Debut: Glyndebourne 1965, as Count Almaviva. Career: Appearances with English National Opera, Scottish Opera and Welsh National Opera; Roles include Guglielmo, Don Alfonso, Don Giovanni, Renato in Un Ballo in Maschera, Count di Luna, Figaro and Bartolo in Il Barbiere di Siviglia, Robert in Le Comte Ory, Marcello, Escamillo, and Count Eberbach in Der Wildschütz by Lortzing; Also sang in the British stage premieres of Prokofiev's War and Peace and The Bassarids by Henze, at the London Coliseum, 1972, 1974; Frequent concert engagements. Address: c/o English National Opera, London Coliseum, St Martin's Lane, London WC2, England.

KITE-POWELL Jeffery T, b. 24 June 1941, Miami, Florida, USA. University Professor; Musicologist. m. Helga A M Bordt, 19 Apr 1973, 3 sons. Education: BM, College-Conservatory of Music, Cincinnati, Ohio, 1963; BS Music Education, University of Cincinnati, 1964; MA Musicology, University of New Mexico, Albuquerque, 1969; PhD Musicology, University of Hamburg, Federal Republic of Germany, 1976. Career: Currently, Director of Early Music Studies and the Early Music Ensembles, Florida State University, Tallahassee, Florida, USA. Publications: The Visby Petri Organ Tablature-Investigation, Critical Edition, Vols 14 & 15 of Quellenkataloge zur Musikgeschichte, 1980; Series Editor of Performer's Guides to Early Music and Editor, contributor to the Renaissance volume, 1994; The New Grove Dictionary of Music and Musicians, 6th Edition, Contributor, 1980; Hamburgische Kirchenmusik im Reformationszeitalter, Leichsenring, Vol 20 in Hamburger Beiträge zur Musikwissenschaft, Editor, 1982; Syntagma musicum III, translation and edition of Michael Praetorius's treatise of 1619, forthcoming. Honours: Invited lecturer, First International Organ Academy, University of Gothenburg, Sweden, 1994; Invited lecturer, Musikwissenschaftliches Synposion, Hamburg, 1995; Keynote speaker, Instrumentalischer Bettlermantl Symposium, University of Edinburgh, 1997. Memberships: President, Early Music of America; Treasurer, Society for Seventeenth-Century Music; American Musicological Society, past president, Southern Chapter; Historical Brass Society. Address: School of Music, Florida State University, Tallahassee, FL 32306-1180, USA.

KITTNAROVA Olga, b. 15 Aug 1937, Prague, Czech Republic. Pedagogue; Journalist. Div., 1 daughter. Education: Musicology, Faculty of Philosophy and History, Charles

University, Prague, 1955-60; PhD, 1971. Career: Editor, Supraphone, 1960-65; Teacher of Music, Music History and Theory, Prague Conservatoire, 1973-91; Pedagogue, Department of Musical Education, Pedagogical Faculty, Charles University, Prague; Permanent Reviewer for newspapers and magazines; Cooperation with 400 programmes for Prague Radio; Interested in musical ecology; Delivered the Women of Europe Award Lecture, The Excess of Sound in Contemporary Music, at Barcelona, 1994. Compositions include: Songs about Music with own texts, piano and Orff's instruments, published, 1995. Publications: Prague Quartet, 1974; Selective Catalogue of Completed Works of Czech Composers of the 20th Century, 1976; Prague Quartet, Memorial Volume, UNESCO Symposium, 1978. Contributions to: Critical Miscellany, Musical Inventor A Hába, 1991; Jarmil Burghauser, 1992; Memorial Volume from Ecological Congress-Warning Memento of Sound Excess, 1995. Memberships: Association of Musical Artists and Musicologists, Committee for Music Ecology; Czech Musical Society; Mozart's Community. Hobbies: Cycling; Canoeing. Address: Benesovska 4, 10100 Prague 10, Czech Republic.

KITTS Christopher (Martin), b. 7 April 1943, London, England. Conductor; Violinist; Educator. m. 16 December 1982. Education: Trinity College of Music, London, 1968; Conducting Studies with Dr Boyd Neel, Toronto, 1964-67, Dr Hans Lert, Virginia, 1966; Violin Studies with Bernard Robbins, New York Philharmonic, Clifford Evans, Toronto. Career: Conductor, Royal Conservatory Orchestra, Toronto, 1967, 1968, 1969; Conductor, Scarborough College Choir and Band, 1970; Concertmaster, North York Symphony Orchestra, 1971, 1972; Freelance Violinist, Toronto, 1972-85; Conducted Tours in England, France, West Germany, Netherlands, with Birchmount Park Collegiate, 1980, 1983, 1987, 1991; Adjudicator, Toronto International Music Festival, 1986, 1987; Music Director and Conductor, Scarborough Philharmonic Orchestra, 1985-93; Guest Conductor, Brampton Symphony, Mississauga Symphony, Scarborough Philharmonic, 1994-95. Address: 3663 Danforth Avenue, Scarborough, Ontario M1N 2GZ, Canada.

KLAES Armin, b. 17 Sept 1958, Koblenz, Germany. Conductor. m. Monika Hachmoller, 16 Mar 1982, 1 son. 1 daughter. Education: Conducting, Reinhard Peters Folkwang-Musikhochschulen Essen; Music pedagody and composition, Musikhochschule, Koln; Musicology, University of Koln; Chamber Music with Gunter Kehr. Debut: Bedford Springs Festival for the Performing Arts, Pennsylvania, USA. Career: Guest conductor with several orchestras since 1978; Founder and regular leader, Kolner Konzertgemeinschaft, 1978-85; Music Director, Mannesmann-Sinfonieorchester Duisburg, 1985-92; Founder and conductor of the Amadeus Kammerorchester, 1991; Since 1992, Artist leader of the Musikgemeinschaft Marl, symphonic orchestra and oratorio chorus. Recordings: Bach, Concert for organ with H Schauerte, Le Carnaval des Animaux. Honours: Folkwang - Forderpries, 1987. Address: Corneliusstrasse 167, 47918n Tonisvorst, Germany.

KLANSKA Vladimira, b. 9 September 1947, Ceské Budejovice, Czech Republic. Hornist. m. Ivan Klansky, 1973-84, 2 sons. Education: Conservatory of Music, Prague, 1965-69; Academy of Music, Prague, 1969-73; Master Classes with Herrmann Baumann, 1976. Debut: Mozart II, Rudolfinum Hall, Prague, 1966. Career: Co-Principal, Prague Symphony Orchestra, 1968-74; Concert Tours Throughout Europe in Duo Recitals with Pianist Ivan Klansky, Mozarteum Salzburg, 1972, Concertgebouw, Amsterdam, 1974; Member, Prague Wind Quintet, 1980; Member, Czech nonet, 1982; Artistic Leader, PWQ and CN, 1991-, Concert Tours with Both Ensembles in Europe, USA and Japan, including Festivals in Salzburg, Edinburgh, Stresa, Sorrento; Radio Recordings in Prague, Stockholm, Brussels, Bremen Geneve, Montreux. Recordings: CD's, both solo and chamber music. Honour: Prize Winner, International ARD Music Competition, Munich, 1973; Juror, International Horn Competitions. Memberships: President, Stich Punto Horn Society, 1989-. Address: Stronjnicka 9, 17000 Praha 7, Czech Republic.

KLANSKY Ivan, b. 13 May 1948, Prague, Czech Republic. Pianist; Piano Lecturer. 4 sons. Education: Conservatory, Prague, 1963-68; Academy of Music, Prague, 1968-73. Debut: Prague, 1960. Career: Over 3000 Solo and Chamber Music Concerts in 5 Continents 1960-97; Head, Piano Department, Academy of Music, Prague; Piano Lecturer, Conservatory Lucerne, Switzerland. Recordings: Shetana, Complete Piano Works; Sanacek, Complete Piano Works; Schubert, Piano Work; Moscheles, Concerto No 3. Honours: 2nd Prize, Bolzano, 1967; 3rd Prize, Napoli, 1968; 2nd Prize, Leipzig, 1968; 2nd Prize, Barcelona, 1970; Finalist, Warsaw, 1970; 2nd Prize, Santander, 1996. Memberships: International Federation of Chopin Societies. Hobbies: Public Transport Timetables. Current Management: Pragoart Concerts, Prague. Address: Pod Devinem 23, Prague 5, Czech Republic.

KLARWEIN Franz, b. 8 March 1914, Garmisch, Germany. Singer, Tenor. m. Sari Barbas. Education: Studied with Fritz

Kerzman and at the Frankfurt Musikhochschule; Further study in Berlin. Career: Sang lyric roles at the Berlin Staatsoper 1937-42; Bayerische Staatsoper Munich from 1942, notably in the world premieres of Capriccio by Strauss 1942 and Hindemith's Die Harmonie der Welt, 1957, and in the German premiere of Raskolnikov by Sutermeister 1949; Salzburg Festival 1942-44, tenor solo in the Choral Symphony and in the unofficial premiere of Strauss's Die Liebe der Danae; Sang with the Munich company at Covent Garden 1953, in the British premiere of Capriccio; Maggio Musicale Florence 1957, as Aegisthus in Elektra. Recordings: Elektra; Der fliegende Holländer and Der Rosenkavalier; Der Waffenschmied by Lortzing; CDs of Die Meistersinger, as Eisslinger, 1964. Address: c/o Bayerische Staatsoper, Postfach 745, D-8000 Munich 1, Germany.

KLAS Eri, b. 7 June 1939, Tallin, Estonia. Conductor. Education: Studied with parents then at the Tallinn Conservatoire with Gustav Ernesaks. Debut: Conducted West Side Story at the Estonian Opera House, 1964. Career: Instrumentalist with the Symphony Orchestra of Estonian Radio from 1964; Studied further at the Leningrad Conservatoire with Nikolai Rabinovich, then at the Bolshoi School, Moscow, Boris Khaikin, 1969-72; Conducted at the Bolshoi from 1972; Musical Director of Tallinn Opera 1975; Founded the Estonian Chamber Orchestra 1977; Guest engagements at the Paris Opera and in Japan; Conductor of the Royal Opera Stockholm, 1985; Conducted Don Giovanni at Stockholm 1988, Eugene Oengin for the Finnish National Opera at Helsinki and Essen, 1989; Music Director, Royal Opera, Stockholm, 1985-89; Chief Conductor, Aarhus Symphony Orchestra, Denmark since 1990; Since 1990 frequent guest conductor of major Symphony Orchestras in USA; Los Angeles, Cleveland, Detroit, Baltimore, Dallas and others; Guest conductor at Hamburg Opera, premiere of Schnittke ballet Peer Gynt, 1989; Debuts with the Los Angeles Philharmonic and the Baltimore Symphony, 1992; Conducted Porgy and Bess at the 1992 Savonlinna Festival; Don Carlos at Helsinki, 1996. Recordings: Recordings for BISA record label includes works by Alfred Schnittke, with the 3rd Symphony, Stockholm Philharmonic and the 4 Violin Concertos, Malmo Symphony. Honours: Order of WASA, Swedish Royal Medal; Order of Finnish Lion, 1992. Current Management: c/o Konserbolaget AB, Kungsgaten 32, S-111 35 Stockholm, Sweden. Address: Nurme 54, EE0016 Tallin, Estonia.

KLEBE Giselher, b. 28 June 1925, Mannheim, Germany. Composer. m. Lore Schiller, 1946, 2 daughters. Education: Berlin Conservatoire; Studied, Boris Blacher. Career: Composer in Berlin until 1957; Professor, Composition & Theory of Music, Nordwestdeutsche Musik-Akademie, Detmold, 1957-; Member, Academy of Fine Arts, Berlin 1964 and Hamburg 1963, Bavarian Academy of Fine Arts, 1978. Composition: Principal Works include: Operas: Die Räuber (Schiller) 1957; Die tödlichen Wünsche (Balzac) 1959; Die Ermordung Caesars (Shakespeare) 1959; Alkmene (Kleist) 1961; Figaro lässt sich scheiden (Oedoen von Horvath), 1963; Jakobowsky und der Oberst (Werfel), 1965; Das Märchen von der Schönen Lilie (Goethe), 1969; Ein Wahrer Held (Synge/Boell), 1975; Rendezvous (Sostschenko) 1977; Der Juengste Tag (Oedoen von Horvath), 1980; Die Fastnachtsbeichte (Zuckmayer), 1983; Gervaise Macquart, 1995; Emile Zola, 1996; Ballets: Signale, 1955; Menagerie, 1958; Orchestral Works: Die Zwitschermaschine 1950; Deux Nocturnes 1952; 5 Sinfonien, 1952, 1953, 1967, 1971, 1977, 1996; Adagio und Fuge (with theme from Wagner's Walküre), 1962; Five Lieder, 1962; Vier Vocalisen für Frauenchor, a Cappella 1963; La Tomba di Igor Strawinsky (oboe and chamber orchestra), 1979; Konzert for organ and orchestra, 1980; Church Music; Missa, 1964; Stabat Mater, 1964; Messe (Gebet einer armen Seele), 1966; Chamber Music: 3 String Quartets, 1949, 1963, 1981; 2 Solo Violin Sonatas, 1952, 1955; 2 Sonatas for Violin & Piano, 1953, 1974; Piano Trio Elegia Appasionata, 1955; Clarinet Concerto, 1984; Notturno for orchestra, 1987; Chamber Music: Soirée für Posaune und Kammerensemble, 1987; Many other musical works. Membership: President of Academy of Fine Arts, Berlin, 1986. Address: Bruchstrasse 16, 4930 Detmold 1, Germany.

KLEE Bernhard, b. 19 April 1936, Schleiz, Germany. Conductor. Education: Studied piano, composition and conducting at the Cologne Conservatoire; Assistant to Otto Auckermann and Wolfgang Sawallisch at the Cologne opera house. Career: Early appointments in Salzburg, Oberhausen and Hanover; Music Director in Lubeck 1966-73; Chief Conductor of the North German Radio in Hanover 1976-79; General Music Director in Dusseldorf from 1977; Chief Guest Conductor of the BBC Philharmonic Orchestra 1985-89; Conducted the orchestra at the 1989 Promenade Concerts, with Berg's Three Pieces from Wozzeck and Mahler's 6th Symphony; Has conducted all the major German and London orchestras, the English Chamber Orchestra, Stockholm and Rotterdam Philharmonics, Zurich Tonhalle, RAI Rome, Vienna Symphony, and NHK Tokyo; US debut 1974, with the New York Philharmonic: has since conducted in San Francisco, Chicago, Detroit and Washington; Regular guest conductor at opera houses in Hamburg, Munich, Berlin, Covent Garden and Geneva; Festival engagements at Edinburgh,

Salzburg, Holland, Hong Kong and Dubrovnik; Promenade Concerts, London 1991, Mozart's Clarinet Concerto and Bruckner's 9th Symphony (BBC Philharmonic). Recordings: Extensive catalogue with Polydor and EMI. Address: c/o Ingpen & Williams Ltd, 14 Kensington Court, London W8 5DN, England.

KLEIBER Carlos, b. 3 July 1930, Berlin, Germany. Conductor. Education: Studied music in Buenos Aires, Chemistry at Zurich University. Career: Worked as repetiteur at the Gärtnerplatz Theatre, Munich, 1952-53; Conducted at Potsdam from 1954, then at the Deutsche Oper am Rhein, Dusseldorf/Duisburg, 1956-64; Zurich Opera 1964-66; Stuttgart Opera from 1966 and Munich Opera from 1968; Vienna Staatsoper debut 1973, Bayreuth Festival 1974, Otello; At Covent Garden (from 1974) has conducted Der Rosenkavalier and Otello; Other operas he has conducted include La Traviata, La Bohème, Der Freischütz, Die Fledermaus, Wozzeck, Carmen and Elektra; Has conducted at the Vienna Festival and the Prague Spring Festival; Engagements with leading orchestras in Europe and North America. Recordings include: Der Freischütz (Dresden Staatskapelle); Beethoven's 4th Symphony (Bavarian State Orchestra) and 5th and 7th Symphonies (Vienna Philharmonic); Schubert Symphonies nos 3 and 8; Brahms Symphony no 4 (Vienna Philharmonic); Dvorak Piano Concerto (Sviatoslav Richter and the Bavarian Radio Orchestra); Die Fledermaus; La Traviata; Tristan und Isolde, with the Dresden Staatskapelle.

KLEIBERG Ståle, b. 8 Mar 1958, Stavanger, Norway. Composer; Associate Professor. m. Åsta Ovregaard, 25 Jun 1982, 1 d. Education: Degree in Musicology, University of Oslo; Diploma in Composing, State Academy of Music, Oslo. Career: In addition to numerous concert performances of his works nearly all have been performed on Norwegian radio; Associate Professor, University of Trondheim. Compositions: 28 Opuses since 1981, including commissions; Compositions include large works for full orchestra and church music as well as chamber works for various ensembles and solo works; String Quartet, 1985; Stilla for Orchestra and Soprano/Tenor, 1986; Two Poems by Montale, 1986; The Bell Reef, Symphony No 1, 1991; The Rose Window, 1992; Dopo for Violoncello Solo and Strings, 1993. Publications: David Monrad Johansen's Musical Thoughts, 1983; Form in Impressionism, 1985; The Music of Hans Abrahamsen, 1986; CPE Bach and The Individual Expression, 1989; Sturm und Drang as Style and Period Designation in Music History, 1991. Membership: Norwegian Society of Composers. Address: Stokkanhaugen 201, N-7048 Trondheim, Norway.

KLEIN Kenneth, b. 5 Sept 1939, Los Angeles, California, USA. Music Director; Conductor. Education: Graduated Magna cum Laude, University of Southern California; Stanford University. Debut: Europe, 1970; Paris, 1974; Moscow, 1974; Vienna, 1975. Career: Conductor, Stuttgart Ballet in Stuttgart and then the Metropolitan Opera in all major cities of the USA; Toured USSR, Romania and Sweden, 1971, 1972; Invited by Pablo Casals to conduct 4 concerts in Puerto Rico, 1974; Conducted Suisse Romande Orchestra, Lamoureux Orchestra, Paris, France, Vienna Symphony, Montreux Festival; Debut with American Symphony Orchestra at Carnegie Hall, New York; Bruckner Orchestra, Austria, 1978; Debut at Rome Festival, 1979; Debut with Philharmonia Orchestra, Royal Albert Hall, London, England, 1979; Florida Philharmonic, Miami, Florida, USA, 1980-81; Edmonton Symphony; Louisville Orchestra; North Carolina Symphony; Kansas City Philharmonic; San Francisco Chamber Orchestra; Music Director, conducting over 60 concerts per season, Guadalajara, Mexico; Music Director, New York Virtuosi, South Dakota Symphony and the Waterville Valley Festival; Has made numerous guest appearances worldwide.

KLEIN Lothar, b. 27 Jan 1932, Hanover, Germany. Composer; Professor of Composition. Education: PhD, Degree in Musicology and Composition, University of Minnesota, 1961. Career: As an undergraduate wrote music for many theatre and film productions; Professor of Composition, University of Toronto; Chairman, Graduate Studies in Music; Guest Lectures for 150th anniversary of Hochschule für Musik, Berlin, American Society for Aesthetics and Fulbright Commission. Compositions include: Stage Works: Canadiana 1980; Last Love 1950-56; Orpheus 1976; The Prodigal Son 1966; Orchestral: Appassionata for Orchestra 1958; The Bluebird 1952; Charivari: Music for an Imaginary Comedy 1966; Epitaphs for Orchestra 1963; Fanfares for Orchestra 1978; Musique a Go-Go 1966; Orchestral Suite from The Masque of Orianna, 1971; Presto for Orchestra, 1958; Rondo Giocoso for Orchestra 1964; Symmetries for Orchestra 1958; Symphonic Etudes (Symphony No 3) 1972; Symphony No 1, 1955; No 2, 1966; Band: Divertimento for Band, 1953; Eroica: Variations on A Promethean Theme 1970; Gloria for Band 1961; Small Orchestra: Janizary Music 1970; Sinfonia Concertante 1956; String Orchestra: Passacaglia of The Zodiac 1971; Soloists with Orchestra: Boccerini Collage for Cello and Orchestra 1978; Concerto for Winds, Timpani and Strings, 1956; Design for Percussion and Orchestra 1970; Ecologues for Horn and Strings, 1954; Invention, Blues and Chase, 1975; Musica Antiqua, 1975; Music for Violin and Orchestra, 1972; Paganini Collage for Violin and Orchestra, 1967; Scenes for Timpani and Strings, 1979; Slices of Time, 1973; Le Tresor des Dieux, 1969; Trio Concertante, 1961; Voices with Orchestra: Dorick Musick, 1973; Herbstlieder, 1962; The Masque of Orianna, 1973; Meditations on The Passyoun, 1961; The Philosopher in The Kitchen, 1974; Voices of Earth; Chorus: 8 Madrigals 1957; An Exaltation, 1960; Good Night, 1970; A Little Book of Hours, 1962; 3 Ancient Folksongs, 1959; 3 Chinese Laments, 1968; 3 Pastoral Songs, 1963; 3 Reflections, 1976; Travellers, 1981; 2 Christmas Madrigals, 1961; numerous works for Solo Voices; Solo Voice with Instrumental Ensemble; Instrumental Ensemble, Instrumental Solos; Piano Works; Concerti Sacro for viola and orchestra, 1980; Symphonic Partita, 1985; Centre-Stage for wind ensemble, 1991; Trocadero for winds and piano, 1994; Hachcava-Memorial Meditations for bass, voice, harps, 3 percussion, 1979; The Jabberwock in Ogden Nash's Dining Room, 1992; Birds, Bells and Bees - an Emily Dickinson Quilt for soprano, alto and pianist, 1986; String Quartet No 2 on piano of Wallace Stevens, 1991; Danceries fopr large orchestra, 1995. Address: PROCAN, 41 Valleybrook Drive, Don Mill, Ontario M3B 2S6, Canada.

KLEIN Mitchell (Sardou), b. 13 Aug 1947, New York, New York, USA. Conductor. m. Patricia Whaley, 20 May 1983. Education: BA, Brandeis University, 1968; BA, Music, College of Notre Dame, Belmont, California, 1972; MA, California State University, Hayward, 1976; Studied cello with Irving M Klein, and conducting with various masters. Career: Associate Conductor, Kansas City Philharmonic, 1979-82; Music Director, Santa Cruz Symphony, 1985-89; Music Director, Peninsula Symphony, California, 1985-; Guest Conductor: Seattle Symphonium, 1984; New Polish Philharmonic, 1993, 1996; San José Symphonium, 1993, 1994, 1996, 1997; Philharmonia Sudecka, Poland, 1997; Many other orchestras; TV Programme, Making Music, 1995; Artistic Director; Irving M Klein International String Competition, 1984-; NPR Radio; Voice of America, US Television. Honours: Bravo Award, 1993; Best Television Performance, 1995; Member, Music Panel, California Arts Council. Memberships: American Symphony Orchestra League; Board Member, Association of Californian Symphony Orchestras; American Symphony Orchestras League. Hobbies: Photography; Sound Equipment; Athletics. Current Management: Conductors' Co-operative Management. Address: 4472 Reinhardt Drive, Oakland, CA 94619, USA.

KLEINDIENST Stella, b. 1957, Germany. Soprano. m. Johannes Schaaf. Education: Studied at the Cologne Opera Studio. Career: Sang at the Bremen Opera, 1981-88, Deutsche Oper Berlin, 1988-89 and the Vienna Staatsoper from 1990; Sang in Musgrave's Voice of Ariadne at the 1981 Edinburgh Festival and in Zemlinsky's Der Kreidekreis at Amsterdam in 1986; Covent Garden in 1987 and 1989 as Cherubino in a production of Figaro by her husband; Further guest appearances at Stuttgart as Ariadne, Geneva and Antwerp; Other roles include Mila in Janácek's Osud, Anne Trulove, Belinda in Dido and Aeneas and Weber's Agathe; Sang Boulotte in Offenbach's Barbe-bleue at Stuttgart, 1996. Address: c/o Johannes Schaaf, Harrison Parrott Ltd, 12 Penzance Place, London, W11 4PA, England.

KLEINERTZ Rainer (Leonhard), b. 18 Dec 1958, Düsseldorf. Musicologist. m. Victoriana Herrador Morillo, 15 July 1988, 2 sons. Education: Diplomas: Viola, Academy of Music, Detmold, 1982; Magister Artium (MA) in Musicology, University of Paderborn, 1987; DrPhil, University of Paderborn, 1992. Career: Research Assistant and Lecturer, University of Paderborn, 1988-92; Visiting Professor, University of Salamanca, 1992-94; Assistant Professor, University of Regensburg, 1994-. Publications: Franz Liszt, Lohengrin et Tannhaüser de Richard Wagner,1989. Contributions to: Zum Problem des Frühwerks bei Franz Liszt in Studia Musicologica 34, 1992; Iphigenia en Tracia: Un zaruela desconocida de José de Nebra in Anuario Musical 48, 1993. Memberships: International Musicological Society; Gesellschaft für Musikforschung. Address: Universität Regensburg, Institut für Musikwissenschaft, D-93040 Regensburg, Germany.

KLEMENS Adam, b. 14 Jan 1967, Prague, Czech Republic. Composer; Conductor. Education: Composition, 1989, Conducting, 1994, Conservatoire, Prague; Composition, Academy of Performing Arts, Prague, 1994. Debut: Composer, Sinfonia Lacrimosa, Piano Concerto, 1989; Conductor, Prague Conservatoire Symphony Orchestra, 1994. Career: Conductor, Amy, with Lynn Barber (US Percussionist); With George Crumb, Night of the Four Moons, 1994; Suk Chamber Orchestra, 1997; Bambini di Praga, 1997; Teacher, Musical Theory, Prague Conservatoire, 1996-. Compositions: Clarinet Sonata, 1987; Sinfonia Lacrimosa, 1989; Perspectives for Oboe Solo, 1992; Music for Four Players, 1993; Piano concerto, 1994; Windy Music for Wind Orchestra, 1995; Fantasy for Wind Quintet and Harp, 1997; Composer of Film and Theatre Music. Honours: 1st Prize, Composers Competition, Generace, 1989, 1990; 3rd Prize, Composers Competition, Czech Ministry of Culture, 1990. Membership: Association of Musical Artists; Jeunesses Musicales of the Czech Republic. Hobbies: Travel; Aircraft; Computing. Address: Chudenicka 1080/12, 02 10200 Praha 10, Czech Republic.

KLERK Albert (De), b. 4 Oct 1917, The Netherlands, Organist; Composer. Education: Amsterdamsch Conservatorium. Career: Organist, St Joseph's Church, Haarlem, 1933-; City Organist, Haarlem, 1956-83; Director of Catholic Choir, Haarlem, 1946-91; Professor of Organ and Improvisation, Amsterdamsch Conservatorium (now Sweelinck Conservatorium), 1965-85. Compositions: Several works for organ including 3 concertos for organ and orchestra, chamber music and liturgical music (7 masses). Recordings: Has made numerous recordings. Honours: Prix d'Excellence, Amsterdam, 1941; Prix du Disque; Prix Edison, 1962. Address: Crayenesterlaan 22, Haarlem, The Netherlands.

KLIMOV Valery (Alexandrovich), b. 16 Oct 1931, Kiev, USSR. Violinist. Education: Studied with Mordkovich in Odessa, then joined David Oistrakh at the Moscow Conservatory, graduated 1959. Career: Prizewinner at competitions in Paris and Prague 1956; Soloist with Moscow Philharmonic 1957; Gold Medal Tchaikovsky Competition Moscow 1958; British debut with BBC Symphony Orchestra at the Royal Festival Hall 1967; Regular visits to America, Canada, Australia, Italy, Germany, Switzerland, Sweden; Appearances with such conductors as Ormandy, Svetlanov, Rozdestvensky, Temirkanov and Arvid Yansons; Other than the standard repertoire, plays music by Prokofiev, Khachaturian, Hindemith and Schnittke; Head of violin studies at the Moscow Conservatory 1975-. Recordings include: CD of the Khachaturian Concerto (Olympia). Honour: National Artist of the RSFSR 1972. Address: c/o Norman McCann International Artists Ltd, The Coach House, 56 Lawrie Park Gardens, London SE26 6XJ, England.

KLINDA Ferdinand, b. 12 Mar 1929, Kosice, Slovak Republic. Concert Organist; Professor. m. Luba Klindova, 2 daughters. Education: Diploma, Bratislava Conservatory, 1950; Med Dr, University of Bratislava, 1952; Concert Diploma, Bratislava Academy of Music, 1954; Studies, Prague, Weimar. Career: Concert tours, master classes in Europe, USA, Japan; Festival performances including Rome, Paris, Vienna, Prague, Helsinki, Budapest, Zurich, Leipzig, Moscow, London, Melbourne; Orchestral concerts with leading conductors including Ancerl, Adler, Baudo, Bour, Dorati, Rozhdestvensky, Herbig, Masur, Matacic, Neumann; Professor, Bratislava Academy of Music, 1962-; Juries, International Organ Competitions, Leipzig, Chartres, St Albans, Nuremberg, Prague and Budapest. Recordings: J S Bach on Historic Organs; Haydn Organ Concertos; Liszt, Messiaen, Slovak Historic Organs. Publications: Slovak Organ Music, Volume I, 1957, II, 1964; Organ Interpretation, 1980; Orgelregistrierung, 1987. Membership: Neue Bachgesellschaft, Leipzig. Current Management: Slovkoncert, Bratislava. Address: Langsfeldova 23, 81104 Bratislava, Slovakia.

KLINKOVA Zhivka, b. 30 July 1924, Samokov, Bulgaria. Composer. Education: Studied at the Sofia Academy and with Wagner-Regeny and Blacher in Berlin, 1960-68. Career: Performances of her stage works in Germany and elsewhere. Compositions include: Ballets and musicals: Kaliakra, 1966, Vietnamese Poem, 1972, Isle Of Dreams, 1978, Cyril And Methodius, 1981, Vassil Levski, 1992; Symphony, 1974; Piano Concerto, 1992; Chamber and keyboard music. Address: c/o Musicautor, 63 Tzar Assen Street, 1463 Sofia, Bulgaria.

KLINT Jorgen, b. 1948, Denmark. Bass-Baritone. Education: Studied at the Odense Conservatory. Debut: Royal Opera Copenhagen in 1975 as the Nightwatchman in Nielsen's Maskarade. Career: Sang Alberich in The Ring at Aarhus, 1983-87, and other Wagner roles include Amfortas, Daland and Titurel; Sang Boris in Shostakovich's Lady Macbeth at Copenhagen in 1991 and Nielsen's Saul in London in 1992; Other roles include Rocco, Ford, Banquo, Gremin and Barre in Penderecki's The Devils of Loudun; Frequent concert engagements. Address: c/o Den Jyske Opera, Thomas Jensens Alle, DK-8000 Aarhus, Denmark.

KLIPSTATTER Kurt, b. 17 Dec 1934, Graz, Austria. Conductor; Music Director. m. Mignon Dunn, 24 July 1972. Education: Conservatory Graz, private studies. Debut: Operahouse Graz, 1954. Career: Coach and Conductor at different opera companies in Austria and Germany; Music Director, Raimundtheater, Vienna, 1968-70; Artistic Director, Memphis Opera, USA, 1972-76; Music Director, Arkansas Orchestra, 1973-80; Faculty and Director of Orchestral Activities, Hartt College, 1977-90; Music Director, Greater Trenton Symphony, 1984-91; Director of Opera, Illinois Opera Theater, 1990-; Guest Conductor, National Opera Bellas Artes, Mexico; Opera Warsaw; City Opera, New York; Chautauqua (Michigan) Opera, Saarbrucken; Kassel Opera. Current Management: Diane Warden and Associates. Address: Krannert Center for the Performing Arts, 500 S Goodwin Avenue, Urbana, IL 61801, USA.

KLIT Lars, b. 9 March 1965, Vestervig, Denmark. 1 daughter. Education: Diploma, Composition, Royal Danish Music Academy, 1991. Compositions: The Last Virtuoso, Opera, 1991-94; Sentinel, 1993-94; Cat Walk, Opera, 1996-97; TN Memoriam Jimi Hendrix II, Concertos for Guitar & Orchestra. Contributions to: Opera Welt. Membership: Danish Composers Society. Address: Teglgaardsvej 627, 2 tv, DK 3050 Humlebaek, Denmark.

KLOBUCAR Berislav, b. 28 Aug 1924, Zagreb, Yugoslavia. Conductor. Education: Studied in Salzburg with Lovro von Matacic and Clemens Krauss. Career: Assistant at Zagreb Opera 1943-51; Conducted at the Vienna Staatsoper from 1953; General Director Graz Opera, 1960-71; Bayreuth Festival, 1968-69, Die Meistersinger and Lohengrin; Metropolitan Opera, 1968, Der fliegende Holländer, Die Walküre and Lohengrin; Music Director, Royal Opera Stockholm, 1972-81; Principal Conductor, Nice Opera, 1983-; Conducted L'amore dei tre re at Palermo, 1989; Many appearances as guest conductor with leading orchestras. Address: Orchestre Philharmonique de Nice, Opéra de Nice, A Rue Saint-Francois de Paule, F-06300 Nice, France.

KLOS Wolfgang, b. 15 July 1953, Vienna, Austria. Viola Professor; Chamber Musician; Soloist. m. Olga Sommer, 20 Feb 1982. Education: Law student, University of Vienna; Violin studies 1969, viola 1971-, Final Diploma with Distinction 1977, Musikhochschule, Vienna; Master courses, M Rostal, U Koch, B Giuranna. Career: Leader, Viola Sections, Tonhalle Orchestra, Zurich, Switzerland, 1977-81; Vienna Symphony Orchestra 1981-89; Teacher, viola, chamber music & orchestra, Vorarlberg State Conservatory of Music, Feldkirch, Austria, 1977-89; Professor, viola and chamber music and master classes, Vienna Musikhochschule, 1988-; Master classes, various locations, Europe and overseas; Soloist throughout Europe, 1981-; Member (numerous concerts, radio, TV recordings worldwide), Vienna String Trio. Recordings include: Continuous recording whole String Trio repertory (5 records to date); Numerous recordings with various orchestras & chamber music groups. Hobbies: Literature; Swimming; Downhill skiing; Cross-country horseriding; Cultural travel.

KLUSAK Jan-Filip, b. 18 Apr 1934, Prague, Czechoslovakia. Composer. m. Milena Kaizrova, 29 Mar 1979, 1 s. Education: Academy of Music, Dramatic Arts, Prague; Studied composition with Jaroslav Ridky and Pavel Borkovec, 1953-57. Compositions include: Published: Four Small Vocal Exercises, 1-11, for flute, 1965; Rondo for Piano, 1967; Published and Recorded: Proverbs for Deep Voice and Wind Instruments, 1959; Pictures for 12 Wind Instruments, 1960; 1st Invention for Chamber Orchestra, 1961; 2nd String Quartet, 1961-62; Variation on a Theme by Gustav Mahler for Orchestra, 1960-62; Sonata for Violin and Wind Instruments, 1965-66; 6th Invention for Nonet, 1969; Invenzionetta per Flauto Solo, 1971; Monody in Memoriam Igor Stravinsky, 1972; 7th Invention for Orchestra, 1973; 3rd String Quartet, 1975; Variations for Two Harps, 1982; Fantasia on Adam Michna of Otradovice for Brass Quintet and Harp, 1983; Six Small Preludes for Orchestra, Vor deinen Thron Tret ich Hiermit, 1984; Opera in 2 Acts, 1984-85; The King with the Golden Mask, ballet, 1986; Hero and Leandros, ballet, 1988; Dämmerklarheit, Songs on Friedrich Rückert, 1988; 4th String Quartet; Mozart-Sickness, Fancy for Chamber Orchestra, 1991; Concerto for Oboe and Small Orchestra, 1991; Tetragrammaton sive Nomina Eius for Orchestra, 1992; Die Kunst des guten Zusammennspiels for Wind, 1992; Ein Bericht für eine Akademie, Opera in 1 Act, 1993-97. Address: Blanicka 26, 120-00 Prague 2, Czech Republic.

KLUSON Jospef, b. 1953, Czechoslovakia. Violist. Education: Studied at the Prague Conservatory and Academy of Fine Arts. Career: Founder member of the Prazak-Quartet, 1972; Tours throughout Europe, America, Japan, Australia and New Zealand; Tours in UK 1982, 1985, 1988, 1989, 1993 (Wigmore Hall, Queen Elizabeth Hall, Huddersfield Contemporary Music Festival); Recitals for BBC, Dutch Radio, Czech Radio, Radio France; Teaching: master classes at Orlando Festival, Mozart European Foundation, Antwerp, Bremen. Recordings: Albums for Supraphon, Orfeo, Ottavo, Harmonia Mundi France. Honours: First Prize in the Czech National String Quartet Competition, 1978; Grand Prix in Evian, 1978; Grand Prix at Prague Spring Competition, 1979. Address: c/o Ingpen and Williams Ltd, 14 Kensington Court, London W8 5DN, England.

KMENTT Waldemar, b. 2 Feb 1929, Vienna, Austria. Singer (Tenor). Education: Studied at the Vienna Musikhochschule with Adolf Vogel, Elisabeth Rado and Hans Duhan. Debut: Vienna 1950, in the Choral Symphony, conducted by Karl Bröhm. Career: Toured Europe with Viennese student group, appearing in Die Fledermaus and Le nozze di Figaro; Vienna Volksoper from 1951, debut as the Prince in The Love for Three Oranges: later roles in Vienna have included Belmonte, Don Ottavio, Ferrando, Idomeneo, Walther, Bacchus and the Emperor in Die Frau ohne Schatten; Sang Jacquino in Fidelio at the opening of the rebuilt Vienna Staatsoper, 1955; Salzburg Festival from 1955, in the premiere of Irische Legende by Egk and as Idamante (Idomeneo), Gabriel in Le Mystère de la Nativité by Martin, Ferrando and

Tamino; Bayreuth Festival 1968-70, as Walther von Stolzing; Further engagements in Milan, Dusseldorf, Paris, Amsterdam, Munich and Stuttgart, and at the Drottningholm and Edinburgh Festivals; Many concert appearances, notably in Das Lied von der Erde by Mahler. Recordings: Salome, Tiefland, Lulu, Bastien et Bastienne, Cosi fan tutte (Philips); Beethoven's Missa solemnis (Electrola); Die Fledermaus, Das Rheingold, Arabella, Tristan und Isolde (Decca); Video of Turandot from the Vienna Staatsoper, 1983. Address: c/o Staatsoper, Opernring 2, A-1010 Vienna, Austria.

KNAIFEL Alexander, b. 28 Nov 1943, Tashkent. Composer. m. Tatiana Melentieva, 31 Dec 1965, 1 daughter. Education: The Secondary Music School at the Leningrad Conservatoire, 1950-61; Moscow Conservatoire, 1961-63; Leningrad Conservatoire, 1963-67. Career: Freelance composer. Compositions: Ainana, 1978; Joan, 1970-78; A Chance Occurrence, 1982; Nika, 1983-84; God, 1985; Agnus Dei, 1985; Litania, 1988; Through the Rainbow of Involuntary Tears, 1987-88; Monodia, Le Chant du Monde, 1990; Lamento, Le Chant du Monde, 1991; Voznoshenije (The Holy Oblation), 1991; Svete Tikhij (O Gladsome Light), 1991; Postludia, 1992; Once Again on the Hypothesis, 1992; Scalae Iacobis, 1992; Chapter Eight, 1993; Maranatha, 1993; Butterfly, 1993; Prayers to the Holy Spirit, 1994-95; Psalm 51(50), 1995; Amicta sole, 1995; the Beatitudes, 1996; Bliss, 1997; Lux aeterna, 1997; Music for 40 films. Recordings: The Canterville Ghost, BBC, 1980; Monodia (Le Chant du Monde, 1990); Le Chant du Monde, 1991); Lamento (Le Chant du Monde, 1991); Vera (Faith), BBC, 1993; A Silly Horse (Melodia, 1988); Passacaglia, 1995; Shramy marsha (Scars of March), 1995; Postludia, 1995; O Heavenly King, 1995; Chapter Eight, 1996; Comforter, 1997. Publications: Two Pieces for ensemble, 1975; Classical Suite, 1976; Five Poems by Mikhail Lermontov, 1978; Musique militaire, 1974; The Canterville Ghost, 1977; Passacaglia, 1990; Lamento, 1979, 1992; The Petrograd Sparrows, 1981; A Silly Horse, 1985; Medea, 1989; Vera (Faith), 1990; Da (Yes), 1991; Comforter, 1997; Bliss, 1997. Honours: DAAD Honoured grant-aided composer, Berlin, 1993; Honoured Art Worker of Russia, 1997. Memberships: Composers Union, 1968-; Cinematographers Union, 1987-. Address: Skobelevski prospekt 5, kv 130, Sankt-Petersburg 194214, Russia.

KNAPP Peter, b. 4 Aug 1947, St Albans, England. Opera Singer (Baritone); Director. m. Mary Anne Tennyson, 2 June 1984, 1 son. Education: St Albans School; St John's College, Cambridge. Debut: Glyndebourne Touring Company. Career: Kent Opera: Monteverdi's Orfeo (televised on BBC); Eugene Onegin; Don Giovanni; La Traviata; English National Opera: Don Giovanni; La Traviata; English National Opera: Don Giovanni; The Marriage of Figaro; Abroad: Sofia, Zurich, Frankfurt, Venice, Florence; Tour of Australia; Regular Broadcasts; 1978 began directing own opera company - La Perichole filmed for BBC TV; 1988/89 2 week season at Sadler's Wells Theatre, London, 1989; sang Mozart's Figaro, 1989, Zelta in The Merry Widow for Scottish Opera, sang Wolfram in Tannhäuser for New Sussex Opera, 1990; Made version of Carmen for Travelling Opera, 1992. Recordings: Monteverdi Vespers; De Falla Master Peter's Puppet Show. Publications: Translations of Cosi fan tutte, The Marriage of Figaro, La Periochole, Orpheus in the Underworld, La Bohème, The Barber of Seville. Honours: First Benson and Hedges Gold Award, 1977. Address: Kaye Artists Management, Barratt House, 7 Chertsey Road, Woking, GV21 5AB, England.

KNEZKOVA Ludmila, b. 22 Apr 1956, Mukacevo, Ukraine. Concert Pianist. m. Bernard Musey, 17 Nov 1990. Education: Tchaikovsky Conservatory, Moscow; Prague Academy of Music; Master classes in Germany and Canada. Career: TV and Radio appearances in Moscow, Prague, Vienna, Austria, Weimar, Germany, New Brunswick, Canada, Italy and the Ukraine. Honours: Prizewinner, Smetana International Piano Competition, 1980; Best Performer, Weimar, Germany, 1987, 1988; Scholarships from Czech Musical Foundation, 1987-89 and Canada, 1992. Hobbies: Travel; Studying; Reading; Swimming. Current Management: Cyrann Ltd, Canada. Address: 840 Grandview Street, Bathurst, New Brunswick, E2A 3R7, Canada.

KNEZKOVA-HUSSEY Ludmila, b. 22 April 1956, Mukacevo, Ukraine. Concert Pianist; Choir Director. m. Bernard Hussey, 17 November 1990, 1 daughter. Education: Lvov Central Music School; Moscow Music School; Tchaikovsky Conservatory, Moscow; Academy of Music, Prague. Career: Several Recitals and Concert Engagements with Leading Orchestras in USA, Canada, Germany, Italy, Russia, Czech Republic, Slovakia, Austria, Hungary, Poland, Ukraine, Switzerland; TV & Radio Appearances in Canada, USA, Czech Republic, Russia, Latvia, Austria, Germany, Italy, Ukraine. Recordings: CD, Canada. Honours include: Smetana International Piano Competition, 1980; Best Performer, Weiman, Germany, 1988; New Brunswick Merit Award, 1995. Memberships: Czech Musicians Association; New Brunswick Musicians Association; American Federation of Musicians; New Brunswick Music Teachers Association. Hobbies: Travel; Reading; Writing. Address: 155 Allison Crescent, Bathurst, NB, E2A 3B4, Canada.

KNIE Roberta, b. 13 May 1938, Cordell, Oklahoma, USA. Singer (Soprano). Education: Studied at Oklahoma University with Elisabeth Parham, Judy Bounds-Coleman and Eva Turner. Debut: Hagen (Germany) 1964, as Elisabeth in Tannhäuser. Career: Sang at Freiburg, 1966-69; Graz Opera, 1969, as Salome, Tosca and Leonore; Zurich and Nice, 1972-73, as Brünnhilde; Metropolitan Opera from 1975; Guest appearances in Kassel, Mannheim, Montreal, Buenos Aires, Brussels, Barcelona, Hamburg, Berlin, Munich and Stuttgart; Other roles include Isolde, Senta, Elsa, Sieglinde, Donna Anna, Elektra, the Marschallin, Lisa in The Queen of Spades, Electra in Idomeneo and both Leonoras of Verdi. Recordings include: Isolde in Tristan und Isolde.

KNIGHT Brenda Mary, b. 13 Dec 1926, London, England. Music Teacher. Education: Royal College of Music, 1943-46; GRSM; ARCM; LRAM; ARCO; A.Cert.C.M. Career: Piano Mistress, Sydenham High School, 1946-51; Music Mistress, St James School, West Malvern, 1951-54; Director of Music, St Audries School, West Quantrose, 1954-90; Founder, Conductor, Quantock Choir, 1987-; Secretary, Royal School of Church Music, Somerset Area, 1989-; Divisional Superintendent, Bandmaster, St Audries School; Nursing Cadets; Vice Chairman, Federation of St John Ambulance Bands; National President, Federation of St John Ambulence Bands, 1993-96. Honours: Serving Sister, Venerable Order of St John of Jerusalem, 1977; Officer Sister, 1983; Shared, GVM Maynard Prize, 1987; Honorary Member, Royal School of Church Music, 1993. Memberships: Incorporated Society of Musicians; Royal College of Music; Royal College of Organists. Hobbies: Gardening; Reading; Family History. Address: Ivy Cottage, Sampford Brett, Taunton, Somerset TA4 4LA, England.

KNIGHT Gillian, b. 1 Nov 1939, Redditch, Worcs, England. Singer (Mezzo-soprano). Education: LRAM, Royal Academy of Music, London; BA, Open University. Career: D'Oyly Carte Opera, 1959-64, sang in contralto roles as Katisha (Mikado), Ruth (Pirates of Penzance), and Lady Jane (Patience); Sadler's Wells/English National Opera as Suzuki in Butterfly, Ragone (Comte Ory), Juno (Semele) and Carmen; Covent Garden from 1970, in the premiere of Maxwell Davie's Taverner, 1972, Der Ring des Nibelungen, Rigoletto, Eugene Onegin and Semele, 1988; Paris Opera debut, 1978, in Die Zauberflöte; US debut, 1979, as Olga in Eugene Onegin at Tanglewood: tours of USA singing Gilbert and Sullivan; Season 1986/87 Gertrude in Hamlet for Pittsburgh Opera; Nurse in Die Frau ohne Schatten for Welsh National Opera, 1989; Sang the Forester's Wife in The Cunning Little Vixen at Covent Garden; France: Rouen, Lile, Nantes, Avignon, Tours, Paris, Toulouse (Carmen, Don Quixote, Werther); Germany; Frankfurt, Ulrica in Ballo in Maschera; Spain: Carmen with Domingo in Valencia and Saragossa; Switzerland: Rigoletto, Geneva; Sang Marguerite in La Dame Blanche at the 1990 Wexford Festival; Sang the title role in the British premiere of Gerhard's The Duenna, Opera North, 1992; Third Maid in Elektra at the First Night of the 1993 London Proms; Sang Annina in La Traviata at Covent Garden, 1996; Concert engagements with conductors such as Bertini, Boulez, Colin Davis, Groves and Solti. Recordings: Six Gilbert and Sullivan roles for Decca; Messiah, Damnation of Faust and Mozart Masses with Colin Davis (Philips); Schoenberg's Moses und Aron with Boulez (CBS); Suor Angelica, Il Tabarro and Madama Butterfly with Maazel (CBS); La Forza del Destino with Levine (RCA). Address: c/o Kaye Artists Management, Barratt House, 7 Chertsey Road, Woking, GV21 5AB, England.

KNIGHT Katherine, b. 1960, USA. Cellist. Education: Johns Hopkins University; New England Conservatory. Career: Co-Founder, Da Vinci Quartet, 1980, under the sponsorship of the Fine Arts Quartet; Many concerts in the USA and elsewhere in a repertoire including works by Mozart, Beethoven, Brahms, Dvorak, Shostakovich and Bartók. Honours: With the Da Vinci Quartet: Grants from the NEA, Western States Arts Foundation and Colorado Council for the Humanities; Artist-in-Residence, University of Colorado. Current Management: Sonata, Glasgow, Scotland. Address: c/o Da Vinci Quartet, 11 Northpark Street, Glasgow G20 7AA, Scotland.

KNIGHT Mark Anthony, b. 24 Apr 1941, Worcestershire, England. Professor of Violin and Viola. m. Patricia Noall, 25 Aug 1965, 1 son, 1 daughter. Education: Guildhall School of Music and Drama, London, 1959-64; Tanglewood International Summer School, Mssachusetts, USA, 1962. Debut: Brighton, 1962. Career: Freelance Violinist, 1965-69, including London Philharmonic Orchestra; Leader, New Cantata Orchestra of London, 1966-69; Senior String Tutor, Wells Cathedral School, Wells, Somerset, 1975-88; Professor of Violin, Viola and Chamber Music, Guildhall School of Music and Drama, London, 1976-; Several radio and TV broadcasts over the years. Compositions: Cadenzas: for Mozart's Violin Concertos No 1 in B flat, K207, and No 2 in D, K211; for Karl Stamitz's Viola Concerto in D; for Hoffmeister's Viola Concerto in D. Recording: A Boy Is Born, as Conductor of Wells Cathedral School Chamber Orchestra, 1977. Publications: Editor: Violin Sonatas Op 5 by Archangelo Corelli, 1991; 42 Violin Studies by Rodolphe Kreutzer, 1992. Contributions to: Regularly to European String Teachers Association's News and Views. Memberships: Incorporated Society of Musicians; European String Teachers Association; Musicians Union. Hobbies: Steam locomotives; Old cars. Address: Great Skewes Cottage, St Wenn, Bodmin, Cornwall PL30 5PS, England.

KNIGHT Timothy John, b. 10 September 1959, Northallerton, Yorkshire, England. Composer; Conductor. Education: York Minster, 1969-73. Career: Director, Wakefield Festival Chorus, 1994; Music Director, Performing Arts College, Leeds, 1993-. Compositions: Winters Rhapsody II; Requeim; Numerous Church & Organ Works. Memberships: Fellow, Guild of Musicians & Singers; Fellow, National College of Music; Associate, Faculty of Church Music. Address: 24 Lidgett Hill, Roundhay, Leeds LS8 1PE, England.

KNIPLOVA Nadezda, b. 18 Apr 1932, Ostrava, Czechoslovakia. Singer (Soprano). Education: Studied at the Prague Conservatory with Jarmila Vavrdova and at the Academy of Musical Arts with K Ungrova and Zdenek Otava. Career: Sang at Usti nad Labem 1956-59 and the Janácek Opera Brno (1959-64), notably as Renata in The Fiery Angel, Katerina in The Greek Passion and Katerina Ismailova; Principal of The Prague National Theatre from 1965: roles include the Kostelnicka in Jenufa, Brünnhilde, Leonore, Milada (Dalibor), Libuse, Emilia Marty, Isolde, Tosca, Aida and Senta; Guest appearances in Salzburg (Brünnhilde, 1967), Barcelona (as Isolde), Turin (in Götterdämmerung) Berlin, Hamburg, New York and San Francisco (Die Walküre); Sang with the Berlin Staatsoper on tour in Japan. Recordings: Jenufa, Libuse, Dalibor, Orfeo ed Euridice (Supraphon); Katya Kabanova (Decca); Der Ring des Nibelungen (Westminster). Honours: Prizewinner at competitions in Geneva (1958), Vienna (1959) and Toulouse (1959); Czech Artist of Merit, 1970. Address: National Theatre, PO Box 865, 11230 Prague 1, Czech Republic.

KNOBEL Marita, b. 1947, Johannesburg, South Africa. Singer (Mezzo-soprano). Education: Studied in Pretoria and at the London Opera Centre. Career: Sanga at the Cologne Opera 1973-85, notably as Auntie in Peter Grimes, Magdalene in Meistersinger and Mother Goose in The Rake's Progress; Guest appearances in Dusseldorf, Dresden, Basle, Barcelona and Edinburgh; Sang at the Munich Staatsoper 1990-91 and at the Vienna Staatsoper from 1992, in such roles as Suzuki, Fidalma (Matrimonio Segreto) and the Witch in Hansel and Gretel. Address: c/o Staatsoper, Opernring 2, A-1010 Vienna, Austria.

KNODT Erich, b. 1945, Germany. Singer (Bass). Education: Studied in Koblenz. Career: Sang at the Stadttheater Koblenz, 1970-72; Wuppertal, 1972-76, Mannheim, 1976-87; Guest appearances at Dusseldorf, Hamburg, Stuttgrt, Brussels, 1989, Paris, Barcelona, Strasbourg and Madrid; Bregenz and Aix-en-Provence Festivals, 1985, 1989, as Sarastro; Wagner repertoire includes King Mark, Liston 1985, King Henry in Lohengrin, 1986, Hunding, Lisbon, 1989, Pogner and Hagen; Hal also sang Mozart's Commendatore, Rocco, King Philip, Boris Godunov, Banquo and Ramphis (Bordeaux 1989); Sang Peneois in a concert performance of Daphne at Rome, 1991; Sarastro at Bordeaux, Pogner at Trieste and Roldano in Franchetti's Christoforo Colombo at the Montpellier Festival, 1992; Sang King Mark in Tristan und Isolde at Trieste, 1996. Many further concert engagements. Address: Nationaltheater, Am Goethplatz, 6800 Mannheim, Germany.

KNOPF Michael, b. 9 Oct 1955, Minnesota, USA. Composer. Education: Studied Composition and Jazz at Wichita State University, Kansas, USA. Career: Freelance composer in Cairns, Queensland, Australia. Compositions include: The Reef, for orchestra, 1987; Places for orchestra, with soprano, 1990; Pandarus in a Mist, for orchestra, 1991; Five Studies for String Quartet, 1990; Great Spirit for guitar, 1992; Three Songs from the Hidden Words, for voice and guitar, 1993; Five Pictures from the Life of the Bab, for violin and guitar, 1993; Earth unto Sky, for violin and string orchestra, 1996; The Turning Point, Cantata for multicultural choir, 1996; Many works for choir; The Mountain of God, for soprano, tenor, baritone, chorus and orchestra, 1997; Commissions from Cairns Civic Orchestra, and others. Address: 12 Cilento Close, White Rock, Qld 4868, Australia.

KNOX Garth (Alexander), b. 8 Oct 1956, Dublin, Republic of Ireland. Violist. Education: ARCM, Royal College of Music, London, 1974-77; Studies with Frederick Riddle; Masterclasses with Paul Doktor and Peter Schidloff. Career: Member of English Chamber Orchestra, 1979-81, and of London Sinfonietta; Dedicatee and 1st performance of Henze's Viola Sonata, Witten, 1981; 1st performance of James Dillon's Timelag Zero, Brighton, 1981; Guest Principal Viola, Opera la Fenice, Venice, 1981-83; Performances of Harold in Italy and Jonathon Lloyd's Viola Concerto with Danish Radio Symphony Orchestra, Copenhagen, 1982; Member of Pierre Boulez's Ensemble Intercontemporain, Paris, 1983-90; Concertos-Luciano Berio and Marc-Andre Dalbavie conducted by Pierre Boulez in Bordeaux, Lisbon, Paris and New York; Concerto by Karl-Amadeus Hartmann, Théâtre du

Rond-Point, Paris, 1987; Tour of USSR with Jan Latham Koenig playing Shostakovich Viola Sonata, 1987; 1st performance of Donatoni's La Souris sans Sourire with Quator Ensemble Intercontemporain, Paris, 1989; Joined the Arditti String Quartet, 1990, premiering quartets by Ferneyhough (No 4), Goehr (No 4), Xenakis' Tetora and Feldman's Quintet; 1st Performance of Ligeti's Loop, for solo viola, 1991. Recordings: Henze's Viola Sonata, Ricordi, 1981; Schoenberg's Verklärte Nacht, supervised by Boulez, CBS; Embellie, for solo viola by Iannis Xenakis. Address: c/o Garth Knox, 6 Willow Road, London NW3 1TH, England.

KNUSSEN (Stuart) Oliver, b. 12 June 1952, Glasgow, Scotland. Composer; Conductor. m. Susan Freedman, 1972, 1 daughter. Education: Purcell School of Music; Private Study, composition, with John Lambert, 1963-68. Debut: Conducting Symphony No 1, London Symphony Orchestra, 1968. Career includes: Study with Gunther Schuller, USA, 1970-73; Koussevitzky Centennial Commission, 1974; Composer-in-residence, Aspen Festival 1976, Arnolfini Gallery 1978; Instructor in composition, Royal College of Music Junior Department, 1977-82; BBC commission, Proms (Symphony No 3), 1979; Guest teacher, Berkshire Music Center, Tanglewood, USA, 1981; Coordinator of Contemporary music activities, Tanglewood, 1986-90; Associate Guest Conductor, BBC Symphony Orchestra, 1989-; Frequent guest conductor, London Sinfonietta, Phiharmonia Orchestra, numerous other ensembles, UK & abroad, 1981-; Co-artistic director, Aldeburgh Festival, 1983-; Conducted Birtwistle's Punch and Judy for Netherlands Opera, 1993. Compositions: Symphony No 1, 1966-67, No 2, 1970-71, No 3, 1973-79; Where the Wild Things Are, opera (Maurice Sendak), 1979-83; Numerous orchestral, chamber, vocal works, including Concerto for Orchestra 1968-70, 1974; Cantata for oboe and string trio 1977; Ocean de la Tenre for soprano and chamber ensemble 1972-73, 1976; Autumnal for violin and piano 1976-77; Four Late Poems and an Epigram of Rainer Maria Rilke for soprano 1988; Piano Variations 1989; Secret Song for solo violin 1990; Whitman Settings for soprano and orchestra, 1992; Horn Concerto, 1994. Recordings: Contract with DGG from 1995 for 20th Century repertory and his own works. Contributor to: Tempo, The Listener. Honours: Winner, 1st Park Lane Group composer award, 1982; CBE, 1994. Memberships: Executive committee, Society for Promotion of New Music, 1978-85; Leopold Stowkowski Society; International Alban Berg Society, New York. Hobbies: Cinema; Foreign Literature; Record collecting & producing. Address: c/o Louise Mitchell, 35 Greenbridge Road, London E9 7DP, England.

KNUTSON David, b. 19 Mar 1946, Wisconsin, USA. Singer (Tenor). Education: Studied in Wisconsin. Career: Has sung in West Germany from 1971; Sang lyric roles at the Deutsche Oper Berlin from 1972; Guest appearances in Hamburg; Munich 1978, in the premiere of Lear by Reimann; Berlin 1975 and 1980, in the local premieres of La Calisto by Cavalli and Hippolyte et Aricie by Rameau; Spoleto Festival 1986, as the Witch in Hansel and Gretel; Sang Bishop Abdisu in Pfitzner's Palestrina, Berlin, 1996. Recordings include: Lear (Deutsche Grammophon). Address: c/o Deutsche Oper Berlin, Richard Wagner Strasse 10, D-1000 Berlin, Germany.

KOBAYASHI Junko, b. Sept 1960, Kobe, Japan. Concert Pianist. Education: Osaka College of Music; Essen Musik Hochschule, Germany; Studied with Maria Curcio and Louis Kentner. Debut: Royal Festival Hall, London, 1988. Career: The Purcell Room Recitals, 1983-93; Appearances in England, Germany, France, Denmark, Bulgaria, USA, Venezuela, Zambia and Japan; Played with orchestras such as the London Philharmonic Orchestra, the Osaka Philharmonic Orchestra, the New Philharmonic Orchestra, The Academy of St Nicholas; Broadcasts on BBC Radio 3, WKAR Televion, USA, ZDF Television, Germany. Contributions: Essays to Kansei Music newspaper. Address: 11 Rosslyn Hill, London NW3 5UL, England.

KOBAYASHI Marie, b. 31 Aug 1955, Kamakura, Japan. Singer (Mezzo-soprano). Education: Arts and Music National University, Tokyo; National Conservatory of Music, Paris. Debut: With 2E2M, International Contemporary Music Festival, Strasbourg, 1983. Career: Appearances: C R Alsina's Prima Sinfonia, Radio France concert with National Orchestra of France, 1985; Satie's La Mort de Socrate, Radio France concert with Nouvel Orchestre Philharmonique, 1989; Smeton in Donizetti's Anna Bolena, Nimes, 1989; Birtwistle's Meridian with Pierre Boulez, Châtelet Theatre, 1990; J Fontyn's Roses des Sable, Radio Brussels (RTBF), 1991; Has sung in many concerts of oratorios by Bach, Handel, Rossini, Mozart, others. Recordings: Les Madrigaux of G Arrgo, 1990; Motets of Vivaldi, 1990; Mozart's Requiem, 1991. Hobbies: Theatre; Films. Address: 49 rue Riquet, Apt 2, 75019 Paris, France.

KOBEKIN Vladimir, b. 22 July 1947, Sverdlovsk, Russia. Composer. Education: Slonimsky at the Leningrad Conservatory, graduating in 1971. Career: Teacher, Urals Conservatory, 1971-80. Compositions include: Swan Song, chamber oper after Chekhov, Moscow, 1980; Dairy of a Madman, mono-opera, Moscow 1980; The Boots, chamber opera, 1981; Pugachyov, musical tragedy, Leningrad, 1983; The Prophet, a Pushkin Triptych, Sverdlovsk 1984; Play about Maximilian, Eleanor and Ivan, Moscow, 1989; The Jester and the King, chamber opera, 1991; The Happy Prince, chamber opera after Wilde, 1991; Instrumental, choral and chamber music. Honours: USSR State Prize, 1987, Honoured Artist of the RSFSR. Address: c/o RAO, Bolchaia Bronnai 6-a, Moscow 103670, Russia.

KOBEL Benedikt, b. 1960, Vienna, Austria. Singer (Tenor). Education: Studied at the Vienna Musikhochschule and the Studio of the Staatsoper. Career: Sang in concert performances of Gurlitt's Wozzeck and Reimann's Gespenstersonate, Vienna 1985; Appearances throughout Austria and the Theater am Gärtnerplatz, Munich, in operettas by Lehar, Zeller, Oscar Straus and Johann Strauss; Vienna Volksoper 1991-92, as Don Ottavio and Camille in Dantons Tod and Tamino, Belmonte, Ferrando, Almaviva, Rinuccio; Vienna Staatsoper 1992, as Cassio in Otello and Narraboth, Flamand (Capriccio), Steuermann (Flying Dutchman). Address: c/o Volksoper, Wahringerstrasse 78, A-1090 Vienna, Austria.

KOBILZA Siegfried, b. 24 Aug 1954, Villach, Carinthia, Austria. Guitarist. m. Vera Kobilza-Schweder, 7 Feb 1983. Education: Finals in Higher Education, Musisch-Padagogisches Realgymnasium, Hermagor, 1973; Diploma in Performance (with distinction), Academy of Music, Vienna, 1981; Pupil of Professor Karl Scheit. Career: 1st concert tour, Austrian cities including Vienna, 1979; Recitals in main Austrian venues including Wiener Musikverein, Wiener Konzerthaus, Grosses Festspeilhaus Salzburg, Mozarteum Salzburg, Brucknerhaus Linz; Soloist with orchestras including Vienna Symphony, Mozarteumorchester Salzburg, Vienna Chamber Orchestra; TV and Radio recordings; Teaching master classes, various European countries and People's Republic of China; Debuts in London, Paris, New York, 1982; Concert tours, Federal Republic of Germany, Switzerland, UK, France, Netherlands, Iceland, Yugoslavia, Hungary, USA, USSR, Czechoslovakia, Turkey, Tunisia, China. Current Management: Sekretariat Siegfried Kobilza. Address: Servitengasse 7/16, A0-1090 Vienna, Austria.

KOBLER Linda, b. 1952, New York City, USA. Harpischordist. m. Albert Glinsky, 10 June 1979. Education: BM, Peabody Conservatory of Music; MM, Juilliard School, 1977. Debut: Carnegie Recital Hall, 1984. Career: Concerto Soloist with: Zurich Chamber Orchestra, New York Chamber Orchestra, Broadway Bach Ensemble, American Baroque Ensemble, Bach Gesellchaft, Seabrook Chamber Players, Cathedral Orchestra, New York Chamber Symphony, Toronto Symphony; Former Member, Ensemble Tafelmusik Quartet; performances in New York, Ohio, New Jersey, California, Washington DC, South Carolina, Louisiana, including Philips Collection, Cleveland Institute, University of California, Carnegie Recital Hall, Merkin Concert Hall, Spoleto Festival, Town Hall, New York City, Metropolitan Museum of Art, Indianapolis, Early Music Festival, Smithsonian Institute; Performances in Switzerland and Germany; Radio appearances in USA; World premiere of works by Zwillich and Persichetti; Faculty, Juilliard School, 1989-96; Harpsichord coach to film star Gwyneth Paltrow, 1994; Commentator, National Public Radio programme, Performance Today, 1997. Recordings: Musical Heritage Society; Works of Christophe Moyreau and Pancrace Royer; Classic Masters; Works of Frescobaldi, Strozzi. Contributions to: Encyclopaedia of the Keyboard. Honours: Winner, Concert Artists Guild New York International Competition, 1983; Grant Awards, Harpischord Music Society, 1984, 1986; Satellite Program Development Fund Grant; Noah Greenberg Award, 1990; Pennsylvania Council on the Arts Fellowship Grant, 1995. Membership: Southeastern Historical Keyboard Society. Address: 4201 Sassafras St, Erie, PA 16508, USA.

KOC Jozik, b. 1968, Oxford, England. Singer (Baritone). Education: Studied at York University and the Guildhall School, London. Career: Concerts and recitals throughout Britain, 1991-92, leading to Wigmore Hall debut 1993; Opera debut as Fiorello in Il Barbiere di Siviglia, and Guide in Death in Venice, for Glyndebourne Touring Opera; Spirit in Monteverdi's Orfeo for English National Opera, Purcell's Aeneas for Opera Factory and Prince Lindoro in Haydn's Pescatrici (Garsington Festival Opera, 1997); Other roles include Mozart's Don Giovanni, Count and Guglielmo, Sancho in Massenet's Don Quichotte, and Schaunard (La Bohème); Concert repertoire includes Bach's B minor Mass, Messiah, Rossini's Petite Messe and the Fauré Requiem; Appearances with the London and Royal Philharmonics, and the English Chamber Orchestra. Recordings include: Baroque Anthems (Hyperion). Address: C&M Craig Services Ltd, 3 Kersley Street, London SW11 4PR, England.

KOCMIEROSKI Matthew, b. 18 Aug 1953, Roslyn, New York, USA. Percussionist; Conductor; Historian; Educator. m. Elaine S Schmidt, 28 Dec 1974. Education: Nassau Community College, 1971-74; Mannes College of Music, 1974-77. Career: Marimba concertos performed with: Atlantic Wind Symphony, New York, Broadway Chamber Symphony, Thalia Chamber Symphony, Seattle, Philharmonia Northwest, Midsummer Musical Retreat Festival Orchestra and The Bainbridge Orchestra; Numerous concerto and recital appearances in the Pacific North West; Chamber music performances include: New Music, Seattle Chamber Music Festival, Bergen International Festival, Goodwill Arts Festival, Seattle Spring Festival of Contemporary Music; Freelance performances with Martha Graham Dance Company, Aeolian Chamber Players, Seattle Symphony, Seattle Opera, Bolshoi Ballet, Joffrey Ballet, Northwest Chamber Orchestra; Instructor of Percussion and Music History, Classical New Music Programme, Cornish College of The Arts, Seattle; Member, New Performance Group, 1981-96; Artistic Director, New Performance Group, Seattle, beginning with the 1984-85 season; Currently Principal Percussionist, Pacific Northwest Ballet Orchestra; Founding Member, Pacific Rims Percussion Quartet, 1995-. Recordings: Paul Dresher's Night Songs, 1984; Atlas Eclipticalis, John Cage conducting, 1986; Janice Giteck's Breathing Songs, and Home; Anthony Braxton's Composition No 96; Bun-Ching Lam, Mountain Clear Water Remote; William Duckworth, Mysterious Numbers; Numerous film scores. Contributions to: Editor of the Guild "Forum" official publication of the IGSOBM. Memberships: International Guild of Symphony Opera and Ballet Musicians; Percussive Arts Society; American Music Center; Artist Trust; ACLU; National Campaign for Freedom of Expression. Address: 12724 19th Avenue NE, Seattle, WA 98125, USA.

KOCSAR Miklós, b. 21 Dec 1933, Debrecen, Hungary. Composer. Education: Studied with Farkas at the Budapest Academy of Music, 1954-59. Career: Teacher, Béla Bartók Conservatory, Budapest, 1972-; Deputy Head of Music, Hungarian Radio, 1983-. Compositions: Horn concerto, 1957; Capriccio for orchestra, 1961; Solitary song for soprano and chamber ensemble, 1969; Variations for orchestra, 1977; Capricorn concerto for flute and chamber orchestra, 1978; Metamophoses for orchestra, 1979; Sequenze for strings, 1980; Elegia for bassoon and chamber ensemble, 1985; Formazioni for orchestra, 1986; Visions of the Night, oratorio for mezzo-soprano solo, mixed choir and orchestra, 1987; Concerto for violoncello and orchestra, 1994; Choral music including I will invoke you, Demon, 1985; Missa in A for equal voices, 1991; Chamber: Wind Quintet, 1959; Brass Trio, 1959; Variziioni for woodwind quintet, 1968; Sestetto d'ottoni, 1972; 7 Variations for viola, 1983; Wind Quintet, No 3, 1984; Quintetto d'ottoni, 1986; Rhapsody for Trombone, piano and percussion, 1989; Trio for strings, 1990; Music for 4 Trombones percussion, 1991; Songs and piano pieces. Honours include: Erkel Prize, 1973, 1980; Merited Artist of the Hungarian People's Republic, 1987; Merited Artist of the Hungarian People's Republic, 1987; Bartók-Pasztory Award, 1992. Address: Artisjus, PO Box 593, H-1538 Budapest, Hungary.

KOCSIS Zoltán, b. 30 May 1952, Budapest, Hungary. Pianist; Composer. m. Adrienne Hauser, 7 Apr 1986. Education: Béla Bartók Conservatory, Budapest, 1967-73; Musical Education: Béla Bartók Conservatory, Budapest, 1964-68; Ferenc Liszt Academy of Music, Budapest, 1968-73. Debut: 1970; US debut 1971, London and Salzburg, 1972; Often heard in Bach and Bartók; in 1988 he played Bartók's 2nd Piano Concerto at the Royal Festival Hall, London. Compositions: Premiere, String Ensemble; 33 December, Chamber Ensemble; The Last But One Encounter, for piano or harpischord; Transcriptions and arrangements for piano and two pianos. Recordings: For Hungaroton, Denon and Philips labels. Contributions to: Mozgó Világ (Budapest) Music Section, 1982-83; Mozgó Világ (Budapest) Music Section, 1982-83, Holmi (Budapest), 1989-. Honours: Liszt Prize, 1973; Kossuth Prize, 1978; Merited Artist, 1984. Current Management: Vigadó-Redoute, Budapest, Hungary. Hobbies: Collecting Records and Tapes. Address: Nárcisz u 29, Budapest H-1126, Hungary.

KOEHNE Graeme (John), b. 1956, Adelaide, South Australia. Composer; University Lecturer. Education: BMus, 1st class honours, MMus, University of Adelaide; Studied composition with Richard Meale, Tristam Cary and Bernard Rands; Composition under Virgil Thomson and Louis Andriessen, School of Music, Yale University, USA. Career: Appointed Tutor in Piano and Composition, University of New England, Armidale, New South Wales, 1978; Collaborated with choreographer Graeme Murphy and Sydney Dance Orchestra; Commissions, Australian Bicentenary, West Australian Ballet Company, Queensland Ballet Company, Australian Chamber Orchestra, Seymour Group (Sydney), Australian Ballet; Currently Lecturer in Composition, University of Adelaide. Compositions: Orchestral: The Iridian Plateau, 1977; First Blue Hours, 1979; Toccata, 1981; Fanfare, 1981; Rain Forest, 1981; riverrun..., 1982; Ballet Suite from The Selfish Giant, 1985; Capriccio for Piano and Strings, 1987; Ensemble: Sextet, 1975; Cantilene, 1978; Crystal Islands, 1982; Divertissement Trois Pièces Bourgeoises, string quartet, 1983; Ricecare and Burletta, string trio, 1984; Miniature, 1985; Voice and ensemble: Cancion, text F Garcia Lorca, 1975; Fourth Sonnet, text S Mallarmé, Suite, 1984; Nearly Beloved, 1986; Nocturnes, 1987; Keyboard Music: Piano Sonata, 1976;

Harmonies in Silver and Blue, piano, 1977; Twilight Rain, piano, 1979; Gothic Toccata, 1984 (aka Toccata Aurora). Address: c/o Boosey & Hawkes (Australia) Pty Ltd, Unit 12/6 (PO Box 188), Artarmon, New South Wales 2064, Australia.

KOETSIER Jan, b. 14 Aug 1911, Amsterdam, Netherlands. Composer; Conductor. m. Margarete Trampe. Education: Academy of Music, Berlin. Debut: As Composer and Conductor, Concertgebouw, Amsterdam, 1937. Career: Second Conductor, Concertgebouw Orchestra, 1942-48; Conductor, Residentieorkest, The Hague, 1949-50; Conductor, Bavarian Radio Symphony Orchestra, Munich, 1950-66; Professor, Musikhochschule, Munich, 1966-76. Compositions include: 3 Symphonies; Orchestral Works; The Man Lot, cantata for Soli, Men's Choir and Orchestra; Opera, Frans Hal; Chamber Music; Various Solo Concertos with Orchestra; Piano Music; Lieder. Recordings: Petite Suite; Brass Quintet; Partita for English Horn and Organ; Concerto for Trumpet, Trombone and Orchestra; Brass Symphony. Current Management: Donemus, Paulus Potterstraat 14, Amsterdam, The Netherlands. Address: Florianhaus, Unterkagn, 84431 Heldenstein, Germany.

KOGAN Semjon, b. 24 Apr 1928, Bobruisk, Ukraine. Conductor. Education: Studied violin and conducting at the St Petersburg Conservatoire. Career: Founded the State Symphony Orchestra at Omsk; Artistic Director, Rostov State Symphony Orchestra, 1976, participating in the 1990 Tchaikovsky International Competition, Moscow; Guest appearances with the USSR State Symphony, Moscow Philharmonic, Moscow Radio and St Petersburg Philharmonic Orchestras and invitations to conduct in Poland, Czechoslovakia and Germany; Repertoire includes Stravinsky and Shostakovich in addition to the standard repertoire; Has given the premieres of works by Denisov, Shchedrin and Khrennikov; Professor, Rostov on Don Conservatoire; Founded Rostov Conservatoire Orchestra, 1993. Recordings: With the Rostov Symphony Orchestra. Current Management: Sonata, Glasgow, Scotland. Address: 11 Northpark Street. Glasgow G20 7AA, Scotland.

KOHLER Axel, b. 1959, Schwarzenberg, Germany. Singer (Countertenor). Education: Studied at the Dresden Musikhochschule. Career: Sang as baritone with the Landesthater Halle from 1984 and after further study made countertenor debut at Halle 1987, as Eustazio in Handel's Rinaldo; Many appearances in Baroque opera at Halle, Innsbruck and Budapest; Sang in Handel's Tamerlano at Washington and New York, in Monteverdi's Poppea at Montpellier, 1989; Engagements with the Akademie fur Alte Musik, Berlin and Musica Antiqua Koln and Munich, Wurzburg, Berlin, London Covent Garden, Antwerp and Ghent opera houses. Address: Opernhaus Halle, Universitätsring 24, 06108 Halle an der Salle, Germany.

KOHN Karl (George), b. 1 Aug 1926, Vienna, Austria. Pianist; Conductor; Music Educator; Composer. m. Margaret Case Sherman, 23 Jun 1950, 2 d. Education: Certificate, NY College of Music, 1944; BA, 1950, MA, 1955, Harvard University; Studied piano with Werschinger, conducting with Prüwer and composition with Piston, Ballantine, Fine and Thompson. Career: Instructor in Music, 1950-54, Assistant Professor, 1954-59, Associate Professor, 1959-65, Professor, 1965-85, William M Keck Distinguished Service Professor, 1985-95 now Professor Emeritus, Pomona College, Claremont, CA; Teaching Fellow, Harvard University, 1954-55; Teacher, Berkshire Music Center, Tanglewood, summers 1954, 1955, 1957; Appearances as Pianist and Conductor. Compositions include: Orchestral: Sinfonia concertante for Piano and Orchestra, 1951; Castles and Kings, suite, 1958; Concerto mutabile for Piano and Orchestra, 1962; Episodes for Piano and Orchestra, 1966; Interlude II for Piano and String Orchestra, 1969; Centone for Orchestra, 1973; The Prophet Bird I, 1976; Time Irretrievable, 1983; Lions on a Banner, Seven Sufi Texts for Soprano Solo, Chorus and Orchestra, 1988; Ode for String Orchestra, 1991; Concert Music for String Orchestra, 1993; End Piece for Chamber Ensemble, 1993; Ternaries for Flute and Piano, 1993; Middle Piece for Chamber Ensemble, 1994; Chamber Music: Encounters I-VI for various instrumental combinations; Choral Works, Songs, Piano pieces and Organ music; Reconnaissance for large chamber ensemble, 1995; Memory and Hope: Essay for Orchestra, 1996; Sax for 4, for saxophone quartet, 1996; More Reflections for clarinet and piano, 1997. Publications: End Piece, 1994; Ternaries, 1995. Address: 674 West 10th Street, Claremont, CA 91711, USA.

KOHN Karl-Christian, b. 21 May 1928, Losheim, Saarbrucken, Germany. Singer. Singer (Bass). Education: Studied with Irene Eden at the Musikhochschule Saarbrucken. Career: Sang at the Deutsche Oper am Rhein Dusseldorf, 1954-57; Städtische Oper Berlin, 1956-58; Sang the title role in Le nozze di Figaro, at the reopening of the Cuvillies-Theater Munich, 1958; Member of the Bayerische Staatsoper Munich from 1958, notably i the 1963 premiere of Die Verlobung in San Domingo by Egk; Schwetzingen Festival, 1961, in the premiere of Elegie für junge Liebende by Henze; Guest appearances in Hamburg, Vienna, Berlin and elsewhere in Europe; Other roles included Mozart's Osmin, Sarastro and Commendatore. Recordings: Der Freischütz, Don Giovanni, Oedipus der Tyrann by Orf (EMI); Arabella, Doktor Faust, Don Giovanni, Wozzeck, Cardillac by Hindemith (Deutsche Grammophon); Bach's Christmas Oratorio. Address: c/o Bayersiche Staatsoper, Postfach 745, D-8000 Munich 1, Germany

KOHOUTEK Ctirad, b. 18 Mar 1929, Zábřeh na Moravě, Czechoslovakia. Composer; Theorist. m. Jarmila Chlebníčková, 8 July 1953, 1 son, 2 daughters. Education: Composition, Brno Conservatory, 1948-49; Janáček Academy of Music Arts, 1949-53; PhD, Palacký University, Olomouc, 1973; CSc, Masaryk University, Brno, 1980. Debut: Munich for orchestra, 1953. Career: Junior, Composition, 1953-59, Fellow, Composition, 1959-65, Senior Lecturer, Composition, Theory of Composition, 1965-80, Janáček Academy of Music Arts, Brno; Professor of Composition, Academy of Music Arts, Prague, 1980-90; Artistic Director, Czech Philharmonic, Prague, 1980-87; Currently full-time Composer, occasional Theorist and Pedagogue. Compositions include: String Quartet, 1959; Concertino, violoncello, chamber orchestra, 1964; Rapsodia eroica, organ, 1965; Inventions, piano, 1965; Miniatures, 4 French horns, 1965; Memento, concerto for percussion and wind instruments, 1966; Teatro del mondo, large orchestra, 1969; Panteon, orchestra, 1970; Festive Prologue, large symphony orchestra, 1971; Celebration of Light, large orchestra, 1975; Symphonic Actualities, orchestra, 1976-78; Tissues of Time, bass clarinet, piano, 1977; Minutes of Spring, wind quintet, 1980; Omaggio a vita, orchestra, 1989; About Cockerel and Little Hen, children's opera, 1989; Motifs of Summer, violin, violoncello, piano, 1990; Funs and Smiles, oboe, clarinet, bassoon, 1991; Winter Silences, brass, percussion, 1993; The Little Peach, mixed choir, piano, percussion, to text by Josef Kainar, 1993; Autumn Songs, 2nd string quartet, 1995; Numerous pieces for choirs. Publications include: Modern Compositional Theories in Music, 1965; Project Musical Composition, 1969; Musical Styles from the Composer's Viewpoint, 1976; Music Composition, 1989. Honours: 1st Prize for The Little Peach, International Composers Competition, Jihlava, 1994. Memberships: Association of Music Artists and Scientists, Prague; Vice-President, Club of Moravian Composers, Brno, 1992-. Address: Helfertova 40, 613 00 Brno - Cerna Pole, Czech Republic.

KOHS Ellis (Bonoff), b. 12 May 1916, Chicago, USA. Composer; Educator. Education: MA, University of Chicago, USA, 1938; Juilliard School of Music, USA, 1938-39; Harvard University, 1939-41. Career: Assistant Professor of Music, Wesleyan University, 1946-48; Associate Professor, Music, College of the Pacific, California, 1948-50; Associate Professor 1950, Professor 1952, Chairman, Theory Department 1966, School of Music, University of Southern California, Retired 1985. Compositions include: 2 Symphonies, 3 String Quartets; Concerto for Orchestra; Etude in Memory of Bartók; Four Orchestral Songs, Studies in Variation; Calumny; Concerto for Percussion Quartet; Concerto for Violin and Orchestra, commissioned by University of Southern California for its Centennial, 1981; Fantasies, Interludes and Canonic Etudes on the name Eudice Shapiro; Orchestral Suite from the Opera, Amerika; Numerous other compositions. Recordings: Chamber Concerto for Viola and Strings; Symphony No 1, String Quartet No 2, XXIII Psalm; Choral Variation No 2 on Hebrew Hymns. Publications: Music Theory, 1961; Musical Form, 1976; Musical Composition, 1980. Current Management: Theodore Presser Music, Bryn Mawr, PA 19010, USA. Address: 8025 Highland Trail, Los Angeles, CA 90046, USA.

KOITO Kei, b. 4 Jan 1950, Kyoto, Japan. Concert Organist; Composer; Professor. Education: Studied organ, philosophy, musical aesthetics and psychology at Tokyo School of Fine Arts; Studied organ with Pierre Segond at the Geneva Conservatory, Analysis, orchestration and composition with Eric Gaudibert; Associated with electro-acoustic studios; Private study of organ with L F Tagliavani, Xavier Darasse and Reinhard Goebel. Debut: Solo recitalist at Victoria Hall, Geneva, Maurice Ravel Auditorium, Lyons. Career: Soloist with symphonic and chamber orchestras, regularly performing at festivals and on radio and TV; Since 1978 has performed over 80 new works for organ, premiering a large number written especially for her; Professor of Organ at the Conservatoire in Lausanne; Adjudicator, guest lecturer and masterclasses in USA, Europe and Asia. Compositions include: Les Tours Du Silence for Narrator and Chamber Ensemble; Labryrinthe Dynamique for Brass Ensemble; Orestes-Stasimon for Choir; Esquisse Alpha for 2 Pianos; Wenn Aus Der Ferne for Organ; Splendid Rotation for 2 Amplified Harpsichords; In Step for String Quartet; Poème Pulvérisé for Voice and Percussion; Meta-Matic No 22 for Tape. Recordings: 6 Trio Sonatas, 5 Concertos, Canonic Variations of JS Bach; Sonatas of CPE Bach and contemporary organ music. Current Management: Europe General: Camille Kiesgen, Bureau International de Concerts et de Conférences, Faubourg Saint-Honoré 252, 75008 Paris, France; USA and Canada: Philip Truckenbrod Concert Artists. Address: Philip Truckenbrod Concert Artists, 300 Asylum Avenue Suite 290, Hartford, CT 06105-4604, USA.

KOIZUMI Kazuhiro, b. 16 Oct 1949, Japan. Conductor; Music Director. m. Masami. Education: University of The Arts, Tokyo; Hochschule für Musik, Berlin; Worked with Seiji Ozawa for 2 years. Career: Assistant Conductor, Japan Philharmonic, 1970-72; Music Director, New Japan Philharmonic, 1975-80, Winnipeg Symphony Orchestra, 1983-; Chief Conductor, Tokyo Metropolitan Orchestra, 1984-; Guest Conductor, Berlin Philharmonic, Chicago Symphony, National Orchestra of France, Royal Philharmonic, Vienna Philharmonic, Toronto Symphony, Tokyo Metropolitan, Kyoto Symphony, Nagoyo Symphony, Montreal Symphony, RAI in Naples and Munich Philharmonic. Recordings: Lalo Concerto Russe/Concerto in F with Radio France, Decca label; Tchaikovsky, Kodály, Dvorák with WSO. Honours: First Prize, 2nd International Conductors Competition (MIN-ONO, 1970); First Prize, von Karajan Competition, 1972; Grand Prix du Disque. Memberships: Advisor, Manitoba Conservatory of Music and Arts. Hobbies: Golf; Pottery; Baseball; Hiking. Current Management: Columbia Artists Management Inc. Address: c/o Columbia Artists Management Inc, New York, USA.

KOJIAN Varujan (Haig), b. 12 Mar 1935, Beirut, Lebanon (of American parentage; Naturalized US citizen, 1967). Conductor. Education: Studied violin, Paris Conservatory, premier prix, 1956, with Ivan Galamian, Curtis Institute of Music, Philadelphia, and with Jascha Heifetz, Los Angeles, 1960; conducting with Sasha Popov; Pupil in conducting of Hans Swarowsky, Vienna, 1971. Career: Assistant concertmaster, 1965-70, Assistant to Zubin Mehta, 1970-71, Los Angeles Philharmonic Orchestra; Assistant conductor, Seattle Symphony Orchestra, 1973-76; Principal Guest Conductor, Royal Opera, Stockholm, 1973-80; Music Director, Utah Symphony Orchestra, Salt Lake City, 1980-83, Chautaugua (NY) Symphony Orchestra, 1981-86, Ballet West, Salt Lake City, 1984-. Recordings: For Andante, Louisville, and Varèse-Sarabande. Honours: 1st Prize, Sorrento conducting competition, 1972.

KOK Nicholas, b. 1962, England. Conductor. Education: Organ Scholar at New College, Oxford; Royal College of Music as Repetiteur. Career: Music Staff of English National Opera from 1989-93; Music Advisor to Contemporary Opera Studio; Has conducted for English National Opera, The Return of Ulysses, The Marriage of Figaro, Cosi fan tutte and King Priam; The Fairy Queen, (Purcell) and Così fan tutte in 1995 and Orfeo in 1996; For English National Opera Bayliss Programmes he conducted Arion and the Dolphin, a new commission by Alec Roth; For Almeida Opera, Mario and The Magician by Stephen Oliver and A Family Affair, a new commission by Julian Grant; He has conducted Cosi fan tutte, The Coronation of Poppea, Reimann's The Ghost Sonata, Xenakis's The Bacchae and Nigel Obsorne's Sarajevo for Opera Factory, London; For Opera Factory Zurich Marschner's Der Vampyr in his own version for Chamber Orchestra and Cavalli's La Calisto; Further engagements with Opera Factory London include Dido and Aeneas and Britten's Curlew River; Other operatic engagements have included Don Giovanni for English Touring Opera, The Barber of Seville for Dublin Grand Opera, Gerald Barry's The Intelligence Park for the Almeida Festival/Opera Factory and Trois Operas Minutes by Milhaud and The Judgement of Paris by Eccles for Trinity College of Music; Has also worked with Scottish Opera; Philharmonia, Ulster Orchestra, London Sinfonietta; Scottish Chamber Orchestra; Royal Scottish National Orchestra; Bournemouth Sinfonietta; Endymion Ensemble; Almeida Ensemble; Cambridge University Chamber Orchestra; London Pro Arte Orchestra and the Philippines Philharmonic Orchestra; A number of Choral Societies; BBC engagements include The Soldier's Tale, The Carnival of the Animals, Reginald Smith Brindle's Journey Towards Infinity, Mondrial by Erollyn Wallen and several television and radio plays; Has arranged and conducted music for ballets by choreographers Robert North and Janet Smith and conducted the Alvin Ailey Dance Theater's season at the London Coliseum; Figaro's Wedding for English National Opera, 1997. Honours include: Countess of Munster Award and Lofthouse Memorial Prize. Address: Allied Artists, 42 Montpelier Square, London SW7 1JZ, England.

KOKKOS Yannis, b. 1944, Athens, Greece. Stage Director and Designer. Education: Studied at National Theatre of Strasbourg. Career: Has created designs for sets and costumes for productions of Macbeth, Lohengrin and Reimann's Lear at Paris Opera Garnier, Pelléas et Mélisandes at La Scala and the Vienna Staatsoper, Don Carlos at Bologna and Elektra at Geneva and San Francisco; Directed the Oresteia by Xenakis in Sicily; Directed and designed Boris Godunov in Bologna and Opera Bastille, Paris, Ariane et Barbe Bleue in Geneva, La Damnation de Faust at the Théâtre du Châtelet, Paris, Nancy Opera with Death in Venice, Festival d'Orange with Carmen, Tosca and Don Giovanni, Welsh National Opera and Scottish Opera with Tristan und Isolde, 1993, and Opera de Bordeaux with Salome; Pelléas et Mélisande and Tristan seen at Covent Garden, 1993; Norma, Opera Bastille, Paris, 1996; Alceste, Scottish Opera, 1996; Tristes Tropiques Aperghis, World premier with Opera Strasbourg, 1996; Elektra, Opera de Lyon, 1997; Clemenza di Tito, Welsh National Opera, 1997; Hänsel and Gretel, Chatelet,

Paris, 1997. Honour: Commandeur des Arts et Lettres, France. Address: 7 Rue Bourdaloue, 75009 Paris, France.

KOLAFA Jirí, b. 26 Feb 1930, Jicín, Czechoslovakia. Composer; Performer (Piano, Harpsichord). m. Vera Cihulová, 1 son. Education: Graduate, State Conservatoire, Prague; Graduate, Academy of Music, Prague. Debut: Song Cycle, 1950. Career: Chamber music performances, Czechoslovakia and abroad, including Germany and Denmark; Reader in Music, Academy of Dramatic Art, Prague. Compositions: About 300 for theatre and film including: Pinocchio, ballet and pantomime; Labyrinth, ballet and pantomime; Chamber music and orchestral works; 2 quintets for wind instruments; Several song cycles; Passacaglia; La Folia e Danza; Racconto for viola and piano; Orbis terrarum for cello and tape; Violin sonata; Panychida; La Folla; Nenies for cello and piano; Struttura di solitudine for chamber ensemble; Sonata per due Boemi; Oratorios: Stabat mater, Canticum, Victimae paschali laudes; A Lyrical Requiem; Generation for trumpet and organ; Piano sonata; Organ works; Madrigalli Boemi for saxophone quartet; Bagatelles for cello and piano; 3 string quartets; Concerto lugubre for harp and string orchestra. Recordings: As member of chamber ensemble. Current Management: OSA, Union protecting Authors' Rights, Prague; Dilia, Theatre Agency, Prague. Address: Cistovická 20, 16300 Prague 6, Czech Republic.

KOLB Barbara, b. 10 Feb 1939, Hartford, Connecticut, USA. Composer. Education: Studied at the Hartt College of Music, MM 1964 and with Lukas Foss and Gunther Schuller at the Berkshire Music Center. Career: Played clarinet in the Hartford Symphony Orchestra 1960-66; Composer-in-residence at the Marlboro Music Festival, 1973, and at the American Academy in Rome, 1975; Taught theory and composition at Brooklyn College and Temple University; Artistic Director of Music New to New York at the Third Street Music School Settlement, 1979. Compositions: Rebuttal for 2 clarinets 1964; Chanson bas for voice, harp and percussion 1965; Three Place Settings for narrator and ensemble, 1968; Trobar clus for 13 instruments 1970; Soundings for 11 instruments and tape 1972 (version for orchestra 1975 and 1977); Frailities for tenor, tape and orchestra, 1971; Spring, River, Flowers, Moon, Night for 2 pianos and tape, 1975; Appello for piano 1976; Musique pour un vernissage for ensemble 1977 (concert version 1979); Songs before an Adieu for flute, guitar and voice 1979; Chromatic Fantasy for narrator and ensemble 1979; 3 Lullabies for guitar 1980; Related Characters for viola and piano 1980; Related Characters for viola and piano 1980; The Point that Divides the Wind for organ and 4 percussionists 1981; Cantico, film score 1982; Millefoglie for ensemble and computer-generated sound, 1985; Time....and Again for oboe, string quartet and tape, 1985; Umbrian Colours for violin and guitar 1986; Yet that things go Round for Chamber Orchestra, 1986-88; Molto Allegra for guitar 1988; The Enchanted Loom for orchestra 1988-89; Extremes for flute and cello, 1989; Voyants for piano and chamber orchestra, 1991; Clouds for organ and piano, recorded tape, 1992. Honours: Rome Prize 1969-71; Fulbright Scholarship 1966-67; MacDowell Colony and Guggenheim Fellowships; Grants from the Ford Foundation and the National Endowment for the Arts (1972-79). Address: Boosey & Hawkes Ltd (promotion), 295 Regent Street, London W1R 8JH, England.

KOLLCZYNSKI Charlotte Ann, b. 8 October 1952, Buffalo, New York, USA. Education: BS, Rosary Hill College, Buffalo, New York, 1974; MM, Music History, State University College at Potsdam, New York, 1978; MLS, Library Science, State University of New York at Buffalo, 1987; Cand phil, Music History, State University of New York at Buffalo. Career: Music Cataloger, Music Library, State University of New York at Buffalo, 1986-87; Monographic Series Librarian, Canisius College, Buffalo, New York, 1987; Music Reference Librarian, Boston Public Library, 1987-. Publications: American Nineteenth Century Broadsides at Buffalo and Erie County Public Library: a catalog and index, MLSs thesis, 1987. Contributions: Reviews for Choice: Current reviews for college libraries, 1987-. Memberships: American Musicological Society; Music Library Association; Music Library Association, New England Chapter. Hobby: Herb Gardening. Address: Research Library, Music Department, Boston Public Library, Box 286, Boston, MA 02117, USA.

KOLLO René, b. 20 Nov 1937, Berlin, Germany. Opera Singer (Tenor). m. 1) Dorthe Larsen, 1967, 2) Beatrice Bouquet, 1982, 1 daughter. Career: Began with Staatstheater, Brunswick, 1965; First Tenor, Deutsche Oper am Rhein, 1967-71; Guest Appearances with numerous leading opera companies, and at annual Bayreuth Wagner Festival, from 1969; Performances include: The Flying Dutchman, 1969, 1970, Lohengrin 1971, Die Meistersinger von Nurnberg 1973, 1974, Parsifal 1975, Siegfried 1976, 1977; Tristan (Zurich) 1980, (Bayreuth 1981); Covent Garden debut 1976, as Siegmund in Die Walküre; Metropolitan Opera debut, 1976, Lohengrin; Sang Otello at Frankfurt, 1988; Returned to Covent Garden 1989, as Siegmund in a new production of Die Walküre conducted by Bernard Haitink; Young Siegfried 1990; Sang Tannhäuser at Hamburg 1990, and as Walther in Die Meistersinger; Season 1991/92 as Peter Grimes at Munich, Tannhäuser at the Deutsche Oper Berlin and in Barcelona; Sang Tannhäuser at the Deutsche Oper, Berlin, 1995. Publication: Imre Fabian im Gespräch mit René Kollo, 1982. Hobbies: Sailing; Tennis; Flying. Address: c/o Personal Artists Management, Wilhelm Str 4, 8000 Munchen 40, Germany.

KOLLY Karl-Andreas, b. 26 May 1965, Switzerland. Pianist. Education: Music Academy, Zurich, 1988; Studied with Karl Engel and Mieczyslaw Horszowski. Debut: Grieg Piano Concerto at Zurich, 1982. Career: Concerto as soloist and chamber musician all over Europe and at several festivals including Lucerne, Zurich, Passau and Davos; Piano Concertos with Tonhalle Orchester Zurich and Symphony Orchestra of Berne; Several radio and television programmes in Switzerland, Germany, Spain and Czech Republic, 1991; Professor, Winderthur Conservatory, 1991-. Recordings: CDs of Schumann piano works including Symphonic Etudes; Brahms, the Piano Trios, with Trio Novanta. Honours: First Prize, Jecklin Competition, 1975; University Competition of Zurich, 1988; Young Musicians Competition, Union of Swiss Banks, 1990; Tschumi prize for best soloist diploma of the year, 1991; Prix Maurice Sandoz, 1990. Hobbies: Travel; Architecture; Films. Address: Burghaldenstrasse 18, CH-5400 Berne, Switzerland.

KOLOMYJEC Joanne, b. 1960, Canada. Singer (Soprano). Career: Appearances in concert and opera throughout Canada, the USA and England from 1985; Opera roles include Mozart's Donna Elvira, Fiordiligi and Countess (all for the Portland and Manitoba companies), and Marguerite; Concert engagements with Toronto Symphony and Calgary Philharmonic Orchestra; Repertoire includes the Mozart and Verdi Requiems, Messiah, Rossini's Stabat Mater, Bruckner's Te Deum, Beethoven's Ninth and Shostakovich's 14th Symphony; Sang David Del Tredici's Alice for the National Ballet of Canada at the London Coliseum, 1987, followed by Zemlinsky's Lyric Symphony; Sang Donna Elvira in a new production of Don Giovanni, at Toronto (1992) and at the Santa Fe Festival. Address: c/o Canadian Opera Company, 227 Front Street East, Toronto, Ontario M5A 1E8, Canada.

KOLTAI Ralph, b. 31 Jul 1924, Berlin, Germany. Stage Designer. Education: Studied in Berlin and London School of Arts and Crafts (now Central St Martin's College of Art and Design). Career includes: Angelique, London Opera Club, 1950; Tannhäuser at Royal Opera House, 1955; Volpone at New Opera Company SW, 1961; Murder in the Cathedral, Sadler's Wells, 1962; Otello and Volo di Notte for Scottish Opera, 1963; Attila for Sadler's Wells, 1963; The Rise and Fall of the City of Mahagonny, 1963; Don Giovanni for Scottish Opera, 1964; Boris Godunov for Scottish Opera, 1965; From the House of the Dead, Sadler's Wells, 1965; The Rake's Progress for Scottish Opera, 1967 and 1971; The Valkyrie, Coliseum ENO, 1970; Elegy for Young Lovers, Scottish Opera, 1970; Götterdämmerung, ENO Coliseum, 1971; Lulu for National Welsh Opera, 1971; Rheingold and Duke Bluebeard's Castle, ENO Coliseum, 1972; Taverner, Royal Opera House, 1972; Tristan and Isolde for Scottish Opera, 1973; Lulu, Kassel, 1973; Siegfried, ENO Coliseum, 1973; Tannhäuser at Sydney Opera House, 1973; Wozzek, Netherlands Opera, 1973; Ring Cycle, touring version, ENO, 1974; Fidelio, Bavarian State Opera, 1974; Don Giovanni, 1975; Midsummer Marriage, Welsh National Opera, 1976; The Ice Break, Royal Opera House, 1977; Threepenny Opera, Aalborg, Denmark, 1979; Anna Karenina, ENO Coliseum, 1981; Die Soldaten at Opera Lyons, 1983; Italian Girl in Algiers, 1984 and Tannhäuser, 1986 at Grand Théâtre de Geneva, 1986; (also directed) The Flying Dutchman 1987 and La Traviata, 1990 at Hong Kong Arts Festival; Pacific Overtures, ENO Coliseum, 1987; The Makropoulos Affair, De Norske Opera, Oslo, 1992; La Traviata, Kungliga Operan, Stockholm, 1993; Otello for Opera Essen, 1994; Madam Butterfly in Tokyo, 1995; Carmen at the Albert Hall, London, 1997. Honour: CBE, 1983. Address: c/o London Management, 2-4 Noel Street, London, W1V 3RD, England.

KOMLOS Péter, b. 25 Oct 1935, Budapest, Hungary. Violinist. m. (1) Edit Fehér, 2 s, (2) Zsuzsa Arki, 1 s. Education: Budapest Music Academy. Career: Founded Komlos String Quartet, 1957; 1st Violinist, Budapest Opera Orchestra, 1960; Leader, Bartók String Quartet, 1963; Extensive tours to Russia, Scandinavia, Italy, Austria, Germany and Czechoslovakia, 1958-64, USA, Canada, New Zealand and Australia, 1970 including Days of Human Rights Concert, UN HQ New York, Japan, Spain and Portugal, 1971, Far East, USA and Europe, 1973; Performed at many festivals including: Ascona, Edinburgh, Adelaide, Spoleto, Menton, Schwerzingen, Lucerne, Aix-en-Provence. Recordings: Beethoven's String Quartets, Budapest; Bartók's String Quartets, Paris. Honours: 1st Prize, International String Quartet Competition, Liège, 1964; Liszt Prize, 1965; Gramaphone Record Prize, Germany, 1969; Kossuth Prize, 1970; Eminent Artist Title, 1980; UNESCO Music Council Plaque, 1981. Hobbies: Model Ship Building; Watching Sport. Address: Törökvész ut 94, Budapest 1025, Hungary.

KOMLOSI Ildiko, b. 1959, Békésszentandra's, Hungary. Singer (Mezzo-soprano). Education: Studied at Szeged Music Academy with Valeria Berdal and at Franz Liszt Academy, Budapest with András Miko; Guildhall School with Vera Rozsa and the Studio of La Scala with Giulietta Simionato. Career: Concert appearances have included the Verdi Requiem in Philadelphia, conducted by Lorin Maazel; Concerts with the BBC Symphony, the Royal Philharmonic with Antal Dorati and the Hungarian Radio and State Television Company; Engagements with the Hungarian State Opera Company, Budapest and the State Operas of Berlin, Vienna, La Scala and in America, San Francisco, Portland, Houston, Columbus, Ohio; Roles include Carmen, Sextus, Leonora in Favorita, Laura, Octavian, Giovanna Seymour (Anna Bolena) and Purcell's Dido; Sang Judit in a concert performance of Duke Bluebeard's Castle with the BBC Philharmonic conducted by András Ligeti, Feb 1991, and at the 1992 Prom Concerts London; Giovanna Seymour at Santiago. Address: Norman McCann International Artists Ltd, The Coach House, 56 Lawrie Park Gardens, London SE26 6XJ, England.

KOMLOSSY Erzsebet, b. 9 July 1933, Salgotarjan, Hungary. Singer (Contralto). Education: Studied at the Bartók Conservatory in Budapest. Career: Member, Hungarian State Opera Budapest; Guest appearances in Moscow, London, Cologne, Edinburgh and elsewhere in Europe; Roles include Azucena (Covent Garden, 1970), Amneris, Ulrica, Preziosilla, Eboli, Carmen, Dalila and parts in operas by Kodály, Szokolay and Erkel. Recordings: Aida, Madama Butterfly, Bank Ban by Erkel, The Spinning Room by Kodály and Blood Wedding by Szokolay (Hungaroton); Hungarian Coronation Mass by Liszt (Deutsche Grammophon); Háry János by Kodály (Decca). Address: c/o Hungarian State Opera House, Népöztársasáy utja 22, 1061 Budapest, Hungary.

KOMOROUS Rudolf, b. 8 Dec 1931, Prague, Czechoslovakia. Composer and Bassoonist. Education: Graduated from Conservatory of Music; Studied composition with Pavel Borkovec at Academy of Musical Arts, Prague. Appointments: Teacher, Central Conservatory of Peking, China, 1959-61; Co-founder, Musica Viva Pragensis, Czechoslovakia; Emigrated to Canada 1969; Associate Professor of Composition and Theory, University of Victoria, 1971-. Compositions: Published by Universal Edition, Vienna and some of them have been issued on Supraphon Records; Mignon for string quartet, 1965; Gone for tape, 1969; Bare and Dainty for Orchestra, 1970; Lady Whiterose Chamber opera, 1971; Anatomy of melancholy for tape, 1974. Honour: Won 1st Prize, Concours International d'Exécution Musicale, Geneva, 1957.

KOMRAKOV Herman (Nickandrovich), b. 29 June 1937, Novgord, Russia. Composer. m. Lukina Alla Urievna, 5 Oct 1962, 1 son, 1 daughter. Education: The Theory of Music, Moscow Conservatory, 1960; Composition, Nizhegorodski Conservatory, 1967. Debut: Symphony No 1, Nizhniy Novgorod, 1967. Career: Teacher, Nizhniy Novgorod Boys Choir, 1954-55; Teacher, Jakutsk Musical College, 1954-55; Pianist, Jakutsk Music Theatre, 1960-62; Pianist, Jakutsk Radio, 1963-64; Professor, Nizhniy Novgorod Conservatory, 1969-85. Compositions: Opera, 4 Ballets, 2 Concerto for piano, Stringed Quartet, a Quartet for wind instruments, Symphony, 10 Oratorios and Cantatas,Sonata for 2 flutes, a Suite for oboe, a Sonatina for a piano, Jakutsk Notebook (12), Organ Alphabet, Sonatina and Suite for accordion, Nizhegorodski Pictures for a folk orchestra. Recordings: A Sonatina for a Piano, Records Firm, Melody, 1981; Quartet for 2 Wood Wind Instruments, Russian Radio; A Sonata for 2 Flute and a Piano, DKC-28358; Suite for Oboe and Instrumental Ensamble, DKC-48433; Nizhegorodsky Pictures for a Folk Orchestra, DKC-41133; Jakutsk Overture for a Folk Orchestra, DKC-41135. Publications include: Suite from the Ballet, The Eagles Fly Northward, 1982; Concert No 2, for a piano with an orchestra, 1982; Nizhegorodsky Pictures, 1984. Contributions to: Musical Life; Soviet Music; Jakutsk Youth. Honours include: Order of the Sign of Honour, 1986. Membership: Union of Composers, Russia, 1968. Hobby: Hunting. Address: Piskunova 45-69, Nizny, Novgord 603005, Russia.

KOMULAINEN Juhani, b, 22 Apr 1953, Jyväskylä, Finland. Composer. Education: BM, University of Miami, Florida, USA, 1975; Composition with Einojuhani Rautavaara, Sibelius Academy, Helsinki, 1978-86. Career: Composes vocal, chamber and stage music. Compositions: Bothnian Dance for String Orchestra; Ballade for Piano; Choral music including Three Landscapes of T S Eliot, Fantaisies Décoratives 1 and 2, Three Sonnets of Shakespeare, Four Ballads of Shakespeare, Shakespearean Settings, Cycle sur Saint Martin, Summer Scenes, Salve. Recording: Three Sonnets of Shakespeare. Honours: Several competition awards including Florilège Vocal de Tours, France, 1996. Address: Pitkänsillanranta 15 B 40, 00530 Helsinki, Finland.

KONECNY Ivan, b. 9 May 1939, Liptovsky Mikulas, Slovakia. Composer; Music Teacher. m. Marta Palanská, 29 May 1971, 1 son, 1 daughter. Education: Conservatory; Second Music

School; Academy of Music in Bratislava, Slovakia. Debut: Overture for Grand Orchestra, 1967. Compositions: Rain - 3 Songs for Mezzosoprano and Piano (text by J Lenko); For piano Op 1, Slovak Musical Foundation, 1975; Six Preludes for Piano, op 2, 1977; Four Bagatelles for Piano, 1978; From My Youth/Three Cycles Compositions for Piano, 1979; Four Bagatelles for Cello and Piano, 1983; Balada for Viola and Piano, 1983, 1991; Tre Intermezzi per Oboe e Piano, 1984, 1987; Memory for Viola Solo, Opus 1989; Phantasy for Piano - 4 Hands. Recordings: Trio for Piano; Concerto For Harpsichord and Chamber Orchestra; Little Suite For Flute, Oboe, Bassoon, Clarinet and French Horn; Outet for 2 Oboes, 2 Clarinets, 2 Cornets, 2 Bassoons; Sonata For Cello Solo; Four Bagatelles For Piano; Three Compositions For Chamber Orchestra. Publications: L Szabadi - I Konecny: Carl Orff's Schulwerk For Elementary School, 1969. Membership: Slovak Musical Union. Hobbies: Musical and fine arts; Literature; Musical and belles-lettres. Address: Starohajska 8, 91700 Trnava, Slovakia.

KONGSTED Ole (Dan), b. 22 Sept 1943, Copenhagen, Denmark. Musicologist; Composer. m. Ida Wieth-Knudsen, 25 Nov 1967, 1 son, 2 daughters. Education: Musicology, University of Copenhagen. Career: Jazz Musician; Holder of Scholarship, Danish State, 1976-80; Freelance Collaborator, Danish Radio, 1976-; Conductor, Choir of the Jeunesses Musicales, 1978-86; Assistant Director, Musikhistorisk Museum and Carl Claudius Samling, Copenhagen, 1980; Choirmaster, Church of the Sacred Heart, Copenhagen, 1983-; Composer; Founder, Leader, Capella Hafniensis, 1990-; Holder of Scholarship, Danish State/Royal Library, 1994. Compositions: 27 opus numbers including: Opus 2, Puer natus est nobis for choir, soloists and organ; Opus 3a, Kyrie fons bonitatis for choir a cappella. Recordings: With Choir of the Jeunesses Musicales; With Ben Webster and Arnved Meyer Band, and Capella Hafniensis. Publications: E turri tibiis canere - Traek af taarnblaesningens historie, in Festskrift Johannes Simons (editor), 1974; Census as Source Material for the History of Music, 1976; Nils Schioerring: Musikkens Historie i Danmark (editor), 1977-78; Music in Denmark at the Time of Christian IV, 1988; Heinrich Schütz und die Musik in Dänemark zur Zeit Christians IV (co-editor), 1989; Kronborg-Motetterne Tilegnet Frederik II og Dronning Sophie 1582, 1990; Kronborg-Brunnen und Kronborg-Motetten, Ein Notenfund des späten 16 Jahrhunderts aus Flensburg und seine Vorgeschichte, 1991; Royal Danish Water Music 1582, 1994. Honour: Organist and Kantor Otto Koebkes Mindelegat, 1992. Address: The Royal Library, Hoejbro Plads 5, 1200 Copenhagen K, Denmark.

KÖNIG Klaus, b. 26 May 1936, Beuthen, Germany. Singer (Tenor). Education: Studied with Johannes Kemter in Dresden. Career: Sang in Cottbus in 1970; Dessau from 1973, as Max, Don Carlos, and Erik in Der fliegende Holländer; Sang at Leipzig 1978-82, Staatsoper Dresden from 1982; Guest appearances in Karlsruhe 1983-85 (Tristan and Tannhäuser), at La Scala and Covent Garden in 1984 (as Tannhäuser) and the Théâtre de la Monnaie Brussels 1985, as Tristan; Sang Max in Der Freischütz, at the opening of the restored Semper Opera House, Dresden (1985); Guest appearances in Paris, Parma, Strasbourg, Madrid, Venice and Barcelona; Other roles include Lensky, Florestan, Radames, Don José, Alvaro in La Forza del Destino, Lohengrin, Walther, Parsifal and Bacchus; Lisbon 1986, as Florestan; Sang Tannhäuser at Cologne and London 1987; Munich Opera 1988, as Menelaos in Die Aegyptische Helena by Strauss; Buenos Aires and Vienna Staatsoper 1988, as Florestan and Bachus; Many engagements in concerts and oratorios. Recordings: Tannhäuser (EMI); Der Rosenkavalier (Denon); Choral Symphony (Philips). Address: c/o Allied Artists Agency, 42 Montpelier Square, London SW7 1JZ, England.

KONISHI Nagako, b. 16 Sep 1945, Agematsu, Nagano, Japan. Composer. Education: Studied at Tokyo National University and with Andrew Imbrie at Berkeley. Compositions include: S'Radda for Children's Choir and Organ, 1975; Five Romances for String Quartet, 1979; Moon Angel for Soprano, Flute and Piano, 1979; Misty Poem for Flute and Harp, 1982; Elegy for Flute and Orchestra, 1983; Away The White for Viola, Clarinet and Piano, 1990. Address: c/o JASRAC, Jasrac House 7-13, 1-Chome Nishishimbashi, Minato-ku, Tokyo 105, Japan.

KONSHINA Yelena, b. 9 Jan 1950, Kirovgrad, Sverdlovsk, Russia. Composer. Career: Resident in Vladimir and composer of religious and other music. Compositions include: A Capella Choral Works, for the Russian Orthodox Church; Cello Sonata, 1973; Piano Concerto, 1975; Trio for Oboe, Bassoon and Cello, 1977; Three Preludes for Piano, 1985. Address: c/o RAO, Bolchaia Bronnai 6-a, Moscow 103670, Russia.

KONSTANTINOV Julian, b. 1966, Sofia, Bulgaria. Singer (Bass). Education: Studied at the Sofia Academy, 1987-93. Career: Sang in The Rake's Progress and Il Barbiere di Siviglia while a student and represented Bulgaria at the 1992 Cardiff Singer of the World Competition; Appearances with the Sofia National Opera in Lucia di Lammermoor, Aida, Rigoletto, Luisa Miller and Turandot (as Timur); Further engagements in Ireland and at the Teatro Colon Buenos Aires, 1995. Recordings: Sarastro in Die Zauberflöte and Commendatore in Don Giovanni. Address: Lies Askonas Ltd, 6 Henrietta Street, London WC2E 8LA, England.

KONSULOV Ivan, b. 29 May 1946, Varna, Bulgaria. Singer (Baritone). Education: Studied with Jossifov in Sofia and with Aldo Protti in Italy. Debut: Opera National Russe (Bulgaria) 1972. Career: Sang in Berne from 1977, as Simon Boccanegra, Marcello (La Bohème), Scarpia, Don Giovanni, Mandryka, Tonio, Pizarro, Don Carlos (La Forza del Destino), Alfio and Iago; Bologna 1980, Zurga in Les pêcheurs de Perles; Philadelphia Opera 1982, Marcello: Bratislava 1984, as Eugene Onegin; Stuttgart and Berlin 1985, Don Giovanni; At the Monte Carlo opera in 1986 sang Gryaznoy in The Tsar's Bride by Rimsky-Korsakov; Engagements at Graz, Barcelona, Madrid and Karlsruhe; Sang Amfortas in Parsifal at Berne, 1989; Season 1992 as the Major-domo in Zemlinsky's Der Zwerg at Trieste. Recordings include: La Bohème-Marcello Opus-Bratislava Stereo with P Dvorsky and TV Film 1980; The Queen of Spades (Tomsky), Musik Mundial-Sofia with International Stars, 1988; Don Carlo-Posa, Balkanton, Sofia, 1988; Opera Recital Arias Balkanton, 1988. Address: c/o Stadttheater Bern, Nägeligasse 1, CH-3011 Bern, Switzerland.

KONT Paul, b. 19 Aug 1920, Vienna, Austria. Composer. 1 son. Education: Conductor's Diploma, 1947, Composer's Diploma, 1948, Vienna Academy of Music. Career: Professor of Composition, 1969-86, Emeritus, 1986-, Vienna Academy of Music. Compositions: Commissioned operas: Lysistrate (for Komische Oper Berlin), 1957; Peter und Susanne (for Austrian Television), 1959; For the Time Being (for Austrian Television), 1965; Celestina (for Stadt-Buhnen, Cologne), 1966; Plutos (for Austrian Government), 1976; Traumleben, musical, 1958; Ballets: Italia Passata; Die Traurigen Jäger; Amores; Il Ballo del Mondo; Monoballette, ballet film; Vom Manne und vom Weibe, oratorio; Symphonies; Concertos; Chamber music; Lieder; Piano Sonatas. Publication: Antianiorganikum. Address: 47 Geusaugasse, Vienna 1030, Austria.

KONTARSKY Alfons, b. 9 Oct 1932, Iserlohn, Germany. Pianist. Education: Studied in Cologne with Else Schmidt-Gohr and Maurits Frank; Further study in Hamburg with Eduard Erdmann, 1955-57. Career: Many appearances with his brother in modern music programmes from 1955, including works by Earle Brown, Kagel, Stockhausen, Pousseur, Berio and Bussotti; Seminar at Darmstadt, 1962-69; Teacher at the Musikhochschule from 1969; Formed Piano Trio with Saschko Gawriloff and Klaus Storck, 1971. Publication: Pro Musica Nova: Studien zum Spielen neuer Musik für Klavier, 1973. Honours include: First prize for Piano Duo at the 1955 Munich Radio International Festival. Recordings include: Bartók's Sonata for two Pianos and Percussion. Address: Stacthiche Hochschule für Musik Rheinland, Degobertstrasse 38, 5000 Köln 1, Germany.

KONTARSKY Alois, b. 14 May 1931, Iserlohn, Germany. Pianist. Education: Studied in Cologne with Else Schmitz-Gohr and Maurits Frank; Further study in Hamburg with Eduard Erdmann. Career: International performances with his brother from 1955 in modern repertoire: Michael Gielen, de Grandis, Henri Pousseur, Berio and Zimmermann; Gave premiere of Stockhausen's Klavierstücke I-XI, Darmstadt 1966; Concerts with the Stockhausen ensemble and duo with the cellist Siegfried Palm; Master class at the Cologne Musikhochschule from 1969. Recordings include: Bartók's Sonata for Two Pianos and Percussion; Klavierstücke I-XI by Stockhausen. Honours include: First prize for Piano Duo at the Munich Radio International Festival, 1955. Addres: Staatliche Hochschule für Musik Rheinland, Degobertstrasse 38, 5000 Köln 1, Germany.

KONYA Ladiszlaus, b. 4 Aug 1934, Rumania. Baritone. Career: Sang in opera throughout Rumania and Eastern Europe from 1953, at Théâtre de la Monnaie at Brussels in 1965 and the Vienna Volksoper, 1967-72; Zurich, 1968-70 and Frankfurt Opera, 1972-86; Further guest appearances at Covent Garden as Luna in Trovatore, Lyon and Toulouse; Other roles have included Don Giovanni, Enrico in Lucia di Lammermoor, Amonasro, Ford, Jack Rance, Kothner in Die Meistersinger, Eugene Onegin and the Forester in The Cunning Little Vixen. Address: c/o Theater der Stadt Frankfurt, Untermáinanlage 11, W-6000 Frankfurt am Main, Germany.

KONYA Sandor, b. 23 Sept 1923, Sarkad, Hungary. Singer (Tenor). Education: Studied at the Budapest Conservatory with Ferenc Szekelyhidy; Further study with Fred Husler in Detmold, and in Milan. Debut: Bielefeld, 1951, as Turiddu. Career: Sang in Bielefeld until 1954, then in Darmstadt; Städtische Oper Berlin 1956, in the premiere of König Hirsch by Henze; Edinburgh Festival, 1956, in Der Barbier von Bagdad by Cornelius; Bayreuth Festival, 1958-71, as Lohengrin and Parsifal; Sang in San Francisco, 1960-65; Metropolitan Opera, 1961-74, as Lohengrin, Radames, Calaf, Pinkerton, Walther von Stolzing, Edgardo, Max in Der Freischütz and Cavaradossi (212 performances in 21 roles); Covent Garden from 1963; Guest appearances in Paris, Milan, Verona, Rome, Munich and Hamburg; Teacher at the Musikhochschule Stuttgart. Recordings: La Bohème, Madama Butterfly, Tosca (Deutsche Grammophon); Die Fledermaus, Lohengrin (RCA); Aida (Hungaroton). Address: c/o Staatliche Hochschule für Musik, Urbanplatz 2, D-7000 Stuttgart, Germany.

KOOPMAN Ton, 2 Oct 1944, Zwolle, Netherlands. Conductor; Organist; Harpsichordist. m. Tini Mathot. Eduction: BMus, University of Amsterdam; Solo Degree Organ, 1969; Solo degree harpsichord, 1970. Career: Founder, Music ensemble Musica da Camera, 1966; Music Antiqua Amsterdam, 1970; Numerous concerts and recordings; Founder, Amsterdam Baroque Orchestra, 1979; Appearances on radio and TV the world over; Solo tours to USA and Japan, and yearly with Amsterdam Baroque Orchestra, to Europe, USA and Japan; Frequently invited as guest conductor, and forms duo with wife; Professor of Harpsichord, Royal Conservatory, The Hague; Season 1997 included Schubert Bicentenary concert in Amsterdam and Bach's B Minor Mass in London. Recordings: Over 150 records as a soloist, of which 40 with the Amsterdam Baroque Orchestra including Buxtehude Cantatas, 4 CDs, 1997. Honours: Toonkunst Award, 1974; Johan Wagenaar Award, 1978; Edison Awards for Recordings; 3M Award for contribution to Ancient Music, 1989; Crystal Award, Osaka Symphony Hall Japan, 1992. Hobbies: Antique Books and Music; Engravings; Paintings; History of 17th & 18th Century; Laurel & Hardy Movies. Address: Amsterdam Baroque Orchestra, Meerweg 23, 1405 BC Bussum, Netherlands.

KOPPEL Lone, b. 20 May 1938, Copenhagen, Denmark. Soprano. Education: Studied at the Royal Danish Academy of Music. Debut: Copenhagen in 1962 as Musetta. Career: Sang at Kiel Opera, 1964-65, and Royal Opera Copenhagen, 1962-95; Guest appearances at Sydney, 1973-78, and Aarhus from 1972 as Leonore in Fidelio and the Trovatore Leonora; Sang Salome at Bonn and Oslo, 1973-74, and Lady Macbeth in Macbeth at Stockholm in 1981; Copenhagen among others Judith in Bluebeard's Castle and Shostakovich's Katerina Ismailova; Other roles include Michal in Saul and David, Wagner's Elisabeth, Kundry, Ortrud and Senta, Elektra, Jenufa, Eboli, Donna Anna and Donna Elvira. Address: c/o Det Kongelige Teator, Box 2185, DK-1017 Copenhagen, Denmark.

KOPTAGEL Yuksel, b. 27 October 1931, Istanbul, Turkey. Pianist; Composer. m. Danyal Kerven, 30 December 1964. Education: Private studies with composer Djemal Rechid; Graduated, Real conservatorio de Music, Madrid, 1955; Diplome Superieur, Schola Cantorum, Ecole Superieure de Musique, Paris, 1958; Certificates on Composition and Spanish Music Interpretation, Santiago, 1959. Debut: First public concert, Istanbul, aged 5. Career: Concerts in Europe (Spain, France, Italy, Switzerland, Czechoslovakia, Germany) USA, India, Pakistan, Russia; Compositions published by Max Eschig, Paris and Bote Bock, Berlin; International concert career with European Orchestras, 1953-; Member of Jury, Schola Cantorum, Paris; Participant, numerous music festivals. Compositions: Tamzara; Toccata; Sonata Menorca; Trois Danses; Pastoral; Etude pour Piano; Deux Chanson du Pecheur Japonais-Hiroshima Lieder; Terezin Lieder (chansons des enfants morts); Zwei Spanische Lieder; Fossil Suite for guitar and piano; Brian's Diary; Epitafio; When We Two Parted, song; Romance de Castille; Prager Lieder. Recordings: Deux Chansons du Pecheur Japonais and Zwei Spanische Lieder, sung by Gunther Leib; Tamzara; Toccata. Contributions to: Filarmoni and Orkestra magazines. Honours: Several mentions and Premiere Prix Schola Cantorum, Paris, 1958-59; 1st Prize for Toccata, Year's Best Piano Competition, Paris, 1959. Memberships: Filarmonic Society, Istanbul; Societe des Auteurs Compositeurs de Musique, France. Hobbies: Photography; Filming; Spanish Literature; Hispano-American Art. Address: Caddebostan Plajyolu 21/32, 81060 Istanbul, Turkey.

KOPYTMAN Mark, b. 6 Dec 1929, Kamenetz-Podolski, USSR. Composer; Pianist. m. Miriam Kopytman, 5 July 1955, 2 daughters. Education: MD, Tchernovitz, USSR, 1952; MMus, Lvow Academy of Music, USSR, 1955; PhD, Moscow Conservatory, USSR, 1958. Career: Senior Teacher, Theory and Composition, USSR State Academies of Music, 1955-72; Chairman of Theory and Composition Department, 1974-76, 1979-82, 1985-, Professor, 1976-, Rubin Academy of Music, Jerusalem, Israel; Deputy Head of Rubin Academy of Music and Dance, Jerusalem, Israel, 1985-; Guest Professor, Hebrew University Musicological Department, Jerusalem, 1979-; Guest Professor of Composition, University of Pennsylvania, USA, 1985 and 1989; Composer in Residence, Canberra School of Music, Australia, 1985. Compositions: Case Mare (Opera), 1966; Songs of Kodr (oratorio), 1966; String Quartet III, 1969; Voices, 1974-75; October Sun, 1974; Monodrama (Ballet), 1975; Concerto for Orchestra, 1976; About an Old Tune, 1977; Rotations, 1979; Cantus II, 1980; Memory, 1981; Kaddish, 1982; Susskind von Trimberg (Opera), 1982-83; Cantus III, 1984; Life of the World to Come, 1985; Variable Structures, 1985-86; Letters of Creation, 1986; Dedication, 1986; Letters of Creation for voice and strings,

1987; Circles for voice, clarinet, cello and piano, 1987; Ornaments for harpischord and orchestra, 1987; Scattered Rhymes for choir and orchestra, 1988; Eight Pages from the Book of Questions for voice solo, 1988; A Poem for the Numbers for the Dead for baritone and chamber ensemble, 1988; Love Remembered for choir and orchestra, 1989; To Go Away for mezzo-soprano and five instruments, 1989. Recordings: Six Moldavian Dances for Orchestra; String Quarteet No 2; About an Old Tune; October Sun; For Harp; Memory; Rotations; Cantus II; Lamentation. Publication: Choral Composition, 1971. Hobby: Graphic Design. Address: 4 Tchernichovsky Str, Jerusalem 92581, Israel.

KORD Kazimierz, b. 18 Nov 1930, Pogorze, Poland. Conductor. Education: Studied piano at the Leningrad Conservatory, composition and conducting at the Cracow Academy. Career: Conducted at the Warsaw Opera, 1960-62; Artistic Director, Cracow Opera, 1962-68 (staged own productions of opera); Music Director, Polish National Orchestra, 1968-73; Metropolitan Opera, 1972, The Queen of Spades: returned for Così fan tutte, Boris Godunov and Aida; San Francisco, 1973, Boris Godunov and Rigoletto; Other opera engagements in London (Eugene Onegin 1976), Amsterdam and Copenhagen; Took the Toronto Symphony Orchestra on its first European tour, 1974: has also conducted the Detroit, Chicago and Cleveland Symphony Orchestras; Artistic Director, Warsaw Phiharmonic from 1977; Chief Conductor of the South West German Radio in Baden-Baden, 1980; Principal Conductor of the Cincinnati Symphony, 1980-82; Has conducted orchestras in Moscow, Leningrad, New York, London, Stockholm, Rotterdam, Pittsburgh, Vienna and Tokyo; Conducted Othello at San Francisco, 1989. Address: c/o Ingpen & Williams Ltd, 14 Kensington Court, London W8 5DN, England.

KORDES Heidrun, b. 1960, Germany. Singer (Soprano). Education: Freiburg Musikhochschule. Debut: Gelsenkirchen Opera. Career: Engagement at the Hessichen Staatstheater, Wiesbaden, from 1986; Roles have included Mozart's Pamina and Susanna, Nedda in Pagliacci, Gilda in Rigoletto and parts in operas by Handel; Guest engagements at Leipzig, Dresden, Mannheim, Frankfurt and the Deutsche Oper am Rhein, Dusseldorf; Frequent concert appearances. Recordings include: Oreste and Xerxes by Handel; Albums of Lieder. Address: c/o Allied Artists, 42 Montpellier Square, London SW7 1JZ, England.

KORF Anthony, b. 14 Dec 1951, New York City, USA. Composer; Conductor. Education: BA, MA, Manhattan School of Music. Career: Artistic Director, Conductor, Parnassus, 1975-; Guest Conductor, Group for Contemporary Music; League ISCM; Co-Founder, Artistic Director, The Riverside Symphony; Commissioned by San Francisco Symphony, American Composers Orchester and others. Compositions: Symphony No 2; Symphony in the Twilight; Oriole; A Farewell; Cantata; Double Take; Brass Quintet; Symphonia; Requiem, 3 Movements for Clarinet Solo. Recordings: A Farewell; Symphony No 2; Conductor: Stefan Wolpe (Koch International); Andrew Imbrie (New World); Babbitt; Davidovsky; Korf; Lundborg; Olan. Publications: Stefan Wolpe Chamber Piece No 2, Editor. Honours: Koussevitsky Commission, 1992; American Academy of Arts and Letters Lieberson Fellowship, 1988. Address: 258 Riverside Drive, 7C, New York, NY 10025, USA.

KORHONEN Ritva-Liisa, b. 1959, Finland. Soprano. Education: Studied in Helsinki and Zurich. Debut: Helsinki in 1984 as Gilda. Career: After further study at the Sibelius Academy sang Musetta and Adina in Helsinki, Fiordiligi at Tampere, Traviata at Oulu and Adele in Die Fledermaus at Lahti; Further appearances at the Savonlinna Festival and in concert. Address: c/o Finnish National Opera, Bulevardi 23-27, SF-00180 Helsinki 18, Finland.

KORN Artur, b. 4 Dec 1937, Wuppertal, Germany. Singer (Bass). m. Sabine Hass. Education: Studied in Cologne, Munich and Vienna with Clemens Glettenberg and Schuch-Tovini. Debut: Cologne Opera Studio 1963, in Un Ballo in Machera. Career: Sang in Graz 1965-68, Vienna Volksoper and Staatsoper from 1968; Glyndebourne Festival 1980-84, as Baron Ochs, Bartolo in Le nozze di Figaro and Waldner in Arabella; Metropolitan Opera from 1984, as Osmin, Bartolo and Ochs; Engagements in Chicago (debut 1984), San Francisco, Detroit, London and Toronto and in Germany, Italy, South Africa and Switzerland; Salzburg Festival 1987, in Schoenberg's Moses and Aron; Sarastro in Magic Flute, Buenos Aires; Ochs in Rosenkavalier, Santiago de Chile; Met Tour, Japan, 1988; State Opera Munich Tour, Japan, 1988; Vienna Festival State Opera Vienna with Hermanns/Harnoncourt (Osmin-Entführung), 1988; Sang 1991/92 as Hagen at Brussels and Mozart's Bartolo at the Salzburg Festival; Often heard in oratorios and Lieder. Recordings include: Alfonso und Estrella by Schubert (PAN); Le nozze di Figaro with Haitink (EMI); Vespro della Beata Vergine with Harnoncourt (Teldec); Video Recordings: Ariadne auf Naxos (Met/Levine); Arabella (Strauss) Glyndebourne/Haitink; Le nozze di Figaro; Die Entführung, Vienna State Opera/Harnoncourt. Address: c/o Staatsoper, Opernring 2, A-1010 Vienna, Austria.

KORN Peter (Jona), b. 30 Mar 1922, Berlin, Germany. Composer; Conductor. Education: Studied at the Berlin Hochschule, with Edmund Ribbra in England and with Stefan Wolpe at the Jerusalem Conservatory, 1936-38; Further study with Schoenberg at UCLA, 1941-42, and with Hanns Eisler, Ernest Toch, Miklos Rozsa and Ingolf Dahl. Career: Founder and conductor of the New Orchestra of Los Angeles, 1948-56; Teacher of composition at the Munich Trapp Conservatory, 1960-61; Visiting Lecturer, at UCLA, 1964-65; Director of the Strauss Conservatory Munich from 1967. Compositions: Opera Heidi in Frankfurt, 1963 (performed Saarbrucken 1978); Orchestral: 3 Symphonies, 1941-46, 1956, 1977; Rhapsody for oboe and strings, 1951; Concertino for horn and strings, 1952; Adagietto, 1954; Variations on a theme from the Beggar's Opera, 1955; Saxophone Concerto, 1956; Verolina Suite, 1959; Variations on a German Folksong for cello and orchestra, 1960; Cello Concerto, 1965; Exorcism of a Liszt Fragment, 1968; 4 Pieces for strings, 1970; Morgenmusik for trumpet and strings, 1973; Beckmesser Variations, 1977; Trumpet Concerto, 1979; Salue to the Lone Wolves for Winds, 1980; Chamber: Cello sonata, 1949; 2 string quartets, 1950, 1963; Horn sonata, 1952; Aloysia-Serenade, 1953; Wind Quintet, 1966; Serenade for 12 strings cellos, 1976; Duo for viola and piano, 1978; ASCAP, ASCAP Building, One Lincoln Plaza, New York, NY 10023, USA.

KORSAKOVA Natasha, b. 29 Jan 1973, Moscow, Russia. Concert Violinist. Education Studied at Central Music School, Moscow. Debut: Concerts with Moscow Chamber Orchestra at the Conservatoire. Career: Has given concerts in Bulgaria, Germany, Greece, Yugoslavia, China, Italy, Belgium and Japan, 1989-; Played at the Panatei Festival, Italy, 1991, and the Bruch Second Concerto with the Russian State Symphony Orchestra, October 1991; Repertoire also includes works by Vivaldi, Bach, Mendelssohn, Mozart, Tchaikovsky and Lalo; Chamber recitals in Japan, 1991 with her mother Iolanthe Miroshnikova as accompanist in works by Brahms, Saint-Saëns, Beethoven and Prokofiev; Based in Germany since 1993. Honours: awards at Wieniawski and Lipinski Competitions, Poland, 1988; Young Violinists International Competition, Kloster Schontal, Germany, 1989. Current Management: Sonata, Glasgow, Scotland. Address: 11 Northpark Street, Glasgow G20 7AA, Scotland.

KORTE Karl (Richard), b. 25 Aug 1928, Ossining, New York, USA. Composer. Education: Studied at the Juilliard School with Otto Luening, Peter Mennin, Vincent Persichetti, Goffredo Petrassi and Aaron Copland. Career: Teacher at Arizona State University, 1963-64 and at Binghamton, New York, 1964-70; Professor of Music, University of Texas at Austin, 1971. Compositions: Orchestral: Concertino on a Choral Theme, 1955; For a Young Audience, 1959; 2 Symphonie, 1961, 1968; Southwest, dance overture, 1963; Concerto for piano and winds, 1976; Chamber: 2 string quartets, 1948, 1965; Quintet for oboe and strings, 1960; Matrix, 1968; Facets, 1969; Rememberances for flute and tape, 1971; Symmetrics, 1973; Piano Trio, 1977; Concertino for base trombone, wind and percussion; The Whistling Wind for mezzo and tape, 1982; Double Concerto for flute, double bass and tape, 1983; Band music and works for chorus including mass for Youth, 1963; Aspects of Love, 1968; Pale is this Good Prince, oratorio, 1973, Of Time and Seasons, 1975. Address: c/o ASCAP, ASCAP Building, One Lincoln Plaza, New York, NY 10023, USA.

KORTEKANGAS Jaakko, b. 1961, Finland. Baritone. Education: Studied at the Sibelius Academy in Helsinki and with Herbert Brauer in Berlin. Career: After further study in Zurich sang at the Freiburg Opera from 1990, notably as Posa in Don Carlos, Belcore, Rossini's Figaro and Billy Budd and Wolfram in Tannhäuser; Guest at Berne in 1992 in Shostakovich's Lady Macbeth and as concert singer in Europe and North America including New York in 1990; Guest at Zürich as Barber of Seville, 1993, and at Finnish National Opera, 1996. Honour: First Prize, 1989 Lappeenranta competition. Address: Rosenstauden 14, 79114 Freiburg im Breisgau, Germany.

KORTEKANGAS Olli, b. 16 May 1955, Turku, Finland. Composer. Education: Studied Composition and Music Theory, Sibelius Academy, 1974-81, West Berlin, 1981-82. Career: Composer; Journalist; Choral Conductor, Pedagogue (Sibelius Academy, National Theatre Academy). Compositions include: TV opera Grand Hotel, 1984-85; Orchestral: Okologie1-Vorspiel, 1983; Okologie, 2; Konzert, 1986-87; Alba, 1988; Amores, 1989; Instrumental Threnody, 1977; Sonata per organo, 1979, Emotion, 1988; Imaggio a M C Escher, 1990, Iscrizione, 1990, Choral MAA, 1984-85, Verbum, 1987, A, 1987-88, Electronic Memoria, 1988-89. Recordings: Has made several recordings of his work (on Finlandia and Ondine labels). Honours: Salzburg Opera Prize, 1989; Gianfranco Zaffrani Prize, 1989. Memberships: Founding Member, Korvat auki Society (society for promotion or new music), Board Member: Society of Finnish Composers, Finnish Composers' Copyright Bureau TEOSTO. Address: Ruohoahdenkatu 20, 00180 Helsinki, Finland.

KOS Bozidar, b. 3 May 1934, Novo Mesto, Slovenia. Composer. m. Milana Karlovac, 29 Apr 1963, 1 daughter. Education: BMus, 1974, BMus 1st Class Honours, Composition, 1975, MMus, 1980, University of Adelaide. Career: Teacher, Cello, Music Theory, State Music School, Novo Mesto, 1943-54; Lecturer in Music, Torrens College of Advanced Education, Adelaide, South Australia, 1975; Tutor in Composition, Electronic Music, 1976-77, Fellow in Composition, 1978-83, University of Adelaide; Lecturer in Composition, 1984-91, Senior Lecturer in Composition, 1992-, Head, Composition Division, 1994-, Sydney Conservatorium of Music, University of Sydney, New South Wales. Compositions: Orchestral: Axis 5-1-5, 1973; Mediations, 1974; Metamorphosis, 1978; Sinfonietta, 1983; Violin Concerto, 1986; Guitar Concerto, 1992; Crosswinds for jazz trumpet, alto saxophone and orchestra, 1993; Ensemble works: Integration, 1972; Chamber Piece, 1973; Little Fantasy, 1978; Quartet, 1980; String Quartet, 1982; Three Movements, 1982; Catena 1, 1985, Quasar, 1987; Catena 2, 1989; Ludus ex Nominum, 1989; Bravissssimo, 1991; Solo works: Reflections, piano solo, 1976; Piano Sonata, 1981; Kolo, piano solo, 1984; Evocations for solo cello, 1994; Instrumental works with synthesiser, computer or tape: Modulations, 1974; Dialogue 1, tape, 1976; Spectrum, 1988. Recordings: Quasar for percussion quartet, CD Synergy Percussion; Piano Sonata, CD The Hands The Dream, Tall Poppies; Violin Concerto, CD Forbidden Colours. Address: Sydney Conservatorium of Music, Macquarie Street, Sydney, New South Wales 2000, Australia.

KOSHAK John, b. 2 May, USA. Conductor; Professor of Music. m. Nancy McKill Koshak, 12 June 1965. Education: BS, Music, Pennsylvania University; MA, Columbia University; Conducting Diploma, Mozarteum, Salzburg, Austria. Career: Conductor, Music Instructor, Department Chair, Smithtown Senior High School, St James, New York, 1960-62, Kaiserslautern American High School, Germany, 1962-64, River Dell Regional Schools, Oradell, New Jersey, 1964-66, Bakersfield High School, California, 1966-71; Music Director, Conductor, Orange County Youth Symphony Orchestra, 1971-; Professor of Music, Chapman University, Orange, 1971-. Publications: The Conductor's Triangle, 1980; The Art of Conducting - Score Study and Preparation, 1984; The Conductor's Check List, 1984; Rehearsal Reminders, 1985; Rehearsal Techniques: The Conductor's Triangle, 1993; The Conductor's Role: Preparation for Individual Study, Rehearsal & Performance, 1997. Contributions to: Bakersfield Californian Newspaper. Honours: Superior Performance Award, US Government, 1963-64; Conducting Competition Winner, Columbia University, New York, 1965; John Koshak Day, Bakersfield, 14 May 1971; ASCAP Awards, Performance of American Music, 1978-79, 1980-81; Orange County Music Educator Association Irene Schoepfle Award, 1982; Chapman University Faculty of the Year, 1996. Memberships: American Association of University Professors; American Federation of Musicians; American Symphony Orchestra League; California Music Educators Association; California Orchestra Directors Association; Conductors Guild; Orange County Music Educators Association; Southern California School Band & Orchestra Association. Address: Chapman Symphony Orchestra, Chapman University, Orange, CA 92666, USA.

KOSHELEV Viacheslav, b. 20 June 1947, Petrozavodsk, Russia. Composer. m. Natalia Khilko, Feb 1989, 1 daughter. Education: Studied at Leningrad Conservatoire, 1972. Debut: Second Sonatina for Clarinet, Bassoon and Piano. Career: Professor of Petrozavodsk Conservatoire. Compositions include: Concert Musik, 4 Dances in Polka Rhythm for orchestra; Sonata for violin solo; Chastushki Suite of Musical Pictures for 2 flutes, 2 clarinets and saxophone; In Modo for brass quintet. Membership: Composers' Union of Russia. Hobbies: Skiing; Running. Address: Anochina Str 37, Apt 28, Petrozavodsk, Russia.

KOSLER Zdenek, b. 25 Mar 1928, Prague, Czechoslovakia. Conductor. m. Jana Svobodova, 1954. Education: Academy of Music and Dramatic Arts, Prague. Career: In Concentration Camp, 2nd world War; Guest Conductor, Prague National Theatre, 1951-, debut with Il Barbiere di Siviglia, 1951; Artistic Director, Olomouc Opera, 1958-62; Chief, Ostrava Opera, 1962-66; Assistant Conductor, New York Philharmonic Orchestra, 1963-64; FOK Orchestra, Prague, 1965-67; Chief Conductor, Berlin Komische Oper, 1966-68; Chief Conductor Opera of the Slovak National Theatre, Bratislava, 1971-76; Artistic Director and Chief Conductor, Prague National Theatre Opera, 1980-85; Conductor, Czech Philharmonic Orchestra, Prague, 1971-80; Concert Tours of Japan, 1968-; Conducted Salome at the Vienna Staatsoper, 1965; Great Britain, 1975, 1977, Austria, France, Italy, Switzerland, 1976, Canada; Concert tours and opera performances in Europe, USA, Canada, Japan with Czech Philharmonic Orchestra, Wiener Symphoniker, Staatskapelle Berlin and Dresden, Wiener Staatsoper, Leningrad Philharmonic, NHK Orchestra 1958; Conducted Martinu's Greek Passion at Wiesbaden and in Paris, 1990; The Bartered Bride at Berne, 1992. Honours: Award, Outstanding Work, 1958; 1st Prize, Young Conductors' Competition, Besancon, 1956; 1st Prize, Gold Medal, D Mitropoulos International Competition, New York, 1963; Artist of Merit, 1974; National Artist, 1984. Address: NAD Sarkou 35, 16000 Prague 6, Czech Republic.

KOSMO Ingeborg, b. 1967, Denmark. Mezzo-Soprano. Career: Frequent concert and opera engagements throughout Scandinavia and Europe; Repertory includes L'Enfant Prodigue by Debussy, the Composer in Ariadne auf Naxos, with songs by Schubert, Strauss and Stravinsky; Contestant at the 1995 Cardiff Singer of the World Competition. Address: Schweigaardsgate 69, 0560 Oslo, Norway.

KOSUT Michal, b. 7 June 1954, Brno, Czechoslovakia. Composer and University Teacher. m. Marie Ruzickova, 10 October 1981, 2 daughters. Education: Janacek's Academy of Performing Arts in Brno, 1973-78, Professor Ctirad Kohoutek. Debut: Symphony Jan Santini Aichel, 1979-80. Career: Compositions performed in Austria, Germany, France, Netherlands, Great Britain, USA, Japan, Denmark, Russia and others; Orchestral/chamber opera, electroacoustic and film music. Compositions: Orchestral works: Jan Santini Aichel, 1979-80; Gepard, 1988; Opera and ballet works: Valery, 1993, Iphygeny, 1996. Recordings: Radio recordings in Switzerland, Netherlands, Germany, France and Great Britain; CD and TV recordings in Czech Republic. Honour: Awarded the Minister of Culture Prize, 1990. Memberships: OSA, Board Member. Hobbies: History; Architecture.

KOSZEWSKI Andrzej, b. 26 July 1922, Poznan, Poland. Composer; Musicologist. m. Krystyna Jankowska, 1 daughter. Education: Studies in Musicology, Poznan University with Adolf Chybinski; Diploma, 1950; Studies in Composition with Theory of Music, State Higher Schools in Poznan with Stefan B Poradowski, Diploma, 1948 and 1953; With Tadeusz Szeligowski, Warsaw, Diploma, 1958. Career: Teacher of Composition and Theory of Music as Professor of Academy of Music, Poznan; Choral works are performed at numerous international festivals and competitions, mainly in Europe, America and Asia. Compositions include: Concerto Grosso, 1947; Suita Kaszubska (Kashubian Suite), 1952; Trzy Kotysanki (Three Cradle Songs), 1952-69; Allegro Symfoniczne, 1953; Sinfonietta, 1956; Sonata Breve, 1954; Muzyka Fa-Re-Mi-Do-Si, 1960; Tryptyk Wielkopolski (Great Poland Triptych), 1963; La espero (The Hope), 1963; Nicolao Copernico dedicatum, 1966; Gry (Games), 1968; Makowe ziarenka, 1969; Przystroje (Ornamentations), 1970; Ba-No-Sche-Ro, 1971-72; Da fischiare, 1973; Canzone e danza, 1974; Trzy koledy (Three Christmas Carols), 1975; Prologus, 1975; 3 Sonatinas, 1978; Ad musicam, 1979; Campana (The Bell), 1980; Angelus Domini, 1981; Three Euphonic Chorales, 1982; Suita Lubuska (Lubusz Suite), 1983; Zaklecia (Incantations), 1983; Strofy trubadura, 1985; Tre pezzi, 1986; Trois chaconnes, 1986; Enigma, 1986; Krople teczy (Drops of a Rainbow) 1988; Wi-La-Wi, 1988-94; Serioso-Giocoso, 1989; Miserere, 1989; 3 Tance polskie (3 Polish Dances), 1989; Canti sacri, 1990; Tristis est anima mea, 1992; Ave Maria, 1992; Trittico di Messa, 1992; Carmina Sacrata, 1992-94; Et lux perpetua, 1992-96; Epitaphium, 1994; Iubilatio, 1994; Non sum dignis, 1996. Recordings: Various recordings. Publications: Author of many publications dealing with Chopinology and Musical Education. Address: ul Poznanska 37 m9, 60-850 Poznan, Poland.

KOSZUT Urszula, b. 13 Dec 1940, Psycszyna, Poland. Singer (Soprano). m. Gerhard Geist. Education: Studied with Maria Eichler-Cholewa in Katowice and with Bogdan Ruskiewicz in Warsaw. Debut: Stuttgart in 1967 as Lucia di Lammermoor. Career: Guest appearances in Germany, Warsaw, Geneva, Zurich, Lisbon, Chicago and Toronto; Roles include Regina in Mathis der Maler, Norma, Gounod's Juliette, Mozart's Donna Anna and Fiordiligi and parts in operas by Strauss, Verdi and Puccini; Concert engagements in works by Beethoven, Bach, Brahms, Handel, Haydn, Mozart and Mahler; Glyndebourne in 1970 as the Queen of Night; Member of the Vienna Staatsoper from 1971; Hamburg Staatsoper in the premieres of Ein Stern geht auf aus Jakob by Burkhard, Staatstheater by Kagel and Under Milkwood by Steffens; Further engagements at Cologne and Stuttgart. Recordings: Beethoven's 9th Symphony, conducted by Kempe; Roles in Don Giovanni, Mathis der Maler, Sutermeister's Romeo and Juliet and Paer's Leonora; Countess de la Roche in Zimmermann's Die Soldaten. Address: Lilienstrasse 26, 6670 St Ingbert, Germany.

KOTCHERGA Anatoly, b. 1947, Ukraine, USSR. Singer (Bass). Education: Studied conducting at the Vinitza Conservatory, then singing at the Tchaikovsky Conservatory, Kiev; Further study with Marguerita Corosio and Giulio Cassaletta, 1975-76. Career: Leading soloist at the Kiev Opera from 1972, notably as Basilio, Mephistopheles, Pimen and Arkel; Guest appearances at La Scala Milan, and in Canada, Spain, France, Bulgaria, Czechoslovakia, East Germany and Australia; Has sung Boris Godunov with the company of Warsaw Opera (also televised, 1986); Vienna Staatsoper 1988-91, as Shaklovity in Khovanshchina and in Don Carlos; Theater an der Wien, Vienna, as the Commendatore in Don Giovanni (1990); Season 1992 as Boris and The Sergeant in Lady Macbeth of the Mtsensk District at the Opéra Bastille, Paris and La Scala Milan; Concert appearances include Rimsky's Mozart and Salieri at the Vienna Konzerthaus and a recital of Russian songs in Lyons; Sang Boris Godunov at Montpellier, 1996. Recording: Khovanshchina by Mussorgsky, conducted by Abbado. Honours: Winner, Glinka Competition 1971 (Prize from the Ukrainian Ministry of Culture); Prize winner at international competitions in Berlin 1973 and Moscow (Tchaikovsky Competition) 1974. Address: c/o Schaddeck Gasse 5/H, Anately 1060 Wien, Austria.

KOTIK Petr, b. 27 Jan 1942, Prague, Czechoslovakia. Composer; Conductor; Flautist. m. 30 Sept 1966, 2 sons. Education: Flute, State Conservatory, Prague, 1956-62; Flute, Music Academy, Prague, 1962-63, 1966-69; Composition, Flute, Music Academy, Vienna, 1963-66. Career: In 1964 performed with John Cage and Merce Cunningham Dance Company in Vienna, Prague and Warsaw; Founder of SEM Ensemble, group dedicated to performance of post-Cagean music including Kotik's compositions, 1970; Since 1972 SEM Ensemble performs yearly concerts, USA and Europe; In 1992 founded Orchestra of the SEM Ensemble, recording CD of works by Cage; Conducted the SEM Orchestra, to critical acclaim, in major concerts at Carnegie Hall, 1992, Schausspielhaus Berlin, Alice Tully Hall at Lincolm Center, Prague Spring Festival and Oji Hall, Tokyo; Performed and conducted at 400 Years of Music in Prague, 1994; Conducted Manhattan Book of the Dead, opera by David First, New York, 1995; Premiered works by Myers, Michell, Lewis and Smith in New York, 1995; Many performances in Europe and the USA with the SEM Ensemble. Compositions include: Music for Three, 1964; Kontrabandt, live electronic music, WDR Cologne commission, 1967; There is Singularly Nothing, text Gertrude Stein, 1971-73; John Mary, text Gertrude Stein, 1973; Many Many Women, text Gertrude Stein, 1975-78; Explorations in the Geometry of Thinking, text R Buckminster Fuller, 1978-80; Solos and Instrumental Harmonies, 1981-83; Wilsie Bridge, WDR Cologne commission, 1986-87; Letters to Olga, text Václav Havel, 1989-91; Quiescent Form for orchestra, 1994-95. Recordings include: 1st record: There is Singularly Nothing Nos 1 and 11, LP, 1975; Entire Music by Marcel Duchamp, LP, 1976; With John Cage, 1991; Petr Kotik: SEM Ensemble. Address: SEM Ensemble, 25 Columbia Place, Brooklyn, NY 11201, USA.

KOTILAINEN Juha, b. 1954, Finland. Baritone. Education: Studied at the Kuopio Academy and the Sibelius Academy in Helsinki. Career: Sang at first in concert, then made opera debut at Helsinki in 1986 as Dandini in La Cenerentola; Has made many appearances as Mozart's Figaro and sang in the premieres of Rautavaara's Vinvent at Helsinki in 1990 and Sallinen's Kullervo at Los Angeles in 1992; Engaged at the Aalto Theatre in Essen where roles have included Besenbinder in Humperdinck's Hansel and Gretel, Krushina in Smetana's The Bartered Bride and Pantalon in Prokofiev's The Love for Three Oranges; Recently he has appeared in title roles of Tchaikovsky's Eugene Onegin, Bartók's Duke Bluebeard's Castle and Gugliemo in Cosi fan tutte; Has also performed in Paul Dessau's opera Die Verurteilung des Lukullus and appeared as Paolo in Verdi's Simon Boccanegra; Title role of Mozart's Don Giovanni at the Aalto Theatre in 1995; Sang the Priest in Dallapiccola's Prigioniero, for Tampere Open, 1996; Repertoire also includes solo songs and bass and baritone parts in great church music works; Has appeared in Bach's St Matthew Passion and the B minor Mass; Has given recitals in Finland, Scandinavia, Germany, Greece and Russia. Recordings: Numerous for various labels. Address: c/o Finnish National Opera, Bulevardi 23-27, SF-00180 Helsinki 18, Finland.

KOTKOVA Hana, b. 3 May 1967, Olomouc, Czech Republic. Violinist. Education: Conservatory Ostrava; Music Academy, Prague; International Menuhin Music Academy, Gstaad; Masterclasses with W Marschner, J Gingold, P Amoyal. Debut: Opava with Opava Chamber Orchestra, 1977. Career: Recitals and solos with orchestras in Czech Republic, Switzerland, Sweden, Italy and France, 1985-; Plays with Camerata Lysy, Yehudi Menuhin and A Lysy in Europe and USA, 1990-93; Chamber Music with N Magaloff, Jeremy Menuhuin, P Coker; Recital in Prague, Rudolfinum (Dvoraks Hall) for Y Menuhin's 80, 1996; Duo with English Pianist S Mulligan, 1996-. Recordings: 1 CD with Enescu and Janacek, Sonatas; 1 CD with Martinu, 3 Sonatas. Honours: Laureat of Kocian's International Competition, 1977; 1st Prize, Beethoven International Competition, 1985; Winner, Prague Spring Competition, 1997; The Gideon Klein Foundation Prize, 1997; City of Prague Prize, 1997. Hobbies: Art; Literature; Mountains. Current Management: ARS Concert Ostrava. Address: Case di Sopra, 6935 Bosco Luganese, Switzerland.

KOTONSKI Wlodzimierz, b. 23 Aug 1925, Warsaw, Poland. Composer. m. Jadwiga Chlebowska, 1951, 1 son. Education: MMus, Warsaw State Highter School of Music. Career: With Experimental Music Studio of Westdeutscher Rundfunk, Cologne, Federal Republic of Germany, 1966-67; Professor of Composition, Head of Electronic Music Studio, Academy of Music, Warsaw, Poland, 1967-; Chief Music Director, Polish Radio and Television, 1974-76; Lecturer on Composition, USA, 1978; 1983-89, President of the ISCM Polish Section. Compositions include: Orchestral and chamber music, electronic and tape music and instrumental theatre. Publications: Goralski and Zbojnicki, 1958; Percussion Instruments in the Modern Orchestra, 1967; Muzyka elektroniczna, 1989. Address: Academy of Music, Okolnik 2, Warsaw 00-368, Poland.

KOTOSKI Dawn, b. 1967, Maryland, USA. Singer (Soprano). Education: Studied in New York. Career: Sang in the YCA concert series in Washington and New York, 1990-91; Further concerts at Carnegie Hall, Avery Fisher Hall, with the Atlanta, Baltimore and Chicago Symphony Orchestras and at the Metropolitan Opera; Sang Mozart's Susanna with the Canadian Opera Company at Calgary, in Handel's Partenope at Omaha and as Massenet's Sophie at St Louis; European engagements as Pamina, Oscar and Musetta at the Vienna Staatsoper, Susanna at Munich, Gilda in Stasbourg and Oscar at the Opera Bastille, Paris; Gilda, Adele in Die Fledermaus, Sophie and Musetta, Zürich Opera season 1996-97; Engaged as Jemmy in a new production of Guillaume Tell in Vienna and as Zdenka in Arabella at Santa Fe; Concert repertory includes Die Schöpfung, by Haydn. Recordings include: Handel's Acis and Galtaea, and Giustino; Lisa in La Sonnambula, with Edita Gruberova. Address: c/o Opernhaus Zürich, Falkenstrasse 1, CH-8008 Zürich, Switzerland.

KOTOUC Jiri, b. 1945, Praha, Czech Republic. Conductor; Harpsichordist; Voice Trainer. Education: Prague Conservatory. Debut: Praha, 1964. Career: Leader, Vocal-Instrumental Ensembles Collegium Flautodolce and Camerata Nova; Tours include Whole of Europe and Canada; Participations in Festivals, Prague Spring, Mozart Open, Czech Republic; Berliner Festtage, Rome; Algarve, Portugal; Alhambra, Spain; Valtice, Czech Republic; Conducting, Pergolesi, La Serva Padrona, Purall, Dido x Aeneas; Monteverdi, Handel. Recordings: Amore, Venere e lersichore, Nuova Era, CD, Italy; Adam Michna: Litanie de Beata Virgine Maria. Hobbies: Opera; Gardening. Address: Ve Smeckach 10, Praha 1, 11000 Czech Republic.

KOUBA Maria, b. 1924, Altenmarkt, Austria. Singer (Soprano). Education: Studied at the Graz Conservatory. Debut: Graz, 1957, as Salome. Career: Sang at Graz, 1957-61, Frankfurt from 1961: roles include Madama Butterfly, Salome, both Leonoras of Verdi, Alice Ford, Jenufa, Senta, Eva, Tosca and Octavian; Guest appearances in Paris, 1962, London 1963 as Salome; Metropolitan Opera 1964-65; Brussels, Vancouver, Santa Fe, Naples, Vienna, Hamburg and Berlin; Other roles include Donna Anna, Liu, and Marenka in The Bartered Bride.

KOUKL George, b. 23 Mar 1953, Origlio, Switzerland. Pianist; Composer. Education: Milan Conservatory; Diploma, Zurich Conservatory; Master classes. Debut: 1972. Career: Radio recordings for BBC London, NRK Oslo, Radio Vienna, SR6 Zurich, SSR Lausanne; TV appearances for Swiss TV; Concerts in Europe, USA, Japan, South America; Festivals; Master classes. Compositions: Pandora's Box; Te Deum; Quartet for wind instruments; Sonata for clarinet and piano; Ideograms, 1991, Radio Lugano. Recordings: Various. Honours: Alienor Award, Washington, 1986. Memberships: Schweizerischer Tonkunstlerverein; Mensa Music, USA. Current Management: Music Play Management, 6947 Vaglio, Switzerland. Address: Casa La Campagnola, 6945 Origlio, Switzerland.

KOUKOS Periklis, b. 3 Jan 1960, Athens, Greece. Composer; Opera Director. Education: Studied Composition with Yannis Papaionnou and Dimitris Dragatakis in Athens, with Hans Werner Henze and Paul Patterson in London. Career: Composer; Teacher of Composition at Athens Conservatory, 1990-; Artistic Director, Greek National Opera. Compositions include: Merlin the Magician, childrens opera, 1987-89; Conroy's Other Selves, opera in 1 act, Athens, 1990; The Manuscript of Manuel Salinas, opera in 3 acts; A Midsummer Night's Dream, opera-ballet, 1982. Address: c/o Greek National Opera, 59-61 Acadimias Str, 106 79 Athens, Greece.

KOUNADIS Arghyris, b. 14 Feb 1924, Constantinople, Turkey. Composer. Education: Studied Piano at Athens Conservatory and with Yanni Papaionnou at the Hellenic Conservatory; Further studies with Wolfgang Fortner in Freiburg. Career: Director of Music Viva concerts at Freiburg from 1963, Professor at Hochschule fur Musik, 1972. Compositions include: Operas: The Return (performed Athens, 1991); Der Gumminsarg, Bonn, 1968; Die verhexten Notenstander, Freiburg, 1971; Teirasias, Heidelberg, 1975; Der Ausbruch, Bayreuth, 1975; Die Bassgeige, Freiburg, 1979; Lysistrate, Lubeck, 1983; Der Sandmann, Hamburg, 1987. Address: c/o Staatliche Hochschule fur Musik, Freiburg im Breisgau, Schwarzwaldstrasse 141, 7800 Freiburg im Breisgau, Germany.

KOUT Jiri, b. 26 Dec 1937, Novedvory, Czechoslovakia. Conductor. Education: Studied conducting and organ at the Prague Conservatory; Further studies at the National Academy of Music in Prague. Career: Resident Conductor, Pilsener Opera and Symphony Orchestra; Principal Conductor of the National Opera in Prague, also appearing with the Prague Symphony Orchestra and the National Radio Orchestra; Principal conductor, Deutsche Oper am Rhein, Dusseldorf, 1978-84; Conducted Der Rosenkavalier at Munich 1985, leading to engagements in Stuttgart, Berlin and Vienna; Debut with the Berlin Philharmonic 1987; Regular appearances in Saarbrucken (The Ring) also Venice, Naples, Florence, Cincinnati and Birmingham; Conducted Katya Kabanova in Paris and Los Angeles, 1988; Lady Macbeth at the Deutsche Oper Berlin (Principal Resident Conductor from 1990), followed by Tristan und Isolde and Mathis der Maler; Bluebeard's Castle at the Vienna Staatsoper; Returned to Los Angeles with Boris Godunov and Parsifal; Metropolitan Opera debut 1991 (Der Rosenkavalier); Season 1992 with Tannhäuser at the Deutsche Oper Berlin and The Makropoulos Case at Los Angeles; Covent Garden debut 1993, Jenufa; Wagner's Ring at the Deutsche Oper, 1997. Honours include: Winner of conducting competitions at Besancon and Brussels, 1965, 1969. Address: c/o Athole Still Ltd, 113 Church Road, London SE19 2PR, England.

KOUTSOBINA Vassiliki, b. 31 July 1964, Athens, Greece. Musicologist; Chemist. m. Argirios Dinopoulos, 30 Oct 1994, 1 son. Education: BSc, Chemistry, University of Athens, 1989; MM, Music History, Hartt School, University of Hartford, USA, 1994; Piano Studies with Arkady Aronov, Manhattan School of Music. Career: Teacher, Music History, Synchrono Conservatory, Athens, 1994-97; Radio Producer, The Composer of the Week, Third Programme, Hellenic Radio, 1997-. Membership: American Musicological Society. Hobbies: Country Walks; Swimming. Address: Terpsitheas 70, 15341 Athens, Greece.

KOVACEVICH Stephen, b. 17 Oct 1940, San Francisco, California, USA. Pianist; Conductor. Education: Studied under Lev Shor and Dame Myra Hess. Debut: London debut, 1961. Career: Appeared at international music festivals in Edinburgh, Bath, Harrogate, Berlin, San Sebastian and Salzburg; Soloist, Henry Wood Promenade Concerts for 14 seasons; Frequent tours in Europe and America; Played Beethoven's Sonatas Op 30 Nos 1 and 2, Op 96 with Kyung Wha Chung, Barbican Centre, 1991; In UK has conducted the City of Birmingham Symphony, BBC Philharmonic, Bournemouth Symphony and the Royal Liverpool Philharmonic Orchestras, Chamber Orchestra of Europe and National Youth Chamber Orchestra (at the 1993 Proms); Conducting abroad in Copenhagen and Lisbon, the Los Angeles Philharmonic at the Hollywood Bowl Festival, 1990; Also works at the Aspen Music Festival each summer, as Pianist and Conductor of the Festival Orchestra and the Student Orchestra; Played Mozart's Concerto K503 and Dvorák's Piano Quintet at the Festival Hall, London, 1997. Recordings: Numerous including CDs of the Grieg and Schumann Concertos (BBC Symphony under C Davis), Mozart Concerto K467 and K503 (London Symphony), Brahms Rhapsodies, Waltzes and Six Piano Pieces, Op 118, Schubert Sonata D960, Beethoven Sonatas Op 90, 101, 111, and Brahms Piano Concertos Nos 1 and 2 (W Sawallisch). Publication: Schubert Anthology. Honours: Winner, Kimber Award, California, 1959; Mozart Prize, London, 1962; Edison Award for recording of Bartók's 2nd Piano Concerto; Gramophone Award for recording of Brahms Piano Concerto No 1, 1993. Hobbies: Table tennis; Chess; Cinema; Indian food. Current Management: Van Walsum Managers. Address: c/o Van Walsum Managers, 26 Wadham Road, London SW15 2LR, England.

KOVACIC Ernst, b. 12 Apr 1943, Kapfenberg, Styria, Austria. Musician; Violinist. m. Anna Maria Schuster, 29 Jun 1968, 4 s. Education: Studied violin, composition and organ, Academy of Music, Vienna. Career: Concerts throughout Europe, USA, Australia, Near, Middle and Far East including performances with LSO, Orchestra RPO, Philharmonia, London Philharmonic, all BBC Orchestras, all German Radio Orchestras, Detroit, Vienna, Prague Symphony, Rotterdam Philharmonic; British premiere of Janacek's Concerto, Liverpool, 1989; Plays British works by Nigel Osborne and Robin Holloway and gave the Concerto by Thomas Wilson at the 1993 London Proms. Recordings: All pieces for violin and orchestra by Mozart; Scottish Chamber Orchestra (Pickwick) Michael Tippett Triple Concerto; 20th Century works including compositions by Krenek, Schwertsik, Eder, Erod, Gruber, Lampersberg; Chamber Music for 2 Violins and Piano. Honours: International Competition Prizes: Geneva 1970, Barcelona 1971, Munich ARD, 1972. Hobbies: Drawing; Football; Composition; Family Life; Reading. Current Management: Ingpen and Williams, 14 Kensington Court, London, W8, England. Address: Im Muehlfeld 3, A-2102 Bisamberg, Austria.

KOVACS Dénes, b. 18 Apr 1930, Vac, Hungary. Violinist. m. 1 son, 1 daughter. Education: Budapest Academy of Music under Ede Zathureczky. Career: 1st Violinist, Budapest State Opera, 1951-60; Leading Violin Professor, Budapest Music Academy, 1957-; Director, Budapest Music Academy, 1967-; Rector, Ferenc Liszt Academy of Music, 1971-80; Dean of String Department, 1980-; Concert tours all over Europe, USA, USSR, Iran, India, China and Japan; Member of Jury in International Competitions: Tchaikovsky, Moscow; Long-Thibaud, Paris; Jean

Sibelius, Helsinki; Joseph Joachim, Vienna; Wieniawski, Warsaw; Tokyo. Honours: Kossuth prize, 1963; Awarded Eminent Artist Title, 1970; Golden Medal of labour, 1974. Address: Music Academy, Liszt Ferenc ter 8, 1061 Budapest VI, Hungary.

KOVACS Endre, b. 5 June 1936, Budapest, Hungary. Organist. Church Music Director. m. Zsuzsa Kiss, 24 Oct 1982, 1 daughter. Education: Ferenc Liszt Academy of Music, Budapest; Courses in Belgium with Anton Heiller and Marie-Claire Alain. Career: Approximately 40-50 concerts a year, Hungary and abroad, including Switzerland, Netherlands, Germany, Austria, Finland, all socialist countries. Recordings: Ferenc Liszt, Complete Organ Works, with S Margittay and G Lehotka. Honours: Grand Prix for Liszt recordings, F Liszt Society of Hungary. Hobbies: Examining structure and mechanism of old organs; Research, organology. Address: Zsókavár u 55.11.9, H-1157 Budapest, Hungary.

KOVACS Janos, b. 1951, Budapest, Hungary. Conductor. Education: Study under Professor Andras Korodi, Ferenc Liszt Academy of Music, Budapest, 1971. Career: Coach, Conductor, Budapest State Opera; Musical Assistant, Bayreuth Festival, 1978, 1979; Frequent Conductor of top Hungarian Symphony Orchestras; Has conducted several guest performances given by the Budapest State Opera at the Dresden Festival and in the Berlin State Opera House; Two guest performances with Hungarian State Symphony Orchestra and festive concert series marking opening of Berlin's reconstructed Neues Konzerthaus, 1984; Conductor of several performances at Vienna Chamber Opera, 1984; Suisse Romande Orchestra, Geneva, Switzerland, 1985. Honour: Liszt Prize, 1985.

KOVARICEK Frantisek, b. 17 May 1924, Litetiny, Bohemia, Czechoslovakia. Composer. m. (1) Vera Fruhaufova, 14 Feb 1957, dec 17 June 1985, (2) Jana Klimtova, 26 Oct 1993. Education: Faculty of Arts, Charles University, 1945-48; Prague Conservatory, 1945-48; Prague Academy of Music, 1948-52. Debut: Overture for Large Orchestra at Rudolfinum, Prague, 1952. Career: All mentioned compositions publicly performed and broadcast many times by Radio Prague; Professor, 1967-85, Director, 1990-91, Prague Conservatory. Compositions: Overture for orchestra, 1951; Songs for low voice and piano; Mourning Music, for large orchestra; The Golden Wave of June, song cycle; The Stolen Moon, lyric comic opera; Mocking Songs for mixed chorus and piano; Capriccio for Chamber Orchestra; Music for Chamber Orchestra, 1982; Concerto for Clarinet and Orchestra; Serenade for Nonet. Recordings: Overture, 1952; Mocking Songs; Posmivanky, 1968; Clarinet Concerto; Capriccio for Orchestra. Hobbies: Literature; History; Geography; Touring. Address: Na Hroude 71, 10000 Prague 10, Czech Republic.

KOVATS Kolos, b. 1948, Hungary. Singer (Bass). Education: Ferenc Liszt Academy of Music, Budapest. Career: Budapest State Opera. Has made numerous appearances including operas The Magic Lute, Eugene Onegin, Boris Godunov, Don Carlos, La forza del destino, Ernani, Simon Boccanegra, Norma and title role in Moses, in concert halls and opera houses around the world; Title role in Bartok's Duke Bluebeard's Castle; Sang Zaccaria in Nabucco at Brussels, 1987; Bluebeard at Turin, 1989; Sang Catalani's La Wally at the 1990 Bregenz Festival; Other roles include Verdi's Philip, Banquo, Sparalucile, Fiesco, Padre Guardiano, Pagno (Lombardi), Fernando, Silva and Ramphis; Also Mozart's Sarastro and Commendatore, Mephistopheles, Creon, Oroveso, Pimen, Gremin and Henry VIII in Anna Bolena; Sang Bluebeard at the Théâtre du Chatelet, Paris, 1996; Has appeared in television and films; Oratorios. Recordings include: Has made numerous records: Medea, Ernani, Don Carlos, Lombardi, Macbeth, Liszt's St Elizabeth, Masses by Mozart and Schubert, Guillaume Tell; Video of Bluebeard's Castle, conducted by Solti. Honours: 1st Prize, Erkel International Voice Contest, 1973; 1st Prize, Rio de Janeiro International Vocal Competition, 1973; 2nd Prize, Moscow Tchaikovsky International Vocal Concours, 1974; Recipient, Liszt Prize; Kossuth Prize, 1992. Address: c/o Hungarian State Opera House, Andrássy u 22, 1061 Budapest, Hungary.

KOWALKE Kim H, b. 25 Jun 1948, Monticello, MN, USA. Professor of Music; Musicologist; Foundation President. m. Elizabeth Keagy, 19 Aug 1978, 1 s. Education: BA, cum laude with special departmental honours in Music, Macalester College, 1970; MA, 1972, MPhil, 1974, PhD, 1977, Yale University. Career: Assistant Professor of Music, 1977-82, Associate Professor, 1982-86, Occidental College, Los Angeles, CA; Professor of Music and Musicology, Eastman School of Music, University of Rochester, NY, 1986-; President of Kurt Weill Foundation for Music Inc; Member of Editorial Board, Kurt Weill Edition, 1992-. Publications: Kurt Weill in Europe, 1979; Accounting for Success: Misunderstanding Die Dreigroschenoper, 1990; Editor: A New Orpheus: Essays on Kurt Weill, 1986, A Stranger Here Myself: Kurt Weill Studien, 1993; Speak Low: The Letters of Kurt Weill and Lotte Lenya, 1995. Contributions to: Chapters in Cambridge Opera Handbook; The Brecht Companion and other books; Articles in Modernism, Modernity, Musical Quarterly, American

Music, Notes, Opera. Hobbies: Tennis; Bridge; Running. Address: 888 Quaker Road, Scottsville, NY 14546-9757, USA.

KOWALOWSKI Zenon Eugeniusz, b. 20 Mar 1939, Biala Podlaska, Poland. Composer. m. Miroslawa Sagan, 24 Dec 1962, 1 son, 1 daughter. Education: Musical Academy, Cracow, 1957-62. Debut: Czestochowa, 1962. Career: Conducted the representative musical group in Siemianowice, 1962-67; Musical Manager, Zagtebia Theatre, Sosnowiec, 1967-71; Lecturer, Silesian University, Cieszyn, 1980. Compositions: Miniatures for Piano, recorded 1959; Frescoes for Two Clarinets, recorded 1961; Lyrical Essays, recorded 1963; Canto, recorded 1965; Monostructures, published 1978; Psalm, published 1978; Concertos Nos I and II for children, published and recorded 1994; Music for theatre, films, and children's and teenager's cartoons for TV or video, 1970-. Recordings include: Theatre music for Boleslaw the Brave by S Wyspienski, Shakespeare's Merchant of Venice, The Unbroken Prince by J Stowachi, The Persians by Aeschylus; Film music for Sisyph, The Flower, Impasse, Following the Mythical Traces, Exodus, The Wolves, Gilgeames; The Anthology of Christmas Carols, instrumental versions. Contributions to: Magazines; Musical Movement; A Guidebook about Culture in Silesia; Reviews on radio and television. Honours: Honoured for Psalm for orchestra, 1964; Award for film compositions for children, Minister of Culture and Art, 1979; Gold Mask Award for theatre music, 1980; Special Award, Vth Art Biennial for Children, Poznan, 1981. Memberships: Authors and Playwrights Union; Union of Polish Composers; Board of Managers, Union of Polish Composers in Silesia. Hobbies: Sport - swimming, sailing, fishing. Address: Baltycka Street 16, 40-779 Katowice, Poland.

KOWALSKI David (Leon), b. 29 Mar 1956, New Haven, Connecticut, USA. Composer; Data Systems Analyst. m. Michelle Disco, 2 Sept 1983, dec 29 Apr 1994. Education: BA, University of Pennsylvania, 1978; MM, Composition, New England Conservatory of Music, 1981; PhD, Composition, Princeton University, 1985; Private studies with Donald Martino, Arthur Berger, Milton Babbitt. Career: Freelance Composer, 1978-. Compositions include: Quintus Obscurus, bass flute, viola, celeste and 2 percussion, 1977; Metamorphosis, jazz trio and orchestra, 1978; Dichotomies, solo viola, 1979, revised 1983; Come Sopra, oboe and cello, 1979; Les Voyageurs, horn and 3 celli, 1979, revised 1991; Quintetino, string quartet and piano, 1980; Concertino, flute/piccolo, clarinet, horn, violin, cello, bass, harp, piano and 2 percussion, 1980; Double Helix, orchestra, 1980, revised 1991; Alle Tode, soprano and piano, 1981; String Quartet No 2, 1982; Chamber Concerto, 1982, revised 1984; Toccata, organ, 1982; Circonspection, soprano and clarinet, 1983; Four Frames, percussion quartet, 1983; Clarinet Quartet, clarinet, violin, cello and piano, 1983; Variations, wind quartet, 1983, revised 1991; Premonitions, piano solo, 1983; Skid Row, computer-generated tape, 1983; Masques, oboe, 1984; Echoes, soprano and computer-generated tape, 1984; Windhover, soprano and piano, 1985; Masques II, solo flute, 1986; Masques III, solo clarinet, 1987; Two Sonnets for soprano and piano, 1988; A Memory of Evening, mezzo and piano, 1989. Recording: Double Helix performed by Silesian Philharmonic, with Joel Suben conducting, CD, 1995. Address: 32 Academy St, PO Box 501, Kingston, NJ 08528, USA.

KOWALSKI Jochen, b. 30 Jan 1954, Wachow, Brandeburg, Germany. Singer (Counter-tenor). Education: Studied at the Berlin Musikhochschule with Heinz Reeh; Further study with Marianne Fischer-Kupfer. Career: Sang at the Handel Festival Halle 1982, in the pasticcio Mucio Scevola; Has appeared with the Komische Oper Berlin from 1983, debut as Feodor in Boris Godunov; Guest appearances at the State Operas of Munich and Hamburg; Paris Opera 1987 as Ptolomeo in Giulio Cesare; Vienna Staatsoper 1987 as Orlofsky in Die Fledermaus; Vienna Volksoper in Giustinio by Handel; Has also sung in Dusseldorf, 1989, Amsterdam and Minneapolis; Sang Gluck's Orpheus with the Komische Oper at Covent Garden 1989, returned as Orlofsky 1990, in performances which also featured Joan Sutherland's retirement; Other roles include Daniel in Handel's Belshazzar, and Annio in La Clemenza di Tito; Sang Farnace in Mozart's Mitridate, Covent Garden 1991; Amsterdam 1992; Ottone in L'Incoronazione di Poppea at the 1993 Salzburg Festival; Sang Britten's Oberon at the Met, 1996-97. Recordings include: Baroque Arias by Prussian composers; Handel and Mozart Arias; Gluck's Orfeo and Euridice; Symphoniae Sacrae by Schütz (Capriccio). Address: Komische Oper, Behrenstrasse 55/57, D-1080 Berlin, Germany.

KOX Hans, b. 19 May 1930, Arnhem, Netherlands. Composer. Education: Studied at Utrecht Conservatory and with Henk Badings, 1951-55. Career: Director of Doetinchem Music School, 1957-71; Teacher at Utrecht Conservatory, 1971-. Compositions include: Over 200 symphonic, operatic and chamber music works including: Dorian Gray, opera, 1974, Lord Rochester, opera, 1978, 3 Symphonies, 1959, 1966 and 1985, Le Songe du Vergier for Cello and Orchestra, 1986, Magnificat I and II for Vocal Ensemble, 1989-90, Das Grune Gesicht, opera,

1981-91, Sonate for Violoncello and Piano, revised 1991, Face to Face, concerto for Altosaxophone and Strings, 1992, Cyclophony XIV, The Birds of Aengus for Violin and Harp, 1992, Oratorium Sjoah, 1993, Violin Concerto No 3, 1993, Orkester Suite Aus der Oper Das Grune Gesicht, 1994, Ballet Suite for Orchestra, revised 1994, Das Credo Quia Absurdum for Soprano Solo, Bass Solo, Choir and Orchestra, 1995. Recordings: 3 CDs: L'Allegria, Oratorium Sjoah and Chamber music "Through a Glass, Darkly". Honours: Visser Neerlandia Prize for Symphony No 1, 1959; Prix Italia for In Those Days, 1970; 1st Prize, Rostrum of Composers for L'Allegria, 1974. Address: c/o Hans Kox Foundation, Vier Heemskinderenstraat 42 hs, 1055 LL Amsterdam, The Netherlands.

KOZAR John, b. 12 June 1946, Indiana, USA. Concert Pianist; Conductor. Education: Academy of Music, Zagreb, Yugoslavia; BMus, MMus, Indiana University, USA. Debut: New York, 1978; British Concerto Debut, 1981. Career: Teacher: University of Kansas, Indiana University, New England College, State University of New York, Ball State University; Recitals: New York city, London, Chicago, Munich, Vienna, Zagreb, Hong Kong, Johannesburg, Paris, Vancouver, Sydney; Concertos: Australia, London Philharmonic, Brooklyn Philharmonic, Pretoria (SA) Symphony; Television: Public Broadcasting Systems, Hong Kong Television, Scottish Television, SABC, CBC, Vancouver; Radio: Numerous radio performances, Nationally and Internationally; Conducting: Music Director, Kentish Opera Group, England; Music Director, Opea Program, State University of New York, Potsdam, 1987-90; Currently Program Director, The Beethoven Foundation, Indianapolis, Indiana; Freelance, Conductor, Opera, Ballet; Founded Piano Productions, 1989; Named a Baldwin Artist by the Baldwin Piano and Organ Company. Recordings: Preamble Records; Orion Rcords. Publication: Annotated Bibliography of American Composer Emerson Whithorne, in progress. Contributions to: Articles in professional journals. Current Management: Talent Centre, PO Box 23220, Cincinnati, OH 45223, USA.

KOZELUHOVA Jitka, b. 19 November 1966, Prague. Composer; Pianist; Singer. m. Marcus Gerhardts, 27 February 1996, 1 son. Education: Conservatory of Prague; Music Faculty of the Academy of Performimg Arts in Prague; Main composition teacher, Ilja Hurnik, Professor Petr Eben; Main piano teacher, Lydmila Simkova; Main singing teacher, Theresic Blumova. Compositions: (recorded by Czech Radio) Sonatine for pianoforte, 1986; Touzeni (Longing) cycle of songs for soprano and pianoforte, 1987; Obrazy (Images), string quartet, 1990-91; Six Songs On The Texts Of The Poems Of Emily Dickinson, cycle for soprano and pianoforte, 1991-92; Three Sentences About The Story Of Christmas, quartet for oboe, clarinet, bassoon and pianoforte, 1992-93; Further recordings: Pierres (Stones) (cycle of womens choirs, 1992; Aus Der Tiefe (de Profundis) for mixed choir with soprano solo, 2 narrators and organ, 1994; Secret Dolour, Fantasy on themes from Schubert's Rondo Op 84, for 4 piano hands, 1994; The Inner Voice, viola solo and symphony orchestra, 1994-95; All You Are Thirsty, Come To The Waters, small cantata for Alto and Baritone solo, English horn, piano and percussions, 1995; For Angels, for 2 flutes, 2 clarinets, string quartet and piano, 1996. Recordings: MC: Behold! I Stand At The Door (trio for flute, violincello, pianoforte), 1992; I Have Seen A Man, 1993; Church Sonata (Partiture (Scores) for winds, organ and percussions; Church Sonata, version restrained for organ and percussion, 1996. Honours: From Generace: 3rd Prize, for Behold! I Stand, 1992; 1st Prize, for Three Sentences, 1993; 3rd Prize, for All You Are Thirsty, 1995; Winner of concours for The Catholic Days, Dresden, 1994. Address: Na Roktyce 30, 18000 Prague 8, Czech Republic.

KOZENA Magdalena, b. 26 May 1973, Brno, Czech Republic. Singer (Mezzo-Soprano). Education: Brno Conservatory, 1987-91; College of Performing Arts, Bratislava, 1991-95; Studies with Christian Elsner, Dresden and Gerald Moore, London. Debut: Vienna Volksoper, 1996. Career: Guest Singer as Dorabella in Mozart's Cosi fan tutte, Janacek Opera House, Brno, 1994-95; Isabella in Rossini's Italiana in Algeri, 1996; International Music Festival, Prague Spring, 1996; Handel's Messiah with Marc Minkowski, 1997; Venus in Rameau's Dardanus with Marc Minkowski, 1997; Regular Appearances for Czech Radio & TV. Recordings: Schumann, Dvorak, Kricka, Sinfonietta, 1995; Bach Arias, Archiv Produktion, 1997. Honours: Winner, International Scheider Competition, 1992; Winner, 66th WA Mozart Competition, Salzburg, 1995; Talent of the Year, Czech Classic 95, 1995. Hobbies: Swimming; Biking; Languages. Current Management: Artimus. Address: Molákova 8, Praha 8, 186 00 Czech Republic.

KOZLOWSKA Joanna, b. 1958, Poznan, Poland. Soprano. Education: Studied at the Poznan Academy. Career: Sang Sandrina in Mozart's Finta Giardiniera at Brussels in 1986 followed by Zerlina, Euridice, Monteverdi's Drusilla and Pamina; Covent Garden in 1986 as Liu in Turandot; Appearances at the Aix-en-Provence Festival, the Scottish Opera at Glasgow as Tatiana in 1988, Hamburg as Ilia in 1990, and the Deutsche Oper Berlin as Micaela in 1988; La Scala Milan debut in 1990 as Marzelline; Sang Mimi at Buenos Aires, 1995; Concert appearances in Baroque music. Address: c/o Théâtre Royale, 4 Leopoldstrasse, B-1000 Brussels, Belgium.

KOZMA Lajos, b. 1938, Lepesny, Hungary. Singer (Tenor). Education: Franz Liszt Academy Budapest; Further study at the Accademia di Santa Cecilia Rome with Giorgio Favaretto and Franco Capuana. Career: First success as Debussy's Pelléas, Budapest, 1962; Appearances from 1964 in Florence, Venice, Rome, Milan, London, Philadelphia, New York and Copenhagen; Amsterdam 1982, as Monteverdi's Orfeo; Teatro San Carlo Naples in Rossellini's La Reine Morte; Further engagements in Paris, Brussels, Aix-en-Provence and Strasbourg; Many concerts in oratorio and Lieder. Recordings include: Lucia di Lammermoor (Eurodisc); Monteverdi Orfeo; Orlando Furioso by Vivaldi (Erato). Address: c/o Hungarian State Opera House, Népóztársaság utja 22, 1961 Budapest, Hungary.

KRAEMER Nicholas, b. 7 Mar 1945, Edinburgh, Scotland. Conductor; Harpsichordist. m. Elizabeth Andreson, 3 sons (1 dec.), 2 daughters. Career includes: Harpsichordist with Academy of St Martin-in-the-Fields and English Baroque Soloists; Founded Raglan Baroque Players, 1978, concerts, numerous radio and TV broadcasts; First Musical Director, Opera 80 (now English Touring Opera); Conducted Mozart at Glyndebourne, 1980-83, English National Opera, 1992; Handel and Monteverdi operas, Paris, Lisbon, Amsterdam, Geneva, Marseille; Associate Conductor, BBC Scottish Symphony Orchestra, 1983-85; Concerts with Polish Chamber Orchestra, Poland, Israel Chamber Orchestra and Frysk Orkest, Netherlands; Artistic Director, Irish Chamber Orchestra, 1986-92, Handel in Dublin concerts, season 1988-89; Concerts with Australian Chamber Orchestra, 1991; Season 1991 with Orchestra of the Age of Enlightenment in Mozart in London; Principal Guest Conductor, Manchester Camerata, 1992-; Debuts, English National Opera, with Magic Flute, 1992, Marseille Opera, with Poppea, 1993; Currently Artistic Director, London Bach Orchestra; Season 1994-95 included visits to Munster Philharmonic and National Arts Centre Orchestra, Ottawa; With Scottish Chamber Orchestra: Purcell's Fairy Queen, Edinburgh and Glasgow, and 2 concerts, Orkney Festival; Appeared with London Classical Players, Salzburg and Vienna, 1995; Season 1995-96 includes concerts with Orchestra of Age of Enlightenment (Purcell series), CBSO and Northern Sinfonia (Purcell's Fairy Queen); Handel's Rodelinda for recording, director, Jonathan Miller; Handel's Messiah with Scottish Chamber Orchestra; Led the Raglan Baroque Players in Rodelinda for Broomhill Opera, 1996. Recordings: Vivaldi Violin Concertos Op 9 with Monica Huggett, Op 8 including The Four Seasons with Raglan Baroque Players; Complete harpsichord concertos of Bach; Complete cello concertos of Vivaldi with Raphael Wallfisch; Locatelli Op 1, Op 3, with Raglan Baroque Players; Vivaldi Wind Concertos, La Stravaganza Op 4 with City of London Sinfonia. Membership: Royal Society of Musicians. Current Management: Ron Gonsalves, 7 New Town, Clapham, London SW4 0JT, England.

KRAFT Jean, b. 9 Jan 1940, Menasha, Wisconsin, USA. Singer (Mezzo-soprano). Education: Studied with Giannini Gregory at the Curtis Institute, Theodore Harrison in Chicago, William Ernst Vedal in Munich and Povla Frijsch in New York. Debut: New York City Opera 1960, in Six Characters in Search of an Author by Weisgall. Career: Sang in Houston, Boston, New Orleans, Philadelphia, Santa Fe, Chicago and Dallas; Metropolitan Opera from 1970, as Flora in La Traviata, Emilia (Otello) 1987, Herodias, Ulrica and Suzuki; Maggio Musicale Florence 1988, as Mrs Sedley in Peter Grimes. Recordings include: Andrea Chénier and Cavalleria Rusticana (RCA). Address: Metropolitan Opera, Lincoln Center, New York, NY 10023, USA.

KRAFT Leo (Abraham), b. 24 July 1922, New York, New York, USA. Composer; Teacher. m. Amy Lager, 16 May 1945, 2 sons. Education: Pupil in composition of Karol Rathaus, Queens College of the City University of New York, BA, 1945, Randall Thompson, Princeton University, MFA, 1947, and Nadia Boulanger, Paris, 1954-55. Career: Faculty Member, Queens College, 1947-. Compositions: Orchestral: Concerto for Flute, Clarinet, Trumpet and Strings, 1951; Variations, 1958; 3 Pieces, 1963; Concerto for Cello, Wind Quintet, and Percussion, 1968; Concerto for 12 Instruments, 1966-72; Music, 1975; Concerto for Piano and 14 Instruments, 1978; Chamber Symphony, 1980; Symphony in One Movement, 1985; Ricercare for Strings, 1985; Concerto for Oboe and Strings, 1986; Chamber: 2 string quartets, 1951, 1959; Sextet, 1952; Partita for Wind Quintet, 1964; Trios and Interludes for Flute, Viola and Piano, 1965; Dialogues for Flute and Tape, 1968; Line Drawings for Flute and Percussion, 1972; Diaphonies for Oboe and Piano, 1975; Dialectica for Flute, Clarinet, Violin, Cello, and Tape, 1976; Conductus Novus for 4 Trombones, 1979; Episodes for Clarinet and Percussion, 1979; Interplay for Trumpet and Percussion, 1983; Strata for 8 Instruments, 1979-84; Piano pieces; Vocal works. Publications: With S Berkowitz and G Fontrier, A New Approach to Ear Training, 1967; Gradus: An Integrated Approach to Harmony, Counterpoint, and Analysis, 1976, 2nd edition, 1987. Address: 9 Dunster Road, Great Neck, NY 11021, USA.

KRAFT William, b. 6 Sept 1923, Chicago, Illinois, USA. Composer. m. 2 sons, 1 daughter. Education: Bachelor's Degree, cum laude, 1951; Master's Degree, 1954; Columbia University; Studied under Jack Beeson, Seth Bingham, Henry Brant, Henry Cowell, Erich Hertzmann, Paul Henry Lang, Otto Luening, Vladimir Ussachevsky. Career: Organised and directed Los Angeles Percussion Ensemble; as percussion soloist performed American premiere of Stockhausen's Zyklus and Boulez's Le Marteau sans Maitre; also recorded Histoire du Soldat under Stravinsky's direction; Conductor of contemporary and other music; Assistant Conductor of Los Angeles Philharmonic, 3 years; served as Musical Director and Chief Advisor, Young Musicians Foundation Debut Orchestra, Los Angeles; appeared frequently at Monday Evening Concerts; Visiting Professor in Composition, USC; Guest Lecturer in Composition, California Institute of Arts, Faculty of Banff Center for Performing Arts; similar residences at University of Western Ontario, Royal Northern College of Music, Manchester, England among others; frequent lecturer at festivals and concert series including Percussive Arts Society International Conference, California State University, Sacramento Festival of New American Music, Res Musica Baltimore concert series; given numerous seminars and master classes at universities and music festivals; Composer-in-Residence, Cheltenham International Music Festival, Cheltenham, England, 1986; Visiting Professor in Composition, UCLA, 1988-89. Compositions include: Dialogues and Entertainments for soprano solo and wind ensemble, 1980; Double Play for violin, piano and chamber orchestra, 1982; Gallery 83, 1983; Timpani Concerto, 1983; Contextures II: The Final Beast, 1984; Interplay, 1984; Weavings for string quartet, 1984; Gallery 4-5, 1985; Quintessence, 1985; Mélange, 1986; Of Ceremonies, Pageants and Celebrations, 1986; Quartet for the Love of Time, 1987; Interplay, 1984; Episodes, 1987; Horn Concerto, 1988; Kennedy Portrait, 1988. Recordings: Many of his compositions recorded for various record companies. Address: 1437 Crest Drive, Altadena, CA 91001, USA.

KRAINEV Vladimir Vsevolodovitch, b. 1 Apr 1944, Krasnoyarsk, Siberia, Russia. Pianist. m. Tatiana Tarasova, 2 Mar 1979. Education: Kharkov Music School, Ukraine; Central Music School, Moscow; Class of Heinrich Neuhaus, Moscow Tchaikovsky Conservatoire. Debut: Haydn Concerto in D Major and Beethoven Concerto No 1 in C Major with Kharkov Philharmonic Orchestra, at age 8. Career: Soloist with world-famous orchestras: London Philharmonic Orchestra, London Symphony Orchestra, London Royal Philharmonic Orchestra, Royal Liverpool Philharmonic Orchestra, BBC Philharmonic, Washington National Symphony, Minneapolis Symphony, Los Angeles Philharmonic, Bavarian Broadcasting Symphony Orchestra, Leipziger Gewandhausorchester, Dresden Philharmonic Orchestra, Sächsische Staatskapelle Dresden, Berlin Symphony Orchestra, Berlin Philharmonic Orchestra, Frankfurt Radio Symphony Orchestra, Tonhalle Orchester Zürich, Berner Symphonie Orchester, NHK Symphony Orchestra, Tokyo Philharmonic Orchestra, all major Russian orchestras; Played with great conductors including Pierre Boulez, Bernard Haitink, Kurt Masur, Carlo Maria Giulini, Evgueni Svetlanov, Guennadi Rohzdestvensky, Yuri Temirkanov, Dmitri Kitaenko, Antal Dorati, Kurt Sanderling, Alexander Dimitriev, Michael Schonwandt; Founder, Chairman, Vladimir Krainev International Young Pianists Competition, Kharkov, and International Vladimir Krainev Charity Fund; Founder, Artistic Director, concert programme Vladimir Krainev, his Friends and Pupils, Moscow Tchaikovsky Conservatoire Large Hall; Professor, Musik Hochschule, Hanover, Germany; Jury Member, international piano competitions, Leeds, Tokyo, Bolzano, Moscow, Clara Haskil, Seoul. Recordings: Prokofiev's 5 Piano Concertos with Frankfurt Radio Symphony Orchestra, conductor Dmitri Kitaenko; Mozart's 27 Piano Concertos with Lithuanian Chamber Orchestra, conductor Saulus Sondezkis; Anthology of Russian Piano Concertos, Shchedrin, Eshpaï, Schnittke. Current Management: Agence Artistique Catherine Petit, 26 rue de la Libération, 92210 Saint-Cloud, France. Address: Hochschule für Musik und Theater, Emmichplatz 1, Hanover, Germany.

KRAINIS Bernard, b. 28 Dec 1924, New Brunswick, NJ, USA. Recorder Player; College Professor. Education: Studied at Denver University, 1946-48 and with Gustav Reese at New York University, 1948-50. Career: With Noah Greenberg founded New York Pro Musica, 1952, with performances until 1959; Toured widely in USA until 1970 with the Krainis Baroque Trio, Krainis Baroque Ensemble and The Krainis Consort; Teacher at Kirkland College, 1969-71, Eastman School Rochester, 1976 and Smith College, 1977-81; Faculty of Mannes College, New York from 1980. Recordings: Early and Baroque music with the New York Pro Musica and his own ensembles. Address: Mannes College of Music, 157 East 74th Street, New York, NY 10021, USA.

KRAJNY Boris, b. 28 Nov 1945, Kromeriz, Czechoslovakia. Pianist. Education: Conservatory Kromeriz, 1959-63; Academy of

Prague, 1963-69. Career: Soloist, Prague Chamber Orchestra, 1972-80 and with Czech Philharmonic, 1982-. Recordings: Bach's Complete Organ Works, and Busoni's Complete Organ Works, and works by Beethoven, Chopin, Ravel, Debussy, Prokofiev, Bartók, Honegger, Roussel, Poulenc, Martinu. Honours: 1st Prize, Piano Competition, Senigallia, 1976; Grand Prix du Disque Charles Gros Paris, 1982. Hobby: Collecting Old Instruments. Address: Czech Philharmony, Dum umelcu, 11000 Prague, Czech Republic.

KRALIK Jan, b. 21 Mar 1947, Lazne Tousen, Bohemia. Mathematician; Musicologist. Education: Graduation in Mathematics, 1970, Philosophical Faculty, 1974, Doctorate in Mathematics, 1983, PhD, 1994, Charles University of Prague; Singing with J O Masák since 1970 and N Kejrova, 1972-83; Theory of Music, Institute of Theatre, Prague, 1977-79. Career: Studies on music and criticism, publishing, 1971-; Radio broadcaster, 1972-; Lecturer on music, 1973-. Recordings: Albums since 1978 and CD in 1989. Publications: Beethoven, 1978; Verdi, 1981; Wagner, 1983; Dvorak, 1985; Smetana, 1990; Novotna, 1991; The Complete Destinn, 1994. contributions to: Gramorevue; Hudebni rozhledy; The Record Collector. Honours: Preis der Deutschen Schallplatten-kritik, 1995. Memberships: Jeunesses Musicales, 1972, Czech President, 1993-95; Czech Chamber Music Society, 1989; Established Emmy Destinn Club in 1992. Address: Mlynska 29, 250 89 Lazne Tousen, Czech Republic.

KRAM David (Ian), b. 17 March 1948, Surrey, England. Orchestral Conductor. m. (1) Toni Anne de Courcy Bennett, 12 December 1970, div 1991, 1 son, 1 duaghter. m. (2) Belinda Saltmarsh, 10 April 1993. Education: Trinity School of John Whitgoft, 1959-65; Royal College of Music, London,; ARCM; Studied with Maestro Luigi Ricci, Rome; Italian Government Scholarship. Debut: Spoleto Festival, Italy, 1969. Career: Music Staff, Centre Lyrique Geneva, Switzerland, 1969-70; Conductor, Stadttheater, Basel, 1970-75; First Conductor, Nationaltheater, Mannheim, Federal Republic of Germany, 1975-77; Resident Conductor, The Australian Opera, 1978-86; Music Director, State Opera of South Australia, 1988-; Artistic Director, Artistic Advisor, Adelaide Chamber Orchestra, 1988; Guest Conductor, Komische Oper, Berlin, Hessisches Staatstheater, Wiesbaden, 1991-92; Musical Director, Ost-West-Jugend-Sinfonie-Orchester, 1992. Hobbies: Bushwalking; Reading; Travel. Current Management: Wolfgang Stoll, München; Glado von May, Frankfurt. Address: c/o Agentur Stroll, Martiusstrasse 3, D-8000 München 40, Germany.

KRAMER Gunter, b. 2 Dec 1940, Neustadt an der Weinstrasse, Germany. Stage Director. Education: Studied at Heidelberg and Freiburg Universities. Debut: First opera production, Krenek's Karl V at Darmstadt, 1979. Career: Head of Drama at Bremen and produced Nono's Intelleranza 60 at Hamburg Staatsoper, 1985; Deutsche Oper am Rhein, Dusseldorf, 1986-87, with Die Tote Stadt and Schreker's Die Gezeichneten; Productions at Deutsche Oper Berlin have included The Makropoulos Case (seen at Los Angeles, 1992); Die Entführung and Die Zauberflöte, 1991; Intendant of the Theatre Company of Cologne, 1990, producing Weill's Die Dreigroschenoper with it at the Spoleto Festival, 1991. Address: c/o Deutsche Oper, Richard Wagnerstrasse 10, Berlin 1, Germany.

KRAMER Jonathon D, b. 7 Dec 1942, Hartford, Connecticut, USA. Composer; Theorist; Educator; Writer; New Music Advisor; Programme Annotator; Composer in Residence; Broadcaster. m. Norma Berson, 28 Aug 1966, 1 son, 1 daughter. Education: BA, magna cum laude, Harvard, 1965; MA 1967; Phd 1969; University of California, Berkeley; Post-doctoral Fellow, School for Criticism and Theory, 1976, University of California, Irvine; Computer Music, Stanford, 1967-68; Music Teachers: K Stockhausen, R Sessions, L Kirchner, A Imbrie, S Shifrin, D Lewin, J Chowning, J Kerman. Career: Assistant Professor and Director of Undergraduate Composition, Yale University, 1971-78; Professor and Director of Electronic Music, University of Cincinnati, 1978-90; Honorary Research Associate, King's College, University of London, 1986; Professor, Columbia University, 1988-; Programme Annotator and New Music Advisor and Composer in Residence, Cincinnati Symphony, 1980-; Broadcaster, WGUC, 1984-88. Compositions: Moments In and Out of Time, orchestra; Music for Piano, No 5 (recorded); Renascence for Clarinet and Electronics (recorded); No Beginning, No End, for orchestra and chorus; About Face, for orchestra; Five Studies on Six Notes, for percussion trio (recorded); The Canons of Blackearth, for percussion quartet and tape (recorded); Atlanta Licks for Chamber Ensemble (recorded). Hobbies: Gourmet Cooking; Abstract Photography. Address: 25 Claremont Avenue, New York, NY 10027, USA.

KRAMER Toni, b. 14 Sept 1935, Malsch, Germany. Singer (Tenor). Education: Studied at the Karlsruhe Musikhochschule. Debut: Stuttgart 1965, in Les Contes d'Hoffmann. Career: Sang in Stuttgart as Pinkerton and Alvaro, and other roles in operas by Puccini and Verdi; Sang Florestan and Erik in Klagenfurt, Parsifal and Lohengrin in Saarbrucken; Stuttgart Staatsoper as Walther in Die Meistersinger, Siegfried, and König Hirsch in the opera by Henze; Munich Staatsoper as Dimitri in Boris Godunov; Bayreuth Festival 1985-86, as Siegfried in Der Ring des Nibelungen; Deutsche Oper Berlin 1987, as Siegfried and Froh in the Ring; Metropolitan 1988, as Siegfried in Götterdämmerung; sang Aegisthus in Elektra at Stuttgart, 1989; Stuttgart Staatsoper 1992, as Bacchus in Ariadne auf Naxos. Recordings include: Lohengrin (CBS); Video of Der Freischütz (Thorn-EMI). Address: c/o Staatsheater Stuttgart, Oberer Schlossgarten 6, D-7000 Stuttgart 1, Germany.

KRAPP Edgar, b. 3 June 1947, Bamberg, Germany. Organist; Harpsichordist; University Professor. m. Dr Maria-Christine Behrens, 22 July 1978, 2 sons. Education: Regensburg Cathedral Church Choir, 1956-64; Studied Organ, College of Music, Munich, 1966-71; Pupil of Marie Claire Alain, Paris, 1971-72. Career: Concerts in Europe, North and South America, Japan; Radio and TV programmes in Germany and Japan; Succeeded Helmut Walcha as Professor of Organ at the Hochschule fur Musik, Frankfurt, 1974; Visiting Professor at the Salzburg Mozarteum, 1982-91; Professor of Organ, Hochschule für Musik, Munich, 1993-; Concerts with conductors such as Rafael Kubelik, Colin Davis, Horst Stein, Christoph Eschenbach. Recordings: Handel: all organ and harpsichord works; Organ recordings in Haarlem (St Bavo Church), Berlin (St Hedwig's Cathedral), Passau Cathedral, historical instruments in East Germany (Brandenburg Cathedral) and South Germany (Benediktbeuern, Ottobeuren Basilica). Honours: 1st Prize, ARD Competition, Munich, 1971; Mendelssohn Prize, Berlin, 1971; German Recording Prizes for Organ, 1981; Harpischord, 1983; Grand Prix du Disque, 1983; Frankfurt Music Prize, 1983. Memberships: Member of Jury of International Organ Competitions at Berlin, Munich, Nürnberg, Linz, Tokyo, Chartes; Member, Bayersiche Akademie der Schönen Künste; Member, Board of Directors, Neue Bachgesellschaft, Leipzig; Artistic Director, Organ Series at New Concert Hall Bamberg. Hobbies: Walking; Family. Address: Hauptstrasse 15, D-82054 Sauerlach-Altkirchen, Germany.

KRASSMANN Jurgen, b. 6 Apr 1933, Gorlitz, Germany. Baritone. Education: Studied at the Dresden Musikhochschule and with Rudolf Bockelmann. Career: Sang with the Dresden Staatsoper, 1956-64 and appeared there and elsewhere in Germany, notably at Halle in operas by Handel, in roles of Cleontes in Alessandro, Gernando in Faramondo, as Scipio, Phoenix in Deidamia, Garibaldo in Rodelinda and Ottone in Agrippina; Sang in Ariodante at Wiesbaden in 1972 and Floridante at Linz in 1987; Further appearances in Leipzig and elsewhere in East Germany as Pizarro, the Dutchman, Rigoletto, Macbeth, Scarpia and Nick Shadow in The Rake's Progress. Address: c/o Landestheater, Promenade 39, A-4010 Linz, Austria.

KRASTEVA Neva, b. 2 Aug 1946, Sofia, Bulgaria. Composer. Education: Studied at the Moscow Conservatory and in Prague and Zurich. Career: Lecturer at the Sofia State Academy from 1974 and founder of Bulgaria's first organ school. Compositions include: Mythological Songs for Soprano and Ensemble, 1976; The Old Icon for Low Voice and Organ, 1987; Apokriff, cantata, 1989; Quantus Tremor, cantata, for Mezzo, Trumpet, Organ and Cello, 1989. Address: c/o Musicautor, 63 Tzar Assen Street, 1463 Sofia, Bulgaria.

KRATOCHVIL Jaromir, b. 28 May 1924, Prague, Czech Republic. Composer; Teacher. m. Sona Brethova, 22 August 1950, 1 son. Education: Faculty of Philosophy, Charles University, Prague; Theory of Composition and Instrumentation, Professor Frantisek Picha. Career: Compositions for Piano in Private Halls. Compositions: The Victorious Life, Musical Poem, 1962; 2 Symphonies; Romantic Suite, for Orchestra, Piano, 1982; Drad Music, for String Orchestra, 1992; Saxophone Quartet, 1996. Recordings: Drad Music, for String Orchestra, 1992; American Master Musicians Collective, 1996; Saxophone Quartet, 1996. Membership: Czech Society of Composers. Hobby: Philosophy. Address: nam. Republiky 1064, 29301 Mlada Boleslav, Czech Republic.

KRAUKLIS Georgij, b. 12 May 1922, Moscow, Russia. Musicologist. m. Irina Shklaeva, 4 Aug 1946, 1 daughter. Education: Musical College, Conservatory of Moscow, 1946-48; Theoretical Studies, Composition Faculty, 1948-53, Postgraduate course in Musical History, 1953-56, Conservatory of Moscow. Career: Consultant to Moscow Philharmonic, 1952-60; Teacher, Choral College, Moscow, 1955-62; Teacher, 1956-67, Docent, 1967-80, Dean, 1978-89, Professor, 1980-, Conservatory of Moscow; Director of Stage, France's Violinists, Sarla, France, 1982. Publications: Piano Sonatas of Schubert, 1963; Operatic overtures of R Wagner, 1964; Symphonic poems of R Strauss, 1970; Symphonic poems of F Liszt, 1974. Contributions include: Bayreuth Music Festival after 116 years, in Musical Academy, 1993. Honours: Prize for article, Ministry of Culture, 1979; Honorary Title of Merited Man (representative) of Russian Art, 1994. Membership: Associate Editor, JALS, USA. Hobbies: Ornithology; Chess. Address: Kostiakova Street 6/5, Ap 81, 125422 Moscow, Russia.

KRAUS Adalbert, b. 27 Apr 1937, Aschaffenburg, Germany. Singer (Tenor). Education: Studied at the Wurzburg Conservatory with H Klink-Schneider. Career: Sang first in concert hall, with repertoire ranging from Baroque to contemporary works; Sang Belmonte in Die Entführung at Giessen, 1968; Lyric roles at the Hanover opera from 1970; Ludwigsburg Festival 1972, as Tamino; Other roles were Mozart's Ferrando, Nemorino, Rossini's Comte Ory, Nureddin in Barbier von Bagdad, Des Grieux in Manon and Florindo in Wolf-Ferrari's Le Donne Curiose; Tour of North and South America 1972, in music by Bach directed by Karl Richter; Concert appearances in London, Rome, Paris and elsewhere in Europe. Recordings: Christmas Oratorio by Schütz; Bach Cantatas; Die Schöpfung by Haydn (Vox); Der Barbier von Bagdad; Zar und Zimmermann (BASF); Die Lustigen Weiber von Windsor (Decca).

KRAUS Alfredo, b. 24 Nov 1927, Las Palmas. Tenor. Debut: In Rigoletto and Tosca, Cairo, 1956. Career: Appearances in Venice, Turin, Barcelona and London, at Stoll Theatre, 1958, in Lisbon in La Traviata with Maria Callas, La Scala, Milan, debut 1958, Covent Garden debut, 1959, as Edgardo in Lucia di Lammermoor; Has sung in all major opera houses in Italy, France and Germany, Vienna, Madrid, Barcelona, Tokyo and Buenos Aires; Appeared in Chicago, 1962, Metropolitan New York, in Rigoletto, 1965; Later appeared in New York as Nemorino, Don Ottavio, Ernesto, Alfredo, Faust, Werther, Tonio (La Fille du Régiment), Gounod's Roméo and Hoffmann; Debut at Paris Opera as Werther and returned for Romeo and Juliet and La Fille du Régiment; Recital at the Teatro Colon, Buenos Aires, 1989; Sang Werther at Lisbon and Rome, 1990; Covent Garden, June 1991, in Les Contes d'Hoffmann; returned, 1992, as Nemorino; Sang Fernand in La Favorite at Madrid, 1992; Werther at Naples, 1996. Recordings: Numerous recordings include Lucia di Lammermoor and a number of video recordings; Werther, Roméo et Juliette, Manon, La Fille du Régiment, I Puritani, La Traviata, Rigoletto, Don Pasquale, La Jolie Fille de Perth, La Muette de Portici. Address: c/o Patricia Greenan, 19B Belsize Park, London NW3 4DU, England.

KRAUS Michael, b. 17 Jan 1957, Vienna, Austria. Baritone. Education: Studied in Vienna with Otto Edelmann and Josef Greindl. Career: After winning various competitions, including the Hugo Wolf in Vienna, sang at Aachen Opera, 1981-84, Ulm, 1984-87, Vienna Volksoper, 1988-91, notably as Papageno; US debut in 1991 at San Francisco Opera; Guest appearances in France, Hungary, Holland, Greece and Israel, as Mozart's Leporello, Guglielmo and Count, Puccini's Marcello and Lescaut, Janácek's Forester, Monteverdi's Ottone and the Count in Lortzing's Wildschütz. Recordings include: Die Zauberflöte; Jonny Spielt auf by Krenek; Der Rosenkavalier; Turandot by Busoni. Address: c/o Volksoper, Wahringerstrasse 78, A-1090 Vienna, Austria.

KRAUSE Monika, b. 1956, Kiel, Germany. Soprano. Education: Studied at the Hamburg Musikhochschule with Judith Beckmann. Career: Engaged at the Gelsenkirchen Opera, 1984-86, at Wiesbaden, notably as Violetta, Norina and Lortzing's Undine; Sang Aennchen in Der Freischütz at the 1991 Eutin Festival, and at Dortmund in 1991 as Donna Elvira; Other roles include Tatiana, Massenet's Sophie and Strauss's Sophie, Pamina, Fiordiligi, Micaela and Pamina. Recordings include: Undine. Address: c/o Städtische Buhnen Dortmund, Kuhstrasse 12, W-4600 Dortmund, Germany.

KRAUSE Tom, b. 5 Jul 1934, Helsinki, Finland. Singer (Baritone). Education: Studied in Hamburg and Vienna and in Berlin with Margot Skoda, Serjo Nazor and Rudolf Bautz. Debut: As Lieder singer in Helsinki, 1957. Career: Stage debut at the Städtische Oper Berlin as Escamillo, 1959; Appearances in Milan, Vienna, Paris, Brussels, Bordeaux, Buenos Aires, Cologne, Munich and Toulouse; Bayreuth 1962, as the Herald in Lohengrin; Glyndebourne and London 1963, as the Count in Capriccio and in Britten's War Requiem; Hamburg Staatsoper from 1962, notably in the premieres of Der Goldene Bock by Krenek, 1964, and Searle's Hamlet, 1967; Metropolitan Opera from 1967, Count Almaviva, Malatesta, Escamillo and Guglielmo; Grand Théâtre Geneva 1983, as Golaud in Pelléas et Mélisande; In Chicago with Lyric Opera, San Francisco Opera and Houston Operas; Other roles include Don Giovanni, Renato, Kurwenal, Amonasro, Germont, Pizarro, Amfortas and Mefistopheles; Sang at the 1985 Savonlinna Festival as King Philip in Don Carlo; Active career as Lieder recital singer and Oratorio Singer; Kammersänger in Hamburg; Salzburg Festival 1992, as Frère Bernard in St François d'Assise by Messiaen; Sang the Music Master in Strauss's Ariadne, Fort Lauderdale, 1996. Recordings: Tristan und Isolde, Le nozze di Figaro, Così fan tutte, Fidelio, Andre Chénier, La Bohème, Don Pasquale, Turandot, Elektra, Salome, Un Ballo in Maschera and Otello; Carmen; Lohengrin; Oedipus Rex; Euryanthe. Honours: Deutsche Schallplatten Prize; Edison Prize; English Gramophone Prize for Sibelius Songs, 1986;

Address: c/o Finnish National Opera, Bulevardi 23-27, SF-00180 Helsinki 18, Finland.

KRAUZE Zygmunt, b. 19 Sept 1938, Warsaw, Poland. Composer; Pianist. Education: Studied with Kazimierz Sikorski and Maria Wilkomirska at the Warsaw Conservatory, MA, 1964; Further study with Nadia Boulanger in Paris, 1966-67. Career: Soloist in recitals of new music in Europe and the USA; Founded the Warsaw Music Workshop, 1967: group consisting of clarinet, trombone, cello and piano, for which 100 composers have written works; Taught piano at Cleveland State University, 1970-71; Lectures at the International Course for New Music at Darmstadt, in Stockholm, Basle and at US Universities; President of the Polish Section of ISCM from 1980; Resident in Paris from 1982; Has worked for IRCAM (Electronic Music Centre) with Boulez; President of the International Society for Contemporary Music, 1987. Compositions: Malay Pantuns for 3 Flutes and Female Voice, 1964; Triptych for Piano, 1964; Esquisse for Piano, 1967; Polychromy, for Clarinet, Trombone, Piano and Cello, 1968; Quatuor pour la Naissance, for Clarinet, Violin, Cello and Piano, 1985; Voices for 15 Instruments, 1968-72; Piece for Orchestra No 1 and 2, 1969-70; 3 String Quartets, 1960, 1969, 1982; Fallingwater for Piano, 1971; Folk Music for Orchestra, 1972; Aus aller Welt Stammende for 10 Strings, 1973; Automatophone for 14 Plucked Instruments and 7 Mechanical Instruments, 1974; Fete Galante et Pastorale, 1975; Piano Concerto, 1974-76; Suite de danses et de chansons for Harpsichord and Orchestra, 1977; The Star, Chamber Opera, 1980; Violin Concerto, 1980; Tableva Vivant for Chamber Orchestra, 1982; Piece for Orchestra No 3, 1982; Arabesque for Piano and Chamber Orchestra, 1983; Double Concerto for Violin, Piano and Orchestra, 1985; Symphonie Parisienne, 1986; Nightmare Tango for Piano, 1987; From Keyboard to Score for Piano, 1987; Sigfried und Zygmunt for Piano and Cello, 1988. Honours include: Chevalier dans l'ordre des Arts et des Lettres, 1984. Address: c/o ZAIKS, 2 rue Hippoteczna, 00 092 Warsaw, Poland.

KRAVITZ Ellen (King), b. 25 May 1929, Fords, New Jersey, USA. Musicologist; Professor. m. Hilard L Kravitz, 9 Jan 1972, 3 stepsons, 1 daughter. Education: BA, Georgian Court College, Lakewood, New Jersey, 1964; MM, 1966, PhD, 1970, University of Southern California. Career: Full Professor of Music History, California State University, Los Angeles, 1967; Researcher in musicology and related arts; Director, Exhibition of Schoenberg's art and music during Schoenberg Centennial Celebration, University of Southern California, 1974; Founder, Friends of Music, 1976, Gala; Chair, 1978-1982; Participant in Faculty Vocal Extravaganza, California State University, Los Angeles, 1981, 1983, 1985, 1987, 1989, 1991, 1993, 1995. Publications: A Correlation of Concepts Found in German Expressionist Art, Music and Literature, 1970; Editor, Journal of the Arnold Schoenberg Institute, Volume I No 3, Volume II No 3; Catalogue of Schoenberg's Paintings, Drawings and Sketches, 1978; Finding Your Way Through Music in World Culture, 1986. Contribution to: Arnold Schoenberg As Artist: Another Look, paper for Musicology Meeting, 1995. Membership: Treasurer, Pacific Southwest Chapter, American Musicological Society, 1995-97. Hobbies: Theatre; Travel; Interior decorating. Address: 526 N Foothill Road, Beverly Hills, CA 90210, USA.

KREBBERS Herman (Albertus), b. 18 Jun 1923, Hengelo, Holland. Violinist. m. A Torlau, 1 son, 1 daughter. Education: Studied at the Amsterdam Musiklyceum with Oscar Back. Debut: Gave first concert in 1932. Career: Soloist with the Concertgebouw Orchestra, 1935; Leader of the Gelderland Orchestra, then the Hague Residentie Orchestra, 1950-62; Leader of the Concertgebouw Orchestra from 1962; Many tours of Europe and the USA as Soloist; Founded the Guarneri Trio, 1963, and played in Violin Duo with Theo Olof; Teacher at the Amsterdam Musiklyceum. Recordings: Bach and Badings Concertos for Two Violins, with Theo Olof and the Hague Philharmonic; Beethoven Concerto with the Hague Philharmonic; Brahms and Bruch Concertos with the Brabant Orchestra; Paganini 1st Concerto with the Vienna Symphony; Haydn Concertos with the Amsterdam Chamber Orchestra. Honours include: Prix d'Excellence, Amsterdam Musiklyceum, 1940; Knight, Oranje Nassau Order; Many prizes from International Competitions. Address: c/o Concertgebouworkest, Jacob Obrechtstraat 51, 1071 KJ Amsterdam, Netherlands.

KREBS Helmut, b. 8 Oct 1913, Dortmund, Germany. Tenor Singer. Education: Berlin Musikhochschule, 1934-37. Career: Began as concert singer; Stage debut, 1937 at the Volksoper, Berlin; Returned to Berlin, 1947; Salzburg Festival, 1949, in the premiere of Orff's Antigonae; Ernesto in Don Pasquale, 1952; Guest appearances in Milan, London, Vienna, Munich, Holland and Belgium; Glyndebourne, 1953 as Mozart's Belmonte and Idamantes; Hamburg Radio, 1954 as Aron in the first performance of Schoenberg's Moses und Aron; Berlin, 1956 and 1965, in premieres of Henze's König Hirsch and Der junge Lord; Also heard as the Evangelist in the Passions of Bach; Professor at the Frankfurt Musikhochschule from 1966; Sang at the Deutsche Oper Berlin, 1988 in From the House of the Dead. Compositions: Orchestral, Operatic, Chamber, Choral and Vocal works published. Recordings: Monteverdi, Orfeo; Henze, Der junge Lord; Bach, Christmas Oratorio; Verdi, Requiem; Stravinsky, Oedipus Rex; Strauss, Ariadne auf Naxos; Schoenberg, Moses und Aron; Wagner, Der fliegende Holländer. Honours: Berliner Künstpreis, 1952; Berliner Kammersänger, 1963. Address: 11 Im Dol 14195 Berlin, Germany.

KREFT Ekkehard, b. 14 July 1939, Sagan/Niederschlesien, Germany. m. Sigrid Schöneberg. Education: Musikhochschule Detmold; Universities of Cologne, Bonn and Marburg; Habilitation, University of Münster, 1974; Professor, 1978. Career: Director, Instituts für Musikpädagogik, 1977-94; Leader, Edvard-Grieg Forschungsstelle, University of Münster, 1995-. Publications: Lehrbuch des Musikwissenschaft, 1985; Kongressbericht, Musikpraxis in der Schule, 1994; Kongressbericht, 1 Deutscher Grieg-Kongress, 1996; Harmonische Prozesse im Wandel der Epochen 1 1995, 2, 1996. Contributions to: Grieg als Wegbereiter der Harmonik des 20 jhs, Studia Musicologica Norvegica, 1993. Membership: Norwegische Akademie der Wissenschaften. Address: Heideweg 5, D48249 Dülmen, Germany.

KREIZBERG Yakov, b. 24 Oct 1959, St Petersburg, Russia. Conductor. Education: Studied privately in St Petersburg and emigrated to the USA in 1976; Conducting fellowships at Tanglewood and the Los Angeles Philharmonic Institute. Career: Music Director of the Mannes College Orchestra, New York, 1985-88; Music Director of the Krefeld Opera and Lower Rhine Symphony, 1988-94; Led Cosi fan tutte and Don Giovanni with Canadian Opera, 1991-92, and Der Rosenkavalier for English National Opera, 1994; Music Director of the Komische Oper Berlin from 1994 and Principal Conductor of the Bournemouth Symphony Orchestra from 1995; Artistic Adviser of Jeunesses Musicales (World Youth Orchestra); Further engagements with the Chicago Symphony, Los Angeles Philharmonic Orchestra, San Francisco Symphony Orchestra, Detroit Symphony Orchestra, Berlin Philharmonic, Royal Concertgebouw, Leipzig Gewandhaus, Philharmonia; At Glyndebourne conducted Jenufa (1992) and Don Giovanni (1995) and engaged for Katya Kabanova, 1998. Address: Harrison Parrott Ltd, 12 Penzance Place, London, W11 4PA, England.

KREJCI Jiri, b. 11 December 1935, Dolni Hbity, Czech Republic. Musician. 2 sons, 1 daughter. Education: Military Music School, Kosice; Concervatory of Music, Prague. Debut: Soloist, Haydn Concerto, Radio Symphony Orchestra, Prague, 1960. Career: Solo Oboist of the Theatre Orchestra, Vinohrady, Prague, 1953-56, Karlin, Prague, 1957-59; Principal Oboe, Radio Symphony Orchestra, Prague, 1959-64; Solo Oboist, Prague Chamber Orchestra without Chef, 1965-77; Artistic Leader, Collegium Musicum Pragense, 1965-90; Member, Czech Nonet, 1977-; Member, Prague Wind Quintet, 1982-93; Live Recordings for the BBC in London. Honours: Prize, Composers Society, 1984; Honorary Award, Ministryof Culture, Czech Republic. Address: Ceskolipska 400/20, 1900 Praha 9, Czech Republic.

KREK Uros, b. 21 May 1922, Ljubljana, Yugoslavia. Composer. m. Lilijana Pauer, 18 June 1960. Education: Classical College, Ljubljana; Music High School, Ljubljana. Debut: 1st Performance of Compositions, Ljubljana, 1945. Career: Performances of compositions on concert stages, radio and television, film, theatre, records and editions. Compositions: Concerto for violin and orchestra; Sinfonietta, Concerto for French horn and orchestra; Concerto for piccolo and orchestra; Rhapsodic Dance for orchestra; Sonata for 2 violins; Five Songs for voice and piano; Movements Concertants, Inventions ferales for violin and strings; Symphony for Strings; Duo for violin and violoncello; La Journee d'un Bouffon for brass quintet; Trio for violin, viola and violoncello; String Quartet; Sur un Melodie for piano; 1 Sonatinas for clarinet; Songs for Eva; Concert Diptych for violoncello and orchestra; Sonata for violoncello and piano; 3 Impromptus for violin solo; Sextet for 2 violins, 2 violas and 2 violoncellos; Espressivo and Appassionato for flute and piano; Songs on Folk Tradition for voice and piano; Canticum Resianum, 1988; Vigoroso for violin and piano, 1991; Cantus gratias agentis for soprano, trumpet and organ, 1994; Reflections, 2nd sonata for violin and piano, 1994; Capriccio notturno for violin and harp, 1996; Chamber music, choir music, film and stage music. Recordings: Numerous recordings of his compositions on CD and cassette for radio and TV. Honours: Preseren Prize, 1952, 1992. Hobbies: Model railways; Mountaineering. Address: SI 4248 Lesce, Na Vrtaci 5, Slovenia.

KREMER Gidon, b. 27 Feb 1947, Riga, Latvia. Violinist. Education: Studied at the Moscow Conservatory with David Oistrakh. Career: Many performances as Concert Soloist in Europe, USA and elsewhere in the standard repertoire and in modern works: often heard in Schnittke, and in May 1986 performed Bernstein's Serenade, London; Duo recitals with the pianist Martha Argerich: sonatas by Franck, Schumann and Bartok, London, 1988; Television appearances include Berg Concerto, with the Bavarian Radio Symphony under Colin Davis; Promenade Concerts, London, 1991, with Gubaidulina's Offertorium, conducted by Simon Rattle; Schubert Contemporary Celebration concert at the Barbican Hall, London, 1997; Premiered Reimann's Concerto at Chicago, 1997. Recordings include: Concertos by Mendelssohn, with Martha Argerich, 1989; Gubaidulina's Offertorium, with the Boston Symphony under Charles Dutoit, Mozart Trio K498 and Duos K423 and K424; Schumann Sonatas, with Argerich. Honours: First Prize of the Latvian Republic, 1963; Winner, Tchaikovsky International Competition, Moscow, 1970. Address: c/o Terry Harrison Management, The Orchard, Market Street, Charlbury, Oxon OX7 3PJ, England.

KRENZ Jan, b. 14 Jul 1926, Wloclawek, Poland. Conductor; Composer. m. Alina Krenz, 1 son. Education: Warsaw and Lodz. Career: Conductor, Lodz Philharmonic Orchestra, 1945; Conductor, Poznan Philharmonic Orchestra, 1948-49; Director and First Conductor, Polish Radio Symphony Orchestra, Katowice, 1953-67; British debut 1961; Conducted Polish Music at the 1967 Cheltenham Festival; Artistic Director, First Conductor, Grand Opera House, Warsaw, 1967-73; General Director, Music, Bonn Orchestra, 1978-; Tours in Hungary, Romania, Czechoslovakia, France, USSR, Germany, Italy, UK, USA, Japan, Australia. Compositions include: Symphony; 2 String Quartets; Noctures for Orchestra; Rozmowa dwoch miast; Rhapsody for Strings, Xylophone, Tam-Tam, Timpani and Celesta, 1952; Concertino for Piano and Small Symphony Orchestra, 1952; Orchestral transcriptions of Microcosmos (B Bartok, 1958); Mythes (Szymanowski), 1964. Recordings: Paderewski's Piano Concerto; Lutoslawski's 1st Symphony and Wieniawski Violin Concertos; Brahms, Mendelssohn and Tchaikovsky Violin Concertos; Chopin Piano Concertos. Hobbies: Painting. Address: Al 1 Armii Wojaska Polskiego 16/38, 00-582 Warsaw, Poland.

KREPPEL Walter, b. 3 Jun 1923, Nuremberg, Germany. Singer (Bass). Education: Studied at the Nuremberg Conservatory. Debut: Nuremberg 1945, as Tommaso in Tiefland. Career: Sang in Nuremberg, 1945-48, Wurzburg, 1948-50; Sang in Heidelberg and Gelsenkirchen, 1953-56, Frankfurt, 1956-59; Member of the Bayerische Staatsoper Munich from 1959, Vienna Staatsoper from 1960 (Rocco in Fidelio, 1962); Bayreuth Festival, 1962, as Fasolt; Salzburg, 1963-64, as Sarastro; Guest appearances in Zurich, London and Amsterdam. Recordings: Kaspar in Der Freischütz, the Commendatore in Don Giovanni; Fasolt in Das Rheingold, conducted by Solti.

KRETH Wolfgang, b. 29 May 1946, Cologne, West Germany. Lutenist. Education: Studied Music, 1967-75 at: Musikhochschule, Köln; Musikhochschule, Düsseldorf; Musikhochschule, Frankfurt; Musikhochschule, Aachen; Musiklehrer-Examen; Staatl Diplom for Lute, summa cum laude. Career: Several Concerts in Europe (Schwetzinger Festspiele, Musica Bayreuth, Dubrovnik-Festival, Wiener Festwochen, Brühler Barock-Fest; Radio Appearances, Interviews. Recordings: Lute Music of Anthony Holborne and Nicolas Vallet; Lute Concerto of Antonio Vivaldi. Contributions to: Several articles in Gitarre und Laute, Köln. Memberships: Lute Society of England; Lute Society of America; Society Nova Giulianiad, Freiburg; Member of EGTA. Address: Theophanoplatz Nr 8, 5 Köln 51, Germany.

KRETSCHMAR Helmut, b. 3 Feb 1928, Kleve, Germany. Singer (Tenor). m. Renate Fischer. Education: Studied in Frankfurt with Kurt Thomas and Hans Emge. Career: Sang first in concerts and oratorios from 1953; At Hamburg in 1954 sang in the first performance (concert) of Schoenberg's Moses und Aron; Sacred music by Bach at the Berliner Festwochen and the Bach Festivals at Luneberg and Heidelberg, 1960-62; Further appearances at the Handel Festival at Göttingen and in Dusseldorf, Japan, Korea, Paris, Madrid, Bombay, London and Ceylon; Lieder recitals with Renate Fischer, Piano; Repertoire includes sacred music by Handel, Haydn and Mendelssohn; Songs by Wolf, Debussy, Schubert and Schumann; Professor at the Detmold Musikhochschule from 1963. Recordings include: Fidelio; Moses und Aron, conducted by Hans Rosbaud; St Matthew Passion, Christmas Oratorio and B Minor Mass by Bach; Beethoven's Missa solemnis; Schubert's Mass in A flat; Die Jahreszeiten by Haydn. Honours: First Prize, German Music High Schools, 1953; Kunstpreis of Nordrhein-Westfalen, 1958.

KREUGER Dana, b. 1947, USA. Mezzo-Soprano. Career: Sang at the Washington Opera from 1973, Houston from 1977 including the 1983 premiere of Bernstein's A Quiet Place, Miami Opera in 1979, New York City Opera, 1979-80 and St Louis, 1982; Roles have included Ragonde in Le Comte Ory, Stravinsky's Mother Goose, Herodias in Salome, Nurse in Boris Godunov and Marthe in Faust. Address: c/o Houston Grand Opera Association, 510 Preston Avenue, Houston, TX 77002, USA.

KRIKORIAN Mari, b. 25 May 1946, Varna, Bulgaria. Opera Singer (Soprano). Education: Secondary School of Music, Varna, 1964; Graduated, 1971, Master's Class, 1972, Bulgarian State

Conservatoire, Sofia; Specialisation course with James King, Vienna, 1977. Debut: As Adalgisa in Norma, Varna National Opera, 1976. Career: 1st Soprano, Varna National Opera, in La Bohème, Simon Boccanegra, Fliegende Holländer, Otello, Don Carlo and Tosca; 1st Soprano, Sofia National Opera, 1983-; Permanent Repertoire includes Norman, Attila, Aida, Il Trovatore, La Forza de Destino, Don Carlos, Otello, La Bohème, Madame Butterfly, Tosca, Liu, Senta, Adriana Lecouvreur, Tatiana in Eugene Onegin, Lisa in Queen of Spades, Yaroslavna in Prince Igor, Verdi's Requiem, Donizetti's Requiem, Bruckner's Requiem, Brahms Deutsches Requiem, Liszt's Christus Oratorio, Rossini's Stabat Mater, Pergolesi's Stabat Mater; Foreign tours, Prague, Budapest, Russia, Armenia, Germany, Italy, France, Spain, Austria, Greece, Egypt, Cyprus, India, Mexico; Film portrait for Bulgarian Television, 1989; Un Ballo in Maschera, 1993; Foreign Tours: Los Angeles (USA) concerts, 1993. Recordings: Opera recital, airs from Bellini, Verdi and Puccini, with Sofia Opera Orchestra, conductor Ivan Marinov, State Recording Company Balkanton, 1984; Attila, digital, compact discs, with Sofia Philharmonic Orchestra, conductor Vladimir Ghiaurov, Attila with Nicola Guzelev; Chants Liturgiques Armeniens CD Edition JADE, Paris, France, 1992; Live and studio recordings for Bulgarian Radio and TV. Honours: 1st Prize, Opera Belcanto Competition, Ostende, Belgium, 1980; Honoured Artist of Bulgaria, 1984. Current Management: SOFIACONCERT, Bulgaria. Address: Druzba 2 bl 213 A, Ap 11, Sofia 1582, Bulgaria.

KRILOVICI Marina, b. 11 Jun 1942, Bucharest, Rumania. Singer (Soprano). Education: Studied with Mdme Vrabiescu-Varianu in Bucharest and with Matia Caniglia and Luigi Ricci in Rome. Debut: National Opera Bucharest, 1966, as Donna Anna. Career: Sang major roles in the Italian repertory with the Bucharest Opera, Covent Garden debut, 1971, as Aida; Chicago Lyric Opera, 1972, as Mimi; Further appearances in Vienna, Berlin, Munich, Montreal, Lisbon, San Francisco and Strasbourg; Hamburg Staatsoper, 1968-76. Recordings include: Cavelleria Rusticana; Donizetti's Il Duca d'Alba.

KRINGELBORN Solveig, b. 1963, Norway. Soprano. Education: Studied at Stockholm Royal Academy. Career: Appearances at the Royal Swedish Opera as Susanna and Papagena, Oslo Opera, 1990-91 as Mimi, Jenufa and Micaela, with further engagements at the Bolshoi, Moscow, Vienna Staatsoper, Strasbourg, Los Angeles as Mozart's Countess in 1993, Brussels in the premiere of Boesmans' Reigen, Salzburg as Fiordiligi in 1993, Bastille as Antonia in 1993, Geneva as Ilia in 1994 and Mozart's Countess in Salzburg in 1995; Other roles include Musetta, Marguerite, Pamina, Nedda, Serpine in La Serva Padrona, and Drusilla in Poppea; BBC Promenade Concerts in 1991, with the premiere of Lutoslawski's Chantefleurs et Chantefables, conducted by the composer, also televised; Wigmore Hall recital debut in 1992; Other concert repertoire includes Haydn's Jahreszeiten in Paris, Nielsen's 3rd Symphony in London under Simon Rattle, Mahler's 2nd Symphony with the Israel Philharmonic and Cleveland Orchestra, and in Los Angeles in 1993; Sang Mozart's Countess at the 1995 Salzburg Festival and for the San Francisco Opera, 1997-98; Fiordiligi at the 1996 Glyndebourne Festival. Recordings include: Grieg Songs conducted by Rozhdestvensky, a Grieg Solo Song disc and Tavener Choral Music conducted by David Hill. Address: c/o IMG Artists, Media House, 3 Burlington Lane, London, W2 2TH, England.

KRISCAK Manuela, b. 1965, Trieste, Italy. Singer (Soprano). Education: Studied at the G Tartini Conservatoire, Trieste. Debut: Musetta in La Bohème at the Teatro Nuovo, Spoleto, 1990. Career: Appearances as Tisbe in Cenerentola at Spoleto and Rome, Bianca in La Rondine and Zerlina at Catania; Gianetta in L'Elisir d'amore for French TV, Un Plaisir in Gluck's Armide at La Scala (1996); Sang Kristina in The Makropoulos Case at Glyndebourne (1995-97) and at Strasbourg and Lisbon; Season 1997-98 as Papagena (Die Zauberflöte) and in Paisiello's Il Barbiere di Siviglia at Trieste. Address: Teatro Comunale, G Verdi di Trieste, Rive Novembre 1, 34121 Trieste, Italy.

KRIVINE Emmanuel, b. 7 May 1947, Grenoble, France. Conductor; Violinist. Education: Studied violin at Grenoble until 1960 and with Henryk Szeryng and Yehudi Menuhin at Paris Conservatoire from 1960. Career: Laureate of Violin competitions during 1960s; Conductor in Belgium from 1964; Chief Guest Conductor of the New Philharmonic Orchestra of Radio France, 1976; Musical Director of the Lorraine Philharmonic Orchestra at Metz, 1981-83; Teacher at Lyon Conservatoire, 1979-81; Chief Guest Conductor, 1983-85, Musical Director, 1987-, of Orchestre National de Lyon; Conducted the premiere of Michel Legrand's Concertoratorio 89, for the bicentenary of the French Revolution. Honours: Prizewinner at violin competitions in Brussels, 1965 and 1968, London, Naples and Bratislava. Address: Orchestra National de Lyon, 82 Rue de Bonnel, F-69431, Lyon Cedex 03, France.

KROLL Mark, b. 13 Sept 1946, Brooklyn, New York, USA. Harpsichordist; Professor of Music. m. Carol Lieberman, 9 July 1975, 1 son. Education: BA, 1968, Graduate School, Musicology, 1968-69, Brooklyn College, City University of New York; MMus, Harpsichord, Yale University School of Music, 1971. Debut: Carnegie Hall, New York City, 1975. Career: Performance in solo recitals, chamber music ensembles and as concerto soloist throughout Europe, South America, USA and Canada; Radio and Television appearances; Numerous television shows for Public broadcasting System and BBC; Currently Professor of Music, Boston University; Conductor, Orchestral works of Rameau, CPE Bach, Vivaldi; Artist-in-Residence, Lafayette College, Conductor and Artistic Director, Opera New England; Visiting Professor: Würzburg Conservatory, Zagreb Music Academy and Belgrade Music Academy. Recordings include: J S Bach, complete sonatas for violin and harpsichord; Handel and Scarlatti, harpsichord works; G F Handel, complete works for recorder and harpsichord; Vivaldi's The Seasons, with Boston Symphony Orchestra; Solo Harpsichord works of J S Bach; Harpsichord works of JNP Royer; Franz Schubert, 3 Sonatinas for violin and fortepiano; M de Falla, El Retablo de Maese Pedro, with Montreal Symphony. Publications: French Harpsichord Music, 1994; 17th Century Keyboard Music, 1997. Contributions to: Numerous articles for Bostonia magazine. Honours: Grants from: NEA, 1984; CIES, 1989; Whiting Foundation, 1993; DAAD, 1996; IREX, 1996. Address: Boston University School of Music, 855 Commonwealth Avenue, Boston, MA 02215, USA.

KROLOPP Wojciech (Aleksander), b. 12 Apr 1945, Poznan, Poland. Musician; Manager; Journalist. Education: Academy of Music Poznan, 1973-77; Pedagogy, 1968-70. Debut: Soloist Soprano, 1957; Soloist Baritone, 1964; Career: Soloist from 1957 (soprano, bass from 1964); Teacher and Conductor, Polish Choir School, Poznan, 1968-; Managing Director, 1969-, Poznan Boys' Choir, and Director of International Boys' Choir Festival, Poznan, 1980-; 3000 concerts with the Poznan Boys' Choir, 400 conducted concerts in 24 countries; Solo parts in major vocal-instrumental works and songs; Camerata, chamber orchestra, 1980-83; Premiere of Mozart opera, Bastien und Bastienne at the Great Theatre in Poznan also in Taiwan and Hong Kong; By end of 1990 nominated as manager and artistic director of the Polish Nightingales. Recordings: Mozart's Coronation Mass and Szymanowski's Stabat Mater, 1991. Publications include: The Poznan Choir School, monography, 1989. Current Management: Polish Artists' Agency, Warsaw and Penta Promotions, Netherlands. Address: Torenstraat 13, B-9160 Lokeren, Belgium.

KROO György, b. 26 Aug 1926, Budapest, Hungary. Music Historian; Music Critic. m. Ilona Balogh, 1 son, 1 daughter. Education: Music Academy of Budapest. Career: Editor, Hungarian Radio Music Department, 1957, Columnist, 1958-; Lecturer in Music History, Budapest Music Academy, 1961-; Professor of Musicology, 1975-; Ford Scholarship to study Bartók Archives, NY, 1967-68; Represents Hungarian Radio at Rostrum of Composers, UNESCO, Paris; Critic for New Music Review, Hungarian Radio, Elet es Irodalom (weekly); Specialist in 19th Century Opera, Bartók and contemproary Hungarian music. Publications: Robert Schumann, 1958; Hector Berlioz, 1960, 1980; Bartók Bela Szinpadi Muvei (The Stage Works of BB), 1962; A Szabadito Opera, 1966; Richard Wagner, 1968; Bartók Kalauz (A Guide To B); A Magyar Zeneszerzes 25 Eve (Thirty Years of Hungarian Composition), 1975; Aladar Rácz, 1979; Heilawâc (four Wagner studies), 1983; Az Elso Zarándokév (The First Year of Pilgrimage, Liszt), 1986; Szabolcsi Bence, 1994. Honours: Erkel Prize, 1963; TUC Award, 1970; Labour Order of Merit, 1986; Szecheyi Prize, 1995. Address: Liszt Ferenc Zenemuveszeti Foiskola, 1061 Budapest, Liszt Ferenc ter 8, Hungary.

KROSNICK Aaron (Burton), b. 28 June 1937, New Haven, Connecticut, USA. Professor of Violin; Artist-in-Residence. m. Mary Lou Wesley, 25 August 1961, 1 son. Education: BA magna cum laude, Yale College, 1959; MS, Juilliard School of Music, 1961; Fulbright Scholar, Royal Conservatory of Music, Brussels, Belgium, 1961-62; Major teachers, Howard Boatwright, Joseph Fuchs, Ivan Galamian, Arthur Grumiaux. Career: Concertmaster (and soloist with orchestras), Springfield, Ohio, Symphony Orchestra, 1962-67; Jacksonville Symphony Orchestra, 1969-80; Sewanee Festival Orchestra, 1969-82; Florida Bicentennial Chamber Orchestra, 1976; Faculty Positions, Wittenberg University, 1962-67; Jacksonville Univerity, 1967-; Summers, Syracuse University, Kneisel Hall Summer School of Ensemble Playing, Sewanee Summer Music Centre, Soloist with extensive concerto repertoire; Appearances with Rome Festival Orchestra, Florida Symphony Chamber Orchestra, Jacksonville University Orchestra and many others; Summers of 1985, 86, Concertmaster and featured Artist, Rome Festival in Italy. Recordings: Music of Frederick Delius, Musical Heritage Society. Address: 13734 Bermuda Cay Court, Jacksonville, FL 32225-5426, USA.

KROSNICK Joel, b. 3 Apr 1941, New Haven, Connecticut, USA. Cellist. Education: Studied with William d'Amato, Luigi Silva and Claus Adam; Further study at Columbia University. Career: Co-founded and directed the Group for Contemporary Music at Columbia University, 1962; Professor at University of Iowa, 1963-66; Cellist in Uniersity String Quartet; Professor at University of Massachusetts, 1966-70; Performed with New York Chamber Soloists and made solo tours to Belgrade, Hamburg, Berlin, London and Amsterdam; New York solo debut, 1970; Has given first performances of works by Babbitt, Subotnick and Ligeti; Taught at California Institute of Arts, 1970-74; Cellist with the Juilliard Quartet from 1974; Worldwide tours in the standard repertoire and contemporary works; Performances in London, 1990 (works by Mozart). Recordings include: Albums with the Juilliard Quartet; Carter's Cello Sonata. Address: c/o Library of Congress, Washington DC, USA.

KROSS Siegfried, b. 24 Aug 1930, Wuppertal, Germany. Professor of Musicology. m. Dorothee Brand, 23 Mar 1962, 2 sons. Education: Studied musicology, German literature, psychology, and experimental physics at Universities of Bonn and Freiburg, Br Gurlitt; DPhil, 1956; Habilitation, 1966. Career: Scholar, Deutsche Forschingsgemeinschaft, Vienna, 1959; Assistant, Beethoven Archives, Bonn; Assistant Professor, 1970, Professor, Dean, Faculty of Humanities, 1988, University of Bonn; Vice-President, Landes-Musikrat. Publications: Die Chorwerke von J Brahms, 1957, 2nd edition, 1963; Das Instrumentalkonzert bei G Ph Telemann, 1969; Dokumentation zur Geschichte des Deutschen Liedes Seit, 1973; Geschichte des Deutschen Liedes, 1989; Briefe Robert und Clara Schumanns, 1978, 2nd edition, 1982; Brahms-Bibliographie, 1983. Contributions to: Die Musikforschung, 19th Century Music, 1982; American Choral Review 25, 1983; Brahms, 1983-87; Festchrift: Beitrage zur Geschichle des Konzerts, 1990. Memberships: American Musicological Society; Gesellschaft für Musikforschung. Address: Musikwissenschaftliches Seminar der Universitat Bonn, Am Hof 34, D-53217 Bonn, Germany.

KRPAN Vladimir, b. 11 Jan 1938, Zelina, Croatia. Concert Pianist; Professor of Piano. Education: Baccalaureate, Zagreb; Diploma, Piano Professor, Zagreb, 1960; Mag.art. Masters Degree, Accademia di Santa Cecilia, Rome, 1967; Honour Diploma Degree, Accademia Musicale Chigiana, Sienna, 1966. Debut: Sienna in 1960. Career: Professor of Piano, Zagreb Music Academy, Skopje Music Academy, and TRU Zagreb; Appearances as concert pianist at festivals in Europe and elsewhere; Teacher at summer courses, masterclasses, in Italy, Slovenia, Germany, Serbia and Montenegro, Austria and USA, Internationale Camp of Jeunesse Musicale, Groznjan, Istria, Croatia; Recitals and concerts with orchestras in most European countries and USA, India, Iran, Pakistan, Syria, Lebanon, Korea and Russia; Over 3000 appearances as soloist in recitals and with various orchestras; Member of piano trio, Orlando; Numerous radio and TV appearances. Compositions: Own Cadenzas for Mozart, K D von Dittersdorf, D V M Puccini concertos, 1970. Recordings include: All Chopin Studies; all Brahms; Paganini Variations; All Beethoven Sonatas and concertos; With Trio Orlando: All Mozart Trios and Quartets with piano; all Piano Trios and Piano Quartets from Brahms; All piano music from Croatian composers, 14 CDs. Publications: Different Studies on Piano Technique and Interpretation. Contributions to: Different studies on education reforms in Croatia and abroad; On piano technique and interpretation; Musical Review; Articles for newspapers and Vecernjilist, Croatia. Honours: 1st Prize, National Competition, 1959; Casagraude Terni, 2nd Prize, 1965; Gold Medal, International Busoni Competition, 1966; Vercelli, 3rd Prize, 1966; Prize of Republic of Croatia, 1974, City of Zagreb, 1994 and Society of Croatian Composers, 1980 and 1995; MOIF, IBC, Cambridge, England, 1995. Memberships include: Founder and President, European Piano Teachers Association, European Council President, 1996-97; Organiser, 19th European Conference of EPTA in Dubrovnik, 1997. Current Management: Koncertina Direkciya Zagreb, Kneza Mislava 18, 10000 Zagreb, Croatia. Address: Basaricekova 3, 10000 Zagreb, Croatia.

KRUGER Anna, b. 1965, USA. Violist. Education: Studies at Manhattan School of Music and at Indiana University with James Buswell. Career: Former principal of New Jersey Symphony; Co-Founder, Lark String Quartet, New York; Recent concert tours to Australia, Taiwan, Hong Kong, China, Germany and Netherlands; US appearances at the Lincoln Center, New York, Kennedy Center, Washington DC and in Boston, Los Angeles, Philadelphia, St Louis and San Francisco; Repertoire includes quartets by Haydn, Mozart, Beethoven, Schubert, Dvorak, Brahms, Borodin, Bartók, Debussy and Shostakovich; Concerts at the Wigmore Hall, London, 1994. Honours include: With Lark Quartet: Gold Medals at 1990 Naumberg and 1991 Shostakovich Competitions; Prizewinner at 1991 London International String Quartet, 1991 Melbourne Chamber Music, 1990 Premio Paulio Borciani, Reggio Emilia and 1990 Karl Klinger Competition, Munich. Current Management: Sonata, Glasgow, Scotland. Address: c/o Lark Quartet, 11 Northpark Street, Glasgow G20 7AA, Scotland.

KRUMM Philip (Edwin), b. 7 Apr 1941, Baltimore, Maryland, USA. Composer. Education: Studied orchestration and composition with Raymond Moses (student of Casals), 1957-59, with Frank Sturchio (student of Puccini), St Mary's University, with Ross Lee Finney, University of Michigan, 1962-64 and Karlheinz Stockhausen, University of California, Davis, 1966. Career: Produced early concert series of major modern works at McNay Art Institute, San Antonio, 1960-61; Performer and Composer at Once Festivals, Ann Arbor, MI, 1962-64; Music Hour, TV with Jerry Hunt, 1964; Sampler, TV programme with Robert Wilson, 1964 and others. Compositions: Paragenesis for 2 Violins and Piano, 1959; Axis; Mumma Mix; Soundtrack score for short film, Angel Of God; Music for Clocks, 1962, Once Festival Chamber Orchestra; Concerto for Saxophone, Phil Rehfeldt, 1964, Bass Clarinet Concerto Performer, Martin Walker, 1972, by Scott Vance and Redlands Ensemble, 1978 and 1986; Farewell To LA, electronic theatre piece, 1975; Sound Machine ('66), 1979; Secret Pleasures, dance suite, 1988-89; No Time At All, electronic-instrumental set, 1989; Short pieces for electronics and instruments: Into The Pines, The Gabrieli Thing; Banshee Fantasia, commissioned by Bay Area Pianists for 100th Anniversary of Henry Cowell's Birth; World Premiere by Blue Gene Tyranny, 3 Day Festival, University of California at Berkeley, 1997. Recordings: Sound Machine, by Dallas Chamber Ensemble, Jerry Hunt, 1966; Concerto for bass clarinet, with Scott Vance and Redlands Ensemble, 1996. Publication: Music Without Notes, 1962. Hobbies: Host of weekly new music radio programme. Address: 103 Erkskine Place, San Antonio, TX 78201, USA.

KRUMMACHER Friedhelm (Gustav-Adolf), b. 22 Jan 1936, Berlin, Germany. Professor. m. Aina Maria Landfeldt, 12 June 1964, 1 son, 1 daughter. Education: Abitur, 1954; Musicology, Philosophy, Germanistics studies, Berlin, Marburg and Uppsala, Sweden; Music Teachers Certificate, 1957; DrPhil, Free University of Berlin, 1964; Habilitation, University of Erlangen-Nurnberg, 1972. Career: Assistant, 1965, Private Docent, 1973, Erlangen-Nurnberg University; Professor, Musikhochschule Detmold, 1975; Professor, Christian Albrechts University, Kiel, 1976-; Professor, Director, Musicological Institute, University of Kiel, in charge of Brahms Gesamtausgabe; Leipziger Mendelssohnausgaben. Publications: Die Uberlieferung..., 1965; Mendelssohn der Komponist, 1978; Die Choralbearbeitung..., 1978; Mahlers III Symphonie, 1991; Editor, Kieler Schriften zur Musikwissenschaft, Vol 22-43, 1978-95; Bach and Jahrgang der Choralkanten, 1995; Musik im Norden, 1996. Contributions to: About 100 in Archiv fur Musikwissenschaft, Die Musikforschung, Kongressberichte, Festchriften. Memberships: Vetenskapssocietet Lund, Sweden, 1975; Jungius-Gesellschaft der Wissenschaften, Hamburg, 1990; Norwegian Academy, 1994; Royal Swedish Academy of Music, 1996. Address: Wippen 1, D-24107 Kiel 1, Germany.

KRUSE Heinz, b. 1940, Schleswig, Germany. Tenor. Education: Studied at the Hamburg Musikhochschule. Career: Sang at the Stuttgart Opera, 1966-68, Hamburg from 1970 in such character roles as Pedrillo and David; Guest appearances in Paris, Toulouse and Bayreuth; Heroic tenor roles from 1987 with Florestan at Mainz, Parsifal at Brunswick, Tristan at Kiel and in concert in London in 1993, and in Hamburg, 1995 and in New York's Carnegie Hall, Siegfried at Hamburg in 1993 and in 1994 in Paris and the Edinburgh Festival; Further engagements as the Emperor in Die Frau ohne Schatten, and Albi in Schreker's Schatzgräber, Hamburg in 1989; Sang Florestan in a concert Fidelio at Edinburgh, 1996. Recordings include: Monostatos in Die Zauberflöte. Address: c/o Staatsoper Hamburg, Grosse Theaterstrasse 34, Pf 302448, W-2000 Hamburg 36, Germany.

KRUTIKOV Mikhail, b. 23 Aug 1958, Moscow, Russia. Singer (Bass). Education: Studies at Moscow State Conservatory and the Opera Studio of Bolshoi Opera, 1982-85; Further Studies with Evgeni Nesterenko. Career: Appearances with Bolshoi Opera, 1985-, as Boris Godunov, Pimen, Mephistopheles, Basilio, Mendosa in Prokofiev's The Duenna and Dunua in The Maid of Orleans by Tchaikovsky; Sang in La Straniera and La cena delle Beffe at Wexford Festival, and with the Bolshoi Company on tour to England, 1990; Season 1991-92 as the Inquisitor in Prokofiev's The Fiery Angel at the Prom Concerts, London, The Love for Three Oranges at Florence, the Commendatore in Dargomizshky's Stone Guest at Salzburg and as King Philip in Don Carlos in Deutsche Oper Berlin; Concert engagements at Elizabeth Hall, London, Shostakovich's 14th Symphony in Vancouver and Lausanne, the Verdi Requiem and Tchaikovsky's Moscow Cantata at the Salle Pleyel, Prokofiev's Ivan the Terrible in Rome and Elijah at Dusseldorf. Recordings include: Holofernes in Serov's Judith, Saison Russe; The Gamblers by Shostakovich. Current Management: Athole Still International Management Limited. Address: Foresters Hall, 25-27 Westow Street, London SE19 3RY, England.

KRUYSEN (Rene) Bernard, b. 28 Mar 1933, Montreux, Switzerland. Baritone. Education: Studied at the Hague Conservatory from 1953 and with Pierre Bernac. Career: Many tours of Europe and the USA in German Lieder and French chansons; Repertoire includes music by Bach, Monteverdi, Schumann, Mussorgsky, Debussy, Poulenc, Fauré and Ravel; Recital partnerships with Noel Lee, Hans Henkemans, Paul Niessing and Poulenc; Operatic appearances in Pagliacci and Halka. Recordings include: Fauré's Requiem; Bach Cantatas; Various song albums. Honours include: Prizewinner, Gabriel Fauré Competition, International Competition of Bois-le-Duc, 1958; Grand Prix du Disque, 1962 for Debussy songs. Address: c/o Royal Conservatory of Music and Dance, Juliana van Stolberglaan 1, 2595 CA Den Haag, Netherlands.

KRYSA Oleh, b. 1 June 1942, Lublin, Poland. Violinist. m. Tatiana Tchekina, 24 December 1966, 3 sons. Education: Lviv Musical School, Ukraine; Moscow Conservatory with David Oistrakh. Debut: Lviv, Ukraine, 1958. Career: Professor of Violin, Kiev Conservatory, Moscow Conservatory, Manhattan School of Music; Eastman School of Music; Solo Recital Tours in USSR, Europe, North America, Far East, Australia, New Zealand; First Violin, Beethoven String Quartet, Moscow; Soloist with Chamber Orchestras of Moscow, Leningrad, Berlin, Leipzig, Dresden, Stuttgart, Warsaw, Prague, Budapest, Bucharest, Belgrade, Torino, London, Stockholm, Bergen, New York, Chicago, Washington, Wellington, Cape Town. Recordings: Violin Concerto by Mozart; Broch Scottish Fantasy; Viotti No 22; Tchaikovsky; Wieniawski No 1; Bloch; Schnittke No 3; Works for Violin and Piano by Ravel, Szymanowski, Schulhoff, Suk, Schnittke, Paganini, Berio, Bazzini; String Quartets by Mozart, Beethoven, Brahms, Shostakovich, Berg, Schnittke, Arensky String Sextet by Tchaikovsky. Honours: Wieniawski Competition 2nd Prize, 1962; Paganini Competition 1st Prize, 1963; Tchaikovsky Competition 3rd Prize, 1966; Montreal Competition 2nd Prize, 1969; Outstanding Artist of Ukrainian Republic, 1970. Hobby: Soccer. Address: 265 Westminster Road, Rochester, NY 14607, USA.

KRZANOWSKA Grazyna, b. 1 Mar 1952, Legnica, Poland. Composer. Education: Studied in Wroclaw. Career: Teacher at the Bielsko-Biala Music School. Compositions include: Melodies, cantata, 1975; Passacaglia for Orchestra, 1976; Drumroll Symphony, 1978; Bonfires for 2 Voices and Chamber Ensemble, 1979; String Quartet No 2, 1980; The Little Choral Symphony, 1985; Silver Line for 15 Strings, 1991. Honours include: Prizewinner at the 1988 Karol Szymanowski Competition. Address: c/o ZAIKS, 2 rue Hipoteczna, 00 092 Warsaw, Poland.

KUBERA Joseph, b. 25 May 1949, Buffalo, NY, USA. Pianist. Education: Studied at the Community Music School in Buffalo and with Walter Hautzig at the Peabody Conservatory, MA, 1970. Career: Has given performances of works by Howard Riley, John Cage, Tcherenin and Carson Kievman; Member of the SEM Ensemble, 1972, New Music Ensemble of the San Francisco Conservatory, 1972-74 and with Steve Reich and Musicians, 1979; Tours of America with the Merce Cunningham Dance Company, 1977-80; Performances of music by Josef Matthias Hauer, originator of a twelve-note theory of composition. Recordings include: Hauer's Atonale Musik, Op 20. Honours include: Fellowship from the Center for The Creative and Performing Arts, 1974-76; NEA Grant to prepare for performance of Music Of Changes by John Cage, 1981.

KUBIAK Teresa, b. 26 Dec 1937, Lodz, Poland. Soprano. Education: Studied at the Lodz Music Academy with Olga Olgina. Debut: Lodz in 1965 as Halka in Moniusko's opera. Career: Sang Michaela in Carmen in 1967; Appeared in the 1969 premiere of The Story of St John and Herod by Twardowski; US debut at Carnegie Hall in 1970 as Shulamith in Goldmark's Die Kōnigin von Saba; Glyndebourne Festival in 1971 as Lisa in The Queen of Spades and Juno in La Calisto by Cavalli-Leppard; Covent Garden in 1972 as Madama Butterfly and Metropolitan Opera from 1973 as Lisa, Jenufa, Giorgietta in Il Tabarro, Tosca and Elisabeth in Tannhâuser; Appearances in San Francisco, Chicago, Houston, Miami, Leipzig, Prague, Venice, Barcelona and Lisbon; Other roles include Aida, Euryanthe, Senta, Tatiana, Tosca and Ellen Orford. Recordings include: La Calisto; Eugene Onegin; Euryanthe. Address: Lodz Music Academy, ul Gdanska 32, 90-716 Lodz, Poland.

KUBICKA Vitazoslav, b. 11 Oct 1953, Bratislava, Czechoslovakia. Composer; Broadcasting Editor Music; Dramaturgist. m. Gabriela Jurolekova, 2 Jul 1988, 1 son, 1 daughter. Education: Composition, University of Music, Bratislava. Debut: Rostrum of Composers, UNESCO, Paris, 1982. Career: Scenic Music for Radio, 130; Television, 20; Films, 12. Compositions include: Orchestral: Dramatic Overture for Large Orchestra, 1980; Concerto for Piano and Orchestra, 1984; Maturing, Overture for Orchestra, 1984; Fantasy for Violoncello and Large Orchestra, 1985; Chamber Opuses: Fantasy for Flute and Piano, 1979; Quintet for Clarinet, Violin, Viola, Violoncello and Piano, 1982; Winter, Sonata for Piano, 1986; Choral: Fugue for Children's Choir, 1982; Electroacoustic: Dedicated to Mussorgski, 1981; Satyr and Nymph, 1985; For Children and Youth: Five Stories for Piano, 1982, 1985. Honours: Jan Levoslav Bella Prize, Slovak Music Fund Bratislava, 1988; Priz Critique Radiomagazin Bratislava, 1989. Membership: Union of Slovak Composer. Hobbies: Nature; Tourism. Address: Drotarska 9, 81102 Bratislava, Slovakia.

KUBIK Ladislav, b. 26 Aug 1946, Prague, Czechoslovakia. Composer. m. Natalie Bartosevicova, 7 Nov 1974, 1 son, 1 daughter. Education: Composition, 1970, Theory of Music, 1972, PhD, 1981, Prague Academy of Music. Career: Music Director, Czechoslovak Radio Prague, 1979-83; General Secretary, Union of Czech Composers and Concert Artists, 1983-. Compositions: Symphonic Works: Symphony, 1970; Drammatic Toccata, 1972; Concerto for Piano and Orchestra, 1974; Hommage a Majakowski, 1976; Concerto for Violin and Orchestra, 1980; Choral Works: Songs of Hope, 1982; Chamber-Cantat: Lament of a Warrior's Wife, 1974; Radio Opera: Solaris, 1975; Ballet: Song of Man, 1984; Vocal Symphony Works: February, 1973; Wolkeriana, 1982; To the Earth of Future, 1985; Songs with Orchestra: Words; Chamber Music: 2 String Quartets, 1981, 1986; Trio Concertante, 1983; Duo Concertante. Recordings: 15 works recorded on record and numerous in Czechosolvak and foreign radio broadcasts. Current Management: Charles University, Prague. Address: Na Brezince 6, 150 00 Praha 5, Czech Republic.

KUBIK Reinhold, b. 22 Mar 1942, Vienna, Austria. Musicologist. 1 son, 1 daughter. Education: Abitur, Humanistic College, Vienna II, 1960; PhD, University Erlangen-Nuremberg, Germany, 1980; Studied Piano, Composition, Conducting wth Hans Swarowsky, Hochschule fur Musik, Vienna. Career: Conductor, Deutsche Oper am Rhein, Dusseldorf (Duisburg) and many European cities including Lille, Barcelona, Ljubljana, 1966-74; Pianist; Composer; Choirmaster; Lecturer, 1980; Proprietor, Hanssler Musik Verlag, Kirchheim, Germany, 1989-; Visiting Professor, Yale University, USA, 1987-91; Production Manager, Universal Edition, Vienna, since 1992; Chief Editor of Gustav Mahler Gesamtausgabe and of Wiener Urtext Edition. Publications: Handels Rinaldo, 1980; About 120 editions including 80 cantatas by J S Bach (Hanssler), EdM 96, 106 and 110, Schubert,Lazarus (Neue Schubert Ausgae II/10). Contributions to: Festschrift Arnold Feil, 1985; KB Stuttgart, 1985; Festschrift Martin Ruhnke, 1986; Veroffentlichungen der International, Handel-Akademie Karlsruhe, vols 2, 3 and 4, 1988; Handel-Symposium Halle, 1989. Address: A-1090 Wien, Liechtenstein Strasse 39/6, Germany.

KUBISCH Christina, b. 31 Jan 1948, Bremen, Germany. Composer. Education: Studied in Bremen and Stuttgart and further at Hamburg, Graz and Zurich, 1969-74. Career: Further study in electrical engineering at Milan and has been active in Germany and abroad as a creator of sound installations; Resident in Berlin from 1987 and teacher at Munster from 1990. Works include: Sound installations at Vienna, The Magnetic Gardens in 1983, Milan in 1985, Amsterdam, Klangzelt in 1986, Sydney, Landscape in 1990 and Kobe, Japan; Sound collages include Liquid Movie, Milan in 1981 and has created further electronic pieces including Night Flights, 1987. Address: c/o GEMA, Postfach 80 07 67, D-81607 Munich, Germany.

KUBITA Jaroslav, b. 13 June 1966, Olomouc, Moravia. Musician (Bassoon Player). Education: Conservatory in Prague, Academy of Music - Music High School in Prague. Career: Solo Bassoonist with Smetana Theatre, Prague, 1984-89; Member of the ensembles in Modo Camerale, Prague Baroque Ensemble, 1986-; Solo Bassonist with Prague Radio Symphony Orchestra, 1989-96; Member of the Czech Philharmonic Orchestra, 1996-. Recordings: Concertos for bassoon by: W A Mozart, C M Weber, J A Rossetti, J N Hummel, J B Vanhal; Sonatas by: C Saint-Saëns, H Dutilleux, E Bozza, W A Mozart, H E Apostel; Trio sonatas by: J D Zelenka; Chamber works as member of the In Modo Chamber Ensemble; Works by: Beethoven, Mozart, Poulenc. Honours: 1st Prizes at the National Competition of the Czech Ministry of Culture, 1986, 1990; 3rd Prize at the C M von Weber Competition, Munich, 1987; 1st Prize at the Wloszakovice Competition for Bassoon, Poland, 1988; 2nd Prize, F Gillet Competition, Manchester, 1989; 1st Prize at the Prague Spring Competition for Bassoon, 1991. Memberships: Fórum Mladých (Youth Forum) Přítomnost; International Double Reed Society, USA. Hobbies: Hiking; Swimming. Address: Na Rokytce 30/1029, 18000 Praha 8 Liben, Czech Republic.

KUBIZEK Augustin, b. 15 Oct 1918, Vienna, Austria. Professor of Music; Composer. m. Alina Gunia, 5 Feb 1992, 2 sons, 2 daughters. Education: Teachers' Training College, 5 years; State Diploma in Singing, 1949; Choral and Orchestral Conducting and Composition, 1955-56. Career: Professor, Academy of Music, Vienna, 1956; University Professor, 1979; Professor Emeritus, 1985. Compositions: Over 200 works including sacred choral works, Neue Messe, 1970; St Michael-Messe, 1970; Missa a Cappella, 1983; Jakobs Stern, 1985; Motets; Memento Homo; Psalmen-Motets, Div Zyklen; Secular works; Symphonic works; Instrumental concerti for clarinet, violoncello, viola and others; Opera, Nathan der Weise, 1994; Oratorios, Stationen; Hadmar der Kuenringer; Works for voice and instruments; Chamber music. Recordings: Numerous works recorded on disc and radio. Address: Schoenburgstrasse 13/27, A-1040 Vienna, Austria.

KUBO Yoko, b. 5 Dec 1956, Nishinomiya, Japan. Composer; Pianist; College Lecturer. Education: BA, 1979, MA, 1981, Osaka College of Music; Diplome d'Etudes Approfondies, University of Paris, France, 1985. Debut: 1979. Career: Many concerts of her compositions, Japan and France, 1979-; Lecturer, Osaka College of Music, 1981-; Associate, Institut Recherche Coordination Acoustique/Musique, Paris, France, 1984-. Compositions: La Sensation de Vingtième Siecle, 12 Percussionists, 1977; Collage, Orchestra, 1978; Objet, 2 Pianos and Percussions, 1979; Play, Violin, Violoncello, Piano, 1979; Crossword, Piano, 1980; Mon parc, String Orchestra, 1980; Quatuor à Cordes No 2, 1980; Concerto pour Violon No 1, 1981; Puzzle, 3 Marimbas, 1981; On the Tree, Soprano, 8 Voices, Piano, 1981; Chikya ni hajimete yuki ga futta hi no koto, Soprano, 8 Voices, Piano, 1981; Quatuor à Cordes No 3, 1981; Concerto pour Orgue, 4 Cuivres et Percussions, 1981; Livre Illustré des chats, String Orchestra, 1982; ...SONG..., 5 Voices and Piano, 1982; Quatuor à Cordes No 4, 1982; Paysage, Flute, Percussion, Piano, 1983; Quatuor pour Flute, Hautbois, Violon et Violoncelle, 1983; Quintette pour Piano No 1, 1983; Marche du roi (extract from Le Roi Nu), String Orchestra, 1984; Espace, 11 Players, 1985; Vision, Piano, 1987; Concerto pour 7 Interprètes, 1987. Address: No 9-25 2-chome, Nigawa-cho Nishinomiya-shi, Hyogo-ken, Japan.

KUCERA Premsyl, b. 18 Apr 1960, Prague, Czech Republic. Composer. Divorced, 1 son. Education: MA, Prague Conservatory, Prague Academy of Performing Arts, composition with J Ceremuga, absolutorium, 1981. Appointments: Collaboration with theatres in Prague, Ostrava, Hradec Králové, Ceské Budejovice and other Czech cities, with Czech Film Studio and Czech TV (for which he composed scenic and film music). Compositions: TV ballets: Statuettes, 1988; Stories, 1996; Also for Laterna Magica; Symphonic works: Balladic Sentences, 1987; Visions, 1989; Chamber music: Brass Trio (trumpet, cornet, trombone), 1989; Vocal cycle, When You Feel Lonely (on poems by V Nezval), 1989. Recordings: TV ballet Statuettes, Balladic Sentences for large orchestras; Music for the theatre; Arthur, serial of animated cartoons, 1997; Songs and music produced and edited in proper digital studio. Honour: The Prize of the Ministry for Culture of the Czech Republic for Balladic Sentences, 1988. Memberships: Association of Czech Composers, Concert Artists and Musicologists; Union of Copyright, OSA. Hobbies: Electronics; Hunting. Current Management: Adastra Agency for production, editing and publication of music. Address: Premsyl Kucera, Jizni II 778, CZ-141 00 Prague 4, Czech Republic.

KUCERA Vaclav, b. 29 Apr 1929, Prague, Czechoslovakia. Composer; Musicologist. m. Maria, née Jeneová, 11 Aug 1951, 2 sons. Education: PhD, Charles University, Prague; Tchaikovsky Conservatory in Moscow: Composition with Vissarion Shebalin, Musicology with L Mazel, V Zuckerman, N Tumanina, graduated with ballet Brigands Fire and a dissertation about Leos Janacek, 1956. Career: Music Department of Radio Prague, 1956-59; Cabinet for New Music Studies, 1959-62; Institute of Musicology, 1962-69; General Secretary, Union of Czech Composers and Concert Artists, 1969-83; Teacher of Composition, 1972-, Professor, 1988-, at Music Faculty of Academy for Performing Arts in Prague. Compositions: About 100 include: The Pied Piper, 1964; Genesis, 1965; Duodrama, 1967; Tableau, 1970; Argot, 1970; Diario, 1971; Salut, 1975; Consciousness of Continuities, 1976; Aphorisms, 1978; Epigrams, 1978; Aquarelles, 1981; Capriccios, 1983; Eruptions, 1984; Duettinos, 1988; Celebrations of Phantasy, 1991; Tuning, 1994; Concierto Imaginativo, 1994; Electroacoustic compositions: Lidice, 1972; Spartacus, 1976. Recordings: Numerous on record and CD. Publications: M P Mussorgsky - Music of Life, 1959; Talent, Mastery, World Outlook, 1962; New Trends in Soviet Music, 1967; Studies: Artistic Featuring in Music, 1965; Experiment in Music, 1973. Contributions to: Articles on music theory, aesthetics, analyses of New Music. Honours: Prize of the Queen Marie-José, Geneva, 1970; Prix d'Italia, 1972; Prize of Union of Czech Composers and Concert Artists, 1983; Prix di Trento, 1994. Memberships: Czech Association of Music Artists and Musicologists; ISCM; AEC; Czech Union for Copyrights. Hobbies: Literature; Fine arts; Film; Television. Address: Jizni II, 778, CZ-141 00 Prague 4, Czech Republic.

KUCHLER Peter, b. 10 May 1940, Dresden, Germany. Tenor Singer. Education: Studied at the Dresden Musikhochschule. Debut: In 1969, at Dresden-Radebeul as Don Curzio in Le Nozze di Figaro. Career: Sang at the Dresden and Leipzig State Operas as Mozart's Pedrillo and Monostatos, Ernesto in Don Pasquale, the Fentons of Nicolai and Verdi, and Truffaldino in The Love for Three Oranges at Dresden in 1990; Many concert engagements. Address: c/o Staatsoper Dresden, Theaterplatz 2, 0-8010 Dresden, Germany.

KUCHTA Gladys, b. 16 Jun 1923, Chicipee, Massachusetts, USA. Singer (Soprano). Education: Studied at Mannes College and the Juilliard School, New York; Further study in Italy. Debut: Florence 1951, as Donna Elvira in Don Giovanni. Career: Sang at Flensburg from 1953, debut as Leonore in Fidelio; Stuttgart Staatsoper as Tosca; Vienna Staatsoper as Elektra; Sang in Berlin from 1958, notably at the Deutsche Oper; Hamburg Staatsoper as Isolde and in other operas by Wagner; Metropolitan Opera 1961, as Chrysothemis in Elektra; Bayreuth Festival, 1968, Sieglinde in Die Walküre; Guest at the Paris Opera, 1972, as the Empress in Die Frau ohne Schatten; Guest appearances in London, Buenos Aires, San Francisco, Tokyo, Dusseldorf and Edinburgh; Retired from stage 1975 and taught in Dusseldorf.

KUDRIASCHOV Vladimir, b. 1947, Russia. Tenor Singer. Education: Studied at the Gnessin Conservatory, Moscow. Career: Sang at the Stanislavsky Theatre in Moscow, 1971-83, then at the Bolshoi Theatre; Roles have included Sobinin in Glinka's Life for The Tsar, Shuisky in Boris Godunov, Count Almaviva, Rodolfo and Sergei in Lady Macbeth of Mtsensk; Guest at Edinburgh in 1991 as Diak in Christmas Eve by Rimsky-Korsakov. Address: c/o Bolshoi Theatre, 103009 Moscow, Russia.

KUDRIAVCHENKO Katerina, b. 2 Mar 1958, Karpnsk, Sverdlovskaya, Russia. Singer (Soprano). m. Paolo Kudriavchenko. Education: Graduated, Tchaikovsky Conservatoire, Moscow, 1985. Career: Member of Bolshoi Opera, 1986-, as Iolanta, Tatiana, Agnes Sorell in The Maid of Orleans, Marfa in The Tsar's Bride, Gilda, Antonida in A Life for the Tsar, Lisa in The Queen of Spades, Prokofiev's The Duenna, Rachmaninov's Francesca, Violetta, Mimi, Liu and Oxsana in Rimsky's Christmas Eve; Western debut as Iolanta at La Scala, 1989; Season 1990-91 with Bolshoi Opera on tour to Spain, Italy, USA (Metropolitan), Japan and Glasgow, Scotland; Freelance Artist debut as Tatiana for New Israel Opera Company at Tel Aviv, 1992; Season 1992-93 as Mimi with Scottish Opera, Liu and Titania at the Bolshoi; Sang Butterfly at Bologna, 1996. Honours include: Gold Medallist, Madam Butterfly Competition, Miami, 1990. Current Management: Athole Still International Management Limited. Address: Athole Still Ltd, Foresters Hall, 25-27 Westow Street, London SE19 3RY, England.

KUDRIAVCHENKO Paolo, b. 12 Aug 1952, Odessa, Crimea, Russia. Singer (Tenor). m. Katerina Kudriavchenko. Education: Studied at Tchaikovsky Conservatory, Odessa. Career: Sang first with Odessa Opera, then Kiev Opera; Bolshoi Opera, Moscow, 1984-, in Rimsky's Invisible City of Kitezh and as Canio, Turiddu, Dimitri in Boris Godunov, Don José and Jeromir in Mlada; Sang Sobinin in A Life for the Tsar with the Bolshoi Company at La Scala and made US debut, 1989, as Manrico for Greater Miami Opera (repeated for Omaha Opera, 1991), as Turiddu and Dimitri; Season 1991-92 as Turiddu at Munich Staatsoper and as Ernani for Welsh National Opera, followed by Manrico for Scottish Opera, Ishmaele in Nabucco at Bregenz Festival, 1993, and Canio at Rouen; season 1993-94 as Calaf and Radames at the Bolshoi; Many concert appearances. Current Management: Athole Still International Management Limited. Address: Athole Still Ltd, Foresters Hall, 25-27 Westow Street, London SE19 3RY, England.

KUEBLER David, b. 23 Jul 1947, Detroit, Michigan, USA. Singer (Tenor). Education: Studied with Thomas Peck in Chicago and Audrey Field in London. Career: Sang in the chorus of the Chicago Opera; Solo career with the Santa Fe Opera from 1972; European debut Berne Opera 1974, as Tamino; Sang Mozart and bel canto roles with Cologne Opera; Glyndebourne Festival, 1976, as Ferrando in Cosi fan tutte; Metropolitan Opera from 1979; Bayreuth Festival, 1980-82, as the Steersman in Der fliegande Holländer; Santa Fe Opera, 1984, in We Come to the River by Henze; Other roles include Don Ottavio, Rodolfo, Pinkerton, Lionel (Martha), Jacquino in Fidelio, Paolino in Il Matrimonio Segreto and Gianneto in La Gazza Ladra; Donizetti's Ernesto and Nemorino; Glyndebourne, 1987-90, Strauss's Flamand and Matteo; Schwetzingen Festival, 1988, as Rossini's Almaviva, (1989 in La Cambiale di Matrimonio); sang Don Ottavio in Rome and Madrid, 1989; Schwetzingen 1990 as Doric in Rossini's La Scala di Seta; Sang in The Spectre's Bride by Dvorak at the 1991 Promenade Concerts, London; Sang the Berlioz Faust at Wellington and Bregenz, 1992; Rome Opera, 1997 in I Vespri Siciliani. Recordings include: Mitridate re di Ponto by Mozart; Fidelio; Videos of La Scala di Seta and Idomeneo, as Idamante. Address: 165 West 57th Street, New York, NY 10019, USA.

KUENTZ Paul, b. 4 May 1930, Mulhouse, France. Conductor. m. Monique Frasca-Colombier, 1956. Education: Studied at the Paris Conservatoire, 1947-50, with Noel Gallon, Georges Hugon and Eugene Bigot. Career: Founded the Paul Kuentz Chamber Orchestra, 1951: many tours of Europe and the USA, including the orchestral works of Bach at Saint-Severin and concert at Carnegie Hall, 1968; Frequent performances of French music, including premieres of works by P M Dubois, J Casterede and J Charpentier; Founded Paul Kuentz Chorus, 1972. Recordings include: Bach's Orchestral Suites, Mass in B Minor and Musikalisches Opfer; Vivaldi's Four Seasons, and other concertos; Flute Concertos by Haydn, Blavet, Mozart, Leclair and Pergolesi; Music by Delalande, Mouret, Gabrieli and Gluck; Mozart's Concerto K299, Requiem, Bastien und Bastienne and Church Sonatas; Harp concertos by Handel, Albrechtsberger, Boieldieu, Wagenseil and Dittersdorf; Haydn Symphonies Nos 85 and 101.

KUERTI Anton (Emil), b. Vienna, 1938. Pianist; Composer. m. Kristine Bogyo, 13 Sept 1973, 2 sons. Education: BM, Cleveland Institute of Music; Diploma, Curtis Institute, 1959; PhD (Hon), York University, 1985, Laurentian University, 1985. Career: Soloist, New York Philharmonic, Cleveland Orchestra, Detroit Symphony, Philadelphia Orchestra, Buffalo Philharmonic, San Francisco Symphony, Denver Symphony, Over 25 appearances with Toronto Symphony and National Arts Centre Orchestra (Ottawa), Dresden Staatskapelle, Leipzig Gewandhaus, London Symphony; Tours worldwide including Soviet Union, Far East, Australia, Latin America; Numerous TV appearances, radio broadcasts; Founder, Festival of Sound, Parry Sound, Ontario. Compositions: Linden Suite for Piano, 1970; String Quartet, 1972; Violin Sonata and Symphony Epomeo, 1975; Piano Man Suite and Piano Concerto, 1985; Clarinet Trio, 1989; Concertino, Jupiter Concerto, 1996. Recordings: Recordings include complete cycle of Beethoven Sonatas and Concerti; Mendelssohn Piano Concerto; Complete Schubert Sonatas. Contributions to: Articles on Carl Czerny in Piano Today and Queen's Quarterly. Honours: Leventritt Award, 1957; Honorary Doctorate, Cleveland Institute of Music, 1996; Toronto Arts Award, 1997. Memberships: Amnesty International; Canadian Scientists and Scholars. Current Management: Concertmasters Incorporated, 22 Linden Street, Toronto, M4Y 1V6. Address: 20 Linden Street, Toronto, Ontario, Canada M4Y 1V6.

KUHLMANN Kathleen, b. 7 Dec 1950, San Francisco, CA, USA. Mezzo-Soprano Singer. Education: Studied at the Opera School of the Lyric Opera Chicago. Career includes: Sang in Chicago from 1979 with debut as Maddalena in Rigoletto; Sang Meg Page in Falstaff at La Scala Milan, 1980 and Charlotte and Rosina at Cologne Opera, 1982; British debut at Covent Garden as Ino and Juno in new production of Semele in 1982; Other Rossini roles include: Arsace in Semiramide, Tancredi at 1986 Wexford Festival, Andromaca in Ermione in Naples, Fallerio in Bianca e Falliero, and Isabella in L'Italiana in Algeri; Metropolitan Opera debut as Charlotte in Werther in 1989; Returned to Covent Garden as Rosina (1986) and in Semele; Carmen and Bradamante in Alcina, 1991-92; Season 1992 included Semper Oper Dresden, BBC Proms, Rossini Arias, Recital at Purcell Room, London, Concert of Nations in Red Square, Moscow; Season 1993 included Carmen at Barcelona, Rossini's Stabat Mater with Dusseldorf Symphony, Beethoven's 9th at Hamburg; Guest artist with many of Europe's premier orchestras; Sang Cornelia in Giulio Cesare at the 1997 Munich Festival and at the Opéra Bastille, Paris. Recordings include: Many for various labels; Several videos including: La Cenerentola from the Glyndebourne Festival, Il Ritorno d'Ulisse in Patria (version by Henze) from the Salzburg Festival, Vivaldi's Orlando Furioso from the San Francisco opera, and L'Incoronzione di Poppea from the Schwetzingen Festival. Honour: Italian Critics Award, 1988. Current Management: Haydn Rawstron. Address: c/o Hadyn Rawstron International Management, 36 Station Road, London SE20 7BQ, England.

KUHN Gustav, b. 28 August 1947, Salzburg, Germany. Conductor. m. Andrea, 6 January 1971, 1 son, 1 daughter. Education: Studies, Academies of Salzburg & Vienna, Universties of Salzburg & Vienna; PhD, 1970. Career: Conducting: Vienna State Opera, 1977, Munich National Theatre, 1978, Covent Garden, London, 1979, Glyndebourne, Munich Opera Festival, Salzburg Festival, 1980, USA Chicago, 1981, Grand Opera, Paris, 1982, Scala Milan, 1984, Arena of Verona, 1985, Rossini Opera Festival, Pesaro, 1987, Salzburg Festival, 1989, Japan, Tokyo, 1991, Salzburg Festival, 1992; Founder, Institut für aleatorische Musik, Salzburg, 1974; Concerts of Contemporary Music in Collaboration with Josef Anton Riedl, 1983-85. Publication: Aus Liebe zur Musik, 1993. Honours: 1st Prize, International Conducting Contest, ORF; Lilly Lehmann Medal, Mozarteum Foundation; Max Reinhardt Medal, Federal Country of Salzburg; Giovanni Zenatello Award, Organisation l'Asco di verona; Senator of Honour, Florence with European Award, Lorenzo il Magnifico; President of Honour, Deutsche Rossini Gesellschaft. Address: Hans Adler, Auguste Viktoria Strabe 64, 14199 Berlin, Germany.

KUHN Laura (Diane), b. 19 Jan 1953, San Francisco, California, USA. Musicologist; Former Assistant Professor. Education: Vocal and piano training, San Francisco, 1975-82; BA, Dominican College, San Rafael, California, 1981; MA, 1986, PhD, 1992, University of California at Los Angeles. Apointments: Member, San Francisco Symphony Chorus, 1980, Oakland Symphony Chorus, 1980-82; Music Critic, Independent Journal, Marin County, California, 1980-82; Reviewer, Los Angeles Times, 1982-87, New York Times, 1986-89; Vocalist, Daniel Lentz Group,

1983-85; Editorial Associate, Nicolas Slonimsky, 1984-95; Associate, John Cage, 1986-92; Assistant Professor, Arizona State University West, Phoenix, 1991-96; Founder-Director, John Cage Trust, New York City, 1993-; Secretary, American Music Center, New York City, 1995-. Publications: Baker's Biographical Dictionary of Musicians (contributing editor), 7th edition, 1984, 8th edition, 1992; A Pronouncing Pocket Manual of Musical Terms (editor), 5th edition, 1995; Baker's Biographical Dictionary of 20th Century Classical Musicians (editor), 1997. Contributions to: Supplement to Music Quarterly; Perspectives of New Music. Membership: American Musicological Society. Address: 10410 North Cave Creek Road, No 2115, Phoenix, AZ 85020, USA.

KUHN Pamela, b. 1960, Oregon, USA. Singer (Soprano). Education: Bachelor of Music, University of Oregon; Master of Music, University of Southern California with Gwendolyn Koldofsky and Margaret Schaper. Debut: London, Wigmore Hall with Graham Johnson, 1984. Career: Recitals at the Purcell Room with Stephen Wilder, Stephen Coombs and Geoffrey Parsons; Isle of Man Festival with Roger Steptoe; Oratorio includes Rossini Petite Messe Solennelle at Queen Elizabeth Hall, Verdi Requiem at Fairfield Halls, Dartington (Diego Masson), Oregon Bach Festival (Helmut Rilling), Penderecki Polish Requiem at Oregon Bach Festival (Penderecki), Brahms Requiem at the Royal Festival Hall and in the USA, Beethoven Missa Solemnis in Lugano, Switzerland, Janacek Glagolitic Mass at Salisbury Cathedral; Opera: Ariadne at Dartington, Aida with Florentine Opera in Milwaukee, Rezia with Scottish Opera at La Fenice, Venice, Soloist in Oberon conducted by Seiji Ozawa at Tanglewood, Edinburgh Festival and Frankfurt Alte Oper, High Priestess with Scottish Opera; Other roles include Micaela, Tosca, Amelia and Sieglinde; Further concert repertory includes operatic evenings with City of Birmingham Symphony Orchestra, Southampton Symphony and Ernest Read Symphony at the Barbican, Shostakovich Symphony 14 with Mark Wigglesworth at St John's Smith Square and Four Last Songs in Nottingham. Address: Lombardo Associates, 61 West 62nd, Suite 6F, New York, NY 10023, USA.

KUHSE Hanne-Lore, b. 28 Mar 1925, Schwann, Mecklenburg, Germany. Singer (Soprano). Education: Studied with Charlotte Menzel in Rostock, at the Stern Conservatory, Berlin and with Paul Lohmann in Potsdam. Debut: Gera 1951, as Leonore in Fidelio. Career: Sang at the Staatstheater Schwerin, 1952-59, Leipzig from 1959; Member of the Staatsoper Berlin from 1963; Guest appearances in Dresden, Budapest, Paris, Moscow, Prague, Cologne, Hamburg and Bayreuth; US debut 1967, as Isolde at Philadelphia; London debut Albert Hall, 1967; Philharmonic Hall, New York, 1967, in the US premiere of Turandot by Busoni; London 1973, as Mita in the British premiere of Der Friedensengel by Siegfried Wagner; Other roles include the Queen of Night, Donna Anna, Lady Macbeth, Tosca, Senta, Venus, Brünnhilde, the Marschallin, Marie in Wozzeck, Kundry, Aida, Abigaille and Ariadne; Guest Professor at the Musikhochschule Weimar, 1973; Professor at the Musikhochschule Berlin from 1974. Recordings: Radamisto by Handel; La Forza del Destino; Der fliegande Holländer; Tiefland; Die Zauberflöte. Address: c/o Deutsche Hochschule für Musik, Otto Grotewohlstrasse 19, D-108 Berlin, Germany.

KUIJKEN Barthold, b. 8 Mar 1949, Dilbeek, Brussels, Belgium. Flautist; Recorder Player; Conductor. Education: Studied at the Conservatoires of Bruges, Brussels and the Hague, with Frans Vester and Frans Brueggen; Self-taught on the Baroque flute. Career: Concerts in Europe, North and South America, Japan, Australia, New Zealand and Israel with his brothers, Lucy van Dael, René Jacobs, Frans Brueggen, Gustav Leonhardt, Bob van Asperen, the Parnassus Ensemble, La Petite Bande and the Collegium Aureum; Teacher of Baroque flute at the Hague and Brussels Conservatories; Repertoire includes music by Telemann, Handel, Haydn, Bach and Mozart; Took part in the Towards Bach concert series on the South Bank, London, August 1989. Recordings: Telemann, W F, J S and C P E Bach, Handel, Leclair sonatas, Haydn trios and quartets, Mozart quartets and concerti, Couperin and Rameau chamber music, Telemann fantasies for transverse flute, German chamber music, J S Bach Suite and Brandenburg Concertos; Various labels. Publication: J S Bach's flute compositions (editor). Address: Zwartschaapstraat 38, B-1755 Gooik, Belgium.

KUIJKEN Sigiswald, b. 16 Feb 1944, Dilbeek, near Brussels, Belgium. Violinist; Conductor. Education: Studied at Bruges Conservatory from 1952; Conservatoire Royale Brussels from 1960 under M Raskin; Self-taught on Baroque violin. Career: Began to re-establish old technique of violin playing in 1969; Played in the avant-garde group Musique-Nouvelle until 1974, and in the Alarius Ensemble from 1964-72; Teacher of Baroque violin at the Hague Conservatory from 1971 and at the Brussels Conservatory from 1994-; Founder of the Baroque orchestra, La Petite Bande in 1972; Tours of Europe, USA, Australia and Japan in chamber music and solo programmes; Debut concert with the Orchestra of the Age of Enlightenment in 1986, Elizabeth Hall London; Collaborations for chamber music mainly with his brothers, Barthold and Wieland, and Robert Kohnen, as well as Gustav Leonhardt; Founded the Kuijken String Quartet in 1986, specializing in Haydn and Mozart; Co Artistic Director of the Towards Bach concert series on South Bank, London, 1989; Conducted La Petite Bande in Haydn's L'Infedeltà Delusa at Antwerp in 1990; Bach's B Minor Mass for the EBU at Antwerp, 1997. Recordings include: Many with La Petite Bande including: Music by Lully, Muffat, Gluck, Haydn's Creation and Symphonies, Mozart's Requiem and Davidde Penitente, Così fan tutte, 1992 and Brandenburg Concertos, 1994; Bach Sonatas with Gustav Leonhardt; 7 Hadyn Symphonies; Mozart Concert Arias; German Chamber Music; Don Giovanni, 1997. Honours include: Deutsche Schallplattenpreis several times; Grand Prix du Disque, France several times; Deutsche Handel Preis, 1994. Address: La Petite Bande, Geert Robberechts Vital Decostestraat 72, 3000 Leuven, Belgium.

KUIJKEN Wieland, b. 31 Aug 1938, Dilbeek, Brussels, Belgium. Viola da Gamba Player; Cellist; Conductor. Education: Studied at the Bruges Conservatory and at the Brussels Conservatoire Royale, 1957-62; Self taught on the Viola de Gamba. Career: Played with the Alarius Ensemble, 1959-72; Played in the avant-garde group Musiques Nouvelles from 1962; Kuijken Early Music Group from 1972; Teacher at the Conservatories of Antwerp, Brussels and the Hague; Master classes in Britain, Innsbruck and the USA; Festival appearances at Flanders, Saintes and the English Bach Festival; Tour of New Zealand and Australia with Gustav Leonhardt, 1979; Cellist with the Kuijken String Quartet from 1986: London debut 1990; Collaborations with his brothers, Frans Brueggen, Alfred Deller and René Jacobs; Repertoire includes music by French, English, Italian and German composers; Performed in the Towards Bach concert series on the South Bank, London, August 1989. Recordings include: Leclair Flute Sonatas, Marais Pièces de Viole du Cinquieme Livre and German Chamber Music. Address: c/o Allied Artists Agency, 42 Montpeiler Square, London, SW7 1JZ, England.

KUJAWINSKA Krystyna, b. 4 Apr 1938, Kalisz, Poland. Soprano. Education: Studied at the Poznan Academy, 1962-67. Debut: Bytom in 1967 as Arabella. Career: Sang at the Poznan Opera from 1970 notably as Elisabeth de Valois, Aida, Desdemona, Micaela, Butterfly, Gioconda and Santuzza; Later roles have included Tosca, the Forza Leonora and Turandot; Guest appearances in France as Electra (Idomeneo), Hamburg as Aida, Parma as Halka, Dresden in Verdi Requiem and Leonora (La forza del destino), in Holland as Tosca and Santuzza and in Germany and Belgium as Abigaille in Nabucco; Has also appeared at the National Theatre Warsaw as Fidelio, Aida and the Trovatore Leonora. Address: c/o Poznan Grand Theatre, Fredry 9, 60-987 Poznan, Poland.

KULESHA Gary (Alan), b. 22 Aug 1954, Toronto, Canada. Composer; Conductor; Pianist. m. Larysa Kuzmenko, 30 Dec 1983. Education: Associate in Piano, 1973, Associate in Composition, 1978, Royal Conservatory of Music, Toronto; Private Studies with John McCabe, London, England and John Corigliano, New York, USA; L Mus, 1976, Fellow 1978, Trinity College, London, England. Career: Composer-in-Residance, Kitchener-Waterloo Symphony, 1989-92; Composer-in-Residence, Candia Opera Company, 1993-95; Guest conducting throughout Canada; Principal Conductor, Festival Theatre, Stratford Festival, Canada; Artistic Director and Principal Conductor, Canadian Contemporary Music Workshops and the Composers Orchestra; Works performed throughout North America, Europe, Iceland, Australia and Latin America. Compositions: Essay for Orchestra; Second Essay for Orchestra; Chamber Concertos 1-5; Duo for Bass Clarinet and Piano; Second Sonata for Piano; Lifesongs for Alto and String Orchestra, text by composer; Nocturne for Chamber Orchestra; Angels for Marimba and Tape, recorded, 1986; Scores for several Shakespearean plays including All's Well That End's Well, Nimrod, Sydney, Australia 1986 and Henry VIII, Stratford 1986; Shama Songs, 1991; Concerto for Recorder, 1992; 3 Essays for Orchestra, 2nd and 3rd Pico Sonata; Concerto for Viola, 1992. Current Management: Nova Ter Artist Inc, Suite 303, 156 Front Street West, Toronto, Ontario, Canada M5J 2L6. Address: 54 Springbrook Gardens, Toronto, Ontario M8Z 3C1, Canada.

KULHAN Jaroslav, b. 7 December 1950, Ceske Budejovice. Cellist of the Panocha Quartet. m. Stepanka Kazilova, 12 August 1978, 1 son, 2 daughters. Education: Prague Conservatory; Academy of Music and Arts in Prague. Appointments: Member of the Panocha Quartet, 1968; Teacher at the Prague Conservatory, 1990-. Recordings: Haydn Op 51, Op 33, Op 55, Op 76; Smetana Quartets 1 and 2; Dvorak's Chamber Music, Martinu's Quartets; Janacek Quartets no 1, Schubert Op 29, 125, 161. Honours: The Grand Prix Academy Charles Cros (Martinu's Quartet nos 4, 6), 1983; Midem Cannes Classical Awards, 1994.

KULINSKY Bohumil, b. 5 May 1959, Prague, Czechoslovakia. Conductor. Education: Prague Conservatory, 1978-81; Prague Music Academy, 1981-84; Music Academy of Janacek-Brno, 1984-86. Career: Conductor, Czechoslovak Children's Choir Bambini di Praga, 1976-; Concert tours: France; Italy; Democratic Republic of Germany, Federal Republic of Germany, Mongolia, Finland; UK; Japan; Appeared on Radio and TV; Conductor, Prague Symphony Orchestra, appearing at Concerts and Festivals, 1984; Conductor, Czech Chamber Philharmonic Orchestra; Concert Tours: Spain and Germany. Recordings: CBS, Sony, Polydor, King Record Japan, Supraphon, Panton; Recordings with Prague Symphony Orchestra. Hobbies: Films (Camera and Direction); Photography. Address: Anenska 2, 11000 Prague 1, Czech Republic.

KULJERIC Igor, b. 1 Feb 1938, Sibenik, Croatia. Composer. Education: Studied at Zagreb Academy of Music, graduated 1965 and the Electronic Music Studios in Milan. Career: Has conducted various orchestras in Zagreb and elsewhere in Croatia; Art Director, Opera Zagreb and Dubrovnik Festival; Art Director, competition for young conductors, L Matacic, Zagreb; Has conducted various orchestras in Croatia, Europe and the USA; Employs electronic and other advanced techniques in his music. Compositions include: The Ballads of Petrica Kerempuh, 1973; Ballets and Incidental Music; Opera: The Power of Virtue, Zagreb, 1977 and Rikard, 2 Acts, after Shakespeare, 1987; Ballad of Petrica Kerempuh, vocal-instrumental, 1973; Canconiere, 1983; Ballet: Ricki Levy, 1991; Croatian Glagolic Requiem, 1996; Chamber music; Music for film and TV; Pop and rock music. Honours: Prizes from radio and TV, 1966, 1969, 1973; Prize of City of Zagreb, 1972, 1987; Prize of State of Croatia, 1987. Membership: Croatian Composers Society. Address: Jagiceva 23, 10000 Zagreb, Croatia.

KULKA Janos, b. 11 Dec 1929, Budapest, Hungary. Conductor. Education: Studied at the Franz Liszt Academy, Budapest, with Janos Ferencsik and Laszlo Somogyi. Career: Repetiteur and Chorus Master at the Budapest Opera from 1950; Conducted Opera in Budapest from 1953 until the 1956 Revolution; Conducted at the Bavarian State Opera, 1957-59, Wurttenberg State Opera, Stuttgart, 1959-61; Principal Conductor of the Hamburg State Opera, 1961-64, Music Director at the Wuppertal Opera, 1964-75; Chief Conductor at Stuttgart from 1976, Nordwestdeutsche Philharmonie, 1976-87; Has worked with leading opera houses in Cologne, Geneva, Paris, Munich, Vienna, Barcelona, Copenhagen, Boston and Buenos Aires; Conducted the premieres of Blacher's Yvonne, Prinzessin von Burgund, 1973, Klebe's Jacobovsky und der Oberst, 1982, and Boehmer's Doktor Faustus, 1985; Has also led operas by Gluck, Mozart, Verdi, Wagner, Schoenberg, Janacek, Dallapiccola and Penderecki; Conducted The Queen of Spades at Berne, 1996. Recordings include: Chopin's 2nd Piano Concerto with Tamas Vasary and the Berlin Philharmonic; Opera recital albums with Grace Bumbry, Thomas Tipton, Walter Berry, Sandor Konya, Brigitte Fassbaender and Teresa Stratas; Il Trovatore. Address: c/o Staatstheater Stuttgart, Oberer Schlossgarten 6, D-70103 Stuttgart, Germany.

KULKA Konstanty (Andrzej), b. 5 Mar 1947, Gdansk, Poland. Violinist. m. 2 children. Education: Higher State School of Music, Gdansk. Career: Participant in 2 music competitions: Paganini Competition, Genoa, 1964, Diploma and Special Prize, Music Competition, Munich, 1966 (1st Prize); Since 1967 has given concerts all over the world and has participated in many international festivals including Lucerne, Prague, Bordeaux, Berlin, Granada, Barcelona; Many recordings, both gramophone and radio/TV. Honours: Prize, Minister of Culture and Art, 1969, 1973; Prize, Minister of Foreign Affairs, 1977; Prize, President of Radio and TV Committee, 1978; Prize Winner, 33rd Grand Prix du Disque International Sound Festival, Paris, 1980; Gold Cross of Merit. Hobbies: Collecting gramophone records; Bridge; Collecting interesting kitchen recipes.

KUN Hu, b. 1963, China. Concert Violinist. Education: Studied at Szechuan and Peking Central Conservatories and at Menuhin International School. Debut: Played with Helsinki Radio Symphony and Helsinki Philharmonic Orchestras, 1979. Career: London debut, 1985, followed by concerts with London Symphony Orchestra and the Philharmonic at the Barbican; Further concerts as Wigmore Hall and on tour to Canada, Japan, Singapore, Hong Kong, Brazil, Australia and Europe; Engagements at Concertgebouw Amsterdam and Zurich Tonhalle; Vienna and Berlin debuts, 1987, with the Beethoven and Sibelius Concertos. Recordings include: Prokofiev First Concerto with the English String Orchestra and the Sibelius and Khachaturian Concertos, both conducted by Yehudi Menuhin. Honours include: Winner, City of Paris Menuhin Competition, 1984,Francescatti Competition, 1987, and Lipizer Competition, Italy, 1988. Address: c/o Anglo Swiss Limited, Suite 35-37, Morley House, 320 Regent Street, London W1R 5AD, England.

KUNAD Rainer, b. 24 Oct 1936, Chemnitz, Germany. Composer. Education: Studied at Dresden Conservatory and at Leipzig, 1956-59. Career: Lecturer at Zwickau Conservatory from 1960, the Director of Incidental Music for Dresden Theatres;

Member of Dresden and Berlin State Operas from 1971; Professor of Composition at Dresden Musikhochschule, 1978; Professor at Salzburg Mozarteum, 1982-84; Emigrated from East Germany, 1984, and settled in Tubingen. Compositions include: Operas and Music Theatre pieces; Bill Brook, Dresden, 1965; Old Fritz, Dresden, 1965; Maitre Pathelin, Dresden, 1969; Sabellicus, after the Faust Legends, Berlin, 1974; Der Eiertanz, 1975, staged Tubingen, 1986; Litauische Claviere, Dresden, 1976; Vincent, based on Van Gogh, Dresden, 1979; Amphitryon, Berlin, 1984; Der Meister und Margarita, Karlsruhe, 1986; Scenic Mystery Play, Die Menschen von Babel, 1986; Orchestral: Aphorismen, 1956; Symphonic Variations, 1959; Symphony, 1984; Sinfonietta, 1969; Concerto for Strings, 1967; Piano Concerto, 1969; Choral and Chamber Music; Piano Pieces and Songs. Address: GEMA, Postfach 80 07 67, D-81607 Munich, Germany.

KUNDE Gregory, b. 1954, Kankakee, Illinois, USA. Singer (Tenor). Education: Studied at Illinois State University and the Opera School of Chicago Lyric Opera. Career: Sang at Chicago from 1979, Washington Opera, 1983, Dallas, 1986, Seattle, 1987; Metropolitan Opera debut, 1987, as Des Grieux in Manon; European engagements at Nice, Théâtre des Champs Elysées, Paris, 1989, and Geneva, in Guillaume Tell; Montpellier, 1990; as Raoul in Les Huguenots; Detroit, 1989, as Gounod's Roméo; Other roles have included Mozart's Belmonte and Tamino, Ernesto, Alfredo, Montreal 1987, Berlin 1991, San Francisco 1993, Carnegie Hall 1995 - sang Arturo in Bellini's Puritani; Other roles include Edgardo in Lucia, Tormo 1993, Leicester in Maria Stuarda, Bologna 1994; Ernesto in Don Pasquale, La Scala 1994, Don Ottavio in Don Giovanni, Geneva 1992, La Scala 1993; Rodrigo in Donna del Lago, La Scala 1993, Rinaldo in Armida, Pesaro 1993; Tonio in Fille du Régiment and Nadir in Les Pêcheurs de Perles; Montpellier and Chicago, 1989, as Des Grieux, and Laertes in Hamlet by Thomas; Sang Lindoro in L'Italiana in Algeri at Berlin, 1992, Idreno in Semiramide at the 1992 Pesaro Festival; Danish Knight in Gluck's Armido to open the 1996-97 season at La Scala. Recordings: Bianca e Fernando; Semiramide; Armide; Hamlet. Address: c/o Robert Lombardo Associates, 61 West 62nd Street, Suite 6F, NY, NY 10023, USA.

KUNDLAK Josef, b. 1956, Bratislava, Czechoslovakia. Tenor. Education: Studied in Bratislava and the European Opera Center in Belgium. Career: Sang with Bratislava State Opera, 1983- in works by Janácek and Smetana, in addition to standard repertory; Sang Nemorino in L'Elisir d'Amore at Teatro Comunale, Bologna, 1987; Ferrando in Così fan tutte at La Scala Milan, 1989 returning in Die Meistersinger in 1990; Sang at Donizetti Festival at Bergamo in 1991 in Elisabetta al Castello di Kenilworth; Further engagements at Teatro San Carlo, Naples and Bayerische Staatsoper, Munich; Appeared as Belmonte in a new production of Die Entführung at Deutsche Oper Berlin in 1991; Sang Rossini's Almaviva at Genoa in 1992. Honours include: Winner, Luciano Pavarotti Competition in Philadelphia, 1985. Address: c/o Deutsche Oper Berlin, Richard Wagnerstrasse 10, D-1000 Berlin, Germany.

KUNKEL Renata, b. 1 Sep 1954, Gdansk, Poland. Composer. Education: Studied at the Warsaw Academy of Music. Career: Lecturer at the Warsaw Academy; Performances of her music in Europe, the USA and Central America. Compositions include: 3 String Quartets, 1979-91; Symphony, 1983; Inner Landscapes for Chamber Orchestra, 1984; Where Worlds Are Naught for String Orchestra, 1987; In A Lit-Up Streak Of Sounds for Ensemble, 1989; The Stream for Orchestra, 1990; Andos for Violin, 1990; Vocal music. Honours include: Prizewinner at the First Lutoslawski International Composers' Competition, 1990. Address: c/o ZAIKS, 2 rue Hipoteczna, 00 092 Warsaw, Poland.

KUNTZSCH Matthias, b. 22 Sept 1935, Karlsruhe, Germany. Conductor (Symphony and Opera). m. Sylvia Anderson, 18 May 1966, 1 son, 1 daughter. Education: Studied Piano, Horn, Conducting, Hochschule fur Musik und Theatre, Hannover; Master courses, Mozarteum, Salzburg, under Lovro von Matacic, Hermann Scherchen, Herbert von Karajan, and Zermatt under Pablo Casals, Karl Engel. Debut: Conducting Don Pasquale, State Theatre, Braunschweig, 1960. Career: Conductor, Jeunesse Musicale Orchestra, Braunschweig, 1957; Musical Assistant, Hannover Opera, 1958; Kapellmeister, Opera Braunschweig, 1959; Assistant to Wolfgang and Wieland Wagner, Bayreuth Festival, 1959-64; Principal Conductor, Bonn Opera, 1962-64, Mannheim Opera, 1964-66, Hamburg State Opera, 1966-69, Staatskapellmeister, Munich State Opera, 1969-73; Generalmusikdirektor, Lübeck Opera and Symphony, 1973-77; Generalmusikdirektor and Operndirektor, Saarbrücken State Opera and Symphony, 1977-85; Conductor, International Youth Festival Orchestra, Bayreuth, 1981-86; Principal Guest Conductor and Artistic Advisor, Basque National Symphony, San Sebastian, Spain, 1986-89; Conducted world premieres of operas, Humphrey Searle's Hamlet, Hamburg, 1968 and Gian Carlo Menotti's Help Help the Globolinks, Hamburg, 1968; Günther Bialas's Aucassin et Nicolette, Munich, 1969; Detlev Mueller-Siemens's Genoveva, Germany TV ZDF; Currently regular Guest Conductor with Utah Symphony and Colorado Symphony. Recordings: With soloists Ruggiero Ricci, Eugene List and others. Honours: Winner, Lower Saxony Prize for Promotion of Young Musicians and granted concert conducting, Hannover Radio Orchestra, 1963; Special Recognition for performing Così fan tutte and Arabella, Orpheus Magazine, 1981. Memberships: Rotary International; Conductors Guild of America; Conductors Guild of California. Hobbies: Reading; Walking; Swimming. Current Management: Stoll, Munich; Kuehnly Stuttgart, Germany; Dorothy Cone, New York City, USA. Address: 123 Nantucket Cove, San Rafael, CA 94901, USA.

KUNZEL Erich, b. 21 Mar 1935, New York, USA. Conductor. Education: Studied at Dartmouth College, AB, 1957 and at Harvard and Brown Universities, AM, 1960. Career: Assistant to Pierre Monteux, 1963-64; Teacher and Director of Choral Music, Brown University, 1958-65; Conducted the Rhode Island Philharmonic, 1960-65; Assistant to Max Rudolf at the Cincinnati Symphony, 1965, Associate Conductor, 1967, Resident Conductor, 1969-74; Led Pergolesi's La Serva Padrona at Santa Fe, 1957, and the US premiere of The Nose by Shostakovich, 1965; Conducted the Cincinnati Opera, 1966; New Haven Symphony Orchestra, 1974-; Founded the Cincinnati Pops Orchestra, 1977 and toured with it to the Far East, 1990; Has also conducted orchestras in Chicago, Boston, Los Angeles, San Francisco, Montreal, Ottawa and Detroit; Music Director of the Indianapolis Symphony Orchestra; Jazz collaborations with Dave Brubeck, Ella Fitzgerald, Duke Ellington, Benny Goodman, George Shearing and Gerry Mulligan. Recordings include: Albums with the Dave Brubeck Trio and the Cincinnati Symphony; Carnaval Roman overture by Berlioz and Pictures at an Exhibition. Address: c/o Cincinnati Symphony Orchestra, 1241 Elm Street, Cincinnati, OH 45210, USA.

KUPFER Harry, b. 12 Aug 1935, Berlin, Germany. Opera Producer. Career: Worked at theatres in Halle, Stralsund and Karl-Marx-Stadt (now Chemnitz); Director, Deutsches Nationaltheater, Weimar, 1963-72; Chief Producer of Staatsoper Dresden, 1972-81; Chief Producer, Komische Oper Berlin from 1981 and Director from 1994; Has produced for Bayreuth: Der fliegende Holländer, 1978, Der Ring des Nibelungen, 1988; Opera Productions for Welsh National Opera at Cardiff, Covent Garden London, Staatsoper and Volksoper Vienna, Amsterdam, San Francisco, Paris, Hamburg, Cologne, Stuttgart and Frankfurt; Important productions include: Orfeo ed Euridice by Gluck, Mozart Cycle, La Damnation de Faust, Pelléas et Mélisande, Moses und Aron, Lear by A Reimann, premiere production of Die schwarze Maske by K Penderecki, Die Soldaten by B A Zimmermann; Has staged Wagner's Parsifal and the Ring, Berlin Staatsoper, 1995-96.

KUPFERMAN Meyer, b. 3 Jul 1926, New York City, USA. Composer; College Professor; Clarinettist. m. Pei-Fen Chin, 26 Jul 1973, 3 sons, 1 daughter. Education: High School of Music & Art, New York City; Queens College, New York; Self-taught, Musical Composition. Debut: Steinway Hall, New York City, 1946. Career: Composer for Symphony, Opera, Concerto, Ballet, Cantata, Films (12 scores), much Chamber Music; Director, Sarah Lawrence Improvisation Ensemble, Music By My Friends Ensemble, Spring Trio Ensemble; Teacher, Compositions & Film Music, Sarah Lawrence College, Bronxville, New York. Compositions: 11 Symphonies; 6 Operas; 7 String Quartets; 3 Piano Concerti; 2 Cello Concerti; Guitar Concerto; 5 Ballet Scores; Torchwine, full length Cantata, Soprano, Basset Horn & Piano. Recordings: Little Symphony; 4th Symphony; Chamber Symphony; Concerto for Cello, Tape & Orchestra; Libretto for Orchestra; Lyric Symphony. Publications: Sonata on Jazz Elements; Little Sonata; Infinities No 22; Partita; In A Garden; Draagenfurt Girl; Sound Phantoms No 7; Fantasy Sonata; 5 Little Zeppelins; Halleluja the Hills. Contributor of: Many articles on Stravinsky, Acrobat of Apollo, in memorial issue, New Perspectives, 1972. Honours: Guggenheim Memorial Grant, 1975; National Endowment for the Arts, 1976-77; Academy & Institute of Arts & Letters, 1981. Memberships: American Society of Composers, Authors and Publishers; American Federation of Musicians. Hobby: Oil Painting. Address: 86 Livingston Street, Rhinebeck, NY 12572, USA.

KUPIEC Ewa, b. 1964, Duszniki. Education: Chopin Conservatory, Warsaw. Career: Soloist. Recordings: Numerous recordings for Polish Radio, BBC London, Austrian Radio and NDR Hamburg. Honours include: First piano recital in Munich acclaimed as Brilliant Debut; First Prize, duo section, Munich Radio Competition, 1992. Address: Hebbelstrabe 61, 50968 Koln, Germany.

KUPREVICIUS Giedrius Antanas, b. 8 Apr 1944, Kaunas, Lithuania. Composer; Carillonist; Pianist. m. Grazina Kupreviciene, 19 Sept 1991, 1 daughter. Education: Vilnius State Conservatory. Debut: Kaunas, 1958. Career: LTV, Vilnius; Ostankino, Moscow. Compositions: Prussians, opera; There, Inside, opera; Symphony; In Chase of Fire, recorded; Kaunas Carillon Music, recorded; The Greenhill's Wolves, recorded; BOROBUDUR Organ Sonata, recorded; Eight Lithuanian Folk Songs for string quartet; The Pagan Cantos for choir; Concerto for violin and organist; Te Deum, concerto for trombone and chamber orchestra. Membership: Lithuanian Musicians Society. Hobbies: Gardening; Cycling. Address: Rokiskio 12, 3005 Kaunas, Lithuania.

KUROSAKI Hiro, b. 1949, Tokyo, Japan. Violinist. Education: Studied at the Vienna Musikhochschule. Career: Solo engagements with the Royal Philharmonic, Dresden Staatskapelle, Salzburg Mozarteum and Vienna Symphony Orchestras; Leader of Les Arts Florissants, under William Christie, and has also played in Baroque and early music ensembles with the Clemencic Consort of Vienna and London Baroque; Teacher at the University of Vienna and the Salzburg Mozarteum. Recordings include: Mozart's violin sonatas, with Linda Nicholson. Honours include: Prizewinner at the Wieniawski and Kreisler Competitions, 1977 and 1979. Address: c/o Les Arts Florissants, 10 Rue de Florence, F-75008 Paris, France.

KURTAG György, b. 19 Feb 1926, Lugos, Romania. Composer. Education: Budapest Music Academy and in Paris. Career: Retired Professor of Chamber Music, Music Academy of Budapest. Compositions: Concerto for Viola, 1954; String Quartet, 1959; Quintet for Wind Instruments, 1959; Eight Pieces for Piano, 1960; Signs for Solo Viola, 1961; Eight Duets for Violin and Cimbalom, 1961; The Sayings of Peter Bornemissza, for Soprano and Piano, 1968; In Memory of a Winter Sunset, Four Fragments for Soprano, Cimbalom and Violin, 1969; Four Capriccios for Soprano and Chamber Ensemble, 1970; Splinters Solo for Cimbalom, 1974; Four Pilinszky Songs, SK Rememberence Noise, Hommage a Mihaly Andras, Twelve Microludes for String Quartet, Herdecker Eurythmie, Guitar Pieces, Omaggio a Luigi Nono, Messages of the Late Miss R V Troussova, Songs of Despondency and Grief, Scenes from a Novel, Attila Jozsef Fragments, Seven Lieder, Eight Tandori Choruses; Kafka Fragments for Soprano and Violin, 1985; Quasi una Fantasia for Piano and Chamber Ensemble; Three Old Inscriptions for Soprano and Piano, 1986; Requiem po drugu for Soprano and Piano, 1987; Introduction, Kyrie A, Hommage à Stockhausen, Trumpet, Double-Bass, Piano, 1992; In Memoriam Thomas Blum, Piano, Celesta, Double-Bass, 1992; Hommage à John Cage, Trumpet, Double-Bass, 1992; Hommage à Tristan, Trumpet, Double-Bass, Piano, Celesta, 1992; Les Adieux in Jacaceks Manier, Piano Solo, 1992; Antiphone in F Sharp, Trombone, Double-Bass, Piano, Celesta, 1992; Kyrie, b, Double- Bass, Piano, 1992; Curriculum vitae, Op 32, 2 Pianos, 2 Basset Horns, 1992; Samuel Beckett: What is the Word, Op 30b; Op 27 No2, Double Concerto; Stele, Op 33; Grabstein für Stephan, Op 15c; Messages for Orchestra; Lettre a Peter Eötvös, Lagebericht, Aus der Ferne; Epilog to Requiem der Versöhnung, 1. Inscription on a Grave in Cornwall, 2. Flowers we are, to Zoltan Koosis. Honours include: Erkel Prize, 3 times; Kossuth Prize, 2nd Degree, 1973; Merited Artist, Eminent Artist's Title; Officier des Arts et des Lettres, Franch State, 1985; Premio Feltrinelli, Accademia dei Lincei, Italy, 1993; Austriasn State Award for European Composers, 1994; Denis de Rougemont Prize, European Associaion of Festivals, 1994. Memberships: Akademie der Kunst, Berlin, 1987; Bayerische Akademie der Schönen Künste, Munich, 1987. Address: 2621 Veröce, Lihegoutca 3, Hungary.

KURTAKOV Krassimir, b. 1953, Sofia, Bulgaria. Bass Baritone. Education: Studied in Sofia. Career: Sang with the National Opera at Sofia from 1979; Guest appearances in Cuba, France, Austria and Eastern Europe, 1980-82; Vienna Kammeroper, 1987-88, as Nicolai's Falstaff and Don Alfonso; Gelsenkirchen from 1990 with further guestings at the Vienna Staatsoper and in Klagenfurt; Other roles include Rocco, King Henry in Lohengrin, King Philip, Ramphis in Aida, Fiesco in Simon Boccanegra, Mephistopheles, Varlaam and Boris Godunov; Bonn 1992 in Rihm's Jakob Lenz. Address: c/o Musiktheater im Revier, Kennedyplatz, Pf 101854, W-4650 Gelsenkirchen, Germany.

KURTZ Eugene (Allen), b. 27 Dec 1923, Atlanta, Georgia, USA. Composer. Education: BA, Music, University of Rochester, 1947; MA, Music, Eastman School of Music, 1949; Study with Arthur Honegger and Darius Milhaud, Ecole Normale de Musique, Paris, France, 1949-51; Study with Max Deutsch, Paris, 1953-57. Career: Guest Professor of Composition, University of Michigan, 1967-68, 1970-71, 1973-74, 1980-81, 1988; Eastman School of Music, 1975; University of Illinois, 1976; University of Texas, 1977-78, 1985-86; Hartt School of Music, 1989; Consultant, Editions Jobert, Paris, 1972-. Compositions: The Solitary Walker, 1964; Conversations for 12 Players, 1966; Ca...Diagramme Pour Orchestre, 1972; The Last Contrabass in Las Vegas, 1974; Mécanique, 1975; Logo, 1979; Five-Sixteen, piano, 1982; World Enough and Time, 1982-; String Trio, Time and Again, 1984-85; From Time to Time, violin and piano, 1986-87; The Broken World, for string quartet, 1993-94; Shadows on the Wind, for 17 players, 1995-96; Icare, for solo flute, 1997. Also film scores and incidental music for radio, theatre and television. Recordings: Mecanique with the French National Orchestra conducted by Alexandre Myrat; Motivations, Books I and II, Piano, Michel Sendrez; The

Contrabass in Las Vegas, Bertram and Nancy Turetzky; Sixteen, Piano, Genevieve Ibanez; Logo I, Richard ...emaker, Clarinet, David Nale, piano, The Continuum ...ussion Quartet, conducted by David Colson; From Time to ..., Adéle Auriol, violin, Bernard Fauchet, piano. Publications: ... Joplin et le Ragtime Classique. Honours: NEA Grantee, ...-83; American Academy of Arts and Letters Award, 1992; ...o Prize, French Academy of Fine Arts, 1997. Memberships: ...été des Auteurs, Compositeurs et Editeurs de Musique. ...ess: 6 rue Boulitte, 75014 Paris, France.

KURYLEWICZ Andrzej, b. 24 Nov 1932, Lvov, Poland. ...poser; Pianist; Trombonist. m. Wanda Warska, 1 daughter. ...cation: Music School, Lvov; Institute of Music, Gliwice; ...ied piano with Henryk Sztompka and composition with ...islaw Wiechowicz, High School of Music, Krakow. Debut: ...tor, Polish Radio Jazz Band, Krakow. Career: Conductor, ...h Radio and TV Orchestra, Warsaw; Founder, Formation of ...emporary Music, 1969-79; Founder of the club of music and ...ature forms, with Wanda Warska, Warsaw Old Town; Has ...n concerts both as conductor and instrumentalist, in Europe, ...h and South America; Co-operation with State University, ...sas. Compositions: Many pieces for symphonic orchestra, ...nber orchestra, song cycles, psalms with Latin texts; Missa ...is, for Roman Missal; Many works for solo instruments ...ding piano, flute and tuba. Honours: Polish Radio and TV ...d, 1965; Award of the City of Warsaw, 1978; Prix Italia, ...; Nominated, composer of Wilhelmshaven, 1984; Medal of ...City of Warsaw, 1997; Many prizes for music composed for ... and theatre. Address: Brodzinskiego 13, 01-557 Warsaw, ...nd.

KURZ Ivan, b. 29 Nov 1947, Prague, Czech Republic. ...poser. m. Zdenka Sklenávová, 21 May 1951, 2 sons, 1 ...ghter. Education: Studied music theory privately with Karel ...nger, 1964-66, composition study with Emil Hlobil, 1966-71 ...postgraduate study with Vaclav Dobias, 1973-76, Academy ...ts and Music, Prague. Career: Dramaturgist for Prague TV, ...-74; Teacher of Music Theory at Academy of Music, 1976-. ...positions include: Orchestral: Concertino for Piano, Flute, ...ussion and Strings, 1974, Slanting Plane, symphonic picture, ..., Allegory, 1982, Symphony No 3, 1986; The Confession, ...erto for bassoon and symphonic orchestra, 1991; Chamber: ...ta for Piano, 1976, Circle Of Notes for String Quartet, 1979, Touch for Piano Trio, 1982, Litanie for Organ and Percussion, ..., Expectation for French Horn and Piano, 1985; Vocal: For Little Mozart, suite for Contralto and Piano, 1975, Got Mint?, ...l and acting etudes for Children's choir, 1982; Instructive ...s: Fiddlers Are Coming for Children's Recitation and Singing, ...; Reverie, electronic music, 1982, Toward You I Come, ...phonic picture, 1989, Evening Meeting, opera, 1989-90. ...y: Theology. Address: Drtinova 26, 150 00 Prague 5, Czech ...ublic.

KUSCHE Benno, b. 30 Jan 1916, Freiburg, Germany. ...-Baritone. Education: Studied in Karlsruhe and with Fritz ...n in Freiburg. Debut: Koblenz in 1938 as Renato. Career: ... in Augsburg, 1939-42; Member of the Bayerische ...tsoper Munich from 1946, and Deutsche Oper an Rhein ...seldorf from 1958; Sang at Salzburg Festival in 1949 in the ...iere of Antigonae by Orff, Covent Garden in 1952 as ...kmesser, and in 1953 as La Roche in the first British ...ormance of Capriccio, Glyndebourne Festival in 1954, ...-64 as Leporello, La Roche and Don Fernando in Fidelio, ...ische Oper Berlin in 1958 as Papageno in Die Zauberflöte ... Metropolitan Opera, 1971-72 as Beckmesser; Guest ...arances in Philadelphia, Amsterdam, Buenos Aires, Zurich, ...nce and Bregenz. Recordings: Die Meistersinger; Die Kluge ...Der Mond by Orff; La Bohème; Lulu. Address: c/o Bayerische ...tsoper, Postfach 745, D-8000 Munich 1, Germany.

KUSIEWICZ Piotr, b. 30 Jun 1953, Gdansk, Poland. ...ist; Singer. Education: Pianist Diploma with Professor ...niew Sliwinski, 1977; Singer Diploma with Distinction, with ...essor Jerzy Szymanski, 1980; Academy of Music, Gdansk. ...er: Singer, Cracow State Opera, 1981-, Teatr STU, 1983-, ...saw Opera House, 1984-, Wroclaw State Opera, 1986-; ...st performances in operas in West Germany, Switzerland, ...ia, Holland, Luxembourg and Italy; Cooperation with ...armonic Societies, chamber ensembles and member of ...l ensemble of ancient music, Bornus Consort; As pianist, ...rmances with leading Polish singers as accompanist in ...nd and abroad, and accompanist in Geneva International ...er Competition, 1978; As singer and pianist, at Festival of ...emporary Music, Warsaw Autumn, 1981, 1983, 1984, 1987, ...ztof Penderecki's Festival in Lusawice, Poland on invitation ...the composer, 1983, and recordings for Polish Radio; Vocal ...er at Academy of Music in Gdansk, 1986. Recordings: GF ...el's Sosarme, Opera Seria in 3 Acts, 2 LPs. Publications: ...uthor, Gdansk Composers, 1980. Address: ul Michala Glinki ...30-271 Gdansk, Poland.

KUTHEN Hans-Werner, b. 26 Aug 1938, Cologne, Germany. Musicologist; Editor, Beethoven Archives. m. Annette Magdalena Leinen, 1 son. Education: Studied Musicology, Bonn University; Bologna; MA 1980; PhD 1985; Bonn University. Publications: On Beethoven Kammermusik mit Blasern, 1969; Article Beethoven Herder, Dad Grosse Lexikon der Musik, 1978; Complete edition, Ouverturen und Wellingtons Sieg, 1974; Critical Report, separately, 1991; Klavierkonzertel, 1984, with Critical Report separately; Klavierkonzerte II(nos 4 and 5), (in preparation); Klavierkonzerte Nr 1-3 (Barenreiter Studienpartituren), 1987; same in practical edition for 2 pianos: no 3 1988, no 1 1990, no 2 1991. Contributions to: Professional publications including: Beethoven Yearbooks, congress reports, scholarly periodicals; International Congress of the Gesellschaft für Musikforschung, Freiburg i.Br, 1993; Gradus ad partituram; Erscheinungsbild und Funktionen der Solostimme ni Beethovens Klavierkonzerten, Congress Report, 1997; Ein unbekanntes Notierungsblatt Beethovens aus der Entstehungszeit der Mondscheinsonate, Prague, 1996; Rediscovery and reconstruction of an authentic version of Beethoven's Fourth Piano Concerto for pianoforte and 5 strings. Memberships: Gesellschft fur Musikforschung; Verein Beethoven Haus Bonn; VG Musikedition. Hobbies: Drawing and Painting; Pianoforte Playing; Family. Address: Konigstr 8, D-5300 Bonn 1, Germany.

KUULBERG Mati, b. 9 Jul 1947, Tallinn, Estonia. Composer; Teacher; Violinist. m. Tiiu Aroella, 27 Jun 1981, 1 d. Education: Tallinn State Conservatoire, 1966-71. Debut: 1966. Career: Estonian State Symphony Orchestra, 1966-75; Tallinn Secondary Music School, 1978-; Head of Information Centre, Estonian Composers Union, 1987-; Jury member for new recordings for Estonian Radio Collection. Compositions: 3 Ballets; 5 Symphonies; 4 Sonatas for Solo Violin; Sonatas for 2 Flutes, 2 Pianos, Solo Clarinet, Piano, Solo Cello; Concerto per Ottoni; Concerto per Fiati; In The Name of Life, oratorio; Wind Quintet; Piano Sextet. Recordings: Wind Quintet, 1973; Sonata No 2 for Solo Violin, 1975; Piano Trio, Sonata for Solo Clarinet, Concert Sonata for Solo Cello, 4 Novelettes for Alto Flute and String Quartet, 1977; Piano Sonata, 1978; Capriccio for 2 Pianos and Percussion, 1984; Saxaphone Quartet, 1987; 3 and 4 Impressions and Giusto for Piano, 1989; Sonatas No 1 and 4 for Solo Violin, 1988; Piano Trio No 2, Reminder for Cello and Piano, Attacca for Solo Trombone, For Tiiu Poem for Violin and Piano, 1991. Address: Weizenbergi 1905, EE0010 Tallinn 10, Estonia.

KUUSISTO Ilkka Taneli, b. 26 Apr 1933, Helsinki, Finland. Composer. m. Marja-Lisa Hanninen, 26 Nov 1972, 2 sons, 2 daughters. Education: Diploma, Precentor-Organist, 1954, Music Teacher, 1958; Studies Composition with Aare Merikanto and Nils-Eric Fougstedt, Sibelius Academy; Studies, School of Sacred Music and Union Theological Seminary, New York under Seth Bingham, 1958-59, Studied in Germany, 1960 and Vienna, 1961. Debut: Conductor, 1955, Composer, 1956. Career: Assistant Head of Music Section, Finnish Broadcasting Corporation; Choral Director, Finnish National Opera; Artistic Director, Fazer Music Corporation, 1982-84; General Director, Finnish National Opera, 1984-92; President, Finnish Copyright Association, 1990-94; Musical Director, Helsinki City Theatre; Conductor, Radio Symphony Chorus. Compositions: 9 Operas; 2 Ballets. Recordings: Suomi-Finland, Songs of Oskar Merikanto, Our Most Beautiful Songs. Honours: World Council of Churches Scholarship, 1958; Scholarship, Finnish State, 1968. Memberships: Composers of Finland; Finnish Light & Film Music Composers. Hobby: Seafaring. Address: Apollonkatu 7, FL-00100, Helsinki, Finland.

KUUSISTO Pekka, b. 1976, Espoo, Finland. Concert Violinist. Education: East Helsinki Music Institute with Geza Szilvay; Sibelius Academy, with Tuomas Haapanaen, from 1985; Indiana University School of Music, Bloomington, with Miriam Fried and Paul Bliss; Steans Institute for Young Artists at the Ravinia Festival, 1995. Career: Many concerts with leading Finnish orchestras, including the Finnish Radio Orchestra and the Helsinki PO; Tour of Japan, season 1996-97; Festival engagements at Helsinki, Turku, Ravinia and Schleswig-Holstein; Concertos with the Stockholm Sinfonietta and Okku Kamu, Orchestra of St John's Smith Square with John Lubbock, BBC Scottish SO under Osmo Vanska and the Malmö SO under Paavo Berglund. Recordings include: Sibelius Concerto, with the Helsinki PO under Leif Segerstram. Honours include: Winner, International Jean Sibelius Violin Competition, Helsinki, and the Kuopio Violin Competition, 1995. Address: c/o Harrison/Parrott Ltd, 12 Penzance Place, London W11 4PA, England.

KUZMENKO Vladimir, b. 1960, Kiev, Ukraine, Russia. Tenor. Education: Studied in Kiev. Career: From 1988 has sung with the National Opera Company of Kiev as Lensky, Rodolfo, Don José, Faust, Dimitri and Count Almaviva; Guest appearances in France, Finland, Austria, Switzerland and Spain; Warsaw Opera in season 1994-95; British debut with the Kiev Opera as Alfredo in La Traviata, on tour in 1995. Address: c/o Sonata Ltd, 11 Northgate Street, Glasgow, G20 7AA, Scotland.

KUZUMI Karina, b. 29 April 1973, Tokyo, Japan. Violinist. Education: Study, Toho Gakuen, Tokyo, 1992; Grad, Pre-College, University of Music & Arts, Tokyo, 1992; Study, Escuela Superior de Musica Reina Sofia, Madrid, 1993; Study, Musikhochschule Lubeck, 1995. Debut: Tokyo City Philharmonic Orchestra, Tokyo, 1986. Career: Concert, Nara, 1992; Radio II Classica, Spain, 1992, NHK-FM, Japan, 1992; Recitals at Auditorio Nacional, Madrid and Tokyo, 1994, Burgos, Melilla, Malaga, Valencia and Santander, 1995; Concert at Tokyo, Gronau and Rheine, 1997. Honours: 1st Prize, All-Japan Student Music Competition, 1988; Scholarship, Foundation Isaac Albeniz, 1994; Scholarship, Culture Department, Japan, 1997; Prize, 33rd Szigeti International Competition, 1997. Hobbies: Travel; Movies. Address: Sanda-cho 4-33-8, Hachioji, Tokyo, Japan.

KVAPIL Jan, b. 1943, Czechoslovakia. Violinist. Education: Studied at Prague Academy of Arts. Career: Member of the Talich String Quartet from 1962; Tours to most European countries and to Egypt, Iraq, North America, Japan and Indonesia; Member of the Chamber Ensemble of the Czech Philharmonic from 1975; Annual visits to France from 1976 and tours of Britain, 1990-91 with concerts at Wigmore Hall, appearances at the Bath and Bournemouth Festivals, Elizabeth Hall and on BBC 2's Late Show, with Janácek's 2nd Quartet; Played Beethoven's Quartet Op 74, the Brahms A minor, Smetana D minor and works by Mozart, in England, 1991; Festival appearances in Vienna, Besançon, Lucerne, Helsinki, Amsterdam, Prague and Salzburg; Repertoire also includes works by Debussy, Bartók (complete quartets recorded), Shostakovich, Ravel and Dvorák. Recordings include: Complete Quartets of Beethoven. Honours include: Grand Prix Charles Cros. Address: c/o Clarion - Seven Muses, 64 Whitehall Park, London, N19 3TN, England.

KVAPIL Radoslav, b. 15 Mar 1934, Brno, Czechoslovakia. Pianist. m. Eva Kvapilova-Maslanova, 11 June 1960, 1 son. Education: Gymnasium Brno, 1944-52; Janacek Academy of Music, Brno, 1952-57; Aspiranteur, Janacek Academy with Prof L Kundera, 1960-63. Debut: Recital, Brno, 1954. Career: Numerous concerts in more than 20 countries including Europe, USA, Canada and Japan, 1956-; Appearances on numerous radio stations including BBC and Radio France; Professor, Conservatory Prague, 1963-73. Recordings: All piano works by A Dvorak, 1967-69, All works J H Vorisek, 1975, Concerto A Reicha, A Dvorak; All piano works of L Janacek, 1969; All polkas of B Smetana, 1969; BIS B Martinu Studies and Polkas, Sonata, 1982; Piano works of Moussorgsky, Calliope: Works of Smetana, and Janacek; Hindemith, Janacek, with Wallace Collection; All piano, violin and violoncello works of L Janacek; 2CD with works of B Martinu/first and last periode; Anthology of Czech piano music: Till end of 95 released 8 volumes containing works of Dvorak, Smetana, Martinu/Paris periode/Vorisek, Fibich, Janacek and Suk, Project will continue; Dvorak: Cypresses, Biblical songs with P Langridge Radio recording BBC includes Dvorak piano concerto, Martinu Concertos No 3, 4, Divertimento, Debussy Phantasie for piano and orchestra. Contributions: Musical Review Prague. Honours: International Competition, Radio CSSR, 1st prize, 1968; Janacek medaile of Ministry culture CSSR, 1978; Honorary Vice President, Dvorak Society of Great Britain; Prize for Czech music, Prague, 1990; CD of the month, Reporter, Paris, 1994-97. Memberships: Chairman, EPTA Czech Republic; Chairman, The South Bohemis Festival Society; Chairman, AMAT Czech Republic; Chairman, Menuhin Live Music Now Czech Republic, 1992; Chairman, Dvorak Society, Prague; Chairman, EPTA C2. Hobby: Chess. Current Management: Audrey Ellison. Address: Hradecka 5, 13000 Praha 3, Czech Republic.

KVARAN Gunnar, b. 1960, Reykjavik, Iceland. Cellist. Education: Studied at the Reykjavik College of Music, at the Copenhagen Conservatory and in Basle and Paris. Career: Solo concerts, recitals and chamber music throughout Scandinavia, France, Germany, Holland and North America; Appearances with the Icelandic Symphony, the Tivoli Orchestra and the Jutland Philharmonic; Professor at the Reykjavik College of Music and member of the Reykjavik Piano Trio. Address: c/o Worldwide Artists, 6 Petersfield Crescent, Coulsdon, Surrey, CR5 2JQ, England.

KVECH Otomar, b. 25 May 1950, Prague, Czechoslovakia. Composer. m. Miluska Wagnerova, 30 Mar 1972, 2 daughters. Education: Composition, Organ, Music Conservatory, Prague, 1965-69; Composition with Professor Pauer, Academy of Music Ats, Prague, 1969-74. Debut: Symphony for Organ and Orchestra, Dvorak's Hall, Prague. Career: Pianist, National Theatre, Prague, 1974-77; Music Producer, 1977-80, Dramaturgist, Editor, 1988-, Radio Praha; Secretary, Organisation of Czech Composers and Concert Artists, 1980-90; Professor, Music Conservatory, Prague, 1990-. Compositions include: 4 symphonies: Organ, 1974, E Flat Major, 1982, D Major, 1984, E Minor with String Quartet, 1987; 5 String Quartets, 1972, 1973, 1974, 1979, 1985; 3 Violin Sonatas, 1974, 1978, 1982; The World Carnival, 1983; Cello Sonata, 1985; Sonata for Organ, 1986; RUR, 1986; Capriccio, concerto, piano trio, orchestra, 1986; Piano Quintet, 1990; Requiem, 1991; 3 songs for voice and organ,

1993-97; Oboe Sonata, 1995; Serenata notturna, 1996; Nokturnale, 1997. Recordings: Piano Trio; The Waltz Across the Room; Symphonies 1, 2; RUR; String Quartet No 5; For Radio Prague: Symphony in E Minor, World Carnival, The Honour to Bach, Capriccio, String Quartets 2, 3, 4; Sonatas for Violin 1, 2, 3, Viola Sonata, Cello Sonata, Wind Quintet; Many works recorded in England, Germany, France. Publications: When the Path Disappeared, song cycle; Three Moments for Accordion; Piano Trio; Prague Panorama; Six Preludes for Flute Solo; String Quartet No 5; Symphony, E Flat Major. Contributions to: Hudebni Rozhledy, Prague; Opus Musicum, Brno. Hobbies: Electric Engines. Address: Korunni 67, 13000 Praha 3, Czech Republic.

KWELLA Patrizia, b. 26 Apr 1953, Mansfield, England. Soprano. Education: Royal College of Music, London. Career: Promenade Concert debut in 1979 with John Eliot Gardiner; Concerts and festivals include Ansbach, Bergen, Innsbruck, Aldeburgh, Bologna, Warsaw, Bath, City of London, Edinburgh and Salzburg; Conductors include Richard Hickox, Peter Maag, Christopher Hogwood and Trevor Pinnock; US debut in 1983 with the San Diego Symphony; Further concerts with the San Francisco, Houston and Washington Symphony Orchestras; Sang in many of the Bach, Handel and Scarlatti tercentenary concerts of 1985; Premiere of Night's Mask by Colin Matthews at the 1985 Aldeburgh Festival; Sang Handel's Alcina at the 1985 Spitalfields and Cheltenham Festivals; Repertoire includes Haydn, Mozart, Brahms, Mahler, Stravinsky and Britten. Recordings: Handel's L'Allegro, Alcina, Alceste, Resurrezione and Esther; Monteverdi's Orfeo and Il Combattimento; Bach's B minor Mass, Magnificat and St John Passion; Mozart's Coronation Mass, Missa Solemnis and Regina Coeli; TV includes many Man and Music appearances for Channel 4. Address: c/o Music and Musicians Artists' Management, 54 Regent's Park Road, London, NW1 7SX, England.

KWILIMBE Bernard, b. 1 September 1955, Nkhotakota, Malawi, Africa. Teacher; Choreographer; Singer; Band Leader. m. Jane Khataza, 3 sons, 1 daughter. Education: Teacher Training, 1976; Diploma, Education, Newcastle Upon Tyne, England, 1981-82; Selftaught Music Education. Career: Malawi Beauty Peagat (Radio), 1979, 1980, 1981; USA American Dance Festival, 1995; International Choreographers Residency Programme Showing Gulewanga Piece, Dance and Music From Malawi. Compositions: Ukhonao, 1980; Apatsa Mosiyana, 1980; Kodi Akalona, 1980; I Love Malawi, 1988. Publications: Music in Malawi Primary Schools, 1982; Looking at Dance and Music. The Malawi Aspect, 1995. Memberships: Malawi Copyright Society; Musicians Association of Malawi. Hobbies: Singing; Dancing. Address: Arts & Crafts Department, Box 264, Lilongwe, Malawi, Africa.

KWON Hellen, b. 11 Jan 1961, Seoul, South Korea. Soprano. Education: Studied in Cologne. Debut: Wiesbaden in 1984 as The Queen of The Night. Career: Has sung at Mannheim, 1985-, Paris Opéra, 1986 in Die Zauberflöte, and Hamburg, 1987; Created the role of Alexis de Lechebot in Liebermann's La Forêt at Geneva, 1987; Sang at Bayreuth Festival in 1988 as a Flower Maiden, Glyndebourne Festival in 1990 as The Queen of Night followed by performances at Bonn and Vienna in 1991; Sang Susanna at Hamburg in 1990, Wellgunde in a concert performance of Götterdämmerung at Rome in 1991 and Blondchen in Die Entführung at Salzburg Festival in 1991; Other roles include Strauss's Sophie and Zerbinetta, Rosina, Norina and Musetta; Sang Susanna at the 1992 Israel Festival, Adele in Die Fledermaus at Hamburg, 1996; Concert tours of USA, France, Italy, Belgium and the Netherlands notably in the B minor Mass and St Matthew Passion of Bach. Recordings include: Nightingale in Die Vögel by Braunfels, 1997. Address: c/o Hamburgische Staatsoper, Grosse Theaterstrasse 34, 2000 Hamburg 36, Germany.

KYHLE Magnus, b. 1959, Sweden. Tenor. Education: Studied at Stockholm College of Music and the State Opera School in Stockholm. Debut: Vadstena Academy in 1983. Career: Engaged at the Royal Opera, Stockholm, 1986-89, Stadttheater Darmstadt, 1989-90 and Landestheater Salzburg, 1990-92; Roles include Mozart's Don Ottavio, Tamino, Monostatos and Ferrando, Pelléas and Paris in La Belle Hélène; Guest appearances at Tenerife and Tokyo; Season 1990-92 as Tamino and Don Ottavio with the Royal Opera Stockholm, Tamino at Salzburg Landestheater and Ferrando at Semperoper Dresden; Season 1992-93 as Beppe in a new production of Pagliacci at Stockholm, and in a new production of Traviata; Stockholm production of The Phantom Of The Opera, 1994-. Address: IM Audio and Music HB, Åsögatan 67VI, S-11829 Stockholm, Sweden.

KYLLONEN Timo-Juhani, b. 1 Dec 1955, Saloinen, Finland. Composer; Accordion Soloist; Conductor. Education: Postgraduate Composition studies, solo accordion, conducting and teaching diplomas, Tchaikovsky Conservatoire and Gnesin Music Institute, Moscow. Debut: Concert of his works at the Tchaikovsky Conservatory, Moscow, April 1986. Career: Biographical programmes, Finnish Television, 1982, 1988;

Several concerts and radio and television programmes in Finland, Sweden, USSR, Peru, Ecuador and Norway; Composer-portrait on Netherlands Radio, 1990, also on Argentinian, Brazilian, Cuban, Israeli and Peruvian radio. Compositions include: Symphony No 1, op 8, 1985-86; Symphony No 2 op 29, 1991-95; Suite for String Orchestra op 27, 1991; Awakening op 23b for string orchestra. Recordings include: Compositions by Timo-Juhani Kyllonen, Finlandia Records; Elegia quasi una sonata, op 15, 1987; Trio No 1, op 9, 1986; Triology for 2 pianos, op 4, 1984; String Quartet No 1 op 3, 1984, Ondine Records; Ciclo para coro mixto op 5. Honours: Pro Musica Award, 1988; Espoo City Arts prize, 1989; Three year Stipendum, Finnish Ministry of Education, 1991-93; 3 different television programmes (personal portraits) on Finnish television. Membership: Finnish Composer's Union. Current Management: Finnish Music Information Centre, Lauttasaarentie 1, 00200 Helsinki, Finland. Address: Joupinmäki 3C49, 02760 Espoo, Finland.

KYNASTON Nicolas, b. 10 December 1941, Morebath, Devon, England. Concert Organist. Education: Accademia Musicale Chigiana, Siena, 1957; Conservatorio Santa Cecilia, Rome, 1958; Royal College of Music, 1960. Debut: Royal Festival Hall, 1966. Career: Organist, Westminster Cathedral, 1961-71; Appointed Consultant Tutor, Birmingham School of Music, 1986-; Travels widely giving regular recitals throughout UK, most European countries and to may exotic places including Barbados, Nassau, Ankara, Istanbul, Tokyo, Hong-Kong, Bangkok, Seoul-Korea and the famous Bamboo Organ of Las Pinas, Philippines and tours of North America; Varied and extensive solo repertoire; Broadcasts regularly on British Broadcasting Corporation Radio and Television and Foreign Networks (particularly West Germany); Teaches Cambridge University; Master Classes in USA, Hong-Kong, Norway, Singapore and Germany; Chairman, National Organ Teacher's Encouragement Scheme, 1993-; Organist of the Athens Concert Hall, May 1995-. Recordings: Numerous commercial recordings for British, French and German companies; 5 nominated Critics Choice; 2 Popular records Great Organ works at Royal Albert Hall earning EMI Sales Award; Bach from Clifton Cathedral nominated Best Solo Instrumental Record of the Year; Received coveted Deutscher Schallplatten preis for Vierne's 6th Symphony (German recording); CD on IMP Masters of Bach Organ Work, 1994. Contributions to: The American Organist; Music and Musicians; Kirche and Musick; RSCM Yearbook; Organ Club Journal and others. Honours: Hon FRCO, 1976; Deutscher Schallplatten preis, 1978; MTA Record Award, 1976. Memberships: President, Incorporated Association of Organists, 1983-85; Honorary Member of the Organ Club. Hobbies: Churches; Pubs. Address: 28 High Park Road, Kew Gardens, Richmond-upon-Thames, Surrey TW9 4BH, England.

KYR Robert (Harry), b. 20 Apr 1952, Cleveland, OH, USA. Composer; Teacher. Education: BA, Yale University, 1974; Royal College of Music, London, 1974-76; MA, University of Pennsylvania, 1978; PhD, Harvard University, 1989. Career includes: Composer-in-Residence, New England Philharmonic, 1985-89; Resident Composer of Extension Works, Composers and Performers Consortium, Boston, MA, 1985-; Teacher of Composition and Theory at Harvard University (teaching fellow), 1985-89, Longy School of Music (Director of Compositional Studies), 1986-, Hartt School of Music (visiting lecturer), Fall 1988. Compositions include: Commissions: Maelstrom (The Fires Of London), 1981, The Greater Changing, Symphony No 2 (Mystic Valley Orchestra, Boston), 1986, A Signal In The Land (Johnson City Symphony Orchestra, TN), 1987, The Fifth Season, Symphony No 3 (Friends Of Music at Yale, Yale Symphony), 1988, Book Of The Hours, Symphony No 1 (New England Philharmonic), 1988, Toward Eternity (Radcliffe Choral Society, Harvard University), 1988, Symphony No 4 (New England Philharmonic), 1989, Symphony No 5 (Pro Arte Orchestra, Boston), 1990; There Is A River for Soprano, Women's Chorus and Orchestra, 1985; Images From Stillness for String Trio, 1986; Images of Reminiscence for Piano, 1987; One for Solo Clarinet. Publication: Complete Works published. Address: 16 Forest Street No 41, Cambridge, MA 02140, USA.

L

LA BARBARA Joan (Lotz), b. 8 June 1947, Philadelphia, Pennsylvania, USA. Composer; Performer; Writer. m. Morton Subotnick, 18 Dec 1979, 1 son. Education: Syracuse University School of Music, 1965-68; Berkshire Music Center, Tanglewood, 1967-68; BS, New York University, 1970. Debut: With Steve Reich and Musicians, Town Hall, New York, 1971. Career: With Steve Reich, 1971-74, Philip Glass, 1973-76, John Cage, premiering Solo for Voice 45 with Atlas Eclipticlis, Winter Music with Orchestra of the Hague, 1976; In Avignon premiere, Einstein on the Beach, 1976; Premiered Subotnick's Double Life of Amphibians, Los Angeles Olympics Arts Festival, 1984; Own work, Houston and San Francisco Symphonies, 1982, Los Angeles Philharmonic, 1983, New York Philharmonic, 1984; Premiered: Subotnick's chamber opera Jacob's Room, American Music Theater Festival and MANCA Festival, Nice, 1993-94, quartet of operas Now Eleanor's Idea (R Ashley), Brooklyn Academy of Music and Avignon Festival, 1994; Many commissions; Newborn vocals for film ALien Resurrection, 1997.Compositions: Most recent: To hear the wind roar, choral, 1989-91; In the Dreamtime, (self portrait, sound painting), 1989; L'albero dalle foglie azzurre, solo oboe with tape, 1989; Awakenings, chamber ensemble, 1991; Klangbild Köln, 1991; 73 Poems to poems by Kenneth Goldsmith, 1994; Calligraphy II/Shadows, voice, dizi, erhu, yangqi, Chinese percussion, 1995; In the shadow and act of the haunting place, voice, chamber ensemble, 1995; Film: Angel Voice, for Date with an Angel, 1987; Score for Anima, 1991; A Trail of Indeterminate Light, for solo cello, 1997. Recordings include: The Art of Joan La Barbara; Sound Paintings; Joan La Barbara Singing through John Cage; 3 Voices for Joan La Barbara (Morton Feldman); Jacob's Room; 73 Poems, CD and CD with book, 1994; Awakenings; L'albero dalle Foglie azzurre; Only: Works for Voice and Instruments, 1996. Contributions to: Grove's Dictionary; Contributing new music editor, Musical America/High Fidelity; Schwann/Opus. Honours: NEA Commissions, 1981, 1982, 1984, 1989, 1991, 1993; Meet the Composer Commission, 1989-91, 1993-94. Memberships: American Society of Composers, Writers and Publishers; Actors' Equity Association; Screen Actors' Guild; American Federation of Television, Radio and Recording Artists. Current Management: Kristina Melcher, Daniel Kosharek, Santa Fe World Music Agency, USA. Address: 121 Coronado Lane, Santa Fe, NM 87501, USA.

LA GRANGE Henry Louis de, b. 26 May 1924, Paris, France. Writer on Music. Education: Studied at Aix-en-Provence and the Sorbonne, Paris; Yale University School of Music, 1941-47; Yvonne Lefébure (piano) and Nadia Boulanger, Harmony, counterpoint, analysis, 1947-53. Career: Music Critic for French and American publications; Guest Lecturer at Columbia, Stanford and Indiana Universities, 1974-81, Geneva, 1982, Leipzig, Juilliard, University of California at Los Angeles, 1985, Budapest, 1987, Hamburg, 1988, Oslo, 1993, also Paris Conservatory, Kyoto, Hong-Kong, Wellington, Sydney, Canberra, Melbourne, elsewhere; Taught a DEA Seminar at the Ecole Normale Supérieure, Paris; Founded the Bibliothèque Musicale Gustav Mahler, Paris, 1986. Publications include: Gustav Mahler: Chronique d'une Vie, 3 volumes, 1979-84; Vienne, Une Histoire musicale, 2 volumes, 1990-91; Mahler, volume I, England and USA, 1973-74. volume II, England and USA, 1994. Honours include: Légion d'Honneur; Officier, Ordre du Mérite; Title of Professor granted by Austrian Government. Address: c/o Bibliothèque Musicale Gustav Mahler, 11 bis, rue de Véezelay, F-75008 Paris, France.

LA MONTAINE John, b. 17 Mar 1920, Chicago, IL, USA. Composer. Education: Studied with Bernard Rogers and Howard Hanson at the Eastman School, with Wagenaar at Juilliard School and with Nadia Boulanger at the American Conservatory, Fontainebleau. Career: Pianist with the NBC Symphony conducted by Toscanini, 1950-54; Composer in Residence at American Academy, Rome, 1962; Visiting Professor at the Eastman School, 1964-65; Nixon Chair at Whittier College, CA, 1977; Currently President of Fredonia Press. Compositions include: Songs of the Rose of Sharon, for soprano and orchestra, 1956; Wonder Tidings for SATB, harp and percussion, 1957; Piano Concerto No.1, 1958; Fragments from the Song of Songs, for soprano and orchestra, 1959; A Trilogy of Medieval Christmas Operas, 1961-9; Birds of Paradise for piano and orchestra, 1964; Sacred Service, 1964-8; Wilderness Journal, after Thoreau, for bass-baritone, organ and orchestra, 1971; The Nine Lessons of Christmas for SATB, harp and percussion, 1975; Be Glad Then America, a Bicentennial opera, 1976; The Lessons of Advent, 1983; Piano Concertos 2, 3, and 4, 1987-9; Arrangement of Bach's Well-Tempered Clavier for Electronic Keyboard, 1991-2; Piccolo Sonata, 1993; A Complete Solution to Elgar's Enigma, for Double Chorus and Two Orchestras, 1995. Recordings include: Piano Concerto No 1 and No 4 (CD); Piano Sonata; Birds of Paradise; Songs of The Rose of Sharon; Flute Concerto (CD); Wilderness Journal (CD); Incantation for Jazz Band (CD); Conversations for Violin and Piano; Six Shakespeare Sonnets; The Nine Lessons of Christmas (CD); The Well-Tuned Keyboard, 2 CDs, after Bach. Publications: Many works published. Honours include: Guggenheim Fellowships; Pulitzer Prize for Piano Concerto, 1959; American Academy of Arts and Letters Award, 1962. Address: 3947 Fredonia Drive, Hollywood, CA 90068, USA.

LA RUE (Adrian) Jan Pieters, b. 31 July 1918, Kisaran, Sumatra. Education: SB, Magna cum laude, Phi Beta Kappa, Paine Fellow, Harvard, 1940; MFA, with distinction, Princeton, 1942; PhD, Dissertation: The Okinawan Classical Songs, Harvard, 1952. Career: Instructor to Associate Professor and Chairman of Music Department, Wellesley College, 1942-43, 1946-57; Profesor of Music, Graduate School of Arts and Science, New York University, 1957-88; Chairman, 1970-71, Executive Dean, 1963-64; Professor Emeritus, 1988; Visiting Professor, 1947; University of Michigan, 1963; Bar Ilan, Israel, 1980, Tokyo, 1988, Indiana, 1990, Queens, Canada, 1995; Research Professor, Austria, 1954-56; 1st Lieutenant, Transportation Corps, Okinawa Campaign, 16 months in Pacific Theatre, 1943-46; Music Curriculum Project, 1966-67; Councillor, Smithsonian Institute, 1967-73; Musicologist-in-Residence, Kennedy Centre, Washington, 1975. Compositions: Concertino, Clarinet and orchestra, 1941; Trio, strings, 1942. Publications: Guidelines for Style Analysis, 1970 (Sp ed 1988), 2nd ed, 1992; Methods and Models for Musical Style Analysis, with Ohmiya, Makoto, 1988; A Catalogue of 18th Century Symphonies, 1988. Contributions to: Die Musik in Geschichte und Gegenwart, 1968; Grove's Dictionary, 6th ed, 1980; Articles in numerous journals and Festschriften, including Festschriften Davison, 1957; Albrecht, 1962; Voetterie, 1968; Geiringer, 1970; Larsen, 1972; Johnson, 1990; Southern, 1992; Ratner, 1992; Editor: Festschriften Reese, 1966; Deutsch, 1968. Honours: Ford Foundation Fellow, 1954; Guggenheim Fellow, 1964-65; ACLS Fellow, 1964-65; NEH Research Grant, 1980-84; LaRue Festschrift Studies in Musical Sources and Style (ed Wolf and Roesner), 1990. Address: Woods End Road, New Canaan, CT 06840, USA.

LA SCOLA Vincenzo, b. 1958, Palermo, Italy. Tenor. Education: Studied with Carlo Bergonzi. Debut: Parma in 1983 as Ernesto in Don Pasquale. Career: Sang in Genoa and Liège, 1984, as Nemorino in Brussels and Rinuccio in Gianni Schicchi and Tonio in La Fille du Régiment in Paris, 1987-88; La Scala debut in 1988 as Nemorino returning 1991-92 as Alfredo and Edgardo in Lucia di Lammeroor; Other roles include Elvino in La Sonnambula at Venice in 1989, Orombello in Beatrice di Tenda, Mascagni's Amico Fritz, the Duke of Mantua and Florindo in Mascagni's Le Maschere; Sang Donizetti's Roberto Devereux at Bologna and Edgardo at La Scala in 1992, and Rodolfo in La Bohème at the Verona Arena in 1992; Sang Edgardo in Lucia di Lammermoor at Florence, 1996. Recordings include: Rossini's Petite Messe Solonelle; Beatrice di Tenda; Rigoletto under Muti; Le Maschere. Address: c/o Teatro alla Scala, Via Filodrammatici 2, I-20121 Milan, Italy.

LAADE Wolfgang, b. 13 Jan 1925, Zeitz, Germany. Ethnomusicologist. m. Dagmar Diedrich, 15 Aug 1962. Education: Musikhochschule Leipzig, 1943; Staatliche Musikhochschule Berlin, 1949-54; PhD, Freie Universitate, Berlin, 1954-60. Career: Research Fellow, Australian Institute of Aboriginal Studies, 1963-67; Research Fellow, Deutsche Forschungsgemeinschaft, 1968-70; Lecturer in Ethnomusicology, University of Heidelberg, 1969-71; Professor of Ethnomusicology, University of Zurich, Switzerland, 1971-90; Guest lectures at German, Austrian, American & Canadian Universities; Guest professorships: Helsinki, Stockholm, Innsbruck, Moscow; Field research in Lapland, Corsica, Tunisia, Australia, Torres Straits, New Guinea, New Britain, India, Sri Lanka, Taiwan, Zimbabwe. Recordings: 10 LP records & 7 CD's. Publications: Books: Die Struktur der korsischen Lamento-Melodik, 1962; Die Situation von Musikleben und Musikforschung in den Laendern Afrikas und Asiens und die neuen Aufgaben der Musikenthnologie, 1969; Neue Musik in Afrika, Asien und Ozeanien; Diskographie und historisch-stilistischer Ueberblick, 1971; Gegenwartsfragen der Musik in Afrika und Asien; eine grundlegende Bibliographie, 1971; Oral traditions & written documents on the history & ethnography of the Northern Torres Strait Islands, Vol 1, 1971; Klangdokumente historischer Tasteninstrumente, orgeln, Kiel-und Hammerklaviere eine Diskographie, 1972; Das Geisterkanu; Suedseemaerchen aus der Torres-Strasse, 1974; Musik der Goetter, Geister und Menschen; die Musik in der mythischen, fabulierenden und historischen Ueberlieferung der Voelker Afrikas, Nordasiens, Amerikas und Ozeaniens, 1975; Musikwissenschaft zwischen gestern und morgen; Das korsische Volkslied; ethnographische und historische Fragen, Gattungen und Stil, 3 vols, 1981-87; Musik und Musiker in Maerchen, Sagen und Anekdoten der Voelker Europas, Vol 1: Mitteleuropa, 1988; Music & Culture in South-East New Britain, in preparation; Compact Discs accompanied by books: Jecklin Disco-JD 652-2, The Confucius Temple Ceremony, Taiwan, 1991; JD 653-2, Taiwan: Music of the Aboriginal Tribes, 1991; JD 654-2, Zimbabwe: The Ndebele People, 1991; JD 655-2, Papua New Guinea: The Coast of the Western Province, 1993. Address: Holzmoosruetistrasse 11, CH-8820 Waedenswil, Switzerland.

LABELLE Dominique, b. 1960, Montreal, Canada. Singer (Soprano). Education: Studied at Boston University and with Phyllis Curtin. Career: Concert appearances with Symphony Orchestras of Dallas, Montreal and Boston; Messiah with Pittsburgh Symphony, Mahler's 2nd Symphony in St Louis and Vaughan Williams's Antarctica Symphony at Indianapolis; Other repertory includes the Verdi Quattro Pezzi Sacri, the Requiems of Mozart and Frank Martin, Mahler's Fourth, Les Nuits d'Eté and Mozart's Exsultate Jubilate; Opera engagements as Donna Anna in the Peter Sellars production of Don Giovanni, Elizabeth Zimmer in Elegy for Young Lovers, Mimi for Glimmerglass Opera, New York, the Countess and Susanna in Le nozze di Figaro at Vancouver (1992); Giulietta in I Capuleti e i Montecchi with Toledo Opera. Recordings include: Elektra, with Boston Symphony; Don Giovanni, on video; Masha and Chloe in The Queen of Spades, conducted by Ozawa. Honours include: Winner, Metropolitan Opera National Council Auditions, 1989. Address: c/o IMG Artists, Media House, 3 Burlington Lane, London W4 2TH, England.

LABEQUE Katia, b. 3 Mar 1950, Hendaye, France. Pianist. Education: Studied with mother, then at Paris Conservatoire. Career: Many appearances with sister, Marielle, in piano duet repertoire; Recitals in London, Paris, New York, Chicago, Boston, Vienna, Tokyo, Berlin, Frankfurt, Birmingham, Zurich; Appearances with the Cleveland Orchestra, Concertgebouw Orchestra, New York Philharmonic, Vienna Philharmonic and London Symphony Orchestra; Festival performances at Hollywood Bowl, Salzburg, Tanglewood, Edinburgh and Berlin; Conductors include: Bychkov, Chailly, Chung, Davis, Dutoit, Herbig, Lopez-Cobos, Mehta, Ozawa, Rattle, Sinopoli, Slatkin and Tilson-Thomas; Jazz collaborations with guitarist John McLaughlin; Featured in BBC TV documentary in 1992. Recordings: Gershwin's Rhapsody in Blue and Concerto in F; Recitals of Brahms, Liszt, Debussy, Ravel and Stravinsky; Rossini's Petite Messe Solenelle with the choir of King's College Cambridge; Bartók's Concerto for 2 Pianos and Orchestra; Symphonic Dances from West Side Story; España, Spanish recital disc; Encores; Love of Colours. Honours include: Gold Disc for Gershwin recording, Dvorák Slavonic Dances, Concertos for 2 Pianos by Bruch and Mendelssohn, and Encore!. Current Management: Trans Art. Address: c/o Trans Art, 8 Bristol Gardens, London, W9 2JG, England.

LABEQUE Marielle, b. 6 Mar 1952, Hendaye, France. Pianist. Education: Studied with mother, then at Paris Conservatoire. Career: Many appearances with sister, Katia, in piano duet repertoire, notably in music by, Bach, Mozart, Brahms, Gershwin, Messiaen, Boulez and Scott Joplin; Recitals in London, Paris, New York, Chicago and Boston; Appearances with the Cleveland Orchestra, Concertgebouw Orchestra, New York Philharmonic, Vienna Philharmonic and London Symphony Orchestra; Festival performances at Hollywood Bowl, Salzburg, Tanglewood, Edinburgh and Berlin; Conductors include: Bychkov, Chailly, Chung, Davis, Dutoit, Herbig, Lopez-Cobos, Mehta, Ozawa, Rattle, Sinopoli, Slatkin and Tilson-Thomas; Jazz collaborations with guitarist John McLaughlin; Featured in BBC TV documentary in 1992. Recordings: Mozart's Concertos K242 and K365 with the Berlin Philharmonic; Carnival of the Animals with the Israel Philharmonic; Poulenc's Concerto for Two Pianos (Philips); Recitals of Liszt, Debussy, Brahms and Stravinsky; Dvorak Slavonic Dances, Concertos to two pianos by Bruch and Mendelssohn (Philips); Encore!, (Sony). Honours include: Gold Disc for Gershwin recording, Dvorák's Slavonic Dances, Concertos for 2 Pianos by Bruch and Mendelssohn, Encore!. Current Management: Trans Art. Address: c/o Trans Art, 8 Bristol Gardens, London, W9 2JG, England.

LABUDA Izabela, b. 1961, Poland. Soprano. Career: Sang Adina in L'Elisir d'Amore and other roles in Poland from 1982; Moved to Germany in 1990 singing at the Essen Opera as Frau Fluth, Janacek's Vixen, and Hanna Glawari in Die Lustige Witwe; Guest at Mannheim Opera, the Vienna Volksoper and the State Opera of Vienna as First Lady in Die Zauberflöte, 1992; Other repertory includes Lucille in Danton's Tod at Volksoper. Address: c/o Staatsoper, Opernring 2, A-1010 Vienna, Austria.

LACHENMANN Helmut, b. 27 Nov 1935, Stuttgart, Germany. Composer. Education: Studied at Stuttgart with Jurgen Uhde (piano) and Johann Nepomuk David (composition); Venice with Luigi Nono. Career includes: Teacher of music theory at Stuttgart Hochschule für Musik, 1966-70, Ludwigsburg Hochschule, 1970-76, Hanover Hochschule für Musik, 1976-81 and Musikhochschule Stuttgart, 1981-; Masterclasses in composition at Basle Music Academy; Instructor at the Ferienkurse in Darmstadt, 1978, 1982, Cursos Latinamericanos de Musica Contemporanae in Brazil, 1978, and Dominican Republic in 1980; Member of Akademie der Kunste, Berlin, Akademie der Schonen Kunste, Munich and Freie Akademie der

Kunste, Hamburg, Leipzig. Compositions include: Souvenir for 41 Instruments, 1959; String Trio, 1966; Les Consolations for Solo Voices, and Orchestra, 1967-68, 1977-78; Tema for Flute, Voice and Cello, 1968; Air for Percussion and Orchestra, 1968-69; Dal Niente for Clarinet, 1970; Klangschatten for 48 Strings and 3 Pianos, 1972; Accanto for Clarinet and Orchestra, 1975; Tanzsuite Mit Deutschlandlied for String Quartet and Orchestra, 1979-80; Harmonica for Tuba and Orchestra, 1981-83; Movement for ensemble, 1983-84; Ausklang for Piano and Orchestra, 1984-85; Allegro Sostenuto for Clarinet, Cello and Piano, 1986-88; II Streichquartett "Reigen Seliger Geister", 1989; Zwei Gefuehle, Musik mit Leonardo for ensemble, 1992; Opera, Das Mädchen mit dem Schwefehölzern, 1997; Das Mädchen mit den Schwefalhoelzern, opera, 1997. Honours: Cultural Prize of Music, City of Munich, 1965; Composition Prize, City of Stuttgart, 1968; Bach Prize, Hamburg, 1972; Siemens Prize, 1997. Address: c/o Breitkopf and Hartel, Walkmuhlstr 52, D- 65195 Wiesbaden, Germany.

LACHMANN Elisabeth, b. 20 Apr 1940, Vienna, Austria. Soprano. Education: Studied in Vienna. Debut: Berne in 1961 as Despina, and Cagliari in Wiener Blut. Career: Sang at Karlsruhe, 1962-64 as Micaela, Marenka, Cherubino and Regina in Mathis der Maler, and Graz, 1964-68 as Pamina, Susanna, Frau Fluth and Zdenka in Arabella; Engaged at Dortmund from 1968 as Mimi, Sophie, Sieglinde, Desdemona, Donna Anna, the Trovatore Leonora, Wagner's Elisabeth, Venus and Brünnhilde, Tosca, Amelia in Un Ballo in Maschera, Aida, Senta, Ariadne and Abigaille; These and other roles in guest appearances at Vienna State Opera, Hamburg, Stuttgart, Frankfurt, Cologne, Zurich and Antwerp; Concert and opera tours to the Netherlands, France, Far East, Africa, South America and Switzerland; Professor at Detmold Musikhochschule, 1984-. Address: Heiligenpesch 18A, D-41069 Mönchengladbach, Germany.

LACHOUT Karel, b. 30 Apr 1929, Prague, Czechoslovakia. Ethnomusicologist; Composer. Education: MusD, Charles University, Prague, Czechoslovakia, 1953; Composition, Academy of Musical Arts in Prague, 1949-54; Private studies. Career: Redacteur of Music Department, Radio Prague, 1953-79; Freelance Composer and Ethnomusicologist, specialising in Latin American Music and Folklore, 1980-. Compositions include: Music for Orchestra, piano pieces, suite Such is Cuba, 1962, 2 string quartets, pieces for dance and light music. Recordings: Origins of Folkmusic in Latin America, a selection of music examples in 2 LP records, with own textbook, Prague, 1987; Folkmusic of Spain, a selection in 2 LPs with own textbook, 1989. Publications: The World Sings, 1957; Music of Chile, 1976; Music of Cuba, 1979; Lexicon of Latin American Music, 1980; Panorama of Spanish Music, 1981; Lullabies from all the World, collection, 1989. Hobbies: Languages (Latin, English, Spanish); Travelling abroad to explore origins of music in foreign countries. Address: Viklefova 11, Prague 3, Czech Republic.

LADE John, b. 8 Apr 1916, Tunbridge Wells, Kent, England. Broadcaster; Writer. m. Susan Ridehalgh-Fisher, 5 Dec 1942, 1 daughter. Education: Licentiate, Trinity College, London, 1946-48. Career: Broadcaster, Music Talks, 1947-; Lecturer, Extra-Mural Department, London University; Producer, 1953, Chief Assistant (Music), Head of Gramophone Programmes, 1972-77, Producer and Initiator, BBC Record Review, 1957 for 1,000 programmes, Organ Gallery, Journeys with Music and others. Publications: Editor, Building a Library and Building a Library 2, based on BBC Record Review, 1979 and 1980; Editor of Series, The Composer as Contemporary; Record Critic, The Tablet; Writer of many record sleeves. Contributions to: Musical Times; Listener; Daily Telegraph; Gramophone. Hobbies: Good food and drink; Reading; Book collecting. Address: Flat 12, 105 Cheyne Walk, London SW10 0DF, England.

LADERMAN Ezra, b. 29 June 1924, Brooklyn, New York, USA. Composer. Education: Studied with Stefan Wolpe, 1946-49; Studied with Miriam Godeon, BA, 1949, Brooklyn College; Columbia University with Douglas Moore and Otto Luening, 1950-52. Career: Teacher, Sarah Lawrence College, 1960-61, 1965-66; State University of New York at Binghampton, 1971-82; Director of the Music program, National Endowment for the Arts, 1979-82; Dean, School of Music, 1989-95, Professor of Music, 1995-, Yale University. Compositions: Dramatic: Jacob and the Indians, opera, 1954; Goodbye to the Clowns, opera, 1956; The Hunting of the Snark, opera-contata, 1958; Sarah, television opera, 1959; Ballets Dance Quartet, esther, Song of Songs, Solos and Chorale; Air Raid, opera, 1965; Shadows Among Us, opera, 1967; Galileo Galilei, opera, 1978; Film and television scores; Orchestral: Piano Concerto, 1939; Leipzig Symphony, 1945; Piano Concerto, 1957; 8 Symphonies, 1964-84; Flute Concerto, 1968; Viola Concerto, 1975; Violin Concerto, 1978; Piano Concerto No 1, 1978; Concerto for String Quartet and Orchestra, 1981; Cello Concerto, 1984; Vocal: oratorios The Eagle Stirred, 1961, A Mass for Cain, 1983; Columbus, cantata, 1975; Chamber: Wind Octet, 1957; Clarinet Sonata, 1958; Double Helix for flute, oboe and string quartet, 1968; Partita for violin, 1982; Double String Quartet, 1983; 8 Symphonies, 1963-93; 9 String Quartets, 1959-95; Marilyn, opera, 1993; The Black Fox, 1968. Recordings: Piano Quintet, RCA; Quartet No 6, RCA; Concerto for Double Orchestra, New World; Pentimento, CRI. Honours include: Oscar for film music, The Eleanor Roosevelt Story, 1965. Address: C/O ASCAP, ASCAP Building, 1 Lincoln Plaza, New York, NY 10023, USA.

LADYSZ Bernard, b. 24 Jul 1922, Vilnius, Poland. Bass Singer. Education: Studied at the Warsaw Conservatory. Career: Sang at the Teatr Wielki Warsaw from 1950 and from 1956 appeared in Chicago, San Francisco, Moscow, Palermo, Naples and Parma; Hamburg Staatsoper in 1969 as Father Barre in The Devils of Loudun by Penderecki; Other roles were Don Giovanni, Boris Godunov, Philip II and the Grand Inquisitor in Don Carlos, Mephistopheles and Szymanowski's King Roger. Recordings include: Raimondo in Lucia di Lammermoor, with Maria Callas; The Devils of Loudun; Penderecki's St Luke Passion and Utrenja.

LAFFAGE Jean-Pierre, b. 26 June 1926, Paris, France. Singer (Baritone). Education: Studied at the Dijon and Paris Conservatories. Debut: Paris Opera 1957, as Valentin in Faust. Career: Sang at the Paris Opera until 1972 and the Opéra-Comique until 1980; Guest appearances throughout France and Italy; Among his best roles were Don Alvar in Les Indes Galantes, Mozart's Figaro, Escamillo, Sharpless, the Villains in Les Contes d'Hoffmann, Ourrais in Mireille, Scarpia, Ford, Amonasro and Oreste in Iphigénie en Aulide; Professor at the Paris Conservatoire, 1977-87. Address: c/o Conservatoire National, 14 Rue de Madrid, F-75008 Paris, France.

LAFITTE Florence, b. 1 July 1961. Two-Piano Duo. Education: Conservatoire National Superieur de Musique, Lyon, France; Liszt Academy, Budapest, Hungary; Manhattan School of Music, New York, USA. Career: Numerous concert appearances in France, Germany, Hungary, USA and Sweden; Tours of Australia, New Caledonia, Indonesia, Brazil, Argentina and Chile. Radio and television appearances at home and abroad. Recordings: Concerto for 2 pianos and orchestra by Poulenc, Orchestre Symphonique Francais, Conductor Laurent Petitgirard, VMG; 2 Piano Recital, Mozart, Liszt, Mendelssohn. Honours: International Music Video Competition, Fuji TV Network, Tokyo, 1987; Honorary Award, Murray Dranoff's Two Piano Competition, Miami, 1990. Current Management: Liliane Weinstadt. Address: 69 B-1180 Brussels, Belgium.

LAFITTE Isabelle, b. 10 July 1961. Two-Piano Duo. Education: Conservatoire National Superieur de Musique, Lyon, France; Liszt Academy, Budapest, Hungary; Manhattan School of Music, New York, USA. Career: Numerous concerts at home and abroad including Germany, Hungary, USA, Stwden; Tours of Australia, New Caledonia, Indonesia, Brazil, Argentina and Chile; Several Radio and Television appearances. Recordings: Concerto for Two Pianos and Orchestra by Poulenc, Orchestre Symphonique Francais, Conductor Laurent Petitgirard; Two Piano Recital, Mozart, Liszt, Mendelssohn. Honours: International Music Video Competition, Fuji TV Network, Tokyo, 1987; Honorary Award, Murray Dranoff's Two Piano Competition, Miami, 1990. Current Management: Liliane Weinstadt. Address: Rue Langeveld 69, B-1180 Brussels, Belgium.

LAFONT Jean-Philippe, b. 4 Feb 1951, Toulouse, France. Bass-Baritone. Education: Studied in Toulouse with Denise Dupleix and in Paris with Gabriel Bacquier. Debut: Toulouse in 1974 as Papageno. Career: Sang at Paris Opéra in 1977 as Nick Shadow in The Rake's Progress, Albi from 1977 as Mozart's Guglielmo and in Grétry's Les Femmes Vengées and Tom Jones, and Paris from 1978 in operas by Gounod, Offenbach, Gluck and Cherubini; Sang in Berlin in the European premiere of Debussy's La Chute de la Maison Usher, at Lyon in 1980 as Choroebus in the French premiere of Les Troyens, and at Aix-en-Provence in 1982 as Boreas in the stage premiere of Rameau's Les Boréades; Guest appearances in Strasbourg, Geneva, Lille, Hamburg, Hanover and Nimes; New York debut in 1983 as Fieramosca in Benvenuto Cellini at Carnegie Hall; Perugia in 1983 in Salieri's Les Daniades, Paris Opéra in 1983 as Rossini's Moise, Brussels and Barcelona in 1984 as Mozart's Count, Rome in 1985 in Cherubini's Demophoon, Aix in 1986 as Leporello in Don Giovanni and sang Amonasro at Bonn in 1989, Debussy's Golaud at Marseilles in 1990, and Alcide in Lully's Alceste at the Théâtre des Champs Elysées, 1991-92; Rigoletto for New Israeli Opera, 1997. Recordings include: Les Boréades; Gounod's Messe Solonelle; La Belle Hélène; Le Postillon de Lonjumeau by Adam. Address: c/o Opéra de Marseilles, 2 Rue Molière, F-13231 Marseille Cedex 01, France.

LAGRANGE Michele, b. 29 May 1947, Conches, Saone-et-Loire, France. Soprano. Education: Studied in Paris. Career: Engaged at Lyon Opera from 1978; Sang at Paris Opéra, 1984-85 in Jerusalem by Verdi and as Alice in Robert le Diable by Meyerbeer; Opéra Comique, 1987 as Donna Anna at the Teatro Colon in Buenos Aires, 1982 as Teresa in Benvenuto Cellini at the Aix-en-Provence Festival, 1989 as Fata Morgana in The Love for Three Oranges; Sang Marguerite in Faust at Avignon and St Etienne, season 1990-91; Montpellier Festival in 1991 in Bizet's Ivan IV, concert performance; Sang Fiorella in Offenbach's Les Brigands at Amsterdam and Isabella in Franchetti's Christoforo Colombo at Montpellier in 1992; Other roles include Musette and Elisabeth de Valois. Recordings include: Poulenc Salve Regina and Stabat Mater; Guercoeur by Magnard; The Love for Three Oranges. Address: c/o Saison Lyrique de St Etienne, 8 Place de L'Hotel de Ville, F-4200 St Etienne, France.

LAGZDINA Vineta, b. 11 Nov 1945, Oldenberg, Germany. Composer; Performer. 1 daughter. Education: BMus, University of Adelaide, 1976; Instrumental Teachers' Certificate, 1979; Computer music studies, Adelaide University Conservatorium, 1980-81. Career: Sound works included in exhibitions in Australia, New Zealand and Japan; Film music includes electronic, computer generated and instrumental, 1978-; Video art music; Grants for experimental music and movement performances, 1981-82; Composer's grant for radio, 1983; Curated Audio-Eyes, exhibition, 1983; Lecturer, Sydney College of The Arts, Music Across the Arts, 1984-; ABC Radio, 1987; The White Bird Music Theatre, 1987; Shock Of The New, video sound track, 1987; Speaking Out, film sound track, 1987. Compositions: Obstruction, computer sound tape for dance, 1981; Noh-Work, a quadrophonic Percussion Tape, 1982; The Black Snake, tape piece for Voice and Electronics, 1983; Double-Dream, Triple fate, video sound tracks, 1984-85; Media Massage, spoken song, 1986. Publications: 22 Contemporary Australian Composers. Contributions to: Article in Art Network, 1983 and in New Music Australia 4, 1985. Address: Flat 11, 26 Pearson Street, Balmain East 2041, Australia.

LAKES Gary, b. 26 Sep 1950, Dallas, TX, USA. Tenor. Education:Vocal studies with William Eddy at Seattle Opera. Debut: Seattle in 1981 as Froh in Das Rheingold. Career: Sang at Mexico City in 1983 as Florestan in Fidelio and Charlotte Opera in 1984 as Samson in Samson et Dalila; Metropolitan Opera debut in 1986 as the High Priest in Idomeneo returning as Tannhäuser and as Siegmund in a new production of Die Walküre; Sang the Emperor in Die Frau ohne Schatten at the Metropolitan in 1989, Radames at New Orleans, Erik in Der fliegende Holländer at the Metropolitan in 1990 followed by Siegmund in New York (also televised) and San Francisco; Sang in Das Lied Von der Erde at the 1991 Promenade Concerts, London; Season 1991-92 as Lohengrin at Buenos Aires and Erik at the Metropolitan; Sang the Berlioz Faust at the Festival Hall, London, 1994; Florestan at the Lincoln Center Festival, 1996. Recordings include: Die Walküre conducted by James Levine. Address: c/o Metropolitan Opera, Lincoln Center, New York, NY 10023, USA.

LAKI Krisztina, b. 14 Sept 1944, Budapest, Hungary. Soprano. Education: Studied at Budapest Conservatory. Debut: Berne, 1976 as Gilda in Rigoletto. Career: Sang with the Deutsche Opera am Rhein, Dusseldorf, in Cologne, and at Bregenz and Edinburgh Festivals; Glyndebourne, 1979-80 as Aminta in Die schweigsame Frau and Sophie in Der Rosenkavalier; Salzburg in 1980 as Lucille in Von Einem's Dantons Tod; Tour of East Germany in 1984 notably in cantatas by Bach; Paris Opéra in 1984 as Sophie; Other roles include Zdenka in Arabella, Mozart's Queen of the Night, Zerlina and Susanna, Carolina in Il Matrimonio Segreto and Nannetta in Falstaff; Sang Marzelline in Fidelio at Hamburg in 1988 and Zdenka at Barcelona in 1989; Sang Marzelline with the company of the Cologne Opera at Hong Hong; Also widely heard in oratorio. Recordings: St Matthew Passion by Bach; Handel's Partenope; Masses by Haydn; Dantons Tod; Concert Arias by Mozart; Bach's Christmas Oratorio; Mozart's C minor Mass; Paisiello's Il Barbiere di Siviglia; Mozart's Schauspieldirektor and Myslivecek's Il Bellerofonte. Address: Oper der Stadt Köln, Offenbachplatz, D-5000 Cologne, Germany.

LAKI Peter, b. 1 February 1954, Budapest, Hungary. Musicologist. m. (1) Judith Frigyesi, 12 April 1978, 1 son, (2) Adrienne Elisha, 10 April 1994. Education: Musicology Diploma, Franz Liszt Conservatory, Budapest, 1979; PhD, Music, University of Pennsylvania, 1989. Appointment: Program Annotator, The Cleveland Orchestra, 1990-. Publication: Bartók and His World (editor), 1995. Membership: AMS (American Musical Society. Hobbies: Hiking; Swimming; Reading. Address: 1393 Willshire, Lyndhurst, OH 44124, USA.

LAKNER Yehoshua, b. 24 Apr 1924, Bratislava, Czechoslovakia. Composer. Education: Studied with Oedoen Partos, Alexander U Boskovich and Frank Pelleg, 1943-48; Studied in USA with Aaron Copland, Tanglewood, Berkshire Music Centre, 1952; Studied at WDR studio for electronic music, Cologne, and with Bernd Alois Zimmermann at Cologne Music Academy, 1959-60. Career: Teacher, Tel-Aviv Music Academy, 1950-63; Composer of music for several theatres, 1965-72; Teacher, Conservatory and Academy of Music, Zurich, 1974-87; Since 1987 has concentrated mainly on Audio-Visual computer composition (AVTS) and has performed his music extensively throughout Europe and Israel. Compositions include: Flute

Sonata, 1948; Sextet for Piano and Wind, 1951; Toccata for Orchestra, 1953; Hexachords for Orchestra, 1960; Figures, ballet, 1962; Dream Of Mohamed for Chorus and Tape, 1968; Kaninchen for Speaker, Percussion and Tape, 1973; Fermatas for Piano, 1977; Circles And Signals for 2 Pianos, 1985; Aleph-Beth-Gimmel for Piano, 1992; Composed "Concrete Music" for various dramatic works at Theater an der Winkelwiese, the Schauspielhaus Zurich (world premiere of Brecht's Turandot, 1969), Theater am Neumarkt; Music for a number of art and commercial films; Composition of AVTS, audio-visual time-structures for computer and screen, 1987-; Musikado, 1987-91; Mini-Mal-Plus; 8 Out Of 59; Die-Das-Den-Die; Black, Bluegreen And Other Sounds; Summary 15; Colored Interruptions; Nowis; Rondo 1993; Unrest for 2 Computers, 1994; Rufe aus dem Dunkel, 1994; 7 Duette für 2 Computers, 1994; Flüchtige Figur, 1994; Chanukiya, 1994; Trilogie 95, 1995; In Memoriam RM, 1995; Klangparalellen, 1995; KLP 6-stimmig, 1995; Kaw we dofek (Line and Pulse), 1995; Tanz der Akzente, 1996; Yagon/Widmung für Selma, 1996; L12c, 1996; SDK, 1996; Alfa-numerisches Ballet, 1997; BX with Variations, 1997; Aufruhr in Mykäne, 1997; Duett der Stillen Berge, 1997. Publication: A New Method of Representing Tonal Relations, 1960. Contributions to: Journals. Honours include: Engel Prize of the Tel Aviv Municipality, 1958; Prize of the Salomon David Steinberg Stiftung, Zurich-Jerusalem, 1970; Komponisten-Werkjahr of the Municipality of Zurich, 1987. Address: Biberlinstr 5, CH-8032 Zurich, Switzerland.

LALANDI Lina (Madeleine), b. Athens, Greece. Festival Director. m. Ralph Emery. Education: Graduated with honours, Athens Conservatory; Privte study in England; Harpsichord and Singing. Career: International career as Harpsichordist, London, Paris, Geneva, Athens; Radio and TV; Founder and Director, English Bach Festival Trust, 1962, specialising now in baroque opera, Purcell, Handel, Rameau, Gluck, Dido and Aeneas and Lully's Bourgeois Gentilhomme, 1995. Honours: OBE, 1975; Officier dans l'Ordre des Arts et des Lettres, France, for services to culture, 1979. Hobbies: Reading; Astrophysics. Address: 15 South Eaton Place, London SW1W 9ER, England.

LALE Peter, b. 1960, England. Violist. Career: Founder Member of the Britten Quartet with debut concert at Wigmore Hall in 1987; Quartet in Residence at the Dartington Summer School in 1987 with quartets by Schnittke; Season 1988-89 includes BBC Lunchtime Series at St John's Smith Square, concerts with the Hermann Prey Schubertiade and collaborations with the Alban Berg Quartet in the Beethoven Plus Series; Season 1989-90 includes debut tours of Holland, Germany, Spain, Austria and Finland, festival appearances at Brighton, City of London, Greenwich, Canterbury, Harrogate, Chester, Spitalfields and Aldeburgh; Formerly resident quartet at Liverpool University; Teaching role at Lake District Summer Music, 1989 and Universities of Bristol and Hong Kong in 1990. Recordings: Beethoven Op 130 and Schnittke Quartet No 3; Vaughan Williams On Wenlock Edge and Ravel Quartet; Britten, Prokofiev, Tippett, Elgar and Walton Quartets. Address: c/o Ingpen and Williams Ltd, 26 Wadham Road, London SW15 2LR, England.

LALLOUETTE Olivier, b. 1970, Paris, France. Singer (Bass). Education: Studied with Marion Sylvstre at the Avignon Conservatoire, Peter Gottlieb at the Paris Conservatoire and Michel Sénéchal at the Ecole d'Art Lyrique, Paris; Further study with René Jacobs and Rachel Yakar at the Opera Studio of the Centre de Musique Baroque at Versailles. Career: Many performances throughout France and Europe in the Mozart, Bel Canto and Baroque repertory; Repertory ranges from Peri's Euridice (1600) to contemporary works, including French 19th century opera; Sang Berardo in Handel's Riccardo Primo with Les Talens Lyriques, Fontevraud, France, 1995. Recordings include: Riccardo Primo (Decca/L'Oiseau Lyre). Honours include: Henri Duparc Prize for Song, 1989. Address: Decca L'Oiseau Lyre (Artists Contracts), Polygram Classics, 1 Sussex Place, London W6 9XS, England.

LALOR Stephen, b. 11 January 1962, Sydney, New South Wales, Australia. Composer; Musical Director. Education: MMus, University of New South Wales, 1988; Tchaikovsky Conservatory, Moscow, 1984-85 and 1988-89. Career: Freelance Composer and Music Education Writer; Director and Arranger for the Sydney Domra Ensemble, 1978-85; Commissions from Macquarie University (1994), among others. Compositions include: Alice: A Musical for Children, 1986; Prelude and Dance for violin and piano, 1988; Six Angels, song cycle for baritone and piano; Three Pieces for Piano, 1989; Three Pieces for Solo Violin, 1989; Damascus, opera, 1990; At the Edhe, for orchestra, 1991; String Quartet, 1991; Maroubra Song Cycle, for soprano, 1991; Capricornia, for string orchestra, 1993; Way Home for soprano or treble, narrator and tape, 1994. Honours include: USSR Government Ukrainian Society Scholarship, 1988. Address: c/o APRA, 1A Eden Street, Crows Nest, NSW 2065, Australia.

LAM Bun-Ching, b. 26 June 1954, Macau. Composer. Education: BA, Chinese University of Hong Kong; MA, PhD, University of California, San Diego. Career: Teacher at Cornish College of the Arts, 1981-86, with performances of her music in Europe, the Far East and the USA; Works featured in music festivals such as ISCM, Steirische Herbst, Austria, Bang on a Can, New York, Tokyo Summer Festival, Japan, New Music America, Hong Kong Arts Festival; Work performed by Vienna Radio Symphony Orchestra, American Composers Orchestra, Women's Philharmonic. Compositions include: Violin Concerto, 1981; Clouds I-IV for Chorus and Ensemble, 1986-94; Impetus, for Chinese orchestra, 1987; Saudades De Macau for Orchestra, 1989; Klang for Solo Percussion, 1990; Last Spring, piano quintet, 1992; Circle for Orchestra, 1992; The Child God, puppet opera, 1993; Sudden Thunder, for pipa and orchestra, 1994; Like Water, for piano, violin and percussion, 1995. Recordings: Mountain Clear Water Remote; Like Water; Run; Klang; E.O.9066; Bittersweet Music I. Honours: National Endowment for the Arts, 1989, 1995; New York Foundation for the Arts Fellowship, 1992; Rome Prize, 1992; Lili Boulanger Award, 1993; Meet the Composer/Lila Wallace Reader's Digest Commission, 1993, 1995. Memberships: BMI; American Music Centre; American Composers' Forum; New York Women Composers' Inc. Address: Notevole Music Publishing Inc, 91 Christopher Street, Montclair, NJ 07042, USA.

LAMA Lina, b. 20 Apr 1932, Faenza, Italy. Concert Violist; Professor of Viola. Education: Diplomas in Violin and Viola, Piano and Composition. Debut: Teatro S Carlo, Naples. Career: Professor at Conservatorio di Musica S Cecilia, Rome, 1959; Appearances on BBC and Italian TV and Radio; Concerts in Germany, Belgium, Italy, Israel, Hungary, Greece, Finland, France, North and South America, Africa, Asia and Japan; Concerts throughout Europe under Italian and foreign Maestri; Sonata per La Gran Viola by Paganini performed at Teatro San Carlo, Naples; Teacher of Viola at Conservatoire of S Cecilia, Roma Festival; International specialisation courses at Festival of Jywaskyla, Finland, Città di Castello, Lanciano, and Mezzolombardo, Italy; Jury Member for international viola competitions: Budapest, 1979, N Paganini, Genova, 1988 and for national viola competition at Vittaorio Veneto, 1986. Honours: Concert Prizes in Italy; Accademico of Accademia di S Cecilia, Roma; Cavaliere al Merito della Repubblica Italiana. Hobby: Painting. Address: Via Ugo de Carolis 31, 00136 Rome, Italy.

LAMARCHINA Robert, b. 3 Sept 1928, New York City, USA. Cellist; Conductor. Education: Paris Conservatoire; Curtis Institute with Piatigorsky and Feuermann. Debut: With St Louis Symphony under Vladimir Golschmann. Career: Played in NBC Symphony Orchestra under Toscanini, 1944; Conductor and Musical Director with Young Musicians Foundation, Los Angeles, 1952-53; Solo Cellist with Chicago Symphony under Fritz Reiner in 1960; Conducted at Metropolitan Opera, La Traviata at Spoleto and Menotti's The Medium at the New York City Opera; Artistic and Musical Director with Honolulu Symphony Society and Hawaii Opera Theatre, 1967-79; Conductor of numerous symphony orchestras and opera companies including New York Philharmonic, St Louis Symphony, Chicago Symphony, Radio Italiana, Zurich Symphony, Vancouver Opera Association and Fujiwara Opera Institute.

LAMB Anthony (Stuart), b. 4 Jan 1947, Woodford, England. Clarinettist. m. Philippa Carpenter-Jacobs, 1 son, 2 daughters. Education: Royal College of Music; ARCM. Debut: With Chamber Ensemble Capricorn at Wigmore Hall in London, 1974. Career: Principal Clarinet with Royal Ballet Orchestra, 1969-71; Founder member of Capricorn (violin, clarinet, cello and piano), 1973 with many concerts and broadcasts; Co-Principal with English National Opera Orchestra, 1976-; Several BBC broadcasts; Freelance Clarinettist with most major British orchestras. Recordings: With Capricorn: Rimsky-Korsakov's Quintet in B flat for Piano and Wind, Glinka's Grand Sextet in E flat for Piano and Strings, 1985. Membership: Musicians Union. Hobby: Tennis. Address: 22 Munster Road, Teddington, Middlesex, TW11 9LL, England.

LAMBERTI Giorgio, b. 9 July 1938, Adria, Rovigo, Italy. Tenor. Education: Studied in Mantua. Debut: Rome in 1964 as Arrigo in I Vespri Siciliani. Career: US debut at Chicago in 1965 as Radames; Rome in 1965 in the premiere of Wallenstein by Zafred; Metropolitan Opera from 1974 as Enzo, Cavaradossi, Radames and Turiddu; Engagements in Paris, Brussels, Budapest, Baltimore, Amsterdam, Helsinki, Florence and Venice; Covent Garden debut, Don Carlos in 1979; Other roles include Pollione, Don José, Jason in Medée, Verdi's Ernani, Alvaro, Manrico and Riccardo, Wagner's Tannhäuser and Lohengrin, Edgardo in Lucia di Lammermoor; Sang Radames at Berlin and Luxor in 1987 and Caracalla Festival, Rome, 1989; Andrea Chénier at Stuttgart in 1988 and appeared as Stiffelio in the first Covent Garden production of Verdi's opera in 1993. Recordings include: Ernani; I Lombardi; Il Corsaro; Gemma di Vergy by Donizetti; Bellini's Zaira. Address: Marks Management, 14 New Burlington Street, London, W1 5HJ, England.

LAMBERTINI Marta, b. 13 Nov 1937, San Isidri, Buenos Aires, Argentine. Composer. Education: Studied at the Catholic University in Argentina and in Buenos Aires. Compositions include: Chamber operas: Alice in Wonderland in 1989 and, Oh, Eternidad...Ossia SMR Bach, 1990; Concertino Serenata in 1981 and Galileo Descubre Las Cuatro Lunas De Jupiter, 1985 for orchestra; Instrumental pieces include Assorted Kochels, 1991 and vocal music, Escena De La Falsa Tortuga, 1993. Address: c/o Lavalle 1547, Apartado Postal Number 11, Sucursal 44-B, 1048 Buenos Aires, Argentina.

LAMBRO Phillip, b. 2 Sept 1935, Wellesley, Massachusetts, USA. Composer; Conductor; Pianist. Education: Studied Music in Boston, later in Miami, Florida; Received scholarship to the Music Academy of the West in California, 1955; Teachers include Donald Pond and György Sandor. Debut: Pianist's Fair, Symphony Hall, Boston, 1952. Career: Composed and conducted music for several motion pictures including documentaries; Major performances now in Israel, Europe and the Orient; His compositions performed by Leopold Stokowski, Philippe Entremont, Santiago Rodriguez, The Philadelphia Orchestra, the Rochester Philharmonic, Baltimore, Indianapolis, Miami, Denver, Oklahoma and New Orleans Symphonies. Compositions include: Miraflores for string orchestra; Dance Barbaro for percussion; Two Pictures for solo percussionist and orchestra; Four Songs for soprano and orchestra; Toccata for piano; Toccata for guitar; Parallelograms for flute quartet and jazz ensemble; Music for wind, brass and percussion; Obelisk for oboist and percussionist; Structures for string orchestra; Fanfare and Tower Music for brass quintet; Night Pieces for piano; Biospheres for 6 percussionists; Trumpet Voluntary; Eight Little Trigrams for Piano. Address: 1888 Century Park East, Suite 1900, Century City, CA 90067-1702, USA.

LAMBROS Simon (David), b. 17 Jan 1960, Mansfield, Nottinghamshire, England. Composer. Education: BSc (Hons), University College, London, 1978; PGCE, Manchester (Victoria) University, 1984; Postgraduate Diploma, Composition, London College of Music; Studied with Tom Williams at Keele University, Simon Parkin at Royal Northern College of Music, Alan Wilson at Goldsmiths and Francis Shaw, National Film and TV School. Career: Thames TV appearance to explain film music techniques to Prince Edward, Nov 1992; Important performances of his works. Compositions include: Magnificat and Nunc Dimittis, 1st performance Worcester Cathedral, 1981; Preludio for orchestra, Thaxted Festival, 1982; Etude for Strings, Bowdon Festival, 1987; Mass of St Francis, Granada TV, 1988; Cello Concerto, Stockport Town Hall with S Callow and Gorton Philharmonic, 1989; Psalm 134 for choir and orchestra, Queen Elizabeth Hall, Oldham, 1990; In Memoriam for choir and orchestra, Stoke-on-Trent, 1991; Clarinet Concerto, University College London with G Denny, 1992; Music, award-winning films: Pirates; A Place in Danger; Blindscape; Music, other films including: Fix und Fertig (German Cinema); Mitologia (Spanish Cinema); Full Throttle (BBC); Queen of the East (BBC); Dream Child (BBC); Ms (Channel 4); Dropping the Baby. Address: Elmina, Old Dashwood Hill, Studley Green, Buckinghamshire HP14 3XD, England.

LAMMERS Gerda, b. 13 Feb 1915, Zeitz, Germany. Soprano. Education: Studied in Berlin with Lula Mysz-Gmeiner and Margret Schwedler-Lohmann. Debut: 1940 as concert singer. Career: Stage debut in 1955 as Ortlinde at Bayreuth; Sang at Kassel, 1956-69 notably as Elektra, Marie in Wozzeck, Wagner's Senta, Isolde and Brünnhilde and Cherubini's Medée, Covent Garden, 1957 and 1959 as Elektra and Kundry, Metropolitan Opera in 1962 as Elektra, and Hamburg Staatsoper in 1959 and 1967. Recordings include: Hindemith's Das Marienleben; Monteverdi's Orfeo.

LAMOREAUX Rosa (Lea), b. 19 Oct 1955, Farmington, New Mexico, USA. Musician-Soprano. m. James L McHugh, 8 Sept 1991. Education: Bachelor of Music, University of Redlands, 1977; ARCM, Royal College of Music, London, England, 1979; Master of Music, University of Redlands, California, 1980. Debut: Kennedy Center. Career: Numerous performances at Kennedy Center, Mozart-Requiem, Exultate Jubilate, Bach-B-minor Mass and Magnificat, Coffee Cantata and Peasant Cantata both staged; Carmel Bach Festival in California, Mozart Bastien Bastienne, Handel Xerxes, role of Romilda, Bach B minor Mass, Haydn Paukenmasse, Lord Nelson Mass, St John passion, Lieder Recitals Bethleham Bach Festival, B minor Mass, St John Passion and Coffee Cantata, Atlanta Symphony with Robert Shaw, B minor Mass, La demoiselle Elue by Debussy, Cincinnati May Festival; Mozart C minor Mass, Reingau Music Festival, Germany. Recordings: Four Centuries of Song Koch Spain in the New World Golden Apple Masters in this Hall Gothic. Honours: Aspen Music Festival Fellowship, Vocal Competition Winner, 1982; Finalist, New York Winner, Early Music Competition, Yugoslavia, 1989; Oratorio Competition, 1984; Marlboro Music Festival Fellowship. Memberships: Sigma Alpha Iota; Cosmos Club. Hobbies: Sews her own concert gowns and costumes; Painting; Studying languages. Address: 5333 North 26th Street, Arlington, VA 22201, USA.

LAMOTHE Donat (Romeo), b. 14 Oct 1935, Keene, New Hampshire, USA. Teacher; Musicologist; Performer on Historical Instruments; Roman Catholic Priest. Education: Precentors Certificate, Gregorian Plainsong, 1955, AB, 1957, Assumption College; MA, Religious Studies, St John's University, Minnesota, 1969; MMus, Musicology, Boston University School of Fine and Applied Arts, 1973; PhD, Music History, Institute of Musicology, University of Strasbourg, 1980; Diplome du 2e degree, Institut Saint-Gregoire-le-grand, Plainsong, Lyons, France, 1960; Ordained Member of Religious Order, Augustinians of the Assumption, 1962. Career: Founder-Director, Salisbury Consort performance group of Medieval and Renaissance music on historical instruments, 1965-; Faculty Member, Music professor, Assumption College, Worcester, Massachusetts, 1963-. Publications: Music in Early Spanish Drama, 1973; Claude Le Jeune (1530-1600) and the Huguenot Psalter, 1980; Matins at Cluny for the Feast of St Peter's Chains, 1987; Editor, Two Psalms of Claude Le Jeune, 1987; Georges Migot: 26 Monodies Permodales, 1990. Contributions to: Revue Internationale de Musique Francaise; Acta Musicologica. Hobbies: Collector of ethnic and antique musical instruments; Stained glass designer and craftsman. Address: Assumption College, Worcester, MA 01615-0005, USA.

LANCE Albert, b. 12 July 1925, Menindie, Australia. Tenor. Education: Studied in Australia and sang minor roles and in operetta. Career: Sang Cavaradossi in Sydney in 1952, Offenbach's Hoffmann in 1954 and in Paris from 1956 at Paris Opéra and Opéra-Comique in operas by Puccini, Gounod and Cherubini; Covent Garden debut in 1958 as the Duke of Mantua opposite Joan Sutherland; Bolshoy Theatre Moscow, 1965-66; Guest appearances in Bordeaux, Lyon, Los Angeles, San Francisco, Vienna, Leningrad, Kiev and Buenos Aires; London Coliseum in 1969 in the first British performance of Roussel's Padmâvati; Teacher at Nice Conservatory from 1974. Recordings include: Werther; Madama Butterfly; Tosca.

LANCELOT James (Bennett), b. 2 Dec 1952, Kent, England. Cathedral organist. m. Sylvia Jane Hoare, 31 July 1982, 2 daughters. Education: St Paul's Cathedral Choir School, 1961-66; Ardingly College, 1966-70; ARCO, 1968; FRCO, 1969; ARCM, Royal College of Music, 1970-71; BA. 1974, MusB, 1975, King's College, Cambridge. Career: Organ scholar, King's College, Cambridge, 1971-74; Assistant Organist, St Clement Danes and Hampstead Parish Church, 1974-75; Sub-organist, Winchester Cathedral, 1975-85; Master of the Choristers and Organist, Durham Cathedral, 1985-; Conductor, Durham University Choral Society, 1987-. Recordings: Numerous with choirs of King's College, Cambridge, Winchester Cathedral and Durham Cathedral; Solo: Great European Organs No 5; The Archbishop's Fanfare. Publications: Durham Cathedral Organs, with Richard Hird, 1991. Honours: Turpin Prize, FRCO, 1969; Stuart Prize, RCM, 1970; Double Distinction, BMus, 1975. Membership: Council Member, Royal College of Organists, 1988-. Hobbies: Railways; Writings of John Buchan. Address: 6 The College, Durham, England.

LANCHBERY John, b. 15 May 1923, London, England. Conductor; Arranger; Composer; Musical Director. m. Elaine Fifield, 17 Dec 1951, 1 d. Education: Alleyn's School, Dulwich, 1934-42; Henry Smart Composition Scholarship to Royal Academy of Music, 1942-43, 1945-48; ARAM; FRAM. Career: Metropolitan Ballet, 1948-50; Sadler's Wells Theatre Ballet, 1951-59; Royal Ballet at Covent Garden, 1960-72; Australian Ballet, 1972-77; American Ballet, 1978-80; Guest Conductor at La Scala Milan, Paris Opera, Staatsoper Vienna, National Theatre Munich, Operan Stockholm, Boston Pops, Houston Symphony Orchestra, Los Angeles Philharmonic, Teatro Municipal Santiago, Bellas Artes Mexico, Teatro Municipao Rio de Janeiro, Toronto Symphony Orchestra; Films: Tales of Beatrix Potter, The Turning Point, Nijinsky, Evil Under The Sun. Compositions: Compositions and Arrangements: La Fille Mal Gardée, The Dream, Don Quixote, A Month In The Country, Monotones, Mayerling, The Sentimental Bloke, The Merry Widow ballet, Rosalinda, Papillon, La Bayadère, The Devil to Pay, Le Chat Botté, Robinson Crusoe, Opportunity Makes The Thief, Figaro, ballet; The Iron Horse, silent film score, 1994; Adaptation, Madame Butterfly, ballet, 1995. Recordings include: La Fille Mal Gardée (twice); A Month in The Country; Don Quixote; Merry Widow Ballet (Gold Record); Complete Tchaikovsky Ballets; Corroborree; Jazz Calendar; La Bayadère. Honours: Bolshoi Theatre Medal, 1961; Carina Ari Medal, 1989; Queen Elizabeth Coronation Award, 1989; OBE, 1990. Membership: Garrick Club, London. Hobbies: Walking; Reading; Travel. Current Management: ICM, New York, USA.

LANCIE John de, b. 26 July 1921, Berkeley, CA, USA. Oboist; Administrator. Education: Curtis Institute, Philadelphia, 1936-40, with Marcel Tabuteau. Career: Played oboe in Pittsburgh Symphony Orchestra, 1940-42; Met Richard Strauss during war service in Europe and encouraged him to write Oboe Concerto; Played with Philadelphia Orchestra from 1946, Principal Oboist , 1954-74; Teacher, 1954-74, Director, 1977-85, Curtis Institute; Commissioned and gave the premieres of Jean

Francaix' Horloge de Flore in Philadelphia in 1961, and the Concerto by Benjamin Lees in 1963; Director at The New World School of Music, 1987.

LANDER Thomas, b. 1961, Sweden. Baritone. Education: Studied at Stockholm College of Music and the State Opera School. Career: Sang with Norrlandsoperan, 1982-83; Engaged at Hamburg Staatsoper, 1986-87, and Vienna Volksoper, 1987-89 as Mozart's Count and Guglielmo; Guest appearances at Aix-en-Provence, Opéra de Lyon and in Italy, Iceland and Israel; Engaged at Hanover, 1990-; Other roles include Mozart's Don Giovanni and Papageno, Malatesta and Harlequin in Ariadne auf Naxos; Sang Christus in Bach's St John Passion at Lucerne Easter Festival in 1993. Address: Nordic Artists Management, Sveavagen 76, S-11359 Stockholm, Sweden.

LANDON H(oward) C(handler) Robbins, b. 6 Mar 1926, Boston, MA, USA. Musicologist. m. Else Radant. Education: BMus, Boston University, 1947. Career: Resident in Europe from 1947; Talks on BBC Radio and TV, 1954-; Guest Teacher, British and American Universities, 1969-; Honorary Professorial Fellow, University College Cardiff, 1972; John Bird Professor of Music, Cardiff; Producer of numerous recordings for the Haydn Society, Vox, Library of recorded Masterpieces. Publications: The Symphonies of Joseph Haydn, 1955; Collected Correspondence and London Notebooks of Haydn, 1959; Essays on Viennese Classical Style, 1970; Beethoven, 1970; Haydn: Chronicle and Works, 5 volumes, 1976-80; Mozart as a Mason, 1983; Edition of Handel's Roman Vespers, 1983; Joseph Haydn, single volume reduction of Chronicle and Works, 1988; 1791: Mozart's Last Year; Mozart: The Golden Years 1781-1791, 1989; Five Centuries of Music in Venice (with John Julius Norwich), 1991; Vivaldi, 1993; The Mozart Essays, 1995; Editor of all Haydn's Symphonies, numerous String Quartets and Operas. Honours: DMus, Boston University, 1969; DMus, Queen's College, Belfast, 1974. Memberships include: President, International Joseph Haydn Stiftung, Eisenstadt. Hobbies: Cooking; Walking; Swimming. Address: Château de Foncoussières, 81800 Rabastens (Tarn), France.

LANDOWSKI Marcel (François Paul), b. 18 Feb 1915, Pont l'Abbe, France. Composer. m. Jacqueline Potier, 1941, 2 sons, 1 daughter. Education: Lycee Janson-de-Sailly; Conservatoire Nationale de Musique de Paris. Career: Director, Conservatoire Boulogne-sur-Seine, 1960-65; Director of Music, Comédie Française, Paris, 1962-66; Inspector-General, Musical Studies, 1964, Director of Music Service, Ministry of Cultural Affairs, 1966-70, Music, Lyric and Dance, 1970-74; Founder, Orchestre de Paris, 1967, Honorary President, 1975-; Inspector-General de l'Instruction Publique, 1974-. Compositions: Numerous orchestral and choral compositions; Film music and music for Cyrano de Bergerac at Comédie Française; Opera, Galina, premiered at Lyon, 1996. Honours: Officer, Legion d'Honneur; Commander des Arts et des Lettres; Croix de Guerre. Membership: Institute of France, Academy des Beaux-Arts, 1975. Address: 10 Rue Max-Blondat, 92100 Boulogne-sur-Seine, France.

LANE Gloria, b. 6 Jun 1930, Trenton, NJ, USA. Mezzo-Soprano; Soprano. m. Samuel Krachmalnick. Education: Studied with Elisabeth Westmoreland in Philadelphia. Debut: Philadelphia in 1950 in the premiere of Menotti's The Consul. Career: Broadway in 1954 in the premiere of Menotti's The Saint of Bleecker Street; British debut in 1958 as Baba The Turk in The Rake's Progress, returning in 1972 as Dorabella in Così fan tutte, Strauss's Ariadne and Lady Macbeth; Covent Garden debut in 1960 as Carmen and sang at Florence in 1966 as Federica in Verdi's Luisa Miller; Guest appearances in Vienna, Paris, Venice, Rome, Palermo, Boston, Chicago and San Francisco; New York City Opera, 1971 as Santuzza in Cavalleria Rusticana. Recordings: The Consul; Rossini's Mosè in Egitto; The Saint of Bleecker Street. Address: c/o New York City Opera, Lincoln Center, New York, NY 10023, USA.

LANE Jennifer (Ruth), b. 25 Nov 1954, Berwyn, IL, USA. Mezzo-Soprano. m. James H Carr, 21 Nov 1987. Education: BMus, Chicago Musical College, Roosevelt University, 1977; MA in Performance, City University of New York, 1980. Debut: Elsbeth in Strauss' Feuersnot, Santa Fe Opera in 1988. Career: Performances with Santa Fe Opera, New York City Opera, Opera Monte Carlo, L'Opéra Français de New York, Opera Omaha, US stage premiere of Handel's Partenope, Milwaukee's Skylight Opera, Opera Ensemble of New York; Prior to operatic career, toured North and South America with the Waverly Consort; Also tours of the Far East with the Gregg Smith Singers; Many concert performances including appearances with the Atlanta Symphony under Robert Shaw, San Francisco Symphony, The National Symphony, St Louis Symphony, and Harrisburg Symphony in Mahler's 2nd and 3rd Symphonies; Many radio broadcasts including Mahler's 3rd Symphony, personal interviews and Radio Canada recital with countertenor, Alan Fast; Sang Alessandro in Handel's Tolomeo at Halle, 1996. Recordings include: JS Bach's St John Passion, Smithsonian Collection of Recordings; Handel's

Theodora with Nicholas McGegan conducting; Bach's Solo Cantata for Alto; John Adams, Grand Pianola Music with composer conducting. Current Management: Byers, Schwalbe and Associates Inc, 584 Broadway, Suite 1105, New York, NY 10012, USA. Address: 514 West 110th Street, Apt 92, New York, NY 10025, USA.

LANE Louis, b. 25 Dec 1923, Eagle Pass, TX, USA. Conductor. Education: Studied at the University of Texas, Eastman School of Music, Rochester and Berkshire Music Center, Tanglewood. Career: Won 1947 competition to become apprentice conductor to George Szell; Assistant Conductor with Cleveland Orchestra in 1956; Principal Conductor with Akron Symphony Orchestra in 1959; Guest conductor with Chicago Symphony and Detroit Symphony; Took Cleveland Orchestra on tour to Europe in 1965 and was resident conductor, 1970-73; Associate Conductor for Blossom Festival, 1968-73; Co-Principal Conductor with Dallas Symphony Orchestra, 1974-77; Principal Conductor with National Symphony Orchestra of the South African Broadcasting Corporation, 1983; Concerts for Ohio Light Opera, 1996.

LANE Piers, b. 1958, London, England. Concert Pianist. Education: Studied with Nancy Weir at the Queensland Conservatorium, Bela Siki in Seattle and Kendall Taylor and Yonty Solomon at the Royal College of Music. Debut: Broadcast recital for ABC, aged 12. Career: Solo and concert appearances in the USA, France, Germany, Spain, Hungary, Italy, India, UK, Australia, Greece, Middle East and New Zealand; Tour of 4 Latin American countries in 1989; Season 1990-91 with visits to Cyprus and Morocco, concerts in UK, 2 visits to Australia and engagements in France and South America, and played Bliss Piano Concerto at the 1991 Promenade Concerts; Has played with such orchestras as the Philharmonia, Royal Philharmonic, BBC Philharmonic, Hallé, City of London Sinfonia and the London Festival Orchestra; Frequent recitals on the BBC and chamber concerts with Kathron Sturrock, the New Budapest Quartet, Alexander Baillie and Julian Lloyd Webber; Many recitals at Wigmore Hall; Contemporary repertory includes Dave Heath's Piano Concerto; Professor of Piano at the Royal Academy of Music. Recordings: Music by Shostakovich, Prokofiev, Schnittke and Rachmaninoff with Alexander Baillie; Moskowski and Paderewski Concertos, the Complete Etudes by Scriabin, and Brahms Piano Quintet; Recitals with violinist, Tasmin Little; Mussorgsky's Pictures at an Exhibition, Stravinsky's Petroushka and Balakirev's Islamey. Honours include: Royal Overseas League Outstanding Musician of The Year, 1982. Memberships: European Piano Teachers Association; The Liszt Society; The Beethoven Pianoforte Society of Europe. Current Management: Patrick Garvey Management. Address: 51 Portland Road, Hove, East Sussex, BN3 5DQ, England.

LANG Aidan, b. 1959, England. Stage Director. Education: Studied English and Drama at Birmingham University. Career: Glyndebourne from 1984, becoming Director of Productions for the Tour in 1991; Currently Principal Associate Director for the Festival; Productions with GTO have included La Bohème (1991, debut), Matthus's Song of Love and Death, The Rake's Progress and Il Barbiere di Siviglia; Premiere of Hamilton's Lancelot at the Arundel Festival, Tamerlano at Göttingen, Carmen for Canadian Opera and Salome at Malaga; Artistic Director of Opera Zuid, Netherlands, with productions of Werther, Ariadne, The Cunning Little Vixen and Don Giovanni; Further engagements include Le Comte Ory for Welsh National Opera, Così fan tutte in Belfast and Cologne, and Tosca at Nice; Die Entführung for Istanbul Festival; Assistant at the Royal Opera, Covent Garden, Opéra de Lyon and Canadian Opera, Vancouver. Address: c/o Glyndebourne Festival Opera, Lewes, Sussex, England.

LANG David, b. 1957, Los Angeles, CA, USA. Composer. Education: Studied at Stanford University and the University of Iowa; Doctorate from Yale School of Music, 1989; Teachers include Jacob Druckman, Hans Werner Henze, Martin Brenick and Henri Lazarof. Career: Freelance composer from 1983; Founded the Bang On A Can Festival, New York City. Compositions: Orchestral: Eating Living Monkeys, 1985, revised 1987, International Business Machine, 1990, Bonehead, 1990; Stage: Judith And Holofernes Puppet Opera, 1989, premiered at the 1990 Munich Biennale; Modern P ainters, 1994, premiered in 1995 by Santa Fe Opera; Chamber and ensemble: Hammer Amour, 1979, revised 1989, Frag, 1985, Spud, 1986, Are You Experienced?, 1987-88, Burn Notice, 1988, Dance/Drop, 1988-89; Solo and Duo: Illumination Rounds for Violin and Piano, 1982, While Nailing At Random for Piano, 1983, Orpheus Over And Under for 2 Pianos, 1989, Vent for Flute and Piano, 1990, The Anvil Chorus for Percussion Solo, 1990, Bitter Herb for Cello and Piano, 1990, My Evil Twin, 1992, Face So Pale, 1992, Cheating, Lying, Stealing, 1993, Music For Gracious Living, 1993, Slow Movement, 1993; By Fire, commissioned by the BBC Singers; Other commissions from City of Munich, Boston Symphony Orchestra, American Composers Orchestra, Cleveland Orchestra, Santa Fe Opera and Saint Paul Chamber Orchestra. Address: Novello and Co Ltd, 8-9 Frith Street, London, W1V 5TZ, England.

LANG Edith, b. 28 Apr 1927, Chicago, USA. Soprano. Education: Studied in Chicago and Italy. Career: Sang in Italy from 1954 with debut as Madama Butterfly, and Hamburg from 1955 as Verdi's Aida, Amelia, Elisabeth de Valois, Leonora and Abigaille, Beethoven's Leonore and Mozart's Donna Anna; Guest appearances in London, Vienna, Milan and Paris; San Francisco in 1959 as the Empress in the US premiere of Die Frau ohne Schatten; Also heard as concert singer; Taught at Lubeck Musikhochschule from 1973. Address: Schleswig-Holsteinische Musikakademie, Jerusalemberg 4, Lubeck, Germany.

LANG Istvan, b. 1 Mar 1933, Budapest, Hungary. Composer. m. Csilla Fülöp, 27 Dec 1966, 1 son. Education: Academy of Music, Budapest. Career: Freelance Composer, 1958-66; Musical Advisor, State Puppet Theatre, 1966-84; Professor of Chamber Music, Academy of Music, Budapest, 1973-; Secretary General, Association of Hungarian Musicians, 1978-90; Member, Ex Committee of International Society for Contemporary Music, 1984-87; Member, Ex Committee of International Music Council, 1989-93. Compositions: Dream about the Theatre, Rounded up TV operas; In memorian NNS; Symphonies Nos 2, 3, 4, 5 and 6; Violin Concerto; Double Concerto for Clarinet and Harp; Concerto Bucolico; Pezzo Lirico; Rhymes; Constellations; Affetti, Intarsia around a Bartók theme; Music 2-3-4; Solo pieces for various instruments; String Quartets Nos 2 and 3; Wind Quintets Nos 1, 2 and 3; Sonata for violin and piano, 1990; Cimbiosis, 1991; Sonata for cello and piano, 1992-93; Off and On for harp and live electronics. Recordings: Several. Honours: Erkel Prize, 1968, 1975; Merit Artist, 1985; Bartok Pázstori Prize, 1994. Membership: Hungarian Composers' Union. Address: Margit Krt 20, H 1027 Budapest, Hungary.

LANG Rosemarie, b. 1955, Grünstädtel, Schwarzenberg, Germany. Singer (Mezzo-soprano). Education: Studied in Leipzig. Career: Sang in opera at Altenburg, then Leipzig; Guest engagements at Dresden as Venus by Wagner, 1988; Berlin Staatsoper as Gluck's Clytemnestra and Wagner's Brangäne, and in premiere of Graf Mirabeau by Siegfried Matthus, 1989 (also televised), and as Azucena by Verdi, 1989; Other roles include Mozart's Dorabella, Cherubino and Sextus, Bellini's Romeo, Rossini's Cenerentola and Rosina, Strauss's Octavian and Composer in Ariadne; Sang Countess Geschwitz in Lulu, 1997; Many concert appearances. Recordings include: Mendelssohn's St Paul; Larina in Eugene Onegin; Schoenberg's Gurre-Lieder; Mozart's Masses; Songs by Schumann and Brahms; Pfitzner's Palestrina as Silla; 8th Symphony by Mahler under Abbado; Rheingold and Walküre (Fricka) by Wagner; Götterdämmerung by Wagner under Barenboim; Guest appearances in Oslo. Address: c/o Staatsoper Berlin, Unter den Linden 7, 10117 Berlin, Germany.

LANGAN Kevin, b. 1 Apr 1955, New York, USA. Singer (Bass). m. Sally Wolf, 16 July 1983. Education: New England Conservatory of Music, 1973-75; Indiana University, 1975-80; BM, MM in Voice; Vocal Instruction with Margaret Harshaw. Debut: New Jersey State Opera in 1979 in Don Carlos. Career: Principal Bass with San Francisco Opera, 1980-; Appeared with New York City Opera, Houston Grand Opera, Philadelphia Opera, Canadian Opera, Miami, Detroit and Dallas Opera, Geneva, Lyon, Winnipeg and St Louis Opera, Colorado, Santa Fe, Edmonton, Vancouver, Seattle, Tulsa, Pittsburgh, San Diego and Washington DC Opera; Appeared with Chicago Lyric and Metropolitan Opera and sang Astofolo in Vivaldi's Orlando Furioso at San Franciscio in 1989, and Colline at San Diego in 1990; Season 1992 as Donizetti's Raimondo at Seattle followed by Rossini's Basilio, and Leporello at the 1992 Santa Fe Festival; Appears on 1993 video of San Francisco Opera production of Turandot in role of Timur; Appeared as Leporello in 1996 Santa Fe festival of Don Giovanni; Sparafucile in 1997 as San Francisco Opera's Rigoletto; Timur in Turandot in 1998 with Dallas Opera and Flanders Opera, Antwerp. Recording: Nozze di Figaro with Nicklaus Harnoncourt, conductor, 1994. Honours: Finalist, National Metropolitan Opera, 1980; 2nd Place, San Francisco Opera Auditions, 1980; Richard Tucker Foundation Award for Advanced Studies, 1984. Hobbies: Fishing; Racquetball. Current Management: Elizabeth Crittenden. Address: Columbia Artists Management Inc, c/o Crittenden Division, 165 West 57th Street, New York, NY 10019, USA.

LANGDON Sophie (Catherine), b. 26 Aug 1958, Hemel Hempstead, Hertfordshire, England. Concert Violinist; Professor of Violin. Education: Royal Academy of Music; Juilliard School, New York, USA; Curtis Institute, Philadelphia, USA; Guildhall School of Music & Drama. Debut: As Soloist, 1981 Spitalfields Festival, London in Kurt Weill's Violin Concerto. Career: Violinist of Trio Zingara, 1980-83, winning Munich International Competition, 1981; Recitals, Concertos, Leading, Directing and Chamber Music Performances and Broadcasts in England at Festivals and all London's major venues and throughout Europe and North America; Teacher, Guildhall School of Music & Drama 1981-86, Central Ostrabothnian Conservatoire, Finland 1986-87, Trinity College of Music 1987-, Menuhin School 1991-92, Chethams School, Manchester 1988-90, Royal Academy of Music 1990-, (currently Professor of Violin at TCM and RAM); Concerto

performances and recordings with the Royal Philharmonic Orchestra, Philharmonia, BBC Symphony Orchestra, BBC National Orchestra of Wales, BBC Scottish Symphony Orchestra, BBC Philharmonic and Berlin Radio Orchestra; Chamber music performances and recordings with, Lontano, Jeux, Aquarius, Music Projects; Langdon Chamber Players and London Sinfonietta; Leader and Director of London Chamber Symphony, Ambache Chamber Orchestra and Academy of London; Guest Leader of City of London Sinfonia, London Mozart Players and Orchestra of St John's Smith Square. Recordings: Dame Ethel Smyth Double Concerto for violin and horn on Chandos label; Mozart Chamber Music with Ambache Chamber Ensemble on Pickwick label. Honours: Associate of the Royal Academy of Music, 1993. Hobbies: Painting; Motorcycling. Address: 84 North Grove, London N15 5QP, England.

LANGER Milan, b. 10 July 1955, Prague, Czechoslovakia. Concert Pianist. m. Marie Sestáková, 30 Jun 1979, 2 daughters. Education: Conservatoire Prague, 1974; Academy of Music, Prague, 1980; 3 Years postgraduate study at Academy of Music Prague, 1986. Career: Freelance pianist, soloist and chamber partner with Ex Ivan Zenaty, violinist; Member of Ars Cameralis Ensemble of Historic Instruments; Collaboration with Czech Symphony Orchestras; Many Radio and TV appearances; Concerts in Czechoslovakia, Germany, UK, France, Belgium, Austria, Switzerland, Greece, Yugoslavia, Spain and Cuba. Recordings: Piano Concerto, Podest; Pezzi Brevi, Filas; Sonata, Amorasa; Kalabis' Sonata for Violin and Piano, Op 58, 1987; Works by Stravinsky, Barber, Prokofiev and Bartók; Radio recordings as soloist in works by Liszt, Schumann, Chopin and Bartók, Prokofiev, and Gothic music. Current Management: Pragokoncert, Praha, Czechoslovakia. Address: Kropackova 559, 149 00 Praha 4-Haje, Czech Republic.

LANGFORD Roger, b. 1965, England. Baritone. Education: Studied at the Royal College of Music and Royal Academy of Music. Career: Soloist with Yorkshire Bach Choir in the St John Passion, Christmas Oratorio, Bach B minor Mass and Monteverdi Vespers; Concerts in France and Germany including Purcell's Aeneas for Cologne Radio; Music theatre includes Eight Songs For A Mad King by Maxwell Davies, Master Peter's Puppet Show and Monteverdi's Combattimento; Visits to Europe with Nigel Rogers's group, Chiaroscuro, performing English and Italian Baroque music; Sang Elijah at Lincoln Cathedral and The Apostles by Elgar at St Albans Abbey; Season 1989-90 as Papageno for British Youth Opera and in Trouble in Tahiti at Edinburgh Festival. Address: c/o Anglo Swiss Ltd, 35-37 Morley House, 320 Regent Street, London W1R 5AD, England.

LANGMAN Krzysztof (Maria), b. 22 July 1948, Cracow, Poland. Flautist. Education: Academy of Music Cracow, 1970-74; Study under S Gazzeloni at Santa Cecilia Academy of Music, Rome, 1976-77. Career: Principal Flautist at State Opera House and Philharmonic Society, Wroclaw; Principal Solo Flute with Baltic Philharmonic Orchestra, Gdansk, 1974-; Currently Assistant Professor of Flute, Academy of Music, Gdansk; Cooperates with Ensemble MW2 Vanguard Group; Concerts in various countries including Austria, Germany, Greece, Norway, Sweden, Denmark, Netherlands, Belgium, UK, Italy, Mexico, Spain, Luxemburg, Switzerland and France. Recordings: Numerous for Polish Radio and TV. Current Management: Polish Artists Agency, Warsaw, Poland. Address: ul Pawla Gdanca 4a-42, 80-336 Gdansk, Poland.

LANGRIDGE Philip (Gordon), b. 16 Dec 1939, Hawkhurst, Kent, England. Tenor. m. Ann Murray, 1981, 1 son, and 1 son and 2 daughters from previous marriage. Education: ARAM, Royal Academy of Music, 1977. Debut: Glyndebourne Festival in 1964. Career: Sang at BBC Promenade Concerts, 1970-, Edinburgh Festival, 1970-, Netherlands Opera, Scottish Opera, Handel Opera amd major opera houses in Britain and abroad; Concerts with major international orchestras and conductors including Boston with Previn, Chicago with Solti and Abbado, Los Angeles with Christopher Hogwood, Sydney with Mackerras, Vienna Philharmonic with Previn, Orchestre de Paris with Barenboim and Mehta and with all major British orchestras; Many first performances with some dedicated to or written for him; Has sung in Osud, Turn of the Screw, Mask of Orpheus, Don Giovanni, Fidelio, Idomeneo, The Rake's Progress, Wozzeck, Castor and Pollux, Rigoletto, Poppea, Lucio Silla, Rossini's Otello, La Donna del Lago, and Cosi fan tutte. Sang in the TV production of Tippett's The Midsummer Marriage in 1989, in Mozart's Idomeneo in a new production at Covent Garden in 1989, Berlioz' Benedict for ENO in 1990, Idomeneo at the 1990 Salzburg Festival, Pelegrin in Tippett's New Year at Glyndebourne, Mozart's Titus at Glyndebourne and the Promenade Concerts in 1991; Season 1992-93 included Aschenbach in a new production of Death in Venice at Covent Garden and Nero in Poppea at Salzburg Festival; Sang in Stravinsky's Pulcinella at 1993 London Proms; Jupiter in Semele at Covent Garden, 1996; Captain Vere in Billy Budd at the Met, 1997. Recordings: Over 50 records, including Moses und Aron. Membership: Music Panel, Arts Council of Great Britain. Hobbies: Collecting Watercolour Paintings and Victorian

Postcards. Address: c/o Allied Artists Agency, 42 Montpelier Square, London, SW7 1JZ, England.

LANKESTER Michael, b. 12 Nov 1944, London, England. Conductor; Musical Director; Professor of Conducting. Education: Royal College of Music; ARCM; GRSM. Career: Musical Director, National Theatre, 1969-75, composing and conducting numerous items to accompany productions; Conductor, Surrey Philharmonic Orchestra, 1972-, and English Chamber Orchestra; Founder of Contrapuncti; Radio and TV broadcasts for BBC and Collaborator with Young Vic Theatre in various productions; Conductor, Cheltenham Festival, Sadler's Wells Theatre and at opening of Royal Northern College of Music, 1973; Made orchestral suite of Britten's The Prince of the Pagodas, and conducted it at the 1979 Promenade Concerts. Recordings include: Gordon Crosse, Purgatory, Ariadne. Honours include: Watney/Sargent Conducting Scholarship, 1967. Membership: Noise Abatement Society. Hobbies: Reading; Walking; Cricket.

LANSING Robert, b. 10 Apr 1915, Chicago, IL, USA. Choral Conductor; Bass Baritone; Voice Teacher. m. Gladys Zeiher, 18 Jun 1943, 1 s, 2 d. Education: University of Illinois, 1932-33; Chicago Conservatory of Music, 1940-42; American Theater Wing, Manhattan School of Music, 1946-49; Studied Voice with Paul Althouse, Friedrich Schorr and Zerline Metzger, and conducting with Hugh Ross. Debut: Town Hall, 1949. Career: Dulcamara opposite Bidu Sayao, Denver Grand Opera, 1950; Member of Metropolitan Opera Chorus, 1945-49 and 1955-60; Sang Escamillo with Boston Opera, 1944; Vocal Teacher, 1950-; Conducted Capitol Opera in Aida, Il Trovatore, Magic Flute and Marriage of Figaro among others, 1950-64; Director of Mountain Bell Singers, 1963-; Directed the Rocky Mountain Singers in 7 international concert tours, 1974-88; Bass Soloist: Messiah, 1984, Elijah, Verdi Requiem, 1985 and Stainer Crucifixion. Memberships: Board of Directors, 1956, AGMA; American Guild of Organists; Musicians Union; AFM. Hobby: Swimming. Address: 940 South Harrison Street, Denver, CO 80209, USA.

LANSKY Paul, b. 18 June 1944, New York, USA. Composer. Education: Studied with George Perle and Hugo Weisgall at Queen's College, NY, BA 1966; Princeton University with Milton Babbitt and Earl Kim, PhD 1969. Career: Teacher, Princeton University from 1969; Associate Editor of Perspectives of New Music, 1972. Compositions: Modal Fantasy for Piano, 1969; String Quartet, 1972-77; Mild Und Leise for Tape, 1974; Crossworks for Piano and Ensemble, 1975; Artifice, on Ferdinand's Reflections, for Tape, 1976; Folk Images for Tape, 1981; As If for String Trio and Electronics, 1982; Folk Images and As It Grew Dark for Tape, 1980-83. Publications include: Affine Music, dissertation, 1969. Honours: League of Composers ISCM electronic music award, 1975; Koussevitsky Foundation Award, 1981. Address: c/o ASCAP, ASCAP Building, One Lincoln Plaza, New York, NY 10023, USA.

LANTOS Istvan, b. 1949, Budapest, Hungary. Pianist. Education: Studied piano under Mme Erzsebet Tusa, Budapest Bela Bartók Conservatory; Ferenc Liszt Academy of Music; Graduate with Distinction, Liszt Academy of Music. Career: Played solo part in Messaien's Turangaêla Symphonie, Bayreuth International Youth Festival, 1970, Hitzacker Festival, Germany, and Bratislava International Rostrum of Young Artists; Numerous appearances in Hungarian concert halls and worldwide; Guest performances at most European Socialist countries and Cuba, Austria, Britain, Canada, Germany, The Netherlands, Ireland, Italy and Switzerland; Has twice toured and held masterclasses in Japan; Soloist with Hungarian State Symphony Orchestra during USA tour; Has toured every 2nd year the major cities in Germany with Hungarian State Symphony Orchestra, 1972-; Also renowned organist; Assistant Professor, Budapest Liszt Academy of Music, 1974-.

LANZA Alcides (Emigdio), b. 2 June 1929, Rosario, Argentina. Nationalized Canadian Citizen. Composer; Pianist; Conductor; University Professor. 2 sons, 2 daughters. Education: Centro Latino Americano de Altos Estudios Musicales Instituto Di Tella, Buenos Aires; Post Graduate Courses, Electronic Music, Columbia University, New York, USA; Studied Composition with Julián Bautista and Alberto Ginastera, Piano with Ruwin Erlich, Conducting with Roberto Kinsky; Further Instruction Courses with various noted artists. Career includes: Concert Tours of Europe, North and South America; Artistic Staff, Teatro Colon, Buenos Aires, 1959-65; Pianist, Lecturer and Conductor, Composers/Performers Group, touring Europe; Composer and Teacher, Columbia-Princeton Electronic Music Centre; Director of Electronic Music Studio and Professor of Composition, McGill University, Montreal, Quebec, Canada, 1971-; Artistic Director, Group GEMS (Group of the Electronic Music Studio). Compositions include: Módulos II, 1982; Módulos III, 1983; Sensors III, for organ and two percussionists, 1982; Eidesis VI, for string orchestra with piano, 1983; Interferences III, for chamber ensemble and electronic sounds, 1983; Acúfenos V, for trumpet, piano and electronic-computer tape, 1980; Ekphonesis VI, actress-singer tape, 1988; ...there is a way to sing it...(solo tape),

1988; un mundo imaginario, choir and computer tape, 1989; vôo, for voice, electroacoustic music and digital signal processing, 1992. Hobbies: Tennis; Swimming; Bicycling; Walking. Current Management: Shelan Concerts. Address: 6351 Trans Island Avenue, Montreal, Quebec, H3W 3B7, Canada.

LAPINSKAS Darius, b. 9 Mar 1934, Kaunas, Lithuania. Composer; Conductor. m. Laima Rastenis, 28 Nov 1970, 1 son. Education: South Boston High School; BA, Composition, Conducting, New England Conservatory, Boston, 1953-57; Akademie fuer Musik und Darstellende Kunst, Vienna, 1957-58; Musik Hochschule, Stuttgart, 1958-60. Career: Musikdirektor, Tuebingen Landestheatre, 1960-65; Kapelmeister, Staatsoper Stuttgart, 1961-65; Schiedsgericht, Composer-Conductor, Mainz TV; Guest Conductor with Stuttgart Symphony Orchestra, Stuttgart Philharmonic, South German Radio Orchestra; Mannheim Opera Orchestra; National Symphony Orchestra of Bogotà, and Symphony Orchestra of Antioquia; Artistic Director of New Opera Company of Chicago. Compositions: Operas: Lokys, Maras, Amadar, Dux Magnus, Rex Amos; Ballet: Laima; Concerto for Piano, Strings and Percussion; Concerto for Violin and Orchestra; Haiku, song cycle; Balyvera, song cycle for Mezzo-Soprano and Orchestra; Les Sept Solitudes, aria for Mezzo-Soprano and Orchestra; Ainiu Dainos, song cycle for Voice and Chamber Orchestra. Recordings: Les Sept Solitudes; Ainiu Dainos; Mergaites Dalia. Honours: BML Prize for Composition, Boston, 1955; Wurttemberg Prize for Composition, 1961; Illinois Arts Council Grant for Composition, 1985, 1986. Hobbies: Tennis; Skiing. Address: 9368 South Longwood Drive, Chicago, IL 60620, USA.

LAPLANTE Bruno, b. 1 Aug 1938, Beauharnois, Quebec, Canada. Singer. 2 sons. Education: 1st Prize in Vocal Art, Conservatoire de Musique du Québec, Montreal. Debut: Cimarosa's The Secret Marriage in Germany. Career: Under scholarships from Canada Arts Council, The Government of Quebec, private foundations and from Goethe Institute in Munich; Worked first in Germany, in Paris under the direction of Pierre Bernac and in Montreal with Lina Narducci; Numerous radio and TV appearances including Susanna's Secret, Gounod's Romeo and Juliette, and Lehar's Merry Widow; Engagements with major Canadian Symphony Orchestras; Les Noces and Carmina Burana with Grands Ballets Canadiens; 30 concerts in Canada for Les Jeunesse Musicales du Canada; A film dealing with his career in the series, Les Nouveaux Interprètes; Stage appearances include Carmen, Il Trittico, Manon, Don Giovanni and many others; Regular tours throughout Europe for concerts and festivals including Festival du Marais, Paris, 1979 and 2 recitals at Festival International de Musique et d'Art Lyrique, Aix-en-Provence. Recordings include: Integrale des 15 Mélodies de Duparc; Mélodies de Lalo et de Bizet; Mélodies de Berlioz; Works by Offenbach, Jules Massenet, Reynaldo Hahn, Charles Gounod, and César Franck among others. Honours: Concours International de Genève, 1966, de Barcelona, 1966, de Montreal, 1967; Grand Prix du Disque, 1977. Membership: Union des Artistes de Montreal.

LAPORTE André, b. 12 July 1931, Oplinter, Belgium. Composer. Education: Studied at Catholic University of Louvain; Organ with Flor Peeters and counterpoint with Marinus de Jong, 1956-58. Career: Producer for Belgian Radio, 1963; Brussels Conservatory from 1968. Compositions: Piano Sonata, 1954; Psalm for 6 Voices and Brass, 1956; Jubilus for 12 Brass Instruments and 3 Percussionists, 1966; Story for String Trio and Harpsichord, 1967; Ascension for Piano, 1967; De Profundis for Mixed Choir, 1968; Le Morte Chitarre for Tenor, Flute and 14 Strings, 1969; Night Music for Orchestra, 1970; La Vita Non E Sogno for Vocalists, Chorus and Orchestra, 1972; Peripetie for Brass Sextet; Chamber Music for Soprano and Ensemble, 1975; Transit for 48 Strings, 1978; Das Schloss, opera in 3 acts after Fr Kafka, 1986; Fantasia-Rondino for Violin and Orchestra, 1988; The Magpie On The Gallows, 1989. Honours: Lemmens-Tinel Award, 1958; Koopal Award from the Belgian Ministry of Culture, 1971 and 1976; Prix Italia, 1976. Address: c/o SABAM, Rue d'Arlon 75-77, 1040 Brussels, Belgium.

LAPPALAINEN Kimmo, b. 1944, Helsinki, Finland. Tenor. Education: Sibelius Academy, 1966-68; Vocal studies with Fred Hustler in Lugano and Luigi Rici in Rome, 1969-70. Career: Finnish National Opera, Helsinki, 1968-72 and Stuttgart Opera from 1972; Sang at Glyndebourne Festival, 1972-74 as Pedrillo in Die Entführung and Idamantes in Idomeneo; Many performances at the Savonlinna Festival in Finland; Sang at Stuttgart in 1983 as Britten's Albert Herring; Also heard in concert. Address: c/o Finnish National Opera, Bailevardi 23-27, SF-00180 Helsinki 18, Finland.

LARA Ana, b. 30 Nov 1959, Mexico City, Mexico. Composer. Education: Studied at the Mexican National Conservatory and at the Warsaw Academy with Witold Ruzinski. Career: President of the Mexican Society for New Music and Director of the ISCM World Music Days at Mexico City, 1994. Compositions include: Icaro for Solo Recorder; Vitrales for Viola, Cello and Double Bass, 1992. Honours include: Fellowship from the Polish Government, 1986. Address: Mayorazgo No 129, Col Xoco, 03330 Mexico D.F., Mexico.

LARA Christian, b. 15 Aug 1946, Merignac, France. Tenor. Education: Studied in Bordeaux. Career: Sang at Lille Opera, 1976-79 and studied further with Michel Senechal in Paris; Sang Juan in Don Quichotte at Venice in 1982, Rodolfo at Nantes, Cavaradossi at Avignon, Faust at Ghent and Antwerp; Theater des Westens, Berlin in 1987 as Sou-Chong in Das Land des Lächelns; Sang Faust at Cologne in 1989 and appeared in La Rondine at Tours in 1991; Concert repertoire includes Mendelssohn's 2nd Symphony; Sang Faust at Vienna in 1991, Ismaele in Nabucco at Karlsruhe, Samson at Besançon, Ruggero in La Rondine at Tours, Cavaradossi in Tosca at Angers, Don José in Carmen at Bregenz and Liège, and Florestan in Fidelio at Tours, all in 1991; In 1992 sang Oedipe Roi by Paul Bastide at Strasbourg, Andrei Khovansky at Strasbourg, Ismaele at Karlsruhe, Florestan at Angers, Don José at the Festival of Bregenz, Jean in Hérodiade at Liège, and Vestale at Nantes; In 1993 sang Luigi in Il Tabarro at Tours, Jean at Toulon and in 1994 sang Des Grieux in Manon and Don José at Bordeaux. Address: 11 Rue Jean Jaurès, 33127 Martignas-sur-Jalle, France.

LARAINE Barbara, b. Hamworthy, Dorset, England. Pianist. m. Peter S Carnt, deceased. Education: Studied Piano with Welton Hickin and Barbara Kirkby-Mason, London; LRAM. Career: Piano Recitals in England, Germany, Switzerland; Broadcasts, Süddeutscher Rundfunk; Accompanist; Teacher. Membership: Incorporated Society of Musicians. Hobbies: Travel; Languages; Dressmaking; Boating. Address: Oberdorfstrasse 32, CH 8335 Hittnau, Switzerland.

LAREDO Jaime, b. 7 June 1941, Cochabamba, Bolivia. Vionlist. m. (1) Ruth Laredo, 1960, divorced 1974, (2) Sharon Robinson. Education: Studied Violin with Antonio de Grassi and Frank Hauser in San Francisco; Josef Gingold and George Szell in Cleveland, and Ivan Galamian at the Curtis Institute, Philadelphia. Career: Orchestral debut San Francisco, 1952; Won Queen Elisabeth of the Belgians Competition 1959 and subsequently appeared with most major orchestras in Europe and America; New York debut Carnegie Hall 1960; London debut Albert Hall 1961; Frequent visitor to summer festivals at Spoleto, Tanglewood, Hollywood Bowl, Ravinia, Marlboro and Edinburgh; Repertoire ranges from Baroque to contemporary works; Gave the premiere of Ned Rorem's Concerto; Director, Soloist, works with St Pauls and Scottish Chamber Orchestras; Director Chamber Music at the 92nd Street NY series in New York; Piano Trio concerts from 1977 with Joseph Kalichstein and Sharon Robinson. Recordings: Trios by Mendelsshn, Brahms and Beethoven for Vox Cum Laude and Pickwick International; Brahms Piano Quartets with Emanuel Ax, Isaac Stern, Yo-Yo Ma. Honours: New York City Handel Medallion, 1960; Stadium in La Paz named after him; Bolivian stamps with his portrait issued in his honour, enscribed with the notes A, D and C (La-re-do). Address: c/o Harold Holt Limited, 31 Sinclair Road, London W14 0NS, England.

LAREDO Ruth, b. 20 Nov 1937, Detroit, Michigan, USA. Concert Pianist. m. 1 June 1960, divorced 1974, 1 daughter. Education: Diploma, Curtis Institute of Music; Philadelphia, BMus, 1960; Studied under Rudolf Serkin at Curtis Institute. Debut: Carnegie Hall with New York Orchestra American Symphony under Leopold Stowkowski. Career: Appeared at Carnegie Hall, the Kennedy Center, Library of Congress and the White House with orchestras the New York Philharmonic, Philadelphia and Cleveland Orchestras, Boston Symphony, St Louis Symphony, Detroit Symphony, National Symphony, the orchestras of Baltimore, Indianapolis, Houston, Buffalo and American Symphony; Participated in The Music from Marlboro Concerts from their inception 1965-; Performed at the Spoleto Festival USA 1983, 1985; Frequent Guest Artist with ensembles, The Tokyo and Shanghai Quartets; Tours with flautist Paula Robison. Recordings: Complete Works of Rachmaninoff; Complete sonatas of Scriabin and works of Barber. Contributions to: Columnist, Keyboard Classics Magazine; Editor, C F Peters Publishing Company. Hobbies: Running; Attending Movies and Ballet; Reading. Current Management: ICM Artists, New York, USA. Address: c/o ICM Artists, 40 W 57th Street, New York, NY 10019, USA.

LARGE Brian, b. 1937, London, England. Musicologist; Pianist; Writer; TV Producer. Education: Studied at Royal Academy of Music and London University. Career: Producer of opera on BBC TV with many other opera television engagements in Europe and the USA. Publications: Books on Smetana, Martinu and Czech Opera; Wrote entry on Martinu in The New Grove Dictionary of Music and Musicians, 1980. Recordings: Many operas on video, including La Cenerentola from the Houston Opera.

LARIN Sergei, b. 1956, Daugavpils, Latvia. Singer (Tenor). Education: Studied at the Vilnius Conservatory. Career: Early roles included Alfredo, Hermann and Vladimir in Prince Igor; Sang at Bratislava Opera from 1989 and guested at Dresden same year in Wagner-Régeny's Prometheus; Further appearances in Paris, at Monte Carlo as Don José and the Vienna Staatsoper as Lensky; Frankfurt 1993, as Sergei in Lady Macbeth of the Mtsensk District, La Scala 1993 as Don Carlo; Many appearances with the Kirov Opera, St Petersburg; Season 1996 with Loris in Fedora at La Scala and Don Jose at the Verona Arena. Address: c/o Teatro alla Scala, Via Filodrammatici 2, 2 Milan 1021, Italy.

LARKIN Christopher (Michael), b. 1 Sept 1947, Wigan, England. Horn Player; Conductor. m. Patricia Stuart, 24 Jan 1970, 1 son, 2 daughters. Education: Thornleigh Salesian College, Bolton, Lancashire, 1958-65; Pupil of James Brown, OBE, at Royal Academy of Music, 1965-68; Member of BBC Training Orchestra, Bristol, 1968-69. Debut: As Conductor, Henry Wood Proms, The London Gabrieli Brass Ensemble, Aug 1991. Career: London Gabrieli Brass Ensemble, joined 1973, Director since 1975; BBC Symphony Orchestra, 1979-. Recordings: Original 19th Century Music for brass; (From The Steeples & The Mountains 20th Century American Brass Music). Publications: Editor in Chief, London Gabrieli Brass Edition, 12 Editions of Original Brass Music, 1991-. Contributions to: Article on Felicien David's Nonetto in C Minor, in volume 5 of Historic Brass Society Journal. Honours: LRAM, 1968; ARCM, 1968; ARAM, 1991. Membership: Royal Society of Musicians. Hobbies: Research into 19th Century Brass Music. Current Management: Helen Sykes Artists Management. Address: 22 Athenaeum Road, London N20 9AE, England.

LARMORE Jennifer, b. 21 June 1958, Atlanta, Georgia, USA. Singer (Mezzo-Soprano). Debut: Sang Sesto in La Clemenza di Tito in France. Career: Many performances in Europe and USA with a repertoire including operas by Mozart, Rossini, Debussy, Handel and Ravel; La Scala debut as Isolier in Le Comte Ory; From 1990 has sung Rossini's Rosina in Paris, Amsterdam, London and Rome, L'Enfant et les Sortilèges at La Scala, Giulio Cesare in Paris, Zerlina in Bonn, Rossini's Isabella and Isolier, in Turin and Milan; Season 1992-93 as Rosina in Bilbao and Berlin, Monteverdi's Ottavia in Bologna and Antwerp, Bellini's Romeo at Geneva and Carnegie Hall, Cenerentola in Florence and Dorabella at Salzburg Festival; Wigmore Hall recital, Mar 1993, with arias by Handel and Massenet and French and Spanish songs; Metropolitan debut as Rosina, Feb 1995; Concerts of Mahler Rückertlieder with R Muti and Vienna Philharmonic, Apr 1995; At Bastille Opera, Paris, as Romeo in I Capuletti and Angelina in La Cenerentola; Season 1996 with Rossini's Isabella at Los Angeles. Recordings include: L'Incoronazione di Poppea; Mozart's C minor Mass; Giulio Cesare; Il Barbiere di Siviglia; Hansel und Gretel; La Cenerentola; Alice in Lucia di Lammermoor; Marianna in Il Signor Bruschino; Arsace in Semiramide; Rossini Songs, Duets and Quartets; Solo CD of Handel and Mozart; Carmen; L'Italiana in Algeri; Solo CD of Travesti arias for Mezzo-Soprano. Honours: Winner, Richard Tucker Award, presentation and Gala at Lincoln Center, Oct 1994. Current Management: Caroline Woodfield and David Foster, ICM, USA; IMG and Tom Graham, London. Address: c/o IMG Artists, Media House, 3 Burlington Lane, Chiswick, London W4 2TH, England.

LARNER Gerald, b. 9 Mar 1936, Leeds, England. Music Critic. m. Celia Ruth Mary White, 2 daughters. Education: BA, New College, Oxford. Career: Assistant Lecturer, Manchester University, 1960-62; Member of the Guardian staff from 1962; Chief Northern music critic from 1965; Translated Wolf's Der Corregidor into English; Wrote libretto for John McCabe's The Lion, The Witch and The Wardrobe, 1971; Artistic Director, Bowden Festival, 1980-84. Contributions to: Musical Times; The Listener. Membership: Critics Circle. Hobbies: Wine Drinking; Art; Glass Collecting. Address: 11 Higher Downs, Altrincham, Cheshire, WA14 2QL, England.

LARROCHA Alicia de, b. 23 May 1923, Barcelona, Spain. Pianist. m. Juan Torra, 1 son, 1 daughter. Education: Studied with Frank Marshall in Barcelona. Career: Performed in public from age 4; Concerto debut in 1934 with the Madrid Philharmonic; British debut in 1953 at Wigmore Hall; US debut in 1955 with the Los Angeles Philharmonic; Formed duo with cellist, Gaspar Cassado in 1956; Solo recitals and concerts with major orchestras in Europe, USA, Canada, Central and South America, South Africa, New Zealand, Australia and Japan; Director, Marshall Academy Barcelona from 1959; Recent British appearances with the City of Birmingham Symphony, Philharmonia and the London Symphony Orchestra; Played Falla's Nights in The Gardens of Spain at the 1986 Promenade Concerts also televised; Barbican Hall recital in 1989; Edinburgh Festival, 1995; Ravel's Concerto in G at the Barbican, 1997. Recordings: Works by Granados, Falla, Albeniz, Mozart and Romantic composers. Honours include: Paderewski Memorial Medal, London, 1961; Decorated Spanish Orders of Civil Merit, 1962 and Isabella la Católica, 1972; Medalla d'oro of City of Barcelona, 1982; Gold Medal of Spanish National Assembly, 1982; Principe de Asturias Prize, 1994; Edison Award, 1968,

1978; Grammy Awards for recordings of Iberia by Albeniz, 1974 and 1989, Ravel Concertos 1975 and Granados Goyescas, 1991; Deutsche Schallplatten Prize, 1979; Grand Prix du Disque, 1991; Musician of the Year, USA, 1978. Current Management: Herbert H Breslin Inc. Address: c/o Herbert H Breslin Inc, 119 West 57th Street 1505, New York, NY 10019, USA.

LARSEN Libby (Brown), b. 24 Dec 1950, Wilmington, Delaware, USA. Composer. Education: Studied at the University of Minnesota with Dominick Argento. Career: Co-founded Minnesota Composers Forum, 1973; Resident Composer with the Minnesota Orchestra, 1983-87 and Artistic Director of the Hot Notes series, 1993; Many commissions from leading orchestras and organizations; Has appeared widely as speaker and teacher. Compositions include: Operas: Frankenstein, The Modern Prometheus, music drama, 1990; A Wrinkle In Time, 1992; Mrs Dalloway, 1993; Symphony, Water Music, 1985; Piano Concerto, Since Armstrong, 1990; Ghosts Of An Old Ceremony for Orchestra, 1991; Sonnets from the Portuguese for Soprano and Chamber Orchestra, 1989; String Quartet: Schoenberg, Schenker and Schillinger, 1991; The Atmosphere As A Fluid System for Flute, Strings and Percussion, 1992; Mary Cassatt for Mezzo, Trombone and Orchestra, 1994; Eric Hermannson's Soul, opera, 1997; String Symphony, 1998. Recordings: Dancing Solo, 1997; Libby Larsen, London Symphony Orchestra, 1997. Honours include: Grammy Award, 1994. Address: c/o ASCAP, ASCAP Building, One Lincoln Plaza, New York, Ny 10023, USA.

LARSON Lisa, b. 1964, Sweden. Singer (Soprano). Education: Vocal studies in Zürich, after a career as flautist. Career: Major roles at the Zürich Operastudio followed by Barbarina in Figaro at the Opera in season, 1996-97; Schubert operas at Potsdam, Barbarina at Lausanne, Amor in Gluck's Orfeo at the Cologne Philharmonic and Papagena under Muti at the opening of the season at La Scala; Komische Oper Berlin, as Barbarina and Papagena, 1996; Adele at Ludwigsburg and Frasquita and Tebaldo at Hamburg; Oscar in Un Ballo in Maschera at Basle, 1997; Concerts include Stockholm Festival appearances with Gosta Winbergh and Messiah in Vienna and at the Vatican. Recordings include: Schubert operas; Orff's Trionfi, under Franz Welser-Most; Schumann's Manfred, under Mario Vanzago; Royal Festival Concert, Stockholm, with Gosta Winbergh. Address: c/o Opernhaus Zürich, Falkenstrasse 1, CH-8008 Zürich, Switzerland.

LARSON Sophia, b. 1954, Linz, Austria. Soprano. m. Hans Sisa. Education: Salzburg Mozarteum with Seywald-Baumgartner; Further study with Ettore Campogalliani. Career: Sang at St Gallen from 1976 as Verdi's Amelia Boccanegra, Mozart's Ilia and Silvia in Mascagni's Zanetto; Sang at Ulm, 1979-80 as Fiordiligi, the Marschallin, Beethoven's Leonore and Katya Kabanova, Bremen, 1980-83, and guest at Hamburg, Stuttgart, Trieste and Rome; Sang at Bologna in 1985 as the Duchess of Parma in Busoni's Doktor Faust, and Turin in 1986 as Puccini's Turandot and in Ghedini's Maria d'Alessandria; Further appearances in South America, Berlin, Berne, Wiesbaden and Bratislava; Bayreuth Festival, 1984-85 as Gutrune in The Ring, and Festival of Verona in 1986 as Minnie in La Fanciulla del West; Studio recordings for French and Italian Radio; Sang Venus in Tannhäuser at Bayreuth Festival in 1987, Gutrune in The Ring at Staatsoper Munich in 1987, Tosca at Turin in 1987, Isolde at Toronto in 1987, War Requiem at Carnegie Hall in 1988, Fedra by Pizzetti at Palermo in 1988, Renata in The Fiery Angel at Grand Théâtre Genève in 1988, Turandot at Zurich in 1988, Senta at Nice and San Francisco in 1988, Sieglinde in Die Walküre at Bayreuth Festival in 1989, Renata at Amsterdam in 1989, Lyrische Symphonie by Zemlinsky at Amsterdam in 1989, Brünnhilde at Linz Brucknerfestival in 1989, Fidelio at Catania in 1989 and Turandot and Tosca at Turin and Zurich in 1990; British debut as Turandot at the London Coliseum, 1995. Address: c/o Opernhaus Zurich, Falkenstrasse 1, CH-8008 Zurich, Switzerland.

LARSSON Carl Edvard, b. 7 Nov 1925, Mõrsil, Jämtland, Sweden. Mouth-Organ Player; Former Blacksmith. m, Selma Maria Mårtensson, 1950, deceased July 1994, 2 sons, 1 deceased, 1 daughter. Career: Performs under name of n'Skogsbylasse; Played mouth-organ as a child, but began officially in 1970s; 1st appearance on Swedish Television in programme Nygammalt, 1977; Has participated in several other television shows, Sweden and Norway; Frequent appearances, Sweden and Norway; Plays early 19th century traditional folk music of legendary musician Lapp-Nils, other old folk music, old dance music and own compositions; Admired for unique technique on diatonic mouth-organ, producing rhythms including bass and guitar. Compositions: About 60 in the genre. Recordings: Numerous, on MC and CD. Honours: 1st nominated National Musician on Mouth Harmonica, Sweden, 1982; Recipient, SKAP Stipendium, 1993; Zorns Gold Badge, 1994. Address: Kall 2714, 83005 Järpen, Sweden.

LARSSON Charlotte, b. 1966, Sweden. Soprano. Education: Studied at the State Opera School in Stockholm from 1989. Debut: Norrlandsoperan as Signe in Stenhammar's Gillet pa Solhaug. Career: Concert appearances including opening of Aarhus Festival, 1991; Sang at Karlstad Opera Festival in 1992 and as Liu in Turandot for Stockholm Folkoperan in 1993; Other roles include Mozart's Pamina and Sandrina, Rosalinda and Dvorák's Rusalka; Engaged at Stockholm Royal Opera, 1994. Address: Nordic Artists Management, Sveavagen 76, S-11359 Stockholm, Sweden.

LASCARRO Juanita, b. 1964, Bogota, Colombia. Singer (Soprano). Education: Studied in Bogota and at the Cologne Musikhochschule, notably with Hartmut Holl and Mitsuko Shirai. Career: Has sung at the Leipzig Opera and at Cologne Opera as Papagena and in Peter Grimes; Markgräflichen Theater Bayreuth in JC Bach's Amadis des Gaules; Appearances at the Teatro Colon Buenos Aires as Adina, Susanna and Micaela; British opera debut as Daphne at Garsington, 1995; Season 1996-97 with Netherlands Opera as Euridice in L'Orfeo, Frasquita and First Flower Maiden at the Opera Bastille and Mahler's 4th Symphony in Germany. Honours include: Winner of the Leipzig Opera, Mendelssohn and Munchner Konzertgesellschaft Competitions (1992-93). Address: c/o Harrison-Parrott Ltd, 12 Penzance Place, London W11 4PA, England.

LASKE Otto, b. 23 Apr 1936, Olesnica, Oels, Silesia, Poland. Composer; Poet; Musicologist. Education: BMus, Akademie fur Tonkunst, Darmstadt; MMus, Composition, New England Conservatory of Music, Boston, USA; PhD, Philosophy, Goethe University, Frankfurt-am-Main, Germany; EdD, Harvard University, USA; Postdoctoral studies at Institute of Sonology, Utrecht, The Netherlands. Debut: Composers Forum, New York City, 1969. Career: Freelance Composer; Professor of Music; Artistic Director, Newcomp Inc, 1981-91. Compositions: 65 Works for instrumental, vocal and electroacoustic music including: Kyrie Eleison, a cappella, 1969, Distances And Proximities for Tape, 1973, Perturbations for Chamber Orchestra, 1979, Terpsichore for Tape, 1980, Soliloquy for Double Bass, 1984, Furies And Voices, 1989, Treelink for Tape, 1992. Publications: Music, Memory and Thought, 1977; Co-Editor, Understanding Music with AI, 1992. Address: 83 Appleton Street, Arlington, MA 02174, USA.

LASSMANN Peep, b. 19 Mar 1948, Tartu, Estonia. Pianist. m. Anne Lassmann, 5 Nov 1982, 1 son. Education: Tallinn Children's Music School, 1957-62; Tallinn Music Secondary School, 1962-66; Tallinn Conservatory, 1966-71 Pianist Diploma, Moscow Conservatory, postgraduate studies, 1971-73. Career: Teacher, 1973; Associate Professor, 1985; Head of Piano Department, 1987; Professor and Prorector, 1991; Rector of Tallinn Conservatory, 1992 (since 1993 Estonian Academy of Music); Many Concert Tours in 23 Countries; Recent Recitals, Complete Piano Works of Messiaen. Recordings: Six LP's and CD's, mainly Estonian Music, also E Tubin Concertino for piano and orchestra, A Rubinstein Sextet for piano and wind instruments; Many recordings in Estonian, Swedish and Moscow Radios. Contributions to: Numerous articles in various Estonian newspapers and magazines. Honours: Various Prizes and Diplomas from The Competitions of Pianists of USSR; The Musician of the Year 1989 of the Estonian Radio Merited Artist of Estonia, 1987. Memberships: Estonian Piano Teachers Association (President); Music Council of Estonia, (President). Hobby: Bird Watching. Address: Trummi 23-26, Tallinn 200026, Estonia.

LASZLO Eösze, b. 17 Nov 1923, Budapest, Hungary. Musicologist. m. (1) Katalin Kerényi, 16 Oct 1948, (2) Margit Szilléry, 24 Sep 1983, 1 s, 1 d. Education: PhD, University of Pázmány, Budapest, 1945; Piano Teacher Certificate, Liszt Academy of Music, Budapest, 1947. Career: Artistic Director, Publishing House, Editio Musica, 1961-87; Executive Secretary, International Kodály Society, 1975-95. Publications: 16 Books including: The Life and Work of Zoltán Kodály, Hungary, England, 1962, Germany, 1964; Zoltán Kodály: His Life in Pictures, Hungary, England and Germany, 1971, 1982; History of Opera, 1960, 1962, 1972; G Verdi, 1961; R Wagner, 1969; Franz Liszt, 119 Roman Documents, 1980. Contributions to: Grove's Dictionary of Music and Musicians; Riemann's Musiklexikon; Hungarian Music Lexikon; Studia Musicologia Hungarica; Magyar Zene, Hungarian Music; Bulletin of International Kodály Society. Address: Attila ut 133, H-1012 Budapest, Hungary.

LASZLO Ferenc, b. 8 May 1937, Cluj, Romania. Flautist; Musicologist; Critic; Lecturer of Chamber Music. m. Ilse Herbert, 6 Feb 1963, 2 sons, 1 daughter. Education: Qualified as Flautist, Secondary Music School, Cluj, 1954 and Academy of Music Cluj, 1959. Debut: As Flautist in 1958; As Musicologist in 1961. Career: Flautist with the Sibiu Philharmonic, 1959-66; Collaborator of Romanian Broadcasting, 1963-85 and Romanian TV, 1970-81; Teacher of Chamber Music at the Secondary Music School, Cluj, 1966-70; Associate Professor of Chamber Music, Academy of Music, Bucharest, 1970-. Publications include: As journalist, 1971-74 and 1976; Bartók Béla, Studies and Testimonies, 1980; Co-author and Editor, Our Way to Kodály, 1984; The 101st Year, About Bartók, Enescu and Kodály, 1984; Béla Bartók, Studies, Articles and Essays, 1984; Béla Bartók's Inheritance in Romania, in progress. Contributions to: Over 2000 contributions to magazines and journals. Address: Casutca Posctala 218, RO-3400 Cluj Napoca, Romania.

LASZLO Magda, b. 1919, Hungary. Soprano. Education: Studied at Franz Liszt Academy, Budapest with Irene Stoasser and Ferenc Szekelyhedi. Debut: Budapest in 1943 as Elisabeth in Tannhäuser and Amelia in Simon Boccanegra. Career: Resident in Rome from 1946; Sang in the radio and stage premieres of Dallapiccola's Il Prigioniero in 1949 and 1950; Sang further in modern works by Ghedini, Casella, Lualdi and Malipiero; Guest appearances in Austria, Germany, France, Holland and Switzerland; Covent Garden in 1954 as Cressida in the premiere of Walton's Troilus and Cressida; Glyndebourne, 1953-54, 1962-63 as Mozart's Cherubino, Gluck's Alceste and as Monteverdi's Poppea; Other roles were Marie in Wozzeck, Wagner's Isolde and Senta, Strauss's Daphne, Busoni's Turandot, Alfano's Sakuntala, Prokofiev's Renata, Handel's Agrippina, Roxana in King Roger, Gluck's Elena and Bellini's Norma. Recordings: Bach Cantatas and St Matthew Passion; L'Incoronazione di Poppea.

LATAL Martin, b. 19 Aug 1964, Olomouc, Czech Republic. Geographical Information Systems Expert; Programmer; Music Composer. m. Zdenka Latalova, 22 August 1986, 3 sons, 1 daughter. Education: Electrical University, Brno; Postgraduate Technical University; Piano Basic School, Olomouc, 1972; Trumpet Basic School, 1976; Organ, Private School, 1985. Career: 8 Organ Concerts, 1983-93; 3 Concerts, 1995; Local Radio Broadcasts; Produced music played at exhibition of Czech painter. Compositions: Improvisations: Double Album, Life With Love, Dreaming Heart; Album, The Desire. Recordings: Album, The Desire, 7 Parts; Double Album, Life With Love, Dreaming Heart, 10 and 11 Parts. Hobbies: Fencing; Cycling; Nature. Current Management: Foresta SG, as Halenkov. Address: Jiraskova 42, 785 01 Sternberk, Czech Republic.

LATARCHE Vanessa (Jayne), b. 3 Apr 1959, Isleworth, Middlesex, England. Concert Pianist; Accompanist; Private Teacher; Director of Latarche Trio. Education: Foundation scholarship to Royal College of Music; Studied with Kendall Taylor, 1977-82; FTCL; LRAM; ARCM. Career: Broadcasts for Radio 3, BBC TV and Cable TV in USA; Piano Teacher at Purcell School and Royal College of Music, Junior Department; Performed at Harrogate International Festival, Battle Festival, various music clubs and concert halls throughout Britain including Fairfield Halls, Croydon, Purcell Room and Queen Elizabeth Hall and Wigmore Hall, London; Recital and concerto appearances. Honours: English Speaking Union, Mayer Scholarship to Aspen Summer Festival, USA, 1982; Martin Musical Scholarship Fund Award to study with Vlado Perlemuter in Paris, and Alexander Kelly in London in 1983; Lisa Fuchsova Prize for Chamber Music, Pianist; Eric Rice Memorial Prize for an Accompanist, Royal Overseas League Competition, 1984. Memberships: Incorporated Society of Musicians; Musicians Union; Ealing and District Music Teachers' Society. Hobbies: Driving; Knitting; Dancing. Address: 10 Ravenswood Gardens, Isleworth, Middlesex, TW7 4JG, England.

LATCHEM Malcolm, b. 28 Jan 1931, Salisbury, England. Violinist. m. 24 June 1964, 1 son, 3 daughters. Education: Royal College of Music, 1947-49, 1951-53; ARCM Performers. Career: Philharmonia Orchestra, 1960-65; Sub-Leader, London Philharmonic Orchestra, 1965-69; Dartington String Quartet, 1969-80; Founder Member, 1959, now Principal and Director, Academy of St Martin-in-the-Fields. Recordings: Chamber music with Academy of St Martin-in-the-Fields Chamber Ensemble; Handel Trio Sonatas; Mozart's Divertimenti; Spohr's Double Quartets; Other chamber music. Honours: Honorary MMus, Bristol University, 1980. Hobby: Gardening. Current Management: ASM (Orchestra) Ltd. Address: Station House, Staverton, Totnes, Devon TQ9 6AG, England.

LATEINER Jacob, b. 31 May 1928, Havana, Cuba. Pianist. Education: Studied in Havana with Jascha Fischermann, 1934-40 and Curtis Institute from 1940 with Isabelle Vengerova; Studied chamber music with Piatigorsky and Primrose. Debut: With the Philadelphia Orchestra under Ormandy in 1945. Career: Tanglewood Festival with Koussevitsky in 1947; New York recital debut in 1948; Tours of Europe, USA and Australia from 1954; Premiered the Concerto by Elliott Carter in 1967 and the Third Sonata of Roger Sessions in 1968; Taught at Mannes College, 1963-70, and Juilliard School, NY, from 1966. Recordings: Works by Beethoven and other 19th Century repertory; Contemporary American works. Address: Juilliard School of Music, Piano Faculty, Lincoln Plaza, New York, NY 10023, USA.

LATHAM-KOENIG Jan, b. 15 Dec 1953, London, England. Conductor; Pianist. Education: Studied at the Royal College of Music with Norman del Mar, Kendall Taylor and Lamar Crowson. Career includes: Regular appearances as conductor with Royal Philharmonic, Philharmonia, London Philharmonic, BBC Symphony, BBC Philharmonic and BBC Welsh Symphony

Orchestras; Guest Conductor of the Los Angeles Philharmonic and St Paul Chamber Orchestras, the Danish and Swedish Radio Orchestras, Stockholm Philharmonic, Maggio Musicale Orchestras, RAI, Italy, Zurich Tonhalle and the Gulbenkian Orchestra in Lisbon; Founded the Koenig Ensemble in 1976; Concert Pianist until 1981; Opera engagements include Giulio Cesare with Royal Swedish Opera in 1985, La Vestale at Genoa in 1984, From the House of the Dead at Venice, 1985-86, Tosca for English National Opera in 1987, The Cunning Little Vixen at Vienna Volksoper in 1992; Festival appearances with La Straniera at Wexford, 1987, Manon and Macbeth at Macerata, 1987-88, world premiere of L'Ispirazione by Bussotti at Maggio Musicale in 1988, and Catalani's Dejanice at Lucca; Has conducted Szymanowski's King Roger for Danish Radio and a cycle of Weill operas and cantatas for West German Radio; Rome Opera in 1988 with the premiere of Busotti's Fedra returning with Donizett's Poliuto to open the 1988-89 season; Debut at Vienna Staatsoper in 1988 in Macbeth; Conducted Leoncavallo's La Bohème at Venice in 1990 and Weill's Mahagonny at the 1990 Maggio Musicale Florence; Permanent Guest Conductor at Vienna State Opera from 1991; Conducted Aida at Covent Garden, 1996; Danish premiere of Poulenc's Carmelites, 1997. Recordings include: Weill's Mahagonny with Anja Silja; Der Zar Lässt sich Photographieren; Walton Concertos with London Philharmonic Orchestra. Address: Unit 2, 39 Tadema Road, London, SW10 0PY, England.

LAUBENTHAL Horst, b. 8 March 1939, Duderstadt, Germany. Singer (Tenor). m. Marga Schiml. Education: Studied in Munich with Rudolf Laubenthal. Debut: Wurzberg, 1967, as Mozart's Don Ottavio. Career: Staatsoper Stuttgart from 1968, in operas by Wagner, Mozart and Beethoven; Guest appearances in Vienna, Hamburg and Barcelona; Bayreuth Festival, 1970, as the Steersman in Der fliegende Holländer; Deutsche Oper Berlin, as Lensky in Eugene Onegin and Pfitzner's Palestrina; Glyndebourne, 1972, as Belmonte in Die Entführung; Paris Opéra, 1977; Turin, 1985, as Tamino in Die Zauberflöte (returned 1987, as Don Ottavio); Often heard as the Evangelist in the Passions of Bach. Recordings: Tannhäuser, Fidelio, Die Meistersinger; Wozzeck and Lulu; Bach Cantatas and Christmas Oratorio; Trionfi by Orff; Konrgold's Violanta; Schubert's Lazarus.

LAUBER Anne (Marianne), b. 28 July 1943, Zurich, Switzerland. Composer; Conductor. Education: Studied at the Lausanne Conservatory and the University of Montreal, 1973-77, with André Prevost. Career: Teacher at French-language universities in Canada and president of the Canadian Music Centre from 1987; Commissions from leading orchestras and soloists. Compositions include: Au-Dela Du Mur Du Son, symphonic tale, 1983; Concertos for String Quartet, 1983, Violin, 1986, and Piano, 1988; Le Songe for Flute and String Quartet, 1985; Jesus Christus, oratorio, 1986; Piano Quintet, 1989; Requiem, 1989; Other vocal music. Address: c/o Canadian Music Centre, 20 St Joseph Street, Toronto, Ontario M4Y 1J9, Canada.

LAUFER Beatrice, b. 27 Apr 1923, New York City, USA. Composer. Education: Studied at Juillard School from 1944 with Roger Sessions, Marion Bauer and Vittorio Giannini. Career: Performances of her music in Germany, Stockholm, China and USA. Compositions include: 2 Symphonies, 1944 and 1961; Opera Ile, after O'Neill's Long Voyage Home, premiered at Stockholm in 1958, revived at Yale School of Music under Phylis Curtin in 1977 and at Shanghai in 1988; Violin Concerto; Concerto for Flute, Oboe Trumpet and Strings, 1962; Lyric for String Trio, 1966; The Great God Brown, ballet, 1966; My Brother's Keeper, biblical opera, 1968; Adam's Rib for Soloists, Chorus and Orchestra; Concertante for Violin, Viola and Orchestra, 1986; Choral music. Address: c/o ASCAP, ASCAP Building, One Lincoln Plaza, New York, NY 10023, USA.

LAUGHLIN Roy, b. 1954, Belfast, Northern Ireland. Conductor; Pianist. Education: Studied at Edinburgh and Durham Universities. Career: Conducted Haydn's L'Infedeltà Delusa at Durham; Head of Music with Opera North, conducting The Magic Flute, Orpheus in The Underworld, La Cenerentola and Der Freischütz; Twice Chorus Master at Wexford Festival and conducted Die Schöpfung in 1989; Assistant Conductor of Halifax Choral Society; Recent engagements with Opera North include Fidelio, The Pearl Fishers, Peter Grimes and the British premiere production of Verdi's Jerusalem in 1990, also La Traviata, Attila and Faust; Season 1992-93 with Falstaff for English Touring Opera and Cimarosa's Secret Marriage for the Cheltenham and Buxton Festivals. Address: Robert Gilder and Co, Enterprise House, 59-65 Upper Ground, London, SE1 9PQ, England.

LAUKVIK Jon, b. 16 Dec 1952, Oslo, Norway. Organist; Harpsichordist. Education: Studied Organ, Church Music and Piano, Conservatory of Oslo, 1972-74; Organ with Professor M Schneider, Harpsichord with Professor H Ruf, Musikhochschule, Cologne, 1974-80; Organ studies with M C Alain, Paris, 1975-77. Debut: Oslo, 1973. Career: Recitals in Western and Eastern Europe, Israel, Japan and USA; Recordings for several European radio stations; Master classes; Jury Member, international competitions. Compositions: Via Crucis; Triptychon; Suite for organ; Anrufung for 2 organs, tape and brass; Euphonie I for organ and 5 percussionists; Euphonie III for cello and organ; Contre-danse for orchestra. Recordings: Neresheim Monastery (works by J S and C P E Bach, Raison, Kittel). Publications: Orgelschule zur historischen Aufführungspraxis, 1990; G F Handel: Organ Concertos op 7 and Nos 13-16 (with W Jacob), 1990; English version, Historical Performance Practice in Organ Playing, 1996. Honours: 1st Prize and Bach Prize, International Organ Week, Nuremberg, 1977. Hobbies: Cooking; Fine wines; Norway. Address: Senefelderstrasse 13, D-70178 Stuttgart, Germany.

LAURENCE Elizabeth, b. 22 Nov 1949, Harrogate, Yorkshire, England. Mezzo-Soprano. Education: Studied clarinet at Trinity College of Music, London. Career includes: Vienna in 1983 in Le Marteau sans Maitre under Boulez; Further concerts with Barenboim, Casadesus, Downes, Jordan and Zender; Made video for French TV, L'Heure Espagnole by Ravel, 1985-86; Sang at Madrid Opera in 1986 as Jocasta in Oedipus Rex, also in Buffalo, USA, with M Valdes, 1991, Paris Opéra as Erda in Siegfried and as Cherubino in Le Nozze di Figaro, returning for the 1989 world premiere of Der Meister und Margarita by Höller; Sang in the 1987 world premiere of The Electrification of the Soviet Union by Nigel Osborne at Glyndebourne Festival; Tour of Italy and Germany in 1987 with Ensemble Intercontemporain, in Pierrot Lunaire, Proms, 1987; Sang in the 1988 premiere of Boulez's revised version of Le Visage Nuptial, La Scala, Milan; Sang Fricka in Das Rheingold at Salle Pleyel, Paris in 1988, and Schoenberg's Op 22 songs and Mahler's 3rd Symphony in Turin under Lothar Zagrosek and Rudolf Barshai; Covent Garden debut in 1989 in the British premiere of Berio's Un Re in Ascolto and in 1991 at La Bastille Opera, Paris; Appeared as Judith in a BBC TV production of Bartók's Bluebeard's Castle in 1989; Contemporary recital of Berio, Bartók, Britten, Reger and Schoenberg at Festival of Montreux; Gurrelieder at Leeds Town Hall in 1989; 1990, sang Erda in Rheingold with D Russell Davies in Bonn opera; 1991, Ligeti's Requiem in Belgium Germany with D Russell Davies; Sang and recorded Le Rossignol, Stravinsky, for the Proms with Boulez; Sang Lady de Hautdesert in the premiere of Birtwistle's Gawain at Covent Garden in 1991; Season 1991-92 as Ravel's Concepcion at Turin and the Duchess of Alba in the premiere of Osborne's Terrible Mouth at the Almeida Theatre; Verdi Requiem, conducted by L Heltay, London, 1992; Season 1993, Die Wuste bat zwolf Ding, Zender, Berlin Opera (concert), Folksongs, Berio, Ulisse Dallapiccola, Salzburg Festival, conducted by Zender; Season, 1994, The Page in Salome, Opera de Marseille, conducted by S Baudo, Toured Germany in Pulcinealla by Stravinsky, Orchestre de Paris; Season 1996, Toured France in Pelléas et Mélisande by Debussy, Flora in La Traviata, Marseille Opera, Nello Santi, Radio France premiered Leucade by L Martin, Salzburg Festival with Ravel's Trois Poèmes de S Mallarmé, Masterclasses on French Contemporary Song at Cité de la Villette, Paris in 1996, Recontres Musicales a Luxéuil les Bains in 1996 and 1997 and participated in Masterclass 2000 in Italy in the presence of Giulietta Simionata in 1997; Recent engagements include: Premiere of Britten's Phèdre in Tblisi, Georgia, with Georgia State Orchestra; L'Enfance du Christ by Berlioz in Malaga, Spain with Cuidad Orchestra conducted by Odón Alonso; French premiere of Gurlitt's Wozzeck in Rouen and Caen Operas; Schoenberg Recital, Academia S Caecilia, Rome; Japanese premiere of Bluebeard's Castle by Bartok in Tokyo conducted by Peter Eötvös; Debut at Théâtre Champs Elysées, Paris, with Les nuits d'été by Berlioz, conducted by R Andreani; Stabat Mater by Rossini conducted by R Gutter in Imola; Concert of symphonic music in 1998, Die Mutter in Lulu, Paris Bastille Opera conducted by Dennis Russell Davis; Regular recitals in Europe. Recordings include: Live recording, Le Marteau sans Maître; Le Visage Nuptial; Bartok's Bluebeard's Castle; Gurlitt's Wozzeck. Current Management: Robert Alfonsi, Mondiale Musique; Robert Gilder & Co, London, Mercedes Sanchez del Rio, Spain. Address: 15 ave Montaigne, 75008 Paris, France.

LAURENS Guillemette, b. 1950, Fontainebleau, France. Mezzo-Soprano. Education: Studied at the Toulouse Conservatoire and the Paris Opéra Studio. Debut: Paris Salle Favart as Anne Trulove in The Rake's Progress. Career: Has performed throughout Europe, the USA and South America; Sang Cybele in Lully's Atys at the Paris Opéra with Les Arts Florissants; Repertoire includes German Lieder, French and Italian Baroque chamber music, Pierrot Lunaire by Schoenberg, La Clemenza di Tito, Giulio Cesare, and I Puritani (Paris Opéra); Appeared with Capriccio Stravagante in America in 1989; Engagements with the Ensemble Sequentia in 12th Century Liturgical Drama; Sang at the Festival of Aix-en-Provence in Iphigénie en Aulide, with John Eliot Gardiner, and Towards Bach concert series on London's South Bank in 1989. Recordings: Monteverdi's Vespers with Philippe Herreweghe; Atys and Il Ballo dell'Ingrate, conducted by William Christie; Bach's B minor Mass with Gustav Leonhardt; Charpentier's Le Malade Imaginaire under Marc Minkowski; Diana in Iphigénie en Aulide under John Eliot Gardiner. Address: Erato Musifrance, c/o WEA Records, PO Box 59, Alperton Lane, Alperton, Middlesex, HA0 1FJ, England.

LAURIE Alison (Margaret), b. 5 Jan 1935, Glossop, Derbyshire, England. Music Librarian. Education: MA, BMus, Glasgow University, 1952-57; PhD, Cambridge University, 1957-60; ARCM. Career: Senior Assistant Librarian, Glasgow University, 1961-63; Music Librarian, Reading University Library, 1963-. Publications: Editions of Purcell, Dioclesian, 1960 and Dioclesian vocal score, 1983; Dido and Aeneas, 1961 and 1979; King Arthur, 1971 and King Arthur vocal score, 1972; Solo songs, 1985; The Indian Queen, 1995. Contributions include: Editor, Neighbour, Music and Bibliography, 1980; Editor, Bent, Source materials and the interpretation of music, 1981; Editor, Spink, Music in Britain: The Seventeenth Century, 1992; Editor, Price, Purcell Studies, 1995; Musical Times. Memberships: Purcell Society, Chairwoman, 1988-; Royal Musical Association; International Association of Music Libraries Archives and Documentation Centres; Library Association. Hobbies: Hill Walking; Gardening. Address: 123 Nightingale Road, Woodley, Reading, Berkshire, RG5 3LZ, England.

LAVENDER Justin, b. 4 June 1951, Bedford, England. Singer (Tenor). Debut: Sang Nadir in Les Pêcheurs de perles at Sydney Opera House, 1982. Career: Has sung Medoro in Haydn's Orlando Paladino at St Gallen, Tamino at Vienna Staatsoper, Pilade (Rossini's Ermione) at Madrid, Le Comte Ory at La Scala, Don Ottavio for Rome Opera and Arnold (Guillaume Tell) and Almaviva at Covent Garden; Appearances in premieres of Il Ritorno di Casanova by Arrigo at the Grand Théâtre Geneva and La Noche Triste by Prodomidès at Théâtre des Champs Elyéeses, Paris; Further engagements as Fernande in La Favorite at Vichy, Almaviva at Pittsburgh (US debut), Belmonte in Vienna and Berlin, Ferrando (Così fan tutte) at Essen, Lindoro at Buxton Festival and Neocles in Le Siège de Corinthe by Rossini at Madrid and the Festival Hall, London; Season 1993 in Il Pirata at Lausanne, Marzio in Mitridate and Arone in Mosè in Egitto at Covent Garden; Sang Don José in Raymond Gubay's Carmen, Albert Hall, 1997; Concert repertoire includes Bartók's Cantata Profana with Georg Solti, Schubert's Mass in E flat with Giulini and Berlin Philharmonic, Schnittke's Faust Cantata under Claudio Abbado and Oedipus Rex conducted by Bernard Haitink; Other conductors have included John Lubbock (Dream of Gerontius), John Pritchard, Menuhin, Alberto Zedda and Leonard Slatkin; Contributions to: The Singer, Rhinegold Publications. Current Management: Magenta Music International Limited. Address: 4 Highgate High Street, London N6 5DJ, England.

LAVIRGEN Pedro, b. 31 July 1930, Bujalance, Adalusia, Spain. Tenor. Education: Studied with Miguel Barrosa in Madrid. Debut: Mexico City in 1964 as Radames. Career: European debut at the Teatro del Liceo, Barcelona as Don José; Sang at Metropolitan in 1969 as Cavaradossi in Tosca, Verona Arena in 1974 and 1976 as Radames, Covent Garden in 1975 and 1978 as Don José and Pollione in Norma, La Scala Milan in 1975 as Don José repeating the role at the 1978 Edinburgh Festival; Other appearances in Hamburg, Munich, Prague, Budapest and Madrid. Recordings include: Il Retablo de Maese Pedro by De Falla.

LAVISTA Mario, b. 3 Apr 1943, Mexico City. Composer. Education: Studied composition with Carlos Chávez, musical analysis with Rodolfo Halffter, National Conservatory of Mexico, 1963-67; Studied in Paris with Jean Etienne Marie, in Cologne with K Stockhausen and Henry Pousseur, 1967-70. Career: Professor of Theory and Composition, National Conservatory of Mexico, 1970-; Founder of group, Quanta, 1970-73; Editor of Pauta, Journal of Music, 1982-. Compositions include: Canto Del Alba in C for Flute; Nocturno in G for Flute; Lamento for Bass Flute; Dusk for Contrabass; Cante for 2 Guitars; Marsias for Oboe and Crystal Cups; Ficciones for Orchestra; Simurg for Piano; Lacrymosa for orchestra; Missa ad Consolationis Dominam Nostram for choir a capella; Reflections Of The Night for String Quartet; Hacia El Comienzo for Mezzo-Soprano and Orchestra, poems by Octavio Paz; Ciucani in B flat for Flute and Clarinet; Madrigal in B flat for Clarinet; Three Nocturnes for Mezzo-Soprano and Orchestra, poems by Alvaro Mutis; Aura, one act opera based on Aura, a short story by Carlos Fuentes; Music for My Neighbor for string quartet; Danza isorrítmica for four percussionists. Memberships: International Society of Contemporary Music; Mexican Editions of Music; Mexican Academy of Arts. Hobby: Billiards. Address: Pirineos 455, Lomas de Chapultepec, 11000, DF, Mexico.

LAWLESS Stephen, b. England. Stage Director. Career: Director of Productions for Glyndbourne Touring Opera, 1986-91; Death in Venice televised and staged at the 1992 Festival; Directed The Pearl Fishers for Scottish Opera, Falstaff at Glyndbourne and Rameau's Les Boreades at the Royal Academy, 1985; Kirov Opera debut with Boris Godunov, 1990, also directed the above at the Vienna Staatsoper and La Fenice Venice, 1994; Figaro and Rosenkavalier for Canadian Opera, Araidne and Ballo in Maschera in Los Angeles, Capriccio in San Francicso and Cosi fan Tuute in Chicago; Hamlet by Thomas at the Vienna Volksoper and a Baroque double bill at Innsbruck: Venus and Adonis, with Dido and Aeneas; Season 1996-97 with Wozzeck in Braunschweig, Carmen for New Israeli Opera, Il Trovatore in Los

Angeles, The Rake's Progress in Pisa and Mozart's Finta Semplice at Potsdam; Has also directed opera in Seoul and Hong Kong. Address: c/o Lies Askonas Ltd, 6 Henrietta St, London WC2E 8LA, England.

LAWLOR Thomas, b. 1938, Dublin, Ireland. Bass-Baritone. Education: BA, National University of Ireland; Dublin College of Music; Guildhall School of Music. Career: Sang with D'Oyly Carte Company, 1963-71 with tours of North America; Glyndebourne, 1971-, in Eugene Onegin, Ariadne, Così fan tutte, Die Entführung, La Bohème, Le nozze di Figaro, Capriccio, Intermezzo, and The Cunning Little Vixen; Engagements with Opera North in A Village Romeo and Juliet, Tosca, Der Rosenkavalier, Der Freischütz, A Midsummer Night's Dream, Manon Lescaut, the premiere of Rebecca by Wilfred Josephs in 1983, Werther, La Cenerentola, Beatrice and Benedict, Jonny Spielt Auf, Die Meistersinger, The Golden Cockerel and Intermezzo; Further appearances with Kent Opera, English Music Theatre, New Sadler's Wells Opera and Opera Northern Ireland, Royal Opera, Dublin Grand Opera; Sang in Rising of The Moon at Wexford Festival in 1990 and Prokofiev's The Duenna; Regular broadcaster on Radio Telefis Eireann and on BBC Radio and TV. Membership: Faculty Member of Summer Conservatory of Music, Bay View, MI, USA. Address: Music International, 13 Ardilaun Road, Highbury. London, N5 2QR, England.

LAWRENCE Amy, b. 1962, Philadelphia, USA. Singer (Soprano). Education: Florida State University, New England Conservatory and Zurich Opera, 1992. Career: Sang in La Forza del Destino and Albert Herring at Zurich, Der Schauspieldirektor by Mozart at Basle; Kiel Opera from 1994, as Dianora in Mona Lisa by Schillings, Adele (Fledermaus), Constanze, Susanna, and Speranza in L'Orfeo in Monteverdi's Orfeo; Concerts include Messiah, Die Schöpfung, and Mozart's C minor Mass; Carmina Burana and Barber's Knoxville Summer of 1915 with the Louisiana PO; Season 1997 with the Mozart's Queen of Night for the Norwegian Opera, Oslo. Honours include: National Finalist, Metropolitan Opera Competition; Semi-finalist, Belvedere Opera Competition, New York. Address: Athole Still Ltd, Foresters Hall, 25-27 Westow Street, London SE19 3RY, England.

LAWRENCE Helen (Ruth), b. 22 July 1942, London, England. OperaSinger (Mezzo-Soprano). m. Abraham Marcus, 1969, 2 children. Education: North London Collegiate School; Royal Academy of Music, London, LRAM; ARAM. Career: Guest Artist: Covent Garden, English National Opera, Handel Opera, Chelsea Opera, Phoenix Opera, Ludwigsburg Festival, Germany; Toured Far East with Royal Opera, 1979; Concerts and recitals: Wigmore Hall, South Bank, Barbican; Major concert halls throughout UK, Germany, Italy, Netherlands, Israel, with Songmakers' Almanac, SPNM, Lotano, Hallé Orchestra, UK Music Clubs and Choral Societies; Roles as Soprano include: Donna Anna, Constanze, Fiordiligi, Médée (Cherubini), Lucrezia Borgia, Lady Macbeth, Violetta, Leonora, Amelia, Abigaille, Tosca, Santuzza, Carmen; Mezzo-Soprano since 1989, with roles including: Carmen, Fidalma, Marcelina and Azucena; Artistic Director and Administrator, New Shakespeare Company's Opera season, Regent's Park Open Air Theatre, 1983; London Masterclasses, 1989-92. Recordings include: BBC Radio: Title roles Giordano's Fedora; Berthold Goldschmidt's Beatrice Cenci; Ginastera's Cantata para American Magica; Discs: Dama in Macbeth; Amme Meme in Goldschmidt's Der Gewaltige Hahnrei, Berlin, 1992; Ornamente by A Krein, 1997. Publication: Life of Mozart, translation from Italian, Great Men Series for Children. Memberships: Equity; Incorporated Society of Musicians. Hobbies: Gardening; Reading; Sewing. Address: 5 Greenaway Gardens, London, NW3 7DJ, England.

LAWRENCE-KING Andrew, b. 1959, Guernsey, Channel Islands. Baroque Harpist and Director. Career: Founder-Member and Director of The Harp Consort, Soloist and Director, appearances with Hilliard Ensemble, Gothic Voices, Hesperion XX, The Kings Singers. Concerts in Europe, Scandanavia, USA, Japan, Australia, New Zealand, South America; Directed Monteverdi's Ulisse at 1992 Swedish Baroque Festival, Malmo; Handel's Almira at Bremen Goethetheatre in 1994, Purcell's Dido and Aeneas in Helsinki in 1995; Solo recital to open 1992 Utrecht Festival, three concerts within 1995 Boston Early Music Festival. Professor of Harp and Continuo, Hochschule für Künste, Bremen, Germany. Recordings: Over 100 titles on Hyperion, Deutsche Harmonia Mundi and others include: The Harp of Luduvico (solo harp music), Luz y Norte (Spanish 17th century dances with guitar band), Purcell's Musick's Hand-Maid and William Lawes' Exquisite Consorts (English ensemble music), Almira (Handel's first opera), The Italian Concerto (Bach, Handel, Vivaldi); Concert programmes include: Luz y Norte (with Spanish dance), Musick's Hand-Maid (vocal and instrumental ensemble), Harp and Double-Harp (solo), as well as orchestral repertoire and operas from Monteverdi to Handel. Publications: Der Harpfenschlaeger (Historical harp technique); Luz y Norte (Spanish and South American harp music); Article in Companion to Medieval and Renaissance Music, Dent 1992. Honours: First Winner of the International Award from Cambridge Early Music Society, 1992. Winner Gramophone Award, 1992. Member, Historical Harp Society, professionally qualified yacht skipper. Current Management: Jane Trewhella. Address: 9 Cliff Street, St Peter Port, Guernsey, Channel Islands.

LAWSON Colin (James), b. 24 July 1949, Saltburn-by-the-Sea, England. Clarinettist; Musicologist; Broadcaster. m. Hilary Birch, 16 Apr 1982, 1 s. Education: ARCM, 1967; Keble College, Oxford; BA (Oxon), 1971; MA (Oxon), 1975; MA, Birmingham University, 1972; PhD, Aberdeen University, 1976. Career: Lecturer in Music at University of Aberdeen, 1973-77; Lecturer and Senior Lecturer in Music, 1978-, Sheffield University: Guest Principal Clarinet, Orchestra of the Age of Enlightenment, 1987-; Professor of Classical Studies and Early Clarinet, Guildhall of Music, London, 1988-91; Principal Clarinet with Hanover Band, 1987-, London Classical Players, 1989- and English Concert, 1991-; Visiting Lecturer, RNCM and RAM, 1992; Current specialisation in historical performance; Member of contemporary ensemble, Lysis; Solo, chamber and orchestral appearances throughout UK, Europe and USA; Performed Mozart Concerto in 1989 on a specially designed boxwood basset clarinet at Cheltenham Festival, London and Oxford venues. Recordings: With Academy of Ancient Music, Albion Ensemble, Classical Winds, CM90, Cristofori, English Concert, The Parley of Instruments, La Petite Bande, L'Ecole d'Orphée and The King's Consort. Publications: The Chalumeau in Eighteenth-Century Music, 1981; Editor, The Cambridge Companion to the Clarinet, 1995. Contributions to: Beethoven and the development of wind instruments, in Beethoven and the Performer, 1994. Hobbies: Travel; Acquisition of early clarinets. Address: 46 Clitheroe Avenue, Harrow, Middlesex, HA2 9UX, England.

LAWSON Peter, b. 11 April 1950, Manchester, England. Pianist. m. Ariane Dandoy, 3 April 1976, 1 son, 1 daughter. Education: Royal Manchester College of Music, 1968-73; Postgraduate Studies, Royal Northern College of Music; GRSM; ARMCM. Career: Piano Soloist, Concertos with BBC Philharmonic,BBC Welsh, RLPO, London Sinfonietta, London Mozart Players; Recitals and Radio in France, Belgium, Holland, Italy, Denmark and throughout England; 20th Century Specialist; Tutor, Chetham's School of Music, Manchester; Examiner, Associated Board of the Royal Schools of Music. Recordings: Satie Piano Music, 1980; New British Piano Music, 1982; American Piano Sonatas (Virgin Classics) vol I, 1991, vol II, 1993; 3 CDs, in preparation. Honours: Silver Disc (Satie Recording), 1989; Churchill Fellowship, 1992. Memberships: European Piano Teachers Association; Musicians Union. Hobbies: Travel; Food. Address: 38 Church Street South, Old Glossop, Derbyshire SK13 9RU, England.

LAWTON Jeffrey, b. 1941, Oldham, Lancashire, England. Tenor. Education: Studied with Patrick McGuigan. Career: With Welsh National Opera has sung Tikhon in Katya Kabanova, also televised, various roles in The Greek Passion by Martinu, Florestan, Huon in Oberon, in Janácek's From The House of the Dead and Jenufa as Laca, Otello, Aeneas in The Trojans and Don José; Sang Siegfried in a new production of The Ring also seen at Covent Garden in 1986, and the Emperor in Die Frau ohne Schatten; Other operatic appearances for Opera North as Erik and Florestan, in Paris, Brussels and Nancy (Otello), and as Siegmund at Cologne; Concert engagements include the Choral Symphony with the Royal Liverpool Philharmonic, Das Lied von der Erde with the BBC Symphony at the Brighton Festival and in Paris, and Mahler's 8th Symphony in Turin; Sang Siegfried in Götterdämmerung in Cologne, Edmund in Lear for English National Opera, Edinburgh Festival in 1990 in Martinu's Greek Passion, Laca in Jenufa for Welsh National Opera and Tristan, 1992-93, Shuisky in Boris for Opera North, 1993-94, Laca for New Israeli Opera and Tristan for Scottish National Opera; Sang Herod in the final scene from Salome at Promenade Concerts in 1993; Sang Pedro in the premiere of Macmillan's Inès de Castro, Edinburgh, 1996; Wagner concert with the Philharmonia, London, 1997. Recordings include: The Greek Passion. Current Management: Music International. Address: Music International, 13 Ardilaun Road, Highbury, London, England.

LAYCOCK Mark, b. 30 Aug 1957, USA. Conductor. m. Emily Muller, 10 Jul 1982, 1 son. Education: New School of Music, Philadelphia, 1975-79; Aspen Music School; Solfege, ear training, 1975; Fellow, St Louis Conservatory, 1977. Debut: Philadelphia Orchestra, 1979. Career: Music Director, Orchestra London, Princeton Chamber Symphony; Philadelphia Orchestra debut in 1979, the Philharmonia Orchestra, Royal Festival Hall and Barbican Centre, London in 1986, and Indianapolis Symphony Orchestra in 1987; Guest Conductor for St Paul Chamber Orchestra, 1986 and 1989, and Moscow Autumn Festival, 1988; Inaugaurated the New Cairo Opera House in 1988; Middle East tour in 1988; Frequent Guest Lecturer with New Jersey Governor's School for the Arts, Trenton State College; Lecturer at Bishop Grosseteste College, Lincoln, England, 1986. Compositions: Published and recorded arranger. Honours: Fellow, Aspen Music Festival, 1977; Winner, Leopold Stokowski Memorial Competition in Association with the Philadelphia Orchestra, 1979; Rupert Foundation International Conducting Awards in London, 1980 and 1982; Outstanding Young Man of America Award, 1986; Finalist, American Symphony Orchestra Stokowski Conducting Competition, 1988. Membership: ASCAP. Address: 520 Wellington St, London, Ontario N6A 3R1, Canada.

LAYTON Richard, b. 1940, Redditch, Worcestershire, England. Violinist. m. 4 children. Education: Studied in London. Career: Freelance musician, then co-leader of the Bournemouth Symphony Orchestra from 1964; Leader of the Bournemouth Sinfonietta, 1969; Soloist in concertos by Bach, Haydn, Mozart, Prokofiev and in the Brandenburg Concertos; Leader of the Silvestri String Quartet, with concerts at Dartington and at Bath Festival; Sub-leader of the London Philharmonic Orchestra, 1973, including appearances with the Glyndebourne Festival; Guest leader with the BBC Welsh Symphony, English National Opera Orchestra, the Park Lane Players and the Philharmonia; Appointed Associate Leader of the Royal Philharmonic Orchestra in 1983. Hobby: Photography. Address: c/o Royal Philharmonic Orchestra, 16 Clerkenwell Green, London, EC1R 0DP, England.

LAYTON Robert, b. 2 May 1930, London, England. Critic; Producer; Writer on Music. m. Ingrid Nina Thompson. Education: Worcester College, Oxford, 1949-53; Universities of Uppsala and Stockholm, 1953-55; Studied composition with Edmund Rubbra and history of music with Egon Wellesz; Further studies with Professor Carl-Allan Mobert. Career: Swedish Film Industry, 1954-55; Teacher in London, 1956-59; BBC Music Division, 1959- (music presentation, 1959, music talks, 1960); General Editor, BBC Music Guides, 1973-; Producer of BBC Lunchtime Concerts at St John's Smith Square, 1984-88. Publications: Franz Berwald, 1959; Jean Sibelius, 1965; Sibelius and His World, 1970; Dvorák Symphonies and Concertos, 1977; Sibelius, 1981; Companion to The Concerto, 1988; Responsible for Scandinavian music in The New Grove Dictionary of Music and Musicians, 1980; Translated Erik Tawaststjerna's Sibelius, volume I, 1976, volume II, 1985, volume III, in preparation; Editor, Companion to The Symphony, in preparation. Contributions to: The Symphony, 1966; The Gramophone; The Listener; The Times; Professional journals in Britain and Sweden. Honours: Finnish State Literary Prize, 1985; Sibelius Medal, 1987; Knight of the Order of The White Rose of Finland, 1988. Address: BBC Radio 3, Broadcasting House, London, WA 1AA, England.

LAYTON Stephen, b. 1962, England. Choral Director; Organist. Education: Chorister at Winchester Cathedral; Music Scholar at Eton College, Organ Scholar at King's College, Cambridge. Career: Appearances with King's College Chapel Choir in Europe, USA and Japan; Conducted Messiah and Gluck's Orfeo at Cambridge; Founder and Director of chamber choir Polyphony, making London Proms debut 1995, with Pärt's Passio and Dido and Aeneas; Musical Director of the Holst Singers; Organist and Director of the Choir at Temple Church, London, from 1996; Engagements with the Philharmonic Chorus, London Philharmonic Choir and BBC SO Chorus; Tour of Brazil with Polyphony and Bournemouth Sinfonietta, 1995; Bach's Christmas Oratorio and Messiah with the Brandenburg Concert in London, 1996; Further concerts in Estonia, Hong Kong, France, Spain and Copenhagen. Recordings include: Macmillan's Seven Last Words from the Cross (BMG Catalyst); Folksongs by Holst and Vaughan Williams (Hyperion). Address: Magenta Music International, 4 Highgate High Street, London N6 5JL, England.

LAYTON Stephen David, b. 23 Dec 1966. Music Company Founder and Director. Education: A H Mann Organ Scholar, King's College, Cambridge. Appointments: Assistant Organist, Southwark Cathedral, 1988-97; Conductor, Guildford Singers, 1988-91; Conductor, Wokingham Choral Society, 1989-97; Choirmaster, St Stephen, Walbrook, 1989-96; Music Director, BBC Daily Service, 1990-94; Music Director, Holst Singers, 1993-; Deputy Chorusmaster, Philharmonia Chorus, 1993-; Tours: Brazil, 1995; Estonia, 1995; Denmark, 1996; BBC Promenade concerts, 1995-97. Recordings: Premieres on CD include Grainger and Britten. Hobbies: Food; Cyberspace; Kite Flying; Gadgets. Address: 13 King's Bench Walk, London, EC4Y 7EN, England.

LAZAR Hans Jurgen, b. 1958, Bad Salzuflen Germany. Singer (Tenor). Education: Studied in Detmold with Sandor Konya. Debut: Detmold 1982, as Mozart's Pedrillo. Career: Sang at the Hagen Opera 1985-87, Essen 1988-91, notably as Wagner's David, Janacek's Fox, Alfred in Fledermaus and Nicolai's Fenton; Frankfurt Opera 1988-91, notably as Britten's Flute; Many concert appearances, including Mozart masses, and Janacek's Diary of One Who Disappeared. Address: Theater der Stadt Frankfurt, Untermainanlage II, W-6000 Frankfurt am Main, Germany.

LAZAREV Alexander, b. 5 July 1945, Moscow, Russia. Conductor. Education: Studied at the Central Music School and the Moscow and Leningrad Conservatories. Career: Has conducted at the Bolshoi Theatre Moscow from 1973, Chief Conductor and Artistic Director, 1987-95; Founded the Ensemble of Soloists of the Bolshoi Theatre, 1978, for the promotion of contemporary music; Regular guest conductor of the St Petersburg Philharmonic and the State Symphony of the Russian Federation; Guest appearances with the Berlin Philharmonic, Bavarian Radio Symphony, Munich, Rotterdam and Netherlands Radio Philharmonics, the Orchestre National de France and the Orchestra of the Accademia di Santa Cecilia, Rome; UK debut, 1987, with the Royal Liverpool Philharmonic; Later engagements with the City of Birmingham Symphony, the Royal Scottish National, Philharmonia and the BBC Symphony Orchestras; Edinburgh Festival, 1987, with the Orchestra of the Bolshoi Theatre; Led the Bolshoi Company in Glasgow with Rimsky-Korsakov's Mlada and Tchaikovsky's Maid of Orleans, 1990; Edinburgh Festival, 1990, 1991; Prokofiev's The Duenna; Conducted the BBC Symphony Orchestra in Henze's Tristan and 7th Symphony at the Barbican Hall, 1991; Promenade Concerts, 1991, 1992, 1993, 1994, 1995; Principal Guest Conductor of BBC Symphony Orchestra, 1992-95; Led the Bolshoi Company on tour to the Metropolitan, New York, 1991; Conducted Salome at Duisburg, 1992; Led Schnittke's adaptation of The Queen of Spades at Bonn, 1996; Recordings: Various recordings on Melodiya, Virgin Classics and Sony Classical. Honours: 1st Prize, Young Conductors' Competition, Moscow, 1971; Winner, Herbert von Karajan Competition, Berlin, 1972. Address: c/o Tennant Artists, Unit 2, 39 Tadema Road, London SW10 0PY, England.

LAZARIDIS Stefanos, b. 28 July 1944, Dire-Daw, Ethiopia. Stage Designer. Education: Studied in Geneva, 1960-62 and at Central School of Speech and Drama, London. Career: Designed Le nozze di Figaro at Covent Garden in 1972 followed by Idomeneò and Werther, 1978-79; Collaborated with John Copley at English National Opera with Die Entführung in 1971 and Il Trovatore in 1972; Further designs for ENO have included Katya Kabanova, Dalibor, Euryanthe, Aida, Der fliegende Holländer, Rusalka, Madama Butterfly, Hansel and Gretel and the Mikado; Collaborations with Yuri Lyubimov for Tristan und Isolde at Bologna in 1983, Rigoletto at Florence in 1984 and Fidelio at Stuttgart in 1985; UK stage premieres of Janácek's Osud in 1984 and Busoni's Doktor Faust in 1986; Designed Tosca at Florence and English National Opera, with Jonathan Miller, in 1986, Nabucco for Opera North and Oedipus Rex and Bluebeard's Castle for Scottish Opera in 1990; Der fliegende Holländer with David Pountney at Bregenz Festival in 1989, Carmen at Earl's Court in London, 1989, and on tour to Japan and Australia; La Fanciulla del West at La Scala in 1991; Pag and Cav at the Berlin Staatsoper, 1996; Associate Artist at English National Opera. Address: English National Opera, St Martin's Lane, London, WC2, England.

LAZARO Francisco, b. 13 Mar 1932, Barcelona, Spain. Tenor. Education: Liceo Conservatory, Barcelona. Debut: Barcelona in 1962 as Gaspare in Donizetti's La Favorita. Career: Sang in Macbeth and Der Rosenkavalier at the 1964 Salzburg Festival, under Karajan; Guest appearances in Berlin, Dusseldorf and Frankfurt, San Francisco in 1965, and Barcelona in 1967 as Calaf in Turandot; Frequent performances at the Munich Staatsoper from 1970; Sang at Hamburg in 1984 as Otello; Other roles include Verdi's Manrico and Radames, Des Grieux in Manon Lescaut, Rodolfo and Don José.

LAZAROF Henri, b. 12 Apr 1932, Sofia, Bulgaria. Composer. Education: Studied with Paul Ben-Haim in Jerusalem; Santa Cecilia Academy in Rome with Petrassi, 1955-57; Brandeis University with Harold Shapero, 1957-59. Career: Teacher at University of California, Los Angeles, 1962-; Artist in Residence at University of West Berlin, 1970-71. Compositions include: Piano Concerto, 1957; Violin Concerto, 1962; Concerto for Piano and 20 Instruments, 1963; Odes for Orchestra, 1963; Double Concerto for Violin, Viola and Chamber Orchestra, 1964; Structures Sonores for Orchestra, 1966; Mutazione for Orchestra, 1967; Cello Concerto, 1968; Events, ballet, 1973; Concertazioni for Orchestra, 1973; Spectrum for Trumpet, Orchestra and Tape, 1975; Chamber Symphony, 1977; Mirrors, Mirrors, ballet, 1980; Sinfonietta, 1981; 3 String Quartets, 1956-80; String Trio, 1957; Wind trio, 1981. Address: c/o ASCAP, ASCAP Building, One Lincoln Plaza, New York, NY 10023, USA.

LAZAROV Stefan (Stefanov), b. 31 Aug 1935, Sofia, Bulgaria. Musicologist. m. Emilia Tsherkozova, 8 Nov 1977, 1 son. Education: Musicology and History of Music at State Conservatoire, Sofia, 1953-58; Diploma, 1958-59; DPhil, 1974; Dr Arts, 1989. Career: Lecturer of Musicology, Philharmonies of Sofia, 1956-61, Plovdiv, 1959-64, Rousse, 1965-66, Opera of Rousse, 1964-65; Professor, 1960, Associate Professor, 1982, University Professor, 1991 in History and Theory of Music, National Academy for Theatre and Film Arts; Professor in History of Opera and Musical Paleography, State Conservatoire, 1963-65; Many public and broadcast lectures; Author of TV plays. Publications include: General History of Music, 11 books, 1958-88; Bulgarian Music: Marin Goleminov, 1971; Pancho Vladigerov and The Theatre, 1974; An Interpetation of the Bulgarian Mediaeval Liturgical Texts, 1974; Die Bogomilen und die Musik, 1975; Pictogrammes et ideogrammes dans l'ecriture musicale Byzantine, 1976; A Mediaeval Slavonic Treatise on Music, 1980; Comparative culturology: The Bogomils, The Music and The Theatre, 1985, Trubadures and the Cathares, 1989, The Bogomils and an Old Musical Tradition in Western Europe, 1990, The Role of the Bogomils and the Cathares in development of European Culture, 1990; Literature for Music, Texts in Original and Translation, 1991. Address: Eline-Peline Str 30, 1421 Sofia, Bulgaria.

LAZARTE Julio (Ricardo), b. 12 July 1956, Tucuman, Argentina. Pianist; Conductor. Education: Medico Degree, National University of Tucuman; Piano and Professor of Piano from School of Musical Arts, National University of Tucuman; Dalcroze Certificate, Carnegie Mellon University, Pittsburgh. Debut: Pianist, Integral version of sonatas and interludes by John Cage, US Embassy, Argentina, 1985; Conductor, Complete version of church sonatas by Mozart, Santisimo Rosario Basilica, Tucuman, 1990. Career: As pianist has performed complete cycles of works for keyboard or chamber music with piano, by Pachelbel, Zipoli, Marcello, Handel, Haydn, Clementi, Mozart, Brahms, Weber, Debussy, Ravel, Satie, Cage, Ginastera and pioneers of Argentinian and Latin American keyboard music; Tours of USA, Spain, Netherlands and Argentina; As conductor founded and is artistic music director for Camerata Lazarte Chamber Orchestra performing widely; Has taught in many academic and cultural institutions. Publication: Author, Lazarte Methodology. Contributions to: Analysis of the Complete Works for Piano Solo of Alberto Ginastera, in Magazine of the Institute of Aesthetic Research. Honours: 1st Prize, Ministry of Social Affairs, Tucuman, 1981; Gold Medal, School of Musical Arts, 1983. Memberships: President, Center of Interdisciplinary Semiotic Studies; Principal Researcher, Institute of Aesthetic Research, National University of Tucuman. Hobby: Painting. Current Management: CESI. Address: c/o CESI, Marcos Paz 250, Tucuman 250, Argentina.

LAZKANO Ramon, b. 26 June 1968, San Sebastian, Basque Country, Spain. Composer. Education: Linguistics, McGill University, Montreal; Conservatoire National Superior de Musique, Paris; Conducting with A Tamayo, Ecole de Hautes Etudes en Sciences Sociales, Paris. Career: Music Played in European Important Festivals, Presences, Paris, 1992, Gaudeamos Muziekweek, Amsterdam, 1992, 1993, Contemporary Music, ARS Musica, Brussels, 1996, International Society for Contemporary Music, Copenhagen, 1996. Compositions: Su-Itzalak, for Cello Octett, 1991; Hitzaurre Bi Concerto, for Piano & Orchestra, 1993; Sorginkeriak, for Ensemble, 1993; Auhen Kantvak, for Choir & Orchestra, 1993-95, 1997. Recordings: Su-Itzalak; Chamber Music. Honours: Gaudeamus Foundation, Special Mention, 1992; Spanish Academy of Fine Arts, Rome, Grant, 1994-95; Prince Pterre de Monaco Prize, 1995; Inaem & College D'Espagne Prize, 1995. Membership: Artistic Director, Ensemble Ostots. Address: 2 Allee D'Andrezeux, 75018 Paris. France.

LAZZARETTI Bruno, b. 1958, Italy. Singer (Tenor). Education: Studied in Bologna. Career: Sang at Bologna from 1980 and appeared in Il Turco in Italia at Reggio Emilia, 1981; La Scale 1982, in Rossignol by Stravinsky, Ariodante and Il Filosofo di Campagna by Galuppi; Further appearances in Andrea Chénier, Vespri Sicilaini and Pergolesi's Lo frate 'nnamorato; Concert performances in Chicago with Daniel Barenboim of Don Giovanni and Cosi fan tutte; Macerata Festival 1991, as Mozart's Titus, Aix 1992, with the tenor solo in Rossini's Stabat Mater; Further engagements at the Verona Arena, Modena, Luca and Palermo; Sang Arbace in Idomeneo at Florence, 1996. Address: c/o Teatro alla Scala, Via Filodrammatici 2, 20121 Milan, Italy.

LE BRIS Michele, b. 1938, France. Soprano. Education: Studied at Conservatoire National, Paris. Debut: Paris Opéra as Marguerite, 1961. Career: Many appearances at such French opera centres as Marseilles, Nantes, Vichy, Strasbourg, Toulouse and Rouen; Strasbourg in 1965 in local premiere of Mozart's La Finta Giardiniera, Amelia in Un Ballo in Maschera, Tokyo, 1972; Sang Halevy's Rachel in London, 1973 and at Barcelona in 1974; Sang at Barcelona in 1976 as Thais; Other roles have included Rossini's Mathilde, Verdi's Desdemona and Trovatore Leonora, Manon Lescaut, Tosca, Mimi, Minnie and Musetta, Massenet's Salome and Sapho, Regina in Mathis der Maler, Mozart's Countess and Donna, Lisa in The Queen of Spades and Janácek's Jenufa. Recordings include: Highlights from Un Ballo in Maschera and Il Trovatore. Address: c/o Theatre National de L'Opera de Paris, 8 Rue Scribe, F-75008 Paris, France.

LE BROCQ Mark, b. 1966, England. Tenor. Education: Studied at St Catharine's College, Cambridge, Royal Academy and National Opera Studio. Career: Principal with English National Opera; Appearances at the Covent Garden and Aix-en-Provence Festivals; Roles include Don Ottavio, Cavalli's Egisto, Paolino in Il Matrimonio Segreto, Berlioz's Benedict, Spirit/Autumn in The Fairy Queen and Odoardo in Ariodante; Concerts in the USA, throughout Europe and in the Middle East with Les Arts Florissants, The Gabrieli Consort and others; Sang in The Prince of Homburg and Don Quixote for English National Opera, 1996. Address: c/o Ron Gonsalves Management, 7 Old Town, Clapham, London, SW4 0JT, England.

LE DIZES Maryvonne, b. 25 Jun 1940, Quimper, France. Violin Soloist; Professor. m. 23 May 1964, 3 sons, 1 daughter. Education: 1st Prize, Violin, National Conservatory of Music, Paris, 1957; 1st Prize, Chamber Music, National Conservatory of Music, Paris, 1958. Debut: Violin Concert. Career: Soloist with Ensemble Intercontemporain, 1978-; Professor at Conservatory of Music, Boulogne Billancourt, France, 1977-. Recordings: Works by Berio, Messiaen, Chapey, Melby, Xenakis, Machover, Carter, Brahms. Honours: Prize, International Thibaud Competition, Paris, 1961; 1st Prize, N Paganini Competition, Genoa, 1962, and International American Music Competition, NY, 1983; SACEM Paris, 1987. Address: CIUP, Maison IAA, 5 Bd Jourdan, 75690 Paris Cedex 14, France.

LE PAGE David, b. 1965, England. Violinist. Career: Co-founder and Second Violinist of the Kreutzer Quartet from 1988; South Bank debut in 1989 followed by Amsterdam Concertgebouw and recital at Palazzo Labia in Venice; 1991 Recital at Lancaster House for Queen Elizabeth; Established repertoire and new compositions with improvisations in The Chamber, featuring live film projection and static coloured images within a darkened set. Honours include: With Kreutzer Quartet: Winner of 1991 Royal Overseas League Competition. Address: Manygate Management, 13 Cotswold Mews, 30 Battersea Square, London, SW11 3RA, England.

LE ROUX Francois, b. 30 Oct 1955, Rennes, France. Baritone. Education: Studied with Francois Loup and at Paris Opéra Studio with Vera Rozsa and Elisabeth Grummer. Career: Sang at the Opera de Lyon, 1980-85 as Mozart's Don Giovanni, Papageno, Guglielmo and Count; From 1985 appeared as Debussy's Pelléas at the Paris Opéra, La Scala, Milan, 1986, Vienna Staatsoper, 1988, Barcelona, Helsinki, 1989, Cologne, 1992, Covent Garden, 1994; Glyndebourne Festival debut in 1987 as Ramiro in L'Heure Espagnole; Hamburg in 1987 as Marcello in La Bohème; Sang Lescaut in a new production of Manon at Covent Garden, 1988, returning as Papageno in 1989; Appeared as Hidraot in Armide at Amsterdam in 1988 and Orestes in Iphigénie at Frankfurt, Ulysse in Il Ritorno at Lausanne, 1989; Also sings Valentin in Faust and has sung Don Giovanni at Paris Opéra and in Zurich under Nikolaus Harnoncourt; Created the title role in the world premiere of Birtwistle's Gawain at Covent Garden, 1991; Season 1992 as Maletesta in Don Pasquale at Covent Garden and the title role in Henze's Der Prinz von Homburg at Munich; sang Pelléas at Covent Garden, 1994; Sang Stravinsky's Nick Shadow at Madrid, 1996. Recordings include: Pelléas et Mélisande, under Claudio Abbado. Honours: Prizewinner at International Maria Casals Competition, Barcelona and the International Competition at Rio de Janeiro. Address: 225 avenue Charles de Gaulle, 92521 Neuilly sur Seine Cedez, France.

LE ROUX Maurice, b. 6 Feb 1923, Paris, France. Conductor; Composer. Education: Studied at the Paris Conservatoire, 1944-52, with Messaien and Fourestier, composition with René Leibowitz and conducting with Dmitri Mitropoulos. Career: Worked on musique concrète project with French Radio, 1951; Music Director of the Orchestre National, 1960-68; Artistic Adviser at the Paris Opéra, 1969-73; Inspector General of Music for the Ministry of Culture, 1973-88; Conductor of leading orchestras in guest engagements in France and abroad; Repertoire has included the Monteverdi Vespers and music by Berg, Schoenberg and Xenakis; Music programme Arcana for French TV from 1968; Film scores for Truffaut, Godard and others. Recordings include: Messiaen Turangalila Symphonie. Publications: Introduction a la Musique Contemporaine, 1947; Claudio Montevedi, 1951; La Musique, 1979; Mussorgsky, Boris Godunov, 1980.

LE SAGE Sally, b. 1937, Farnborough, England. Soprano; Professor of Singing. Education: Studied at the Royal College of Music and with Pierre Bernac on a scholarship in Paris. Career: Sang with Deller Consort, 1964-67; Concert appearances throughout Britain, Europe and USA which included the Vienna, Aix, Ghent and Three Choirs Festivals; Many BBC concerts and recitals; Other concert repertoire included L'Enfant et Les Sortilèges in Leeds with Simon Rattle, Haydn Nelson Mass at Carnegie Hall, NY, USA, Beethoven's 9th for Dutch TV in Amsterdam, Mozart's C minor Mass at Royal Festival Hall with Charles Groves, A Child of Our Time in Stockholm under Michael Tippett, Messiah with the Hallé in Manchester, and Mahler's 8th Symphony at the Albert Hall in London; Opera appearances with Scottish Opera as The Woodbird in Siegfried, Covent Garden and Glyndebourne, Teofane in Handel's Ottone at Sadler's Wells Theatre and Ann Trulove in The Rake's Progress at Cambridge Arts Theatre. Recordings: Various. Honours: 1st Prize Vocal Concours, s'Hertogenbosch, Holland, 1967. Hobbies: Painting; Crafts; Swimming; Gardening. Address: 13 Observatory Road, East Sheen, London, SW14 7QB, England.

LE TEXIER Vincent, b. 1957, France. Singer (Bass-baritone). Education: Studied privately at the Grenoble Conservatory and at the studio of the Paris Opéra. Career: Appearances at the Paris Opera in Orphée aux Enfers and with the Opéra-Comique in From the House of the Dead; Sang Goland in the Russian premiere of Pelléas et Mélisande and appeared at the 1989 Aix Festival, in The Love for Three Oranges; Lyon, as Schaunard in La Boheme, the four devils in Les Contes d'Hoffmann, the King from Debussy's Rodrigue et chimene (wordly creation); In Bordeaux, as Leporello in Don Giovanni, Escamillo in Carmen, the Count in Le Nozze di Figaro, Frere Laurentin in Roméo at Juliette by Berlioz; In Rouen, as Basilio in Il Barbiere di Siviglia, Kaspar in Freischütz (French version by Berlioz), the Count in Capriccio, the Spectre in Zauberflöte, Mephisto in Faust, Sade in Teresa by Darius Constant, Wozzeck in Wozzeck by Gurlitt (French version); Appearances at the Paris Opera in Madame Butterfly, and in Pelléas et Melisande; Golaud in Impressions de Pelleas, from Peter Brook and Darius Constant, in Paris and on tour around Europe, 1991-92; Created the role of Ethnologist from Georges Apeighis' Tristes Tropiques, Strasbourg, 1996. Recordings include: The Love for Three Oranges; Alcyone by Marais; Salome, Strauss; Psalm 129, Guy Ropartz; Messa di Gloria, Donizetti; Platée by Rameau; La Caravave du Caine by Giêtry; L'enfant et les Portileges by Ravel; Mélodies by Duparc, Ropaitx and Fauré. Honour: Grand Critics' Prize, 1997. Address: 30 rue Darceau, 93100 Montreuil, France.

LEA Yvonne, b. 1960, Cheshire, England. Singer (Contralto). Education: Studied at Royal Northern College of Music with Frederick Cox and at the National Opera Studio, London. Career: Appearances with Glyndebourne Festival in Die Zauberflöte, Hippolyta in A Midsummer Night's Dream, Rosina in Il Barbiere di Siviglia and Linette in The Love for Three Oranges; Royal Opera House, Covent Garden, in Der Rosenkavalier and Third Lady in Die Zauberflöte; Sang Suzuki with Welsh National Opera and appeared at Batignano and Spitalfields Festivals in Cesti's La Dori; Recent engagements in Graham Vick's version of The Ring for the City of Birmingham Touring Opera, as Hippolyte at the 1991-92 Aix Festivals and Grimgerde in Die Walküre for Scottish Opera; Tour of France with A Midsummer Night's Dream, 1994; Sang Mother Goose in The Rake's Progress for Welsh National Opera, 1996; Concert repertoire includes Messiah, Elgar's Sea Pictures, Elijah and Beethoven's Mass in C. Recordings include: Williamson's Six English Lyrics. Address: c/o IMG Artists, Media House, 3 Burlington Lane, London W4 2TH, England.

LEA-COX Graham (Russell), b. 15 Feb 1957, Bulawayo, Rhodesia. Conductor. Education: Christ Church Cathedral School, Oxford, England, 1965-75; London University; Royal College of Music, London; Magdalen College, Oxford; MA(Oxon); ARCM, ARCO(CHM), MTC, 1975-81. Debut: Carnegie Hall, New York, 1983. Career: Artistic Director, Texas Boys Choir, USA, 1983-85; Freelance Conductor, Performer, 1985-; Tours of USA, Canada, Japan, Hong Kong, New York, Kambara, Tokyo; Conducting and solo and chamber recitals in Europe, Scandinavia, Africa; Artistic Director, English Performing Arts Ensemble, 1988-; Conductor and Artistic Director, Elizabethan Singers of London, regular foreign tours of Europe and Scandinavia; Artistic Director and Conductor of Festivals including the South Bank, London. Compositions: Choral and Instrumental Music; Incidental Music for Stage and Recordings of poetical/Literary compilations. Recordings: Film and television music; Chamber music and song from The Court of Queen Victoria; Warchild Festival Highlights, Festival Hall, London; William Boyce: Secular Masque; Ed, Lea-Cox. Publication: Research for Publication: Gluck: The Swedish opera Mss, Kungliga Teatra 1770-1815. Hobbies: Photography Travel; Wine. Current Management: Hadyn Rawstron Ltd, 36 Station Road, London SE20 7BQ, England.

LEACH Mary (Jane), b. 12 June 1949, St Johnsbury, Vermont, USA. Composer; Performer. Education: BA, Theatre, Music, University of Vermont; Postgraduate, Composition, with Mark Zuckerman, Columbia University. Career: Appeared: Experimental Intermedia Foundation (New York), 1982, 1984, 1987, 1992; Relache (Philadelphia), 1984, 1987; Music Gallery (Toronto), Metronome (Barcelona), Newband (New York), 1985; Roulette, New York, 1985, 1995; Charles Ives Center (Connecticut), Logos (Gent, Belgium), 1986, 1987; BACA Downtown (Brooklyn), New Music America (Philadelphia), Palais des Beaux Art (Brussels), Sankt Peter (Cologne), Apollohuis (Eindhoven, Holland), 1987; Clock Tower (New York), 1988; Real Ways (Hartford, Connecticut), Franenzeichen Festival (Cologne), Ton Gegen Ton (Vienna), New Music America (New York), 1989; Kunsthalle Bremen, Romanische Summer Festival (Cologne), Music Today (Tokyo), 1990; Experimentelle Music (Munich), 1991; Sound Symposium (Newfoundland), Ijsbreker (Amsterdam), Corn Palace (Minneapolis), 1992; Bang on a Can Festival (New York), 1992, 1993; Interpretations Series (New York), Walker Art Center, 1993; Subtropics Festival (Miami), 1994; Radio: John Schaeffer's New Sounds, 3MBS Australia, Radio Bremen, WDR-Köln, Earworks; CBC, 1992; Radio Cultura (Sao Paulo), Radio 2 (Brussels), 1994; First Art, 1995; TV: WDR Köln. Compositions: Note Passing Note, 1981; Solar Spots, 1983; Held Held, 1984; 8x4, 1985; Bare Bones, Bruckstück, Pipe Dreams, Sephardic Fragments, 1989; The Upper Room, 1990; Kirchtraum, 1991; Feu de Joie, 1992; Ariadne's Lament, He Got Dictators, Xantippe's Rebuke, 1993; Corrina Ocarina, 1994; Tricky Pan, Windjammer, 1995. Recordings: 4BC, 1984; Green Mountain Madrigal, Trio for Duo, 1985; Lake Eden, 1986; Ariel's Song, Mountain Echoes, Guy de Polka, 1987; Her 1001 Nights, 1988; Celestial Fires, 1993; Xantippe's Rebuke, 1995. Address: 90 LaSalle Street #13H, New York, NY 10027, USA.

LEADBETTER Martin (John), b. 6 April 1945, London, England. Composer. m. Ivy G, 7 June 1969, 2 sons. Education: Studied at Associate and Licentiate Trinity College of Music, London; Studied with Dr Alan Bush, 1982-88. Career: TV Flim, Anglia TV, BBC 3 Music Weekly and BBC 4 Womans Hour. Compositions include: 2 Symphonies, 3 String Quartets, An English Requiem, Songs, Instrumental and Choral Works; Laudate Dominium, 1992, Performed Fontainebleau, France, 1993; Some 150 Works to Date. Publications include: Soliloquy; Little Prelude and Fugue. Honour: Commissioned By Radio Victory to Compose String Trio. Memberships: Performing Right Society; Composers Guild. Address: Ivy Lodge, 2 Priory Lane, Little Wymondley, Hertfordshire SG4 7HE, England.

LEAH Philip John, b. 23 Oct 1948, Dulwich, London, England. Music Educator. 2 sons. Education: Studied at the Northern School of Music, Manchester, 1968-71; GNSM, 1971; Padgate College of Education, Warrington, 1971-72; PGCE, 1972; Studies: Flute, Piano, Composition. Career: Peripatetic Music Teacher, Glamorgan, 1972-73, City of Birmingham, 1973-90; Lecturer, North Worcestershire College of Education, 1977-, University of Wolverhampton, 1982-; Founderand Musical Director, West Birmingham Schools Wind Band, 1985-, Halesowen Symphony Orchestra, 1986-; Examiner, Guildhall School of Music and Drama, 1988-. Compositions include: Conversations for Flute and Piano; Fanfare for a Golden Jubilee; Concertino for Bass Tuba and Orchestra; Prelude and Scherzo for String Quartet; Suite for Chamber Orchestra; Various Arrangements for Woodwind Instruments. Honour: 1st Prize, Horatio Albert Lumb Composition Competition. Memberships: Royal Society of Musicians of Great Britain; Incorporated Society of Musicians; Musicians' Union. Hobbies: Astrology; Social Sciences; Pre-Raphaelite Art; Watching football and cricket; Drinking real ale. Address: 23 New England, Halesowen, West Midlands B62 9EG, England.

LEAPER Adrian, b. 1953, England. Conductor. Education: Studied at the Royal Academy of Music and with George Hurst. Career: Assistant Conductor at the Halle Orchestra in season 1986-87 and has subsequently worked with all leading British orchestras, and the Vienna, Prague and Moscow Symphonies, and the Belgium National Orchestra; Music Director of the Orquesta Filarmonica de Gran Canaria from 1994. Recordings include: Albums of Sibelius, Elgar, Holst, Havergal Brian, Tchaikovsky and Nielsen. Address: Olivia Management, 28 Sheffield Terrace, London, W8 7NA, England.

LEAR Evelyn, b. 8 Jan 1926, Brooklyn, New York, USA. Soprano. m. (1) 1 son, 1 daughter, (2) Thomas Stewart. Education: New York University; Hunter College; Juilliard Opera Workshop; Fulbright Scholar to Germany, 1955. Career: UK debut in Four Last Songs with London Symphony Orchestra, 1957; Stage debut as the Composer in Ariadne auf Naxos, Berlin, 1959; Deutsche Oper Berlin, 1961, creating title role in Klebe's Alkmene; Jeanne in premiere of Egk's Die Verlobung in San Domingo, Munich, 1963; Covent Garden debut, 1965, as Donna Elvira; Lulu in Berg's opera at Vienna Opera House, 1962, and Sadler's Wells Theatre, 1966; Metropolitan Opera debut in premiere of Levy's Mourning Becomes Electra, 1967; La Scala debut, 1971, in Wozzeck; Performed regularly with leading opera companies and orchestras in Europe and USA; Guested with Berlin Opera and Vienna State Opera; Soloist with leading US orchestras including New York Philharmonic and Los Angeles Philharmonics, Philadelphia Orchestra, and Chicago, Boston and San Francisco Symphonies; Many recitals and orchestral concerts and operatic performances with Thomas Stewart; Major roles include Marie in Wozzeck, Marschallin in Der Rosenkavalier, Countess in Figaro, Fiordiligi in Così fan tutte, Desdemona, Mimi, Dido in The Trojans, Donna Elvira in Don Giovanni, Marina in Boris Godunov, Tatiana in Eugene Onegin, Lavinia in Mourning Becomes Electra, and title role in Lulu; Appeared in film Buffalo Bill, 1976; Sang in premieres of The Seagull by Pasatieri, 1974, Robert Ward's Minutes to Midnight, 1980, and Kelterborn's Der Kirschgarten, Zurich, 1984; The Met, 1985, as the Marschallin; Countess Geschwitz in Lulu at Florence, 1985, Chicago, 1987, and San Francisco, 1989; Miss Dilly in Bernstein's On the Town at the Barbican Hall, London, 1992. Recordings include: Wozzeck; Lulu; The Flying Dutchman; Magic Flute excerpts; Boris Godunov; Eugene Onegin; Der Rosenkavalier; Bach's St John Passion; Pergolesi's Stabat Mater; Children's Songs from Around the World; Songs of the Sea; Song recitals include: Vivaldi, Fauré, Strauss, Bizet, Debussy, Wolf, Chausson, Sondheim, Copland, Ives and Porter; Evelyn Lear & Thomas Stewart sing Strauss and Wagner; Evelyn Lear - a celebration of 20th Century Song; Evelyn Lear - Songs my mother taught us; Russian Art Songs - Tchaikovsky to Rachmaninoff; Evelyn Lear Sings Songs by Richard Strauss. Honours: Concert Artists' Guild Award, 1955; Kammersängerin Award by Berlin Senate, 1963. Address: 15101 Rosecroft Road, Rockville, MD 20853, USA.

LEATHERBY Carol Ann, b. 1948, Barking, London, England. Singer (Mezzo-Contralto); Director of Victoriana (Victorian Musical Entertainment). Education: Morley College with Ilse Wolf, 1968-69; Guildhall School of Music and Drama, 1969-71; Vienna with Eugenie Ludwig, 1981-82; Private study in London with Lyndon Van der Pump, 1972-. Debut: Purcell Room, London, 1973. Career: Welsh National Opera, 1973-75; Covent Garden Opera, 1975-78; Glyndebourne Festival Opera, 1979-80; New Opera, 1981; Music in Camera, Southern TV, UK, 1980; Delius Talk on Radio London, 1980; Broadcasts for BBC, London and Cardiff; Recitals at Purcell Room, Wigmore Hall; Concerts at Festival Hall and Queen Elizabeth Hall; Memorial concert for Princess Grace of Monaco at Queen Elizabeth Hall, 1983; Specialist in the songs of Frederick Delius; Athens Festival, 1985; Alte Oper, Frankfurt, 1985, 1986; Purcell Room concerts as member of Quintessence founded in 1984, presenting Victorian and Edwardian entertainment in costume and performing music by Gershwin and Cole Porter, 1984, 1985 and 1986; The Vampyr, soap opera for BBC2 TV, music by Heinrich Marschner, 1992. Recordings: Czech songs by Foerster, Smetana and Dvorák, 1983; Songs of Praise, BBC TV; Sita-Mother Earth-Holst recorded at St John's Smith Square in conjunction with the Holst Society. Hobbies: Cooking; Violin Restoring; Walking; Crossword Puzzles. Current Management: Crescendo Concert Agency, 25 Summer House, Bonfield Road, London, SE13 6BY, England. Address: 278 Monega Road, Manor Park, London, E12 6TS, England.

LEAVINS Arthur, b. 14 July 1917, Leicester, England. Violinist. m. Mary Baddeley, 2 sons. Education: Royal Academy of Music; LRAM; ARAM. Debut: New Zealand, 1925. Career: Played with Catterall Quartet; Leader, Royal Philharmonic Orchestra; Sub-leader, BBC Symphony Orchestra; Leader, BBC Concert Orchestra; Now retired. Recordings: Stravinsky's L'Histoire du Sodat. Honours: Jonathan North Medal. Membership: Royal Society of Musicians. Hobbies: Reding; Gardening; Golf. Address: 17 Highfield Drive, Bromley, Kent, England.

LEBARON Anne, b. 30 May 1953, Baton Rouge, Louisiana, USA. Composer. m. Edward J Eadon, 6 July 1982, 1 daughter. Education: BA, Music, University of Alabama, 1974; MA, Music, State University of New York, Stony Brook, 1978; Darmstadt, 1980; Köln Musikhochschule, 1980-81; National Classical Music Institute, Korea, 1983; DMA, Columbia University, 1989. Career includes: Featured on National Public Radio, 1989, 1990; Artist-in-Residence, PASS Studio, 1991; Composer-in-Residence (Meet The Composer New Residencies), Washington, District of Columbia, 1993-96. Compositions: The E & O Line, chamber opera; Orchestral: Strange Attractors; Southern Ephemera, 1994; Lasting Impressions, 1995; Mambo, 1995; Chamber music: Telluris Theoria Sacra; The Sea and the Honeycomb; Noh Reflections; Metamorphosis; Rite of the Black Sea; Planxty Bowerbird; I Am An American...My Government Will Reward You; Lamentation-Invocation; Concerto for Active Frogs; Dish; Waltz for Quintet; Three Motion Atmospheres; Southern Ephemera; Devil in the Belfry; Light Breaks Where No Sun Shines; Story of My Angel; Sachamama, 1995. Recordings include: Rana, Ritual and Revelations; The Music of Anne Le-Baron, 1992; Phantom Orchestra: The Anne LeBaron Quintet, 1992; The Musical Railism of Anne LeBaron, 1995. Honours: National Endowment for the Arts Composer Fellowships, 1986, 1990; Guggenheim Fellowship, 1991; Fromm Foundation Award, 1992. Address: 3338 17th Street NW, Washington, DC 20010, USA.

LEBHERZ Louis, b. 14 Apr 1948, Bethesda, Maryland, USA. Singer (Bass). Education: Studied at Indiana University. Debut: Memphis Opera, as Padre Guardiano in La Forza del Destino, 1974. Career: Many appearances at opera houses in North and South America (Caracas, 1981); European engagements at Frankfurt, 1981, Karlsruhe, 1984-85, Berne, 1985-86, Geneva, 1988; Sang Melothal in Guillaume Tell at Covent Garden and the Grand Inquisitor in Don Carlos at Los Angeles, 1990; Appeared in Massenet's La Navarraise with Long Beach Opera, 1990, as Basilio, the Commendatore in Don Giovanni at Los Angeles Music Center, 1991; Sang Rocco at New Orleans, 1992; Other roles include Sarastro, King Mark, Fasolt, Baldassare in La Favorita, Verdi's Zaccaria, Nabucco and Fiesco, Colline, and Don Diego in L'Africaine. Recordings include: Verdi's Aroldo; Jone by Petrella.

LEBIC Lojze, b. 23 Aug 1934, Prevalje, Slovenia. Composer; Conductor; Professor of Music Theory. m. Jelena Ukmar, 2 Aug 1961, 1 daughter. Education: Diploma in Archaeology, University of Ljubljana, 1957; Academy of Music,

Ljubljana, 1972; Studies in Darmstadt. Career: Conductor, RTV Ljubljana, 1962-72; Appeared at Musica Antiqua Europae Orientalis Festival, Bydgoszcz, Poland, 1968; Festival van Vlaanderen, 1968; Ohrid Festival, 1968; Jihlava Festival, Czechoslovakia, 1969; Zagreb Biennale, 1969; Dubrovnik Festival, 1969; University of Ljubljana, 1985-. Compositions include: Symphonic music; Voice: November songs, Korant, Sentence, Tangram; Queensland Music Symphony with Organ; Burnt Grass, cantata; Ajdna for choirs, recorders and percussion instruments; Fauvel 86, vocal instrumental scene; Chamber music: Quartet for Percussion; String Quartet; Ateliers I-III; Vocal music, solo instrument, electronic, choral music. Recordings: Various as conductor and composer. Publications: The Basis of Music Art, book, 1982; Sound and Silence, Compositional Synthesis of the Eighties, Music Biennale Zagreb, 1985. Honours: Winner, Class Trophy (Contemporary Music), Let the People Sing, BBC, 1972; Preseren's Fund Prizes, 1966, 1970, 1987; Preseren's Prize, Ljubljana, 1994. Memberships: International Society for Contemporary Music, Secretary, Yugoslavian Section 1981-91; Society of Slovene Composers; Slovene Academy of Sciences and Arts, 1991. Hobbies: Archaeology; Travel. Address: Bratov Ucakar 134, 61000 Ljubljana, Slovenia.

LEBRECHT Norman, b. 11 July 1948, London, England. Writer on Music. m. Elbie Spivack, 1977, 3 daughters. Education: Barllan University, Israel. Career: Radio and TV Producer, 1969-78; Writer and Lecturer, 1978-. Publications: Discord, 1982; Hush! Handel's in a Passion, 1985; The Book of Musical Anecdotes, 1985; Mahler Remembered, 1987; The Book of Musical Days, 1987 The Maestro Myth, 1991; Music in London, 1992; The Companion to Twentieth Century Music, 1992; The Music Business, 1996. Contributions to: Sunday Times; The Times; Daily Telegraph; Classical Music; Opera News; Melbourne Age. Memberships: Society of Authors. Address: 3 Bolton Road, London NW8 0RJ, England.

LECHNER Gabriele, b. 8 Mar 1961, Austria. Singer (Soprano). Education: Studied at the Hochschule für Musik und Darstellende Kunst in Vienna. Career: Sang Sulamith in The Queen of Sheba with the Graz Opera, appeared later in Don Giovanni, Mefistofele, La Forza del Destino, Otello and Don Carlos; Amelia in Un Ballo in Maschera at the Vienna Staatsoper with Pavarotti) followed by such operas as Simon Boccanegra, Rusalka, Elektra, Der Rosenkavalier, Capriccio and Die Walküre; Engagements with the Zürich Opera as Elsa in Lohengrin, Senta, Die Fliegender Holländer, the Marsckallin in Der Rosenkavalier, both Verdi Leonoras, Tosca, the Empress (Die Frau ohne Schatten), Ariadne, Alice Ford, Aida, Giulietta in Contes d'Hoffmann, Andrea Chenier, Maddalena; Guest appearances at Madrid, Barcelona, Berlin, Paris, Frankfurt, Hamburg, Cologne, Amsterdam, Prague, Florence, Rome, Edinburgh and Glasgow; Conductors have included Abbado, Bernstein, Mehta, Maazel, Barenboim, Dohnanyi and Sinopoli; Other roles include Carlotta in Die Gezeichneten by Schreker (at Zürich). Honours include: Several major competition awards. Address: c/o Opernhaus Zürich, Falkenstrasse 1, CH-8008 Zürich, Switzerland.

LECIAN Krystof Filip Albert, b. 22 May 1974, Prague, Czech Republic. Student. Education: Cello, Prague Conservatoire, 1988-94; Cello, Academy of Performing Arts, 1994-. Debut: Prague Lichtenstein Palace, Niccolo Paganini 24 Caprices in Transcription, 1996. Career: Festival of A Dvorak, Pribram, 1997. Recordings: Niccolo Paganini 24 Caprices in Transcription for Cello, 1997. Honour: Prize, Bohuslav Martinu Society, 1986. Membership: Club of Niccolo Paganini, 1998-. Hobby: Transcriptions for Cello. Address: Mrstikova 47, 100 00 Praha 10, Czech Republic.

LEDBETTER Steven (John), b. 13 Dec 1942, Minneapolis, Minnesota, USA. Musicologist. m. Mary Lee Stewart, 10 Sept 1966, 1 son, 1 daughter. Education: BA, Music, Pomona College, 1964, studying voice (baritone) with Margery Smith Briggs, 1961-64, and conducting with W F Russell; MA, Musicology, 1968, PhD, Musicology, 1971, New York University; Voice with Edith Bers, New York, 1969-72. Career: Instructor, 1969-71, Assistant Professor of Music, 1971-72, New York University; Assistant Professor of Music (music history), Choral Conductor, Dartmouth College, 1972-79; Director of Publications (title changed to Musicologist and Programme Annotator in 1984), Boston Symphony Orchestra, 1979-; Freelance Writer; Record Producer. Recordings: As Producer: John K Paine, Chamber Music, 1986; Chamber Works of George W Chadwick, 1998. Publications include: 100 Years of the Boston Pops, 1985; Sennets and Tuckets: A Bernstein Celebration, 1988; Editor: Ornithoparcus, Dowland, A Compendium of Musical Practice, 1973; Luca Marenzio, The Secular Works, vol 7, 1978, vol 17, 1991; George W Chadwick, Songs to Poems by Arlo Bates, 1979; George F Bristow, Rip Van Winkle, 1991; Gilbert and Sullivan, Trial by Jury, 1993. Contributions to: Liner notes for 90 recordings. Address: Symphony Hall, Boston, MA 02115, USA.

LEDEC Jan, b. 8 Mar 1922, Prague, Czechoslovakia. Musicologist; Editor; Music Writer. m. Dagmar Capková, 9 Mar 1950. Education: Faculty of Philosophy, Charles University, Prague, 1945-49; Prague Conservatory, 1945-47; Diploma, Choir Conducting, Academy of Music and Dramatic Arts, 1947; PhD, 1952. Career: Music Teacher, Choirmaster, Music Producer, Liberec, 1945-53; Music Administrator, Editor, Head of Music Department, Institute of Cultural Activities, Prague, 1953-65; Music Administrator, Prague Symphony Orchestra, 1965-67; Freelance Writer on Music, specialising in contemporary music and music for choir, 1967-72; Executive Manager, Music Information Centre of Czech Music Fund, Prague, 1972-87; Freelance Musicologist, Music Adviser, 1987-; Secretary, Association for Contemporary Music Pritomnost, Present time, 1991-93; Freelance Musicologist, Music Adviser, 1993-. Publications: Editor, Sborovy repertoár, 20 volumes, 1960-68; Various cycles for Radio Prague, 1968-75; Nástin Vyvoje ceské soudobé hudby po roce 1945, 1972; Editor in Chief, Music News from Prague, 1978-87. Contributions to: Music News from Prague, 1987-. Address: Seifertova 25, 130-00 Prague 3-Zizkov, Czech Republic.

LEDGER Philip (Stevens), b. 12 Dec 1937, Bexhill-on-Sea, England. Conductor; Organist; Academy Principal. m. Mary Erryl Wells, 15 Apr 1963, 1 son, 1 daughter. Education: King's College, Cambridge, 1956-61; MA, MusB (Cantab); FRCO. Career: Master of the Music, Chelmsford Cathedral, 1962-65; Director of Music, 1965-73, Dean, School of Fine Arts and Music, 1968-71, University of East Anglia, Norwich; Director of Music, King's College, Cambridge, 1974-82; Principal, Royal Scottish Academy of Music and Drama, Glasgow, 1982-. Recordings: Many as Director of Music with Choir of King's College, Cambridge, English Chamber Orchestra, Benjamin Britten, Janet Baker, Robert Tear, Pinchas Zukerman and others including CDs of Elgar's Coronation Ode, Orlando Gibbons Church Music and Organ Music from King's. Publications: Tallis to Wesley, volume 8 William Byrd, 1968; Editor: Anthems for Choirs 2 and 3; The Oxford Book of English Madrigals, 1978. Honours: FRCM, 1983; Honorary RAM, 1984; CBE 1985; Honorary LLD, University of Strathclyde, 1987; FRNCM, 1989; Honorary GSM, 1989; FRSE, 1990; Honorary Professor, University of Glasgow, 1993. Memberships: President, Royal College of Organists, 1992-94; President, Incorporated Society of Musicians, 1994-95; Chairman, Committee of Principals of Conservatories, 1994-98; Sette of Odd Volumes. Hobbies: Swimming; Theatre. Address: Royal Scottish Academy of Music and Drama, 100 Renfrew Street, Glasgow, G2 3DB, Scotland.

LEE Chan-Hae, b. 8 Oct 1945, Seoul, Korea. Composer. Education: Studied at Yonsei University and the Catholic University of America, Washington, District of Columbia. Career: Lecturer at Yonsei University. Compositions include: Hyesang and Chosaeng (1980-81) for voices and ensemble; Galpiri for clarinet, 1986; Three Fragments for flute, 1989; The Cross for chorus, 1988; Martyr for string orchestra, 1990; Glorification for three percussion instruments, 1991. Address: c/o 2,3/F Samjeo Building, 236-3 Nonhyeon-dong, Kangnam-gu, Seoul, Korea.

LEE Dennis (Ean Hooi), b. 2 Dec 1946, Penang, Malaysia. Pianist. m. Chee-Hung Toh, 16 Aug 1990. Education: BMus, London University; MMus, with Angus Morrison, Royal College of Music, London, 1964-68; Studied with Josef Dichler, Vienna Hochschule, 1968-69; Studied with Ilonka Deckers in Milan. Debut: Purcell Room, London, and Kennedy Center, Washington DC. Career: Concerts (recitals, chamber music and orchestral appearances), TV and radio recordings, UK, Europe, USA, Canada, South America, Hong-Kong, Japan, South-East Asia, Australia, New Zealand; Radio braodcasts include live transmissions for BBC Radio 3; Festivals include Adelaide, Montreux, Spoleto, Cheltenham, Brighton, Lincoln, Newbury, Warwick, Mananan, Arundel; Orchestral appearances include BBC Regional, Hallé, Wiener Symphoniker, London Mozart Players, RAI Milan, Polish and Slovak Chamber Orchestras. Recordings: Szymanowski Piano Pieces; Ravel Duets with Philippe Entremont. Honours: Prizes: BBC Competition, 1971; Casagrande, Italy, 1975, 1977; Sydney, 1977; Busoni, Italy, 1978. Address: Flat 5, 12 St Quintin Avenue, London W10 6NU, England.

LEE Douglas (Allen), b. 3 November 1932, Carmel, Indiana, USA. Professor of Musicology. m. Beverly Haskell, 2 September 1961. Education: BMus, DePauw University, 1954; MMus 1958, Rackham Fellow, 1961-63, PhD 1968, University of Michigan; National Endowment for the Humanities Seminar in Editing Early Music, 1985; Piano Studies with Theodore Lettvin and Gyorgy Sandor. Career: Instructor, Mount Union College, Alliance, Ohio, 1959-61; Professor, Music, Wichita State University, Kansas, 1964-86; Professor, Musicology, Vanderbilt University, Nashville, Tennessee, 1986-; Faculty, Mount Union College, University of Michigan, International Music Camp-Interlochen, Wichita State University, Vanderbilt University; Editor, American Music Teacher, 1968-70; The C P E Bach Edition, 1985-; Sonneck Society Newsletter, 1988-90. Publications: The Works of Christoph Nichelmann, 1971; Christoph Nichelmann-Two Concertos, 1977; Six Sonatas of Franz Benda, with Embellishments, 1981; Franz Benda - A Thematic Catalogue, 1984; Chapters in Great Lives in Music-Renaissance to 1800, 1989; 2 chapters in Great Events in History, Arts and Culture, 1993; C P E Bach: Six Keyboard Concertos (Collected Works). Contributions to: 23 articles, New Grove Dictionary of Music and Musicians. Hobbies: Photography; Sports Car Mechanics. Address: Vanderbilt Unviersity, Blair School of Music, 2400 Blakemore Avenue, Nashville, TN 37212, USA.

LEE Hope K W, b. 14 Jan 1953, Taiwan, Republic of China. Canadian Citizen. Composer. m. David M Eagle, 23 Aug 1980. Education: BSc, University of Toronto, Canada, 1973; BMus, 1978, MMus, 1981, McGill University; Darmstadt Ferienkurs Neue Musik, 1978; Staatliche Hochschule für Musik, Freiburg, 1981-83. Career: Works heard regularly on CBC and Radio Canada; Work performed in Music Today '85 Festival, Tokyo; ISCM World Music Days, 1987, Germany; Invited to 1st International Women Composers' Conference, Berlin, 1982; Invited Guest Composer, Boswil Kunstlerhaus, Switzerland, 1985. Compositions include: Instrumental Ensemble: Nabripamo, 1982; M-Nabri, 1983; Nohr, 1983; Luminare, 1984-85; Konductus, 1985; Jygge-Somebody's, 1987; Jygge-Somebody's and Nobody's, 1987; ...I, Laika..., 1988-89; In The Beginning Was The End, 1989; Hsieh Lu Hsing, 1991; Tangram, Harpsichord, Bass Clarinet and Tape, 1992; March 3rd, 1911, Bass Clarinet, Piano with/without Tape, 1993; Instrumental Ensemble with Voices: Ballad of Endless Woe, 1978-79; In A Mirror of Light, 1988; Voices in Time for Flute, oboe, Clarinet, Bass Clarinet, Trumpet, French Horn, Harp, Accordion, Percussion, 2 Violins, Viola, Cello, double Bass, Tape and Live Electronics, 1992-94; Solo Works: Dindle for Piano, 1979; Melboac for Harpsichord, 1983; Flake Upon Flake Upon...1989, for Piano; Entends, Entends le passé qui marche, Piano and Tape, 1992; von einem Fremden Stern for Organ, 1993; Orchestral Works: Onomatopoeia, 1979-81; Electronic Works: Study Chant IV, V, 1979; Collaboration Chant VI, 1979; Performances: Aspekte Salzburg Festival, 1990; Scotia Festival of Music, 1991; Voices in Time, orchestral version, 1995; Gently Rings in Autumn Wind, organ, 1995; Across the Veiled Distances, piano and axio optional, 1996; Shadows of an Uncounted Journey, chamber ensemble, soprano, axio, 1997; Arrows of Being Arrows of Becoming, string quartet, 1997. Recordings: New Music for Harpsichord from Canada and the Netherlands. 1988; Emotion: Acoustic and Electroacoustic Works by David Eagle and Hope Lee, 1994; Polaris, pianist Colleen Athparia plays music by Canadian composers, 1996. Honours: First Prize for Nabripiano in the Scotia Festival of Music, Boulez Year Composers' Competition, 1991. Memberships: International League of Women Musicians; Canadian League of Composers; Association of Canadian Women Composers. Address: c/o Furore Verlag, Naumberger Strasse 40,D-34127 Kassel, Germany.

LEE Lynda, b. 1969, Ireland. Soprano. Education: Studied at the Dublin College of Musicians. Career: Opera engagements with Opera Northern Ireland, Wexford Festival, Musica nel Chiostro and at the Covent Garden Festival as Irene in Tamerlano; Concerts with the Ulster Orchestra, at the Glasgow Mayfest, Bath Festival and in Jonathan Miller's production of the St Matthew Passion; Represented Ireland at the 1993 Cardiff Singer of the World Competition. Recordings include: St Matthew Passion, Wallace's Maritana. Address: c/o Ron Gonsalves Management, 7 Old Town, Clapham, London, SW4 0JT, England.

LEE Mi-Joo, b. 7 July 1959, Seoul, Korea. Pianist. m. Klaus Hellwig. Education: Folkwanghochschule, Essen; Hochschule der Künste, Berlin; New England Conservatory, Boston; Mozarteum, Salzburg. Career: Stage appearances with orchestra and solo recitals at Berlin Philharmonic Hall, Schauspielhaus, Munich, Dresden, Paris, Milan, Brussels, Tokyo, Seoul, various European countries and many German cities; Television and radio appearances: WDR, NDR, RIAS Berlin, Deutschlandfunk, Deutschland Radio Berlin, Radio France, BRT Brussels, Czechoslovak broadcast, Korean Broadcast, DeutscheWelle, Südwestfunk 3. Recordings: C Saint-Saëns op 72, 52, 111; Humoresken (Schumann, Reger, Dohnany, Rachmaninoff); M Ravel Concerto G-Major; R and C Schumann Op 105, 121, Op 22; Beethoven Op 13, Chopin, Liszt and 6 Paganini Études; R Schumann Op 3, 10, 14. Honours: Lilli-Lehman Medal (International Foundation Mozarteum); Prizes at international competitions: Viotti (Vercelli), 1st Prize, 1985; Tokyo, 4th Prize, 1986; Brussels, Queen Elizabeth Silver Medal, 1987. Memberships: Jury of International Piano Competitions, Viotti (piano and chambermusic), 1996; Orléans, 1998. Current Management: Konzertdirektion Martin Müller. Address: Mommsenstr 58, 10629 Berlin, Germany.

LEE Michelle, b. 31 May 1952, London, England. Flautist. 1 daughter. Education: Bartok Conservatory, Budapest, Hungary, 1970-71; Royal College of Music, London, 1971-75; Robert Schumann Institute, Dusseldorf, Germany, 1975-76, 1977-78; Franz Liszt Academy, Budapest, Hungary, 1978-80; ARCM, Flute & Recorder and Piano; Examiner of Music for Trinity College, London. Career: Regular Recitals in Great Britain and Europe;

Recorded for Hungarian Radio; Soloist for BBC Radio 3 and given many first performances including the World Premiere of György Kurtag's Seven Bagatelles, Op 14B, 1982 at her Wigmore Recital on 14 June 1982; First Broadcast performance of Fauré's Morceau de Concours for Flute and Piano on BBC Radio 3, May 1985; First UK Broadcast of György Kurtag's Seven Bagatelles, Op 14B on BBC Radio 3, October 1987. Composition: Scarlet Runner, for Flute, Percussion, Prerecorded Tape and 5 Synthesizers. Recordings: Soloist, German Record of Contemporary Music with Live Electronics, VMS 1021; Morton Feldman Flute Concerto with Moscow Philharmonic Orchestra, 1992. Memberships: Incorporated Society of Musicians; Royal College of Music Society; British Flute Society. Address: 223 Mellis Road, Thornham Parva, Eye, Suffolk IP23 8ET, England.

LEE Ming Cho, b. 3 Oct 1930, Shanghai, China. Stage Designer. Education: Studied at Occidental College and University of California at Los Angeles, 1950-54. Career: Theatre and ballet designs in New York, 1955-59; Peabody Arts Theater, Baltimore, 1959-63, with designs for Il Turco in Italia, Mahagonny, Werther, Hamlet and Les Pêcheurs de Perles; Designed Tristan und Isolde for Baltimore Civic Opera and Butterfly for the Opera Company of Boston, 1962; Resident Designer at San Francisco Opera from 1961, Juilliard School, New York, 1964-70; Metropolitan Opera, 1965-, with Figaro, Boris Godunov, Lohengrin and Khovanshchina (1985); Premiere of Ginastera's Bomarzo for the Opera Society of Washington, 1967, Giulio Cesare and Lucia di Lammermoor for Hamburg Staatsoper, 1969, 1971; Teacher of set design at Yale Drama School from 1968. Address: c/o Metropolitan Opera, Lincoln Center, New York, NY 10023, USA.

LEE Noël, b. 25 Dec 1924, Nanking, China. Composer; Concert Pianist. Education: BA cum laude, Harvard University, Cambridge, Massachusetts, USA, 1948; Artist's Diploma, New England Conservatory of Music, Boston, 1948. Career: Numerous concert tours and appearances in North and South America, Europe, Australia; Engagements on every European State Radio; Vast solo, concerto and chamber repertoire. Compositions include: Caprices on the name Schönberg, piano and orchestra; 8 études, piano; Dialogues, violin and piano; Convergences, flute and harpsichord; Chroniques, piano; Errances, band; 5 songs on Lorca, soprano, flute, guitar; Songs of Calamus, voice, clarinet, cello, percussion; Triptyque, violin, piano and orchestra; Dance Fantasy, orchestra; 5 Preludes prolonged, piano; Partita, quintet piano and winds; Le tombeau d'Aaron Copland, sextet; Azurs, voice and piano 4 hands, plus 7 other song cycles; Variations antiques, flute and piano; 3 Fantasy pieces, flute and guitar. Recordings include: 180 LPs and CDs of solo, piano 4-hand, chamber, and vocal works of Schubert, 19th-century French composers, Debussy, Ravel, Stravinsky, Bartók, Copland, Carter and other American composers. Publication: Critical edition of Debussy's Two Piano works, 1989. Honours: Prix de Composition Lili Boulanger, 1953; Louisville Orchestra Young Composers' Award, 1954; National Academy of Arts and Letters Award, 1959; Grand Prix du Disque, 1959, 1974, 1985, 1989, 1993, 1995; Grand Prix des Disquaires Français, 1978; Prizewinner, Arthur Honegger Competition Contest, 1986; Charles Oulmont Foundation Award, 1991. Membership: American Music Center. Current Management: Patrick Ponce Organisation, France; Joyce Rohr Management, USA and Scandinavia. Address: 4 Villa Laugier, 75017 Paris, France.

LEE Sung-Sook, b. 1948, Korea. Singer (Soprano). Education: Studied in Korea and at the Juillard School, New York. Debut: Premiere of Menotti's Tamu Tamu, Chicago, 1973. Career: Sang at Spoleto Festival and San Francisco, 1974; La Scala and Covent Garden 1975; Frankfurt Opera 1976-77; Seattle Opera and Miami from 1978; New York City Opera 1975-76; Concert appearances with the Buffalo Philharmonic, Seattle, Dallas and Pittsburgh Symphonies; Repertoire has included music by Puccini and Rossini (Stabat Mater). Address: c/o New York City Opera, Lincoln Center, New York, NY 10023, USA.

LEE Yi, b. 3 Mar 1957, Shanghai, China. Classical Musician; Violinist. m. Anita C Gao, 25 May 1986. Education: Shanghai Conservatory of Music, Shanghai; Midwest Institute, Crete, Nebraska, USA; University of Illinois, Champaign-Urbana; New England Conservatory of Music, Boston. Career: Zong Zheng Symphony, Beijing, 1974-81; Lincoln Symphony and Lincoln Chamber Orchestra, Nebraska, USA, 1982; Symphony Nova Scotia, Halifax, Canada, 1985-; Coach of Nova Scotia Youth Orchestra, Halifax, 1990-; Appearance on CBC Radio Morningside, 1991 and MITV Halifax, 1991; Daily News Sunday Magazine, March 3rd 1991; 1st Violin of Halifax Library Players, 1992-; Violin Instructor, Acadia University, Wolfville, 1993-94. Memberships: American Federation of Musicians. Hobbies: Sports; Running; Swimming; Travel; Investing In Stock Market. Address: 38 Birchwood Terrace, Dartmouth, Nova Scotia, Canada B3A 3W3.

LEE Young-ja, b. 4 June 1936, Wonju, Korea. Composer. Education: Studied in Seoul, at the Paris and Brussels Conservatoires and the Manhattan School of Music. Career: Performances of her work in Europe, Korea and Central America. Compositions include: Suite for orchestra, 1971; Movement symphonique for orchestra, 1972; Piano concerto, 1973; Piano sonata, 1985; Three Love Songs for soprano and harp, 1991; Gae-chun for orchestra, 1991; Quintet for flute, harp and string trio, 1992. Address: c/o KOMCA, 2,3/F Samjeon Building, 236-3 Nonhyeon-dong, Kangnam-gu, Seoul, Korea.

LEECH Richard, b. 1956, Binghamton, California, USA. Singer (Tenor). Career: Sang first as baritone, then sang Offenbach's Hoffmann while a student; Many concert and opera appearances from 1980, notably at Cincinnati, Pittsburgh, Baltimore, Houston and Chicago; European debut at the Deutsche Oper Berlin, 1987, as Raoul in Les Huguenots; Chicago Lyric Opera, 1987, and La Scala, 1991, as Rodolfo; Has sung Gounod's Faust at San Diego, 1988, and at the Orange Festival and Metropolitan Opera, 1990; Pinkerton in Washington DC and Florence and La Scala (debut 1990), 1987 and 1989; Donizetti's Edgardo and Nemorino at the Deutsche Oper Berlin, 1988-89, and the Duke of Mantua at the New York City Opera (1988) and Metropolitan Opera, 1990; Season 1991/92 as Raoul in a new production of Les Huguenots at Covent Garden (debut), Pinkerton at Chicago and the Duke of Mantua at the Met; Rodolfo at the Met, 1994; Sang Faust at the Met, 1997; Concert engagements include Beethoven's Ninth and Verdi Requiem. Recordings: Les Huguenots; Fledermaus; Salome; Faust; Rosenkavalier. Address: c/o Metropolitan Opera, Lincoln Center, New York, NY 10023, USA.

LEEDY Douglas, b. 3 Mar 1938, Portland, Oregon, USA. Composer; Conductor; Educator. Education: BA, Pomona College, 1959; MA, University of California, Berkeley, 1962; Karnatic vocal music with K V Narayanaswamy. Career: French horn, Oakland Symphony Orchestra, San Francisco Opera, Ballet Orchestras, Cabrillo Festival Orchestra, 1969-65; Music faculty, University of California, Los Angeles, 1967-70; Reed College, 1973-78; Professor of Electronic Music, Centro Simon Bolivar, Caracas, Venezuela, 1972; Musical Director, Portland Baroque Orchestra, 1984-85; Complete performances of Handel's Jephtha and Theodora, Portland Handel Festival, 1985. Compositions: Usable Music I for Very Small Instruments with Holes, 1968; The Twenty-Fourth Psalm for chorus and orchestra, 1971; Fantasy on Wie schön leuchtet der Morgenstern for organ and voice; Canti/Music for contrabass and chamber ensemble; Music for Meantone Organ; Hymns from the Rig Veda for chorus and Javanese or American gamelan; Pastorale (Horace) for chorus and just-tuned piano, 4-hands, 1993. Recordings: Entropical Paradise: 6 Sonic Environments, Seraphim. Publications: Harpsichord Book III (just tuning); Chansons from Petrucci in Original Notation, 1983. Contributions to: Interval; The Courant; MLA Notes; The New Grove Dictionary of American Music. Memberships: Music Library Association; International Heinrich Schütz Society. Hobbies: Gardening; Classical philology. Address: PO Box 140 Oceanside, OR 97134, USA.

LEEF Yinam (Arie), b. 21 Dec 1953, Jerusalem, Israel. Composer. m. Tanya Fonarev, 23 Nov 1978, 1 son, 1 daughter. Education: BMus, Artist Diploma, Rubin Academy of Music, Jerusalem; MA, PhD, University of Pennsylvania; Composition Fellow, Tanglewood, 1982. Career: Visiting Lecturer, Swarthmore College, USA, 1982-84; Philadelphia College of the Performing Arts, 1984; Teaching, University of Pennsylvania, 1984-85; Lecturer, Senior Lecturer, Jerusalem Rubin Academy of Music and Dance, 1985-. Compositions: Gilgulim, woodwind trio, 1976, for string trio, 1980; Three Pieces, piano; Fireflies, soprano, flute, harpsichord, 1977; String Quartet No 1, 1978; KO, solo oboe, 1978; Ha'Bor, 1978; Laments, chamber orchestra, 1979; Flowers, Insects and a Very Thin Line, flute, oboe, piano trio, 1979; Canaanit Fantasy, piano, 1981; The Invisible Carmel, soprano and 5 players, 1982; Violin concerto, 1983; Octet, 1984; A Place of Fire, mezzo and 11 players, 1985; Fanfares and Whispers, trumpet and string orchestra, 1986; Sounds, Shadows for choir, 1987; How Far East, How Further West?, piano, 1988; Trio for oboe, violin, horn, 1988; Scherzos and Serenades, orchestra, 1989; Elegy, harpsichord, 1990; Tribute, orchestra, 1991; Elegy for string quartet, 1991; Symphony No 1, 1992; Sea Songs, equal voice choir, 1993; Cantilena, guitar, 1993; Threads of Time and Distance, alto, oboe and string orchestra, 1995; Visions of Stone City, symphony no 2, orchestra, 1995; Vizkor, flute, 1995; Said His Lover, alto and clarinet, 1996; Night Light orchestra, 1996; Viola Concerto, 1997; Recordings: Numerous for Israel Broadcasting Authority; Commissions including Fromm Music Foundation at Harvard, Swarthmore Music and Dance Festival, Concerto Soloists Chamber Orchestra of Philadelphia, Penn Contemporary Players, Jerusalem Symphony Orchestra, Israel Sinfonietta Be'er Sheva, Jerusalem Dance Workshop, Rinat Choir. Honours: ACUM Prize, 1992; Israel Prime Minister Prize, 1993. Memberships: ACUM; League of Composers in Israel. Address: 1 Ramban Street 10, Jerusalem 92422, Israel.

LEEK Stephen, b. 8 Oct 1959, Sydney, New South Wales, Australia. Composer; Conductor. Education: Study with Larry Sitsky, 1979-83; BA (Music), Canberra School of Music, 1983; ABC Young Composers Workshop, 1985. Career: Tasmanian Dance Company, 1982-85; Director, Arts Now; Artistic Director, Conductor, The Australian Voices; Commissions from Seymour Group, Chamber Made Opera, Brisbane Biennial Festival, among others; Residencies with St Peters Lutheran College, 1988, 1989, 1996, and Tasmanian Dance Theatre, 1993; Part-time Lecturer, Composition and Improvisation, Queensland Conservatorium. Compositions include: At Times.... Stillness, for organ, 1985; Thought, for female chorus, flute and piano, 1988; Once on a Mountain, and Songs of Space, Sea and Sky, for choir, 1988-89; Killcallow Catch, music theatre, 1990; Stroke, music theatre in 1 act, 1990; Voyage, for chorus, 1990; Five Songs, for female chorus, 1990; Five Song of the Sun, for orchestra, 1991; As You Like It, for piano, 1992; Great Southern Spirits, for chorus, and vocal soloists, 1993; Island Songs, for chorus, female soloists and piano, 1994. Honours include: Sounds Australian Awards, 1991. Address: P O Box 839, Indooroopilly, Qld 4068, Australia.

LEEKE David, b. 10 May 1957, Shropshire, England. Organist; Conductor; Writer; Examiner; Adjudicator. m. Tina M Daler. Education: Privately with the late A S W Baker; Royal College of Music. Career: Assistant Organist, Croydon Parish Church, 1977-79; Organist and Master of the Music, Folkestone Parish Church, 1979-90; Assistant Music Teacher, St Augustine's College, Westgate-on-Sea, 1980-87; Director of Music, St Mary's College, Folkestone, 1987-90; Director of Music, Maidstone Grammar School, 1990-; Organist and Choirmaster, St Mary's, Kemsing, 1990-94; Conductor and Musical Director, East Malling Singers, 1991-; Canterbury Diocesan Music Consultant and Adviser, 1994-; Conductor, Musical Director, Linden Ensemble, 1994-; Assistant RSCM Regional Director for Kent and Northwest Europe, 1996-; Examiner, Associated Board, Royal School of Music, 1996-. Compositions: Hymn tunes; Anglican chants; Anthems. Recordings: An Organ Celebration, Folkestone Parish Church, 1980; A Festival of Lessons and Carols, Folkestone Parish Church Choir, 1983; Music from Maidstone Grammar School, 1996. Publications: Let's Make Music, Music For All, 1992. Memberships: Royal College of Organists; Royal College of Music Society; Association of British Choral Directors; Music Masters and Mistresses Association; Incorporated Society of Musicians; Elgar Society. Hobbies: Old English pubs; English history; Driving; Swimming; Biographies. Address: Chequer Tree Farm, Bethersden, Kent TN26 3JR, England.

LEES Benjamin, b. 8 Jan 1924, Harbin, China. Composer. Education: University of Southern California with Halsey Stevens, Ingolf Dahl; With George Antheil and in Europe. Career: Teacher, Peabody Conservatory, 1962-64, 1966-68; Queens College, New York, 1964-66; Manhattan School, 1972-74; Juilliard, 1976-77; Commissions, Tokyo String Quartet, Dallas, Delaware, Wichita and Pittsburgh Symphonies, Philadelphia and Louisville Orchestras, Chamber Music America. Compositions: 5 Piano Sonatas; 4 String Quartets; 5 Symphonies; 3 Violin Sonatas; Sonata, 2 pianos, 1951; Profile, orchestra, 1952; Declamations, strings, piano, 1953; 5 Symphonies; 3 Violin Sonatas; Concertos: Piano, 1955, 1966, Violin, 1958, Orchestra, 1959, Oboe, 1963, String Quartet, Orchestra, 1965, Chamber Orchestra, 1966, Woodwind Quintet, Orchestra, 1976, Brass, Orchestra, 1983, French Horn, Orchestra, 1992; The Oracle, music drama, 1955; Divertimento burlesca, orchestra, 1957; Concertante breve, 1959; Visions of Poets, cantata after Whitman, 1962; Spectrum, orchestra, 1964; The Gilded Cage, opera, 1964; Silhouettes, wind, percussion, 1967; Medea of Corinth, vocalists, wind quintet, timpani, 1970; Odyssey 1, piano trio, 1971, 2, solo piano, 1980; The Trumpet of the Swan, narrator, piano, 1972; Collage, string quartet, woodwind quintet, percussion, 1973; Etudes, piano, orchestra, 1974; Variations, piano, orchestra, 1976; Passacaglia, orchestra, 1976; Scarlatti Portfolio, ballet, 1979; Mobiles, orchestra, 1979; Double Concerto, piano, cello, 1982; Fantasy Variations, piano, 1984; Portrait of Rodin, orchestra, 1984; Mirrors, piano solo, 1992-94; Borealis, orchestra, 1993; Echoes of Normandy, tenor, orchestra, 1994. Recordings: Symphonies 2, 3, Concerto for Orchestra, Louisville Orchestra; Concerto for String Quartet and Orchestra, Royal Philharmonic; Violin Concerto, American Symphony; 4th Piano; 4th Piano Sonata, Gary Graffman; Complete Violin Works, Ellen Orner violin, Joel Wizansky piano. Honours include: Guggenheim Fellow, 1954, 1966; Fulbright Fellow, 1956-57; Sir Arnold Bax Medal, 1958; Lancaster Symphony Orchestra Composer Award, 1985. Address: 2451-A Birdie Way, Palm Springs, CA 92264, USA.

LEFANU Nicola (Frances), b. 28 Apr 1947, Wickham Bishops, Essex, England. Composer; Professor of Music. Education: MA(Oxon). Career: Broadcasts and performances in UK, America, Europe and Australia; Professor of Music at University of York. Compositions: Over 50 vocal, choral, solo, chamber, orchestral, theatre and ballet works including: Variations for Oboe Quartet, The Same Day Dawns for Soprano and Chamber Ensemble, Columbia Falls for Orchestra, But Stars Remaining for Soprano; Operas: Dawnpath, 1977, The Story of Mary O'Neill, radio opera for 17 voices, 1989; The Green Children, 1990; Blood Wedding, 1992; The Wildman, 1995. Honours: Cobbett Chamber Music Prize, 1968; 1st Prize, British

Broadcasting Corporation Composition Competition, 1971; Mendelssohn Scholarship, 1972; Gulbenkian Dance award, 1972; Harkness Fellowship, 1973; Honorary Fellow, St Hilda's College, Oxford, 1993; Honorary DMus, Durham, 1995. Membership: Council, Society for Promotion of New Music. Current Management: Novello (Music Sales). Address: 5 Holly Terrace, York YO1 4DS, England.

LEFEBVRE Claude, b. 11 November 1931, Ardres, Calais, France. Composer. m. Ingeborg Giese, 1 May 1965, 2 daughters. Education: Prizes in Harmony, Counterpoint and Fugue, 1955-57, Composition with Darius Milhaud, 1959-60, Paris Conservatory; Composition with Pierre Boulez, Musikakademie Basel, Switzerland, 1961-62. Career: Teacher of Analysis and Composition, Metz Conservatory, France, 1966-; Founder and Artistic Director, Centre Européen pour la Recherche Musicale and the International Meeting of Contemporary Music, Metz; Artistic Director of his electro-acoustic studio, Lorraine, 1976-; Lectures in Contemporary Music, Metz University, 1978-. Compositions Include: Cheminements, 1969; Naissances Pour Quatre Joueurs, 1971; Musiques en Liberté, 1971; Sous le Regard du Silence, 1973; Durchdringen der Nacht, 1976; Verzweigungen-Ramifications, 1976; Ivresse-Absence, 1977; Dérives Nocturnes, 1978; Tourbillonnements, 1979; Mémoires Souterraines, 1980; Océan de Terre, 1981; Lorraine, 1983; Oregon, 1984; Mosella, 1984; La Chute, 1985; Sur le lac...la main, saison, 1991-92; Sur le Seuil...Inenfant, 1991; Quand les Verres Éclatent...; X...1994; 1992-93; Seule la Peau..., saison, 1991-92. Recordings: D'Un Arbre de Nuit, 1971; Etwas Weiter, 1972; (Le Chant du Monde); Océan de Terre; Vallée; Orégon; Verzweigungen; Savoure; Mosella (Harmonia Mundi HM 83). Address: 9 Rue Claude Debussy, F 57103 Jouy-aux-Arches, France.

LEFEBVRE Pierre, b. 1959, Drummondville, Quebec, Canada. Tenor. Education: Studied in Montreal and Italy. Career: Sang at first in such roles as Edgardo and Rodolfo; Guest appearances in Lucca, Rome and Montreal; La Scala Milan in Fidelio, Traviata and Don Carlos; Frankfurt Opera 1991, in Franchetti's Cristoforo Colombo; Further appearances in Giovanna d'Arco at Bologna, and in Don Carlos and Die Zauberflöte at Turin. Recordings include: Video of Giovanna d'Arco (Teldec). Address: c/o Teatro alla Scala, Via Filodrammatici 2, 20121 Milan, Italy.

LEFKOWITZ Mischa, b. 17 Mar 1954, Riga, Latvia. Concert Violinist. m. Irini Lefkowitz, 15 June 1980. Education: Special School of Music, Riga; Moscow Conservatory of Music; Wayne State University, Detroit, USA; Mozarteum Academy, Salzburg. Debut: New York, 1984; Paris, 1985. Career: Radio Show, KPFK; Radio Appearances, KPFC, Los Angeles, KCRW, Los Angeles; TV Appearances on CBS; Orchestral appearances with major orchestras and recitals. Compositions: (Recorded) Mozart Concerto A Major; Giardini Concerto A Major; Bloch Concerto; Works by Sarasate, Prokofiev. Recordings: Laurel and Sequence Records; Recorded with London Philharmonic and English Chamber Orchestras. Contributions to: New York Times; Boston Globe; LA Times. Honours: City of Paris Prize, 1985; Carnegie Hall American Music Prize, 1983. Memberships: Chamber Music America; College Music Society. Hobbies: Writing; Basketball; Swimming. Current Management: ICA Management. Address: 3435 Bonnie Hill Drive, Los Angeles, CA 90068, USA.

LEFORT Bernard, b. 29 July 1922, Paris, France. Singer (Baritone); Administrator. Education: Studied at the Paris Conservatoire and with Aureliano Pertile in Milan, Hermann Wiessenborn in Berlin and Elisabeth Rado in Vienna. Career: Sang at Salle Gaveau during the 1940s and was often heard in music by Auric, Honegger, Milhaud and Poulenc; Sang in the premiere of Tailleferre's Concerto pour Baryton and appeared from 1953 at the Théâtre du Châtelet, Paris, in operettas; Performed at the Lucerne Opera, notably as Don Giovanni and retired from the stage 1960, becoming artistic director of the Lausanne Festival; Director of the Marseille Opera, 1965-68 reviving such operas as La Gioconda, Lucrezia Borgia, Henze's Prince of Homburg and Britten's The Turn of the Screw; Artistic Director of the Theatre de Ville Paris, 1969-78; Festival of Aix-en-Provence, 1973-80; General Administrator of the Paris Opera, 1980-82; Teacher at Mannes College New York and at the Academy of Vocal Art at Philadelphia; Produced Gounod's Mireille at the Juilliard Opera School, New York, 1986. Address: c/o Juilliard School of Music (Opera Dept), Lincoln Plaza, New York, NY 10023, USA.

LEFTERESCU Petre, b. 1 May 1936, Bistrita, Rumania. Violinist; Professor. m. Ogneanca Tomici, 27 Sept 1958. Education: Bucharest Music Academy, 1953-58; Postgraduate courses, Moscow Conservatory, USSR, at D Oistrakh Violin Chair, 1967. Career: Solo concerts and chamber music tours as violinist, Rumania, 1958-; Violin professor, Cluj Music Academy, 1958-69; Professor of Chamber Music, Bucharest Academy of Music, 1969-; 1st violin, Forum String Quartet, 1985; Appearances, Rumanian television. Recordings: Rumanian and universal music. Contributions to: Muzica Contemporanul. Current Management: ARIA, Rumanian Artists' Management Company. Address: Calea Victoriei Nr 83, et IX, ap 37, Bucharest 70176, Rumania.

LEGA Luigi, b. 7 Apr 1940, Bordighera, Italy. Singer (Tenor). Education: Studied in Rome, Basle and Mannheim. Debut: Overhausen, as Pinkerton, 1961. Career: Many appearancea at such German opera centres as Munich, Hamburg, Stuttgart, Mannheim, Berlin (Deutsche Oper) and Wuppertal; Further engagements at Amsterdam, Palermo, Barcelona, Rio de Janeiro, Trieste and Vienna as Verdi's Radames, Duke of Mantua, Alvaro, Alfredo, Don Carlos, Manrico and Riccardo; Also a noted interpreter of Don José, Edgardo, Florestan, Andrea Chénier, Turiddu, Rodolfo, Cavaradossi and Des Grieux in Manon Lescaut; Teacher of singing in Wuppertal. Address: c/o Wuppertal Buhnen, Spinnstrasse 4, 5600 Wuppertal, Germany.

LEGANY Denes, b. 14 May 1965, Budapest, Hungary. Composer; Pianist; Conductor; Professor. m. Eva Toth, 23 Aug 1990, 2 sons, 1 daughter. Education: BM, Bartok Conservatory of Music; MM, DMA, Liszt Academy of Music. Career: Professor, Budapest University School of Music, 1987-94; Professor, Vice President, Budapest Conservatory of Music, 1993-; Visiting Professor, Several Colleges and Universities; Recitals in 3 continents; Lectures on TV and radio. Recordings: Hommage à Bartok CD, 1995; Works recorded by Hungarian and foreign record companies. Publications: Easy Piano Pieces for Children; Festival Music, for band; Trios for French Horn; Suite for Trumpet; Trombone Quartets; Saxophone Quartet; Air, for saxophone and piano; Flute Duos; Three Childrens Choruses; Fragments, for saxophone solo. Honours: 15 international and national composition contest prizes; Award of Artisjus, Budapest; Award, Soros Foundation, New York, (three times). Address: Apahida Utca 11, H-1112 Budapest, Hungary.

LEGANY Dezsö, b. 19 Jan 1916, Szombathely, Hungary. Musicologist. m. Erzsébet Hegyi, 23 Sept 1961, 2 sons. Education: LLD, University of Pécs; Composition, Liszt Academy of Music, Budapest; DMusSc, Hungarian Academy of Sciences, Budapest. Career: Professor, Liszt Academy of Music, Budapest, 1951-58; Professor, Bartók Conservatory of Music, Budapest, 1958-73; Head of Hungarian Music Department, Institute for Musicology, Hungarian Academy of Sciences, 1973-83. Publications: Henry Purcell, 1959, 2nd Edition, 1981; A Chronicle of Hungarian Music: A Thousand Years of Music History in Documents, 1962; Works of F Erkel, 1975; Liszt in Hungary 1869-1873, 1976; Letters of Z Kodály, 1982; Liszt and His Country, 1869-1873, 1983; F Liszt Unbekannte Presse und Briefe aus Wien 1822-1886, 1984; Liszt in Hungary 1874-86, 1986; Liszt and His Country, 1874-1886, 1992. Contributions to: New Grove Dictionary; New Grove Dictionary of Opera; Sohlmans Musiklexikon; The Concise Oxford Dictionary of Opera; Zenei Lexikon; Studia Musicologica; Magyar Zene; The New Hungarian Quarterly; Bulletin of the International Kodály Society; Grazer Musikwissenschaftliche Arbeiten; Journal of the American Liszt Society; Periodica Musica; Vigilia; Nuova Rivista Musicale Italiana; The Liszt Society Journal, London; Liszt Saeculum, Sweden; Dictionary of Opera, London, 1992. Honours: Grand Prize of the Artistic Foundation, 1982; Prize of the American Liszt Society, 1984; Prize of the Cziffra Foundation, 1984; Erkel Ferenc Prize, 1988. Memberships: Board Member, Hungarian Liszt Society; Honorary Member, American Liszt Society; Patron, Swedish Liszt Centre. Address: Apahida u 11, H-1112 Budapest, Hungary.

LEGGATE Robin, b. 18 Apr 1946, West Kirby, Cheshire, England. Singer (Tenor). Education: Studied at Queen's College, Oxford (1964-67) and the Royal Northern College of Music. Career: Royal Opera House, Covent Garden from 1977, as Cassio in Otello (conducted by Zubin Mehta, Christoph von Dohnányi and Colin Davis); Elemer (Arabella), Narraboth (Salome), the Painter in Lulu and Tamino in a new production of Die Zauberflöte, 1979; Has also sung in Prince Igor and Il Trovatore at Covent Garden; Appearances with the Netherlands Opera and at the Hamburg Staatsoper from 1978; South Australian Opera, 1982, as Ferrando in Cosi fan tutte; Théâtre du Châtelet, Paris, as Tamino, 1983; Other Mozart roles include Belmonte and Don Ottavio, which he has sung with most of the regional British companies; Recent engagements in Le nozze di Figaro in Madrid, Weber's Oberon with Scottish Opera, Eisenstein in a new production of Die Fledermaus for Scottish Opera, and the premiere of André Laporte's Das Schloss, in Brussels; Has sung at the Festival Hall from 1976 (debut with the London Symphony in Pulcinella); In 1981 sang in Mendelssohn's Elijah at Florence and appeared in Mozart's C minor Mass with the London Philharmonic, conducted by Solti; Sang in the stage premiere of Gerhard's Duenna, Madrid, 1992; Sang in world premiere of Life with an Idiot by Schnittke at Netherlands Opera, 1992; Opéra Bastille (St François d'Assise) and at Salzburg Festival (Salome), 1993; Sang in first production of Stiffelio (Verdi) at Royal Opera House, 1993; Cassio at Covent Garden, 1994; The Scribe (Khovanshchina) at La Monnaie Brussels. Recordings include: La Fanciulla del West from Covent Garden; Haydn's Armida; The Light of Life by Elgar. Current Management: Lies Askonas Ltd. Address: 6 Henrietta Street, London WC2 8LA, England.

LEHANE Maureen, b. 19 Sept 1932, London, England. Concert and Opera Singer Mezzp-soprano). m. Peter Wishart, 1966 (deceased 1984). Education: Queen Elizabeth's Girls' Grammar School, Barnet; Guildhall School of Music and Drama; Studied under Hermann Weissenborn, Berlin, and John and Aida Dickens; Gained Arts Council Award to Study in Berlin. Career includes: Has sung numerous leading roles, (Operas including Arianna and Faramondo) with Handel Opera Societies of England and America, in London and in Carnegie Hall, New York, also in Poland, Sweden and Germany, gave a numer of Master Classes on the interpretation of Handel's vocal music (notably at s'Hertogenbosch Festival, Holland, 1972, 1973); Debut at Glyndebourne, 1967, as Melide in Cavalli's L'Ormindo; Festival appearances include Stravinsky Festival, Cologne; City of London; Aldeburgh; Cheltenham; Three Choirs; Bath; Oxford Bach; Göttingen Handel Festival; Toured North America, 3 month tour of Australia, 2 month tour of Far East and Middle East, 1971; Sang in Holland and for Belgium TV; Visits to Berlin, Lisbon, Poland and Rome, 1979-80; Warsaw, 1981; Title role of Handel's Ariodante, Sadler's Wells, 1974; Wishart's Clytemnestra, London, 1974; Purcell's Dido and Aeneas, Netherlands Opera, 1976; Started an annual music festival dedicated to the memory of Peter Wishart, 1986-; Great Elm Music Festival (Jackdaws, Great Elm, devoted to music education). Recordings: Made numerous recordings, Bach, Haydn, Mozart, Handel. Publications: Songs of Purcell edited with Peter Wishart. Memberships: Jury, International Singing Competitions', Hertogenbosch Festival, Holland, 1982-, and Llangollen International Eisteddfod from 1991. Hobbies: Cooking; Gardening; Reading.

LEHMANN Hans Ulrich, b. 4 May 1937, Biel, Switzerland. Composer; Professor. m. Ursula Lehmann. Education: BA, 1956; Universities of Berne, Zurich and Basle, 1956-67; Diplomas: Violoncello, 1960, Music Theory, 1962; Master classes in Composition with Boulez and Stockhausen, 1960-63. Career includes: Lecturer, Zurich University, 1969-90; Professor, Theory, Composition, 1972-, Director, 1976-, Musikhochschule, Zurich; President, SUISA (Swiss Authors Association), 1991-. Compositions include: Quanti, 1962; Mosaik, 1964; Noten, 1964-66; Spiele, 1965; Rondo, 1967; Instants, 1968; Konzert, 1969; Régions III, 1970; discantus I and II, 1970; Sonata da chiesa, 1971; Tractus, 1971; zu streichen, 1974; zu blasen, 1975; Tantris, 1976-77; Motetus Paraburi, 1977-78; Kammermusik I, 1978-79; Kammermusik II, 1979; Duette, 1980; Lege mich wie ein Siegel auf dein Herz, 1980-83; Canticum I and II, 1981; Stroking, 1982; Mirlitonnades, 1983; battuto a tre - tratto, 1983; Mon amour, 1983; Triplum, 1984; -ludes, 1985; Alleluja, 1985; In Memoriam Nicolai de Flue, 1986-87; Fragmente, 1986-87; Streichquartett, 1987-88; Osculetur me, 1988-89; de profundis, 1988-89; Esercizi, 1989; Wandloser Raum, 1989; ad missam Prolationum, 1989-90; etwas Klang von meiner Oberfläche, 1989-90; Nocturnes, 1990-91; ut signaculum, 1991-92; el mar, 1993; Prélude à une étendue, 1993-94. Contributor to: Professional journals. Honours include: Composers Prize, Swiss Musicians Association, 1988; Music Prize, City of Zurich, 1993. Memberships: Numerous professional organisations. Address: Haldenstrasse 35, CH-8615 Wermatswil, Switzerland.

LEHMANN Wilfred, b. 1929, Melbourne, Victoria, Australia. Composer; Violinist; Conductor. Education: Studied in Australia and London; Violinist with the Birmingham Orchestra, 1958-60; Conductor, Tokyo Philharmonic Orchestra, 1960-70; Assistant Conductor Queensland Symphony Orchestra, 1972; Nashville Symphony, and Chamber Orchestra, 1976-79; Conductor ABC Sinfonia, Australia, 1982; Member of Sydney String Quartet; Commisions include: Song of Mululu, 1977; Two String Quartets (2nd 1988); Bacchanals, for orchestra, 1988; Concerto for Two Pianos and Percussion, 1991. Honours include: First Prize, Carl Flesch International Violin Competition (London), 1958; Fellowship in Composition, Tennessee Arts Commission, 1979. Recordings include: Bacchanals, and 2nd String Quartet (ABC). Address: c/o APRA, 1A Eden Street, Crows Nest, NSW 2065, Australia.

LEHNHOFF Nikolaus, b. 20 May 1939, Hanover, Germany. Opera Producer and Designer. Education: Trained as assistant stage director at the Deutsche Oper Berlin, and at Bayreuth and the Metropolitan Operas, 1963-71. Career: Staged Die Frau ohne Schatten at the Paris Opéra, 1971; Director of several opera productions in Germany and Switzerland; San Francisco, 1985, Der Ring des Nibelungen; Produced Katya Kabanova at Glyndebourne and Der fliegende Holländer at Santa Fe, both in 1988; Returned to Glyndebourne, 1989, Jenufa; Idomeneo at the Salzburg Festival, 1990; Munich Opera, 1990, Der fliegende Holländer; Elektra at Leipzig, 1991; Season 1991/92 with Lohengrin at Frankfurt and Henze's Der Prinz von Homburg at the Munich Festival; Produced The Makropoulos Case by Janácek at Glyndebourne, 1995; Pfitzner's Palestrina at Covent Garden,

1997. Address: c/o Glyndebourne Festival Opera, Lewes, Sussex BN8 5UU, England.

LEHR Edit, b. 1954, Budapest, Hungary. Singer (Soprano). Education: Studied at the Budapest School of Music and at the Cologne Musikhochschule. Career: Sang at uppertal Opera, 1980-82, the Freiburg Opera 1982-86, then at Gelsenkirchen; Guest appearances in Heidelberg, Vienna, Basel and Budapest; Among her best roles are Gilda, Violetta, Musetta, Donna Anna, Lauretta, Rosina, Fiordiligi, Susanna, Gretel, the Princess in Der Zwerg by Zemlinsky; Frequent concert appearances throughout Europe. Address: c/o Musiktheater im Revier, Kennedyplatz, Pf 101854, 45881 Gelsenkirchen, Germany.

LEHRBAUMER Robert, b. 20 July 1960, Vienna, Austria. Pianist; Conductor. Education: Studied Piano, Organ, Conducting, Composition, Vienna School of Music and Dramatic Art; Diplomas with highest distinction, Organ, Piano, 1987, 1988. Career: Played with Vienna Philharmonic Orchestra, Vienna Symphonic Orchestra, Austrian Broadcasting Corporation Orchestra and other major orchestras; Conductors: Claudio Abbado, Yehudi Menuhin, André Previn, Sandor Vegh; Appeared with Wolfgang Schneiderhan, Anton Dermota, Walter Berry, Philippe Entremont; Concerts in most European countries, Korea, Japan, Thailand, Indonesia, Malaysia, Mexico, Argentina, USA (including Schubert Festival, Washington, and Carnegie Recital Hall, New York, Kenya, Uganda); International festivals, Vienna, Lucerne, Nurnberg, Prague Spring Festival, Bruckner Festival, Linz Festival and Cervantino, Mexico; Many radio and television performances; Teaching, summer academies, Austria and abroad; World premieres of new works; Specialist, Schubert piano works, Haydn, Mozart, Beethoven piano concertos, A Berg, F Schmidt, E Schulhoff, K Szymanowski. Recordings: LPs and CDs: Baroque, Romantic and contemporary piano music (Liszt, Schumann, Tchaikovsky, Brahms, Schubert, Weissensteiner, Schollum, Albinoni, Pachelbel, Muffat, Kerll). Current Management: Freunde der Claviermusik. Address: Freunde der Claviermusik, Penknergasse 21, A-3150 Wilhelmsburg, Austria.

LEHRMAN Leonard (Jordan), b. 20 Aug 1949, Kansas, USA. Conductor; Composer; Pianist; Accompanist; Translator; Director. m. Karen S Campbell, 31 July 1978, div. 1986. Education: Private study with Elie Siegmeister, 1960-69; Fontainebleau Conservatoire, 1969; BA, Harvard College, 1971; Ecole Normale de Musique, Paris, 1971-72; Salzburg Mozarteum, 1972; Opera conducting, Indiana University, 1975-76; MFA, 1975, DMA, Composition, 1977, Cornell University; ML-LS, Long Island University, 1995. Debut: As Pianist, Carnegie Recital Hall, 1979; As Conductor, Bremerhaven and Berlin, 1981, 1983. Career: Assistant Chorus Master and Assistant Conductor, Metropolitan Opera, 1977-78; Assistant Conductor, Heidelberg Festival, 1979, Augsburg Städtische Bühne, 1980, and Basler Theater, 1980-81; Conductor, Schauspielhaus Wien, 1981; Kapellmeister, Stadttheater Bremerhaven, 1981-83; Chief Coach, Conductor, Theater des Westens, 1983-85; Laureate Conductor, Jewish Music Theatre of Berlin; President, Long Island Composers Alliance, 1991-96; Has appeared on ZDF, WTIU and WCIC TV and various other TV and radio stations; Faculty, Jewish Academy of Fine Arts; Music Director, North Shore Synagogue (Syoset) and Community Presbyterian Church Malverne. Compositions: Tales of Malamud; 2 1-act operas: Idiots First (completion of work begun by Marc Blitzstein) and Karla; Sima; Hannah; The Family Man; Flute Concerto; Violin Concerto; Growing Up Woman; Let's Change the World. Address: 10 Nob Hill Gate, Roslyn, NY 11576, USA.

LEIB Gunther, b. 12 Apr 1927, Gotha, Thuringen, Germany. Singer (Baritone); Professor. Education: After violin studies entered vocal class at the Weimar Conservatory. Career: First violin in Landeskapelle at Gotha from 1949; Stage debut at Kothen, 1952, as Bartolo in Il Barbiere di Siviglia. Career: Sang at Kothen, Meinigen and Nordhausen; Stadttheater Halle, 1956-57; Staatsoper Dresden from 1957, Berlin from 1961; Sang Christus in Bach's St John Passion in Italy, 1957, conducted by Franz Konwitschny; Annual appearances at the Handel Festivals, Halle; Salzburg Easter Festival, 1974-75, as Beckmesser in Die Meistersinger, conducted by Karajan (also at the Met, 1976); Guest engagements at the Paris Opéra, Moscow Bolshoi, Hamburg Staatsoper, National Operas of Warsaw, Prague and Budapest, Sofia, Stockholm and Helsinki; Other roles were Guglielmo, Raimondo, Papageno, Don Pasquale and Germont; Professor at the Carl Maria von Weber Hochschule, Dresden, 1964-76; Currently Professor at the Musikhochschule Berlin. Recordings: Così fan tutte; Die Zauberflöte; Ein Deutsches Requiem; Lucia di Lammermoor; Don Pasquale; La Traviata; St Matthew Passion; Der Dorfjahrmarkt by Benda; La Bohème; Einstein by Dessau. Address: Hochschule für Musik Hanns Eisler, Otto-Grotewohlstrase 19, 1008 Berlin, Germany.

LEIDEL Wolf-G, b. 14 Dec 1949, Königsee, Thuringia, East Germany. Professor of Music Theory. m. Sabine Sonsalla, 29 June 1972. Education: Studied Conducting and Composition, 1968-73. Debut: World premiere of his Symphony No 1 with Jena Philharmonic, 1974. Career: Kapellmeister, Theater Weimar, 1974-83; Meisterschuler Berlin, Akademie der Künste, East Berlin, 1983-85; Assistant, Music Theory, 1985-93, Professor, Music Theory, 1993, Hochschule für Musik, Weimar; Many world and other premieres of numerous compositions, especially music for organ. Compositions include: Zi Bims Barenreiter, a feast of organ exuberance, for organ; Meinem Rosengarten for organ and violin. Recordings: Zi Bims Barenreiter played by Kerin Bowyer; Meinem Rosengarten, played by Bittotmann (violin) and W Gleidel (organ). Contributions to: Orgelmusik; Orgelgutachten; Other publications. Honours include: 1st Prize in National Improvisation Competition, 1976. Memberships include: GdO; Olivier-Messiaen Association; VDK; Museum für Orgelbau, Thuringia. Hobbies include: Organ; Composition; Astrophysics; Cosmology; Theology. Address: Bauhausstr 12, D-O 5300 Weimar, Germany.

LEIFERKUS Sergei, b. 4 Apr 1946, Leningrad, Russia. Singer (Baritone). Education: Studied at the Leningrad Conservatoire, with Barsov and Shaposhnikov. Career: Joined the Leningrad Maly Theatre, 1972: sang in Eugene Onegin, Iolanta, Il Barbiere di Siviglia and Don Giovanni; Joined Kirov Theatre Leningrad, 1977, and sang Prince Andrei in War and Peace by Prokofiev; Sang with Berlin Philharmonic under Kurt Masur, 1983; Wexford Festival 1982-86, in Grisélidis and Le Jongleur de Notre Dame by Massenet, Hans Heiling by Marschner and Königskinder by Humperdinck; Scottish Opera from 1985, as Don Giovanni, Germont and Eugene Onegin, 1988; Covent Garden 1987, as Eugene Onegin and Tomsky in The Queen of Spades, with the Kirov Company; English National Opera 1987, as Zurga in Les Pêcheurs de Perles; US debut 1987, in Symphony No 13 by Shostakovich, with the Boston Symphony; In 1989 gave Wigmore Hall debut recital, sang Luna in a new production of Il Trovatore at Covent Garden and appeared in a concert performance of Giovanna d'Arco at the Festival Hall; Concert performance of Mlada by Rimsky-Korsakov, at the Barbican Hall; Season 1989-90 included US Opera debut at San Francisco, as Telramund in Lohengrin, and the title role in a new production of Prince Igor at Covent Garden; Sang Rangoni in Boris Godunov at the Kirov Theatre, St Petersburg, 1990 (also televised); Luna at the Teatro Colon, Buenos Aires, Mazeppa at the Bregenz Festival and Netherlands Opera, Amsterdam, Ruprecht in Prokofiev's Fiery Angel at the BBC Promenade Concerts, London; Tomsky in The Queen of Spades in Boston and New York with the Boston Symphony (also recorded for BMG) under Ozawa; In 1992, he sang Onegin in Montreal, Ruprecht in St Petersburg (also video taped), Tomsky at Glyndebourne and Vienna State Opera, Rangoni at San Francisco, Iago at Covent Garden under Solti and at the Metropolitan; In 1993, he sang Carlo in La Forza del Destino for VARA Radio at the Amsterdam Concertgebouw, Shostakovich 13th Symphony with the New York Philharmonic under Masur (also recorded for Teldec), Scarpia, Amonasro, Escamillo and Luna (new production under Mehta) at the Vienna State Opera, Telramund in Cologne, Igor and Onegin for VARA in Amsterdam with the Kirov Company, Mazeppa for the Opera Orchestra, New York, recorded Iago for DG in Paris with Placido Domingo, a new production of Onegin at Covent Garden, under Gergiev, recorded volumes of Mussorgsky and Shostakovich songs for Conifer/BBC and DG, appeared at the Tanglewood Festival; Gave Masterclasses at the Britten/Pears School, Aldeburgh, sang Ruprecht with the Kirov in St Petersburg and Japan, a recital at the Wigmore Hall, London, appeared in concerts and recorded Rangoni for Sony in Berlin with the Philharmonic under Abbado and Scarpia at Covent Garden; In 1994, he made his first appearance at La Scala in a new production of The Fiery Angel under Chailly, further performances as Iago at the Metropolitan, New York, Scarpia at Opera Bastille, Paris, recorded Telramund for BMG in Munich under Colin Davis, sang Mephistopheles in La Damnation de Faust with Ozawa and the Berlin Philharmonic in Berlin, recorded Pizarro in Fidelio under Harnoncourt with the Chamber Orchestra of Europe for Teldec, the title role in Nabucco at the Bregenz Festival, recorded more Shostakovich Songs for DG and a Rakhmaninov Album for Chandos, sang Ruprecht in San Francisco and gave recitals across America, Escamillo at the Teatro Colon, Buenos Aires and Prokofiev's Ivan the Terrible under Muti at La Scala; In 1995, he sang Iago again at Covent Garden, Mazeppa at Netherlands Opera, Amsterdam, Shostakovich's 13th Symphony under Masur in Leipzig with the Gewandhaus Orchestra, Gryaznoy in The Tsar's Bride for Opera Orchestra of New York in Carnegie Hall, Escamillo in a gala performance of Carmen with Jose Carreras in Stuttgart, Iago at the Vienna State Opera, recitals at Cologne and Graz, Amonasro at the Berlin State Opera under Mehta, recorded albums of Mussorgsky and Glinka songs for Conifer/BMG and Scarpia alongside Luciano Pavarotti as Cavaradossi at the Ravinia Festival; Sang Count Luna in Pfitzner's Palestrina; Boccanegra in the original version of Verdi's opera and Telramund in Lohengrin at Covent Garden, 1997. Address: c/o Allied Artists, 42 Montpelier Square, London SW7 1JZ, England.

LEIGH Adèle, b. 15 June 1928, London, England. Singer (Soprano). Education: Studied in New York with Julius Gutmann. Career: Sang first in USA; Covent Garden from 1949, as Xenia in Boris Godunov, Mozart's Cherubino and Pamina, Strauss's Sophie and Massenet's Manon; Sang in the premieres of Vaughan Williams's Pilgrim's Progress and Tippett's The Midsummer Marriage; Boston, 1959, as Musetta in La Bohème; New York City Center Opera, 1960, as Sophie in Werther; Zurich Opera, 1961-; Operetta performances at the Vienna Volksoper from 1965; Brighton Festival, 1984, in Offenbach's La Vie Parisienne; Sang in Sondheim's Follies (London 1987); Senior Tutor in Opera Stagecraft at the Royal Northern College of Music, 1992. Address: Royal Northern College of Music (Opera Faculty), 124 Oxford Road, Manchester M15 6FY, England.

LEIGH David (Anthony), b. 3 Apr 1953, London, England. Harpsichordist; Fortepianist. Education: BA, Reading University, 1975; Guildhall School of Music. Debut: Wigmore Hall, 1975. Career: Recitals all over the UK, Canada, USA, Netherlands, Belgium, Austria; Lectures in USA and Austria; Masterclasses in USA and UK; Radio broadcasts in UK, Canada and USA; Known for knowledge of early keyboard instruments and their restoration. Recordings: Several. Publications: Book on early pianos in preparation; Encyclopaedia articles on harpsichord and clavichord. Contribution to: Antique Collector, on square pianos. Hobbies: Collecting old piano and harpsichord records; Theatre; Film; Arts; Antiques; Food and wine. Address: Greystones, The Slade, Charlbury, Oxford OX7 3SJ, England.

LEISNER David, b. 22 Dec 1953, Los Angeles, California, USA. Guitarist; Composer; teacher. Education: Studied privately with John Duarte, David Starobin, Richard Winslow, Virgil Thompson and David Del Tredici, Wesleyan University; BA, 1976. Career: Teacher of Guitar at Amherst College, 1976-78; New England Conservatory from 1980; Manhattan School of Music from 1993; New York debut at Merkin Hall, 1979; Solo and Chamber Music Recitals in USA, Canada and Europe; Concerto Soloist with L'Orchestre de la Suisse Romande, Australian Chamber Orchestra, New York Chamber Ensemble and others; Compositions performed by the Fresno Philharmonic, Amarillo Symphony, Colonial Symphony, Springfield Symphony Orchestra, Fairfield Orchestra, Sanford Sylvan, Paul Sperry, Benjamin Verdery, Eugenia Zukerman, The Saturday Brass Quintet and the Los Angeles Guitar Quartet. Compositions include: Embrace of Peace, orchestra, 1991; Dances in the Madhouse, violin (or flute) and guitar, 1982; Orchestrated, 1989; Battlefield Requiem, percussion quartet and solo cello; Ad Majoren Dei Gloriam, brass quintet, 1992; Confiding, for voice and piano, voice and guitar, 1985-86; Candles in Mecca, piano trio, 1988. Recordings: The Viennese Guitar, Titanic. Honours: 2nd Prize, Toronto International Guitar Competition, 1975; Silver Medal, Geneva International Guitar competition, 1981; Aaron Copland Fund for Music Grant, 1996. Memberships: Pro Musicis Awards Advisory Committee; Board of Directors, Guitar Foundation of America. Current Management: Aaron Concert Management. Address: 1926 Broadway, 6th Floor, New York, NY 10023, USA.

LEIXNER Vladimir, b. 1953, Czechoslovakia. Cellist. Education: Studied in Prague with members of the Smetana Quartet. Career: Cellist in various Czech ensembles from 1970; Co-Founder and Cellist of the Stamic Quartet, Prague, 1977; Performances at the Prague Young Artists and the Bratislava Music Festivals; Tours to Spain, Austria, France, Switzerland, Germany and Eastern Europe; Tour of the USA in 1980 with debut concerts in Britain at London and Birmingham in 1983; Further British tours in 1985 and 1988 (Warwick Arts Festival) and 20 concerts in 1989; Gave the premiere of Helmut Eder's 3rd Quartet in 1986; Season 1991-92 with visit to the Channel Islands with Festival of Czech Music, to Holland, Finland, Austria and France, Edinburgh Festival and debut tours of Canada, Japan and Indonesia. Recordings: Shostakovich No 13; Schnittke No 4; Mozart's K589 and K370; Dvorák, Martinu and Janácek's Complete Quartets. Honours: With Stamic Quartet: Prizewinner, International Festival of Young Soloists, Bordeaux, 1977, Winner ORF Austria International String Quartet Competition, 1986, followed by live broadcast from Salzburg Mozarteum, Academie Charles Cros Grand Prix du Disque, 1991 for Dvorák Quartets. Address: c/o Anglo Swiss Management, 4-5 Primrose Street, 1a Sharpleshall Street, London, NW1 8YW, England.

LEJET Edith, b. 19 July 1941, Paris, France. Composer; Professor. Education: Conservatoire National Superieur de Musique de Paris. Compositions: Monodrame, pour violon et orchestre, 1969; Journal D'Anne Frank, oratorio, 1970; Quatuor De saxophones, 1974; Harmonie Du Soir, 1977; Espaces Nocturnes, 1976; Gemeaux, 1978 and Balance, 1982, for guitar; Triptyque for organ, 1979; Volubilis for Violoncello, 1981; Aube Marine, 1982; L'Homme Qui Avait Perdu Sa Voix, Théâtre Musical, 1984; Ressac, 1986; Les Rois Mages, oratorio, 1989; 7 Chants Sacrés for female chorus and organ, 1990; Améthyste for 12 strings, 1990; Trois Eaux-Fortes, for piano, 1992; Trois Noëls, for children's chorus, 1994; Océan Pathétique, for 5 different instruments, 1994; Des Fleurs in Forme de Diamants, for guitar and 7 instruments, 1997. Publications: Pedagogic Books: La Precision Rythmique Dans la Musique 3 volumes. Honours: Numerous 1st Prizes at Paris Conservatory, Vocation Foundation, 1967; Grand Prix de Rome, 1968; Prix Florence Gould, 1970; Prix

Herve Dugardin, 1974; Grand Prix de la Musique de Chambre de la SACEM, 1979. Address: 11-13 rue Cino Del Duca, 75017 Paris, France.

LELIE Martinus Christoffel (Christo), b. 28 Dec 1956, Dordrecht, Netherlands. Writer on Music; Solo Concert Organist; Pianist. Education: Piano, 1982, Organ, 1984, Rotterdam Conservatory. Career: Organist, Musical Director, Reformed Churches, The Hague and Delft; Critic, Trouw newspaper; Pianist, Rotterdamse Dansacademie; Editor, EPTA Piano Bulletin and Franz Liszt Kring; Freelance Writer on music; Numerous organ recitals; Played Liszt organ works in Liszt Cycles, Rotterdam, 1990; Accompanist (piano, organ, harpsichord) in vocal, instrumental concerts and dance performances, Netherlands, Germany; Staff, Liszt Festivals, Utrecht, 1988, Amsterdam, 1990; Staff, Gina Bachauer Audition, Amsterdam, 1991; Lectures on Liszt, Scarlatti, Italian organs; BRT radio commentary on harpsichord and fortepiano, Bruges, Belgium, 1986. Compositions: Choral Preludes for organ; Roman Variations; Study 87, piano; Several religious works for choir; Renaissance Dances transcribed for organ; Fantasy in E minor, organ; Passacaglia, organ. Publications: 1685 Europa en de Muziek, Scarlatti, 1985; Liszt in Amsterdam, festival book, 1991; Van Piano tot Forte, history of the early piano, 1994.

LEMANN Jean (Juan), b. 7 Aug 1928, Vendôme, France. Composer; Pianist; Professor of Composition. m. Maria Luisa Herreros, 28 Sep 1957, 2 daughters. Education: BA, Mathematics, 1948; Architecture, Catholic University of Chile, 1948-50; Piano studies, 1942-54, Postgraduate, 1955-59, University of Chile, National Conservatory of Music; Composition at University of Chile, Catholic University of Chile, privately; Visiting Fulbright Scholar, Juilliard School of Music, NY, 1970-71. Career: Professor of Piano, Music Theory, Choral Conductor, Experimental School of Arts, 1957-61; Professor of Piano, Composition, 1961-91, Vice-Dean, 1981-82, Faculty of Arts, University of Chile; Adviser, cultural and artistic institutions; Pianist, Lecturer, Adjudicator, Composer and Professor of Composition at Faculty of Arts, University of Chile. Compositions include: Orchestral, chamber, choral, mime, theatre, ballet, and film music including Leyenda Del Mar; Sonata Para Arpa; El Cuerpo La Sangre; Variaciones Para Piano; Puentes (words, P Neruda); Eolica Para Cello Solo; Akustika for Recorder; Obertura de Concierto for orchestra, 1986; Maestranza de Noche for alto, violin, clarinet, cello and piano, 1987; Fantasia Concertante, piano and orchestra, 1988; Rapsodia for guitar, 1996; Viola da Gamba and Piano, 1992, Barrio Sin Luz for Soprano Voice and Piano, 1992; Recordings include: El Cuerpo Y La Sangre; Mass, Veni Domine; Ironias Musicales; Variaciones Para Piano; Tres Variables Para Piano; Leyenda Del Mar; Homenaje A Leng; Corranda De La Gacela; Aleluya; Ojitos De Pena. Contributions to: Anales de la Universidad de Chile; Revista Musical Chilena. Memberships: Academia Chilena de Bellas Artes; Sociedad Nacional de Compositores de Chile. Hobby: Photography. Address: Laura de Noves 460, Las Condes, Santiago, Chile.

LEMELIN Stéphane, b. 2 Apr 1960, Rimouski, Quebec, Canada. Pianist. Education: BM 1982, MM 1983, Peabody Conservatory, USA; Doctor of Musical Arts, Yale University, 1990. Career: Performed with orchestras across Canada and in the USA; Frequent CBC and NPR broadcasts; Recitals across Canada, in USA, France and UK; Piano Faculty, Yale University, USA, 1986-90 and University of Alberta, Canada, 1990-. Recordings: Schubert Sonata in A, D959; Schumann Waldszenen, Op 82, Fantasiestücke, Op 111, 1991; Complete Nocturnes by Fauré. Honours: Prizewinner, Casadesus International Competition, 1983. Current Management: Marie Rakos Concert Management. Address: RR #1, New Hamburg, Ontario N0B 2G0, Canada.

LENDVAY Kamillo, b. 28 Dec 1928, Budapest, Hungary. Composer; Professor and Head of Music Theory Department. m. 6 June 1972, 1 daughter. Education: Ferenc Liszt Academy of Music, Budapest, 1959. Career: Musical Leader, State Puppet Theatre, 1960-66; Musical Director, Artistic Ensemble, Hungarian People's Army, 1966-68; Conductor and Artistic Director, Operetta Theatre, Budapest; Musical Lector, Hungarian Radio, 1962-; Composer; Professor and Head of Music Theory Department, Ferenc Liszt Academy of Music, Budapest, 1973-; President, Artisjus, Bureau for Protecting Protecting Authors' Rights. Compositions include: Orogenesis, oratorio, 1969-70; Cantatas: Cart-Drive into the Night, 1970; Scenes from Thomas Mann's Joseph and His Brothers, 1978-81; Orchestral works: Mauthausen, symphonic poem, 1958; Four Invocations, 1966; The Harmony of Silence, 1980; Chaconne for Orchestra, 1988; Concertos: Concertino, 1959; Violin Concerto No 1, 1961-62; Pezzo Concerto, 1975; Violin Concerto No 2, 1986; Concerto semplice, 1986; Expressions for 11 strings, for chamber orchestra, 1974; Chamber music; Solo pieces; Several works for wind orchestra and choir; Music for films and stage; Stabat Mater. Recordings: Numerous. Honours: Erkel Musical Prize, 1962, 1964, 1978; Trieste Competition, 1975; Title of Merited Artist, 1981; Grand Prix Inernational du Disque Lyrique for opera The

Respectable Street-Walker, 1983; Bartók-Pasztory Prize, 1989. Membership: President, Association of the Hungarian Composers. Address: 1137 Szt Istvan Park 23, Budapest, Hungary.

LENHART Renate, b. 1942, Austria. Singer (Soprano). Education: Studied at the Vienna Conservatory. Career: Concert tour of South America, 1966-67; Subsequent engagement at Zürich Opera: roles there included Micaela, Marzelline in Fidelio, Mozart's Pamina and Zerlina, Constanza in Henze's Il Re Cervo, Julia Farnese in Ginaster's Bomarzo, Miranda in The Tempest by Frank Martin and Lisa in The Queen of Spades; Further roles at Zürich and as guest in Munich, Paris, Amsterdam and Vienna have included Alice Ford, Ludmilla, Glauce in Médée, Sophie and Frau Fluth in Die Lustigen Weiber von Windsor; Appearances in Monteverdi's Poppea and Ulisse at Bregenz and in the Jean-Pierre Ponnelle cycle at Zürich; Most frequently heard as Pamina, also sang First Lady in the Ponnelle production of Die Zauberflöte. Address: c/o Opernhaus Zürich, Flakenstrasse 1, CH-8008 Zürich, Switzerland.

LENTZ Daniel (Kirkland), b. 10 Mar 1942, Latrobe, PA, USA. Composer. m. Marlene Helen Wasco, 24 Aug 1964, 1 daughter. Education: BS, Music, St Vincent College, 1962; MFA, Ohio University, 1965; Brandeis University, 1965-67; Tanglewood, summer, 1966; Musicology, Stockholm University, Sweden, 1967-68. Career: Founder, Director of ensembles, California Time Machine, 1969-73, The San Andreas Fault, 1974 and 1976, The Daniel Lentz Ensemble, 1978-80, Lentz, 1983-85 and Daniel Lentz and Group, 1986-; 10 European tours and major/premiere performances: Gaudeamus Foundation, 1972, New Music America Festivals in 1983 and 1986, LA Olympic Arts Festival, 1984, Wild Turkeys at Carnegie Hall, 1986, The Crack In The Bell, LAPhil New Music Group, 1986. Compositions include: Canon And Fugle, 1971; Loverise, 1971; King Speech Song, 1972; Song(s) Of The Sirens, 1973; Missa Umbrarum, 1973; O-Ke-Wa, 1974; Sun Tropes, 1975; Requiem Songs, 1976; Three Pretty Madrigals, 1976; Composition In Contrary And Parallel Motion, 1977; Elysian Nymph, 1978; Wolf Is Dead, 1979, 1982; Uitoto, 1980; Music By Candlelight, 1980; Dancing On The Sun, 1980; Point Conception, 1981; Adieu, 1983; On The Leopold Altar, 1983; Lascaux, 1984; Is It Love, 1984; Bacchus, 1985; Topanga Tango, 1985; Time's Trick, 1985; Wild Turkeys, 1985; The Crack In The Bell, 1986. Recordings: Several. Address: Box 311, US Route 30, Latrobe, PA 15650, USA.

LEON Tania (Justina), b. 14 May 1943, Havana, Cuba. Composer. Education: Studied in Havana and at New York University. Career includes: Resident in USA from 1967 and creative association with the Dance Theatre of Harlem; Teacher at Brooklyn College, 1985-; Vice Chair, Board of Directors, 1994, Artistic Advisor, New Residencies Program, 1994, Meet the Composer; Professor, Brooklyn College Conservatory of Music, 1994; Visiting Lecturer, Harvard University, 1994; Revson Composer Fellow, New York Philharmonic, 1993-; Visiting Professor, Yale University, 1993; Artistic Adviser, Latin American Project, American Composers Orchestra, 1992; Numerous conducting engagements include: Savannah Symphony Orchestra, Georgia, 1996; Charlotte Symphony Orchestram North Carolina, 1996; Associate Conductor for The Voyage, Metropolitan Opera, 1996; Residencies include: Composer, Scripps College, Claremont, California, 1996. Compositions include: Ballets The Beloved (1972) and Bele (1981); Opera Scourge of Hyacinths, 1994; Kabiosile, piano concerto, 1988; Carabali (1991) and Indigena for orchestra; Son sonore for flute and guitar (1992) and other chamber music; Instrumental and vocal music, including Batey for vocal soloists and 2 percussion, 1989. Recordings: Momentum, piano solo; Indigena, chamber works by Tania León; Paisanos Semosi, Ana Maria Rosado; Batey, The Western Wind; De Orishas, The Western Wind. Publications: Momentum, for solo piano, 1986; Paisanos Semosi for solo guitar, 1986; Parajota Delate for mixed quintet, 1992; Ritual for solo piano, 1991. Honours include: NEH Recording Grant, 1992; Copland Fund for Music Recording Grant, 1993; BMW Music Theater Prize for best composition, Munich Biennale, 1994; NYSCA Commission Award, 1994; Meet the Composer/Reader's Digest Commission Award, 1995. Address: c/o ASCAP, ASCAP Building, One Lincoln Plaza, New York, NY 10023, USA.

LEONARD Lawrence, b. 22 Aug 1928, London, England. Conductor. m. (1) Josephine Duffey, 1 son, 1 daughter, (2) Katharina Wolpe, (3) Dr Rose Walker. Education: Royal Academy of Music, London; LRAM; L'Ecole Normale de Musique; Studied privately with Ansermet and Kleiber. Career: Assistant Conductor, BBC Northern Orchestra, 1 year; Assistant Conductor, Hallé Orchestra, 5 years; Music Director, Edmonton Symphony Orchestra, Canada, 5 years; Worldwide Freelance concerts. Compositions: 4 pieces for orchestra; Group Questions for orchestra; Symphonic Poem for orchestra; Mezoon (for the Sultan of Oman); Pictures From an Exhibition (Moussorgsky/Leonard); Various arrangements; Carnival of the Animals (Saint-Saëns/Leonard). Recordings: Francesca Da Rimini;

Sleeping Beauty Suite; Complete Harpsichord Concerti, Bach; Telemann Flute Suite; Pictures From an Exhibition. Publications: Horn of Mortal Danger; Pictures from an Exhibition. Honours: FRAM; FGSM. Memberships: Composers' Guild, Chairman, 1977. Hobbies: Chess. Address: Boxhurst, Old Reigate Road, Near Dorking, Surrey RH4 1NT, England.

LEONARD Lysiane, b. 1957, Belgium. Singer (Soprano). Education: Studied with Jules Bastin in Brussels, at the Juillard School and with Hans Hotter in Munich. Career: Has sung at the Liège Opera from 1982, notably as Fenena in Nabucco, Elvira (Rossini) Norina, Siebel (Faust), Frasquita (Carmen) and Liu; Guest appearances at Rouen in Les Indes Galantes, the Paris Opéra-Comique in La Belle Hélène and at Montpellier in Schumann's Faust (1985) concert repertory also includes Les Nuits d'été by Berlioz (Aix, 1983); Further concerts in music by Vivaldi, Bach, Handel, Haydn and Telemann. Address: c/o Opera Royale de Wallonie, 1 Rue des Dominicains, B-4000 Liège, Belgium.

LEONARD Sarah (Jane), b. 10 Apr 1953, Winchester, England. Singer (Soprano). m. Michael Parkinson, 5 Apr 1975, div., 1 son, 1 daughter. Education: Music Department, Winchester School of Art, 1969-71; GGSM Diploma, Guildhall School of Music and Drama, London, 1971-76. Career: Member, BBC Singers, 1976-81; Member, London Sinfonietta Voices; High Soprano; Broadcasts with BBC Singers, Endymion Ensemble and London Sinfonietta; Television appearances, Video Alice, Channel 4 TV, and The Middle of the Road Hour, Channel 4 TV; Sang the Mad Boy in Goehr's Sonata about Jerusalem, Aldeburgh Festival, 1990; Sings with Michael Nyman Band; Guest appearances with Hilliard Ensemble; Sang at La Scala, Milan, 1989 and 1992; International Soloist in 20th century repertoire; Sang in the premiere of Lachenmann's Das Mädchen, Hamburg, 1997. Recordings include: Drusilla in L'Incoronazione di Poppea; Miserere by Arvo Pärt with Hilliard Ensemble; My Heart is Like a Singing Bird, English Song Company. Honours: Susan Longfield Award, Guildhall School of Music and Drama, 1976; Winner, Young Artists and 20th Century Music, Park Lane Group, 1984. Membership: Incorporated Society of Musicians. Hobbies: Theatre; Swimming; Knitting; Sewing. Current Management: Allied Artists. Address: 42 Montpelier Square, London SW7 1JZ, England.

LEONHARDT Gustav, b. 30 May 1928, Graveland, The Netherlands. Harpsichordist; Organist; Conductor. Education: Schola Cantorum Basle, 1947-50, with Eduard Muller. Debut: Vienna in 1950 with Bach's The Art of Fugue on the harpsichord. Career: Professor of Harpsichord at Vienna Academy of Music, 1952-55; Teacher at Amsterdam Conservatory from 1954; Organist at Waalse Kerk, Amsterdam until 1981, since then organist at Nieuwe Kerk, Amsterdam; Founded Leonhardt Consort in 1955; Played the organ and harpsichord and acted the part of JS Bach in a 1967 film, The Chronicle Of Anna Magdalena Bach; Visiting Professor at Harvard University, 1969-70; Work as conductor includes Monteverdi's L'Incoronazione di Poppea, Amsterdam in 1972; Extensive tours of USA and Europe as harpsichordist, notably in the works of Bach, Frescobaldi, Sweelinck, Froberger and Louis Couperin. Recordings: About 150 including Bach's Goldberg Variations, as harpsichordist. Publications: Editions of The Art of Fugue, 1952 and keyboard music by Sweelinck for the Dutch Critical Edition. Honours: Erasmus Prize, 1980; Honorary Doctorates, 1982, 1983 and 1991. Address: Music Conservatory, Amsterdam, Netherlands.

LEOSON Markus, b. Linköping, Sweden. Solo Percussionist; Solo Timpanist. Education: Royal Conservatory of Music, Stockholm. Debut: Stockholm Concert Hall, Apr 1995. Career: Live radio concert, Stockholm and Reykjavik, Iceland, 1995; Artist in Residence, Swedish Radio, 1996, also solo concerts, Norrtelje Festival, Stockholm, Linköping with wind orchestra; Soloist with Tampere Philharmonic Orchestra; Portrait in TV programme NIKE, Copenhagen; Solo concert, Gothenburg; Solo, Stockholm, 1997, also soloist with Swedish Radio Symphony Orchestra, Kalmar; 1998 engagements with Gothenburg Symphony Orchestra, Helsingborg Symphony Orchestra, St Petersburg, Braunschweig; Solo Timpanist with Royal Opera Orchestra, Stockholm. Recordings: Markus Leoson, Percussion; Numerous for Swedish Radio P2 as Artist in Residence, 1996-97. Honours: 1st Prize as Soloist, Sweden, 1995; 2nd Prize, Nordic Soloist Competition, 1995; 2nd Prize, ARD, Munich, 1997; 1st Prize, EBU IFYP Competition, Bratislava, 1997. Membership: Percussion Creative, Germany. Hobby: Cimbalo playing. Address: Rosenlundsgatan 20, S-11853 Stockholm, Sweden.

LEPORE Paolo, b. 1958, Italy. Conductor. Education: Studied at the Bari Conservatoire and with Gabriele Ferro and Franco Ferrara. Career: Artistic Director of the Orchestra di Bari, 1985-94; Orchestra Sinfonica Siciliana from 1985; Artistic Director of the Orchestra Sinfonica di Bari from 1994; Guest appearances in France, Hungary, Mexico and Italy. Hobbies: Historical conservation; Cuisine Cooking; Horse Riding. Address: c/o

Worldwide Artists, 6 Petersfield Crescent, Coulsdon, Surrey CR5 2JQ.

LEPPARD Raymond (John), b. 11 August 1927, London, England. Conductor; Harpsichordist; Composer. Education: Trinity College, Cambridge. Career: Fellow, Trinity College, University Lecturer in Music, 1958-68; Honorary Keeper of the Music, Fitzwilliam Museum, Cambridge, 1963; Conductor, Covent Garden (debut 1959, Handel's Solomon), Sadler's Wells, Glyndebourne, (debut 1964, L'Incoronazione di Poppea); Various overseas orchestras; Principal Conductor, BBC Northern Symphony Orchestra, 1972-80; Principal Guest Conductor, St Louis Symphony Orchestra, 1984-; Music Director, Indianapolis Symphony Orchestra, 1987; London Proms, 1993, with Tchaikovsky's Second Symphony and Ravel's Shéhérazade. Publications: Realisations of Monteverdi: Il Ballo delle Ingrate, 1958; L'Incoronazione di Poppea, 1962; L'Orfeo, 1965; Il Ritorno d'Ulisse, 1972; Realisations of Francesco Cavalli: Messa Concertata, 1966; L'Ormindo, 1967; La Calisto, 1969; Magnificat, 1970; L'Egisto, 1974; L'Orione, 1983; Realisation of Rameau's Dardanus, 1980; British Academy Italian Lecture, 1969 (Proceedings, Royal Musical Association); Raymond Leppard on Music, 1993. Honours: Commendatore al Merito della Repulica Italiana, 1974; Commander, Order of British Empire (CBE), 1983. Hobbies: Music; Theatre; Books; Friends. Address: c/o Colbert Artists Management, 111 West 57th Street, NY 10019, USA.

LEPRINCE Franck, b. 7 May 1957, Dover, England. Violinist. Education: Poole College, Dorset; Dortmund University, Germany; Trinity College, London; Frankfurt Conservatoire; Royal Military School of Music. Debut: British Embassy, Paris, 1979. Career: Leader, HM Royal Artillery Orchestra, Germany, 1980-93; Leader, Army Air Corps Orchestra, 1993-; Various Television appearances and session work; Radio broadcasts; South Coast Opera; Member, The Lutz Quartet, Germany; Shows for Roger Whittaker, Nigel Kennedy, Rosalind Plowright, Horst Jankowski, Moira Anderson, Harry Secombe, Eve Boswell. Contributions to: Journal into Melody. Memberships: Incorporated Society of Musicians; P@mra. Hobbies: Equine Sports; Fine Arts. Current Management: A Rosenfeld, Glissando Music, C A Music. Address: 12 Portarlington Court, 15 Portarlington Road, Westbourne, Bournemouth, Dorset BH4 8BU, England.

LERDAHL Fred, b. 10 Mar 1943, Madison, WI, USA. Composer; Music Theorist. m. 29 Nov 1980, 3 daughters. Education: BMus, Lawrence University, 1965; MFA, Princeton University, 1967. Career: Professor of Music at University of California at Berkeley, 1969-71, Harvard University, 1971-79, Columbia University, 1979-85, and University of Michigan, 1985-; Residency at IRCAM, 1981 and at American Academy in Rome, 1987; Works commissioned by the Fromm Music Foundation, the Koussevitzky Music Foundation, the Juilliard Quartet, the Pro Arte Quartet and the Spoleto Festival. Compositions: String trio, 1966; Wake for Soprano and Chamber Ensemble, 1968; Chords for Orchestra, 1974-83; Eros for Mezzo-Soprano and Chamber Ensemble, 1975; First String Quartet, 1978; Waltzes for Chamber Ensemble, 1981; Second String Quartet, 1982; Beyond The Realm Of Bird for Soprano and Chamber Orchestra, 1984; Fantasy Etudes for Chamber Ensemble, 1985; Cross-Currents for Orchestra, 1987; Waves for Chamber Orchestra, 1988. Recordings: Fantasy Etudes; First String Quartet; Second String Quartet; Eros; String Trio. Publication: Co-Author, A Generative Theory of Tonal Music, 1983. Current Management: Musical Associates of America. Address: 1210 West Liberty Street, Ann Arbor, MI 48103, USA.

LERNER Mimi, b. 1954, Poland. Mezzo-Soprano. Education: Studied at Queen's College, New York and Carnegie-Mellon University. Debut: New York City Opera as Sextus in La Clemenza di Tito, 1979. Career: Sang at various American opera houses and at Glyndebourne in 1984 as Marcellina in Le nozze di Figaro; La Scala in 1985 as Alcina, Théâtre Châtelet Paris in 1986 as Isabella in L'Italiana in Algeri, and at Amsterdam in 1987 as Eboli in Don Carlos; Sang with New Orleans Opera Association, 1989-90 as Amneris and Adalgisa; Sang Ruggiero in Alcina at Vancouver in 1990, Rosina at Pittsburgh and Despina at Toronto in 1991; Santa Fe Festival in 1991 as Carlotta in Die schweigsame Frau; Sang Marcellina in Figaro at Orchestra Hall, Chicago, 1992; Other roles include Smeton in Anna Bolena, Suzuki, Siebel and Cenerentola. Recordings include: Second Lady in a video of Die Zauberflöte, from the Metropolitan. Address: c/o New Orleans Opera Association, 333 St Charles Avenue, Suite 907, New Orleans, LA 70130, USA.

LESNA Martina, b. 12 June 1969, Piestany, Slovakia. Musician (Flute and Baroque Flute). Education: Bratislava Conservatory; Academy of Music in Bratislava, Slovakia; Conservatoire Nationale Superieur de Musique de Paris (First Prize, 1996). Career: Member of chamber orchestra, Musica Aeterna, Bratislava, 1987-; Soloist of Musica Aeterna, 1996; Participated in Samedis Musiqaux Versailles, 1988; Oude Muziek Festival, Utrecht, 1993; Bach's Tage, Berlin, 1995. Recordings: Played flute in Muscia Aeterna (chamber orchestra) in Bratislava, Capella Saravia (Hungary), Musica Florea (Prague). Honour: Prize in radio competition, Concerto Praga, Czech Republic, 1986. Membership: Gustav Mahler Youth Orchestra (Claudio Abbado), 1987. Hobbies: Laguages; Sports. Address: Jelacicova 3, 821 08 Bratislava, Slovakia.

LESOVICHENKO Andrey, b. 20 Sept 1960, Caluga, Russia. Musicologist. m. Fall Geleua, 11 July 1987, 2 daughters. Education: Musical College, Theory Department, 1979; Musicologists Faculty, Musical academy, Novosibirsk, 1984; Postgraduate, Moscow Conservatory. Career: Candidate of Arts Sciences, Moscow Conservatory, 1992; Professor of History of Music, High School Committee, Moscow, 1995; Professor of History of Music, Novosibirsk Conservatory, 1990-. Publications: The Questions of Development Between Cult Arts and Ideology of Middle Ages, 1990; Western Musical Tradition and Medieval Religion Cognition, 1992; Periphery in Culture, 1994. Contributions to: Musical Review, Moscow; Tuporurations of All-Russian Musical Society, Moscow; Music, Kijev. Honours: Laureate of All-Union (USSR) Competition of Musicologists-lectors, Moscow, 1989. Memberships: All-Russian Musical Society; All-Russian Society Knowledge. Hobbies: History of philosophy; Singing medieval songs. Address: 630081 Partizanskaya 35-1, fl 7, Novosibirsk, Russia.

LESSARD John (Ayres), b. 3 July 1920, San Francisco, California, USA. Composer; Professor Emeritus. m. Sarah Fuller, 12 June 1973, 6 daughters. Education: Piano with Elise Belenky; Composition with Henry Cowell, Ernst Levy, Nadia Boulanger; Diploma, Harmonie, Contrepoint, Fugue, Ecole Normale de Musique, Paris, 1938-39; Diploma, Composition, Longy School of Music, Cambridge, Massachusetts, 1940. Compositions Include: Ariel, 1939; Sonata for Piano, 1940; Box Hill Overture (Orchestra), 1946; Full Fathom Five, 1948; When as in Silk My Julia Goes, 1951; Octet for Wind Instruments, 1952; Sonata for Cello and Piano, 1956; Rose Cheek Laura, 1960; Sinfonietta Concertante (Orchestra), 1961; Epithalamion, 1962; Concerto for Harp and Orchestra, 1963; 12 Songs from Mother Goose, 1964; Trio in Sei Parti; Fragments from the Cantos of Ezra Pound for Baritone and 9 Instruments, 1969; Brass Quintet, 1971; Pastimes and an Alleluia (Orchestra), 1974; Movements for Trumpet and Various Instruments I-VIII, 1976-84; Threads of Sound Recalled, 1980; Concert Duo for Viola and Guitar, 1981; Divertimento for Solo Guitar, 1981; Music for Guitar and Percussion, 1982; Stars, Hill, Valley, Song, 1983; Duet for Piano and Percussion, 1984; Pond In A Bowl (Soprano, Percussion, Piano), 1984; Four Pieces for Viola and Percussion, 1985; Album for Guitar, 1986; Bagatelles for Piano I, II, III, IV, 1986-91; Drift, Follow, Persits (Solo Horn, Piano, Percussion), 1988; An Assembled Sequence for a Solo Percussionist, 1989; The Seasons (Soprano, 2 Percussionists), Piano, 1992. Current Management: American Composers Alliance. Address: 15 Scotts Cove Lane, East Setauket, New York, NY 11733, USA.

LESSER David Thomas, b. 15 Jan 1966, Birmingham, England. Composer; Lecturer; Pianist. m. Clare Ward. Education: Royal College of Music, London, 1985; Huddersfield University, 1991-93. Debut: St Pauls, Birmingham, 1986. Career: Concert Performances, 1986-; Lecturer, University of Warwick, 1994. Compositions: Scape, Solo, 1986; Orkney Aphorisms, 1993; Tränen.., 1994; Snare, 1994; O ignis spiritus, 1997. Memberships: PRS, 1993; ISM, 1993. Hobbies: Reading; Films. Address: 351 Station Road, Dorridge, Solihull, West Midlands B93 8EY, England.

LESSER Laurence, b. 28 Oct 1938, Los Angeles, California, USA. Cellist. m. Masuko Ushioda, 23 Dec 1971, 1 son, 1 daughter. Education: BA, Harvard University, 1961; Fulbright Scholar, Cologne, with Gaspar Cassadò; Studied with Gregor Piatigorsky in Los Angeles. Career: Concert performances in USA, Europe, Japan and South America; Appearances with Boston Symphony, Los Angeles Philharmonic, London Philharmonic and other major orchestras; Assistant to Piatigorsky, University of Southern California, Los Angeles; Teacher at Peabody Institute, Baltimore; Visiting Professor at Toho School of Music, Tokyo; Teacher, appointed President, 1983, New England Conservatory, Boston, Massachusetts, retired 1996; Full-time Cello and Chamber Music Faculty, NEC. Recordings: Schoenberg/Monn Concerto; Lazarof Concerto; Chamber Music in Heifetz- Piatigorsky Series. Honours: Cassadó Prize, Siena, Italy, 1962; 4th Prize, Tchaikovsky Competition, Moscow, 1966. Memberships: Overseer, Boston Symphony Orchestra; Trustee, WGBH Educational Foundation, Boston; Advisory Council, Chamber Music America; Phi Beta Kappa. Address: New England Conservatory, 290 Huntington Avenue, Boston, MA 02115, USA.

LESSING Kolja, b. 15 Oct 1961, Karlsruhe, Germany. Violinist; Pianist; Composer. Education: Violin lessons, 1964-, piano, 1966-, with mother; Violin studies, Hansheinz Schneeberger masterclasses, Diploma with Distinction, 1982, Basel, Switzerland, 1978-; Piano studies with Peter Efler, Diploma, 1983, Basel, 1979-83. Debut: Violin recital at Ettlingen Castle in 1981; Piano, Lausanne in 1982. Career: Concerts throughout Europe; Solo violin recitals and chamber music concerts; Orchestral concerts with Dresdner Philharmonic, Nationaltheaterorchester Mannheim, Radio Sinfonieorchester Basel and others; Several premieres and numerous recitals, violin solo and piano solo with thematic programmes; Founder Member with Rainer Klaas and Bernhard Schwarz, Trio Alkan, 1988-; Professor, Musikhochschule Wurzburg, 1989-. Compositions: Mostly recorded, German and Swiss Radio Stations; Various works for solo violin, solo clarinet, 2 clarinets and violin, 1978-. Recordings include: Works by Franz Berwald, Walther Geiser, Karl Michael Komma, Isang Yun; Numerous radio recordings, some first recordings, extensive repertoire in Germany, Switzerland and Sweden; Playback recording of Fauré's 2nd Sonata for Violin and Piano, 1989.

LESTER Richard, b. 1959, England. Cellist. Education: Studies at the Royal College of Music with Ameryllis Fleming. Career: Member of Domus from 1979; Performances in a portable white geodesic dome on informal locations in Europe and Australia; Public workshops, discussion groups and open rehearsals in a wide repertoire; Frequent performances in London at the Wigmore Hall and on the South Bank, throughout the UK and on Radio 3; Festival engagements at Bath, Cheltenham, Salisbury, Sheffield and the City of London; Tours of South America, Canada, Spain, Italy, Germany, Ireland and Norway; 1991 tours of the Netherlands and New Zealand; Solo concerts and recitals throughout Britain and tours of Europe, Japan and the Middle East; Concerto performances with the Chamber Orchestra of Europe at Carnegie Hall and in Berlin and Vienna; Salzburg Camerata Academica in Austria, Germany and Italy under Sandor Vegh. Recordings include: Piano Quartets by Fauré, Dvorák, Brahms, Mozart and Mendelssohn; Schubert's Trout Quintet and Adagio and Rondo Concertante with pianist, Chi-Chi Nwanoku; Works by Martinu, Suk, Kodály and Dohnányi; Complete cello repertoire of Mendelssohn. Honours include: Deutsche Schallplattenpreis, 1986 and Gramophone Magazine Award for Best Chamber Music Record of 1986 for Fauré Piano Quartets; Prizewinner at International Scheveninges Cello Competition, 1987. Address: Unit 2, Tadema Road, London, SW10 0PY, England.

LESURE François, b. 23 May 1923, Paris, France. Musicologist. m. Anik Devriès, 26 Jan 1987. Education: Archiviste-paléographe, Ecole des Chartes; Licencié-es-Lettres, Sorbonne; Conservatoire de Paris. Career: Director, Department of Music, Bibliothèque Nationale, 1950-88; Directeur d'études a l'Ecole des Hautes Etudes, depuis 1970; Professor, Brussels University, 1965-77; Chargé du Musée de la musique de La Villette, 1989-91. Publications: Music and art in Society, 1968; Musique et musiciens francais du XVIe siècle, 1977; Catalogue de l'oeuvre de C Debussy, 1977; Editor des Chansons polyphoniques de C Janequin, 6 volumes, et Rédacteur en chef des Oeuvres complètes de C Debussy, 6 volumes published since 1986; Claude Debussy, Biographie critique, 1994. Contributions to: Number of articles in Revue de musicologie; Cahiers Debussy; Fontes artis musicae; Annales musicologiques. Honour: Légion d'honneur, Arts et Lettres, Mérite. Memberships: American Academy of Arts and Sciences; Académie royale de Belgique; Président, 1971, 1988, Société francaise de musicologie. Address: 66 Rue d'Assas, 75006 Paris, France.

LETHIEC Michel, b. 11 Dec 1946, Poitiers, France. Clarinettist. Education: Studied in Bordeaux and at the Paris Conservatoire. Career: Concerto engagements with the Monte Carlo Philharmonic, Radio France Philharmonic, Ensemble Orchestre de Paris and the Lausanne Chamber Orchestra; British appearances with the English Chamber Orchestra, Academy of St Martin in the Fields and the Scottish Ensemble; Recitals and chamber concerts with Leonard Rose, Aurèle Nicolet, Karl Engel, Joseph Suk, Elly Ameling, Philippe Entremont and the Talich, Vermeer, Takacs and Sibelius Quartets; Has premiered works by Ballif, Boucourechliev, Marco, Corigliano and Scolari; Festival engagements include Edinburgh and the Eastern Music Festival, USA; Concert repertoire includes music by Copland, Crusell, Hindemith, Krommer, Mercadante, Mozart, Pleyel, Spohr, Stamitz and Weber; Boulez Domaines and Busoni Concertino; Double Concertos by Bruch with viola, Strauss with bassoon, Danzi with flute and Devienne with clarinet; With string quartets plays works by Mozart, Brahms, Weber, Reger, Reicha, Hindemith, Birtwistle, Yun and Bloch; Director of the Pau Casals Festival in Prades. Honours include: Interpretation Prize at the International Competition in Belgrade; Grand Prix du Disque, 1978 for Asceses by Jolivet; Chevalier de L'Ordre National du Merite, Professeur an Conservatoire de Paris. Address: Les Templiers, 06790 Aspremont, France.

LETTVIN Theodore, b. 29 Oct 1926, Chicago, Illinois, USA. Concert Pianist. m. Joan Rorimer, 2 sons, 1 daughter. Education: MusB, Curtis Institute of Music. Debut: Ravinia Festival, 1951. Career: First appearance as concert pianist in 1931; Appeared with Chicago Symphony Orchestra, 1938; Solo orchestral engagements at Gallery Art, Washington, Philadelphia, Pops

Orchestra, Saratoga Springs, Tanglewood, Grant Park Symphony and Florida orchestras among others, 1938-64; Radio appearance, Bell Telephone Hour in 1948; Apprentice to conductor, William Steinberg, Buffalo Symphony Orchestra, 1951; Concert Artist, National Music League, Europe and North Africa and at other concerts in France, Corsica, Tunisia, Algeria, Switzerland, Belgium and Germany, 1952; Artist in Residence at University of Colorado, 1956; Head of Piano Department, Cleveland Music School Settlement, 1958-68; Professor of Music, New England Conservatory of Music, Boston, 1968; Assistant Artist, Marlboro Music Festival, 1963; New York Philharmonic Promenade Concerts, 1970, 1972; American Pianist Olympics, 1972; Performed at Salzburg Festival in 1974, also at Chautauqua and Ravinia Festivals; Appeared with New York, Cleveland, Minneapolis, Boston, Atlanta, Pittsburgh and Cincinnati Orchestras; Town Hall Concerts in New York City; Professor of Piano at University of Michigan, Ann Arbor, 1977-87; Director of Doctoral Programme in Performance, The Music Department, Rutgers, State University of New Jersey, 1987-92, Teacher of Piano and Chamber Music, 1992-. Address: 12 Bernard Road, East Brunswick, NJ 08816, USA.

LEUCHTMANN Horst, b. 26 Apr 1927, Brunswick, Germany. Musicologist. m. Brita-Angela von Wentzel, 28 Nov 1952, 1 son, 2 daughters. Education: PhD, State Music School, Brunswick, University of Munich, 1957; Honorary Professor, Musikhochschule Munich, 1986. Career: Editor, Musikhistorische Kommission, Bayerische Akademie der Wissenschaften; Lecturer, University of Munich and Musikhochschule Munich; Ordentliches Mitglied der Bayerischen Akademie der Schönen Kunst, 1989. Publications: Editor, Complete Works of Orlando di Lasso; Editor, Musik in Bayern; Books; Editions; Dictionaries; Translations. Honours: Award, Bayerische Club, Munich, 1979; Festschrift, 1993; Award, Bayerische Akademie der Wissenschafteu, 1995; Order of Merit, Federal Republic of Germany, 1996. Membership: Der Bayerische Club. Address: Markgrafenstrasse 50, D-81827 Münich 82, Germany.

LEVAILLANT Denis, b. 3 Aug 1952, Paris, France. Pianist; Composer; Musical Director. m. Christine Rigaud, 21 Oct 1972, 1 son, 1 daughter. Education: MPhil, 1973; Piano studies since age of 5 years and composition studies since age of 12 years at Nancy, France; Advanced study at Paris, France. Debut: As pianist in concert in 1969; First composition recorded, Radio France, 1975. Career: Many occupations as producer and artistic director. Compositions: 60 including Le Baigneur, opéra-bouffe, 1976; Piano Transit, for piano and tape, 1983; Les Pierres Noires, for chamber choir, 1984; OPA MIA, opera, 1987-89; Les Couleurs de la Parole, for orchestra, 1990-91; Tombeau de Gesualdo, for chamber choir, 1993-95; Echo de Narcisse, concerto for piano and orchestra, 1995-96; Le Clair l'Obscur, string quartet #2, 1996-97. Recordings: 12 CDs. Publications: L'Improvisation Musicale, 1981; Le Piano, 1986. Contributions to: Le Monde de la Musique, 1981-1983. Honours: Villa Medicis, 1983; Prix Italia, 1988. Memberships: SACEM; SACD; SPEDIDAM; ADAMI. Hobbies: Sports de Montagne. Current Management: Bleu 17. Address: Bleu 17, 21 Paris-Forêt, 77760 Achères La Forêt, France.

LEVARIE Siegmund, b. 24 July 1914, Austria. Musician; Educator; Author; Conductor. m. Norma Levarie, 26 Mar 1945, 1 daughter. Education: Conductor's Diploma, New Vienna Conservatory, 1935; PhD, University of Vienna, 1938. Career: Faculty, Founder of Collegium Musicum, Conductor, Director of Concerts, University of Chicago, USA, 1938-52; Dean, Chicago Music College, 1952-54; Executive Director, Fromm Music Foundation, 1952-56; Chairman, Music Department, 1954-62, Professor of Music, 1954-84, Brooklyn College; Professor of Music, Graduate School, City University of New York, 1963-90; Visiting Professor, University of Pisa, Italy, 1984, 1991; Scuola Normale Superiore, Pisa, 1990, 1991. Publications: Mozart's Le nozze di Figaro, 1952, reprint, 1977; Fundamentals of Harmony, 1954, reprint, 1962, 1984; Guillaume de Machaut, 1954, reprint, 1970; Musical Italy Revisited, 1963, reprint, 1973; Tone, co-author Ernst Levy, 1968, 2nd edition, 1980, reprint, 1981; Musical Morphology, 1983; Editor, Lucy Van-Jung Page, 1977; About 80 articles and reviews, also translations. Membership: American Musicological Society, National Council for 6 years. Address: 624 Third Street, Brooklyn, NY 11215, USA.

LEVCHENKO Grigory (Semenovich), b. 12 Aug 1933, Poltava, Ukraine. Choir Master; Professor. m. Dorogan Ganna Ivanovna, 12 Mar 1981, 1 daughter. Education: High Trade Union School of Culture, Leningrad, 1963-68; Poltava Music College, 1956-60. Debut: Poltava, Philharmonic Society Concert Hall, conducted a choir during the final examination in Music College, 1960. Career: Kiev Palace of Culture, 1982, 1983; Drama Theatre in Velikotyrnovo, Bulgaria, 1984; St Maria Cathedral, St Mariekirchen, 1990; Wiener Konzerthaus Grosser Saal, 1991; Festival Wiener Musiksommer szene Rathaus; Cathedral "Herz Jezu", Zingen, Germany, 1992; Bolshoi Theater, Moscow, 1993; Philharmonic Society Concert Hall of Leuven, Belgium, and the Theatre de Beausobre Morges, Switzerland, 1994; Film, Meeting Spring, Ukrtelefilm, Kiev, 1988; Film, Choeurs en Balade, Lausanne, Une coproduction de la Television Suisse Romande (TSR) 1995. Compositions: 13 original choir compositions; 31 arrangements of Ukrainian People's Songs; 25 Concert Programmes. Recordings: Colours of Poltavschina, 1987; Ukrainian Voices, 1993; Ukrainian Voices Kalena, 1995. Publications: Selection of Songs, 1985, 1986; Conduction of a Choir, 1995. Honours: Honoured Arts Worker of Ukraine; Prize Winner of Republican, 1992 and Regional 1981 Festivals. Membership: Ukrainian Music Union. Hobby: Gardening. Address: Artema St 13, Apt 23, Poltava 314014, Ukraine.

LEVI Yoel, b. 16 Aug 1950, Stomar, Rumania. Naturalised US Citizen, 1987. Conductor. m. Jacqueline Levi, 3 sons. Education: MA, Violin and Percussion, University of Tel Aviv, Israel, 1975; Graduate degree, Jerusalem Academy of Music, 1976; Diploma, Guildhall School of Music and Drama, London, 1978; Studied with Mendi Rodao, Franco Ferrara, Siena, and Kirill Kondrashin, Hilversum; Accademia di Santa Cecilia, Rome. Career: Percussionist, Israel Philharmonic Orchestra, 1975; Conducting Assistant, 1978-80; Resident Conductor, 1980-84, Cleveland Orchestra, USA; Music Director and Conductor, Atlanta Symphony Orchestra, 1988-; Guest Conductor with major North American and European orchestras; Season 1997 with the Yomiuri Nippon Symphony Orchestra, Tokyo and KBS Symphony, Korea; La Faneiulla del West at Florence; Director of the Israel Festival, 1997, 1998. Recordings: For several labels. Honours: 1st Prize, Conductors' International Competition, Besançon, France, 1978. Address: c/o Atlanta Symphony Orchestra, 1280 Peachtree Street NE, Atlanta, GA 30306, USA.

LEVI MINZI Carlo, b. 10 Dec 1954, Milan, Italy. Pianist. Education: Giuseppe Verdi Conservatory, Milan; Piano Diploma, 1974; Piano Certificate, Tchaikovsky Conservatory, Moscow, 1975 and from Curtis Institute of Music, Philadelphia, 1978. Career: Recitals and appearances with various orchestras in Europe and USA, 1972-; TV and Radio appearances on national stations in Italy, Switzerland, France, Spain, Austria, Germany, Poland, Bulgaria, USA and Mexico. Compositions: Completion Of Schubert's F Sharp Minor Sonata, 1983, with Quirino Principe; First Performance, Town Hall, NY, 1984; First Radio Recording, WDR, Koln, 1985. Recordings: Several. Contributions to: Various journals. Membership: Vice President, Classical Frontiers, NY, USA.

LEVIN Robert D, b. 13 Oct 1947, Brooklyn, New York, USA. Pianist; Musicologist; Theorist. m. (1) Christine Noël Whittlesey, 18 May 1974, div. 1991, (2) Ya-Fei Chuang, 30 July 1995. Education: AB magna cum laude with highest honours, Music, Harvard University, 1968; Private studies with Nadia Boulanger, 1960-64; Conducting with Hans Swarowsky, 1966. Career: Solo and chamber appearances throughout Europe, USA and Japan, 1970-; Pianist, New York Philomusica, 1971-. Compositions: Mozart Completions: Requiem, Concerto for piano, violin, orchestra in D; Quintet for clarinet and strings in B flat; Symphonie concertante for flute, oboe, horn, bassoon and orchestra in E flat; Larghetto and Allegro in E flat for 2 pianos; Oboe concerto in F (all published, 4 latter works recorded); Horn Concertos in E flat and in D; Sonata Movement in G. Recordings: Mozart Sonatas for piano 4 hands, with Malcolm Bilson; Music for 2 pianos, with Malcolm Bilson; Hindemith, Complete Viola/Piano Sonatas, with Kim Kashkashian; Beethoven Piano Concertos with Orr and John Eliot Gardiner; Mozart Concertos, with AAM and Christopher Hogwood; Many others. Publications: Who Wrote the Mozart Four Wind Concertante?, 1988; Sightsinging and Ear Training Through Literature (with Louis Martin), 1988; Other texts in harmony and counterpoint published privately. Contributions to: Mozart-Jahrbuch; Early Music; Various musicological congress reports; Performance Practice, The New Grove; The Mozart Compendium; Eighteenth Century Keyboard Music. Honours: Grant in Composition, Copley Foundation, 1961; Prize, Lili Boulanger Fund, 1966, 1971. Memberships include: Internationale Stiftung Mozarteum; Neue Bachgesellschaft; GEMA. Hobbies: Trams and electric traction; Hiking. Current Management: ARTRA, Chicago, USA. Address: Music Department, Harvard University, Cambridge, MA 02138, USA.

LEVIN Walter, b. 6 Dec 1924, Berlin, Germany. Violinist; College Professor. Education: Studied at the Juilliard School with Ivan Galamian. Career: Co-founded the La Salle String Quartet at the Juilliard School, 1949, with many concerts featuring modern composers and the quartets of Beethoven, and with European debut in 1954; Composers who have written for the ensemble include Hans Erich Apostel, Earle Brown, Henri Pousseur, Mauricio Kagel, György Ligeti, Penderecki and Witold Lutoslawski; Quartet in Residence at Colorado College, 1949-53, then at the Cincinnati College, Conservatory of Music (also Professor there); Quartet disbanded in 1988. Recordings include: Works by Berg, Schoenberg, Webern and Zemlinsky; Beethoven's Late Quartets.

LEVINE Gilbert, b. 22 January 1948, New York City, USA. Conductor. Education: Reed College, 1965-67; Juilliard School of Music, 1967-68; Studied music history with Arthur Mendel and Louis Lockwood; Conducting with Jacques-Louis Monod; Music Theory with Milton Babbitt and J K Randall; AB, Princeton University, 1971; MA, Music Theory, Yale University, 1972; Conducting with Franco Ferrara, Siena. Debut: Nouvel Orchestre Philharmonique de Radio France, Paris, 1973. Career: Guest Conductor with various major North American and European Orchestras including: North German Radio Symphony Orchestra, Hamburg, 1977; Royal Philharmonic Orchestra, London, 1978; (West) Berlin Radio Symphony Orchestra, 1980; Minnesota Orchestra, 1984; Toronto Symphony; New York Philharmonic Orchestra; Dresden State Orchestra; San Francisco Symphony; Philadelphia Orchestra, 1986; Music Director, Karkow Philharmonic Orchestra, 1987-. Address: 1 Gracie Terrace, Apt 2F, New York, NY 10028-7956, USA.

LEVINE James, b. 23 June 1943, Cincinnati, Ohio, USA. Conductor; Pianist. Education: Piano with Rosina Lhevinne, Rudolf Serkin; Conducting with Jean Morel, Fausto Cleva, Max Rudolf; Style and Interpretation with Walter Levin; Vocal Repertoire with Jennie Tourel, Pierre Bernac, Hans Hotter, Martial Singher, Mack Harrell; Student, the Juilliard School, 1961-64. Career: Piano Debut 1953 with Cincinnati Symphony; Conducting Debut 1961 at Aspen Festival; Cleveland Orchestra, Assistant Conductor to George Szell, 1964-70; Metropolitan Opera, Principal Conductor, 1974-, Music Director, 1976-, Artistic Director, 1986-; Ravinia Festival (summer home of Chicago Symphony Orchestra), Musical Director, 1973-93; Cincinnati May Festival, Music Director, 1973-77; Frequent Guest both as Conductor and Pianist throughout US and Europe including Vienna Philharmonic, Berlin Philharmonic, Chicago Symphony; Conducted Metropolitan Opera Premieres of Verdi's I Vespri Siciliani, Stiffelio, I Lombardi, Weill's The Rise and Fall of the City of Mahagonny, Stravinsky's Oedipus Rex, Berg's Lulu, Mozart's Idomeneo and La Clemenza di Tito, Gershwin's Porgy and Bess, Schoenberg's Erwartung; Inaugurated the Live from the Met TV Series for PBS; Conducted the first complete cycles of Wagner's Ring at the Met in 50 years (Spring 1989); Salzburg Festival Premieres of Offenbach's Les Contes d'Hoffman (1980) and Schoenberg's Moses und Aron (1987); Centennial production of Parsifal at the Bayreuth Festival, 1982-88; World Premiere of The Ghosts of Versailles (Corigliano), 1991; Ring cycle at the Met, 1997. Recordings include: Since 1973 over 100 albums of symphonic works, chamber music, Lieder and song recitals and solo piano music as well as 3 dozen complete operas. Honours: Hon Dr, University of Cincinnati; First Recipient of the Cultural Award of the City of New York; Musical America's Musician of the Year Award; Nine-Time Grammy Award Winner; Hon Dr, New England Conservatory, 1992, Northwestern University, 1992. Address: c/o Ronald Wilford, Columbia Artists Management Inc, 165 West 57th Street, NY 10019, USA.

LEVINSKY Ilya, b. 1965, Baku, Russia. Singer (Tenor). Education: Studied at the Baku Academy of Music, until 1989. Career: Soloist with the Baku Opera, from 1987; Israel Philharmonic summer opera, from 1991; Member of the Komische Opera Berlin with leading roles in Falstaff, La Traviata, Don Giovanni, Così fan Tutte and Die Zauberflöte, until 1998; Season 1996-97 as Dimitri in Boris Gudunov with the Frankfurt Opera, in The Nose by Shostakovich for Netherlands Opera and as Sinodal in Rubinstrin's The Demon at the Bregenz Festival; Season 1997-98 as Tamino at Frankfurt, Dimitri at Toulouse and Sinodal at the Vienna Konzerthaus; Concerts with the Gothenburg Symphony (Skriabin 1), Cologne WDR Orchestra and the Detroit SO. Recordings include: Lady Macbeth of Mtsensk and Shostakovich Japanese Songs, Rachmaninov Aleko and Francesca da Rimini; Tchaikovsky Songs; Kalman's Die Herzogin von Chicago, under Richard Bonynge. Address: c/o Lies Askonas Ltd, 6 Henrietta St, London WC2E 8LA, England.

LEVY Edward (Irving), b. 2 May 1929, Brooklyn, NY, USA. Composer. Education: BA, City College New York, 1957; Princeton University with Milton Babbitt; EdD, Columbia University Teachers College, 1967; Further study with Ralf Shapey and Stefan Wolpe. Career: Teacher at CW Post College, Long Island University, 1961-67; Professor of Music at Yeshiva University, 1967. Compositions include: Duo for Violin and Cello, 1950; 2 Songs for Mezzo and Piano, 1951; Clarinet Sonata, 1956; String Trio, 1959; Trio for Clarinet, Violin and Piano, 1961; Images for Soprano and Piano, 1961; Quintet for Flute and Ensemble, 1967; Variations On A Theme by Brahms for Flute, Clarinet and Horn, 1979; Concatenations for 2 Flutes, Clarinet and Cello, 1980; Movement for Brass Quintet, 1980; Works for chorus and for chamber orchestra. Address: c/o ASCAP, ASCAP Building, One Lincoln Plaza, New York, NY 10023, USA.

LEVY Gerardo, b. 1920. Berlin, Germany. Flautist; Conductor; Teacher. Education: Graduate, Collegium Musicum, Buenos Aires, Argentina; BMus Magna Cum Laude, Boston University, Massachusetts, USA. Debut: Buenos Aires, Argentina, 1942. Career: Soloist, various Chamber Ensembles, USA, Europe, South America; Principal Flautist, Orquesta Filarmonica, Radio Nacional Orquesta Sinfonica, Amigos de la Musica;

Director of Woodwind Studies, New York University; Principal Flautist, White Plains Symphony Orchestra and Clarion Orchestra; Co-Principal Flautist, New York City Opera; Faculty, Sessione Senese per La Musica e l'Arte in Siena, Italy; Florence, Italy; Director and Conductor, Caecilian Chamber Ensemble of New York. Recordings: Cri Vox; Vanguard. Memberships: Board of Directors, New York Flute Club; National Flute Association. Hobby: Philately. Address: 123 West 93 Street, Apt 8F, New York, NY 10025, USA.

LEVY Marvin (David), b. 2 Aug 1932, Passaic, NJ, USA. Composer. Education: BA, New York University, 1954· MA, Columbia University, 1956. Career includes: Archivist, American Opera Society, 1952-58; Music Critic for a number of leading publications including Opera News, Musical America, American Record Guide, New York Herald Tribune and Composer. Compositions include: Opera: The Tower, 1956, Escorial, 1958, Sobata Electra, 1957, Mourning Becomes Electra, 1967; Vocal: Echoes, 1956, For The Time Being, 1959, One Person, 1962, Sacred Service For The Sabbath Eve: Shir Shel Moshe, 1964, Masada, 1973, In Memoriam WH Auden, 1984; Orchestra: Caramoor Festival Overture, 1958, Symphony, 1960, Kyros, 1961, Piano Concerto, 1970, Trialogus, 1972, Canto De Los Maranos, 1977, Pascua Florida, 1988; Instrumental: String Quartet, 1955, Rhapsody, 1956, Chassidic Suite, 1956, Arrows Of Time, 1988. Honours: 2 Prix de Rome Scholarships, 1962, 1965; 2 Guggenheim Fellowships, 1960, 1964; Grants include Ford Foundation, 1965, Damrosch, 1961, National Endowment for The Arts, 1974, 1978; Recipient, Scroll, City of New York. Membership: ASCAP. Current Management: Sheldon Softer Management. Address: c/o Sheldon Softer Management, 130 West 56, New York City, NY 10019, USA.

LEWIN David (Benjamin), b. 2 July 1933, New York, USA. Composer; Theorist. Education: Studied with Edouard Steuermann, 1945-50; MFA, Princeton University, 1958, with Milton Babbitt, Roger Sessions and Earl Kim. Career: Junior Fellowship at Harvard, 1958-61; Computer music at the Bell Laboratories, Murray Hill, New Jersey; Teacher at the University of California at Berkeley, 1961-67, Stony Brook, New York, 1967-80, Yale University, 1979-85 and Professor at Harvard University, 1985-. Compositions include: Viola Sonata, 1958; Essay On A Subject By Webern for Chamber Orchestra, 1958; Classical Variations On A Theme by Schoenberg for Cello and Piano, 1960; Fantasia for Organ, 1962; Fantasy-Adagio for Violin and Orchestra, 1963-66; Quarter Piece for String Quartet, 1969; Woodwind Trio, 1969; Computer Music, 1971; Fanfare, 1980, for Piano, 1982; Generalized Musical Intervals and Transformations, 1987. Publications include: Studies of Parsifal, Moses und Aron and Rameau's Traité de l'Harmonie. Contributions to: Journal of Music Theory; Perspectives of New Music. Address: Harvard University, Music Building, Harvard, Cambridge, MA 02138, USA.

LEWIN Michael, b. 1 Dec 1948, Epsom, Surrey, England. Professor of Guitar. m. Marylyn Troth, 31 Jul 1982, 1 son, 2 daughters. Education: Royal Academy of Music, London, 1967-71; LRAM, Performer; DipRAM; FRAM. Career: Head of Guitar, Royal Academy of Music; Performances on guitar and lute for Royal Shakespeare Company, Ballet Rambert, English Music Theatre, English National Opera, Scottish Opera, Royal Opera House, Covent Garden, also with Praetorius Consort of London, Monteverdi Orchestra, English Baroque Soloists, English Chamber Orchestra and Orchestra of La Piccola Scala, Milan; Broadcasts for BBC, Thames TV, Yugoslav, Belgian, French and West German radio and European Broadcasting Union. Recordings: Various. Publication: Editor, Trinity College Guitar Grade Syllabus and Albums, 1986-89, published 1985, 1989 and 1990-93. Address: c/o Royal Academy of Music, Marylebone Road, London, NW1 5HT, England.

LEWIS Brenda, b. 2 Mar 1921, Harrisburg, PA, USA. Soprano. Education: Studied in Philadelphia. Career: Sang in The Bartered Bride with the Philadelphia Opera Company; Sang with New York City Opera, 1943-67 with debut as Santuzza in Cavalleria Rusticana, in San Francisco in 1950 as Salome, at Metropolitan Opera from 1952 as Musetta in La Bohème, Marina in Boris Godunov, Barber's Vanessa and Rosalinde in Die Fledermaus, and at Chicago in 1965 as Marie in Wozzeck; Guest appearances in South America. Address: c/o New York City Opera, Lincoln Center, New York, NY 10023, USA.

LEWIS Daniel, b. 10 May 1925, Flagstaff, AZ, USA. Conductor. Education: Studied composition with Nino Marcelli in San Diego, 1939-41; BM, San Diego State College, 1949; Further study with Eugen Jochum in Munich, 1960. Career: Leader of the Honolulu Symphony during war service; Assistant Conductor with San Diego Symphony, 1954-56; Leader and Associate Conductor, 1956-59; Music Director of the Pasadena Symphony, 1972-83 notably in neglected 18th century and American music; Guest Conductor with the Los Angeles Philharmonic, Oakland Symphony, Atlanta Symphony, Minnesota Orchestra, Utah Symphony, Seattle Symphony, Los Angeles Chamber Orchestra and the Louisville Orchestra; Chairman of the Conducting Studies Department at the University of Southern California. Address: Music Department, UCLA, Los Angeles, California, USA.

LEWIS Jeffrey, b. 28 November 1942, Port Talbot, South Wales. Composer. 1 son, 1 daughter. Education: BMus 1st class honours 1965, MMus 1967, University College, Cardiff; PhD, University of Wales, 1977; ARCM Organ Performers; Studied composition with Boguslaw Schäffer, Krakow, Poland, with Don Banks, London, with Stockhausen and Ligeti, Darmstadt, Germany, 1967-68. Career: Pianist, Paris Chamber Ensemble, 1967-68; Lecturer in 20th Century Composition Techniques and Experimental Music, City of Leeds College of Music, England, 1969-72; Lecturer, Department of Music, University College of North Wales, Bangor, 1973-; Lecturer, 1973-87, Senior Lecturer, 1987-93, Department of Music, University College of North Wales, Bangor. Compositions: Orchestral: Piano Concerto; Mutations I; Antiphony; Fanfares with Variations; Aurora; Memoria; Limina Lucis; Instrumental: Mutations II; Esultante; Momentum for Organ; Threnody for Piano; Trilogy for Piano; Tableau; Fantasy for Piano; Chamber: Epitaph for Abelard and Heloise; Antiphon; Litania; Stratos; Ritornel; Mobile II; Time-Passage; Wind Quintet: Sonante; Piano Trio; Choral: Carmen Paschale; Pro Pace; Hymnus Ante Somnum; Westminster Mass; Lux Perpetua. Recordings: Commercial CD (Sea of Glass, Lontano Records Ltd); Dreams, Dances and Lullabies for Harp. Publications: Article: The Current State of British Cathedral Music, Choir & Organ, 1993. Honours: Welsh Arts Council Composition Bursary, 1967-68; 1st Prize, International Organist, Composer Competition, Zwolle, Holland, 1972; 1st Prize, Stroud Festival International Composers' Competition, 1972. Memberships: Association of Professional Composers; Composers Guild of Great Britain; Incorporated Society of Musicians; Performing Right Society; Mechanical Copyright Protection Society. Address: Crafnant, Park Crescent, Llanfairfechan, Gwynedd LL33 0AU, Wales.

LEWIS Keith, b. 6 Oct 1950, Methven, New Zealand. Tenor. Education: Studied in New Zealand and in London from 1976. Career includes: Sang in premiere of Tavener's Thérèse at Covent Garden returning as Rossini's Almaviva and as Bellini's Tebaldo and Tamino in Magic Flute; Appearances worldwide in such operas as Don Giovanni, Armide, La Clemenza di Tito, Eugene Onegin, as Mozart's Ferrando, Belmonte, and Monteverdi's Giove; Concert engagements in Damnation of Faust, Haydn's Creation, Schumann's Paradies und der Peri, The Dream of Gerontius, Bach B minor Mass, and Beethoven's 9th with such conductors as Solti, Giulini and Abbado; Further appearances include Mendelssohn's Elijah with Colin Davis, Verdi's Requiem, Mozart's Requiem and Bach Mass in B minor; Sang in the opening concert of the 1991 Promenade Concerts, in Idomeneo at Glyndebourne in 1991, in Britten's Serenade in London, and Haydn's Creation under Sinopoli; Sang Alwa in Berg's Lulu at the Berlin Staatsoper, 1997. Recordings include: Rossini's Tancredi, Otello and Moses; Gluck's Alceste; Don Giovanni conducted by Haitink; Messiah under Solti; Masses by Haydn under Marriner; Paradies und der Peri under Albrecht; Berlioz Lelio, Te Deum and Requiem under Inbal; Berlioz Requiem under Bertini; Mozart Requiem; Beethoven's 9th, Wand and Giulini; Salome under Mehta. Current Management: IMG Artists Europe. Address: c/o IMG Artists Europe, Media House, 3 Burlington Lane, Chiswick, London, W4 2TH, England.

LEWIS Michael, b. 1948, Adelaide, South Australia. Baritone. Education: Studied in Adelaide and at the London Opera Centre. Career: Sang first at Wexford Festival, then with Glyndebourne Festival and Touring Operas, Welsh National and Scottish Operas, Frankfurt Opera and companies in Australia; Resident principal with Opera North and Australian Opera; Season 1992-93 as Verdi's Luna, Amonasro, Rigoletto and Renato in Australia, Rigoletto at La Fenice Venice, Rossini's Figaro for English National Opera; Performances of L'Africaine and Tiefland in Berlin, I Masnadieri and Macbeth in Australia and Bizet's Zurga in San Diego; Other roles include Mozart's Guglielmo, Alfonso, the Count and Papageno, Malatesta, Lescaut in Manon, Riccardo in I Puritani, Marcello and Don Carlo in La Forza del Destino; Concert repertoire includes Carmina Burana, Belshazzar's Feast and Elijah. Address: c/o IMG Artists, Media House, 3 Burlington Lane, London, W4 2TH, England.

LEWIS Oliver, b. 12 May 1966, London, England. Education: Purcell School of Music, London; Konservatorium für Musik, Bern, Switzerland; Studied with Carl Pini, David Takkeno, Sandor Vegh, Aaron Rosand, Igor Ozim, Wen Xun Chen. Debut: British Concerto debut with National Children's Orchestra of Great Britain, age 12. Career: Solo concert tours, England, France, Spain, Portugal, Switzerland, Germany, Austria, Netherlands, Georgia; Broadcasts worldwide, including German TV and Radio, Swiss Radio, BBC Radio 3, Classic FM Radio; Swiss Concerto debut with Bern Symphony Orchestra, Casino Berne, 1990; Became Concertmaster and Soloist, Heidelberg Chamber Orchestra, 1991; Directs an annual chamber music festival, St Moritz, Switzerland; Gives masterclasses at Dartington International Summer School. Recordings: CDs including world premiere recordings of rare English music; English Romanticism, music by Ferguson, Goossens and Ireland; English Romanticism II, music by Elgar and Goossens. Current Management: Audrey Ellison International Artists Management. Address: 14 Woodmansterne Road, Carshalton Beeches, Surrey SM5 4JL, England.

LEWIS Paul, b. 1943, Brighton, England. Composer. m. Marie-Genevieve, 1977, 1 daughter. Education: Brighton College. Career: Composer, British TV, 1963-; TV Scores include, Arthur of the Britons, 1972, Spring and Autumn, 1973-74, Kings Royal, 1981-82, Lady Killers, 1980-81, Swallows and Amazons Forever, 1983, The Prisoner of Zenda, 1989, The Dark Angel, 1988, Woof, 1988-; Numerous Concert and Chamber Works, including Norfolk Concerto for Flute, harp and strings, based on The Vanishing Hedgerows TV Score; Woof, Variations on a Mongrel Dog for harmonica and orchestra; Subject of a 25 minute Documentary by HTV in the Series Music Writers on TV, 1995; Was one of BBC Radio 2's Legends of Light Music, 1997. Hobby: Mediaeval and Renassiance art and architecture. Address: Court House, Church Street, Martock, Somerset TA12 6JL, England.

LEWIS Robert Hall, b. 22 Apr 1926, Portland, OR, USA. Composer; Conductor; Professor. m. Barbara Bowersock, 8 Aug 1959, 1 daughter. Education: BM, Distinction, 1949, MM, 1951, PhD, 1964, University of Rochester, Eastman School; Conducting Diploma, Paris Conservatoire, 1953; Composition Diploma, Vienna Academy of Music, 1957; Monteux School of Conducting, summer 1954. Career: Principal Trumpet with Oklahoma Symphony Orchestra, 1951-52; Assistant Principal Trumpet, Rochester Philharmonic Orchestra, 1953-55; Guest Conductor with Baltimore Symphony Orchestra, Indiana University Orchestra, and National Gallery Orchestra; Conducted recordings of own music with London Symphony, Royal Philharmonic, London Sinfonietta and Philharmonia Orchestras; Professor of Music at Goucher College, Baltimore; Professor of Composition at Peabody Institute, Johns Hopkins University. Compositions include: String Quartets I-IV; Music for Twelve Players; Music for Brass Quintet; Osservazioni for Flutes, Piano and Percussion; Monophony I-IX for Solo Winds; Concerto for Chamber Orchestra; Symphony No 2; Nuances II for Orchestra; Moto; Atto for String Orchestra. Recordings: Divertimento for 6 Instruments; Toccata for Violin and Percussion; Symphony No 2; Nuances II for Orchestra; Three Prayers Of Jane Austen; Concerto for Chamber Orchestra; Serenades for Piano Solo; Moto for Orchestra; Atto for String Orchestra; Combinazioni I, II, III, IV. Contributions to: Professional journals. Hobby: Study of Foreign Languages. Address: 328 Broadmoor Road, Baltimore, Maryland, USA.

LEWIS William, b. 23 Nov 1935, Tulsa, OK, USA. Tenor. Education: Studied at Fort Worth and New York. Debut: Fort Worth in 1953 in Gianni Schicchi. Career: Early appearances in Cincinnati, San Francisco and Dallas; New York City Opera in 1957 in Die Fledermaus, Metropolitan Opera from 1958 in Salome, Elektra, Boris Godunov, Jenufa, The Queen of Spades, La Bohème and Francesca da Rimini; Sang Aeneas in the 1983 New York production of Les Troyens and at Spoleto in 1959 in the premiere of Barber's A Hand of Bridge; Sang at San Francisco, 1984-85 as Loge in The Ring, Wexford Festival and La Scala, 1986-87 in Humperdinck's Königskinder and the title role in the premiere of Testi's Riccardo III; Spoleto Festival in 1989 as Aegisthus in Elektra; Sang Arbace in Idomeneo at San Francisco in 1989 and in the premiere of Blimunda by Azio Corghi at the Teatro Lirico Milan in 1990; Other roles include Pollione in Norma, the Emperor in Die Frau ohne Schatten, Don José, Offenbach's Hoffmann, Radames, Gabriele Adorno in Simon Boccanegra and Strauss's Guntram. Recordings include: Adolar in Euryanthe. Address: c/o San Francisco Opera, War Memorial Opera House, San Francisco, CA 94102, USA.

LEWKOVITCH Bernhard, b. 28 May 1927, Denmark. Composer; Organist. Education: Graduate in Music Theory, 1948, Organ, 1949, Royal Danish Conservatry of Music; Composition teachers were Poul Schierbeck and Jorgen Jersild; Studied in France. Career includes: Organist, 1947-63, Cantor, 1953-63, Sankt Ansgar Catholic Church, Copenhagen; Organist and Cantor, Church of Holy Sacrament, Copenhagen, 1973-; Founder and Leader of Schola Gregoriana Men's Choir, Schola Cantorum Mixed Choir, both now under the name Schola Cantorum. Compositions include: Vocal music and instrumental music for orchestra, ensemble, piano and organ including: Mass for 2 Corui and Mixed Choir, Songs Of Solomon for Tenor and Clarinet, Coruo and Bass Trombone, Deprecations for Tenor, Horn and Bass Trombone, Preacher And Singer for Tenor and Piano; Six Partitas for 5 Brass Instruments, volumes I-II; Improperia Per Voce (Good Friday); 3 Tasso Madrigali for Mixed Choir; Responsoria for Mixed Choir (Good Friday); Helligandskoraler (Holy Ghost Chorales) for 4 Brass Players, 1980, numerous organ chorales and liturgical works. Address: Bredgade 69, 1260 K Copenhagen, Denmark.

LI Hong-Shen, b. 1960, Beijing, China. Singer (Tenor). Education: Studied at the Central Conservatory of Beijing and the Juilliard School with Ellen Faull. Career: Joined the San Francisco

Opera Merola Program, 1987, performing Rinuccio in Gianni Schicchi and Lindoro in L'Italiana in Algeri; Further appearances as the Duke of Mantua, Aufidio in Mozart's Lucio Silla, the Italian Singer, Alfredo, Tebaldo, Pirro in Ermione and Leukippos in Daphne with the San Francisco Opera; Other roles include Rossini's Count Almaviva, Steuermann in Fliegende Holländer (debut with the Metropolitan Opera), Nadir, Macduff, Nemorino and Idreno in Semiramide; Concert repertoire includes the Verdi Requiem and Mozart's Requiem, Beethoven's 9th Symphony and Rossini's Stabat Mater. Honours include: Highest Fellowship Scholarship at Central Conservatory of Beijing; Winner, 1991 Metropolitan Opera Competition Nationals; George London Award; Adler Fellow with the San Francisco Opera, 1989-91. Address: c/o IMG Artists, Media House, 3 Burlington Lane, London, W4 2TH, England.

LI Tian-Sheng, b. 14 Aug 1948, Tianshui, Gansu, China. Cellist; Viola da Gamba Player. m. Jian-Hua Chen, 20 Mar 1976, 2 daughters. Education: Diploma, School of Music attached to Central Conservatory, Peking, China, 1959-67; MMus, Cello Performance, School of Music, Indiana University, Bloomingotn, 1984; DMA, Cello Performance, Memphis State University. Debut: Central Ballet Theatre, Peking, China, 1978. Career: Cellist with Symphony Orchestra of Central Ballet Theatre, 1968-80; Student of Distinguished Professor of Cello, Janos Starker, 1981-84; Cello and Re-Bu, chinese instrument solo, Indianapolis TV Arts Network, 1983; Cellist with Memphis Symphony, USA, 1984-; Cello Instructor at Memphis State University, Suzuki String Program, 1985-. Recordings: Two Cello Solo recordings: Violoncello recital of Chinese Cello Music and Violoncello recital of World Famous Cello Music, 1981. Address: c/o The Department of Music, Memphis State University, Memphis, TN 38152, USA.

LIANG Ning, b. 1957, Peking, China. Singer (Mezzo-soprano). Education: Studied in Gwangdong and Peking; Further studies at Juilliard School and American Opera Center in New York. Debut: Central Conservatory Peking, 1983 as Cherubino. Career: Wigmore Hall Recital, London, 1983; Sang at Peking and Shanghai as Carmen and Rosina, Cenerentola at the 1987 Aspen Festival; Philadelphia and Helsinki, 1988 as Dorabella and Carmen; Studied further at the Juilliard School, 1986-89; Sang Cherubino in London and Hamburg, 1989-91; La Scala, Milan 1990, as Suzuki in Butterfly; Sang Rosina at Toronto and at the Vienna Festival, 1992; Concert engagements include Beethoven's Ninth in Lisbon and Bellini's Il Pirata in New York; Opera engagements include, Ottavia in L'Incoronazione di Poppea (Marseille and Amsterdam), Stephano in Roméo et Juliette (Hamburg), Octavian (German Opera Berlin and Hamburg) and Sesto in La Clemenza di Tito (Stuttgart). Recordings Include: Carmen and Le nozze di Figaro. Honours: Numerous Prizes in American Competitions: Metropolitan Opera National Council Competition, Musicians Emergency Competition, Rosa Ponselle International Vocal Competition, Loren L Zachery Competition and the Luciano Pavarotti Competition. Address: c/o Hamburgisches Staatsoper, Grosses-Theaterstrasse 34, 2000 Hamburg 36, Germany.

LIAO Naixiong, b. 27 Jun 1933, Shanghai, China. Director, The Institute for Music Research. m. Dec 1954, 1 daughter. Education: Studied composition and music theory, 1951-54, and piano, 1954-58, Shanghai Conservatory. Career: Assistant for Piano, 1958-74, Researcher at the Institute for Music Research, 1974-78, Lecturer, 1978-80, Associate Professor, 1980-86, Vice-Director, 1982-84, Director, 1984-, Professor, 1986-, Shanghai Conservatory; Research Fellow, Alexander von Humboldt Foundation, Germany, 1982-84; Currently working on History of The European Opera and on Carl Orff. Publications: The German Liederalbum, 1959; Chopin, 1981; Grieg, 1982; Musik Durch die Man Zu Den Quellen Steigt, 1985; Quo Vadis The Opera in China?, 1987. Contributions to: The Ocean of Words; The Great Chinese Encyclopedia; People's Music; Articles on music; China im Aufbau; Art of Music; China - Report; Art of Opera; Radio programmes in Shanghai, Peking, West Berlin, Munich and Cologne. Address: Shanghai Conservatory, Feng Yang Road 20, Shanghai, China.

LICHTMANN Theodor (David), b. 25 Dec 1938, Bern, Switzerland. Pianist; University Professor. Education: Teacher's Diploma, University of Zurich; Akademie für Musik, Vienna, Austria; Hochschule für Musik, Munich, Germany; MMus, University of Texas, USA; Piano studies with Irma Schaichet, Zurich, and Leonard Shure, New York City. Debut: Bern in 1954. Career: Recitals in Zurich, Berlin, Vienna, Hamburg, London and smaller cities in Switzerland; Co-founder and pianist of Mendelssohn Trio; Broadcasts on Swiss Radio and TV; US recitals in Philadelphia, Denver, Austin, and Roswell; Broadcasts on radio and TV in Denver, Colorado; Professor at School of Music and Chairman of Piano Department, University of Denver, Distinguished Faculty-Artist. Recordings include: Fair Play; Summit Brass; Complete works by Hindemith for Brass and Piano. Contributions to: ARBA; Libraries Unlimited. Memberships: College Music Society; Colorado Mountain Club. Hobbies:

Literature; Photography; Mountaineering. Address: 3005 East Cedar Lane, Denver, CO 80209, USA.

LIDDELL Nona (Patricia), b. 9 Jun 1927, London, England. Musician. m. Ivor McMahon, 15 Jul 1950 (deceased), 1 d. Education: Royal Academy of Music. Career: Leader, English String Quartet, 1957-73; Leader, Richards Piano Quintet, 1964-79; Leader, London Sinfonietta, 1970-94; Professor, Trinity College of Music. Recordings: Violin Concerto, Kurt Weill; Phantasie by Schoenberg with John Constable; Gemini by Roberto Gerhard with Joan Constable; Chamber Music by Martinu, Chausson, Herbert Howells; Brahms's Horn Trio with Schiller Trio; Stravinsky's Soldier's Tale; Chamber Music by Schoenberg. Honour: MBE; Fellow of The Royal Academy of Music. Membership: Incorporated Society of Musicians. Hobbies: Reading; Cooking. Address: 28B Ravenscroft Park, Barnet, Hertfordshire, EN5 4NH, England.

LIDL Vaclav, b. 5 Nov 1922, Brno, Czechoslovakia. Composer. m. Eva Hromadkova, 1 son. Education: Graduate Business Academy; Brno Conservatoire. Career: Writer of many musical scores for films and television. Compositions include: Divertimento for flute, clarinet and bassoon; 3rd string quartet; Dandelions, for flute, soprano and harp; 1st Symphony for Grand Orchestra; Cantus Variabilis for violin, clarinet and piano; Hic Homo Sum, Cantata for mixed choir, tenor, piano and percussion; Our Little Drummer, Cantata for child's voice and Grand Orchestra; 2nd Symphony for Chamber Orchestra; 3rd Symphony for Grand Orchestra; Many compositions for various types of choirs; Ballade on a June Morning (Lidice 1942), for Grand Orchestra; Concerto for trumpet and orchestra. Honour: Antonin Zapotocky Prize for the Ballade on a June Morning, 1984. Membership: Association of Musicians and Musicologists. Hobby: Skiing. Current Management: Music Information Centre, Besedni 3, 118 00 Praha 1, Czech Republic. Address: Soukenicka 14, 110 00 Praha 1, Czech Republic.

LIEBERMAN Carol, b. 18 Aug 1943, New York, New York, USA. Musician; Violinist; Baroque Violinist. m. Mark Kroll, 9 July 1975, 1 son. Education: BA, City College of New York, 1965; MMus, 1967, DMA, 1974, Yale University School of Music; Violin studies with Raphael Bronstein and Broadus Erle. Debut: Carnegie Recital Hall, New York, 1975. Career: Faculty, Boston University School of Music, 1979-; Concertmaster, Masterworks Chorale Orchestra, 1980-; Concerts throughout USA and in Rome, Italy, Antwerp, Caracas, Lisbon and Canada; Broadcasts for WGBH Radio-TV and WBUR Radio, Boston, including 6 part simulcast series for Maine Public Television; Radio and Television Programmes for Canadian Broadcasting Corporation; Former Member, Israel Philharmonic Orchestra and Toronto Symphony; Assistant Professor, College of Holy Cross, 1985-88; Associate Professor, 1989-; Co-Diretor, Holy Cross Chamber Players, 1985-; Broadcasts for Radio National de Espana, Madrid, 1985; Soloist with Connecticut Early Music Festival, 1985-. Recordings: CD's: Schubert Sonatinas for Violin and Fortepiano; Dohnanyi Sonata for Violin, Piano and Second Piano Quintet; Numerous recordings for various labels. Memberships: Co-Director, Holy Cross Chamber Players; Violinist with Early Music Ensemble of Boston; Violinist of Lieberman/Kroll Duo. Address: Department of Music, College of the Holy Cross, PO Box 151A, Worcester, MA 01610, USA.

LIEBERMANN Lowell, b. 22 Feb 1961, New York, USA. Composer; Conductor; Pianist. Education: BM, 1982, MM, 1984, DMA, 1987, The Juilliard School, NY; Composition with David Diamond and Vincent Persichetti; Conducting with Laszlo Halasz; Piano with Jacob Lateiner. Debut: Carnegie Recital Hall, New York City, 1978. Compositions: Symphony Op 9; Piano Concerto Op 11; 2 Piano Sonatas Op 1 and 10; Sechs Gesänge Nach Gedichten von Nelly Sachs for Soprano and Orchestra Op 18; Sonata for Viola and Piano Op 13; Missa Brevis for Chorus and Organ; Song Cycles; Chamber Music; Sonata for Flute and Piano Op 24; Quintet for Piano, Clarinet and String Trio Op 26; Domain of Arnheim Op 33; Quintet for Piano and Strings Op 34; Nocturnes Op 20, 31, 35; Gargoyles Op 29; Piano Concerto No 2 Op 36, 1992; Concerto for Flute and Orchestra Op 39, 1992; Songs and Piano Pieces; The Picture of Dorian Gray, opera, Op 45, 1995; Sonata for Violin and Piano Op 46, 1994; Album for the Young for Piano Op 43, 1994; Revelry for Orchestra, Op 47, 1995; Longfellow Songs Op 57; Loss of Breath Op 58; Flute and Harp Conerto Op 48. Recordings: Piano Music of Lowell Liebermann, Musical Heritage Society; Many recordings on various labels. Membership: Director of Yaddo Colony; ASCAP; NARAS. Address: 820 West End Avenue Apt #10B, New York, NY 10025, USA.

LIEBERMANN Rolf, b. 14 Sep 1910, Zurich, Switzerland. Musician; Administrator; Composer. Education: Zurich Conservatoire and University of Zurich. Career: Member of Musical Department at Swiss Radio Corporation, 1945-50; Head of Orchestra Department, Swiss Radio Station Beromünster, 1950-57; Musical Director, North German Broadcasting System, Hamburg, 1957-59; General Manager of Hamburg State Opera,

1959-72 and Théâtre National de L'Opéra, Paris, 1973-80; Guest Professor at Salzburg Mozarteum, 1982; General Manager of Hamburg State Opera, 1985-. Compositions include: Operatic: Leonore, 1952, School For Wives, 1955, The Forest, 1987; Orchestral: Polyphonic Studies, 1943, Volkslieder Suite, Furioso, 1947, The Song Of Life And Death, 1950, Concerto for Jazzband and Symphony Orchestra, 1954, Symphonie des Echanges for Business Machines, 1964, Piano Quintet, 1987, Monologue of Medea for Soprano, Choir and Orchestra, 1989, Concerto for Violin and Orchestra, 1993. Honours: Dr hc of the University of Spokane and Berne; Commander Legion d'Honneur, 1974; Commander of L'Ordre des Arts et des Lettres; Commander de L'Ordre de la Légion d'Honneur. Memberships: L'Académie des Beaux Arts de Berlin and of Hamburg; Honorable Member of the Hochschule Mozarteum of Salzburg and of the Royal Academy of Fine Arts, London. Address: Hamburg Staatsoper, Hamburg, Germany.

LIEBERSON Peter, b. 25 Oct 1946, NY, USA. Composer. m. Ellen Kennedy, 3 daughters. Education: Studied at New York University, Columbia University and Brandeis University; Composition teachers were Milton Babbitt, Charles Wvorinen, Donald Martino, and Martin Boykan. Compositions include: Worlds Turning; Drala; Lalita; Ziji; Raising The Gaze; Variations for Violin and Piano; Piano Fantasy; Flute Variations; Concerto for 4 Groups of Instruments. Recordings: Piano Concerto; Bagatelles; Lalita; Raising The Gaze; Piano Fantasy; Concerto for 4 Groups of Instruments. Honours: Charles Ives Fellowship; National Endowment for The Arts; American Academy of Arts and Letters; Brandeis University Creative Arts Award. Membership: BMI. Hobby: Golf. Address: 47 Anchor Drive, Halifax, Nova Scotia, Canada, B3N 3E4.

LIEBL Karl, b. 16 Jun 1915, Schiltberg, Germany. Tenor. Education: Studied with Paul Bender in Munich and with Albert Meyer in Augsburg. Debut: Regensburg in 1950. Career: Sang in Wiesbaden from 1951, Cologne Opera, 1955-59 notably as Huon in Oberon, and Vienna Staatsoper, 1956-59; Sang the Cardinal in Mathis der Maler under Hindemith; Sang at Metropolitan Opera, 1959-68 as Wagner's Lohengrin, Tristan, Loge, Walther, Siegfried, Siegmund and Parsifal; Guest appearances in Munich, Hamburg, Chicago, Baltimore, Brussels, Zurich, Venice and Madrid; Teacher at University of Mainz from 1967. Recordings: Der fliegende Holländer; Die Zauberflöte; Lohengrin; Die Meistersinger; Oberon. Address: c/o Staatliche Hochschule für Musik, Bingerstrasse 26, 6500 Mainz, Germany.

LIEBOLD Angela, b. 15 Aug 1958, Dresden, Germany. Singer. Education: Studied at Dresden Musikhochschule. Career: Appearances at the Dresden Opera from 1985 in the title role of the premiere of Weise Von Liebe und Tod Des Cornets Christopher Rilke by Siegfried Matthus; Lieder recitals in Russia, Hungary, France and Germany; Engagements in opera elsewhere in Germany; Teacher of Singing at the Dresden Musikhochschule from 1983. Honours include: Prize Winner at the Walter Gruner Lieder Competition, Bach International, Maria Callas Competition, Athens, and Robert Schumann Competition. Address: c/o Semper Oper, 8012 Dresden, Germany.

LIEDBECK Sixten, b. 28 Oct 1916, Karlsborg, Sweden. Composer. Education: Instrumentalist, Organ, Piano Composer; Composing Studies, Z Kodaly, Budapest. Debut: Concert Hall, Stockholm. Career: Conductor, Opera House and Oscar's Theatre. Compositions: Suite for Strings; Ballet Music for Orchestra; Musical Isola Bella; Symphonic Prologue for Orchestra; Concertino for Flute and Strings. Recordings: Marcia Burlesca/Clarinet Quintet; Esquisse Stringorch. Honour: City Hall Award, 1950. Membership: Society of Swedish Authors. Hobby: American Cars. Address: Batsbacken 10, 746 91 Balsta, Sweden.

LIELMANE Rasma, b. 1958, Latvia, Russia. Concert Violinist. Education: Studied with David Oistrakh at the Moscow Conservatoire. Career: Appearances with the leading orchestras of Europe and North America; Collaborations with the Munich Philharmonic, Berlin Symphony and the Dresden Philharmonic; Appearances in London, Hamburg, Toronto, Montreal, Nice and Milan. Honours: First Prize, International Violin Competition, Sofia; Prizewinner at the Vianna de Motta Competition in Portugal, Nicola Paganini in Italy, and Maria Canals Competition in Montreal; Tibor Varga Prize in Switzerland. Address: Norman McCann International Artists Ltd, The Coach House, 56 Lawrie Park Gardens, London, SE26 6XJ, England.

LIFCHITZ Max, b. 11 Nov 1948, Mexico City, Mexico. Composer; Conductor; Pianist. Education: Studied at the Juilliard School of Music, New York, and Harvard University, Cambridge, Massachusetts, also Berkshire Music Center. Debut: Mexico City, 1955. Career: Pianist, Juilliard Ensemble; Lecturer, National Music Camp, Michigan; Faculty, Manhattan School of Music; Assistant Professor in Music, Columbia University; Executive Director, Conductor, North South Consonance Inc; Associate Professor in Music, State University of New York; Chair, Music Department, State University of New York at Albany, 1995-.

Compositions include: Intervencion for Violin and Orchestra; Night Voices #13 for cello and orchestra; Kaddish, Choir and Chamber, Ensemble, Tiempos; Tientos, Accordion. Recordings: Affinities, Piano Solo; Transformation, Cello; Yellow Ribbons No 2; Canto de Paz; Yellow Ribbons No 21; Consorte; Winter Counterpoint, Flute, Oboe, Bassoon, Viola; Exceptional String Quartet; 3 Piano Albums of American Piano Music; Of Bondage and Freedom. Publications: String Quartets and Piano Sonatas by Carlos Chávez for G Shirmer Inc Honours: 1st Prize, Gaudeamus Competition, 1976. Hobbies: Sports; Photography. Current Management: North/South Concerts. Address: North/South Concerts, PO Box 5081, Albany, NY 12205-0081, USA.

LIFSHITZ Constantin, b. 1977, Ukraine. Concert Pianist. Education: Gnessin School Moscow, from 1982; Currently studying with international piano teachers at International Piano Foundation, Lago di Como. Career: Concerts in the West from 1990; Collaboration with violinist Vladimir Spivakov, including tour of Japan with the Moscow Virtuosi; Further concerts with the Monte Carlo Philharmonic, Moscow Philharmonic in Munich, Moscow State Symphony Orchestra (concerto debut) and the St Petersburg Philharmonic on tour to Europe, with Yuri Temirkanov, 1997; Chamber music with Lynn Harrell, Gidon Kremer and Mischa Maisky; Contracted to appear at Shostakovich Festival in Tokyo, performing Shostakovich Piano Concerto No 1, and also for a recital tour of Japan including a performance with the Tokyo Symphony Orchestra. Recordings include: Recital discs. Honours include: Russian Cultural Foundation New Name Scholarship, 1990; Winner, German Echo Classic Record Prize, 1995. Address: c/o IMG Artists, Media House, 3 Burlington Lane, London W4 2TH, England.

LIGABUE Ilva, b. 23 May 1932, Reggio Emilia, Italy. Soprano. m. Paolo Pedani. Education: Giuseppe Verdi Conservatory Milan and the Scala Opera School. Debut: Milan, 1933-53, as Marina in I Quattro Rusteghi. Career: Sang at Glyndebourne, 1958-65 as Mozart's Donna Elvira and Fiordiligi, Verdi's Alice Ford and Donizetti's Anna Bolena, Chicago in 1961 as Margherita in Mefistofele, and La Scala in 1961 as Bellini's Beatrice di Tenda; Guest appearances in Buenos Aires, Dallas, Hamburg, Brussels and Aix-en-Provence; American Opera Society in 1963, Verona Arena, 1971-72, and Covent Garden in 1963 and 1974 as Alice Ford, Donna Elvira and Elisabeth de Valois. Recordings: L'Italiana in Londra by Cimarosa; Falstaff; Ascanio in Alba by Mozart; Cherubini's Lodoiska and L'Osteria Portoghese. Address: c/o Teatro alla Scala, Via Filodrammatici 2, I-20121 Milan, Italy.

LIGENDZA Catarina, b. 18 Oct 1937, Stockholm, Sweden. Soprano. m. Peter Ligendza. Education: Studied in Vienna and Wuerzburg with Henriette Klink, Stuttgart with Trudi Eipperle and Saarbrücken with Josef Greindl. Debut: Linz in 1963 as Mozart's Countess. Career: Sang in Brunswick and Saabrücken, 1966-69 as Verdi's Elisabeth de Valois and Desdemona and Strauss' Arabella; Sang at Hamburg Staatsoper from 1967, Deutsche Oper Berlin and Staatsoper Stuttgart from 1970, and Staatsoper Wien from 1971 with Wagner's Ring, Isolde with Carlos Kleiber, Lisa in The Queen of Spades, and Elsa in Lohengrin with Placido Domingo; Sang at Staatsoper München in Fliegende Holländer and Lohengrin from 1978 and Götterdämmerung; Sang Arabella at La Scala in 1970 and at Salzburg Easter Festival under Karajan; Metropolitan Opera debut in 1971 as Beethoven's Leonore; Bayreuth Festival, 1971-77 as Brünnhilde and Isolde, 1986-87 as Elsa in Lohengrin and Isolde; Covent Garden debut in 1972 as Senta in Der fliegende Holländer; Sang in Wagner's Ring with Deutsche Oper Berlin in 1987 in Japan; Retired from the stage in 1988; TV productions and opera films: Der fliegende Holländer, Lohengrin, Elsa, Freischütz, Agathe, and Elektra, Chrysothemis with conductors Sawallisch, Russell Davies and Karl Böhm. Recordings: Third Norn in Götterdämmerung; Arias by Handel; Eva in Meistersinger von Nürnberg; Lars Erik Larsson, Förkläddgud; Three Songs, Rangström.

LIGETI András, b. 1953, Hungary. Conductor. Education: Franz Liszt Academy, Budapest, violin diploma, 1976; Conducting with Andras Korodi. Career: Orchestra Leader, Hungarian State Opera House, 1976-80; Regular concerts as solo violinist in Europe and Canada; Associate Conductor, with György Lehel, of the Budapest Symphony Orchestra, 1985, with tours of Britain, Europe and America; Regular conductor at the Budapest Opera; British debut in 1989 with the BBC Symphony Orchestra, returning to conduct the BBC Scottish Symphony Orchestra and BBC Philharmonic in 1991, with Bartók's Duke Bluebeard's Castle, Weber's 2nd Piano Concerto and Mahler's 5th Symphony. Address: c/o Norman McCann International Artists Ltd, The Coach House, 56 Lawrie Park Gardens, London, SE26 6XJ, England.

LIGETI György (Sandor), b. 28 May 1923, Romania. Composer. m. Dr Vera Spitz, 1957, 1 son. Education: Budapest Academy of Music with Ferenc Farkas and Sándor Veress. Career: Taught at Budapest Academy of Music, 1950-56; Left Hungary in 1956; Guest Professor at Stockholm Academy of Music, 1961-71; Composer in Residence at Stanford University, California in 1972; Worked in Electronic Studios, Cologne, Germany; Active in music composition at Cologne, Vienna, Stockholm and Darmstadt; Professor of Composition, Hamburg Music Academy, 1973-89; Festival of Music, including Le Grand Macabre on London's South Bank, 1989; Concert series Clocks and Clouds, London, 1997. Compositions include: Artikulation, tape piece, 1958; Atmosphères for Orchestra, 1960; Poème Symphonique for 100 Metronomes, 1962; Requiem for Soprano, Mezzo-Soprano, 2 Choirs and Orchestra, 1963-65; Concerto for Cello and Orchestra, 1966; Ten Pieces for Wind Quintet, 1968; String Quartet No 2, 1968; Melodien for Orchestra, 1971; Clocks And Clouds for 12 Female Voices and Orchestra, 1973; Monument, Selbstportrait, Movement for 2 Pianos, 1976; Le Grand Macabre, opera, 1977; 3 Phantasies After Hölderin, 1982; 6 Etudes for Piano, 1985; Nonsense Madrigals for 6 Voices, 1988; Violin Concerto, 1990; L'escalier du diable for piano, 1993. Recordings: Complete works recorded on 16 CDs, from 1996. Honours: Orden Pour Le Mérite, Bonn, 1975; Prix Ravel, 1984; Prix Honegger, 1985; Grawemeyer Award, 1986; Doctor hc, Hamburg University, 1988; Commandeur dans l'Ordre National des Arts et Lettres, France, 1988; Prix Prince Pierre de Monaco, 1988. Memberships: Swedish Royal Academy of Music, 1964; Academy of Arts Berlin, 1968; Free Academy of Arts, Hamburg, 1972; Bavarian Academy of Fine Arts, Munich, 1978; American Academy and Institute of Arts and Letters, 1984. Address: Mövenstrasse 3, D-2000 Hamburg 60, Germany.

LIKA Peter, b. 1949, Germany. Singer (bass-baritone). Education: Studied in Munich. Career: Sang with the Augsburg Opera 1972-81 and later joined the Bavarian Chamber Opera for performances of Baroque opera; a noted interpreter of sacred music by Bach and Mozart, appearing in Cologne (1989), Berlin and the Ludwigsburg Festival; Tour of Japan 1987, with Haydn's Die Jahreszeiten; Brussels 1991, in Mozart's Requiem.

LIKIN Jurij, b. 11 Nov 1967, Minsk, Belarus (Former USSR). Oboist. m. Anna Jermolowitch, 7 Mar 1987, 1 daughter. Education: Music Lyceum, Belarusian State Music Academy, Minsk; 1 year stage in Paris, Class of Maurice Bourgue, Prague Mozart Academy, 1994. Debut: Age 16, Stage of Belarusian Philharmonic, Minsk. Career: Ekaterinburg, Moscow, Minsk, Kaliningrad, Prague, Berlin, Brunswick, 1991-94; Trieste, 1993; Stresa, Italy, 1994; Paris Théâtre des Champs-Elysées, 1994; Marseille, 1995; Les Grands Heures de Saint-Emilion, France, 1995; Principal Oboist of State Symphony Orchestra of Belarusian Philharmonic, since 1994; Soloist of Prague Symphony Orchestra, Prague Chamber Philharmonic and Member of Prague Wind Quintet. Recordings: (CD's): B Martinu; A Reicha; E Bozza; Max Stern; F Poulenc Sonata, Sextet. Honours: 1st Prizes in National Competitions of USSR, 1986, 1987. Address: Trytova 1120, 19800 Prague 9, Czech Republic.

LILBURN Douglas (Gordon), b. 2 November 1915, Wanganui, New Zealand. Composer; Professor of Music. Education: Canterbury University College, Christchurch, New Zealand; Studied with Vaughan Williams,Royal College of Music, London, England. Career: Freelance Composer; Composer-in-Residence, Cambridge Summer Music Schools, 1946-49, 1951; Part-time Tutor in Music, 1947-49, Lecturer 1949-55, Senior Lecturer 1955-63, Associate Professor 1963-70, Professor with a personal Chair, 1970; Director of Electronic Music Studies, Victoria University, Wellington, New Zealand. Compositions include: Overture, Aotearoa, 1940; A Song of Islands, 1947; 3 Symphonies, 1949, 1951, 1961; String Quartet and String Trio; 3 Violin Sonatas; A range of works for piano and chamber music ensembles; Electronic Music. Honours include: Cobbett Prize, RCM, 1939; 3 New Zealand Centennial Awards, 1940; Philip Neill Memorial Prize, 1944; Hon DMus, University of Otago, 1969; Composers Association of New Zealand Citation for Services to New Zealand Music, 1978; Several Awards from APRA and Queen Elizabeth II Arts Council; Order of New Zealand, 1988. Address: 22 Ascot Terrace, Wellington I, New Zealand.

LILL John (Richard), b. 17 Mar 1944, London, England. concert Pianist. Education: FRCM; FLCM. Debut: 1st concert, age 9; debut, 1963, Royal Festival Hall. Career: Recitals worldwide; Soloist, many leading orchestras throughout UK, Europe, USA, Japan, Far East, Australia, New Zealand, Canada, Scandinavia; Complete cycle of Beethoven sonatas, Queen Elizabeth Hall, 1982, Barbican Centre, 1986, Tokyo, 1987, California; Season 1989/90 included concerts with the Royal, Tokyo and Helsinki Philharmonics; Season 1990-91, Beethoven Concerto cycle (Hong Kong), toured Japan and Australia, concerts with Scottish National and Hallé Orchestras, Prokofiev Sonatas at Queen Elizabeth Hall; Beethoven concertos with City of Birmingham Symphony (under Walter Weller), Royal Philharmonic and Royal Scottish National Orchestras; Both Brahms concertos with Hong Kong Philharmonic; Concert in Madrid with St Petersburg Philharmonic, recitals, Royal Festival Hall and Vienna Konzerthaus, Prokofiev series (Châtelet, Paris); Bath Festival, Colmar, BBC Proms, 1992/93; NHK Symphony/Tokyo, Royal Scottish Orchestra (Weller); Celebrity Recital, Symphony Hall, Birmingham; Recital/concert in St Petersburg with St Petersburg Symphony and Leipzig Symphony Orchestras; Brahms B flat Concerto at 1993 Proms; Season 1993/94, UK tour with Yomiuri Nippon Symphony (Tokyo), Spain tour with Royal Scottish National Orchestra and Weller, also Hong Kong Philharmonic, BBC Proms, Royal Philharmonic, RLPO; Royal Festival Hall recital (50th birthday); 1994/95, Dallas Symphony, European tour with NHK Symphony and Inbal, Switzerland with RSNO/Weller; US tour with BBC Symphony Orchestra and Andrew Davis, autumn 1995; Played Tchaikovsky's Concerto with the CBSO, 1997. Recordings include: All Beethoven Piano Sonatas, Concertos and Bagatelles; Both Brahms Piano Concertos; Tchaikovsky Piano Concerto No 1 with London Symphony Orchestra; Complete Prokofiev Sonatas, 1991; Rachmaninov complete solo piano works and concertos with BBC Welsh Orchestra/Otaka. Honours include: Hon FTCL; Hon FLCM; 1st Prize, Royal Overseas League Competition, 1963; International Tchaikovsky Competition, Moscow, 1970; Dinu Lipatti Medal; Chappel Gold Medal; OBE, 1978; Hon DSc, Aston, 1978; Hon DMus, Exeter, 1979. Hobbies: Chess; Amateur radio; Walking. Current Management: Harold Holt Ltd. Address: Harold Holt Ltd, 31 Sinclair Road, London W14 0NS, England.

LILLIEQVIST Karl Torbjorn, b. 29 April 1945, Malmoe, Sweden. Opera Singer; Opera Director. Education: Intalian Music History, University of Lund; Akademie fur Musik, Wien, 1966-69; Accademia di Santa Cecilia, Rome, 1969-70; College of Music & Drama, Stockholm, 1971-74; Masterclasses with Gerald Moore, Erik Werba; Singing Studies with Erik Saedén, Eugene Ludwig, Vera Rosza. Debut: Drottningholm Court Theatre, 1971. Career: Regularly Performing at the Royal Opera Stockholm, Drottningholm Court Theatre, Gothenburg Opera, Malmoe Music Theatre; Specialized in Character Roles including Mozarts Basilio, Garo, Mime, Bardolfo, Frosch; Several Roles in Television Operas; Regularly Performing with Stockholm Royal Philharmonic Orchestra, Gothenburg Symphony Orchestra, Malmo Symphony Orchestra, including Stage Concerts of Operas; Concert Tour of Moscow, St Petersburg; Song Recitals in Sweden and Abroad; Producer of a Childrens Opera at the Festival of the Arts, Wellington, New Zealand; Artistic Leader, International Vadstena Academy, 1981-85; Guest Professor at Various Colleges of Music in Sweden and Abroad. Honours: Italian State Scholarship, 1971; Svenska Dagbladets Opera Prize, 1989; Drottningholm Court Theatre Scholarship, 1995. Honour: Council, International Vadstena Academy. Hobbies: Cooking; Swimming. Current Management: Nordic Artist AB, Stockholm, Sweden. Address: Hagagatan 38, S-11347 Stockholm, Sweden.

LILOVA Margarita, b. 26 July 1935, Tscherwen, Bulgaria. Mezzo-Soprano. Education: Studied in Sofia with Maria Zibulka and Michail Jankov. Debut: Varna Opera in 1959 as Maddalena in Rigoletto. Career: Sang in Varna as the Countess in The Queen of Spades and Azucena, and Covent Garden and Vienna Staatsoper debuts in 1962 and 1963 as Amneris; Guest appearances at the Paris Opéra, Komische Oper Berlin and the Teatro Colón, Buenos Aires, also at Los Angeles, Berlin, Montreal and Moscow; Member of the Vienna Staatsoper from 1963 including a tour of Japan in 1986, as Marcellina in Le nozze di Figaro and Annina in Der Rosenkavalier; Sang at Salzburg Festival, 1965-67 as the Hostess in Boris Godunov under von Karajan, La Scala Milan in 1973 as Ulrica in Un Ballo in Maschera returning in 1988 as Mary in Der fliegende Holländer; Many concert appearances and song recitals. Recordings: Les Contes d'Hoffmann; Boris Godunov; Der Rosenkavalier; Bruckner Te Deum and Mass No 2; Verdi Messa da Requiem; Video, Maidservant in Elektra conducted by Abbado. Honour: Kammersängerin, 1984, Staatsoper Wien. Membership: Professor, Hochschule für Musik und Dorstellende Kunst, Wien, 1993. Address: c/o Staatsoper, Opernring 2, A-1010 Vienna, Austria.

LILTVED Oystein, b. 20 Jan 1934, Arendal, Norway. Bass Singer. m. Virginia Oosthuizen. Education: Studied with Maria Hittorf in Vienna, Luciano Donaggio in Trieste and Frederick Dalberg in Kapstad, South Africa. Debut: Basle in 1959 as Konshak in Prince Igor. Career: Many appearances at the opera houses of Oslo, Stockholm, Dusseldorf, Kassel and Barcelona; Sang in South Africa at Cape Town and at Johannesburg; Sang at Seattle Opera as Hagen in Götterdämmerung; Other roles have been Wagner's Daland, Landgrave and Fafner, Verdi's King Philip and Fiesco, Mozart's Osmin and Sarastro, Mephistopheles, Varlaam in Boris Godunov, Oroveso, Rocco, Raimondo in Lucia di Lammermoor and Swallow in Peter Grimes; Many appearances in concerts and oratorios.

LIM Liza, b. 30 August 1966, Perth, Western Australia. Composer; Lecturer. Education: BA, Victoria College of the Arts, 1986; Study with Ton de Leeuw, 1987; MMus, University of Melbourne, 1993. Career: Lecturer in Composition, University of Melbourne, 1991; Commissions from Duo Contemporain, The Seymour Group; Intercontemporain (Paris), ABC/BBC, Ensemble Modern (1995) and others. Compositions include: Blazefor mezzoand ensemble, 1986; Pompes Funebres for string quartet, 1987; Koan, for alto saxophone and percussion, 1987; Tarocchi, for 3 guitars, double bass and percussion, 1988; Voodoo Child for soprano and ensemble, 1989; Constellations, for violin and string orchestra, 1989; Garden of Earthly Desire, for ensemble, 1989; Diabolical Birds, for ensemble, 1990; Amulet, for viola, 1992; Hell, for string quartet, 1992; The Oresteia, opera for 6 voices, 11 instruments and 1 dancer, 1993; Koto, for ensemble, 1993; Lin Shang Yin for coloratura soprano and 15 instruments, 1993; Cathedral, for orchestra, 1994; Sri Vidya for chorus and orchestra, 1994-95. Honours: Sounds Australian Award, 1990. Address: c/o APRA, 1A Eden Street, Crows Nest, NSW 2065, Australia.

LIM Soon-Lee, b. 3 Aug 1957, Singapore. Violist; Conductor. m. 23 June 1983. Education: Licentiate, Royal Schools of Music (Violin and Viola); BM with distinction, Eastman School of Music, University of Rochester. Debut: Paganini, Grand Viola Sonata, Kilburn Hall, Eastman School of Music. Career: Sub-Principal, Singapore Symphony Orchestra; Assistant Conductor, Singapore Youth Orchestra; Conducted Singapore Symphony Orchestra for the opening and closing ceremonies of the 17th South East Asia Games, 1993; Music Director, Resident Conductor, National University of Singapore Concert Orchestra. Honours: 1st Prize, Viola/Cello Open, Singapore National Music Competition, 1981. Memberships: Conductors' Guild; American Viola Society; American String Teachers' Association; Singapore National Arts Council, Member of Arts Resource Panel. Hobby: Running. Address: 69 Bodmin Drive, Singapore 1955.

LIMA Luis, b. 12 Sep 1948, Cordoba, Argentina. Tenor. Education: Studied voice with Carlos Guicchandut in Buenos Aires and with Gina Cigna in Italy. Debut: Lisbon in 1974 as Turiddu in Cavalleria Rusticana. Career: Guest appearances in Mainz, Munich, Stuttgart and Hamburg; Sang at La Scala Milan in 1977 as Edgardo in Lucia di Lammermoor; Further appearances in Strasbourg and Spain as Rodolfo, Cavaradossi and Faust in Mefistofele; US debut in 1976 in a concert performance of Donizetti's Gemma di Vergy at Carnegie Hall; Metropolitan Opera debut in 1978 as Alfredo in La Traviata; Sung at New York City Opera in 1979 in La Bohème and Rigoletto, Salzburg Festival in 1984 as Verdi's Macduff, Maggio Musicale Florence, 1985-86 as Don Carlos and as Riccardo in Un Ballo in Maschera, and Covent Garden in 1985 as Nemorino and Don Carlos, returning to London in 1988 as Edgardo; Salzburg Easter Festival in 1988 as Cavaradossi and sang Faust at the opening of the season at the Teatro Colón Buenos Aires in 1990; Sang Don José in a new production of Carmen at Covent Garden in 1991 and Verdi's Don Carlos at San Francisco in 1992; Madrid in 1992 as Don José and New York Metropolitan in 1994 as Cilea's Maurizio; Season 1996 with Rodolfo at Covent Garden; Don Carlos at the New York Met, 1997. Recordings include: Gemma di Vergy; Le Roi de Lahore; Video of Don Carlos and of Carmen, both from Covent Garden. Address: c/o Stafford Law Associates, 6 Barham Close, Weybridge, Surrey, KT13 9PR, England.

LIMA Paulo (Costa), b. 26 Sept 1954, Salvador, Bahia, Brazil. Composer; Professor of Music. m. Ana Margarida Cerqueira Lima e Lima, 2 sons. Education: Music School, UFBa, 1969-76; BM, Composition, 1978, MS, 1978, University of Illinois, Urbana, USA; PhD, UFBA, 1998. Career: Professor of Music at Universidade Federal da Bahia, 1979; Head of Music Department, UFBa, 1986-88; Director of Music School, UFBa, 1988-92; Participation as composer at many national and international events; Festivals: Campos de Jordao, Sao Paulo, UFRJ; Director of Music School, Universidade Federal da Bahia, 1988-92; International events at Dresden and Urbana; Assistant President, Universidade Federal da Bahia, 1996-98. Compositions: Bundle for Solo Flute, 1977, FCEBa, 1981; Ubaba, O Que Diria Bach, 1983, Funarte for Chamber Orchestra; Atôtô-Balzare, UFBA for Percussion and Piano; Cuncti-Serenata, 1983, Funarte UFBA for Piano Solo; Fantasia, 1984, Funarte UFBA for Piano Solo; Pega Essa Nega e Chera, for piano solo, 1993; Corrente de Xango, for cello, 1995; Ponteio, for piano solo, 1995; Atoto do L'homme armè, for chamber orchestra, 1996; Ibejis, for flute and clarinet, 1996; Frevo, for piano solo, 1997. Recordings: Compositores Da Bahia, 5, 7 and 8; Outros Ritmos, 1997; Impressionem, 1997. Publications: Editor of Art, Music Periodical, 1981-91. Contributions to: Musical and academic journals. Honours: Composition Prize, Max Feffer, Sao Paulom 1995; Fellowship in Composition, Vitae Foundation, 1995; Copene Prize, 1996. Address: R Sabino Silva 304, ap 401, Chame 40155-250, Salvador, Brazil.

LIN Cho-Liang, b. 21 Jan 1960, Taiwan. Violinist. Education: Studied violin from age 5; Sydney Conservatoire, 1972-75; Juilliard School, 1975-78, with Dorothy DeLay. Debut: Played with the Philadelphia Orchestra under Ormandy and with the London Symphony Orchestra under Previn, 1976. Career: Many performances with leading orchestras in Europe and America; Season 1993-94 with concerts in UK, North America, Finland, Germany, Belgium, France and Far East; United Kingdom, Holland, France, Finaldn and Spain, 1995; Plays a 1707 Stradivarius once owned by Samuel Dushkin. Recordings: Mendelssohn Concerto with the Philharmonia Orchestra conducted by Michael Tilson Thomas; Mozart's 5 Concerti with the English Chamber Orchestra under Raymond Leppard; Concertos by Sibelius and Nielsen conducted by Esa-Pekka Salonen; Bruch Violin Concerto and Scottish Fantasy with Chiacgo Symphony conducted by Leonard Slatkin; Stravinsky, Prokofiev 1 and 2 violin concertos with Los Angeles Philharmonic conducted by Esa-Pekka Salonen. Address: c/o ICM Artists (London) Ltd, Oxford House, 76 Oxford Street, London, W1N 0AX, England.

LIN Hua, b. 8 Aug 1942, Shanghai, China. Composer; Professor. Education: Graduated with honours, Shanghai Conservatory of Music, 1966; Piano and composition with Sang Tong, Wang Jianzhong and Chen Mingzhi. Career: Composer for Shanghai Wind Band, 1967-76, Shanghai Opera and Ballet House, 1976-79; Associate Professor, Counterpoint, Fugue, Shanghai Conservatory of Music, 1979-; Consultant, Shanghai Philharmonic Association, 1982-. Compositions include: Bright Mountain Flowers In Full Bloom, ballet, 1976; Fantasy for Piano and Accordion, 1978; Love Of The Great Wall for Piano and Accordion, 1978; Farewell Refrains At Yang Gate Pass for Piano Quartet, 1978; Beauty Of Peking Opera for String Quartet, 1979; Album Of Woodcuts for Piano Quintet, 1979; Amid Flowers Beside A River Under The Spring Moon for 4 Harps, 1979; Flower And Song, concertino for Soprano and Orchestra, 1980; Suite Tragedy for Chamber Symphony, 1988; 24 Preludes and fugues on reading Sikong Tu's Shipin (Personalities of Poetry in Tang Dynasty), 1990; Album of World Folk Songs for Piano, 1991; Stage, film and TV music. Publications: Guide The Teaching of Polyphony by Using Creative Psychology, 1980; Stravinsky Techniques in Polyphonic Writing, 1987; The Sense of Ugliness and Its Application in Western Music, 1988; Abstraction of Art and Abractionism, 1989. Address: 20 Fenyang Road, Shanghai, China.

LIND Eva, b. 14 Jun 1965, Innsbruck, Austria. Singer (Soprano). Education: Studied in Vienna. Debut: Landestheater Innsbruck, 1983, as a Flowermaiden in Parsifal. Career: Sang Lucia di Lammermoor at Basle, 1985 and the Queen of Night at Vienna and Paris, 1987; Salzburg Festival 1986 and 1987, as the Italian Singer in Capriccio; Vienna Staatsoper from 1986, as Lucia (Lucia di Lammermoor) and Sophie in Werther; Stuttgart Staatsoper as Adele in Die Fledermaus; British debut as Nannetta in Falstaff, Glyndebourne, 1988; Gounod's Juliette at Zurich, 1990 followed by Sophie in Der Rosenkavalier at Vienna, Brussels and Berne Opera; Concerts with Francisco Araiza at the Teatro Colon, Buenos Aires, 1990; Sang Mozart's Blonde at Catania, 1996. Recordings: Die Fledermaus, conducted by Placido Domingo; Naiad in Ariadne auf Naxos, with the Leipzig Gewandhaus Orchestra conducted by Kurt Masur; Coloratura arias, including Elisabeth ou La Fille proscrit by Donizetti; Papagena in Die Zauberflöte, conducted by Marriner; Olympia in Tales of Hoffmann, with Jeffrey Tate; Opera duets with Francisco Araiza; Aennchen in Der Freischütz, conductor, Colin Davis.

LINDBERG Christian, b. 1958, Stockholm, Sweden. Trombone Soloist. m. 4 children. Education: Studied trumpet as teenager, then trombone; Further studies in Stockholm, London, Los Angeles, 1978-83. Career: Member, Royal Stockholm Opera Orchestra, 1977-78; Currently gives over 100 concerts yearly as trombone soloist with world's major symphony orchestras; Solo programmes including music theatre; Appearances with Per Lundberg, piano, and with Hakan Hardenberger, trumpet; Repertoire includes contemporary music, baroque music played on original instruments, classical and romantic music; Works composed for him include concertos by Schnittke, Xenakis, Takemitsu and Arvo Part; Played at several UK festivals and Pitea Festival, North Sweden, summer 1993; Season, 1993-94 with concerts in Germany, Switzerland, Iceland, Denmark, Sweden, Israel; Tours, USA and with Scottish Chamber Orchestra, Scotland; Schnittke's Dialogue with Nash Ensemble, London; Performances with Prague Symphony Orchestra, Czech Republic, and Gothenburg Symphony Orchestra, Sweden; Carnegie Hall debut with Zwillich Trombone Concerto and world premiere of Trombone Concerto by Toru Takemitsu with St Paul Chamber Orchestra, USA; Several German festivals and Japan tour, summer 1994; 1994-95 season included performances of Trombone Concerto by Iannis Xenakis, new works by Kalevi Aho and Arvo Part, also tours, Australia, France, Japan; Masterclasses; Designs instruments and mouthpieces for CONN Instrument Company. Recordings include: British Trombone Concerti; American Concerti; Italian repertoire for Trombones, Voice and Chamber Organ; Gemeaux by Takemitsu; Frank Martin's Ballade with Concertgebouw Orchestra and Riccardo Chailly. Current Agent: Clarion/Seven Muses, 47 Whitehall Park, London N19 3TW, England. Address: Valhallavagen 110, 114 41 Stockholm, Sweden.

LINDBERG Magnus, b. 27 Jun 1958, Helsinki, Finland. Composer; Pianist. Education: Studied at the Sibelius Academy, Helsinki; Further studies with Globokar in Paris, Donatoni in Siene and Ferneyhough at Darmstadt. Compositions include: Three Pieces for Horn and String Trio; Arabesques for Wind Quintet; Quintet for Piano and Wind; De Tartuffe je Croi for String Quartet and Piano; Drama for Orchestra; Sculpture II for Orchestra; Linea d'Ombra for Flute and Ensemble; Action Situation Signification for Horn or Clarinets and Ensemble (1982); Ritratto for Orchestra; Zona for Ensemble; Metal Work for Accordion and Percussion; Kraft for Orchestra (1985); UR for 5 Players and Live Electronics; Twine for Piano; Trios Sculptures for Orchestra; Tape: Etwas Zarter; Ohne Audruck; Faust; Ensemble triptych Kinetics, Marea and Joy (1988-90); (orrente II, 1991); Aura, 1994; Arena, 1995; Cello Concerto. Honours include: Prix Italia for Faust; Nordic Music Prize for Kraft. Address: c/o Boosey and Hawkes Ltd, 295 Regent Street, London W1R 8JH.

LINDE Hans-Martin, b. 24 May 1930, Werne, Germany. Recorder Player; Flautist; Conductor. m. Gudrun Olshausen, 1 son, 2 daughters. Education: Staatliche Hochschule fur Musik, Freiburg, 1947-51, with Konrad Lechner (conducting) and Gustav Scheck (flute). Career: Solo flautist of the Cappella Coloniensis of West German Radio, Cologne; Concert tours in Europe, USA, South America, Middle and Far East from 1955; Teacher of Baroque Flute, Recorder and Conducting from 1957; Conductor of Vocal Ensemble, 1965-; Conductor of Chamber Orchestra, 1970- of the Schola Cantorum Basiliensis, Basle; Co-Editor, Zeitschrift für Spielmusik, 1966-; Concert associations with August Wenzinger and Frans Brueggen; Conducted with Basler-Linde Concert in Vivaldi's La Griselda at Ludwigshafen, 1989. Recordings include: Flute Concertos by Leclair, Stamitz, Dittersdorf and Mozart; Recorder Concertos by Sammartini and Vivaldi; English Consort Music and Chamber Music by Bach, Handel, Haydn with the Linde-Consort; Conductor of the Linde-Consort and the Cappella Coloniensis; Guest Conductor of several orchestras and choirs in different European countries and in the USA; Recordings as a conductor include: Bach; Masses, Brandenburg Concertos, Orchestral Suites; Schütz: Exequien; Handel: Water-Music, Music for the Royal Fireworks, Concerti grossi op 6, Keiser's Der Grossmutige Tomyris. Publications: Kleine Anleitung zum Verrzieren alter Musik, 1958; Handbuch des Blockflötenspiels, 1962.

LINDENSTRAND Sylvia, b. 24 Jun 1942, Stockholm, Sweden. Singer (Mezzo-Soprano). Education: Studied at the Opera School of the Royal Opera, Stockholm. Debut: Stockholm 1962, as Olga in Eugene Onegin. Career: Has sung at the Royal Opera, Stockholm as Dorabella, Cherubino, Marina in Boris Godunov, Octavian, Brangäne, Fricka in the Ring and Cenerentola; Sang Tchaikovsky's Maid of Orleans, 1986 and sang in Singoalla by Gunnar de Frumerie 1988; Guest appearances at Bayreuth, 1964, Copenhagen and the Moscow Bolshoi; Glyndebourne 1975 and 1979, as Dorabella and Amaranta in La Fedeltà Premiata; Aix-en-Provence, 1976, Zerlina in Don Giovanni; Sang Idamante in Idomeneo at Drottningholm; Royal Opera Stockholm, 1991 as Dionysus in the premiere of Backanterna by Daniel Börtz (production by Ingmar Bergman); Many concert engagements. Recordings include: Songs by Liszt. Honours include: Swedish Court Singer, 1982. Address: c/o Kungliga Teatern, P O Box 16094, S-102 51 Stockholm, Sweden.

LINDERMEIER Elisabeth, b. 1923, Munich, Germany. Singer (Soprano). m. Rudolf Kempe (died 1976). Education: Studied at Munich Musikhochschule. Debut: Bavarian State Opera, Munich, 1946, as the Sandman in Hansel and Gretel. Career: Many appearances in Munich in the lyric soprano repertory: appeared with the company at Covent Garden in the British premiere of Strauss's Die Liebe der Danae, 1953; Berlin and Dresden 1956, as Leonora in Il Trovatore; Glyndebourne Festival 1956, Donna Elvira; Sang Freia and Gutrune in Ring cycles at Covent Garden and appeared also in a stage version of Handel's Samson, 1958; Further engagements in Vienna, Frankfurt and Amsterdam; Strauss performances at the Munich Festival. Recordings: Die Zaubergeige by Werner Egk, Hansel and Gretel; Daphne by Strauss, Munich, 1950; Finale of Götterdämmerung. Address: c/o Bayerische Staatsoper, Postfach 745, D-80336 Munich 1, Germany.

LINDHOLM Berit (Maria), b. 18 Oct 1934, Stockholm, Sweden. Opera Singer (Soprano). m. Hans Lindholm, 2 daughters. Education: Studied at Stockholm Opera School. Debut: Countess in Le nozze di Figaro, Stockholm, 1963. Career: Performances all over the world including, New York Met, Carnegie Hall, San Francisco, Chicago, London, Paris, Hamburg, Berlin, Munich, Moscow, Naples, Madrid, Geneva, Zürich, Dusseldorf, Vienna, Barcelona, Bayreuth; Repertoire includes, Isolde, Brünnhilde, Kundry, Tosca, Salome, Elektra, Turandot, Fidelio, Dyer's Wife in Die Frau ohne Schatten. Recordings include: Les Troyens; Die Walküre; Songs by Swedish Composers. Memberships: Swedish Royal Academy of Music. Honours: Opera Singer by Appointment of the King of Sweden. Address: Artistsekretariat Ulf Törnqvist, Sankt Eriksqatan 100, S-11331 Stockholm, Sweden.

LINDLEY Simon Geoffrey, b. 10 October 1948, Barnehurst, Kent, England. Organist. m. Carel Louise McMiram,

1974, 3 sons, 1 daughter. Education: Magdalen College School, Oxford; Royal College of Music. Debut: Westminster Cathedral, 1969. Career: Deputy Organist, Westminster Cathedral, 1969-73; Assistant Master of Music, Cathedral & Assey Church of St Alban, 1970-75; Director of Music, St Albans School, 1971-75; Master of Music, Organist, Leeds Parish Church, 1975-; City Organist, Leeds, 1976-; Senior Assistant Music Officer, Leeds, 1987-; Music Director, St Peters Singers & Chamber Orchestra, 1977-; Resident Music Director, Principal Conductor, Yorkshire Evening Post Band, 1995-; Special Commissioner, RSCM, 1975-; Examiner, Associated Board, 1976-. Compositions: Come Sing and Dance, 1977; Ave Maria, 1979; Evening Prayer, 1986; O God, My Heart is Ready, 1990; Carols, 1995; On Easter Morn, 1995; Now the Green Blade Riseth, 1995; Jacob's Ladder, 1995; Anthems for Unison & Two Park Singing; Hilariter, 1996. Recordings: Numerous as Organist and Conductor. Publication: Muse and the Mass, 1990. Contributions to: Listener; Musical Times; Organists Review; Dalesman; Church Music Quarterly; Choir & Organ. Honours: Geoffrey Tankard Prize, 1968; ARSCM, 1987; Hon FGMS, 1996. Memberships: Royal College of Organists; Incorporated Society of Musicians; Cathedral Organists Association. Hobbies: Walking; History; Typography. Address: 8 The Chandlers, The Calls, Leeds LS2 7EZ, England.

LINDNER Brigitte, b. 1959, Munich, Germany. Singer (Soprano). Education: Studied in Munich. Debut: Gärtnerplatz-Theater Munich as a Boy in Die Zauberflöte. Career: Sang Gretel in Humperdinck's opera (also televised) and in Mozart's Bastien and Bastienne; Adult debut at the Ludwigsburg Festival 1980, as Barbarina in Le Nozze di Figaro; Bayreuth Festival 1985, as the Shepherd boy in Tannhäuser; Sang Despina in Così fan tutte for Kiel Opera, 1990; Other roles include Papagena and parts in operettas by Lehar and Johann Strauss; Concert appearances in oratorios by Bach, Haydn and Mozart. Recordings: Hansel and Gretel, Die Zauberflöte.

LINDROOS Peter, b. 26 Feb 1944, Pojo, Finland. m. Anja Hilleri Kervinen, 1963, 4 children. Education: Studied in Helsinki, with Jolanda di Maria Tetris, 1966-68, and with Luigi Ricci in Rome and Mario del Monaco in Treviso. Debut: Cantor, Organist from Sibelius Academy, 1964; Helsinki, 1968, as Rodolfo in La Bohème; Gothenburg, 1969, notably as Verdi's Otello; Member of the Royal Opera Copenhagen from 1971, Staatsoper Stuttgart from 1974; Covent Garden, 1975-76 as the Duke of Mantua and Bacchus; Guest appearances in Berlin, Munich, San Francisco, London and Vienna; Cologne Opera, 1983, as Parsifal; Other roles include Verdi's Manrico and Gabriele Adorno, Don José, Janacek's Laca, David in Nielsen's Saul and David, and Apollo in Strauss's Daphne, Don Carlo, Otello, Alfredo, Cavaradossi; Helsinki 1985, in the premiere of Rautavaara's Thomas; Sang at the Edinburgh Festival, 1987 in Juha by Merikanto; Lausanne and Graz, 1987 as Bacchus and in the premiere of Cerha's Der Rattenfänger; Sang Apollo in Daphne at Munich, 1988; Radames at the Savonlinna Festival, 1989. Guest as Don José at Buenos Aires, 1993; Dimitri, Boris Godunov, Paris Grand Opera, Bacchus at the Opéra-comique, Armide by Gluck in Madrid and Barcelona, Des Grieux at the Edinburgh Festival and Montreal, Apollo in Daphne at La Scala, Lohengrin in Copenhagen and Edmonton; Sang Bacchus at Copenhagen, 1992. Recordings include: Liszt's Christus. Honours: The White Rose of Finland, The Knight of the Ivass, 1983; Order of Dannebrog, Denmark, 1982. Address: c/o Royal Danish Theatre, Box 2185, DK 1017, Copenhagen, Denmark.

LINDSAY L Christeene, b. 2 Mar 1951, San Diego, California, USA. Opera Singer (Soprano). divorced, 2 sons, 4 daughters. Education: Studied voice with Robert Austin, 1974-86; with Larra Browning Henderson, 2 years. Debut: With Pacific Chamber Opera as Laetitia in Old Maid, 1981. Career: Despina, Cosi fan Tutte, 1982; Sister Marguerite, Sound of Music, 1982; Gretel, Hansel & Gretel, 1982; Fanny in Rossini's Cambiale, 1984; Lucieta in Il Quattro Rusteghi, 1984; Maturina, Don Giovanni-Gazzaniga; Martha, Flotow's Martha; Little Match Girl, 1985; Adele, Fledermaus, 1986; Saffi, Gypsy Baron, 1987; Marietta, Naughty Marietta, 1988; Managing Director, Pacific Chamber Opera, 1986-88. Address: 7807 Artesian Road, San Diego, CA 92127, USA.

LINDSKOG Par, b. 1962, Kungelv, Sweden. Singer (Tenor). Education: Vocal studies at Gothenburg, from 1981. Career: Secondary roles at the Opera Studio and Theatre in Gothenburg; Berlin Staatsoper as Max in Der Freischütz, Narraboth (Salome), Steva (Jenufra) and the Steersman in Der Fliegende, Holländer, from 1987; Further engagements in Lisbon, Salzburg, Dresden and Leipzig; Season 1995/96 as Young Man in Moses und Aron under Pierre Boulez at Amsterdam and Salzburg, and under Christoph von Dohnanyi with the Philharmonia Orchestra at the Festival Hall, London; Further roles include Tamino, Don Ottavio and Barinkay in Der Zigeunerbaron, Vienna, 1996. Honours include: Bayreuth Scholarship, 1993. Address: c/o Deutsche Staatsper Berlin, Unter den Linden 7, 0-1060 Berlin, Germany.

LING Jan Nils, b. Apr 1934, Orebro, Sweden. Musicologist; Professor. m. (1) Britt Nyberg, Jun 1958, 1 son, 1 daughter. m. (2) Monica Lauritzen, Dec 1981. Education: Piano studies, Swedish Royal Academy of Music, 1955-59; Ph Candidate, 1959; MA, 1961, PhD, 1967. Career: Professor of Musicology, University of Goteborg. Publications: Svensk Folkmusik, 1964; Nyckleharpen (Keyed Fiddle), 1967; Levin Christian Wiedes Vissamling: i 1800-talets Folkligpa Vissang (Study of Folksong in 19th Century Sweden), 1965; Folkmusikboken, 1980; Europas Musikhistoria-1730, 1983; Europas Musikhistoria, Folkmusiken, 1989; Also articles on Music History, Sociology of Music, Folk Music, various journals, different languages. Honour: Musical prize, Expressen Spelmannen (The Player), 1983. Memberships: Royal Swedish Academy of Music; Kungl Vitterhetssamfundet i Goteborg. Hobby: Music. Address: Anggardsgatan 31, 413 19 Goteborg, Sweden.

LINGE Ruth, b. 13 Oct 1927, Porsgrunn, Norway. Opera Singer; Lyrical Soprano. m. Tormod Linge. Education: Private, Oslo, Stockholm, Vienna. Debut: As Norina in Don Pasquale, Oslo, 1951. Career: Norsk Operaselskap, 1951-58; Member, Den Norske Opera, 1958-; Main roles include Zerlina, Donna Elvira, Donna Anna, Cherubino, Papagena, Adina, Gilda, Rosina, Musetta, Olympia; Appearances in TV opera productions, radio concerts. Memberships: Secretary, Board Society of Norwegian Opera Singers; Society of Norwegian Musica Artists.

LINGWOOD Tom, b. 15 Sept 1927, Guildford, Surrey, England. Stage Director and Designer. Education: Studied at Guildford School of Art and the St Martin's School of Art, London. Career: Designs for Martin y Soler's Una Cosa Rara, Jeannetta Cochrane Theatre, 1965 and Manon Lescaut at Covent Garden, 1968; For Australian opera has designed La Bohème and La Forza del Destino, 1970, Nabucco, 1971; War and Peace for the opening of the Sydney Opera House, 1973 followed by Salome and Don Pasquale, 1976, 1978; Teacher at the New South Wales Conservatorium of Music and the National Institute of Dramatic Art. Honours: Emmy Award, 1989, for La Bohème. Address: c/o Australian Opera, Sydney Opera House, Sydney, NSW, Australia.

LINJAMA Jouko, b. 1934, Finland. Composer. Education: Sibelius Academy; Musicology and Literature, Helsinki University; Further studies in Composition, Cologne, 1962-64; Staatliche Hochschule für Musik; Composers Seminar, Kölner Kurse für Neue Musik. Career: Organist, St Henrik's Catholic Church, 1958-60; Cantor-Organist, Parish of Tuusula, 1964-. Compositions include: Orchestra: 2 Symphonies from oratorio Homage to Aleksis Kivi, 1972; La Migration d'Oiseaux Sauvages, 1977; Choral Works: How It Is, oratorio, 1968; Homage to Aleksis Kivi, symphonic oratorio, 1970, 1974, 1976; Missa De Angelis, 1969; La Sapienza, oratorio da camera, 1980; Mailman Algusta ia Loomisesta, oratorio, 1983; Chamber Music: String Quartet No 1, 1978; No 2, 1979; Concerto for Organ, Marimba, Vibraphone, 2 Wind Quartets, 1981; Works for Organ: Sonatina supra B-A-C-H, 1968; Magnificat for Organ, 1970; Partitasonata Veni Creator Spiritus, 1969; Missa Cum Jubilo for Organ, 1977; Organum supra B-A-C-H, 1982; Toccata in D, 1985; Reflections, duet for Organ, 1991; Cappella Choral Works: Two Cantio Motets, 1973; 4 Madrigals for Male Voice Choir, 1977, 1982; Partita per coro, 1979; On The Road to Splendour, 1980; Has composed numerous solo songs and music for Shakespeare's play, As You Like It, 1972. Recordings: Numerous recordings of his work. Address: Teosto, Lauttasaarentie 1, 00200 Helsinki 20, Finland.

LINKE Fritz, b. 15 May 1923, Claussnitz, Germany. Singer (Bass). Career: Sang in Chemnitz from 1950; Dresden Staatsoper, 1951-56; Staatsoper Stuttgart, 1956-86; Guest appearances in Hamburg, Munich, Paris, Barcelona, Venice, Rome, Bologna, Mannheim, Cologne, Zurich and Karlsruhe; Bayreuth Festival, 1963-70; Roles include Mozart's Osmin and Sarastro, Verdi's Padre Guardiano and King Philip, Wagner's Daland, Fafner, Hunding and Landgrave, Beethoven's Rocco and Baron Ochs in Der Rosenkavalier. Address: c/o Staatstheater Stuttgart, Oberer Schlossgarten 6, D-7000 Stuttgart 1, Germany.

LINN Robert, b. 11 Aug 1925, San Francisco, California, USA. Composer. Education: Studied with Darius Milhaud at Mills College; MM, 1950, University of California at Los Angeles, with Roger Sessions, Bernard Stevens and Ingolf Dahl. Career: Faculty member at University of California at Los Angeles, 1958; Chairman of the department of music theory and composition, 1973-. Compositions: Clarinet Sonata, 1949; String Quartet, 1951; Four Pieces for concert band, 1954; 2 Piano Sonatas, 1955, 1964; Symphony, 1956; Concerto Grosso, 1961; Brass Quintet, 1963; Woodwind Quintet, 1963; Hexameron for piano and orchestra, 1963; Elevations for wind, 1964; Concertino for violin and wind octet, 1968; Sinfonia for strings, 1967, revised, 1972; Pied Piper of Hamelin, oratorio, 1968; Fantasia for cello and strings, 1976; Twelve, 1977; Concerto for flute and winds, 1980; Partita for winds, 1980; Concertino for woodwind quintet and strings, 1982; Concerto for piano and wind, 1984; Vocal music, including Songs of William Blake for chorus, 1981. Honours: Commissions and grants from the American Guild of Organists, the Louisville Orchestra and the Huntingson Hartford Foundation. Address: c/o ASCAP, ASCAP Building, One Lincoln Plaza, New York, NY 10023, USA.

LINOS Glenys, b. 29 Sept 1941, Cairo, Egypt. Singer (Mezzo-soprano). Education: Athens Conservatory; London Opera Centre. Career: Sang in Mainz, Ulm and Wiesbaden from 1970; Guest appearances in most major German opera houses; Bayreuth and Salzburg Festivals; Toulouse, 1983, as Carmen; Festival Hall, London, 1983, in the Verdi Requiem; Ghent, 1984, as Santuzza in Cavalleria Rusticana; Zurich, 1984-85, as Pensithelia in the opera by Schoeck; Paris Opéra-Comique, 1985, in The Stone Guest by Dargomizhsky; Lausanne and La Scala Milan, 1986, as the Sorceress in Dido and Aeneas and Geneviève in Pelléas et Mélisande; Rome Opera, 1986, as Ermengarda in Agnese di Hohenstaufen by Spontini; Sang Clairon in Capriccio at Bologna, 1987; Auntie in Peter Grimes at the Zurich Opera, 1989; Clytemnestra in Elektra at the Teatro Nuovo, Spoleto, 1990; Television appearances include Adriano in Rienzi, Wiesbaden Opera. Recordings include: Monteverdi's Orfeo. Address: c/o Opernhaus Zurich, Falkenstrasse 1, CH-8008 Zurich, Switzerland.

LIPKIN Malcolm (Leyland), b. 2 May 1932, Liverpool, England. Composer; Lecturer. m. Judith Frankel, 5 Aug 1968, 1 son. Education: Liverpool College, 1944-48; Royal College of Music, London, 1949-53; Privately with Mátyás Seiber, 1954-57; DMus, London, 1972; ARCM; LRAM. Debut: Gaudeamus Foundation, Netherlands, 1951. Career: Numerous broadcast and public performances of own compositions of orchestral, choral, vocal, chamber and instrumental music in many countries, 1951-. Compositions: Sinfonia di Roma, Symphony No 1; The Pursuit, Symphony No 2; Sun, Symphony No 3; Two Violin Concertos, Piano Concerto, Flute Concerto; Oboe Concerto; Psalm 96 for Chorus and Orchestra; Four Departures for Soprano and Violin; Five Shelley Songs; Clifford's Tower for instrumental ensemble; String Trio; Harp Trio; Five Piano sonatas; Violin sonata; Wind Quintet; Metamorphosis for Harpsichord; Naboth's Vineyard for Recorders, Cello and Harpsichord; Interplay; Pastorales for Horn and Strings; Piano Trio; Prelude and Dance for Cello and Piano; Nocturne for Piano; Bartók Variations for String Quartet; Dance Fantasy for Solo Violin; Five Bagatelles for Oboe and Piano, 1993; Duo for Violin and Cello, 1994; Second Violin Sonata, 1997. Recordings: Clifford's Tower; Pastorale, string trio recorded by Nash Ensemble, 1986; Piano Trio recorded by English Piano Trio on Kingdom Label, 1992. Contributions to: Musical Times; Musical Opinion; Classical Music. Hobbies: Long country walks. Address: Penlan, Crowborough Hill, Crowborough, Sussex TN6 2EA, England.

LIPKIN Seymour, b. 14 May 1927, Detroit, Michigan. USA. Pianist; Conductor. Education: Studied at the Curtis Institute, 1938-47, with David Sapert, Rudolf Serkin and Horsowski; Conducting studies with Koussevitsky at the Berkshire Music Center and as apprentice to George Szell at the Cleveland Orchestra, 1947-48. Debut: Conducted the Cleveland Little Symphony, 1948. Career: Soloist with the New York Philharmonic, 1949; Concerts with leading American orchestras; Teacher of conducting at the Berkshire Music Center, 1951-54; Conducted the New York City Opera, 1958, New York Philharmonic, 1959, Long Island Symphony, 1963-79; Joffrey Ballet, 1966-79; Teacher of piano at the Curtis Institute from 1969, Manhattan School from 1972; Resumed solo piano career in New York, 1981. Honours include: Winner, Rachmaninov Piano Competition, 1948. Address: c/o Manhattan School for Music, 120 Claremont Avenue, New York, NY 10027, USA.

LIPMAN Michael, b. 15 Mar 1954, Meriden, Connecticut, USA. Cellist; Educator. Education: Paul Olefsky, Hartt College of Music; Ronald Leonard and Paul Katz, Eastman School of Music; Leonard Rose, Blossom Music Festival; BMus, 1976, MMus in Performance and Literature, 1978, Eastman School of Music. Debut: Recital, Pittsburgh, 1985. Career: Soloist, Aspen Philharmonia Orchestra, 1977; Cello, Rochester Philharmonic, 1977-78; Principal Cello, Aspen Chamber Symphony, 1978-80; Associate Principal Cello, New Haven Symphony, 1978-79; Cello, Pittsburgh Symphony, 1979-; Soloist, Pittsburgh Symphony, 1985, 1993; Recitals and chamber music concerts throughout USA; Participant, Aspen Music Festival, 1976-80, New York String Seminar, 1976-77, Cleveland Chamber Seminar, 1977-78, Grand Teton Music Festival, 1982; Artist Lecturer in Cello, Carnegie-Mellon University, 1986-; Cellist and Founding Member, The California University of Pennsylvania String Quartet, 1986; Full-length radio broadcast of Pittsburgh debut recital, WQED, 1986; Solo and chamber music performances in Beijing, China, and Moscow, Russia, 1987, 1989; Faculty, Duquesne University School of Music, 1994-; Founding Member, The Dalihapa Ensemble, 1995-. Honours: 1st Prize, Aspen Concerto Competition, 1977; Passamaneck Award, Pittsburgh (Pennsylvania) Y Music Society, 1985. Hobbies: Racquetball; Golf; Running; Reading. Address: 4011 Boulevard Drive, Pittsburgh, PA 15217, USA.

LIPOVETSKY Leonidas, b. 2 May 1937, Montevideo, Uruguay. Concert Pianist; Lecturer; Educator. m. Astrid Eir Jonsson, 14 Apr 1973, 1 son, 2 daughters. Education: Juilliard School of Music, NYC, USA; Studied Piano with Wilhelm Kolischer, The Kolischer Conservatory, Montevideo, Uruguay and with Rosina Lhevinne and Martin Canin. Debut: National Symphony, Montevideo, Uruguay, 1959; NYC, 1967; Recital, NYC, 1964. Career: South American premiere of Britten's Piano Concerto in D Montevideo, 1959; Concert tours in UK, Europe, Russia, Scandinavia, USA, Canada, Central and South America; Soloist on tour with Czech Philharmonic, Leos Janacek in Spain and Czechoslovakia and with English Chamber Orchestra in USA National Symphony Orchestra, Mexico; National Orchestra Association, NYC, USA; Juilliard Orchestra, NYC, USA; Winnipeg Symphony, Canada; Royal Liverpool Philharmonic, UK; Seville Philharmonic, Spain; National Symphony of Iceland, Reykjavik; Chicago Chamber Orchestra, Chicago; Cedar Rapids Symphony, Iowa; National symphony of Columbia, Bogota, South America; Ossodre, Montevideo, Uruguay, South America; Mexico National Conservatory, Mexico; Broadcasts include BBC, London, UK; TV appearances and Special Guest Artist, UN General Assembly; Lectures at Trinity College of Music and Dartington College, UK and at the Juilliard School of Music, New York City, USA; Moscow Conservatory, Moscow, Russia; The High Museum of Art, Atlanta, GA; The Appleton Museum, Ocala, FL as well as in universities, Colleges and Systems of Education in the USA, Alaska, Canada, Puerto Rico, Central and South America; Creator of Project, Music and The Arts; Associate Professor of Piano, School of Music, The Florida State University, USA. Current Management: Project Music & The Arts, 1802 Atapha Nene, Tallahassee, FL 32301, USA. Address: 1802 Atapha Nene, Tallahassee, FL 32301, USA.

LIPOVSEK Marjana, b. 3 Dec 1946, Ljubljana, Slovenia. Singer (Mezzo-soprano). Education: Studied in Ljubljana and at the Music Academy in Graz. Career: Started in Vienna, then Hamburg, then Munich; Has sung in Munich, Marie (Wozzek), La Forza del Dastino; Nurse (Frau ohne Schatten); Kundry (Parsifal); Has sung at the Bavarian State Opera, Munich, from 1983, notably as Konchakovna in Prince Igor and Fricka in Der Ring des Nibelungen; Bregenz Festival from 1988, as Dalila and Carmen (1991); Has sung at the Vienna Staatsoper and in Berlin, Stuttgart, Frankfurt, Hamburg, Madrid and Milan; Has sung in the USA with Chicago and San Francisco Opera; Covent Garden debut, 1990, as Clytemnestra in Elektra, conducted by Georg Solti; Other roles include Ulrica, Orfeo, Octavian, Dorabella, Mistress Quickly, Azucena, Amneris, Brangaena, Marfa in Khovanshchina and Marie in Wozzeck; Concert engagements with Abbado, Horst Stein, Harnoncourt, Helmuth Rilling, Colin Davis, Sinopoli, Maazel, Sawallisch and Haitink; Beethoven's Missa Solemnis under Michael Gielen (also televised); London debut, 1988, in Das Lied von der Erde with the London Symphony; Salzburg Festival recitals from 1985; Other recitals at the Schleswig-Holstein and Hohenems Festivals, in Brussels, Amsterdam, Vienna and Germany and at the Wigmore Hall, London (1990); Season 1990/91 US concert debut with the New York Philharmonic conducted by Ozawa and the Boston Symphony Orchestra; Sang the Nurse in Die Frau ohne Schatten at the 1992 Salzburg Festival; Sang Clytemnestra at the 1996 Florence Maggio Musicale. Recordings include: Bach's Passions; Orfeo by Gluck and Messiah; Beethoven's 9th Symphony; Fricka in Das Rheingold and Die Walküre; Orlofsky in Die Fledermaus; The Witch in Hansel and Gretel under Jeffrey Tate; Clytemnestra in Elektra under Sawallisch. Honours include: Grand Prix du Disque for recording of Martin's Cornet. Address: c/o Lies Askonas Ltd, 6 Henrietta Street, London WC2, England.

LIPP Wilma, b. 26 Apr 1925, Vienna, Austria. Singer (Soprano). Education: Studied in Vienna and with Toti dal Monte in Milan. Debut: Vienna, 1943, as Rosina in Il Barbiere di Siviglia. Career: Member of the Vienna Staatsoper from 1945, notably as Mozart's Queen of Night; Salzburg Festival from 1948, as Mozart's Servilia, Blondchen, Donna Elvira and Queen of Night; Covent Garden, 1951, as Gilda in Rigoletto; La Scala Milan, 1950, and Glyndebourne, 1957, as Constanze in Die Entführung; US debut at San Francisco, 1962, as Nannetta in Falstaff; Guest appearances in London, Hamburg, Munich, Berlin and Paris; Returned to Salzburg, 1983-84, as the Duenna in Der Rosenkavalier (also at Turin, 1986). Recordings: Brahms Ein Deutsches Requiem; Die Zauberflöte; Die Entführung; Fra Diavolo; Die Fledermaus; Fidelio; Der Rosenkavalier. Address: c/o Staatsoper, Opernring 2, A-1010 Vienna, Austria.

LIPPERT Herbert, b. 1963, Germany. Singer (Tenor). Career: Sang at the Lubeck Opera 1987-91, in such roles as Pedrillo and Albert Herring; Bregenz Festival 1989, as Ferrando in Così fan tutte, followed by Tamino in Vienna, Munich and Cologne; Salzburg Festival from 1990, in Fidelio, Die Zauberflöte and Die Frau ohne Schatten; Naples and Aix Festival 1992 as Wagner's Steersman and as Don Ottavio; Further engagements at the Stuttgart and Leipzig Operas; Sang Wagner's David at Covent Garden, 1997; Concert repertory includes Bach's St Matthew Passion. Recordings include: Don Ottavio in Don Giovanni under Solti. Address: c/o Salzburg Festival (Opera). PO Box 140, A-5010 Salzburg, Austria.

LIPPERT Marion, b. 24 Sept 1939, Munich, Germany. Singer (Soprano). Education: Studied with the late Annelies Kupper in Munich; Further study in Padua. Debut: Hagen, 1956, as Aida. Career: Augsburg, Cologne and Stuttgart, 1959-62; Member of the Bavarian State Opera, Munich; Guest appearances in Germany, Austria, Italy, France and South America; Metropolitan Opera, 1969, as Puccini's Turandot; Other roles have included Verdi's Lady Macbeth, Abigaille, Leonora and Amelia, Wagner's Brünnhilde, Venus and Senta, Mozart's Donna Anna, the Marschallin in Der Rosenkavalier, Beethoven's Leonore and the Empress in Die Frau ohne Schatten. Address: c/o Bayerische Staatsoper, Postfach 745, D-8000 Munich, Germany.

LIPPMANN Friedrich, b. 25 July 1932, Dessau, Germany, Musicologist. m. Gudrun Schuppa, 1 child. Education includes: PhD, 1962. Career: Member, Joseph Haydn Institute, Cologne, 1962-64; Director, Music History Department, German Historical Institute, Rome, Italy, 1964. Publications include: J Haydn Harmoniemesse (editor), 1966; Vincenzo Bellini und die italienische Opera Serie seiner Zeit, 1969, Italian version, 1981; Versificazione italiana e ritmo musicale, 1985. Contributions to: Various professional journals; Editor, Analecta Musicologica and Concentus Musicus. Memberships: International Musicological Society; German Society for Music Research; Italian Musicological Society. Hobbies: Literature; Art. Address: Oberer Lindweg 20, D-53129 Bonn, Germany.

LIPTAK David, b. 18 Dec 1949, Pittsburgh, Pennsylvania, USA. Composer; Pianist; Teacher. m. Catherine Tait, 1 daughter. Education: Duquesne University, 1967-71; BM, Eastman School of Music, 1973-76; MM, DMA, Composition. Career: Composition and Theory Faculties, Michigan State University, 1976-80; University of Illinois, 1980-87; Eastman School of Music, 1986-, including Chairman of Composition Department, 1993-. Compositions: Duo, 1979, 1992; Seven Songs, 1984; Arcs, 1986; Loner, 1989; Trio, 1990; Shadower, 1991; Rhapsodies, 1992; Ancient Songs, 1992. Recordings: Seven Songs, 1984; Illusions, 1989. Publications: Compositions. Address: Composition Department, Eastman School of Music, 26 Gibbs Street, Rochester, NY 14064, USA.

LIPTON Daniel B, b. 1950, Paris, France. Conductor; Artistic Director. m. Olga Lucia Gaviria, 7 Mar 1983. Education: High School of Music and Art; Manhattan School of Music; Juilliard School; Mannes College; Ecole Normale Supérieure; Accademia Chigiana. Career: Appeared as Conductor, Settimane Senese, American Ballet Theater, Denver Symphony, Holland Festival (Concertgebouw), Teatro Comunale Bologna, Maggio Musicale Fiorentino (Florence), Zurich Opera, Liceo Barcelona, Madrid Opera, Teatro La Fenice (Venice), Châtelet (Paris), Sadler's Wells London, Houston Grand Opera, Utah Opera, San Antonio Festival, Hamburg Staatsoper, throughout North and South America, Paris Opera Orchestra and Bayerische Staatsoper (Munich); Artistic Director, Bogotà, Colombia (Colombia Symphony Orchestra and Opera de Colombia), 1975-83, Opera Hamilton, Ontario, Canada, 1986-, San Antonio Festival, San Antonio, Texas, 1987-; Conducted world premiere of Gian Carlo Menotti's The Wedding; Die Zauberflöte for Opera Hamilton, 1996. Recordings: Tosca, Puccini; Recital of Montserrat Caballé and José Carreras at Gran Teatre del Liceo in Barcelona; Video tapes: Donizetti, Don Pasquale; Giordano, Andrea Chénier; Leoncavallo, Pagliacci; Mascagni, Cavalleria Rusticana; Mozart, Nozze di Figaro; Ponchielli, Gioconda; Puccini, La Bohème, Tosca, Turandot; Verdi, Aida, Ballo, Forza, Rigoletto, Trovatore. Current Management: European: Carlos Caballe, Ioan Holender; Canadian: Rosario Farro (Impresario); USA: Robert Lombardo; James Harwood Management (New York).

LIPTON Martha, b. 6 Apr 1916, New York, USA. Singer (Mezzo-soprano). Education: Studied at the Juilliard School, New York. Debut: New Opera Company, New York, 1941, as Pauline in The Queen of Spades. Career: New York City Opera, 1944, in Martha; Metropolitan Opera from 1944, as Siebel in Faust, Verdi's Emilia, Amneris and Maddalena, Bizet's Mercedes and Humperdinck's Hansel; 298 performances in 36 parts, Rio de Janeiro, 1950; Carnegie Hall, 1952, in a concert performance of Wolf's Der Corregidor; Chicago, 1956, as Herodias in Salome; Other roles include Verdi's Meg Page and Ulrica, Mozart's Cherubino and Strauss's Octavian; Also heard as Lieder singer and in oratorio. Recordings: Mother Goose in The Rake's Progress; Orlofsky in Die Fledemaus; Handel's Messiah. Address: c/o Metropolitan Opera, Lincoln Center, New York, NY 10023, USA.

LISICHENKO Yuri, b. 1 Feb 1954, Lvov, USSR. Solo Concert Pianist; Professor. m. Irina Plotnikova, 20 Sept 1974, 1 son, 1 daughter. Education: Lvov Special Music School; Moscow Conservatory. Debut: With Philharmonic Orchestra, Hall of Lvov Philharmonia. Career: Professor, Moscow Conservatory; Performed: The Great Hall, 1973, 1975, The Small Hall, 1988, 1989, Moscow Conservatory; Milan, Turin, Verona, Italy, 1991; Basel, Switzerland, with violinist Tatiana Grindenko, 1991; Many TV and Radio appearances including TV film Avantgarde in Music (Company of Musical Programmes), 1989. Recordings: Chopin Sonata, A Rubinstein Sonata, Schumann; Melody, compact disc; Baroque music with Chamber Orchestra under Tatiana Grindenki, 1990; Ondine, Finland. Honours: 3rd Prize, Marguerite Long and Jacques Thibaud Competition, Paris, 1975; Honorary Diploma, Tchaikovsky Competitions, 1978. Memberships: Union of Musicians, Moscow. Hobby: Mountain Skiing. Current Management: Gosconcert, USSR; Matteo Tradardi, Itaca, Italy. Address: Teply Satn styr 25 K1, Apt 244, Moscow 117133, Russia.

LISITSYAN Pavel, b. 6 Nov 1911, Vladikavkas, Russia. Singer (Baritone); Teacher. Education: Studied in Leningrad, 1932-35. Career: Sang first in Leningrad, then at Erivan, Armenia; Appeared as leading baritone at the Bolshoy, Moscow, from 1940; Roles included Tchaikovsky's Yeletsky (Queen of Spades) and Eugene Onegin, Escamillo and Napoleon in War and Peace; Mazepa in Tchaikovsky's Mazepa; Robert in Tchaikovsky's Iolanta; Valentin in Gounot's Faust; Jermont in Verdi's Traviata; Mr Ford in Verdi's Falstaf; Concert tour of USA in 1960, appearing at the Metropolitan Opera as Amonasro; Tours of Western Europe, Asia, Japan, 1945-70; Sang in vocal quartet with his three children in the USSR and abroad, 1965-1975; Teacher at Erivan Conservatory, 1967-73; Teacher at Moscow State Philharmonia, Bolshoy, masterclasses in Western Europe, 1965-96; Professor from 1970. Recordings include: Aida, Carmen, Pagliacci, War and Peace, Rimsky-Korsakov's Sadko. Address: c/o Bolshoy Theatre, Pr Marxa 8/2, 103009 Moscow, Russia.

LISNEY James, b. 1960, England. Pianist. Debut: Wigmore Hall, 1986. Career: Regular appearances at the Royal Festival and Barbican Halls; Performances with Major Orchestras such as the Royal Philharmonic, The London Mozart Players, the European Community Chamber Orchestra and the Bournemouth Sinfonietta; Many prestigious recital series and festivals, and invitations to perform in the USA, France, Italy, Germany, Romania and Poland. Recordings: Tchaikovsky for IMP Classics. Honours: Only Artist to be selected by the Young Concert Artist Trust, Young Instrumentalists of Outstanding Potential. Address: 90 Fulwell Road, Teddington, Middlesex TW11 0RQ, England.

LISSITSIAN Rouben, b. 9 May 1945. Singer. Education: Central Music School, Moscow, 1953-60; Russian Music Academy, Moscow, 1965-69. Debut: Great Hall of Conservatory, Moscow, 1965. Career: Soloist-Vocalist, Cellist, Flautist, Madrigal Ensemble, 1965-69; Part of Evangelist From Mattäuspassion by Bach, Great Hall of Philharmonic, St Petersburg, 1973; Part of Samson From Oratorio Samson by Händel, Great Hall of Conservatory, Moscow, 1974; Part of Tenor From War Requeim by Britten, Wrozlaw-Festival, 1974; Part of Tenor From Symphony by Beethoven, Paris Congres de Palais, 1974; Rubajat by Gubaidulina With Schönberg Ensemble in Amsterdam, 1996; Tours of Germany, Israel, France, Finland, Netherlands, Hungary, USA, Canada, Poland. Recordings: P Cornelius, Weihnachtslieder; R Schumann, Lieder; W A Mozart, Requiem; J Brahms, Walzer; S Gubaidulina, Perception; Pärt, Stabat Mater. Honours: 1st Prize, Gold Medal, International R Schumanns Competition, Germany, 1969. Memberships: President, German-Russian Cultural and Educational Academy; Art Director, Russian Dramatic Theatre, Cologne. Hobby: Travel. Address: Ossendorfer Weg 37, 50827 Cologne, Germany.

LISTER Marquita, b. 1961, Washington DC, USA. Singer (Soprano). Education: New England Conservatory of Music; Oklahoma City University. Career: Appearances with Houston Opera as Fiordiligi, Micaela, Vitellia and Gershwin's Bess; Further engagements at San Francisco as Vitellia, 1993, and Aida, 1997, Portland Opera (Verdi's Alice and Elisabetta), Teatro Bellas Artes, Michagan Opera Theater (Aida), Utah and Pittsburgh Operas (Aida) and Baltimore (Liu in Turandot); European appearances at Verona (Nedda and Musetta), Staatstheater Stuttgart (Liu and Mimi), London, Milan, Paris, Berlin and the 1997 Bregenz Festival (all as Bess); Concerts with the Boston Pops, Leipzig Radio Orchestra, Bilbao Orkestra Sinfonika and the Academy of St Martin in the Fields; Gala Concert at Houston Grand Opera with Placido Domingo; Gala Concert, Johnstown Symphony Orchestra with Justino Diaz. Recordings include: Excerpts from Porgy and Bess, and Gershwin's Blue Monday (Cincinnati Pops). Honours include: Female Artist of the Year, Pittsburgh Opera. Address: c/o John J Miller Artist Management, 801 West 181st Street #20, New York, NY 10033, USA.

LISTOVA Irene, b. 1960, Moscow, Russia. Violinist. Education: Studied at the Moscow Conservatoire with Leonid Kogan. Career: Member of the Prokofiev Quartet (founded at the Moscow Festival of World Youth and the International Quartet Competition at Budapest); Many concerts in the former Soviet Union and on tour to Czechoslovakia, Germany, Austria, USA, Canada, Spain, Japan and Italy; Repertoire includes works by Haydn, Mozart, Beethoven, Schubert, Debussy, Ravel,

Tchaikovsky, Bartók and Shostakovich. Current Management: Sonata, Glasgow, Scotland. Address: 11 Northpark Street, Glasgow G20 7AA, Scotland.

LITSCHAUER Walberga, b. 15 Oct 1954, Klagenfurt, Austria. Musicologist. Education: Klagenfurt High School; Musicology, Philosophy and Theatre Sciences, University of Vienna; Piano studies, Vienna Conservatory, completed 1979; PhD, thesis The Italian Song in Vienna from 1750 to 1820, University of Vienna, 1980. Career: Member of Editorial Board, Director of Vienna Office, Neue Schubert Ausgabe, compendium of all Schubert's compositions; Has edited volumes of Schubert's piano music. Publications: Neue Dokumente zum Schubert-Kreis, volume 1, 1986, volume 2, 1993; Schubert und das Tanzvergnügen, with Walter Deutsch, 1997; About 70 publications on Schubert, Bruckner and music history. Contributions to: Bruckner und des romantische Klavierstücke, 1989; Schuberts Gesellschaftsmusik, 1991. Honour: Franz Schubert Grand Prix, for special achievements in Schubert research. Memberships: Board Member, several national and international Schubert societies. Address: Neue Schubert-Ausgabe, Österreichische Akademie der Wissenschaften, Dr Ignaz Seipel-Platz 2, A-1010 Vienna, Austria.

LITTLE Tasmin, b. 1965, London. Violinist. m. Michael Hatch, 31 Jul 1993. Education: Studied at the Yehudi Menuhin School, The Guildhall School of Music and with Lorand Fenyves in Canada. Career: Many solo engagements with leading orchestras, including appearances with the Leipzig Gewandhaus, the Berlin Symphony Orchestra, the Royal Philharmonic, Philharmonia BBC Symphony, Royal Danish and Royal Liverpool Philharmonic; Conductors include Kurt Masur, Vladimir Ashkenazy, Leonard Slatkin, Charles Groves, Vernon Handley, James Loughran, Edward Downes, Sian Edwards, Yehudi Menuhin, Jan Pascal Tortelier, Richard Hickox and Andrew Davis; Performances in East Germany from 1986, including the Delius Concerto and the Concerto by Dvorak; British engagements at the South Bank Centre, Barbican and Harewood House and the Henley, Chester, Chichester, Cambridge and Salisbury Festivals; Three Choirs Festival 1989, Returned 1993 with the Elgar Concerto; Concerto and recital performances in France, Germany, Denmark, Canada, China, Oman, Zimbabwe, Hong Kong and India; BBC Symphony debut 1990, returning to premiere the concerto by Robert Saxton at the Leeds Festival; French debut 1990 with the Haydn C major and Bach A minor concertos; Promenade Concerts 1990 in the London premiere of the concerto by Janacek conducted by Charles Mackerras; Season 1990-91 included debut with the London Symphony and Bournemouth Symphony Orchestras and a return to the Promenade Concerts, with the Dvorak Concerto; Walton Concerto at the 1993 Proms. Recordings include: Bruch and Dvorak Concertos with the Liverpool Philharmonic; Sonatas by George Lloyd, with Martin Roscoe; Delius Violin and Double Concertos with Rafael Wallfisch and Charles Mackerras; Brahms and Sibelius Concertos; Vaughan Williams's The Lark Ascending conducted by Andrew Davis. Honours include: Finalist, 1982 BBC Young Musician of the Year; Gold Medal, Guildhall School of Music, 1986; Cosmopolitan Magazine's Woman of Tomorrow in the Arts. Hobbies: Theatre; Languages; Swimming; Cooking. Address: c/o Ingpen and Williams Limited, 14 Kensington Court, London W8 5DN, England.

LITTLE Vera, b. 10 Dec 1928, Memphis, Tennesee, USA. Singer (Contralto). m. Professor S Augustithis. Education: Studied in Paris, Rome, Copenhagen and Germany. Debut: New York City Opera 1950, as Preziosilla in La Forza del Destino. Career: Guest appearances in Israel, Germany and Italy; Deutsche Oper Berlin 1958-85, notably as Carmen and as Melanto in Dallapiccola's Ulisse and in the 1965 premiere of Henze's Der Junge Lord; Vatican Concert 1959, in a Bach Cantata for the Pope; Salzburg Festival 1966 as Beroe, in the premiere of The Bassarids by Henze. Recordings: Gaea in Daphne by Strauss and Begonia in Der Junge Lord.

LITTON Andrew, b. 16 May 1959, New York City, USA. Conductor. Education: Juilliard School of Music. Career: Assistant Conductor at La Scala, Milan after Graduation; Has conducted Oslo Philharmonic, Swedish Radio Orchestra; Stockholm Philharmonic; Goteberg Symphony Orchestra, Berlin Radio Symphony Orchestra, WDR Koln, Chicago Symphony, Pittsburgh Symphony, Los Angeles Philharmonic, Philadelphia Orchestra, Utah, Washington National Symphony Orchestra; Appointed Principal Guest Conductor, 1986 and Principal Conductor and Artistic Adviser from 1988 of Bournemouth Symphony Orchestra; Metropolitan Opera debut in 1989 with Eugene Onegin; Conducted Bournemouth Symphony in Bernstein's Age of Anxiety and Sibelius's Second Symphony at 1991 Promenade Concerts, London; Covent Garden debut in 1992 with the house premiere of Porgy and Bess; London Proms in 1993 with Walton's Violin Concerto and Tchaikovsky's Fourth Symphony; Music Director and Conductor of Dallas Symphony, 1994-; Led Porgy and Bess at the 1997 Bregenz Festival. Recordings include: Over 30 including: Elgar Enigma Variations, Mahler Symphony No 1 and Das Lied von der Erde, Tchaikovsky's Symphonies Nos 1-5, Shostakovich's Symphony No 10, Rachmaninov Symphonies Nos 1, 2 and 3. Honours: Winner, Rupert Foundation International Conductors' Competition, 1982; Winner, Bruno Walter Conducting Scholarship, Juilliard School. Current Management: IMG Artists. Address: c/o IMG Artists, Media House, 3 Burlington Lane, London, W4 2TH, England.

LITZ Gisela, b. 14 Dec 1922, Hamburg, Germany. Singer (Soprano). Education: Studied in Hamburg. Career: After singing in Wiesbaden joined the Hamburg State Opera: visited Edinburgh with the company, 1952; Sang in the 1954 stage premiere of Martinu's The Marriage; Bayreuth Festival, 1953-54; Often heard in operetta and in Bach's cantatas; Guest engagements in Buenos Aires, Rome, Lisbon, Munich and Brussels; Professor at Hamburg Musikhochschule from 1969. Recordings: Lortzing's Der Waffenschmied and Die Opernprobe; Nicolai's Die Lustige Weiber von Windsor; Le nozze di Figaro; Hansel and Gretel; Scenes from operettas. Address: Hochscule für Musik and Darstellende Kunst, Harvestehuderweg 12, 2000 Hamburg 13, Germany.

LIU Gui Teng, b. 15 March 1955, Dandong, Liaoning, China. m. Yan-yu Wang, 30 September 1981, 1 son. Publication: Dangu Music Study, 1991. Contributions to: Musicology in China; Music Study. Honour: 1st Class Prize, First Middle-Aged and Youth Music Thesis, China, 1996. Memberships: Chinese Musicians Association; China Manchu Music Research Institute. Hobbies: Writing; Manchu Musical Instruments. Address: Cultural Bureau of Dandong City, No 118 7th Jing Street, Dandong City, Liaoning 118000, China.

LIU Zhuang, b. 24 Oct 1932, Shanghai, China. Composer. Education: Studied at the Shanghai Conservatory, Career: Teacher at the Peking Central Conservatory and composer with the Central Philharmonic Society; Collaborated with others in the 'Yellow River' piano concerto, 1971. Compositions include: Violin concerto, 1963; Plum Blossom Triptych for orchestra, 1979; Moon Night by the Spring River, woodwind quintet, 1978; Three Trios for flute, cello and harp, 1987; Impressions of Tashgul-Kan for orchestra, 1987. Address: c/o Music Copyright Society of China, 85 Dongsi Nan Jajie, Beijing 100703, China.

LIVELY David, b. 27 June 1953, Ironton, Ohio, USA. Pianist. Education: Ecole Normale de Musique de Paris Licence de Concert, 1970; Studied Privately with Wilhelm Kempff, Claudio Arrau. Debut: St Louis Symphony Orchestra, 1968. Career: Soloist with: Cleveland Symphony Orchestra; Baltimore Symphony Orchestra; Kennedy Center, Washington, DC; English Chamber Orchestra; Royal Philharmonic Orchestra, 1979; Vienna Symphony Orchestra; Bavarian Radio Orchestra; Berlin Symphony Orchestra; Orchestre National de France; Orchestre National de Monte Carlo; La Scala; Orchestre de la Suisse Romande; Director, St Lizier Festival, France. Recordings: Numerous on major labels. Contributor to: Analyse Musicale Master Classes: Royal Scottish Academy, Glasgow, Hochschule, Vienna. Honours: Prizewinner, Queen Elisabeth Competition, Brussels 1972; Tchaikovsky, Moscow 1974, Geneva 1971, Marguerite Long 1971; Dino Ciani Award, La Scala, 1977. Current Management: Liliane Weinstadt, Brussels, Belgium. Address: c/o Liliane Weinstadt, Rue Langeveld 69, 1180 Brussels, Belgium.

LIVENGOOD Victoria, b. 1961, USA. Singer (Mezzo-soprano). Education: BM, University of North Carolina at Chapel Hill, 1983; MM, Honours, Opera, Boston Conservatory, 1985. Career: Sang Gertrude in Hamlet for Miami Opera (1987) followed by Beauty in Beauty and the Beast by Oliver at St Louis; New York Academy of Music 1988, as Juno in Platée; Charlotte in Werther, Seattle Opera, 1989; Meg Page in Falstaff, Calgary Opera, 1991; Europe debut 1991, as Mozart's Idamante at Nice; Guest appearances as Dorabella for Hawaii Opera (1990) and Carmen at Cologne (1992); Metropolitan Opera debut 1991, as Laura in Luisa Miller; Isoliero in Il Conte Ory, Spoleto Festival, Charleston, 1993; Maddalena in Rigoletto, Cologne and Edmonton, 1994; Lola, Cavalleria Rusticana, Metropolitan Opera, 1994; Girl in Mahaghonny for Met Opera, 1995; Carmen, Edmonton Opera, 1995; Dalila, Baltimore Opera, 1995; Giulietta in Tales of Hoffmann, Santiago, Chile, 1995; Preziosilla in La Forza del destino for Met Opera, 1996; Isabella in The Voyage and Maddalena in Rigoletto, for Met Opera, 1996; Hippolyta in A Midsummer Nights Dream, 1996; Waltraute in Die Walkyre, 1997; Giulietta in Les Contes d'Hoffmann, 1998; Sonyetka, Lady Macbeth of Mtsensk; Recitalist, Kennedy Centre, 1986; Carnegie Hall debut, 1986; Recitalist, Smithsonian Institute, Washington DC, 1986; New York City recital debut, 1987; Soloist with symphonies of Atlanta, Cologne, San Diego, Baltimore, Minnesota and Washington; Cincinnati May Festival, and Lincoln Centre Chamber Music Society, 1996; Verdi's Requiem Soloist, Carnegie Hall, 1998. Recordings include: Puck in Oberon; Solo CD, Haydn Canzonettas. Honours: Winner, Metropolitan Opera Competition, 1985; Winner, Rosa Ponselle Competition, 1987; Grant recipient, Sullivan Foundation, 1987; Winner, Luciano Pavarotti Competition, 1988; Grant, National Institute Music Theatre, 1989; Named Distinguished Alumni of University of North Carolina at Chapel Hill, 1996. Address: c/o Metropolitan Opera, Lincoln Center, New York, NY 10023, USA.

LIVINGSTONE Kathleen (Mary), b. 26 Dec 1951, Helensburgh, Scotland. Singer (Soprano). m. Neil Mackie (Tenor), 14 Jul 1973, 2 daughters. Education: Royal Scottish Academy of Music and Drama, 1969-73; Royal College of Music, 1973-75; Diploma, MusEd, Royal Scottish Academy of Music and Drama; Diploma, Royal Scottish Academy of Music and Drama; Wigmore Hall, London, 1976. Career: World Wide Concert appearances; Radio and TV Broadcasts in France, Spain, Italy. Honours: Countess of Munster Award, 1974, 1975; Caird Scholarship, 1973; Royal College of Music Scholar, 1973; Earl of Dalhousie Award, 1975; Silver Medal, Worshipful Company of Musicians, 1975; Major Prizewinner, Royal Scottish Academy of Music & Drama and Royal College of Music, 1969, 1975; Professor of Singing, Royal College of Music, 1993. Memberships: Incorporated Society of Musicians; Equity. Hobbies: Gardening; Cooking; Dressmaking. Address: 70 Broadwood Avenue, Ruislip, Middlesex HA4 7XR, England.

LIVINGSTONE Laureen, b. 3 Feb 1946, Dumbarton, Scotland. Singer (Soprano); Teacher. 1 s, 1 d. Education: Royal Scottish Academy of Music, 1963-66; London Opera Centre, 1967-69; DipMusEd; RSAM. Career: Wide variety of operatic, concert and TV appearances in UK and abroad; BBC Proms; Recitals including Wigmore Hall and 1st BBC Lunchtime recital in 1976; Guest appearances with London Symphony Orchestra, Hallé, English Sinfonia, Northern Sinfonia, Scottish National and Scottish Chamber Orchestras; Operatic roles include: Zerlina, Pamina, Gretel, Lucia in Rape of Lucretia with Scottish Opera, Susanna, Sophie and Vrenchen in A Village Romeo and Juliet with English National Opera North, Gilda in Rigoletto and Sophie in Der Rosenkavalier for English National Opera, 1988; Major roles with the New Sadler's Wells Opera, Handel Opera and others; Engagements abroad include Woglinde at Teatro di San Carlo, Naples, 1980 and Gilda for Royal Flemish Opera in Antwerp, 1985; Professor of Singing at Trinity College of Music, London. Recordings: Several recital programmes for BBC; Countess Maritza; Gianetta in The Gondoliers, 1st colour production for BBC TV; Ninetta in The Love for Three Oranges, BBC TV, 1980; Elsie in The Yeoman of the Guard, Channel 4 video; Amore in Il Ritorno d'Ulisse in Patria, Glyndebourne, video 1973. Honours: Caird Scholarship, 1967; Winner, Peter Stuyvesant Scholarship, 1969. Address: 12 Pymmes Brook Drive, New Barnet, Hertfordshire, EN4 9RU, England.

LLEWELLYN Grant, b. 29 Dec 1960, Tenby, Wales. Conductor. m. Charlotte Imogen Rose, 7 Apr 1984. Education: Cheetham's School of Music, Manchester, 1972-79; Gonville and Caius College, Cambridge, 1980-83; Royal College of Music, London; Tanglewood Music Center, 1986. Career: Has conducted City of Birmingham Symphony Orchestra, English Chamber Orchestra, Scottish National Orchestra, Royal Liverpool Philharmonic Orchestra, Northern Sinfonia, Scottish Chamber Orchestra, City of London Sinfonia and BBC Symphony, Philharmonic and Welsh Orchestras; Took Stockholm Sinfonietta on UK tour, 1986 and conducted at Spoleto, Charleston and Jeunesse Musicale World Orchestra at Berlin Festival; London Proms debut 1993, with the BBC Welsh Symphony in Mendelsssohn's Violin Concerto and Beethoven's Seventh Symphony; Conducted BBC National Orchestra of Wales Opera Gala, 1996. Honours: Royal College of Music Tagore Gold Medal, 1984; Tanglewood Conducting Fellowship and English-Speaking Union Scholar, 1985; Leeds Conductors' Competition, 1986 (first prize). Hobbies: Association Football (awarded Blue for Cambridge University, 1982); Travel. Current Management: Van Walsum Management, 40 St Peter's Road, London W6 9BH, England. Address: Bassett Cottage, 43 Main Road, Long Hanborough, Oxfordshire, England.

LLOVERAS Juan, b. 6 Apr 1934, Barcelona, Spain. Tenor. Education: Studied at the Conservatorio del Liceo, Barcelona. Debut: Tev Aviv in 1966 as Rodolfo. Career: Sang in Israel until 1969, Krefeld, 1970-71, Essen, 1971-74 and Cologne from 1977; Staatsoper Hamburg from 1973 in 200 performances in the Italian repertory; US debut as Manrico at the San Francisco Opera in 1975; Metropolitan Opera debut in 1979 as Turiddu followed by the Duke of Mantua and Manrico; Deutsche Oper Berlin, 1977-83; Further engagements at Dusseldorf, Stuttgart, Lille, Lyon, Paris, and Houseon, 1982, Amsterdam and Covent Garden London in 1981; Other roles have included Edgardo, Enzo, Riccardo, Don Carlos, Macduff, Andrea Chenier, Werther, Laca in Jenufa and Henry in Die schweigsame Frau. Address: c/o Deutsche Oper Berlin, Richard Wagnerstrasse 10, D-1000 Berlin, Germany.

LLOYD David, b. 29 Feb 1920, Minneapolis, Minnesota, USA. Singer (Tenor). Education: Minneapolis College of Music; Curtis Institute, Philadelphia; Berkshire Music Center. Career: After 1947 debut sang with New York City Opera, then with New England Opera Company; Athens Festival, 1955; Glyndebourne, 1957, as Tamino in Die Zauberflöte and Bacchus in Ariadne auf Naxos; Other roles were Mozart's Belmonte and Idomeneo,

Flamand in Capriccio, Rodolfo, Jacquino and Gonslave in L'Heure Espagnole; Also heard in concert and oratorio; Artistic Director, Hunter College, New York; Director of the Lake George Opera Festival, USA, 1974.

LLOYD David (Bellamy), b. 22 Nov 1937, Stockport, Cheshire, England. Piano Accompanist. Education: ARMCM (Performance and Teaching). Debut: Recital with Heddle Nash, Wigmore Hall, 1956. Career: Accompanist to Jan Peerce, Festival Hall, London and tour of France, Germany, Switzerland, Austria and Netherlands; Television appearances with Jack Brymer, Adele Leigh and Charlotte Rimmer. Former accompanist to Jack Brymer, Leon Goossens and Elizabeth Harwood in recitals and broadcasts, Singapore, Hong Kong, India, New Zealand, Spain, Canada and USA; Senior Lecturer, Royal Northern College of Music and Professional Accompanist, 1967-93; Examiner, Associated Board of Royal Schools of Music, 1969-. Compositions: Schubert Arpeggione Sonata, arranged by David Lloyd, published. Recordings: Brahms Clarinet Sonata Op 120/1, Weber Duo Concertante; Brahms Clarinet Sonata Op 120/2; Schubert Arpeggione Sonata arranged for Clarinet; Schumann Phantasiestücke Op 73; Hurlstone Four Characteristic Pieces; Art of Leon Goossens. Honours: Hilary Haworth Prize, RMCM, 1958; Membership: Incorporated Society of Musicians. Hobbies: Opera; Travel; Railways; Photography; Motor cars. Address: Cynghanedd, 8 Brynci, Penybont, Llandrindod Wells, Powys LD1 5SW, Wales.

LLOYD George, b. 28 Jun 1913, Cornwall, England. Composer; Conductor. m. Nancy Juvet, 22 Jan 1937. Education: Studied violin with Albert Sammons and composition with Harry Farjeon. Debut: As conductor with Bournemouth Municipal Orchestra, 1933. Career: Has performed at the Lyceum Theatre, London, 1935, BBC Symphony Orchestra, 1935; The Serf performed by Royal Opera Covent Garden, 1938; John Socman at the British Hippodrome, 1951; BBC broadcast of 8th Symphony, 1977; Principal Guest Conductor of Albany Symphony Orchestra, 1989-91. Compositions: 3 Operas, 12 symphonies, 4 piano concertos, 2 cantatas: The Vigil of Venus and A Symphonic Mass, 2 violin and piano sonatas and piano solos. Recordings include: 12 Symphonies; 4 Piano concertos; The Vigil of Venus; A Symphonic Mass; Violin and Piano sonatas; Piano solos; Works for brass band. Honour: Honorary DMus, Salford University, 1992. Membership: Association of Professional Composers. Current Management: Albany Records, UK. Address: c/o Albany Records, PO Box 12, Carnforth, Lancashire, LA5 9PD, England.

LLOYD Jonathan, b. 30 Sep 1948, London, England. Composer. Education: Composition lessons with Emile Spira; Studied at Royal College of Music, London, with Edwin Roxburgh and John Lambert; Worked with Tristram Cary at Electronic Music Studio. Career: Twentieth Century Ensemble, 1968; Awarded Mendelssohn Scholarship and lived in Paris, 1969-70; Occasional work as performer, busker, street musician, 1974-77; Composer-in-Residence, Dartington College Theatre Department, 1978-79. Compositions include: Orchestral: Cantique, 1968, 5 Symphonies, 1983-89, Rhapsody for Cello and Orchestra, 1982, Viola Concerto, 1979-80, Everything Returns for Soprano and Orchestra, 1977-78, Mass for 6 Solo Voices, 1983, Missa Brevis, 1984, Toward the Whitening Dawn for Chorus and Chamber Orchestra, 1980, Revelation for 8 Voices, 1990, Marching to a Different Song for Soprano and Chamber Orchestra, 1991, Ballad for The Evening of a Man for Mixed Quartet, 1992; Dramatic: The Adjudicator, community opera, 1985, Music for Alfred Hitchcock's Blackmail, 1993; Recently: Tolerance for Orchestra, 1994, People Your Dreams for Voice and Ensemble, 1994, Blessed Days of Blue for Solo Flute and Strings, 1995, Violin Concerto, 1995; Piano Concerto, 1995. Recordings: Mass; Second Symphony, 1992; Largo. Address: c/o Boosey and Hawkes Ltd, 295 Regent Street, London, W1R 8JH, England.

LLOYD Robert (Andrew), b. 2 Mar 1940, Southend-on-Sea, Essex, England. Opera Singer (Bass). m. 22 Feb 1964, 1 son, 3 daughters. Education: BA Hons, Modern History, Keble College, Oxford; Graduate, Modern History, Oxford University, 1962; Private Study with Otakar Kraus, London Opera Centre, 1968-69. Debut: Fernando in Beethoven's Leonore, Collegiate Theatre, London, 1969. Career: English National Opera, 1969-72; Covent Garden, 1972-83; Freelance in all major opera houses, 1983-; Met debut, 1988; Principal roles, Boris Godunov; Philip II; Sarastro, Gurnemanz, Fiesco; Mephistopheles, Osmin, altogether 120 roles; Appearances with most leading orchestras; Film: Parsifal, Director, Hans Jurgen Syberberg; Video: Notably Don Carlos, Coronation of Poppea, and Tales of Hoffmann, Boris Godunov and Fidelio; First British Bass to sing Boris Godunov at Kirov Opera, 1990 (also televised); Vienna Staatsoper, 1990, as King Henry in Lohengrin; At Covent Garden sang Georgio Walton, Arkel and Commendatore, 1993; Sang in Britten's version of The Beggar's Opera at the 1993 Aldeburgh Festival; Season 1997 with Chérubin and Lohengrin at Covent Garden, Die Zauberflöte at Salzburg; Sang Gurnemanz for Netherlands Opera, 1997. Recordings: Over 50 recordings with all the major companies, Parsifal, Entführung, Barbiere di Siviglia, Nozze di Figaro, Messiah, Mozart Requiem, Il Trovatore, Macbeth, Rigoletto; Romeo and Juliette and Damnation de Faust in Denon's Berlioz Cycle, Elgar's Apostles. Contributions to: Frequent contributions to magazines and BBC Radio and TV. Honours: Grammy (Mozart Requiem); Grammy Nomination (Figaro); Prix Italia; R P Society Award for BBC's Bluebeard's Castle, 1989; CBE, 1991; Elected Honorary Fellow, Keble College, Oxford. Membership: Garrick Club, London. Hobbies: Sailing; Hill Walking. Current Management: Lies Askonsas Limited. Address: Lies Askonas Ltd, 6 Henrietta Street, London, WC2, England.

LLOYD DAVIS John, b. 1958, England. Stage Director and Designer. Education: Studied at Bristol University. Career: Directed Le nozze di Figaro for Pavillion Opera, then supervised 1983 tour of England; Staff Producer, English National Opera from 1984; Freelance productions include: The Cunning Little Vixen, Gianni Schicchi and L'elisir d'Amore; Season 1988-89 with Wozzeck at the Almeida Theatre, Don Giovanni at the Kammeroper Vienna and Assistant to Tim Albery with Les Troyens at Nice and the Scottish Opera; Co-directed Falstaff at ENO and Rusalka for the Frankfurt Opera, with David Pountney; Der fliegende Holländer at the 1989 Bregenz Festival, Die Zauberflöte and Rigoletto for the Kammeroper 1990-91; Madama Butterfly at Ludwigshafen and Dublin, Christmas Eve at the Guildhall School, 1990; Scottish Opera, 1991, with The Cunning Little Vixen; Produced Der Wiederspenstigen Zähmung by Götz at the 1991 Wexford Festival, Figaro at Dublin, Zauberflöte at Klagenfurt and Zar und Zimmermann at Aachen, 1992-93; Produced and designed The Rake's Progress for the New Sussex Opera, 1992. Current Management: Athole Still International Management Limited. Address: Athole Still Ltd, Forresters Hall, 25-27 Westow Street, London SE19 3RY, England.

LLOYD ROBERTS Carys, b. 1969, Wales. Soprano. Education: Studied at the Welsh College of Music and Drama. Career: Engagements with the Welsh National Opera, Musica nel Chiostro and City of Birmingham Touring Opera as Papagena, First Lady, Barbarina and Hansel; Purcell's King Arthur with Les Arts Florissants at Covent Garden and The Fairy Queen with the Northern Sinfonia; Concerts include the Jonathan Miller production of the St Matthew Passion and appearances at Llandaff Cathedral and St Martin-in-the-Fields, London. Address: c/o Ron Gonsalves Management, 7 Old Town, Clapham, London, SW4 0JT, England.

LLOYD WEBBER Andrew (Sir), b. 22 Mar 1948, London. Composer. m. (1) Sarah Jane Hugill, 1971 (divorced 1983), 1 son, 1 daughter. m. (2) Sarah Brightman, 1984 (divorced 1990). m. (3) Madeleine Gurdon, 1991, 2 sons. Education: Westminster School; Oxford University; Royal College of Music, FRCM, 1988. Compositions: Joseph and the Amazing Technicolor Dreamcoat (lyrics by Tim Rice, 1968, rev 1973 and 1991); Jesus Christ Superstar (lyrics by Tim Rice, 1970); Jeeves (lyrics by Alan Ayckbourn, 1975); Evita (lyrics by Tim Rice, 1976; stage version, 1978); Tell Me On a Sunday (lyrics by Don Black, 1980); Cats (based on poems by TS Eliot, 1981); Starlight Express (lyrics by Richard Stilgoe, 1984); The Phantom of the Opera, (lyrics by Richard Stilgoe and Charles Hart, 1986); Aspects of Love (Don Black and Charles Hart, 1989); Sunset Boulevard (book and lyrics by Don Black and Christopher Hampton, 1993); Requiem, 1985; Variations on a theme of Paganini for Orchestra, 1986; Deviser of children's board game Calamity! The International High-Risk Insurance Game. Publications: Evita (with Timothy Rice, 1978); Joseph and the Amazing Technicolor Dreamcoat (with Rice, 1982). Honours: Numerous including: Laurence Olivier, Tony, Drama Desk and Grammy Awards; Praemium Imperiale Award for Music, 1995; Knighted 1992. Hobby: Architecture. Address: 22 Tower Street, London WC2H 9NS, England.

LLOYD WEBBER Julian, b. 14 Apr 1951, London, England. Musician (Cellist). m. (1) Celia Mary Ballantyne, 29 Jun 1974 (divorced 1989). m. (2) Zohra Mahmud Ghazi, 1 Jul 1989. Education: University College School, 1964-67; Royal College of Music, 1968-72; Study with Pierre Fournier, 1973. Debut: Queen Elizabeth Hall, London, 1972. Career: Appears regularly with world's leading orchestras, including Berlin Philharmonic, Czech Philharmonic, English Chamber, London Symphony, Royal Philharmonic with such conductors as Solti, Maazel, Menuhin and Neumann; Many TV and Radio performances including Elgar and Dvorak Concertos, Face the Music and South Bank Show, 1989. Recordings: More than 25 world premiere recordings of works by Arnold, Britten, Holst, A Lloyd Webber, Rodrigo, Sullivan and Vaughan Williams; Complete cello music of Delius; Concertos by Dvorak, Elgar, Lalo, Saint-Saëns, Honneger, Haydn; Sonatas by Britten, Debussy, Ireland, Rachmaninov, Shostakovich. Publications: Classical Cello, 1980; Romantic Cello, 1981; French Cello, 1981; Pieces of Frank Bridge, 1982; Young Cellist's Repertoire Books 1, 2 and 3, 1984; Holst's Invocation, 1984; Travels with my Cello, 1984; Song of the Birds, 1985; Recital Repertoire for Cellists, Vols 1, 2, 3, 4, 1986. Contributions to: The Times; Sunday Times; The Composer; Music and Musicians. Honours: Suggia Gift, 1968; Seymour Whinyates Award, 1971; Percy Buck Award, 1972; Gold Disc for Variations Recording, 1978; Spanish Ministry of Culture Award for world premiere recording of Rodrigo Cello Concerto, 1982; Best British Classical recording of 1986 for Elgar Cello Concerto - BPI Awards; Professional societies committee member, solo performers section, Incorporated Society of Musicians, 1982. Hobbies: Topography (especially British); Turtle Keeping; Leyton Orient Football Club. Address: c/o Kaye Artists Management, 7 Chertsey Road, Woking GU21 5AB, England.

LLOYD-HOWELLS David, b. 11 Jan 1942, Cardiff, Wales. Composer. Education: Ealing Music Centre, London, 1960-64; Trinity College of Music, 1967; Pontypridd Technical College 1972-73; South Gwent College 1974; BMus, Honours, Wales, 1977-80; FTCL, FLCM, Diplomas, 1979-80; MMus, Distinction, University of London, 1981-83; York University, 1984-85. Career: Tutor in Music, Gwent, 1971-77; Adult Education, 1980-83; Community Musician, 1984; Freelance Composer, Conductor, Artistic Director, Adjudicator; Works mainly with electronic-live media; Music Theatre, Modern Dance Groups, Cedar Dance Theatre Company, London, 1983; D.L.H. Productions, music for film, video and self-therapy, 1990. Compositions include: Sound Spaces 1,2,3; Solo Piano, Fine Line; 3 Sound-scapes, Piano Solo, World Premier String Quartet, 1978 op 52 Germany, 1991; Choirs and Dialogues for Fifteen Strings and Electronics, 1987, Performed LRO 1989; Pinocchio, Music Theatre for adults and children in school, commissioned LEA, 1990; Symphony No 3, 1978-80; The Promenade, music theatre, 1983; Wind Quartet, 1986; String Quintett, 1988, Music for Brass trio, commissioned by Welsh Brass trio; Funk Street Bum at the Celtic Health Farm, 1991; Passions for a Moving Image, tape, 1992; Nightcity Pulses, 1992; The Insects Convention for Madrid Radio, 1992 and Tangerine Radio Moscow, 1993; Saxophone Quartet, 1993. Recording: Piano Sonata 2, 1978. Publications: Various commissions including folk opera, The Earthdream. Contributions to: Insightionomic Perception and Musical Creativity, Composer and Computer Sonic Arts Journal. Honours: Walford Davies Prize, 1980; Elected Fellow, Royal Society of Arts, 1980; Scored donated, National Library of Wales, 1992. Memberships: Sonic Arts Network; International Directory of Electronic Art, Paris. Current Management: DLH Creations. Address: 24 Kensington Road, Chichester, West Sussex PO19 2XN, England.

LLOYD-JONES David (Mathias), b. 19 Nov 1934, London, England. Musician. m. Anne Carolyn Whitehead, 1964, 2 sons, 1 daughter. Education: Westminster School; Magdalen College, Oxford. Career: Chorus Master, New Opera Co, 1961-64; Conducted at Bath Festival, 1966, City of London Festival, 1966, Wexford Festival, 1967-70, Scottish Opera, 1968, Welsh National Opera, 1968, Royal Opera, Covent Garden, 1971; Sadler's Wells, Opera Co (now English National Opera), 1969-; Artistic Director, Opera North, 1978-90; Conductor for TV Operas (Eugene Onegin, The Flying Dutchman, Hansel and Gretel) for operas in Amsterdam and Paris; Conducted The Queen of Spades at Nice, 1989; Don Pasquale for Opera North, 1990; Guildhall School of Music, March 1990, La Vida Breve and Angélique; The Love for Three Oranges at New Israeli Opera, Boris Godunov at Santiago and Tchaikovsky's Yolanta for Opera North at the Edinburgh Festival, 1992; Appearances with most British Symphony Orchestras. Publications: Boris Godunov, translation; Vocal Score, Eugene Onegin; Translation, Vocal Score, Boris Godunov - Critical Edition of Original Full Score; numerous contributions to publications including Grove's Dictionary of Music and Musicians, Musik in Geschichte und Gegenwart, Music and Letters, The Listener. Hobbies: Theatre; French Cuisine; Rose Growing. Address: 94 Whitelands House, Cheltenham Terrace, London SW3 4RA, England.

LLOYD-ROBERTS Jeffrey, b. 1968, Wales. Singer (Tenor). Education: Studied at the Royal Northern College of Music with Barbara Robotham and at Lancaster University. Career: Appearances with Welsh National Opera in The Makropoulos Case, as Nemorino with English Touring Opera in Le Roi malgré Lui for Chelsea Opera and in Aroldo at the Buxton Festival; Season 1995 as Lindoro in La fedelta premiata for Garsington Opera and concerts of Korngold's Ring of Polycrates, the B Minor Mass, the Verdi Requiem, Mahler's 8th Symphony and The Dream of Gerontius. Address: c/o Harold Holt Ltd, 31 Sinclair Road, London W14 0NS.

LOBANOV Vassily, b. 1947, Moscow, USSR. Composer; Pianist. Education: Studied at the Tchaikovsky Conservatoire, Moscow, 1963-69, with Leo Naumov, Sergei Balasanyan and Alfred Schnittke. Career: Has accompanied Natalia Gutman and Oleg Kagan individually and as member of trio; Interpreter of modern works at festivals in Moscow, Witten, Vienna and Kuhmo, Finland; Premiered his Second Piano Sonata at the Moscow Autumn Festival, 1980; Has partnered Sviatoslav Richter in duets; December Nights concert in the Pushkin Museum Moscow, 1981; Soloist with the Moscow Philharmonic from 1982. Compositions include: Oratorio Lieutenant Schmidt, 1979; Opera Antigone, 1985-88; Orchestra: Symphony for Chamber Orchestra, 1977;

Piano Concerto 1981; Cello Concerto, 1985; Sinfonietta, 1986; Concerto for Viola and Strings, 1989; Chamber: 5 String Quartets, 1966, 1968, 1978, 1987, 1988; Twelve Preludes for Piano, 1965; Partita for Piano, 1967; 2 Cello Sonatas, 1971, 1989; 2 Piano Sonatas, 1973, 1980; 3 Suites for Piano; Seven Pieces for Cello and Piano, 1978; Variations for Two Trumpets, 1979; Seven Slow Pieces for Piano, 1978-80; Flute Sonata, 1983; Clarinet Sonata, 1985; Fantasia for Solo Cello, 1987; Violin Sonata, 1989; Vocal: Three Haikus for Low Voice and Piano, 1963; Three Romances (bass), 1965; Five Romances, 1971; Four Poems to texts by Alexei Parin (bass), 1984; Eight Poems (soprano), 1984; Stravinsky's Italian Suite adapted for Cello and Chamber Orchestra, 1985. Address: c/o Boosey & Hawkes Limited, 295 Regent Street, London W1R 8JH, England.

LOCKE Peter, b. 1 Feb 1937, Wolverhampton, England. Accompanist; Pianist; Voice Coach. Education: LRAM, 1956; MA, King's College, Cambridge, 1960; Diploma di Perfezionamento, Accademia di Santa Cecilia, Rome, 1962. Debut: Civic Hall, Wolverhampton, 1954. Career: Actor, Pitlochry, Leicester, Nottingham, Arts Theatre, London, 1963-70; Maestro Collaboratore, Teatro La Fenice, Venice, 1971-81; Voice Coach for Tito Gobbi's Opera Workshop, Villa Schifanoia, Fiesole, Italy, 1979-81; Music Director, Intermezzi Ensemble, London, 1981-84; Repetiteur, The Opera House, Belfast, 1982-84; Principal Repetiteur, Lyric Opera, Brisbane, Australia, 1984; Chorus Master, Icelandic Opera, Reykjavik, 1986-89; Principal Repetiteur, Voice Coach, Victoria State Opera, Melbourne, Australia, 1986-89; Formal piano duo with Brian Stacey, Australia, 1989; Pianist, Conductor, Chamber Made Opera, Australia, in Fall of the House of Usher (Glass), Greek (Turnage), Sweet Death (Greenwell), 1990-92; Chorus Master, Voice Coach, Die Csárdásfurstin, Icelandic Opera, 1993; Recital with Helen Noonan at Downes Warehouse, London and The Open University, Milton Keynes, 1993; Vocal coaching, Royal Academy of Music, London, 1993; Musical Director, Conductor, Robert Ashley's Improvement, Melbourne, 1994; Chorus Master, Voice Coach, La Forza del Destino, National Theatre, Iceland, 1994; Vocal Coach, Royal Opera Schools of London, 1994-95; Musical Director, The Burrow, opera about Franz Kafka, Melbourne, 1995. Recordings: Mona Vanna, Rachmaninov, Chorus Master, Icelandic Opera, 1990; Chorus Master, Icelandic Symphony and Opera Chorus, Music of Jón Leifs, 1994; Pianist, Woman's Song, with Helen Noonan, 1994. Membership: Incorporated Society of Musicians. Current Management: Performance Management, 120 Johnson Street, Fitzroy 3065, Victoria, Australia. Address: 9 Emperor's Gate, London SW7 4HH, England.

LOCKHART Beatriz, b. 17 Jan 1944, Montevideo, Uruguay. Composer. Education: Studied at the Montevideo Conservatory and in Buenos Aires. Career: Teacher at the Caracas Conservatory (1974-88), University of Montevideo, and elsewhere. Compositions include: Ecos for orchestra; Concerto Grosso; Masia muju for flute and orchestra (1987); Theme and variations for piano; Ejercio I for tape and other electronic music; Vision de los vencidos for voice and orchestra, 1990. Address: c/o AGADU, Calle canelones 1122, Montevideo, Uruguay.

LOCKHART James, b. 16 Oct 1930, Edinburgh, Scotland. Conductor; Accompanist. m. Sheila Grogan, 25 Sept 1954, 2 sons, 1 daughter. Education: Edinburgh University; Royal College of Music, London. Debut: Yorkshire Symphony Orchestra, 1954. Career: Assistant Conductor, Yorkshire Symphony Orchestra; Repetiteur, Städtische Bühnen Münster, 1955-56; Bayerische Staatsoper München, 1956-57; Director, Opera Workshop, University of Texas, 1957-59; Repetiteur, Glyndebourne Opera, 1957-79; ROH Covent Garden, 1959-60; Assistant Conductor, BBC Scottish Symphony, 1960-61; Conductor, Sadler's Wells Opera, 1961-62; Conductor at ROH Covent Garden, 1962-68; Professor, Royal College of Music, 1962-72; Music Director, Welsh National Opera, 1968-73; General Music Director, Staatstheater Kassel, 1972-80, Rheinische Philharmonie and Koblenz Stadttheater, 1981-91; Director of Opera, RCM London, 1986-92; Director of Opera, London Royal Schools Vocal Faculty, 1992-96; Opera Consultant, Royal Academy and Royal College of Music, London, 1996-; Guest Professor of Conducting, Tokyo National University of Fine Arts and Music, 1998-; Conducted at the Welsh National Opera 50th Anniversary Gala, 1996. Recordings include: Dittersdorf: Doktor and Apotheker; Brahms, Schumann, French and Spanish Songs with Margaret Price; Le Flem, and Schmitt with the Rheinische Philharmonie; Royal Philharmonic Orchestra: Beethoven Symphonies 2 and 8, Mozart Symphonies, 36 and 39. Honours: BMus, 1950; ARCM, 1951; FRCO (CHM), 1951; Solti Scholarship for Most Promising Young British Musician, 1964; FRCM, 1987; Hon, RAM, 1993. Membership: ISM. Hobbies: Mountain hiking; Swimming; Travel; Languages. Current Management: Portland Wallis. Address: 105 Woodcock Hill, Harrow, Middlesex HA3 0JJ, England.

LOCKLAIR Dan (Steven), b. 7 Aug 1949, Charlotte, North Carolina, USA. Composer; Organist. m. Paula Welshimer, 23 July 1983. Education: BM cum laude, Mars Hill College, North Carolina, 1971; SMM, School of Sacred Music, Union Theological Seminary, New York City, 1973; DMA, Eastman School of Music, 1981; Studied Composition with Joseph Goodman, Ezra Laderman, Samuel Adler, Joseph Schwantner. Career: Broadcasts of his compositions, National Public Radio (including performances on St Paul Sunday Morning, Performance Today, Pipe Dreams), Canadian Broadcasting Corporation (Arts National) and Voice of America; Composer-in-Residence, Associate Professor of Music, Wake Forest University. Compositions include: The Breakers Pound, harpsichord; When Morning Stars Begin to Fall, orchestra; Constellations, organ, percussion; Inventions, organ; Prism of Life, orchestra; In The Autumn Days, chamber orchestra; On Cats, choir; A Christmas Carol, choir; Ecstasy in Jericho, guitar; Visions In The Haze, piano; ...the moon commands..., chamber ensemble; In The Almost Evening, chamber ensemble; Break Away!, choir; Scintillations, ballet; Good Tidings From The Holy Beast, 1-act opera; Lairs of Soundings, soprano, double string orchestra; Flutes, solo flutes, 1 player; Changing perceptions, & Epitaph, choral cycle; Creation's Seeing Order, prelude, orchestra; Clusters's Last Stand, on the ground, harpsichord; The Columbus Madrigals, treble voices, piano; Alleluia, double choir; Rubrics, organ, 1988, published 1992; Voyage, organ, 1991, published 1992; Windswept (the trees), choral cycle in 9 movements, choir, woodwind quintet, piano, 1992; Hues, 3 Tone Poems, orchestra, 1993; Dream Steps, dance suite, flute, viola, harp, 1993; Brief Mass, SSAATTBB choir a cappella, 1993. Recordings: 10 CDs of his works including All-Locklair Choral CD featuring Choral Art Society of Portland, Maine, 1995. Honours: Top Prize, Barlow International Composition Competition, 1989. Address: 827 Roslyn Road, Winston-Salem, NC 27104, USA.

LOCKWOOD Annea (Ferguson), b. 29 Jul 1939, Christchurch, New Zealand. Composer; Performer; University Lecturer. Education: BMus, University of Canterbury, New Zealand, 1961; Royal College of Music, London, 1961-63, LRAM, ARCM Piano Performance; Musikhochschule Cologne, 1963-64; Institute for Sound and Vibration Research, psychoacoustical research, postgraduate, Southampton University, UK, 1971-73. Career: Major performances of own compositions: Cheltenham Festival, UK, 1965, 1969; Commonwealth Festival, UK, 1965; Parie Biennale, 1965; Fylkingen Festival, Stockholm, 1970; Queen Elizabeth Hall, London, 1971; Lincoln Center Plaza, New York, 1974; New Music America Festivals, 1979, 1982, 1986; Autunno Musicale a Como, Italy, 1979; Sydney Biennale, 1982; Westdeutscher Rundfunk, Meet the USA Festival, 1982; Asia Pacific Festival, 1984; Westdeutscher Rundfunk, Ives & Co, 1988; New York-Cologne Festival, 1989. Compositions include: Recorded: Glass Concert; World Rhythms; Tiger Balm; Published: Malaman; Spirit Catchers; Humming; Delta Run; Sound Map of the Hudson River; Glass Concert, World Rhythms, Tiger Balm, Malolo, A Sound Map of the Hudson River. Publications: Malaman, Spirit Catchers, Humming, Delta Run, Amazonia Dreaming, Tiger Balm, Glass Concert. Honours: National Endowment for the Arts Composition Fellow, USA, 1979; CAPS Composition Fellowship, USA, 1979; Arts Council of Great Britain, 1972; Gulbenkian Foundation Grants, 1972. Memberships: Composers Forum, New York (Board Member); American Composers Alliance; BMI Inc. Address: Baron de Hirsch Road, Crompond, NY 10517, USA.

LOCKWOOD Lewis, b. 16 Dec 1930, New York, USA. Musicologist. Education: Queens College, New York, BA 1952; PhD Princeton University, 1960. Career: Instructor at Princeton from 1958, Professor 1968-80; Professor, Harvard University, 1980-; Editor, Journal of American Musicological Society, 1963-66; Consultant Editor for New Grove Dictionary of Music and Musicians, 1980; President of the American Musicological Society, 1987-88; Founding Editor, Beethoven Forum, 1992-. Publications include: Music in Renaissance Ferrara, 1984; Beethoven: Studies in The Creative Process, 1992. Honours: Recipient of Einstein and Kinkeldey Awards of American Musicological Society; Elected Honorary Member of American Musicological Society, 1993. Address: Harvard University, Music Building, Harvard, Cambridge, MA 02138, USA.

LOEBEL David, b. 7 Mar 1950, Cleveland, OH, USA. Conductor. m. Jane Cawthorn, 7 Jul 1977. Education: BS 1972, MMus 1974, Northwestern University. Career: Assistant Conductor, Syracuse Symphony Orchestra, 1974-76; Music Director, Binghamton Symphony Orchestra, 1977-82; Music Adviser, Anchorage Symphony Orchestra, 1983-86; Assistant, 1982-86, Associate Conductor, 1986-90, Cincinnati Symphony Orchestra; Associate Conductor, 1990-94, Associate Principal Conductor, 1994-, St Louis Symphony Orchestra. Honours: 3rd Prize, 1976, Co-winner, 1978, Baltimore Symphony Orchestra Young Conductors' Competition; ASCAP Award, Adventuresome Programming, 1981; Seaver, NEA Conductors Award, 1992. Address: c/o St Louis Symphony Orchestra, 718 North Grand Blvd, St Louis, MO 63103, USA.

LOEVAAS-GERBER Kari, b. 13 May 1939, Oslo, Norway. Singer (Soprano). m. Manfred Gerber, 1968, 1 daughter. Education: Conservatory Oslo; Musikakademie Wien; Studies with KMSGR Erna Westenberger, Frankfurt. Debut: Nuri, Oslo, 1959. Career: Opera Houses in Dortmund and Mainz; Festivals at Salzburg, Vienna, Lucerne, Bergen, Ludwigsburg, Schwetzigen, Athens, Flandern; Television includes Fischer und seine Fru/Schoeck, 1981 and Peer Gynt, W Egk, 1983; All major radio stations in Germany, Austria, Norway, Switzerland, France and Italy. Recordings include: Debut record: Lieder (Grieg, Mussorgski, Sibelius) with Erik Werba; Petite Messe Solenelle, Rossini; Die Feen, Wagner; War Requiem, Britten; more than 30 records. Honours: Deutsche Grammophon Sonderpreis, Vienna, 1960. Hobby: Painting. Current Management: Sudwestdeutsche Konzertdirektion Russ, Stuttgart. Address: Gugerhalde 10, CH 8207 Schaffhausen, Switzerland.

LOGIE Nicholas, b. 12 May 1950, Hemel Hempstead, Hertfordshire, England. Musician (viola); Orchestra Manager. m. Marina Orlov, 4 Sept 1972, 2 sons. Education: Yehudi Menuhin School, 1963-67; Royal College of Music, London; Northwest Deutsche Musikakademie, Detmold, Germany; Santa Cecilia, Rome, Italy. Debut: Wigmore Hall, London, 1984. Career: Member of Vienna Symphony Orchestra. 1973-78; Chilingirian String Quartet, 1978-81; Orchestra Manager, Glyndebourne Touring Opera, 1990; Baroque Viola, London Baroque, 1985-; Senior Lecturer, Royal Northern College of Music. Recordings: Schubert Cello Quintet; 6 Mozart Quartets with Chilingirian Quartet. Contributions to: 5 Sketches for Solo Viola by Elizabeth Maconchy; Newsletter No 24, The Viola Society, March 1985. Address: Lott's End, Highgate, Forest Row, Sussex RH18 5BE, England.

LOH Lisa, b. 6 Jan 1967, Hong Kong. Pianist. Education: Diploma, Management Studies; Associate, Licentiate, Guildhall School of Music and Drama; Licentiate, Royal Academy of Music; Associate, Royal College of Music. Debut: Purcell Room, South Bank, London, 1993. Career: Appearances in Concerts and Recitals, Fairfield Halls, South Bank and Barbican Centre; Broadcasts on ITV, RTHK Radio Hong Kong. Honours: Several Prizes, UK Competitions. Membership: Fellow, Guild of Musicians and Singers. Hobbies: Cookery; Travel. Address: 83 Andrews House, Fore Street, London EC2Y 8AY, England.

LOJARRO Daniela, b. 1964, Italy. Singer (Soprano). Education: Studied with Carlo Bergonzi, among others. Debut: Sang Gilda at Bussetto. Career: Sang Adina at Parma and Cleone in the first modern revival of Rossini's Ermione (Pesaro 1987); Martina Franca Festival in Acis and Galatea and Susanna in Paisiello's Nina at Savona; Lucerne Opera as Lucia di Lammermoor (1988), Zurich as Marie in La fille du régiment (1988, 1991), Covent Garden 1990 as Clorinda in La Cenerentola, Amina in La sonnambula at Liège, 1992; Other roles include Nannetta, Gluck's Amor and Oscar in Un ballo in maschera (at Naples). Recordings include: Crispino e la Comare, (Nuova Era). Address: Gladbachstrasse 52, CH 8044 Zurich, Switzerland.

LOMBARD Alain, b. 4 Oct 1940, Paris, France. Conductor. Education: Studied at the Paris Conservatoire with Line Talleul (Violin) and Gaston Poulet (Conducting). Debut: Salle Gaveau, Pais, aged 11 with the Pasdeloup Orchestra. Career: Assistant, the Principal Conductor with Lyon Opera, 1961-65; American Opera Society, 1963, with Massenet's Hérodiade; Conducted New York Philharmonic and at Salzburg Festival, 1966; Musical Director, Miami Opera, Florida, 1966-74; Metropolitan Opera, 1967, Gounod's Faust; Director of the Strasbourg Philharmonic, 1972-83; Opéra du Rhin, 1974-80; Guest conductor with Schveningen Festival, Holland, Hamburg Opera, L'Orchestre de Paris and other leading orchestras; Conducted Die Zauberflöte at Bordeaux, 1992; Conducted Falstaff at Catania, 1996. Recordings include: Mozart's Così fan tutte, with Strasbourg Ensemble; Berlioz Symphonie Fantastique, Harold in Italy and Roméo et Juliette; Verdi Requiem; Prokofiev Violin Concertos (Amoyal) and Ballet Suites; Bartók Concerto for Orchestra and Miraculous Mandarin; Ravel Piano Concerto, Queffelec, and Daphnis et Chloe No 2; Gounod Roméo et Juliette. Honour: Gold Medal, Dimitri Mitropoulos Competition, 1966. Address: c/o S A Gorlinsky Limited, 33 Dover Street, London W1X 4NJ, England.

LOMBARDO Bernard, b. 15 Nov 1960, Marseille, France. Tenor. Education: Studied in Marseille and Treviso. Career: Sang widely in France including Bruno in I Puritani at the Paris Opera-Comique, 1987; Tour of Australia, 1988-89, notably as Turiddu at Sydney and Melbourne; St Gallen in 1988 as Edgardo and Opéra Bastille in France in 1990 as Cassio in Otello; La Scala Milan debut in 1991, as Floreski in Cherubini's Lodoiska; Season 1992 as Hoffmann at Kaiserslautern and Roland in Esclarmonde at St Etienne; Other roles include Jacopo in I Due Foscari, Tybalt in Roméo et Juliette at Zurich, Ismaele in Nabucco and Gabriele Adorno at Geneva. Recordings include: Lodoiska and Lucia di Lammermoor. Address: c/o Teatro alla Scala, Via Filodrammatici 2, 20121 Milan, Italy.

LOMON Ruth, b. 7 Nov 1930, Montreal, Canada. Composer. m. Earle Lomon, 4 Aug 1951, 1 s, 2 d. Education: McGill University; New England Conservatory. Debut: Piano,

Montreal, Canada. Career: 2 Piano team with Iris Graffman Wenglin with appearances on radio and TV, performing and lecturing on works by women composers, playing contemporary and classical repertoire, 1973-83; Commissioned works for ALEA III, Boston University Festival, Opus II and III, Michigan University, Canadian Contemporary Music Festival, Music Teachers National Association, National Women's Studies Association, Ohio University. Compositions include: Published: Esquisses for piano solo; Seven Portals of Vision for Organ, 5 Songs on poems by William Blake for Contralto and Violin, Dust Devils for Harp, Janus for String Quartet, Diptych for Woodwind Quintet, Metamorphoses for Cello and Piano, Songs for a Requiem for Soprano, Piano or Woodwinds, Equinox for Brass Quartet, Celebrations for 2 Harps, Bassoon Concerto, Dialogue for Harpsichord and Vibraphone, Requiem Mass for Full Chorus and Brass Accompaniment; Butterfly Effect for String Quartet, 1990, Terra Incognita for Orchestra, 1993, and Shadowing for Piano Quartet, 1993. Recordings include: Five Ceremonial Masks for Piano; Soundings and Triptych for two pianos, 1992; Terra Incognita with Warsaw Philharmonic Orchestra under Jerzy Swoboda, 1993; Bassoon Concerto in 3 movements, with bassoonist Gretzer under Gerard Schwarz with Prague Radio Symphony Orchestra. Honours: New Mexico Arts Division and NEA, 1990; New England Foundation for The Arts, MA Council on the Arts and Humanities, Helene Wurlitzer Foundation Grant, Radcliffe College, Harvard University; Bunting Institute Fellowship, 1995. Membership: Vice President of American Women Composers. Address: 2A Forest Street, Cambridge, MA 02140, USA.

LONDON Edwin, b. 16 Mar 1929, Philadelphia, Pennsylvania, USA. Composer. Education: Studied at Oberlin College Conservatory and the University of Iowa, PhD, 1961; With Gunter Schullar at Manhattan School of Music and with Milhaud and Dallapiccola; Conducting studies with Izler Solomon. Career: Teacher at Smith College, Northampton, 1960-68; University of Illinois, 1973-83; Chairman of the Music Department at Cleveland State University, 1978-; Founder and leader of the Cleveland Chamber Orchestra. Compositions: Santa Claus, Mime Opera, 1960; 3 Settings of Psalm 23 for Choruses, 1961; Woodwind Quintet, 1958; Sonatina for Viola and Piano, 1962; Brass Quintet, 1965; Portraits of Three Ladies, Theatre Piece, 1967; Four Proverbs, 1968; The Iron Hand, Otarorio, 1975; The Death of Lincoln, Opera, 1976; Psalms of These Days, 1976-80; Metaphysical Vegas, Musical 1981. Honours: Guggenheim Foundation Grant; NEA Grants; Hamburg Opera Contemporary Festival Grant. Address: c/o ASCAP, ASCAP Building, One Lincoln Plaza, New York, NY 10023, USA.

LONGHI Daniela, b. 1956, Italy. Soprano. Education: Studied in Verona and Mantua. Career: Sang at the Verona Arena from 1981, as the Priestess in Aida and Liu in Turandot; Guest appearances at Turin as Micaela, Liège as Violetta and Thais and Parma as Leonore in the French version of Il Trovatore, 1990; Marseille and Madrid, 1990-91 as Anna Bolena, Montpellier in 1991 as Elizabeth I in Roberto Devereux by Donizetti; Other roles include Manon and Mimi; Sang Violetta at Detroit, 1996. Address: c/o Opéra de Montpellier, 11 Boulevard Victor Hugo, F-34000 Montpellier, France.

LONGTIN Michel, b. 20 May 1946, Montreal, Canada. Composer; Teacher. Education: Acting I, Mime Certificate, 1964; BA, College des Eudistes, 1967; Computer Science Diploma, 1969; Musical Studies with Dolin, Hambraeus, Hetu, Lanza, Pedersen, Prevost Garant (Montreal and Toronto), 1968-73; BMus, 1973, MMus, 1975, DMus, Composition, 1982, Universite de Montreal. Career: Adjunct Professor of Composition and Contemporary Musical Analysis, University of Montreal, 1987-. Compositions include: Recorded: Deux Rubans Noirs III for Ensemble, 1979; La Trilogie de la Montagne, Electronic Music, 1980; Kata: San Shi Ryu for Ensemble, 1982; Pohjatuuli, Hommage a Sibelius for Ensemble, 1983; Autour d'Ainola for Orchestra, 1986. Honours: Broadcast Music Inc Award to Student Composers, New York, 1972; Canadian Choral Alliance Prize for Composition, 1974; Canadian Composers League Prize for Composition, 1975; Prix Jules-Leger for Pohjatuuli, 1986. Memberships: Centre de Musique Canadienne; LCC; Founding Member, ACREQ. Hobbies: Cycling; Science; Reading. Address: Faculty of Music, Universite de Montreal, CP 6128, Succ A, Montreal, Quebec, Canada H3C 3J7.

LONSDALE Michael (James), b. 11 October 1961, Newcastle, New South Wales, Australia. Composer. Education: New South Wales Conservatory, 1985-87; Study with Nigel Butterley 1984-85 and Bozidar Kos, 1986-88. Career includes: Faculty Member, Barker College, Hornsby; Commissions from David Forrest (1986) and Warringah Council, 1989-91. Compositions include: Calm Obstables, Mouna, and Pais, all for piano, 1985-86; Celeritas for string trio, piano and wind trio, 1985; Fulgur Arbor for tenor trombone, 1986; I See Past the River.... for chorus and orchestra, 1988; Lung Gompa for piano, 1993; It Stirs Beneath, for chorus, 1994; Time is the Loser, for string quartet, 1994; Viper for contra bassoon, 1995. Honours include: ABC/Department of Education Young Composer of the Year Award, 1979. Address: c/o APRA, Locked Bag 3665, St Leonards, NSW 2065, Australia.

LOOSLI Arthur, b. 23 Feb 1926, La Chaux d'Abel, Berner, Jura, Switzerland. Concert Singer. m. Theresia Rothlisberger, 2 sons. Education: Conservatoire of Berne with Felix Loeffel; Studies with Mariano Stabile, Venice and Arne Sunnergard, Stockholm, Sweden. Debut: Berne, 1958. Career: Performances in Switzerland, Belgium, Sweden, Netherlands, Germany and Italy; Guest Artist at Stadttheater, Berne. Recordings: Elegie, Lieder (Othmar Schoeck); Winterreise (Schubert); Schwanengesang (Schubert); Johannes - Passion (Bach). Publications: Illustrations of Franz Hohler's Tschipo and Der Granitblock im Kino. Honours: Recipient, 1st Prize, International Singers Competition, Bass Baritone, 'sHertogenbosch, Netherlands, 1959; Further professional activities. Memberships: Othmar Schoeck Association; Swiss Music Teachers Association. Hobbies: Painting and Graphics; Drawing Master at Gymnasium, Thun, Switzerland. Address: Gurtenweg 31A, 3074 Muri, Switzerland.

LOOTENS Lena (Helena-Alice), b. 14 April 1959, Genk, Belgium. Soprano. m. Matthias Muller, 3 December 1988, 1 daughter. Education: Royal Atheneum of Maasmechelen; Conservatories of Brussels and Gent; Private studies with Vera Rozsa, London; Margreet Honig, Amsterdam; Kristina Deutekom, Amsterdam. Career: Appearances with numerous orchestras; Concert tours to Belgium, Netherlands, Germany, England, Switzerland, Israel and Poland; Appearances on Radio and Television includes, BRT, BBC, WDR, NDR, SDR; Opera engagements in Innsbruck, Monte Carlo, Antwerp, Montpellier, Liège and Versailles. Recordings: L'Infedeltà Delusa; Concert Arias; Flavio of Handel, Deutsche Schallplattenpieis; L'Incoronazione di Poppea of Monteverdi; Die Israeliten in der Wüste, C P E Bach; Requiem/Mozart; La Guiditta/Almeida; Die Heirat Widerwillen/Humperdinck. Honours: 1st Prize Singing, National Competition for the Youth of Belgium; Alex Devries Scholarship, Roeping Foundation. Address: Platte-Lostr 341, B03010 Kessel-Lo, Belgium.

LOPARDO Frank, b. 1958, New York, USA. Singer (Tenor). Education: Studied in New York. Debut: St Louis, 1984, as Tamino. Career: Season 1985-86 at Dallas and Naples, Don Ottavio at Aix and La Scala, Milan; Sang Fenton in Falstaff at Amsterdam 1986, Ferrando at Glyndebourne, 1987; Vienna Staatsoper from 1987, notably as Belfoire in Il Viaggo a Reims, conducted by Abbado; Sang Elvino in La Sonnambula and Rossini's Almviva at Chicago, 1989; Sang Lindoro in L'Italiana in Algeri, Covent Garden, 1989; Season 1991 as Elvino and Ferrando at Florence, Don Ottavio at San Francisco; Sang Rossini's Lindoro at San Francisco, 1992; Alfredo at Covent Garden, 1995; Lensky in Paris, 1996. Recordings include: Mozart's Requiem and Don Giovanni; L'Italiana in Algeri; Falstaff. Address: Metropolitan Opera, Lincoln Center, New York, NY 10023, USA.

LOPEZ-COBOS Jesus, b. 25 Feb 1940, Toro, Spain. Conductor. m. Alicia Lopez-Cobos, May 1987, 3 s. Education: PhD in Philosophy, 1964; Diploma in Composition, Madrid Conservatory, 1966; Diploma in Conducting, Vienna Academy, Austria, 1969. Debut: Concert, Prague, 1969; Opera, La Fenice, Venice. Career includes: Debuts at: Deutsche Oper in 1970 with La Bohème and San Francisco, USA in 1972 with Lucia di Lammermoor; Conducted Carmen at Covent Garden, 1975, Adriana Lecouvreur at the Metropolitan, 1978, Der Ring with Deutsche Oper Berlin on tour to Japan, 1987; Principal Guest Conductor with London Philharmonic, 1982-86; Principal Conductor and Artistic Director of Spanish National Orchestra, 1984-89; Music Director of Cincinnati Orchestra, 1986- and Lausanne Chamber Orchestra, 1990-; Concerts with many leading orchestras in Britain, USA, Germany, Amsterdam, Vienna, Switzerland, Norway and Israel. Opera productions at Royal Opera House, Covent Garden, and La Scala; Conducted La Serva Padrona at Lausanne, 1996. Recordings include: Franck's Symphony in D minor, Ravel's Bolero and Bruckner's Symphonies Nos 4, 6 and 7 with Cincinnati Orchestra; Donizetti Lucia di Lammermoor, Rossini's Otello, Recital and operatic discs with José Carreras and Liszt Dante Symphony, Falla, Three-Cornered Hat, Chabrier Espana. Honours: 1st Prize, Besançon International Conductors Competition, 1969; Prince of Asturias Award, from the Spanish Government, 1981; First Class Cross of Merit of Germany, 1989. Hobby: Tennis. Current Management: Terry Harrison Artists Management. Address: The Orchard, Market Street, Charlbury, Oxon, OX7 3PJ, England.

LOPEZ-YANEZ Jorge, b. 1963, Mexico. Tenor. Education: Studied in Mexico City and California. Debut: Long Beach Opera in 1986 as Rossillon in Die Lustige Witwe. Career: European debut at Hanover in 1988 as the Duke of Mantua; Dusseldorf and Stuttgart, 1988-89 as Ramiro in La Cenerentola; Further engagements as Fenton at Los Angeles and Bordeaux, Oronte in Alcina at the Paris Châtelet, Rossini's Almaviva at Munich, Donizetti's Tonio at Zurich and Alfredo in La Traviata at the Vienna Staatsoper, 1992; Glyndebourne debut in 1995 as Pyrrhus in the British stage premiere of Rossini's Ermione; Sang Nemorino at Santiago. Address: Robert Gilder & Co; Enterprise House, 59-65 Upper Ground, London SE1 9PQ, England.

LORAND Colette, b. 7 Jan 1923, Zurich, Switzerland. Singer (Soprano). Education: Musikhochschule Hanover; Zurich with Frau Hirzel. Debut: Basle 1946, as Marguerite in Faust. Career: Frankfurt Opera 1951-56, notably as the Queen of Night; Hamburg Opera from 1955, often in operas by Henze, Penderecki and Orff; Edinburgh Festival 1955; Lisbon 1961, as Constanze in Die Entführung; Deutsche Oper Berlin 1972, in the premiere of Fortner's Elisabeth Tudor; Created roles in Orff's De Temporum fine Comoedia, Salzburg Festival, 1973, and Reimann's Lear, Munich 1978 (as Regan, repeated at the Paris Opera, 1982). Recordings: Lear and De Temporum fine Comoedia; Orff's Prometheus. Address: c/o Bayerische Staatsoper, Postfach 745, D-8000 Munich, Germany.

LORANGE Nicole, b. 28 Nov 1942, Montreal, Canada. Soprano. Education: Studied with Pierrette Alarie and at the Vienna Music Academy with Erik Werba. Career: Sang at first in concert and made stage debut at the Linz Landestheater in 1969 as Desdemona; Further appearances with the Canadian Opera Company as Musetta in 1972, and Opéra Montreal as Tosca in 1980; Metropolitan Opera, 1982-84 as Butterfly, Adriana Lecouvreur and Francesca da Rimini; Other roles include Donna Elvira and Offenbach's Giulietta; Many concert appearances. Address: c/o L'Opéra de Montreal, 260 de Maisonneuve Boulevard West Montreal, Province Québec H2H 1Y9, Canada.

LORD Bernadette, b. 1965, Derby, England. Singer (Soprano). Education: Studied at the Guildhall School and with Suzanne Danco in Florence; Further study at the European Arts Centre, 1988. Career: Joined Opera Wallonie, Liège and sang Helena in Schubert's Der Häusliche Krieg in Belgium, Holland and Paris; Glyndebourne and Covent Garden debuts as Cis in Albert Herring; Other roles include Despina for British Youth Opera at the Cheltenham Festival, Miss Wordsworth in Albert Herring, Lucia in The Rape of Lucretia, Gretel for Opera East, Susanna and Barbarina in Le nozze di Figaro; Sang Jano in Jenufa at Covent Garden, 1993. Address: c/o Royal Opera House (Contracts), Covent Garden, London WC2, England.

LORENTZEN Bent, b. 11 Feb 1935, Oerum, Denmark. Composer. m. Edith Kaerulf Moeller, 2 Aug 1958, 1 son, 3 daughter. Education: Royal Academy of Music, Copenhagen, 1960. Career includes: Performances throughout Europe of works including Euridice, Die Music kommt mit äusserst bekannt vor!, Eine Wundersame Liebesgeschichte, Stalten Mette, Toto, Fackeltanz, Samba, Pianoconcerto Nordic Music Days, Saxophone Concerto, two choral songs to Enzensberger, 1991, Bill and Julia (opera), The Magic Brilliant, (The Danish National Opera), 1993; The Scatterbrain, Royal Theatre, 1995. Compositions include: Purgatorio, choral; Granite; Quartz; Syncretism; Colori; Concerto for oboe; Samba; Paradiesvogel; Graffiti; Genesis; New Choral Dramatics; Ammen Dammen Des; Round; 5 easy Piano Pieces, Olof Palme for mixed choir; Comics, 3 Latin Suites, Tordenskiold. Recordings include: The Bottomless Pit; Visions; Cloud-Drift; Mambo, Intersection, Puncti, Triplex, Groppo, Nimbus, Cruor, Umbra, Paesaggio, Dunkelblau, Round, Cyclus I-IV, Mars; Piano and oboe concertos; Regenbogen; Comics; Lines; Tears; Orfeo Suite; Intrada; Alpha and Omega. Publications: Ej Sikkelej, 1967; Recorder System, 1962-64; Musikens AHC, 1969; Mer om Musiken, 1972; Introduction to Electronic Music, 1969. Honours: Prix Italia, 1970; First prize, Nyon Film Festival, 1973, as well as awards in Poland, Austria, and Messiaen-prize, Bergamo, 1988; Composer of the Year, 1990; Recording Award 1991 for Piano Concerto; Carl Nielsen Award, 1995. Memberships: Danish Composers Society. Hobbies: Gardening. Current Management Edition Wilhelm Hansen, Bornholmsgade 1, 1266 Kobenhavn K, Denmark. Address: Sotoften 37, 2820 Genofte, Denmark.

LORENZ Andrew (Bela), b. 17 Oct 1951, Melbourne, Victoria, Australia. Violinist. m. Wendy Joy Lorenz, 1 son. Education: DSCM Performers Diploma and Teachers Diploma, Sydney Conservatory of Music, 1970. Career: Recitals; Concerto, radio and television performances; Deputy Leader, Melbourne Elizabethen Trust Orchestra, 1972; Led for D'Oyly Carte Opera Company, Sadler's Wells, England, 1973-74; Leader, New England Ensemble (resident piano quartet) and Lecturer, Music Department, University of New England, Armidale, New South Wales, Australia, 1975-82; Founding Member and Leader, New England Sinfonia; World tours with New England Ensemble; Associate Concertmaster, Adelaide Symphony Orchestra, 1983-86; Leader, Australian Piano Trio, 1983-87; Currently: Senior Lecturer in Strings, University of Southern Queensland, Toowoomba, Queensland; Leader, Darling Downs Trio; Director, McGregor Chamber Music School. Recordings: Works by Beethoven, Turina, Margaret Sutherland, Mozart, Fauré, John McCabe, Mendelssohn, Goossens; Mary Lageau; 6 LPs/CDs including: Sundry chamber works and Concerto Soloist with many of Australia's leading orchestras and Slovak Radio Symphony; Australian premieres of Benjamin, McCabe and Myslivecek Concertos. Honours include: Winner, Victorian ABC Concerto Competition, 1972. Hobbies: Sport; Reading. Address: 6 Merlin Court, M/S 852 Toowoomba Mail Servce, Queensland 4352, Australia.

LORIMER Heather, b. 1961, Wallasey, Cheshire. Singer (Soprano). m. Gerard Quinn. Education: Studied at the Royal Northern College of Music, Manchester with Frederick Cox and now with Iris Dell'Acqua. Career: Scottish Opera Go Round, Mimi in La Bohème, 1987; Glyndebourne Festival and Touring Opera, Constanze, Die Entführung aus dem Serail, 1988; Countess, Le nozze di Figaro, 1989; Opera 80, Tatiana in Eugene Onegin in 1989 and Hanna Glawari in The Merry Widow, 1990; Travelling Opera, Mimi; Countess; Donna Elvira; Don Giovanni; Fiordiligi in Cosi fan tutte; Violetta in La Traviata and Micaela in Carmen; English Touring Opera, Mimi, 1994; Education tours for Glyndebourne, Opera 80 and English National Opera's Lillian Bayliss Programme; Other roles performed include: Giorgetta, Il Tabarro; Liu, Turandot; Norina, Don Pasquale; Rosina, Il Barbiere di Siviglia; Rosalinde, Die Fledermaus; Rosario, Goyescas; Dirce, Medea; Leila, The Pearl Fishers and in 1993 she created the title role in Michael Finnissy's Thérèse Raquin, for the Royal Opera's Garden Venture; Concert repertoire includes, Verdi Requiem; Rossini Stabat Mater; Dvorak Requiem; Elijah; Carmina Burana; Brahms Requiem; Fauré Requiem; Sea Symphony and The Kingdom. Honours include: International Opera and Bel Canto Duet Competition, Antwerp, Gerard Quinn; Scottish Opera John Noble Competition. Address: 92 Sturla Road, Chatham, Kent ME4 5QH, England.

LORIOD Jeanne, b. 13 July 1928, Houilles, France. Ondes Martenot Player. Education: Studied with Maurice Martenot at the Paris Conservatoire, from 1946. Debut: Academy of Santa Cecilia, Rome, 1950. Career: Appearances with the Berlin Philharmonic, London Symphony, Boston SO, Cleveland Orchestra, Amsterdam Concertgebouw, Orchestre de Paris, Chicago and San Francisco SOs, St Petersburg, New York and Los Angeles Philharmoics; Teacher at the Paris Conservatoire from 1970, founded Sextuor Jeanne Loriod 1974; Performances of works by more than 350 composers, including works by Murail, Bussotti, Jolivet, Tomasi and Barraudi; Frequently heard in music by Messiaen. Recordings include: Messiaen's Turangalila-Symphonie and Trois Petites Liturgies. Publications: Three-Volume, La Technique de L'Onde Electronique. Honours include: Grand Prix du Disque (ten times); Ondes Martenot Medal at the Paris Conservatoire. Address: Allied Artists, 42 Montpellier Square, London SW7 1JZ, England.

LORIOD Yvonne, b. 20 Jan 1924, Houilles, Seine-et-Oise, France. Pianist. m. Olivier Messiaen, dec 1992. Education: National Conservatory of Music, Paris. Career: Solo Recitals in most European countries, North and South America, and Japan with leading orchestras; 1st Performaces in Paris of 21 Concerti by Mozart and Concerti by Bartok and Schoenberg and many works by Jolivet and all Messiaen works with piano including Visions de l'Amen, 1943, Turangalila Symphonie 1948, Catalogue d'Oiseaux 1958, Des Canyons aux Etoiles 1974; Professor of Piano, Paris Conservatoire of Music; Master Classes at summer schools, Darmstadt and Bayreuth, France and USA. Recordings: Numerous works issued. Honours: Officer, Legion of Honour; Grand Prix du Disque.

LORRAIN Denis, b. 29 July 1948, Ithaca, New York, USA. Composer. m. Jacqueline Quiniou, 1 Aug 1970, 1 daughter. Education: Baccalaureate, Serie Philosophie, 1967; BMus, Composition, University of Montreal, 1971; MMA, Composition, McGill University, 1973; Doctorat, Musique et esthetique, University of Paris, Sorbonne, 1983. Career: Assistant, IRCAM, Paris, 1978; Associate Professor, Faculty of Music, University of Montreal, 1980; Maitre Assistant, IRCAM, Paris, 1982; Professor, Conservatoire National Superieur de Musique, Lyon, 1988. Compositions: Huit Pieces Pour Piano; Arc, String Orchestra; P-A, Voices; P-A, Version Luminy; L'Angelus, Clarinet and Tape; Suite Pour Deux Guitares; Sequence, Organ; Polyphrase, Orchestra; Generiques, Tape; Contra Mortem, Clarinet; Droite, Homage to Le Corbusier, Tape; Le Talon d'Achille, Flute; Extrema, Organ and Percussion; Les Portes du Sombre Dis, Tape; Di Mi Se Mai..., Brass Quintet, Percussion and Tape; The Other Shape, Percussion and Tape; ... Black It Stood as Night, Tape; La Nuova Ricordanza, Two Harpsichords. Address: SONVS-CNSM de Lyon, CP 120, 3 Quai Chaveau, 69266 Lyon Cedex 09, France.

LOTHIAN Helen, b. Scotland. Singer (Mezzo-soprano). Education: Studied at the Royal Scottish Academy and the Guildhall School; Further study with Patricia Hay in Scotland. Career: Concert appearances throughout Britain in music by Verdi, Bruckner, Beethoven, Mozart and Haydn; Recitals at the Covent Garden Festival, Clonter Opera Farm and elsewhere; Sang the Lady Artist in Berg's Lulu with the BBC SO, 1995; Opera engagements include Christoph Rilke's Song of Love and Death by Matthus, for Glyndbourne Touring Opera; Dorabella, Carmen and Cherubino for British Youth Opera, Dardane in Haydn's L'Incontro Improvviso at Garsington and Mozart's Third Lady at the Covent Garden Festival; Romeo in Bellini's I Capuleti e i Montecchi for Castleward Opera, 1995; Royal Opera and Scottish Opera debuts as Flora in La Traviata, 1996. Address: c/o Lies Askonas Ltd, 6 Henrietta St, London WC2E 8LA, England.

LOTT Felicity (Ann) (Dame), b. 8 May 1947, Cheltenham, Gloucestershire, England. Singer, Soprano. m. (1) Robin Golding, 22 Dec 1973, (2) Gabriel Woolf, 19 Jan 1984, 1 daughter. Education: BA, Hons, French, Royal Holloway College, London University, 1965-69; LRAM, Royal Academy of Music, 1969-73. Debut: English National Opera, 1975 as Pamina in Die Zauberflöte. Career: Principal roles with Glyndebourne, Covent Garden, ENO, WNO, SNO, Paris Opera, Brussels Opera, Hamburg, Munich, Chicago, New York Metropolitan, San Francisco, Vienna, Dresden; Founder Member of Songmakers' Almanac; Wide concert and oratorio and recital repertoire; Glyndebourne debut 1977, as Anne Trulove in The Rake's Progress; TV appearances in Rake's Progress, Zauberflöte, Midsummer Night's Dream, Intermezzo; Roles include Strauss, Arabella, Christine, Octavian, Marschallin and Countess in Capriccio; Mozart, Pamina, Fiordiligi, Donna Elvira, Countess, Xiphares in Mitridate; Amadeus Soundtrack; Royal Wedding, 1986. Recordings include: Countess in La Nozze di Figaro; Ellen Orford in Peter Grimes; Fiordiligi in Cosi fan Tutte; Elvira in Don Giovanni; Many recital discs with Graham Johnson and duets with Ann Murray. Honours: Fellow, Royal Academy of Music, 1987; Honorary Doctor of University of Sussex, 1989; Commander of the Order of the British Empire, New Year's Honours, 1990; Chevalier Dans L'Ordre Des Arts et Des Lettres, 1992; Honorary Fellow, Royal Holloway College, 1995; Honorary Doctorate, Loughborough University, 1996; Dame of the Order of the British Empire, 1997; Honorary Doctorate, University of Loughborough, 1996; Honorary DMus, University of London, 1997. Memberships: Equity; Incorporated Society of Musicians. Current Management: Lies Askonas Limited. Address: c/o Lies Askonas Limited, 6 Henrietta Street, London, WC2E 8LA.

LOUGHRAN James, b. 30 June 1931, Glasgow, Scotland. Musician. m. (1) Nancy Coggon, 20 September 1961, (2) Ludmila Navratil, 15 April 1985, 2 sons. Debut: Royal Festival Hall, London, 1961. Career: Associate Conductor, Bournemouth S.O, 1962-65; Principal Conductor, BBC Scottish S.O, 1965-71; Principal Conductor and Musical Adviser, Hallé Orchestra, 1971-83; Principal Conductor, Bamberg S.O, 1979-83; Guest Conductor of Principal Orchestras in Europe, America, Australasia and Japan; Tours with Munich Philharmonic, BBC Symphony, Stockholm, London and Japan Philharmonic and Scottish Chamber Orchestras; Permanent Guest Conductor, Japan Philharmonic Symphony Orchestra, 1993. Recordings include: Symphonies by Beethoven, Brahms and Elgar, as well as works by Mozart, Berlioz, Schubert, Dvorak, Rachmaninov, Havergal Brian, Walton, Holst and McCabe. Honours: Philharmonia Orchestra Conducting, First Prize, 1961; FRNCM, 1976; FRSAMD, 1983; Freeman, City of London, 1991; Liveryman, Musicians' Company, 1992; Hon DMus, Sheffield, 1983; Gold Disc, EMI, 1983. Hobbies: Golf; Travel. Current Management: Interartists Holland BV. Address: The Rookery, Bollington Cross, Macclesfield, Cheshire SK10 5EL, England.

LOUIE Alexina (Alexi), b. 30 July 1949, Vancouver, British Columbia, Canada. Composer; Pianist. Education: Studied at the University of British Columbia and at San Diego with Pauline Oliveros. Career: Teacher in Pasadena and Los Angeles, 1974-80; Commissions from leading Canadian orchestras; Teacher in Canada from 1980. Compositions include: Journal, music theatre, 1980; Music for a Thousand Autumns for orchestra, 1983; The Eternal Earth (1986) and The Ringing Earth (1986) for orchestra; Piano concerto, 1984; Thunder Gate for violin and orchestra, 1991; Piano quintet Music from Night's Edge (1988) and other chamber music; Love Songs for a Small Planet, for soprano, chamber choir and ensemble (1989) and other vocal music. Address: c/o 41 Valleybrook Drive, Don Mills, Ontario M3B 2S6, Canada.

LOUKIANETS Viktoria, b. Kiev, Russia. Singer (Soprano). Education: Studied at the Kiev Music School and Kiev Conservatoire. Career: Soloist with the Ukrainian Opera in Kiev from 1989; Guest appearances in France, Portugal, Czech Republic, Italy and Switzerland; Principal with the Vienna Staatsoper, singing Adina (L'Elisir d'Amore), Elvira (L'Italiana in Algeri), Rosina the Queen of the Night and Olympia (Contes d'Hoffman) from 1994; Oscar in Ballo in Maschera at Naples, 1994, and the Deutsche Oper Berlin; Appearances as Violetta at the Salzburg Festival, New York Met, debut 1996, also at the Opera Bastille, Paris, 1998; La Scala Milan debut as the Queen of Night, 1995; Season 1996-97 at Covent Garden as Medora in Il Corsaro and Gilda in Rigoletto; Other roles include Donna Anna (at Salzburg) and Wagner's Woglinde (at La Scala, under Muti). Honours include: Winner, Mozart Bicentennial Competition, Italy, 1991; Winner, Maria Callas Competition at Athens, 1991. Address: c/o Lies Askonas Ltd, 6 Henrietta St, London WC2E 8LA, England.

LOUP François, b. 4 Mar 1940, Estavayer-le-lac, Switzerland. Singer (Bass). Education: Studied piano organ, composition and singing at Fribourg. Career: Sang at the Geneva Opera 1964-66, notably in the premiere of Monsieur de Pourceaugnac by Martin; Directed various vocal ensembles for which he harmonised motets, madrigals and Swiss folk songs; Soloist with the Ensemble Instrumental de Lausanne, under Michel Corboz; Many performances of Baroque music, notably with the Societa Cameristica di Lugano and with the Opera de Lyon, in Orfeo by Monteverdi; Oratorio performances in many European countries; Sang in Bizet's Docteur Miracle at the 1975 Spoleto Festival; Sang Bartolo in Le nozze di Figaro at Houston 1988, repeated at Glyndebourne 1989, later at the Albert Hall, London; San Diego and the Opera de Lyon 1989, as Don Pasquale and as Balducci in Benvenuto Cellini; Season 1992 with Mozart's Bartolo at San Diego, Don Pasquale at Vancouver and the Sacristan in Tosca at San Francisco; Sang in La Bohème at the Met, 1994; Bailiff in Werther at Tel Aviv, 1996. Other roles include Leporello, Figaro, Dulcamara, Masetto, Arkel, Pimen, Frère Laurent in Roméo et Juliette and Sarastro; Dedicatee of several contemporary compositions, and teacher of singing; Pupils include François Le Roux. Address: c/o Metropolitan Opera, Lincoln Center, New York, NY 10023, USA.

LOVE Shirley, b. 6 Jan 1940, Detroit, MI, USA. Singer (Mezzo-soprano). Education: Studies with Avery Crew in Detroit and Margaret Harshaw in New York. Debut: Metropolitan Opera in 1963 in Die Zauberflöte. Career: Remained in New York for 20 seasons, as Carmen, Dalila, Verdi's Maddalena, Amneris and Emilia, Rossini's Angelina and Rosina, Siebel in Faust, Pauline in The Queen of Spades and in operas by Ravel, Menotti and Bernstein; Guest appearances in Cincinnati, Chicago, Miami and Philadelphia; Sang at Baltimore in 1962, in the premiere of Kagen's Hamlet; Concert appearances in Amsterdam, Bologna and Florence. Address: c/o Metropolitan Opera, Lincoln Center, New York, NY 10023, USA.

LOVEDAY Alan (Raymond), b. 29 Feb 1928, England. Violinist. m. Ruth Stanfield, 1952, 1 son, 1 daughter. Education: Private study; Royal College of Music, prizewinner. Debut: Childhood debut, age 4; Debut in England, 1946. Career: Numerous concerts, broadcasts, television appearances, Britain and Overseas; Played with all leading conductors & orchestras. Ranges from Bach, on un-modernised violin, to contemporary music; Professor, Royal College of Music, 1955-72; Soloist, Academy of St Martin-in-the-Fields. Hobbies: Chess; Bridge. Address: c/o Academy of St Martin-in-the-Fields, Raine House, Waine Street, Wapping, London E1 9RG, England.

LOVELAND Kenneth, b. 12 Oct 1915, Sheerness, Kent, England. Music Critic. m. Anne Edwards. Career: Music Critic; Various professional publications; Own music magazine, Radio Wales, Cardiff; Music programmes for Radio Telefis Eireann, Dublin, Republic of Ireland; BBC Kaleidoscope. Contributions to: The Times; Opera; Musical Times; Country Life. Honours: Golden Statue of Vienna, 1970; Cavliere, Italian Govenment, 1970; Guild for the Promotion of Welsh Music Award, 1985; Honorary MMus, University College of Wales, 1986. Memberships: Critics Circle; Guild of British Newspapers Editors, President 1962; National Training Council, President, 1968. Hobbies: Watching Cricket and Soccer; Travel; Food and wine. Address: 20 Monmouth House, Cwmbran, Gwent, NP44 1QT, wales.

LOVETT Terence (George), b. 2 July 1922, London, England. Conductor. m. Selina Dorothy Clark; 3 sons. Education: Royal Academy of Music; FRAM; LRAM. Debut: London, 1941. Career: Organist and choirmaster for numerous choirs; Conductor and Atristic Director Hull Philharmonic Society; Plays piano, viola, horn, trumpet and organ; Guest conductor in Sweden, with BBC Symphony and in Europe, Middle and Far East. Memberships: Royal Philharmonic Society; ISM; RCM Club; Le Petit Club Francais. Honours: Royal Academy of Music Prize, 1942. Hobbies: Fencing; Reading; Cooking. address: 15 Beauchamp Road, E Moseley, Surrey, KT8 OPA, England.

LOVING Rita, b. New York, New York, USA. Pianist; Singer; Voice Teacher; Opera Coach. m. Maurice Stern, 1965, divorced 1978, 2 stepsons, 1 stepdaughter. Education: Bachelor's degree, Oberlin Conservatory, Oberlin, Ohio; MMus, Manhattan School of Music, New York City; Opera School, Mannes School of Music, New York City. Career: Concerts as Pianist-Accompanist and Singer, USA and Europe, solo and with husband; Engagements in European Opera Houses as Opera Coach and occasional small roles, 1969-91: Städtische Bühne, Flensburg, Germany, 1969-71, Hessische Staattheater, Wiesbaden, Germany, 1971-75, Opera Forum, Enschede, Netherlands, and Nederlands Stichting Opera House, Amsterdam, 1976-78; Currently Opera Coach, Bayerische Staatsoper, Munich. 1978-; Teacher, various opera programmes including AIMS, Graz, Austria, 1981-87, Israel Opera Programme, 1989, 1990,

Bayreuther Seminar, 1990, 1991, Munich Seminar, 1997; Musical specialty, One Woman Show, singing and playing music of George Gershwin and Cole Porter, on concert stage in Munich, Austria, USA, Switzerland, Denmark; Masterclasses given at Manhattan School of Music, Mannes School of Music and Oberlin Conservatory. Hobbies include: Reading; Swimming; Hiking; Biking. Address: Liebigstrasse 13, 80538 Munich, Germany.

LOWENTHAL Jerome, b. 11 Feb 1932, Philadelphia, Pennsylvania, USA. Concert Pianist. m. Ronit Amir, 7 July 1959, 2 daughters. Education: BA, University of Pennsylvania, 1953; MS, Juilliard School of Music, 1956; Premier License de Concert, Ecole Normale de Musique; Piano studies, Olga Samaroff, William Kapell, Eduard Steuermann, Alfred Cortot. Debut: Philadelphia Orchestra, 1945. Career: Appearances with orchestras of: New York, Philadelphia, Boston, Cleveland, Israel Philharmonic, Stockholm, Chicago, Los Angeles, Detroit, Pittsburgh; Conductors: Monteux, Stokowski, Bernstein, Ormandy, Giulini, Tennstedt, Mehta, Ozawa, Barenboim, Comissiona;Tours of Southeast Asia, New Zealand, Latin America, Western Europe, USSR, Poland, Romania; Piano Faculty, Juilliard School, 1990-. Recordings: Rorem Concerto no 3, Louisville-Mester; Tchaikovsky Concerti 1, 2 and 3, London Symphony Orchestra Comissiona; Liszt Opera Paraphrases; Gershwin Concerto in F and Rhapsody in Blue, Utah Symphony Orchestra; Sinding, Sonata & short pieces for solo piano; Liszt Concerto No 1, No 3, Totentanz, Malediction: Vancouver Symphony, Commissiona. Honours: Laureat, Darmstadt Competition 1957; Busoni Competition 1957; Reine Elizabeth 1960. Current Management: Herbert Barrett. Address: 865 West End Avenue, Apt 11A, NY 10025, USA.

LU Siqing, b. 26 Nov 1969, Qingdao, China. Violinist. Education: Juilliard School of Music, NY; Central Conservatory of Music, Beijing; Yehudi Menuhin School, London. Debut: With Royal Philharmonic Orchestra, Fairfield Hall, 1983. Career: Regular concert appearances in Asia, Europe, South America, North America; Soloist with: Royal Philharmonic Orchestra; Symphony Orchestra of Genoa Opera House; Vancouver Symphony Orchestra; Bern Symphony Orchestra; National Orchestra of Columbia, 1988; Toured with China Broadcasting Symphony Orchestra in 7 countries, Europe; Numerous appearances, TV and Radio, including Swiss Radio. Recordings: Exclusive recording for Chinese company; CD release by Philips for Asian distribution; 2 CDs, China, 1982; Numerous concert and recital works on tape and CDs. Honours: Silver Medal, Royal Amateur Philharmonic Society; 1st Prize, 34th International Paganini Violin Competition, Italy, 1987; Many other International Prizes. Hobbies: Football; Tennis; Reading; Food; Stereo; Cars. Address: c/o Curzon and Kedersha, 330 East 39th Street, Suite 28E, New York, NY 10016, USA.

LUBBOCK John, b. 18 Mar 1945, Hertfordshire, England. Conductor. Education: Chorister at St George's Chapel, Windsor then Royal Academy of Music; Conducting studies with Sergiu Celibidache. Career: Founder, Camden Chamber Orchestra, 1967 becoming in 1972 the Orchestra of St John's Smith Square; Frequent concerts at St John's Church in Westminster and on tour in Britain, Europe, USA and Canada; Guest Conductor with City of Birmingham Symphony, London Philharmonic, BBC Scottish Symphony, Bournemouth Symphony and Sinfonietta, London Mozart Players, Irish Chamber Orchestra, Stuttgart Symphony Orchestra and Netherlands Chamber Orchestra; Works regularly with the Ulster Orchestra and as Principal Conductor with Belfast Philharmonic Society and the Oxford University Orchestra; Worked with the Hallé Orchestra in 1992 and again in 1995; Conducted Berio's Sinfonia at Barbican Hall, 1985 and the premiere of Meirion Bowen's orchestration of Tippett's The Heart's Assurance; Schumann's Requiem and Dvorak's Symphonic Variations at St John's, 1997. Recordings include: Arnold Guitar Concerto and Rodrigo Concierto de Aranjuez; Haydn Symphony Nos 44 and 49; Mendelssohn Symphony Nos 3 and 4; Schubert Symphony No 5; Stravinsky Apollo and Orpheus; Tchaikovsky Serenade; Vivaldi Concerti op 10, all with the Orchestra of St John's Smith Square. Current Management: Owen-White Management. Address: c/o Owen-White Management, 14 Nightingale Lane, London, N8 7QU, England.

LUBET Alex (Jeffrey), b. 9 June 1954, Harvey, IL, USA. Composer; Theorist; Educator. m. Iris Misae Shiraishi, 9 Aug 1981, 1 daughter. Education: BMus, Composition, Chicago Musical College of Roosevelt University, 1975; MA 1977; PhD 1979, Composition, Univesity of Iowa. Career: Assistant Professor of Music Theory and Composition, 1979-86; Associate Professor of Music Theory and Composition, 1986-; University of Minnesota; Major performances include: St Paul Chamber Orchestra; Ars Nova Festival, Donaueschingen, Institut für Neue Musik, Freiburg, Festival Musical du Chateau de Pourtales, Strasbourg; Broadcasts on Sudwestfunk and National Public Radio, USA. Compositions: Two Octave Etudes; Lament; Ma Tovu; Psalm 139; M'ein Sheva; La Armonia del Mundo; Rhythm Changes; God's Love Dancing Between The Shadows; Three Short Pieces After Webern; 123454; Jaltgrang; The Song of The Jain Temples; Shabbat Shalom; Masada. Recordings: Two octave Etudes; Ma Tovu. Address: School of Music, 100 Ferguson Hall, University of Minnesota, Minneapolis, MN 55455, USA.

LUBIN Steven, b. 22 Feb 1942, New York, USA. Pianist; Musicologist. m. Wendy Lubin, 2 June 1974, 2 sons. Education: AB, Harvard College; MS, Juilliard School of Music; PhD, New York University; Piano studies with Lisa Grad, Nadia Reisenberg, Seymour Lipkin, Rosina Lhevinne and Beveridge Webster. Debut: Carnegie Recital Hall, New York, 1977. Career: Soloist, Mostly Mozart Festival, Summerfare and other festivals; Concert tours in North America and Europe, 1977-; Soloist and Conductor of continuing series, the Metropolitan Museum, New York City; Filmed as soloist in Mozart and Beethoven works for British TV documentary, in London and Vienna, 1986; Repeated appearances at Mostly Mozart Festival, Lincoln Center, New York, Metropolitan Museum series, Alice Tully Hall, Y series, Kennedy Center, Ravinia Festival; Director of the Mozartean Players, a chamber group performing on 18th century period instruments; Faculty appointments have included Juilliard, Vassar, Cornell; Concerto performances with Los Angeles and St Paul Chamber Orchestras, as well as the Academy of Ancient Music. Recordings: Ongoing cycle of Mozart piano concertos as soloist and conductor; Cycle of Beethoven piano concertos, soloist with Christopher Hogwood and the Academy of Ancient Music, 1987; Also works of Mozart, Beethoven, Schubert and Brahms; Albums of solo and duo sonatas by Mozart; 6 Trios by Haydn with the Mozartean Players. Current Management: New World Classics, 1 Riverdale Avenue, Suite 4, Riverdale, NY 10463, USA. Address: Music Division, School of the Arts, SUNY, Purchase, NY 10577, USA.

LUBLIN Eliane, b. 10 Apr 1938, Paris, France. Soprano. Education: Studied in Paris then at the Verdi Conservatory in Paris. Debut: Aix-en-Provence as Debussy's Mélisande. Career: Paris Opéra-Comique; Monte Carlo Opera in Menotti's The Medium; Paris Opéra from 1969 in Les Dialogues des Carmélites, as Massenet's Manon, Marguerite in Faust, Ellen Orford in Peter Grimes and in the 1981 French premiere of Ligeti's Le Grande Macabre. Recordings include: Sapho by Gounod. Address: c/o Théâtre National de L'Opéra de Paris, 8 Rue Scribe, F75009 Paris, France.

LUBOTSKY Mark, b. 18 May 1931, Leningrad, Russia. Violinist. Education: Moscow Conservatory from 1953, with A Yampolsky and D Oistrakh. Debut: Bolshoi Hall of Moscow Conservatory, 1950, Tchaikovsky Concerto. Career: Solo recitals and concerts with major orchestras in Britain, Scandinavia, Germany, Holland, Italy, USA, Australia, Japan and Israel; Many television and radio performances; Teacher, Gnessin Institute, Moscow, 1967-76; Professor, Sweelinck Conservatory, Amsterdam, 1976-; Professor, Hochschule für Musik, Hamburg, 1986-; British debut, 1970, Britten's Concerto at the Promenade Concerts. Receordings: Concertos from the Baroque by Mozart, Britten, Schnittke, Tubin; Solo Sonatas by Bach; Sonatas by Brahms, Mozart, Shostakovich, Schnittke. Honours: Mozart International Competition, Salzburg, 1956; Tchaikovsky International Copetition, Moscow, 1958. Current Management: Encore Concerts Limited. Address: Caversham Grange, The Warren, Mapledurham, Berkshire RG4 7TQ, England.

LUCA Sergiu, b. 4 Apr 1943, Bucharest, Rumania. Violinist; Teacher. Education: Studied at the Bucharest Conservatory 1948-50, with Max Rostal in London and at the Berne Conservatory; Curtis Institute with Galamian. Debut: With the Philadelphia Orchestra conducted by Eugene Ormany, playing the Sibelius Concerto, 1965. Career: Founder and Director, Chamber Music Northwest Festival in Portland, 1971-80; Professor of violin at the University of Illinois 1980-83; Starling Professor of Classical violin and violinist-in-residence at the Shepherd School of Music, Houston, 1983-; Music Director of the Texas Chamber Orchestra, 1983-88; Founder and General Director of Da Camera, in Houston, Texas, an Arts Organisation producing approximately 50 concerts a year of small ensemble repertoir, from Renaissance to Jazz, 1988-; Solo performances in the USA, Europe, and Japan; Recitals of the unaccompanied works of Bach with authentic instrument and bow; Mozart sonatas with Malcolm Bilson. Recordings: Bach sonatas partitas for unaccompanied violin; Bartok works for violin and piano. Honours: Finalist, 1965 Leventritt Competition; Winner, 1965 Philadelphia Orchestra Youth Auditions. Address: Shepherd School of Music, Rice Univesity, Houston, Texas, USA.

LUCHETTI Veriano, b. 12 Mar 1939, Viterbo, Italy. Singer, Tenor. m. Mietta Sighele. Education: Studied with Enrico Piazza and in Milan and Rome. Debut: Wexford festival 1965, as Alfredo in La Traviata. Career: Spoleto 1967, as Loris in Fedora and in Donizetti's Il Furioso all'isola di San Domingo; Guest appearances in Palermo, Parma, Venice, Vienna, Munich, Paris, Mexico City, Dallas and Houston; Maggio Musicale Florence 1971, 1974, in L'Africaine and Agnes von Hohenstaufen by Spontini; La Scala 1975, in Verdi's Attila; Covent Garden 1973-76, as Rodolfo, Pinkerton and Gabriele Adorno in Simon Boccanegra; Aix-en-Provence 1976, as Jason in Cherubini's Médée, Verona 1984, in Verdi's I Lombardi; Vienna Staatsoper 1988, as Foresto in Attila; Sang Radames at Turin 1990, Don José at the Verona Arena; Also heard in concert, Verdi's Requiem at Covent Garden, 1976. Recordings: Médée, Hungaroton; Nabucco and Verdi Requiem; Piccinni's La Cecchina; Griselda by Scarlatti; 2 further recordings of the Verdi Requiem. Address: c/o S A Gorlinsky Ltd, 33 Dover Street, London, W1X 4NJ, England.

LUCHSINGER Ronald, b. 7 Nov 1940, Dubuque, Iowa, USA. Stage Director; Producer; Principally in Opera; Music Theatre. Education: BA, University of Dubuque, 1964; Graduate Studies: Wayne State Univesity, Detroit, Michigan, 1964-65; MM, Hartt School of Music, 1972. Career: Faculty, Oakland University, Michigan, 1964-65; Faculty, Detroit Music Settlement School, 1965-66; Assistant Stage Director, Hartt Opera Theatre, Hartford, Connecticut, 1969-70; Principal Stage Director, Opera Arts Association, Florida, 1973-76; Stage Director, California Music Center, 1973-83; Faculty, Hartt School of Music, 1975-85; Faculty, Mannes College of Music, 1978-79; Artistic Director, Troupers Light Opera, Connecticut 1978-92; Resident Director, Simsbury Light Opera, 1985-; Stage Director, New Britain Opera, 1981-88; Stage Director, Dallas Lyric Opera, 1985-91; General Director, Opera North, 1992-. Memberships: State Governor, Connecticut, Massachusetts and Rhode Island, National Opera Association. Hobbies: Student of History. Address: 13 Dartmouth College Hwy, Lymer, NH 03768, USA.

LUCIC Zeljko, b. 24 February 1968, Zrenjanin, Yugoslavia. Opera Singer. m. Gordana, 23 March 1991, 2 sons. Education: Faculty of Music, Belgrade; Academy of Arts, Novi Sad. Debut: National Opera House, Novi Sad. Career: Belgrade Opera House; Novi Sad National Opera House; Teatro del Liceu, Barcelona; Constanza Opera House, Romania; Athenaeum Festival, Athens. Recordings: F Cilea: A Lecouvrer, Michonet; G Puccini: La Boheme, Marcello; W A Mozart: Le nozze di Figaro, Caunt Almaviva; G Puccini: Madame Butterfly, Charples; G Donizetti: Lucia di Lamermoor, Lord Enrico. Honours: 1st Prize, International Vocal Competition, Francisco Vinas, Barcelona, 1997. Memberships: National Society of Professional Musicians in Yugoslavia. Hobby: Basketball. Current Management: Hoallender-Calih, Vienna. Address: c/o Radivoje Lucic, Stevice Jovanovica St No 7, 23000 Zrenhanin, Yugoslavia.

LUCIER Alvin, b. 14 May 1931, Nashua, New Hampshire, USA. Composer. m. Wendy Wallbank Stokes, 27 Aug 1979, 1 daughter. Education: Nashua, New Hampshire, Parochial and Public Schools; The Portsmouth Abbey School; BA, Yale University, 1954; MFA, Brandeis University, 1960; Fulbright Scholarship, Rome, 1960-62. Career: Choral Director, Brandeis Univesity, 1962-70; Professor of Music, Wesleyan University, 1970-, Chair of Department, 1979-84; Co-Founder, Sonic Arts Union, 1966-77; Music Director, Viola Farber Dance Company, 1972-77. Compositions: Action Music for Piano, 1962, BMI Canada; Music for Solo Performer, 1965 for enormously amplified brain waves and percussion; Vespers, 1967; Chambers, 1968; I Am Sitting in A Room, 1970; Still and Moving Lines of Silence in Families of Hyperbolas, 1972-; Bird and Person Dyning,1975; Music in A Long Thin Wire 1977; Crossings, 1982-84; Seesaw, 1984; Sound on Paper, 1985. Numerous recordings including: Bird and Person Dyning; The Duke of York, Cramps Records, Italy. Publications: Chambers in collaboration with Douglas Simon, 1980. Contributions to: Professional publications. Hobbies: Fly Fishing in the American West; Salmon Fishing in Iceland. Address: Music Department, Wesleyan University, Middletown, CT 06457, USA.

LUCIUK Juliusz (Mieczyslaw), b. 1 Jan 1927, Brzeznica, Poland. Composer. m. Domicela Dabrowska, 10 Nov 1956, 2 daughters. Education: Academy of Music, Krakow; Studied with Nadia Boulanger and Max Deutsch in Paris, 1958-59. Debut: 3 songs performed, 1954. Career: Various works recorded by Polish Radio, BBC, Sender freies Berlin, ORTF France, Italian Palermo, Netherlands Radio. Compositions: Numerous including: 3 Passion Songs for soprano and organ; Concertino for piano and small symphony orchestra; Concerto for double bass and symphony orchestra; Image, Preludes and Tripticum Paschale for organ; Sonata for bassoon and piano; Variations for cello and piano; Monologues and Dialogues for soprano recorders; Ballets: Niobe; Death of Euridice; Medea; L'Amour d'Orphée, opera-ballet; Demiurgos, chamber opera; Works for solo voice and chamber ensemble: Floral dream; Le Souffle du Vent; Portraits Lyriques; Works for solo voice and chamber orchestra: Tool of the Light; Poéme de Loire; Wings and Hands; Oratorios: St Francis of Assisi; Gesang am Brunnen; Sanctus Adalbertus flos purpureus; Polish Litany, The Polish Mass for mezzo-soprano, mixed choir and wind orchestra; Choral works include: 4 Antiphonae and vespera in Assumptione Beatae Mariae Virginis for men's choir; The Mass for men's choir and organ; The Mass, Hymnus de Caritate and Magnificat for mixed choir; Apocalypsis for 4 soloists and mixed choir; Osiers, 5 pieces for string chamber orchestra; Orchestral works: Concertino for piano and small symphony orchestra; Concerto for double bass and symphony orchestra;

Four Symphonic Sketches; Symphonic Allegro; Composition for Four Orchestral Ensembles; Speranza Sinfonica; Lamentuzioni in memoriam Grazyma Bacewicz; Warsaw Legend (Quasi Cradle Song). Address: Os Kolorowe 6 m 10, 31-938 Krakow, Poland.

LUCKY Stepán, b. 20 Jan 1919, Zilina, Slovakia. Composer. Education: Prague Conservatory, 1936-39; Studied with Ridky, 1945-47; Musicology at Prague University, 1945-48. Career: Member of Czech resistance; Committee member of Pritomnost Association for Contemporary Music, 1946-48; Music Critic for Prague papers; Head of Music for Czech TV, 1954-58; Taught at Prague Academy, 1956-61; PhD, Charles University Prague, 1990. Compositions: Divertimento for 3 Trombones and Strings, 1946; Cello Concerto, 1946; Piano Concerto, 1947; Opera Midnight Surprise, 1959; Violin Concerto, 1965; Octet for Strings, 1970; Double Concerto for Violin, Piano and Orchestra, 1971; Nenia for Violin, Cello and Orchestra, 1974; Concerto for Orchestra, 1976; Fantasia Concertante for Bass Clarinet, Piano and Orchestra, 1983; Much film music, 1950-88; Chamber and Instrumental music. Honours include: State Order for Outstanding Accomplishment, 1969; Artist of Merit, 1972. Hobbies: Travel; Swimming; Chess. Address: Lomena 24, 162 00 Prague 6, Czech Republic.

LUCY Janet Rose, b. 10 June 1960, Hempstead, New York, USA. Musician. Education: Masters Degree, Secondary Education, Hofstra University, LI, New York, USA; Studied at Juilliard Pre-College; Received Bachelor's of Music, Manhattan School of Music; Studied as Graduate Student, SUNY at Stony Brook, New York, USA. Career: Has appeared with Manhattan Chamber Orchestra at Alice Tully Hall, Golden Center and on WNCN in New York; Other appearances include: Carnegie Hall, Tilles Center and on Tour to Seoul, Korea. Recordings include: Recorded an all Cowell and an all Hohvahness CD with Manhattan Chamber Orchestra; Other CD's with MCO include a Violin Concerto by David Amram and various works by William Grant Still on the Koch or Newport Classic Labels. Memberships: American Federation of Musicians; Chamber Music America; MENC/NYSSMA. Hobbies: Golf; Swimming; Reading; Movies. Address: 101 Cooper Street #5J, New York, NY 10034, USA.

LUDGIN Chester, b. 20 May 1925, NY, USA. Singer, Baritone. Education: Studied in NY with William S Brady. Debut: Experimental Opera Theatre NY as Scarpia in Tosca. Career: NYC Opera from 1961, notably in the premieres of The Crucible by Ward and The Golem by Ellstein; Guest appearances in Baltimore, Boston, Chicago, Miami, Toronto, Montreal, Mexico City, San Diego and Milwaukee; San Francisco 1966, in the US premiere of Janacek's The Makropoulos Case; Other roles include Escamillo in Carmen, Mephistopheles in Faust, and Rossini's Figaro; Sang at Houston in the 1988, in the US premiere of Dead Souls; Horace Tabor in The Ballad of Baby Doe at Detroit, 1988. Address: c/o Opera Company of Boston, PO Box 50, Boston, MA 02112, USA.

LUDWIG Christa (Deiber), b. 16 Mar 1928, Berlin, Germany. Singer, Mezzo-Soprano. m. 1. Walter Berry, 2. Paul-Emile Deiber, 3 Mar 1972, 1 son. Education: German Abitur, 1944; Studies with mother, Eugenie Besalla, singing. Debut: Frankfurt, Germany, 1946. Career: After Frankfurt, Darmstadt, Hanover; Vienna Staatsoper, 1955-94; All important Opera Houses, London Covent Garden, Amneris and Carmen; Scala, Milan; Tokyo; Chicago; San Francisco; Berlin; Munich; Some opera and concerts, TV, Films, concerts all over the world; Salzburg Festival from 1954, debut as Cherubino, sang Mistress Quickly in Falstaff 1981; Metropolitan Opera 1959-90, as the Dyer's Wife in Die Frau ohne Schatten, Cherubino, Dido in Les Troyens, Fricka and Waltraute in the Ring, Ortrud, Kundry, Charlotte, Clytemnestra and Marshallin; Sang in concert performances of Bernstein's Candide at the Barbican, 1989, Clytemnestra in Vienna, Berlin, New York, Paris; in Elektra at Innsbruck 1990; Other roles have included Eboli, Leonore, Dalila, Lady Macbeth, Marie in Wozzeck and Ottavia in L'Incoronazione di Poppea; Gave Lieder recital at the Wigmore Hall, London, 1991, Von Einem, Wolf, Strauss and Schubert; Farewell recitals in London and the USA, 1993. Recordings: with Böhm: Cosi fan tutte, Marriage of Figaro, Missa Solemnis; with Karajan: Götterdämmerung, Tristan and Isolde, Verdi's Requiem, Das Lied von der Erde; Rosenkavalier-Octavian; with Bernstein: Rosenkavlier - Marschallin, Das Lied von der Erde, Brahms - Recital; With Giulini: Verdi's Requiem; With Klemperer: Wesendonck Lieder, Das Lied von der Erde; Farewell to Salzburg, recital 1993. Publications: Paul Lorenz; Christa Ludwig, Walter Berry; Eine Kunstler Biographie. Honours include: 1st prize Radio Frankfurt, 1948, 1962; Kammersängerin Staatsoper Wien, 1962; Osterreich Grosses Verdienstkreuz 1 Classe fur Kunst and Wissenschaft, 1980; Ehrenmitglied Staatsoper Wien and Goldenen Ehrenring Ehrenmitglied Konzerthaus Wien-Silberne Rose der Wiener Philharmoniker, 1980; Wolf, Mozart, Mahler Medals; Grammy Awards and many other different prizes; Chevalier Legion D'Honneur, France, 1989; Commandeur de L'Ordre des Arts Et des Lettres, France, 1989; Medaille Ville de Paris and Shibuya-Preis, Japan, 1993; Echo Deutscher Schallplattenpreis and Berliner Bär and Karajan-Preis, 1994; Musician of Year, Musical America, 1994; Professor E H Stadt Berlin and Ehrenmitglied Wiener Philharmoniker, 1995. Hobbies: Reading; Cooking. Address: Calliope, 162 Chemin du Santon, F-06250 Mougins, France.

LUFF Enid, b. 21 Feb 1935, Ebbw Vale, Glamorgan, Wales. Composer. m. Alan Luff, 30 June 1956, 3 sons, 1 daughter. Education: LRAM, Piano Teacher's Diploma, 1965; BMus, Honours, 1971, MMus, 1974, University of Wales; Advanced Composition with Elisabeth Lutyens and Franco Donatoni. Career: Composer, 1971-; Runs Primavera self-publishing company with Julia Usher, 1980-. Compositions: Four piano pieces, Tapestries for chamber group; Symphony No 1; Mathematical Dream, solo harp; Wind Quintet: The Coastal Road; Sheila NaGig, for soprano and pianoforte; Dream Time for Bells for chamber group; Sky Whispering for solo piano; Sonata: Storm Tide for piano; Come the Morning, for chamber ensemble; RAGS, music for mime, electronic tape, 1990; Peregrinus, Trilogy for organ, 1991; Listening for the Roar of the Sun, for oboe, speaker, dance and slide projection, 1992; Symphony 2, 1994. Recordings: Several works recorded on BBC Recordings and Danish Radio Recordings. Memberships: Composers Guild of Great Britain; PRS; MCPS; Women in Music. Hobbies: Learning languages; Swimming. Address: 119 Selly Park Road, Birmingham B29 7HY, England.

LUITZ Josef, b. 2 August 1934, Vienna, Austria. Solo Cellist. m. Sonja Edelgard Mayerhofer, 4 August 1962, 1 son, 1 daughter. Education: School for Musical Instruments Makers, Vienna; Cello Studies with Professor W Kleinecke, Konservatorium, Vienna; Master-Course with Professor N Hubner, Santiago de Compostella. Debut: Musikverein, Vienna, 1957. Career: 1st Cellist, Tonkuenstler Orchestra, 1957-61; Solo Cellist, 1962-; Member, Haydn Quartet, 1965-72, Ensemble Kontrapunkta, 1968-75; Philharmonia Quintet, 1971-77; Professor, Cello, Konservatorium, Vienna, 1972-; Chairman, Tonkuenstler Chamber Orchestra, 1978-; Concordia Trio, 1979-; Chairman, International Chamber Music Festival, Austria, 1978-. Recordings: Chamber Music Series for Musical Heritage Society Inc, New York; Spohr Octet with Vienna Octet; With Tonkuenstler Chamber Orchestra; many Radio Productions as Soloist. Honours: Professor, Austrian Government, 1985. Hobbies: Hiking; Reading.

LUKACS Ervin, b. 1928, Budapest, Hungary. Conductor. Education: Bela Bartok Conservatory, 1950-51; Conductor's Diploma, Ferenc Liszt Academy of Music, 1956. Career: Conductor, Hungarian People's Army Artistic Ensemble, 1954-56; Principal Conductor, Miskolc Opera House and Miskolc Symphony Orchestra, 1956-57; Professor, Department of Conducting, Liszt Academy of Music, Budapest, 1956-59; Conductor, Budapest State Opera, 1957-; Master Class held by Franco Ferrara in Venice and Accademia di Santa Cecilia, Rome, Italy, 1961, 1962; As conductor has made several extensive tours with Hungarian State Symphony Orchestra. Honours: 2st Prize, Santa Cecilia International Concours for Conductors, 1962; Liszt Prize; Merited Artist of the Hungarian People's Republic. Address: c/o Hungarian State Opera, Budapest, Hungary.

LUKAS Laslo, b. 1964, Budapest, Hungary. Singer (Baritone). Education: Franz Liszt Music Academy, Budapest. Career: Sang with the Budapest State Opera four seasons, then with the Prague State Opera; Trier Opera from 1991, including Tcherikov in the first production this century of Zemlinsky's first opera, Sarema; Guest appearances in Germany and elsewhere as Rigoletto, Scarpia Jochanaan in Salome, Macbeth, Posa, Count Luna, Kaspar, Cadillac, and the Man in Hindemith's Mörder, Hoffnung der Frauen; Simone in Zemlinsky's Florentinische Tragödie, at the Prague State Opera. Recordings include: Sarema (Koch International). Address: c/o Theater der Stadt Trier, Am Augustinerhof, D-5500 Trier, Germany.

LUKAS Zdenek, b. 21 Aug 1928, Prague, Czechoslovakia. Composer. Education: Tutorials led by Miloslav Kabelac, 1961-70. Career: Worked for Czech Radio 1953-65; Choral conductor in Pilsen 1955-65; Teacher, Prague Conservatoire' Choirmaster, Czechoslovak State Song and Dance Ensemble; Freelance Composer from 1965. Compositions include: Radio Opera Long Live the Dead Man 1968; Home Carnival, 1-act opera 1968; Orchestral: Piano Concerto 1955; Violin Concerto 1956; Cello Concerto 1957; 4 Symphonies 1960-66; Concerto Grosso for string quartet and orchestra 1964; Symphonietta solemnis 1965; Sonata concertata for piano, winds and percussion 1966; Concerto for violin, viola and orchestra 1969; Variations for piano and orchestra 1970; Postludium for strings 1970; Choral music includes Adam a Eva, oratorio 1969; The Spring is Coming, cycle for male choir and solo violin, 1975; The Message of Music, 4-voice girls' choir with piano accompaniment, 1982; Chamber: 3 String Quartets 1960, 1965, 1973; Partita semplice for 4 violins and piano 1964; Wind Quintet 1969; Saxophone Quartet 1970; Electronic work You do not Kill 1971; Trio for Violin, Violoncello and Piano, Op 106, 1974; Prague Pastorale for Organ Solo, Op 158, 1981; Rondo for Bassoon and Piano, Op 168, 1981; 3 Duets for 2 Violins Op 188, 1984; Duo di basso, violoncello and double-bass, op 210, 1987; 4th String Quartet Op 213, 1987. Address: Murmanska 13, 100 00 Praha 10, Czech Republic.

LUKE Ray, b. 30 May 1926, Fort Worth, TX, USA. Composer; Conductor. Education: Studied at Texas Christian University and at the Eastman School of Music, Rochester with Bernard Rogers. Career: Taught at the East Texas State College 1951-62; Oklahoma City University from 1962; Associate Conductor, Oklahoma City Symphony 1969-73; Principal Guest Conductor 1974-78. Compositions: Opera Medea 1979; Ballet Tapestry 1975; 4 Symphonies 1959-70; Bassoon Concerto, 1965; 2 Suites for Orchestra 1958, 1967; Symphonic Dialogues for violin, oboe and orchestra 1965; String Quartet 1966; Piano Concerto 1970; Septet 1979. Honours: Grand Prix Gold Medal Queen Elisabeth of the Belgians Competition, for Piano Concerto, 1970. Address: c/o ASCAP, ASCAP Building, One Lincoln Plaza, NY 10023, USA.

LUKOMSKA Halina, b. 29 May 1929, Suchedniow, Poland. Singer, (Soprano). Education: State Opera High School, Poznan, 1951-54; Warsaw State Music High School; Further study with Toti dal Monte in Venice. Career: Wide appearances as concert singer from 1960, notably in works by Webern, Serocki, Boulez, (Pli selon Pli), Maderna, Schoenberg, Nono and Lutoslawski; Festival engagements at Edinburgh, Perugia, Vienna, Toulouse, and Warsaw; Holland Festival 1967, in Monteverdi's Orfeo; North American tour with Cleveland Orchestra 1973. Recordings: Works by Berg, (Altenberglieder) and Webern; Pli Selon Pli; Confitebor Domine by JC Bach; Boris Godunov. Honours: Winner, s-Hertogenbosch Competition, 1956.

LUMSDAINE David, b. 31 Oct 1931, Sydney, NSW, Australia. Composer. m. Nicola Lefanu, 1 s, 2 d. Education: NSW Conservatorium of Music; Sydney University; Studied with Matyas Seiber, Royal Academy of Music, London; DMus, 1981. Career: Composer; Teacher of Composition and Music Editor, London, England; Lecturer in Music, Durham University, 1970-; Founder, Electronic Music Studio, Durham; Lecturer, King's College, London, 1981-93. Compositions include: Orchestral: Episodes, 1969, Looking Glass Music, 1970, Sunflower for Chamber Orchestra, 1975, Shoalhaven, 1982, Mandela V for Symphony Orchestra, 1988; Vocal: The Ballad of Perse O'Reilly for Tenor, Male Chorus and 2 Pianos, 1953-81, Annotations of Auschwitz for Soprano and Ensemble, 1964, 1970, Aria for Edward Eyre for Soprano and Double Bass Soloists, Chamber Ensemble, Narrators, Tape and Electronics, 1972, Tides For Narrator, 12 Voices and Percussion, Caliban Impromptu for Piano Trio, Tape and Electronica, 1972, Empty Sky, Mootwingee for Ensemble, 1986, Round Dance for Sitar, Table, Flute, Cello and Keyboard, 1989; Piano Works: Canberra, piano solo, 1980, Wild Ride to Heaven, with Nicola Lefanu, for Electronics, 1980; Garden of Earthly Delights, 1992; Kali Dances, 1994. Current Management: Sounds Australian, PO Box N690, Grosvenor Place, Sydney, NSW 2000, Australia. Address: 5 Holly Terrace, York, YO1 4DS, England.

LUMSDEN David (James) (Sir), b. 19 Mar 1928, Newcastle-upon-Tyne, England. m. Sheila Gladys Daniels, 28 Jul 1951, 2 s, 2 d. Education: Dame Allan's School; Selwyn College, Cambridge; MA, 1955; DPhil, 1957. Career: Fellow, Organist at New College Oxford; Rector, chori, Southwell Minster; Founder and Conductor of Nottingham Bach Society; Director of Music, Keele University; Visiting Professor at Yale University; Principal: Royal Scottish Academy of Music and Drama and Royal Academy of Music; Hugh Porter Lecturer at Union Theologial Seminary, NY, 1967. Publications: An Anthology of English Lute Music, 1954; Thomas Robinson's Schoole Musike 1603, 1971. Contributions to: The Listener; The Score; Music and Letters; Galpin Society Journal; La Luth et sa Musique; La musique de la Renaissance. Honours: Kt, 1985; Honorary DLitt, 1990. Memberships: Incorporated Society of Musicians, President, 1984-85; Royal College of Organists, President, 1986-88; Incorporated Association of Organists, 1966-68; Honorary Editor, Church Music Society, 1970-73; Chairman, National Youth Orchestra of GB, 1985-94; Chairman, Early Music Society, 1985-89; Board, Scottish Opera, 1977-83; Board, ENO, 1983-88. Hobbies: Photography; Hill Walking; Reading; Theatre; Travel. Address: Melton House, Soham, Cambridgeshire, CB7 5DB, England.

LUMSDEN Ronald, b. 28 May 1938, Dundee, England. Pianist. m. 1. Annon Lee Silver, deceased, 1 son, 2. Alison Paice Hill, 1975, 1 son, 1 daughter. Education: Harris Academy, Dundee; Royal College of Music, London; ARCM; LRAM. Career: Pianist in Residence, University of Southampton, 1965-68; Henry Wood Promenade Concerts, 1973, 1974; Soloist in Arts Council Contemporary Music Network, 1974-76; Visiting Piano teacher, 1976-; Honorary Director of School of Music, 1984-, Reading University; Frequent broadcasts and recitals in United Kingdom. Recordings: Messiaen's Canteyodjaya for Gaudeamus Foundation; Open University's Modern Music. Contributions to:

Bartók, in Makers of Modern Culture, 1981. Honours: 1st Prize Winner, International Competiton for Interpreters of Contemporary Music, Utrecht, 1968. Memberships: Executive Committee, Society for Promotion of New Music, 1975-78; Incorporated Society of Music; European Piano Teachers Association. Address: 50 Grosvenor Road, Caversham, Reading, Berkshire, RG4 0EN, England.

LUND Tamara, b. 1941, Finland. Singer, Soprano. Career: Sang with Finnish National Opera from 1967, notably in the 1968 local premiere of Berg's Lulu, title role; Member of the Teater am Gärtnerplatz Munich from 1973, with tours to Berlin, Komische Oper and Theater des Westerns; the Theater an der Wien, Vienna; Engageed at the Zurich Opera, 1979-83; Helsinki 1973, as Daphne in the premiere of Apollo and Marsyas by Rautavaara; Other roles have included Carmen, Musetta, Janacek's Vixen and Jenny in Aufsteig und Fall der Stadt Mahagonny; Sang Juno in the incidental music to The Tempest by Sibelius, Savonlinna 1986; Many appearances in operetta.

LUNDBERG Gunnar, b. 1958, Sweden. Singer, Baritone. Education: Studied at the State Opera School Stockholm and in Salzburg. Debut: Vadstena Accademy, 1984. Career: Member of the Royal Opera Stockholm from 1988, notably as the Herald in Lohengrin, Escamillo, Valentin, Mozart's Count and Figaro, Don Giovanni and Rossini's Figaro; Season 1991 as Barelli in the European premiere of The Aspern Papers by Argento; Engaged for seasons 1992-94 as Silvio in Pagliacci and Marcello in La Bohème; Concert repertoire includes Ein Deutsches Requiem, the Bach Passions and B Minor Mass; St John Passion at the 1993 Lucerne Easter Festival.

LUNDBERG Robert, b. 25 Jun 1948, CA, USA. Lutemaker. m. Linda Toenniessen, 2 d. Career: Apprenticeship in violin making with Paul Schuback, a Mirecourt trained master maker; Journeyman work in 1973 with Jacob van de Geest in Vevey, Switzerland; Established a workshop in Portland, OR, in 1974, Master maker; Travelled to major European museums measuring, photographing and analyzing ancient lutes; To date has built over 500 instruments of which 300 are lutes, and restored instruments in many private and public collections; Lecturer; Conservator of musical instruments, Smithsonian Institute, Washington DC, 1980-85. Publications: Written over 50 essays, articles and reviews on the history and construction of the lute and related topics including, Sixteenth and Seventeenth Century Lute Making, The Historical Lute Construction; Essay, In Tune with the Universe: The physics and metaphysics of Galileo's Lute, 1992. Memberships: Lute Society of America, Ed Board; The Lute Society; American Musical Instrument Society; Galpin Society; FOMRHI; AIC; IIC. Hobbies: Collecting Antiques, NW Regional Art and Textiles; Bookbinding. Address: 3344 NE Oregon Street, Portland, OR 97232, USA.

LUNDBORG Charles (Erik), b. 31 Jan 1948, Helena, Montana, USA. Composer. m. Zinta Bibelnieks, 14 Nov 1981. Education: BM, New England Conservatory of Music, Boston; MA, 1974, DMA, 1985, Columbia University. Career: Performances & Commissions by Houston Symphony Orchestra, American Composers Orchestra, Ursula Oppens, Piano, Speculum Musicae, Group for Contemporary Music, Parnassus, New Music Consort, Pittsburgh, New Music Ensemble, Light Fantastic Players, Composers Ensemble, Light Fantastic Players, Composers Ensemble, New Jersey Percussion Ensemble, many others. Compositions: Passacaglia, Two Symphonies, from Music Forever, No 2 Piano Concerto; Soundsoup; Solotremolos. Recordings: Passacaglia from Music Forever No 2; Soundsoup. Contributions to: Milton Babbitt, String Quartet No 3, Contemporary Music Newsletter, 1974. Honours: Guggenheim, 1976-77; NEA Fellowships, 1975, 1981, 1983. Memberships: BMI; American Composers Alliance, Board Member, 1980-82; Board, ISCM, League of Composers, 1975-78. Address: 2465 Palisade Ave, 8F, Riverdale, NY 10463, USA.

LUNDGREN Stefan, b. 5 May 1949, Hogsby, Sweden. Lutenist; Composer; Editor. Luemusic. m. Henrike Brose, 21 Mar 1985. Education: Studied music: Music School, Oskarshann, Sweden, 1972-74; Lund University, 1974-77; Schola Cantonum Basiliensis, Basel, 1977-79. Career: Teacher; Performer; Composer; Publisher; Lute Music, 1979-; Director, Annual Lute Course, Ried im Zillertal, Austria, 1983-; Teacher, Summer Courses, Svenska Gitarr och lutasallskapets, 1985. Compositions: Sonatas 1-3 for solo lute, 1981-84; Sonata No 4, for solo lute, 1986. Publications: New School for the Renaissance Lute, 1985; Publishers of: 50 English Duets in 4 volumes; Charles Mouton; Suite in G Minor; J A Losy, Two Suites; Little Book for Lute 1 for Renaissance Lute; Little Book for Lute 2, Baroque Lute, J S Bach, Complete works for lute. Address: Barerstrasse 70, D 8000 Munchen 40, Germany.

LUNDQUIST Torbjörn Iwan, b. 30 Sept 1920, Stockholm, Sweden. Composer; Symphonist. m. (1) Maud Lagergren, 2 sons, 1 daughter, (2) Marianne Lagergren. Education: Studied Composition with Dag Wiren, Conducting with Otmar Suitner, and Musicology at the Uppsala University. Debut: As Composer and Symphonist with his Symphony No 1, Stockholm, 1956. Career: Conductor and Artistic Director at the Drottningholm Palace Theatre, 1949-56; Guest Conductor in Sweden and Europe; Full-time symphonic writing, 1970-. Compositions: 8 symphonies; Piano Concerto (Hangar Music), 1967; Confrontation for large orchestra, 1968; 2 String quartets, 1969; Moment of Eternity, 1-act opera, 1974; Concerto Grosso for violin, cello and strings, 1974; Piano Trio, 1975; Irish Love Songs (James Joyce) 7 songs for baritone and piano, 1992; Chamber Music (James Joyce) 9 songs for baritone, cello and piano, 1994; Pour l'Eternite (Jean-Luc Caron) 7 songs for baritone and piano, 1995; Symphony No 9, 1996. Recordings: Symphony No 1, 1956; Evocation, 1964 Sisu for 6 percussion, 1976; Symphony No 3, 1976; Windpower for symphonic band, 1978; Violin Concerto, 1978; Arctic, 1984; 7 Rilke Songs for soprano and orchestra, 1985; Symphony No 7, Humanity, 1988; New Bearings for baritone and piano, 1990. Honours: Ture Rangström Scholarship, 1975; Swedish State Award for Artists (for life), 1976; Kurt Atterberg Scholarship, 1986; Hugo Alfvén Scholarship, 1992. Memberships: The Society of Swedish Composers; The Swedish Society of Composers, Authors and Editors. Current Management: Swedish Music Information Center, Stockholm, Sweden. Address: Litslena Hällby, S-740 81 Grillby, Stockholm, Sweden.

LUNDSTEN Ralph, b. 6 October 1936, Ersnäs, Sweden. Composer; Filmmaker; Artist; Owner of Swedens most famous picture and electronic music studio, Andromeda, including the Love Machine and other invented synthesizers. Career: 500 opus, 60 records, 12 short films, art exhibitions, a book with CD; Worked for the Opera House in Stockholm and Oslo, the Modern Museum and the National Museum in Stockholm, the Louvre and the Biennale in Paris, the Triennale in Milan and the Museum of Contemporary Crafts in New York; Subject of a number of Radio and TV portraits, 1971-93 and a special portrait-exhibition at the Music Museum in Stockholm, 1991-92. Compositions include: Nordic Nature Symphony No 1, The Water Sprite; No 2, Johannes and the Lady of Woods; No 3, A Midwintersaga; No 4, A Summer Saga; No 5, Bewitched; No 6, Landscape of Dreams; Erik XIV and Gustav III (2 ballets about Swedish Kings); Cosmic Love; Ourfather; Nightmare; Horrorscope; Shangri-La; Universe; Discophrenia; Alpha Ralpha Boulevard; Paradise Symphony; Cosmic Phantazy; The Dream Master; The Gate of Time; The Ages of Man; Sea Symphony; Mindscape Music; Nordic Light; The Symphony of Joy (dedicated to the United Nations 50 years anniversary); The Symphony of Light; The Symphony of Love. Address: Frankenburgsväg 1, S-13242 Saltsjö-Boo, Sweden.

LUNELL Hans, b. 12 Apr 1944, Skellefteå, Sweden. Composer; Computer Scientist. Education: Fil kand, Uppsala University, 1967; Fil dr (PhD), Linköping University, 1983; Musicology, Uppsala University; Music Theory and Composition, Royal College of Music, Stockholm; Piano study with Greta Erikson. Career: Assistant Professor, Linköping University, 1971-83; Associate Professor, KTH, Stockholm, 1983-86; Director of Institute for Electro-Acoustic Music in Sweden, 1989-93. Compositions: Intensità for piano trio, 1981-82; La notte in Sicilia for soprano, bass clarinet and vibraphone, 1984; Affinities I for piano solo, 1985. Contributions to: Numerous articles, many to Nutida Musik. Memberships: Society of Swedish Composers; International Confederation for Electro-Acoustic Music; STIM. Address: Teknikvägen 105, 175 75 Järfälla, Sweden.

LUNETTA Stanley, b. 5 June 1937, Sacramento, CA, USA. Composer. Education: BA Sacramento State College; MA University of CA at Davis, with Jerome Rosen and Larry Austin; Further study with John Cage, David Tudor and Karlheinz Stockhausen. Career: Founded New Music Ensemble, 1963; Editor of Source: Music of the Avant Garde 1971-77; Percussionist and teacher in Sacramento. Compositions: Many Things for Orchestra 1966; Piano Music 1966; A Piece for Bandoneon and Strings 1966; Free Music 1967; Ta Ta for chorus and mailing tubes 1967; The Wringer, mixed media 1967; Funkart 1967; Twowomanshow, theatre piece 1968; Spider Song with Lartry Austin, 1968; Mr Machine for flute and tape 1969; A Day in the Life of the Mooscak Machines 1972; The Unseen Force theatre piece with dancers 1978; From 1970 much music from a series of self-playing electronic sound sculptures, e.g. Mooscak Machine, Sound Hat and Cosmic Cube. Address: c/o ASCAP, ASCAP Building, One Lincoln Plaza, NY 10023, USA.

LUPERI Mario, b. 1954, Sardinia, Italy. Singer, (Bass). Education: Studied in Calgliari, Verona and Siena. Debut: Perugia 1979, in Olympie by Spontini and in Cherubini's Requiem. Career: Palermo and Florence 1981, as Publio in La Clemenza di Tito and as Thoas in Iphigénie en Tauride; La Scala from 1982, as the Emperor in The Nightingale, Simone in Gianni Schicchi and Pluto in the Monteverdi Orfeo; Macerata Festival 1984-86, as Colline and Timur, Salzburg Easter Festival 1986, as the Grand Inquisitor; Sang Ramphis in Aida at the Munich Staatsoper 1986, Luxor 1987; Season 1986-87 as Verdi's Pistol at Brussels, Oroe in Semiramide and Oroveso in Norma at Naples; North American debut 1988, as Timur at Pittsburgh; Sang Colline at Genoa, 1990, Giorgio in I Puritani in Marseilles, 1991; Mozart's Bartolo in Venice 1991 and in Fra Diavolo at La Scala, 1992; Many concert appearances; including the Commendatore in Don Giovanni at the Festival Hall, London, 1996. Address: c/o Teatro alla Scala, Via Filiodrammatici 2, 20121 Milan, Italy.

LUPO Benedetto, b. 3 July 1963, Bari, Italy. Pianist; Piano Teacher in the N Piccinni Conservatoire, Bari, Italy. Education: Studied at N Piccinni Conservatoire with Michele Marvulli, Pierluigi Camicia. Teachers: Maria Teresa Somma, Aldo Ciccolini. Debut: Beethoven 1st Concerto with Bari Symphony Orchestra, December, 1976. Career: Antwerp: A De Vries, Foundation; Naples: Academy San Pietro a Majella, RAI A Scarlatti Orchestra; Milan: Angelicum Symphony Orchestra; Marseille: Lundis Du Conservatoire; Nantes: Orchestre Philharmonique des Pays de Loire, conductor Pierre-Michel Durand; Lourmarin; Castle Festival; St Jean de Luz, Orchestre du Capitole de Toulouse, Conductor Michel Plasson; Madrid: National Radio Recitals Season; Cordoba, Sevilla, Granada, Burgos, Cleveland: Severance Hall and IMC Orchestra; Salt Lake City; Utah Symphony, conductor Joseph Silverstein; Temple Square Series; Rio de Janeiro; Brazilian Symphony; Salvador: Castro Alves Theatre; Stresa: International Festiva. Honours: 1st Prize in the following International Competitions: Senigallia; International Meetings 1977; Milan: Alfred Cortot, Competition, 1980, 26th City of Jaen International Competition, Spain, 1982; 2nd prize in R Casadesus, International Competition, Cleveland, 1985. Address: Via Caravaggio, 1-70021 Acquaviva Delle Fonti-Ba, Italy.

LUPTACIK Jozef, b. 10 Jan 1947, Vysoka pri Morave, Slovakia. Musician (Clarinet). m. Eva, 11 November 1972, 1 son, 1 daughter. Education: Musical Conservatory, Bratislava, 1962-69; Academy of Music, Bratislava, 1969-73; Summer courses with Professor V Riha, Prague, 1970-71. Debut: A Copland, Concerto, Music Festival, Bratislava, 1973. Compositions: E Suchon, Concertino (1st performance), with Czech Philharmonic, Prague, 1978; Mozart, Weber, Kramar, Concerto with Slovak Philharmonic. Recordings: E Suchon, Concertino; Weber/Mozart, Kvinteto (B Major, A Major); Weber, Concert in F Minor, E Major; Brahms/Beethoven, Trio; J Brahms, Sonata in E Major, F Minor; Mozart, Clarinet Concerto; J Hummel, Clarinet Quartet. Honours: Finalist with Diploma, competition in Budapest, 1970; 4th Prize, Beograd, 1971; Member of international juries, international clarinet competitions. Memberships: Slovak Philharmonic Orchestra, 1sr clarinet Bratislava; Associate Professor, Academy of Music, Bratislava. Address: Hlavna 36, 900 66 Vysoka pri Morave, Slovakia.

LUPTACIK Jozef, b. 3 Aug 1974, Bratislava. Education: Musical Conservatory, Bratislava, 1990-93; Academy of Music, Bratislava, 1993-97. Debut: C Debussy, Rhapsodie with Slovak Philharmonic, Bratislava, 1994. Appointment: 1st clarinet in Slovak Philharmonie Orchestra, Bratislava. Compositions: W A Mozart Concert, 1992; R Strauss Duet Concertino, 1995; F Kramar Concert for 2 Clarinets. Recording: Slovak Woodwind Quintet. Hobby: Sport. Address: Hlavna 36, 900 66 Vysoka Pri Morave, Slovakia.

LUPU Radu, b. 30 Nov 1945, Galati, Romania. Classical Pianist. Education: First piano lessons, 1951; Scholarship, 1961, Graduated, 1969, Moscow Conservatoire. Career: Leading Interpreter for German classical composers; Frequently appears with all major British orchestras; Toured Europe with London Symphony Orchestra; American debut, 1972; Gave world premiere of André Tchaikovsky's Piano Concerto, London, 1975; Brahms D Minor Concerto with the Berlin Philharmonic at the 1996 London Proms. Recordings: For Decca including complete Beethoven cycle with Israel Philharmonic and Zubin Mehta, 1979; Mozart sonatas for violin and piano, with Szymon Goldberg; Brahms Piano Concerto No 1 with Edo de Waart and the London Philharmonic Orchestra; Mozart Piano Concerto K467 with Uri Segal and the English Chamber Orchestra; Various Beethoven and Schubert sonatas; Mozart and Beethoven wind quintets in E Flat, Mozart Concerto for 2 pianos, concerto for 3 pianos transcribed for 2 pianos, with Murray Perahia and the English Chamber Orchestra; Schubert Fantasia in F Minor and Mozart in D for 2 pianos, with Murray Perahia; 2 discs of Schubert Leider with Barbara Hendricks, EMI; Schubert Duets with Daniel Barenboim, Teldec. Honours: First Prize, Van Cliburn Competition, 1966; Enescu International Competition, Bucharest. 1967; Leeds International Competition, 1969. Hobbies: Chess; Bridge; History. Current Management: Terry Harrison Artists Management. Address: The Orchard, Market Street, Charlbury, Oxon OX7 3PJ, England.

LUTHER Mark, b. 14 November 1961, Bristol, England. Singer (Tenor). Education: Studied at the National Opera Studio, and at the Guildhall School with Noelle Barker. Deubt: St John's Smith Square, 1989, in Elijah. Career: Concert appearances include Opera Gala Evening at Covent Garden, Vivaldi's Gloria with the Northern Symphonia and showings at the Purcell Room and the Elizabeth Hall; Opera engagements include touring performances with British Youth Opera as Rodolfo; Other roles include: Idomeneo, Don Ottavio and Remendado (Carmen); Macduff and Arturo in Lucia di Lammermoor for Welsh National Opera, Don José at Rotterdam and the Verdi Requiem in Holland; Don Ottavio in Schönbrunn Vienna. Current Management: Athole Still International Management Limited. Address: Foresters Hall, 25-27 Westow Street, London SE19 3RY, England.

LUTZE Gert, b. 30 Sept 1917, Leipzig, Germany. Singer, Tenor. Education: Sang in the choir of St Thomas's Leipzig from 1928. Career: Bach's St Matthew Passion conducted by Gunter Ramin; Many appearances as concert and oratorio singer; Opera roles included Puccini's Pinkerton and Rodolfo, Mozart's Ferrando and Rimsky-Korsakov's Sadko; Engagements as Bach singer in Schaffhausen, Zurich, Basle, Berne, Helsinki, Paris, Brussels and Luxembourg; Sang in Prague and China 1955; St Matthew Passion in Bologna and Florence 1957; Further concerts with Karl Richter as conductor.

LUXON Benjamin, b. 24 March 1937, Cornwall, England. Singer (Baritone). m. Sheila Amit, 1969, 2 sons, 1 daughter. Education: Westminster Training College, Guildhall School of Music and Drama. Debut: English Opera Group, 1963. Career: Sang with the English Opera Group, 1963-70; Royal Opera House, Covent Garden, and Glyndebourne Festival Opera, 1971-; Netherlands Opera, 1976-; Frankfurt Opera House, 1977-; Roles include Monteverdi's Ulisse, Janacek's Forester, Mozart's Don Giovanni and Papageno, Tchaikovsky's Onegin, Verdi's Posa and Falstaff and Wagner's Wolfram, Alban Berg's Wozzeck, Los Angeles, 1988; Recitals and Folk Singing; Paris Opera, 1980; La Scala, Milan, 1986; Television appearances include title role in Giulio Cesare by Handel, Theater an der Wien, Vienna, 1985, conducted by Nikolaus Harnoncourt; Sang Falstaff at Los Angeles, 1990; Other roles include Count Almaviva and Sherasmin in Oberon, Edinburgh, 1986 and Falstaff for ENO, 1992; Vocal coach at Tanglewood, USA, 1996. Recordings include: Mahler's 8th Symphony and Schubert's Song Cycles. Honours include: FGSM, 1970; Hon RAM, 1980; Hon DMus, Exeter, 1980; CBE, 1986. Address: Lower Cox Street Farm, Detling, Maidstone, Kent ME14 3HE, England.

LVOV Boris, b. 1928, Moscow, Russia. Concert Pianist. Education: Studied at the Central School of Music and at the Moscow Conservatoire. Debut: First public concert aged nine years. Career: performed at the Moscow Conservatoire in 1946; Many concerts in the former Soviet Union, Eastern Europe and China from 1948; Appearances with David Oistrakh, Rostropovitch, Kondrashin and Emil Gilels; Former Professor of Piano, Moscow Conservatoire, then emigrated to Israel and is currently Professor at the Rubin Academy of Music in Jerusalem; Recent concert tours to Europe, Japan, Scandinavia and United States, both in recital and concert; Repertoire includes music by Haydn, Mozart, Schumann, Liszt, Prokofiev, Bartók and Stravinsky. Honours: Winner, Beethoven Cometition for performance of the Hammerklavier Sonata. Address: 11 Northpark Street, Glasgow G20 7AA, Scotland.

LYMPANY Moura, (Dame), b. 18 Aug 1916, Saltash, Cornwall, England. Concert Pianist. Debut: Performance at Harrogate, 1929. Mendelssohn's First Concerto. Career: Has played in USA, Canada, South America,Australia, New Zealand, India and most European countries including Russia; Has often been heard in music by Khachaturian, Rachmaninov, Ireland, Delius, Rawsthorne, Cyril Scott and Chopin; Played Mendelssohn at the 1991 Promenade Concerts, London. Recordings: Numerous on major labels. Honours: Commander Order of the British Empire; Fellow, Royal Academy of Musicians, 1948; DBE, 1992; FRCM, 1995. Address: Chateau Perigord 2, Appt 81, Monte Carlo, Monaco.

LYONS Graham John, b. 17 July 1936, London, England. Composer; Publisher. 1 son, 3 daughters. Education: Guildhall School of Music, 1958-62. Career: Instruments Played, Bassoon, Saxophone, Clarinet, Flute, Piano; Composer, Arranger, BBC Light Music; Musician, Arranger, New Zealand Television, 1 year. Compositions: Sonata for Clarinet & Piano; 60 Albums of Educational Wind Music. Publications: Take Up The Clarinet, Take Up The Flute, 1982; Useful Carinet Solos, Useful Flute Solos, 1984. Memberships: Incorporated Society of Musicians; Association of Professional Composers. Hobby: Philosophy of Science. Address: 37 Gloucester Drive, London N4 2LE, England.

LYSIGHT Michel (Thierry), b. 14 October 1958, Brussels, Belgium. Composer; Conductor; Professor. Education: Candidate in Musicology, Free University of Brussels, 1978; Academy of Schaerbeek; Conservatoire Royal de Musique, Mons; Conservatoire Royal de Musique, Brussels; Advanced Diplomas, Solfege 1980, Chamber Music 1988, Composition 1989. Career: Professor, Academies of Schaerbeek, 1979-89, Woluwe Saint-Pierre, 1981-90, Professor, 1989-90, Deputy Director 1990-, Academy of Brussels; Founder, Michel Lysight Ensemble for Contemporary Music, 1991; Director, Pedagogical Collection,

Alain Van Kerckhoven Publisher. Compositions include: Chamber music, orchestral music, piano, percussion including, Reflexion, clarinet or bassoon and piano; Soleil Bleu, 1 wind instrument and piano; Trois Croquis, violin or flute or clarinet or cello or bassoon or saxophone and piano or string orchestra, 1990-93; Chronographic I for wind quintet; Quatrain, flute, oboe, clarinet, bassoon, 1990; Chronographie II for string orchestra, 1992-93; Vedanta for clarinet, bassoon and piano, 1993; Chronographie III for flute, clarinet, bassoon, violin, viola, cello, double bass and piano, 1993. Recordings: XXth Century Belgian Works for Clarinet and Piano by Ronald Vanspaendowck and Leonardo Anglani (Reve Gailly Productions); Sit Down and Listen, by Mireille Gleizes, (Alan Van Kerckhoven Productions). Honours: Priz Irene Fuerison, Royal Academy for Fine Arts of Belgium; Silver Medal, International Academy of Lutece. Memberships include: Belgian Composers Union; Association for the Diffusion of the Belgian Music; Belgian Centre for Music Documentation. Address: Servranckxplein 3, 1932 Sint Stevens, Woluwe, Belgium.

LYSY Alberto, b. 11 Feb 1935, Buenos Aires, Argentina. Violinist; Teacher. Divorced, 4 children. Education: Studied with Ljerko Spiller in Argentina; Further study in Paris and London. Career: Solo recitals and performances with orchestras in Italy, France, Israel, Japan, India, USA, USSR, South America; Founder of chamber orchestra in Buenos Aires, 1965; Director of Camerata Lysy, Gstaad; Director, International Menuhin School, Gstaad. Honours: Prizewinner, Queen Elisabeth of Belgium International Competition, 1955. Hobbies: Cross Country Skiing; Chess; Football. Address: Chalet Anegla, Gstaad, Switzerland.

LYSY Antonio, b. 1963, Rome, Italy. Education: Studied with his father, the violinist Alberto Lysy; Menuhin School with Maurice Gendron and William Pleeth; Menuhin Academy with Radu Aldulescu; Royal Northern College of Music with Ralph Kirshbaum. Career: Concert engagements in Austria, Argentina, France, germany, Israel, Italy and Spain; British venues include the Royal Festival Hall, Wigmore Hall, Queen Elizabeth Hall and St John's Smith Square; Chamber concerts with Radu Aldulescu, Gidon Kremer, Lamar Crowson and Yehudi and Jeremy Menuhin; Principal Cellist with the Chamber Orchestra of Europe and appearances with the Manchester-based Goldberg Ensemble; Camerata of Salzburg 1988, with Sandor Vegh as conductor; Solo performances of Tchaikovsky's Rococo Variations in Buenos Aires and Italy; Further engagements with the Philharmonia Orchestra and at the Brighton Festival; Artistic Director of Chamber Music Festival in Tuscany, Incontri Musicali in Terra di Siena, from summer 1989. Recordings: Bloch's Prayer and Tchaikovsky's Souvenir de Florence with the Camerata Lysy. Address: c/o Anglo-Swiss Artists Management Ltd, 4-5 Primrose Mews, 1a Sharpleshall Street, London NW1 8YW, England.

LYUBIMOV Yuri (Petrovich), b. 30 Sept 1917, Yaoslal, Russia. Stage Director. Career: Actor at the Moscow Arts Theatre and Vakhtangov Theatre; Artistic Director of the Taganka Theatre, Moscow, 1964-84; Opera productions have included The Queen of Spades at the Paris Opera, Don Giovanni in Budapest, Khovanshchina at La Scala, Rigoletto in Florence and Tristan und Isolde at Bologna; Produced Mussorgsky's Salammbo in Paris and Naples, 1986; Royal Opera House, Covent Garden 1986 and 1988, with Jenufa and Das Rheingold; Produced the Queen of Spades at Karlsruhe 1990, The Love for Three Oranges at the Bayerische Staatsoper, Munich, 1991; Staged The Queen of Spades, adapted by Alfred Schnittke, at Bonn, 1996. Address: c/o Bayerische Staatsoper, Postfach 100148, 8000 Munich 1, Germany.

M

MA Yo Yo, b. 7 Oct 1955, Paris, France. Cellist. m. Jill Horner, 1978, 1 son, 1 daughter. Debut: Aged 5. Career: Performed with all major orchestras including Berlin Philharmonic, Boston Symphony, Chicago Symphony, Israel Symphony, London Symphony; Regularly appears at Tanglewood, Salzburg, Edinburgh and other major festivals; Plays regularly in Chamber Music ensemble with Isaac Stern and in a duo partnership with Emanuel Ax; Premiered the Concerto by H K Gruber, Tanglewood 1989; Beethoven Cello Sonatas from the Edinburgh Festival televised BBC, 1991; Recital tour with Emanuel Ax celebrating 20th anniversary of their partnership, 1995-96; Bach's suites for solo cello at the Barbican Hall, London, 1995. Recordings: Numerous including: Six Bach Suites for unaccompanied cello, CBS, 1984; CDs of Haydn's Cello Concerto in D, English Chamber Orchestra; Schubert's String Quintet, with the Cleveland Quartet; Shostakovich Concerto No 1, Philadelphia Orchestra; Barber Concerto and Britten Cello Symphony, Baltimore Symphony; Brahms Double Concerto, Isaac Stern and the Chicago Symphony; Schumann Works for Cello, Emanuel Ax, Bavarian Radio Symphony. Honours: Avery Fisher Prize, 1978; Grammy Award, 1984. Current Management: ICM Artists Limited. Address: c/o ICM Artists Limited, 40 West 57th Street, NY 10019, USA.

MAAG Peter, b. 10 May 1919, St Gall, Switzerland. Conductor. m. 1 son. Education: Theology and Philosophy Studies at Zurich and Basel Universities; Studied piano with Alfred Cortot. Career: Began conducting in small theatre; Assistant to Wilhelm Furtwängler; Assistance to Ernest Ansermet, Orchestra de la Suisse Romande; Dusseldorf Opera 1952-55; Chief Conductor Bonn Opera 1956-59; Volksoper, Vienna 1962; Teatro Regio, Turin 1974; Berne Symphony Orchestra 1984-; Former Principal Guest Conductor, Radiotelevisione Italian RAI; now Orquesta Nacional, Madrid; Regular Guest Conductor at La Scala, Milan; Metropolitan Opera, Don Giovanni, 1972, NY; Teatro Colon, Buenos Aires, Venice; Royal Opera House, Covent Garden; Also at various festivals including Aix-en-Provence, Zurich, Netherlands, Vienna, Salzburg; Conducted Cosi fan tutte, and played harpsichord continuo at the Gran Teatre del Liceu, Barcelona, 1990; Conducted Idomeneo at the Madrid Mozart Festival, 1996. Recordings: Mozart Symphonies, Piano Concertos, with Katchen, Gulda and Klien, Posthorn Serenade and Masonic Music; Complete Schubert Symphonies; Britten and Dvorak Violin Concertos; Mendelssohn's 3rd Symphony and Midsummer Night's Dream Music; Myslivecek's oratorio Abraham and Isaac, with the Czech Philharmonic; CDs of Saint-Saëns's 3rd Symphony, d'Indy's Symphonie Cevenole and Martinu's Rhapsody Concerto for viola and orchestra with the Berne Symphony, Conifer. Honours: Toscanini Medal, Parma 1969; Verdi Medal 1973. Hobbies: Theology. Address: Casa Maag, 7504 Pontresina, Switzerland.

MAAZEL Lorin, b. 6 Mar 1930, Neuilly, France. American Conductor and Musician. m. Dietlinde Turban, 3 sons, 4 daughters. Education: Music studies with Vladimir Bakaleinikoff; Philosophy major, University of Pittsburgh. Career: Composer, Conductor, American symphony orchestras, 1938-; European debut, 1953; Violin Recitalist; Conductor of operas including new productions, Metropolitan Opera, New York, Teatro alla Scala, Milan, Royal Opera House, London, Paris Opera; Festivals include Bayreuth (The Ring), Salzburg, Edinburgh, Lucerne: Tours, South America, Australia, former USSR, Japan, China; Artistic Director, Deutsche Oper Berlin, 1965-71; Musical Director, Radio Symphony Orchestra, Berlin, 1965-75; Associate Principal Conductor, New Philharmonia Orchestra, London, 1970-72; Director, Cleveland Orchestra, 1972-82; Director, Vienna State Opera, 1982-84; Music Director, Pittsburgh Symphony Orchestra, 1988-96; Music Director, Bavarian Radio Symphony Orchestra, 1993-; Since 1987 participation in over 25 benefit concerts, many to benefit international relief organisations such as UNHCR, UNICEF, World Wildlife Fund; Ninth New Year's Day concert with the Vienna Philharmonic, 1996; Led the premiere of Penderecki's Seven Gates of Jerusalem, 1997. Recordings: Over 350 including full cycles of Beethoven, Mahler, Rachmaninov, Sibelius, Tchaikovsky symphonic works; Puccini opera cycle; Music visualisation: Holst, Planets and Vivaldi, Four Seasons, Mozart, Don Giovanni, Bizet, Carmen. Hobbies: Swimming; Tennis; Reading. Address: c/o Z des Aubris, Tal 15 5th Fl, D-80331 Munich, Germany.

MACAK Ivan, b. 26 Aug 1935, Gbelce, Czechoslovakia. Education: Faculty of Arts, Comenius University, Bratislava. Career: Editorial Staff, L'udova Tvorivost and Nasa praca; Music department, Historical Institute of the Slovak National Museum, Bratislava, 1965; College of Music, Academy of Music and Drama; Musico-Folklorist Department, Slovak Academy of Sciences; Researcher, Musical Instrumentary of Indians and Eskimos, Canada, 1972; Competition of Makers of Folk Musical Instruments, Detva, 1977; Musico-Instrumental Programmes, Under-Polana Folk Festival, Detva, 1977-85. Publications: Annual Bibliography of European Ethnomusicology, 11 volumes, 1966-80; Musicologia, 2 volumes; Contributions to the Study of Traditional Musical Instruments in Museums.

MACAL Zdenek, b. 8 Jan 1936, Brno, Czechoslovakia. Conductor. Education: Brno Conservatory, 1951-56; Janacek Academy 1956-60. Debut: Czech Philharmonic Orchestra 1966, at the Prague Spring Festival; British Debut, 1969, with the Bournemouth Symphony: US debut with the Chicago Symphony 1972. Career: Conductor of the Moravian Symphony Orchestra at Olomouc, 1963-67; Tours to Hungary, Bulgaria, West Germany, Austria and Switzerland; Music Director of the Cologne Radio Symphony Orchestra 1970-74; Chief Conductor of the Orchestra of Hanoever Radio from 1980; Music Director, Milwaukee Symphony from 1986, Sydney Symphony, 1986-93; Conducted Prince Igor at the Grant Park Concerts, Chicago, 1990. Recordings: Dvorak's Cello and Piano Concertos; Brahms Alto Rhapsody, Soukupova; Mozart Piano Concertos K488 and K595; Schoeck's Penthesilea; CD of Dvorak's 9th Symphony and Symphonic Variations, Classic for Pleasure. Honours: Winner, International Conductors Competition at Bescançon, 1965; Mitropoulos Competition, NY, 1966. Address: c/o Harold Holt Ltd, 31 Sinclair Road, London W14 ONS, England.

MACANN Rodney, b. 1950, New Zealand. Singer, Baritone. Debut: European debut as The Speaker in The Magic Clute, with Welsh National Opera. Career: Sang with New Zealand Opera before studying singing and theology in London; Appearances with Opera North as Don Alfonso, Sharpless and Jochanaan, and in La Cenerentola and Samson et Dalila; English National Opera as Tchaikovsky's Mazeppa, Ariodates in Xerxes by Handel, Don Alfonso, Klingsor in Parsifal; Scarpia and Escamillo; With the Royal Opera Covent Garden has sung in Andrea Chenier, King Priam, Les Contes d'Hoffmann and Tosca; Engagements in France, Norway and Italy, as Arthur in The Lighthouse by Peter Maxwell Davies; Adelaide Festival, South Australia as Ruprecht in The Fiery Angel; Sang Cuno in Der Freischütz at Covent Garden, 1989, the Music Master in Ariadne for ENO, 1990; Concerts with all the leading British orchestras and frequent performances of Christus in the Bach Passions; Further concerts in Bergen, Florence, NY, and Toulouse; Sang Mozart's Figaro at Wellington, New Zealand, 1995. Recordings: Video of Andrea Chenier, Covent Garden, 1984. Address: c/o Stafford Law Associates, 6 Barham Close, Weybridge, Surrey KT13 9PR, England.

MACDONALD Hugh, b. 31 January 1940, Newbury, Berks, England. Professor. m. (1) Naomi Butterworth, 1963, 1 son, 3 daughters, (2) Elizabeth Babb, 1979, 1 son. Education: MA, 1966; PhD, 1969, Pembroke College, Cambridge. Career: General Editor, Complete works of Berlioz, 1965; Lecturer, Cambridge University, 1966-71; Oxford University, 1971-80; Visiting Professor, Indiana University, 1979; Gardiner Professor of Music, Glasgow University, 1980-87; Avis Blewett Professor of Music, Washington University, St Louis, 1987-. Publications: Editor, New Berlioz Edition, 1967; Skryabin, 1978; Berlioz, 1982; Berlioz: Selected Letters, 1995. Contributions to: The New Grove Dictionary of Music and Musicians; The New Grove Dictionary of Opera. Honours: Szymanowski Medal; FRCM. Address: Department of Music, Washington University, Campus Box 1032, St Louis, MO 63130, USA.

MACDONALD Kenneth, b. 1938, Iona, Hebrides. Singer, (Tenor). Education: Studied at the Guildhall School of Music, London with Dino Borgioli. Career: Sang in the chorus at Covent Garden from 1946; Solo appearances from 1952, notably as Don Ottavio, and in the 1961 British premiere of Strauss's Die schweigsame Frau and in many character roles; Guest engagements with the Light Opera Company, Sadler's Wells Opera, Welsh National Opera and the English Opera Group; Concert repertoire has included Irish and Scottish Folk Songs; The Steersman in Der fliegende Holländer, conducted by Klemperer. Recordings: Fidelio quartet and Stravinsky's Mavra; Salome; Messiah.

MACDONALD Malcolm (Calum), b. 26 Feb 1948, Nairn, Scotland. Writer on Music; Journalist. Education: Downing College, Cambridge. Career: Freelance Writer for Musical Journals; Music Copyist; Editor; Managing Editor, Tempo Magazine; Compiler, Gramophone Classical Catalogue. Compositions; Surface Measure and Before Urbino, 2 songs with orchestra; At the Firth of Lorne and other songs with piano; Piano Pieces; Arrangements of various contemporary works. Publications: Havergal Brian; Perspective on the Music, 1972; John Foulds; His Life in Music, 1975; Schoenberg, 1976. Contributions to: The Listener, Musical Times, Tempo, Musical Events; Records and Recordings. Address: 95 King Henry's Road, Swiss Cottage, London NW3, England.

MACDOUGALL Jamie, b. 25 Jan 1966, Glasgow, Scotland. Singer, Tenor. Education: Studied at the Royal Scottish Academy of Music and the Guildhall School of Music; Italy with Carlo Bergonzi. Career: Appeared with Songmakers' Almanac 1988 at the Nottingham Festival, at the Buxton Festival and in London in Handel's Israel in Egypt and Mozart's C minor Mass; Season 1990-91 with Haydn's Creation in Aberdeen and at the Usher Hall, Edinburgh; Bach's Magnificat and Purcell's King Arthur at the Elizabeth Hall; Mozart's C Minor Mass conducted by Frans Brueggen; Handel's Belshazzar; Orlando Paladino by Haydn at Garsington Manor; Bach's Magnificat and B Minor Mass in Belgium; Recital in the Szymanowski series at the Purcell Room; Operatic engagements include the Prologue and Quint in The Turn of the Screw and Gluck's Alceste with the English Bach Festival in Monte Carlo and at Covent Garden; Season 1996 with Septimus in Theodora at Glyndebourne, Fernando in Handel's Almira at Halle, Bach's Magnificat in Manchester and Mozart's Ottavio for GTO. Recordings: King Arthur conducted by Trevor Pinnock. Honours: Jean Highgate Scholarship and Lieder Prize at RSAM; Finalist in the Kathleen Ferrier Singing Competition, 1986. Address: Harrison/Parrott Ltd, 12 Penzance Place, London W11 4PA, England.

MACGREGOR Joanna, b. 16 July 1959, London, England. Concert Pianist; Composer. Education: Studied at Cambridge, Royal Academy of Music and the Van Cilburn Piano Institute, Texas. Career: Concert appearances with the London Symphony Orchestra, Royal Philharmonic, London Mozart Players, CBSO, BBC Symphony, Royal Scottish, ECO, Royal Liverpool; Festival engagements at Shrewsbury, Harrogate, Bath, Edinburgh and Salisbury; Tours of Africa and the Philippines under the British Council; Tivoli Festival Copenhagen recital, 1988; Season 1988-89 with the BBC Scottish Symphony, the City of Birmingham Symphony and the English Chamber Orchestra; Promenade Concerts London, 1990, 1991; International piano series recitals at the South Bank, London, 1990-91; Celebrity Recital Barbican Centre, 1992; Other contemporary repertoire includes works by Berio, Xenakis, Ligeti, Tristan Murail, Takemitsu and James Dillon; Composer of music for various theatre companies, television and radio; Play for radio based on Satie's writings, Memoirs of an Amnesiac; Played in Messiaen's Turangalila Symphony at the 1993 London Proms; Founded Contemporary Music Festival, Platform at ICA, 1991-93; World premiere, Hugh Wood's Piano Concerto Proms, 1991; World premiere, Birtwistle's Antiphonies with Boulez and Philharmonia, 1993; Played Messiaen's Vingt Regards at the Barbican Hall, London, 1997. Recordings: American Piano Classics; Britten Concerto, Satie recital, the Gershwin Songbook and music by Bach, Scarlatti, Bartók, Debussy, Ravel and Messiaen. Address: c/o Ingpen and Williams Ltd, 26 Wadham Road, London SW15 2LR, England.

MACHA Otmar, b. 2 Oct 1922, Ostrava, Czechoslovakia. Composer. m. Marta Hrochová, 20 Sept 1947, 1 son, 1 daughter. Education: Graduated, Music High School, Prague, 1948. Career: Music Dramaturgist, Radio Prague, 1945-61; Full-time Composer, 1962-. Compositions include: String Quartets, 1943, 1982, 1990; Violin Sonatas, 1948, 1987; The Lac Ukereve, opera, 1963; Variations on a Theme by Jan Rychlik, 1964; Sinfonietta No 1, 1971, No 2, 1982; Metamorphoses Promethei, opera, 1981; Infidelity Trapped, opera; Night and Hope, symphonic poem; Comenius Testament, oratorio; Seikilos Variations, violin solo, 1991; Sinfonietta da Camera, 1993. Honours: State Prize, 1967; Merited Artist, 1982. Membership: International Music Festival, Prague. Address: Hradecká 22, 13000 Prague 3-Vinohrady, Czech Republic.

MACHL Tadeusz, b. 22 Oct 1922, Lwów, Poland. Composer; Organist; Professor. m. Irena Paszkiewicz-Machl, 2 children. Education: State College of Music, Krakow, 1949-52, under guidance Professor Malawski and Professor Rutkowski. Career: Works recorded in Poland, played through Poland and abroad; Professor, Prorector, 1969-72, Academy of Music, Krakow; Director of Chair of Composition, 1966-72; President of Disciplinary Committee of Pedagogical Staff, 1972-89. Compositions: For great symphony orchestra: 6 Symphonies: 1947, 1948, 1948, 1954, 1963, 1997; 7 Organ Concertos, 1950, 1952, 1953, 1957, 1969, 1983; Concerto for 3 Organs, 1979; 9 Instrumental Concertos: Concerto for Voice, 1958; Violin Concerto, 1960; Harpischord Concerto, 1962; Piano Concerto, 1964; Arpa Concerto, 1965; Concerto for Piano and Harpischord, 1966; Violoncello (or Viola) Concerto, 1967; Concerto for 2 Pianos and Organ, 1969; Concerto for Bugle-horn, 1971; 4 Cantatas: Work Day, 1948; Concerto for Youth, 1954; Icar's Flight, 1968; Blue Cross, 1974; Rapsod, 1996; Transcriptions for organ compositions of J S Bach: Prelude and Fugues, 1956; Fantasy G, 1993; Poems: Jubilee Poem, 1979, My Town, 1992, Dirge, 1994; Lyric Suite, 1956; Requiem, 1980; Symphonic Scherzo, 1986; Symphonic Poem, 1996; Chamber Music: 4 string quartets, 1950, 1957, 1961, 1972; Lyric Suite, 1955; Herbarium, 1980; Triptych - Heartiness Landscapes, 1993; Organ Music: 5 Virtuoso etudes, 1950; Deux pieces pour grand orgue, 1964; Mini Suita, 1967; Triptych, 1968; 10 Compositions pour orgue, 1970; Landscapes I, 1976, II, 1978, III, 1982; Great Fantasy with B-A-C-H Fugue, 1980; Rupicaprae, 1982; 15 Rosary Poems, 1983; Disonatio, 1989; Poem, 1992; Choruses; Songs; Piano Music; Music for cinema, theatre and ballet; 45 organ choral supplements to Polish elegiac songs, 1997. Honours: Award: Special Mention for String Quartet in Liège, 1956, 1959; Active Man of Culture, 1970; Bachelors and Officers, Polonia Restituta, 1972, 1988; Merit Teacher of Poland, 1989; 1st Degress Ministry of Culture and Art, 1971 and 1990. Membership: Union of Polish Composers and ZAiKS, Warsaw. Hobbies: Aviation; Motoring; Mountains; Dogs. Address: ul Bol Chrobrego 29/27, 31-428 Krakow, Poland.

MACHOVER Tod, b. 24 Nov 1953, NY, USA. Composer; Cellist. m. June Kinoshita. Education: BM, 1975, MM, 1977, Doctoral Studies, Juilliard School of Music; University of California at Santa Cruz, 1971-73; Columbia University, 1973-75. Career: Composer-in-Residence, Institut de Recherche et Coordination Acoustique/Musique, Paris, 1978-79; Director, Musical Research, 1979-85; Faculty member, Associate Professor of Music and Media, Director of Experimental Media Facility, Media Laboratory, Massachusetts Institute of Technology, 1985-, Co-Director of research consortium, 1994-; Invented technology named hyperinstruments, 1986, began instrument design for this technology, 1991; Brain Opera, first performance, Lincoln Centre Festival, 1996; Forthcoming tours with his repertoire in United States, Europe and Asia; Music performed by many prominent musicians, such as Yo-Yo Ma, and ensembles. Compositions include: Fusione Fugace, 1981-82; Electric Etudes, 1983; Hyperstring Trilogy, 1991-93; Bounce, 1992; Wake-up Music, 1995; Brain Opera, 1995-96; He's Our Dad, 1997; Resurrection, forthcoming. Publications: Numerous including: Hyperinstruments: A Progress Report, 1992; subject of many books, chapters and articles on the subject of hyperinstruments and his compositions. Contributions to: Book chapters and articles learned musical journals. Honours include: Gaudeamus Prize, 1977; Grant, Gulbenkian Foundation, 1980; Grants from National Endowment for the Arts, 1981, 1983, 1985; Prix de la Creation, French Culture Ministry, 1984; Friedheim Award, Kennedy Centre, 1987; Grant, Aaron Copland Fund for music, 1994; Chevalier de l'Ordre des Arts et des Lettres, 1995. Address: MIT Media Laboratory, 20 Ames Street, E15 494, Cambridge, MA 02139, USA.

MACIAS Reinaldo, b. 1 Sept 1956, Cuba. Singer (Tenor). Education: Studied in the USA and at the Geneva Conservatory. Career: Sang at first in concert, notably with Messiah, Haydn's Schöpfung and Jahreszeiten and the Requiems of Dvorak, Britten and Mozart; Verdi Requiem in Paris, 1989; Opera roles from 1989, with Almaviva in Vienna and Zurich, Don Ottavio and Ferrando in Holland, the Berlioz Iopas at Zurich and Gounod's Romeo in Liège (1993); Other roles include the Duke of Mantua, Tamino and Lindoro (all in Zurich, 1991-92). Address: c/o Opernhaus Zurich, Falkenstrasse 1, CH-8008 Zurich, Switzerland.

MACKAY Penelope (Judith), b. 6 Apr 1943, Bradford, Yorkshire, England. Singer (Soprano). Education: Secretarial College, Lycée Francais, London; Guildhall School of Music and Drama. Debut: Glyndebourne, 1970. Career: Sang at Glyndebourne, 1970-72, with English Opera Group, 1973-75, English Music Theatre, 1976-78, English National Opera, 1980-83; Freelance work in Britain, Europe and USA; Over 20 leading roles; Sang in premieres of Lutyens's Time Off, 1971, Britten's Death in Venice, 1973; British Premieres of Hans Werner Henze's La Cubana in the title role, 1978; Krenek's Jonny Spielt Auf (Anita), 1984, Ligeti, Le Grand Macabre (Miranda), 1982; Austrian premiere in modern times of Fux's Angelica, Vincitrice di Alcina (Angelica), Graz, 1984, and British premiere in modern times of Handel's Rodrigo (Rodrigo), 1985. Memberships: Incorporated Society of Musicians; British Voice Association. Hobbies; Human potential; Painting; Reading; Good food and good company. Current management: Jeffrey and White. Address: 9-15 Neil Street, London WC2, England.

MACKENZIE Jane (Leslie), b. 1956, British Columbia, Canada. Singer, Soprano. Education: Studied at the University of Victoria and with Frances Adaskin. Debut: Opera debut as Donna Elvira with Kent Opera. Career: Concerts throughout Britain and North America, notably with the Stockholm Bach Choir at the Elizabeth Hall, London, with Trevor Pinnock at Aldeburgh, at the Wigmore Hall with Roger Vignoles and the last night of the 1984 Promenade Concerts; English National Opera as Mozart's Countess and Marzelline in Fidelio; Scottish Opera from 1986 as Micaela, Pamina and the Countess; Appearances with Opera North as Pamina, Anne Trulove, Euridice and Fiordiligi; Welsh National Opera debut 1987, as Mimi; Has returned to Vancouver 1986 and 1988 as Pamina and the Governess in The Turn of the Screw. Honours: Prize winner at competitions in Guelph, Canada, the Belvedere in Vienna and Benson and Hedges at Snape. Address: c/o Korman International Management, Crunnells Green Cottage, Preston, Herts SG4 7UQ, England.

MACKERRAS (Alan) Charles (MacLaurin) (Sir), b. 17 Nov 1925, Schenectady, USA. Conductor. m. Helena Judith Wilkins, 1947, 2 daughters. Education: Principal Oboist, Sydney Symphony Orchestra, Australia, 1943-46; British Council Scholar, Prague Academy of Music, Czech Republic, 1947-48. Debut: Die Fledermaus, Sadler's Wells Opera, 1948. Career: Staff Conductor, 1949-53, Musical Director, 1970-77, Conducted first British performance of Janácek's Katya Kabanova, 1951, Sadler's Wells Opera - later English National Opera; Principal Conductor, BBC Concert Orchestra, 1954-56; Freelance conductor with concert tours to USSR, South Africa, North America, Australia, 1957-66; Principal Conductor, Hamburg State Opera, Germany, 1966-69; Chief Guest Conductor, BBC Symphony Orchestra, 1976-79; Chief Conductor, Sydney Symphony Orchestra, Australian Broadcasting Commission, 1982-85; Frequent Guest Conductor, Vienna State Opera, Geneva and Zurich Opera, Royal Opera House, Covent Garden, English National Opera, San Francisco Opera; Frequent radio and television broadcasts and appearances at international festivals and opera houses, Has conducted several operas by J C Bach; Musical Director, Welsh National Opera, 1987-91; Conducted Lohengrin at San Francisco, 1989, new production of Der Rosenkavalier for WNO 1990 followed by Cosi fan tutte in Vienna, Burgtheater edition of 1790, and Handel's Xerxes for ENO in tour to Russia; Falstaff at the 1990 Glyndebourne Festial, Idomeneo for WNO 1991 (also at the Proms); Fidelio in concert at the 1995 Edinburgh Festival. Recordings include: Handel Series, DGG; Janácek Operas, Deccca. Publications: Ballet arrangements: Sullivan's Pineapple Poll, Verdi's Lady and the Fool; Reconstruction of Sullivan's lost Cello Concerto; Contributor to: Opera magazine; Where we are Now (interview) 1990; Music and Musicians; Contributed four appendices to Charles Mackerras, a Musician's Musician, by Nancy Phelan, 1987; etc. Honours include: CBE, 1974; Gramophone Record of the Year, 1977, 1980; Janácek Medal, 1978; Knighthood, 1979; Fellow, Royal College of Music, 1987. Hobbies: Languages; Yachting. Current Management: Marks Management Limited.

MACKEY Steven, b. 1956, Frankfurt, Germany. Composer. Education: PhD, Composition, Brandeis University. Career: Commissions from the Koussevitzky and From Foundations, the Kronos and Concord Quartets and soprano Dawn Upshaw; Professor of Music, Princeton University. Compositions include: Among the Washington, soprano and string quartet, 1989; On All Fours, string quartet (Vermeer Quartet), 1990; On the Verge/Troubadour Songs, for electric guitar and string quartet, 1992; TILT for orchestra, 1992; Physical Property, for electric guitar and string quartet, 1992; Eating Greens, 1994; Deal, concerto for electric and guitar drumset. 1995. Honours include: Guggenheim, Lieberson and Tanglewood Fellowships. Address: c/o Boosey and Hawkes Limited, 295 Regent Street, London W1R 8JH, England.

MACKIE David, b. 25 Nov 1943, Greenock, Scotland. Repetiteur; Accompanist; Conductor. Education: Royal Scottish Academy of Music, 1961-64; Glasgow University, 1969-72; Birmingham University, 1972-75; MA; BMus; Dip MusEd; RSAM; ARCM. Career: Repetiteur, D'Oyly Carte Opera, 1975-76; Chorus Master and Associate Conductor, 1976-82; Music Associate for BBC Complete Gilbert and Sullivan Operas, 1989; Wrote and presented 14 interval talks; Accompanist and Conductor; Tours of USA and Canada in concerts of Gilbert and Sullivan. Compositions include: Arthur Sullivan, Cello Concerto Reconstruction, with Charles Mackerras. Recordings include: The Gondoliers, 1977; Cox and Box/The Zoo, 1978; The Yeomen of the Guard, 1979, as chorusmaster to the D'Oyly Carte Opera Company; Arthur Sullivan - cello concerto in D, joint reconstruction in collaboration with Sir Charles Mackerras, 1986; Sullivan, Cello Concerto. Publications: Sullivan Cello Concerto, 1986; Piano Reduction, 1987; Arthur Sullivan - cello concerto in D reconstruction, with Charles Mackerras. Memberships: ISM; RSM. Hobby: Cartology. Address: 187A Worple Road, Raynes Park, London, SW20 8RE, England.

MACKIE Neil, b. 11 Dec 1946, Aberdeen, Scotland. Singer, Tenor. Debut: London with the English Chamber Orchestra under Raymond Leppard. Career: European engagements at the Flanders and Savonlinna Festivals, Concertgebouw Orchestra, in Rome for RAI and in Scandinavia; Tours of Holland and Belgium with La Petite Bande conducted by Sigiswald Kuijken; Association with Peter Maxwell Davies includes premieres of The Martyrdom of St Magnus, 1977, The Lighthouse 1980 and Into the Labyrinth 1983; Sang Ejomatz in Mozart;s Zaide at Wexford, 1981; Premiered Henze's Three Poems of WH, Auden at Aldeburgh, 1984; Appeared at Cheltenham and Aldeburgh Festivals; UK engagements with the Halle, Bournemouth Sinfonietta, BBC Symphony and Scottish Chamber Orchestras, and with the London Sinfonietta under Simon Rattle; June 1988, Into the Labyrinth at the Ojai Festival in America; 1988-89 tour of USA with the Scottish Chamber Orchestra and appearances with the Orchestre National de Paris; Professor of Singing, Royal College of Music, London, 1985; Head of Vocal Studies, Royal College of Music, 1993. Recordings: Mozart's Requiem and Haydn's Die Schöpfung with La Petite Bande; Mozart Masses with the King's College Choir; Britten's Serenade, with premiere of Now Sleeps the Crimson Petal and unpublished songs. Honours: FRSAMD, 1992; Hon D Mus, Aberdeen, 1993; CStJ, 1996. Hobbies: Reading; Charity Work; Occasional Gardening. Address: c/o Lies Askonas Ltd, 6 Henrietta Street, London WC2E 8LA, England.

MACKINTOSH Catherine, b. 1948, England. Violinist. Debut: Concert at St John's Smith Square, London, 1984. Career: Extensive tours and broadcasts in France, Belgium, Holland, Germany, Austria, Switzerland, Italy and Spain. Tours of the United States and Japan, 1991-92; British appearances include four Purcell concerts at the Wigmore Hall, 1987, later broadcast on Radio 3; Repertoire includes music on the La Folia theme by Vivaldi, Corelli, CPE Bach, Marais,A Scarlatti, Vitali and Geminiani; Instrumental works and songs by Purcell, music by Matthew Locke, John Blow and Fantasias and Airs by William Lawes; 17th Century virtuoso Italian music by Marini, Buonamente, Gabrieli, Fontana and Stradella; J S Bach and his forerunners, Biber, Scheidt, Schenk, Reincken and Buxtehude. Recordings: Six record set on the La Folia theme; Purcell sonatas by Vivaldi and Corelli; Frequent engagements with other ensembles. Memberships: Purcell Quartet.

MACMILLAN James, b. 1959, Kilwinning, Ayrshire, Scotland. Composer; Lectuter in Music. Education: Studied at the Universities of Edinburgh and Durham. Career: Formerly lecturer in the music departments of Edinburgh and Manchester Universitites; Lecturer at the Royal Scottish Academy of Music and Drama; Performances of his music by the New Music Group of Scotland, Circle, Nomos, Lontano and the Scottish Chamber Orchestra; Commissions from the Edinburgh Contemporary Arts Trust, The Traverse Theatre, Scottish Chamber Orchestra, the Paragon Ensemble, Cappela Nova and the Scottish Chamber Choir; Prom Commission, The Confession of Isobel Gowdie, BBC Scottish Symphony Orchestra; Featured Composer, 1990 Musica Nova Festival, Glasgow; Seven Last Words from the Cross premiered on BBC TV Easter, 1994. Compositions: Study on Two Planes for cello and piano 1981; Three Dawn Rituals for ensemble 1983; Beatus Vir for chorus and organ 1983; The Road to Ardtalla for ensemble 1983; Songs of a Just War for soprano and ensemble 1984; Piano Sonata 1986; Two Visions of Hoy for oboe and ensemble 1986; The Keening for orchestra 1986; Festival Fanfares for brass band 1986; Litanies of Iron and Stone for ensemble with tape 1987; Untold for ensemble 1987; Visions of a November Spring for string quartet 1988; Busqueda for 8 actors, 3 sopranos, speaker and ensemble 1988; Into the Ferment for Orchestra 1988; Cantos Sagrados for chorus and organ 1989; The Exorcism of Rio Sumpul for Chamber Ensemble 1989; As Mothers See Us, for ensemble 1990; The Berserking, Piano Concerto, 1990; The Confession of Isobel Gowdie for orchestra 1990; Soweton Spring for wind band 1990; Catherine's Lullabies for chorus and ensemble 1990; Scots Song for Soprano and Ensemble 1991; Tuireadh for clarinet and string quartet 1991; Sinfonietta 1991; Tourist Variations, 1 act chamber opera 1992; Opera Ines de Castro, 1993; Visitatio Sepulchri for 7 singers and chamber orchestra, 1993; Trumpet Concerto, 1993; Vs for orchestra, 1993; Seven Last Words from the Cross for choir and strings, 1994; Ines de Castro, opera, 1996; Clarinet Concerto, 1997. Address: c/o Boosey & Hawkes, 295 Regent Street, London, W1R 8JH, England.

MACNEIL Cornell, b. 24 Sept 1922, Minneapolis, Minnesota, USA. Singer, Baritone. Education: Studied at Hartt School, Hartford, with Friedrich Schorr; NY with Virgilio Lazzari and Dick Marzollo; Rome with Luigi Ricci. Debut: Philadelphia 1950, in the premiere of Menotti's The Consul. Career: NYC Opera debut, 1953, as Germont; San Francisco 1955, as Escamillo; Chicago, 1957, in Manon Lescaut; Metropolitan Opera from 1959-87, as Verdi's Rigoletto, Amonasro, Nabucco, Iago and Luna, Puccini's Scarpia and Michele, and Barnaba in La Gioconda, 460 performances in 26 parts; La Scala Milan 1959, as Carlo in Ernani; Covent Garden debut 1964, as Verdi's Macbeth; Verona Arena 1971; Guest appearances in Caracas, Mexico City, Vienna, Buenos Aires, Barcelona, Rome and Naples. Recordings: Un Ballo in Maschera, Rigoletto, Aida, Cavalleria Rusticana, Luisa Miller, La Fanciulla del West, La Gioconda, La Traviata, Falstaff. Address: c/o Metropolitan Opera, Lincoln Center, New York, NY 10023, USA.

MACNEIL Walter, b. 1957, New York, USA. Singer (Tenor). Education: Studied with his father, Cornell MacNeil. Career: Sang at the San Francisco Opera from 1983, as Froh, Rodrigo in Otello and Alfredo; Sang Alfredo at New Orleans 1984, with his father as Germont père; Carnegie Hall 1985, in Semele, and Don Ottavio at Milwaukee 1986; Glyndebourne 1987-88 and Metropolitan 1989, as Alfredo; Sang Aubry in Der Vampyr by Marschner at the 1992 Wexford Festival; Other roles include Tamino (Connecticut Opera, 1991), Ruggiero in La Rondine and Nadir in Les pecheurs de Perles (Honolulu 1987). Address: c/o Metropolitan Opera, Lincoln Center, New York, NY 10023, USA.

MACURDY John, b. 18 Mar 1929, Detroit, Michigan, USA. Singer, Bass. m. Justine May Votypka, 1 son, 1 daughter. Education: Wayne State University, Detroit; Vocal Study with Avery Crew, Detroit. Debut: New Orleans, 1952, in Samson et Dalila; Appearances in Baltimore, Houston, Philadelphia, San Francisco and Santa Fe; NYC Opera debut 1959, in Weill's Street

Scence; Metropolitan Opera from 1962 as the Commendatore, Crespel in Les Contes d'Hoffmann and Rocco in Fidelio; Sang in the premieres of Antony and Cleopatra, 1966 and Mourning Becomes Elektra, 1967; 1st local Performance of Les Troyens, 1973; Paris Opera 1973, as Arkel in Pelléas et Mélisande; La Scala Milan 1974, as Rocco in Fidelio; Salzburg Festival 1977-78, as the Commendatore in Don Giovanni; Milan 1984 as the Landgrave in Tannhäuser; Seattle Opera 1986, as Hagen and Hunding in the Ring; Metropolitan 1987, as Fasolt in Das Rheingold; Hunding at San Francisco 1990; Appearances at Aix and Orange Festivals, Hollywood Bowl, Miami Opera and Scottish Opera; Season 1992 in Billy Budd at the Met, as Trulove in The Rake's Progress at Aix-en-Provence, as Fiesco in Simon Boccanegra Montpellier, The Flying Dutchman in Buenos Aires as Daland and L'Africaine in Marseille; 995 performances as Leading Bass; Over 1500 operatic performances; Sang Fafner in Das Rheingold at Marseille, 1996; Hunding at the Met, 1996. Recordings: Don Giovanni; Beatrice et Benedict; Otello; The Rev Hale in Ward's The Crucible. Honours: City of Detroit Medal, 1969; Rockefeller Foundation Grant, 1959; Presently only American to be listed in the Wagnerian Annals for singing all the Bass Roles in the Ring Cycle; Inducted into the Academy of Vocal Arts Hall of Fame. Membership: Bohemian Club. Hobbies: Antiques; Gardening; Tennis; Golf. Address: Tall Oaks Court, Stamford, CT 06903, USA.

MADDALENA James, b. 1954, Lynn, Massachussetts, USA. Singer, Baritone. Education: Studied at the New England Conservatory of Music. Debut: Rogers and Hammerstein medley with the Boston Pops Orchestra, 1974. Career: From 1974 has appeared in a complete cycle of Bach's cantatas at Emmanuel Church Boston, conducted by Craig Smith; Founder member of the Liederkreis Ensemble, Naumburg Awad, 1980; Association with director Peter Sellars from 1981 includes the title role in Don Giovanni and Leading roles in Handel's Orlando, American Repertory Theatre, 1982; Cosi fan tutte, Castle Hill Festival, 1984; Haydn's Armida, New Hampshire Symphony, 1983; Giulio Cesare and the Brecht Weill Kleine Mahagonny, Pepsico Summerfare, 1985; Soloist in Messiah at Carnegie Hall 1984, with Banchetto Musicale; Sang the title role in the world premiere of Nixon in China by John Adams, Houston, 1987, repeated at Edinburgh 1988 and The Captain in the premiere of Adams's The Death of Klinghoffer, Brussels 1991, and at Lyon, Vienna and NY; Has appeared as Mozart's Count in the Sellars version of Le nozze di Figaro, seen at Purchase, NY and Papageno at Glyndebourne, 1990; Created Merlin in Tippett's New Year at Houston 1989 and in the British premiere at Glyndebourne; Season 1992 in Nixon in China at Adelaide and Frankfurt, Don Alfonso at Glyndebourne; Sang in Susa's Transformations at St Louis, 1997. Recordings. Brahms Liebeslieder Waltzes, with Liederkreis; Nixon in China and The Death of Klinghoffer. Address: c/o Houston Grand Opera Association, 510 Preston Avenue, Houston, TX 77002, USA.

MADDISON Dorothy, b. 12 Jan 1956, Fergus Falls, Minnesota, USA. Lyric Coloratura Soprano. m. 29 Dece 1979, Ian Maddison. Education: BMus, St Olaf College, Minnesota, 1977; Guildhall School of Music & Drama, London, England, 1977-79; Britten-Pears School, Aldeburgh; Private study with Audrey Langford and Andrew Feidld, Cantica Voice Studio, London. Debut: Purcell Room, London, April 1986 with Graham Johnson, piano. Career: Freelance concert and operatic singer; Operatic roles include The Queen of Night in The Magic Flute; Zaide; Madames Herz and Silberklang in The Impressario, Mozart; Norina in Don Pasquale; Adina in Elixir of Love; Rita by Donizetti; Tytania in Midsummer Night's Dream, Britten; Mable, Pirates of Penzance; Zerbinetta, Ariadne auf Naxos, Strauss; The Nightingale, Stravinsky; Oratorio repertoire: includes works by Bach, Handel, Haydn, Mozart, Mendelssohn, Orff; Recital Repertoire: Standard works by European composers, also songs from the American Midwest, a programme featuring works by Minnesota composers Argento, Dougherty, Franklin, Larsen, Paulus, first given in April 1988, Purcell Room, London with Robin Bowman, piano; Recent appearances with: English Bach Festival, New Sadler's Wells Opera Company, Opera Factory, London Opera Players. Honours: Honours and Distinction, St Olaf College, Walter Hyde Memorial Prize, Guildhall School. Membership: Equity. Address: 95 Tanfield Avenue, London NW2 7SB, England.

MADER-TODOROVA Marina, b. 20 Aug 1948, Silistra, Bulgaria. Singer (Soprano). Education: Studied in Varna, Sofia and Vienna. Career: Sang at first in opera at Varna then Mainz and Bremen, 1976-77 as Desdemona and Micaela; Gelsenkirchen 1977-80 as Elisabeth de Valois, Ariadne and Tosca; Further appearances at Dortmund, 1980-83, Hamburg, Stuttgart, Frankfurt and Basle; Engaged at the Deutsche Oper am Rhein, 1984-86, Graz, 1984-89, notably as Eva, Amelia in Ballo in Machera, Leonara in Il Trovatore, Agathe and Ariadne; Further appearances at the Deutsche Oper Berlin, Budapest, Mannheim, Palermo, Zurich, Copenahgen and Liège; Other roles have included Butterfly, Elisabeth in Tannhäuser, Elsa, Mozart's Fiordiligi and Countess, Mimi and Arabella; Many concert appearances. Address: Vereinigte Buhnen, Kaiser Josef Platz 10, A-8010 Graz, Austria.

MADRA Barbara, b. 1958, Koszian, Poznan, Poland. Singer (Soprano). Education: Studied in Poznan. Career: Sang at first with the Poznan Opera then from 1980 at the Brussels Opera, notably as Mimi, Violetti, Fiordiligi, Elisabeth de Valois, Mozart's Vitellia and Arminda, the Trovatore Leonora and Amelia Grimaldi; Guest appearances in Geneva, Lausanne, at the Holland Festival, Buenos Aires, Barcelona and Toulouse (Donna Elvira, 1990); Sang Tatiana at Zurich 1990 and at La Scala in Rimsky's Tale of Tsar Saltan and as Eva in Die Meistersinger. Address: c/o Théâtre Royale, 4 Leopoldstrasse, B-1000 Brussels, Belgium.

MADROSZKIEWICZ Joanna Dorota, b. 22 March 1956, Szczecin, Poland. Violinist. 1 son, 2 daughters. Education: Magister of Art; Akademia Muzyczna Gdansk; Hochschule für Musik, Vienna. Career: Engagements at Geneva, Prague, Lublin, Naples; Concerts with Vienna Symphony Orchestra, Polish National Philharmonie, London Mozart Players, Residentre Orkest, Austria Radio Orchestra, Deutsche Kammerakad; Numerous Recitals; Debut at Salzburg Festspiele with Vienna Philharmony Orchestra. Recordings: Schubert, Haydn, Beethoven. Honours: Best Young Artist of Poland Award, 1977; Commander of the Order of Polonia Restituta, 1994. Hobbies: Poetry; Gardening. Current Management: Hörtnagel, Germany. Address: Kielmansegg 26, A-2340 Mödling, Austria.

MADZAR Aleksandar, b. 1968, Belgrade, Yugoslavia. Concert Pianist. Education: Belgrade Academy of Music, with Eliso Virsaladze in Moscow, at the Strasbourg Conservatory and with Daniel Blumenthal in Brussels. Career: Frequent appearances from 1985 with leading orchestras in France, Germany, Italy, Spain, Scandinavia and Britain; Berlin Philharmonic debut 1990 and further engagements with the Chamber Orchestra of Europe, Royal Philharmonic, Leipzig Gewandhaus, Bremen PO and Czech Philharmonic (1996); Recitals at Salzburg, Davos, Bad Kissingen and Ivo Pogorelich Festivals; Chamber music collaborations in Boston, New York (Carnegie Hall), Milan, Amsterdam Concertgebouw, Vienna Musikverein, and South Africa. Recordings include: Prokoviev Violin Sonatas with Kyoko Takezawa (BMG); Chopin Concertos and solo works by Ravel (BMG); Two concertos by Erwin Schulhoff (Decca). Honours include: Prize winner, 1996 Leeds International Piano Competition; Winner, Ferruccio Busoni Competition, 1989; Winner, Barenreiter Prize at the International Mozart Competition, Salzburg, 1985. Address: Harrison/Parrott, 12 Penzance Place, London W11 4PA, England.

MAE Vanessa (Vanessa Mae Nicholson), b. 27 October 1978, Singapore. Concert Violinist. Education: Studied with Lin Yao Ji, Central Conservatoire, Beijing; Felix Andrievsky, Royal College of Music, London. Career includes: First National Tour of Britain 1990, featuring the Tchaikovsky Concerto; First International Tour with the London Mozart Players, 1990; Over 300 Live Performances in 35 countries; The Classical Tour, 1997, visiting Sheffield, Birmingham (Symphony Hall), Leicester, London (Barbican) and Manchester (Bridgewater Hall); Frequent Television Appearances and participant in 'crossover' concerts. Recordings include: Tchaikovsky and Beethoven Concertos, 1990; Compilation Albums, including arrangement of Bach Toccata and Fugue. Honours include: Winner, BAMBI Top International Classical Artist Award and ECHO Klassik Award for Bestselling Album of the Year, 1995 (3 million recordings sold worldwide to date). Address: c/o Trittico Ltd, 34 Philimore Walk, London W8 7SA, England.

MAEGAARD Jan (Carl Christian), b. Copenhagen, Denmark. Composer; Musicologist. m. Kirsten Offer Andersen, 14 Aug 1973, div, 2 daughters. Education: Royal Danish Conservatory; Dr phil, University of Copenhagen, 1972. Career: Freelance Musician, 1949-56; Music Critic, 1952-60; Teacher, Royal Danish Conservatory of Music, 1953-58; Teaching Assistant, 1959-61, Associate Professor, 1961-71, Professor, 1971-, University of Copenhagen; Guest Professor, State University of New York, USA, 1974; Professor of Music, University of California, Los Angeles, 1978-81. Compositions include: Musica riservata no 1, op 52, string quartet; Two choruses, op 57, nos 2 and 3; Musica riservata no 2, op 61, for oboe, clarinet, bassoon and saxophone; Pastorale, op 63, for 2 clarinets; Labirinto 1, op 77, viola solo; Orchestration of P Heise, Dyvekes Sange I-VII, op 78, for soprano and orchestra; Labirinto II, op 79, for guitar; Partita, op 89, for organ; Cello Concerto, op 98. Recordings include: Chamber Concerto no2, op 38; Octomeri, op 40, for violin and piano; Musica riservata no 1 op 52; Trio Serenade, O alter Duft aus Märchenzeit, op 36, for violin, cello and piano. Publications: Books: Musikalsk Modernisme, 1964; Studien zur Entwicklung des dodekaphonen Satzes bei Arnold Schonberg I-III, 1972. Contributions to: Numerous articles to magazines and journals including: The Nomenclature of Pitch-Class Sets, 1985; Die Komponisten der Wiener Schule und ihre Textdichter sowie das Komponisten-Dichter-Verhaltnis heute, 1988; Zur harmonischen Analyse der Musik des 19 Jahrhunderts, Eine theoretische Erwägung, 1990; Kuhlau Kanons, 1996. Memberships include: Royal Danish Academy, 1986; Norwegian Academy of Science and Letters, 1988; International Musicological Society, 1982. Address: Duevej 14 6, 2000 Frederiksberg, Denmark.

MAFFEO Gianni, b. 30 Mar 1939, Vigevano, Milan, Italy. Singer, Baritone. Education: Studied at the Liceo Musiale di Vercelli. Debut: Sang Tonion in Pagliacci with the Associazione Lirico Compagnia, 1961. Career: Many appearances at such opera centres as La Scala Milan, Genoa, Palermo, Turin and Verona, 1973; Sang Schaunard in the Zeffirelli/Karajan Bohème at La Scala, 1963; Guest engagements at Vienna, Prague, Rouen, Monte Carlo, Brno, Lisbon, Munich and the NYC Opera; Further appearances at Toulouse, Nice, Bordeaux and Frankfurt as Marcello, Sharpless, Germont, Count Luna and Rigoletto. Recordings: Madama Butterfly; La Bohème. Address: Teatro Alla Scala, Via Filodrammatici 2, 20121 Milan, Italy.

MAGA Othmar, b. 30 June 1929, Brno, Czechoslovakia. Conductor. Education: Studied at the Stuttgart Hochschule für Musik, 1948-52; Tubingen University, 1952-58; Accademia Chigiana at Siena with Paul van Kempen, 1954-55; Further studies with Sergiu Celibidache, 1960-62. Career: Conducted the Göttingen Symphony Orchestra, 1963-67, Nuremberg Symphony, 1968-70; General Music Director at Bochum, 1971-82; Artistic Director of the Odense Symphony Orchestra, Denmark, and Permanent Conductor of the Orchestra of the Pomeriggi Musicali de Milano, 1987; Also Conductor of the Folkswangschule at Essen; Guest Conductor with leading orchestras in Europe and tour of Japan with the NHK Symphony Orchestra; From 1992 Chief Conductor of the KBS-Symphony Orchestra in Seoul, Korea. Current Management: Konzertdirektion Jürgen Erlebach, Hamburg, Germany. Address: Merlos 19, 36323 Grebenau, Germany.

MAGAZINER Elliot A, b. 25 Dec 1921, Springfield, MA, USA. Violinist; Conductor; Educator. m. Sari Magaziner, 2 d. Education: National Orchestra Association, 1937-40; Princeton University, 1943; Juilliard School of Music, New York, 1946-50. Debut: Town Hall, New York, 1952. Career: Staff Artist, Concertmaster, CBS TV and Radio Networks, with conductors Reiner, Ansermet, Beecham and Stokowski; Conductor, Senior Violin Instructor, Westchester Conservatory of Music; Professor of Music, Conductor, Manhattanville College Community Orchestra; Head of Chamber Music and Strings; Affiliated Artist Teacher, State University of New York; Visiting Conductor, Dubuque Symphony; Soloist with the New York Philharmonic and Symphony, Symphony of the Air, Chicago, Fort Myers, Dubuque, York and St Petersburg symphony orchestras; Recitals in New York, Washington, Detroit, Amsterdam, Paris and Jerusalem; Starred in The Violin, CBS TV. Recordings: Charles Ives Sonata No 2; Charles Ives Trio, with Frank Glazer and David Weber; Vivaldi's Concerto in C and Concerto in B Flat, with Orchestre Symphonique de Paris. Address: 250 Garth Road Apt 2B3, Scarsdale, NY 10583, USA.

MAGEAU Mary, b. 4 Sept 1934, Milwaukee, Wisconsin, USA. Composer; Harpischordist. Education: BMus, DePaul University, Chicago, 1963; MMus, University of Michigan, 1969. Career: Faculty Member, Queensland Conservatory, 1987-91; Queensland University of Technology, 1992-95; Founder Member of the Brisbane Baroque Trio. Compositions include: Concerto for harpischord and strings, 1978; Australia's Animals, for piano, 1978; Concert Pieces for violin, cello and piano, 1984; Indian Summer, for youth orchestra, 1986; Concerto Grosso, 1987; Australis 1788, music drama, 1987; Triple Concerto, for violin, cello, piano and orchestra, 1990; Suite for Strings, 1991; An Early Autumn's Dreaming for orchestra, 1993; Dialogues, for clarinet, viola, cello and piano, 1994; The Furies, for piano and orchestra, 1995. Honours include: 4th Alienor Harpischord Composition Awards, 1994. Address: c/o APRA, 1A Eden Street, Crows Nest, NSW 2065, Australia.

MAGEE Barry, b. England. Singer (Baritone). Education: Studied at the Guildhall School and the National Opera Studio. Debut: Opera North as Schaunard in La Bohème, 1995. Career: Appearances as Eugene Onegin for British Youth Opera, Papageno for Scottish Opera and Masetto for Mid-Wales Opera; Guglielmo for Central Festival Opera, Mozart's Figaro for Opera Omnibus and Schaunard at the Albert Hall, 1996; Almeida Festival apperances and concert with the London SO in West Side Story; Season 1996-97 as Sharpless in Butterfly at Santiago, in Billy Budd at the Opéra Bastille, Paris, Gugliemo for Opera North; Royal Opera debut as Silvio in Pagliacci, 1997-98. Honours include: Prizewinner, Kathleen Ferrier Awards, 1995. Address: c/o Harrison/Parrott Ltd, 12 Penzance Place, London W11 4PA, England.

MAGNES Frances, b. 27 Apr 1919, Cleveland, OH, USA. Violinist. Education: Studied with Herman Rosen. Debut: With Cleveland Orchestra under Rodzinski, 1933. Career: Studied further with Louis Persinger and Adolf Busch in NY then toured the USA with the Busch Chamber Players, 1946-46; Recital debut at the Carnegie Hall, 1946, followed by concerts in England, France, and Israel; Concert tours of South America, Canada and USA under such conductors as Boult, Bernstein, Mitropoulos and Monteux; Premiered Wolpe's Violin Sonata, 1949 and Tibor Serly's Sonata for solo violin 1950; Dohnányi's 2nd concerto 1952, and again at the Carnegie Hall, 1981; Leader of the Westchester Symphony Orchestra under Newell Jenkins, 1963-64, and the Baroque Chamber Orchestra of Scarsdale, 1966-80. Recordings: Bach Concerto for two violins, with Adolf Busch; Wolpe's Violin Sonata and Serly's Sonata for solo violin.

MAGNUSON Elizabeth, b. 1968, Chicago, USA. Singer (Soprano). Education: Studied in Chicago and with Lucille and Robert Evans in Salzburg. Career: Appearances with the Zürich Opera as the Queen of Night, Amanda in Ligeti's Le Grand Macabre, Genio in Haydn's Orfeo and Euridice and Marzelline in Fidelio, from 1992. Concert engagements in the Missa Solemnis, Carmina Burana, Henze's Being Beauteous and Bach's Christmas Oratorio; Concert tours to St Petersburg and South America, with further opera appearances at the Wurzburg Festival, the Deutsche Oper Berlin (Queen of Night, 1996), and Zürich, Oberto in Alcina and Mozart's Constanze, season 1996-97; Conductors include Christoph Eschenbach, Rolf Beck, Jesus Lopez Cobos (Messiah in Lausanne) and Ingo Metzmacher (Strauss's Burger als Edelmann, in Stuttgart). Honours include: Winner, Chicago Belcanto Competition, 1991. Address: c/o Opernhaus Zürich, Falkenstrasse 1, CH-8008 Zürich, Switzerland.

MAGNUSSON Lars, b. 10 Mar 1955, Gothenburg, Sweden. Opera Singer, Tenor. Education: Studied at University of Gothenburg and the Opera School in Stockholm. Career: Principal tenor at the Royal Opera, Stockholm, from 1982; Roles have included, the Italian Tenor in Der Rosenkavalier, Lensky, the Duke of Mantua, Alfredo, David in Die Meistersinger and Rodolfo in La Bohème; Sang Pedrillo in a new production of Die Entführung at Covent Garden in 1987. Further performances in Monte Carlo, Nice, Strasborg, Vienna, Staatsoper, and San Francisco, 1990; Metropolitan Opera debut 1990 as Pedrillo, returning as David, 1992; Royal Opera Stockholm, Gabriele in Verdi's Simon Boccanegra, 1991; Further engagements as David in Paris, Vienna and Marseilles, and the Steersman in Der fliegende Holländer in Geneva; Sang David in a new production of Die Meistersinger at the Metropolitan, 1993, also San Francisco. Address: c/o Athole Still Ltd, Foresters Hall, 25-27 Westow Road, London SE19 3RY, England.

MAGOMEDOVA Ludmilla, b. 23 May 1961, Ukraine, Russia. Singer (Soprano). Education: Studied in Moscow. Career: Made concert tour of Siberia, 1986-87, and made stage debut 1987, as the Trovatore Leonara at Kuibishev; Verdi birthday concert in Moscow (1988) and Staatsoper Berlin from 1989, as Tosca and Leonora; Sang Norma at Graz in 1989, Aida at the Split Festival 1990; Other roles include Violetta, Lisa in The Queen of Spades and Amelia (Un ballo in maschera). Address: c/o Staatsoper Berlin, Unter den Linden 7, 0-1060 Berlin, Germany.

MAGUIRE Hugh, b. 2 August 1926, Dublin, Ireland. Violinist; Conductor. Education: College of Music, Dublin; Royal Academy of Music, London; Studies with George Enescu in Paris, 1949-50. Debut: Dublin, 1938. Career: London Debut, Wigmore Hall, 1947; Leader of the Bournemouth Municipal (Symphony) Orchestra, 1953-56, London Symphony Orchestra, 1956-62, BBC Symphony, 1962-67; Leader of the Allegri Quartet, 1968-76; Performances of contemporary British composers including Nicola LeFanu, Sebastian Forbes and Elizabeth Maconchy; Leader of the Melos Ensemble, 1977; Co-Leader of the Orchestra of The Royal Opera House, Covent Garden, 1983-91; Tours of British universities giving concerts and lectures under the auspices of the Radcliffe Trust; Professor at the Royal Academy of Music, London; Director of the Orchestra and Director of String Studies at the Britten-Pears School. Honours: FRAM, 1960; MMus, The University of Hull, 1975; DLitt, University of Ulster, 1986; DMus, The National University of Ireland, 1992. Recordings: Works by Britten, Sherlaw Johnson, Maconchy, Forbes, Elgar, Alexander Goehr and Frank Bridge with the Allegri Quartet. Address: Manor Farm, Benhall Green, Saxmundham, IP17 1HN, England.

MAGYAR Gabriel, b. 5 Dec 1914, Budapest, Hungary. Cellist; Teacher. m. Julie Dora Magyar, 17 July 1952. Education: Student, National School of Music, Budapest; Master's degree, Royal Hungarian Franz Liszt Conservatory, Budapest, 1936. Debut: Darius Milhaud, Budapest, 1938. Career: Concert Cellist, Europe, 1932-41; South America, 1947-49; Concert Cellist, USA, 1949-; Teacher, Solo Cellist, 1949-56; Professor of Cello and Chamber Music, University of Oklahoma, 1951-56; Cellist, Hungarian String Quartet, 1956-72; Professor of Chamber Music: Colby College, summers 1962-72; Banff Art Centre, summers 1972-83; Professor of Cello and Chamber Music, 1973-80, Emeritus, 1980-, University of Illinois, Urbana; Vice-President, Conservatory of Central Illinois, 1986-87. Recordings: For several

labels. Honours: Recipient, Bartók Belá-Pasztory Ditta Award, Bartók Kuratorium, 1987; Grand Prix du Disque, Paris. Hobbies: Drawing; Painting; Photography. Address: 101 W Windsor No 3103, Urbana, IL 61801, USA.

MAHLER Hellgart, b. 7 May 1931, Vienna, Austria. Composer; Music Teacher. Education: Associate of the Royal College of Music, London. Career: Freelance composer; Music teacher, 1954-. Compositions include: Three Galactic Fragments, for piano, 1966, 1980; Mira Ceti for violin and orchestra, 1973; Albedo for symphony orchestra, 1965, 1973; Glassscapes, 1976; Equations for trumpet and percussion, 1980; And the Desert Shall Blossom for small orchestra, 1980; The Icknield Quartett II for string quartet and flute, 1978; Zero-G for winds, brass, 6 percussion, harp, piano and violin, 1982; Skyscapes for Five Players, 1989; Scherzo and Quatro for violin, 1989; Divertimento for guitar, 1989; How Beautiful Are Thy Dwelling Places, for flute; Quintet, 1991; Sonnets for strings, vol 1, for cello, 1991; Isochasm, for violin, cello and piano, 1991; Sound Sculptures for clarinet, bass clarinet and bassoon, 1994; Commissions from Silver Harns, 1977, Geoffrey Tozer, 1988, Jan Sedivka, 1989, John Bussey (1994) and Gabriella Smart (1994-95), among others. Address: c/o APRA, 1A Eden Street, Crows Nest, NSW 2065, Australia.

MAIER Franz-Josef, b. 27 Apr 1925, Memmingen, Germany. Violinist; Conductor. Education: Studied at the Augsburg Conservatory, at the Munich Academy of Music and the Music Gymnasium Frankfurt. Debut: Violin recital at Munich, 1942. Career: Soloist with the Reichs Symphony Orchestra on tour of Germany 1942; Studied further at Saarbrucken and after war service at the Hochschule fur Musik, Cologne with Philip Jarnach; Played in Schaffer Quartet and the Schubert Trio; Lecturer at the Robert Schumann Conservatory Dusseldorf 1949-59; Professor and leader of the violin master classes at the Cologne Musikhochschule 1959; Performances of contemporary, Baroque and early classical music; Co-founded the Collegium Aureum 1964, becoming conductor and leader of the ensemble on violin; Concerts played on original instruments or copies; Leader of the Collegium Aureum Quartet 1970. Recordings: Suites from Campra's Les Fêtes Venetiennes and Lully's Amadis; Bach Suites, Brandenburg Concertos; Pergolesi La Serva Padrona; Mozart Serenades, Divertimenti, Piano Concertos and Symphonies, Coronation Mass, Requiem and Solemn Vespers; Beethoven 3rd Symphony, 4th Piano Concerto and Triple Concerto; Handel Concerti Grossi Op 3, Alexander's Feast, Water Music, Music for the Royal Fireworks and Organ Concertos, (Harmonia Mundi and BASF).

MAILMAN Martin, b. 30 June 1932, NY, USA. Composer; Teacher. m. Mary Nan Hudgins, 22 Aug 1959, 1 son, 1 daughter. Education: BM, 1954, MM, 1955, PhD, 1960, Eastman School of Music, University of Rochester. Career: Composer in Residence, Ford Foundation Young Composers Project, 1959-61; Composer in Residence, East Carolina University, 1961-66; Regents Professor of Music and Composer in Residence, North Texas State University, 1966. Compositions: The Hunted, opera, 1959; Liturgical Music, 1964; Requiem, Requiem, 1970; Decorations, 1974; Symphony No 2, 1979; Concerto for Violin and Orchestra, 1982; Exaltations, 1981; Symphony No 3, 1983; Trio, 1985; Cantata, 1984; Love Letters from Margaret for soprano and orchestra, 1991. Recordings: Autumn Landscape. Honours: Queen Marie Jose Prize for Violin Concerto, 1983; ABA-Ostwald Prize for Exaltations, 1983; Edward Benjamin Award for Autumn Landscape, 1955; Annual ASCAP Awards; Prizes: Ostwald-ABA Award for Exaltations in 1983; Symphony No 3, Fantasies, 1983; Trio for Violin, Cello and Piano, 1985; Precious Friends hid in Death's Dateless Night, 1988. Memberships: ASCAP; PKL; TMEA; American Bandmasters Association. Address: College of Music, University of North Texas, Denton, TX 76203, USA.

MAISKY Mischa, b. 10 Jan 1948, Riga, Latvia. Concert Cellist. m. M Kay Lipman, 1 Jan 1983, 1 son 1 daughter. Education: Moscow Conservatory; Studied with Mstislav Rostropovich; Masterclasses with Gregor Piatigorsky. Debut: Leningrad Philharmonic Orchestra, 1965. Career: Appearances at Carnegie Hall, Royal Festival Hall, Berlin Philharmonic Hall; Recitals with Martha Argerich, Radu Lupu, Boris Belkin, Malcolm Frager; Television and radio, Japan, UK, Germany, Netherlands, France, Spain, Mexico, USA, Israel, USSR; Various films; Played the Walton concerto at the Festival Hall, London, 1993. Shostakovich 1st Concerto at the 1993 Proms. Recordings: Bach Sonatas, with Martha Argerich; Bach, 6 Cello Solo Suites; Schumann Cello Concerto with Vienna Philharmonic, Leonard Bernstein; Brahms Double Concerto with Gidon Kremer, Vienna Philharmonic, Leonard Bernstein; Haydn Concertos with the Chamber Orchestra of Europe. Honours: All Russian Cellists Competition, 1965; Tchaikovsky International Competition, Moscow, 1966; Gaspar Cassado International Competition, Florence, 1973; Grand Prix du Disque, Paris; Record Academy Prize, Tokyo, 1985 and 1989. Hobbies: Music. Current Management: Intermusica Artists Management, London, England. Address: 138 Meerlaan, 1900 Overijse, Belgium.

MAISURADZE Badry, b. 1967, Georgia, Russia. Singer (Tenor). Career: Frequent recitals, concerts and opera appearances throughout Europe and in Russia; Contestant at the 1995 Cardiff Singer of the World Competition; Repertory includes Donizetti's Il Duca d'Alba, Carmen, Tosca, Verdi's Il Corsaro and songs by Rachmaninov. Address: c/o Cardiff Singer of the World, BBC Wales, Music Department Broadcasting House, Llandaff, Cardiff CF5 2YQ, Wales.

MAIXNEROVA Martina, b. 20 Sept 1947, Prague, Czechoslovakia, now Singapore Citizen; Solist; Chamber Pianist; Professor of Piano. m. Pavel Pranti, violinist, 24 June 1972, 2 sons. Education: Graduated with Distinction, Conservatory of Music, Prague, 1966; Master's Degree with Distinction, Academy of Musical Arts, Prague, 1972. Career: Professor of Piano in Singapore, 1980; Assistant Professor of Piano at the Academy of Musical Arts, Prague, 1975-80; Professor of Piano at the Music School for Especially Gifted Children in Prague, 1970-73; Adjudicator at the First Rolex Piano Competition in Singapore, 1987; Festival appearances in England, Germany, Czechoslovakia, Austria, Poland, USA and Korea; Solo appearances with orchestras including: Guest soloist with the Prague Chamber Orchestra without a Conductor, 1980; Guest soloist with the Singapore Symphony Orchestra, 1981, England, Sweden, Czechoslovakia and Japan. Memberships: ARS Cameralis Ensemble, 1976-80; Prague Baroque Ensemble, 1973-80. Address: 110 Wishart Road, 03-07 Pender Court, Singapore 0409.

MAJOR Malvina (Lorraine) (Dame), b. 28 Jan 1943, Hamilton, New Zealand. Opera Singer (Soprano). m. Winston William Richard Fleming, 16 Jan 1965, dec 1990, 1 son, 2 daughters. Education: Grade VIII, Piano, Singing, Theory, Convent at Ngaruawahia, Waikato; Singing continued under Dame Sister Mary Leo, St Mary's Music School, Auckland, 1960-65 and Ruth Packer, Royal College of Music, London, London Opera Centre, UK, 1965-67. Debut: Camden Town Festival, 1968 in Rossini's La Donna del Lago. Career includes: Performances as: Belle, Belle of New York, New Zealand, 1963; Pamina, Magic Flute, London Opera Centre, 1967; 1st non Mormon Soloist to sing with Mormon Tabernacle Choir, 1987; Matilda in Elisabetta Regina d'Inghilterra, Camden Town, 1968; Rosina, Barber of Seville, Salzburg (conductor, Claudio Abbado), 1968-69; Gala Concert, King & Queen of Belgium, Centenary Antwerp Zoological Society, 1969; Marguerite, Gounod's Faust, Neath & London, 1969; Bruckner's Te Deum, conductor Daniel Barenboim, 1968; Cio Cio San, Madam Butterfly; Widow, The Merry Widow; Gilda in Rigoletto; Tosca; Constanze in Die Entführung; Arminda in La Finta Giardiniera, Brussels, 1986; Donna Elvira, Don Giovanni, Brighton Festival, 1987; Donna Anna in Don Giovanni at Sydney, Australia, 1987; Operas include recent productions of Rosalinda (Die Fledermaus) and Lucia di Lammermoor, Mimi in La Bohème and Constanze in New York and Australia; Sang Arminda at Lausanne, 1989, Constanze with the Lyric Opera of Queensland; Season 1992-93 with Lucia at Adelaide, Arminda at Salzburg, Violetta and Gilda at Wellington; Sang in Eugene Onegin and Don Giovanni with Wellington City Opera, 1997. Recordings: To The Glory of God, 1964; L'amico Fritz, opera (Caterina), 1969; Songs for All Seasons, Mahler Symphony No 4, 1970; Scottish Soldiers Abroad, 1975; Alleluia, 1974; Operatic Arias, conductor John Matheson, 1987; La Finta Giardiniera, Brussels. Contributions to: London Sunday Times (article by Desmond Shawe-Taylor). Honours: New Zealand Mobil Song Quest, 1963; Melbourne Sun Aria, Australia, 1964; Kathleen Ferrier Scholarship, London, 1966; OBE, 1985; DBE, 1991; Hon D Litt, 1993; Hon D Waik, 1993. Hobbies: Golf; Family. Address: P O Box 4184, New Plymouth, New Zealand.

MAJOR Margaret, b. 1932, Coventry, England. Violist. Education: Royal College of Music. Debut: Wigmore Hall, London, 1955 with Gerald Moore. Career: Principal Viola, Netherlands Chamber Orchestra, 1955-59; Oromonte Trio, 1958-65; Principal Viola, Philomusica of London, 1960-65; Viola, Aeolian String Quartet, 1965-81; Professor of Viola, Royal College of Music, London, 1969-. Recordings: Complete String Quartets of Haydn; Late Beethoven Quartets; Ravel and Debussy Quartets; Complete Mozart Viola Quintets. Honours: Lionel Tertis Prize, 1951; International Music Association Concert Award, 1955; MA, University of Newcastle upon Tyne, 1970; FRCM, 1992. Hobby: Good Food. Address: 13 Upper Park Road, Kingston Hill, Kingston-upon-Thames, Surrey, KT2 5LB, England.

MAKINO Yutaka, b. 5 July 1930, Tokyo, Japan. Composer. Education: Studied with Koscak Yamada. Career: Freelance composer of operas and instrumental works. Compositions: Operas Ayame, Radio Opera, CBS, 1960; Mushrooms, comic opera, Tokyo, 1961; Benkei in the Boat, Tokyo, 1962; Hanjo, Tokyo, 1963; Snow-Woman, Yokohama, 1964; The Origin of the Deer Dance, Tokyo, 1967; The Millionaire Ayaginu, comic opera, Tokyo, 1979; The Tale of Ogetsu, 1990. Honours: Argentine Music Festival Prize, 1955; National Arts Festival Grant Prize, 1960; Spanish Radio Prize, 1962. Address: c/o JASRAC, Jasrac

House 7-13, 1-Chome Nishishimbashi, Minato-ku, Tokyo 105, Japan.

MAKLAKIEWICZ Tadeusz (Wojciech), b. 20 October 1922, Mszczonow, Poland. Composer. m. Maria Pawluskiewicz, 4 June 1952, 3 daughters. Education: Department of Law, Jagiellonian University, Krakow, 1949; State High School of Music, 1958. Debut: Festival of Polish Music, Warsaw, 1951. Career: Dean of Music Education Faculty, 1968-69; Deputy Rector, 1969-71, State High School of Music, Warsaw; Head of Music Education Department, 1973; Rector, 1975-78. Compositions: The Kurpie Suite, for Soprano and Mixed Choir a Cappella, 1957; Cantata: Peace; Friendship; Work; Epitaphium for Symphony Orchestra, 1959; Rondo for Clarinet and Piano or Orchestra; Vienna, Vocalisation for Soprano and Orchestra, 1964; Polonais of the Tank Corps; The Clocks are Ringing; Songs for Children for Voice and Piano; Mazovian Dance for Piano, 1977; Hands Friendly With Hands, for Mixed Choir and Organ, 1977; Quintet for Flute, 2 Clarinets, Bassoon and Harp, 1977; Above Clouds, for Mixed Choir, 1978; March for Brass Band, 1979; Salvum Fac, for Mixed Choir, 1981; The Bible Triptych, for 2 Clarinets and Bassoon, 1982; Suite for Cello, 1983; The Gorals Mass, for Mixed Choir and Organ, 1983; Chryzea Phorminx Ode for 4 Trombones, 1984; Arch of Triumph, for Woodwind Quintet, 1984; Wistful Songs for Baritone and Piano, 1985; Love Letters, Variations for String Orchestra, 1985; Ave Maria, for 3 Violins, 1986; At Zelazowa Wola, 3 Stanzas for Baritone, Flute, Alto, Horn and Harp, 1986; Violin Concerto for Children, 1987; A Memory, for 3 Cellos, 1987; A Flag for Female Choir, 1988; Credo, Motet for Mixed Choir and Organ, 1992; Ave Maria in Honour of Notre Dame of Lourdes, for Soprano and Organ, 1993; Romantic Swans, for Soprano and Piano, 1994; Aria for Soprano and Orchestra, 1995. Memberships: President, Authors Agency Limited, Warsaw, till 1985; Union of Polish Composers; President, Society of Authors ZAIKS, Warsaw, 1993-97; Vice-President, Polish Board of Société Européene de Culture, 1994-. Hobbies: History and Culture of Ancient Greece and Rome. Address: Smolna 8/90, 00-375 Warsaw, Poland.

MAKRIS Andreas, b. 7 Mar 1930, Salonika, Greece. Composer. m. Margaret Lubbe, 12 June 1959, 2 sons. Education: Phillips University, Enid, Oklahoma, USA, 1950; Postgraduate studies, Kansas City Conservatory, Missouri, and Mannes College of Music, 1956; Aspen Music Festival; Fontainebleau School, France; Studied with Nadia Boulanger. Career: Compositions premiered and performed, USA, Canada, Europe, South America, Japan, USSR; Appeared twice with premieres, national TV networks, USA, 1978, 1984; Composer-in-residence, National Symphony Orchestra, 1979-90; Advisor to Matislav Rostropovich for new music, 1979-90; His complete short works performed on Voice of America Radio, 1980, 1982. Compositions include: Scherzo for Violins, 1966; Concerto for Strings, 1966; Aegean Festival, 1967; Concertino for Trombone, 1970; Anamnesis, 1970; Viola Concerto, 1970; Efthymia, 1972; Five Miniatures, 1972; Mediterranean Holiday, 1974; Fantasy and Dance for saxophone, 1974; Sirens, 1976; Chromatokinesis, 1978; In Memory, 1979; Variations and Song for orchestra, 1979; Fanfare Alexander, 1980; 4th of July March, 1982; Life-Nature Symphonic Poem, 1983; Concerto Fantasia for Violin and Orchestra, 1983; Caprice Tonatonal, 1986; Intrigues for solo clarinet and wind ensemble, 1987; Concertante for Violin, Cello, French Horn, Clarinet, Percussion and Orchestra, 1988; Sonata for Cello and Piano, 1989; Symphony to Youth, 1989; Trilogy for Orchestra, 1990; Alleluia for mixed chorus and brass quintet, 1990; Concertino for organ, flute and string quartet, 1992; A Symphony for soprano and strings, 1992; Woodwind Quintet, 1993; Decalog - Ten Songs for Young Students, 1995; Various works for violin, string quartets, voice quintets, duets, arrangements of Paganini and Bach; Compositions for special anniversaries and festival openings. Address: 11204 Oak Leaf Drive, Silver Spring, MD 20901, USA.

MAKRIS Cynthia, b. 1956, Sterling, CO, USA. Singer (Soprano). Education: Studied at the University of Colorado and Adams State College. Career: Sang Alice Ford, Donna Elvira and Tosca while a student; European debut at Graz as Violetta; Stadttheater Freiburg, 1980-82 as Constanze, Pamina, Violetta and Saffi in Zigeunerbaron; Sang at Bielefeld from 1982 as Donna Anna, Agathe, Marenka, Lucia di Lammermoor and Manon Lescaut and in revivals of Schreker's Irrelohe and Max Brand's Maschinist Hopkins; Member of the Dortmund Opera from 1986 as Desdemona, Leonora in Il Trovatore, Amelia in Un Ballo in Maschero, and Arabella; Other roles include Marietta in Die Tote Stadt at Dusseldorf and at Antwerp, 1995, Marie in Wozzeck at Karlsruhe, Mozart's Countess, Wagner's Eva and Freia and the Empress in Die Frau ohne Schatten; Has sung the title role in Salome at Dortmund, Berlin Staatsoper and Deustche Opera, Tokyo and Scottish Opera at Glasgow, 1990. Address: c/o Opernhaus, Kuhstrasse 12, D-4600 Dortmund, Germany.

MAKSYMIUK Jerzy, b. 9 Apr 1936, Grodno, Poland. Conductor. Education: Studied Violin, piano, conducting, composition, Warsaw Conservatory, Poland. Career: Conducted, Warsaw Grant Theatre where later founded Polish Chamber Orchestra; Principal Conductor, Polish National Radio Orchestra, 1975-77; Touring Eastern Europe and USA; United Kingdom debut with Polish Chamber Orchestra, 1977, since appearing in Western Europe, Scandinavia, Japan, Australia, New Zealand, Salzburg and Edinburgh Festivals, festivals at Aix, Flanders, Granada, Lucerne, Vienna, BBC Promenade Concerts in London; Guest Conductor, Northern Sinfonia, Scottish Chamber Orchestra, BBC Philharmonic Orchestra, 1980-; Chief Conductor, BBC Scottish Symphony Orchestra, 1983-93; Guest Conductor, London Symphony Orchestra, London Philharmonic Orchestra, Tokyo Metropolitan Orchestra, Indianapolis Symphony, Sydney Symphony; Conducted Don Giovanni for English National Opera, 1991 (debut), Die Fledermaus, 1993; Led Premiere of Macmillan's The Confession of Isobel Gowdie, Proms, 1990 and Robin Holloway's Violin Concerto, 1992; Season 1992-93 with the Royal Liverpool Philharmonic, the Residentié and Limburg Orchestra and the Hong Kong Philharmonic. Recordings: Haydn, Bach, Vivaldi, Tchaikovsky, Mendelssohn (EMI); Music for Pleasure; Schumann with London Philharmonic Orchestra and Devoyon; Shostakovich Piano Concerto with Dimitri Alexeev and the English Chamber Orchestra (Classics for Pleasure). Honours: Honorary DLitt, Strathclyde University, 1990; Gramophone Award for Contemporary Music, 1993; Honorary Title, Conductor Laureate, BBC Scottish Symphony. Current Management. IMG Artists. Address: Media House, 3 Burlington Lane, Chiswick, London W4 2TH, England.

MALACHOVSKY Martin, b. 23 Jan 1968, Bratislava, Slovakia. Opera Singer (bass). m. Iveta Pasková, 1 daughter. Education: Academy of Arts, Bratislava, 1986-92; Hochschule für Musik und darstellende Kunst in Vienna, Masterclasses - E Nesterenko, 1990; Conservatoire National superieur de Paris (Prof Gottlieb), 1991. Debut: Slovak National Theatre, 1991. Career: J Massenet, Don Quixote; G Rossini, Il Barbiere di Siviglia (Don Basilio); G Puccini, La Bohème (Colline), Slovak National Theatre, Bratislava; J Offenbach: Les Contes d'Hoffman (Luther Crespel), Opera Comique, Paris, 1996; W A Mozart, Le nozze di Figaro, Bartolo, 1995; Mozart Festival, Madrid, 1992; Maifestspiele, Wiesbaden, 1996; Ch Gounod: Faust (Wagner), National Theatre Prague, 1996. Recordings: La Damnation de Faust - H Berlioz - Director Jerome Kaltenbach. Honour: 3rd Place, International A Dvorak's Singing Competition in Carlsbad, 1988. Membership: Slovak Music Union. Hobby: Travel. Address: Interartists, Slovakia. Address: Gorkého 13, 811 01 Bratislava, Slovakia.

MALAGNINI Mario, b. 1959, Salo, Italy. Singer, Tenor. Education: Studied at the Brescia Conservatory and the Giuseppe Verdi Conservatory, Milan with Piermirando Ferraro; Further study with Tito Gobbi and Giuseppe di Stefano. Career: Sang in Frankfurt and Milan, La Scala, 1985, as Radames, and in IL Corsaro; Returned to La Scala 1986-87, as Alfredo and Ismaele in Nabucco; Verona Arena from 1987, as Foresto in Attila, Pinkerton, Riccardo and Radames; Appeared as Don José at Glyndebourne 1987, and in a concert performance of La Battaglia di Legnano at Carnegie Hall, as Arrigo; Further engagements at Florence, as Pinkerton and Gabriele Adorno, Nimes and Monte Carlo, Pollione in Norma, Vienna, Berlin, Houston, Budapest and Seoul, 1988; Teatro La Fenice Venice, 1990 as Rodolfo in Leoncavallo's Bohème. Recordings: Emilia di Liverpool, with the Philharmonia Orchestra, Opera Rara; Norma conducted by Emil Tchakarov. Honours: Winner, Tito Gobbi Competition, 1983; Concorso Enrico Caruso and Belvedere Competition, Vienna, 1984. Address: c/o Arena di Verona, Piazza Bra 28, 1-37121 Verona, Italy.

MALANIUK Ira, b. 29 Jan 1923, Stanislava, Poland. Singer, Mezzo-Soprano. Education: Studied with Adam Didur in Lwow and with Anna Bahr-Mildenburg in Vienna; Salzburg Mozarteum. Debut: Graz 1945. Career: Sang in Zurich from 1947, notably in The Rake's Progress, 1951; Bayreuth Festival 1951-53, as Brangaene, Magdalena, Fricka and Waltraute, Munich Opera from 1952, as Orpheus, Lady Macbeth and Bartók's Judith; Vienna Opera from 1956; Covent Garden 1953, as Adelaide in Arabella, with the Munich Company; Paris Opera 1956, in Das Rheingold; Salzburg Festival from 1956, notably in the 1958 local premiere of Barber's Vanessa; Concert performances from 1966; Professor at the Graz Conservatory from 1971. Recordings: Die Meistersinger, Arabella, Aida, Cosi fan tutte, Le nozze di Figaro; Waltraute in Götterdämmerung, conducted by Clemens Krauss, Bayreuth 1953; Brangaene in Tristan und Isolde, under Karajan, Bayreuth, 1952.

MALAS Spiro, b. 28 Jan 1933, Baltimore, Maryland, USA. Bass-baritone. m. Marlene Kleinman. Education: Studied with E Nagy, Peabody Conservatory of Music, Baltimore; E Baklor and D Ferro, NY; Coached by I Chicagov. Debut: Marco, Gianni Schicchi, Baltimore Civic Opera, 1959. Career: NYC Opera debut, Spinellocchio in Gianni Schicchi, 1961; Toured Australia with Sutherland-Williamson International grand Opera Co 1965; Covent Garden debut, London as Sulpice in La fille du Régiment, 1966; Chicago Lyric Opera debut as Assur in Semiramide, 1971; Metropolitan Opera debut NY as Sulpice, 1983; Other roles have been the Sacristan in Tosca, Zuniga, Mozart's Bartolo and Frank in Die Fledermaus; Sang Frank Maurrant in the British premiere of Weill's Street Scene, Glasgow 1989; Don Isaac in Prokofiev's Duenna at the 1989 Wexford Festival; Vancouver 1990, as Baron Zeta in The Merry Widow; Many concert engagements; Teacher, Peabody Conservatory of Music. Recordings. For Decca-London. Honours: Winner, Metropolitan Opera Auditions, 1961. Address: c/o Columbia Artists Management Inc, 165 West 57th Street, NY 10019, USA.

MALAS-GODLOEWSKA, b. 1955, Warsaw, Poland, Singer, Coloratura Soprano. Education: Studied in warsaw. Career: Sang at the Warsaw Opera from 1978 as Zerbinetta, the Queen of Night, Rosina, Norina, and Constanze in Die Entführung; Leading roles at the Vienna Volksoper, Paris Opera-Comique, Nantes, Olympia, Basle, Berne, Wiesbaden and Dresden; Sang Celia in Mozart's Lucio Silla, at Nanterre and Brussels, 1986; Sang Madeleine in Le Postillon de Longjumeau at the Grand Theatre Geneva, 1990; Queen of Night in new productions of Die Zauberflöte at Houston and Paris, Opera Bastille, 1991; Théâtre du Châtelet Paris in L'Enfant et les Sortilèges; Concert performances in Britain, Switzerland, Poland, Germany, Holland, Belgium, and France, Gstaad Festival, 1987 in Beethoven's Ninth, conducted by Yehudi Menuhin. Honours: Winner, Toulouse International Competition, 1978. Address: c/o Opera de la Bastille, 120 Rue de Lyon, F-75012 Paris, France.

MALASPINE Massimiliano, b. 17 May 1925, Fara Novarese, Italy. Singer, Bass. Education: Studied with Lina Pagliughi. Career: Appearances from 1959 at such Italian Opera centres as La Scala Milan, Teatro San Carlo Naples, Teatro Fenice Venice and the Teatro Regio Parma; Further engagements at Genoa, Turin, Brussels, Munich Staatsoper, Montreal, Toulouse, Frankfurt, Rio de Janeiro, Paris, Barcelona and Miami; Roles have included Colline in La Bohème, Oroveso in Norma; Ptolomey in Giulio Cesare; Sarastro and Verdi's Padre Guardiano; Banquo and Ramphis; Teacher of singing in Milan after retiring from stage. Address: c/o Teatro alla Scalla, Via Filodrammatici 2, 20121 Milan, Italy.

MALCOLM Carlos (Edmond), b. 24 Nov 1945, Havana City, Cuba. Composer; Pianist. 1 son, 1 daughter. Education: Pre-university studies, Vedado Institute, Havan, 1963. Started Musical education, 1957; Piano Graduate, Amadeo Roldan Conservatory; Degree in Musical Composition, The Superior Institute of Arts, Havana, 1983. Debut: National Theatre, Cuba, 1964. Career: Composer and Pianist; National Modern Dance Ensemble, 1964-68; Cuban Institute of Radio, occasionally Cuban Institute of Film, 1968-70; Belongs to The Staff of Composers of The Ministry of Culture of Cuba, 1970-; Toured throughout Mexico, Jamaica, Equador, playing own works, teaching and lecutring; Works have been played in New Music Concerts, Warsaw Autumn, Berlin's Biennalle, Japan, Argentina, Hungary. Compositions: Quetzalcoat!, Song of the Feathered Serpent, for flute and piano; Beny More redivivo, for string quartet; Adagio for piano, 4 hands; El Remediano; Eclosion; Articulations for piano; 13 studies for piano; Songs set to texts by Caribbean Poets; Rumours, for violin, cello and piano; Meditation for piano, all composed between 1963-90; New Music Concerts: ACCORDES quartet played, Benny More redivivo; Played with flautist Robert Aitken, Quetzalcoat! for flute and piano; Other compiositions for piano solo,at Toronto's Premier Grand Theater, Royal Conservatory of Music; Bayreuth's Festival of Music; AMBER Trio, Israel, played piano trio, Rumours and first performance of Meditation for piano solo, Germany, 1990; University La Salle of Philadelphia. Address: ul Piekna 16, m2, 00-539 Warsaw, Poland.

MALFITANO Catherine, b. 18 Apr 1948, New York City, New York, USA. Singer (Soprano). Education: High School of Music and Art; Manhattan School of Music; With violinist father and dancer/actress mother. Debut: Nannetta in Falstaff, Central City Opera, 1972. Career: With Minnesota Opera, 1973, New York City Opera, 1973-79, debut as Mimi/La Bohème; Netherlands Opera: Susanna in Figaro, 1974, Eurydice, 1975, Mimi, 1977; Salzburg Festival: Servilia in Tito, 1976, 1977, 1979, 3 Hoffmann roles, 1981, 1982, Salome, 1992, 1993, Elvira in Giovanni, 1994, 1995; Met debut as Gretel, 1979, returning for many other roles; Vienna Staatsoper: Violetta, 1982, Manon, 1984, Grete in Schreker's Der Ferne Klang, 1991, Salome and Butterfly, 1993; Maggio Musicale Florence: Suor Angelica, 1983, Jenny in Weill's Mahagonny, 1990, Salome, 1994; Teatro Comunale, Florence: Antonia in Hoffmann, 1980-81, Mimi, 1983, Faust, 1985, Butterfly, 1988, Poppea, 1992; Munich: Berg's Lulu, 1985, Mimi, 1986, Daphne, 1988; Covent Garden: Susanna, Zerlina, 1976, Butterfly, 1988, Lina (Stiffelio), Tosca, Tatyana, 1993, Salome, 1995; Berlin Deutsche Oper: Butterfly, 1987, Amelia in Boccanegra, Mimi, Susanna, 1989, Salome, 1990; Berlin Staatsoper, Marie (Wozzeck), 1994, Leonore (Fidelio), 1995; Geneva: Fiorilla (Turco), 1985, Poppea, Manon, 1989, Leonore, 1994; La Scala: Daphne, 1988, Butterfly, 1990; Lyric Opera, Chicago: Susanna, 1975, Violetta, 1985, Lulu, 1987, Barber's Cleopatra, 1991, Butterfly, 1991-92, Liu, 1992; Engaged as Jenny in Mahagonny for the 1998 Salzburg Festival; World premiere roles created: Conrad Susa's Transformations, 1973, Bilby's Doll (Carlisle Floyd), 1976, Thomas Pasatieri's Washington Square, 1976, William Bolcom's McTeague, 1992. Recordings: Rossini Stabat Mater, conductor Muti; Gounod Roméo et Juliette, conductor Plasson; Strauss's Salome, conductor Dohnányi; Music for Voice and Violin with Joseph Malfitano; Others; Videos include Tosca with Domingo; Stiffelio with Carreras and Salome. Honours: Emmy, Best Performance in Tosca film. Current Management: Tom Graham, IMG Artists Europe, Media House, 3 Burlington Lane, London W4 2TH, England; Rita Schütz, Artists Management Zürich, Rütistrasse 52, 8044 Zürich-Gockhausen, Switzerland.

MALGOIRE Jean-Claude, b. 25 Nov 1940, Avignon, France. Conductor; Oboist. Education: Studied in Avignon and at the Paris Conservatory, prizes for oboe and chamber music, 1960. Career: 1966 founded La Grande Ecurie et la Chambre du Roy, for the performance of Baroque music; Founded Florilegium Musicum de Paris; Concerts of medieval and Renaissance Music; Handel's Rinaldo at the Festival Hall, London; Rameau's Hippolyte et Aricie for the English Bach Festival at Covent Garden; Campra's Tancrède for the Copenhagen Royal Opera and at the Aix-en-Provence Festival 1986; L'Incoronazione di Poppea at the Stockholm Opera; Rameau's Les Indes Galantes at the Versailles Opera Royal; Conducted Cephale et Procris by Elisabeth Jacquet de la Guerre at St Etienne, 1989, Kreutzer's Paul et Virginie at Tourcoing; Season 1992 with Lully's Alceste at the Théâtre des Champs-Elysées, Paris, a Vivaldi pastiche, Montezuma, at Monte Carlo and Gnecco's Prova di un'opera seria at Montpellier; Conducted Salieri's Falstaff at Tourcoing, 1996. Recordings: Rinaldo; Handel's Xerxes; Hippolyte et Aricie and Les Indes Galantes; Tancrède; Cavalli's Ercole Amante; Handel Concerti Grossi Op 3 and 6, Water and Fireworks Music; Lully Alceste, Psyché and Le Bourgeois gentilhomme; Vivaldi Beatus Vir, Gloria and flute concertos; Charpentier Messe de Minuit; Renaissance music with the Florilegium Musicum de Paris. Honours: Prix Internationale de Geneve, Oboe, 1968. Address: La Grand Ecurie et la Chambre du Roy, 9 Place des Federées, F-93160 Noisy le Grand, France.

MALIPIERO Riccardo, b. 24 July 1914, Milan, Italy. Composer. Education: Studied at the Milan Conservatory, 1930-1937 and with his uncle Gian Francesco Malipiero, at the Venice Conservatory 1937-39. Career: Began career as a pianist, interrupted by WWII; After WWII began as Composer and Music Critic; Organized the first International Congress of Dodecaphonic Music, Milan 1949; Lectured in USA 1954 & 1959; Master classes at the Di Tella Institute Buenos Aires, 1963 and the University of Maryland, 1969; Director of the Varese Liceo Musicale 1969-, 1984. Compositions: Operas Minnie la candida 1942; La Donna e Mobile 1954; TV opera Battono alla Porta 1962; L'Ultima Eva, 1995; Orchestral: Piano Concerto, 1937; 2 Cello Concertos, 1938 and 1959; Balletto 1939; Piccolo Concerto for piano and orchestra, 1945; Antico sole for soprano and orchestra 1947; Cantata sacra for soprano, chorus and orchestra 1947; 3 Symphonies 1949, 1956, 1959; Violin Concerto 1952; Studi 1953; Overture-Divertimento del Ritorno 1953; Concerto for piano and ensemble, 1955; Concerto Breve for ballerina and chamber orchestra 1956; Cantata di Natale for soprano, chorus and orchestra 1959; Concerto per Dimitri for piano and orchestra, 1961; Nykteghersia 1962; Cadencias 1964; Muttermusik 1966; Mirages 1966; Carnet de Notes 1967; Rapsodia for violin and orchestra 1967; Serenata per Alice Tully 1969; Monologo for male voice and strings 1969; Concerto for Piano Trio and orchestra 1976; 2 Piano Concertos 1974; Requiem 1975; Ombre 1986; Go Placidly for baritone and chamber orchestra 1975; Loneliness for soprano and orchestra 1987; Due Arie for soprano and orchestra, 1990; Lieder études for soprano and piano, 1991; Chamber: Musik 1 for cello and 9 instruments 1938; 3 String Quartets 1941, 1954, 1960; Violin Sonata 1956; Piano Quintet 1957; Musica da camera for wind quintet 1959; Oboe Sonata 1959; 6 Poesie di Dylan Thomas 1959 for soprano and 10 instruments; Mosaico for wind and string quartets, 1961; Preludio, Adagio e Finale for soprano, 5 percussionists and piano 1963; In Time of Daffodils, Cummings, for soprano, baritone and 7 instruments 1964; Nuclei for 2 pianos and percussion 1966; Cassazione for string sextet 1967; Piano Trio 1968; Ciaccona di Davide for viola and piano 1970; Giber Folia for clarinet and piano 1973; Memoria for flute and harpsichord 1973; Winter quintet for quintet 1976; Apresmiro for 11 instruments 1982; Voicequintet for soprano and string quartet 1988; Piano Music. Address: Via A Stradella 1, 20129, Milano, Italy.

MALIPONTE Adriana, b. 26 Dec 1938, Brescia, Italy. Singer (Soprano). Education: Conservatoire de Mulhouse with Suzanne Stappen Bergmann and with Carmen Melis in Milan; Protegée of Rosa Ponselle, Baltimore. Debuts: Paris Opera as Micaela in Carmen, 1962-63; Gran Teatro Liceo, Barcelona with Massenet's Manon, 1964. Career: Sang in San Carlo Naples, Lisbon, Milan, Marseille, Tokyo and in all major operas of the world; Has wide repertoire of some 60 roles; UK debut, 1967, at Glyndebourne Festival in Elisir d'amore; La Scala debut in Manon with Pavarotti, Mar 1970, returning in I Masnadieri, 1978, and La Bohème, Elisir d'amore, Carmen, Turandot, (Liu), Luisa Miller; Metropolitan Opera debut in La Bohème with Pavarotti, 1971; Japan, in La Bohème, (Mimi), Traviata and Carmen, 1975, returning in La Bohème, with Carlos Kleiber director, 1981; Pagliacci with Placido Domingo, Covent Garden, 1976; La Bohème and Traviata, Vienna Staatsoper and at Mozart Festival, director Karl Böhm, 1977; Iris at Newark Symphony Hall; La Traviata with A A Krauss, Pretoria, 1983; Maria Stuarda, director Santi, and Guglielmo Tell, Zurich, 1986-87, 1990; Debut in Adriana Lecouvreur, Tenerife, 1989-90; Recent concerts in Taipei, also Carmen, Turandot and Liu, 1994; Gave recital at Salle Gaveau, Paris, 1994. Recordings include: Micaela in Carmen, with Bernstein, 1973; Le Villi (Puccini), RCA; Les Pêcheurs des Perles; Pagliacci with Placido Domingo, video. Honours: Winner, Génève International d'Execution Musicale, 1960; Prix Villabella, Grand Prix du Disque, 1965; Grammy, USA, 1973; Maschera d'Argento, Campione d'Italia, 1976; Premio Illica, 1983; Rosa d'Oro, 1984; Vittoria Alata, Brescia, 1985; Chevalier des Arts et des Lettres, Académie de France. Address: Via Macchi 75, Milan, Italy.

MALIS David, b. 1961, USA. Singer (Baritone). Career: Many appearances in concert and opera in North America and Europe, from 1985; Season 1995 with performances in Athens, Buenos Aires from Pittsburgh; Metropolitan Opera in Peter Grimes and La Bohème; Sang Belcore at San Diego, 1996. Honours include: Winner, 1985 Cardiff Singer of the World Competition. Address: c/o Metropolitan Opera, Lincoln Center, New York, NY 10023, USA.

MALMBERG Urban, b. 29 Mar 1962, Stockholm, Sweden. Singer, Baritone. Education: Sang in the Boy's Choir of the Stockholm Opera and appeared as First Boy in the 1974 Bergman movie version of Die Zauberflöte; Studied in Stockholm with Helge Brilioth and Erik Saeden. Career: Sang at Stockholm in works by Peter Maxwell Davies and Janake Hillerud; Hamburg Staatsoper from 1983, as Malatesta, Don Pasquale, Masetto, Papageno, Schaunard in La Bohème, Harlequin in Ariadne and in Nono's Intolleranza and Die Gespenstersonate by Reimann; Guest appearances in Dusseldorf, Las Palmas, London, Moscow, San Francisco and Tokyo; Other roles have included Guglielmo and Donner, Brussels and Bonn, 1990, Belcore, Marcello and Lescaut; Season 1992 with Malatesta at Vancouver and Frère Leon in Messiaen's St François d'Assise at the Salzburg Festival; Concert repertoire includes the St Matthew Passion, Beethoven's Ninth, Ein Deutsches Requiem and Peer Gynt. Recordings: Ariadne auf Naxos and Les Contes d'Hoffmann; The Count in Schreker's Der Schatzgräber, with Hamburg forces. Address: Hamburgische Staatsoper, Grosse-Theaterstrasse 34, D-2000 Hamburg 36, Germany.

MALMBORG Gunila, b. 26 Feb 1933, Lulea, Sweden. Singer, Soprano. m. Lars af Malmborg. Education: Royal Stockholm Academy of Music. Debut: Stockholm 1960, as Marzeline in Fidelio. Career: Guest appearances in Copenhagen, Oslo, Monte Carlo, Cologne and Kiel; Munich 1968, as Salome and Aida; Glyndebourne 1965, as Lady Macbeth; Well known in Wagner roles and as Verdi's Abigaille and Amelia, Mozart's Donna Anna, Puccini's Tosca and Turandot and Offenbach's Giulietta. Memberships: Stockholm Opera from 1960. Address: c/o Kungliga Teatern, PO Box 16094, S-10322 Stockholm, Sweden.

MALONE Carol, b. 16 July 1943, Grayson, Kentucky, USA. Singer, Soprano. Education: Studied at the University of Indian at Bloomington, at the Hamburg Musikhochschule and with Joseph Metternich in Cologne. Debut: Cologen 1966, as Aennchen in Der Freischütz. Career: Many appearances at such German opera centres as the State Operas of Hamburg, Munich and Stuttgart, Deutsche Oper am Rhein Dusseldorf, Nationaltheater Mannheim and Frankfurt; Further engagements at Brussels, Vienna Volksoper, Salzburg, San Francisco, Amsterdam, Venice and the Edinburgh Festival; Sang with the Deutsche Oper Berlin in the premiere of Love's Labour Lost by Nabokov, Brussels, 1973 and as Zerlina in Don Giovanni, Berlin, 1988; Other roles have included Marzelline, Nannetta, Despina, Susanna, Blondchen, Sophie, Adele in Die Fledermaus and Adelaide in Blacher's Preussiches Märchen; Many concert appearances. Recordings: Trionfo d'Afrodite by Orff. Address: c/o Deutsche Oper Berlin, Richard Wagnerstrasse 10, D-1000 Berlin, Germany.

MALSBURY Angela (Mary), b. 5 May 1945, Preston, Lancashire, England. Clarinettist. m. David Pettit, 24 July 1965, 1 son. Education: Beauchamp School, Kibworth, Leicester, 1960-62; Associated Board Scholar, Royal College of Music, London, 1962-66; ARCM, Clarinet Teacher and Piano Teacher; LRAM, Clarinet Performer. Debut: Concert debut, Royal Festival Hall, with London Mozart Players, 1976. Career: Concerto Soloist with major orchestras world wide; Clarinet Quintets including classical and contemporary repertoire; Member of De Saram Trio and Cameristi of London, Musicians of the Royal Exchange and Albion Ensembles, Principal Clarinet of London Mozart Players; Clarinet Professor, Royal Academy of Music. Recordings: Richard Baker's Musical Menagerie, Cameristi of London. Recordings: Mozart Serenade for 13 Wind Instruments (Academy of St Martins, Albion and LMP); Mozart, Clarinet Quintet with the Coull String Quartet (LDR); Mozart, Clarinet Concerto, London Mozart Players and Jane Glover (ASV). Honours: Philip Cardew Memorial Prize, 1963; Marjorie Whyte Prize, 1964; Mozart Memorial Prize, 1974; Hon. RAM, 1991. Memberships: Musicians Union. Hobbies: Cooking; Swimming. Current Management: John Wright. Address: 40 Greenford Avenue, Hanwell, London W7 3QP, England.

MALTA Alexander, b. 28 Sept 1942, Visp, Wallis Canton, Switzerland. Singer, Bass. Education: Studied with Desider Kovacz in Zurich, Barra-Carracciolo in Milan and Enzo Mascherini in Florence. Debut: Stuttgart 1962, as the Monk in Don Carlos. Debut: US 1976, with the San Francisco Opera. Career: Sang in Brunswick, Munich, Berlin, Vienna, Frankfurt, Geneva, Paris and Venice from 1966; Chicago Lyric Opera in Ariadne auf Naxos; Seattle Opera as Osmin in Die Entfuhrung; Brussels Opera from 1979, notably in Wozzeck, Lulu and Schubert's Fierrabras; Rome Opera as Orestes in Elektra; Maggio Musicale Florence as Wagner's Fasolt and Landgrave; La Scala Milan in Handel's Ariodante; Hamburg Opera as Golaud, Pelléas et Mélisande, Colline in La Bohème, Die Fledermaus, Munich State Opera, Hoffmann, Mèse, Adriana Lecouvreur, Deutsche Oper Berlin as Nicolai's Falstaff, Gounod's Mefistofele and Rocco in Fidelio; Salzburg Festival in Carmen and Don Giovanni, conducted by Karajan; Covent Garden 1985, in Tippett's King Priam, title role; Sang the Voice of Neptune in Idomeneo at the 1990 Salzburg Festival. Recordings: Lady Macbeth of the Mtsenk District; Carmen, Don Giovanni and the Bruckner Te Deum; Rigoletto; Zar und Zimmermann; Wozzeck. Address: c/o Harrison/Parrot Ltd, 12 Penzance Place, London, W11 4PA, England.

MALTA Alvaro, b. 19 May 1931, Lisbon, Portugal. Singer (Bass). Education: Studied in Lisbon. Career: Has sung at the Teatro San Carlos Lisbon, as Figaro, Papageno, Mephistophélès and Klingsor further appearances until 1984 as the Commendatore, Wurm in Luisa Miller, Ramphis and Trulove in The Rake's Progress; Guest engagements in Italy and France and at the Wexford Festival (1977-79) in Herodiade, Tiefland and L'Amore dei tre Re; Other roles have included Monterone, Colline and Des Grieux. Address: c/o Teatro Sao Carlos, Rua Serpa Pinto 9, 1200 Lisbon, Portugal.

MALTMAN Christopher, b. England. Singer (Baritone). Education: Studied at the Royal Academy of Music and with Sesto Bruscantini and Thomas Hampson. Career: Concert engagemnts include Haydn's St Nicholas Mass with the English Chamber Orchestra, Elgar's The Apostles, under Vernon Handley, the Fauré Requiem at the Albert Hall and the Vaughan Williams Serenade to Music with the CBSO; Recitals at the Châtelet, Paris, 1996, and the Wigmore Hall, 1997; Opera includes Silvio in Pagliacci and Billy Budd, for Welsh National Opera, 1997; Hadyn's L'Isola Disabitata and Hasse's Solimano at the Berlin Staatsoper, Tarquinius in The Rape of Lucretia at Montpellier and Raimbaud in Le Comte Ory for Glyndbourne Touring Opera, season 1997-98. Recordings include: Paris in Roméo et Juliette; Serenade to Music; Beethoven Folk Songs; Warlock Songs; Ireland Songs. Honours include: Queen's Commendation for Excellence at the RAM. Address: c/o Lies Askonas Ltd, 6 Henrietta St, London WC2E 8LA, England.

MAMLOK Ursula, b. 1 Feb 1928, Berlin, Germany. Composer. Education: Studied in Berlin and Ecuador, NY with Szell at Mannes College and Manhattan School of Music with Vittorio Viannini; Further study with Wolpe, Steuermann, Shapey and Sessions. Career: Teacher, NYU, 1967-76, Kingsborough Community College, 1972-75, Manhattan School, 1976-; Represented USA at the 1984 International Rostrum of Composers. Compositions: Concerto for strings, 1950; Grasshoppers: 6 Humoresques, 1957; Oboe Concerto, 1974; Concertino for wind quartet, 2 percussion and string orchestra, 1987; Woodwind Quintet, 1956; String Quartet, 1962; Capriccios for oboe and piano, 1968; Variations and Interlude for percussion quartet 1971; Sextet 1978; String Quintet, 1981; From my Garden for violin or viola, 1983; Akarina for flute and ensemble, 1985; Bagatelles for clarinet, violin and cello, 1988; Rhapsody for clarinet, viola and piano, 1989; Stray Birds for soprano, flute and cello, 1963; Hiku settings for soprano and flute, 1967; Der Andreas Garten for mezzo, flutes and harp, 1987; Sunflowers for ensemble, 1990; Five Intermezzi for guitar, 1992; Piano music and pieces for tape. Recordings: Walter Hinrischen Award, American Academy and Institute of Arts and Letters, 1989. Address: c/o ASCAP, ASCAP Building, One Lincoln Plaza, NY 10023, USA.

MANAGER Richetta, Singer (Soprano). Education: Bachelor, Applied Voice, Washburn University of Topeka, Kansas. Career: Leading Artists with Gelsenkirchen Opera, appeared in the Roles of Violetta in La Traviata, Amelia in Un Ballo in Maschera, Alice Ford in Falstaff, Elena in I Vespri

Siciliani, Leonora in La Forza del destino, Nella in Gianni Schicchi, Mimi in La Boheme, Leonore in Fidelio, Tosca, Elsa in Lohengrin, Venus and Elisabeth in Tannhäuser, Agathe in Der Freischütz, The Countess in Le Nozze di Figaro, Donna Anna in Don Giovanni, die Erste Dame in Die Zauberflöte, Cleopatra in Händels Giulio Cesare, and Title Role in Alcina, Giulietta in Les Contes d'Hoffmann, Marie in The Bartered Bride, Rosalinde in Die Fledermaus, Saffi in Der Zigeunerbaron, The Duchess of Parma in Busoni's Dr Faustus, Ariadne, Arabella, The Countess in Cappricio, Denise in Tippett's The Knot Garden; Performed at Numerous Festivals with Several Professional Orchestras. Honours: 1st Prize, Metropolitan Opera Guild Auditions; 1st Prize, Federated Music Clubs Competition; Gelsenkirchen's Alfred Weber Prize of Excellence. Address: Grenzstr 131, 45881 Gelsenkirchen, Germany.

MANASSEN Alex (Jacques), b. 6 Sept 1950, Tiel, Netherlands. Composer. Education: Studied composition at Sweelinck Conservatory, Amsterdam, with Ton de Leeuw, 1972-79. Career: Performances live, on radio and television in the Netherlands; Performances in Italy, France, England, Germany, Israel, Sweden, USA, Poland; Commissions for all important Dutch funds; Teacher of Contemporary and Electronic Music, Sweelinck Conservatory, Amsterdam, 1991; Co-founder, Composer, Manager, Delta Ensemble; Teacher of Music and Informatica, Utrecht Conservatory, 1990; Dean, Director, Teacher of Composition, Swolle Conservatory, 1991-. Compositions: Katarsis-Arsis for organ, 1973; Prelude, for strings and harpsichord, 1973/95; Mei, for flute and string quartet, 1974; Citius, Altius, Fortius, Variable instrumentation, 1979; Pandarus Sings, for mezzo soprano, flute, clarinet and piano, 1980; Pandarus Sings, Higher, for soprano, flute, clarinet and piano, 1980; De Waal, for 1 or more instruments, especially for beginners, 1980; Interlude 1, Sextet, for oboe, bassoon, french horn and string trio, 1980; Bass Clarinet Concerto, for bass clarinet and orchestra, 1982; Helix for marimba, 1983; Denkmal an der Grenze des Fruchtlandes, for soprano and chamber ensemble, 1983; Air for Orchestra, 1985; Air for electronic music, 1986; Air-Facilmente, clarinet, violin, cello and piano, 1986; Songs and Interludes, for soprano and chamber ensemble, 1979-88; A Call to La Source Possible, for soprano and chamber ensemble, 1988; Air Conditioned, computer controlled player piano, 1988; Lamento for a landscape, electronic music, 1988; Moordunkel, for soprano, accordion, bass clarinet and percussion, 1990; Two Ears to Hear Two Eyes to See, contralto, tenor and piano, 1990, and for soprano, clarinet and piano, arranged Paul van Ostaijen, 1993; Hallo, Hallo, computer controlled sound generating object on request of the Art Foundation Neerijnen; commissioned by the Amsterdam Fund for the Arts and the Province of Gelderland, 1991; Evening Beach Piano, 1991; Farewell to a Landscape, for high voice and clarinet, 1994; Lamento for the Hanze Towns, 1994; Requiem for a Landscape, based on The Tree Bible by William van Toorn, Gerrit Noordzij and others; Elegy in Memoriam Chris Walraven for 8 celli, 1996; Commissioned by the Fund for the Creation of Music. Address: Ankummerdijk 6, NL 7722, XJ Dalfsen, Netherlands.

MANCINELLI Aldo, b. 29 July 1928, Steubenville, Ohio, USA. Concert Pianist; Professor of Music. m. (1) 1 son, 1 daughter, (2) Judith Elaine Young, 1 June 1971, 1 son, 1 daughter. Education: Graduated, 1952, Graduate Study, 1953, Oberlin Conservatory of Music; Graduated, Accademia Nazionale di Santa Cecilia, Rome, Italy, 1955; Studied with Claudio Arrau, Rudolf Firkusny and Carlo Zecchi. Debut: Beethoven 1st Piano Concerto, with Wheeling (West Virginia) Symphony, 1941. Career: Recitals throughout Europe, North Africa, Middle East, North America; Appeared as Soloist with major symphony orchestras throughout Europe and USA, including Cleveland Symphony, San Antonio Symphony, La Scala (Milan), Royal Liverpool Philharmonic, Santa Cecilia Orchestra (Rome), NDR Orchestra (Hamburg). Recordings: Piano Music of Charles Griffes, Musical Heritage Society; Beethoven's Concerto No 5 (Emperor); Many recordings for Radiotelevisione Italiana; French North Africa Radio, Tunis; Romanian Radio, Bucharest. Contributions to: Charles Griffes, An American Enigma, in Clavier, 1985. Honours: 1st Prize Winner, Ferruccio Busoni, International Piano Competition, Bolzano, Italy, 1950; Laureate, Liverpool International Piano Concerto Competition, 1959; Laureate, Casella, International Piano Competition, Naples, 1953. Address: 341 Timber Place, Decatur, IL 62521, USA.

MANCINI Caterina, b. 1920, Italy. Singer, Soprano. Education: Studied in Milan and elsewhere in Italy. Career: Many appearances from 1948 at such Italian opera centres as Bologna, Venice, Rome, Leonora in Il Trovatore; The Baths at Caracalla; La Scala Milan from 1951, debut as Donizetti's Lucrezia Borgia; Sang Agathe at Rome, 1952, and appeared at the Maggio Musicale Florence and the Verona Arena, 1956; Guest engagements in concert and opera elsewhere in Europe. Recordings: La Battaglia di Legnano, Ernani and Il Trovatore; Santuzza in Cavalleria Rusticana and Anaide in Rossini's Mosè in Egitto; Guillaume Tell; Attilia; Il Duca d'Alba by Donizetti. Address: c/o Teatro alla Scalla, Via Filodrammatici 2, 20121 Milan, Italy.

MANDAC Evelyn, b. 16 Aug 1945, Malaybalay, Mindanao, Philippines. Singer, Soprano. Education: Oberlin College Conservatory; Juilliard School New York. Debut: Mobile, Alabama, 1968 in Orff's Carmina Burana. Career: Santa Fe 1968, in the US premiere of Henze's The Bassarids; Washing DC 1969, as Mimi in La Bohème; Toured with Juilliard Quartet, 1969, in Schoenberg's 2nd Quartet; Seattle Opera 1972, in the premiere of Pasatieri's The Black Widow; Sang in the US premiere of Berio's Passaggio; San Francisco 1972, as Inez in L'Africaine; Glyndebourne 1974-75, as Susanna and Despina; Houston Opera 1975, as Lauretta in Gianni Schicchi; Baltimore Opera 1976, in the premiere of Pasatieri's Inez de Castro; Lisa in The Queen of Spades for US TV, 1977; Guest appearances in Toulouse, Turin, Rome, Salzburg Festival and Geneva. Recordings: Carmina Burana, conducted by Ozawa.

MANDANICI Marcella, b. 15 Apr 1958, Genoa, Italy. Composer. m. Giuseppe Venturini, 22 Dec, 1978. Education: Piano diploma, Brescia, 1979; Harpsichord Diploma 1984, Composition Diploma 1986, Milan; Composition Diploma, Santa Cecilia Academy, Rome, 1988. Career: Autumn Musicale, Como, 1984; Aspekte, Salzburg, 1986; Nuove Musica Italiana, Rome, 1987-88; Settimana di Musica Contemporanea Desenzano, 1987-88; Musica Rave, Milano, 1985; Spazio Musica, Cagliari, 1988. Compositions: Author of many compositions for solo instruments, chamber ensemble and orchestra including: Invenzione a Cinque, for flute, clarinet, viola, cello and piano, 1982; Edipan Steps for piano, 1983; Rugginenti; Senza Testo, for voice, 1987. Recordings: Invenzione a Cinque; Senza Testo. Honours: Steirischer Herbst Selection, Graz, 1986; IGNM Selection, Koln, 1987, both with steps; Antologia Radiotre Selection, Rome, 1988, with Double Path. Memberships: Founded, Nuovi Spazi Sonori, Italian Association for Contemporary Music, Artistic Director, 1987-. Address: Via Vittorio Emanuele 11-60, 25122 Brescia, Italy.

MANDEL Alan (Roger), b. 17 July 1935, New York, USA. Concert Pianist; Professor of Music; Artistic Director. m. Nancy Siegmeister, 1 June 1963, divorced 1989. Education: BS 1956, MS 1957, Juilliard School of Music; Diploma in Piano and composition, Akademie Mozarteum, Salzburg, Austria, 1962; Diploma, Academia Monteverdi, Bolzano, Italy, 1963. Debut: Town Hall, New York City, 1948. Career: Over 305 International Concert Tours in 50 Countries; Noted for his repertoire of esoteric and seldom-played masterpieces; Professor of Music, The American University, Washington DC; Artistic Director, Washington Music Ensemble; Chairman of the Music Division, The American University, Washington DC, 1992. Compositions: Composed a Symphony, piano concerto, many piano compositions and songs. Recordings include: The Complete Piano Works of Charles Ives (4 record albums); Louis Moreau Gottschalk; Forty Works for the Piano (4 record albums); Anthology of American Piano Music 1790-1970 (3 record albums); Three Sides of George Rochberg; Carnival Music; Elie Siegmeister; Sonata No 4 for Violin and Piano; American Piano (CD); Rags and Riches, CD, Premiere Recordings Inc, New York, 1992. Publications: Charles Ives: Study No 5 for Piano, edited by Alan Mandel with Preface Performance notes, Editorial notes and Analytical notes, 1988. Current Management: Guy Friedman, 37 Robins Crescent, New Rochelle, NY 10801, USA. Address: 3113 Northampton St NW, Washington DC 20015, USA.

MANDELBAUM Mayer (Joel), b. 12 Oct 1932, NY, USA. Composer. Education: Studied with Welter Piston, Irving Fina and Harold Shapero; BA, Harvard, 1953; PhD Indiana University, 1961. Career: Teacher, Queen's College, NY, 1961; Director of the Aaron Copeland School of Music; Fellow, MacDowell Colony 1968. Compositions: Operas: The Man in the Man-Made Moon 1955; The Four Chaplains, 1956 and The Dybbuik, 1971; Light Opera: As you Dislike It, 1973; Orchestra: Concovation overture 1951; Piano Concerto 1953; Sursum Corda 1960; Sinfonia Concertante for oboe, horn, violin, cello and small orchestra, 1962; Memorial for string orchestra, 1965; Trumpet Concerto, 1970; Chamber: Wind Quintet, 1957; 2 string quartets, 1959, 1979; Oboe sonata, 1981; Clarinet sonata, 1983; Piano Sonata, 1958; Mass for men's voices and organ, 1954; Choruses, Songs, Musicals and Incidental Music. Address: c/o ASCAP, ASCAP Building, One Lincoln Plaza, NY 10023, USA.

MANDUELL John (Sir), b. 1928. Composer; Principal, Royal Northern College of Music, 1971-96. m. Renna Kellaway, 1955, 3 s, 1 d. Education: Haileybury College; Jesus College, Cambridge, University of Strasbourg; Royal Academy of Music; FRAM 1964; FRNCM 1974; FRCM 1980; FRSAMD 1982; FWCMD 1991; Hon FTCL 1973; Hon GSM 1986. Career includes: BBC Music Producer, 1956-61; Governor, National Youth Orchestra, 1964-73 and 1978-; Chief Planner, The Music Programme, 1964-68; Director of Music, University of Lancaster, 1968-71; Associated Board of Royal Schools of Music, 1971-; Governor of Chetham's School, 1971-; Principal, Royal Northern College of Music, 1971-96; Honorary Lecturer in Music, University of Manchester, 1976-; Programme Director of Cheltenham Festival, 1969-95; Director, Young Concert Artists' Trust, 1983-, and Lake District Summer Music Festival, 1984-; President of European Association of Music Academies, 1988-; Opera Board, 1988- and Board, 1989-, Royal Opera House; Board of Manchester Arts, 1991-; Engagements and tours as composer, conductor and lecturer in Canada, Europe, Hong Kong, South Africa and USA; Chairman of numerous committees; Chairman or member of many international musical competition juries. Compositions: Overture, Sunderland Point, 1969; Diversions for Orchestra, 1970; String Quartet, 1976; Prayers from the Ark, 1981; Double Concerto, 1985. Contributions to: The Symphony, 1966. Honours include: 1st Leslie Boosey Award, Royal Philharmonic Society and PRS, 1980; CBE, 1982; Kt, 1989; Chevalier de l'Ordre des Arts et des Lettres, France, 1990; Honorary DMus at Lancaster, 1990 and Manchester, 1992. Hobbies: Cricket; Travel; French Life, Language and Literature. Address: c/o Royal Northern College of Music, 124 Oxford Road, Manchester, M13 9RD, England.

MANIATES Maria (Rika), b. 30 Mar 1937, Toronto, Canada. Musicologist. Education: Associate, Royal Conservatory of Toronto (solo piano), 1958; BA Music, University of Toronto, 1960; MA, Musicology, 1962, PhD 1965, University of Columbia. Career: Professor Emeritus of Musicology, Chairman, Department of History and Literature of Music, 1973-78, Faculty of Music, Fellow of Victoria College, University of Toronto; Specialist, Renaissance period and philosophy of music; Director and performer, Renaissance Music Group, CBC TV Show, 1969; Visiting Professor of Music, Columbia University, 1967, 1976; Associate Dean, Humanities, School of Graduate Studies, University of Toronto, 1990-92; Vice Dean, School of Graduate Studies, 1992-95. Publications: Combinative Techniques in Franco-Flemish Polyphony, 1965; Mannerism in Italian Music and Culture 1530-1630, 1979; Music and Civilization: Essays in Honor of Paul Henry Lang, 1984; The Combinative Chanson: An Anthology, 1989; Ancient Music Adapted to Modern Practice: Nicola Vicentino, 1996; Music Discourse from Classical to Early Modern Times, 1997. Honours: Connaught Senior Fellowship, 1982-83; ASCAP-Deems Taylor Award, 1986. Memberships: American Musicological Society; International Musicological Society. Address: Faculty of Music, University of Toronto, Canada, M5S 1A1.

MANION Michael (Lawrence), b. 6 Aug 1952, Grand Rapids, Michigan, USA. Composer. Education: BMus, Oberlin Conservatory, 1977; M.Mus, University of IL, 1983; D.Phil, in progress, University of Sussex, 1988; Jenkintown Conservatory, 1966-68; Private Student, Ramon Zupko, 1973; Musikhochschule, Cologne, 1981. Career: Percussionist; American Youth Symphony, 1969-70; Grand Rapids Symphony, 1970-74; Freelance, Chicago, San Francisco, Cologne, 1979-82; Freelance Composer, 1980-; Development of Computer Music Software, 1980-86; Performances in West Germany, Holland and USA. Compositions: Echoes, Densities, 1974; Orbis Musica, 1975; Combinations, 1976; Wheels, 1976; Meta, 1977; Delta, 1976; Screen, 1979; Islands, 1982; Music for Flute, Bass, Clarinet and Tape, 1986. Publications: Stockhausen in Den Haag, Editor, 1984. Honours: Guest Composer, Institute for Sonology, Utrecht, 1984. Memberships: American Federation of Musicians. Address: 29A St George Road, Brighton, BN2 1ED, East Sussex, England.

MANN Robert, b. 19 July 1920, Portland, Oregon, USA. Violinist; Composer; Conductor; Teacher. m. Lucy Rowan. Education: Juilliard School of Music with Edouard Dethier, Adolfo Beti, Felix Salmond, Edgar Schenkman, Bernard Wagenar and Stefan Wolpe. Debut: Violin recital NY 1941. Career: Joined faculty of Juilliard School after wartime service; Founded Juilliard String Quartet 1948; Many concert engagements in Europe and USA; Established 1962 as quartet-in-residence under the Whittall Foundation at the Library of Congress, Washington, DC; Quartet-in-residence at Michigan State University from 1977; First performances of Quartets by Carter, Kirchner, Schuman, Sessions, Piston, Babbitt, Copland and Foss; First US Quartet to visit USSR, 1961; Repertory of 600 wroks; Conductor of contemporary music; Has performed and lectured at the Aspen Music Festival; President of the Naumburg Foundation 1971; Chairman of Chamber Music panel 1980; Coach to Concord, Tokyo, LaSalle and Emerson String Quartets; Formed Duo with son Nicholas Mann 1980; Visited London with the Juilliard Quartet, 1996. Recordings: Complete Beethoven Quartets and Mozart's Quartets dedicated to Haydn; Contemporary works. Address: c/o Violin Faculty, Juilliard School of Music, Lincoln Plaza, NY 10023, USA.

MANNING Jane, b. 20 Sept 1938, Norwich, England. Singer (Soprano); Lecturer. m. Anthony Payne, 24 Sept 1966. Education: LRAM, 1958; GRSM, 1960; ARCM, 1962. Career: 20th century music specialist, more than 300 world premieres; Sings in leading concert halls and festivals worldwide; BBC broadcasts since 1965, and Promenade concerts; Wexford Festival Opera, 1976; New Opera Company, 1978; Scottish Opera, 1979; Brussels

Opera, 1981; Garden Venture, 1991, 1993; Founder, Jane's Minstrels (ensemble), 1988, regular appearances in London and Europe, for BBC, also many CDs; Visiting Professor, Mills College, California, 1982-86; Visiting Lecturer, University of York, 1987; Visiting Professor, Royal College of Music, London, 1995-; Honorary Professor, University of Keele, 1996-99. Recordings include: Complete song cycles of Messiaen; Schoenberg's Pierrot Lunaire, Moses und Aron; Ligeti Aventures Nouvelles Aventures; Complete vocal works of Erik Satie, 1994; Jane Manning, 1995. Publications: Book chapter in How the Voice Works, 1982; New Vocal Repertory-An Introduction, 1986, Volume 1, reissued, 1994, Volume 2, 1997 Contributions to: A Messiaen Companion, 1995; Articles to Composer, Music and Musicians, The Independent. Honours include: Special Award, Composers' Guild of Great Britain, 1973; FRAM, 1978; DUniv, University of York, 1988; OBE, 1990. Memberships: Vice-President, Society for Promotion of New Music; Executive Committee, Musicians' Benevolent Fund; Chairman, Nettlefold Festival Trust; ISM; Equity. Hobbies: Cinema; Ornithology; Philosophy. Address: 2 Wilton Square, London N1 3DL, England.

MANNING Peter, b.17 July 1956, Manchester, England. Violinist. Education: Chathams School 1969-73; Royal Northern College of Music; Indiana University, USA 1973-81. Debut: Concert at Wigmore Hall, 1987. Career: Solo appearances with Philharmonia Orchestra, Hallé Orchestre, City of Birmingham Symphony; Co-leader, London Philharmonic Orchestra; Professor, Royal Northern College of Music; Quartet in Residence at the Dartington Summer School, with quartets by Schnittke; Season 1988-89 in the Genius of Prokofiev series at Blackheath and BBC Lunchtime Series at St John's Smith Square; South Bank Concerto conducted by Neville Marriner concerts with the Hermann Prey Schubertiade and collaborations with the Alban Berg Quartet in the Beethoven Plus series; Tour of South America 1988, followed by Scandinavian debut; Season 1989-90 with debut tours of Holland, Germany, Spain, Austria and Finland; Tours from 1990 to the Far East, Malta, Sweden and Norway; Schoenberg-Handel Concerto with the Gothenburg Symphony; Festival appearances at Brighton, the City of London, Greenwich, Canterbury, Harrogate, Chester, Spitalfields and Aldeburgh; Collaborations with John Ogdon, Imogen Cooper, Thea King and Lynn Harrell; Formerly resident quartet at Liverpool University; Teaching role at Lake District Summer Music 1989; Universities of Bristol, Hong Kong 1990. Recordings: Beethoven Op 130 and Schnittke Quartet no 3; Vaughan Williams On Wenlock Edge and Ravel Quartet; Britten, Prokofiev, Tippett, Elgar and Walton Quartets; Exclusive contract with EMI from 1990. Address: c/o Ingpen and Williams Ltd, 26 Wadham Road, London SW15 2LR, England.

MANNINO Franco, b. 25 Apr 1924, Palermo, Italy. Conductor; Composer; Pianist. Education: Piano with R Silvestri, Composition with V Mortari, Academy of Santa Cecilia, Rome; Graduated in Piano, 1940, Composition, 1947. Debut: As Composer, 1932; As Pianist, 1940; As Conductor, 1955. Career: 1st American tour as Pianist, 1946, as Conductor with Maggio Musicale Fiorentino, 1957; Artistic Director, 1969, 1970, Artistic Advisor, 1974, Teatro San Carlo, Naples; Numerous Guest Conductor appearances including with Leningrad Orchestra, Orchestras of Peking and Shanghai; Major US Orchestras, etc; Many years as Principal Guest Conductor, Opera of Monte Carlo; Principal Conductor, Artistic Advisor, 1982-86, Principal Guest Conductor, 1986-89; National Arts Centre Orchestra, Ottawa; Numerous US tours; Toured Hong Kong and Japan with National Arts Centre Orchestra, 1985; His works performed by many leading orchestras. Compositions: Over 320 works including opera, ballet, oratorios, symphonies, chamber music, music for theatre; Music for over 100 films of directors such as Huston, Visconti, Moguy. Recordings: Conductor of own works and works of Bach, Mendelssohn, Mozart, Liszt, Wagner, Schubert, Schumann, Puccini, Franck, Chopin, Verdi, Scarlatti, for Conevox, Melodya, USSR, Curci, CBC, RCA, Fontana, Phillips and other labels; Artistic Director, Visconti Record Album, CBS-Sony. Honours: Recipient of numerous awards and other honours. Address: Via Citta di Castello 14, 00191 Rome, Italy.

MANNION Rosa, b. 1960, Liverpool, England. Singer, Soprano. Education: Studied at the Royal Scottish Academy. Debut: 1984 as Adina (L'Elisir d'amore) Scottish Opera; Glyndebourne Festival debut 1987, as Constanze. Career: Has sung with Scottish Opera as Gilda, Adina, Pamina, Dorinda, Handel's Orlando, Sophie in Werther and Susanna, 1989; English National Opera from 1987 as Sophie in Der Rosenkavalier, Anna in the world premiere of Holloway's Clarissa, Cordelia in King Lear, Oscar, Atalanta, Xerxes and Nannetta; Has sung Magnolia in Show Boat with Opera North and Gilda (Rigoletto), Asteria (Tamburlaine) and Minka (La Roi Malgré Lui); Concert appearances with the Manchester Camerata, the Scottish Chamber and National Orchestras, the Hallé, the City of London Sinfonia, Les Arts Florissants, Rundfunk Symphony Orchestra, Berlin, and the London Mozart Players; ECO, BBC Philharmonic; Conductors include Raymond Leppard, Jeffrey Tate, Richard Hickox and Jane Glover, Philippe Herreweghe, Charles Mackerras, Yehudi Menuhin; Neeme Jarvi at the Edinburgh Festival; Season 1992 as Atalanta at ENO, Dorabella under John Eliot Gardiner at Amsterdam and Lisbon, Gilda for Opera North; Royal Opera debut as Pamina, 1993; Aix-en-Provence debut 1993 as Dorinda (Orlando); American debut 1996 with Orlando in New York; Sang Maria in Schubert's Lazarus, RCM, London, 1997. Recordings: Mozart's Ascanio in Alba, with Musique en Sorbonne; Cosi fan tutte; Die Zauberflöte; Missa Solemnis; Orlando; Entführung. Honours: Winner, Scottish Opera International Singing Competition; John Scott Award, Scottish Opera. Address: c/o IMG Artist Management, Media House, 3 Burlington Lane, Chiswick, London W4 2TH, England.

MANNOV Johannes, b. 1965, Copenhagen, Denmark. Singer, Baritone. Education: Studied at the Conservatoires of Freiburg and Karlsruhe. Career: Sang with the boys' choir Kobenhauns-Drengekor before adult study; Has sung with the Kassel Opera from 1987 as Mozart's Papageno, Masetto and Figaro; Concert performances under such conductors as Helmuth Rilling, Luigi Nono, George Malcolm, Frans Bruggen, Segerstram and Hans Martin Schneidt; Has performed Mozart's Requiem in Bremen, the Christmas Oratorio in Cologne and Frankfurt and an Italian tour with Bach's St John Passion, 1991-92; Britten's War Requiem in Frankfurt; Sang Mozart's Figaro for Opera Northern Ireland 1991. Recordings include: Keresmin in Holger Danske by Kunzen, 1996. Honours: Prizewinner, s'Hertogenbosch Competition, 1986; Helsinki Competition, 1989. Address: Anglo Swiss Ltd, Suite 35-37, Moley House, 320 Regent Street, London W1R 5AD, England.

MANSON Anne, b. 1960, USA. Conductor. Education: Studied at Harvard University, King's College London, the Royal College of Music with Norman del Mar and James Lockhart and the Royal Northern College of Music. Career includes: As Music Director of Mecklenburgh Opera has conducted The Emperor of Atlantis by Viktor Ullmann, Die Weisse Rose by Udo Zimmermann, Manekiny by Rudzinski, The Soldier's Tale at Almeida Theatre London; First woman to conduct Vienna Philharmonic Orchestra in a rehearsal of Boris Godunov in 1991 also first woman to conduct at the Salzburg Festival in 1994; Conducted John Hawkin's Echoes at the Riverside Studios for the Covent Garden Project, 1991 and English Touring Opera in Don Pasquale and Don Giovanni; Conducted the Endymion Ensemble in the premiere of Nicola Lefanu's Blood Wedding for the Women's Playhouse Trust in London, (1992) and the British premiere of Petrified by Juraj Benes; Assistant to Claudio Abbado at 1992 Salzburg Festival in From the House of the Dead and in Lohengrin at Vienna Staatsoper; Conducted at La Monnaie Brussels in 1993 in a triple bill of works by Monteverdi and Judith Weir; Concerts with the Wiener Kammerorchester; Conducted in Boris Godunov with the Vienna Philharmonic and Sam Ramey in 1994; US debut at Washington Opera with Samuel Barber's Vanessa in 1995; Conducted Royal Scottish National Orchestra in Dvorák and Stravinsky, 1997; Engaged for Dangerous Liaisons by Susa at Washington, 1998. Honours include: Fellow in Conducting, Royal Northern College of Music; Marshall Scholarship; Prizes at the RCM and RNCM. Current Management: Ingpen and Williams Ltd. Address: c/o Ingpen and Williams Ltd, 26 Wadham Road, London SW15 2LR, England.

MANSOURI Lotfollah (Lotfi), b. 15 June 1929, Tehran, Iran. Opera Stage Director. m. Marjorie Anne Thompson, 18 Sept 1954, 1 daughter. Career: Assistant Professor, University of California, Los Angeles, USA, 1957-60; Dramatic Coach, Music Academy of the West, Santa Barbara, California, 1959; Resident Stage Director, Zurich Opera, Switzerland, 1960-65; Director of Dramatics: Zurich International Opera Studio, 1961-65, Centre Lyrique, Geneva, 1967-72; Chief State Director, Geneva Opera, 1965-75; Artistic Advisor, Tehran Opera, 1973-75; Opera Advisor, National Arts Centre, Ottawa, Canada, 1977; Operatic Consulting Director, MGM film Yes, Giorgio, 1981; Opera Sequence in Norman Jewison's film Moonstruck, 1987; General Director, San Francisco Opera, 1988-; Guest Director, various opera companies including New York Metropolitan, San Francisco Opera, La Scala, Verona, Vienna Staatsoper, Vienna Volksoper, Salzburg Festival, Covent Garden, Amsterdam Opera, Holland Festival, L'Opéra de Nice, Festival d'Orange, Australian Opera, Kirov Opera, Lyric Opera Chicago; Dallas Opera; With Surtitles TM initiated above-stage projection of simultaneous opera texts, 1983; Presided over the redevelopment of the War Memorial Open House, gala re-opening, Sept 1997. Publication: An Operatic Life (co-author), 1982. Memberships: Board of Directors, Opera America, 1979-91, 1993-96; American Guild of Musical Artists; AFTRA; Canadian Actors' Equity Association. Address: War Memorial Opera House, 301 Van Ness Ave, San Francisco, CA 94102-4509, USA.

MANSUR Cem, b. 1957, Istanbul, Turkey. Conductor. Education: Studied at the Guildhall School in London and with Leonard Bernstein in Los Angeles. Career: Conductor of the Istanbul State Opera, 1981-89, also giving orchestral concerts; London debut 1985, with the English Chamber Orchestra; Further engagements with orchestras and opera companies in Holland, Italy, Romania, Russia, France and Czechoslovakia; Kirov Opera at St Petersburg 1993 and 1994 for several operas; Principal Conductor of the City of Oxford Orchestra from 1989, including tours to Vienna, Zurich, Prague and Budapest; Led Debussy's Le Martyre de Saint Sebastian at St John's Smith Square and Katya Kabanova at Nancy, 1995; Further concerts with the Royal Philharmonic, Georges Enescu Philharmonic, Scottish Chamber Orchestra, London Mozart Players and the Hungarian State Orchestra. Address: c/o Atholl Still Ltd, Foresters Hall,25-27 Westow Street, London SE19 3RY.

MANTEL Gerhard (Friedrich), b. 31 Dec 1930, Karlsruhe, Germany. Concert Cellist. m. Renate Mantel, 1 son. Education: Music Academies in Mannheim and Paris; Musikhochschule Saarbrucken; Studied with August Eichhorn and Pierre Fournier. Career: Solo cellist, Bergen Symphony, Norway; WDR Orchestra,, Cologne; Worldwide recital tours, mainly with pianist Erika Friesar; Professor, Frankfurt Musikhochschule, 1973-; Assistant Director 1975-. Recordings: With Erika Friesar, Sonatas by Mendelssohn, Strauss, Grieg. Publications: Cello Technik 1973. Memberships: European String Teachers Association. Honours: Kulturpreis der Stadt Karlsruhe, 1955. Hobbies: Reading; Family. Address: 6236 Eschborn 2, Felderbergstrasse 44, Germany.

MANTLE Neil (Christopher), b. 16 Mar 1951, Essex, England. Conductor. m. Inga Wellesley, 17 Oct 1980, 1 son, 1 daughter. Education: Royal Academy of Music, London, 1969-70; Royal Scottish Academy of Music, 1970-73. Career: Conducting with Scottish Sinfonia, 1970-, Edinburgh Opera Company, 1975-81, Sinfonia Opera, 1983-84; Guest Conductor, Scottish National Orchestra, 1984;- Guest Conductor, BBC Scottish Symphony Orchestra, 1986-. Honours: Hugh S Robertson Conducting Prize, Royal Scottish Academy of Music, 1973; 2nd prize, Leeds Conductors Competition, 1986. Memberships: Elgar Society. Hobbies: Old, preferably black and white films; Collecting old records. Current Management: Anglo-Swiss Artists Management, PO Box 719, London, N6 5UX, England.

MANUGUERRA Matteo, b. 5 Oct 1924, Tunis, Tunisia. Singer, Baritone. Education: Studied in Buenos Aires, Argentina, with Umberto Landi. Debut: As tenor in Mozart's Requiem. Career: Sang in Europe from 1962, debut at Lyon as Valentin in Faust; Paris Opera from 1965, as Rigoletto, Escamillo, Germont and Enrico in Lucia di Lammermoor; US debut Seattle 1968, as Gerard in Andrea Chenier; Metropolitan Opera debut 1971, as Enrico; Returned to NY 1983 as Barnaba in La Gioconda, Carlo in La Forza del Destino, and Amonasro; Verona Arena 1980-85; Frankfurt 1986, in a concert performance of La Gioconda; Guest appearances Vienna, Hamburg, London, Geneva, Athens and Santiago; Sang Carlos in La Forza del Destino at Hanover, 1987; Naples 1989, as Renato in Un ballo in Maschera; Sang Rigoletto at Covent Garden, 1991 and the Metropolitan and Santiago, 1992. Recordings: Tosca; Le Villi; Nabucco; La Bohème; Il Barbiere di Siviglia; Werther; I Puritani; La Battaglia di Legnano; Stiffelio; Il Trovatore; Francesca da Rimini.Address: c/o Patricia Greenan, 19B Belsize Park, London NW3 4DU, England.

MANZ André, b. 15 Dec 1942, Chur, Switzerland. Organist; Pianist; Harpsichordist; Teacher. m. Irene Pomey. Education: Music Academy Zurich; Conservatory Winterhur; Hochschule für Musik, Cologne, Germany; Masters degree in Organ and Piano; Concert Diploma in Organ. Debut: 1964. Career: Organ recitals in Switzerland, Germany, Italy, Denmark, Japan, Poland, USA, Canada, Spain and Austria; Various radio series; Piano Duo with Irene Manz-Pomey. Composition: Play b-a-c-h for 6 organists and assistants, 1971. Recordings include: Swiss Baroque Soloists; Several organ solo recordings including the complete organ works by Franz Liszt; 2 CDs: Variations on National Anthems, Battles and Thunderstorms for Organ, and Four Hands Organ-Playing Throughout Five Centuries. Contributions to: Various musical journals. Honours: Many musical prizes and scholarships; Annual Prize of Eastern Swiss Radio and TV Association, 1994; Annual Cultural Prize of Canton Thurgau Government, 1996. Memberships: Schweizer Tonkunstlerverein, STV; Schweizer Musikpadagogischer Verband, SMPV; President of Thurgau Organists Association; Rotary Club. Hobbies: Collecting records of great pianists; Long distance running; Figure skating; Cats. Address: Brunnenfeldstrasse 11, CH-8580 Amriswil, Switzerland.

MANZ Wolfgang, b. 6 Aug 1960, Dusseldorf, Germany. Pianist. m. Julia Goldstein, 2 Aug 1985, 2 sons, 1 daughter. Education: Studied with Professor Drahomir Toman, Prague and Professor Karlheinz Kaemmerling at High School of Music, Hanover. Career: Performed at Promenade Concerts in London, England with the BBC Symphony Orchestra, 1984; Gilels Memorial Concert in Dusseldorf, 1986; Recital at Karajan Foundation in Paris, 1987 and Concert Tours, recitals, Broadcasts and Concerto performances all over Europe; Concert tours since 1988 in Japan; teacher, Karlsruhe Music High School, 1994-. Recordings: Beethoven Triple Concerto with English Chamber Orchestra and Saraste, Dohnanyi Piano Quintet op 1 with Gabrieli String Quartet (Chandos Records); Chopin Studies (Pavane

Records); Russian Piano Music for 2 Pianos (EMS). Honours: First Prize, Mendelssohn Competition, Berlin, 1981; Second Prize, Queen Elisabeth Competition, Brussels, 1983; Second Prize, Leeds Piano Competition, 1981; Van Cliburn International Piano Competition, Texas, USA, Jury Discretionary Award, 1989. Memberships: Chopin Society, Hanover; Mozart Society, Dortmund, 1989-. Current Management: J Hannemann, Husumer Strasse 16, D-20251 Hamburg, Germany. Address: Pasteurallee 55, D-30655 Hanover, Germany.

MANZINO Leonardo, b. 24 Feb 1962, Montevideo, Uruguay. Pianist; Musicologist. Education: Piano Diploma, Kolischer Conservatory, Montevideo, 1978; Licentiate in Musicology, University of Uruguay, 1986; Master of Music in Piano Performance, 1988, PhD Musicology-Latin American Music, The Catholic University of America, 1993. Debut: Sala Martins Pena, Brasilia, 1983. Career: International Summer Music Festivals of Brasilia, 1983-84; Uruguayan Music Students Association, 1983; Jeunesses Musicales of Uruguay Series, 1984-85; Argentine Music Foundation Series, 1986; Professor, School of Music, University of Uruguay, 1993; Director, Musicanga Classics, 1995. Publications: Composers of the Americas, vol 20, editor, 1993; Uruguayan Music in the 1892 celebrations for the IV Centenary of the Encounter of Two Worlds, Latin American Music Review, 1993. Honours: Winner, Uruguayan Music Students' Piano Competition, 1983; Winner, Jeunesses Musicales of Uruguay Piano Competition, 1984. Hobbies: Swimming; Gardening; Reading. Address: Brito del Pino 1423, Montevideo 11600, Uruguay.

MANZONE Jacques (Francis), b. 4 Jun 1944, Cannes, France. Violinist; Professor of Music. Education: Studied at Nice Conservatoire with Henri Mazioux; Paris Conservatoire with Roland Charmy and Jacques Fevrier; Further study with Eugène Bigot and Henryk Szeryng. Career: Soloist with the French Radio Orchestra and Société des Concerts du Conservatoire; Co-founded Ensemble Instrumental de France, Paris, 1966; Soloist with Orchestra of Paris, founded by Charles Munch, 1967; Professor, Nice Conservatoire, 1977; Soloist, Nice Philharmonic Orchestra; Professor of Chamber Music, Nice International Summer Academy; Musical Director, Chamber Orchestra of Nice, 1984; Plays a Maggini violin; Musical Director, Chamber Opera of France. Recordings: About 30 records as soloist or conductor. Address: 7 Avenue des Fleurs, 06000 Nice, France.

MANZONI Giacomo, b. 26 Sept 1932, Milan, Italy. Composer; Teacher. m. Eugenia Tretti, 1960, 1 son. Education: Liceo Musica Laudamo, Messina and Conservatorio Verdi, Milan (Composition); Foreign Languages, Università Bocconi, Milan; Piano Diploma, Milan; -. Career: Teacher of Composition, Conservatorio Verdi, Milan, 1962-64, 1968-69, 1974-91, Conservatorio Martini, Bologna, 1965-68, 1969-74, Masterclass, Composition, Scuola di Musica, Fiesole, 1988-, and Accademia Pescarese, 1992-; Composer, international festivals, Amsterdam, Berlin, Osaka, Prague, Warsaw, Venice. Compositions: Operas: La Sentenza (Bergamo), 1960; Atomtod (Piccola Scala, Milan), 1965; Per Massimiliano Robespierre (Bologna), 1975; Doktor Faustus, by Thomas Mann (La Scala, Milan), 1989; Orchestral includes: "Insiemi", 1967; Masse: omaggio a E Varèse, piano, orchestra, 1977; Modulor, 1979; Ode, 1982; Scene Sinfoniche per il Dr Faustus, 1984; Dedica, texts by B Maderma, flute, bass, orchestra, choir ad lib, 1985; Chorus, orchestra: 5 Vicariote, 1958; Ombre, to memory of Che Guevara, 1968; Parole da Beckett, 1971; Hölderlin (frammento), 1972; Il deserto cresce (Nietzsche), 1992; Chamber includes: Musica notturna, 7 instruments, 1966; Quadruplum, 4 brass instruments, 1968; Spiel, 11 strings, 1969; String quartet, 1971; Percorso GG, clarinet, tape, 1979; D'improvviso, percussion, 1981; Klavieralbum 1956; Incontro, violin, string quartet, 1983; Opus 50 (Daunium), 11 instruments, 1984; 10 versi di E Dickinson, soprano, harp, strings, 1988. Recordings: Masse: omaggio a E Varèse; Parole da Beckett; Ode; Dedica; Quadruplum; Musica notturna; 10 Versi di E Dickinson; Scehe Filufoniche; Musica per Poutorma, per puastetto d'archi; Other chamber music. Publications: Guida all'ascolto della musica sinfonica, 1967; A Schoenberg - L'uomo, l'opera, i testi musicati, 1975; Per M Robespierre - Testo e materiali per le scene musicali (with L Pestalozza and V Puecher), 1975; Scritti, 1991; Tradizione e Utopia, 1994; Translations: many works by T W Adorno and A Schönberg. Contributions to: Music critic, L'Unità, 1958-66; Many Italian and foreign periodicals. Address: Viale Papiniano 31, 20123 Milan, Italy.

MARAN George, b. 25 July 1926, Massachusetts, USA. Singer, Tenor. Education: Studied at Harvard University and New York. Career: Sang in sacred music at the Salzburg Festival, 1951-66; European tour 1956 with the Salzburg Festival Company in Mozart's La Finta Semplice, directed by Bernhard Paumgartner; Sang at the Darmstadt Opera 1956-94, notably as Titus by Mozart; Death in Venice by Britten, 1983; Appearances at the Aldeburgh Festival, 1959-60, in The Rape of Lucretia and in the premiere of A Midsummer Night's Dream; Concert and oratorio engagements in Germany, England and Austria, all European Countries. Recordings: La Finta Semplice; Messiah, conducted by Adrian Boult, and Elijah under Josef Krips. Address: c/o Staatstheater, Postfach 111432, 64283 Darmstadt, Germany.

MARANGONI Bruno, b. 13 Apr 1935, Rovigo, Italy. Singer, Bass. Education: Studied with Campogalliani and in Venice. Debut: Venice 1960, as Anselmo in La Molinarelli by Puccinni. Career: Many apearances at the Teatro Fenice Venice, Teatro San Carlo Naples, Teatro Massimo Palermo and in Turin, Triste and the Caracalla Baths, Rome; Verona Reana, 1973, 1978, 1983-84; Guest engagements at Aix-en-Provence, Lisbon, Barcelona and Chicago; Other roles have included Geronimo in Il Matrimonio Segreto, Mozart's Leporello, Osmin and Sarastro, Marcel in Les Huguenots, Bartolo in Paisiello's Il Barbiere di Siviglia, Uberto in Pergolesi's La Serva Padrona, Alvise La Gioconda and Wagner's Daland, Pogner and Hunding; Television appearances in La Pietra del Paragone, as Asdrubal, L'Elisir d'Amore, Don Carlos, Il Trovatore, Guillaume Tell and Aida. Address: c/o Arena di Verona, Piazza Bra 28, 37121 Verona, Italy.

MARBE Myriam-Lucia, b. 9 Apr 1931, Bucharest, Romania. Composer. m. Aristide Poulopol, 14 Feb 1963, 1 daughter. Education: Piano studies with Angela Marbe, Florica Muzicescu and Silvia Capatana; Graduate, Music Conservatory of Bucharest; Studied Composition with Leon Klepper, Mihail Jora and Mihail Andricu. Career: Musical Editor, Bucharest Film Studio, 1953-54; Associate Professor, 1972-; Assistant Lecturer, Associate Professor, Academy of Music, Bucharest, 1954-88; Appearances at concerts and conferences; Radio and TV broadcasts. Compositions: Recorded: Incantatio, clarinet solo; Ritual for the Thirst of the Earth for choir and percussion; Jocus secundus; Eine Kleine Sonnenmusik - Serenata for chamber orchestra; Saxophone concerto; Trommelbass, string trio; Harpsichard concerto; Le temps retrouve; La parabole du grenier I for piano, harpsichord and celestra; Cyclus I for flute, guitar and percussion; Chiuituri for children's choir, flute and percussion: Quator for strings No 1; Fra-Angelico-Chagall-Voronet-Requiem; Shepherd's Pavane with birds (organ); Sonate for cello and organ; Paos for clarinet and viola; Quatuor for strings II; La parabole du grenier II for harpsichord and chamber ensemble Tapes: Sonata for 2 violas; En souvenir for choir and orchestra; Quatuor for strings I and II; Concerto for viola; Sonata per due for flute and viola, 1985; Des-Cantec, for wind quintet, 1985; An die Sonne, for voice, 1986; Lui Nau, Streichquartett Nr3, 1988; Ur-Ariadne-Sinfonie Nr 1, for mezzosopran, saxophone and orchestra, 1988; Dialogi-Nicht nur ein Bilderbuch für Christian Morgenstern, for Bass clarinet, piano, speaker ad libitum with percussion, 1989; Diapente, for five violoncelli, 1990; Yorick for clarinet, violin and piano, 1993; Passages in the wind for tenor clarinet, cello and harpsichord, 1994; Le temps inévitable for chamber ensemble, 1994; 5M for guitar, 1995; Sym-phonioa, for chamber ensemble and voice, 1996; The Song of Ruth for five violoncelli, 1996; Ariel, sontat for violoncello solo, 1996; Le Jardin enchante, for flutes, percussion and tape for 1 instrumentalist, 1994; La Parabole du gremier I for piano, harpsichord and celestra, 1975-79; E-Y-The, for clarinet and violoncelli, 1990; Pretuitorul, Der Schatzer, 1990; Stabat mater, for 12 voices and ensemble, 1991. Address: Str Gri-Alexandrescu nr 32, 71128 Bucharest, Romania.

MARC Alessandra, b. 1959, Berlin, Germany (American Citizen). Singer (Soprano). Education: Studied in the USA. Debut: Waterloo Festival 1983, as Mariana in Wagner's Das Liebesverbot. Career: Sang Gluck's Iphigénie (en Aulide) 1984, Tosca at the Connecticut Opera 1987; Wexford Festival 1987, as Lisabetta in La cena delle beffe; Santa Fe 1988, as Maria in Strauss's Friedenstag, followed by Adriadne 1990; Chicago and San Francisco as Aida, which she also sang on her Metropolitan Opera debut; Other roles include the Empress in Die Frau ohne Schatten (Holland Festival, 1990), Sieglinde and Silvana in La Fiamma by Respighi; Turandot at Philadelphia and Covent Garden (1994); Sang Turandot at the 1996 Macerata Festival; Concert repertoire includes the Verdi Requiem and Beethoven's Ninth; Also a noted recitalist (Wigmore Hall, London, 1990). Recordings include: Two versions of Elektra, as Chrysothemis under Barenboim, 1996, and the title role under Sinopoli, 1997. Address: c/o Lies Askonas Ltd, 6 Henrietta Street, London WC2E 8LA, England.

MARCELLINO Raffaele, b. 1964, Sydney, New South Wales, Australia. Composer. Education: BMus, New South Wales Conservatory, 1985; Dip Ed, Sydney College of Advanced Education, 1987. Career: Faculty Member, St Vincent's College, Potts Point, 1990-94; University of Tasmania, 1995; Resident Composer, Sydney Youth Orchestra, 1992. Compositions: Woodwind Quintet, 1983; Cathedrale for 7 brass instruments, 1984; Five Bells for string quartet and percussion, 1984; Five Bells for string quartet and percussion, 1984; Incunabula, for orchestra, 1985; Responsorio for chorus, 1987; Antipodes, for orchestra, 1987; Suite Etuis for orchestra, 1988; Whispers of Fauvel, for clarinet and percussion, 1988; The Remedy, 1 act opera, 1989; Nona for violin, 1991; Prester John, for ensemble, 1991; Don Juan, dance theatre, 1992; Corbaccio, for trombone and orchestra, 1993; Leviathan, for trombone, 1994. Honours include: Australian Composers National Opera Award, 1988. Address: c/o APRA, 1A Eden Street, Crows Nest, NSW 2065, Australia.

MARCHAND Jacques, b. 1 December 1948, Quebec, Canada. Education: BAC in Composition, McGill University, Montreal; BAC in Piano, Vincent D'Indy Music School, Montreal. Career: Nearer the Stars, Ballet for Violin Solo (Colorado Ballet Company), 1981; Founder, Orchestre Symphonique Regional d'Abitibi-Temiscamingue, 1986. Compositions: Nearer the Stars, 1981; Suite Pour Orchestre, 1987; Fantaisie Pour Orchestre, 1989; Impromptu Pour Piano et Orchestre, 1993; Un Dimanche A Poznan (Poème Symphonique), 1993. Recordings include: Cassette, Jacques Marchand Compositeur, 1988. Honours: Citoyen d'Honneur de la Societe Nationale des Quebecois, 1992; Hommage de la Chambre de Commerce de Rouyn-Noranda, 1993. Memberships: SOCAN; SODRAC; AOC. Address: 22, 8 Rue Rouyn-Noranda, Quebec J9X 2A4, Canada.

MARCHI Claudia, b. 1967, Bologna, Italy. Singer (Mezzo-soprano). Education: Studied with Elvina Ramella. Career: Appearances at Savona from 1992 as Isabella (L'Italiana in Algeria), Verdi's Maddalena and as Sigismonda in the opera by Rossini, under Richard Bonynge, 1992; Australian tour, with Luciano Pavarotti in Verdi's Requiem, 1994; Season 1995 as Fenena in Nabucco and Azucena in Trovatore, at Marseilles; Season 1996-97 as Isabella in Genoa and Isaura in Rossini's Tancredi at the Zürich Opera; Further engagements as Rosina and in works by Jommelli, Bach, Mozart and Pergolesi. Honours include: Prizewinner at the Verdi Competition in Parma and the Luciano Pavarotti International Voice Competition. Address: c/o Opernhaus Zürich, Falkenstrsse 1, CH-8008 Zürich, Switzerland.

MARCHWINSKI Jerzy (Wladyslaw), b. 6 Jan 1935, Truskolasy, Warsaw. Pianist. m. Ewa Podles, 17 July 1980, 2 daughters. Education: Frédéric Chopin Academy of Music, Warsaw; Further studies with Carlo Zecchi. Debut: Moscow, 1957. Career: Solo and chamber performances in major cities in Europe, America and Australia; Partner of many instrumentalists and singers, especially violinist Konstanty Kulka, Maureen Forrester and Ewa Podles; Currently Professor at Warsaw Academy of Music. Recordings: About 25 LPs and CDs. Publication: An Accompanist: An attempt to define him in light of contemporary requirements, 1976. Contributions to: Ruch Muzyczny, Warsaw. Honours: Polish Radio Prize; Minister of Culture of Poland. Memberships: Société des Artistes Musiciens Polonais; Frédéric Chopin Society. Hobby: Mountain climbing. Address: ul Szafirowa 60, 04-954 Warsaw, Poland.

MARCINGER Ludovit, b. 21 December 1932, Malacky, Slovakia. Pianist; Pedagogue. m. Maria Marcingerova, 7 May 1977, 2 daughters. Education: State Conservatoire, Bratislava; Academy of Music and Drama, Bratislava; Ferencz Liszt Academy of Music, Budapest. Debut: Recital, Dresden, 1958. Career: Recitals: Prague, 1965; Havana, 1980; With Orchestra, Prague, 1964; J Cikker, Concertino for Pf and Orchestra; Carlsbad, 1966; Grieg, Concert in A Minor, Bratislava, 1967; A Rubinstein, Concerto No 5 in D Minor; Piano Accompaniment of the Vocalists: Peter Dvorsky, Tenor, Song Recitals, Oper d Stadt, Bonn, 1983; Grosser Musikvereinssaal, Vienna, Teatro alla Scala, Milano, Brucknerhaus Linz, Slovak National Theatre Bratislava, 1984; Deutsche Oper Berlin, Theatre de L'Athénée Paris, 1986; Suntory Hall tokyo, 1989; Peter Mikulas-Bass, Songs Recitals, Mexico City, Caracas, Managua, San Jose, 1992, Bratislava Music Festival, 1994, Prague, 1996; With Other Vocalists, Peking, 1987, Buenos Aires, 1996. Recordings include: A Dvorak, Biblical Songs, Op 99, Tchaikovsky, Songs-Peter Mikulas, Bass, 1990; R Schumann, Frauenliebe und Leben, A Dvorak, 4 Songs, Op 2 V narodnim tonu; F Schubert, Lieder, Peter Mikulas, Bass, 1997. Honours: Several Prizes in Music Competitions. Memberships: Slovak Music Union; Association of Concert Artists of Bratislava. Hobby: Photography. Address: Vysoka skola muzickych umeni, Zochova 1, 81103 Bratislava, Slovakia.

MARCO-BUHRMESTER Alexander, b. 1963, Basle, Switzerland. Singer (Baritone). Education: Studied in Basle and Berne. Debut: Berne 1985, as Weber's Abu Hassan. Career: Toured Switzerland as Dandini in La Cenerentola and sang at the Biel Opera 1986 as Marcello in La Bohème; Essen Opera 1989-92, Dortmund from 1992, notably in the premiere of Caspar Hauser by Reinhard Febel. Address: c/o Städtische Buhnen, Kuhstrasse 12, W-4600 Dortmund, Germany.

MARCUS Ada (Belle Gross), b. 8 July 1929, Chicago, Illinois, USA. Composer; Pianist. m. Isadore Marcus, 2 daughters. Education: DePaul University Music School, Chicago, 1939-44; Studied Composition, American Conservatory of Music, 1954, Roosevelt University, 1959 and with various masters. Career: Concerts, midwest, 1947-; Soloist with major symphonies; Performances of own compositions throughout USA and on TV, 1954-88; Former Faculty, Chicago Conservatory College; Several of her compositions were chosen for exhibition at the 1974 International Society for Contemporary Music World Days, Rotterdam, Holland. Compositions include: Snow, chamber opera; Shakespearean Duo; Song for Flute, 1970; Symphony of the Spheres; Zen; Outward Bound; Textures for piano, flute and strings; Song Cycles; numerous piano pieces and songs; Highlights Suite, composed 1986; World Premiere, Brevities, with Chicago Chamber Orchestra, 1989; Sonata for violin and piano, presented New Music Chicago Festival, 1992; Composed: Commission from Chicagoo Chamber Orchestra, Overture to Unity, Sonata for strings for string orchestra, 1990. Recording: Symphony of the Spheres, 1995. Publications: International Encyclopedia of Women Composers, current issue; Contemporary Concert Music by Women, A Directory of the Composers and their Works, current issue. Honour: ASCAP (American Society of Composers Award Publishers, 4 special awards, 1991, 1992, 1993, 1995. Current Management: Independent Concert Management. Address: 9374 Landings Lane, Des Plaines, IL 60016, USA.

MARCUSSEN Kjell, b. 19 May 1952, Arendal, Norway. Composer. Education: Studied at the Agder Music Conservatorium; Diploma in Guitar and Composition, Guildhall School of Music, London with Robert Saxton. Debut: Cardiff Festival of Music, 1982. Compositions: Cantatas; Orchestral works; Guitar Concerto; Solo and Chamber works; Festival Overture for Symphonic Band, 1994. Recordings include: CD, Woodcut for Violin, Flute and Cello; CD, Festival Overture; CD, Tordenskjold Kantate. Publications: Guitar Sonata No 1, 1988; Woodcut for Violin, Flute and Cello, 1988; Partita Jubilante for Brass, 1993; Early Part of Summer for Flute and Harp; Introduction and Allegro for Guitar Duo. Honour: Special Mention at 15th Concorso internazionale di composizione originale per banda Corciano, 1994. Membership: Norwegian Composers' Society. Address: Skoleveien 6, 1380 Heggedal, Norway.

MARDER Samuel, b. 11 Dec 1930, Czernowitz, Romania. Violinist. m. 1959. Education: BMus 1955, MMus, EdM, Manhattan School of Music, NY; Studied with Hubert Aumere, Ralphael Bronstein, Louis Persinger, Nathan Milstein. Debut: Lincoln Center, NY, 1983. Career: First performance of Ben Haim Sonata in London and Vienna; First Performance of Earnest Lubin Sonata on radio in WNYC and in New York; Radio performances in Madrid, Helsinki, La Paz, and other cities; Televised concerts in Seoul, Korea, 1988; Concert tours throughout USA, Canada, Israel, South America, Spain, Finland, Bulgaria and South Korea. Honours: Hon Award from Mayor, City of Arequipa, Peru 1980; First Place, Violin Competition, Czernowitz, Soviet, 1940. Memberships: President, Intern Artists Alliance; Director, Riverdale Music Society. Hobbies: Writing; Philosophy. Address: c/o International Artists Alliance Inc, PO Box 3242, Rockefeller Station, NY 10185, USA.

MARECEK Karol, b. 1 May 1928, Bratislava, Slovakia. Soloist in Opera. m. Eva Markusits, 2 sons. Debut: Don Giovanni (Mozart). Career: Operas: Carmen (Escamilo), Onegin (Onegin); Bohemia-Marcel and Shounard; Madame Bouterfly-Scharples; Faust-Valentine and various memberships with radio, TV. Memberships: Slovak Philharmony. Hobbies: Cooking; Reading; Nature. Address: Orgovanova 2, Kosice, 04001, Slovakia.

MARESTIN Valerie, b. 1962, Pau, France. Singer (Mezzo-soprano). Education: Studied in Lyon with Eric Tappy and in Paris. Debut: Théâtre de Paris 1987, as La Bella Helene. Career: Guest appearances throughout France, including Carmen at Angers (1988); Sang Debussy's Geneviève at Moscow (1987) and Mistress Quickly at Limoges; Other roles include Maddalena, Rossweise, Marcellina in Figaro, Rossini's Isabella (at Rheims and Tours), Massenet's Dulcinée and Fenena in Nabucco; Bregenz Festival 1991, as Carmen; Frequent concert appearances. Address: c/o Bregenz Festival, Postfach 311, A-6901 Bregenz, Austria.

MAREZ OYENS Tera de, b. 5 Aug 1932, Velsen, Netherlands. Composer. m. M S Arnoni, 8 Mar 1975 (deceased), 2 s, 2 d. Education: Diploma, Conservatorium Amsterdam, 1953; Studied composition with Hans Henkemans, conducting with Frits Kox, electronic music University of Utrecht. Career: Composer of about 200 works for orchestra, chamber music, choral, electronic music, most performed in Netherlands, England, Germany, Israel, USA; Conductor, choirs and orchestras; Performances as pianist; Own music programmes and serial broadcast on radio; Docent in Composition and Contemporary Music, Conservatorium Zwolle, until 1988; Compositions: Orchestral Music: Structures and Dance for Violin and orchestra, 1985; Litany of the Victims of War for Orchestra, 1985; Symmetrical Memories for Cello and Orchestra, 1988; Confrontations for Piano and Orchestra, 1990; Linzer Concert for Accordion and Orchestra, 1991; Chamber Music: Nam San for Marimba Solo, 1993; Dublin Quartet, 1989; If Only for Soprano and Percussion, 1991; From a Distant Planet for Baritone and Piano, all recorded. Publications: Werken met moderne klanken, 1978, Canto di Parole, 1968; Edited songbooks for children. Contributions to: Articles about electronic music, music education, notation, women and music, Dutch magazines and International Society of Music Education publications. Honours: Composer in Residence, GA State University, Atlanta; Grant of "Meet The Composer", New York; 1st Prize for Vignettes, Dublin, 1990; Commission for Orchestral Work for celebration 50 years United Nations in Rotterdam, 1995. Memberships include: League of Dutch Composers. Hobbies: Music; Travel; Reading. Address: Celebeslaan 13, 1217 GT Hilversum, Netherlands.

MARGGRAF Wolfgang, b. 2 Dec 1933, Leipzig, Germany. Musicologist. m. Anne-Marie Lorz, 4 Jan 1975, 2 sons. Education: Studied at Universities of Leipzig and Jena, 1952-57; PhD, Leipzig, 1964. Career includes: Professor, 1987; Rector, Musikhochschule Weimar, 1990-93. Publications: Franz Schubert, 1967, 2nd edition, 1978; Giacomo Puccini, 1977; Franz Liszt, Schriften zur Tonkunst, 1980; Giuseppe Verdi, 1982; Franz Liszt in Weimar, 1985; Bach in Leipzig, 1985. Memberships: The Liszt Society, Weimar, 1984-; Gesellschaft für Musikforschung, 1991-. Address: Barfußerstrasse 12, Eisenach, Germany.

MARGIONO Charlotte, b. 1965, Holland. Singer (Soprano). Education: Studied at the studio of Netherlands Opera. Career: Appearances with Netherlands Opera from 1983, as Kate Pinkerton, Fiordiligi, Pamina, Liu and Amelia Grimaldi; Komische Oper Berlin 1985 as Marenka in The Bartered Bride; Berne and the Aix Festival 1988, as Mozart's Countess and Vitellia; Repeated Vitellia at Salzburg 1991 and sang Pamina at Bordeaux, 1992; Strauss's Four Last Songs at the 1995 Prom Concerts, London; Beethoven concert with Roger Norrington at Bremen, 1995 (also televised). Recordings include: Die Zauberflöte, as First Lady (Erato); Beethoven's Mass in C and Missa Solemnis (DGG); Ein Deutsches Requiem (Philips); Cosi fan tutte and La Finta giardiniera (Teldec). Address: c/o De Nederlandse Opera, Waterlooplein 22, 1011 PG Amsterdam, Netherlands.

MARGISON Richard (Charles), b. 16 July 1953, Victoria, BC, Canada. Operatic Tenor. m. Valerie Mary Kuinka, 12 Aug 1989. Education: University of Victoria, Victoria Conservatory of Music: AVCM; Banff School of Fine Arts; Voice Teacher: Selena James; Coaches Leopold Simoneau, Frances Adaskin. Debut: The Bartered Bride with the Pacific Opera Company, Victoria BC. Career: Has performed with many orchestras, including: Vancouver 1989, Toronto 1989, Montreal 1990, London Philharmonic 1991, Chicago 1991, Victoria 1991; Regularly appeared with Opera Companies including: English National Opera, 1989 and 1991 as Verdi's Riccardo and as Vakula in Rimsky's Christmas Eve, Montreal Opera 1991, Canadian Opera Company, 1991, Santiago Opera (Teatro Municipal) 1991, Den Norske Opera (Norway) 1991, Calgary Opera 1991 as Nadir in Les Pêcheurs de Perles; Other roles include Mozart's Ferrando (Ottawa) and Tito, Pinkerton (Edmonton), Fenton in Falstaff, Faust (at Houston), Don Carlos (San Francisco, 1992), Nemorino, Edgardo, Alfredo, Rodolfo and Lensky; Season 1992/93 as Riccardo at Antwerp, Don José at Brussels, Don Carlos at Melbourne and Cavaradossi at Covent Garden; Many appearances on radio and television in opera, oratorio and concert; Engaged as Cavaradossi in Tosca at the re-opening of the San Francisco Opera, 1997. Recordings: Beethoven 9th with London Philharmonic Orchestra, Yehudi Menuhin conducting, RPO Records 1991; Les Grand Duos D'Amour from French Operas: Quebec Symphony, Simon Streatfield conducting, 1988. Hobbies: Fishing; Tennis; Sailing. Current Management: Columbia Artists: Zemsky Green Division, New York, USA. Address: 42 Aberdeen Avenue, Toronto, Ontario, M4X 1A2, Canada.

MARGITA Stefan, b. 3 Aug 1956, Kosice, Czechoslovakia. Singer (Tenor). Studied in Kosice and was member of the National Theatre Prague 1986-91 Notably as Hoffmann; Guest appearances in Moscow, Genoa, Stuttgart, Paris and Budapest; Wexford Festival 1991, as Lucentio in The Taming of the Shrew by Goetz; Season 1991-92 as Don Ottavio at the Savonlinna Festival and Bellini's Tebaldo at Budapest; Sang Lensky at Trieste, 1996. Recordings include: Bellerofonte by Myslivecek and Mahler's Das klagende Lied (Supraphon). Address: c/o National Theatre, PO Box 865, 11230 Prague 1, Czech Republic.

MARGOLINA Yelena, b. 1964, Lvov, Ukraine. Concert Pianist. Education: Studied in Lvov and at the St Petersburg State Conservatoire. Debut: Beethoven's Second Concerto, Lvov, 1974. Career: Notable performances at Moscow, Kiev, Khabarovsk, Lvov and Dnepropetrovsk; Western debut playing Prokofiev's Third Concerto, Berlin Schauspielhaus, 1985; Concerts at the Prokofiev Centenary Festival in Scotland, 1991; Performs in chamber concerts and as solo recitalist in a repertoire including works by Haydn, Mozart, Liszt, Beethoven, Debussy and Shostakovich; Concerto repertoire includes: Beethoven 1-4, Schumann, Chopin, Tchaikovsky, Ravel and Prokofiev; Currently resident in Germany. Honours include: Scottish International Piano Competition Winner, 1990; Casals Monferrato in Italy, 1990. Address: c/o Sonata, 11 Northpark Street, Glasgow, G20 7AA, Scotland.

MARIANI Lorenzo, b. 1950, NY, USA. Stage Director. Education: Studied at Harvard and the University of Florence, Italy. Debut: Maggio Musicale Florence, 1982, Bluebeard's Castle. Career: Directed L'Heure Espagnole at Florence, La Traviata, Luisa Miller and Offenbach's Barbe-Bleue, 1994 at Bologna; Montepulciano Festival with the Henze-Paisiello Don Chisciotte, Greek by Mark Antony Turnage and Puccini's Edgar; Recent productions include La Forza del Destino at Florence, Massenet's Esclarmonde in Turin, I Quatro Rusteghi in Geneva, La Bohème in Chicago and Don Giovanni in Tel Aviv; Revived Antoine Vitez's production of Pelléas et Mélisande for Covent Garden, 1993; Aida at Florence, 1996. Address: c/o Teatro Comunale di Firenze, via Solferino 15, 50123 Florence, Italy.

MARIMPIETRI Lydia, b. 1932, Italy. Singer (Soprano). Education: Studied in Italy. Career: Sang at La Scala Milan from 1959, at first as Nella in Gianni Schicchi, and as Micaela; Further appearances in Rome, Venice, Parma (Pamina, 1974) and Covent Garden (Nedda and Nannetta, 1973-75); Glyndebourne Festival 1962-65, as Drusilla in Poppea and Susanna; Other roles have included Mimi (at the Vienna Staatsoper), Marguerite, Manon, Bizet's Leila, Donna Elvira, Butterfly (Dallas, 1966) and Rossini's Elvira; Sang Mimi at Rome, 1976. Recordings include: L'Incoronazione di Poppea (EMI). Address: c/o Teatro dell'Opera di Roma, Piazza B Gigli 8, 00184 Rome, Italy.

MARIN Ion, b. 8 July 1960, Bucharest, Romania. Conductor. Education: Studied at the George Enescu Music School Bucharest, the Mozarteum Salzburg, Accademia Chigiana in Siena and the |International Academy, Nice. Career: Music Director, Transylvania Philharmonic, 1981, appearing in Rumania, East Germany, Czechoslovakia,Greece, Italy and France; Resident Conductor, Vienna Staatsoper, 1987-91, with repertoire from Mozart to Berg; Season 1991-92, in Japan for concerts with Margaret Price and Ruggiero Raimondi, Gala Concert in Prague and Le nozze di Figaro at the Teatro la Fenice, Venice; London debut with the LSO, 1991, English Chamber Orchestra with Yo-Yo Ma as soloist, 1992; US debut conducting L'Elisir at Dallas 1991, San Francisco, 1992, with Il Barbiere di Siviglia; Led Roman Polanski's production of Les Contes d'Hoffmann at the Opéra Bastille, Paris, 1992; Metropolitan Opea, 1992-93, Semiramide and Ariadne auf Naxos, Magic Flute; Further engagements in L'Italiana in Algeri at Venice, 1992, and with Houston Grand Opera; Concerts with the City of Birmingham Symphony, Philadelphia Orchestra, Santa Cecilia, Rome, BBC Symphony, Rotterdam Philharmonic, Montreal Symphony, 1993; Season 1997 with Scottish Chamber Orchestra, Orchestre National de France and the Yomiuri Nippen SO, Japan; Tour of Australia with the ABC. Recordings: Lucia di Lammermoor, with Studer and Domingo, series of Rossini one-acters starting with Il Signor Bruschino, Semiramide and sacred music for DGG; Various for other major labels including Mozart arias with Barbara Hendricks and the ECO, 1997. Honours: Awards Deutsche Schallplatten; Critics Award, 1992, 1994; Nominations for Grammy award. Address: c/o Harold Holt Ltd, 31 Sinclair Road, London, W14 ONS, England.

MARINELLI Carlo, b. 13 Dec 1926, Rome, Italy. Musicologist; Discographer. 1 son, 1 daughter. Education: Degree in Letters, University of Rome, 1948. Career: Founder and Editor, Microsolco magazine, 1952-59; Professor, History of Music, 1970-, Associate, 1985-, Associate, History of Modern and Contemporary Music, 1992-, Department of Comparative Culture, Faculty of Letters, University of L'Aquila. L'Aquila. Publications: Le cantate profane di J S Bach, 1966; La musica strumentale da camera di Goffredo Petrassi, 1967; Lettura di Messiaen, 1972; Cronache di Musica Contemporanea, 1974; L'opera cèca, l'opera russa, l'opera in Polonia e Ungheria, 1977; Opere in disco. Da Monteverdi a Berg, 1982; Goffredo Petrassi, An Anthology, 1983; Faust e Mefistofele nelle opere sinfonico-vocali, Discografia, 1986; Le opere di Mozart su libretti di Da Ponte, Discografia, 1988; Mozart, Singspiele, Discografia, 1993. Editor: Quaderni IRTEM, Discografie Mozart, Rossini, Monteverdi, Donizetti, Bellini, Verdi, Puccini; Repertori fonti sonore audiovisive italiane Mozart, Rossini; Notizie Videoarchivo Opera e Balletto; Notizie Archivo Sonoro Musica Contemporanea. Memberships: President, IRTEM; President, AIASA; Board Member, IMZ; International, American, Australian, French, Spanish and Italian Musicological Societies; IASA; IAML; ARSC; ASRA; AFAS; AISNA; ADUIM. Address: Via Francesco Tamagno 67, 00168 Rome, Italy.

MARINOV Swetoslav, b. 21 Sept 1945, Lom, Bulgaria. Leader; Solo Concert Violinist. m. Elena Maeva, 10 Aug 1967, 2 sons. Education: Music school of Sofia, Bulgaria; Bulgarian State Conservatoire, Sofia; Studied with V Tatrai in Budapest, with Mischa Geler in Moscow Conservatoire, with Yfrah Neaman at the Guildhall School of Music and Drama. Debut: Violinist, Orpheus String Quartet, 1969. Career: Performed with the Tilev String Quartet from 1973, and the Bulgarian RT String Quartet, 1975; Leader of Sofia Soloist Chamber Orchestra, 1981 and Leader of Bremerhaven's Opera, Germany, 1988; Other concert activity includes violinist and violist of Bulgarian RT String Quartet and

Sofia Chamber Orchestra; Concert tours in Europe, Asia, Australia, South America; In duo violin piono, concerts with Katia Evrova in France, Cycle of Mozart 16 sonatas, 1990, 1991 and Beethoven, Schubert, C Franck sonatas, 1992; Brazil 1993; In solo viola concert tour with G Tilev, violin, in Symphonie Concertante by Mozart with Niederheinischen Sinfoniker, Mönchengladbach. Recordings: With Radio Sofia, Warsaw, Moscow and Paris. Honours: Prize winner of competition for string quartets in Kolmae, 1978 and Evian, France, 1980. Address: Rosenweg 5, 27607 Langen, Germany.

MARK Peter, b. 31 Oct 1940, New York, New York, USA. Conductor. m. Thea Musgrave. Education: BA, Musicology, Columbia University, 1961; Juilliard School of Music, with Jean Morel, Joseph Fuchs, Walter Trampler, MS, 1963. Career: Boy soprano soloist, Children's Chorus, New York City Opera and Metropolitan Opera, 1953-55; Principal freelance and string quartet violist, Juilliard Orchestra, Princeton Symphony, Trenton Symphony, Tiemann String Quartet, Beaux Arts and Los Angeles String Quartet, Santa Barbara Symphony, Lyric Opera Chicago, 1960-68; Assistant principal violist, Los Angeles Philharmonic Orchestra, 1968-69; Solo Violist, Europe, South America and US tours, 1965-77; General Director, Conductor, Virginia Opera Association, 1975-; Conductor, Chamber Players, Santa Barbara Chamber Orchestra, 1976-77; Guest Conductor, Wolf Trap Orchestra, 1979, New York City Opera 1981, Los Angeles Opera Repertory Theater 1981, Royal Opera House, London, 1982, Hong Kong Philharmonic Orchestra 1984; Jerusalem Symphony Orchestra, 1988; Tulsa Opera, 1988; Opera Nacional de Mexico, 1989; Conductor, local premiere of Porgy and Bess, Buenos Aires and Sao Paulo, 1992; Guest Conductor, Opera Nacional de Mexico, 1989, 1992; Orlando Opera Company, 1993; Richmond Symphony, 1993; New York Pops, Carnegie Hall, 1991; Conducted La Bohème at the 1996 Torre del Lago Festival. Recordings: As conductor: Mary, Queen of Scots, 1979; A Christmas Carol, 1980; Moss Music Group 301, Moss Music Group 302; Handel's Julius Caesar, 1997; Also numerous recordings as violist. Honours: Recipient Elias Lifchey viola award Juilliard School of Music, 1963; Rosa Ponselle Gold Medal, 1997. Memberships: Phi Beta Kappa; Musicians Union, New York, London, Los Angeles, Norfolk, Virginia. Address: c/o Virginia Opera, PO Box 2580, Norfolk, VA 23501, USA.

MARKAUSKAS Arvydas, b. 25 Sept 1951, Kaunas, Lithuania. Singer (Baritone). Education: Studied at the Vilnius Conservatory. Career: Sang at the Vilnius Opera from 1979, making his debut as the Count in Lortzing's Der Wildschütz; Guest appearances throughout Russia and eastern Europe and with the Lithuanian Opera in the USA (notably in Chicago); Other roles include Belcore, Posa, Eugene Onegin, Amonasro, Iago, Nabucco and Marcello; Concert repertoire includes Handel's Samson, the War Requiem, Carmina Burana and Kabalevsky's Requiem. Address: c/o Lithuania State Opera, Vienuolio 1, 232600 Vilnius, Lithuania.

MARKERT Annette, b. 1957, Kaltensundheim,Germany. Singer, Mezzo-soprano. Education: Studied in Leipzig with Helga Forner and with Hannelore Kuhse and Eleanore Elstermann. Debut: British Debut, Dec 1989 in the Alto Rhapsody with the BBC Philharmonic under Kurt Sanderling. Career: Has sung with the Landestheater Halle as Handel's Floridante, Rinaldo and Tamerlano, Gluck's Orpheus and Carmen; Bach oratorios on German radio and oratorio performances and Lieder recitals throughout Germany. Honours: Second Prize, Maria Canals Competition, Barcelona, 1985; Handel Prize 1989. Address: c/o Landestheater Halle, Universitatsring 24-25, D-4020 Halle, Germany.

MARKEVITCH Dimitry, b. 16 Mar 1923, La Tour-de-Peilz, Switzerland. Cellist. Education: Studied with Maurice Eisenberg and Nadia Boulanger at Ecole Normale de Paris, and in the USA with Gregor Piatigorsky. Recordings include: 6 Bach Suites; 7 Beethoven Cello Sonatas; Beethoven Kreutzer Sonata, Op 47, Czerny version; Kodály Sonata Op 8; Shostakovich Sonata Op 40. Publications: Beethoven Op 64, 2nd edition, 1992; 6 Bach Suites, 3rd edition, 1995; Cello Story, The Solo Cello, both being reprinted. Memberships: American Violoncello Society; Viola da Gamba Society of America; Violin Society of America; American Musicological Society; American Musical Instrument Society; American Beethoven Society; Catgut Acoustical Society of America; Shrine to Music Museum of America; Société Française de Musicologie; Château Chillon, Montreux, Switzerland; Société Paderewski, Switzerland. Address: 87 Rue du Lac, CH-1815, Clarens, Switzerland.

MARKHAM Ralph, b. 1949, Canada. Pianist. Career: Studied at the Royal Toronto Conservatory of Music, and at the Cleveland Institute of Music with Vronsky and Babin; Formed Piano Duo partnership with Kenneth Broadway and has given many recitals and concerts in North America and Europe; BBC Debut recital 1979 and further broadcasts on CBC TV, Radio France Musique, The Bavarian Radio Hilversum in Holland; Stravinsky's Three Dances from Petrushka at the Théâtre des Champs Elysées, Paris, 1984; Season 1987-88, included 40 North American recitals; Concert with the Vancouver Symphony and New York debut on WQXR Radio; Season 1988-89 included the concertos for Two Pianos by Mozart and Bruch in Canada and a recital tour of England and Germany; Recent performances of the Bartók Sonata for two pianos and percussion, with Evelyn Glennie and a 1990-91 tour of North America, Europe and the Far East; Festival appearances include Newport USA 1988. Recordings: Duos by Anton Rubinstein; Vaughan Williams Concerto for Two Pianos; Saint-Saëns Carnival of the Animals. Honours: Young Artist of the Year, Musical America Magazine, 1980, with Kenneth Broadway. Address: c.o Robert Gilder and Co, Enterprise House, 59-65 Upper Ground, London SE1 9PQ, England.

MARKHAM Richard, b. 23 June 1952, Grimsby, England. Pianist. Education: Privately with Shirley Kemp and Max Pirani, RAM; ARAM; LRAM; ARCM; RAM Recital Diploma. Debut: Queen Elizabeth Hall, 1974. Career: Recitals and Concerto Performances throughout England and abroad; Several London appearances at Royal Festival Hall, Royal Albert Hall, Queen Elizabeth Hall, Wigmore Hall, Barbican Hall and Purcell Room; the Henry Wood Promenade Concerts; Appearances at Festivals in Aldeburgh, Bath, Berlin, Cheltenham, Harrogate, City of London, Schleswig-Holstein and York; Regular broadcasts of recitals and concerts for BBC and numerous TV and Radio Stations abroad; Has performed with the Philharmonia Orchestra, LSO, RPO, LPO, ECO, SNO, London Mozart Players, Bournemouth Sinfonietta, Hallé, Ulster and BBC Philharmonic and Scottish Symphony Orchestras; Frequent appearances and tours with piano duo partner, David Nettle in Europe, North America, Far East and Middle East. Recordings: Kabalevsky, Stravinsky and Rachmaninov with Raphael Wallfisch (cello), Bernstein (Arr. Nettle and Markham), Bennett and Grainger (2 Pianos); Holst, The Planets (2 Pianos) and Stravinsky, Petrushka and Le Sacre du Printemps (piano duet) with David Nettle; Elgar, Holst, Grainger and Rossini with CBSO Chorus; Saint-Saëns Carnival of the Animals with Aquarius (Collins Classics); South of the Border, a Latin American Collection with Jill Gomez (Hyperion); Nettle and Markham in England (Pickwick); Arnold, Concerto for Two Pianos and Concerto for Piano Duet (Conifer). Honours: Silver Medal, Geneva International Competition, 1972; Calouste Gulbenkian Foundation Music Fellowship, 1976-78. Memberships: Incorporated Society of Musicians; Royal Academy of Music Club. Hobbies: Travelling; Cooking; Theatre; Cinema; Playing Cards; Naturism. Address: The Old Power House, Atherton Street, London SW11 2JE, England.

MÄRKL Jun, b. 1959, Munich, Germany. Conductor; Musical Director. Education: Studied piano, violin and conducting, with degrees in violin and conducting, Music Academy, Hannover, 1978; Further studies with Kees Bakels, Sergiu Celibidache and Gustav Meier, University of Michigan at Ann Arbor, USA. Career: Member, Junge Deutsche Philharmonie, 1980-84; Season 1991-92, Principal Conductor and Music Director, Saarland State Theatre; Conducted performances of Tosca, Marriage of Figaro, and Dvorak's Dmitrij; Conducted premiere of Detlev Glanert's Der Spiegel des großen Kaisers, 1995; Season 1995-96, London debut at Royal Opera House, Covent Garden, with Götterdammerung; Season 1996-97, with Bavarian State Opera in Munich, included new production of Smetana's Bartered Bride, Aida, Madame Butterfly, La Traviata, Peter Grimes; With Berlin State Opera, productions of Lohengrin, Salome, The Flying Dutchman, 1996-97; Also engagements in the same season with La Clemenza di Tito in Stuttgart and Falstaff in Bern, Madame Butterfly, Manon, Tales of Hoffmann, Tosca, Turandot and Hindemith's Cardillac; Premiere of Babylon by Detlef Heusinger, Schwetzinger Festspiele, 1997; Forthcoming engagements include tours to Japan and Australia in 1998 and a debut at the Metropolitan Opera, New York. Honours: Conducting Competition winner, German Music Council, 1986; Scholarship for study at Tanglewood with Leonard Bernstein and Seiji Ozawa, with the Boston Symphony Orchestra. Address: c/o Nationaltheater Mannheim, Goetheplatz, 68161 Mannheim, Germany.

MARKOV Albert, b. 8 May 1933, Kharkov, USSR. Violinist; Composer. Education: Kharkov Music School; Moscow Gnessin Conservatory; Graduate Master Diploma, 1957; Doctor, 1960. Career: Concert Tours in USSR, Eastern and Western Europe, America, Solo with Leningrad Philharmonic, Moscow Philharmonic, major orchestras in Belgium, America, Holland, Sweden, England, Denmark, Portugal, Poland, Germany, Yugoslavia and other countries, 1978-; Professor, Manhattan School of Music, USA. Compositions: 3 Violin Sonatas; 3 Violin Rhapsodies; Concerto Caprices; Duo Sonata for two violins; Chamber Symphony; Formosa, suite for violin and orchestra. Recordings: Paganini Concerto No 2; Other recordings with orchestras and solo compositions by Bach, Veracini, Schubert, Pagannini, Prokofiev, Shostakovich, about 30. Publications: Sonata for Violin Solo, Violin Technique 1984; Duo-Sonata Edition of The Tchaikovsky Violin Concerto; Three Rhapsodies for violin and orchestra "Little Mermaid" (method). Contributions to: Sovetskaya Musica, USSR; Novoye Russkoe Slovo, Russian Daily, USA. Honours: Gold Medal, Violin National Competition, Moscow, 1957, in Brussels, 1959; Ysaye Medal, Belgium. Memberships: Rondo Music Society, President; Music Director, Albert Markov Summer Music Festival, Nova Scotia, Canada. Hobbies: Inventor; Patent Holder. Address: 3 Farm Creek Road, Rowayton, CT 06853, USA.

MARKOVA Juliana, b. 8 July 1945, Sofia, Bulgaria. Pianist. m. Michael Roll, 1 son. Education: Sofia Conservatory; Verdi Conservatory Milan with Ilonka Deckers. Career: After success in Enescu and Marguerite Long Competitions she performed on both sides of the Atlantic; Berlin Festival, Boston Symphony Orchestra and Andrew Davis and the Los Angelese Philharmonic under Zubin Mehta; Concerto engagements with all major orchestras in the USA and recitals at Lincoln Center NY and in Los Angeles; Recent performances in Atlanta, Cleveland, Chicago, Philadelphia, Detroit, Dallas, Montreal, Toronto and Milwaukee; European tours have included Berlin, Florence and Milan; London concerts with the London Symphony Orchestra, Royal Philharmonic and the Philharmonia, with Claudio Abbado and Simon Rattle; Regional engagements with the City of Birmingham Symphony and Royal Scottish Orchestra; British tour with the Sofia Philharmonic; Season 1991-92 with tour of Japan and debut with the San Francisco Symphony; Repertoire includes concertos by Beethoven, Haydn, Mozart, Prokofiev and Saint-Saëns. Address: c/o Harold Holt Ltd, 31 Sinclair Road, London W14 ONS, England.

MARKS Alan, b. 14 May 1949, Chicago, IL, USA. Concert Pianist. Education: Studied Piano with Shirley Parnas Adamas, Juilliard School of Music with Irwin Freundlich; BMus, 1971; Studied at Peabody Conservatory Baltimore with Leon Fleischer, 1971-72. Career: New York debut in 1971 followed by tour of US schools, prisons and hospitals with violinist Daniel Heifetz; Tours as soloist throughout USA and in Europe and Japan; British debut in 1979; Chamber music performances at the Marlboro and Santa Fe Festivals; Premiered Seven Pieces and Caprichos by Carlos Chavez, 1975, 1976; Teacher at the 92nd Street "Y" in New York, 1972-80 and Lincoln Center Institute, 1979-81. Honours include: Winner of Concert Artists Guild Piano Competition, 1970. Address: c/o Lincoln Center Institute, Lincoln Center, NY 10023, USA.

MARKUS Urs, b. 29 Sept 1941, Villmergen, Aargau, Switzerland. Singer, Baritone. Education: Studied in Zurich, Milan and Fribourg. Career: Sang as a bass at the Biel-Solothurn Opera, 1979-81, baritone roles at Trier, 1983-86; Engaged at Brunswick 1986-88, Nationaltheater Mannheim from 1988; Guest engagements at Geneva, Nancy and Metz; Roles have included Pizarro and Gluck's Agamemnon, Mozart's Count and Alfonso, Verdi's Amonasro and Iago, Telramund, the Dutchman and Hans Sachs, Escamillo and Gerster's Enoch Arden; Concert appearances throughout Switzerland in Berlin, Venice and Copenhagen.

MARLEYN Paul, b. 1965, England. Concert Cellist. Education: Studied with David Strange at the Royal Academy of Music, from 1981, with Lawrence Lesser in Boston and Aldo Parisot at Yale University. Career: Recital and solo appearances from 1988 throughout Europe, Canada and the United States, Jordan Hall Boston, Merkin Hall NY, Chamber Music East and Cape and Island's Music Festivals; Wigmore Hall, London; Tour of Europe 1985 as solo-cellist with the European Community Youth Orchestra under Claudio Abbado; Radio and television engagements in Britain, the USA and Switzerland; Tours of Japan, South Korea and Switzerland, 1991. Honours: Suggia Scholarship, Dove Prize and Thomas Igloi Trust Prize at the RAM; First Prize, Hudson Valley National String Competition, NY, 1988. Address: c/o Anglo-Swiss Management, Suite 35-37 Morley House, 320 Regent Street, London W1R 5AD, England.

MAROS Miklos, b. 14 Nov 1943, Pecs, Hungary. Composer; Teacher; Chamber Orchestra Leader. m. Ilona Maros. Education: Composition and Theory, Academy of Music, Budapest; Composition, State College of Music, Stockholm. Career: Leader, Maros Ensemble; Compositions frequently performed in Europe and USA. Compositions include: Turba, choir; Denique, soprano and orchestra; Symphonies Nos 1-3; Oolit, chamber orchestra; Divertimento, chamber orchestra; Concerto for Harpsichord and Chamber Orchestra; Concerto for Trombone and Orchestra; Sinfonietta; Concerto for Alto Saxophone and Orchestra; Concerto for Clarinet and Orchestra; Chamber music; Electronic music. Recordings: Descort, soprano flute and double bass; Manipulation No 1, bassoon and live electronics; Divertimento, chamber orchestra; Oolit; Circulation, strings; Dimensions, percussion; Quartet for Saxophones; Symphony No 1; Stora grusharpan, radio opera; 4 songs from Gitanjali, soprano and chamber ensemble; Concerto for Trombone and Orchestra; Capriccio, guitar; Undulations, alto saxophone and piano; Passacaglia, soprano and organ; Turba, choir; Schattierungen, violincello; Praefatio, organ; Concerto for Alto Saxophone and Orchestra; Sinfonia concertante (Symphony No 3); Trifoglio, harp. Honours: Composer-in-Residence, West

Berlin (DAAD/Berliner Künstler programme); Lifetime Artists' Award, Swedish Government, 1990. Memberships: Society of Swedish Composers; Imternational Society for Contemporary Music, Swedish Section; Society for Experimental Music and Arts. Address: Krukmakargatan 18, S-11851 Stockholm, Sweden.

MAROSI Laszlo, b. 11 Oct 1960, Sarvar. Education: Piano, Trombone, Secondary Music School, 1974-78; Conducting Studies, Pál Karch, At Tama's Breitner, L F Academy of Music, Budapest, 1978-82; Musical History Research at Palkarch MM and Studies, 1988-93. Debut: Hungarian Radio Wind Symphony Concert and Recording, 1982. Career: Leader Conductor, Central Band of the Hungarian Army, 1983-95; Head of Wind Conducting, University of Music, 1987; Conductor, Wind Symphony of BP Academy of Music, 1993; Founder Conductor, Budapest Wind Symphony, 1993. Compositions: Several arrangements for wind symphony, Editio Musica, Budapest; Fam Music Publisher Budapest, Musica Mundana Deurne. Recordings: Hungarian Wind Music, 1985; Liszt Marches, 1986; Hungarian Historical Marches, 1992; Variations for Winds, 1994; Hungarian Wind Symphony Music, 1995; In medias res, 1996; The Magic Potion, 1996; Frigyes Hidas: Requiem, 1996; The Lehár Dynasty Marches, 1997; László Dubrovay: New Wind Music, 1997. Publications: The History of Military Music in Hungary, 1994; Conductors 1741-1945. Contributions to: Die Militarmusik des Freiheits Kampfes 1848-49; Die Gegenwartige Situation der Militarmusik, 1995. Honours: Award of the Association of Hungarian Composers, 1992, 1996. Memberships: IGEB; WASBE. Hobbies: Gardening; Sport. Current Management: Fon-Trade. Address: 1134 Budapest, Gidofalvy u 29 VIII 6 Hungary.

MARQUEZ Marta, b. 1955, San Juan, Puerto Rico. Singer (Soprano, since 1994 Mezzo-Soprano). Education: Studied at the Juilliard, New York, and with Tito Gobbi in Florence. Debut: New York City Opera, as Oscar in Un Ballo in Maschera. Career: Sang at Saarbrucken from 1979, notably as Constanze, Frau Fluth, Mimi, Violetta, Susanne and Zdenka in Arabella; Spoleto Festival, 1982, as Sylvie in Gounod's La Colombe; Deutsche Oper am Rhein, Düsseldorf, from 1984, with notable roles including Poppea, Hänsel, Cherubino, Idamantes, Cenerentola and Rosina (Barbiere), and further engagements throughout Germany; Puerto Rico at the Pablo Casals Festival and appearances in Moscow with the Düsseldorf company; Other roles include Nedda and Musetta; Frequent concert appearances; Guest appearances at Royal Opera House, Covent Garden (Zerlina, Musetta), and Bavarian State Opera, Munich (Susanna, Aennchen); Sang the title role in the premiere of Klebe's Gervaise Macquart, Dusseldorf, 1996. Address: Neusserweg 72, 40474 Düsseldorf, Germany.

MARRINER Andrew (Stephen), b. 25 Feb 1954, London, England. Clarinettist. m. Elizabeth Ann Sparke, 17 Dec 1988, 1 son. Education: Kings College Choir School, Cambridge, 1962-67; Kings School, Canterbury, 1967-71; Oxford University, 1972-73; Musichochschule, Hannover, Germany, 1973-77. Debut: Solo chamber and orchestral work, 1977-. Appointments: Principal Clarinet, London Symphony Orchestra, 1986-; Prinicipal Clarinet Academy, St Martins, 1987-; First performances of pieces written for him by: John Taverner, 1997, Robin Holloway, 1997, Dominic Muldowney, 1997. Recordings: Mozart Quintet and Concerto (London Proms, 1997); Weber Concerto; Finzi Concerto; Taverner. Honour: Hon RAM, 1995. Membership: Lords Taverner. Hobby: Cricket. Current Management: Ingpen and Williams. Address: 67 Cornwall Gardens, London, SW7 4BA, England.

MARRINER Neville (Sir), b. 15 Apr 1924, Lincoln, England. Musician; Conductor. m. Elizabeth M Sims, 1958, 1 son, 1 daughter. Education: Lincoln School; Royal College of Music. Career: Director, Academy of St Martin in the Fields, 1959; Musical Director, Los Angeles Chamber Orchestra, 1969-78; Director, South Bank Festival of Music, 1975-78; Director, Meadowbrook Festival, Detroit, 1979-84; Music Director, Minnesota Orchestra, 1979-86; Music Director, Stuttgart Radio Symphony Orchestra, 1986-89; Conducted Béatrice et Bénédict at the Festival Hall, 1989. Recordings include: CDs of Dvorák Serenades, Haydn Violin Concerto in C; Mozart Serenade K361; Il Barbiere di Siviglia; Schubert 4th and 5th Symphonies; Baroque Favourites, with Yehudi Menuhin, The English Connection (Vaughan Williams The Lark Ascending, Elgar Serenade and Tippett Corelli Fantasia); Trumpet Concertos with Hakan Hardenberger; Mendelssohn Piano Works with Murray Perahia, Mozart Haffner Serenade; 200 other recordings include Bach Concertos, Suites and Die Kunst der Fuge; Vivaldi, The Four Seasons and other concertos; Concerti Grossi by Corelli, Geminiani, Torelli, Locatelli and Manfredini, Mozart Symphonies, Concertos, Serenades and Divertimenti, Handel Messiah, Opera overtures and Water and Fireworks music; Die Zauberflöte, 1980; Handel Arias with Kathleen Battle; Il Turco in Italia and Don Giovanni; Verdi's Oberto, 1997. Honours: CBE; FRCM; KBE, 1985; Tagore Gold Medal; Six Edison Awards, Netherlands; Two Mozart Gemeinde Awards, Ausdtria; Grand Prix du Disque, France, three times; 2 Grammy Awards, USA; FRAM; Shakespeare Prize; KT of Polar Star. Address: 67 Cornwall Gardens, London SW7, England.

MARROCCO William (Thomas), b. 5 Dec 1909, West New York, NJ, USA. Professor.m. 15 Sept 1937, 1 son, 1 daughter. Education: BM, 1934, MA, 1940, Eastman School of Music, University of Rochester; PhD, University of California, Los Angeles, 1952; Licentiate and Magistrate Diplomas, R Conservatory of Music, Naples, Italy. Career: Instructor, Violin, University of Iowa, 1945; Associate Profesor, University of Kansas, Lawrence, 1946-49; Professor, University of California, 1949-77; Associate Director of the Education Abroad Program in Hong Kong during 1976-77. Recordings: With the Roth String Quartet; String Quartet in C, by Vernon Duke, 1959; Quartet: Op 74, Ernst Toch, 1961; Quintets in G and C, by Michael Haydn, 1959. Publications: Music in America, with Harold Gleason, 1964; Polyphonic Music of the Fourteenth Century, 6 volumes, 1967-78; Medieval Music, with Nicholas Sandon, 1977; Memoirs of a Stradivarius, 1988; Major Article, Anthonius Arena, Master of Law and Dance of the Renaissance, Studi Musicali XVIII, 1989; 9 other publications. Address: 2101 Buck Street, Eugene, OR 97405, USA.

MARS Jacques, b. 25 Mar 1926, Paris, France. Singer, Bass. Career: Sang at the Paris Opera from 1955; Other roles include the Commendatore in Don Giovanni, King Philip in Don Carlos, Boris Godunov and Mephistopheles in La Damanation de Faust; Paris Opéra-Comique, 1965, as the villians in Les Contes d'Hoffmann; Glyndebourne Opera, 1969-70, as Golaud in Pelléas et Mélisande; Sang in the premiere of Daniel-Leseur's Andrea del Sarto, Marseilles, 1969; Monte Carlo, 1979, as Massenet's Don Quichotte; Appearances at La Scala Milan and the Maggio Musicale Florence. Recordings: Persée et Andromède by Ibert; Les Abencérages by Cherubini; Pelléas et Mélisande; Sang in the premiere of Daniel-Lesur's Andrea del Sarto, Marseilles, 1969; Monte Carlo, 1979, as Massenet's Don Quichotte; Appearances at La Scala Milan and the Maggio Musicale Florence. Recordings: Persée et Andromède by Ibert; Les Abencérages by Cherubini; Pelléas et Mélisande; Les Pêcheurs de Perles. Address: c/o Opera de Monte Carlo, Place du Casino, Monte Carlo, Monaco.

MARSALIS Wynton, b. 18 Oct 1961, New Orleans, Louisiana, USA. Trumpeter. Education: Trained in classical music and played with the New Orleans Philharmonic aged 14; Juilliard School, NY, USA. Career: Joined Art Blakey and the Jazz Messengers 1980; Toured with Herbie Hancock, 1981; Formed own group 1982 with brother Branford Marsalis on tenor saxophone; Grammy Awards 1984 for Jass album and for Concertos by Haydn, Hummel and Leopold Mozart; Appearances with New York Philharmonic, Cleveland Orchestra, Los Angeles Philharmonic, London Symphony and other major European orchestras; Conductors include, Lorin Maazel, Zubin Mehta, Leonard Slatkin and Esa-Pekka Salonen. Recordings: Exclusive contracts with CBS Masterworks and CBS Records. Honours: Awards include Grammy, USA; Grand Prix du Disque, France. Address: c/o Van Walsum Management, 40 St Peter's Road, London W6 9BH, England.

MARSCHNER Wolfgang, b. 23 May 1926, Dresden, Germany. Violinist. Education: Studied violin, piano, composition and conducting, Conservatory Dresden and Mozarteum Salzburg. Debut: At age 9 with Tartini's Devil's Trill sonata. Career: Professor, Folkwang-School, Essexn, 1956; Professor, Music Conservatory, Cologne, 1958; Professor, Music Conservatory, Freiburg, 1963-; Regular Mastercourses in Warsaw and Weimar; Director of Pfluger-Foundation for young violinists, freiburg; International soloist career, concerts in Edinburgh Festival and with Berlin Philharmonic and Royal Philharmonic, London; Premiere, Schoenberg's Violin Concerto in many cities including London, Vienna and Zurich; Founder of: International Ludwig Spohr Violin Competition; Jacobus Stainer Violin Maker's Competition; International Youth Violin Competition; German Spohr Academy; Festival Wolfgang Marschner, Hinterzarten. Compositions: Various works for orchestra; 2 concerti for violin and orchestra; Sonata for solo violin; Canto notturno for violin and organ; Rhapsody for viola solo. Honours: Kranichsteiner prize for contemporary music, 1954; English record prize for interpretation of Schoenberg's Violin Concerto, Bundesverdienstkreuz, 1986. Address: Burgunder Strasse 4, D-7800 Freiburg, Germany.

MARSH Jane, b. 25 June 1944, San Francisco, USA. Singer, Soprano. Education: Studied with Ellen Repp at Oberlin College and with Lili Wexburg and Otto Guth in NY, USA. Debut: Spoleto Festival 1965, as Desdemona. Career: Sang in Essen, Hamburg, Moscow, Prague, Naples, Trieste and Johannesburg: Further appearances in Pittsburgh, San Antonio and San Francisco, 1968; Deutsche Oper am Rhein Dusseldorf from 1968; Salzburg 1973, in the premiere of Orff's De Temporum fine Comoedia; Often heard as Mozart's Donna Anna, Queen of Night and Constanze. Recordings: De Temporum fine Comoedia; The Invisible City of Kitezh; Alfonso und Estrella; Penthesilea by Schoeck; Der Vampyr by Marschner, Voce.

MARSH Robert Wayne Edward, b. 9 Feb 1956, Salford, Lancashire, England. Organist; Conductor; Composer; Teacher; Writer. Education: Organ Scholar, Keble College, Oxford; Postgraduate Studies, Jesus College, Cambridge; Royal Manchester College of Music; Royal Northern College of Music; Royal College of Music. Debut: Organ Continuo Player with Winchester Cathedral Choir and Waynflete Singers, Winchester Cathedral, 1978. Career: Assistant Director of Music, 1978-79, Director of Music, 1979-86, Reigate Grammar School; Conductor, Dorking Choral Society, 1979-81; Member, General Committee, The Leith Hill Musical Festival, 1979-81; Organist, St Clement's Church, King Square, London, 1984-86; Assistant Organist, Ripon Cathedral, Director of Music, Ripon Cathedral Choir School, 1986-; Acting Organist and Master of the Choristers, Ripon Cathedral, 1994; Organist in Residence and Master of the Choristers, Malsis School, 1998-; Many Appearances on TV and Abroad. Recordings: The White Doe; Sing Joyfully; Cathedral Music From the Twentieth Century; The Organ of Ripon Cathedral. Publication: A Short History of the Organs of Ripon Cathedral, 1994. Contributions to: Independent Schools Association Incorporated Magazine; Ackrill Newspapers Ltd. Honours: ARCO, 1975; FRCO, 1977; BA(Oxon), 1977; Certificate in Education, University of Cambridge, 1978; ARCM, 1979; MA(Oxon), 1981. Memberships: Royal College of Organists; Incorporated Society of Musicians; Incorporated Association of Organists. Current Management: Ann Longmuir Services to the Arts. Hobbies: Cinema; Swimming; Travel; Photography; Reading; Politics. Address: Malsis School, Crosshills, North Yorkshire BD20 8DT, England.

MARSH Roger, b. 10 Dec 1949, Bournemouth, England. Composer; Lecturer. m. (1) Christina Rhys, 24 Jul 1976, 2 s, 1 d, (2) Anna Myatt, 19 Sep 1992, 1 s. Education: BA, 1971, DPhil, 1975, University of York; Studied with Bernard Rands. Career: Harkness Fellow, 1976-78, University of CA, San Diego; Lecturer, Keele University, 1978-88; Lecturer, Senior Lecturer, University of York; Member of Midland Music Theatre; Director of Black Hair contemporary music ensemble. Compositions: Not a Soul But Ourselves for 4 Amplified Voices, 1977; The Big Bang, music theatre, 1989; Stepping Out for Piano and Orchestra, 1990; Kagura, 1991; Love on The Rocks, music theatre, 1988; Espace for Orchestra, 1994. Recordings include: Not a Soul But Ourselves; Numerous radio broadcasts; CDs: Love on The Rocks and Ferry Music. Publications: Various. Honours include: Arts Council Composition Bursary, 1993. Memberships: SPNM Reading Panel, 1991-92; BBC Reading Panel, 1987-. Current Management: Novello; Mycaenas Music. Address: Ball Hall Farm, Storwood, York, YO4 4TD, England.

MARSH-EDWARDS Michael (Richard), b. 7 April 1928, Westgate-on-Sea, Kent, England. Composer; Conductor. m. (1) Stella K Parrott, 9 April 1952, 1 daughter, (2) Ann Wardleworth, 11 November 1971, (3) Srinuan Suwan, 9 January 1981, 1 son, 1 daughter. Education: Trinity College, London University, Associate and Licentiate Diplomas, Hon PhD, DMus. Career: Conductor, Luton Bach Orchestra, 1949-63; Conductor 1952-63, currently Vice President, Luton Symphony Orchestra; Director of Music, Luton Industrial Mission and Luton Community Centre, 1957-62; Conductor, Halton Orpheus Choir, 1973-75; Freelance Conductor and Lecturer; Consultant, Bangkok Symphony Orchestra. Compositions: Toccata for Percussion and Orchestra; Variations, 8 percussionists; 3 Studies, 12 percussionists; Dance Overture; Birthday Overture; Revolutionary Overture, 1956; Chester Overture; Celebration Overture; Music 1, 60 strings; Music 2, strings and percussion; Music 3, strings and brass; Music 4; Oppositions, 2 orchestras; Structures; Fantasy on the Waltz of Diabelli; Thai Dances; Balinese Dances; Petite Suite pour le Tombeau d'Erik Satie; Treurzang; Suite Guernesiaise; Concerto for 11 instruments; Horn Concerto; Devouring Time, high voice and piano; Mischievous Ditties, high voice and piano; Elegy on the Name of Havergal Brian, piano or string orchestra; Peter Goldberg Variations, wind quintet; Concertino for harpsichord and string orchestra; Incantations, for flute, oboe, viola and piano; Toccata on One Note, for piano; Numerous other instrumental, vocal and electronic pieces; Music for children. Publications: Author of Concert Notes; Author and Presenter of Radio Scripts. Honours: Medal, American Biographical Institute, 1986; Alfred Nobel Medal, 1991. Memberships: Life Member, Former Vice-Chairman, British Music Society and Havergal Brian Society; Composers' Guild of Great Britain; Performing Rights Society. Address: 5/2440 Muban Prachachuen, Pakkred, Nontaburi 11120, Thailand.

MARSHALL Ingram (Douglas), b. 10 May 1942, NY, USA. Composer. Education: BA, Lake Forest College, 1964, Columbia University with Ussachevsky, electronic music, 1964-66, with Morton Subotnick in NY and California, and traditional Indonesian music at the California Institute of the Arts. Career: Taught at the California Institute of the Arts until 1974; Performances in Java, Bali and Scandinavia. Compositions: Transmogrification for tape, 1966; Three Buchla Studies for synthesizer 1969; Cortez, text-sound piece 1973; Vibrosuperball for 4 amplified percussion 1975; Non Confundar for string sextet, alto flute, clarinet and electronics, 1977; Spiritus for 6 strings, 4 flutes, harpsichord and vibraphone, 1981; Frog Tropes for brass sextet and tape, 1982; Voces resonae for string quartet, 1984. Address: ASCAP, ASCAP Building, One Lincoln Plaza, NY 10023, USA.

MARSHALL J Richard, b. 28 July 1929, Schenectady, NY, USA. Opera Conductor; Director. Education: BA, University of Rochester, 1951; MMus, 1953, DMus, 1963, Indiana University; Arts Management Diploma, Harvard University, 1967. Career: Head, Opera and Choral Music, University of Buffalo, NY, 1959-62; Head, Opera, Boston Conservatory, 1965-68; Founder, Director, New England Regional Opera, 1967-76; General Director, Charlotte Opera, Charlotte, North Carolina, 1976-82; Founder, President, Southern Opera Conference; Founder, Director, Center for Contemporary Opera, NYC, 1982-. Honours: Award for Service to Opera in New England, Performing Arts Association, Boston, 1975. Memberships: President, Southern Opera Conference; Central Opera Service; National Opera Association. Hobbies: Photography; Travel. Address: 475 Riverside Drive, Room 936, NY 10115, USA.

MARSHALL Margaret (Anne), b. 4 Jan 1949, Stirling, Scotland. Concert & Opera Singer, Soprano. m. Graeme Griffiths King Davidson, 2 daughters. Education: DRSAMD, Royal Scottish Academy of Music and Drama. Debut: Covent Garden, 1980; Vienna Staatsoper, 1988, Mozart's Countess; North America Opera debut in Toronto as Vitelia. Career: Performances in Festival Hall, Barbican, Covent Garden; Concerts & Opera in major European events; Has sung Gluck's Euridice and Mozart's Countess at Florence; Sang Fiordiligi at La Scala and Salzburg, 1982; Sang Fiordiling, La Scala, 1982 and Salzburg 1982-85 and 1990-91; Season 1990-91 with Countess in Hong Kong and Donna Elvira for ENO; Season 1991-92 included Violetta at Frankfurt, Mozart Bicentenary Gala at Covent Garden, followed by Fiordiligi and Vitellia in La Clemenza di Tito at the Salzburg Festival; Sang in Mozart's La Finta Giardiniera at the 1995 Montpellier Festival; Mozart's Countess of Flanders, 1995. Recordings: Mozart's C Minor Mass and Haydn's Masses, conducted by Marriner; Vivaldi's Tito Manlio and Canatas, Negri; Handel's Jephtha and Saul; Gluck Orfeo, Muti; Haydn Die Schöpfung and Bach St Matthew Passion, Erato; Pergolesi Stabat Mater, Abbado; Mozart Davidde Penitente and Die Schuldigkeit des Ersten Gebotes; Vaughan Williams Sea Symphony, Virgin Classics; Elgar The Kingdom, Chandos; Hypermestra in Les Danaides by Salieri. Honour: 1st prize, Munich International Competition, 1974. Hobbies: Squash; Golf. Address: Woodside Main Street, Gargunnock, Stirling, FK7 OPL, Scotland.

MARSHALL Nicholas, b. 2 Jun 1942, Plymouth, Devon, England. Composer; Teacher. m. Angela Marshall, 21 Jul 1982, 1 s, 1 d. Education: MA, University of Cambridge, 1964; Royal College of Music, 1964-65. Career: Pianist; Conductor; Teacher; Chairman and Artistic Director, Ashburton Festival, 1980-84. Compositions include: Section: Partita for Guitar; Three Japanese Fragments for guitar; Seven Folksongs for voice, recorder and piano; Arion and The Dolphins, Junior Operetta; Inscriptions for A Peal of Eight Bells for SATB; Suite for Guitar, Flute, Clarinet, Violin and Cello; Four Haiku for Solo Recorder; Trio for Recorders; Sonatina for Solo Flute; Jump for Flute and Piano; Five West Country Folk Songs for SATB; Two West Country Folk Songs for SATB; A Playford Garland for SATB; The Young King, Children's Opera; Five Country Dances for orchestra, Cool Winds for Cello and Guitar; The Virgin's Song for SATB; Carol for Christmas Eve for SATB. Recordings: On CD: Original music for Cello and Guitar, EMEC; Three Japanese Fragments for Guitar, EMEC. Membership: Composers' Guild of Great Britain. Address: Under Hill House, Slapton, Kingsbridge, Devon, TQ7 2PN, England.

MARSHALL Robert (Lewis), b. 12 Oct 1939, New York, New York, USA. Musicologist. m. Traute Maass, 9 Sept 1966, 1 son, 1 daughter. Education: AB, Columbia University, 1960; MA, 1962, PhD, 1968, Princeton University; French Horn with Gunther Schuller, High School of Music and Art, New York. Career: Faculty Member, 1966-83, Chair, 1972-78, Music, University of Chicago; Visiting professor at Princeton University, 1971-72; Columbia University, 1977; Faculty, 1983-, Incumbent Endowed Chair: Louis, Frances and Jeffrey Sachar Professor, Chair, 1985-92, Music, Brandeis University. Publications: The Compositional Process of J S Bach, 1972; Studies in Renaissance and Baroque Music in Honour of Arthur Mendel, 1974; Critical Editor, Cantatas for 9th and 10th Sundays after Trinity, 1985; J S Bach Cantata Autographs in American Collections, 1985; The Music of J S Bach: The Sources, The Style, The Significance, 1989; Mozart Speaks: Views on Music, Musicians and The World, 1991; Eighteenth Century Keyboard Music, 1994; Dennis Brain on Record: A Comprehensive Discography, 1996. Contributions to: Musical Quarterly; Journal of American Musicological Society. Honours: Otto Kinkeldey Award, American Musicological Society, 1974; First Incumbent, Harold Spivacke Consultant to Music division, Library of Congress, 1985; ASCAP-Deems Taylor Award, 1990. Memberships: American Bach Society; Neue Bach-Gesellschaft.

Hobbies: Hiking; Travel. Address: 100 Chestnut Street, West Newton, MA 02165, USA.

MARSHALL Wayne, b. 31 Jan 1961, Oldham, Lancashire, England. Concert Organist; Conductor. Education: ARCM Chetham's School Manchester; FRCO Royal College of Music, 1978-83; Austrian Government Scholarship 1983, to study at the Vienna Hochschule. Career: Organ scholar at Manchester Cathedral and St George's Chapel Windsor; Recitals at St Paul's Cathedral, Westminster Abbey, Festival Hall, Leeds and Birmingham Town Halls, and King's College, Cambridge; Tours of the USA and Yugoslavia; Windsor and Hong Kong Festivals; 1986, worked as repetiteur for Glyndebourne production of Porgy and Bess: Appeared as Jasbo Brown the jazz pianist; Assistant Chorus Master at Glyndebourne 1987; 1988-89 Seasons included Promenade Concert debut with the Poulenc Concerto and appearances with the City of Birmingham Symphony under Simon Rattle and the BBC Symphony under Paul Daniel; Conducted the premiere of Wilfred Joseph's Alice in Wonderland at the Harrogate Festival 1990; Carmen Jones in the West End, London, 1991; Last Night of the 1997 London Proms; Conductor of Porgy and Bess at the Bregenz Festival, 1997-98; Recital repertoire includes works by Bach, Dupré, Franck, Liszt, Messiaen, Reger, Schmidt and Vierne. Address: c/o Harold Holt Ltd, 31 Sinclair Road, London W14 ONS, England.

MARSHALL-DEAN Deirdre Pauline, b. 28 Feb 1965, Melbourne, Australia. Ethnomusicologist. m. Terry Dean, 14 Jan 1995, 1 son. Education: Studied Classical Singing with Junewyn Jones and Bettine McCaughan; BEd, Music, 1983-87, MA, 1988-94, Monash University; Studies, University of New England. Debut: Victoria State Opera Youth Company, 1985. Career: Teacher, Music, 1988; Founder, Dean Educational Services, 1994-. Recordings: 4 Teachers handbook and Tape using Indonesian Music and Western Classroom Instruments. Publications: YAP Islands; Maori Music in Australia. Contributions to: Musicology Australia. Memberships: International Council for Traditional Music; Musicological Society of Australia. Address: 30 Edithvale Road, Edithvale, Victoria 3196, Australia.

MARTA Istvan, b. 14 June 1952, Budapest, Hungary. Composer. 2 daughters. Education: Course in Composition in Yugoslavia led by W Lutoslawski, 1979; Diploma in Composition and Teaching from Ferenc Liszt Academy of Music, Budapest, 1981. Career: Folk Music Collecting Tour in Moldavia, Romania, 1973; Over 30 pieces of stage and film music composed; Teacher of History of Classical Music and Analysis of 20th Century Music, Jazz Department, Bela Bartok School of Music, Budapest, 1981-83; Organiser of Planum and Rendezvous, festivals of international contemporary music, 1982 and 1984; Music Director, National Theater, New Theater, Budapest, 1990-95; Director, Art Valley Multicultural Festival, 1995. Compositions: Text and Music, stage performance based on Samuel Beckett's radioplay, 1978; King of the Dead, cantata 1979; Christmas Day - 24th Lesson, Music for Chamber ensemble, 1980; Our Heats, movements for chamber choir and chamber orchestra, 1983; Visions, ballet performed by the ballet corps of the Hungarian State Opera, 1984; Dolls House Story, composition for percussion instruments, 1985; Workers' Operetta, musical 1985; per quattro tromboni, 1986; Kapolcs Alarm, a videoclip, 1987; Slips and Streams, a ballet for tape, 1989; Doom, A Sigh, string auartet, 1989; The Glassblower's Dream, string quartet, 1990; Anatomy of a Scream, ballet for tape, 1990; Blasting in the Bird Cage for tape, 1990; The Temptation of St Anthony, ballet for tape, 1992; Don't Look Back, ballet for tape, 1995; Faust, ballet for tape, 1995. Recordings: Our Hearts, Hungaroton, 1985; Alte und Neue Musik, Thorofon, Hannover 1984; The Wind Arises, Krem, Hungaroton, 1987. Honours: Hungarian Television Excellence Prize, 1975; Hungarian Radio Audience Prize, 1982 and 1987; Prize of the Tribune Internationale des Compositeurs, Paris, 1982 and 1987; Erkel Prize, Hungary, 1987. Memberships: Hungarian Music Union; Group of 180, 1980-83; Mandel Quartet, playing old and new music on harpsichord, synthesizer and percussion, 1982-. Hobbies: Old houses; Video. Current Management: Interkoncert, Budapest. Address: Ferenciektere 7-8, H-1053 Budapest, Hungary.

MARTIN Adrian, b. 1958, England. Singer (Tenor). Education: Studied at the London Opera Centre and the National Opera Studio. Debut: With Opera for All as Ramiro and Tonio. Career: Sang small roles at Covent Garden in Parsifal, Salome and Die Zauberflöte, then the Dancing Master in Ariadne and Pong in Turandot; Glyndebourne Festival as Tamino and Idamante; Appearances with English National Opera as Cassio, Alfred, the Steersman, Anatol (War and Peace), Don Ottavio, Vincent (Mireille), Tamino, Ferrando and Rodolfo, Nadir, Jenik in The Makropoulos Case and Erik in Fennimore and Gerda; Welsh National Opera as Lensky in Serban's production of Eugene Onegin; Scottish Opera in La Scala di Seta and La Cambiale di Matrimonio by Rossini; Has sung with Opera North as Rodolfo, Alfredo, Camille, Ismaele (Nabucco), Sali in a Village Romeo and Juliet, Tamino, Jacquino, Nadir and Ernesto; Overseas engagements at St Gallen (Hoffmann and Don Ottavio); Hamburg

and Zurich (Hoffmann); Paris (Tybalt in Roméo et Juliette at the Opéra) and Queensland (Nadir and Rodolfo at the Lyric Opera). Current Management: Athole Still International Management Limited, Forresters Hall, 25-27 Westow Street, London SE19 3RY, England.

MARTIN Andrea, b. 9 Mar 1949, Klagenfurt, Germany. Singer, Baritone. Education: Studied in Vienna and at the Santa Cecilia Academy in Rome; Teachers included Anton Dermota, Hans Hotter, Ettore Campogallian, Mario del Monaco and Giuseppe Taddei. Debut: Treviso 1979, as Malatesta in Don Pasquale. Career: Sang with the Wiener Kammeroper and in Klagenfurt, Salzburg, Graz and Munich; Further Italian engagements at Rome, Palermo, Bologna, Venice, Naples and Verona; Ravenna Festival as Michonnet in Adriana Lecouvreur; Has sung in Maria di Rudenz by Donizetti at Venice and Wiesbaden, as Luna in Trovatore at the Dresden Staatsoper; Guest appearances at the Théâtre des Champs-Elysées, Paris, Liège, Barcelona, Lisbon and Vienna; Concert tours of Japan, Korea, the USA and Brazil. Recordings: Imelda de Lambertazzi and Alina, Regina di Golconda by Donizetti, Salieri's Axur, and Così fan tutte. Address: c/o Teatro La Fenice, Campo S Fantin 2519, 1-30124 Venice, Italy.

MARTIN George (Whitney), b. 25 Jan 1926, New York, USA. Writer. Education: BA, Harvard College, 1948; Trinity College, Cambridge, 1950; LLB, University of Virginia Law School, 1953. Career: Practised Law, 1955-59; Full-Time Writer, 1959-. Publications: The Damrosch Dynasty, America's First Family of Music, 1983; The Companion to Twentieth-Century Opera, 3rd edition, 1989; Verdi, His Music, Life and Times, 4th edition, 1992, Chinese (pirated) edition, 1982, Spanish edition, 1984; Aspects of Verdi, 2nd edition, 1993; Verdi at The Golden Gate, Opera and San Francisco in the Gold Rush Years, 1993; The Opera Companion, 5th edition, 1997. Address: 21 Ingleton Circle, Kennett Square, PA 19348, USA.

MARTIN Janis, b. 16 Aug 1939, Sacramento, California, USA. Singer, Soprano. m. Gerhard Hellwig. Education: Studied with Julia Monroe in Sacramento and Lili Wexberg and Otto Guth in New York. Debut: San Francisco, 1960 as Annina in La Traviata. Career: Returned to San Francisco as Marina, Venus and Meg Page; New York City Opera debut 1962, as Mrs Grose in The Turn of the Screw; New York Metropolitan Opera from 1962-66, at first in mezzo roles then from 1973 as Sieglinde, Marie in Wozzeck and Kundry; Bayreuth Festival 1968-73, as Magdalene, Eva, Sieglinde and Kundry; Chicago 1971, as Tosca; Deutsche Oper Berlin 1971-88; Covent Garden 1973, as Marie; La Scala 1980, as The Woman in Erwartung; La Scala, Marie; Geneva Opera 1985 as Isolde; Other roles include Wagner's Senta, Brünnhilde, Isolde, Venus and Kundry; Tosca; Fidelio, Santuzza and Strauss's Ariadne, Dyer's Wife, Salome, Elektra, and Marschallin; Cologne Opera 1988, as the Dyer's Wife; Turin and Bayreuth, 1989, as Brünnhilde; Sang Beethoven's Leonore at Dusseldorf, 1990; Season 1991-92, as the Götterdämmerung Brünnhilde at Brussels and Senta at Naples; Sang Orpheus at the Accademia di Santa Cecilia, Rome, 1996. Recordings: Adriano in Rienzi; Der fliegende Holländer; Erwartung; Sancta Susanna by Hindemith. Address: c/o Deutsche Oper am Rhein, Heinrich-Heine Allee 16, D-4000 Dusseldorf, Germany.

MARTIN Kathleen, b. 28 Feb 1948, Texas, USA. Singer, Soprano. Education: studied at UCLA and at California State University Long Beach. Debut: San Francisco Opera as Madama Butterfly. Career: England at the Lubeck Opera, 1974-80, as Fiordiligi, Donna Elvira, Nedda, Mimi, Desdemona, the Trovatore Leonora, Elsa, Tatiana and Katya Kabanova; Sang at the Frankfurt Opera 1980-83, guest engagements at the Theater am Gärtnerplatz, Munich; Sang at Toulouse as Jordane in the 1985 premiere of Landowski's Montségur and appeared at the Paris Opéra, 1987. Address: c/o Teatre du Capitole, Place du Capitole, F-31000 Toulouse, France.

MARTIN Philip (James), b. 27 Oct 1947, Dublin, Ireland. Concert Pianist; Composer. m. 22 Aug 1970, 1 son, 1 daughter. Education: St Marys College, Rathmines, Dublin; Patricia Read Pianoforte School, Dublin; Private Studies with Mabel Swainson, Dublin; Royal Academy of Music, London; Private Studies with Louis Kentner, London, and Yvonne Lefebure, Paris. Debut: Wigmore Hall, London, 1970. Career: Regular Performances with Major British Orchestras; Royal Festival Hall and Royal Albert Hall Debut, 1977; BBC Prom Concerts, 1985, 1987 Recorded Live on Omnibus at the Proms, BBC Television. Compositions: 2 Piano Concertos; Harp Concerto; Beato Angelico, for Large Orchestra; 3 Piano Trios; Various Chamber Music and Over 150 Songs. Recordings: 3 Volumes of Piano Music of Louis Moreau Gottschalk; 2 CD's of Chamber Music; 2 CD's of Music by Percy Grainger; Piano Music and Songs. Honours: FRAM, London; AOSDANA, Ireland; UK-US Bicentennial Arts Fellowship. Memberships: Incorporated Society of Musicians; Composers Guild; PRS. Hobbies: Reading; Walking; Art. Address: Chapel House, Theobalds Green, Calstone Calne, Wiltshire SW11 8QE, England.

MARTIN Ruth (Kelley), b. 14 Apr 1914, Jersey City, USA. Writer; Musician; Translator; Librettist. m. Thomas Philipp Martin, 17 June 1939, 1 son, 3 daughters. Education: AB, Smith College, 1937; Language Study, Columbia University, University of Munich, Summers, 1934-35; Private Study of Violin, 1921-31; Voice Study, Lausanne, 1931-32, Smith College, 1932-36; Violin Study at Smith College, 1932-37. Career: Premieres of Translations & Adaptions: The Magic Flute, 1941; Abduction from the Seraglio, 1946; Così fan tutte, 1950; Metropolitan Opera; Marriage of Figaro, 1948; The Trial, von Einem, 1953; Golden Slippers, 1955; Die Fledermaus, 1953; Don Giovanni, 1963; Danton's Death, 1966; Daughter of the Regiment, 1975; Grand Duchess of Gerolstein, 1982, New York City Opera. Compositions: 100 songs for Silver Burdett Children's Schools Series; 50 English Translations of Opera and Operettas; Adaptations and Original with Thomas Martin including Carmen, Gypsy Baron, A Night in Venice, Barber of Seville, La Bohème, Girl of the Golden West, Die Tote Stadt, Tales of Hoffmann. Recordings: The Magic Flute; Così fan tutte; Highlights from Die Fledermaus; A Night in Venice; Mozart Operatic arias. Publications: Legend of a Musical City by Max Graf, Translator; Philosophical Library, 1945; The Great Operas of Mozart, 1962; A Treasury of Opera Liberettos, 1962. Hobbies: Mountain Climbing; Print and Autography, Musicians, Collecting. Address: 219 West 13th Street, Apt 1, NY 10011, USA.

MARTIN Vivian, b. 1945, Detroit, Michigan, USA. Soprano. Education: BS, Wayne State University; Student, Detoit Conservatory of Music. Debut: Leonora in La Forza del Destino. Career: Soloist, Munich Philharmonic and Nuremberg Symphony and Philharmonic Choir, 1970; Rezia in Weber's Oberon at Wexford, Republic of Ireland, Opera Festival, 1972; Royal Opera Ghent, Stadt Opera Essen; Badische Opera, Karlsruhe; Stadt Opera, Bonn; Mainz Opera; Royal Opera Lisbon, Portugal; Stadtheater Bremen; Television broadcasts for BBC, BRT Belgium, Bratislava, Czechoslovakia; Philharmonic Orchestra and Opera; Soloist Gavelborg Symphony, Gayle, Sweden, 1978; Symphony Radio Concert Paris, 1978; Warsaw Symphony Orchestra; Tour of India, Iran, Afghanistan, USA State Department, 1976; Toured with Gavelborg Symphony Orchestra, Sweden, 1981-84; Appeared in opera concert on radio and TV Bucharest, 1979; Sang Leonora in Il Trovatore in opera festival at Constanze, Romania, 1979; Concerts in Belgrade, Tivoli Gardens, Copenhagen, Denmark, Zagreb, Yugoslavia, 1979; Opera concert tour of Sweden with Gayle Symphony Orchestra, 1979; Appeared in Aida and as Bess, Porgy and Bess, Bratislava, 1979; As Cio-Cio San in Madam Butterfly and Leonora in Il Trovatore, Constanze, 1980. Recordings: Has made numerous recordings. Honours: Recipient, numerous scholarships and awards. Memberships: Actors Equity; AFTRA, American Guild Musical Artists.

MARTINCEK Dusan, b. 13 June 1936, Presov, Slovakia. Composer. m. Magdalena Kockova, 1961, 1 son. Education: Piano and Composition, Bratislava Conservatory, 1951-56; Bratislava Academy of Music and Drama, 1956-61. Career: Assistant, Music Theory, 1961-72; Associate Professor, Theory, 1973-86; Freelance Artist, 1987-92; Professor, Composition, Bratislava Academy of Music and Drama, Bratislava, 1993. Compositions include: Dialogues in the Form of Variations for piano and orchestra, 1961; Simple overture for small orchestra, 1961; 8 piano sonatas, 1967-1981; String Quartet, 1982-84; Animation for 35 solo strings, 1983-86; Continuities for large orchestra, 1987-88; Communications for violin and piano, 1988; Interrupted Silence for large orchestra, 1989-90; Contradiction for String Quintet, 1989-90; 10 Movements for piano, 1992; New Nocturnes for piano, 1993-94; Compositions for flute and piano, for solo guitar, and so on. Honours: J L Bella Prize, 1981; Certificate of Merit, 1993; Man of the Year, 1993; Performances throughout Europe and overseas; Best analyses of his works: Tempo, No 179 (Boosey and Hawkes); Dusan Martincek: An Introduction to His Music (David Babcock). Memberships: Numerous musical institutions. Hobbies: Visual arts; Philosophy; Theatre; Chess. Address: Lipskeho 11, 84101 Bratislava, Slovakia.

MARTINEAU Malcolm, b. 1960, Edinburgh, Scotland. Pianist. Education: Studied at St Catharine's College, Cambridge, and at the Royal Academy of Music with Kendall Taylor and Geoffrey Parsons; Further study with Joyce Rathbone. Career: Has accompanied wuch leading singers as Janet Baker, Della Jones, Marie McLaughlin, Julia Migenes, Stephen Varcoe and Thomas Allen; Concerts in Fredensborg Palace in Denmark with Laurence Dale, at the Concertgebouw with Sarah Walker and at the Châtelet in Paris with Lorna Anderson; Engagements with clarinettist Emma Johnson; Has played in master classes at the Pears-Britten School for Suzanne Danco, Elisabeth Schwarzkopf, Ileana Cotrubas and Kurt Equiluz; Festival appearances and series of concerts at St John's Smith Square featuring songs by Debussy and Poulenc; Recitals at the Wigmore Hall and on South Bank; Paris, Belgium, Italy and throughout the UK. Recordings: Complete Fauré songs with Sarah Walker; Recital with Della Jones. Honours: Walter Gruener International Lieder Competition, 1984. Address: Lies Askonas Ltd, 6 Henrietta Street, London WC2, England.

MARTINEZ Odaline de la, b. 31 October 1949, Matanzas, Cuba. Composer; Conductor; Pianist. Education: BFA, Tulane University, 1968-72; Royal Academy of Music, 1972-76; GRSM (Composition and Piano); MMus (Composition), University of Surrey, 1975-77; Postgraduate Research (Computer Music), 1977-80. Career: Compositions broadcast by BBC, Radio Istanbul, Radio Cork, Radio Belgrade, KPFA San Francisco; Music Director, Cardiff Festival, 1994, conductor of Dame Ethel Smyth's Opera, The Wreckers, Proms BBC in 1994 (revival after over 50 years). Compositions include: After Sylvia (Song cycle); Phasing for Chamber Orchestra; A Moment's Madness for Flute and Piano; Sister Aimee, Opera; 2 American Madrigals for Mixed Chorus; Conductor of Lontano and London Chamber Symphony; Many performances of Contemporary Music; Conducted the premiere of Berthold Goldschmidt's Beatrix Cenci, 1988; Directed series of Latin American concerts on South Bank, 1989; Conducted Lontano at St John's London, 1997. Recordings: British Women Composers, Vol I and II, Villa Lobos Chamber and Choral Music, Boulez sans Boulez all on Lorelt label; 2 CD's major revivals of Ethel Smyth: Conifer CD of The Wreckers; Chandos CD of Orchestral Serenade and Double Concertos. Publication: Mendelssohn's Sister. Memberships: SPNM, Women in Music. Honours: 1st Woman to conduct BBC Prom Concerts at the Royal Albert Hall; Danforth Fellowship; Marshall Scholar; Watson Fellow; National Endowments for the Arts, USA; Joyce Dixie Prize; Villa-Lobos Medal, 1987; Manson Scholarship; Outstanding Alumna Tulane University, FRAM. Hobbies: Travel; Eating Out; Films. Current Management: Denise Kantor Management. Address: c/o Lontano, Toynbee Studios, 28 Commercial Street, London E1 6LS, England.

MARTINEZ Ruben, b. 1962, Argentina. Singer (Tenor). Career: Many opera engagements in South America and Europe, notably in Donizetti's L'Elisir d'amor and Gounod's Roméo et Juliette; also sings chansons by Fauré; contestant at the 1995 Cardiff Singer of the World Competition. Address: Street 27 No 1221 La Plata (CP1900), Buenos Aires, Argentina.

MARTINEZ-IZQUIERDO Ernest, b. 11 June 1962, Barcelona, Spain. Conductor and Composer. Education: Clarinet and Piano Studies; Diplomas in Composition and Orchestra Conductor, 1986. Debut: Barcelona 1985 with his Ensemble "Barcelona 216". Career: Principal Conductor of the Ensemble Barcelona 216; Assistant Conductor of JONDE (Youth Spanish Orchestra), 1985-87; Assistant Conductor of ONE (Spanish National Orchestra), 1988; Assistant Conductor of the Ensemble Inter-Contemporain, 1988-90; Concerts with foreign orchestras like Philharmonic Orchestra of Minsk, Ensemble Contemporain de Montreal, Orchestra of The Teatro Comunale di Bolonia or Avanti Orchestra of Helsinki; Concerts with the mainly Spanish orchestras as OBC (Symphonic Orchestra of Barcelona), ONE (Spanish National Orchestra), Cadaqués Orchestra, Symphonic Orchestra of Tenerife, Symphonic Orchestra of Granada; As Guest Conductor or with his own Ensemble, he has conducted in the principal European cities as Paris, Prague, Bordeaux, Amsterdam, Palermo, Luxembourg, Madrid, Rome and in some of the most important festivals, Festival Internacional de Alicante, Festival de Torroella de Montgri, Zagreb's Biennal, Festival Castell de Perelada, Festival de Cadaqués, Holland Festival, Helsinki's Biennal, Barcelona's Festival de Musica del Segle XX, Festival Aujourd 'hui Musiques of Perpignan. Compositions: Música para orquesta de cuerdas, 1986; Música para 10 vcl y orquesta, 1991; Música per a un festival, 1992; Norte-Sur, 1993; Alternanqa, 1995. Recordings include: Album de Colien, Spanish and Portuguese Contemporary Piano Music, 1995; Music for the film Metropolis by Martin Matalon, 1995; Composers of Cercle Manuel de Falla, 1995; Xavier Benguerel: 7 Fables de La Fontaine, 1995. Honours: Several. Memberships: The Associacio Catalena de Compositors. Address: Muntaner 511 #6, 08022 Barcelona, Spain.

MARTINIS Carla, b. 1921, Danculovice, Yugoslavia. Singer, Soprano. Education: Zagreb Conservatory, with Professor Martinis. Career: Sang first in Zagreb and Prague; New York City Opera 1950-53, debut as Turandot; Vienna Staatsoper from 1951, debut as Aida conducted by Karajan; Salzburg Festival 1951, as Desdemona conducted by Furtwängler; Paris Opera 1951, as Amelia in Un Ballo in Maschera; La Scala Milan, Aix-en-Provence, Naples and Florence, 1952; San Francisco Opera, 1954; Sang La Gioconda at Trieste, 1956. Recordings: Otello from Salzburg; Donna Anna in Don Giovanni; La Forza del Destino; Tosca.

MARTINO Donald (James), b. 16 May 1931, Plainfield, New Jersey, USA. Composer; Clarinettist; Educator; Publisher. Education: BM, Syracuse University, 1952; MFA, Princeton University, 1954; MA, Harvard University (honorary) 1983; Fulbright Grant for study with Luigi Dallapiciola, Florence, Italy, 1954-55, 1955-56. Career: Associate Professor of Music, Yale University, 1958-69; Chairman of Composition, New England Conservatory, 1969-79; Irving Fine Professor, Brandeis University, 1979-82; Walter Bigelow Rosen Professor, Harvard University, 1983-93, Professor Emeritus, 1993-. Compositions include: Published: Contemplations for Orchestra, 1956; Concerto for Wind Quintet, 1964; Concerto for Piano and Orchestra, 1965; Notturno, flute, clarinet, violin, violoncello, percussion, piano, 1973; Paradiso Choruses, chorus, soloists, orchestra, tape, 1974; Ritorno for Orchestra, 1975; Triple Concerto for Clarinet, Bass Clarinet and Contrabass Clarinet with Chamber Ensemble, 1977; Fantasies and Inpromptus, piano solo, 1981; Divertisements for Youth Orchestra, 1981; String Quartet, 1983; The White Island, chorus, chamber orchestra, 1985; Concerto for Alto Saxophone and Chamber Orchestra, 1987; From the Other Side, flute, violoncello, percussion, piano, 1988; Twelve Preludes for Piano, 1991; Three Sad Songs, viola and piano, 1993; Conerto for violin and orchestra, 1996. Recordings include: Donald Martino: Piano Music; Donald Martino: Chamber Music; Donald Martino: Piano and Chamber Music; Donald Martino: A Jazz Set. Publications: Editor: 178 Chorale Harmonizations fo J S Bach: A Comparative Edition for Study, 1984. Contributions to: The Source Set and its Aggregate Formations, Journal of Music Theory, 1961; Notation in General Articulation in Particular, 1966; An Interview by James Boros, 1991; Perspectives of New Music. Honours: Pulitzer Prize, 1974; Kennedy Center-Friedheim Award, 1985; Mark M Horblit Award, Boston Symphony, 1987. Memberships: American Academy of Arts and Letters; American Academy of Arts and Sciences; Founder, American Society of Composers; Broadcast Music Inc. Hobby: Tennis. Current Management: Dantalian Inc, USA. Address: 11 Pembroke Street, Newton, MA 02158, USA.

MARTINOTY Jean-Louis, b. 20 Jan 1946, Etampes, France. Stage Director. Career: Radio producer for ORTF, then critic for L'Humanité; Assistant to Jean-Pierre Ponnelle, notably in works by Mozart and Monteverdi at Zurich; Baroque repertoire includes productions for the Karlsuhe Handel Festival; Production of Ariande auf Naxos seen at the Paris Opéra 1983, Covent Garden 1985; General Administrator of the Paris Opera at the Palais Garnier 1986-89; Productions in season 1990-91 included Ziegeunerbaron at the Zurich Opera, La Clemenza di Tito at the Deutsche Oper Berlin; Produced Tamerlano at the 1993 Handel Festival, Karlsruhe; Boris Godunov at Montpellier, 1996. Address: c/o Opéra de Montpellier, 11 Boulevard Victor Hugo, F-34000 Montpellier, France.

MARTINOVIC Boris, b. 1953, Croatia. Singer (Bass-baritone). Education: Studied at the Juilliard School, New York. Debut: Avery Fisher Hall New York, in Refice's Cecilia. Career: Charleston 1977, in The Queen of Spades; European appearances at Trieste, Rome and Naples; Teatro Regio Parma in Lucia di Lammermoor, Semiramide, Gerusalemme by Verdi and Roméo et Juliette; Pesaro Festival as Rossini's Mosè, Colline at the Paris Opera, Vienna and Zurich as Escamillo, at Zurich as Onegin and Pesaro 1991 as Orbazzano in Rossini's Tancredi; Bregenz Festival 1992, Escamillo. Recordings include: Prince Igor, Ivan Susanin by Glinka and Boris Godunov, as Rangoni (Sony); Crespel in Les Contes d'Hoffmann (Philips). Address: c/o Robert Gilder and Co, Enterprise House, 59-65 Upper Grand, London SE1 9PQ, England.

MARTINPELTO Hillevi, b. 9 Jan 1958, Alvalden, Sweden. Singer, Soprano. Education: Studied at the Stockholm Opera School. Career: Sang Pamina in Die Zauberflöte with the Folksopera in Stockholm and at the Edinburgh Festival; Norrlands Opera from 1987 in Ivar Hallström's Den Bergtagno, also on Swedish TV and at the York Festival; Tatiana in Eugene Onegin and Marguerite; Royal Opera Stockholm debut 1987, as Madama Butterfly; Sang the title roles in Gluck's Iphigénie operas at the Drottningholm Festival, 1989-90; Théâtre de la Monnaie Brussels from 1990 as Fiordiligi and the Countess in Le nozze di Figaro; Season 1991-92 with Fiordiligi at the Hamburg Staatsoper, Wagner's Eva at Nice, Donna Anna at Aix-en-Provence; Season 1992-93 included: Don Giovanni, Aix-en-Provence Festival, France; Così fan tutte, Hamburg State Opera, Germany; Das Rheingold, Lyric Opera of Chicago, USA; Le nozze di Figaro, Toulouse Opera, France; Châtelet, Monteverdi and Wagner's Eva in Tokyo with Deutsche Oper Berlin; Further engagements include Verdi's Desdemona in Helsinki; Concert engagements with Dvorak's Requiem, Scottish National Orchestra, 1987; Residentie Orchestra of The Hague in Mozart; Belgian Radio Orchestra; Philharmonia of London in The Creation, conducted by Claus Peter Flor; Sang Donna Anna in Don Giovanni, at Glyndebourne, 1994-; Agathe in Der Freischütz for the Royal Danish Opera at Copenhagen, 1997; Further engagements include: Don Giovanni and Clemenza di Tito (Munich) and Idomeneo (Lausanne); Concert appearances with the National Orchestra of Wales, City of Birmingham Symphony Orchestra, the Gesellschaft der Musikfreunde in Vienna and the Vienna Symphony Orchestra amongst others. Recordings: Elettra in Idomeneo, conducted by John Eliot Gardiner; Countess in Figaro with Gardiner. Address: Artists Sekretariat Ulf Tornqvist, Sankt Eriksgatan 100, 2 tr S113 31 Stockholm, Sweden.

MARTINS Maria de Lourdes, b. 26 May 1926, Lisbon, Portugal. Composition Professor, Conservatório Nacional, Lisbon. Education: Graduate, National Conservatory of Music, Lisbon, Piano and Composition; Advanced studies in Composition with H Genzmer, Music High School, Munich, Germany, 1959-60; Diploma Orff Institute of the Mozarteum, Salzburg, 1964-65. Career includes: Piano Concerts on National and German Radio; TV performances in Portugal; 1st Opera, S Carlos National Theatre, Lisbon, July 1986; Professor of Music Education and Composition, National Conservatory in Lisbon, 1970-96, now retired; Lectures and seminars in Portugal, Argentina, USA, Japan, Germany, Switzerland, Poland and Spain. Compositions: Numerous including: Encoberto de F Pessoa, 1965; O Litoral de A Negreiros, 1971-; Rondó for Wind Orchestra, 1978; Portuguese Christmas Songs for Wind Orchestra, 1978; Portuguese Dances, 1978; Sonatinas 1 and 2 for Piano; Catch, 1981; Ritmite, 1983; Musica de Piano Para Criancas Ed Valentim de Carvalho; Opera: Tres Máscaras, 1983; Simetria for Clarinet Solo, 1984; 4 Poemas de F Pessoa, 1984; Moments of Peace by J Gracen Brown, 1989; II String Quartet, 1989; Concerto de piano, 1990; Divertiment on Mozart Themes, 1991; Kinder Opera "Donzela Guerreira", 1995; Musica para piano, pianist, Erszebet Tusa; Suite para Quinteto. Recordings: Educo Edition; Wind Quartet; 12 Choral Port Songs; Piano Works; Decca, Historia de Natal. Publication: Pizzicato. Honours: Composition Prizes: National Prize Carlos Seixan, 1959; YMP, 1960; C Gulbenkian Foundation, 1965, 1971. Memberships: ISME; APEM. Hobbies: Travel. Address: R Trindade Coelho 108, 2775 Pareded, Portugal.

MARTINUCCI Nicola, b. 28 Mar 1941, Tarent, Italy. Singer, (Tenor). Education: Studied with Sara Sforni in Milan. Debut: Teatro Nuovo Milan 1966, as Manrico. Career: Sang at La Scala and at the Teatro La Fenice, Venice; Deutsche Oper am Rhein Dusseldorf from 1973; Florence, 1974 as Filippo in a revival of Spontini's Agnese di Hohenstaufen; Verona Arena 1982-86, as Radames, Calaf and Andrea Chenier; Covent Garden debut 1985, as Dick Johnson in La Fanciulla del West; Appearances in Dublin, Teheran, Budapest and Salzburg; Rome Opera, 1989 as Poliuto; Sang Calaf in London, 1990; Pollione at Catania, Manrico at Parma; Season 1992 as Enzo in La Gioconda at Rome and Calaf at the Festival of Caracalla; Sang Andrea Chenier there, 1996. Recordings: Video of Turandot, from Verona; Donizetti's Poliuto. Address: Stafford Law Associates, 6 Barham Close, Weybridge, Surrey KT13 9PR, England.

MARTLAND Steve, b. 1958, Liverpool, England. Composer. Education: Graduated from Liverpool University, 1981; Royal Conservatory, The Hague, Holland, with Louis Andriessen; Tanglewood USA with Gunther Schuller. Career: Works with students and musicians outside the classical tradition; Pieces for informal Dutch ensembles, the Jazz Orchestra Loose Tubes and the band Test Department multi-media project for BBC TV. Joint premiere of Babi-Yar with the Royal Liverpool Philharmonic and the St Louis Symphony Orchestra; American Invention performed in the USA and Japan; Performances with the Steve Martland Band, including the 1994 South Bank Meltdown Festival (returned 1997). Compositions: Remembering Lennon for 7 players, 1981-85; Lotta Continua for orchestra 1981-84; Duo for trumpet and piano 1982; Canto a la Esperanza for soprano, electric guitar and chamber orchestra 1982; Kgakala for piano 1982; Babi Yar for orchestra 1983; Orc for horn and small orchestra 1984; American Invention for 13 players 1985; Shoulder to Shoulder for 13 players 1986; Dividing the Lines for brass, wind band 1986; Remix for jazz ensemble 1986; Big Mac I, II for 4-8 players 1987; Divisions for electronic tape 1986-87; Drill for 2 pianos 1987; Glad Day for voice and ensemble 1988; Albion for tape and film 1987-88; Terra Firma for 5 voices, with amplification and video 1989; Crossing the Border for Strings, 1991; The Perfect Act for ensemble and voice, 1991; Beat the Retreat, for eleven players, 1997; Kick, for eleven players (1995-96); Eternal Delight for eleven players, 1997. Honours: 1981 Mendelssohn Scholarship; 1985 Government Composition Prize, Holland. Address: Schott and Co Ltd, 48 Great Marlborough Street, London W1V 2BN, England.

MARTON Eva (Heinrich), b. 18 June 1943, Budapest, Hungary. Soprano. m. Zoltan Marton, 1 son, 1 daughter. Education: Graduate, Franz Lizst Academy. Debut: Budapest Opera, 1968. Career: Soprano with various opera Companies, including Frankfurt Opera, Vienna State Opera, Hamburg State Opera, Metropolitan Opera, La Scala, Chicago Lyric Opera, San Francisco Opera, Teatro Colon, Buenos Aires, Bayreuth and others. Roles include: Empress in Frau ohne Schatten; Salome; All three Brünnhildes in Ring Cycle; Elisabeth and Venus in Tannhäuser; Elsa and Ortrud in Lohengrin; Senta in Der fliegende Holländer; Title roles of Turandot, Tosca, Manon Lescaut, Fedora, Gioconda, Aida; Amelia in Ballo in Maschera; Leonora in Trovatore; Lady Macbeth in Macbeth; Elisabetta in Don Carlo; Leonore in Fidelio; Maddalena in Andrea Chénier; Leonora in La Forza del Destino; Covent Garden debut 1987, Turandot, returned 1990 as Elektra; Sang Tosca in Budapest, 1989, Elektra at Barcelona, 1990; Vienna Staatsoper 1991, as Salome; Season 1992 with Turandot for the Royal Opera at the Wembley Arena and at Chicago, the Walküre Brünnhilde at Bonn, Salome at Barcelona and the Dyer's Wife in Die Frau ohne Schatten at Salzburg; Elektra in a new production for Washington Opera, 1997; TV films: Two Turandots, Vienna and Met; Toscas, Verona and Florence; Tannhäuser, Lohengrin, Trovatore, all at the Met; Andrea Chénier, La Scala. Recordings: Violanta, Turandot, Fedora, Andrea Chénier, Bluebeard's Castle, Gioconda; Album of Wagner Scenes; Album of Puccini arias; Album of Richard Strauss songs; Final scene from Salome; Brünnhilde in The Ring conducted by Haitink; Videos of Elektra conducted by Abbado and Il Trovatore from the Met. Contributions to: Interview with Alan Blyth, People, Opera Magazine, Feb 1990. Address: c/o Royal Opera House, Covent Garden, London, WC2, England.

MARTTINEN Tauno, b. 27 Sept 1912, Helsinki, Finland. Composer. Education: Studied Music, Viipuri, 120's; Studied Music, Helsinki, 1930's. Career: Director, Hameenlinna Music Institute, 1950-75. Compositions: The Cloak, 1962-63; The Engagement, 1964; Burnt Orange, 1968; Maitre Patelin, 1969-72; Shaman's Drum, 1974-76; The Earl's Sister, 1977; The Pharoah's Letter, 1978-80; Song of the Great River, 1982-84; Seven Brothers by Aleksis KIVI, Op 263, 1976-86; Ballets: A Portrait of Dorian Gray, 1969; Snow Queen, 1970; The Sun Out of the Moon, 1975-77; The Ugly Duckling, 1976, 1982-83; Orchestra: Symphony No 1, 1958; Symphony No 2, 1959; Symphony No 3, 1960-62; Symphony No 4, 1964; Symphony No 7, 1977; panu, God of Fire, 1966; Symphony No 8, 1983; Symphony No 9, 1986; The Maid of Pohjola, 1982; Solo Instrument Concerto for piano and orchestra, 1964; Concerto for flute and orchestra, 1972; Concerto for Clarinet and Orchestra, 1974; Concerto for two pianos and orchestra, 1981; Concerto for piano and orchestra No 4 Op 241, 1984; Chamber Music: Delta, 1962; Alfa op 16, 1963; Visit to the Giant Sage Vipunen, 1969; String Quartet No 2, 1971; Divertimento, 1977; Intermezzo, 1977-78; Le Commencement, 1979; Trio, 1982; Solo Instrument: Titisee for piano, 1965; Adagio for organ, 1967; Sonatina for piano; Nore dame, 1970; The Cupola, for organ, 1971; Sonata for piano, 1975; Impression for cello, 1978; Prophet for organ, 1984. Honours: Honourary Professor conferred by the State, 1972. Address: TEOSTO, Lauttasaarentie 1, 00200 Helsinki 20, Finland.

MARTURET Eduardo, b. 19 Sep 1953, Caracas, Venezuela. Conductor; Composer. Education: Music Degree, Anglia University; Further studies in Cambridge, Siena and Rome. Debut: Caracas in 1978. Career: Artistic Director, Sinfonietta Caracas, 1986; Music Director with Teatro Teresa Carreño, 1984-76, and Orq Sinfonica Venezuela, 1987-95; Has conducted major orchestras in Germany, Holland, USA, Scandinavia and Hungary. Compositions include: Canto Llano; Music For Six And Sax; Tres Tiempos; Casa Bonita. Recordings: Brahms Complete Symphonies, Overtures and Concertos; With Berliner Symphoniker, Mozart Symphonies and Complete Violin Concertos; Concertgebouw Chamber Orchestra. Publications: Casa Bonita: Catalogue of The Exhibition, 1988; Article, Perspectives of Mozart's Symphonic Music, 1991. Honours include: Orden Diego De Losada, 1992; Best Conductor, 1992; Best Classical Record, 1992; Orden Andres Bello, 1992. Memberships: SPNM, London; American Symphony Orchestra League; Conductors' Guild, USA. Hobbies: Fishing; Wines; Yachting. Current Management: John Gingrich, New York, USA. Address: PO Box 2912, Caracas, Venezuela.

MARUZIN Yuri, b. 8 Dec 1947, Perm, Russia. Singer, Tenor. Education: Studied in Leningrad. Debut: Maly Theatre, Leningrad, 1972. Career: Appearances with the Kirov Opera Leningrad, St Petersburg from 1978 notably as Hermann in The Queen of Spades and Dimitri in Boris Godunov and touring to Covent Garden, 1987 as Lensky; Sang the Tsarevich in Rimsky's The Tale of Tsar Saltan at La Scala and Reggio Emilia, 1988; Galitsin in Khovanshchina at the Vienna Staatsoper, 1989; San Francisco Opera as Anatol in War and Peace, Andrei Khovansky in Khovanshchina at Edinburgh, 1991; Other guest engagements at Turin, Nice, Madrid and Toronto; Other roles include Faust, Pinkerton, Rodolfo, Don Carlos, Don Alvaro, Alfredo and the Duke of Mantua; Sang Hermann at Glyndebourne, 1992; New Israeli Opera, 1997 in Lady Macbeth of the Mtsensk District. Address: Kirov Opera and Ballet Theatre, St Petersburg, Russia.

MARVIA Einari, b. 21 Nov 1915, Tuusniemi, Finland. Composer; Musicologist. m. Lisa Aroheimo, 28 June 1984, 2 sons, 1 daughter. Education: Sibelius Academy, Helsinki; Music studies, Vienna, 1951; MA, 1955; PhLic, 1973. Debut: Composition Concert, Helsinki, 1945. Career: Director of Publications, Edition Frazer, Helsinki, 1946-80. Compositions: Taru, symphonic poem; Piano Sonata in D flat major; Many songs and choral works including: Unhon maa, song cycle; 6 songs to words of Katri Vala. Publications: Fazerin Musikkikauppa, 1987-47, 1947; Suomen Saveltajien 25 vuotta, 1970; Sibeliuksen rituallimusikki, 1984; Suomen Saveltajia I-II, editor, 1965-66; Documenta Musicae Fennicae I-XVI, editor. Contributions to: Many articles on Finnish music hisotyr notably academic music and orchestra history. Honours: Award Winner, Viotti Song Competition, Vercelli, 1951; Award of Honour, Foundation for the Support of Finnish Music, 1985; Pro Finlandia Medal; Finland's Cross of Freedom; Verdienstkreuz vom Deutschen Adler. Memberships: Society of Finnish Composers. Hobbies: Old Finnish Books.

MARVIN Frederick, b. 11 June 1923, California, USA. Pianist; Musicologist; Professor. Education: Curtis Institute of Music, Philadelphia; Southern California Conservatory, Los Angeles. Debut: Carnegie Hall, 1949. Career: Toured USA, 1949-54; Concerts in every major capital of Europe from 1954, solo recitals, and concert lectures; Master Classes; Professor of Piano, 1968-, Professor Emeritus and Artist in Residence, 1990, Syracuse University. Recordings include: George Antheil Piano Sonata No 4; Liszt Album, Sonatas by Moscheles and L Berger, 3 LPs of sonatas by Dussek; Schubert Album; Three CD albums of Sonatas by JL Dussek; Sonatas by Soler, 3 albums; 4 Villancicos by A Soler; Liszt, CD. Publications: 63 Sonatas by Soler; Four Villancicos and Salve, Lamentation, Soler; Edited 8 volumes Sonatas, and Choral works, Padre Soler; 2 sonatas, J L Dussek; Contributions to music magazines. Honours: Carnegie Hall Award, Most Outstanding Debut in New York City, 1948; Schnabel Gold Medal, London, 1955; Orden del Mérito Civil (Commander), Spanish Government, 1969; Croix de Commandeur, Medille de Vermiel, Arts-Sciences, Lettres, France, 1974. Address: c/o Ernst Schuh, 246 Houston Avenue, Syracuse, NY 13224, USA.

MARVIN Roberta (Montemorra), b. 29 July 1953, Massachusetts, USA. Musicologist. m. Conrad A Marvin, 30 June 1973. Education: BM, Boston Conservatory of Music, 1975; MA, Tufts University, 1986; PhD, Brandeis University, 1992. Appointments: Lecturer, Tufts University, 1991-92; Visiting Assistant Professor, Boston University, 1992-93; Assistant Professor, University of Alabama, 1993-97; Associate Professor, University of Iowa, 1997-. Publications: Artistic Concerns and Practical Considerations in the Composition of I masnadieri, Studi Verdiani 7, 1992; A Verdi Autograph and the Problem of Authenticity, Studi Verdiani 9, 1993; Shakespeare and Primo Ottocento Opera: The Case of Rossini's Otello, The Opera and Shakespeare, 1994; Aspects of Tempo in Verdi's Early and Middle Period Italian Operas, Verdi's Middle Period: Source Studies, Analysis and Performance Practice (1949-59), 1997; Verdi The Student - Verdi The Teacher; Giuseppe Verdi's I masnadieri, critical edition (editor). Contributions to: The New Grove Dictionary of Opera, 1992; and The New Grove Dictionary of Music and Musicians, revised edition. Honours: Premio Internazionale 'Giuseppe Verdi', 1991; Fulbright Research Fellowships, 1988, 1993; American Philosophical Society, 1992; NEH Summer Stipend, 1993. Memberships: American Musicological Society; Royal Musical Association. Address: University of Iowa, School of Music, Voxman Music Building, Iowa City, IA 52242, USA.

MÄRZENDORFER Ernst, b. 26 May 1921, Salzburg, Austria. Conductor. Education: Studied with Clemens Krauss at the Salzburg Mozarteum. Career: Conducted opera in Salzburg from 1940; Graz Opera, 1945-51; Professor, Salzburg Mozarteum, 1951; Conducted at the Teatro Colon Buenos Aires, 1952-53; Conductor of the Mozarteum orchestra, 1953-58, including tour of the USA, 1956; Conducted at the Deutsche Oper, Berlin from 1958 and at the Vienna Staatsoper from 1961, premiere of Henze's Ballet Tancredi 1966; Recorded the 106 symphonies of Haydn with the Vienna Chamber Orchestra, 1967-71; Premiered his completion of Bruckner's 9th Symphony at Graz, 1969; Conducted first performances of Einem's Turandot, 1954 and Medusa, 1965; Led Mona Lisa by Max von Schillings at the Vienna Volksoper, 1996. Recordings: Early Mozart symphonies, Concerto K299 and Divertimento K334; Mendelssohn Concerto for violin and piano; Donizetti L'Elisir d'Amore, with the Berlin Symphony Orchestra; Eine Nacht in Venedig, Hungaroton; Haydn Complete Symphonies, Musical Heritage Society. Address: c/o Vienna Volksoper, Währingerstrasse 78, A-1090 Vienna, Austria.

MASCIADRI Milton (Walter), b. 15 Nov 1959, Montevideo, Uruguay. Double Bass Player. m. Rosanna Urbani, 19 Dec 1986. Education: Studies with Milton Romay Masciadri, Uruguay and Brazil; Master's degree, University of Hartford, with Gary Karr; Doctorate, State University of New York, with Julius Levine, Lawrance Wolfe. Career: Formerly: Assistant Principal Bass, Porto Alegre Symphony Orchestra, Brazil; Assistant Professor, Federal University of Rio Grande do Norte, UFRN; Solo Bass, UFRN Chamber Orchestra; Professor, Federal University of Santa Maria; Presently: Associate Professor of Double Bass, University of Georgia, Athens, USA; Assistant Principal Bass, Charleston Symphony Orchestra; Principal Bass, Macon Symphony Orchestra; Frequent appearances as Solo Bassist with Orchestra and recitals, USA, Uruguay, Argentina, Brazil, Mexico, Central America, Italy, Greece, Germany; Broadcasts: Public Radio, USA; Public Radio and TV, Brazil and Uruguay, American Italian RAI TV; Professor of Double Bass, Several music festivals; Teaches at International Music Festival, Brasilia, International Festival, Vale Veneto and Victoria, Brazil, Georgia Music Festival,

USA; Lectures extensively on Double Bass, American and Latin American Universities; Has premiered compositions of American and Latin American composers. Address: University of Georgia, School of Music, Athens, GA 30602, USA.

MASHEK Michal, b. 17 Sept 1980, Usti Nad Labem, Czech Republic. Pianist. Education: Music Conservatory, Teplice; Music Conservatory in Prague. Career: TV documentary, Goldbergs variations; Radio Prague recordings, Goldberg variations and Beethoven Sonata Op 81a. Recordings: Fantaisie and Toccata by B Martinu (CD); Goldberg Variations by J S Bach (CD). Honours: First Prize, International Piano Competition "Virtuosi Per Musica di Pianoforte"; First Prize in International Beethover piano competition. Hobbies: Cars; Dogs. Address: Vodarska 128, 40331 Usti nad Labem, Czech Republic.

MASLANKA David (Henry), b. 30 Aug 1943, Maryland, USA. Composer. Education: Studied at the New England Conservatory 1959-61, Oberlin College, BMus, 1965, and Michigan State University, PhD, 1965-70. Career: Teacher, State University of New York at Geneseo, 1970-74; Sarah Lawrence College, 1974-80; Kingsborough College, City University of New York, 1981-90; Freelance Composer, 1990-. Compositions include: Orchestra: Symphony no 1, 1970; Five songs for soprano, baritone and orchestra, 1976; In Lonely Fields, for percussion and orchestra, 1997; Percussion: Crown of Thorns, 1991; Montana Music: Three Dances for Percussion, 1993; Chamber: Duo for flute and piano, 1972; Quintet no 1 for wind, 1984; Sonata for alto saxophone and piano, 1988; Sonata for horn and piano, 1996; Wind ensemble: Concerto for piano, winds and percussion, 1976; A Child's Garden of Dreams, 1981; Symphony no 2, 1987; In Memorium, 1989; Symphony no 3, 1991; Symphony no 4, 1993; Mass, 1995; Sea Dreams: Concerto for Two Horns and Wind Orchestra, 1997; Vocal: Anne Sexton Songs for soprano and piano, 1975; The Hungry Heart, for chorus, 1996; Black Dog Songs, for tenor and piano, 1996. Recordings: David Maslanka Wind Quintets; Wind Music of David Maslanka; Tears; Mass; Percussion Music of David Maslanka; When Angels Speak; Prevailing Winds. Honours: MacDowell Colony Fellowships; Grants from National Endowment for the Arts, Martha Baird Rockefeller, ASCAP, National Symphony Orchestra. Address: 2625 Strand Avenue, Missoula, Montana 59804, USA.

MASON Anne, b. 1954, Lincolnshire, England. Singer, Mezzo-soprano. Education: Studied at the Royal Academy of Music with Marjorie Thomas and at the National Opera Studio. Career: Welsh National Opera Chorus, 1977-79; Opera North from 1982 as Fenena in Nabucco, and in Madama Butterfly; English National Opera 1983, as a Valkyrie in a new production of Die Walküre; Innsbruch Early Music Festival 1983, in Cesti's Il Tito, conducted by Alan Curtis; Kent Opera and Scottish Opera 1984, in new productions of King Priam by Tippett and Edward Harper's Hedda Gabler; Covent Garden appearances in Carmen, as Mercedes; Otello, Emilia; Das Rheingold, Madam Butterfly, Die Walküre, La Clemenza di Tito, Cenerentola, Rosenkavalier, Traviata and Götterdämmerung; Glyndebourne Tour 1987, as Dorabella in Così fan tutte; Recent engagements as Annius in La Clemenza di Tito at Aix, Casoi fan tutte with Welsh National Opera and as Marcellina in Le nozze di Figaro in Madrid; Season 1992 as Donna Clara in the stage premiere of Gerhard's The Duenna, at Madrid, as Henrietta Maria in I Puritani at Covent Garden and Cornelia in Julius Caesar for Scottish Opera; Second Maid in Elektra at the First Night at the 1993 London Proms; Sang Gertrude in Hansel and Gretel for Scottish Opera, 1996; Concerts in Britain, Germany, France, Austria and Belgium, notably in The Dream of Gerontius and Verdi's Requiem. Recordings: Video of HMS Pinafore; Helen in King Priam; Second Bridesmaid in Le nozze di Figaro, conducted by Solti; Marcellina, Figaro, with Haitink; Emilia di Liverpool, Opera Rara. Honours: Gerhardt Lieder Prize, the Recital Diploma and the Countess of Munster Award, at the Royal Academy of Music; Finalist in the 1983 Benson and Hedges Gold Award; ARAM of Royal Academy of Music. Address: c/o Harrison Parrott Ltd, 12 Penzance Place, London W11 4PA, England.

MASON Barry, b. 6 Sept 1947, Cottingham, Yorkshire, England. Lutenist; Guitarist; Musical Director. m. Glenda Simpson, 1 Oct 1983. Education: Hull College of Technology; Royal Academy of Music with Anthony Rooley and David Munrow, 1969-74; Royal College of Music with Dian Poulton, 1974-75. Debut: Purcell Room, 1973. Career: Director, Camerata of London, 1974; Director, 1st Early Music Centre Festival, London, 1977; Director, Progress Instruments Tours, Japan, Europe and USA, 1978; The Wicked Lady film, BBC Shakespeare Films: Director, The Guitarist's Companion, 1986. Recordings: Popular Music From The Time of Elizabeth I; The Muses Garden of Delights; Music For Kings and Courtiers'; The Queens Men; Thomas Companion; Elizabethan Ayres and Duets; Contributions to: Guitar International; Early Music News; Early Music Magazine; Music in Education. Honours: Peter Latham Award for Musicology, Royal Academy of Music, 1971; 1996 Britten Award for Composition. Current Management: Francesca McManus. Memberships: Council Member, Early Music Centre. Address: Francesca McManus, 71 Priory Road, Kew Gardens, Richmond, Surrey, TW9 3PH, England.

MASON Marilyn, b. 29 June 1925, OK, USA. Organist. Education: Studied in OK State University, at the University of Michigan, Union Theological Seminary NY, and with Nadia Boulanger, Maurice Duruflé and Arnold Schoenberg. Career: Teacher at the University of Michigan, 1947, Chairman of organ department, 1962, Professor 1965; Recital tours of North America, Europe, Australia, Africa and South America; Concerts with the Detroit and Philadelphia Orchestras; 60 Commissions for such composers as Krenek, Cowell, Albright, Ulysses Kay, Sowerby and Ross Lee Finney. Recordings: Albums of music by Sessions, Satie, Schoenberg and Virgil Thomson; Currently recording the music of Pachelbel for the Musical Heritage Society. Address: The University of Michigan, School of Music, Ann Arbor, MI 48109, USA.

MASSARD Robert, b. 15 Aug 1925, Pau, France. Singer, Baritone. Education: Conservatories of Pau and Bayonne. Career: Sang the High Priest in Samson et Dalila at the Paris Opera, 1952; Thoas in Iphigénie en Tauride at Aix, 1952; Sang Ashton in Lucia di Lammermoor at the Paris Opera 1957; Glyndebourne 1958, in Alceste; Orestes in Iphigénie en Tauride with the Covent Garden Company at Edinburgh, 1961; Sang Fieramosca in Benvenuto Cellini with the Royal Opera in London; Bolshoy Theatre Moscow 1962, as Rigoletto; La Scala Milan 1967, as Valentin in Faust; Paris 1974, as Sancho Panza in Massenet's Don Quichotte; Other roles include Nero in L'Incoronazione di Poppea, the Count in Capriccio, Milhaud's Orpheus, Escamillo and Ravel's Ramiro. Recordings: Iphigénie en Tauride; Mireille; Thais; Rigoletto; Benvenuto Cellini; Raimbaud in Le Comte Ory, Chant du Monde. Address: c/o Philipps, Polygram Classics, PO Box 1420, 1 Sussex Place, Hammersmith, London W6 9XS, England.

MASSEUS Jan, b. 28 Jan 1913, Rotterdam, Netherlands. Composer. Education: Studied piano at the Rotterdam Conservatory with Willem Pijper; Studied composition with Henk Badings. Career: Music Critic in Rotterdam, 1956-60; Electronic music studios of the Delft Technical High School, 1958-59; Director, Leeuwarden Music School, 1961-72. Compositions: 2 Violin Sonatas, 1946, 1950; Quintet for Piano and Strings, 1952; Sinfonietta, 1952; Violin Concerto, 1953; Gezelle liederen for Soprano, Alto, Piano 4 hands and Percussion, 1955; Concerto for 2 Flutes and Orchestra, 1956; Partita for Violin and Piano, 1956; Flute Sonata, 1957; Piano Concerto, 1966; Skirmishes for Chorus and Orchestra, 1975; Iowa Serenade for Youth Symphony Orchestra, 1981; Concerto for Euphonium and Brass Band, 1983; Aquarius for Brass Band, dedicated to Marilyn Ferguson; Nada Brahma for Piano 4 hands and Wind, 1988; Pandora for Solo-Percussionist and Wind, 1990; Wayang-Liedereb (poems) for Declamator and Percussion, 1991; Claviator for Brass Band, 1994. Honour: Visser-Neerlandia Prize, 1956. Address: Serviceflat "Het Oosten", Rubenslaan 1 Flat 7, 3723 BM Bilthoven, Netherlands.

MASSEY Andrew (John), b. 1 May 1946, Nottingham, England. Orchestral Conductor. m. Sabra A Todd, 29 May 1982, 1 son, 1 daughter. Education: BA, Merton College, Oxford University, 1968; MA, Analysis Contemporary & Conducting techniques, 1969; Dartington Summer School with Hans Keller, Witold Lutoslawski, Luciano Berio. Debut: Cleveland, 1978. Career: Assistant conductor, Cleveland Orchestra, USA, 1978-80; Associate Conductor, New Orleans Symphony Orchestra, 1980-86, San Francisco Symphony Orchestra, 1986-; Music director, Rhode Island Philharmonic, 1986-; Art adviser, prime guest conductor, Fresno Philharmonic, 1986-; Music Director, 1987-; Music Director, Toledo Symphony, Ohio, 1990-; Guest appearances with National Symphony, Pittsbsurgh, Vancounver Symphony and others. Memberships: American Federation of Musicians. Hobbies: Trees; Computers; Philosophy of Sir Karl Popper. Current Management: John Gingrich Management, PO Box 1515, NYC, NY 10023, USA.

MASSEY Roy (Cyril), b. 9 May 1934, England. Organist. m. Ruth Carol Craddock Grove, 1975. Education: BMus, University of Birmingham; Private Study with David Willcocks, FRCO(chm), ADCM, ARCM. Career: Organist: St Alban's, Conybere Street, Birmingham, 1953-60; St Augustine's, Edgbaston, 1960-65; Croydon Parish Church, 1965-68; Conductor, Croydon Bach Society, 1966-68; Special Commissioner, Royal School of Church Music, 1964-; Organist to the City of Birmingham Choir, 1954-; Organist, Master of Choristers, Birmingham Cathedral, 1968-74; Director of Music, King Edward's School, Birmingham, 1968-74; Conductor, Hereford Choral Society, 1974-; Organist, Master of Choristers, Hereford Cathedral, 1974-; Conductor-in-Chief, alternate years Associate Conductor, Three Choirs Festival, 1975-; Adviser on Organs to Dioceses of Birmingham & Hereford, 1974-. Honours: FRSCM 1971, DMus (Cantuar) 1991, for distinguished services to Church Music in recognition of work as a Cathedral Organist, as a Conductor of the Three Choirs Festival, and for work and influence in other musical spheres. Memberships: Royal Society of Musicians, 1991. Address: 1 College Cloisters, Hereford HR1 2NG, England.

MASSIS Annick, b. 1960, France. Singer (Soprano). Education: Studied at the Francis Poulenc Conservatoire, Paris. Debut: Toulouse, 1991. Career: Engagements include Ophelie in Hamlet and Philene in Mignon by Thomas at Compiègne; Rosina, Micaela and Anna in The Merry Wives of Windsor at the Opera-Comique, Paris; Carloina in Il Matriomonio Segreto at Nantes and Aricie (Hippolyte et Aricie by Rameau) at the Paris Opéra Garnier and the Brooklyn Academy of Music; Lucia di Lammermoor at Rouen and as Countess Adèle in Le Comte Ory at the 1997 Glyndebourne Festival; Season 1997-98 as Gluck's Eurydice and Marie in La Fille du Régiment at Geneva; Bizet's Leila at Toulouse and Countess Adèle at Florence and Montpellier. Address: c/o Grand Théâtre de Genève, 11 Boulevard du Théâtre, CH-1211 Geneva 11, Switzerland.

MASSIS René, b. 1946, Lyon, France. Singer (Baritone). Education: Studied in Lyon and Milan. Debut: Marseille 1976, as Silvio in Pagliacci. Career: Sang in L'Heure Espagnole at La Scala (1978) and has appeared throughout France and Italy; Lucca 1985 in Dejanice by Catalani, Paris Opéra 1988, as Valentin in Faust; Paris Opéra-Comique 1990, in Auber's Manon Lescaut at Nice Opéra 1990-91, in Wozzeck and as Guglielmo; Other roles include Rossini's Figaro (Glyndebourne Touring Opera, 1989), Mozart's Count, Belcore, Verdi's Ford and Posa, Fieramosca in Benvenuto Cellini, Eugene Onegin and the Marquis in Massenet's Grisélidis; Sang the title role in the premiere of Goya by Prodromidès, Montpellier, 1996. Recordings include: Chausson's Le Roi Arthus (Erato) Iphigénie en Aulide and La Juive (Philips). Address: Théâtre de L'Opéra de Nice, 1a 6 Rue St François de Paule, F-06300 Nice, France.

MASSON Askell, b. 21 Nov 1953, Reykjavik, Iceland. Composer; Musician. Education: Reykjavik Children's School of Music, 1961-63; Reykjavik College of Music, 1968-69; Private Studies, London, England, with Composition, Patrick Savill, 1975-77; Percussion with James Blades, 1975-76. Debut: Icelandic Television playing own music, 1969. Career: Commenced composing 1967; Composer, instrumentalist, National Theatre of Iceland, 1973-75; Producer, Icelandic State Radio, 1978-83; General Secretary, Icelandic League of Composers, 1983-85; Chairman, STEF, Iceland Performing Rights Society, 1989-; Currently working solely on composition. Compositions include: Opera: The Ice Palace, 1995; Sinfonia Trilogia, 1992; Piano Concerto, 1985; Concert Piece for snare drum and orchestra, 1982; Sonata for violin and piano, 1993; Woodwind Quintet, 1991; Trio for piano trio, 1995; Meditation, organ, 1992; Sindur (Sparks), percussion quartet, 1989; Okto November, strings, 1982; Run, orchestra, 1994. Recordings: Marimba Concerto; Clarinet Concerto; Trio; Sonata; Partita; Hrim; Snow; Helfro and others. Current Management: Iceland Music Information Centre, Reykjavik. Address: PO Box 821, 121 Reykjavik, Iceland.

MASSON Diego, b. 21 June 1935, Tossa, Spain. Conductor. Education: Paris Conservatoire, 1953-59; Study with Leibowitz, Maderna and Boulez. Career: Worked as percussionist in Paris with the ensemble Domaine Musicale; Founded Musique Vivante, 1966; Conducted premieres of Stockhausen's Stop and Setz die Segel zur Sonne; Early performances of works by Boulez including Domaines and .. explosante fixe.. and Berio; Musical Director of Marseilles Opera and Ballet-Theatre Contemporian, Angers; Conducted the Company at Sadler's Wells, London, 1971 and 1973; Guest engagements as orchestral conductor in France and elsewhere in Europe; Conducted La Bohème for Opera North, 1989, premiere of Caritas by Robert Saxton, 1991; Premiere of Il giudizio Universidade by Claudio Ambrosini at Citti dilastelle, 1996; Stavinsky concert at St John's, London, 1997. Recordings: Boulez, Domaine; Globokar, Fluide and Ausstrahlungen; Berio, Laborintus II; Boulez Le Marteau sans maitre, with Yvonne Minton; Stockhausen Aus den sieben tagen, and Liaison; Keuris Alto saxophone concerto. Address: Ingpen and Williams Ltd, 26 Wadham Road, London SW15 2LR, England.

MASSON Gerard, b. 12 Aug 1936, Paris, France. Composer. Education: Largely self-taught; Some study with Henri Pousseur and with Earle Browne and Stockhausen in Cologne, 1965-66. Compositions: Piece for 14 instruments and percussion 1964; Dans le deuil des vagues 1 and 11 for 10 instruments and for voice and orchestra 1968, 1970; Bleu Loin for 12 strings 1970; Ici c'est la Tyrannie for orchestra 1973; String Quartet 1973; Hypnopsie for orchestra 1974; Phonies and Phoenemes for chorus and orchestra 1975. Address: SACEM, 225 avenue Charles de Gaulle, 92521 Neuilly sur Seine Cedex, France.

MASTERS Rachel, b. 9 Sept 1958, Purley, Surrey, England. Harpist. Education: Junior Student, Guildhall School of Music and Drama, 1971-75; National Youth Orchestra, 1972-76; Scholar, Royal College of Music, 1976-80; ARCM, Honours. Debut: Wigmore Hall, 22 June 1982. Career: Joint Winner, SE Arts Young Concert Artists Award, 1979; Joint 2nd Prize, Mobil

Oil Harp Competition, 1980; Incorporated Society of Musicians Young Concert Artist, 1981; Principal harp in London Philharmonic Orchestra, since 1989; Professor at Royal College of Music. Recordings: Mozart Flute and Harp Concerto, with Phillipa Davies, City of London Sinfonia and Richard Hickox; Chandos: Harp pieces by Debussy, Ravel, Glière, Ginastera and Alwyn; Britten: Ceremony of Carols with King's College, Cambridge. Honours: Jack Morrison, Elisabeth Coates, Harp Prizes, Royal College of Music. Hobbies: Tennis; Walking; Cinema. Address: 31 Westfield Road, Surbiton, Surrey, KT6 4EL, England.

MASTERS Robert, b. 16 Mar 1917, Ilford, Essex, England. Violinist. Education: Royal Academy of Music, London. Career: Leader, Robert Masters Piano Quartet, 1940-63; Professor of Violin, Royal Academy of Music, London, 1947-64; Leader, Bath Festival Orchestra and Menuhin Festival Orchestra, 1960-75; Leader, London Mozart Players, 1961-78; Director of Music, Yehudi Menuhin School, England, 1968-80; Co-Director, Menuhin Music Academy, Gstaad, Switzerland, 1980-84; Guest Professor, Taiwan Universities, 1980-; Beijing and Shanghai Conservatories of Music, Banff Arts Centre; Artistic Director, Menuhin International Violin Competition, Folkestone, 1983-95; Artistic Director, New Zealand International Violin Competition, 1992; Director of Music, Hattori Foundation for Music and Art, 1992. Recordings: Robert Masters Piano Quartet, Fauré Piano Quartets (Argo); Walton Piano Quartet (Argo); Skalkottas Piano Trio, with Marcel Gazelle and Derek Simpson. Honour: FRAM. Address: 72d Leopold Road, London SW19 7JQ, England.

MASTERSON Valerie, b. 3 June 1937, Birkenhead, England. Singer (Soprano). m. Andrew March, 1 son, 1 daughter. Education: Royal College of Music, London; Milan, Won Countess of Munster Scholarship; Gulbenkian Scholarship. Career: Performances in Falstaff, Il Turco in Italia and Der Schauspieldirektor, Landestheater, Salzburg; D'Oyly Carte Opera Company including film version of Mikado; Member, English National Opera, 1972-; Roles include, Manon, Traviata, Mimi, Juliet, Louise, Pamina, Gilda, Countess and Susanna in Figaro; Seraglio, Constanza; Cleopatra in Julius Caesar; Mireille; Debut in Covent Garden, 1974, in Das Rheingold; Traviata, Fidelio, We Come To The River by Henze; Semele, Faust (Marguerite), Carmelites, Micaela in Carmen; The King Goes Forth to France (Sallinen); Guest Appearances in Concerts and Opera in many major cities of the world including Paris, Aix, Milan, Munich, New York, Chicago, San Francisco, Barcelona, Geneva, South America; Sang Marguerite in Faust and Mozart's Countess at the London Coliseum, 1990; Fiordiligi for Welsh National Opera and Ilia in Idomeneo for the English Bach Festival at Covent Garden; Season 1992-93 with the Countess at Dublin and the Marschallin at Liège; President of British Youth Opera; Professor of Singing; Honorary, Academy of Music, London. Honours: SWET Award, 1983; CBE, 1988; FRCM awarded in 1992; FRCM, 1993; Honorary RAM, 1994. Address: c/o English National Opera, St Martin's Lane, London WC2, England.

MASTILOVIC Daniza, b. 7 Nov 1933, Negotin, Serbia. Singer, Soprano. Education: Belgrade Conservatory with Nikola Cvejic. Career: Sang operetta in Belgrade, 1955-57; Minor roles at Bayreuth from 1956; Joined Georg Solti at Frankfurt Opera, 1959, debut as Tosca; Guest appearances in Hamburg, Dusseldorf, Zagreb, Vienna and Munich; Teatro Colon Buenos Aires 1972, as Abigaille in Nabucco; Zurich 1973, as Ortrud in Lehengrin; Covent Garden 1973-75, as Elektra; Metropolitan Opera 1975, as Elektra; Commemorated the 50th anniversay of Puccini's death with a performance of Turandot at Torre del Lago, 1974; Landestheater Salzburg 1987, as Clytemnestra in Elektra. Address: c/o Landestheater, Schwarstrasse 22, A-5020 Salzburg, Austria.

MASTROMEI Giampietro, b. 1 Nov 1932, Camoire, Tuscany, Italy. Singer, Baritone. Education: Studied in Buenos Aires with Apollo Granforte, Mario Melani and Hilda Spani. Career: Sang at the Teatro Colon, Buenos Aires for 13 seasons from 1952; European debut, 1962, appearing in France and Italy, and at the Covent Garden, 1973, as Renato, Un Ballo in Maschera and Amonasro; Verona Arena, 1971-86, as Amonasro and Scarpia; Further appearances at Caracas, Bilbao, Tokyo, Barcelona, Hamburg, Madrid, San Francisco, Dallas and Philadelphia; Also since Verdi's Iago and Rigoletto and roles in operas by Pergolesi, Scarlatti and Dallapiccola. Recordings: Simon Boccanegra; Il Corsaro; Aida.

MASUR Kurt, b. 18 July 1927, Brig, Silesia. Conductor. Education: National Music School, Breslau, 1942-44; Leipzig Conservatory, 1946-48. Career: Repetiteur and conductor at the Halle National Theatre, 1948; Conductor at Erfurt City Theatre, 1951-53 and Leipzig City Theatre, 1953-55; Conductor of Dresden Philharmonic 1955; General Music Director, Mecklenburg Staatsheater, 1958; Musical Director Dresden Philharmonic, 1967-72; Conductor, Leipzig Gewandhaus Orchestra, 1970; Tours of Europe, South America, Japan, USA, Canada and Middle East; British debut, 1973 with the New Philharmonia Orchestra; US debut 1974, with the Cleveland Orchestra; Conducted the London Philharmonic Orchestra in the Choral Symhony at the 1989 Promenade Concerts in London; Britten's War Requiem, 1990; London Proms 1993, with the Gewandhaus Orchestra in Schubert 8 and Bruckner 4, Brahms B flat concerto and A Midsummer Night's Dream by Mendelssohn; Principal Conductor, New York Philharmonic Orchestra, 1990. Recordings: Symphonies by Mendelssohn, Bruckner, Beethoven, Schumann and Tchaikovsky; Prokofiev's Piano Concertos; Beethoven's Missa Solemnis. Address: Norman McCann Ltd, The Coach House, 56 Lawrie Park Gardens, London SE26 6XJ, England.

MASUROK Yuri, b. 18 July 1931, Krasnik, Poland. Ukrainian Singer, Baritone. Education: Studied at Lvov Institute and Moscow Conservatoire. Career: Sang at the Bolshoy, Moscow, from 1963, debut as Eugene Oengin; Vienna Staatsoper as Scarpia, Luna and Escamilio; Aix-en-Provence, 1976, as Germont in La Traviata; Covent Garden debut 1975, as Renato in Un Ballo in Maschera; Returned to London as Posa in Don Carlos, Eugene Onegin and Count di Luna; US debut at Metropolitan Opera 1975, with Bolshoy Company; San Francisco, 1977, as Renato; Metropolitan debut as Germont, 1978; Covent Garden 1983 and 1986, as Luna and Germont; Sang at Wiesbaden 1987 as Scarpia, Budapest as Robert in Iolanta, with the company of the Bolshoi Theatre; Gran Teatre del Liceu Barcelona 1989, as Eugene Onegin; Concerts in Great Britain have included Wigmore Hall recitals and Festival Hall concert conducted by Svetlanov; Song repertory includes music by Ravel, Debussy, Schumann and Henze; Other operatic roles include Andrei Bolkonsky in War and Peace, Mazeppa, Rossini's Figaro and Yeletsky in The Queen of Spades; Sang Onegin at Milwaukee, 1992; Scarpia at Metropolitan, New York, 1993 and at Moscow, 1996. Recordings: Eugene Onegin, Tosca, The Queen of Spades and Iolanta on Russian labels; Tosca, Il Trovatore and Boris Godunov, Address: c/o Bolshoi Theatre, Ochotnyj Rjad 812, 103009 Moscow, Russia.

MATEJCEK Jan Vladimir, b. 29 Dec 1926, Hamburg, Germany. Administrator; Writer. m. Hanja Jindrova, 29 Apr 1950, 1 son, 1 daughter. Education: Doctorate of Laws, Charles University, Prague, 1951; Piano, Composition, Musicology. Career: In Czech Republic: Foreign Relations Secretary, Guild of Czechoslovak Composers, 1954-61; Managing Director: Prague Symphony Orchestra FOK, 1961-62, Music Department, Czechoslovak Theatrical and Literary Agency, 1962-64, PANTON Music Publishers, Prague, 1964-68; In Canada: Consultant, Canadian Music Centre, 1969-70; Executive Director, Ontario Symphony Orchestra Federation and Ontario Choral Federation, 1970-71; Founding Board Member, Association of Canadian Orchestras, 1971; Executive Assistant, Composers Authors and Publishers Association of Canada, 1971-77; Chief Executive Officer, Performing Rights Organization of Canada (PROCAN), 1980; First Chief Executive Officer, SOCAN, 1990-92; Representative, Schott Music International for Canada; Consultant, Prague Spring Festival; Visiting Lecturer, Law Faculty, Charles University, Prague; Writer. Publications include: Contemporary Czechoslovakian Piano Music Vols 1, 2, Cologne, 1968; History of BMI Canada and PROCAN: Their role in Canadian Music, Toronto, 1996; Alfred Maria Jelinek: A Profile of a Composer (in Czech), 1884-1932, 1997. Contributions to: International music magazines. Honours: Honourary Life Member, Association of Canadian Orchestras, 1992; Annual Jan V Matejcek SOCAN Award, Most Successful Canadian Concert Music Composition, 1992. Membership: Administrative Council and Executive Bureau, International Confederation of Societies of Authors and Composers (CISAC), 1982-92. Hobbies: Music; Golf; Outdoors. Address: 28 Tarlton Road, Toronto, Ontario M5P 2M4, Canada.

MATHER Bruce, b. 9 May 1939, Toronto, Canada. Composer; Pianist. m. Pierrette LePage. Education: Studied composition at the Royal Conservatory of Music in Toronto, in Paris with Roy Harris, Boulez, Milhaud and Messiaen, Universities of Stanford and Toronto, PhD, 1967. Career: Teacher at McGill University Montreal from 1966; Solo piano recitals and piano duet performances with Pierrette LePage. Compositions: Five Madrigals for soprano and ensemble, 1967-73; Music for Vancouver, 1969; Musique pour Rouen for string orchestra 1971; Music for Organ, Horn and Gongs, 1973; Eine Kleine Blassermusik, 1975; Au Chateau de Pompariain for Mezzo and Orchestra, 1977; Musique pour Champigny for vocal soloists and ensemble 1976; Ausone for 11 instruments 1979; Musigny for orchestra, 1980; Barbaresco for viola, cello and double bass, 1984; Scherzo for orchestra 1987; Dialogue pour trio basso et orchestre, 1988. Songs. Address: c/o SOCAN, 41 Valleybrook Drive, Don Mills, Ontario M3B 2S6, Canada.

MATHER Martin, b. 6 October 1927, Harrow, England (Australian National). Composer. Education: BA (Hons), University of London, 1948; Royal College of Music, with Herbert Howells and Frank Merrick, 1952-55. Career: Resident in Australia from 1956; Public Library of New South Wales, 1958-72; Freelance composer. Compositions include: Last Voyage of Matthew Flanders for soprano, tenor, chorus and orchestra, 1965; ANZAC Requiem for soloists, chorus and orchestra, 1967; Sextet, 1975; Fourteen Lieder for baritone and piano, 1986; Homage to Pushkin for baritone and piano, 1988; Twenty Four Preludes for piano, 1994. Recordings include: ANZAC Requiem, with the Adelaide SO; Sounds Australian, 1976. Honours include: Patrons Fund Award, RCM, 1954. Address: c/o APRA, 1A Eden Street, Crows Nest, NSW 2065, Australia.

MATHES Rachel (Clarke), b. 14 Mar 1941, Atlanta, Georgia, USA. Opera Singer; College Processor. Education: BA, Music, Birmingham-Southern College, 1962; MM, Vocal Performance, 1988, DMA, Vocal Performance, 1991, University of South Carolina; Study at Akademie für Musik und Darstellende Kunst, Vienna, Austria, 1962-63. Debut: Aida at Basel, Switzerland, 1965. Career: Deutsche Oper am Rhein, Dusseldorf, Germany, 1965-71; Freelance throughout Europe, 1971-74; Metropolitan Opera, New York, 1974-77, Debut as Donna Anna; New York City Opera, 1975, debut as Turandot; Wolf Trap Festival, Verdi's Requiem, 1975; Glasgow Opera, as Donna Anna, 1975. Recordings: Highlights from Mozart's Don Giovanni with the Glasgow Opera, 1975. Address: c/o Augustana College Music Department, Rock Island, IL 61201, USA.

MATHIESEN Thomas (James), b. 30 Apr 1947, Roslyn Heights, New York, USA. Musicologist. m. Penelope Jay Price, 11 Sept 1971. Education: BMus, Willamette University, 1968; MMus, 1970, DMA, Honours, 1971, University of Southern California. Career: Lecturer in Musicology, University of Southern California, Los Angeles, 1971-72; Professor of Music and Head Musicology Area, 1972-86, Associate Dean, Honours and General Education, 1986-88, Brigham Young University, Provo, Utah; Professor of Music, Indiana University, 1988-. Publications: Thesaurus Musicarum Latinarum, Project Director; A Bibliography of Sources for The Study of Ancient Greek Music, 1974; General Editor, Greek and Latin Music Theory, 1982-, currently 10 volumes; Aristides Quintilianus on Music in Three Books: Translation, with Introduction, Commentary and Annotations, 1983; Ancient Greek Music Theory: A Catalogue Raisonné of Manuscripts, 1988; Editor, Festa Musicologica: Essays in Honor of George J Buelow, 1995. Contributions to: Acta Musicologica; Fontes Artis Musicae; Journal of Musicology; Journal of Music Theory; Festival Essays for Pauline Alderman; Mousikologia; International Musicological Society Report for the 12th Congress; Musical Humanism and Its Legacy: Essays in Honor of Claude V Palisca; Articles for New Grove Dictionary of Music and Musicians, 2nd edition. Honours: ACLS Grant, 1977; NEH Fellowship, 1985-86; Guggenheim Fellowship, 1990-91; National Endowment for the Humanities, 1992-94, 1994-96. Memberships: American Musicological Society; Society for Music Theory; Music Library Association. Address: 1800 Valley View Drive, Ellettsville, IN 47429-9487, USA.

MATHIS Edith, b. 11 Feb 1938, Lucerne, Switzerland. Singer, Soprano. m. Bernhard Klee. Education: Studied at the Lucerne Conservatory and in Zurich with Elisabeth Bosshart. Debut: Lucerne 1956, in Die Zauberflöte. Career: Sang in Cologne from 1959, Berlin from 1963; Salzburg Debut 1960, in concert; Glyndebourne, 1962-65, as Cherubino and as Sophie in Der Rosenkavalier; Metropolitan Opera debut 1970, as Pamina; Returned to New York as Ännchen in Der Freischütz, Sophie, and Zerlina in Don Giovannia; Covent Garden, 1970-72, as Mozart's Susanna and Despina; Other roles include Ninetta in La Finta Semplice, Salzburg; Beethoven's Marzelline, Debussy's Mélisande, Verdi's Nannetta and Mozart's Aminta; Mozart's Countess; Weber's Agathe, Der Freischütz, Strauss Arabella and the Marschallin in Der Rosenkavalier; Sang in the premieres of Henze's Der junge Lord, Berlin 1965 and Sutermeister's Le Roi Bérenger, Munich 1985; Barcelona 1986, as Agathe; Debut as the Marschallin at the Berne City Opera, 1990; Concert appearances in Baroque music and as Lieder singer; Sang Lieder by Mendelssohn, Brahms and Schubert at the Wigmore Hall, London, 1997. Recordings: Le nozze di Figaro; Die Zauberflöte; Fidelio; Die Freunde von Salamanka of Schubert, Der Wildschutz, Lortzing; Frau Fluth, Nicolai's Lustige Weiber von Windsor; Mozart's Ascanio in Alba, Il Re Pastore, Il Sogno di Scipione and Apollo et Hyacinthus; Bach Cantatas; Haydn's Il Mondo della Luna and L'Infedelta Delusa; Handel's Ariodante. Address: Ingpen and Williams Ltd, 26 Wadham Court, London SW15 2LR, England.

MATORIN Vladimir, b. 1950, Russia. Singer (Bass). Education: Gnessin High School, Moscow, until 1974. Career: Sang leading bass roles at the Moscow Music Theatre, 1974-89; Soloist with the Bolshoi Opera from 1991, with Rossini's Basilio, Ivan Susanini, Rene in Iolanthe and Galitsky in Prince Igor; Mussorgsky celebration concerts 1989, Boris Godunov at Geneva and Chicago 1994; Tchaikovsky's Gremin at the Teatro Zarzuela, Madrid; Appearances at the Wexford Festival 1993 and 1995, in Cherivichki by Tchaikovsky and Rimsky-Korsakov's May Night; Songs by Mussorgsky, Rachmaninov and Tchaikovsky at the Deutsche Opera, Berlin, 1995. Address: Allied Artists, 42 Montpelier Square, London SW7 1JZ, England.

MATOUSEK Bohuslav, b. 1949, Czechoslovakia. Violinist. Education: Jaroslav Pekelsky Vaclav Snitil; Further study with Arthur Grumiaux, Nathan Milstein and Wolfgang Schniderhan. Career: Soloist with the Tokyo Symphony Orchestra, 1977-78; Co-founder and leader of the Stamic Quartet of Prague 1980; Performances at the Prague Young Artists and the Bratislava Music Festivals; Tours to Spain, Austria, France, Switzerland, Germany and Eastern Europe; Tour of the USA 1980, debut concerts in Britain at London and Birmingham, 1983; Further British tours 1985, 1987, 1988, Warwick Arts Festival, and 1989, 20 concerts; Gave the premiere of Helmut Eder's 3rd at the Channel Islands, Festival of Czech Music; Holland, Finland, Austria and France; Edinburgh Festival and debut tours of Canada, Japan and Indonesia. Recordings: Shostakovich No 13, Schnittke No 4, Panton; Dvorak, Martinu and Janacek complete quartets; Haydn Violin Concertos 1-6 Supraphon, Schubet Sonatinas and Grand Duo, Denon; Brahms, Bruch Concertos; Dvorak Concerto; Brahms's Sonatas, Bayuer R E; Dvorak Complete violin and piano; Martinu Duo Concertante; B Martinu Complete violin and piano. Honours: With Members of Stamic Quartet: Prize winner, Winner 1986 ORF, Austrian Radio, International String Quartet Competition followed by live broadcast from the Salzburg Mozarteum; Academie Charles Cros Grand Prix du Disque, 1991, for Dvorak quartets; 1 Prix International Violin Competition Prague, as soloist, 1972. Current Management: UK, R Gilder. Address: Dvorakova 311, 25264 Velké Prilepy, Czech Republic.

MATOUSEK Lukas, b. 29 May 1943, Prague, Czechoslovakia. Composer; Clarinettist; Performer of Medieval Instruments. m. Zuzana Matouskova, 28 June 1966, 2 daughters. Education: Prague Conservatory of Music; Private Study with Mil Kabelac, Composition, Janacek Academy of Music, Brno. Career: Artistic Director, Ars carmeralis Ensemble; Many concerts and recordings for braodcasting and TV throughout Europe; Recordings as performer, and of own works. Compositions: For Orchestra: Radices Temporis, Stores, Concerto for percussion and winds, Metamorphoses of Silence for strings; Chamber Music: Sonata for violin and piano; Sonata for double-bass and chamber ensemble; Wind-Quintet; Aztecs for percussion, Intimate Music for viola or cello, Recollection of Mr Sudek for brass-sextet, Sonatina for clarinet and piano; Vocal: Two Cantatas, Colours and Thoughts, The Flower from the Eden, Several Children's Choir Pieces. Recordings: CD, Gothic Music in Bohemia; Music of Charles University; Machaut-Chansons. Address: Vapencova 10, 14700 Prague 4, Czech Republic.

MATSUDA Nobuya, b. 12 Aug 1931, Kobe, Japan. Composer; Conductor; Pianist; Organist; Music Educator. m. Michiko Tokiwa, 3 May 1956, 2 sons, 1 daughter. Education: BA, Tokyo Art University, 1955; MA, Southern Illinois University, 1957; DMA, American Conservatory of Music, 1965; Studied Conducting with Hideo Saito, Tokyo, 1947-52, Thor Johnson, Chicago, 1958-61, Pierre Monteux, Summer School; Composition with Tomojiro Ikenouchi, Tokyo, Roy Harris, Carbondale, Illinois, 1957, Paul Hindemith, Yale University, Leo Sowerby, American Conservatory of Music, Chicago, Elliott Carter and Roger Sessions, Tanglewood Festival. Career: Guest Conductor: Former Tokyo Symphony Orchestra, Tokyo Glee Club, Fish Creek Music Festival Orchestra; Fellow Conductor, Tanglewood Music Festival; Conductor, Founder, Sioux County Orchestra, Sioux Center, Iowa; Conductor, Westmont College Orchestra; Performed own compositions at concerts; Piano and Organ recitalist; Guest Conductor, Southern Illinois University Orchestra with Roy Harris; Faculty: American Conservatory of Music, Chicago, 1965-80; Faculty, Dordt College, 1984-86; Faculty, Westmont College, Santa Barbara, California, 1986-95. Publications: Harmony, Theory and Practice; Strict Counterpoint; Sightreading book. Memberships: American Musicological Society; Society of Composers Inc; College Music Society. Address: 220N Maple Street, Hedron, ND 58638, USA.

MATSUNAGA Harunori, b. 23 Nov 1952, Tokyo, Japan. Assistant Professor, Ibarako Women's Junior College; Writer of Music. Education: Master Degree, Tokyo-Gakugei College, 1977. Career: Performed Works for 2 Pianos in Tokyo, 1981-; Performed Strauss-Godowsky's Fledermaus by Own Arrangement for 2 Pianos, 1997; Writer of Many Music Notes for CD's. Publications: A Dictionary of Piano-Duo Works, 1991; The Fun of Piano-Duo, 1993. Hobby: Collecting piano-duo works, especially out-of-print works. Address: 30-4 Kameido 7-chome, Koto-ku, Tokyo 136, Japan.

MATSUZAWA Yuki, b. 1960, Tokyo, Japan. Concert Pianist. Education: Studied with: Akiko Iguchi and Hiroshi Tamura at Tokyo University of Fine Arts; Further study with Vladimir Ashkenazy in Europe. Career: Concert engagements in Europe, Asia and USA; Radio and television engagements in Britain, Ireland, Holland, Greece, USA, Japan; Irish debut, 1990 with the Berlin Radio Symphony Orchestra; London debut, 1990 at Wigmore Hall; London appearances at: Wigmore Hall, Barbican Hall, St John's Smith Square; Concerto appearances with: Royal Philharmonic Orchestra, BBC Symphony Orchestra, Montreal Symphony Orchestra, Athens Radio Symphony Orchestra, Berlin Radio Symphony Orchestra, NHK Symphony Orchestra, New London Orchestra; Chamber music appearances with Suk Quartet in Britain and Czechoslovakia and with Martinu Quartet in Britain; Tours of Britain and Europe; Concerts with: English Chamber Orchestra, Brno Philharmonic, and Bournemouth Sinfonietta. Recordings: Exclusive recording contract with Novalis Records. Honours: Prizewinner at such competitions as Queen Elizabeth, Brussels, Maria Canals, Barcelona, and Montreal International, Canada. Address: Norman McCann International Artists Ltd, 56 Lawrie Park Gardens, London, SE26 6XJ, England.

MATTEUZZI William, b. 1957, Bologna, Italy. Singer, Tenor. Education: Studied with Paride Venturi. Debut: Sang Massenet's Des Grieux in Milan. Career: Season 1987 sang Rossini's Ramiro at Bologna, Nemorino at Bergamo and Evander in Alceste at La Scala; Rossini's Comte Ory at Venice, 1988, La Scala, 1991; Pesaro Festival, 1988, in La Scala de Seta, as Roderigo in Rossini's Otello, 1991; Count Almaviva on Metropolitan Opera debut 1988 and at Barcelona, 1991; Sang Lindoro in L'Italiana in Algeri, at Monte Carlo, 1989; Medoro in Orlando Furioso by Vivaldi at San Francisco; Other roles include Flamand in Capriccio and Ernesto in Don Pasquale. Recordings: Francesca da Rimini; Borsa in Rigoletto; Edmondo in Manon Lescaut and in Barbiere di Siviglia; Rossini's Zelmira; Tonio in La Fille du Régiment, Carlo and Goffredo in Rossini's Armida. Honours: Winner, Caruso International Competition, Milan. Address: c/o Teatro alla Scala, Via Filodrammatici 2, 201212 Milan, Italy.

MATTHEW-WALKER Robert, b. 23 July 1939, Lewisham, London, England. Musician. m. Lynn Sharon Andrews, 27 Dec 1969, 1 son. Education: London College of Printing; Goldsmith's College; London College of Music; Private Composition study with Darius Milhaud, Paris, 1962-63. Career: Composer, Record Company Executive, Author, Critic. Compositions: Symphonies 1-6, 1955, 1958, 1959, 1964, 1968 (2); Violin Concerto, 1962; Piano Sonatas 1-4, 1976 (2), 1980, 1982; Piano Trio, 1978; Horn Concerto, 1980; Cello Sonata, 1980; String Quartet, 1980; Sinfonia Solemnis, 1981. Recordings: Le Tombeau de Milhaud; Divertimento on a Theme of Mozart. Publications: Rachmaninoff: His Life and Times, 1980; Madonna - The Biography, 1989; Havergal Brian, 1995; Heartbreak Hotel - The Life and Music of Elvis Presley, 1995; Editor: The Keller Column, 1990; The Symphonies of Robert Simpson, 1991. Contributions to: Editor, Music and Musicians, 1984-88; National Dictionary of Biography, Musical Times, other publications. Memberships: Performing Right Society; Critics' Circle. Hobbies: History; Politics. Address: 1 Exford Road, London SE12 9HD, England.

MATTHEWS Andrea, b. 6 Nov 1956, Needham, MA, USA. Singer (Soprano). Education: AB, Princeton University, 1978. Debut: Marriage of Figaro as Susanna at Virginia Opera, 1984. Career: Semele in Semele; Gretel in Hansel and Gretel, Virginia Opera; Gilda in Rigoletto, Piedmont Opera; Zerlina in Don Giovanni, Greensboro Opera; Euridice in Orfeo ed Euridice, Violetta in La Traviata, Susanna in Marriage of Figaro, Marie in Bartered Bride and Ilia in Idomeneo at The Stadttheater Aachen, Germany; Other roles: Musetta, Mimi in La Bohème, Pamina in Magic Flute, Lauretta in Gianni Schicchi, Marzelline in Fidelio, Lucy in The Telephone, Marguerite in Faust, Nannetta in Falstaff; Soloist with many orchestras and companies including: St Louis Symphony; Houston Symphony; Baltimore Symphony; Atlanta Symphony; Stuttgart Philharmonic, Prague Autumn Festival, Philadelphia Orchestra, Puerto Rico Symphony, Honolulu Symphony, National Symphony at Wolf Trap, Los Angeles Master Chorale, Dessoff Choirs, Oratorio Society of New York, Mostly Mozart Festival, New Mexico Symphony, Kalamazoo Symphony, Utah Symphony, St Paul Chamber Orchestra, American Ballet Theater, American Symphony, Raleigh Symphony and Cincinnati Symphony; Art-Song recitals in many American States. Recordings: Vaughan Williams's Serenade to Music; Handel's Siroe, Muzio, Berenice, Tolomeo; Christmas Album; Victor Herbert's Thine Alone (songs); Ned Rorem's Three Sisters. Current Management: Thea Dispeker Artists Representative. Address: c/o Thea Dispeker, 59 East 54th Street, New York, NY 10022, USA.

MATTHEWS Colin, b. 13 Feb 1946, London, England. Composer. Education: Nottingham University; Composition with Arnold Whittall and Nicholas Maw. Career: Collaborated with Deryck Cooke on performing version of Mahler's 10th Symphony; Taught at Sussex University, 1972-73, 1976-77; Assistant to Britten in last years; Cortège premiered under Bernard Haitink at Covent Garden, 1989, Machines and Dreams by the London Symphony Orchestra, 1991. Compositions: Ceres for nonet, 1972; Sonata No 4 for orchestra, 1975; Partita, violin, 1975; Five Sonnets to Orpheus, tenor and harp, 1976; Specula for quartet, 1976; Night Music for small orchestra, 1977; Piano Suite, 1979; Rainbow Studies for quintet, 1978; Shadows in the Water, tenor and piano, 1979; String Quartet No 1, 1979; Sonata No 5, Landscape for orchestra, 1977-81; Oboe Quartet, 1981; Secondhand Flames, 5 voices, 1982; Divertimento, double string quartet, string orchestra, 1982; The Great Journey, baritone and ensemble, 1981-86; Toccata Meccanica for orchestra, 1984; Triptych for piano quintet, 1984; Cello Concerto, 1994; Three Enigmas, cello and piano, 1985; String Quartet No 2, 1985; Suns Dance, 10 players, 1985; Monody for Orchestra, 1987; Two Part Invention for chamber orchestra, 1987-88; Pursuit, 16 players, 1987; Fuga, 8 players, 1988; Cortège for orchestra, 1989; 2nd Oboe Quartet, 1989; Hidden variable, 15 players, 1989; Quatrain, wind, brass and percussion, 1989; Chiaroscuro for orchestra, 1990; Machines and Dreams, full or small orchestra and children, 1990; Broken Symmetry for Orchestra, 1992; Contraflow, 14 players, 1992; Memorial for Orchestra, 1993; String Quartet No 3, 1994; Cello Concertono 2, 1996; Renewal for chorus and orchestra, 1996. Recordings: The Great Journey; Cello Concerto, Landscape; Broken Symmetry, 4th Sonata, Suns Dance. Honours include: Chamber Music Prize, BBC, 1970; Ian Whyte Award, 1975; Park Lane Group Composer Award, 1983. Address: c/o Faber Music Ltd, 3 Queen Square, London WC1N 3AU, England.

MATTHEWS David (John), b. 9 Mar 1943, London, England. Composer; Writer. Education: BA, Classics, Nottingham University; Private study in composition with Anthony Milner. Career: Worked with Deryck Cooke on completion of Mahler's 10th Symphony; Assistant to Britten, 1966-69; Musical Director, Deal Festival. Compositions include: 4 Symphonies; In the Dark Time for orchestra; The Music of Dawn for Orchestra; Romanza for Cello and Small Orchestra; Capriccio for Two Horns and Strings; Chaconne for Orchestra; From Sea to Sky for Small Orchestra; Serenade for Small Orchestra; A Vision and a Journey for orchestra; Oboe Concerto; Violin Concerto; Variations for Strings; Introit for Two Trumpets and Strings; Cantiga for Soprano and Orchestra; Marina for Baritone, Basset Horn, Viola and Piano; 4 Hymns for Chorus; The Company of Lovers for Small Chorus; The Ship of Death for chorus; 7 String Quartets, 1970-95; The Flaying of Marsyas for Oboe Quintet; Clarinet Quartet; 2 Piano Trios; String Trio; Piano Sonata; Three Studies for Solo Violin; Winter Journey for solo violin; From Coastal Stations for Voice and Piano; The Golden Kingdom for voice and piano; Vespers for Mezzo Soprano and Tenor Solo, Chorus and Orchestra; A Congress of Passions for Voice, Oboe and Piano; Skies now are Skies for Tenor and String Quartet; A Little Threnody for Cor Anglais. Recordings: The Company of Lovers; Romanza; Cantiga; September Music; Introit; The Flaying of Marsyas; A Little Threnody; Winter Journey; Piano Sonata; Symphony No 4; Piano Trio 1; The Golden Kingdom; Vespers for mezzo, tenor, chorus and orchestra, 1994. Publications include: Editor, Mahler, Symphony No 10, 1976; Michael Tippett, 1980; Landscape into Sound, 1992; Editor, Beethoven arr Mahler, String Quartet op 95. Contributions to: Tempo; TLS. Membership: Association of Professional Composers. Hobbies: Walking; Drawing. Address: c/o Faber Music Ltd, 3 Queen Square, London WC1N 3AU, England.

MATTHEWS Michael Gough, b. 12 July 1931, London, England. Pianist; Teacher. Education: Royal College of Music, open scholarship 1947; ARCM, FRCM 1972; ARCO. Debut: Wigmore Hall, 1960. Career: Pianist; Recitals; Broadcasts and Concerts in UK, Europe and Far East; Adjudicator international competitions; Masterclasses; Lecture Recitals; Piano Teacher; Supervisor; Junior Studies; RSAMD, 1964-71; Royal College of Music; Director, Junior Department and Professor of Piano, 1972-75; Registrar, 1975; Vice-Director, 1978-84; Director, 1985-93; Director Associated Board of the Royal Schools of Music, 1985-93; Director, Royal Music Foundation Inc, USA, from 1985; Consultant to H M the Sultan of Oman, Jaguar Cars Sponsored Concerts; Piano recitals, lectures and masterclasses in the UK and abroad. Recordings: 2 CDs of piano music by Fauré; 8 nocturnes; 9 preludes; 2 barcarolles; Thème et variations; Mazurka. Publications: Various musicala entertainments; Arranger of Educational Music. Honours:Gold Medal, RCM, 1953; FRCM, 1972; Prize, Chopin International Piano Competition, 1955; Chopin Fellowship, 1959; FRSAMD, 1986; FRNCM, 1991; Hon GSM, 1987; Hon RAM, 1979. Memberships: Royal Philharmonic Society; Comité d'Honneur Presence de l'Art, Paris; Vice President, RCO; Honorary Vice President, Royal Choral Society; Vice President, Royal College of Music, 1997. Hobby: Gardening. Address: Laurel Cottages, South Street, Mayfield, East Sussex TN20 6DD, England.

MATTHUS Siegfried, b. 13 Apr 1934, Mallenuppen, Germany. Composer. m. Helga Matthus-Spitzer. Education: Deutsche Hochschule für Musik, 1952-58, with Wagner-Régeny; Study with Hanns Eisler at the Germany Academy of Arts. Career: Freelance Composer since 1958; Permanent musician for TV, Radio, Film from 1958; Composer-in-Residence at the Komische Oper Berlin from 1964; Works performed in all European Countries, Japan, North and South America, Australia; Since 1991, Artistic Director, Chamber Opera Festival, Rheinsburg; Professor 1985. Compositions: Operas: Lazarillo vom Tormes, 1964; Der Letzte Schuss, 1967; Noch ein Loffel Gift, Liebling, 1972; Omphale, 1976; Judith, 1982-84; Die Weise von Liebe und Tod des Cornets Christoph Rilke, 1983-84; Graf Mirabeau, 1987-88; Desdemona and her Sisters, 1991-92; Orchestral:

Kleines Orchesterkonzert, 1963; Inventionen, 1964; Violin Concerto, 1968; Dresdner Sinfonia, 1969; Piano Concerto, 1970; Serenade, 1974; Cello Concerto, 1975; 2nd Symphony, 1976; Responso, Concerto for Orchestra, 1977; Visions for Strings, 1978; Flute Concerto, 1978; Concerto for Trumpet, Kettledrums and Orchestra, 1982; The Wood, Concerto for Kettledrums and Orchestra, 1984; Divertimento for Orchestra, 1985; Oboe Concerto, 1985; The Bride of the Wind, Concerto for Orchestra, 1985; Nächtliche Szene im Park for Orchestra, 1987; Tief ist der Brunnen der Vergangenheit, Four Pieces for Symphonic Orchestra, 1991-92; Sinfonie (Gewandhaussinfonie), 1992-93; Piano Concerto (based on Opus 25 by Johannes Brahms) 1992; Manhattan Concerto, 1993; Concerto for Horn and Orchestra, 1994; Blow out, Concerto for organ and orchestra, 1995; Das Land Phantasien, for orchestra, 1996 Vocal: Weisen von Liebe, Leben und Tod, (Text R M Rilke), Lieder für Countertenor (Alt) und Orchester, 1993; Vocal: 5 Orchestra Lieder, 1962; Wir Zwei, 1970; 5 Liebeslieder des Catull, 1972; Laudate PACEM, 1974; Vocal: Hyperion-Fragmente, 1978-79; Holofernes-Portrait for Baritone and Orchestra, 1981; Die Liebesqualen des Catull, 1985-86; Nachtlieder für Baritone, String Quartet and Harp, 1987; Wem ich zu gefallen suche-Lieder und Duette für Tenor, Baritone and Klavier, 1987; Chamber: Octet, 1970; String Quartet, 1972; Trio for Flute, Viola and Harp, 1972; Octet, 1989; Windspiele für Violiue, Viola und Violon Cello; Lichte Spiele, 1996; Das Mädchen und der Tod, 1996. Honours: Hanns Eisler Prize, 1969; Arts Prize, DDR, 1970; National Prize, DDR, 1972, 1984. Memberships: Academy of Arts, Berlin-East; Academy of Arts, Berlin-West; Bayerischen Akademie der Schönen Künste in Munich. Hobby: Travel. Address: Elisabethweg 10, 13187 Berlin, Germany.

MATTILA Karita, b. 5 Sept 1960, Somero, Finland. Singer, Soprano. Education: Studied in Helsinki with Liisa Linko-Malmio; Pupil of Vera Rozsa from 1984. Career: Won 1983 Singer of the World Competion in Cardiff; Concert appearances with Abbado, Albrecht, Colin Davis, Dohnányi, Giulini, Salonen and Sinopoli; Orchestras include: Vienna Philharmonic, Vienna Symphony, Cleveland, London Symphony and the Staatskapelle Dresden; Operatic roles include Fiordiligi at the 1985 and 1987 Munich Festivals; Covent Garden debut 1986, as Fiordiligi; Returned for Pamina in Die Zauberflöte; Mozart's Elvira with Washington Opera, US debut; Scottish Opera, Hamburg Opera and Chicago Lyric Opera; Wagner's Eva In Brussels; Sang Emma in Schubert's Fierrabras in Vienna, with Abbado; Other engagements include Elvira and Eva at the Metropolitan Opera, 1990; Sang Ilia in Idomeneo at San Francisco, 1989, Agathe in Der Freishütz at Covent Garden; Sang Donna Elvira at the Vienna Festival, Amelia Grimaldi in Simon Boccanegra at the Geneva Opera, 1991; Sang Sibelius's Hostkvall and Luonnotar at the 1991 Prom Concerts, London; Appeared as Eva in a new production of Die Meistersinger at the Metropolitan, 1993; Sang songs by Grieg at the 1993 Prom Concerts; Appearances at the Salzburg Festival and with the Berlin Philharmonic Orchestra, 1993; Sang Elsa in Lohengrin at San Francisco (1995) and Covent Garden, 1997. Recordings: Portrait Record with Pritchard; Bruckner's Te Deum with Haitink; Cosi fan tutte and Don Giovanni with Marriner; Recordings for Deutsche Grammophon with Abbado and for Supraphon with Gerd Albrecht; Le nozze di Figaro with Mehta and Beethoven's Ninth conducted by Marriner. Address: IMG Artists, Media House, 3 Burlington Lane, London W4 2TH, England.

2)MATTINSON David, b. 1964, England. Singer, Bass-baritone. Education: Choral Scholar, Trinity College, Cambridge; Guildhall School of Music with Thomas Hemsley; Further study with Rudolf Pierney. Career: Concert repertoire includes the B minor Mass, Messiah, The Creation, Requiems of Brahms, Verdi and Fauré, The Dream of Gerontius and A Child of Our Time; Appearances with the City of London Sinfonia, the Bournemouth Symphony and the London Philharmonic Orchestras; Further concerts include Elijah at the Albert Hall; Christus in the St Matthew Passion at the Festival Hall; Mozart's Requiem, and Beethoven's Ninth in Koblenz; Song recitals with the accompanist Clare Toomer in Winterreise, Dichterliebe, La Bonne Chanson and the Songs of Travel by Vaughan Williams: Appearances with the New Songmakers and the Mistry String Quartet and at the Buxton, Malvern and Warwick Festivals; Operatic roles include Gualtiero in Musgrave's The Voice of Ariadne, Mozart's Figaro, Germont, and Glover in La Jollie Fille de Perth; Scottish Opera debut 1991, as Zuniga in Carmen; Debut as Mozart's Figaro, Opera North, 1992; Season 1992 as Villotto in Haydn's La Vera Costanza for Garsington Opera and in Billy Budd for Scottish Opera; Sang Mozart's Figaro for Central Festival Opera, 1996. Recording: Bach St John Passion. Honours: Gold Medal Rosebowl and the Worshipful Company of Musicians' Silver Medal, GSM; Gold Medal in the 1988 Royal Overseas League Music Competition; Prizewinner, Walter Gruner International Lieder Competition; Elly Ameling International Lied Concours; 1st prize, 1990 BP Peter Pears Award. Address: Kaye Artists Management Ltd, Barratt House, 7 Chertsey Road, Woking, Surrey GU21 5AG, England.

MATTIOTTO Claudia, b. 21 Jan 1959, Torino, Italy. Pianist. m. Guido Scano, 1 Aug 1985, 1 son. Education: High School for Training of Primary Teachers; Piano Diplomas: Verdi High Conservatory, Torino and Ecole Internationale de Piano, Lausanne, Switzerland; Mozarteum, Salzburg, Austria; Manhattan School of Music, New York, USA. Debuts: Solo, 1981; Piano Duo, 1985; With orchestra, 1988. Career: Concerts in all Italy and in France, Germany, Egypt, India, Slovenia, Rumania; Conductor and special teacher in musical courses and seminars; Many European broadcasting appearances. Recordings: 4 Steps im 4 Hands, series of 15 weekly programmes, Monte Carlo, Bucharest, Marseille, Trieste Radio and TV Broadcasting. Publication: In Musica, piano teaching methodology text, 1986. Honours: Teaching Certificate, Manhattan School of Music, 1991; 1st Prize, Genova Competition, 1986. Membership: President, International Centre for Musical Research. Hobbies: Photography; Swimming. Address: Via Bonomea 217, 34136 Trieste, Italy.

MATTON Roger, b. 18 May 1929, Granby, Quebec, Canada. Composer. Education: Studied in Arthur Letondal's class, Conservatoire de musique du Quebec, Montreal; Studied composition under Claude Champagne; Studied under Andree Vaurabourg-Honegger and Nadia Boulanger, Ecole normale superieure de musique; Attended Olivier Messiaen's analysis classes, Conservatoire de Paris; Studied ethnomusicology under Marius Barbeau, National Museum of Canada, Ottawa. Career: Joined Archives de folklore, Laval, Quebec; Teacher, History Department, Laval, Quebec City; Composer of music having received commissions from Canadian Broadcasting Corporation; l'orchestre symphonique de Quebec, Montreal Symphony Orchestra, Le Grand Theatre de Quebec. Compositions: Orchestral: Danse Bresillienne 1946; Danse Lente 1947; L'Horoscope 1958; Mouvement Symphonique 1, 1960, 11 1962, 111 1974, IV 1978; Pax 1950, Soloists with Orchestra: Concerto pur deux pianos et orchestre, 1964; Concerto pour saxophone et orchestre a cordes 1948; Voices with Orchestra: L'escaouette 1957; Te Deum 1967; Chamber Music: Esquisse pour quatuor a cordes 1949; Etude pour clarinette et piano 1946; Piano: Berceuse 1945; Trois Preludes pour piano 1949; Two Pianos: Concerto pour deux pianos et percussion 1955; Danse bresilienne 1946; Organ: Suite de Paques, 1952; Te es Petrus, 1984. Recordings: Berceuse; Concerto pour deux pianos et orchestre; Concerto pour deux pianos et percussion; Danse breilienne; l'horoscope; Movement Symphonique 1, 11; Suite de Paques; Te Deum; Trois Preludes pour piano. Honours: Awarded distinction at Seventh Gala du Quebec, Montreal for choral suite l'Escaouette 1965; Received Prix du Disque Pierre Mercure for Concerto pour deux pianos et orchestra 1966; Presented with Prix Calixa Lavallee by St Jean Baptiste Society for contribution to French-Canada 1969. Membership: Canadian League of Composers. Address: c/o SOCAN, 41 Valleybrook Drive, Don Mills, Ontario M3B 2S6, Canada.

MATUSKY Patricia (Ann), b. 20 July 1944, Detroit, Michigan, USA. Ethnomusicologist. m. Howard A Yamaguchi, 11 Jan 1981, 1 son. Education: Private piano study; National Music Camp, Interlochen, Michigan; BMus, University of Michigan, 1966, AMLS, 1969; MA, Musicology, Hunter College, City University of New York, 1974; PhD, Ethnomusicology, University of Michigan, 1980. Appointments: Librarian, New York Public Library, Music Division, Lincoln Centre; Senior Lecturer, Ethnomusicology, University of Malaya, Kuala Lumpur, 1983-86, LaSalle College of the Arts, Singapore, 1991-94; Head, School of Music, LaSalle College of the Arts, Singapore, 1992-94; Associate Professor, Music, University Sains Malaysia, 1994-97. Publications: Music in the Malay Shadow Puppet Theater, 1980; Instruments and Major Forms of Malay Music, 1989; Malaysian Shadow Play and Music, 1993, 1997; Muzik Malaysia, 1997. Contributions to: West Magazine; Garland Encyclopaedia of World Music; Asian Music; Sarawak Museum Journal; Asian Folklore Studies; American Musical Instrument Society Journal. Honours: John D Rockefeller Fund Fellowship, 1975-76; Fulbright-Hays Professor in Music, 1981-82. Memberships: Society for Ethnomusicology; Society for Asian Music; American Musical Instrument Society. Address: 1220 Villanova Drive, Davis, CA 95616, USA.

MATUSZCZAK Bernadeta, b. 10 Mar 1937, Torum, Poland. Composer. Education: Studied with Szeligowski and Sikorski at the Poznan and Warsaw Conservatories: Paris with Nadia Boulanger. Compositions: Julia i Romeo, chamber opera, Warsaw 1970; Humanae Voces, radio oratorio, 1972; Mysterium Heloizy, opera, 1973-74; The Diary of a Madman, monodrama after Gogol, Warsaw 1978; Apocalypsis, radio oratorio, 1979; Prometheus, chamber opera after Aeschylus, 1981-83. Address: c/o ZAIKS, 2 rue Hipoteczna, 00 092 Warsaw, Poland.

MATUZ Istvan, b. 21 Jan 1947, Nagykoros, Hungary. Flautist. m. Katalin Vas, 13 Mar 1976, 2 sons. Education: Budapest Music High School, Hungary; Conservatoire Superieur de Musique, Brussels, Belgium. Career: Assistant, Conservatoire, Brussels, 1971-72; Solo flautist, Opera de Wallonie, Liege, Belgium; Professor of flute, Music High School, Liszt Ferenc, Debrecen, 1975-; Soloist, Hungarian Philharmonic Society, 1978-; Solist, Ensemble Intercontemporain, Paris, 1980-81. Recordings: 20th Century works for flute; New flute recording withnew flute technique Hungaroton; Matuziada, flute and electronic guitar, Dubrovay; Approximately 12 Hungarian records, Hungarian works. Hobbies: Languages. Address: 1124 Budapest, Tamasi Aron u 23, Hungary.

MATYS Jiri, b. 27 Oct 1927, Bakov, Nachod area, Czechoslovakia. Composer. Education: Graduated Brno Conservatory, 1947, studied with Kvapil at the Janacek Academy of Music in Brno. Career: Teacher, Janacek Academy, 1953-57, then Head of the School of Music at Kralove Pole in Brno, 1957-60. Compositions: Viola Sonata, 1954; 5 String Quartets, 1957-90; Variations on Death for narrator, horn and string quartet of a poem by Milan Kundera, 1959; Morning Music, 1962; Solo viola sonata, 1963; Music for string quartet and orchestra, 1971; Suite for viola and bass clarinet, 1973; Symphonic Overture, 1974; Dialogue for cello and piano, 1976; Suite for flute and guitar, 1981; Music for strings, 1982; Chamber Music includes: Divertimento for Four Horns, 1981; Suite for Wind Quintet, 1984; Compositions for Solo instruments; Sonata for Violin Solo, 1977; Music for Piano, 1985; Poetic Movements V, four compositions for four guitars, 1988; String Quartet No 5, 1989-90; Sonata for Violin Solo, 1991; Night Thoughts, A cycle of piano compositions in five parts, 1992; Sonata for Violin Solo, 1993. Address: c/o OSA, Cs Armady 20, 160-56 Prague 6 Bubenec, Czech Rpublic.

MAUCERI John F, b. 12 Sept 1945, NY, USA. Conductor; Music Director. m. Betty Weiss, 15 June 1968, 1 son. Education: M.Phil, 1971, BA, 1967, Yale University; Tanglewood, 1972. Career: Music Director: Yale Symphony, 1968-74; American Symphony Orchestra, 1984-87; Washington Opera, 1979-82; Kennedy Center, 1973-; Scottish Opera, 1987-93; Consultant, Music Theater, Kennedy Center, 1982-; Co-Producer, On Your Toes, Musical Play, Broadway and London's West End, 1982; Lyric Opera of Chicago debut, La Bohème, 1987; Music Director, WNET Gala of Stars, A Musical Toast, 1987; Conducted, the New York Philharmonic Metropolitan Opera Orchestra and Empire Brass, Carnegie Hall, 1987; British premiere of Weill's Street Scene, 1989; Conducted new production of La Forza del Destino for Scottish Opera, 1990, followed by revivals of Salome and Madama Butterfly; Les Troyens in Glasgow and London; Conducted own edition of Blitzstein's Regina at Glasgow, British Premiere, 1991; Madama Butterfly at Turin, 1996. Recordings: Recordings: Original Cast: Candide, 1973, On Your Toes, 1983; New York City Opera, Candid, 1985; Original Cast, Song and Dance, 1985; My Fair Lady, with Kiri Te Kanawa and Jerry Hadley. Contributions to: Opera Magazine, 1985. Honours: Antoinette Perry, Outer Critics Circle, Drama Desk Awards, Best Opera Recording, Candide, 1987. Current Mangement: Columbia Artists. Address: c/o Columbia Artists Management, 165 West 57th Street, NY 10019, USA.

MAUEROVA-GAJEROVA Nada, b. 11 March 1928, Brno, Czech Republic. Writer; Actress. m. M Vacek, 17 June 1988, 1 son, 2 daughters. Education: Private Music School. Debut: Bonet Prediari, Cycle of Concert Songs for Soprano and Chamber Orchestra. Career: Extensive Art Activities in All Mentioned Media, 1946-. Compositions: Concert Songs, Zena, Mledam Te, Mixed Choir, Zeme Ma, Musical Monologue, Sleeping Beauty; Opera Cibretto, Jan Zelivsky, Bratr Zak; Romance, Pro Kridlovkc, Kocour. Recordings: Bratr Zak, 1983; Kocour Mikes, 1986; Romance, Pro Kridlovkc. Honours: Prize, Union of Composers for Song Cycle, 1978; 1st Prize, Jiklare Competition. Memberships: Union of Writers, Prague; Association of Music Artists & Scientists; Actors Association. Hobbies: Music; Literature; Gardening; Dogs. Address: Dedinska 894, 161 00 Prague 6, Czech Republic.

MAUNDER Charles (Richard Francis), b. 23 Nov 1937, Portsmouth, England. m. 3 sons. Lecturer; Musicologist; Early Music Practitioner. Education: Jesus College, Cambridge, 1955-61; MA, PhD, Cambridge, 1962. Career: Fellow of Christ's College, Cambridge, 1964-; Lecturer at Univesities in Britain, Cambridge, London, Reading, Leeds, and the USA, Philadelphia, Chicago, Northwestern, Northern Illinois, and at musicological conferences, International Mozart Congress, Salzburg, 1991; Performer on the bass viol, Cambridge Consort of Viols, baroque, classical viola, Cambridge Early Music; Violone, concerts in Cambridge and elsewhere include Messiah, St John Passion, Brandenburg Concertos, Bach Christmas Oratorio and Monteverdi Vespers; Has restored early keyboard instruments, including square piano by Johannes Zumpe, London 1766, for Emmanuel College, Cambridge; Instruments built includes copies of two-manual harpsichord by Thomas Hitchcock and Mozart's forepiano; Founder of the Cambridge Classical Orchestra, 1990. Publications: Mozart's Requiem: On Preparing a New Edition, 1988; Numerous editions of 17th and 189th Century music, including 13 of the 48 volumes of J C Bach's Collected Works; Mozart's Requiem K626, C minor Mass K 427 and Vesperae. Contributions: Galpin Society Journal, Musical Times, Early Music, Journal of the Royal Musical Association, Music and Letters, Notes, Mozart-Janrbuch. Address: 54 High Street, Sawston, Cambridge, CB2 4BG, England.

MAUNDER Stuart, b. 1957, Australia. Stage Director. Career: Productions for Australian Opera include Nabucco, Die Fledermaus, Don Pasquale and Romeo et Juliette; La Traviata, Barber of Seville and Iolanthe for Victorian State Opera; Die Entführung and Don Pasquale for Lyric Opera Queensland; Music theatre pieces by Bernstein, Sondheim and Sullivan throughout Australia; Resident in Britain from 1990, staging Rigoletto and Hoffmann for Stowe Opera and Figaro at the Hong Kong Academy; Staff Director at Covent Garden, reviving La Bohème, L'Elisir d'amore and Guillaume Tell for Lisbon, and featuring in ROH/BBC TV Top Score presentations; Season 1996-97 with Die Zauberflöte for British Youth Opera, Hindemith and Monteverdi one-actors for Stopera, Canberra, and Gales at the Sydney Opera House. Address: C&M Craig Services Ltd, 3 Kersley Street, London SW11 4PR, England.

MAURER Elsie, b. 1938, Germany. Singer (Mezzo-soprano). Career: Sang at the Aachen Opera from 1963, Pforzheim 1964-67, Frankfurt Opera from 1968; Among her best roles have been Meg Page, Olga in Eugene Onegin and Mary in Fliegender Holländer; Guest appearances at Brunswick, Oldenburg and elsewhere as Ortrud, Amneris, Herodias and Preziosilla; Sang Countess Geschwitz in Lulu for Essen Opera as guest at Barcelona (1969) and Trieste (1971); Also guested at the Vienna State Opera. Recordings include: Die Soldaten by Zimmermann (Teldec).

MAURO Ermanno, b. 20 Jan 1939, Trieste, Italy. Singer, Tenor. Education: Studied at the Toronto Conservatory with Herman Geiger-Torel. Debut: Canadian Opera Company 1962, as Tamino in Die Zauberflöte. Career: Sang Manrico in Toronto 1965; Covent Garden from 1967, debut in Manon Lescaut; Guest appearances with Welsh National Opera, Scottish Opera and at Glyndebourne; New York City Opera, 1975 as Calaf in Turandot; BBC TV as Paco in La Vida Breve; Metropolitan Opera from 1978, as Canio, Manrico, Ernani, Pinkerton, Paolo in Zandonai's Francesca da Rimini and Des Grieux; La Scala and Rome 1978; San Francisco 1982; Vienna 1983; Brussels 1984, as Manrico; Dallas Opera 1985, as Otello; Other roles include Male Chorus in The Rape of Lucretia; Donizetti's Edgardo, Gounod's Faust, Verdi's Radames, Riccardo, Alfredo and Gabriele Adorno; Don José, Cavaradossi, Dick Johnson and Enzo in La Gioconda; Sang Cavaradossi at the Met 1986, Turiddu 1989; Calaf at the Deutsche Oper Berlin 1987; San Francisco and Barcelona 1989, as Otello and Enzo; Sang Manrico with Zurich Opera 1990, Maurizio in Adriana Lecouvreur at Montreal; Season 1992 at Radames at Dallas, Puccini's Des Grieux at Miami, Calaf at Philadelphia and Turiddu at the Teatro Colon, Buenos Aires; Sang Loris in Fedora at Montreal, 1995. Address: c/o Metropolitan Opera, Lincoln Center, NY 10023, USA.

MAUS Peter, b. 1948, Germany. Singer, Tenor. Debut: Bayreuth Youth Festival, 1972, in Wagner's Das Liebesverbot. Career: Sang in the 1981 premiere of Kagel's Aus Deutschland; Bayreuth Festival from 1982, with minor roles in Parsifal and Die Meistersinger; Shepherd in Tristan, 1993; Teacher of Singing at the Hochschule für Kunste in Berlin, from 1987. Recordings: Das Liebesverbot; Die Meistersinger; Masses by Schubert, Donizetti Mass and Wolf's Der Corregidor; Esquire in Parsifal, conducted by Barenboim. Memberships: Deutsche Oper Berlin from 1974, in such character roles as Wenzel in The Bartered Bridge, Sparlich in Lustigen Weiber, Peter Ivanov in Zar und Zimmermann, Pong, the Count in Zimmermann's Die Soldaten, Fatty in Mahagonny and Eljeya in From the House of the Dead. Address: c/o Deutsche Oper Berlin, Richard Wagnerstrasse 10, D-1000 Berlin 10, Germany.

MAW (John) Nicholas, b. 5 Nov 1935, Grantham, England. Composer. m. Karen Graham, 1960, 1 s, 1 d. Education: Royal Academy of Music; Study with Nadia Boulanger and Max Deutsch, Paris, 1958-59; Fellow Commoner in Creative Arts, Trinity College, Cambridge, 1966-70. Career: Incomplete premiere of Odyssey at 1987 Promenade Concerts, complete with the City of Birmingham Symphony under Simon Rattle in 1990, American Games premiered at 1991 Proms; Commission for opera, Sophie's Choice, for opening season of refurbished Covent Garden theatre, 1999-2000. Compositions include: Operas: One Man Show, 1964, The Rising of The Moon, 1970; Orchestral Works: Sinfonia, 1966, Serenade for Small Orchestra, 1973, 1977, Odyssey, 1974-87, Spring Music, 1983, The World in the Evening, 1988, American Games for Wind Ensemble, 1991, Shahnama, 1992; Instrumental Solos with Orchestra: Sonata Notturna for Cello and String Orchestra, 1985; Voice and Orchestra: Nocturne, 1958; Chamber Music: String Quartet, 1965, No 2, 1983, No 3, 1994, Chamber Music for Wind and Piano Quintet, 1962, Violin Concerto, 1993; Instrumental Music: Sonatina for Flute and Piano, 1957, Personae for Piano, Nos I-III, 1973, Nos IV-VI, 1985; Vocal Music: 5 Epigrams for Chorus, 1960, The Voice of Love for Mezzo Soprano and Piano, 1966, Reverdie, 5 songs for Male Voices, 1975, Nonsense Rhymes, Songs and Rounds for Children, 1975-76, The Ruin, 1980, Five American Folksongs for High Voice and Piano, 1988; Roman Canticle for Medium Voice and Chamber Ensemble, 1989, Sweté Jesu, 1990, The Head of Orpheus, for soprano and 2 clarinets, 1992. Honours: Midsummer Prize, Corporation of London, 1980; Sudler International Wind Band Prize, 1991; Stoeger Prize for Chamber Music, 1993. Address: c/o Faber Music Ltd, 3 Queen Square, London, WC1N 3AU, England.

MAX Robert, b. 7 Feb 1968, London, England. Solo Cellist; Cellist with Barbican Piano Trio. m. Zoë Solomon, 21 Mar 1993. Education: Royal Academy of Music, 1984-87; GRSM, Honours 1st Class; LRAM, Diploma RAM, Royal Northern College of Music, 1987-89; Juilliard School, New York, 1990-92. Career: Concerts throughout UK, Europe, North and South America and the Far east; String Finalist, BBC Young Musician of the Year, 1984; Music Director for Nonesuch Orchestra; Music Director for Zemel Choir. Recording: Barbican Piano Trio: Mendelssohn D Minor with works by Alan Bush and John Ireland, 1989, Complete Piano Trios of E Lalo. Honours: 1st Prize, European Music for Youth Cello Prize, 1984; Edward Boyle Memorial Scholarship to Banff Centre for the Arts; Julius Isserlis Scholarship for Study Abroad; Winner, String Section of International Young Concert Artists Competition, 1989; Royal Overseas League Prize, 1989. Memberships: Incorporated Society of Musicians; European String Teachers Association; Association of British Choral Directors. Address: 5 Asmuns Hill, London, NW11 6ES, England.

MAXWELL Donald, b. 12 Dec 1948, Perth, Scotland. Baritone Singer. m. Alison Jayne Norman. Education: Studied Geography at Edinburgh University. Debut: With Scottish Opera in Musgrave's Mary, Queen of Scots, 1977. Career: Has sung Rossini's Figaro and Zurga, in Les Pêcheurs de Perles with Scottish Opera, Cavalli's Egisto, Janácek's The Cunning Little Vixen, From the House of the Dead; With Welsh National Opera: Verdi's Iago, Renato, Rigoletto, Don Carlo, in Ernani; Covent Garden debut 1987, in British premiere of Sallinen's The King Goes Forth to France; Appearances with Opera North as The Dutchman and Scarpia, Vancouver as Rigoletto and at La Monnaie, Brussels; Major Roles: Falstaff, Paris, Tokyo, Milan, Vienna, New York, and on TV; Iago for TV and Paris Opera; Wozzeck for TV; Rigoletto, Flying Dutchman, Scarpia, Gunther, Figaro, Renato, Pizarro, Don Carlo, Don Alfonso, Zurga, Eisenstein, Golaud; Sang the Athlete in Lulu at the 1996 Glyndebourne Festival; Many appearances in light music particularly as member of The Music Box. Recordings include: Notably Carmina Burana. Address: c/o Music International, 13 Ardilaun Road, London, N5 2QR, England.

MAY Marius, b. 1950, England. Cellist. Education: Studied with Andre Navarra in Paris and with Pierre Fournier in Geneva. Debut: Wigmore Hall, 1973, followed by recital and concerto appearances throughout Britain; Festival Hall 1976, with the Schumann Concerto and the Philharmonia Orchestra. Career: Has played in public from age 10, giving a recital at the Royal College of Music, London, and playing the Saint-Saëns A minor Concerto in Edinburgh; Edinburgh and Bath Festivals, 1976; Soloist with leading orchestras in Europe; Several tours of Germany have included Berlin Philharmonic concert 1980; Concerts with Yehudi Menuhin at the Gstaad Festival, Switzerland. Has recently played the Elgar Concerto with the London Philharmonic and the Finzi Concerto at the Three Choirs Festival with the Royal Philharmonic; Has taught at the University of California in Los Angeles; BBC TV concerts include the Tchaikovsky Rococo Variations and a Gala from the Edinburgh Festival. Address: c/o Ingpen and Williams Ltd, 26 Wadham Road, London SW15 2LR, England.

MAYER Richard, b. 9 June 1948, Brno, Czech Republic. Composer. Education: Faculty of Arts, University of Brno; Piano, Composition, Conservatory, Brno; PhD, Musicology, 1975. Debut: Brno, 1969, Zlin, 1980. Career: Records of compositions on Czech TV and radio; Piano Fantasy, Iceland, the Premiere, USA, 1990. Compositions include: Sonata for Violin and Piano; Concerto for 2 Pianos and Tromba; Quartet for Clarinet, Violin, Viola and Cello; Variation for Clarinet and Piano; Reykjavik, Sonata for Viola and Cello; Variation for Tromba and Piano; Iceland, Fantasy for Piano Solo; Saga of Northern Night, A Cycle of Compositions for Alto and Bassoon; Drama Musicum Sine Verbis - Chronikon Mundi, 1st Symphony for Chamber Orchestra; Magna Missa Millennia Islandica: Great Magnificent Mass for large orchestra, organ, narrator, solos and choir, dedicated to the forthcoming anniversary of 1000 years of accepting Christianity in Iceland. Recordings: Several. Contributions to: Opus Musicum. Memberships: Nordic Society of Prague; Bohemian Music Association; Club of Moravian Composers. Hobbies: History of Iceland; Literature of Iceland. Address: Cihlarska 14, 602 00 Brno, Czech Republic.

MAYER Thomas, b. 1907, Germany. Conductor. Education: Studied conducting and composition, State Academy of Music, Berlin. Debut: USA, Metropolitan Opera, NY, 1947. Career: Opera Theatres of Beuthen, Leipzig, Teplitz and Aussig; Assistant to Erich Kleiber, Fritz Busch and Arturo Toscanini, Teatro Colon, Beunos Aires; Director, German Opera season, Santiago, Chile; Director, State Symphony Orchestra, Montevideo; Conducted Salome with Astrid Varnay, Cincinnati, 1948; Tristan und Isolde with Flagstad, Caracas; First Foreign Director, Venezuelan Symphony Orchestra; Conductor, Halifax Orchestra, Canada; Ottawa Orchestra became National Orchestra of Canada; Guest conductor, London Symphony, Royal Philharmonic, Chicago, Buffalo, Toronto, Montreal, Cincinnati, Munich Philharmonic, Essex and all the major Australian orchestras, as well as opera in Hamburg, Stuttgart and Australia; Conductor, Sinfonie Orchestra Berlin, 1974-; Frequent guest, Berlin Symphony, East. Address: c/o Norman McCann Ltd, The Coach House, 56 Lawrie Park Gardens, London SE2 6XJ, England.

MAYER William (Robert), b. 18 Nov 1925, New York, USA. Composer. Education: BA, Yale University, 1949; Studied with Roger Sessions at Julliard, 1949 and at the Mannes College of Music, 1949-52. Career: Secretary, National Music Council, 1980. Compositions: Stage: The Greatest Sound Around, children's opera, 1954; Hell World children's opera, 1956; One Christmas Long Ago, opera in act, 1964; Brief Candle, micro-opera, 1964; A Death in the Family, opera 1983; The Snow Queen, ballet, 1963; Orchestra: Andante for strings, 1955; Hebraic Portrait, 1957; Overture for an American, 1958; Two Pastels, 1960; Octagon for piano and orchestra, 1971; Inner and Outer Strings for string quartet and string orchestra, 1982; Of Rivers and Trains, 1988; String Quartet and other chamber music; Piano Sonata Choruses and song. Honours; Guggenheim Fellowship, 1966; National Institute for Musical Theater Award, 1983. Address: ASCAP, ASCAP Building, One Lincoln Plaza, NY 10023, USA.

MAYES Samuel (Houston), b. 11 Aug 1917, Missouri, USA. Cellist. Education: Studied with Felix Salmond at the Curtis Institute, 1929-37. Career: Philadelphia Orchestra 1936, principal from 1939; Principal Cellist of the Boston Symphony Orchestra, 1948-64, Philadelphia Orchestra, 1964-73; Played with the Los Angeles Philharmonic, 1974-75; Many appearances as soloist, notably the US premiere of Kabalevsky's First concerto with the Hartford Symphony and the Boston Symphony, 1953; Former teacher at the New England Conservatory and Bost University, University of Michigan from 1975. Recordings: Prokofiev's Symphony-Concerto with the Boston SO and Don Quixote with the Philadelphia Orchestra. Address: Michigan State University, School of Music, East Lansing, MI 48824, USA.

MAYFORTH Robin, b. 1965, USA. Violinist. Education: Studied at the Juilliard School, New York. Career: Appearances with I Solisti Veneti, under Claudio Scimone; Co-founded the Lark Quartet, USA; Recent concert tours to Australia, Taiwan, Hong Kong, China, Germany, Holland; US appearances at the Lincoln Center, New York, Kennedy Center, Washington DC and in Boston, Los Angeles, Phildelphia, St Louis and San Francisco; Repertoire includes quartets by Haydn, Mozart, Beethoven, Schubert, Dvorak, Brahms, Borodin, Bartók, Debussy and Shostakovich. Honours: (With Lark Quartet): Gold Medals at the 1990 Naumberg and 1991 Shostakovich Competitions; Prizewinner, 1991 London International String Quartet, 1991 Melbourne Chamber Music, 1990 Premio Paulio Borciani (Reggio Emilia) and 1990 Karl Klinger (Munich) Competitions. Current Management: Sonata, Glasgow Scotland. Address: c/o The Lark Quartet, 11 Northpark Street, Glasgow G20 7AA, Scotland.

MAYNOR Kevin (Elliott), b. 24 July 1954, Mt Vernon, New York, USA. Classical Singer. Education: Diploma, Manhattan School of Music, 1970-72; BME, Bradley University, 1972-76; MM, Northwestern University, 1976-77; MV, Moscow Conservatory, 1979-80; Indiana University, 1980-83; DM, 1988. Debut: Carnegie Hall, 1983; Avery Fisher Hall, Fidelio, 1985; New York City Opera, Akhnaten, 1985. Career: Chicago Lyric Opera; Santa Fe Opera; Virginia Opera; Nashville Opera; Long Beach Opera; Chicago Opera Theater; Mobile Opera; Apprenticeship, 1st from the West, Bolshoi Opera, 1979-80. Honours; Richard D Tucker Grant; Fulbright Award, 1979; George London Career Grant, 1986; William Sullivan Award, 1983; NATS Winner, 1984; 1st International Singing Competition, South Africa, 1984; National Arts Club Award, 1984. Membership: NAACP. Current Management: Herbert Barrett Management. Address: 201 Egmont Avenue, Mt Vernon, NY 10552, USA.

MAZURA Franz, b. 22 Apr 1924, Salzburg, Austria. Singer (Bass-Baritone). Education: Studied with Fred Husler in Detmold. Debut: Kassel 1955. Career: Sang at Mainz and Brunswick until 1964; Mannheim 1964-89; Salzburg 1960, in La Finta Semplice; Pizarro in Fidelio, 1970; Member of Deutsche Oper Berlin 1963; Paris Opera from 1973, as Wagner's Wotan, Alberich and Gurnemanz; Sang Dr Schön in the 1979 premiere of the 3-act version of Berg's Lulu; Bayreuth Festival from 1971, as Biterolf, Alberich, Gunther, Gurnemanz, Klingsor and the Wanderer in the 1988 Ring Cycle directed by Harry Kupfer; Hamburg Opera from 1973; Israel Festival, Caeserea, as Moses in Schoenberg's Moses und Aron; Guest appearances in Vienna, Buenos Aires, San Francisco, Nice and Strasbourg; Metropolitan Opera debut 1980, as Dr Schön, returned to New York as Klingsor, Alberich, Gurnemanz, Creon in Oedipus Rex, Pizarro, Doctor in Wozzeck, Frank in Die Fledermaus, Rangoni in Boris Godunov and the

Messenger in Die Frau ohne Schatten, 1989; Bayreuth Festival, 1988-89 as Klingsor and the Wanderer; Season 1991-92 as Voland (the Devil), in Höller's Meister und Margarita at Cologne and Klingsor at the Met and the Bayreuth Festival; Narrated Henze's Raft of the Medusa, Festival Hall, London, 1997. Recordings include: Dr Schön, Jack the Ripper in Lulu (Grammy Award 1980) (Deutsche Grammophon); Gunther in Götterdämmerung (Philips); Schoenberg's Moses (Philips). Address: c/o Ingpen & Williams Ltd, 26 Wadham Road, London SW15 2LR, England.

MAZURKEVICH Yuri (Nicholas), b. 6 May 1941, Lvov, USSR. Professor of Violin; Concert Violinist. m. Dana Mazurkevich, 4 July 1963, 1 daughter. Education: School of Gifted Children, Lvov, 1948-60; Moscow State Conservatoire, with D Oistrakh, 1960-65, Postgraduate course, Artist Diploma; Masters degree in Performance, 1965-67. Career: Concert Violinist appeared all over the world; Recorded for Radio Moscow, France, BBC, ABC (Australia), CBC (Canada), Sender Freies (West Berlin), WGBH (Boston) and many others; Assistant Professor, Violin, Kiev State Conservatory, 1967-73; Associate Professor, Violin, University of Western Ontario, 1975-85; Professor of Violin, Chairman of String Department, 1985-, Boston University; Member of Quartet Canada, 1980-. Recordings: Works by Beethoven, Paganini, Tartini, Handel, Spohr, Leclair, Prokofiev, Sarasate, Honegger, Telemann and others in Moscow, Toronto and Montreal, Canada. Honours: Prize Winner of 3 International Violin Competitions, Helsinki 1962, Munich 1966 and Montreal 1969. Memberships: Music Council of Canada. Hobbies: Sport; All kinds of outings. Address: 56 Mason Terrace, Brookline, MA 02146, USA.

MAZZARIA Lucia, b. 1964, Gorizia, Poland. Singer (Soprano). Education: Studied in Trieste and Rome. Debut: Venice 1987, as Mimi. Career: Hamburg Opera 1987, as Mimi, Liu and Micaela; La Scala Milan debut 1988, as Lauretta in Gianni Schicchi, returning as Liu, Euridice and Violetta; Cologne Opera 1991, as Amelia Boccanegra; Further appearances at Monte Carlo, Covent Garden (London), Houston and Vienna; Venice 1990, as Mimi in Leoncavallo's Bohème; Further tours of Russia, Japan and Korea; Sang Desdemona at the 1996 Holland Festival. Recordings include: Leoncavallo's Bohème (Nuova Era). Address: c/o Oper der Stadt Köln, Offenbachplatz, Pf 180241, W-5000 Cologne 1, Germany.

MAZZOLA Denia, b. 1956, Bergamo, Italy. Singer (Soprano). Education: Studied with Corinna Malatrasi. Career: Sang Amina in La Sonnambula at Brescia, then Lucia di Lammermoor, and Adina at Florence and Milan; Landestheatre Salzburg 1984, as Gilda, St Gallen 1985 as Violetta; Sang at the Zurich Opera 1985-87, notably as Elvira in I Puritani; Appearances as Lucia at Naples, 1988-89, New York City Opera; La Scala Milan, 1987, Sole in Fetonte by Jommelli; Further engagements at Houston, Alice Ford, San Francisco, in Maria Stuarda, Bergamo, Amelia in Elisabetta al Castello di Kenilworth by Donizetti, 1989, Reggio Emilia, Violetta, Barcelona, Elvira, 1990 and the 1990 Montpellier Festival, Palmide in a concert performance of Meyerbeer's Il Crociato in Egitto; Sang Mimi at the 1996 Torre del Lago Festival. Recordings include: Lucia di Lammermoor, with forces of the San Carlo, Naples (Nuova Era). Address: Teatro San Carlo, Via San Carlo 98F, I-80132 Naples, Italy.

MAZZOLA Rudolf, b. 1941, Basle, Switzerland. Singer (Bass). Education: Studied in Basle and Zurich. Debut: Commendatore in Don Giovanni at St Gallen. Career: Sang at St Gallen until 1971, Basle, 1971-75; Engaged at the Vienna Volksoper from 1975, debut in Wolpert's version of Molière's Le Malade Imaginaire; Sang Osmin in Die Entführung at the Vienna Staatsoper, 1977, returning as Sarastro, Gremin, Pimen, Padre Guardiano and the Grand Inquisitor; Bregenz Festival 1980 and 1984, as Osmin and the Sacristan in Tosca; Salzburg Festival 1981 in the premiere of Cerha's Baal, Paris Opera 1983, as Truffaldino in Ariadne auf Naxos; Sang the Doctor in Wozzeck at Barcelona 1984, Rossini's Basilio at Liège 1988; Toronto, Don Alfonso in Così fan tutte, 1992; Nice, La Roche, Capriccio, 1993; Created roles in Einem's Tulifant and Krenek's Kehraus um St Stephan, Ronach Theater Vienna, 1990, and sang Mozart's Bartolo at the Theater an der Wien, 1991; Guest appearances at Frankfurt, Hamburg, Munich, Budapest, Turin and Zurich; Frequent concert and oratorio appearances. Address: c/o Staatsoper Opernring 2, A-1010 Vienna, Austria.

MCALISTER Barbara, b. 1944, Oklahoma, USA. Singer (Mezzo-soprano). Education: Studied at Oklahoma University and at Los Angeles. Career: Sang at Koblenz Opera from 1976, in The Medium, as Stravinsky's Mother Goose and Verdi's Ulrica; Sang at Passau 1980-81, Flensburg 1981-83 and Bremerhaven 1983-87; Roles have included Preziosilla, Carmen, Herodias, and Orlofsky; Guest at Monte Carlo 1987, as Meg Page; Concert repertoire includes Messiah, Beethoven's Ninth, the Kindertotenlieder and the Alto Rhapsody. Address: c/o Stadttheater Bremerhaven, Theodor-Heuss-Platz, Pf 120541 W-2850 Bremerhaven, Germany.

MCALPINE William, b. 3 Dec 1922, Stenhaosemuir, Scotland. Singer (Tenor). Debut: First Jew in Salome at Covent Garden, 1951. Career: Sang at Covent Garden as Jacquino, Andres in the first British staging of Wozzeck, Don Basilio and in the premieres of Britten's Billy Budd and Gloriana, 1951, 1953; Glyndebourne Festival, 1956-69, as Idamantes, the Italian Singer and Bacchus; Sadler's Wells English National Opera, 1956-74, as Don Ottavio, Rinuccio, Tamino, Alfredo, Belmonte, Boris in Katya Kabanova, Pinkerton, Cavaradossi, Erik and Hoffmann; Appearances with Scottish Opera, 1965-74, as Cassio, Faust and Bob Boles in Peter Grimes; Overseas engagements at Vancouver, Paris, Florence, Hamburg, Berlin and Aix; Sang at Covent Garden, 1960-75, as Grigory (Boris), Alfredo and Hoffmann. Recordings include: Handel's Messiah. Address: c/o English National Opera, St Martin's Lane, London WC2, England.

MCCABE John, b. 21 Apr 1939, Huyton, Lancashire, England. Classical Musician. Education: Manchester University; Royal Manchester College of Music; Hochschule für Musik, Munich, Germany; BMus, FRMCM, FLCM, FRCM, Hon RAM, FRNCM, FTCL. Career includes: Piano recitals, wide repertoire but specialising in contemporary music and Haydn; English premiere, Corigliano's Piano Concerto; Danish premiere, Delius Piano Concerto; Director, London College of Music, 1983-90. Compositions: Operas, ballets, symphonies, concertos, choral and keyboard works, TV and film music; Works include, Chagall Windows (orchestra); Notturni ed Alba (soprano & orchestra); Cloudcatcher Fells (brass band); Concerto for Orchestra, US premiere, 1984; Rainforest 1, 1984; Fire at Durilgai (orchestra), premiered BBC Philharmonic Orchestra, Manchester, later performances Prague, London Promenade Concerts, 1989; Flute Concerto, 1990; Red Leaves for small orchestra, 1991; Tenebrae for piano, 1993; Edward II, full-length ballet, Stuttgart, 1995, UK premiere, Birmingham Royal Ballet, 1997. Recordings: Wide range from Scarlatti, Clementi, Bax, Walton, Hindemith, Howells and Grieg to contemporary British, American, Australian composers, including own piano music and complete Haydn piano music (12 CD's). Honours include: Commander, Order of British Empire, 1985. Memberships: Association of Professional Composers. Hobbies: Books; Films, especially Westerns; Cricket; Snooker; Bonfires. Address: c/o Novello & Company, 8/9 Frith Street, London W1V 5TZ, England.

MCCALDIN Denis (James), b. 28 May 1933, Nottingham, England. Conductor. m. Margaret Anne Smith, 1 s, 1 d. Education: BSc, PhD, Nottingham University; BMus, Birmingham University. Career: Professor and Director of Music, Lancaster University; Guest appearances as Conductor, Royal Liverpool Philharmonic Orchestra, London Mozart Players, Royal Philharmonic Orchestra, Hallé Orchestra, Haydn Orchestra and others, 1970-; BBC Radio programmes including series on virtuoso chamber orchestras. Recordings: Haydn and Schubert Masses; Haydn Society Chorus and Orchestra. Publications: Stravinsky, 1972; Mahler, 1981; Haydn Mass in F Major, 1993; Editor, Berlioz Te Deum; Editor, Haydn Little Organ Mass, 1988; Haydn Te Deum 1800, 1992; Haydn Mass in F, 1993; Haydn Nelson Mass, 1996. Contributions include: Beethoven Companion; Music Review; Music Times; Music and Letters; Music in Education; Times Higher Education Supplement; Soundings. Memberships: Board of Directors, North West Arts Board, Manchester, 1991; Granada Foundation, Manchester, 1993; Lansdowne Club. Hobbies: Good Food; Music. Address: Department of Music, University of Lancaster, Bailrigg, Lancaster, LA1 4YW, England.

MCCANN Norman, b. 24 Apr 1920, London, England. Concert Agent. Education: Royal Academy of Music, London. Career: Appeared in opera, concerts, musical shows, Shakespeare, and on radio and television; Administrative and Artistic Director, British Opera Company; Director of Productions, Hintlesham Festival of the Arts; Artistic Adviser, Battle Festival; Executive Director, Children's Opera Group; Concerts Organiser, International Eisteddfod; Concert Manager, London Bach Society and Goldsmiths' Choral Union; Chairman, Minerva Ballet Trust; Concerts Manager and Artistic Adviser, South and North Wales Association of Choirs; President, British Association of Concert Agents; Manager and Business Adviser to distinguished artists including Kurt Masur, Kurt Sanderling, Gunther Herbig, Peter Schreier; Executive Member, Visiting Orchestras Consultative Association; Mounted West Side Story, Festival of Szeged, Hungary; Curator of International Music Museum; Artistic Adviser, Dyfel Management. Honours: Kyril and Methodius, Bulgarian Government; ARAM, Royal Academy of Music; Fellow, Royal Society of Arts; Fellow, Institute of Directors. Memberships: British Institute of Management; President, English Singers and Speakers Association; President and Chairman, Lewisham Chamber of Commerce. Address: c/o International Artists Limited, The Coach House, 56 Lawrie Park Gardens, London SE26 6XJ, England.

MCCARTHY Fionnuala, b. 1963, Ireland. Singer (Soprano). Education: Studied in Johannesburg and at Detmold, Germany. Debut: Kaiserslautern 1987, as Mimi. Career: Sang at the Mannheim Opera from 1988, debut as Wagner's Woglinde with further appearances as Lauretta, Euridice, Echo, Marzelline, Pamina, Zerlina and Mozart's Countess; Sang Marguerite at Giessen (1990) and appeared with the Deutsche Oper am Rhein 1990-92; Sang Donna Elvira with Pimlico Opera at Tullnally, Ireland, 1996; Ighino in Pfitzner's Palestrina at the Deutsche Oper, Berlin, 1996. Address: c/o Deutsche Oper am Rhein, Richard-Wagner-Strasse 10, 10585 Berlin, Germany.

MCCARTHY John, b. 1930, England. Choral Director; Director of Music. Career: Musical Director of the Ambrosian Singers and Ambrosian Opera Chorus and many other famous Choral Groups; Director of Music, Carmelite Priory; Former Chorus Master, Royal Opera House, Covent Garden; Professor, Royal College of Music; Choral Director to nearly all the greatest conductors in the world; Director of many hundreds of very successful recordings and broadcasts. On television has been Choral Director for many operas and music programmes; In London Theatre has been involved in a number of musicals and revivals and several Royal Command Performances; Shows include: Mame; The Great Waltz; Gone With The Wind, Drury Lane; Showboat; The King and I; Choral Director for hundreds of films including the Oscar winning Oliver, Tom Jones, Goodbye My Chips, Scrooge, Cromwell, Fiddler on the Roof, The Great Waltz, Man of la Mancia, Close Encounters; Chariots of Fire; Amadeus. Recordings include: Over 150 recordings of operas in French, German, Italian, Russian and English; Conductor of 3 award winning LP's for European Grand Prix du Disques; Fauré Requiem; Lucia di Lammermoor; Beethoven's 9th Symphony; Vivaldi's Gloria. Publications include: Editor, series of Tudor and Renaissance Music. Honours include: OBE, 1990; 5 Nominations for USA Grammy award for Choral Direction; National Academy of Performing Arts Awards. Address: c/o Ambrosian Singers, 4 Reynolds Road, Beaconsfield, Buckinghamshsire HP9 2NJ, England.

MCCARTNEY (James) Paul (Sir), b. 28 June 1942, Liverpool, England. Songwriter; Performer. m. Linda Eastman, 1969, 1 son, 3 daughters. Education: Self-taught in playing guitar, piano, organ, trumpet. Career: Wrote first fong, 1956 and numerous songs with John Lennon, joined pop group The Quarrymen, 1956; Appeared under various titles until formation of the Beatles, 1960; Appeared with The Beatles in the following activities, performances in Hamburg, The Cavern, Liverpool; Worldwide Tours, 1963-66; Attended Transcendental Meditation Course, Maharishi's Academy, India, 1968; Founded Apple Limited, after the collapse of the Apple Corp Limited, left the Beatles, 1970 and formed MPL Group of Companies; First solo album, 1970; Formed own group, Wings, 1971-, touring Britain and Europe, UK, Australia and the USA; Released film, album, Give My Regards to Broad Street, 1984; Tour of Scandinavia, 1989. Recordings include: With The Beatles: Please Please Me, 1963; A Hard Days Night, 1964; Beatles for Sale, 1965; Help!, 1965; Rubber Soul, 1966; Revolver, 1966; Sgt Pepper's Lonely Hearts Club Band, 1967; Magical Mystery Tour, 1967; The Beatles, 1968; Yellow Submarine, 1969; Abbey Road, 1969; Let It Be, 1970. Wings: McCartney, 1970; Ram, 1971; Wild Life, 1971; Red Rose Speedway, 1973; Band On The Run, 1973; Venus and Mars, 1975; Wings at the Speed of Sound, 1976; Wings Over America, 1976; London Town, 1978; Wings Greatest, 1978. Solo: Back To The Egg, 1979; McCartney II, 1980; Tug of War, 1982; Pipes of Peace, 1983; Give My Regards to Broad Street, 1984; Press To Play, 1986; All the Best!, 1987; CHOBA B CCCP, 1988; Flowers in the Dirt, 1989; Tripping the Live Fantastic, 1990; Unplugged: The Official Bootleg, 1991; Paul McCartney's Liverpool Oratorio, 1991, written by Carl Davis; Flaming Pie, 1997; Standing Stone, symphonic work, 1997. Honours include: MBE, 1965; Numerous Grammy Awards; Ivor Novello Awards include: for International Achievement, 1980, for International Hit of the Year (Ebony and Ivory), 1982, for Outstanding Contribution to Music, 1989; Guiness Book of Records; Triple Superlative Award; Freeman of the City of Liverpool, 1984; KBE, 1997. Address: c/o MPL Communications Ltd, 1 Soho Square, W1V 6BQ, England.

MCCARTY Patricia, b. 16 July 1954, Wichita, Kansas, USA. Viola Soloist; Recitalist; Chamber Musician. m. Ronald Wilkison, 29 Aug 1982. Education: BMus, University of Michigan, 1974; MMus, University of Michigan, 1976. Debut: New York, 1978; Wigmore Hall, London, England, 1986; Beethovenhalle, Bonn, 1991; Japan Tour, 1993. Career: Viola Soloist, Recitalist and Chamber Musician in performances throughout the United States, Europe and Japan; Appearances include Detroit, Houston, Brooklyn, Boston Pops, Beethovenhalle, Suisse Romande, Kyoto and Shinsei Nihon Tokyo orchestras; Recitals in New York, San Francisco, Detroit, Boston and London; Chamber Music performances at Marlboro, Aspen, Tanglewood, Hokkaido and Sarasota festivals; Faculty the Boston Conservatory. Recordings: Viola Works of Rebecca Clarke; Songs of Charles Martin Loeffler; Brahms Viola Quintets; Dvorak String Sextet; Keith Jarrett

Concerto. Current Management: Ashmont Music. Address: c/o Anne Thomas, 25 Carruth Street, Boston, MA 02124, USA.

MCCAULEY Barry, b. 2 Jue 1950, Altoon, Pennsylvania, USA. Singer (Tenor). Education: Studied at Eastern Kentucky University and Arizona State University. Debut: San Francisco Spring Opera 1977, as Don José. Career: San Francisco Opera 1977, as Faust; Further appearances in Houston and San Diego; European debut Frankfurt 1979, as Edgardo in Lucia di Lammermoor; New York City Opera from 1980; Aix-en-Provence Festival, 1980 as Don Ottavio; Paris Opera from 1982, Teatro Comunale Florence, 1983 (debut as Wilhelm Meister in Mignon); Théâtre de la Monnaie Brussels, 1984 and 1986, as Idamante and Belfiore in La Finta Giardiniera; Glyndebourne Festival, 1985-88, as Don José and Boris in Katya Kabanova; Metropolitan Opera debut 1985, as Jacquino; Vienna Staatsoper, 1984, Don Ottavio; Has sung Offenbach's Hoffmann at the Spoleto Festival, 1989 and Seattle and Geneva, 1990; Other roles include Alfredo, Seattle, 1988, Maurizio in Adriana Lecouvreur, Trieste, 1989, Belmonte, Gluck's Admete, Nemorino, Robert Dudley in Maria Stuarda, the Duke of Mantua, Fenton, Pinkerton, Gerald in Lakmé, Nadir, Lensky and Froh in Das Rheingold; Debut as Parsifal at Amsterdam, 1991. Address: Seattle Opera Association, PO Box 9248, Seattle, WA 98109, USA.

MCCAULEY John J, b. 16 Nov 1937, Des Moines, Iowa, USA. Pianist. Conductor; Teacher. Education: MS MusEd Honours, 1960, 1961, University of Illinois at Urbana; Conducting studies, Tanglewood and Aspen, 1960-64; MS, Piano, Juilliard School of Music, 1964; Diplomas in Piano, Chamber Music, Conducting Mozarteum Summer Academy, Salzburg, Austria, 1968-74. Debut: Carnegie Recital Hall, New York City, 1975. Career: Numerous concerts also chamber music US Coast East and Midwest also in Europe; Frequent radio and television appearances; Recitals, of piano solos and chamber music include, Lincoln Center, 1967-89, Juilliard School of Music Recital Hall, Wave Hill Concert Series; Bronx Symphony Orchestra as concerto soloist, Lincoln Center Mozart Festival, Research Assistant, 1988; Radio Station WQXR, The Listening Room with Robert Sherman. Compositions: Columbia Artists Management Recital Accompanist, Community Concerts throughout USA 1983-84, 1984-85. Bronx Symphony Orchestra, Lehman Center for the Performing Arts, Guest Conductor, 1985; Des Moines Metro Opera, Des Moines, IA, Assistant Conductor, Musical Coach, 1984-89, Arizona Opera, Tuscon and Phoenix, AZ, Assistant Conductor Brooklyn Philharmonic, Brooklyn Academy of Music, New York, NY, Associate Conductor, 1985; Eastern Opera Theater, New York, NY, Conductor of East Coast Tours, 1982-84; Bel Canto Opera, New York, NY, Conductor, 1979-1982.

MCCAWLEY Leon (Francis), b. 12 July 1973, Cheshire, England. Concert Pianist. m. Anna Paik, 3 June 1996. Education: Chetham's School of Music, Manchester; Graduated, Curtis Institute, Philadelphia, 1995; Studied with Heather Slade-Lipkin, Eleanor Sokoloff and Nina Milkina. Career: Performances from 1993 with the City of Birmingham and Vienna Symphonies, BBC Philharmonic Orchestra, Philharmonia, London Philharmonic and Royal Philharmonic Orchestras, tours in 1995 to Japan and New Zealand; Recitals at the Wigmore Hall, Queen Elizabeth Hall and elsewhere, with festival engagements at Helsinki, Bath, Harrogate and Spoleto; London Proms debut 1995, with Mozart's Concerto K449; Season 1997 with the Auckland Philharmonia, Minnesota Orchestra, Dallas Symphony and BBC Orchestra of Wales. Recordings include: Barber, Music for Solo Piano. Honours: BBC Young Musician Piano Section, 1990; LPO Pioneer Young Soloist, 1990; 1st Prize, Beethoven International Piano Competition, Vienna, 1993; 2nd Prize, Leeds International Piano Competition, 1993. Current Management: Harold Holt Ltd. Address: 31 Sinclair Road, London W14 0NS, England.

MCCOLL William (Duncan), b. 18 May 1933, Port Huron, Michigan, USA. Clarinettist; Bassett Hornist. m. Sue McColl, 1 son. Education: 2 years at Oberlin; 1 year at Manhattan School of Music; Graduate with Reifezeugnis, State Academy of Music and Representational Arts, Vienna. Career: Solo Clarinettist with US Seventh Army Symphony Orchestra, 1957-58 and Philharmonia Hungarica, Vienna, 1959; Clarinettist, Festival Casals; Solo Clarinettist with Puerto Rico Symphony Orchestra and Clarinet Instructor for Puerto Rico Conservatoire, 1960-68; Clarinettist, Soni Ventorum Wind Quartet, 1963-; Professor, University of Washington, 1968-; Bass Clarinettist, Orquestra Filarmonica de las Americas, Mexico City, summers 1976-78. Recordings: Villa-Lobos, Trio for Bassoon, Clarinet, Oboe and quarter ditto with flute; Reicha Quintet in G major; Haydn Clock Organ pieces, arranged for wind quintet; Beethoven, Clock Organ pieces, arranged for wind quintet; Reicha Quintet in E minor; Danzi Quintet in F major; Poulenc Duo for Clarinet and Basson; Villa-Lobos Trio for Clarinet, Bassoon and Piano; Numerous other compositions and arrangements. Address: c/o School of Music, University of Washington, Seattle, WA 98195, USA.

MCCORMACK Elizabeth, b. 1964, Fife, Scotland. Singer (Mezzo-soprano). m. Douglas Vipond, 21 July 1990. Education:

BA, Glasgow University; Royal Scottish Academy with Duncan Robertson and at London Opera Studio. Career: Edinburgh Festival debut 1986 with Alan Ramsay's The Gentle Shepherd; Concert performances include Handel's Messiah, Samson and Coronation Anthem; Mozart Requiem, Beethoven Missa Solemnis and CPE Bach Magnificat; Stravinsky's Pulcinella with the English Chamber Orchestra at the Barbican; Sang De Nebra's Requiem and Handel's Dixit Dominus with La Chappelle Royale and Philippe Herreweghe 1989; Haydn's Theresian Mass with the Orchestra of the Age of Enlightenment at the Elizabeth Hall; Has also sung in Elgar's The MusicMakers, Vivaldi's Gloria and the Duruflé Requiem; English National Opera debut, 1989 in The Mikado; Scottish Opera 1990 in the premiere of Judith Weir's The Vanishing Bridegroom; Season 1994-95 as Cenerentola for Castleward Opera and Iolanthe for Scottish Opera; Season 1997 at the Opéra Bastille, Paris, in Parsifal and as Mozart's Annius. Honours: Scottish Opera John Noble Bursary, 1987; Decca-Kathleen Ferrier Prize, 1987; Isobel Baillie Performance Award, 1987; Scottish Opera John Noble Award, 1987; Royal Overseas League, 1987; English Speaking Union, 1988; Caird and Munster Scholarships, 1987-89. Current Management: Harold Holt Ltd. Address: 31 Sinclair Road, London W14 0NS, England.

MCCRAY James, b. 21 Feb 1939, Warren, Ohio, USA. Singer (Tenor). Education: Studied with Raymond Buckingham. Debut: Stratford Festival, Canada in Weill's Aufstieg und Fall der Stadt Mahagonny. Career: Appearances in Seattle, Kansas City, Miami, San Francisco and the New York City Opera; Guest with Tel-Aviv Opera, Israel; Roles include Verdi's Ismaele, Radames and Manrico, Wagner's Siegmund and Siegfried, Don José, Samson, Ponchielli's Enzo and Puccini's Calaf, Dick Johnson and Cavaradossi; Sang Florestan at Montreal, 1999; Young Siegfried in the first modern Polish production of the Ring, Warsaw, 1989; Wuppertal 1989, as Tristan. Address: c/o Wuppertaler Bühnen, Spinnstrasse 4, D-5600 Wuppertal, Germany.

MCCREADY Ivan, b. 1963, England. Cellist. Education: Studied at the Royal Academy of Music with Derek Simpson. Career: Member of the Borante Piano Trio from 1982; Concerts at the Wigmore Hall and in Dublin and Paris; Beethoven's Triple Concerto at the Festival Wien Klassik, 1989; Season 1990 at the Perth and Bath Festivals and tour of Scandinavia, Russia and the Baltic States; Cellist of the Duke String Quartet from 1985; Performances in the Wigmore Hall, Purcell Room, Conway Hall and throughout England; Tours of Germany, Italy, Austria and the Baltic States; South Bank series 1991, with Mozart's early quartets; Soundtracks for Ingmar Bergman documentary The Magic Lantern, Channel 4 1988; Features for French television 1990-91, playing Mozart, Mendelssohn, Britten and Tippett; Brhams Clarinet Quintet for Dutch Radio with Janet Hilton; Live Music Now series with concerts for disadvantaged people; The Duke Quartet Invites... at the Derngate, Northampton 1991, with Duncan Prescott and Rohan O'Hara; Resident quartet of the Rydale Festival 1991; Residency at Trinity College, Oxford, tours to Scotland and Northern Ireland and concert at the Elizabeth Hall 1991. Recordings include: Quartets by Tippett, Shostakovich and Britten (Third) for Factory Classics. Honours include: Awards include the Harold Craxton at the RAM and the Leche Scholarship. Address: Anglo-Swiss Management, Suite 35-37, 320 Regent Street, London W1R 5AD, England.

MCCREESH Paul D, b. 24 May 1960, London, England. Conductor; Baroque Cellist. m. Susan Jones, 23 Jul 1983. Education: University of Manchester. Career: Director, Gabrieli Consort and Players, founded 1982; Frequent performances and recordings of Baroque and Renaissance in UK and abroad; Led the first modern performance of Maurice Greene's Jephtha, 1997. Recordings include: Video, music for San Rocco. Honour: Gramophone Award, 1990 and 1993; ABC Record of the Year, 1991; Dutch Edison Award, 1991 and 1995; Grammy nomination, USA, 1994; Diapason D'Or, France, 1994; Echo Prize, Germany, 1995. Hobbies: Walking; Travel. Current Management: Gasweli Management. Address: Forester's Hall, 25-27 Weston Street, London SE19 3RY, England.

MCCULLOCH Jenifer (Susan), b. 3 Aug 1957, London, England. Opera Singer (Lyrico-Spinto Soprano); Voice Teacher. Education: Royal College of Music, 1975-82; ARCM honours, 1979; National Opera Studio, 1985-86. Debut: As Countess Almaviva in Mozart's Marriage of Figaro with English National Opera, 1986. Career: Concerts at the major London venues and at festivals in Edinburgh, Cambridge, Henley and Manchester; Appeared in oratorio all over UK and Europe; Has sung Brahms's Requiem with David Willcocks and Mendelssohn's Infelice with Solti; Recorded Mozart's Exultate Jubilate and Strauss's Four Last Songs for BBC; American debut in the Four Last Songs, with San Jose Symphony Orchestra; Verdi's Requiem at the Three Choirs Festival and Usher Hall, Edinburgh; Beethoven's Ninth under Laszlo Heltay at 1992 Kenwood Summer Season opening; Appearances in opera include Donna Anna in Don Giovanni for English National Opera; Glyndebourne Festival debut as Vitellia in La Clemenza di Tito, followed by Musetta in La Bohème and Donna Anna for the Touring Opera; Tosca in Dublin, Mozart's

Marcellina in Hong Kong, Netherlands (Opera Zuid and Amsterdam), Lisbon, Paris, Ludwigsburg and London; Various TV broadcasts including 2 episodes of Inspector Morse; Professor of Singing, Trinity College of Music, London. Recordings: Marriage of Figaro; A Victorian Christmas; Gilbert and Sullivan. Hobbies: Calligraphy; Cooking; Entertaining; Reading. Current Management: Robert Gilder & Co. Address: Flat One, 80 Sunnyhill Road, Streatham, London SW16 2UL, England.

MCCULLY James K, b. 19 October 1958, Hot Springs, Arkansas, USA. Opera and Music Theater Administrator; Coach; Director. Education: Private Study with Wagnerian Soprano Marjorie Lawrence, 1974-78; BA, Music, BA, Radio, TV and Film, University of Arkansas, 1985; General Managers Training Program, American Symphony Orchestra League, Avery Fisher Hall, Lincoln Center for the Performing Arts, New York City, 1987; Graduate Certificate, Arts Administration, American University, Washington, DC, 1994. Career includes: Performing Artist, Hot Springs National Park Foundation for the Performing Arts, 1977-79; Production Coordinator, Central City Opera House Association, Denver, Colorado, 1984; Opera Music Theater Fellow, National Endowment for the Arts, Washington, DC, 1985; Executive Director, National Center for the Arts, Washington, DC, 1986-88; Music Theater Instructor, National Conservatory of Dramatic Arts, Washington, DC, 1988-90; Musical Director, Troika Organization, Rockville, Maryland, 1990-92; Vocal Coach, Olney Theatre Center for the Performing Arts, Maryland, 1993; On-Site Evaluator, National Endowment for the Arts, Washington, DC, Pittsburgh Opera, Virginia Opera, Opera Carolina, San Francisco Mime Company, Tennessee Repertory Theatre, 1993-94; General Director, Opera Music Theater International, Arlington, Virginia, 1991-. Publications: A Guide to Operatic Excellence, 1987; The Scientific Development of Voice, 1990. Honours include: International Bravo Award, Opera Music Theater Institute, Washington, DC, 1995; Award of Excellence, Musical Support, US Department of Defense, Washington, DC, 1995; Trustee, National Opera Associations Vocal Competition, Boston, 1996; Chairman, National Opera Association, Washington DC, 1998; International Forums on: Composing, Conducting, Master Class series; Singer Training; Women in Opera and Music Theatre; African Americans in Opera; Canadian Embassy Reception, hosted by Raymond Chretien; Marjorie Lawrence International Vocal Competition, 1998; Musical America official sponsor. Honours include: Arts and Humanities Award Grant, Music Criticism, 1985; Award of Excellence, International Society of Performing Arts Administrators Congress, London, 1987; Helen Hayes Award nomination, Outstanding Resident Musical, 1992. Memberships: Opera America; International Society of Performing Arts Administrators; National Opera Association; Cultural Alliance of Greater Washington; Phi Mu Alpha. Address: Opera Music Theater International, 1818 North Ode Street, Arlington, Virginia, USA.

MCDANIEL Barry, b. 18 Oct 1930, Lyndon, Kansas, USA. Singer (Baritone). Education: Juilliard School, New York; Stuttgart Musikhochschule with Alfred Paulus and Hermann Reutter. Debut: Sang in recital at Stuttgart in 1953. Career: Mainz Opera, 1954-55; Stuttgart Opera, 1957-59; Karlsruhe, 1960-62; Deutsche Oper Berlin from 1962, notably in Baroque and contemporary works, also Mozart and Wagner; Sang in the premieres of Henze's Der junge Lord, 1965 and Reimann's Melusine, 1971; Salzburg Festival, 1968; Metropolitan Opera, 1972 as Debussy's Pelléas; Other roles include the Barber in Die schweigsame Frau and Olivier in Capriccio; Guest appearances in Schubert Lieder and as Christus in the St Matthew Passion. Recordings: Bach, Christmas Oratorio; Ariadne auf Naxos, Dido and Aeneas, La Finta Giardiniera and Der junge Lord, Deutsche Grammophon; Orff's Trionfi, BASF. Address: c/o Deutsche Oper Berlin, Richard Wagnerstrasse 10, D-1000 Berlin, Germany.

MCDERMOTT Vincent, b. 5 Sep 1933, Atlantic City, NJ, USA. Composer; Professor. Education: Composition studies with C Vauclain, D Milhaud, G Rochberg and K Stockhausen; BFA, 1959, PhD, 1966, University of Pennsylvania; MA, University of California, Berkeley, 1961. Career: Performances of major works in Zagreb, London, Stockholm, Jakarta, Vancouver, Chicago, Cincinnati, Cleveland, Washington, Seattle, San Antonio, Portland, Milwaukee, New York and Dallas. Compositions include: He Who Ascends by Ecstasy, piano tape, 1972; Pictures at an Exhibition, tape slides, 1974; Siftings upon Siftings for Orchestra, 1976; A Perpetual Dream, mono-opera, 1978; Slayer of Time for Chorus and Instruments, 1977; Solonese Concerto for Piano Chamber Ensemble, 1979; Laudamus for Chorus, 1980; The King of Bali, opera, 1990; Fugitive Moons for String Quartet, 1991; Mata Hari, opera, 1993; Titus Magnificus for Orchestra, 1994. Recordings: The Bells of Tajilor; The Dark Laments of Ariadne and of Attis; Fiddles, Queens and Laddies; Sweet Breathed Minstrel. Contributions to: A Conceptual Musical Space in Journal of Aesthetics and Art Criticism, 1968. Honours: National Endowment for the Arts; 3 Commissions: 1986, Fiddles, Queens and Laddies, 1987, The King of Bali, opera and 1992, The Death of Karna, opera; Master's Fellowship, Oregon Arts Commission, 1989. Memberships: BMI; American Music Center; College Music

Society; Society of Composers. Address: Music Department, Lewis and Clark College, Portland, OR 97219, USA.

MCDONALD Margaret, b. 1964, Grimsby, England. Singer (Mezzo-soprano). Education: Royal Northern College of Music, and in Milan. Career: Early experience with Glyndebourne Festival and Touring Opera; Engagements with Opera North as Carmen, and in Mason's Playing Away, Oberon (1985), Rebecca by Josephs and Gianni Schicchi; Eboli in Don Carlos for Scottish Opera Go Round, Ascanio in Benvenuto Cellini and Bizet's Djamileh for Chelsea Opera Group; Further appearances with English National Opera, English Bach Festival and Buxton Festival; Concerts include the Three Choirs, Quimper, Spitalfields, Saintes and Dublin Contemporary Festivals; Extensive oratorio repertory at concert halls and cathedrals throughout Britain, including works by Henze and Boulez. Recordings include: Isoletta in Bellini's La Straniera, with the Northern Sinfonia; She-Ancient in Tippett's Midsummer Marriage (Nimbus). Honours: Curtis Gold Medal at the RNCM. Address: Musicmakers, Little Easthall, St Paul's Walden, Nr Hitchin, Herts, SG4 8DH, England.

MCDONALL Lois, b. 7 Feb 1939, Larkspur, Alberta, Canada. Singer (Soprano). Education: Studied in Edmonton, Vancouver and Toronto and with Otakar Kraus in London. Debut: Toronto 1969 in Wolf-Ferrari's Il Segreto di Susanna. Career: Sang in Ottawa and Toronto, then Flensburg, Germany; Sadler's Wells/English National Opera from 1970, notably as Handel's Semele and in the title role of Hamilton's Anna Karenina (1981); Other roles include Mozart's Countess, Constanze and Fiordilig, Massenet's Manon and the Marschallin; Sang the Comtesse de Coigny in Andrea Chénier at Toronto, 1988; Currently teaching at University of Toronto; Freelance singing roles include Fedora, Opera in concert, Anna in Anna Karenina as guest of ENO. Recordings include: Freia in The Ring (HMV) and Donizetti's Maria Padilla. Memberships: National British Equity, ACTRA Canadian Society. Address: c/o Canadian Opera Co, 227 Front Street East, Toronto, Ontario, M5A 1EB, Canada.

MCDONNELL Thomas (Anthony), b. 27 Apr 1940, Melbourne, Australia. Singer (Baritone). m. Mary Jennifer Smith. Education: Melba Conservatorium, Melbourne, with Lennox Brewer. Debut: Belcore in L'Elisir d'Amore at Brisbane, 1965. Career: Sadler's Wells/English National Opera from 1967, as Mozart's Figaro, Verdi's Germont, Escamillo and in the first British stage performance of Prokofiev's War and Peace (1972) and Henze's The Bassarids (1974); Sang in War and Peace at the opening of the Sydney Opera House, 1973; Created roles in Crosse's The Story of Vasco, 1974, Henze's We Come to the River and Tippett's The Ice Break (both at Covent Garden); Iain Hamilton's The Royal Hunt of the Sun and Nicola LeFanu's Dawnpath (both 1977); London Collegiate Theatre 1977 in the British premiere of Nielsen's Saul and David; Well known as Mozart's Papageno and Tchaikovsky's Onegin; Sang Mozart's Commendatore with Opera Factory, Elizabeth Hall, 1990 and Silva in Ernani for Chelsea Opera Group; Sang Lictor in The Coronation of Poppea for Opera Factory, 1992. Recordings include: Israel in Egypt; La Fanciulla del West; Tancredi; Donizetti rarities. Honours include: Showcase Australia, 1965; Leverhulme Youth and Music Scholarship to Rome. Hobbies: Shakespeare; Chamber Music; Poetry; Architecture; Jogging; Tennis. Address: c/o Opera Factory, 8a The Leather Market, Weston Street, London SE1 3ER, England.

MCFADDEN Claron, b. 1961, Rochester, New York, USA. Singer (Soprano). Education: Studied at the Eastman School, Rochester. Career: Has sung in concert, opera and oratorio from 1984; Opera debut 1985 in Hasse's L'Eroe Chinese conducted by Ton Koopman; Regular appearances with William Christie in Europe and North and South America, notably as Amour in Rameau's Anacréon at the Opéa Lyrique du Rhin; Netherlands Opera debut 1989, as Zerbinetta in Ariadne auf Naxos; Season 1991 included Mozart's Impresario at the Salzburg Festival and on South Bank, Acis and Galatea with the King's Consort and Rameau's Les Indes Galantes with Les Arts Florissants in Montpellier; Has also worked in concert with the Schoenberg Ensemble and composers Gunther Schuller, Louis Andriessen and Steve Reich; Carmina Burana conducted by Leopold Hager and L'Enfant et les Sortilèges under Sergiu Comissiona; Sang in Purcell's Fairy Queen with Les Arts Florissants at the Barbican Hall, 1992; King Arthur at Covent Garden, 1995; Sang in Bach's B Minor Mass at St John's London, 1997; Lulu at the 1996 Glyndebourne Festival. Recordings: Acis and Galatea and Handel's Ottone with the King's Consort; Haydn's Orfeo with La Stagione Frankfurt; Vocal works by Glenn Gould (Sony Classical); Les Indes Galantes. Honours include: Prize Winner at the 1988 International Competition, s-Hertogenbosch. Address: c/o Glyndebourne Festival Opera, Lewes, Sussex, England.

MCFARLAND Robert, b. 1958, Canada. Singer (Baritone). Season 1987 as Donner in Das Rheingold at the Metropolitan and Amonasro at Miami and Houston; European debut Nice 1988, as Jack Rance (repeated for Opera North at Leeds, 1990); Further guest appearances at Miami (Luna in Trovatore), Lisbon (Iago, 1990), Toronto (Escamillo, 1990) and Monte Carlo (Nottingham in Roberto Devereux); Other roles include the villains in Les Contes d'Hoffmann; Renato at Antwerp, 1992 and Tonio (Miami, 1991). Address: c/o Greater Miami Opera, 1200 Coral Way, Miami, FL 33145, USA.

MCFARLANE Clare, b. 24 July 1963, Lancashire, England. Violinist; Teacher. m. Leland Chen, 12 Aug 1987, 2 sons. Education: Yehudi Menuhin School, 1973-82; Guildhall School of Music and Drama, 1982-87; Teachers: Margaret Norris, John Glickman, Peter Norris, Hans Keller; ARCM, Honours. Career: BBC Young Musician of the Year, String Section Winner, 1980; Performed in all major concert halls in Londoon; Soloist with RPO, Hallé, Northern Sinfonia, London Mozart Players, Orchestra of St John's, Smith Square; Performed in USA, Canada, India, China and Europe; Duo with Leland Chen for 2 Violin and violin/viola works; Performed a cycle of all Beethoven Sonatas in Purcell Room, 1989; Professor of Violin, London College of Music, 1985-89; Violin Teacher, Chetham's School of Music; Chosen for Representation by YCAT; Has given masterclasses and teaches privately. Address: 11 Mayfield Road, Kersal, Salford, Lancashire M7 3WZ, England.

MCGEGAN Nicholas, b. 14 Jan 1950, Sawbridgeworth, Hertfordshire, England. Conductor. Education: BA, Corpus Christi College, Cambridge, 1969-72; MA, Magdalen College, Oxford, 1972-76. Career: Professor of Baroque Flute, 1973-79, Professor of Music History, 1975-79, Director of Early Music, 1976-80, Royal College of Music; Artist-in-Residence, Washington University, St Louis, Missouri, 1979-85; Music Director, Philharmonia Baroque Orchestra, San Francisco, 1985-; Music Director, Ojai Music Festival, Ojai, California, 1988; Baroque Artistic Consultant, Santa Fe Chamber Music Festival, 1990-92; Music Director, Gottingen Handel Festival, Gottingen, Germany, 1991-; Artistic Director and Founder, Arcadian Academy, San Francisco, 1992-; Principal Conductor, Drottningholm Court Theatre, Sweden, 1993-96; Principal Guest Conductor, Scottish Opera, 1993; Appearances as Guest Conductor include San Francisco Symphony, Los Angeles Philharmonic, City of Birmingham Symphony Orchestra, Halle Orchestra, Sydney Symphony, Melbourne Symphony. Recordings: (as a soloist) CPE Bach's Quartets (flute); JC Bach's Sonatas Op1 18 (flute) with Christopher Hogwood); JS Bach's Anna Magdelena Notebook (harpsichord); Music For Two Flutes By The Bach Family with Stephen Preston; Haydn's London Trios (flute), Piano Trios (piano and flute); Vivaldi's Concertos For Two Flutes; (as conductor) JS Bach's Cantatas and around 20 operas and oratorios by Handel, of which Susanna and Ariodante have both won Gramophone Awards, and works by Arne, Corelli, P Humfrey, Matteis, Monteverdi, Mozart, Purcell, Rameau (including 3 operas), A Scarlatti, Telemann, Uccellini, Vivaldi. Publications: Editions, Philidor's Tom Jones, 1978. Contributions to: Articles include Handel, Musical Times, 1994. Honours: 2 Diapson d'Or Awards for recordings with the Arcadian Academy; Handel Prize, Halle Handel Festival, Germany; Drottningholmsteaterns Vanners Hederstecken, honorary medal of the Friends of the Drottningholm Theatre. Memberships: Advisory Boards, Maryland Handel Festival and London's Handel House. Hobbies: Gardening; History. Address: Schwalbe and Partners, 170 East 61 Street #5N, New York, NY 10021, USA.

MCGIBBON Roisin, b. 1960, Northern Ireland. Singer (Soprano). Education: Studied with Margaret Lensky at the Guildhall School of Music and at the National Opera Studio. Career: Represented Northern Ireland in the Cardiff Singer of the World Competition, 1985; Appearances for Radio Telfis Eireann include Lieder by Schumann and Liszt; Wexford Festival 1986, in Humperdinck's Kőnigskinder and Rossini's Tancredi; Has also sung the Composer in Ariadne auf Naxos; Concert engagements in Messiah at Armagh, Britten's War Requiem in Belfast, Savitri by Holst at Aix and Elgar's Apostles in Nottingham. Address: c/o Magenta Music International, 64 Highgate High Street, London N6 5HX, England.

MCGLAUGHLIN William, b. 3 Oct 1943, Philadelphia, Pennsylvania, USA. Conductor; Radio Broadcaster; Trombonist. Education: BM 1967, MM 1969, Temple University; Studied conducting with Wm R Smith, Robert Page, Max Rudolph. Career: Assistant 1st Trombonist, Philadelphia Orchestra, 1967-68; Co-Principal Trombonist, Pittsburgh Symphony, 1969-75; Exxon-Arts Endowment Conductor, 1975-78, Associate Conductor 1978-82, St Paul Chamber Orchestra; Music Director, Eugene, Oregon, Symphony 1981-85, Tucson Symphony 1982-87, Kansas City Symphony 1986-, San Francisco Chamber Orchestra 1986-; Host, Music Director of St Paul Sunday Morning, American Public Radio, 1980-87; Guest Conductor, St Louis, Denver, Houston and Pittsburgh Symphonies, Minnesota Orchestra, Los Angeles and Denver Chamber Orchestras. Honour: Exxon-Arts Endowment Conducting Grant with St Paul Chamber Orchestra, 1975-78. Current Management: American International Artists Inc, 515 East 89th Street, Suite 6B, New York, NY 10128, USA.

MCGREEVY Geraldine, b. England. Singer (Soprano). Education: Studied at the University of Birmingham; Royal Academy of Music; National Opera Studio. Career: Concert repertoire includes: Schoenberg's Pierrot Lunaire; Villa Lobos' Bachianas Brasileiras No 5; Berg's Orchestral Extracts from Wozzeck with Gennadi Rozhdestvensky; Britten's Les Illuminations; Strauss' Vier Letze Lieder; Operatic roles: Donna Anna, for British Youth Opera; First Lady, Mistress Page, Sir John in Love; Casilda, Gondoliers; Fiordiligi with Sir Colin Davis; Galatea by Handel and Laurette in Bizet's Le Docteur Miracle. Recordings: John Blow; Spanish Renaissance; BBC Radio 3 broadcasts, for Young Artists Forum, 1995, and Composer of the Week, 1997; 2 world premieres by Koechlin; Purcell Room debut, 1997; Wigmore Hall debut, 1997. Honours include: Worshipful Company of Musicians medal, 1995; RAM Shinn Fellowship, 1996; Winner, Kathleen Ferrier Award, 1996. Address: c/o Lies Askonas Ltd, 6 Henrietta St, London WC2E 8LA, England.

MCGUIRE Edward, b. 15 Feb 1948, Glasgow, Scotland. Composer. Education: Composition study with James Iliff, Royal Academy of Music, 1966-70; Studied with Ingvar Lidholm at The State Academy of Music, Stockholm, Sweden, 1971; ARCM; ARAM. Career: Radio broadcasts on BBC Radio 3 include: Symphonic Poem, Calgacus, 1976, Symphonic Poem, Source, 1979; Euphoria performed by The Fires of London, 1980, Edinburgh International Festival; Debut at London Proms, 1982; BBC Radio 3 series features trilogy, Rebirth, Interregnum, Liberation, 1984; Wilde Festival commission (String Trio) for performance by The Nash Ensemble, 1986; Premiere of Guitar Concerto, 1988; Peter Pan for Scottish Ballet, 1989. Compositions: A Glasgow Symphony, 1990; The Loving of Etain, 1990 for Paragon Opera; Trombone Concerto, 1991; The Spirit of Flight, ballet, 1991; Cullercoats Tommy, opera, 1993. Recordings: His music has featured on CDs including Paragon Premieres, 1993 and Scotland's Music, 1993. Honours: Hecht Prize, RAM, 1968; National Young Composers Competition, Liverpool University, 1969; Competition for Test Piece for Carl Flesch International Violin Competiton, 1978; Competition for a String Quartet for performance at SPNM 40th Anniversary Gala Concert, Barbican, 1983; Featured composer, Park Lane Group Purcell Room series, 1993; BBC Radio 3 Composers of The Week, 1995. Memberships: Whistlebinkies Folk Music Group, 1973-; Scottish Arts Council Music Committee, 1980-83. Address: c/o Scottish Music Information Centre, 1 Bowmont Gardens, Glasgow, G12 9LR, Scotland.

MCINTIRE Dennis K(eith), b. 25 June 1944, Indianapolis, Indiana, USA. Historian (Music and Literature); Lexicographer. Education: Indiana University. Appointments: Research Editor, various general reference works, 1965-79; Editorial Associate, Nicolas Slonimsky, 1979-95; Advisor, The Oxford Dictionary of Music, 1985, 2nd edition, 1994, The New Grove Dictionary of American Music, 1986, The New Everyman Dictionary of Music, 1988, Brockhaus Riemann Musik Lexikon: Ergänzungsband, 1989, 2nd edition, 1995, Dictionnaire biographique des musiciens, 1995, The Hutchinson Encyclopaedia of Music, 1995. Publications: Baker's Biographical Dictionary of Musicians (contributing editor), 7th edition, 1984, (associate editor), 8th edition, 1992; International Who's Who in Music and Musicians' Directory (consultant editor), 12th edition, 1990, (appendices editor), 13th to 15th editions, 1992-96; Baker's Biographical Dictionary of 20th Century Classical Musicians (associate editor), 1997; International Authors and Writers Who's Who (consultant editor), 15th edition, 1997, 16th edition, forthcoming; International Who's Who in Poetry and Poets' Encyclopaedia (consultant editor), 8th edition, 1997, 9th edition, forthcoming. Contributions to: The New Grove Dictionary of American Music, 1986; Supplement to Music Since 1900, 1986; The New Grove Dictionary of Opera, 1992; Music Since 1900, 5th edition, 1994; The New Grove Dictionary of Music and Musicians, revised edition, forthcoming. Honour: Advisor, Encyclopaedia Britannica, 1996-. Memberships: High Churchman (Conservative); Freemason; Ancient Accepted Scottish Rite; American Musicological Society; Music Library Association; Sir Thomas Beecham Society, USA. Address: 9170 Melrose Court, Indianapolis, IN 46239, USA.

MCINTYRE Donald (Conroy) (Sir), b. 22 Oct 1934, Auckland, New Zealand. International Opera Singer, Baritone. m. Jill Redington, 29 Jul 1961, 2 d. Education: Auckland Teachers Training College; Guildhall School of Music, London. Debut: Welsh National Opera, as Zachariah in Nabucco, 1959. Career includes: Principal Bass, Sadler's Wells Opera, 1960-67, Royal Opera House, Covent Garden, 1967-; Annual appearances at Bayreuth Festival, 1967-81 as Wotan in the Ring and frequent international guest appearances; Sang Amfortas at Bayreuth, 1987-88, Monterone in a new production of Rigoletto at Covent Garden, 1988, followed by Prospero in British premiere of Berio's Un Re in Ascolto, 1989, Wotan in Die Walküre for Australian Opera, 1989; debut as Balstrode in Peter Grimes at Covent Garden, 1989, Hans Sachs in New Zealand premiere of Die Meistersinger, Wellington, 1990; Telramund, Teatro San Carlos, Lisbon, 1990; Wagner's Hans Sachs at Covent Garden, 1993 and in Lady Macbeth of Mtensk at Munich, 1993; Sang Gurnemanz in Parsifal at Antwerp, 1996; Other roles include: the Wanderer in Der Ring, Barak in Die Frau ohne Schatten, Pizarro in Fidelio, Golaud in Pelléas et Mélisande, Kurwenal in Tristan und Isolde, Heyst in Victory, Jochanaan in Salome, Scarpia in Tosca, Nick Shadow in The Rake's Progress, Doctor Schön in Lulu. Recordings: Pelléas et Mélisande, Oedipus Rex, Il Trovatore; Video of Der Ring des Nibelungen, from Bayreuth. Honours: Fidelio Medal from the International Association of Opera Directors and Intendants for Oustanding Service to the Royal Opera House, 1967-89; OBE, 1975; CBE, 1985; KBE, 1992. Hobbies: Sport particularly Golf, Tennis and Swimming; Gardening; Languages; Farming; Carpentry. Address: Foxhill Farm, Jackass Lane, Keston, Bromley, Kent, England.

MCINTYRE Joy, b. 24 Sept 1938, Kinsley, Kansas, USA. Singer (Soprano). Education: Studied at the New England Conservatory and the Salzburg Mozarteum. Career: Sang at the Saarbrucken Opera 1964-66, Dortmund 1966-74 and Munich Staatsoper 1976-81; Roles have included Suzuki, Brangaene, Leonore, Venus, Ortrud, the Dyer's Wife, Marie, Abigaille, Santuzza, Turandot, Judith in Bluebeard's Castle and Lady Macbeth; Guest appearances at the Vienna Staatsoper, Lyon, Strasbourg, Brussels, Hamburg and Glasgow (Scottish Opera). Address: c/o Bayerische Staatsoper, Max Joseph Platz. Pf 100148, W-8000 Munich 1, Germany.

MCKAY Elizabeth (Norman), b. 21 Nov 1931, London, England. Musicologist; Pianist. m. Gilbert Watt McKay, 7 Dec 1960, 1 s, 2 d. Education: BSc, Bristol University, 1949-52; LRAM, Pianoforte Performer, 1952; Somerville College Scholar, DPhil, Oxford University, 1958-61. Career: Musicologist, Pianist, chamber music, accompanist, coach, theatre work; Teacher; Lecturer in Musical History. Publications: Schubert's Music for the Theatre; Proceedings of The Royal Musical Association, 1966-67; Schubert as a Composer of Operas, Schubert Studies, 1982; The Impact of The New Pianoforte: Mozart, Beethoven and Schubert, 1987; Franz Schubert's Music for the Theatre, 1991; Schubert's Klaviersonaten von 1815 bis 1825, in Franz Schubert Reliquie-Sonate, 1992; Schubert biography, 1997. Contributions to: The New Grove Dictionary of Opera; Enzyklopadie des Musik Theaters, 1994; The Music Review; Musical Times; Osterreichische Musikzeitschrift; Music and Letters; The Beethoven Newsletter. Honour: Honorary Member of the Board of International Franz Schubert Institute. Address: Gamrie, Swan Lane, Long Hanborough, Witney, Oxon, OX8 8BT, England.

MCKAY James (Rae), b. 4 Oct 1944, Toronto, Canada. Professor of Music; Conductor; Bassoonist. Education: BA Hons, Music, Trinity College, University of Toronto, 1967; MA, Musicology, University of Chicago, USA, 1971. Career: Chairman, Performance Department, University of Western Ontario, London, Ontario; Past Chairman,Department of Music, York University, North York, Ontario; Conductor, Music Director, Toronto Community Orchestra; Guest Conductor, Mount Orford, Quebec Symphony, Canada, Orchestra London, Canada; Bassoon Soloist with McGill Chamber Orchestra, Chamber Players of Toronto, Contemporary Chamber Players of Chicago, Canadian Broadcasting Corporation; Director, Decoustics/ACS Centre for Acoustical Research at York University. Recordings: Three for All, Golden Crest CRS-4217; Solo Bassoon and Piano, Golden Crest; Stravinsky's L'Histoire du soldat, Ultra; Sessions, Concertino, Desto. Contributions to: The Breval Manuscript; New Interpretations in Cahiers Debussy Nouvelle Series No 1, 1977, 1978; Le Trio, op 120 de Fauré; Une esquisse inconnue du troisième mouvement, Etudes Fauréennes, Paris, 1982. Address: Faculty of Music, University of Western Ontario, London, Ontario N6A 3K7, Canada.

MCKAY Marjory (Grieve), b. 23 June 1951, Edinburgh, Scotland. Opera Singer (Soprano). m. Frederick Charles McKay, 17 July 1981. Education: Trinity Academy, Edinburgh, 1956-69; Royal Manchester College of Music, 1969-74; Royal Northern College of Music, 1974-75. Debut: As Esmeralda, Scottish Opera, 1980. Career: Scottish opera roles, concerts and recitals; Esmeralda in Bartered Bride, Belleza in L'Egisto and Feklusa in Katya Kabanova; Scottish Opera Go Round, Violetta; Welsh National Opera Workshop, Violetta in La Traviata; Many concerts and recitals in Scotland and the north of England; Now living in Sydney, Australia; Debut in Australian Opera as Gerhilde in Die Walküre, 1985 and Xenia in Boris Godonuv, 1986; debut with Western Australian Opera as Madame Butterfly, 1987; Created the title role in Alan Holley's new opera, Dorothea; Les Huguenots Video (Joan Sutherland's Farewell), 1990. Hobbies: Dressmaking; Knitting; Picture framing; Bakers clay modelling; Various handicrafts; Gardening; Swimming; Creating rag dolls. Current Management: Opera Australia. Address: 4 Pelican Street, Gladesville, Sydney, New South Wales 2111, Australia.

MCKEE Gerald, b. 1928, USA. Singer (Tenor). Career: Sang widely in Germany from 1959, first at Regensburg and Frankfurt then Kassel 1964-66; Roles have included Wagner's Erik, Tannhäuser, Tristan, Siegmund and Siegfried, Manrico, Otello, Bacchus Laca in Jenufa and Samson; Guest appearances in London, Turin, Hamburg, Palermo and Naples. Recordings: Siegfried in the Ring (Westminster).

MCKELLAR FERGUSON Kathleen, b. 1959, Stirling, Scotland. Singer (Mezzo-soprano). Education: Studied at the Royal Scottish Academy and the Royal College of Music; Further study with Margaret Hyde. Career: South Bank debut 1987, with the London Bach Orchestra; Beethoven's Ninth at the Gstaad Festival, 1990 and with the Ulster Orchestra; Other repertoire includes Mozart's Requiem, the Brahms Alto Rhapsody, Mahler's 8th, Songs of the Auvergne and A Child of our Time; Season 1990-91 with Haydn's Nelson Mass and the English Chamber Orchestra, Messiah with the Liverpool Philharmonic; Also sings Elgar's Sea Pictures and Music Makers, St Matthew Passion (Fairfields Hall) and Elijah; Concerts with Yehudi Menuhin at Festival Halls; Opera repertoire includes Florence Pike in Albert Herring (Aldeburgh 1986), Maketaten in Aknaten by Philip Glass for ENO 1987, Mozart's Marcellina and Third Lady for Pavillion Opera, Cherubino, and Handel's Bradamante (Alcina) for Flanders Opera 1991, Second Lady (Magic Flute) at Théâtre Royale de la Monnaie, Brussels, 1993, Suzuki (Madam Butterfly) for Opera Forum in Nederlands, 1994-, and Bradamante (Alcina) with Nikolaus Harnoncourt at Zurich Opera; Second Lady at Festival of Aix en Provence. Address: IMG Artists Europe, Media House, 3 Burlington Lane, Chiswick, London W4 2TH, England.

MCKERRACHER Colin, b. 1960, Falkirk, Scotland. Singer (Tenor). Education: Studied with Joseph Ward at the Royal Northern College of Music and with Nicolai Gedda. Career: Has sung with Glyndebourne Touring Opera and the Festival in Simon Boccanegra and Capriccio, 1986-87; Appearances with Scottish Opera-Go-Round as Steva in Jenufa, Beppe and Turiddu (Cav and Pag) and Don Carlos; Lensky in Eugene Onegin for Opera 80 followed by Monostatos in The Magic Flute and Ernesto in Don Pasquale; English National Opera and Covent Garden debuts season, 1990-91, as Ferrando and in Così fan tutte. Honours: Prizewinner, 1989 Rio de Janiero International Singing Competition. Address: Anglo Swiss Ltd, 3 Primrose Mews, 1a Sharpleshall Street, London SW1 8YW, England.

MCKINNEY Thomas, b. 5 May 1946, Lufkin, Texas, USA. Singer (Baritone). Education: Studied in Houston, Hollywood and New York. Debut: Houston, 1971 as Tchelkalov in Boris Godunov. Career: Sang in opera in Cincinnati, Houston, San Diego and San Francisco; European engagements at the Wexford Festival (Thaisi), the Vienna Volksoper and the Theatre Royale de la Monnaie, Brussels; Other roles have included Pelléas, Guglielmo, Don Giovanni, Mozart's Count, Papageno, Rossini's Figaro, Eugene Onegin, Hamlet, Belcore, Massenet's Herode and Athanael (Thais), Verdi's Posa and Ford and Peachum in The Beggar's Opera; San Diego, 1972 in the premiere of Medea by Alva Henderson; Frequent concert appearances. Address: c/o Volksoper, Wahringerstrasse 78, A-1090 Vienna, Australia.

MCLACHLAN Murray, b. 6 Jan 1965, Dundee, Scotland. Concert Pianist. m. Mary Russell, 6 Mar 1993. Education: Studied at Chetham's School and at Cambridge with Peter Katin and Norma Fisher. Debut: Free Trade Hall, Manchester, 1983. Career: Performed extensively throughout Britain as a recitalist and concerto soloist with Royal Philharmonic Orchestra, Scottish Chamber Orchestra, BBC Scottish Orchestra, Manchester Camerata; Toured Belorussia, 1991; Has performed complete cycle of 32 Beethoven sonatas from memory in Glasgow, Dundee and Aberdeen. Recordings include: Complete sonatas of Prokofiev, Myaskovsky and Kabalevsky and solo works of Khatchaturian; Piano concerto of Ronald Stevenson. Honours: Piano Prize, Chetham's Cambridge Instrumental Exhibition' Penguin Rosette Award, for CD of music from Scotland. Membership: Adjudicator, British Federation of Festivals. Hobbies: Hill walking; Films; Cookery; Reading. Current Management: Siva Oke Music Management. Address: Banrye Cottage, 5 Holburn Place, Aberdeen AB1 6HG, Scotland.

MCLAIN John (Anthony Lain), b. 5 June 1933, Chingford, London, England. Composer; Songwriter. Education: BSc, Mathematics, London University, 1955. Career: National Service, REME, 1955-57; CAV Ltd, 1957-59; Royal Society for the Prevention of Accidents, 1959-70; ICI (Plastics), 1970-85; British Aerospace, 1985-87. Compositions: Our Father, Who Art in Heaven (Lord's Prayer); Why Don't They Write the Songs?; Now You Have Gone; Dream Awhile; The Poop Scoop Song; Television: Our Father, Who Art in Heaven, performed by the Gibside Singers Ladies' Choir, Tyne Tees TV. Recording: Now You Have Gone, by Tony Jacobs with Jim Barry (piano). Memberships: Performing Right Society Ltd; BASCA; Mensa; Robert Farnon Society. Hobbies: Country Walking; Golf. Address: 42 Osidge Lane, Southgate, London N14 5JG, England.

MCLAUGHLIN Marie, b. 2 Nov 1954, Hamilton, Lanarkshire, Scotland. Singer (Soprano). Education: Studied at the London Opera Centre and the National Opera Studio. Career: Sang Susanna and Lauretta while a student; English National Opera from 1978, in The Consul, Dido and Aeneas, A Night in Venice and Rigoletto; Royal Opera Covent Garden from 1980 as Barbarina and Susanna in Le nozze di Figaro, Zerlina, Iris in Semele, Marzelline in Fidelio, Nannetta in Falstaff, Zdenka in Arabella and Tytania in A Midsummer Night's Dream; Glyndebourne Festivals as Micaela (Carmen) and Violetta, 1985, 1987, Salzburg Festival as Susanna, conducted by James Levine; Scottish Opera in Orfeo ed Euridice and Le Nozze di Figaro; Deutsche Oper Berlin as Susanna and Marzelline; Hamburg, Susanna, Marzelline; Chicago Lyric, Zerlina, Despina; Washington, Susanna; Met New York as Marzelline; La Scala, Milan, Adina; Paris Opéra in Roméo et Juliette; Sang Zdenka in Arabella at Covent Garden, 1990; Marzelline in Fidelio at the 1990 Salzburg Festival, Zerlina at the Vienna Festival; Geneva Opera 1992, as Despina, and Jenny in Mahagonny; Sang Jenny at the Opéra Bastille, Paris, 1995; Donna Elvira at Lausanne, 1996. Concert appearances in London, Edinburgh, New Work, Chicago, Berlin, Spain, France, Belgium and Germany; Conductors worked with include Maazel, Bernstein, Haitink, Barenboim, Davis, Leppard, Celibidache, Harnoncourt, Mehta and Levine; Season 1992-93, as Blanche in the Carmelites at Geneva, Susanna on tour with the Royal Opera to Japan, Ilia in Idomeneo at Barcelona and Ivy in On the Town at the Barbican Hall. Recordings include: Video of Covent Garden Fidelio (Virgin), Handel's L'Allegro, il Pensieroso ed Il Moderato; Die Zauberflöte and Dido and Aeneas; Cosi fan tutte (Levine), Mozart, Requiem (Bernstein), (Phonogram); Videos of Rigoletto, Carmen, Traviata, Mozart's C Minor Mass and Haydn's Mass in Time of War. Address: c/o Harrison/Parrot Ltd, 12 Penzance Place, London W11 4PA, England.

MCLEAN Barton (Keith), b. 8 Apr 1938, New York, New York, USA. Composer. m. Priscilla McLean, 28 Aug 1967. Education: BS, Music Education, State University College, Potsdam, New York, 1960; MM, Music Theory, Eastman School of Music, 1965; MusD, Composition, Indiana University, 1972. Career: Teacher: State University College, Potsdam, 1960-66, Indiana University, South Bend, 1969-76, University of Texas, Austin, 1976-83; Teacher, Ear Studios, 1987-88, 1990-92, Director, Ear Studios, 1987-88, Rensselaer Polytechnic Institute. Compositions: Numerous including: Dimensions I, violin, tape, 1973, II, piano, tape, 1974, III, saxophone, tape, 1978, IV, saxophone, tape, 1979, VIII, piano, tape, 1982; Metamorphosis, orchestra, 1975; Heavy Music, 4 crowbars, electronic, 1979; Ixtlan, 2 pianos, 1982; The Last Ten Minutes, computer generated, 1982; The Electric Sinfonia, 1982; String Quartet, from the Good Earth, 1985; In the Place of Tears, chamber ensemble, voice, 1985; In Wilderness is the Preservation of the World, environmental-electronic, 1986; Voices of the Wild - Primal Spirits, orchestra, 1987; Visions of a Summer Night, computer tape, 1989; Rainforest, 1989; Rainforest Images, computer tape, 1992; Rainforest Reflections, electronic processed soloist and orchestra, 1993; Rainforest Images I and II, video, 1993; Forgotten Shadows, computer tape, 1994; Jambori Rimba, 1996; Desert Spring, 1996; Dawn Chorus, 1996; Forgotten Shadows, 1996. Recordings: Visions of a Summer Night, 1992; Rainforest Images, 1993; Demons of the Night, Fireflies, Earth Music, 1994; The Electric Performer; The McLean Mix and the Golden Age of Electronic Music. Honours: Virgil Thompson Foundation Grant, 1987; Asian Cultural Council Grant, 1996. Contributions to: Adirondac; Sounds Australian; SEAMUS Journal; Leonardo Music Journal; Experimental Musical Instruments. Honours: Electric Sinfonia Prize, Bourges Electroacoustic Music Festival, 1983; Several fellowships and grants. Address: Coon Brook Road, Petersburgh, NY 12138, USA.

MCLEAN Priscilla (Taylor), b. 27 May 1942, Fitchburg, Massachusetts, USA. Composer; Performer. m. Barton Keith McLean, 26 Aug 1967. Education: BEd, State College, Fitchburg, 1963; BMusEd, University of Lowell, Massachusetts, 1965; MM Composition, Indiana University, 1969. Career: Concerts, The McLean Mix (husband-wife duo performing own electronic acoustic music), Holland, Belgium, Zagreb Muzicki Biennale, 1981; Amsterdam, Holland Radio, Oslo, Finland, Sweden, 1983; Australia, New Zealand, Hawaii, 1990; Tours, USA, 1981-95, yearly; Canada, 1986; Guest Composer, Kennedy Center for the Performing Arts, 1977; Gaudeamus Musiekweek, Holland, 1979; Guest Professor and Composer/Performer, University of Hawaii, 1985; Guest Soprano Soloist, Cleveland Chamber Orchestra (Wilderness), 1989; Guest composer/performer (residency), University of Sarawak, Malaysia, 1996; Tunugan Festival of Asian music, Philippines, 1997. Compositions Include: Variations and Mozaics on a Theme of Stravinsky; Dance of Dawn; Invisible Chariots; The Inner Universe; Fantasies for Adults and Other Children; Beneath the Horizon I, III; Night Images; Messages; Fire and Ice; Elan!; 3 Pieces for In Wilderness is the Preservation of the World; In Celebration; Wilderness; A Magic Dwells, (Orchestra and Tape), 1986; Voices of the Wild, Orchestra and Soloist (Electronic Music), 1988; The Dance of Shiva, (Electronic Tape and Multiple Slides), 1990; Rainforest (Coil with B McLean), 1990; Everything Awakening Alert and Joyful, (full Orchestra and Narrator), 1991; In the Beginning, 1995; Rainforest Images, 1993; Desert Spring with Barton McLean, 1996; Jambori Rimba with

Barton McLean, 1997. Recordings include: Dance of Dawn 1975; Interplanes, 1978; Variations and Mozaics on a Theme of Stravinsky, 1979; Invisible Chariots, 1979; Electronic Music from the Outside In, 1980; Beneath the Horizon III and Salt Canyons, 1983; In Wilderness is the Preservation of the World, 1987; Rainforest Images II; The Electric Performer; Gods, Demons and the Earth; McLean Mix and the Golden Age of Electronic Music. Memberships: BMI; American Music Center; Seamus; SCI. Current Management: The McLean Mix/MLC Publications. Address: 55 Coon Brook Road, Petersburgh, New York, NY 12138, USA.

MCLEOD John, b. 8 Mar 1934, Aberdeen, Scotland. Composer; Conductor; Lecturer. m. Margaret Murray (pianist), 12 Aug 1961, 1 s, 1 d. Education: Royal Academy of Music, 1957-61; Composition pupil of Lennox Berkeley; Conducting pupil of Adrian Boult. Career: Freelance Composer, Conductor and Lecturer, 1970-74; Director of Music, Merchiston Castle School, Edinburgh, 1974-85; Visiting Lecturer, Royal Scottish Academy of Music and Drama, 1985-89; Visiting Lecturer in Composition and Contemporary Music at Napier University of Edinburgh, 1989-94; Visiting Composer, Lothian Specialist Music Scheme, 1986-92; Ida Carroll Research Fellow, Royal Northern College of Music, 1988-89; Guest Conductor for various Scottish orchestras including Royal Scottish National Orchestra; Director of postgraduate course in composing for film and television at Thames Valley University and London College of Music, 1991-97; Visiting Professor, Royal Academy of Music, 1993-97. Compositions include: The Gokstad Ship for Orchestra, National Youth Orchestra of Scotland Commission, 1982; Stabat Mater for Soloists, Choir and Orchestra, Edinburgh Royal Choral Union Commission, 1986; Percussion Concerto, Evelyn Glennie Soloist, National Youth Orchestra of Scotland Commission; The Song of Dionysius for Percussion and Piano, premiered at the 1989 London Proms with Evelyn Glennie and Philip Smith; Film scores for many TV and cinema films including, Another Time, Another Place; Works now performed and recorded by leading artists, orchestras and at major international festivals. Honours: FRAM; FRSA; FTCL; LRAM; ARCM; LTCL; Guinness Prize for British Composers, 1979; UK Music Education Award, 1982. Hobbies include: Travel; Books; Art; Films; Theatre; Walking; Gardening; Cooking. Address: Hill House, 9 Redford Crescent, Colinton, Edinburgh, EH13 0BS, Scotland.

MCMASTER Brian (John), b. 9 May 1943, Hitchin, England. Opera Administrator. Education: Wellington College, 1955-60; LLB, Bristol University, 1963. Career: International Artists Department, EMI, 1968-73; Controller, Opera Planning, English National Opera, 1973-76; General Administrator, Welsh National Opera, Cardiff, Wales, 1976-92; Artistic Director, Vancouver Opera, British Columbia, Canada, 1983-89; Director, The Edinburgh Festival, 1992. Address: 21 Market Street, Edinburgh EH1 1BW, Scotland.

MCMASTER Zandra, b. 1960 Ballymena, N Ireland. Singer (Mezzo-soprano). Education: Studied at the Trinity College of Music and London Opera Centre. Debut: Purcell Room, London, 1983. Career: Sang Mahler's 4th Symphony at Madrid 1984 and has been resident in Spain singing in concert with most leading Spanish Orchestras; Salzburg Mozarteum 1989-91, Concertgebouw Amsterdam 1990 and US debut 1991, in Bernstein's 1st Symphony at Colorado; Seville World 'Expo concert 1992 and Beethoven's Ninth in Berlin; Further repertoire includes the St Matthew Passion, Rossini's Stabat Mater and the Kindertotenlieder. Address: Helen Sykes Management, Fourth Floor, Parkway House, Sheen Lane, East Sheen, London SW14 8LS, England.

MCNAIR Sylvia, b. 23 June 1956, Mansfield, Ohio, USA. Singer (Soprano). Education: Studied at India University. Career: Sang in Messiah at Indianapolis, 1980; Euroean debut in the premiere of Kelterborn's Ophelia, Schwetzingen, 1984; Concert appearances in Cleveland, Baltimore, San Francisco, Detroit, Montreal, Indianapolis, Atlanta, St Louis, Washington and Los Angeles; New York at the Carnegie, Avery Fisher and Alice Tully Halls; Season 1991-92 with the Chicago Symphony under Solti, Berlin Philharmonic under Haitink, City of Birmingham Symphony under Rattle, Concentus Musicus under Harnoncourt and London Philharmonic under Masur; Mozart's Ilia and Servilia with the Monteverdi Choir and Orchestra conducted by John Eliot Gardiner; US opera appearances as Pamina at Santa Fe, Ilia; Hero (Béatrice et Benédict) and Morgana in Alcina at St Louis; Sang Ilia in Lyon and Strasbourg and Susana with Netherlands Opera; Pamina at the Deutsche Oper Berlin and the Vienna Staatsoper; Glyndebourne Festival 1989 as Anne Trulove; Covent Garden and Salzburg debuts as Ilia in Idomeneneo; Season 1991-92 with Bastille Opera (Paris) and Metropolitan Opera (as Marzelline in Fidelio) debuts; Covent Garden 1992, in Rossini's Il Viaggio a Reims; Sang Poppea at the 1993 Salzburg Festival and returned for Pamina in Die Zauberflöte, 1997; Engaged as Blanche Dubois in Previn's A Streetcar Named Desire, San Francisco, 1998. Recordings: Albums with Neville Marriner, Roger Norrington, John Eliot Gardiner, Colin Davis, Kurt Masur, James Levine and Bernard Haitink; Idomeneo with John Eliot Gardiner (Deutsche Grammophon). Address: Lies Askonas Ltd, 6 Henrietta Street, London WC2, England.

MCNEIL-MORALES Albert John, b. 14 Feb 1925, California, USA. Professor; Conductor. m. Helen Rambo, 29 Dec 1953, 1 son. Education: BA, University of California; MA, DMA, University of Southern California. Debut: Europe 1968. Career: Founder, Albert McNeil Jubilee Singers, 1964; Has travelled to 64 countries and performed over 3,000 concerts, with major performances in Berlin Philharmonie, Salle Gaveau, Paris; Mozarteum, Salzburg; Conservatory de St Cecilia, Rome; Mann Auditorium, Tel Aviv; Alice Tully Hall, New York; Dorothy Chandler Pavillion, Los Angeles. Publications: Co-author, Silver Burdett Music (series), 1979-86; Albert McNeil Choral Series, Articles in the Choral Journal and Voice (Chorus America). Honours: Almunus of the Year, UCLA, 1991; Sterling Patron, My Phi Epsilon, 1990. Memberships: Phi Mu Alpha; Association of Professional Vocal Ensembles; American Choral Directors Association. Current Management: Walter Gould, Century Artists Bureau Inc. Address: 447 Herondo St 210, Hermosa Beach,CA 90254, USA.

MCTIER Duncan (Paul), b. 21 Nov 1954, Stourbridge, Worcestershire, England. Double Bass Soloist; Teacher. m. Yuko Inoue, 11 Jan 1984. Education: King Edward VI Grammer School, Stourbridge; Bristol University, 1972-75; BSc (Hons), Mathematical Sciences; ARCM (Hons), 1974. Career: Member, BBC Symphony Orchestra, 1975-77; Principal Bass, Netherlands Chamber Orchestra, 1977-84; Senior Double Bass Tutor, Royal Northern College of Music, 1984-; Professor of Double Bass, Royal College of Music, 1987-91; Double Bass Consultant, Royal Scottish Academy of Music & Drama, 1991-; Solo appearances with Netherlands Chamber Orchestra, Concertgebouw Chamber Orchestra, Bournemouth Sinfonietta, Netherlands Philharmonic Orchestra, Orchestre Regional d'Auvergne, Barcelona Municipal Orchestra, Northern Sinfonia Orchestre de Chambre Detmold, Nippon Telemann Ensemble of Osaka, Lausanne Chamber Orchestra, BBC Concert Orchestra, Scottish Chamber Orchestra, Bournemouth Symphony Orchestra; World Premieres of Concertos written by Peter Maxwell Davis, John Casken and Derek Bourgeois; Recitals and master classes throughout Europe and Japan. Recordings: Solo recordings: Bottesini Grand Duo for Philips; Various pieces with Paganini Ensemble for Denon; Dutch TV recordings of Bottesini Grand Duo and 2nd Concerto; Dvorak String Quintet and Waltzes with Chilingirian Quartet (Chandos); Extensive radio recordings. Honour: 1st Prize Winner, Isle of Man International Double Bass Competition, 1982. Hobbies: Golf; Carpentry. Current Management: Music Productions, London. Address: c/o Manager, Music Productions 'J' House, 6 Studland Street, London W6 0JS, England.

MCVEAGH Diana (Mary), b. 6 Sept 1926, Ipoh, Malaya. Writer on Music. m. Dr C W Morley, 7 Oct 1950, dec 1994. Education: Malvern Girls' College, 1936-44; Royal College of Music, 1944-47, ARCM, GRSM. Career: Assistant Editor, Musical Times, 1965-67; Executive Committee of the New Grove, 1970-76; Contributor to The Times, 1947-69, also to Musical Times, The Listener, Records and Recordings; Executive Committee of the GKN English Song Award, 1982-89. Publications: Elgar (Dent) 1955; Contributor to New Grove Dictionary of Music (article on Elgar), Twentieth-Century English Masters (MacMillan) 1986. Memberships: Royal Musical Association Council, 1961-76, Vice President, Elgar Society. Address: Ladygrove, The Lee, Great Missenden, Bucks HP16 9NA, England.

MCVICAR David, b. 1965, Glasgow, Scotland. Stage Director. Education: Studied at the Royal Scottish Academy of Music and Drama. Career: College productions Rimsky's Mozart and Salieri, Die Zauberflöte and Semele; Stravinsky's Soldier's Tale at the Edinburgh Festival and Harrogate, Aberdeen and London Opera Festivals; Mozart's Il Re Pastore for Opera North (1993), followed by Thomas' Hamlet, 1995. Address: Performing Arts, 6 Windmill Street, London W1P 1HF.

MEAD Philip (John), b. 8 Sept 1947, Chadwell St Mary, Essex, England. Pianist. m. Gillian Mead, 2 Aug 1969, 3 daughters. Education: ARCM, Performing 1966, FTCL 1982, LRAM 1968, GRSM 1969, Royal Academy of Music; Honorary degree ARAM, 1993. Debut: Purcell Rome, 1973. Career includes: Performances, major festivals, England and overseas; Specialist, 20th century piano music; Commissioned works include works for piano and electronics by Dennis Smalley, Jonathan Harvey, Tim Souster and others; Featured soloist at London South Bank's 1987 Electric Weekend; Soloist, BBC Symphony Orchestra Ives Festival, 1996; Founded the first British Contemporary Piano Competition, Cambridge 1988; Professor, London College of Music; Repetoire includes Messiaen, Tippett, Stockhausen and George Crumb. Recordings: Numerous for BBC and European Stations, including Stephen Montague, Slow Dance on a Burial Ground; Recorded 8 CDs of electronic music; Contributions to: Electro Acoustic Music; Classical Piano. Honours: 5 prizes, Royal Academy of Music; Research Awards; Prizewinner, Gaudeamus International Competition for Interpreters of Contemporary Music, 1978; ARAM, RAM, 1993; Artistic Director, Contemporary Piano Competition. Memberships: Sonic Arts; Society for the Promotion of New Music; EPTA. Hobbies: Jogging; Reading. Current Management: Magenta Music International Ltd. Address: 31 Lingholme Close, Cambridge CB4 3HW, England.

MEALE Richard, b. 24 Aug 1932, Sydney, Australia. Composer. Education: New South Wales Conservatorium of Music; University of California at Los Angeles. Career: Programme Planning Officer for the Australian Broadcasting Commission, 1962-68; Senior Lecturer in the Department of Music at the University of Adelaide from 1969; Active as Pianist from 1955, notably in the music of Messiaen. Compositions: Stage: The Hypnotist Ballet, 1956; Incidental Music to King Lear; Juliet's Memoirs, opera, 1975; Operas Voss, 1986 and Mer de Glace, 1991; Orchestral: Flute Concerto, 1959; Sinfonia for piano and strings, 1959; Homage to Garcia Lorca for double string orchestra, 1964; Images, 1966; Very High Kings, 1968; Clouds Now and Then, 1969; Soon it Will Die, 1969; Evocations, 1973; Viridian, 1979; Instrumental: Divertiemnto for Piano Trio, 1959; Flute Sonata, 1960; Les Alboradas for flute, horn, violin and piano, 1963; Wind Quintet, 1970; Incredible Floridas for flute, clarinet, violin, cello, piano and percussion, 1971; 2 String Quartets, 1974, 1980; Fanfare for brass ensemble, 1978; Keyboard: Sonatina Patetica, 1957; Orenda, 1959; Coruscations, 1971. Honours: 1971 Member of the British Empire; Composers Fellowship awarded by the South Australian Government, 1972-75. Memberships: Adelaide Festival Centre Trust, 1972; President of the Australian Branch of ISCM, 1977; Chairman of the composition Panel of the Music Board of the Australia Council. Address: c/o Universal Edition, 2/3 Fareham Street, London W1V 4DU, England.

MECKNA Michael, b. 13 Feb 1945, Long Beach, California, USA. Musicologist. m. Eva Kartinen, 18 February 1976. Education: BA, California State University, Long Beach, 1967; PhD, Santa Barbara, University of California, 1984; Horn study with Fred Fox. Appointments: Assistant Professor, Ball State University, 1984-90; Associate Professor, Texas Christian University, 1990-. Publications: Austrian Cloister Symphonists (with R Freeman), 1982; The Rise of the American Composer-Critic, 1984; Virgil Thomson: A Bio-Bibliography, 1986; 20th Century Brass Soloists, 1994. Contributions to: Articles in American Music, Musical Times, Musical Quarterly, Oesterreichische Musikzeitshrift; 3 of the Grove Dictionary series. Honours: Young Artist Award, Long Beach Symphony, 1965; Aspen Fellow, Music Critics Association, 1980; Sinfonia Foundation Research Grant, 1984; NEH Research Grants, 1985, 1987; Outstanding Academic Book, Choice Magazine, 1987. Memberships: American Musicological Society; College Music Society; Sonneck Society. Hobby: Ballroom dancing. Address: Department of Music, Texas Christian University, Fort Worth, TX 76129, USA.

MEDCALF Stephen, b. 1960, England. Stage Director. m. Susan Gritton, 1 son. Education: London Drama School. Career: Graduated 1983 and became associate director at Glyndebourne 1988, working with Peter Sellars, Peter Hall and Trevor Nunn; Resident Producer at Guildhall School of Music from 1991, including UK stage premiere of Prokofiev's Duenna; Director of Productions for English Touring Opera from 1991, with Elisir d'Amore; Season 1994 with Le nozze di Figaro at Glyndebourne, La Finta Giardiniera for GSM, Haydn's L'Incontro Improvviso at Garsington and Orfeo ed Euridice for English Touring Opera; Season 1995 with Rape of Lucretia at GSM, Handel's Ezio at the Théâtre des Champs Elysées, Paris, Die Zauberflöte at Parma with John Eliot Gardiner; Elisir d'Amore with West Australian Opera and Rimsky's May Night at Wexford; The Marriage of Figaro for English Touring Opera, 1997. Recordings: Videos: Cosi fan tutte, with John Eliot Gardiner; Le nozze di Figaro, Glyndebourne Festival Opera and Channel 4; Die Zauberflöte. Address: Performing Arts, 6 Windmill Street, London W1P 1HF.

MEDEK Ivo, b. 20 July 1956, Brno, Czech Republic. Composer. m. Zuzana Medová, 11 Aug 1986, 2 sons. Education: Computers and Structural Mechanics (Dipl ing), Technical University; Master Composition, 1989, PhD, Composition and Theory, 1997, Janacek Academy of Music and Dramatic Art in Brno. Career: About 60 compositions of orchestral, chamber, electroacoustics music, many recorded on television, broadcasts and festivals in the Czech Republic, Europe and USA, 1990, 1994; Docent of Darmstadt courses, lectures in Brno, Austria, Poland, Holland, Portugal; Assistant Professor of Janacek Academy of Music in Brno. Compositions: Adledaivan, 1988; Pangea, 1989; Triads, 1989; Cephedidy, 1991; Flow, 1992; Postludio, 1994; Persofonie, 1995. Recordings: Adai; Adeldaivan; Flow; Cepheidy; Postludio; Fests; Pangea; Wandering in Well-known Landscape; Persofonie. Publications: Basic General Composing Principles, 1989; Processuality as a Complex Composing Method, 1996. Contributions to: About 100 articles, Opus Musicum, Czech Music, The Silence. Honour: Czech Music

Fund Prize, 1993. Memberships: Camerata Brno "Q" Society, Czech Music Council. Hobbies: Tennis; Skiing; Literature. Address: Sirotkova 67, 61600 Brno, Czech Republic.

MEDEK Tilo, b. 22 Jan 1940, Jena, Germany. Composer. Education: Studied in Berlin with E Meyer and Wagner Regeny. Career: Moved to West Germany in 1977. Compositions include: Operas Einzug, 1969; Icke und die Hexe Yu, 1971; Appetit auf Frukirschen, 1972; Katharina Blum, 1991; Gritzko und der Pan, 1987; Balled David and Goliath, 1972; Orchestral: Tiade 1964; Dad Zogernde Lied, 1970; Flute concerto, 1973; Piccolo Concerto, 1975; Konig Johann, concert overture, 1976; Marimba Concerto, 1976; 2 Cello Concertos, 1978, 1984; Organ Concerto, 1979; Violin Concerto, 1980; Eisenblatter for organ and orchestra, 1983; Rheinische Sinfonie, 1986; Chamber: Flute Sonata, 1963; 3 Wind Quintets, 1965-79; String Trio, 1965; Divertissement for wind quintet and harpsichord, 1967; Schwanengesang for clarinet, trombone, cello and piano, 1973; Nonet, 1974; Tagtraum for 7 instruments, 1976; Giebichestein for 8 instruments, 1976; Reliquienschrein for organ and percussion, 1980; Vocal: Altägyptische Liebeslieder for 2 voices and orchestra, 1963; Sintflutbestanden for tenor, horn and piano, 1967;Gethsamane, cantata, 1980; Piano and organ music. Address: c/o GEMA, Postfach 80 07 67, D-81607 Munich, Germany.

MEDELSKY Borivoj, b. 29 February 1956, Bratislava, Slovakia. Musicologist; Violin Celist; Composer. m. Eva Medelska-Pavova, 1 February 1986, 2 sons. Education: Faculty of Philosophy, Comenius University, Bratislava, 1978-82; PhD, Musicology, 1982. Career: Active Member, Slovak National Theatre, Bratislava Opera Orchestra, 1977-78. Compositions: 10 Songs. Recordings: 2 Songs. Contributions to: Newspapers and Muscial Magazines. Memberships: Slovak Music Association; Slovak Syndicate of Journalists. Hobbies: Sport; Culture; Nature. Address: Obchodna 12, 811 06 Bratislava, Slovakia.

MEDJIMOREC Heinz, b. 1940, Vienna, Austria. Pianist. Education: Studied in Vienna. Career: Performances of Haydn and other composers in Vienna and elsewhere from 1968; Co-founder, Hydn Trio of Vienna, 1968 and has performed in Brussels, Munich, Berlin, Zurich, London, Paris and Rome; New York debut in 1979 and has made frequent North American appearances with concerts in 25 states; Debut tour of Japan 1984, with further travels to the Near East, Russia, Africa, Central and South America; Series at the Vienna Konzerthaus Society from 1976, with performances of more than 100 works; Summer Festivals at Vienna, Salzburg, Aix-en-Provence, Flanders and Montreux; Master Classes at the Royal College and Royal Academy in London, Stockholm, Bloomington, Tokyo and the Salzburg Mozarteum. Recordings include: Complete piano trios of Beethoven and Schubert, Mendelssohn D minor, Brahms B major, Tchaikovsky A minor, Schubert Trout Quintet; Albums of works by Haydn, Schumann, Dvorak and Smetana. Address: Haydn Trio, Sue Lubbock Concert Management, 25 Courthorpe Road, London NW3 2LE, England.

MEDLAM Charles, b. 1949, England. Conductor; Cellist. Education: Studied the cello in London, Paris (with Maurice Gendron at the Conservatoire), Vienna and Salzburg (performance practice with Nikolaus Harnoncourt). Career: Lectured and played in the resident string quartet at the Chinese University of Hong Kong; Founded London Baroque with Ingrid Seifert 1978; Directs the group as chamber orchestra and conducts when larger forces are required; Conducted the first performance of Scarlatti's Une villa di Tuscolo and a revival of Gli Equivoci Sembiante, for the BBC; Season 1990-91 include Dido and Aeneas at the Paris Opera, Blow and Lully at the Opera-Comique; Aci, Galatea e Polifemo in Spain, Holland and England, and cantatas by Handel and Rameau in Austria, Sweden and Germany with Emma Kirkby; Other recent repertoire includes Charpentier's Messe de Minuit; 4 violin music by Telemann, Vivaldi and Wassenaar; Bach Brandenburg Concertos; Monteverdi Tancredi and Clorinda; Salzburg Festival debut 1991, with music by Mozart; Further festival engagements at Bath, Beaune, Versailles, Ansbach, Innsbruck and Utrecht; Conducted London Baroque in Handel's Op 6 no 6 and Purcell's Come, Ye Sons of Art Away at the 1993 Proms. Recordings: Marais La Gamme, Theile Matthew Passion, Bach Trio Sonatas, Charpentier Theatre Music, Handel Aci, Galatea e Polifemo, Venus and Adonis, Purcell Chamber Music (Harmonia Mundi); Purcell Fantasias, Bach Violin Sonatas, Monteverdi Orfeo, Handel German Arias (EMI); A Vauxhall Gardens Entertainment; English Music of the 18th Century; Francois Couperin Chamber Music; The complete trio sonatas of Corelli, Handel, Purcell, Lawes; Gamba sonatas by CPE Bach, harpsichord concertos by JC Bach/WA Mozart. Hobby: Writing Short Stories. Address: Brick Kiln Cottage, Hollington, Nr Newbury, Berkshire RG20 9XX, England.

MEDVECZKY Adam, b. 1941, Budapest, Hungary. Conductor. Education: Timpanist Graduate, Bela Bartok Conservatory; Department of Conducting, Liszt Academy of Music, Budapest, 1968; Master Class, Maestro Franco Ferrara, Italy. Career: Timpanist, Hungarian State Symphony Orchestra for 9 years; Conductor, Budapest State Opera, 1974; Numerous guest appearances in Bulgaria, Germany, Greece, The Netherlands, Poland, Italy, Romania, Russia and USA; Professor, Ferenc Liszt Academy, Budapest, 1981-. Recordings: Has made numerous recordings. Honurs: Liszt Prize, 1976; 2nd Prize, Hungarian Television International Concours for Young Conductors, 1974.

MEEK Clarissa, b. 1970, England. Singer (Mezzo-soprano). Education: Guildhall School of Music and Drama. Career: Appearances with Scottish Opera in The Merry Widow, Street Scene, Figaro, The Magic Flute, Death in Venice, Jenufa and Salome; Iolanthe in the opera by Sullivan (also broadcast); Glyndebourne Festival as Mdme Larina in Eugene Onegin, Pauline (The Queen of Spades), Glasha (Katya Kabanova) and two roles in the premiere production of Birtwistle's Second Mrs Kong (1994); Season 1996-97 with Haydn's Stabat Mater at Aldeburgh, Thisbe (Cenerentola) in Japan and Maddalena in Rigoletto at Guernsey; Concerts include Messiah in Hanover and The Dream of Gerontius; Other operas include Les Boréades by Rameau, Tchaikovsky's The Enchantress and Monteverdi's Ulisse (as Penelope). Honours include: Erich Vietheer Memorial Award at Glyndebourne, 1995. Address: c/o C&M Craig Services, 3 Kersley Street, London SW11 4PR, England.

MEEK James, b. 29 July 1957, Winchester, England. Singer (Baritone). Education: Studied at the Guildhall School of Music. Career: Sang for three seasons at the Buxton Festival and appeared as Owen Wingrave at Aldeburgh; Other roles include Escamillo, Rossini's Figaro, Mozart's Count and Guglielmo, Valentin in Faust and the Doctor in Debussy's posthumous Fall of the House of Usher (Elizabeth Hall 1989); Sang in Haydn's La Vera Costanza in Germany; Concert repertoire includes Elijah, the Petite Messe Solennelle, Handel's Judas Maccabeus (Flanders Festival) Israel in Egypt and Dixit Dominus; Bach's Christmas Oratorio at the Snape Maltings, St John and St Matthew Passions; Britten's War Requiem in Germany and Yugoslavia and the Requiems of Mozart, Fauré and Brahms; Sang Messiah at the National Concert Hall Dublin, Pulcinella at the Barbican and the Missa Solemnis at Guilford Cathedral; Songs by Henri Dutilleux at Aldeburgh and concerts with the Songmakers' Almanac at the Bath, Nottingham, Buxton and Derby Festivals; Recitals on South Bank in the Schoenberg Reluctant Revolutionary Series, 1989 and Schubert directed by Hermann Prey, accompanied by Iain Burnside; Sang Starveling in A Midsummer Night's Dream at Aix-en-Provence, 1992.Address: c/o Ron Gonsalves Management, 5-7 Old Town, Clapham, London SW4 0JT, England.

MEER Rud van der, b. 23 Jun 1936, The Hague, Holland. Singer (Baritone), Education: Studied oboe and conducting at Royal Conservatory, The Hague; Vocal teachers include Pierre Bernac. Debut: As singer, 1967. Career: Played oboe in Hague Philharmonic Orchestra; Teacher at various grammar schools; Conductor of Choir in Holland; Recitalist and oratorio soloist in major centres including London, New York, Berlin, Paris, Vienna and Warsaw; Recitals for the BBC and at the Holland, Helsinki and English Bach Festivals; Bregenz Festival and The Belgian Festival of Flanders; Conductors include: Gerd Albrecht, Berio, Michel Corboz, Jean Fournet, Harnoncourt, Leitner, Pritchard and Hans Vonk; Performances with Elly Ameling in New York and London of Wolf's Italienisches Liederbuch and Spanisches Liederbuch; Moscow debut 1988 in the Sviatoslav Richter Festival at the Pushkin Museum; Tour of Russia in May 1989; BBC Recital, 1997; Permanent member of the jury of the International Singing Competiton of Hertogenbosch. Recordings: 30 discs of Lieder and Oratorio; 40 Bach Cantatas; Bach's St John Passion. Honours: Laureate of International Vocal Competitions of Hertogenbosch, Toulouse and Barcelona; Grand Prix du Disque, 1970 for St John Passion. Hobby: Ice Hockey. Address: c/o Music International, 13 Ardilaun Road, Highbury, London, N5 2QR, England.

MEGYERI Lajos, b. 5 May 1935, Backo Gradiste, Yugoslavia. Composer; Conductor; Professor. m. Toth Maria, 5 September 1959, 1 daughter. Education: Music Academy, Composing Line, Belgrade. Debut: Symphonic Movement with Introduction, Subotica, 1963. Career: Appearances in Germany, 1968, 1970, USA, 1972, Holland, 1973; Autor's Concerts in Subotica, 1969, 1995; Conductor, National Theatre Orchestra, Subotica, 1977-81. Compositions: Quatuor; Symphonic Movement with Introduction; Sonatina; Scherzo; Capriccio; Adagio; Variation; Suite, for Piano, 1989-91; Missa Hungarica, 1995. Recordings: Piano Album - Autor's LP, 1991; Sonatina, for Piano, 1994; Quatuor, 1995; Missa Hungarica, 1995-96. Honours: 1st Prize, Accordion Trio, World Festival, Luzern, 1968; 1st Prize, Gold Medal, Accordion Orchestra, Grand Prix European de L'Accordeon, France, 1972. Memberships: Organization of Composers in Yugoslavia; Alliance of Estrade Artists. Hobby: Electronics. Address: Nusiceva 2a, 24000 Subotica, Yugoslavia.

MEHNERT Thomas, b. 1966, Chemitz, Germany. Singer (Bass), Education: Studied at the Richard Strauus Conservatory, Munich, from 1991, The Munich Singschule. Career: Concert performances at the 1995 Rheingau Music Festival, and the Mozart Festival at Wurzburg; Engagement at the Cottbus Opera as Colline, Colas in Mozart's Bastien und Bastuenne, the Hermit in Der Freischütz Figaro and Banquo, from 1995; Guest appearances with Netherlands Opera as Pluto in Monteverdi's Orfeo and Fifth Solo Voice in Moses und Aron, Under Pierre Boulez (also at the Salzburg Festival); Royal Festival Hall, London, in Moses und Aron with the Philharmonia Orchestra under Christoph von Dohnányi, 1996. Honours include: Deutsche Buhnvereins Grant, 1993. Address: c/o Staatsoper Cottbus, Karl Liebnecht Strasse 136, 0-7500 Cottbus, Germany.

MEHTA Ramanlal C, b. 31 Oct 1918, Surat, India. Musician; Professor of Music. m. Shribala, 1 son, 2 daughters. Education: BA; DMus (Hon Cau). Career: Programme Executive, Music, All India Radio, Bombay-Ahmedabad-Baroda, 1945-53; Principal, College of Indian Music, Dance and Dramatics and Professor of Music, MS University, Baroda, 1954-76. Publications: Psychology of Music (Ed), 1980; Essays in Musicology, (Ed), 1983; Studies in Musicology, (Ed), 1983; Music and Mythology, (Ed), 1989; On Music, (Ed), 1989; Thumri-Tradition and Trends, (Ed), 1990. Contributions to: Journal of The Indian Musicological Society and others. Honours: Honorary Doctorate in Music, conferred by Akhil Gandharva Mahavidyalaya, Bombay, 1968; Emeritus Fellow, (Music), Government of India, 1984-86; Gujarat State Award for Music, 1978; Sarangdev Fellowship, Bombay, 1988; Award of Shreshtha Sangeet Acharya, Raipur, 1993. Memberships: Founder and Secretary, Indian Musicological Society; Vice Chairman, Gujarat Sangeet Natak Akademi, Gujarat, 1993. Current Management: Secretary, Indian Musicological Society, Jambu Bet, India. Address: Jambu Bet, Dandia Bazar, Baroda 390001, India.

MEHTA Zubin, b. 29 Apr 1936, Bombay, India. Conductor; Musician. m. (2) Nancy Diane Kovack, 19 July 1969, 1 son, 1 daughter from first marriage. Education: St Xavier's College, Bombay, India, 1951-53; State Academy of Music, Vienna, 1954-60. Career: Music Director, Montreal Symphony, Canada, 1961-67; Music Director, Los Angeles Philharmonic, 1962-78; Music Director for Life, Israel Philharmonic, 1969-; Music Director, New York Philharmonic, 1978-; Frequent Guest Conductor with: Philadelphia Orchestra, Berlin Philharmonic, Vienna Philharmonic, L'Orchestre de Paris, Maggio Musicale Fiorentino; Conducted Il Trovatore and Don Giovanni at Florence, 1990; Baths of Caracalla 1990, with three well known tenors; Conducted Wagner's Ring at Chicago, 1993; Season 1992 with a live Tosca at Rome for world-wide television, Aida with the Israel Philharmonic, Tosca at Covent Garden, La Forza del Destino and Le nozze di Figaro at the Maggio Musicale; Moses und Aron, 1994; Turandot and Ariadne auf Naxos, 1997. Recordings: Salome (Sony); Video of Tosca; CDs of Mozart's Sinfonia Concertante K364 and Concertone K190 (Israel Philharmonic), Tchaikovsky's 1st Piano Concerto and Violin Concerto (Gilels/Zukerman/NYPO); Khachaturian Violin Concerto (Perlman); Saint-Saëns 3rd Symphony (Los Angeles Philharmonic); Puccini La Fanciulla del West (Royal Opera House) and Turandot (Sutherland and Pavarotti); Bellini's I Puritani (Gruberova and Merritt). Honours: 1st Prize, Liverpool England International Conductors Competition, 1958; Decorated Padma Bhushan of India, 1967; Commendatore of Italy; Medaille d'Or Vermeil of the City of Paris; Honorary Citizen of Tel Aviv, 1986. Hobby: Cricket. Address: c/o Cynthia Meister, 27 Oakmont Drive, Los Angeles, CA 90049, USA.

MEI Eva, b. 1969, Fabiano, Italy. Singer (Soprano). Education: Studied at the Luigi Cherubini Conservatory, Florence. Career: Sang Mozart's Conztanze at the Vienna Staatsoper, 1990; Engaged at Zürich as Donna Anna, Alcina, Mozart's Countess and Luitgarde in Schubert's Des Teufels Lustschloss; Covent Garden debut as the Queen of The Night, Berlin Staatsoper as Violetta; La Scala debut as Amenaide in Tancredi, 1993; Rossini Festival at Pesaro as Fanny in La Cambiale di Matrimonio and Berenice in L'Occasione fa il ladro, 1995-96; Vienna Festival as Genio in Haydn's Orfeo ed Euridice, 1995; Concert engagements at the Amsterdam Concertgebouw, Queen Elizabeth Hall (London), Academia di Santa Cecilia (Rome) and halls in Buenos Aires, Vienna, St Petersburg and Moscow. Recordings include: A Mezzanote, songs by Bellini, Rossini and Donizetti; Rossini's Tancredi and Mozart's Il re Pastore. Honours include: Caterina Cavalieri Prize at the 1990 Mozart Competition, Vienna. Address: c/o Opernhaus Zürich, Falkenstrasse 1, CH-8008 Zürich, Switzerland.

MEIER Jaroslav, b. 7 Dec 1923, Hronov, Czechoslovakia. Composer. m. Marta Kurbelova, 1950, 2 sons. Education: Organ, Academy of Music, Prague, 1939-44; Organ and Composition, Academy of Music, Bratislava, 1947-49. Career: Head of Music Department, Radio Bratislava, 1949-56; Head of Music Department, Czechoslovakia TV, Bratislava, 1956-; Music Designer (a lot of TV and radio plays and films). Compositions:

Opera Erindo (rewriting opera by baroque composer J S Kusser); TV opera The Night before Immortality (libretto after A Arbuzov); Opera, The Wooden Shoes (libretto after Guy de Maupassant); Orchestral works, Dances from my Country; Songs from my Country; What a Smell (song cycle based on Stefan Zary's poems); Concerto da Camera for organ and orchestra, 1982. Recordings: Chamber Music, Trois Impromptus; Prelude and Double Fugue; Divine Love; The Cycle Nocturnal Songs; Toccata et fuga, Fantasia concertante. Publications: Obrazovka pina hudby, (The Screen full of Music), 1970; Johann Sigismund Kusser, 1986. Contributions to: Slovenska hudba (Slovak Music); Hudebni zivot (Music Life); Czeskoslovenska televize (TV weekly paper). Honours: Prize of Critics at the International TV Festival The Golden Prague, 1976, for TV opera The Night before Immortality. Memberships: Union of Czechoslovak Composers; IMZ. Address: Palackého 407, 54931 Hronov, Czech Republic.

MEIER Johanna, b. 13 Feb 1938, Chicago, USA. Singer (Soprano). m. Guido Della Vecchia. Education: Studied at the University of Miami with Arturo di Filippi and at the Manhattan School with John Brownlee. Debut: New York City Opera 1969, as the Countess in Capriccio. Career: Sang with the City Opera as Donna Anna, Senta, Louise and Tosca; Metropolitan Opera from 1976, as Marguerite, Ariadne, the Marschallin, Ellen Orford, Chrysothemis, Elisabeth, Brünnhilde in Die Walküre and Kaiserin; Guest engagements in Seattle, Washington, Philadelphia, San Diego, Ottawa and Chicago; Other roles include Sieglinde, Musetta, Mozart's Countess, Amelia (Un ballo in Maschera), Agathe and Eva; Bayreuth Festival debut 1981, as Isolde; Vienna Staatsoper from 1983, Fidelio and Senta; Tour of Japan 1986, as Isolde and the Marschallin; Barcelona and Buenos Aires 1987, as Elisabeth in Tannhäuser and Chrysothemis; Sang Turandot at Dallas and New Orleans, 1987-88; Ariadne at Trieste, 1988; Pittsburgh Opera, 1989, as Chrysothemis; The Dyer's Wife in Die Frau ohne Schatten at the 1990 Holland Festival. Address: c/o Metropolitan Opera, Lincoln Center, NY 10023, USA.

MEIER Jost, b. 15 Mar 1939, Solothurn, Switzerland. Composer; Conductor. Education: Studied at the Berne Conservatory and with Frank Martin in Holland. Career: Conducted at the Biel Opera, 1968-79, Basle, 1980-83. Compositions include: Sennentuntschi, dramatic legend, Freiburg, 1983; Der Drache, opera in 2 acts, Basle, 1985; Der Zoobar, opera in 4 scenes, Zurich, 1987; Augustin, opera in 4 scenes, Basle, 1988; Dreyfus, opera, Berlin (Deutsche Oper), 1994. Address: c/o Deutsche Oper Berlin, Richard Wagnerstrasse 10, D-1000 Berlin, Germany.

MEIER Waltraud, b. 9 Jan 1956, Wurzburg, Germany. Singer (Mezzo-soprano). Education: Studied with Dietger Jacob in Cologne. Career: Sang in Wurzburg from 1976 as Cherubino, Dorabella, Nicklaus in Les Contes d'Hoffmann and Concepcion in L'Heure Espagnole, Mannheim 1978-80, as Carmen, Fricka, Waltraute and Octavian; Dortmund 1980-83, as Kundry in Parsifal, Eboli in Don Carlos and as Santuzza in Cavalleria Rusticana; Guest appearances in Cologne, Hamburg, Buenos Aires, Opera de Paris, Staatsoper Wien, Scala di Milano, San Francisco Opera, Munich, Bayreuth from 1983; Sang Kundry in Götz Friedrich's production of Parsifal, Brangäne in Tristan und Isolde, and Waltraute in Harry Kupfer's 1988 production of The Ring; Covent Garden debut 1985, as Eboli, returned to London 1988, as Kundry; Made her Metropolitan Opera debut in 1987 as Fricka in Rheingold and Walküre; Other roles include Azucena (Il Trovatore), Venus (Tannhäuser), the Composer (Ariadne auf Naxos); Sang Venus at Hamburg, 1990; Debut at the Teatro San Carlos, Lisbon, 1990 as Ortrud in Lohengrin; Théâtre du Châtelet, Paris, 1990 as Marguerite in La Damnation de Faust; Sang Waltraute at the Bayreuth Festival, 1988-92, Tchaikovsky's Maid of Orleans at Munich; Season 1992-93 as Kundry at La Scala and the Metropolitan, Berg's Marie at the Théâtre du Châtelet, Paris, and since 1993 as Isolde at Bayreuth; Sang Sieglinde at the Vienna Staatsoper and La Scala, Milan, 1994; Carmen at the Metropolitan, 1997; Engaged as Leonore at Munich, 2000; Also heard as a concert singer, in Brahms, Mahler and Verdi. Recordings include: Opera: Dittersdorf's Doktor und Apotheker; Venus and Kundry; Brahms Alto Rhapsody; Fricka in James Levine's Die Walküre, Wesendonk and Kindertotenlieder, Missa Solemnis, Mozart Requiem; Wagner recital with the Symphonieorchester des Bayerischen Rundfunks under Lorin Maazel, 1997. Honours: Recipient of several prestigious prizes; Holds titles of Bayerische Kammersängerin at the Bavarian State Opera and Kammersängerin at the Vienna State Opera. Address: PO Box 100262, Bayreuther Festspele, 95402 Bayreuth, Germany.

MEIGS Melinda (Moore), b. 28 Nov 1953, Michigan, USA. Singer; Harpsichordist; Teacher; Performer. Education: BA, Smith College, Massachusetts, 1975; BMus, 1975; Studies with Ilse Wolf, Ronald Murdoch, Lory Wallfisch; Masterclass with Gustav Leonhardt. Debut: Lieder Recital, Boston, Massachusetts, 1975; Harpsichord Concert, Northampton, Massachusetts, 1975. Career: Tours throughout Europe, USA and Canada as Soloist, Accompanist and Soprano Soloist in Vivaldi Gloria and Bach Magnificat with choir; Appearances on Athens TV; Broadcast on Paris Radio. Compositions: Glissando, for tape recorder, 1981; Spirit Healer, for voices and voice and cello, 1986. Recordings: Spanish Villancicos on Diverse Winds, cantatas of Boismortier, Caldara and Telemann. Honour: Phi Beta Kappa, 1975. Membership: Incorporated Society of Musicians. Hobbies: Travel; Reading; Walking. Address: 261 Grove Street, London SE8 3PZ, England.

MEKLER Mani, b. 1951, Haifa, Israel. Singer (Soprano). Education: Studied in Italy. Career: Sang Leonora in Il Travatore at Stockholm and with Welsh National Opera, 1976, 1977; Glyndebourne debut 1978, as First Lady in Die Zauberflöte; Wexford Festival 1979, as Giulia in Spontini's La Vestale; Deutsche Oper am Rhein, Dusseldorf, from 1979 as Janacek's Jenufa and Mila (Osud) and Chrysothemis; Further appearances at Drottningholm, Zurich and Milan, La Scala (premiere of Testi's Riccardo III, 1987); Other roles include Puccini's Manon Lescaut, Tosca and Butterfly, Strauss's Salome and Ariadne, and Goneril in Reimann's Lear.

MELBY John B, b. 3 Oct 1941, Wisconsin, USA. Composer. m. Jane H Thompson, 15 June 1978, 2 sons, 1 daughter. Education: Diploma, 1964, BMus, 1966, Curtis Institute of Music; MA, University of Pennsylvania, 1967; MFA, 1971, PhD, 1972, Princeton University. Career: Currently Professor of Music, University of Illinois, Urbana. Compositions include: ...Of Quiet Desperation for computer-synthesized tape, 1976; Concerto No 1 for violin and computer-synthesized tape, 1979, No 2, 1986; Layers for computer-synthesized tape, 1981; Wind, Sand, and Stars for 8 instruments and computer-synthesized tape, 1983; Concerto for violin, English horn and computer-synthesized tape, 1984; Concerto for computer-synthesized tape and orchestra, 1987; Symphony No 1, 1993; The rest is silence... for organ, 1994; Other concerti, songs and keyboard works. Recordings include: 91 Plus 5 for brass quintet and computer-synthesized tape; Forandre: 7 variations for digital computer; Two Stevens Songs for soprano and computer-synthesized tape; Concerto for violin, English horn and computer-synthesized tape; Concerto No 1 for violin and computer-synthesized tape; Concerto Nos 1 and 2 for flute and computer-synthesized tape; Chor der Steine; Chor der Waisen. Publications: Some recent developments in computer-synthesized music, 1973; Proceedings of the 1975 Music Computation Conference (edited with James Beauchamp), 1976; 'Layers': An approach to composition for computer based upon the concept of structural levels, 1983; 'Computer' Music or Computer 'Music', 1989. Contributions to: Reviews to Contemporary Music Newsletter, 1969-71. Honours include: 1st Prize, 7th International Electroacoustic Music Awards, Bourges, France, 1979; Guggenheim Fellowship; American Academy of Arts and Letters Award. Memberships: BMI; American Composers' Alliance. Address: School of Music, 2136 Music Building, 1114 West Nevada, University of Illinois, Urbana, IL 61801, USA.

MELBYE Mikael, b. 15 Mar 1955, Frederiksberg, Denmark. Baritone; Stage Director; Designer. Education: Royal Danish Conservatory, Copenhagen. Debut: As Guglielmo in Così fan tutte, Royal Danish Opera, 1976. Career: Vast repertoire of mostly lyric baritone roles including Mozart, Rossini, Donizetti, Verdi and Puccini; First appearance outside Denmark was in the Spoleto Festival, 1981 as Danilo in The Merry Widow; He has since appeaed in opera houses all over the world including La Scala di Milano, Paris Opera, Aix en Provence Festival, Théâtre du Châtelet, Covent Garden, Munich, Hamburg, Metropolitan Opera (Papageno, 1995), Dallas Civic Opera, Santa Fe Opera; Currently pursuing, in addition to his singing, a career as Director and Stage Designer; Directed, designed and performed in Così fan tutte at the Royal Danish Opera, 1995; Directed and designed the first ever performance of Turandot at the Royal Danish Opera, 1995; Director, Arabella, in 1997. Recordings include: Carmen (Karajan), Die Zauberflöte (Colin Davis). Honours: Won Golden Pegasus Award, Italy; Oberdörfer Preis, Germany; Gladsaxe Music Award; OV Award for best production (Turandot), Denmark. Address: c/o Lies Askonas, 6 Henrietta Street, London WC2E 8LA, England.

MELCHER Wilhelm, b. 5 Apr 1940, Hamburg, Germany. Violinist. Education: Studied in Hamburg and Rome. Career: Leader of the Hamburg SO, 1963; Former Member of Karl Munchinger's Stuttgart Chamber Orchestra, Heilbroon; Co-Founder, Melos Quartet of Stuttgart, 1965; Represented West Germany at the Jeuness Musicales in Paris, 1966; International concert tours from 1967; Bicentenary concerts in the Beethoven Haus at Bonn, 1970; British concerts and festival appearances from 1974; Cycle of Beethoven quartets at Edinburgh Festival, 1987; Wigmore Hall, St John's Smith Square and Bath Festival, 1990; Associations with Rostropovitch in the Schubert Quintet and the Cleveland Quartet in works by Spohr and Mendelssohn; Teacher, Stuttgart Musikhochschule. Recordings include: Complete quartets of Beethoven, Schubert, Mozart and Brahms; Quintets by Boccherini with Narciso Ypes and by Mozart with Frank Beyer. Honours: Grand Prix du Disque and Prix Caecilia, Academie du Disque, Brussels (with Melos Quartet). Address: c/o Ingpen & Williams Ltd, 26 Wadham Road, London SW15 2LR, England.

MELCHERT Helmut, b. 24 Dept 1910, Kiel, Germany. Singer (Tenor). Education: Studied at the hamburg Musikhochschule. Debut: Began as a concert singer, 1936. Career: Sang at Wuppertal Opera from 1939; Member of Hamburg Opera, 1943-77, notably in Wagner roles and as the Elector in the 1960 premiere of Henze's Der Prinz von Homburg; Guest appearances in Berlin, London, Dusseldorf, Munich and Amsterdam; Edinburgh 1956, as Stravinsky's Oedipus; Zurich 1957, as Aron in the stage premiere of Schoenberg's Moses und Aron; Salzburg Festival 1966, in the premiere of Henze's The Bassarids; Taught singing at the Hamburg Musikhochschule. Recordings: Salome (HMV); Wozzeck and Die Verurteilung des Lukullus by Dessau; Moses und Aron; Karl V by Krenek. Address: c/o Hamburgische Staatsoper, Grosse Theaterstrasse 34, D-2000 Hamburg 36, Germany.

MELIS György, b. 2 July 1923, Szarvas, Hungary. Singer (Baritone). Education: Studied at the Budapest Academy of Music, with Olga Relevhegyi. Debut: Budapest Opera 1949, as Morales in Carmen. Career: Many appearances in the major baritone roles of Mozart and Verdi; Sang Don Giovanni at Glyndebourne in 1961, and in Brussels, Berlin and Moscow; Further engagements in Edinburgh, (Bartok's Bluebeard 1973), Vienna and South America; Sang Don Giovanni at Wiesbaden 1987, as guest with the Hungarian State Opera (Bluebeard at Covent Garden 1989); Also heard in concert and oratorio; Song recitals include music by Bartok and Kodaly. Recordings: Kodaly's Hary Janos and Budavari Te Deum; Don Giovanni; Rigoletto; Szokolay's Samson; Title role in Bluebeard's Castle by Bartók, conducted by Fricasy; Scala Milano, Bartok's Bluebeard, 1978. Honour: Kossuth Prize 1962. Address: Hungarian State Opera, Népöztarsasag utja 22, 1061 Budapest, Hungary.

MELKUS Eduard, b. 1 Sept 1928, Baden, Austria. Violinist. m. Marlis Melkus-Selzer, 4 children. Education: Studied violin with Ernst Moravec 1942-53, Firmin Touche, Alexander Schaizhet and Peter Rybar; Musicology at Vienna University with Erich Schenk. Debut: Vienna 1944. Career: Founded Eduard Melkus Ensemble and Capella Academia, 1965, playing mainly on original instruments of the 18th Century; Professor of Violin and Viola at the Vienna Hochschule für Musik from 1958; Concerts in all Europe, USA, Australia, Japan, South America; Visiting Professor, University of Georgia, USA, 1973-74, University of Illinois and others; Lectures and master classes in many Universities all over the world. Recordings: Concertos by Bach, Tartini, Vivaldi, Haydn; sonatas by Biber, Corelli, Bach, Mozart and Handel; Solo violin music by Bach, Haydn's La Vera Costanza at the Schönbrunn Palace, Vienna, 1984 (TV). Publications: Die Violine, Schott, many articles on interpretation. Honours include: Kornerpreis 1967; Edison Prize, Prix Academia Charles C Gross; Great Cross of Honour of the Republic of Austria. Memberships: Ex-President, Austria ESTA. Hobbies: Studies of fine art; Music; Collecting old Violins and Fine Art. Address: 1020 Wien 2, Obere Donaustrasse 57/14, Austria.

MELLERS Wilfrid (Howard), b. 26 April 1914, Leamington, Warwickshire, England. Composer; Author; University Professor (retired). m. (1) Vera Muriel Hobbs, (2) Pauline PeggyLewis, 3 daughters, (3) Robin Stephanie Hildyard; Education: BA (Cantab), 1936; MA (Cantab), 1939; DMus, University of Birmingham, 1960; DPhil, City University, 1980; FGSM, 1982; Studied with Egon Wellesz and Edmund Rubbra. Career: College Supervisor in English, Lecturer in Music, Downing College, Cambridge, 1945-48; Staff Tutor in Music, Extra-Mural Department, University of Birmingham, 1948-59; Andrew Mellon Professor of Music, University of Pittsburgh, 1960-63; Professor of Music, University of York, England, 1964-81; Visiting Professor, City University, 1984-; Organiser, Attingham Park Summer School of Music, 13 years; Lecturer in Australia, USA, Canada; Work for radio and TV. Compositions: About 50 including Life Cycle, 3 choirs, 2 orchestras; A May Magnificat; Sun-flower; Rosae Hermeticae; Spells, soprano, chamber ensemble; The Ancient Wound, monodrama; Venery fir Six Plus; Chants and Litanies of Carl Sandberg; Yeibichai, coloratura soprano, scat singer, jazz trio, orchestra, tape (Proms commission). Recordings include: Voices and Creatures; The Wellspring of Loves; Rose of May; Life-Cycle. Publciations: 20 books including Studies in Contemporary Music, 1948; Francois Couperin, 1950, revised and expanded edition, 1984; Man and His Music, 2 vols, numerous editions and translations; The Masks of Orpheus, 1987; Vaughan Williams and the Vision of Albion, 1989; Le Jardin Retrouvé: Homage to Federico Mompou, 1990; The Music of Percy Grainger, 1992; Francis Poulenc, 1993. Contributions to: Currently writes regularly for the Times Literary Supplement. Honours: Honorary DPhil, City University, 1981; Hon FGSM, 1982; OBE, 1982; Professor Emeritus, University of York, 1984. Membership: Sonneck Society. Address: Oliver Sheldon House, 17 Aldwark, York YO1 2BX, England.

MELLES Carl, b. 15 July 1926, Budapest, Hungary. Conductor. m. Gertrud Dertnig, 1 son, 1 daughter. Career: Studied in Budapest. Career: Conductor of the Hungarian State Orchestra, 1951; Conductor of the Symphony Orchestra of Hungarian Radio and Television; Professor at the Budapest Academy of Music, 1954-56; Left Hungary during the revolution of 1956; Conductor of the Radio Orchestra of Luxembourg, 1958-60; Conductor of major orchestras including New Philharmonia and the Vienna and Berlin Philharmonics; Salzburg and Bayreuth Festivals; Concert tours of Japan, South Africa and Europe; Regular conductor of the Vienna Symphony Orchestra and on Austrian Radio. Recordings: Mozart Piano Concertos K459 and K466 (Ingrid Haebler, Vienna Symphony Orchestra). Honour include: Franz Liszt Prize, Budapest, 1956. Address: Grundbergstrasse 4, 1130 Vienna, Austria.

MELLNAS Arne, b. 30 Aug 1933, Stockholm, Sweden. Composer. 1 son. Education: Royal College of Music, Stockholm; Further study with Boris Blacher, Max Deutsch and György Ligeti, 1959-62. Career: Active at the San Francisco Tape Music Center, 1964; Teacher, Stockholm Citizens School, 1961-63; Royal College of Music, 1963-86; Chairman, ISCM Swedish Section, 1984-96; President, ISLM, 1997. Compositions include: Orchestral works: Collage, 1962; Aura, 1964; Transparence, 1972; Moments musicaux, 1977; Capriccio, 1978; Symphony No 1, Ikaros, 1986; Passages, 1989; Intimate Games, Concerto for flute and chamber orchestra, 1992; Chamber music: Quasi niente for string trio, 1968; Sub luna for soprano and ensemble, 1973; Rendez-vous 1-5, Duo works for various instruments, 1979-97; Nocturnes for mezzosoprano and ensemble, 1980; Riflessioni for clarinet and tape, 1981; Stampede for saxophone quartet, 1985; Gardens for ensemble, 1986; Enymion for ensemble, 1993; String Quartet no 1, Hommages, 1993; Like raindrops, pearls on velvet, for ensemble, 1996; Mixed choir a cappela: Succsim, 1967; Aglepta, childrens choir, 1969; Dream, 1970; Bossa buffa, 1973; A wind has blown, 1973; 10 Proverbs, 1981; L'Infinito, 1982; Laude, 1994; Kosmos, 1994; Sweet Spring, 1994-97; Operas: The Canterville Ghost, chamber opera, 1980; Bed of Roses, chamber opera, 1984; Doktor Glas, 1990. Membership: Royal Swedish Academy. Address: c/o Swedish MIC, P O Box 27327, S-102 54 Stockholm, Sweden.

MELLON Agnès, b. 17 Jan 1958, Epinay-sur-Seine, France. Singer (Soprano). m. Dominique Visse. Education: Studied in Paris and San Francisco. Career: Sang with the Paris Opéra and the Opéra-Comique; Later appearances in the Baroque repertoire, notably as Tibrino in Cesti's Orontea at the 1986 Innsbruck Early Music Festival, Eryxene in Hasse's Cleofide, 1987 and Telaire in Rameau's Castor et Pollux at the 1991 Aix-en-Provence Festival; Sang the title role in Rossi's Orfeo at the Queen Elizabeth Hall, London, with Les Arts Florissants, 1990; Sang on Mondonville's Les Festes de Paphos at Versailles, 1996. Recordings include: Rossi's Orfeo, Cavalli's Xerxes, Lully's Atys, Charpentier's Médée and David et Jonathas, Hasse's Cleofide, Rameau's Anacréon and Zoroastre; Labels include Erato and Harmonia Mundi.

MELLOR Alwyn, b. 1968, Rawtenstall, Lancashire, England. Singer (Soprano). Education: Royal Northern College of Music, with further study in Italy and St Petersburg. Career: Roles with Welsh National Opera (from 1992) have included Tatiana, Ginevra in Ariodante, Liu, Fiordiligi, Marguerite; Anne Trulove, and Micaela; Donna Elvira for WNO and Glyndebourne Touring Opera, Fiordiligi at Sante Fe (1997); Concerts include Edinburgh Festival with the Scottish Chamber Orchestra; Die Schöpfung in Amsterdam with the Bach Soloists under Marc Minkowski, 1993; US debut with the Kansas City Camerata, 1996; Season 1997 with Britten's Spring Symphony (Rotterdam PO under Donald Runnicles). Recordings include: Elsie in Yeomen of the Guard, with WNO. Honours include: Awards from the Peter Moores Foundation. Address: c/o Ingpen & Williams Ltd, 26 Wadham Road, London SW15 2LR, England.

MELNIKOV Alexander, b. 1973, Russia. Concert Pianist. Education: Moscow Tchaikovsky Conservatory, with Lev Naumov, from 1991. Career: Regular guest at international festivals, including the Schleswig-Holstein (Germany), Yehudi Menuhin (Switzerland), Styrian Festival (Austria) and the Bashmet Festival at Bonn; Recitals throughout Europe, America and the Far East, concertos with such conductors as Gergiev, Lazarev and Fedoseyev; Chamber music with Vadim Repin, Boris Pergemenschikov and the Shostakovich Quartet; Performs regularly in Japan in recitals and concertos with the Japan Philharmonic, recitals in Toronto with Vodim Repin (violin); Solo recitals in the USA, Luxembourg, London, Paris and Moscow; Repertoire includes Beethoven, Grieg, Schumann and Schubert. Honours include: Laureate of the Robert Schumann Competition, Zwickau, 1989; Queen Elizabeth of Belgium Competition, Brussels, 1991. Address: c/o IMG Artists, Media House, 3 Burlington Lane, London W4 2TH, England.

MELNYK Lubomyr (Eugene), b. 22 Dec 1948, Munich, Germany. Composer; Pianist. m. Karin Haerdin, 8 May 1978, 2 d. Education: MA, Queen's University, Kingston, 1971; BA, University of Manitoba, 1969; ARCT, Conservatory of Music, Toronto. Career: Pioneered the Continuos Technique for piano; Recorded over 15 works for radio in Canada and Europe; Has written full length score for 6 modern ballets premiered in Lyon, New York, Stockholm and Paris; Over 200 concerts given to date. Compositions: Major ballet works include Voice of Trees, The Eastern Horn, Islands, Page Music, 4 Symphonies; Over 90 pieces for piano or piano ensemble; 2 String Quartets in the Continuous mode. Recordings: KMH; Poslaniye, Lund-St Petri Symphony; The Song of Galadriel; Concert Requiem; A Portrait of Petlurs on The Day he Was Killed. Publications: Open Time: The Art of Continuous Music, 1981; Circular Pieces: 22 Etudes for Piano, 1982. Address: c/o Haerdin, Kadettu 3-F, 19040 Roserberg, Sweden.

MENARD Pierre, b. 1945, Quebec, Canada. Violinist. Education: Studied at Quebec Conservatory and at Juilliard with Dorothy DeLay, Ivan Galamian and the Juilliard Quartet. Career: Solo appearances in Canada and the USA; Former Concertmaster of the Aspen Festival Orchestra and the Nashville Symphony; Co-Founder and Second Violinist of the Vermeer Quartet from 1970; Performances in most North American centres, Europe, Israel and Australia; Festival engagements at Tanglewood, Aspen, Spoleto, Berlin, Edinburgh, mostly Mozart (New York), Aldeburgh, South Bank, Santa Fe Chamber Music West, and the Casals Festival; Resident Quartet for Chamber Music Chicago; Master classes at the Royal Northern College of Music, Manchester; Member of the Resident Artists Faculty of Northern Illinois University. Recordings: Quartet by Beethoven, Dvorak, Verdi and Schubert (Teldec); Brahms Clarinet Quintet with Karl Leister (Orfeo). Honours: 1st Prize in Chamber Music, Quebec Conservatory; Winner, National Festival of Music Competition; Prix d'Europe from the Quebec Government. Address: Allied Artists, 42 Montpelier Square, London SW7 1JZ, England.

MENESES Antonio, b. 23 Aug 1957, Refice, Brazil. Concert Cellist. Education: Studied with the late Antonio Janigro in Dusseldorf and Stuttgart. Career: Has appeared widely in Europe and America from 1977; Appearances with the Berlin Philharmonic conduced by Karajan, with the London Symphony Orchestra in London and the USA, and with the Israel Philharmonic, Vienna Philharmonic and Concertgebouw Orchestras; Other conductors include Abbado, Previn, Maazel and Muti; Tours of Australia 1984, 1987; Engagements at the Lucerne and the Salzburg Easter Festivals, with the Berlin Philharmonic. Recordings include: Brahms Double Concerto, with Anne-Sophie Mutter; Strauss Don Quixote, conducted by Karajan (Deutsche Grammophon). Honours include: 2nd Prize at International Competitions in Barcelona and Rio de Janeiro; 1st Prize at ARD Competition, Munich, 1977; Gold Medal, Tchaikovsky International Competition, Moscow, 1982.

MENKOVA Irina, b. 1960, Moscow, Russia. Violinist. Career: Co-founder, Glazunov Quartet, 1985; Concerts in the former Soviet Union and recent appearances in Greece, Belgium, Poland, Germany and Italy; Works by Beethoven and Schumann at the Beethoven Haus in Bonn; Further engagements in Canada and Holland; Teacher, Moscow State Conservatoire and Resident at the Tchaikovsky Conservatoire; repertoire includes works by Borodin, Shostakovich and Tchaikovsky, in addition to the standard works. Recordings: Tchaikovsky on Olympia label. Honours: Prizewinner, Borodin Quartet and Shostakovich Chamber Music Competitions, with the Glazunov Quartet. Current Management: Sonata, Glasgow, Scotland. Address: 11 Northpark Street, Glasgow G20 7AA, Scotland.

MENOTTI Gian Carlo, 7 July 1911, Cadegliano, Italy. Composer; Stage Director. 1 son (adopted). Education: Curtis Institute of Music, Philadelphia, Pennsylvania. Career: Went to USA 1928; Member of Teaching Staff, Curtis Institute of Music, 1941-45; Founder and President, Festival of TwoWorlds, Spoleto, Italy and Charleston, South Carolina; Die Frau ohne Schatten and Handel's Semele at the 1997 Spoleto (Italy) Festival. Compositions include: Operas: Amelia Goes To The Ball; The Old Maid And The Thief; The Island God; The Telephone; the Medium; The Consul; Amahl and The Night Visitors; The Labyrinth (own libretti); The Saint of Bleecker Street 1954; The Last Savage 1963; Martin's Lie 1964; Help, Help, The Globolinks (Space Opera for Children) 1968; The Most Important Man in The World 1971; Tamu Tamu 1973; Hero 1976; La Loca 1979; Song of Hope (Cantata) 1980; St Teresa 1982; The Boy Who Grew Too Fast 1982; Goya - premiere at Washington Opera 1986; The Wedding, premiere at Seoul, South Korea 1988; Ballet: Sebastian; Film: The Medium (Producer); Vanessa (libertto) 1958; The Unicorn, The Gorgon and The Manticore - a Madrigal Fable, Maria Golovin 1959; The Death of The Bishop of Brindisi (Cantata) 1963; Chamber Music Songs: For The Death of Orpheus, for tenor, chorus and orchestra, 1990. Honours: Hon BM (Curtis Institute of Music); Guggenheim Award 1946, 1947; Pulitzer Prize 1950, 1955; Kennedy Centre Award 1984; New York City Mayor's Liberty Award, 1986; Hon Association national Institute of Arts and Letters 1953; Richard Tucker Award, 1988. Address: ASCAP Building, One Lincoln Plaza, NY 10023, USA.

MENTZER Susanne, b. 21 Jan 1957, Philadelphia, USA. Singer (Mezzo-soprano). Education: Juilliard School, New York and with Norma Newton. Debut: Houston Opera 1981, as Albina in La Donna del Lago. Career: Appeared with Dallas Opera 1982, in Gianni Scicchi and Das Rheingold; Washington Opera as Cherubino; Chicago Lyric Opera, Phladelpha Opera and New York City Opera as Rosina in Il Barbiere di Siviglia; Houston Opera as Rossini's Isolier, and at Rossini Festival Pesaro, Italy, the Composer in Ariadne auf Naxos and Giovanna Seymour in Anna Bolena; European debut with Cologne Opera 1983, as Cherubino, later Massenet's Cendrillon; La Scala Milan as Zerlina in Don Giovanni; Vienna Staatsoper as Cherubino; Covent Garden debut 1985, as Rosina, returned as Giovanna Seymour 1988, and Dorabella in Cosi fan tutte 1989; Metropolitan Opera debut 1989, as Cherubino; Monte Carlo 1988, as Adalgisa in Norma; Sang Octavian at the Théâtre des Champs-Elysées, Paris 1989; Annius in La Clemenza di Tito at La Scala, 1990 and Sesto in the Chicago premiere of Mozart's opera, 1991; Salzburg Festival, Cherubino and Zerlina, Metropolitan Opera, Idamante, 1991; In Les Contes d'Hoffmann as Nicklausse, Octavian in Der Rosenkavalier, Composer in Ariadne auf Naxos, Metropolitan Opera, 1992-93; Geneviève in Pelléas et Mélisande at the Palais Garnier, Paris, 1997; Romeo at the Opéra Bastille. Recordings include: Anna Bolena with Sutherland and Bonynge and Bruckner Te Deum on Philips label, Mozart Masses with King's College Choir; Barber of Seville, EMI, (Rosina); Idomeneo, Philips, (Idamante); Don Giovanni, EMI (Zerlina). Current Management: IMG Artists Europe. Address: c/o IMG Artists Europe, Media House, 3 Burlington Lane, Chiswick, London W4 2TH, England.

MENUHIN Jeremy, b. 2 Nov 1951, San Francisco, California, USA. Pianist. Education: Paris with Nadio Boulanger, Israel with Mindru Katz (piano), Vienna with Hans Swarowsky (conducting). Career: Public performances from 1965; New York recital debut, 1984; Berlin Philharmonic, 1984; Dame Myra Hess series, Chicago, 1985; Regular recitals, Kennedy Center (Washington DC), Berlin Philharmonie, Amsterdam Concertgebouw, La Salle Pleyel; US tours with Czech Philharmonic and Prague Chamber Orchestra, 1989; Guest appearances, San Francisco and Houston Symphonies; European orchestras include BBC, Royal and Amsterdam Philharmonics, Salzburg Mozarteum, Orchestre National de France; 1987-88 season included Windsor Festival concert with English Chamber Orchestra; Beethoven's 1st concerto with Leningrad Philharmonic conducted by Yehudi Menuhin; 1989 European concert tour with Toulouse Chamber Orchestra; Chamber music with cellists Colin Carr, Steven Isserlis, Marius May; Recitals with sopranos Edith Mahis and Arleen Auger, Aldeburgh, 1987; With Hallé Orchestra, Zurich Tonhalle Orchestra, Sinfonia Varsovia, 1994; Tour of Germany, Czech Republic and Poland with Philharmonia Hungarica (Schumann, Bartók's 3rd Piano Concerto); Bath Festival with English Symphony Orchestra; Beethoven's 5th Piano Concerto with Orchestra of St John's Smith Square; Tour of Russia and further concerts throughout Europe, 1995; St Nazaire Festival, Wigmore Hall, and other festivals. Recordings include: Works by Schubert, Mozart, Debussy, Beethoven; Bartok's 2 violin sonatas with father, Yehudi Menuhin; Dvorák Quartet and Quintet with Chilingirian Quartet. Honours: Grand Prix de Disque, 1981. Address: c/o Diana Walters Artists Management, Ivey Cottage, 3 Main Stret, Keyham, Leicestershire LE7 9JQ, England.

MENUHIN Yalta, b. 7 Oct 1921, San Francisco, California, USA. Concert Pianist. m. Joel Ryce, 2 sons. Education: Studied piano with Marcel Ciampi in Paris and with Carl Friedberg at the Juilliard School, New York. Career: Has appeared worldwide as soloist and with leading instrumentalists; Duo pianist with husband Joel Ryce; Appearances at leading European festivals; TV appearances in Paris, London, New York and Geneva. Recordings: Several solo and duo piano works for Everest, EMI, World Record Club and Deutsche Grammophon. Honours: 1st Prize with Joel Ryce, Harriet Cohen International Music Award, 1962.

MENUHIN Yehudi (Lord), b. 22 Apr 1916, New York, USA. Violinist; Conductor. m. (1) Nola Ruby Nicholas, 1938, 1 s, 1 d, (2) Diana Rosamond Gould, 1947, 2 s. Education: Privately in USA and Europe; Studied with Sigmund Anker, Louis Persinger, Georges Enesco, Romania, and Adolph Busch, Basel. Debut: New York, 1925; Paris, 1927; Berlin, 1929, with Bruno Walter and The Berlin Philharmonic. Career includes: First world tour 1935; Appeared as soloist in orchestras under many leading conductors; Researched and restored many neglected compositions; Gave numerous benefit concerts during and after World War II; Gave premiere of Bartók's Solo Violin Sonata, 1944; Since 1945: Toured extensively worldwide; Made documentary musical films in Europe and USA; Founded Yehudi Menuhin School, Surrey, 1963; Yearly Festival at Gstaad, 1957-, Bath 1959-68, Windsor, 1969-72; Appeared in film, Raga, 1974; Founder Chairman, Live Music Now, 1977; President, Royal

Philharmonic, 1982-; Recent conducting engagements include Beethoven Symphony series with the Warsaw Sinfonia (1997). Recordings include: CDs of Baroque Favourites (Vivaldi and Corelli; Classics for Pleasure); Elgar Music for Strings (Arabesque); Menuhin Birthday Edition (5 CD's), released April 1991, for 75th birthday; Concertos by Sibelius, Nielsen, Bloch, Berg, Bartók (No 1 and Viola), Beethoven and Mendelssohn; Ravel, Piano Trio, Brahms Horn Trio and chamber music by Debussy, Schubert and Mendelssohn (HMV/EMI). Publications include: The Violin - Six Lessons with Yehudi Menuhin, 1971; The Violin, 1976; Sir Edward Elgar: My Musical Grandfather, 1976; Autobiography, Unfinished Journey, 1977; The King, The Cat and The Fiddle, 1983; Life Class, 1986. Honours: Order of Merit; KBE, UK; President, Hallé Orchestra, 1992; Elevated to Peerage, 1993. Memberships: President, Trinity College of Music, 1971 and RPO; Elgar Society, 1984-; Goodwill Ambassador of UNESCO, 1992. Current Management: SYM Music Company Ltd. Address: c/o SYM Music Company Ltd, P O Box 6160, London, SW1W 0XJ.

MENUT Nicole, b. 21 Aug 1937, Toulouse, France. Singer (Soprano). Education: Studied at the Paris Conservatoire with Jean Giradeau. Career: Sang in Paris from 1962, Opéra-Comique 1965, notably as Lauretta, Mimi, Mélisande and Euridice; Paris Opera from 1965, with guest appearances at Nice, Toulouse, Strasbourg (1974) and Tours (1975); Aix-en-Provence Festival 1967-68; Many concert appearances and broadcast engagements.

MENZEL Peter, b. 31 Jan 1943, Dresden, Germany. Singer (Tenor). Education: Studied at the Dresden Musikhochschule. Career: Sang with the Dresden Opera from 1968; Berlin Staatsoper from 1977, notably in the 1979 premiere of Leonce und Lena by Dessau; Other roles have included Monostatos, Oronte in Alcina, Jacquino, Mime, Pang in Turandot, the Captain in Wozzeck, and Bardolph; Many concert appearances, notably with the Thomas Choir Leipzig on tour to Switzerland, Italy and Japan. Address: c/o Staatsoper Berlin, Center der Linden 7, 0-1060 Berlin, Germany.

MERCER Alexandra, b. 12 May 1944, Gravesend, Kent, England. Singer (Mezzo Soprano). m. Philip Mercer, 2 Oct 1965, 2 twin daughters. Education: Studied with Maestro Antonio and Lina Riccaboni Narducci in Milan, 1963-65, 1967-69; Royal Scottish Academy of Music, 1965-67. Debut: Barga Festival, 1970. Career: Has appeared in opera throughout UK and Europe, with companies such as English Bach Festival Trust, Kent Opera, Royal Opera House Covent Garden, Opera Rara, and Barber Institute; Roles include Poppea, Despina, Dorabella, Rosina, Hansel, Ascanius, Smeton, Isabella, Mrs Sedley, The Sorceress and Samson; Festival appearances: Barga, 1970, Edinburgh, 1978 and 1979, Bath 1981, Wexford, 1984; Regular appearances in concert, oratorio and recital; BBC Soloist for Radio 3 and 2 with BBC debut in 1984. Recordings: Opera Rara, 100 Years of Italian Opera 1800-1910. Honours: 2 Vaughan Williams Trust Awards, 1972 and 1973. Membership: Equity. Hobbies: Politics; Fashion; Travel; Languages; Family. Current Management: Norman McCann International Artists Ltd, London, England. Address: 25E Frognal, London, NW3 6AR, England.

MEREDITH Morley, b. 8 Feb 1922, Winnipeg, Manitoba, Canada. Singer (Baritone). Education: Studied with W H Anderson in Canada and with Boris Goldowsky at Tanglewood; Further study with Alfredo Martini in New York. Debut: New York City Opera 1957, as Escamillo. Career: Metropolitan Opera from 1962, in Les Contes d'Hoffmann and as Zuniga (Carmen), Klingsor, Faninal (Der Rosenkavalier), the Emperor in The Nightingale, Doctor in Wozzek and the Speaker in Die Zauberflöte; Carnegie Hall 1971, in the US premiere of Handel's Ariodante; Guest appearances with Scottish Opera and in Geneva, Chicago, San Francisco and Philadelphia; Sang in Billy Budd at the Metropolitan, 1992. Address: c/o Metropolitan Opera, Lincoln Center, NY 10023, USA.

MERIGHI Giorgio, b. 20 Feb 1939, Ferrara, Italy. Singer (Tenor). Education: Studied at the Rossini Conservatory, Pesaro. Debut: Spoleto Festival 1962, as Riccardo in Un Ballo in Maschera. Career: Many appearances on Italian stages, including the Verona Arena and at the Florence Festival (Meyerbeer's Robert le Diable 1968); Covent Garden 1971 and 1974; Metropolitan Opera debut 1978, as Manrico in Il Trovatore; Guest engagements in Berlin, Monte Carlo, Barcelona, Marseilles and Brussels; Geneva 1984, as Pollione in Norma; Wiesbaden Festival 1985, as the Duke of Mantua; Italian TV as Pinkerton in Madama Butterfly; Munich and Palermo 1987-88 as Maurizio in Adriana Lecouvreur; Sang Luigi in Il Tabarro at the Met 1989, Maurizio at Bonn; Season 1992 with Don José at Genoa, Andrea Chénier at Turin and concert in memory of Mario del Monaco at the Torre del Lago Festival; Sang Ismaele in Nabucco at Verona, 1996. Address: c/o S A Gorlinsky Ltd, 33 Dover Street, London W1X 4NJ, England.

MERILÄINEN Usko, b. 27 Jan 1930, Tampere, Finland. Composer. Compositions include: Epyllion for orchestra, 1963; Piano Sonata No 2, 1966; Papillons for 2 Pianos, 1969; Concerto for Piano and Orchestra No 2, 1969; Symphony No 3, 1971; Concerto for 13 Instruments, 1971; Piano Sonata No 3, 1972; Concerto for Double Bass and Percussion, 1973; Psyche, ballet in 2 acts, 1973; Piano Sonata No 4, 1974; Concerto for Cello and Orchestra, 1975; Dialogues for Piano and Orchestra, 1977; Mobile, ein Spiel for Orchestra, 1977; Simultus for 4 Instruments, 1979; (Suvisoitto) Summer Sounds for Flute and Grasshoppers, 1979; Kyma for String Quartet, 1979; Paripeli for Cello and Piano, 1980; Quattro notturni per Arpa, 1984-85; ...but this is a landscape, Monsieur Dali!, 1986; Exodus for Choir and Orchestra, 1988; Concerto No 2, Aikaviiva (Timeline) for Orchestra, 1989; Letter to a Cellist for Cello Solo and Ensembles, 1990; Concerto for Guitar and Orchestra, 1991; Piano Sonata No 5, 1992; String Quartet No 3, 1992; Geasseija niehku, summer concert for Chamber Orchestra, 1993-94; Fetes d'Henriette for Flute, Cello and Piano, 1995; Kehrä for orchestra, 1996. Recordings include: Visions and Whispers with Mikael Helasvuo on flute; Ku-Gu-Ku, electroacoustic works; Timeline, Concerto No 2 under Leif Segerstram; Papillons, Piano Sonatas 2, 4 and 5 with Jaana Kärkkäinen and Ilmo Ranta. Honours: Wihuri Foundation International Sibelius Prize, 1965; Prof hc, Doctor hc, Sibelius Academy, 1997. Membership: Chairman, Association of Finnish Composers, 1981-92. Address: Nokiantie 102, 33300 Tampere, Finland.

MERRILL Nathaniel, b. 8 Feb 1927, Massachusetts, USA. Stage Director. Education: Trained with Boris Goldovsky at New England Conservatory of Music and with Gunther Rennert, Herbert Graf and Carl Ebert in Europe. Debut: Boston 1952, with the US premiere of Lully's Amadis. Career: Metropolitan Opera New York from 1955, resident stage director from 1960, with productions of Turandot, Meistersinger, Les Troyens, Aida, Rosenkavalier, Adriana Lecouvreur, Luisa Miller, Parsifal, Porgy and Bess, 1985, Il Trovatore, Samson et Dalila and L'Elisir d'amore (collaborations with designer Robert O'Hearn); Other stagings at Strasbourg, Vancouver, Verona, San Francisco, New York City Opera and the Vienna Staatsoper. Address: c/o Metropolitan Opera, Lincoln Center, NY 10023, USA.

MERRILL Robert, b. 4 June 1919, Brooklyn, New York, USA. Singer (Baritone). m. (1) Roberta Peters, (2) Marion Machno, 1954, 1 son, 1 daughter. Education: Studied with mother and with Samuel Margolis in New York. Career includes: Sang over 800 performances with Metropolitan Opera as: Verdi's Renato, Don Carlo, Iago, Di Luna, Rigoletto and Posa, Puccini's Marcello and Scarpia, Gounod's Valentin and Rossini's Figaro; Sang for both Houses of Congress on the occasion of President Roosevelt's funeral, 1945; Performed for every subsequent US president including Reagan; Guest appearances in Chicago, San Francisco, Milan, and Venice; Sang Germont at Covent Garden, 1967; Performed as Tevye in Fiddler on the Roof in over 800 performances, 1970-74; Tour of Japan with Metropolitan Opera, 1975; Concerts in London, Bournemouth, Geneva and Israel, 1975; Official singer with New York Yankees from 1969-. Recordings: Cavalleria Rusticana; La Bohème; La Traviata; Carmen; Il Barbiere di Siviglia; La Gioconda; Aida; Falstaff; La Forza del Destino; Il Trovatore; Rigoletto; Manon Lescaut; Il Tabarro; Un Ballo in Maschera; Bloch's Sacred Service; Carousel; Kismet; Fiddler on the Roof. Publications: Once More From the Beginning, 1965; Between Acts, 1976; The Divas, 1978. Honours include: Harriet Cohen International Music Award, 1961; Handel Medal, City of New York, 1970; The National Medal of The Arts, USA, 1993; Honorary Music Doctorates, Gustavus Adolphus College, 1970, CUNY, 1996; International Dor L'Dor B'Nai B'rith, 1994; Lawrence Tibbett Award in Guild of Music Artists Relief Fund, 1996. Memberships: AGMA; AGVA; AFTRA; SAG; Actors' Equity, 1945-; Friar's Club, Monk, 1968-. Hobbies: Golf; Baseball; Fine Art. Current Management: Gurtman and Murtha Associates, 450 Seventh Avenue #603, New York, NY 10123, USA. Address: Robert Merrill Associates Inc, 79 Oxford Road, New Rochelle, NY 10804, USA.

MERRIMAN Nan, b. 28 Apr 1920, Pittsburgh, USA. Singer (Mezzo-soprano). m. Tom Brand. Education: Studied with Alexia Bassian in Los Angeles and with Lotte Lehmann. Career: Debut in concert, 1940; Opera debut as La Cieca in La Gioconda, Cincinnati, 1942; Sang in Toscanini's NBC broadcasts as Maddalena in Rigoletto, Gluck's Orpheus and Meg Page in Falstaff; Glyndebourne 1953, 1956, as Baba the Turk in The Rake's Progress and Dorabella in Così fan tutte; Sang at Aix-en-Provence as Dorabella, at the Holland Festival and La Scala Milan (1955); Piccola Scala 1958, in the local premiere of Dargomizhsky's The Stone Guest; Guest engagements in Paris, Geneva, Amsterdam, Chicago and San Francisco. Many appearances in concert. Recordings include: Così fan tutte conducted by Karajan (Columbia). Honours include: 1st Prize, National Federation of Music Clubs, 1943.

MERRITT Chris, b. 27 Sept 1952, Oklahoma City, USA. Singer (Tenor). Education: Studied at Oklahoma City University; Apprentice Artist at the Santa Fe Opera. Career: Sang in Augsburg as Idomeneo, Rossini's Otello, Rodolfo and Julien in Louise; New York City Opera debut 1981, as Arturo in I Puritani; Appeared in Rossini's Tancredi at Carnegie Hall, Il Viaggio a Reims at the Vienna Staatsoper, Ermione in Naples and Maometto II at San Francisco Opera; Paris Opera debut 1983, in Rossini's Moise; Sang Uberto in La Donna del Lago at Covent Garden; Season 1985-86 in Il Viaggio a Reims at La Scala, as Rodrigo (La Donna del Lago) in Paris, Idreno in a concert performance of Semiramide at Covent Garden; Leukippos in Daphne at Carnegie Hall; Maggio Musicale Florence 1986, as Benvenuto Cellini; Aeneas in Les Troyens in Amsterdam; Nemorino in L'Elisir d'Amore at Orlando, Florida; Opened the 1988-89 season at La Scala in Guillaume Tell by Rossini; Title role in Robert le Diable at Carnegie Hall; Sang in I Puritani at the Rome Opera, 1990; Arnold in a new production of Guillaume Tell at Covent Garden, 1990; Sang Admète in Alceste at the opening of the 1990-91 season at Chicago; Benvenuto Cellini at Geneva, 1992; Season 1992-93 as Leicester in Rossini's Elisabetta at Naples, Arnold at Covent Garden and San Francisco, Rodrigo in La Donna del Lago at La Scala and Conte di Libenskof in Il Viaggio a Reims at Pesaro; Season 1996-97 as Schoenberg's Aron in Amsterdam and Paris and in the premiere of Henze's Venus and Adonis at Munich; Featured Artists (People no 183) Opera Magazine Fesitval issue, 1992; Concert engagements in Verdi's Requiem; Haydn's Creation and the Choral Symphony in Israel; Rossini's Petite Messe Solennelle in Amsterdam. Recordings: Rossini's Stabat Mater, Ermione and Il Viaggio a Reims; Donizetti's Emilia di Liverpool; I Puritani; Faust, conducted by Michel Plasson. Address: c/o Harrison/Parrott Ltd, 12 Penzance Place, London W11 4PA, England.

MERTENS Klaus, b. 25 Mar 1949, Kleve, Germany. Singer. m. Ingrid Mertens, 14 May 1986, 1 son, 3 daughters. Education: Diploma, 1976. Career: Numerous Radio Recordings and TV Productions; Oratorio Work and Song Recitals, 1976-. Recordings: Bach, St Matthew Passion, St John Passion, Christmas Oratorio, Mass in B Minor; Complete Recordings of all Cantatas. Membership: Bach-Gesellschaft. Address: Buschhovener Straße 2, Alfter, Germany.

MESHIBOVSKY Alexander, b. 15 Apr 1949, Kharkov, Russia. Concert Violinist; Associate Professor. Education: Special School of Music for Gifted Children, Kharkov, 1955-65; Kharkov Conservatory, 1965-70; Masterclasses with Boris Goldstein, Moscow, 1971-74. Career: Concertmaster, Soloist, Moscow Chamber Orchestra, Russian Concert Agency, 1971-72; Soloist, Moscow Concert Agency, 1972-74; Dozent, Innsbruck Conservatory, 1975-76; Concerts in many European Countries, USA; Associate Professor, East Tennessee State University, 1984-; Associate Professor, West Virginia University, 1988. Compositions: Paganini Variations; Transcriptions of works by Debussy, Gershwin, Rachmaninoff and many others. Hobbies: Fine Arts; Sport. Current Management: Alpha Attractions Inc, New York, USA. Address: 82-46 Lefferts Blvd, Apt 2D, Kew Gardens, NY 11415, USA.

MESPLÉ Mady, b. 7 Mar 1931, Toulouse, France. Singer (Soprano). Education: Studied in Toulouse and with Janine Micheau in Paris. Debut: Liège 1953, as Lakmé; Paris Opéra-Comique from 1956, Opéra from 1958, notably as the Queen of Night, Gounod's Juliette, Ophelia in Hamlet, Philine in Mignon, Donizetti's Norina and Lucia and Sophie in Der Rosenkavalier; Aix-en-Provence 1966, as Ariadne; Metropolitan Opera debut 1973, as Gilda; Guest appearances in Buenos Aires, Moscow, Rome and Naples; Concert performances include Schoenberg's Die Jakobsleiter in London, conducted by Boulez. Recordings: Lakme; Socrate by Satie, Barbiere di Siviglia and Guillaume Tell; Operettas by Lecoq, Messager, Planquette, Hahn and Offenbach. Address: c/o Conservatoire National de Musique de Lyon, 3 Quai Chauveau, 69009 Lyon, France.

MESSENGER Thomas, b. 15 Oct 1938, Edinburgh, Scotland. University Head of Department and Senior Lecturer. m. Joan Helen Kelly, 22 Mar 1965, 2 sons. Education: ARCM, Piano Teacher, George Heriot's School, Edinburgh, 1957; BMus, Hons, Organ Scholar, University of Glasgow, 1961; ARCO, 1960; Fulbright Scholar, Washington University, USA, 1961-62; PhD, University of Wales, 1979. Career: Graduate Assistant, Washington University, USA, 1961-62; Lecturer, Royal Scottish Academy of Music, 1962-68; Conductor, New Consort of Voices, 1966-68, Monteverdi Singers, 1970-79; Examiner, Associated Board of the Royal Schools of Music, 1969-; Lecturer, Music Department, University College of North Wales, 1968-79; Lecturer, 1979-83, Senior Lecturer and Administrative Head of Department of Music, 1990, Head of Department of Music, 1992-, University of Surrey, England; Various broadcasts as Conductor; Broadcast talk on John Lloyd's Missa O Quam Suavis, 1982; Broadcast performance of his edition of Lloyd's Mass, Taverner Choir, Conductor Andrew Parrott. Publications: Two Part Counterpoint from the Great Masters, 1970; Editions: Three Chansons for Three Recorders, 1971; Five Imitations for Three Recorders, 1971; Two Books of Canzonets for Four Recorders, 1971, 1979. Hobbies: Hill Walking; Opera; Swimming. Address: 5 St Mildred's Road, Guildford, Surrey GU1 1TX, England.

MESSIEREUR Petr, b. 1937, Czechoslovakia. Violinist. Education: Studied at Prague Academy of Art. Career: Leader of the Talich String Quartet from 1972; Tours to most European countries, Egypt Iraq, North America, Japan, Indonesia; Camber Ensemble of the Czech Philharmonnic from 1975; Annual visits to France from 1976; Tours of Britain 1990-91, with concerts at the Wigmore Hall, appearances at the Bath and Bournemouth Festivals, Elizabeth Hall and on BBC2's Late Show, with Janacek's 2nd Quartet; Also played Beethoven's Quartet Op 74, the Brahms A minor, Smetana's D minor and works by Mozart in England; Festival appearances in Vienna, Besancon, Dijon, Helsinki, Amsterdam, Prague and Salzburg; Repertoire also includes works by Debussy, Bartok (complete works recorded by Supraphon), Shostakovich, Ravel and Dvorak. Recordings include: For the French companies Sarastro and Calliope, with the complete quartets of Beethoven; Albums for Collins Classics. Honours include: Grand Prix Charles Cros. Address: c/o Clarion/Seven Muses, 64 Whitehall Park, London N19 3TN, England.

MESSITER Malcolm, b. 1 Apr 1944, Kingston, Surrey, England. Oboist. m. Christine Messiter. Education: Paris Conservatoire 1967; Royal College of Music, London; ARCM. Debut: Purcell Room, London, 1971. Career: Principal Oboe, BBC Concert Orchestra, 1972-77; Solo concert engagements; Many appearances as chamber music player. Honours include: Royal College of Music Oboe Prize, 1970. Hobbies: Model Aircraft; Winemaking. Address: 67 Crescent Way, Hadley Wood, Herts EN4 0EQ, England.

MESTER Jorge, b. 10 Apr 1935, Mexico City, Mexico. Education: MA, Juilliard School of Music, New York, 1958; Studied with Leonard Bernstein, Berkshire Music Center, Tanglewood, summer 1955; Albert Wolff, the Netherlands. Career: Teacher of Conducting, Juilliard School of Music, 1955-67; Music Director, Louisville Orchestra, 1967-79; Music Director, Aspen (Colorado) Music Festival, 1970-; Musical Adviser and Principal Conductor, kansas City (Missouri(Philharmonic Orchestra, 1971-74; Music Director, Casals Festival, Puerto Rico, 1979-; Teacher of Conducting, Conductor of School Ensembles, 1980-; Chairman, Conducting Department 1984-87, Juilliard School; Music Director, Pasadena (California) Symphony Orchestra, 1984-; Guest Conductor in North America and overseas; Chief Conductor of the West Australia Symphony and Principal Guest conductor of the Adelaide Symphony Orchestra; Conducted Der Rosenkavalier at Sydney, 1992. Recordings: For Cambridge; Columbia; Composers Recordings Inc; Desto; Louisville; Mercury; Vanguard including Dallapiccola Piccola musica notturna, Hindemith Concert Music for viola and Kammermusik No 2; Bruch's 2nd Symphony; Penderecki De Natura Sonoris; Shostakovich Hamlet Music; Strauss's Six Songs Op 68; Milhaud Symphony No 6; Martin Cello Cencerto. Honour: Naumburg Award, 1968; Alice M Distwon Award for Conductors, 1985. Address: c/o The Juilliard School, Lincoln Center, New York, NY 10023, USA.

MESZOLY Katalin, b. 1950, Hungary. Contralto. Education: Studied singing under Professor Jenö Sipos, Budapest; Professor Paula Lindberg, Salzburg, Austria. Career: Budapest State Opera, 1976-, from debut, leading contralto of Budapest Opera; Performed title role of Carmen 129 times at Budapest and overseas; Azucena, Il Trovatore; Amneris, Aida; Ulrica, Un Ballo in Maschera; Preziosilla, La forza del destino, Marfa in Khovanshchina; Judith, Bluebeard's Castle, at La Scala 1981; Sang Britten's Mrs Herring at Budapest, 1988, Herodias in Salome, 1989; Ulrica (Un Ballo in Maschera) for Opera de Montreal, 1990; Has appeared in oratorios including Verdi's Requiem, Mozart's Requiem; Gives song recitals; Guest performer in numerous countries and Operas including Milan Scala, Austria, West Germany, Spain, France, Mexico, Egypt and others. Honour: Liszt Prize. Address: Hungarian State Opera House, Népötarsasag utja 22, 0161 Budapest, Hungary.

METCALF John (Philip), b. 13 Aug 1946, Swansea, Wales. Composer. m. Gillian Alexander, 14 Sept 1972, 2 sons, 1 daughter. Education: BMus First Class Honours, University of Cardiff, 1967. Career: Commissions from Festivals of Cardiff, Swansea and North Wales, Bath and Cheltenham, England and Frankfurt, Germany, also from BBC, Gulbenkian Foundation, London Sinfonietta and Welsh National Opera; Currently Associate Artistic Director and Composer-in-Residence, Banff Centre, School of Fine Arts, Alberta, Canada; Opera, Kafka's Chimp, premiered at Banff, 1996. Compositions: Horn Concerto, 1972; PTOC, 1973 Auden Songs, 1973-77; 5 Rags for Charlotte, 1975; Ave Maria, choral, 1977; The Journey, opera, 1981; Music of Changes, orchestra, 1981; Two Carols, 1981; Clarinet Concerto, 1982; The Crossing, music theatre, 1984; The Boundaries of Time, cantata, 1985; Also music for dance, film and television; Piano Trio, 1988; Opera, Tornrak, 1989; Orchestra Variations, 1990; Opera, Kafka's Chimp, 1996. Honours: Gulbenkian Dance Fellow, 1973; UK-USA Bicentennial Arts Fellow, 1977-78; University of Wales Creative Arts Fellow, 1984. Address: Ty YforY, Llanfair Road, Lampeter, Dyfed SA48 8JZ, Wales.

METCALFE John, b. 1964, England. Violist. Education: Studied at the Royal Northern College of Music with Simon Rowland-Jones, at the Guildhall School of Music, and with Bruno Giuranna at Berlin Hochschule. Career: Concerts, Europe, USA, Japan, and on Channel 4 and Canadian TV; Principal viola with the Kreisler String Orchestra; Member of Durutti Column, 1984-88; Violist with Duke String Quartet from 1985; Performances in the Wigmore Hall, Purcell Room, Conway Hall and throughout Britain; With Duke Quartet, tours with Rosas throughout Europe and to Brazil; South Bank series, 1991, with Mozart's early quartets; Soundtrack for Ingmar Bergman documentary The Magic Lantern, Channel 4, 1988; BBC debut feature; Features for French TV, 1990-91, playing Mozart, Mendelssohn, Britten and Tippett; Brahms Clarinet Quintet for Dutch Radio with Janet Hilton; Live Music Now series with concerts for disadvantaged people; The Duke Quartet invites...at the Derngate, Northampton, 1991, with Duncan Prescott and Rohan O'Hara; Resident quartet, Rydale Festival, 1991; Residency, Trinity College, Oxford, tours to Scotland and Northern Ireland and concert at the Elizabeth Hall, 1991; Season 1993/94 with Duke Quartet at Casa Manilva Festival, Spain, and tour of Britain; Founded Factory Classical Label, 1988. Compositions: Arranger for Pretenders, Blur, Cranberries, Morrissey, Lloyd Cole; Compositions for TV; With Duke Quartet, composing music for Union Dance Co. Recordings include: Quartets by Tippett, Shostakovich and Britten (Third); Other albums including music by Dvořák, Barber and Glass; 3 world premieres by Kevin Volans. Honours include: Martin Musical Trust Award; South East Arts Scholarships. Current Management: Lorraine Lyons. Address: 81b Sarsfield Road, London SW12, England.

METHVEN Jean, b. 1940, St Andrews, Fife, Scotland. Coloratura Soprano. m. Ian C Moore, 7 June 1980. Education: ARCM; LRAM; Studied withEna Mitchell, Roy Henderson and Denis Dowling. Debut: Scottish Opera, 1965; Sadlers Wells Opera 1969; English National Opera, 1974. Career: Appearances with Scottish Opera, Sadlers Wells Opera, ENO, including roles of the Queen of Night in Mozart's The Magic Flute and Olympia in Offenbach's The Tales of Hoffmann; Concerts, oratorios and recitals. Honours: Sir James Caird Scholarships, 1967-69. Memberships: Incorporated Society of Musicians; British Actors Equity. Hobbies: Gardening; Photography; Dress Making. Address: Morven, The Ridgeway, High Wycombe, Bucks HP13 5BE, England.

METTERNICH Josef, b. 2 June 1915, Hermuhlheim, Nr Cologne, Germany. Singer (Baritone). Education: Studied in Berlin and Cologne. Career: Sang with the opera chorus at Cologne and Bonn; Solo debut 1945, as Tonio in Pagliacci at the Berlin Stadtische Oper; Covent Garden debut 1951, as the Dutchman; Metropolitan Opera 1953-56, as Carlo (La forza del destino), Amfortas, Wolfram, Kurwenal, Tonio, Luna, Renato and Amonasro; Further appearances in Paris, Vienna, Hamburg and Edinburgh; Bayerische Staatsoper Munich from 1954, notably as Johannes Kepler in the premiere of Hindemith's Die Harmonie der Welt (1957) and as Kothner in Die Meistersinger at the reopening of the Nationaltheater, 1963; Professor at the Cologne Musikhochschule from 1965, retired as singer 1971. Recordings include: Pagliacci (HMV); Hansel und Gretel (Columbia); Salome (Philips); Lohengrin, Fidelio and Der fliegende Holländer (Deutsche Grammophon).

METTERS Colin (Raynor), b. 22 Jan 1948, Plymouth, Devon, England. Conductor. m. Susan Furlong, 28 Jun 1980, 2 d. Education: ARCM, Violin and Conducting, Royal College of Music, 1966-71; Studied Conducting under Vernon Handley and George Hurst, 1966-71; Liverpool Seminar under Charles Groves, 1969; Master classes with Nadia Boulanger, 1968. Career: Musical Director, Ballet Rambert, 1972-74; Conductor, Sadler's Wells Royal Ballet, 1974-82; Teacher of Conducting, Canford Summer School of Music, 1973-83; Musical Director, East Sussex Youth Orchestra, 1979-; Guest Conductor with London Schools Symphony Orchestra, British Youth Symphony Orchestra, National Centre for Orchestral Studies; Freelance Conductor, 1982-; Director of Conducting, Royal Academy of Music, 1983-; Conducted major UK, Provincial and BBC Orchestras; Conducted extensively abroad. Recordings: BBC Radio and Television and various. Honour: Honorary RAM conferred at RAM Graduation, 1995. Current Management: Helen Sykes Management. Address: Fourth Floor, Parkway House, London SW14 8LS, England.

METTRAUX Laurent, b. 27 May 1970, Fribourg, Switzerland. Composer. Education: Literature Section, St Michael's College; Piano, Violin, Singing, Complete Theoretical Studies with Professor René Oberson, Conservatoire de Fribourg; Composition with Professor Eric Gaudibert, Conducting with Professor S-L Chen, Geneva; Studies in Ancient Music, Musicology, Music History, Organ. Debut: 1st compositions at age 12. Career includes: Symphonie pour orchestre de chambre first performed by Orchestre de Chambre de Lausanne, conductor Jesus Lopez-Cobos; Directed first performance of his composition Lysistrata; first performance of Concerto for 15 solo strings under Tibor Varga at opening concert, Tibor Varga Festival 1994; Numerous commissions. Compositions include: Lysistrata, after Aristophanes, 1993-94; Concerto for 15 solo strings, 1994; Fantasia for solo violin, 1994-95; Vers le Soleil Couchant, oratorio, 1995-96; Trio No 2, for piano, violin and cello, 1995-96; Sonata for flute and piano, 1996; Concerto for violin, 1996; String Quartet, commission for Talich Quartet. Honour: Symphonie pour orchestre de chambre won 1st Prize and Public Prize, 1st Competition for Young Composers, 1993. Membership: Swiss Musicians Association, 1995-. Address: Route Principale 160, CH-1791 Courtaman, Switzerland.

METTRE Raimundo, b. 1949, Brazil. Singer (Tenor). Education: Studied in Berlin and Milan. Career: Sang at the Piccola Scala Milan 1982, in Ariodante; Appearances at Zurich as Almaviva and the Duke of Mantua (1985-86), Basle (Rodolfo, 1987), at Rio de Janeiro as Werther and Don José and at Barcelona as Mozart's Ferrando and Don Ottavio; Other roles include Percy in Anna Bolena (at Lisbon), Belmonte (at Tel Aviv); US debut at Philadelphia, as Ernesto in Don Pasquale; Concert repertoire includes the Verdi Requiem, Puccini's Messa di Gloria, Rossini's Stabat Mater and oratorios by Handel. Address: Opernhaus Zurich, Falkenstrasse 1, CH-8008 Zurich, Switzerland.

METZ Catherine, b. 1965, USA. Violinist. Education: Studied in New York. Career: Recitalist, Lincoln Center's Alice Tully Hall, 92nd Street 'Y' and appearances with major orchestras; Chamber Musician at the Santa Fe Festival, Spoleto Festival and Lockenhaus Kammermusikfest and the International Musicians Seminar in Prussia Cove; Co-Founder, Orion Quartet and has given concerts at Washington DC's Kennedy Center, at Boston Gardner Museum and throughout the USA; Carnegie Hall recital, 1991 and as part of the Centenial Celebration tribute; Concerts as Turku Festival in Finland. Address: Orion Quartet, Ingpen & Williams Ltd, 26 Wadham Road, London SW15 2LR, England.

MEVEN Peter, b. 1 Oct 1929, Cologne, Germany. Singer (Bass). Education: Studied at the Cologne Musikhochschule with Robert Blasius. Debut: Hagen, Westfalen, 1957, as Ferrando in IL Trovatore. Career: Sang in Mainz, Wiesbaden and Oldenburg from 1959; Deutsche Oper Berlin from 1964; Many guest appearances in Germany and engagements in Amsterdam, Basle, Lisbon, Stockholm, Moscow and San Francisco; Covent Garden London, Gurnemanz in Parsifal; Bayreuth 1971, as Fafner; Salzburg 1974, as Sarastro in Die Zauberflöte; Paris Opera as Daland in Der fliegende Holländer, 1981; Brussels 1983-85, as Kaspar in Der Freischütz and Pogner in Die Meistersinger (also at the Metropolitan 1976-77); Sang Lodovico in Schreker's Die Gezeichneten for Austrian Radio; Sang Hagen and Hunding in the Ring at Geneva, 1988; King Heinrich in Lohengrin at Santiago, 1988, Hagen at the 1989 Holland Festival; Sang Rocco in Fidelio at Dusseldorf, 1990. Recordings: Sacred music by Bruckner; Der Freischütz (Deutsche Grammophon); Mathis der Maler by Hindemith (HMV); Fidelio (Eurodisc). Address: Deutsche Oper am Rhein, Heinrich Heine Allee 16, D-4000 Dusseldorf, Germany.

MEWES Karsten, b. 18 Mar 1959, Pirna, Saxony, Germany. Singer (Baritone). Education: Studied at the Hanns Eisler Musikhochschule Berlin. Career: Sang at the Potsdam Opera and the Komische Oper Berlin, 1985-88; Berlin Staatsoper from 1985, notably in the 1989 premiere of Graf Mirabeau by Siegfried Matthus; Guest appearances in Dresden and elsewhere as Mozart's Count, Masetto, Guglielmo and Papageno, Lotzing's Zar, Silvio, Escamillo and Hans Scholl in Udo Zimmermann's Die weisse Rose; Concert repertoire includes works by Bach, Handel, Brahms and Fauré; Lieder recitals in Germany, Finland, Norway, Czechoslovakia, Poland and France. Honours: Competition Prize Winner at Zwickau, Verona, Hamburg, Rio de Janeiro, 1985-87.

MEYER Felix, b. 24 May 1957, St Gallen, Switzerland. Musicologist. m. Rosmarie Anzenberger, 28 Nov 1986, 1 son, 1 daughter. Education: Musicology, English and German Literature, University of Zurich; PhD, Musicology, 1989; Violin studies in St Gallen; Piano studies with Hans Steinbrecher in St Gallen, Werner Bärtschi in Zurich, Ian Lake in London. Career: Secretary, Swiss Youth Music Competition, 1984-85; Curator of Music Manuscripts at Paul Sacher Foundation, Basel, 1986, duties including Director of concert series Klassizistische Moderne, Basel, 1996, and Director of exhibition of music manuscripts at Pierpont Morgan Library, New York City, 1998. Publications: A Study of Charles Ives's Concord Sonata, 1991; Editor, contributor, Quellenstudien II: Zwölf Komponisten des 20. Jahrhunderts, 1993; Editor, contributor, Klassizistische Moderne, 1996; Co-editor, 2 facsimile editions of works by Igor Stravinsky. Contributions to: Music Analysis; Revista de musicología; Neue Zürcher Zeitung; Others. Memberships: Swiss Musicological Society; German Musicological Society. Hobbies: Skiing; Swimming. Address: Augustinergasse 5, CH-4051 Basel, Switzerland.

MEYER Henry, b. 29 June 1923, Dresden, Germany. Violinist; College Professor. Education: Studied at Prague Music Academy in Paris with George Enescu and at the Juilliard School with Ivan Galamian. Career: Co-Founded the Lasalle String Quartet at the Juilliard School, 1949; Many concerts featuring modern composers and the quartets of Beethoven; European debut 1954; Composers who wrote for the ensemble include Hans Erich Apostel, Earle Brown, Henri Pousseur, Mauricio Kagel, György Ligeti, Penderecki and Witold Lutoslawski; Quartet-in-Residence and Professor, Cincinnati College-Conservatory of Music; Quartet disbanded 1988; Has since given masterclasses in the USA, Europe, Israel, Australia and Japan. Recordings include: Works by Berg, Schoenberg, Webern and Zemlinsky; Beethoven's Late Quartets; Brahms; Wolf. Address: c/o Cincinnati College-Conservatory of Music, Cincinnati, OH 45221, USA.

MEYER Kerstin, b. 3 Apr 1928, Stockholm, Sweden. Opera Singer (Mezzo-Soprano); Rector Emerita; University Professor. m. Björn G Bexelius, 23 Dec 1974. Education: Royal Swedish Conservatory, Stockholm, 1948-50; Swedish University College of Opera, 1950-52; Accademia Chigiana, Italy; Mozarteum, Austria. Debut: Royal Opera, Stockholm, 1952, as Azucena in Il Trovatore. Career: Orchestra appearances with the Hallé Orchestra; London Philharmonic, Berlin and Vienna Philharmonics, La Suisse Romande, Santa Cecilia, Chicago, ABC, BBC, NZBC television; Leading roles in most of the important Houses and Festivals in Europe, North and South America, Far East, such as Royal Opera House Covent Garden, Welsh and Scottish Operas, Glyndebourne and Edinburgh Festivals; La Scala, Milan, La Fenice and Santa Cecilia, Italy, Vienna and Salzburg, Austria; Munich, Berlin, Cologne and Hamburg, Germany; Paris, Marseilles, France, Moscow, Tashkent, Tallin, Riga, USSR, Metropolitan Opera House, San Francisco, Santa Fe, Tulsa, USA; Teatro Colon, Argentina; Mexico City, Tokyo, Hong Kong; Sang in first British performances of operas by Henze and Einem at Glyndebourne and in the world premieres of operas by Goehr and Searle (Hamburg), Henze's The Bassarids at Salzburg, 1966 and Ligeti's Le Grand Macabre at Stockholm, 1978; President, Swedish University College of Opera, 1984-94; Advisory Director, European Mozart Academy, Cracow and New York. Recordings: Operas, recitals with von Karajan, Barbirolli, Solti, Hans Schmidt-Isserstedt and Sixten Ehrling. Honours include: Royal Swedish Court Singer, 1963; Swedish Vasa Order; Swedish Litteris et Arbitus; Swedish Illis Quorum, 1994; Commander of the British Empire, 1985; German Cross of Honour 1st Class; Italian Order of Merit. Memberships include: Board Member, STIM; Board member, Umeå University; Assessor, HEFCE, London. Address: Porsvaegen 48, 16570 Haesselby, Sweden.

MEYER Krzysztof, b. 11 Aug 1943, Krakow, Poland. Composer; Music Theorist; Pianist. 1 son, 1 daughter. Education: High School of Music, Krakow; American Conservatory, Fontainebleau. Debut: Warsaw in 1965. Career: Professor: High School of Music, Krakow, 1966-87 and High School of Music, Cologne, 1987-; President of Union of Polish Composers, 1985-89. Compositions include: Stage Works: Cyberiada, opera, premiere in 1986, The Gamblers, completion of Shostakovich's opera, premiere 1983, The Maple Brothers, children's opera, premiere 1990; Orchestral: 4 Symphonies, Hommage à Johannes Brahms; Musica incrostate; Concertos for: Piano, Violin, Violoncello, 2 for Oboe, Trumpet, Saxophone, 2 for flute, Double concerto for Harp and Cello, Symphony in Mozartean style, Caro Luigi for 4 Cellos and Orchestra; For Choir and Orchestra: Epitaphium Stanislaw Wiechowicz in memoriam, (Symphony No 2), Symphoniec d'Orphée (Symphony no 3), Liryc Triptych for Tenor and Chamber Orchestra, Mass for Choir and Organ; Chamber Works: Clarinet Quintet, Piano Quintet, 10 String Quartets, Piano Trio, String Trio; For Various Ensembles: Concerto Retro; Hommage à Nadia Boulanger, Capriccio, Canzona and Sonata for Cello and Piano; For Piano: 5 Sonatas, 24 Preludes; Solo Sonatas for: Cello, Cembalo, Violin, Flute, Fantasy for Organ. Recordings include: String Quartets Nos 1-9; Hommage à Brahms; Symphonies 1-6; Clarinet Quintet; The Gamblers, and others. Publication: Dimitri Shostakovich, 1973; Shostakovich, 1995. Contributions to: Various Journals. Honours: Grand Prix, Prince Pierre de Monaco, 1970; Award, Minister of Culture and Art, Poland, 1973, 1976; Medal, Government of Brazil, 1975; Gottfried von Herder Preis, Wien, 1984; Award, Polish Composers Union, 1992; Jurzykowski Foundation, New York, 1993. Address: Kurt Schumacher Str 10 W-51, 51427 Bergisch Gladbach, Germany.

MEYER Paul, b. 5 March 1965, Mulhouse, France. Clarinettist; Conductor. Education: Studied at the Paris Conservatoire and the Basle Musikhochschule. Debut: Orchestre Symphonique du Rhin, 1978. Career: Concerts in New York, 1984; Formed association with Benny Goodman; Engagements with the Orchestre National de France, BBC SO, Royal Philharmonic, Tokyo SO, Salzburg Mozarteum, Suisse Romade, Zurich Tonhalle and ABC Australia; Modern repertory includes works by Boulez (Domains), Gould and Henze; Premiere of Concerto by Gerd Kuhr at the Sinfonia Varsovia, 1994; Premiered Penderecki's arrangement of Viola Concerto, 1996, and the Concerto by Berio, with the Concertgebouw Orchestra, 1997; Tour of the USA with Yo-Yo Ma, Emmanuel Ax and Pamela Frank, playing Brahms and Schoenberg, 1995; Further partnerships with Eric Le Sage, Barbara Hendricks, Gidon Kremer, Maria Jao Pires, Jean-Pierre Rampal, Rostropovitch, Heinrich Schiff and Isaac Stern; Quintet with the Carmina, Cleveland, Emerson and Takacs String Quartets; Concerts as conductor with the Munich CO, English CO and with Carmen in the South of France, 1997. Recordings include: Concertos by Mozart, Copland and Busoni, with the English CO; Weber and Fuchs wth the Carmina Quartet; Mendelssohn and Reinecke, with Eric Le Sage. Honours include: Winner, French Young Artists Competition, 1982; USA Young Artists Competition, 1984. Address: c/o Harrison/Parrott Ltd, 12 Penzance Lane, London W11 4PA, England.

MEYER Sabine, b. 30 March 1959, Crailsheim, Germany. Clarinettist. Education: Studied with her father, Karl Meyer, with Otto Hermann in Stuttgart and Hans Deinzer in Hanover. Career: Joined the Bavarian Radio Symphony Orchestra from 1983, at first under Herbert von Karajan then Claudio Abbado; Trio partnership with her brother Wolfgang, and Reiner Behle, notably in the Trios with Clarinet by Beethoven and Brahms; Further Collaborations with Pianist Rudolf Buchbinder, Cellist Heinrich Schiff and the Cleveland and Brandis Quartets; Regular concerts in the Divertimenti and Serenades of Mozart with members of the Berlin Philharmonic; Premieres of Octet for Winds by Edison Denisov (1991) and the Romance for clarinet and orchestra by Richard Strauss (1991). Honours include: Winner, ARD Competition at Munich. Address: c/o Berlin Philharmonic Orchestra, Philharmonie, Matthäukirchstrasse 1, D-1000 Berlin 30, Germany.

MEYER-WOLFF Frido, b. 22 Apr 1934, Potsdam, Germany. Singer (Bass-baritone). Education: Studied in Berlin, Paris and Hamburg. Debut: Stralsund 1955, as Mozart's Figaro. Career: Appearances at Trier, Hamburg, Kassel, Kiel and the Deutsche Oper Berlin; Opera Comique Paris, 1963, in the premiere of Menotti's The Last Savage; Spoleto Fesitval, 1964; As Ochs in Der Rosenkavalier; Aix en Provence Festival, 1963, 1964, Marseilles from 1961, Brussels, 1965, Monte Carlo 1967-94, Nice 1962-89, Lausanne 1987; Decorated Chevalier des Arts et Lettres by the French Government, 1985; Direction of open-air theatre Jean Cocteau Cap d'All near Monaco, created and conducted a new chamber orchestra from 1989; Other roles include parts in operas by Verdi, Wagner, Puccini, Strauss, Rossini, Smetana and Moussorgsky; Sang in Wozzeck, Samson et Dalila, and Das Schloss by Reimann, first performance, 1992 at Deutsche Oper Berlin; Frequent concert appearances. Honour: Chevalier dans l'Ordre des Palmes Academiques, 1997. Current Management: Concertino. Address: c/o Berliner Str 40, D-14467 Potsdam, Germany.

MEYEROWITZ Jan, b. 23 Apr 1913, Beslau, Germany. Composer. Education: Studied in Berlin with Zemlinsky and in Rome with Respighi and Casella. Career: Resident in Belgium, 1938-46; Naturalized US Citizen, 1951; Taught at the Berkshire Music Center, Tanglewood, 1948-51 and at Brooklyn 1954-61 and City 1962-80 Colleges of the City University of New York. Compositions include: Operas, The Barrier, 1950; Eastward in Eden, 1951; Simoon, 1950; Bad Boys in School, 1953; Esther, 1957; Port Town, 1960; Godfather Death, 1961; Die Doppelgängerin, 1967; Orchestral, Silesian Symphony, 1957; Symphony Midrash Esther, 1957; Flemish Overture, 1959; Flute Concerto, 1962; Oboe Concerto, 1963; Sinfonia Brevissima, 1965; 6 Pieces for Orchestra, 1967; 7 Pieces for Orchestra, 1972; 6 Songs for Soprano and Orchestra, 1979; Cantatas and other choral music; Chamber, Woodwind Quintet, 1954; String Quartet, 1955; Violin Sonata, 1960; Flute Sonata, 1961; Piano Sonata, 1958; Songs. Publications: Monograph on Schoenberg, 1967 and Der echte Judische Witz, Berlin, 1971. Address: ASCAP, ASCAP Building, One Lincoln Plaza, NY 10023, USA.

MEYERS Anne Akiko, b. 1970, San Diego, California, USA. Violinist. Education: Indiana University with Josef Gingold; Colburn School of Performing Arts with Alice and Eleanor Schoenfeld; Dorothy DeLay and Masao Kawasaki at Juilliard School, New York. Career: Debut as concerto soloist, age 7; Later appeared with Los Angeles Philharmonic, New York Philharmonic conducted by Mehta and New York String Orchestra at Carnegie Hall; Far East engagements with Japan Philharmonic and NHK Symphony Orchestra; Summer festivals include Aspen, Ravinia, Tanglewood, Hollywood Bowl; Tours: St Louis Symphony with Leonard Slatkin, Australian Chamber Orchestra, Baltimore Symphony with David Zinman, Moscow Philharmonic; Appeared on TV with John Williams and Boston Pops; Played with Minnesota Orchestra, Prague Symphony Orchestra, Hallé Orchestra, Orchestre de Paris and Jerusalem Symphony; Appearances in Montreal Symphony, Boston Symphony, St Louis Symphony, Philadelphia Orchestra, Toronto Symphony, Swedish Radio Orchestra, Moscow Philharmonic, Belgian Radio Orchestra; Berlin Radio Symphony. Recordings include: Concertos by Barber and Bruch with Royal Philharmonic Orchestra and Christopher Seaman; Lalo Symphonie Espagnole and Bruch Scottish Fantasy with Royal Philharmonic Orchestra, Lopez-Cobos, Cesar Franck and Richard Strauss Sonatas; Mendelssohn with Philharmonia and Andrew Litton; Salut d'Amour for RCA. Contributions to: Featured, Strad Magazine. Honours: Youngest to sign with Young Concert Artists; Sole recipient of Avery Fisher Career Grant, 1993. Current Management: ICM Artists, 40 W 57th St, New York, NY 10019; Jasper Parrott, London; Japan Arts, Tokyo. Address: c/o Harrison/Parrott Ltd, 12 Penzance Place, London W11 4PA, England.

MEYERSON Janice, b. 1950, Omaha, Nebraska, USA. Mezzo-soprano. m. Raymond Scheindlin, 5 Apr 1986. Education: BA, Washington University, St Louis, Missouri, 1973; MM, New England Conservatory, 1975; Fellowship, Berkshire Music Center (Tanglewood), 1976-77. Career: Carmen (title role), New York City Opera and Théâtre Royal de la Monnaie, Brussels; Amneris in Aida, Teatro Colón, Buenos Aires and Frankfurt Opera; Santuzza in Cavalleria Rusticana, New York City Opera; Judith in Bluebeard's Castle, New York Philharmonic and Palacio de Bellas Artes, Mexico City; Brangaene in Tristan and Isolde, Leonard Bernstein conducting Philadelphia Orchestra; Soloist, Mahler's 3rd Symphony, American Symphony, Carnegie Hall; Soloist, Boston Symphony, Milwaukee Symphony, Minnesota Orchestra, New Orleans Symphony, National Symphony, Dallas Symphony, Washington Opera, Houston Grand Opera, Montreal Opera, Opera Company of Philadelphia, Aspen Festival, Spoleto USA, Marlboro, Tanglewood, Wolf Trap, Schleswig-Holstein Music Festival, Deutsche Oper Berlin, Moscow State Symphony Orchestra. Recordings: For the Night to Wear, with Boston Musica Viva, 1994. Address: 420 Riverside Drive, Apt GC, New York, NY 10025, USA.

MEYFARTH Jutta, b. 1933, Germany. Singer (Soprano). Career: Sang at Basle in 1955; Aachen Opera 1956-59; Member of Frankfurt Opera from 1959; La Scala Milan debut 1960; Maggio Musicale Florence 1961, as Elsa in Lohengrin; Bayreuth Festival 1962-64, as Freia, Gutrune and Sieglinde; Munich Opera 1965, as Donna Anna; Guest appearances in Buenos Aires, Brussels, Rome, London, Lisbon, Athens, Lyon and Antwerp; Other roles included Wagner's Isolde,The Empress in Die Frau ohne Schatten, Aida, and Martha in Tiefland.

MEZO Laszlo, b. 1940, Hungary. Cellist. Education: Studied at the Franz Liszt Academy, Budapest. Career: Cellist of the Bartók Quartet from 1977; Performances in nearly every European country and tours of Australia, Canada, Japan, New Zealand and the USA; Festival appearances at Adelaide, Ascona, Aix, Venice, Dubrovnik, Edinburgh, Helsinki, Lucerne, Menton, Prague, Vienna, Spoleto and Schwetzingen; Tour of Britain 1986 including concerts at Cheltenham, Dartington, Philharmonic Hall, Liverpool, RNCM, Manchester and the Wigmore Hall; Tours of Britain 1988 and 1990 featuring visits to the Sheldonian Theatre, Oxford, Wigmore Hall, Harewood House and Birmingham; Repertoire includes standard classics and Hungarian works by Bartók, Durko, Bozay, Kadosa, Soproni, Farkas, Szabo and Lang. Recordings include: Complete quartets of Mozart, Beethoven and Brahms; Major works of Haydn and Schubert (Hungaraton); Complete quartets of Bartók (Erato). Honours: With Members of Bartók Quartet, Kossuth Prize, Outstanding Artists of the Hungarian People's Republic 1981; UNESCO/IMC Prize 1981. Address: c/o Ingpen & Williams Ltd, 26 Wadham Road, London SW15 2LR, England.

MICHAEL Audrey, b. 11 Nov 1949, Geneva, Switzerland. Singer (Soprano). Education: Studied with father, Jean-Marie Auberson, and in Milan and Hamburg. Career: Sang with the Hamburg Staatsoper, 1976-81, Deutsche Oper am Rhein Dusseldorf, 1981-86; Guest appearances throughout Europe; Roles have included Gluck's Amor in Orpheus, Ilia (Idomeneo), Mozart's Pamina, Susanna, Countess and Papagena, Elvira (L'Italiana in Algeri), Adina, Lauretta, Zdenka, Mélisande and Elisabeth Zimmer in Elegy for Young Lovers by Henze; Sang at Hamburg in the premieres of Kommen und gehen by Heinz Holliger, 1978, William Ratcliff by Ostendorf, 1982 and Jakob Lenz by Wolfgang Rihm, 1979; Théâtre Municipal Lausanne, 1991 as Sextus in Gluck's La Clemenza di Tito; Sang Sextus at the Théâtre des Champs Elysées, Paris, 1996; Concert engagements in the Baroque and modern repertory throughout Switzerland and in Berlin, Stuttgart, Paris, Lisbon and Buenos Aires. Recordings include: Monteverdi Orfeo, L'Enfant et les Sortilèges, Masses by Schubert and Beethoven; Rigoletto, Luisa Miller and Parsifal; Monteverdi Ballo delle Ingrate and Vespers of 1610. Address: c/o Opéra de Lausanne, PO Box 3972, CH-1002 Lausanne, Switzerland.

MICHAEL Beth, b. 1962, Gwent, Wales. Singer (Soprano). Education: Studied at the Welsh College of Music and Drama and the RAM, London. Debut: Pheadra in Cavalli's L'Egisto for Scottish Opera, 1982. Career: Roles with Opera 80/English Touring Opera include Cenerentola, Carmen, Gretel, Frasquite, the Merry Widow and Lucia; Further engagements as Manon

Lescaut, Butterfly (Surrey Opera), Tosca (Regency Opera) and at Wexford, Bayreuth and London (English National Opera); Appearances with the Royal Opera, Covent Garden, in Death in Venice, The Cunning Little Vixen, Turandot, Der Rosenkavalier, La Traviata and Die Walküre; Countess Ceprano in Rigoletto, 1997; Many concert appearances, and engagements on radio and television. Address: c/o English National Opera (contracts), St Martin's Lane, London WC2, England.

MICHAEL Nadja, b. 1969, Leipzig, Germany. Singer (Mezzo-soprano). Education: Studied in Stuttgart and in USA with Carlos Montane. Debut: Ludiwgsburg Festival 1993, as Third Lady in Die Zauberflöte. Career: Appearances at Wiesbaden as Amastris (Xerxes) and Eustazio (Rinaldo), Dulcinée in Don Quixote at St Gallen and Tchaikovsky's Olga at Glyndebourne; Strauss's Dryad at the Dresden Semper Oper and Handel at the Berlin Staatsoper; Season 1997-98 as Varvara in Katya Kabanova at Covent Garden (debut), Ottavia in Poppea at Munich, Wagner's Venus at Naples and Mahler's Rückert Lieder and Second Symphony; Further concerts include Elijah, Messiah, Berio's Folk Songs and Mahler's Das Lied von der Erde (Swiss TV); Appearances in Carmen in Italy and at St Gallen and Tokyo. Address: Balmer & Dixon Management, 8006 Zurich, Granitweg 2, Switzerland.

MICHAELIDES Nefen, b. 14 February 1939, Caucasian Origin. Musicologist; Piano Pedagogue. m. Stelios Michaelides, 24 February 1960, 1 son. Education: Graduate, #Conservatory of Felix Mendelssohn Bartholdy, Leipzig, Germany, 1966; PhD, Martin Luther University, Halle, Germany, 1972. Career: Representative of Cyprus in International Music Conferences; Jury Member, International Music Competitions; Liaison Officer, ICTM (UNESCO), 1982-; Founder, Non Profit Making School in Limassol, 1982; National Committee, International Repertory of Music Literature Centre, New York, 1995-. Honours: Numerous Prizes & Awards, including 4th Prize, International Piano Competition, Senigollia, Italy, 1994; 1st Prize, International Piano Competition, Palermo, Italy, 1995. Address: Professional Music School, Piano Department, 16 Philopimenos Street, Limassol 3075, Cyprus.

MICHAELS-MOORE Anthony, b. 8 Apr 1957, Essex, England. Singer (Baritone). Education: Studied at Newcastle University with Denis Matthews and at Royal Scottish Academy; Further study with Eduardo Asquez and Neilson Taylor. Career includes: Principal Baritone at Covent Garden from 1987 in Jenufa, Boris Godunov, Turandot, Rigoletto, Pagliacci, Der Freischütz and La Bohème; English National Opera from 1987 as Zurga, Marcello and the Count in new production of Figaro, 1991; Sang Escamillo, Creon in Oedipus Rex and Figaro; US debut with Philadelphia Opera 1989 as Guglielmo, followed by Missa Solemnis in Los Angeles, 1990; Other appearances include: Germont and Posa in new production of Don Carlos in 1993 for Opera North; Concert engagements include Mehul's Uthal conducted by Neeme Järvi; London concert debut in Duruflé Requiem at the Elizabeth Hall; Also sings The Kingdom, Belshazzar's Feast, Carmina Burana, Rossini's Stabat Mater, Elijah and The Creation; Sang Don Fernando in the world premiere production of Gerhard's The Duenna at Madrid, 1992; Season 1992-93 as Marcello and Forester in Vixen at Covent Garden and in a Rossini concert at Turin; Opened 1993-94 season at La Scala as Licinius in La Vestale by Spontini; Lescaut, Belcore and Figaro at Vienna Staatsoper, 1994 and Sharpless and Orestes at Paris Bastille, 1994; Sang Stankar in Stiffelio, and Simon Boccanegra, ROH, 1995; Macbeth in the 1847 version of Verdi's opera at Covent Garden, 1997. Recordings: Carmina Burana under Previn with Vienna Philharmonic; La Vestale at La Scala; Die Walpurgisnacht; Szymanowski's Stabat Mater; Puccini Highlights, ROH. Honour: Joint Winner of Luciano Pavarotti Opera Company of Philadelphia Competition. Address: Harold Holt Ltd, 31 Sinclair Road, London, W14 0NS, England.

MICHAILOV Maxim, b. 1961, Moscow, Russia. Singer (Bass). Education: Studied at the Gnessin Conservatory, Moscow. Career: Sang with the Bolshoi company, Moscow, from 1987 as Sarastro, Ivan Khovantsky in Khovanshchina, Tsar Dodon in The Golden Cockerel and Zaccaria in Nabucco; Edinburgh Festival 1991 on tour with the Bolshoi in Eugene Onegin and Rimsky's Christmas Eve; Guest appearances in opera and concert throughout Russia; Sang Sarastro at Schönbrunn, Vienna, 1996. Address: c/o Bolskoi Theatre, 103009 Moscow, C1S, Russia.

MICHALICA Peter. Violinist. Education: Conservatory of Music, Bratislava, 1959-65; VSMU Academy Superior of Musical Arts, Bratislava, 1965-69; PI Tchaikovsky Conservatory, Moscow, 1971-74; Royal Conservatory of Music, Brussels, 1975. Career: Associate Professor, 1969-71, Professor, 1976-83, Professor, 1989-, Academy Superior of Music, Bratislava; Professor, Conservatory of Music, Bratislava, 1977-83, 1993-; Guest Professor, 1982, Fulbright Professor, 1983, Michigan University, Lansing, USA; Fulbright Professor, 1985-87, Visiting Professor, 1987-88, Wayne University, Detroit, USA; Regular Concerts on

Four Continents, including, Italy, Germany, Hungary, Spain, Czech Republic, India, Russia, Switzerland, Bulgaria, Yugoslavia, Austria, Romania, China, Cuba, Tunisia, Poland, Norway, Canada, Belgium, England, France, USA; Numerous International Festivals. Recordings: LP's, CD's and for TV and Radio. Honours: 1st Prize, National Competitions, Prague and Bratislava, 1961, 1962, 1968; Prize, Carl Flesch International Violin Competition, England, 1966; Golden Medals and Diplomas, International Laureates Days, K Popova, Pleven, Bulgaria, 1970, 1972; Premier Prix avec Grande Distinction, Royal Conservatory, Brussels, 1975; F Kafenda prize, Slovak Music Foundation, 1976; Prize, International Prix Musical de Radio, Brno, 1978; Awards of Czech Radio and TV, 1978, 1980; National Prize, Slovak Government, 1982; Meritorious Artist of Czechoslovakia, Government of Czechoslovakia, 1986. Memberships include: Honorary President, International Summer Music Festival, Bojnice, Slovakia; Board Director, Jan Cikker Foundation; Rotary Club, Bratislava; Honorary President, Association of Friendship Slovakia/Israel. Address: Stefanikova 7, SK-811 06 Bratislava, Slovakia.

MICHALKO Jan (Vladimir), b. 6 May 1951, Myslenice, Slovakia. Musician; Concert Organist; Teacher. m. Marta Kacianova, 7 Jun 1985, 1 s, 1 d. Education: University of Munich, 1973; Evangelical Theological Faculty of Comenius University, ThM, 1974; Conservatorium Bratislava, 1975; Graduate School of Performing Arts, Bratislava, MusM, 1979. Career: Associate Professor and Chair Department of Church Music, Graduate School of Performing Arts, Bratislava; Teacher of Organ Improvisation, Conservatorium, Bratislava; Senior Organist at the Lutheran Great Church in Bratislava; President of the Church Music Committee for the Lutheran Church in Slovakia; Concert tours in Finland, Austria, Hungary, Germany, USA, UK, Italy, Russia, France, Poland, Rumania, Latvia, Lithuania and Bulgaria; Chamber Cembalo Player; Appearing on Czechoslovak Television, Gala Concert, 1987 and 1988; International Music Festival MELOS-Ethos Bratislava, 1991; International Music Festival, Atelier, Praha, 1993; 2nd International Slovak Historic Organs, 1993; Bratislava Music Festival, 1993; Recitals; Soloist with Slovak Philharmonic, 1985 and 1987, Slovak Chamber Orchestra, 1987 and State Philharmonic Kosice, 1989. Compositions: Music for theatre plays, Theatre Nitra, Bratislava; Stage music for TV, films and Slovak Television, 1994. Recordings: 6 LP records and 6 CDs. Publication: Hudobna vychova (Musical Education), textbook, 1987. Honour: Annual Interpretation Frico Kafenda Prize, 1990. Current Management: Slovkoncert. Address: 81103 Bratislava, Konventná 11, Slovakia.

MICHALOVA Eva, b. 9 August 1939, Banska Bystrica, Slovakia. Chief, Universal Department. m. Ivan Michal, 12 August 1961, 2 daughters. Educawtion: Musical Department, Couienius University, Bratislava. Contributions to: Major Slovak Magazines. Honours: Doctor of Pedagogic, Charles University, Prague. Membership: Slovak Musical Society. Hobby: Literature. Address: Svermova 1, 974 01 Banska Bystrica, Slovakia.

MICHALOWSKA Krystyna, b. 13 July 1946, Vilnius, Poland. Singer (Mezzo-soprano). Education: Studied in Gdansk. Debut: Bydgoszcz 1970, as Azucena. Career: Engagements in Szczecin, Poznan and Gdansk; Guest appearances in Germany, Bulgaria, Rumania, Russia and Czechkoslovakia. Appearances at Bielfeld and elsewhere in Germany from 1980, as Leonora in La Favorita, Carmen, Eboli, Lady Macbeth, Ulrica, Fides, Rosina, Konchakovna, Olga and Larina in Eugene Onegin, Dalila, Laura in La Gioconda, Sara in Roberto Devereux and the Nurse in Die Frau ohne Schatten; Bielefeld 1991, in Yerma by Villa-Lobos, as Ortrud and in the premiere of Katharin Blum by Tilo Medek; Frequent concert appearances. Address: c/o Stadtisches Buhnen, Brunnenstrasse 3, 4800 Bielefeld 1, Germany.

MICHEL Winfried, b. 21 Apr 1948, Fulda, Germany. Flautist;Composer. Education: Studied at the Royal Conservatorie as a student of Frans Bruggen. Debut: Kassel Palais bellevue, 1974. Career: Solo performances at Flanders Festival, Concertgebouw Amsterdam, Tage fur Alte Musik Kassel, and Radio BRT Bruxelles, BBC London and Radio Hilversum. Compositions include: Piano Trio, 1990; TU-I for recorder and harpsichord; Horen and Sehen for violoncello; 20 volumes of chamber music. Recordings include: Corelli and Vivaldi Concertos; Simonetti, trio sonatas; Kasseler Avantgarde with own compositions; Telemann, 4 sonatas. Publications: JJ Quantz, Solfeggi, 1980; V Eych, 1982; J Haydn, first publication of 6 sonatas, 1993. Honours: Coupe du Conseil d'Ile de France, 1992. Memberships: European Recorder Teachers Association; Professor, Akademie Kassel and the Conservatoire in Munster. Hobbies: Mountain Tours. Address: Wiener Str 65a, D-48145 Munster, Germany.

MICHELI Lorenzo, b. 13 June 1975, Milan, Italy. Guitarist. Education: Classical Lycée Certificate, full marks; Studied under Paola Coppi at Milan; Graduated, full marks, Conservatory of Trieste; Studied at F Zigante, Lausanne, and with O Ghiglia, Accademia Chigiana, Siena, Musik-Akademie, Basel; Currently

studying Greek, Latin and Medieval Literatures, University of Milan. Debut: Recital, Milan, 1994; With Turin Philharmonic Orchestra, Alessandria, 1997. Career: Many solo recitals and chamber music concerts throughout Italy. Recordings: Works by J Rodrigo, A Piazzolla, Tansman and Barrios; Dionisio Aguado's Complete Works, forthcoming. Honours: 1st Prize, TIM, Rome, 1996; Finalist, Prix Pro Musicis, Paris, 1996; 1st Prize, Gargano, 1996; 2nd Prize, Maria Camals, Barcelona, 1997; 1st Prize, Alessandria, 1997. Address: Via Berguzzo 5, 20148 Milan, Italy.

MICHELOW Sybil, b. 12 Aug 1925, Johannesburg, South Africa. Singer (Contralto). m. Dr Derek Goldfoot, 18 Apr 1950. Education: Music Diploma, Witwatersrand University, South Africa; Private studies with Franz Reizensten and Mary Jarred. Debut: London, 1958. Career: Concert performances in UK and aboard, especially of Handel's Messiah; Frequent radio and television appearances, notably in Rule Britannia at the Last Night of the Proms; Singing Instructor, Royal Academy of Dramatic Art, 1956-. Compositions include: Incidental music for Royal Academy of Dramatic Art production of Brecht plays Chalk Circle and Mother Courage; Children's stories with music, South African Broadcasting Corporation. Recordings include: Music of Court Homes, volume 4, and Bach Cantatas 78 and 106; Bliss Pastoral; Dallapiccola Sicut Umbra. Memberships: Royal Society of Musicians of Great Britain, Governor, 1982-85, 1988-93; Incorporated Society of Musicians. Hobbies: Piano in chamber music groups; Calligraphy. Address: 50 Chatsworth Road, London NW2 4DD, England.

MICHELS Maria, b. 1931, Germany. Singer (Soprano). Career: Sang at the Syadtishe Oper Berlin from 1955 and appeared further in opera at Kiel, Mannheim and Frankfurt; Essen 1963-66, Munich Staatsoper 1966-69, then the Hanover Opera; roles have included Cherubini's Médée, the Queen of Night, Strauss's Sophie and Zerbinetta, Lulu, Lucia di Lammermooor, Musetta and Olympia; Guest appearances at the Vienna and Stuttgart State Operas, Florence and Brussels (in Arabella), Paris Opera and Barcelona (as Lulu), 1969).

MICHIELS Jan Prosper, b. 10 Oct 1966, Izegem, Belgium. Solo Concert Pianist. m. Inge Spinette, 16 Aug 1991. Education: Izegem College; Royal Conservatory, Brussels, 1984-88; With Hans Leygraf, Hochschule der Künste, Berlin. Career: Professor of Piano, Royal Conservatory, Brussels; Worked with conductors as Peter Eötvös, Hans Zender, Alexander Rahbari. Recordings: Several CDs with works of Brahms, Beethoven, Mendelssohn, Debussy, Ligeti, Huybrechts, Poulenc, Weber, Benjamin; Ligeti, Etudes I-XIV; Brahms, op 116-119; Debussy, Préludes, Images. Honours: Prizewinner, several competitions including Queen Elizabeth Competition, Brussels, 1991. Hobby: Contemporary Art. Current Management: Lyons Management, London, England. Address: Achterstraat 22B, B-9310 Meldert (Aalst), Belgium.

MICHNIEWSKI Wojciech, b. 4 Apr 1947, Lodz, Poland. Conductor; Composer. Education: Conducting, Theory of Music, Composition, Warsaw Academy of Music, 1966-72; Honours degree with distinction, 1972. Career: Assistant Conductor 1973-76, Conductor 1976-79, Warsaw National Philharmonic Orchestra; Artistic Director, The Grand Opera Theatre, Lodz, 1979-81; Musical Director, Modern Stage, Warsaw Chamber Opera, 1979-83; Principal Guest Conductor, Polish Chamber Orchestra and Sinfonia Varsovia, 1984-; Conductor, concerts in most European countries, South America, Asia; Appeared West Berlin Philharmonic Hall, La Scala, Milan, Teatro Colon in Buenos Aires; Participant in numerous international festivals including Steyrischer Herbst, Graz, Austria; International May Festival, Barcelona, Spain; Recontres Musicales, Metz, France; International May Festival, Wiesbaden, Germany; Bemus Festival, Belgrade, Yugoslavia; Dimitria Festival, Thessaloniki, Greece; Warsaw Autumn Festival; Wratisalvia Cantans Music Festival; International Biennale, East Berlin; Polish Chamber Orchestra and Sinfonia Varsovia, 1984-86; General and Artistic Director, The Poznan Philharmonic Orchestra, 1987-; Others. Recordings: Gramophone Records; CBS Japan; EMI; Pavane Olympia; Polskie Nagrania Muza; Polton; Tonpress; Radio and TV Recordings. Hobbies: Climbing; Skiing; Sailing; Painting. Current Management: Polish Artists Agency PAGART. Address: ul Braci Zauskich 3/77, 01 773 Warsaw, Poland.

MICKA Vit, b. 1 December 1935, Prague, Czech Republic. Conductor; Composer. m. 1966. Education: Academy of Music, Prague. Debut: National Theatre, Prague. Career: Conductor, Moravian Philharomy, 1968-81; Director, Pilsen Radio Orchestra, 1981-90; Professor, Academy of Music, Prague. Compositions: Concerto, for Piano, Strings, Trumpets; Concert, for Violin & Orchestra; Lonely Statues, for Organ & Strings. Recordings: Contemporary Music. Honour: Prize, Competition for Young Violinists, 1977. Membership: Composers Guild, Prague. Address: Holeckova 19, 15000 Prague 5, Czech Republic.

MIDDENWAY Ralph, b. 9 September 1932, Sydney, NSW, Australia. Composer; Music Critic. Education: New South Wales Conservatory, 1951-57; BA, University of Sydney, 1958. Career includes: Faculty of Music, University of Adelaide, 1977-82; Music Critic, 1970-86; Horticulturist, from 1989. Compositions include: The Child of Heaven, for chorus, brass sextete and percussion, 1971; Stone River, for medium voice and 4 percussion, 1984; Stream of Time, for soprano, bass clarinet and piano, 1984; Sinfonia Concertante for brass quintet and orchestra, 1985; Sonata Capricciosa, for piano, 1986; Mosaics for orchestra and saxophone ensemble, 1986; The Letters of Amalie Dietrich, 1 act opera, 1986, Barossa, Singspiel in 2 acts, 1988; The Lamentations of Jeremiah for chorus, 1990; The Eye of Heaven for baritone and string quartet, 1991; Seven Sogns of John Donne for baritone and chamber orchestra, 1994; Sonata-East River for piano, 1995. Commissions from University of Adelaide Foundation and Adelaide Chamber Orchestra, among others. Address: c/o APRA, 1A Eden Street, Crows Nest, NSW 2065, Australia.

MIDORI, b. 25 October 1971, Osaka, Japan. Violinist. Education: Studied with her mother, Setsu Goto, and at Juilliard with Dorothy DeLay, Jens Ellerman and Yang-Ho Kim. Debut: Gala Concert with the New York Philharmonic, 1982. Career: Appearances at the White House, Kennedy Center, Carnegie Hall, the Musikverein, the Philharmonic in Berlin and other major centres; Orchestras include the Berlin Philharmonic, the Boston and Chicago Symphony Orchestras, London Symphony, the Orchestre de Paris, Israel Philharmonic and the Philadelphia Orchestra; Conductors have included Abbado, Ashkenazy, Barenboim, Bernstein (Serenade), Mehta and Rostropovitch; Appeared at the Concertgebeow, Amsterdam; Founded the Midori Foundation to promote the learning and education of classical music to children of all ages all over the world; Played the Tchaikovsky Concerto on debut at the London Proms, 1993. Recordings include: Dvorák Concerto with the New York Philharmonic; Complete Paganini Caprices; Bartók's Concertos with the Berlin Philharmonic and a live recording of Carnegie Hall Recital Debut (Sony Classical); CD, Encore, released by Sony Classical. Address: c/o ICM Artists, 40 West 57th Street, New York, NY 10019, USA.

MIGENES Julia, b. 13 Mar 1949, New York, USA. Singer (Soprano). Education: New York High School for Performing Arts and the Juilliard School; Cologne with Gisela Ultman. Career: Appeared on Broadway and at the New York City Opera from 1965 (debut in The Saint of Bleecker Street); Vienna Volksoper 1973-78; Roles included Mozart's Despina, Blonchen and Susanna, Schmidt's Esmeralda, Strauss's Sophie and Olympia in Les Contes d'Hoffmann; Metropolitan Opera from 1979, in Mahagonny, Lulu, Pagliacci and La Bohème; Geneva Opera 1983 as Salome; Vienna Staatsoper as Lulu; TV appearances in Germany and on Channel 4, England; Appeared in Francesco Rossi's 1984 film of Carmen; Covent Garden debut 1987, as Manon; Sang Tosca at Earl's Court London, 1991; concert with Domingo at Buenos Aires, 1992. Recordings: Notre Dame; Videos of Carmen and La Voix Humaine. Honours include: Golden Bambi Awards from German TV, 1980, 1981. Address: c/o Stafford Law Associates, 6 Barham Close, Weybridge, Surrey KT13 9PR, England.

MIHELCIC Pavel, b. 8 Nov 1937, Novo Mesto, Yugoslavia. Composer. m. Majda Lovse, 10 Apr 1965, 2 daughters. Education: Diploma, 1963, Special Class 1967, Academy of Music, Ljublijana. Career: Professor, Conservatory of Music, 1982-; Manager, Department of Smyphonic Music, Ljubljana Broadcasting Corporation, 1982-. Compositions include: Orchestral works: Bridge for strings; Asphalt ballet; Concerto for horn and orchestra; Sinfonietta; Musique Funèbre for violin and orchestra; Chamber works: Limite; Blow Up; Take-off for piano; Sonatine; Sonata 80; Chorus, 1,2,3,4,5,10,13; Games and Reflections; Double Break; Published by Edition DSS, Ljubljana and Edition Peters, Leipzig; Recorded: Quinta Essentia for brass quintet; Timber-line for chamber orchestra; Exposition and Reflections for 9 horns; Stop-time for horn and chamber orchestra; Team for woodwind quintet; Introduction and Sequences for orchestra; Scenes From Bela Krajina; Fading Pictures; Snow of First Youth for orchestra. Contributions to: Standing Music Critic, Delo, Ljubljana; Zvuk, Sarajevo. Honours: Preseren Prize, 1979; Zupancic Prize, 1984. Memberships: President, Slovenian Composers Society, 1984-. Address: Melikova ul 10, 61108 Ljubjana, Slovenia.

MIKHAILOV Maxim, b. 1956, Moscow. Singer (Bass-baritone). Education: Gnessin Institute, Moscow, until 1988. Career: Soloist at the Bolshoi Theatre from 1987; Recitalist and guest opera appearances in Italy, Germany, Denmark, Hungary and elsewhere; Season 1993-94 in Rossini's La Scala di Seta and Massenet's Chérubin at the Wiener Kammeroper, in the Mozart Festival at Schönbrunn and in Rachmaninov's Miserly Knight at the Bolshoi; Seaso 1995 with Orlik in Mazeppa at Amsterdam, concert performance of Prokoviev's War and Peace at the Vienna Konzerthaus, and Rimsky's May Night at the Wexford Festival; Season 1996-97 with Prince Khovansky in Khovanshchina at Nantes and Mozart's Masetto at Covent Garden. Address: Allied Artists, 42 Montpelier Square, London SW7 1JZ, England.

MIKI Minoru, b. 16 Mar 1930, Tokushima, Shikoku, Japan. Composer. Education: Studied composition with Ifukube at the Toyko National University of Fine Arts and Music, 1951-55. Career: Founder and Artistic Director, Ensemble Nipponia, later Pro Musica Nipponia, ensemble of traditional Japanese instruments, 1964; Foreign tours with the Ensemble from 1972; Founded the opera theatre ensemble Utaza, 1986; Founded the multi-culture ensemble YUI Ensemble, 1990; Founded the Orchestra Asia, 1993. Compositions include: Eurasian Triology including Symphony for Two Worlds, 1969-81; Shunkin-Sho, opera in 3 acts, Tokyo, 1975; Ada (An Actor's Revenge). opera in 2 acts, English Music Theatre at the Old Vic, London, 1979; The Monkey Poet, folk opera, 1983; Joruri, opera in 3 acts, St Louis. 1985; Yomigaeru, musical-opera, Tokyo, 1989; Wakahime, opera in 3 acts, Okayama, 1991; Shizuka and Yoshitsune, opera in 3 acts, Kamakura, 1993. recordings: Works Selections I-IV of Minoru Miki including Eurasian Triology, Camerata Records. Publications: The Method of Japanese Instruments, 1995. Honours: Grand Prize of the National Art Festival, 1970; Giraud Opera Prize for composition of Shunkin-sho, 1976; National Purple Ribbon, 1994. Memberships: Vice President, Japan Federation of Composers; Director, Kurashiki City Cultural Foundation; Director, Yonden Cultural Foundation. Current Management: Japan Arts Corporation, Tokyo. Address: 1-11-6 Higashi Nogama, Komae-shi, Tokyo 201, Japan.

MIKULA-DRABEK Marzena Maria, b. 21 June 1949, Zabrze, Poland. Pianist; Composer; Musical Director. m. Andrzej Drabek, 1984, 2 sons. Education: Piano Diploma, Music Lyceum, Katowice. Debut: International Music Competition, Geneva, 1972. Career: Concert Tours with Paris Chamber Ensemble in Southern France and Switzerland; Collaboration, Wyspianski Theatre, Katowice; Musical Director, State New Theatre, Zabrze, 1974-. Compositions: Shakespeare - Richard III; Plaut - The Merchant; Moliere - The Miser; Fredro - Zemsta, The New Don Kichot (co-writer); Slowacki - Balladyna; Jonson - Volpone; Czechow - The Peewit. Recordings: Several Songs including Oh Lady, You Are Charming. Honours: Gold Mask of The Evening, 1981; Medal of Merit for Silesia, 1981; Silver Cross of Merit, 1984. Memberships: Society of Authors and Composers; ZAIKS. Hobby: Collecting Antiques and curios. Address: de Gaulle 43/6, 41-800 Zabrze, Poland.

MIKULAS Peter, b. 1955, Czechoslovakia. Singer (Bass). Education: Studied at the College of Music and Drama in Bratislava with Viktoria Stracenska. Career: Soloist with the Slovak National Theatre in Bratislava, 1978-; Roles have included Kecal in The Bartered Bride, Dulcamara, Gremin, Raimondo, Fiesco (Sinon Boccanegra), Don Alfonso and Sarastro; Guest appearances with the National Theatre Prague, the Berlin Staatsoper and other leading European theatres; Concert engagements with the Czech and Slovak Philharmonic Orchestras and at the Bratislava, Prague Spring and Carinthian Summer Festivals; Has sung in Vienna, Salzburg, Leipzig, Berlin, Tokyo, Lisbon, Madrid, Liverpool and most Italian centres. Honours: Prizewinner at the 1977 Antonin Dvorak International Singers Competition, Carlsbad; Tchaikovsky Competition, Moscow, 1982; Mirjam Helin Competition, Helsinki, 1984; Prize of the Union of Slovak Performing Artists for appearance in Suchon's Svatopluk. Address: Music International, 13 Ardilaun Road, London N5 2QR, England.

MILAN Susan, b. 1947, England. Flautist. m. 2 sons. Education: Junior Exhibitioner, Royal College of Music; Studied with John Francis at the Royal College of Music and Geoffrey Gilbert at the Guildhall School of Music; Attended the Marcel Moyse Masterclasses in Switzerland; Graduated from the Royal College of Music with Honours. Career: Principal Flute of the Bournemouth Sinfonietta, 1968, 1972; Principal Flute of the Royal Philharmonic Orchestra, 1974-82; Developed Solo Career; Many Commissions, the latest, 1992 Concerto by Robert Simpson; Quintet Charicciso J Feld; Tours wide world as Soloist and Recitalist; Runs two annual masterclass courses; Professor of Flute, Royal College of Music, London; Ensembles: London Sonata Group; Instrumental Quintet of London; Recital duo with Ian Brown; Recently premiered concerto composed for her by Robert Simpson at the Malvern Festival. Recordings: Records for Chandos Label and Upbeat Classics. Publications: Publishes editions for Boosey & Hawkes, and Pan Educational Music. Memberships: Lady Chairman, British Flute Society, 1990-94. Current Management: Upbeat Management. Address: 18 St Albans Avenue, Weybridge, Surrey KT13 8EN, England.

MILANOV Michail, b. 1949, Sofia, Bulgaria. Singer (Bass). Education: Studied in Sofia. Career: Sang in Bulgaria from 1974; Throughout Germany from 1977, notably at the Theater am Gärtnerplatz, Munich, from 1988 (Dosifey in Khovanshchina, 1992); Other roles have included Mefistofele, King Philip, Rocco, Hagen, King Mark, and Colline in La Bohème (Verona Arena, 1982); Many concert appearances and lieder recitals. Address: c/o Staatstheater am Gärtnerplatz, Gärtnerplatz, W-8000 Munich 5, Germany.

MILANOVA Stoika, b. 5 Aug 1945, Plovdiv, Bulgaria. Concert Violinist. Education: Studied with father Trendafil Milanova and with David Oistrakh at the Moscow Conservatory. Career: Appearances with principal UK orchestras from 1970; Engagements in most European countries; Yomiuri Nippon Symphony Orchestra, Japan, 1975; Concerts with the Hallé Orchestra and at the Hong Kong Festival; Tour for Australian Broadcasting Commission, 1976; US and Canadian debuts 1978; Tours of Eastern Europe 1985-86; Duo recitals with Radu Lupu and the late Malcolm Frager. Recordings: Balkanton (Bulgaria), some released by Harmonia Mundi, including the complete Brandenburg Concertos with Karl Munchinger and Prokofiev's Violin Concertos; Sonatas with Malcolm Frager (BASF). Honours include: 2nd Prize, Queen Elisabeth Competition, Belgium, 1967; 1st Prize, City of London International Competition (Carl Flesch), 1970; Grand Prix du Disque, 1972. Address: Terry Harrison Artists Management, The Orchard, Market Street, Charlbury, Oxon OX7 3PJ, England.

MILASHKINA Tamara (Andreyevna), b. 13 Sept 1934, Astrakhan, USSR. Singer (Soprano).Education: Studied with Elena Katul'skaya at the Moscow Conservatory. Debut: Bolshoy Theatre 1957, as Titania in Eugene Onegin. Career: Has sung Lisa in The Queen of Spades, Zarina in The Legend of Tsar Saltan, Yaroslavna in Prince Igor and Natasha (War and Peace) with the Bolshoy Company; Guest appearances at La Scala (Lida in La battaglia di Legnano, 1962), Helsinki, Paris, Wuppertal and in North America; Vienna Staatsoper 1971, as Lisa; Deutsche Oper Berlin 1974, as Tosca; Other roles include Fevronia (The Invisible City of Kitezh), Maria (Tchaikovsky's Mazeppa) and Lyuba (Prokofiev's Semyon Kotko) and Verdi's Elisabeth de Valois and Leonora (Il Trovatore). Recordings include: Mazeppa, Tosca, The Queen of Spades and The Stone Guest. Address: c/o Bolshoy Theatre, Pr Marxa 8/2, 103009 Moscow, Russia.

MILBURN Ellsworth, b. 6 Feb 1938, Greensburg, Pennsylvania, USA. Composer. Education: Studied with Scot Huston at the University of Cincinnati College-Conservatory of Music, 1956-58, with Roy Travis and Henri Lazarof at the University of California at Los Angeles, 1959-62, and with Milhaud at Mills College in Oakland, 1966-68. Career: Teacher, University of Cincinnati College-Conservatory of Music, 1970-75, Rice University, Houston, from 1975. Contributions include: Opera Gesualdo 1973; 5 Inventions for 2 flutes, 1965; Massacre of the Innocents, chorus, 1965; Concerto, piano and chamber orchestra,1967; String Trio, 1968; Soli, 5 players on 10 instruments, 1968; String Quintet, 1969; Soli II for 2 players on flutes and double bass, 1970; Voussoirs for orchestra, 1970; Soli III for clarinet, cello and piano, 1971; Soli IV, flute, oboe, double bass and harpsichord, 1972; Violin Sonata, 1972; Lament, harp, 1972; Spiritus mundi for high voice and 5 instruments, 1974. Address: Rice University, Shepherd School of Music, PO Box 1892, Houston, TX 77251, USA.

MILCHEVA-NONOVA Alexandrina, b. 27 Nov 1936, Shoumen, Bulgaria. Singer (Mezzo-soprano). Education: Studied with G Cherkin at the Sofia Conservatory. Debut: Warna 1961, as Dorabella in Cosi fan tutte. Career: Sang at theBulgarian National Opera in Sofia from 1968; Guest appearances in Vienna, Brussels, Paris, Amsterdam, Berlin (Komische Oper), London and Zurich; Munich 1979 and 1984; Verona Arena 1980 and 1984; Maggio Musicale Florence 1983, in Suor Angelica, Teatro Liceo Barcelona 1983, as Preziosilla in La Forza del Destino; La Scala Milan as Marfa in Khovanshchina, repeated at the Paris Opera 1984; Geneva 1984, as Adalgisa in Norma; Other roles include Azucena, the Princess in Adriana Lecouvreur, Dalila, Carmen and Cenerentola. Recordings include: Carmen, Boris Godunov and Khovanshchina (Balkanton); Aida and songs by Mussorgsky (Harmonia Mundi); Leoncavallo's La Bohème (Orfeo).

MILES Alastair, b. 1961, England. Singer (Bass). Education: Studied flute and voice at Guildhall School and National Opera Studio. Debut: Sang Trulove, in The Rake's Progress, for Opera 80, 1985. Career: Appearances from 1986 with Glyndebourne Festival and Touring Opera in Capriccio, Katya Kabanova, The Rake's Progress and Die Zauberflöte; Welsh National Opera as Basilio, Sparafucile, Raimondo and Silva, in Ernani; Royal Opera, Covent Garden in Parsifal, Viaggio a Reims, I Capuleti, Fidelio, Rigoletto, La Cenerentola and La Bohème; Other engagements in Vancouver, Amsterdam, San Francisco, Lyon and Deutsche Oper Berlin; Concert appearances under Gardiner in Beethoven's Missa Solemnis, Mozart's Requiem, Handel's Saul and Agrippina and Verdi Requiem; Under Harnoncourt in Handel's Samson and Bach Cantatas; With Kurt Masur in Elijah and the St Matthew Passion; Berlioz, La Damnation de Faust and Romeo and Juliette under Colin Davis; Bartolo in Figaro with Simon Rattle and the CBSO; Messiah under Helmut Rilling; Damnation of Faust under Chung; Season 1993 in the Choral Symphony under Giulini and title role in Le nozze di Figaro under Harnoncourt for Netherlands Opera; Sang Sir George Walton in I Puritani, Met, 1997. Recordings include: Lucia di Lammermoor; Saul and Agrippina; Elijah; La Traviata; Rigoletto; Verdi Requiem; Die Zauberflöte; Don Giovanni; Berlioz

Roméo et Juliette; Le nozze di Figaro; La Cenerentola. Address: IMG Artists Europe, Media House, 3 Burlington Lane, London, W4 2TH, England.

MILES-JOHNSON Deborah, b. England. Singer (Mezzo-soprano). Career: Concerts include: Handel's Israel in Egypt on tour to Spain, Elijah in Toronto, St Matthew Passion under Andrew Parrott, Mozart's C Minor Mass at the Barbican and Elgar's Music Makers at Peterborough Cathedral; Opera roles include: Bianca in The Rape of Lucretia, Mrs Peachum in The Beggar's Opera, Mdme Popova in Walton's Bear (Thaxted Festival), Orlofsky in Fledermaus (Haddo House) and Mrs Sedley in Peter Grimes; Royal Opera Covent Garden in Birtwistle's Gawain; Dido and Aeneas with the English Bach Festival; Season 1997 with Schubert and Haydn in Switzerland, Handel's Il Parnasso in Festa and Stravinsky's Requiem Canticles with the CBSO under Simon Rattle; Further concerts with Klangforum at the Vienna Konzerthaus (Barraqué's au dela du hasard...) and at the Wigmore Hall with Fretwork: debut there in Upon Silence by George Benjamin. Recordings include: Resurrection by Peter Maxwell Davies; Rutti's Magnificat; Pärt's Stabat Mater, with Fretwork, under Parrott. Address: 19 Gorham Drive, St Albans AL1 2HU, England.

MILKINA Nina, b. 27 Jan 1919, Moscow, USSR. Concert Pianist. m. Alastair Robert Masson Sedgwick, 1943, 1 son, 1 daughter. Education: Musical studies with the late Leon Conus, Moscow Conservatoire; Paris Conservatoire; Private study with Professors Harold Craxton, Tobias Matthay, London, England. Debut: 1st public appearance, age 11, with Lamoureux Orchestra, Paris. Career includes: Broadcasting, television, touring in Great Britain and abroad; Commissioned by BBC broadcast series of all Mozart's piano sonatas; Invited to give Mozart recital, bicentenary celebration of Mozart's birth, Edinburgh Festival; Widely noted for interpretation of Mozart's piano works. Recordings: For Westminster Company, New York; Pye Record Company and ASV Ltd, London; Mozart, Haydn, Scarlatti, Brahms Piano Trios, Scriabin, Rachmaninov, Prokofiev, Complete Chopin Mazurkas. Publications: Works for Piano; Early Compositions (Age 11). Honour: Honorary Member, Royal Academy of Music. Hobbies: Chess; Fly Fishing. Current Management: Marketing and the Arts. Address: 17 Montagu Square, London, W1H 1RD, England.

MILL Arnold van, b. 26 Mar 1921, Schiedam, Holland. Singer (Bass). Education: Studied at Rotterdam Conservatory. Debut: Brussels Théâtre de la Monnaie, 1946. Career: Sang in Holland and Belgium; Antwerp Opera 1950; Wiesbaden 1951-53; Staditsche Oper Berlin 1952, as Zaccaria in Nabucco; Maggio Musicale Florence 1953, in Agnese di Hohenstaufen; Hamburg Opera from 1953, notably in the 1969 premiere of Penderecki's The Devils of Loudun; Bayreuth Festival 1955-60, as Daland, Titurel,Fasolt and Fafner; Edinburgh Festival 1956, in The Barber of Bagdad and Oedipus Rex; Guest appearances in Vienna, Paris, Lisbon and Rio de Janeiro; Sang in Mahler's 8th Symphony with the LSO under Horenstein, 1959. Recordings: Tristan und Isolde, Die Walküre, Parsifal, Aida, Don Giovanni (Decca); Die Entführung and The Devils of Loudun (Philips).

MILLER Clement A, b. 29 Jan 1915, Cleveland, Ohio, USA. Musicologist. m. (1) Jean Miller (dec.), 2 sons, 1 daughter, (2) Nancy Voigt, 25 Sept 1983. Education: BM, Piano, 1936, MM, Music Theory, 1937, Cleveland Institute of Music; MA, Western Reserve University, 1942; PhD, Musicology, University of Michigan, 1951. Career: Instructor, Head of Music Department (History), Dean of Faculty, Acting Director, Cleveland Institute of Music, Ohio, 1937-65; Professor of Music, Fine Arts Department, John Carroll University, 1967-79. Publications: Heinrich Glarean: Dodecachordon, 1965; Franchinus Gaffurius: Musica Practica, 1968; Johannes Cochlaeus: Tetrachordum Musices, 1970; Sebald Heyden: De Arte Canendi, 1972; Hieronymus Cardanus: Writings on Music, 1973; Le Gendre, Maille, Morpain: Collected Chansons, 1981; Nicolaus Burtius: Musices Opusculum, 1983; Co-editor: A Correspondence of Renaissance Musicians, 1990; Commentary and Translation: Musica Practica by Bartolomeo Ramis de Pareia, 1993. Contributor to: The Musical Quarterly; Journal of the American Musicological Society; Die Musik in Geschichte und Gegenwart; New Grove Dictionary of Music and Musicians. Honours: Guggenheim Fellowship, 1974-75; Outstanding Educator of America, 1975. Memberships: American Musicological Society; Renaissance Society of America; Music Library Association; Musica Disciplina. Address: 7922 Bremen Avenue, Parma, OH 44129, USA.

MILLER D Douglas, b. 2 July 1941, Algona, Iowa, USA. Professor of Music; Conductor. m. Grace Ann Fogle, 6 June 1964, 1 son, 1 daughter. Education: Bachelor, Music Education, Drake University, 1963; Master of Music in Composition, Drake University, 1965; Doctor of Musical Arts in Choral Conducting, Indiana University, 1973. Appointments: Graduate Assistant, Indiana University, Bloomington, 1965-68; Instructor, University of Southern Maine, Gorham, 1968-69; Professor of Music, University Park, Penn State University, 1969-; Music Director/Conductor of ensembles: Penn State Philharmonic, 1969-82; Musica da Camera Chamber Orchestra, 1971-84; State College Choral Society, 1971-; Penn State Chamber Singers, 1982-; Penn State Concert Choir, 1983-; Pennsylvania Chorale, 1984-; Pennsylvania Chamber Chorale, 1992-. Publication: Heinrich Schütz - A Bibliography (co-author), 1986. Honour: Choice for outstanding academic book award for Heinrich Schütz - A Bibliography, 1986. Memberships: American Choral Directors Association, PA President, 1993-95, 1996-97; American Musicological Society; Society for Seventeenth Century Music; College Music Society; Chorus America; International Federation for Choral Music; Music Educators National Conference. Hobbies: Gardening; Building. Address: 330 Henderson Road, Julian, PA 16844, USA.

MILLER Jonathon, b. 21 July 1934, London, England. Stage Director. Education: Studied Natural Sciences, St John's College, Cambridge; MD 1959. Career: Director, Theatre Productions, including: Merchant of Venice; Three Sisters; The Seagull; Eugene O'Neill's Long Day's Journey into Night; The Emperor; The Taming of the Shrew, Royal Shakespeare Company, 1987; Artistic Director, Old Vic, 1988; Director, Opera, British Premiere of Arden Must Die; Orfeo; Janacek's Cunning Little Vixen; The Marriage of Figaro, English National Opera, 1978; Associate Producer, English National Opera, 1980; Productions with the company include: Arabella, Otello, Rigoletto, Don Giovanni, Magic Flute, Tosca; The Mikado, The Barber of Seville, Der Rosenkavalier and Carmen; Director, Tosca, Maggio Musicale, Florence, 1986; Numerous TV appearances, including series on the history of medicine, The Body in Question; Director 12 plays, BBC's Shakespeare Series, 1980-81; Producer, Mozart's Cosi fan tutte, 1985-86; Produced Don Giovanni at Florence, 1990, Le nozze di Figaro at the Vienna Festival, 1991; Season 1992 with Donizetti's Roberto Devereux at Monte Carlo, Manon Lescaut at La Scala, also at Trieste; Le nozze di Figaro at Florence; Covent Garden debut with Cosi fan tutte, 1995; Lecturer; Mitridate for the Salzburg Mozartwoche, 1997; Directed Strauss's Ariadne auf Naxos at the Maggio Musicale in Florence, 1997. Publications: The Body in Question; States of Mind; The Human Body; The Facts of Life; Subsequent Performances, 1986; Beyond The Fringe. Contributions: A Profile of Jonathon Miller by Michael Romain, 1992. Honour: Honorary DLit by Cambridge University, 1996. Address: c/o English National Opera, London Coliseum, St Martin's Lane, London WC2, England.

MILLER Kevin, b. 1929, Adelaide, Australia. Singer, Tenor. Education: Studied at Elder Conservatory, Adelaide. Career: Sang with the Australian National Theatre Company, Melbourne in operas by Mozart, Rossini and Vaughan Williams; Studied further in London, and in Rome with Dino Borgiloi and toured with the Australian Opera, 1955; Glyndebourne Festival, 1955-57, as Pedrillo, Monostatos and Scaramuccio in Ariadne auf Naxos; Welsh National Opera from 1958, notably as Rossini's Ramiro, Vanja in Katya Kabanova, Sellum in The Rake's Progress and Offenbach's Orpheus; Toured West Germany & Australia, 1962 with Orpheus in the Underworld and The Rake's Progress. Recordings: The Rake's Progress, conducted by the composer.

MILLER Lajos, b. 23 Jan 1940, Szombathely. Singer; Dramatic Bariton. m. Susanna Dobranszky, 31 Apr 1964, 1 son. Education: Diploma, Hungarian State Academy of Music, 1968. Debut: Hungarian State Opera House, 1968, in Szokolay's Hamlet. Career: Singer, major companies in Budapest, Vienna, Milan, Rome, Florence, Paris, Toulouse, Aix-en-Provence, Munich, Hamburg, Bonn, West Berlin, Brussels, Liège, Wexford Festival, Glasgow, Liverpool, Houston, Buenos Aires, New York, Carnegie, Philadelphia, Caracas; Roles include: Verdi Simon Boccanegra, Renato, Ballo, Luna Il Trovatore, Germont La Traviata, Rigoletto, Carlo in Ernani, Carlo in Forza, Miller, Giacomo in Giovanna d'Arco; Posa, Don Carlo; Macbeth, Rolando in Battaglia; Puccini; Scarpia in Tosca, Marcello in Tabarro, Sharpless in Butterfly; Sang Ivo in Berio's La Vera Storia at the Paris Opera, 1985; Teatro Colon Buenos Aires 1987, as Grigor, in The Tsar's Bride by Rimsky-Korsakov; Metropolitan 1989-90, as Luna in Il Trovatore; Opera de Montreal, 1990, as Verdi's Renato; Sang Yeletsky in The Queen of Spades at La Scala Milan, 1990; Films & TV Films include: Rigoletto; Pagliacci; Olympiade; Verdi's Ernani; Don Carlos; Simon Boccanegra; Attila; (Ezio); Puccini's; Butterfly as Sharpless; Boito, Nerone (Fanuel); Mercadante Il Giuramento, (Manfredo); One record of Verdi baritone arias. Honours: Budapest, 3 P. Erkel, 2P. Kodaly, 1972; Toulouse, Grand Prize, 4 extra Prizes, Paris, 1974; Budapest, Kossuth Prize, 1980. Address: 28-A Balogh Adam Utca, 1026 Budapest II, Hungary.

MILLER Leta (Ellen), b. 30 Sep 1947, Burbank, CA, USA. Musicologist; Flautist; Professor. m. Alan K Miller, 29 Jun 1969, 1 s, 1 d. Education: BA, 1969, PhD, 1978, Stanford University; MM, Hartt College of Music, 1971. Career: Professor, University of California, Santa Cruz; Recitalist of baroque and modern flute. Recordings: Modern Flute: The Prismatic Flute, by Lou Harrison, David Cope and Gordon Mumma, with Ensemble Nova, 1988, Solstice, Canticle No 3 Ariadne by Lou Harrison, with A Summerfield Set, 1990, Music of Germaine Tailleferre, 1993, Birthday Celebration by Lou Harrison, 1994, Chansons de Bilitis and other French Chamberworks, by Debussy, 1995; Baroque Flute: 6 Sonatas for Flute and Continuo and Flute Unaccompanied by CPE Bach, 1988, 6 Sonatas for Flute and Continuo, The Earlier Sonatas, 1990, 4 Sonatas for Flute and Keyboard, 1992, Josef Bodin de Boismortier, Music for 1-4 Flutes, in press, New Music for Old Instruments, in press; Renaissance Flute: Les Plaisirs d'amour - Sixteenth Century Chansons from the French Provinces, 1993. Publications: Music in the Paris Academy of Sciences 1666-1793, with A Cohen, 1979; Music in the Royal Society of London 1660-1806, with A Cohen, 1987; Editor: Chansons from The French Provinces 1530-1550, volume 1, 1980, volume 2, 1983, Thirty Six Chansons by French Provincial Composers 1529-1550, 1981, Gioseppe Caimo: Madrigali and Canzoni for Four and Five Voices, 1990. Contributions to: Music and Letters, 1985; Journal of The Royal Musical Association, 1990; Studies in the History of Music, 1992; Journal of Musicology, 1993; Early Music, 1995. Address: Porter College, University of California, Santa Cruz, CA 95064, USA.

MILLER Margaret, b. 1960, Indiana, USA. Violist. Education: Studied at Indiana and Wisconsin Universities. Career: Principal Violist with the Colorado Springs Orchestra and Co-founded the Da Vinci Quartet, 1980, under the sponsorship of the Fine Arts Quartet; Many concerts in the USA and elsewhere in a repertoire including works by Mozart, Beethoven, Brahms, Dvorak, Shostakovich and Bartók. Honours: (with the Da Vinci Quartet): Awards and grants from the National Endowment for the Arts, The Western States Arts Foundation and the Colorado Council for the Humanities; Artist in Residence, University of Colorado. Current Management: Sonata, Glasgow, Scotland. Address: 11 Northpark Street, Glasgow G20 7AA, Scotland.

MILLER Mildred, b. 16 Dec 1924, Cleveland, OH, USA. Recital Soloist; Impresario. m. Wesley W Posvar, 30 Apr 1950, 1 son, 2 daughters. Education: BMus Cleveland Institute of Music, 1946; Artist's Diploma, New England Conservatory, 1948. Debut: Metropolitan Opera, 1951. Career: Metropolitan Opera, 1951-74 as Siebel, Faust, Nicklausse in Les Contes d'Hoffmann, Susuki, Meg Page and Magdelena in Die Meistersinger, 253 performances in 21 parts; TV debut, Voice of Firestone, 1952; Appearances at San Francisco, Chicago Lyric, Cincinnati, San Antonio, Pasadena, Pittsburgh, Kansas City, Fort Wrorth, Omaha, Vienna, Berlin, Munich, Frankfurt Operas, 1959-73; Film: Merry Wives of Windsor; Musical Comedy, Pittsburgh Civic Light Opera. Recordings: Musical Heritage, Westminster, Strand and Metropolitan Opera Records. Contributions: Opera News; Bravo Magazine. Memberships: Director, Gateway to Music; Pittsburgh Opera; Honorary President, Women's Association, University of Pittsburgh; Founder, Artistic Director, Pittsburgh Opera Theater, 1978-. Address: Pittsburgh Opera Theatre, PO Box 110208, Pittsburgh, PA 15232, USA.

MILLET Gilles, b. 1965, England. Violinist. Education: Studied in London and with Feodor Droujinin, violist of the Beethoven Quartet. Career: Many concerts throughout Britain in works by Shostakovich, Fauré and English composers; Venues include Aldeburgh Festival (Quartet in Residence), Middle Temple (London), Huddersfield and Andover. Honours: with members of the Danel Quartet) Prizewinner in competitions at Florence, St Petersburg, Evian and London, 1991-94. Address: Manygate Management, 13 Cotswold Mews, 30 Battersea Square, London SW11 3RA.

MILLGRAMM Wolfgang, b. 16 Apr 1954, Ostseebad Kuhlungsborn, Germany. Singer (Tenor). Education: Studied with Gunter Leib in Berlin; Musikhochschule, Berlin. Debut: Semperoper in Dresden, 1992 as Graf Elemer in Arabella. Career includes: Deutsche Staatsoper, Berlin, singing the Steersman in Fliegender Holländer, Walther in Tannhäuser and Alfred in Die Fledermaus; Visited Japan, Hungary and Switzerland with Deutsche Staatsoper; Solo appearances in Yugoslavia, Romania and the former Soviet Union; Chamber Singer in 1988; Sang the Steersman at Bregenz Festival, 1988, 1989, and in concert for Radio France, 1990; Season 1992-93 was engaged at the City of Nuremberg Theatre where he made guest appearance in 1991 as Adolar in Euryanthe; Other roles include: Erik in Holländer, José in Carmen; During that period also sang the Drum Major in Wozzeck and Max in Freischütz; Further appearances: Frankfurt-am-Main as Alfred in Fledermaus; Parsifal in Nuremberg and Hoffmann at Gärtnerplatz in Munich, 1995; Eleazar in La Juive, Aegisth in Elektra , Florestan in Fidelio at Dortmund in season 1995-96. Recordings include: Ariadne auf Naxos and First Prisoner in Fidelio, conducted by Haitink. Current Management: Buhnen und Konzertagentur, Sigrid Roslock. Address: Eugen-Schonhaar-Strasse 1, 10407 Berlin, Germany.

MILLING Stephen, b. 1965, Denmark. Singer (Bass). Career: Many appearances with the Royal Danish Opera, Copenhagen, and elsewhere in Scandinavia; Repertory includes Die Zauberflöte (Sarastro) and Don Carlos (King Philip); Also sings Lieder by Brahms; Contestant in the 1995 Cardiff Singer of the World Competition; Guest at Covent Garden, London, with the

Royal Danish Opera in Prokofiev's Love for Three Oranges. Address: Sundevedsgade 2, st tv, 1751 Copenhagen V, Denmark.

MILLIOT Sylvette, b. 6 June 1927, Paris, France. Violoncellist; Musicologist. Education: Doctor of Musicology; Studied Violoncello, National Conservatory of Music, Paris. Career: Research Assistant, Museum of the National Conservatory of Music, Paris; Soloist, Radio France; Various concert tours; Head of Research, CNRS, French National Centre for Scientific Research in Musicology and Musical Iconography. Publications: Documents inédits sur les Luthiers parisiens du 18 siécle, 1970; La Sonate, 1978; Le Violoncelle en France au XVIIIe Siécle, 1981; Le Quatuor, 1986; Marin Marais, 1991; Entretiens-Avec-Navarra, 1991; History of Parisian Violin Making from the XVIIIth Century to 1960, Vol I, The Family Charnot-Chardon, 1994, vol II, The Violin Makers of the XVIIIth Century, 1997. Contributions to: Revue Française de Musicologie; Recherches sur la Musique française classique; the STRAD; Articles on Lutherie Française, 1992, 1993, 1995. Honours: 1st Prize for Violoncello, National Conservatory of Music; Héléne Victor Lyon Prize; Solo Artist's Guild Prize. Memberships: French Musicology Society; French Society of 18th Century Studies. Hobbies: History of art; Psychology. Address: 6 Villa del la Reunion, 75016 Paris, France.

MILLO Aprile, b. 14 Apr 1958, NY, USA. Singer, Soprano. Education: Studied with her parents and with Rita Patane. Debut: Salt Lake City 1980, as Aida. Career: Gave concert performances in Los Angeles and made La Scala Milan and Welsh National Opera debuts at Elvira in Ernani; Metropolitan Opera debut 1984, as Amelia Boccanegra; returned to NY as Elvira, Elisabeth de Valois and Aida; Guest appearances in Hamburg and Vienna; Other roles include Leonaro in Il Trovatore and La Forza del Destino; Sang Aida and Liu at the Metropolitan 1987, followed by Elvira in Ernani, Elisabeth de Valois and Imogene in Il Pirata; Carnegie Hall 1987, Il Battaglia di Legnano, as Lida, Verona Arena and Caracalla festival 1988-90; Sang Aida at Washington 1990, Luisa Miller at Rome; Season 1991-92, as Marguerite at Chicago, debut, Elisabeth de Valois at the Met and Verona and Aida at the Festival of Caracella; Sang Maddalena in Andrea Chenier at Rome, 1996. Recordings: Luisa Miller and Don Carlos conducted by James Levine; Met productions of Aida on video; Un Ballo in Maschera. Address: c/o S A Gorlinsky Ltd, 33 Dover Street, London, W1X 4NJ, England.

MILLS Alan, b. 21 July 1964, Belfast, Northern Ireland. Composer; Pianist. Education: Ulster College of Music, 1978-81; Music, Churchill College, Cambridge University, 1983-86; MA (Cantab); Advanced Composition, Guildhall School of Music and Drama, London, 1986-87. Career: As Pianist and Accompanist for BBC Radio Ulster, Dutch Television and Radio France, 1987-. Publications include: 25 songs for voice and piano, 1986-; Daybreak over Newgrange for large orchestra and chorus, 1987; Three Irish poems for baritone and small orchestra, 1991; Sonatina for piano, 1993, published 1995; Incantation for trombone and piano, 1993, published 1993; Hymn to the Aten for chamber choir and harp, 1993, published 1994; Romanza for horn and piano, 1994, published 1995; In converse with the mountains for a cappella vocal ensemble, 1995; Capriccio for harpsichord, published 1995. Recording: Hymn to the Aten, by Concert de L'Hostel-Dieu, Lyons. Honours: Special Youth Prize, Lloyds Bank Composer's Award, 1988; Lower Machen Festival Prize, 1993. Membership: Composers' Guild of Great Britain. Hobby: Collecting antiquities. Address: 87 Palmerston Road, Wood Green, London N22 4QS, England.

MILLS Betty, b. Shanghai, China. Solo and Orchestral Flautist; Solo Pianist. m. Antony Gray. Education: Hunmanby Hall School, Yorkshire; Royal Academy of Music, London; Studied piano with Harold Craxton, organ with C H Trevor and flute with Gerald Jackson; ARAM; GRSM. Career: Professor of Flute, Royal Academy of Music; Principal Flute, Sadler's Wells Opera and Royal Ballet at Covent Garden; Solo Flautist in Oriel and Oriana trios; Recitals as Flautist and solo pianist for BBC, music clubs and Universities and Schools throughout England; In Spain for Radio Nacional Espana; Has performed concertos for flute and piano in London and in provincial concerts; Freelance orchestral work with BBC Symphony and BBC regional orchestras and various London orchestras; Also with Hallé and visiting foreign opera and ballet orchestras; Associated Board Examiner in United Kingdom and Far East; Visiting Teacher, Winchester College, Sherborne, Haileybury, King's College, Taunton; Adjudicator, Examiner for Guildhall School of Music and International Baccalaureate. Hobbies: Travel; History; Tennis; Swimming; Photography. Address: Ferndene, Bracken Close, Storrington, West Sussex RH20 3HT, England.

MILLS Bronwen, b. 1960, England. Singer, Soprano. Education: Studied at London University, The Guildhall School of Music and with Joy Mammon. Career: Opera engagements include Dido and Aeneas with Opera Restor'd at the 1986 Edinburgh Festival; Elizabeth Hall 1989 in The Death of Dido by Pepusch and Dibdin's Ephesian Matron; Season 1989-90, with Traviata for New Israeli Opera and Dublin Grand Opera; Elizabeth Zimmer in Henze's Elegy for Young Lovers in London; Norina in Don Pasquale and Madeline in Fall of the House of Usher by Glass in Wales; Donna Anna in Don Giovanni for Opera North, 1992; Man Who Mistook his Wife for a Hat, Michael Nyman, for Music Theatre Wales, 1992-93; Other roles include Mozart's Countess and Fiordiligi, Opera 80, the Governess and Miss Jessel in the Turn of the Screw, and Micaela; Opera North as the Queen of Shemakah in The Golden Cockerel, Strauss's Daphne and Blondchen in Die Entführung; Concert engagements with the Scottish Chamber Orchestra in Handel's Dixit Dominus and Bach's B minor Mass; St Matthew Passion in Stratford and Haydn's Stabat Mater at St John's Smith Square; Mozart's C minor Mass with the Northern Sinfonia, Beethoven's Missa Solemnis at Canterbury Cathedral and the Christmas Oratorio in Belgium; Wexford Festival, 1990, in Handel's L'Allegro, il Penseroso ed il Moderato; Tour of English Cathedrals with London Festival Orchestra in 1991, Messiahs in Germany, Norway in 1992 also Messiahs in Lithuania and Moscow, Kremlin, with Yehudi Menuhin; Further appearances at the Malvern, Music at Oxford, Cambridge and Sully-sur-Loire Festivals. Recordings: Solomon by John Blow, Hyperion; Beggar's Opera, Polly Peachum, Hyperion; Dibdin Operas, Hyperion; 100 years of Italian Opera, Opera Rara; Emilia di Liverpool, Opera Rara.

MILLS Erie, b. 22 June 1953, Granite City, IL, USA. Soprano. Education: National Music Camp, Interlochen, MI; BMus, MA, University of IL; Studied with Karl Trump, Grace Wilson and Elena Nikolai. Debut: St Louis 1978, in the US premiere of Martin y Soler's L'Arbore di Diana; Ninette in Love for Three Oranges, Chicago Lyric Opera, 1979. Career: Sang New York City Opera debut as Cunegonde, Candide, 1982; Metropolitan Opera debut, New York as Blondchen, Die Entführung aus dem Serail, 1987; New York recital debut, 1989; Guest appearances with Cincinnati Opera; Cleveland Opera; San Francisco Opera; Minnesota Opera; Opera Society of Washington DC; Santa Fe Opera; Houston Grand Opera; Hamburg State Opera; Teatro alla Scala, Milan; Vienna State Opera; Sang Marie in La Fille du Regiment at New Orleans, 1989, Blondchen in Die Entführung for Opera de Montreal, 1990; Sang Zerlina at Milwaukee, 1996; Soloist with many leading orchestras; Numerous recitals; Television appearances; Roles include Rossini's Rosina; Offenbach's Olympia; Donizetti's Lucia; J Strauss's Adele; R Strauss's Zerbinetta. Recordings: For New World Records. Address: c/o Metropolitan Opera, Lincoln Center, New York, NY 10023, USA.

MILLS Richard (John), b. 14 Nov 1949, Toowoomba, Queensland, Australia. Composer; Conductor. Education: University of Queensland; Queensland Conservatorium; Guildhall School of Music, London, England. Career: Regular Guest Conductor of all major Australian Orchestras; Artist-in-Residence, Australian Ballet, 1987-88; Artist-in-Residence, Australian Broadcasting Corporation, 1989-90; Artistic Director, Adelaide Chamber Orchestra, 1991-97; Artistic Advisor, Queensland Symphony Orchestra, 1991-94; Artistic Advisor, Brisbane Biennial International Music Festivals, 1995-97; Artistic Director, West Australian Opera, 1997-. Compositions: Principal Works: Music for Strings, Concerti for Trumpet and Percussion; Bamaga Diptych; Fantastic Pantomines; Flute Concerto (written for James Galway); Concerto for Violoncello and Orchestra; Violin Concerto (for Carl Pini, 1992); Summer of the Seventeenth Doll, 1994. Honours: National Critics Awards, 1988, 1991; Sir Bernard Heinze Award, 1997. Current Management: Arts Management, 180 Goulburn Street, Darlinghurst, New South Wales 2010, Australia. Address: 22 Gray Road, Hill End, Queensland 4101, Australia.

MILNE Hamish, b. 27 Apr 1939, Salisbury, England. Pianist. m. Margot Gray, 1 son, 2 daughters. Education: Royal Academy of Music, London; Guido Agosti, Rome, Siena. Debut: 1963. Career: Concerto, Recital, Chamber Music in UK, Europe, USA & USSR; Over 100 BBC Broadcasts; Proms Debut, 1978; Professor, Piano, Royal Academy of Music, London. Recordings: Piano works by Chopin, Liszt, Haydn, Medtner, Mozart, Reubke, Schumann, Weber. Publications: Bartok, 1981; Heritage of Music, Contributor, 1982. Contributions: Medtner-Centenary Appraisal, 1981. Honours: Collard Fellowship, 1977; FRAM, 1978. Address: 111 Dora Road, London, SW19 7JT, England.

MILNE Lisa, b. Scotland. Singer (Soprano). Education: Studied at the Royal Scottish Academy of Music. Career: From 1994 appearances throughout Scotland in concert and recital; Member of Scottish Opera from 1994, as Gianetta in L'Elisir d'Amore (debut role), Mozart's Susanna, Zerlina and Ilia, the Dew Fairy in Hansel and Gretel and Coryphée in Alceste; Season 1996 in recitals at Covent Garden and Aix en Provence and City of London Festivals; Concerts with the National Youth Orchestra of Scotland, Scottish Chamber, Royal Philharmonic, London Philharmonic and Royal Liverpool Philharmonic Orchestras; Season 1997-98 as Servilia in La Clemenza di Tito for Welsh National Opera, Atalanta in Xerxes at Göttingen and Handel's Rodelinda at Glyndebourne. Recordings include: Handel and Vivaldi with the King's Consort (Hyperion); Vaughan Williams Serenade to Music (Decca). Honours include: Winner, 1993 Maggie Teyte Prize and 1996 John Christie Award. Address: c/o Lies Askonas Ltd, 6 Henrietta St, London WC2E 8LA, England.

MILNER Anthony (Francis Dominic), b. 13 May 1925, Bristol, England. Composer. Education: Composition with Matyas Seiber, 1944-48; Royal College of Music, 1945-47; DMus, London; FRCM. Career: Tutor, Music Theory and History, Morley College, London, 1946-64; Extension Lecturer, 1958-65, University of London, 1954-65; Staff Member, 1961-, including Principal Lecturer, 1980-89, Royal College of Music, London; Lecturer, King's College, University of London, 1965-71; Senior Lecturer, 1971-74, Principal Lecturer, 1974-80, Goldsmiths' College, University of London; Visiting Lecturer, USA, 1964-88; Composer-in-Residence, Summer School of Liturgical Music, Loyola University, New Orleans, 1965, 1966; Director, Harpsichordist, London Cantata Ensemble baroque music group, 1954-65. Compositions: Variations for Orchestra, 1958; April Prologue, overture, 1961; Divertimento, string orchestra, 1961; Sinfonia Pasquale, string orchestra, optional wind, brass, 1963; Chamber Symphony, 1968; Symphonies Nos 1, 2, 3, 1972, 1978, 1986; Concerto for Symphonic Wind Band, 1979; Concerto, string orchestra, 1982; Chorus, orchestra: 5 Cantanas, 1948, 1955, 1956, 1969, 1974; The Water and the Fire, oratorio, 1960-61; Festival Te Deum, 1967; Motet for Peace, 1973; The Gates of Summer, 1990; Chorus, Organ: Anthems, 1958, 1968, 1971, 1976; Processional, 1980; Responsorial Psalm, 1982; Chorus a cappella: Mass, 1951; 2 motets, 1955, 1959; Cantata, 1956; 2 partsongs, 1957, 1974; Turbae for the Passion, according to St John, 1968, according to St Matthew, 1962; Instrumental: Quartet, oboe, strings, 1953; Rondo Saltato, organ, 1955; Fugue for Advent for Organ, 1958; Quintet for Wind Instruments, 1964; String Quartet No 1, 1975; Voice with instrumental accompaniment: The Song of Akhenaten, 1954; Midway, 1974; Out Lady's Hours, song cycle, 1957; Music for children; Music for radio, etc: Congregational music. Recordings: Cantatas Salutatio Angelica and Roman Spring, 1975; Symphony No 1; Variations for Orchestra. Publications: Harmony for class teaching, 2 vols, 1950; Piano Sonata 1989; Cantata, The Gates of Summer, 1990; Antony Milner, A Bio-Bibliography by James Siddons; Several book-chapters. Contributions: Musical Quarterly; Proceedings of the Royal Musical Association; The Musical Times. Honours: Appointed Knight of St Gregory, Pope John Paul II, 1985. Address: 147 Heythorp Street, Southfields, London, SW18 5BT, England.

MILNER Howard, b. 1953, England. Singer, (Tenor). Education: Studied at Cambridge University and the Guildhall School of Music. Career: Glyndebourne Opera from 1985, including tour to Hong Kong, 1986 and appearances in Albert Herring and Capriccio; Kent Opera title role in Le Comte Ory, Jacquino in Fidelio and Eumeus in The Return of Ulysses; Sang Arnalta in L'Incoronazione di Poppea; Monostatos for Early Opera Project; Pedrillo, Die Entführung and Camille in The Merry Widow, for Scottish Opera; Covent Garden 1990-91 in Die Meistersinger and Capriccio; English National Opera, Squeak in Billy Budd; Haydn's Lo Speziale with the Aix-en-Provence Chamber Opera; Don Curzio in Marriage of Figaro with Opera Factory; Frequent concerts in Britain and Europe, Promenade Concerts debut 1988; Arnalta in Coronation of Poppea for Opera Factory, 1992; Sang Mozart's Monostatos with Opera Factory, 1996. Recordings: Bach's B minor Mass and Monteverdi's Orfeo with John Eliot Gardiner, Deutsche Grammophon; Beethoven's Choral Fantasia conducted by Roger Norrington; Video of ENO Billy Budd. Current Management: C & M Craig Services Ltd, 3 Kersley Street, London, SW11 4PR, England. Address: c/o Korman International Management, Crunnells Green Cottage, Preston, Herts, SG4 7UQ, England.

MILNES Rodney, b. 26 July 1936, Stafford, England. Music Critic; Magazine Editor. Career: Music Critic, Queen Magazine, later Harpers and Queen, 1968-87; Opera Critic, The Spectator, 1979-90; Opera Critic, London Evening Standard, 1990-92; Chief Opera Critic, The Times from 1992; Reviews for Opera Magazine from 1971, Associate Editor, 1976; Editor from 1986. Publications: Numerous opera translations; Under original name, Rodney Blumer, has translated such operas as Osud,Tannhäuser, Rusalka and The Jacobin; Consultant Editor, Viking Opera Guide, 1993. Address: c/o Metropolitan Opera, Lincoln Center, New York, NY 10023, USA.

MILNES Sherrill, b. 10 Jan 1935, Hinsdale, IL, USA. Opera Singer, Baritone. m. Nancy Stokes 1969, 1 son, 1 son, 1 daughter by first marriage. Education: MMUS, ED, Drake University, Northwestern University; Studied with Boris Goldovsky, Rosa Ponselle, Andrew White, Hermanes Baer with Goldovsky Opera Company, 1960-65; NY City Opera Company, 1964-67. Debut: Metropolitan Opera, NY 1965, as Valentin in Gounod's Faust. Career: Leading Baritone 1965-, as Verdi's Miller, Renato, Amonasro, Don Carlo, Germont, Simon Boccanegra, Iago, Macbeth, Montfort, Paolo, Posa and Rigoletto; Has also appeared in NY as Wagner's Herald, Lohengrin and Donner, Rossini's Figaro, Don Giovanni, Barnaba, Jack Rance, Scarpia, Riccardo in I Puritani and Alphonse in La Favorite; Has performed with all American City Opera Companies and major American Orchestras, 1962-73; Performed in Don Giovanni, Vespri Sicillani and all standard Italian repertory baritone roles; San Francisco Opera; Hamburg Opera; Frankfurt Opera; La Scala, Milan; Covent Garden, London; Teatro Colon; Buenos Aires; Vienna State Opera; Paris Opera; Chicago Lyric Opera, including Puccini's Scarpia and Verdi's Posa, Boccanegra, Iago and Don Carlo; NYC Opera 1982, as Hamlet in the Opera by Thomas, returned 1990; Season 1991-92, with debut as Falstaff, Jack Rance at the Met and Scarpia at Buenos Aires; Sang Cilea's Michonnet at the Met, 1994; Sang Nemico della patria at the Met Opera gala, 1996. Recordings: 60 Albums, 1967-; Videos of Il Trovatore from the Met; Tosca in the Original Locations. Honours: 3 Hon Degrees, Order of Merit, Italy, 1984. Memberships: Chairman of Board, Affiliate Artists Inc.

MILOJKOVIC-DJURIC Jelena, b. 2 Dec 1931, Belgrade. Musicologist. m. Dusan Djuric, 24 Sep 1955, 2 d. Education: MA 1963, PhD 1982, University of Belgrade. Career: Lecturer, University of Belgrade, 1963-65; Research Associate, Musicological Institute, Belgrade, 1963-65; Lecturer, Slavic Languages, University of Colorado, 1968; Lecturer, Russian and German, Texas A and M University, 1972-74; Research Associate, Soviet and Eastern Studies, University of Texas, 1987-; Fellow, Interdisciplinary Group for Historical Literary Study. Publications: Books: The Music of Eastern Europe, 1978, Tradition and Avant-Garde: The Arts in Serbian Culture Between the Two World Wars, 1984, Tradition and Avant Garde: Literature and Arts in Serbian Culture 1900-1918, 1988, Aspects of Soviet Culture: Voices of Glasnost 1960-1990, 1991, Panslavism and National Identity in Russia and in The Balkans 1830-1880: Images of The Self and Others, 1994; Also book chapters and articles. Honours include: Association of Composers and Writers of Yugoslavia Award, 1969; Mihailo Dordevic Prize for her book Panslavism and National Identity, 1994. Memberships: American Musicological Society; American Association for The Advancement of Slavic Studies. Hobby: Collecting Art. Address: 1018 Holt Street, College Station, TX 77840, USA.

MILOSI Rodrigue, b. 7 Sept 1935, Clichy, France. Violinist; Music Professor. Education: Higher studies, Conservatoire National Superieur de Musique, Paris; Certificate qualifying as teacher in National Conservatories. Career: Tours in France, Belgium, Italy, Rumania, Bulgaria, Argentina, Brazil, Chile, Bolivia, Ecuador, Paraguay, Panama; Various contemporary works for violin dedicated to him; Jury Member, Conservatoire Superieur de Musique, Paris; Pedagogical courses, Touquet, Flaine, and Universite d'Orsay, Paris; Artistic Director, Festival of Provence; Professor, National Conservatory of the Caen Region; Violin Soloist, Caen Chamber Orchestra. Recordings: Complete Grieg Sonatas, with pianist Noel Lee, ADDA, France. Honours: Emile Francaise Prize, 1952; Pablo de Sarasate Prize, 1952; 1st Prize & Prize of Honour, Violin, Conservatoire National Superieur de Musique, Paris. Hobbies: Collecting objets d'arts, paintings and drawings of all periods. Address: 4 Square La Fontaine, 75016 Paris, France.

MILVEDEN J Ingmar G, b. 15 Feb 1920, Gothenburg, Sweden. Composer; Assistant Professor. m. Ulla Milveden, 1 son, 1 daughter. Education: Licentiate of Philosophy, 1951; PhD, 1972; Musical Theory, Counterpoint, Composition, with Dr S E Svensson, Uppsala; Musicology with Professor C A Moberg; Schola Cantorum Basiliensis, Basel. Debut: Serenade for Strings, Philharmonic Orchestra of Gothenburg, conductor Issay Dobrowen, 1942. Career: Assistant Professor of Musicology, University of Uppsala. Compositions: Great Mass for Uppsala Cathedral, 1969; Pezzo Concertante for orchestra and soloists, 1971; Clarinet Concerto, 1972; Now, cantata to Linnean texts for choir and orchestra; Gaudeat Upsalia, cantata for 500th anniversary of University of Uppsala, 1977; Musicae in honorem Sanctae Eugeniae, 1982. Publications: Zu den liturgischen Hystorie in Schweden; Liturgie- und choralgeschichtliche Untersuchungen, 1972. Honours include: Uppsala Landstings Kulturpris, 1969; Scholarship, Royal Swedish Academy of Music, 1972, 1973. Memberships: Royal Swedish Academy of Music; Royal Academy of Arts and Sciences of Uppsala; Rotarian; Chairman, Musikaliska Konstföreningen. Hobby: Swedish church life. Address: Torkelsgatan 16B, S-753 29 Uppsala, Sweden.

MILYAEVA Olga, b. 1967, Moscow, Russia. Violist. Education: Studied at the Central Music School, Moscow. Career: Co-Founder, Quartet Veronique, 1989; Many concerts in the former Soviet Union and Russia, notably in the Russian Chamber Music Series and the 150th Birthday Celebrations for Tchaikovsky, 1990; Masterclasses at the Aldeburgh Festival, 1991; Concert tour of Britain in season 1992-93; repertoire includes works by Beethoven, Brahms, Tchaikovsky, Bartók, Shostakovich and Schnittke; Resident Quartet, Wilwaukee University, USA. Honours include: (With Quartet Veronique): Winner, All-Union String Quartet Competition, St Petersburg, 1990-91; Third Place, International Shostakovich Competition, St Petersburg, 1991. Current Management: Sonata, Glasgow, Scotland. Address: c/o Sonata (Quartet Veronique), 11 Northpark Street, Glasgow G20 7AA, Scotland.

MIMS Marilyn, b. 1962, USA. Soprano. Education: Studied at Indiana University with Virginia Zeani. Career: Sang at Kentucky Opera from 1987 as Lucia and Violetta, New Orleans Opera from 1990 and at the Metropolitan Opera in 1990 as Donna Anna and Fiordiligi; Guest appearances with Hawaii Opera as Constanze in 1988, and Fiordiligi at Santa Fe; Sang at San Francisco Opera, 1990-92 as Donna Anna and Anna Bolena. Recordings include: Ortlinde in Die Walküre, conducted by James Levine. Address: San Francisco Opera, War Memorial Opera House, San Francisco, CA 94102, USA.

MINDE Stefan P, b. 12 Apr 1936, Leipzig, Germany. Conductor. m. Edith Halla, 8 July 1961, 2 sons. Education: Member of Thomanerchor, Leipzig, 1947-54; MA, Mozarteum, Salzburg, Austria, 1958. Debut: State Theatre, Wiesbaden, Germany, Krenek: Life of Orestes. Career: Civic Opera Frankfurt am Main under Sir Georg Solti; Hessisches Staatstheater Wiesbaden under Sawallisch; Principal Conductor at Civic Theatre Trier, Mosel; Berkshire Music Festival at Tanglewood, Massachusetts, USA, with Eric Leinsdorf; Chorusmaster and Conductor, San Francisco Opera; General Director and Conductor at Portland Opera Association, Oregon, 1970-84; Founder, Music Director and Conductor of Sinfonia Concertante, Chamber Orchestra, Portland, Oregon; Guest appearances with New York City Opera, Philadelphia, Pittsburgh, Cincinnati, San Diego, Phoenix, Los Angeles, Seattle, Vancouver, British Columbia, Toronto, Edmonton, Calgary, Lisbon, Portugal, Saarbrucken, Cologne, Nuremberg, Hawaii Opera, Eugene Opera, Utah Opera, Sapporo, Japan, Seoul (South Korean National Theatre) and others; Guest Professor at Portland State University, Pacific Lutheran University, Tacoma, Washington and Florida State University; Conducted Wagner's Ring at Flagstaff, Arizona, 1996, engaged to repeat in 1998. Honours: C D Jackson Prize for Conducting, Tanglewood, 1968; For his contribution to opera in the United States, National Opera Association, 1982. Memberships: Oregon Public Broadcasting; Honorary Member, International Alliance of Theatrical Employees; Honorary Member, Imperial Brass Society, Portland. Current Management: Anthony George, Artists Management, 250 West 77th Street, New York, NY 10024, USA. Address: 1640 SE Holly Street, Portland, OR 97214, USA.

MINDEL Meir, b. 25 Dec 1946, Lvov, Russia. Composer. m. Tzippi Bozian, 25 Dec 1968, 4 daughters. Education: Harmony, Counterpoint, Electronic Music with Itzhak Saday, 1970-71; Rubin Music Academy, Tel Aviv, 1971-75; Composition with Abel Ehrlich, 1975-77. Debut: Concert in Rubin Academy, Agony for Flute, 1974. Career: Radio appearances: Israeli Young Composer, The Blue and the White, 1982, Circle, A Maya Prophecy, 1987, Together with..Meir Mindel, An hour of M M Compositions, 1988, Israel Broadcasting Authority; Represented Israel at World Festival of Jewish Music, Montreal, Canada, 1983; Genesis with Morli Consort, Israel Defence Forces Army Broadcasting, 1984; General Director, Secretary, Kibbutz Composers' Organisation; Secretary of Management and Board of Israel Composers' League; Founder, Open-Air Museum Project, Kibbutz Negba; Attempted to develop a new musical "language" for recorders; Music performed in Israel and abroad. Compositions include: The Tie, strings, 1980; Grotesque, piano, 1983, recorders, 1985; Genesis, recorders, 1983; A Maya Prophecy, mixed choir a cappella, 1985; Agony, flute, 1986; The Courting Muse, trombone, 1986; Tamar, flute, horn, piano, 1988; Poem, horn, 1988; My City, 2 choirs; The Family Tree, singers ensemble, 1989; Iri, 2 choirs, 1989; Koli, songs, 1989; The Shadow, children's choir, 1989; Murmurs, trumpet, flugelhorn, 1989; Between Rosh Pina and Safed, song; Music for Michal Gretz-Mindel's poem A White Lie, for children's choir, 1994; Symbiosis, for clarinet, bass clarinet and magnetic tape; Circles; The Catch; Where Are You All?; SugiHara, for shakuhachi Japanese bamboo flute, eastern percussion instruments and orchestra, 1995; Sounds of Strings, 18 arrangements for string quartet, 1996. Recordings: Negba 40; Bereshit (Genesis), 1987; Song of Songs 85-Duo Beersheba; A Maya Prophecy, Tel-Aviv Philharmonic Choir; Murmurs, A Courting Muse, in Composers in search of their roots; Tamar (1st CD by a single Israeli composer); Israeli Sounds of Strings, 18 arrangements of folk songs, 1998. Honours include: Prize, Eliezer Young Composers' Competition, Israel Music Institute, 1982; Israel Music Institute Musician Prize, 1987; Acum Prize, 1988; National Council for Culture and Art Prize, 1994; Recipient, Prime Minister's Grant for composition, 1995. Hobbies: Original poetry/music combinations; Historical research; Psychology. Address: Kibbutz Negba, 79408, Israel.

MINEVA Stefka, b. 1949, Stara Zagora, Bulgaria. Singer, (Mezzo-Soprano). Education: Studied in Sofia. Debut: Staga Zora 1972, as Berta in IL Barbiere di Siviglia. Career: Sang Suzuki, Olga and Amneris at Stara Zagora; Sofia Opera from 1977, notably as Marfa in Khovanshchina. Guest appearances throughout Europe; Metropolitan Opera, 1986-88, as Marfa; Sang Konchakovna in Prince Igor at Perugia, 1987, Liubasha in The Tsar's Bridge at Rome and Kabanicha in Katya Kabanova at Florence, 1989; Other roles include Marina in Boris Godunov, Eboli, Adalgisa and Leonora in La Favorita; Sang Fenena in Nabucco at the 1991 Verona Arena. Recordings: Rimsky-Korsakov's Vera Sheloga and Prokofiev's War and Peace; Madama Butterfly. Honours: Prize Winner, 1976 Sofia and 1977 Osten International Competitions. Address: c/o Arena di Verona, Piazza Bra 28, 37121 Verona, Italy.

MINGARDO Sara, b. 1970, Venice, Italy. Singer (Contralto). Education: Academia Chigiana of Siena. Career: Many performances at leading Italian opera houses, including Teatro Comunale of Bologna, La Scala Milan, Teatro Comunale Florence, Teatro Regio Turin and Teatro San Carlo, Naples; Further engagements in Puccini's Trittico under Riccardo Chailly, as Emilia in Otello under Claudio Abbado in Berlin and Salzburg (1996); Sang title role in revival of Handel's Riccardo Primo with Les Talens Lyriques under Christophe Rousset at Fontevraud, France, 1995. Recordings include: Riccardo Primo (Decca/L'Oiseau Lyre). Address: c/o Deutsche Oper Berlin, Bismarckstrasse 35, D-1000 Berlin 10, Germany.

MINICH Peter, b. 1928, St Polten, Switzerland. Singer, (Tenor). Education: Studied at the Horak Conservatory, Vienna. Debut: St Polten 1951, in Millöcker's Bettelstudent. Career: Engaged at St Gallen 1951-55, Graz, 1955-60; Vienna Volksoper from 1960, notably as Eisenstein in Fledermaus on tour to Japan, 1985; Salzburg Festival 1962-63, in Die Entführung: Other roles have included the Baron in La Vie Parisienne, Paquilo in La Perichole, René in Graf vom Luxembourg by Lehar and Jim Mahoney in Mahagonny; Frequent concert and television appearances. Address: c/o Volksoper, Wahringerstrasse 78, A-1090 Vienna, Austria.

MINKOFSKI-GARRIGUES Horst, b. 23 July 1925, Dresden, Germany. Concert Pianist; Composer; Professor. m. Edeltraud Peschke, 1 son, 2 daughters. Education: Music Academy & Conservatory, Dresden; Studies with Professor Herbert Wuesthoff, Romana Lowenstein, Karl Knochenhauer, Hermann Werner Finke, Schneider-Marfels. Debut: State Orchestra, Dresden. Career: Numerous appearances, concerts and radio broadcasts throughout the world. Compositions: For Orchestra: Klaviermusik, op 15, Piano Concerto, Variations over a theme by Tchaikovsky, op 8, Expo '67 to 2 pianos and orchestra; For piano solo; Impromptus, Preludes, Sonatinas, Sonata op 23 and Scherzo, op 37; For piano, four hands; Eight Miniatures, op 27, Introduction, Theme and Variations for 2 Pianos & Cello, op 14, Andante for 2 pianos, Expo '67 for 2 Pianos op 28, Pictures of a Child for 2 Pianos op 30; Chamber Music includes: Song Cycle; Love and Deception, op 41, works for flute & piano, organ, op 38. Recordings: World Premiere Recording of the Complete works for Piano, four hands by Franz Schubert, 11 albums, in collobration with former student, Lothar Kilian; Also compositions for 4 hands by Beethoven, Brahms, Tchaikovsky, Saint-Saëns, Dvorak and Smetana; With Orchestra: Concerto for 2 pianos by Bach; Concerto in D-Major by Haydn, Klaviermusik, op 15 by Minkofski-Garrigues; Numerous solo and chamber music recordings including Schubert's Sonatas for Violin and Piano with Wolfgang Marschner. Hobbies: Antiques; Gardening; Swimming; Jogging. Address: 205 Edison Ave, St Lambert, Montreal, Quebec, Canada, J4R 2P6.

MINKOWSKI Marc, b. 4 Oct 1962, Paris, France. Conductor. Education: Studied at the Hague Conservatory and at the Pierre Monteux Memorial School, USA. Career: Founder of and has performed with, Les Musiciens du Louvre, 1984; Has conducted works by Handel including Riccardo Primo, 1991 for the English Bach Festival and Gluck's Iphigénie en Tauride at Covent Garden; French repertoire includes Charpentier's Malade Imaginaire, Alcyone by Marin Marais, Mouret's Les Amours de Ragonde and Titon et l'Aurore by Mondonville, Rameau's Hippolyte et Aricie, Gluck's Armide; Lully's Phaëton, Opéra de Lyon, 1993; Ariodante by Handel, Welsh National Opera, 1994; Agrippina by Handel, Semper Oper, Dresden, 1994; Dido and Aeneas by Purcell, Houston Grand Opera, 1995; Orchestre de Chambre de Genève, 1995; Amsterdamse Bach Solisten, 1995; Rotterdam Philharmonic, 1995; Idomeneo by Mozart, Opéra de Paris-Bastille, 1996; Orfeo ed Euridice by Gluck, National Opera, Netherlands, 1996; Armide by Gluck, Opéra de Nice, 1996; L'Inganno Felice by Rossini, Poissy, France, 1996; Acis et Galatée, summer tour, 1996; Engaged for Die Entführung at the 1997 Salzburg Festival; Music Director of the Flanders Opera, from 1997. Recordings: Les Amours de Ragonde by Mouret; Mondonville's Titon et l'Aurore; Stradella's San Giovannia Battista; Grétry's La Caravane du Caire; Alcyone by Marin Marais; Le Malade Imaginaire by Charpentier; Platée by Rameau; Rebel's Les Elemens; Handel's Amadigi; Handel's Teseo; Il Trionfo del Tempo by Handel; Concerti Grossi op 3, by Handel; Rameau's Hippolyte et Aricie, 1994; La Resurrezione by Handel, 1995. Honours: 1st prize, 1st International Concert of Ancient Music, Bruges, 1984. Address: Les Musiens du Louvre, 163 Rue Saint-Honoré, 75001 Paris, France.

MINOR Andrew C, b. 17 Aug 1918, Atlanta, Georgia, USA. Musicologist. m. Catherine Hogan, 2 daughters. Education: BA, Emory University, 1940; MMus 1947, PhD 1950, University of Michigan. Recordings: As conductor of Cellgium Musicum, University of Missouri-Columbia, 2 masses by J Michael Haydn, Handel's Joshua, Gossec's Messe des Morts. Publications: General editor, American Institute of Musicology's Joan Mouton's Opera Omnia, 4 volumes, 1967-74; Associate editor, Accademia Musicale, 17th century vocal and instrumental music, 10 volumes, 1970. Contributions to: Grove's Dictionary, 6th edition. Memberships: American Musicologial Society; Music Teachers National Association; Missouri Music Teachers Association; American Choral Revie, Associate Editor. Address: 919 Timberhill Road, Columbia, MO 65201, USA.

MINTER Drew, b. 11 Jan 1955, Washington DC, USA. Singer, (Countertenor). Education: Studied at Indiana University and with Rita Streich, Erik Werba and Marcy Lindheimer. Career: Performed in concert with various early music ensembles, including the Waverly Consort of New York; Stage debut as Handel's Orlando at the St Paul's Baroque Festival, 1983; Further appearances in early opera at Boston, Brussels and Los Angeles; Omaha and Milwaukee 1988, as Arsace in Handel's Partenope and Otho in L'Incoronazione di Poppea; Santa Fe 1989, in the US premiere of Judith Weir's A Night at the Chinese Opera and as Endimione in La Calisto by Cavalli; Television appearances include Ptolemeo in Handel's Giulio Cesare, directed by Peter Sellars; Sang the title role in Handel's Ottone, Göttingen, 1992; Endymion in Cavalli's Calisto at Glimmerglass, 1996. Recordings: Ottone in Handel's Agrippina and the title role in Floridante, conducted by Nicholas McGegan. Address: c/o Santa Fe Opera, PO Box 2408, Sant Fe, NM 87504, USA.

MINTON Yvonne (Fay), b. 4 Dec 1938, Sydney, Australia. Mezzo Soprano Singer. m. William Barclay, 21 Aug 1965, 1 s, 1 d. Education: Sydney Conservatorium. Career: Soloist with major Australian orchestras; In 1964 appeared in premiere of Nicholas Maw's One Man Show; Soloist with Royal Opera, Covent Garden, notably as Mussorgsky's Marina, Mozart's Dorabella, Wagner's Waltraute and Thea, in premiere of Tippett's Knot Garden, 1970; Has appeared with most major symphony orchestras in the world and at all major opera houses; Sang Octavian at the Metropolitan, (1973); Brangaene at Bayreuth Festival, (1974); Fricka and Waltraute in Centenary Ring, 1976; Octavian at Paris Opéra, 1976; Countess Geschwitz in premiere of the 3 act version of Lulu; Kundry at Covent Garden, in a new production of Parsifal; Waltraute at Turin Opera, (1988); Sang Fricka in Die Walküre at Lisbon, 1989; Leokadja Begbick in Mahagonny at 1990 Maggio Musicale, Florence; Season 1993-94 as Marguerite in La Damnation de Faust at Wellington and Mme Larina, in Eugene Onegin at Glyndebourne. Recordings: Concert recordings with Chicago Symphony Orchestra; BBC Symphony Orchestra and others; Opera recordings include: Rosenkavalier; La Clemenza di Tito; Wagner's Ring; Tristan and Isolde and others. Honours: Honorary RAM, 1977; CBE, 1981. Hobbies: Gardening; Reading. Current Management: Ingpen and Williams Ltd. Address: 6 Manor House Court, Heath Road, Reading, RG6 1NA, Berkshire, England.

MINTZ Shlomo, b. 30 Oct 1957, Moscow, USSR. Violinist. m. Corina Ciacci Mintz, 2 sons. Education: Diploma, Juilliard School of Music. Career: Music Advisor to Israel Chamber Orchestra, 1989-; Conducts and performs with this orchestra in Israel and abroad; Recitals and Chamber Music Concerts throughtout the World; Performed with: Israel Philharmonic; Berlin Philharmonic; Vienna Philharmonic; London Symphony; New York Philharmonic; Chicago Symphony; Philadelphia Orchestra; Boston Symphony; Los Angeles Philharmonic; Played the Mendelssohn Concerto with the Royal Philharmonic, London, 1997. Recordings: Works by Bach; Bartok; Bruch; Debussy; Dvorak; Franck; Kreisler; Mendelssohn; Mozart; Paganini; Prokofiev; Ravel; Sibelius; Vivaldi; Beethoven; Brahms; Fauré; Lalo; Vieuxtemps. Honours: Grand Prix du Disque, 1981, 1984, 1988; Premio Accademia Musicale Chigiana Siena, 1984. Management: ICM Artists Ltd. Address: ICM Artists Ltd, 40 West 57 Street, New York, NY 10019, USA.

MINUTILLO Hana, b. 1963, Jihlava, Czechoslovakia. Singer (Mezzo-soprano). Education: Studied at the Pardubice Conservatory. Career: Sang at Liberec in Nabucco, Manon and Rusalka; Opera Studio of the National Theatre Prague from 1989, as Carmen, Rosina and Arsamene in Handel's Serse; Further study in Belgium and with Svatava Subrtova, followed by Mozart's Clemenza di Tito in Darmstadt (1993-94 season) and concert performances of Les Troyens under Michel Plasson in Toulouse and Arhens; Bregenz Festival in Francesca da Rimini and Nabucco; Season 1994-95 as Carmen and The Fox in The Cunning Little Vixen, under Mackerras, at the Théatre du Chatelet, Paris; Further engagements as the Witch in Rusalka at Essen, The Diary of One who Disappeared, by Janácek, with Peter Schreier in Leipzig, Olga in Eugene Onegin at Amsterdam and Mozart's Annio (Clemenza di Tito) at Wiesbaden; Flowermaiden at Zurich, 1997. Recordings include: Rusalka, conducted by Charles Mackerras. Address: c/o Opernhaus Zurich, Falkenstrasse 1, CH-8008 Zurich, Switzerland.

MIREA Marina, b. 1941, Bucharest, Rumania. Soprano. Education: Studied at the Bucharest Conservatory. Career: Sang at the Bucharest National Opera from 1969, notably as Violetta, Constanze, Pamina, Lucia di Lammermoor, Olympia, Lakmé and Gilda; Guest engagements at the Berlin and Budapest State Operas, at Tel-Aviv and in France, Russia, West Germany and Greece. Address: Bucharest National Opera, Bucharest, Rumania.

MIRICIOIU Nelly, b. 31 Mar 1952, Romania. Singer, Soprano. Education: Studied in Bucharest and Milan. Debut: Sang the Queen of Night in Die Zauberflöte at Iasi, Romania, 1974. Career: Appeared with the Brasov Opera 1975-78; Scottish Opera 1981, as Tosca and Violetta; Covent Garden debut 1982, as Nedda in Pagliacci, returning as Musetta in La Bohème, Marguerite and Antonia in Les Contes d'Hoffmann; Further engagements in Toronto, San Diego, San Francisco, Paris, Rome, Hamburg, Milan La Scala and Verona; Amsterdam 1988 as Rossini's Armida; In 1989 sang Violetta in Monte Carlo and Ravenna and Yaroslavna, Prince Igor, at Munich; Season 1992 as Violetta at Philadelphia; Maria Stuarda, Lucrezia Borgia, Semiramide and Ermione at the Amsterdam Concertgebouw and Amenaide in Tancredi at the Salzburg Festival; Other roles include Puccini's Butterfly, Mimi and Manon Lescaut and Lucia di Lammermoor; Sang Elisabeth in the French verison of Don Carlos, Brussels, 1996. Address: c/o IMG Artists, Media House, 3 Burlington Lane, London W45 2TH, England.

MIROGLIO Thierry (Jean-Michael), b. 1 Sept 1963, Paris, France. Percussionist. Education: Baccalaureat; Studied Musical Acoustics with Iannis Xenakis, Paris University, Sorbonne; Percussion with J P Drouet and Sylvie Gualda, National Conservatory, Versailles; Harmony & Counterpoint, Chamber Music, National Conservatory of Boulogne, Billancourt. Career: Researcher & Soloist with ensembles: Musique Vivante; Atelier Ville d'Avray; Orchestra Opera de Paris; Orchestre Radio France; Musica Insieme etc, Soloist, concerts in Festivals of Radio France, Angers, Besancon, Orleans, Nice, Salzburg, Athens, Paris, Wurzburg, Venice, Bamberg, Rouen, Munich, Trento, Cremona also in South America; Artistic Director, Percussion Season of the French Society of Contemporary Music; Radio broadcasts; Masterclasses, lectures, seminars on the volution of Percussion style from the origin until our time, numerous countries; Masterclasses, South America, 1990; World or Grand Premieres of works of Cage, Ohana, Boucourechiev, Ballif, Pousseur, Denisov, Stahmer, Donatoni, Kelemen, Henze, several dedicated to him. Recordings: For French, German, Austrian, Italian, Canadian and Greek radio. Honours: 1st prize, Percussion, National Conservatory, Versailles; Prize for Chember Music, National Conservatory of Boulogne. Address: 6 rue Leclerc, F-75014, Paris, France.

MIRSHAKAR Zarrina, b. 19 Mar 1947, Dushanbe, Tajikstan. Composer; Teacher. Education: Studied at the Moscow State Conservatory. Compositions include: String Quartet; 24 music pieces for piano; Three Frescos of Pamir for violin and piano, published 1979; Sonata for clarinet solo, published 1982; Sonata for oboe solo; Respiro for violin, chamber orchestra and timpani; Six pieces for piano, published 1987; Music for documentary film, Our Baki; Colours of Sunny Pamir, symphonic poem, published 1989; Sonata for oboe solo; Symphonietta for string orchestra; Symphony for chamber orchestra; Three Inventions for piano quintet. Recordings include: 24 music pieces for piano; Sonata for clarinet solo; Sonata for oboe solo; Cycle of songs for children on M Mirshaker's poems. Honours include: Lenin Komsomol Prize Laureate, 1985. Memberships: Union of Composers of Tajikstan, 1992; Union of Soviet Composers, 1974-92. Address: Pionersky St proezd I 12, 734003 Dushanbe, Tajikstan.

MIRTOVA Elena, b. 1962, South West Siberia, Russia. Singer, Soprano. Education: Studied at the Leningrad Conservatory, graduated 1988. Debut: Sang at the Musical Academy and Philharmonic Hall in Prague while a student. Career: Sang Maria in Rimsky-Korsakov's The Tsar's Bridge in Moscow and Leningrad; Series of concerts in Moscow and Leningrad, 1984; Principal soloist at the Kirov Theatre in Leningrad, St Petersburg from 1988; Rimsky's Olga and Maria, Tchaikovsky's Tatiana and Iolanta and Violetta; Sang in the 14th Symphony of Shostakovich with the Chamber Orchestra of the Lithuanian Philharmonia at the Berliner Philharmonie, 1989; Sang Iolanta at Frankfurt 1990 and Leonora in Il Trovatore with Omaha Opera 1991. Honours: Winner, Glinka Competition, 1984; First prize, Dvorak Voice Competition, Karlovi Vari, 1987; Winner, Fidenza, Parma Verdi Competition, 1990. Address: c/o Athole Still Ltd, Foresters Hall, 25-27 Westow Street, London SE19 3RY, England.

MIRZOYAN Edward, b. 12 May 1921, Gori, Georgia, USSR. Composer. m. Elena Stepanyan, 1 June 1951, 1 son, 1 daughter. Education: Musical College, Yerevan, 1928-36; Yerevan Conservatoire, 1936-41; Postgraduate, Moscow Concervatoire, 1946-48. Debut: Yerevan, 1938. Career: Lecturer, 1949; Professor, 1965-; Head, Chair of Composition, 1972-8, Yerevan Conservatoire; Secretary, 1950-52, Chairman, 1956-; Armenian Composer's Union; Chairman, 1952-56; Armenian Musical Foundation. Compositions: Sako from Lahore, symphonic poem, 1941; Symphonic Dances, suite, 1946; String quartet, 1947; Overture, 1947; Introduction & Perpetuum Mobile; Violin & Orchestra, 1957; Symphony, 1962; Cantatas, 1948, 1949, 1950; Cello Sonata, 1967; Piano pieces, 1983; Epitaph, symphonic poem, 1988. Recordings: Introduction & Perpetuum Mobile; Symphony, Symphonic Dances; String Quartet; Cello Sonata; Romances; Piano Poem. Memberships: Armenian & CIS Composers' Societies. Current Mangement: Armenian Composers' Union. Address: c/o Armenian Composers' Union, Demirchyan str, 25, Yerevan 375002, Armenia, CIS.

MISKELL Austin, b. 14 Oct 1925, Shawnee, OK, USA. Professor; Singer. Divorced, 2 s. Education: Oklahoma City University, 1946-47; Hochschule für Musik, Zurich, 1955-65; Mozarteum of Salzburg, 1955-65; LRAM, Royal Academy of Music, London. Career: Featured soloist with Elizabethan Consort of Viols, London, Anglian Chamber Soloists London, Ricecare, Ensemble for Ancient Music, Zurich, Arte Antica Zurich; Sang in 25 countries, 1950-86; Performances with Tonhalle Orchestra, Zurich, Orchestra de la Academia Santa Cecilia Rome, London Symphony Orchestra, Pro Arte, London, Stuttgarter Synfoniker and others; Participant at music festivals including: Sagra Musicale, Perugia, Italy, Settimane Musicali, Ascona, Salzburg Bach Festival, Britten, Purcell Festival, Buenos Aires, Mozart Festival, Munich, Bergen Festival, Norway, 1970-80; Assistant Professor of Voice at National University of Colombia, Bogotà, 1976-82; Head of Voice at Conservatory of Tolima, Ibague, Colombia, 1978-82; Teacher of Voice, Italian Opera, Teatro Colon, National Opera Company, Bogotà, 1978-81; Lecturer in Voice, University of New Mexico, 1982-83; Professor of Voice, College of Santa Fe, 1982-85. Recordings: Numerous including: I Sing America, 1969, Radha Krishna, 1971, Pergolesi Requiem, 1972; Ballades Rondeaux and Virelais, 1973. Publication: Poetry - The Salt Cathedral, 1981. Address: PO Box 204 Manhasset, Long Island, NY 11030, USA.

MISSENHARDT Gunter, b. 29 Mar 1938, Augsburg, Germany. Singer, Bass. m. Agnes Baltsa, 1974. Education: Studied at the Augsburg Conservatory and with Helge Roswaenge. Career: Sang at the Bayerische Staatsoper Munich, 1965-68; Frankfurt, 1968-72; Berne, 1973-78; Appearances from 1978 at Aachen, Bremen and Brussels, 1986; Since 1984, State Opera Vienna (Ochs, Osmin, Varlaam, Colline); 1984, Grand Opera Paris (Ochs); Covent Garden, London, since 1985, Bartolo, Varlaam, Ochs, Rocco; 1994 Scala di Milano (Osmin); Dusseldorf, 1988; Théâtre des Champs Elysées Paris, 1989, as Ochs in Der Rosenkavalier; Season 1987-88 as the Doctor in Wozzeck at Strasbourg and Schigolch in Lulu at Brussels; Other roles have included Kecal, Osmin, Bett in Zar und Zimmerman, Masetto, Mozart's Figaro and Varlaam in Boris Godunov; Sang Osmin in Die Entführung at Geneva, 1996. Address: c/o Deutsche Oper am Rhein, Heinrich Heine Allee 16, 4000 Duseeldorf, Germany.

MITCHELL Clare, b. 1960, England. Costume and Stage Designer. Education: Studied at the Bristol Old Vic Theatre School. Career: Assistant Costume Designer, Royal Shakespeare Company, Stratford; Costumes for premiere of Rebecca by Wilfred Josephs at Leeds, 1983; English National Oper for Madama Butterfly, Scottish Opera Don Giovanni, and Jenufa in production by Yuri Lyubimov at Zurich and Covent Garden, 1986-93; Costumes and sets for Ulisse by Monteverdi and Handel's Flavio at the Batignano Festival, Rigoletto for Opera 80 and Donizetti's Tudor trilogy for Monte Carlo Opera; Costumes for Traviata at English National Opera, 1996. Address: c/o English National Opera, St Martin's Lane, London WC2, England.

MITCHELL Donald (Charles Peter), b. 6 Feb 1925, London, England. Writer on Music; Critic. m. Kathleen. Education: Durham University, 1949-50, with Arthur Hutchings and A E F Dickinson. Career: Founder, 1947, Co-Editor, 1947-52, Music Survey; Music Critic, The Musical Times, 1953-57; Editor of Tempo, 1958-62; Head of Music Department, Faber and Faber, 1958; Managing Director, 1965-71, Chairman, 1977-86, Faber Music; Music Staff of Daily Telegraph, 1959-64; Professor of Music, 1971-76, Visiting Professor, 1976-, Sussex University; Chairman, Performing Right Society, 1989; Director of study courses at the Britten-Pears School, Snape; Visiting Professor, York University, 1991; Visiting Professor, King's College, London University, 1995. Publications include: Benjamin Britten (joint editor), 1952; The Mozart Companion (joint editor), 1956; Author of 3 volumes of a projected 4 on the life and music of Mahler, 1958-86; The Language of Modern Music, 1963; Benjamin Britten, 1913-76: Pictures from a Life (with J Evans), 1978; Britten and Auden in the Thirties, 1981; Benjamin Britten: Death in Venice, 1987; Letters from a Life: Selected Letters and Diaries of

Benjamin Britten, Vols 1 and 2, 1923-1945 (with Philip Reed); Cradles of the New: Writings on Music 1951-1991, 1995. Contributions to: Music Survey, The Chesterian, Tempo, Musical Times, Music and Letters, Opera; Articles on Reger, Schoenberg, Weill, Berg, Malcolm Arnold, Hindemith, Britten, Prokofiev and Stravinsky. Honours: PhD (Southampton); Honorary MA (Sussex); Doctor of University of York; Mahler Medal, 1987. Address: 83 Ridgmount Gardens, London WC1E 7AY, England.

MITCHELL Geoffrey (Roger), b. 6 Jun 1936, Upminster, Essex, England. Counter Tenor; Conductor; Choral Manager. Education: Studied with Alfred Deller and Lucy Manen. Career: Counter tenor, lay clerk, Ely Cathedral, 1957-60; Westminster Cathedral, 1960-61; Vicar-choral, St Paul's Cathedral, 1961-66; Founder and conductor, Surrey University Choir, 1966; Manager, John Alldis Choir, 1966-; Cantores in Ecclesia, 1967-77; Conductor, New London Singers, 1970-86; Professor, Royal Academy of Music, 1974-; Singing Teacher, King's College, and St John's College, Cambridge, 1975-85; Conductor, Geoffrey Mitchell Choir, 1976-; Conductor, London Festival Singers, 1987-; BBC Choral Manager, 1977-92; Guest Conductor, Camerata Antigua of Curitiba, Brazil. Recordings: Various with: John Alldis Choir; Cantores in Ecclesia; Pro Cantione Antigua; Opera Rara. Honours: Honorary Associate, Royal Academy of Music, 1981; Vice Chairman, Federation of Cathedral Old Chorister Associations, 1987-92, Chairman, 1992-; Honorary Fellow, Trinity College, London. Membership: British Broadcasting Corporation Club. Hobbies: Collecting antique prints; Swimming; Food. Address: 49 Chelmsford Road, Woodford, London, E18 2PW, England.

MITCHELL Ian, b. 14 Feb 1948, South Yorkshire, England. Clarinettist. m. Vanessa Noel-Tod, 5 Sept 1970, 1 son, 1 daughter. Education: Royal Academy of Music, 1966-70; GRSM; London University, Goldsmiths' College, 1976-79; BMus, London. Debut: Purcell Room, London, 1971. Career: Solo appearances throughout Britain, Europe, Middle East, USA (4 tours) Australia, North Korea; Chamber Concerts widely in Europe; Solo Broadcasts BBC, Swedish, New York, Belgian, Austrian, German Radio Stations; Soloist on British TV and in film of composer Cornelius Cardew; Numerous first performances, many works written for him; Director of Gemini Leading 20th Century Ensemble which is a pioneer in music education; Member of Dreamtiger, Eisler Ensemble of London, Entertainers Clarinet Quartet, AMM; Part-time Tutor in Performance, Exeter University, 1996-. Recordings: Works of Nicola LeFanu (with Gemini); Works of Oliver Knussen; Draughtman's Contract, The Masterwork and others with Michael Nyman Band; Eisler with Dagmar Krauze; Works by David Lumsdaine, John White, Fashion Music; Numerous chamber ensemble recordings. Publications: Structure and Content of Lessons; Preparing for Performance. Contributions to: Musical Times; Clarinet and Saxophone; Contact; Musical Performance. Honour: Hon ARAM, 1997. Membership: ISM. Hobbies: Family; Reading; Badger Watching. Address: 137 Upland Road, East Dulwich, London SE22 0DF, England.

MITCHELL Lee, b. 27 Apr 1951, Wilmington, Delaware, USA. Composer; Pianist; Educator. Education: BMus, Peabody Institute, Johns Hopkins University, 1970; Studies, University of California, Santa Barbara; PhD, University of Berne, Switzerland, 1976. Debut: Wilmington, Delaware. Career: Professor, Music Theory and History, Academy of Music, Biel, Switzerland, 1973-76; Professor of Music Theory and History, Peabody Institute, Johns Hopkins University, Baltimore, 1976-86; Chairman, Theory, Hopkins, 1984-86; Adjunct Professor of Music, Goucher College, Towson, Maryland, 1980-83; Lecturer, University of Esztergom, Hungary, 1980, 1981, 1983; Profesor of Music, Johns Hopkins University, School of Continuing Studies, 1986-; Television appearances, Baltimore, 1969; Radio broadcasts, Budapest, 1981, Switzerland, 1993; Piano Concerts, USA, Switzerland, Germany, Holland, Greece, Hungary; Compositions performed in the USA, Peru, Europe. Compositions include: Baltimore Reflections for flute and piano, 1989; Variations and Toccata for organ; Fantasy Allegro for flute and organ, 1993; Ballade for violin, viola and piano, 1994; Four Jewish Melodies for clarinet and piano, 1995. Honours: Rockefeller Grant in Composition, 1965; Winner, Dame Myra Hess Memorial Concert Series Award, Chicago, 1987; Artist Fellow in Musical Composition, State of Delaware, 1991; Meet the Composer Grants, 1992, 1993, 1994, 1996. Memberships: Sonneck Society; American Musicological Society. Address: Comanche Circle/Warwick Park, Millsboro, DE 19966, USA.

MITCHELL Leona, b. 13 Oct 1949, Enid, OK, USA. Singer, (Soprano). Education: Studied at University of OK and in Santa Fe and San Francisco; With Ernest St John Metz in Los Angeles. Debut: San Francisco, 1972, as Micaela in Carmen; Metropolitan Opera from 1975, as Micaela, Pamina, Puccini's Manon, Liu and Mini, Elvira in Ernani and Leonora in La Forza del Destino; Barcelona 1975, as Mathilde in Guillaume Tell; Guest appearances in Houston, Washington, Stuttgart and Geneva; Covent Garden debut 1980, as Liu in Turandot; Sydney Opera, 1985, as Leonora in Il Trovatore; Nice Opera, 1987 as Salome in Massenet's Herodiade; Paris Opéra-Comique in Puccini's Trittico, all 3 soprano leads; Verona 1988, Aida; Sang Elvira in Ernani at Parma, 1990, the Trovatore Leonora at the Teatro Colon Buenos Aires; Season 1992 as Aida for New Israeli Opera; Sang Strauss's Ariadne at the Sydney Opera House, 1997. Recordings: Gershwin's Bess. Address: c/o Teatro Regio, Via Garibaldi 16, 1-43100 Parma, Italy.

MITCHELL Madeleine Louise. Concert Violinist. Education: Junior Exhibitioner, Royal College of Music, 1969-75; Foundation Scholar, 1975-79; GRSM, 1st class hons, 1978; ARCM, Teachers honours and performers honours, 1979; Eastman and Juilliard Schools, New York, MMus, Violin performance, 1981. Debut: London, recital South Bank, 1984. Career: BBC 1, TV Music Time, 1979; London South Bank recitals include Awards by Park Lane Group, Worshipful Company Musicians, Kirckman Society; Numerous solo tours in concertos and recitals in Britain, Germany, Spain, Czechoslovakia, Italy, USA, Canada; World Tour, British Council, 1989 and 1990; Violinist Fires of London, 1985-87; Several solo works written for her; Numerous international Festival appearances including: ISCM Masters of 20th Century Music, Warsaw, Cardiff, Harrogate, Brighton, Malta, Kiev, Huddersfield, Dartington; Malvern, Aspen, Bath, Belfast, Dvorak CCSR; Schwetzingen, Toronto; Soloist on tour with Wurttemberg, Munich Chamber Orchestras; Ulster, Czech Radio Symphony, (Plzen), Malaga Symphony of Spain, Academy of London; London Festival Orchestra; Karlsbad SO CSSR; Wigmore Hall debut recital, 1989; Solo tour South America, 1991; Concertos with City of London Orchestra, QEH, London 1992, Royal Philharmonic Orchestra, London, 1993; Polish Radio Symphony 94, Kiev Radio/TV Orchestra, 94; Ulster Orchestra; Tours also include Poland, Ukraine, South Bank Recitals, 1993, 1994, 1995, 1996, Recitals, New York, 1994, 1997, Wigmore Hall, 1995, 1997; Professor of Violin, Royal College of Music, numerous masterclasses worldwide; Artistic Director, London Chamber Ensemble; BBC Proms, 1996; Artistic Director, Bed Violin Festival, Cardiff (Patron: Yehudi Menuhin), several BBC broadcasts; Works specially written for her by Brian Elias, Stuart Jones, Piers Hellawell, Anthony Powers, Vladimir Runshak, James MacMillan, John Woolrich, Michael Nyman, John Hardy. Recordings: Broadcasts in Poland, Ukraine, Hong Kong, Colombia, Australia - ABC and Channel 7 TV, Germany, Britain, Singapore, Italian TV, Canada; Czechoslovakia; SABC; Broadcasts also include BBC Radio and TV; Messiaen Quartet for the End of Time for Collins Classics with Joanna MacGregor, 1994; Broadcasts also include BBC Radio and TV. Honours: ITT/Fulbright Fellowship, USA, 1979-81; Performance Arts Achievement Awd for Women in UK under 35, 1991. Hobbies: Fine Art; Dancing; Swimming; Cycling. Address: 41 Queens Gardens, London, W2 3AA, England.

MITCHELL Scott, b. 1964, Perth, Scotland. Pianist. Education: Studied at the Royal Academy of Music with Alexander Kelly and John Streets; Further study with members of the Amadeus Quartet. Career: Member of the Borante Piano Trio, 1982-; London Performances at the Purcell Room and Wigmore Hall in the trios of Beethoven; Tours to Dublin, Paris and Vienna, Beethoven's Triple Concerto at the 1989 Festival Wiener Klassik; Concerts in Tel Aviv and Jerusalem and association with the Israel Piano Trio at the 1988 Dartington Summer School; Season 1990 at the Perth and Bath Festivals, tour of Scandinavia, Russia and the Baltic States; Television appearances on Channel 4 and BSB; Duo partnerships with Laurence Jackson (violin) and Duncan Prescott (clarinet) with concerts at the Wigmore and Purcell Room; Accompanist to Yvonne Howard (mezzo soprano) and Barry Banks (tenor), including tour of France, Spain and Portugal, 1989. Recordings: Albums for Chandos with Duncan Prescott and Collins Classics with Jennifer Stinton (flute). Honours include: Leverhulme Scholarship; English Speaking Union Scholarship; Lisa Fuchsova Prize, Royal Overseas League Competition, 1990. Current Management: Scott Mitchell Management. Address: The Old Stable, Shudy Camps Park, Shudy Camps, Cambs CB1 6RD, England.

MITCHINSON John (Leslie), b. 31 Mar 1932, Blackrod, Lancashire, England. Opera and Concert Singer, Tenor; Administrator. m. Maureen Guy, Mezzo-Soprano, 8 Mar 1958, 2 sons. Education: Royal Manchester College of Music; ARMCM; FRMCM; Studied singing with Frederick Cox, Heddle Nash and Boriska Gerab. Debut: TV Series with Eric Robinson, Music for You; Stage debut as Jupiter in Handel's Semele at Sadler's Wells Theatre, 1959. Career: Senior Lecturer, Royal Norther College of Music, 1987-92; Head of Vocal Studies, Welsh College of Music and Drama, 1992-; Many Radio, TV, Concert and Opera appearances worldwide, ENO, WNO, Scottish Opera, Basle Opera, Prague Opera; Most of the world's Music Festival; Roles include: Idomeneo, Aegisthus, Luca in From the House of the Dead, Manolios in The Greek Passion; Dalibor, Florestan, Siegmund; Sang Svatopluk Cech in the first British production of Janacek's The Excursions of Mr Broucek, ENO, 1978; Wagner's Tristan and Peter Grimes for Welsh National Opera; Opera North and Buxton Festival, 1983 as Max in Der Freischütz and Gualtiero in Vivaldi's Griselda; Menelaus in Belle Hélène, Scottish Opera, 1995; Director of Vocal Studies at the Welsh College of Music and Drama, Cardiff. Recordings: Mahler 8th Symphony, Bernstein; Mahler 8th Symphony, Wyn Morris; Lied von der Erde, Alexander Gibson, Beatrice et Benedict, Berlioz (Colin Davis); Lelio, Berlioz (Pierre Boulez); Tristan und Isolde, Wagner (Reginald Goodall); Glagolitic Mass Janacek (Simon Rattle); Glagolitic Mass (Kurt Masur), Gewandhaus Orchestra, 1990; Lied von der Erde, Raymond Leppard; Lied von der Erde, Horenstein; Dream of Gerontius, Simon Rattle and CBSO. Honours: Queens Prize and Royal Philharmonic Kathleen Ferrier Prize 1956-57; Curtis Gold Medal, RMCM, 1953; Ricordi Opera Prize 1952. Hobbies: Cooking; Boats. Address: The Verzons Granary, Munsley, Ledbury, Herefordshire, England.

MITIC Nikola, b. 27 Nov 1938, Nis, Serbia. Singer, (Bass-Baritone). Education: Studied in Belgrade and with V Badiali in Milan. Career: Many appearances at the Belgrade National Opera from 1965; Guest engagements with the company at Copenhagen, 1968, Barcelona, 1972. Further appearances at the Vienna Staatsoper, Philadelphia, 1970; Dusseldorf, Perugia Festival, 1973, Rome 1975 and Dublin; Roles have included Rigoletto, Mozart's Figaro, Eugene Onegin, Mazeppa, Riccardo in I Puritani, Posa in Don Carlos and Enrico in Lucia di Lammermoor. Address: c/o Teatro dell'Opera di Roma, Piazza B, Gigli 8, 00184 Rome, Italy.

MITO Motoko, b. 13 June 1957, Kyoto, Japan. Violinist. m. Yoske Otawa, 17 Mar 1989. Education: Toho School of Music, Tokyo; Hochschule Mozarteum, Salzburg, Austria. Debut: Salzburg. Career: Concertmaster, International Music Art Society Orchestra, Tokyo, 1980-81; Soloist, International Mozart Week, Salzburg, 1984; Many recitals and appearances with Professor Erika Frieser, Piano, throughout Europe and Japan, 1984-; Member, Salzburger Streichquartett, 1987-. Recordings: Preiser Record, 1 Salzburger Streichquartett; Preiser Record, 2 Salzburger Streichquarttet. Current Management: Sound Gazely, Tokyo, Japan. Address: Kamiyasumatsu 11, Tokorozawa, Japan.

MITTELMANN Norman, b. 25 May 1932, Winnipeg, Manitoba, Canada. Opera Singer, Baritone. m. 24 Feb 1979, 2 daughters. education: Curtis Institute of Music, with Martial Singher, Ernzo Mascherini, diploma, 1959. Debut: Toronto Opera Company. Career: Opera houses, Germany; Italy; Austria; Puerto Rico; Canada; USA; Poland; Switzerland. Roles include: Amonasro, (Aida), Zurich, 1967; William Tell, May Festival, Florence, 1969; Rigoletto, Chicago Opera Theatre, 1977; Scarpia, (Tosca), Venice, 1979; John Falstaff, Hamburg and Berlin, 1979; Nelusko, (L'Africaine), San Francisco Opera; Mandryka, (Arabella), La Scala; Sang at Zurich until 1982. Recordings: Video of La Gioconda, from San Francisco, 1979. Honours: Gellow, Rockefeller Foundation, 1956-59; Award, Fischer Foundation, 1959. Hobbies: Gardening. Current Management: Robert Lombardo Associates, 61 West 62nd Street, Suite F, New York, NY 10023, USA.

MIYAZAWA Junichi, b. 23 Nov 1963, Gunma, Japan. Music Critic; Writer; Translator; Researcher of Russian and Canadian Literatures. Education: Bachelor of Political Science, Aoyama Gakuin University, Tokyo, 1986; BA, 1988, MA, 1990, Waseda University, Tokyo. Career: Assistant, 1993-95, Lecturer, 1995-, Waseda University; Music Critic, GQ Japan, 1993-94; Record Geijutsu, 1995-; Hosei University, 1996-;Keio University, 1997-. Publications: Editor, Glenn Gould, 1988; Co-Translator, Glenn Gould, Pluriel, 1991; Co-Author, Glenn Gould Studies, 1991; Translator, Glenn Gould: A Life and Variations, 1992; Co-Translator, A Book on Andrei Tarkovsky's The Mirror, 1994; Co-translator, Writing About Music, 1994; Translator, Glenn, 1995; Translator, Glenn Gould: Portraits of the Artist as a Young Man, 1995; Numerous articles, liner notes and translations. Hobbies: Jogging; Zen Meditation. Address: Apt 207, 4-38-18 Shimo-Takaido, Suginami-Ku, Tokyo 168, Japan.

MIZELLE Dary John, b. 14 June 1940, Stillwater, OK, USA. Composter. Education: Studied at the California State University and University of California at Davis, PhD, 1977. Career: Tutor, University of Florida, 1973-75, Oberlin College, 1975-79, State University at Purchase, New York, 1990. Composition: Polyphonies, I-III, 1975-78; Polytempus I for trumpet and tape, 1976; Primavera-Heterphony for 24 cellos, 1977; Samadhi for quadrophonic tape, 1978; Quanta II and Hymn of the World for 2 choruses and ensemble, 1979; Lake Mountain Thunder for cor anglais and percussion ensemble, 1981; Thunderclap of time, music for a planetarium, 1982; Requiem Mass for chorus and orchestra, 1982; Sonic Adventures, 1982; Quintet for Woodwinds 1983; Contrabass Quartet, 1983; Indian Summer for string quartet and oboe, 1983; Sounds for orchestra, 1984; Concerto for contrabass and orchestra, 1974-85; Genesis for orchestra, 1985; Blue for orchestra 1986; Percussion Concerto 1987; Parameters for percussion solo and chamber orchestra, 1974-87; Earth Mountain Fire, 1987-; Fossy: A Passion Play music theater, 1987; Chance Gives me What I Want, dance, 1988. Address: ASCAP, ASCAP Building, One Lincoln Plaza, NY 10023, USA.

MIZZI Alfred (Freddie Paul), b. 12 Oct 1934, Valletta, Malta. Musician, Clarinettist. m. 24 June 1953, 2 daughters. Education: ALCM, 1966. Debut: As soloist with the Malta National Orchestra, 1961. Career: Belfast Arts Festival, 1967; Member, World Symphony Orchestra performances in New York, Washington & Florida, 1971; Soloist in concerts in Bucharest, Mannheim, Mozart Castle, Darmstadt, Wigmore Hall & Barbican Centre, London, 1973-83; Concerts in France & Greece as part of the Mediterranean Arts Festival, 1985; Concerts at the Czechoslovakia Arts Festival, 1986; Soloist with: Stamitz Symphony Orchestra, West Germany; Watford Chamber Orchestra, England; Zapadocesky Symphony Orchester, Czechoslovakia and others. Soloist with string quartets: The Brevis String Quartet, Malta; Salzburg String Quartet, Austria; Sinnhoffer String Quartet, West Germany; Quartetto Academica, Rumania; The Rasumovsky String Quartet, Great Britain and others; Television appearances and radio broadcasts in Malta, Rumania, BBC Germany, USA, France, Greece, Italy. Honours: Phoenicia International Culture Award, 1985; Malta Society of Arts Award, 1986. Memberships: Performing Rights Society, London. Hobbies: Paintings; Football. Current Management: Corinthia Group of Companies. Address: Il Klarinett, Ursuline Sisters Street, G'Mangia, Malta.

MOBBS Kenneth (William), b. 4 Aug 1925, Northamptonshire, England. Keyboard Specialist; Tutor. m. (1) Barbara McNeile, 2 Sep 1950, (2) Mary J Randall, 18 May 1979, 3 d. Education: Clare College, Cambridge; Royal College of Music; Private Study with Greville Cooke and M P Conway. Debut: Organ Recital, King's College, Cambridge, 1949. Career: Lecturer, Senior Lecturer of Music, University of Bristol, 1950-83; Freelance Keyboard Performer, including Harpsichord Concerto, Solo Piano, Fortepiano Recitals and numerous accompaniments on BBC Radio; Director, Mobbs Keyboard Collection. Compositions include: Engaged!, comic opera, 1963. Recordings include: Mobbs Keyboard Collection, Volume 1; Golden Age of The Clarinet. Contributions to: Encyclopaedia of Keyboard Instruments, 1993; Early Music; Galpin Society Journal; English Harpsichord Magazine. Hobbies: Photography; Bird Watching. Address: 16 All Saints Road, Bristol, BS8 2JJ, England.

MÖDL Martha, b. 22 Mar 1912, Nuremberg, Germany. Singer, Soprano & Mezzo-Soprano. Education: Studied in Nuremberg and with Otto Mueller in Milan. Debut: Sang Humperdinck's Hansel at Remschied in 1943. Career: Dusseldorf Opera 1945-49 in mezzo roles; Sang at Hamburg from 1949 as a soprano; Covent Garden debut 1950, as Carmen; Returned 1966 as Strauss's Clytemnestra and 1972 in Die schweigsame Frau; Bayreuth, 1951-67 as Kundry, Brünnhilde, Sieglinde, Waltraute, Gutrune and Isolde; 1955 sang Beethoven's Leonore at the reopening of the Vienna State Opera; Metropolitan Opera debut 1957, as Brünnhilde; 1963 sang the Nurse in the production of Strauss's Die Frau ohne Schatten at the reopening of the Munich Opera; Sang in the premieres of Reimann's Melusine, 1971 and Ghost Sonata 1984, Fortner's Elisabeth Tudor 1972, Von Einmen's Kabale und Liebe 1978 and Cerha's Baal 1981; Sang the Countess in the Queen of Spades at Nice, 1989 and at Essen 1990; Sang Bazouga in the premiere of Klebe's Gervaise Macquart, Dusseldorf 1995. Recordings: Der Ring des Nibelungen and Fidelio, conducted by Furtwängler; Elektra; Oedipus Rex; Parsifal; Die Frau ohne Schatten, Deutsche Grammophon. Address: c/o Theater Essen, Rolandstrasse 10, D-4300 Essen, Germany.

MOE Bjorn (Kare), b. 10 Aug 1946, Hegra, Norway. Concert Organist. m. Kristine Kaasa, 21 June 1975. Education: Trondheim School of Music, 1963-67; Musik-Akademie der Stadt Basel Abteilung Konservatorium and Schola Cantorum Basiliensis 1968-73, Eduard Muller and Wolfgang Neininger; Paris, Gaston Litaize and Praha, Jiri Reinberger. Career: Professor at Trondelag Musik-konservatorium, Trondheim 1973-84; Full-time Concert Organist 1985-; Concerts with the complete works of Olivier Messiaen, the main works of Max Reger and other organ music from all periods; World premiere of several new works from Switzerland, Iceland and Norway, 45 minutes work of Ketil Hvoslef Revelations of John in the Bergen International Festival 1986; Co-operates with other arts as theatre, dance and poetry, Exultate, concert with dance recitation and organ, performed 20 times in the main cities in the Nordic countries; Organ Expert; Counseller. Address: Postboks 16, N-7084 Melhus, Norway.

MOENNE-LOCCOZ Philippe, b. 21 Mar 1953, Annecy, France. Musician; Composer. m. 30 Aug 1986, 1 son. Education: Studies in electro-acoustic Composition, 20th century analysis, string bass, contemporary, classical and popular music. Debut: At age 10. Career: Teaches aspects of music through animation at special children's centre; teacher of Guitar and Electro-acoustic Music; Teacher of electro-acoustic music, Conservatoire de Geneva, Switzerland; Director, Collectif et Compagnie (studio for research, creative work and music education), Annecy. Compositions: Electro-acoustic works: Boucles; Réves opaques; Oscillation; Petit musique du Soir; Mixed works, electro-acoustic and traditional instruments; Le cri des idées sur l'eau; Recontre; Mixage 4; Oscillation No 1,2,6; Chaos for tape only; Aspérites (CDO2), 1992; Fermez la porte, 1992; Inventions, 1991. Recordings: Réves opaques, cassete C1; Le cri des idées sur l'eau, Radio Suisse Romanda, CD's, Trola, Chutts, 1989. Membership: Association for Electro-acoustic Music, Geneva. Address: 16 Impasse des Tablettes, 74940 Annecy Le Vieux, France.

MOEVS Robert (Walter), b. 2 Dec 1920, La Crosse, Wisconsin, USA. Composer; Professor. m. Maria Teresa Marabini, 1 Oct 1953, 1 son, 1 daughter. Education: BA, Harvard College, 1942; Conservatoire National, Paris, France, 1947-51; MA, Harvard University, 1952. Career: Fellow, American Academy in Rome; Professor, Harvard University, USA, 1955-63; Professor, Rutgers, 1964-91; Professor Emeritus, 1991. Compositions: Numerous works for solo instruments, chorus, orchestra, chamber music. Recordings: Numerous works recorded. Publications: Numerous works published in Paris, Italy and USA. Contributions to: Musical Quarterly; Perspectives of New Music; Journal of Music Theory. Honours: Award, National Institute of Arts and Letters, 1956; Recipient, Guggenheim Fellowship, 1963-64; Several ASCAP Awards. Memberships: Founding Member, American Society of University Composers; Executive Committee, International Society for Contemporary Music; National Associate, Sigma Alpha Iota. Address: 1640 River Road, Blackwell's Mills, Belle Mead, NJ 08502, USA.

MOFFA Robert A, b. 7 June 1941, Philadelphia, USA. Composer; Conductor; Pianist. m. Mercedes Sheets Moffa, 8 August 1964, 3 daughters. Education: BA, Music; Piano, Harmony, Theory, Richard Caruso, 1948-59; Composition, Hayle Carpenter, Ryan University, 1960. Debut: Conductor, Composer, 1st Major Works, Berlin Suite for Orchestra, 1963. Career: Appeared on Major Television Stations, NBC, ABC, CBS, and Locals; Conducted Major Symphony Orchestras Worldwide; Founder, American Symphony Orchestra of Florida; Composer of Music to Recognize People, Events, Freedom and Mankind. Compositions include: Berlin Suite, Orch 20 mm, 5 Movements, 1963; Poland Today, Orch 20 mm, 4 Movements, 1982; The American Farmers Suite, 20 mm, 1986. Recordings: Piano Works, Concerto Rapsody; Romance Fa Prano; La Nova Vita; Nova Romantrea; Looking Back. Publications: The 99th Congress of USA Published Music Efforts in the Congressional Record, 14 August 1986. Contributions to: Articles in Musical Compositions in Over 30 National Magazines. Honours include: Recognition From President Kennedy, 1963; Artistic Award, State of Florida, 1982. Memberships: ASCAP; MENC; Sym-Association. Hobby: Sailing. Current Management: RAM Musical Productions. Address: 1414 33rd Street South East, Ruskin, FL 33570, USA.

MOFFAT Julie, b. 1966, Leicester, England. Singer (Soprano). Education: Studied at the Royal College of Music, 1984-88, with Marion Studholme; Further study with Pamela Cook and Paul Hamburger. Debut: London 1987, in Elliott Carter's A Mirror on Which to Dwell. Career: British premiere of Jonathon Harvey's From Silence, 1989; Appearances with such contemporary music groups as Klangforum Wien, Ensemble Inter Contemporain, Ensemble Moderne of Frankfurt and the BBC Singers; Repertoire has included works by Zender, Barraqué, Webern, Zimmerman, Nono, Beat Furrer and Varèse; Requiem for Reconciliation with Helmuth Rilling at the 1995 Stuttgart Music Festival; Frequent engagements in oratorios by Bach, Beethoven, Haydn, Mozart, Rossini, Mendelssohn and Schubert; Season 1996-97 at the Vienna Konzerthaus, the Bregenz, Salzburg and Schleswig-Holstein Festivals, with the Geneva Chamber Orchestra, at the Berlin Festival and with London Sinfonietta. Recordings: Albums with Klangforum Wien, Stuttgarter Bach Akademie and Ensemble Inter-Contemporain; Music by Zimmermann and Dallapiccola. Honours include: Foundation Scholarship to the RCM, 1984. Address: Owen/White Management, 39 Hillfield Avenue, London N8 7DS, England.

MOFFO Anna, b. 27 June 1932, Wayne, Pennsylvania, USA. Singer (Soprano). Education: Studied at the Curtis Institute with E Giannini-Gregory; Rome with Luigi Ricci and Mercedes Llopart. Debut: Sang Norina in Don Pasquale at Spoleto in 1955. Career: Madama Butterfly on Italian TV, 1956; Sang Mozart's Zerlina at Aix in 1956 and Verdi's Nannetta at Salzburg, 1957; Metropolitan Opera from 1959 as Verdi's Violetta and Gilda, Donizetti's Lucia and Adina, Puccini's Liu, Mozart's Pamina, Massenet's Manon, Gounod's Marguerite and Juliette, the soprano roles in Les Contes d'Hoffmann and Debussy's Mélisande; Covent Garden debut 1964, as Gilda; Guest appearances in Berlin, Vienna and Buenos Aires; Sang Thais at Seattle, 1976 and Adriana Lecouvreur at Parma, 1978. Recordings: La Bohème, Le nozze di Figaro, Capriccio, Carmen and Falstaff (Columbia); Lucia di Lammermoor, Hänsel und Gretel, Iphigènie en Aulide (Eurodisc); Madama Butterfly, Il Filosofo di Campagna, La Serva Padrona, Luisa Miller (RCA); Film version of La Traviata. Address: c/o Metropolitan Opera, Lincoln Center, NY 10023, USA.

MOHLER Hubert, b. 1922, Augsburg, Germany. Singer, Tenor. Education: Studied in Augsburg. Career: Sang in the choir of the Augsburg Stadttheater, 1946-52; Appeared in solo roles at Gelsenkirchen, 1952-57; Oberhausen, 1957-61; Augsburg, 1961-64; Many appearances at the Cologne Opera, 1964-89, as Mozart's Pedrillo, Monostatos and Basilio, Mime in the Ring, David in Die Meistersinger, Valzacchi, Rosenkavalier, the Captain in Wozzeck, the character roles in Les Contes d'Hoffmann and Adam in The Devils of Loudun; Many appearances in Germany and abroad as concert singer. Recordings: Mozart Masses; Les Brigands by Offenbach. Address: c/o Oper der Stadt Köln, Offenbachplatz, 5000 Cologne, Germany.

MOHR Thomas, b. 17 Oct 1961, Neumunster, Holstein, Germany. Singer, Baritone. Education: Studied in Lubeck, graduating in 1985, and in Hamburg. Debut: Lubeck 1984, as Sivio in Pagliacci. Career: Sang at Lubeck and Detmold, 1984-85, Bremen, 1985-87, Nationaltheater, Mannheim, from 1987; Guest appearances at the Schleswig-Holstein Festival, 1987, and at Cologne, Hamburg and Ludwigsburg; Other roles include Mozart's Count and Papageno, Rossini's Figaro, Lortzing'z Zar and Count, Der Wildschütz, Wolfram and Billy Budd; Many concerts and Lieder recitals. Honours: Winner, 1984 s'Hertogenbosch Competition; 1985 German Lied Competition, London. Address: Nationaltheater, Am Goetheplatz, 6800 Mannheim, Germany.

MOLDOVEANU Eugenia, b. 19 Mar 1944, Bursteni, Rumania. Singer, Soprano. Education: Studied at the Ciprian Porumbescu Conservatory and in Bucharest with Arta Florescu. Debut: Bucharest 1968 as Donna Anna in Don Giovanni. Career: Guest appearances in Belgrade, Sofia, Athens, Amsterdam, Trieste, Stuttgart, Dresden and Berlin; Repertoire includes roles in operas by Mozart, Verdi and Puccini; Sang Mozart's Countess while on tour to Japan with Vienna Staatsoper, 1986; Season 1987 sang Mozart's Countess at La Scala Milan, Butterfly at Verona and Donna Anna at Turin, Countess, 1989. Address: Teatro Regio di Torino, Piazza Castello 215, 1-10124 Turin, Italy.

MOLDOVEANU Nicolae, b. 20 July 1962. Conductor. Education: Musikhochschule Zurich, Switzerland; Royal Academy of Music, London. Career: Resident Conductor, Bournemouth Orchestra. Honours: Edwin Samuel Dove Prize, Royal Academy of Music, London, 1993. Membership: Associate, Royal Academy of Music, London, 1997. Current Management: Von Walsum Management Ltd. Address: 4 Addison Bridge Place, London W14 8XP, England.

MOLDOVEANU Vasile, b. 6 Oct 1935, Konstanza, Rumania. Singer, (Tenor). Education: Studied in Bucharest with Constantin Badescu. Debut: Bucharest 1966, as Rinuccio in Gianni Schicchi. Career: Stuttgart debut 1972, as Donizetti's Edgardo; Munich Opera from 1976, as Rodolfo and the Duke of Mantua; Deutsche Oper Belin and Chicago Lyric Oper 1977; Hamburg Opera 1978, as Don Carlos; Metropolitan Opera from 1979, as Pinkerton, Turiddu, Gabriele Adorno, Luigi in IL Tabarro and Henri in Les Vêpres Siciliennes; Covent Garden 1979, as Don Carlos; Zurich Opera 1980, in Verdi's Attila; Monte Carlo 1982, in Lucia di Lammermoor; Guest appearances in Helsinki, Brussels, Barcelona, Dresden, Cologne, Frankfurt and Athens; Other roles include Mozart's Don Ottavio, Pedrillo and Tamino; Stuttgart Staatsoper and Nice 1988, as Cavaradossi and as Puccini's Dick Johnson; Sang Pinkerton at Rome, 1990. Address: c/o Lies Askonas Ltd, 6 Henrietta Street, London, WC2, England.

MOLINO Pippo, b. 10 June 1947, Milan, Italy. Composer. m. Giovanna Stucchi, 22 July 1972, 1 son, 2 daughters. Education: Degree, Composition and Choral Music. Debut: Venezia Opera Prima Festival Competition, 1981. Compositions: Replay 1, 11, piano, 1978; Tres, violin and viola, 1978; Litanie, orchestra, 1979; Il Canto Ritrovato, orchestra, 1980; Il Cavalier Selvatico, oratorio, 1981; Cantabile, flute piano, 1983; Jeu, oboe, 1984; Da Lontan, harp, 1985; Per la Festa Della Dedicazione, organ, 1986; Harmonien, wind quintet, 1989; Radici, clarinet, 1991; Ricordando, twelve instruments, 1992; Quintetto, clarinet, string quartet, 1993; Itinerari, string orchestra, 1994; Angelus, soprano, alto and string orchestra, 1997. Recordings: Il Pensiero Dominante; Nel Tempo. Publications: Articles in La Musica, Musica e Realta, Reggio Emilia, Il Giornale della musica. Honours: Rimini Aterforum, 1979; Venezia Opera Prima, 1981; Roodeport International Eisteddfod of South Africa, 1983. Memberships: SIMC; Societa Italiana Musica Contemporanes. Hobbies: Tennis. Current Management: BMG Ariola, Rugginenti. Address: Via Pistrucci 23, 20137 Milano, Italy.

MOLL Clare, b. 1960, Northumberland, England. Singer, (Mezzo Soprano). Education: studied at the Royal Academy of Music. Career: Sang in Henze's La Cubana with English Music Theatre and Dorabella with Scottish Opera-go-Round; Opera 80 as Rosina and Mozart's Marcelina; Has sung with Scottish Opera in Die Meistersinger, Magdalena; L'Egisto by Cavalli and L'Enfant et les Sortilèges; With Opera North appeared as Mrs Peachum in The Threepenny Opera and toured for Welsh National Opera in a show featuring Ivor Novello; English National Opera in The

Magic Flute, Parsifal and Orpheus in the Underworld; Covent Garden debut 1985, as a Dryad in Ariadne auf Naxos; Concert repertoire ranges from Bach and Handel to Gilbert and Sullivan and musicals. Address: c/o Korman International Management, Crunnells Green Cottage, Preston, Herts SG4 7UQ, England.

MOLL Kurt, b. 11 Apr 1938, Buir, Germany. Singer, Bass. Education: Studied at Cologne Hochschule and with Emmy Mueller. Debut: Lodovico in Otello, Aachen 1961; Sang at Mainz and Wuppertal in 1960s; Bayreuth Festival 1968- as Fafner, Pogner, Gurnemanz and Marke; Member of the Hamburg Opera from 1970 and took part in the premiere of Bialas's Der gestiefelte Kater at the 1975 Schwetzingen Festival; 1972 Osmin in Die Entführung at La Scala; US debut San Francisco 1974, as Gurnemanz; Covent Garden debut 1977, as Kaspar in a new production of Der Freischütz, Metropolitan Opera debut 1978, as the Landgrave in Tannhäuser; Later sang Beethoven's Rocco, Osmin and Ochs in Der Rosenkavalier; Visited Japan with the Hamburg Opera in 1984; Returned to Covent Garden 1987, as Osmin; San Francisco 1988, Gurnemanz in Parsifal; Metropolitan 1990, as the Commendatore in Don Giovanni, returned 1992, as Gurnemanz; Sang Pogner in Meistersinger at the 1997 Munich Festival. Recordings: Die Entführung, Der Schauspieldirektor, Parsifal, Der Freischütz, Missa Solemnis, Salome, Tristan und Isolde, Die Lustigen Weiber von Windsor, Der Rosenkavalier (Deutsche Grammophon); St John Passion, Die Zauberflöte, Intermezzo, Abu Hassan, Die Zwillinngsbruder, Bastien und Bastienne(Deutsche Grammophon); Don Giovanni, Les Contes d'Hoffmann, Lulu, Le nozze di Figaro, Die Meistersinger, Otello, Der Freishütz, Der fliegende Holländer, Tannhäuser, Winterreise, Video of Die Zauberflöte from the Met. Address: c/o Lies Askonas Ltd, 6 Henrietta Street, London WC2, England.

MOLL Maria, b. 1949, Northumberland, England. Singer, Soprano. Education: Studied at the Royal Academy of Music with Marjorie Thomas and at the London Opera Centre. Career: Sang Mozart's Countess and the Femal Chorus in The Rape of Lucretia at Sadler's Wells Theatre; Glyndebourne Festival Opera from 1975, as Second Lady in Die Zauberflöte, Beethoven's Leonore and Musetta; Appearances as Leonora in La Forza del Destino for Welsh National Opera; Tosca for Scottish Opera and Musetta and Abigaille for Opera North, Fata Morgana in The Love for Three Oranges, 1990; Covent Garden debut 1983, in the Stravinsky/Ravel double bill; Engagements in Don Carlos at Brussels and Macbeth at the Hong Kong Festival; English National Opera from 1987, in Lady Macbeth of Mtsenk and Reimann's Lear; Has also sung in musical theatre; Season 1992 in Die Königskinder for ENO. Honours: Isobel Jay Prize for Operatic Sopranos and the Robert Radford Prize at the RAM. Address: c/o Korman International Management, Crunnells Green Cottage, Preston, Herts SG4 7UQ, England.

MOLLER Anthea Mary, b. 27 Jan 1939, Dunedin, New Zealand. Musician; Voice Teacher. m. div. 1 son, 1 daughter. Education: Piano with Mr D J Palmer, Timaru; Voice Teachers: Grace Wilkinson, Joan Davies, Mary Adams Taylor. Debut: St Matthew Passion, Christchurch. Career: Il Trovatore, Verdi; Television: Old Maid and the Thief, Menotti; Gianni Schicchi, Puccini; Dr Miracle; National Artist for Radio New Zealand; Artist for Australian Broadcasting Commission; Bluebeard's Castle, Sydney Opera House; Hansel and Gretel, Victorian State Opera; Many other operas and oratorio, contemporary music andlieder; Many recordings for Radio New Zealand; Concerts with the New zealand Symphony Orchestra including, Verdi Requiem, Mahler 8th and Mahler 2nd, Kullervo by Sibelius. Recordings: Kiwi; Music by Ronald Tremain; The Flame Tree; Music by Douglas Lilburn. Hobbies: Swimming; Walking. Address: 44 Rambler Crescent, Beachoven, Auckland, New Zealand.

MOLLER Niels, b. 4 Sept 1922, Gorlev, Denmark. Singer, Tenor; Administrator. Education: Studied in Copenhagen, latterly at the Opera School of the Royal Opera. Debut: Sang Rossini's Figaro in Copenhagen, 1953. Career: Changed to tenor roles 1959 and sang in Copenhagen until 1975 as Florestan, Tannhäuser, Don José, Aegisthus, Shuisky, the Drum Major in Wozzeck and Zeus in Monteverdi's Ulisse; Bayreuth Festival, 1962-65, as Melot and Erik; Guest appearances at Brussels, Vienna, Oslo, Geneva, Venice, Barcelona, 1968, Lisbon, 1972 and Bordeaux; Baritone roles included Renato in Un Ballo in Maschera, Dandini, and Tarquinius in The Rape of Lucretia; Sang the title role in the premiere of Macbeth by H Koppel and retired as singer, 1975 after appearing as Aegisthus; Director of the Royal Opera Copenhagen 1978-83; Frequent concert engagements. Recordings: Schoenberg Gurrelieder; Parsifal, Bayreuth, 1962; Saul and David by Nielsen. Address: c/o Det Kongelige Teater, Box 2185, DK-1017 Copenhagen, Denmark.

MOLLET Pierre, b. 23 Mar 1920, Neuchâtel, Switzerland. Singer, Baritone. Education: Studied in Neuchâtel, Lausanne and Basle. Career: Performed as concert singer in France and Switzerland from 1948; Opéra-Comique, Paris from 1952, notably as Debussy's Pelleas; Aix-en-Provence 1952, in Iphigénie en Tauride by Gluck; Paris Opera, 1954, in Gounod's Roméo et Juliette; Geneva 1963, in the premiere of Martin's Monsieur de Pourceaugnac, repeated at the Holland Festival; As a concert singer often appeared in the cantatas of Bach and in music by Honegger, which he studied with the composer. Recordings: Pelléas et Mélisande, Roméo et Juliette and L'Enfant et les Sortilèges; La Damnation de Faust; Iphigénie en Tauride.

MOLLOVA Milena, b. 19 Feb 1940, Razgrad, Bulgaria. Concert Pianist; Professor of Piano. 1 son, 2 daughters. Education: Studied piano with Pavla Jekova; Studied with composer and pianist Dimitar Nenov, 1947; Studied with Professor Panka Pelisheck from 1949; Studied at the Bulgarian Music Academy with Professor Pelischeck from age 14; Studied in the class of Professor Emil Gilels at the Moscow State Conservatory, 1960-61. Debut: First piano concert at age 6. Career: Soloist in Sofia State Orchestra with the Beethoven third piano concerto, directed by Professor Sasha Popov; During her education gave numerous concerts in Bulgaria and successful participation in international competitions in Moscow, Paris and Munich; Concert tours in USSR, 1958, 1959, 1960, in Czechoslovakia, Poland, Belgium and Yugoslavia; Appointed Assistant to Professor Pelisheck at the Bulgarian Music Academy, Sofia 1963 and as a concert pianist to the Bulgarian Concert Agency; Conducted own class of young piano students, 1969-; Tour of Japan and Cuba, 1973; Appointed Reader 1976 and Professor 1989 in the Bulgarian Music Academy; To celebrate 40 years on stage, played in Sofia and Varna the whole 32 Beethoven sonatas in 9 concerts, recorded on compact disks. During last few years has conducted Master Classes in Essen, Germany and Manfredony, Foggia, Italy. Recordings: Numerous recordings of piano works from Bach to modern composers.

MOLNAR András, b. 1948, Hungary. Singer (Tenor). Education: Hungarian Radio Children's Choir; Studied singing, 1976. Career: Member, Choir of The Hungarian Radio and Television, 1977-78; Soloist at Budapest State Opera, 1979-; Appeared in title roles in Erkel's László Hunyadi, Mozart's Magic Flute, Verdi's Ernani and in La Forza del destino, Don José in Carmen, 1981-82, Title role in Lohengrin, 1981-82; Invited to sing title role in Theo Adam's new production of Wagner's Lohengrin at Berlin State Opera, 1983; Regular appearances with Budapest State Opera including the premiere of Ecce Homo by Szokolay, 1987; Sang at Teatro Colón Buenos Aires, 1987 as Donello in La Fiamma by Respighi; Budapest 1988-90, in Erkel's Hunyadi László and as Tannhäuser; Frequently participates in oratorio performances; Other performances in: Florestan in Fidelio, Budapest, 1984, Zurich and Graz in 1994; Wagner's Meistersinger at Budapest, 1985, Der fliegende Holländer at Bonn 1986, Zurich, 1987 and Liège in 1995; Tristan at Budapest in 1988, Parsifal in Budapest, 1982 and Antwerp in 1987; Tannhäuser in Rouen, 1992, Limoges in 1994; Radames in Aida, Budapest in 1994; Die Walküre, Budapest with YuriSimonow, 1995. Honours: 1st Prize, Treviso Toti dal Monte International Vocal Competition, 1980; Kossuth Prize - First Hungarian Cultural Prize, 1994. Current Management: Interkoncert, Katalin Kirici. Address: 1051, Budapest, Vorosmarty Tér 1, Hungary.

MOLNAR Nicolette, b. 1959, London, England. Stage director. Education: Columbia University, New York, USA; Hamburg Musikhochschule, with Gotz Friedrich. Career: Assistant to David Pountney at ENO and the Bregenz Festival (Nabucco, Fliegende Holländer), and has worked with Wexford Festival (Balfe's The Rose of Castile, 1991), Dublin Grand Opera (Lakmé, 1993), ENO (Così fan tutte, 1994) and Castleward Opera Ireland (I Capuleti e i Montecchi, 1995 and Ariadne auf Naxos, 1996). Address: Performing Arts, 6 Windmill Street, London W1P 1HF.

MOLNAR-TALAJIC Liljana, b. 30 Dec 1938, Bronsanski, Brod, Yugoslavia. Singer, Soprano. Education: Studied in Sarajevo. Debut: Sarajevo, 1959, as Mozart's Countess. Career: Sang at Sarajevo and Zagreb, 1959-75; Guest appearances at the Vienna Staatsoper, Florence and San Francisco, 1969; Philadelphia from 1970, Naples 1971; Verona Arena, 1972-73, as Aida and the Forza Leonora; Sang at Covent Garden, 1975, 1977, Metropolitan Opera, 1976, Aida; Further appearandces at Barcelona, Nice and the Deutsche Oper Berlin, 1977-78, Milan, Rome and Marseilles; Other roles have included the Trovatore Leonora, Amelia in Ballo in Maschera, Desdemona and Norma. Recordings: Verdi Requiem. Address: c/o Arena di Verona, Piazza Bra 28, 37121 Verona, Italy.

MOLSBERGER Friedrich, b. 30 June 1961, Dusseldorf, Germany. Singer (Bass). Education: Studied in Dusseldorf and Berlin. Career: Deutsche Oper Berlin from 1988, in operas by Mozart, Puccini, Verdi, Strauss and Donizetti; Notable roles have been Sarastro, Masetto, Mozart's Publio and Bartolo, Banquo, Arkel and Colline; Sang in the 1990 premiere of Henze's Das verratene Meer; Guest engagements at Hamburg, Karlsruhe, Bonn (Minister in Fidelio, 1992) and Nice; Concert appearances in music by Bach, Verdi, Brahms and Haydn. Address: c/o Deutsche Oper Berlin, Bismarckstrasse 35, W-1000 Berlin 10, Germany.

MONELLE Raymond (John), b. 19 Aug 1937, Bristol, England. Critic; University Lecturer. m. Hannelore E M Schultz 1964, divorced 1983, 2 daughters. Education: Pembroke College, Oxford; Royal College of Music 1964-66, BMus, London, 1st class honours; PhD, Edinburgh, 1979. Career: Senior Lecturer, Bedford College of Physical Education, 1966-69; Lecturer in Music, University of Edinburgh, 1969-; Music Critic, The Scotsman, 1972-88; Music Critic; The Independent, 1986-; Critic, Opera Magazine, 1984-. Compositions: Much educational choral music published; Several commissioned works, eg Missa Brevis 1979; Cantata, Ballattis of Luve, 1983. Contributions to: Music Review; Music and Letters; British Journal of Aesthetics; Music Analysis, Comparative Literature, International Review of the Aesthetics and Sociology of Music. Book: Linguistics and Sematics in Music, Published in 1992. Hobbies: Square-rigged sailing ships. Address: 3 Livingstone Place, Edinburgh, EH9 1PB, Scotland.

MONETTI Mariaclara, b. 1965, Italy. Concert Pianist. Education: Studied in Turin, at the Venice and Lucerne Conservatoires and the Salzburg Mozarteum; Teachers included Geza Anda and Vladimir Ashkenazy. Career: Many appearances in 18th century repertoire in Italy and throughout Europe; British appearances with the London Symphony at the Barbican and recital at the Purcell Room, South Bank. Recordings include: Mozart concertos K466 and K595, with the Royal Philharmonic; Paisiello 8 Piano Concertos, with the English Chamber Orchestra. Honours include: Gold Medal, Viotti International Competition. Address: Manygate Management, 13 Cotswold Mews, 30 Battersea Square, London SW11 3RA, England.

MONK Allan, b. 19 Aug 1942, Mission City, British Columbia, Canada. Singer (Bass-Baritone). Education: Studied in Calgary with Elgar Higgin and in NY with Boris Goldovsky. Debut: Western Opera, San Francisco, 1967 in Menotti's The Old Maid and The Thief. Career: Has sung in Portland, St Louis, Chicago, Hawaii and Vancouver; Canadian National Opera, Toronto, 1973 in premiere of Wilson's Abelard and Heloise; Metropolitan Opera from 1976 as Schaunard in La Bohème, The Speaker in Die Zauberflöte, Berg's Wozzeck, Wagner's Wolfram and Verdi's Posa and Ford; Sang Macbeth at Toronto 1986, followed by Carlo in La Forza del Destino; Opéra de Montreal, 1988 as Don Giovanni; Sang Nick Shadow in The Rake's Progress for Vancouver Opera, 1989; Wozzeck and Iago at Toronto in 1990; Sang Simon Boccanegra for Long Beach Opera, 1992. Recordings include: Andrea Chénier; La Traviata; Allan Monk with Calgary Philharmonic Orchestra. Honours: Artist of the Year, 1983; Officer of The Order of Canada, Canadian Music Council, 1985. Address: 97 Woodpark Close SW, Calgary, Alberta, Canada, T2W 6H1.

MONK Meredith (Jane), b. 20 Nov 1942, New York, New York, USA. Composer; Singer; Director; Filmmaker. Education: BA, Sarah Lawrence University, 1964; Hon Doctorate, Bard College, 1988, University of the Arts, 1989. Voice: Vicki Starr, John Devers, Jeanette Lovetri; Composition Study, Ruth Lloyd, Richard Averre, Glenn Mack; Piano, Gershon Konikow. Debut: Washington Square Galleries, New York City, 1964. Career: Performed worldwide with own vocal ensemble; Appearances include: Carnegie Hall; Town Hall; Guggenheim Museum; Public Theater, New York City; Festivals in London, Paris, Tokyo, Jerusalem, Rome, Stockholm, Munich, Frankfurt, Cologne. Compositions: Key; Our Lady of Late; Songs from the Hill; Tablet; Dolmen Music; Vessel: An Opera Epic; Quarry: An Opera; Book of Days; Turtle Dreams; Education of the Girlchild: An Opera; Specimen Days; The Games; Acts from Under and Above; Paris; Chacon; Facing North, premiere, 1990; Atlas: An Opera in three parts, premiere, Houston Grand Opera, 1991; New York Requiem, 1993; Volcano Songs, 1994; American Archeology #1, 1994; The Politics of Quiet, 1996; Steppe Music, 1997. Recordings include: Monk and the Abbess: The Music of Meredith Monk and Hildegard von Bingen; Facing North, ECM New Series, 1992; Atlas: An Opera in three parts, 1993; Volcano Songs, 1997. Publication: Art and Performance Series: Meredith Monk, edited by Deborah Jowitt, 1997. Honours include: Dance Magazine Award, 1993; The John D and Catherine T MacArthur Foundation Award, 1995; Scripps Award, 1996; Outstanding Alumnus Award, 1996. Memberships: ASCAP; American Music Centre; Board of Directors, The Kitchen. Hobbies: Horse Riding; Gardening. Current Management: The House Foundation for the Arts. Address: 228 West Broadway, New York, NY 10013, USA.

MONK Peter (Anthony), b. 17 June 1946, Hetton-le-Hole, Durham, England. Composer; Teacher. m. Diana Worthington, 18 Dec 1976, 1 son, 1 daughter. Education: Teaching Certificate, Bede College of Education, Durham, 1968; Premier Prix, Conservatoire Royale de Musique, Liège, Belgium, 1975; MMus, King's College, London, 1984; Studied Composition with Henri Pousseur, Centre de Recherches Musicales de Wallonie, Liège. Career: Works performed extensively in Western Europe and Japan; Most works have been broadcast on Belgian Radio, several on BBC Radio 3; Funds from Arts Council to write Emperor's New Notes for Brass Quintet, from Eastern Arts to write Railway Parade for Clarinet and Piano, from Greater London

Arts Association for Signor Glissando for Harpsichord. Compositions: Numerous including: The Emperor's New Notes; The Golden Spike; Troisième Vue sur les Jardins Interdits; Appeelkins; Lasagna da Caccia; Percy, Signor Glissando; Salute to the Third Age, Streamliner; Thel Met Pousseur in Rue Forgeur Blues; Danse Sacrée et Danse au Contraire; Nine Gentlemen of Verona, for Gli Ottoni di Verona. Hobbies: Poetry; O Gauge model railways. Address: Fir Tree House, 169b St James's Road, Croydon, Surrey CR0 2BY, England.

MONNARD Jean-Francois, b. 4 Nov 1941, Lausanne, Switzerland. Conductor. m. Lia Rottier. Education: LLM, University of Lausanne; Music Academy, Lausanne; Folkwang Hochschule, Essen, German Federal Republic; Orchestral Conducting Diploma, 1968; International Conductors Course with Jean Fournet, Hilversum, Holland. Career: Conductor of Operas, Kaiserslautern; Graz, Austria; Trier, Aachen and Wuppertal; Currently Music Director in Osnabruck; Guest Conductor: Tonhalle Orchestra, Zurich; BRT-PhiPharmonic Orchestra, Brussels; Bournemouth Sinfonietta; ORF Symphony Orchestra, Vienna; Orchestre de la Suisse Romande, Geneva; Leipzig Opera; Dortmund Opera; Bordeaux Opera. Contributions to: Revue des Musiciens Suisses. Membership: Association Suisse des Musiciens. Address: Chemin de l'Eglise, 1066 Epalinges, Switzerland.

MONOSOFF Sonya, b. 11 Jun 1927, Ohio, USA. Violinist; Professor of Music, Cornell University. m. Carl Eugene Pancaldo, 8 Dec 1950, 4 daughters. Education: Artists Diploma, Juilliard Graduate School, 1948. Debut: New York City, USA. Career: Concerts and Master Classes: USA, Canada, Europe, Israel, Australia and New Zealand. Recordings: Heinrich Biber, Mystery Sonatas and 1681 Sonatas; JS Bach, Sonatas for Violin and Harpsichord; Mozart, Sonatas. Contributions to: Notes: Early Music; The New Grove; The Musical Times. Honours: Stereo Review, Best Record of the Year (Bach), 1970; Fulbright Lectureship, New Zealand, 1988; Bunting Institute, 1967-68; Smithsonian Institute, 1971. Memberships: Early Music America, Steering Committee; American Musical Instrument Society, Editorial Board. Hobby: Chamber Music. Current Management: Curzon & Kedersha, New York. Address: Cornell University, Music Department, Lincoln Hall, Ithaca, New York 14853, USA.

MONOSZON Boris, b. 1955, Kiev, Russia. Violinist; Conductor. Education: Graduate, Moscow Conservatoire, 1979. Career: Made several concert tours of European and Latin American countries as concert master, Prague Symphony; Interpreted Concerto for Violin and Orchestra by Sibelius, Royal Festival Hall, London, England. Soloist, Teplice State Philharmonic Orchestra, 1982-. Honours: Laureate, Tibor Varga International Competition, Switzerland, 1981.

MONOT Pierre-Alain, b. 7 Mar 1961, Fleurier, Switzerland. Trumpeter; Composer. m. Esther Herrmann, 23 Sept 1988. Education: Diplome professionnel de trompette; Diplome de virtuosite, Teacher, Andre Besancon. Career: 1st Trumpet, Winterthur Symphony Orchestra; Member of NOVUS Brass Quartet Concert in Europe, Zurich, Rome, Paris, Lausanne, Far East, Japan, China. Compositions: Quatuor 1980 for Brass Quartet; Trois douces Rèveries Medievales; SR 1986 for Vibraphone and Brass Quintet; La Neige orange for brass quartett; Dans le Chateau de la Fee fluide brass quartet; Trois Ayres de Cour for brass quartet and orchestra. Recordings: Novus, 1986; La Neige Orange, 1988. Honours: 1st prize, Competition of Union Bank of Switzerland, 1987; 1st Prize, Concours de la Pierre d'Hauterive, 1983. Memberships: Association des musiciens suisses, AMS. Hobbies: Photography. Current Management: Mrs Indira Tasan.

MONOYIOS Ann, b. 28 Oct 1949, Middletown, CT, USA. Singer (Soprano). Education: Studied at Princeton University and with Oren Brown. Career: Concert performances in Baroque music with the Folger Consort, Washington DC; Stage debut with the Concert Royal of New York, in Rameau's Les Fêtes d'Hébé; European debut at the 1986 Göttingen Festival, in Handel's Terpsichore with the English Baroque Soloists conducted by John Eliot Gardiner; Opéra Comique Paris and Aix-en-Provence Festival, 1987, as Lully's Sangaride (Atys) and Psyché; Sang Elisa in Mozart's Il Re Pastore at the Nakamichi Festival in Los Angeles, 1990; Further engagements at Salzburg, Spoleto and Frankfurt. Recordings: Iphigénie en Aulide with the Opéra de Lyon; Purcell's Dioclesian and Timon of Athens, 1996.

MONTAGUE Diana, b. 8 Apr 1953, Winchester, England. Singer, (Mezzo-Soprano). Education: Studied at the Royal Manchester School of Music with Ronald Stear, Frederic Cox and Rupert Bruce-Lockhard. Debut: With Glyndebourne Touring Opera 1977, as Zerlina. Career: Member of the Royal Opera Covent Garden, 1978-83, as Laura in Luisa Miller, Kate Pinkerton, Annius in La Clemenza di Tito, Nicklausse, Cherubino and Parseis in Esclarmonde with tour of the Far East; Bayreuth debut 1983, as Wellgunde and Siegrune in Der Ring des Nibelungen, Chicago 1984, in the Missa Solemnis conducted by Solti; Edinburgh Festival 1985, as Mélisande; Salzburg Festival 1986, as Cherubino; Metropolitan Opera debut 1987, Sextus in La Clemenza di Tito; Returned to New York as Dorabella and as Nicklausse in Les Contes d'Hoffman; German operatic debut 1987, Dorabella in a new production of Cosi fan tutte at the Frankfurt Opera; Appearances with Scottish Opera as Cherubino and Orlofsky and with English National Opera as Cherubino and Prosperina in Monteverdi's Orfeo; Promenade Concerts London 1988, in Pelléas et Mélisande; Glyndebourne Opera 1989, Gluck's Orfeo; Sang The Fox in The Cunning Little Vixen at Covent Garden, 1990; Idamante in Idomeneo at the 1990 Salzburg Festival; Cherubino at the Vienna Staatsoper 1990, Lucio Silla 1991; Glyndebourne 1991 as Sextus in La Clemenza di Tito, also at the Promenade Concerts, London; Season 1992 sang Gluck's Iphigénie en Tauride for Welsh National Opera, and Dorabella for ENO; Snag Isolier in Le Comte Ory at Glyndebourne, 1997; Concert engagements in the Mozart Requiem, Bach B Minor Mass, Rossini's Stabat Mater and The Damnation of Faust by Berlioz. Recordings: Title role in Iphigénie en Tauride, Mozart's C Minor Mass; Handel arias with Simon Preston and Monteverdi's Orfeo, Deutsche Grammophon; Clothilde in Norma; Cunning Little Vixen; Romeo in I Capuleti ei Montecchi; Armando in Meyerbeer's Il Crociato in Egitto. Address: c/o Harrison/Parrott Ltd, 12 Penzance Place, London W11 4PA, England.

MONTAGUE Stephen (Rowley), b. 10 Mar 1943, Syracuse, New York, USA. Composer; Pianist. m. Patricia Mattin, 10 May 1986, 1 son, 1 daughter. Education: AA, St Petersburg Junior College, Florida, 1963; BM, Honours, 1965 MM, Theory, 1967, Florida State University; DMA, Composition, Ohio State University, 1972; Postgraduate work, Conducting, Mozarteum, Salzburg, 1966; Fulbright, Warsaw, Poland, 1972-74; Computer Music, IRCAM, Paris, France, 1982; CCRMA, Stanford University, 1986. Debut: Wigmore Hall, London, England. 1975. Career includes: Warsaw Autumn Festivals, 1974, 1980, 1989, 1991, 1995; Metz Festival, 1976; New Music America, 1987, 1988, 1990; Montague/Mead Piano Plus first tour of the USA, 1986; Frequent European and North American tours to present; Chairman, Sonic Arts Network, United Kingdom, 1987-88; Almeida Festival, London, 1988; Guest Professor, University of Texas at Austin, 1992, 1995; Featured Composer, Speculum Festival, Norway, 1992; World tours with Maurice Agis' inflatable sculpture, Colourspace, 1987-95; Centre Pompidou premiere, 1995; Composer-in-Association with the Orchestra of St John's Smith Square, London, 1995-96; Cheltenham Festival, 1995; Ultima 95 Festival, Oslo. Compositions include: Varshavian Spring, 1973; Eyes of Ambush, 1973; Sound Round, 1973; Paramell Va, 1981; Duo, 1982; At the White Edge of Phrygia, 1983; String Quartert No 1, 1989-93; Behold a Pale Horse, 1990; Silence: John, Yvar and Tim, 1994; Snakebite, 1995. Recordings include: Stephen Montaque Orchestra and Chamber Works, CD, Continuum CDs Limited. Honours include: Ernst von Dohnanyi Award, 1995; 1st Prize, Bourges Electronic Music Competition, 1994. Memberships include: Chairman, Society for the Promotion of New Music, 1993-95. Current Management: Magenta Music International. Address: 2 Ryland Road, London NW5 3EA, England.

MONTAL Andre, b. 18 Nov 1940, Baltimore, USA. Singer. Tenor. Education: Studied at the Eastman School, The Music Academy of the West at Santa Barbara and the Curtis Institute. Debut: American Opera Society New York, 1964, as Tebaldo in I Capuleti e i Montecchi. Career: Has sung at opera houses in Boston, Chicago, Philadelphia, San Francisco and Vancouver; Metropolitan Opera from 1974; Further engagements with Australian Opera at Sydney; Other roles have included Donizetti's Ernesto, Nemorino, Tonio and Edgardo, Oronte in Alcina, Gounod's Romeo, Rossini's Almaviva, Lindoro, and Idreno in Semiramide, Mozart's Ferrando, Belmonte and Don Ottavio; Mephistopheles in Prokofiev's Fiery Angel, Verdi's Duke, Pinkerton and the Italian Singer in Rosenkavalier.

MONTANO David R, b. 2 December 1951, Lafayette, Indiana, USA. Educator; Pianist. m. Valerie Lewin Montano, 6 August 1978, 1 son, 1 daughter. Education: LTCL, Trinity College of Music, London, 1974; BM, Indiana University, 1975; MM, University of Arizona, 1977; DMA, University of Missouri, 1983. Career: Graduate Assistant, University of Arizona, 1975-77; Faculty, Pina Community College, Tucson, Arizona, 1977-78; Graduate Assistant, University of Missouri, 1978-81; Faculty, University of Denver, 1981-; Faculty Recitals and Concerto Performances, University of Denver. Publications: 24 Karat Piano Skills, 1993. Contributions to: Colorado Music Educator; Teaching Music; Missouri Journal of Research in Music Education; Colorado Music Educator; Ars Musica Denver. Honours: Pi Kappa Lambda, 1973; Phi Kappa Phi, 1981; Graduate Achievement Award, University of Missouri, 1983; Alumni Award, Excellence in Performance and Teaching, University of Arizona, 1995. Memberships: American Musicological Society; College Music Society; International Society for Music Education; Music Educators National Conference; Music Teachers National Association. Hobbies: Travel; Computer Programming. Address: School of Music, University of Denver, 7111 Montview Boulevard, Denver, CO 80220-1687, USA.

MONTARSOLO Paolo, b. 16 Mar 1925, Portici, Naples, Italy. Singer, Bass; Producer. Education: Studied with Enrico Conti in Naples and at the La Scala Opera School. Debut: La Scala 1954. Career: Guest appearances in Italy in operas by Rossini, Donizetti, Wolf-Ferrari and Mozart; Bergamo 1955, in a revival of Donizetti's Rita; Verona 1956; Glyndebourne Festival from 1957, as Mustafa in L'Italiana in Algeri, Selim in Il Turco in Italia, and Mozart's Osmin, Leporello and Don Alfonso; Florence, 1966, in Luisa Miller; Deutsche Oper am Rhein Dusseldorf 1973; Paris Opera 1977, as Don Magnifico in La Cenerentola; Geneva Opera 1984, in L'Italiana in Algeri; Engagements in Moscow, Lisbon, New York, Naples and Rio de Janiero; Sang Don Magnifico at the Berlin Staatsoper, 1987; Mustafa at Covent Garden, debut 1988; Salzburg Festival 1988-89, as Mozart's Bartolo and Don Magnifico; Staged and sang Don Pasquale at the Dallas Opera, 1989, Covent Garden, 1990; Sang Donizetti's Dulcamara at the Royal Opera, 1992; Engaged in Manon Lescaut at the 1997 Glyndebourne Festival. Recordings: La Cenerentola; Il Barbiere di Siviglia; Rita and Viva La Mamma; La Serva Padrona; Madama Butterfly. Address: c/o Renata Skotto Opera Academy, Via Gentile, 25-17012 Albissola Marine, Savona, Italy.

MONTÉ Ruth, b. 3 Dec 1958, Galatzi, Romania. Concert Harpsichordist; Organist; Pianist. m. Noel Monté, 26 Oct 1986. Education: Summa cum laude, Academy of Music, Bucharest; Juilliard School of Music, New York; Studies with Rozalyn Tureck, Trevor Pinnock, John Weaver, Peter Husford, Frederick Neemann, Peter Williams, Lukas Foss. Debut: Bucharest, Romania, 1973. Career: Bucharest, Romania, 1977, Weimar, Germany, 1978; TV and Radio Appearances in Romania; Lecturer, Performer, Bach on Harpsichord, Piano, Organ in North America; Lecturer, Performance, 50th Anniversary of the UN, New York Academy of Sciences. Recordings: Integral of Bach's Keyboard Music on Harpsichord, Piano and Organ. Honours: Laureate, National Youth Music Festival, Romania, 1973. Memberships: Chamber Music America; Early Music and Gramophone. Hobby: Scuba Diving. Address: 923 Fifth Avenue #17B, New York, NY 10021, USA.

MONTEFUSCO Licinio, b. 30 Oct 1936, Milan, Italy. Singer, (Baritone). Education: Studied in Milan. Debut: Teatro Nuovo Milan 1961, As Zurga in Les pecheurs de Perles. Career: Sang Renato in Un Ballo in Maschera at Florence, 1963, followed by appearances throughout Italy, notably at the Teatro Reggio Turin; Guest appearances at the Vienna Staatsoper from 1964, Deutsch Oper Berlin from 1966; US debut Philadelphia 1965; La Scala Milan, 1970, as Montfort in I Vespri Siciliani; Sang at Monte Carlo 1967-68, Brussels and Strasbourg, 1972-74, Verona 1972 as Amonasro, Marseilles, 1979; Sang Francesco Foscari in I Due Foscari at Turin, 1984 and Posa in Don Carlos, 1985; Other roles have included Verdi's Germont, Luna, Rigoletto, Macbeth, Carlos and Ford, Enrico in Lucia di Lammermoor, Alfonso in La Favorita, Marcello, Gerard and Valentin. Address: c/o Dublin Grand Opera Society, John Player Theatre, 276-288 Circular Road, Dublin 8, Ireland.

MONTENEGRO Roberto, b. 18 Sept 1956, Montevideo, Uruguay. Conductor. Education: Hamburg Musikhochschule; Studied with Guido Santorsola, Gerhard Markson, Aldo Ceccato and Sergiu Celibidache. Debut: Santa Barbara Festival Symphony Orchestra, California, 1985. Career: Conducted the world premiere of Francisco Rodrico's Guitar Concerto with the Venezuelan National Orchestra, 1992, and world premiere of Cesar Cano's Piano Concerto with the Spanish National Orchestra, 1993; Teacher of masterclasses in Uruguay and Argentina, Italy (European Community Music High School) and Spain (Santiago de Compostela's International Conducting Masterclasses); Assistant to Aldo Ceccato in Hamburg and Hannover; Jury, Young Concert Artists, New York, USA; Artistic and Musical Director, SODRE, Uruguay, 1991-95; Guest Conductor: Spain, France, Argentina, Venezuela, Czech Republic, USA, Canada, Israel. Honours include: Man of the Year, American Biographical Institute, 1993; Honorary Member, Young Concert Artists, 1994; Baron, Royal Order of the Bohemian Crown, 1995. Address: Avenida del Libertador 1684, Apt 1202, PO Box 1552, Montevideo, Uruguay.

MONTEUX Claude, b. 15 Oct 1920, Brookline, MA, USA. Conductor; Flautist. Education: Studied flute with Georges Laurent. Career: Solo debut 1940; Played with Kansas City Philharmonic 1946-; Conductor of the Ballets Russes 1949-; Guest conductor with the London Symphony and with continental orchestras; Conductor of Columbus Ohio Orchestra 1953-56; Music Director of the Hudson Valley Philharmonic, New York, 1959-75; Director of the conducting department at the Peabody Conservatory, Baltimore. Memberships: Harpsichord Quartet 1947-54.

MONTGOMERY Kathryn, b. 23 Sept 1952, Canton, Ohio, USA. Singer, (Soprano). Education: Studied at the University of

Bloomington, Indiana. Debut: Bloomington 1972, as Elvira in Ernani. Career: Sang at Norfolk from 1978 as Frasquita, and in the premiere of Musgrave's Christmas Carol; European debut at Cologne 1980, as Leonore in Fidelio; Sang at Cologne and Zurich 1980-82, Mannheim 1981-85; Guest engagements at Venice, Edinburgh, Barcelona and Brussels; Metropolitan Opera debut 1985, as Chrysothemis; Pretoria, South Africa, 1984 as Salome; Other roles include Wagner's Elsa, Senta and Sieglinde, Tosca, Donna Anna, Berg's Marie, Donna Elvira and the Empress in Die Frau ohne Schatten; Sang Aksinya in Lady Macbeth of Mtsensk at the Deutsche Oper Berlin, 1988; Frequent concert appearances. Address: c/o Deutsche Oper Berlin, Richard Wagnerstrasse 10, D-1000 Berlin 1, Germany.

MONTGOMERY Kenneth, b. 28 Oct 1943, Belfast, Ireland. Conductor. Education: Royal Belfast Academical Institution; Royal College of Music, London. Debut: Glyndebourne Festival 1967; Staff Conductor, Sadler's Wells, English National Opera 1967-70; Assistant Conductor, Bournemouth Symphony Orchestra and Sinfonietta from 1970; Conducted Weber's Oberon at Wexford, 1972; Strauss's Ariadne and Capriccio for Netherlands Opera, 1972, 1975; Director, Bournemouth Sinfonietta, 1974-76; Covent Garden debut 1975, Le nozze di Figaro; Principal Conductor, Dutch Radio Orchestra from 1976; Musical Director, Glyndebourne Touring Opera 1975-76; Guest appearances with Welsh National Opera, Canadian Opera; Concert performance of Donizeti's Anna Bolena at Amsterdam, 1989; Hansel and Gretel for Netherlands Opera, 1990; Conducted Tosca and The Magic Flute for Opera Northern Ireland at Belfast, 1990; Season 1991 with Alcina for Vancouver Opera, Figaro in Belfast and The Passion of Jonathon Wade for the Monte Carlo Royal Opera (repeated at San Diego, 1996). Honours: Silver Medal, Worshipful Company of Musicians, 1963; Tagore Gold Medal, Royal College of Music, 1964. Hobby: Cooking. Address: c/o Robert Gilders Co, Enterprise House, 59-65 Upper Ground, London SE1 9PQ, England.

MONTRESOR Beni, b. 31 Mar 1926, Bussoloegno, Italy. Opera Designer and Producer. Career: Designs for Barber's Vancessa seen at Spoleto 1961; Pelléas et Mélisande Glyndebourne 1962; Die Zauberflöte New York City Opera 1966; Metropolitan Opera with Menotti's The Last Savage and La Gioconda; Lohengrin for San Francisco Opera; Designs for Massenet's Esclarmonde, San Francisco 1976, were seen also at the Metropolitan and Covent Garden; Falstaff for the opening of the season at the Rome Opera, 1989, Samson et Dalila at Houston, 1990; Other productions have included L'elisir d'amore and Benvenuto Cellini at Covent Garden, 1966 and 1976, Madama Butterfly at Verona, 1978, and Zelmira by Rossini at Rome, 1989; Pacini's Saffo at the 1995 Wexford Festival. Address: c/o Houston Grand Opera, 510 Preston Avenue, Houston, TX 77002, USA.

MOODY Howard, b. 7 May 1964, Salisbury, Wiltshire, England. Conductor; Pianist; Composer. m. Emily Blows, 1 daughter. Education: Chorister, Salisbury Cathedral School; Music Scholar, Canford School; Organ Scholar, New College, Oxford; Guildhall School of Music and Drama. Appointments: Artistic Director of the Sarum Chamber Orchestra, 1986-; Worked as conductor with many of the major British orchestras, Netherlands Radio Chorus, Opera Factory, Salisbury Festival Chorus. Compositions: Score for Station House Opera, funded by the Arts Council of Great Britain, 1997; Weigh Me The Fire, choral work commissioned by Southern Cathedrals Festival, 1997. Recordings: as pianist: Beethoven Cello Sonatas, with David Watkin (cello), recorded on original fortepianos, 1996; Francis Pott Cello Sonata, with David Watkin, 1997. Honour: FRCO, 1985. Address: 64 Whistler Street, London, N5 INJ, England.

MOODY Ivan (William George), b. 11 Jun 1964, London, England. Composer. m. Susanna Simoes Diniz, 2 Sep 1989. Education: Royal Holloway College, London University; BMus, 1985; Studies with John Tavener, 1984-86. Career: Works performed and broadcast in UK, Austria, Denmark, Portugal, Italy, Germany, Finland, Estonia, Netherlands, Brazil and USA; Lecturing for music festivals in UK, Netherlands and Finland and courses in UK and Portugal; Conducting of various choirs in Europe in Orthodox and Renaissance sacred repertoire; Works performed throughout East and West Europe, Brazil and USA. Compositions include: Lithuanian Songs, 1986; Cantigas de Amigo; Canticle at The Parting of The Soul; Burial Prayer; Miserere, 1988; Hymn of The Transfiguration; Lament for Christ, 1989; Liturgy of St John Chrysostom, 1991; Cantigas do Mar, 1991; Anamnisis; Hymn of Joseph of Arimathea; Hymn to Christ the Saviour, 1991; Vigil of the Angels, 1991; Passion and Resurrection, 1992. Recordings: As Conductor: Ippolitov - Ivanov, Divine Liturgy, Ikon, Tavener, various works, Ikon. Publications: Editions of Renaissance polyphony for Mapa Mundi, 1989, 1991, Chester Music, 1990-, Fundacao Calouste Gulbenkian, 1991. Address: c/o Vanderbeek and Imrie Ltd, 15 Marvig, Lochs, Isle of Lewis, HS2 9QP, Scotland.

MOOG Robert (Arthur), b. 23 May 1934, Flushing, NY, USA. Designer of electronic instruments. Education: Studied at Queens College, New York and Columbia University; PhD Engineering Physics, Cornell University 1965. Career: Founded R A Moog Company, 1954, for the manufacture of electronic musical instruments; 1st synthesizer modules, 1964; Portable monophonic instrument and Minimoog 1970; Moog Music established 1971 at Buffalo, NY, 1973; Founded Big Briar Company, 1978, producing devices for the control of synthesizers; Has lectured widely on synthesizers and similar products in the US and Europe; Consultant for Kurzweil Music Systems of Boston, 1984, becoming Chief Scientist; Collaborations with Wendy Carlos and various rock musicians. Address: c/o Kurzweil Music Systems, Main Street, Buffalo, Massachussetts, USA.

MOORE Barbara (Patricia Hill), b. 28 Dec 1942, St Louis, Missouri, USA. Soprano; Professor. m. Leandrew Moore, 27 Aug 1966, 1 daughter. Education: MS, University of Illinois. Career: Professor of Voice, Southern Methodist University, Dallas, Texas, 1974-; Chair, Department of Voice, 1975-92; Guest appearances: Greensboro, N Carolina Symphony; Nuremberg Symphony; Irving, Texas Symphony, Pennsylvania Opera; Beaumont Symphony; Dallas Youth Orchestra; Dallas Chamber Opera; Dallas Symphony; Dallas Civic Symphony; Berlin-Theater Des Westens; Milwaukee, Wisconsin-Florentine Opera, 1989-90; Guttenberg, Germany, 1989, 1990, 1991; Muenster University Concert, 1990-91; Stuttgart-Theater Des Westens, 1990; Weilheim, Germany, 1990-91; Saarbrucken, Germany, 1991; Saarlouis, Germany, 1990-91; Eutin Summer Concert Series, 1983-92; Hanover, Germany; Aboard MS Europa, concerts in Japan, Hawaii, Central America, Panama, Brazil, and Norway, 1989, 1991; Recitals include: Eutin Civic Summer Concert Series, West Germany, 1983-86; Malenta, West Germany, 1985; Cologne, West Germany, 1985; Salzburg College and Salzburg College and Salzburg Seminar, Austria, 1984, 1985; Concerts and recitals 1995-98 in Verlin, Bremen, Bad Ryrmont, Stuttgart, Essen, Zurich, Montreux, Lenk, Bad Rogar, Avignon, Aix les Bains, Nimes and Marseilles. Recording: Jump Back! African American Poetry in Song, with Richard Gordon accompanying. Memberships: National Association of Teachers of Singing, President Elect, Dallas-Ft Worth Chapter, 1998-; National Opera Association; Pi Kappa Lambda; Sigma Alpha Iota. Current Management: Fischer v d Made, Parkweg 5, 31789 Hameln, Germany. Address: 1821 Carmel Cove, Plano, TX 75075, USA.

MOORE Carman (Leroy), b. 8 Oct 1936, Lorain, Ohio, USA. Composer; Conductor. Divorced, 2 sons. Education: BS Music, Ohio State University, 1958; MS Music, Composition, Juilliard School of Music, 1966; Studied composition with Hall Overton, Luciano Berio, Vincent Persichetti. Career: Commissioned performances by New York Philharmonic, San Francisco Symphony, Rochester Philharmonic; Performances by Cleveland Orchestra, Nexus Ensemble, Aeolian Chamber Players; Founder, Composer, Conductor, Skymusic Ensemble, 1978; Taught at Yale School of Music, Queens and Brooklyn Colleges, Manhattanville; Music Critic, Columnist, The Village Voice, 1966-76; Master Composer, Young Choreographers and Composers Project, American Dance Festival, 1986-. Compositions: Wildfires and Field Songs; Gospel Fuse; Hit: A Concerto for Percussion and Orchestra; Mass for the 21st Century; Concertos, The Theme is Freedom, for Skymusic Ensemble; Wild Gardens of the Loup Garou, and The Last Chance Planet opera; Paradise Lost, musical; Four Movements for A Five Toed Dragon for Orchestra and Chinese Instruments; Berenice Variations, for clarinet, piano, violin and violoncello; Love Notes to Central Park, mixed media for Skymaic Ensemble, 1996; Journey to Benares, musical, 1997; Gethsemane Park, opera, 1998. Recordings: Youth in a Merciful House, Sextet, Folkways; Berenice: Variations on A Theme of G F Handel; Four Movements for A Fashionable 5-Toed Dragon, Hong Kong Trade Development Council; Lyrics to all songs on Felix Cavaliere, Bearsville. Publications: Somebody's Angel Child: The Story of Bessie Smith, 1970; Rockit. Contributions to: Frequently to New York Times, Vogue, others. Hobbies: Tennis; Reading. Current Management: Brownhouse Management/Grant Center, 2160 No Central Road, Ft Lee, NJ 07024, USA. Address: 152 Columbus Avenue, 4R, New York, NY 10023, USA.

MOORE Charles (Neil), b. 1940, Wolverhampton, England. Conductor; Violinist; Musical Director; Lecturer; Teacher. m. Hilary Derricott, 1 son, 1 daughter. Education: Tettenhall College, Staffordhsire; Birmingham School of Music; Royal College of Music; Private Teaching with Michael Zabludow, Max Rostal and Adrian Boult. Career: Music Staff, Wolverhampton College of Technology, 1966-69; Member of Music Staff, Wolverhampton Education Authority, 1966-71; Visiting Teacher, Westhouse School, Birmingham, 1971-76; Visiting Teacher, Denstone College, 1983-84; Lecturer, Wolverhampton Polytechnic, 1983-88; Leader, English Philharmonic Orchestra, 1973-79; Principal Conductor and Musical Director, English Philharmonic Orchestra, 1979-; Has appeared as Violinist with every major British Orchestra, frequent Guest Conductor throughout England, Canada and USA as well as on Continent; Regularly conducts Malaga Symphony Orchestra, Spain. Recordings: Many recordings and Conductor for BBC, Independent Radio and Television. Contributions to: Regular contributor to newspaper articles as well as broadcast talks. Memberships: Royal Air Force Association; Rotary. Hobbies: Collecting Classic Cars; Riding; Walking. Address: c/o Sound & Music Ltd, 70 Lea Road, Wolverhampton WV3 0LW, England.

MOORE F Richard, b. 4 Sept 1944, Uniontown, Pennsylvania, USA. Professor of Music. divorced, 1 son, 2 daughters. Education: BFA, Music Composition, 1966, BFA, Music Performance, Piano, Percussion, 1966, Carnegie Mellon University; Music Composition and Theory, University of Illinois, 1966-67; MS 1975, PhD, 1977, Computer Engineering, stanford University. Career: Acoustics Research, AT & T Bell Laboratories, 1966-79; Developed MUSIC V and GROOVE computer music systems with Max V Mathews, Currently Professor of Music; Director, Computer Audio Research Laboratory CARL, University of California, San Diego, UCSD, Author of music synthesis programme. Compositions: Computer generated art films,with Lillian Schwartz and Ken Knowlton; Pixillation, 1970, Apotheosis, 1971, Affinities 1971, Mathoma 1971, Enigma 1972, Galaxies 1975. Computer Music: Requiem for computer generated tape. Publications: Realtime Interactive Computer Music, PhD dissertation, 1977; Programming in C with a Bit of UNIX, Prentice Hall 1985; Elements of Computer Music, Prentice Hall, 1990. Contributions to: CARL Startup Kit; Carnegie Technical; Communications of the Association for Computing Machinery ACM; Computer Music Journal. Address: Center for Research in Computing and The Arts, CRCA-0037, University of California, San Diego UCSD, La Jolla, CA 92093, USA.

MOORE Jonathan, b. 1960, England. Actor; Writer; Stage Director. Career: Worked in the Theatre and for Television; Co-librettist and Director of Greek by Mark-Anthony Turnage, premiered at the 1988 Munich Biennale and seen later at the Edinburgh Festival, at the London Coliseum, 1990, directed the version on BBC television; Directed Henze's Elegy for Young Lovers, La Fenice, Venice; Wrote the Libretto for Horse Opera, a TV Film opera for Channel Four, Music by Stewart Copeland; Staged the premiere of Hans Jurgen von Böse's 63 Dream Palace at Munich, 1990 and the premiere of Michael Berkeley's Baa Baa Black Sheep, Opera North, 1993; British Premiere of Schnitke's Life With an Idiot, ENO London Coliseum, 1995; Further Projects: Libretto and Direction of premiere East and West, by Ian McQueen (Almeida 1995); Libretto and Direction of premiere Mottke the Thief by Bernd Franke, Munich, 1997; The Nose (Shostakovich), ENO London Coliseum, 1996; Staged the premiere of Macmillan's Inès de Castro, Edinburgh, 1996. Honours: Best Libretto Award, Munich, for Greek, 1988; Best Director Award, for 63 Dream Palace, Munich, 1990; Royal Philharmonic Society Award and the Midem Award, Cannes, 1991; Nominated for Olivier Award, for Greek, ENO Coliseum, 1991; BMW Award, for Die Vier Himmelsrichtungen, Munich, 1994. Address: c/o Ingpen & Williams Limited, 26 Wadham Road, London SW15 2LR, England.

MOORE Kermit, b. 11 Mar 1929, Akron, Ohio, USA. Cellist; Conductor; Composer. m. Dorothy Rudd, 20 Dec 1964. Education: BMus, Cleveland Institute of Music, 1951; MA, New York University, 1952; Paris Conservatory, 1953-56. Debut: New York Town Hall, 1949. Career: Cello recitals in Paris, Brussels, Vienna, Cologne, Hamburg, Munich, Geneva, Basel, Amsterdam, Tokyo, Seoul, New York, Boston, Chicago and San Francisco; Guest Conductor of Detroit Symphony, Brooklyn Philharmonic, Symphony of New World; Festival Orchestra at the United Nations; Berkeley (California) Symphony; Dance Theater of Harlem; Opera Ebony. Compositions: Music for cello and piano; Music for Viola, percussion and piano; Many Thousand Gone, strings, chorus and percussion; Music for timpani and orchestra; Music for flute and piano; Five Songs for DRM. Recordings: Brahms: Sonata in E Minor, Dorothy Rudd Moore; Dirge and Deliverance, Performance Records; Mendelssohn, Sonata in D Major, Kermit Moore: Music for Cello and Piano, Performance Records; Karl Weigl Sonata, Love Song and Wild Dance, Orion records. Publication: Chapter in The Music Makers, 1979. Hobby: Hiking. Current Management: Rud/Mor Corporation. Address: 33 Riverside Drive, New York, NY 10023, USA.

MOORE Timothy, b. 19 Feb 1922, Cambridge, England. Composer. Education: Trinity College, Cambridge, 1939-41, 1945-46; MA; BMus; Royal College of Music, London, 1946-48. Career: Director of Music, Dartington Hall School, 1950-82. Compositions: 3 two-part Inventions for Piano; Andante for Cor Anglais and Piano; Suite in G for 3 Recorders; Night Song for SA and Piano; Sing Lullaby for SSATB; West Country Variations for 2 Cellos and Piano; Trumpet Concerto, 1948; Suite in F for Orchestra, 1949; Clarinet Concerto, 1956; Horn Sonata, 1970; Partita for 2 Pianos, 1985; Orchestral Variations on a Theme by Fauré, 1987; Piano Duet Concerto, 1989; Variations for Piano and Orchestra on a Theme by Mozart, 1992; String Quartet in D Minor, 1994. Recording: Suite in G. Publications: Lullaby for SSATB, 1947; Three 2 part Inventions for Piano, 1948; Andante for Cor Anglais and Piano, 1949; Suite in G for 3 Recorders, 1950; Night Song for SA and Piano, 1967; West Country Variations for 2 Cellos and Piano, 1979; Brass Quintet, 1991. Honours: Madrigal Society's Prize, 1947; Farrar Prize, 1947; Royal Philharmonic Society Prize, 1948; 1st Prize, Duets for Beginners, Composition Competition, International Piano Duo Association, 1990. Memberships: Composers' Guild; PRS. Address: 86 Chesterton Road, Cambridge, CB4 1ER, England.

MOORMAN Madeleine (Charlotte), b. 18 Nov 1933, Little Rock, Arkansas, USA. Cellist. Education: BMus, Centenary College, Shreveport, 1955; Julliard School with Leonard Rose, 1957-58. Career: Member of Jacob Glick's Boccherini Players, 1958-63; The American Symphony Orchestra, until 1967; Founded the Annual New York Avant Garde Festival, 1963; Colloborations with composer and video artist Nam June Paik from 1964, including Cello Sonata No 1 for Adults Only, 1965, Opera Sextronique, 1967, TV Bra for Living Sculpture, 1969, TV Cello, 1971 and Global Groove, 1973; The People of the State of New York against Charlotte Moorman performed 1977; Performances of the cello wrapped in cellophane, in a gondola and in an oildrum, and underwater; Has performed works by John Cage. Address: c/o Nam June Paik, ASCAP, ASCAP Building, One Lincoln Plaza, NY 10023, USA.

MORA Barry, b. 1944, New Zealand. Baritone Singer. Education: Studied in London with Otakar Kraus and John Matheson. Career includes: Sang at Gelsenkirchen, 1977-79 as: Verdi's Posa and Luna; Mozart's Speaker and Figaro; Sang at Frankfurt from 1979 as Tamare, in Die Gezeichneten and Ford, in Falstaff; Festival Hall debut, 1979 as Schumann's Faust; Covent Garden Debut 1980 as Donner, in Das Rheingold; Scottish Opera in 1983 as the Traveller, in Death in Venice; Welsh National Opera from 1986 as Donner, Gunther, The Forester in The Cunning Little Vixen and Frank in Die Fledermaus, 1991; Netherlands Opera, 1991; Engagements at Deutsche Oper Berlin, Zurich Opera, Aachen, Dusseldorf, Barcelona, Wellington and Canterbury, New Zealand; Also sang in 1992: Rosenkavalier, Sydney; La Traviata, Barcelona; Parsifal, Frankfurt; Cosi fan tutte, Wellington; Un Ballo in Maschera, Brussels; Concert repertoire includes, Puccini's Messa di Gloria, Bach's B minor Mass and St John Passion; Carmina Burana, Stravinsky's Canticum Sacrum, Lieder eines fahrenden Gesellen by Mahler, Lulu at Buenos Aires, Così fan tutte at Barcelona Opera, La Cenerentola, Australian Opera, 1994; Current roles with Australian Opera as Dr Schön, in Lulu, Alidoro, in La Cenerentola; Tales of Hoffmann, 1995; Wellington Opera: Ping, in Turandot, 1994; Balstrode, in Peter Grimes, 1995; Father, in Hansel and Gretel, 1995. Address: c/o Haydn Rawstron Ltd, 36 Station Road, London SE20 7BQ, England.

MORALES Abram, b. 30 Nov 1939, Corpus Christi, TX, USA. Singer (Tenor). Education: BME, MM, Southern Methodist University; Study for DMA, North Texas State University. Career: Dallas Opera, San Francisco Opera, Town Hall in New York City, Seattle Opera, Alice Tully Hall in New York City, Minneapolis Opera; On tour with: Metropolitan Opera Company in role of Lindoro in Rossini's L'Italiana in Algeri, 1986, Buxton Festival, England singing Count Alberto in Rossini's L'Occasione fa Il Ladro, 1987; Concert Opera Orchestra of Manhattan at Town Hall, New York City, as Belfiore in Il Viaggio a Reims, 1987. Hobby: Film Festivals. Current Management: Columbia Artists, 165 West 57th Street, New York, NY 10019, USA. Address: 3002 Glenview Road, Wilmette, IL 60091, USA.

MORAN Robert, b. 8 Jan 1937, Denver, Colorado, USA. Composer. Education: Studied with Hans Erich Apostel and Roman Haubenstock Ramati in Vienna, Luciano Berio and Darius Milhaud at Mills College. Career: Founded and co-directed the New Music Ensemble, San Francisco Conservatory; Performances throughout USA and Europe as Pianist; Lecturer on contemporary music. Compositions: Silver and The Circle of Messages, for chamber orchestra, 1970; Emblems of Passage for 2 orchestras, 1974; Angels of Silence for viola and chamber orchestra, 1975; The Last Station of the Albatross, for 1-8 instruments, 1978; Survivor from Darmstadt, 1984; Mixed media works and stage works including Let's Build a Nut House, chamber opera, 1969; Erlösung dem Erlöser, music drama, 1982; LeipzigerKerzenspiel, 1985; The Juniper Tree, 1985; Desert of Roses, 1992; From the Towers of the Moon, 1992; Dracula Diary, 1994. Address: c/o BMI, 320 West 57th Street, New York, NY 10019, USA.

MORAVEC Antonin, b. 29 April 1928, Brno, Czech Republic. Violinist; Composer. m. Karla Moravcova, 15 July 1950. Education: Conservatory of Brno; Janacek Academy of Musical Art, Brno; Moscow Conservatory of P J Tchaikovsky; Study at V Prihoda. Career: Professor, Music Academies and Universities: Janacek Academy, Brno, Music Academy Prague, Mastercourses at Kunitachi Music Academy in Tokyo, Tchaikovsky Concertatory in Moscow, Mozarteum in Salzburg, Basel-Muttenz, Castle of Lancut in Poland, Castle of Pommersfelden in Germany; Member, 35 Juries of International Violin Competitions; Recitals on Radio and Television Worldwide. Compositions: Polonaise; Arietta; A Starry Night; Capriccio for Violin and Piano; 15 Cadenzas for Violin Concertos by Viotti, Haydn, Mozart, Slavik, Pagannini. Recordings: Complex Violin Sonatas by B Martinu, D Shostakowich, S Prokofiev; Piano Trio by M Istvan. Honours: Honorary Professor, Kunitachi Music Academy, Tokyo, 1961; Medal of L Janacek, Ministry of Culture, Czech Republic, 1978; Medal of the City of Prague, 1978; Prize, Union of Czech Composers, 1982; Honorary Title of Merited Artist, Czech Government, 1979; Golden Merit of Janacek Academy of Music, 1982. Membership: Association of Music Artists & Scientists, Prague. Address: Taussigova 1152, 182 00 Praha 8, Czech Republic.

MORAVEC Vincent (Paul), b. 2 Nov 1957, Buffalo, NY, USA. Composer; Professor of Music; Electronic Music Synthesist; Conductor. Education: BA magna cum laude, Music, Harvard University, Cambridge, Massachusetts, 1980; MA Music Composition, 1982, DMA Music Composition, 1987, Columbia University, New York. Career: Currently Assistant Professor of Music, Dartmouth College, Hanover, New Hampshire. Compositions: Missa Miserere, 1981; Ave Verum Corpus, 1981; Pater Noster, 1981; Sacred Songs, 1982; Three Anthems, 1983; Songs for Violin and Piano, 1983; Music for Chamber Ensemble, 1983; Wings, 1983; Spiritdance, 1984; Innocent Dreamers, 1985; Four Transcendent Love Songs, 1986; Prayers and Praise, 1986; Whispers, 1986; The Kingdom Within, 1987. Current Management: JL Music Productions, 250 West 100th Street Suite 104, NY 10025, USA. Address: c/o Music Department, Dartmouth College, Hanover, NH 03755, USA.

MORAWETZ Oskar, b. 17 Jan 1917, Czechoslovakia. Composer;Professor. m. 1958, 1 son, 1 daughter. Career: Professor of Music, University of Toronto; Orchestral compositions performed frequently by Canadian Orchestras, Canadian Broadcasting Corporation and in USA, Europe and Australia; Among major orchestras abroad, his compositions have been performed by the Philadelphia, Chicago, Detroit, Minneapolis, Indianapolis, Washington and Aspen Festival Orchestras in USA and major orchestras in France, Sweden, Norway, Belgium, Holland, Italy, Czechoslovakia and Greece; Conductors who have programmed his works include, William Steinberg, Zubin Mehta, Karel Ancerl, Kubelik, Walter Susskind, Seiji Ozawa, Adrian Boult, Izler Solomon, Sixten Ehrling and Ernest MacMillan; Artists such as Glenn Gould, Rudolf Firkusny and Anton Kuerti have premiered his piano compositions and Maureen Forrester, Jon Vickers, Louis Marshall, Dorothy Maynor, Louis Quilico and Lillian Sukis have included compositions in programmes in Canada, USA, Europe and Australia. Compositions: Memorial to Martin Luther King for cello and orchestra; Sinfonietta For Winds and Percussion, From The Diary of Anne Frank; Fantasy in D; Piano Concerto. Recordings: Many of his compositions have been recorded by various record companies. Address: c/o OSA, Cs armady 20, 160-56 Prague 6, Bubenec, Czech Republic.

MORAWSKI Jerzy, b. 9 Sept 1932, Warsaw, Poland. Musicologist. m. Katarzyna. Education: Theory, 1957, Piano, 1961, Warsaw Conservatory; MA, Institute of Musicology, Warsaw University, 1958; PhD, Institute of Arts, Polish Academy of Sciences, 1970; D habil, Jagiellonian University, Krakow, 1997. Career: Assistant, Department of Theory and History of Music, 1956-70, Doctor, Head, History Music Section, 1970-79, Vice-Director, Institute of Arts and Polish Academy of Sciences, 1979-81; Lecturer, Warsaw University, 1968-70; Academy of Catholic Theology, Warsaw, 1970-73; Jagiellonian University, Krakow, 1971-82. Publications include: Research on Liturgical Recitative in Poland, 1973, 1986, 1992, 1995; The Problems of the Tropes Techniques, 1976, 1979; Polish Hymns, 1991; Editor-in-Chief of serial publications: Monumenta Musicae in Polonia and Musica Medii Aevi; Books: Musical Lyric Poetry in Medieval Poland, 1973; Theory of Music in the Middle Ages, 1979; Liturgical Recitative in Medieval Poland, 1996; Editor, Musica Antiqua Polonica: Anthology, The Middle Ages, 1972; The Rhymed History of St Jadwiga, 1977; The Rhymed History of St Adalbert, 1979; The Polish Cistercian Sequences, 1984; Jan Stefani's Six Partitas for Wind Instruments, 1993. Contributions to: Professional publications. Memberships include: Past Vice-Secretary and President, Polish Composers' Union, Musicological Section; International Musicological Society. Address: ul Dluga 24 m 43, 00-238 Warsaw, Poland.

MORDKOVITCH Lydia, b. 1950, Saratov, USSR. Concert Violinist. Education: Studied at the Odessa Conservatory and with David Distrakh in Moscow. Career: Emigrated to Israel 1974, later resident in London; British debut 1979, with the Halle Orchestra under Walter Suskind; Appearances with the Philharmonia, London Symphony, London, Royal and Liverpool Philharmonics, Scottish National, City of Birmingham Symphony and all the BBC Symphony Orchestras; US debut with the Chicago Symphony under Solti; Returning to play the Brahms Concerto with the Philadelphia Orchestra under Muti; Promenade Concerts debut 1985, returning 1988 with Szymanowski's 2nd Concerto; Further engagements in Finland, Norway, Italy and the Canary Islands; Conductors include Kurt Sanderling, Stanislaw Skrowaczewski, Charles Groves and Marek Janowski. Recordings: Shostakovich Concertos with the Scottish National under Neeme Järvi; Complete works for solo violin by Bach; Concertos by Bruch, Prokofiev and Brahms; Moeran Concerto with the Ulster Orchestra under Vernon Handley, Chandos; CD: Solo Sonatas by Ysaÿe. Honours: Prize Winner, National Young Musicians Competition, Kiev; Long-Thibaud International Competition, Paris; Gramophone Award for Best Concerto Recording, 1990; Diaspason d'or, France, for Prokofiev Concertos. Address: c/o Norman McCann International Artists Ltd, The Coach House, 56 Lawrie Park Gardens, London, SE26 6XJ, England.

MOREHEN John (Manley), b. 3 Sept 1941, Gloucester, England. Lecturer; Musicologist; Organist; Conductor. m. Marie Catherine Jacobus, 26 July 1969, 1 son, 1 daughter. Education: Clifton College; Royal School of Church Music; New College, Oxford; College of Church Musicians, Washington DC; King's College, Cambridge; MA, Oxon and Cantab; PhD, Cantab; FRCO (Chm); FRCCO. Career: Assistant Director of Music at St Clement Danes and Hampstead Parish Church; Organist to Hampstead Choral Society, Martindale Sidwell Choir and London Bach Orchestra, 1964-67; Lecturer, College of Church Musicians, Washington Cathedral and the American University, Washington DC, 1967-68; Sub-Organist, St George's Chapel, Windsor Castle, 1968-72; Lecturer in Music, University of Nottingham, 1973-82; Senior Lecturer, 1982-89; Professor of Music, 1989; Conductor, Nottingham Bach Society, 1983-90; BBC Recitalist, 1964-; Tours of Europe and North America; Freeman of the City of London, 1991; Liveryman, Worshipful Company of Musicians, 1991; Justice of the Peace, Nottinghamshire, 1991; Member of the Humanities Research Board Music Panel, 1994-97; HEFCE Subject Assessor (Music), 1994-95; Music Adviser to the Commonwealth Scholarship Commission, 1996-. Recordings: With choirs of New College, Oxford and Hampstead Parish Church. Publications: Many editions of 16th and 17th Century English Music; Articles in the New Grove Dictionary, 6th edition and Musical Periodicals; Major editions of the music of Richard Nicolson, 1975, Christopher Tye, 1979, William Byrd, 1987, Thomas Morley, 1991, 1997. Address: Wynstay, Clipstone Lane, Normanton-on-the-Wolds, Plumtree, Nottinghamshire NG12 5NW, England.

MOREL Francois, b. 14 Mar 1926, Montreal, Canada. Composer. Education: Studied piano with private teacher; Studied composition with Clude Champagne, Conservatoire de Muique, Montreal. Career: Working for Radio-Canada writing background music for theatre, radio and television, 1956-81; Professor of composition, orchestration and analysis; l'Ecole de musique, Universite Laval, Quebec City; President of publishing firm, Les Editions Quebec-Musique, Montreal; Received commissions for compositions from Canadian Broadcasting Corporation, First International Festival of Contemporary Music for Wind Symphony Orchestra, Edmonton Symphony Orchestra; McGill Chamber Orchestra, Societe de Musique Contemporaine du Quebec, Guitar Society of Toronto 1976; Olympic Games Committee; Montreal International Competition among others. Compositions: Orchestral: Antiphonie 1953; Boreal 1959; Departs 1968-69, Diptyque 1948, revised 1955-56; Esquisse 1947-47; L'Etoile noire 1961-62; likkii 1971; Jeux 1976; Litanies 1955-56, revised 1970; Melisma 1980; Le mythe de la roche percee 1960-61; Neumes despace et reliefs 1967; Prismes-anamorphoses 1967; Radiance 1970-72; Requiem for Winds 1962-63; Rituel de l'espace 1958-59; Sinfonia 1963; Spirale 1956; Trajectoire 1967. Instrumental Ensemble: Cassation 1954; Etude en forme de toccate 1965; Quatuor No 1, 1952, No 2, 1962-63; Quintette pour cuivres 1962; Rhythmologue 1970; Symphonie pur cuivres 1956. Instrumental Solo and Vocal Solos. Address: c/o CAPAC Canada, PRS Limited, Berners Street, London W1, England.

MORELLE Maureen, b. 1937, Hampshire. Singer, Mezzo-Soprano. Education: Studied at the Royal College of Music. Career: Sang in the original London Cast of West Side Story; Opera debut as Smeton in Anna Bolena at the 1960 Glyndeboure Festival; Later appearances as Geneviève in Pelléas et Mélisande, Marcellina in Le Nozze di Figaro, and Madam Larina in Eugene Onegin; Sadler's Wells Opera: Rosina, Barber of Seville; Dorabella in Cosi fan tutte; Pippa in Thieving Magpie; Cherubino in Figaro; English National Opera as Ottavia, Coronation of Poppea; Wagner's Fricka, First Norn and Flosshilde, in The Ring conducted by Reginald Goodall; Rosina, Dorabella and Lady Essex in Gloriana; Sang in A Midsummer Night's Dream and Birtwistle's Punch and Judy, world premiere, 1968, for English Opera Group and toured to San Francisco, Brussels, Paris and Montreal; Engagements with Welsh National Opera and Opera North include Cherubino, Fenena in Nabucco, Mrs Sedley in Peter Grimes, and the Hostess in Boris Godunov, 1989; Season 1987-88 as The Mayor's Wife in Jenufa at Covent Garden and Verdi's Azucena for ENO and Scottish Opera; Regular appearances on BBC's Friday Night is Music Night and Melodies for You; ROH Season, 1992-93, Mayor's Wife, Jenufa; Opera North, Larina, Eugene Onegin. Honours: Queen's Prize at the RCM. Address: c/o Korman International Management, Crunnells Green Cottage, Preston, Herts SG4 7UQ, England.

MORELLI Adriana, b. 1954, Italy. Singer, Soprano. Education: Studied at Regiio Calabria. Debut: Spoleto 1978, as Musetta. Career: Sang Sophie in Werther at Bergamo 1979, Lauretta in Gianni Schicchi at Lucca, 1981; Further engagements as Butterfly and Mimi at Spoleto and Lille, Elisabeth de Valois at Dijon, Amsterdam, Amelia, Un Ballo in Maschera, at Trieste; Sang Margherita in Mefistofele and Tosca at Genoa, 1987-88, Giorgetta in Il Tabarro at Florence 1988 and Maria Stuarda at Piacenza, 1990; La Scala debut, 1990, as Nedda in Pagliacci; Sang Silvia in Mascagni's Zanetta at Florence, 1996; Stage and concert appearances in South America. Address: c/o Teatro alla Scala, Via Filodrammatici 2, Milan, Italy.

MORGAN Arwel Huw, b. 1950, Ystalyfera, Swansea, Wales. Singer, Bass. Career: Joined the chorus of Welsh National Opera in 1978; Solo roles in Wales have included Don Fernando, Fidelio; Ladas in The Greek Passion; Angelotti in Tosca; Hobson, Peter Grimes; The Parson in The Cunning Little Vixen; Created the role of Maskull for New Celtic Opera's Voyage to Arcturus; English National Opera from 1987 in Lady Macbeth of Mtsensk and The Cunning Little Vixen; Toured Britain 1988, as Osmin in Opera 80's Die Entführung aus dem Serail; Season 1992 as Leporello, and as Carl Olsen, in Weill's Street Scene for ENO; Fabrizio in The Thieving Magpie for Opera North; Sang Leporello in a new production of Don Giovanni for Welsh National Opera, 1996. Recordings: Polonius in Hamlet by Ambroise Thomas, conducted by Richard Bonynge. Address: c/o Ingpen and Williams Ltd, 26 Wadham Road, London SW15 2LR, England.

MORGAN Beverly, b. 17 Mar 1952, Hanover, New Hampshire, USA. Soprano. Education: Mt Holyoke College, 1969-71; BMus, Honours, New England Conservatory of Music, 1971-73; MMus, Honours, 1973-75, New York. Debut: Recital debut as winner of Concert Artists Guild Award, 1978. Career: Operatic Appearances with Wiener Staatsoper, San Francisco Opera, Netherlands Opera, Opera Company of Boston, Pittsburgh, Omaha and Philadelphia Operas, Kennedy Center in Washington and Scottish National Opera; Sang in the premiere of Glass's Satyagraha at Amsterdam, 1980, and in the US Premiere of Zimmermann's Die Soldaten, Boston, 1982; Other appearances in Bernstein's A Quiet Place at La Scala and in Vienna at Santa Fe in the US Premieres of Henze's English Cat and Penderecki's Die schwarze Maske, 1985, 1988; Scottish Opera as Berg's Lulu, 1987; Other roles include Tatiana and Violetta at Seattle and Fusako in Henze's Das Verratene Meer, Berlin and Milan; Concert appearances with Boston Symphony, San Francisco Symphony, Chamber Society of Lincoln Center, American String Quartet, Marlboro Music Festival, American Composers Orchestra; Performances under Leonard Bernstein, Seiji Ozawa and Herbert Blomstedt. Recordings: DGG. Hobbies: Backpacking; Vegetarian Cooking. Current Management: Columbia Artists Management Incorporated, NY, USA. Address: c/o Crittenden Division, Columbia Artists Management Incorporated, 165 West 57th Street, NY 10019, USA.

MORGAN David, b. 18 May 1932, Ewell, Surrey, England. Composer; Musician (Cor anglais). Education: New South Wales Conservatory, 1946-52; Study in London with Norman Del Mar and Matyas Seiber, 1955-56; BMus, University of Durham, 1970. Career: Cor anglais player in the Sydney Symphony Orchestra; Composer and Arranger with the South Australian Department of Education, 1975-93; Commissions from the Adelaide Chamber Orchestra and Musica da Camera, among others. Compositions include: Mass in B Major, 1948; Horn Concerto, 1957; Violin Concerto, 1957; Concerto for Viola and Strings, 1958; Little Suite for Wind, 1976; Concerto Grosso No 2 for string trio and string orchestra, 1978; Sinfonia for 11 string players, 1978; Loss for 4 percussion, 1982; Suite for String Orchestra, Percussion and Piano, 1985; Fun and Games for 4 percussion, 1986; Jubilee Overture, 1986; Harpischord Sonata, 1992; Concerto for Orchestra No 1, 1993, No 2, 1994; Trumpet Concerto, 1995. Honours include: British Council Bursary. Address: c/o APRA, 1A Eden Street, Crows Nest, NSW 2065, Australia.

MORGAN Michael (DeVard), b. 17 Sept 1957, Washington, DC, USA. Conductor. Education: Oberlin College Conservatory of Music; Berkshire Music Centre, Tanglewood, 1977. Debut: Operatic, Vienna State Opera, 1982. Career: Apprentice Conductor, Buffalo Philharmonic, 1979-80; Assistant Conductor, St Louis Symphony, 1980-81; Assistant Conductor, Chicago Symphony, 1986-; Guest Conductor: New York and Warsaw Philharmonics, Vienna, Baltimore, Houston, New Orleans Symphony Orchestras; National Symphony, Washington; Deutsche Staatsoper, Berlin; Summer Opera Theater, Washington, DC; Orchestras in Italy, Denmark and Holland. Honours: 1st prize, Hans Swarowsky International Conductors Competition Vienna, 1980; Prizes in Conducting Competitions at Baltimore, 1974; San Remo, 1975; Copenhagen, 1980. Current Management: Sheldon Soffer Management Inc, NY; Alex Saron, Blaricum, Holland, Europe. Address: 1220 Decatur Street, NW, Washington, DC 20011, USA.

MORGAN Morris, b. 26 Sept 1940, Berlin, Germany. Singer (Baritone). Education: Studied in Dusseldorf, Cologne and Wiesbaden, 1955-71. Career: Sang at Cologne in the 1965 premiere of Die Soldaten by Zimmermann; Kiel Opera 1965-68, notably in the 1965 premiere of Reimann's Traumspiel; Wiesbaden 1968-71, Bern 1971-79, Freiburg 1978-81; Further engagements at Dusseldorf, Mannheim, Stuttgart, Bremen, Saarbrucken, Lubeck and Klagenfurt; Returned to Berne 1985, as Marcello in La Bohème; Concert appearances in baroque music and as Lieder singer. Recordings include: Die Soldaten; Zemlinsky's Kleider Machen Leute; Israel in Egypt and Carmina Burana. Address: Stadttheater Bern, Nageligasse 1, CH-3011 Bern, Switzerland.

MORGAN Robert P, b. 28 July 1934, Nashville, Tennessee, USA. Professor of Music (Music Theory). m. 12 June 1965. Education: BA, 1956, PhD, 1969, Princeton University; MA, University of California, Berkeley, 1958; Hochschule für Musik, Munich, Germany, 1960-62. Career: Professor of Music (Music Theory), Yale University. Compositions: Numerous works for orchestra, chamber ensembles and voice. Recording: Trio for Flute, Cello and Harpsichord. Publications: Twentieth Century Music; Music: A View from Delft, Selected Essays of Edward T Cone (editor). Contributions to: Numerous articles to Musical Quarterly; Journal of Music Theory; 19th Century Music; Perspectives of New Music. Honours: Woodrow Wilson Fellowship, 1956-57; German Government Grant, 1960-62; Senior Fellow, National Endowment of Humanities, 1983-84. Memberships: Society for Music Theory, Executive Board Member 1985-86; American Musicological Society, Council Member 1982-85; College Music Society. Hobbies: Tennis; Skiing. Address: Department of Music, Yale University, New Haven, CT 06520, USA.

MORIARTY John, b. 30 Sept 1930, Fall River, Massachusetts, USA. Administrator; Educator. Education: BM, New England Conservatory, 1952; Mills College with Egon Petri, summers, 1949, 1950 and 1952; Brandeis University, 1954-55. Career: Most recent recordings include Tamerlano by Handel, 1970; 6 records as conductor of Chamber Orchestra, Copenhagen and 3 records as piano accompanist, Cambridge; Ballad of Baby Doe; Artistic Administrator, Opera Society of Washington, 1960-62, Santa Fe Opera, New Mexico, 1962-65; Director, Wolf Trap Co, Vienna, Virginia, 1972-77; Principal Conductor, Central City Opera, Denver, 1978-; Artistic Director, 1982-; Panelist, Connecticut Arts Council, 1982 and 1984; Adjudicator, various contests including Metropolitan Opera Auditions, 1965-; Chairman, Opera Department of New England Conservatory. Publication: Author, Diction, 1975. Honour: DM, Hon, New England Conservatory, 1992. Address: New England Conservatory, 290 Huntington Avenue, Boston, MA 02115, USA.

MORISON Elsie, b. 15 Aug 1924, Victoria, Australia. Singer, Soprano. m. (1) Kenneth Stevenson, 1950, (2) Rafael Kubelik, 1963, dec 1996. Education: Melba Conservatorium, Australia; Studied with Clive Carey at the Royal College of Music, London. Debut: London debut in Acis and Galatea at the Albert Hall in 1948; Melbourne, 1994, in the Messiah. Career: Acis and Galatea, Albert Hall, 1948; Sadler's Wells Opera, 1948-54, notably as Fiordiligi, Lauretta, Nannetta; Covent Garden, 1954-62; Pamina, Susanna, Mimi, Marenka in Bartered Bride, and 1958, Blanche in British Premiere of Dialogues des Carmelites, by Poulenc. Glyndebourne, 1953-59 in The Rake's Progress and Fidelio; Many appearances at International Festivals as a concert singer. Recordings: Haydn The Seasons and Handel, Oratorio Solomon; Handel's Messiah; Mahler's 4th Symphony; Entire Gilbert and Sullivan operas; Mahler's 4th Symphony. Honours: Melba Scholarship. Address: Im Sand, CH 6047 Kastanienbaum, Switzerland.

MORK Truls, b. 25 Apr 1961, Bergen, Norway. Concert Cellist. Education: Studied with: His father; Frans Helmerson, Swedish Radio Music School; Later study with Heinrich Schiff, Austria and Natalia Schakowskaya, Moscow. Career includes: Extensive tours of Europe, Russia, USA and Far East, 1984-; Performances with Oslo Philharmonic, Royal Philharmic, Orchestre National de France, City of Birmingham Symphony, Moscow Philharmonic, Moscow Radio Symphony, Israel Philharmonic, Gothenburg Symphony, Hamburg Philharmonic, London Symphony, Scottish Chamber and Zurich Tonhalle; Recital Debuts in: London's Wigmore Hall, 1988; New York's Town Hall, 1986; Tours of Australasia with the Adelaide, Sydney and Melbourne Symphony Orchestras; Numerous recitals in New Zealand; Other engagements include tours of USA, Japan and Spain; Concerts with the Gulbenkian and Berlin Symphony Orchestras, Bergen Philharmonic and Atlanta and Detroit Symphony Orchestras; Nordic tours with solo recitals and piano quartet recitals; Chamber Festivals include Casals Festival, Kuhmo, Korsholm and Naantali; Founder and Artistic Director: International Chamber Music Festival, Stavanger; Also participated in many festivals including Flanders, Rouen, Bergen International, Spoleto, Seattle; Plays a Domenico Montagnana Cello; Played Brahms and Shostakovich at the Wigmore Hall, London, 1997. Recordings include: Haydn Cello Concertos; Schumann, Elgar and Saint-Saëns Concertos; Dvorák Cello Concertos; Tchaikovsky Rococo Variations; 2 Recital discs of Cello works by Grieg and Sibelius, and Brahms; Works by Shostakovich and Prokofiev. Honours: Numerous awards in national and international competitions. Address: c/o IMG Artists Europe, Media House, 3 Burlington Lane, London, W4 2TH, England.

MOROZOV Alexander, b. 1950, USSR. Singer, Bass. Education: Studied at the Leningrad Conservatory. Career: Joined the Kirov Opera, Leningrad, 1983 and has sung Don Basilio, Mephistopheles, Pimen, Boris Godunov and Surin in The Queen of Spades; Sang at Covent Garden 1987 with the Kirov, as Surin, Pimen and Boris; Tours to Zurich and France; Sang Zemfira's father in a concert performance of Rachmaninov's Aleko at the Santa Cecilia, Rome, 1989; Amsterdam 1989, as Pimen; Dolokhov in War and Peace for Seattle Opera, 1990; Scottish Opera 1990 as Padre Guardiano in La Forza del Destino; Covent Garden company as Basilio, and Fiesco in a new production of Simon Boccanegra conducted by Georg Solti, 1991. Recordings include: Lord Rochefort in Anna Bolena, 1996. Honours: First Prize at competitions in Rio de Janeiro and Moscow, Tchaikovsky International. Address: Allied Artists, 42 Montpelier Square, London, SW7 1JZ, England.

MOROZOV Igor, b. 1948, Moscow, USSR. Singer, Baritone. Education: Studied at the Moscow Conservatory. Career: First engagement at the Kirov Theatre Leningrad, then sang at the Bolshoi, Moscow, from 1976 as Eugene Onegin, Count Luna, Germont, Yeletzky, The Queen of Spades; Robert in Tchaikovsky's Iolanta; Sang in Shchedrin's Dead Souls at Boston, 1988; Guest engagements in Finland and Hungary as concert and opera atrist; British debut at Covent Garden, 1988. Address: Allied Artists, 42 Montpelier Square, London, SW7 1JZ, England.

MOROZOV Vladimir (Mikhailovich), b. 1933. Opera Singer, Bass. Education: Leningrad Conservatory. Career: Soloist with Kirov Opera 1959-, roles include: Varlaam in Boris Godunov; Ivan The Terrible in The Maid of Pskov; Grigory in Quiet Flows the Don; Peter the Great, Peter I. Honours: Glinka Prize, 1974; RSFSR People's Artist, 1976; USSR People's Artist 1981. Membership: CPSU, 1965-. Address: c/o Kirov Opera Company, St Petersburg, Russia.

MORREAU Annette (Scawen), b. 4 Feb 1943, Altrincham, England. Writer; Broadcaster; Producer. Education: BA, Durham University; University of IN, Bloomington, USA. Career: Founder, The Contemporary Music Network, UK; Music Officer, Arts Council of Great Britain until 1987; Assistant Editor Arts at Channel 4 TV; Executive Director, Morreau Productions; Independent TV Producer of music programmes; Devised, Not Mozart series on BBC2 TV, 1991; Independent Radio Producer of music programmes for BBC Radio 3: Feuermann Remembered, Diary of a Composition, William Kapell Remembered. Contributions to: Tempo; Contact; Classical Music; BBC Music Magazine; Guardian; Independent; BBC Domestic and World Service Radio. Honour: First Female Recipient to win Durham/Bloomington scholarship exchange. Memberships: IARP; BACA. Hobbies: Cooking; Collecting Oil Lamps; Sailing; Cello. Address: 15 Callcot Road, London, NW6, England.

MORRIS Andrew (William), b. 18 Dec 1948, Kent, England. Director of Music; Conductor; Organist. Education: Chorister of Westminster Abbey; Royal Academy of Music; Goldsmiths' College, University of London; The Institute of Education; MA, BMus (London); GRSM; FTCL; ARCO (CHM); LRAM; ARCM. Career: Conductor, University of London Choir, 1970-72; Director of Music, Christ's College, Finchley, 1972-79; Organist and Director of Music, The Priory Church of St Bartholomew-the-Great, Smithfield, London EC1, 1971-79; Founder and Artistic Director, St Bartholomew's Festivals, 1973, 1977, 1978, 1979; Musical Director, The New English Singers, 1974-79; Director of Music, Bedford School, 1979-; Member, Executive Committee, 1978-88, Honorary Treasurer, 1980-84, Chairman, 1984-87, The New Macnaghten Concerts; Examiner to The Associated Board of the Royal Schools of Music, 1980-; Founder and Director, New Bedford Singers, 1983-93. Recordings: In Quires and Places No 13, with St Bartholomew-the-Great Choir; Mozart's Church Music, with St Bartholomew-the-Great Choir. Honours: ARAM, 1989. Memberships: Royal Academy of Music Club; Royal College of Organists; MMA, Committee 1988, Honorary Secretary 1990-95, President-Designate 1995; Freeman of the City of London, 1978-. Hobbies: Cricket (Member of MCC); History; Architecture; Sailing. Address: The Music School, Bedford School, Bedford MK40 2TU, England.

MORRIS Colin, b. 17 Nov 1952, Sheerness, Kent, England. Singer (Baritone). Education: BA, 1974, PhD, 1978, Geography,

Exeter University; ARCM Performers, 1977; Private Study with Derek Hammond-Stroud. Debut: Edinburgh Festival with Kent Opera, 1979. Career: Many concert and recital appearances in UK and Netherlands; Lieder repertoire of over 300 songs; Toured UK and USA with Pavilion Opera, London Opera Players, Regency Opera, D'Oyly Carte, Crystal Clear Opera; Penang Festival; Overseas opera debut, Singapore, 1992; Main roles are Don Alfonso, Leporello, Magnifico, Bartolo, Pasquale, Dulcamara; Falstaff, Rigoletto, Sharpless, Scarpia and Tonio; Operetta, especially "patter" roles in Gilbert and Sullivan. Recordings: Several song recitals on British Broadcasting Corporation, Radio Kent; Commercial recordings of Noel Coward, Jerome Kern. Memberships: Mensa; Equity; Incorporated Society of Musicians, Performers and Composers Section. Hobbies: Gilbert and Sullivan; Works of Noel Coward; Siamese Cats. Current Management: Music International, 13 Ardilaun Road, Highbury, London, N5 2QR, England. Address: 49 Winstanley Road, Sheerness, Kent, ME12 2PW, England.

MORRIS Gareth (Charles Walter), b. 13 May 1920, Clevedon, Somerset, England. Flautist. m. (1) 1954, 1 d; (2) Patricia Mary Murray, 18 Dec 1975, 1 s, 2 d. Education: Bristol Cathedral School and privately; Royal Academy of Music, London. Career: Soloist; Professor, Royal Academy of Music, 1945-85; Principal Flautist, Philharmonia Orchestra, London, 1948-72. Recordings: Numerous. Publications: Flute Technique, 1991; Numerous articles in journals. Honours: ARAM, 1945; FRAM, 1949; FRSA, 1967. Memberships: Royal Society of Arts, Member of Council, Chairman, Music Committee; Royal Society of Musicians, Governor. Hobbies: Antiquarian Horology; Reading; Collecting books. Address: 4 West Mall, Clifton, Bristol BS8 4BH, England.

MORRIS James, b. 10 Jan 1947, Baltimore, Maryland, USA. Singer, (Bass-Baritone). m. Susan Quittmeyer. Education: Studied with Rosa Ponselle in Baltimore, with Frank Valentino and Nicola Moscona in New York. Debut: Baltimore Civic Opera 1967, as Crespel in Les Contes d'Hoffmann; Metropolitan Opera from 1971, as Mozart's Commendatore and Don Giovanni, 1975; Verdi's Procida, Padre Guardiano, Grand Inquisitor and Philip II, and the villains in Les Contes d'Hoffmann; Glyndebourne debut 1972, as Verdi's Banquo; At the Salzburg Festival he has sung Guglielmo in Cosi fan tutte and Mozart's Figaro, 1986; Received coaching from Hans Hotter and sang Wagner's Wotan in San Francisco and Vienna 1985; Other roles include Gounod's Mephistopheles, Britten's Claggart and Donizetti's Henry VIII; Sang the Dutchman at the Metropolitan 1989, Mephistopheles and Wotan, also televised, 1990; Sang Mephistopheles at Cincinnati 1990, with hife wife as Siebel; Covent Garden 1990, as the Wanderer in a new production of Siegfried; Season 1992, as the Dutchman in New York and at Covent Garden, Claggart in Billy Budd at the Met and Boris Godunov at San Francisco; Sang Iago at the Met, 1995, returned for Mozart's Figaro, 1997. Recordings: Wotan in Ring cycles conducted by James Levine and Bernard Haitink, 1988-90. Address: c/o Lies Askonas Limited, 6 Henrietta Street, London, WC2, England.

MORRIS Joan (Clair), b. 10 Feb 1943, Portland, Oregon, USA. Singer; Teacher. m. William Bolcom, 28 Nov 1975. Education: Gonzaga University, 1963-65; Diploma, American Academy of Dramatic Arts, 1968. Debut: Wigmore Hall, 1993. Career: Performed at the Boston Pops, 1976; Polly Peachum in The Beggar's Opera, Guthrie Theatre, Minneapolis, 1979; Soloist, World Premiere of William Bolcom's Songs of Innocence and Experience, Stuttgart Opera, 1984 and at New York Premiere, 1987; Weill Recital Hall, Carnegie Hall, 1987; Soloist, world premiere of William Bolcom's 4th Symphony with the St Louis Symphony 1987; Played the Nurse in world premiere of Casino Paradise, 1990; Alice Tully Hall, Lincoln Center, 1976, 1977, 1978, 1980, 1983, 1995; Ewart Hall, American University in Cairo, 1988; 20th Anniversary Concert with guest Max Morath at Hunter College, 1993; Church of Santo Spirito, Florence, 1989; Since 1981, Assistant Adjunct Professor of Musical Theater at University of Michigan. Compositions include: Songs: Carol, 1981; Tears at the Happy Hour, 1983, both with William Bolcom. Recordings include: After The Ball: A Treasury of Turn-of-the-Century Popular Songs, 1974; Songs by Ira and George Gershwin, 1978; Blue Skies, 1985; Let's Do It: Bolcom and Morris Live at Aspen, 1989; Orchids in the Moonlight, with tenor Robert White, 1996; 19 albums recorded to date, including Songs of Rodgers and Hart, Jerome Kern and Leiber and Stoller. Publications: Contributor to the New Grove Dictionary of American Music. Honour: Grammy Nomination, After the Ball, 1975. Membership: Azazels, University of Michigan. Hobbies: Photography. Current Management: ICM Artists, 40 W 57th Street, New York, NY 10019, USA. Address: 3080 Whitmore Lake Road, Ann Arbor, MI 48105, USA.

MORRIS Richard Frances Maxwell, b. 11 September 1944, Sussex, England. Chief Executive. m. Marian Sperling, 9 April 1983, 2 daughters. Education: Eton College, Windsor; New College, Oxford; College of Law, London; Private Singing Lessons with Maureen Morelle, John Hauxvell, Kenneth Woollam. Career includes: Solicitor, Farrer & Co, 1967-71; Manager, Grindlay Brandts, 1971-75; General Manager, SG Warburg & Co, 1975-79; Finance Director, Joint Managing Director, Hodder & Stoughton, 1979-91; Trustee, Kent Opera, 1985-90; Chief Executive, Associated Board of the Royal Schools of Music, 1993-; Founder, Almaviva Opera, 1989-. Memberships: Incorporated Society of Musicians; Music Masters and Musicians Association. Hobbies: Singing; Golf; Visual Arts. Address: Holdfast House, Edenbridge, Kent TN8 6SJ, England.

MORRIS Robert (Daniel), b. 19 Oct 1943, Cheltenham, England. Composer; Music Theorist; Professor. m. Ellen Koskoff, 10 June 1979, 1 son, 2 daughters. Education: BM, with distinction, Eastman School of Music; MM 1966; DMA 1969; University of Michigan. Career: Instructor, University of Hawaii, 1968-69; Assistant Professor, 1969-75, Director, Yale Electronic Music Studio, 1973-78; Associate Professor, 1975-78; Chairman, Composition Department, 1974-78, Yale University; Associate Professor, 1977-80, Director, Electronic and Computer Music Studio, 1977-80, University of Pittsburgh; Associate Professor, 1980-85; Professor, 1986-, Eastman School of Music. Compositions: Continua for Orchestra, 1969; Thunders of Spring Over Distant Mountains, Electronic Music, 1973; In Different Voices for 5 Wind Ensembles, 1975-76; Plexus for Woodwinds, 1977; Passim, 1982; Echanges, piano and computer generated tape, 1983; Cuts, wind sensemble, 1984. Recordings: Phases for two-pianos and electronics; Motet On Doo-dah; Hamiltonian Cycle; Inter Alia; Karuna. Publications: Composition with Pitch-Classes: A Theory of Compositional Design, 1986. Contributions to: Reviews and Articles in Journal of Music Theory, Perspectives of New Music; Musical Quarterly; JAMS; In Theory Only. Hobbies: Study in Mathematics; Buddhist Scripture; South Indian Classical Music; Philosophy; Camping.

MORRIS Stephen, b. 1970, Bridlington, Yorkshire, England. Violinist. Education: Studied with Yfrah Neaman in London and with Manoug Parikian and Maurice Hasson at the Royal Academy of Music. Career: Leader of the RAM symphony orchestra 1988; Further study with Howard Davis; Leader of the Pegasus and Thames Chamber Orchestra; As soloist plays Bruch, Bach, Mendelssohn and Lalo; 2nd violin of the Duke String Quartet from 1985; Performances in the Wigmore Hall, Purcel; Room, Conway Hall and throughout Britain; Tours to Germany, Italy, Austria and the Baltic States; South Bank series 1991, with Mozart's early quartet's; Soundtrack from Ingmar Berman documentary and The Magic Lantern, Channel 4 1988; BBC Debut feature; Features for French television 1990-91, playing Mozart, Mendelssohn, Britten and Tippett; Brahms Clarinet Quintet for Dutch Radio with Janet Hilton; Live Music Now series with concerts for disadvantaged people; The Duke Quartet invites... at the Derngate, Northampton, 1991, with Duncan Prescott and Rohan O'Hara; Resident quartet of the Rydale Festival 1991; Residency at Trinity College, Oxford, tours of Scotland and Northern Ireland and concert at the Elizabeth Hall 1991. Recordings: Quartets by Tippett, Shostakovich and Britten 3rd for Factory Classics. Honours: Awards at the RAM include the John Waterhouse Prize; London Orchestral Society Prize; Poulet Award; Inter-collegiate Quartet Prize. Address: c/o Anglo-Swiss Management, Suite 35-37, Morley House, 320 Regent Street, London W1R 5AD, England.

MORRIS Victor, b. 14 July 1934, England. Education: Royal Manchester College of Music, 1951-55. Career: English National Opera, 1959-64; Chorus Master and Conductor, 1964-75; Head of Music Staff, Conductor, 1975-89; Head of Auditions, 1989-94; Artistic Director, Ronald Dowd National Summer School for Singers, Bathurst, NSW; Vocal Course Director at Brereton International Music Symposium; Visiting Repetiteur Tutor at Guildhall School of Music & Drama; Visiting Tutor for Singers & Repetiteurs at Welsh College of Music and Drama; Maintains coaching studios for Singers and Repetiteurs in London and in Sydney, Australia. Recordings: Clarinet and Piano Duo Repertoire with John Denman; Clarinet Concertos, directing from harpsichord, with John Denman and ENO Orchestra; Live Concert with Rita Hunter, now reissued on CD; Harpsichord and Spinet on the soundtrack for A Man For All Seasons; Various Excerpt Recordings. Honour: FRMCM. Hobbies: Animal Welfare; Environment Issues. Address: 45 Madrid Road, London SW13 9PQ, England.

MORRIS Wyn, b. 14 Feb 1929, Wales, Conductor; Musical Director. m. Ruth Marie McDowell, 1962, 1 son, 1 daughter. Education: Royal Academy of Music; Mozarteum, Salzburg, Austria. Career: Apprentice conductor, Yorkshire Symphony Orchestra, 1950-51; Musical Director, 17th Training Regiment, Royal Artillery Band, 1951-53; Founder & conductor, Welsh Symphony Orchestra, 1954-57; Koussevitsky Memorial Prize, Boston Symphony Orchestra, 1957; Observer, on invitation George Szell, Cleveland Symphony Orchestra, 1957-60; Conductor, Ohio Bell Chorus, Cleveland Orpheus Choir, Cleveland Chamber Orchestra, 1958-60; Choir of Royal National Eisteddfod, Wales, 1960-62; London Debut, Royal Festival Hall with Royal Philharmonic Orchestra, 1963; Conductor to Royal Choral Society, 1968-70, Huddersfield Choral Society, 1969-74; Ceremony of Investiture for Prince Charles as Prince of Wales, 1969, Royal Choral Society tour of USA, 1969; Chief Conductor, Musical Director, Symphonica of London, Current: Specialist, conducting works of Mahler. Recordings: Des Knaben Wunderhorn, with Janet Baker and Geraint Evans; Das klagende Lied; Symphonies 1, 2, 5, 8; No 10 in Deryck Cooke's final performing version. Honours: August Mann's Prize, 1950; Fellow, Royal Academy of Music, 1964; Mahler Memorial Medal, Bruckner & Mahler Society of America, 1968. Hobbies: Chess; Rugby; Football; Climbing; Cynghanedd; Telling Welsh Stories. Address: c/o Manygate Management, 1 Summerhouse Lane, Harmondsworth, Middlesex UB7 OAW, England.

MORRISON Bryce, b. 27 Nov 1938, Leeds, Yorkshire, England. Teacher; Pianist; Critic; Lecturer. Education: MA (Oxon); MA, Dalhousie; MMus, SMU; Music Scholar, Kings School, Canterbury, 1952; Studied with Ronald Smith, Kings School and at Guildhall School of Music and Drama. Career: Has interviewed many world class pianists including Horowitz, Rubinstein and Clifford Curzon; Musical Advisor to EMI for 2 disc album The Art of Eileen Joyce; Jury Member of many national and international piano competitions including the Naumberg in New York; Chairman, First Terence Judd International Award, 1982; His students have been international prize winners; Has lectured and given Master Classes in Australia, Poland, America, Great Britain, China and Japan; Television appearances in Great Britain and Australia; Extensive broadcasts for BBC, ABC and CBC; also in Poland, USA, and New Zealand; Professor, Royal Academy of Music. Publications: Published extensively in: The Times; The Times Literary Supplement; Observer; Gramophone and others; also in America and Australia; Major Contributor to Phaidon Book of The Piano; 2 BBC Talks published in John Lade's Building a Library; Short biography of Liszt and commenced study of the Cuban pianist Jorge Bolet; Written over 300 annotations for Decca, EMI, CBS, in England and America, including personal tributes to Solomon and Terence Judd. Honours: Held the Corina Frada Pick Chair of Advanced Piano Studies, Ravinia Festival, Chicago, 1988; Honorary ARAM, 1995. Address: Flat 19, 11 Hinde Street, London, W1M 5AQ, England.

MORTIER Gerard, b. 25 Nov 1943, Ghent, Belgium. Opera Director. Education: Student of Law, 1961-66, Journalism and Communications, 1966-67, University of Ghent. Career: Administrative Assistant, Festival de Flandre, 1968-72; Assistant Administrator, Oper de Stadt Frankfurt am Main, 1973-77; Director, Artistic Production, Hamburg Staatsoper, 1977-79; Technical Programme Consultant, Théâtre National de l'Opera de Paris, 1979-81; Director General, Opera National, Brussels, 1981-91; Director of the Salzburg Festival from 1992; Has commissioned operas from leading composers: Philippe Boesmans, La Passion de Gilles, Andre Laporte, Das Schloss, and Hans Zender, Stephen Climax; Associated with Director Peter Sellars at Brussels, premiere of The Death of Klinghoffer by John Adams, 1991; Salzburg, Messiaen's St François d'Assise, 1992. Address: c/o Festspielhaus, Salzburg, Austria.

MORYL Richard, b. 23 Feb 1929, Newark, NJ, USA. Composer; Conductor. Education: Studied at Montclair State College, New Jersey and Columbia University, MA 1959; Further study with Boris Blacher and Arthur Berger. Career: Teacher, 1960-72; Founder, New England Contemporary Music Ensemble, 1970; Director, Charles Ives Center for American Music, 1979. Compositions: Ballons for percussion, orchestra, radios and audience, 1971; Volumes for piano, organ and orchestra, 1971; Chroma, 1972; Loops for large orchestra with any instruments, 1974; Strobe for large orchestra with any instruments, 1974; The untuning of the Skies, 1981; The Pond, flute and chamber orchestra, 1984; Instrumental music including Rainbows, I and II, 1982-83 and The Golden Phoenix for string quartet and percussion, 1984; Vocal: Flourescents for 2 choruses, 2 percussion and organ, 1970; Illuminations for soprano, 43 choruses and chamber orchestra, 1970; De morte cantoris for soprano, mezzo and ensemble, 1973; Das Lied for soprano and ensemble, 1975; Stabat Mater, 1982; Come, Sweet Death, chorus and piano, 1983; Mixed media works including Passio avium, 1974; Atlantis, 1976; Visiones mortis, 1977; Music of the Spheres, 1977; An Island on the Moon, 1978; A Sunflower for Maggie, 1979; Music for tape, electronics. Address: ASCAP, ASCAP Building, One Lincoln Plaza, NY 10023, USA.

MOSCA Silvia, b. 1958, Italy. Singer, Soprano. Education: Studied in Naples. Debut: Mantua Teatro Sociale as the Trovatore Leonara. Career: Has sung at opera houses throughout Italy and appeared as Luisa Miller at the Metropolitan 1988; Leonora at Liège and Miami 1988-89; Sang Aida at Buenos Aires and the Savonlinna Festival, 1989; Elvira in Ernani at Rome and Venice, 1989-90. Address: c/o Teatro La Fenice, Campo S Fantin 1965, 30124, Venice, Italy.

MOSCATO Jacques, b. 1945, France. Conductor; Clarinettist. Debut: Municipal Orchestra as Clarinettist, 1955. Career: Director, Public conert, Switzerland, 1962; In charge, Music Department, International University, City of Paris from

1968; Director, Charleville Mezieres Conservatorium from 1969; Conductor, Concerts in West Germany, Belgium and France, 1971; Guest Conductor, Australian Broadcasting Commission, 1976, 1978; Conductor, Monte Carlo Symphony, the Salle Garnier of Monte Carlo, 1979-94; Guest Conductor, Istanbul Symphonic Orchestra, Symphony Orchestra, Pays Loire, France, 1984, 1989. Composition: Music for film, Symphonic Interdite, 1983; A Music Ballet, Resonances, 1989. Recordings: Albums, Symphony no 2, plus eleven Viennese Dances (Beethoven), 1977, Les Musiciens Monegasquesm, 1981. Honours: First prize of Versailles, 1967; Named a Director Academie de Musique, Prince Rainier III, Monaco, 1979. Memberships: International Jury, Enna Piano Competition, Sicily, 1985, Stresa, Italy, 1986; Scriptwriter, L'Effet Vicaldi (translated by Anthony Burgess), 1985; L'Ode a La Vie (Beethoven's Life), 1992. Address: Academie de Musique, Prince Rainier III de Monaco, 1 Boulevard Albert 1er, Monaco.

MOSER Edda, b. 27 Oct 1938, Berlin, Germany. Singer (Soprano). Education: Studied at the Berlin Conservatory with Hermann Weissenborn and Gerty Konig. Debut: Berlin Stadtische Oper 1962, in Madama Butterfly. Career: Sang at Hagen and Bielefeld from 1964; Began musical association with Hans Werner Henze at Brunswick in 1967 and sang in the premiere of Das Floss der Medusa, Vienna 1971; 1968 sang Wellgunde in Das Rheingold at the Salzburg Festival and at the Metropolitan; Later New York appearances as Mozart's Donna Anna, Queen of Night and Constanze, Puccini's Musetta and Liu and Handel's Armida, Rinaldo, 1984; Guest appearances in Russia, Berlin, Vienna, Salzburg, Aspasia in Mozart's Mitridate at Hamburg (Lucia 1974) and South America; Modern repertory includes music by Nono, Fortner, Zimmermann and Stravinsky, (The Nightingale); Sang Strauss's Ariadne at Rio de Janeiro, 1988; Marie in Wozzeck at the Teatro Valli, Reggio Emilia, 1989. Recordings: Der Ring des Nibelungen, Orfeo ed Euridice, Rappresentazione di Anima e di Corpo, Das Floss der Medusa, Deutsche Grammophon; Don Giovanni, also filmed; Idomeneo, Die Zauberflöte, Das Paradies und die Peri, Leonore, Beethoven; Abu Hassan, Der häusliche Krieg by Schubert, Genoveva by Schumann, Die Abreise, (Electrola). Address: Ingpen and Williams Ltd, 26 Wadham Road, London SW15 2LR, England.

MOSER Thomas, b. 27 May 1945, Richmond, Virginia, USA. Singer, Tenor. Education: Richmond Professional Institute; Curtis Institute Philadelphia; California with Martial Singher, Gerard Souzay and Lotte Lehmann. Career: After success at the 1974 Metropolitan Auditions sang in Graz from 1975; Munich Opera, 1976, as Mozart's Belmonte; Vienna State Opera from 1977, as Mozart's Tamino, Ottavio, Titus and Idomeneo, Strauss's Flamand and Henry; Achilles in Iphigénie en Aulide, conducted by Charles Mackerras; New York City Opera 1979, as Titus; Salzburg Festival 1983, in La Finta Semplice; La Scala Milan, 1985, as Tamino; Rome Opera, 1986, as Achilles; Paris Opéra Comique, 1987 as Mozart's Idomeneo and Tito; Sang the Tenor in the premiere of Berio's Un Re in Ascolto, Salzburg, 1984; Vienna Staatsoper, 1987, as Achilles in Iphigénie en Aulide, Schubert's Fierabras at the Theater an der Wien, 1988; Sang Florestan in Fidelio at La Scala and Salzburg, 1990; New production of Lucio Silla at Vienna, 1991, the Emperor in Die Frau ohne Schatten at Geneva, 1992; Season 1992-93, with Florestan at Zurich and the Emporor at Salzburg; Sang title role in Pfitzner's Palestrina at Covent Garden, 1997; As concert singer in Beethoven's Choral Symphony and Missa Solemnis, Britten's War Requiem, the Bach Passions, Schmidt's Das Buch mit Sieben Siegeln and Mozart's Requiem; Conductors include Giulini, Colin Davis, Mehta, Leinsdorf, Leopold Hager and Horst Stein. Recordings: Roles in Stiffelio, Verdi; Mozart and Salieri, Rimsky-Korsakov; Zaide; La Finta Giardiniera and Don Giovanni, Mozart; Die Freunde von Salamanka, Schubert; Genoveva, Schumann; Oedipus Rex, Stravinsky; Handel's Utrecht Te Deum and Dvorak's Requiem. Address: c/o Lies Askonas Ltd, 6 Henrietta Street, London WC2, England.

MOSES Don V, b. 21 Dec 1936, Kansas, USA. Conductor. m. Ann Swedish, 28 Jan 1973, 1 son, 1 daughter. Education: BME, Fort Hays, Kansas State College, 1959; MM, 1961, DMA, 1968, Indiana University. Career: Associate Professor of Music, Indiana University, 1964-73; Professor, Music, 1986-88, Director, School of Music, 1988-, University of Illinois; Music Director of Classical Music Seminar, Eisenstadt, Austria, 1976-. Recordings: Liebeslieder Waltzes, Brahms; Harmoniemesse, Haydn; Mass in B flat, Hummel. Publications: Face to Face With An Orchestra, 1984; The Complete Conductor, 1995. Contributions to: American Choral Directors Hournal. Honours: Guest, International Choral Festival, New York City, 1972; Conductor of 30 all-state Festivals; Guest Conductor, Györ Philharmonic Orchestra, Hungary, 1983; Medal of Honour, State of Burgenland Austria, 1994. Memberships: American Choral Directors Association; American Choral Foundation; National Association of Music Executives of State Universities. Hobbies: Golf. Address: 1914 Byrnebruk Road, Champaign, IL 61820, USA.

MOSES Geoffrey, b. 24 Sept 1952, Abercynon, Wales. Singer, (Bass). Education: Emmanuelle College, Cambridge; Guildhall School of Music and with Otakar Kraus and Peter Harrison. Debut: Welsh National Opera, 1977, as Basilio in Il Barbiere di Siviglia; Other roles include Seneca, L'Incoronazione di Poppea, Sarastro and Padre Guardiano in La Forza del Destino; Covent Garden debut 1981, in Les Contes d'Hoffmann; Returned in a new production of Otello; Glyndebourne Festival debut 1984; Sang Fiesco in Simon Boccanegra 1986; Brussels Opera in Hoffmann and Boccanegra; Welsh National Opera in Peter Stein's production of Falstaff; Season 1990-91, with WNO in Figaro, Carmen and Falstaff, also on tour to Japan; Concert engagements include: La Damnation de Faust in Frankfurt and the Choral Symphony with the Scottish National Orchestra; Sang in Strauss's Die Liebe der Danae for BBC Radio 3, conducted by Charles Mackerras. Recordings: Rigoletto. Address: c/o Harrison Parrott Ltd, 12 Penzance Place, London W11 4PA, England.

MOSES Leonard, b. 6 Jan 1932, New York City, NY, USA. Composer. m. Alice Irma Prather, 11 April 1954, 1 son, 1 daughter. Education: Studied with: 3rd Generation Master-Student of Brahms; 2nd Generation Master-Student of Glazunov; Howard Hanson and Louis Menini, Eastman School of Music; Thad Jones, Catholic University of America; Musical: BMUs, BMusEd, 1955; MMus, 1962; Doctoral Candidate, 1964. debut: Composer, Philadelphia, 1943. Career: Washington DC, Good Music Station, a RKO Radio Station, 1987.. Compositions: Ode to Judith Ivie; In Flanders Fields, 1987; Major Commissions: Under the Auspices of Maryland, State Council of Arts: When I was One and Twenty, and 11 other Vocal Works, 1984; American Sonatina for Piano and Heenay Mahtov Variations for Violin and Piano, 1985; Symphonic Brass Quintet, 1986; Goodbye My Fancy, A Dance Work with Chamber Orchestra, 1987; Other Major Commissions: Sonata For Flute and Harp; Trio in D for Oboe, Flute and Piano, 1986; The Oratorio, Sermon On the Mount for Soloists, Chorus and Orchestra, 1987; String Quartet No 1, The Folk, 1988; Three Songs for Soprano, Oboe and Piano, 1988; Ballet: Flatland, 1989. Publications: Ode to Judith Ivie, 1988; In Flanders Fields, 1988. Address: 16 Southgate Avenue, Annapolis, MD 21401, USA.

MOSHINSKY Elijah, b. 8 Jan 1946, Shanghai, China. Opera Producer. m. Ruth Dyttman, 1970, 2 sons. Education: BA, Melbourne University, Australia; St Anthony's College, Oxford University, UK. Career: Original Productions at Covent Garden of: Peter Grimes, 1975; Lohengrin, 1977; The Rake's Progress, 1979; Macbeth, 1981; Samson and Delilah, 1981; Other opera productions include: Wozzeck, 1976; A Midsummer Night's Dream, 1978; Boris Godonuv, 1980; Un Ballo in Maschera, Metropolitan Opera, New York, 1980; Il Trovatore, Australian Opera, 1983; For English National Opera, Le Grand Macabre, 1982; Mastersingers of Nuremberg, 1984; Bartered Bride, 1985; La Bohème, 1988 for Scottish Opera; For Royal Opera: Tannhäuser, 1984; Samson, 1985; Otello, 1986, Die Entführung aus dem Serail, 1987; Productions at National Theatre; Troilus and Cressida, 1976; Productions on the West End; Television film of Michael Tippett's The Midsummer Marriage, 1988; Produced La Forza del Destino for Scottish Opera, 1990; Attila at Covent Garden; Lohengrin revival by Royal Opera 1997 and taken to New York Met, season, 1998. Contributions to: Opera Magazine, 1992, Verdi: A Pox on Post-Modernism. Hobbies: Painting; Conservation. Address: 28 Kidbrooke Grove, London, SE3 OLG, England.

MOSLEY George, b. 1960, England. Singer (Baritone). Education: Studied with Laura Sarti at the Guildhall School, at the Academia Chigiana in Siena, the Munich Hochschule für Musik and the National Opera Studio, London. Career: Performed in many operas including: Dandini in La Cenerentola, 1987, and Onegin in Tchaikovsky's Eugene Onegin, 1989, both for Opera 80; Orlofsky in Strauss's Die Fledermaus, Scottish Opera, 1990; Marco in Puccini's Gianni Schicchi, 1990, The Sportsman in Delius's Fennimore and Gerda, 1990 and the Duke of Albany in Reimann's Lear, 1991, all for the English National Opera; Patroclus in King Priam, Opera North, 1991; Malatesta in Don Pasquale and Guglielmo in Così fan tutte, 1991 and Dandini in La Cenerentola in 1992, all for Teatro Verdi, Pisa, Italy; Schaunard in La Bohème for Scottish opera, 1993; Ottone in Incoronazione di Poppea and Count in Le nozze di Figaro, both for Teatro Verdi, Pisa, Italy, 1993; Father in Baa Baa Black Sheep for Opera North and BBC Television, 1993; Count in Le nozze di Figaro for Concert Hall, Athens, 1993; Papageno in the Magic Flute for Scottish Opera, 1994; Sang Berardo in Riccardo Primo at the 1996 Handel Festival at Göttingen. Recordings include: Schumann's Dichterliebe and Liederkreis Op 39; Aeneas in Dido and Aeneas conducted by John Eliot Gardiner. Honours include: Schubert Prize and French Song Prize, and First Prize, International Mozart Competition, Salzburg, 1998. Current Management: Robert Gilder and Company, London. Address: Enterprise House, 59/65 Upper Ground, London SE1 9PQ, England.

MOSTAD Jon, b. 21 Apr 1942, Oslo, Norway. Composer. m. Ase S Folleras, 1 son, 2 daughters. Education: MDivinity; Intermediate Grade of Music, University of Oslo, 1969; Diploma in Composition, Music Academy of Oslo, 1974. Compositions include: I Forassol; Den Sommeren; Sanger I den siste Tid for Mixed Chorus and Organ; Towards Balance for Symphony Orchestra, 1977-78; Concerto for Violoncello and Orchestra, 1988-90; Choral, orchestral, instrumental, piano, organ, electroacoustical and chamber works; Works broadcast by Norwegian, Swedish, Yugoslavian and British radio and on Norwegian TV; Performances by the symphony orchestras of Oslo, Bergen and Trondheim. Recordings: Song for Symphony Orchestra; Towards Balance; The Light Shines in the Darkness for Orchestra; House for Orchestra; Concerto for Violoncello and Orchestra. Contributions to: Und Chopin ist Auch Dabei, Ballade, 1982. Honours: Norwegian Broadcasting Competition Prize for Compositions for Childrens and Youth Choirs, 1972; 3rd Prize, Competition for Male Chorus Composers, 1981. Memberships: Norwegian Composers Association; Chairman, Fredrikstad Section, National Committee, Ny Musikk, 1976-80; Norwegian Branch of ISCM. Hobbies: Forest and Mountain Walking; Skiing; Gardening. Address: Skovbolev 3, N-1605 Fredrikstad, Norway.

MOSUC Elena, b. 18 Jan 1964, Iasi, Rumania. Singer (Soprano). Education: Studied at the George Enescu Conservatory, Bucharest. Debut: Tasi Opera 1990, as Mozart's Queen of Night. Career: Further appearances as Lucia di Lammermoor, Gilda and Violetta; Concerts with the Moldau Philharmonic and in Mozart masses at Bucharest; Theater am Gärtnerplatz Munich, Vienna Staatsoper and Deutsche am Rhein 1990, as the Queen of Night; Zurich Opera from 1991, as Lucia and Donna Anna. Address: Zurich Opera, Falkenstrasse 1, CH-8008 Zurich, Switzerland.

MOTHERWAY Fiona, b. 1967, Western Australia. Singer (Soprano). Education: Studied in Australia and at the Royal Academy of Music (graduated 1994). Career: Performances with British Youth Opera and elsewhere as Fiordiligi; Cambridge Handel Opera Group as Melissa in Amadigi di Gaula; other Handel roles include Semele, Atalanta (Xerxes), Cleopatra and Ginevra (Ariodante); Also sings Mozart's Countess, Susanna and Pamina, Musetta, Gilda and Purcell's Dido; Season 1996-97 with Olympia in Contes d'Hoffman for Stowe Opera and Naiade in Ariadne for Castleward Opera; Concerts include Strauss Four Last Songs, Haydn's Creation and Nelson Mass, Messiah, Bach B minor Mass, Mozart's C minor Mass and Requiem; Mahler's 4th Symphony under Colin Davis; Concert tour of Australia, 1996-97. Address: C&M Craig Services Ltd, 3 Kersley Street, London SW11 4PR, England.

MOTLIK Jaroslav, b. 20 Apr 1926, Chuderín. Violist. m. Milada Zídkova, 2 sons. Education: Conservatory, 1942-48; Academy of Fine Arts, 1948-52; Study at Sergiu Celibidache, 1967-73. Debut: Czech Chamber Orchestra, Professor Vaclav Talich, 1945. Career: Czech Chamber Orchestra, 1945-58; Czech Philharmonic Orchestra, principal viola, 1948-90; Academy of Fine Arts, Prague, 1973-, Professor, 1991. Recordings: Sonatas by Brahms op 120, Martinu, Debussy, Vycpálek Suite with viola solo, Stamic, Stravinsky; Chamber music by Bach, Beethoven, Mozart, Rejcha; Mozart, Sinfonia Concertante; Martinu, Rhapsody Concerto. Membership: Intergram. Address: Luzická 30, 12000 Prague 2, Czech Republic.

MOTT Louise, b. Barnet, Hertfordshire, England. Singer (Mezzo-soprano). Graduated 1996, Royal College of Music Opera Department. Career: Opera roles include Handel's Xerxes, Juno & Ino (Semele) and Medarse in Siroe, for the London Handel Society at the RCM; Orlofsky, Ragonde (Le Comte Ory), Rosina, Mozart's Sesto, and Isabella in L'Italiana in Algeri; Concerts include Mozart's Requiem at the Albert Hall, Messiah at St John's Smith Square, Elgar's Dream of Gerontius and The Music Makers, Dvorák Requiem, Elijah, and the Stabat Maters of Haydn and Rossini; Wigmore Hall debut 1996, with the Young Songmakers' Almanac series; Season 1997 with Mozart's Requiem at Bath Abbey, Handel's Ariodante at the Covent Garden Festival and Marlinchen in the premiere of Roderick Watson's The Juniper Tree, at Munich and the Almeida Theatre, London. Honours include: Lies Askonas Singing Prize, Peter Pears Exhibition and Keith Falkner Prize for Bach and Handel, at the RCM.

MOTUZAS Alfonsas, b. 22 Nov 1955, Siauliai, Lithuania. Tutor. m. Genovaite Motuziene, 8 Dec 1980, 1 son, 1 daughter. Education: Music Academy. Career: International Conference. Compositions: 3 Audio Recordings. Publications: The Stations of Calvary of Lowlands; Religious Songs for the Dead, 1993; The Instruments and National Music of Minor Lithuania, 1994; National Musical Instruments - Their Place in Religious Songs and Sacred Music of the Nation. Membership: Lithuanian Catholic Academy of Science. Hobby: Travelling. Address: Mogiliovo 6-48, 5822 Klaipeda, Lithuania.

MOULDS Christopher, b. 1967, Halifax, England. Conductor; Keyboard Player. Education: Studied at City University, the Guildhall School and Royal College of Music. Career: Conducted Figaro and The Rake's Progress at the RCM; Member of Music Staff, English National Opera, 1991-95, working with productions of Billy Rudd, Carmen, Wozzeck, Orfeo, Lohengrin and Street Scene; Harpischord continuo for ENO's Xerxes and Ariodante; Chorus Master at Glyndebourne Festival from 1995, conducting Figaro 1997; Further engagements with British Youth Opera, Opera Company Tunbridge Wells (Barber and Figaro), European Community Youth Orchestra and London Sinfonietta (as orchestral keyboard player); Conducted The Magic Flute for ENO, 1996, 1997-98. Address: Flat 549, Manhattan Buildings, Fairfield Road, London E3 2UL, England.

MOULSON John, b. 25 July 1928, Kansas City, Missouri, USA. Singer, (Tenor). Education: Studied in Atlanta. Debut: Berlin Komische Oper 1961 as Cavaradossi. Career: Sang at the Komische Oper until 1982 as Alfredo, Traviata, Hoffmann, the Steersman in Fliegende Holländer, 1969-72, as Lensky, Gabriele Adorno and Oedipus Rex; Sang at Boston 1988, in the US premiere of Dead Souls by Shchedrin; Further guest engagements in Germany, England, Italy, Poland, Russia and the USA.

MOUND Vernon, b. 1954, England. Opera Director. Education: Studied at London University. Career: Has worked with the Royal Opera, the Scottish Ballet, the Swan Theatre, Opera North and the Black Theatre of Prague as Stage Manager; Administrator; Company Manager; Assistant Director; Staff producer at Opera North 1983-88, assisting on new productions and directing revivals; Workshops for children and adults, including community piece Quest of the Hidden Moon; Directed small-scale touring version of Carmen; The Gondoliers for New Sadler's Wells Opera, 1988; Directed the Opera Informal and the Sondheim Workshop at the Royal College of Music, 1989-91; Directed Handel's Ariodante for the Birmingham Conservatoire, 1990 and The Marriage Contract and Le Pauvre Matelot for Morley Opera; Productions of Amahl and the Night Visitors at the Barbican Centre and Alice, the Musical at St Martin-in-the-Fields; La Finta Giardiniera for the Opera Hogskolan in Stockholm, Mar 1991, and Pedrotti's Tutti in Maschera at the Britten Theatre; La Fille du Régiment, 1992; Associate Director Carmen Jones at The Old Vic. Address: c/o Norman McCann International Artists Ltd, The Coach House, 56 Lawrie Park Gardens, London SE26 6XJ, England.

MOUNTAIN Peter, b. 3 Oct 1923, Shipley, Yorkshire, England. Violinist. 1 son. 2 daughters. Education: Royal Academy of Music, London. Debut: Wigmore Hall, London, 1942. Career: Leader, Soloist, Symphony Orchestra, Tours of Europe and Far East; Member, Philharmonia Orchestra; Leader, Royal Liverpool Philharmonic Orchestra, 1955-66; Concertmaster, BBC Training Orchestra, 1968-75; Head of Strings, Royal Scottish Academy of Music and Drama, 1975-90; Soloist, Guest Leader, Many British Orchestras; Coach, Youth Orchestras. Honours: Fellow, Royal Academy of Music, London, 1963; Adjudicator and Examiner; Fellow, Royal Scottish Academy of Music and Drama, 1988; Honorary LLD, University of Bradford, 1995. Memberships: Committee, Scottish Arts Council; Chairman, Scottish Society of Composers. Address: 93 Park Road, Bingley, West Yorkshire BD16 4BY, England.

MOUTSOPLOULOS Evanghelos A. b. 25 January 1930, Athens, Greece. University Professor; Member of Academy of Athens. m. Michèle Montaigne. Education: MA, University of Athens; State PhD, University of Paris, France; Composition, Athens and Paris. Compositions: Suites for Orchestra; Chamber Music; Lieder. Publications: Over 50 books and over 450 articles including: La Musique dans l'Oeuvre de Platon, 1959; Rhythms and Dances of Greeks and Bulgarians, 1959; Aesthetic Categories: An Introduction to the Axiology of the Aesthetic Object, 1970; Platon, Dictionnaire de la Musique, Volume II, 1970; La Philosophie de la Musique dans la Dramaturgie Antique: Formation et Structure, 1975; The Aesthetics of J Brahms: An Introduction to the Philosophy of Music, 2 vols, 1986; Poiésis et Techné. Idées pour une Philosophie de l'art, 3 vols, 1994. Contributions to: Revue Philosophique; Diotima; Les Etudes Philosophiques; Others. Memberships: Société Française de Musicologie; Union of Greek Composers. Address: 40 Hypsilantou Street, Athens 11521, Greece.

MOWES Thomas, b. 7 Sep 1951, Halle, Germany. Baritone. Education: Studied at the Weimat Hochschule. Career: Sang as Bass-Baritone at the Magdeburg Opera from 1977, and Baritone roles at Halle from 1988, Leipzig and Dresden from 1990; Roles have included Busoni's Doktor Faust, Nekrotzar in Le Grand Macabre and Orestes in Elektra; Guest engagements as Basle as Verdi's Posa, and at Frankfurt as Faninal in Der Rosenkavalier; Other roles include Handel's Polyphemus, Don Alfonso, Ottokar in Der Freischütz, Luna, Nabucco, Rigoletto, Wolfram and Escamillo; Many concert appearances. Address: Frankfurt Opera, Frankfurt am Main, Germany.

MOXON BROWNE Kicki, b. 19 Dec 1945, Katrineholm, Sweden. Piano Teacher; Performer. m. Robert Moxon Browne, 26 June 1968, 1 son, 1 daughter. Education: Uppsala University; Piano Pedagogy, Stockholms Borgarskola; Studies with Gottfrid Boon, Edith Vogel, Kenneth van Barthold; LRAM; LGSM Career: Piano Teacher, Hampstead School and several others in the English State Comprehensive System, 1971-91; Private Practice, London, 1991-; Accompanist, Solo Performer. Contributions to: Times Literary Supplement. Memberships: ISM; Musicians Union. Hobbies: Film; Theatre. Address: 37 Mowbray Road, London NW6 7QS, England.

MOYER Frederick, b. 1957. Pianist. Debut: New York, 1982. Education: Curtis Institute of Music; Bmus, Indiana University. Career: Performed in nearly all the states of USA; Frequent tours of Europe, Asia and South America; Solo Appearances with Orchestras include: Philadelphia, Houston, Milwaukee, Boston, Cleveland, Baltimore, Minnesota, St Louis, Dallas, Indianapolis, Pittsburgh, Utrecht, London, Rio di Janeiro, Montevideo, Singapore, Hong Kong, Tokyo and the major orchestras of Australia; Participant of numerous Music Festivals. Recordings: 14 commercial recordings for major labels. Address: c/o Betsy M Green Associates, Artists Management, 36 Hampshire Road, Wayland, MA 01778, USA.

MOYLAN William (David), b. 23 Apr 1956, Virginia, Minnesota, USA. Professor; Composer; Recording Producer. m. Vicki Lee Peterlin, 18 Dec 1976. Education: BMus, Composition, Peabody Conservatory, Johns Hopkins University, 1979; MMus, Composition, University of Toronto, Canada, 1980; Doctor of Arts in Theory and Composition, Ball State University, USA, 1983. Career: Professor, Sound Recording Technology, College of Fine Arts, University of Massachusetts, Lowell. Compositions: Published works include: On Time - On Age, for soprano, flute, trumpet, piano and 4-channel tape, 1978; Concerto for Bass Trombone and Orchestra, 1979; Brass Quintet, for brass quintet and tape, 1979; Two Movements for String Orchestra, 1980; Duo for Flute and Tape, 1980; Seven Soliloquies, for trumpet, 1981; Metamorphic Variations, for clarinet, 1983; The Now, for high voice, horn and piano; Trio for Trombones, for alto, tenor and bass trombones, 1984; Three Interplays for Trumpet Duo, 1984; Wind Quintet No 2, 1985; Stilled Moments for solo violin, 1988; Evocations for Guitar, 1988; La Liberté, for soprano and piano, 1989; Eroica, a Piano Sonata, 1989; Two Suspended Images, for wind controller, 1990; Ask Your Mama, 1990; The Dream Deferred, for 2-channel tape, 1990; Mother Earth and Her Whales, 1993; The Stolen Child, 1995; For a Sleeping Child, 1996. Recording: For a Sleeping Child, 1997. Publication: The Art of Recording: The Creative Resources of Music Production and Audio, 1992. Memberships: AES; BMI; CMS; NARAS; SPARS. Address: College of Fine Arts, University of Massachusetts at Lowell, Lowell, MA 01854, USA.

MOYLE Richard (Michael), b. 23 Aug 1944, Paeroa, New Zealand. Ethnomusicologist. m. Linden Averil Evelyn Duncan, 1 s, 2 d. Education: Licentiate, Trinity College, London, 1965; MA, 1967; PhD, 1971, University of Auckland. Career: Visiting Lecturer in Anthropology, Indiana University, USA, 1971-72; Assistant Professor in Music, University of Hawaii, 1972-73; Research Fellow, Ethnomusicology, 1974-77, Research Grantee, 1977-82, Australian Institute of Aboriginal Studies; Senior Research Fellow, Faculty of Arts, University of Auckland, New Zealand, 1983-86; Lecturer then Senior Lecturer in Ethnomusicology and Director of Archive of Maori and Pacific Music, University of Auckland, 1986-. Recordings: The Music of Samoa; Traditional Music of Tonga; Compiler, Tonga Today. Publications: Fagogo: Fables from Samoa, 1979; Songs of the Pintupi, 1981; Alyawarra Music, 1985; Tongan Music, 1987; Traditional Samoan Music, 1988; Sounds of Oceania, 1989; Polynesian Song and Dance, 1991. Contributions to: Numerous professional journals. Address: Department of Anthropology, University of Auckland, Private Bag, Auckland, New Zealand.

MOYSE Louis (Joseph), b. 14 Aug 1912, Scheveningen, Netherlands. Musician; Professor. m. 1. 2 sons, 2 daughters, 1. Janet White, 27 July 1974. Education: Flute with Philippe Gaubert and Marcel Moyse, Piano with Joseph Benvenuti and Isidore Philipp, Paris Conservatory of Music. Career: Professor of flute, Paris Conservatory; Flautist, French Radiodiffusion and Concerts Lamoureux; Emigrated to USA, 1949; Co-Founder, Marlboro School of Music Festival, USA; Co-Founder, Brattleboro Music Center, Vermont; Professor of Flute, Piano and Chamber Music, Marlboro College, Vermont and University of Toronto, Canada; Guest Professor, University of Boston; Master classes, seminars, concerts, USA, Canada and Overseas. Compositions: Major works include: Ballad of Vermont for narrator, soloists, chorus and orchestra; Divertimento for 14 instruments; Woodwind Quintet; Quintet for 5 flutes; Sonata for flute and piano; 3 concerti grossi for various instruments and orchestras; Suite in old style for flute ensemble; 4 pieces for 3 flutes and piano; Suite for 2 flutes, alto and bass flute and piano; Pieces for flute alone; Duets, trios; Many transcriptions for young flautists. Recordings: International Prize with Moyse Trio, Paris, 1936. Publications: Colloborating with Mrs Joan Bauman on book about his father Marcel Moyse. Contributions to: Various articles in Flute Magazines. Honours: 1st Prize, Paris Conservatory of Music, 1932. Memberships: Moyse Trio, for many years. Hobbies: Drawing. Address: RR 2, Box 2446, Westport, NY 12993, USA.

MOYSEOWICZ Gabriela (Maria), b. 4 May 1944, Lwow, Poland. Composer; Pianist; Choir Director. Education: Lyceum of Music, Cracow, Poland, 1962; Academies of Music, Cracow and Katowice, Poland; MA, 1967. Debut: Playing own piano concerto, Cracow, 1957. Career: Piano recitals; Public performances of own compositions throughout Poland; Radio appearances, discussions and interviews. Compositions include: Media vita, for 2 violins, cello, soprano and bass recitativ; 9 Moments Musicaux, for piano and strings; Rhapsody No 1 for piano; Marche Funebre, for cello and piano; Deux Caprices, for violin solo; Ave Maria, for 2 mixed choirs a capella; Sonata No 1, for cello and piano; Two Canzonas, for viola de gamba solo; Piano Sonata numbers 3 to 8 including the 6th Noumenon and 8th Concatenatio; Sonata Polska, for violin and piano; Alleuja for choir; Credo for 4 voice choir, 1991; Trio for piano, violin and violoncello, 1992, 1993; Discours, with Miss H Steingroever, for flute and piano, 1993; Passacaglia for violin, 1994; Shadow symphony for large orchestra; Churchmusic: Media Vita, Dies irae, Ave Maria, Pater noster, Kyrie, Alleluja, Amen Credo. Recordings: Piano recitals and chamber music on German broadcasting. Publications: Diploma: Exemplification of the own aesthetic - based on the 2nd piano concerto, 1967; Eva Weissweiler: omponistinnen aus 500 Jahren, 1981; Martella Gutiérrez-Danhoff: Ein Portrait der Komp G Moyseowicz, 1983-84; Ein Portraitder Komp G Moyswowicz by Bettina Brand, 1988. Honours: 2 years Scholarship and Rector Prize, Poland. Membership: GEMA. Current Management: Composer, Pianist, Church-Musician (Organ). Address: Schlossstrasse 50, D-14059 Berlin 19, Germany.

MOZES Robert, b. 1950, Romania. Violist. Education: Studied at the Cluj Academy of Music and the Tel Aviv Rubin Music Academy. Career: Member of and solo appearances with the Israel Philharmonic; Chamber music concerts in Israel, the USA, Canada and Japan; Co-Founder, Jerusalem String Trio, 1977, performing in Israel and in Europe from 1981; Repertoire includes string trios by Beethoven, Dohnányi, Mozart, Reger, Schubert and Tanyev; Piano Quartets by Beethoven, Brahms, Dvorak, Mozart and Schumann; Concerts with Radu Lupu and Daniel Adni. Recordings: Albums for Meridian, Channel Classics Studio, Holland and CDI, Israel. Address: c/o Anglo-Swiss Ltd, Suites 35-37, Morley House, 320 Regent Street, London W1R 5AD, England.

MOZETICH Marjan, b. 7 Jan 1948, Gorizia, Italy. Composer. Education: Began piano training at age 9; Studied piano and theory with Reginald Bedford; Studied with John Weinzweig and Lothar Klein; ARCT Piano Performance Diploma, 1971; BMus, University of Toronto, 1972; Further studies with Luciano Berio in Rome and Franco Donatoni in Siena. Career: Teacher of composition, Queen's University, Kingston, Ontario, 1991-. Compositions: Sonata for flute and harp; Songs of Nymphs for harp; Procession, El Dorado, Dance of the Blind and Fantasia, all recorded. Honours: String quartet Changes recognised as outstanding work at Student Composers Symposium, Montreal, 1971; Wind quintet awarded 2nd Prize at International Gaudeamus Composers Competition, Amsterdam, 1976; String orchestra piece, Nocturne, received 1st Prize in CAPAC - Sir Ernest Macmillan Award, 1977; Viola solo work Disturbances chosen by CBC Radio to represent Canada at 25th Anniversary of International Rostrum of Composers, Paris 1978. Hobbies: Avid reader; Gardener. Address: 654 North Shore Road, Howe Island, Ontario K7G 2V6, Canada.

MOZHAYEV Fyodor, b. 1958, Voroshilovgrad, Ukraine. Singer (Baritone). Education: Studied at the Kharkov Conservatoire. Career: Sang first at the Moldavian State Opera and at the Perm Opera 1982-93; Member of the Bolshoi Opera from 1994, with Mozart's Figaro, 1995; Guest engagements with the Kirov Opera, Kharkov Opera and in Kiev; Has also sung widely in France and in Poland, Budapest and Malta; Other roles include Verdi's Iago, Renato, Luna and Germont, Scarpia, Ruprecht in The Fiery Angel, Lionel in The Maid of Orleans, Escamillo and Rubinstein's Demon. Honours include: Prizewinner at 1979 Riga Song Competition. Address: Sonata Ltd, 11 North Park Street, Glasgow G20 7AA, Scotland.

MRACEK Jaroslav (John Stephen), b. 5 June 1928, Montreal, Canada. Professor of Music, Musicology, Emeritus, 1991 of San Diego State University. m. 5 Aug 1963, 2 sons. Education: Assoc Dip, Royal Conservatory of Music, Toronto, 1948; BMus, University of Toronto, 1951; MA 1962, PhD 1965, Indiana University, studied with Willi Apel, John R White, Paul Nettl, Walter Kaufmann, Bernard Heiden, Marie Zorn, harpsichord; Studied piano with Alberto Guerrero, Toronto. Career: Taught instrumental, vocal music English and History at Lisgar Collegiate Institute, Ottawa, Canada, 1953-59; Lecturer: University of Illinois, Urbana 1964-65; Assistant, Associate, Full Professor, San Diego State University, 1965-91; General Director, the Smetana Centennial, International Conference and Festival of Czechoslovak Music, San Diego State University, 1987;

Conducted at Canadian Music Festival, San Diego State University, 1987. Publications: Seventeenth-Century Instrumental Dance Music, 1976; 5 articles, New Grove Dictionary of Music & Musicians, 1980; Papers published in proceedings: International Musicological Congress-Bach, Handel, Schütz-Stuttgart, 1985; Musica Antiqua Congress, Bydgoszcz, 1985; Rudolf Firkusny at 75, Musical America, 1987; Smetana Centennial, Musical America, 1985. Honours: Rudolf Firkusny n Medal, 1992. Address: 5307 W Falls View Dr, San Diego, CA 92115, USA.

MUCZYNSKI Robert, b. 19 Mar 1929, Chicago, IL, USA. Composer; Professor of Music. Education: BM, 1950, MM, 1952, DePaul University, Chicago; Academy of Music, Nice, France, 1961. Career: Visiting Lecturer, DePaul University, Chicago, summers 1954-56; Head of Piano Department, Loras College, Dubuque, Iowa, 1956-58; Visiting Lecturer, Roosevelt University, Chicago, 1964-65; Professor, Head of Composition, University of Arizona, Tucson, 1965-87; Professor Emeritus, 1988-. Compositions: Over 40 published works including: Concerto for Piano and Orchestra; First Symphony; Suite for Orchestra; Concerto for Alto Saxophone and chamber Orchestra; 3 Piano Sonatas; 3 piano trios; String trio; Sonatas for Cello, for Alto Saxophone, for Flute and Piano; Time pieces, for clarinet, piano; Scores for 9 documentary films; Commission: Dream Cycle, for solo piano, 1983; Quintet for Winds, 1985; Third Piano Trio, 1986-87; Moments, for flute and piano; Desperate Measures (Paginini Variations for piano). Recordings: In release: Compact Disc recordings of Concerto No 1 for Piano & Orchestra; A Serenade for Summer; The Three Piano Trios; Trio for Violin, Viola, Cello; Alto Saxophone Concerto; Sonata for Flute and Piano; Second Piano Concerto. Hobbies: Films; Reading; Writing; Dogs. Address: 2760 N Wentworth, Tucson, AZ 85749, USA.

MUFF Alfred, b. 31 May 1949, Lucerne, Switzerland. Singer (Bass-Baritone). Education: Studied with Werner Ernst in Lucerne, Elisabeth Grümmer and Irmgard Hartmann-Dressler in Berlin. Debut: Don Ferrando in Fidelio, Lucerne, 1974. Career: Member of the opera companies in Lucerne, Linz, Mannheim and since 1986 Zurich; Opera roles include, Philip II, Don Carlo; Boris Godunov; Falstaff; Der fliegende Holländer; Barak in Die Frau ohne Schatten; Hans Sachs in Die Meistersinger von Nuernberg; King Marke and Kurwenal in Tristan und Isolde; Appeared as Wotan and Wanderer in Ring des Nibelungen; King Heinrich in Lohengrin; Jochanaan in Salome; Orestes in Elektra; Musiklehrer in Ariadne auf Naxos; Ochs in Der Rosenkavalier; Osmin in Die Entführung aus dem Serail; Pizarro in Fidelio and Scarpia in Tosca at the Opernhaus Zurich, since 1986; Appearances also include: Barak at Milan's La Scala, Munich Festival; Title part of Der fliegende Holländer Barcelona's Teatro del Liceu, Bruckner Festival, Linz, and at the Deutsche Oper Berlin and for a recording; Philip II in the original (French) version of Don Carlo at the Paris Opera, in the Italian version at the Théâtre de la Monnaie in Brussels and at the Munich State Opera; Stravinsky's Oedipus Rex under Erich Leinsdorf in Geneva; Beethoven's Ninth Symphony under Kurt Sanderling in Geneva, under Pinchas Steinberg in Vienna and under Horst Stein in Basel; Jochanaan, Salome at the Vienna State Opera, at the Semper Oper in Dresden, in Barcelona and at the Festival of Taormina (under Giuseppe Sinopoli); Dvorak's Te Deum, in Vienna and at the Prague Spring Festival; Beethoven's Missa Solemnis (under Rudolf Barschai) on a tour of Switzerland, in Turin, Cologne and Vienna (under Hans Vonk); Mahler's Eighth Symphony in Bonn; Schoenberg's Gurrelieder under Gerd Albrecht in Barcelona and under Eliahu Inbal in Torino; Schnittke's Faust Kantate under Claudio Abbado in Vienna; Haydn's Paukenmesse with the Israel Philharmonic Orchestra under Zubin Mehta; Wotan, Die Walküre at the Munich Opera Festival, at the Vienna State Opera and in a new production at the Cologne Opera; Gurnemanz in Parsifal at the Brucknerfest in Linz; Wanderer in a new production of Siegfried and Wotan in a revival of Rheingold at the Hamburg State Opera; Die Schöpfung under Wolfgang Sawallisch for a TV Concert; Pizarro, Fidelio under Peter Schneider at the RAI Torino; Barak in a new production of Die Frau ohne Schatten under Christoph von Dohnanyi at the Zurich Opera; Opera roles in the 1996-97: Adolfo in Alfonso and Estrella, Wiener Festwochen; Salle Pleyel Landgraf in Tannhäuser, Paris; Orest in Elektra, Wotan in Rheingold, Hamburg; Albert in Werther, Robert in Des Teufels Lustschloss, Kreon in Oedipus Rex, Gurnemanz in Parsifal, Holländer in Der fliegende Holländer, Osmin in Die Entführung aus dem Serail, Zurich; Barak in Frau ohne Schatten, Dresden; Dvorak Requiem in Prague. Recordings include: First complete version of Die Frau ohne Schatten under Wolfgang Sawallisch; Die Zauberflöte under Armin Jordan; Der fliegende Holländer under Pinchas Steinberg; Die Walküre under Christoph von Dohnanyi; Adorno in Schreker's Die Gezeichneten; Paul Dessau, Hagadah. Honours: Kunstpreis of the City of Lucerne. Address: c/o Opernhaus Zurich, Falkenstrasse 1, CH-8008 Zurich, Switzerland.

MULDOWNEY Dominic, b. 19 July 1952, Southampton, England. Composer. m. Diane Trevis, 3 Oct 1986, 1 daughter. Education: BA, BPhil, York University. Career: Composer in Residence, Southern Arts Association, 1974-76; Composer of Chamber, Choral, Orchestral Works including work for theatre and TV; Music Director, National Theatre, 1976-. Compositions include: An Heavyweight Dirge, 1971; Driftwood to the Flow for 18 String, 1972; 2 String Quartets, 1973, 1980; Double Helix for 8 players, 1977; 5 Theatre Poems after Brecht: The Beggar's Opera, realization, 1982; Piano Concerto, 1983; The Duration of Exile, 1984; Saxophone Concerto, 1985; Sinfonietta, 1986; Aus Subtilior, 1987; Lonley Hearts, 1988; Violin Concerto, 1989-90; On Suicide, for voice and ensemble, 1989; Un Carnival Cubiste for 10 bass players and metronome, 1989; Percussion Concerto, for Evelyn Glennie, 1991; Oboe Concerto, 1992; Trumpet Concerto, 1993; Concerto for 4 violins and strings, 1994; Concerto Grosso, 1997; Music for King Lear, 1997. Recordings include: Piano, Saxophone and Oboe Concertos. Memberships: APC. Hobbies: France. Current Management: Cavlin Music Corp. Address: c/o National Theatre, London SE1 1PX, England.

MULLER Barbel, b. 1968, Duisburg, Germany. Singer (Mezzo-soprano). Education: Studied at the Frankfurt Musikhochschule and with Laura Sarti and Elsa Cavelti. Career: Sang in concert from 1987 and made opera debut at Linz 1991, singing the Composer (Ariadne), Dorabella and Carmen; Further appearances as Sesto (Clemenza di Tito), Orlofsky, Charlotte and Octavian (Strasbourg, 1995); Concert repertoire includes Mozart's Requiem (at Stuttgart), the Christmas Oratorio (Ulm and Amsterdam), St Matthew Passion (Tubingen), Elijah (Zurich) and Bach's B Minor Mass (Frankfurt). Address: Atholl Still Ltd, Foresters Hall, 25-27 Westow Street, London SE19 3RY.

MÜLLER Rufus, b. 5 Feb 1959, Kent, England. Singer (Tenor). Education: Choral Scholar, New College, Oxford; Currently studying with Thomas LoMonaco, New York. Career: Worked with many established conductors including: Ivor Bolton, Richard Hickox, Joshua Rifkin, Andrew Parrott and Ivan Fischer; Opera and concert appearances throughout Europe, Japan and the USA; Roles performed include: Bastien in Mozart's Bastien und Bastienne; Aminta in Peri's Euridice; Tersandre in Lully's Roland; Giuliano in Handel's Rodrigo; Lurcanio in Handel's Ariodante; Recitals in Wigmore Hall and Barbican, London, and on radio for BBC, in Munich, Tokyo, Madrid, Utrecht, Salzburg and New York; Recent engagements include Schubert's Die Schöne Müllerin, Munich; Jonathan Miller production of St Matthew Passion at Brooklyn Academy of Music; Mendelssohn's St Paul with the Leipzig Gewandhaus Choir; Beethoven's Ninth Symphony and Handel's Messiah with the Swedish Chamber Orchestra; Televised tour of Messiah in Spain with Trevor Pinnock and the English Concert; Forthcoming engagements include: World première, Rorem's Song Cycle Evidence of Things Not Seen, Carnegie Hall, New York, and Washington DC; St Matthew Passion in Sweden, Germany and Switzerland; Castor in Rameau's Castor et Pollux; Mendelssohn's Elijah in New York; Monteverdi's Il Ritorno d'Ulisse in Athens and Florence; Recital, Musée d'Orsay, Paris. Recordings include: Bach's St John Passion; Die Zauberflöte; Beethoven's Choral Fantasia; Dowland's First Book of Airs; Haydn's O Tuneful Voice; 19th Century Songs; The Evangelist in Bach's St Matthew Passion; Telemann's Admiraltätsmusik and Solo Cantatas. Address: The Garden Flat, 26 Oliver Grove, London SE25 6EJ, England.

MÜLLER-LORENZ Wolfgang, b. 24 Nov 1946, Cologne, Germany. Singer (Tenor). Education: Studied in Cologne. Career: Sang as Baritone, at the Mannheim Opera, 1972; Engagements at Munich, Nuremburg, Karlsruhe, Frankfurt and Mannheim as Papageno, Rossini's Figaro and Dvorak's Jacobin; Studied further with Hans Hopf and sang at the Graz Opera from 1980 as Lohengrin, Cavardossi, Calaf and Loge; Siegmund and Siegfried in a Ring cycle, 1989; Sang with the Deutsche Oper Berlin on tour to Washington, 1989, and as Bacchus in the original version of Ariadne auf Naxos at the Landestheater, Salzburg, 1991; Other roles have included Otello, Dimitri in Boris Godunov, Parsifal, The Marquis in Lulu, Erik, Herman and Fra Diavolo, Zurich Opera, 1989; Frequent concert appearances notably in contemporary works. Address: c/o Landestheater, Schwarstrasse 22, A-5020 Salzburg, Austria.

MULLER-MOLINARI Helga, b. 28 Mar 1948, Pfaffenhofen, Bavaria, Germany. Singer (Mezzo-soprano). Education: Studied with Felicie Huni-Mihaczek in Munich and with Giulietta Simionato in Rome. Career: Sang at Saarbrucken, 1972-73; La Scala Milan, 1975 in L'Enfant et Les Sortilèges, Piccola Scala 1979 in Vivaldi's Tito Manlio; Further appearances at the Salzburg Festival, as Annina, 1983, Barcelona, as Cheubino 1984, Turin as Carmen, 1988 and Monte Carlo, Portrait de Manon by Massenet, 1989; Roles in operas by Rossini, Mozart and other composers at Nancy, Dublin, Pesaro and elsewhere; Trieste 1991 as Werther. Recordings include: Der Rosenkavalier, Ariadne auf Naxos, Mozart Requiem, Bruckner Te Deum, Oronte by Cesti, Monteverdi Madrigals; Handel Partenope; L'Arcadia in Brenta by Galuppi, Rossini's Aureliano in Palmira and La Gazza Ladra. Address: Teatro Comunale di Trieste, Riva Novembre 1, 34121 Trieste, Italy.

MULLOVA Viktoria, b. 27 Nov 1959, Moscow, Russia. Violinist. Education: Studied with V Bronin, Central School of Music, Moscow. Career: Appearances with many of the World's most renowned orchestras including: Berlin Philharmonic, London Symphony, Royal Philharmonic, Boston Symphony, Pittsburgh and Toronto Symphonies; Worked with conductors including: Abbado, Boulez, Haitink, Maazel, Marriner, Masur, Ozawa, Previn, Muti; Appeared in many festivals including: Marlboro, Tanglewood, Edinburgh, Lucerne; Appearances with London Symphony Orchestra in Germany, Cleveland Orchestra, Dallas Syphony, Los Angeles Philharmonic, Berlin Philharmonic, Israel Philharmonic; Performances with the Mullova Chamber Ensemble from 1994; Season 1996-97 with the Munich Philharmonic, Philharmonia and Los Angeles Philharmonic. Recordings include: Exclusively for Philips; Debut release of Tchaikovsky and Sibelius with Ozawa and the Boston Symphony was awarded the Grand Priz du Disque; Vivaldi's Four Seasons with Abbado and the Chamber Orchestra of Europe; Solo works of Bartók, Bach, Paganini; Shostakovich Concerto No 1 and Prokofiev No 2 with André Previn and the Royal Philharmonic; Paganini Concerto No 1 and Vieuxtemps No 5 with Neville Marriner and the Academy of St Martin in the Fields; Brahms, Violin Concerto, Berlin Philharmonic, Claudio Abbado. Honours: 1st Prize, Sibelius Competition, Helsinki, 1981; Gold Medal, Tchaikovsky Competition, Moscow, 1982; International Prize of the Accademia Musicale Chigiana in Siena, 1988. Current Management: Harold Holt Limited. Address: c/o Harold Holt Limited, 31 Sinclair Road, London W14 0NS, England.

MUMELTER Martin, b. 12 May 1948, Innsbruck, Germany. Violinist. m. Magdalena Pattis, 28 October, 2 sons, 2 daughters. Education: Konservatorium Innsbruck; Philadelphia Musical Academy. Career: Mainly with 20th Century Music & Wiener Symphoniker, Staatskapelle Berlin, RSO Vienna, SO des Bayerischen Rundfunks, Mozarteum Orchestra Salzburg; Appearances at Musikbiennale Berlin, Bregenzer Festspiele, Sagar Musicale Umbra, Festwochen der Alten Musik Innsbruck. Recordings: 200 Radio Recordings, Several CD's Publication: Ums Leben spielen (book), 1994. Honours: Preis der Kritik Musikbiennale Berlin, 1979; Berlanda Preis des Landes Tirol, 1985. Hobbies: Skiing; Hiking. Address: Pizach W 31, A-6073 Sistrans, Austria.

MUMFORD Jeffrey, b. 1955, Washington, USA. Composer. Career:Commissions from, Robert Evett Fund of Washington, DC, 1977, Cellist Fred Sherry, 1981, Aspen Wind Quintet, 1983, McKim Fund, Library of Congress, 1986, New York New Music Ensemble, 1987, Violist Marcus Thompson, 1989, Amphion Foundation for the Da Capo Chamber Players, 1989, Frommm Music Foundation, 1990, Roanoke Naumburg Foundation, 1991, Abel/Steinberg/Winant Trio, 1991, Roanoke Symphony Orchestra, 1992, Cellist Joshua Gordon, 1994, Cincinnati Radio Station WGUC, 1994, National Symphony Orchestra, 1995; Works Extensively Performed in the USA and abroad, including Performances at the Library of Congress, Aspen Music Festival, Bang On A Can Music Festival, Seattle Chamber Music Festival, London's Purcell Room, Helsinki Festival, Musica Nel Nostro Tempo Festival, Milan and by Saint Paul Chamber Orchestra. Compositions include: Fragments From the Surrounding Evening; A Flower in Folding Shadows, for Piano and Four Hands; Linear Cycles VII, for Solo Violin; Echoes in a Cloud Box, for Violin and Cello; Jewels Beyond the Mist; Diamonds Suspended in a Galaxy of Clouds, Soprano Solo; Lullaby, for Soprano and Piano; In Forests of Evaporating Dawns; A Pond Within the Drifting Dusk. Contributions to: Quadrivium Music Press; Perspectives of New Music. Honours include: Guggenheim Fellowship; Awards from, Minnesota Composers Forum, American Music Center, Alice M Ditson Fund. Address: c/o Jecklin Associates, 2717 Nichols Lane, Davenport, IA 52803, USA.

MUMMA Gordon, b. 30 Mar 1935, Framingham, Massachusetts, USA. Composer; Performer; Author; Professor of Music. Career includes: Composer and Performer of electroacoustic and instrumental music with performances and recordings in North and South America, Europe and Japan; TV and film performances, Germany and USA; Visiting Lecturer, various colleges and universities; Composer and Performing Musician, Sonic Arts Union, New York City, and Merce Cunningham Dance Company, 1966-74; Professor of Music, 1975-95, Professor Emeritus, 1995-, University of California, Santa Cruz; Visiting Professor of Music, University of California, San Diego, 1985-87. Compositions include: Music from The Venezia Space Theatre; Dresden Interleaf 13 Feb 1945; Mesa; Hornpipe; Schoolwork; Cybersonic Cantilevers; Pontpoint. Recordings: All listed compositions plus performance of music by Robert Ashley, David Behrman, George Cacioppo, John Cage, Mauricio Kagel and Christian Wolff. Contributions to: Numerous books and journals including: James Klosty's Merce Cunningham; Appleton and Perera's Development and Practice of Electronic Music; Gilbert Chase's Roger Reynolds: A Portrait; Journal of Audio Engineering Society; Darmstadt Beitrage zur neue Musik; Neuland I; Sound Recording, major article to The New Grove Dictionary of American Music, 1986. Memberships: Society for

Ethnomusicology; Braodcast Music Inc. Current Management: Artservices, 325 Spring Street, New York, NY 10013, USA. Address: Porter College, University of California, Santa Cruz, CA 95064, USA.

MUNCASTER Clive, b. 24 Jan 1936, Hove, Sussex, England. Composer; Conductor; Violinist; Pianist; Music Therapist. m. (1) 5 sons, (2) Dulcie Bull, 27 Sept 1997. Education: LRAM, Royal Academy of Music, 1954; BM, 1971, MM, 1973, Florida University; DMA, University of Missouri, Kansas City, 1984. Debut: The Happy Hypocrite with Oxford Chamber Ensemble, Queen Elizabeth Hall, London, 1967. Career: Numerous Broadcasts of Compositions, The Enthusiasts, BBCTV (Southern), 1970; Founder, Director, Churchill Memorial Concerts, Blenheim Palace; Founder, Governor, The Music Therapy Charity; Director of Music Therapy Programme, University of Miami, Florida, 1976-77, Maryville College, St Louis, 1977-81, College of St Teresa, Winona, Minnesota, 1985-88; Radio Announcer, KXTR Kansas City; Host for Radio Show, Sounds Health, KQAL, Winona; Chairman, Fine and Performing Arts Division, College of St Teresa, 1986-88; Music Director, Virginia School of the Arts, Lynchburgh, 1989-91; Music Director, Liberty University Symphony Orchestra and String Professor, Liberty University, 1991-94; Founder, Director, Dr Clive Muncaster's Music Clinics, 1993-. Honours: Ford Foundation Fellowship, University of Missouri, Kansas City, 1981; Pi Kappa Lambda, 1983. Memberships: Royal Musical Association; Composers Guild for Great Britain; National Association for Music Therapy. Hobbies: Tennis; Sailing. Address: 119 Commonwealth Court, Apt 1, Princeton, NJ 08540, USA.

MUNDT Richard, b. 8 Sept 1936, Illinois, USA. Singer (Bass). Education: Studied in New York and Vienna. Debut: Saarbrucken 1962, as the Commendatore in Don Giovanni. Career: Appearances at Kiel, Dortmund, Darmstadt, Graz, Liège and the Spoleto Festival; American engagements at the New York City Opera, San Francisco, Portland, Chicago and Cincinnati; Other roles have included Mozart's Osmin, Don Giovanni, Figaro and Sarastro, Rocco, Arkel in Pelléas et Mélisande, Ramphis, King Philip, Padre Guardiano and Wagner's Marke, Daland, Fasolt, Pogner, Hunding and Landgrave.

MUNI Nicholas, b. 1960, USA. Stage Director. Career: Artistic Director, Tusla Opera, 1988-; Has directed over 150 opera productions with leading US companies; Season 1989-90, with Il Trovatore at Seattle, transferring to Houston, Toronto and Vancouver; French version of Verdi's opera at Tulsa, with new production of The Juniper Tree by Philip Glass and Robert Moran; New York City Opera debut with La Traviata, 1991; World premiere of Frankenstein the Modern Prometheus, by Libby Larsen, for Minnesota Opera; US premiere of Rossini's Armida at Tulsa, 1992; Complete version of Lulu for Canadian Opera and Ariadne auf Naxos at Opera Theater of St Louis; World premiere of Moran's The Shining Princess at Minnesota, 1993; Staging of Norma for Seattle and Houston; Los Angeles, 1996. Address: c/o Athole Still International Management Ltd, Foresters Hall, 25-27 Westow Street, London, SE19 3RY, England.

MUNKITTRICK Mark, b. 1951, Boston, Massachusetts, USA. Singer (Bass). Education: Studied at Fresno State College, California. Career: Sang in Carnegie Hall concert performances of Donizetti's Gemma di Vergy and Puccini's Edgar, 1976-77; New York City Opera 1977, as Daland and Pogner; Guest appearances in Washington, Baltimore, Los Angeles and Atlanta, as Leporello, Alfonso, Raimondo and Monteverdi's Seneca; Sang at Karlsruhe, 1978-87, as Mephistopheles, Rocco, Basilio, Kecal, Banquo, King Philip, Ramphis, the Landgrave in Tannhäuser and Fafner; Madrid, 1984, as Handel's Giulio Cesare; Dresden Staatsoper 1989 as Morosus in Die schweigsame Frau; Member of the Stuttgart Staatsoper from 1985; Guest engagements throughout Germany and Europe; Other roles include Arthur in The Lighthouse by Maxwell Davies, Kaspar and Henry VIII in Anna Bolena; Sang Taddeo in L'Italiano in Algeri at Stuttgart, 1996; Wide concert repertory including bass solo in the Missa Solemnis. Recordings include: Gemma di Vergy and Edgar. Address: c/o Stuttgart Staatsoper, Oberer Schlossgarten 6, 7000 Stuttgart, Germany.

MUNOZ Daniel, b. 1951, Buenos Aires, Argentina. Singer (Tenor). Education: Studied in Buenos Aires. Career: Sang at the Teatro Colon Buenos Aires from 1979, Teatro de la Zarzuela Madrid from 1980; Studied further in Milan and sang from 1982 at opera houses in Spain, Portugal and South America; Nancy Opera 1983, as Cavaradossi, Liège 1986 as Pinkerton and the Berne Stadtheater, 1988; Sang Cornil Schut in Pittore Fiamminghi at Trieste and Calaf at the Szeged Festival, Hungary, 1991; Other roles include Don José, Faust, Werther, Don Carlos and Des Grieux in Manon Lescaut; Sang Andrea Chenier at Buenos Aires, 1996; Frequent concert appearances. Address: Teatro Comunale, Riva Novembre 1, 34121 Trieste, Italy.

MUNSEL Patrice, b. 14 May 1925, Spokane, Washington, USA. Singer (Soprano). Education: Studied with Charlotte Lange, William Herman and Renato Bellini in New York. Debut: Metropolitan Opera 1943, as Philine in Mignon. Career: Sang in New York until 1958, as Adele in Die Fledermaus, Offenbach's Périchole, Lucia di Lammermoor, Rosina, Olympia in Les Contes d'Hoffmann, the Queen of Shemakha, Zerlina, Despina and Gilda; European Tour 1948; Starred in 1953 film Melba; Appeared in musical comedy after leaving the Metropolitan.

MURA Peter, b. 21 June 1924, Budapest, Hungary. Conductor. m. Rose Tóth, 1 daughter. Education: High School of Music, Budapest. Debut: Hungarian State Opera House, 1948. Career: Solo Repetiteur, 1945-, Conductor of the Stagione, 1950-53, Hungarian State Opera House; Director and Chief Conductor, Miskolc National Theatre Opera Company, 1953-57; State Opera Conductor, Warsaw, Poland, 1957-58; Conductor, Silesian Opera, Bytom, Poland, 1958-61; Director and Chief Conductor, Miskolc Symphony Orchestra, Hungary, 1961-84; Conductor, Hungarian State Opera, 1984-87; Professor, High School of Music, Budapest, 1986-; Conductor, Wiener Kammeroper, 1990-91. Recordings: Mozart: Idomeneo Overture and Ballet, Symphony in A, 1974. Honours: Ferenc Liszt Prize, 1966; Merited Artist of the Hungarian People's Republic, 1972. Current Management: Pentaton Ltd, Budapest, Hungary. Address: Podmaniczky U 63, H-1064 Budapest, Hungary.

MURAI Hajime (Teri), b. 31 July 1953, San Francisco, California, USA. Conductor. Education: Aspen School of Music, 1971; Institut des Hautes Etudes Musicales, Crans; Switzerland, 1973; BA Music 1974, MA Music 1976, University of California, Santa Barbara; California Institute of the Arts, 1975-76. Career: Currently, Ruth Blaustein Rosenberg Director of Orchestral Activities, Peabody Conservatory of Music; Music Director, Peabody Symphony and Concert Orchestras since 1991; Associate Professor of Orchestra and Conducting, College Conservatory of Music, University of Cincinnati, 1976-91; Music Director and Conductor, Cincinnati Youth Symphony Orchestra, 1978-91; has conducted the Baltimore Symphony, Cincinnati Symphony, Detroit Symphony, Florida Symphony, Phoenix Symphony, Fort Wayne Philharmonic, San Jose Chamber Orchestra, Indiana Chamber Orchestra, Symphony of the Mountain, Hamilton-Fairfield Symphony; Presented 1st performance in English of Shostakovich's Symphony No 13, Babi Yar, 1983. Address: 604 Shelley Road, Towson, MD 21286, USA.

MURGATROYD Andrew, b. 1955, Halifax, Yorkshire, England. Singer (Tenor). Education: Studied singing with Barbara Robotham at Lancaster University and with Rudolf Pierney; Lay-Clerk at Christ Church Cathedral, Oxford. Career: Concert engagements include Israel in Egypt for John Eliot Gardiner in Stuttgart, Milan, Paris, Rome, East Berlin and Turin; Handel's Esther for WDR in Cologne and Acis and Galatea for Swiss television; Monteverdi Vespers and Alexander's Feast at Aix-en-Provence; Performances of Bach's St John Passion in London, Cambridge and Spain, and the St Matthew Passion at the Festival Hall, 1990; Debussy's Rodrigue et Chimène in London and Manchester; Beethoven's Ninth with the Hanover Band in London and Germany; Contemporary Music Network Tour with Richard Bernas, 1990; Sang in Haydn's St Nicholas Mass and Stabat Mater at St John's, London, 1997. Recordings include: Beethoven's Missa Solemnis and Ninth Symphony (Nimbus); Monteverdi Vespers with The Sixteen (Hyperion); Campra's Tancrède (Erato); Leclair Scylla et Glaucus; John Tavener, We Shall See Him As He Is, (Chandos); Antonio Teixeira, Te Deum (Collins Classics). Address: c/o Hazard Chase Ltd., Richmond House, 16-20 Regent Street, Cambridge CB2 1DB, England.

MURGU Corneliu, b. 1948, Timisoara, Rumania. Singer (Tenor). Education: Studied in Rumania, in Florence and with Marcello del Monaco in Treviso. Debut: Wiener Staatsoper with Cavalleria Rusticana (Turiddu), 1978. Career: Following appearances until 1982: Deutsche Oper Berlin, Munich, Hamburg, Stuttgart, Düsseldorf, Zürich and Graz; In 1982 made his debut at the Met with Ballo in Maschera (Riccardo); In the same year, appearances in Naples, Rome and Andrea Chenier in Bonn; Norma (Pollione) in Lyon, Carmen and Turandot in Caracalla, Rome, 1983-85; La Scala debut with Aida (Radames), 1986; Andrea Chenier and Samson in Rio de Janeiro and Cavalleria Rusticana in Barcelona, 1987-89; Otello in Opéra Bastille in Paris, 1990; Cavalleria Rusticana/Pagliacci and Carmen in Rotterdam, 1994-95; Debut in Verona with Otello, 1994, and Covent Garden debut with Calaf in Turandot. Recordings include: Otello with Renato Bruson, Fanciulla del West with Gwyneth Jones, Cavalleria Rusticana/Pagliacci, Carmen. Address: Les Achantes, 6 Avenue des Citronniers, 98000 Monte Carlo.

MURPHY Heidi Grant, b. 1962, USA. Singer (Soprano). Education: Studied in New York. Career: Member of the Met Opera's Young Artist Development Program, from 1988; Met debut in Die Frau ohne Schatten (1989) followed by Xenia (Boris Godunov), Papagena, Oscar, Nannetta, Sophie in Der Rosenkavalier, Soeur Constance (Carmélites) Ilia; Servilia (La Clemenza di Tito), Pamina and Susanna in season 1997-98; Santa Fe debut 1991, as Susanna; European debut at Brussels 1991, in La Favorita, followed by Monteverdi's Drusilla with Netherlands Opera, Mozart's Celia (Lucio Silla) and Ismene (Mitridate) at Salzburg, Servilia at the Paris Opera and Ilia at Frankfurt; Concerts include Mozart's C Minor Mass (Houston Symphony), Mahler's Eighth Symphony (Atlanta Symphony and Vienna Philharmonic; New York Philharmonic debut 1996, in Honegger's Jeanne d'Arc au Bucher; Conductors have included Levine, Ozawa, Robert Shaw, Masur, Michael Tilson Thomas and Charles Dutoit. Recordings include: Idomeneo, from the Met (DGG); Haydn's Die Schöpfung (Teldec). Honours include: Winner, 1988 Metropolitan National Council Auditions. Address: c/o Lies Askonas Ltd, 6 Henrietta St, London WC2E 9LA, England.

MURPHY Suzanne, b. 15 Oct 1941, Limerick, Ireland. Singer (Soprano). Education: Studied with Veronica Dunne at the College of Music in Dublin, 1973-76. Career: Has sung with Welsh National Opera from 1976 as Constanze, Amelia (I Masnadieri and Un Ballo in Maschera), Elisabeth de Valois, Leonora (Il Trovatore), Elvira (Ernani and I Puritani), Violetta, Norma, Lucia di Lammermoor and Musetta; Has sung Constanze and Donna Anna for English National Opera; Donna Anna and the soprano roles in Les Contes d'Hoffmann for Opera North and Constanze for Scottish Opera; German debut 1985, as Norma in a concert performance of Bellini's opera in Munich; Returned 1988 for Amelia (Un Ballo in Maschera); Vienna Staatsoper debut 1987, as Electra in Idomeneo; Invited to return 1988-89 (Armenian Gala Benefit Concert); Has sung Reiza in Oberon at Lyon and Donna Anna at the Aix-en-Provence Festival; North American engagements include Norma at the New York City Opera, Amelia (Ballo), Elvira (Puritani) and Lucia in Vancouver, Fiordiligi, Ophelia (Hamlet) and Violetta in Pittsburgh; Sang Alice Ford in the Peter Stein production of Falstaff for Welsh National Opera (repeated in New York and Milan 1989); Sang Norma for the Dublin Grand Opera Society 1989, Hanna Glawari in The Merry Widow for Scottish Opera; Title role in La Fanciulla del West for Welsh National Opera, 1991; Electra in Idomeneo at the Albert Hall (Proms) and in Wales with WNO, 1991; Season 1992 with Elvira in Ernani and Tosca, in new productions for UNO; Concert appearances in Austria, Sweden, Denmark, Belgium and Portugal; Sang Leonore in Fidelio on South Bank, London, 1989 and at Belfast, 1996. Address: c/o Ingpen & Williams Ltd, 26 Wadham Road, London SW15 2LR, England.

MURRAY Ann, b. 27 Aug 1949, Dublin, Ireland. Singer (Mezzo-soprano). m. Philip Langridge. Education: Studied at the Royal College of Music in Manchester with Frederick Cox and at the London Opera Centre (1972-74). Debut: Aldeburgh 1974, with Scottish Opera as Alceste in the opera by Gluck. Career: Wexford Festival 1974-75 as Myrtale in Thaïs by Massenet and Queen Laodicea in Cavalli's Eritrea; English National Opera in Le Comte Ory and as Cenerentola; Covent Garden from 1976, as Cherubino, Siebel (Faust), Ascanio, Tebaldo in I Capuleti e i Montecchi, the Child in L'Enfant et les Sortilèges, Idamante and the Composer in Ariadne auf Naxos; Sang Octavian at Covent Garden 1989 and returned 1991 as Sifare in a new production of Mitridate for the Mozart bicentenary; US debut 1979 with the New York City Opera as Sextus in La Clemenza di Tito, repeating the role at the Metropolitan in 1984; Salzburg Festival 1981, as Nicklausse in Les Contes d'Hoffmann; Glyndebourne Festival 1979, as Minerva in Il Ritorno di Ulisse, returned to Salzburg 1985 to sing the role in Henze's version of Monteverdi's opera; Milan La Scala 1983 as Dorabella in Così fan tutte, returned 1984 as Cecilio in Mozart's Lucio Silla; In 1989 sang Cenerentola at Salzburg; English National Opera 1990 as Berlioz's Beatrice; Sang Cecilio in a new production of Lucio Silla at the Vienna Staatsoper, 1991; Season 1992-93 appeared as Ruggiero in a new production of Handel's Alcina at Covent Garden, Xerxes for ENO, Cecilio at Salzburg and in The Beggar's Opera at Aldeburgh; Title role in Giulio Cesare at Munich, 1994; Many concert appearances including Stravinsky's Pulcinella at the 1993 London Proms; Season 19996-97 included Brangaene in Munich and Ruggiero at the Vienna Festival; Giulio Cesare for the Royal Opera, 1997. Recordings include: St Matthew Passion, Handel and Mozart arias, Roméo et Juliette, Mozart's Requiem; Haydn's Stabat Mater; Purcell's Dido and Aeneas; Les Contes d'Hoffmann; Così fan tutte, Videos of Xerxes and Mitridate.

MURRAY John Horton, b. 1960, West Berlin, Germany. Singer (Tenor). Education: Studied at Curtis Institute in Philadelphia. Career: Concert engagements in Beethoven's Ninth with the Atlanta Symphony, Mahler's 8th with Bournemouth Symphony and Janacek's Glagolitic Mass with Royal Philharmonic, 1993; Bach's Magnificat for PBS television in USA; Performances of Salome with Boston Symphony and Idomeneo at Tanglewood; Appearances at Metropolitan Opera from 1991 in Les Contes d'Hoffmann, Lucia di Lammermoor, Die Zauberflöte, Das Rheingold; Sang Max in Der Freischütz with Opera Orchestra of New York and has appeared frequently with Lyric Opera of Chicago; Carnegie Hall debut with Vienna Philharmonic; Sang Don José at the Verona Arena, 1996. Honours: National Institute for Music Theater Prizes; George London Award, 1988; Finalist in 1989 Metropolitan National Council Auditions. Address: c/o

IMG Artists, Media House, 3 Burlington Lane, London W4 2TH, England.

MURRAY Margaret, b. 11 Mar 1921, Lille, France. Lecturer; Accompanist; Cellist; Recorder Player. Education: Wycombe Abbey, Bucks; RCM; ARCM; LRAM. Career: Several public concerts; Music Mistress, Marlborough College, 1942-43, Wycombe Abbey, 1946-52; Secretary, Orff Society, 1964-; Editor, Orff Times, 1979-97. Recordings: Music for Children, Orff, Schulwerk. Publications: Orff Schulwerk, 5 volumes, 1958-66; Translator, Gunild Keetman's Elementaria, 1974; Barbara Haselbach's Dance Education; Carl Orff's The Schulwerk. Honour: Pro Merito, Carl Orff Foundation, 1990. Memberships: ISM; Society for Research in Psychology of Music & Music Education; Orff Society. Hobbies: Films; Reading. Address: 7 Rothesay Avenue, Richmond, Surrey TW10 5EB, England.

MURRAY Niall, b. 22 Apr 1948, Dublin, Ireland. Opera Singer (Baritone). m. Barbara F M Murray, 1 daughter. Education: Royal Academy of Music, Dublin. Debut: Boy Soprano in Pantomime, Dublin. Career: Appearances as Curly in Oklahoma, Dublin, 1970; Opera debut, Bomarzo, Coliseum, London, 1976; Baritone Lead in over 52 musicals including, English National Opera, London; TV and Radio appearances, England and Ireland frequently; Also appeared in Cabarets and Musicals, major opera appearances include Papageno, Schaunard, Figaro (Barber of Seville), and Lescaut (Manon); Sang lago at the Basle City Theatre 1988 (under the name Mario di Mario). Recordings: Niall Murray Sings (Irish Songs); Danilo; The Merry Widow; Robert in La Fille du Régiment. Address: c/o English National Opera, London Coliseum, St Martin's Lane, London WC2, England.

MURRAY William, b. 13 Mar 1935, Schenectady, New York, USA. Singer (Baritone). Education: Studied at Adelphi University and in Rome. Debut: Spoleto 1957, in Il segreto di Susanna by Wolf-Ferrari. Career: Appearances in Munich, Salzburg, Amsterdam and Frankfurt; Member of the Deutsche Oper Berlin from 1969; Sang Dallapiccola's Ulisse at La Scala in 1970, and took part in the premiere of Nabokov's Love's Labour Lost, Brussels 1973; Other roles include Don Giovanni, Verdi's Macbeth, Luna, Rigoletto and Germont, Puccini's Scarpia and Lescaut, Wagner's Wolfram and parts in We Come to the River by Henze, Orff's Antigonae and Paisiello's Re Theodoro in Venezia. Honours include: Fulbright Scholarship, 1956; Kammersänger of the Deutsche Oper Berlin. Address: c/o Deutsche Oper Berlin, Richard Wagnerstrasse 10, D-1000 Berlin, Germany.

MUSACCHIO Martina, b. 11 Feb 1956, Aosta, Italy. Singer (Soprano). Education: Studied in Geneva with Ursula Buckel and in Florence, Munich and Zurich. Career: Sang at Zurich Opera 1981-82, Lucerne 1982-85; Guest appearances at Geneva, Dusseldorf, Venice, Mantua, Lausanne and Ravenna; Roles have included Mozart's Susanna, Zerlina, Despina, Pamina and Papagena, Donizetti's Norina and Adina, Martha, Micaela, Euridice, Orff's Die Kluge and Ismene in Honegger's Antigone; Sang Lisetta in La Rondine at Monte Carlo, 1991; Concert appearances throughout Switzerland and in Hamburg, Munich, Stuttgart, Paris, Venice and Madrid, notably in Baroque repertoire. Address: c/o Opéra de Monte Carlo, Place du Casino, Monte Carlo.

MUSGRAVE Thea, b. 27 May 1928, Edinburgh, Scotland. Composer. m. Peter Mark, 1971. Education: Edinburgh University; Paris Conservatoire under Nadia Boulanger. Career: Lecturer, Extra-Mural Department, London University, 1958-65; Visiting Professor, University of California, Santa Barbara, USA, 1970; Distinguished Professor, Queen's College, City University of New York, 1987. Compositions include: Chamber Concertos 1, 2 and 3; Concerto for Orchestra, 1967; Clarinet Concerto, 1968; Beauty and the Beast, ballet, 1969; Night Music, 1969; Horn Concerto, 1971; The Voice of Ariadne, chamber opera, 1972-73; Viola Concerto, 1973; Mary Queen of Scots, opera, 1976-77; A Christmas Carol, opera, 1978-79; Harriet, A Woman Called Moses, 1980-84; Peripateia for orchestra, 1981; An Occurrence At Owl Creek Bridge, radio opera, 1981; Space Play, 1984; The Golden Echo I and II, 1985-86; Rainbow for orchestra, 1990; Wild Winter for ensemble, 1993; Autumn Sonata, concerto for bass-clarinet and orchestra, 1993; Simón Bolívar, opera in 2 acts, 1993; Journey Through a Japanese Landscape, concerto for marimba and wind orchestra, 1993-94; On the Underground Set No 1 - On gratitude, love of madness, SATB, 1994; On the Underground Set No 2 - The strange and the exotic, SATB, 1994; Helios, concerto for oboe and orchestra, 1995; Chamber music; Songs; Choral music; Orchestral music. Honours: Koussevitzky Award, 1972; Guggenheim Fellow, 1974-75, 1982-83; Honorary DMus, Council for National Academic Awards, Smith College and Old Dominion University. Hobbies: Cinema; Reading. Address: c/o Novello and Co Ltd, 8/9 Frith Street, London W1V 5TZ, England.

MUSTONEN Olli, b. 7 June 1967, Helsinki, Finland. Concert Pianist; Composer. Education: Studied piano, harpsichord and composition from age 5; Later studies with Ralf Gothoni, Eero Heinonen (piano) and Einojuhani Rautavaara (composition). Career: From 1984, appearances with most major orchestras in Finland and with the Oslo Philharmonic, City of Birmingham Symphony Orchestra and the Royal Philharmonic Orchestra; Festivals include Helsinki, Berlin, Lucerne and Schleswig-Holstein; US debut 1986 at the Newport Festival; Los Angeles Philharmonic at the Hollywood Bowl and New York recital in Young Concert Artists series; London debut April 1987 at the Queen Elizabeth Hall; Concerto performance with the London Philharmonic; Paris debut with the Orchestre de Paris conducted by Kurt Sanderling; 1989 season on Far East tour with the Stockholm Philharmonic and further engagements in the USA; Regular chamber concerts with Heinrich Schiff, Sabine Meyer, Dmitry Sitkovetsky and Steven Isserlis; Soloist in his own two piano concertos; Recital debuts at the Amsterdam Concertgebouw and Chicago's Orchestra Hall, 1990-91; Prom Concerts, London 1991; Beethoven's 1st Concerto 1993; Nonet for two string quartets and double bass premiered at the Wigmore Hall, 1995. Recordings include: Duo recital with Isabelle van Keulen (Philips); Shostakovich Preludes and works by Aiken; Prokofiev Concertos, 1997-98. Honour: Prizewinner in 1984 Geneva Competition for Young Soloists. Address: c/o Harrison/Parrott Ltd, 12 Penzance Place, London W11 4PA, England.

MUTI Riccardo, b. 28 July 1941, Naples, Italy. Orchestra Conductor. m. 3 children. Education: Milan Conservatory. Career: Principal Conductor, Orchestra Maggio Musicale, Florence, Italy, 1969-81 notably in operas by Rossini, Meyebeer, Spontini and Verdi; Principal Conductor, 1973-82, Music Director, 1979-82, Philharmonia Orchestra, London, England; Principal Guest Conductor, 1977-80, Music Director, 1980-92, Philadelphia Orchestra, USA; Music Director, La Scala, Milan, 1986-; Guest Conductor, numerous orchestras, Europe, USA; Conductor of Opera, Florence, Milan, London, Vienna, Munich, Salzburg, Covent Garden debut, Aida, 1977; Conducted I Vespri siciliani at the opening of the season at La Scala, 1989, La Clemenza di Tito and La Traviata 1990; Cosi fan tutte at the 1990 Salzburg Festival; Season 1992-93 with Parsifal and La Donna del Lago at La Scala, Pagliacci at Philadelphia; Engaged for concert performance of Verdi's Nabucco with the Israel Philharmonic; Season 1996-97 with Gluck's Armide in Milan and Così fan tutte at the Vienna Festival. Recordings: Symphonic and operatic recordings, EMI, including La Traviata (Scotto) I Puritani (Caballé), Don Pasquale, Attila; Dvorak's Violin Concerto, Scriabin's 1st Symphony; Rigoletto; Guillaume Tell (Studer), Tosca (Vaness). Honour: Winner, Guido Cantelli International Contest, 1967. Current Management: Columbia Artists Management, New York, USA. Address: c/o Columbia Artists Management, 165 West 57th Street, New York, NY 10019, USA.

MUTTER Anne-Sophie, b. 29 June 1963, Rheinfeldin, Germany. Concert Violinist. m. Dithelf Wunderlich, 1989. Education: Studied in Germany and Switzerland with pupils of Carl Flesch. Career: Attracted the attention of Karajan at the 1976 Lucerne Festival and appeared at the 1977 Salzburg Festival; British debut 1977, at the Brighton Festival with the English Chamber Orchestra under Daniel Barenboim; US debut with the National Symphony Orchestra of Washington; Moscow debut March 1985; Several return visits to Russia and Eastern Block Countries; Aldeburgh Festival 1985, playing Beethoven Trios with Rostropovitch and Bruno Giurrana; British concerts with the Philharmonia (Tchaikovsky Concerto) and the Royal Philharmonic under Kurt Masur; Gave the premiere of Lutoslawski's Chaine 2 in 1986; Lullaby for Anne Sophie written for her 1988; Former Chair of Violin at the Royal Academy of Music, London; Played the Brahms Concerto at the London Barbican, 1996; World tour with Beethoven Sonatas, 1998. Recordings include: Standard repertoire and works by Stravinsky and Lutoslawski (Partita and Chaine). Honours: Citizen of Honour, Wehr, 1989; Bundesverdienstkreuz First Class, awarded by the Bundespraesident; Appointed first holder of the International Chair of Violin Studies, Royal Academy of Music. Address: c/o Kaye Artists Management, Barratt House, 7 Chertsey Road, Woking GU21 5AB, England.

MYERS Michael, b. 1955, USA. Singer (Tenor). Education: Studied at Curtis Institute, Philadelphia. Debut: Central City Opera 1977, in The Bartered Bride. Career: US appearances in Minnesota, Tulsa, Cleveland, San Francisco, Los Angeles and Des Moines; Season 1981-82 as Belmonte in Ottawa, Alfred in Die Fledermaus for Charlotte Opera, Faust for Providence and Virginia Operas and Jenik in Kentucky and Augusta; Highlights of 1982-83 were debuts at the New York City Opera, as Rodolfo, Santa Fe Opera as Quint (Turn of the Screw), Monteverdi's Nerone with Canadian Opera and the Duke of Mantua for Hawaii Opera Theatre; Sang Nick in the premiere of The Postman Always Rings Twice for St Louis Opera (1982) and repeated the role at the 1983 Edinburgh Festival; Scottish Opera debut 1984, as Idomeneo, returning as the Duke in Rigoletto and Cavalli's Orione; Season 1984-85 included Percy to Joan Sutherland's Anna Bolena for Canadian Opera, Flotow's Lionel in Portland and Lord Puff in the US premiere of Henze's The English Cat, at Santa Fe; Season 1985-86 featured debuts with Seattle Opera (Des Grieux in Manon), in Toulouse (Gounod's Romeo), Long Beach Grand Opera (Belmonte), Montpellier (Rimsky's Mozart) and with the Mostly Mozart Festival (Belfiore in La Finta Giardiniera); Active during 1986-87 at Philadelphia (Wagner's Steersman), Pittsburgh (Edgardo in Lucia di Lammermoor) with the Canadian Opera as Dimitri in Boris Godunov and the Mostly Mozart Festival as Ageonore in Il Re Pastore; From 1987 has sung Berg's Painter with the Chicago Opera, the Berlioz Faust with Lyon Opera, Sergei in Lady Macbeth of Mtsensk with Canadian Opera, Boris in Katya Kabanova at Glyndebourne and Ismael in Nabucco in Philadelphia and New York; Season 1992 as Tom Rakewell at Brussels and Percy in Anna Bolena at Santiago; Tom Rakewell at Madrid, 1996; Concert engagements include Rossini's Stabat Mater (Cincinnati May Festival) and Huon in Oberon for Radio France. Honours include: First Prize 1979 Merola Program of the San Francisco Opera. Address: c/o Columbia Artists Inc, 165 West 57th Street, New York, NY 10019, USA.

MYERS Pamela, b. 1952, Baltimore, USA. Singer (Soprano). Debut: San Francisco Western Opera, 1977 as Mozart's Countess. Career: Sang the title role in Stephen Oliver's The Duchess of Malfi, Santa Fe 1978; Appearances at New York City Opera from 1979, Scottish Opera 1980-81, as Lucia; Giessen 1981 in the title role of Menotti's La Loca, Amsterdam 1983 as Mozart's Constanze, Innsbruck Early Music Festival 1984 in Handel's Rodrigo; Sang at Marseille 1988 and 1991 as Desdemona and Ellen Orford; Other roles have included Aennchen in Der Freischütz, Zerlina, Zerbinetta, Micaela, Luisa Miller, Violetta, Liu and Lady Macbeth; Noted concert artist. Address: c/o Opera de Marseille, 2 Rue Molière, F-1321 Marseille, France.

MYERS Peter (Joseph), b. 3 February 1962, Werribee, Victoria, Australia. Composer. Education: BA (Hons), 1984, MA, 1990, La Trobe University. Career: Faculty Member, La Trobe University, 1984-90; Pascoe Vale Girls' Secondary College, 1993-. Compositions include: Transformations, for oboe, 1983; Aftermath for concert band Octet for Winds, 1984; Scintilla, for orchestra, 1986; Of Minds and Minds for Ensemble, 1987; Antipathy for mezzo and ensemble, 1988; Towards the Equinox for chamber ensemble, 1986; Vex for violin, 1988; Homage to the Ancient, for trombone, percussion, and piano; Pasar, for piano, 1991; Bilanx for violin, cello, piccolo, clarinet and piano, 1991; Demons Within, for orchestra, 1993; Paroxysms, for string quartet, 1993. Address: APRA, 1A Eden Street, Crows Nest, NSW 2065, Australia.

MYERSCOUGH Clarence, b. 27 Oct 1930, London, England. Violinist. m. Marliese Scherer, 1 son, 1 daughter. Education: Royal Academy of Music, London; Premier Nommé a l'Unanimité, Paris Conservatoire. Career: Professor, Violin, Royal Academy of Music, 1964-; Soloist, Recitalist and Chamber Music Player; Appeared in Many International Music Festivals including Ascona, Segovia, Madrid, Badajoz and Cardiff; Several tours in USA and Far East; Broadcasts for BBC, IVT, RTE, HK TV and Major European Stations; Founder Member, Fidelio Quartet. Recordings: String Quartets of Britten, Tippett, Delius, Arriaga; Violin Sonata by Hoddinott with Martin Jones. Honours: Winner, All England Violin Competition, National Federation of Music Festivals and Albert Sammons Prize, 1951; 2nd Prize, Carl Flesch International Violin Competition, 1952; Fellow, Royal Academy of Music. Memberships: Incorporated Society of Musicians; Royal Society of Musicians of Great Britain. Hobbies: Astronomy; Microscopy. Address: 17 Salterton Road, London N7 6BB, England.

MYERSCOUGH Nadia, b. 29 July 1967, London, England. Violinist. Education: Royal Academy of Music, London; Studies with her father, Clarence Myerscough; Indiana University, Bloomington, USA; Studies with Franco Gulli, Rostislav Dubinsky, Luba Edlina, Shigeo Neriki. Career: Soloist, Recitalist and Chamber Music Player; Member, The Rogeri Trio; Broadcasts on BBC Radio 3, Classic FM and France Music; Appearances at South Bank, Wigmore Hall, City of London Festival, Wexford Festival; Soloist with the Lucerne Festival Strings, London Soloists, Oxford Harmonic Society, Kent Concert Orchestra, Bangkok Philharmonic. Recordings: Dvorak, Suk, Smetana CD; The Festival Strings Lucerne Vivaldi Concerto CD; Chamber Music Works by Alan Rawsthorne. Honours: Associate, Royal Academy of Music; B J Dale Prize; Countess of Munster Award; Several scholarships; English Speaking Union Fellowship. Memberships: New Helvetic Society; RAM Club. Hobby: Gardening. Address: M&M Management, 17 Salterton Road, London N7 6BB, England.

N

NAAF Dagmar, b. 1934, Munich, Germany. Singer (Mezzo Soprano). Education: Studied in Munich. Career: Sang in Opera at Freiburg, 1958-63, Munich, 1963-66, Wiesbaden, 1963-66 and Hanover, 1966-70; Engaged at Cologne, 1967-69, Graz, 1970-72, Staatsoper Munich, 1974-76; Guest appearances at Brussels, Berne, Marseilles, Rio de Janeiro, Amsterdam, Octavian, 1965, Barcelona and Vienna, 1972; Other roles have included Monteverdi's Ottavia, Handel's Cornelia, Gluck's Paride, Dorabella, Brangaene; Strauss's Composer and Clairon; Verdi's Preziosilla, Azucena, Amneris and Eboli; Noted concert artist. Address: c/o Bayerische Staatsoper, Postfach 100148, 8000 Munich, Germany.

NADAREISHVILI Zurab, b. 4 January 1957, Poti, Georgia. Composer. m. Niho Shawdia, 23 November 1985, 1 son, 1 daughter. Education: Theoretical Department, Music School, Poti; Tbilisi State Conservatoire. Debut: Tbilisi, 1985. Career: Performed in St Petersburg, 1987, Moscow, 1988, Amsterdam, 1992, USA, 1993. Compositions: 2 String Quartets; Brass Quintet; Orchestral Minatures; Symphonic Poem; Hymns, for Chamber Orchestra; Variations, for Piano; Variations, for Piano and Orchestra; Instrumental Pieces. Recording: Hymns, for Chamber Orchestra, 1988. Publications: The Way to Music, 1987; Musical Georgia, 1997. Honours: Moscow Composers International Competition, 1987; Georgian Composers Union Award, 1992; 3rd Place, Moscow Prokofiev Competition, 1997. Memberships: Georgian Composers Union. Address: Street No 20, fl 41, Tbilisi 380071, Georgia.

NADLER Sheila, b. 1945, New York City, USA. Mezzo-Soprano. Education: Studied at the Manhattan School of Music, at the Opera Studio of the Metropolitan Opera and Juilliard School. Career: Sang at San Francisco and New York City Opera from 1970, Baltimore from 1972, notably in 1975 in the premiere of Inez de Castro by Pasatieri, Metropolitan Opera from 1976; Sang Anna in Les Troyens at La Scala in 1982, and Clytemnestra in Elektra at Santiago in 1984; Further appearances as Fricka and Waltraute in The Ring, at Marseilles, Lyon and Brussels and as Erda, Herodias, Jocasta in Oedipus Rex, Azucena, Ulrica, Mistress Quickly, Cornelia, Giulio Cesare and La Cieca in La Gioconda; Sang Clytemnestra in Elektra at Seattle, 1996. Address: c/o Baltimore Opera Company, 527 North Charles Street, Baltimore, MD 21201, USA.

NAEF Yvonne, b. 1965, Switzerland. Singer (Mezzo-soprano). Education: Studied in Zurich, Basle and Mannheim. Career: Concert and recital appearances from 1987; Opera debut as Rossini's Cenerentola, followed by an engagement at St Gallen, as Ulrica, Ariodante, Gluck's Orfeo and Sara in Roberto Devereux, from 1992; Wiesbaden from 1993, as Preziosilla, Rosina, Suzuki, Fricka, Brangaene and Adalgisa; Monte Carlo 1994, as Giovanna Seymour in Anna Bolena, and La Scala Milan as Offenbach's Giulietta; Invalid Woman in Schoenberg's Moses and Aron at Amsterdam, Salzburg and the Festival Hall, London (1996); Appearances as Verdi's Amneris at St Gallen, Wiesbaden and the Deutsche Oper Berlin; Concert engagements in Prokofiev's Alexander Nevsky (at Naples), Mahler's Second Symphony (Venice), Bach's B Minor Mass (Lausanne) and Das Lied von der Erde (Toulouse); Bayreuth Festival 1997, as Waltraute and Second Norn, in The Ring. Honours include: Second Prize, Lieder and Oratorio section, 1987 Maria Callas Competition, at Athens. Address: c/o Opernhaus Zurich, Falkenstrasse 1, CH-8008 Zurich, Switzerland.

NAEGELE Philipp (Otto), b. 22 Jan 1928, Stuttgart, Germany. Violinist; Violist; Professor. 1 son. Education: BA, Queens College, New York, USA, 1949; MA 1950, PhD 1955, Princeton University, New Jersey. Career: Violinist and Violist, Marlboro Music Festival, Marlboro, Vermont, 1950-; Violinist, Cleveland Orchestra, 1956-64; Member, Resident String Quartet, Kent State University, Kent Ohio, 1960-64; Violin Faculty, Cleveland Institute of Music, 1961-64; Assistant Professor, 1964-68, Associate Professor, 1968-72, Professor, 1972-78, William R Kenan Jr Professor of Music, 1978-, Smith College, Northampton, Massachusetts; Member, Vegh String Quartet, 1977-79; Violist, Cantilena Piano Quartet, concerts USA and abroad, 1980-; Numerous concerts: Music from Marlboro series, USA, independently, Europe; Residences: National Arts Center, Ottawa; Yehudi Menuhin School, England; Freiburg Hochschule für Musik; Banff Center for the Arts; Rubin Academy, Tel Aviv University; Teacher, Chamber Music Ensembles, Musicorda Summer School, Mount Holyoke College, 1987-. Recordings: Numerous recordings of violin/viola solos and chamber music for Columbia Records, Marlboro Recording Society, Da Camera Schallplatten (Mannheim), Musical Heritage Society, Nonesuch, Pro Arte, Arabesque, Spectrum, Stradivari Records, Bis Records, Sony Classical and Bayer Records, including 6 LPs as part of complete recorded edition of chamber works of Max Reger for his centennial, Da Camera, 1973. Publications: Gustav Mahler and Johann Sebastian Bach; August Wilhelm Ambros in Grove's Dictionary of Music and Musicians. Address: 57 Prospect Street, Northampton, MA 01060, USA.

NAFE Alicia, b. 4 Aug 1947, Buenos Aires, Argentina. Singer (Mezzo-soprano). Education: Studied in Buenos Aires with Ferruccio Calusio and in Europe with Luigi Ricci and Teresa Berganza. Career: Sang in Barcelona after winning competition there, debut in Verdi's Requiem; Sang in Toledo and at the Bayreuth Festival, 1975; Member of the Hamburg Opera, 1977-81; Geneva Opera, 1981, in La Cenerentola; Lyon 1981, in Beatrice et Benedict by Berlioz; Sang Rosina with the Cologne Opera at the 1981 Edinburgh Festival; La Scala 1984, as Idamante in Idomeneo; Covent Garden 1985, as Rosina; Guest engagements in Spain, South America, France, Germany and China; Other roles include Carmen and Dorabella; Sang Adalgisa at Covent Garden, 1987; Metropolitan Opera debut 1988, as Sextus in La Clemenza di Tito and Ramiro in La Finta Giardiniera; Sang Massenet's Charlotte at the Teatro Regio Parma, 1990; Also heard in oratorios and as song recitalist. Recordings: Mercedes in Carmen and La Vida Breve (Deutsche Grammophon); Monteverdi Madrigals (RCA); Così fan tutte (Decca). Address: c/o Teatro Regio, Via Garibaldi 16, I-43100 Parma, Italy.

NAGANO Kent (George), b. 22 Nov 1951, Morro Bay, California, USA. Conductor. Education: BA 1974 and studied with Grosvenor Cooper, University of California, Santa Cruz; MM, San Francisco University, 1976; Studied piano with Goodwin Sammel; Conducting with Laszlo Varga, San Francisco. Career: Opera Company of Boston, 1977-79; Music Director, Berkeley (California) Symphony Orchestra, 1978; Ojai (California) Music Festival, 1984; Chief Conductor, Opera de Lyon, 1989-; Guest Conductor with many orchestras in the USA and Europe; Conducted Madama Butterfly at Lyon, 1990 followed by Dialogues des Carmélites and a French version of Strauss's Salome; Associate Principal Guest Conductor of the London Symphony Orchestra, 1990; Music Director of the Hallé Orchestra from 1992; Season 1992 with Busoni's Turandot at Lyon, Madame Butterfly at Symphony Hall Birmingham (Lyon Company) and The Rake's Progress at Aix-en-Provence; Conducted Carmen at Lyon, 1996. Recordings include: The Love for Three Oranges, Dialogues des Carmélites, Salome (Virgin Classics). Honours: Co-recipient, Affiliate Artist's Seaver Conducting Award, 1985; Gramophone Magazine Record of the Year Award for The Love of Three Oranges, 1990; Winner, with Opéra de Lyon, the 1995 Grammy Award for Best Opera Recording for Carlisle Floyd's Susannah. Address: The Hallé Orchestra, Heron House, Albert Square, Manchester M2 5HD, England.

NAGY Janos B, b. 1943, Debrecen, Hungary. Singer (Tenor). Education: Bartok Conservatory, Budapest. Career: Sang with Hungarian Territorial Army choir on tour, 1967-70; Stage debut at Budapest, 1971, as Don José in Carmen; Many performances in operas by Verdi and Puccini; Berlin 1978, in the Verdi Requiem; Warsaw national Opera 1979; Member of Deutsch Oper am Rhein, Dusseldorf from 1981; Other roles include Puccini's Des Grieux, Cavaradossi and Calaf, Verdi's Manrico, Duke of Mantua, and Macduff, Nemorino in L'Elisir d'Amore and Pollione in Norma; Guest appearances at opera houses in Germany and Switzerland; Sang Radames with the Deutsche Oper am Rhein, Dusseldorf, 1989. Recordings: Boito's Nerone (Hungaroton); Kodály's Te Deum; Psalmus Hungaricus and Missa Brevis; Christus by Liszt; Mose in Egitto; Szokolay's Blood Wedding; Simon Boccanegra. Address: c/o Hungarian State Opera House, Nepöztarsasay utja 22, 1061 Budapest, Hungary.

NAGY Robert, b. 3 Mar 1929, Lorain, Ohio, USA. Singer (Tenor). Education: Cleveland Institute of Music. Career: Metropolitan Opera from 1957, as Canio in Pagliacci, Beethoven's Florestan, Herod in Salome and the Emperor in Die Frau ohne Schatten; With the Met and the New York City Opera (from 1969) has sung in 1000 opera performances; Guest appearances in Chicago, Baltimore, San Diego, Seattle, Montreal and New Orleans; Repertoire includes roles by Wagner, Verdi, Barber, Bizet and Puccini.

NAHAY Paul, b. 31 May 1958, Camden, New Jersey, USA. Composer; Music Theorist; Pianist; Music Director; Professor. Education: BMus, Composition, University of Maryland, College Park, 1979; MMus, Composition, University of Maryland, College Park, 1980; DMA, Composition, Stanford University, 1983. Career: Lecturer, General Honours, Associate Music Director, Opera Theatre, Music Director, Baroque Ensemble, University of Maryland, 1983-84; Lecturer, Music Theory, Music Director of Alea II, Ensemble for New Music, Stanford University, 1984-86; Music Software Developer. Compositions: Terra Nova for chorus and orchestra, 1995. Publications: Fanfare for Brass Quintet, 1980; Duet for Flutes, 1981; Canon for Two Flutes, 1981; Sonnet for Mixed Chorus and Flute Quartet, 1981; For Flute and Tape, 1981; ScoreInput (Music software), 1990. Honours: First Prize, University of Maryland Composition Competition for Etude for Orchestra, 1980; Graduate Fellowship, Stanford University, 1981-83. Memberships: ASCAP. Hobbies: Personal computer programming; Racquetball; Puzzle invention. Address: 5117 West Shoreline Drive, Floyds Knobs, IN 47119, USA.

NAKARAI Charles Frederick Toyozo, b. 25 Apr 1936, Indianapolis, Indiana, USA. Music Educator; Adjudicator. Education: BA, cum laude, Butler University, 1958; MM, Butler University, 1967; Postgraduate work, University of North Carolina, 1967-70. Career: Organist, Director of Choirs, Northwood Christian Church, Indianapolis, 1954-57; Minister of Music, Allisonville Christian Church, Indianapolis, 1957-58; Assistant Professor of Music, Milligan College, Tennessee, 1970-72, Private Teacher of Music, Durham, North Carolina, 1972-; Faculty, Piano Camp, University of North Carolina, Greensboro, 1996-97. Compositions: 3 Movements for Chorus, 1971; Bluesy, 1979. Publication: Vinquist and Zaslaw, Performance Practice: A Bibliography, 1970. Honours: Various Scholarships & Military Awards. Memberships: American Musicological Society; College Music Society; American Guild of Organists; Music Teachers National Association; North Carolina Music Teachers Association; Durham Music Teachers Association; Organ Historical Society. Address: 3520 Mayfair Street, Apt 205, Durham, NC 27707-2673, USA.

NAN Sheli, b. 23 Nov 1950, New York, USA. Pianist; Harpsichordist; Percussionist; Composer; Educator. Education: Studied with Vivian Rivkin; Julliard School of Music; University of Wisconsin; Conservatorio Luigi Cherubini, Italy. Career: The Music Studio, 1975-. Compositions: La Musica Nos Cuenta Una Historia; Over 40 Other Compositions for Solo Piano, Harpsichord, Ensemble. Recordings: Heart-Felt Piano Music; Acoustic Piano Excursions; Sarah and Hagar; Tech-Ethnic; Music For a Vanished Tribe; The Last Gesture and Other Works for Harpsichord. Publications: Bienvenidos! Welcome to the Musical World of Sheli Nan!; La Musica Nos Cuenta Una Historia; The Composers Tool Kit; The Sheli Nan Method, forthcoming. Memberships: ASCAP; Music Sources; MTA; SFEMS. Hobbies: Improvisation; Salsa Dancing. Current Management: Russ Jennings Productions. Address: 150 Vicente Road, Berkeley, CA 94705, USA.

NAPIER Marita, b. 16 Feb 1939, Johannesburg, South Africa. Singer (Soprano). Education: Studied first in South Africa, then Detmold. Debut: Bielefeld 1969, as Venus in Tannhäuser. Career: Sang in Essen, Hanover and Hamburg; San Francisco, 1972-75, as Wagner's Sieglinde, Eva and Freia; Covent Garden, 1974; Bayreuth Festival, 1974-75, as Sieglinde and Eva; Verona Festival, 1979; Engagements in Vienna, Frankfurt, Stockholm, Chicago, Philadelphia and Rome; Other roles have included Elsa, both Verdi's Leonoras, Santuzza, Ariadne and Elisabeth de Valois; Met Opera New York in Turandot, Hansel and Gretel and The Ring; Gurrelieder under Boulez and Feuersnot for RAI, Italy; Director of PACT Opera Training Centre at Pretoira, 1992; Sang Isolde at Cape Town, 1992; Giulietta in Les Contes d'Hoffmann, 1995. Recordings include: Gurrelieder, Boulez; Feuersnot, Rai; Walküre, Met; Beethoven's 9th Symphony (Philips); Das Rheingold (Eurodisc). Address: Capab Opera, PO Box 4107, Cape Town, South Africa.

NAPOLI Jacopo, b. 26 Aug 1911, Italy. Composer. Education: S Pietro a Majella Conservatoire of Music, Naples; Obtained diplomas in Composition, Organ and Piano. Career: Held Chair of Counterpoint and Fugue at Cagliari Conservatoire and at Naples Conservatoire; Director, S Pietro a Majella Conservatoire of Music, Naples, 1955, 1962; Director, Giuseppe Verdi Conservatoire of Music, Milan, 1972, then Director, St Cecilia Conservatory, Rome; Director, Scarlatti Arts Society, 1955-; Works performed in Germany, Spain and on Italian Radio. Compositions: (Operas): Il Malato Immaginario, 1939; Miseria e Nobilta 1946; Un Curioso Accidente 1950; Masaniello 1953; I Pescatori, 1954; Il Tesoro, 1958; (Oratorio) The Passion of Christ; Operas Il Rosario, 1962 and Il Povero Diavolo, 1963; Il Barone avaro 1970; Piccola Cantata del Venerdi Santo, 1964; (Orchestral Works) Overture to Love's Labours Lost, 1935; Preludio di Caccia, 1935; La Festa di Anacapri, 1940.

NASEDKIN Alexei, b. 20 Dec 1942, Moscow, Russia. Concert Pianist. Education: Studied at Central Music School and the Conservatoire, Moscow. Debut: Public concerts from 1951, aged 9. Career: Has toured extensively in Russia and throughout the world, playing works by Haydn, Scarlatti, Mozart, Beethoven, Schubert, Chopin, Prokofiev and Shostakovich; Professor in Piano at Moscow Conservatoire from 1968; Vladimir Ovchinikov has been among his pupils. Compositions: Works for piano and orchestra. Recordings: Many. Honours: Gold Medal at competitions in Vienna and Munich, 1967; Prizewinner at Leeds, 1966, and Moscow, 1962. Address: c/o Sonata, 11 Northpark Street, Glasgow G20 7AA, Scotland.

NASH Graham (Thomas), b. 21 Jun 1952, London, England. Conductor. Divorced, 1 s. Education: LRAM, Royal Academy of Music, 1970-74. Debut: Conducting, Royal Albert

Hall, 1980, Cracow Radio Symphony Orchestra, Poland, 1988 and London Philharmonic Orchestra, 1985. Career: Conducting, Victor Hochhauser, Opera Gala Nights at Royal Albert Hall, Royal Festival Hall, Barbican, 1980-89; Guest Conductor, London Festival Ballet; Music Director, London City Ballet, 1986-88; Kuopio Orchestra debut in Finland, 1987. Composition: In Memoriam, Lord Mountbatten for Large Orchestra, 1979. Honours: North London Orchestral Society Prize for Conducting, 1974; Blake Memorial Prize for Flute, Ensemble Prize, 1974. Membership: Incorporated Society of Musicians. Address: 53 Faraday Avenue, Sidcup, Kent, DA14 4JB, England.

NASH Peter Paul, b. 1950, Leighton Buzzard, Bedfordshire, England. Composer. Education: Cambridge University, with Robin Holloway. Career: Composition Fellow at Leeds University, 1976-78; Composer in Residence at the National Centre for Orchestral Studies, 1983; Producer, BBC Radio 3, 1985-87; Critic and Broadcaster, (presenter of Music Week on Radio 3); Symphony premiered at the 1991 Promenade Concerts, London. Compositions: String Trio, 1982; Wind Quintet; Insomnia for chamber ensemble; Etudes for Orchestra (On the Beach, Percussion Study, Parting) 1983-84; Figures for harp; Earthquake, scena for narrator and six players, quintet, 1987; Symphony, 1991. Address: c/o Faber Music Ltd, 3 Queen Street, London WC1N 3AU, England.

NASIDZE Sulkhan, b. 17 Mar 1927, Tbilisi, Georgia. Composer. m. Lali Surguladze, 20 July 1963, 1 son, 1 daughter. Education: Tbilisi Conservatory. Debut: Concert for Piano and Symphony Orchestra, Tbilisi, 1954. Career: Chamber, Symphony, Chamber-Instrumental, Chamber-Vocal, Choral, Ballet, Film Music Interpreted in Concert Halls & Opera Houses; TV & Radio, 1954-97. Compositions: Chamber Symphony, 1969; Symphony, Pirosmani, 1977; Symphony, Dalai, 1979; Concert for Violin, Cello & Chamber Orchestra, 1982; Ballet, King Lear, 1988; Concert for Cello & Symphony Orchestra, 1990; Stringed quartet No 2, no 3, Epitaph No 4, No 5; Con sordino; Piano concert No 3, Autumn Music; Piano Quintet; Piano Quartet, Metamorphosis; Piano Trio, Antiphonia. Recordings: Chamber Symphony, Melodia Panton; Symphony, Pirosmani Melodia; Symphony, Passione Melodia; Symphony, Dalai Melodia. Publications: Particularities of Gurian Folk Polyphony Songs, 1970; Polyphonic Processes in Z Paliachvifiil Opera, 1971; Some Words About Modern Music, 1974. Honours: Shota Rustaveli Prize, Georgia, 1978; State Prize, Russia, 1986. Memberships: Union of Composers, Georgia. Hobbies: Rambles; Sport. Address: Kazbegi Avenue 20, Apt 6, Tbilisi 380077, Georgia.

NATANEK (Adam) Tadeusz (Ted), b. 23 July 1933, Cracow, Poland. Conductor. m. Danuta Florek, 27 July 1966. Education: Department of Pedagogy, 1957; Department of Composition and Conducting, 1960; Academy of Music, Cracow, 1960. Debut: Cracow Philharmonic Orchestra, 1960. Career: Musical Conducting Assistant, 1961-62; Conductor, 1962-69; Director, Artistic Manager and Chief Conductor, 1969; Guest Conductor, Warsaw National Philharmonic, The Great Symphony Orchestra of Polish Radio and TV, Cracow and USSR, Czechoslovakia, Rumania, the Netherlands, Germany, Switzerland, Austria, Sweden, Italy, Norway and Spain; Professor of Maria Sklodowska-Curie University, Lublin; Guest Conductor, Havana, Cuba; Director, Artistic Manager and Chief Conductor of the Lublin Philharmonics, 1989-90; Artistic Director of the Symphonic Orchestra in Valladulid, Spain, 1990; Guest Conductor in nearly all European countries and in the USA. Recordings: Numerous radio and TV recordings. Contributions to: Promoter and Reviewer, Maria Sklodowska-Curie University, Lublin and Academy of Music, Warsaw and Poznan. Address: ul Szczerbowskiego 13/10, 20-012 Lublin, Poland.

NATRA Sergiu, b. 12 Apr 1924, Bucharest, Romania. Composer. Education: MA, National Music Academy, Bucharest, 1952; Studied Composition with Leo Klepper. Career: Commissions of Symphony Works, Chamber Music, Stage and Film Music in Romania; Major commissions in Israel by the Israel Festival, Israel Philharmonic Orchestra, Israel Radio, Israel Composers Fund; Professor, Composition; Examiner for the higher musical education, Israel Ministry of Education and Culture, 1964-71; Commission for Testimonium, 1968. Compositions: 3 Corteges in the Street, 1945; Suite for Orchestra, 1948; Sinfonia for Strings, Music for Violin and Harp, Music for Harpsichord and 6 Instruments, 1964; Music for Oboe & Strings, 1965; Sonatina for Harp, 1965; Song of Deborah, 1967; Variations for Piano and Orchestra, 1966; Prayer for Harp, 1972; Sonatina for Trumpet, 1973; Sonatina for Trombone Solo, 1973; Sacred Service, 1976; From the Diary of a Composer, 1978; Variations for Harpsichord, 1978; Hours for mezzo-soprano violin, clarinet and piano, 1981; Music for Harp and three Brass Instruments, 1982; Divertimento for harp and strings, 1983; Ness Amim, Cantata for solo voices, choir, chamber orchestra with harpsichord, 1984; Music for Violin and Piano, 1986; Sonatina for piano, 1987; Music for NICANOR for Harp Solo and Chamber Ensemble, 1988; Developments for viola solo and chamber orchestra, 1988. Recordings: Suite for Orchestra, 1948; Music for Harpsichord and 6 Instruments; Song of Deborah; Sonatina for Harp; Trio for Violin Violoncello and Piano; Developments, for viola and chamber orchestra. Address: 10 Barth St, Tel-Aviv 69104, Israel.

NAUHAUS Gerd (Ernst Hermann), b. 28 July 1942, Erfurt, Gerrmany. Musicologist. m. Ursula Karsdorf, 15 Aug 1965, 2 sons, (1 deceased), 1 daughter. Education: Matriculation, 1961; Diploma, Musical Education, 1965, Diploma, Musicology, 1969, PhD, 1980, Martin Luther University, Halle-Wittenberg. Career: Dramaturg at Zwickau Opera House, 1967; Musicologist, 1970-, Vice-Director, 1980-, Robert Schumann House, Zwickau; Director, 1993. Publications: Robert Schumann, Diaries and Household Books, complete scholarly edition, volume III, 1982, volume II, 1987; Clara Schumann 3 part Songs After Poems by Geibel, 1989; Piano Sonata in G minor, 1991 (first editions); Mardi in E Flat Major (after G Minor), 1997; Honours: Schumann Prize, Zwickau Town Council, 1986. Memberships: Vice-Chairman, Scientific Secretary, Robert Schumann Society, Zwickau; German Musicological Society. Hobbies: Literature; Architecture; Walking tours; Travel. Address: Robert-Schumann-Haus, Hauptmarkt 5, D-08056 Zwickau/Saxony, Germany.

NAYLOR Peter, b. 5 Oct 1933, London, England. Composer. Education: MA, Cambridge, 1957; BMus, London, 1961; Fellow, Royal College of Organists, London, 1961; Associate, Royal College of Music, London, 1962. Career: Lecturer, City Literary Institute, London, 1963-65; Lecturer, Harmony and Counterpoint, History, Royal Scottish Academy of Music and Drama, 1965-71; Organist, Ashwell Festival, Herts, 1964-69; Associate Organist, Glasgow Cathedral, 1972-85; Music Associate, Scottish Opera for Youth, 1975-80; Repetiteur, Shepway Youth Opera, Kent, 1982-85. Compositions: Symphony in One Movement, Tides and Islands; Beowulf for Symphonic Wind Band; Odysseus Returning, three act opera; Pied Piper, one act opera; The Mountain People, workshop opera; Earth was Waiting, cantata; Wassail Sing We for SA Chorus, Piano and Percussion; A Hero Dies for 22 Voices and Clarsach; Movement for Organ; Toccata for Organ; Air and Variations for 2 Pianos; Clarinet Quintet; Love and Life (5 songs); Carols and Anthems. Recordings: Elizabethan Singers, Louis Halsey; Eastern Monarchs, Choir of St John's College, Cambridge, George Guest; Now the Green Blade Riseth, SATB Choir of Glasgow Cathedral, John R Turner; Clarinet Quintet, Colin Bradbury and the Georgian Quartet. Honours: London University Convocation Trust Prize, 1959; Aschenberg Composition Prize, 1959. Memberships: Composers Guild of Great Britain; Scottish Society of Composers. Hobbies: English literature; Walking. Address: Greenacres, Brady Road, Lyminge, Folkestone, Kent, CT18 8HA, England.

NAYLOR Steven, b. 1956, Gwent, Wales. Pianist; Accompanist; Vocal Coach. Education: University College, Cardiff, at the National Opera Studio and the Royal Academy, London; BMus (Hons); ARAM; Further piano studies with Geoffrey Parsons. Career: Accompanist and opera coach at many venues in Britain and abroad; Music Staff Member, Glyndebourne Festival Opera from 1989 (Senior Coach for Le Comte Ory, 1997, also televised on Channel 4); BBC Radio 3 broadcasts; Further engagements at the Wexford and Buxton Festivals, the Munich Festival and the Hans Werner Henze Summer Academy in Germany; Canadian Opera, Singapore Arts Festival, Royal Opera House Covent Garden, English National Opera and Paris (Opéra and Chatelet); Netherlands Opera, Amsterdam. Honours: Prizes for piano accompaniment at the RAM, and the Countess of Munster Musical Trust Scholarship; Jani Strasser Award, Glyndebourne, 1993. Address: c/o Glyndebourne Festival Opera, Glyndebourne Lewes, East Sussex, BN8 5UU, England.

NAZZARENO Antinori, b. 1949, Anzio, Italy. Singer (Tenor). Education: Studied at the Accademie di Santa Cecilia, Rome. Sebut; Rome, 1978. Career: Sang Pinkerton at the Rome Opera, 1979, and has appeared at the opera houses of San Remo, Naples, Trieste, Bonn and Verona; Macerata and Torre del Lago festival, La Scala Milan, 1991, as Foresto in Attila; Other roles include Verdi's Ismaele, Alfredo, Macduff and Don Carlo, Rodolfo, Cavaradossi, Steva in Jenufa and Maurizio in Adriana Lecouvreur. Recordings include: Tosca and Madama Butterfly (Balkanton). Address: c/o Teatro alla Scala, Via Filodrammatici 2, 20121 Milan, Italy.

NEAMAN Yfrah, b. 13 Feb 1923, Sidon, Lebanon. Concert Violinist. m. 16 Mar 1963, 1 son, 1 daughter. Education: Conservatoire National Supérieure de Musique, Paris; Further studies with Carl Flesch, Jacques Thibaud, Max Rostal. Debut: Soloist with London Symphony Orchestra, London, 1944. Career: Professor, Violin, Head, Advanced Solo Studies, Guildhall School of Music and Drama, London, England; Recitals; Concerts with orchestras; Radio and TV appearances; Masterclasses in Europe, USA, Canada, Japan, China, South America, Africa and Asia; Artistic Consultant, London International String Quartet Comeptition; Artistic Adviser, Wells Cathedral School, England. Recordings: Concertos: Roberto Gerhard, Racine Fricker, Don Banks; Sonatas: John Ireland, Franck; Trios: John Ireland; Bloch, Fauré and Ravel. Publications: Editions of several musical works including: Beethoven Violin Concerto; Tartini Devil's Trill Sonata; Beethoven Violin and Piano Sonatas. Honours: 1st Prize for Violin, Paris Conservatoire, 1937; FGSM, 1964; Freedom of the City of London, 1980; OBE, 1983; Order of Madarsky Kohnik, Bulgaria, 1993; Cobbett Medal, London, 1997; Gutenberg Plaquette, Mainz, Germany, 1997. Membership: Freeman, Worshipful Company of Musicians. Address: 11 Chadwell Street, London EC1R 1XD, England.

NEARY Martin (Gerard James), b. 28 Mar 1940, London. Organist and Master of Music, Westminster Abbey; Organ Recitalist and Conductor; Founder and Conductor, Martin Neary Singers; Conductor, Wayflete Singers. m. Penelope Jane Warren, 1967, 1 son, 2 daughters. Education: HM Chapels Royal, St James's Palace; Cith of London School; Gonville and Caius College, Cambridge (Organ Scholar, MA); FRCO. Career: Assistant Organist 1963-65; Organist and Master of Music 1965-71; St Margaret's Westminster; Professor of Organ, Trinity College, London, 1963-72; Organ Advisor to Diocesan of Winchester, 1975-; Conductor, Twickenham Musical Society, 1966-72; Founder and Conductor, St Margaret's Westminster Singers, 1967-71; Director of Southern Cathedrals Festival, 1972, 1975, 1978, 1981, 1984, 1987; Organist and Master of Music, Winchester Cathedral, 1972-95, Westminster Abbey, 1995-; Organ Recitalist and Conductor; Founder and Conductor, Martin Neary Singers, 1972-; Conductor, Waynflete Singers, 1972-; Many organ recitals and broadcasts in England, including Royal Festival Hall and music festivals; has conducted many premieres of music by British composers including John Tavener's Ultimos Ritos, 1979, Jonathan Harvey's Hymn, 1979, and Passion and Resurrection, 1981, with Martin Neary Singers performing Madrigals and Graces at 10 Downing Street, 1970-74; Toured US and Canada, 1963, 1968, 1971, 1973, 1975, 1977, 1979, 1982, 1984; BBC Promenade Concerts, 1979, 1982; Conductor with ECO, 1978, 1980, 1981; LSO, 1979, 1980, 1981; Bournemouth SO and Sinfonietta 1975-; Many European Tours; Artist-in-Residence, University of California at Davis, 1984; President, Cathedral Organists Association. Recordings: Many recordings including Lloyd Webber's Requiem (Golden Disc). Hobby: Watching Cricket. Address: Westminster Abbey, London, W1, England.

NEBE Michael, b. 28 July 1947, Nordenbeck, Waldeck, Germany. Cellist. Education: Educational Diploma and Teaching qualifications, Dortmund Conservatorium; MMus, King's College, University of London, England, studied under Thurston Dart, Brian Trowell, Antony Milner, Geoffrey Bush; Licentiate, Royal Academy of Music, studying with Florence Hooton and Colin Hampton; Conducting, private studies in Germany and at Morley College under Lawrence Leonard; International Conductors' Seminar, Zlin, Czech Republic, 1991 and 1993, under Kirk Trevor, Jiri Belohlavek and Zdenek Bilek. Debut: Wigmore Hall, London, 1977. Career: Member, London Piace Consort, London Piace Duo, chamber music, London; Numerous performances throughout UK; Tours, Federal Republic of Germany, Netherlands, USA, Canada, Australia; Conductor and Musical Director of Civil Service Orchestra, 1990; Associated Conductor of Surrey Sinfonietta; Musical Director, Fine Arts Sinfonia, 1994; Teacher, freelance musician, soloist, conductor, translator, writer, lecturer and adjudicator; Has made numerous recorded radio and television appearances. Publications: Translation into German, Eta Cohen's Violin Tutor, 1979; Cello Tutor, 1984. Memberships: Dvorak Society; Incorporated Society of Musicians; Musicians' Union. Hobbies: Reading; Composition; Theatre and opera. Current Management: Thornton Management. Address: c/o Thornton Management, 24 Thornton Avenue, London SW2 4HG, England.

NEBLETT Carol, b. 1 Feb 1946, Modesto, California, USA. Singer (Soprano). Education: Studied with Lotte Lehmann and Pierre Bernac. Career: Sang with Roger Wagner Chorale from 1965; Stage debut as Musetta, New York City Opera 1969; Returned as Marietta in Die Tote Stadt, Poppea, and Margherita and Elena in Boito's Mefistofele; Chicago 1975, as Chrysothemis in Elektra; Veinna Staatsoper debut 1976 as Minnie in La Fanciulla del West, Covent Garden 1977; Metropolitan Opera debut 1979, as Senta in Der fliegende Holländer; Returned as Tosca, Amelia (Un Ballo in Maschera), Manon Lescaut and Alice Ford in Falstaff; Appearances in Dallas, Turin, Leningrad, Pittsburgh, Baltimore and San Francisco; Other roles include Violetta, Minnie in La Fanciulla del West, Mozart's Countess, Charpentier's Louise and Antonia in Les Contes d'Hoffmann; Salzburg Festival as Vitelia in La Clemenza di Tito (has also appeared as Vitelia in Jean-Pierre Ponnelle's film of the opera); Teatro Regio Turin 1987, in Respighi's Semirama; Sang Mme Lidoine in Les Dialogues des Carmélites at San Diego, 1990; Debut as Norma for Greater Miami Opera 1990; Aida for Cincinnati Opera; Season 1992 as Tosca for Opera Pacific at Costa Mesa, Queen Isabella in Franchetti's Cristoforo Colombo at Miami and as Amelia in Un Ballo in Maschera at Dublin; Sang the title role in Blitzstein's Regina at Costa Mesa, 1990. Recordings include: Die Tote Stadt (RCA); La Fanciulla del West

(Deutsche Grammophon); La Bohème (HMV). Address: c/o Stafford Law Associates, 6 Barham Close, Weybridge, Surrey KT13 9PR, England.

NEDELKA Michal, b. 13 May 1964, Brandys nad Labem, Czech Republic. Music Teacher. Education: Piano, Conservatory of Music, Plzen; Music, Russian, Postdoctoral Study, Faculty of Education, Charles University, Prague. Publications: Polyphony in Folksong, 1993; Handbook of Piano Improvisation, 1997. Contributions to: Music Education; Cantus. Membership: Czech Music Society. Hobbies: Gardening; Cooking. Address: Hrozneho 20, 289 22 Lysa nad Labem, Czech Republic.

NEGRI Vittorio, b. 16 Oct 1923, Milan, Italy. Conductor. Education: Studied composition, conducting and violin at the Milan Conservatory. Career: Assistant Conductor to Bernhard Paumgartner at the Salzburg Mozarteum, 1952; Guest Conductor with leading orchestras in Europe; Appearances at festivals in Flanders, Salzburg, Montreux, Orange and Versailles; Engagements at La Scala, Milan and with the Orchestre National de France, the Dresden Staatskapelle and the Boston Symphony Orchestra. Recordings: Music by Mozart, Vivaldi and composers of the Venetian Baroque, including the sacred choral works of Vivaldi, with Margaret Marshall, Ann Murray, Linda Finnie, Anne Collins, Felicity Lott, Sally Burgess, Robert Hall and Anthony Rolfe Johnson (Philips). Honours: Numerous awards for recordings. Address: Chemin des Cuarroz 8, 1807 Blonay, Switzerland.

NEGRIN Francisco (Miguel), b. 1963, Mexico. Opera Director. Education: Studied cinematography in France notably at Aix-en-Provence. Career: Staff Producer at Théâtre Royal de la Monnaie, Brussels; Has assisted directors such as Patrice Chereau, K E Herrmann and Graham Vick; Associations with many opera houses including: Paris Châtelet, Salzburg Landestheater and Seattle Opera; Directed the premiere of his version of Debussy's The Fall of the House of Usher, Christ Church, Spitalfields, 1986, and at London International Opera Festival and Lisbon Opera, 1989; Has produced Werther at Opera de Nice, 1990, Orlando Paladino at Garsington Manor, 1990, La Traviata and the Mozart pasticcio The Jewel Box at Opera North, 1991 being the first outside production to be invited by Glyndebourne to be performed there, 1991, Così fan tutte at Seattle Opera, Don Carlos at Victoria State Opera, Melbourne, L'Heure Espagnole and La Colombe at the Guildhall School of Music, 1993, and Handel's Julius Caesar at Australian Opera in Sydney, 1994 and Melbourne, 1995; World premieres of Tourist Variations and Visitatio Sepulchri by James Macmillan at Glasgow's Tramway and at the Edinburgh Festival, Una Cosa Rara by Martin y Soler at the Drottningholm Festival; Schoeck's Venus at Geneva, 1997. Recordings: Julius Caesar on CD and Video. Current Management: IMG Artists. Address: c/o Diana Mulgan, IMG Artists, Media House, 3 Burlington Lane, London, W4 2TH, England.

NÉGYESY János, b. 13 Sept 1938, Budapest, Hungary. Violinist. Education: State Examination, Franz Liszt Music Academy, Budapest. Career: Concertmaster, Berlin Radio Orchestra, Federal Republic of Germany, 1970-74; Professor of Music, University of San Diego, USA, 1979-; Soloist in all major European festivals including Berliner Festwochen, Royan Festival, Donaueschingen, Paris, Witten Chamber Music Festival, Meta Music Festival Berlin, Metz Festival; Soloist in festivals in New York, San Francisco, Washington DC, Baltimore, Vancouver, Tokyo, Buenos Aires, Mexico City, Tehran, Helsinki, Stockholm, Zürich, Paris, Torino, Ferrara, Buedapest, elsewhere. Compositions: Latest multimedia works for Electronic Violin System: Digitales, 1993; Igitur, 1993; en route, 1995. Recordings: All Violin Sonatas by Charles Ives, 1975; Dedications to János Négyesy, 1978; John Cage: Freeman Etudes I-XVI for solo violin, 1984; Personae, Violin Concerto by Roger Reynolds, 1992; The Complete Violin Duos by Béla Bartók, with Päivikki Nykter, 1993; The Complete Freeman Etudes for Solo Violin by John Cage, 1995; Dedications 2, Solo Violin works written for and dedicated to János Négyesy, 1995. Publications: New Violin Technique, 1978. Memberships: New York Academy of Sciences; American Association for the Advancement of Science; International Platform Association. Hobbies: Photo-montages and collages (exhibitions); Computer graphics (exhibitions in Finland, Argentina, USA). Address: 344 Prospect Street, La Jolla, CA 92037, USA.

NEHER Patrick, b. 5 Apr 1959, Los Alamos, Mew Mexico, USA. Professor of Music; Soloist; Composer; Chamber Musician. Divorced, 1 daughter. Education: Eastman School of Music, 1976; BM, MM, Juillard School, 1977-81; Diploma from International Rabbath Institute, 1996. Debut: New York, 1981; Parma, Italy, 1989; Perth, Australia, 1992; Sydney, 1994; Paris, 1996. Appointments: Professor of Music, University of Arizona, for 13 years; Principal Bassist, Tucson Symphony for 10 years; Principal Bass of Santa Fe Pro Musica for 8 years; Guest Artist, Chamber Music Festival for 15 years; Travelled as Clinician to Australia, Europe, South America, Canada. Compositions include: Your Eyes, for soprano, double bass and piano; Accept! for soprano and double bass; The Frog Prince Continued..., for soprano, tenor, double bass and violin; Sonatina No 3, for double bass and piano; Gjauticurratifiticus, for dancer, double bass and trio; Dance In The Clouds, for 12 dancers and 12 double basses. Recordings: CD: Bass Ascending, The Music Of Patrick Neher, 1998. Publications: The New Revoloution in Double Bass, 1992; Interlochen 93, Bloomington 95 (highlights of the ISB conference, video productions, 1993, 1995; From the Student's Perspective, 1994. Contributions to: Double Bass Forum Editor, for American String Teacher Magazine, 1992-94. Memberships: International Society of Bassists; Chamber Music America; College Music Society. Hobbies: photography; Videography. Current Management: Self-managed. Address: School of Music, University of Arizona, Tucson, AZ 85721, USA.

NEIDHART Elke, b. 1940, Germany. Stage Director. Education: Studied at the Stuttgart Drama and Opera School. Career: Assistant at the Zurich Stage Opera, 1964; Resident Director of Australian Opera from 1977, staging Fidelio, Cav and Pag, Lohengrin and Salome; Has also staged Fidelio for Lyric Opera of Queensland, Puritani and Flying Dutchman for Victorian State Opera; From 1990, Director of Productions at Cologne Opera, assisting on and restaging The Ring, From the House of the Dead, Don Giovanni, Der Prinz von Homburg and La Finta Semplice; Il Trovatore at Sydney, 1996. Address: c/o Atholl Still Ltd, Foresters Hall, 25-27 Westow Street, London SE19 3RY, England.

NEIGHBOUR Oliver (Wray), b. 1 April 1923. Retired Music Librarian, Reference Division of The British Library. Education: Eastbourne College; BA, Birbeck College, London, 1950. Career: Entered Department of Printed Books, BM, 1946; Assistant Keeper in Music Room, 1951; Deputy Keeper, 1976; Music Librarian, Reference Division of The British Library, 1976-85. Publications: (with Alan Tyson) English Music Publishers' Plate Numbers, 1965; The Consort and Keyboard Music of William Byrd, 1978; (ed), Music and Bibliography: Essays in Honour of Alec Hyatt King, 1980; Article on Schoenberg in New Grove Dictionary of Music and Musicians, 1980; Editor of First Publications of Works by Schumann, Schoenberg and Byrd. Honours: Fellow, British Academy. Hobbies: Walking; Ornithology. Address: 12 Treborough House, 1 Nottingham Place, London W1M 3FP, England.

NEIKRUG Marc (Edward), b. 24 Sept 1946, New York City, USA. Composer; Pianist. Education: Studied with Giselher Klebe in Detmold 1964-68; Stony Brook State University of New York; MM in Composition 1971. Career: Commissions from the Houston Symphony and the St Paul Chamber Orchestra (Consultant on Contemporary Music 1978); Los Alamos premiere at the Deutsche Oper Berlin, 1988; Duo partnership with Pinchas Zukerman; Visited London, 1989; British premiere of Violin Concerto at South Bank and duo recital at the Barbican Hall. Compositions: Piano Concerto 1966; Solo Cello sonata 1967; Clarinet Concerto 1967; 2 String Quartets 1969, 1972; Viola Concerto 1974; Suite for cello and piano 1974; Rituals for flute and harp 1976; Concertino for ensemble 1977; Fantasies for violin and piano 1977; Continuum for cello and piano 1978; Cycle for 7 pianos 1978; Kaleidoscope for flute and piano 1979; Eternity's Sunrise for orchestra 1979-80; Through Roses, theatre piece 1979-80; Mobile for orchestra 1981; Violin Concerto 1982; Duo for violin and piano 1983; Los Alamos opera, 1988. Honours: NEA Awards 1972 and 1974; Prizes for Through Roses at the Besancon Film Festival 1981, and the International Film and Television Festival, New York, 1982. Address: c/o ASCAP, ASCAP Building, One Lincoln Plaza, NY 10023, USA.

NEJCEVA Liljana, b. 1945, Silistra, Bulgaria. Singer (Mezzo-soprano). Education: Studied at the music schools in Ruse and Sofia. Career: Sang at the Leipzig Opera 1969, as Amastris in Xerxes, Ulrica, Lady Pamela in Fra Diavolo, Fidalma in Il Matrimonio Segreto and Konchakovna in Prince Igor; Member of Bayerische Staatsoper Munich, 1973-78, as Azucena, Maddalena, Marina in Boris Godunov and Cherubino; Has sung with Nationaltheater Mannheim, 1981-; Guest appearances include Hamburg (as Eboli), Berlin Staatsoper (Dorabella), Vienna Volksoper (Carmen) and Cologne (Suzuki); Also sings Luisa Miller; Travelled to Japan and Cuba; Concert engagements in Munich, Prague, Rome, Frankfurt and Paris. Address: Music International, 13 Ardilaun Road, London N5 2QR, England.

NEL Anton, b. 29 Dec 1961, Johannesburg, South Africa. Pianist; Professor of Piano. Education: BMus, University of the Witwatersand, South Africa, 1983; Performers Diploma, MMus 1984, DMus 1986, University of Cincinnati, USA. Debut: Carnegie Recital Hall, New York, 1986. Career: Performances with major orchestras including Chicago, Seattle, Cincinnati, Brooklyn; Recitals and chamber music concerts throughout USA, Canada, Europe, Parts of Africa; Recitals in Alice Tully Hall, New York; Barbican Centre and Queen Elizabeth Hall, London; Many appearances at summer festivals including Aspen, Ravinia; Professor of Piano, Eastman School of Music, Rochester, New York. Recordings: Saint-Saëns, Carnival of the Animals; Haydn-4 Sonatas. Honours: 1st Prize, Walter W Naumburg International Piano Competition; 1st Prize, Joanna Hodges International Piano Competition; Prizes at Leeds and Pretoria International Piano Competition. Memberships: Pi Kappa Lambda. Hobbies: Reading; Board Games; Cooking. Current Management: Walter W Naumburg Foundation.

NELSON John, b. 6 Dec 1941, San José, Costa Rica. Conductor. Education: Studies at Juilliard School, NY. Career: Conductor, Berlioz's Les Troyens, New York, 1972; Conductor, New York City Opera, 1972-; From 1973 at Metropolitan Opera, conducting Cavalleria Rusticana, Pagliacci, Jenufa, Il Barbiere di Siviglia, Carmen and L'Incoronazione di Poppea; Conducted US premiere of Britten's Owen Wingrave, Santa Fe Opera; Music Director, Indianapolis Symphony Orchestra, 1977-88; Music Director St Louis Opera, 1981-91, continuing as Principal Guest Conductor; Caramoor Festival, New York; Tour of Europe, 1987; Guest engagements with leading orchestras in North America and Europe; Debut with Lyon Opera, 1991 conducting Béatrice and Bénédict; Conducted Benvenuto Cellini at Geneva Opera, 1992; Offenbach's The Tales of Hoffmann at the Bastille; Recent productions include Handel's Xerxes, Massenet's Don Quichotte with Chicago Lyric Opera, Béatrice and Bénédict with Welsh National Opera, Faust at Geneva Opera, Benvenuto Cellini with Rome Opera, Don Carlos at Lyon Opera and A new opera at Lyon Opera by Marcel Landowski; Verdi's Vespri Siciliani at Rome, 1997. Recordings: Béatrice and Bénédict; CD, Bach Arias with Kathleen Battle; Gorecki's Beatus Vir with Czech Philharmonic; Handel's Semele with English Chamber Orchestra and Kathleen Battle, awarded Grammy Award, Best Operatic Recording of 1993; CD of Works of Paul Schönfield, 1994; Gorecki's Miserere with Chicago Symphony and Chicago Lyric Opera Choruses. Honour: Diapason d'Or Award for Erato recording of Béatrice and Bénédict, 1992. Address: c/o IMG Artists Europe, 3 Burlington Lane, Chiswick, London, W4 2TH, England.

NELSON Judith, b. 10 Sep 1939, Chicago, IL, USA. Singer (Soprano). m. Alan H Nelson, 5 Aug 1961, 1 s, 1 d. Education: BA, Music, St Olaf College, Northfield, MN, 1961; Studied piano 12 years; Principal Teachers of Voice: Thomas Wikman, Chicago; James Cunningham, Berkeley; Martial Singher, Santa Barbara. Debut: Paris, 1973. Career: Radio: BBC, France, Belgium, Holland, Germany, Italy, Austria, Scandinavia; Several BBC Promenade Concerts; Television: Series, Music in Time, Open University Handel's Messiah, BBC; ITV; Performances with major symphonies including: San Francisco Symphony; Los Angeles Philharmonic; Baltimore Symphony; Atlanta Symphony; St Louis Symphony. Recordings: Various recordings including: Belinda in Dido and Aeneas, (Chandos), Handel's Alceste and La Resurrezione; Haydn: Canzonets and Cantatas, with Koch International. Honours: Alfred Hertz Memorial Fellowship, 1972-73; Honorary Doctorate, St Olaf College, 1989. Current Management: Christopher Tennant Management, London, England. Address: 2600 Buena Vista Way, Berkeley, CA 94708, USA.

NELSON Martin, b. 1950, London. Singer (Bass). Education: Studied at Caius College, Cambridge and with Tito Gobbi and Peter Harrison. Career: Has sung principal roles for Opera North, Kent Opera, English Music Theatre, Travelling Opera, Birmingham Music Theatre and Musica nel Chiostro; Appearances at the Buxton and Wexford Festivals and concerts in Tours, Versailles and Israel; Engagements as Christus in the St John and St Matthew Passions of Bach; Stravinsky's Pulcinella on BBC 2; Has sung in the West End (Sondheim's A Little Night Music) and in music theatre (Royal Opera Garden Venture); Founder of Scrap and Scratch Opera, using recycled materials; With New Israel Opera appeared as Alidoro in La Cenerentola. Address: c/o Korman International Management, Crunnells Green Cottage, Preston, Herts SG4 7UQ, England.

NELSON Ron, b. 14 Dec 1929, Joliet, Illinois, USA. Composer; Professor of Music. m. Helen Mitchell (deceased), 1 son, 1 daughter. Education: BM, 1952, MM, 1953, DMA, 1956, Eastman School of Music, Rochester; Ecole Normale de Musique, Paris, France, 1955-56. Career: Professor Emeritus, 1993. Compositions: Opera, The Birthday of the Infanta, 1956; The Christmas Story, 1958; Toccata for Orchestra, 1963; What is Man?, 1964; Rocky Point Holiday, 1969; This is the Orchestra, 1969; Prayer for an Emperor of China, 1973; Five Pieces for Orchestra after Paintings of Frank Wyeth, 1975; Four Pieces after the Seasons, 1978; Three Autumnal Sketches, 1979; Mass of LaSalle, 1981; Nocturnal Pieces, 1982; Three Settings of the Moon, 1982; Medieval Suite, 1983; Aspen Jubilee, 1984; Te Deum Laudamus, 1985; Danza Capriccio for saxophone, 1988; Three pieces after Tennyson, 1989; Fanfare for the Hour of Sunlight, 1989; Morning Alleluias, 1989; The Deum Laudamus, 1991; To the Airborne, 1991; Passacaglin (Homage on B-A-C-H), 1992; Lauds (Praise High Day), 1992; Epiphanies, fanfares and chorales, 1994; Chaconne (In memoriam...), 1994. Recordings include: Behold Man, Reference Recordings; Pebble Beach Sojourn, Reference Recordings; Savannah River Holiday,

Mercury records; Morning Alleluas, Kosie Recordings; Passacaglia (Homage on B-A-C-H), EMI Records; Sarabande: For Katharine in April, Mercury Records. Publications: Te Deum Laudamus, 1991; To The Airborne, 1991; Lauds, 1992, Passaglia (Homage on B-A-C-H), 1993; Sonoran Desert Holiday, 1995; Epiphanies (Fanfares and Chorales), 1995. Honours include: Lifetime Achievement Award, CBDNA, 1993. Address: Sonoran Highlands, 28412 N 97th Way, Scottsdale, AZ 85262, USA.

NELSOVA Zara, b. 23 Dec 1918, Winnipeg, Manitoba, Canada. Concert Cellist. m. Grant Johannesen, 1963. Education: Studied at the London Violoncello School with Herbert Walenn; Further studies with Casals. Debut: London 1932, in Lalo's Concerto. Career: Played in Canadian Trio with two sisters; US debut 1942, New York Town Hall; US Citizen from 1955; Numerous recitals with Grant Johannesen; Appearances in Italy, Spain, Portugal, Switzerland, Holland, England, USA and Scandinavian countries; Performed Bloch's Suites for Solo Cello on the BBC, 1957;Tour of Russia, 1966; Early performances of works by Barber, Hindemith and Shostakovich. Honours include: Canadian Centennial Medal of the Confederation, 1967.

NELSSON Woldemar, b. 4 Apr 1938, Kiev, Ukraine. Conductor. Education: Studied with his father in Kiev, then at the Novosibirsk Conservatory and in Moscow and Leningrad. Career: Assistant to Kyrill Kondrashin at the Moscow Philharmonic, 1972; Conducted leading orchestras in the USSR, with such soloists as Rostropovitch, David Oistrakh and Gidon Kremer; Emigrated to West Germany 1977 and conducted major orchestras in Hamburg, Munich, Berlin, Frankfurt, Vienna, London, Geneva, Amsterdam, Tel Aviv, Jerusalem and Montreal; Directed the premiere of Henze's ballet Orpheus, Stuttgart 1979, and took the production to Washington and the Metropolitan Opera New York; Guest Conductor with Stuttgart Opera from 1980; General Music Director of the State Theatre in Kassel; Has conducted opera productions in Paris, Philadelphia, Japan, Vienna and Barcelona; Bayreuth Festival, 1980-85, Lohnegrin and Der fliegende Holländer; Conducted the world premiere of Penderecki's opera Die schwarze Maske, Salzburg 1986; Currently Music Director of the Royal Opera, Copenhagen. Recordings include: Lohengrin (CBS); Der fliegende Holländer (Philips). Honours include: Max Reger Prize. Address: c/o Staatstheater Stuttgart, Oberer Schlossgarten 6, D-7000 Stuttgart 1, Germany.

NEMESCU Octavian, b. 29 Mar 1940, Pascani, Rumania. Composer; University Lecturer. m. Erica Nemescu. Education: Bucharest Conservatory, DMus 1978. Compositions include: Sonata for clarinet and piano, 1962; Triangle for orchestra, 1964; Ego (multi-media performance) 1970; The Play of Senses, music for a pair of ears, of eyes, of hands, a nose and a mouth, 1973-76; Cromosom, imaginary music, 1974; Natural !!!, music in space, 1974; Calendar, permanent music for the environment of a room, 1976; Semantica, metamusic for lovers of music, 1978; Natural-Cultural for chamber ensemble and tape, 1984. Honours include: Aaron Copland Composition Prize, 1970. Membership: Composers Union of Rumania. Address: Bu Dinicu Golescu 23-25, BL B Scara 3, Ap 65, Sector VII, Codul 77112, Bucharest, Rumania.

NEMET Mary Ann, b. 10 June 1936, Budapest, Hungary. Violinist. 3 children. Education: AMusA, University Conservatorium, Melbourne; Studied with Stella Nemet, Max Rostal and Arthur Grumiaux. Debut: Beethoven Violin Concerto with Sydney Symphony Orchestra, 1955. Career: Concert tours, radio and TV appearances in Australia and Far East; Toured most European countries with pianist Roxanne Wruble (Duo Landolfi); Appointed to Sydney Conservatorium, 1970; Soloist, East Germany, 1972; Leader of Nemet String Trio and Piano Quartet, London; Chamber music and solo work throughout Australia; Lecturer in Strings, Victorian College of the Arts, 1976-90; Specialist Violin Tutor, University of Southern Queensland; Frequent Recitalist for ABC Radio; Senior String Examiner, Australian Music Examinations Board. Recordings: Numerous. Contributions to: Australian Music Teacher. Memberships: Australian String Teachers' Association; Musical Society of Victoria. Address: 7 Merlin Court, Toowoomba, MS 852 Queensland 4350, Australia.

NEMETH Geza, b. 1930, Hungary. Violist. Education: Studied at the Franz Liszt Academy, Budapest. Career: Violist of the Bartok Quartet from 1957; Performances in nearly every European country and tours to Australia, Canada, Japan, New Zealand and the USA; Festival appearances at Adelaide, Ascona, Aix, Venice, Dubrovnik, Edinburgh, Helsinki, Lucerne, Menton, Prague, Veinna, Spoleto and Schwetzingen; Tour of Britain 1986 including concerts at Cheltenham, Dartington, Philharmonic Hall Liverpool, RNCM Manchester and the Wigmore Hall; Tours of Britain 1988 and 1990, featuring visits to the Sheldonian Theatre Oxford, Wigmore Hall, Harewood House and Birmingham; Repertoire includes standard classics and Hungarian works by Bartók, Durko, Bozay, Kadosa, Soproni, Farkas, Szabo and Lang. Recordings include: Complete quartets of Mozart, Beethoven and Brahms; Major works of Haydn and Schubert (Hungaroton); Complete quartets of Bartók (Erato). Honours: (with members of Bartók Quartet) Kossuth Prize, Outstanding Artist of the Hungarian People's Republic, 1981; UNESCO/IMC Prize 1981. Address: c/o Ingpen & Williams Ltd, 26 Wadham Road, London SW15 2LR, England.

NENDICK Josephine, b. 1940, Kent, England. Singer (Soprano). Education: Studied at the Royal College of Music, the Guildhall School of Music with Audrey Langford. Career: Sang first at the Aldeburgh Festival, then premiered works by Boulez and Bo Nilsson at Darmstadt; Has sung with such ensembles as Capricorn, Domaine Musical, Ensemble Musique Nouvelles, Music Group of London, Les Percussions de Strasbourg; Festival engagements at Avignon, Berlin, Cheltenham, London (English Bach), Edinburgh, Prades, Royaun, Warsaw; Conductors include Pierre Boulez, Ernest Bour, Charles Bruck, Colin Davis, Michael Gielen, Norman Del Mar, Bruno Maderna, Manuel Rosenthal; Repertoire includes Berg, Der Wein; Berio Magnificat, Chamber Music, Circles; Four Popular Songs, Sequenza; Boulez Improvisations sur Mallarmé, Le Marteau sans Maitre, Le Soleil des Eaux; Birtwistle Entractes and Sappho Fragments; Bussotti Le Passion selon Sade; Ravel Chansons Medécasses and 3 Poemes de Stephane Mallarmé; Schoenberg Pierrot Lunaire and Das Buch der Hängenden Gärten; Webern Songs Op 8 and Op 13; Bartók Village Scenes; Works by Barraqué, Smith Brindle, Finnissy, Dillon, Cage, Crumb, Dallapiccola, Stravinsky, Babbitt, Ives and Satie; Sang in Bach's Christmans Oratorio, Berlioz Les Troyens (Ascanius), Delius A Mass of Life; Mahler Das Lied von der Erde, Monteverdi L'Incoronazione di Poppea (Drusilla, at Bremen) and Mozart's Requiem and C minor Mass. Recordings include: Boulez Le Soleil des Eaux (EMI); Lutyens Quincunx, with the BBC SO (Argo); Barraqué Sequence and Chant après Chan (Valois).

NENTWIG Franz Ferdinand, b. 23 Aug 1929, Duisburg, Germany. Singer (Bass-Baritone). Debut: Bielefeld 1962, as Ottokar in Der Freischütz. Career: Sang in Darmstadt and Hanover and at the Vienna Volksoper, Vience 1983, as Amfortas in Parsifal; Wagner performances in Munich, Berlin and Hamburg; Tour of Japan 1984 with the Hamburg Company; Metropolitan Opera 1984 as Telramund in Lohengrin; Barcelona 1986 also in Lohengrin; Further appearances in Cologne, Frankfurt, Karlsruhe, Stuttgart and Mannheim; Other roles include Pizarro in Fidelio, Escamillo, Strauss's Jochanaan and Mandryka, Mozart's Count and Don Alfonso, Verdi's Rigoletto and Amonasro and Wagner's Dutchman, Wotan and Gunther; Sang Hans Sachs with the Berlin Staatsoper on tour to Japan, 1987; Salzburg Festival and Turin 1987, as Schoenberg's Moses and as Wotan; Sang Dr Schön in Lulu and Dr Vigilius in Schreker's Der ferne Klang, 1988; Wotan in the first Polish production of the Ring, 1989; Brussels 1990, as Shishkov in From the House of the Dead; Sang La Roche in a new production of Capriccio at Covent Garden, 1991; season 1991-92 as Wotan at Brussels and Beckmesser at Spoleto. Recordings include: Schreker's Der Schatzgräber (Capriccio). Address: c/o Théâtre Royal de la Monnaie, 4 Leopolstrasse, B-1000 Brussels, Belgium.

NERSESSIAN Pavel, b. 26 Aug 1968, Ramenskoye, Moscow, Russia. Concert Pianist. Education: Studied at Central Music School, Moscow and at Tchaikovsky Conservatory, Graduated 1987. Career: Concert tours of Russia from 1972 and more recent appearances in Spain, Hungary, Italy, France and Ireland; Season 1992-93 in Cannes and Dublin, tour of Japan and appearances in Austria, England, Ireland, Canada, and the USA; Professor of Piano at Moscow Conservatory. Honour: 2nd Prize, Beethoven Competition in Vienna, 1985. Address: c/o Ingpen & Williams Ltd, 26 Wadham Road, London SW15 2LR, England.

NES Jard van, b. 15 June 1948, Holland. Singer (Mezzo-soprano). Debut: Sang in Mahler's 2 Symphony under Bernard Haitink at Concertgebouw, 1983. Career: Appearances in Bach's St Matthew Passion under Nikolaus Harnoncourt and in Mahler's 8th Symphony; Tour of North America with Minnesota Orchestra and Edo de Waart, 1987-88; Further concerts in Paris, London, Oslo, Montreal and Ludwigsburg; Stage debut with Netherlands Opera 1983, as Bertarido in Rodelinda; Double bill of Hindemith's Sancta Susanna and Mörder, Hoffnung der Frauen 1984; Season 1986-87 with parts in Il Ritorno di Ulisse, Die Meistersinger, (Magdalena) and Tristan und Isolde as Brangaene; Sang in Ligeti's Le Grand Macabre at the Paris Châtelet and the Salzburg Festival, 1997. Recordings: Mozart Requiem, Brahms Alto Rhapsody, Mahler 2nd Symphony and Zemlinsky Lieder; Messiah; Beethoven's Ninth; Handel's Theodora and Das Lied von der Erde. Address: c/o Lies Askonas Ltd, 6 Henrietta Street, London WC2, England.

NESCHLING John, b. 1945, Rio de Janeiro, Brazil. Conductor. Education: Studied in Vienna with Hans Swarowsky; Further study with Leonard Bernstein in the USA. Career: Engagements with the London, Vienna and Berlin Radio Symphony Orchestras, New York and Israel Philharmonic, the Tonhalle, Zurich and the Italian Radio at Naples and Milan; Opera appearances at Berlin (Deutsche Oper and Staatsoper), Stuttgart, Hamburg and Stockholm; Principal Conductor of the San Carlo Lisbon 1981-88; Music Director of the Teatro Sao Paulo and at St Gallen in Switzerland (Die Zauberflöte 1989); Engaged for Trovatore, Figaro, Pagliacci and Gianni Schicchi at St Gallen; Lucia di Lammermoor, Butterfly, Andrea Chénier and Il Barbiere di Siviglia as guest conductor at the Vienna Staatsoper; Conducted Il Guarany by Gomes at Bonn, 1994. Recordings include: Il Guarany, 1996. Honours include: Winner, International Competition for young conductors in Florence, London Symphony Orchestra International Competition. Address: Walter Beloch srl, Artists Management, Via Melzi D'Eril, 26 20154 Milan, Italy.

NESS Arthur J, b. 27 Jan 1936, Chicago, Illinois, USA. Musicologist. m. Charlotte A Kolczynski, 29 Dec 1982. Education: BMus, Music Theory, University of Southern California, 1958; AM, Music, Harvard University, 1963; PhD, Musicology, New York University, 1984. Career: Assistant Professor, University of Southern California, 1964-76; Associate Professor, Daemen College, 1976-83; Visiting Lecturer, State University of New York, Buffalo, 1983-87; Editor and Music Engraver, 1990-; General Editor, Monuments of the Lutenist Art, 1992-94. Composition: Three Poems by Kenneth Patchen, for alto and piano. Publications: Lute Works of Francesco Canova da Milano (1497-1543), 1970; The Herwath Lute Tablatures, 1984; The Königsberg Manuscript (with John M Ward), 1989. Contributions to: Major contributor, New Grove Dictionary of Music, 1980, New Harvard Dictionary of Music, 1986. Also periodicals: Journal of American Musicological Society; Le Luth et sa Musique II, 1985; Music in Context: Essays for John M Ward, 1985; New Grove Dictionary of American Music, 1986. Honours: Fulbright Fellow, University of Munich; Healey Award, 1984. Hobby: Gardening. Address: 2039 Commonwealth Avenue, Suite 10, Boston, MA 02135, USA.

NESTERENKO Evgeny, b. 8 Jan 1938, Moscow, Russia. Singer (Bass). Education: Studied at the Leningrad Conservatory. Debut: Maly Theatre, Leningrad, 1963 as Gremin in Eugene Onegin. Career: Sang at Maly and Kirov Theatres until 1971, when he joined the Bolshoy, Moscow; Roles there have included Mussorgsky's Boris Godunov and Dosifey and Borodin's Khan Konchak; Vienna Staatsoper and Metropolitan Opera debuts as Boris Godunov, 1974, 1975; La Scala Milan 1978, as King Philip in Don Carlos; Covent Garden 1978, as Don Basilio; Verona Festival 1978, 1985, 1989, 1991; Barcelona 1984, as Zaccaria in Nabucco; Bregenz Festival 1986; Wiesbaden and Savonlinna Festival, 1987 as Boris and Ivan Khovanski; Sang Bartók's Bluebeard at Budapest 1988; Munich and La Scala, Milan 1989, as Konchak in Prince Igor and as Ivan Susanin; Sang Basilio at Munich 1990, King Philip in Don Carlos at the 1990 Orange Festival and at Helsinki, 1995; Appeared as Verdi's Attila at Antwerp 1993; Concert engagements in music by Mussorgsky and Shostakovich. Recordings: Glinka's Ruslan and Ludmilla and Ivan Susanin; Tchaikovsky's Mazeppa, Iolanta and Eugene Onegin; Rachmaninov's Francesca da Rimini; Songs by Shostakovich and Mussorgsky; Suite on Poems of Michelangelo and 14th Symphony by Shostakovich; Verdi Requiem, Nabucco and Trovatore; Gounod Faust; Donizetti Don Pasquale and L'Elisir d'Amore; Verdi - Attila and Bela Bartók Bluebeard's Castle. Publication: Evgeny Nesterenko, Thoughts on My Profession, 1985. Honours: People's Artist of the USSR, 1976; Prize City of Vercelli (Italy) Viotti d'Oro, 1981; Golden Disc, Melodia, USSR, 1 Prize984; City of Verona Giovanni Zenatello, Italy, 1986; Chaliapin Prize, 1992; Wilhemn Furtwängler Prize, 1992; Austrian Member, Academy of Endeavours Work, Moscow, Russia. Address: Riemergasse 10/14, A-1010 Vienna, Austria.

NETTL Bruno, b. 14 Mar 1930, Prague, Czechoslovakia. Musicologist. m. Wanda White, 2 daughters. Education: BA, 1950, MA, 1951, PhD, 1953, Indiana University, Bloomington, USA; MALS, University of Michigan, Ann Arbor, 1960. Career: Instructor in Music, 1953-54, Assistant Professor of Music, 1954-56, 1959-64, Wayne State University, Detroit, Michigan; Associate Professor of Music, 1965-67, Professor of Music and Anthropology, 1967-, University of Illinois, Urbana; Visiting Professor of Music, Harvard University, 1990; Distinguished Albert Seay Professor of Music, Colorado College, 1992; Visiting Hill Professor of Music, University of Minnesota, 1995; Benedict Distinguished Visiting Professor of Music, Carleton College, 1996. Publications include: Music in Primitive Culture, 1956; An Introduction to Folk Music in the US, 1960; Cheremis Musical Styles, 1961; Theory and Method in Ethnomusicology, 1964; Folk and Traditional Music of the Western Continents, 1965, 2nd edition, 1972; Daramad of Chahargan, A study of the performance practice of Persian music, 1972; Contemporary Music and Music Cultures, with C Hamm and R Byrnside, 1975; Eight Urban Musical Cultures, 1978; The Study of Ethnomusicology, 1983; The Western Impact on World Music, 1965; The Radif of Persian Music, 1987, 1992; Blackfoot Musical Thought: Comparative Perspectives, 1989; Comparative Musicology and Anthropology of Music, 1991; Heartland Excursions: Ethnomusicological Reflections of Schools of Music, 1995; Editor, Ethnomusicology, 1961-65. Honours: Honorary DHL, University of Chicago, 1993; Koizumi prize for Ethnomusicological Research and Teaching,

Tokyo, 1994; Honorary DHL, University of Illinois, 1996; Fellow, American Academy of Arts and Sciences, 1997. Membership: Honorary Member, American Musicological Society, 1995. Address: 1423 Cambridge Drive, Champaign, IL 61821, USA.

NEUBAUER Margit, b. 1950, Austria. Singer (Mezzo-soprano). Education: Studied in Vienna. Career: Sang at Linz Landestheater, 1975-77, notably in 1976 premiere of Der Aufstand by Helmut Eder; Engagements at Frankfurt Opera from 1977, Zurich, 1978-79, Hamburg, 1980-83, Deutsche Oper Berlin, 1982-85; Bayreuth Festival 1981-86, as Sigrune in Die Walküre and a Flowermaiden in Parsifal; US tour with Deutsche Opera, 1985; Roles have included Cherubino, Flosshilde, Brigitte in Korngold's Tote Stadt, Annina, Rosenkavalier and the title role in Miss Jule by Bibalo; Many concert appearances, notably in Baroque music. Recordings: Parsifal, Bayreuth, 1985; Bach B minor Mass and Handel Utrecht Te Deum.

NEUBURGER Roberto P, b. 22 Nov 1949, Buenos Aires, Argentina. Singer (Baritone). m. Alicia Del Carmen De Rosa, 27 Feb 1974, 1 son, 1 daughter. Education: University of Buenos Aires; Private instruction: Singing and Vocal Technique with Professors Galperin, Souza, Maranca; Piano, Harmony, Counterpoint. Debut: Schütz, St Matthew Passion (Evangelist), 1977. Career: Regular appearances in chamber music performances or music-theatre presentations from early music (German Renaissance lute songs) to premières of contemporary vocal compositions including Dufour's Jeu Delicieux, Olaizola's Ondo, others, 1977-; 1st performances in Buenos Aires of works by Xenakis, Cage, Stockhausen, Crumb, Kagel, Berio, Roqué Alsina, De Pablo, Bussotti, at Centro Cultural Recoleta, Teatro Colón, (Salón Dorado), other venues. Recording: Olaizola, Ondo for solo voice, chorus and percussion, after poem by Oliverio Girondo. Contributions to: Essays on psychoanalysis and music in: Contexto en Psicoanalisis; Agenda de Letra Viva; others. Memberships: Performs for: Asociación Argentina de Compositores; Cultrum-Compositores Asociados; Agrupación Nueva Musica. Hobbies: Paddle Tennis; Study of psychoanalytic theory especially Lacanian contributions; Study and practice of languages (English, Spanish, German, French, Italian, Russian, Latin, Modern Greek). Address: Tronador 3719, 1430 Buenos Aires, Argentina.

NEUENFELS Hans, b. 1941, Krefeld, Germany. Stage Director. Debut: Produced Il Trovatore at Nuremberg, 1974. Career: Frankfurt Opera, 1976-80, with Macbeth, Aida, Die Gezeichneten by Schreker and Busoni's Doktor Faust; Productions at Deutsche Oper Berlin, 1982-86 have included La Forza del Destino, Rigoletto and Zimmermann's Die Soldaten; Paris Opera 1989 with the premiere of York Höller's Der Meister und Margarita, the last production at the Palais Garnier before the opening of the Opéra Bastille; Il Trovatore at the Deutsche Oper, 1996. Address: c/o Deutsche Oper Berlin, Bismarckstrasse 35, D-1000 Berlin 10, Germany.

NEUGEBAUER Hans, b. 17 Nov 1916, Karlsruhe, Germany. Singer (Bass); Stage Director. Education: Studied in Mannheim and Hamburg. Debut: Karlsruhe 1946, as Bett in Zar und Zimmermann. Career: Sang Buffo and other roles at Karlsruhe until 1951, Frankfurt Opera, 1951-60, notably as the King in Aida and Mozart's Figaro; Producter of opera from 1955, first at Frankfurt and Heidelberg, then Kassel, 1962-64; Staged premiere of Zimmermann's Die Soldaten at Cologne, Der Rosenkavalier at Glyndebourne, 1965; Guest engagements as Producer at Dusseldorf, Kassel, Mannheim, Basle, Trieste and Chicago. Address: c/o Oper der Stadt Koln, Offenbachplatz 5000 Cologne, Germany.

NEUHOLD Günter, b. 2 Nov 1947, Graz, Austria. Conductor. m. Emma Schmidt, 1 s. Education: Hochschule für Musik, Graz; Graduated 1969; Conducting Studies with Franco Ferrara in Rome and Hans Swarowsky in Vienna. Career includes: Worked in various German Opera Houses; 1st Kapellmeister in Hannover and Dortmund, 1972-1980; Guest conductor, Vienna Philharmonic and Radio Orchestras in Italy; Music Director, Teatro Regio, Parma, 1981-85; Orchestra Sinfonica dell'Emilia Romagna: Verdi's Requiem; Choral Symphony; Mahler's 2nd and 5th Symphonies; Principal Guest Conductor, Staatskapelle Dresden, performances include Tannhäuser, Ariadne, Electra; 1st performance worldwide of Strauss's Romance for Cello and Orchestra, 1985; TV engagements: France, Germany, Austria, Spain, Moscow, Beethoven's Missa Solemnis at the Vatican, Eurovision, 1985; Guest appearances: Vienna State Opera, Die Fledermaus and La Scala, Milan, Zauberflöte; Philadelphia Opera, Don Giovanni; Opera tours to: Moscow, Japan, USA; Music Director, Chief Conductor, Royal Philharmonic of Flanders, 1986-90; Music Director, Badisches Staatstheater, Karlsruhe, 1989-95; Australian debut, 1989 with Melbourne Symphony Orchestra; Il Trovatore, Elektra for Leipzig Opera, 1990; Tours of Austria and Britain with Royal Philharmonic Orchestra of Flanders; From 1995: Conducted Henze's Prinz von Homburg at Toulouse, 1997; General Music Director and Opera Director, Bremen, Germany. Recordings include: Bruckner 4th Symphony; La Damnation de Faust; Wagner's Ring; Mahler 1, 2, 5; Brahms 1; Le sacre du printemps; Berg Op 6. Honours: First Prize, Conducting: Florence, 1976; San Remo, 1976; Salzburg, 1977. Address: Bartensteinerstrasse 42, 28329 Bremen, Germany.

NEUMANN Vereslav, b. 27 May 1931, Czech Republic. Composer. m. (1) Jana Hoskova 1958, (2), Hana Kapinusova, 1989. Education: Graduate, Academy of Musical Arts, Prague, 1954. Career: Professor, Popular Conservatory, Prague, 1969-91; Co-Owner, Edit Records and Publishing Ltd, Prague, 1990-; Director, Prague Conservatoire, 1991-. Compositions: The Chimney Opera, 1965; Story of the Old Armchair, Full-Length Lyrical Comedy Opera, 1987; Panorama of Prague, 1962; Symphonic Dances for Full Orchestra, 1984; Little Singers Christmas, 1976; String Quartet, 1969; 5 Dramatic Sequences for Cello and Piano, 1978; Portraits of a Man, for Violin and Piano, 1987; The Lament of Ariadne Abandoned, 1970; Atlantis, 1985; Rhymes, 5 Ditties for Soprano, Flute and Piano, 1980; When Birds Fall Silent, 4 Songs for Medium-Range Voice and Piano, 1985; Farewell Amadeus!, Sonatina for Soprano, Flute and Piano, 1987. Honours: Prize, International Choral Competition, Tours, 1982; Award, Panton Publishing House, Prague, 1987; Czech Composers and Concert Artists Prize, 1987. Address: Na Petrinach 1896/31, 162 00 Prague 6, Czech Republic.

NEUMANN Wolfgang, b. 20 June 1945, Waiern, Austria. Singer (Tenor). Education: Vocal studies in Essen and Duisburg. Debut: Bielefeld 1973, as Max in Der Freischütz. Career: Sang at Augsburg from 1978, Mannheim from 1980; Maggio Musicale Florence 1983, as Tannhäuser; Appearances in Zurich, Bologna, Munich and Hamburg; Other roles include Wagner's Erik, Rienzi, Schoenberg's Aron (at Barcelona), Tristan, Lohengrin and Siegfried, Verdi's Otelo, the Emperor in Die Frau ohne Schatten, Turiddu in Cavalleria Rusticana, Puccini's Calaf and Edgar in Reimann's Lear; Concert repertoire includes Schoenberg's Gurrelieder and Das Lied von der Erde by Mahler; Metropolitan opera debut as Siegfried in the Met's new production of Siegfried by Otto Schenk/James Levine, 1988; Sang the Cardinal in Mathis der Maler at Munich, 1989; Teatro Colon Buenos Aires 1990, as Rienzi in a concert performance of Wagner's opera. Address: c/o Ingpen & Williams Ltd, 26 Wadham Road, London SW15 2LR, England.

NEUMANN-GLUXAN Dagmar, b. 25 Dec 1961, Bohumin, Czech Republic. Musicologist; Violinist. m. (1) Robert Neumann, 31 Jan 1987, 1 son, (2) Dr Christian Gluxan, 29 June 1996, 1 son, 1 daughter. Education: Conservatory, Czech Republic; Musicology, University of Brno, Vienna. Career: Interpretation of 18th Century Music; Founder of Ensemble le Monde Classique, Vienna on original instruments; Repertoire: Archive research in Europe; Concerts, TV Recordings, CD Recording; Emphasis on unknown composers. Recordings: First complete recording of Frantisek V Mica oratorium, Abgesungene Betrachtungen 1727, 1994 (Supraphon); First complete recording of Frantisek V Mica opera L'Origine di Jaromeriz 1730, 1994; Regular cooperation with Czech TV. Publications: Die spieltechnischen Besonderheiten der Violinstimmmen in Mozart's Betulia Liberata; Das unbekannte Stimmenmaterial zu Gluck's Don Juan in der Wiener Nationalbibiothek; Das Prinzip der Nachahmung instrumentaler Idiomatik im 17 und frühen 18 Jahrhundert; Bemerkungen zur Violinskordatur im 18 Jahrhundert; Die Violinskordatur in der Musikaliensammlung des Erzbischofs Carl Liechtenstein-Castelcorn in Kremsier (Diss). Contributions: Die Oper L'Origine di Jaromeriz, von Fr V Mica. Honours: Prize granted by Minister of Education of Czech Republic, 1986; Prize of the Golden Harmony for the best Czech recording of the year 1994. Memberships: International Gluck Society; Austrian Society for Musical Research. Hobbies: Arts; Literature; Botany; Violin Tutor. Address: Schottenfeldg 55-7, 1070 Vienna, Austria.

NEUNTEUFEL Michael, b. 9 Apr 1958, Vienna, Austria. Pianist; Composer; Pedagogue. m. Corinna Neunteufel, 28 Dec 1978, 2 sons, 2 daughters. Education: Degree in Music Education with distinction, Hochschule fur Musik und Darstellende Kunst in Vienna, 1978; Military Service, Gardemusik - Oboe; Further studies at university and in instrumental pedagogics, MA, Hochschule für Musik und Darstellende Kunst Mozarteum in Salzburg, 1987-90. Career: Music teacher, Feldkirch 1978-93 and Bregenz, 1981-; Professor, Vorarlberger Landeskonservatorium at Pedagogical lectures; Lecturer, international symposia on improvisation and composition, 1996, and the role of music in a changing world, 1997; Concert appearances on piano and harpsichord; Participation at International Choir and Orchestra Workshops; Lecturer at Music-Pedagogical courses and juror at music competitions, 1988; Radio appearances since 1982; Premiere performance of compositions at the International Kammermusik Festival Austria, Stift Altenburg, 1995. Compositions: Chamber: Meloi, Bläsertrio, Kammermusik, Ohne Titel, Gavotte, Redundanz, Perpetuum, Sonata Longa, Triangel, Klaviertrio, Streichquartett, Sonata; Piano: Fantasia Meditation, Impressionen; Vier Klavierstücke The Laws; Tagttraeume, for solo piano; Vocal: Liederzyklen, Motette Peace for Mixed Choir, Sacred Music for Male Choir Im Reiche der Herrlichkeit, Verborgene Worte for mixed choir and soloist in German and English language; Music for String Orchestra: Sonatine Sinfonietta, Suite; Music for children, wind instruments, guitars and violoncello. Recordings: Songs for Soprano and Piano by Joseph Marx and Hugo Wolf; Own Compositions: Ohne Titel, Impressionen, Meloi, Gavotte, Redundanz, Sonata Longa, Im Reiche der Herrlichkeit. Honours: Various honours and awards including composition prizes, 1st Prize at Salzburg, 1984, and 2nd Prize at Dornbirn, 1986. Membership: AGMOE. Hobbies: Sports; Hiking; Family; Travel. Address: Langenerstrasse 14a, A-6900 Bregenz, Austria.

NEVILLE Margaret, b. 3 Apr 1939, Southampton, Hampshire, England. Soprano. Education: Studied with Ruth Packer and Olive Groves in London, Maria Carpi in Geneva. Debut: Covent Garden in 1961 in Die Zauberflöte. Career: Appearances at Sadler's Wells, Scottish Opera, Welsh National Opera, Barcelona, Aix, Berlin and Hamburg; Glyndebourne, 1963-64 in Die Zauberflöte and L'Incoronazione di Poppea; Roles included Mozart's Zerlina, Despina and Susanna, Verdi's Gilda, Donizetti's Norina and Humperdinck's Gretel; Sang in the 1967 BBC production of Cavalli's L'Erismena. Recording: Hansel and Gretel. Honour: Mozart Memorial Prize, 1962. Hobby: Walking with Basset hound called Henry. Address: 74 Orchards Way, Highfield, Southampton SO17 1RE, England.

NEVSKAYA Marina, b. 1 Oct 1965, Moscow, Russia. Organist; Composer; Music Teacher. Education: Central Music School, 1984; Moscow Tchaikovsky State Conservatory, 1989; Postgraduate, Moscow Conservatory, 1989-91; Studies, Royal Carillon School, Mechelen, Belgium, 1993-94. Debut: Organ Concert, Moscow, 1986. Career: Festival of Young Composers, Moscow, 1985; Recitals, Moscow Conservatory, 1987, 1988, Dnepropetrovsk and Yalta, Ukraine, 1989, Festival of Young Organists, Polotsk, Byelorussia, 1989; Participation, Organ Forum, Kazan, 1990, International Summer Organ Course, The Organ Art of Flor Peeters, Mechelen, 1990, 1991; International Organ Week, Vlaardingen, Netherlands, 1991, 1993; Recitals, Vlaardingen, 1991, Biyelaya Tserkov, Ukraine, 1991, 1992, Dnepropetrovsk and Yalta, 1992, Krasnoyarsk, 1993; Concert tours, Belgium and Netherlands, 1993, 1994, Italy, 1993, Siberia, 1994; Recitals, St Petersburg, 1994, Yalta, 1995, 1996, Tver, 1992-; Participation, Yearly Music Festivals, Tver and Moscow. Compositions: Symphoniette; String Quartet; 2 Piano Sonatas; Sonata for Trumpet and Piano; Sonata for Violin and Organ; Suite for Organ; Poem for Viola and Piano; Vocal and Piano Cycles; Pieces for Wind Instruments; Pieces for Carillon and Other Chamber Works. Recordings: Italian, French and German Organ Music of the 17th-18th Centuries; Organ Recital, 5th International Bach Festival, Tver, 1997; Playing in the British Bach Film, 1993. Contributions to: Organnoye iskusstvo. Honours: Laureate, 2nd and 3rd Prizes, All-Union Contest of Young Composers, Moscow, 1985; Laureate, 2nd Prize, International Flor Peeters Organ Contest, Mechelen, 1990. Memberships: Russian Union of Composers; Russian Authors Society. Hobbies: Philosophy; Writing poems and stories; Painting. Current Management: Academy of Fine Arts, Moscow. Address: Tver Philharmonic, Teatralnaya pl 1, 170000 Tver, Russia.

NEWAY Patricia, b. 30 Sep 1919, Brooklyn, NY, USA. Soprano. m. Morris Gesell. Education: Studied at Mannes College of Music and with Morris Gesell. Debut: Chautauqua in 1946 as Fiordiligi in Così fan tutte. Career: New York City Center Opera from 1948 notably as Berg's Marie, in Britten's The Rape of Lucretia and in the 1954 premiere of Copland's The Tender Land; Created roles in Menotti's The Consul in 1950 and Maria Golovin in 1958; Sang at Aix-en-Provence Festival in 1952 in Iphigénie en Tauride, Paris Opéra-Comique, 1952-54 notably as Tosca and Katiusha in Alfano's Risurrezione and with American companies in works by Poulenc, Hoiby and Weisgall; Formed Neway Opera Company in 1960. Recordings: The Consul; Cantatas by Buxtehude; Iphigénie en Tauride.

NEWBOULD Brian (Raby), b. 26 Feb 1936, Kettering, Northamptonshire, England. University Professor. m. (1) Anne Leicester, 1960, 1 son, 1 daughter, (2) Ann Airton, 1976, 1 daughter. Education: BA, General Arts, 1957, BMus, 1958, MA, 1961, Bristol. Career: Lecturer, Royal Scottish Academy of Music, 1960-65; Lecturer, University of Leeds, 1965-69; Professor of Music, University of Hull, 1979-; Gave 3 talks on Schubert's Symphonic Fragments on BBC Radio 3, 1983. Compositions: Realisations of Schubert Symphonies No 7 in E D729, No 10 in D D936A; Completion of Schubert Symphony No 8 in B minor D759; Orchestration of Schubert's other symphonic fragments; Patrick for narrator and small orchestra. Publications: Schubert and the Symphony: A New Perspective, 1992. Contributor to: 19th Century Music; Current Musicology; Music Review; Musical Times; Music and Letters. Membership: Royal Society of Arts. Hobbies: Travel; Walking; Badminton. Address: Department of Music, University of Hull, Hull HU6 7RX, England.

NEWLAND Larry, b. 24 Jan 1935, Winfield, Kansas, USA. Conductor. m. Paula Kahn, 18 Feb 1977, 2 daughters. Education: BM, Oberlin Conservatory, 1955; MM, Manhattan School of Music, 1957. Career: Violist and keyboard player with New York Philharmonic, 1960-74; Assistant Conductor, New York Philharmonic, 1974-85; Music Director, Harrisburg, Pennsylvania Symphony, 1978-94; Guest Conductor with New York City Ballet and orchestras worldwide, 1974-; Chair, Music Department and Director of Ensembles, Adelphi University, Garden City, New York, 1990-; Faculty, International Opera Workshop, Czech Republic, 1997, Associate Artistic Director, forthcoming appointment. Recordings: Numerous broadcasts with New York Philharmonic and other orchestras. Contributions to: Articles in Apprise. Honours: Harold Bauer Award, 1957; Koussevitzky Conducting Prize, 1961; Leonard Bernstein Conducting Fellowship, 1962; City of Harrisburg, and Pennsylvania, Governor's citations, 1982; Pennsylvania, House of Representatives citation, 1988; Pennsylvania senate citation, 1994. Memberships: President, Conductors Guild; American Symphony Orchestra League; American Federation of Musicians; Chamber Music America. Hobbies: Tennis; Hiking; Sailing. Address: 300 West End Avenue G-B, New York, NY 10023, USA.

NEWLIN Dika, b. 22 Nov 1923, Portland, OR, USA. Musicologist; Composer. Education: BA, Michigan State University, 1939; MA, UCLA, 1941; PhD, Columbia University, 1945; Composition studies with Schoenberg and Sessions. Career: Teacher at Western Maryland College, 1945-49, Syracuse University, 1949-51, Drew University, 1952-65, North Texas State University, 1963-75, and Virginia Commonwealth University, 1978-. Compositions: Sinfonia for Piano, 1947; Piano Trio, 1948; Chamber Symphony, 1949; Fantasy On A Row for Piano, 1958; Study In Twelve Tones for Viola D'Amore and Piano, 1959; Atone for Chamber Ensemble, 1976; Second-Hand Rows for Voice and Piano, 1978; Three Operas; Piano Concerto; Symphony for Chorus and Orchestra. Publications: Bruckner - Mahler - Schoenberg, 1947, 1978; Schoenberg Remembered 1938-76, 1980; Translations of Leibowitz's Schoenberg et son Ecole, 1949, Schoenberg's Style and Idea, 1951, and Rufer's Das Werk Arnold Schoenberg, 1962.

NEWMAN Anthony, b. 12 May 1941, Los Angeles, CA, USA. Harpsichordist; Organist; Composer; Fortepianist; Conductor. m. Mary Jane Flagler, 10 Sep 1968, 3 sons. Education: BS, Mannes College; MA, Harvard University; DMA, Boston University; Diplome Superieure, Ecole Normale de Musique, Paris. Debut: Carnegie Recital Hall. Career: Performing artist in USA and Europe from 1967 with Detroit Symphony, Boston Symphony, Los Angeles Symphony, New York Philharmonic and as conductor with Los Angeles Chamber, Y Chamber, NY, Scottish Chamber, and St Paul Chamber Orchestras; Appearances with Israel Symphony, Calgary Symphony, Colorado Symphony, New Jersey Symphony, Youth Chamber Orchestra and Vienna Boys Choir, and St Stephens Cathedral, Vienna, Krakow Festival, 1991, 1992. Compositions include: Concertino for Piano and Winds; Concerto for Viola and Strings; Symphony for String Orchestra; Grand Hymns Of Awakening for Chorus, Orchestra and Bagpipes; Works for organ solo, piano quintet, quartets for flutes and various smaller works; On Fallen Heroes, sinfonia for Orchestra, 1988; Symphony for Strings and Percussion, 1987; 12 Preludes and Fugues for piano; Symphony No 1 and 2 for Organ Solo. Recordings: Over 100 including Bach, Baroque and Classical repertoire; On Fallen Heroes, Brandenburg Concerti. Publications: Bach and The Baroque, 1985; Symphony No 1 for Organ and No 2 for Organ; Three Preludes and Fugues for Organ, 1990; Variations on Bach; 12 Preludes and Fugues for Piano; Sonata for Piano, 1992. Current Management: ICM, 40 West 57th Street, New York, NY 10019, USA. Address: State University of New York, Purchase, NY 10577, USA.

NEWMAN Leslie, b. Canada. Flautist. Education: BMus, University of Toronto; Studies with the late Thomas Nyfenger at Yale University and Julius Baker at Juilliard School of Music; Also studied at Mozarteum in Salzburg; Scholaship student with András Adorján, Peter Lukas-Graf and Wolfgang Schulz. Debut: Performed Carl Nielsen's Flute Concerto with the Toronto Symphony Orchestra, aged 18. Career: Performances at Lincoln Center's Alice Tully Hall, Salzburg Festival, Wigmore Hall, London; Soloist, Toronto Symphony Orchestra Tour to 1988 Winter Olympics Arts Festival at Calgary; Performed major flute concerti with orchestras throughout Canada; Recitalist on Classic FM in England and CBC Radio in Canada; Duo with pianist John Lenehan, debuted at Wigmore Hall, London; Appearances at Canadian National Competitive Festival of Music. Recordings include: 2 solo CDs; Four concerti with CBC Vancouver Orchestra. Honours: Winner, Canadian National Competitive Festival of Music, aged 17; Canada Council Grant; Outstanding Performance Major, Yale University; Top Prizewinner, CBC National Young Performer's Competition; Finalist, New York's Pro Musicis International Competition. Address: c/o Latitude 45/Arts Promotion Inc, 109 St Joseph Blvd West, Montreal, Quebec H2T 2P7, Canada.

NEWMAN William S, b. 6 Apr 1912, Cleveland, OH, USA. Professor of Music; Writer; Pianist. m. 20 Dec 1947. Education: Western Reserve University; Cleveland Institute of Music; PhD in Musicology, Columbia University, 1939. Career: Teacher, Cleveland Public Schools and Western Reserve University, 1935-39; Officer, Army Air Forces Intelligence, World War II; Music Faculty, 1945-55, Professor, 1955-62, Alumni Distinguished Professor of Music, 1962-77, Professor Emeritus, 1977-, University of North Carolina; Courses at Bennington College, Columbia Teachers' College, Juilliard School of Music, SUNY in Binghamton, Northwestern University, University of Alberta; Soloist with numerous orchestras; Chamber groups; Recitalist throughout America. Publications: 9 Books including: The Pianist's Problems, 1950, 4th edition, 1984, Understanding Music, 1953, 2nd edition, 1961, paperback 1967, The Sonata in The Baroque Era, volume I, 1959, 4th edition, 1983, The Sonata in The Classic Era, volume II 1963, 3rd edition, 1983, The Sonata Since Beethoven, volume III, 1969, 3rd edition, 1982, paperback, 1967, Performance Practices in Beethoven's Piano Sonatas, 1971; Beethoven on Beethoven - Playing His Piano Music His Way, 1988. Address: c/o Music Department, University of North Carolina, Chapel Hill, NC 27514, USA.

NEWSTONE Harry, b. 21 Jun 1921, Winnipeg, Canada. Conductor. 1 s. Education: With Dr Herbert Howells, 1943-45; Guildhall School of Music and Drama, 1945-49; Accademia di Santa Cecilia, Rome, 1954-1956. Debut: Chamber Orchestra with Haydn Orchestra at Conway Hall, London, 1949; Full orchestra at Royal Festival Hall Philharmonic Orchestra, 1959. Career: Formed Haydn Orchestra in 1949; BBC broadcasts from 1951 with Hadyn Orchestra, London Philharmonic Orchestra, London Symphony Orchestra, Philharmonia, RPO, BBC Symphony and other BBC orchestras; Guest appearances in Berlin, Copenhagen, Hamburg, Budapest, Prague, Jerusalem, Toronto, Vancouver, Mexico City, Liverpool Philharmonic, and Bournemouth Symphony Orchestra; Musical Director of Sacramento Symphony Orchestra, CA, 1965-78; Director of Music, University of Kent, 1979-86; Professor of Conducting at Guildhall School of Music, 1979-87; Visiting Lecturer, University of the Pacific, Stockton, CA, 1988-89. Recordings: Bach Brandenburg Concertos; Clavier Concertos with Mindru Katz; Haydn Symphonies, 49, 73, 46, 52; Haydn and Mozart Arias with Jennifer Vyvyan and Peter Wallfisch; Mozart Symphony 41 and Serenata Notturna; Stravinsky Dumbarton Oaks Concerto; Mozart Opera Overtures; Clarinet and Orchestral works by Copland, Arnold, Lutoslawski and Rossini with Gary Gray. Publications: Editions of works by Bach, Mozart and Haydn for Eulenburg Edition Miniature Scores, including new edition of Haydn's 12 London Symphonies from 1983-. Hobbies: Photography; Painting. Address: 4 Selborne Road, Ilford, Essex, IG1 3AJ, England.

NEWTON Norma, b. 20 Mar 1936, Dolgeville, New York, USA. Singer (Soprano). Education: Studied in Austin (Texas) and Paris. Career: Sang at the Dallas Civic Opera 1962-63, City Opera New York 1964 and 1966 as Donna Elvira and Mozart's Countess; Member of the Kiel Opera, Germany, 1966-72, Graz 1972-73; Sang Butterfly with Welsh National Opera 1973 and appeared widely as guest as Mozart's Pamina, Fiordiligi and Susanna, Eurydice, Katya Kabanova and Berg's Marie; Teacher in Houston from 1980.

NGUYEN (Thuyet) Phong, b. 15 Jul 1946, Vinh Binh, Vietnam. Professor; Musician. Education: BA, Philosophy and Literature, University of Saigon, 1974; PhD, Ethnomusicology, Sorbonne University, Paris, France, 1982; Studied Vietnamese traditional music and Buddhist chant (voice, stringed instruments, percussion), with Master Tram Van Kien and Venerable Thien Dao in South Vietnam, from age 5. Debut: As professional musician at age 10. Career: Performances of traditional Vietnamese music in Asia, Europe and USA including NHK TV in 1975, UNESCO Auditorium, Paris in 1980, Palais du Lac, Vichy, France, 1981, Cosful Theatre, Frankfurt in 1984, Metropolitan Museum of Art, NY in 1985, Memorial Art Gallery, Rochester, USA in 1986, Northwest Folklife Festival in USA, 1988 and about 25 American university auditoriums. Composition: Dan Tranh, 7 Improvisations, 1986. Recordings: Eternal Voices - Vietnamese Traditional Music in the US; Traditional Music of Vietnam; Vietnamese Music in France and United States; Dan Tranh, 7 Improvisations, Music for Meditation; Traditional Instrumental and Vocal Music of Vietnam. Publications: Ritual Music Ensemble and Traditional Custom in South Vietnam, 1974; From Rice Paddies and Temple Yards: Traditional Vietnamese Music, 1989; Music for Children, 1989; World of Sounds in Vietnam: 12 Contemporary Issues, 1989; Searching for a Niche - Vietnamese Music at Home in America, 1995. Address: 207 Bowman Drive, Kent, OH 44240, USA.

NICA Grigore, b. 14 Oct 1936, Ploiesti, Romania. Composer. m. Constantinescu Anca Rodica, 31 Jan 1970, 1 son, 1 daughter. Education: Musical Conservatory, Ciprian Porumbescu, Bucharest. Career: Violin Professor, Musical High School, Tulcea; Musical Editor, Radio; Has had broadcasts of work on radio and TV, 1968-88. Compositions: Four Songs for Voice and Piano, Op 5, 1965; The Brave Soldier Svejk, sequences for Voice and Chamber Music (and others), Op 13, 1971; Symphonic piece for orchestra, Aegyssus Op 28, 1978. Recordings: Suite for Orchestra, Op 16, 1972-73; Three Sketches for Orchestra, Op 9, 1969-70; Cantata, The Banner Op 14, 1972. Membership: Composers Union of Romania. Hobbies: Football; Swimming; Volleyball; Table Tennis; Bicycling. Address: 7227 Crest Road, Rancho P-V, CA 90274, USA.

NICHITEANU Liliana, b. 1962, Bucharest, Romania. Singer (Mezzo-Soprano). Education: Studied at the Bucharest Academy. Career: Numerous engagements including Oslo as Rosina, 1989; Berliner Philharmonie, Fjodor in Boris Godunov, concerts and recordings (CD) with Claudio Abbado, 1993; Vienna, Rossini, Messa di Gloria, 1995; Seasons 1995-97, sang Octavian at Frankfurt; Zerlina at the Mozart Festival, Madrid; Cherubino and Despina with Harnoncourt in Zürich; Sang Te Deum, Bruckner, in Edinburgh Festival concert; Sang at Salzburg Festival with Valery Gergiev; Concert repertory: Bach: Magnificat; Johannes Passion; Brahms Alto Rhapsody; Mahler; Concert appearances worldwide in Bach B minor Mass; Mozart, Requiem and C minor Mass; Honneger, Jeanne d'Arc; Mahler, Des Knaben Wunderhorn; Mahler, 8th Symphony; Rossini, Stabat Mater and Messa di Gloria; Hindemith, Die junge Magd, Sieben Lieder for orchestra and alto. Honours: Belvedere Contest, 2 prizes and 6 special prizes, Vienna, 1989; Geneva CIEM contest, 2 prizes and Suisse Prize, 1991. Address: c/o Zurich Opera, Falkenstrasse 1, CH-8008 Zurich, Switzerland.

NICHOLAS James, b. 25 Jan 1957, Valley Stream, NY, USA. Cellist. Education: BM in Cello Performance, 1979, MM, Cello Performance, 1982, Master of Early Music, 1988, DMus, 1988, Indiana University. Career: Freelance Cellist and Baroque Cellist; Announcer and Producer, Connecticut Public Radio WPKT Meriden, WNPR Norwich and WEDW Stamford and Greenwich. Compositions: Concerto for Natural Horn (Romantic), 1984; Panikhida (Mnemosynon) for Unaccompanied Natural Horn, 1987; 3 Sonatas for Natural Horn and Piano, 1985, 1993, 1995; Son of Horn Concerto, 1988; Corni Duos, 1991; Grande fantaisie en forme de potpourri, pour cor à pistons en fa et pianoforte (ca 1838), 1991; Psalsima (Chants) for Natural Horn and Small Orchestra, 1991; Return of The Shoe Quintet: The Sequel for Horn and Strings, 1994; Mozart: Horn Concerto in Eb, K370b and 371, a reconstruction, 1994; Mozart: Horn Concerto in E, K494a, a reconstruction, 1995. Publications: J S Bach - Six Sonatas and Partitas, An Urtext edition for Viola, 1986; J S Bach - Six suites for Cello, an attempt at an Urtext for Viola, 1986; J S Bach - Suite No 6 S1012, a performing version for the 4 Stringed Cello, 1986; Edition of Horn Concerti from the Lund Manuscript, 1989. Contributions to: The Horn Call. Honour: Performer's Certificate, Indiana University, 1978. Hobbies: Animals; Gardening; Photography; Language Study. Address: c/o Birdalone Books, 9245 East Woodview Drive, Bloomington, IN 47401-9101, USA.

NICHOLLS David (Roy), b. 19 Nov 1955, Birmingham, England. Musicologist; Composer. m. Tamar Hodes, 28 July 1984, 1 son, 1 daughter. Education: St John's College, Cambridge with Hugh Wood, 1975-78, 1979-84; Degrees: BA, Honours, 1978, MA, 1982, PhD, 1986, all Cantab. Career includes: Keasbey Fellow in American Studies, Selwyn College, Cambridge, 1984-87; Lecturer in Music, 1987-, Head of Department of Music, 1990-, Senior Lecturer in Music, 1992, Professor of Music, 1995, Keele University. Compositions include: Pleiades for 3 Groups of Instruments, 1979-80; The Giant's Heart for Singers and Instrumentalists, 1983; 2 Japanese Miniatures for 8 Instruments, 1988-89; Winter Landscape with skaters and birdtrap, string quartet, 1989-90; Cantata: Jerusalem, soprano, double choir, double wind band, 1990-91; String Quartet, NMC D006, 1992, Bingham String Quartet. Publications: American Experimental Music, 1890-1940, 1990; new edition of Henry Cowell's New Musical Resources, 1995; Editor, The Whole World of Music: A Henry Cowell Symposium, 1997. Contributions to: Musical Times; Journal of American Studies; American Music; Musical Quarterly; Reviews in newspapers and journals; BBC Music Magazine. Memberships: Society for the Promotion of New Music; Sonneck Society for American Music; Performing Rights Society; Mechanical Copyright Protection Society. Hobbies: Food; Wine; Literature; Theatre; Films. Address: c/o Department of Music, Keele University, Keele, Staffordshire, ST5 5BG, England.

NICHOLLS Hyacinth, b. 10 Sep 1956, Trinidad. Mezzo-Soprano. Education: Studied at the Guildhall School of Music and the National Opera Studio. Career: Sang Cherubino, Octavian, Dorabella, Carmen and Dalilah while a student; Professional debut in 1985 at Wigmore Hall; Sang in the European premiere of Virgil Thomson's Four Saints in three acts, Belgium, 1983; Glyndebourne Festival from 1986 in Porgy and Bess, Sang Purcell's Sorceress at Battersea Arts Centre, 1995; L'Enfant et les Sortilèges, Die Entführung, La Traviata, The Electrification of the Soviet Union as Natasha in the premiere, and as Varvara in Katya Kabanova; Tour of Italy in 1989 with Albert Herring; Other roles include Fenina in Nabucco and Humperdinck's Gretel; Sang in the Royal Opera's Garden Venture in 1989; Has performed the role of Carmen for several opera companies including English National Opera's Baylis Programme and the Royal Opera House's Education Programme; Other roles include the title role in Gluck's Orfeo, Dalila, Third Lady (Magic Flute) and Suzuki (Madama Butterfly); Has recently returned from Syria where she sang the role of Dido in a production of Syria's first ever opera; Further roles include Carmen and Serena (Porgy and Bess); Concert repertoire includes Schumann Lieder with recital at St John's with Iain Burnside, Beethoven's Mass in C, the B minor Mass and the St Matthew Passion. Honours include: Ricordi Opera Prize; Susan Longfield Award; Winner, Maggie Teyte International Competition, 1985. Current Management: Helen Sykes Artists Management. Address: 4th Floor, Parkway House, Sheen Lane, East Sheen, London SW14 8LS, England.

NICHOLLS Simon, b. 8 Oct 1951, London, England. Pianist. m. Lorraine Wood, 10 May 1976. Education: Junior Exhibitioner, 1963-69, Foundation Scholar, 1969-74, Royal College of Music; Diplomas: GRSM, ARCM and LRAM. Career: Performances in London, St John's Smith Square, Wigmore Hall, South Bank, Snape Maltings, Aldeburgh and at music clubs throughout Britain; Broadcasts on BBC and ITV and Radio; Tours and broadcasts in France, Holland, Germany, Eire, Greece and USA; Piano Teacher at Yehudi Menuhin School, 1976-86 and Professor at Royal College of Music, 1985-. Recording: Simon Nicholls Plays Scriabin. Publications: The Young Cellist's Repertoire, Recital Repertoire for Cellists with Julian Lloyd Webber. Contributions to: Piano Journal; Music and Musicians; Tempo. Memberships: Musicians Union; EPTA. Hobbies: Languages; Reading; Swimming; Record Collecting. Address: 49 Grove Road, London, N12, England.

NICHOLSON George (Thomas Frederick), b. 24 Sep 1949, Great Lumley, County Durham, England. Composer; Pianist. m. Jane Ginsborg, 14 Jun 1984, 1 s, 1 d. Education: BA, Honours, 1971, DPhil, 1979, University of York. Career: Freelance teacher, Guildhall School of Music and Drama, Morley College, London, 1978-88; Recitals with Jane Ginsborg, Soprano and with Philip Edwards, Clarinet, Triple Echo; Associate Composer with Lysis, 1984-; Lecturer, Keele University, 1988-. Compositions: Orchestral Works: 1132; The Convergence of the Twain; Blisworth Tunnel Blues for Soprano and Orchestra; Chamber Concerto; Cello Concerto; Flute Concerto; Chamber works include: Winter Music; Ancient Lights; Movements; Stilleven; 2 String Quartets; Piano Sonata; Brass Quintet; The Arrival of the Poet in the City (melodrama) for actor and 7 musicians; Vocal Music includes: Aubade; Vignette; Peripheral Visions; Alla Luna for Soprano, Clarinet and Piano. Contributions to: Articles in Composer Magazine. Honours: Yorkshire Arts Composers' Award, 1977; Young Composer, Greater London Arts Association, 1979-80; Triple Echo, 4th Prize, Gaudeamus Competition, Rotterdam, 1982. Membership: Association of Professional Composers. Hobbies: Photography; Jazz; Winemaking. Address: Department of Music, Keele University, Keele, Staffordshire, ST5 5BG, England.

NICHOLSON Linda, b. 1955, England. Fortepiano Player. Career: Member of the London Foretpiano Trio from 1978; Duo with Violinist, Hiro Kurosaki; Solo recitals and concertos, performances of the Viennese classics on original instruments at major festivals and concert series throughout Europe including Italy, Belgium, France, Germany, Britain and the Netherlands; 12 Concert series of the complete piano trios of Haydn in London 1982, to mark the composer's 250th anniversary; Complete piano trios of Beethoven at the Wigmore Hall in 1987; Season 1991 with Mozart Trios and quartets in London, tour on the early Music Network and lunchtime recitals at the Elizabeth Hall; Played Mozart in Barcelona, Lisbon and Germany; Frequent radio broadcasts. Recordings: Complete Trios by Mozart; Trios by Haydn and Beethoven; Mozart Concertos; Complete Violin Sonatas by Mozart, with Hio Kuoselui. Address: 21 Clapham Common Northside, London, SW4 0RG, England.

NICKLIN Celia (Mhry), b. 28 Nov 1941, Malmesbury, Wiltshire, England. Musician; Oboist. m. Howard Gough, 8 Feb 1964, 3 daughters. Education: Cheltenham Ladies College; Royal Academy of Music, London; Hochschule für Musik Detmold, Germany. Career: Principal Oboe, City of Birmingham Symphony Orchestra 1962-63, London Mozart Players 1970, Academy of St Martin in the Fields 1970; Professor, Royal Academy of Music, London. Recordings: Vaughan Williams, Handel, Vivaldi Oboe Concertos with Academy of St Martin, Mozart with London Mozart Players; Many hundred more. Honour: FRAM. Address: 19 Park Hill, Carshalton, Surrey SM5 3SA, England.

NICOLAI Claudio, b. 7 Mar 1929, Kiel, Germany. Baritone. Education: Vocal studies with Clemens Kaiser-Breme in Essen and Serge Radamsky in Vienna. Debut: Theater am Gärtnerplatz, Munich, 1954. Career: Early engagements as a tenor then as baritone from 1956; Appearances at Bregenz Festival, Vienna Volksoper and in Stuttgart, Hamburg, Brussels, Munich, Berlin, Paris, London, Stockholm, Oslo, Prague, Bucharest, Budapest, Zurich and Amsterdam; Member of the Cologne Opera from 1964; Sang in the 1965 premiere of Zimmermann's Die Soldaten and visited London in 1969 for the British premiere of Henze's Der Junge Lord; Sang with Oper der Stadt Köln from 1966; Roles include Giovanni, Count, Papageno and Guglielmo; Tel Aviv in 1984 in Die Zauberflöte, Metropolitan Opera in 1988, sang Don Alfonso at Brussels and Barcelona in 1990 and Don Alfonso under John Eliot Gardiner at Amsterdam in 1992; Professor at the Musikhochschule Cologne; Salzburg Festival, 1976-79; Nozze di Figaro, Giovanni, Vienna Staatsoper; 15 years guest at the Berlin Staatsoper and three times in Japan; Così fan tutte in Paris with J E Gardiner. Recordings: Der Freischütz; Die Fledermaus; Die Kluge; Highlights from Die Soldaten. Address: c/o Staatliche Hochschule für Musik, Degobertstrasse 38, 5000 Köln 1, Germany.

NICOLESCO Mariana, b. 28 Nov 1948, Brasov, Romania. Soprano. Education: Music and Violin in Romania, age 6-18, graduating with Bruch Concerto; Voice with Jolanda Magnoni, Conservatorio Santa Cecilia, Rome; Later with Elisabeth Schwarzkopf and Rodolfo Celletti. Debut: TV concert, Voci Rossiniane International Award, Milan, 1972. Career: Sang Violetta in La Traviata, Teatro Comunale, Florence, 1976, Gran Teatro del Liceu, Barcelona, 1976, 1978, 1981, also San Francisco Opera, 1991; Violetta at Metropolitan Opera, 1978, where she also appeared as Gilda in Rigoletto, 1978, and Nedda in Pagliacci, 1979, 1986, Donna Elvira in Don Giovanni, Teatro dell'Opera, Rome, 1984, Munich Staatsoper and Munich Festival, 1986-93, Tokyo, 1988, La Scala, Milan, 1987, 1988, 1993; Also at La Scala, world premiere of Berio's La Vera Storia, 1982, and Un Re in Ascolto, 1986; Dargomishky's Stone Guest, 1983, Mozart's Lucio Silla, 1984, Luigi Rossi's L'Orfeo, 1985, Jommelli's Fetonte, 1988, 3 recitals, 1988-93; Elettra in Idomeneo, Salzburg Festival, 1990, 1991, Japan, 1990, Dresden Semper Oper, 1991; A true dramatic coloratura: Bellini's Beatrice di Tenda, La Fenice, Venice, 1975, Donizetti's Maria di Rohan, Martina Franca Festival, 1988, Elisabeth Queen of England in Roberto Devereux, Monte Carlo, 1992, Anna Bolena, Munich, 1995; Performed at leading opera houses worldwide; Concerts: Royal Festival Hall London, Carnegie Hall New York, Musikverein Vienna, Boston Symphony Hall, Concertgebouw Amsterdam, Teatro Real Madrid, Cleveland Symphony Hall, Teatro alla Scala. Recordings: Bellini: Beatrice di Tenda; Donizetti: Maria di Rohan; Verdi: Simon Boccanegra; Puccini: La Rondine; Mozart: Le nozze di Figaro; World premiere: Meyerbeer cantata Gli Amori di Teolinda, Ravel cantatas Alcyone, Alyssa. Honours: Chevalier, Order of Arts and Letters, France, 1985; Honorary Citizen, Bucharest, 1991; UNESCO Medal, Artistic Accomplishments, 1992; Honorary Member: Romanian Academy and Romanian National Committee for UNICEF, 1993; President, Founder, Romanian Atheneum International Foundation, New York. Address: c/o Wolfgang Stoll, Martius Str 3, 80802 Munich, Germany.

NICOLET Aurèle, b. 22 Jan 1926, Neuchâtel, Switzerland. Flautist; Professor of Music. m. Christiane Gerhard. Education: Studied in Zurich with André Jaunet and Willy Burkhard; Paris Conservatoire with Marcel Moyse and Yvonne Drapier. Career: First Flute in Winterhur Orchestra, 1948-50; Solo flautist with Berlin Philharmonic, 1950-59; Professor at Berlin Musikhochschule, 1950-65; Later taught in Freiburg and Basle; Concert appearances throughout Europe as soloist with orchestra and with chamber ensembles; Works written for him by composers including Denisov, Takemitsu, Kelterborn and Huber. Recordings include: Works by Bach conducted by Karl Richter; Quartets and Concertos by Mozart. Honours: First Prize, Paris Conservatoire; First Prize, International Competition at Geneva, 1948; Music Critics' Prize, Berlin, 1963.

NICOLL Harry, b. Coupar Angus, Perthshire, Scotland. Tenor. Education: Studied at the Royal Scottish Academy of Music and Drama. Career: Sang with Scottish Opera Go Round from 1979 as Nemorino, Ferrando, Alfredo and Ramiro; Appearances with Welsh National Opera as Valetto in L'Incoronazione di Poppea, Vasek, the Idiot in Wozzeck and Brighella and the Dancing Master in Ariadne; Sang with English National Opera in Pacific Overtures, Street Scene and The Mikado and with Scottish Opera in their Rossini Double Bill, as The Lover in the premiere of Judith Weir's The Vanishing Bridegroom in 1990, as Bardolph and as Almaviva; Other engagements with Opera North in Acis and Galatea and L'Heure Espagnole, Park Lane Group in La Finta Semplice, Glyndebourne Touring Opera as Pedrillo in Die Entführung, English Bach Festival in Versailles as Thespis in Rameau's Platée, Kammeroper Berlin in The Lighthouse, Il Re Pastore and Il Matrimonio Segreto; La Fenice Venice in Zaide, Frankfurt and Jerusalem as Roderigo in Otello, Cologne Opera as Vasek, The Bartered Bride, Opera Voor Vlaanderen, Pedrillo in Die Entführung, New Israeli Opera, Tel Aviv, Idiot in Boris, Vasek in Bartered Bride, and as Almaviva, Barbiere; Théâtre des Champs Elysées as Medor in Roland by Lully; Has sung in several operas at the Batignano Festival; Concert appearances in the UK and abroad. Address: 5-7 Old Town, Clapham, London SW4 0JT, England.

NICULESCU Stefan, b. 31 July 1927, Moreni, Romania. Composer; Musicologist; Professor. m. Colette Demetrescu, 22 June 1952. Education: Conservatory of Music, Bucharest; Studio Siemens for Electronic Music, Munich, Germany. Debut: Bucharest in 1953. Career: Professor of Compositions and Music Analysis, Bucharest Conservatory of Music; Guest, Deutscher Akademischer Austauschdienst, Berlin, 1971-72. Compositions: 3 Symphonies, 1956-84; 3 Cantatas, 1959-64; Unisonos for Orchestra, 1970; The Book With Apolodor, opera for children, 1975; Omaggio A Enescu E Bartok for Orchestra, 1981; Invocatio, for 12 voices, 1989; Axion, for saxophone and women's choir, 1992; Psalmus, for 6 voices, 1993; Deisis, Symphonie no 4, 1995; Litanies, Symphony no 5, 1997. Recordings: Formants for Orchestra; Scenes for Orchestra; Symphonies for 15 Soloists; Inventions for Clarinet and Piano; Aphorismes D'Héraclite for Choir; Triplum 2 for Clarinet, Cello and Piano; Ison 1 for 14 Soloists; Ison 2 for Winds and Percussion; Echos for Violin; Synchronie 1 for 2-12 Instruments; Symphony No 2; Heteromorphie for Orchestra; Tastenspiel for Piano; Cantos, Symphonie no 3, for saxophone and orchestra, 1990. Publications: Co-Author, George Enescu, monography, 1971; Reflections About Music, 1980. Contributions to: Muzica; Revue Roumaine D'Histoire de L'Art; Arta; Studii de Muzicologie; Muzyka. Honours: Romanian Academy Prize, 1962; French Academy Prize, 1972; Prizes, Romanian Composers Union, 1972, 1975, 1979, 1981, 1982, 1984, 1994; Festival Montreux Prize, International Record Critics Award, 1985; Herder Prize, Vienna, 1994. Memberships: Romanian Composers Union, 1958; SACEM, Paris, 1969; Romanian Academy, 1993. Address: Intrarea Sublocotenent Staniloiu 4, 73228 Bucharest 39, Romania.

NIEHAUS Manfred, b. 18 Sep 1933, Cologne, Germany. Composer. Education: Studied with Zimmermann at Cologne. Career: Dramaturg and Director at Wurttemberg Landesbuhne, Esslingen am Neckar, 1963-65; Editor for Westdeutsche Rundfunk, Cologne from 1967 and freelance composer from 1989. Compositions: Music theatre works Bartleby, Cologne and Berlin, 1967; Die Pataphysiker, Kiel, 1969; Maldoror, Kiel, 1970; Die Badewanne, Bonn, 1973; It Happens, Bonn, 1973; Sylvester, Stuttgart, 1973; Tartarin Von Tarascon, Hamburg, 1977; Die Komponiermaschine, Nuremberg, 1980; Das Verlorene Gewissen, Gelsenkirchen, 1981; Das Christbaumbrettl, Cologne, 1983; Die Geschichte Vom Riesen Und Dem Kleinen Mann Im Ohr, Emmerich, 1984. Honour: Cologne Forderpreis, 1966. Address: c/o GEMA, Postfach 80 07 67, D-81607 Munich, Germany.

NIEHOFF Beatrice, b. 1952, Mannheim, Germany. Soprano. Career: Sang at Karlsruhe and Darmstadt, 1977-82; Later appearances in Hamburg, Zurich, Berlin and Vienna notably as Mozart's Constanze, Countess, Pamina and Fiordiligi, Dvorák's Rusalka, Weber's Agathe and Wagner's Elsa; Modern repertory includes operatic roles in Fortner's Bluthochzeit, Zemlinsky's Der Kreidekreis, Hindemith's Mathis der Maler and Schoeck's Massimilia Doni; In 1988 sang Eva in a new production of Die Meistersinger at Essen and the Protagonist in the German premiere of Berio's Un Re in Ascolto at Dusseldorf; Returned to Dusseldorf in 1989 as Cleopatra in Giulio Cesare by Handel.

NIELSEN Bent Christoffer, b. 8 Sept 1923, Landet, Taasinge, Denmark. Teacher; Musician. m. Tove Melhedegaard, 11 September 1949, 1 son, 2 daughters. Education: Graduate, Farmers School, 1946; Teachers Training College, 1951-55; Musical Studies, Clarinet, 1939-46, Bassoon, 1946-48. Career: Farmer, 1939-51; Member, Local Orchestra, 1942; Member, Local Symphony Orchestra, 1943; Fynske Musikantere, 1946-; Assistant, Several Amateur Orchestras; Member, Baroque Group, Svendborg, 1963-67; Own Quartet for Danish Fiddlers Music, 1969-; Sub-Editor, Hjemstavnsliv, Fiddlers and Folkdancers Paper, 15 years; Member, Team Preparing RISM Catalogue of Music Collection at the Castle of Valdemarslot, 1980-85. Publications: Music Section of Gamie Danse fra Bornholm, 1971; Music Section of Vesteregnens gamle danse, 1982; 358 Danske Folkedansermelodier (2 violins, clarinet A bass), 1985. Contributor to: Hjemstavnsliv; Fyns Amts Avis. Membership: Danske Folkedanseres Spillemandskreds, Vice Chairman, 1963-67. Hobbies: Biology; Treatises in Botany, Psychology and Primitive Art; Collecting Older Musical Instruments & Notebooks to Exhibit. Address: Enkesaedet Skovballevej 21, Taasinge, 5700 Svendborg, Denmark.

NIELSEN Inga, b. 2 June 1946, Holbaek, Seeland, Denmark. Singer (Soprano). m. Robert Hale, 3 daughters. Education: Music Academy, Vienna; Musikhochschule Stuttgart. Debut: Gelsenkirchen, Germany, 1973. Career: Sang in Munster, 1974-75; Bern, 1975-77; Member of Frankfurt Opera, 1978-83; Ludwigsburg Festival, 1978, as Zerlina in Don Giovanni; Dusseldorf, 1980, as Blonde in Die Entführung and Norina in Don Pasquale; New York City Opera, 1980, as Johann Strauss's Adele and Nannetta in Falstaff; Schwetzingen, 1983, in the premiere of Henze's The English Cat; Stuttgart, 1984, as Donna Elvira in Don Giovanni; Guest appearances in Hamburg, Aachen and Oslo; has sung Donizetti's Lucia in Pittsburgh, Oslo and Hamburg, 1984-87; Wexford Festival, 1986, as Amenaide in Rossini's Tancredi; Palermo 1987, as Marguerite; sang Mozart's Constanze at Salzburg and Covent Garden, 1987-89; Cologne and Strasbourg, 1989, as Ilia and Fiodiligi; sang Christine in the Italian premiere of Strauss's Intermezzo, Bologna, 1990; Munich Festival, 1990, as Aspasia in Mitridate; Season 1992 as Marzelline at Zurich and Gilda at Oslo; Covent Garden 1995, as Ursula in Hindemith's Mathis der Maler; Engaged for Schubert's Des Teufels Lustschloss, Vienna Festival, 1997. Recordings: Zerlina in Don Giovanni, from Luwigsburg; Flowermaiden in Parsifal (Deutsche Grammophon); The Seven Last Words on the Cross by Haydn; Zemlinsky's Der Zwerg (Schwann). Address: Pflugstevistr 20, CH-8703 Erleubech, Switzerland.

NIELSEN Svend, b. 20 Apr 1937, Copenhagen, Denmark. Composer. Education: Studied Music, University of Copenhagen; Music Theory, Royal Academy of Music, Copenhagen. Debut: Copenhagen, 1962. Career: Teacher, Royal Academy of Music, Aarhus, 1967-. Compositions: Orchestral: Metamorphoses, 1968; Nuages, 1972; Symphony, 1978-79; Nocturne, 1981; Concerto for Violin and Orchestra, 1985; Nightfall for Chamber Orchestra, 1989; Voice and Instruments: Three of Nineteen Poems, 1962; Duets, 1964; Romances, 1970-74; Chamber Cantata, 1975; Sonnets of Time, 1978; Ascent Towards Akseki, 1979; Choral Music: Motets, 1982; Imperia, 1982; Jorden, 1983; Piano Music: Romantic Piano Pieces, 1974; 5 Inventions, 1983; Chamber: Rondo for Flute Quintet, 1986; String Quartet, 1987; Black Velvet, Clarinet Quintet, 1988; Variations for Double Quintet, 1989; Windscapes for Brass Quintet, 1990; Aria for Orchestra, 1991; Aubade for Orchestra, 1994; Sinfonia Concertante for Cello and Chamber Orchestra, 1994; Shadowgraphs for 10 Instruments, 1995. Recordings: Carillons; Sinfonia Concertante; Nightfall. Honour: Carl Nielsen Prize, 1981. Address: Royal Academy of Music, 8210 Aarhus V, Denmark.

NIELSEN Tage, b. 16 Jan 1929, Frederiksberg, Denmark. Professor; Composer. m. Aase Grue-Sorensen, 14 Oct 1950, 1 son, 2 daughters. Education: Musicology, University of Copenhagen, 1947-55; Additional studies in Israel 1972, Italy 1974, USA 1975. Debut: As Composer, 23 October 1949, UNM Festival, Stockholm. Career: Deputy Head of Music Department, Radio Denmark, 1957-63; Director, Professor, Royal Academy of Music, Aarhus, 1963-83; Chair of Board, Danish State Art Foundation, 1971-74; Director, Accademia di Danimarca, Rome, 1983-89; Managing Director, The Society for Publication of Danish Music, 1989-93. Compositions: Two Nocturnes, piano, 1961; Il gardino magico, orchestra, 1968; Three Character Pieces and an Epilogue, piano, 1972-74; Passacaglia, orchestra, 1981; Laughter in the Dark, opera, 1987-91; Paesaggi, 2 pianos, 1985; Three Opera Fragments, 13 instruments, 1986; The Frosty Silence in the Gardens, guitar, 1990; Lamento and Chorale Fantasy, organ, 1993-95; Fegiardino Magico, for orchestra; Passacaglia, for orchestra; Two nocturnes for piano; Three Opera Fragments, for 13 instruments; The Frosty Silence in the Gardens, guitar solo. Publications: Fra on Langgaard, Alban Berg's Lulu and Lutoslawski and others in Dansk Musiktidsskrift. Honours: The Anker Prize, 1975; The Schierbeck Prize, 1992. Membership: Danish Composers Society. Hobby: PHotography. Address: Peter Bangsvej 153, 2000 Frederiksberg, Denmark.

NIEMAN Alfred (Abbe), b. 25 Jan 1913, London, England. Composer; Pianist. m. Aileen Steeper, 2 sons. Education: RAM; RAM; ARAM; FGSM. Career: Concert appearances in a two piano team and performances with British Broadcasting Corporation for 5 years; Professor of Composition and Piano and Lecturer at Guildhall School of Music. Compositions include: 2nd Piano Sonata; 9 Israeli Folksongs; Paradise Regained for Cello, Piano and Chinese Cymbals; Symphony No 2; Variations and Finale for Piano; Adam, cantata for Tenor, 4 Trombones, 5 Percussion and Piano; Various songs; Sonata for Guitar, commissioned from Gilbert Biberian through The Arts Council and first performed at Purcell Room in 1986; Soliloquy for Solo Cello, commissioned by Stefan Popov and first performed at St John's Smith Square in 1986 and a further 6 times in Bulgaria; Suite for Piano; Three Expressions for Unaccompanied Chorus; Chromotempera, concerto for Cello and Piano. Recordings: Canzona for Quintet, Flute, Oboe, Clarinet, Violin and Piano. Publications: Schumann; Tension In Music; The Earth It Is Your Shoe for Solo Guitar. Contributions to: A Fresh Look at Webern, in The Composer, No 30. Honours include: McFarren Gold Medal. Memberships: CGGB; British Association of Music Therapy; Consultant, National Association for Gifted Children. Hobby: Cricket. Address: 21 Well Walk, London, NW3, England.

NIEMELA Hannu, b. 17 Apr 1954, Lohtaja, Finland. Baritone. Education: Graduated from Sibelius Academy, Helsinki, 1983; Further study with Kim Borg and Hans Hotter. Debut: Zurich Opera in 1985 as Marullo in Rigoletto. Career: Member of Karlsruhe Opera, 1985-89 and Staatstheater Mainz from 1989; Guest engagements at Savonlinna and Schwetzingen Festivals and at Berne, Basle, Mannheim, Dresden, Prague, Leningrad and Strasbourg; Karlsruhe in 1986 in the premiere of Der Meister und Margarita by Rainer Kunad; Other roles have included Mozart's Count, Papageno and Don Giovanni, Gluck's Orestes, Escamillo, Wozzeck and Demetrius in A Midsummer Night's Dream, and Verdi's Macbeth and Falstaff; Sang the title role in the German premiere of Le Roi Arthus by Chausson, Cologne, 1996; Noted concert artist. Address: c/o Staatstheater, Gutenbergplatz 7, 6500 Mainz, Germany.

NIENSTEDT Gerd, b. 10 Jul 1932, Hanover, Germany. Bass-Baritone. Education: Studied with Otto Kuhler in Hanover. Debut: Bremerhaven in 1954. Career: Sang in Gelsenkirchen, 1955-59, Wiesbaden, 1959-61, Cologne, 1961-72, Vienna Staatsoper, 1964-73, Bayreuth Festival, 1962-75 as Klingsor, Biterolf, Kothner, Donner, Hunding and Gunther and sang Wozzeck in Wieland Wagner's last production at Frankfurt in 1966 and in the 1965 premiere of Die Soldaten by Zimmermann at Cologne; Intendent of the Landestheater Detmold, 1985-87; Guest appearances in Milan, Berlin, Paris, Buenos Aires, Chicago, San Francisco, Montreal and Zurich; Also heard as concert singer; Worked as administrator at Bielefeld Opera House from 1973 and Detmold Landestheater, 1985-. Recordings: Tannhäuser; Parsifal; Die Meistersinger; Die Walküre; Das Rheingold from Bayreuth; Mozart's Requiem; Mahler's Das klagende Lied; Salome. Address: c/o Landestheater, 4930 Detmold, Germany.

NIES Otfrid, b. 5 May 1937, Giessen, Germany. Violinist; Writer on Music. m. Christel Nies-Fermor, 7 Sep 1961, 2 sons, 2 daughters. Education: Violin studies with Max Rostal, 1960-64, and chamber music with Rudolf Kolisch. Career: Member of National Theatre Orchestra, Mannheim, 1964-66; Leader, Stadttheaterorchester Hagen, 1966-71 and leader for Staatstheaterorchester Kassel, 1971-; Presentation of music for player piano by Conlon Nancarrow at Documenta 7, Kassel, 1982; Founder of Archiv Charles Koechlin, 1984. Recordings: Quintets, Op 80 for Piano and Strings, Op 156 for Flute and Harp, by Charles Koechlin; Music for Violin and Player Piano by Conlon Nancarrow. Publications: Orchestration of Quartre Interludes, Op 214 for The Ballet Voyages, Op 222, 1947, by Charles Koechlin, 1986. Contributions to: Many articles on Charles Koechlin in Das Orchester, Neue Zeitschrift fuer Musik, Fonoforum. Memberships: Association Charles Koechlin, Paris; Internationale Schoenberg-Gesellschaft, Vienna. Hobbies: Unknown Music and Composers; Contemproary Music. Address: Saengerweg 3, D-3500 Kassel, Germany.

NIGG Serge, b. 6 June 1924, Paris, France. Composer. m. Micheline Nourrit, 1950, 1 daughter. Education: Paris Conservatory with Messiaen, 1941-46; Studied with Leibowitz, 1945-48. Career: Freelance Composer; Professor of Orchestration at the Paris Conservatory. Compositions include: 3 Sonatas for piano; 1 sonata for violin solo; 1 sonata for violin and piano; 4 Melodies on poems of Paul Eluard; Concerto for viola and orchestra; 2 Piano Concertos; Concerto for flute and strings; Mirrors for William Blake for orchestra; Fulgur for orchestra; Milton d'Oiseaux d'Or for orchestra; Du Clair au Sombre song-cycle for soprano and orchestra to poems by Paul Eluard; Symphony poems Timour and Pour uin poéte captif; Violin concerto; Jérome Bosch-Symphony; Poéme Pour Orchestre. Recordings: 1st Piano Concerto (Orchestre National de France); Violin Concerto (Christian Ferras); Visages d'Axel; Le Chant du Depossede; Jérome Bosch-Symphony; Arioso for Violin and Piano; String Quartet; Poéme for orchestra; Million d'Oiseaux d'Or, Orchestre de Paris. Contributions to: Discours de reception a l'Academie des Beaux Arts, 1990; Revue "Diapason": Les Quatuors de Bela Bartok, 1991; Communication a l'Academie des Beaux-Arts: Peut-on encore, composition musicale?. 1992; 4 Sonatas. Publications: Published discourses from academic seminars and symposia. Honours include: Officer de l'Ordre du Merite, President d'Academie des Beaux Arts, 1995; Chevalier de la Légion d'honneur. Memberships: President, Societe Nationale de Musique, 1989; Elu membre de l'Academie des Beaux-Arts, 1989; President de l'Academie and President de l'Institut de France, 1995. Address: 15 bis rue Darcel, 92100 Boulogne sue Seine, France.

NIIMI Tokuhide, b. 5 August 1947, Nagoya, Japan. Composer. Education: Graduated University of Tokyo 1970 and studied at the Tokyo National University of Fine Arts and Music, 1971-78. Career: Faculty Member, Toho Gauden School of Music, Tokyo; Board Member, Directors of the Japanese Composers Society. Compositions include: Percussion Concerto, 1973; Enlacage I for chorus and orchestra, 1977; Enlacage II for 3 percussionists (1978) and III for 2 marimbas and 2 percussionists (1980); 2 Symphonies, 1981, 1986; Three Valses for piano duet, 1986; 2 Piano Concertos, 1984 and 1993 (Eyes of the Creator); Under Blue Skies, for children's chorus, mixed chorus and orchestra, 1986; Ohju for cello, 1987; Kazane, for clarinet, violin and cello, 1989; Au-Mi for soprano, violin, cello and piano, 1989; Heteorhthmix for orchestra, 1991; Chain of Life for chamber orchestra, 1993; Planets Dance for 6 percussionists, 1993; String Quartet, 1994. Address: c/o JASRAC, 3-6-12 Uehara, Shibuya-ku, Tokyo 151, Japan.

NIKKANEN Kurt, b. Dec 1965, Hartford, Connecticut, USA. Concert Violinist. Education: Began violin studies aged 3; Boston University Prep Division with Roman Totenberg; Juilliard School, New York, with Dorothy DeLay, graduated 1986. Career: Won first competition, 1976; Carnegie Hall debut, 1978, playing the Saint-Saëns Introduction and Rondo Capriccioso; 1980, played the Paganini 1st Concerto with the New York Philharmonic; Bruch 1st Concerto with the Boston Pops; Appearances with the Hartford Symphony, Colorado Philharmonic, New Jersey Chamber Orchestra and Aspen Chamber Symphony; European debut, 1981, with recital tour of Finland; Cleveland Orchestra debut in the Glazunov Concerto, July 1988; UK debut playing the Elgar Concerto with the Royal Liverpool Philharmonic conducted by Libor Pesek, Sept 1988; Toured in Venezuela; Debuted at the Kennedy Center in Washington DC; Further engagements with the Helsinki Philharmonic under James DePreist, and an orchestral/recital tour of Japan; Season 1990-91, made debuts in London, Munich and Barcelona; Season 1991-92, engagements with the San Francisco, New Orleans and Portland Symphonies; Recital debuts in Vancouver, Berlin and Paris; Played the Glazunov Concerto at the 1991 Promenade Concerts, London; 1995, BBC Scottish Symphony, Bergen Philharmonic, Seattle International Festival, Hallé Orchestra, Khumo Festival, Resedentie Orchestra of Holland; Premiered John Adams Concerto in Sweden with the Stockholm Philharmonic, John Adams conducting, January 1995; Season 1996-97 included the Adams Concerto with the Hallé Orchestra, the New Zealand Symphony Orchestra and the Cincinnati Symphony, Dvorak and Brahms on Far East tour. Recordings include: Tchaikovsky and Glazunov Concertos. Hobbies: Tennis; Physical fitness. Address: c/o Harrison/Parrott Ltd, 12 Penzance Place, London W11 4PA, England.

NIKODEMOWICZ Andrzej, b. 2 Jan 1925, Lvov, Poland. Composer; Pianist. m. Kazimiera Maria Grabowska, 6 July 1952, 1 son, 1 daughter. Education: Studied with Adam Soltys, Faculty of Composition, Conservatory of Lvov, 1950; Studied with Tadeusz Majerski, Faculty of Piano, 1954. Career: Professor of Composition and Piano, Conservatory of Lvov, 1951-73; Dismissed by reason of religious convictions; 1980-: Professor of Faculty of Music, University of Maria Curie-Sklodowska in Lublin; Professor, Faculty of Church Musicology, Catholic University, Lublin. Compositions: Extensive list of compositions including: Piano works, Ekspresje, 66 miniatures for piano solo, 1959-60; Violin works; Songs for voice and piano; Chamber Concerto, 1968; Composizione sonoristica, for violin, violoncello and piano, 1966-71; Musica concertante per tre for flute, viola and piano, 1966-67; 3 nocturns for trumpet and piano, 1964; Symphonic music, 1974-75; Concertos for violin and symphony orchestra, 1973; choir music including 500 Polish Christmas carols; Theatre Music, (Pantomime) Glass Mountain, 1969; 35 religious cantatas including: Magni ficat for choir of women and orchestra, 1977-78; Evening Offering, 1980; Hear My Cry, O God, 1981; 5 Lullabies for violin and piano, 1991; 4 songs for soprano, trumpet and organ, text: George Herbert, 1992; Variations, Ave maris Stella, for organ, 1993; Concerto for piano and symphony orchestra, 1994. Recordings: Two cantatas, cycle of songs. Contributions to: Several reviews in Ruch Muzyczny. Honour: Prize of Saint Friar Albert. Membership: Polish Composers Society; ZAIKS. Hobbies: Astronomy; Painting; Folk Music. Address: ul Paryska 4/37, 20-854 Lublin, Poland.

NIKOLAJEV Vladimir, b. 15 Dec 1953, Nikolajev Town, Russia. Composer. m. Alparova Nailja, 6 Jun 1987, 1 s. Education: School of Arts, Ufa, 1971-76; Gnesin Musical Institute, Moscow, 1976-81; Aspirant, Moscow Conservatoire, 1982-85. Debut: Moscow, 1981. Career: Gnesin Concert Hall, Moscow, 1981; Many songs broadcast on radio, 1987-; Art Institute Concert Hall, Ufa, 1984; Participant, Saratov International Competition of Young Composers, 1988; Meeting on Moscow TV, 1989; Participant, Lutoslawski Competition, Warsaw, 1991; Music for The Blue Eye of Siberia, documentary film about Lake Baikal. Compositions: Hymn for Violin Solo, 1987; Cry and Choral for Violin and Piano, 1988; Serenade, capriccio for Accordian, 1990; Legend About Beautiful Maiden Salimakai, 1991. Recordings: Ballade for Accordian and Orchestra, record, 1989; Over 10 song recordings for radio. Contributions to: Soviet Musik magazine, 1989; Newspapers. Honours: Winner, Magic Cristall, Russia Modern Song Competition, 1989; 4th Place, Concerto for Orchestra, First Lutoslawski Competition, 1991; 1st Prize, Lili Boulanger Memorial Fund, Boston, USA, 1992. Membership: Union of Composers, Russia. Address: Dirizabielnaja 24 ap 6, Dolgoprudny, Moscow Area 141700, Russia.

NIKOLOV Nikola, b. 1924, Sofia, Bulgaria. Tenor. Education: Studied in Sofia. Debut: Varna in 1947 as Pinkerton. Career: Sang at Varna until 1953 then studied further in Moscow and sang at Sofia National Opera from 1955; Appearances in Moscow and Leningrad in the 1950s, La Scala Milan in 1958 as Jenik in The Bartered Bride; Season 1958-60 at Wexford Festival, Vienna Staatsoper and Covent Garden as Radames; New York Metropolitan in 1960 as Don José, and State Operas of Berlin and Hamburg and Naples in 1963 as Vasco da Gama in L'Africaine.

Sang further in Munich, Barcelona, Geneva, Belgrade, Budapest and Bucharest; Other roles included Manrico, Turiddu, Cavaradossi, Calaf and Don Carlos. Recordings: Aida; Carmen; Boris Godunov; L'Africaine. Address: c/o Bayerische Staatsoper, Postfach 100148, 8000 Munich 1, Germany.

NIKOLOV Victor, b. 8 March 1976, Pleven, Bulgaria. Pianist. Education: Music School of Pleven; Music Academy of Sofia. Debut: Recital, Art Gallery Hall, Pleven, 1984. Career: Visitor to Japan as a Participant in a Representative Group of Young Talents; Numerous Concerts; Festivals include, March Musical Days, Rousse; Laureate Days, Katia Popova, Pleven; The Golden Diana, Yambol; Reviews of the Art of Performance and Music; Concerts as Soloist of the Pleven Philharmonic Orchestra and Radio Orchestra, Sofia. Recordings: Records for Bulgarian National Radio, Czech Radio, Japan Radio, Television in Bulgaria, Germany, Italy and Japan. Honours: 1st Prize, National Competition S Obretenov, Provadia, 1986; 1st Prize, National Competition D Nenov, Razgrad, 1987; 1st Prize, International Competition Virtuosos of the Piano, Czech Republic, 1987; 3rd Prize, International Competition for Piano Players, Marsala, Italy, 1990; 1st Prize, First Private Competition for Chamber Music, Pleven, 1992; 1st Prize, National Competition for Chamber Accompaniments, Pleven, 1994; 2nd Prize and Award, International Competition Albert Russel, 1994. Hobby: Swimming. Address: Kiril i Metodi Str 24, Pleven 5800, Bulgaria.

NIKOLSKY Gleb, b. 1959, Moscow, Russia. Singer (Bass). Education: Studied at the Moscow conservatory and at La Scala, Milan. Career: Soloist at the Bolshoi Theatre, Moscow, as Verdi's King Philip, Ramphis, Fiesco and Padre Guardiano, Boris, Dosifey, Ivan Susanin and Gounod's Mephistopheles; Guest appearances in Italy, the USA and Zurich (Gremin in Eugene Onegin, 1990); Carnegie Hall 1990, as the Archbishop in Tchaikovsky's The Maid of Orleans; Metropolitan Opera from 1991. Address: Bolshoi Theatre, 103009 Moscow, Russia.

NILON Paul, b. 1961, Keighley, Yorkshire. Singer (Tenor). Education: Studied with Frederic Cox at the Royal Northern College of Music. Career includes: Appearances with Opera 80 as Don Ottavio, the Duke of Mantua and Sellem in The Rake's Progress; La Fenice, Venice, as Sellem; Musica nel Chiostro in Batignano, Italy, as Jacquino in Beethoven's Leonora; Has sung Strauss's Scaramucchio and Mozart's Belmonte for Opera Northern Ireland, 1987-88; Mario and the Magician, Stephen Oliver, world premiere Batignano, 1988; With City of Birmingham Touring Opera has sung Fenton in Falstaff and Mozart's Tamino; Has sung with Opera North from 1988 as Hylas in The Trojans, Kudras (Katya Kabanova), Belfiore (La Finta Giardiniera), Leander in Nielsen's Maskarade (British premiere), Ferrando and Don Ottavio; Engagements with New Israel Opera and English National Opera, 1990-92 as Ferrando, Narraboth (Salome) and Telemachus in The Return of Ulysses; Tamino ENO, 1992-93, Duel of Tancredi and Clorinda; Tamino Scottish Opera, 1992, ENO, 1993; In Ariodante ENO, as Lurcanio, 1993; Many concert appearances; Almaviva, Barbiere, ENO and New Israeli Opera; King Ouf in L'Etoile; Paolino in Secret Marriage; Benedict in Beatrice and Benedict, Welsh National Opera; Pirro in Rossini's Ermione at Glyndebourne 1996; Alfredo for GTO. Recordings include: L'Assedio di Calais by Donizetti and Volume II and III in One Hundred Years of Italian Opera (Opera Rara); Medea in Corinta by Mayr; Orazi e Curiazi, Mercadante (Opera Rara). Current Management: IMG Artists Europe. Address: Media House, 3 Burlington Lane, London W4 2TH, England.

NILSON Göran W, b. 5 Jan 1941, Halmstad, Sweden. Conductor; Pianist. m. Catharina Ericson, 20 June 1965, 1 son, 1 daughter. Education: Royal High School of Music, Stockholm; Further studies in Paris, London and New York. Debut: As Pianist at age 15, Stockholm Concert Hall, 1956. Career: As Pianist, tours in Europe and USA; Conductor, Royal Opera, Stockholm, 1963-69; Chief Conductor, Örebro and Gävle, 1974-93; Guest Conductor, Europe, USA, Asia and Mexico. Recordings: Many recordings of Swedish music with different Swedish orchestras. Honour: Jeton Reward from Royal High School of Music, Stockholm, 1956. Membership: Royal Swedish Academy of Music, 1986-. Hobby: Airplanes. Current Management: Konsertbolaget AB, Stockholm, Sweden. Address: Tantogatan 47-I, S-11842 Stockholm, Sweden.

NILSSON Anders, b. 6 July 1954, Stockholm, Sweden. Composer. m. Elzbieta Mysliwiec, 11 Feb 1989, 2 daughters. Education: Private musical studies; Music High School, Stockholm, 1971-73; Birkagården Folk High School, Stockholm, 1973-75, 1977-78; Composition, State College of Music, Stockholm, 1979-83. Debut: 1st of Trois Pièces pour grand orchestre, with Danish Radio Symphony Orchestra, Copenhagen, 15th Jan 1981. Career: Composer, Conductor, Swedish National Theatre Centre and Stockholm City Theatre, 1975-78; Full-time Composer, 1983-; Represented at International Society for Contemporary Music World Music Days, 1990, 1993, and elsewhere. Compositions include: Trois Pièces pour grand orchestre, 1980-88; Ariel for oboe, tape and string orchestra, 1985; Reflections for soprano and chamber ensemble, 1982; Cadenze for chamber orchestra, 1987; Concerto for organ and orchestra, 1987; Sinfonietta for orchestra, 1992; Divertimento for chamber ensemble, 1991; KRASCH for saxophone quartet and percussion-ensemble, 1993; Concerto Grosso for saxophone quartet and orchestra, 1995; Symphony no 1, 1996; Titanics for orchestra, pianoconcerto, 1997. Recordings: Ariel; Cadenze; Concerto for organ and orchestra; Five Orchestral Pieces for piano; Reflections; KRASCH; Divertimento; Aria. Publications: Scores: Resonance for piano, 1985; Reflections, 1986; Ariel, 1990; Five Orchestral Pieces for piano, 1993; Mountains for organ, 1994; Divertimento for chamber ensemble, 1995. Contributions to: Numerous articles to Nutida Musik, Swedish magazine for contemporary music. Honours include: Rosenborg Prize, Gehrmans Music Publishers, 1988; 1st Prize, Grand Prix de Saint-Rèmy-de-Provence, for Mountains, 1992. Memberships: Swedish Composers' League; International Society for Contemporary Music. Address: Fyrskeppsvägen 128, S-121 54 Johanneshov, Sweden.

NILSSON Birgit (Fru Bertil Niklasson), b. 17 May 1918, Karup, Sweden. Soprano. m. Bertil Nicklasson. Education: Stockholm Royal Academy of Music. Career: With Stockholm Opera, 1946-58; Sang at Glyndebourne as Mozart's Electra in 1951, at Bayreuth, Munich, Hollywood Bowl, Buenos Aires and Florence, Covent Garden London as Brünnhilde, Turandot, Elektra and Isolde, at La Scala Milan, Naples, Vienna, Chicago and San Francisco, Metropolitan Opera, NY, and Moscow; Sang in Turandot at Paris in 1968, Tosca at New York in 1968, Elektra at London in 1969 and was particularly well known for her Wagnerian roles as Brünnhilde and Isolde and as Strauss's Elektra, Salome and Dyer's Wife; Appeared at the Met Opera Gala, New York, 1996. Last stage performance in 1982; Gala performances at the Metropolitan in 1983; Currently gives masterclasses in England and elsewhere. Recordings include: Aida; Der Freischütz; Salome; Un Ballo in Maschera; Don Giovanni; Der Ring des Nibelungen; Oberon; Tannhäuser; Tristan; La Fanciulla del West. Honours: Medal Litteris et Artibus, 1960; Medal for Promotion of Art of Music, Royal Academy of Music, Stockholm, 1968; Austrian and Bavarian Kammersängerin; Honorary Member of the Vienna State Opera, 1968; First Commander Order of Vasa, 1974; Honorary Member, Royal Musical Academy, London; Honorary Doctorates; Swedish Gold Medal, CL 18 Illis Quorum. Address: c/o Kungliga Teatern, PO Box 16094, S-10322 Stockholm, Sweden.

NILSSON Bo, b. 1 May 1937, Skelleftehamn, Sweden. Composer. Divorced, 2 daughters. Education: Piano under Micha Pedersen, 1945-50; Audiology under K G St Clair Renard, 1951-54; Counterpoint and instrumentation under Karl Birger Blomdahl, 1955-57. Debut: Composer, Cologne, 1956. Career: Freelance Artist, 1976-; Compositions played worldwide; Author. Compositions include: Brief an Gösta Oswald, 1958-59; Drei Szenen, 1960-61; Swedenborg Dreaming for Electronic Music, 1969; Deja Vu for Woodwind Quartet, 1967; Deja connu, deja entendu for Wind Quintet, 1976; We'll Be Meeting Tomorrow for Mixed Choir, Soprano, Celesta and Triangles, 1970; Fatumeh for Speaker, Soloists, Mixed Choir, Electronics and Large Orchestra, 1973; La Bran for Soprano, Saxophone, Mixed Choir, Orchestra and Electronics, 1975; Fragments for Marimba, 5 Thai-gongs, 1975; Floten aus der Einsamkelt for Soprano, 9 Players, 1976; Bass, bass, tuba solo, 6 Javanian tuned gongs, Chinese Gong, 1977; Plexus for Brass Instruments, Piano and Percussion, 1979; Wendepunkt-Infrastruktur-Endepunkt, brass quintet, 1981; Autumn Song for Baritone and Orchestra, 1984; My Summerwind is Yours, for Baritone and Orchestra, 1984; Brief an Gösta Oswald; Arctic Romance, 1995; A Spirit's Whisper in Swedenborg's Gazebo, 1996; Film music; Songs; Jazz. Recordings: Introduction and Midsummer Tune; Quantitaten, Raga Rena Rama; Rendez-vous; You; Illness; Walz in Marjoram; Blue-Black Samba; The Last Lass; To Love; Lidingo Airport; Forward Waltz; The Swinging World of Bo Nilsson; The Missile; In The Loneliness of The Night; Ravaillac; A Spirit's Whisper, 1997; Many Others. Publications: Spaderboken, 1962; Missilen eller Livet i en mossa, 1994. Honours: Christopher Johnson Grand Prize, 1975; Hilding Rosenberg Prize, 1993; State Artist's Salary, 1974-. Address: Kocksgatan 48, 4 tr, 116 29 Stockholm, Sweden.

NILSSON Pia-Marie, b. 1961, Sweden. Soprano. Education: Studied at Stockholm College of Music and the State Opera School. Debut: Stockholm Folkoperan in 1985 as the Queen of Night. Career: Sang at Royal Opera Stockholm and the Drottningholm Theatre, 1986-88 and Frankfurt Opera from 1989 as Sandrina in La Finta Giardiniera, Servilia in La Clemenza di Tito, Pamina, Oscar in Ballo in Maschera, Gilda and Sophie; French debut in 1991 as Donna Anna at Nancy; Concert engagements in Scandinavia, Italy, Switzerland, Germany and Austria; Engaged as Oscar for the Théâtre de la Monnaie, Brussels, 1995; Season 1994-95, Ring Cycle, Frankfurt; Season 1995-96, Susanna, Frankfurt; Broadcasting commitments in Scandinavia.

NILSSON Raymond, b. 26 May 1920, Mosman, Sydney, Australia. Tenor. Education: Studied at the New South Wales Conservatorium and at the Royal College of Music in London. Career: After early experience in Australia sang with the Carl Rosa Company, the English Opera Group and Sadler's Wells; Royal Opera House Covent Garden from 1952 as Don José, Alfredo, Germont and Pandarus in Troilus and Cressida; Guest appearances in Wiesbaden and elsewhere in Germany as concert artist, with further tours to USA and Holland; Australian tours with the Elizabethan Opera Company in 1958 and Sadler's Wells in 1960; Other roles included Turiddu, Rodolfo, Narraboth in Salome and Luigi in Il Tabarro; BBC performances of Schoenberg's Gurrelieder, Hindemith's Mathis der Maler, Oedipus Rex and Kodaly's Psalmus Hungaricus; Sang in Janácek's Glagolitic Mass with ABC, Australia. Recordings: Bob Boles in Peter Grimes; Psalmus Hungaricus. Address: c/o Australian Opera, PO Box 291, Strawberry Hills, New South Wales 2012, Australia.

NIMSGERN Siegmund, b. 14 Jan 1940, St Wendel, Germany. Baritone. Education: Vocal studies with Paul Lohmann and Jakob Staempfli. Debut: Lionel in Tchaikovsky's Maid of Orleans, Saarbrucken, 1967. Career: Sang in Saarbrucken until 1971 then Deutsche Oper am Rhein, Dusseldorf, 1971-74; London Promenade Concerts in 1972 as Mephistopheles in La Damnation de Faust; La Scala Milan and Paris Opéra in 1973, Covent Garden in 1973 as Amfortas in Parsifal; Paris, 1977-82 as the Speaker in Die Zauberflöte, Creon in Oedipus Rex, Telramund in Lohengrin and Beethoven's Pizarro; Metropolitan Opera in 1978 as Pizarro and Bayreuth Festival, 1983-85 as Wotan in the Peter Hall production of Der Ring des Nibelungen; Often heard as concert singer; Chicago Lyric Opera in 1988 as Scarpia and sang Wotan in Das Rheingold at Bonn in 1990, Don Pizarro in Fidelio at La Scala and Telramund at Frankfurt in 1991. Recordings: St John Passion by Bach; Masses by Haydn and Hummel; Pergolesi's La Serva Padrona; Cantatas by Bach and Telemann; Bach's Magnificat; St Matthew Passion and Bach B minor Mass; Alberich in Das Rheingold; Mosè in Egitto; Die Schöpfung; Marschner's Der Vampyr. Address: c/o Ingpen and Williams Ltd, 26 Wadham Road, London SW15 2LR, England.

NIN-CULMELL Joaquin (Maria), b. 5 Sept 1908, Berlin, Germany. Composer. Education: Studied at Schola Cantorum in Paris, Paris Conservatory with Paul Dukas and private study with Manuel de Falla in Granada. Career: Instructor, Middlebury College, Vermont, USA, 1938-40 and Williams College, 1940-50; Professor of Music, University of California at Berkeley, 1949-74, Emeritus Professor, 1974-; Has appeared as Pianist and Conductor in USA and Europe. Compositions: Piano Concerto, El Burlador de Sevilla, ballet; Piano Quintet, Three Impressions, Sonata Breve, Tonadas and 12 Cuban Dances for piano; Three Old Spanish Pieces for Orchestra; Diferencias for Orchestra; Concerto for Cello and Orchestra after Padre Viola; Mass in English for Mixed Chorus and Organ; La Celestina, opera; Cantata for Voice and Harpsichord or Piano and Strings, after Padre Jose Pradas; Le Rêve de Cyrano, ballet; Symphony of the Mysteries, for organ and gregorian chant; Canciones de la Barraca, for voice and piano; Songs and choral pieces; Guitar and organ pieces. Recording: Tonadas, volumes I-IV, Maria Luisa Cantas. Publications: Editor, Spanish Choral Tradition; Prefaces in English and French for Anais Nin's Early Diaries. Membership: Corresponding Member of Royal Academy of Fine Arts of San Fernando, Madrid. Address: 5830 Clover Drive, Oakland, CA 94618, USA.

NIRQUET Jean, b. 15 Aug 1958, Paris, France. Countertenor; Conductor; Musicologist. Education: Baccalauréat of Sciences; Licence, History, Sorbonne University, Paris; Flute, bassoon, piano and theory studies at Strasbourg Music High School and Conservatory until 1964; Harmony and conducting with Claude-Henry Joubert, singing with Jacqueline Bonnardot at Conservatory of Orléans until 1978; Music analysis with Betsy Jolas, singing with Christiane Eda-Pierre at Conservatory of Paris. Career includes: Engagements at opera houses of Paris, Lyon, Nice, Strasbourg, Karlsruhe amd Helsinki; Radio appearances in France, Germany and Holland and at numerous festivals; Film for Südwestfunk 2, Pasticcio of Handel-Martinoty, 1985. Recordings: Handel's Alessandro; Cavalli's Serse; Charpentier's Vespers of the Annunciation, Te Deum and David et Jonathas; Gilles' Requiem; Prodomidès' H H Ulysse. Publications: Rose et Colas de Monsigny, 1982; L'Irato de Méhul, 1984; La Dramaturgie des Opéras de Lully Dans L'Etude des Tempi; Analyse d'Epiphanie d'André Caplet. Current Management: Anglo Swiss, London, England; Rainer-Poilvé, Paris, France; Kempf, Munich, Germany. Address: c/o Anglo Swiss Ltd, Suites 35-37, Morley House, 320 Regent Street, London W1R 5AD, England.

NISHIDA Hiroko, b. 17 Jan 1952, Oita, Japan. Soprano. Education: Studied in Tokyo. Career: Sang with the Bonn Opera, 1979-81; Appearances at Zurich Opera as Butterfly, Berne, Mimi, St Gallen, Micaela and the Forza Leonora at Berlin, Munich, Cologne, Frankfurt, Dusseldorf, Stuttgart and Mannheim; Sang Butterfly with Opéra de Lyon in 1990; Further guest appearances at San Diego, Enschede and Amsterdam, Vienna Staatsoper; Hamburg; Prague; Sofia; Vancouver; Tokyo; Other roles include Arminda in La Finta Giardiniera, Pamina, Manon Lescaut, Lauretta, Elisabeth de Valois and Kunigunde in Lortzing's Hans Sachs; Concert repertoire includes works by Bach, Handel, Mozart, Schubert, Beethoven, Bruckner and Mahler. Address: Magnihalde 11, CH-9000 St Gallen, Switzerland.

NISKA Maralin, b. 16 Nov 1930, San Pedro, CA, USA. Soprano. Education: Studied with Lotte Lehmann. Career: Sang widely in California from 1955; Sang at San Diego Opera in 1965 as Mimi in La Bohème, sang Floyd's Susannah with the Met National Company, at New York City Opera in 1967 as Mozart's Countess returning as Turandot, Tosca, Salome and Janácek's Emilia Marty, and at Metropolitan Opera, 1970-77 as Tosca, Musetta and Hélène in Les Vêpres Siciliennes; Italian debut as Marie in Wozzeck at Maggio Musicale Florence, 1978; Other roles have included Violetta, Madam Butterfly, Donna Elvira, Manon Lescaut and Marguerite in Faust.

NISSEL Siegmund (Walter), b. 3 Jan 1922, Munich, Germany. Musician. m. 5 Apr 1957, 1 son, 1 daughter. Education: External Matriculation, Honours Degree, London University; Private violin study with Professor Max Weissgarber until 1938, then with Professor Max Rostal in London. Debut: With Amadeus Quartet at Wigmore Hall in London, 1948. Career: Founder Member of the Amadeus Quartet; Innumerable BBC Radio and TV and ITV appearances; International concert career; Quartet disbanded in 1987. Recordings: Mozart, Beethoven, Schubert and Brahms Quartets; Benjamin Britten; Brahms Sextets. Honours: Honorary DMus, London and York Universities; OBE; Verdienstkreuz für Musik in Germany and Austria; Honorary LRAM. Memberships: ISM; ESTA. Hobby: Chess. Address: 29 The Park, London, NW11 7ST, England.

NISSMAN Barbara, b. 31 Dec 1944, Philadelphia, Pennsylvania, USA. Concert Pianist. Education: BMus, 1966, MMus, 1966, DMus Arts, 1969, University of Michigan; Studied with Pianist, György Sandor. Debut: American Orchestral Debut with Philadelphia Orchestra, Ormandy, 1971. Career: Appearances with London Philharmonic, Royal Philharmonic, Rotterdam Philharmonic, L'Orchestre de la Suisse Romande, BBC Symphony, Netherlands, Chamber, Munich Philharmonic, Bavarian Radio Orchestra; United States; Philadelphia, Pittsburgh, Minnesota, Chicago, Cleveland, St Louis, New York Philharmonic Orchestras; With Ormandy, Muti, Mata, Skrowaczewski, Zinman, Slatkin; Concert tours of the Far East, Latin America and Soviet Union; Presented Dutch Premiere of Ginastera Piano Concerto, 1978 in Concertgebouw; Soloist at Gala 60th birthday concert for Ginastera with Suisse Romande, 1976; Third Piano Sonata, 1982, of Ginastera, dedicated to Ms Nissman. Recordings: Complete Solo and Chamber Music of Alberto Ginastera; Music of Franz Liszt; Complete piano sonatas of Prokofiev, 3 volumes. Publication: Alberto Ginastera - Piano Sonata No 3, 1982. Contributions to: Keynote Magazine, 1983, Interview with Alberto Ginastera; Piano Today; Musical Times. Honours: Stanley Medal, University of Michigan, 1966; Martha Baird Rockefeller Grant, 1971 and 1981; Alumnae Athena Award, 1981; Citation of Merit Award, University of Michigan, 1996. Hobbies: Listening to old recordings; Reading; Hiking in West USA mountains. Current Managements: Joan Regalbuto, USA; Audrey Ellison, UK. Address: Rte 2, Box 260, Lewisburg, WV 24901, USA.

NITESCU Adina, b. 1965, Romania. Singer (Soprano). Education: Studied at the George Enescu Conservatoire, Bucharest, and in Munich; Stipendium from Georg Solti, 1991-92. Career: Roles with the Opera Studio of the Bavarian State Opera included Mozart's Countess and Fiordiligi; Bucharest Opera debut as Mimi in La Bohème, 1993; Further engagements as Donna Anna at Leipzig, Saarbrucken and Essen; Mimi at Cologne and Wiesbaden, Marzelline in Fidelio at the 1996 Bregenz Festival and Gounod's Marguerite at the Deutsche Oper, Berlin, First Lady in Die Zauberflöte, and in Gluck's Armide to open the 1996 season at La Scala, Milan; Glyndebourne Festival 1997, as Manon Lescaut in a new production of Puccini's opera. Address: Planie 7, 72764 Reutlingen, Germany.

NITSCHE Horst, b. 22 Mar 1939, Vienna, Austria. Singer (Tenor). Education: Studied at the Bruckner Conservatory, Linz. Career: Sang at the Landestheater Salzburg from 1970, Vienna Staatsoper 1972; Appearances in Vienna (also at Volksoper) as Monostatos, Don Curzio, Jacquino, Zorn in Meistersinger, Flavio in Norma and Missail in Boris Godunov; Sang in the 1976 premiere of Kabale und Liebe by Einem; Salzburg Festival from 1977, in Salome, Don Carlos, Die Zauberflöte and Le nozze di Figaro. Recordings: Character roles in Il Trovatore, Der Rosenkavalier, Die Zauberflöte and Don Carlos (EMI and RCA). Address: Vienna Staatsoper, Opernring 2, A-1010 Vienna, Austria.

NIXON June, b. 1942, Boort, Victoria, Australia. Composer; Organist; Choral Conductor. Education: BMus, University of Melbourne; FRCO; ARCM. Career: Organist and Director of Music at St Paul's Anglican Catherdral, Melbourne, 1973; Teaching Staff, University of Melbourne, 1961. Compositions: Numerous compositions for organ and choir. Honours include: 1st Prize, Australian National Organ Competition, 1968; AEH Nickson and Lizette Bentwich Scholarships, 1970; John Brooke Prize, Royal College of Organists, 1971; Percy Jones Award, Catholic Archdiocese of Melbourne, 1995. Address: 115 Canterbury Road, Middle Park, 3206 Australia.

NIXON Marni, b. 22 Feb 1930, Altadena, CA, USA. Soprano; Teacher. Education: Studied at the University of Southern California with Carl Ebert, Stanford University with Jan Popper and the Berkshire Music Center with Boris Goldovsky and Sarah Caldwell. Career: Has sung in musical comedy, programmes for children's television, concerts, opera and film sound tracks; Provided the singing voices for Deborah Kerr in The King and I, Natalie Wood in West Side Story and Audrey Hepburn in My Fair Lady; Has appeared in Los Angeles, San Francisco, Tanglewood and Seattle as Mozart's Blondchen, Constanze and Susanna, Philine in Thomas' Mignon, and Strauss's Zerbinetta and Violetta; Concert engagements in Cleveland, Toronto, Los Angeles, Israel and London; Modern repertory includes works by Webern, Ives, Hindemith and Stravinsky; Teacher at California Institute of Arts, 1969-71 and Music Academy of The West, Santa Barbara, from 1980. Recordings include: Webern Complete Works, conducted by Robert Craft. Address: c/o Music Academy of The West, 1070 Fairway Road, CA 93109, USA.

NIXON Roger, b. 8 Aug 1921, Tulare, CA, USA. Composer. Education: Studied at University of California, Berkeley, PhD in 1952, notably with Roger Sessions, Arthur Bliss, Bloch and Schoenberg. Career: Teacher at Modesto Junior College, 1951-59 and San Francisco State University from 1960. Compositions: Opera: The Bride Comes To Yellow Sky, 1968; Orchestral: Air for Strings, 1953, Violin Concerto, 1956, Elegaic Rhapsody for Viola and Orchestra, 1962, Viola Concerto, 1969, San Joaquin Sketches, 1982, California Jubilee, 1982, Golden Jubilee, 1985; Chamber: String Quartet No 1, 1949, Conversations for Violin and Clarinet, 1981, Music for Clarinet and Piano, 1986; Vocal: Christmas Perspectives for Chorus, 1980, Festival Mass for Chorus, 1980, Chaunticleer for Male Chorus, 1984, The Canterbury Tales for Chorus, 1986, The Daisy for Chorus, 1987; Song Cycles include, A Narative Of Tides for Soprano, Flute and Piano, 1984. Honours: Grants and commissions from the San Francisco Festival of The Masses and American Bandmasters Association. Address: c/o ASCAP, ASCAP Building, One Lincoln Plaza, New York, NY 10023, USA.

NOBLE Jeremy, b. 27 Mar 1930, London, England. Musicologist; Critic; Broadcaster. Education: Worcester College, Oxford, 1949-53; Private music studies. Career: Music Critic for The Times, 1960-63, and The Sunday Telegraph, 1972-76; Research Fellow, Barber Institute Birmingham, 1964-65; Associate Professor at State University of New York, Buffalo, 1966-70 and from 1976; Fellow, Harvard Institute for Renaissance Studies, Florence, 1967-68; Leverhulme Research Fellow, 1975-76; Many broadcasts for BBC Radio 3. Publications: Articles on Josquin, Debussy and Stravinsky for the Musical Times; Purcell and The Chapel Royal, in Essays on Music, 1959; Mozart: A Documentary Biography, translation of O Deutsch with E Blom and P Branscombe, 1965; Entries on Josquin and, jointly with EW White, Stravinsky for The New Grove Dictionary of Music and Musicians, 1980. Address: Department of Music, State University of New York, Buffalo, NY 14260, USA.

NOBLE John, b. 2 Jan 1931, Southampton, England. Singer (Baritone). Education: MA (Hons), Cambridge; Privately with Clive Carey CBE and Boriska Gereb. Career: Concerts and Oratorio with major orchestras throughout UK; Tours in Europe and USA; Guest Artist in opera with Covent Garden and other companies; Many broadcasts for BBC in wide range of music including several first performances; Professor of Singing at Royal Northern College of Music, Manchester. Recordings: Vaughan Williams, The Pilgrim's Progress, title role, conductor Boult; Britten, Albert Herring (Vicar), conductor Britten; Delius, Sea Drift, conductor Groves. Memberships: Past Chairman, Solo Performers, Incorporated Society of Musicians; Councillor, British Actors' Equity Association. Address: 185 Syon Lane, Isleworth, Middlesex TW7 5PU, England.

NOBLE Timothy, b. 1945, Indianapolis, IN, USA. Baritone. Career: Sang supporting roles in Carmen, Turandot and Wozzeck with San Francisco Opera in 1981; Houston Opera from 1982 as Ping, Leporello and Falstaff; Colorado Springs Festival in 1982 as Rigoletto and Fort Worth and Opéra-Comique Paris in 1983 as Sharpless and Germont; Season 1985-86 at Santa Fe in the premiere of John Eaton's The Tempest, as Falstaff in Amsterdam and as Simon Boccanegra at Glyndebourne returning in 1988 as Germont; San Francisco in 1987 as Tomsky in The Queen of Spades, Venice in 1988 in Verdi's Stiffelio; Sang Shaklovity in Khovanshchina at the Metropolitan in 1988 and San Francisco in 1990 returning to New York in 1991 as Leporello; Opera Pacific at Costa Mesa and the Santa Fe Festival in 1991 as Renato and as Jack Rance in La Fanciulla del West; Other roles include William Tell, Amonasro, Macbeth, Iago, Tonio, Alfio, Di Luna and Scarpia; Sang Columbus in the premiere of The Voyage by Philip Glass at New York Metropolitan in 1992; Iago at the 1996 Holland Festival; Further engagements in musicals and as concert artist. Address: c/o Caroline Woodfield, ICM, 40W 57th Street, New York, NY 10019, USA.

NÖCKER Hans Gunter, b. 22 Jan 1927, Hagen, Germany. Bass-Baritone. Education: Studied in Brunswick and with Hans-Hermann Nissen and Willi Domgraf-Fassbaender in Munich. Debut: Munster in 1952 as Alfio in Cavalleria Rusticana. Career: Many appearances in Germany particularly at Hamburg, Munich and Stuttgart; Bayreuth Festival, 1958-60, Munich 1963 in the premiere of Egk's Die Verlobung in San Domingo and Schwetzingen 1966 in Gluck's Armide; Sang at Deutsche Oper Berlin in the 1972 premiere of Fortner's Elisabeth Tudor, La Fenice Venice in 1983 as Klingsor in Parsifal, and Berlin in 1984 in the premiere of Reimann's Gespenstersonate; Guest appearances in Florence, Brussels, Palermo, London and Edinburgh; Sang at Munich in the 1986 premiere of D Kirchner's Belshazzar; Sang in Orff's Trionfo di Afrodite at Munich Festival in 1990; Sang in the premiere of Böse's Schlachthof 5, Munich, 1996. Recordings: Orff's Trionfo di Afrodite; Oedipus der Tyrann; Götterdämmerung. Address: c/o Bayerische Staatsoper, Postfach 745, D-8000 Munich 1, Germany.

NODA Ken, b. 5 Oct 1962, New York, USA. Concert Pianist (retired); Musical Assistant to Artistic Director, Artistic Administration, Metropolitan Opera. Education: Private studies with Daniel Barenboim. Career: London debut in 1979 with the English Chamber Orchestra and Daniel Barenboim; Later engagements with the Philharmonia, Berlin Philharmonic, Orchestre de Paris, Rotterdam Philharmonic, New York Philharmonic and Chicago Symphony; Conductors include Abbado, Chailly, Andrew Davis, Kubelik, Leinsdorf, Levine, Mehta, Ozawa and Previn; Recitals in London, Toronto, Chicago, Lincoln Center New York, Hamburg and La Fenice Venice; Festival appearances at Mostly Mozart, NY, Ravinia and Tanglewood; 1986 debut with the Vienna Philharmonic in Salzburg; Season 1986-87 in concerts with the Berlin Philharmonic, the Hallé and the Philharmonia; 1988 concerts with the Rotterdam Philharmonic playing Mozart under James Conlon, Beethoven's Triple Concerto with Pinchas Zukerman and Lynn Harrell at Ravinia; Toured Japan with Ozawa and the New Japan Philharmonic. Recordings include: Concertos by Beethoven, Chopin, Haydn, Liszt and Schumann. Address: c/o Metropolitan Opera, Lincoln Center, New York, NY 10023, USA.

NOEL Rita, b. 21 Nov 1943, Lancaster, South Carolina, USA. Singer (Mezzo Soprano). Education: Studied at Eastman School, at Queens College, Charlotte, South Carolina and in New York and Vienna. Career: Played violin and viola with the Vienna Chamber Orchestra and the Berlin Symphony; Stage debut with the Metropolitan National Opera Company, 1966, as Flora in Traviata; Further appearances at the Theater am Gärtnerplatz Munich, Bielefeld, Amsterdam and Miami; Other roles have included Mozart's Cherubino and Sextus, Cornelia in Giulio Cesare, Carmen, Rosina, Octavian, Nickausse, Azucena and Santuzza; Frequent concert engagements. Address: c/o Staatstheater am Gärtnerplatz, Gärtnerplatz 3, 8000 Munich, Germany.

NOELTE Rudolf, b. Mar 1921, Berlin. Stage Director. Education: Studied at Berlin University. Career: Assisted Jurgen Fehling, Erich Engel and Walter Felsenstein at the Hebbel Theatre Berlin; Produced Max Brod's adaptation of The Castle by Kafka in 1953; Productions of classic plays in Germany and Vienna; First opera production, Lulu in Frankfurt; Has directed Don Giovanni in West Berlin, Eugene Onegin in Munich and The Queen of Spades in Cologne, The Bartered Bride and La Traviata for Welsh National Opera, Der Freischütz in Bremen, Ariadne auf Naxos at the Bayerische Staatsoper in Munich and Otello in Frankfurt; Covent Garden debut in 1987 with Massenet's Manon. Address: Allied Artists Ltd, 42 Montpelier Square, London, SW7 1JZ, England.

NOLAN David, b. 1949, Liverpool, England. Violinist. Education: Studied with Yossi Zivoni and Alexander Moskowski at the Royal Manchester College of Music; Studied in Russia, 1972-76. Debut: Played the Mendelssohn Concerto, 1965. Career: Joined the London Philharmonic Orchestra, 1972, leader from 1976; Many appearances with the London Philharmonic Orchestra and other orchestras in concertos by Bach, Beethoven, Brahms, Bruch, Glazunov, Korngold, Mozart, Paganini, Saint-Saëns, Stravinsky, Tchaikovsky and Walton; Played the Schoenberg Concerto with the BBC Scottish Symphony conducted by Matthias Bamert, 1988. Recordings: The Lark Ascending by Vaughan Williams; The Four Seasons by Vivaldi. Honours: RMCM performances, diploma, distinction. Address: 126 Turney Road, Dulwich, London, SE21 7JJ, England.

NOLEN Timothy, b. 9 Jul 1941, Rotan, TX, USA. Baritone. Education: Studied at the Manhattan School of Music and with Richard Fredericks and Walter Fredericks. Debut: New Jersey Opera Newark as Rossini's Figaro. Career: Sang Marcello in La Bohème with San Francisco Opera in 1968; Appearances in Chicago, Houston, Boston and Minneapolis; European debut at Rouen in 1974 as Pelléas; Sang at Amsterdam in 1974 in the premiere of The Picture of Dorian Gray by Kox, at Cologne, 1974-78 and Paris, Bordeaux, Aix and Nantes as Mozart's Count, Figaro and Guglielmo, Donizetti's Malatesta and Belcore, Monteverdi's Orpheus, and Dandini in La Cenerentola, Puccini's Gianni Schicchi, the Emperor in The Nightingale by Stravinsky and Ford in Falstaff; Sang in the premieres of Carlisle Floyd's Willie Stark and Bernstein's A Quiet Place, Houston in 1981 and 1983; Further engagements at Florence, Geneva, Miami, New York, City Opera and Philadelphia; Santa Fe Festival in 1992 as Mr Peachum in The Beggar's Opera and Frank in Die Fledermaus; Sang Malatesta at Chicago, 1995.

NONI Alda, b. 30 Apr 1916, Trieste, Italy. Soprano. Education: Studied in Trieste and Vienna. Debut: Ljubljana in 1937 as Rosina in Il Barbiere di Siviglia. Career: Sang first in Yugoslavia then joined the Vienna Staatsoper in 1942; Sang Mozart's Despina and Verdi's Gilda and Oscar; Appeared as Zerbinetta in a 1944 performance of Ariadne auf Naxos to celebrate the 80th birthday of Richard Strauss; Sang in Milan, Rome, Venice and Turin from 1945 and at Cambridge Theatre London in 1946 as Norina in Don Pasquale opposite Marino Stabile; La Scala from 1949 in Cimarosa's Il Matrimonio Segreto and Piccinni's La Buona Figliuola; Sang Zerlina, Nannetta and Papagena with the company of La Scala during its 1950 visit to London; Glyndebourne, 1950-54 as Blondchen, Despina and Clorinda in La Cenerentola; Guest appearances in Berlin, Paris at the Opéra-Comique, Lisbon, Madrid and Rio de Janeiro. Recordings include: Ariadne auf Naxos; Don Pasquale; L'Elisir d'Amore; Lucia di Lammermoor; Il Matrimonio Segreto; Le nozze di Figaro; La Cenerentola.

NORAS Arto Erkki, b. 12 May 1942, Turku, Finland. Cellist. Education: Sibelius Academy; Paris Conservatoire, 1962-64. Career: Appearances with Major Orchestras Worldwide; Founder, Member, Sibelius Academy Quartet; Founder, Artistic Director, Naantali Music Festival; Founder, International Paulo Cello Competition; Professor, Cello, Sibelius Academy, 1970-. Recordings: Numerous. Honour: Runnerup, Tchaikovsky Competition, 1966. Address: Patrick Garvey Management, Top Floor, 59 Lansdowne Place, Hove, East Sussex BN3 1FL, England.

NORBERG-SCHULZ Elisabeth, b. Jan 1959, Norway. Soprano. Education: Studied at Accademia di Santa Cecilia, Rome, the Pears-Britten School at Snape and with Elisabeth Schwarzkopf in Zurich. Career: Gave lieder recitals and sang Britten's Les Illuminations at Snape in 1981; Sang supporting roles in Italy and elsewhere at first, then sang Gilda and Lucia di Lammermoor; Has appeared under such conductors as Georg Solti, Riccardo Muti and Claudio Abbado, notably at La Scala Milan; Sang Musetta in La Bohème with La Scala on a visit to Japan in 1988 and at Rome Opera in 1989 as Barbarina in Le nozze di Figaro; Maggio Musicale Fiorentino in 1989 as Ilia in Idomeneo and sang Pamina in Die Zauberflöte at the Salzburg Landestheater in 1991 as part of the Mozart bicentenary celebrations; Season 1992 as Norina at Naples, Guardian of the Threshold in Die Frau ohne Schatten and Servilia in La Clemenza di Tito at Salzburg; Covent Garden debut 1995, as Liu in Turandot; Sang Cimarosa's Carolina at Rome, 1996. Address: c/o Teatro alla Scala, Via Filodrammatici 2, I-20121 Milan, Italy.

NORBY Erik, b. 9 Jan 1936, Copenhagen, Denmark. Composer. Education: Copenhagen Boys' Choir and Tivoli Band; Copenhagen Conservatory; Diploma in Composition, 1966. Career: Teacher, North Jutland Conservatory until 1975 then freelance composer. Compositions include: Orchestra: Folk Song Suite, 1962, Music for 6 Sextets, 1966, The Rainbow Snake, 1975, Illuminations, Capriccio, 1978, 3 Dances, 1983; Chamber: Illustrations, 1965, Schubert Variations, 1974, Partita, 1981, Tivoli Collage, 1983, Ravel: Le Tombeau De Couperin, 1984; Solo Instrument: 12 Danish Folk Songs for Piano, 1961, Chromaticon, partita in 8 movements, 1971, Five Organ Chorales, 1976-78; Choral: March, 1972, Winter Twilight, 1973, Nightingale, 1973, Song Near The Depth Of Spring, 1973, Festival Cantata, on the occasion of the 150th anniversary of Copenhagen Cathedral, 1979, Edvard Munch Triptych, 1978-79; Solo Voice: Two Songs, 1963, Six Shakespeare Sonnets, 1981, 13 Elizabethan Love Songs, The Ballad About My Life, 1984; Music for educational use: Three Suites, 1961, Three Small Suites, 1962, Little Sonatina, Three Humoresques, Evening Song, Suite No 2, 1963. Recordings: Numerous recordings of his work. Current Management: Koda, Maltegårdsvej 24, 2820 Gentofte, Denmark. Address: Kochsvej 13, 3tv, DK- 1812 Frederiksberg C, Denmark.

NORDAL Jon, b. 1926. Composer; President, Reykjavik College of Music. Education: Studied with Arni Kristjansson, Jon Thorarinsson and Dr V Urbancic at Reykjavik College of Music, Iceland; Studies with W Frey and W Burkhard at Zurich, Switzerland, 1949-51 and in Paris and Rome; Darmstadt summer courses, 1956-57. Career includes: President, Reykjavik College of Music. Compositions: Orchestral: Concerto Lirico for Harp and Strings, Concerto for Orchestra, 1949, Concerto for Piano and Orchestra, 1956, Sinfonietta Seriosa, 1956, A Play Of Fragments, 1962, Adagio for Flute, Harp, Piano and Strings, 1965, Stiklur, 1970, Canto Elegiaco, 1971, Leidsla, 1973, Epitaphio, 1974, The Winter Night, 1975, Twin Song for Violin, Viola and Orchestra, 1979, Dedication, 1981, Choralis, 1982, Concerto for Cello and Orchestra, 1983; Chamber: Sonata for Violin and Piano, Fairy Tale Sisters for Violin and Piano, Chorale Prelude for Organ, 1980, Duo for Violin and Cello, 1983; Choir Music: Seven Songs for Male Chorus, 1955. Address: STEF, Laufasveji 40, Reykjavik, Iceland.

NORDEN Betsy, b. 17 Oct 1945, Cincinnati, OH, USA. Soprano. Education: Studied at Boston University. Career: Member of Metropolitan Opera Chorus from 1969; Solo appearances at the Metropolitan from 1972 in Le nozze di Figaro and as Papagena, Elvira in L'Italiana in Algeri, Constance in the Carmelites, Oscar and Despina in Cosi fan tutte, 1990; Sang in The Cunning Little Vixen at Philadelphia season, 1980-81, Constance at San Francisco in 1983 and Gretel at San Diego, 1985; Many concert appearances. Address: c/o Metropolitan Opera, Lincoln Center, New York, NY 10023, USA.

NORDGREN Pehr (Henrik), b. 19 Jan 1944, Saltvik, Finland. Composer. Education: Studied composition under Professor Joonas Kokkonen, musicology at Helsinki University and composition and traditional Japanese music at Tokyo University of Arts and Music, 1970-73. Career: Assistant at Helsinki University. Compositions include: Euphonie 1 Op 1, 1967; 7 String Quartets, 1967-92; Ten Ballades To Japanese Ghost Stories By Lafcadio Hearn, 1972-77; As In A Dream, Op 21, 1974; Symphony Op 20, 1974; Autumnal Concerto for Traditional Japanese Instruments and Orchestra, 1974; Wind Quintet No 2, Op 22, 1975; Butterflies, 1977; Summer Music Op 34, 1977; Symphony for Strings Op 43, 1978; In Patches, 1978; Piano Quintet Op 44, 1978; In The Palm Of The King's Head for Soprano, Baritone, Chams and Orchestra, 1979; Three Cello Concertos, 1980-92; The Lights Of Heaven for Soprano, Tenor, Chorus and Ensemble, 1985; Symphony No 2, 1989; Cronaca for Strings, 1991. Recordings: Hoichi Earless Op 17; Ballades. Address: TEOSTO, Lauttasaarentie 1, 0020 Helsinki 20, Finland.

NORDHEIM Arne, b. 20 Jun 1931, Larvik, Norway. Composer. Education: Studied with Conrad Baden and Bjarne Brustad at Oslo Conservatory and with Vagn Holmboe in Copenhagen in 1955. Career: Critic for Dagbladet of Oslo, 1960-68; Lecturer on and performer of live electronic music. Compositions include: Epigram for String Quartet, 1954; String Quartet, 1956; Canzona for Orchestra, 1961; Katharsis, ballet on legend of St Anthony for Orchestra and Tape, 1962; Kimare, ballet, 1963; Epitaffio for Orchestra and Tape, 1963; Favola, musical play, 1965; Three Responses, 1967; Eco for Soprano, Chorus and Orchestra, 1968; Incidental music for Peer Gynt, 1969; Dinosaurus for Accordion and Tape, 1971; Doria for Tenor and Orchestra, 1975; Ballets: Strender, Ariadne And The Tempest, 1974-79; Tempora Noctis for Soprano, Mezzo, Orchestra and Tape, 1979; Aurora for soloists, Chorus, 2 Percussion and Tape, 1984; Varder for Trumpet and Orchestra; Maema for Orchestra, 1988; Monolith for Orchestra, 1990. Address: c/o 4 Galleri Oslo, Toyenbekken 21, Postboks 9171, Gronland, 0134 Oslo 1, Norway.

NORDIN Birgit, b. 22 Feb 1934, Sangis, Norrbotten, Sweden. Soprano. Education: Studied at the Stockholm Opera School and with Lina Pagliughi in Italy. Debut: Stockholm in 1957 as Oscar in Un Ballo in Maschera. Career: Annual visits to the Drottningholm Opera from 1960 notably in operas by Mozart; Sang at Wexford Festival in 1963 and 1965, and Glyndebourne Festival in 1968 as Blondchen in Die Entführung; Sang Jenny in Weill's Mahagonny at Copenhagen in 1970, Berlin in 1970 as soloist in Bach's St Matthew Passion and Christmas Oratorio; Television appearance as Berg's Lulu and sang the Queen of Night in Bergman's film version of The Magic Flute in 1974; Oratorio engagements in Scandinavia, Germany, England and Austria; Has sung with the Royal Opera Stockholm on tour to Covent Garden in 1990 and the Edinburgh Festival; Other roles include Mozart's Susanna and Pamina, Gilda, Rosina, Sophie in Der Rosenkavalier and Mélisande. Recordings: Die Zauberflöte; Madrigals by Monteverdi; Video of Don Giovanni, as Donna Elvira. Honour: Swedish Court Singer, 1973. Address: c/o Kungliga Teatern, PO Box 16094, S-10322 Stockholm, Sweden.

NORDIN Lena, b. 18 Feb 1956, Visby, Sweden. Soprano. Education: Studied voice and piano at the College of Music in Malmo and Stockholm, and in Salzburg, Florence and Siena. Debut: Verdi's Luisa Miller. Career: Member of soloist ensemble of the Royal Opera in Stockholm, 1987; Has performed numerous roles including: Cleopatra, Donna Anna, Antonia, Lauretta, Marguerite, Konstanze, Violetta, Maria Stuarda, Norma and Sophie; Has also sung at the Drottningholm Court Theatre (Dido and Regina in Soler's Cosa Rara); Has guested Wexford Opera Festival twice, including as Aspasia in Mozart's Mitridate, 1989; Other roles include Adele, Countessa di Folleville in Rossini's Il viaggio a Reims and Donna Elvira; Has also sung in Dresden, Copenhagen, London, Moscow and Seville; Concert engagements include performances in USA, France, Germany and in Scandinavia. Recordings: Title roles in Berwald's Estrella di Soria, Hallman's Solitär and in Naumann's Gustav Wasa; Carmina Burana; Arias by Mozart, Verdi and Gounod; Mary Stuart, Queen of Scots; CD of Mozart Concert Arias, 1996. Honours: Christina Nilsson Prize, 1959; Birgit Nilsson Prize, 1987; Svenska Dagblacket, Prize, 1987; Jussi Björling Prize, 1997. Current Management: Allied Artists. Address: Östermalmsg 3, 11424 Stockholm, Sweden.

NORDMO-LOVBERG Aase, b. 10 Jun 1923, Malselv, Norway. Soprano; Administrator. Education: Studied with Hjaldis Ingebjart in Oslo. Debut: Concert debut in 1948, and operatic debut in 1952 as Imogen in Cymbeline by Arne Eggens. Career: Member of the Royal Opera Stockholm, 1953-69 with debut as Elisabeth in Tannhäuser; Vienna Staatsoper in 1957 as Sieglinde in Die Walküre; Concert appearances in London, Philadelphia and Paris, 1957; Metropolitan Opera, 1959-61 as Elsa in Lohengrin, Eva, Sieglinde and Leonore; Bayreuth Festival, 1960 as Elsa and Sieglinde; Sang at the Stora Theatre Gothenburg in 1963 and 1967 as Elisabeth and Tosca; Engagements at the Drottningholm Court Theatre included Angelica in Handel's Orlando; Professor at the Oslo Music School from 1970 and Director of The Oslo Opera, 1978-81. Recordings include: Excerpts from the 1960 Bayreuth Festival. Honours: Gold Medal for Singing, Harriet Cohen International Music Award, 1958; Orde Van Oranje-Nassau, 1963; Officer of L'Ordre de Leopold II, 1964; Commander, St Olavs Orden, 1981; Commander, Kungl Nordstjerne Orden, 1986. Address: Skjellerüder 7, 2600 Lillehammer, Norway.

NORDSTRØM Hans-Henrik, b. 26 June 1947, Nakskov, Denmark. Composer. m. Anne Kristine Smith, 1 son. Education: Royal Danish Academy of Music, Copenhagen, 1965-70. Debut: Copenhagen, 1990. Compositions: Songlines, The Mountains of Monesties, Space/Room, String Quartet No 2 (Faroese), Carnac, M 31, Sonata per l'Inverno, Seven Vignets From Susa, La Primavera, Images d'automne, To the Winter and La rosa, la noche y el tiempo. Recordings: Portrait, CD with Moyzes Quartet; The Jutland Ensemble; Anna Klett and Lin Ensemble. Honours: Grant, Danish Art Foundation, 1990-; Artistic Director, Contemporary Music in Susaa Festivals, 1992-. Membership: Danish Composers Society. Address: 26 Tyvelsevij, DK 4171 Glumso, Denmark.

NORDWALL Eva (Marie), b. 4 Oct 1944, Uherské Hradiste, Czechoslovakia. Harpsichord Soloist. m. Ove Nordwall, 30 Dec 1973, 2 sons. Education: Piano solo, Brno Conservatory, 1959-63; Piano with Professor Stina Sundell, Harpsichord with Margit Theorell, Swedish Royal High School of Music, 1964-73. Debut: As Harpsichord Soloist, Stockholm, 1972. Career: Concerts and tours of Sweden, Norway, Denmark, Poland, Austria, Germany, Canada, USA, Puerto Rico, 1972-; Numerous television and radio appearances in Sweden and abroad; Solo harpsichord music written for by some 30 Swedish and international compoers including Ligeti. Recordings: Several recordings of mostly contemporary music, solo harpsichord music in Sweden, Canada and Puerto Rico. Honours: Recipient of several including Swedish State Award for Artists, 1980, 1981, 1986, 1989. Memberships: Swedish Union of Musicians; Musikcentrum. Current Management: Sforzando Produktion, Granvägen 6, S-640 50, Björnlunda, Sweden. Address: Österlan2gatan 14 1, S-11131 Stockholm, Sweden.

NOREJKA Virgilius, b. 22 Sep 1935, Siaulai, Lithuania. Tenor; Administrator. Education: Studied in Volnius. Debut: State Opera of Vilnius, 1957 as Lensky in Eugene Onegin. Career: Sang in Lithuania as Alfredo, the Duke in Rigoletto, Werther, Don José, Almaviva and The Prince in The Love For Three Oranges; Guest appearances in Moscow, Leningrad, Kiev and Kharkov; Gave recitals and sang Russian folksongs, in addition to operatic repertoire; Further engagements at the Berlin Staatsoper and in Poland, Bulgaria, Denmark, Finland, Italy, Austria, Hungary, USA and Canada; Sang Radames at Hamburg Staatsoper and also appeared in operas by Lithuanian composers; Director of the Vilnius Opera, 1975-. Recordings: Various. Address: Av Rómulo Gallegos, Edf Residencias, Santa Rosa, Apt 4-B, Sebucan, Caracas 1071, Venezuela.

NORGÅRD Per, b. 13 Jul 1932, Gentofte, Denmark. Composer. Education: Degrees in Music History, Music Theory and Composition, Royal Danish Academy of Music, 1952-55; Studied with Nadia Boulanger, Paris, France, 1956-57. Career: Teaching positions at Odense Conservatoire, 1958-61, Royal Academy of Music, 1960-65, Royal Academy of Music, Aarhus, 1965. Compositions include: Operas: Gilgamesh, 1971-72,

Siddharta, 1974-79, The Divine Circus, 1982; Orchestral: Symphony No 1, 1953-55, Voyage Into The Golden Screen, 1968-69, Twilight, 1976-77, Symphony No 3 in 2 Movements, 1972-75, No 4, 1981, No 5, 1990, Spaces Of Time, 1991; String and Wind orchestras: Metamorphosis, 1953, Modlys, 1970; Chamber: Fragment V, 1961, Prelude And Ant Fugue (With A Crab Cannon), 1982, Lin for Clarinet, Cello and Piano, 1986; Solo keyboard: Sonata in One Movement, 1953, Canon, 1971; Choral: Evening Land, 1954, Frost Psalm, 1975-76, Interrupted Hymn, Scream, Drinking Song; Solo instruments and orchestra: Between, 3 movements for Cello and Orchestra, 1985, Helle Nacht, violin concerto, 1987, King, Queen and Ace for Harp and 13 Instruments, 1989; Percussion: Iching, solo, 1982. Recordings: Much of his work recorded and available on CD. Honours: Numerous honours including Nordic Council Prize for Music for opera Gilgamesh, 1974; Holds several Honorary posts. Address: Koda, Maltegårdsvej 24, 2820 Gentofte, Denmark.

NORHOLM Ib, b. 24 Jan 1931, Copenhagen, Denmark. Composer. Education: The Royal Danish Academy of Music, Copenhagen. Career: Music Critic with several major Copenhagen Newspapers; Professor of Composition, The Royal Danish Academy of Music; Organist in Copenhagen. Compositions include: Stanzas And Fields; Strofer Og Marker; Trio Op 22; Fluctuations, The Unseen Pan; Exile, Music For A Composition for Large Orchestra; From My Green Herbarium; September-October-November; After Icarus; Tavole Per Orfeo; Invitation To A Beheading, 1965; Isola Bella, 1968-70; Den Unge Park, 1969-70; Day's Nightmare, 1973; Violin Concerto, 1974; Heretic Hymn, 1975; The Garden Wall, 1976; The Funen Cataracts, 1976; Essai Prismatique, 1979; Lys, 1979; Decreation, 1979; The Elements; Moralities - Or There May Be Several Miles To The Nearest Spider; Ecliptic Instincts; Apocalyptic Idylls, 1980; Before Silence, 1980; Haven Med Steir Der Deler Sig, 1982. Recordings: Much of his work recorded. Current Management: Koda, Maltegårdsvej 24, 2820 Gentofte, Denmark. Address: Henningsens Allé 30B, DK-2900 Hellerup, Denmark.

NØRHOLM Kaj, b. 4 Sept 1943, Hjørring, Denmark. Birgitte Norholm, 9 Jan 1965, 2 sons. Education: Teacher Education, Studies of Management and Direction; Graduate, Music Academy, Aalborg, 1972. Career: Senior Master, 1972-94, Headmaster, 1994-, Upper Secondary School; Guest Conductor, Danish Radio Girls Choir, 1981; Conductor, Choirs, Orchestras and Big Band. Compositions: Vensyssel Festival Fanfare, 1975; Hjørring Jubilee Cantata, 1993; Several arrangements for choir and orchestra. Publications: The Song Book I, 1988; The Elements of Music, 1988; The Opera Song Book, 1995; The Song Book II, 1996. Memberships: IMC; EMC; Danish Music Council; Nordic Music Committee; Danish Music Information Centre. Hobbies: Travel; Culture. Current Management: Vestfyns Gymnasium. Address: Glenshojparken 77, 5620 Glamsbjerg, Denmark.

NORMAN Jessye, b. 15 Sept 1945, Augusta, Georgia, USA. Concert and Opera Singer (Soprano). Education: BM cum laude, Howard University, Washington DC; Peabody Conservatory, 1967; MMus, University of Michigan, 1967-68. Career: Operatic debuts: Deutsche Oper, Berlin, 1969: La Scala, Milan, 1972; Royal Opera House, Covent Garden, 1972; New York Metropolitan Opera, as Cassandra in Les Troyens, 1983; American debut, Hollywood Bowl, 1972; Lincoln Center, New York City, 1973; First Covent Garden recital, 1980; Debut at Barbican, 1983; Tours include North and South America, Europe, Middle East, Australia and Israel; Many international festivals including Aix-en-Provence, Aldeburgh, Berlin, Edinburgh, Flanders, Helsinki, Lucerne, Salzburg, Tanglewood, Spoleto, Hollywood, Ravinia; Roles include Verdi's Aida, Wagner's Elisabeth and Strauss's Ariadne; Opened the season at Chicago in 1989, as Gluck's Alcestis; Sang Sieglinde in Die Walküre at the Metropolitan, 1990 (also televised); Sang Janacek's Emilia Marty at the Met, 1996; Concert repertory includes Les Nuits d'été by Berlioz. Recordings include: Le nozze di Figaro, La Finta Giardiniera, Fidelio, Carmen, Haydn's La Vera Costanza, Ariadne, Verdi's Un Giorno di Regno and Il Corsaro, Schubert Lieder, Das Lied von der Erde (Philips); Alceste, Oedipus Rex, Debussy's La Demoiselle Elue (Orfeo); Mahler's 2nd Symphony (CBS); Les Contes d'Hoffmann, Euryanthe (EMI); Fauré's Pénélope (Erato); Die Walküre (Eurodisc); Elektra, conducted by Claudio Abbado (Deutsche Grammophon). Address: c/o Shaw Concerts Incorporated, 1995 Broadway, New York, NY 10023, USA.

NORRINGTON Roger (Arthur Carver) (Sir), b. 16 Mar 1934, Oxford, England. Musical Director. m. (1) Susan Elizabeth McLean, May 1964, divorced 1982, 1 son, 1 daughter, (2) Karolyn Mary Lawrence, Jun 1984. Education: Dragon School, Oxford; Westminster; BA, Clare College, Cambridge; Royal College of Music. Debuts: British, 1962, BBC Radio, 1964, TV, 1967, Germany, Austria, Denmark, Finland, 1966, Portugal, 1970, Italy, 1971, France and Belgium, 1972, USA, 1974, Holland, 1975, Switzerland, 1976. Career: Freelance Singer, 1962-72; Musical Director for Schütz Choir of London, 1962-, London Baroque Players, 1975-, London Classical Players, 1978-97; Principal Conductor for Kent Opera, 1966-84 and Bournemouth Sinfonietta, 1985-89; Guest Conductor for many British, European and American Orchestras; Many TV specials and broadcasts in UK and abroad; Conducted the British stage premiere of Rameau's Les Boréades, Royal Academy of Music, 1985, Die Zauberflöte at the 1990 Promenade Concerts and a series of Beethoven Symphonies on BBC TV, 1991; Conducted the London Classical Players in Mozart's Prague Symphony and Requiem at Prom Concerts in 1991; Season 1992 with Rossini Bicentenary concert at Fisher Hall, NY; Conducted Beethoven's Missa Solemnis at the Albert Hall, London, December 1995; Mozart's Mitridate at Salzburg (1997) and Haydn songs with the LPO at South Bank. Recordings: Numerous with London Classical Players including Die Zauberflöte, Beethoven's 2nd and 8th Symphonies, Schütz St Matthew Passion and Resurrection, Bruckner Mass No 2, and Don Giovanni in 1993. Contributions to: Occasional articles and reviews in musical journals. Honours: Order of The British Empire, 1979; Cavaliere, Order al Merito della Repubblica Italiana, 1981; Gramophone Award, 1987; Opus Award, 1987; Ovation Award, 1988; KBE, 1996. Hobbies: Reading; Walking; Sailing.

NORRIS David Owen, b. 16 June 1953, Northampton, England. International Concert Pianist; Broadcaster. 2 sons. Education: First Class Honours in Music, Organ Scholar, Keble College, Oxford, 1972-75; RAM, 1975-77, Paris, 1977-78. Career: Professor, RAM, 1978-; Repetiteur at Covent Garden and Assistant MD at RSC until 1980; TV appearances across Europe and North America; Performances at Wood Promenade Concerts; Chairman of Faculty, Steans Institute for Singers, Chicago, 1992-; Artistic Director of Cardiff Festival, 1992-; Gresham Professor of Music, 1993-. Honours: Fellow, Royal Academy of Music, 1988; First ever Gilmore Artist, 1991. Memberships: Fellow, Royal College of Organists; ISM. Address: 60 Old Oak Lane, London, NW10 6UB, England.

NORRIS Geoffrey, b. 19 Sept 1947, London, England. Critic; Musicologist. Education: ARCM, 1967; BA, University of Durham, 1969; University of Liverpool, 1969-70, 1972-73; Institute of Theatre, Music and Cinematography, Leningrad, 1971. Career: Music Critic for The Times, Daily Telegraph and The Sunday Telegraph; Lecturer in Music History, Royal Northern College of Music, 1975-77; Commissioning Editor, New Oxford Companion to Music, 1977-83; Music Critic, The Daily Telegraph, 1983; Chief Music Critic, 1995-, Daily Telegraph. Publications include: Encyclopedia of Opera, co-author, 1976; Rachmaninoff, 1976, 2nd edition, 1993; Shostakovich: The Man and His Music, co-author, 1982; A Catalogue of the Compositions of S Rachmaninoff, co-author, 1982. Contributions to: New Grove Dictionary of Music and Musicians, 1980; Musical Times; Music Quarterly; Tempo; Music and Letters; BBC Broadcasts. Membership: Royal Musical Association; The Critics' Circle. Address: D44 Du Cane Court, London SW17 7JH, England.

NORTH Nigel, b. 1954, London, England. Lutenist; Guitarist; Professor of Lute. Education: Guildhall School of Music, 1964-70; Royal College of Music, 1971-74; Classical guitar with John Williams and Carlos Bonell, viols with Francis Baines; Postgraduate course in early music at the GSM, 1974-75 and baroque lute studies with Michael Schaffer in Germany, 1976. Career includes: Performances from 1973 with the Early Music Consort of London, Academy of Ancient Music, Schütz Choir of London and Early Opera Project with Roger Norrington, Kent Opera, English Concert with Pinnock, Taverner Players, London Baroque, Trio Sonnerie, Raglan Baroque Players, and The Sixteen Choir and Orchestra; Professor of Lute at the Guildhall School from 1976; Solo debut at Wigmore Hall in 1977 with Bach recital on lute and played at Bach 300th anniversary concerts in London, 1985 with Maggie Cole; Solo recitals and tours from 1977 worldwide; Accompanist to such singers as Alfred Deller and Emma Kirkby; Summer Academies include The Lute Society of America, 1980-88 and Trio Sonnerie Summer School, 1989; Masterclasses, lectures and workshops in Sardinia, Rome, Venice, Vancouver, New York and San Francisco. Recordings: As soloist, music by Robert de Visee, Dowland, Bach and Vivaldi; Albums of Monteverdi, Handel, Purcell, Corelli and Vivaldi with London Baroque, Taverner Players, The English Concert, Academy of Ancient Music, Raglan Baroque Players, Trio Sonnerie and The Sixteen Choir and Orchestra (Monteverdi Vespers, 1988). Publications: Lute Music By William Byrd, 1976; Lute Music by Alfonso Ferrabosco, 1979; Continuo Playing on Lute, Archlute and Theorbo, 1987.

NORTH Roger (Dudley), b. 1 Aug 1926, Warblington, Hampshire, England. Composer; Writer; Tutor. m. Rosamund Shreeves, 3 Apr 1965, 2 daughters. Education: Oxford University, 1943-44; Royal Academy of Music, 1947-51; LRAM, 1951. Career: Various small choir and orchestra conductorship posts, 1950-56; Evening Institute teaching, 1951-; Morley College, 1963-91; Approximately 100 broadcast talks for BBC, 1960-70. Composition: Sonata for Clarinet and Piano, published around 1956; Salle d'Attente Suite, 1977; Film Music: Music for Dance and Theatre; 1 Act Opera (performed but not published). Recording: Salle d'Attente, ballet suite, 1977. Publication: The Musical Companion, Book I, 1977; ABC of Music (Musical Companion), 1979; Wagner's Most Subtle Art, 1996. Contributions to: Thematic Unity in Parsifal to Wagner Society Magazine; The Rhinegold - The Music to English National Opera Guide, 1985. Honours: William Wallace Exhibition, Royal Academy of Music, 1949; Battison Haynes Prize for Composition, Royal Academy of Music, 1949; Oliviera Prescott Gift for Composition, Royal Academy of Music, 1950. Membership: Composers' Guild. Hobby: Walking. Address: 24 Strand on the Green, London W4 3PH, England.

NORTHCOTT Bayan (Peter), b. 24 Apr 1940, Harrow-on-the-Hill, Middlesex, England. Music Critic; Composer. Education: BA, Dip ED, University College, Oxford; BMus, University of Southampton. Career: Music Critic for the New Statesman, 1973-76, Sunday Telegraph, 1976-86 and The Independent, 1986-. Compositions include: Hymn to Cybele, 1983; Sextet, 1985; Concerto for horn and ensemble, 1996; Instrumental music and songs. Publications include: Study of Alexander Goehr. Contributions to: New Grove Dictionary of Music and Musicians, 1980; Music and Musicians; The Listener; Musical Times; Daily Telegraph; Guardian; Tempo; Dansk Musiktidsskrift; BBC Music Magazine. Membership: Music Section, Critics Circle, 1974-92. Address: 52 Upper Mall, London, W6, England.

NORUP Bent, b. 7 Dec 1936, Hobro, Denmark. Baritone. Education: Studied with Kristian Rils in Copenhagen, with Karl Schmitt-Walter in Munich and with Herta Sperber in New York. Debut: Copenhagen in 1970 as Kurwenal in Tristan und Isolde. Career: Sang at The Royal Theatre of Copenhagen, 1970-73, Brunswick, 1973-78, Nuremburg, 1978-, Hannover, 1981-, Bayreuth Festival, 1983, San Antonio Festival, 1985 and guest appearances in leading roles worldwide including Vienna, London, Paris, Hamberg, Berlin, Dusseldorf, Hannover, France, Spain, Holland, Poland, Ireland and USA; Roles include Holländer, Telramund, Amfortas, Klingsor, Wotan, Sachs, Pizarro, Jochanaan, Iago, Scarpia, and Borromeo; Sang Telramund in Lohengrin at Venice in 1990, and Klingsor at Aarhus in 1992; Sang Telramund in Logengrin at Naples, 1995; Well known as concert singer. Recordings include: Orestes in Elektra. Address: Royal Opera, Copenhagen, Denmark.

NOTARE Karen, b. 1961, USA. Singer (Soprano). Education: Manhattan School of Music, New York. Debut: Madama Butterfly for New York City Opera, 1987. Career: European debut as Leoncavallo's Zaza, at the 1990 Wexford Festival; Tosca with Greater Miami Opera and the Royal Danish Opera, Mimi at Nive, Desdemona in Hong Kong and Mariella in Mascagni's Piccola Marat at the 1992 Wexford Festival; Bonn Opera from 1994, as Manon Lescaut, Donna Elvira, and Lisa in The Queen of Spades; Concerts with the Pittsburgh and Cincinnati Symphonies, Verdi Requiem with the Eastern Connecticut SO; Season 1996 with the Trovatore Leonora for Fort Worth Opera, and Tosca with Opera Zuid, Netherlands. Address: Athole Still Ltd, Foresters Hill, 25-7 Westow Street, London SE19 3RY, England.

NOTT Jonathon, b. 1963, Solihull, England. Conductor. Education: Choral scholar at St John's College, Cambridge, 1981-84; Royal Northern College of Music, 1984-86; National Opera Studio, 1986-87. Career: Repetiteur then Conductor at the Frankfurt Opera from 1988; First Kapellmeister of Wiesbaden Opera and Symphony Orchestra 1991-, with repertoire of leading works from composers such as Verdi, Mozart, Puccini, Rossini, Wagner; Conducted premieres of Elektra, Tosca, Aida; Conducted Der Ring des Nibelungen with Siegfried Jerusalem and Janis Martin as part of Centenary Maifestspiele; Music Director, Luzern Opera and Symphony Orchestra, 1997-; Founding Conductor, Dresden Symphoniker, 1998; Guest appearances with major German orchestras, Bergen Philharmonic and London Sinfonietta; Regular concerts with Ensemble Modern and Ensemble Intercontemporain; Russian and French premieres of Henze Requiem; World premieres include Brian Ferneyhough, Wolfgang Rhim and Rolf Rhiem; Frequent collaborator with Ligeti and a major exponent of his works. Recordings: With ASKO Ensemble and Moscow Philharmonic. Address: Luzerner Theater, Theaterstraße 2, CH 6002, Lucerne, Switzerland.

NOVAK Vlastislav, b. 17 November 1931, Ricky, Czech Republic. Conductor; Professor. m. Olga Novakova, 29 June 1957, 1 son, 1 daughter. Education: University of Pardubice; Music School J Kocian; Academy of Music, Praha. Career: Founder, Academic Choir at University Pardubice, 1950; University Lecturer, Pardubice, 1957; Founder, International Competition IFAS and the Childrens Choir Competition, Pardubice, 1968; Conservatory Professor, Conducting, 1970; Assistant Professor, 1994; Jury Member, International Choir Competitions in Germany, USA, Italy, Greece, Lithuania, Russia, Poland. Compositions: An Arrangement of Folk Songs. Recordings: B Britten, Cantata Academica; B Martinu, Czech

Madrigals; Songs of PDS; Czech Christmas Carols; Iuventus Cantans. Publications: Czech Choral Music; Czech Composers Smetana, Dvorak, janacek, Martinu in Choral Music; Czech Choral Music for Children. Honours: Merit Artist, Czech Republic; Prizes, B Smetana, 1984, Comenius, 1985, F Lysek Conductors Prize, 1995, G Mahler, 1997. Memberships: Czech Composers & Artists Association; Czech Choir Conductors Association. Hobbies: Management; Weekend Craft Works. Address: Trida Miru 71, 530 02 Pardubice, Czech Republic.

NOVIKOV Alexander Vyacheslavovich, b. 20 February 1952, Nogliki, Sakhalin Island, Russia. Composer. m. Elena Novikova. Education: Khabarovsk Academy of Railway Transport; Novosibirsk Conservatory, 1985. Debut: Novosibirsk, 1982. Recordings: Mass for Choir & Symphony; Conductor, Viktor Tits; Concertino for Harpsichord, 2 Violins & Symphony. Publications: Library of Choirmaster, 1984; Siberian & Russian Far East Composers Choir Music. Honours: Winner, All-Soviet Competition for Student Composers, 1982; Prize, Competition, Khabarovsk Regional Administration. Memberships: Union of Soviet Composers. Current Management: Michael Lachman Arts Management. Address: 3/15 Frunze Street, Khabarovsk 680000, Russia.

NOVOA Salvador, b. 30 Oct 1937, Mexico City, Mexico. Opera Singer; Tenor; Voice Teacher. m. 16 Aug 1968, 3 sons, 1 daughter. Education: School of Music, The University of Mexico, 1957-62; Voice with Felipe Aquilera Ruiz, 1957-66; Kurt Baum, 1972-80. Debut: As Pinkerton in Madame Butterfly, Mexico Opera Company, 1960. Career: Erik in Der fliegende Holländer with the Philadelphia Lyric Opera; Several roles in various operas with the New York City Opera including: Don José and Cavaradossi, the title roles in Bomarzo and Don Rodrigo, Faust in Mefistofele and Edgardo in Lucia di Lammermooor; He has appeared with opera companies widely including San Diego Opera, Houston Grand Opera, Boston Opera, Cincinnati Opera, Teatro Colon, Argentina, Opera Municipal de Marseille, Stuttgart Opera Company, Tehran; His repertoire includes: Radames, Andrea Chenier; Bomarzo (Pier Francesco), Carmen (Don José), Cavalleria Rusticana (Turiddu); Don Rodrigo, Faust, Macbeth, Macduff, Faust in Mefistofele; Pollione in Norma; Samson in Samson and Delilah; Numerous other roles in various operas; Symphonic repertoire includes, Beethoven's Ninth Symphony and Verdi's Messa da requiem. Recording: Bomarzo by Alberto Ginastera, CBS Records. Honour: 2nd Prize, Metropolitan Opera Regional Auditions, Mexico City, 1959. Address: 248 West 88th Street, New York, NY 10024, USA.

NOVOTNY Jan, b. 15 Dec 1935, Prague, Czechoslovakia. Pianist. m. 26 Apr 1985, 2 daughters. Education: Conservatory Praha, 1950-55; Academy of Music Arts, Praha, 1955-59. Debut: Praha, 1954. Career: Concert performances worldwide with frequent appearances at Prague Spring Festival, Festival de Bonaguil, France and on Radio Prague, Bern, Gothenburg, Brussels, Paris and TV Prague; Chairman of the Jury, Smetana Piano Competition, Czechoslovakia; Head, Piano Classes Department, Prague Conservatory, 1988-. Recordings: Beethoven's Sonatas Op 10 No3, Op 22, Op 28, Op 31 No1; Smetana's Complete Piano Works, 10 records; Schumann's Phantasie C major Op 17; FX Dussek's Piano Concertos; Jan L Dusik and Dussek: Last Piano Sonatas; Jaroslav Jezek's Complete Piano Works; Ignaz Moscheles' Concerto No 5 Op 87 in C minor; JL Dussek's Piano Concertos and Selection, both with Prague Radio Symphony Orchestra. Publication: Smetana: Piano Compositions, in 7 volumes, complete edition 1st time in history. Contributions to: Gramorevue, Praha. Honours: State Prize, 1984; Annual Prize of Panton Editor, Praha, 1987. Membership: President, Smetana Society, 1991. Address: Rosickych 6, Prague 5 CZ-150 00, Czechoslovakia.

NOWACK Hans, b. 1930, Waldenburg, Germany. Singer (Bass). Education: Completed vocal studies 1956. Career: Sang at heidelberg Opera from 1959, Bielefeld 1961 and Bremen Opera 1963-66; Essen Opera from 1967, with guest engagements at Vienna, Barcelona, Mexico, Venice, Lisbon and New Orleans; Roles have included Osmin, Sarastro, Kaspar in Der Freischütz, Gurnemanz, Hunding, Rocco and Ochs; Further visits to Hamburg, Munich, Berlin and Warsaw, as Jupiter in Rameau's Platée, Marke, the Commendatore, Daland, Boris Godunov and Hindemith's Cardillac. Address: Theater Essen, Rolandstrasse 10, W-4300 Essen 1, Germany.

NOWAK Grzegorz, b. 1951, Poland. Conductor. Education: Studied conducting, violin and composition at the Poznan Academy of Music; Later at Eastman School of Music, Rochester and at Tanglewood with Bernstein, Ozawa, Leinsdorf and Markevitch. Career: Music Director for Slupsk Symphony Orchestra, 1976-80; Won first prize in 1984 at Ansermet Conducting Competition, Geneva; Engagements followed with London Symphony, Montreal Symphony and Orchestre National de France; Has also appeared with orchestras of Rome, Oslo, Stockholm, Copenhagen, Helsinki, Monte Carlo, Jerusalem, Madrid, Lisbon, Baltimore, Cincinnati, San Diego, Vancouver, Ottawa, Tokyo, Hong Kong, Geneva, Zurich, Baden-Baden, Milan, Saarbrücken, Rotterdam, Florence, Göteborg, Malmö, Birmingham, Liverpool, Bournemouth, Manchester, Belfast and Glasgow; Currently Music Director of the Biel Symphony Orchestra, Switzerland. Recordings: Ravel's Daphnis et Chloe and Bartók's Dance Suite with the London Symphony Orchestra. Honours: American Patronage Prize, 1984; Europaischen Förderpreis für Musik, 1985. Address: c/o Harrison-Parrott Ltd, 12 Penzance Place, London, W11 4PA, England.

NOWAK Maria Malgorzata, b. 7 June 1977, Poznan, Poland. Violinist. Education: Julius Stern Institute, 1992-97; Ignacy Jan Paderewski Academy of Music, 1995-97; Hochschule Der Kunste, Berlin, 1997-. Debut: Poznan, 1995. Career: Played in Concerts at Poland, Germany, England, France, Holland, Belgium, Spain. Recordings: Polish Radio and Television Compositions of H Wieniawski, M Ravel, E Chausson, P Sarasate, A Vivaldi, A Dvorak. Honours include: 1st Prize, National Violin Competition for Young Musicians, Olsztyn, Poland, 1989, Lublin, 1990; 1st Prize, International Violin Competition, Lublin, 1991. Hobbies: Poetry; Culture. Address: ul Newtona 16A/40, 60 161 Poznan, Poland.

NUCCI Leo, b. 16 Apr 1942, Castiglione dei Pepoli, Bologna, Italy. Baritone. m. Adriana Anelli. Education: Studied with Giuseppe Marchesi and Ottaviano Bizzarri. Debut: Spoleto in 1967 as Rossini's Figaro. Career: Sang Puccini's Schaunard at Venice in 1975, at La Scala Milan in 1976 as Figaro, at Covent Garden in 1978 as Miller in Luisa Miller and Metropolitan Opera from 1980 as Renato in Un Ballo in Maschera, Eugene Onegin, Germont, Amonasro and Posa in Don Carlos; Sang at Paris Opéra in 1981 as Renato and at Pesaro in 1984 in a revival of Rossini's Il Viaggio a Reims; Wiesbaden in 1985 as Rigoletto, at Salzburg Festival, 1989-90 as Renato, Turin in 1990 as Silvio in Pagliacci and Parma as Di Luna in Il Trovatore; Sang Iago in concert performances of Otello at Chicago and New York in 1991; Season 1992 as Luna at Turin, Tonio at Rome, Iago at Reggio Emilia, the Forza Don Carlo at Florence and Rossini's Figaro at the Festival of Caracalla; Sang Dulcamara at Turin, 1994; Sang Rossini's Figaro at the Verona Arena, 1996. Recordings: Donizetti's Maria di Rudenz; Ford in Falstaff; Il Viaggio a Reims; Aida; Simon Boccanegra; Otello; Rigoletto; Michonnet in Adriana Lecouvreur; Video of Il Barbiere di Siviglia, from the Metropolitan. Address: c/o Allied Artists Agency, 42 Montpelier Square, London, SW7 1JZ, England.

NUNEMAKER Richard E, b. 30 Nov 1942, Buffalo, New York, USA. Clarinettist; Saxophonist. m. Lynda Perkins, 15 Aug 1964, 1 son, 1 daughter. Education: BS, Education, Clarinet, State University of New York College at Fredonia, 1964; MM, Clarinet, University of Louisville, 1966; Studied with Clark Brody, Jerome Stowell, James Livingston, Allen Sigel, William Wilett. Career includes: Bass Clarinet, Saxophone, Houston Symphony, 1967-; Clarinet, Saxophone, Houston Pops, 1970-85; Cambiata Soloists, 1970-84; Faculty, Clarinet, Saxophone, Assistant Director, Wind Ensemble, University of St Thomas, Houston, 1970-92; Clarinet, Saxophone, Music America Chamber Ensemble, 1977-92; Clarinet, Saxophone, Pierrot Plus Ensemble, Rice University, 1987-92; Clarinet and saxophone concertos with Lawrence Foster, Jorge Mester, Sergiu Comissiona, other conductors; Frequent Recitalist and Soloist with chamber music ensembles on radio and TV, including new music; Principal Clarinet, Orquesta Filarmonica de la Ciudad de Mexico, 1987; Clarinet and Saxophone Opus 90, New Directions in American Chamber Music, 1990; Carnegie debut, New and Traditional Music Concert, music of Willian Thomas McKinley, 1994; European debut, tour with Camerata Bregenz, conductor Christoph Eberle, Austria, 1994; Clarinet, Bass Clarinet, Saxophone, CUBE, New Music Chicago. Recordings: America Swings I, II. A Tribute to Benny Goodman; A Tribute to Artie Shaw, with Houston Symphony; From the Great Land; Continuum Percussion Quartet, Eugene Kurtz, Logo 1; Golden Petals/Richard Nunemaker; Beauty/Paul English. Publications: If The Shoe Fits, 1979. Memberships include: International Clarinet and Saxophone Congresses; Clarinetwork Inc; International League of Women Composers. Hobbies: Running; Gardening; Photography. Current Management: Lyn-Rich Management. Address: c/o Lyn-Rich Management, 1617 Fannin Street 2519, Houston, TX 77002, USA.

NYGAARD Jens, b. 26 Oct, 1931, Stephens, Arizona, USA. Conductor; Pianist. Education: Studied with parents, at Louisiana State University and at Juilliard School, MS, 1957. Career: Conducted Mozart 200th birthday concert, 1956; Conductor of Music, In Our Time series of concerts at Columbia University, 1964-66; Founder of Westchester Chamber Chorus and Orchestra, 1965; Beethoven Concerts as Pianist and Conductor in Vienna, 1970; Soloist in complete Mozart piano concertos at Washington Heights Young Men's Hebrew Association, NY, 1974-75; Conducted Mozart's Il Re Pastore and USA premiere of Pergolesi's La Contadina Astuta; Co-founder of the Jupiter Symphony Orchestra in New York, 1979; Music Director of the Naumberg Symphony Orchestra in 1980; Teacher at Columbia University Teachers College, 1981-82; Conductor of Rutgers University Symphony Orchestra, 1982. Address: c/o Columbia University Teachers College, 703 Dodge, New York, NY 10027, USA.

NYIKOS Markus (Andreas), b. 9 Dec 1948, Basel, Switzerland. Cellist. m. Verena Kamber, 8 Dec 1982, 1 daughter. Education: Musik Akademie, Basel with Paul Szabo; Konservatorium Luzern with Stanislav Apolin; Masterclasses with Zara Nelsova, Pierre Fournier, Sandor Vegh and Janacek Quartet. Career: Cello solo at Festival of Strings Lucerne, 1974-79 and with Philharmonische Virtuosen Berlin, 1983-; Professor, Hochschule der Kunste Berlin, 1979-; Guest Professor at Shanghai Conservatory; Numerous concerts and radio appearances worldwide. Recordings: Vivaldi; Cello Concertos with Radio Sinfonie Orchestra Berlin; Brahms Sonatas in E minor and F major, with pianist, Gerard Wyss; Schubert's Arpeggione-Sonata in A minor with Gerard Wyss; With La Groupe Des Six, compositions by Auric, Poulenc, Honegger, and Milhaud, with pianist, Jaroslav Smykal. Address: c/o Robert Gilder, Anglo Swiss Artists Management, Suites 35-37, Morley House, 320 Regent Street, London W1R 5AD, England.

NYKRYN Jan, b. 8 Nov 1974, Prague, Czech Republic. Violist. Education: Conservatory in Prague; Lawrence University, USA; Kato Havas Courses, England; Pedagogical Faculty, Charles University, Prague. Debut: Prague, 1995. Career: Telemann, Concerto in G Major with Fox Valley Youth Orchestra, 1992; Northwoods Twilight Concert Tour, USA, 1992; Stamic, Concerto in D Major with Chamber Ensemble, Prague, 1995; Czech Nonet Concert Series, 1995, 1996, 1997. Recordings: For Czech Radio: S Barber Quartet; For Harmonia Mundi: Schubert Octet, Martinu Nonet, Roussel Trio, Roussel Serenade, Mozart Oboe Quartet. Honour: Young Artists Audition Award, Milwaukee, 1992. Membership: INTERGRAM. Hobbies: Political Science; Internet Programming. Address: Lesnicka 8, 150 00 Prague 5, Czech Republic.

NYMAN Michael, b. 23 Mar 1944, London, England. Composer. Education: Studied with Alan Bush at Royal Academy of Music, 1961-65, King's College, London, 1964-67, and with Thurston Dart. Career: Writer and Music Critic, 1968-78. Compositions include: Film music for Peter Greenaway creations, The Falls, 1977, The Draughtsman's Contract, A Zed and Two Noughts, Drowning By Numbers and Prospero's Books; The Piano, 1992; Renaissance Masque for cabaret chanteuse, rock singer and opera star; Ballet scores for choreographers Rosemary Butcher and Siobhan Davies; Works for cabaret artiste Ute Lemper and the Balanescu Quartet; Concerto and Where The Bee Dances for saxophonist John Harle; Songs For Tony for Saxophone Quartet, premiered in 1993; Festival Hall concert 1997, with the Philharmonia and the Michael Nyman Band; Compositions include: The Kiss, video-duet, 1984; The Man Who Mistook His Wife For A Hat, chamber opera, London, 1986; Vital Statistics, London, 1987; Orpheus' Daughter, Rotterdam, 1988; La Princesse De Milan, dance opera after The Tempest, Avignon, 1991; Letters, Riddles And Writs, TV opera in Not Mozart series, BBC TV, 1991; Piano Concerto, 1993. Recordings: The Michael Nyman Songbook; The Essential Michael Nyman Band; String Quartet Nos 1-3; Where The Bee Dances; The Man Who Mistook His Wife For A Hat. Publications: Libretto for Birtwistle's Dramatic Pastoral, Down by the Greenwood Side, 1968-69; Experimental Music: Cage and Beyond, 1974. Address: c/o PRS Ltd, Member Registration, 29-33 Berners Street, London, W1P 4AA, England.

NYQUIST Kristian (Benedikt), b. 16 Oct 1964, Los Angeles, USA. Harpsichordist. m. Judith Nyquist, 10 Aug 1991, 1 son, 1 daughter. Education: Staatliche Musikhochschule, 1983-88; Conservatorie National de Région Rueil-Malmaison, 1988-92. Debut: Ernst Toch Saal, Mannheim, Germany, 1986. Career: Concerts as Recitalist, Continuo Player, Duo Partner and Soloist in Germany, France, Belgium, Netherlands, Poland, Czech Republic, Switzerland, Russia, USA, Brazil. Recordings: Chamber Music by J B de Boismortier; Solo Debut CD, Cembalo Impressionen, 1996; C P E Bach, 5 Sonatas for Harpsichord and Flute, 1996; J S Bach, 5 Flute Sonatas, 1997; D'Anglebert Harpsichord Music, 1998. Publictions: Realizations of Figured-Bass Parts; Trio-Sonatas by Tartini;; Sonata Pastorale by Campioni, Zimmermann, Verlag. Honours: 1st Prize, Concours Musical de Region d'Ile de France, 1991; Prague Spring Competition, Honorary Mention, 1994. Memberships: Deutscher Tonkunstler-Verband, Stuttgart Section; France Action Musique. Hobbies: Reading; Travel; Languages. Address: Soonwaldstrasse 27, D-55566 Bad Sobernheim, Germany.

NYSTEDT Knut, b. 3 Sept 1915, Oslo, Norway. Composer; Conductor; Organist. m. Brigit Nystedt, 20 June 1942, 1 son, 2 daughters. Education: Examen, Artium, 1935; Organ with Arild Sandvold, Oslo Conservatory of Music, and Ernest White, New York, 1947; Composition with Bjarne Brustad, Oslo, and Aaron Copland, New York, 1947. Debut: Organist, 1938; Conductor, Oslo Philharmonic, 1945. Career: Organist, Torshov Church, Oslo, 1946-82; Conductor, Norwegian Soloist Choir, 1950-90, performances worldwide; Professor of Choral Conducting, Oslo University, 1964-85. Compositions: 5 String Quartets, 1938, 1948, 1955, 1966, 1988; Piano variations, 1948; Symphony for Strings, 1950; Lucis Creator Optime, soli, chorus, orchestra, 1968; With Crown and Star, Christmas opera, 1971; Pia memoria, 9 brass instruments, 1971; Music for 6 Trombones, 1980; Exsultate, 1980; Mountain Scenes, concert band, 1981; A Hymn of Human Rights, chorus, harp, string quartet, 1982; For a Small Planet, chorus, recitation, harp, string quartet, 1982; Sinfonia del Mare, 1983; Ave Maria, chorus, violin solo, 1986; Songs of Soloman, church opera, 1989; Ave Christe, women's chorus, orchestra, 1991; Messa per Percussione, 1991; Concerto Arctandriae, strings, 1991; 4 Grieg Romances, chorus a capella, 1992; The Conch, male quartet with counter tenor, 1993; Concerto Sacro, violin, organ, 1993; Miserere, 16-part chorus of mixed voices, 1994; One Mighty Flowering Tree, chorus, brass, 1994; Gebete für Mitgefangene (Bonhoeffer), soprano, organ, 1994; Kristnikvede, 1000th anniversary of Christianity in Norway, chorus, orchestra, 1994; Libertas Vincit, 50th anniversary of liberation from German occupation, recitation, chorus, orchestra, 1994; A Song as in The Night (Esaiah), soprano and baritone solo, chorus and string orchestra, 1996. Recordings: Numerous. Honours: Knight, Order of St Olav, 1966; Distinguished Service Citation, Augsburg College, USA, 1975; Music Prize, Norwegian Council for Cultural Affairs, 1980; Professor Honorario, Mendoza University, Argentina, 1991; Lindeman Prize, 1993; Fanny Elsta Prize, Bergen Music Festival, 1994. Membership: Society of Norwegian Composers. Address: Vestbrynet 25 B, 1160 Oslo, Norway.

O

O'BRIEN Eugene, b. 24 Apr 1945, Paterson, NJ, USA. Composer; Teacher. Education: Studied at University of Nebraska, MM 1969, with Bernd Alois Zimmermann at Cologne, Indiana University with John Eaton and Iannis Xenakis, and Donald Erb at the Cleveland Institute of Music, DMA, 1983. Career: Teacher, 1973-81, Composer-in-Residence, 1981-85, Cleveland Institute; Associate Professor at Catholic University of America in Washington DC, 1985-87, and at Indiana University School of Music, 1987-. Compositions: Orchestral: Symphony, 1969, Cello Concerto, 1972, Dedales for Soprano and Orchestra, 1973, Rites Of Passage, 1978, Dreams And Secrets Of Origin for Soprano and Orchestra, 1983, Alto Saxophone Concerto, 1989; Chamber: Intessitura for Cello and Piano, 1975, Embarking For Cythera for 8 Instruments, 1978, Tristan's Lament for Cello, Allures for Percussion Trio, 1979, Psalms and Nocturnes for Flute, Viola da Gamba and Harpsichord, 1985, Mysteries of the Horizon for 11 Instruments, 1987; Vocal: Requiem Mass for Soprano, Chorus and Wind Ensemble, 1966, Nocturne for Soprano and 10 Instruments, 1968, Elegy for Bernd Alois Zimmermann for Soprano and Ensemble, 1970, Lingual for Soprano, Flute and Cello, 1972; Taking Measures, ballet, 1984. Honour: Guggenheim Fellowship, 1984-85. Address: c/o ASCAP, ASCAP Building, One Lincoln Plaza, New York, NY 10023, USA.

O'HORA Ronan, b. 9 Jan 1964, Manchester, England. Pianist. m. Hannah Alice Bell, 5 Jan 1991. Education: GMus, Honours, Royal Northern College of Music, 1985. Career: Recitals and concerts in UK, USA, Australia, New Zealand, Germany, France, Italy, Austria, Switzerland, Spain, Denmark, Norway, Sweden, Belgium, Holland, Portugal, Ireland, Yugoslavia and Czechoslovakia; Concerts with Philharmonia, Royal Philharmonic, BBC Symphony, Hallé, Bournemouth Symphony, Royal Liverpool Philharmonic, BBC Philharmonic, BBC Scottish, Zurich Tonhalle Orchestra, Netherlands Radio Symphony and Chamber Orchestras, Philharmonia Hungaria, Indianapolis Symphony, and Florida Philharmonic. Recordings: Concertos by Tchaikowsky, Grieg and Mozart with the Royal Philharmonic Orchestra; Britten complete music for two pianos with Stephen Hough; Numerous radio recordings in UK, USA, France, Holland, Poland, Czechoslovakia, Portugal and Ireland; Senior tutor at Royal Northern College of Music. Honours: Silver Medal, Worshipful Company of Musicians, 1984; Dayas Gold Medal, 1985; Stefania Niedrasz Prize, 1985. Hobbies: Reading; Theatre. Current Management: Robert Gilder and Company. Address: 11 Daresbury Road, Chorlton, Manchester M21 9NA, England.

O'LEARY Thomas, b. 3 Sep 1924, Punxsutawney, PA, USA. Bass Singer. Education: Studied with Alexander Kipnis in New York. Debut: San Jose in 1947 as Kecal in The Bartered Bride. Career: Sang at Nuremberg, 1960-65, Vienna Volksoper, 1962-75 with further engagements at Munich, Hamburg, Rome, Bologna, Berlin, Barcelona, Zurich, Marseilles and Frankfurt; Appearances at Boston, Baltimore and New Orleans from 1967, Chicago in 1977, and San Francisco, Houston and San Diego; Other roles have included Sarastro, Rocco, King Philip, Zaccaria, Mephistopheles, Arkel, Boris and Pimen in Boris Godunov, Wagner's Mark, Daland, Pogner, Hunding, Hagen and Gurnemanz; Frequent concert performances. Address: c/o Volksoper, Wahringerstrasse 78, A-1090 Vienna, Austria.

O'NEILL Charles, b. 22 Sep 1930, Ridgefield Park, NJ, USA. Tenor. Education: Studied in New York. Debut: Fort Worth Opera in 1958 as Radames. Career: Appearances at opera houses in Santa Fe, Cincinnati, Hamburg, Stuttgart, Berlin, Cologne, Frankfurt, Dusseldorf and Zurich; Member of the Theater am Gärtnerplatz Munich, with guest engagements at Toronto, Vancouver, Belgrade and Basle; Other roles have been Florestan, Don José, Don Carlos, Alvaro, Manrico, Otello, Turiddu, Samson, Cavaradossi, Rodolfo, Calaf, Andrea Chénier, Oedipus Rex by Stravinsky, Bacchus and Siegmund.

O'NEILL Dennis, b. 25 Feb 1948, Pontarddulais, Wales. Tenor. Education: Studied privately with Frederick Cox, Campogalliani and Ricci. Career: State Opera of South Australia, 1975-77, then principal tenor for Scottish Opera; Debuts with Covent Garden in Norma in 1979, Glyndebourne at the Italian Singer in Der Rosenkavalier in 1980, USA at Dallas in Lucia di Lammermoor in 1983, and Vienna Staatsoper as Alfredo in La Traviata in 1983; Has sung internationally including Hamburg, Berlin, Paris, Brussels, Marseilles, Nice, Munich, Cologne, Oslo, Barcelona, Zurich, Chicago, San Francisco, Metropolitan Opera, Vancouver, San Diego and Copenhagen; Long association with the Royal Opera House, Covent Garden in many roles including Rodolfo in La Bohème, the Duke in Rigoletto, Edgardo in Lucia di Lammermoor, Riccardo in Un Ballo in Maschera, and Foresto in Attila; Season 1992 with British Youth Opera Gala at Covent Garden, as Manrico in Munich, Riccardo at the Opéra Bastille and Radames at Tel Aviv; Covent Garden 1994-95, as Radames in Aida; Returning 1997 as Macduff in the 1847 version of Macbeth; Engaged as Radames at the Met, 1999. Recordings include: Opera Gala Recital, 1991. Address: c/o Ingpen and Williams Ltd, 26 Wadham Road, London, SW15 2LR, England.

O'NEILL Fiona, b. 1958, England. Soprano. Education: Studied at the Royal Northern College of Music; Masterclasses at Aldeburgh. Career: Solo roles have included Musetta, Norina and Donna Anna for Travelling Opera, Mabel in The Pirates of Penzance for New D'Oyly Carte, Serpetta in La Serva Padrona at the Northcutt Theatre in Exeter, and Salome for the Stockholm Folkopera at the Edinburgh Festival; English National Opera, 1990-91 as Papagena and as Gerda in Fennimore and Gerda; Sang the title role in Lakmé and Louise at the Bloomsbury Theatre and Pedrotti's Tutti in Maschera at the Britten Theatre; Concert engagements include Kurt Weill songs at the Cheltenham and Edinburgh Festivals; Premiere of Goehr's Sing Ariel, at the 1990 Aldeburgh Festival and Handel's Solomon at Birmingham in 1990; Festival Hall debut with the Philharmonia Orchestra in 1990 and debut at the Barbican with the RPO in 1991; Sang Mimi for Castleward Opera, 1996. Address: c/o Norman McCann International Artists Ltd, The Coach House, 56 Lawrie Park Gardens, London, SE26 6XJ, England.

O'REILLY Brendan, b. 1935, Dublin, Ireland. Violinist. Education: Studied at Belvedere College Dublin, with David Martin at the Royal Academy of Music and with Andre Gertler in Brussels. Career: Played with the Radio Eireann String Quartet in Cork, then freelanced with the Royal Philharmonic and the English Chamber Orchestra; Co-founded the Gabrieli Quartet in 1967 touring Europe, North America, the Far East and Australia; Festival engagements in Britain, including Aldeburgh, City of London and Cheltenham; Concerts every season in London, participation in the Barbican Centre's Mostly Mozart Festival and resident artist at the University of Essex from 1971; Has co-premiered works by William Alwyn, Britten, Alan Bush, Daniel Jones and Gordon Crosse, 3rd Quartet of John McCabe in 1979 and the 2nd Quartets of Nicholas Maw and Panufnik, 1983-80; British premiere of the Piano Quintet by Sibelius in 1990. Recordings: 5 CDs including early pieces by Britten, Dohnányi's Piano Quintet with Wolfgang Manz, Walton's Quartets and the Sibelius Quartet and Quintet, with Anthony Goldstone. Address: c/o Anglo Swiss Ltd, Suite 35-37, Morley House, 320 Regent Street, London W1R 5AD, England.

O'REILLY Graham (Henry Meredith), b. 4 Sep 1947, Parkes, New South Wales, Australia. Singer; Conductor; Musicologist. m. (1) Jill Barralet, 2 Sep 1972, divorced, 1 son, 1 daughter, (2) Brigitte Vinson, 27 Dec 1986, 2 daughters. Education: BA, Honours, University of Sydney, 1968; Associate, Sydney Conservatorium of Music, 1966; Licentiate, Trinity College, London, 1969. Debut: Messiah at Sydney Town Hall in 1971. Career: Music Teacher in Sydney, 1970-73; Researcher of late Restoration stage music, 1973- and pitch in Renaissance vocal music, 1979-; Concert and session singer in London, 1973-82; Director for early music ensembles, 1976- and for The Restoration Musick, 1980-81, Psallite, 1981-86 and Ensemble William Byrd, 1983-; Singing Teacher, 1980-; Member of Groupe Vocal de France, 1982-86; Solo oratorio and ensemble singer specialising in early music. Recordings: With Psallite: Music by Tallis, Byrd and Gibbons and Collected Works of Jon Dixon; With Groupe Vocal de France: Sacred Music of Giacinto Scelsi; With Ensemble William Byrd: English Music of The Seventeenth Century, Volume I: Orlando Gibbons, Volume 2: Welcome Vicegerent, music of Henry Purcell; Palestrina: Canticum Canticorum; Handel: Music for Cannons, Vol 1-3, Chandon anthems. Publication: Editor, Eccles: Music to Macbeth, Cathedral Music, 1978. Honour: Frank Busby Musical Scholarship, Sydney University, 1967. Hobbies: Children; French Cuisine. Address: 10 rue Massenet, 93600 Aulnay-Sous-Bois, France.

O'SHAUGHNESSY J Michael, b. 15 Apr 1940, Evanston, Illinois, USA. Trade Book Publisher; Executive. m. Marianne Farrell O'Shaughnessy, 16 June 1979, 3 daughters. Education: BA, Liberal Arts, University of Notre Dame, 1963; MS, International Graduate School of Business, Glendale, Arizona, 1971; Photography and Films Studies, Columbia College, 1979-82. Career: Board of Directors, Milkweed Editions, Minneapolis, Minnesota, 1986-95; Board of Directors, Victory Gardens Theatre, Chicago, Illinois, 1986-91; Board of Directors, Accion International, Somerville, Massachusetts, 1986-; Board of Directors, Santa Fe Chamber Festival, 1988-91; Board of Directors, Santa Fe Opera, 1988-94; Board of Directors, Chamber Music America, 1991-; Board of Directors, Chamber Music Chicago (now Performance Arts Chicago); National Association of African-America Heritage Preservation, Indianapolis, Indiana, 1995-; I A O'Shaughnessy Foundation, St Paul, Minnesota, 1997-Address: 924 Canyon Road #5, Santa Fe, NM 87501-6122, USA.

OAKLEY-TUCKER John, b. 1959, Canada. Singer (Baritone). Education: Studied at Guildhall School of Music, Britten-Pears School, Ravel Academy with Peter Pears, Gerard Souzay, Elisabeth Schwarzkopf and Thomas Hampson; Continues to study with David Pollard. Career: Operatic début in the title role of Britten's Owen Wingrave, conducted by Steuart Bedford, Aldeburgh, 1984; Sang in Glyndebourne Opera Festival Chorus in Jenufa, Arabella, Le nozze di Figaro and Falstaff, 1988-90; Operatic roles include: Lead role, Tom in Hans Werner Henze's The English Cat, conducted by the composer, Berlin, 1989, Italy, 1990 and Barbican, London, 1991 as part of the Henze BBC Festival; 2 lead roles for the Royal Opera House 'Garden Venture' project, 1991; Toured the Middle and Far East, singing Marcello in La Bohéme, 1992 and Belcore in L'Élisir d'Amore, 1993; Title role in Eugene Onegin, Co-Opera, London, 1993; Lead role of Pluto in the world premiere of Hilda Paredes' chamber opera, The Seventh Pip, Mexico City, 1993; Belcore with Island Opera, 1994; English tour with Camberwell Opera as Il Conte, 1994-95, both directed by Mark Tinkler; Pluto in The Seventh Pip, San Diego, 1995; Further roles include Don Giovanni, Gugliemo, Papageno, Sid (Albert Herring) and Billy Budd; Concert performances include: Bach's St John's and St Matthew's Passion, Duruflé's Requiem, Dvorak's Requiem, Elgar's Apostles, Fauré's Requiem, Handel's Messiah, Mozart's Requiem, Orff's Carmina Burana, Rossini's Petite Messe Solenelle and Vaughan Williams Sea Symphony; Toured United Kingdom, Spain, Portugal, singing Mahler's Kindertotenlieder for the Ballet Rambert, 1988-89; Recital début with Graham Johnson, Schumann's Dichterliebe and English Song, Purcell Room, 1987; Performances with the Songmakers' Almanac; Schubert's Winterreise with Nicholas Bosworth, Purcell Room, 1992; Recital tour of the Middle East with Iwan Llewelyn-Jones, 1993; Schubert's Die schöne Müllerin with Iwan Llewelyn-Jones, Purcell Room, 1994; Other recitals in Britain and abroad. Recordings: Tom in Hans Werner Henze's The English Cat, German Television, Tristar, 1991; Pluto in Hilda Paredes' The Seventh Pip, with Arditti String Quartet, CD, Modus Records, New York, 1995. Honours include: AGSM; Countess of Munster Musical Trust Scholarship. Current Management: Judith Newton, 75 Aberdare Gardens, London NW6 3AN. Address: 8 Whiteley Close, Dane End, Near Ware, Hertfordshire SG12 0NB, England.

OBATA Machiko, b. 23 Feb 1948, Sapporo, Japan. Soprano. Education: Studied in Tokyo and Cologne. Career: Appearances with the Cologne Opera as Mozart's Pamina and Servila, Marzelline in Fidelio, Gretel, Liu and Flora in The Turn of The Screw; Sang the Woodbird in Siegfried in 1991; Guest engagements at Strasbourg, Munich and the Opéra Comique in Paris; Salburg Easter and Summer Festivals in 1991 as Barbarina in Le nozze di Figaro; Frequent concert appearances. Address: c/o Oper der Stadt Köln, Offenbachplatz, 5000 Cologne, Germany.

OBERHOLTZER William, b. 1947, Bloomington, IN, USA. Baritone. Education: Studied at Indiana State University. Debut: Indiana in 1972 in Herakles by John Eaton. Career: Sang Marcello at St Gallen in 1976 then at Saarbrucken, 1978-81, Gelsenkirchen, 1981-86, and Kassel from 1986, St John in Wolfgang von Schweinitz' Patmos in 1990; Engaged at Munster, 1986-88 and made guest appearances at Dusseldorf as Marcello, Linz, Krefeld and Hannover; Other roles include Mozart's Count and Don Giovanni, Valentin, Renato, Rigoletto, Ford, Paolo, Wagner's Wolfram and Amfortas, Strauss's Jochanaan and Mandryka and Wozzeck; Concert engagements include Bach's St John Passion in Berlin and Carmina Burana.

OBERLIN Russell, b. 11 Oct 1928, Akron, OH, USA. College Professor; Retired Countertenor; Lecturer. Education: Artists Diploma in Voice, Juilliard School, 1951. Career: Founding member of New York Pro Musica Antiqua and soloist with many orchestras including New York Philharmonic, Chicago Symphony and Buffalo Philharmonic; Little Orchestra Society, Clarion Concerts, Smithsonian Institute Concert Series, CBS Radio Orchestra; Masterclasses throughout USA; Opera appearances in major roles at Covent Garden in Midsummer Night's Dream, San Francisco Opera, at Edinburgh and Vancouver Festivals and American Opera Society; Solo recitalist throughout USA; Radio and TV appearances; Thomas Hunter Professor of Music, Hunter College and The Graduate Center of the City University of New York, 1966-. Recordings include: A Russell Oberlin Recital; Russell Oberlin, Handel Arias; Russell Oberlin, Baroque Cantatas; Soloist with New York Philharmonic, Handel's Messiah; Bach's Magnificat in D; Soloist with New York Pro Musica, The Play of Daniel; Thomas Tallis's Sacred Music; Josquin des Pres' Missa Pange Lingua; Walton's Façade with Hermione Gingold; Numerous other recordings including recently reissued CDs including: Troubadour and Trouvére Songs. English Polyphony of the 13th and Early 14th Centuries, The French Ars Antiqua and William Byrd Music for Voice and Viols. Honours: Numerous honours and awards. Memberships: National Association of Teachers of Singing; Academia Monteverdiana; Founding Board Member, Waverly Consort, Berkshire (Mass) Concert Series, Soho Baroque Opera Company; American Academy of Teachers of Singing. Address: c/o Hunter College, City University of New York, 695 Park Avenue, New York City, NY 10021, USA.

OBERMAYR Christine, b. 30 May 1959, Wiesbaden, Germany. Mezzo-Soprano. Education: Studied in Mainz with Josef Metternich. Debut: Theater am Gärtnerplatz Munich in 1983 as Cherubino. Career: Sang a Flowermaiden at Bayreuth Festival in 1984; Roles in Munich have included Hansel, Flotow's Nancy, Nicklausse and Orlofsky; Engagements at Wiesbaden, 1984-89 as Carmen, Emilia, Otello, Olga, Janácek's Fox, the Composer in Ariadne and Ottavio in L'Incoronazione di Poppea; Further appearances at the Theater an der Wien, the Paris Opéra and the Teatro Regio Turin; Sang Lyubasha in Rimsky's Tsar's Bride in 1985 and Mary in Der fliegende Holländer at Naples in 1992; Many concert and lieder performances. Honours: Prizewinner in competitions at Vienna, Wiesbaden and Berlin.

OBERSON René, b. 27 Jun 1945, La Tour-de-Treme, Fribourg, Switzerland. Composer; Organist; Professor. m. 2 sons, 1 daughter. Education: Teachers' Training College, Schools of Music in Fribourg, Berne and Geneva. Career: Organist at concerts in Switzerland and abroad notably at Notre-Dame, Paris, France and Symphony Hall, Osaka, Japan; Professor, School of Music, Fribourg. Compositions include: L'Exilée (The Exiled Woman), 1983; Concerto for Pan Pipes, 1984; Le Grand Cercle (The Great Circle), 1985; Homo Somniens, 1988; Au Seuil De L'Ere Du Verseau (On The Threshold Of The Era Of Aquarius), 1988; Jumière Divine, Omniprésente, Invulnerable for Organ, 1990; Espoirs for 2 Trumpets, 2 Trombones and Organ, 1990. Recordings include: Numerous works have been recorded by the Lausanne Chamber Orchestra, the Berne Symphony Orchestra, The Netherlands National of Jeunesses Musicales Orchestra; Also radio recordings. Contributions to: Has reconstructed the Fourth Concerto for Organ or Harpsichord and String Orchestra by the Swiss composer, Meyer von Schauensee, 1720-1798. Hobbies: Reading; Chess; Walking; Swimming. Address: Pavillon Trobère Miraval, CH-1756 Lovens, Switzerland.

OBRADOVICH Aleksandar, b. 22 Aug 1927, Bled, Yugoslavia. Composer; Professor of Composition. m. Biljana, 2 Aug 1953, 1 son. Education: Academy of Music, 1952; Grants to spec. in London and New York. Career: Assistant Professor, Associate Professor, Professor, Faculty of Music Art, Belgrade, 1954-91; General Secretary of Union of Composers of Yugoslavia, 1962-66; Rector, University of Arts, Belgrade, 1978-83; President of Senate, 1981-82, President, 1982-83, of Union of Yugoslavian Universities. Compositions: 8 Symphonies, 5 concertos, 5 cantatas; Wind Of Flame, Green Knight, Stradum, cycles of songs; A Springtime Picnic At Dawn, ballet; Many other symphonic works, 15 vocal, instrumental and chamber works, music for 7 films and for 9 radio dramas; Electronic music and chorale works; Compositions have been performed in 32 different countries. Recording: Radio-Televizja Belgrade. Publications: Orchestration I-II, 1978, III in preparation; Electronic Music and Electronic Instruments, 1978. Contributions to: Over 350 articles and music critiques. Honours: 25 Prizes including October Prize of Belgrade in 1959 for Symphonic Epitaph, 4th July Prize in 1972 for IV Symphony and 7th July Prize in 1980 for his whole work. Membership: Society of Serbian Composers. Address: Branka Djonovica 8, Belgrade 11 040, Yugoslavia.

OBRAZTSOVA Elena (Vasilyevna), b. 7 July 1939, Leningrad, USSR. Singer (Mezzo-soprano). Education: Leningrad Conservatoire, studied under Professor A Grigorijeva. Debut: As Marina Mnisek in Boris Godunov, The Moscow Bolshoi Theatre, 1963. Career: Member of the Moscow Bolshoi Theatre, 1964-; Repertoire includes: (Russian) Countess in The Queen of Spades, 1965; Lyubasha in The Tsar's Bride, 1967; Konchakovna in Prince Igor, 1968; Marfa in Khovanshina, 1968, Lyubva in Sadko, 1979; (Italian and French) Amneris in Aida, 1965; Azucena in Il Trovatore, 1972; Eboli in Don Carlos, 1973, Santuzza in Cavalleria Rusticana, 1977; Ulrica in Un Ballo in Maschera, 1977; Adalgiza in Norma, 1979; Giovanna Seymour in Anna Bolena, 1982; Orfeo in Orfeo and Eurydice, 1984; Neris, Medea, 1989; Leonora in La Favorita, 1992; Aunt Princess in Suor Angelica, 1992, Carmen, 1972, Charlotte in Werther, 1974, Dalilah in Samson and Dalilah, 1974, Herodiade, 1990; Opera of the 20th century: Britten's A Midsummer Night's Dream, 1965; Molchanov's Dawnsare Quiet Here, 1975; Bartok's Duke Bluebeard's Castle, 1978; Stravinsky's Oedipus Rex, 1980; Respighi, La Fiamma, 1990; Prokofiev's Semion Kotko, 1970; War and Peace, 1971; The Gambler, 1996; Appearances in most leading Opera Houses of Europe and America; Tours throughout Russia and the world; Repertoire of recitals includes the music of more than 100 composers of 18th, 19th and 20th centuries; Professor of the Moscow Conservatoire, 1984; Has staged Werther at the Moscow Bolshoi Theatre, 1986; Television appearances include 12 music films. Recordings: Over 50 of operas, oratorios, cantatas, solo discs of arias and chamber music. Honours: Gold Medals at Competitions, 1962, 1970; Medal of Granados, Spain, 1971; Gold Pen of Critics, Wiesbaden, 1972; State Prize of Russia, 1974; Lenin Prize, 1976; People's Artist of the USSR, 1976; Gold Verdi, Italy, 1978; Memorial Medal of Bartok, Hungary, 1982; Gold Star, Hero of Labour, 1990. Address: c/o Bolhoi Theatre, Moscow, Teatralnaya pl 1, 103009, Russian Federation.

OCHMANN Wieslaw, b. 6 Feb 1937, Warsaw, Poland. Tenor. Education: Studied in Warsaw with Gustav Serafin and Sergiusz Nadgryzowski. Debut: Bytom in 1959 as Edgardo in Lucia di Lammermoor. Career: Warsaw Opera from 1964 with roles including Jontek in Halka, Tchaikovsky's Lensky, Cavaradossi, Dmitri in Boris Godunov and Arrigo in Les Vêpres Siciliennes; Guest appearances at the Staatsoper Berlin, Paris Opéra, Covent Garden, Hamburg and Prague; Glyndebourne, 1968-70 as Tamino, Lensky and Don Ottavio; Metropolitan Opera from 1975 as Henri, Dmitri, Lensky and Golitsin in Khovanschina; Further appearances in Moscow, Chicago, Vienna, San Francisco and Geneva; Sang Grigory in Boris Godunov at the Metropolitan in 1982, Fritz in Schreker's Der Ferne Klang at Brussels in 1988, Hermann in the Queen of Spades and Idomeneo at San Francisco in 1987 and 1989; Sang the Shepherd in Szymanowski's King Roger at Buenos Aires in 1981 and at the Festival Hall London in 1990; Sang Grigory in Boris Godunov at the Berlin Staatsoper, 1996. Recordings: Moniuszko's Halka and Ghost Castle; Penderecki's Requiem and Te Deum; Idomeneo; Mozart's Requiem; Bruckner's D minor Mass; Salome; Jenufa; Rusalka. Address: c/o San Francisco Opera, War Memorial House, San Francisco, CA 94102, USA.

OCTORS Georges, b. 1940, Zaire, Africa. Conductor. Education: Studied violin at first, then composition with Francis de Bourguignon at the Brussels Conservatory; Conducting studies with André Cluytens. Career: Founded and conducted the Antwerp Bach Society Chamber Orchestra; Assistant to Cluytens at the National Orchestra of Belgium, 1967; Music Director, 1975-83, Resident Conductor, 1983-86, Conductor and Musical Adviser of Gelders Orchestra in Arnhem, 1986-; Musical Director of the Chamber Orchestra of Wallonia, 1990; Guest appearances in Amsterdam, Leningrad, London with LSO at the Barbican Hall in 1990, and elsewhere; Featured soloists have included Jessye Norman, Yehudi Menuhin, Igor Oistrakh, Uto Ughi, Paul Tortelier, Kyung Wha Chung and Vladimir Ashkenazy. Honours include: Winner of various competitions as violinist. Address: Anglo Swiss Management Ltd, Suite 35-37, Morley House, 320 Regent Street, London W1R 5AD, England.

ODDIE Mildred Graham, b. 26 September 1925, Birch Vale, Derbyshire, England. Education: LRAM, Piano, 1946; ARCM, Piano, 1950; Ridgeway School, Lymington. Career: Private Teacher, 1980-; Visiting Piano Teacher, Walhampton School, 1981-92. Membership: Incorporated Society of Musicians. Hobbies: Riding; Tennis; Cycling. Address: Squirrels, 94 Osborne Road, New Milton, Hants BH25 6AA, England.

ODNOPOSOFF Ricardo, b. 24 Feb 1914, Buenos Aires, Argentina. Violinist; Educator. m. (1) 1 daughter, (2) Irmtraut Baum, 20 Mar 1965. Education: MMus, High School Music, Berlin, 1932. Career: Violinist, playing in concerts throughout the world, 1932-; Teacher, University of Caracas, Venezuela, 1943-47; Taught summer courses Mozarteum, Salzburg, 1955-60; International Summer Academy, Nice, France, 1959-73; Professor, High School for Music, Vienna, 1956-, Professor Emeritus 1975-; Teacher, High School for Music, Stuttgart, Germany, 1964-94; Music High School, Zurich, 1975-84. Recordings: All of his former LP's are re-edited on CD's. Honours: Decorated Chevalier des Arts et Lettres, France; Chevalier de l'Ordre Rose Blanche, Finland; Comdr Order of Leopold II, Belgium; Grosses Verdienstkreuz des Verdienstordens, Germany; Mun Hwa Po Chang, South Korea; Medal for Merit, Argentina; Medal of Honor in Silver, City of Vienna, 1979; Ehrenkreuz fur Wissenshaft und Kunst i Klasse, Austria; Medal of Merit in Gold, Government Baden-Wurttemberg, West Germany; Gold Ring of Honor by the Wiener Philharmoniker; Honour Member, Academie of Music, Stuttgart. Membership: Freemason. Address: 27 Singerstrasse, 1010 Vienna, Austria.

OELZE Christiane, b. 1965, Cologne, Germany. Singer (Soprano). Education: Studies with Klesie-Kelly Moog and Erna Westenberger. Debut: Despina, Ottawa. Career: Sang with Sir Neville Marriner, Frans Brüggem, Helmuth Rilling, Roger Norrington, Horst Stein, Nikolaus Harnoncourt, Pierre Boulez, Simon Rattle, Esa-Pekka Salonen, Riccardo Muti, Charles Mackerras, Seji Ozawa; Roles include: Pamina, in Leipzig and Lyon; Konstanze, in Salzburg and Zürich; Anne Trulove at Glyndebourne; Pamina in Zauberflöte and Marzelline in Leonore under John Eliot Gardiner; Regina in Mathis der Maler; Zdenka in Arabella and Zerlina in Don Giovanni at the Royal Opera House, Covent Garden; Mitridate at the Salzburg Festival in 1997. Recordings: Goethe-Lieder by Schubert, Wolf; Concert arias and C Minor Mass by Mozart; Webern Songs and Cantatas; Zauberflöte with John Eliot Gardiner. Honour: Winner, Hugo Wolf Contest 1987. Current Management: Artists Management. Address: c/o Artists Management, Künstlersekretariat Pieter G Alferink, Apollolaan 181 - 1077 AT Amsterdam, Netherlands.

OERTEL Christiane, b. 22 Dec 1958, Potsdam, Germany. Mezzo-Soprano. Education: Studied at the Leipzig Hochschule, 1975-82. Career: Member of the Komische Oper Berlin from 1988 as Cherubino, Olga, Dorabella and Carlotta in Die schweigsame Frau; Debuts at Covent Garden, Hamburg and in 1991 as Cherubino; Hamburg Cherubino; Japan visit with Covent Garden, Cherubino, 1992; Engagement Theater Erfurt, 1982-88; Debut as La Cenerentola, G Rossini, Komische Oper, 1994; Concert with Gewandhaus Leipzig under Kurt Masur; Many concert appearances. Address: c/o Komische Oper Berlin, Behrenstrasse 55-57, D-10117 Berlin, Germany.

OGAWA Noriko, b. 28 Jan 1962, Kawasaki, Japan. Pianist. Education: Tokyo College of Music High School, 1977-80, Juilliard School, New York, 1981-85; Piano studies with Benjamin Kaplan, 1988-. Career: Concerto soloist from 1976 playing works by Mendelssohn, Tchaikovsky, Liszt, Schumann and Chopin; New York recital debut in 1982, London Wigmore Hall debut in 1988 playing Schumann's Fantasy and Liszt's Sonata; Recitals throughout England and Ireland; Major appearances worldwide include the Harrogate Festival and the Tokyo and Yokohama Festivals; She has recorded several times for the BBC including Tchaikovsky B flat minor and Prokofiev No 3 Concertos with Rozhdestvensky and the State Symphony Orchestra of the Russian Ministry of Culture; Has appeared outside the UK with Tokyo Symphony and Philharmonic, the Yomiuri Nippon Symphony Orchestra (with Jan Pascal Tortelier) and the Singapore Symphony; Formed a duo with clarinettist, Michael Collins in 1988, performing at Wigmore Hall and various festivals; 1991 included performances with Philharmonia Orchestra at the Festival Hall, the Ulster Orchestra and Bournemouth Symphony; Gave world premiere of a work by Lyn Davies at Lower Machen Festival and live BBC solo broadcast. Recordings: Czerny Etudes; Liszt; Prokofiev; Finzi Bagatelles. Honours: 2nd Prize, International Music Competition of Japan, 1983; Gina Bachauer Memorial Scholarship, Juilliard, 1984; 3rd Prize, Leeds International Piano Competition, 1987. Address: c/o Clarion Seven Muses, 64 Whitehall Park, London, N19 3TN, England.

OGDON Wilbur L, b. 19 Apr 1921, USA. Composer; Professor of Music Theory, Literature and Composition. m. Beverly Jean Porter, Aug 1958, 1 son, 2 daughters. Education: BM, University of Wisconsin, 1942; MA, Hamline University, St Paul, Minnesota, 1947; PhD, Indiana University, 1955; Further study, University of California, Berkeley, 1949-50, Ecole Normale de Musique, 1952-53; Studied composition with Ernst Krenek, Roger Sessions, Rene Leibowitz. Career: Professional positions and teaching: University of Texas, 1947-50; College of St Catherine, St Paul, 1956-57; Illinois Wesleyan University, 1957-65; Music Director, Pacifica Foundation, Berkeley, 1962-64; University of Illinois, 1965-66; University of California, San Diego, 1966-; Founding Chair, Music Department, 1966-71; Emeritus, UCSD, 1991-. Compositions: 3 Piano Pieces, 1950; Capriccio for Piano, 1952; Seven Piano Pieces, 1987; Voice: 3 Baritone Songs, 1950-56; Two Ketchwa Songs, 1955; Le Tombeau de Jean Cocteau, I, II and III, 1964, 1972, 1976; By the ISAR, 1969; Winter Images, 1981; Summer Images, 1985; The Awakening of Sappho (chamber opera), 1980; Chorus: Statements; 3 Sea Songs; Instrumental: 7 Pieces and a Capriccio for violin and piano, 1988-89; 6 Small Trios, trumpet, marimba, piano, 1980; 5 Preludes, violin, piano, 1982; 5 Preludes, violin, chamber orchestra, 1985; Capriccio and 5 Comments, symphony orchestra, 1979; Serenade No 1 for Wind Quintet, 1987; Serenade No 2 for Wind Quintet, 1990; Palindrome and Variations, string quartet, 1962; 3 Trifles, cello, piano, 1958; Two Sea Chanteys, soprano, baritone and two percussionists, 1988; Four Chamber Songs, soprano with viola, cello, flute, oboe and harp, 1989; Four Tonal Songs, 1988-90; A Modern Fable, 2 soprano, baritone with violin, cello, clarinet, bass clarinet and percussion; Serenade 2, Wind Quintet, 1994; 13 Expressions, solo violin and six instruments, 1993; Variation Suite, flute, viola (also violin, viola), 1995. Publications: Series and Structure, 1955; Horizons Circled (with Ernst Krenek and John Stewart), 1974; How Tonality Functions in Webern's Opus 9, Extempore, 1990. Contributions to: On Webern's Op 27, II, in Journal of Music Theory; Journal of Schoenberg Institute; An Unpublished Treaties by Rene Leibowitz; How Tonality Functions in Schoenberg's op 11, No 1. Address: 482 15th Street, Del Mar, CA 92014, USA.

OGNIVTSEV Alexander (Pavlovich), b. 27 Aug 1920, Petrovoskoy, Russia. Bass Singer. Education: Studied at the Kishinev Conservatory. Debut: Bolshoi Theatre, Moscow, 1949 as Dosifey in Khovanshchina. Career: Has sung major roles in the Russian bass repertory such as Rimsky Korsakov's Ivan the Terrible and Tchaikovsky's Prince Gremin and Renée in Iolanta; Has also performed Philip II in Don Carlos, Mephistopheles, Don Basilio and the General in Prokofiev's The Gambler (also on the Bolshoy's visit to the Metropolitan in 1975); Sang in the premieres of Shaporin's The Decembrists in 1953 and Kholminov's An Optimistic Tradegy in 1967; Guest appearances in Italy at La Scala, Austria, France, Rumania, Canada, Poland, India, Turkey, Hungary and Japan; Appeared in 1953 film version of the life of Shalyapin and sang Aleko in a film of Rachmaninov's opera. Honours include: People's Artist of Russia, 1965.

OHANESIAN David, b. 6 Jan 1927, Bucharest, Rumania. Baritone. Education: Studied in Budapest with Aurel

Costescu-Duca and in Cluj with Dinu Badescu. Debut: Cluj in 1950 in Pagliacci. Career: Sang Tonio at Bucharest in 1952 and remained at the National Opera until 1977 as Verdi's Iago, Rigoletto, Amonasro and Luna, Eugene Onegin, Telramund, Scarpia, Escamillo and Rossini's Figaro, in Meyerbeer's Margherita d'Anjou and Tchaikovsky's Mazeppa; Noted as Enesco's Oedipe, which he sang in Bucharest and as guest abroad; Engagements in Hamburg, Moscow, Prague, Lyon, Paris, Barcelona, Budapest, Leningrad, Warsaw and Tel Aviv. Recordings include: Oedipe and Cavalleria Rusticana. Publication: Passion of Music, with I Sava, Bucharest, 1986.

OHLSSON Garrick, b. 3 Apr 1948, Bronxville, NY, USA. Pianist. Education: Westchester Conservatory; Juilliard School with Sascha Gorodnitsky, and later with Olga Barabini and Rhosa Lhevinne. Career includes: Over 10 tours of Poland and appearances with major symphony orchestras in Europe, USA, Japan, and New Zealand; Recent appearances with Cleveland, Chicago, Philadelphia, Pittsburgh, and San Francisco Orchestras; European engagements with Munich Philharmonic, Northern German Radio, Rotterdam Philharmonic and all major London Orchestras; Appearances at City of London Festival, South Bank Summer Music, and the Promenade Concerts with BBC Symphony Orchestra, and at festivals, recitals and concerts in Bergen, Prague, Sofia, Dubrovnik and Tivoli. Recordings: Brahms Concerto No 1; Liszt Concerti; Solo works by Chopin; Scriabin Piano Concerto with the Czech Philharmonic. Honours: Prizewinner at Busoni Piano Competition, Italy, 1966, Chopin International Piano Competition, Warsaw, 1970, and Montreal International Piano Competition, 1970. Current Management: Harold Holt Ltd. Address: Harold Holt Ltd, 31 Sinclair Road, London, W14 0NS, England.

OHTANI Kimiko, b. 10 July 1941, Kyoto, Japan. Professor. Education: Musicology & Ethnomusicology, Tohogakuen School of Music, BA, 1965; Dance Ethnology, University of Hawaii, USA, MA, 1981; Ethnomusicology & Social Anthropology, Queens University, Belfast, PhD, 1994; Studies of Piano, Indian Classical Dance & Mridangam (Indian Drum). Publications: Bharata Notyam, Rebirth of Dance in India, 1992; Japanese Approaches to the Study of Dance, 1992. Memberships: International Council for Traditional Music; Society for Ethnomusicology. Hobby: House Plants. Address: Diapalace Masugata 801, 4-28 Masugata, Kochi 780, Japan.

OHTSUKA Shozo, b. 23 July 1926, Tokyo, Japan. Vocalist; Chorus Leader; Writer. m. Yuriko, 29 Aug 1948. Education: Graduate, Faculty of Economics, University of Tokyo, 1948; Private Singing Lessons, Dina Notargiacomo, Tokyo, 1948-53; Musicology, Tomojiro Ikenouchi, 1961; Private Singing Lessons, Jeanne Fort-Badard, Paris, 1965; General Music Education, Akeo Watanabe, 1960-80. Debut: Recital, Swedish Art Songs, Tokyo, 1964. Career: Swedish TV with Nordic Choral Society, Japan, 1964; Soloist, NHK Tokyo Radio, 1965; Finnish TV with NCSJ, 1968; TBS Tokyo, 1969; TBS TV Emperor Showa in Denmark, 1971; Swedish Broadcasting Corporation, 1997. Compositions: Hisame no Furuhi (It's Raining Freezing Cold), Choral Work, 1950, 1992. Recordings: Life, Music, Memories, Talk and Solo Singing; Asia Soundtek, 1997; Joint Recital, Nordic Choral Society of Japan and Schola Cantorum, 1997. Publications: Swedish Choral Works, 1964; John Horton, Scandinavian Music, 1971; Harukanaru Hokuovni, 1979. Contributions to: Comedy in Black Frame; The God in Disguise. Honours: Sankt Olaf Medaljien, Norway, 1971; Honorary Life Member, Schola Cantorum, University of Oslo, 1993. Memberships: Japan Federation of Musicians; Nordic Choral Society of Japan; Grieg Society of Japan; Council Assembly of International Edvard Grieg Society. Hobby: Cookery. Current Management: Kreis Planning. Address: 2-46-5 Eifuku, Suginami-ku, Tokyo 168-0064, Japan.

OHYAMA Heiichiro, b. 31 Jul 1947, Kyoto, Japan. Violinist; Violist; Conductor. m. Gail J Ohyama, 1 son. Education: Toho Music High School; Toho College of Music; Guildhall School of Music and Drama; AGSM, Indiana University, USA. Debut: New York City, USA. Career: Professor of Music at University of California, Santa Barbara; Assistant Conductor and Principal Violist with Los Angeles Philharmonic; Music Director, Santa Barbara Chamber Orchestra and Crossroads Chamber Ensemble; Music Director and Artistic Director with La Jolla Chamber Music Festival. Recordings: Various. Contributions to: Marlboro Music Festivals; Santa Fe Chamber Music festivals; Round Top Music Festivals. Honours: Carl Flesch International Competition, 1968; Indiana University, 1971; Winner, Young Concert Artist, 1975. Membership: Musicians Union, England. Hobbies: Skin Diving; Kendo. Address: 6305 Via Cabrera, La Jolla, CA 92037-5636, USA.

OISTRAKH Igor (Davidovich), b. 27 Apr 1931, Odessa, Russia. Violinist. Education: Music School and State Conservatoire, Moscow; Student at State Conservatoire, 1949-55. Career: Many foreign tours, several concerts with father, David Oistrakh, notably in music by Spohr, Leclair and Bach; 60th Birthday Concert at the Barbican Centre, London, 1991 playing concertos by Mozart and Mendelssohn; Played the Shostakovich 1st Concerto at the Festival Hall, 1997. Honours: 1st Prize in Violin Competition in Budapest, 1952 and Wieniawski Competition, Poznán; Honoured Artist of RSFSR. Address: State Conservatoire, 13 Ulitsa Herzen, Moscow, Russia.

OKADA Hiromi, b. 24 Sept 1958, Obihiro, Japan. Pianist. m. Sachiko Sugaya, 20 Oct 1983. Education: Toho Gakuen School of Music, Tokyo; Maria Curcio, London. Debut: Wigmore Hall, 1985. Career: Touring Extensively in Europe, Japan, South Korea; Recitals, Wigmore Hall, 1986, 1987, 1990, 1994, 1995, 1997; Bach Plus Series at St Laurence Jewry in the City, 1991 and Hiromi Okada's Micro Cosmos Series, Tokyo, 1995-; Festivals include Exeter, 1989, Rousse, Bulgaria, 1992, Mayfest, Glasgow, 1992; Appearances as Soloist with The Philharmonia, BBC Concert Orchestra, ECO, RPO, NSO; Numerous Radio and TV Broadcasts. Recordings: Liszt Album; Hammerklavier. Honours: 1st Prize, International Piano Competitions, Barcelona, 1982, Tokyo, 1983, Pretoria, 1984; Chopin Society of Japan Award, 1994. Hobbies: Cats; Wildlife. Current Management: International Artists Management. Address: 46 The Netherlands, Coulsdon, Surrey CR5 1ND, England.

OKADA Yoshiko, b. 5 Oct 1961, Japan. Pianist. m. Grzegorz Cimoszko, 1 son. Education: Ecole Normale de Musique, Paris, 1976-80; Studied in Paris with Yvonne Loriod, 1980-82, in London with Maria Curcio and in Switzerland with Nikita Magaloff. Debut: Carnegie Hall, New York in 1991. Career: Touring in recital and as soloist with orchestras throughout USA, Canada, Poland, Denmark, Belgium, Switzerland and France. Recordings: Japan: CDs of Mozart Sonatas and Concertos with Warsaw Chamber Orchestra. Hobbies: Literature; International Cuisine; Fashion Designing. Current Management: Albert Kay Associates Inc. Address: Albert Kay Associates Inc, Concert Artists Management, 58 West 58th Street, New York, NY 10019-2510, USA.

OKE Alan, b. 1954, London, England. Baritone, since 1992 Tenor Singer. Education: Studied at Royal Academy of Music, Glasgow and in Munich with Hans Hotter, Career: Sang first in concert and in oratorios; Stage debut with Scottish Opera; Roles include: Papageno in Die Zauberflöte, Schaunard in La Bohème, and Olivier in Capriccio; Sang in Cavalli's L'Egisto in Frankfurt, Venice and Schwetzingen, 1983; Covent Garden, 1984 in Taverner by Maxwell Davies; Took part in British premiere of Weill's Street Scene, Glasgow, 1989; Guest appearances with English National Opera and Opera North; Sang Malatesta, in Don Pasquale, Stratford-Upon-Avon, 1990; Sang Macheath in The Threepenny Opera, Leeds, 1990; Season 1992 with Pluto in Orpheus in the Underworld, for Opera North; Tenor roles include Alfredo in La Traviata for Opera North; Gaston in La Traviata for GTO at Glyndebourne, 1996. Recordings include: Giuseppe in The Gondoliers. Address: c/o Opera North, The Grand Theatre, 46 New Briggate, Leeds, Yorkshire, LS1 6NU, England.

OLAFIMIHAN Tinuke, b. 1961, London, England. Soprano. Education: Studied at the Colchester Institute, at Morley College and the National Opera Studio in London; Further study with Elisabeth Schwarzkopf. Debut: Despina at the Elizabeth Hall in 1989 with the National Opera Studio. Career: Has sung Zerlina in Don Giovanni at the Snape Maltings, Messiah with The Sixteen under Harry Christophers and appearances with the Vivaldi Concertante at St John's Smith Square and in the St John Passion at Belfast; Sang Susanna in a production of Figaro by Colin Graham and Barbarina for Opera Northern Ireland and in Aix-en-Provence; Sang Carmina Burana at the Elizabeth Hall in 1990 and Clara in the Covent Garden premiere of Porgy and Bess in 1992. Honours include: Peter Stuyvesant Foundation Scholarship; Walter Legge/Elisabeth Schwarzkopf Society Award; Finalist, 1988 Richard Tauber Competition.

OLAFSSON Kjartan, b. 18 Nov 1958, Reykjavik, Iceland. Composer. 2 daughters. Education: BM, Reykjavic College of Music, 1984; Institute in Sonology, Holland, 1984-86; Licentiate of Music, PhD, Sibelius Academy, 1995. Debut: Reykjavik, 1985. Compositions: Reflex for Orchestra, 1988; Bribraut for Clarinet Trio, 1993; Summary for tape, 1994; Utstrok for Orchestra, 1995. Recordings: Reflex for Orchestra; Utstrok for Orchestra; Bribraut for Clarinet Trio; Dimma for Viola and Piano; Summary for Tape; Dark Days for electronics and live performance. Publications: Calmus Theory Books, 1,2,3,4. Contributions to: CALMUS (Calculated Music). Honours: Prize, Competition for Young Composers; Grants, Ministries of Iceland & Finland. Membership: Society of Composers in Iceland. Address: PO Box 03352, IS-123 Reykjavik, Iceland.

OLAH Tiberiu, b. 2 Jan 1928, Arpasel, Transylvania, Romania. Composer. m. Yvonne Olah, 28 Mar 1959. Education: Academia de Musica, Cluj, 1946-49; Tchaikovsky Conservatory, Moscow, 1949-54; Composition Diploma, magna cum laude. Debut: Trio, Cluj, 1955. Career: Performance of Cantata for Female Choir and Ensemble at Prague in 1962, Warsaw and Budapest in 1963, Warsaw in 1966, West Berlin STB Orchestra in 1967, Darmstadter Ferienkurse in 1968; Performance of Columna by Infinita Orchestra; World's first performance and commissioned works: West Berlin, 1971, Perspectives, Paris, 1971, Ed Salabert's ORTF Orchestra, Translations for 16 Strings, New York Lincoln Center, Washington Kennedy Center, 1974; Time Of Memory to the memory of N and S Koussevitsky, Berlin Festwochen, 1988; Concerto Delle Coppie; Bucharest: The International Week of New Music, 1991; Obelisque For Wolfgang Amadeus for Saxophone and Orchestra, Karlsruhe, Germany, 1992; Concertante commissioned by Land Baden, Wurttemberg. Recordings: Numerous. Publications: Editor: Muzicale, Bucharest, Salabert, Paris, Schott, Germany, Muzyka, Moscow. Hobby: Travel. Address: Bulevard Dacia 11, 70185 Bucharest, Romania.

OLCZAK Krzysztof (Robert), b. 26 May 1956, Lodz, Poland. Composer; Solo Concert Accordionist. m. 21 Jun 1980, 1 son, 1 daughter. Education: Diploma in Accordion, Fr Chopin Academy of Music, Warsaw, 1979; Diploma, honourable mention, Composition, Academy of Music, Gdansk, 1986. Career: Solo and chamber concerts in Poland from 1978; Played with National Philharmonic, 1985, 1986 and Bialystok, Gdansk, Koszalin, Lodz, Opole, Poznan, Wroclaw, Austria, Finland, Germany, Italy, Norway, Sweden and Russian Philharmonic Orchestras; Appearances at contemporary music festivals include Styrian Autumn, Austria, Warsaw Autumn, Poznan Spring, Gdansk Encounters of Young Composers; Conservatorium Legnica, 1987, 1991, Musik Biennale, Berlin in 1987, Musica Polonica Nova, Wroclaw in 1988, and Internationale Studienwoche, Bonn in 1991; Tour of Scandinavia with American Waterways Wind Orchestra in 1990; Currently Lecturer at Gdansk Academy of Music. Compositions include: Accordion Solos: Manualiter, 1977, Phantasmagorien, 1978, Winter Suite, 1980, Fine Pluie, 1980, Berceuse, 1984, Rondino, 1985, Pozymk for 4 performers, 1982, Sea Spaces for Soprano and Prepared Piano, 1982, Cantata for Soprano, 2 Accordions, 1984, Sinfonietta Concertante for Percussion and Orchestra, 1985-86, Belt The Bellow for Tuba and Accordion, 1986, Trio, Hommage to Karol Szymanowski, 1987, Intervals for Organ and 2 Accordions, 1987, Concerto for Accordion and Orchestra, 1989, Concerto Grosso for Wind Orchestra, 1990. Hobby: Tennis. Address: 11 Listopada 79, 80-180 Gdansk, Poland.

OLDFIELD Mark, b. 1957, Sheffield, England. Baritone. Education:Studied at School of Music, Colchester with Rae Woodland and at Royal College of Music; Further study with Kenneth Woollam. Career: Operatic work has included Metcalf's Tornrak at Banff Centre in Canada, and Papageno for London Opera Players; London International Opera Festival in 1989 in The Fisherman by Paul Max Edlin; Sang Purcell's Aeneas and Eugene Onegin at the Royal College of Music; Concert repertoire includes the Brahms Requiem, Snape Maltings, Bach's Magnificat, Las Palmas and Cantata No 11, Handel's Chandos Anthems with the English Chamber Orchestra under Charles Mackerras, Vaughan Williams's Five Mystical Songs, Carmina Burana, Monteverdi Madrigals and the Brahms Liebeslieder in Northern Italy; Sang Mercurio in Cavalli's La Calisto in Provence; Eiriksdottir's I Have Seen Someone at the Riverside Studios, London, 1996. Address: c/o Anglo Swiss Ltd, Suites 35-37, Morley House, 320 Regent Street, London W1R 5AD, England.

OLDHAM Arthur, b. 6 Sept 1926, London, England. Composer; ChorusMaster. 2 sons, 2 daughters. Education: Royal College of Music; Private pupil of Benjamin Britten, 8 years. Debut: Mercury Theatre, London, 1946. Career: Conductor, Ballet Rambert, 1946-47; Director of Music, St Mary's Catholic Cathedral, Edinburgh, 1956; Chorus Master, Scottish Opera; Chorus Master, Edinburgh Festival Chorus, 1965-94; Chorus Master, London Symphony Orchestra Chorus; Chorus Master, Concertgebouw Orchestra; Chorus Master, Orchestre de Paris. Compositions: Opera: Love in a Village; Song cycles: Five Chinese Lyrics, The Commandment of Love, Choral and orchestral; Psalms in Time of War (premiered at Edinburgh Festival, 1977); Le Testament de Villon, for 3 soloists, chamber choir, full chorus and full orchestra, 1997. Recordings: Major portion of choral and operatic repertoire. Honours: Officier de l'Ordre des Arts et des Lettres, France, 1986; 3 Grammy Awards; OBE, 1989. Membership: Incorporated Society of Musicians. Hobbies: Gardening; Golf. Address: Fontaine Melon, 58230 Gouloux, France.

OLDING Dene Maxwell, b. 11 Oct 1956, Melbourne, Australia. Violinist. m. Irina Morozova, 10 Dec 1987, 1 son. Education: Juilliard School, New York. Debut: Wigmore Hall, 1984. Appointments: Over 40 Concerto Works with Orchestras in Australia, New Zealand, USA. Recordings: Concertos by Barber, Martin, Hindemith, Milhaud; Complete Quartets of Sculthorpe; Numerous CD's with Australia Ensemble and Sonata CD. Contributions to: Strad Magazine. Honours: Laureate, Queen Elisabeth of Belgium International Violin Competition, 1985; Winston Churchill Memorial Fellowship, 1985. Current Management: Arts Management. Address: 63 Probert Street, Newtown 2042, Australia.

OLEDZKI Bogdan, b. 25 June 1949, Stupsk, Poland. Conductor. m. Ewa Glowacka, 12 Aug 1981. Education: Warsaw Music Academy, 1974. Debut: National Philharmonic Orchestra, Warsaw in 1974. Career: Conductor in Warsaw, Radom and Poznan, 1974-82; Principal Conductor for Rzeszow Philharmonic Orchestra, 1982-84; Conductor for Great Opera, Warsaw, 1984-; Guest Conductor with Philharmonic Orchestra, Poland and Salzburg-Aspecte, Edinburgh and Skopje Festivals. Current Management: Polish Artistic Agency (PAGART), Warsaw, Poland. Address: Bandrowskiego 8 m 60, 01-496 Warszawa, Poland.

OLEFSKY Paul, b. 4 Jan 1926, Chicago, IL, USA. Cellist; Teacher. Education: Studied at Curtis Institute with Gregor Piatigorsky, 1943-47, with Pablo Casals and with Karajan and Monteux (conducting). Career: Former First Cellist of Philadelphia Orchestra and Detroit Symphony Orchestra; Concert soloist with leading orchestras in USA and abroad; Recitalist in North America and Europe with solo works by Kodaly and Bach and the premieres of works by Milhaud, Tcherepnin, Virgil Thomson and Shapleigh; Professor of Cello and Chamber Music at University of Texas, Austin, 1974-. Recordings: Solo recordings with the English Chamber Orchestra as cellist and conductor. Honours: Naumberg Award, 1948; Michaels Memorial Award of the Young Concert Artists, 1953. Address: University of Texas, Department of Music, Austin, TX 78712, USA.

OLEG Raphael, b. 8 Sept 1959, Paris, France. Concert Violinist. Education: Paris Conservatoire from 1972 with first prizes for violin and chamber music, 1976. Career: International reputation as recitalist and with Europe's major symphony orchestras; Lucern Festival in 1986 with the Czech Philharmonic and Vaclav Neumann; First Prize in Tchaikovsky International Competition in 1986; British debut in 1987 playing the Brahms Concerto with the London Symphony Orchestra under Jeffrey Tate; 1987 tour of European Festivals with the Orchestre National de France and Lorin Maazel; Engagements with the Concertgebouw under Chailly, Orchestre de Paris under Bychov, the Philadelphia Orchestra under Maazel and the Munich Staatsorchester under Sawallisch; UK appearances with the Philharmonia, English Chamber Orchestra, Northern Sinfonia, Scottish Chamber Orchestra and City of London Sinfonia; Japanese debut in 1989 at Suntory Hall; Engagements in 1989-90 season included a tour of Italy with ECO and Tate, and a tour of France and Switzerland with the Academy of St Martin-in-The-Fields and Marriner; Gave recitals at Prague Spring Festival and Paris, concerts with the Orchestre National de France, and Polish Chamber Orchestra; 1990-91 toured Germany with Chamber Orchestra of Europe and Berglund, and Japan with the Nouvel Orchestre Philharmonique. Address: Van Walsum Management Ltd, 4 Addison Bridge Place, London W14 8XP, England.

OLEJNICEK Jiri, b. 11 Feb 1937, Brno, Czechoslovakia. Tenor. Education: Studied at the Brno Conservatory from 1954. Career: Sang at Opava Opera from 1962, and Janácek Opera in Brno from 1964; Roles have included Tamino, Alvaro, Rodolfo, the Prince in Rusalka, Stahlav in Smetana's Libuse and Dmitri in Boris Godunov; Guest appearances in Florence in 1967 and Barcelona as Lensky in 1976; Frequent concert engagements. Address: c/o Janácek Opera, Dvorákova 11, 657-70 Brno, Czech Republic.

OLESCH Peter Otto, b. 10 Sep 1938, Andreashutte, Oberschlesien, Germany. Bass-Baritone. Education: Studied in Dresden with Rudolf Bockelmann. Debut: Berlin Staatsoper in 1963 as a Flemish Deputy in Don Carlos. Career: Sang at the Berlin Staatsoper until 1982 in such roles as Masetto, Monterone, Bartolo, Pistol, Falstaff, Alberich, Alfio in Cavalleria Rusticana, Vaarlam and Rangier in Penderecki's The Devils of Loudun; Sang at Leipzig Opera in 1989 as Don Pasquale; Many concert performances. Recording: Puntila by Dessau. Address: c/o Städtische Theater, 7010 Leipzig, Germany.

OLIVEIRA Elmar, b. 28 Jun 1950, Waterbury, CT, USA. Violinist. Education: Hart College of Music, Hartford, CT; Manhattan School of Music. Career: Appearances with orchestras including New York Philharmonic, Cleveland, Baltimore, Chicago Symphony, Dallas, Montreal and Moscow Philharmonic. Recordings include: Sonata by Husa. Honours: First Prize, Naumberg Competition, 1975; Gold Medal, Tchaikovsky International Competition, 1978. Hobbies: Antiques; Art; Collecting String Instruments; Pool; Billiards.

OLIVER Alexander, b. 27 Jun 1944, Scotland. Tenor. Education: Royal Scottish Academy; Further studies in Vienna and with Rupert Bruce-Lockhart. Career: Netherlands Opera from 1971 in The Love For Three Oranges, Intermezzo, Peter Grimes, L'Ormindo and The Turn of the Screw; Scottish Opera in A Midsummer Night's Dream, Wozzeck, The Bartered Bride, Eugene Onegin and Mahagonny; Opera North as Nemorino in L'Elisir d'Amore; Glyndebourne Opera in Il Ritorno d'Ulisse, Ariadne auf Naxos and Albert Herring in 1985; Covent Garden in Eugene Onegin, Le nozze di Figaro, Andrea Chénier, Manon and Albert Herring, 1989; Zurich Opera from 1978 in L'Incoronazione di Poppea and Les Contes d'Hoffmann; Brussels Opera in 1982 as Arbace in Idomeneo, returning for the world premiere of Le Passion de Gilles by Boesmans; Antwerp Opera and Canadian Opera debuts in 1983 in Death in Venice and Poppea; La Fenice Venice in Curlew River, La Scala Milan in the premiere of Riccardo III by Flavio Testi and sang Mime in a new production of Siegfried at Covent Garden in 1990; Sang Shapkin in From the House of the Dead at Brussels in 1990, and at Salzburg in 1991 in Le nozze di Figaro; Sang Schmidt in Werther for Netherlands Opera, 1996; Concert engagements with the Concertgebouw Orchestra in the St John and St Matthew Passions of Bach and Stravinsky's Pulcinella; Houston Symphony and Chicago Symphony and frequent appearances with the Songmakers' Almanac. Recordings include: Videos of Gilbert and Sullivan's The Sorcerer and Pirates of Penzance. Address: c/o Harrison Parrott Ltd, 12 Penzance Place, London, W11 4PA, England.

OLIVER John (Edward), b. 21 Sept 1959, Vancouver, Canada. Composer. Education: MMus, 1984, DMus, 1992, Composition, McGill University, Montreal; BMus Composition, University of British Columbia; Studies: Composition, Guitar, Piano, Voice, San Francisco Conservatory of Music, 1977-79. Career: Works performed by: New Music Concerto, Toronto 1982, 87, Vancouver New Music, 1982, 1990, Societé de Musique Contemporaine de Quebec, 1989, Canadian Opera Company, 1991; Composer-in-Residence, Banff Centre, Leighton Artist Colony, 1989, 1990 and Music Department, 1990, 1991, Canadian Opera Company, 1989, 1991, Vancouver Opera, 1992-. Compositions: Gugcamayo's Old Song and Dance, Canadian Opera Company, 1991; El Reposo del Fuego, 1987; Aller Retour, 1988; Marimba Dismembered, 1990; Before the Freeze, 1984. Recordings: El Reposo del Fuego; Marimba Dismembered; Before the Freeze. Publication: New Music in British Columbia in Soundnotes, Fall, 1992. Honours: Canada COuncil Arts Awards, 1984-87, 1991; 8th CBC National Radio Competition for Young Composers, 1988; Two prizes, 1989 PROCAN Young Composers Competition. Memberships: Society of Composers, Authors and Music Publishers of Canada; American Federation of Musicians; Canadian Electroacoustic Community. Hobbies: Reading; Skiing; Hiking; Dining.

OLIVER Lisi, b. 13 Dec 1951, Frankfurt am Main, Germany. Stage Director; Translator. Education: BA, Smith College, 1973; ALM Harvard University, 1988; PhD in Linguistics, 1995. Career: Stage Manager, Bolshoi Opera US Tour, 1974; Inaugural Gala for President Carter, 1978; Production Stage Manager, Assistant Director, Opera Company of Boston, 1975-78; Assistant Director, Komische Oper Berlin, 1979-80; Director, Opera Company of Boston, Opera New England, Skylight Comic Opera, Des Moines Metro Opera, Atlanta Opera, Baldwin-Wallace Conservatory, Opera Company of the Philippines, Massachusetts Institute of Technology, Wolftrap Farm Park, City of Boston First Night, 1980-90; Director of Opera Studio, New England Conservatory, 1988-90; First projected titles at Bolshoi Opera, 1991; Director, Atlanta Opera Studio, 1989; Title Supervisor, Atlanta Opera, Boston Lyric Opera; Director of Raymond Street Translations, Titles Rental Company; Professor of Mediaeval Studies and Linguistics, Louisiana State University. Publications: Translations of Surtitles used by many American Companies. Honours: Yvonne Burger Award, Smith College, 1973; Merit Award, Komische Oper, 1980; National Opera Institute Grant, 1978-80; Whiting Fellowship, Harvard University, 1994-95. Hobbies: Linguistic Research; Golf; Tennis; Sailing. Address: 2021 Cedardale Avenue, Baton Rouge, LA 70808, USA.

OLIVERO Alberto, b. 8 Oct 1952, Turin, Italy. Composer; Music Teacher. Education: Diploma, Vocal Composition, Conservatory of Music of Milan, 1977; Specialisation courses in Medieval Musicology, 1981. Debut: 1973. Career: Medieval Harp and Recorder Player with early music consorts: Studio di Musica Antica, 1973-77, Ars Antiqua, 1978-, Lyocorne Early Music Consort, 1980-; Teacher of Choral Practice and Music Theory. Compositions: Chromophonie for Solo Recorder; Scharade for 3 Recorders; Kryptographie for Recorder and Harpsichord; Song For Faith for Soprano and Guitar; Madrugada for Tenor and Piano; Vide-Runt Omnes for 3 Choirs and 3 Mixed Instrumental Groups. Recording: Medioevo and Rinascimento, with Lyocorne Early Music Consort. Publications: Carissimi - Judicium Salomonis Revision, 1986; Anon Sec XII - Ordo ad Representandum Herodem, Transcription; Anon Sec XIII - Laude Del Cod Magh 11.1.122 and Cortona 91, 1985. Contributions to: Concert programmes for Settembre Musica, Festival di Aosta, Accademia Stefano Tempia and many other concert societies. Memberships: American Musicological Society; Società Italiana di Musicologia; Internationale Musikwissenschaftsgesellschaft; Sociedad Espanola de Musicologia. Address: Via Meucci 2, 10121 Torino, Italy.

OLIVERO Magda, b. 25 Mar 1912, Saluzzo, Turin, Italy. Soprano. Education: Studied in Turin with Luigi Gerussi, Luigi Ricci and Ghedini. Debut: Turin in 1933 as Lauretta in Gianni Schicchi. Career: La Scala in 1933 in Nabucco; Sang widely in Italy as Adriana Lecouvreur, Puccini's Liu, Suor Angelica and Minnie, Violetta, Zerlina, Poppea and Sophie in Der Rosenkavalier; Retired in 1941 but returned to stage in 1951 to sing Adriana at the composer's request; Sang at Stoll Theatre in London as Mimi in 1952 with further appearances in Edinburgh, Paris, Brussels, Amsterdam and Buenos Aires; Other roles included Fedora, Mascagni's Iris, Zandonai's Francesca, Puccini's Giorgetta and Tosca and parts in operas by Poulenc and Menotti; US debut at Dallas in 1967 as Médée, Metropolitan Opera in 1975 as Tosca. Recordings: Turandot; Fedora; Francesca da Rimini; La Fanciulla del West; Il Tabarro; Risurrezione by Alfano; Médée; Madama Butterfly.

OLIVEROS Pauline, b. 30 May 1932, Houston, TX, USA. Composer; Performer. Education: BA, San Francisco State College, 1957. Career: Director, San Francisco Tape Music Center, 1966, Expo '67 Montreal, Canada, 1967, and Expo '70 Osaka, Japan, 1970; Professor of Music, University of California, San Diego, 1970; Summer Olympics, Los Angeles, 1984; Works performed and solo performances worldwide and with numerous orchestras. Compositions: Roots For The Moment; Tara's Room; The Well And The Gentle; Tashi Gomang; Rose Moon; Sonic Meditations; Horse Sings From Cloud; Rattlesnake Mountain; Lullaby For Daisy Pauline; Spiral Madala; Bonn Feier; Double Basses At 20 Paces; 3 Songs for Soprano and Piano; To Valerie Solanas and Marilyn Monroe; Jar Piece; Sound Patterns. Recordings: The Well And The Gentle; The Wanderer; Accordion And Voice; Vor Der Flüt. Publication: Software for People, 1984. Contributions to: Numerous. Honours: Foundation Gaudeamus Prize, 1962; Guggenheim Award, 1973; Beethoven Prize, Bonn, Germany, 1977; Pauline Oliveros Day and 30 Year Retrospective, Houston, TX, 1983; Retrospective at JF Kennedy Center for Performing Arts, Washington DC, 1985; Honorary DMA, University of Maryland, 1986. Memberships: Founding Director, Pauline Oliveros Foundation; Board of Directors, American Music Center; Founding Co-Director, Good Sound Foundation; Board of Governors, New York Foundation for Arts. Current Management: Stidfole and Pratt Associates. Address: c/o ASCAP, ASCAP Building, One Lincoln Plaza, New York, NY 10023, USA.

OLLESON (Donald) Edward, b. 11 Apr 1937, South Shields, England. University Lecturer; Writer on Music. m. Eileen Gotto, 2 sons, 1 daughter. Education: BA, Hertford College, Oxford, 1959; MA, 1963; DPhil, 1967. Career: Assistant Lecturer, Hull University, 1962-63; Research Lecturer, Christ Church, Oxford, 1963-66; Faculty Lecturer, Oxford University, 1966-72; Fellow, Merton College, 1970-; University Lecturer in Music, 1972-. Publications: Editor, Proceedings of The Royal Musical Association, volumes 94-100; Essays, with Nigel Fortune and FW Sternfeld, on Opera and English Music in honour of Sir Jack Westrup, 1975; Participation in Everyman Dictionary of Music, 5th edition, 1975; Modern Musical Scholarship, 1978; Co-editor, Music and Letters, 1976-86. Hobbies: Gardening; Cooking. Address: Faculty of Music, St Aldate's, Oxford, OX1 1DB, England.

OLLI Kalevi, b. 1951, Finland. Bass-Baritone Singer. Education: Studied at the Sibelius Academy in Helsinki. Career: Sang Silvano in Un Ballo in Maschera at Helsinki in 1977 and sang at the Frankfurt Opera, 1978-84; Appearances at the Savonlinna Festival as the Dutchman and concert engagements, including Lieder recitals, in Germany, Switzerland and elsewhere. Honours include: Prizewinner in competitions at Savonlinna, Lappeenranta and Geneva, 1977-81. Address: Finnish Opera, PL 176, SF-00251 Helsinki, Finland.

OLLMANN Kurt, b. 19 Jan 1957, Racine, WI, USA. Baritone. Education: Studied with Gerard Souzay, among others. Career: Sang with the Milwaukee Skylight Opera, 1979-82; Engagements in Santa Fe, Washington DC, Milan and Brussels in operas by Debussy and Mozart; Pepsico Summerfare New York in 1987 as Don Giovanni, in the Peter Sellars version of Mozart's opera; Sang under Bernstein in the Viennese premiere of A Quiet Place in 1986 and as Maximilian in a concert performance of Candide at the Barbican in London, 1989; Seattle Opera in 1988 as Mercutio in Gounod's Roméo et Juliette; St Louis Opera, 1989-90, as Purcell's King Arthur and Mozart's Count; Many concert appearances; Season 1992 in On The Town at the Barbican Hall and the title role in the US premiere of Bôse's The Sorrows of Young Werther at Santa Fe. Recordings: Count Paris in Roméo et Juliette, conducted by Michel Plasson; Candide and West Side Story conducted by the composer; Mercutio in Roméo et Juliette, under Leonard Slatkin, 1996. Address: Opera Theater of St Louis, PO Box 13148, St Louis, MO 63119, USA.

OLMI Paolo, b. 1953, Italy. Conductor. Education: Studied with Massimo Pradella and Franco Ferrara in Rome. Career: Frequent appearances with major orchestras in Italy and abroad from 1979; Opera debut at Teatro Communale di Bologna, 1986; Conducted Rossini's Mosè in Egitto at Rome 1988, later at the Bayerische Staatsoper, Munich; Deutsche Oper am Rhein Dusseldorf with Traviata, Théâtre des Champs Elysées with

Rossini's Guillaume Tell; British debut 1991, with Royal Philharmonic in a concert performance of Nabucco; Bellini's Zaira at Catania, 1990; Concerts of the Schleswig-Holstein Festival, the Philharmonic Berlin, the Frankfurt Alte Oper and the Philharmonie in Munich; English Chamber Orchestra with Rostropovitch as soloist; Appointed Principal Conductor of the RAI Rome 1991; Deutsche Oper Berlin 1992 with La Forza del Destino, tour of Italy with the Royal Philharmonic 1993, Verdi Requiem at the Festival Hall 1994; Engagements with Liverpool Philharmonic in season 1992-93 and conducted Mosè at Covent Garden 1994; Madama Butterfly at Copenhagen, 1996. Address: c/o IMG Artists, Media House, 3 Burlington Lane, London W4 2TH, England.

OLOF Theo, b. 5 May 1924, Bonn, Germany. Violinist. Education: Studied with Oskar Back in Amsterdam. Debut: Amsterdam in 1935. Career: Tours of Europe, the United States and Russia from 1945 as soloist; Leader of the Hague Residentie Orchestra, 1951-71; Duo partnership with Hermann Krebbers included premieres of concertos written for them by Geza Frid, 1952, Henk Badings in 1954 and Hans Kox in 1964; Leader of the Concertgebouw Orchestra, 1974-85; Recitals with pianist, Janine Dacosta, and Gerard van Blerk until 1985 and teacher at the Hague Conservatory; Has given first performances of works by Bruno Maderna and Hans Henkemans. Address: de Lairessestraat 12 B, 1071 PA Amsterdam, Netherlands.

OLSEN Derrick, b. 30 Mar 1923, Berne, Switzerland. Bass-Baritone; Administrator. Education: Studied in Berne, Geneva and Lucerne. Career: Sang at Grand Théâtre Geneva, 1944-69, Basle, 1950-55, with guest engagements at Holland and Schwetzingen Festivals, Buenos Aires, Milan, Berlin Staatsoper, Zurich, Lucerne and Marseilles; Roles included Mozart's Count, Masetto and Alfonso, Pizarro, Rossini's Basilio and Bartolo, Iago, Germont and Melitone, Wagner's Dutchman, Telramund and Klingsor, Jochanaan, Malatesta and Achilles in Penthesilea by Schoeck; Sang at Basle Opera in 1952 and 1958 in the premieres of Leonore by Liebermann and Titus Feuerfuchs by Sutermeister; Concert premieres of oratorios by Honegger, Cantate de Noel, 1953, Kelterborn and Frank Martin, Mystère de la Nativité, 1958 and Martinu, Gilgamesh, 1958; Sang in the British premiere of Schoenberg's Von Heute auf Morgen, Festivall Hall, 1963; Member of the Quatuor Vocale de Geneve and Artistic Director of the Radio Orchestra Beromunster at Zurich, 1958-70. Recordings: Pelléas et Mélisande; Monteverdi's Combattimento; Sutermeister's Schwarze Spinne; Martin's Le Vin Herbé; Handel's Apollo e Dafne. Address: c/o Opernhaus Zurich, Falkenstrasse 1, CH-8008 Zurich, Switzerland.

OLSEN Frode, b. 10 Apr 1952, Oslo, Norway. Bass Singer. Education: Studied at Opera State Conservatory in Oslo and Düsseldorf. Debut: Düsseldorf, 1982. Career: Sang at Deutsche Oper am Rhein Düsseldorf, 1982-86, notably as Mozart's Masetto and Don Alfonso; Badisches Staatstheater Karlsruhe from 1986, as Sarastro, Pimen, Gremin, Zaccaria, Wagner's Pogner, King Mark and Landgrave, Orestes and Basilio; Guest engagements at: Dresden, Leipzig, Strasbourg, Dortmund, Berne, Vienna, Volksoper, Oslo; Fasolt, in The Ring at Brussels, 1991; Salzburg Festival debut 1992, as a Soldier in Salome; Further appearances as: Sarastro at Brussels, 1992, King Ludwig, in Euryanthe at Music Festival in Aix-en-Provence, 1993, Doctor, in Wozzeck at Frankfurt, Gremin, in Eugene Onegin at the reopened Glyndebourne Opera House, 1994; Other roles include: Raimondo, the Commendatore in Don Giovanni, Colline, Timur, Elmiro in Rossini's Otello; Concert repertoire includes: Verdi's Requiem, Rossini's Petite Messe Solennelle, Stabat Mater, Messiah, Bach's Christmas Oratorio, St Matthew Passion, Elijah, Die Schöpfung; Melchtal in Guillaume Tell in Pesaro-Rossini Festival, 1995; Sang Gurnemanz, in Parsifal for first time, Rouen, France; For 1996 at Glyndebourne, Valens in Handel's Theodora, and Gremin in Onegin. Address: c/o Athole Still International Management Ltd, Foresters Hall, 25-27 Westow Street, London, SE19 3RY, England.

OLSEN Keith, b. 1957, Denver, CO, USA. Tenor. Education: BM, San Francisco Conservatory; MM, University of Tennessee and professional study at the the Juilliard School of Music. Debut: US: New York City Opera, 1982, in Die Lustige Witwe; European: Staatstheater Karlsruhe as Rodolfo in 1987. Career: Sang at San Francisco as Capriccio, Helsinki, Los Angeles, Barcelona as Alfredo, Pretoria as Hoffmann and as Rodolfo in Hamburg, London, Arena di Verona, Frankfurt, Dusseldorf, Wiesbaden, Hannover and Toronto, with Manrico in Berlin and Leipzig, Hans in Stuttgart and MacDuff in Bologna; Other guest appearances include Radames in Rome and Radio France with Dick Johnson, Turiddu and Hoffmann in Bonn; Film credits include Puccini's Des Grieux, 100th anniversary performance, RAI, Turiddu, South African Broadcasting Corporation and Beethoven's Ninth Symphony with Kurt Masur, Mittel Deutsche Rundfunk; Has sung for three years at the Royal Opera House Covent Garden, with debut as Rodolfo and subsequently as Pinkerton and Boris in Katya Kabanova; (Boris, 1997). Recording: Giuliano in Handel's Rodrigo. Address: c/o San Francisco Opera, War Memorial Opera House, San Francisco, CA 94102, USA.

OLSEN Stanford, b. 1959, Salt Lake City, Utah, USA. Singer (Tenor). Education: Studied with the Metropolitan Opera Development Program. Career: For the Metropolitan Opera in New York has sung Arturo in Puritani, Don Ottavio, Ferrando, Belmonte, Idreno (Semiramide), Count Almaviva, Ernesto and Fenton; European career includes Don Ottavio at the Deutsche Oper Berlin, Rossini's Comte Ory for Netherlands Opera and Belmonte under John Eliot Gardiner; Concert at the Mostly Mozart Festival New York, in Boston and elsewhere for the Handel and Haydn Society (Messiah and The Creation), for the Berlin Philharmonic (Berlioz Requiem, 1989) and at the Salzburg Festival with the International Bach Academy; New York recital debut at Alice Tully Hall 1990, with Die schöne Müllerin; Season 1993-94 at the Ravinia Festival in Fidelio, with the Houston Symphony in Britten's War Requiem and a tour of Spain with Messiah, conducted by Helmuth Rilling; Sang Iopas in Les Troyens at La Scala, 1996. Address: c/o Atholl Still Ltd, Foresters Hall, 25-27 Westow Street, London SE19 3RY, England.

OLVIS William, b. 12 Feb 1928, Hollywood, USA. Tenor; Baritone. Career: Sang at Boston in 1956 in the premiere of Bernstein's Candide; Sang at New York City Opera from 1957, and Metropolitan Opera from 1958; Roles have included Steuermann, Narraboth, Ismaele, Radames, Don José and Pinkerton; Sang at Deutsche Oper am Rhein, Dusseldorf, 1963-66; Has sung widely in Germany as Gabriele Adorno, Calaf, Cavaradossi, Bacchus and the Emperor in Die Frau ohne Schatten; Sang at Bayreuth Festival in 1965 as Froh and Erik; Baritone roles at Gelsenkirchen, 1971-74 and sang Jupiter in Monteverdi's Ulisse with Long Beach Opera in 1988. Recordings include: Judas Maccabeus, Handel Society. Address: c/o Long Beach Opera, 6372 Pacific Coast Highway, Long Beach, CA 90801, USA.

OMACHI Yoichiro, b. 22 Aug 1931, Tokyo, Japan. Conductor. Education: Studied at Tokyo Academy of Music, 1948-54, with Akeo Watanabe and Kurt Woss; Academy of Music, Vienna with Karl Bohm, Franco Ferrara, and Herbert von Karajan. Career: Toured Japan in 1957 with Karajan and the Berlin Philharmonic; Guest conductor with the Berlin Philharmonic, Tonkunstler Orchestra, Vienna, 1959; Chief Conductor, Tokyo Philharmonic Orchestra, 1961; Founded Tokyo Metropolitan Symphony, 1964; Guest conductor with Vienna Symphony Orchestra, 1964-67; Permanent Conductor of the Dortmund Opera, 1968-73; East Asian tour with the Tokyo Philharmonic, 1973; Season 1976-77 conducted Aida at Mannheim, Fidelio in Prague, Madama Butterfly at the Berlin Staatsoper and The Merry Widow in Tokyo; Concerts in Japan, South America, 1978-79; Madama Butterfly at the Vienna Staatsoper in 1980, Permanent Conductor, 1982-84, including Attila on Austrian TV and ballet performances; Professor in Opera Faculty at the Tokyo Academy of Music. Recordings: Various with the Tokyo Philharmonic.

OMAN Julia Trevelyan, b. 11 July 1930, London, England. Stage Designer. Education: Studied at Royal College of Art with Hugh Casson. Career: Television Designer with the BBC 1955-67; Royal Opera House, Covent Garden with designs for Eugene Onegin 1971, La Bohème 1974 and Die Fledermaus 1977; Hamburg Staatsoper 1973 in Un Ballo in Maschera, Royal Opera Stockholm 1982, Otello, The Consul for Connecticut Opera 1985; Designed Arabella at Glyndebourne 1984. Honours: Royal Designer for Industry, 1977; CBE, 1986. Address: c/o Royal Opera House, Covent Garden, London WC2, England.

OMBUENA Vicente, b. 1949, Valencia, Spain. Tenor. Education: Studied in Valencia. Career: Sang at first in concert then with Mainz Opera, 1989-91 as Don José, Erik, Cassio and Lysander in A Midsummer Night's Dream; Sang at Hamburg Staatsoper from 1991 notably as Ernesto in Don Pasquale. Recordings include: Franchetti's Cristofor Colombo. Address: Staatsoper Hamburg, Grosse Theaterstrasse 34, Pf 302448, W-2000 Hamburg 36, Germany.

OMILIAN Jolanta, b. 1956, Warsaw, Poland. Soprano. Education: Studied at the Chopin Academy in Warsaw. Debut: Venice in 1979 as Violetta. Career: Sang widely in Germany including Bonn and Dortmund and at the 1985 Macerata Festival as Elisabetta in Roberto Devereux; Sang in Maria Stuarda at Palermo in 1989, Donizetti's Parisina at Basle in 1990 and Norma at Rio de Janeiro; Other roles include Dorabella and Leonora in Trovatore, Amenaide in Tancredi, Fiorilla in Il Turco in Italia, and Anaide in Mosè in Egitto. Recordings include: Adriano in Siria by Pergolesi; Il Bravo by Mercadante. Address: Montpellier Opéra, 11 Boulevard Victor Hugo, F-34000 Montpellier, France.

ONAY Gülsin, b. 1954, Istanbul, Turkey. Concert Pianist. Education: Studied at the Paris Conservatoire with Pierre Sancan and Nadia Boulanger and with Monique Haas and Bernhard Ebert. Career: Solo appearnaces with the Berlin Radio Symphony Orchestra, Austrian, Bavarian and North German Radio orchestras; Copenhagen Symphony, Staatskapelle Dresden, Mozarteum Orchestra Salzburg and the Tokyo Symphony; Repeated tours of west and east Europe, the Far East, in particular Japan; International Festival appearances: Steirischer Herbst, Warsaw autumn, Berliner Festtage, Mozartfest Würzburg, Istanbul Festival, Schleswig-Holstein Festival; Repertoire includes all the concertos of Beethoven, Brahms, Chopin, Liszt, Grieg, Schumann and Rachmaninov and A A Saygun; Mozart K414, K466, K467, K488, K491, K503 and K595 and for 2 pianos and orchestra; Saint-Saëns 2, Tchaikovsky 1, Bartok 2 and 3, Prokofiev 1 and 3, Ravel and Weber F minor; Dvorak piano concerto, de Falla (Nights in Gardens of Spain). Recordings include: Solos by Franck, Schubert (Harmonia Mundi); Chopin, Debussy, Ravel (KLAVINS); Bartok. Address: Schlossgasse 20, 79112 Freiburg, Germany.

ONCINA Juan, b. 15 Apr 1925, Barcelona, Spain. Singer (Tenor). Education: Studied in Oran, Barcelona with Mercedes Caspir and in Milan with Augusta Oltrabella. Debut: Barcelona 1946, as Des Grieux in Manon. Career: Sang opposite Tito Gobbi in Il Barbiere di Siviglia at Barcelona; Paris 1949 in Il Matrimonio Segreto; Florence 1949-50, in Cherubini's Osteria Portoghese and Lully's Armide; Glyndebourne 1952-65, as Don Ramiro in Cenerentola, Ferrando, Comte Ory, Scaramuccio in Ariadne auf Naxos, Rossini's Almaviva, Fenton in Falstaff, Don Ottavio, Lindoro in L'Italiana in Algeri and in Anna Bolena; Palermo 1959, in Belini's Beatrice di Tenda; Verdi and Puccini roles from 1963; Guest appearances in Monte Carlo, Venice, Triste and Florence; Vienna Staatsoper 1965; Hamburg 1971-74. Recordings: Le Comte Ory and La Cenerentola from Glyndebourne (HMV); Don Pasquale (Decca); L'Arlesiana by Cilea; Un Giorno di Regno by Verdi; Donizetti's Roberto Devereux; Sacchini's Oedipe a Colonne. Address: c/o Hamburgische Staatsoper, Gross-Theaterstrasse 34, D-2000 Hamburg 36, Germany.

OPALACH Jan, b. 2 Sept 1950, Hackensack, New Jersey, USA. Singer (Bass-Baritone). Education: Studied at Indiana State University. Career: Sang at various regional USA operatic centres, New York City Opera from 1980 as Bartolo, Papageno, Schaunard, Kingfisher (Midsummer Marriage) and Leporello; Caramoor Festival, 1980, as Viltotta in the USA premiere of Haydn's La Vera Costanza; St Louis 1986 in USA premiere of Rossini's Il Viaggio a Reims; Sang at Seattle Opera, 1991-92, as the Music Master in Ariadne auf Naxos and Guglielmo in Cosi fan tutte; New York City Opera, 1991 as the Forester in The Cunning Little Vixen, Mozart's Figaro at Toronto; Sang in Rossini Gala Opera at New York's Fisher Hall, 29 February 1992; New York Premiere, A Zimmerman's Die Soldaten, Wesener, NYCO, 1992; New York Premiere, Tippetts' Midsummer Marriage, King Fisher, 1993; World Premiere, Glass's The Voyage, Metropolitan Opera, 1992; American Premiere, Schnittke's Faust Cantata, American Symphony Orchestra with Botstein; Rossini's Italiana in Algeri, Taddeo, Netherlands Opera. Recordings: Solo Bach Cantatas and Bach Ensemble; 2 world premiere recordings R Beaser's Seven Deadly Sins, D Russell, American Composers' Orchestra (ARGO); Syringa, Elliott Carter; Speculum Musicae (Bridge). Honours: NEA Recital Grant, 1986; W M Naumburg Vocalist Award, 1989; Metropolitan Opera Nationals Award; Hertogenbosch Vocalisten Concours, 1981. Current Management: Janice Mayer and Associates. Address: 201 West 54 Street, Suite 1c, New York, NY 10019, USA.

OPEKAR Ales, b. 31 October 1957, Prague, Czechoslovakia. Musicologist. m. Olga Kovarikova, December 1985, 2 daughters. Education: Philosophic Faculty of the Charles University, Prague; CSc (equivalent of PhD), Branch of Theory and History of Music. Publications include: Eccentrics in Ground Floor, 1989; Encyclopedia of Jazz and Modern Popular Music, 1987, revised, 1990; Analysis of a Rock Album, 1992. Contributions: Towards the History of Czech Rock Music, 1993; Analysis of a Rock Album: Flamengo, Chicken in the Watch, 1993; Big Beat Footsteps, 1996. Memberships: Executive Committee Member, 1993-97, General Secretary, 1995-97, International Association for the Study of Popular Music (IASPM); Association of Musical Artists and Scientists; Union of Authors and Performers (SAI). Address: Institute of Musicology, Puskinovo Nam 9, 1600 Prague 6, Czech Republic.

OPIE Alan, b. 22 Mar 1945, Redruth, Cornwall, England. Singer (Baritone). Education: Guildhall School of Music, London; London Opera Centre with Vera Rosza. Debut: Sadler's Wells Opera 1969, as Papageno in Die Zauberflöte; Appearances with English National Opera, Welsh National Opera, Aldeburgh Festival and Santa Fe Opera; Other roles include Mozart's Guglielmo, Rossini's Figaro, Verdi's Germont, Britten's Demetrius and Charles Blount (Gloriana) and Massenet's Lescaut; Sang Wagner's Beckmesser with English National Opera 1984 and at Bayreuth, 1987, 1988, Berlin, 1990, Munich, 1994; Sang Germont with ENO, 1990 and the title role in Busoni's Doctor Faust; Glyndelbourne Festival 1990, as Sid in Albert Herring; Season 1992 as The Fiddler in Königskinder for ENO, Balstrode in Peter Grimes at Glyndebourne, Melitone in The Force of Destiny and Papageno at the Coliseum; Balstrode at New York Metropolitan,

1994; Pauga in Don Quichotte, Paolo in Munich, 1995; Sang Rossini's Taddeo for ENO, 1997; Balstrode in Peter Grimes at the New York Met, 1998. Recordings include: Maria Stuarda by Donizetti (EMI); The Bear, Rape of Lucretia, Troilus and Cressida, Barber of Seville; Hugh the Drover. Address: c/o Allied Artists Agency, 42 Montpelier Square, London SW17 1JZ, England.

OPPENHEIM David J, b. 13 Apr 1922, Detroit, Michigan, USA. Musician (Clarinettist); University Dean. m. 1) Judy Holiday, 1948, 2) Ellen Adler, 1957, 2 sons, 1 daughter, (3) Patricia Jaffe, 1987. Education: Interlochen National Music Camp, Michigan; Juilliard School of Music, New York, 1939-40; University of Rochester Eastman School of Music, 1940-43. Career: Director, Master Works Division, Columbia Records, 1950-59; Producer, Director, Writer, Network News, CBS Television, 1962-68; Executive Producer, Public Broadcasting Laboratory, 1968-69; Co-Producer of Saul Bellow's Last Analysis, Broadway, New York, 1962; Producer of documentary films on Stravinsky and Casals, CBS; Executive Producer, Cultural Programming, Public Broadcasting Laboratory; Clarinet soloist, Prades, France, 1957, San Juan, Puerto Rico, 1959; Performed under Koussevitsky, Toscanini, Leinsdorf, Steinberg, Bernstein, Stokowski, Stravinsky; Performed chamber music with Casals, Serkin and Casadesus; Tony Awards Nominating Committee, 1983-87; Artist-in-Residence, New Mexico, Music Festival. Recordings: Brahms Clarinet Quintet with Budapest Quartet; Mozart Clarinet Quintet in A Major with Budapest Quartet; L'histoire du Soldât, Octet, Septet, conducted by Stravinsky; Bernstein Sonata, Clarinet and Piano (dedicated to David Oppenheim); Copland Sextet with Juilliard Quartet; Douglas Moore Quintet with New Music Quartet. Hobbies: Mycology; Gardening; Theatre; Literature; Travel. Address: 1225 Park Avenue 6A, New York, NY 10128, USA.

OPPENS Ursula, b. 2 Feb 1944, New York City, USA. Concert Pianist. Education: BA, Radcliffe College, 1965; Juilliard School 1966-69, with Rosina Lhevinne, Guido Agosti and Leonard Shure. Debut: New York, 1969. Career: Performances with Boston Symphony, New York Philharmonic and other leading American orchestras; Recitals at Tully Hall, Kennedy Center; Appearances at Aspen, Berkshire and Marlboro Festivals; Tours of Europe and US as soloist and as member of Speculum Musicae; Performances of contemporary music; Engagements with the Chamber Music Society of Lincoln Center and the Group for Contemporary Music; Conposers who have written for her include Rzeweski, Wolff, Carter and Wuorinen; Teacher at Brooklyn College, City University of New York. Recordings include: Busoni, Mozart and Rzewski. Honours: Winner, Busoni International Piano Competition, 1969; Avery Fisher Prize, 1976. Current Management: Colbert Artists Management, 111 West 57, New York, NY 10019, USA. Address: 777 West End Avenue, New York, NY 10025, USA.

OPRISANU Carmen, b. 1964, Brasov, Romania. Singer (Mezzo-soprano). Education: Studied at the Cluj Music Academy. Career: Sang with the Rumanian Opera at Cluj, 1986-93, and gave concerts with the Bucharest Radio Symphony Orchestra and the Georges Enescu Philharmonic (tours of Italy and Spain); Bucharest State Opera 1993, as Carmen and Rosina; Lucerne State Theatre 1993-96, as Carmen, Suzuki, Isabella in L'Italiana in Algeri, the Composer (Ariadne auf Naxos), Ramiro in La Finta Giardiniera and Adalgisa; Season 1995 as Isabella at the Deutsche Opera Berlin and Sigismondo in the German premiere of Rossini's opera, at Wildbad; Season 1996-97 as Carmen in a co-production of the opera between La Scala and Covent Garden; Charlotte in Werther, Rosina and Maddalena with the Zurich Opera. Honours include: Prize winner at the 1992 Vienna Belvedere Competition and the 1995 Placido Domingo Operalia Competition, in Madrid. Address: c/o Opernhaus Zurich, Falkenstrasse 1, CH-8008 Zurich, Switzerland.

ORAMO Sakari, b. 1966, Helsinki, Finland. Conductor; Violinist. m. Anu Komsi. Education: Studied at the Sibelius Academy and the Utrecht Conservatoire. Career: Founder Member of the Avanti Chamber Orchestra, 1982-89; Violin Leader of the Finnish Radio Symphony Orchestra, 1991 and Co-Principal Conductor from 1994; Further engagements with major Scandinavian Orchestras, City of Birmingham Symphony, BBC Symphony and Philharmonic, London Sinfonietta and Rotterdam Philharmonic; Danish Radio Symphony from 1994, tour of Australia; Principal Conductor for the City of Birmingham Symphony, 1997. Address: Harrison Parrott Ltd, 12 Penzance Place, London W11 4PA, England.

ORBAN Gyorgy, b. 12 July 1947, Tirgu-Mures, Romania. Hungarian Composer. Education: Studied at Cluj Conservatory, 1968-73. Career: Teacher of Theory at Cluj Conservatory until 1979; Moved to Hungary and became Editor of the Editio Musica Budapest; Teacher of Composition at Music-Academy, Budapest. Compositions: Orchestra: Five Canons to Poems by Attile Joszef for soprano and chamber ensemble, 1977; Triple Sextet, 1980; 2 Serenades, 1984, 85; 4 Duos with soprano and clarinet, 1979; Soprano and double bass, 1987; Soprano and Violoncello, 1989; Soprano and Violin, 1992; Sonata Concertante for clarinet and piano, 1987; Wind Quintet, 1984; Brass Music for Quintet No 1, 1987; Sonata for bassoon and piano, 1987; Sonata for violin, 1970; 2 Sonatas for Violin and Piano, 1989, 91; Suite for piano, 1986; 4 Piano Sonatas, 1987, 88, 89; Chorus and Orchestra: Rotate Coeli, oratorio, 1992; Regina Martyrum, oratorio, 1993; Missa No 2, 1990, No 4, 1991, No 6, 1993; Chorus and Chamber Ensemble: Missa No 7, 1993; Flower Songs for Female Choir, 1978; Chorus Book in Memory of S A No 1, 1984; Chorus Book No 2; Book of Medallions, cycle of 9 choruses, 1987; Stabat Mater, 1987; About 40 little latin motets for mixed and female chorus. Address: c/o H-1016 Budapest, Mészáros u. 15-17, Hungary.

ORCIANI Patrizia, b. 1959, Fano, Urbino, Italy. Soprano. Education: Studied at the Bologna Conservatory. Debut: Fano in 1983 as Mimi in La Bohème. Career: Has sung widely in Italy notably as Liu at the 1991 Verona Festival and as Handel's Cleopatra at the Valle d'Istria Festival; Sang at the Bonn Opera, 1991-92; Other roles include Donizetti's Adina and Norina, Rossini's Elvira, Micaela and Giulietta in Les Contes d'Hoffmann. Recordings include: Cimarosa's L'Italiana in Londra; Nina by Paisiello; Il Signor Bruschino. Address: c/o Bonn Opera, Am Boeselagerhof 1, Pf 2440, W-5300 Bonn, Germany.

ORDONEZ Antonio, b. 27 Oct 1948, Madrid, Spain. Singer (Tenor). Education: Studied in Madrid with Miguel Garcia Barrosa. Career: Concert appearances in Spain and USA from 1980; Opera debut at Teatro Zarzuela Madrid 1982, as Pinkerton, Sang Don Carlos at Liège 1986 and at Deutsche Oper Berlin 1988; Teatro Liceo Barcelona 1986, in Paccini's Saffo, with Montserrat Caballé; Further guest appearances as Cavaradossi at Dallas 1987, Calaf at Ravenna Festival 1988 and as Alvaro in La Forza del Destino at Washington 1989; San Francisco Opera 1991 as Foresto in Attila; Other roles include Rodolfo, Deutsche Oper 1989, Alfredo, Riccardo, Gabriele Adorno and Edgardo in Lucia di Lammermoor, Liège 1987; Sang Don José in Carmen at Earl's Court, London 1991. Address: c/o San Francisco Opera, War Memorial Opera House, San Francisco, CA 94102, USA.

ORE Cecilie, b. 1954, Oslo, Norway. Composer. Education: Piano studies at Norwegian State Academy of Music and in Paris; Studied Composition with Ton de Leeuw at Sweelinck Conservatory, Amsterdam, and at Institute of Sonology in Utrecht. Career: Frequent performances at Nordic and international festivals; Commissioned by BBC Symphony Orchestra. Compositions: Orchestral music: Porphyre, 1986; Nunc et Nunc, 1994; Chamber music: Helices, for wind quintet, 1984; Preasems Subitus, for string quartet, 1989; Erat Erit Est, for ensemble, 1991; Futurum exactum, for string ensemble, 1992; Lex Temporis, for string quartet, 1992; Ictus, for 6 percussionists, 1997. Recording: Codex Temporis, 1996. Honour: 1st and 2nd Prize, International Rostrum for Electro-acoustic Music, 1988. Membership: Society of Norwegian Composers. Address: Ullevålsvn 61 B, 0171 Oslo, Norway.

ORGONASOVA Luba, b. 22 Jan 1961, Bratislava, Czechoslovakia. Singer (Soprano). Education: Studied at Bratislava Conservatory. Career: Concert and operatic engagements in Czechoslovakia 1979-83; Hagen Opera, West Germany, 1983-88 as Mozart's Ilia and Pamina, Gilda and Violetta, Lauretta and Sophie in Der Rosenkavalier; Guest appearances in Nuremberg, Essen, Hamburg and Zurich; Vienna Volksoper 1988-89; Sang Pamina and Donna Anna at Aix-en-Provence Festival, 1988-89; Opera de Lyon 1988 as Madame Silberklang in Der Schauspieldirektor; Sang Constanze at Deutsche Oper Berlin and in Lisbon 1991, with concert performances of Die Entführung under John Eliot Gardiner in London and Amsterdam; Other roles include Susanna, Atalanta in Handel's Serse, Marzelline, Cendrillon and Antonio, Les Contes d'Hoffmann; Sang Donna Anna at Chicago, 1995; Concert repertoire includes Janacek's Glagoltic Mass, Bruckner's Te Deum and the Missa Solemnis, all at Zurich, Haydn's Harmonie Mass at Bremen and Oratorios by Bach, Handel and Dvorak. Recording: Die Zauberflöte. Address: c/o Chicago Light Opera, 20 North Wacker Drive, Chicago, IL 60604, USA.

ORKIS Lambert (Thomas), b. 20 Apr 1946, Philadelphia, Pennsylvania, USA. Pianist; Chamber Music Artist; Soloist; Educator. m. Janice Barbara Kretschmann, 19 Feb 1972. Education: Diploma and BM, Piano Performance, Curtis Institute of Music; MM, Piano Performance, Temple University. Career: Worldwide performances; Premiered solo works of George Crumb, Richard Wernick, Maurice Wright and James Primosch, including Wernick's Piano Concerto, Washington DC and Carnegie Hall, New York, with National Symphony Orchestra, 1991; Recitals with cellist Mstislav Rostropovich, 1981-, with violinist Anne-Sophie Mutter, 1988-, with soprano Arleen Augér, 1987-90, with soprano Lucy Shelton, 1981-; Founding Member, fortepianist, Castle Trio, 1988-; Pianist, Smithsonian Chamber Players, 1983-; Pianist, Library of Congress Summer Chamber Festival, 1986-89; Pianist, American Chamber Players, 1986-89; Pianist, 20th Century Consort 1976-87; Judge, Carnegie Hall International American Music Competition for pianists, 1985; Judge, Kennedy Center Friedheim Awards, 1991; Soloist in Residence, 1983; Principal Keyboard, National Symphony Orchestra, Washington DC, 1982-; Professor of Piano, Co-ordinator of Master of Music programme in piano accompanying and Chamber Music. Recordings: Solo: Music of Louis Moreau Gottschalk, 1988; Schubert Impromptus, 1990; Schubert Moment Musicaux & 3 Klavierstücke, 1993; George Crumb, A Little Suite for Christmas, Richard Wernick, Sonata for Piano, 1986; With Anne-Sophie Mutter: Berlin Recital, 1996; With Anner Bylsma: Works by Franchomme and Chopin, 1994, works by Brahms and Schumann, 1995; With Arleen Augér: Schubert Lieder, 1991; With Castle Trio: Beethoven Cycle of Piano Trios, 1989-92. Honour: Grammy Award nomination, Best Chamber Music Performance, 1997. Current Management: Solo; Sheldon/Connealy at Columbia Artists Management; Castle Trio: Joanne Rile Artists Management. Address: c/o LOJO, 1931 South George Mason Drive, Arlington, VA 22204, USa.

ORLANDI MALASPINA Rita, b. 28 Dec 1937, Bologna, Italy. Singer (Soprano). m. Massimiliano Malaspina. Education: Studied with Carmen Melis in Milan. Debut: Teatro Nuovo Milan, 1963 as Verdi's Giovanna d'Arco. Career: Sang widely in Italy, and at Covent Garden, London, Munich, Hamburg, Paris, Nice, Barcelona, Vienna and Buenos Aires; Metropolitan Opera debut 1968; Other roles included Puccini's Tosca and Suor Angelica, Wagner's Elsa, Giordano's Maddalena and Verdi's Aida, Odabella, Leonora, Amelia, Abigaille, Desdemona, Luisa Miller, Elisabeth and Lucrezia (I Due Foscari); Also heard in concert. Address: c/o Teatro alla Scala, Via Filodrammatici 2, Milan, Italy.

ORLOFF Claudine, b. 6 Jan 1961, Brussels, Belgium. Pianist. m. Burkard Spinnier, 1 Oct 1983, 2 sons. Education: Diplome superieur, Piano, class of J C Vanden Eunden, 1985, Diplome superieur, Chamber Music, class of A Siwy, 1987, Conservatoire Royal de Musique, Brussels; Private studies with B Lemmens, 1985-88. Career: Recording for RTB, 1978; Regular appearances as soloist and in chamber music; Often includes contemporary works in recital programmes, including Van Rossum's 12 preludes, 1986; Many concerts on 2 pianos (with Bukard Spinnier), Belgium, France, Germany, including Musique en Sorbonne, Paris, July 1991; Radio engagement, Hommage a Milhaud, live, RTB Brussels, Oct 1992. Honours: Ella Olin Prize, Brussels, 1985. Current Management: F E de Wasswige Music Management. Address: 82 rue des Garonnes, 1170 Brussels, Belgium.

ORMAI Gabor, b. 1950, Hungary. Violist. Education: Studied with Andras Mihaly at the Franz Liszt Academy, Budapest, with members of the Amadeus Quartet and Zoltán Szekely. Career: Founder member of the Takacs Quartet, 1975; Many concert appearnaces in all major centres of Europe and the USA; Tours of Australia, New Zealand, Japan, South America, England, Norway, Sweden, Greece, Belgium and Ireland; Bartók Cycle for the Bartók-Solti Festival at South Bank, 1990; Great Performers Series at Lincoln Center and Mostly Mozart Festival at Alice Tully Hall, New York; Visits to Japan 1989 and 1992; Mozart Festivals at South Bank, Wigmore Hall and Barbican Centre, 1991; Bartók Cycle at the Théâtre des Champs Elysées, 1991; Beethoven Cycles at the Zurich Tonhalle, in Dublin, at the Wigmore Hall and in Paris, 1991-92; Resident at the University of Colorado, Resident at the London Barbican, 1988-91, with masterclasses at the Guildhall School of Music; Plays Amati instrument made for the French Royal Family and loaned by the Corcoran Gallery, Gallery of Art, Washington DC. Recordings: Schumann Quartets Op 41, Mozart String Quintets (with Denes Koromzay), Bartók 6 Quartets, Schubert Trout Quintet (with Zoltán Kocsis) Hungaroton; Haydn Op 76, Brahms Op 51 nos 1 and 2, Chausson Concerto (with Joshua Bell and Jean-Yves Thibaudet); Works by Schubert, Mozart, Dvorák and Bartók. Honours: Winner, International Quartet Competition, Evian, 1977; Winner, Portsmouth International Quartet Competition, 1979. Address: c/o Lies Askonas, 6 Henrietta Street, London WC2E 8LA, England.

ORR Buxton (Daeblitz), b. 18 Apr 1924, Glasgow, Scotland. Composer; Conductor. m. (1) Isobel Roberts, 1954, (2) Jean Latimer, 1968. Education: University College School, London; BSc, Physiology, 1st Class Honours, 1946, MBBS, 1948, Middlesex Hospital; FGSM, Guildhall School of Music and Drama, 1971. Career: Film and Theatre Music, 1955-61; Conductor, London Jazz Composers Orchestra, 1970-80; Founder, Director, Conductor, Guildhall New Music Ensemble, 1975-91; Composer in Residence, Banff, Alberta, Canada, 1984-85. Compositions: Opera, The Wager, 1961; Music Theatre, Unicorn, 1981; The Last Circus, 1984; Ring in The New, 1986; Chamber, Vocal and Orchestral Music; Works for Brass and Wind Ensembles including concertos for Trumpet, Trombone and a John Gay Suite for Symphonic Wind Band; Sinfonia Ricercante, 1988; Refrains VI for Chamber Orchestra, 1992-; Narration for Symphonic Wind Orchestra, 1994. Recordings: Vocal and Piano Music; 3 Piano Trios; Various Vocal Settings. Contributions to: Composer; The Listener; New Grove Dictionary; ENO Opera Guides; BBC Talks.

Honours: Commissions from: McEwen, Glasgow; BBC London and Scotland; City of London Festival; Merseyside Arts; Seagrams Award, American National Music Theater Network, 1988. Memberships: Executive Council, Composers Guild; Park Lane Group; Editorial Board, Composer Magazine; Reading Panels, SPNM, BBC; Association of Professional Composers. Address: Church House Barn, Llanwarne, Hereford, HR2 8JE, England.

ORR Robin (Robert Kemsley), b. 2 June 1909, Brechin, Scotland. Composer. m. (1) Margaret Ellen Mace, 29 Dec 1937, 1 son, 2 daughters, (2) Doris Ruth Winny-Meyer, 14 July 1979. Education: Royal College of Music, London; Organ Scholar, Pembroke College, Cambridge University; MA; MusD; Studied with Casella in Siena and Boulanger in Paris. Career: Organist, St John's College, Cambridge, 1938-51; Flight Lieutenant, RAFVR, 1941-45; University Lecturer in Music, 1947-56, Professor of Music, 1965-76, Cambridge University; Professor of Music, Glasgow University, 1956-65; Chairman, Scottish Opera, 1962-76; Director, Arts Theatre, Cambridge, 1970-76; Director, Welsh National Opera, 1977-83. Compositions include: Symphony in 1 movement (Edinburgh Festival and Promenade Concerts), 1963; Full Circle, opera in 1 act (Scottish Opera), 1967, 1968; Symphony No 2 (Edinburgh Festival), 1971; Hermiston, opera in 3 acts (Scottish Opera, Edinburgh Festival), 1975; Symphony No 3 (Llandaff Festival commission), 1978; On the Razzle, opera in 3 acts, libretto by composer after the play by Tom Stoppard (RSAMD Glasgow), 1988; Sinfonietta Helvetica (BBC commission), 1990; Numerous other works including church music. Honours: CBE, 1972; Honorary DMus, Glasgow, 1972; Honorary LLD, Dundee, 1976; FRCM, 1965; Honorary RAM, 1966; Honorary FRSAMD, 1985; Honorary Fellow, St John's College, Cambridge, 1987; Honorary Fellow, Pembroke College, Cambridge, 1988. Address: 16 Cranmer Road, Cambridge CB3 9BL, England.

ORREGO-SALAS Juan A, b. 18 Jan 1919, Santiago, Chile, South America. Composer; Professor of Music; Architect. m. Carmen Benavente 1943, 4 sons, 1 daughter. Education: BA 1938, MA 1943, State Uniersity of Chile. Career includes: Conductor, Catholic University Choir, 1938-44; Professor of Musicology, Faculty of Music, State University of Chile, 1942-61; Editor, Revista Musical Chilena, 1949-53; Music Critic, El Mercurio, 1950-61; Director, Instituto de Extension Musical, Chile, 1957-59; Chairman, Music Department, Catholic University, Chile, 1951-61; Professor of Music, Director of Latin American Music Centre, Indiana University, USA, 1961-. Compositions include: Orchestral: Variaciones serenas for strings, 1971; Volte for chamber orchestra, 1971; Symphony No 2, 1966; Violin Concerto, 1983; Second Piano Concerto, 1985; Cello Concerto, 1992; Chamber Music: Trio No 2, 1977; Presencias, 1972; Tangos, 1982; Balada for cello and piano, 1983; Partita, 1988; Vocal Music: Missa in tempore discordige, 1969; The Days of God, 1974-76; Bolivar for narrator, chorus and orchestra, 1982; The Celestial City, 1992; Stage Music: The Tumbler's Prayer (ballet), 1960; Widows (opera), 1989. Publications include: Latin American Literary Review, 1975; Music of the Americas (co-editor), 1967; Encyclopedia Americana, 1970. Contributions to: Musical Quarterly; Tempo; Revista Musical. Address: 490 S Serena Lane, Bloomington, IN 47401, USA.

ORTH Norbert, b. 1939, Dortmund, Germany. Singer (Tenor). Education: Studied in Hamburg and Cologne and at the Dortmund Opera House School. Career: Sang in Enschede, Holland, then at opera houses in Dusseldorf, Nuremburg, Munich, Paris, Berlin and Stuttgart; Metropolitan Opera 1979, as Pedrillo in Die Entführung; Augsburg 1981, as Max in Der Freischütz; Appearances at the Salzburg and Bayreuth Festivals; Loge in Das Rheingold 1984; Sang Walther in Die Meistersinger at Hanover 1986; Sang Tannhaüser at Kassel 1988, Lohengrin at Hanover and Wiesbaden; Walther in Die Meistersinger at the rebuilt Essen Opera, 1988; Théâtre du Châtelet, Paris 1990, as Walther; Season 1992 as Berg's Alwa at Dresden and Parsifal at Turin; Also heard in the concert hall, as Lieder and oratorio singer. Recordings: Die Entführung (Eurodisc); Schubert's Die Freunde von Salamanka (Deutsche Grammophon); Augustin Moser in Die Meistersinger, Bayreuth 1974 (Philips). Address: c/o Niedersächsische Staatsheater, Opernplatz 1, D-300 Hannover 1, Germany.

ORTIZ Cristina, b. 17 Apr 1950, Bahia, Brazil. Pianist. Education: Studied at the Conservatory in Rio de Janeiro, then with Magda Tagliaferro in Paris; After becoming first woman to win the Van Cliburn Competition (1969) resumed studies at the Curtis Institute, Philadelphia with Rudolf Serkin. Career: New York recital debut 1971; Moved to London 1972 and has since played with most of the world's leading orchestras: Vienna Philharmonic, Berlin Philharmonic, New York Philharmonic, Concertgebouw, Chicago Symphony, Israel Philharmonic and Los Angeles Philharmonic; Tours with Royal Philharmonic and Philharmonia Orchestras in Europe and Latin America; Conductors include Previn, Mehta, Kondrashin, Ashkenazy, Leinsdorf, Chailly, Masur, Salonen, Colin Davis, Janssons, Fedoseyev; Season 1997 with the NHK Symphony, the Bergen Philharmonic and the Philharmonia under Janowski. Recordings: Extensive repertoire with many labels including works by Clara Schumann (1997). Address: c/o Harrison/Parrott Ltd, 12 Penzance Road, London W11 4PA, England.

ORTIZ Francisco, b. 1948, Spain. Singer (Tenor). Education: Studied in Barcelona and Madrid. Debut: Barcelona 1973, as Foresto in Attila. Career: Further appearances as Foresto in London, Paris, 1974, Madrid and Venice, 1976, Toulouse, 1979; New York City Opera 1973, as Turiddu, Nice 1974, as Radames, Geneva 1975, as Puccini's Des Grieux; Sang Pollione in Norma at Amsterdam, Barcelona and Vienna 1978-80; Théâtre de la Monnaie Brussels 1981, as Cavaradossi, Sydney Opera 1982, as Manrico; Further engagements at Hamburg, Santiago, Ernani 1979, Paris, Rio de Janeiro and the Vienna Staatsoper, Alvaro in La Forza del Destino; Appeared with Canadian Opera Company at Toronto as Pollione 1991; Performances in Zarzuela and as concert artist. Address: c/o Canadian Opera Company, 227 Front Street East, Toronto, Ontario MFA 1E8, Canada.

ORTIZ William, b. 30 Mar 1947, Salinas, Puerto Rico. Composer. m. Candida Ortiz, 26 Mar 1988, 3 d. Education: Puerto Rico Conservatory of Music; MA, PhD, State University of New York, Stony Brook; State University of New York at Buffalo. Career: About 100 works for orchestra, chamber ensembles, solo works, songs, opera and electronic music. Compositions include: Trio Concertante en 3 Realidades; Unknown Poets from the Full-Time Jungle; Loaisai; Nueva York Tropical; Caribe Urbano; Garabato; A Sensitive Mambo in Transformation; Suspension de Soledad en 3 Tiempos. Recordings: 1245 E 107th Street; Amor, Cristal y Piedra; William Ortiz Chamber Music; Abrazo; New Music for Four Guitars. Publications: Du-Wop and Dialectics, in Perspectives of New Music, 1988; Musical Snobbism, Latin American Music Conference; Music Critic to San Juan Star. Honours: Music Composition Prize, Ateneo Puertorriqueno, 1989; Guest Composer, Latin American Music Festival, Caracas, Venezuela, 1991-92; Premiered Composer, 1995 Casals Festival. Memberships: Society of Composers; American Composers Alliance; American Music Center; Composers Forum. Address: Calle Jaguey D-43, El Plantio, Toa Baja, Puerto Rico 00949.

OSBORNE Charles, b. 24 Nov 1927, Brisbane, Australia. Critic; Author. Education: Studied piano with Archie Day and Irene Fletcher and voice with Vido Luppi and Browning Mummery. Career: Assistant Editor, London Magazine, 1957-66; Assistant Literary Director, Arts Council of Great Britain, 1966-71, LiteraryDirector, 1971-86; Member of Editorial Board, Opera Magazine; Broadcaster on musical subjects on BBC Radio 3; Currently Theatre Critic for the Sunday Telegraph. Publications: Opera 66, 1966; The Complete Operas of Verdi, 1969; Editor, Letters of Giuseppe Verdi, 1971; The Concert Song Companion, 1974; Wagner and his World, 1977; The Complete Operas of Mozart, 1978; The Dictionary of Opera, 1983; The Operas of Richard Strauss, 1988. Contributions to: Opera; London Magazine; Spectator; Times Literary Supplement; Encounter; New Statesman; Observer; Sunday Times. Hobby: Travel.

OSBORNE Conrad L(eon), b. 22 July 1934, Lincoln, Nebraska, USA. Music Critic; Vocal Coach. Education: Studied at Columbia University, Singing with Cornelius Reid and Acting with Frank Corsaro. Career: Private Teacher of Singing and Arts; Management Consultant; Former actor in theatre and on television, former baritone with minor opera companies in the New York area; Chief Critic of vocal music of High Fidelity, 1959-69; New York Music Critic for the Financial Times, 1962-69; Advisory Editor of the Musical Newsletter, 1970-77. Publications: Discographies for the operas of Verdi, Mozart and Wagner for High Fidelity; Articles and reviews for Opus Magazine from 1984. Address: Financial Times Ltd (Arts), Bracken House, Cannon Street, London EC4, England.

OSBORNE Nigel, b. 23 June 1948, Manchester, England. Composer. Education: Oxford University with Kenneth Leighton and Egon Wellesz; Warsaw with Witold Rudzinski, 1970-71. Career: Swiss Radio Prize 1971 for seven Words; Lecturer at Nottingham University, 1978-; Conducted the premiere of The Sun of Venice at the Festival Hall, London, 1992. Compositions: Seven Words, cantata, 1971; Heaventree for chorus, 1973; Remembering Esenin for cello and piano, 1974; The Sickle for soprano and orchestra, 1975; Chansonier for chorus and ensemble, 1975; Prelude and Fugue for ensemble, 1975; Passers By for trio and synthesizer, 1978; Cello Concerto, 1977; I Am Goya for baritone and quartet, 1977; Vienna Zurich Constance for soprano and quintet, 1977; Figure/Ground for piano, 1978; Kerenza at the Dawn for oboe and tape, 1978; Orlando Furioso for chorus and ensemble, 1978; Songs from a Bare Mountain for women's chorus, 1979; In Camera for ensemble, 1979; Under the Eyes for voice and quartet, 1979; Quasi una fantasia for cello, 1979; Flute Concerto, 1980; Gnostic Passion for chorus, 1980; Poem without a Hero for four voices and electronics, 1980; Mythologies for sextet, 1980; The Cage for tenor and ensemble, 1981; Piano Sonata, 1981; Choralis I-III, for six voices, 1981-82; Sinfonia I, 1982; Sinfonia II, 1983; Cantata piccola for soprano and string quartet; Fantasia for ensemble, 1983; Wildlife for ensemble, 1984; Alba for mezzo-soprano, ensemble and tape, 1984; Zansa for ensemble, 1985; Hell's Angles, Chamber Opera, 1985; Pornography for mezzo-soprano and ensemble; The Electrification of the Soviet Union, opera after Pasternak, 1986; Lumiere for string quartet and 4 groups of children, 1986; The Black Leg Miner for ensemble, 1987; Esquisse I and II for strings, 1987; Stone Garden for Chamber Orchestra, 1988; Zone for oboe, clarinet and string trio, 1989; tracks for 2 choirs, orchestra and wind band, 1990; Eulogy (for Michael Vyner), 1990; Canzona for brass, 1990; Violin Concerto, 1990; The Sun of Venice (after Turner's visions of Venice), 1991; Terrible Mouth, opera, 1992; Sarajevo, opera, 1994. Address: c/o Universal Edition Ltd, 2 Fareham Street, London W1, England.

OSKARSSON Gudjon, b. 1965, Reykjavik, Iceland. Singer (Bass). Education: Studied in Iceland and Italy (Osimo and Milan). Career: Member of the Norwegian Opera from 1990, as Colline, Zuniga, Sparafucile and Raimondo (Lucia di Lammermoor); Fafner, Hunding and Hagen in The Ring, 1993-96 (also at Norwich, 1997); Further appearances at Mozart's Commendatore at Glyndebourne and Covent Garden (1996-97), as Raimondo at Munich and Fafner in Das Rheingold at La Scala (1996); Concerts include: Tosca and Otello with the Israel PO (1995-97), Act I of Die Walküre with the LSO, Rocco in Fidelio under Carlo Rizzi and the Berlioz Messe Solenelle with the Gothenburg SO; Further concerts with the Oslo and Bergen Philharmonics and the Trondheim SO. Address: c/o Norwegian Opera, PO Box 8800, Youngstorget, N-0028 Oslo, Norway.

OSKOLKOV Sergei (Alexandrovich), b. 9 Mar 1952, Donetsk, Ukraine. Composer; Pianist. m. Natalia Semionovna Oskolkova, 23 Apr 1986, 2 sons. Education: Poetry and Painting lessons; Piano class of Galina Sladkovskaya, Donetsk Music College, 1967-71; Piano class of Pavel Serebryakov, 1971-77, Composition class with Professor Vjacheslav Nagovitsin and Professor Yuri Falik, 1976-81, Leningrad Conservatory. Debuts: As Pianist with Donetsk Philharmonic Orchestra, October 1972; Performance of vocal compositions, Leningrad, 1975. Career: Publishing poetry and selling paintings and graphics, 1972-; Participant as Composer and Pianist at international festivals in Berlin, Kazan, St Petersburg and Kalingrad, 1985; Concert tours, Germany, France, Belgium, Ukraine, Kazakhstan, Latvia. Compositions: 2 String Quartets, recorded 1976, 1979; Sinfonietta for string orchestra, recorded 1979; 2 Concertos for piano and orchestra, recorded 1981, 1988; Count Nulin, opera, recorded Leningrad Radio, 1983; Set of Pieces and 2 Sonatas for piano, recorded 1994, published; Music for Russian folk instruments; Music for theatre and film. Recordings: Offenbach, Liszt, as pianist with St Petersburg Quartet, CD, 1994; 2nd Piano Sonata and cycle of songs by Oskolkov, 1996; Mussorgsky and Tchaikovsky, as pianist, Radio St Petersburg, 1996. Membership: Union of Composers of Russia, 1988. Hobby: Cars. Address: St Petersburgsky Prosp 51, ap 5, Petrodvorets, St Petersburg 198903, Russia.

OSOSTOWICZ Krysia, b. 1960, England. Violinist. Education: Studied with Yehudi Menuhin and Sandor Vegh. Career: Founder Member of Chamber Ensemble Domus and Leader of the Endymion Ensemble; Many performances as soloist and chamber musician with repertoire from Baroque to Bartok. Address: c/o Connaught Artists Ltd, 39 Cathcart Road, London SW10 9JG, England.

OSTEN Sigune von, b. 8 Mar 1950, Dresden, Germany. Singer (Soprano). Education: Studied in Hamburg and Karlsruhe and with Elisabeth Grümmer and Eugen Rabine. Debut: Sang John Cage's Aria at Hanover 1973. Career: Noted interpreter of 20th century repertoire at the Dresden and Salzburg Festivals, the Bonn and Vienna Festivals at Venice, Berlin, Donaueschingen, Madrid, Strasbourg, St Petersburg, Moscow and Tokyo; Concert tours, radio and television recordings of Europe, the USA, Japan and South America and opera engagements at Stuttgart, Wiesbaden, Paris, Venice and Lisbon; Repertoire includes Berg's Marie and Lulu and the Woman in Schoenberg's Erwartung; Shostakovich, Lady Macbeth; Sang Fusako in Henze's Des verratene Meer at Wiesbaden, 1991 and the Mother in Turnage's Greek, Wuppertal 1992; Worked with composers such as Halffter, Penderecki, Denisov, Messiaen, Cage, Scelsi and Nono. Recordings: Penderecki Luke Passion; Messiaen, Harawi; Noche pasiva by Halffter and Dittrich's Engführung; Songs by Ives, Satie, Cage. Address: c/o Hessisches Staatstheater, Postfach 3247, 8200 Wiesbaden, Germany.

OSTENDORF John, b. 1 Nov 1945, New York, USA. Singer (Bass-baritone). Education: Studied at Oberlin College with Margaret Harshaw. Debut: Chautauqua Opera 1969, as the Commendatore in Don Giovanni. Career: Appearances at San Francisco, Houston, Baltimore, Toronto and Philadelphia; Amsterdam 1979 in the premiere of Winter Cruise by Henkeman; Repertoire includes Don Alfonso, Basilio, Escamillo, Ramphis in

Aida and Handel's Julius Caesar; Many concert performances, notably in the Baroque repertoire. Recordings: Bach's St John Passion and Handel's Imeneo, Joshua and Acis and Galatea. Address: c/o San Francisco Opera, War Memorial Opera House, San Francisco, CA 84102, USA.

OSTHOFF Wolfgang, b. 17 Mar 1927, Halle Saale, Germany. Musicologist. m. Renate Goetz, 3 sons. Education: Frankfurt Conservatory with Kurt Hessenburg and others; Universities of Frankfurt and Heidelberg with H Osthoff, T Georgiades and others. Career: Assistant Lecturer, Munich University, 1957-68; Professor, 1968-, Emeritus, 1995, Wurzburg University. Publications: Das dramatische Spätwerk Claudio Monteverdis, 1960; Beethoven Klavier Konzert c-moll, 1965; Theatergesang und darstellende Musik in der Italienischen Renaissance, 2 volumes, 1969; Heinrich Schütz, 1974; Stefan George and "les deux Musiques", 1989; Briefwechsel Hans Pfizner-Gerhard Frommel, 1990. Contributions to: Musicology journals. Memberships include: International Musicology Society. Address: Institut für Musikwissenschaft, University of Würzburg, Residenzplatz 2, D-97070 Würzburg, Germany.

ÖSTMAN Arnold, b. 24 Dec 1939, Malmo, Sweden. Conductor; Musical Director. Education: Studied art history, Lund University; History of music, Paris and Stockholm Universities. Career includes: General Administrator and Artistic Director, Court Theatre, Drottningholm, Sweden, productions there on period instruments include Mozart's Don Giovanni, Cosi fan tutte, Nozze di Figaro and Die Zauberflöte; Conducted Mozart's oratorio La Betulia Liberata at La Fenice, Venice, 1982; Series of Purcell's The Fairy Queen throughout Italy; Il Matrimonio Segreto at Cologne Opera, Washington Opera and Sadler's Wells Theatre, London, 1983; Covent Garden Debut, 1984 with Don Giovanni; Il Barbiere di Siviglia, Kent Opera, 1985; La Siège de Corinthe, Rossini, Paris Opera, 1985; Conducted Mozart's Lucio Silla, Vienna Staatsoper, 1990; Concerts with Netherlands Radio Chamber Orchestra, Stuttgart Philharmonic, Cologne Orchestra of WDR and Dusseldorf Symphony, 1990-; Season 1992 with Rossini's La Donna del Lago at the Concertgebouw and Orfeo ed Euridice at Drottningholm. Recordings include: Cosi fan tutte; Le nozze di Figaro; Don Giovanni; Die Zauberflöte for Decca Records' Florilegium Label; Video recordings of Mozart's operas based on performances at Drottningholm. Honours include: Edison Prize, Netherlands; Cecilia Prize of Belgian critics. Current Management: Haydn Rawstron Limited, London. Address: c/o Haydn Rawstron Ltd, 36 Station Road, London SE20 7BQ, England.

OTAKA Tadaaki, b. 8 Nov 1947, Kamakura, Japan. Orchestra Conductor. m. Yukiko Otaka, 23 Nov 1978. Education: Toho-Gakuen School of Music, Japan; Hochschule für Musik, Vienna, Austria. Career includes: Music Faculty, Toho-Gakuen School of Music, 1970-; Principal Conductor, Tokyo Philharmonic Orchestra, 1974-; Principal Conductor, Sapporo Symphony Orchestra, 1981; Principal Conductor, BBC Welsh Symphony Orchestra; Promenade Concerts London 1991, with Tchaikovsky's Violin concerto, excerpts from Romeo and Juliet, Tippett's Piano Concerto and Ein Heldenleben; Made his Welsh National Opera debut in 1991 conducting Strauss's Salome; Conducted the BBC in New York and Baltimore at the United Nations Day concert in 1994; Appointed first Music Advisor and Principal Conductor, Kioi Sinfonietta, Tokyo; Conducted the Orchestra's debut in 1995; Currently engaged with Royal Liverpool Philharmonic, Residentie Orchestra, and with concerts with BBC National Orchestra of Wales and BBC Symphony Orchestra; Seasons 1997-98, and 1998-99, include debuts with the London Symphony, Bamberg Symphony and Olso Philharmonic. Recordings include: Rachmaninov Symphonies with BBC National Orchestra of Wales; Further projects with BBC NOW, Yomiuri Nippon Symphony and Kioi Sinfonietta Tokyo. Honours: Suntory Music Awd, 1992; Fellowship, Welsh College of Music and Drama, 1993; Honorary Doctorate, University of Wales. Address: c/o BBC Welsh Symphony Orchestra, Broadcasting House, Llandaff, Cardiff CF5 2YQ, Wales.

OTT Karin, b. 13 Dec 1945, Wädenswil, Zurich, Switzerland. Singer (Soprano). Education: Studied in Zurich and Germany. Career: Sang first with the opera house of Biel-Solothurn; Appeared in Mussorgsky's Sorochintsy Fair at Brunswick 1970; Zurich 1970, as Tove in Schoenberg's Gurrelieder; Paris Opéra as the Queen of Night in Die Zauberflöte; Salzburg Festival 1979-81; Venice 1981, in the premiere of Sinopoli's Lou Salomé; Engagements at Stuttgart, Berlin, Zurich, Amsterdam and Vienna. Recordings include: Die Zauberflöte, conducted by Karajan (Deutsche Grammophon). Address: c/o Opernhaus Zurich, Falkenstrasse 1, CH-8008 Zurich, Switzerland.

OTTENTHAL Gertrud, b. 1957, Bad Oldesloe, Schleswig-Holstein, Germany. Singer. Education: Studied in Lubeck. Career: Sang at Wiesbaden Opera 1980, Hamburg 1981-82; Engagements at Vienna Volksoper 1982, Salzburg Festival 1984, Vienna Festival 1986-88; Sang Mozart's Countess at Klagenfurt 1984, Komische Oper Berlin 1986, returned to Berlin 1990 as Mimi; Further appearances at Theater am Gärtnerplatz Munich, Barcelona and the Schwetzingen Festival; Other roles include Agathe, Fiordiligi, Sandrina in La Finta Giardiniera, Rosalinde, Antonio and Arianna in Giustino by Handel; Concert repertoire includes works by Bach, Handel, Mozart, Bruckner and Schubert. Recordings: Werther, Der Rosenkavalier and Der Wildschütz; Mrs Ma in Der Kreidekreis by Zemlinsky; Donna Elvira in Don Giovanni, conducted by Neeme Järvi. Address: c/o Komische Oper Berlin, Behrenstrasse 55-57, 1086 Berlin, Germany.

OTTER Anne Sofie von, b. 9 May 1955, Stockholm, Sweden. Singer (Mezzo-Soprano). Education: Stockholm Royal Conservatory and Guildhall School of Music and Drama, London; Vocal Studies since 1981 with Vera Rozsa. Career: Basle Opera from 1982 as Hansel, Alcina in Haydn's Orlando Paladino, Mozart's Sextus and Cherubino (Le nozze di Figaro) and Gluck's Orpheus; Aix-en-Provence Festival (La Finta Giardiniera-Don Ramiro) 1984; In 1985 sang Mozart's Dorabella (Cosi fan tutte) in Geneva and Cherubino at Covent Garden; US debut 1985, with the Chicago Symphony, Bach's B Minor Mass in Philadelphia; Cherubino at the Metropolitan Opera; Guest appearances in Milan, Berlin, Munich, Stockholm, Geneva and Lyon; La Scala Milan 1987; Season 1992 as Romeo in I Capuleti e i Montecchi at Covent Garden, Ramiro in La Finta Giardiniera at Salzburg; Conductors include John Eliot Gardiner, Solti, C Davis, Giulini, Levine, Sinopoli and Muti; Sang in the Met Opera Gala, conducted by James Levine, 1996. Recordings: Cosi fan tutte; Orfeo ed Euridice, Idomeneo and La Clemenza di Tito conducted by Gardiner, Olga in Eugene Onegin and Cherubino in Figaro under Levine; Les Contes d'Hoffmann and Hansel and Gretel with Tate, Der Rosenkavalier under Haitink; Mozart and Verdi Requiem (Gardiner) and C minor Mass (Marriner), Bach Matthew Passion and Christmas Oratorio (Gardiner) and B minor Mass (Solti) Messiah and Dido and Aeneas (Pinnock); Brahms Alto Rhapsody (Levine) Messiah and Elijah (Marriner); Songs by Grieg, Mahler, Brahms (DGG), Sibelius (BIS) and Stenhammar; Handel's Jephtha, Gluck's Le Cinesi, Schubert's Rosamunde and Berg Songs with Abbado; Title role in Ariodante (1997). Address: IMG Artists, 3 Burlington Lane, Chiswick, London W4 2TH, England.

OTTO Lisa, b. 14 Nov 1919, Dresden, Germany. Singer (Soprano). m. Albert Blind. Education: Dresden Musikhochschukle, with Susane Steinmetz-Pree. Debut: Beuthen 1941, as Sophie in Der Rosenkavalier. Career: Sang in Beuthen 1941-44; Nuremburg 1945-46; Dresden 1946-51; Städtische (later Deutsche) Oper Berlin from 1951; Took part in the 1965 premiere of Henze's Der junge Lord; Salzburg 1953-57, as Blondchen and Despina; Glyndebourne 1956, as Blondchen in Die Entführung; Guest appearances in Vienna, Milan and Paris; Other roles include Mozart's Papagena and Susanna, Beethoven's Marzelline, and Ighino in Palestrina; Many engagements as concert singer. Recordings: St John Passion by Bach (HMV); Der junge Lord (Deutsche Grammophon); Die Zauberflöte; Cosi fan tutte.

OUNDJIAN Peter, b. 21 Dec 1955, Toronto, Ontario, Canada. Violinist. Education: Studied at the Juilliard School with Ivan Galamian and Dorothy DeLay. Career: Leader of the Tokyo Quartet from 1981; Regular concerts in the USA and abroad; First cycle of the complete quartets of Beethoven at the Yale at Norfolk Chamber Music Festival, 1986; Repeated cycles at the 92nd Street Y (New York), Ravinia and Israel Festivals and Yale and Princeton Universities; Season 1990-91 at Alice Tully Hall and the Metropolitan Museum of Art, New York, Boston, Washington DC, Los Angeles, Cleveland, Detroit, Chicago, Miami, Seattle, San Francisco, Toronto; Tour of South America, two tours of Europe including Paris, Amsterdam, Bonn, Milan, Munich, Dublin, London, Berlin; Quartet-in-Residence at Yale University, University of Cincinnati College-Conservatory of Music. Recordings: Schubert's major Quartets; Mozart Flute Quartets with James Galway and Clarinet Quintet with Richard Stolzman; Quartets by Bartok, Brahms, Debussy, Haydn, Mozart and Ravel; Beethoven Middle Period Quartets (RCA). Honours: Grand Prix du Disque du Montreux; Best Chamber Music Recording of the Year from Stereo Review and the Gramophone; Four Grammy nominations. Address: Intermusica Artists Management, 16 Duncan Terrace, London N1 8BZ, England.

OUSSET Cécile, b. 23 Jan 1936, Tarbes, France. Concert Pianist. Career: Studied Paris Conservatoire with Marcel Ciampi; Graduated 1950 with First Prize in piano; British debut at Edinburgh Festival 1980; Many appearances with leading orchestras in Britain and abroad; French debut with the Orchestre de Paris, followed by appearances with all major French orchestras; First recital at the Théâtre des Champs-Elysées in season 1987-88; US debut with the Los Angeles Philharmonic Orchestra, 1984; Later engagements with the Minnesota and Boston Symphony Orchestras; Debut tour of Japan 1984; Repertoire includes Brahms, Beethoven, Rachmaninov and French music; Played Debussy's Preludes on BBC TV 1988. Recordings: Brahms 2nd Concerto, with the Leipzig Gewandhaus Orchestra; Concertos by Rachmaninov, Liszt, Saint-Saëns, Grieg, Ravel and Mendelssohn; Recitals of Chopin, Liszt and Debussy (EMI). Honours include: Prizewinner at Van Cliburn, Queen Elisabeth of Belgium, Busoni and Marguerite Long-Jacques Thibaud Competitions; Grand Priz du Disque for Brahms Concerto recording. Address: c/o Intermusica Artists' Management, 16 Duncan Terrace, London N1 8BZ, England.

OUZIEL Dalia, b. 28 Sept 1947, Tel Aviv, Israel. Pianist. m. Jerrold Rubenstein, 1 July 1969, 1 son, 1 daughter. Education: Rubin Academy, Tel Aviv; Royal Conservatories, Mons and Brussels, Belgium. Career: Soloist and Chamber Artist; Performs at festivals and is known through her numerous recordings. Recordings include: Beethoven Variations, Piano Solo; Mozart Concerti, Double Piano Concerti, Sonatas for Violin and Piano, complete Piano Duos; Violin-Piano Sonatas of Mozart, Brahms, Fauré, Copland, Ives, Mendelssohn, Ravel, Grieg, Villa-Lobos, others; Piano Trios of Fauré, Schubert, Brahms, Mendelssohn, others; Fauré Piano Quartets; Chausson Concerto; Schubert Trout; Mendelssohn Sextet; Beethoven Lieder. Address: Avenue de la Rose des Vents 4, 1410 Waterloo, Belgium,

OVCHINIKOV Vladimir, b. 1960, Belebey, USSR. Concert Pianist. Education: Studied in Moscow with Anna Artobolevskaya and Alexey Nazedkin. Career: International engagements from 1980, including Aldeburgh, Cheltenham, Edinburgh, Lichfield and Schleswig Holstein Festivals; Recitals in London (debut at the Barbican Hall, 1987), Chicago, Toronto, Munich and Rotterdam; Season 1989- includes tour of Japan and London concerto debut with the Philharmonia Orchestra at the Festival Hall; Glyndebourne recital for the Brighton Festival; Western debut in Trio with Alexander Vinnitsky and Alexander Rudin at the Wigmore Hall, May 1989. Recordings include: Trios by Rachmaninov and Shostakovich; Tchaikovsky's 1st Piano Concerto, with the London Philharmonic conducted by Yuri Simonov (Collins Classics). Honours: Runner up (to Ivo Pogorelich) Montreal Competition 1980; Joint Silver Medal (with Peter Donohoe) Tchaikovsky Competition Moscow 1982; Winner, Leeds International Piano Competition 1987. Address: Artist Management International, 12/13 Richmond Buildings, Dean Street, London W1V 5AF, England.

OVENS Raymond, b. 14 Oct 1932, Bristol, England. Violinist. m. Sheila Margharet Vaughan Williams, 1 son, 1 daughter. Education: Royal Academy of Music; ARAM. Debut: Wigmore Hall, London, 1950. Career: Leader, London Symphony Orchestra, 1951; Principal 2nd Violin, Royal Philharmonic Orchestra, 1956; Assistant Leader, 1972; Leader until 1980, BBC Scottish Symphony Orchertra; Leader, Philharmonia Orchestra 1980-85, Orchestra of the English National Opera from 1985; Has played concertos with the BBC Scottish Symphony, the Vancouver Symphony and the Philharmonia Orchestra; Concerts and Recitals for BBC; Leader, Lyra String Quartet; Leader, Ceol Rosh Chamber Group. Honour: FRAM. Hobbies: Painting; Golf.

OWEN Barbara, b. 25 Jan 1933, Utica, New York, USA. Organist and Musicologist. Education: MusB, Westminster Choir College, 1955; MusM, Boston University, 1962; Additional study at North German Organ Academy and Academy of Italian Organ Music. Career: Music Director of First Religious Society, Newburyport, 1963-; Freelance Researcher, Lecturer, Recitalist, Teacher and Organ Consultant. Publications include: Editions of Music: A Century of American Organ Music, 4 volumes, 1975, 1976, 1983, 1991; A Century of English Organ Music, 1979; A Handel Album, 1981; The Candlelight Carol Book, 1981; 4 Centuries of Italian Organ Music, 1994; A Pachelbel Album, 1994; Books written: The Organs and Music of King's Chapel, 1965, 1993; The Organ in New England, 1979; E Power Biggs, Concert Organist, 1987; Co-editor, Charles Brenton Fisk, Organ Builder, 1986; The Registration of Baroque Organ Music, 1997. Contributions include: Grove's Dictionary, 6th Edition; Grove's Dictionary of Musical Instruments; New Grove Dictionary of American Music; Harvard Dictionary of Music. Memberships: American Guild of Organists; Organ Historical Society, President, 1997-; American Musical Instrument Society; Sonneck Society. Hobbies: Gardening; Cats. Address: 28 Jefferson Street, Newburyport, MA 01950, USA.

OWEN (Rasmussen) Lynn, b. 1936, Kenosha, Wisconsin, USA. Concert and Opera Singer (Soprano); Voice Teacher, Barnard College and privately. m. Richard Owen, 4 June 1960, 3 sons. Education: Northwestern University; BS, MS with honours 1958, Juilliard School of Music; Diplomas in Voice and Opera (highest honours), Vienna Academy of Music, Austria, 1960. Debut: Constanza in Abduction from the Seraglio, New Orleans Opera, USA. Career: La Fanciulla del West (Minnie), Fliegende Holländer (Senta), Metropolitan Opera, New York; Don Carlos (Elisabetta), Forza del Destino (Leonora), Il Trovatore (Leonore), Prince Igor (Jaroslavna), Zurich, Switzerland; Il Trovatore, Turandot, Fidelio (Leonora), Krefeld Opera, Hamburg and Frankfurt, Germany; Fanciulla del West, Central City, Fliegende Holländer, Aspen, USA; Ballo in Maschera, Othello, Calgary,

Canada; Il Trovatore, Caracas, Venezuela; Siegfried (Brünnhilde), Art Park, New York; Isolde, Mexico City Opera; Concerts and recitals throughout USA and Europe. Recordings: Serenus Records; Vanguard Records. Contributions to: Music Journal. Hobbies: Tennis; Skiing; Sailing. Address: 21 Claremont Avenue, New York, NY 10027, USA.

OWEN Stephen, b. 1961, USA. Singer (Bass-Baritone). Career: Concert appearances at Carnegie Hall, New York and in Dallas, Cleveland, Orlando, Seattle and Honolulu; European debut as Gunther in Götterdammerung at Salzburg, 1990; Further appearances as Wagner's Dutchman at Kassel and Aachen, Don Pizarro, Escamillo and Jochanaan; Roles at Aachen Opera have included the Villains in Les Contes d'Hoffmann, Tonio and Scarpia; Graz Opera as Luna, Kurwenal and Mephistophélès; Teatro Colon Buenos Aires 1993, as the Ring Master in Lulu. Address: c/o Atholl Still Ltd, Foresters Hall, 25-27 Westow Street, London SE19 3RY, England.

OWENS Anne-Marie, b. 1955, Tyne and Wear, England. Singer (Mezzo-Soprano). Education: Studied at the Newcastle School of Music, the Guildhall School and the National Opera Studio. Career: Sang Gluck's Orpheus, Dido, Dalila and Angelina (La Cenerentola) while student; Professional debut as Mistress Quickly on the Glyndebourne Tour; For English National Opera has sung Charlotte, Rosina, Maddalena, Suzuki (Madame Butterfly), Bianca (The Rape of Lucretia), Solokha in the British premiere of Rimsky-Korsakov's Christmas Eve, 1988, and Magdalene; Covent Garden 1989, as Third Lady in Die Zauberflöte and Rossweise in a new production of Die Walküre; Visit to the Vienna Staatsoper with the company of the Royal Opera, 1992; Sang Jocasta in Oedipus Rex for Opera North, followed by the title role in Ariane and Bluebeard by Dukas, 1990; Season 1992 in Les Contes d'Hoffmann at Covent Garden, as Baba the Turk in The Rake's Progress at Brussels and Preziosilla in The Force of Destiny for ENO; Other roles include Arnalta in Monteverdi's Poppea (Glyndebourne Festival); Clotilde in Norma and the Hostess in Boris Godunov (Royal Opera); Baba the Turk (Brussels); Fidalma in Il Matrimonio Segreto (Lausanne); Sang Venus in a new production of Tannhäuser for Opera North; Concert appearances with the City of Birmingham Symphony, BBC Symphony, London Mozart Players, Royal Liverpool Philharmonic; Has sung at the London Proms, Aix-en-Provence, San Sebastien, Rouen and Detroit (US debut with Messiah). Address: Foresters Hall, 25-27 Westow, London SE19 3RY, England.

OWENS David (Bruce), b. 16 Oct 1950, USA. Composer. m. 23 Jun 1974, 1 s, 2 d. Education: Eastman School, Rochester, NY; Manhattan School, NY. Compositions: Sonatina for Percussion Solo, 1969; Quartet for Strings, 1969; Encounter for Orchestra, 1970; Gentle Horizon for Chamber Ensemble, 1972; Ricercar for Band, 1978; Concerto for Viola and Orchestra, 1982; The Shores of Peace for Chorus and Chamber Orchestra, 1984; Fantasy on a Celtic Carol for Viola and Piano, 1985; Jonah, opera in 3 acts, 1986-89; One in Heart, processional for Organ or Orchestra or Band, 1988; My Frozen Well for SATB Chorus, 1991; Echoes of Edo for Piano Solo, 1993; Trio for Violin, Horn and Piano, 1995; Choral, piano, organ pieces and songs. Contributions to: Columns and articles on 20th Century music, also reviews of many books in music; The Christian Science Monitor; Ovation; Musical America. Honour: ASCAP/Deems Taylor Award for Distinguished Criticism, for Christian Science Monitor column, Inside 20th Century Music, 1983. Membership: American Society of Composers, Authors and Publishers. Address: 75 Travis Road, Holliston, MA 01746, USA.

OXENBOULD Moffatt, b. 18 Nov 1943, Sydney, Australia. Artistic Director, Opera Australia. Education: Studied at the National Institute for Dramatic Art. Career: Stage Manager with Elizabethan Trust Opera, 1963-65, Sutherland Williamson Opera, and at Sadler's Wells, London, 1966-67; Planning Coordinator with Elizabethan Trust Opera-Australian Opera, 1967-73; Artistic Administrator, Australian Opera, 1974-84, Artistic Director from 1984; Productions include: The Rape of Lucretia, 1971, Il Trittico, 1978, La Clemenza di Tito, 1991, Idomeneo, 1994, and Madam Butterfly, 1997. Publication: Joan Sutherland: A Tribute, 1989. Contributions to: Various Australian publications. Honours: Order of Australia, 1985; Dame Joan Hammond Award, 1986. Hobbies: Gardening; Collecting theatre ephemera. Address: c/o Opera Australia, PO Box 291, Strawberry Hills, New South Wales 2012, Australia.

OXLEY James, b. England. Singer (Tenor). Education: Royal College of Music (as Cellist), Oxford University, and with Rudolf Piernay. Debut: Royal Albert Hall 1991, under David Willcocks. Career: Concerts include Les Illuminations, and the Brahms Experience on South Bank (1992) and Edinburgh Festival, 1993; Season 1995-96 with Messiah (CBSO and Ulster Orchestras), and Alexander's Feast by Handel with the Brandenburg Consort; A Child of our Time in Oxford and Sweden, L'Enfance du Christ in Spain, and Britten's War Requiem; Bach's B Minor Mass on tour to France with Le Concert Spirituel; Opera

roles include Tamino (at Durham), Ottavio, Rodolfo and Alfredo; Title roles in Britten's Prodigal Son, with Kent Opera; Season 1996-97 with Purcell's King Arthur in France and The Fairy Queen at Schlossbruhl; Werther at Wexford, the Christmas Oratorio under Marc Minkowski, the Missa solemnis at the Festival Hall, London, and Messiah with the CBSO. Honours include: First Prize at the 1994 International Vocalisten Councours's-Hertogenbosch. Address: c/o Hazard Chase Ltd, Richmond House, 16-20 Regent Street, Cambridge CB2 1DB, England.

OZAWA Seiji, b. 1 Sept 1935, Shenyang, China. Conductor, Music Director, Boston Symphony Orchestra. m. Vera Motoki-Ilyin, 1 son, 1 daughter. Education: Student, Toho School of Music, Tokyo, Japan, 1953-59; Studied with Hideo Saito, Eugene Bigot, Herbert von Karajan, Leonard Bernstein, at the invitation of Charles Munch studied at Tanglewood, 1960. Career: One of three assistant conductors, New York Philharmonic, 1961-62 season; Music Director, Ravinia Festival, 1964-68; Music Director, Toronto Symphony Orchestra, 1965-69; Music Director, san Francisco Symphony Orchestra, 1970-76; Artistic Advisor, Tanglewood Festival, 1970-73; Music Director, Boston Symphony Orchestra, 1973-; Guest Conductor, major orchestras throughout the world including Philadelphia, Chicago Symphony Orchestras, New York Philharmonic, Berlin Philharmonic, Orchestre de Paris, New Philharmonia, Paris Opéra, Orchestre National de France, La Scala, New Japan Philharmonic, Central Peking Philharmonic, Vienna Philharmonic; Led Boston Symphony Orchestra Cultural Exchange in Peking and Shanghai, China, 1979; Conducted the world premiere of Olivier Messiaen's St Francis of Assisi, Nov 1983, at Paris Opéra, which was subsequently awarded the Grand Prix de la Critique, 1984, in the category of French world premieres; Conducted the Boston Symphony in Beethoven's 8th and the Symphonie Fantastique at the 1991 Promenade Concerts, London; Conducted the Berlin Philharmonic in Russian Nights concert at Moscow, 1995; 50th Anniversary performance of Peter Grimes at Tanglewood, 1996. Recordings: Philips, Telarc, CBS, Deutsche Grammophon, Angel/EMI, New World, Hyperion, Erato and RCA Records, including the Berg and Stravinsky Violin Concertos (Perlman); Saint Francois d'Assise; Schoenberg's Gurrelieder; Messiaen Turangalila Symphony; Stravinsky Firebird, Rite of Spirng and Petrushka; Ives 4th Symphony; The Queen of Spades (RCA). Honours: Recipient Emmy Award for Outstanding Achievement in Music Direction for Boston Symphony's Evening at Symphony PBS TV Series; Grand Prix du Disque for recording of Berlioz Romeo et Juliette; 1st Prize, International Competition of Orchestra Conductors, France, 1959. Current Management: Columbia Arts Management Inc, 165 W 57th Street, NY 10019, USA. Address: Music Director, Boston Symphony Orchestra, Symphony Hall, 301 Massachusetts Avenue, Boston, MA 02115, USA.

OZIM Igor, b. 9 May 1931, Ljubljana, Yugoslavia. Violinist; Professor of Violin. m. Breda Volovsel, 1963, 1 son, 1 daughter. Education: State Academy of Music, Ljubljana; Diploma RCM, London; Private study with Max Rostal, London. Debut: Ljubljana, 1947. Career: Tours of Europe, USA, South America, Australia, New Zealand and Japan; Broadcasts in all European countries. Recordings: Numerous. Publications: Editor of numerous contemporary violin works; Editor, Pro Musica Nova, 1974; Editor, Complete Violin Concertos by Mozart, for Neue Mozart Ausgabe, Bärenreiter Edition. Honours: Carl Flesch Medal, International Competition, London, 1951; 1st Prize, German Broadcasting Stations International Competition, Munich, 1953. Hobbies: Photography; Table Tennis. Current Management: Konzertdirektion Hörtnagel, Munich, Germany. Address: Breibergstrasse 6, D-50939 Köln 41, Germany.

OZOLINS Arthur (Marcelo), b. 7 Feb 1946, Lübeck, Germany. Concert Pianist. Education: Faculty of Music, University of Toronto, Canada, 1962-63; BSc, Music, Mannes College of Music, New York, USA, 1964-67; Studies with: Pablo Casals, Jacques Abram, Nadia Boulanger, Nadia Reisenberg, Vlado Perlemuter. Debut: Toronto Symphony Orchestra, Toronto, 1961. Career: Soloist with Royal Philharmonic, Hallé Orchestra, Stockholm and Oslo Philharmonic, Leningrad Philharmonic, Montreal Symphony, Toronto Symphony; Recitals, New York, London, Paris, Moscow, Leningrad, Buenos Aires, Sydney, San Paulo; 7 Tours, USSR; TV and Radio Performances, CBC, BBC, Swedish Radio; Concerto repertoire included works by Bach, Brahms, Beethoven, Mozart (K414, K466 and K503), Rachmaninov, Prokofiev, Tchaikovsky and Tippett (Handel Fantasy). Recordings: The Complete Piano Concerti and Paganini Rhapsody of Rachmaninov with Mario Bernardi and the Toronto Symphony plus Dohnanyi's Variations on a Nursery Song, Healey Willan's Piano Concerto and Strauss Burleske; Numerous Solo recordings. Honours: 1st Prizes, Edmonton Competition, 1968, CBC Talent Festival, 1968; Juno Award, Best Classical Record, 1981; 7 Canada Council Awards. Memberships: AFM; English Speaking Union. Hobbies: Swimming; Study of Philosophy and Psychology. Current Management: Richard von Handschuh, Toronto; Robert Gilder & Co, London. Address: 159 Colin Avenue, Toronto, Canada M5P 2C5.

OZOLINS Janis (Alfreds), b. 29 Sept 1919, Riga, Latvia. Violoncellist; Concert Singer; Orchestral Conductor. m. Adine Uggla, 15 May 1951, 2 sons, 1 daughter. Education: Diploma, Solo Violoncello, Conservatory of Latvia, 1944; Studied with Professor E Mainardi, Rome, 1947-48; Studied Composition, Riga, and Royal Academy of Music, Stockholm, Singing Teachers Examination, Stockholm, 1958; Examinations in Musicology, University of Uppsala, 1962. Debut: Violoncello, Riga, 1933. Career: Concert radio recitals, solo performances with orchestra, Latvia, Sweden, Denmark, UK, Italy, Switzerland; Music Master, 1956-; Conductor, Landskrona Symphony Orchestra, Sweden, 1957; Bass Soloist, Beethoven's 9th Symphony with H Blomstedt, Norrköping, Sweden, 1961; Director, Växjö Municipal School of Music and Municipal Music Dor, Växjö, Sweden, 1964-84; Conductor, operas and ballets, Växjö. Contributions to: Sohlmans Musiklexicon. Honours: National Prize of Latvia, 1944; Culture Prize, Växjö Lions Club, 1976; Royal Gold Medal, Swedish Orchestra National Federation, 1977, 1984. Hobbies: Languages; Globetrotting; Gastronomy. Address: Via Sicilia 1, I-63039 San Benedetto del Tronto (AP), Italy.

P

PABST Michael, b. 1955, Graz, Austria. Singer (Tenor). Education: Studied in Graz and Vienna. Career: Principal Tenor at Vienna Volksoper, 1978-84, singing operetta and lyric opera roles; Dramatic repertoire from 1985, including: Max, in Der Freichütz, Munich; Bacchus, at Philadelphia, Stuttgart, Frankfurt and Houston; Lohengrin, at Hamburg and Zurich; Walther, at Cape Town and Trieste; Erik, at La Scala and Buenos Aires; Huon, Oberon, at La Scala; Florestan at the Savonlinna Festival and Siegmund at Liège; Guest appearances at Vienna Staatsoper from 1991, with Florestan The Drum Major, in Wozzeck, Max, Jenik in The Bartered Bride, Erik; Other roles include Hoffmann, Pedro in Teifland, Luigi in Il Tabarro; Schubert's Fierabras; Sergei, in Lady Macbeth; Strauss's Matteo, Aegisthus, Burgomaster, in Friedenstag and Apollo. Recordings include: Heinrich in Schreker's Irrelohe, 1995. Address: c/o Athole Still International Management Ltd, Foresters Hall, 25-27 Westow Street, London, SE19 3RY, England.

PACANOVSKY Ivan, b. 13 July 1934, Levoca, Czechoslovakia. m. Milena Pacanovska, 22 August 1970, 1 son, 1 daughter. Education: Pedagogical University, Bratislava, Slovakia.

PACCAGNINI Angelo, b. 17 Oct 1930, Castano Primo, Milan, Italy. Composer. Education: Studied at Milan Conservatory 1949-53 and with Berio and Maderna. Career: Teacher of electronic music at the Milan Conservatory, 1969-80; Former Director of the Mantua and Verona Conservatories. Compositions: Le Sue Ragioni, opera in 1 act, Bergamo, 1959; Mosè, radio opera, 1963; IL Dio, radio opera, 1964; Tutta la Voglono, tutti la Spogliano, opera in 3 acts, Venice; Un Uomo da Salvare, Milan, 1969; Partner, electronics scena, Turin, 1969; E L'Ora, radio opera, 1970; La Misura, il Mistero, Milan, 1970; C'Era una Volta un re, television opera, 1974; Olivo Verdevivo, television opera, 1977. Honour: Prix Italia 1964 for IL Dio di oro. Address: SIAE, (Sezione Musica), Viale della Letteratura n 30, 00144 Rome, Italy.

PACE Carmelo, b. 17 August 1906, Valletta, Malta. Music Teacher; Composer. Education: Fellow, London College of Music, England; Licentiate, Royal Schools of Music. Career: Founder, Conductor, Malta Cultural Institute Concerts, 1948-; Lecturer, History and Theory of Music. Compositions include: Works for pianoforte, solo and various other instruments; Orchestral, choral and vocal solos and chamber music; Operas including Caterina Desguanez, 1965, I Martiri, 1967, Angelica, 1973 and Ipogeana, 1976; Incidental music for stage works includes, La Predestinata, 1954; Il Natale di Cristo, 1955; San Paolo, 1960; Space Adventure, 1962; Il-Kappella tal-Paci, 1973; Il-Francizi f'Malta, 1978; Oratorios and Cantatas include, Alba Dorata (opera oratorio in 3 parts), 1964; Eternal Triumph, 1966; The Seven Last Words, 1978; Cantico di Salomone, 1982; Cantate Domino, 1982; Stabat Mater, 1982; Te Deum, 1983; Sultana tal-Vittorji, 1985; Sejha, 1986; Alter Christus - San Frangisk, 1986; Gloria, 1989; Ballet, Ballet Hongrois, 1940; Ruth, 1979. Publications: Carmelo Pace - A Maltese Composer who collected some Maltese Folk Music; His Fantasia Maltensina was premiered in 1931. Membership: Performing Right Society, London. Hobbies include: Reading. Address: 14 St Dominic Street, Sliema, SLM 06, Malta.

PACE Patrizia, b. 1963, Turin, Italy. Singer (Soprano). Education: Studied at Turin Conservatory. Debut: La Scala 1984 as Celia in Mozart's Lucio Silla. Career: Has appeared in Milan as Micaela, Mozart's Despina, Susanna and Zerlina, Oscar, Lisa in La Sonnambula and in premiere Il Principe Felice by Mannino, 1987; Guest appearances at Deutsche Oper Berlin, Spoleto Festival and the Vienna Staatsoper as Oscar and Rossini's Elvira, 1986 and 1988 Gilda, Nannetta in Falstaff and Yniold; Further engagements at Hamburg Staatsoper as Liu, Florence, Genoa, Palermo and Covent Garden 1991 and 1993 as Gilda and Yniold in Pelléas et Mélisande; Other roles include Rosina and Sofia in Il Signor Bruschino; Engaged as Nannetta in Falstaff for the Royal Opera, 1998. Recordings: Barbarina in Le nozze di Figaro and Mozart's Requiem; Mozart's C minor Mass. Address: c/o Teatro alla Scala, Via Filodrammatici 2, Milan, Italy.

PACIOREK Grazyna, b. 11 Dec 1967, Zyrardow, Poland. Composer. Education: Degree in Violin, State School of Music, Warsaw, 1987; Currently studying Composition under Professor M Borkowski, Academy of Music, Warsaw; International courses for young composers, Polish Section, ISCM, Kazimierz Dolny, Poland, 1989, 1990, 1991; Computer course and workshops, Studio of Electroacoustic Music, Academy of Music, Cracow, 1991. Career: Many performances at the composers concerts in Warsaw (Academy of Music, Royal Castle) and in Cracow, 1987-91; Composed music for film aired on Polish TV, 1991; Works presented in radio programme at Gdansk Meeting of Young Composers, Oct 1991 and 5th Laboratory of Contemporary Chamber Music, 1991. Compositions include: Monologue for Oboe Solo; Te-qui-la for 6 percussion group; Toccata for violin, cello and piano, string quartet; Muzyka Mapothana for oboe and accordiov; Concert for viola and orchestra; Electronic Music, film music. Honours: June 1991, Academy of Music in Warsaw applied to Minister of Culture and Fine Arts for her artistic scholarship in 1991. Memberships: Polish Society for Contemporary Music; Polish Composers' Union Youth Circle. Hobbies: Sailing; Dancing. Address: ul Sienkiewicza 28/4, 05-825 Grodzisk Maz, Poland.

PACKER Janet, b. 14 Aug 1949, New York, New York, USA. Violinist. m. Samuel Rechtoris, 19 Feb 1995. Education: Diploma, Eastman School of Music, 1966; BA, History, magna cum laude, Wellesley College, 1970; MA, History of Ideas, Brandeis University, 1972; Violin with Millard Taylor, Broadus Erle, George Neikrug; Chamber Music with György Sebok, Sandor Vegh, Guarneri String Quartet. Career: Extensive Performance of 20th Century Music with Dinosaur Annex Music Ensemble, 1976-86; Violin and Piano Recitals throughout USA, 1991-; Artistic Director, Preparatory Division, Longy School of Music, Cambridge, Massachusetts, 1985-; Classical Violin with Pianoforte Recitals, 1987; New York City Debut, Weiler Hall, 1993, Paris Debut, American Embassy, 1993; President, Pro Violino Foundation, 1995-; Numerous solo appearances with orchestras. Recordings: Vittorio Rieti, Serenata for Violino Concertante e Piccola Orchestra; Ezra Sims, All Done From Memory for Violin; Two for One for Violin and Viola; Sextet; Lee Hyla, Trio for Violin, Viola and Cello; Hayg Boyajian, Epistles for Violin, Oboe and Bassoon; Gardner Read, Five Aphorisms op 150, for Violin and Piano; William Thomas McKinley, Violin Concerto. Honours: Winner, Young Artists Competition, Rochester, New York, 1966; Billings Performance Award, Wellesley College, 1970; Artist on the Massachusetts Touring Roster, 1997. Memberships: American String Teachers Association; National Music Teachers Association; American Composers Forum; American Music Center; Early Music America. Address: 10 Chester Street #7, Cambridge, MA 02140, USA.

PACLT Jaromir, b. 24 Feb 1927, Hradec Kralove, Bohemia. Musicologist; Violinist. Education: Ph, Dr, University of Prague, 1953; CSc, University of Prague, 1966; DSc, 1993. Career: Editor, Kniznice Hudebnich rozhledu, 1955-60; Director, Exposition Hall, Theatre of Music, Prague, 1961-63; Czechoslovakian Academy of Sciences, 1963-. Publications: Editor, Tri Kapitoly o Z Nejedlem, 1957; Editor, Stravinsky u nas, 1957; Editor, Tvurci moderni hudby, 1965; Editor, Kresba a zvuk, 1969; Editor, Hudba v ceském divadle a cinohre, 1972; Editor, Slovnik svetovych skladatelu, 1971; Editor, E F Burian, 1981; Redactor and editor of the synthetic work: History of the Czech Musical Theatre (1848-1945); Editor, Conception of colour-music in the work of Czech modern composer M Ponc (1902-1976), 1986; Editor, The Artists of the Czech Musical Theatre (dictionary); Editor, M Ponc (monograph), 1990; Editor, Tableaux vivants, 1990; Editor, Musical Theatre of Horror, 1991; Editor, V Talich in Sweden, 1992; Editor, Prag als Asylstadt (1918-1938), 1993, (Germany); Editor, Denni Repertoár Movèho Nemeckèho Divadla V Praze, 1885-1927, Zemrel, 1994. Honours: 1st Prize, Czechoslovakian Radio 1967; 2nd Prize, International Music Competition, Radio Brno, 1970; Prize Supraphon, 1982. Hobbies: Painting; Motoring. Address: 19 U Nesypky, 150 00 Prague 5, Czech Republic.

PADILLA AnnaMaria, b. 30 Sept 1978, Santa Fe, New Mexico, USA. Performing Artist; Classical and Flamenco Guitarist; Vocalist. Education: BA, summa cum laude, St Marys College, California; MA, St John's College, New Mexico, expected 1999; University of New Mexico; College of Santa Fe. Debut: John F Kennedy Performing Arts Center, Washington, DC. Career: Soloist, Guitar, Concierto de Aranjuez, St Francis Auditorium, Santa Fe; Soloist, Guitar, Vivaldi Concerto in D, New Mexico Symphony Orchestra; TV/Film work: Lazarus Man; Gypsy Girl, Gypsy Girl, Australian National Art Gallery; ABC TV; EWTN; QVC. Compositions: El Ave; Rose of the Wine; Flamenco Padre Nuestro; Flamenco Ave Maria. Recordings: CD's & Cassettes. Publications: Why Wait? Graduate!, 1994. Contributions to: Hispanic Business Magazine; Hispanic Magazine; Sassy; Twin Circle; La Opinion; You!. Honours: RT Miller Award, 1994; Le Fevre Award, Performing Arts, St Marys College; Outstanding Graduate, Distance Education Council; New Mexico Entrepreneur of the Year. Memberships: Phi Theta Kappa; Metropolitan Opera Guild; Spanish Colonial Arts Society; National Association of Female Executives. Hobbies: Historical Spanish Art Research; X-C Skiing. Current Management: Musica Mundial Productions. Address: PO Box 6097, Santa Fe, NM 87502, USA.

PADMORE Elaine (Marguirite), b. 1945, Haworth, Yorkshire, England. Opera House Director; BBC Producer and Presenter; Singer. Education: BMus, MA, University of Birmingham, 1965-69; LTCL Piano Diploma; Scholarship for piano accompaniment, Guildhall School of Music; Studied singing privately with Helen Isepp. Career: Editor with Oxford University Press; BBC Producer of music programmes and major series for Radio 3; BBC Chief Producer of opera, 1976-82; Artistic Director, Wexford Festival, 1982-94; Radio Broadcaster and Singer appearing in concerts and opera; Lecturer in Opera at Royal Academy of Music, London; Artistic Director, Dublin Grand Opera, 1989-93; Artistic Director of Classical Productions, London, 1990-92 with Tosca in 1991 and Carmen in 1992; Artistic Consultant for London International Opera Festival, 1991-92; Director of Royal Danish Opera, Copenhagen, 1993-. Publications: Wagner, in the series The Great Composers, 1970; Chapter on Germany, in Music in The Modern Age, 1973. Contributions to: Grove's Dictionary; Various British professional journals. Honours: Pro Musica Prize, Hungarian Radio, 1975; Prix Musical de Radio Brno, 1976; Honorary Associate, Royal Academy of Music, 1981; Sunday Independent Arts Award for Services to Music in Ireland, 1985; Knight of The Royal Danish Dannebrog Order, 1994. Membership: Incorporated Society of Musicians. Address: 11 Lancaster Avenue, Hadley Wood, Hertfordshire, England.

PADMORE Mark Joseph, b. 8 Mar 1961, London, England. Singer. m. Josette Simon, 27 Oct 1996. Education: Kings College, Cambridge, 1979-82; Studied with Erich Vietheer, Gita Denise, Janice Chapman and Diane Forlano. Career: Singer at Major Festivals including Aix-en-Provence, Edinburgh, BBC Proms, Salzburg, Spoleto, Tanglewood, New York; Opera House debuts: Teatro Comunale, Florence, 1992; Opera Comique, Paris, 1993; Theatre du Chatelet, 1995; Royal Opera House, Covent Garden, 1995; Scottish Opera, 1996; Opera de Paris, 1996. Recordings: Chabrier Briseis; Charpentier, Medee; Handel, Messiah; Esther, Samson; Haydn, Masses; Purcell, Fairy Queen and King Arthur; Rameau, Hippolyte et Aricie. Hobbies: Theatre; Cycling. Current Management: Van Walsum Management. Address: 4 Addison Bridge Place, London W14 8XP, England.

PADOUROVA-HAVLAKOVA Lydie, b. 30 Aug 1957, Prague, Czech Republic. Singer (Mezzo Soprano). m. Jan Padour, 1 June 1979, 1 son. Education: Conservatoire of Prague; University of Music in Prague. Debut: National Theatre in Prague, 1986. Career: Prague National Theatre: L Janáček's Kata Kabanova (Varvara); Prokofiev's Obrucenije v Monasture (Betrothal in a Monastery-(Klara); Tchaikovsky's Queen of Spades (Pavlina and Dafnis), 1987; W A Mozart's Le nozze di Figaro, as Cherubino, 1988; H Purcell's Dido and Aeneas (Dido). Recordings: Arias By Mascagni: Santuzza; Bizet's Carmen; Mozart's Dorabella; Thomas's Mignon; Purcell's Dido; Donizetti's Orsini (Lucrezia Borgia); Complete Opera: S Prokofiev s Betrothal in a Monastery. Hobbies: Music; Theatre; Dogs; Sports. Current Management: Na Lysinach 461/30, 14700 Prague, Czech Republic.

PADROS David, b. 22 Mar 1942, Igualada, Barcelona, Spain. Composer; Pianist. Education: Municipal Music School, Barcelona, 1966; Musikhochscule Trossingen, Freiburg, Germany, 1966-69; Konservatorium, Basel, 1969-72; Zurich, Switzerland, 1972-75. Compositions: Styx, Chamber Ensemble; Heptagonal, piano; Crna Gora, Chamber Ensemble; Khorva, orchestra; Cal Ligrama (F1 in G, piano); 2 Legendes, organ; Batalla, piano, harpsichord and strings; Musik im Raum, chamber ensemble; Jo-Ha-Jyu, orchestra; Arachne, Chamber ensemble; Maqam, piano; Trajectories, violin; Confluences, brass ensemble, percussion, tape; Chaconne, string quartet, harpsichord; El Sermo de R Muntaner, 4 mixed voices, 4 old wind instruments, organ; Ketjak, pianists quartet; Recordant W A M, clarinet and organ; La Sala de la Suprema Harmonia, chamber ensemble, 1991; Jdeb, recorder quartet, 1992; 6 Differencies, organ, 1992; Ghiza-i-ruh, flute, clartinet, piano, 1993; Nocturne, flute, viola, clarinet, 1992; Gjatams, piano quartet, 1993; Xucla el silenci noctum, flute, clarinet, violin, cello, 1994. Recordings: Musik in Raum, Association of Catalan Composers; Arachne, Catalunya Musica; Confluencies, AS; Chamber Music, 6 works, on CD, Nova Era. Contributions to: Revista Musical Catalana. Honours: Hans-Lenz-Preis, Germany, 1969; Komposition-Preis det Stiftung Landis and Gyr, Switzerland, 1976. Membership: Associacio Catalana de Compositors. Address: Rosello 213, 1-1 E-08008 Barcelona, Spain.

PADROS Jaime, b. 26 Aug 1926, Igualada, Spain. Composer; Pianist. m. Eva Marie Wolff, 1962, 1 son, 2 daughters. Education: Baccalaureat, Monastery of Montserrat, Barcelona; Formation, Escolania de Montserrat, 1939-; Piano, organ and musical studies with Dom David Pujol; Piano studies with Frank Marshall & Alicia de Larrocha, Academia Marshall, 1941; Composition with Josep Barbera, Cristobal Taltabull, Barcelona, Darius Milhaud, Paris. Debut: As Composer, Ballet Fantasia de circo, 1954. Career: Concerts in all major cities and radio stations in Spain, Paris, Prague and many German cities; First pianist to rediscover several of the works of the 18th Century Spanish Composers Antonio Soler and Narcis Casanoves; First to play complete piano works of Arnold Schoenberg, Alban Berg, Anton Webern and other contemporary composers in Spain; Piano Teacher, Academy of Music, Trossingen, West Germany, 1964-94; Numerous commissioned works, 1954-. Compositions: Chamber music for different casts of instruments: Tannkas del somni 1950; Sonata para piano, 1954; Quintet per a quartet d'arc i piano, 1962; Planctus, 1977; Cancionero del lugar, 1978; Policromies, 1980; Several settings of folk songs for choir; Poemas de fragua, 1984; Musica cambiante (piano solo and string orchestra), 1986. Recordings: Contrapuntos sobre canciones populares castellanas, 1962; Sternverdunkelung, 1960; Llibre d'alquimies I, 1967; Serenata, 1978; Trama concentrica, 1982; Paseo y contradanza, 1985. Honours: Premio Juventudes musicales, 1954; Premi Orfeo catala, 1962. Address: Seelengraben 30, 89073 Ulm, Germany.

PAGE Christopher (Howard), b. 8 Apr 1952, London, England. Medievalist. m. Régine Fourcade, 15 Sept 1975. Education: BA, English, Oxford University; DPhl, York University. Career: University Lecturer in Medieval English, University of Cambridge; Frequent Broadcaster on BBC Radio 3, both as Lecturer and as Director of his Ensemble, Gothic Voices; Presenter of Radio 4 Arts programme, Kaleidoscope. Recordings: Directed Gothic Voices in Sequences and Hymns by Abbess Hildegard of Bingen; The Mirror of Narcissus; Songs by Guillaume de Machaut; The Garden of Zephirus; Courtly Songs of the Early 15C; The Castle of Fair Welcome; Courtly Songs of the late 15C; The Service of Venus and Mars; A Song for Francesca; Music for the Lionhearted King. Publications: (Book) Voices and Instruments of the Middle Ages; Sequences and Hymns by Abbess Hildegard of Bingen; The Owl and the Nightingale; Musical Life and Ideas in France, 1100-1300. Contributions to: Many academic and scholarly contributions to Early Music; Galpin Society Journal; Proceedings of the Royal Musical Association; New Oxford History of Music; Cambridge Guide to the Arts in Britain; Early Music History; The Historical Harpsichord. Honours: British Entrant and Prizewinner, Innsbruck International Radio Prize, 1981; Several Awards for Record of Hildegard; Gramophone Awards for three records; Fellow, Fellowship of Makers and Restorers of Historical Instruments; senior Research Fellow in Music, Sydney Sussex College, Cambridge. Hobbies: Research and Performance. Address: Sidney Sussex College, Cambridge University, Cambridge, England.

PAGE Kenneth, b. 8 Dec 1927, Birmingham, England. Musician; Violinist; Violist; Conductor. m. Brenda Gane, 10 Oct 1953. Education: Birmingham Conservatoire; Studied with Ernest Element, Yfrah Neaman, Max Rostal. Career: BBC Radio 3 and 4; BBC TV; Violinist with Amati Quartet, 1951-53; Violinist and Violist with Element Quartet, 1953-60; Violinist and Violist with Voces Intimae Quartet, 1960-; Violinist with Archduke Trio, 1961; Founder, Music Director and Conductor of Orchestra da Camera; Conductor of Birmingham Philharmonic Orchestra, 1959-86. Recordings: Wilfred Josephs Piano Concerto No 2; Christmas Music from Hereford Cathedral; Violin Concerto and Music for Strings by John Jeffreys. Honours: Honorary MMus, Leicester University, 1975; Honorary MSc, University of Aston, 1983. Hobbies: Photography; Model Railways. Address: 41 Fishponds Road, Kenilworth, Warwickshire, CV8 1EY, England.

PAGE Paula, b. 24 Sept 1942, Corinth, Mississippi, USA. Singer (Soprano). Education: Studied at Indiana University, Bloomington and on a Fulbright Scholarship in Europe. Debut: Inez in Il Trovatore, Hamburg, Staatsoper, 1968. Career: Hamburg Staatsoper 1968-72; Appearances at Wuppertal, Aachen, Bremen, Santa Fe, Norfolk, Antwerp, Liege, Bordeaux, Lison, Venice, Dusseldorf; Berlin, Frankfurt-am-Main Opera from 1983; Repertory includes lyric roles and parts in modern operas; Presently Professor of Voice, Staatliche Hochschule für Musik. Honours: Prizewinner, New York Metropolitan Auditions of the Air, 1967; WGN Auditions of the Air, 1967; Geneva International Competition, 1968; S-Hertogenbush Holland, 1968; Martha B Rockefeller Grant, 1977. Address: Königsberger Strabe 25, D-6239, Germany.

PAGE Steven, b. 1950, England. Singer (Baritone). Education: Studied with Margaret Hyde and at the Opera Studio, London. Career: Sang Don Alfonso and Nick Shadow with Opera 80, (now English Touring Opera); For English National Opera he has sung the title role in Mozart's Don Giovanni, Tarquinius in The Rape of Lucretia, Albert in Werther, Paolo in Simone Boccanegra, Valentine in Faust and the Count in Marriage of Figaro and most recently the role of Figaro; For Scottish Opera he has appeared as Guglielmo in Cosi fan tutte, Marcello in La Bohème, Chorèbe in Les Troyens, Ford in Falstaff and the title role of Don Giovanni and the Count in Marriage of Figaro; He has also taken part in four seasons at the Buxton Festival in leading roles and has appeared with Opera Factory as Don Giovanni at the Queen Elizabeth Hall; For Glyndebeourne Touring Opera has sung Nick Shadow in Rake's Progress, Leporello in Don Giovanni, Anubis in Harrison Birtwistle's The Second Mrs Kong and Coyle in a anew production by Robin Philips of Britten's Owen Wingrave; Made his debut Glyndebourne Festival as Nick Shadow in 1994 and returned as Leporello in Don Giovanni and Anubis; Sang Geronio in Rossini's Il Turco in Italia, Garsington, 1996. Address: c/o Stafford Law Associates, 6 Barham Close, Weybridge, Surrey KT13 9PR, England.

PAHUD Emmanuel, b. 1969, France. Flautist. Education: Premier Prix at the Paris Conservatoire, 1990; Further study with Aurele Nicolet. Career: Principal Flute of the Berlin Philharmonic, and many concerts as solo artist appearances at leading international festivals and chamber music societies throughout Europe and Japan; Recitalist in International Rising Stars Series in season 1997-98, with concerts at Carnegie Hall and in Europe. Recordings include: Mozart Concertos with the Berlin Philharmonic and Abbado; French repertory with pianist Eric Le Sage (EMI Classics). Honours: Prize Winner at several international competitions. Address: c/o Harold Holt Ltd, 31 Sinclair Road, London W14 0NS, England.

PAIK Byung-dong, b. 26 Jan 1936, Seoul, Korea. Professor. m. Wha-ja Woo, 4 Oct 1969. Education: Graduated, Shin-Heung High School, Jeon-joo; Department of Composition, College of Music, Seoul National University, 1961-63; Stadtliche Hochschule fur Musik, Hanover, Germany, 1971-79. Debut: Annual Korean New Composers Prize with Symphonic Three Chapters, 1962. Career: 6 composition recitals since 1st recital, 1960-; Has presented his works several times with National Symphony Orchestra, Seoul Philharmonic Orchestra and other ensembles; Professor, Personnel Management Member, College of Music, Seoul National University; President, Perspective Composers Group. Compositions: Major works, Symphonic Three Chapters, 1962; Un I, II, III, IV, V, VI for Instrumental Ensemble; Drei Bagetellen fur Klavier, 1973; Concerto for Piano and Orchestra, 1974; Veranderte Ehepaar, 1986; In September for Orchestra, 1987; Contra, 1988. Recordings: Ein kleine Nachtlied fur Violine und Klavier, SEM, Seoul, 1978; Guitariana for two Guitars, SEM, 1984; Byul-Gok 87, Jigu Record Corporation, Seoul, 1987. Publications: Musical Theory, 1977; Essays: Seven Fermatas 1979; Essays: Sound or Whispering, 1981; Harmony, 1984; Music for Culture, 1985; College Musical Theory, 1989; The Streams of Modern Music, 1990. Address: 214-1 Sangdo 1 dong, Dongjakgu, A-202 Sangdo Villa, Seoul, Korea.

PAIK Kun-Woo, b. 10 May 1946, Seoul, South Korea. Classical Pianist. m. Mi-Ja Son, 14 Mar 1976, 1 daughter. Education: High School of Performing Arts, New York City, USA, 1965; Diplomas, Juilliard School of Music, New York, 1965-71; Studied with Rosina Lhevine; Further studies with Ilona Kabos, London, with Wihelm Kempff and Guido Agosti, Italy. Debut: As soloist, Grieg Concerto with National Orchestra of Korea, Seoul, at age of 10; New York Orchestral Debut with James Conlon and National Orchestra, Carnegie Hall, 1972; London Debut, 3 recitals, Wigmore Hall, 1974. Career: Recitalist, Alice Tully Hall, New York City, 1971; Recitals, concerts, USA, Europe, South Korea, 1971-; Performed at numerous major festivals, USA and Europe including Berlin, Spoleto, Edinburgh, Paris, Aix-en-Provence; Appearances with major orchestras include London Philharmonic, Paris Orchestre Nationale, Berlin Radio, Suisse Romande, Frankfurt Radio Symphony; US West Coast solo debut with recitals, Los Angeles and San Francisco. Recordings: Ravel's complete solo works and 2 concerti, Orfeo and Seon; Moussorgsky's complete piano solo works, RCA; Sonata D960, Schubert, Seon. Honours: Special Prize, Dmitri Mitropoulos Competition, 1969; 1st Prize, Walter Naumburg Piano Competition, New York, 1971; Finalist, Leventritt Competition, 1971; Joseph Lhevine Award; Franz Listzt Award. Hobbies: Photography; Cinema; Travel; Food; Drawing; Reading. Address: 7 rue Villebois-Mareuil, 94300 Vincennes, France.

PAIK Nam June, b. 20 July 1932, Seoul, South Korea. Education: Studied at University of Tokyo; Music theory with Thrasybulos Georgiades in Munich and with Wolfgang Fortner in Munich. Career: Worked with Stockhausen at Electronic Music Studio in Cologne, 1958-60; Summer seminars for new music at Darmstadt, 1957-61; Moved to New York 1964, Los Angeles 1970; Performance of music involves total art, including duo recitals with topless cellist Charlotte Moorman in which composer's spine serves as cellist's fingerboard. Compositions: Ommaggio a Cage, involving the destruction of piano and raw eggs, and the painting of hands in jet black, 1959; Symphony for 20 Rooms, 1961; Global Groove, high-velocity collage using video tape, 1963; Variations on a Theme of Saint-Saëns for piano and cellist in oil drum; Performable Music, in which performer is required to cut left forearm with a razor, 1967; Opera Sextronique, 1967; Opera Electronique, 1968; Creep into a Whale; Young Penis Symphony, 1970; Earthquake Symphony, with grand finale, 1971; Video Buddha, 1974; The More The Better, 1988; Video Opera, 1993. Address: c/o ASCAP, ASCAP Building, One Lincoln Plaza, NY 10023, USA.

PAILLARD Jean-François, b. 28 Apr 1928, Vitry-le-Francois, France. Conductor; Musicologist. m. Anne Marie Beckensteiner, 3 sons. Education: First Prize in Music History, Paris Conservatoire; Studied conducting with Igor Markevitch, Salzburg; Graduated from the Sorbonne in mathematics. Career: Founded the Jean-Marie Leclair Instrumental Ensemble, 1953; Many tours of Europe, USA and the Far East with the Jean-François Paillard Chamber Orchestra, notably in French music of the 17th and 18th centuries; Organiser and Teacher of Conducting Courses, Spring and Summer, France. Publications: La Musique Francaise Classique, 1960, 1973; Archives de la Musique Instrumentale; Archives de la Musique Religieuse. Recordings include: Bach, Brandenburg Concertos, Suites for Orchestra, Harpsichord Concertos and Musical Offering; Handel Alexander's Feast, Water and Fireworks Music, Dettingen Te Deum, Concertos for oboe, organ and harp; Couperin Les Nations; Delalande Symphonies; Charpentier Te Deum, Magnificat and Messe de Minuit, Baroque trumpet concerto (Maurice André); Rameau Les Indes Galantes; Mozart Divertimenti; Flute and Violin concertos, concerto K 299. Honours: Many Grand Prix du Disque (Academie Charles Cros, Disque Francais Disque Lyrique); Prix Edison, Holland; German Record Prize; Gold Record, Japan. Memberships: French Musicological Society; French Society of the 18th Century. Hobbies: Piloting Aircrat; Sailing; Mountaineering. Address: 23 Rue de Marly, 7860 Etang la Ville, France.

PAITA Carlos, b. 10 Mar 1932, Buenos Aires, Argentina. Conductor. m. Elisabeth de Quartbarbes, 7 children. Education: Studied with Juan Neuchoff and Jacobo Fischer. Debut: Teatro Colon, Buenos Aires. Career: Conducted the National Radio Orchestra in Argentina; Verdi Requiem, 1964, Mahler's 2nd Symphony, 1965; Stuttgart Radio Symphony from 1966; Appearances in London, Paris, Edinburgh and the USA (debut 1979, with the Houston Symphony Orchestra). Recordings: Festival Wagner; Grands Overtures; Verdi Requiem; Beethoven's Eroica Symphony; Rossini Overtures; Mahler's 1st Symphony; Symphonie Fantastique by Berlioz. Honours: Grand Prix, Academie Charles Cros, Paris, 1969; Grand Prix de L'Academie Francaise, 1978. Address: 15 Chemin du Champ d'Anier, 1209 Geneva, Switzerland.

PAKSA Katalin, b. 8 Feb 1944, Zalaergerszeg, Hungary. Ethnomusicologist. div., 1 daughter. Education: Liszt Ferenc Academy of Music, Budapest. Debut: Museum for Ethnography, Budapest, 1968. Career: Folk Music Research Group, 1971, Institute of Musicology, 1974, Chief Investigator, Head of Folk Music Department, Institute of Musicology, 1997, Hungarian Academy of Sciences. Recording: Anthology of Hungarian Folk Music IV - Great Hungarian Plain, original archival recordings, 1989. Publications: The Ornamentation of the Hungarian Folk Song, 1993; Corpus Musicae Popularis Hungaricae - Collection of Hungarian Folk Music, Vol X, 1997. Memberships: Committee of Musicology, Scientific Qualification Board, Hungarian Academy of Sciences; International Council for Traditional Music. Hobbies: Reading; Listening to music. Address: MTA Zenetudományi Intézet Pf 28, H-1250 Budapest, Hungary.

PAL Tamas, b. 16 Sept 1937, Gyula, Hungary. Conductor. Education: Studied with Janos Viski and Andreas Korody at the Franz Liszt Academy Budapest. Career: Conducted the Budapest State Opera 1960-75, notably at the Edinburgh Festival (1973) and the Wiesbaden May Festival (1974); Principal Conductor of the Szeged Symphony Orchestra and Opera, 1975-83; Permanent Conductor of the Budapest Opera, 1983-85; Artistic Director of the open air summer music festival at Budapest, 1987; Has conducted operatic rarities such as Salieri's Falstaff, Liszt's Don Sanche and Il Pittor Parigino by Cimarosa. Recordings include: Liszt Piano Concerto No 2 with the Hungarian State Orchestra; Brahms Symphony No 3 and Academic Festival Overture with the Budapest Symphony Orchestra; Il Pittor Parigino (premiere recording). Address: c/o Hungarian State Opera House, Nepoztarsasag uta 22, 1061 Budapest, Hungary.

PALACIO Ernesto, b. 19 Oct 1946, Lima, Peru. Singer (Tenor). Education: Studied in Peru and Milan, Italy. Debut: Sang Almaviva in San Remo, Italy, 1972. Career: Sang lyric roles in Milan, Rome, Venice, Trieste, Bologne, Turin, Genoa, Palermo, Naples, Parma, Catania; Guest appearances in London (Covent Garden), New York (Metropolitan and Carnegie Hall), Buenos Aires (Colon), Berlin (Philharmonic), Edinburgh, Marseilles, Bordeaux, Lille, Nancy, Lyon, Strasbourg, Houston, Dallas, Zurich, Dusseldorf, Munich, Caracas, Chile; Other roles include 18 operas of Rossini, Don Giovanni, Cosi fan tutte, Re Pastore, Die Zauberflöte, Finta giardiniera, Finta Semplice (Mozart); Elisir d'amore, Don Pasquale, La fille du Régiment, Esule di Roma, Torquato Tasso (Donizetti); Sang in a revival of Ciro in Babilonia of Rossini at Savona, 1988; Appeared as Argirio in Tancredi opposite Marilyn Horne at Barcelona, May 1989, Bilbao, Jan 1991; Bonn Opera 1990, as Almaviva. Recordings: Mosè in Egitto (Philips); Il Turco in Italia (CBS); Miserere by Donizetti (Voce); Adelaide di Borgogna by Rossini; Vivaldi's Serenata a Tre (Erato); Torquato Tasso; Catone in Utica by Vivaldi (RCA); Unpublished arias by Rossini, conducted by Carlo Rizzi; Prince Giovanni in Una Cosa Rara (Astrée/Auvidis). Address: c/o Via Del Gelso 1, 20070 Dresand, Milan, Italy.

PALACIO Pedro Antonio, b. 15 Apr 1961, La Rioja, Argentina. Composer. 1 son. Education: Diplomas: Master of Guitar, 1979, Master of Musical Composition, 1985, Cordoba, Argentina; Master of Composition and Musical Analysis, France, 1987. Debut: Variations for Piano performed at National Festival for Contemporary Music, Argentina, 1984. Career: Performance of works: Teatro Colon, Argentina; Festival Antidogma Musica, Italy; Mengano Quartett and WNC Ensemble, Cologne, and Turmheim Ensemble, Germany; Ensemble Stringendo, Ensemble Aleph at Festival of Evreux, BMA Ensemble at Nantes, Wozzeck Trio, ENMD-Montreuil Ensemble, France; World Music Days Festival, Zurich, Switzerland; Poland Broadcasting Symphony Orchestra; Symphony Orchestra of Cordoba. Compositions: Axis; Triolaid; Quintolaid; Latidos; Yugoslavia Burning; Omphalo; Dämmerung; Laughs of Tokyo; Histoire d'Oiseaux Mathématiques. Recordings: CDs: Dämmerung; Laughs of Tokyo. Publication: Roman-B for guitar, 1987. Honours: Essec-Invention, France, 1986; Icons, Italy, 1988; Trinac, Argentina, 1989; André Jolivet, France, 1991; Kazimierz Serocki, Poland, 1996; Alberto Ginastera, Argentina, 1996. Membership: SACEM, France. Hobby: Tennis. Address: 56 avenue Jean-Jaurès, 75019 Paris, France.

PALAY Elliot, b. 18 Dec 1948, Milwaukee, Wisconsin, USA. Singer (Tenor). Education: Studied at Indiana University, Bloomington with Charles Kullmann; Further study with Clemens Kaiser-Breme in Essen. Debut: Lubeck 1972, as Matteo in Arabella. Career: Sang in Freiburg, Dusseldorf, Munich and Stuttgart; Komische Oper Berlin 1977, in Aufstieg und Fall der Stadt Mahagonny; Returned to USA and sang at the New York City Opera; Santa Fe and Seattle 1983, as Siegfried in Der Ring des Nibelungen; Antwerp and Ghent 1983, as Siegmund in Die Walküre; Dresden 1984, in Wozzeck; Other roles include Wagner's Tristan and Walther, Verdi's Radames and Ismaele, the Emperor in Die Frau ohne Schatten and Boris in Katya Kabanova; Sang Siegfried with the Jutland Opera at Aarhus, 1987. Address: c/o Den Jydske Opera, Musikhuset Arkus, Thomas Jensens Alle, DK-8000 Aarhus, Denmark.

PALECZNY Piotr Tadeusz, b. 10 May 1946, Rybnik. Concert Pianist. m. Barbara Kurnik, 31 March 1975, 1 son. Education: Chopin Music Academy, Warsaw. Career: Numerous Concerts with Orchestras Like Chicago Concert Gebouw, Tonhalle Rai, Gewandhaus, BBC, Santa Cecilia; Recitals on 6 Continents; Masterclasses in Paris, Tokyo, Buenos Aires, Lugano, Warsaw; Jury, International Piano Competitions, Cleveland, London, Warsaw. Recordings: Piano Concertos. Honours: Many High Polish State Distinction Prizes of Ministry of Culture, Polish Radio & TV; Order of Aztec Eagle, Mexico. Membership: Chopin Society, Warsaw. Hobbies: Painting; Travel. Address: Ligonia 57, 01498 Warsaw, Poland.

PALEY Alexander, b. 9 Jan 1956, Kishinev, USSR. Concert Pianist. m. 29 July 1978, 1 daughter. Education: Master's Degree, PhD, Moscow Conservatory. Debut: Kishinev, 2 Apr 1969. Career: Performed with Moscow Virtuosi (U Spivakov), 1985-90; Bolshoi Theatre Orchestra, 1986; With Monte Carlo Philharmonic, 1989; With Colorado Symphony, 1991; Recitals, Chatelet, Paris, 1990, Auditorium de Halles, 1991, Strasbourg, Moscow, Prague, Berlin, Sofia; Appeared with National Symphony Orchestra, Wolf Trapp Festival, 1991 and Boston Pops, 1991; Chamber music with Fine Arts Quartet, New York Chamber Soloists also with V Spivakov, Bella Davidovich, Oleg Krysa, D Sitkovetsky and B Pergamentshikov; Musical Director, Cannes-sur-Mer Festival, France. Recordings: Talent, Belgium; Liszt, all 4 Mephisto valses, other pieces; National Public Radio, USA; Radio France; Melodia, Moscow, 1990. Honours: Bach International Competition, Leipzig, 1984; 1st Prize, Vladigekov International Competition, Bulgaria, 1986; Grand Prix, Young Artist Debut, New York, 1988; 1st Prize, Alex de Vries Prize, Belgium, 1990. Hobbies: Reading Classical and Philosophical Literature; Museums; Theatre; Opera; Ballet. Current Management: Melvin Kaplan Inc. Address: 850 West 176th Street, Apt 4 D, New York, NY 10033, USA.

PALISCA Claude (Victor), b. 24 Nov 1921, Rijeka, Croatia. Professor of History of Music. m. (1) Jane Pyne, 1 son, 1 daughter, (2) Elizabeth Keitel, 1987. Education: BA, Queens College, Flushing, New York, 1943; MA, Harvard University, 1948; PhD, Harvard University, 1954; MA (Honorary), Yale University, 1964. Career: Instructor, Assistant Professor in Music, University of Illinois, 1953-59; Associate Professor of History of Music 1959-64; Professor of History of Music 1964-92; Emeritus, 1992-; Director of Graduate Studies in Music, 1967-70, 1987-92; Chairman, Department of Music, 1969-75, of Renaissance Studies, 1977-80, Yale University. Publications: Girolamo Mel: Letters on Ancient and Modern Music to Vincenzo Galilei and Giovanni Bardi, 1960, 1977; 17th Century Science and the Arts (with 3 others), 1961; Musicology (with others), 1963; Baroque Music, 1968, 1991; Translated with Guy Marco, Zarlino, The Art of Counterpoint, Le istitutioni harmoniche, 1558, Part III, 1968; Norton Anthology of Western Music, 1980, 2nd edition, 1988, 3rd edition, 1996; History of Western Music (with D J Grout), 3rd edition, 1980, 4th edition, 1988, 5th edition, 1996; Humanism in Italian Renaissance Musical Thought, 1985; The Florentine Camerata, 1989; Studies in the History of Italian Music and Music Theory, 1994. Honours include: Guggenheim Fellowships, 1960-61, 1980-81; Prize of International Musicological Society for Humanism, 1987; Fellow, American Academy of Arts and Sciences, Academia Filarmonica of Bologna. Memberships include: President, National Council of the Arts in Education, 1967-69; Vice-President, New Haven Symphony Incorporated, 1969-71; President, American Musicological Society, 1970-72; Vice-President, International Musicological Society, 1977-82. Address: 954 Prospect Street, Hamden, CT 06517, USA.

PALKOVIC Jan, b. 6 Nov 1957, Bratislava, Slovakia. Musical Dramaturgist. m. Eva Palkovicova, 31 July 1982, 2 daughters. Education: Faculty of Art, Comenius University; Diploma. Career: Records and Publishing House, Opus, 1983-89; Slovak Radio, Bratislava, 1989-91; Private Radio Rock FM, 1991-97; National Radio Station, Slovak Radio, 1997; Popmusic Dramaturgist, Opus. Contributions to: Musical Life; Literarny tyzdennik; Bluesline Magazine; Radio programmes. Memberships: Slovak Blues Society; Slovak Musical Union. Address: Jana Stanislava 43, 841 05 Bratislava, Slovakia.

PALM Matsi, b. 13 Jan 1942, Tallinn, Estonia. Bass Singer. Education: Studied at the Tallinn Conservatoire, in Moscow and at La Scala. Career: Has sung with the Estonian State Opera from 1967 notably as Boris, Kaspar, Basilio, King Philip, Ivan Khovansky and the Dutchman; Guest appearances from 1980 in Helsinki as Attila, the Savonlinna Festival as the Dutchman, Paris Opéra in 1988 as Pimen and at Karlsruhe in 1992 in Khovanshchina; Buenos Aires from 1991 in Iolanta and Lohengrin; Further appearances in Moscow, St Petersburg, Prague and Berlin with many concerts. Address: c/o Estonian State Opera, Estonia Boulevard 4, E10517 Tallinn, Estonia.

PALM Siegfried, b. 25 Apr 1927, Barmen, Germany. Cellist; Professor of Music; Administrator. m. Brigitte Heinemann. Education: Studied with father and in Enrico Mainardi's master classes at Salzburg. Career: Principal Cellist, Lubeck City Orchestra, 1945-47, Hamburg Radio Symphony, 1947-62, Cologne Radio Symphony, 1962-67; Played with Hamann Quartet 1950-62; Formed Duo with Aloys Kontarsky 1965; Joined Max Rostal and Heinz Schroter in Piano Trio, 1967; Professor at Cologne Musikhochschule, 1962, Director from 1972; Teacher at Darmastadt from 1962; Has also taught at the Royal Conservatory Stockholm, Dartmouth College USA, Marlboro USA and the Sibelius Academy Helsinki; Intendant of the Deutsche Oper Berlin, 1977-81; Many recitals and appearances with leading orchestras; Engagements at Holland Festival, Warsaw Autumn Festival, Prague Spring Festival and Barcelona Festival; First performances of works by Stockhausen, Zimmermann, Penderecki, Xenakis, Zillig, Blacher, Feldman, Ligeti, Fortner, Yun, Kelemen and Kagel. Publication: Pro musica nova: Studien zum Spielen neuer Musik für Cello, 1974. Honours include: German Record Prize, 1969. Address: c/o Ingpen & Williams Ltd, 26 Wadham Road, London SW15 2LR, England.

PALMER Felicity (Joan), b. 6 Apr 1944, Cheltenham, England. Singer (Mezzo-Soprano). Education: Guildhall School of Music and Drama; Hochschule Musik, Munich; AGSM, Teacher and Performer; FGSM. Debut: Purcell's Dido with Kent Opera, 1971; In USA, Marriage of Figaro, Houston, 1973; At La Scala, Milan in world premiere of Riccardo III, 1987. Career includes: Major appearances at concerts in Britain, America, Belgium, France, Germany, Italy, Russia and Spain; Operatic appearances include: The Magic Flute, 1975, Alcina, Bern, 1977, Idomeneo, Zürich, 1980, Rienzi, ENO, 1983, King Priam, Royal Opera, 1985, Albert Herring, Glyndebourne, 1985; Recitals in Amsterdam, Paris and Vienna, 1976-77; Concert tours to Australasia, Far East and Eastern Europe, 1977-; Sang in Flavio Testi's Riccardo III at Milan, 1987; Has sung Kabanicha at Chicago and Glyndebourne; Sang title role in the stage premiere of Roberto Gerhard's The Duenna, Madrid, 1992; Season 1992 as Clytemnestra for Welsh National Opera and the Countess in The Queen of Spades at Glyndebourne; In 1993 sang in Pelléas and Mélisande for Netherlands Opera, and at Orlando and Aix-en-Provence, Fille du Régiment for San Francisco Opera, and Katya Kabonova, Toronto; In 1994 sang in The Rake's Progress, Chicago, Elektra at Dresden and La Scala, Milan; In 1995 sang in Ballo in Maschera at Catania, and in Elektra in Japan with Sinopoli; Clytemnestra in Elektra at Covent Garden, 1997. Recordings include: Messiaen's Poèmes pour Mi, with Pierre Boulez; French songs with John Constable and Simon Rattle with the Nash Ensemble; Andromache in King Priam with David Atherton; Title role in Gluck's Armide. Honours: Kathleen Ferrier Memorial Prize, 1970; CBE, 1993. Current Management: AOR Management Ltd. Address: Westwood, Lorraine Park, Harrow Weald, Middlesex HA3 6BX, England.

PALMER John, b. 25 Sept 1959, Avalon, England. Composer. Education: Humanities and Classical Studies, University of London and Florence; Composition Studies with Jonathan Harvey, Uinko Globokar, Edison Denisov; Graduate, Piano Studies, Conservatory of Music, Lucerne, Switzerland; Postgraduate, Composition, Trinity College, London; PhD, Composition, City University, London. Career: TV Appearance, Featured Composer in Electroshock Program, Moscow; Russian TV Radio Interviews, ORF (Austria), BBC (UK), Colour Bleu (Switzerland) Wired for Sound (Canada), 104-Mh2 Sydney (Australia). Compositions include: Legend, You, Chamber Ensemble; String Quartet I; Theorem, Piano Trio; Orchestral and vocal works; Electroacoustic: Beyond The Bridge; Vision; Renge-Kyo; Phonai; Spirits; Reflections; Eternity; Epitaph. Recordings: Beyond The Bridge; Vision; Renge-Kyo; Spirits. Honours: 1st Prize, Cultural Prize, City of Lucerne with Omen for Orchestra and Amplified Voices, 1994; 2nd Prize, Bourges International Competition with Beyond The Bridge for Cello and Electronics, 1994; 1st Prize, Surrey Sinfonietta Orchestral Competition with Concertino, 1995; 2nd Prize, City of Klagenfurt with String Quartet I, 1996; 2nd Prize, Tokyo International Chamber Music Competition with Theorem for Piano and Trio. Address: Music Department, University of Hertfordshire, College Lane, Hatfield AL10 9AB, England.

PALMER Larry, b. 13 Nov 1938, Warren, Ohio, USA. Harpsichordist; Organist. Education: Studied at Oberlin College Conservatory and Eastman School at Rochester, DMA 1963; Harpsichord with Isolde Ahlgrimm at Salzburg Mozarteum and with Gustav Leonhardt at Haarlem. Career: Recitalist on Harpsichord and Organ throughout the USA and Europe, with premieres of works by such composers as Vincent Persichetti and Ross Lee Finney; Harpsichord Editor of The Diapason from 1969; Professor of Harpsichord and Organ at Southern Methodist University in Dallas, 1970. Publications: Hugo Distler and his Church Music, 1967; Harpsichord in America: A 20th Century Revival, 1989 (2nd Ed 1992). Recordings: Organ works of Distler and harpsichord pieces from the 17th to the 20th centuries. Address: c/o Southern Methodist University, Meadows School of the Arts, Dallas, TX 75275, USA.

PALMER Peter, b. 7 Mar 1945, West Bridgford, Nottinghamshire, England. Writer on Music; Opera Director. Education: Exhibitioner in Modern Languages, Gonville and Caius College, Cambridge, 1963-66, MA; Apprentice Stage Director, International Opera Studio, Zurich, 1967-69. Career: Founder and Artistic Director, East Midlands Music Theatre; First British stage productions of works by Janácek, Krenek, John Ogdon, Schoeck. Publications: Translations include: From the Mattress Grave, song cycle by David Blake, 1980; Wagner and Beethoven by Klaus Kropfinger, 1991; Late Idyll: The Second Symphony of Johannes Brahms by Reinhold Brinkmann, 1995; Essays on the Philosophy of Music by Ernst Bloch, 1985; Johann Faustus, libretto by Hanns Eisler. Contributions to: Reviews and articles in Die Tat, Zurich; Music and Musicians; German Life and Letters; Tempo; The Musical Times; Talks for BBC Radio 3. Honour: Music and Letters Award, 1991. Memberships: Founding Member, Carl Nielsen Society of Great Britain; Life Member, Othmar Schoeck Gesellschaft. Hobbies: Cats; Crosswords. Address: 2 Rivergreen Close, Beeston, Nottinghamshire, NG9 3ES, England.

PALMER Rudolph (Alexis), b. 5 Aug 1952, New York City, USA. Conductor; Composer; Pianist. m. Madeline Rogers, 21 June 1981. Education: BA, Russian, French, Bucknell University, 1973; BS, Composition, Mannes College of Music, 1975; MM, Juilliard, Composition, 1977; DMA, Juilliard, Composition, 1982. Career: Conducting and Composition Faculty, Mannes College of Music, 1982-; Director, Great Neck Choral Society, 1983-84; Orchestra Director, Horace Mann School, 1988-93; Associate Conductor, Amor Artis Chamber Choir, Fairfield County Chorale; Conductor, North Jersey Music Educators Orchestra, Brewer Chamber Orchestra; Palmer Chamber Orchestra; Palmer Singers. Compositions: Contrasts for Four Bassoons (recorded Leonarda Records); O Magnum Mysterium (Albany Records); Commissions: Songs of Reflection; The Vision of Herod; The Immortal Shield; Orchestration of Leonard Bernstein's Touches; Numerous other works for chamber groups, chorus and orchestra, including 2 string quartets, 1 symphony, Dance-Music (a ballet), orchestral overtures and several dramatic cantatas. Recordings: Accompanist: Lieder, (by women composers), Leonarda; The Unknown Dvorak, Erasmus; Conductor; Baroque Cantatas of Versailles, Erasmus; The Romantic Handel, Leonarda; Handel's Imeneo, Vox Cum Laude; Telemann's Pimpinone; Handel's Berenice; Handel's Siroe; Pergolesi's La Serva Padrona, Omega; Handel's Joshua; Handel's Muzio; A Scarlatti's Ishmael; F Joseph Haydn's La Canterina; Handel Arias, Julianne Baird; Chorusmaster, Bach, St John Passion. Hobbies: Theatre; Concerts; Baseball (New York Yankees); Travel; Wine Collector. Address: 215 West 88th Street, Apt 7E, New York, NY 10024, USA.

PALOLA Juhani, b. 25 Nov 1952, Helsinki, Finland. Violinist. m. Liisa-Maria Lampela, 27 Sept 1977, 2 daughters. Education: Violin Studies, Oulu Music Institute, Sibelius Academy, Privately in Munich with Professor Takaya Urakawa. Deubt: Soloist, Oulu Symphony Orchestra, 1968. Career: Concerts as Soloist and Chamber Musician, Finland, Sweden, 1968-, Norway, Ukraine, Romania, Albania, Germany, Switzerland, USA, Austria; Professor of Violin, Teachers Training College, Rorschach, Switzerland; First Violin in Arioso Quartet, St

Gallen. Recordings: Several for Radio and TV; Classic 2000. Membership: ESTA. Address: Salen 248, 9035 Grub AR, Switzerland.

PALOMBI Antonello, b. 1965, Umbria, Italy. Singer (Tenor). Education: Studied in Italy. Debut: Sang Pinkerton in Germany, 1990. Career: Appearances as Dourmont in La Scala di Seta at Pistoia and as the Duke of Mantua in Austria; Edoardo in La Cambiale di Matrimonio at Macerata, Ferrando at avenna, Macduff at Livorno and Attalo in Rossini's Ermione in Berlin; Teatro Comunale, Pisa, as Alfredo, Ramiro (La Cenerentola), Don José and Monteverdi's Telemaco (Ritorno di Ulisse); Nemorino at San Gimmingano, the Duke of Mantua in Tokyo and Sou Chong in Das Land des Lächelns at Florence; Sang Edmondo in a new production of Manon Lescaut at Glyndebourne, 1997; Concerts include Pulcinella, at Pisa and Modena. Address: Teatro Comunale G Verdi, Via Palestro 40, 56200 Pisa, Italy.

PÅLSSON Hans, b. 1 Oct 1949, Helsingborg, Sweden. Pianist; Professor. m. Eva Pålsson, 14 Apr 1980. 2 sons, 1 daughter. Education: Staatliche Hochschule für Musik und Theater, Hanover, Germany, 1968-72; Graduated as Soloist, 1972. Debut: Stockholm, Sweden, 1972. Career: Concerts in approximately 20 countries; Performed in 24-part TV series Dead Masters, Live Music, 1994-97; Dedicatee of 50 solo pieces and piano concertos; Professor, Lund University, 1987; Juror at international piano competitions, Masterclasses. Recordings: Approximately 25 CDs. Honours include: Swedish 1st Prize, Nordic Music Prizes Competition, 1972; Swedish Phonogram Award, 1987. Membership: Royal Swedish Academy of Music. Hobbies: Reading; Art; Cooking. Current Management: Svensk Konsertdirektion, Gothenburg, Sweden. Address: Gotlandsvägen 4, S-22225, Sweden.

PAMPUCH Helmut, b. 1939, Grossmahlendorf, Oberschlesien, Germany. Singer (Tenor). Education: Studied at Nuremberg with Willi Domgraf-Fassbaender, 1957-62. Career: Sang at Regensburg from 1963; Appearances in Brunswick, Wiesbaden and Saarbrucken; Member of the Deutsche Oper am Rhein Dusseldorf 1973-, notably in character and buffo roles; Bayreuth debut 1978, later appeared as Mime in Das Rheingold, 1990; Paris Opera 1979, in the premiere of the full version of Berg's Lulu, conducted by Pierre Boulez; Has sung Mozart's Monostatos at La Scala 1985, and Mime in Ring cycles at San Francisco 1984-90 and Zurich 1989; Further engagements at the State Operas of Hamburg, Munich and Stuttgart; Deutsche Oper Berlin and the Grand Théâtre Geneva; Sang Mime in Das Rheingold at Bayreuth, 1992 and at Buenos Aires, 1995; Many concert appearances. Recordings include: Lulu (Deutsche Grammophon); Das Rheingold (Philips). Address: c/o Deutsche Oper am Rhein, Heinrich-Heine Allee 16, D-4000 Dusseldorf, Germany.

PANENKA Jan, b. 8 July 1922, Prague, Czechoslovakia. Pianist. Education: Studied with frantisek Maxian in Prague and with Serebryakow in Leningrad. Debut: Prague 1944. Career: Member of the Suk Trio, 1957-; Duo recitals with Josef Suk; Chamber concerts with the Smetana Quartet; Soloist with the Czech Philharmonic Orchestra from 1959; Performances in Eastern Europe, West Germany, England and Australia; Professor of Piano at the Prague Academy. Recordings: Beethoven Concertos; Dvorak Piano Trios; Violin Sonatas by Suk and Debussy. Honour: Winner, International Piano Competition Prague, 1951; Grand Prix du Dusque, 1959; Artist of Merit, 1972.

PANERAI Rolando, b. 17 Oct 1924, Campi Bisenszio, Florence, Italy. Singer (Baritone). Education: Studied in Florence with Raoul Frazzi and in Milan with Armani and Giulia Tess. Debut: Naples in 1947 as Faraone in Rossini's Moses. Career: Sang at La Scala from 1951, debut in Samson et Dalila; Venice 1955 in the stage premiere of Prokofiev's The Fiery Angel; Aix in 1955 as Mozart's Figaro; Salzburg from 1957 as Ford in Falstaff, Masetto in Don Giovanni, Guglielmo in Cosi fan tutte and Paolo in Simon Boccanegra; Sang in the Italian premiere of Hindemith's Mathis der Maler, Milan, 1957; Covent Garden debut 1960 as Figaro; Other roles include Verdi's Luna and Giorgio Germont, Henry Ashton in Lucia di Lammermoor and Marcello in La Bohème; Appearances in Verona, Florence, Rome, San Francisco (1958), Moscow, Rio de Janeiro, Athens, Berlin, Munich and Johannesburg; Returned to Covent Garden in 1985 as Dulcamara in L'Elisir d'Amore; Maggio Musicale Florence, 1988 as Puccini's Gianni Schicchi; Sang Michonnet in Adriana Lecouvreur at the 1989 Munich Festival; Douglas in Mascagni's Guglielmo Ratcliff at Catania, 1990; Returned to Covent Garden, 1990 as Dulcamara. Recordings: I Puritani; Così fan tutte; Il Trovatore; Falstaff; Il Barbiere di Siviglia; La Bohème; Aida; Verdi's Oberto; Parsifal with Maria Callas. Address: c/o Royal Opera House, Covent Garden, London, WC2, England.

PANHOFER Walter, b. 3 Jan 1910, Vienna, Austria. Pianist. m. Getraut Schmied 1956, 2 sons. Education: Vienna State Academy of Music and Dramatic Art. Career: Concert tours throughout Europe and overseas as soloist and as chamber music performer; Professor of Music, University of Vienna, 1971-. Recordings: Various works including Schubert's Trout Quintet, with members of the Vienna Octet on the Decca label. Honour: Austrian Cross of Honour, for science and art. Hobbies: Books; Skiing; Mountains. Address: Erdbergstrasse 35, A-1030 Vienna, Austria.

PANKRATOV Vladimir, b. 1958, St Petersburg, Russia. Singer (Bass). Education: Studied at the St Petersburg Conservatoire. Career: Sang with the Kirov Opera in St Petersburg and on tour to Edinburgh, Italy, Sweden, France and Japan in Prince Igor, War and Peace and Khovanshchina; Italian roles include Sparafucile, Philip II, Fiesco, Dulcamara, Basilio, Sarastro, Leporello and Mozart's Commendatore; Guest engagements with Heidelberg Opera until 1995; Debut with Theatre du Capitole Toulouse, 1996; Concert repertoire includes songs by Borodin, Glinka and Tchaikovsky, and the Requiems of faure, Mozart and Verdi; Frequent concerts in Israel, where he also teaches at the Rubin Academy. Address: Atholl Still Ltd, Foresters Hall, 25-27 Westow Street, London SE19 3RY, England.

PANNELL Raymond, b. 25 Jan 1935, London, Ontario, Canada. Composer; Pianist. Education: Studied piano with Steuermann and composition with Wagenaar and Giannini at Juilliard. Career: Taught at Toronto Royal Conservatory from 1959, Directed opera workshops at Stratford Festival, Ontario, 1966; Assistant Director and Resident Conductor at Atlanta Municipal Theater, 1960 and Director of Youth Experimental Opera Workshop, 1969; Co-founder and General Director of Co-Opera Theatre in Toronto, 1975. Compositions: Stage works: Aria da Capo, opera in 1 act, Toronto 1963; The Luck of Giner Coffey, opera in 3 acts; Go, children's opera, 1975; Midway 1975; Push, developmental opera in 1 act, Toronto 1976; Circe, masque, Toronto 1977; Aberfan, video opera, CBC 1977; N-E-U-S, radio opera 1977; Souvenirs, opera in 1 act, Toronto 1979; Refugees, vaudeville, Little Rock, Arkansas, 1986 (revised version); The Downsview Anniversary Song-Spectacle Celebration Pageant 1979; Harvest, television opera, CBC 1980; The Forbidden Christmas, musical 1990. Honour: Salzburg Television Opera Prize for Aberfan, 1977. Address: c/o SOCAN, 41 Valleybrook Drive, Don Mills, Ontario M3B 2S6, Canada.

PANNI Marcello, b. 24 Jan 1940, Rome, Italy. Composer; Conductor. m. Jane Colombier, 3 Dec 1970, 1 daughter. Education: Roma Liceo Classico; Roma Accademia Santa Cecilia, 1961-65; Paris Conservatoire National Superieur, 1965-68. Debut: Venice 1969. Career: Teacher, (Milhaud Chair), Composition and Conducting, Mills College, Oakland, California, USA, 1979-85; Guest Conductor, major stages in Italy; Rome Opera; La Scala, Milan; San Carlo, Naples; La Fenice, Venice; Paris Opera, 1985; Vienna Staatsoper, 1986; Hamburg Staatsoper, 1977; Zurich, 1986; Berlin Deutsche Oper, 1988; New York Metropolitan Opera House, 1988; London Covent Garden, 1989; Concerts: Roma Accademia Santa Cecilia, 1970-; Radio Symphony Orchestras, Italy; Season 1992 with L'Elisir d'amore at Barcelona and The Fall of the House of Usher by Philip Glass at Florence; Season 1993, Trittico by Puccini; Wildschütz by Lortzing at the opera of Bonn; First Guest Conductor, Bonn Opera, 1993. Compositions: Klangfarbenspiel, performed at Milan Piccola Scala, in conjunction with director Mario Ricci and painter Piero Dorazio, 1973; La Partenza dell'Argonauta, directed by Memé Perlini, performed at Florence Maggio Musicale, 1976. Current Management: Stage Door, Via Giardini 941, Modena 41040, Italy. Address: 3 Piazza Borghese, 00186 Rome, Italy.

PANOCHA Jiri, b. 1940, Czechoslovakia. Violinist. Education: Studied at the Prague Academy of Arts. Career: Leader of International Student Orchestra in Berlin, under Karajan; Co-founded the Panocha Quartet, 1968; Many concert appearances in Europe, the USA, Canada, Iraq, Mexico, Cuba and other countries; Repertoire includes works by Smetana, Janacek, Dvorak, Martinu, Haydn, Mozart, Beethoven, Schubert, Bartok and Ravel. Recordings include: Dvorak late quartets and Terzetto; Haydn Op 33 nos 1-6, D Major Op 64; Martinu Complete Quarters; Mendelssohn Octet (with Smetana Quartet); Mozart Oboe Quartet, Clarinet Quintet and Horn Quintet; Schubert Quartettsatz D703 (Supraphon). Honours include: Prize winner (with members of Panocha Quartet) at Kromeriz, 1971; Weimar 1974; Prague 1975; Bordeaux 1976; Grand Prix du Disque, Paris, 1983 for Martinu recordings. Address: Pragokoncert, Malterzska nam 1, 118112 Prague 1, Czech Republic.

PANTILLON Christopher (David), b. 26 Jan 1965, Neuchatel, Switzerland. Cellist. Education: Baccalaureat es Lettres, Humanities, Neuchatel, Switzerland, 1983; Studied with Heinrich Schiff, Conservatory, Basle, 1984-88; Diploma of Cello, 1988; Studied with Valentin Erben, Hochschule für Musik, Vienna. Career: Numerous appearances as soloist or chamber player; Member, Trio Pantillon (with 2 brothers); Concerts in Geneva, Zurich, Bern, Vienna, Paris, Rome, England, France, Germany, Holland; Appeared on Swiss television and radio. Recordings: Kabalevsky: Cello-Concerto No 1 in G Minor. Honour: 2nd Prize, Swiss Youth Competition, Lucerne, 1983. Membership: ESTA. Current Management: Music Management International. Address: La Chanterelle, CH-2022 Bevaix, Switzerland.

PANUFNIK Roxanna, b. 1968, London, England. Composer. Education: Studied at the Royal Academy, with Paul Patterson and Henze. Career: BBC Researcher and Interviewer; Visiting teacher of composition at various schools in England and Barbados; First ever Composer-in-Residence for the Royal County of Berkshire; Performances of her music at most of London's main concert venues throughout Britain, with further performances in France, Italy, Warsaw, Canada, Barbados, Australia, the Far East and Vienna. Compositions include: Dance Suite for the chamber orchestra, Florilegium; Eight Deadly Sins for Recorder; Around Three Corners, Piano Trio; Mass for Westminster Cathedral Choir, Westminster Mass, and various choral and chamber works; Olivia, variation also with children's choir; String Quartet; Orchestrated Samuel Arnold's opera Inkle and Yarico (1787) for its first modern performance, Barbados, 1997; Future commissions include a chamber opera for the Broomhill Trust, Polish carol arrangements for children's choir and orchestra and piano music for the Mark Baldwin Dance Company. Address: Helen Sykes Management, Fourth Floor, Parkway House, Sheen Lane, East Sheen, London, SW14 8LS, England.

PANULA Jorma, b. 10 Aug 1930, Kauhajoki, Finland. Composer; Conductor; Professor of Conducting. Education: Studied at the Helsinki School of Church Music, at the Sibelius Academy and with Dean Dixon in Lund; Further study with Franco Ferrara at Hilversum, and in Austria and France. Career: Conducted at theatres in Lahti and Tampere 1953-58, Helsinki 1958-62; Founded the chamber orchestra of the Sibelius Academy and conducted the Helsinki Philharmonic Orchestra 1965-67 and the Aarhus City Orchestra in Denmark 1973; Guest appearances in the USSR, USA and Europe; Notable for his interpretations of late Romantic and early 20th Century music; Professor of Conducting at the Sibelius Academy, 1973-; Stockholm Musik Hogskolen, 1981-88; Copenhagen Royal Conservatorium, 1988-91; Professor for many summer courses in conduction including Yale University and Bartok Seminar in Hungary. Compositions include: Violin Concerto 1954; Jazz Capriccio for piano and orchestra 1965; Steel Symphony 1969; Choral and vocal works. Recordings include: Madetoja's Symphony No 3 and Opera Pohjalaisia; Englund's Piano Concerto and Palmgren's Piano Concerto No 2, with the Helsinki Philharmonic (EMI) Address: c/o Sibelius Academy, P Rautatiekatu 9, 00100 Helsinki 10, Finland.

PANZARELLA Anna Maria, b. 1970, France. Singer (Soprano). Education: Studied in Grenoble and Geneva, at the Royal College of Music and at the National Opera Studio. Debut: Sang Fransquita in Carmen with Geneva Opera. Career: Appeared in La rondine for Opera North, as Frasquita in Lisbon, and Stephano in Roméo et Juliette at Covent Garden; Season 1995-96 as Puccini's Lauretta in Brussels, First Lady (Die Zauberflöte) at Aix and Amore in the world premiere of Goehr's Arianna at Covent Garden; Season 1996-97 as DOnna Elvira for Opera Zurich, Balkis in Haydn's L'Incontro Improvviso at Lausanne and Rameau's Aricie in Paris and New York; Season 1997 as Adele in Le Comte Ory for GTO and Despina at the Bastille, Paris. Recordings include: Mozart's Requiem with Les Arts Florissants and William Christie (Erato). Address: c/o Harold Holt Ltd, 31 Sinclair Road, London W14 0NS, England.

PAP Janos, b. 25 December 1957, Budapest. Musical Acoustician. m. Eva Raffay, 5 July 1980, 1 d. Education: Maths, Phys, Eotvos University, Budapest. Career: Doctor of University, 1986; Scholarship, Hungarian Academy of Sciences, 1986-89; Scholarship, DAAD, 1988-89; Assistant Professor, Liszt Academy of Music, 1990-; DAAD Scholar, 1994. Publications: Fundamentals of Musical Acoustics, 1992; Fundamentals of Acoustics of Musical Instruments; Die Klauiere von Franz Liszt. Membership: ISME. Address: F Liszt Academy of Music, Liszt Ter 8, H-1061 Budapest, Hungary.

PAPE Gerard (Joseph), b. 22 Apr 1955, Brooklyn, New York, USA. Composer. m. Janet Smarr Pape, 23 Aug 1981, 2 sons. Education: BA, Columbia, University, 1976; MA, 1978, PhD, 1982, University of Michigan; Studied composition with George Cacioppo and William Albright. Career: Director, Composer-in-Residence, Sinewave Studios, 1980-91; Music presented in over 25 concerts in Ann Arbor, Michigan; Produced the annual Festival of Contemporary Orchestral, Ensemble and Electronic Music, Ann Arbor, twice, 1986-91; Since 1991, Director, Les Ateliers, UPIC Paris, France (Electronic Music Studio). Compositions include: Ivan and Rena for 4 Vocal Soloists and Orchestra, 1984; Cosmos for Large Orchestra, 1985; The Sorrows of The Moon for Baritone and Tape, 1986; Folie à Deux for Violin and Piano, 1986; Exorcism for Baritone and Orchestra, 1986; Catechresis for Soprano and Orchestra, 1987; Cerberus for Organ and Tape, 1987; Vortex (String Quartet No 2), 1988; Three Faces of Death for Orchestra, 1988; Piano Concerto, 1988;

Xstasis for Ensemble and Tape, 1992; 2 Electro-Accoustic Songs for Voice, Flute and Tape, 1993; Le Fleuve du Désir (String Quartet No 3), 1994; Monologue for bass voice and tape, 1995; Battle for 4 solo voices and tape, 1996; Makbenach for saxophone, ensemble and tape, 1996; Feu Toujours Vivant, for large orchestra and live electronics, 1997. Recording: Mode 26, 6 pieces of Music by Gerard Pape, 1992. Contribution to: Complexity, Composition, Perception, published in Currents in Musical Thought, 1994. Honours: Various grants to produce the Sinewave series of concerts, Michigan Council for The Arts; Meet The Composer, 1989; 6 ASCAP Standard Awards, 1992-97. Membership: ASCAP. Address: 62 Rue Michel Ange, 75016 Paris, France.

PAPE René, b. 4 Sept 1964, Dresden, Germany. Singer (Bass-baritone). Education: Member of Dresden Kreuzchor 1974-81, tours to Japan and Europe; Dresden Musikhochschule from 1981. Debut: Berlin Staatsoper 1987, as the Speaker in Die Zauberflöte. Career: Sang in 1989 premiere of Siegfried Matthus's Graf Mirabeau at Berlin Staatsoper and has appeared there and elsewhere in Germany as Mozart's Figaro and Alfonso, Verdi's Banquo, Procida and King in Aida, Gremin in Eugene Onegin and Galitzky in Prince Igor; Guest engagements at Frankfurt and Vienna Staatsoper; Salzburg Festival 1991, as Sarastro in Die Zauberflöte; Many concert appearances, notably in Mozart's Requiem for the bi-centenary performances in 1991; Sang the Speaker in Die Zauberflöte at the Met, 1995; Appeared in Lohengrin at Covent Garden, 1997. Address: c/o Allied Artists Agency, 42 Montpellier Square, London SW7 1JZ, England.

PAPERNO Dmitry, b. 18 Feb 1929, Kiev, USSR. Concert Pianist; Professor of Piano. m. Ludmila Gritsay, 21 May 1966, 2 daughters. Education: Graduated, Central School of Music for Especially Gifted Children (affiliated with Tchaikovsky Conservatory), Moscow, 1946; Honours degree, Moscow Tchaikovsky Conservatory, 1951; Postgraduate (Aspiranture), 1955; Studied with professor Alexander Goldenweiser. Debut:Recital, Moscow, 1955. Career: Concert career: Pianist-Soloist, Mosconcert; About 1500 solo recitals and performances in the former Soviet Union, Eastern and Western Europe and Cuba including The USSR State Orchestra, (Moscow, Leningrad and Brussels, Belgium EXPO 1958), Gewandhaus Orchestra, (Leipzig, 1960), Hallé Orchestra, (Manchester, 1967), and many others 1955-76; Numerous concerts in USA, 1977-, also Holland, France, Belgium, Majorca and Portugal, 1985-; Sonata recital with Mstislav Rostropovich, Pasadena, California, USA, 1989; Teaching: Moscow State Gnesin Institute, 1967-73; DePaul University, Chicago, USA, 1977-; Full Professor of Piano, 1985; Many masterclasses in the USA and Europe including Tchaikovsky Conservatory, Moscow. Recordings include: Melodia, USSR , 5 recordings: works by Chopin, Liszt, Grieg, Schumann, Bach-Busoni, Debussy, Medtner; 2 videotapes for Moscow television - piano recital and Chopin F minor concerto with Moscow Radio and Television Orchestra under Gennady Rozhdestvenski; Musical Heritage Society, USA, 2 recordings: Selected Works of Scriabin, 1978, and Tchaikovsky's The Seasons, 1982; 5 CDs, USA; Russian Piano Music, 1989; Works of Bach-Busoni, Beethoven, Schubert, Brahms, 1990; Uncommon Encores, 1992; Chopin Live, including the 5th Chopin Competition, Warsaw, 195, 1997; Selected works from the 1960s and 1970s, 1998. Publications: 2 books in Russian; Notes of a Moscow Pianist, 1983; Post Scriptum, 1987; Articles and reviews in USSR and USA. Hobbies: Books; Chess; Stamps. Address: 2646 North Wayne Unit A, Chicago, IL 60616, USA.

PAPINEAU-COUTURE Jean, b. 12 Nov 1916, Outremont, Québec, Canada. Composer. m. Isabelle Baudoin (dec. 1987). Education: Conducting with Francis Findley, Composition with Quincy Porter, Piano with Beveridge Webster; BMus, New England Conservatory of Music, Boston, 1941; Composition and Harmony under Nadia Boulanger at Madison, Wisconsin, Lake Arrowhead and Santa Barbara, California. Career: Teaching Piano, Jean-de-Brebeuf College, Montreal, 1943-44; Teacher of Music, Conservatoire de Musique et d'Art Dramatique de la Province de Québec, Montreal, 1946-52; Professor, 1951-, Faculty Secretary, 1952-67, Vice Dean, 1967, Dean, 1968-73, Faculty of Music, University of Montreal; Commissions from Canadian Broadcasting Corporation, Montreal Symphony Orchestra, others. Compositions include: Suite Lapitsky, orchestra, 1965; Dialogues, 1967; Sectuor, 1967; Nocturne, 7 instruments, 1969; Oscillations, orchestra, 1969; Chanson de rahit, voice, ensemble, 1972; Obsession, 1973; Trio in 4 movements, 1974; Slano, 1975; Le débat du coeur et du corps de villon, voice, ensemble, 1977; Prouesse, viola, 1986; Nuit Polaire, contralto, 10 instruments, 1986; Vers l'Extinction, organ, 1987; Thrène, violin, piano, 1988; Courbes, organ, 1988; Les arabesques d'Isabelle, flute, cor-d'anglais, clarinet, bassoon, piano, 1989; Celebrations, woodwinds, 5 brass percussions, piano, strings, 1990; Quasipassacaille, C'est bref, organ, 1991; Tournants, organ, 1992; Automne, flute oboe, clarinet, bassoon, horn, string quintet, 1992; Vents capricieux sur le clavier, flute, oboe, clarinet, bassoon, piano, 1993; Chocs sonores, marimba, cymbal and tom; Glanures, soprano, chamber orchestra, 1994; Fantasque, violoncello solo, 1995. Recordings: Many on various labels. Honours: Canadian Governor-General's Prize, 1994. Address: 4694 Lacombe, Montreal, Quebec, Canada H3W 1R3.

PAPPANO Antonio, b. 30 Dec 1959, London, England (US Citizen). Conductor. Education: Studied in America with Norma Verrilli, Arnold Franchetti and Gustav Meier. Career: Repetiteur and Assistant Conductor at New York City Opera, Barcelona, Lyric Opera of Chicago and Bayreuth (Tristan and The Ring, with Barenboim); Concerts with the Oslo PO, Orchestra de Paris, Gurzenich Orchestra (Cologne), Tokyo PO, Chicago SO, Cleveland Orchestra and Los Angeles PO; Opera debut at the Norwegian Opera, Oslo, with guest appearances at English National Opera, Covent Garden and the Berlin Staatsoper; Music Director of the Théatre Royal, Brussels, from 1992, leading Salome, Die Meistersinger, Un Ballo in Maschera, Ariadne and Otello; Vienna Staatsoper debut with Siegfried (1993) returning 1998 for I Vespri Siciliani; Season 1996 with the original Don Carlos in Brussels and at the Paris Châtelet; Season 1997 with Salome at Chicago and Eugene Onegin at the Metropolitan; Engaged for Lohengrin at Bayreuth, 1999. Recordings include: Don Carlo and La Bohème; As Pianist, accompanying Rockwell Blake in song recital. Address: Allied Artists, 42 Montpelier Square, London SW7 1JZ, England.

PAQUETTE Daniel, b. 1930, Morteau, Doubs, France. Professor Emeritus of History of Music. m. Madeleine Mougel, 22 Aug 1957, 1 son, 1 daughter. Education: Licence, Degree in History of Art and Archaeology, University of Dijon, 1962; Doctorate, 3rd cycle, University of Dijon, 1969; Doctor of Letters, University of Paris IV, Sorbonne, 1978; 1st prize in Musical Composition, National Conservatoire of Dijon, 1961; 1st prize for Violincello and History of Music, National Conservatoire of Saint Etienne, 1951. Career: Teacher of Musical Education, Lycees in Angiers, 1952, Dijon, 1953-64; Assistant, Institute of Musicology, University of Strasbourg, 1964-69; Lecturer, University of Dijon, 1970-72; Professor, Univeristy of Lyon, 1972-; Head, Musicology Section, Universities of Besancon and Dijon (Audio-visual education), St Etienne; Leader, Philharmonic Choirs of Dijon and Voix Amies Dijon, 1953-64; Leader, University Orchestra, Strasbourg, 1964-69. Compositions: Les Dames des Entreportes, symphonic poem; Operetta for children; Les Fantomes du Val au Faon; A cappella choral music based on ancient music of 16th-18th century; Film and chamber music; Films, J J Rousseau et la musique; J Ph Rameau, musicien sensible et savant rigoureux. Publications: L'Instrument de musique dans la Grece Antique, 1984; Jean Phillipe Rameau musicien bourguignon, 1983; Musique baroque, Aspects dela musique en France et a Lyon au XVIII, since 1990; Articles in Dictionaire de la Musique, 1976-86 and Die Musik in Geschichte und Gegenwart, 1970. Address: Les Furtins, 71960 Berze-la-Ville, France.

PARATORE Anthony, b. 17 June 1946, Boston, Massachusetts, USA. Concert Pianist. Education: BM, Boston University, 1966; BM, MS, Juilliard School, New York, 1970. Debut: Metropolitan Museum, 1973. Career: Guest appearances with New York Philharmonic, Chicago, San Francisco, Detroit, Washington National, Denver, Indianapolis, Atlanta, San Diego, BBC London, Vienna Philharmonic, Berlin Philharmonic, Vienna Symphony, RAI Orchestra, Nouvel Philharmonique, Warsaw Philharmonic, Amsterdam Philharmonic, Rotterdam Philharmonic, Norwegian Chamber Orchestra, English Chamber Orchestra, Prague Chamber Orchestra, Bavarian Radio Orchestra; Festival appearances, mostly Mozart, Salzburg, Berlin, Lucerne, Istanbul, Adelaide Festival in Australia, and Spoleto. PBS television special, The Paratores, Two Brothers, Four Hands; NPR radio, All Things Considered and A Note To You. Compositions: Premiers of new compositions; Wolfgang Rihm, Maskes; Manfred Trojan, Folia; William Bolcom, Sonata for two pianos in one movement. Recordings: Pictures at an Exhibition, Mussorgsky; Opera Festival for Four Hands; Mendelssohn Concerti for two pianos and orchestra; Variations for Four Hands; Schoenberg Chamber Symphony op 9; Stravinsky, Sacre du Printemps; Ravel; Bolero, Ma Mère L'Oye, Rapsodie Espagnole; Gershwin; Rhapsody in Blue, Concerto in F. Contributions to: Keyboard Classics; Clavier magazine. Honours: 1st Prize, Munich International Music Competition, Duo-Piano Category, 1974. Memberships: Boston Musician's Association; Dante Alighieri Society. Current Management: Hans-Ulrich Schmid, Hannover, Germany. Address: Schmiedestrasse 8, 30159 Hannover, Germany.

PARATORE Joseph D, b. 19 Mar 1948, Boston, Massachusetts, USA. Concert Pianist. Education: BM, Boston University, 1970; MS, Juilliard School, 1972. Debut: Metropolitan Museum of Art, 1973. Career: Guest appearances with New York Philharmonic, Chicago Symphony, San Francisco, Detroit, Indianapolis, Atlanta, Washington National, Denver, San Diego, BBC, Vienna Philharmonic, Berlin Philharmonic, Vienna Symphony, RAI, Nouvel Philharmonique, Warsaw Philharmonic, Amsterdam Philharmonic, Rotterdam Philharmonic, Norwegian Chamber Orchestra, English Chamber Orchestra, Prague Chamber Orchestra, Bavarian Radio Orchestra; Festival appearances, Lucerne, Istanbul, Adelaide Festival in Australia, Salzburg, Berlin, Spoleto, mostly Mozart; Television: WGBH-PBS Television Special The Paratores, Two Brothers/Four Hands; Radio: NPR All Things Considered and A Note to You. Compositions: Premiers of new compositions: Wolfgang Rihm, Maskes; Manfred Trojan, Folia; William Bolcom, SOnata for two pianos in one movement. Recordings: Mussorgsky - Pictures at an Exhibition and Opera Festival for Four Hands; Mendelssohn Concerti for Two Pianos and Orchestra; Variations for Four Hands; Schoenberg, Chamber Symphony op 9; Stravinsky, Sacre du Printemps; Ravel; Bolero, Ma Mère L'Oye, Rapsodie Espagnole; Gershwin; Rhapsody in Blue, Concerto in F. Contributions to: Keyboard Classics - The Art of Transcribing Mussorgsky; Clavier Magazine - Master Class - Ravel Ma Mère L'Oye. Honours: 1st Prize, Munich International Music Competition, Duo-Piano Category, 1974. Memberships: Boston Musician's Association; Dante Alighieri Society. Current Management: Hans-Ulrich Schmid, Hannover, Germany. Address: Schmiedestrasse 8, 30159 Hannover, Germany.

PARDEE Margaret, b. 10 May 1920, Valdosta, Georgia, USA. Violinist; Voilist; Teacher of Violin and Viola. m. Daniel R Butterly, 5 July 1944. Education: Diploma, 1940, Post Graduate Diploma, 1942, Institute of Musical Art, Juilliard School; Diploma, Juilliard Graduate School, 1945; Studied with Sascha Jacobsen, 1937-42, Albert Spalding, 1942-44, Louis Persinger, 1944-46, Ivan Galamian, 1948-56. Debut: New York Town Hall, 1952. Career: Toured as Soloist and in String Quartet and Duo Recitals as Violinist and Violist, USA; Soloist with Symphony Orchestra; Faculty Member, Juilliard School, 1942-; Concert Master, Great Neck Symphony, New York, 1954-85; Faculty Member and Director, Meadowmount School of Music, 1956-85, 1988-92; Adjunct Professor, Queens College, New York, 1978-, State University of New York, Purchase, 1980-; Jury Member, National and International Competitions; Faculty Member, Estherwood Festival and School, Dobbs Ferry, New York, 1984-85, Estherwood Festival and Summer School, Oneonta State University, 1986; Faculty, Bowdoin Summer Music Festival, Bowdoin College, Brunswick, Maine, 1987; Taught in Conservatory of Music of the Simon Bolivar Orchestra in Caracas, Venezuela, 1988, 1989; Invited to teach in Caracas, Venezuela for Municipal Orchestra and Symphonica, 1991-; On Faculty at Killington Chamber Music Festival, Killington, 1993-. Address: c/o Juilliard School, Lincoln Center Plaza, New York, NY 10023, USA.

PARIK Ivan, b. 1955, Czechoslovakia. Conductor. Education: Studied with Hans Swarowsky in Vienna and with Arvid Jansons and Kurt Masur in Weimar; Munich Staatsoper with Wolfgang Sawallisch. Career: Has appeared with leading orchestras in Czechoslovakia and elsewhere in Eastern Europe; Conductor at Ostrava Opera from 1980, leading works by Mozart, Verdi, Puccini, Weber, Gounod, Wagner, Bizet, Strauss, Shostakovich and Czech composers; Guest Conductor at Vienna Volksoper, notably with The Bartered Bride, Die Entführung, Die Zauberflöte and Dvorak's Jacobin; Guest appearances in Dresden with Rusalka and Lohengrin; Bilbao and Prague with Così fan Tutte; Conducted Rigoletto at Gars am Kamp, Austria, 1992; Musical Director of the Klagenfurt Opera from 1992; Concert engagements in works by Mozart, Schubert, Berlioz, Brahms, Dvorak, Janacek, Debussy, Stravinsky and Strauss. Address: c/o Pragokoncert, Maltezske nam 1, 11813 Prague 1, Czech Republic.

PARIK Ivan, b. 17 Aug 1936, Bratislava, Slovakia. Composer. m. Magdalena Barancoková, 2 Oct 1970, 1 daughter. Education: Completed Composition and Conducting studies, Bratislava Conservatory, 1958; Composition, Academy of Music and Dramatic Arts, Bratislava, 1958-62; Habilitation as Associate Professor of Composition, 1976; Degree of Professor, 1990. Debut: Music for 4 strings. Career: Lecturer, 1962-, Pro-Rector, 1990-94, Rector, 1994-97, Academy of Music and Dramatic Arts, Bratislava. Compositions: Orchestral including: Music for Ballet, 4 scenes for large orchestra, 1968; Fragments, suite for ballet, 1969; Musica pastoralis for large orchestra, 1984; Music for Flute, Viola and Orchestra, 1987; Two Arias on text fragments of Stabat mater for higher voice and orchestra; Chamber including: Sonata for flute, 1962; Songs about Falling Leaves for piano, 1962; Time of Departures, diptych for soprano and piano, 1976; Seen Closely Above the Lake for reciter, wind quintet, piano and string quartet, also version for orchestra, 1979; Pastorale for Organ, 1979; Music for Milos Urbásek for string quartet, 1981; Duet for Violas, 1981; How It Is Drunken from a Well, music to poem by Milan Rúfus for reciter and chamber orchestra, 1990; Choral including Among the Mountains, ballad for mixed choir, 1973; Electroacoustic music including: Music to Opening II for flute solo and tape, 1970; Im memoriam Ockeghem, 1971; Hommage to Hummel, 1980; Scenic and film music including: Fragment, ballet in 1 act on motifs of Kobo Abbe's novel Sand Woman, 1969; King Lear, 1969; Three Sisters, 1981; Medea, 1983. Publications: Some Remarks on the Problems of Education in Composition, habilitation thesis, 1974; Co-author, How to Read a Score, 1986; Many articles. Honours: Honorary Medal, Slovák Philharmonic Orchestra, 1986; Gold Medal, Academy of Music, Prague, 1997. Memberships:

Chairman, Music Foundation; Slovak Music Union. Address: Gajova 17, 81109 Bratislava, Slovakia.

PARIS Alain, b. 22 November 1947, Paris, France. Conductor. m. Marie-Stella Abdul Ahad, 23 June 1973. Education: Licence in Law, Paris, 1969; Studied Piano with Bernadette Alexandre-Georges, Ecriture with Georges Dandelot; Conducting with Pierre Dervaux (Licence de concert, Ecole Normale de Musique, 1967), Louis Fourestier, Paul Paray. Debut: 1969. Career: Guest Conductor, with major French orchestras including, Orchestre de Paris, Orchestre National, Orchestre de Lyon, Toulouse, Strasbourg; Performed with various orchestras abroad including, Dresdner Philharmonic, Slovak Philharmonic, Orchestre de la Suisse Romande, Philharmonia Hungarica, Philharmonie George Enesco (Bucarest), Orchestra de la BRT (Brussels), Milan, Saint Petersburg, Germany, Luxembourg, Greece, Iraq; Assistant Conductor, Orchestre du Capitole de Toulouse, 1976-77; Associate Conductor, 1983-84, Permanent Conductor, 1984-87, Opéra du Rhin, Strasbourg; Producer, Musical Broadcasts for Radio France, 1971-; Professor of Conducting, Strasbourg Conservatory, 1986-89. Publications: Dictionnaire des interprètes et de l'interprétation musicale, Paris, Robert Laffont, 1982, 4th edition 1995; Spanish Translation, Turner, Madrid, 1989; German Translation, Bärenreiter/dtv, Kassel-Munich, 1992; Les Livrets d'opéra, Paris, Robert Laffont, 1991; Editor, French Edition of the New Oxford Companion to Music (Dictionnaire encyclopédique de la musique, Robert Laffont 1988) and Baker's Biographical Dictionary of Musicians (Dictionnaire biographique des musiciens, Robert Laffont 1995). Contributions to: Encyclopaedia Universalis; Retz; Quid; Scherzo; Courrier musical de France. Honours: Licence de concert, Ecole Normale de Musique, Paris, 1967; 1st Prize, concours international de Besancon, 1968. Memberships: Société Française de Musicologie. Hobbies: Tennis. Address: 33 Rue de Constantinople, 75008 Paris, France.

PARISOT Aldo (Simoes), b. 30 Sept 1920, Natal, Brazil. Cellist. Education: Studied with Thomazzo Babini and with Ibere Gomes Grosso; Further study at Yale University. Debut: With the Boston Symphony at the Berkshire Music Center, 1947. Career: Principal Cellist, Pittsburgh Symphony, 1949-50; Tours of Europe, Asia, Africa, South America and throughout the USA from 1948; Plays solo works by Bach and the sonatas of Brahms and Beethoven in recital; Joined faculty of Peabody Conservatory 1956-58, Yale University 1958, Mannes College 1962-66, New England Conservatory 1966-70; Music Director of Also Parisot International Cello Course and Competition in Brazil, 1977; Artist-in-Residence, Banff Center for the Arts, Canada, 1981-83; Has given the premieres of works by Quincy Porter, Villa-Lobos (concerto no 2 1955), Claudio Santoro (concerto 1963), Leon Kirchner (concerto for violin, cello and orchestra 1960), Alvin Etler (concerto 1971), Yehudi Wyner (De novo 1971) and Donald Martino.

PARKER Jon Kimura, b. 25 Dec 1959, Vancouver, Canada. Concert Pianist. Education: Master's in Music, 1983 and Doctor of Musical Arts, 1989, Juilliard School; Teachers: Adele Marcus, Lee Kum-Sing, Edward Parker and Marek Jablonski. Debut: New York, 1984 and London 1984. Career: Performed with London Symphony, London Philharmonic, Toronto Symphony, Cleveland Orchestra, Minnesota Orchestra, Los Angeles Philharmonic, Scottish National Orchestra, Berlin Radio Symphony, NHK Orchestra, Japan, and all Canadian Orchestras; Recital tours in Europe, Canada, North and South America, Far East and Australia; Command performance for Queen Elizabeth II and Prime Minster of Canada, 1984; Featured on CBC TV documentary show The Journal, Local Boy Makes Great in 1985; Benefit performance of Beethoven's Emperor Concerto at Sarajevo, New Year's Eve, 1995. Recordings: Tchaikovsky Piano Concerto No 1; Prokofiev Piano Concerto No 3 with André Previn and Royal Philharmonic Orchestra, 1986; Solo Piano Music of Chopin, 1987; Two Pianists are Better Than One, with Peter Schickele, 1994. Honours: 1st Prize and Princess Mary Gold Medal, Leeds International Piano Competition, 1984; Canadian Governor General's Performing Arts Award, 1996; Numerous other first prizes in international competitions. Hobbies: Old Jazz Recordings; Producing home videos with original plots. Address: c/o ICM Artists Ltd, 40 West 57th Street, New York, NY 10019, USA.

PARKER Moises, b. 1945, Las Villas, Cuba. Singer (Tenor). Education: Studied in Munich, at Juilliard School and Verdi Conservatory Milan; Teachers included Tito Gobbi, Richard Holm and Hermann Reutter. Debut: New York City Opera 1976 as Don José. Career: Sang at Strasbourg Opera 1978-80 as Tamino, Hoffmann and Ratansen in Roussel's Padmavati; Season 1981-82 with Welsh National Opera and Scottish Opera as Rodolfo and Alvaro; Brunswick and Augsburg 1982-83 as Don José and Alvaro; Deutsche Oper Berlin as Pinkerton; Sang Otello at Coburg 1984 and at Stuttgart and Klagenfurt 1989; Theater des Westens Berlin 1988-89, as Gershwin's Porgy, Wurzburg 1990 as Bacchus; Member of Kiel Opera from 1988, notably as Turiddu in Cavalleria Rusticana and Win-San-Lui in Leoni's L'Oracolo, 1990;

Concert repertoire includes Messiah, Beethoven's Ninth and the Missa Solemnis, Elijah, Rossini's Stabat Mater and Messe Solennelle, Verdi's Requiem. Honours: Prize Winner at 1974 Voci Verdiane Competition at Bussetto, 1975 Francisco Vinas at Barcelona. Address: c/o Buhnen des Landeshaupt, Rathausplatz, 2300 Kiel, Germany.

PARKER Roger, b. 2 Aug 1951, London, England. Writer on Music. Education: Studied at London University with Margaret Bent and Pierluigi Petrobelli. Career: Professor at Cornell University, USA, 1982-94; Coordinating Editor of Donizetti Critical Edition, 1988; Founding Co-Editor, Cambridge Opera Journal, 1989; University Lecturer in Music and Fellow of St Hugh's College, Oxford, 1994. Publications: Critical Edition of Verdi's Nabucco, 1987; (with A Groos) Giacomo Puccini; La Bohème, 1986, and Reading Opera, 1989; Studies in Early Verdi, 1989; Analyzing Opera: Verdi and Wagner (with C Abbate), 1989; Articles on Verdi and his operas in The New Grove Dictionary of Opera, 4 volumes, 1992; Oxford Illustrated History of Opera, editor, 1994. Honours: Dent Medal, 1991. Address: Faculty of Music, St Aldate's, Oxford OX1 1DB, England.

PARKER-SMITH Jane (Caroline Rebecca), b. 20 May 1950, Northampton, England. Concert Organist. m. John Gadney, 24 October 1996. Education: Royal College of Music, 1967-71; Postgraduate Study with Nicolas Kynaston, England and Jean Langlais, Paris. Career: Westminister Cathedral, 1970; Royal Festival Hall, 1972; BBC Promenade Concert, 1972; Solo Recitals, Jyvasklya Festival, Finland, 1977, Stockholm Concert Hall, 1980, Hong Kong Arts Festival, 1988, Roy Thomson Hall, Toronto, 1989, City of London Festival, 1992, Festival Paris Quartier D'Ete, 1995, American Guild of Organists Centennial Convention, New York, 1996. Recordings: Widor Symphonies, Music for Trumpet & Organ with Maurice Andre; Liszt Organ Works, Saint-Saëns Organ Symphony No 3, Janacek Glagolitic Glass; Baroque Organ Concertos with Prague Chamber Orchestra. Honours: ARCM, 1966; Winner, National Organ Competition, 1970; LTCL, 1971; Hon FGMS, 1996, Hon FNMSM, 1997. Memberships: Incorporated Society of Musicians; Royal College of Organists; Incorporated Association of Organists. Current Management: Karen McFarlane Artists Inc, Cleveland, USA. Address: 141 The Quadrangle Tower, Cambridge Square, London W2 2PL, England.

PARKIN Simon, b. 3 Nov 1956, Manchester, England. Composer; Pianist; Teacher. Education: Yehudi Menuhin School, 1967-74; MusB, University of Manchester, 1977; Graduate, Royal Northern College of Music, 1978; Associate, Royal College of Music, 1973. Career: Performances in St John's, Smith Square, London, Wigmore Hall and Queen Elizabeth Hall, London; Performances as duo-partner in Budapest, Liszt Academy and Berlin (Otto Braun Saal); Resident Pianist at ISM, LDSM and Lenk courses; Compositions performed in London, New York, Frankfurt, Germany; Broadcasts on German radio; Teaching Posts: Royal Northern College of Music; Yehudi Menuhin School. Compositions: Ted Spiggot and the Killer Beans (Opera); Le Chant des Oiseaux (choral work); Laughter and Tears (Requiem, choir and orchestra) Piano trio, string quartet, chamber concerto; Composer of several sonatas for solo instruments and piano. Honours: Recipient various university and college prizes; Morley College Centenary Concerto Prize for chamber concerto. Hobbies: Reading; Writing; Giraffes. Address: 39 Crompton Road, Burnage, Manchester M19 2QT, England.

PARKINSON Del R, b. 6 Aug 1948, Blackfoot, Idaho, USA. Pianist; University Professor. m. Glenna M Christensen, 6 Aug 1986. Education: BM, 1971, MM, 1972, Performers Certificate, 1972, DM, 1975, Indiana University; Postgraduate Diploma, The Juilliard School 1977; Fulbright Hays Grant for graduate study in London, England, 1974-75. Debut: Wigmore Hall, London, 1976; Carnegie Recital Hall, New York, 1981. Career: Concerto appearances with Chicago Civic Orchestra, Utah Symphony, Boise Philharmonic and Guadalajara Symphony; Solo recitals in USA, England and Mexico; Chamber Music in USA and aboard Royal Viking Cruise Line; Teaching Career: Assistant Professor at Furman University, 1975-76, Piano Coordinator at Ricks College, 1977-85, Professor at Boise State University, 1985-; Performed with American Piano Quartet throughout USA, Asia and Europe, 1989-95. Recording: With American Piano Quartet. Publication: Selected Works for Piano and Orchestra in One Movement, 1821-53, Indiana University Doctoral Dissertation, 1975. Contributions to: Record review for Journal of American Liszt Society of Charles Koechlin piano music, 1984. Address: Music Department, Boise State University, Boise, ID 83725, USA.

PARKINSON Paul (Andrew), b. 26 Mar 1954, Wallasey, Cheshire, England. Composer. Education: Royal Academy of Music, 1973-78; Mendelssohn Scholar, 1978-79; Studies with Nadia Boulanger, Paris, France and Peter Racine Fricker, Santa Barbara, California, USA. Career: Lecturer, Royal Academy of Music, London, England, 1979-83; Composer-in-Residence, Lincolnshire and Humberside Arts, 1984; Freelance Composer, Lecturer, 1985-. Compositions: Oboe Sonata, 1976; Sinfonia for

Orchestra, 1977; String Trio, 1977; Wind Quintet, 1978; Four Love Songs, 1979; Transit One (flute, oboe and piano), 1979; Dance Poems for Chamber Orchestra, 1982; String Quartet, 1982; Capriccio (harp), 1983; Dream Gold (cantata), 1984; Prayer Before Birth, 1984; Brass Reflections, 1984; Three Donne Songs, 1985; Hymn, 1985; Piano Sonata, 1986; Passion for Double String Orchestra, 1989; Release for Orchestra, 1991. Address: 37c Allen Road, Stoke Newington, London N16 8RX, England.

PARNAS Leslie, b. 22 Nov 1932, St Louis, Missouri, USA. Concert Cellist; Professor of Music. m. Ingeburge Parnas, 2 sons. Education: Curtis Institute of Music, Philadelphia, with Piatigorsky. Debut: New York Town Hall, 1959. Career: Solo Cellist, annual world wide concert tours with leading orchestras; Director, Kneisal Hall Summer Music School, Blue Hill, Maine; Teacher at the St Louis Conservatory of Music, from 1982. Recordings: Has recorded for Columbia and Pathé-Marconi Records. Honours: Pablo Casals Prize, Paris, 1957; Primavera Trophy, Rome, 1959; Prizewinner, International Tchaikovsky Competition, Moscow, 1962. Memberships: Chamber Music Society of Lincoln Center, New York. Hobbies: Languages; Photography; Tennis. Address: c/o Columbia Artists Management, 165 West 57th Street, New York, NY 10019, USA.

PARR Patricia (Ann), b. 10 June 1937, Toronto, Canada. Musician (pianist); Educator. 2 sons. Education: Curtis Institute of Music, Philadelphia, Pennsylvania, USA; Studied Piano with Isabelle Vengerova; Composition with Gian-Carlo Menotti; Diploma, 1957; Postgraduate studies with Rudolf Serkin. Debut: Toronto Symphony age 9. Career: Soloist with Philadelphia, Cleveland, Pittsburgh, Toronto Orchestras and others; New York Town Hall debut; Soloist and Chamber Musician appeared extensively in Canada and USA; In Trio Concertante toured Australia, 1975 and 1978; Festival appearances include Marlboro, Stratford, Fontana, Marin County, Festival of the Sound; Founding Member, Amici (a chamber ensemble); Faculty, Duqueshe University, 1967-74, University of Toronto, 1974-, Royal Conservatory of Music, 1982-90. Recordings: Summit Records with AMICI; Musica Viva Series with Clarinettist Joaquin Valdepenas; Arbor Discs with Violinist Lorand Fenyves; CBC Records with Hornist Eugene Rittich; Centrediscs with Marc Dubois, tenor. Address: 57 Woodlawn Ave West, Toronto, Ontario M4V 1G6, Canada.

PARRIS Robert, b. 21 May 1924, Philadelphia, Pennsylvania, USA. Composer. Education: Studied at University of Pennsylvania (MS 1946) with Peter Mennin and William Bergsma at Juilliard (BS 1948) with Ibert and Copland at Berkshire Music Center and with Honegger at the Ecole Normale in Paris. Career: Has taught at Washington State College and University of Maryland; George Washington University 1963, Professor, 1976-. Compositions include: Orchestra: Symphony, 1952; Piano Concerto, 1953; Concerto for 5 kettledrums and orchestra, 1955; Viola Concerto, 1958; Violin Concerto, 1958; Flute Concerto, 1964; Concerto for trombone and chamber orchestra, 1964; Concerto for percussion, violin, cello and piano, 1967; The Phoenix, 1969; The Messengers, 1974; Rite of Passage, 1978; The Unquiet Heart for violin and orchestra, 1981; Chamber Music for orchestra, 1984; Vocal: Night for baritone string quartet and clarinet, 1951; Alas for the Day, cantata, 1954; Hymn for the Nativity for chorus and brass ensemble, 1962; Dreams for soprano and chamber orchestra; Cynthia's Revell's for baritone and piano, 1979; Chamber: 2 String Trios, 1948, 1951; 2 String Quartets, 1951, 1952; Sonata for solo violin, 1965; The Book of Imaginary Dreams, Parts I and II for ensemble, 1972, 1983; Three Duets for electric guitar and amplified harpsichord, 1984. Honours include: NEA Grants, 1974, 1975; Commissions from Detroit Symphony Orchestra and the Contemporary Music Forum. Address: c/o ASCAP, ASCAP Building, One Lincoln Plaza, NY 10023, USA.

PARRISH Cheryl, b. 6 Nov 1954, Pasadena, Texas, USA. Singer (Soprano). Education: Graduated Baylor University, 1977 and studied at Vienna Musikhochschule, 1978-79. Career: Has sung at San Francisco Opera from 1983, as Sophie in Rosenkavalier and Werther and Mozart's Blondchen and Susanna (season 1990-91); Miami Opera, 1987 and 1991, as Ophelia in Hamlet and as Despina; Sang Adele in Die Fledermaus at Toronto, 1987 and San Diego, 1991; Sophie in Der Rosenkavalier at Zurich Opera, 1988 and has guested further at Florence and Santa Fe; Shepherd in Tannhäuser at Austin, Texas, 1996; Frequent concert appearances. Address: c/o San Francisco Opera, War Memorial Opera House, San Francisco, CA 94192, USA.

PARROTT Andrew, b. 10 Mar 1947, Walsall, England. Conductor. Education: Merton College, Oxford (Director of Music and research into performance practice of early music). Career: Formed Taverner Choir at the invitation of Michael Tippett for a 1973 Bath Festival concert; Subsequently founded Taverner Consort and Players; Promenade Concert debut 1977 with Monteverdi's Vespers; Guest Conductor with English and Scottish Chamber Orchestras, London and Bournemouth Sinfoniettas, the

BBC Philharmonic and Orchestras in Canada, Czechoslovakia, Holland, Norway, Switzerland, USA and Austria; Conducted world premiere of Judith Weir's A Night at the Chinese Opera for Kent Opera 1987; Performances of music by Britten, Nono, Henze, Stravinsky and Varese; Has been Musical Assistant to Tippett and a Member of Electric Phoenix; Season 1992-93, Figaro for Opera North, Monteverdi's Orfeo in Boston, Die Zauberflöte at Covent Garden (debut), the premiere of a symphony by Vladimir Godar and music by Tippett in Norway. Recordings: Orchestral music, opera and major choral masterpieces for EMI and other companies including CDs of Bach B Minor Mass and St Johns Passion, Monteverdi Vespers, Purcell Dido and Aeneas, Handel Carmelite Vespers, Vivaldi concertos; Choral music by Gabrieli, Josquin, Mozart, Schütz, Tallis and Taverner. Contributions to: Early Music; New Oxford Companion to Music, 1983; New Oxford Book of Carols (co-editor), 1992. Address: c/o Allied Artists Ltd, 42 Montpelier Square, London SW7 1JZ, England.

PARROTT Ian, b. 5 Mar 1916, London, England. Professor of Music, Retired. m. Elizabeth Olga Cox, 2 s. Education: Royal College of Music, 1932-34; New College, Oxford University, 1934-37; Associate, Royal College of Organists, 1936; DMus, Oxford University, 1940; MA, 1941. Compositions include: The Black Ram, opera, 1957; Several orchestral works including 5 symphonies; Chamber music and songs; Ceredigion for Harp, 1962; Flamingoes, song; Soliloquy and Dance, for harp; Welsh Folk Song Mass, 1973-74; Duo Fantastico No 2 for Violin and Piano, 1990. Recordings include: Contemporary Welsh Choral Music, 1969; Contemporary Music for Harp and Flute, 1969-70; Contemporary Welsh Chamber Music, 1971; Trombone Concerto, 1974. Publications include: Elgar, 1971; The Crying Curlew, (Peter Warlock, Family and Influences), 1994; The Music of Rosemary Brown, 1978; Cyril Scott and His Piano Music, 1991. Contributions to: Various professional journals. Honours include: 1st Prize for Luxor, Royal Philharmonic Society, 1949; Harriet Cohen International Musicology Medal, 1966. Memberships include: Vice-President, Elgar Society; Vice-President, Peter Warlock Society. Address: Henblas Abermad, near Aberystwyth, Dyfed, SY23 4ES, Wales.

PARRY Susan, b. Bedfordshire, England. Singer (Mezzo-soprano). Education: Studied at Birmingham University and the Royal Academy of Music. Career: Welsh National Opera from 1987, as the Witch in Hansel and Gretel, and Kate Pinkerton; English National Opera debut 1992, in the premiere of John Buller's The Bacchae; Company Principal with ENO from 1995, as the Kitchen Boy in Rusalka, Brangaene (first major role, 1996), Janacek's Fox, Strauss's Octavian and Composer, and Dorabella, (1997); Concerts include the Brahms Liebeslieder Waltzes under Antal Dorati, Messiah at the Albert Hall and Beethoven's Ninth at the Festival Hall; Season 1996 included concert of Gluck's Iphigénie en Tauride with the Orchestra of the Age of Enlightenment, Covent Garden debut in Alzira, and Tebaldo in Don Carlos at the London Proms; Falla's El Amor Brujo with the BBC PO, Henze's La Cubana with the Ballet Rambert and an orchestration of Alma Mahler Lieder at Maastricht; Imelda in Verdi's Oberto at Covent Garden (1997), Pierotto in Donezetti's Linda di Chamounix with the OAE and Hansel in concert with the CBSO under Mark Elder. Address: c/o ENO Press Office, English National Opera, St Martin's Lane, London WC2N 4ES, England.

PÄRT Arvo, b. 11 Sept 1935, Paide, Estonia. Composer. Education: Studied at the Tallinn Conservatory with Heino Eller. Career: Music Division of Estonian Radio, 1958-67; Settled in West Berlin, 1981. Compositions include: Orchestral: Nekrolog, 1959; 3 Symphonies, 1963, 1966, 1971; Wenn Bach Bienen gezüchtet hätte, 1977; Fratres for String Orchestra, 1980; Vocal: Our Garden, cantata, 1959; Credo, for solo piano, choir and orchestra, 1968; St John Passion, 1981-82; Stabat Mater, for vocal and string trios, 1985; Miserere, for 5 solo voices, chorus and orchestra, 1989; The Beatitudes, for chorus and organ, 1989; Berlin Mass, for chorus and string orchestra, 1990; Mother of God and Virgin for chorus, 1990; Chamber Music: Quintettino, for wind quintet, 1964; Fratres, for violin and piano, 1977; Summa, string quartet, 1991; Psalom, string quartet, 1991; Sarah was Ninety Years Old, for 3 voices, percussion and organ, 1990; Mirror in Mirror, for violin and piano, 1978; Adagio for piano trio, 1992; Silouan's Song for string orchestra, 1991; Vocal: Litany, for 4 solo voices, chorus and orchestra, 1994. Memberships: Ehrendoktor of the Tallinn Conservatory; Swedish Royal Music Academy. Current Management: Universal Edition (London) Limited. Address: H Schott Ltd, 48 Great Marlborough Street, London W1V 2BN, England.

PARTRIDGE Ian H, b. 12 June 1938, London, England. Tenor; Teacher. m. Ann Glover, 4 July 1959, 2 sons. Education: Clifton College, 1952-56; Royal College of Music, 1956-58; Guildhall School of Music, 1961-63. Debut: Bexhill, 1958. Career: Concerts & Recitals Worldwide; Covent Garden debut, 1969; Numerous Broadcasts for BBC & Worldwide Television; Appearances include, St Nicolas for Thames Television. Recordings: Schone Mullerin, Schubert; Dichterliebe and Liederkreis op 39-Schumann; On Wenlock Edge & Other Songs, V Williams; The Curluew, Peter Warlock; Songs by Faure, Duparc, Delius, Gurney. Honours: Harriet Cohen Award, 1967; Prix Italia, 1977; CBE, 1992; Hon RAM, 1996. Memberships: Garrick Club; Governor, RSM; Director, PAMRA. Hobbies: Bridge; Cricket. Address: 127 Pepys Road, London SW20 8NP, England.

PASATIERI Thomas, b. 20 October 1945, New York, USA. Composer. Education: Studied with Giannini and Persichetti at Juilliard and with Darius Milhaud at the Aspen Music School. Career: Freelance Composer, 1965-; Commissions from National Educational Television, Houston Grand Opera, Baltimore Opera, Michigan Opera Theater, University of Arizona, Evelyn Lear and Thomas Stewart. Compositions: Operas: The Women, Aspen 1965; La Divine, New York, 1966; Padrevia, New York, 1967; The Trial of Mary Lincoln, NET 1972; Black Widow, Seattle, 1972; The Seagull, Houston, 1974; Signor Deluso, Vienna, 1974; The Penitentes, Aspen, 1974; Inez de Castro, Baltimore, 1976; Washington Square, Detroit, 1976; Three Sisters, 1979; Before Breakfast, New York, 1980; The Goose Girl, Fort Worth, 1981; Maria Elena, Tucson, 1983; Invocations for Orchestra, 1968; Heloise and Abelard for Soprano, Baritone and Piano, 1971; Rites de passage for low voice and Chamber Orchestra, 1974; Three Poems of James Agee, 1974; Far from Love for Soprano, Clarinet and Piano, 1976; Permit Me Voyage, Cantata, 1976; Mass for 4 Solo Voices, Chorus and Orchestra, 1983; Piano Music; 400 Songs. Address: c/o ASCAP, ASCAP Building, One Lincoln Plaza, New York, NY 10023, USA.

PASCANU Alexandru, b. 3 May 1920, Bucharest, Romania. Composer; Professor. Education: Faculty of Law; Academy of Music. Debut: 1947. Career: Assistant, Theory and Solfeggi, 1952-55, Lecturer, Score Reading and Theory of Instruments, 1955-60, Reader, Harmony and Orchestration, 1960-66, Professor of Harmony, 1966-; Music Conservatoire of Bucharest; Councillor Direction Creative People, 1952; Councillor, Electrecord, 1971-. Compositions: Choral Music (Old Laments, Kyndya, Festum, Hibernum); Chamber Music (Suite for Piano, Nocturnes for Piano, Horn, Cello, Balade for Clarinet); Symphonic Music; Poem of the Carpatians; In Memoriam; Black Sea; Toccata for Orchestra. Recordings: Suite Diptich for string orchestra; Pro Humanitate. Publications: Principles of Harmony (in collaboration); About the Musical Instruments, 3 editions, 1959, 1966, 1980; Armonia (Harmony), 2 volumes, 1974, 1975, 1977, 1982. Contributions to: Muzica; Contemporanul; Cronica; Essays; Educational Broadcasting Cycles. Hobbies: Humourist; Photography. Address: Str O Cocarascu 102, 78182 Bucharest, Romania.

PASCHER Hartmut, b. 1956, Vienna, Austria. Violist. Education: Studied at the Vienna Academy of Music. Career: Member of the Franz Schubert Quartet from 1979; Many concert appearances in Europe, the USA and Australia, including the Amsterdam Concertgebouw, the Vienna Musikverein and Konzerthaus, the Salle Gaveau Paris and the Sydney Opera House; Visits to Zurich, Geneva, Basle, Berlin, Hamburg, London, Rome, Rotterdam, Madrid and Copenhagen; Festival engagements include Salzburg, Wiener Festwochen, Prague Spring, Schubertiade at Hohenems, the Schubert Festival at Washington DC and the Belfast and Istanbul Festivals; Tours of Australasia, USA; Frequent Concert Tours of Britain: Frequent appearances at the Wigmore Hall and Cheltenham Festival; Teacher of the Graz Musikhochschule; Masterclasses at the Royal Northern College of Music at Lake District Summer Music. Recordings include: Schubert's Quartet in G, D877; Complete Quartets of Dittersdorf; Mozart: String Quartet in D, K575, String Quartet in B Flat, K589, Tchaikovsky String Quartets No 1 and 3 op. 11 D major and op. 30 E flat minor. Address: Unit 2, 39 Tadema Road, London SW10 0PY, England.

PASCOE John, b. 1949, Bath, England. Artistic Director; Founder, Bath and Wessex Opera. Debut: Designed Julius Caesar for English National Opera, also seen in San Francisco, Geneva, the Metropolitan and on television, 1979. Career: Designed Lucrezia Borgia at Covent Garden and Alcina at Sydney, both with Joan Sutherland, Tosca for Welsh National Opera, 1980; Producer and Designer: La Bohème in Belfast, Solomon at the Göttingen Festival, 1984; Producer and Designer: Rameau's Platée in Spoleto Festival, also seen in BAM, New York; Designer: Orlando at San Francisco and Chicago; Così fan tutte in Dallas; Anna Bolena, with Joan Sutherland, in Toronto, Chicago, Detroit, Houston and San Francisco, 1985-86; Designer: Amahl and the Night Visitors; Norma, in Santiago, 1987; Producer and Designer: Anna Bolena at Covent Garden; Norma in Los Angeles and Detroit, both with Joan Sutherland, 1988; Producer and Designer: La Bohème in Bath; Designed: Tosca in Nice; Apollo and Hyacinthus at Cannes Festival, Madrid, Paris, 1991, 1992; Producer and Designer: La Traviata in Bath; Designer: Anna Bolena in Washington DC, 1993. Honours include: Evening Standard Award for Julius Caesar, 1979. Address: c/o Athole Still International Management Ltd, Foresters Hall, 25-27 Westow Street, London, SE19 3RY, England.

PASCOE Keith, b. 1959, England. Violinist. Career: Founder Member of the Britten Quartet, debut concert at the Wigmore Hall, 1987; Quartet in Residence at the Dartington Summer School, 1987, with quartets by Schnittke; Season 1988-89 in the Genius of Prokofiev series at Blackheath and BBC Lunchtime Series at St John's Smith Square; South Bank appearances with the Schoenberg/Handel Quartet Concerto conducted by Neville Marriner, concerts with the Hermann Prey Schubertiade and collaborations with the Alban Berg Quartet in the Beethoven Plus series; Tour of South America 1988, followed by Scandinavian debut; Season 1989-90 with debut tours of Holland, Germany, Spain, Austria, Finland; Tours from 1990 to the Far East, Malta, Sweden, Norway; Schoenberg/Handel Concerto with the Gothenburg Symphony; Festival appearances at Brighton, the City of London, Greenwich, Canterbury, Harrogate, Chester, Spitalfields and Aldeburg; Collaborations with John Ogdon, Imogen Cooper, Thea King and Lynn Harrell; Formerly resident quartet at Liverpool University; Teaching role at Lake District Summer Music 1989; Universities of Bristol, Hong Kong 1990. Recordings: Beethoven Op 130 and Schnittke Quartet no 3 (Collins Classics); Vaughan Williams On Wenlock Edge and Ravel Quartet (EMI); Britten, Prokofiev, Tippett, Elgar and Walton Quartets (Collins Classics); Exclusive Contract with EMI from 1991. Address: c/o Ingpen & Williams Ltd, 26 Wadham Road, London SW15 2LR, England.

PASHLEY Anne, b. 5 June 1937, Skegness, England. Singer (Soprano). m. Jack Irons, 1 son, 1 daughter. Education: Guildhall School of Music, London. Career: Took part as sprinter in 1956 Olympic Games, at Melbourne; State debut in Semele, with Handel Opera Society, 1959; Glyndebourne debut 1962, in Die Zauberflöte; Covent Garden debut 1965, as Barbarina in Le nozze di Figaro; Guest appearances with English National Opera, Scottish Opera, Welsh National Opera and at Edinburgh and Aldeburg Festivals; Foreign engagements in France, Germany, Portugal, Spain, Belgium, Italy, Israel; Leading roles in 8 BBC TV operas and numerous radio broadcasts; New Opera Company, London, in the British premiere of Hindemith's Cardillac, 1970. Recordings include: La Morte de Cléopatre, Berlioz; Magnificat, Bach; Albert Herring and Peter Grimes, Britten. Contribution to: The Listener. Membership: Equity. Hobbies: Winemaking; Table Tennis; Art Collecting; Interior Design. Address: 289 Goldhawk Road, London W12, England.

PASKALIS Kostas, b. 1 Sept 1929, Levadia, Boeotia, Greece. Singer (Baritone). m. Marina Krilovici. Education: Studied at the National Conservatory Athens. Debut: Athens 1954, as Rigoletto. Career: Vienna Staatsoper from 1958, debut as Renato in Un Ballo in Maschera; Tour of North America 1960; Glyndebourne 1964-72, as Macbeth and Don Giovanni; Metropolitan Opera debut 1965, as Don Carlos in La Forza el Destino; Rome Opera 1965-66 as Rigoletto and Posa, in Don Carlos; Salzburg Festival 1966, as Pentheus in the premiere of Henze's The Bassarids; La Scala Milan 1967, as Valentin in Faust; Guest appearances in Leningrad, Kiev, Berlin and Moscow; Sang Nabucco at Brussels 1987; New Jersey Opera 1988, as Don Giovanni; Director of the National Opera of Greece from 1988. Recordings: Escamillo in Carmen (HMV); Alfonso in Donizetti's Lucrezia Borgia. Address: National Union of Greece, 18-A Harilaou Trikoupi Street, 106 79 Athens, Greece.

PASKUDA Georg, b. 7 Jan 1926, Ratibor, Germany. Singer (Tenor). Career: Sang small roles in various German theatres from 1951; Bayreuth Festival from 1959, notably as Frch and Mime; Paris Opera 1960; Bavarian State Opera Munich from 1960, notably in operas by Strauss, Puccini, Lortzing, Wagner, Verdi and Mozart; Munich 1967, as Don Carlos and 1986 in the premiere of V.D Kirchner's Belshazzar. Recordings: Parsifal, Tannhäuser and Arabella; Die Frau ohne Schatten; Das Rheingold and Der fliegende Holländer, from Bayreuth. Address: c/o Bayerische Staatsoper, Postfach 745, D-8000 Munich 1, Germany.

PASQUIER Bruno, b. 10 Dec 1943, Neuilly-sur-Seine, France. Violist. Education: Studied at the Paris Conservatoire 1957-63 with Etienne Ginot and his father, Pierre Pasquier. Career: Mix à Munich, 1965; Queteur à cadas, string quartet, 1972-83; Leader, viola section in the orchestra of the Paris Opera, 1972; Soloist with the Orchestre Nat ional de France, 1984-89; With Regis Pasquier and Roland Pidoux founded the New Pasquier Trio, 1970; Solo performances with leading orchestras in france and abroad; Professor of Viola and of Chamber Music at the Paris Conservatoire, 1983; Plays a Maggilli viola, ca 1620. Honour: Chevalier de l'Ordre des Arts et Lettres, 1991. Address: Conservatoire National Superieur de Musique, 109 Av Jean Jaurs, 17019 Paris, France.

PASQUIER Regis, b. 10 Oct 1945, Fontainebleau, France. Violinist. Education: Studied at the Paris Conservatoire, gaining first prize in violin and chamber music aged 12; Further study with Isaac Stern. Career: Concert tours of Belgium, Holland and Luxembourg 1958; New York recital 1960; Many concerts with leading orchestras in Europe and America; Soloist with the

Orchestre National de France, 1977-86; With Bruno Pasquier and Roland Pidoux formed the New Pasquier Trio, 1970; Sonata recitals with pianist Jean-Claude Pennetier; Concerto repertoire ranges from standard classics to works by Xenakis and Gilbert Amy (Trajectoires); Plays a Montagnana instrument; Professor of Violin and of Chamber Music at the Paris Conservatoire, 1985. Address: Conservatoire National Superieur de Musique, 14 Rue de Madrid, 75008 Paris, France.

PASTILLE William, b. 30 Apr 1954, Providence, Rhode Island, USA. Musicologist. m. Janice M Macaulay, 31 May 1986. Education: AB, Music, Brown University, 1976; MA, Musicology 1979, PhD, Musicology 1985, Cornell University. Career: Visiting Professor of Music History, University of Wisconsin, Madison, 1985-86; Faculty, St John's College, Annapolis, Maryland, 1986-. Publication: Ursatz: The Musical Philosophy of Heinrich Schenker, 1985. Contributions to: Heinrich Schenker, Anti-Organicist, 19th Century Music, 1984; (translation) Franz Schubert: Ihr Bild by Heinrich Schenker, Sonus, 1986; Review of Federhofer, Heinrich Schenker, Journal of the American Musicological Society, 1986; Schenker's Brahms, The American Brahms Society Newsletter, 1987; Counterpoint and Free Composition, Theoria, 1988; The Spirit of Musical Technique by Heinrich Schenker (a translation), Theoria, 1988; Music and Morphology: Goethe's Influence on Schenker's Ontology in Schenker Studies, 1990; The Development of the Ursatz in Schenker's Published Works, in Trends in Schekerian Research, 1990; Johannes Brahms by Heinrich Schenker, The American Brahms Society Newsletter, 1991; Music Theory and the Spirit of Science, ex tempore, 1995; The God of Abraham, Aquinas, and Schenker: Faith in an Age of Unbelief, Indiana Theory Review, 1995; Schenker's Value-Judgemnents, Music Theory On-Line, 1995; National Endowment for the Humanities Summer Stipend, 1986. Memberships: American Brahms Society; American Musicological Society; Society for Music Theory. Address: St John's College, PO Box 2800, Annapolis, MD 21404-2800, USA.

PATACHICH Ivan, b. 3 June 1922, Budapest, Hungary. Composer. m. Ibolya Markovics, 10 Nov 1951, 1 daughter. Education: Ferenc Liszt Academy of Musik, 1941-47; Composition, A Siklos; Conducting, J Ferencsik. Debut: Opera House, Budapest. Career: Musical Director, MAFILM, Budapest, 1952-. Compositions: Concerto per Arpa, 1956; Tre pezzi, 1961; Petite Suite, 1961; Theomachia, 1 Act Opera, 1962; Fuente Ovejuna, 3 Act Opera, 1971; Symphonietta Savariansis, 1965; Contorni per Arpe, 1968; Concerto per Violino per Pianoforte, 1969; Concerto per Organo, 1973; Spettri, electronic music, 1974; Ritmi Dispari, 1966; Music of the Bible, Cantata, 1968. Recordings: Quartettino per Sassofoni, 1972; Musical Electroalchemy, 1981; Sonata per Zymbalum, 1975; Ludi Spaziali, 1986; Funzione Acustica, 1979; Ta Foneenta, 1979; Metamorphosi per Marimba, 1981; On Filmmusic, 1971; MELOS, 1978 Eine neue Notation electronischer Musik. Honours: International Electroacoustic Prize, Bourges, 1978;World Youth Festival Prize, Moscow, 1957; Niveau Prize, Hungarian TV, 1972; CIME Grand Prix, France, 1984. Memberships: Hungarian Artisjus; Computer Music Association, San Francisco, USA. Address: 1016 Budapest, Naphegy ter 9, Hungary.

PATAKI Eva, b. 19 Oct 1941, Budapest, Hungary. Pianist. m. T Batny, 27 Aug 1971. Education: Diploma, Concert Performance, Pedagogy, Academy of Music, Budapest; Studied with Carlo Zecchi in Salzburg. Debut: Recital, Budapest, 1965. Career: Assistant, Mozarteum, Salzburg, 5 years; Coach, Royal Opera, Stockholm, 1967-; Concerts, radio and TV, with Helena Doese, Catarina Ligendza, C-H Ahnsjö, Nicolai Gedda, Gösta Winbergh, others, all over Europe and in Moscow, St Petersburg and other venues, 1967-; Producer, concerts at Royal Opera, Stockholm, 1985-. Recordings: Several. Hobbies: Psychology. Address: Artistsekretariat Ulf Tornqvist, Sankt Eriksgatan 100 2 tr, S-113 31 Stockholm, Sweden.

PATCHELL Sue, b. 1948, Montana, USA. Singer, Soprano. Education: Studied in Montana and at University of California at Los Angeles. Career: Engaged at Graz Opera, 1974, Gelsenkirchen, 1979-86; Wiesbaden, 1986-, notably as Elsa in Lohengrin, 1988, and Elisabetta in Don Carlos at Wiesbaden Festival, 1990; Hamburg Staatsoper as Tatiana in Eugene Oengin, Barcelona, 1989 and 1990, as Eva and Chrysothemis, Antwerp Opera as Elisabeth in Tannhäuser and Ariadne; Other roles include Marguerite, Mozart's Countess and Donna Elvira, Frau Fluth and Rosalinde; Sang Isolde at Trieste, 1996; Concert repertoire includes Das Buch mit Sieben Siegeln by Franz Schmidt. Recordings: Das Dunkle Reich by Pfitzner. Address: c/o Hessisches Staatstheater, Postfach 3247, 6200 Wiesbaden, Germany.

PATON Iain, b. 1960, Scotland. Singer, Tenor. Education: Studied at Royal Scottish Academy and with David Keren in London. Career: Appearances with Glyndebourne Festival and touring Opera in Capriccio, Death in Venice and Le nozze di Figaro, Don Curzio; Sang in Judith Weir's The Vanishing Bridegroom for Scottish Opera at Glasgow and Covent Garden; Season 1992-93, as Pedrillo in Die Entführung and in The Makropoulos Case, season 1993-94, as Vanya in Katya Kabanova, Tamino and the Shepherd in Tristan und Isolde; Sang Leicester in Maria Stuarda for Scottish Opera-Go-Round, 1992; City of Birmingham Touring Opera in Mozart's Zaide; Concert repertoire includes Liszt's Faust Symphony and appearances with Scottish Early Music Consort in Northern Ireland, Germany and Poland; Sang Eurimachos in Dallapiccola's Ulisse for BBC, 1993; Season 1995-96 in Purcell's King Arthur and as Mozart's Pedrillo with Les Arts Florissants and Boris in Katya Kabanova at Dublin; Season 1997 with Ferrando for Flanders Opera and Scottish Opera. Honours: Eric Vertier Award, at Glyndebourne. Address: c/o Harold Holt Ltd, 31 Sinclair Road, London W14 ONS, England.

PATRIARCO Earle, b. 1965, USA. Singer (Baritone). Career: Many concert and recital engagements in Europe and the USA, with songs by Poulenc and Strauss; Opera repertory includes Cosi fan tutte and The Queen of Spades; Contestant at the 1994 Cardiff Singer of the World Competition. Address: 1716 Kennedy Drive, Milpitas, CA 95025, USA.

PATTERSON Paul (Leslie), b. 15 June 1947, Chesterfield, England. Composer; Educator. m. Hazel Wilson, 1981, 1 son, 1 daughter. Education: Royal Academy of Music; FRAM, FRSA, 1980. Career: Freelance Composer, 1968-; Art Council Composer-in-Association, English Sinfonia, 1969-70; Director, Contemporary Music, Warwick University, 1974-80; Composer-in-Residence,SE Arts Association, 1980-82, Bedford School, 1984-85; Professor of Composition, 1970-, Head of Composition/20th Century Music, 1985-, Royal Academy of Music; Artistic Director, Exeter Festival, 1991; Composer-in-Residence, 1990-91. Compositions: Te Deum, 1988; Symphony, 1990; The Mighty Voice, 1991; Performances worldwide by leading orchestras, soloists, ensembles, also film and television music. Publications: Rebecca, 1968; Trumpet Concerto, 1969; Time Piece, 1972; Kyrie, 1972; Requiem, 1973; Comedy for 5 Winds, 1973; Requiem, 1974; Fluorescences, 1974; Clarinet Concerto, 1976; Cracowian Counterpoints, 1977; Voices of Sleep, 1979; Concerto for Orchestra, 1981; Canterbury Psalms, 1981; Sinfonia, 1982; Mass of the Sea, 1983; Deception Pass, 1983; Duologue, 1984; Mean Time, 1984; Europhony, 1985; Missa Brevis, 1985; Stabat Mater, 1986; String Quartet, Harmonica Concerto, Magnificat & Nunc Dimitus, 1986; Te Deum, 1988; Tunnell of Time, 1988; The End, 1989; Violin Concerto, 1992; Little Red Riding Hood, 1993; Magnificat, 1994; Royal Eurostar for the opening Channel Tunnel, 1994. Honours: Medal of Honour, Polish Ministry of Culture, 1986; Leslie Boosey Award, 1996. Memberships: ADC; RSA; SPNM. Hobbies: Sailing; Croquet. Current Management: Helen Sykes. Address: 31 Cromwell Avenue, Highgate, London N6 5HN, England.

PATTERSON Susan, b. 1962, USA. Soprano. Career: Sang widely in USA and made European debut in 1988 with the Welsh National Opera as Violetta; Sang at San Francisco in 1988 and 1991 as Anne Trulove and Constanze; Sang Gilda at Vancouver in 1989 and in Cherubini's Lodoiska at La Scala, 1990-91; Sang at Rome Opera in 1991 as Adele in Le Comte Ory, Fiordiligi at Cologne and Berenice in Rossini's L'Occasione fa il Ladro at Schwetzingen and Paris; Sang Aspasia in Mozart's Mitridate at Amsterdam in 1992; Magda in La Rondine at St Louis, 1996; Frequent concert appearances. Address: c/o San Francisco Opera, War Memorial Opera House, San Francisco, CA 94102, USA.

PATTON Chester, b. 1965, Columbia, MS, USA. Singer (Bass). Education: Studied at the San Francisco Conservatory of Music. Career: Appearances with San Francisco Opera from 1993, as Don Basilio, the King of Egypt in Aida, First Nazarene in Salome, Colline, Raimondo and Lord Walton in I Puriatni; Bay Area credits include further appearances with West Bay Opera, Opera San José, Pocket Opera and Berkeley Contemporary Opera; Title role in the US premiere of Tippett's King Priam, San Francisco Opera Center; Debut with Opera Pacific as Basilio, Beethoven's Pizarro at Lyon, High Priest in Nabucco at the Opéra Bastille and Timur in Turandot (1997); Hawaii Opera Theater as Ferrando in Trovatore, Sparafucile and Colline. Recordings include: Mandarin in San Francisco Opera production of Turandot. Address: c/o San Francisco Opera, War Memorial House, Van Ness Avenue, CA 94102, USA.

PAUER Jiri, b. 22 Feb 1919, Libusin, Kladno, Czechoslovakia. Composer; Administrator. Edcuation: Studied with Alois Haba at Prague Conservatory, 1943-46, and at Academy of Musical Arts. Carer: Professor of Composition at Prague Academy, 1965-89; Head of Opera at Prague National Theatre, 1951-55, 1965-67, Director 1979-89; Director of Czech Philharmonic, 1958-79. Compositions include: Operas: Prattling Slug, for children, 1958; Zuzana Vijirova, 1958; Little Red Riding Hood, Olomouc, 1960; Matrimonial Counterpoints, Ostrava, 1962; The Hypochondriac (after Moliere), Prague, 1970 revised version, Prague, 1988; Swan-Song, monodrama, Prague, 1974; Ballet: Ferdy the Ant, 1975; Orchestral: Comedy Suite, 1949; Bassoon Concerto, 1949; Rhapsody, 1953; Oboe Concerto, 1954; Horn Concerto, 1958; Symphony, 1963; Commemoration, 1969; Trumpet Concerto, 1972; Initials, 1974; Symphony for Strings, 1978; Marimba Concerto, 1984; Suite, 1987; Chamber: Divertimento for 3 clarinets, 1949; Violin Sonatina, 1953; Cello Sonata, 1954; 4 String Quartets, 1960, 1969, 1970, 1976; Divertimento for Monet, 1961; Wind Quintet, 1961; Piano Trio, 1963; Characters for brass quintet, 1978; Episodes for string quartet, 1980; Trio for 3 horns, 1986; Violin Sonata, 1987; Nonet No 2, 1989; Piano music, cantatas and songs. Address: c/o National Theatre, PO Box 865, 11230 Prague 1, Czech Republic.

PAUK György, b. 26 Oct 1936, Budapest, Hungary. Concert Violinist. m. 19 Jul 1959, 1 s, 1 d. Education: Franz Liszt Music Academy, Budapest, being youngest pupil of Professors Zathureczki, Weiner and Kodály. Career: Many concerts in Hungary and throughout Eastern Europe; Moved to London in 1961 and gave his recital and orchestral debuts there in the same year; Has performed worldwide with all major orchestras of London and on the continent under leading conductors including Pierre Boulez, Antal Dorati, Lorin Maazel, Tennstedt, Georg Solti, Simon Rattle; American debut with Chicago Symphony Orchestra and has played with several US Orchestras; Appearances at such festivals as Aspen, Ravinia, Hollywood Bowl and Saratoga; Formed a trio with Peter Frankl and Ralph Kirshbaum achieving worldwide acclaim; Conductor and soloist with English Chamber Orchestra, Mozart Players and Academy of St Martin-in-the-Fields; Masterclasses; Professor at Royal Academy of Music, London, 1987-; Director, Mozart Bicentenary Festival, 1991; 25th Anniversary concerts with the Pauk-Frankl-Kirschbaum Trio, 1997. Recordings include: Alban Berg's Chamber Concerto, a Bartók Album and Tippett's Triple Concerto (Record of Year 1983); Complete Sonatas by Handel; Complete Violin Concertos by Mozart; 3 Brahms Sonatas; Mozart Quintets (viola part); All Bartók works for Violin, Piano, Solo Violin and orchestra, (1st Bartók record nominated for Grammy Award), 1995. Honours include: Honorary Fellow, Guildhall School of Music; Honorary RAM, 1990. Hobbies: Sport; Family. Current Management: Clarion Seven Muses, 47 Whitehall Park, London, N19 3TW, England. Address: 27 Armitage Road, London, NW11 8QT, England.

PAUL Steven (Everett), b. 6 Dec 1937, Atlanta, Georgia, USA. Producer; Editor; Musicologist; Broadcaster; Flautist. m. Sophie Arbenz, 6 Oct 1981, 2 sons. Education: BA, Columbia, 1958; MA, Yale, 1959; PhD, Musicology, King's College, Cambridge, England, 1981; Juilliard School of Music; Trinity College of Music, London, England; Harvard Law School, USA. Career: Performances in chamber ensembles and orchestras in New York, Boston, London, Cambridge, Hamburg; Producer, CBS Records, New York, 1966-72; Editor, Deutsche Grammophon (Polydor) Hamburg, 1975-79; Executive Producer, Deutsche Grammophon, 1979-; Broadcasts on BBC Radio 3, WNCN (NY), WFMT (Chicago), NPR (National Public Radio, USA), NDR (Norddeutscher Rundfunk Hamburg), DLF (Deutschlandfunk Cologne); Lectures at International Music Conferences (Washington 1975, Vienna 1982), and Universities (Cambridge, Oxford, Warwick, England and Minnesota, USA). Publications: Author of sleeve notes for CBS, DGG and RCA Recordings; Introduction and Notes for The Scatological Songs and Canons of W A Mozart, 1969; The Musical Suprise; A Discussion of the Element of the Unexpected in the Humour of Haydn, 1975; Comedy, Wit and Humour in Haydn's Instrumental Music, in Haydn Studies, 1981; Wit and Humour in the Operas of Haydn in Proceedings of the International Joseph Haydn Congress, 1986; Several published interviews with musicians; Music Arrangements (Chappell/Intersong). Contributions to: Professional publications and concert programmes. Address: c/o Polygram, Alte Rabenstrasse 2, D-2000 Hamburg 13, Germany.

PAUL Thomas, b. 22 Feb 1934, Chicago, IL, USA. Singer, Bass. Education: Studied at the Juilliard School with Beverly Johnson and Cornelius Reid. Debut: NY City Opera 1962, as Sparafucile in Rigoletto. Career: Sang in NY, Pittsburgh, Washington, Vancouver, San Francisco and Montreal as Mozart's Figaro and Sarastro, Pogner in Die Meistersinger, Bartók's Duke Bluebeard, Padre Guardiano, La forza del destino; Ptolemy in Giulio Cesare by Handel; Sang at Central City Colorado in the premiere of Robert Ward's Lady from Colorado, 1964; Many concert performances; Teacher at the Eastman School, Rochester, and the Aspen School, Colorado. Recordings: Brander in La Damnation de Faust, Deutsche Grammophon.

PAULI Hansjörg, b 14 Mar 1931, Winterthur, Switzerland. Musicologist; Writer; Filmmaker. m. Federica Staub, 22 Sept 1960, 1 son, 1 daughter. Education: Abitur Oberrealschule, Winterthur, 1949; Winterthur Conservatory of Music, 1953-56; Private Studies with Hans Keller, London, 1956-57; DPhil, University of Osnabrück, Germany, 1987. Career: Producer, 20th Century Music, Zurich Radio, 1960-65; Music Producer, Hamburg Television, 1965-68; Freelance, 1968-; Teaching: Filmhochschule Munchen, 1969-; Accademia di Musica della Svizzera Italiana, 1980-; Filmakademie Berlin, 1981-; Zurich University, 1984;

Musikhochschule Freiburg, 1987; Bern Conservatory, 1988; Frankfurt University, 1989; Zurich University, 1992-93. Compositions: As Writer/Director some 30 TV Films on Contemporary Music, Art, Literature; Some 200 Radio Broadcasts; 2 Major Exhibitions on Hermann Scherchen, Berlin, 1986; On Stravinsky/Schlemmer/Scherchen Les Noces, Lugano, 1988. Publications: Für wen komponieren Sie eigentlich?, 1971; Filmmusik: Stummfilm, 19£1; Hermann Scherchen, Musiker, 1891-1966, with Dagmar Wünsche, 1986. Contributions to: Numerous articles in worldwide publications; Contributions to various anthologies. Address: Sentiero al Calvario 20, CH 6644 Orselina, Switzerland.

PAULUS Stephen (Harrison(, b. 24 Aug 1949, Summit, New Jersey, USA. Composer. m. Patricia Ann Stutzman, 18 July 1975, 1 son. Education: Alexander Ramsey High School, 1967; BA, 1971, MA, Music Theory and Composition, 1974; PhD, Music Theory and Composition, 1978, University of Minnesota. Career: Co-Founder, Minnesota Composer's Forum, 1973-85; Composer-in-Residence, Minnesota Orchestra, 1983-87; Vice-President, Minnesota Composer's Forum, 1983-. Compositions: Operas: The Village Singer; The Postman Always Rings Twice; The Woodlanders, 1984; Harmoonia, 1990; Orchestral, Suite from The Postman Always Rings Twice; Symphony in Three Movements; Reflections; Ordway Overture; Concerto for Orchestra; Spectra; Chorus and Orchestra: So Hallow'd Is The Time; Letter For The Times; Canticles, North Shore; Chorus: Too Many Waltzes; Jesn Carols; Echoes Between the Silent Peaks; Chamber Ensembles: Partita for Violin and Piano; Music for Contrasts, String Quartet; Courtship Songs, Flute, Oboe, Cello, Piano; Wind Suite, WW Quartet; Voice, Letters from Colette, Soprano and Chamber Ensemble; All My Pretty Ones, Soprano and Piano; Artsongs, Tenor and Piano; Mad Book; Shadow Book, Tenor and Pianoforte; Three Elizabethan Songs, Soprano and Pianoforte. Recordings: So Hallow'd Is The Time, for Chorus, Orchestra and Soloists; Symphony in Three Movements, Neville Marriner/Minnesota Orchestra. Memberships: American Society of Composers, Authors and Publishers; Minnesota Composers' Forum. Hobbies: Tennis; Hiking; Reading. Address: c/o Opera Theater of St Louis, PO Box 13148, St Louis, MO 63119, USA.

PAUSTIAN Inger, b. 1937, Denmark. Singer (Mezzo-Soprano). Education: Studied in Copenhagen. Career: Engaged at Kiel Opera, 1965-67, Hanover, 1967-69, Frankfurt, 1969-78; Guest appearances at Hamburg, 1970, Munich, 1971, and Valencia, 1976, as Ortrud in Lohengrin; Bayreuth Festival, 1968-71, as Siegrune, Wellgunde and a Flowermaiden; Sang at Zurich Opera, 1976-77; Other roles included Monteverdi's Penelope, Mozart's Marcellina, Magdalene, Brangaene, Herodias and the Nurse in Die Frau ohne Schatten; Verdi's Azucena, Amneris and Eboli, Guilietta in Les Contes d'Hoffmann, Larina in Eugene Onegin and Agave (The Bassarids by Henze); Frequent concert performances. Address: c/o Opernhaus Zurich, Falkenstrasse 1, CH-8008 Zurich, Switzerland.

PAUTZA Sabin, b. 8 February 1943, Calnic, Rumania. Composer; Conductor. m. Corina Popa, 2 October 1974, 2 daughters. Education: Conducting, Bucharest Academy of Music, 1964; Composition, Accademia Musicale Chigiana, Siena, Italy, 1970. Debut: Rumanian Athenee, Rumania, 1964. Career: Professor of Harmony and Conducting, Iassy Academy of Music, 1965-84; Conductor, Iassy Academy of Music Orchestra, 1969-84; Appearances, Bayreuth Wagner Youth Festival, 1974, 1977, 1978, Carnegie Hall, New York, 1984; Music Director, Conductor, Plainfield Symphony Orchestra, New Jersey, USA, 1987-. Compositions: Symphony No 1, In Memoriam; Symphony No 2, Sinfonia Sacra; Offering to the Children of the World for double choir; Games I, II, III and IV for orchestra; 3 String Quartets; Double Concerto for viola, piano and orchestra; Ebony Mass for choir, organ and orchestra; Another Love Story, opera for children; Laudae for chamber orchestra; Five pieces for large orchestra; Nocturnes for soprano and orchestra; Haiku for soprano and chamber orchestra; Simfonietta, 1994; Rita Dove Triptych, 1994; Chimes for percussion instruments, 1995. Honours: George Enesco Prize for Composition, Romanian Academy, 1974; Romanian Union of Composers Prize, 1977; Martin Luther King Jr Prize for "Chimes, 1995. Address: 240 Locust Avenue, Locust, NJ 07760, USA.

PAVAROTTI Luciano, b. 12 Oct 1935, Modena, Italy. Singer (Tenor). m. Adua Veroni, 1961, 3 d. Education: DMus, Istituto Magistrale; Tenor Range. Debut: As Rodolfo in La Bohème, at Reggio nell' Emilia, 1961; As Edgardo in Lucia di Lammermoor in Miami, USA, 1965. Career: Appearances include: Staatsoper Vienna, Royal Opera House of London, 1963, La Scala European tour, 1963-64, La Scala, 1965, Metropolitan Opera House, NY, 1968, Paris Opéra and Lyric Opera of Chicago, 1973; Many recitals and concerts worldwide from 1973; Appeared in MGM film, Yes, Giorgio, 1981; Sang Manrico in TV simulcast from the Met, 1988, in a new production of Rigoletto, 1989, Nemorino in L'Elisir d'Amore at Covent Garden, 1990; Concert at Glasgow, 1990; Sang Manrico at 1990 Maggio Musicale Florence and appeared with 2 other tenors at World Cup Concert, Caracalla; Concert performances of Otello at Chicago, 1991; Sang Otello and Nemorino in NY, 1991-92; Debut as Verdi's Don Carlos at the opening of the 1992-93 season at La Scala; Returned to Covent Garden in 1992 as Cavaradossi; Metropolitan Opera, 1994 as Arvino in I Lombardi; Sang Gustavus (Ballo in Maschera) at Covent Garden, 1995 and at the Metropolitan, 1997. Recordings include: La Bohème, Madama Butterfly, Beatrice di Tenda, Lucia di Lammermoor, La Fille du Régiment, Maria Stuarda, Un Ballo in Maschera, Luisa Miller, Macbeth, Mefistofele, Idomeneo, Aida, Norma, Tosca, Otello. Publication: Pavarotti: My Own Story, with William Wright. Honours include: Honorary Degree, Pennsylvania, 1979; Grand Officier, Italy; Noce d'Oro National Prize; Luigi Illica International Prize; First Prize Gold Orfeo (Academie du Disque Lyrique de France). Hobbies: Painting; Equitation. Address: Via Giardini 941, 41040 Saliceta, Modena, Italy.

PAVIOUR Paul (Sir), b. 14 April 1931, Birmingham, England. Composer; Community Musician. Education: Studied in London with Herbert Howells, Vaughan Williams and Adrian Boult (MMus, University of London, 1962). Career: Faculty Member, All Saints College, Bathurst, 1969-75; Conductor, Goulburn Consort of Voices, 1975-; Commissions from Goulburn Festival of the Arts, Australian Government, and others; Goulburn College of Advanced Education, 1975-84; Organist and Conductor with Argyle Operatic Society, 1977-. Compositions include: Horn Concerto, 1970; Missa Australis, 1971; Take Kissing as a Natural Law, for female voices and flute, 1971; Four Carols, 1972; A New Australian Mass, 1973; All Systems Go for chorus and orchestra, 1980; An Urban Symphony (No 2), 1982; This Endris Nyghte, Christmas Cantata, 1982; Concerto for Oboe, Strings and Percussion, 1983; Symphony No 5, 1985. Honours include: Knighted 1994, for services to community music in Australia. Address: 4 Beppo Street, Goulburn, NSW 2580, Australia.

PAWLAK Ireneusz (Jakub), b. 22 Mar 1935, Wrzesnia, Poland. Catholic Priest; Scholar; Composer. Education: Theology, Seminary of Gniezno, 1960; MA, 1964, Music and Musicology, 1965, Doctorate, 1976, Privatdocent, 1990, Catholic University, Lublin. Career: Choirmaster in Gniezno, 1965; Director of Schola Gregoriana in Lublin, 1974-; Director of chair of Gregorian Chant, Catholic University of Lublin. Compositions: Two liturgical masses, some liturgical songs for common use. Publications: Petricovian Graduals as document of Polish Gregorian Chant after Trent Council, 1988; Spiewy Uwielbienis (Cantica Laudis), 1993. Contributions to: About 100 articles on music in Polish periodicals: Stduia Gnesnensia, Msza Swieta, Homo Dei, Ruch Biblijny i Liturgiczny, Encyklopeedia Katolicka, Encyklopedia Muzyczna PWM. Memberships: Zwiazek Kompozytorow Polskich; Towarzystwo Naukowe KUL; Society of Church Music Lecturers; Episcopal Commission of Church Music. Address: ul Niecala 8/93, 20-080 Lublin, Poland.

PAYER-TUCCI Elisabeth, b. 1944, Germany. Soprano. Career: Sang at the Berne Opera, 1968-70 and at the Cologne Opera until 1976; New York in 1980 as Irene in a concert rendition of Rienzi; Sang the Siegfried Brünnhilde at the Metropolitan, Isolde at Rome and Ariadne at Lisbon; Sang at Verona Festival as Turandot, Brünnhilde at Barcelona and Senta at Rio de Janeiro (1987); Other roles have included Verdi's Amelia in Un Ballo in Maschera, the Forza Leonora, and Santuzza in Cavalleria Rusticana.

PAYNE Anthony (Edward), b. 2 Aug 1936, London, England. Composer. m. Jane Manning, 24 Sept 1966. Education: Classics, Dulwich College, London; Music, Durham University, 1958-61. Career: Freelance Writer, Musicologist, Lecturer, part-time composing, 1962-73; Composer, 1973-. Compositions: Paraphrases and Cadenzas, 1969; Paean for solo piano, 1971; The Spirits Harvest, full orchestra, 1972-85; Concerto for Orchestra, 1974; World's Winter, soprano and ensemble, 1976; String Quartet, 1978; The Stones and Lonely Places Sing, septet, 1979; Song of the Clouds, oboe and orchestra, 1980; A Day in the Life of a Mayfly, sextet, 1981; Evening Land, soprano and piano, 1981; Spring's Shining Wake, orchestra, 1982; Songs and Dances, strings, 1984; The Song Streams in the Firmament, septet, 1986; Half Heard in the Stillness, full orchestra, 1987; Consort Music, string quintet, 1987; Sea Change, septet, 1988; Time's Arrow, full orchestra, 1990; The Enchantress Plays, bassoon and piano, 1990; Symphonies of Wind and Rain, chamber ensemble, 1992; Orchestral Variations: The Seeds Long Hidden, 1993; Empty Landscape - Heart's Ease, sextet, 1995; Commissioned by the BBC to realise Elgar's Sketches for his Third Symphony for the 1998 Proms season. Recordings: The World's Winter; Paean; Phoenix Mass; The Music of Anthony Payne, BBC Records; Adelstrop; NMC. Publications: Schoenberg, 1968; The Music of Frank Bridge, 1984. Contributions to: Musical Times; Tempo; Music and Musicians; The Listener; Daily Telegraph; The Times; The Independent; Country Life. Honours: Radcliffe Prize, 1975; Concerto for Orchestra chosen for ISCM Festival, Boston, 1976. Memberships: Composers' Guild; Association of Professional Composers; Society for the Promotion of New Music. Hobbies: English countryside; Films. Current Management: J W Chester. Address: 2 Wilton Square, London N1 3DL, England.

PAYNE Nicholas, b. 1945, Kent, England. Administrator. m., 2 sons. Education: Eton (King's Scholar), 1958-63; Trinity College, Cambridge, 1963-66. Career: Paterson Concert Management, 1967; Arts Council Administration Course, 1967-68; Finance Department, Royal Opera House, Covent Garden, 1968-70; Subsidy Officer, Arts Council, 1970-76; Financial Controller, Welsh National Opera, 1976-82; General Administrator, Opera North, 1982-93; Director of Opera at Royal Opera House, Covent Garden, from 1993. Address: c/o Royal Opera House, Covent Garden, London WC2E 9DD, England.

PAYNE Patricia, b. 1942, Dunedin, New Zealand. Singer (Mezzo-Soprano). Education: Studied in Sydney and London. Debut: Covent Garden, 1974, as Schwertleite in Die Walküre: returned as Ulrica in Un Ballo in Maschera, Azucena, Erda in Das Rheingold, First Norn in Götterdämmerug and Filippyevna in Eugene Onegin, 1989; Barcelona, 1974-75, as La Cieca in La Gioconda and as Erda; Bayreuth Festival and San Francisco Opera, 1977; La Scala, Milan, 1978 as Ulrica; Verona Festival, 1980; Guest appearances at Frankfurt Opera and the Metropolitan, New York (debut 1980 as Ulrica, sang in La Gioconda, 1983); Has sung Gaea in the British premiere of Strauss's Daphne, Opera North, 1987; Appearances with English National Opera in The Love for Three Oranges, Salome and The Magic Flute; Sang Prokofiev's Princess Clarissa with Opera North at the 1989 Edinburgh Festival; Season 1992 as Herodias in Salome at Wellington; Sang the Witch in Hansel and Gretel and Auntie in Peter Grimes at Wellington, 1996; Concert repertoire includes the Wesendonck Lieder, Bach's St John Passion (in Paris), the Alto Rhapsody and Beethoven's 9th (Spain), Alexander Nevsky and the Mozart Requiem (London, Festival Hall). Recordings include: Un Ballo in Maschera and Peter Grimes; Beethoven's Missa Solemnis. Honours: Sidney Sun Aria Winner, 1966; Prize Winner, s'Hertogenbosch Competition, 1972. Address: c/o Harrison/Parrott Limited, 12 Penzance Place, London W11 4PA, England.

PAYNTER John (Frederick), b. 17 Jul 1931, England. University Professor. m. Elizabeth Hill, 1956, 1 daughter. Education: GTCL, Trinity College of Music, London, 1952; DPhil, York, 1971. Career: Teacher, Primary and Secondary Schools, 1954-62; Lecturer, Music, CF Mott College of Education, Liverpool, 1962-65; Principal Lecturer/Head, Department of Music, Bishop Otter College, Chichester, 1965-69; Lecturer 1969, Senior Lecturer 1974-82, Professor of Music Education/Head, Department of Music, University of York, 1982-. Compositions: Choral & Instrumental Works including: Landscapes, 1972; The Windhover, 1972; May Magnificat, 1973; God's Grandeur, 1975; Sacraments of Summer, 1975; Galaxies for Orchestra, 1977; The Voyage of St Brendan, 1978; The Visionary Hermit, 1979; The Inviolable Voice, 1980; String Quartet No 1, 1981; Cantata for the Waking of Lazarus, 1981; The Laughing Stone, 1982; Contrasts for Orchestra, 1982; Variations for Orchestra and Audience, 1983; Conclaves, 1984; Piano Sonata, 1987; Four Sculptures of Austin Wright, for Orchestra, 1991, 1994; String Quartet, No 2; Time After Time, 1991. Publications include: Sound & Silence, with P Aston, 1970; Hear and Now, 1972; The Dance & The Drum with E Paynter, 1974; All Kinds of Music, volumes 1-3, 1976, volume 4, 1979; Sound Tracks, 1978; Music in the Secondary School Curriculum, 1982; Sound and Structure, 1992; Editor, Series, Resources of Music; Joint Editor, British Journal of Music Education; Companion to Contemporary Musical Thought. Honours: OBE, 1985; Honorary GSM, 1986. Membership: FRSA. Address: Westfield House, Newton upon Derwent, York Y04 5DA, England.

PAZDERA Jindrich, b. 25 July 1954, Zilina, Slovak Republic. Violinist and Teacher. m. 23 Jan 1982, 1 son. Education: Moscow State Conservatory, 1974-79; Violin Class by Leonid Kogan, graduated with honours, 1979. Debut: Bratislava, Violin Concerto No 2, by Karol Szymanowski, with the Slovak Philharmonic Orchestra, 1974. Career: Concerts in 24 countries in Europe, America and Asia, as soloist with orchestras and as a chamber musician (violin and piano, Bohemia Piano Trio); Teacher: Bratislava Secondary Music School, 1983-94; Prague Academy of Arts, 1991-; Reader of Violin, 1995-; Repertoire: 25 violin concertos and many recital programmes; Numerous first night performances of contemporary Slovak and Czech works. Recordings: CD: As Violinist: Violin Concertos, Vivaldi, 1990; Le Quattro Stagioni, Vivaldi, 1992; Piano Trio works by Beethoven, Dvorak, 1995; Violin works by W A Mozart, 1997; As Conductor: Chamber Orchestra works by Suk, Barber, Bruckner and Shostakovich, 1993. Publications: A Reconstruction of a W A Mozart's Sinfonia Concertante in A, for Violin, Viola and Cello (K104-320), A World Premiere, 1991, CD Rec, 1997; Translations of Methodical and Muspsychological Works of Russian Authors (V P Bronin, G Kogan). Honour: A Frico Kafenda Slovak National Music Award, 1985. Memberships: Slovak Music Association; Czech Association of Music Artists and Scientists. Hobbies:

Woodworking; Growing fruit trees. Address: Luzická 8, 120 00 Prague, Czech Republic.

PEACOCK Lucy, b. 21 Jun 1947, Jacksonville, Florida, USA. Singer (Soprano). Education: North West University, USA, and at the Opera Studio of the Deutsche Oper Berlin. Debut: Berlin 1959, in Der Rosenkavalier. Career: Sang in Berlin as Flotow's Martha, Mozart's Pamina, Countess and Servilia, Cavalli's Calisto, Micaela in Carmen and Rosina in Il Barbiere di Siviglia; Guest appearances in Dusseldorf, Vienna, Munich, Hamburg, Turin, Geneva, Paris and London; Bayreuth 1985, as Freia in Das Rheingold and in Die Walküre and Götterdämmerung; Sang Eva in Die Meistersinger at the 1988 Festival; Sang Mathilde in Guillaume Tell at Catania, 1987; Deutsche Oper Berlin as Marenka in The Bartered Bride and as Myrtocle in Die Toten Augen by d'Albert; Created the title role in Desdemona und ihre Schwestern by Siegfried Matthus, Schwetzingen 1992; Princesse de Bouillon in Adriana Lecouvreur at Adelaide, 1994; Television appearances include Martha, in Flotow's opera. Address: Ingpen and Williams Ltd, 26 Wadham Road, London SW15 2LR, England.

PEARCE Alison (Margaret), b. 5 Aug 1953, Bath, England. Singer (Soprano). Education: AGSM, distinction in Performance, Guildhall School of Music and Drama, 1972-77; With Pierre Bernac, Paris, 1977-78, Gerhard Husch, Munich, 1980-81. Debut: Wigmore Hall, London. Career: International soloist, oratorio, concert, opera; Regular performances, all major British choirs, orchestras and conductors including Colin Davis, Charles Groves, David Willcocks, James Lockhart, Steuart Bedford, Sylvian Cambreling, Libor Pesek; Major festivals: Three Choirs, Cheltenham, Llandaff, Brighton, Flanders, France, Norway, Philippines; Soloist, world premieres: Sinfonia Fidei (A Hoddinott), Six Psalms (D Muldowney), Music's Empire (J McCabe); Regular BBC appearances include 1995 Fairest Isles series, Eugenie (The Rising of the Moon, N Maw), Diana (The Olympians, A Bliss), Bronwen, (Bronwen, J Holbrooke); TV debut, 1982, Hallé Orchestra; Opera debut UK, title role in Lucia di Lammermoor, 1982; Other roles include Violetta (La Traviata), Abigaille (Nabucco), Manon (Manon Lescaut), Elisabeth (Tannhäuser), Tosca, Fidelio; 1995-96 season includes Mahler 8th, Britten War Requiem, Verdi Requiem, Elgar The Kingdom, Beethoven Missa Solemnis, Penderecki Te Deum, Nabucco, Manon Lescaut, Four Last Songs (R Strauss), in UK, France, Belgium, Norway, Netherlands, Israel. Current Management: Ariette Drost, Netherlands. Address: PO Box 223, 27 Endell Street, Covent Garden, London WC2H 9BY, England.

PEARCE George Geoffrey, b. 19 September 1943, Cottingham, Yorkshire, England. Teacher; Organist; Choirtrainer. Education: ALCM (Pno P), 1960; ARCM (OP/OT), 1962-63; FTCL, 1964; GRSM, 1965; ARCO, 1965; Studied, Royal College of Music, London, 1962-65. Career: Music Teacher, Kingston upon Hull including: Head of Music, Hull Grammar School, 1965-73; Assistant Organist, Beverley Minster, 1969-73; Instructor of Piano, Harlaw Academy, Aberdeen, 1973-83; Conductor, Aberdeen Orpheus Choir, 1974-83; Organist, Master of Choristers, St Andrew's Episcopal Cathedral, Aberdeen, 1975-83; Organist, Master of Choristers, Bridlington Priory, Yorkshire, 1984-87; Director of Music, Selby Abbey, Yorkshire, 1987-94; Teacher of Piano, North Riding College of Education, Scarborough, 1985-88; St Peters School, York, 1984-93; Performer and private teacher, 1994-. Composition: A Set of Preces and Responses for the Church Service, 1976. Recordings: O Sing Joyfully, 1978; Organ and Choral Music From Aberdeen Cathedral, 1980; Favourite Hymns From Bridlington Priory, 1985; Organ Music From Selby Abbey, 1991; TV and Radio Broadcasts as Organist and Conductor. Honour: RCO Sawyer Prize, 1965. Hobbies: Swimming; Gardening; Hill Walking; Reading Thrillers. Address: Woodlands, Garden Lane, Sherburn in Elmet, North Yorkshire LS25 6AT, England.

PEARCE Michael, b. 1945, Chelmsford, Essex, England. Singer (Baritone). Education: Choral Scholar at St John's College, Cambridge; Study with Otakar Kraus and Elizabeth Fleming. Career: Concert appearances in China, Canada, Brazil and throughout Europe; Repertory includes Mozart Requiem (at Bruges), Monteverdi Vespers (Maastricht), Bach B Minor Mass (Turin and Edinburgh), Messiah (London and Brighton) and Brahms Requiem (Royal Festival Hall); Haydn's Theresienmesse at Windsor, The Creation at the London Barbican and Schöpfungsmesse at the Elizabeth Hall; Opera roles include Ortel in Meistersinger and 5th Jew in Salome, both at the Royal Opera House, Claudius in Handel's Agrippina with Midsummer Opera, Lysiart in Weber's Euryanthe with New Sussex Opera and Beethoven's Rocco; Season 1996-97 with A Child of our Time by Tippett, the Berlioz Messe Solennelle and Elijah in Norway; Mozart's Requiem and Carmina Burana in Spain; Verdi Requiem at Canterbury Cathedral and Messiah with David Willcocks; Christus in Bach's St John Passion in London, St Matthew Passion at Salisbury and the B Minor Mass at Beverley Minster. Recordings include: Handel Coronation Anthems under Simon Preston; Bach B Minor Mass, Edinburgh 1990. Honours include: Winner, first English Song Award at the Brighton Festival. Address: 1 Homelands Copse, Fernhurst, Haslemere, Surrey GU27 3JQ, England.

PEARCE Michael, b. 25 Mar 1954, Windsor, New South Wales, Australia. Composer. Education: BA, 1978, BMus (Hons), 1979 (study with Peter Sculthorpe), University of Sydney; Sussex University, with Jonathan Harvey, 1980. Career: Faculty Member, New South Wales Conservatory, 1981-; University of Sydney, 1990; Active interest in urban aboriginal music. Compositions include: Kynesis, for string quartet, flute, guitar and harpsichord, 1978; Eulogy, for flute, percussion and piano, 1979; Interiors, for violin, cello, flute, carinet and percussion, 1981; Deserts I for 4 percussion, 1982; Deserts II and III for ensembles, 1982-83; Chamber Symphony, 1987; Canciones, for soprano and 7 instruments, 1990; Oh Tierra, Esperame for soprano and piano, 1991; Chamber Symphony No 2, 1991; Commissions from Synergy and Seymour Group. Honours include: Sarah Makinson Prize for Composition, 1979. Address: c/o APRA, 1a Eden Street, Crows Nest, NSW 2065, Australia.

PEARLMAN Martin, b. 21 May 1945, Chicago, USA. Conductor; Harpischordist; Composer. Education: Studied with Karel Husa at Cornell University (BA 1967) and with Gustav Leonhardt, harpischord, in the Netherlands, 1967-68; MM in composition with Yehudi Wyner at Yale University (1971) and further harpischord study with Ralph Kirkpatrick. Career: Founder and director of early music group, Banchetto Musicale, 1973 (named Boston Baroque from 1992); Faculty member at University of Massachusetts at Boston, 1976-81; Many tours as harpischordist in repertory which includes D Scarlatti and Couperin family; US premieres of works by Handel, Rameau and other Baroque composers, as conductor; Handel's Semele at the Kennedy Center, Washington DC, 1995. Publications include: Performing editions of Monteverdi's L'Incoronazione di Poppea, Purcell's Comical History of Don Quixote, and Mozart's fragment, Lo Sposo Deluso; Complete edition of the harpischord music of Armand-Louis Couperin. Honours include: Erwin Bodky Award, 1972; Prize-winner at 1974 Bruges Competition. Address: c/o Washington Opera (Artists Contracts), John F Kennedy Center for the Arts, Washington DC 20566, USA.

PECCHIOLI Benedetta, b. 1949, Italy. Singer (Mezzo-Soprano). Debut: Piccola Scala, as Clarina in La Cambiale di Matrimonio, 1973. Career: Appearances at Monte Carlo from 1974, Rouen, 1974-75, Maggio Musicale, Florence, 1976-77, in Henze's Il Re Cervo and as Fenena in Nabucco; Spoleto Festival, 1976, as Cenerentola, Geneva, 1980 and 1986, Brussels, 1982 and 1987; Metropolitan Opera debut, 1983, as Rosina; Further engagements at Teatro Reggio Turin, Bilbao Festival, Teatro Massimo Palermo and Aix-en-Provence Festival (Meg Page, 1971); Concert appearances in the Ring at Paris, and at Carnegie Hall, New York; La Scala, Milan, 1989, in Rossi's Orfeo; Other roles include Fidalma in Il Matrimonio Segreto, Liseta in Il Mondo della Luna, Erilda in Le Pescatrici by Haydn, Maddalena, Federica in Luisa Miller, Donizetti's Smeton in Anna Bolena and Orsini in Lucrezia Borgia, and Genevieve in Pelléas et Mélisande. Recordings include: Il Guiramento by Mercadante; Demetrio e Polibio by Rossini; Donizetti's Pia de Tolomei. Address: c/o Teatro alla Scala, Via Filodrammatici 2, Milan, Italy.

PECHACEK Stanislav, b. 15 February 1951, Dolní Dobrouc. Music Teacher; Choir Conductor; Editor-in-Chief. Education: Czech and Music, Faculty of Philosophy, Olomouc, 1974; PhD, Theory and History of Music, 1978; 10 years violin at Music Basic School (MBS); 5 years piano at MBS, 5 years at the Faculty Courses of Choir Conducting. Debut: Choir Conductor, 1978. Appointments: Teacher at Pedagogical Grammar School (PGS), Prague, 1975; Conductor of Girls Choir at PGS, 1978-90; Senior Lecturer at the Faculty of Pedagogics, Music Department, Prague, 1984; Conductor of Women's Choir, Puella Pragenses, 1990-94; Conductor of Children's Choir, Mladi (The Youth), Prague, 1994-; Hundreds of concerts with all choirs in Prague; Czech Republic and abroad (England, Spain, Belgium, Holland, Sweden, Denmark, Switzerland, Germany, Italy, Hungary, France); Many International Choir Festivals in Czech Republic and abroad. Publications: Practical Tasks in Music Didactic, 1991; Guitar Accompaniments of Folksongs, 1993; Fundamentals of Conducting Techniques, 1994. Contributions to: Editor-in-Chief of Cantus (magazine for choir art), 1993-; Texts about choir art and music education in magazines: Cantus and Music Education. Memberships: Association of Choir Conductors; Association of Czech Choirs (member of Presidium); Agec Arbeitsgemeinschaft Europaischer Chorverbne (member of music committee). Hobbies: Cycling; Skiing; Tourism. Address: Katerinska 24, CZ-12800, Prague 2, Czech Republic.

PECKOVA Dagmar, b. 4 Apr 1961, Chrudim, Czechoslovakia. Singer (Mezzo-Soprano). Education: Studied at Prague Conservatory and in Dresden. Career: Sang at Dresden Staatsoper, 1987-, as Cherubino, Rosina and a Dryad in Ariadne auf Naxos; Berlin Staatsoper, 1989-, as Dorabella, Konchakovna in Prince Igor, Hansel, and in Der Kaiser von Atlantis by Ullmann; Guest appearances elsewhere in Germany and in Czechoslovakia; Season 1992 as Jenny in Aufstieg und Fall der Stadt Mahagonny at Stuttgart Staatsoper and Olga in Eugene Onegin at the Théâtre du Châtelet, Paris; Concert repertoire includes Requiems by Mozart, Dvorak and Verdi, Mahler's 2nd Symphony and Debussy's Le Martyre de St Sebastien. Address: c/o Stuttgart Staatsoper, Oberer Schlossgarten 6, 7000 Stuttgart, Germany.

PECMAN Rudolf, b. 12 Apr 1931, Staré Mesto u Frydku (Frydek-Místek), Czechoslovakia. Professor of Masaryk University, Brno. Education: Philosophy Faculty of Masaryk University, Brno, Czech Republic, Musicology and Aesthetics, 1950-55. Appointments: Assistant, 1955, Docent, 1984, Ordinary Professor, 1990, Philosophy Faculty, Masaryk University. Publications: Books: Josef Myslivecek und Sein Opernepilog, Brno, 1970; Beethoven Dramatik (Beethoven the Dramatic Composer), Hradec Králové, 1978; Beethovens Opernpläne, Brno, 1981; Josef Myslivecek, Prague, 1981; Georg Friedrich Handel, Prague, 1985; Eseje o Martinu (Essays about Martinu), Brno, 1989; F X Richter Und Eine "Harmonischen Belehrungen", Michaelstein/Blankenburg, 1991; Style and Music 1600-1900 (in Czech), Brno 2nd Ed, 1996; The Attack on Antonín Dvorak (in Czech), Brno, 1992. Membership: Czech Music Society, G-F-Handel-Gesellschaft, Halle (Saale). Hobbies: Literature; Philosophy. Address: 638 00 Brno, Czech Republic.

PECORARO Herwig, b. 1959, Bludenz, Switzerland. Tenor. Education: Studied at the Bregenz Conservatory. Career: Sang at the Graz Opera, 1985-90 and Bregenz Festival from 1985 as a Priest in Die Zauberflöte and the Steuermann in Fliegende Holländer; Sang at Vienna Staatsoper from 1991 notably as Pedrillo and Steuermann; Other engagements at Nice and the Smetana Theatre in Prague; Appeared at the Vienna Volksoper in 1992 in Dantons Tod. Address: c/o Vienna Staatsoper, Opernring 2, A-1010 Vienna, Austria.

PEDANI Paolo, b. 1930, Italy. Singer (Bass). Education: Studied in Milan. Career: Sang in Cherubini's L'Osteria Portoghese and Falla's Vida Breve at La Scala, 1950-51; Appearances at Bologna, Genoa, Trieste and Venice from 1954, Wexford Festival, 1956-59, Spoleto, 1961; Aix-en-Provence Festival from 1959, in Haydn's Mondo della Luna and as Masetto; Venice, 1966, in premiere of La Metamorfosi di Bonaventura by Malipiero; Florence, 1976, in the Italian premiere of Henze's Il Re Cervo; Guest appearances at Barcelona, Catania, Mexico City and Antwerp; Other roles included Rossini's Alidoro, Don Magnifico, Taddeo and Basilio, Don Pasquale, Don Alfonso, Melitone in La Forza del Destino and Paisiello's Basilio; Character roles from 1970.

PEDERSON Monte, b. 1960, Sunnyside, Washington, USA. Singer (Bass-Baritone). Education: Studied in USA and with Hans Hotter in Munich. Debut: San Francisco Opera, as M Gobineau in Menotti's The Medium, 1986. Career: Engaged at various opera houses in USA and at Bremen, 1987-88, notably as Szymanowski's King Roger; Montpellier and Bregenz, 1988-89, as Wagner's Dutchman; Minister in Fidelio at Orange, Deutsche Oper Berlin and Stuttgart, 1989-90; Sang Pizarro in a new production of Fidelio at Covent Garden, 1990, followed by concert performance at the Festival Hall, conducted by Lorin Maazel; Season 1990-91 as Shishkov in From the House of the Dead at Cologne, Orestes in Elektra at San Francisco and Amfortas at La Scala; Salzburg Festival, 1992, as Shishkov, Houston Opera, 1992, as Amfortas in a production of Parsifal by Robert Wilson; Other roles include Jochanaan in Salome, Basle, 1989, and Angelotti. Recordings include: Video of Covent Garden Fidelio; Sang Nick Shadow at the 1996 Salzburg Festival; Golaud in Pelléas at Brussels. Address Théâtre Royale de la Monnaie, 4 Léopoldstrasse, B-1000 Brussels, belgium.

PEDICONI Fiorella, b. 1950, Italy. Singer (Soprano). Education: Studied at Conservatorio Giuseppe Verdi, Milan. Career: Appeared at first in Il Barbiere di Siviglia and I Puritani at opera houses in Italy; Sang Violetta at Glyndebourne, 1988, Gilda at Covent Garden, 1989; Appeared in Bussotti's L'Ispirazione at Turin, 1991, as Sandrina in La Finta Giardiniera at Alessandria; Has also sung in operas by Haydn, Pergolesi, Rossini, Respighi, Cimarosa and Donizetti at such opera centres as La Scala, Milan; San Carlo, Naples; La Fenice, Venice; Teatro dell'Opera, Rome; Grand Théâtre, Geneva; Théâtre des Champs Elysées, Paris and the Gran Liceo, Barcelona.

PEDUZZI Richard, b. 28 Jan 1943, Argentan, France. Stage and Costume Designer. Education: Studied Scultpure at Academie de Dessin, Paris. Career: Collaborations with producer Patrice Chéreau have included L'Italiana at Spoleto, 1969, and Les Contes d'Hoffman and Lulu at the Paris Opera, 1974, 1979; Der Ring des Nibelungen at Bayreuth, 1976; Lucio Silla for La Scala, Théâtre des Amandiers in Nanterre and Théâtre de laMonnaie, Brussels, 1984-85; Co-Artistic Director with Chéreau of Théâtre des Amandiers, 1982-89; Stage designs for Tony Palmer's production of Les Troyens at Zurich, 1990, Don Giovanni at Rome, 1991; Costume designs for War and Peace at San Francisco, 1991, Le nozze di Figaro (designs), Salzburg, 1995. Address: c/o Teatro dell'Opera, Piazza B Gigli 8, 00184 Rome, Italy.

PEEBLES Anthony (Gavin Ian), b. 26 Feb 1946, Southborough, England. Concert Pianist. m. Frances Clark, 1982, 2 sons, 2 daughters. Education: Trinity College, Cambridge; Piano with Peter Katin. Debut: Wigmore Hall, London, 1969. Career: Has given concerts in 109 countries; Many BBC recordings: Soloist with London Symphony, Royal Philharmonic, Philharmonia, Hallé, Royal Liverpool Philharmonic, City of Birmingham Symphony, BBC Philharmonic and BBC Welsh Symphony Orchestras. Recordings: Copland Fantasy; Bartók Studies; Dallapiccola Quaderno Musicale di Anna Libera; Ravel Gaspard de la Nuit, Miroirs, Sonatine, Pavane; Recital of Liszt operatic transcriptions. Honours: 1st Prize, BBC Piano Competition, 1971; 1st Prize, Debussy Competition, 1972. Hobby: Tennis. Address: 18 Geneva Road, Kingston-upon-Thames, Surrey KT1 2TW, England.

PEEBLES Charles (Ross), b. 31 Aug 1959, Hereford, England. Conductor. Education: ARCM, MA (Cantab), Trinity College, Cambridge, 1980; Guildhall School of Music and Drama, 1980-81; Conducting Fellow, Tanglewood, 1982, Career: Orchestras worked with include City of London Sinfonia, City of Birmingham Symphony, Bournemouth Sinfonietta, European Community Chamber Orchestra, London Mozart Players, English Chamber Orchestra, BBC Symphony Orchestra, Scottish Chamber Orchestra, Nash Ensemble, Composers Ensemble, London Sinfonietta, Vienna Chamber Orchestra; Since 1992 all major orchestras of Spain including Orquesta Nacional de Espana; Opera work includes Opera 80/English Touring Opera and Garsington Opera; La Serva Padrona for Broomhill Opera, 1996. Recordings: Orchestral Works by M Berkeley and Leighton, also Honegger's Amphion. Honours: Winner, 1st Prize, 1st Cadaques International Conducting Competition, Spain, 1992. Hobbies: Cinema; Cricket; Literature. Current Management: Norman McCann International Artists, The Coach House, 56 Lawrie Park Gardens, London SE26 6XJ, England. Address: 71 Bartholomew Road, London NW5 2AH, England.

PEEL Ruth, b. 29 Mar 1966, Rinteln, Germany. Singer (Mezzo-soprano). Education: Royal Northern College of Music. Career: Opera roles have included Third Lady in Die Zauberflöte at Geneva and the 1994 Aix Festival, Kate Pinkerton at Antwerp and the Page in Salome at Covent Garden; Kate in Britten's Owen Wingrave for Glyndebourne Touring Opera, the title role in The Rape of Lucretia, under Stuart Bedford, and the Countess of Essex in Gloriana for Opera North; Concerts include recitals in the Covent Garden Festival, Wigmore Hall, Glasgow, Manchester and St John's Smith Square, London (Young Songmakers' Almanac, with Graham Johnson); Concerts include Pergolesi's Stabat Mater at the Barbican Hall, Mahler's 2nd Symphony in Lithuania, Beethoven's 9th in Japan under Ozawa and Holst Songs for the BBC. Recording: Brahms recital. Honours include: Claire Croiza French Song Prize, at the RNCM; Kathleen Ferrier Decca Prize, 1993; Lieder Prize, RNCM. Address: Cinema Binatang, 141 King Henry's Road, London NW3 3RD, England.

PEGG Carole (Anne), b. 19 Sept 1944, Nottingham, England. Ethnomusicologist; Musician (Singer, Fiddle Player). 1 daughter. Education: BA, Social Anthropology, 1979; PhD, Social Anthropology, 1985, Cambridge University; Traditional English Folk Fiddle learned in the field; Mongolian Horse-Head Fiddle from Mongolian Musicians. Debut: Queen Elizabeth Hall. Career: As Mr Fox, Queen Elizabeth Hall; As Carolanne Pegg, The Roundhouse half-hour TV programme Sounding Out; Many TV and Radio performances; Currently Ethnomusicologist specialising in Mongolian traditional music, song and dance; Compiled and introduced half-hour programme on Mongolian music, Radio 3; Co-Editor, the British Journal of Ethnomusicology, 1993. Compositions: Recorded: The Gay Goshawk, 1970; Mendle, 1971; Clancy's Song, Man of War, Winter People, The Lizard, Wycoller, The Lady and The Well, Fair Fortune's Star, The Sapphire, Mouse and the Crow, A Witch's Guide to the Underground, 1973. Publications: Book on Mongolian Music and Ethnicity in preparation. Address: Mongolia and Inner Asia Studies Unit, University of Cambridge, Faculty of Oriental Studies, Sidgwick Avenue, Cambridge CB3 9DA, England.

PEHRSON Joseph (Ralph), b. 14 Aug 1950, Detroit, Michigan, USA. Composer; Pianist. m. Linda Past, 13 July 1985. Education: BA 1972, MM 1973, DMA 1981, University of Michigan; Graduate Studies, Eastman School of Music. Career includes: Harmonic Etude for Solo Horn at Merkin Concert Hall, NY, 1988 performed by Francis Orval; Hornucopia by the Francis Orval Horn Ensemble, Budapest, Hungary, 1989; Several works at Greenwich House, New York City, 1992 including Tonreiter, Lewis Carroll Songs, Etheroscape and Windwork; Several works performed by Goliard Concerts at their Warwick Music Festival, NY, 1992 including Ariadne, Caprice and Thanatopsis and

subsequently presented on tour in USA, 1992-93; Guest composer at University of Akron, 1993; Exhilarations for Clarinet, Cello and Piano was performed by Composers Concordance, 1993; Thanatopsis was performed by Long Island Composers Alliance, 1994; Commission by St Luke's Chamber Ensemble for a piece for trumpet and strings, entitled Trumpet in a New Surrounding, performed 1997 at the Dia Center for the Arts, Manhattan; Commission by the Archaeus Ensemble, Romania, for a new piece for nine players, Wild, Wild, West, performed 1997, Bacau, Romania. Compositions include: For Orchestra: Chromakkordion, 1995; Chamber Ensemble: Concerto for Horn and 8 Instruments, 1987; Confessions of the Goliards for Tenor Voice, Flute, Violin and Cello, 1992; Hornorarium for Four Horns, 1994; Forest of Winds, for Wind Ensemble, 1994; Trios and duos include: Arecibo for Piano and Percussion, 1976; Exhilarations for Clarinet, Cello and Piano, 1993; Jollity for Violin and Harp, 1994; For Solo Instruments: Three Pianopieces, 1991; Panoply for Solo Flute, 1992; Lake Fantasy for Solo Oboe, 1993. Recording: Thanatopsis. Publications: Works published through Seesaw Music Inc and Soundspells Inc. Honours: Standard Awards, 1976-, American Society of Composers Authors and Publishers. Membership: Co-director, Composers' Concordance, Manhattan. Address: c/o Composers Concordance, P O Box 20548 (PABT), New York, NY 10129, USA.

PEINEMANN Edith, b. 3 Mar 1939, Mainz, Germany. Violinist; Professor. Education: Guildhall School of Music, London; Violin lessons with father, Robert Peinemann, Heinz Stanske, Max Rostal. Career: 1st Prize at ARD Competition, Munich; Appearances resulting with Solti, Szell, Steinberg, Karajan, Herbig, Tennstedt, Dohnányi, Boulez, Yan Pascal Tortelier, Kempe, Keilberth, Munch, Barbirolli, Sargent with leading orchestras worldwide; Carnegie Hall debut with Szell and Cleveland Orchestra, 1965; Festivals including Salzburg, Lucerne, Marlboro Chamber Music; Professor, Academy of Music, Frankfurt, 1976-; Performances of the Beethoven Concerto with the Detroit Symphony, the Mendelssohn in Chicago, and the Pfitzner in Cleveland and with the BBC Philharmonic, 1991. Recordings: with DGG. Honour: Plaquette Eugene Ysaye, Liège. Hobbies: Reading; Hiking; Fine Arts; Cooking; Cross Country Skiing. Address: c/o Pro Musicis, Ruetistrasse 38, CH-8032 Zurich, Switzerland.

PELINKA Werner, b. 21 Jan 1952, Vienna, Austria. Composer; Pianist; Teacher. m. Liliane Flühler, 26 Mar 1976, 2 daughters. Education: Hochschule für Welthandel, Vienna; University of Michigan; Konservatorium der Stadt Wien; MA, Hochschule für Musik und darstellende Kunst, Vienna, 1985; DPhil, University of Vienna, 1985. Career: Concerts with horn player Roland Horvath (member of Vienna Philharmonic) as Ensemble Wiener Horn; His own compositions played in Grosser Musikvereinssaal and Grosser Konzerthaussaal in Vienna and on television; Teaching, Toho-Vienna Music Academy; Since 1992, Manager of Viennese Children's Music Festival, Kinderklang; Formation of a Tomatis Institute in Vienna (training in Paris), 1994-95. Compositions: Op 1-32 e.g. Op 1: Pater Noster; Op 5: Sinfonietta con Corale; Op 9: Trio Reflexionen; Op 14: Passio Silvae; Op 24: Concerto for Jon; Op 28: Die Erbsenprinzessin, Oper frei nach H Chr Andersen (Libretto, Martin Auer), 1995. Recordings: Horn und Klavier 4, (with op 2 op 5 and op 8) Werner Pelinka (piano) and Roland Horvath (horn); Österreichische Komponisten der Gegenwart, (with op 12) Brigitte Hübner (contralto), Werner Pelinka (piano); Passio Silvae, (with op 14) with Johannes Jokel (bass voice), Roland Horvath (horn) and Werner Pelinka (piano); Horn und Klavier 5 with op 24; New Music for Orchestra VMM with op 5 (ORF Symphonic Orchestra conducted by Christo Stanischeff, Soloist, Erwin Sükar, Horn); Trio Arabesque op 26 (oboe, bassoon, piano - Tonkünstler Ensemble); Diagonal, concert pieces for strings, op 27, Ruse Philharmonic conducted by Tsanko Delibozov, CD. Publication: Die Vertonungen des lateinischen Paternoster der nachklassischen Zeit (Diss 1985, Vienna). Contributions to: Gebet und Kunst (in Singende Kirche 1985); Eine Atom-Oper als Warnung (in Morgen 1986). Memberships: AKM, 1986-; ÖKB, 1987-. Address: Gusenleithnergasse 30, A-1140 Vienna, Austria.

PELL William, b. 1946, USA. Singer (Tenor). Education: Studied in Baltimore and at Manhattan School of Music. Career: Sang at first as Baritone, notably, Don Giovanni, Mozart's Figaro (Toronto) and Germont (San Francisco); Tenor roles, 1975-, debut as Rodolfo; Sang in Amsterdam, 1983, Spoleto, 1987, as Parsifal; Deutsche Oper Berlin, 1982, notably in the 1987 premiere of Rihm's Oedipus; As Siegfried, 1988, and Kudriash in Katya Kabanova; Trieste and Hanover, 1988, as Bacchus and as Alwa in Lulu; Bayreuth Festival, 1989-91, as Parsifal and Walter von der Vogelweide; Frankfurt Opera, 1990, as Jimmy in Mahagony, Cologne, 1991, in From the House of the Dead; Other roles include Gounod's Romeo, Matteo in Arabella, Andres (Wozzeck), Desportes (Die Soldaten) and Jean in Miss Julie by Bibalo. Recordings Include: Walther von der Vogelweide in Tannhäuser. Address: c/o Deutsche Oper Berlin, Richard Wagnerstrasse 10, D-1000 Berlin, Germany.

PELLEGRINI Maria, b. 15 Jul 1943, Pescara, Italy. Singer (Soprano). Education: Studied at the Opera School of the Royal Conservatory in Toronto. Debut: With the Canadian Opera Company as the Priestes in Aida, 1963. Career: Sang Gilda 1965; Appearances in Montreal, Toronto and Vancouver; Sadler's Wells Opera from 1967, Covent Garden from 1968, notably as Violetta, Micaela in Carmen and Madama Butterfly; Guest appearances in Genoa, Bologna, Parma and Trieste and with the Welsh National Opera; US debut Pittsburgh, 1975. Recordings include: Carmen.

PELLEGRINO Ron(ald Anthony), b. 11 May 1940, Kenosha, Wisconsin, USA. Composer; Performer. Education: Studied at Lawrence University (BM, 1962) and with Rene Leibowitz and Rudolph Kolisch at University of Wisconsin (PhD, 1968). Career: Electronic Music Studio at University of Wisconsin from 1967; Director of the Electronic Music Studios at Ohio State University, 1968-70, and Oberlin Conservatory, 1970-73; Associate Professor at Texas Tech University, Lubbock, 1978-81; Founded electronic music performance ensembles Real Electric Symphony and Sonoma Electro-Acoustic Music Society. Compositions include: Electronic and Mixed Media; S&H Explorations, 1972; Metabiosis, 1972; Figured, 1972; Cries, 1973; Kaleidoscope, Electric Rags, 1976; Setting Suns and Spinning Daughters, 1978; Words and Phrases, 1980; Siberian News Release, 1981; Spring Suite, 1982; Laser Seraphim and Cymatic Music, 1982; Tape and Instruments: The End of the Affair, 1967; Dance Drama, 1967; Passage, 1968; Markings, 1969; Leda and the Swan, 1970; Phil's Float, 1974; Wavesong, 1975; Issue of the Silver Hatch, 1979. Publications include: An Electronic Music Studios Manual, 1969. Honours include: National Endowment for the Arts and National Endowment for the Humanities grants for founding the Leading Edge contemporary music series. Address: c/o ASCAP, ASCAP Building, One Lincoln Plaza, New York, NY 10023, USA.

PELLETIER Louis-Philippe, b. 1945, Montreal, Canada. Pianist; Professor. Education: Studies with Lubka Kolessa, Claude Helffer, Harald Boje, Aloys Kontarsky. Appointments: Professor of Piano, Chair, Department of Piano, McGill University. Recordings: Piano Works, Bach, Beethoven, Schumann, Brahms, Debussy, Boulez, Messiaen, Stockhausen, Xenakis, Schoenberg, Berg, Webern, Vivier, Papineau-Couture, Garant. Honours: 1st Prize, Arnold Schoenberg Piano Competition, Rotterdam, 1979; Artist of the Year, Canadian Music Council, 1980. Address: Latitude 45, Arts Promotion Inc, 109 St Joseph Blvd West, Montreal, Quebec H2T 2P7, Canada.

PELTZ Charles (Harvey Jones), b. 30 Jul 1959, Bath, New York, USA. Conductor; University Professor. 1 son, 2 daughters. Education: BM, Ithaca College; MM, Conducting Performance, New England Conservatory. Debut: Rome, 1982, Boston, 1986, New York, 1987; Hamilton, Ontario, 1989. Career: Broadcasts on NPR, APR and Euroradio; Guest Conductor: New Jersey Ballet, 1988, Pacific Symphony, 1992, Buffalo Philharmonic, 1993; Appeared: Musicisti Americani, Italy, 1984-87, North American New Music Festival, 1988, 1993; Hamilton Philharmonic, 1989, Buffalo Opera Sacra, 1991-; Faculty, State University of New York, Buffalo. Recordings: World Premiere Recording: Honneger, Christoph Colomb '93, Opera Sacra. Honours: Plesur Excellence in Teaching Award; Distinction in Performance, New England Conservatory; Pi Kappa Lambda. Membership: Conductors Guild. Hobby: Equestrian. Address: 222 Baird Hall, SUNY at Buffalo, Buffalo, NY 14260, USA.

PEMBERTON JOHNSON Anne, b. 3 Sept 1958, New York City, New York, USA. Singer (Soprano). Education: Studied at New England Conservatory and Peabody Institute. Career: Sang in Heinz Holliger's Not I at Frankfurt, Paris and Almeida Festival, London; Appearances at Munich in George Crumb's Star Child conducted by Paul Daniel and at Salzburg Festival with the Ensemble Modern under Hans Zender; Premieres of works at Library of Congress and Kennedy Center, Washington DC; Recent engagements of Pli selon Pli by Boulez and Berg's Altenberg Lieder with RAI Milan and BBC Philharmonic Orchestras; Season 1992-93 with Stravinksy's Rossignol in The Hague, conducted by Edward Downes and opening concert of Luigi Nono Festival of the Venice Biennale, 1993; Other conductors include Matthias Bamert and Peter Eötvös. Address: c/o Ingpen & Williams Limited, 26 Wadham Road, London SW15 2LR, England.

PENA Paco, b 1 Jun 1942, Spain. Musician; Flamenco Guitar Player. m. Karin Vaessen, 1982, 2 daughters. Education: Cordoba, Spain. Career: Flamenco Guitar Player, 1954-; Founded Paco Pena Flamenco Company, 1970; Founded Centro Flamenco Paco Pena, Cordoba, 1981. Honour: Ramon Montoya Prize, 1983. Address: 4 Boscastle Road, London NW5, England.

PENBERTHY James, b. 3 May 1917, Melbourne, Australia. Composer. Career: Musical Director of Australian National Ballet, 1947-50; Studied further in Europe and returned to Australia in 1952; Performances of stage works in Hobart, Perth and Canberra. Compositions include: Operas: The Whip, 1952, Larry,

1955, Ophelia Of The Nine Mile Beach, Hobart, 1965, The Earth Mother, 1957, The Bullock Driver, 1958, Dalgerie, Perth, 1959, The Miracle, Perth, 1964, The Town Planner, 1965, Swy, Canberra, 1975, Stations, 1975, Henry Lawson, 1989, The Creation Of The World, 1990; Ballets and concert music. Address: c/o Western Australia Opera Company, PO Box 7052, Cloisters Square, Perth, WA 6000, Australia.

PENDACHANSKA Alexandrina, b. 1970, Bulgaria. Singer (Soprano). Education: Studied with her mother, Valeri Popova. Debut: Sang in concert at Sofia, 1987, with Violetta's Act 1 aria. Career: Concert tour of West Germany, 1989; Performances of Traviata in Sofia and Bilbao; Performances of Lucia in Cairo and Sofia; Performances of Gilda in a new production of Rigoletto for Welsh National Opera, 1991; Concert engagements with the Sofia Philharmonic and other orchestras in Bulgaria, Moscow and Kiev; Lucia di Lammermoor (title role) in Dublin, Ophelia in Hamlet with Monte Carlo Opera, 1991-92; Sang Marie in La Fille du Régiment at Monte Carlo, 1996. Recordings: Antonida in A Life for the Tsar by Glinka. Honours: Second Prize, International Competition, Bilbao, 1988; Winner, 23rd International Dvorak Competition in Prague, 1988; Pretoria Music Competition, 1st Prize, 1990. Address: Harold Holt Limited, 31 Sinclair Road, London W14 0NS, England.

PENDERECKI Krzysztof, b. 23 Nov 1933, Debica, Poland. Composer; Educator. m. Elzbieta Solecka, 1965, 1 son, 1 daughter. Education: State Academy of Music, Krakow, Poland. Career: Professor, Krakow Academy of Music, Poland, 1958; Lecturer, Folkwang Academy, Essen, 1966-68; Scholarship to Berlin, Deutscher Akademischer Austauschedienst, 1968; Principal, Rector, Professor Docent, State Academy of Music, Krakow, 1972-; Professor, Yale University, 1973-78; Principal Guest Conductor, NDR-Orchestra, Hamburg, 1988-. Compositions: Dimensions der Zeit und der Stille, 1960; String Quartet No 1, 1960; Anaklasis, 1960; Threnos for the Victims of Hiroshima, 1961; Polymorphia, 1961; Canon, 1962; Stabat Mater, 1962; Fluorescences, 1962; Capriccio for Oboe and Strings, 1964; Passio et Mors Domini Nostri Jesu Christi, secundum Lucam, 1966; De natura sonoris I, 1966; Dies Irae, 1967; Capriccio for Violin and Orchestra, 1967; Pittsburgh Overture, 1967; Capriccio per Siegfried Palu, 1968; The Devils of Loudun, Opera, 1969; Quartetto per Archi No 2, 1968; Kosmogonia, 1970; Prelude, 1971; Utrenja, Grablegung und Auferstehung Christi, for 5 Soloists, 2 Choirs, Orchestra, 1971; De Natura Sonoris No 2, 1971; Concerto Violoncello and Orchestra, 1966-72; Partita for Harpsichord and Orchestra, 1971; Ecloga VIII, for 6 Singers, 1972; Canticum Canticorum Salominis for 16 Part Chorus and Chamber Orchestra, 1973; Symphonie No 1, 1973; Magnificat, 1974; Awakening of Jacob, for Orchestra, 1974; Violin Concerto, 1977; Paradise Lost (Rappresentazione), 1978; (Christmas) Symphony No 2, 1980; Te Deum, 1980; Lacrimosa, 1980; Cello Concerto No 2, 1982; Viola Concerto, 1983; Polish Requiem, 1983-84; The Black Mask, Opera, 1986; Song of Cherubim, 1986; Veni creator, 1987; Symphony No 4, 1989; Symphony No 3, 1990-95; Ubu Rex, Opera, 1991; Symphony No 5, 1992; Sinfonietta per archi, 1992; Flute Concerto, 1992; Sinfonietta No 2 for clarinet and strings, 1994; Violin Concerto No 2, 1995; Hymne au den heiligeu Daniel, 1997; The Seven Gates of Jerusalem for soloists, chorus and orchestra, 1997. Honours: North Rhine-Westphalia Award, 1966; Sibelius Award, 1967; Prix d'Italie, 1967, 1968; 1st Class State Award 1968; Gustav Charpentier Prize, 1971; Gottfried von Herder Prize, 1977; Arthur Honegger Music Award for Magnificat, 1978; Grand Medal of Paris, 1982; Dr L C Mult, Wolf Prize, 1987; Commander's Cross of the Order of Merit of the Federal Republic of Germany, 1990; University of Louisville Grawemeyer Award of Music Composition, 1992. Address: c/o Schott Musik Int, Weihergarten 5, D-55116 Mainz, Germany.

PENDLEBURY Sally, b. 1960, England. Cellist. Education: Studied at Chetham's Schhol of Music, in Dusseldorf and at New England Conservatory. Career: Led Cello Section of the European Community Youth Orchestra, 1982-85; Currently member of the Chamber Orchestra of Europe; Recitals with Natalia Gutman and Yuri Bashmet; Co-founded Vellinger String Quartet, 1990; Participated in master classes with Borodin Quartet at Pears-Britten School, 1991; Concerts at Ferrara Musica Festival, Italy and debut on South Bank with London premiere of Robert Simpson's 13th Quartet; BBC Radio 3 Debut, December 1991; Season 1992-93 with Concerts in London, Glasgow, Cambridge, at Davos Festival, Switzerland and Crickdale Festival, Wiltshire; Wigmore Hall with Haydn (Op 54 no 2), Gubaidulina and Beethoven (Op 59 no 2), Purcell Room with Haydn's Last Seven Words. Address: c/o Georgina Ivor Associates (Vellinger Quartet), 66 Alderbrook Road, London SW12 8AB, England.

PENHERSKI Zbigniew, b. 26 Jan 1935, Warsaw, Poland. Composer. m. Malgorzata, 1 son. Education: Composers Diploma, Warsaw Conservatory of Music, 1959. Compositions include: Musica Humana for baritone, choir and symphony orchestra, 1963; Missa Abstracta for tenor, reciting voice, choir and symphony orchestra, 1966; Street Music, chamber ensemble,

1966; Samson Put on Trial, radio opera, 1968; 3 Recitativi for soprano, piano and percussion, 1968; 3M-H1, electronic piece, 1969; Instrumental Quartet, 1970; Incantationi 1 Sextet for Percussion Instruments, 1972; The Twilight of Peryn, opera in 3 parts, 1972; Masurian Chronicles 2, for symphony orchestra and magnetic tape, 1973; Radio Symphony for 2, 1975; Anamnesis for symphony orchestra, 1975; String Play for string orchestra, 1980; Edgar: The Son of Walpor, opera in 3 parts, 1982; Jeux Partis for saxophone and percussion, 1984; 3 impressions for soprano, piano and four percussions, 1985; Scottish Chronicles for symphony orchestra, 1987; The Island of the Roses, chamber opera, 1989; Signals for Symphony orchestra 1992; Cantus for mixed choir, 1992. Address: Al Wojska Polskiego 20, 01-554 Warsaw, Poland.

PENICKA Miloslav, b. 16 April 1935, Ostrava, Czechoslovakia (Australian Citizen). Composer; Percussionist. Education: Dip Comp, High Distinction, Prague Academy of Music and Arts, 1964; Violin Studies with Jindrich Feld. Career: Abbotsleigh School, Wahroonga, 1969-75; Percussionist with the Sydney Symphony Orchestra, 1967-76. Compositions include: 2 String Quartets, 1962, 1969; Piano Concerto, 1963; Symphony, 1964; Clarinet Quintet, 1967; Piano Quartet, 1974; Clarinet Concerto, 1977; Sonatina for Strings, 1980; Piano Sonata no 2, 1980; Partita for 2 violins and cello, 1987; Sonatina for Piano, 1989; Kookaburra's Friends for piano, 1990; Nocturne for string orchestra, 1991; Winter Pastorale: Summer Hill, for small orchestra, 1992; Ballade for flute and piano, 1992; Gemini Suite for small orchestra, 1994; Lt Clark's March for orchestra, 1994; Cavatina for cello and piano, 1994; Santa Clauses for violin and piano, 1994; Commissions from Lane Cove Youth Orchestra, and others. Address: 9 Warraroon Road, Lane Cove 2066, Australia.

PENKOVA Reni, b. 28 Oct 1935, Tarnovo, Bulgaria. Singer (Mezzo-soprano). Education: Studied with Nadia Aladjem and Elena Doskova-Ricardi in Sofia. Debut: Burgass 1960, as Olga in Eugene Onegin. Career: Member of the National Opera Sofia from 1964; Guest appearances in Holland and England; Glyndebourne Festival 1971-77 as Olga, Pauline in The Queen of Spades, Dorabella in Così fan tutte and Meg Page in Falstaff; Other roles include Gluck's Orpheus, Cherubino, Octavian in Der Rosenkavalier, Amneris, and Angelina in La Cenerentola; Also heard in concert and oratorio; Member of the Bulgarian National Opera, Sofia till 1991; Presently, Vocal Professor, State Musical Academie, Sofia; Further roles include Bartok, (Bluebeard's Castle), Judith, 1975; Britten, (Midsummer Night's Dream), Oberon, 1982; Verdi (Nabucco), Fenena, 1976; Bellini, (Norma), Adalgisa, 1984; Donizetti, (La Favorita), Leonora, 1985; Cilea, (Adriana Lecouvreur), La Princesse de Bouillon, 1987. Recordings include: Prince Igor by Borodin (HMV). Address: 1202 Bulgaria Blvd, Slivnitza 212-A, Sofia, Bulgaria.

PENN William (Albert), b. 11 Jan 1943, Long Branch, New Jersey, USA. Composer. Education: Studied with Henri Pousseur and Maurico Kagel at the State University of New York at Buffalo, MA, 1967, and at Michigan State University, PhD, 1971; Further Study at Eastman School with Wayne Barlow. Career: Faculty member of Eastman School, 1971-78; Staff Composer at New York Shakespeare Festival, 1974-76; Folger Shakespeare Theatre and Sounds Reasonable Records in Washington from 1975. Compositions include: String Quartet, 1968; At Last Olympus, Musical, 1969; Spectrums, Confusions and Sometime for Orchestra, 1969; The Pied Piper of Hamelin, Musical, 1969; Chamber Music No 1 for Violin and Piano, 1971, for Cello and Piano, 1972; Symphony, 1971; The Boy Who Cried Wolf is Dead, Musical, 1971; Ultra Mensuram 3 Brass Quintets, 1971; The Canticle, Musical, 1972; Inner Loop for Band, 1973; Niagura 1678 for Band, 1973; Night Music for Flute and Chorus, 1973; Miriors sur le Rubaiyat for Piano and Narrator, 1974; Incidental Music and Songs. Honours include: American Society for Composers, Authors and Publishers Awards and National Endowment for the Arts Fellowship. Address: c/o ASCAP, ASCAP Building, One Lincoln Plaza, New York, NY 10023, USA.

PENNARIO Leonard, b. 9 Jul 1924, Buffalo, New York, USA. Concert Pianist. Education: Studied with Guy Maier, Olga Steeb and Ernest Toch. Debut: With the Dallas Symphony Orchestra, 1936, playing the Grieg Concerto. Career: Soloist with the Los Angeles Philharmonic, 1939; Played Liszt's E flat Concerto with the New York Philharmonic under Artur Rodzinski, 1943; Tour of Europe, 1952, in the popular Romantic repertory; Chamber Concerts with Jascha Heifetz and Gregor Piatigosky in Los Angeles; Premiered the Concerto by Miklos Rozsa with the LA Philharmonic under Zubin Mehta, 1966.

PENNETIER Jean-Claude, b. 16 May 1942, Chatellerault, France. Pianist; Conductor. Education: Studied at Paris Conservatoire. Career: Numerous Solo appearances in Europe and elsewhere, 1968-; Chamber Musician with Regis Pasquier (Violin) and Trio with E Krivine and F Lodeon; Recitals with Piano Four Hands; Duo with Clarinettist Michel Portal 1979-80; Member of such ensembles as Domaine Musical, Musique Vivante, Ars Nova, Itineraire and Musique Plus; Performer of Contemporary

Music at the Roayn and La Rochelle Festivals; Has conducted the Ensemble InterContemporain and the orchestras of French Radio; Premiered Maurice Ohana's 24 Preludes (1973) and Piano Concerto, 1981; Nikiprovetski's Piano Concerto, 1979; Professor of Chamber Music at the Paris Conservatoire, 1985-. Honours include: Winner, Prix Gabriel Fauré and International Competition Montreal, 2nd Prize, Long-Triubaud Competition; Winner, Geneva International Competition, 1968. Address: Conservatoire National Superieur de Musique, 14 Rue de Madrid, 75008 Paris, France.

PENNY Andrew (Jonathan), b. 4 Dec 1952, Hull, Yorkshire, England. Conductor. m. Helga Robinson, 3 Sept 1988, 1 son, 1 daughter. Education: ARNCM, GRNCM, Royal Northern College of Music, Manchester, after Clarinet and Conducting studies; Studied Conducting on Rothschild Scholarship with Sir Charles Groves and Timothy Reynish; Studied with Edward Downes on courses in Netherlands and later at BBC Conductors' Seminar. Career: Riders to the Sea (Vaughan Williams), Sadler's Wells Theatre, London; Conductor of Sheffield Philharmonic Orchestra, 1979-89; Musical Director, Hull Philharmonic Orchestra, 1982-; Broadcasts with the BBC. Recordings: 20 CDs for Marco Polo including premiere recordings of Sullivan's ballet and theatre music, symphonies by C Armstrong Gibbs, Edward German and film music by Vaughan Williams and William Walton; Premiere recordings of 11 overtures by Castelnuovo-Tedesco with the West Australian Symphony Orchestra, Perth, 1994; Recordings in Kiev, 1994; Cycle of Malcolm Arnold Symphonies with the National Symphony Orchestra, Dublin, 1995; With Queensland Symphony Orchestra, Brisbane, 1995. Honours: Ricordi Prize, Royal Northern College of Music, 1976. Address: 14 South Lane, Hessle, East Yorkshire, England.

PENROSE Timothy (Nicholas), b. 7 Apr 1949, Farnham, Surrey, England. Singer. m. (1) Shirley Margaret Bignell. m. (2) Carol Heather Oake, 15 Nov 1986. Education: Licentiate and Fellow, Trinity College, London. Debut: Opera - Holland Festival, 1974. Career: Numerous solo concert appearances throughout UK and most European countries; Visits to North and South America; Tours with Pro Cantione Antique of London, Solo Recitals for BBC and European Radio Stations; Concerts with Medieval Ensemble of London and London Music Players. Recordings: Handel's Semele; Purcell's The Fairy Queen, with John Eliot Gardiner; Others with Pro Cantione Antiqua, Medieval Ensemble of London, London Music Players and London Early Music Group. Honour: Recipient, Greater London Arts Association, Young Musicians Award, 1975. Memberships: Gentlemen-in-Ordinary, Her Majesty's Chapel Royal, 1972-75; City Glee Club, London. Hobbies: Motorcycling; Organ Playing. Address: 83 Langdale Avenue, Mitcham, Surrey CR4 4AJ, England.

PENTLAND Barbara, b. 2 Jan 1912, Winnipeg, Canada. Composer. Education: Studied composition with Cecile Gauthiez, Paris; Studied under Frederick Jacobi and Bernard Wagenaar at Juilliard School of Music, New York and Aaron Copland at Berkshire Music Centre. Career: Instructor, Royal Conservatory of Music, Toronto, 1942; Worked at MacDowell Colony, 1947-48; Taught Theory and Composition, Music Department, University of British Columbia, Vancouver, 1949-63; Performed as Pianist throughout Canada, USA and Europe and in broadcasts for CBC and BBC; Has composed music and has received commission from Canadian Broadcasting Corporation, Winnipeg Symphony Orchestra, University of British Columbia, Purcell String Quartet, International Institute of Music of Canada, Vancouver New Music Society, New Music Concerts, among others. Compositions include: Stage Works: Beauty and The Beast, 1940, The Lake, 1952; Orchestral: Arioso and Rondo, 1941; Ave Atque Vale, 1951; Cinescene, 1968; Symphony No 1, 1945-48, No 2, 1950; Symphony For Ten Parts, No 3, 1957; Symphony No 4, 1959; Variations on a Boccherini Tune, 1948; String Orchestra: 5+, Simple Pieces for Strings, 1971; Res Musica, 1975; Ricercar for Strings, 1955; Strata, 1969; Soloist with Orchestra: Colony Music, 1947; Concerto for Organ and Strings, 1949; Concerto for Piano and Strings, 1956; News, 1970; Variations Concertantes, 1970; Instrumental Ensemble: Canzona, 1961; Cavazzoni for Brass, 1961; Duo for Viola and Piano, 1960; Eventa, 1979; Interplay, 1972; Mutations, 1972; Occasions, 1974; Septet, 1967; Sonata for Cello and Piano, 1943; Sonata for Violin and Piano, 1946; String Quartet No 1, 1945, No 2, 1953, No 3, 1969, No 4, 1980, No 5, 1985; Triance, 1978; Trio Con Alea, 1966; Instrumental Solo: Phases for Solo Clarinet, 1977; Reflections, 1971; Solo Violin Sonata, 1950; Sonata for Solo Flute, 1954; Variations for Viola, 1965; Chorus: Epigrams and Epitaphs, 1952; Saluation of The Dawn, 1954; Three Sung Songs, 1965; What Is Man, 1954; Solo Voice: At Early Dawn, 1945; Disasters of The Sun, 1976; Sung Songs 1-3, 1964, 4-5, 1971; Keyboard: Aria, 1954; Arctica, 1971-73; Caprice, 1965, revised 1977; Dirge, 1948; Echoes I and II; Ephemera, 1974-78; Fantasy, 1962; From Long Ago, 3 Little Pieces, 1946; Hands Across the C, 1965; Maze/Labyrinthe and Casse-Tete/Puzzle, 1968, 1964; Music of Now, 1969-70; Tenebrae, 1976; 3 Pairs, 1964; Toccata, 1958; Variations, 1942; Vita Brevis, 1973. Recordings: Many recordings on various labels.

Address: Performing Rights Organisation of Canada Limited, 41 Valley Brook Drive, Don Mills, Ontario M3B 2S6, Canada.

PEPPERCORN Lisa (Margot), b. 2 Oct 1913, Frankfurt, Main, Germany. Brazilian Citizen of German Origin. Musicologist. m. Lothar Bauer, 9 Apr 1938. Education: Abitur; Degree, History of Music, Royal Conservatory, Brussels. Debut: London. Career: Worked in London until 1938; From 1938 in Rio de Janeiro as Music Correspondent for New York Times, for Musical America, 1939-46, as Market Researcher for RCA Victor, NJ, 1940-47, and other US Companies 1946-52; Researching, The Villa-Lobos biography travelled in Latin America and The US, 1959-60; Research work on Villa-Lobos in Zurich, Switzerland, 1961-. Publications: Numerous studies on Villa-Lobos including: A Villa Lobos Opera, 1940, Musical Education in Brazil, 1940, Violin Concerto by Villa-Lobos, 1941, New Villa-Lobos Works, 1942, Villa-Lobos in Paris, volume 6, 1985, all published in USA; H Villa-Lobos, Leben und Werk des Brasilianischen Komponisten, Atlantis, Zurich, 1972 (out of print); Various other studies on Villa-Lobos published in Brazil, Germany, Italy, Holland, Switzerland and Belgium; Published in Great Britain: Villa-Lobos in The Illustrated Lives of the Great Composers, 1989, also being prepared in Chinese and Portuguese, Villa-Lobos, The Music, 1991; Villa-Lobos: Collected Studies, 1992; Letters, 1994. Address: Schulhaus Strasse 53, 8002 Zurich, Switzerland 138.

PERAHIA Murray, b. 19 Apr 1947, New York City, New York, USA. Pianist; Conductor. Education: Graduate, Mannes College; Studied with Jeanette Haien, Artur Balsam, Mieczyslaw Horszowski. Career: Debut: Carnegie Hall 1968 won Leeds International Competition, 1972; London debut 1973. Guest Pianist and Conductor, all major orchestras including; New York, Boston, Chicago, Philadelphia, Cleveland, Los Angeles, London, Paris, Berlin, Amsterdam Symphony Orchestras; Performed with Budapest, Guarneri and Galimir String Quartets; Participant, Marlboro Music Festival, Aldeburgh, Edinburgh and Vienna Music Festivals; Recitaltours, USA, Canada, Europe, Japan; From 1982 through 1989 he was co-artistic director of the Aldeburgh Festival, England; Played Mozart's Concerto K491 with the Philharmonia, Festival Hall, 1997. Recordings: Sony Classical, Masterworks; including all Mozart Concertos as Pianist-Conductor with English Chamber Orchestra; Beethoven Concerti with Concertgebouw Orchestra, Chopin with the Israel Philharmonic, Concertos by Mendelssohn, Schumann and Grieg; Solo works by Schubert, Schumann, Mendelssohn, Chopin, Beethoven and Bartók (Sonata for two pianos and percussion, with Georg Solti); Schubert's Winterreise with Dietrich Fischer-Dieskau. Honours: Avery Fisher Artist Award, 1975; Kosciusko Chopin Prize. Current Management: IMG Artists, 22 East 71 Street, New York, NY 10021, USA.Address: Frank Salomon Associates, 201 West 54 Street, Suite 1C, New York, NY 10019, USA.

PERDIGAO Maria (Madalena Azeredo), b. 28 Apr 1923, Figueira Da Foz, Portugal. Director of The Department of Artistis Creation and Art Education of the Calouste Gulbenkian Foundation. m. Dr José De Azeredo Perdigao, 1 son. Education: Graduate in Mathematics, Coimbra University, 1944; Graduate in Piano, Conservatorio Nacional, Lisbon, 1948; Studied in Paris with Marcel Ciampi, Professor of National Conservatory of Paris. Career: Lectures on musical subjects; Head of Music Department, Calouste Gulbenkian Foundation, 1958-74; Created the Gulbenkian Orchestra, 1962, The Gulbenkian Choir, 1964, The Gulbenkian Ballet, 1965 and organised the Gulbenkian Music Festivals, 1958-70; President, International Music Festival of Lisbon, 1983; Piano Recitals and Concert Performances; Assessor to the Ministry of Education for Artistic Education, Lisbon, Portugal, 1978-84; Director of the Department of Artistic Creation and Art Education of The Calouste Gulbenkian Foundation. Address: R Marques de Fronteira, 8, 2° D, 1000 Lisbon, Portugal.

PEREIRA Clovis, b. 14 May 1932, Caruaru, Brazil. Composer. m. Rizomar Pereira, 18 Feb 1955, 2 sons, 2 daughters. Education: Studies with Guerra Peixe, 1951; School of Arts, Boston University, 1991. Debut: Conductor, Lamento e Dansa Brasileira, 1968. Career: Arranger, Radio Jornal do Commercio, 1950; Head, Music Department, Television, 1960; Chairman, Conservatorio Pernambucano de Musica, 1983; Tour of USA as Brazilian Representative and Conductor of University of Paraiba Chorus, 4th International Choir Festival, 1974; Teacher, University da Paraiba, Rio Grande do Norte e Pernambuco, 1994. Compositions: Grande Missa Nordestina para Coro, Solistas e Orquestra; 3 Peças Nordestinas; Terno de Pifes; Cantiga; Velame; Cantata de Natal; Poetas Nordestinos, Songs for Voice and Piano; Concertino para Violino e Orquestra de Camara, 1994. Honours: 1st Prize, Primeiro Concurso Nacional de e Orq de Camara, 1964; Trofeu Cultural Cidade do Recife, 1997. Hobbies: Audio; Football. Address: Rua Pe, Bernardino Pessoa, 395 Apt 102, Recife 51020-210, Brazil.

PEREIRA Paulo (Sergio de Graça Torres), b. 28 Nov 1954, Castro, Parana, Brazil. Conductor; Violinist; Professor. 2 daughters. Education: Parana School of Music and Fine Arts Conservatory, 1972; BSEd, Music Education, Tennessee Technological University, 1978; MM, Applied Music, Andrews University, 1990; DMA, Applied Music, Michigan State University, 1992. Debut: Soloist, Teatro Nacional, Brasilia, 1967; Conductor, St Michael the Great Orchestra, England, 1992; Brazilian Chamber Orchestra, 1994-95. Career includes: Concertmaster and/or Assistant Concertmaster: Curitiba Opera Company, Campos de Jordao I International Music Festival, Parana State Symphony (and Assistant Conductor), Parana State Chamber and Londrina VIII Music Festival Orchestras, Parana Soloists, Brazil; Caracas and Mérida Philharmonics, Mérida Chamber Orchestra, Venezuela; St Joseph Pro Musica Chamber, Michiana Symphony (Assistant Conductor, Guest Conductor), Michigan State University Symphony (Assistant and Guest Conductor); Newbold Summer Music Festival Orchestra; ASTA International Workshop String Orchestra, Switzerland; St Michael the Great Symphony and Chamber Orchestras; Assistant Concertmaster, 1st Violinist: Sao Paulo State Symphony, Parana Federal University Symphony, Camerata Antiqua of Curitiba (and Music Director, Guest Connductor); Tennessee Technological Community, Nashville, Virginia Commonwealth University, Richmond and Greater Lansing Symphonies, Renaud Chamber Orchestra; Music Director, Conductor, Venezuelan National Youth Symphony; Guest Conductor: Curitiba Chamber Orchestra, Michigan New Music Ensemble. Address: R Amintas de Barros 470 Apt 1003, Curitiba, PR 80060-200, Brazil.

PERERA Ronald (Christopher), b. 25 Dec 1941, Boston, Massachusetts, USA. Composer. Education: Studied with Leon Kirchner at Harvard, MA 1967, and at the electronic studios of Utrecht University. Career: Teacher at Syracuse University, 1968-70, Dartmouth College, 1970, Smith College, Northampton, 1971; Currently, Elsie Irwin Sweeney Professor of Music at Smith College. Compositions include: Instrumental: Improvisation for Loudspeaker, 1968, Alternate Routes for Electronics, 1971, Fantasy Variations for Piano and Electronics, 1976, Tolling for 2 Pianos and Tape, 1979; Choral: Mass, 1967, Three Night Pieces, 1974, Everything that Hath Breath, 1976; Songs: Dove sta amore for Soprano and Tape, 1969, Apollo Circling, 1972, Three Poems of Gunther Grass for Mezzo, Chamber Ensemble and Tape, 1974, The White Whale for Baritone and Orchestra, 1981; The Canticle of the Sun for Chorus, 1984; The Yellow Wallpaper, chamber opera, 1989; Music for Flute and Orchestra, 1990; The Saints for Orchestra, 1990; The Outermost House, cantata for Mixed Chorus, Narrator, Solo Soprano and Chamber Orchestra, 1991; S, opera based on novel by John Updike, 1995. Recordings include: Earthsongs on CD. Publications include: Co-editor, Development and Practice of Electronic Music, 1975; Sleep Now for High Voice and Piano, 1994 and a further 30 pieces published. Address: Department of Music, Smith College, Northampton, MA 01063, USA.

PERESS Maurice, b. 18 Mar 1930, New York, USA. Conductor. Trumpeter. Education: Studied at New York University and Mannes College (conducting with Philip James and Carl Bamberger). Career: Played trumpet before appointed by Bernstein as Assistant Conductor of the New York Philharmonic, 1961; Conducted revivals of Candide, Los Angeles, 1966, and West Side Story, New York, 1968; Music Director of the Corpus Christi Symphony Orchestra, 1962-75, the Austin Symphony, 1970-73 and the Kansas City Philharmonic, 1974-80; Guest Conductor in Brussels, Hong Kong, Vienna, Jerusalem and Mexico City; Conducted the premiere of Bernstein's Mass at the opening of the Kennedy Center, Washington DC, 1971, and at the Vienna Staatsoper, 1981; Led the US premiere of Einem's Der Besuch der alten Dame at the San Francisco Opera, 1972; Has orchestrated, edited and conducted jazz music by Duke Ellington, Eubie Blake and Gershwin (60th anniversary concert of the Rhapsody in Blue, New York, 1984); Has taught at New York University, the University of Texas at Austin and Queens College, New York. Recordings include: Bernstein's Mass (musical director); Organ Concertos 1 and 2 by Rheinberger, with E Power Biggs and the Columbia Symphony Orchestra. Memberships include: President, Conductors' Guild of the American Symphony Orchestra League. Address: Music Faculty, Queen's College, City University of New York, New York, USA.

PEREZ Jose-Maria, b. 1934, Spain. Tenor. Education: Studied in Spain and Switzerland. Career: Sang at the Lucerne Opera, 1959-60, then at Innsbruck and Basle; Sang at Graz Opera, 1963-84 in such roles as the Duke of Mantua, Don Carlos, Rodolfo, Calaf, Radames, Cavaradossi, Andrea Chénier, Alfredo and Turiddu; Guest appearances in Switzerland and elsewhere as Vasco da Gama, Faust, Pelléas, Sergei in Lady Macbeth of Mtensk and Albert Gregor in The Makropoulos Case; Also active in operetta at Berlin, Barcelona and Vienna. Address: c/o Graz Opera, Vereingte Buhnen, Kaiser Josef Platz 10, A-8010 Graz, Austria.

PEREZ-GUTIERREZ Mariano, b. 11 Sept 1932, Palencia, Spain. Professor; Principal Director; Director of Orchestra and Choirs. m. Mary Cruz Bianco. Education: Licentiate, Doctorate Arts, University of Sevilla; Diploma, 1st Class, Graduate Awards, Conservatorio of Madrid, Piano, Conterpoint and Fugue, Composition, Organ; Licentiate in Chant Gregorian & Musicological Studies, Paris, 1963, 1964. Career: Canon, Cathedral of Santiago de Compostela, 1964; Choir Master, 1964; Director of Orchestra, Choirs, Chapel of the Cathedral; Professor, Aesthetics & History of Music, Higher Conservatory of Music of Sevilla, 1969, Head of Studies, 1972, Vice Principal, 1974, Principal Director, 1978; Professor, History of Music, Royal Higher Conservatory of Music, Madrid, 1985; Vice-Principal, National Musicological Society, 1984; President, International Society for Music Education, 1986; Editor, of Journal Musica and Educacion, from 1988-. Compositions include: Elegia Cromatica for Violin and Piano; Secuencias Ciclicas for Orchestra; Canto a Santiago for Choir Organ and Orchestra. Recordings: Misa Jubilar. Publications include: Musica Sagrada y Lenguas Modernas, 1967; Origen y Naturaleza del Jubilus Alelyuatico, 1972; Comprende y ama la Musica, 1979; El Universo de la Musica, 1980; Falla y Turina, 1982; Diccionario de la Musica y los Musicos, 3 Volumes, 1985; Estélica Musical de Ravel, 1987; Falla y Paris; A Si Canta Palencia, 1994; Asi Canta Espana, 1994; Ed Zarzuela Gran Via, by F Chuecos, 1994. Hobbies: Private Collection of Ancient and Exotic Instruments. Address: Revisrie Musica y Educacion, Escosora 27-50, 28015 Madrid, Spain.

PERGAMENSHIKOV Boris, b. 1948, St Petersburg. Cellist. Education: St Petersburg Conservatory (wiith Professor Emmanuel Fischmann). Career: Concerts with leading orchestras of Moscow and St Petersburg; Emigrated to the West in 1977; Played concerts worldwide and guest in cities and music festivals from Berlin to Tokyo and from Salzburg to Jerusalem; new York debut in 1984; Recent appearances include: Concerts with the Berlin Philharmonic, the Vienna Symphony, the Symphony Orchestra of Bavarian Radio, the BBC Symphony Orchestra, the Orchestre National de France and the NHK Symphony Orchetsra, Tokyo; Since 1995 appeared at festivals including: Edinburgh, BBC Promenade concerts in London, the Schleswig Holstein Music Festival, the Prague Spring Festival, the Menuhin Festival, Gstaad, Casals Festival in Puerto Rico and Kremerata Lockenhaus; Performed with musicians including: Claudio Abbado, the Amadeus and Alban Berg Quartets, Gidon Kremer, Elizabeth Leonskaja, Rafael Kubelik, Witold Lutoslawski, Dmitri Sitkovetsky, Yehudi Menuhin, Kryzysztof Penderecki, András Schiff, Wolfgang Schneiderhan and Sandor Végh; Conducted master classes, at the Cologne Music Academy, 1977-92; Programme planning of the Chamber Music Festival "Finale", at Philharmonie Cologne; Founder of European Chamber Music Association; Extensive repertoire ranging from Baroque performance practice to modern cello techniques; Has worked closely with leading contemporary composers such as Lutoslawski, Penderecki and Halffter; Recent engagements include concerts in Vienna, Berlin, Munich and London with appearances at the Salzburg Festival, Lucerne Festival and Berlin Festival. Recordings: Works by Penderecki. Honours: First Prize, Gold Medal, 5th Tchaikovsky Competition. Address: Columbia Artists Management Ltd, 28 Cheverton Road, London N19 3AY, England.

PÉRISSON Jean-Marie, b. 6 Sep 1924, Arcachon, France. Conductor. Education: Studied with Jean Fournet in Paris and with Igor Markevitch in Salzburg. Career: Conducted the orchestra of the Salzburg Mozarteum in Austria and Germany then led the French Radio Orchestra at Strasbourg, 1955-56; Permanent Conductor at the Orchestre Philharmonique of Nice and Musical Director of the Nice Opera; Conducted cycles of The Ring and the French premieres of Katerina Ismailova by Shostakovich in 1964, Elegy for Young Lovers by Henze in 1965 and Prokofiev's The Gambler in 1966; Gave Janácek's Katya Kabanova at the Salle Favart, Paris, and conducted the Monte Carlo Opera, 1969-71; Directed the Presidential Symphony Orchestra, 1972-76, and worked in the French repertory at the San Francisco Opera; Conducted Carmen at Peking in 1982. Address: c/o San Francisco Opera, War Memorial Opera House, San Francisco, CA 94102, USA.

PERKINS John (MacIvor), b. 2 Aug 1935, St Louis, Missouri, USA. Composer; Teacher. Education: Studied at Harvard University (BA, 1958) and New England Conservatory (BMus, 1958); Further study with Nadia Boulanger in Paris, Roberto Gerhard and Edmund Rubbra in London and Arthur Berger and Irving Fine at Brandeis University. Career: Teacher at University of Chicago, 1962-65, Harvard, 1965-70, and Washington University at St Louis (Chairman of Music Department), from 1970. Compositions include: Divertimento, Chamber Opera, 1958; Andrea del Sarto, Music Theatre, 1980; Instrumental: Canons for 9 Instruments, 1958; Intermezzo, Variations for Piano, 1962; Five Miniatures for String Quartet, 1962; Quintet Variations, 1962; Music for Orchestra, 1964; Music for Brass, 1965; Music for 13 Players, 1966; Cadenza, 1978; Eight Songs, 1956-62; Three Studies for Chorus, 1958; Alleluia, 1971; After a Silence-Alph, 1976. Honours include: Commissions from the Fromm Foundation, St Louis Bicentennial and the Smithsonian Bicentennial. Address: c/o ASCAP, ASCAP Building, One Lincoln Plaza, New York, NY 10023, USA.

PERL Alfredo, b. 1965, Santiago, Chile. Concert Pianist. Education: Studied at the Universidad de Chile with Carlos Botto; Cologne Musikhochschule with Günter Ludwig; With Maria Curcio in London. Career: Concerts throughout South America and Europe, with the Filarmonica de Santiago and the Zagreb Symphony; Liszt Années de Pèlerinage for the BBC, 1990; Season 1990-91 with Amsterdam recital and London debut at the Purcell Room, Beethoven and Liszt; Schumann and Mendelssohn for Radio France, Schubert at the Bishopgate Institute, London; Recitals at the Herkulessaal, Munich, May 1991; Recital, Queen Elizabeth Hall, London, as part of the International Piano series, 1992; Concerts with the Royal Philharmonic and the Noord-Nederlands Orchestra, 1992; Beethoven 5th Concerto with the Residentie Orchestra at the Hague, 1991-92 season; Leipzig Gewandhaus recital and in Prague, 1993, also US debut with the Florida Philharmonic, a recital at Ravinia; 1993-94 season, recitals in Hamburg, Hannover, Moscow Conservatoire, with the Medici Quartet in London and the Lebanon; 1994-95 season, recitals in Prague, London's Queen Elizabeth and Wigmore Halls, Moscow Conservatoire, Dusseldorf, Bologna; Beethoven sonata series at the Wigmore Hall, 1996-97; Spring 1997, gave a series of recitals appearing in Germany's main cultural centres including the Berlin Schauspielhaus, Hamburg Musikhalle, Leipzig Gewandhaus, Düsseldorf Tonhalle, Frankfurt Alte Oper and Munich Prinzregententheatre; 1997 Debut as Royal Albert Hall with BBC Philharmonic Orchestra. Recordings: Fantasias by Schumann, Liszt and Busoni; Brahms Sonatas for clarinet and piano, with Ralph Manno; Complete Beethoven sonatas and Diabelli Variations; Grieg Concerto and Szymanowski, Symphonie Concertante. Honours: Prizewinner at such competitions as Vina del Mar (Tokyo), Ferruccio Busoni at Bolzano and the Beethoven in Vienna; 1st Prize, International Piano Competition in Montevideo. Address: c/o Harold Holt Ltd, 31 Sinclair Road, London W14 0NS, England.

PERLE George, b. 6 May 1915, Bayonne, New Jersey, USA. Composer; Author. m. (1) Laura Slobe, 1940,(2) Barbara Phillips, 1958, 2 daughters, (3) Shirley Gabis Rhoads, 6 June 1982. Education: BMus, DePaul University, 1938; MMus, American Conservatory of Music, 1942; PhD, New York University, 1956. Career: Professor Emeritus, City University of New York; Major Compositions performed by Chicago Symphony, Boston Symphony, BBC Symphony, Royal Philharmonic Orchestra, Philadelphia Symphony, San Francisco Symphony, Juilliard Quartet; Bavarian State Radio Orchestra; Da Capo Chamber Players; Cleveland Quartet; Dorian Wind Quintet; Goldman Band. Compositions include: Quintet for strings, 1958; Concerto for cello and orchestra, 1966; Songs of Praise and Lamentation for soloists, chorus and orchestra, 1974; Sonata for cello and piano, 1985; Sonata a Cinque, 1986; Dance Fantasy for orchestra, 1986; Concerto for piano and orchestra, 1990; Sinfonietta II, 1990; Transcendental Modulations for orchestra, 1993; Phantasyplay for piano, 1994. Recordings include: Concerto No 2 for piano and orchestra; Two Rilke Songs, 1941; Four Wind Quintets, 1967-84; Fantasy Variations for piano, 1971; Dickinson Songs, 1978; Concertino for piano, winds and timpani, 1979; Ballade for piano, 1980; 6 New Etudes for piano, 1984. Publications: Serial Compositions & Atonality, 1962, 6th Edition 1991; Twelve-Tone Tonality, 1977, 2nd edition, 1995; The Operas of Alban Berg, vol 1, Wozzeck, 1980; Vol II, Lulu, 1985; Co-author, New Grove Second Viennese School, 1983; The Listening Composer, 1990; The Right Notes, 1995; Style and Ideas in the Lyric Suite of Alban Berg, 1995. Contributions to: Professional journals. Honours: Guggenheim Fellowships, 1966, 1974; Pulitzer Prize for Wind Quintet IV, 1986; MacArthur Fellowship, 1986; Elected to American Academy & Institute of Arts & Letters, 1978, American Academy of Arts & Sciences, 1985. Memberships: Various professional organizations. Current Management: E C Schirmer, Boston. Address: 138 Ipswich Street, Boston, MA 02215, USA.

PERLEMUTER Vlado, b. 26 May 1904, Kowno, Poland. Pianist; Professor. m. Jacqueline Deleveau, 1938, deceased 1987.. Education: Studied with Moszkowski and Cortot. Career: Learnt Ravel's Piano Music, 1925-27 and played it to the composer; Notable exponent of French music and of Chopin; Professor at the Paris Conservatoire from 1950-76; Appearances in all major European cities; Tours of Canada, USA and Japan; Masterclasses in Canada and Japan, the Dartington Summer School and at the Royal Academy of Music, London; Retired from public performance, 1993; Continues to teach privately. Recordings include: Complete piano works of Ravel; Chopin's 24 Etudes; 12 Nocturnes, Piano Sonatas, and 4 Ballads; All Mozart sonatas; Works by Beethoven, Schumann, Liszt and Debussy. Publication: Ravel d'après Ravel, with Helene Jourdan-Morhange, 1953. Honours: All Prizes for piano, Paris Conservatoire; Grand Prix du Disque for Chopin Recital, 1972; Grand Prix de l'Academie du Disque Charles-Cros for Chopin Etudes, 1981; Grande Officier de la Légion d'Honneur, 1992. Address: c/o Maureen Garnham, 8 St George's Terrace, London, NW1 8XJ, England.

PERLMAN Itzhak, b. 31 Aug 1945, Tel Aviv, Israel. Violinist. Education: Shulamit High School, Tel Aviv; Juilliard School, New York. Debut: in USA, at Carnegie Recital Hall, 1963, in London, with London Symphony Orchestra, 1968. Career: Tours extensively in Europe and USA; Masterclasses at Meadowbrooks Festival, USA, 1970; Salzburg Festival debut 1972, with Mozart's Concerto K218, under Abbado; Season 1997 with Daniel Barenboim; Recitals in France and Italy with Bruno Canino. Recordings: Records for EMI, CFP and DG; Most Major Concertos including, Bartok, Berg, Stravinsky; Chamber Music including, Beethoven Piano Trios. Honours: Honorary MusD, University of South Carolina, 1982; Medal of Liberty, 1986; EMI Artist of the Year, 1995. Address: c/o Sheldon Gold, ILM Artists Limited, 40 West 57th Stret, New York, NY 10019, USA.

PERLONGO Daniel, b. 23 September 1942, Gaastra, MI, USA. Composer. Education: Studied with Leslie Bassett and Ross Lee Finney at the University of Michigan (MM 1966) and with Goffredo Petrassi at the Academia di Santa Cecilia, Rome, 1966-68. Career: Resident at the American Academy in Rome, 1970-72; Professor of composition and theory at Indiana University of Pennsylvania, 1980-. Compositions include: Piano Sonata, 1966; Myriad for orchestra, 1968; Intervals, for string trio, 1968; Missa Brevis, 1968; Movement in Brass, for 12 instruments, 1969; Changes for wind ensemble, 1970; Ephemeron, for orchestra, 1972; Variations for chamber orchestra, 1973; Voyage for chamber orchestra, 1975; 2 String Quartets, 1973, 1983; Ricercar, for oboe, clarinet and bassoon, 1978; A Day at Xochimiloo, for wind quintet and piano, 1987; Lake Breezes, for chamber orchestra, 1990; Piano Concerto, 1992; Arcadian Suite for horn and harp, 1993; Three Songs for chorus, 1994; Shortcut from Bratislava for orchestra, 1994; Two Movements for orchestra, 1995; Sunburst, for clarinet and orchestra, 1995. Honours include: NEA Fellowships, 1980 and 1995. Address: c/o ASCAP, ASCAP Building, One Lincoln Plaza, New York, NY 10023, USA.

PERNEL Orrea, b. 9 Jul 1906, St Mary's Platt, Kent, England. (US Citizen, 1949). Solo Violinist. Education: Private studies, violin, Venice, from age 6; Further studies, Adila Fachiri, London; Chamber Music, Lily Henkel; Edouard Naduad, Paris Conservatoire. Career includes: Tours, recitals, soloist with all major orchestras, UK and Europe; Represented England, ISCM Festival, Prague, and soloist with the Helsinki Philharmonic and Radio Orchestras (also played to Sibelius by invitation), 1935; 1st US tour, 1937; Tours, Holland, Belgium, USA (including series, Beethoven Sonatas, with Dean Bruce Simonds, Yale), 1939; Concerts and teaching (including Bennington College), USA, 1940-68; Bach Festival, Prades (sent by Pablo Casals's US Committee), 1950, 1953; Sonata recitals, Finland, 1951; Various European tours, 1950's; Teacher, Royal College of Music, London, 1966-67; BBC Broadcasts, Promenade Concerts, various chamber groups, UK, 1960's-70's; Dartington Hall Summer School; Master classes, Dartington, London, Glasgow, International Cello Centre, UK, 1968-. Honour: Premier Prix, Paris Conservatoire (1st Briton), 1924. Membership: Emeritus Member, International Society of Musicians. Address: 34 High Street, Bideford, North Devon EX39 2AN, England.

PERRIERS Danièle, b. 24 Jun 1945, Beaumont-le-Roger, Eure, France. Singer (Soprano). Education: Studied in Paris with Janine Micheau, Roger Bourdin and Fanelu Revoil. Debut: Marseille, 1968, as Sophie in Werther. Career: Has appeared in France at the Paris Opéra and the Opéra-Comique, and in Nice, Bordeaux, Lyons, Rouen, Toulouse and Strasbourg; Also engaged at the Grand Théâtre de la Monnaie, Brussels and in Liège and Monte Carlo; Glyndebourne Festival 1972-73 and 1976, as Despina and Blondchen; Widely known in the Coloratura and light lyrical repertory and in operattas; Sang also in works by Bizet, Boieldieu, Lecocq, Offenbach, Rossini and Richard Strauss. Recordings: Les Brigands by Offenbach; Die Entführung, Glyndebourne 1972; L'Amant jaloux by Grétry.

PERRY Douglas R, b. 19 Jan 1945, Buffalo, NY, USA. Tenor. Career: Sang at the New York City Opera from 1970 with his debut as Mozart's Basilio, and at Santa Fe Festival from 1971, notably in the US premieres of Reimann's Melusine in 1972 and Weir's A Night at the Chinese Opera in 1989; Sang in the premieres of Glass's Satyagraha at Stuttgart in 1980 and The Voyage at the Metropolitan in 1992; Other modern repertory has included Menotti's Tamu Tamu at Chicago in 1973 and Bernstein's A Quiet Place at Houston in 1983; Has also sung Rameau's Platée, M. Triquet in Eugene Onegin and Scaramuccio in Ariadne auf Naxos; Sang Quint in The Turn of the Screw at Montreal, 1996. Recordings: Satyagraha; A Quiet Place. Address: c/o Santa Fe Opera, PO Box 2408, Santa Fe, NM 87504, USA.

PERRY Elisabeth, b. 1955, England. Concert Violinist. Education: Graduated, Menuhin School, 1972 and studied further with Dorothy DeLay and Oscar Shumsky at Juilliard. Debut: South Bank, London, 1978. Career: Concerts in Cincinnati, Florida, Chicago, Colorado and San Francisco and showings at Carnegie Hall with Alexander Schneider; Bartok's Second Concerto in

Chicago; Further engagements in France, Switzerland, Italy and Germany; Leader of Deutsche Kammerakademie, 1987; Concerts in Sviatoslav Richter's Festival of British Music at Moscow and Leningrad, 1987; US premire of Schnittke's Quasi una Fantasia at Alice Tully Hall and the Berg Chamber Concerto at Elizabeth Hall under Lionel Friend; Recital tour of New Zealand, 1990, and the Berg Violin Concerto in London; Plays a Giovanni Grancini Violin on loan from Yehudi Menuhin. Recordings include: Bach's Double Concerto, with Menuhin; Kirschner's Duo for Violin and Piano. Honours include: Winner, Concert Artists Guild Competition, New York. Address: c/o Anglo Swiss Limited, Suite 35-37, Morley House, 32 Regent Street, London W1R 5AD, England.

PERRY Eugene, b. 1955, Nashville, TN, USA. Singer (Baritone). Education: Studied in New York. Debut: Sang St Ignatius in Four Saints in Three Acts by Virgil Thomson, with the Opera Ensemble of New York, 1986. Career: Sang Tarj in premiere of Under the Double Moon, by Anthony Davis, St Louis, 1989; Don Giovanni in the Peter Sellars production of Mozart's opera at Purchase and elsewhere; European debut as Alidoro in La Cenerentola at Nice, 1989; Season 1990-91 at New York City Opera, as Shiskov in US stage premiere of From the House of the Dead and as Stolzius in Die Soldaten by Zimmermann; Appeared as the Devil in Dvorak's Devil and Kate at St Louis, 1990; Théâtre de la Monnaie, Brussels, 1991, as Mamoud in premiere of The Death of Klinghoffer by John Adams (repeated at Brooklyn Academy of Music, New York); Sang Mercutio in Cavalli's Calisto at Glimmerglass Opera, 1996. Recordings include: Video of Don Giovanni; The Death of Klinghoffer. Honours include: George London Award from National Institute of Music Theater, 1986. Address: c/o New York City Opera, Lincoln Center, New York, NY 10023, USA.

PERRY Herbert, b. 1955, Nashville, TN, USA. Baritone. Education: Studied with his twin brother, Eugene, in Texas and Arizona. Career: Sang at the Houston and St Louis Operas from 1984; Sang at the Spoleto Festival at Charleston in 1987 as Citheron in Rameau's Platée, at Pepsico Summerfare in 1989 as Leporello in Don Giovanni, at Chicago Opera, Nice and Santa Fe in 1991 in I Puritani, as Mozart's Figaro and as Masetto, and sang Leporello at Toronto in 1992; Sang Mozart's Don Alfonso at Toronto, 1995. Recordings include: Video of Don Giovanni, in the production by Peter Sellars. Address: Lyric Opera Chicago, 20 North Wacker Drive, Chicago, IL 60606, USA.

PERRY Janet, b. 27 Dec 1947, Minneapolis, Minnesota, USA. Singer (Soprano). m. Alexander Malta. Education: Curtis Institute, Philadelphia, with Euphemia Gregory. Debut: Linz 1969, as Zerlina in Don Giovanni; Appearances in Munich and Cologne as Norina (Don Pasquale), Adina (L'Elisir d'Amore), Blondchen (Die Entführung), Zerbinetta (Ariadne auf Naxos) and Olympia (Les Contes d'Hoffmann); Guest engagements in Vienna, Frankfurt, Stuttgart and at the Aix-en-Provence Festival; Glyndebourne 1977, as Aminta in Die schweigsame Frau; Numerous opera and operetta films for German TV; Salzburg Festival; Sang Zerbinetta in Ariadne auf Naxos, RAI Turin, 1989; Violetta at the 1990 Martina Franca Festival; Season 1992 as Gluck's Eurydice at Bonn and Cleopatra in Giulio Cesare at the Halle Handel Festival. Recordings: Papagena in Die Zauberflöte, conducted by Karajan; Falstaff, Der Rosenkavalier, Beethoven's Ninth, Bruckner Te Deum; Nannetta in Falstaff; Egk's Peer Gynt. Address: c/o Harrison/Parrott Limited, 12 Penzance Place, London W11 4PA, England.

PERRY Jennifer, b. 1969, Rotterdam, The Netherlands. Soprano. Education: Studied at the Royal Academy and the Guildhall School of Music. Career: Concerts include Handel's Dixit Dominus on tour with the Tallis Scholars and regular appearances with other leading choral societies; Other repertoire includes Mozart's C minor Mass and songs by Schubert and Duparc; Operatic roles include Despina, Susanna and First Lady. Address: c/o Ron Gonsalves Management, 7 Old Town, Clapham, London, SW4 0JT, England.

PERRY Ross, b. 1954, Montreal, Canada. Stage Director; Choreographer. Education: Studied in Atlanta and Jacksonville. Career: Resident Assistant Director for Houston Grand Opera from 1986, working with such operas as Boris Godunov, Così fan tutte, Turandot, Figaro, Salome and Faust; Assistant at the Los Angeles Music Center with Idomeneo and at Santa Fe and Spoleto; Has worked further as Director and/or Choreographer at Houston, with Hansel and Gretel, The Mikado, Mefistofele and Desert of Roses by Robert Moran; Further engagements with Australian Opera (Così fan tutte, 1992), Victoria State Opera (Carmen) and Washington Opera (Mefistofele, 1995). Address: Atholl Still Ltd, Foresters Hall, 25-27 Westow Street, London SE19 3RY, England.

PERTUSI Michele, b. 1965, Parma, Italy. Singer (Bass). Education: Studied in Parma with Carlo Bergonzi. Debut: Modena, as Silva in Ernani, 1984. Career: Appearances at Teatro Donizetti, Bergamo, Ravenna Festival and Teatro Comunale, Bologna;

Teatro Regio, Parma, 1987-, notably as Dulcamara, 1992; Season 1992 as Mozart's Count at Orchestra Hall, Chicago, and Figaro at Florence; Sang Talbot in Maria Stuarda at Barcelona, Assur in Semiramide at Pesaro; Other roles include Raimondo in Lucia di Lammermoor, Pagano in I Lombardi, and Rossini's Maometto; Sang Don Giovanni at Lausanne, 1996. Recordings include: Mozart's Figaro, Assur, Alidoro, Silva, Lodovico in Otello; La Wally by Catalani. Address: c/o Teatro Regio, Via Garibaldi 16, 43100 Parma, Italy.

PERUSKA Jan, b. 1954, Czechoslovakia. Violist. Education: Studied in Prague with members of the Smetana Quartet. Career: Co-Founder and Violist of the Stamic Quartet of Prague, 1977; Performances at the Prague Young Artists and the Bratislava Music Festivals; Tours to Spain, Austria, France, Switzerland, Germany and Eastern Europe; Tour of the USA 1980, debut concerts in Britain at London and Birmingham, 1983; Further British tours, 1985, 1987, 1988 (Warwick Arts Festival) and 1989 (20 concerts); Gave the premiere of Helmut Eder's 3rd Quartet, 1986; Season 1991-92 with visit to the Channel Islands (Festival of Czech Music), Holland, Finland, Austria and France, Edinburgh Festival and debut tours of Canada, Japan and Indonesia. Honours: (with members of Stamic Quartet): Prize Winner, International Festival of Young Soloists, Bordeaux, 1977; Winner, 1986 ORF (Austrian Radio) International String Quartet Competition (followed by live broadcast from the Salzburg Mozarteum); Academie Charles Cros Grand Prix du Disque, 1991, for Dvorak Quartets. Recordings: Shostakovich No 13, Schnittke No 4; Mozart K589 and K370; Dvorak, Martinu and Janacek complete quartets. Address: c/o Anglo-Swiss Management, Suite 35-37, Morley House, 320 Regent Street, London W1R 5AD, England.

PERUSSO Mario, b. 16 Sept 1936, Buenos Aires, Argentina. Conductor; Composer. Career: Deputy Conductor at Teatro Colon, Buenos Aires, giving his own opera Escorial in 1989 and Puccini's La Rondine, 1990; Conducted Otello and Turandot at La Plata, season 1990-91. Compositions include: Operas: La Voz del Silencio, 1 act, Buenos Aires, 1969; Escorila, 1 act, Buenos Aires, 1989; Sor Juana Ines de la Cruz, 1991-92, premiered, 1993; Conducted Tosca at La Plata, 1995. Recordings include: La Voz del Silencio. Address: c/o Teatro Colon, Buenos Aires, Cerrito 618, 1010 Buenos Aires, Argentina.

PERUZZI Elio, b. 14 Oct 1927, Malcesine, Verona, Italy. Clarinettist; Conservatory Teacher. Education: Canetti Institute, Vicenza; B Marcello Conservatory, Venice. Debut: Olympic Theatre, Vicenza. Career: Soloist with Virtuosi di Roma, Solisti Veneti, Solisti di Milano, 1950-; String Quartets of Milan, Ostrava, Brno, Prague and Zagreb, and with Brno Philharmonic Orchestra, Bozen Orchestra, Padua Chamber Orchestra, Filarmonico di Bologna, 1960-; Founder, Bartók Trio (clarinet, violin, piano), 1958, Piccola Camerata Italian (mediaeval, renaissance and baroque instruments), 1967; Performances, Europe, USA, South America, USSR, Canada, 1960-. Recordings: Mozart Clarinet Quintet with Moravian Quartet, 18th and 19th century music with Virtuosi di Roma. Publications: Esercizi e Studi Method for Recorder, 1972; Editor, various works including: Sonatas by Robert Valentine for 2 Recorders, 1973; G Rossini Variations for Clarinet and Orchestra, 1978; A Ponchielli's Il Convegno for 2 Clarinets and Piano, 1988. Honours: Accademia Tiberina, Rome. Hobby: Photography. Current Management: Francesca Diano, Via Vallisnieri 13, 35100 Padova, Italy. Address: Via Monte Solarolo 9, 35100 Padova, Italy.

PESEK Libor, b. 22 June 1933, Prague, Czechoslovakia. Conductor. Education: Graduate. Academy of Musical Arts, Prague. 1056. Career: Founder, Prague Chamber Harmony, 1959; Founder, Sebastian Orchestra, Prague, 1965; Musical Director, State Chamber Orchestra, Czechoslovakia, 1969-77; Frysk Orkest, Netherlands, 1969-75; Overijssels Philharmonic Orkest, Netherlands, 1975-79; Slovak Philharmonic Orchestra, 1981-82; Conductor-in-Residence, Czech Philharmonic Orchestra, Prague, 1982-; Principal Conductor, Musical Advisor, Royal Liverpool Philharmonic Orchestra, England, 1987-; Regular Guest Appearances with Philharmonia Orchestra, London, England; Films include: Dvorak's Rusalka, Munich, 1976; Stravinsky's Pulcinella, Television, Prague, 1983; Stravinsky's L'Histoire du soldât, television, Prague, 1982; Benda's Medea, 1975; Tchaikovsky's Swan lake, 1970; Guest Conductor with orchestras in Paris, Naples, Brussels, Berlin, Amsterdam, Vienna, Warsaw, Basel, Lisbon, USA, Russia, Montreal; Conducted the RLPO at the 1991 Promenade Concerts, London; Elgar's Cello and Beethoven's C Minor Concertos; Suk's Asrael Symphony and Tchaikovsky's Pathétique; President of the Prague Spring Festival. Recordings include: Suk's Ripening, Asrael Symphony and Summer's Tale; Wagner's Wesendonck Lieder; Schmidt's 3rd Symphony; Massenet, Werther, complete opera; Bruckner's 7th Symphony; Complete Symphonies of Dvorak for Virgin Classics. Memberships: Union of Czech Composers and Performing Artists. Current Management: IMG Artists Europe. Address: Media House, 3 Burlington Lane, London W4 2TH, England.

PESKO Zoltan, b. 15 Feb 1937, Budapest, Hungary. Composer; Conductor. Education: Diploma, Liszt Ferenc Music Academy, Budapest, 1962; Master Courses in Composing with Goffredo Petrassi, Accademia di S Cecilia, Rome, Italy and in Conducting, Pierre Boulez, Basel, Switzerland and Franco Ferrara, Rome, Italy, 1963-66. Debut: As Composer and Conductor, Hungarian TV, 1960. Career: Work with Hungarian TV, 1960-63; Assistant Conductor to Lorin Maazel, West Berlin Opera and Radio Orchestra, West Berlin, 1969-73; Performances at Teatro alla Scala, 1970; Professor, Hochschule, West Berlin, 1971-74; Chief Conductor, Teatro Communale, Bologna, Italy, 1974-; Conducted Wagner's Ring at Turin, 1988; Concert performance of Mussogsky's Salammbo at the 1989 Holland Festival; Teatro Lirico Milan 1990, premiere of Blimunda by Azio Corghi; Has also led the premieres of Bussotti's Il Catalogo è questo, 1960; Donatoni's Voci, 1974, In Cauda, 1982, Tema 1982, Atem 1985; Jolivet's Bogomile suite 1982; Dies by Wolfgang Rihm, 1985; Fünf Geistliche Lieder von Bach by Dieter Schnebel, 1985; Season 1992 with Der fliegende Holländer at Naples and Le Grand Macabre at Zurich; Conducted Fidelio at Rome, 1996. Compositions: Tension, String Quartet, 1967; Trasformazioni, 1968; Bildinis einer Heligen, Soprano and Children's Choir, Chamber Ensemble, 1969; Jelek, 1974. Recordings: Various for CBS Italiana. Contributions to: Melos. Honours: Prize for Composition, Academia di S Cecilia, Rome, Italy, 1966; Premio Discografico, for recording debut as Conductor, Italian Critics, 1973. Current Management: Musart, 20121 Milan, Via Manzoni 31, Italy. Address: 40125 Bologna, Teatro Communale, Largo Respighi, Italy.

PESKOVA Inna, b. 1960, Moscow, Russia. Violist. Education: Studied at Moscow Conservatoire with Alexei Shislov. Career: Co-founder, Glazunov Quartet, 1985; Many concerts in Russia and recent appearances in: Greece; Poland; Belgium; Germany; Italy; Works by Beethoven and Schumann at Beethoven Haus in Bonn; Further engagements in Canada and Netherlands; Teacher at Moscow State Conservatoire and Resident at Tchaikovsky Conservatoire; Repertoire includes works by: Borodin; Shostakovich; Tchaikovsky in addition to standard works. Recordings include: CD's of the six quartets of Glazunov. Honours: With Glazunov Quartet: Prizewinner of Borodin Quartet and Shostakovich Chamber Music Competitions. Address: c/o Sonata (Glazunov Quartet), 11 Northpark Street, Glasgow, G20 7AA, Scotland.

PETCHERSKY Alma, b. 1950, Argentina. Concert Pianist. Education: Studied with Roberto Caamano in Buenos Aires; Maria Curcio in London and with Magda Tagliaferro and Bruno Seidlhofer of the Vienna Academy. Debut: Teatro Colon Buenos Aires with Bartok's 3rd Concerto. Career: Concert and broadcasting engagements in Russia, USA, Canada, Spain, Germany, Brazil, Czechoslovakia, Mexico and the Far East; London appearances at the Wigmore Hall. Recordings: Works of the German, French and Russian schools, latin-American and Spanish Romantic Composers; Complete piano music by Ginastera; Recordings for the BBC, London and CBC, Canada. Current Management: M Gilbert Management. Address: 516 Wadsworth Avenue, Philadelphia, PA 19119, USA.

PETER Fritz, b. 7 Nov 1925, Camorino, Switzerland. Singer (Tenor). Education: Studied in Winterthur, Zurich and Stuttgart, 1945-55. Career: Sang at Ulm Stadttheater, 1955-61, Zurich Opera from 1961, notably in premieres of Martinu's Greek Passion, 1961, Sutermeister's Madame Bovary, 1967, and Kelterborn's Ein Engel kommt nach Babylon, 1977; Guest appearances at Geneva, Lucerne, Munich, Hamburg, Frankfurt, Cologne, Nice, Milan, Helsinki, Vienna and Edinburgh, as Ernesto, Max and Tristan; Many concert performances. Recordings include: Monteverdi's Poppea and Ulisse conducted by Nikolaus Harnoncourt. Address: Opernhaus Zurich, Falkenstrasse 1, CH-8008 Zurich, Switzerland.

PETERS Johanna (McLennan), b. 1932, Glasgow, Scotland. Singer (Mezzo Soprano); Professor of Singing; Head of Opera Studies. Education: National School of Opera, London. Debut: Glyndebourne, 1959, as Marcellina in Le Nozze di Figaro. Career: Sang at Royal Opera House, Covent Garden, Sadler's Wells Opera, Welsh National Opera, Scottish Opera, Glyndebourne Festival Opera, English Opera Group and Phoenix Opera; Professor of Singing, Head of Vocal Studies at the Guildhall School of Music, London, 1989-. Recordings include: Albert Herring by Britten. Hobbies: Travel; Archaeology; Cooking. Address: c/o Music International, 13 Ardilaun Road, London, N6 2QR, England.

PETERS Reinhard, b. 2 Apr 1926, Magdeburg, Germany. Conductor. Education: Studied at the Hochschule fur Musik in Berlin and in Paris with Enescu, Thibaud and Cortot. Career: Repetiteur at the Berlin Staatsoper 1946-49; Conducted the Berlin Stadtische Oper from 1952 (debut with Rigoletto); Concerts with the Berlin Philharmonic from 1952; Conductor of the Deutsche Oper am Rhein Dusseldorf, 1957-60; Generalmusikdirektor at Munster 1961-70; Permanent guest conductor at the Deutsche Oper Berlin from 1970; Musical Director of the Philharmonia Hungarica 1975-79; Guest conductor with orchestras in Europe and the Americas; Salzburg, Spoleto, Edinburgh and Glyndebourne Festivals; Conducted the first performances of Blacher's Zwischenfalle bei einer Notlandung, 1966, Sutermeister's Madame Bovary, 1967, Reimann's Melusine, 1970, Derives by Grisey, 1974 and Symphony no 1 by Isang Yun, 1984. Recordings: Suites from Dardanus, Amadis de Gaule and King Arthur, with the Collegium Aureum (RCA); Handel Organ Concerto, Praise of Harmony and Look Down, Harmonius Saint, with Theo Altmeyer, and three Italian cantatas, with Elly Ameling; Symphonies by Haydn and Mozart; Viola Concertos by Paganini, Stamitz and Hoffmeister, with the Philharmonia Hungarica; Le Postillion de Lonjumeau by Adam (Eurodisc). Address: c/o Deutsche Oper Berlin, Richard Wagnerstrasse 10, D-1000 Berlin, Germany.

PETERS Roberta, b. 4 May 1930, New York City, USA. Singer (Soprano). Education: Studied with William Herman in New York. Debut: Metropolitan Opera, 1950 as Zerlina in Don Giovanni. Career: With Metropolitan Opera until 1985 as the Queen of Night, Rosina, Mozart's Barbarina, Despina and Susanna, Verdi's Oscar, Nanetta and Gilda, Donizetti's Norina, Lucia and Adina, Strauss's Sophie and Zerbinetta, and Olympia in Les Contes d'Hoffmann; Covent Garden 1951, in The Bohemian Girl, under Beecham; Salzburg Festival 1963-64, as the Queen of the Night; Sang in Leningrad and Moscow, 1972; Other roles included Violetta, Mimi and Massenet's Manon; Sang on Broadway in The King and I, 1973; Appeared with Newark Opera 1989 as Adina in L'Elisir d'amore. Recordings: Il Barbiere di Siviglia; Un Ballo in Maschera; Ariadne auf Naxos; Cosi fan tutte; Die Zauberflöte; Lucia di Lammermoor; Orfeo ed Euridice. Publication: Debut at the Met, 1967. Address: c/o Metropolitan Opera, Lincoln Center, New York, NY 10023, USA.

PETERSEN Dennis, b. 11 May 1954, Iowa, USA. Singer (Tenor). Education: Studied at University of Iowa and with San Francisco Opera's Merola Programme. Career: Concert appearances in Mozart's Requiem, Messiah and Bach's Magnificat with St Paul Chamber Orchestra; Haydn's Theresienmesse at Spoleto Festival in Charleston; Sang in Tippett's A Child of Our Time at Carnegie Hall and concerts with New Jersey and Baltimore Symphonies under David Zinman and Calgary Philharmonic under Mario Bernadi; Engagements with San Francisco Opera, 1985- including: Don Quichotte, Captain in Wozzeck, Mime in Der Ring des Nibelungen, Die Meistersinger, and Tybald in Roméo et Juliette; Lyric Opera of Chicago debut in season 1992-93 as Mime in Das Rheingold under Zubin Mehta; Sang Carlo in Donizetti's Il Duca d'Alba at Spoleto Festival; Season 1994-95 at Chicago Lyric Opera in Boris Godunov, and Mime in Siegfried; Metropolitan Opera in Lady Macbeth of Mtsensk (debut) and as Bob Boles in Peter Grimes; Season 1995-96 at San Francisco Opera in Anna Bolena and Madama Butterfly, Chicago Lyric Opera, Andrea Chenier - The Ring Cycle and Miami Opera in Ariadne auf Naxos. Current Management: IMG Artists. Address: c/o IMG Artists, Media House, 3 Burlington Lane, London, W4 2TH, England.

PETERSEN Nils (Holger), b. 27 Apr 1946, Copenhagen, Denmark. Composer; Minister of The Danish Church. m. Frances Ellen Hopenwasser, 11 Sept 1971, div 1989, 1 son, 1 daughter. Education: Degree in Mathematics, University of Copenhagen, 1969; Postgraduate studies in Mathematics, Universities of Copenhagen and Oslo; Studies in Theology, Copenhagen University; Piano studies with Elisabeth Klein, composition with Ib Norholm; PhD in Theology, University of Copenhagen, 1994. Career: Minister of The Danish Church, 1974-; Research Fellow, 1990-, Research Lecturer, 1995, University of Copenhagen; External Professor of Gregorian Studies, University of Tronheim, Norway, 1997-; Freelance Composer with compositions performed on Danish, Swedish, Norwegian and Dutch Radio and on Danish TV, at Nordic Music Days and various concerts in many countries. Compositions: Piano and Guitar solo works, published and recorded; Fools Play, opera, 1970 first performed in 1985; Vigil for Thomas Beckett, liturgical opera, 1989; Church Cantatas, 1971, 1974 and 1976; Antiphony for Good Friday for 9 Instruments and Voice; 2 Wind Quintets; Solo works for violin, piano and organ; The Lauds of Queen Ingeborg, liturgical opera, 1991; Fragments of a Distant Voice, Electrophonic work for the Danish State Radio, 1992; Concerto for Clarinet in B and Octet, 1994; A Plain Song, piano. Recordings: Various instrumental works on major labels. Publications: Kristendom i Musikken, 1987; Liturgy and the Arts in the Middle Ages, 1996. Contributions to: Various articles on Theologico-musical aspects of the western culture in musical and theological papers. Honour: Hakon Borresen Memorial Prize, 1993. Memberships: Danish Composers Society; Board of the Nordic Society for Interart Studies. Hobby: Mountain Hiking. Address: Mimersgade 56, 1 tv, DK-2200 Copenhagen N, Denmark.

PETERSON Claudette, b. 15 Jul 1953, Lakewood, Ohio, USA. Singer (Soprano). Education: Studied at San Francisco Conservatory. Career: Sang at San Francisco Opera from 1975;

Washington Opera, 1979, as Blondchen in Die Entführung, Boston, 1980, as Dunyasha in War and Peace, Chicago, 1982, as Adele in Fledermaus; New York City Opera, 1985-86, as Manon and Lisette in La Rondine; Sang Yum-Yum in The Mikado for Canadian Opera at Toronto, 1986; Other roles have included Lucia (Arizona Opera) and Gilda (Shreveport); Further engagements at Buffalo, Houston, Geneva and Honolulu; Frequent concert appearances. Recordings include: Musgrave's A Christmas Carol. Address: c/o New York City Opera, Lincoln Center, New York, NY 10023, USA.

PETERSON Glade, b. 17 Dec 1928, Fairview, Utah, USA. Singer (Tenor). Education: Studied with Carlos Alexander in Salt Lake City and with Enrico Rosati and Ettore Verna in New York. Debut: NBC Opera New York, 1957, as Pinkerton. Career: Sang at such American centres as Dallas, Baltimore, San Francisco, Houston, Pittsburgh, San Antonio and Santa Fe; European engagements at Brussels, Amsterdam, Basle, Bordeaux, Geneva, Munich, Hamburg, Stuttgart and Milan; Many appearances at the Zurich Opera, including the premiere of Martinu's Greek Passion, 1961; Metropolitan Opera, 1973; Other roles have included Florestan, Riccardo, Don Alvaro (La Forza del Destino), Walther, Loge, Cavaradossi, Don José and Hermann in The Queen of Spades; Lyric roles have been Mozart's Ferrando, Belmonte and Tamino; Puccini's Rodolfo and Rinuccio; Edgardo in Lucia di Lammermoor and Tonio in La Fille du Régiment; Massenet's Des Grieux and Bizet's Nadir; Verdi's Fenton and Alfredo; Many concert appearances; Founded Utah Opera at Salt Lake City, 1978. Recordings include: Duets from Madama Butterfly and Manon, with Felicia Weathers. Address: c/o Utah Opera Company, 50 West Second South, Salt Lake City, UT 84101, USA.

PETERSON John Murray, b. 14 January 1957, Wollongong, New South Wales, Australia. Composer. Education: BMus, honours, 1990, MMus, 1994, Sydney University; PhD, Sydney University (current). Career: Orchestral Works Performed by Queensland Philharmonic Orchestra and Tasmanian Symphony Orchestra; Broadcasts on ABC Classic FM and BBC Radio 3. Compositions: Walking On Glass, Piano Solo; A Voice From The City, Voice and Small Ensemble; The Still Point, Cello; Rituals in Transfigured Time, Orchestra; Of Quiet Places, Voice and Guitar. Recordings: Greenbaum Hindson Peterson, 1995. Honours: Semi-Finalist, Masterprize, London, 1997. Memberships: Australian Music Centre; Musicological Society of Australia. Hobbies: Films; Tennis. Address: 67 Kingsclear Road, Alexandria, NSW 2015, Australia.

PETERSONS Ingus, b. 12 Feb 1959, Gulbene, Latvia. Tenor. Education: Studied at the Riga Academy. Debut: Riga in 1985 as Lensky in Eugene Onegin. Career: Sang at the Riga Opera as the Duke of Mantua, Alfredo, Don Carlo and Nemorino; Sang at Wexford Festival in 1987 as Arturo in La Straniera by Bellini, Opera North Leeds in 1988 as Edgardo in Lucia di Lammermoor and sang Hoffmann at the Folksoperan Stockholm in 1991; Engaged at the Landestheater Kiel from 1991; Other roles have included Des Grieux in Massenet's Manon and the Italian Singer in Der Rosenkavalier. Address: c/o Landestheater Kiel, Opernhaus am Kleinen Kiel, Pf 1660, W-2300 Kiel, Germany.

PETIT Jean-Louis, b. 20 Aug 1937, Favrolles, France. Conductor; Harpsichordist; Composer. Education: Studied in Paris with Igor Markevitch, Pierre Boulez and Olivier Messiaen. Career: Organised and conducted various ensembles in the regions of Champagne, 1958-63 and Picardy, 1964-70; Performaces on Radio and Television, tours of Europe and the United States; Co-directoed the Paris Summer Festival, 1972-77; Founder member of the contemporary music group Musique Plus; Director of the Association musicale international d'echange (AMIE); Director of the Ecole Nationale de Musique de Ville d'Avray. Compositions include: Au-dela du signe for Orchestra; De Quelque Part Effondree de l'homme for Quartet; Continuelles discontinues for Percussion; (82 Opus) Transcriptions of early music. Recordings include: Works by Boismortier, Leclair, Marais, Rameau, Lully, Mouret, Devienne, Campra, Francoeur, Couperin and Mondonville; Roussel's Sinfonietta; Les Troqueurs by d'Auvergne; 2nd Symphonie of Gounod; Chamber Music by Saint-Saëns.

PETIT Pierre, b. 21 Apr 1922, Poitiers, France. m. (3) Liliane Fiaux, 1974, 4 sons, 1 daughter from previous marriages. Education: Lycée Louis-le-Grand, Université de Paris à la Sorbonne and Conservatoire de Paris. Career: Head of Course, Conservatoire de Paris, 1950; Director of Light Music, Office de Radiodiffusion et Télévision Française (ORTF), 1960-64; Director of Music Productions, ORTF, 1964-70; Chamber Music, 1970-; Producer, Radio-Télévision Luxembourgeoise (RTL), 1980; Director-General, Ecole Normale de Musique de Paris, 1963; Music Critic, Figaro. Compositions include: Suite for 4 Cellos, 1945; Zadig (Ballet), 1948; Ciné-Bijou (Ballet), 1952; Feu Rouge, Feu Vert, 1954; Concerto for Piano and Orchestra, 1956; Concerto for Organ and Orchestra, 1960; Furia Italiana, 1960; Concerto for 2 Guitars and Orchestra, 1965. Publications: Verdi 1957, Ravel 1970. Honours: Chevalier, Légion d'honneur, Officier des Art et Lettres, Ordre nationale du Mérite, Officier de l'Ordre du Cèdre du Liban; Premier Grand Prix de Rome, 1946. Membership: Gov Council Conservatoire de Paris. Address: 28 Rue Cardinet, 75017 Paris, France.

PETKOV Dimiter, b. 5 Mar 1939, Sofia, Bulgaria. Singer (Bass). m. Anne-Lise Petkov. Education: Sofia Music Academy with Christo Brambarov. Debut: Sofia as Ramfis and Zaccaria, 1964. Career: Guest appearances, Glyndebourne Festival, 1968, 1970, as Osmin and Gremin; Rostropovich Festival, Aldeburgh, 1983; Earl's Court, London, 1988; Birmingham Arena, 1991; Daytona Festival with London Symphony Orchestra, 1993; Arena di Verona as Philipp II, 1969, As Zaccaria, 1981, as Ramfis, 1986, 1987; Appearances: Vienna State Opera, 1972-86, 1990, as Philip II, Ramfis, Boris, Khovansky, Mephisto; Madrid, Barcelona, 1978-86, 1990; Chicago, 1980; Bologna, 1980-83, 1988; Catania, Palermo, Lecce, 1981, 1984, 1986; La Scala, Milan, 1981, 1984, 1989; Washington DC, 1982, 1984; Carnegie Hall, New York City, 1982, 1984, 1989; Zurich, Hamburg, Bonn, 1984-85, 1990; Naples, 1984, 1991; Rome, 1987, 1992; Florence, 1986-89, 1991; Monte Carlo, 1986, 1989; Paris, 1986, 1988; Deutsche Oper Berlin, 1988-93; Dallas, 1989, 1993; Opera Bastille, Paris, 1990-93; Appeared with Berlin Philharmonic, London Symphony Orchestra, National Symphony Washington DC, Boston Symphony Orchestra at Tanglewood, Israel Philharmonic (Zubin Mehta) at Tel-Aviv, Montreal Symphony Orchestra, RAI Orchestras in Milan, Rome, Naples, Orchestre de Paris, Orchestre National de France, Concertgebouw Amsterdam, St Petersburg Philharmonic Jerusalem Symphony, San Francisco Symphony; In demand for all the Verdi roles: Philipp, Zaccaria, Fiesco; Bellini, Rossini, Donizetti; Mephisto by Gounod in French repertoire; All main roles in Russian repertoire: Boris Godunov, Ivan Khovansky, Ivan Susanin, others; Sang Shishkov in From the House of the Dead, Opéra du Rhin, 1996. Recordings: EMI, Lady Macbeth of Mtsensk; EMI, Shostkovich 13th Symphony with London Symphony Orchestra; Aleko by Rachmaninov; Khovanshchina by Mussorgsky; Erato, Yolanta by Tchaikovsky, Mussorgsky cycles and Boris arias, 1989; Koch, Shostakovich cycles, 1993; Sony, Boris Godunov, 1992; Verdi Requiem at Eckphrasis Records, New York, 1994; Has sung with such conductors as Abbado, Mehta, Bartoletti, Previn, Molinari-Pradelli, Rostropovich, Ozawa, Rozdestvensky, Prêtre, Bernstein, Pritchard, Maazel, Giulini in Werner Herzog's Fitzcarraldo sang Ernani at Manaus. Address: Rue du Conseil-Général 6, 1205 Geneva, Switzerland.

PETRASSI Goffredo, b. 16 July 1904, Zagarolo, Italy. Composer. m. Rosetta Acerbi, 1962, 1 daughter. Education: Conservatorio S Cecilia, Rome. Career: Supt Teatro Fenice, Venice, 1937-40; President, International Society for Contemporary Music, 1954-56; Professor of Composition, Accadamie S Cecilia. Compositions include: Orchestral: Partita 1932, First Concerto, 1933, Second Concerto 1951, Recreation Concertante (Third Concerto) 1953, Fourth Concerto 1954, Fifth Concerto 1955, Invenzione Concertata 1957, Quartet 1957; Operas and Ballets: Follia di Orlando 1943, Ritratto di Don Chisciotte 1945, Il Cordovano 1948, Morte dell'Aria 1950; Choral Works: Salmo IX 1936, Magnificat 1940, Coro di Morti 1941, Noche Oscura 1951, Mottetti 1965; Voice and Orchestra Quattro Inni Sacre 1942; Chamber Music: Serenata 1958, Trio 1959, Suoni Notturni 1959, Propos d'Alain 1960, Concerto Flauto 1960, Seconda Serenata-Trio 1962, Settimo Concerto 1964, Estri 1966-69, Ottavo Concerto 1970-72, Elogio 1971, Nunc 1971, Ala 1972, Orationes Christi 1975, Alias 1977, Grand Septuor 1978, Violasola 1978, Flou 1980, Romanezetta 1980, Poems 1977-80, Sestina d'Autunno 1981-82, Laudes Creaturarum 1982; Duetto for violin and viola, 1985. Address: Via Ferdinando di Savoia 3, 00196 Rome, Italy.

PETRE Leonardus (Josephus), b. 27 Jan 1943, Saint Triniden, Belgium. Professor of Trumpet. m. Maes Arlette, 24 Jul 1965, 2 sons. Education: Bachelor of Medicine, University of Leuven, 1962; Music schools of St Trinden en Hasselt, First prizes in Music-Reading and Trumpet; Royal Music Academy (Conservatoire Royal) Brussels, First Prizes in Music Reading, Transposition, Trumpet and Musical History. Career: Teacher of trumpet and several other brass instruments in several music schools; Professor of Trumpet at the Lemmens Institute, Leuven; Many appearances as member of orchestra or soloist on the Belgian and German Radio and TV; Soloist at many classical concerts in Belgium, France, Holland and Germany; Trumpet-Soloist with The New Music Group, and Collegium Instrumentale Brugense; Member of the Xenakis Ensemble, Holland; Creator and leader of The Belgian Brass Quintet 2, 1973-79; Conductor of brassband and fanfare; Specialist in playing Bach-trumpet (piccolo) and copies of very old trumpets. Recordings: Several cantatas of J S Bach with La Chapelle des Minimes, Brussels. Contributions to: Several articles concerning the trumpet and brass playing in local music magazines. Membership: International Trumpet Guild. Hobbies: Gardening; Reading about natural healing methods. Address: Smoldersstraat 44, 3910 Herk de Stad, Belgium.

PETRI Michala, b. 7 July 1958, Copenhagen, Denmark. Recorder Player. m. Lars Hannibal, 4 July 1992. Education: Studied with Professor Ferdinand Conrad, Staatliche Hochschule für Musik und Theater, Hanover, Germany. Debut: Danish Radio, 1964. Career: Appearances as Soloist with Orchestra Tivoli, Copenhagen, 1969; Over 2000 concerts in Europe, USA, Japan and Australia; Numerous appearances at festivals and performances on TV and Radio; Performs frequently with lutenist and guitarist Lars Hannibal throughout the world. Recordings: More than 30 albums including: 12 with the Academy of ST Martin-in-the-Feilds, Bach Sonatas and Handel Sonatas with Keith Jarrett, Vivaldi Concertos with Heinz Hollinger, Henryk Szeryng, Contemporary Concerts with English Chamber Orchestra; 2 albums with Lars Hannibal; Has inspired and initiated various contemporary compositions by Malcolm Arnold, Vagn Holmboe, Per Norgaard, Thomas Koppel and Gary Kulesha amongst others. Honours: Jacob Gade Prize, 1969, 1975; Critics Prize of Honour, 1976; Nording Radio Prize, 1977; Niels Prize, 1980; Tagea Brandts Prize, 1980; Maarum Prize, 1981; Schroder Prize, 1982; Knight of Dannebrog, 1995; Deutsche Schallplattenpreis, 1997; Honorary Artist, Soro International Organ Festival, 1992. Address: Nordskraenten 3, 2980 Kokkedal, Denmark.

PETRIC Ivo, b. 16 June 1931, Ljubljana. Musician; Composer; Conductor. Education: Music Academy Ljubljana. Debut: First performances, Piano Trio, May 1952. Career: Conductor of Slavko Osterc Ensemble (for contemporary music), 1962-82; Editor-in-Chief of Composers Editions, 1970-; Artistic Director, Slovenian Philharmonic, 1979-95. Compositions: Orchestral music; Concertos for various instruments; Chamber Music; Sonatas for various instruments with piano (3 Symphonies, 1954, 1957, 1960); Trumpet Concerto, 1986; Dresden Concerto for Strings, 1987; Trois Images, 1973; Dialogues Entre Deux Violons, 1975; Jeux Concertants for Flute and Orchestra, 1978, Toccata Concertante for 4 Percussionists and Orchestra, 1979, Gallus Metamorphoses, 1992; Scottish Impressions, 1994; The Song of Life, 1995; The Four Seasons, 1995; The Autumn Symphony, 1996. Recordings: Several works of orchestral, chamber and solo music. Honours: Slovene State Preseren Foundation Prize, 1971; 1st Prize, Wieniawski International Composition Competition for Violin, 1975; Ljubljana Prize for Artists, 1977; Oscar Espla International Competition, First Prize, 1984. Membership: Association of Slovene Composers. Address: Bilecanska 4, 61000 Ljubljana, Slovenia.

PETRINSKY Natascha, b. 1966, Germany. Singer (Soprano). Education: Studied at the Karlsruhe Musikhochschule and the Rubin Academy, Tel Aviv. Career: Has sung in oratorio throughout Germany and other concert appearances in Israel; Opera repertoire includes Donna Elvira (New Israeli Opera, 1994) and Countess Almaviva. Recordings include: Mercédès in Carmen, under Sinopoli, 1996. Address: Atholl Still Ltd, Foresters Hall, 26-27 Westow Street, London SE19 3RY, England.

PETRO Janos, b. 5 Mar 1937, Repceszemere, Hungary. Conductor; Chief Music Director. m. 27 Aug 1959, 1 son, 1 daughter. Education: Conductor and Composer, Academy of Music, Budapest, 1959. Debut: As Composer, Vienna, 1959. Career: Opera and Concerts in Budapest, Vienna, Berlin, Dublin, Bratislava, Frankfurt, Hamburg, Graz; Radio Budapest; Vienna Symphonic Record Register; Television Budapest and Vienna. Recordings include: Goldmark: Concerto for Violin and Orchestra; Mendelssohn: Concerto for Violin and Orchestra; Haydn: Scena di Berenice and Concert Arias; P Karolyi; Epilogus; P Karolyi: Consolatio; Bizet: Symphony C-major; Bizet: Suite L'Arlesienne; Beethoven: Egmont Overture; Liszt: Les Préludes; Haydn: Symphony No 104. Honours: F Liszt Prize, Conductor, Budapest, 1983; World Young Composer Prize, Vienna, 1959; State Prize, Budapest, 1982. Membership: Musicians Alliance, Budapest, President and Member. Hobby: Stamp Collecting. Current Management: Interkoncert Budapest, Vorosmarty ter 1, Austrokonzert, Vienna. Address: Martirok tere 8, H-9700 Szombathely, Hungary.

PETROBELLI Pierluigi, b. 18 Oct 1932. Padua, Italy. Musicologist; University Teacher. Education: Studied Composition with A Pedrollo, Padua, 1954-57; Laurea in Lettere, University of Rome, 1957; MFA, Musicology, under O Strunk and A Mendel, Princeton University, USA, 1961; Studied Musicology under W Waite, Harvard Summer School. Career: Librarian, Archivist, Verdi Institute, Parma, 1964-69; Librarian, G Rossini Conservatory, Pesaro, 1970-73; Teacher of Music History, Parma University, Cremona Extension, 1970-72; Lecturer in Music, 1973-75, Reader in Musicology, 1976-80, King's College, University of London; Member of Organising Committee for Xth Congress of International Society of Musicology in Copenhagen, 1972; Director, Istituto nazionale di studi Verdiani, Parma, 1980-; Professor of Music History, University of Perugia, 1981-83; Professor of Music History, La Sapienza University of Rome,

1983-. Publications: Giuseppe Tartini: le fonti biografiche, 1968; Tartini, le sue idee e il suo tempo, 1992; Music in the Theater - Essays on Verdi and Other Composers, 1994; Studi verdiani Yearbook, editor, 1981-; Critical Edition of Mozart's Il pastore, with Wolfgang Rehm, 1984; Carteggio Verdi-Ricordi 1880-1881, Co-editor, 1988. Contributions to: Acta Musicologica; Nuova Rivista Musicale Italiana; Tempo; Mozart Jahrbuch; Studi Verdiani; Chigiana. Honours: Corresponding Member, American Musicological Society, 1989; Member of the Academia Europaea, 1992; Honorary Foreign Member, Royal Musical Association, 1997. Address: 34 Via di S Anselmo, I-00153 Rome, Italy.

PETROCZI Karol, b. 5 March 1944, Lucenec, Slovakia. Concert Master; Conductor; Teacher of Music. m. Maria, 1 son, 1 daughter. Education: Conservatorio Kosice, Slovakia, 1958-64; Postgraduate, Academy of Arts, Prague, 1972-77. Debut: Bratislava, 1969. Career: Concert Master, Radio Orchestra, Kosice, 1964-69, State Philharmonic Orchestra, Kosice, 1969-, Cairo Symphony Orchestra, 1972-73, Prchestra Symphonicas de Astori, Spain, 1991-92; Solo Violin Performances, Germany, Spain, Denmark, Poland, Russia, Hungary, Bulgaria, Egypt, Switzerland; Choir Master of Teachers Choir, Kosice, Collegium Technicum, Kosice; Concerts in the Whole of Europe; Regular Radio and Television Appearances in Slovakia. Recordings: Early Compositions of J Straus (solo violin). Honours: Choral Competitions, 1st Prize, Grand Prix, Slovakia, 1997, 2 1st Prizes, Teesside International Eisteddfod, 1997. Memberships: ESTA; Union of Concert Artists in Slovakia. Hobby: Fine Arts. Address: Clementisova 1, 04000 Kosice, Slovakia.

PETROFF-BEVIE Barbara, b. 2 June 1934, Hamburg, Germany. Lyric Artist (Soprano). Professor of Music. m. Joseph Petroff, 17 May 1973, 1 son, 1 daughter. Education: University; Master classes, Hochschule für Musik, Hamburg; Opera classes, Bern and Geneva Conservatories; Diploma. Debut: As Constance in Entführung aus dem Serail, Stadttheater Luneberg, 1959, and as Clarice in Haydn's Il mondo della luna, Stadttheater Bern, 1960. Career includes: Main appearances: Aarhus, Denmark; Bern and Geneva, Switzerland; The Hague, Netherlands; Royal Opera Ghent, Belgium; Linz, Austria; Kiel, Germany; Grand Theatre, Geneva; Sang as Carolina in Il matrimonio segreto, Gilda in Rigoletto, Blondchen and Constanze in Entführung, Musetta, Sophie in Der Rosenkavalier, Ännchen in Freischütz, Susanna in Figaro, Despina in Così fan tutte, Adele in Die Fledermaus, Rosina in Barbiere di Siviglia and Adina in L'Elisir d'amore; Operettas: Maritza in Gräfin Maritza and Evelyne in Graf von Luxemburg. Address: 12 rue de Chêne-Bougeries, CH 1224 Geneva, Switzerland.

PETROV Andrey (Pavlovich), b. 2 Sept 1930, Leningrad, Russia. Composer. Education: Studied at Leningrad Conservatory, 1949-54. Career: Editor at Muzgiz Music Publishers, Teacher at Leningrad Conservatory, 1961-63; Chairman of Leningrad/St Petersburg Composers Union from 1964. Compositions include: Operas: Peter the First, Leningrad, 1975; Mayokovsky Begins, Leningrad, 1983; Ballets: The Magic Apple Tree, 1953; The Station Master, 1955; The Shore of Hope, 1959; The Creation of the World, 1971; Pushkin: Reflections on the Poet, 1978; Orchestral: Pioneer Suite, 1951; Sport Suite, 1953; Radda and Lioko, Symphonic Poem, 1954; Songs of Today, 1965; Poem, in memory of the Siege of Leningrad, 1965; Patriotic vocal music; Film music and popular songs. Honours: USSR State Prizes. Address: c/o RAO, Bolchaia Bronnai 6-a, Moscow 103670, Russia.

PETROV Ivan, b. 23 Feb 1920, Irkutsk, USSR. Singer (Bass). Education: Glazunov Music College Moscow, 1938-39, with a Mineyev. Career: Sang with Ivan Kozlovsky's opera group from 1939; Concert engagements with the Moscow Philharmonic, 1941; Bolshoy Theatre, Moscow, from 1943; Sang there in the 1953 premiere of Shaporin's The Decembrists; Paris Opéra, 1954, as Boris Godunov; Concert tour of Europe, 1954-55; Other operatic roles include Glinka's Ruslan, Dosifey in Khovanshchina, Mepistopheles in Faust, Verdi's King Philip and Basilio in Il Barbiere di Siviglia. Recordings: Eugene Onegin; Rachmaninov's Aleko; Prince Igor; Ruslan and Ludmilla; Boris Godunov; Verdi Requiem; The Tale of Tsar Saltan by Rimsky-Korsakov, Tchaikovsky's Mazeppa and Roméo and Juliette. Recordings include: Title role in Prince Igor, conducted by Mark Ermler. Address: c/o Bolshoi Theatre, Pr Marxa 8/2, 103009 Moscow, Russia.

PETROV Marina, b. 27 Dec 1960, Kiev, Russia. Recital Pianist; Piano Lecturer. Education: Central Music School for Gifted Children, Belgrade, 1966-76; Central Music School for Gifted Children, Kiev, 1976-77; College of Music, Belgrade, 1977-79; Graduate course in Performance, Teaching and Accompaniment, Moscow Conservatoire, 1979-84; Advanced solo studies at Belgrade Academy of Music, 1985-87. Debut: In Belgrade, 1969. Career: Recital Pianist, 1969-; First appearance on TV and Radio in Belgrade in 1969; Subsequently played in Kiev and Moscow; Tours in Yugoslavia; Has also played in Norway and in UK at venues including London, Dartington Hall and Bristol, 1990-; Lecturer in Piano. Contributions to: The Times; Rutland and Stamford Mercury; West Country Tribune; Politica, Yugoslavia. Honours: 1st Prize, Republican Festival for Gifted Children, Yugoslavia, 1970, 1972 and 1973; 1st Prize, 1972, 3rd Prize, 1973, 2nd Prize, 1978, Federal Competition for Young Pianists; 1st Prize, Republican Competition for Young Pianists, 1978. Membership: Incorporated Society of Musicians. Hobbies include: Reading; Swimming; Theatre; Arts. Address: 53A Berriman Road, London, N7 7PN, England.

PETROV Nikolai, b. 14 Apr 1943, Moscow, USSR. Pianist. Education: Graduated Moscow Conservatory, 1967; Postgraduate studies with Yakov Zak. Career: Public career from 1962; Many appearances with leading orchestras in Europe, Turkey, Canada, Japan, Mexico, the USA and USSR; Soloist with the Moscow Philharmonic Orchestra from 1968; Often heard in Tchaikovsky and Rachmaninov. Honours: Second Prize Van Cliburn International Competition, 1962; Second Prize Queen Elisabeth of the Belgians Competition, 1964. Address: c/o The Entertainment Corporation, 9 Great Newport Street, London WC2H 7JH, England.

PETROV Petar (Konstantinov), b. 23 Jun 1961, Stara Zagora, Bulgaria. Composer and Pianist. Education: Musical School, St Zagora, 1975-80; State Musical Academy, Sofia, 1983-88. Debut: New Bulgarian Music, 1984. Career: Manager and Pianist in Chilorch-choire, Sofia, 1988-91; Honorary Professor of Contrapunct in Bulgarian State Academy, 1990-93; Professor of Contrapunct and Composition in Music School, St Zagora; Composition Master Class of Profesor Anatol Vieru-Rumenia, 1993-95; Many appearances as Chamber Pianist with Rosed Idealov - Clarinet. Compositions: Lamento for String Orchestra, 1987,BR; Concert for Violin and Orchestra, 1987 BR, BTV; Improvisions for Concert for Piano, 1990, BTV; Katarsis for Chamber Orchestra, 1990, BR. Recordings: Sonata-Partita for Violin Solo, 1986, BTV; Concerto Piccolo for Flute, Violin and Piano, 1987, BR; Studium 2 for Flute Solo, 1989, BR; Concerto Piccolo No 4, for Strings, Cembalo and Piano, 1994, BR; Dialoge mit der Stiele, for Clarinet and Violoncello, 1995, BR, BTV. Honours: Diploma from Second International Competition for Junior Pianist and Composers, Equador, 1988; Second Prize, Second International Competition for Composers, Music and Earth, Sofia, 1994. Memberships: Union of Bulgarian Composers. Address: ul Chr. Morfova No 2 ych, V Et 3 m Ap 42, Stara Zagora, 6000 Bulgaria.

PETROVA Elena, b. 9 Nov 1929, Modry Kamen, Slovakia. Composer; Poet. m. Hanus Krupta, deceased, 1 child, deceased. Education: Four-term study of Musicology and Aesthetics at the Charles University, Prague; Piano at the High School of Music, Bratislava; Composition, Janacek's Academy of Music, Brno; Studied in USA. Debut: Graduation concert (Cantata To Night), Prague, 1970. Career: Works performed at home and abroad (Italy, Germany, Spain, Great Britain, Sweden, Russia, USA); Ballet Sunflower staged in Paris and Pilsen; Cooperates with Czech radio and televison and with a Prague art company Lyra Pragensis (organises concerts and poetry readings); Teacher of composition and improvisation at the Ceske Budejovice University and Charles University, Prague. Compositions include: 3 Symphonies, 1968, 1972, 1986; Symphonic Interludes, 1983; Si Le Soleil Ne Revenait Pas (full length opera), 1989; Comedy dell'arte for Reciter and Harpsichord (own poems), 1991; 4 String Quartets, 1968, 1972, 1989, 1992; Sun Sonata for soprano and orchestra or piano, 1992; Caprices and Dawning both for female choir a capella, 1993; Etudes for Fourhanded Piano, 1996; 3 Ballets for Orchestra, 1996; Trio for Flute, Clarinet and Piano, 1996. Honours: Second Prize, String Quartet, International Competition in Philadelphia, 1968; First Prizes, Czech National Competition, 1971, 1972; First Prize, International Competition in Denver for Inspiration for fourhanded piano, 1975; Honorary Mention in Jihlava, 1973; Honorary Mention, Women Composers Competition in Mannheim for Madrigals and Reliefs, 1976, 1978. Hobbies: Reading; Travelling. Address: Vitova 23, 186 00 Prague 8, Karlin, Czech Republic.

PETROVICS Emil, b. 9 Feb 1930, Nagybecskerek, Yugoslavia. Composer; Professor of Composition. 1 daughter. Education: Studied with Ferenc Farkas, Liszt Ferenc Academy of Music, Budapest, Hungary. Career: Professor, Academy of Dramatic and Film Arts; Professor of Composition and Head of Composition Faculty, Liszt Academy of Music; Director of Hungarian State Opera, 1986-. Compositions: Opera: C'est la Guerre, Lysistrata, Crime and Punishment; Ballet: Salome; Oratorios: The Book of Jonah, 6 cantatas; Cantat No 7, Pygmalion, 1995; Symphonic Works: Symphony for String Orchestra, Concerto for Flute and Orchestra; Vörösmarty Overture, 1993; Concertio for Trumpet and Orchestra, 1990; Two Intermezzi for strings, 1997; Chamber Works: String Quartet, Wind Quintet, Cassazione for 5 Brass, Passacaglia in Blues for Bassoon and Piano, Nocturne, Mouvement en Ragtime for 1 and 2 Cymbals; String Quartet No 2, 1991; Three Poems for tenor voice and piano, 1996; All above works recorded; Hungarian Children's Songs for Flute and piano, recorded in Canada; Four Self Portraits in Masks for Harps. Memberships: President, ARTISJUS; Bureau hongrois pour la protection des droits d'auteurs, Budapest. Address: Attila ut 39, Budapest, H-1013, Hungary.

PETRUSHANSKY Boris, b. 3 Jun 1949, Moscow, Russia. Concert Pianist. Education: Studies at Central School of Music and Moscow Conservatoire. Career: Many concert tours of Russia and appearances in Italy, Hungary, UK, Germany, France, Japan and Australasia; Repertoire includes works by: Beethoven; Brahms; Liszt; Prokoviev; Shostakovich; Schnittke; Gubaidulina; Professor at Academica Pianistica in Italy. Recordings include: Works by: Schnikkte; Gubaidulina. Honours include: Prizewinner in competitions at: Leeds, 1969; Moscow, 1970; Munich, 1971; Casagrande, 1975. Address: c/o Sonata, 11 Northpark Street, Glasgow, G20 7AA, Scotland.

PETRUTSHENKO Natalia, b. 21 Aug 1963, Ulan-Ude, Russia. Pianist. Education: Basic Musical Education, Kemerovo; Completed High Music School, Nikolaev, Ukraine, 1983; Diploma with highest honours, graduating from class of Professor Dorenski, 1991, PhD, 1993, P I Tchaikovski Moscow Conservatoire. Career: Comprehensive repertoire with orchestra and solo; Participant, 1st S V Rachmaninoff International Competition for Pianists, Moscow and International Competition for Young Performers, Japan, 1993; Guest performance tour to Japanese towns; Numerous concerts in major cities in Russia, Ukraine, Belarus, the Baltic States, Bulgaria and Romania; Professor, High Music School, Kurgan, Russia, 1994; Soloist, District Philharmonic Society, Nikolaev, Ukraine, 1995; Living in Varna, Bulgaria, 1996-; European tour in preparation. Honour: Prizewinner, 1st S V Rachmaninoff International Competition for Pianists, 1993. Address: Tchaika Housing Quarters, block 38 ap 24, Varna 9010, Bulgaria.

PETTAWAY Charles (Henry) Jr, b. 7 June 1949, Philadelphia, Pennsylvania, USA. Concert Pianist; Educator. m. Terri Lynn, 5 Oct 1985, 1 son, 1 daughter. Education: BMus Cum Laude, Philadelphia Musical Academy; MMus Cum Laude, Temple University; Private Studies, Master Classes, various teachers. Debut: Orchestral, Guest Soloist, Capital Orchestra, Toulouse, France, 1974. Career includes: Performances, Washington DC; Philadelphia; New York; Israel; France; USSR; Tour, Switzerland, 1981; Guest Soloist, numerous major and community orchestras throughout USA; Radio and TV performances; Master Classes, various colleges; Visiting Lecturer, Piano, Lincoln University, Pennsylvania, 1988-89; Assistant Professor of Music, Lincoln University, Pennsylvania. Recording: Charles Pettaway Performs Russian Piano Music. Honours include: Selected participant, Tchaikovsky International Competition, USSR, 1974, 1978; 1st Prize, Robert Casadesus International Competition, Paris, France; Named DeBose Artist 1997, for the National Piano Competition held at Southern University at Baton Rouge, Louisiana. Current Management: Lumaria Ricks Blakeney. Address: 2007 Upland Way, Philadelphia, PA 19131, USA.

PETUKHOV Mikhail, b. 24 Apr 1954, Varna, Bulgaria. Concert Pianist. Education: Studied in Kiev and at Moscow Conservatoire with Tatiania Nikolayeva. Career: Many concerts in Russia, Italy, Belgium, Netherlands, Czechoslovakia and Germany; Played with Royal Scottish Orchestra, 1992, followed by Tchaikovsky First Concerto with City of Birmingham Symphony under Yuri Simonov; Repertoire has also included works by Purcell, Ravel, Handel, Stravinsky, Mendelssohn, Schumann, Schoenberg and Ives; Professor in Piano at Moscow Conservatoire. Honours include: 3rd Prize at J S Bach Competition, Leipzig, 1972; Queen Elizabeth Competition at Brussels, 1975. Address: c/o Sonata, 11 Northpark Street, Glasgow, G20 7AA, Scotland.

PFAFF Luca, b. 25 Aug 1948, Olivone, Switzerland. Conductor. m. Dominique Chanet, 1986, 2 sons. Education: Basel University; Conservatorio G Verdi, Milan; Musikakademie, Vienna; Accademia Santa Ceàlia, Rome. Career: Director, Orchestre Symphonique du Rhin, France; Director, Carme, Milan; Founder, Ensemble Alternance, Paris; Guest Conductor, major orchestras, Europe. Recordings: Scelsi; Donatoni; Dusapin, Opera Romeo et Juliette; Mozart, Gran Partita. Contributions to: Monde de la Musique; Harmonie; Rivista Musicale; Diapason d'Or, 1985; Best CD of 1988; Donatoni, CHOC, Monde de la Musique. Hobbies: Himalayas; Skiing; Driving Collection Cars. Current Management: Valmalete, Paris, France. Address: Aeschenvorstadt 15, CH-4051 Basel, Switzerland.

PFISTER Daniel, b. 6 Nov 1952, St Gallen, Switzerland. Composer. Education: Teachers' Training College, 1970-74. Music Education: Konservatorium Winterthur (Conservatoire), 1974-78; Teachers' Diploma piano, 1978; Musikhochschule Zurich, music theory with Hans Ulrich Lehmann, 1977-78; Hochschule für Musik und darstellende Kunst in Vienna, composition with Prof Alfred Uhl, 1978-84; Diploma composition, 1984; Hochschule für Musik und darstellende Kunst in Wien, conducting with Prof Otmar Suitner, 1984-87. Career: Freelance Composer; Private teacher for music theory composition and piano, 1982-. Compositions: Saitenspiel, 1982 for 2 guitars; Concerto for String orchestra, 1982-87; Aeon for soprano and piano, 1983; Aeon for soprano and orchestra, 1983-84; Canto for soprano or flute or saxophone, 1985-88; Canto for soprano (flute), clarinet and vibraphone, 1986; Neun und Zehne auf einen Streich, for guitar, 1988; Touches for flute, oboe, clarinet, bassoon, horn, trumpet, snare drum, gong, xilorimba, vibraphone, guitar, piano, violin, viola, violincello, 1988-89; Bruchstuecke aus Touches, 1988, 880 un satiesme, instrument is free, 1988; 12 kleine Odien for flute and guitar, 1987-89; Max and Moritz for reciter and guitar, 1990-91. Membership: SMPV Schweizerischer Musikpaedagogischer Verband. Address: Lehnstrasse 33 CH-9014, St Gallen, Switzerland.

PHARR Rachel (Elizabeth Caroline), b. 15 Apr 1957, Picayune, Mississippi, USA. Harpsichordist. m. Bernard Gerard Kolle, 1 Jan 1989. Education: BMus Summa Cum Laude, Piano Performance major, 1978, MMus, Piano Performance major, 1980, University of Southwestern Louisiana, Lafayette; Aspen Music School, Aspen Festival, 1980, 1981; MMus, Harpsichord Performace major, Arizona State University, Tempe, 1982; Banff Centre School of Fine Arts, Canada, 1987-89. Career: Harpsichordist with Houston Baroque Ensemble, 1983-87, with Texas Chamber Orchestra in Houston, Texas, 1985-87; Numerous concerts, Banff Centre, Banff, Alberta, Canada, 1987-89; Performed at Aspen Music Festival, 1981, Breckenridge Music Institute, 1982, 1983; Featured Soloist in Houston Harpsichord Society's presentation of the entire J S Bach Well-Tempered Clavier for Bach Tercentenary, 1985; New Music America concerts, 1986; Tours as Solo Harpsichord, 1986, with Liedermusik Ensemble, 1987; Harpsichord Accompanist, Banff Centre, 1988-89; Radio performances, KLEF, Houston and WWNO, New Orleans; TV performance, NBC-Channel 4, Denver. Hobbies: Studying French; Reading; Jogging; Cross-country Skiing. Address: c/o Newton T Pharr, 314 Dodson Street, New Iberia, LA 70560, USA.

PHILIP Robert (Marshall), b. 22 Jul 1945, Witney, Oxfordshire, England. Freelance Music Critic; BBC Television Producer. m. Maria Lukianowicz, 3 Jan 1976, 2 daughters. Education: Royal College of Music, 1962-64; Peterhouse, Cambridge, 1964-68; University (now Wolfson) College, Cambridge, 1968-72; ARCM; MA; PhD. Career: Junior Research Fellow at University Wolfson College, Cambridge, 1972-74; Producer, BBC Television, Open University Department, 1976-; Freelance Music Critic and Broadcast Talks; Early Recordings and Musical Style, 1992. Contributions to: Records and Recording; BBC Record Review; Broadcast Series includes: The Long Playing Era (Radio 3); The Developing Musician (Radio 3); Composer and Interpreter (BBC World Service); Musical Yearbook (BBC World Service); Vintage Years (Radio 3). Honour: Organ Scholarship, Peterhouse, Cambridge, 1964; Visiting Research Fellowship, Open University, 1995-98. Membership: Royal Musical Association. Address: BBC Open University Production Centre, Walton Hall, Milton Keynes, MK7 6BH, England.

PHILIPS Daniel, b. 1960, USA. Violinist. Career: Winner of Young Concert Artists International Auditions and recitalist at Lincoln Center's Alice Tully Hall, 92nd Street 'Y' and appearances with major orchestras; Chamber musician at Santa Fe Festival, Spoleto Festival, Lockenhaus Kammermusikfest and the International Musicians Seminar in Prussia Cove; Co-founded the Orion Quartet and has given concerts at Kennedy Center, Washington DC, at Gardner Museum, Boston and throughout USA; Carnegie Hall recital, 1991 as part of the Centennial Celebration tribute to next 100 years of music making; Concerts at Turku Festival in Finland; Professor of Violin at State University of New York and Faculty member at Aaron Copland School of Music. Address: c/o Ingpen & Williams Limited, 26 Wadham Road, London SW15 2LR, England.

PHILIPS Leo, b. 1960, England. Violinist. Education: Studied at Yehudi Menuhin School and with Sandor Vegh, Dorothy DeLay and Shmuel Ashkenasi. Career: Concerts as Chamber Musician and Soloist; Former member of the Chamber Orchestra of Europe; Currently Leader and Principal Director of East of England Orchestra; Co-founder Vellinger String Quartet, 1990; Participated in master classes with Borodin Quartet at Pears-Britten School, 1991; Concerts as Ferrara Musica Festival, Italy and debut on South Bank with London premiere of Robert Simpson's 13th Quartet; BBC Radio 3 Debut, December 1991; Season 1992-93 with concerts in London, Glasgow, Cambridge, at Davos Festival, Switzerland and Crickdale Festival, Wiltshire; Wigmore Hall with Haydn (Op 54 no 2), Gubaidulina and Beethoven (Op 59 no 2), Purcell Room with Haydn's Last Seven Words. Recordings include: Elgar's Quartet and Quintet, with Piers Lane. Address: c/o Georgina Ivor Associates (Vellinger Quartet), 66 Alderbrook Road, London SW12 8AB, England.

PHILLIPS Jean (Susan), b. 24 May 1942, London, England. Concert Pianist; Harpsichordist; Teacher. Divorced, 2 d. Education: Junior Exhibitioner, 1952-58, Senior Exhibitioner, 1958-63, ARCM, 1961, Royal College of Music. Debut: Wigmore Hall, London, 1965. Career: Concert Pianist at Queen Elizabeth Hall, Purcell Room, Wigmore Hall and major venues in England; Founder of Concerts for Children and Parents, Purcell Room, South Bank, London, 1971 giving concerts with Gerard Benson for 19 years; Television performances for ITV and national and local radio; Visiting Lecturer in Piano and Harpsichord, Christchurch College, Canterbury; Concert tours abroad in Belgium, France, Kenya, Cyprus and Jersey, 1988; Concerts in Iceland and Australia including two broadcasts for ABC, 1990. Recording: For National Trust on Broadwood Square Piano of 1788, 1992. Current Management: Don Goodell. Address: Gothic Cottage, 22 Orchard Street, Canterbury, Kent, CT2 8AP, England.

PHILLIPS John (Alan), b. 14 Apr 1960, Adelaide, South Australia, Australia. Musicologist. Education: BMus (Hons), 1983, PhD, Musicology, in progress, University of Adelaide; Conducting, Composition, Vienna Konservatorium and Hochschule, 1983-85. Career: Active Choral Conductor, Adelaide; Involved on major research project on Bruckner's 9th symphony finale, 1989-, its new performing version completed with Nicola Samale, Rome, May 1991, first performed, Linz, Austria, by Bruckner Orchestra, Dec 1991, first recorded by same orchestra, 1993; Lectures, conference papers, Australia, Europe; Press conferences, Australian, German, Austrian, US newspapers; Interviews, Australian, German, Austrian Radio. Compositions: Many unpublished works; Choral arrangements. Recording: 2-piano recording, Bruckner 9th Symphony Finale with Edward Kriek, ABC Radio, Dec 1990. Publications: Bruckner's 9th Symphony Revisited. Towards the re-evaluation of a 4-movement symphony, dissertation, 1995; Editor: Anton Bruckner: 9th Symphony in D Minor: Finale: Reconstruction of the Autograph Score from the Surviving Manuscripts: Performing Version by Nicola Samale, John A Phillips and Giuseppe Mazzuca, with the assistance of Gunnar Cohrs, 1992; Anton Bruckner Gesamtausgabe: Zu Band IX; Finale: Rekonstruktion der Autograph-Partitur nach den erhaltenen Quellen. a) aller dem Finale der IX Symphonie zugehörigen Manuskripte, 1994. Hobby: Body building. Address: 107 Fourth Avenue, Joslin, SA 5070, Australia.

PHILLIPS Margaret (Corinna), b. 16 Nov 1950, Exeter, Devon, England. Concert Organist; Harpsichordist. Education: Royal College of Music, 1968-72; FRCO; GRSM; ARCM, organ performing with honours; Studied privately with Marie-Claire Alain in Paris, France, 1972-73. Debut: Royal Festival Hall, 1972. Career: Director of Music, St Lawrence Jewry next Guildhall, London, 1976-85; Professor of Organ and Harpsichord, London College of Music, 1985-91; Tutor in Organ Studies, Royal Northern College of Music, 1993-; President, Incorporated Association of Organists, 1997-99; Recitals throughout: Europe, USA, Mexico, Australia; Radio broadcasts in: UK, Sweden, Denmark, Netherlands, Australia; Performances with: London Choral Society, BBC Singers, The Sixteen and London Mozart Players; Lecturer, English Church and Organ Music. Recordings: Festliche Orgelmusik; English Organ Music from Queen Elizabeth I to Queen Elizabeth II; D Buxtehude; Orgelmusik i Karlskoga kyrka; Klosters Orgel; Organ Music of Saint-Saens; 18th Century English Organ Music; 19th Century English Organ Music; Wesley, Music for Organ; Dances for Organ. Hobbies: Reading; Walking; Playing The Violin. Address: 83 Church Street, Milborne Port, Sherborne, Dorset, DT9 5DJ, England.

PHILLIPS Paul (Schuyler), b. 28 Apr 1956, New Jersey, USA. Conductor. m. Kathryne Jennings, 23 Nov 1986, 1 daughter. Education: BA, cum Laude, Music, Columbia College, 1978; MA, Composition, Columbia University, 1980; MM, Conducting, College-Conservatory of Music, University of Cincinnati, 1982; Eastman School, 1974-75; Mozarteum, Salzburg, 1977; Aspen, 1979, 1980, 1981; LA Philharmonic Institute, 1982; International Conductors Course, NOS, Netherlands, 1983; Tanglewood, 1985; New York Philharmonic Conductors Symposium, 1987; Music Academy of the West, 1986; Workshops, 1987, 1991, 1992; Masterclass, 1992, American Symphony Orchestra League; Weiner Meisterkurse, 1990. Debut: Conducting Brown Orchestra (with Dave Brubeck Quartet), Carnegie Hall, 1990 (with Itzhak Perlman), Avery Fisher Hall, 1992. Career: Frankfurt Opera, 1982-83; Kapellmeister, Luneberg Stadttheater, 1983-84; Associate Conductor: Greensboro Symphony, 1984-86, Savannah Symphony, 1986-89, Rhode Island Philharmonic, 1989-92; Assistant Conductor, Greensboro Opera, 1984-86; Music Director: Young Artists Opera Theatre, 1984-85, Brown University Orchestra, 1989-, University of Rhode Island Opera Ensemble, 1990-91, Worcester Youth Symphony, 1991-, Holy Cross Chamber Orchestra, 1993-; Youth Concert Conductor, Maryland Symphony, 1985-; Director, Savannah Symphony Chorale, 1987-89; Artistic Director, Brown Opera, 1992-; Guest Conductor, Netherlands Radio Chamber Orchestra and Choir, Pro Arte Orchestra of Vienna, US Orchestras; Music Director, Pioneer Valley Symphony, 1994-; Lecturer in Music, Brown University, 1989-. Compositions: For Orchestra, Chamber Ensembles, Voice, Piano, Theatre, Film, TV. Contributions to: The Enigma of Variations: A Study of Stravinsky's Final Work for Orchestra, Music Analysis, 1984. Address: Brown University, Box 1924, Providence, RI 02912, USA.

PHILLIPS Peter, b. 15 Oct 1953, Southampton, England. Choral Director. Education: Studied at Winchester College and St John's College, Oxford. Career: Has taught at Oxford University and Trinity College of Music and the Royal College of Music; Founded the Tallis Scholars, 1978 and Gimell Records, 1981; Regular concerts in Britain and abroad. including USA from 1988 and Australia from 1985 (Byrd's Five-Part Mass at the Sydney Opera House); From 1989 the Far East and Promenade Concert debut with Victoria's Requiem; Documentary feature on ITV South Bank Show, 1990; United Kingdom concerts include Bath Festival, Buxton Festival and Edinburgh Festival, 1995-96. Recordings include: Lassus Music for Double Choir; Sarum Chant; John Sheppard Media Vita; Gesualdo Tenebrae Responsories; Cornysh Stabat Mater, Salve Regina and Magnificat; Clemens non Papa Missa Pastores Quidnam vidistis; Victoria Requiem and Tenebrae Responsories; Cardoso Requiem; Josquin Masses; Byrd The Great Service and Three Masses; Medieval Christmas Carols and Motets; Palestrina Masses, 4 CDs; Tallis Complete English Anthems and Spem in Alium; Allegri Miserere and Mundy Vox Patris Caelestis; Taverner Missa Gloria Tibi Trinitas; Russian Orthodox Music; Ikon of Light by John Tavener; CD based on South Bank Show feature; Isaac Missa de Apostolis; Tomkins The Great Service; Tallis Lamentations of Jeremiah. Contributions to: Music and Letters; The Listener; The Spectator; The Guardian; Advisory Editor, Proprietor, The Musical Times, 1995-. Honours include: (with Tallis Scholars): Record of the Year, Gramophone Magazine, 1987; Gramophone Award for Early Music Record of the Year, 1987, 1991, 1994. Memberships: Athaeneum; Chelsea Arts Club; MCC. Address: c/o The Administrator, Tallis Scholars Trust, Fenton House, Banbury Road, Chipping Norton, Oxon OX7 5AW, England.

PHILLIPS Todd, b. USA. Violinist. Education: Juilliard School with Sally Thomas and at the Salzburg Mozarteum with Sandor Vegh. Career: Leader with the Orpheus Chamber Orchestra and solo performances with the Pittsburgh SO (debut aged 13), the Brandenburg Ensemble, Camerata Academica of Salzburg, and leading American orchestras; Chamber music at the Santa Fe, Marlboro and Mostly Mozart festivals; Joint leader of the Orion String Quartet, with concert tours throughout North America and to London, Vienna and Amsterdam; 'Fourteen Musicians from Marlboro' tours; Season 1996-97 with Chamber Music Society of Lincoln Center, including premiere of George Perle's Quintet for horn and strings; Member of the violin and chamber music faculties at the Mannes School of Music. Recordings include: Mozart's Sinfonia Concertante K364, with the Orpheus Chamber Orchestra (DGG). Address: Orion String Quartet, Ingpen & Williams Ltd, 14 Kensington Court, London W8 5DN, England.

PHILOGENE Ruby, b. England. Singer (Mezzo-soprano). Education: Studied at the Curtis Institute, Philadelphia, and the Guildhall School of Music and Drama. Career: Concert engagements with the San Francisco SO, London Philharmonic and City of London Sinfonia; Season 1994-95 included Mahler 2 with the Liverpool Philharmonic, Messiah under Yehudi Menuhin, Bach B Minor Mass and Schumann's Scenes from Faust with the LPO, Janacek's Glagolitic Mass and Les Nuits d'Eté by Berlioz; Opera appearances as Britten's Hermia (with the LSO under Colin Davis), in Biber's Arminio at Innsbruck, the Page in Salome (Covent Garden 1997), in Handel's Orlando with the Gabriele Consort and as Goehr's Arianna; Season 1997-98 as Dorabella in Cosi fan tutte for Opera North and a new production of Parsifal in Brussels; Other repertory includes the Sorceress in Dido and Aeneas (Staatsoper Berlin) and Smeraldine in The Love for Three Oranges, at Lyon and San Francisco. Recordings include: A Midsummer Night's Dream; Arianna. Honours include: Winner, 1993 Kathleen Ferrier Memorial Prize. Address: c/o Lies Askonas Ltd, 6 Henrietta St, London WC2E 8LA, England.

PIAN Rulan Chao, b. 20 Apr 1922, Cambridge, Massachusetts, USA. Professor Emeritus. m. Theodore Hsueh-huang Pian, 1 daughter. Education: BA, Music, 1944, MA, Music, 1946, PhD, Musicology, Far Eastern Languages, 1960, Radcliffe College; Private Lessons in Piano, Cello, Japanese Court Music, Chinese Zither. Career: Teaching Assistant, Chinese, 1947-58, Instructor, Chinese, 1959-61, Lecturer, Chinese, 1961-74, Professor, East Asian Languages and Civilisations Music, 1974-92, Departments of East Asian Languages and Civilisations and of Music, Master of South House, 1975-78, Harvard University; Numerous Field Trips on Music to Far East; Visiting Professor, Music, Chung Chi College, Chinese University of Hong Kong, 1975, 1978-79, 1982, 1994; Visiting Professor, Taiwan, Tsing Hua University, 1990, Central University, 1992. Publications: A Syllabus for the Mandarin Primer, 1961; Sonq Dynasty Musical Sources and Their Interpretation, 1967; Complete Musical Works of Yuen Ren Chao (compiler), 1987. Contributions to: Numerous articles to music publications. Honours: Caroline I Wilby Prize for Dissertation, Radcliffe College, 1960; PBK, 1961; O Kinkeldy Award for Book, American Musicological Society, 1968; Medal, Distinguished Achievement, Radcliffe Graduate Society, 1980; Various Grants, 1958-79; Honorary Professor, Central China University of Science and Technology, Wuhan, 1990, Academician, Academia Sinica, Taiwan, 1990, Central-South University of Science and Technology, Changsha, Hunan, 1991, Southwest Jiaotong University, Chengdu, 1994, Sashih University, Hubei, 1996; Research Fellow of Several Institutes. Memberships include: Association for Asian studies; International Council for Traditional Music; Past Executive Board Member, Chinese Language Teachers Association; Editorial Boards of Musicology in China, Beijing and Chinese Theatrical Forum, Lanzhou; Charter Member, Association for Chinese Music Research. Address: 14 Brattle Circle, Cambridge, MA 02138, USA.

PIANA Dominique, b. 5 Jul 1956, Eupen, Belgium. Harpist; Teacher; Performer; Composer and Arranger. m. Will Joel Friedman, 26 May 1985, 1 son. Education: Royal Conservatory of Music, Brussels, 1974-80; Claremont Graduate School, California, 1982-85; Special training in Music Education Methods, Music & Movement, and the Concept of Life Energy in Music. Career: Professor of Harp, La Sierra University, Riverside, California, USA, 1982-; Professor of Harp, University of Redlands, California, 1985-; As performer: Solo and lecture recitals, Chamber Music, Concerti. Compositions: Mélodies imaginaires, for solo harp, 1995. Recordings: Harpiana Productions: Fancy, entertaining music for harp, 1984; Lulling the Soul, Carols of Love and Wonder, 1992; The Harp of King David, songs of Longing and Hope, 1994; Beyond Dreams, the Spirit of Reconciliation, 1996. Contributions to: Revue Musicale Belge, Belgium; Lumiere, France. Memberships: American Harp Society, Programme Chairman, 1992 National Conference; American String Teachers Association; World Harp Congress; American Musicological Society. Hobbies: Creative Writing; Translating; Nature; Spiritual Healing. Address: 30765 Palo Alto Drive, Redlands, CA 92373, USA.

PIATTI Polo (Osvaldo Ernesto), b. 25 Jan 1954, Buenos Aires, Argentina. Composer; Concert Pianist; Contemporary Classics Improvisor; Music Director. m. Martina Mars, 31 Aug 1988. Education: Baccalaureate in Biological Sciences, Buenos Aires; Anthroposophish Pädagogisches Seminar, West Berlin, Germany; Professor Nacional de Musica; National Academy of Music, Buenos Aires; Studies in Composition, Electronic Music and Musicology, Université de la Sorbonne, Paris, France. Career: Performer of Musik der Bilder, first non-jazz improvisations solo concert in Europe, Stuttgart, 1987; Numerous Piano Improvisat Concerts, including, Moments in Time, Austria, Italy, France, Holland, 1975; Piannissimo, Spain, Poland, 1976; Musica Nueva, Argentina Tour and National Broadcast; Another Sky, Bolivar Hall, London, 1992; The Terrestrial Trilogy, Bloomsbury Theatre, London, 1993; Anybody Out There?, St James, Piccadilly, London, 1994; Numerous musical directions for theatres and academies in Europe and England. Compositions: For Theatre, Narrenherbst, Stuttgart, 1986; Schuld und Sühne, Basel, 1987; Der Satierkreis, Stuttgart, 1987; Narren Auf Eis, Stuttgart, 1987; Kofferzirkus, Stuttgart, 1988; Ein Traumspiel, Zurich, 1988; Faust, Stuttgart, 1989; Arzt Wider Willen, Stuttgart, 1989; Murder in the Cathedral, Stuttgart, 1989; Dornröschen, Stuttgart, 1990; Peer Gynt, Stuttgart, 1990; For Dance, Fata Morgana, for dramatic dance, Stuttgart, 1989; Seasons, Stuttgart, 1989; Colours, Stuttgart, 1989; For Contemporary Dance, Six Dances, for ballet, London, 1994; Compositions for Films, L'Escalier and Les Montres, director Michel Duffois, Paris, 1975; Mes Marriages/Meine Hochzeiten, director Didier Bay, West Berlin, 1979; Lifestyle, director Nessan Cleary, London, 1991. Publications: The Magical Sound, on music and cosmology, 1993-95. Contributions to: Numerous articles from 1986. Address: World Centre of Performing Arts, The International University, The Avenue, Bushey, Herts WD2 2LN, England.

PIAU Sandrine, b. 1969, France. Singer (Soprano). Education: Studied with Julius Rudel in Paris and with Rachel Yakar and Rene Jacobs at Versailles. Career: Concert appearances in Bach's Passions and Magnificat under Philippe Herrweghe and Mozart's Exultate Jubilate with Jean-Claude Malgoire; Has also appeared under William Christie in Rossi's Orfeo, Mozart's Davidde Penitente, Campra's Idomenee and Purcell's King Arthur (Covent Garden and Paris, 1995); Has also sung in Purcell's Fairy Queen, Rameau's Les Indes Galantes and Castor et Pollux (at Aix), Handel's Scipione (as Berenice) and Pergolesi's Stabat Mater; Sang Almirena in Handel's Rinaldo under Christophe Rousset, Beaune, 1996. Address: c/o Les Arts Florissants, 10 Rue de Florence, F-25008 Paris, France.

PICCONI Maurizio, b. 1957, Italy. Bass-Baritone. Education: Studied at Osimo. Career: After winning competitions such as the Concours Bellini in 1983 and the Philadelphia International in 1985, sang widely in Italy; Roles have included Rossini's Taddeo, Gianni Schicchi, Bartolo, Dulcamara, Belcore and Malatesta; Sang at Zurich in 1988 as Sulpice in La Fille du Régiment, at Bonn in 1992 as Leporello and further appearances at Dublin, Bilbao, Amsterdam, Strasbourg and Philadelphia; Sang Rossini's Bartolo at Pavia, 1995. Recordings include: Il Furioso all'Isola di San Domingo by Donizetti. Address: c/o Bonn Opera, Am Boeselagerhof 1, Pf 2440, W-5300 Bonn, Germany.

PICHLER Guenter, b. 9 Sep 1940, Austria. Violinist. Education: Studied in Vienna. Career: Leader of the Vienna Symphony Orchestra, 1958; Leader of Vienna Philharmonic, 1961; Professor, Hochschule für Musik, Vienna, 1963-; Guest Professor, Hochschule für Musik, Cologne, 1993-; Founder, leader of the Alban Berg Quartet from 1971; Annual concert series at the Vienna Konzerthaus, the QEH London, Théâtre des Champs Elysées Paris, Opera Zurich and festival engagements worldwide; Associate Artists at the South Bank Centre, London; US appearances: first performances include Berio, von Einem, Schnittke, Rihm in Washington DC, Los Angeles, San Francisco and New York (Carnegie Hall). Recordings include: Complete quartets of Beethoven, Brahms, Berg, Webern and Bartok; Late quartets of Mozart, Schubert, Haydn and Dvorak; Ravel, Debussy and Schumann Quartets; Live recordings from Carnegie Hall (Mozart, Schumann); Konzerthaus in Vienna, Complete Beethoven; Brahms, Dvorak, Smetana, Rihm, Schnittke, Berio, Janacek; Opéra-Comique Paris, (Brahms). Honours include: Grand Prix du Disque; Deutscher Schallplatenpreis; Edison Prize; Japan Grand Prix; Gramophone Magazine Award; International Classical Music Award, 1992; Honorary Member of the Vienna Konzerthaus. Address: Intermusica Artists' Management, 16 Duncan Terrace, London N1 8BZ, England.

PICHT-AXENFELD Edith (Maria), b. 1 Jan 1914, Freiburg, Germany. Pianist; Organist; Harpsichordist; Educator. m. Professor Dr Georg Picht, 4 sons, 1 daughter. Education: Studied piano with Paula Roth-Kastner, 1920-32, 1932-34 with Anna Hirzel-Langenhan, Rudolph Serkin, 1934-35; Abitur, Freiburg, 1931; Private Music teaching Examination, 1932; Studied organ with Albert Schweitzer, USA. Debut: Freiburg 1927. Career: Piano and Harpischord Concerts throughout Europe, Britain, South America, South Africa and Asia, 1935-; Participant, International Festivals including English Bach Festival; Chamber music partnership with Aurele Nicolet and Heinz Holliger; Piano Trio with Nicolas Chumachenco and Alexandre Stein; Professor, Staatliche Hochschule für Musik, Freiburg, 1947-. Recordings include: Bach, Goldberg Variations and Six Partitas; Baroque Sonatas for oboe and basso continuo; Bach Wohltemperiertes Klavier Books I and II, English Suites. Honour: Chopin Prize, Warsaw, 1937. Memberships: Deutscher Musikrat; European Piano Teachers Association. Address: Altbirkelhof, D-79856 Hinterzarten, Germany.

PICK Karl-Heinz, b. 18 Aug 1929, Rothenburg/Lausitz, Germany. Pianist; Composer; Piano Teacher. m. Elisabeth Buckisch, 3 Sept 1949, 2 daughters. Education: Felix Mendelssohn Bartholdy College of Music, Leipzig. Career: Concert Pianist in Europe, Asia, Near East; Composer; His 2 concertos for piano and orchestra performed in Leipzig (Gewandhaus); Professor of Piano, Felix Mendelssohn Bartholdy College of Music, Leipzig; Director, Piano Department, Leipzig College, 1969-85; Professor of Piano, Hochschule für Musik Und Theater, Leipzig, now Emeritus, 1994-; Jury Member: Sofia Festival Competition, 1969; J S Bach Competition, Leipzig, 1977, 1980; Tchaikovsky Competition, Moscow, 1978; Vianna da Motta Competition, Lisbon, 1979; Viotti Competition, Vercelli, 1979, 1980, 1981, 1984; Robert Schumann Competition, Zwickau, 1981; Queen Elisabeth Competition, Brussels, 1983, 1987; Marguerite Long-Jacques Thibaud Competition, Paris, 1983; Maria Callas Competition, Athens, 1985; Frédéric Chopin Competition, Warsaw, 1985, Darmstadt, 1989, 1992, Göttingen, 1990, 1993; Prague Spring Competition, 1988; President, Piano Jury, J S Bach Competition for Students. Compositions include: Piano works: Zwei Konzerte und ein Concerto piccolo für Klavier und Orchester; Toccata; Vier tänzerische Stücke für Klavier; Huldigungen; Trois pièces pour piano; Erste Sonate; Suite zu dritt und Polonaise; Fantastisches Nocturne; Klaviergeschichten des Burattino und Märchensuite nach Märchen der Gebrüder Grimm; Songs; Cantatas; Chamber music; Violin Concerto. Memberships: Elected President, Chopin Society, Democratic Republic of Germany, 1986; President, Deutsche Chopin-Gesellschaft, 1990, erneute Wahl, 1995; Member of Presidium, International Federation of Chopin Societies, 1990. Address: Heinrich-Buchner-Strasse 2, D-04347 Leipzig, Germany.

PICK-HIERONOMI Monica, b. 1940, Cologne, Germany. Singer (Soprano). Education: Studied at Rheinischen Musikschule with Diether Jakob. Career: Sang first in Oberhausen, then Gärtnerplatztheater Munich; Sang at Nationaltheater Munich, 1977-88; Has appeared elsewhere in Germany, and in Holland, Belgium, Austria and Switzerland; British appearances with Welsh National Opera and Opera North and at Buxton Festival; Roles have included Mozart's Constanze, Donna Anna, Electra, Vitellia and Countess; Verdi's Leonora (Il Trovatore), Luisa Miller, Violetta and Desdemona; Ariadne, the Marschallin, the Empress in Die Frau ohne Schatten and Elektra; Mathilde in Guillaume Tell, Zurich; Prima Donna in Donizetti's Viva la Mamma, Amelia (Ballo in Maschera) and Leonora (Forza del Destino); Concert engagements include Christ at the Mount of Olives by Beethoven, with the Orchestra de Lyon, under Serge Baudo; Season 1988-89 included Donna Anna in Liège and Handel's Belshazzar in Karlsruhe; Puritani at Brescia and Aida at the Verona Arena. Address: Music International, 13 Ardilaun Road, London N5 2QR, England.

PICKENS Jo Ann, b. 1955, USA. Singer (Soprano). Education: Studied in USA and Europe. Career: Concert appearances with the Chicago Symphony under Solti, Los Angeles Philharmonic under Kurt Sanderling and Baltimore Symphony; German debut in 1984 appearing later in Porgy and Bess; Toured France in 1987 with the Orchestre Symphonique de Paris, in Verdi's Requiem; British appearances with the Scottish Chamber, Scottish National, Royal Philharmonic, Ulster, Royal Liverpool Philharmonic Orchestras, London Mozart Players, English Chamber and Halle Orchestras; Conductors include: Antal Dorati, Penderecki, Rattle, Norrington and Libor Pesek; Sang in Liszt's Christus at the Festival Hall, 1990 under Brian Wright, A Child of Our Time under Richard Hickox at the City of London Festival; Concert performance of Nabucco with the Chorus and Orchestra of Welsh National Opera at St David's Hall; Sang in Les Troyens at the Berlioz Festival Lyon with Serge Baudo, Armide at the Buxton Festival and as Purcell's Dido, in France; Other appearances with the Chicago Lyric Opera and in Spain. Recordings include: Verdi Quattro Pezzi Sacri with the Chicago Symphony; My Heritage, Negro spirituals and songs by Black American composers with American pianist, Donald Sulzen. Honours: Winner of Concours International de Chant, Paris; Benson and Hedges Gold Award for Concert Singers; Metropolitan Regional Auditions, Paris. Current Management: Neil Dalrymple, Music International. Address: c/o Music International, 13 Ardilaun Road, London, NW3 1RR, England.

PICKER Martin, b. 3 Apr 1929, Chicago, Illinois, USA. Professor; Musicologist. m. Ruth Gross, 21 June 1956, 1 son, 2 daughters. Education: PhB, 1947, MA, 1951, University of Chicago; PhD, University of California, Berkeley, 1960. Career: Instructor, University of Illinois, 1959-61; Assistant Professor, Rutgers University, 1961-65; Associate Professor, 1965-68, Professor, 1968-97, Chairman of Music Department, 1973-79, Emeritus Professor, 1997-, Rutgers College. Publications: The Chanson Albums of Marguerite of Austria, 1965; Introduction to Music, with Martin Bernstein, 3rd edition, 1966, 4th edition, 1972; Fors Seulement: 30 Compositions, 1981; The Motet Books of Andrea Antico, 1987; Johannes Ockeghem and Jacob Obrecht: A Guide to Research, 1988; Henricus Isaac, A Guide to Research, 1991; Editor-in-Chief, Journal of the American Musicological Society, 1969-71. Memberships: American Musicological Society; International Musicological Society. Address: Music Department, Mason Gross School of the Arts, Douglass Campus, Rutgers University, New Brunswick, NJ 08903, USA.

PICKER Tobias, b. 18 July 1954, New York. Composer. Education: Studied with Charles Wuorinen at the Manhattan School of Music (BM 1976) and with Elliott Carter at Juilliard (MM 1978). Career: Composer-in-Residence with the Houston Symphony Orchestra, 1985-87; Commissions from the American Composers Orchestra, San Francisco SO, St Paul Chamber Orchestra, and Ursula Oppens; Opera, Emmeline, premiered at the Santa Fe Festival, 1996. Compositions include: 4 Sextets for various instruments, 1973, 1973, 1977, 1981; Rhapsody for violin and piano, 1979; 3 Piano Concertos, 1980, 1983, 1986; Violin Concerto, 1981; 3 Symphonies, 1982, 1986, 1989; Serenade for piano and wind quintet, 1983; Piano-o-rama, for 2 pianos, 1984; Encantadas, for narrator and orchestra, 1984; Dedication Anthem for band, 1984; Old and Lost Rivers, for orchestra, 1986; String Quartet, New Memories, 1987; Piano Quintet, 1988; Romances and Interludes, after Schumann, for oboe and orchestra, 1990; Two Fantasies, for orchestra, 1991; Bang, for piano and orchestra, 1992; Violin Sonata, Invisible Lilacs, 1992; Emmeline, opera, 1996. Honours include: Charles Ives Scholarship, 1978; Guggenheim Fellowship, 1981. Address: c/o ASCAP, ASCAP Building, One Lincoln Plaza, New York, NY 10023, USA.

PICKETT Philip, b. 17 Nov 1950, London, England. Director; Performer of Early Wind Instruments. Education: Introduced to variety of early wind instruments by Anthony Baines and David Munrow: experienced on recorder, crumhorn, shawm, rackett and others; Professor of Recorder at the Guildhall School of Music, 1972, helping to organise the School's early music department; Fellow of the GSM, 1985; Soloist with leading ensembles, including the Academy of St Martin in the Fields, Polish Chamber Orchestra, London Mozart Players, City of London Sinfonia, London Bach Orchestra and the English Concert; As Director of the New London Consort has appeared at major festivals and concert halls in Finland, France, Germany, Greece, Holland, Hong Kong, Israel, Belgium, Spain, Italy, Latin America, Switzerland, USSR and Yugoslavia; British appearances include five Early Music Network tours; Medieval Christmas Extravaganza on the South Bank and concerts for the 21st anniversary of the Elizabeth Hall; Director of the South Bank Summerscope Festival of Medieval and Renaissance Music (Pickett's Pageant), 1988; Regular engagements at the Bath, Edinburgh, King's Lynn, Edinburgh and City of London Festivals; BBC Programmes include music for half the complete Shakespeare play series, BBC2; Music in Camera showings and regular concerts on Radio 3; Composed music for A Meeting in Vallodolid (Shakespeare and Cervantes) for Radio 3, 1991; Promenade Concerts include Bonfire of the Vanities (Medici Wedding Celebrations of 1539), 1990; Oswald von Wolkenstein concert at the Purcell Room, London, 1997 and Miracles of Mary at the QEH. Recordings include: Dances from Terpsichore by Michael Praetorius; Medieval Carmina Burana; The Delights of Posilipo (Neopolitan Dances); Instrumental music by Biber and Schmelzer; Monteverdi Vespers and Orfeo; Cantatas and concertos by Telemann and Vivaldi; Medieval pilgrimage to Santiago; CD of Virtuoso Italian Vocal Music with Catherine Bott: de Rore, Cavalieri, Luzzaschi, G Caccini, Rasi, Gagliano, Marini, Frescobaldi, Monteverdi, F Caccini, Bernardi, Rossi and Carissimi (Il lamento in morte di Maria Stuarda); Biber Requiem. Address: c/o Jessica Atkinson, Polygram Classics (Publicity), P O Box 1420, 1 Sussex Place, Hammersmith, London W6 9XS, England.

PIDOUX Roland, b. 29 Oct 1946, Paris, France. Cellist. Education: Studied at the Paris Conservatoire from 1960, with André Navarra, Jean Hubeau and Joseph Calvet. Career: Co-founded the Ensemble Instrumental de France; Played with the orchestra of the Paris Opéra from 1968; Member of the Via Nova Quartet, 1970-78; Joined Regis and Bruno Pasquier, 1972, to form the Pasquier Trio; Directed the record collection Les Musiciens for Harmonia Mundi, 1979; Soloist with the Orchestra National of France, 1979-87; Professor of Cello at the Paris Conservatoire, 1987; Plays a Stradivarius of 1692. Address: Conservatoire National Superieur de Musique, 14 Rue de Madrid, 75008 Paris, France.

PIECZONKA Adrianne, b. 1963, Canada. Singer (Soprano). Education: Studied in Canada and with Vera Rosza in London. Career: Concert engagements include Mozart's C minor Mass at the opening of the 1991 Edinburgh Festival, also at Gstaad and both conducted by Menuhin; Concerts with orchestras in Vienna, Amsterdam, Warsaw and Toronto; Recitals in UK, Switzerland, France, Brazil, USA and Canada; Appearances at Vienna Volksoper and Staatsoper include Tatyana in Eugene Onegin, Donna Elvira, Agathe, Laura in Der Bettelstudent, Micaela, Countess Almaviva and Freia in new production of Das Rheingold, 1992; Sang in premiere of Reimann's Das Schloss, 1992; Sang Countess also at Deutsche Oper Berlin, Staatsoper Dresden, Zurich and Munich, 1994-95; London Proms debut singing Beethoven's Ah Perfido with Neville Marriner, 1994; Sang in Gounod's Faust at Volksoper and Hindemith's Cardillac at Staatsoper in Vienna; Sang Mimi in Stuttgart and Toronto, 1994, Tatyana, 1994, Donna Elvira in Don Giovanni at Glyndebourne, 1995, Title role of Arabella at Glyndebourne, Eva in Meistersinger and Antonia in Hoffmann at Wiener Staatsoper, 1995; Sang Schoeck's Venus at Geneva, 1997. Recordings include: First Lady in Die Zauberflöte conducted by Solti. Honours include: Winner, 's Hertogenbosch, Netherlands and Pleine-sur-Mer, France, International Vocal Competitions. Address: c/o IMG Artists, Media House, 3 Burlington Lane, London, W4 2TH, England.

PIENCIKOWSKI Robert, b. 26 May 1951, Bremen, Germany. Musicologist. m. Evangelia Eleftheriou, 3 Jan 1980. Education: Université de Genève; Conservatoire de Musique, Genève. Debut: Studio de Musique Contemporaine de Genève, 1973; IRCAM, Paris, 1980. Career: In charge of Information Department at the SMC (Geneva), 1973-77; Music Analysis lectures at IRCAM, Paris, 1980-90; Musicologist, Paul Sacher Foundation, Basel, 1990-. Publications: René Char et Pierre Boulez, 1980; Nature morte avec guitare, 1985; Inschriften: Ligeti, Xenakis, Boulez, 1997. Address: Münsterplatz 4, CH-4051 Basel, Switzerland.

PIERARD Catherine, b. England. Career: Many appearances in Great Britain and Europe, with the Jerusalem SO, City of London Sinfonia, Scottish Chamber Orchestra and Concertgebouw; Opera roles have included Tatiana in Eugene Onegin, Fiordiligi and Donna Elvira with English Tourin Opera (1994), Papagena in Die Zauberflöte at the 1990 London Proms, Purcell's Dido (Spitalfields Festival 1993), Gluck's Alceste, Iphigénie and Euridice; Engagements with Roger Norrington in Orfeo at the Bath Festival and Purcell's Fairy Queen in Florence; Drusilla and Fortune in Monteverdi's Poppea under Richard Hickox; Season 1995-96 in Mozart's C Minor Mass, Messiah with the Ulster and London Bach Orchestras & Ravel's Sheherazade with the Bournemouth SO; Biber's Arminio at the Salzburg and Innsbruck Festivals, Bach's Magnificat at Ottawa and Handel's Belshazzar with Nicholas Kraemer. Recordings include: Monteverdi Arias (Hyperion) Dioclesian and The Fairy Queen (EMI); Britten's Rape of Lucretia (Chandos). Address: c/o Magenta Music International, 4 Highgate High Street, London N6 5JL, England.

PIGNEGUY John Joseph, b. 8 Jul 1945, Shoreham-by-Sea, Sussex, England. Freelance Horn Player. m. Ruth Smith, 16 Jun 1973. Education: Royal Academy of Music, 1963-66; Studied with James Brown OBE. Career: 1st Horn, London Mozart Players, 1968-70; 1st Horn, Royal Opera House, Covent Garden, 1972-74; Member, Merlot Trio; Founder Member, Nash Ensemble, broadcasting on Radio and TV and Promenade Concert appearances; Member, Philip Jones Brass Ensemble, 1979-83; Regular Adjudicator for BBC TV Young Musician of The Year competition; Musical Director, Sound of Horns and Horns Unlimited; Invited by Yehudi Menuhin to appear with Merlot Trio, Gstaad Festival, Switzerland, 1978; Extensive studio work for films, TV, and records; Former Professor of Horn, Trinity College of Music, London. Recordings: Numerous records with: Nash Ensemble, Philip Jones Brass Ensemble, Locke Brass, and Sound of Horns. Membership: Associate of The Royal Academy, 1990. Hobbies: Archaeology; Cycling; Walking Holidays; Gardening; General interest in sport. Address: 21 Brechin Place, London, SW7 4QD, England.

PIKE Jeremy, b. 20 Nov 1955, London, England. Composer. m. Teresa Majcher, 15 Aug 1981, 1 daughter. Education: Abingdon School, 1966-73; MA, King's College, Cambridge, 1973-76; Junior Exhibitioner, Royal Academy of Music, 1969-73; Postgraduate Composition and Conducting, Royal Academy of Music, 1976-77; LRAM, Piano, 1979. Career: British Council Scholarship to study composition with Henryk Gorecki in Poland, Katowice Academy of Music, 1978-79, and with Tadeusz Baird at the Warsaw Academy, 1979; Director of Contemporary Music, University of Warwick, 1981-; Teaching posts held at, Bedford School, 1981-82 and Stamford School, 1982-. Compositions include: Time and Tide, Chorus and Orchestra; 2 Piano Concertos; 2 Chamber Symphonies; Shorter Orchestral Works include, the Voice; Overture; Fugue; 5 String Quartets; Oboe Quartet; Clarinet Quartet; Quintet for 5 Clarinets; Fantasy for Nonet; 6 Piano Sonatas and other Piano works; Guitar Sonata; Vocal works. Hobbies: Photography; Walking; Railways. Address: University of Warwick, Coventry, West Midlands CV4 7AL, England.

PIKE Julian, b. 1958, England. Singer (Tenor). Education: Studied at the Royal College of Music and with Pierre Bernac in France. Career: Sang Don José in Peter Brook's version of Carmen in Paris, Zurich, Stockholm, Copenhagen and New York, 1982-84; Sang Michael in productions of Stockhausen's Donnerstag aus Licht in Holland, Germany, Italy and London (Covent Garden, 1985); Tour with the European Community Youth Orchestra under Matthias Bamert, 1985; Wexford Festival, 1985, in Mahagonny; Appearances with Kent Opera in Poppea and Rameau's Pygmalion; Has sung in Henze's English Cat in Frankfurt, at the Edinburgh Festival and for the BBC; Premiere productions of Montag aus Licht in Milan, Amsterdam, Frankfurt and Paris, from 1988; Sang Roderick in The Fall of the House of Usher by Glass with Music Theatre Wales, 1989; Ligeti Festival at the South Bank, 1989; Other roles include the Dancing Master in Ariadne and Piet the Pot in Le Grand Macabre (Stockholm, 1991); Season 1992 as Michael in the premiere of Stockhausen's Dienstag aus Licht at Lisbon and later at Amsterdam; Recitals at the Bath, City of London, Camden and Aldeburgh Festivals: repertoire includes, Bach, Monteverdi and contemporary music; Tours of France, Germany, Belgium, Holland, Poland, Finland and Austria (Salzburg); Appearances with the Songmakers' Almanac and Fortune's Fire Lute Song Ensemble. Address: Allied Artists, 42 Montpelier Square, London SW7 1JZ, England.

PILAND Jeanne, b. 3 Dec 1945, Raleigh, North Carolina, USA. Singer (Mezzo-Soprano). Education: Bachelor's Degree, University of North Carolina; Further studies in New York with Gladys White and Professor Carolyn Grant. Debut: New York City Opera, 1972. Career: New York City Opera, 1974-77; Sang at the Deutsche Oper am Rhein from 1977 as Cherubino; Composer, Ariadne, Octavian, Der Rosenkavalier, Silla in Palestrina and the Child in L'Enfant et les Sortilèges; Hamburg from 1981, Munich from 1985; Ludwigsburg Festival 1984, as Dorabella, Vienna Staatsoper, 1984, 1987, 1991 as Composer and Dorabella; Sang the Composer in Paris, Dresden, Hamburg, Vienna, Nice, Monte Carlo, Amsterdam, 1987, Ariadne auf Naxos at Covent Garden and Aix-en-Province, 1985; Returned to Aix 1986 and 1988, as Mozart's Idamante and Sextus, Composer and Octavian; Has appeared as Octavian at Dresden 1986 for 75th Anniversary of World premiere, Cologne, Zurich, Nice 1986, and Monte Carlo 1987, Santa Fe, 1988; Aix-en-Province, Munich, Hamburg 1988, as Idamante and Octavian; Sang Octavia in L'Incoronazione di Poppea Annius, La Clemenza di Tito, at Geneva, 1989; Other roles include Rosina and Cenerentola, Preziosilla, Smeaton (Anna Bolena), Zerlina and Massenet's Charlotte, Rosina, Concepcion, (L'Heure Espagnole), Elena (La Donna del Lago), Marguerite (Damnation de Faust), Clytemnestra, Iphigenia in Aulis, La Scala Milan, Cherubino, 1981; Houston and Los Angeles, Dorabella; Vancouver, Adalgisa, Norma, 1991 - Carmen; Sang Charlotte in Werther for Florida Grand Opera, 1996; Repertoire includes, Berlioz, Les Nuits d'Eté, Shéherazade, Mahler's Symphonies and Lied-Cycles. Address: c/o Grand Théâtre de Geneve, 11 Boulevard de Theatre, CH-1211 Geneva 11, Switzerland.

PILARCZYK Helga, b. 12 Mar 1925, Schoningen, Brunswick, Germany. Singer (Soprano). Education: Studied in Brunswick and Hamburg. Career: Brunswick, 1951-54, debut as Irmentraud in Lortzing's Der Waffenschmied; Hamburg Staatsoper, 1954-68, notably as Berg's Marie and Lulu, the Mother in Dallapiccola's Il Prigioniero, Jocasta in Oedipus Rex, Renata in The Fiery Angel; Städtische Oper Berlin, 1956, in the premiere of Henze's Il Re Cervo; Glyndebourne, 1958, 1960, as the Composer in Ariadne auf Naxos and Columbina in Arlecchino; Covent Garden, 1959, as Salome; US debut Washington, 1960, as the Woman in Erwartung; Metropolitan Opera, 1965, as Marie in Wozzeck. Publication: Kann Man die Moderne Opern Singen?, 1964. Recordings: Erwantung; Pierrot Luniare. Address: c/o Hamburgische Staatsoper, Grosse-Theaterstrasse 34, D-2000 Hamburg 36, Germany.

PILAVACHI Anthony, b. 1962, Cyprus. Stage Director. Education: Guildhall School of Music and Drama, 1984-86. Debut: Pergolesi's La Serva Padrona at Monte Carlo, 1983. Career: Director and Assistant at the Bonn Opera, 1987-92, notably with Falstaff (1991); Director and Assistant, Cologne Opera, 1992-95, notably with Peter Grimes, 1994; Carmen at Bergen (1992); Il Barbiere di Siviglia and Traviata at Bogota (1994); Season 1995 with Un Ballo in Maschera at Freiburg, Carmina Burana at Dresden in the Zwinger Courtyard, Handel's Tolomeo with the Hallé and Lulu at Lubeck, 1996; Season 1997 in Freiburg with Orpheus in the Underworld and The Love of Three Oranges, for the reopening of the theatre; Tales of Hoffmann at Lubeck; Engaged for 1998-99 season for Poro at the Komische Oper Berlin and for Daphne at the Deutsche Oper Berlin. Honours include: Princess Grace of Monaco Scholarship, 1983. Address: c/o Haydn Rawstron Ltd, 36 Station Road, London SE20 7BQ, England, and Konzertagentur Hans-Ulrich Schmid, Schmiedestrasse 8, D-30159 Hannover, Germany.

PILBERY Joseph, b. 30 Mar 1931, London, England. Conductor; Orchestral Administrator. m. 1970, 1 son. Education: Royal Academy of Music, with Ernest Read; Trinity College of Music, with Trevor Harvey, Peter Gellhorn and Harry Blech. Debut: Royal Albert Hall, December 1954. Career: Has given concerts in all major London Concert Halls, notably with the London Mozart Players and the Royal Philharmonic Orchestra; Has conducted all 10 Mahler Symphonies, including the Resurrection Symphony at the Festival Hall; Lectures for the University of Maryland, the Elgar Society and the London Symphony Orchestra Club; Foreign engagements in Zurich, Vienna and the Salzburg Festival, 1982; Repertoire includes Carmina Burana, Sullivan's Golden Legend and Ivanhoe, Aida, La Bohème, Die Meistersinger, The Bartered Bride, Holst's The Perfect Fool, and Tosca; Founded the Vivaldi Concertante, 1983. Recordings include: Serious music by Arthur Sullivan, Music Rara, 1975. Contributions to: Music and Musicians; Classical Music. Honours: Diploma, Services to Italian Music, 1989. Hobbies: History; Cinema. Address: Allegro 35 Laurel Avenue, Potters Bar, Herts EN6 2AB, England.

PILGRIM Shirley, b. 1957, London, England. Singer (Soprano). Education: Studied at the Royal Academy of Music with Ilse Wolf and Patricia Clark; Further study at the National Opera Studio. Career: Sang with the Glyndebourne Festival and Touring Opera choruses; Solo debut as Helena with the Touring Opera, in A Midsummer Night's Dream; Appearances in Hong Kong, 1986, and at the Buxton and Wexford Festivals; With Opera East has sung Mimi, and the Female Chorus in The Rape of Lucretia, 1991; Scottish Opera as Despina, and cover for various roles; New D'Oyly Carte Opera Carte, 1988, in Yeoman of the Guard and Iolanthe; Oratorio and concert engagements, notably at the Barbican Hall, London, and recitals including lighter American music; Sang in Born Again at the 1990 Chichester Festival; Other recent roles include: Countess in The Marriage of Figaro, Fiordiligi in Così fan tutte, Tosca in Tosca, Mimi in La Bohème. Honours: ARCM, 1979; Dip RAM, 1981. Current Management: Judith Newton, OCA. Address: 85 Chichester Road, Edmonton Green, London N9 9DH, England.

PILKOVÁ Zdenka, b. 15 June 1931, Prague, Czechoslovakia. Musicologist. m. Dr Jiří Pilka, 27 June 1951, 2 daughters. Education: Diploma, Charles University, Prague, 1955; PhD 1969; Private piano studies, 1938-53. Career: Editor in Music Department of Czechoslovak Radio Broadcasting, Prague, 1954-64; Research Worker, Musicological Institute, Czechoslovak/Czech Academy of Sciences, Prague, 1964-97; Visiting Lecturer, Charles University, Prague, 1987-88; Specializes in 18th Century Music; Lectures and Seminars at overseas universities. Publications include: Dramaticka' tvorba Jiřího Bendy (Dramatic Works of Georg Benda), 1960; Co-Author of Hudba v Českych dýjinách (Music in Czech History), 1983,

1988; Co-Author, Hudební věda (Musicology) I-II, 1988; Böhmische Musiker am Dresdner Hof 1710-1840; Various score editions as editor or co-editor including Böhmische Violinsonaten I, II 1982, 1985. Contributions to: Various music Lexica, congress reports and journals including: New Grove Dictionary of Music and Musicians; Musikforschung, Haydn Studies, Bachstudien, Zelenka-studien; Series of programmes for broadcasting. Memberships include: International Musicological society; Czech Early Music Society (Board Member); Gesellschaft für Musikforschung. Hobbies: Gardening. Address: Nám J. Machka 9, 15800 Prague 5, Czech Republic.

PILOU Jeannette, b. Jul 1931, Alexandria, Egypt. Singer (Soprano). Education: Studied with Carla Castellani in Milan. Debut: Milan in 1958 as Violetta. Career: Sang widely in Italy as Mélisande, Mimi, Liu, Susanna, Manon, Nedda, Micaela, Marguerite and Nannetta; Appearances in Barcelona, Buenos Aires, Hanover, Hamburg and Wexford; Vienna in 1965 as Mimi; With Metropolitan Opera from 1967-86 with debut as Gounod's Juliette; Covent Garden, 1971 as Madama Butterfly; Sang at Monte Carlo 1973 in the premiere of Rossellini's La Reine Morte; Other roles have included the female leads in Von Einem's Der Prozess, Gluck's Euridice, Marzeline in Fidelio and Magda in La Rondine; US appearances in Houston, Chicago, San Francisco, New Orleans and Philadelphia. Recordings include: Micaela in Carmen.

PILZ Gottfried, b. 1944, Salzburg, Austria. Stage and Costume Designer. m. Isabel Ines Glathar, 1 son. Education: Academy of Arts, Vienna, 1962-66; Assistant at the Vienna State Opera to Wieland Wagner, Luchino Visconti, Teo Otto, Luciano Damiani, Rudolf Heinrich and others, 1965-69; Assistant to Filippo Sanjust, 1969-72. Debut: Reimann's Melusine world premiere at Berlin, Edinburgh and Schwetzingen Festival, staged by Gustav Rudolf Sellner. Career: Operas, Dramatic Theatre and Ballets in Austria, Belgium, Great Britain, Netherlands, USA and Switzerland, principal in Germany; Exhibitions in Berlin, Kunsthalle Bielefeld, Düsseldorf, Kunsthalle Kiel and Wuppertal (Reflexe I-III, Aus-Grenzen I-III); Debut as a Producer with Rameau's Hippolyte et Aricie at Oper Leipzig, 1993; Collaborations with John Dew, 1979-92 (Wagner's Ring, Krefeld, 1981-85, The Unknown Repertory at Bielefeld, 1983-91, Les Huguenot's Deutsche Oper Berlin, 1987 as well as Royal Opera House, Covent Garden, 1991 and others); With Götz Friedrich (Der Rosenkavalier, Un Ballo in Maschera, Deutsche Oper Berlin, 1993) with Gunther Krämer since 1990 at Kölner Schauspiel, with Nikolaus Lehnhoff at Oper Frankfurt and Leipzig; at Munich as well as at Zürich, Henze's new version of Der Prinz von Homburg, 1992 and 1993; With Christine Mielitz, Rienzi at Komische Oper Berlin, 1992, engaged for Henze's The Bassarids at Hamburg Oper, 1994 and also for 1994 at Oper Leipzig, Moses and Aron staged by George Tabori; Designs for the premiere production of Böse's Schlachthof 5, at the 1996 Munich Festival. Address: Leipzig Opera, Augustusplatz 12, 0-7010 Leipzig, Germany.

PILZ Janos, b. 1960, Hungary. Violinist. Education: Studied at the Franz Liszt Academy of Budapest and with Sandor Devich, György Kurtag and Andras Mihaly. Career: Member of the Keller String Quartet from 1986, debut concert at Budapest, March 1987; Played Beethoven's Grosse Fuge and Schubert's Death and the Maiden Quartet at Interforum 87; Series of concerts in Budapest with Zoltan Kocsis and Deszö Ranki (piano) and Kalman Berkes (clarinet); Further appearances in Nurembourg at the Chamber Music Festival La Baule and tours of Bulgaria, Austria, Switzerland, Italy (Ateforum 88 Ferrara), Belgium and Ireland; Concerts for Hungarian Radio and Television. Recordings: Albums for Hungaroton from 1989. Honour: 2nd Prize, Evian International String Quartet Competition, May 1988. Address: c/o Artist Management International, 12/13 Richmond Buildings, Dean Street, London W1V 5AF, England.

PIMLOTT Steven (Charles), b. 18 Apr 1953, Manchester, England. Director of Opera, Theatre, Musicals. m. Daniela Bechly, 27 Jul 1991, 2 s, 1 d. Education: MA, English, Cambridge University; Studied Oboe. Career: Staff Producer, ENO, 1976; Began long working relationship with Opera North, 1978, including productions of Nabucco, The Bartered Bride and Prince Igor; Associate Director, Sheffield Crucible Theatre, 1987-88; Other opera works include: Samson and Delila, Bregenz, 1988, Carmen, Earls Court, 1989 and La Bohème, 1993; Musicals: Carousel, Royal Exchange Theatre, 1985, Carmen Jones, Sheffield Crucible, 1986, Sunday in the Park with George, National Theatre, 1990. Hobby: Playing the Oboe. Current Management: Harriet Cruickshank. Address: 97 Old South Lambeth Road, London, SW8 1XU, England.

PINI Carl, b. 2 Jan 1934, London, England. Violinist. Education: Studied with his father, cellist Anthony Pini (1902-89) and in London. Career: Former leader of the Philomusica of London, English Chamber Orchestra and Philharmonia Orchestras (1974-); Leader of the London String Quartet from 1968 and the Melbourne Symphony Orchestra from 1975; Many chamber recitals in English works and the established repertory. Address: Manygate Management, 13 Cotswold Mews, 30 Battersea Square, London, SW11 3RA, England.

PINKHAM Daniel, b. 5 June 1923, Lynn, Massachusetts, USA. Composer. Education: AB, 1943, MA, 1944, Harvard University; Private studies with Nadia Boulanger. Career: Faculty Member, New England Conservatory, 1957-; Music Director of King's Chapel, Boston, 1958-. Compositions: 4 symphonies; Concertos for trumpet, violin, organ, piano, piccolo; Theatre works and operas; Chamber music; Songs; Electronic music; Television film scores. Recordings: Christmas Cantata; Signs of the Zodiac; Symphonies 2, 3 and 4; Angels are everywhere; Serenades; Miracles; Epiphanies; Magnificat; Proverbs; Diversions; Concertante for violin and harpsichord soli, strings and celesta; Inter alia; Advent Cantata; Wedding Cantata; String Quartet; Versets; Holland Waltzes. Address: 150 Chilton Street, Cambridge, MA 02138-1227, USA.

PINNOCK Trevor (David), b. 16 Dec 1946, Canterbury, Kent, England. Musician; Conductor/Harpsichordist. Education: Canterbury Cathedral Choir School; Simon Langton Grammar School, Canterbury; Foundation Scholarship, Royal College of Music, 1966-68. Debut: London Solo Debut: Purcell Room, 1968. Career: Galliard Harpsichord Trio (with Stephen Preston, Flute; Anthony Pleeth, Cello), 1966-71; Founder/Current Musical Director, The English Concert, 1972-; Recitals throughout Europe, Canada, USA and Japan; Artistic Director and Principal Conductor of the National Arts Centre Orchestra of Canada, 1991-. Recordings: Over 70 with The English Concert including Bach: Complete Orchestral Works and Harpsichord Concerti; CPE Bach: Orchestral Works; Handel: Messiah; Purcell: Dido and Aeneas; Haydn: Nelson Mass; Handel: Concerti Grossi op 3, no 6 and Organ Concertos; Boyce: Symphonies; Haydn: Symphonies; Vivaldi: Concertos; Handel: Acis and Galatea; Purcell: King Arthur; Mozart: Complete Symphonies; Purcell: Dioclesian and Timon of Athens; Rameau: Complete Keyboard Works; Bach: Partitas, Goldberg Variations; Handel: Harpsichord Suites; Scarlatti: Sonatas. Honours: Grand Prix du Musique, Edison Pries, Deutsche Schallplattenpreis, the Gramophone Prize; CBE, 1992. Current Management and Address: c/o Ms Jan Burnett, 8 St George's Terrace, London NW1 8XJ, England.

PINSCHOF Thomas, b. 14 Feb 1948, Vienna, Austria. Musician (Flautist). Education: Artist and Teacher Diploma, Conservatorium of Vienna with Camillo Wanausek; Studies with Aurèle Nicolet; Master Classes with Karl-Heinz Zöller, Jean-Pierre Rampal, Severino Gazzelloni; Postgraduate Studies, Indiana University, USA. Debut: Wiener Musikverein, Brahms-Saal, 1965. Career: Member, Vienna Symphony Orchestra, 1971-72; Berkshire Music Festival, Tanglewood, USA (with Scholarship Boston Symphony Orchestra), 1969; Founder, ENSEMBLE I, 1971-; Artist-in-Residence, with ENSEMBLE I, Victorian College of the Arts, Melbourne, Australia, 1976; Acting Head, Woodwind Department, Lecturer in Flute and Chamber Music, Victorian College of Arts, Melbourne, until 1988; Lecturer, Canberra School of Music, Melbourne University. Recordings: Deutsche Grammophon, Adel-Cord, Philips. Publications: Music editions for various publishers including, own series, Pinschofon, with Zimmermann. Contributions to: The Flautist; Flutenotes; Musikerzeihung; Österreichishce Musikzeitschrift; Kunst und Freie Berufe. Honours: 2nd Prize, International Flute Competition, Severino Gazzelloni, 1975; Alban Berg Foundation Award, 1971; Australia Council Music Board Grantee, 1984-85 for project with Prof Nikolaus Harnoncourt. Hobbies: Flying; Tennis; Swimming; Skiing. Address: Mozart Circle, Donvale, VIC 3111, Australia.

PIRES Filipe, b. 26 June 1934, Lisbon, Portugal. Composer. m. Ligia Falcao, 29 Mar 1958. Education: Piano Superior Course, 1952; Composition Superior Course, 1953, National Conservatory, Lisbon; Piano and Composition, Hannover Music High School, 1957-60. Career: Professor of Composition, Porto National Conservatory, 1960-70; Professor of Composition, Lisbon National Conservatory, 1972-75; Music Specialist, UNESCO, Paris, 1975-79; Concert tours in Europe (Pianist and Composer); Professor of Composition, Porto High School of Music, 1993-; Artistic Director, National Orchestra, Porto, 1997-. Compositions: Figurations I - flute; Sonatine, violin and piano; Piano Trio; Figurations II, piano; Figurations III, 2 pianos; 3 Poems by Fernando Pessoa, high voice and piano; String Quartet; Ostinati, 6 percussionists. Recordings: Piano Trio; Figurations I; Figurations IV; Ostinati; Figurations III; String Quartet; Canto Ecumenico, tape music; Litania, tape music; Homo Sapiens, tape music; 20 Choral Songs; Portugaliae Genesis, baritone, mixed choir and orchestra; Sintra; Akronos; Are, Wolfsburg: Sonata, 1954. Publication: Theory of Counterpoint and Canon, 1981. Membership: Vice-President, Portuguese Authors Society. Address: R Costa Cabral, 2219-4D, 4200 Porto, Portugal.

PIRES Maria Joao, b. 23 July 1944, Lisbon, Portugal. Concert Pianist. Education: Lisbon Academy of Music with Campos Coelho; Studied composition and theory with Francine Benoit; Further study with Rosl Schmid in Munich and Karl Engel in Hanover. Career: First recital aged 4; Concerto debut in Mozart aged 7; Early concert tours of Portugal, Spain and Germany; International career from 1970, with performances in Europe, Africa and Japan; Career interrupted by ill-health; British debut, 1986, at the Elizabeth Hall, London; Canadian debut, 1986, with the Montreal Symphony conducted by Charles Dutoit; debut tour of North America, 1988, appearing with the New York Philharmonic, Houston Symphony, Toronto Symphony and the National Arts Centre Orchestra, Ottawa; Season 1988-89 with concerts in Vienna with Claudio Abbado; Munich with Carlo Maria Giulini; Carnegie Hall debut recital; Played Mozart's Concerto K271 at Symphony Hall, Birmingham, 1997; Repertoire includes Mozart, Schubert, Schumann, Beethoven and Chopin. Recordings include: Complete Mozart Piano Sonatas; Concertos by Mozart. Honours:- First Prize, Beethoven International Competition, Brussels, 1970; Edison Prize, Prix del l'Academie du Disque Français and Prix de l'Academie Charles Cros for Mozart Sonata Recordings. Current Management: Herzberger Artists. Address: 't Woud 1, 3862 PM Nijkerk, Netherlands.

PIRONKOFF Simeon (Angelov), b. 18 June 1927, Lom, Bulgaria. Composer. Education: Graduated from State Music Academy at Sofia, 1953. Career: Violinist at National Youth Theatre, Sofia, 1947-51, later working as Conductor, Bulgarian Film Studios from 1961, Vice-President of Union of Bulgarian Composers, 1980. Compositions include: Opera: Socrates' Real Apology, Monodrama, Sofia, 1967; The Good Person of Szechwan (after Brecht), Stara Zagora, 1972; The Life and Suffering of Sinful Sophronius, Oratorio, Sofia, 1977; The Motley Bird, Ruse, 1980; Oh, My Dream, Ruse, 1987; Orchestral: Symphony for Strings, 1960; Movements for Strings, 1967; Night Music, 1968; Requiem for an Unknown Young Man, 1968; A Big Game for little orchestra, 1970; Ballet Music in Memory of Igor Stravinsky, 1972; Music for Two Pianos and Orchestra, 1973; Concerto Rustico for Cello and Orchestra, 1982; Entrata and Bulgarian Folk Dance, 1983; Lyric Suite for Strings, 1983; In the Eye of the Storm for Tenor and Orchestra, 1986; Symphonic Sketch on a Popular Melody, 1986; Flute Concerto, 1987; Passaglia for Symphonic Orchestra, 1991; Chamber: 3 Trios, 1949, 1950, 1987; 3 String Quartets, 1951, 1966, 1985; Sonata for Solo Violin, 1955; Berceuse for Clarinet and Piano, 1983; Theme and Variations for Violin and Piano, 1985; Symphony for 11 Soloists, 1990; Songs of Life and Death, Poetry of Emily Dickinson for Woman's Voice and Chamber Assembly, 1988; Tree Movements for Harp Solo, 1992; Piano Music, Choruses and Songs; Bosnian Lullaby, 1993; The Green Rain for mixed choir, 1994; Four capriccios by Paganini transcribed for string ensemble; The Memory of a Piano, symphonic music for piano and orchestra; El Tango, variations for symphonic orchestra; Fantasy, on poetry of Heinrich Heine for baritone, piano and cello; The Flight of the Beetle, Rosakov, transcription for four saxophones; Film and Theatre Music. Address: Vitoscha Blvd 56, 1463 Sofia, Bulgaria.

PISCHNER Hans, b. 20 Feb 1914, Breslau, Germany. Teacher; Harpsichordist; Musicologist; Intendant; Retired. Education: Musicology studies at University of Breslau; Keyboard studies with Bronislav von Pozniac and Getrud Wertheim; Professor, 1949, PhD, 1961. Career: Head of Radio Music Department, 1950-54, Head of Music Department, 1954-56, Ministry of Culture; Representative, Ministry of Culture, 1956-62; Intendant, Deutsche Staatsoper, Berlin, 1963-89; Numerous appearances as soloist and accompanist in Europe, America and Japan, now retired. Recordings: Numerous works by Bach, both as soloist and continuo player; Bach Sonatas with David Dibrach. Publications: Music in China, 1955; Die Harmonielehre Jean-Philippe Rameaus, 1967; Premier en eines Lebens, autobiography, 1986. Contributions to: Several articles for professional journals. Honours include: Handel Prize, Halle, 1961; National Prize, 3rd class, 1961; Johannes R Becher, 1962; National Prize, 1st Class. Memberships: Chairman, Neue Bach-Gesellschaft, Leipzig. Address: Friedrichstrasse 105C, D-10117 Berlin, Germany.

PITFIELD Thomas (Baron), b. 5 Apr 1903, Bolton, Lancashire, England. Composer; Artist; Author. m. 26 Dec 1934. Education: Royal Manchester College of Music, 1924-25. Career: Engineering, 1917-24; Tettenhall College, 1935-45; RMCM, 1947-72; RNCM, 1972-73. Compositions include: Numerous compositions for Orchestra; Brass Band; Choral; Chamber Music; Piano Solos; State Works. Publications: The Poetry of Trees; No Song, No Supper (Autobiography), 1986; Recording a Region, 1987; My Words, 1988; A Song After Supper (vol 2 of autobiography); A Cotton Town Boyhood, 1991; A Wayfarers Chronical, 1991; 26 Songs British Heritage Series; Johnny Robins Nonsense Verse and Drawings; Limusics, 40 limericks with drawings. Contributions to: Musical Times; Listener; Country Life; The Countryman; The Artist. Honours: Hon Fellow (FRMCM), 1943; OUP Choral Prize, 1943; Welsh National Chamber Music Prize. Memberships: Composers Guild of Great Britain; Hon Member, the Association of Professional Composers, 1993. Hobbies: Crafts; Nature Study, especially trees and bird-song.

Address: Lesser Thomas, 21 East Downs Road, Bowdon, Altrincham, Cheshire WA14 2LG, England.

PITTMAN Richard (Harding), b. 3 June 1935, Baltimore, Maryland, USA. Conductor. m. 10 Sept 1965, 1 son. Education: BMus, Peabody Conservatory, 1957; Private study in conducting with Laszlo Halasz, NY, 1960-63, Sergiu Celibidache, Accademia Musicale Chigiana, Siena, Italy, 1962, W Brueckner Ruggeberg, Hamburg, 1963-65 and Pierre Boulez, Basel, Switzerland, 1970. Career includes: Instructor, of Conducting and Opera, Eastman School of Music, 1965-68; Teacher of Orchestral Conducting and Orchestra Conductor, New England Conservatory, 1968-85; Music Director, Conductor, Concord Orchestra, 1969-; Music Director of Boston Musica Viva, 1969-; Guest Conductor of National Symphony, Washington DC, BBC Symphony, London, BBC Philharmonic, BBC Scottish Symphony, BBC Welsh Symphony, London Sinfonietta, Frankfurt Radio Symphony, Germany, Hamburg Symphony, BBC Concert Orchestra, Virginia Philharmonic, Norfolk, Chattanooga Symphony, Tennessee, American Repertory Theatre, Cambridge, Massachusetts, Hartford Chamber Orchestra, Connecticut, Boston Lyric Opera, Tulsa Opera, Opera Omaha, Huntingdon Theatre Company, Boston, City of London Symphonia, Ulster Orchestra, Belfast, Nebraska Chamber Orchestra, Lincoln, Dutch Ballet Orchestra, Amsterdam, and Kirov Opera Orchestra, St Petersburg, Russia; Additional Guest Conductor, Banff Arts Festival, Canada; BBC Singers; American Repertory Theatre, Cambridge, Massachusetts; Currently, Music Director, New England Philharmonic, Boston, 1997-. Recordings: Music by Ives, Berio, Davidovsky, Harris, Schwantner, Henry Brant, Wilson, Lieberson, Rands, Ellen Taaffe Zwilich, Shifrin, Musgrave, Crawford and Seeger; William Kraft; John Thow; Ronald Perera; John Harbison; Ezra Sims. Honours: Laurel Leaf Award from American Composers Alliance, New York, 1989; Peabody Conservatory Distinguished Alumni Award, 1996. Current Management: Helen Sykes Artists Management. Address: 41 Bothfeld Road, Newton Center, MA 02159, USA.

PITTMAN-JENNINGS David, b. 1949, Oklahoma, USA. Baritone. Career: Studied in America. Career: Sang Lensky at Graz Opera in 1977 and was engaged at Bremen, 1981-85; Sang at Paris Opéra, 1982-83, as Don Fernando in Fidelio and Schaunard in La Bohème; Sang Germont at Tel-Aviv in 1988, and Wozzeck at Reggio Emilia in 1989; Member of the Karlsruhe Opera from 1990 singing Amfortas in Parsifal at Strasbourg in 1991; Season 1992 in Dallapiccola's Il Prigioniero, and as Mandryka in Arabella at the Vienna Staatsoper; Other roles have included Guglielmo, the Count in Capriccio, Mozart's Count and Figaro, Lescaut, Chorèbe in Les Troyens, Marcello and Gluck's Orestes; Sang in Schoeck's Venus at Geneva, 1997; Concerts include Beethoven's Ninth, Elijah, Ein Deutsches Requiem and L'Enfance du Christ. Address: c/o Staatstheater Karlsruhe, Baumeisterstrasse 11, Pf 1449, W-7500 Karlsruhe, Germany.

PIZARRO Artur, b. 1968, Lisbon, Portugal. Concert Pianist. Education: Studied with Sequeira Costa in Lisbon and at the University of Kansas; National Conservatory of Music in Lisbon. Career: Numerous concert performances in Europe from 1987; London debut 1989, at the Wigmore Hall, followed by concerts with the London Mozart Players at the Elizabeth Hall; Has also played with the RAI-Torino Symphony, the Gulbenkian Orchestra and the Moscow Philharmonic; Rachmaninov's 3rd Concerto with the City of Birmingham Symphony in Leeds and the BBC Symphony under Andrew Davis in London, 1990; Further engagements with the London Symphony (de Burgos), Royal Liverpool Philharmonic (Pesek), Los Angeles Philharmonic at Hollywood Bowl, English Chamber Orchestra, City of London Sinfonia, Hallé and BBC Symphony (Proms 1991); Recitals in Britain, Japan, Australia and the USA; Played the Ravel Concerto in G at the 1991 Promenade Concerts, London; Recital in International Piano Series at South Bank, 1997. Honours: Winner 1987 International Vianna de Motta Competition, Lisbon; Greater Palm Beach Symphony Invitational Piano Competition, Florida, 1988; First Prize, 1990 Harvey Leeds International Pianoforte Competition. Address: Harrison/Parrott Limited, 12 Penzance Place, London W11 4PA, England.

PIZER Elizabeth (Faw Hayden), b. 1 Sept 1954, Watertown, New York, USA. Composer; Musician. m. Charles Ronald Pizer, 10 July 1974. Education: High School Diploma, New York State Regents Diploma, Watertown High School, 1972; Boston Conservatory of Music, Boston, Massachusetts, 1972-75. Career: Numerous major concert performances of her compositions internationally including, San Jose State University Symphonic Band, 1979; Members of Honolulu Symphony Orchestra, String Quartet, 1980; Lincoln Centre, New York, Charleston, South Carolina; Jacksonville, Florida, Donne in Musica Festival, Rome, 1982; San Francisco Chamber Singers, Nevada City, San Francisco, Berkeley and Ross, California, 1982; Piccolo Spoleto Festival, 1983; University of Michigan, 1983; Mexico City, 1984; Heidelberg, West Germany, 1985; Oakland, California, 1986; Many major broadcasts of compositions, throughout the USA, 1979-86 and a live concert broadcast including pre-recorded material in Australia, 1986. Compositions: Expressions Intimes, for Solo Piano, 1975, recorded by pianist Max Lifchitz, 1992; Quilisoly, for Flute and Piano, or Violin and Piano, 1976; Look down, Fair Moon, for Voice and Piano, 1976; Elegy, (formerly known at Interfuguelude) for String Orchestra, or String Quartet or Wind Quartet, 1977; Fanfare Overture, Symphonic Band, 1977-79; Five Haiku, for Soprano and Chamber Ensemble, 1978; Five Haiku II, for Mezzo-Soprano and Piano, 1979; Madrigals Anon, A Capella Choir, 1979; Sunken Flutes, Electronic Tape, 1979; String Quartet, 1981; Lyric Fancies, Solo Piano, 1983; Kyrie Eleison, A Capella Chorus, 1983; Strains and Restraints, solo piano, 1984, recorded by Max Lifchitz, 1992; Nightsongs, voice and piano, 1986; Arlington, electronic tape, 1989; Embryonic Climactus, electronic tape, 1989; Aquasphere, electronic tape, 1990; Elegy in Amber (In Memoriam Leonard Bernstein) string orchestra, 1993, recorded by the Slovak Radio Symphony Orchestra conducted by Robert Stankovsky, 1996. Address: 19458 Southshore Road, Point Peninsula, Three Mile Bay, New York, NY 13693, USA.

PIZZI Pier Luigi, b. 15 June 1930, Milan, Italy. State Director and Designer. Education: Studied architecture at Milan Polytechnic. Debut: Designed Don Giovanni at Genoa, 1952. Career: Designs and productions for such Baroque operas as Handel's Ariodante, La Scala, 1982, and Rinaldo (seen at Reggio Emilia, Paris, Madrid and Lisbon); Rameau's Hippolyte et Aricie and Castor et Pollux, Aix-en-Provence, 1983, 1991; Gluck's Alceste for La Scala, 1987; Other work has included Les Troyens, to open the Opera Bastille at Paris in 1990, followed by Samson et Dalila, 1991; I Capuleti e i Montecchi at Covent Garden, 1984, Don Carlos at Vienna, 1989; La Traviata seen at Monte Carlo, Venice and Lausanne; Rossini productions at Pesaro include Otello and Tancredi, 1991; Staged Gluck's Armide at La Scala to open the 1996-97 season; Rossini, Guillaume Tell, Rossini Opera Festival, 1995; Gluck Armide opening season, Scala de Milano, 1996; Verdi, Macbeth, Arena di Verona, 1997. Honour: Legion d'Honneur. Address: c/o Opera de Monte Carlo, 98000 Principaute de Monaco.

PLA GARRIGOS Adolf, b. 4 Oct 1960, Sabadell, Spain. Musician; Pianist. m. Roser Farriol. Education: Superior Diploma, Public Conservatoire of Barcelona, 1984; Postgraduate, Franz Liszt Academy, Budapest, 1988; Meisterklassen Diploma, Würzburg, Germany, 1992. Career: Invited to the International Festivals of Barcelona, Madrid, Havana and St Petersburg, also at Pau Casals Festival in Spain, El Salvador and Prades, France; Appeared in concerts in Italy, Germany and Hungary and on Spanish National Radio, Russian National Radio and Catalan TV. Recording: CD of music by Schumann, Granados and Ravel as soloist, Ma De Guido, 1995. Honours: Scholarships from Barcelona University, Sofia Puche Foundation and Valencia Diputacion and Robert Wagner Foundation; First Prize, Young Pianist Performance of Catalonia, 1984; First Prize, Civtat de Manresa, International Competition. Memberships: Director of Professional Conservatoire of Sabadell, 1989-93, 1996-97; Council Member, Catalan Association of Performance, 1994-. Current Management: Felip Pedrell. Address: c/o Felip Pedrell 24, E 08208 Sabadell, Spain.

PLACIDI Tommaso, b. 29 March 1964, Rome, Italy. Conductor. Education: Geneva Conservatory; Vienna Academy of Music; Academia Musicale Chigiana, Siena, Italy. Appointments: Assistant Conductor, London Symphony Orchestra; Guest conductor, in Europe, of the London Symphony Orchestra, Orchestre National du Capitole de Toulouse, Orchestre Philharmonique de Strasbourg, Orchestre Philharmonique des Pays de Loire, Orchestre de la Suisse Rohande, Orchestre de Chambre de Lausanne, Wiener Kammerorchester, Orchestra Sinfonica RAI, Turin, Orchestra del Teatro Regio, Turin, Orchestra della Toscana, Florence, Orchestre Sinfonica Haydn Bolzano, Trento, Orchestra of Bratislava Opera House, Philharmonisches Staatorchester Halle. Recordings: Tchaikovsky's Violin Concerto, Piano Concerto No 1; Weber's Clarinet Concertos, Münchner Rundfunkorchester, Germany, 1997. Honours: 1st Prize, Besançon Conducting Competition, 1992; 1st Prize, Donatella Flick Conducting Competition, London, 1966. Current Management: CAMI, New York. Address: 5 Chemin Taverney, 1218 Geneva, Switzerland.

PLAGGE Wolfgang (Antoine Marie), b. 23 Aug 1960, Oslo, Norway. Composer; Pianist. m. Lena Rist-Larsen, 25 June 1993. Education: Began Piano, age 5; Piano with Robert Riefling and Jens Harald Bratlie, Norway, Composition with Oistein Sommerfeldt and Johan Kvandal; Piano with Evgenij Koroliev, Composition with Werner Krützfeld, Musikhochschule, Hamburg, graduated 1983. Debut: Pianist, Oslo, 1972. Career: 1st published work at age 12; Commissions. Compositions include: Music for 2 Pianos, 1982-89; Piano Sonata V, 1985-86, VI, 1988-91; Vesaas-Sange: Baryton og Piano, 1989-90; A Litany for the 21st Century: Sonata for Horn and Piano, 1989; Festival Music, symphonic band, 1989, 1994 Version, symphonic orchestra; Concerto: Horn and Orchestra, 1990; Canzona: Brass Quintet and Pianoforte, 1990; Concerto: Violin and Orchestra, 1991; Concerto: 2 Pianos and Orchestra, 1991; Solarljod: Solsanger fra Norron Middelalder, 1992; Sonata II, Bassoon and Pianoforte, 1993; Hogge i Stein, A Portrait of Trondenes Church and Her People, narrator, choir, 3 soli, orchestra, 1994; Concerto for Trumpet and Orchestra, 1994. Recordings: Canzona, Wolfgang Plagge, piano, and Arctic Brass; Bassoon sonata, Robert Rønnes, bassoon, Eva Knardahl, piano; Concerto for Horn and Orchestra, Froydis Reed Wekre, horn, Trondheim Symphony Orchestra, conductor Ole Kristian Ruud; Contemporary Music for Brass: Canzona, Wolfgang Plagge, piano, and Arctic Brass; Eivind Groven; Piano Concerto, Wolfgang Plagge, piano, Trondheim Symphony Orchestra, conductor Ole Kristian Ruud. Honours: Winner, Young Pianists National Championship, 1971; National and international piano prizes; Forsberg's Music Prize, 1979; Composer of the Year, Norway, 1995. Memberships: Norwegian Composers' Association; Guild of Performing Artists. Hobbies: Astronomy; Geology. Current Management: Ad Libitum, Oslo, Norway, Address: Seljefloyten 39, N-1346 Gjettum, Norway.

PLAISTOW Stephen, b 24 Jan 1937, Welwyn Garden City, England. Pianist; Critic; Broadcaster. Education: ARCM, Clare College, Cambridge. Career: Freelance Journalist from 1961; BBC Music Producer, 1962-74; Chairman British Section of ISCM and Music Section of ICA, 1967-71; Member, Music Panel, Arts Council of Great Britain, 1972-79; Chief Assistant to Controller of Music, BBC, 1974-79; Chairman, British section of ISCM and Arts Council Contemporary Music Network, 1976-79; Editor, Contemporary Music, BBC, 1979-92; Deputy Head of Radio 3 Music Department, BBC, 1989-92. Contributions to: The Gramophone; Guardian; Musical Times; Tempo. Address: 5 Gloucester Court, 33 Gloucester Avenue, London NW1 7TJ, England.

PLANCHART Alejandro (Enrique), b. 29 Jul 1935, Caracas, Venezuela. Music Historian; Composer. Divorced, 1 daughter. Education: MusB, 1958, MusM, 1960, Yale University School of Music; PhD, Harvard University, 1971. Career: Freelance Arranger, Composer, New York and New Haven, 1960-64; Instructor/Assistance Professor, Yale, 1967-75; Associate Professor, University of Victoria, 1975-76; Associate Professor, University of California at Santa Barbara, 1976-; Visiting Professor, Brandeis, 1982-83. Compositions: Divertimento for Percussion Trio; Five Poems of James Joyce for Soprano and Piano. Recordings: 20 recordings of medieval and renaissance music with the Cappella Cordina, Lyrichord and Musical Heritage Society. Publications: The Repertory of Tropes at Winchester, 2 volumes, Princeton, 1977; Beneventanum Troporum Corpus, with John Boe co-editor, 10 volumes in press. Contributions to: Guillaume Dufay's Masses: Notes and Revisions, in Musical Quarterly, 1972; Fifteenth-Century, Masses: Notes on Chronology and Performance, in Study Musicali 10, 1983; About 50 other titles. Address: 1070 Via Regina, Santa Barbara, CA 93111, USA.

PLASSON Michel, b. 2 Oct 1933, Paris, France. Conductor. Education: Studied at the Paris Conservatoire and in the USA with Leinsdorf, Monteux and Stokowski. Career: Musical Director in Metz, 1966-68; Director of the Orchestra and of the Théâtre du Capitole in Toulouse, 1968-83; Operatic performances in Toulouse include Salome, Aida, Die Meistersinger, Faust, Parsifal, Carmen and Montségur by Landowski (world premiere, 1985); Conductor of the Orchestre National du Capitole de Toulouse from 1983; At the Palais Omnisport de Paris-Bercy has conducted Aida, Turandot, the Verdi Requiem and Nabucco, 1984-87; Guest engagements with the Berlin Philharmonic Orchestra, London Philharmonic, Orchestre of the Suisse Romande, and the Gewandhaus Orchestra Leipzig; Paris Opéra, Geneva Opera, State Operas of Vienna, Hamburg and Munich, Zurich Opera, Covent Garden, Metropolitan Opera, Chicago and San Francisco; Principal Guest Conductor of the Zurich Tonhalle Orchestra from 1987; Conducted new production of Guillaume Tell at Covent Garden, 1990; Il Trovatore at the Halle aux Grains, Toulouse, 1990; Faust at the 1990 Orange Festival; Returned to Covent Garden, 1991, Tosca; Season 1991-92 with Lucia di Lammermoor at Munich, Guillaume Tell at Covent Garden, Don Quichotte at Toulouse and Carmen at Orange; Conducted La Forza del Destino at Orange, 1996. Recordings include: La Vie Parisienne; La Grande Duchesse de Gérolstein; Chausson's Symphony; Saint-Saëns Piano Concertos; Premiere pressings of Roussel's Padmâvati, Magnard's Symphonies and Guercoeur, Symphonic poems by Chausson; Les Pêcheurs de Perles; Faust. Address: c/o SA Gorlinsky Ltd, 33 Dover Street, London W1X 4NJ, England.

PLATT Ian, b. 1959, Fleetwood, England. Singer (Baritone). Education: Studied with John Cameron at Royal Northern College of Music. Career: Sang Rossini's Figaro, Guglielmo, Papageno and Junius in The Rape of Lucretia for Royal Northern College of Music; Professional debut for Kent Opera, in La Traviata and Il Barbiere di Siviglia; Engagements with Opera 80 as Don Magnifico in La Cenerentola and Baron Zeta in The Merry Widow; New Sadler's Wells Opera as Agamemnon in La Belle Helene; Sang Tom in Henze's The English Cat at Hebbel Theatre, Berlin and toured with Travelling Opera as Schaunard and Mozart's Figaro; Welsh National Opera and Scottish Opera, 1991, in La Traviata; Alcindoro in La Bohème for Glyndebourne Touring Opera, 1991; Pirate King, D'Oyly Carte, 1993; Don Magnifico, Welsh National Opera, 1993-94. Recordings include: Il Crociato in Egitto by Meyerbeer, Opera Rara. Address: Robert Gilder & Co, 59-65 Upper Ground, London, SE1 9PQ, England.

PLATT Norman, b. 29 Aug 1920, Bury, Lancashire, England. Singer; Opera Director. m. (1) Diana Franklin Clay, 1942, 1 son, 1 daughter, (2) Johanna Sigrid Bishop, 1963, 1 son, 2 daughters. Education: BA, King's College, Cambridge, 1939-41; Studied Singing with Elena Gerhardt and Lucy Manen. Career: Principal, Sadler's Wells, 1945-47; English Opera Group, 1948; Vicar Choral, St Paul's Cathedral, London, 1948-52; Freelance Recitalist, Actor, Opera Singer and Broadcaster in UK and Europe; Member of Deller Consort, 1950-64; Visiting Instructor in Vocal Studies, Morley College, Goldsmiths' College and Royal School of Church Music, London, 1956-76; Founder, Director and Principal Producer, Kent Opera, 1969-89, refounded, 1992, productions there include The Return of Ulysses, The Marriage of Figaro, Iphigenia in Tauride, Agrippina, Dido and Aeneas, and Peter Grimes; Toured with Britten's Prodigal Son, 1995; Triple Bill of Britten's Church Operas, 1997; Director of first Acting in Opera course, 1989. Recordings: For 2 labels. Publications: Translations of songs and operas including Don Giovanni, Fidelio and The Coronation of Poppea. Contributions to: Numerous articles on music to various publications. Honours: OBE, 1985; Honorary Doctorate, University of Kent, Canterbury, 1980. Address: Pembles Cross, Egerton, Ashford, Kent, England.

PLATT Richard (Swaby), b. 14 May 1928, London, England. Musicologist. m. (1) 2 sons, 1 daughter, (2) Diane Ibbotson, 3 Dec 1977, 1 son, 1 daughter. Education: Associate, Royal College of Art, 1953; Studied privately with Walter Bergmann, 1965-, Hugh Wood, 1966-68. Career: Painter, Printmaker, exhibiting at Royal Academy, London Group and others, 1953-61; One man show of works, Leicester Galleries, 1956; Musicologist, specialising in 18th Century English Music, 1969. Editions, William Boyce, 12 Overtures; Thomas Arne, 4 Symphonies; Works by Croft, Roseingrave, Mudge, Fisher; Semele by John Eccles; Gli Equivoci, by Stephen Storace; Peleus and Thetis by William Boyce. Recordings: Editions of music Boyce (Solomon), Arne and Roseingrave. Publications: Contributor of chapters, New Grove, 1980 and Grove Opera 1992; Theatre Music 1700-1760 in Blackwell's History of Music in Britain volume 4; The Symphony, 1720-1840, 1983; Eccles, Judgement of Paris, 1984. Contributions to: BIOS 17, on Gerard Smith Organ Contract. Memberships: Royal Musical Association. Address: 3 Stratton Place, Falmouth, Cornwall TR11 2ST, England.

PLATT Theodore, b. 8 Sept 1937, Moscow, Russia. Conductor; Composer; Double Bassist; Harpsichordist. Education: Degree in Double Bass Performance, Composition and Music Education, Ippolitov-Ivanov Conservatory of Music, 1956; Doctorate, Moscow Conservatory of Music, 1962. Career: Founder and Director, 4 chamber ensembles including first baroque and classical ensembles in USSR (Moscow), 1968-81, and New York Concertino Ensemble, 1981; Live concerts on major classical music radio stations in US; 8 years as Double Bass Soloist of Moscow Chamber Orchestra under Rudolf Barshay (performance with Gilels, Menuhin, Oistrakh, Rostropoivch, others); Discovered and premiered lost baroque works; Teacher and Coach of String Instruments and Voice. Compositions: 2 Symphony Concertos; Cycles of Vocal Compositions; 1 Quartet. Recordings: Baroque, Romantic and modern works as Double Bass Soloist of Moscow Chamber Orchestra under Rudolf Barshay; Baroque-Early Romantic repertoire (Mozart, Boccherini, Bach, Schubert, others) as Music Director and Soloist with New York Concertino Ensemble. Memberships: Conductors Guild; College Music Society. Hobbies: Film; Current Events; Cooking. Current Management: Ishikawa Foundation. Address: Sai Wai-Cho 5-7, Kanazawa-shi, Ishikawa-ken, 920-0968 Japan.

PLATZ Robert H P, b. 16 Aug 1951, Baden-Baden, Germany. Composer; Conductor. Education: Studies with Wolfgang Fortner, Karlheinz Stockhausen, Francis Travis; IRCAM computer workshop for Composers. Career: Founded new music group Ensemble Köln, 1980; Own concert series with Ensemble Köln, 1982; Appeared in new music festivals such as Musik der Zeit WDR and Musica Viva series of Munich, Donaueschingen and La Rochelle; Performed at Salzburg Festival, Metz; All works recorded by Radio Stations in Germany. Compositions: Schwelle, Full Orchestra and Tape; Chlebnicov, Ensemble and Tape; Maro & Stille, Soprano, Violin and Piano Solos, plus Ensembles and Choirs; Raumform, Clarinet Solo; Flotenstücke - 7 Pieces for Flute and Ensemble; Requiem for Tape; Pianoforte 2; Closed Loop, Guitar; Verkommenes ufer, opera (texts Heiner Müller); Quartett (Zeitstrahl) for String Quartet, 1986. Publications: Musikalische Prozesse, 1979; Uber Schwelle, 1980; Uber Schwelle II, 1981; Uber Tasten, 1983; Versuch einer Asthetik des Kleinen, 1984; Blumroder, Nicht Einfach, Aber Neu, 1980; Formpolyphone Musik, 1981; Stegen: Robert HP Platz, 1982; Van den Hoogen: Komplizierte Horbarkeit, 1982; Blumröder: Maro, 1984; Van den Hoogen: Raumform, 1984; Allende-Blin: Uber Chielnicov, 1984; Record Maro, Irvine Arditi, Violin.

PLAVIN Zecharia, b. 7 June 1956, Vilnius (Vilna), Lithuania. Pianist. m. 12 June 1984, 1 son, 1 daughter. Education: BMus, MMus, Ciurlionis School of Arts, S Rubin Academy of Music, University of Tel Aviv, Israel. Career: Concerts with Israel Philharmonic Orchestra, Jerusalem Symphony Orchestra, Symphonietta of Beer-Sheva, Haifa Symphony Orchestra, others; Recitals on all major stages in Israel; Concerts in Western Europe from 1988; Numerous recordings for Israel Broadcasting Authorities; Work for Israel Concert Bureau Omanuth Laam. Recordings: Various. Publication: The Metamorphoses by O Partos. Honours: 1st Prize, S Rubin Academy of Music Competition, 1978; National François Shapira Prize, 1980; Diploma, Israel Broadcasting Competition, 1985. Current Management: International Music Consultants.

PLAZAS Mary, b. 9 Sept 1966, Wallingford, England. Singer (Soprano). Education: Studied at Royal Northern College of Music with Ava June and at National Opera Studio. Career: Solo recitals at Wigmore Hall, Purcell Room, Birmingham Town Hall and Royal Exchange Theatre, Manchester; Concerts at Cheltenham and Aldeburgh Festivals; Opera engagements include Poulenc's La Voix Humaine at Aix-en-Provence, Nannetta at Aldeburgh and Despina for Mid-Wales Opera; English National Opera debut, 1992, as Heavenly Voice in Don Carlos; Opera North, 1992-, as the Gypsy in UK premiere of Gerhard's The Duenna, Barbarina and Susanna in Figaro and Tebaldo in Don Carlos; Sang in Opera Factory's Nozze di Figaro for Channel 4 Television and appeared as Echo in Ariadne auf Naxos for Garsington Opera; Joined English National Opera as Company Principal, Aug 1995 and sang Echo in Ariadne auf Naxos, 1997. Honours include: Winner, Kathleen Ferrier Memorial Scholarship, 1991. Address: c/o Owen-White Management, 14 Nightingale Lane, London N8 7QU, England.

PLEASANTS Henry, b. 12 May 1910, Wayne, Pennsylvania, USA. Writer on Music. Education: Philadelphia Musical Academy; Curtis Institute of Music. Career: Music Critic, Philadelphia Evening Bulletin, 1930-42; Central European Music Correspondent for New York Times, 1945-55; London Music Critic for International Herald Tribune, Paris, 1967; London Editor for Stereo Review, New York, 1967-; Guest Lecturer at numerous institutions in USA and UK; Participant in musical TV and radio programmes for BBC and in USA, Canada and Europe. Publications: The Agony of Modern Music, 1955; Death of a Music, 1961; The Great Singers, 1966; Serious Music - and All That Jazz!, 1969; The Great American Popular Singers, 1974; Opera in Crisis, 1989; Translator and editor: Vienna's Golden Years of Music (Eduard Hanslick), 1950; The Musical Journeys of Louis Spohr, 1961; The Musical World of Robert Schumann, 1965; The Music Criticism of Hugo Wolf, 1979; Piano and Song (Friedrich Wieck), 1988. Contributions to: Major US and UK music magazines; Encyclopaedia Britannica; New Grove Dictionary of Music and Musicians, 1980. Address: Roebuck House, London SW1E 5BE, England.

PLECH Linda, b. 1951, Vienna, Austria. Singer (Soprano). Education: Studied in Vienna and at Salzburg Mozarteum. Career: Sang as Mezzo at Klagenfurt Opera, 1976-77; Oldenburg, 1980-84; Soprano roles at Kaiserslautern, 1985-86, Hamburg Staatsoper, 1987-88 as Donna Anna and Elisabeth de Valois; Cologne, 1989, as Jenufa, Bregenz Festival, 1988-89, as Senta in fliegende Holländer; Sang the Trovatore Leonore at Deutsche Oper Berlin, 1989, Ariadne auf Naxos at Antwerp; Season 1991-92 as Senta at Geneva, Elisabeth in Tannhäuser at Barcelona; Other roles include Marenka in The Bartered Bride and Giulietta in Les Contes d'Hoffmann. Address: c/o Grand Théâtre de Genève, 11 Boulevard du Theatre, CH-1211 Geneva, Switzerland.

PLEETH William, b. 12 Jan 1916, London, England. Cellist; Professor. m. Margaret Good, 1 son, 1 daughter. Education: London Academy; London Cello School; Leipzig Conservatory with Julius Klengel. Debut: Leipzig, 1932. Career: Played at Grotrian Hall, London, 1933; Performances on BBC TV and Radio; Concerts in London, UK, Netherlands, Germany, France, Italy, Australia and New Zealand; Sonatas with Margaret Good; Member of Blech Quartet, 1936-41, Allegri Quartet, 1952-67; Additional cellist for Amadeus and other string quartets; Professor of Cello at the Guildhall School of Music, London, 1948-78; Anthony Pleeth and Jacqueline de Pré were among his pupils. Recordings: Cello and piano sonatas by Brahms, Grieg and Mendelssohn; Schubert's String Quintet; Messiaen's Quatuor pour la fin du temps; Brahms Sextets. Honours: OBE, 1989. Publications: Cello, Menuhin Series, 1982, now published in many languages. Memberships: Incorporated Society of Musicians; ESTA. Hobbies: Gardening; Collecting Early English furniture. Address: 19 Holly Park, London N3 3JB, England.

PLESHAK Victor (Vasilievich), b. 13 Nov 1946, Leningrad, Russia. Composer. 2 sons. Education: Choral College of Chapel; Choir Conductors Department, St Petersburg Conservatoire (with B Tischenko). Debut: Many-coloured Balls, song cycle for children, verses by Akimya, Leningrad Radio. Compositions: Over 17 musicals and operas including: The Red Imp, musical, 1980; The Knight's Passions, 1981; The Glass Menagerie, opera, 1987; A Tale of a Blot, New Year operetta, 1988; Caution Baba-Yaga, ecological opera; Inspector, an opera after Gogol, 1993; Choral Cycle, About Friendship, Love and Brotherhood, to verses by R Burns, 1983; Over 100 published songs including: V Pleshak, Songs for voice and piano (guitar, accordion), in Soviet Composer, 1988. Recordings: The Tale of a Dead Tsarevna and Seven Epic Heroes, opera in 2 acts; The Wodow of Valencia, musical after the play by Lope de Vega; Oh These Pretty Sinners, musical farces after Lasage and Rabelais; The Booted Cat, musical after the play by Pierrot. Honours: All-Union Competition of Songs for Students Choir, 1972; Winner, Leninsky Komsomol Prize, All-Union Songs Competition, All-World Festival of Youth and Students, 1985. Memberships: Composers Union of St Petersburg. Hobby: Football. Address: Gorokhovaya St (formerly Dzerzhinskaya) 53 kv 29, 190031 St Petersburg, Russia.

PLETNEV Mikhail, b. 1957, Russia. Concert Pianist; Conductor; Composer. Career: Performs throughout Russia, Europe, Japan and the USA with the world's leading orchestras; Season 1993-94 included recitals in London, Berlin, Paris, Milan, Zurich, Munich and others; Founded Russian National Orchestra in 1990 and now tours with them as conductor in Europe, Japan, North and South America; Also conducts Philharmonia Orchestra, Deutsche Kammerphilharmonie, Norddeutsche Rundfunk Symphony Orchestra, London Symphony Orchestra; With RNO represented Russia in the Cultural Olympiad of the centennial Olympic Games in Atlanta and performed at the London BBC Proms and the Edinburgh Festival; Continues to tour as a pianist and gives concerts abroad and in Russia; Has performed with Haitink, Maazel, Chailly, Tennstedt, Sanderling, Blomstedt, Järvi, Thielemann and the Berlin Philharmonic, the Bayerische Rundfunk Symphony, Philharmonia, London Symphony, Orchestre National de France, Israel Philharmonic, San Francisco Symphony and Pittsburgh Symphony; Played with the Russian National Orchestra at the Festival Hall, London, 1997. Recordings include: As Pianist: Rachmaninov's 1st Concerto and Paganini Rhapsody, works by Hadyn, Beethoven, Chopin, Tchaikovsky, Mussorgsky, Scarlatti (Scarlatti sonatas Instrumental Category of 1996 Gramophone Awards) and clarinet sonatas with Michael Collins; Tchaikovsky's 6th Symphony as conductor with Russian National Orchestra (voted runner-up in orchestral category of 1992 Gramophone Awards). Honours: Gold Medal, Tchaikovsky International Piano Competition, Moscow, 1978. Address: c/o Columbia Artists Management Ltd, 28 Cheverton Road, London, N19 3AY, England.

PLISHKA Paul, b. 28 Aug 1941, Old Forge, Pennsylvania, USA. Singer (Bass). Education: Studied at Montclair State College and with Armen Boyazjian. Debut: Paterson Lyric Opera, 1961. Career: Metropolitan Opera from 1967, as King Marke in Tristan, Procida in Les vêpres Siciliennes, Varlaam and Pimen in Boris Godunov, Oroveso in Norman, Leporello and the Commendatore in Don Giovanni, Banquo in the Peter Hall production of Macbeth, and Philip II in Don Carlos; La Scala, 1974, in La Damnation de Faust; San Francisco, 1984, as Silva in Ernani; Teatro Liceo Barcelona, 1985; Orange Festival, 1987, as Phanüel in Massenet's Hérodiade; Sang Daland in Der fliegende Holländer at the Metropolitan, 1989; Procida at Carnegie Hall, 1990; Opera Company of Philadelphia, 1990, as the Mayor in La Gazza Ladra, Fiesco in Simon Boccanegra at the Metropolitan; Grand Park concerts Chicago, in Prince Igor; Season 1991-92 as Giorgio in Puritani at Chicago, the Pope in Benvenuto Cellini at Geneva and Zaccaria at Montreal; Sang Mozart's Bartolo at the Met, 1997. Recordings: Crespel in Les Contes d'Hoffmann and Henry VIII in Anna Bolena; Norma; Le Cid and Donizetti's Gemma di Vergy; Faust; Wurm in Luisa Miller. Address: c/o Ingpen and Williams Limited, 26 Wadham Road,London SW15 2LR, England.

PLOWRIGHT Jonathan, b. 24 Sept 1959, Doncaster, South Yorkshire, England. Concert Pianist. m. Diane Shaw, 18 Aug 1990. Education; Birmingham University, 1978-79; Royal Academy of Music, London, 1979-83; Peabody Conservatory, Baltimore, 1983-84. Debut: Carnegie Recital Hall, New York, 1984; Purcell Room, South Bank, 1985. Career: World Premiere performance: Constant Lambert Piano Concerto, St Johns Smith Square, 1988; Royal Concert for HRH Princess Alexandra, St James' Palace, 1988; Royal Concert for the Sultan of Oman, 1990; Soloist with the Halle, the Royal Philharmonic Orchestra, the English Chamber Orchestra and the BBC Concert Orchestra; Performed for conductors Colin Davis, Neville Marriner, Owain Arwell Hughes, Paul Daniel and Martin Brabbins; Numerous South Bank and Wigmore Hall recitals; Numerous BBC broadcasts; major UK festivals: Edinburgh, European Arts Festival, Covent Garden International, City of London, Brighton and Chichester; Chamber music with the Scottish Ensemble,

Guildhall String Ensemble, the Coull Quartet and own group Capital Virtuosi; Appearances abroad in Majorca, France, Portugal, Spain, South America, Ireland, Australia, Norway, Luxembourg, Germany, Austria, Belgium, South Africa, Canada, Singapore and Holland. Recordings: Brahms, solo piano; East European Recital; Capital Virtuosi Ensemble; Chopin, solo piano. Honours: McFarren Gold Medal, Recital Diploma, RAM, 1983; Fulbright Scholarship, 1983; Commonwealth Musician of the Year, 1983; Winner, European Piano Competition, 1989; Associate, Royal Academy of Music, 1990. Current Management: Mayer Artist Management, Vienna. Address: 281 Eastern Road, Brighton, BN2 5TA, England.

PLOWRIGHT Rosalind (Anne), b. 21 May 1949, Worksop, England. Soprano. Education: LRAM, Royal Northern College of Music, Manchester. Debut: As Page in Salome, English National Opera, 1975. Career includes: Miss Jessell, Turn of the Screw, ENO, 1979; Debut, Covent Garden as Ortlinde, Die Walküre, 1980; With Bern Opera, 1980-81, Frankfurt Opera and Munich Opera, 1981; US debuts, Philadelphia, San Diego, also Paris, Madrid, Hamburg, 1982; La Scala, Milan, Edinburgh Festival, San Francisco, New York, 1983; With Deutsche Opera, Berlin, 1984; Houston, Pittsburgh, Verona, 1985; Teatro Communale, Florence, 1986; Tulsa, Lyon, Buenos Aires, Israel, 1987; Lausanne, Geneva, Bonn, 1988; Copenhagen, Lisbon, 1989; Sang Wagner's Senta at Covent Garden, 1986; Gluck's Alceste at La Scala, Milan, 1987 (followed by Desdemona in London); Season 1988 as Médée in Lausanne, Elisabeth de Valois in Geneva and Norma in Bonn; 1988-89 as Médée and the Trovatore Leonora at Covent Garden; Vienna Staatsoper debut 1990 as Amelia (Un Ballo in Maschera); Season 1990-91 as Lady Macbeth in Frankfurt and Israel, Desdemona in Munich and Tchaikovsky's Tatyana at Pittsburgh; Tosca at Torre del Lago, Italy; Recitals, Concerts, UK, Europe, USA; Featured Artist (People No 180) Opera Magazine, 1992; Season 1992-93, as Elisabeth de Valois at the London Coliseum and Nice, Gioconda for Opera North; Sang Tosca for ENO, 1994; Other Roles: Ariadne; Elizabeth I, Maria Stuarda; Elena, Sicilian Vespers; Manon Lescaut; Aida; Suor Angelica; Giorgetta, Il Tabarro; Violetta, La Traviata; Norma; Madama Butterfly; Maddalena, Andrea Chénier; Leonora, La Forza del Destino; Sang Santuzza at the Berlin Staatsoper, 1996. Honours include: SWET Award, 1979; 1st Prize, 7th International Competition for Opera Singers, Sofia, 1979; Prix, Fondation Fanny Heldy, Academie Nationale du Disque Lyrique, 1985. Address: c/o Barratt House, 7 Chertsey Road, Woking, Surrey GU21 5AB, England.

PLOYHAROVA-PREISLEROVA Vlasta, b. 25 Jan 1928, Zbynice, Klatovy, Czech Republic. Singer (Soprano). m. Frantisek Preisler Senior, 8 Apr 1972, 1 son, 1 daughter. Education: Conservatory of Prague; Corso Academia Musicale Siena, Italy (Professor Gina Cigna), 1960, 1961, 1962, 1963. Debut: In Smetana's Bartered Bride at Janacek Theatre, Brno, 1958. Career: Appeared at Theatre Olomouc, 1956-84, Theatre Brno, 1960-64, Theatre Ostrava, 1967-77; Operatic repertoire includes: Puccini's Turandot and Madame Butterfly, Strauss' Rosenkavalier (as Sophie), Tchaikovsky's Eugene Onegin, Jolanta, Massenet's Manon, Verdi's Rigoletto, Bizet's Carmen, Gounod's Faust, Gluck's Orfeo and Euridice, Beethoven's Fidelio, Mozart's Don Juan, Cosi fan tutte, Offenbach's Tales of Hoffman and Janacek's Cunning Little Vixen and From the House of the Dead; also operas by Skroup, Dvorak, Fibich, V Novak, V Blodek, B Martinu, Smetana, B G Pergolesi, C M Weber, G Rossini, F Flotow, J F Halevy, G A Lortzing, Rimsky-Korsakov, R Leoncavallo, N Zajc, A Honegger; Concert repertoire includes: Bach's Magnificat, Beethoven's 9th Symphony, Mahler's 4th Symphony. Honour: International Concorso, Toulos, Franca, Silver Medal, 1957. Address: Brno, Jánska 16 60200 Czech Republic.

PLUISTER Simon, b. 12 Nov 1913, Obdam, The Nederlands. Composer; Conductor; Organ and Piano Teacher. m. Jacoba Maria Leentvaar, 1943, 1 son, 1 daughter. Education: Studied Composition with Daniel Ruyneman, and at Amsterdam Conservatory with Hendrik Andriessen and Ernest W Mulder; Studied Pianoforte with André Jurres. Debut: As Composer, Amsterdam, 1936. Career: Composer for Dutch Broadcasting, NCRV, 1950-57; Conductor, The Harold Shamrock Concert Orchestra, Radio Tivoli Orchestra and Vocal Ensemble with instruments, 1955-66; Organ Teacher, Music School, Emmeloord, 1969-79. Compositions: For Orchestra: 15 Psalms and Hymns, 3 Suites, Punch-and-Judy Show, 3 Cascades, Rhapsody in Beer - tonality; For Solo, Choir and Orchestra: Psalm 65, 121, 137, 138, Cantata St Luke 24, Concerto da chiesa The Acts II; 3 Operettas; 2 Works, Voice with Orchestra; 3 Works for Sting-Orchestra; 75 Works for Small-Orchestra (Short pieces and suites); Concertino for Piano and Orchestra, Ricercare and Ciga for Organ and String-Orchestra; Chamber Music, Donemus, Amsterdam, Holland; Music for Pianoforte 2 hds, 4 hds and for 2 Pianofortes; Calvinus Sinfonia for Strings 1987; Commission NCRV; To Silvestre Revueltas, from Mexico, at his death, for Choir (mixed voices) and Orchestra, 1987, (choir singing and speaking); Five Brown Songs, for Soprano, Flute, Alto Saxophone and Pianoforte, 1988; Larghetto for Strings, 1988; The Days after the Crucifixion, Prologue from the Opera, Bar Abbas, for Soli, Female-Choir and Orchestra, 1986, (also as Cantata); Opera Bar Abbas, for Soli Choir and Orchestra, 1986-88; Concerto da Chiesa for 2 Recorders, V-Cello and Organ, 1990; Ant Brothers (fruit nursery) Musical for Soli Choir and Orchestra, 1990-91; Chronicle of an Eyewitness, Electronic Music for a Broadcast-Play; Super Flumina Babylonis for Soprano-Solo, Male-Choir and Pianoforte, 1992; Ave Verum Corpus and Gloria for Baritone-Solo, Male Choir and Organ, 1992; Duo Facile for Violin, V-Cello; Fantasia for Trio (Violin, Viola and V-Cello), 1993; Requiem for strings, flute, clarinet, sax, trumpet, trombone, organ and choir, 1995. Membership: GENECO (Society of Dutch Composers). Address: Zwartemeerweg 23, 8317 PA Oud-Kraggenburg, Nop, The Netherlands.

PLUSH Vincent, b. 18 Apr 1950, Adelaide, South Australia. Composer. Education: BM, University of Adelaide; Studied computer music, University of California, San Diego, USA. Career: Staff, Music Department, Australian Broadcasting Commission; Teacher, NSW State Conservatorium of Music, 1973-80; Tutor, Music Department, University of NSW, 1979; Founder, The Seymour Group, University of Sydney, 1976; Consultant for many arts bodies on Federal, State and Municipal levels; Composer-in-Residence, Musica Viva, 1985; Artistic Director, The Braidwood Festival, 1989 and 1991; Composer-in-Residence, ABC Radio, 1987. Compositions: Work for Orchestra, Pacifica, 1986, rev 1987; Works for Ensemble: On Shooting Stars-Homage to Victor Jara, 1981; Facing the Danger, 1982; The Wakefield Convocation, 1985; Helices, from The Wakefield Chronicles, 1985; The Love Songs of Herbert Hoover, 1987; Works for Solo Instrument and Ensemble; Aurores, from O Paraguay!, 1979; Bakery Hill Rising, 1980; Gallipoli Sunrise, 1984; FireRaisers, 1984; Works for Brass Band: The Wakefield Chorales, 1985-86; March of the Dalmations, 1987; Works for Narrator and Accompaniment: The Wakefield Chronicles, 1985-86; The Maitland and Morpeth String Quartet, 1979-85; The Musie of Fire, 1986-87; Instrumental Works: Chu no mai, 1974-76; Encompassings, 1975; Chrysalis, 1977-78; Stevie Wonder's Music, 1979; The Wakefield Invocation, 1986; The Wakefield Intrada, 1986; Works for Tape: Vocal Works; Choral Works; Music Theatre Works and Arrangements. Address: c/o Australian Music Centre, P O Box 49, Broadway 2007, Australia.

PLUYGERS Catherine, b. 20 Nov 1955, Colchester, Essex, England. Oboist; Artistic Director. Education: BMus, Honours, University of London, 1978; ARCM, Performance, 1978, ARCM, Teaching, 1979, Royal College of Music; Banff Centre School of Fine Arts, Canada, 1984; Goldsmiths College, 1991. Career: Freelance orchestral player with BBC, Royal Ballet Orchestra, Ulster Orchestra; Founder Member, Thomas Arne Players, with Purcell Room debut, 1985, Wigmore Hall debut, 1986; Recital tour, oboe and organ music, South Norway, sponsored by Norwegian Arts Council, 1982; Formed New Wind Orchestra (NEWO), 1985 and New Wind Summer School, 1988; Premiered Sonata No 2, opus 64, oboe and piano, dedicated to self by Dr Ruth Gipps, 1986; BBC World Service broadcast, 1986; NEWO South Bank Premiere, Queen Elizabeth Hall, 1986. Compositions: Gloryland, Mixed Media one woman show on subject of War and The Square, A Mixed Media piece performed in Purcell Room, 1990, by the Group Interartes and Hong Kong City Hall, 1990. Recordings: English Music for Oboe and Piano, with accompanist Matthew Stanley, 1984. Current Management: Self: New Wind Management Ltd. Address: 119 Woolstone Road, Forest Hill, London, SE23 2TQ, England.

PODESVA Jaromir, b. 8 Mar 1927, Brno, Czechoslovakia. Composer. Education: Studied at the Brno Conservatory (1946-47) and with Kvapil at the Janácek Academy of Music, Brno (1947-51); Further study with Aaron Copland at Tanglewood and with Henri Dutilleux in Paris. Career: Faculty Member, Ostrava Conservatory, 1969-87. Compositions include: 10 Symphonies, 1951, 1961, 1966, 1967, 1967, 1970, 1983, 1986, 1989, 1993; 6 String Quartets, 1950, 1951, 1955, 1960, 1964, 1976; 2 Nonets, 1955, 1972; Violin Santa 1958; Wind Quintet, 1961; Flute Concerto, 1965; Bambini di Praga, pantomine, 1968; Suite for viola and piano, 1969; Concerto for string quartet and orchestra, 1971; Piano Concerto, 1973; Concertino for 2 violins and piano, 1973; Beskydy Suite for orchestra, 1974; Violin Concerto, 1975; Trumpet Concerto, 1975; Homage to Leos Janacek, for orchestra, 1977; Quartet for violin clarinet, cello and piano, 1977; Sonata for solo viola, Circle, 1982; Clarinet Quintet, 1984; Clarinet Sonatina, 1984; Sinfonietta Festival, 1984; Viola Concerto, 1986; Fantasia Quasi una sonata for violin and piano, 1987; Trio for violin, cello and piano, 1990; Movement for viola and piano, 1992; Five Pieces for string ensemble, 1994. Publications include: Current Music in the West, Prague, 1963; The Possibilities of Cadences in the Twelve Note System, Prague, 1974. Address: c/o OSA, Cs armady 20, 160-56 Praha 6 Bubenec, Czech Republic.

PODLES Eva, b. 26 Apr 1952, Warsaw, Poland. Mezzo-Soprano. Education: Studied at the Warsaw Music Academy. Debut: Warsaw Chamber Opera in 1975 as Dorabella. Career: After winning prizes at Athens and Geneva in 1977, Moscow in 1978 and Toulouse in 1979, sang widely in Europe as Rosina, Cenerentola and Carmen; Sang at the Metropolitan Opera in 1984 as Handel's Rinaldo, at Trieste and Warsaw as Jaroslavna in Prince Igor, at Covent Garden in 1991 as Edvige in Guillaume Tell, and at the Opéra Bastille, Paris as Dalila in Samson et Dalila; Other noted roles have been Rossini's Arsace and Isabella, Leonora in La Favorita, Ragonde in Comte Ory and Tancredi (Antwerp, 1991); Sang the Marquis in La Fille du Regiment at La Scala, 1996. Recordings include: Verdi Requiem; Penderecki's Te Deum. Address: c/o Opéra Bastille, 120 Rue de Lyon, F-75012 Paris, France.

PODMORE Audrey Grace, b. 18 April 1944, Castle Donnington, England. Music Teacher; Facilitator. Education: Chiswick Music Center; NEETCSA, Colchester Institute; Trinity College of Music, London; Composition Studies with Diana Burrell, Michael Finnissy, Daryl Runswick; Studies in clarinet, playing and pedagogy, with Pamela Weston. Career: Pioneered Use of Microtechnology in Music Education, Featured on Music Now, BBC World Service, 1986; Musical Chair, BBC Radio 2, 1996; Presentations at Colloquium/Exhibition Events; Facilitated for Many Disabled Musicians, Working for Equal Opportunities in Music Education; Instrumental in the Establishment of new provision for children and adults. Publications: Computer-Assisted Learning Materials for NCET Publications, 1987. Contributions to: Extending Horizons. Membership: Incorporated Society of Musicians. Hobbies: Gardening; Rambling. Address: 9 Mallard Close, Haslemere, Surrey GU27 1QU, England.

POGACNIK Miha, b. 31 May 1949, Kranj, Yugoslavia. Concert Violinist; Music Director; President of Idriart. m. Judith Csik, 31 Jan 1974, 1 son, 1 daughter. Education: Artists' Diploma with distinction, DAAD Scholar, Cologne Conservatory of Music (Musikhochschule), 1967-72; Fulbright Scholar, Indiana University School of Music, 1973-74; Professors Veronek, Ozim, Gingold, Rostal, Szeryng. Career: Over 100 Concerts per season 1977- in: USA, Canada, Mexico, South America, Australia, New Zealand, China, Scandinavia, Western and Eastern Europe; Music Director of Chartres Festival d'Ete, 1981-; President and Founder, IDRIART International, Geneva (Institute For The Development of Intercultural Relations Through The Arts) now represented in 30 countries, 1983-; Music Director of past 20 IDRIART Festivals on 5 continents. Recordings: Have chosen to refuse all offers to record in order to further live communication with audiences.

POGORELICH Ivo, b. 20 Oct 1958, Belgrade, Serbia. Pianist. m. Aliza Kezeradze, 1980. Education: Studied with Aliza Kezeradze at the Moscow Conservatory. Career: International success from 1980, after elimination from the Chopin International Piano Competition; Solo recitals and appearances with major orchestras in Europe, USA, Japan, Australasia; Plays Chopin, Rachmaninov and other Romantics; Records exclusively for Deutsche Grammophon; Settled in England, 1982. Recordings include: CD of Prokofiev's 6th Sonata and Gaspard de la Nuit by Ravel; Works by Chopin. Honours: 1st Prize, Casagrande Competition at Terni, 1978; 1st Prize, Montreal International Competition, 1980; Created Ambassador of Goodwill at UNESCO in 1987 (only musician to be bestowed this honour). Address: c/o Kantor Concert Management & Public Relations, 67 Teignmouth Road, London NW2 4EA, England.

POGSON Geoffrey, b. 1966, England. Tenor. Education: Studied at Cambridge and Trinity College of Music. Career: Appearances with Glyndebourne Festival in The Queen of Spades in 1995, English National Opera, Scottish Opera and Opera North; Roles include Monostatos, Augustin Moser, Vere in Billy Budd, Quint in The Turn of the Screw and Cornwall in Lear. Recordings include: Remendado in Carmen conducted by Abbado. Address: c/o Ron Gonsalves Management, 7 Old Town, Clapham, London, SW4 0JT, England.

POHL Carla, b. 1942, Johannesburg, South Africa. Singer (Soprano). Education: Studied in South Africa and at the Wiesbaden Conservatory. Career: Sang at Pforzheim from 1970; Freiburg from 1979, notably as Tosca, Maddalena in Andrea Chenier, Marenka in The Bartered Bride and Stauss's Chrysothemis; Wiesbaden, 1979-81; Deutsche Oper am Rhein Dusseldorf from 1981, as Wagner's Elisabeth, Eva and Sieglinde, the Empress in Die Frau ohne Schatten, Strauss's Ariadne and Marschallin, and Leonore in Fidelio; Guest appearances in Mannheim, Berlin, Nancy, Karlsruhe, Stuttgart, Vienna State Opera, Munich State Opera, Milan, Rome and Brunswick; Tour of South Africa, 1985; Deutsche Oper am Rhein 1987, as Rezia in Oberon; Deutsche Oper Berlin and Santiago Chile 1988, as Chrysothemis and Elsa. Address: c/o Deutsche Oper am Rhein, Heinrich-Heine Allee 16, D-4000 Dusseldorf, Germany.

POKA Balazs, b. 1955, Hungary. Baritone. Education: University of Medicine, 1976. Career: Hungarian State Opera House; Has made several films on television in works of Rossini, Menotti, Lortzing and Puccini; Sang role of Schaunard in Puccini's La Bohème; Participant in concert and opera performances broadcast by Hungarian Radio; Numerous appearances on concert stage in oratorios; Has performed in numerous countries including, Federal Republic of Germany; France, Belgium, The Netherlands, Czechoslovakia, Bulgaria, Austria, Ireland and Italy; Roles include: Dandini in La Cenerentola; Valentin in Faust, Silvio in Pagliacci; Malatesta in Don Pasquale; Albert in Werther; Igor in Prince Igor; Di Luna in Il Trovatore; Carlos in La Forza del Destino; Germont in La Traviata; Renato in Un Ballo in Maschera; Onegin in Onegin; Ping in Turandot; Figaro in Il Barbiere di Siviglia; Rodrigo in Don Carlos; Escamillo in Carmen; Marcello in La Bohème. Honours: Silver Diploma, Pula International Opera Competition.

POLA Bruno, b. 1945, Rovereto, Trento, Italy. Singer (Baritone). Education: Berlin Conservatory, 1963-68. Career: Engaged at Kaiserslatern Opera 1968-71, Kiel 1972-73, Cologne 1974-77, Zurich Opera 1978-81; Recitals and concerts throughout Germany, Holland, Switzerland and Austria; From 1982 engagements at such major opera centres as Milan, Rome, Lisbon, Vienna, Munich and Hamburg; Metropolitan Opera from 1988, in Cavalleria Rusticana, Il Barbiere di Siviglia, Gianni Schicchi, Rigoletto, Don Giovanni, La Fanciulla del West, Falstaff, Simon Boccanegra, and L'Elisir d'Amore; Season 1996-97 in Cavalleria Rusticana and La Forz del Destino at the Met; Dulcamara at Vienna and Covent Garden, 1995-97; Amonasro in Aida at Santiago, Arena di Verona and Covent Garden; Further opera appearances at Turin, Ascona, Montreal, Pittsburgh, Florence, Geneva and Houston. Address: Via al Ronco 7, 6933 Muzzano, Switzerland.

POLASKI Deborah, b. 26 Sept 1949, Richmond Centre, Wisconsin, USA. Singer (Soprano). Education: Conservatory of Music Ohio; American Institute of Music Graz. Career: Sang at Gelsenkirchen, Karlsruhe and Ulm from 1976; Further appearances at opera houses in Hanover, Munich, Hamburg and Freiburg; Festival of Waiblingen 1983, in a revival of Croesus by Reinhard Keiser; Oslo 1986, as Elektra; Other roles include Leonore in Fidelio, Wagner's Isolde and Sieglinde and Marie in Wozzeck; Bayreuth Festival, 1988, as Brünnhilde in the Ring cycle directed by Harry Kupfer; Sang Brünnhilde at Rotterdam 1988, Cologne 1990; Stuttgart Staatsoper 1989, as Elektra (also at the Teatro Nuovo Spoleto, 1990); Season 1992 as the Dyer's Wife in Die Frau ohne Schatten at Amsterdam and Brünnhilde at Bayreuth; Sang Brünnhilde in new Ring Cycle at Covent Garden, 1994-95, returned 1997 as Elektra; Engaged to sing Isolde under Abbado at Salzburg, 1999. Recording: Wolf-Ferrari's Sly (RCA); Brünnhilde's Immolation with the Chicago Symphony (Erato). Address: Oper der Stadt Köln, Offenbachplatz, D-5000 Cologne, Germany.

POLAY Bruce, b. 22 Mar 1949, Brooklyn, New York, USA. Conductor; Composer. m. Louise Phillips, 17 Dec 1983, 2 sons, 3 daughters. Education: BM, Composition, University of Southern California, 1971; MA, Composition, California State University, 1977; DMA, Instrumental Music, Arizona State University, 1989; Conducting studies with Herbert Blomstedt, Jon Robertson, Murray Sidlen, Alberto Bolet. Debuts: Conducting: US, Lakewood (California) Chamber Orchestra, 1972; Europe, Filarmonica de Stat Sibiu, Romania, 1993. Career: Currently Music Director, Knox-Galesburg (Illinois) Symphony, 1983-; Associate Professor of Music, Knox College; Recent guest conducting in USA, Romania, Russia, Spain and Ukraine. Compositions: Encomium for 3-part children's chorus, narrator and orchestra, 1987; Concerto for Tenor Trombone, 1991; Three Wood Paintings for a cappella chorus, 1991; Cathedral Images for orchestra, 1993; Concerto-Fantasie for piano and orchestra, 1997; Anniversary Mourning, for acappella choir, 1996; Sound Images: Pictures for an Exhibition, for solo piano, 1995; Bondi's Journey: An Orchestral Rhapsody on Jewish Themes, 1994. Recording: Cathedral Images, CD, 1996. Honour: Illinois Conductor of the Year, 1997-98. Memberships: Foundation for New Music, Advisory Board, 1995-; Illinois Council of Orchestras, Board of Directors, 1994. Current Management: International Artists Alliance. Address: 1577 N Cherry Street, Galesburg, IL 61401, USA.

POLEGATO Brett, b. 1968, Canada. Singer (Baritone). Career: Frequent concert and recital engagements in North America and Europe, with songs by Schubert and Schumann; Opera repertory includes Don Pasquale, Billy Budd and Le nozze di Figaro; Contestant at the 1995 Cardiff Singer of the World Competition. Address: c/o Hart/Murdock Artists' Management, 204a St George Street, Toronto, Ontario M5R 2N6, Canada.

POLGAR Laszlo, b. 1 Jan 1947, Somogyszentpal, Hungary. Singer (Bass). Education: Studied at the Franz Liszt Academy of Music, Budapest. Career: Sang at the Budapest Opera from 1972, as Rocco, Osmin, Sarastro and Leporello; Professor of Singing at the Liszt Academy from 1978; Brussels debut 1981, as Colline in La Bohème; Covent Garden debut 1982, as Rodolpho in La Sonnambula; Hamburg Staatsoper as Osmin and Basilio; US debut Philadelphia 1982, as Colline; Has sung Gurnemanz (Parsifal) in Budapest and Berlin; Concert appearances as Bartók's Bluebeard in Hungary, Ireland, Russia, Italy, France and Canada; Promenade Concerts London 1984, 1987, as Bluebeard and in Pulcinella by Stravinsky; Carnegie Hall New York 1987, in the Choral Symphony; Die Schöpfung and the Dvorák Requiem at La Scala, Milan; Operatic engagements in Paris (Varlaam in Boris Godunov), Vienna, Munich (Leporello, 1984) and Zurich; sang Padre Guardiano in La Forza del destino at Budapest, 1990; Member of the Zurich Opera from 1991; Season 1992 as Rossini's Basilo at Brussels and Vienna, Bartók's Bluebeard at the Prom Concerts London; Sang in Schubert's Alfonso und Estrelle at the 1997 Vienna Festival. Recordings include: Il Barbiere di Siviglia and works by Haydn and Liszt (Deutsche Grammophon); Alphonse in La favorita by Donizetti. Honours: Winner, Dvorák International Singing Competition, 1974; Winner, Hugo Wolf Competition Vienna (1980) and Pavarotti Competition Philadelphia (1981); Liszt Prize, Hungary, 1982. Address: c/o Hungarian State Opera House, Népöztársaság utja 22, 1061 Budapest, Hungary.

POLGAR Tibor, b. 11 Mar 1907, Budapest, Hungary. Composer; Conductor; Pianist; Professor of Music. m. Ilona Nagykovacsi, 10 July 1947. Education: University degree in philosophy; Diploma in composition, Royal Academy of Music, Budapest, 1925. Debut: Concerts and radio broadcasts, Budapest, 1925. Career: Conductor, Composer in residence, Hungarian Broadcasting Corporation, 1925-48; Artistic Director, Hungarian Radio, 1948-50; Associate Conductor, Philharmonia Hungarica, Marl-Westphalen, Germany, 1962-64; Teaching Staff, Opera Department, University of Toronto, Canada, 1966-75; Course Director, York University, Toronto, 1976-77. Compositions include: A European Lover, musical satire in one act; The Glove, one act opera; The Troublemaker, comic opera; The Suitors, opera; A Strange Night, opera; The Last Words of Louis Riel, cantata from Canadian history; Notes on Hungary, suite concert band; Ilona's Four Faces, for Clarinet; Lest We Forget the Last Chapter of Genesis, Cantata; Pentatonia; Festive Fanfare; Passacaglia; Concerto romantico for Harp; Concertino for Trumpet with Symphonies Orchestra, Two Symphonic Dances in Latin Rhythum for Trumpet solo and Concert Band; The Voice of the Soul, A Fantasy in 3 movements for Concert Band; 200 feature and documentary film scores; music for CBC radio and television plays. Address: 21 Vaughan Road, Apt 1903, Toronto, Ontario, M6G 2N2, Canada.

POLIANICHKO Alexander, 1948, Russia. Conductor. Education: Violin studies at the Rostov Conservatory, conducting at the Leningrad Conservatoire, under Ilya Musin. Career: Violinist with the Leningrad PO, under Evgeny Mravinsky; Former artistic director of the St Petersburg Orchestra; Director of the Opera at the Kirov Theatre; Artistic Director of the Belorussian CO in Minsk from 1987, and many guest appearances with leading Russian orchestras; Conducted the Kirov Company at the 1991 Edinburgh Festival (The Marriage), Los Angeles 1993 (The Nutcracker) and Tel Aviv 1996 (Khovanshchina); Further visits to France, South Korea and Japan; English National Opera from 1994, with Eugene Onegin and Carmen; Season 1994-95 La Bohème at Oslo, The Fiery Angel in San Francisco and tour of Australia for the ABC; Season 1996 with La Bayadere at the Paris Opera and in New York, and debut with the Bournemouth Sinfonietta; Principal Conductor, Bournemouth Sinfonietta, 1997-98 onwards, has conducted revival of Eugene Onegin at ENO, 1997-98. Recordings include: Albums for Melodiya. Address: Ingpen & Williams Ltd, 26 Wadham Road, London SW15 2LR, England.

POLIANSKY Valerig K, b. 19 Apr 1949, Moscow, USSR. Conductor. m. Olga P Lapuso, 1 son, 1 daughter. Education: State Conservatoire Tchaikowsky, Moscow, graduated in Choir Conducting, 1971, Orchestra Conducting, 1974. Debut: Moscow Operetta. Career: Conducted, Shostakovich's Katerina Ismailowa at Bolshoi Theatre. Recordings: Rachmaninov Vespers, Liturgia of St John Chrysostom, A Schnittke, Choir Concert; A Bruckner, Geistliche motetten, L Cherubini, Requiem in C minor, P Tchaikovsky, Liturgia of St John Chrysostom, Various chorus; Orchestral Serenade. Contributions to: Soviet Music; Music Life; Music in the USSR. Honours: Arezzo Prize for best conductor, 1975; Honoured Artist of the People of Russia until 1996. Address: Begovay 4 allegro 3-40, 125040 Moscow, Russia.

POLISI Joseph W, b. 1947, USA. President, The Juilliard School. Education: BA, Political Science, University of CT, 1969; MA, International Relations, Fletcher School of Law and Diplomacy, Tufts University, 1970; MMus, 1973, MMA, 1975, DMA, 1980, Yale University; Studies with Maurice Allard, Conservatoire National de Paris, 1973-74. Career: Currently President, The Juilliard School, New York City; Extensive solo and chamber bassoon performances throughout USA; Chairman, Seaver Institute, National Endowment for The Arts Conductors Program; Member, National Committee on Standards in The Arts; Scholarship Committee, Presser Foundation; Co-Chair, Music Professional Training Panel, National Endowment for The Arts, 1984-87; Former Accreditation Evaluator for National Association of Schools of Music. Recording: A Harvest of 20th Century Bassoon Music, 1979; Honours: Doctor of Music, Curtis Institute of Music, Philadelphia, PA, 1990; Honorary Member, Royal Academy of Music, London, England, 1992. Address: The Juilliard School, 60 Lincoln Center Plaza, New York, NY 10023, USA.

POLIVNICK Paul, b. 7 Jul 1947, Atlantic City, NJ, USA. Conductor. m. Marsha Hooks, 20 Jun 1980. Education: BM, Juilliard School of Music, NY, 1969; Aspen Music School, CO, summers 1961, 1968, 1970, 1972; Berkshire Music Center, Tanglewood, MA, summers, 1965, 1966 and 1971; Accademia Musicale Chigiana, Siena, Italy, summer 1969. Career: Conductor, Debut Orchestra, Los Angeles, 1969-73; Associate Conductor, Indianapolis Symphony Orchestra, 1977-80; Associate Principal Conductor, Milwaukee Symphony Orchestra, 1981-85; Music Director, Alabama Symphony Orchestra, Birmingham, 1985-. Recordings: Several. Honour: Honorary Doctorate, Montevallo University, 1986. Membership: American Symphony Orchestra League. Hobbies: Working Out; Reading; Backpacking; Cooking; Travel. Current Management: Maxim Gershunoff Attractions Inc. Address: c/o Alabama Symphony Orchestra, 1814 First Avenue North, Birmingham, AL 35209, USA.

POLLARD Mark, b. 14 February 1957, Melbourne, Victoria, Australia. Composer; Music Director. Education: BA (Hons) 1981, MA 1984, La Trobe University. Career includes: Senior Tutor, La Trobe University, 1983-85; Lecturer, Victoria College of the Arts, 1986-; Music Director of various contemporary ensembles; Commissions from Seymour Group, Australian Chamber Soloists, New Audience, and others. Compositions include: Quinque II for tape, 1979; Krebs for piano, 1983; A Sympathetic Resonance for guitar, 1989; Bass Lines for amplified double bass, 1990; Carillon for Sacha for piano, 1991; Two Drummings for Joe, for choir, 1991; The Quick or the Dead, for string quartet, 1992; A View from the Beach, for orchestra, 1994; The Art of Flirting for clarinet, 1994; Inherit the Wind, for English horn, 1994. Honours include: Spivakovsky Awards, 1993. Address: c/o APRA, 1A Eden Street, Crows Nest, NSW 2065, Australia.

POLLASTRI Paolo, b. 12 July 1960, Bologna, Italy. Oboist. m. Christine Dechaux, 24 Sept 1988, 1 daughter. Education: Scientific Diploma, Bologna, 1979; Oboe Diploma, Bologna, 1977; Oboe Diploma 1982, Baroque Oboe Diploma 1982, Brussels; Diploma D'Onore (Accademia Chigiana, Siena), 1977. Career: 1st Oboe, Orchestra Giovanile Italiana, 1977; Genova, 1979; Rai Roma, 1981; Orchestra Regionale Toscana-Firenze, 1982-89; Accademia di S Cecilia, Roma, 1989; Solisti Veneti, 1984-89; TV and Radio appearances with RAI 1, 2, 3 (Solisti Veneti); TV Australiana (Solisti Veneti); Radio Israeliana (Accademia Bizzantina); BBC (Solisti Veneti); Played at Festivals in Montreux, Salzburg, Zagreb and Belgrade, Martigny and Vevey, Toulouse, Paris, Stuttgart, Edinburgh, Sydney, Melbourne and Canberra. Recordings: Respighi, Solisti Veneti, Erato; Vivaldi, Oboe concertos, Accademia Bizantina, Frequenz; Malipiero, Respighi, Ghedini, Rota, Woodwind Quintet, Fonè. Contributions to: Il Dopo Concerto, 1980-81; The Italian Academy of Woodwinds, 1988-89. Current Management: Modena International Music. Address: Paolo Pollastri, Via di Mugnana 3, 50027 Strada in Chianti, Firenze, Italy.

POLLET Françoise, b. 10 Sept 1949, Boulogne Billancourt, near Paris, France. Singer (Soprano). Education: Studied at Versailles Conservatory and in Munich. Debut: Lubeck, as the Marschallin, 1983. Career: Sang at Lubeck until 1986, as Santuzza, Fiordiligi, Donna Anna, Elisabeth in Tannhäuser, Amelia in Ballo in Maschera, Alice Ford, Giulietta, Ariadne and Arabella: Appearances as Agathe at Marseilles, Vitellia in La Clemenza di Tito at Opéra-Comique, Paris, and Dukas' Ariadne at Théâtre du Châtelet in a production by Ruth Berghaus, 1991; At Montpellier has sung Reizia in Oberon, Meyerbeer's Valentine, Catherine of Aragon in Saint-Saëns's Henry VIII, Elisabeth, and Magnard's Berenice; Hamburg, 1990, in premiere of Liebermann's Freispruch für Medea; Covent Garden, 1991, as Valentine; Other roles include Cassandra in Les Troyens, at Brussels, and Mozart's Countess; Concert repertoire includes Schumann's Liederkreis and Les Nuits d'Eté by Berlioz. Recordings include: 4th Symphony by Guy Ropartz; La Vièrge in Jeanne d' Arc au Bûcher by Honegger, conducted by Ozawa.

POLLETT Patricia (Engeline Maria), b. 13 Oct 1958, Utrecht, Holland. Violist; Senior Lecturer and Musician in Residence at University of Queensland. m. Dr Philip Keith Pollett, 28 Jan 1978, 1 son. Education: BMus, Honours, University of Adelaide, 1979; ARCM, Royal College of Music, 1980; Hochschule der Kunst, West Berlin, 1988; Teachers: Beryl Kimber, Peter Schidlof, Margaret Major, Bruno Giuranna. Career: Member of I Solisti Veneti, 1983-84; Founder Member of Perihelion, contemporary ensemble; Resident at University of Queensland, 1988-; Concerto Soloist with Gulbenkian Orchestra, Lisbon, 1984, Queensland Philharmonic Orchestra, 1989 and 1995, Queensland Symphony Orchestra, 1990, 1991 and 1994, Sydney Symphony Orchestra, 1991, and Mozart Symposium at University of Otago, New Zealand, 1991. Compositions: Commissioned new works for viola by Colin Spiers, Andrew Schultz, Nigel Sabin, Philip Bracanin, Ross Edwards, Colin

Brumby (world premiere performances of these works), Robert Davidson, Stephen Cronin, Mary Mageau, Andrew Ford and Elena Kats-Chernin. Recordings: Tapestry, and Points of Departure; Chamber Music of Andrew Schultz; Anthology of Australian Music; Evocations; Patricia Pollett: Viola Concerti; Solo: Viola Power, Australian works for viola. Address: 21 Almay Street, Kenmore, Queensland 4069, Australia.

POLLINI Maurizio, b. 5 Jan 1942, Milan, Italy. Pianist; Conductor. Education: Studied with Carlo Lonati, and with Carlo Vidusso at the Milan Conservatory. Career: Has played with Berlin and Vienna Philharmonic Orchestras, Bayerischer Rundfunk Orchestra, London Symphony Orchestra, Boston, New York, Philadelphia, Los Angeles and San Francisco Orchestras; Has played at Salzburg, Vienna, Berlin, Prague Festivals; Plays Boulez, Nono and Schoenberg, in addition to the standard repertory; Has conducted operas by Rossini at Pesaro from 1981 (La Donna del Lago); World tour with Bach's Well-Tempered Clavier, 1985; Played the 2nd Sonata of Boulez and Beethoven's Diabelli Variations, London 1990; Beethoven Sonata series at the Festival Hall, 1997; Also at La Scala, Carnegie Hall and Vienna. Recordings: For Polydor International, including CDs of Bartók Piano Concertos 1 and 2 (Chicago Symphony/Abbado); Chopin 1st Concerto (Philharmonic/Kletski) and Sonatas Op 35, Op 58; Beethoven Late Sonatas; Brahms Piano Quintet (Quartetto Italiano); Schoenberg piano music; Stravinsky Petrushka Three Movements, Webern Variations, Boulez 2nd Sonata, Prokofiev 7th Sonata. Honour: First Prize, International Chopin Competition, Warsaw 1960. Address: c/o Harrison/Parrott Ltd, 12 Penzance Place, London W11 4PA, England.

POLOLANIK Zdenek, b. 25 October 1935, Brno, Czechoslovakia. Composer. Education: Graduated 1961, Janácek Academy of Music, Brno. Career: Freelance Composer from 1961. Compositions include: Variations for organ and piano, 1956; Sinfonietta, 1958; String Quartet, 1958; Divertimento for 4 horns and strings, 1960; 5 Symphonies, 1961, 1962, 1963, 1969; Concentus resonabilis for 19 soloists and tape, 1963; Musica Spingenta I-III, 1961-63; Horn sonata, 1965; Piano Concerto, 1966; Concerto Grosso I and II, 1966, 1988; Missa Brevis, 1969; Song of Songs, oratorio, 1970; Snow Queen, ballet, 1978; Lady Among Shadows, ballet, 1984; Summer Festivities for chorus and 2 pianos, 1985; Easter Way, 14 songs for soprano and ensemble, 1990; Small Mythological Exercises, melodrama, 1991; Ballad for cello and piano, 1992; Christmas Triptych for bugle and 4 trombones, 1993; First One Must Carry the Cross, chamber oratorio for medium voice and synthesizer, 1993; Eulogies, Psalms for chorus, 1993; Cantus Laetitae, Psalms for Women's chorus, 1993. Address: c/o OSA, Cs armady 20, 160-56 Praha 6 Bubenec, Czechoslovakia.

POLOZOV Vyacheslav M, b. 1950, Mariupol, Ukraine, USSR. Singer (Tenor). Education: Studied at the Kiev Conservatory. Debut: Kiev Opera 1977, as Alfredo in La Traviata. Career: Leading tenor at the Saratov Opera 1978; Leading tenor at Minsk Opera 1980; Bolshoi Opera Moscow, 1982, Alfredo and Turiddu, opposite E Obraztsova; Sang Pinkerton at La Scala 1986; US debut with Pittsburgh Symphony Orchestra 1986, as Cavaradossi, opposite R Scotto (Great Wood Festival), conductor M Tilson Thomas; US stage debut the Chicago Lyric Opera 1986, as Rodolfo in La Bohème, opposite K Ricciarelli; Further appearances at Washington DC (1986, as Lykov, in The Tsar's Bride, under M Rostropovich, director-G Vishnevskya), New York (Met 1987, as Pinkerton, opposite R Scotto); Palm Springs, as Cavaradossi with R Scotto; San Antonio (as Cavaradossi under Julius Rudel); Met (as Rodolfo, 1987, summer park concerts); Washington DC, as Dimitri in Boris Godunov, under M Rostropovich; season 1987/88 with Calaf in New City Opera, repeated at the Bayerische Staatsoper Munich; Rome Opera as Lykov and the Metropolitan as Verdi's Macduff; Michigan Opera Theatre as Rodolfo in La Bohème, (1988 debut); Further debuts at the San Francisco Opera (1988 as Enzo, in La Gioconda), Carnegie Hall (1988, as Andrea Chénier, conducted by Eve Queler), Canadian Opera Company (1989 as Cavaradossi), Greater Miami Opera (1989, as Alvaro in La Forza); Sang Pinkerton in San Francisco, 1989, Lyon Opera (debut 1990), as Pinkerton, repeated in the Greater Miami Opera, director R Scotto; appearance, at the 1990 Caracella Festival, Rome, and Turiddu and Lensky with the Chicago Lyric Opera, 1990; Calaf with the Greater Miami Opera; Cavaradossi in the Houston Grand Opera, 1991; as Lensky in Hamburg; as Don Carlo in Denver at the Opera Colorado. Recordings include: Aleko by Rachmaninov (Melodia); Boris Godunov (Erato, under M Rostropovich), TY broadcast Canadian Opera Company, Tosca. Honours: Winner, All-Russia Glinka Competition 1981; Sofia Competition, Bulgaria, 1984 (for the Duke of Mantua); Madam Butterfly Competition, Tokyo, 1987. Address: 367 Columbus PKWY, Mineola, New York 11501, USA.

POLSTER Hermann Christian, b. 8 Apr 1937, Leipzig, Germany. Education: Studied with his father and at the Universityof Leipzig. Career: Sang with the Dresden Kreuzchor while a boy; Many engagements with the Leipzig Bach Soloists, the chorus of St Thomas's Leipzig and the Leipzig Gewandhaus Orchestra; Guest appearances Berlin; Munich, Frankfurt, Hamburg, Roma, Milano, Torino, Amsterdam (St Matthew Passion); Halle (Shostakovich 14th Symphony); Tokyo, Osaka (Bach: St Matthew and St John Passion, Beethoven's Ninth); Paris (Fidelio), Moscow, Buenos Aires, Rio de Janerio, Aix-en-Provence, Venice, Dubrovnik, Prague (Beethoven's Ninth); Other repertoire includes Monteverdi's Vespers; Buxtehude Cantatas, Telemann Cantatas, Psalms, Serenades; Handel Saul, Acis and Galatea, Samson, Belshazzar, Judas Maccabeus, Solomon, Jephtha, Hercules and Messiah; Bach Cantatas and Oratorios; Haydn Oratorios; Mozart Masses, Requiem, Solemn Vespers and Die Zauberflöte (Sarastro); Beethoven Missa Solomnis, Mass in C and Christus am Olberg; Mendelssohn Elijah, St Paul, Erste Walpurgisnacht; Schumann Paradies und die Peri; Verdi Requiem; Brahms Ein Deutsches Requiem; Mahler 8th Symphony; Janácek Glagolitic Mass; Stravinsky Oedipus Rex; Wagner Die Meistersinger (Pogner); Tchaikovsky Eugene Onegin (Gremin); Blacher The Grand Inquisitor; Shostakovich 13th Symphony, Songs of Michelangelo; Professur für Gesang Musikhochschule Leipzig, International Masterclasses, Juror by international competitions (Brussels, Moscow, Berlin, Leipzig). Recordings: St Matthew Passion and Bach Cantatas (Eurodisc); Elijah and Orff's Die Kluge (Philips); Beethoven: Fidelio (1804 version), Missa solemnis (Eterna); Shostakovitch Michelangelo Songs (Eterna); Mozart Litaneien (Philips); Concert works conducted by Karl Böhm, Karajan, Herbert Kegel, Neville Marriner, Wolfgang Sawallisch and Kurt Masur. Honours: Kammersänger, Kunstpreisträger. Memberships: Deutscher Musikrat, Bundesverband Deutscher Gesangspädagogen (Vizepräsident); Neue Detusche Bachesellschaft. Address: c/o Gewandhausorchester, Augustusplatz 8, 0-4109 Leipzig, Germany.

POMERANTS-MAZURKEVICH Dana, b. 11 Oct 1944, Kaunas, USSR. Concert Violinist; Professor of Violin. m. Yuri Mazurekvich, 4 July 1963, 1 daughter. Education: MMus, 1961-65, Artist Diploma 1965-68, Moscow State Conservatory. Career: Performed as the Mazurkevich Violin Duo member and also as a soloist in: USSR, Poland, USA, Canada, Australia, England, France, Belgium, East and West Germany, Hong Kong, Taiwan, Switzerland, Italy, Roumania, Mexico and other countries; Recorded for Radio Moscow, France, ABC (Australia), WGGH (Boston); CBC (Canada); BBC (England); Sender Freies (W Berlin), and others. Recordings: Works by Telemann, Prokofiev, Honegger, Sarasate, Spohr, Rawsthorne, Wieniawski, Shostakovich, Leclair, Handel and others; Masters of the Bow, Toronto, Canada; SNE, Montreal, Canada. Current Management: Robert M Gewald Management. Address: School of Music, Boston University, 855 Commonwealth Avenue, Boston, MA 02215, USA.

POMMIER Jean-Bernard, b. 17 Aug 1944, Beziers, France. Concert Pianist; Conductor. Education: Began piano studies aged 4; later studied with Yves Nat, Eugene Istomin and Eugen Bigot (conducting); 1958-61 Paris Conservatoire. Career: Has performed widely from 1962, notably in Europe, the USA, Far East, the USSR, Israel and Scandinavia; Salzburg debut with Karajan 1971; Berlin Philharmonic 1972; US debut in season 1973-74 with the New York Philharmonic and the Chicago Symphony; Engagements with the Concertgebouw under Haitink, the Orchestre de Paris under Barenboim, the St Paul Chamber Orchestra and Zukerman; Festival appearances at Edinburgh, South Bank Music, Ravinia and Mostly Mozart (New York); Director/soloist with English Chamber Orchestra in Salzburg and Vienna and with Scottish Chamber Orchestra in France, Belgium and Holland; Season 1987-88 solo appearances with the London Philharmonic, the Hallé and Royal Philharmonic; conducting Bournemouth Symphony and Ulster Orchestras and the Northern Sinfonia on a tour of Spain; Appointed Music Director of the Melbourne Summer Music Festival for 1990; Chamber music with Casals, Schneider, Richter, Oistrakh and Stern and with the Guarneri and Vermeer Quartets; Season 1991-92 appearances with the Northern Sinfonia in North America, Bournemouth Symphony, the Philharmonia and Ulster Orchestra and conducted the Hallé and Royal Liverpool Philharmonic. Recordings: Poulenc's Piano Concerto with the City of London Sinfonia and Sonatas by Brahms with Leonard Rose and Jaime Laredo (Virgin). Honour: First Diploma of Honour at the 1962 Tchaikovsky Competition Moscow; Poulenc's Piano Concerto with the City of London Sinfonia and Sonatas by Brahms with Leonard Rose and Jaime Laredo (Virgin). Address: c/o Harold Holt Ltd, 31 Sinclair Road, London W14 0NS, England.

POMPILI Claudio, b. 12 May 1949, Gorizia, Italy. Composer. Education: BMus, University of Adelaide, 1983; Study with Richard Meale and Tristram Cary in Australia (1980-82) and with Franco Donatoni and Salvatore Sciarrino in Italy (1984-85); IRCAM studios, Paris, 1984. Career includes: Faculty Member, University of Adelaide, 1983-84, University of New England, 1987-97; Associate Professor and Director, Conservatorium of Music, University of Wollongong, 1998-; Commissions from Duo Contemporain, Perihelion and others. Compositions include: Medieval Purity in a Bed of Thorns, for tape, 1981-84; The Star Shoots a Dart, for flute, clarinet, violin and cello, 1985; Polymnia Triptych for soprano and large ensemble, 1986; Songs for Ophelia for soprano, 1989; Scherzo alla Francescana, for double bass, 1990; Trio for violin, guitar and double bass, 1990; Zeitfluss: teuflicher kontrapunkt, for wind quintet, 1990; Lo spazio stellato si riflette in suoni, for baroque flute, 1990; Ah, amore che se n'ando nell'aria, for clarinet, viola and cello, 1991; String Quartet, 1992; El viento lucha a obscura con tu sueno, 1993; Fra l'urlo e il tacere, for bass clarinet, 1993. Honours include: Adolf Spivakovsky Scholarship, 1990. Address: Conservatorium of Music, University of Wollongong, P O Box 62, Keiraville, NSW 2500, Australia.

POND Celia (Frances Sophia), b. 5 Jan 1956, London, England. Cellist. m. Ambrose Miller, 4 Apr 1981. Education: BA 1974-77, MA 1981, Girton College, Cambridge University; LRAM, Royal Academy of Music, London, 1977-78; Staatliche Hochschule für Musik, Rheinland, 1978-81. Career: Principal Cello, European Community Chamber Orchestra, 1981-; Artistic Adviser; Many recitals throughout Europe with Trio Gardellino, 1983-86; Cello and Piano Duo, Celia and Mary Pond; Recitals in Britain and Far East including Hong Kong and Peking. Recordings: Antonio Duni; Cantate da Camera Dedicate Alla Maesta di Giovanni V. Contributions to: Early Music, 1978; Solo Bass Viol Music in France. Honours: Edith Helen Major Prize, Cambridge, 1976; West German Government Scholarship, 1978. Membership: Incorporated Society of Musicians. Hobbies: Cooking; Travel. Address: Fermain House, Dolphin Street, Colyton, Devon EX13 6LU, England.

PONET Luc Ghislain Johan, b. 28 Nov 1959, Hasselt, Belgium. Professor of Organ; Organist. m. Gilissen Regina, 20 Aug 1983, 3 sons. Education: MMus, College of Music "Lemmensinstituut", Leuven, Organ Performance, 1982; Diplome Superieure, 1985; Post-graduate work: Studies with Dr H Haselböck-Hochschule für Musik und Darstellende Kunst in Vienna, 1986-87. Career: Professor for Organ, Lemmensinstitute, College of Music, Leuven, 1982-; Director of Music, Organist at the Basilica of Tongeren, 1988-; Faculty Member, Guest Professor of the Concordia University, River Forest, Illinois, USA, 1996-; Recitals and concerts (as soloist and/or with orchestras) in most European countries, Japan, USA, Mexico; also masterclasses and lectures; Conductor of the Basilica-Choir and the Kleine Cantorij (Tongeren) with the emphasis on the baroque and classical repertoire for choir and orchestra. Recordings: Numerous recordings (CD, radio and television) on organs in Belgium, Europe and the USA. Membership: Rotary International, 1992-. Hobbies: Enjoying life and the family on a farm in the country; Horse-riding; Reading books on philsophical, esoteric and musical topics. Current Management: Forum Musicale. Address: St Geertruistr 92, B-3700 Tongeren, Belgium.

PONIATOWSKA Irena, b. 5 Jul 1933, Góra Kalwaria, Poland. Musicologist. m. Andrzej Poniatowski, 14 Nov 1953 (dec 1994), 1 d. Education includes: Diploma, Musicology, Warsaw University, 1962; PhD, 1970; Qualification to Assistant Professor, 1983; Habil; Qualification to Professor, 1994. Career: Tutor, 1970, Vice Director, 1974-79; Assistant Professor, 1984, Extraordinary Professor, 1991, Institute of Musicology, Vice Dean, Faculty of History, 1988-90, 1993-, Warsaw University; President, Council, 1976-84, Vice President, 1986-91, Chopin Society; President: Congress, Musica Antique Europae Orientalis, Poland, 1988, 1991, 1994; Polish Chopin Academy, 1994; Editor of many encyclopaedias including: Polish Encyclopaedia of Music, Volumes 1, 11, 111, IV, 1979-; Various offices in Union of Polish Composers, Section of Musicologists; Dean, Faculty of History, Warsaw University, 1988-90, 1993-. Publications: Beethoven Piano Texture, 1972; The Chronicle of the Important Musical Events in Poland 1945-72, 1974; Piano Music and Playing in XIX Century Artistic and Social Aspects, 1991; Dictionary of Music for Schools, 1991; History and Interpretation of Music, 1993, 2nd edition, 1995; Editor, Musical Work: Theory History, Interpretation, 1984; Maria Szymanowske 25 Mazurkas, 1993; Many articles in collective works. Contributions to: Muzyka; Ruch Muzyczny; Rocznik Chopinowski; Chopin Studies; Hudobny Zivot; Quadrivium. Honours: Golden Cross of Merit, 1979; Prize, Minister of National Education, Poland, 1992. Memberships include: International Musicological Society; Union of Polish Composers; Polish Society of Contemporary Music; Liszt Society; Board, Internationale Chopin Gesellschaft-Wien; Les Amis de Nicolas Chopin, Marainville, France. Address: Filtrowa 63-38, 02-056 Warsaw, Poland.

PONKIN Vladimir, b. 1951, Irkutsk, Siberia, Russia. Conductor. Education: Studied at Gorky Conservatoire and with Rozhdestvensky in Moscow. Career: Assistant conductor at Bolshoy Theatre and at Moscow Chamber Theatre; Conductor with Yaroslavl Philharmonic Orchestra, later with Russian State Cinema Orchestra; Guest engagements with St Petersburg Philharmonic and Russian State Academic Symphony Orchestra; Chief Conductor and Music Director of Russian State Maly Symphony from 1991; Currently, Music Director of New Moscow State Symphony Orchestra; Has toured to Italy, Hungary,

Germany, Austria, Spain and Denmark; Repertoire has included much contemporary music as well as standard works. Recordings include: CDs on the Chant du Monde. Honours include: Winner, 1990 Rupert Foundation Conducting Competition, London. Address: c/o Sonata, 11 Northpark Street, Glasgow, G20 7AA, Scotland.

PONOMARENKO Ivan, b. 1955, Ukraine, Russia. Baritone. Education: Studied at the Odessa Conservatory and with Irina Arkhipova. Career: Sang first with Odessa State Opera Theatre as Escamillo, Don Giovanni, Renato in Un Ballo in Maschera, Germont and Amonasro; Member of the Kiev Opera from 1981 touring with company to Germany, Spain, The Netherlands, Hungary, France and Spain; Sang at Strasbourg Festival in 1993 as Nabucco; British debut on tour in 1995; Recitalist with a wide repertoire. Address: c/o Sonata Ltd, 11 North Park Street, Glasgow, G20 7AA, Scotland.

PONS Juan, b. 1946, Ciutadella, Menorca. Singer (Baritone). Education: Studied in Barcelona. Career: Sang at the Teatro Liceo Barcelona, at first as a tenor; Covent Garden 1979, as Alfio in Cavalleria Rusticana; Barcelona 1983, Herod in Massenet's Hérodiade; Paris Opéra 1983, as Tonio in Pagliacci; Guest appearances in Munich, Madrid and at the Orange Festival; Verona Arena 1984-85, Amonasro; La Scala Milan 1985, as Rigoletto and as Sharpless in Madama Butterfly; Metropolitan Opera 1986, as Scarpia in Tosca; Well known as Verdi's Falstaff; (Munich Staatsoper 1987), San Francisco and Rome 1989; Also sings Renato in Un Ballo in Maschera and roles in operas by Donizetti; sang Verdi's Germont at Chicago 1988; Sharpless in Madame Butterfly at La Scala, 1990; Barcelona 1989, as Basilio in Respighi's La Fiamma (also at Madrid); Season 1992 as Tonio in Pagliacci at Philadelphia, Scarpia at San Francisco and Luna at Madrid; Sang Amonasro at the Verona Arena, 1994; Tonio at Los Angeles, 1996. Recordings: Aroldo by Verdi (CBS); Pagliacci (Philips). Address: c/o Teatra alla Scala, Via Filodrammatici 2, Milan, Italy.

PONSONBY Robert (Noel), b. 19 Dec 1926, Oxford, England. Arts Administrator. m. Lesley Black, 23 Apr 1977. Education: Trinity College, Oxford, 1948-50; MA Hons (Oxon). Career: Staff Member, Glyndebourne Opera, 1951-55; Artistic Director, Edinburgh Festival, 1956-60; General Administrator, Scottish National Orchestra, 1964-72; Controller of Music, BBC, 1972-85; Artistic Director, Canterbury Festival, 1986-88; Administrator, Friends of Musicians Benevolent Fund, 1987-93. Publication: Short History of Oxford University Opera Club, 1950. Contributions to: Numerous magazines and journals. Honours: CBE, 1985; Honorary RAM, 1975; Janácek Medal, Czech Government, 1980. Memberships: Fellow, Royal Society of Arts. Hobbies: Music; Fell walking. Address: 11 St Cuthbert's Road, London NW2 3QJ, England.

PONTES-LEÇA Carlos de, b. 26 Nov 1938, Coimbra, Portugal. Writer on Music and Music Manager. Education: Law Graduate, Coimbra University; Journalist Graduate, University of Navarra, Spain; Piano and Composition, Music Conservatories of Lisbon and Coimbra, with Croner de Vasconcellos and M Lourdes Martins, among other teachers. Career: Assistant Director, Music Department, Calouste Gulbenkian Foundation; Associated Editor (for Music and Dance) of the cultural magazine Coloquio-Artes, Lisbon, 1971-96; Artistic Director of the Leiria Music Festival; Author of musical Programmes on Portuguese Television and Broadcasting, Essays on History of Music and Musical Aesthetics and programme notes for Gulbenkian Foundation, San Carlos Theatre (Lisbon National Opera) and CD recordings; Commentator of Opera Performances on Radio and Television. Contributions to: The New Grove Dictionary of Music and Musicians, London; Gulbenkian Dictionary of Portuguese Music and Musicians, Lisbon; Verbo Encyclopedia, Lisbon. Address: Calouste Gulbenkian Foundation, 1093 Lisbon, Portugal.

PONTINEN Roland, b. 1963, Stockholm, Sweden. Concert Pianist. Education: Studied at Stockholm Music Academy and with Menahem Pressler, Gyorgy Sebok and Elisabeth Leonskaya. Debut: Stockholm, with Bartok's 2nd Concerto, 1983. Career: Many appearances with leading orchestras, including all major Swedish ensembles, Oslo Philharmonic, Jerusalem Symphony, BBC Symphony, Slovak Philharmonic and Accademia Santa Cecilia, Rome; Festival engagements include Bergen, Schleswig-Holstein, Ludwigsburg, Ravenna, Edinburgh and Newport, USA; Promenade Concerts, London 1989, and Aldeburgh Festival; Recitals throughout Scandinavia, Western Europe, Australia and New Zealand; Chamber concerts and Lieder evenings with Hakan Hardenberger, Nobuko Imai, Chritian Lindberg, Arve Tellefsen, Barbara Hendricks and Sylvia Lindenstrand. Recordings include: Albums as accompanist to singers and instrumentalist and Concertos by Grieg and Tchaikowsky, with Bamberg Symphony Orchestra conducted by Leif Segerstram. Address: c/o Anglo/Swiss Ltd, Ste 35-37 Morley House, 320 Regent Street, London W1R 5AD, England.

PONTVIK Peter, b. 29 Apr 1963, Copenhagen, Denmark. Swedish Citizen. Composer; Ensemble Leader. 1 son. Education: Languages: German, Spanish, French, Swedish; Private tuition in Composition with Marino Rivero, 1983-86; Musicology, Choir Conducting, National Conservatory, Montevideo, 1984-86; Composition with Sven-David Sandström, Royal Academy of Music, Stockholm, 1989-92, and with Wolfgang Rihm, Academy of Music, Karlsruhe, Germany, 1992-94; Ferienkurse für Neue Musik, Darmstadt, 1994. Debut: 1st performance of Reencuentro con Misiones for bandoneon at Taller de Música Contemporánea, Montevideo, 1985. Career: Grew up in Uruguay; UNM Festival (Young Nordic Music): selected works at Helsinki, 1990, Stavanger, 1993, Malmö, 1994; Founder and Artistic Leader of Ensemble Villancico, Stockholm, 1994; Radio appearances, several works, Swedish and German Broadcasting, 1994-97. Compositions: Amen for mixed choir, 1989; Three Images for Three Recorders, 1990; Candombe for wind orchestra, 1990-91; Yeikó for bandoneon, percussion and dancer, 1992-93; Allelu for mixed choir, 1993; En kort mässa-Missa brevis for choir and brass quintet, 1994; Ur Sagitra, for choir and percussion, 1996-97. Recording: Cancionero de Uppsala 1556, with Ensemble Villancico. Contributions to: Uruguay - ett land utan UR-musik?, article to Kontrast magazine, Stockholm, 1994. Honour: 1st Prize, International Competition for Choir Composition, Tolosa, Spain, 1989. Membership: FST (Society of Swedish Composers). Address: Tantogatan 59-2 tr, 118 42 Stockholm, Sweden.

POOLE John, b. 1934, Birmingham, England. Choral Director. m. Laura McKirahan, 22 July 1987, 3 sons. Education: Studied at Oxford University. Career: Former Organist of London University Church and Music Director at University College, London; Founded the Bloomsbury Singers and Players; Director of the BBC Singers, 1972-90 and has directed the BBC Symphony Chorus and Singers in many concerts throughout Britain and abroad; Music Director of the Groupe Vocal de France, 1990-95 and currently Chief Guest Conductor of the BBC Singers, with frequent performances of modern repertory; Guest Director, worldwide. Recordings: Giles Swayne, Cry, with BBC Singers; Martin-Mass, Britten, A Boy Was Born, BBC Singers, Westminster Cathedral Choristers; Chants d'Eglise with Groupe Vocal de France. Membership: FRCO. Address: Helen Sykes Management, First Floor, Parkway House, Sheen Lane, East Sheen, London, SW14 8LS, England.

POOT Sonja, b. 3 Dec 1936, Gravenzande, Netherlands. Singer (Soprano). Education: Studied in Salisbury (Rhodesia), Amsterdam and Vienna. Career: Sang at Bonn Opera, 1964-71, notably as Constanze in Entführung, and Donizetti's Lucia and Maria de Rohan; Nuremberg, 1971-73, Stuttgart Staatsoper, 1973-78; Guest engagements at Basle, Amsterdam (Elsa 1978), Vienna Volksoper, Rome, Geneva (Elettra in Idomeneo, 1973), Barcelona and Ottawa; Other roles have included Mozart's Donna Anna, Queen of Night and Pamina, Anna Bolena, Lucrezia Borgia, Violetta, Amelia in Ballo in Maschera and Norina in Don Pasquale; Many concert performances. Address: c/o Staatsoper Stuttgart, Oberer Schlossgarten 6, 7000 Stuttgart, Germany.

POPE Cathryn, b. 1960, England. Singer (Soprano). Education: Studied with Ruth Packer at the Royal College of Music; Further study at the National Opera Studio. Career: With English National Opera has sung Papagena and Pamina in The Magic Flute, Anna (Moses), Susanna, Zerlina, Sophie (Werther), Leila (The Perl Fishers), Gretel and Werther; Sang Oksana in the first British production of Christmas Eve by Rimsky-Korsakov, 1988; Sang Amor in Orpheus and Euridice for Opera North; Royal Opera Covent Garden as Gianetta (L'Elisir d'Amor), Frasquita (Carmen) and a Naiad (Ariadne auf Naxos). Recordings include: Anne Trulove in The Rake's Progress; Barbarina in Le nozze di Figaro; Sang Gretel with Netherlands Opera 1990, Pamina at the London Coliseum; Sang in new productiions of The Marriage of Figaro and Königskinder at the Coliseum, 1991-92; Gilda in a revival of Rigoletto, 1992/93; Featured Artist, Opera Now magazine, Feb 1992. Recordings include: Video of Rusalka (as Wood Nymph). Address: c/o English National Opera, St Martin's Lane, London WC2, England.

POPE Michael Douglas, b. 25 Feb 1927, London, England. Musician; Producer; Choral Conductor; Writer. m. (1) Margaret Jean Blakeney, 1954, 1 son, (2) Gillian Victoria Peck, 1967, 1 son, 1 daughter. Education: Guildhall School of Music and Drama, 1949-53. Career: Served in Army, 1945-48; Joined BBC, 1954; Assistant, Music Division, 1960; Producer, Music Programmes and Music Talks, 1966-80; Planned and produced many programmes and series with BBC Chorus, subsequently BBC Singers; Responsible for revival of works by Elgar, Stanford, Bantock (Omar Khayyám trilogy, 1979), Bennett, Rootham, Hurlstone, Boyce (Solomon, 1979), Parry (Prometheus Unbound, 1980) and other composers; Missing Music, 1972; The Direction of Modern Music, 1979, transmitted, 1980; Musical Director, London Motet and Madrigal Club, 1954-93; Guest Conductor, RTE; Honorary Secretary, Royal Philharmonic Society, 1983-85. Publications include: King Olaf and the English Choral Tradition in Elgar Studies, 1990. Contributions to: DNB; Royal College of Music Magazine. Memberships: Royal Musical Association; Incorporated Society of Musicians; Association of British Choral Directors; Elgar Society, Chairman 1978-88, Vice-President 1988. Hobbies: Reading; Theatre; Athletics history. Address: Quarry Farm House, Chicksgrove, Salisbury, Wiltshire SP3 6LY, England.

POPESCU Constantin, b. 22 July 1955, Focsani, Romania. Musician. m. Rodica Brune, 1995, 1 son, 1 daughter. Education: BA, MA, Music Conservatory, Bucharest, 1975-79; Professional Studies, Juilliard School of Music, 1991-92. Career: Solo Appearances in Connecticut; Teacher, Connecticut; Founder, Bottesini Double Bass Duo; Tours of Sapin, 1980, Spain and Italy, 1982, Spain, United States and Canada, 1983, United States, 1989. Honours: Winner, International Bassists Society Solo Competition, 1990. Memberships: International Society of Bassists; Board Director, American String Teachers Association. Address: 19 Ferris Drive, Old Greenwich, CT 06870, USA.

POPIELSKI Zbigniew Bogdan, b. 18 May 1935, Bialystok, Poland, Composer; Teacher of Music. m. Marianna Dub, 17 Aug 1963, 2 daughters. Education: Piano and Organ, Secondary Music School, Warsaw, 1959, 1964. Graduated in Composition, Frederic Chopin Academy of Music, Warsaw, 1964. Debut: Annual concert of pupils of Secondary Music School, Warsaw, June 1958. Career: Kain, ballet music, staged in Bialystok, 1981; Participated, Festival of Polish Music, Montreal, Canada, 1995; Teremin Days, Music Festival of Electronic Works, St Petersburg, Russia, 1996. Compositions: Kain, ballet music; Triptych for Reeds; Capriccio e Fuga for 5 Clarinets. Recording: Kain. Contributions to: Bialystok newspapers. Honours: 3rd Prize, for Triptych for Reeds, All Polish Composers Competition for Chamber Music, 1988; 3rd Prize Winner, for Capriccio e Fuga, Japan International Competition for Chamber Music, Tokyo, 1997. Memberships: Polish Composers Union; Association of Polish Music Artists; Association of Authors ZAIKS. Hobbies: Learning English; Cars and driving on highroads. Address: 13 Poleska str 10, 15-476 Bialystok, Poland.

POPLE Ross, b. 11 May 1945, Auckland, New Zealand. Conductor; Cellist. m. (1) Anne Storrs, 25 June 1965, div., 3 sons, 1 daughter, (2) Charlotte Fairbairn, July 1992, 1 son. Education: Royal Academy of Music, London; Recital Medal, Honorary RAM; Paris Conservatoire. Debut: London, 1965. Career: Principal Cello, Menuhin Festival Orchestra; BBC Symphony Orchestra, 1976-86; Director of London Festival Orchestra, 1980-; Founder, Cathedral Classics, Festival of Music in Cathedrals, UK, 1986-; London South Bank series, Birthday Honours, 1988-; Founder and Developer of The Warehouse, Waterloo (home to London Festival Orchestra and recording studio), 1993. Recordings: Haydn, Boccherini, Mozart, Mendelssohn, Schoenberg, Vaughan Williams, Holst, Strauss, Arnold, Franck, Bach and others, for various labels. Hobbies: Tennis; Golf; Sailing; Farming. Address: Sellet Hall, Stainton, Kendal LA8 0LE, England.

POPOV Stefan, b. 1940, Bulgaria. Cellist. Education: Studied in Sofia, the Moscow Conservatory with Sviatoslav Knushevitsky and Mstislav Rostropovitch, 1961-66. Debut: Sofia 1955. Career: Many concert appearances in Europe, North America, Asia notably at London, Moscow, Boston, Florence, Geneva, Dublin, Genoa, Milan, Budapest; Concerto repertoire includes works by Vivaldi, Haydn, Boccherini, Beethoven, Schumann, Dvorák, Brahms, Elgar, Hindemith, Milhaud, Honegger, Kabalevsky and Shostakovich; Don Quixote by Strauss; Respighi Adagio with Variations; Prokofiev Symphonie Concertante; Bloch Schelomo; Sonata collaborations with the pianist Allan Schiller; Has taught at Boston University, the New England Conservatory of Music. Honours: Winner of competitions in Moscow 1957, Geneva 1964, Vienna 1967, Florence 1969; 1966 Techaikovsky International Competition, Moscow. Address: Sofia-concert, Bulgarian Artistic Agency, 3 Volov Street, Sofia, Bulgaria.

POPOV Valery, b. 1965, Kharkov, Ukraine. Tenor. Education: Studied at the Kharkov Institute of Arts. Career: Has sung at the Kiev and Kharkov Opera Houses and from 1994 as Principal at the Brno Opera Theatre, Czechoslovakia; Roles have included Cavaradossi, Don Alvaro, Don Ottavio, Don Carlos, Turridu, Samson and Alfredo; Sang Don José on tour to France in 1992; Further appearances throughout Europe and North America. Honours include: Prizewinner, Belvedere International Competition, Vienna. Address: c/o Sonata Ltd, 11 North Park Street, Glasgow, G20 7AA, Scotland.

POPOV Vladimir, b. 29 Apr 1947, Moscow, Russia. Singer (Tenor). Education: Studied at Tchaikovsky Conservatory, Moscow. Career: Sang at Bolshoi Opera, Moscow, 1977-81; Studied further in Milan and emigrated to USA, 1982, singing Ramirez in La Fanciulla del West at Portland; Metropolitan Opera debut, 1984, as Lensky in Eugene Onegin; Further engagements as Calaf at Houston, 1987, as Cavaradossi at Philadelphia, 1987, as Dimitri in Boris Godunov at Covent Garden, 1988, and Hermann in The Queen of Spades at Washington, 1989; Sang

Calaf with Covent Garden Company at Wembley Arena, 1991, Samson at Detroit and Canio in Pagliacci at Buenos Aires, 1992; Other roles include Ernani, Gabriele Adorno, Don José and Radames (San Francisco, 1989).

POPOVA Valeria, b. 1945, Bulgaria. Singer (Soprano). Education: Studied with father Sacha Popov, in Sofia and with Gina Cigna. Debut: Sang Lauretta in Gianni Schicchi at National Theatre, Belgrade. Career: Sang at Plovdiv Opera, 1971-76, Sofia from 1976; Guest engagements in former Soviet Union, Germany, Rumania and Cuba; Other roles include Violetta, Manon, Mozart's Countess, Jenufa, Fiordiligi, Marguerite, Donna Anna, Pamina and Leonora in La Forza del Destino; Sang Amelia in Ballo in Maschera at Milwaukee, 1990; Also teacher of singers: daughter Alexandrina Pendachanska has been among her pupils. Recordings include: Arias by Puccini, Verdi, Massenet and Bellini. Address: c/o Alexandrina Pendachanska, Harold Holt Ltd, 31 Sinclair Road, London W14 0NS, England.

POPOVICI Dorum, b. 17 Fe 1932, Resita, Romania. Composer. Education: Studied in Timosoara, 1944-50, at Bucharest Conservatory, 1950-55, and Darmstadt, 1968. Career: Editor of Romanian Radio and Television, 1968. Compositions: Operas: Promethu, Bucharest, 1964; Mariana Pineda, Iasi, 1969; Interrogation at Daybreak, Galati, 1979; The Longest Night, Bucharest, 1983; Firmness, composed 1989; Orchestral: Triptyque, 1955; 2 Symphonic Sketches, 1955; Concertino for strings, 1956; Concerto for orchestra, 1960; 4 Symphonies, 1962, 1966, 1968, 1973; Poem Bizantin, 1968; Pastorale Suite, 1982; Chamber: Cello sonata, 1952; Violin Sonata, 1953; String Quartet, 1954; Fantasy for String Trio, 1955; Sonata for 2 cellos, 1960; Sonata for 2 violas, 1965; Quintet for piano, violin, viola, cello, clarinet, 1967; Piano Trio, 1970; Madrigal for flute, clarinet, string trio and trombone; Cantatas, piano music, choruses, songs. Address: Vaselor 3A sect 2, Bucharest, Rumania.

POPPLEWELL Richard (John), b. 18 Oct 1935, Halifax, England. Organist; Choirmaster; Recitalist; Composer; Accompanist; Teacher. m. Margaret Conway, 1 s. Education: Chorister, organ scholar at King's College, Cambridge; Clifton College, Bristol; Royal College of Music; FRCO; FRCM. Career includes: Regular broadcasts; Soloist, Henry Wood Promenade Concert, 1965; Recitalist in Britain; Tours of Canada, Netherlands, France, Portugal; Assistant Organist, St Paul's Cathedral, 1958-66; Professor of Organ, Royal College of Music, 1962-; Director of Music, St Michael's Cornhill, 1966-79; Assistant Conductor and Accompanist, Bach Choir, 1966-79; Organist, Choirmaster and Composer, Her Majesty's Chapels Royal, St James' Palace, 1979-; A Conductor at various royal weddings. Compositions include: Organ Suite; Puck's Shadow; Chorale Preludes; Easter Hymn and Down Ampney; Elegy; Variations on a New Year's Carol, There is No Rose; Concerto in D for Full Orchestra and Organ; Christening Anthems for Royal Occasions; Jubilee March for Organ; Concerto in F for Full Orchestra and Organ; Anthem for 250th Anniversary, Royal Society of Musicians; National Anthem, dedicated by Gracious Permission to HM Queen Elizabeth II. Recordings: Own Compositions; Carols with Bach Choir; Organ Music from St Michael's, Cornhill. Publications: Triumphal March for Organ; Two Amens. Honours: ARCO Sawyer Prize at age 14; Prizes, Royal College of Music, 1955, 1956; Fellow, ibid, 1982; MVO, 1990. Memberships: Royal College of Organists; Incorporated Society of Musicians; Musicians Union. Hobbies: Reading; Swimming; Walking. Address: 23 Stanmore Gardens, Richmond, Surrey, TW9 2HN, England.

PORTELLA Nelson, b. 1945, Brazil. Singer (Baritone). Education: Studied in Rio de Janeiro. Career: Sang widely in South America opera houses from 1970, Teatro Liceo Barcelona from 1980, Naples from 1983 and Venice from 1985; Caracalla Festival, 1986, Ravenna, 1988; Roles have included Don Giovanni, Leporello, Masetto, Germont, Iago, Sharpless, the Count in Capriccio and Wozzeck. Recordings include: Scarpia, in Tosca (Balkanton); Mascagni's Le Maschere (Cetra).

PORTER Andrew, b. 26 Aug 1928, Cape Town, South Africa. Writer on Music. Education: MA, Oxford University, England. Career: Wrote for Manchester Guardian, 1949 and The Times, 1951; Music Critic for Financial Times, 1953-74, The New Yorker, 1972-92 and The Observer, 1992-97; Editor, The Musical Times, 1960-67; Visiting Fellow, All Souls College, Oxford, 1973-74; Bloch Professor, University of CA, Berkeley, CA, USA, 1980-81; Opera translation performances include, Verdi's Don Carlos, Rigoletto, Othello, Falstaff, Macbeth, The Force of Destiny, Nabucco, King for a Day, Wagner's The Ring, Tristan and Isolde, Parsifal, Handel's Ottone, Haydn's Deceit Outwitted and The Unexpected Meeting, Mozart's Mithradates, Lucio Silla, The Abduction from the Seraglio, Idomeneo, The Impresario, Figaro's Wedding, Cosi fan tutte, Don Giovanni and The Magic Flute, Gluck's Orpheus, Richard Strauss's Intermezzo, Rossini's The Turk in Italy and The Voyage to Rheims, Puccini's La Bohème. Recordings: The Ring; Othello, English translation. Publications: A Musical Season, 1974; Music of Three Seasons, 1978; Music of Three More Seasons, 1980; Musical Events: A Chronicle, 1986, 1991; Editor with David Rosen, Verdi's Macbeth: A Sourcebook, 1984. Contributions include: Music and Letters; Musical Quarterly; Musical Times; Proceedings of the Royal Musical Association; Atti del Congresso Internazionale di Studi Verdiani. Honours: Deems Taylor Award, American Society of Composers, Authors and Publishers, 1975, 1978, 1981; Corresponding Fellow, American Musicological Society. Memberships include: Vice-President, Donizetti Society; Royal Musical Association; American Institute of Verdi Studies. Address: c/o The Observer, 119 Farringdon Road, London, EC1R 3ER, England.

PORTER David (Hugh), b. 29 Oct 1935, New York, New York, USA. Pianist and Harpischordist; Educator; College President. m. (1) Laudie E Dimmette, 21 June 1958, deceased, 3 sons, 1 daughter, (2) Helen L Nelson, 24 Aug 1987. Education: BA, summa cum laude, Swarthmore College, 1958; PhD, Princeton University, 1962; Philadelphia Conservatory of Music, 1955-61; Private Piano Study with Edward Steuermann, 1955-62; Harpischord with Gustav Leonhardt, 1970, 1977. Debut: Philadelphia, 1955. Career: Piano and Harpischord Recitals and Lecture-Recitals throughout USA, 1966-; In London and Edinburgh, 1977; Performances on Radio and TV, 1967-; Professor of Classics and Music, Carleton College, 1962-; President, Carleton College, 1986-87; President, Skidmore College, 1987-; Author: Only Connect: Three Studies in Greek Tragedy, Horace's Poetic Journey, The Not Quite Innocent Bystander: Writings of Eduard Steuermann. Contributions to: Articles in Music Review and Perspectives of New Music; Numerous articles in classical journals. Honours: Steuermann Scholarship, Philadelphia Conservatory of Music, 1955-. Address: Skidmore College, Saratoga Springs, NY 12866, USA.

POSCHNER-KLEBEL Brigitte, b. 1957, Vienna, Austria. Singer (Soprano). Education: Studied in Vienna with Gerda Scheyrer and Gottfried Hornik. Career: Sang with Vienna Staatsoper, 1982-, Volksoper, 1983-; Guest appearances at Aix-en-Provence Festival, 1988-89, Fiordiligi, La Scala, Milan as Pamina, 1986, Venice, Amsterdam and Tokyo; Sang Susanna in Khovanshchina at Vienna Staatsoper, 1989; Other roles include Hansel, Rosalinde, Esmerelda, Sophie in Der Rosenkavalier, Xenia in Boris Godunov and Lucy in The Beggar's Opera; Frequent concert appearances. Recordings: Khovanshchina; Video of Elektra conducted by Abbado, as a Maidservant. Address: c/o Staatsoper, Opernring 2, A-1010 Vienna, Austria.

POSMAN Lucien, b. 22 March 1952, Maldegem. Composer. m. Karen Coussement, 10 August 1991, 2 daughters. Education: Ghent Royal Conservatory; Antwerp Royal Conservatory. Compositions: Hercules Haché; The Adventure of a Professor; Wheel Within Wheel; The Last Haycart; O! Zon. Recordings: The Last Haycart; Marsyas Swan Song on Sax. Honour: Muirelhuis Prize for Chamber Music. Address: Bylokevest 39, Ghent, Belgium.

POSPISIL Juraj, b. 14 June 1931, Olomouc, Czechoslovakia. Composer. Education: Studied at the Olomouc School of Music (1949-50), Janacek Academy, Brno (1950-52) and with Cikker at the Bratislava Academy (1952-55). Career: Lecturer in theory and composition at the Bratislava Academy of Music and Drama, 1955-91. Compositions include: The Mountains and the People, symphonic poem, 1954; 5 Symphonies, 1958, 1963, 1967, 1978, 1986; Sonata for strings, 1961; Song About a Man, symphonic variations, 1961; Trombone Concerto, 1962; 4 String Quartets, 1970, 1979, 1985, 1990; Inter Arna, cycle of 3 operas, 1970; Violin Concerto, 1968; Clarinet Concerto, 1972; To Bratislava, for baritone and orchestra, 1973; Symphonic Frescoes I-III, 1972, 1976, 1981; Concerto Eroico, for horn and orchestra, 1973; Chamber Sinfonietta, 1974; November Triptych, for chamber chorus, wind and piano, 1977; 2 Trios for piano, violin and cello, 1977, 1987; Concerto for soprano and orchestra, 1984; Dulcimer Concerto, 1989; Sonata for alto trombone and strings, 1991; Bass Quintet, 1991; The Lord's Prayer of the Hussites, sacred cantata, 1991; Manon Lescaut, scenic drama, 1993; Bass Tuba concerto, 1994; Autumn Bottling, for bass voice and string quartet, 1994. Address: c/o SOZA, Rastislavova 3, 821 08 Bratislava, Slovak Republic.

POSSEMEYER Berthold, b. 1950, Gladbeck, Westfalen, Germany. Singer (Baritone). Education: Studied in Cologne with Josef Metternich. Career: Sang at first in concert and gave Lieder recitals, notably at Paris, New York, Jerusalem, Hamburg, Turin and Venice; Stage career from 1978, at first at Oldenburg, then from 1979 at Essen, as Rossini's Figaro, Papageno, Guglielmo, Eugene Onegin and Silvio in Pagliacci; Sang at Gelsenkirchen Opera, 1984-86, then returned to concerts; Repertoire includes works by Bach, Mozart, Mendelssohn and Distler. Address: c/o Musiktheater im Rivier, Kennedyplatz, 4650 Gelsenkirchen, Germany.

POSTNIKOVA Viktoria, b. 12 Jan 1944, Moscow, USSR. m. Gennadi Rozhdestvensky 1969. Concert Pianist. Education: Studied at the Moscow Central School of Music with E B Musaelian, 1950-62; Further study with Yakov Flier at the Moscow Conservatoire. Career: Many concert appearances in Europe, Russia and the USA from 1966; Repertoire includes music by Bach, Handel, Scarlatti, Haydn, Mozart, Liszt, Chopin, Mendelssohn, Schumann, Brahms and Rachmaninov; Modern repertoire includes music by Busoni, Ives, Britten and Shostakovich; Played in the UK premiere of Schnittke's Concerto for piano duet and orchestra in London 1991. Recordings: Tchaikovsky Concertos (Decca); Busoni Concerto and complete piano works by Janácek and Tchaikovsky (Erato); Violin sonatas by Busoni and Strauss (Chandos); Complete piano concertos of Brahms, Chopin and Prokofiev (Melodiya). Honours include: Prize winner at competitions in Warsaw (1965), Leeds (1966), Lisbon (1968) and Moscow (1970). Address: Allied Artists, 42 Montpelier Square, London SW7 1JZ, England.

POTT Francis (John Dolben), b. 25 Aug 1957, Oxfordshire, England. Composer; Pianist; Baritone; University Lecturer. m. Virginia Straker, 19 Sept 1992, 1 son. Education: Chorister, New College, Oxford; Music Scholar, Winchester College and Magdalene College, Cambridge; Composition with Robin Holloway, Hugh Wood; Piano with Hamish Milne, London; MA, MusB, University of Cambridge. Career: Assistant Director of Music, Exeter School, 1980; Director of Music, New College School, Oxford, 1982; Acting Assistant Director, Abingdon School, 1986; Freelance composition/performance; Tutor in Compositional Techniques, Oxford University, 1987-89; Lecturer in Music, St Hugh's College, 1988; Lecturer in Music, Director of Foundation Studies, West London Institute, 1989-91; John Bennett Lecturer in Music, St Hilda's College, Oxford, 1991-; Visiting Tutor in Composition, Winchester College, 1991-96; Piano recitalist and accompanist; Toured Brazil with Winchester Cathedral Choir, 1991, and USA, 1995. Compositions: Organ: Mosaici di Ravenna, 1981; Empyrean, 1982; Fenix, Music for Lincoln Minster, Organ, Brass, Percussion, Timpani, 1985; Passion Symphony, Christus, 1986-90, premiered Westminster Cathedral, 1991; Toccata for Organ, 1991; choral (church) and other works; Piano Quintet, premiered by The Twentieth Century Consort, Smithsonian Institute, USA, 1993; Piano, Chamber Sonata for cello and piano, premiered Wigmore Hall, London, 1996, Piano Concerto, in progress; Also commissioned for 30 minute choral and orchestral work for Three Choirs Festival, Worcester Cathedral, 1999; Many TV and radio broadcasts; Works performed in 15 countries worldwide. Honour: Toccata for Piano, dedicated to Marc-André Hamelin, awarded First Prize, 2nd International Prokofiev Composition Competition, Moscow, March 1997. Address: Thurlows, Main Road, Littleton, Winchester, Hampshire SO22 6PS, England.

POTURLJAN Artin (Bedros), b. 4 May 1943, Kharmanli, Bulgaria. Composer. m. Akopjan Anahid Aram, 28 June 1974, 2 sons. Education: Theoretical Faculty with speciality in Musical Pedagogy, State Academy of Music, Sofia, 1967; Composition at Yerevan State Conservatoire Komitas, 1974. Career: First public performance of compositions in Yerevan, Moscow and Tbilisi, 1970-74; Performances of Symphonies Nos 1 and 2 in Sofia, 1976 and 1978; Member of Bulgarian Composers Union, 1978; Regular appearances in New Bulgarian Music Festival, 1980-97; Authorial recital of chamber compositions at Yerevan, Armenia in 1987 and Sofia in 1991; Performances of Four Spiritual Songs for Organ in Austria at Vienna, Klagenfurt and Anif, 1991; Participation in Holland-Bulgarian Music Festival, Sofia, 1992; Teacher of Polyphony in State Musical Academy, Sofia. Compositions: Concerto for Violin and Symphony Orchestra; Music for 3 Flutes, 2 Pianos, Tam-Tam and Strings; Klavier Quintet, Sonata for Violin and Piano; Four Spiritual Songs on Themes by Nerses Shanorhali for Organ; Opera, Women's Cry, in one act, 1979; Poem for Organ and Symphony Orchestra, 1980; Fantasia for Piano and Symphony Orchestra, 1990; Mosaici for Symphony Orchestra, 1993; Klavier Trio, 1995; Songs. Recordings: Arabesques for Piano; The Confession for Piano; Fantasia, Worlds for 2 Pianos; Symphony No 2, documentary; Concerto for Violin and Symphony Orchestra, documentary; Mosaici, 1994; Others on Bulgarian Radio. Honours: 1st Prize in Composition Competition, Pazardjik, 1985; Prizes of Bulgarian Composers Union for Arabesques, 1983 and Violin Concerto, 1989. Membership: Society for Contemporary Music in Bulgaria, 1992-. Hobby: Chess. Address: Iztok Bl 4 vch B, 1113 Sofia, Bulgaria.

POULENARD Isabelle, b. 5 July 1961, Paris, France. Singer (Soprano). Education: Studied at L'Ecole de l'Opera de Paris. Career: Sang at Tourcoing in operas by Mozart, Paisello, Monteverdi, Scarlatti and Vivaldi, conducted by Jean-Claude Malgoire; Has performed in operas at the festivals of Carpentras and Avignon; Hippolyte et Aricie under William Christie at the Opéra-Comique; Les Dialogues des Carmélites at the Opéra du Rhin; Cesti's Orontea at the Innsbruck Festival, under René Jacobs; Sang Gluck's Iphigénie en Aulide with the City of London Sinfonia at the Spitalfields Festival; Other repertoire includes Paisiello's Il Re Teodoro in Venezia, Handel's Alessandro and Massenet's Grisélidis; Concert appearances throughout France and in Venice, Flanders, Innsbruck and Stuttgart; British engagements at the Barbican, London and for Music at Oxford; Season 1992 as Teutile in the Vivaldi pastiche Montezuma at Monte Carlo and in Conti's Don Chisciotte at the Innsbruck Festival of Early Music; Sang Bita in Cimarosa's Il Mercato di Malmantile, Opéra du Rhin, 1996. Recordings: Music by Cesti, Rameau, Couperin, Schütz, Cavalli, Bach and Vivaldi; Monteverdi's Il Combattimento di Tancredi e Clorinda; Lully's Armide, La Malade imaginaire by Charpentier and Die Zauberflöte (Erato); Handel's Tamerlano (CBS); Le Cinesi by Gluck and Les Indes Galantes by Rameau, (Harmonia Mundi). Address: c/o Opéra du Rhin, 19 Place Broglie, F-07008 Strasbourg, France.

POULET Michel, b. 1960, France. Cellist. Education: Studied at the Paris Conservatoire with Jean-Claude Pennetier and with members of the Amadeua and Alban Berg Quartets. Career: Member of the Ysaÿe String Quartet from 1986; Many concert performances in France, Europe, America and the Far East; Festival engagements at Salzburg, Tivoli (Copenhagen), Bergen, Lockenhaus, Barcelona and Stresa; Many appearances in Italy, notably with the Haydn Quartets of Mozart; Tours of Japan and the USA 1990 and 1992. Recordings: Mozart Quartet K421 and Quintet K516 (Harmonia Mundi); Ravel, Debussy and Mendelssohn Quartets (Decca). Honours: Grand Prix Evian International String Quartet Competition, May 1988; special prizes for best performances of a Mozart quartet, the Debussy quartet and a contemporary work; 2nd Prize, Portsmouth International String Quartet Competition, 1988. Address: c/o Lies Askonas Ltd, 6 Hennrietta Street, London WC2E 8LA, England.

POULSON Lani, b. 7 Mar 1953, Tremonton, Utah, USA. Mezzo Soprano. Career: Sang as Charlotte, Ramiro, Carmen, Octavian and The Composer, Countess Geschwitz in Lulu; Sung at the Hamburg Staatsoper as Cherubino, Court Theatre at Drottingholm as Sextus in La Clemenza di Tito, Montpellier in 1988 as Dorabella, Stuttgart in 1991 in world premiere, as Andromeda in Perseo ed Andromeda by Sciarrino; Appearances at Essen, Lausanne, Stravanger, Frankfurt, Orleans, Munich, Strasbourg and in Der Rosenkavalier at Mannheim, Tel-Aviv, Budapest and Bonn; Concert repertory includes: the St Matthew Passion, Mozart's Requiem and Beethoven's Mass in C; In season 1993-94 sang performances of Sesto in Dresden, also as part of the Dresden Musikfestspiele; Season 1994-95 included the world premiere of Rihm's Das Schweigen der Sirenen at the Staatstheater in Stuttgart returning to Dresden for futher performances of La Clemenza di Tito; World premiere concert performance of L'Icone Paradoxale by Gerard Grisey, 1996, and also in Strasbourg, Frankfurt and Reggio Emilia; Season 1997-98, Ottavia in L'Incoronazione di Poppea, Utah Opera and debut as Magdalene in Meistersinger in Lisbon; Season 1998-99, new production of Al gran sole carico d'amore by Luigi Nono at Stuttgart. Honours: Prizewinner of the Concours International de Chant de la Ville de Toulouse, 1984; Grand Prizewinner, the first prize Mezzo and winner of the Elly Ameling Prize for Lieder at the 's-Hertogenbosch International Vocal Competition. Address: c/o Haydn Rawstron Ltd, 36 Station Road, London SE20 7BQ, England.

POULTON Robert, b. 1960, Brighton, England. Singer (Baritone). Education: Studied with Rudolf Piernay, Guildhall School of Music and Drama; Further study, European Opera Centre, Belgium and National Opera Studio, London. Career: Sang The Ferryman in Britten's Curlew River for Nexus Opera at the 1986 Bath Festival; Repeated at the Promenade Concerts; With Glyndebourne Touring Opera has appeared in L'Heure Espagnole, L'Enfant et Les Sortilèges, La Traviata, Le nozze di Figaro, Katya Kabanova and Jenufa, (last two also televised); Oratorio repertoire includes Purcell, Haydn's Creation, Vaughan Williams, Bach's St John Passion, Handel's Messiah, Elgar's The Kingdom and Finzi; Concerts in Singapore, Italy, Belgium and Israel; Created roles of Doctor, Policeman and Stranger in Judith Weir's The Vanishing Bridegroom, Scottish Opera, 1990; Created title role in Gassir the Hero by Theo Loevendie for Netherlands Opera, 1991; ENO Debut, Leander in Love for Three Oranges, 1991; Engaged as Figaro (Mozart) Scottish Opera; Ned Keene, Peter Grimes, Glyndebourne Festival, 1992; Sang Punch in Birtwistle's Punch and Judy for Netherlands Opera, 1993; Count Almaviva in Figaro's Wedding for ENO, 1994; Ned Keene, (Grimes), ENO, Nantes, Cologne and Copenhagen; Created Mr Dollarama in Birtwistle's The Second Mrs Kong, Glyndebourne Tour 1994 and festival, 1995; Douphol in Traviata for GTO at Glyndebourne, 1996. Recordings: Baron Zeta in Die Lustige Witwe, EMI, 1993. Honours include: Silver Medal for Singing and Lord Mayor's Prize, Guildhall School of Music. Current Management: Musicmakers International Artists Representation. Address: Little Easthall, St Paul's Walden, Hertfordshire SG4 8DH, England.

POUNTNEY David, b. 10 Sept 1947, Oxford, England. Opera Producer. Education: Radley College and Cambridge University. Career: First opera production Cambridge 1967, Scarlatti's Trionfo dell'Onore; Wexford Festival 1972, Katya Kabanova; Director of Productions for Scottish Opera 1975-80, notably with Die Meistersinger, Eugene Onegin, Jenufa, The Cunning Little Vixen, Die Entführung and Don Giovanni; Australian debut 1978, Die Meistersinger; Netherlands Opera 1980, world premiere of Philip Glass's Satyagraha; Principal Producer and Director of Productions, English National Opera, 1982-93: work includes The Flying Dutchman, The Queen of Spades, Rusalka, The Valkyrie and Lady Macbeth of Mtsensk; American debut with Houston Opera, Verdi's Macbeth: returned for the world premiere of Bilby's Doll by Carlisle Floyd, Katya Kabanova and Jenufa; Produced Weill's Street Scene for Scottish Opera, 1989; Other productions include From the House of the Dead in Vancouver, Dr Faust in Berlin and Paris, and The Fiery Angel at the State Opera of South Australia, Adelaide; The Flying Dutchman, Nabucco and Fidelio for the Bregenz Festival, The Excursions of Mr Broucek for the Munich State Opera, the World Premiere of Philip Glass's The Voyage at the Met, and the Fairy Queen for ENO; Season 1995-96 included Aida in Munich and libretto and direction of Peter Maxwell Davies's new opera The Doctors of Myddfai for Welsh National Opera; Season 1997-98 with Martinu's Julietta for Opera North and Rigoletto at Tel Aviv; Numerous opera translations from Russian, Czech, German and Italian. Address: IMG Artists, Media House, 3 Burlington Lane, London W4 2TH, England.

POUSSEUR Henri, b. 23 June 1929, Malmedy, Belgium. Composer. Education: Studied at the Liege Conservatory, 1947-52; Brussels Conservatory, 1952-53. Career: Worked at the Cologne and Milan electronic music studios, notably with Stockhausen and Berio; Taught music in Belgian schools, 1950-59; Founded in 1958 and directed the Studio Musique Electronique APELAC in brussels; Lecturer in courses of new music, Darmstadt, 1957-67, Cologne, 1962-68, Basle, 1963-64, and the State University of New York at Buffalo, USA, 1966-69; Lecturer at the Liège Conservatory; Professor of Composition, 1971, Director of the Institution, 1975-94; Teacher at Liege University, 1983-94; Directed the organisation of the New Institut de Pedagogie Musicale in Paris. Compositions: Symphonies, for 15 soloists, 1954; Mobile, for 2 pianos, 1958; Trois visages de Liège, electronic, 1961; Votre Faust, fantasy in the opera genre, with Michel Butor, 1960-68; Petrus Hebraicus, chamber music/theatre, for Schoenberg's centenary, 1973-74; La Rose de Voix, for 4 speakers, 16 solo voices, 4 choirs, 8 instruments, 1982; Traverser la forêt, for speaker, 2 solo voices, chamber choir and 12 instruments, 1987; Dichterliebesreigentraum, for 2 solo voices, 2 solo pianos, choir and orchestra, 1993. Publications include: Books: Ecrits d'Alban Berg, selected and translated with commentary, 1956; Fragments théoriques I Sur la musique experimentale, 1970; Musique sémantique Societe, 1972; Die Apotheose Rameaus (Versuch zum Problem der Harmonik), 1987; Schumann le Poète (25 Moments d'une lecture de Dichterliebe), 1993. Honours: Doctor Honoris Causa, Universities of Metz and Lille. Current Management: Icare. Address: 38 Avenue Wellington, B-1410 Waterloo, Belgium.

POWELL Claire, b. 1954, Tavistock, Devon, England. Singer (Mezzo-Soprano). Education: Royal Academy of Music; London Opera Centre. Career includes: Sang Alceste and Cherubino at Sadler's Wells while with London Opera Centre; London debut recital Wigmore Hall, 1979; Early appearances with Glyndebourne Festival Opera: has sung in Il Ritorno d'Ulisse, Falstaff, La Fedeltà Premiata and A Midsummer Night's Dream; Appearances with Welsh National Opera, Scottish Opera, Opera North and English National Opera, roles include, Berlioz, Didon, Beatrice and Marguerite, Carmen, Verdi's Ulrica and Preziosilla, Mussorgsky's Marina, Mozart's Cherubino and Idamante, Gluck's Alceste and Orfeo, Handel's Cornelia and Cyrus, Ponchielli's Laura, Saint-Saëns's Dalila, Ravel's Concepcion and Tchaikovsky's Pauline; Covent Garden from 1980, Les Contes d'Hoffmann, Midsummer Night's Dream, Otello, Lulu, Rigoletto, Die Zauberflöte, Ariadne auf Naxos, A Florentine Tragedy, Don Carlos (Eboli 1989); Médée (Neris), Rigoletto (Maddalena), Orlofsky, Fledermaus and Samson et Dalila; US debut 1990, as Maddalena at San Francisco; Sang Pauline in The Queen of Spades at Madrid, 1990; Guest appearances in Frankfurt, San Francisco, Barcelona, Madrid, Toronto, Paris, Rome, Brussels, Liège and Lisbon; Sang Eboli in a new production of Don Carlos for Opera North, 1993; April 1995, role of Auntie, Peter Grimes, Royal Opera House; Guest appearances in Munich and Hamburg as Carmen and Eboli, and Lausanne as Mistress Quickly; Title role in Gerhard's The Duenna, Leeds, 1996; Sang Quickly in new production of Falstaff in Cologne with Conlan and Carsen, 1997; Emilia in new production of Otello in Brussels with Pappano and Decker, 1997; Auntie in Peter Grimes, Tokyo with Otaka, Savonlinna with Royal Opera House, new production, San Francisco with Rurrides and Alder, 1998; Concert repertoire includes St Matthew Passion, Verdi Requiem, Das Lied von Erde, La Mort de Cleopatre, Stabat Mater, Petite Messe Solenelle by Rossini, Messiah and Elijah. Recordings include: Title role in The Duenna; Rosenkavalier conducted by Bernard Haitink; Video of Les Contes d'Hoffmann (as Nicklausse) and A Midsummer Night's Dream; El amor Brujo, Der Rosenkavalier, Il Ritorno di Ulisse in Patria; Video of Otello with Solti, Royal Opera House. Honours: Richard Tauber Memorial Prize, 1978. Address: c/o Lies Askonas, 6 Henrietta Street, London WC2E 8LA, England.

POWELL Kit (Christopher Bolland), b. 2 Dec 1937, Wellington, New Zealand. Composer; Lecturer in Music. m. Brigitte Bänninger, 14 Dec 1966, 1 s, 1 d. Education: MSc, Diploma of Teaching; BMus. Career: Teacher of Mathematics and Music, New Zealand High School, 1962-75; Lecturer, Christchurch Teachers College, 1975-84; Studied in Europe, 1980-81; Has written experimental music for choruses and percussion and 5 song cycle settings of poems by Michael Harlow and 3 major works of experimental music, theatre; Computer Music, Swiss Computer Music Centre, 1985; Atelier UPIC, Paris, 1987. Compositions: The Evercircling Light for Choir SATB and Percussion, 1980; Christophorus for Children's Choir and Orchestra, 1981; Galgenlieder, 1982; Les Episodes for Soprano, Bass Soloists and Orchestra, 1987; Concerto for 2 Violins, String and Percussion, 1989; Hauptsache man geht Zusammen hin, chamber opera, SATB, Speaker and Instrumental Ensemble, 1989-93; Gargantua for Wind Orchestra, 1990. Recordings: Devotion to The Small, 1980; The Evercircling Light, 1982; Hubert The Clockmaker, 1982; Whale, 1994; Chinese Songs, 1995. Publications: Workbook for University Entrance Prescription, 1973; Musical Design, 1975; Musik mit gefundenen Gegenständen, 1982; Suite for Solo Trombone. Memberships: Composers Association of New Zealand; Swiss Tonkünstlerverien. Hobby: Arts. Address: Nigelstrasse 11, 8193 Eglisau, Switzerland.

POWELL Mel, b. 12 Feb 1923, NY, USA. Composer. m. Martha Scott, 23 Jul 1946, 1 s, 2 d. Education: MusB, MA, Yale University, 1952; Studied piano with Sara Barg and Nadia Reisenberg; Composition with Paul Hindemith. Career: Chairman, Yale University Composition Faculty, 1954-69; Dean, California Institute of The Arts School of Music, 1969-72; Provost (CalArts), 1972-76; Professor and Fellow of The Institute, 1976-. Compositions: Filigree Setting for String Quartet; Haiku Settings for Voice and Piano; String Quartet, 1982; Woodwind Quintet; Modules for Chamber Orchestra; Strand Settings for Mezzo Soprano and Electronics; Duplicates, a concerto for Two Pianos and Orchestra, 1990; Many other orchestral pieces, vocal, chamber music and electronic works including Computer Prelude, 1988. Recordings: The Music of Arnold Schöenberg and Mel Powell; The Music of Milton Babbitt and Mel Powell; The Chamber Music of Mel Powell; Mel Powell: Six Recent Works. Publications: Compositions, essays and articles. Contributions to: Perspectives of New Music; Journal of Music Theory; American Scholar. Honours: Guggenheim Fellowship, 1960; National Institute of Arts and Letters Grant Award, 1964; Works chosen to represent USA in International Society for Contemporary Music Festivals, 1960 and 1984; Pulitzer Prize, 1990. Memberships: President, American Music Center, 1957-60; Consultant, National Endowment for The Arts, 1970-73; Awarded Honorary Life Membership in Arnold Schöenberg Institute. Address: c/o California Institute of The Arts, Valencia, CA 91355, USA.

POWER Patrick, b. 6 Jun 1947, Wellington, New Zealand. Singer (Tenor). Education: Studied at Universities of Otago and Auckland, New Zealand; Studied at University of Perugia, Italy. Career: Principal lyric tenor with: the Norwegian Opera in Oslo; Gärtnerplatz, Munich and Krefeld; Covent Garden debut, 1983, as the Simpleton in Boris Godunov, followed by Britten's Serenade for the Royal Ballet; Has Sung Alfredo for Kent Opera, Rodolfo and Almaviva for Scottish Opera; Glyndebourne Festival as Flute and Des Grieux in Manon for Opera North; Wexford Festival in title role of Massenet's Le Jongleur de Notre Dame; Overseas engagements as The Italian Tenor in Rosenkavalier and Fenton for Royal Danish Opera; Don Ottavio, Tamino and Rodolfo in Cologne; Belmonte in New Zealand and at Drottningholm; Le Comte Ory and Huon in Oberon at in Lyons and Alceste in Paris; Alfredo, Tamino and Don Ottavio in Canada; Almaviva in San Francisco; Season 1988-89, as Nadir in Les Pêcheurs de Perles in Pisa; Faust with Victorian State Opera; Returned to Australia as Pinkerton, Hoffmann, Rodolfo and the Duke of Mantua; Sang Nadir at Adelaide, 1996. Recordings include: Beethoven's 9th Symphony conducted by Roger Norrington; Balfe's Bohemian Girl conducted by Richard Bonynge. Address: c/o Athole Still International Management Ltd, Foresters Hall, 25-27 Westow Street, London, SE19 3RY, England.

POWERS Anthony, b. 1953, London, England. Composer. Education: Studied with Nadia Boulanger in Paris and with David Blake and Bernard Rands at York. Career: Composer-in-Residence, Southern Arts; Composer-in-Residence, University of Wales, Cardiff College. Compositions include: Piano Sonata No 2, 1985-86; Stone, Water, Stars, 1987; Horn Concerto, 1989; Cello Concerto, 1990; String Quartet No 2, 1991. Current Management: Oxford University Press, London, England. Address: Oxford University Press, Music Department, 3 Park Road, London NW1 6XN, England.

PRABUCKA-FIRLEJ Anna, b. 8 Mar 1950, Elblag, Poland. Piano Soloist; Chamber Pianist; Teacher. m. Jan Firlej, 27 Mar

1971, div 1991, 1 son. Education: Diploma with distinction, Music Lyceum, Gdansk, 1969; MA, 1974, Doctorate (Adjunct qualification), 1980, Academy of Music, Gdansk; Habilitation (Docent qualification), Academy of Music, Lodz, 1987. Debut: Piano soloist with orchestra at age 11, Elblag. Career: Piano soloist (symphony concerts, recitals) and chamber pianist, performances in Poland, Finland, Sweden, UK, Germany, Iceland, Austria, Greece, Czechoslovakia, Hungary, Bulgaria, USSR, Italy, Switzerland; As accompanist appearances with Eduard Melkus (Austria)-violin, Peter Damm (Germany)-horn, William Bennet (UK) flute, Marina Tschaikovskaja (Russia)-cello, Peter Leisegang (Switzerland)-cello, Siegfried Palm (Germany)-cello; Radio and TV recordings; Teaching: Professor of Chamber Music, Academy of Music, Gdansk; Guest Professor and Accompanist, Music Master Classes, Mynämäki, Finland, 1976, International Music Seminar, Weimar, Germany, 1984-91, Mattheiser Sommer-Akademie, Sobernheim, Germany, 1988-95, Chamber Music Seminar, Kozani, Greece, 1990-94. Recordings: CD, Slavic Music, 1994. Publications: Realisation of the piano part of instrumental baroque sonatas on basis of selected contemporary editions, 1988; Remarks on realisation of accompaniment for piano extract from the selected works of vocal-instrumental scores by J S Bach, 1989. Hobbies: Painting; Literature; History; Languages. Address: ul Leszczynskich 1g 24, 80-464 Gdansk, Poland.

PRANDELLI Giacinto, b. 8 Feb 1914, Lumezzane, Brescia, Italy. Singer (Tenor). Education: Studied with Fornarini in Rome and with Grandini in Brescia. Debut: Bergamo 1942, as Rodolfo in La Bohème. Career: Sang at La Scala in May 1945, in a performance of the Choral Symphony conducted by Toscanini; Appeared in Milan 1947 and 1954, in the local premieres of Peter Grimes and Menotti's Amelia al Ballo; Engagements at the Verona, Edinburgh and Florence Festivals; Metropolitan Opera 1951; London debut 1957 as Edgardo in Lucia di Lammermoor at the Stoll Theatre. Recordings include: Amelia al Ballo and La Bohème (Decca); Adriana Lecouvreur, Fedora and Francesca da Rimini (Cetra); Mefistofele and Il Tabarro (HMV); Lodoiska by Cherubini (MRF).

PRANTL Pavel, b. 21 Apr 1945, Susice, Czechoslovakia. Concertmaster; Professor of Violin. m. Martina Maixnerova, 24 June 1972, 2 sons. Education: Conservatory of Music, Kromeriz, 1960-65; Master's degree with Distinction, Academy of Musical Arts, Prague, 1965-72; Master classes with Maestro David Oistrakh, 1966, 1971. Debut: Czechoslovak Broadcasting Coroporation, 1956. Career: Member, First Violin Group, 1967-76, Assistant Concertmaster, 1976-78, Czech Philharmonic Orchestra; Concertmaster, Artistic Director, Prague Chamber Orchestra Without a Conductor, 1978-80; Founder, Artistic Leader, Prague Baroque Ensemble, 1973-80; Concertmaster, Singapore Symphony Orchestra, 1980-93; Guest Soloist with: Prague Symphony Orchestra, 1968; Moravian Philharmonic Orchestra, 1975; Radio Pilsen Symphony Orchestra, 1977; Singapore Symphony Orchestra, 1981-87; Numerous tours abroad including festivals in Salzburg, Montreux, Edinburgh, Wurzburg, Japan (Tokyo, Hokkaido), Korea (Seoul), USA (Cornell University, University of California at Los Angeles, San Diego); Head of String Department, Hong Kong Academy for Performing Arts, 1993-95; Director, Singapore Professional String Centre, 1995-. Recordings: Ivo Blaha's Violin Concerto, 1970; Czech Chamber Music, Czech Classical Violin Concertos, 1991. Honours: Honorary Professor, Paris and Brussels; Honorary DFA, London Institute. Memberships: Czechoslovak Society for Arts and Sciences, USA, 1982-; Dvorák Society, England, 1981-; International Parliament for Safety and Peace (United Nations), Deputy Member 1990-. Address: 110 Wishart Road, 03-07 Pender Court, Singapore 0409.

PRATICO Bruno, b. 1962, Aosta, Switzerland. Bass-Baritone. Education: Studied at the opera school of La Scala. Career: Sang Rossini's Mustafa and Bartolo under Abbado at La Scala; Bologna in 1987 as Belcore, Reggio Emilia in 1988 as Gaudenzio in Il Signor Bruschino; Has sung widely in Italy and guest appearances elsewhere include Opéra de Lyon in 1989, in Salieri's Prima La Musica poi le Parole, and Marseille in 1990 as Leporello; Other repertory includes The Mikado (Macerata Festival), Zurga in Les Pêcheurs de Perles and Geronimo in Cimarosa's Il Matrimonio Segreto. Recordings include: Leoncavallo's La Bohème; Lakmé and Paisiello's Don Chisciotte; Cimarosa's I Due Baroni di Rocca Azzurra. Address: c/o La Scala Milan, Via Filodrammatici 2, I-20121 Milan, Italy.

PRATLEY Geoffrey (Charles), b. 23 Mar 1940, Woodford, Essex, England. Accompanist. m. 1) Wendy Eathorne, 27 Mar 1965, 1 daughter, 2) Vija Rapa, 20 June 1987, 1 daughter. Education: Royal Academy of Music, 1958-63; LRAM, ARCM, 1960; GRSM, 1961; BMus, Dunelm, 1969. Career: Numerous Concerts throughout the World with many international artists including Baker, Domingo, Tortelier, Goossens, Brymer, Holmes, Streich and Milanova; Professor, Royal Academy of Music, from 1965-; Professor, Trinity College of Music, 1990-. Compositions: Dorothy Parker Poems for female voice and piano; Five Irish Folk-Songs; Five English Folk-Songs. Recordings: Ivor Gurney Songs with C Keyte; numerous BBC Recordings for Radio and TV. Publications: Handel Operatic Repertory BK2: Arias for tenor and piano (Stainer and Bell); Concert Master Series: Book 1 - Tchaikovsky Violin solos with piano (Faber); William Walton's Viola Concerto, new viola/piano score (OUP). Honours: ARAM, 1967; FRAM, 1977. Memberships: Incorporated Society of Musicians; Royal Society of Musicians. Address: The Willows, Bambers Green, Bishops Stortford CM22 6PE, England.

PRATT Stephen (Philip), b. 15 Jun 1947, Liverpool, England. Composer; Lecturer; Broadcaster; Conductor. m. Monica Mullins, 14 Oct 1972, 1 s, 3 d. Education: Certificate of Education, Christ's College, Liverpool, 1965-68; Royal Manchester College of Music, 1968-69; BA, Honours, University of Reading, 1969-71; BMus, University of Liverpool, 1971-72. Career: Broadcaster, BBC Radio Merseyside, 1971-; Senior Lecturer in Music, 1972-, Head of Music, 1991-, Liverpool Institute of Higher Education; Freelance Conductor, 1975-; Part time Lecturer, Open University, 1976-78; Part time Lecturer, Lancashire Polytechnic, 1983-; Part time Lecturer, Liverpool University, 1984-86; Fellow, University of Liverpool, 1993-; Broadcaster, BBC Radio 3, 1994-. Compositions include: Star and Dead Leaves; Winter's Fancy, 1978; Some of Their Number for Orchestra, 1980; Fruits of The Ground for Horn Trio, 1982; The Judgement of Paris for Orchestra, 1985; Strong Winds, Gentle Airs for Concert Band, 1987; String Trio, 1988; Uneasy Vespers for Mixed Choir, Soloists and Orchestra, 1991; At The Turn of The Year for Piano, 1993; About Time for Small Ensemble with Tape, 1995. Recording: Star and Dead Leaves, 1977. Contributions to: Arts Alive, 1972-; Reviewer, 1976-78, The Guardian; Classical Music, 1975-78. Honours: Chandos Composition Prize, Musica Nova, Glasgow, 1981. Hobbies: Football; Painting. Address: 43 Hallville Road, Mossley Hill, Liverpool, L18 0HP, England.

PRAUSNITZ Frederik (William), b. 26 Aug 1920, Cologne, Germany. Conductor. m. Margaret Britten Grenfell, 1 son, 1 daughter. Education: Juilliard Graduate School, 1945. Debut: Conducted Detroit Symphony Orchestra, 1944. Career: Guest Conductor with BBC Symphony Orchestra, London Symphony, New Philharmonia, London Philharmonic, Royal Philharmonic, English Chamber Orchestra and many orchestras on the continent; First European performances of music by Carter, Schuman, Sessions and Wolpe; Associate Director, Public Activities, 1947-49, Assistant Dean, 1949-61, Juilliard School of Music; Conductor, New England Conservatory Symphony Orchestra, Boston, 1961-69; Music Director, Syracuse Symphony, 1971-74; First US performances of works by Schoenberg, Stockhausen, Varèse, Webern and Dallapiccola; Director of The Peabody Conservatory Symphony Orchestra, 1976-80; Director of Conducting Programs, 1980-97; Conductor Laureate; Director of the Contemporary Music Ensemble at Peabody; Visiting Lecturer at Harvard and Sussex Universities. Recordings: Walton's Façade; Works by Roger Sessions and other modern composers. Publications: Score and Podium: A Complete Guide to Conducting, 1983, 1998; Roger Sessions: A Critical Biography, 1998. Honours include: Honorary Fellow, University of Sussex, 1970; Gustav Mahler Medal of Honour of The Bruckner Society of America, 1974. Address: 103 Dove Drive, Lewes, DE 19958, USA.

PRECHT Ulrika, b. 1959, Sweden. Singer (Mezzo-soprano). Education: Studied in Opera Studio 67 and Stockholm State Opera, Stockholm. Debut: Royal Opera, Stockholm, as Cherubino, 1990. Career: Sang Dalila with Folkoperan Stockholm, 1991, and Nancy in Martha for Dublin Opera, 1992; Season 1992-93 in Rossini's Il Signor Bruschino at Frankfurt, Eboli in Don Carlos at Stockholm and title role of Carmen at Sodertaleoperan; Concert engagements throughout Scandinavia. Address: Nordic Artists Management, Svervagen 76, S-11359 Stockholm, Sweden.

PŘEDOTA Stanislav, b. 28 June 1963, Ceske Budejovice, Czech Republic. Singer (Tenor). Education: Academy of Music, Prague. Career: Member, Schola Gregoriana Pragensis, 1988-, with recordings and concerts including Il canto delle pietre, Italy and Switzerland, 1993, Festival van het Gregorians, Watou, Belgium, 1994, 1997, Voix et routes romaines, Strasbourg, France, 1995, Prague Spring Festival, 1995-97, Festival de musique sacrée de Fribourg, Switzerland, 1996, Klangbogen Festival, Vienna, Austria, 1996, Mémoire de baptême de Clovis Festival, Reims, France, 1996, International Festival of Santander, Spain, 1997; Member, Musica Antiqua Praha, 1991-96, with recordings and concerts including Lufthansa Baroque Music Festival, London, 1991, 1993, Early Music Festival, York, England, 1993, Tage Alter Musik, Herne, Germany; Solo recordings and concerts of baroque music; Guest Solo Singer with other ensembles including Musica Florea. Recordings: Solo CDs: Janácek, Moravian Folk Poetry in Songs, Folk Poetry from Hukvaldy, 1993, Dvorák, Songs, 1995; With Musica Antiqua Praha: Baroque Music from the Kromeriz Archives, 1991, Italian Music of Early Baroque, 1992, Christmas Music of Baroque Bohemia, 1993, Alessandro Grandi and Masters of Italian Baroque, 1995; With Schola Gregoriana Pragensis: Bohemorum sancti, 1994, Rosa mystica, 1995, In Pragensi Ecclesia, 1996, Anno Domini 997, 1997, Liturgical Year, 1997; Anticae Moderna, 1998; With Musica Florea: J D Zelenka, Missa sanctissimae trinitatis, 1994; Many other CDs with Gothic, Renaissance and Baroque music. Honours include: Golden Harmony Award for year's best Czech recording, 1995. Address: Pod Lysinami 13, 14700 Prague 4, Czech Republic.

PREECE Margaret, b. 1965, England. Singer (Soprano). Career: Appearances with English National Opera as Zerlina, Janacek's Vixen, Ninetta (Love for Three Oranges) and Nymph in Monteverdi's Orfeo; Elisabeth de Valois for Opera-Go-Round, in The Ring Saga for City of Birmingham Touring Opera and Oriana in Handel's Amadigi with Opera Theatre Dublin (also on tour to France); Alice Ford, Fiordiligi and Adina for English Touring Opera; Donizetti's L'Ajo nel Imbarazzo and Provenzale's Lo Schiavo di sua Moglie at Musica nel Chiostro, Batignano; Season 1997 with the Queen of Night for Opera Theatre Dublin and Despina Papagena for Opera North; Concerts include Mozart's Davidde Penitente (at Seville), Beethoven's Missa solemnis, Dvorak Requiem and Paul Patterson's Mass of the Sea; Further opera roles include Oscar (Ballo in Maschera), Cordelia in Reimann's Lear, Susanna, Mozart's Countess, Anne Trulove, and Gilda. Address: C&M Craig Services Ltd, 3 Kersley Street, London SW11 4PR, England.

PREGARDIEN Christoph, b. 18 Jan 1956, Limburg, Germany. Singer (Tenor). Education: Studied at the Frankfurt Hochschule für Musik and in Milan and Stuttgart. Career: Sang first with the Limburg Cathedral Choir; Operatic engagements in Frankfurt, Gelsenkirchen, Stuttgart, Ludwigshafen, Hamburg, Antwerp and Karlsruhe; parts include Almaviva, Tamino, Fenton and Don Ottavio; Concert appearances in the festivals of Flanders, Holland, Israel, Paris, Aix, Ansbach, Innsbruck and Göttingen; Conductors include Sigiswald Kuijken, Gustav Leonhardt, Ton Koopman, Philippe Herreweghe, Roger Norrington, Ivan Fischer, Hans-Martin Linde, Wolfgang Gönnenwein, Frans Brueggen, Helmuth Rilling, Ferdinand Leitner and Michael Gielen; Sang in production of the St Matthew Passion for Belgian television; Towards Bach and Haydn concert series on London's South Bank, 1989; Sang in L'Infedeltà Delusa by Hadyn for Flanders Opera 1990; Debut recital at the Wigmore Hall, London, 1993, returned in Schubert's Winterreise, 1997. Recordings include: St John and St Matthew Passion conducted by Leonhardt; St John Passion, Bach's Magnificant; L'Infedeltà Delusa by Haydn; Mozart Concert Arias conducted by Kuijken; Buxtehude Cantatas and Mozart Requiem under Ton Koopman; Bach Lutheran Masses under Herreweghe; Symphoniae Sacrae by Schütz; Grimoaldo in Rodelinda (Harmonia Mundi). Address: c/o Lies Askonas Ltd, 6 Henrietta Street, London WC2E 8LA, England.

PREIN Johann (Werner), b. 3 Jan 1954, Trofaiach, Leoben, Austria. Singer (Bass-baritone). Education: Studied with Herma Handl-Wiedenhofer in Graz. Career: Sang in concerts and recitals from 1979; Stage career from 1984, notably at Graz and Vienna; Bayreuth Festival, 1984-85, as Donner in Das Rheingold; Engaged at Gelsenkirchen from 1986; Guest appearances at the Vienna Staatsoper, Dusseldorf and Barcelona; Wiesbaden 1988, as King Henry in Lohengrin; At Gelsenkirchen in 1989 sang Wagner in the first German production of Busoni's Doktor Faust, in the completion by Antony Beaumont; Other roles include: Mephistopheles (Faust); 4 villains in Les Contes d'Hoffmann; the Speaker in Die Zauberflöte; Biterolf and the Landgrave in Tannhäuser; Wotan in Der Ring des Nibelungen; Achilles in Penthesilea by Schoeck. Recordings include: Lieder by Joseph Mathias Hauer (Preiser); Der Konthur in Schulhoff's Flammen, 1995. Address: Musiktheater im Revier, Kennedyplatz, D-4650 Gelsenkirchen, Germany.

PREISLER Frantisek (Senior), b. 29 Apr 1948, Opava. Opera Stage Manager (Producer). m. Vlastimila Plosharova Preislerova, 8 Apr 1972, 1 son. Education: Janacek's Academy, Brno. Debut: Smetana's Two Widows at the Theatre Olomouc, 1973. Career: Producer at: Theatre Olomouc, 1973-80; Theatre Maribor, Ljubljana, 1980-83; College Lecturer, Janaceks Academy, Brno, 1982-92; Janacek Theatre, Brno, 1983-92; Director, Janacek's Opera, Brno, 1985-92; Productions in Czechoslovakia of over 60 operas from the Slav repertoire (Smetana's Bartered Bride, Two Widows and The Secret, Dvorak's Rusalka, Janacek's Jenufa, Cunning Little Vixen and Kata Kabanova, Mussorgsky's Boris Gudunov and Khovanstina, Tchaikovsky's Eugene Onegin, Borodin's Prince Igor) and also Bizet's Carmen, Puccini's Madama Butterfly, La Bohème, Gershwin's Porgy and Bess, and Strauss's Rosenkavalier, Mozart's La nozze di Figaro and Don Giovanni, Gounod's Faust, Rossini's Il Barbière di Siviglia, Donizetti's L'Elisir d'Amore; Verdi's La Traviata; Massenet's Werther, and numerous others. Honours: Ljubljana Festival, Porgy and Bess, Estonia, 1982. Membership: Free Artist.

PREISLER Frantisek (Junior), b. 23 Oct 1973, Olomovc, Czech Republic. Conductor; Dirigent. Education: Janacek's Conservatory, Brno; Jancek's Academy, Brno; Wiener Meisterkurs für Dirigentem, Austria. Debut: Janacek's Katja Kabanova, Janacek's Theatre Brno, 1993. Career: The first Czech version of Jesus Christ Superstar; Chief Conductor of Musical Theatre Karlin, Prague; Conductor in the National Theater, Prague; Chief Conductor of Janacek's Symphony Orchestra, Prague, 1997-; Conducted operas and musicals including Smetana's The Kiss and the Two Widows, Mozart's Così fan tutte, Die Zauberflöte, Don Giovanni, Beethoven's Fidelio, Rossini's Il Barbiere di Seviglia, Verdi's Nabucco, Aida, La Traviata, Rigoletto, Macbeth, Otello and La Forza del Destino, Puccini's Turandot, La Bohème and Tosca, Leoncavallo's I Pagliacci, Mascagni's Cavalleria rusticana, Dvorak's Rusalka, Meyerbeer's Les Huguenots, Strauss' Die Fledermaus. Compositions: Instrumental arrangements; film music. Recordings: Complete Orchestral works of Joseph Bulogne, Chevalier de Saint Georges; Live recording: Andrew Lloyd Webber's Requiem; B Smetana, Two Widows, radio and television. Membership: National Theater of Prague. Hobbies: Singing; Trombone. Current Management: GOJA agency. Address: National Theatre of Prague, Ostrovni, Prague 1 11230, Czech Republic.

PREMERU Donata, b. 4 June 1939, Nagybecskerek, Yugoslavia. Musicologist; Music Writer; Broadcaster; Lecturer; Journalist; Promotion Manager. m. Jovan Premeru, 17 March 1962, 1 son, 1 daughter. Education: History of Arts, University of Zagreb; Language Diplomas from Cambridge, Italy, France; State Musical School; Diploma, Musicology, Academy of Music, Zagreb; Postdiploma, London University. Career: Lecturer, Zagreb; Music Editor, Radio Belgrade; Freelance Editor; Numerous Appearances on Radio and Television in Belgrade and Novi Sad. Publications: On Childrens Operas, 1997. Contributions to: Oko; Il Mondo della Musica; Pro Femina; Pro Musica; Rec; Continuo; Projekat; Politika. Honours: 1st Prize, Radio Belgrade, 1965; Golden Microphone, Radio Belgrade, 1990. Memberships: Union of Yugoslav Composers; Union of European Journalists. Hobbies: Artistic Photography; Cinema; Cooking; Swimming; Walking. Address: Prol Brigada 52 (Krunska), 11000 Beograd, Yugoslavia.

PREMRU Raymond (Eugene), b. 6 June 1934, Elmira, New York, USA. Composer; Musician; Divorced, 2 daughters. Education: BMus, Composition (Performers), Certificate of Trombone, Eastman School of Music, University of Rochester, New York, 1956. Career: Member, Phillip Jones Brass Ensemble, 1960-; Commissions from Cleveland Orchestra (Lorin Maazel), Pittsburgh Symphony (André Previn), Philadelphia Orchestra (Riccardo Muti), Philharmonia Orchestra (Lorin Maazel), London Symphony Orchestra (Previn), Royal Choral Society (Meredith Davies), International Trumpet Guild, York Festival, Cheltenham Festival, Camden Festival, Philip Jones Brass Ensemble; Visiting Professor, Trombone, Guildhall School of Music, Eastman School of Music, Rochester, 1987. Compositions: Music from Harter Fell; Quartet for 2 Trumpets, horn and Trombone; Divertimento for Ten Brass; Concertino for Trombone, flute, oboe, clarinet and bassoon; Tissington variations. Recordings: Easy Winner, Argo/Decca Records; Modern Brass, Philip Jones Brass Ensemble. Contributions to: International Trombone Association Journal; Instrumentalist Magazine. Hobby: Tennis. Address: Eastman School of Music, University of Rochester, 26 Gibbs Street, Rochester, NY 14604, USA.

PRESCOTT Duncan, b. 1964, England. Clarinettist. Education: Studied at the Royal Academy of Music with Anthony Pay, and with Karl Leister. Career: Recitals at the Wigmore Hall and on the South Bank; Member of the Nash Ensemble, with whom he has broadcast the Brahms, Reger and Weber Clarinet Quintets; Mozart Clarinet Concerto with the London Sinfonietta and the English String Orchestra; Performances at many jazz venues, including Ronnie Scott's; Member of the Boronte Ensemble and duo partnership with pianist Scott Mitchell; Further engagement in Germany, America, Israel, Russia, Japan, Hong Kong and Italy. Recordings: Virtuoso pieces with Scott Mitchell (Chandos). Honours: Capitol Radio Music Prize; Lambeth Music Award; Frank Britton Award; Malcolm Sargent Music Award; Scholarships from the Myra Hess Trust, Countess of Munster Trust and the English Speaking Union. Address: c/o Anglo-Swiss Management, Suite 35-37 Morley House, 320 Regent Street, London W1R 5AD, England.

PRESSLER Menahem, b. 16 Dec 1923, Magdeburg, Germany. Pianist; Professor of Music. m. Sara Szerzen, 1 son, 1 daughter. Education: Educated in Israel; Studied with Petri and Steuermann. Career: Distinguished Professor, Indiana University, USA, 1955-; Soloist under Stokowski, Dorati, Ormandy, Mitropoulos; Co-founder, The Beaux Arts, Trio, 1955, which performs yearly in the Capitals of Europe and Americas; Appearances at Festivals in Edinburgh, Salzburg, Paris; Since 1984 in Residence at the Library of Congress in Washington, DC; Subscription concerts in New York, Metropolitan Museum and at Harvard University. Recordings: Most of the Trio Repertoire; More than 50 records for Philips. Publications: Several publications. Honours: Winner of Debussy Prize in San Francisco; 3 Grand Prix du Disques, Gramophone Record of the Year Award; Prix d'honneur Montreux Prix Mondial Du Disques. Current Management: Columbia Artists Management, New York. Address: 1214 Pickwick Place, Bloomington, IN 47401, USA.

PRESTON Katherine (Keenan), b. 7 December 1950, Hamilton, Ohio, USA. Music Historian; Associate Professor Music. m. Daniel F Preston, 8 October 1971, 1 son. Education: University of Cincinnati, 1969-71; BA, The Evergreen State College, Olympia, Washington, 1974; MA, Musicology, University of Maryland, 1981; PhD, Musicology, Graduate Center, City University of New York, 1989. Career: Taught at University of Maryland, Catholic University, and Smithsonian Institution; Currently Associate Professor, College of William and Mary, Williamsburg, Virginia, 1989-. Publications: Books: Scott Joplin, Juvenile Biography, 1987; Music for Hire: The Work of Journeymen Musicians in Washington DC 1875-1900, 1992; Opera on the Road: Traveling Opera Troupes in the United States, 1820-1860, 1993; The Music of Toga Plays (Introduction) in Playing Out The Empire: Ben Hur and other Toga Plays and Films, 1883-1908, edited by David Mayer, 1994; Editor of Irish American Theater, Volume 10 in Series Nineteenth-Century American Musical Theater, 1994. Contributions include: Various Articles including: The 1838-40 American Concert Tour of Jane Shirreff and John Wilson, British Vocal Stars in Studies in American Music, 1994; Popular Music in the Gilded Age: Musicians' Gigs in Late Nineteenth-Century Washington DC, in Popular Music, 1985; Music and Musicians at the Mountain Resorts of Western Virginia, 1820-1900, in A Celebration of American Music, 1989; Numerous articles in The New Grove Dictionary of American Music, 1986 and The New Grove Dictionary of Opera, 1992. Memberships: American Musicological Society; Sonneck Society for American Music. Address: 137 Pintail Trace, Williamsburg, VA 23188, USA.

PRESTON Simon (John), b. 4 Aug 1938, Bournemouth, England. Musician; Organist; Conductor. Education: BA 1961, MusB 1962, MA 1964, King's College, Cambridge University; Fellow, Royal College of Music; Fellow, Royal Academy of Music. Career: Sub-Organist, Westminster Abbey, 1962-67; Acting Organist, St Albans Abbey, 1968-69; Organist and Tutor in Music, Christ Church, Oxford, 1970-81; CUF Lecturer in Music, Oxford University, 1972-81; Organist/Master of Choristers, Westminster Abbey, London, 1981-87. Recordings: Organ Music by Handel and Liszt and Masses by Haydn with the Christ Church Choir; Handel: Choral works with Westminster Abbey Choir; Series of Bach's Organ Works; Liszt Fantasia on Ad nos, ad Salutarem Undam, Reubke Sonata on the 94th Psalm; Choral works for Palestrina, Allegri, Anerio, Nanino and Giovannelli. Honours: Dr Mann Organ Student, King's College, Cambridge; Honorary Fellow, Royal College of Organists; Edison Award, 1971; Grand Prix du Disque, 1979; International Performer of the Year (New York Chapter of the American Guild of Organists), 1987. Memberships: Member of the Jury for Organ Competitions at: St Albans 1983, Lahti Finland 1985, Bruges Belgium 1986, Dublin Ireland 1990, Calgary Canada 1990; Chairman, Performer of the Year Award (Royal College of Organists), 1988; Patron of the University of Buckingham; Member, Music Panel of the Arts Council, 1968-72; Member, BBC Music Advisory Committee, 1965-67; Royal Society of Musicians; Vice President, Organ Club; Vice President, Organists' Benevolent League; Chairman, Herbert Howells Society; Fellow, Royal Society of Arts. Hobbies: Theatre; Croquet. Address: Little Hardwick, Langton Green, Kent TN3 0EY, England.

PRETRE Georges, b. 14 Aug 1924, Waziers, France. Conductor. m. Gina Marny, 1 son, 1 daughter. Education: Lycée and Conservatoire de Douai, Conservatoire National Supérieur de Musique de Paris and Ecole des chefs d'orchestra. Career: Director of Music, Opera Houses of Marseilles, Lille and Toulouse 1946-55, Director of Music, Opéra-Comique, Paris, 1955-59, at l'Opéra 1959-; Director-General of Music at l'Opéra, 1970-71; Conductor of the symphonic associations of Paris and of principal festivals throughout the world; also conducted at La Scala, Milan, and major American orchestras; Conductor, Metropolitan Opera House, New York, 1964-65, La Scala, Milan, 1965-66, Salzburg, 1966; Appointed First Guest Conductor, Wiener Symphoniker, Vienna, 1986; Concerts at the 1995 Lucerne Festival. Recordings: Several complete opera sets with Maria Callas; Lucia di Lammermoor, La Traviata, Tosca, Iphigénie en Tauride; Poulenc Sinfonietta, Les Biches, Suite Française and Piano concerto; La Damnation de Faust; Saint-Saëns 3rd Symphony; Berg Chamber Concerto and Violin Concerto (Christian Ferras); Symphonie Fantastique; Franck Psyché et Eros; Faust (Domingo/Freni); Samson et Dalila (Vickers/Gorr). Honours: Chevalier, Légion d'honneur, 1971; Haute Distinction République Italienne, 1985, Commdr République Italienne, 1980; Officer, Légion d'honneur, 1984. Address: Chateau de Vaudricourt, a Naves, par Castres, 81100 France.

PREVIN André, b. 6 Apr 1930, Berlin, Germany. Conductor; Composer; Pianist. m. 4 Jan 1982, 4 sons, 3 daughters. Education: Conducting, Pierre Monteux; Composition, Mario Castelnuovo-Tedesco. Career: Music Director of Houston Symphony, 1967-69, London Symphony, 1968-79, Pittsburgh Symphony, 1976-84, Royal Philharmonic, 1985-91, Los Angeles Philharmonic, 1985-89; Guest Conductor at Salzburg and Edinburgh Festivals, all major orchestras in Europe and USA; Conductor Laureate, London Symphony Orchestra, 1992. Compositions include: Reflections for Orchestra; Triolet for Brass; Song Cycle; Invisible Drummer for Piano; Every Good Boy Deserves Favour, for Orchestra and Actors, play by Tom Stoppard; Honey and Rue, songcycle on text by Toni Morrison, 1992; Cello Sonata, 1993; Sally Chisum Remembers Billy The Kid, songcycle on text by Michael Ondaatje, 1994; Violin Sonata, 1994; Trio for Piano, Oboe and Bassoon, 1994; Four Songs for Soprano, Cello and Piano, text by Toni Morrison, 1994; Commission from the San Francisco Opera for A Streetcar Named Desire, 1998. Recordings include: Over 150 recordings as conductor and 25 as pianist, including CDs of Elgar's 2 Symphonies, Orff's Carmina Burana, Prokofiev's Symphonies and Piano Concertos (Ashkenazy), Shostakovich's Symphonies, Vaughan Williams 9 Symphonies, Walton's 1st Symphony, Die Fledermaus with Vienna Philharmonic, Complete Orchestral Works Richard Strauss with Vienna Philharmonic. Publications: Face to Face, 1971; Orchestra, 1979; Guide to Music, 1983; No Minor Chords, autobiography, 1992. Honours: Academy Award, 4 times; Grammy Award, 6 times; Honorary Fellow, Royal Academy and Guildhall; Honorary Doctorates from various US universities and Curtis Institute, Philadelphia; KBE, HM Queen Elizabeth II, 1996. Memberships: Academy of Motion Picture Arts and Sciences; Dramatists Guild; Composers Guild; National Composers and Conductors League. Address: c/o Ronald Wilford, Columbia Artists Inc, 105 W 57th Street, New York, NY 10019, USA.

PREVITALI Fabio, b. 1961, Venice, Italy. Baritone. Education: Studied at the Venice Conservatory. Debut: Luca in 1987 in Salieri's Falstaff. Career: Sang at Treviso in 1987 as Albert in Werther, Frank in Die Fledermaus and in Linda di Chamounix; Season 1988 at opera houses in Paris, Verona and Reggio Emilia; Other roles in Don Giovanni, Maria Stuarda, La Bohème, Eugene Onegin and Semele. Recordings include: Franchetti's Cristoforo Colombo, taped at Frankfurt in 1991. Address: Reggio Emilia Opera, Teatro Municipale, Piazzo Martini 7 Luglio, 42100 Reggio Emilia, Italy.

PREVOST André, b. 30 July 1934, Hawkesbury, Ontario, Canada. Composer. Education: Conservatoire de Musique de Montréal; Studied under Olivier Messiaen at Paris Conservatoire and Henri Dutilleux at Ecole Normale, Paris; Studied electronic music under Michel Philippot, ORTF; Studied under Aaron Copland, Zoltán Kodály, Gunther Schuller and Elliott Carter at Berkshire Music Center, Tanglewood, Massachusetts. Career: Professor of composition and analysis, Faculty of Music, University of Montreal; composed music played throughout Canada and also France, USA, England, Yugoslavia, India and New Zealand; commissions have been received from Jeunesse Musicales du Canada, Quintette de Cuivres de Montreal, Charlottetown Festival, Ten Centuries Concerts, Canadian Broadcasting, McGill Chamber Orchestra, l'Orchestre symphonique de Quebec, Communaute Radiophonique des Pays de Langue Francaise, London (Ontario) Symphony Orchestra, Société de Musique Contemporaine du Québec, Canadian Music Centre among others. Compositions include: Orchestral: Célébration 1966; Chorégraphie I, 1972, II 1976, III 1976, IV 1978; Cosmophonie 1985; Diallele 1968; Evanescence 1970; Fantasmes 1963; Hommage 1970-71; Ouverture 1975; Scherzo 1960; Soloists with Orchestra: Concerto pour Violoncelle et Orchestre 1976; Le Conte de l'Oiseau 1979; Hiver dans l'Ame 1978; Paraphase 1980; Chamber Music: Improvisation Pour Violon Seul 1976; Improvisation pour Violoncelle Seul 1976; Improvisation pour Alto Seul 1976; Mobiles 1959-60; Mouvement pour Quintette de Cuivres 1963; Musique pour l'Ode au St Laurent 1965; Mutations 1981; Quatuor 1958, No 2 1972; Sonate pour Alto et Piano 1978; Sonate No 1 pour Violoncelle et Piano 1962; No 2 Pour Violoncelle et Piano 1985; Suite pour Quotuor a Cordes 1968; Triptyque 1962; Trois Pieces Irlandaises 1961; Solo Voice: Geoles 1963; Improvisation pour Voix et Piano 1976; Musique Peintes 1955; Chorus: Ahimsa 1984; Missa de Profundis 1973; Psalm 148 1971; Keyboard: Cinq Variations sur un Thème Grégorien 1956; Improvisation pour piano 1976; Variations en passacaille 1984. Address: c/o SOCAN, 41 Valleybroo Drive, Don Mills, Ontario M3B 2S6, Canada.

PREY Claude, b. 30 May 1925, Fleury-Sur-Andelle, France. Composer. Education: Studied with Milhaud and Messiaen at the Paris Conservatoire, with Migone in Rio de Janiro and at the Laval University. Compositions include: Lettres Perdues, Opera Episolaire, RFT, 1961; Le Coeur Revelateur, Chamber Opera After Poes Tel Tale Heart, Paris, 1964; L'Homme Occis, Opera Clinique composed, 1963, Staged Rouen, 1978; Jonas Opera Oratorio, ORTF, 1966; Les Mots Croises, composed, 1965,

Staged Paris, 1978; Donna Mobile, Opera d'Appartement, composed 1965, Staged Tours 1985; Metamorphose D'Echo Opera de Concert, Prague, 1967; La Noirceur Du Lait, Opera Test, Strasbourg, 1967; On Veutt La Lumiere, Allonsy, Opera Parodie, Angers, 1968; Fetes de la Faim, Opera Pour Dames, Avignon, 1972; Les Liaisons Dangereuses, Strasbourg, 1974; Young Libertad, Opera Study, Lyons, 1976; La Grand Mere Francaise, Opera Illustre, Avignon, 1976; Utopopolis, Opera Chanson, Paris, 1980; L'Escalier de Chambord, Dramma Melodico, Tours, 1981; Lunedi Blue, Opera Breve, Paris, 1982; Pauline, Chamber Opera, Touring, 1983; O Commeeau, Opera Madrigalesque, Paris, 1984; Le Rouge et le Noir, Opera in 2 Acts After Stendhal, Aix en Provence, 1989; Sommaire Soleil, Opera Composed, 1990; Theatrephonie for 12 Voices and Piano, 1971. Address: SACEM, 225 avenue Charles de Gaulle, 92521 Neuilly sur Seine Cedex, France.

PREY Florian, b. 1959, Hamburg, Germany. Singer (Baritone). Education: Studied with father, Hermann Prey, and at Munich Musikhochschule. Career: Gave Lieder recitals and appeared in concert from 1982; Opera debut as the Count in Schreker's Der ferne Klang, Venice, 1984; Sang in a staged version of St Matthew Passion at Teatro La Fenice, 1984; Silvio for Vienna Kammeroper, 1986; Stadttheater Aachen, 1988-, as Harlekin in Ariadne auf Naxos, Falke and Papageno; Writer of stage pieces and film scripts (Montag eine Parodis, 1985). Address: c/o Stadttheater, Theaterstrasse 1-3, 5100 Aachen, Germany.

PREY Hermann, b. 11 July 1929, Berlin, Germany. Opera and Concert Singer (Baritone). m. Barbara Pniok 1954, 1 son, 2 daughters. Education: Humanistisches Gymnasium Zum Grauen Kloster Berlin and Staatlich Musikhochschule, Berlin. Career: Appeared at State Opera, Wiesbaden 1952, also Hamburg, Munich, Berlin, Vienna; Created Meton in Krenek's Pallas Athene Weint, Hamburg, 1955; Guest appearances at La Scala, Milan, Metropolitan Opera, New York, Teatro Colón, Buenos Aires, San Francisco Opera; New York debut, 1960; Covent Garden debut, 1973; Rossini's Figaro; Has sung at Festivals at Salzburg, Bayreuth, Edinburgh, Vienna, Tokyo, Aix-en-Provence, Perugia, Berlin; now with Munich State Opera; best known as Mozart's Papageno, Figaro and Guglielmo, and Wagner's Wolfram and Strauss's Storch (Munich 1990); Returned to Metropolitan 1987, in Ariadne auf Naxos; Sang Beckmesser at Covent Garden 1990 and at the 1990 Munich Festival; Appeared as Beckmesser in a new production of Die Meistersinger at the Metropolitan, 1993; Engaged as Papageno for the 1997 Salzburg Festival; Noted recitalist, in Lieder by Schubert, Brahms and Schumann. Publication: Premierenfieber (memoirs) 1981. Honours include: Winner Meistersänger-Wettbewerb, Nuremberg 1952. Hobbies: Riding; Films. Address: 8033 Krailling vor München, Fichtenstrasse 14, Germany.

PRIBYL Lubos, b. 29 Oct 1975, Prague, Czech Republic. Pianist. Education: Conservatoire in Prague with Professor Radomír Melmuka, 1990-96; Academy of Music in Prague with Professor Emil Leichner, 1997-. Debut: Zlín, performance in the concert of the Zlín Symphony orchestra, 1989-. Career: Recital in the Beethoven festival in Teplice, 1992-; Concerts in Bolzano, Brixen, Italy, 1994; Concert tour in Japan (Tokyo, Sapporo, Obihiro, Asahikava), 1996; Played Tchaikovsky's Concert no 1, with orchestra of the Prague Conservatoire, 1997; Short portrait on Czech television, 1997. Recordings: A few recordings in Czech Radio (Chopin, Tchaikovsky, Rachmaninov, Martinu, Jezek); CD, piano recital (Hadyn, Liszt, Semtana, Rachmaninov, Martinu, Jezek). Honours: Competition, Virtuosi per musica di pianoforte, Czech Republic, 1st Prize, 1988; Competition "Citta di Senigallia", Italy, 5th prize, 1991; Beethoven Competition in Hradec nad Moravicí, Czech Republic, 1st Prize, 1992; F P Neglia Competition in Enna, Italy, 2nd Prize, 1993; Dr Václav Holzknecht Competition in Prague, 1st Prize, 1995; Mavi Marcoz Competition in Aosta, Italy, 5th Prize, 1995. Current Management: Agency Pragokoncert. Address: Smeralova 34, 170 00 Praha 7, Czech Republic.

PRICE Curtis (Alexander), b. 7 Sept 1945, Springfield, Missouri, USA. Musicologist. Education: Studied at Southern Illinois University, 1963-67, and at Harvard with John Ward and Nino Pirotta (PhD, 1974). Career: Teacher at Washington University, St Louis, Missouri, 1974-81, and at King's College, London; Reader, 1985, Professor, 1988; Appointed Principal of Royal Academy of Music, 1995. Publications include: The Critical Decade for English Music Drama, 1700-1710, Harvard, 1978; Music in the Restoration Theater: with a Catalogue of Instrumental Music in the Plays, 1665-1713, Ann Arbor, 1979; Henry Purcell and the London Stage, Cambridge, 1984; H Purcell: Dido and Aeneas (editor), New York, 1986; Italian Opera and Arson in Late Eighteenth-Century London, 1989; The Impresario's Ten Commandments: Continental Recruitment for Italian Opera in London 1763-4 (with J Milhous and R D Hume), London, 1992; Man and Music: The Early Baroque Era (editor), London 1993; Presided over Arthur Jacobs Memorial Gathering, Duke's Hall, RAM, 1997. Address: Royal Academy of Music, Marylebone Road, London NW1 5HT, England.

PRICE Gwyneth, b. 1945, Bath, England. Soprano. Education: Studied in London with E Herbert-Caesari. Career: Many appearances at opera houses throughout the UK, including Royal Opera, Covent Garden as the Priestess in Aida, Fortune Teller in Arabella, Milliner and Duenna in Rosenkavalier, Villager in Jenufa, 1993; Sang title role in Menotti's The Old Maid and The Thief at Norfolk Festival, 1992; Concert repertoire includes Verdi's Requiem, conducted by Colin Davis; Council member of Friends of Covent Garden. Address: c/o Royal Opera House (Friends), Covent Garden, London, WC2, England.

PRICE Henry, b. 18 Oct 1945, Oakland, CA, USA. Tenor. Career: Many seasons at the New York City Opera where he sang Telemaco in Monteverdi's Ulisse, Tamino, Almaviva, Narciso in Il Turco in Italia, Gennaro in Lucrezia Borgia and operetta roles; Other appearances in Philadelphia and Miami, at the US Spoleto Festival and from 1983 in Europe, notably at the Mainz and Linz Operas. Address: c/o New York City Opera, Lincoln Center, New York, NY 10023, USA.

PRICE Janet, b. 1938, Abersychan, Pontypool Gwent, South Wales. Singer (Soprano). m. Adrian Beaumont. Education: University College of Cardiff, South Wales; BMus (1st class honours) and MMus (Wales); LRAM (Singing Performer); ARCM (Piano Performer); LRAM (Piano Accompanist); Special study of French Music with Nadia Boulanger, Paris; Studied Singing with Olive Groves, Isobel Baillie and Hervey Alan. Career: Singer in concerts with leading orchestras and conductors throughout Britain and Western Europe; Numerous premieres, including the Belgian premiere of Tippett's Third Symphony, Festival of Flanders, 1975; Has sung opera with Glyndebourne Festival Opera, Welsh National Opera Company, Kent Opera Company, Opera Rara, Handel Opera Society, San Antonio Grand Opera, Texas, BBC TV; Has made a speciality of resurrecting neglected heroines of Bel Canto period, being the first person to sing a number of these roles in the modern era; Highlights include: Live commercial recording of Beethoven's 9th Symphony with Haitink and the Concertgebouw Orchestra and Chorus; Tippett's 3rd Symphony with Haitink and the London Philharmonic Orchestra; Stravinsky's Les Noces, with Rozhdestvensky and the BBC Symphony Orchestra and Chorus; Sang role of Hecuba in Kent Opera's production of Tippett's King Priam (video). Recordings: For several labels. Contributions to: Haydn's Songs from a Singer's Viewpoint, article to The Haydn Yearbook, 1983. Honours: Winner, British Art Council First Young Welsh Singers' Award, 1964. Hobbies: Fell-walking; Tapestry work; Gardening. Address: 73 Kings Drive, Bishopton, Bristol BS7 8JQ, England.

PRICE Leontyne, b. 10 Feb 1927, Laurel, Mississippi, USA. Soprano Singer. Education: Central State College, Wilberforce, Ohio and Juilliard School of Music. Career: Appeared as Bess (Porgy and Bess), Vienna, Berlin, Paris, London, New York, 1952-54; Recitalist, Soloist, 1954-; Soloist, Hollywood Bowl, 1955-59, 1966; Opera Singer NBC-TV, 1955-58, San Francisco Opera Co, 1957-59, 1960-61, Vienna Staatsoper, 1958, 1959-60, 1961; Recording Artist RCA-Victor, 1958-; Appeared Covent Garden, 1958-59, 1970, Chicago, 1959, 1960, 1965, Milan, 1960-61, 1963, 1967, Metropolitan Opera, New York, 1961-62, 1963-70, 1972, as both Leonoras of Verdi, Madame Butterfly, Fiordiligi, Puccini's Tosca, Minnie, Liu and Manon, Ariadne and Pamina; Paris Opéra as Aida, 1968, Metropolitan Opera as Aida, 1985 (Retired as opera singer but still active in concert). Recordings: Numerous recordings, notably The Essential Leontyne Price, 11 CDs, 1996). Honours: Fellow, American Academy of Arts and Sciences; Hon DMus (Howard University, Central State College, Ohio); Hon DHL (Dartmouth); Hon Dr of Humanities (Rust College, Mississippi); Hon DHum Litt (Fordham); Presidential Medal of Freedom, Order of Merit (Italy), National Medal of Arts, 1985. Address: c/o Columbia Artists Management Inc, 165 West 57th Street, New York, NY 10019, USA.

PRICE Margaret (Berenice) (Dame), b. 13 Apr 1941, Tredegar, Wales. Soprano Opera Singer. Education: Trinity College of Music, London. Debut: Operatic debut with Welsh National Opera in Marriage of Figaro, 1963. Career: Renowned for Mozart Operatic Roles; Has sung in world's leading opera houses and festivals; Many radio broadcasts and television appearances; Major roles include: Countess in Marriage of Figaro, Pamina in The Magic Flute, Fiordiligi in Così fan tutte, Donna Anna in Don Giovanni, Constanze in Die Entführung, Amelia in Simon Boccanegra, Agathe in Freischütz, Desdemona in Otello, Elisabetta in Don Carlo, Aida and Norma; Sang: Norma at Covent Garden, 1987, Adriana Lecouvreur at Bonn, 1989, Elisabeth de Valois at the Orange Festival; Sang Amelia Grimaldi in a concert performance of Simon Boccanegra at the Festival Hall, 1990; Season 1993-94 in Ariadne auf Naxos at Opera de Lyon and Staatsoper Berlin. Recordings: Many recordings of opera, oratorio, concert works and recitals including, Tristan und Isolde, Le nozze di Figaro, Elgar's The Kingdom, Don Giovanni, Così fan tutte, Judas Maccabeus, Berg's Altenberglieder, Mozart's Requiem and Die Zauberflöte; Jury Member, Wigmore Hall International Song Competition, 1997. Honours: CBE; Honorary Fellow, Trinity College of Music; Elisabeth Schumann Prize for Lieder, Ricordi Prize for Opera, Silver Medal of The Worshipful Company of Musicians; DMus, University of Wales, 1989; DBE, 1993. Memberships: Fellow of The College of Wales, 1991; Fellow of The College of Music and Drama of Wales, 1993. Hobbies: Cookery; Reading; Walking; Swimming. Address: c/o Lies Askonas Ltd, 6 Henrietta Street, London WC2, England.

PRICE Perry, b. 13 Oct 1942, New York, Pennsylvania, USA. Singer (Tenor). m. Heather Thomson. Education: Studied at University of Houston, in London with Otakar Kraus and in New York. Debut: San Francisco, as Des Grieux in Manon, 1964. Career: New York (City Opera), Houston, Philadelphia, San Diego and Portland; Sang further at Montreal, Vancouver, Toronto, Lisbon and Stadttheater Augsburg; Other roles have included Mozart's Ferrando, Don Ottavio and Tamino, Rossini's Almaviva and Lindoro, the Duke of Mantua, Edgardo, Nemorino, Faust and Hoffmann; Active in concert and as teacher.

PRICK Christof, b. 23 Oct 1946, Hamburg, Germany. Conductor. Education: Studied in Hamburg with Wilhelm Bruckner-Ruggebourg. Career: Assistant at the Hamburg Staatsoper; Permanent conductor at Trier Opera, 1970-72, Darmstadt, 1972-74; Musical Director at Saarbrucken, 1974-77, Karlsruhe, 1977-84; Staatskapellmeister at the Deutsche Oper Berlin, 1977-84 (returned to conduct the premiere of Wolfgang Rihm's Oedipus, 1987); Conducted Così fan tutte at Los Angeles 1988 and Arabella at Barcelona, 1989; Music Director, Los Angeles Chamber Orchestra, 1992-; Conducted Fidelio and Tannhäuser at the Metropolitan, 1992; Music Director City of Hannover, Germany, as of 1993-94 Season. Address: Los Angeles Chamber Orchestra, 315 W 9th Street, Suite 801, Los Angeles, CA 90015, USA.

PRIDAY Elisabeth, b. 1955, Buckingham, England. Singer (Soprano). Education: Studied at the Royal Academy of Music. Career: Joined the Monteverdi Choir 1975: concerts at the Aix Festival, and BBC Promenade; Sang in Handel Opera's Giustino 1983 and Hasse's L'Eroe Cinese at the 1985 Holland Festival; Appearances with Roger Norrington for the Maggio Musicale Florence (Speranza in Orfeo) and Amor in Gluck's Orfeo with the Scottish Chamber Orchestra; Dido and Aeneas with the English Concert in Germany, London and the Brighton Festival Concert performances of Bach's B minor Mass in King's College, Cambridge, Handel's Carmelite Vespers with the European Baroque Orchestra, Alexander's Feast for RAI in Italy and Messiah at the Festival de Beaune in France and also QEH; Monteverdi Vespers in St John's Smith Square, Bristol, St Albans; Concerts in France and England with Chiaroscuro and Climene in Gluck's La Corona at the City of London Festival; Paris 1991 with the Deller Consort. Recordings: Bach Motets with the Monteverdi Choir; Purcell's King Arthur, Music for the Chapels Royal and the Fairy Queen; Handel's Israel in Egypt, Semele and Dixit Dominus with the Winchester Cathedral Choir; Motets by Schütz and Monteverdi; Rameau's Les Boréades; Vivaldi Glorias (Nimbus); Dido and Aeneas with Trevor Pinnock and also with John Elliot Gardiner.

PRIESTMAN Brian, b. 10 February 1927, Birmingham, England. Conductor; Music Director; Professor. m. Ford McClave, 2 March 1972, 1 daughter. Education: BMus, 1950, MA, 1952, University of Birmingham; Dipl Sup, Brussels Conservatoire, 1952. Career: Has held Musical Directorships of Royal Shakespeare Theatre and with Symphony Orchestras in Edmonton, Canada, Baltimore, Denver & Miami; Principal Conductor, New Zealand Symphony Orchestra & Malmö, SO; Former, Dean and Professor, University of Cape Town; Currently Artist-in-Residence, University of Kansas, USA. Recordings: For Westminster, RCA and Musique en Wallonie. Honours: DHL, University of Colorado, 1972. Memberships: Board Member, Conductors' Guild. Hobbies: Cooking; Reading. Current Management: Mariedi Anders Artists Management, San Francisco, USA. Address: 3700 Clinton Parkway No 1307, Lawrence, KS 66047, USA.

PRIETO Carlos, b. 1 January 1937, Mexico City, Mexico. Concert Cellist. m. Maria Isabel, 28 December 1964, 2 sons, 1 daughter. Education: BS, Metallurgical Engineering, 1958, BS, Economics, 1959, Massachusetts Institute of Technology, USA; Russian, Lomonosov University, Moscow, USSR, 1962; Master of Engineering, CESSID, Metz, France, 1963; Mexico City Concervatory of Music, under Imre Hartman, 1942-54; Studied with: Pierre Fournier, Geneva, 1978; Leonard Roase, New York, USA, 1981, 1982. Career: Member of Trio Mexico, 1978-81; International career as Concert Cellist; Many world tours, USA, Canada, Western and Eastern Europe, USSR, Latin America, China, Japan, India, 1981-; Performances in Carnegie Hall and Lincoln Center, New York; Kennedy Center, Washington; Salle Pleyel and Salle Gaveau, Paris; Philharmonic Hall, Leningrad; Concertgebouw, Amsterdam; Has performed at International

Music Festivals; Played at world premieres of many cello concerti including those of Carlos Chavez, Joaquin Rodrigo. Recordings include: Complete Bach Suites for Cello Solo, 1985; Works by Paganini, Ponce, Rachmaninov, Fauré, Mendelssohn, Tchaikovsky. Publications: Alrededor del Mundo con el Violonchelo (Around the World with the Cello), autobiography, 1987; Russian Letters, 1965. Honours: Outstanding Soloist of 1981 given by Mexican Association of Music Critics, 1982. Current Management: Gurtman & Murtha Associates Inc, New York City, USA; Choveaux Management, Mancroft Towers, Oulton Broad, Lowestoft, Suffolk, England. Address: c/o Gurtman and Murtha Associates Inc, 450 7th Floor #603, New York, NY 10123-0101, USA.

PRIMROSE Claire, b. 2 Oct 1957, Melbourne, Victoria, Australia. Singer (Mezzo-Soprano). Education: Graduate, Victorian College of Arts; Studied voice with Joan Hammond, Melbourne; Studied interpretation of French Song with Gerard Souzay, Paris. Debut: As Mezzo Soprano in Australia; As Soprano from 1990, as the sister in Holloway's Clarissa, English National Opera. Career includes: Mezzo Soprano: Krista in The Makropolous Case; Meg Page in Falstaff; Mercedes in Carmen; Cornelia, in Giulio Cesare; Title role in Cendrillon at Wexford Festival; Charlotte in Werther at Montpellier; Giulietta in Les Contes d'Hoffmann at Lille; Salud in La Vida Breve at Liège; Suzuki in Madame Butterfly for Opera North; Orlofsky in Die Fledermaus at the Hong Kong Festival; Dorabella in Cosi fan tutte; Sesto in La Clemenza di Tito for Opera Forum, Holland; Soprano: Leonore in Fidelio; Medea in Teseo, Athens Festival and Sadlers Wells; Dido in Dido and Aeneas at Bologna; Title role in Alceste, Monte Carlo Festival and Covent Garden; Elettra, in Idomeneo, Valencia Festival, 1991; Chrysothemis, State Opera of South Australia and Festival of Melbourne; Leonore, in Fidelio, Australian Opera, 1992-93; Paris Debut as Alceste, at Châtelet; Scandinavian Debut as Elettra, in Idomeneo, Helsinki and with the New Israeli Opera in Tel Aviv, 1992; Fiordiligi, Lyric Opera of Queensland; Santuzza, Australian Opera, 1994 and 1996; Numerous concert appearances include a Wigmore Hall recital with Roger Vignoles in Berlioz's Romeo et Juliette, Salle Pleyel, Paris and Leonara, in La Forza del Destino, Scottish Opera. Honours include: Winner, Metropolitan Opera Competition; Winner, Pavarotti International Competition, Philadelphia. Address: Athole Still Intl Management Ltd, Foresters Hall, 25-27 Weston Street, London, SE19 3RY.

PRINCE-JOSEPH Bruce, b. 30 August 1925, Beaver Falls, Pennsylvania, USA. Conductor; Composer; Organist; Harpsichordist; Pianist. Education: BMusA, Yale University, 1946; MMusA, University of Southern California, 1952; Conservatoire Nationale de Musique, Paris, France, 1953. Career: Staff Pianist, Organist, Harpsichordist, New York Philharmonic, 1955-74; Professor, Chairman, Department of Music, Hunter College of the City University of New York, 1955-78. Recordings: 6 Sonatas for Violin and Harpsichord, RCA, 1965; Glagolitic Mass, Janácek, 1967, Ode to St Cecillia, Handel, 1958, Columbia Records. Honours: Grammy Nomination, 1965, for 6 Sonatas for Violin and Harpsichord; Associate Fellow, Berkeley College, Yale University, 1978-83. Address: 6540 Pennsylvania Avenue, Kansas City, MO 64113, USA.

PRING Katherine, b. 4 June 1940, Brighton, England. Singer (Mezzo-Soprano). Education: Studied at the Royal College of Music with Ruth Packer; Further study with Maria Carpi in Geneva and Luigi Ricci in Rome. Debut: Geneva 1966, as Flora in La Traviata. Career: Sang at Sadler's Wells from 1968, notably as Carmen, Dorabella, Poppea, Eboli, Azucena and Waltraute; Sang in the 1974 British stage premiere of Henze's The Bassarids; Covent Garden debut 1972, as Thea in The Knot Garden; Bayreuth 1972-73, as Schwertleite in Die Walküre; Glyndebourne 1978, as Baba the Turk in The Rake's Progress; Other modern roles include Kate in Owen Wingrave and Jocasta in Oedipus Rex. Recordings: Fricka and Waltraute in The Ring conducted by Reginald Goodall (EMI); The Magic Fountain by Delius (BBC Artium). Address: c/o Trafalgar Perry Ltd, 4 Goodwin's Court, St Martin's Lane, London WC2N 4LL, England.

PRING Sarah, b. 1962, England. Singer (Soprano). Education: Studied at Guildhall School, in Florence with Suzanne Danco, and with Johanna Peters. Career: Sang Norina, Susanna, Concepcion and Martinu's Julietta while a student in London, the Trovatore Leonora in Belgium; Professional debut at Glyndebourne, 1988, as Alice in Falstaff, returning as Barena in Jenufa; Glyndebourne Touring Opera as Glasha in Katya Kabanova, First Lady in Die Zauberflöte and Dorabella; Opera North debut, 1989, as Concepcion, Scottish Opera, 1991, as Mimi; Concert appearances at Festival Hall (Jenufa), Greenwich Festival (Judas Maccabeus), Belfast (Beethoven's Ninth) and Purcell Room; Sang Gluck's Euridice for Opera West, 1991; English National Opera debut, 1993, Princess Ida, Don Pasquale; ENO, 1993, Norina, Don Pasquale; ENO, 1994, Nannetta, Falstaff, also Glyndebourne Touring Opera, Second Niece, Peter Grimes. 1995, Second Niece, Paris Châtelet; Covent Garden debut 1996 as a Rhinemaiden in Götterdämmerung. Honours include: Joint winner, 1990 John Christie Award. Address: Little Easthall Farmhouse, St Paul's Walden, Nr Hitchin, Hertfordshire, SG4 8DH, England.

PRINGLE John, b. 17 Oct 1938, Melbourne, Victoria, Australia. Singer (Baritone). Education: Graduated as Pharmaceutical Chemist, 1961; Studied Singing in Melbourne and with Luigi Ricci in Rome. Debut: Australian Opera, as Falke in Die Fledermaus, 1967. Career: Many appearances with Australian Opera as Mozart's Don Giovanni, Count and Papageno, Verdi's Posa, Ford, the Lescauts of Puccini and Massenet, Rossini's Barber, Britten's Death in Venice, Mozart's Figaro, Don Alfonso, Debussy's Golaud; Nick Shadow in The Rake's Progress, Andrei in War and Peace, Janácek's Forester and Robert Storch in Intermezzo (Glyndebourne, 1984); Also sings Olivier in Capriccio and appeared at Paris, Brussels and Cologne, 1980-85; Sang Beckmesser in Meistersinger for Australian Opera, 1988-89, Comte de Nevers in Les Huguenots, 1990; Appeared in Los Angeles and San Diego, 1992; Sang Prus in The Makropoulos Case at Sydney, 1996. Recordings include: Video of Les Huguenots; Videos of Intermezzo and Love for Three Oranges (both Glyndebourne); Die Meistersinger (Australian Opera). Honours: Member, Order of Australia, 1988. Address: c/o Australian Opera, PO Box 291, Strawberry Hills, New South Wales 2012, Australia.

PRIOR Benjamin, b. 1943, Venice, Italy. Singer (Tenor). Career: Sang widely in Italy from 1967, with Edgardo at La Fenice Venice in 1969; Wexford Festival, 1971, in La Rondine and Vienna Staatsoper, 1972, as Verdi's Riccardo; Barcelona 1971, as Percy in Anna Bolena, San Francisco 1980 (Alfredo), Buenos Aires 1981 (Pinkerton) and New Orleans Opera 1981-88; Sang Pinkerton at Verona (1983) and has also sung Verdi's Rodolfo (Luisa Miller) and Foresto, Nemorino, Faust, Macduff, the Duke of Mantua and Des Grieux. Address: New Orleans Opera, 333 St Charles Avenue, Suite 907, New Orleans, LA 70130, USA.

PRIOR Claude, b. 8 June 1918, Geneva, Switzerland. Composer. m. Anne-Marie Pharabod, 1 Aug 1940, 1 son, 3 daughters. Education: Universitat Munich; Conservatoire, Paris. Career: Radiodiffusion Francaise, Club d'essai, Concerts of UNESCO, 1948; Club Francais du dique, 1953; Resonances, 1957; Teaching, 1967; Director, Music School and Festival of St Malo, 1968; Director of Studies, Dijon, 1972; Independent conducting and teaching, 1984-. Compositions include: Uniting Messiaen's Harmony and Stravinsky's Counterpoint: Melodies, Choir and Orchestra; Bateau Ivre, Paris, 1957; Song of songs, Koln, 1957; Symphonie Concertante-Organ Concertino-Musical Tales, Sydney 59; The Snow Queen-La petite Sirene-Magnificat, soloists, choir & Orchestra or soloists, choir & Organ Trio and 5 instruments; Seagulls, Concerto for Saxophone and Wind; Operas: L'heure sicilienne; No Orchids; Wuthering Heights; Concertos for piano and violin; Piano Preludes; Wuthering Heights, Opera in 3 Acts, adaptation of novel by Emily Brontë, also poems by Emily, Charlotte and Anne Brontë. Recordings: La Petite Sirene; Petit Poucet; Musical Tales. Address: 38 rue de Vaugirard, 75006 Paris, France.

PRITCHARD Edith, b. 1962, Edmonton, Canada. Singer (Soprano). Education: Studied at University of Toronto and Royal Northern College of Music. Career: Represented Canada at the 1991 Cardiff Singer of the World Competition; Sang Fiordiligi at the 1991 Glyndebourne Festival and the Countess in Cornet Rilke by Siegfried Matthus with the 1993 Glyndebourne Tour; Other roles include First Lady in Die Zauberflöte at Covent Garden, 1992-93, Licenza in Mozart's Sogno di Scipione at Buxton Festival and the Heavenly Voice in Don Carlos for Opera North. Honours include: Brigitte Fassbaender Prize for Lieder, Royal Northern College of Music, and 1992 John Christie Award, Glyndebourne. Address: c/o Harold Holt Ltd, 31 Sinclair Road, London W14 0NS, England.

PRITCHARD Gwyn (Charles), b. 29 Jan 1948, Richmond, Yorkshire, England. Composer; Conductor; Cellist. m. Claudia Klasicka, 23 June 1967, 2 daughters. Education: Royal Scottish Academy of Music and Drama, 1966-69; Studied cello with Joan Dickson, Composition with Dr Frank Spedding; DRSAM. Career: Director of Music, Salisbury Cathedral School, 1969-70; Contract for documentary Young Composer, 1972-73; Cellist with Medusa Ensemble, 1976-78; Artistic Direc tor and Conductor, Uroboros Ensemble, 1981-; Compositions performed worldwide including Warsaw Autumn Festival, Mexico Festival, Huddersfield Contemporary Music Festival, International Composers Forum, USA, Eastern and Western Europe, and Australia; Featured Composer at Southampton International New Music Week, 1989. Compositions: Concerto for Viola and Orchestra, 1967, revised 1984; Tangents, 1970; Spring Music for Chamber Orchestra, 1972; Enitharmon, 1973; Becoming, 1974; Five pieces for Piano, 1975; Ensemble Music for Six, 1976; Nephalauxis, 1977; Strata, 1977; Jardenna, 1978; Objects in Space, 1978; Mercurius, 1979; Duo, 1980; Earthcrust, 1980; Visions of Zosimos, 1981; Sonata for Guitar, 1982; Moondance, 1982; Lollay, 1983; Dramalogue, 1984; Chamber Concerto, 1985; Madrigal, 1987; La Settima Bolgia, 1989; Eidos, 1990; Janus, 1991; Wayang, 1993; Demise, 1994. Membership: Society for the Promotion of New Music. Address: 13 Nevil Road, Bishopston, Bristol BS7 9EG, England.

PROBST Dominique (Henri), b. 19 Feb 1954, Paris, France. Percussionist; Composer; Conductor. Education: Baccalaureat, Philosophy Studies, La Sorbone, Paris, 1971; Paris Conservatoire National Superieur de Musique, 1st Prize Percussion, 198; Prize, Composition, Lili & Naida Boulanger Foundation, 1979. Career: As Musician at La Comedie Francaise, and many other great Parisian theatres, 1974-; Titulary Member, Concert Colonne & Ensemble Percussion 4; Assistant, CNSM, Paris, 1978-; Professor, Levallois Conservatory of Music, 1984-. Compositions: Numerous pieces for Theatre: King Lear, 1978; Dom Juan, Tete d'or Berenice, 1979; Macbeth; Les Caprices de Marianne, Les Plaisirs de L'Ile Enchantée, 1980; Les Cenci, 1981; Marie Tudor, 1982; L'Esprit des Bois; Dialogues des Carmélites, 1984; La Mouette, L'Arbre des Tropiques, Le Cid, 1985; L'Hote et le Renegat; Thomas More' Richard de Gloucester' Bacchus, 1987; Ascese-A-Seize, 6 percussion players; Les Plaisirs de l'Ile Enchantee, for recorder, violin, guitar & percussion; Coda & Variation IV, guitar. Contributions to: Professional journals including La Revue Musicale. Honour: Prize Marcel Samuel Rousseau, Académie des Beaux-Arts of Paris, 1986, for Opera, Maximilien Kolbe. Hobby: Chess. Address: 39 Rue Durantin, 75018 Paris, France.

PROCHAZKOVA Jarmila, b. 27 February 1961, Trebic. Musicologist. Education: Piano, Conservatoire in Brno; Masaryk University in Brno; Faculty of Musicology. Appointments: Scholarship-holder of the Leos Janacek Fund, practice at Janacek Archives; Custodian, Janacek Archive of the Music History Department of Moravian Museum in Brno. Publictions: Leos Janacek, Album for Kamila Stösslova, in Czech and German, 1994, in English, 1996; Jarmil Prochazkova, Bohumir Volny, Leos Janacek, born in Hukvaldy, Czech and English versions, 1995. Contributions to: About 20 on Jancek's composition method, folk inspirations, sociological aspects; On The Genesis of Janacek Symphony Dunaj, 1993; Leos Janacek and the Czech National Band, 1995. Memberships: Commission to edit Janacek's Musical Works. Hobbies: Racing cars; Motorcycles. Address: Foltynova 6, CZ-635 00, Brno, Czech Republic.

PROCTER Norma, b. 15 Feb 1928, Cleethorpes, Lincolnshire, England. Career includes: International Concert Singer - Contralto, now retired; Vocal studies with Roy Henderson; Musicianship with Alec Redshaw, Lieder with Hans Oppenheim and Paul Hamburger; London debut at Southwark Cathedral, 1948; Specialist in concert works, oratorio and recitals; Appeared with all major festivals in UK and Europe; Operatic debut as Lucretia in Britten's Rape of Lucretia, Aldeburgh Festival, 1954, 1958; Covent Garden debut in Gluck's Orpheus, 1960; Performed in Germany, France, Spain, Portugal, Norway, Sweden, Denmark, Finland, Holland, Belgium, Austria, Israel, Luxembourg, South America. Recordings include: Messiah; Elijah; Samson; Mahler's 2nd, 3rd and 8th Symphonies, Das klagende Lied; Hartmann 1st Symphony; Julius Caesar Jones-Williamson; Nicholas Maw's Scenes and Arias; BBC, Last Night of the Proms; Premiere recording Brahms, Mahler, Ballads; Conductors include: Bruno Walter, Bernstein, Rafael Kubelik, Karl Richter, Pablo Casals, Malcolm Sargent; Charles Groves, David Willcocks, Alexander Gibson, Charles Mackerras and Norman del Mar. Memberships: President, Grimsby Phil Society. Honour: Honorary RAM, 1974. Hobbies: Sketching; Painting; Tapestry. Address: 194 Clee Road, Grimsby, Lincolnshire, England.

PROFETA Laurentiu, b. 12 Jan 1925, Bucharest, Romania. Composer. m. Nicole Profeta, 6 Nov 1956. Education: Philosophical Degree, 1948; Bucharest and Moscow Conservatories, 1955. Debut: Puppet Suite, awarded Enescu Prize, 1946. Compositions include: Songs for Children and Youth, 1968; Prince and Pauper, Ballet, 1970; Gypsy Songs, 1971; Adventure in the Garden, Oratorio for Children's Choir and Symphony Orchestra, 1973; 6 Humorous Pieces, Suite for Children's Choir and Small Orchestra, 1974; Madrigal, for Choir and Small Orchestra, 1975; Songs, 1982; The Triumph of Love, Ballet, 1983; Chosen Melodies, 1983; Music for Artistic Pictures; The Story of Peter Pan, Opera for Children, 1984; Rica's, One-Act Ballet, 1986; Hershale, Musical, 1989; The Losers, musical, 1990; Of The Carnival, Ballet, 1991; Turandot, Musical, 1992; Maria Tanase, Musical, 1992; Eva-Now, Musical, 1993; Romanian Christmas Carols for Children's Choir and Orchestra, 1994; Symphonic Pop-Music for Synthesizers (audio cassette), 1995; Shalom Alehem's Musical World - Jewish Songs, (audio cassette), 1997. Recordings: 7 Long Playing records; Adventure in the Garden, 1984; The Story of Peter Pan, 1986; Romanian Christmas Carols, audio cassette, 1996. Contributions to: Muzica Review and other professional publications. Honours: Prize of the Union of Composers and Musicologists of Romania, 1993. Memberships: The Director Council of Composers Union, 1990. Address: Str Take Ionescu No 8, 70154 Bucharest, Romania.

PROKINA Elena, b. 16 Jan 1964, Odessa, Russia. Soprano. Education: Studied in Odessa and at the Leningrad Theatre Institute and Leningrad Conservatory. Career: Kirov Theatre Leningrad from 1988 as Emma in Khovanshchina, Violetta, Marguerite, Natasha in War and Peace (seen on BBC TV), Tatyana, Desdemona, Pauline in The Gambler, Jaroslavna in Prince Igor, Iolanta and Maria in Mazeppa; Tours with the Kirov Company in Europe and Kirov Gala at Covent Garden, 1992-; Shostakovich No 14 with the LSO under Rostropovitch, 1993; Covent Garden debut in 1994 as Katya Kabanova in a production by Trevor Nunn, returning 1995 as Desdemona; Katya at Covent Garden in 1997. Address: c/o Royal Opera House, Covent Garden, London, WC2, England.

PROMONTI Elisabeth, b. 9 July 1942, Budapest, Hungary. Opera and Concert Singer; Music Educator. 1 son. Education: Diploma, Choir Conducting Faculty, Franz Liszt Music Academy, Budapest; Diploma with 1st class honours, Opera, Song, Oratorio, Akademie Mozarteum, Salzburg; Studied with Zoltan Zavodsky, Viorica Ursuleac, Friederike Baumgartner, Elisabeth Grümmer International Opera Studio, Opera Zurich, 1970-71. Debut: As Aida, Bielefeld Municipal Theatre, 1967. Career: Opera Singer, Bielefeld, Oberhausen, Kiel, Bremen, Heidelberg, Bordeaux, Vienna, Zurich, 1967-75; Concert Singer, 1975-; Appearances on radio and TV; Tours in various European countries, USA and Canada; Director, Swiss Kodály Institute, 1983-95; President, Swiss Kodály Society, 1991-96. Recordings: Zoltan Kodály, Epigrammes, 1991; Folk Songs arranged by Great Composers, 1993; Masterclasses and Presentation in Europe, USA and Canada. Address: PO Box 4051, CH-6002 Lucerne, Switzerland.

PROSTITOV Oleg, b. 7 September 1955, Stavropol, Russia. Composer. m. Grishina Lyudmila, 22 May 1976, 1 son, 1 daughter. Education: Rimsky-Korsakov State Conservatoire, Leningrad (Petersburg), 1979; Postgraduate courses with Professor Mnatsakanyan, pupil of Shostakovich, Leningrad (St Petersburg) Conservatoire, 1983. Debut: Stavropol, 1972. Career: Participant of 3 international music festivals, Baku, 1987; Sofia, 1990; St Petersburg, 1991; Sonata-fantasy, Amadeus. Compositions: 5 symphonies, 2 piano concertos, a violin concerto, 5 children musicals, a great number of chamber and vocal instrumental works (sonatas, suites, string quartets, cantatas, romances), about 100 songs. Recordings: Sonata-fantasy, Amadeus; Sonata for trombone, violin and piano performed in Moscow, St Petersburg, Florida, Stutgart, Paris, A Black Man, monopera for baritone, mixed choir, large symphony orchestra based on the poem by S Esenin. Honours: 1st Prize for vocal cycle on the poems by S Esenin for baritone and piano, Young Musicians' Competition, Leningrad (St Petersburg), 1978. Membership: Union of the Composers of Russia, since 1979. Hobby: Painting. Current Management: Chairman, Krasnoyarsk Department, Union of the Composers of Russia. Address: Krasnoyarsky Rabochy, 124-A Apt 25, 660095 Krasnoyarsk, Russia.

PROTSCHKA Josef, b. 5 Feb 1946, Prague, Czechoslovakia. German Singer (Tenor). Education: Philology and Philosopy at Universities of Tubingen and Bonn; Cologne Musikhochschule with Erika Köth and Peter Witsch. Career: Giessen, 1977-78, Saarbrücken, 1978-80, leading tenor at Cologne Opera from 1980, singing all main tenor parts in Ponnelle's Mozart cycle, Lionel (Martha), Tom Rakewell, Faust, Max, Lensky, Hans, José, Hermann (Queen of Spades), Loge, Erik, Eisenstein; Freelance from 1987; Important debuts: Salzburg Festival and Vienna State Opera (Hans), 1985; La Scala and Semperopera Dresden (José), 1986; Bregenz Festival (Hoffmann), Maggio Musicale, Florence (Flamand) and Zürich Opera, 1987; Wiener Festwochen (Fierrabras-Schubert), 1988; Hamburg State Opera as Florestan/Elis in Schreker's Schatzgräber, 1989, Idomeneo, 1990; Royal Opera, Brussels, 1989, as Florestan/Lohengrin, 1990; Florestan at Covent Garden and Tokyo NHK, 1990; US debut, Houston (Song of the Earth), 1991; Now appears regularly on stage at all famous festivals and opera houses with leading conductors and producers; Also lieder recitals, concerts, radio and TV productions; Professor, Hochschule für Musik Köln, Aachen Division, and Det Kongelige Danske Musikkonservatoriet, Copenhagen, 1993-. Recordings include: Haydn Die Schöpfung; Schubert Fierrabras; Schubert Schöne Müllerin; Mendelssohn Lieder, complete; Fiedelio (Florestan) and Flying Dutchman (Erik) with Vienna Philharmonic and Dohnányi; Mozart Lieder, complete; Videos: Fidelio, Covent Garden; Tales of Hoffmann, Bregenz Festival; Fierrabras, Theater an der Wien; Schatzgräber, Hamburg Opera; Missa solemnis, Uracher Musiktage; Lieder recital, Urach. Address: Ringstrasse 17B, 50765 Köln, Germany.

PROUVOST Gaetane, b. 21 July 1954, Lille, France. Violinist. m. Charles de Couessin, 6 July 1985, 2 sons. Education: Baccalaureat; 1st Prize, Violin and Chamber Music, Cycle de Perfectionnement, Conservatoire National Superieur, Paris; Studied: With Ivan Galamian, Juilliard School of Music, New York; Chigiana, Siena, Italy; With D Markevitch, Institut des hautes etudes musicales, Montreux; Pupil of Zino Francescatti. Debut: Carnegie Hall, 1974. Career: Soloist with Radio-France Orchestra, Orchestre Lamoureux, Bucharest Philharmonic; Gdansk Philharmonic, Ensemble Intercontemporain, Ensemble Forum; Performed under conductors J Conlon, K Nagano, G Bertini, P Boulez, A Tamayo, S Baudo, R Kempe; Recitals with M Dalberto, N Lee, P Barbizet, B Rigutto, A Queffelec; Premiered: Olivier Greif's Sonate; M Rateau's Offrande lyrique, Paris, 1984; Participated in Etienne Perrier's film Rouge Venitien; Professor, Conservatoire National Superieur de Musique, Paris. Recordings: Prokofiev, Sonatas op 80 and 94 for violin and piano (with A R el Bacha); Szymanowski, Complete works for violin and piano. Honours: Prizewinner, Carl Flesch International Competition, London; Award for Best Record, France, 1987. Memberships: Alumni Association of Conservatoire National Superior de Musique, Paris. Current Management: Ch de Colsessin, France. Address: 7 rue des Volontaires, 75014 Paris, France.

PROUZA Zdenek, b. 3 Aug 1955, Prague, Czechoslovakia. Cellist. m. Katherine H Allen, 25 Apr 1987. Education: Conservatory of Music, Prague; Academy of Performing Arts, Prague; Hochschule für Musik, Wien; Mozarteum, Salzburg; Accademia Musicale Chigiana, Siena. Debut: Recital debut in Prague, 1973. Career: Principal Cellist with Czech Chamber Orchestra and Nurnberg Symphony Orchestra; Co-Principal with Vienna Chamber Orchestra and Munich Chamber Orchestra; Solo appearances in Czechoslovakia, West Germany, Belgium, France, Italy, Austria, USA and Canada. Recordings: Pauer, Radio Prague; Suk, Czech TV; Suk, ORTF; Vivaldi, RAI; Saint-Saëns, Colosseum; Musical Heritage Society. Honours: Concertino Praga, 1970; Beethoven Cello Competition, 1972; Czech Cello Competition, 1976; Contemporary Performance Award, Czech Music Foundation, 1977, 1978. Membership: American Cello Society. Hobby: Computers; Financial Markets. Current Management: The Added Staff. Address: 820 West End Avenue, Suite 3C, New York, NY 10025, USA.

PROVOST Serge, b. 1952, Saint-Timothée de Beauharnois, Quebec, Canada. Composer; Performer; Professor. Education: Studied composition and analysis under Gilles Tremblay, organ with Bernard Lagacé; Studied writing, electracoustics, orchestration, piano and harpischord, Conservatoire de Musique, Montréal 1970-79; Studied composition and analysis under Claude Ballif, Paris 1979-81. Career: Professor of analysis, Trois-Rivières and Hull Conservatories; took part in Banff Centre's Composers Workshop 1979 and Rencontres Internationales de la Jeunesse at Bayreuth Festival; given organ recitals in France, Germany and Canada. Compositions include: Les Isle du Songe, for choir, orchestra and percussion; Cretes, a piece for 2 harpischords which Swiss duo Esterman-Gallet commissioned and played in 1980; Tetrarys, 1988, saxophone, harp, flute, piano; Les Jardins Suspendus, 1989, 4 ondes martenots, piano. Honours: Won 1st Prize in composition for choir, orchestra and percussion with Les Isle du Songe, 1979; Won First Prize in analysis at Conservatoire de Paris 1981. Address: c/o SOCAN, 41 Valleybrook Drive, Don Mills, Ontario M3B 2S6, Canada.

PROWSE Philip, b. 29 Dec 1937, Worcestershire, England. Stage Director and Designer. Education: Studied at Slade School of Fine Art, London. Career: Teacher at Birmingham College of Art and Slade School of Fine art; Designed ballets for Covent Garden, followed by Orfeo ed Euridice, 1969, and Ariadne auf Naxos, 1976; Director of Citizens Theatre, Glasgow, 1970-; Produced and Designed Handel's Tamerlano for Welsh National Opera, 1982, and Les Pêcheurs de Perles for English National Opera, 1987; Designs for Jonathan Miller's production of Don Giovanni at English National Opera, 1985 and The Magic Flute for Scottish Opera; Work as Producer and Designer for Opera North includes Orfeo ed Euridice, Die Dreigroschenoper and Aida, 1986, UK premiere of Strauss's Daphne, 1987 and La Gioconda, 1993; Staged the house premiere of Verdi's Giovanna d'Arco, Covent Garden, 1996. Address: c/o The Citizens Theatre, Gorbals Street, Glasgow, G5 9DS, Scotland.

PRUETT James (Worrell), b. 23 Dec 1932, Mount Airy, North Carolina, USA. Music Librarian; Musicologist. Education: PhD, University of North Carolina, 1962. Career: Reference assistant at North Carolina University Library 1955, Music Librarian 1961-76; Music Department 1963, Professor of Music and Chairman 1976; Chief of Music Division, Library of Congress, 1987. Memberships: Member, American Musicological Society; Member, Music Library Association (President 1973-75), Editor of Notes (Journal of the Music Library Association) 1974-77. Publications include: Studies in Musicology, 1969; Many journal and encyclopaedia articles, book and music reviews. Address: 325 6th Street SE, Washington, DC 20003, USA.

PRUETT Jerome, b. 22 Nov 1941, Poplar Bluff, Missouri, USA. Singer (Tenor). Education: Studied with Thorwald Olsen in St Louis and with Boris Goldovsky in West Virginia. Debut: Carnegie Hall New York 1974, in a concert performance of Donizetti's Parisina d'Este. Career: Sang with New York City Opera then followed a career in Europe: Vienna Volksoper, 1975, in the premiere of Wolpert's Le Malade Imaginaire; Théâtre de la Monnaie Brussels, 1983, as Julien in Louise and as Boris in Katya Kabanova; Geneva Opera, 1984, as Debussy's Pelléas; Sang at Nancy, 1984, in Henze's Boulevard Solitude; Other roles include Mozart's Belmonte and Tamino, Nicolai's Fenton, Tonio in La Fille du Régiment and Ernesto in Don Pasquale; Amsterdam and Paris, 1988, as Boris in Katya Kabanova and Faust; Sang Ferrando in Cosi fan tutte at the Gran Teatre del Liceu Barcelona 1990. Recordings: Louise (Erato). Address: c/o Harrison/Parrott Ltd, 12 Penzance Place, London W11 4PA, England.

PRUSLIN Stephen (Lawrence), b. 16 Apr 1940, Brooklyn, New York, USA. Pianist; Writer on Music. Education: Studied at Brandeis University (BA 1961) and Princeton (MFA 1963); Piano studies with Eduard Steuermann. Career: Taught at Princeton until 1964, then moved to London; Recital debut as pianist at Purcell Room, South Bank, 1970; Concert appearances with BBC Symphony and Royal Philharmonic; Recital accompanist to Bethany Beardslee, Elisabeth Söderström and the late Jan DeGaetani; Appearances with London Sinfonietta and the Fires of London (Co-founder), 1970-87; Repertoire has included works by Elliott Carter, Maxwell Davies (premiere of Piano Sonata), late Beethoven, Bach and John Bull; Collaborated with Davies on music for Ken Russell's film The Devils and has written other film and theatre music, including Derek Jarman's The Tempest; Articles on contemporary music, translation of Schoenberg's Pierrot Lunaire and librettos for Birtwistle's Monodrama, 1967, and Punch and Judy, 1968. Recordings include: Award-winning albums as solo and ensemble pianist. Publications include: Peter Maxwell Davies: Studies from Two Decades (editor), London, 1979. Address: c/o Universal Edition, Warwick House, 9 Warwick Street, London W1R 5RA, England.

PRYCE-JONES John, b. 1946, Wales. Conductor. Education: Studied in Penarth and Worcester and at Corpus Christi College, Cambridge (Organ Scholar). Career: Assistant Chorus Master and Conductor at Welsh National Opera, 1970-; Freelance conductor in the United Kingdom and abroad until 1978; Chorus Master and Conductor with Opera North, 1978-; Head of Music, Scottish Opera, 1987; Debut with English National Opera in The Mikado; Music Director of The New D'Oyly Carte Opera, 1990-92; First US visit of the Company with The Mikado and The Pirates of Penzance; Artistic Director of the Halifax Choral Society; Has conducted the Oslo Philharmonic, the Bergen Symphony and the Norwegian Broadcasting Orchestra; Debut with Icelandic Opera, 1991, with Rigoletto; Principal Conductor and Musical Director, with Northern Ballet Theatre, 1992; Rigoletto, with Opera North, 1992; La Bohème with Welsh National Opera, 1993; Conducted CBSO, BBC Welsh Symphony Orchestra. Recordings: Pirates of Penzance; Mikado; Iolanthe; Gondoliers. Honours: ARCO; MA. Address: 4 Croft Way, Menston, West Yorkshire, CS29 6LT, England.

PRYOR Gwenneth, b. 7 Apr 1941, Sydney, New South Wales, Australia. Concert Pianist. m. Roger Stone, 10 Dec 1972, 1 son, 1 daughter. Education: Diploma, New South Wales Conservatorium of Music; ARCM, Royal College of Music. Debut: Wigmore Hall, London. Career: recitals and concerts in major cities in United Kingdom, Europe, North and South America and Australia; Many records and radio broadcasts, both solo and chamber music; Teaching, Morley College. Recordings: Moussorgsky's Pictures at an Exhibition; Schumann's Carnaval and Papillons; Gershwin's Rhapsody in Blue and Concerto; Several discs with clarinettist Gervase de Peyer; Malcolm Williamson Concertos. Honours: Prize for Most Outstanding Student, New South Wales Conservatorium, 1960; 1st Prize, Australia House, 1963; Gold Medal, Royal College of Music, 1963. Memberships: Incorporated Society of Musicians; Royal Society of Musicians. Hobbies: Cooking; Reading. Current Management: Roger Stone Artist Management. Address: West Grove, Hammers Lane, London NW7 4DY, England.

PRZEREMBSKI Zbigniew Jerzy, b. 3 February 1952, Szczecin, Poland. Musicologist; Doctor of The Arts. m. Violetta Przerembska, 25 June 1987, 1 son. Education: Institute of Musicology, Warsaw University; Institute of Church Musicology, Catholic University, Lublin. Career: Research Worker, Institute of Art, Polish Academy of Sciences. Publications: Melodic Styles and Melodic Forms of Polish Folk Songs, 1994. Contributions to: Muzyka; Wychowanie Muzyczne W Szkole; Ruch Muzyczny; Tworczosc Ludowa; Polish Art Studies; Rodovid. Memberships: International Council for Traditional Music; European Seminar in Ethnomusicology. Hobby: Tourism. Address: Institute of Art, Polish Academy of Sciences, ul Dluga 26/28, PL-00-950 Warsaw, Poland.

PRZYBYLSKI Bronislaw (Kazimierz), b. 11 December 1941, Lodz, Poland. Composer. Education: Studied at the Lodz Stage College of Music, 1964-69, with Boleslaw Szabelski in Katowice, and with Roman Haubenstock-Ramati at the Vienna Hochschule für Musik, 1975-76. Career: Faculty Member, Lodz State College of Music, from 1964. Compositions include: Wind Quintet, 1967; String Quartet, 1969; Quattro Studi for orchestra, 1970; Suite of Polish Dances, 1971; Scherzi musicali for strings,

1973; Midnight, monodrama for actor and chamber ensemble, 1973; Concerto Polacco for accordion and orchestra, 1973; Voices for 3 actors and chamber ensemble, 1974; Requiem for soprano, 2 reciters, boys' chorus and orchestra, 1976; Sinfonia da Requiem, 1976; Arnold Schoenberg In Memoriam for string quartet, 1977; Sinfonia Polacca, 1974-78; The City of Hope, for bass, chorus and 2 orchestras, 1979; Sinfonia-Affresco, 1982; Concerto for harpischord and strings, 1983; Return, quasi symphonic poem, 1984; Miriam, ballet, 1985; Concerto Classico for accordion and orchestra, 1986; Wawelski Smok, ballet, 1987; Lacrimosa 2000 for strings, 1991; Autumn Multiplay for 6 instruments, 1994; Jubilaums Sinfonie, 1995; solo songs; choruses. Address: c/o ZAIKS, 2 rue Hipoteczna, 00 092 Warsaw, Poland.

PTASZYNSKA Marta, b. 29 Jul 1943, Warsaw, Poland. Composer; Percussionist; Teacher. m. Andrew Rafalski, 9 Nov 1974, 1 daughter. Education: Warsaw Lyceum and MA, Music, Academy of Music, 1967; MA, Music, 1967, Percussion in 1967 and Composition in 1968, all with distinction; Studied composition with Nadia Boulanger in Paris and L'ORTF Music Centre; Artist Diploma from the Cleveland Institute of Music, 1974. Career: Performances at International festivals including ISCM World Music Days, and International conventions; Radio and TV appearances in Poland and USA; Teacher of Composition and Percussion at Warsaw Higher School of Music and in USA, including the Indiana University in Bloomington, 1970-. Compositions: Symphonic music, chamber music, instrumental solo works, music for children, TV opera, including: Madrigals for Chamber Ensemble, 1971, Oscar Of Alva, 1972, Spectri Sonori for Orchestra, 1973, Siderals for 10 Percussionists and Light Projection, 1974, Space Model for 1 Percussionist, 1975, Epigrams, 1976-77, Dream Lands, Magic Spaces for Violin and Percussion Ensemble, 1979, Sonnets To Orpheus for Mezzo-Soprano and Chamber Orchestra, 1981, La Novella D'Inverno for String Orchestra, 1984, Concerto for Marimba and Orchestra, 1985, Moon Flowers for Cello and Piano, 1986. Recordings: Polskie Nagraina; Un Grand Somnieil Noir, 1979; La Novella D'Inverno, 1985; Moon Flowers, 1986; Space Model; Epigrams; Many archive recordings at Polish Radio and also Moon Flowers at BBC in 1986. Publications: Many works published. Contributions include: Cum Notis Variorum. Hobbies: Art; Theatre. Address: 48 Aspen Way, Brookfield, CT 06804, USA.

PUDDY Keith, b. 27 Feb 1935, Wedmore, England. Music Professor; Clarinettist; Researcher. m. Marilyn Johnston, 14 Feb 1950, 1 son. Education: Studied at Royal Academy of Music, London. Career: Principal Clarinet for Hallé Orchestra under Barbirolli, at age 23; Returned to London for solo and chamber music; Former member of The Gabrieli Ensemble, The Music Group of London, The New London Wind Ensemble; Now plays with The London Wind Trio and London Music Phoenix; Awarded Leverhulme Trust Fellowships in 1983 and 1988 to study and research clarinets; Principal Clarinet and Wind Advisor on period instruments to the New Queen's Hall Orchestra, London; Performs and records on both modern and period instruments; Professor at the Royal Academy of Music and Trinity College of Music, London; Member of the London Wind Trio and NSW Queens Hall Orchestra; Freelance Clarinettist, playing solo and chamber and also performing on early period instruments. Recordings: Major chamber repertoire on various labels; Brahmns Sonatas; Brahmns Quintet; Mozart Concerto; Mozart Quintet; Beethoven Septet; Numerous solo period recordings. Honours: Honorary FTCL, 1970; FRAM, 1995. Hobby: Mediaeval art. Address: 20 Courtnell Street, London W2 5BX, England.

PUERTO David Del, b. 30 April 1964, Madrid, Spain. Composer. m. Karin Anita Burk, 24 June 1991. Education: Private studies in Madrid with: Alberto Potin (guitar); Jesus Maria Corral (harmony); Francisco Guerrero (composition); Luis de Pablo (composition). Career: Major works in: Almeida Festival, London, 1985; Ensemble Intercontemporain Season, Paris, 1989; Geneva Summer Festival, 1989; Alicante Festival, 1991, 1996; Ars Musica Festival, Brussels, 1992, 1993, 1996; Gaudeamus Week, Amsterdam, 1993, 1996; Takefu Festival, Japan, 1993. Compositions: Corriente Cautiva for Orchestra, 1991; Concerto for Oboe and Chamber Ensemble, 1992; Etude, for wind quintet, 1993; Vision Del Errante, for 12 mixed voices, 1994; Concerto for Marimba and 15 Instruments, 1996; Concerto For Violin and Orchestra. Recordings: Concerto for Oboe, by Ernest Rombout, Xenakis Ensemble and Diego Masson (conductor); Invernal and En La Luz, by Orquestra Del Teatre Lliure, Concuctor, J Pons; Consort, by Quartet de Bec Frullato; Verso III, by José Vicente (percussion); Verso I, Isabelle Duval (flute). Contributions to: Proceso Formativoy Creativo en La Industria de la Musica, 1996. Honours: Prize: Gaudeamus (Amsterdam) for Concerto for Oboe, 1993; Prize, El Ojo Critico, Spanish National Broadcasting, 1993. Membership: Sociedad General de Autores y Editores (SGAE), Spain. Hobbies: Nature; writing poetry. Address: c/o SGAE, Fernando IV 4, 28004 Madrid, Spain.

PUFFETT Derrick (Robert), b. 30 Nov 1946, Oxford, England. Musicologist. Education: BA, New College, Oxford, 1968; DPhil, 1977, Wolfson College, Oxford. Career: Research Fellow, Wolfson College, Oxford, 1973-84; Member, Oxford University Music Faculty, 1978-84; Lecturer, Hertford College, Oxford, 1978-81; St Hilda's College, 1979-84; St Edmund Hall, 1979-84; Christ Church, 1981-84; Lecturer: Cambridge University Music Faculty, 1984-; Fellow and Lecturer of St John's College, Cambridge, 1984-; Associate Editor, Music Analysis Journal, 1984-86; Editor, 1986-. Publication: The Song Cycles of Othmar Schoeck, 1982. Contributions to: Articles to professional journals. Memberships: British Royal Music Association; Advisory Board, Music Analysis Journal.

PULESTON Faith, b. 1942, England. Singer (Mezzo-soprano). Education: Studied with Eva Turner at the Royal Academy of Music and in Germany. Career: Sang at the Saarbrucken Opera from 1966, Deutsche Oper am Rhein at Dusseldorf from 1968; Roles have included Carmen, Eboli, Fricka and Mozart's Sextus; Bayreuth Festival, 1970-71, as Grimgerde, and Verdi's Amneris at Covent Garden; Sang Brangaene at the Stadttheater Hagen, 1991. Address: Stadttheater Hagen, Elberfelderstrasse 65, W-5800 Hagen, Germany.

PULIEV Michael, b. 27 Mar 1958, Sofia, Bulgaria. Singer (bass-baritone). Education: Studied in Sofia with Boris Christoff. Career: Sang at the National Opera, Sofia, 1984-86, then gave concerts in Bulgaria, China, Korea, Germany and Switzerland; Sang at Stadttheater Bern, 1986-87, Liège-, as Mars in Orphée aux Enfers, Frère Laurent in Roméo et Juliette and roles in Mascagni's Nerone, Die Zauberflöte, Le nozze di Figaro, La Traviata and Andrea Chenier. Honours: Winner, Bulgarian young singers competitions; Prize winner, Maria Callas Competition at Athens, 1984, Geneva International, 1987.

PURCELL Kevin John, b. 9 Sept 1959, Melbourne, Victoria, Australia. Composer; Author; Conductor. Education: BA (Music), La Trobe University, 1980; MMus, University of Melbourne, 1991; GradDipMus, New South Wales Conservatory, 1993; Janacek Academy, Brno, 1994; Composition with Brenton Broadsctock, 1989-91; Conducting with Myer Fredman, 1993. Career: Conductor in Australia and England; Faculty Member, University of Melbourne, 1990-92; Resident in London. Compositions include: Symphony No 1: The Monk of St Evroul, 1990; Three Brass Monkeys, for trumpet, horn and bass trombone, 1990; An Umbrella for Inclement Weather, for flute, oboe and clarinet, 1991; Kite Songs for a Crescent Moon, for mezzo and large ensemble, 1992; Symphony No 2: The Enchanter of Caer-Myrddin, 1992; The Thirty-Nine Steps, 1-act chamber opera, 1993-95. Honours include: Sir Charles Mackerras Conducting Award, 1995. Address: c/o APRA, 1A Eden Street, Crows Nest, NSW 2065, Australia.

PURCELL Patricia (Elizabeth Harley), b. 7 Sept 1925, Egham, Surrey, England. Pianist; Teacher. Education: Royal College of Music, London, 1944-47; ARCM, 1945; Pupil of Frank Merrick; Disciple of Leschetizky & Viennese School. Debut: Royal Albert Hall, London, 1958. Career: Various recital/concerto appearances including Wigmore Hall, London, 1969; Polish Tour, Frederic Chopin Society, 1972, including Chopin's birthplace, 27th Chopinowski International Festival at Duszniki, and appearances on Polish Radio and TV; Private Teacher. Honour: Winner, 1st Prize, Piano Concerto Class, London Musical Competition Festival, 1956. Membership: Incorporated Society of Musicians. Hobbies: Cooking; Psychology; Nature. Address: c/o National Westminster Bank plc, 81 Aldwick Road, West Bognor Regis, West Sussex, PO21 2NS, England.

PURVES Christopher, b. 1960, England. Bass-Baritone. Education: Choral scholar at King's College, Cambridge. Career: Appearances with English and Welsh National Operas and Opera Northern Ireland as Mozart's Figaro, Leporello, Masetto, the Speaker and Papageno; Other roles include Don Pasquale, the Sacristan in Tosca, Dandini in La Cenerentola, Janácek's Forester and Melibeo in La Fedeltà Premiata (Garsington, 1995); Concerts with such conductors as Colin Davis, Pesek, Rattle, Hickox, Christopher and Herreweghe. Recordings include: Israel in Egypt, with Gardiner; Purcell and Charpentier albums. Address: c/o Ron Gonsalves Management, 7 Old Town, Clapham, London, SW4 0JT, England.

PUSAR Ana, b. 1954, Celje, Yugoslavia. Soprano. Education: Studied in Celje and at School of Music, Ljubljana. Career: Sang in Ljubljana from 1975 as Rosina, Manon, Tatiana, Dido, Nedda, Micaela, Desdemona and Poppea; Berlin Komische Opera, 1979-85; Appearances at the State Operas of Berlin and Dresden; Guest appearances in Japan, Prague, Moscow, Leningrad, Edinburgh, Venice and Madrid; Roles have included: Mozart's Fiordiligi and Countess, Agathe, Araidne, Elsa, Madama Butterfly and Ellen Orford; Sang the Marschallin at reopening of Dresden Semper Oper, 1985, Vienna Staatsoper from 1986 as Donna Anna, Arabella, Agathe and the Marschallin, Munich Staatsoper in Daphne, as the Countess in Figaro and Capriccio and Donna Anna; Has also sung in Barcelona, Venice, Hamburg, Montreal, Geneva, Stuttgart, Lisbon, Toulouse, Graz and Cologne; Season 1992 with Sieglinde in Die Walküre at Bonn; Concert appearances in most major European centres; Has worked with such conductors as Peter Schneider, Gerd Albrecht, John Pritchard, Nikolaus Harnoncourt and Lorin Maazel; From 1992 sang: Tatiana at Venice, 1993, Katya Kabanova at Zurich, 1994 and Graz, 1994 in Stiffelio at Lima; Gertrud at Palermo, 1995. Recordings include: Der Rosenkavalier, Semper Opera; Bontempi Requiem; Dvorak Stabat Mater; Così fan tutte; Hugo Wolf, Lieder, 1990; Rachmaninov Lieder und Romances; Orfeo, 1994. Honours include: Winner, Toti dal Monte Competition and Mario del Monaco Competition, 1978; National Award of Slovenia, 1979. Current Management: Music International. Address: c/o Music International, 13 Ardilaun Road, London, N5 2QR, England.

PUTILIN Nikolai, b. 1953, Russia. Singer (Baritone). Career: Principal with the Kirov Opera at the Mariinsky Theatre, St Petersburg; Roles have included Verdi's Iago, Posa, Rigoletto, Amonasro, Germont and Don Carlo (Forza); Scarpia, Escamillo, Eugene Onegin, Figaro, Tomsky (The Queen of Spades), Rubinstein's Demon, Prince Igor, Ruprecht (The Fiery Angel), Rangoni (Boris Godunov) and Mizgir in The Snow Maiden; Guest with the Kirov at the Metropolitan New York, Milan, Hamburg and Japan; Edinburgh Festival, 1995, in Rimsky's Sadko and Invisible City of Kitezh; Boris Godunov at the 1995 Birmingham Festival, and the posthumous premiere of Karetnikov's Apostle Paul's Mystery; Scarpia at the 1995 Savonlinna Festival; Drury Lane, London, 1997, with the Kirov Company, as Boris. Address: Lies Askonas Ltd, 6 Henrietta Street, London WC2E 8LA, England.

PUTKONEN Marko, b. 1947, Finland. Singer (Bass). Education: Studied at the Sibelius Academy, Helsinki. Career: At the Finnish National Opera has sung Mozart's Bartolo, Nicolai's Falstaff, in Katerina Ismailova, Sallinen's Red Line and the 1990 premiere of Rautavaara's Vincent (as Gauguin); Guested at Los Angeles, 1992, in the premiere of Kullervo by Sallinen; Further guest appearances at the Savonlinna Festival (Rocco, 1992), Zurich and Geneva. Address: Finnish National Opera, 23-27 Bulevardi, SF-00180 Helsinki, Finland.

PUTNAM Ashley, b. 10 Aug 1952, NY, USA. Singer, Soprano. Education: University of Michigan, with Elizabeth Mosher and Willis Patterson. Career: Norfolk Opera, Virginia, from 1976 as Donizetti's Lucia and the title role in the US premiere of Musgrave's Mary Queen of Scots; NYC Opera debut, 1978, as Violetta; Later sang Bellini's Elvira, Verdi's Gieslda, Thomas' Ophelia and Donizetti's Maria Stuarda; European debut 1978 as Musetta at Glyndebourne; Returned for Arabella 1984; Lucia with Scottish Opera; Mozart's Fiordiligi at Venice and for BBC TV, Sifare in Mitridate at Aix, Donna Anna in Brussels and Countess Almaviva in Cologne; Covent Garden debut 1986, as Janacek's Jenufa; Appearances at Santa Fe in Thomson's The Mother of us All and in the title role of Die Liebe der Danae, 1985; Metropolitan Opera debut 1990, as Donna Elvira; Florence 1990, as Katya Kabanova; Sang Ellen Orford in Peter Grimes at the Geneva Opera and Vitellia in La Clemenza di Tito at the 1991 Glyndebourne Festival; Season 1991-92 as Fusako in the US premiere of Henze's Das Verratere Meer, at San Francisco, and the Marshallin at Santa Fe; Sang St Teresa I in Thomson's Four Saints in Three Acts, Houston and Edinburgh, 1996; Concert engagements with the Los Angeles Philharmonic, New York Philharmonic and Concertgebouw Orchestras; Regular concerts at Carnegie Hall. Recordings: The Mother of us All; Mary Queen of Scots; Musetta in La Bohème. Address: c/o Lies Askonas Ltd, 6 Henrietta Street, London WC2, England.

PUTTEN Thea van der, b. 1950, Eindhoven, Netherlands. Singer (Soprano). Education: Studied at the Hague Conservatory. Career: Sang in the 1980 Holland Festival and with Netherlands Opera in La Cenerentola, Hansel and Gretel, Die Zauberflöte and La Vie Parisienne; Nedda in Pagliacci, 1985; Komische Oper Berlin, 1988, as Donna Elvira, and in the 1986 premiere of Ketting's Ithaka, at the opening of the Amsterdam Muziektheater; Many concert engagements; Teaches singing at the Royal Conservatory, The Hague. Recordings include: Die Zauberflöte (RCA). Address: Netherlands Opera, Waterlooplein 22, 1001 PS Amsterdam, Netherlands.

PÜTZ Ruth-Margret, b. 26 Feb 1931, Krefeld, Germany. Singer (Soprano). Education: Studied with Bertold Putz in Krefeld. Debut: Cologne 1950, as Nuri in Tiefland by d'Albert. Career: Sang at Hanover 1951-57; Stuttgart from 1957, notably as Gilda and Zerbinetta; Bayreuth Festival 1960, as Waldvogel; Salzburg Festival 1961, as Constanze in Die Entführung; Russian Tour with the Capella Coloniensis 1961; Hamburg Staatsoper 1963-68; Guest appearances in Buenos Aires, Helsinki, Frankfurt, Munich, Nice, Rome, Venice, Naples and Barcelona. Recordings: Bach's Magnificat; Die Lustigen Weiber von Windsor; Lortzing's Undine; Il Barbiere di Siviglia; Queen of Night in Die Zauberflöte; Trionfo by Orff (BASF). Address: c/o Bayerische Staatsoper, Postfach 745, D-8000 Munich 1, Germany.

PUYANA Rafael, b. 4 Oct 1931, Bogotá, Colombia. Harpsichordist. Education: Studied under Wanda Landowska. Career: Now lives in Spain but gives performances throughout the world; Festival appearances at: Berlin; Ansbach; Holland; Aldeburgh; Harrogate; Besançon; Aix-en-Provence; BBC television, 1985, with Sonatas by Scarlatti. Recordings: Records for Philips and CBS labels. Hobbies: Collecting Old Keyboard Instruments. Address: c/o Miss M Garnham, 8 St George's Terrace, London, NW1 8XJ, England.

PY Gilbert, b. 9 Dec 1933, Sete, France. Singer (Tenor). Debut: Verviers, Belgium, 1964 as Pinkerton in Madama Butterfly. Career: Paris Opera from 1969, notably as Manrico, Don José, Samson, Florestan, Tannhäuser, Lohengrin and in La Damnation de Faust; Paris Opéra-Comique 1969, in the title role of Les Contes d'Hoffmann; Nice Opéra in the local premiere of Sutermeister's Raskolnikov; Toulouse 1970, in Gounod's La Reine de Saba; Guest appearances in Vienna, Munich, Verona, Florence, Barcelona, New Orleans and Budapest; Turin 1973, as Lohengrin; Sang at the 1987 Orange Festival as Jean in Massenet's Hérodiade; Aeneas in Les Troyens at Marseilles 1989. Recordings include: Carmen (RCA); La Vestale by Spontini. Address: Opéra de Marseille, 2 Ruè Moliére, F-1323 Marseille Cedex 01, France.

PYATT David, b. 1974, England. Horn Player. Career: Former Principal Horn, National Youth Orchestra and National Youth Chamber Orchestra of Great Britain; From 1988 has performed with the London Symphony and Halle Orchestras, English Chamber Orchestra and London Mozart Players; Tours of Germany and Japan with the BBC National Orchestra of Wales; Played the Second Concerto by Strauss at the 1993 London Proms; Repertoire ranges from Telemann, Haydn and Mozart to contemporary composers; Broadcast on BBC and Independent television and radio; Television recital with Martin Jones and the Young Composer Workshop, 1996; Season 1998 includes a performance of Mozart Concertos at the Salzburg Mozartwoche Festival under Trevor Pinnock and with the Isreal Chamber Orchestra. Recordings include: Strauss Concerti; Britten Serenade; English Rare Concerti; Mozart Concerti. Honours include: Gramophone Magazine's Young Artist of the Year, 1996. Address: c/o Harold Holt Ltd, 31 Sinclair Road, London W14 0NS, England.

PYPER George (Earl), b. 5 Jun 1927, Toronto, Ontario, Canada. Violinist, Orchestral and Soloist; Instructor; Music Journalist; Theatre and Arts Critic. Education: Graduate, Jarvis Collegiate Institute, Toronto, 1945; Studied at Ontario College of Art with Eric Friefeld and Harley Parker, 1948; Acting with Burton James at Banff School of Fine Arts; At Toronto Conservatory of Music with Jack Montague, Kathleen Parlow, Chamber Music, Alexander Brott at McGill Conservatorium in Montreal; Studied violin with Alexander Chuhaldin in Toronto, and Counterpoint with Dr Healey Willan. Debut: Soloist, Tomorrow's Concert Stars, CBC, 1944. Career: Resident Concertmaster, Royal Alexandra Theatre, Toronto, 1947-54; Performing Member of London Symphony Orchestra, 1956-57, Toronto Symphony Orchestra, 1958-63; Violin Instructor, Lakefield College School, 1970-74; Concertmaster, Peterborough Symphony Orchestra, 1972-77, also soloist at Trent University; Instructor at Sir Sandford Fleming College, Peterborough, Ontario; Solo Violin concert in British Columbia, Canada, Gabriola, Victoria, Surrey and at most LDS chapels, Vancouver Island; Member, First American Violin Congress, Yehudi Menuhin, Washington DC, 1987; Solo engagements, West Coast featuring Bach Partitas for Solo Violin. Hobbies: Landscape Painter; The Arts.

Q

QUARTARARO Florence, b. 31 May 1922, San Francisco, USA. Singer (Soprano). Education: Studied with Elizabeth Wells in San Francisco and Pietro Cimini in Los Angeles. Debut: Hollywood Bowl 1945, as Leonora in Il Trovatore. Career: Metropolitan Opera from 1946, as Micaela (Carmen), Pamina, Verdi's Violetta and Desdemona and Nedda (Pagliacci); San Francisco 1947, as Donna Elvira in Don Giovanni; Guest appearances at Philadelphia and elsewhere in the USA; Arena Flagrea, Naples, 1953 as Margherita in Mefistofele; Many concert appearances.

QUASTHOFF Thomas, b. Nov 1959, Hildesheim, Germany. Singer (Baritone). Education: Studied with Charlotte Lehmann in Hanover and with Carol Richardson; Law degree at the University of Hanover. Career: Many appearances at the world's leading concert halls in Oratorio and Lieder; Season 1995 with US debut at the Oregon-Bach Festival and Japan debut with the Internationale Bachakademie under Helmuth Rilling; Season 1995-96 at the Schleswig-Holstein Festival, the Herkulessaal in Munich and in Paris and Madrid; Britten's War Requiem at the Edinburgh Festival under Donald Runnicles; Season 1996-97 with the English Chamber Orchestra, Berlin Philharmonic under Rattle and the Chamber Orchestra of Europe under Abbado; Schubert Bicentenary concerts 1997, including Wigmore Hall recital and Winterreise for television. Recordings include: Bach Cantatas (Bayer); St John Passion and Schumann Lieder (BMG); Schubert Goethe-Lieder, Fidelio under Colin Davis and Mozart Arias (BMG). Honours include: Grand Prix Gabriel Fauré, Paris, for Schumann Lieder. Address: c/o Ingpen & Williams Ltd, 26 Wadham Road, London SW15 2LR, England.

QUEFFÉLEC Anne, b. 17 Jan 1948, Paris, France. Concert Pianist. m. 2 children. Education: Studied at the Paris Conservatoire and in Vienna with Paul Badura-Skoda, Jörg Demus and Alfred Brendel. Career: Solo recitals and orchestral concerts from 1969 in Europe, Japan, USA, Israel and Canada; Conductors include James Conlon, Rudolf Barshai, Colin Davis, Pierre Boulez, Theodor Guschlbauer, Charles Groves, Heinz Holliger, Armin Jordan, Raymond Leppard, David Zinman, Neville Marriner, Jerzy Semkov and Stanislav Skrowaczewski; British appearances with all the BBC Symphony Orchestras, the Royal Liverpool Philharmonic, Bournemouth Symphony, Hallé, Scottish Chamber, Northern Sinfonia, Royal Philharmonic, City of Birmingham Symphony and the London Symphony; Concerts at the Proms in London, Cheltenham, Bath, King's Lynn Festivals; Chamber music recitals with Pierre Amoyal, Augustin Dumay, Régis Pasquier, Frederic Lodéon, the Chilingrian Quartet and Imogen Cooper (piano duo). Recordings: Works by Scarlatti, Chopin, Schubert, Liszt, Ravel, Mendelssohn, Fauré, Hummel and Debussy; Complete solo works of Satie and Ravel, Poulenc's Concerto for Two Pianos. Honours: 1st Prizes for piano and for chamber music at the Paris Conservatoire, 1965, 1966; Winner, Munich International, 1968; 5th Prize, Leeds International, 1969; Victoire de la Musique Awards, Best French Classical Artist of the Year, 1990. Hobbies: Reading; Philosophy; Cooking; Friends; Cycling; Jogging. Address: c/o Christopher Tennant Management, Unit 2, 39 Tadema Road, London SW10, England.

QUELER Eve, b. 1 Jan 1936, NY, USA. Conductor; Director of Opera. m. Stanley N Queler, 1 s, 1 d. Education: High School of Music and Art, NY; City University of New York; Mannes College of Music, NY; Graduate Conducting studies with Joseph Rosenstock, at American Institute of Conducting under auspices of St Louis Symphony, with Walter Susskind and Leonard Slatkin and at Concours de Monte Carlo with Igor Markevitch and Herbert Blomstedt; Accompanying studies with Paul Ulanovsky and Paul Berl; Analysis with Paul Emerich. Career includes: Founder, Director and Conductor of Opera Orchestra of New York, 1968-; National Opera Orchestra workshop created for her by University of Maryland, 1978; Guest Conductor for Cleveland and Philadelphia Orchestras, symphonies of Edmonton, Toledo Jacksonville, Kansas City, New Jersey, Hartford, Chautauqua, Montreal, Puerto Rico and Colorado Springs, Michigan Chamber Orchestra and Fort Wayne Philharmonic; Opera Companies include Gran Teatro Liceo, Barcelona, St Louis, Chattanooga, Providence, Shreveport, San Diego, Sydney Australia, Opera South, Opera de Nice, Oberlin Opera Festival in Lyon, Opera Metropolitan in Caracas, National Theatre of Czechoslovakia, Orchestra Lyrique on Radio France and New York City Opera; conducted Rossini's Armida at Carnegie Hall, 1996. Recordings include: Puccini's Edgar; Donizetti's Gemma di Vergy; Verdi's Aroldo; Boito's Nerone. Contributions include: An American Conductor in Prague. Honours include: Martha Baird Rockefeller Fund for Music Study Grant, 1970; Honorary Doctorates from Russell Sage College, 1978 and Colby College, 1983. Current Management: Herbert Barrett Management, 1776 Broadway, Ste 504, New York, NY 10019, USA. Address: Vincent and Robbins Associates, 124 East 40th Street, Ste 304, New York, NY 10016, USA.

QUILICO Gino, b. 29 Apr 1955, New York, USA. Singer (Baritone). Education: Graduated University of Toronto 1978; Vocal studies with Lina Pizzolongo and his father. Career: Canadian debut 1978, in a TV performance of The Medium; Member of the Paris Opéra from 1980, in operas by Rossini, Britten, Poulenc, Puccini, Gounod, Massenet, and Gluck; UK debut with Scottish Opera at the 1982 Edinburgh Festival, as Puccini's Lescaut; Covent Garden debut 1983, as Valetin in Faust; later London appearances as Puccini's Marcello, Donizetti's Belcore, Rossini's Figaro, Escamillo and Posa in Don Carlos (1989); Aix-en-Provence Festival 1985 and 1986, as Monteverdi's Orfeo and Mozart's Don Giovanni; Metropolitan Opera debut 1987, as Massenet's Lescaut; Malatesta in Don Pasquale at Lyon; Sang Dandini in La Cenerentola at the 1988 and 1989 Salzburg Festivals; Rome Opera 1990, as Riccardo in I Puritani; Sang Gluck's Oreste at the 1994 Vienna Festival; Sang Iago at Cologne, 1996. Recordings include: Lescaut in Manon (EMI); Dancairo in Carmen (Deutsche Grammophon); Mercutio in Roméo et Juliette (EMI); Marcello in La Bohème and Malatesta in Don Pasquale (Erato); Video of 1988 Salzburg Cenerentola. Address: IMG, Media House, 3 Burlington Lane, London W4 2TH, England.

QUILOCO Louis, b. 14 Jan 1929, Montrel, Quebec, Canada. Opera Singer (Baritone); Professor. m. (1) 29 Oct 1949, 1 son, 1 daughter, (2) Christina Petrowska, 30 Nov 1993. Education: Quebec Conservatory; Mannes School of Music, New York, USA. Debut: New York City Opera. Career: New York City Opera, 1949; Spoleto Festival, 1959; San Francisco Opera, 1955; Metropolitan Opera Audition of the Air, 1953; Covent Garden Opera, London, England, 1960; Paris Opera, France, 1962; Vienna Opera, Austria, 1964; Canadian Opera Company, 1959; CBC TV, Canada, Television France, Live from the Metropolitan Opera House of New York, 1982, 1983, 1984, 1985 (New York roles included Golaud, Rigoletto, Iago, Macbeth, Posa, Falstaff, Scarpia, Renato and Germont); Sang Michonnet in Adriana Lecouvreur for Opéra de Montréal, 1990; Professor, Toronto University. Recordings include: Live from the Met, video disc; Un Ballo in Maschera and Don Carlo. Honours: Honorary Doctor Immeritum, Quebec University; Companion, Order of Canada. Hobbies: Building model radio controlled aeroplanes; Electric trains; Photography; Video recording. Current Management: Ann Summers Management, Box 188 Station A, Toronto, Ontario, Canada M5W 1B2. Address: 25 Berryman Street, Toronto, Canada M5R 1M7.

QUING Miao, b. 1955, China. Singer (Mezzo-soprano). Education: Studied at the Peking Conservatory. Career: Sang Carmen under the direction of Jacqueline Brumaire at Peking, 1982; Studied further at the Nancy Conservatoire and sang Butterfly from 1986 at Basle, Berlin, Lausanne, Toulon and Covent Garden; Guested with the Peking Opera at Savonlinna as Carmen, sang Donna Elvira at Brunswick (1991) and in Ariadna and Zauberflöte at the Bonn Opera; Many concert engagements. Address: Oper der Stadt Bonn, Am Boeselagerhof 1, Pf 2440, W-5300 Bonn, Germany.

QUINN Gerard, b. 1962, Irvine, Scotland. Singer (Baritone). m. Heather, 1 d. Education: Studied flute at Napier College, Edinburgh; Singing at The Royal Northern College of Music, Manchester with Patrick McGuigan; The National Opera Studio, London; In Vienna with Otto Edelmann and presently with Iris Dell'Acqua. Career: Early appearances as Golaud, Pelléas et Mélisande, Escamillo, Mozart's Count and Junius in The Rape of Lucretia; Buxton Festival Opera 1985; Glyndebourne Festival debut 1987, in Capriccio; Glyndebourne Tour, 1988, in La Traviata; Scottish Opera debut 1989, Donner, (Das Rheingold); English National Opera debut 1990, as Pantaloon, (The Love for Three Oranges), also for New Israeli Opera; Royal Opera, Covent Garden debut Flemish Deputy, (Don Carlo), 1989; Meru, (Les Huguenots), 1991 and in 1994 Le Comte in the British premiere of Massenet's Chérubin, and sang various roles with the New Garden Venture in world premieres of Biko Survival Song and The Menaced Assassin; Welsh National Opera debut, 1993, Enrico, (Lucia di Lammermoor), 1995, Father, Hansel and Gretel, Germont, (La Traviata); Bath and Wessex Opera, title role Rigoletto, 1994; English Touring Opera, 1994, Marcello, La Boheme; European Chamber Opera 1993, Count di Luna, Il Trovatore (also recorded), 1994 Count Alamaviva, Le nozze di Figaro and Rigoletto; Crystal Clear Opera, Sharpless, Madam Butterfly, 1995; Other roles performed include Nabucco, Germont, Ford, Michele, Il Tabarro, Tonio, Pagliacci, Zurga in The Pearl Fishers, Malatesta, Don Pasquale, Danilo in The Merry Widow, Don Giovanni and Eugene Onegin; Concert repertoire includes Elijah, Carmina Burana, Sea Symphony, Dream of Gerontius, Brahms Requiem and Britten's War Requiem. Honours include: International Opera and Bel Canto Duet Competition, Antwerp, with his wife, the soprano, Heather Lorimer; South East Arts Young Musicians Platform; Sir James Caird Travelling Scholarship; Awards from the Vaughan Williams Trust, Countess of Munster and The Peter Moores Foundation. Address: c/o International Opera and Concert Artists, 75 Aberdare Gardens, London NW6 3AN, England.

QUITTMEYER Susan, b. 1955, USA. Singer (Mezzo-soprano). m. James Morris. Education: Studied at Wesleyan University, Illinois, and at the Manhattan School of Music. Career: Sang with the America Opera Project, notably in the premiere of John Harbison's A Winter's Tale, at San Francisco, 1979; Guested at St Louis (debut in a revival of Martin y Soler's L'Arbore di Diana, 1978), and sang further at San Francisco from 1981; Sang in Montreal from 1983, Los Angeles 1984; Santa Fe 1984-88, notably in the US premiere of Henze's We Come to the River; Further US appearances in Philadelphia, Cincinnati and San Diego; Sang the Messenger in Monteverdi's Orfeo at Geneva (1986) and Sesto in Giulio Cesare at the Paris Opera, 1987; Further European engagements as Octavian for Netherlands Opera, Cherubino and Annius at Munich and Zerlina at the Vienna Staatsoper; Salzburg Festival debut 1991, as Idamantes in Idomeneo; Concerts with the Los Angeles Philharmonic and the Symphony Orchestras of Oakland, Sacremento and San Francisco; Metropolitan Opera from 1987 as Nicklausse in Les Contes d'Hoffmann and Dorabella; Sang Varvara in Katya Kabanova and Siebel with James Morris, 1991; Other roles include Meg Page, Cherubino, the Composer in Ariadne, Carmen, Pauline (The Queen of Spades) and Zerlina (Miami 1988); Engaged as Siebel at San Francisco, 1995; Many concert appearances. Address: c/o Metropolitan Opera, Lincoln Center, New York, NY 10023, USA.

QUIVAR Florence, b. 3 Mar 1944, Philadelphia, USA. Singer (Mezzo-Soprano). Education: Philadelphia Academy of Music; Juilliard School New York. Career: Concert appearances with the New York, Los Angeles and Israel Philharmonics, the Cleveland, Philadelphia and Mostly Mozart Festival Orchestras and the Boston Symphony; Conductors include Mehta, Bernstein, Leinsdorf, Boulez, Muti and Colin Davis; Metropolitan Opera debut 1977, as Marina in Boris Godunov: returned to New York for Jocasta (Oedipus Rex); Isabella (L'Italiana in Algeri), Fides (Le Prophète) and Serena in Porgy and Bess; Guest appearances in Berlin, Florence, Geneva, Montreal and San Francisco; Recent engagements include La Damnation de Faust in Geneva, the Wesendonk Lieder in Madrid and London, the Verdi Requiem with the Philharmonia Orchestra, Mahler's 3rd Symphony with the New York Philharmonic and performances with the Berlin Philharmonic under Giulini; Festival appearances with the Israel Philharmonic in Salzburg, London, Lucerne, Florence and Edinburgh; Sang Ulrica in Un ballo in maschera at the 1990 Salzburg Festival (also televised); Season 1990/91 with Mahler's 2nd and 3rd symphonies (La Scala and New York, and in Japan); Met Opera as Federica in Luisa Miller; Gurrelieder under Zubin Mehta; London Proms 1991, in The Dream of Gerontius; Sang in the Met Opera Gala concert, 1996. Recordings: Rossini's Stabat Mater (Vox); Mahler's 8th Symphony under Seiji Ozawa (Philips); Mendelssohn's Midsummer Night's Dream (Deutsche Grammophon); Berlioz's Romeo and Juliet (Erato); Virgil Thomson's Four Saints in Three Acts (Nonesuch); Verdi Requiem; Un ballo in maschera conducted by Karajan (Deutsche Grammophon); Luisa Miller (Sony); Schoenberg's Gurrelieder. Address: Kaye Artists Management, Barratt House, 7 Chertsey Road, Woking, Surrey GU21 3AB, England.

R

RAAD Virginia, b. 13 Aug 1925, Salem, West Virginia, USA. Concert Pianist; Musicologist. Education: BA, Wellesley College; New England Conservatory; Diploma, Ecole Normale de Musique, Paris; Doctorate, highest honours, University of Paris. Career: Numerous concerts, lectures, master classes, including: Alliance Francaise, Pittsburgh and University of Pittsburgh; Walsh College, Ohio; Special Summer Artist; Middlebury College, Vermont; Wellesley College, Massachusetts; University of Michigan-Dearborn; Elmira and Manhattanville Colleges, New York; Rollins College, Florida; College of William and Mary, Virginia; University of Notre Dame, Indiana; Marietta College, Ohio; Huntington Galleries, West Virginia; Music Teachers' Association Convention, Houston; Musician in Residence, North Carolina Arts Council and Community Colleges; Mount Mary College, Wisconsin; Portland State University, Oregon; Seton Hill College, Pennsylvania; Mount Union College, Ohio; Berea College, Kentucky; Community concerts, music clubs, TV, radio, USA, Europe; Adjudicator, Grant Reviewer. Recordings: The Piano Works of Claude Debussy, 1994, 1995. Publications include: L'Influence de Debussy: Amerique (Etats-Unis), in Debussy et l'evolution de la musique au XXe siècle, 1965; Claude Debussy, Gabriel Faure, both in New Catholic Encyclopaedia, 1967. Contributions to: Musical Courier, 1961; The American Music Teacher, 1968, 1971, 1976, 1977, 1981, 1986; Piano Guild Notes, 1973, 1995; Clavier, 1979, 1986; The Piano Sonority of Claude Debussy, 1994. Honours: Travel Grant, American Council of Learned Societies; Government grants; Outstanding West Virginia Woman Educator, Delta Kappa Gamma; Biography, Study in pioneering music methods, placed in Arthur and Elizabeth Schlesinger Library on History of Women in America, Radcliffe College. Memberships: American, International and French Musicological Societies; College Music Society; American Society for Aesthetics; Music Teachers' National Association, Musicology Programme Chair, 1983-87. Address: 60 Terrace Avenue, Salem, WV 26426, USA.

RABES C-A Lennart, b. 1938, Eskilstuna, Sweden. Pianist; Harpsichordist; Organist; Conductor; Lecturer; Editor; Examiner. Education: Music Academy, Zurich; Accademia Chigiana, Siena; ARCM, London; Studied Piano with Professor S Sundell, Stockholm, E Cavallo, Milan, B Siki, Zurich, M Tagliaferro, Paris; J von Karolyi, Munich; Studied Conducting with C von Garaguly, Stockholm, P von Kempen, Siena, Sir Adrian Boult, London; BA, Music, Pacific Western University, Los Angeles, California, 1992. Debut: As Pianist and Conductor, Stockholm, 1951. Career: Performances in major cities of Europe, Canada and USA; Many recordings for Swedish, Austrian, French, Swiss and German broadcasting companies; Director, International Liszt Centre, Stockholm; Organist, various churches, Munich, 1960-66, Swiss Church, London, 1966-78; Founder, Musical Director, Deal Summer Music Festival, Deal, Kent, England, 1981-83, Sabylund Festival, Sweden, 1985-; Repetiteur at Norrlandsopera, Umea, 1985-88; Has given concerts at historical places including On Wagner's Erard at the Wagner Museum, Tribschen, Lucerne, Switzerland, 1985; Lecturer for research associations, universities radio and conservatories; Examiner, Associated Board, Royal Schools of Music, London; Currently working at Operastudio 67, Stockholm. Recordings: Piano works by Liszt. Publication: Liszt's Scandinavian Reputation, in Liszt and His World, 1998. Contributions to: Liszt Saeculum. Honours: Hungarian Liszt Medal, 1986; 1st Place for record of Piano Music by Liszt, ABIRA Artistic Competition Award, 1992; Medal of Excellence, American Liszt Society, 1997. Memberships: SYMF; International Association of Music Libraries; Music Library Association. Address: Synalsvagen 5, S-16149 Bromma, Stockholm, Sweden.

RABIN Shira, b. 1 Apr 1970, Tel-Aviv, Israel. Violinist. Education: Studied at the Juilliard School with Dorothy DeLay. Debut: Played with the Israel Philharmonic 1979. Career: Appeared in the International Huberman Week with Isaac Stern and the Israel Philharmonic 1983; Toured Europe 1983, Canada coast-to-coast tour 1985; Played with Henryk Szeryng during Israel Philharmonic Jubilee Season 1987; Soloist in the Stradivarius Year in Cremona; Israel representative in Italian Nights of Music with Zubin Mehta; Gala concert at Carnegie Hall with Isaac Stern; Musical Discovery of 1989 in Italy, after recital debut in Milan; German debut Feb 1991, with the Bavarian Radio Symphony Orchestra; US debut 1992 with the Philadelphia Orchestra under Riccardo Muti; Further concerts with the Pittsburgh Orchestra under Lorin Maazel. Address: IMG Artists Europe, Media House, 3 Burlington Lane, Chiswick, London W4 2TH, England.

RABSILBER Michael, b. 8 Sept 1953, Stassfurt, Magdeburg, Germany. Singer (Tenor). Education: Studied at Leipzig Musikhochschule. Debut: Stadttheater Halle 1980 in Wagner-Regeny's Die Burger von Calais. Career: Sang at Halle until 1984 then joined the Komische Oper Berlin, with guest appearances in Leipzig and Dresden; Roles have included Mozart's Belmonte and Don Ottavio, Lensky, Ferrando Tamino, Max in Der Freischütz, Nicolai's Fenton and Pinkerton; Sang Zhivny in a production by Joachim Herz of Janacek's Osud, Dresden 1991; Frequent concert engagements. Address: c/o Komische Oper Berlin, Behrenstrasse 55-57, 1086 Berlin, Germany.

RACETTE Patricia, b. 1967, San Francisco, USA. Singer (Soprano). Education: Studied with the Merola Opera Program, San Francisco. Career: Has sung with the San Francisco Opera from 1990, as Alice Ford, Rosalinde, Freia, Micaela, Mimi, Antonia and Mathilde in Guillaume Tell, 1997; Other roles include Musetta for Netherlands Opera and at the Metropolitan (1994), Ellen Orford for Vancouver Opera and Gluck's Iphigénie en Tauride at Saint Louis; Further appearances with the New York City and Vienna State Operas; Concerts include the Messa per Rossini and Stephen Albert's Flower in the Mountain, at San Francisco; Sang Emmeline Mostover in the premiere of Tobias Picker's Emmeline, Santa Fe, 1996. Address: c/o Harrison Parrott Ltd, 12 Penzance Place, London W11 4PA, England.

RADETA Zdenko, b. 16 Sept 1955, Kragujevac, Yugoslavia. Composer; Conductor. m. Miroslava Jankovic, 28 Sept 1980, 2 sons, 1 daughter. Education: Department of Composition and Orchestration and Department of Conducting, Faculty of Music, Belgrade; Advanced studies at Tschaikovsky Conservatoire, Moscow, 1991-92. Debut: Four Sketches for chamber ensemble, 1974. Career: Singer in Choir, Radio Television Belgrade; Producer, Radio Belgrade; Professor of Harmony and Counterpoint, Mokranjac Intermediate School, Belgrade. Compositions: 9 Piano pieces, 1972-90; Solo songs, 1974-84; 12 works for choirs, 1974-87; 1st String Quartet, 1980; Caleidoscope for 15 strings, 1985; Caleidoscope 2 for symphony orchestra, 1988. Recordings: Permanent recordings for Radio Television Belgrade including Caleidoscope 2, 1st String Quartet, Remembrance for flute and piano, Wedding for mixed choir, and ballet Verities. Honours: October Prize, City of Belgrade, 1974; SOKOJ Awards, 1983, 1984; 6 Awards from Association of Composers of Serbia. Memberships: Association of Composers of Serbia; SOKOJ. Address: Jurija Gagarina 186/4, 11070 Novi Beograd, Yugoslavia.

RADIGUE Eliane, b. 24 Jan 1932, Paris, France. Composer. m. Arman, 17 Feb 1953 (div 1971), 1 son, 2 daughters. Education: Studied with Pierre Schaeffer, Pierre Henry; School of the Arts, New York University, University of Iowa, California Institute of the Arts, USA. Career includes: Work with electronic sounds on tape; Recent performances: Salon des Artistes Decorateurs, Paris; Foundation Maeght, St Paul de Vence; Albany Museum of the Arts, New York; Gallery Rive Droite, Paris; Gallery Sonnabend, New York; Gallery Yvon Lambert, Paris; etc; Festivals including: Como, Italy; Paris Autumn; Festival Estival, Paris; International Festival of Music, Bourges, France; New York Cultural Center; Experimental Intermedia Foundation, New York; Vanguard Theater, Los Angeles; Mills College, Oakland, California; University of Iowa; Wesleyan University; San Francisco Art Institute. Compositions include: Environmental Music, 1969; OHMNT-Record Object, 1971; Labyrinthe Sonore, tape music, 1971; Chry-ptus, 1971; Geelriandre, 1972; Biogenesis, 1974; Adnos, 1975; Adnos II, 1980; Adnos III, 1982; Prelude a Milarepa, 1982; 5 songs of Milarepa, 1984; Jetsun Mila, 1986. Recordings: Songs of Milarepa, New York; Mila's Journey Inspired by a Dream; Jetsun Mila, cassette, New York. Contributions to: Musique en Jeu, 1973; Art Press, 1974; Guide Musical, 1975. Address: 22 rue Liancourt, 75014 Paris, France.

RADNOFSKY Kenneth (Alan), b. 31 July 1953, Bryn Mawr, Pennsylvania, USA. Saxophonist. m. Nancy Abramchuk, 1 May 1977, 2 daughters. Education: BM cum laude, University of Houston, Texas; MM, with honours, New England Conservatory of Music, Boston. Career: Carnegie Hall debut, 1985 Performance of Gunther Schuller Saxophone Concerto written for Radnofsky; European debut, 1987 with Leipzig Gewandhaus Orchestra as first ever Saxophone Soloist under direction of Kurt Masur; First ever saxophone soloist with Dresden Staatskapelle Orchestra and Pittsburgh Symphony Orchestra; Solo works premiered or dedicated to Radnofsky by Milton Babbitt, Donald Martino, Gunther Schuller, Morton Subotnick, Lee Hoiby, David Amram, Alan Hovhaness and John Harbison; Saxophonist with Boston Symphony, 1977-; Soloist with BBC, Boston Pops and numerous USA orchestras. Recordings: With Boston Symphony as saxophone in Berg Violin Concerto; Soloist with New York Philharmonic in debussy Rhapsody with Masur on Teldec, 1996; Bass clarinet in Schoenberg Kammersymphonie with Felix Galimir; Soprano Sax in works by Roger Bourland. Contributions to: Numerous articles in Saxophone Journal. Honours: Appointed youngest member of Faculty, New England Conservatory, 1976. Address: PO Box 1016, E Arlington, MA 02174, USA.

RADOVAN Ferdinand, b. 26 Jan 1938, Rijeka, Yugoslavia. Singer (Baritone). Education: Studied in Belgrade. Debut: Belgrade National Opera 1964 as Germont. Career: Sang at Ljubljana 1965-67, Graz 1967-74, Dortmund 1974-77; Guest appearances at Vienna Volksoper, Dusseldorf, Essen, Bordeaux ad Prague and the States Operas of Hamburg and Munich; Returned to Yugoslavia 1977; Other roles have included Escamillo, Mozart's Count and Don Giovanni, Verdi's Rigoletto, Nabucco, Amonasro, Renato, Luna and Iago; Prince Igor, Scarpia, Barnaba in La Gioconda, Nelusko in L'Africaine, Jochanaan, Enrico, Gerard and Milhaud's Christophe Colombe; Concert and oratorio engagements. Address: Slovensko Narodno Gledalisce, Zupancicava 1, 61000 Ljubljana, Slovenia.

RAE Caroline Anne, b. 7 Jan 1961, Leeds, England. Pianist; Musicologist. m. Peter Whittaker, 20 Aug 1993, 2 sons. Education: BA, 1982, MA, 1986, DPhil, 1990, Somerville College, Oxford; Hochschule für Musik und Theaater, Hannover, Germany, 1985-88, DiplMus (First), 1988; Piano studies with Fanny Waterman, David Wilde, Yvonne Loriod, masterclasses with Karl-Heinz Kämmerling; French Government Scholarship, 1982-83; ARCM, 1984. Debut: 1982. Career: As pianist: Recitals, lecture-recitals, chamber music, masterclasses in UK, Germany and France; Two-piano duo with Robert Sherlaw Johnson; Appearances for BBC TV and Channel 4; As musicologist: College Tutor, Oxford University, 1984-88; Lecturer in Piano, Oxford Polytechnic, 1984, 1988; Lecturer, Department of Music, University of Wales, Cardiff, 1989-; Radio France Broadcast, 1992; Visiting Lecturer, University of Rouen, France, 1993. Publications: The Music of Maurice Ohana, forthcoming; Articles on 20th Century French music published in English, French and German. Contributions to: New Grove Dictionaries; Musical Times; Les Cahiers Debussy; Les Cahiers Du C Irem; NZM; Revista Musica; Contemporary Composers. Membership: Royal Musical Association. Address: Department of Music, Corbett Road, University of Wales, Cardiff CF1 3EB, Wales.

RAE (John) Charles Bodman, b. 10 Aug 1955, Catterick, England. Composer. m. Dorota Kwiatkowska, 14 Apr 1984. Education: Cambridge University, 1974-78; Chopin Academy of Music, Warsaw, 1981-83; Piano studies with Miss Fanny Waterman; Composition studies with Edward Cowie, Robert Sherlaw Johnson and Robin Holloway; MA (Cantab); PhD (Leeds); ARCM. Career: Broadcaster: Contributions as Writer, Presenter for BBC Radio 3 including Glocken, Cloches, Kolokola (6-hour series on European Bells); An Affair with Romanticism, features on Penderecki and Lutoslawski; Lecturer, Composition and Analysis, 1979-81, 1983-92, Head of School of Creative Studies, 1992-, City of Leeds College of Music; Visiting Composer, University of Cincinnati College-Conservatory of Music, Ohio, USA, 1993. Compositions: Six Verses of Vision, 1976; String Quartet, 1981; Jede Irdische Venus, 1982; Fulgura Frango, 1986; Donaxis Quartet, 1987. Publications: The Music of Lutoslawski, 1994; Muzyka Lutoslawskiego, 1995; Die Musik von Lutoslawski, 1995; Bells in European Music, in progress. Contributions to: Many articles on music of Lutoslawski to journals. Memberships: Royal Musical Association; Fellow, Royal Society of Arts; Composers' Guild of Great Britain. Address: Crossbeck House, Crossbeck Road, Ilkley LS29 9JN, West Yorkshire, England.

RAE-GERRARD Colleen (Margaret), b. 7 Jan 1938, Auckland, New Zealand. Pianist; Fortepianist. m. Ronald Joseph Gerrard, 16 Sept 1961, 1 son, 1 daughter. Education: Licenciate, Royal School of Music, 1958; BMus, 1972; BMus Honours, 1977. Debut: Auckland, 1955. Career: Appearances as recitalist, concerto soloist, accompanist and chamber music player in New Zealand, Australia, UK and Vienna, Austria; Network artist for radio New Zealand and ABC Australia; Appearances for TVNZ - Television New Zealand; Specializes in early piano and has given many concerts on a Stein copy in Australia and New Zealand; Toured for New Zealand Music Federation, 1981 and 1982; Concerts also in Brussels, Greece, Holland. Recordings: Solo piano, Haydn, Debussy, Villa-Lobos, Ode Record, 1972; The Colonial Piano, played on 2 historic pianos, 1978; On Wenlock Edge with tenor Anthony Benfell and a string quartet of NZSO players, 1981; Romanza with soprano Anna Langston and clarinettist Deborah Rawson, 1983; Haydn's Arianna a Naxos with contralto Flora Edwards. Honours: Auckland Star Piano Concerto, 1959; Waikato Times Piano Concerto Contest, 1959; Queen Elizabeth II Arts Council Study Awards, 1977 and 1983. Hobby: Yachting. Address: 91 Fox Street, Ngaio, Wellington, New Zealand.

RAEKALLIO Matti (Juhani), b. 14 Oct 1954, Helsinki, Finland. Pianist; Professor. m. Sinikka Alstela, 7 May 1977, 1 s, 1 d. Education: Turku Institute of Music, 1967-72; Private lessons with Maria Diamond Curcio, London, 1972-73 and with Dieter Weber, Vienna Music Academy, Austria, 1974-76; Leningrad Conservatory, 1977-78; Diploma, Sibelius Academy, Finland, 1978. Debut: As orchestra soloist, Turku, 1971; Solo, Helsinki, 1975. Career: Extensive tours with all professional Finnish symphony orchestras, 1971-; Recitals in Nordic countries, 1971-, in Finland, 1975-, in Central Europe, 1979-; Recitals in USA, 1981-; First American tour as orchestra soloist with Helsinki

Philharmonic Orchestra, 1983; Visiting Professor, Western MI University, 1984-85; Recitals in America, 1988, Helsinki Festival, 1981-87, Savonlinna Opera Festival, 1988; Beethoven Complete Sonatas in 5 Finnish cities, 1989-90; Concerto repertoire includes over 40 works for Piano and Orchestra; Professor, Royal Swedish College of Music, Stockholm, 1991; Associate Professor, Sibelius Academy, Helsinki, 1994-. Recordings include: Complete Prokofiev Sonatas; About 20 CDs; Numerous for the archives of the Finnish Broadcasting Company. Contributions to: Several Finnish journals of music. Membership: Board of Directors, Society for Finnish Concert Soloists. Hobbies: Chess; Literature. Current Management: Jonathan Wentworth Associates Ltd, USA. Address: c/o Sibelius Academy, Pl 86, Fin-00251, Helsinki, Finland.

RAES Godfried-Willem, b. 3 Jan 1952, Ghent, Belgium. Musicmaker. m. Moniek Darge, 15 Sept 1973. Education: Masters Degree in Musicology 1973, Ghent University; Masters Degree in Philosophy 1975; Doctors Degree in Musicology 1993; Piano, Clarinet, Composition, Avant-Garde Music, Royal Conservatory of Music, Ghent. Debut: With Logos-ensemble 1968. Career: Concert Manager for Philharmonic Society, Brussels 1973-88; Leader of The Logos-Ensemble 1968-; Director of The Logos-Foundation 1977-; Professor of Experimental Music Composition and Performance at The Ghent Royal Conservatory 1982-. Compositions: Bellenorgel; Attitudes; Epitafium; Cues; Fortepiano; Holosound; A Book of Fugues; A Book of Chorals; Symphony for Singing Bicycles; Compositions for traditional and newly invented instruments: Pneumafoon, Junks, Sirene; Sound sculptures Radar-harps and automats; Hex (a concerto for violin and full automated orchestra), A Book of Moves, for non-impact instruments of his own design. Recordings: All major international radio and television stations; Records on IGLOO Label; Bellenorgel, Improvisation/Composition, Pneumafoon. Publications: Creative Music Making in an Anti-Creative Society? (Essay 1976); Improvisation 1981-93; An Invisible Musical Instrument (doctoral dissertation, 1993). Honour: Louis Paul Boon Prize, 1982; Tech-Art Prize, 1990. Hobbies: Digital and analog microelectronics, computer, programming and architecture. Address: c/o Logos Foundation, Kongostraat 35, B-9000 Ghent, Belgium.

RAFFAELLI Piero, b. 8 Apr 1949, Cesena, Italy. Violin Teacher and Concertist. m. Santarelli Mariangela, 18 May 1975, 2 daughters. Education includes: Violin Studies, Diploma, Conservatory of Music, G B Martini, Bologna, 1971; Viola Studies; Primary School Teachers Diploma, 1968; Master Courses with various teachers. Debut: 7 February 1968, Italy. Career: Radio appearances in Italy and Norway; Italian and European Concerts with Ensemble I Cameristi di Venezia; Solo Concerts with Capella Academica of Vienna, Italy; Chamber Music Group Layer & Soloist, Italy; Europe, North America with Italian Ensembles, 1971-73; Leader, Guitar Trio Paganini (also a viola player); Duo Recitals, Barcelona, Vienna, Berlin W, Olso, Trondheim, Greece, Italy; Violin Teacher, Conservatory of Music, Bologna, 1978-. Recordings: With Ensemble E Melkus; Wien; Solo Violin Works by M Kich (Yugoton) dedicated to him, 1981; Contemporary Violin Chamber Music Recording, 1982. Publications: Revisions of Violin Works in First Printing for Zanibon and Violoncelo, 1979; A Vivaldi Concerto F 1 n 237 in D for violin, strings, cembalo, 1980; N Paganini 3 Duetti Concertanti for Violin and Violoncello, 1982. Address: Via Filli Latini 112, 1-47020, S Giorgio di Cesena, Italy.

RAFFANTI Dano, b. 5 Apr 1948, Lucca, Italy. Singer (Tenor). Education: Studied at the La Scala School. Debut: Scala School 1976, in Bussotti's Nottetempo. Career: Verona 1978, in Orlando Furioso: Dallas 1980, in the US premiere of Vivaldi's opera; San Francisco 1980, as Almaviva in Il Barbiere di Siviglia; Houston 1981-82, as Giacomo in La Donna del Lago by Rossini; Metropolitan Opera from 1981, as Alfredo, Rodolfo, the Duke of Mantua, Edgardo, Goffredo in Handel's Rinaldo and the Italian Singer in Der Rosenkavalier; Teatro San Carlos Naples and Covent Garden, 1983 and 1984, as Tebaldo in I Capuleti e i Montecchi by Bellini; Guest appearances in Hamburg, Berlin, Santiago, Bilbao and at the Landestheater Salzburg; Maggio Musicale Florence 1989, as Idomeneo; Sang the Duke of Mantua at Turin, Dec 1989; Florence 1990, as Ugo in Donizetti's Parisina; Season 1992 as Cléomène in La Siège de Corinthe by Rossini at Genoa. Recordings include: Fra Diavolo (Cetra); I Capuleti e i Montecchi (EMI); La Donna del Lago (CBS). Address: c/o Harrison/Parrott, 12 Penzance Place, London W11 4PA, England.

RAFFEINER Walter, b. 8 April 1947, Wolfsberg, Germany. Singer (Tenor). Education: Studied in Vienna and Cologne. Debut: Sang at Hagen in Germany as a Baritone. Career: Sang at Darmstadt as a Tenor, 1979 and appeared at Frankfurt from 1980 as Max, Parsifal, Florestan, Stolzius in Die Soldaten and the Painter and Negro in Lulu; Sang at Rouen and the Paris Opera 1982, as Siegmund and Lohengrin; Guest appearances in Hamburg, Freiburg, Vienna, Dusseldorf and Munich; Salzburg Festival 1986, as Silvanus Schuller in the premiere of Penderecki's Schwarze Maske; Appeared as Siegmund with the Kassel Opera at the restored Amsterdam Opera House; Other roles have included Tristan, Pedro in Tiefland, Ivanovich in The Gambler, Sergei in Katerina Ismailova, Shuisky, Herod, Yannakos in Martinu's Greek Passion and Tichon in Katya Kabanova; Sang in the premiere of Lampersberg's Einöde der Welt, Bonn, 1995. Recording: Drum Major in Wozzeck.

RAFFELL Anthony, b. 1940, London, England. Baritone Singer. Career: Sang first with a touring company with the works of Gilbert and Sullivan; Opera debut at Glyndebourne 1966, in Werther by Massenet; Sang at Gelsenkirchen, Karlsruhe and Bremen; Debut, Covent Garden as Pantheus in The Trojans, 1969; Member of the Stuttgart Opera from 1985; Metropolitan Opera debut 1983, as Kurwenal, in Tristan und Isolde, returning as Hans Sachs, 1985; Appearances in Ring Cycles with the English National Opera and in Seattle; Further appearances as Klingsor in Turin, Wotan in Rome, Jochanaan in Rio de Janeiro, Falstaff in Lisbon and at Parma, Trieste and Nancy; Metropolitan Opera 1989, as Gunther, in Götterdämmerung; Sang Telramund at Buenos Aires, 1991; Regularly at Vienna State Opera, Hamburg, Berlin and Stuttgart; More recently in Buenos Aires in Tales of Hoffmann, as a guest, 1993. Recordings include: Der Ring des Nibelungen, conducted by James Levine, also on video. Address: 14 Stevenson Drive, Abingdon, Oxon, OX14 1SN, England.

RAFOLS Alberto (Pedro), b. 7 July 1942, Guantanamo, Cuba. Pianist/Professor of Music. Education: BM 1967; MM 1969; University of Illinois; DMA, University of Washington 1975; Fulbright Scholar; Academia Marshall, Barcelona, Spain, 1970-72; Academia Chigiana, Siena, Italy, Summer, 1971; Teachers: Alicia de Larrocha, Bela Siki, Howard Karp. Career: Performances: Throughout the United States, Canada, Peru, Bolivia, Portugal, Spain and Colombia including Alaska, Hawaii and Azores Islands; Academic Appointments: University of Illinois 1969-70; University of Washington, Seattle, 1975-84; University of Alaska (part-time) 1982-84; University of Texas in San Antonio 1984-. Recordings: Live Broadcasts, Nationwide; Radio Television: Espanola, Madrid 1981; Barcelona 1984. Hobbies: Visual Arts/ Literature. Address: 4203 Cabell Drive #322, Dallas, TX 15204, USA.

RAFTERY J Patrick, b. 4 Apr 1951, Washington DC, USA. Singer (Baritone). Education: Studied with Armen Boyajian. Debut: Chicago Lyric Opera 1980, as Shchelkalov in Boris Godunov. Career: European debut 1982, at the Théâtre du Châtelet, Paris, as Zurga in Les Pêcheurs de Perles; Glyndebourne 1984, as Guglielmo; Santa Fe, New Mexico, 1984 in Verdi's Il Corsaro and Gwendoline by Chabrier; Covent Garden debut 1985, as Mozart's Count; Further appearances with the New York City Opera and in Hamburg, Brussels, and Cologne; Santiago 1988, as Luna in Il Trovatore; Rome Opera 1988, as Puccini's Lescaut; Sang Belcore in L'Elisir d'Amore at Genoa in 1989; Other roles include Escamillo, Mercutio (Roméo et Juliette), Eugene Onegin, Valentin (Faust), Yeletsky in The Queen of Spades and Rossini's Figaro; Sang Rossini's Figaro at Vancouver, 1991.

RAFTIS Alkis, b. 31 October 1942, Athens, Greece. University Professor. 1 son. Education: Degrees, General Sociology, Political Sociology Management, Engineering; Sociology and Ethnography of Dance. Recordings: Editor, 20 Greek Dances, 20 Macedonian Dances, Pontic Dances, Cretan Dances and Songs, Loupsiko, Konitsa Wedding Songs and Dances. Publications: The World of Greek Dance; Encyclopedia of Greek Dance; Dance and Poetry; Danse et poésie; Dances of the Whole World. Contributions to: 100 articles in 6 languages in professional journals. Membership: President, Greek Dance Theatre. Hobby: Dance. Address: Greek Dances Theatre, 8 Scholiou Street, GR 10558 Athens, Greece.

RAGACCI Susanna, b. 1959, Stockholm, Sweden. Singer (Soprano). Education: Studied in Florence. Career: Sang first at Rome as Rossini's Rosina, then appeared at Florence, Venice, Palermo, Turin and La Scala Milan; Sang Gilda in Dublin and at the Wexford Festival in Cimarosa's Astuzie Femminili; Opera de Wallonie at Liège 1987-88 as Rosina and as Egloge in Mascagni's Nerone; Sang at Bologna in the 1987 Italian premiere of Henze's English Cat and at Florence as the Italian Singer in Capriccio; Théâtre du Châtelet Paris 1992 as Sofia in Il Signor Bruschino. Recordings: Vivaldi's Catone in Utica and La Caduta di Adamo by Galuppi; I Pazzi per Progresso by Donizetti; L'Elisir d'amore.

RAGATZU Rosella, b. 1964, Cagliari, Sardinia. Singer (Soprano). Education: Studied at the Cagliari Conservatory and with Magda Olivero and Claudio Desderi. Career: Sang Fiordiligi at Spoleto (1987) and Donna Anna at Treviso, 1989; Toured Italy, 1990, as Mozart's Countess and sang this role with Donna Anna at the 1991 Macerata Festival; Further guest appearances at the Leipzig Opera, Teatro Regio Turin (in Don Carlos) and at Frankfurt in a concert of Franchetti's Cristoforo Colombo (1991), as Queen Isabella. Honours include: Winner, 1987 Concorso Sperimento di Spoleto and 1989 Concorso Toti dal Monte, Treviso.

RAGIN Derek Lee, b. 17 June 1958, West Point, New York, USA. Singer (Counter-tenor). Education: Arts High School, Newark, New Jersey; Newark Boys Chorus School, 1969-72; Piano Scholarship, Newark Community Center of Arts, 1970-75; Piano, BM, MMT, Oberlin Conservatory of Music, 1980. Debut: Opera - Festwoche der Alten Musik, Innsbruck, Austria, 1983. Career: Recital Debut, Wigmore Hall, London, 1984; Debut Recital, Aldeburgh Festival, 1984; Sang title role in Handel's Tamerlano, both at Lyon Opera, France and at Göttingen Handel Festival; BBC Debut Recital, 1984; Debut at the Metropolitan Opera in Handel's Giulio Cesare, September 1988; Recitals and Oratorio continued in Frankfurt, Munich, Stuttgart, Cologne, Venice, Milan, Bologna, New York, Amsterdam, Maryland Handel Festival, London, Washington DC, Atlanta, Boston, San Francisco; Made Salzburg debut in Gluck's Orfeo, 1990; Gluck's Orfeo in Budapest, 1991; Season 1992 in Conti's Don Chisciotte at Innsbruck and as Britten's Oberon at Saint Louis; Sang in Ligeti's Le Grand Macabre at the Paris Châtelet and the Salzburg Festival, 1997; Hasse's Attilio regolo at Dresden, 1997. Recordings: Role of Spirit in Purcell's Dido and Aeneas (Philips Label), 1985; Title role in Handel's Tamerlano (Erato Label), 1985; Handel's Flavio and Tolomeo in Giulio Cesare, Harmonia Mundi; Handel's Saul, Philips Label; Vivaldi Cantatas, Etcetera Label and CBS. Hobbies: Dancing; Movie-goer; Reader of all kinds of magazines. Current Management: Colbert Artists Management, New York, USA. Address: 106 1/2 9th Avenue, Newark, NJ 07107, USA.

RAGNARSSON Hjalmar (Helgi), b. 23 Sept 1952, Isafjordur, Iceland. Composer. m. Sigridur Asa Richardsdottir, 2 sons, 1 daughter. Education: Isafjordur School of Music, 1959-69; Reykjavik College of Music, 1969-72; BA, Brandeis University, USA, 1974; Rijksuniversiteit Utrecht-Instituut voor Sonologie, Netherlands, 1976-77; MFA, Cornell University, USA, 1980. Compositions include: Six songs to Icelandic Poems for voice and chamber ensemble, 1978-79; Romanza for flute, clarinet and piano, 1981; Canto for mixed choirs and synthesizer, 1982; Mass for mixed choir, 1982-89; Trio for clarinet, cello and piano, 1983-84; Five Preludes for piano, 1983-85; Tengsl for voice and string quartet, 1988; Spjotalög for orchestra, 1989; Raudur Thradur, ballet music for orchestra, 1989; Rhodymenia Palmata, chamber opera, 1992; Concerto for organ and orchestra, 1997; Music for theatre including Icelandic National Theatre and Reykjavik Municipal Theatre; Music for films: Tears of Stone, 1995; Music for TV films, Iceland State Television Service and Swedish State Television. Recordings: Conductor, Icelandic Choral works with the University Choir of Iceland; Own choral works for Hljomeyki Chamber Choir. Publications: Jon Leifs, Icelandic Composer: Historical Background, Biography, Analysis of Selected Works, MFA thesis, 1980; A Short History of Icelandic Music to the Beginning of the Twentieth Century, 1985; Film script: Tears of Stone, co-author, 1995. Memberships: Composers Society of Iceland, President 1988-92; President, Federation of Icelandic Artists, 1991-. Address: Laekjarhjalli 22, 200 Kopavogur, Iceland.

RAICHEV Rouslan, b. 2 May 1924, Milan, Italy. Conductor. Education: Studied the piano in Milan, then with Leopold Reichwein, Emil Sauer and Karl Böhm in Vienna (until 1944). Career: Assistant at the Vienna Staatsoper 1942-43; Chief Conductor at the Königsberg Opera 1943-44; Conductor of the Varna Opera, Bulgaria, 1946-48; Conductor of the Sofia Opera 1948-89 (Musical Director 1981-89); Conducted the State Orchestra of Plovdiv 1968 and directed stage works at the Schleswig-Holstein Festival 1974-78; Guest conductor at the Vienna Staatsoper, La Scala Milan and the Paris Opéra. Recordings include: Rachmaninov Aleko (AVM).

RAILTON Dame Ruth, b. 14 Dec 1915, Folkestone, Kent, England. Musician; Pianist; Conductor. m. Cecil Harmsworth King, 1962. Education: Royal Academy of Music, London; Pupil of Rachmaninov, Myra Hess and Schnabel; Conducting with Sir Henry Wood; LRAM; ARAM; FRAM. Career: Director of Music or Choral Work for many schools and societies 1937-48; Founder and Musical Director, National Youth Orchestra, 1946-66; Adjudicator, Federation of Music Festivals; Governor Royal Ballet School, 1966-74; Director, National Concert Hall, Dublin, 1981-86; President, Ulster College of Music; Chairman, National Children's Orchestra, 1989. Publication: Daring to Excel, 1992. Honours: OBE, 1954; DBE, 1966; Honorary LLD, Aberdeen University; Honorary FRCM, FTCL and RMCM; Professor, Chopin Conservatoire, Warsaw; Professor Conservatoire of Azores. Memberships: ISM; University Womens Club. Address: Ardoyne House, Pembroke Park, Dublin 4, Republic of Ireland.

RAIMONDI Gianni, b. 13 Apr 1923, Bologna, Italy. Singer (Tenor). Education: Studied with Gennaro Barra-Caracciolo and with Ettore Campogalliani in Milan. Debut: Bologna 1947, as the Duke of Mantua. Career: Sang Pinkerton at Budrio, 1947; Bologna 1948, as Ernesto in Don Pasquale; Florence 1952, in Rossini's

Armida, with Callas; London, Stoll Theatre, 1953; Naples 1955, in the premiere of Madame Bovary by Pannain; La Scala Milan from 1956, notably as Alfredo and as Lord Percy in Anna Bolena, opposite Callas, and in Mosè and Semiramide (1958, 1962); US debut San Francisco 1957; Verona Arena from 1957; Guest appearances in Vienna from 1959, Munich from 1960; Metropolitan Opera from 1965, as Rodolfo, Cavaradossi and Faust; Hamburg Staatsoper 1969-77; Other appearances in Paris 1953, Chicago, Dallas, Lisbon, Edinburgh, Geneva, Zurich and Helsinki; Other roles included Gabriele Adorno, Ismaele (Nabucco), Arrigo in Les Vêpres Siciliennes, Pollione, and Edgardo. Recordings: La Favorita (Cetra); La Traviata (Deutsche Grammophon); Linda di Chamounix; Maria Stuarda, with Callas; I Puritani; Armida. Address: c/o Teatro alla Scala, Via Filodrammtatici 2, Milan, Italy.

RAIMONDI Ruggero, b. 3 Oct 1941, Bologna, Italy. Singer (Bass). m. Isabel Maier. Education: Student, Theresa Pediconi, Rome, 1961-62; Armando Piervenanzi, 1963-65. Debut: Spoleto, 1964. Career: Appeared Rome Opera; Principal opera houses in Italy; Metropolitan Opera, 1970; Munich; La Scala; Lyric Opera; Chicago; Paris Opera; Sang Don Giovanni at Glyndebourne, 1969, and throughout the world; Covent Garden, 1972, as Fiesco in Simon Boccanegra; Vienna Staatsoper, 1982, as Don Quichotte; Hamburg, 1985, as Gounod's Mephistopheles; Sang Selim in Il Turco in Italia; Chicago, 1987, as Mozart's Count; Pesaro, 1985 and Vienna as Don Profondo in Il Viaggio a Reims; Sang in the opening concert at the Bastille Opéra, 1989; Don Giovanni, 1986; 25th Anniversary Celebration at the Barbican Hall, 1990; Scarpia in a televised Tosca from Rome, 1992; Il Barbiere di Siviglia, 1992; Sang Rossini's Mosè at Covent Garden, 1994; Donizetti's Don Pasquale; Iago in Otello, Salzburg, 1996; Don Quichotte at Rome. Recordings: 2 Verdi Requiems; Complete operas Attila, I Vespri Siciliani, La Bohème, Aida, Don Carlos, Forza de Destino, Il Pirata, Norma, Don Giovanni, Carmen, Nozze di Figaro, Mosè, Italiana in Algeri, Boris Godunov, Pelléas et Mélisande, Turandot, Barbiere di Siviglia, Cenerentola, Simon Boccanegra, Macbeth, Nabucco, I Lombardi; Sang Don Giovanni in Joseph Losey's film of Mozart's opera; Sang Escamillo in Francesco Rosi's Carmen; Maurice Béjart's 6 Characters in Search of a Singer; Boris in Zylawsky's film Boris Godunov; Played in Alain Resnais' Life is a Bed of Roses; Opera production since 1986. Honours: Recipient, Competition Award, Spoleto; Officier des Arts et lettres in France; Commendatore Della Republica in Italy; Chevalier de l'ordre de Malte; Citizen of Honour, City of Athens, Greece. Address: 140 bis, rue Lecourbe, F-75015 Paris, France.

RAIMONDO Ildiko, b. 11 Nov 1962, Arad, Rumania. Singer (Soprano). Education: Studied at the Arad Conservatory. Career: Sang at Chemnitz from 1983 and from 1988 at the Vienna Kammeroper, in Dresden and at the Landestheater Linz; Bregenz Festival 1991 (as Micaela) and further appearances at the Vienna Volksoper and Staatsoper; Other roles have included Mozart's Zerlina, Susanna, Despina and Pamina, Sophie in Der Rosenkavalier and Walter in La Wally; Concerts include Masses by Mozart and Rossini, Die Schöpfung, the Verdi Requiem and Ein Deutsches Requiem; Marzelline in Fidelio at the 1996 Edinburgh Festival. Address: c/o Staatsoper Vienna, Opernring 2, A-1010 Vienna, Austria.

RAINER Alice and Clarice (Twins), b. 28 Aug 1932, Opp, Alabama, USA. Concert Piano-Duettists. Education: Diploma, Opp High School, 1950; BMus Degree, University of Montevallo School of Music 1954; Aspen Music School, Aspen, Colorado, 1958-59; Private Study with Vronsky and Babin, Duo-Pianists 1960-61. Debut: Judson Hall, New York City. Career: Concert also broadcast, National Gallery of Art, Washington DC; Haarlem Philharmonic Society of New York City; Woman to Woman, National TV, Los Angeles, California; Philadelphia, PA; Chicago, IL; Minneapolis, MN; Oklahoma, OK; Mobile, AL; Jackson, MS; Memphis, TN; Charleston, SC; West Palm Beach, FL; Richmond, VA; Ft Wayne, IN; Colorado Springs, CO; Winston-Salem, NC. Contributions to: Music Journal, Viva le Piano Duet!; Music Journal, Piano Duet Treasure Chest; Piano Technicians Journal, The Unseen Artist. Hobbies: Constant Research into Original Piano Duet Repertoire and Little Known Duets; Twin Toy Poodles; Flowers and Plants. Current Management: The Alkahest Agency, Atlanta, GA, USA. Address: 409 Sellars Drive, Opp, AL 36467, USA.

RAITIO Pentti, b. 4 June 1930, Pieksamaki, Finland. Composer; Music Educator. Education: Studied composition with Joonas Kokkonen, 1961-63; Erik Bergman, 1963-66; Diploma, Sibelius Academy, Helsinki, 1966. Career: Director, Hyvinkaa School of Music, 1967-; Chairman, Lahti Organ Festival, 1981-85; Association of Finnish Music Schools, 1986-. Compositions: Orchestral: 13, 1964; Audiendum, 1967; 5 Pieces for String Orchestra, 1975; Petandrie, 1977; Noharmus, 1978; Noharmus II, 1980; Canzone d'autunno, 1982; Flute Concerto, 1983; Due figure, 1985; Yoldia arctica, 1987; Chamber: Small Pieces for Brass Instruments, 1984; Wind Quintet, 1975; Nocturne for Violin and Piano, 1977; Vocal: 3 Songs for Soprano, 1962; the River, 7 Songs for Soprano and 7 instruments, 1965; Along the Moonlit Path, 3 songs for Soprano and 4 Instruments, 1965; Orphean Chorus, 3 songs for Baritone and Men's Chorus, 1966; 3 Songs for Baritone and String Quartet, 1970; One Summer Evening for Men's Chorus, 1971; Song for Men's Chorus, 1972; Song for a Rain Bird for Baritone and Piano, 1974; I'm Looking at the River, 6 songs for Women's or Youth Chorus, 1986. Address: c/o Hyvinkaa School of Music, 05800 Hyvinkaa, Finland.

RAJMON Radko, b. 27 January 1936, Jicin, Bohemia, Czechoslovakia. Music Master and Educationalist; Musicologist. m. Eva Cihlarova, 5 August 1967, 4 sons. Education: Elementary School of Music; Musicology, University, Brno. Career: Teacher, secondary schools; Research Worker, Research Institute of Pedagogy, Prague; Publicist, Editor, Radio and Textbook-Author, GS/Cz Music Society; Private Teacher; now retired. Publications: Music at the primary school, 5 re-edited repeatedly since 1980; Music at the special school, 4/5 (co-author), 1984, re-editions. Contributions to: Contributions to journals Hudebnivychova, 1968-70, Estaticka vychova, 1964-1985. Memberships: Czechoslovakia Music Society; Czechoslovakia Society for Music Education. Hobbies: Arts; Family; Nature. Current Management: Cooperation with a private conservatoire of dance. Address: Kropackova 563, 149 00 Praha 4, Czechoslovakia.

RAJNA Thomas, b. 21 Dec 1921, Budapest, Hungary. Pianist; Composer; Lecturer. Education: 1944-47 Liszt Academy of Music with Kodály, Sandor Veress and Leo Weiner; Royal College of Music with Herbert Howells and Angus Morrison. Career: Professor of Piano and Composition, Guidhall School of Music, 1963; Lecturer, Keyboard History and Studies, University of Surrey, 1967; Senior Lecturer at Cape Town University from 1970; Appointed Associate Professor, 1989; Numerous performances as pianist in Europe and South Africa of music by Stravinsky, Messiaen, Scriabin, Liszt, Granados and Rajna. Compositions include: Dialogues for Clarinet and Piano, 1947; Preludes for Piano, 1944-49; Music for cello and piano 1957; Capriccio for keyboard 1960; Piano Concerto No 1 1962; Movements for Strings 1962; Cantilenas and Interludes for Orchestra 1968; Three Hebrew Choruses, 1972; Four African Lyrics for high voice and piano 1976; Piano Concerto No 2, 1984; Concerto for Harp and Orchestra, 1990; Amarantha (opera) 1991-1995; Video Games, 1994; Rhapsody for Clarinet and Orchestra, 1995; Fantasy for Violin and Orchestra, 1996; Suite for Violin and Harp, 1997. Recordings: Complete piano works of Stravinsky and Granados; works by Messiaen, Bartók, Scriabin, Liszt and Schumann; Rajna: Piano Concerto No 1; Music for Violin and Piano; Preludes for Piano; Serenade for 10 Wind Instruments, Piano and Percussion; Divertimento Piccolo for Orchestra; Piano Concerto No 2; Concerto for harp and orchestra; The Hungarian Connection, music by Dohnanyi and Rajna, 1997; Video Games. Contributions to: The Composer. Honours: Liszt Prize, Franz Liszt Academy, 1947; Dannreuther Prize, Royal College of Music, 1951 ARTES Award (SA Broadcasting Corp), 1981; Fellow, University of Cape Town, 1981; Doctor of Music (UCT), 1985; Award of Merit, Cape Tercentenary Foundation, 1997. Address: 10 Wyndover Road, Claremont, Cape 7700, South Africa.

RAJTER Ludovit, b. 30 Jul 1906, Pezinok, Slovakia. Conductor; Composer. m. Elisabeth Rajter, 14 Jul 1967, 1 s, 1 d. Education: Studied with Franz Schmidt, Joseph Marx (Composition), Clemens Krauss, Alexander Wunderer (Conducting), Academy of Music, Vienna, 1929; Study with E von Dohnányi, Liszt Academy, Budapest. Debut: Vienna, 1929. Career: 1st Conductor, Hungarian Radio, Budapest, 1933-45; Chief Conductor, CS Radio Bratislava, 1945-50, 1968-77; 1st Conductor, Slovak Philharmonic, Bratislava, 1949-76; Guest Conductor, Radio Basel, 1969-70; Professor, Ferenc Liszt Academy of Music, 1938-45, Academy of Music, Bratislava, 1949-76; Honorary Conductor, Savaria Symphony Orchestra, Szombathely, 1992-. Compositions: Sinfonietta, 1929; Divertimento for Orchestra, 1932; Balett (Maiales), Budapest, 1938; String Quartet No 1, Vienna; Quintet, Serenade, for Flute, Oboe, Clarinet, Horn and Bassoon; Sonata per Contrabasso e Pianoforte; Suite for Violoncello Solo Nos 1 and 2; Divertimento for Winds; Several works for Choir; Suite for Violin Solo, 1992; Sinfonietta, Bratislava, 1993; Partita for 8 Cellos, 1995; Musica Alternativa for 8 Cellos, 1995; Fantasia for cello solo, 1995. Recordings include: Brahms Symphonies 1-4; Franz Schmidt Symphonies 1-4, and Piano Concerto in E flat major; Variations on a Theme by Beethoven; A von Zemlinsky Symphony in D minor; Others by various composers. Contributions to: Hudobny Zivot, Slovak Music, Bratislava. Honour: Bartók - Pásztory Prize, 1994. Memberships: Honorary President, Franz Liszt Society, Bratislava; Honorary Member, Hungarian Interpreters' Society, Budapest. Address: Fandlyho 1, SK-81103 Bratislava, Slovak Republic.

RAMEY Phillip, b. 12 September 1939, Elmhurst, Illinois, USA. Composer. Education: Studied composition with A Tcherepnin at the International Academy of Music in Nice (1959) and at De Paul University, Chicago (BA 1962); Further study with Jack Beeson at Columbia University, New York (MA 1965). Career: Program Editor for the New York Philharmonic, 1977-93; Freelance composer, with premieres at New York, Sacramento and Chicago. Compositions include: 6 Piano Sonatas, 1961, 1966, 1968, 1968, 1974, 1988; Concert Suite for piano and small orchestra, 1962 (revised 1984); Music, for brass and percussion, 1964; Orchestral Discourse, 1967; Night Music, for percussion, 1967; Suite for violin and piano, 1971; 3 Piano Concertos, 1971, 1976, 1994; A William Blake Trilogy for soprano and piano, 1980; Moroccan Songs to Words of Paul Bowles, for high voice and piano, 1982-86; Concerto for horn and strings, 1987; Rhapsody for cello, 1992; Trio Concertant for violin, horn and piano, 1993; Tangier Portraits, for piano, 1991-94; La Citadelle for horn and piano, 1994; Praeludium for 5 horns, 1994; Color Etudes for piano, 1994. Address: c/o ASCAP, ASCAP Building, One Lincoln Plaza, New York, NY 10023, USA.

RAMEY Samuel, b. 28 Mar 1942, Kolby, Kansas, USA. Singer (Bass-Baritone). Education: Wichita State University, with Arthur Newman; New York with Armen Boyajian. Debut: New York City Opera 1973, as Zuniga in Carmen: returned as Mephistopheles (Gounod and Boito), Attila, Don Giovanni, Henry VIII (Anna Bolena) and Massenet's Don Quichotte; Glyndebourne debut 1976, as Mozart's Figaro; Nick Shadow in The Rake's Progress 1977; Guest appearances in Hamburg, San Francisco, Chicago and Vienna, as Colline in La Bohème, Figaro, and Arkel, in Pelléas et Mélisande; Covent Garden debut 1982: returned to London for a concert performance of Semiramide, 1986 and as Philip II in Don Carlos, 1989; Metropolitan Opera debut 1984, as Argante in Rinaldo, 1986-87 as Walton in I Puritani and Escamillo; Pesaro 1984, in a revival of Rossini's Il Viaggio a Reims; Bartók's Bluebeard 1989, at the Met; Pesaro Festival 1986 (Maometto II) and 1989 (La Gazza Ladra); Munich 1988, as Mephistopheles; Don Giovanni at Salzburg from 1987, Metropolitan and Maggio Musicale, Florence 1990; Season 1992/93 as Attila at San Francisco and Geneva, Rossini's Basilio at the Met, Philip II in Venice and New York, the Hoffmann Villains and Berlioz Mephistopheles at Covent Garden and Nick Shadow at Aix-en-Provence; Sang Mephistopheles in a new production of Faust at the Vienna Staatsoper, 1997; Other roles include the villains in Les Contes d'Hoffmann, Verdi's Renato and Banquo, and Mozart's Leporello; Covent Garden, 1997, as Verdi's Fiesco and Oberto. Recordings: Bach B Minor Mass, I Due Foscari, Un Ballo in Maschera, Ariodante, Lucia di Lammermoor, Maometto II, Petite Messe solenelle, Haydn's Armida (Philips); Le nozze di Figaro, The Rake's Progress (Decca); Il Turco in Italia, La Donna del Lago (CBS); Il Viaggio a Reims, Don Giovanni (Deutsche Grammophon). Address: c/o Harrison/Parrott Ltd, 12 Penzance Place, London W11 4PA, England.

RAMICOVA Dunya, b. 1950, Czechoslovakia. Costume Designer. Education: Studied at Yale School of Drama. Career: Has collaborated with Director Stephen Wadsworth on Jenufa and Fliegende Holländer for Seattle Opera, Fidelio for Scottish Opera and La Clemenza di Tito for Houston Grand Opera; Costume designs for Peter Sellars production of Die Zauberflöte and The Electrification of the Soviet Union at Glyndebourne, Tannhäuser at Chicago, Nixon in China for Houston and St François d'Assise at Salzburg, 1992; Premiere of The Voyage by Philip Glass at the Metropolitan, 1992, production by David Pountney; Covent Garden, 1992, costumes for Alcina; Costumes for the house premiere of Mathis der Maler, Covent Garden, 1995. Address: c/o Metropolitan Opera, Lincoln Center, New York, NY 10023, USA.

RAMIREZ Alejandro, b. 2 Sep 1946, Bogota, Columbia. Singer (Tenor). Education: Qualifies as Doctor of Medicine, then studied singing at Conservatory of Bogota; Further study at the Musikhochschule Freiburg, 1973-75; Completed studies with Annelies Kupper in Munich and Gunther Reich in Stuttgart. Career: Sang in Pforzheim, 1975-77, Kaiserslautern, 1977-80; Member of Mannheim Opera, 1980-82, Frankfurt from 1982; Covent Garden, London, 1984 as Nemorino in L'Elisir d'Amore; Vienna Staatsoper, 1985 as Alfredo; Salzburg Festival in 1985 in the Henze/Monteverdi Il Ritorno d'Ulisse; Other roles include Belmonte, Don Ottavio, Tamino, Ferrando, Jacquino in Berlin 1984, Elvino in La Sonnambula, Rossini's Almaviva and Lindoro, Strauss's Narraboth and Flamand, Rodolfo and Edgardo; Concert repertoire includes the Evangelist in the Bach Passions, and works by Handel, Bruckner, Schumann, Dvorák, Beethoven and Verdi; Bavarian State Opera as Don Ottavio, Frankfurt, 1980-85; La Scala Milan in 1988 as Henry Morosus in R Strauss's Schweigsame Frau, 1990; Season 1992 as Rodolfo at Bonn and Tamino at Dusseldorf; Professor of Singing at the Musikhochschule of Mannheim, Germany. Recordings include: Schumann's Manfred; St John Passion and Christmas Oratorio by Bach; Sacred Music by Schubert, Mendelssohn and Charpentier; The Seven Last Words by Schütz; Mozart's Nozze di Figaro under Riccardo Muti. Address: Andersenstrasse 55, 68259 Mannheim, Germany.

RAMIRO Yordi, b. 1948, Acapulco, Mexico. Singer (Tenor). Debut: Mexico City, 1977, as Pinkerton. Career: Sang at the Vienna Staatsoper from 1978 and guested at the San Francisco Opera, 1979, as Rinuccio in Gianni Schicchi; Further appearances at Seattle as Alfredo, Barcelona as Rodolfo (1980) and Mexico City as Edgardo; Strasbourg, 1983, as Gounod's Romeo; Covent Garden, 1984, in Der Rosenkavalier and Arturo in I Puritani at the 1985 Bregenz Festival; Metropolitan Opera debut, 1985, as Paco in La Vida Breve; Other roles include Ernesto in Don Pasquale, Nemorino, the Duke of Mantua and Tebaldo in I Capuleti by Bellini. Recordings include: Rigoletto and La Traviata (Naxos). Address: c/o Staatsoper Vienna, Opernring 2, A-1010 Vienna, Austria.

RAMPAL Jean-Pierre (Louis), b. 7 Jan 1922, Marseille, France. Flautist. m. Françoise-Anne Bacqueyrisse, 1947, 1 son, 1 daughter. Education: University of Marseille. Career: Worldwide tours, 1945-; Participant in major festivals including in Rio de Janeiro, Aix, Menton, Salzburg, Edinburgh, Prague, Athens, Zagreb, Granada and Tokyo; Editor for Ancient and Classical Music, International Music Company, New York City, 1958-; Professor, Conservatoire National Supérieur de Musique de Paris, France, 1969-82; Has premiered concertos by Jolivet (1950), Rivier (1956), Nigg (1961), Françaix (1967) and Martinon (1971). Publications: La Flûte, 1978; Music, My Love. Honours: Commandeur, Legion d'honneur; Commandeur de l'Ordre des Arts et des Lettres de France; Grand Prix du Disque, 1954, 1956, 1959, 1960, 1961, 1963, 1978; Oscar du Premier Virtuose Français, 1956; Prix Edison, 1969; Léonie Sonning Danish Music Prize, 1978; Prix d'honneur, Prix Mondial du Disque de Montreux, 1980; Commandeur de l'Ordre National du Mérite; Order of Sacred Treasure Japan. Memberships: French Musicological Society; President, Association de Musique et Musiciens, 1974-92. Hobbies: Tennis; Deep-sea diving; Movie making. Current Management: Bureau de Concerts, M de Valmalete, 11 Av Delcassé, 75008 Paris, France. Address: 15 Avenue Mozart, 75016 Paris, France.

RAN Shulamit, b. 21 October 1949, Tel Aviv, Israel. Composer; Pianist. Education: Studied in Tel-Aviv, and with Norman Dello Joio (composition) at the Mannes College of Music, New York (graduated 1967); Further study with Dorothy Taubman and Ralph Shapey. Career: Many concert tours of Europe and the USA as concert pianist; Teacher at the University of Chicago, composer-in-residence with the Chicago Symphony 1991; Visiting Professor at Princeton University, 1987; Works premiered at New York, Jerusalem, Philadelphia, Chicago, Berkeley and Los Angeles. Compositions include: Capriccio for piano and orchestra, 1963; Symphonic Poem for piano and orchestra, 1967; Quartet for flute, clarinet, cello and piano, 1967; Structures for piano, 1968; Seven Japanese Love Poems for voice and piano, 1968; O the Chimneys for mezzo-soprano and tape, 1969; Concert Piece for piano and orchestra, 1971; Ensembles for Seventeen, for soprano and 16 instruments, 1975; Double Vision for woodwind quintet, brass quintet and piano, 1976; Piano Concerto, 1977; Apprehensions for voice, clarinet and piano, 1979; 2 String Quartets, 1984, 1989; Concerto da Camera I for woodwind quintet, 1985; Concerto for Orchestra, 1986; Concerto da Camera II for clarinet, string quartet and piano, 1987; Symphony No 1, 1990; Mirage for 5 players, 1990; Chicago Skyline for brass and percussion, 1991; Inscriptions for violin, 1991; Legends for orchestra, 1993; Three Fantasy Movements for cello and orchestra, 1993; Invocation, for horn, timpani, and chimes, 1994; Between Two Worlds: The Dybbuk, opera, 1994-95. Honours include: Pulitzer Prize (for Symphony No 1, 1991); First Prize, Kennedy Center Friedheim Awards, 1992. Address: c/o ASCAP, ASCAP Building, One Lincoln Plaza, New York, NY 10023, USA.

RANACHER Christa, b. 12 Dec 1953, Dollach in Kärnten, Austria. Singer (Soprano). Education: Studied in Vienna and attended master classes by Mario del Monaco and Elisabeth Schwarzkopf. Career: Sang at Regensburg, 1984-85, Monchengladbach from 1985, Leonore in Fidelio, 1989; Further appearances at Gelsenkirchen, Mannheim, Munster, Hanover, the Deutsche Oper Berlin, Staatsoper Munich and Zurich; Season, 1992, as Salome at Dusseldorf and Shostakovich's Katerina Ismailova at Berne; Other roles include Mozart's Countess and Donna Anna, Agathe, Marenka in The Bartered Bride, Senta, and Ada in Wagner's Die Feen, Tosca, Santuzza, Zdenka, Arabella, Judith in the opera by Siegfried Matthus, Sophie in Cerha's Baal and Andromache in Troades by Reimann; Sang Stella in Goldschmidt's Der Gewaltige Hahnrei, Bonn, 1995; Noted concert performer. Address: c/o Deutsche Oper am Rhein, Heinrich Heine Allee 16, 4000 Dusseldorf, Germany.

RANDLE Thomas, b. 21 Dec 1958, Hollywood, California, USA. Singer (Tenor). Education: Studied at the University of Southern California. Career: Concert appearances in the USA and Europe with the London Philharmonic Orchestra, Boston Symphony Orchestra and the Leipzig Radio Symphony Orchestra; Conductors include Helmuth Rilling, Gennadi Rozhdestvensky, Michael Tilson Thomas and André Previn; Has sung Berg and Stravinsky, and the US and world premieres of works by Tippett, Heinz Holliger and William Kraft with the Los Angeles Philharmonic; Often heard in Bach, Handel and Mozart; Bach's Christmas Oratorio in Leipzig; Operatic repertoire includes all the major tenor roles of Mozart, Rossini and Donizetti, and French roles of Massenet and Thomas; British debut as Tamino in Nicholas Hytner's production of The Magic Flute (English National Opera, 1988, returned, 1989); European opera debut at the Aix-en-Provence Festival, France, in Purcell's The Fairy Queen; Sang Monteverdi's Orfeo at Valencia, 1989; Ferrando in Brussels and with Scottish Opera; Sang Tamino at Glyndebourne, 1991; Sang Dionysius in the premiere of John Buller's The Bacchae and as Pelléas, English National Opera, 1992; Sang title role in reduced version of Pelléas et Mélisande with Peter Brook in Paris and European tour, Netherlands Opera in world premiere of Peter Schaat's opera Symposion, based on Life of Tchaikovsky, in 1994; Season 1994 returned to English National Opera to sing Tippett's King Priam and appeared in Britten's Gloriana at Covent Garden; Fairy Queen at ENO, 1995; Sang Idomeneo for Scottish Opera, 1996. Recordings: Purcell's Fairy Queen with Les Arts Florissants; Tippett's The Ice Break with London Sinfonietta; Britten's War Requiem with BBC Scottish Symphony Orchestra; Liugi Nono, Canti di Vita e d'Amore with Bamberg Symphony Orchestra; Mozart's Requiem with German National Youth Orchestra; Handel's Esther with Harry Christophers and the Sixteen; Requiem of Reconciliation with Helmuth Rilling and the Israel Philharmonic Orchestra; Handel's Messiah with the Royal Philharmonic Orchestra. Address: c/o IMG Artists Europe, Media House, 3 Burlington Lane, Chiswick, London W4 2TH, England.

RANDOLPH David, b. 21 Dec 1914, New York, New York, USA. Conductor; Author; Lecturer; Broadcaster. m. Mildred Greenberg, 18 July 1948. Education: BS, City College of NY; MA, Teachers College, Columbia University. Career: Conductor, The Masterwork Chorus and Orchestra, St Cecilia Chorus and Orchestra, at Carnegie Hall, Avery Fisher Hall, Kennedy Center, Washington DC; Numerous choral works including: Bach's B Minor Mass, Christmas Oratorio, Brahms' Requiem, Mozart's Requiem, Vaughan Williams's Sea Symphony and Hodie, Dona Nobis Pace, Mass in G Minor, Haydn's Mass in Time Of War, Orff's Carmina Burana, Beethoven's Mass in C and Missa Solemnis, Mozart's Mass in C Minor, Mendelssohn's Symphony No 2, Elijah and Die erste Walpurgisnacht, Poulenc's Gloria, Kodály's Te Deum, 170 Complete performances of Handel's Messiah; Guest Conductor: The Philharmonia Orchestra, Barbican Centre, London, Brahms's Requiem, 1988; Pre-concert Lecturer: New York Philharmonic, Cleveland Orchestra, Vienna Symphony Orchestra; Conductor, David Randolph Singers; Radio Broadcasts, The David Randolph Concert, WNYC Radio, 1946-79; Guest Critic, First Hearing, WQXR Radio and 60 stations throughout USA, 1986-; Host, Lincoln Center Spotlight, WQXR Radio; Lecturer, New York University, The New School; Professor of Music, State University of New York, New Paltz, Fordham University, Montclair State College, New Jersey; Conductor, Concert tour of Spain, with four American choruses and The Radio Television Orchestra of Moscow, Russia, 1992. Composition: A Song for Humanity. Recordings: Works by: Monteverdi, Schütz, Handel's Messiah; Writer, Narrator, The Instruments of the Orchestra, CD, 1995; Madrigals of Weelkes, Bateson, Wilbye, Gesualdo, 13 Modern American Madrigals. Publication: This Is Music: A Guide to The Pleasures of Listening, 1964, new edition, 1997. Honours: Distinguished Alumni Award, Columbia University, 1982; Certificate of Appreciation, Mayor of City of New York, Carnegie Hall, 1991; St Cecilia Chorus endowed the David Randolph Distinguished Artist-in-Residence Programme at the New School, New York, 1996; Townsend Harris Medal, College of the City of New York, 1996. Address: 420 East 86th Street, Apt 4C, New York, NY 10028, USA.

RANDOVA Eva, b. 31 Dec 1936, Kolin, Czechoslovakia. Singer (Mezzo-soprano). Education: Studied with J Svanova at Usti nad Labem, and at the Prague Conservatory. Career: Sang first at Ostrava, as Eboli, Carmen, Amneris, the Princess in Rusalka, and Ortrud; Prague National Opera from 1969; Nuremberg and Stuttgart from 1971; Bayreuth Festival from 1973, as Gutrune, Fricka and Kundry; Salzburg Festival, 1975, Eboli in Don Carlos, conducted by Karajan; Covent Garden debut, 1977, as Ortrud; Returned to London as Marina, Venus, the Kostelnicka in Jenufa, 1986, and Azucena in a new production of Il Trovatore, 1989; Metropolitan Opera, 1981, 1987, as Fricka and Venus; Orange Festival, 1985, as Marina in Boris Godunov; Vienna, 1987, in Rusalka; Sang Ortrud at San Francisco, 1989, Stuttgart, 1990; Sang Marina in Boris Godunov at Barcelona, 1990; Season 1992 as Clytemnestra at Athens; Covent Garden, 1994, as Kabanicha in Katya Kabanova (returned 1997); Frequent concert engagements. Recordings: Bach cantatas; Santuzza in Cavalleria Rusticana; Mahler's Resurrection Symphony; Glagolitic Mass by Janácek; Sarka by Fibich; The Cunning Little Vixen and Jenufa, conducted by Charles Mackerras. Address: c/o Lies Askonas Ltd, 6 Henrietta Street, London WC2, England.

RANDS Bernard, b. 2 Mar 1935, Sheffield, Yorkshire, England. Composer; Conductor. Education: BMus, 1956, MMus, 1958, University of Wales, Bangor; Study in Italy with Dallapiccola, Boulez, Maderna and Berio. Career: Instructor at the music department of York University, 1968-74; Fellowship in Creative Arts at Brasenose College, Oxford, 1972-73; Professor of Music at the University of California, San Diego, from 1976; Visiting professor at the California Institute of the Arts in Valencia, 1984-85; Has worked at electronic music studios in Milan, Berlin, Albany (New York) and Urbana; Appearances as conductor of new music, notably with the London Sonor ensemble; Founder-member of music theatre ensemble CLAP. Compositions: Serena, music theatre, 1972-78; Orchestral: Per Esempio, 1968; Wildtrack I-III, 1969-75; Agenda, 1970; Mesalliance, 1972; Ology for jazz group, 1973; Aum, 1974; Serenata 75b, flute, chamber orchestra, 1976; Hirath, cello, orchestra, 1987; ...Body and Shadow..., 1988; Instrumental: Espressioni, series of piano pieces, 1960-70; Actions for Six, 1962; Formants I, II, 1965-70; Tableau, 1970; Memo 1-5, solo pieces, 1971-75; Dejà I, 1972; As all get out, 1972; Etendre, 1972; Response, double bass, tape, 1973; Scherzi, 1974; Cuaderna for string quartet, 1975; Madrigali, 1977; Obbligato, string quartet, trombone, 1980; ...In the Receding Mist..., flute, harp, string trio, 1988; Vocal: Ballad 103, 1970-73; Metalepsis 2 for mezzo, 1971; Lunatici, soprano, ensemble, 1980; Dejà 2, soprano, ensemble, 1980; Sound Patterns, various combinations with voices; Canti del Sole, tenor, orchestra, 1983; London Serenade, 1984; Le Tambourin, suite 1, 2, 1984; Ceremonial, 1, 2, 1985-86; Serenata 85, 1985; Requiescat, soprano, chorus, ensemble, 1985-86; ...Among the Voices..., chorus, harp, 1988. Honours: Pulitzer Prize for Canti del Sole, 1984. Address: c/o Universal Edition, 2/3 Fareham Street, London W1, England.

RANGELOV Svetozar, b. 1967, Bulgaria. Singer (Bass). Education: Graduated, State Musical Academy, Sofia, 1994. Career: Many concert and opera engagements in Bularia and elsewhere in Europe; Opera debut as Ferrando in Il Trovatore with the Bulgarian National Opera, 1995; Repertory also includes Le nozze di Figaro, Verdi's Vespri Siciliani and songs by Glière, Cui and Borodin; Contestent at the 1995 Cardiff Singer of the World Competition. Address: j.k. Druzba, bl.43, entr 7, ap 114, Sofia 1592, Bulgaria.

RANKI Dezsö, b. 8 Sept 1951, Budapest, Hungary. Pianist. Education: Béla Bartók Conservatory; Ferenc Liszt Academy of Music; Graduated with distinction, 1973. Career: Has given numerous guest performances including: Kremlin Conservatory, Moscow, USSR; Royal Festival Hall, London, England; Deputised for Rubinstein in Milan and for Benedetti-Michelangeli at Menton; Appearances at International Festivals of Antibes, Helsinki, Lucerne, Menton, St Moritz, Paris and Prague; Carinthian Summer Festival, Ossiach, Villach; Solo part, Bernstein's The Age of Anxiety, Carinthian Festival, 1975; Regular appearances worldwide. Honours: Kossuth Prize; Liszt Prize; 1st Prize, Robert Schumann International Piano Competition, Zwickau, 1969; Recipient, 1st Prizes, National Piano Competitions, 1965, 1967, 1969.

RANKI György, b. 30 Oct 1907, Budapest, Hungary. Composer. m. Anna Dékány, 13 Nov 1940, 1 son, 1 daughter. Education: Ferenc Liszt Academy of Music, Budapest; Studied Composition under Zoltán Kodály. Career: World publicity on some compositions: King Pomade Suite; Pentaerophonia; Serenade of the Seven Headed Dragon; His ballet comedy Magic Drink world premiered in Wiesbaden. Compositions: Operas: King Pomade's New Clothes, 1953; The Tragedy of Man, 1970; The Boatman of the Moon, 1979; 5 ballets including: Cantus Urbis, 1944; Cain and Abel, 1989; 12 symphonic scores including 2 symphonies, concertos and suites; Chamber music including: Pentaerophonia for woodwind quartet; Serenade for brass septet; String Quartet; Two Wonder Oxen, story with music; Vocal and instrumental; Theatre and film music. Recordings: King Pomade's New Clothes I Suite (Louisville Symphony Orchestra); The Tragedy of Man; 1st Symphony; Concertos; Historical Tableaux; Three Nights; Don Quixote; Cain and Abel, 1989. Honours: Kossuth Prize, 1854; Erkel Prize; Named Merited Artist, Pro Arte, 1950-77; Bartók-Pasztory Prize, 1987. Current Management: Artisjus, Vörösmarty-Tér 1, Budapest 1051, Hunary. Address: 36 Gülbaba-utca, 1023 Budapest, Hungary.

RANKIN Nell, b. 3 Jan 1926, Montgomery, Alabama, USA. Singer (Mezzo-soprano). Education: Studied with Jeanne Lorraine at the Birmingham Conservatory and with Karin Branzell in New York. Debut: New York Town Hall recital, 1947. Career: Stage debut, Zurich, 1949, as Ortrud in Lohengrin; Sang, 1949-50, in 126 performances; La Scala Milan, 1951, in the Verdi Requiem, to celebrate 50 Commemoration of Verdi's death; Metropolitan Opera from 1951-76, as Amneris, Laura, Marina, Azucena, Ulrica, Gutrune, Ortrud, Carmen, Eboli, Santuzza, Brangaene and Fricka; Covent Garden, 1953-54, as Carmen, Amneris, Ortrud and Azucena; Appearances at San Francisco, 1955, and Vienna; Sang at Cincinnati, 1956, in the US premiere of Britten's Gloriana; La Scala Milan, 1960, as Cassandre in Les Troyens; San Carlo Opera, Naples, 1961, sang Eboli in Don Carlo; Carnegie Hall, 1983, celebrated 30th anniversary since debut at Metropolitan Opera as Queen Gertrude in Thomas' Hamlet; Headed, Music Dept, Academy of Vocal Arts, Philedelphia, 1979-86. Recordings include: Suzuki in Madama Butterfly; Cassandre in Les Troyens (La Scala); Brahm's Lieder recital; Amneris in Aida (Herbert Von

Karajan); Verdi Requiem (La Scala); Laura in Gioconda; Azucena in Trovatore; Amneris in Aida and Marina in Boris Godonov (Metropolitan Opera); and Werther (New Orleans Opera); Les Troyens; Lieder recital. Honour: 1st Prize, Internationale Concours de Musique, Geneva, Switzerland, 1950. Address: 1040 Park Avenue, New York, NY 10028-1032, USA.

RANKINE Peter (John), b. 11 Mar 1960, Queensland, Australia. Composer; Conductor. Education: BMus, Queensland Conservatory, 1984; GradDipMus, 1985; MMus, University of Queensland, 1996. Career: Faculty Member, University of Queensland, 1987; Queenland University of Technology, 1988-94; Commissions from Queensland Wind Soloists, Australian Broadcasting Commission, Dance North, Opera Queensland, Canticum and others. Compositions include: Bunyip!, chamber opera, 1985; Three Movements for Orchestra, 1986; Eulogy for windquintet, 1987; Symphonia Dialectica, 1988; From Fire by Fire for Wind octet, 1989; Celtic Cross for violin and chamber orchestra, 1990; Time and the Bell: Clarinet Concerto, 1990; John Brown, Rose, and the Midnight Cat, for ensemble, 1992; Surya Namaskar, Chaand Namaskar, for horn and percussion, 1993; Please No More Psalms, ballet score, for oboe, clarinet, percussion, violin and cello, 1994; Media Vita, for choir, clarinet, trombone and percussion, 1997. Honours include: Sounds Australian Awards, 1990-91. Address: 3/15 Bellewe Terrace, St Lucia, Qld 4067, Australia.

RAPER Marion (Eileen), b. 18 Feb 1938, Birmingham, England. Pianist; Accompanist. m. 28 July 1962, div. 1979. Education: Licentiate, Royal Academy of Music, 1957-59; University of London Teaching Certificate, Goldsmiths' College, University of London, 1959-61; BA, Honours, Open University. Career: Recitals throughout England with singers and instrumentalists; Broadcasts for BBC and Capital Radio; Teaching, Guildhall School of Music; Master classes in London; Tour of Canada with Jennifer Hillman, piano duo, 1987; Appearances on television (ITV and Channel 4); Member of the Ridings Piano Quartet; Second tour of Canada with Jennifer Hillman, 1989. Membership: Incorporated Society of Musicians. Address: 3 Cavendish Drive, Guiseley, Leeds LS20 8DR, England.

RAPF Kurt, b. 15 Feb 1922, Vienna, Austria. Conductor; Musician; Composer. m. Ellen Rapf, 2 Dec 1961, 1 daughter. Education: Graduate in Piano, Organ and Conducting, Music Academy, Vienna. Career: Founder and Conductor, Collegium Musicum Wien (Vienna String Symphony), 1945-56; Assistant Conductor to Hans Knappertsbusch, Opera House Zurich, Switzerland; Accompanist for famous singers and instrumentalists; Director of Music, Innsbruck, 1953-60; Broadcast and television activities; Numerous tours in Europe, USA, Canada, Middle and Far East; Many appearances at festivals in Europe; Professor, Chief of Music Department, City of Vienna, 1970-87; Head of Austrian Composers' Guild, 1970-83; Founder and Music Director of Vienna Sinfonietta, 1986. Compositions: Over 140 works for orchestra, choir, chamber orchestra, organ and piano solo, chamber music and vocal works. Recordings: Over 70 records as conductor, harpsichordist, organist, pianist, and composer. Hobby: Swimming. Address: Bossigasse 35, A-1130 Vienna, Austria.

RAPHANEL Ghilaine, b. 19 Apr 1952, Rouen, France. Singer (Soprano). Education: Studied at the Rouen Conservatory and at the Paris Conservatoire with Janine Micheau. Career: Sang Rosina in Il Barbiere di Siviglia at the Opera Studio of the Paris Opera; Stadttheater Basle from 1980 as Gilda, Constanze, Juliette, Manon, and Titania in A Midsummer Night's Dream; Guest appearances in Lyon and Nantes; Hamburg Staatsoper, 1985, as the Queen of Night and Zerbinetta; Aix-en-Provence Festival, 1985, Zerbinetta; Sang at Mézières, 1988, as Amor in Orfeo ed Euridice; At Nancy, 1989, as Susanna. Recordings include: Pousette in Manon, L'Etoile by Chabrier; Fiorella in Les Brigands by Offenbach; Marguerite de Valois in Les Huguenots; Sang Nicolais Frau Fluth at the Paris Opéra-Comique, 1995-96. Address: c/o Opéra de Nancy et de Lorraine, Rue Ste Catherine, F-54000 Nancy, France.

RAPPE Jadwiga, b. 1957, Poland. Singer (Contralto). Education: Studied in Warsaw and Breslau. Career: Sang at first in concert and made stage debut at Warsaw in 1983; Has sung throughout Europe in concert, notably with masses by Mozart, Bach and Beethoven and Szymanowski's Stabat Mater; Performances of Erda in Wagner's Ring at the Deutsche Oper Berlin, Warsaw and Covent Garden from 1988; Concerts of La Gioconda in Amsterdam and Strauss's Daphne (as Gaea) in Geneva, 1990-91; Other roles include Ulrica, Orpheus and Juno in Semele. Address: Warsaw National Opera, Grand Theatre, Place Teatrainy 1, 00-950 Warsaw, Poland.

RASMUSSEN Karl Aage, b. 14 Dec 1947, Kolding, Denmark. Composer; Conductor; Professor of Music. m. Charlotte Schiotz. 7 May 1975. Education: Composition with Per Norgaard, degrees in Music History, Theory and Composition, Academy of Music, Aarhus. Career includes: Teacher: Academy of Music, Aarhus, 1970-, Royal Academy, Copenhagen, 1980-; Director, Conductor, Chamber Ensemble, The Elsinore Players, 1975-; Numerous duties at the New Music Department, Danish Radio, co-editing The Danish Music Magazine; Lectures, many European countries, USA; Artistic Director, NUMUS Festival, Aarhus, also Esbjerg Ensemble (1991-). Compositions include: Stage: Jephta, 2-act opera, 1976-77; Majakovskij, 2-act scenic concert piece, 1977-78; Jonas, musical play for radio, 1978-80; 'Our Hoffmann', opera, 1986; The Sinking of the Titanic, opera, 1994; Orchestral: Symphony Anfang und Ende, 1973; Contrafactum, concerto for cello and orchestra, 1980; A Symphony in Time, 1982; Movements on a Moving Line, 1985; Phantom Movements, 1989; Chamber: Protocol and Myth, 1971; Genklang, 1972; A Ballad of Game and Dream, 1974; Lullaby, 1976; Berio Mask, 1977; Le Tombeau de Père Igor, 1977; Parts Apart, 1978; Capricci e Dance, 1979; Italiensk Koncert, 1981; Ballo in Maschera, 1981; Pianissimo Furioso, 1982; A Quartet of Five, 1982; Solos and Shadows, 1983; Fugue/Fuga (Encore VIII), 1984; Surrounded by Sales, 1985; Still, string quartet, 1988; Solo instrument: Invention, 1972; Antifoni, 1973; Paganini Variations, 1976; Fugue/Fuga, 1984; Triple Tango, 1984; Etudes and Postludes, piano, 1990; Vocal: Love Is In The World, 1974-75; One And All, 1976; Encore Series I-XI, 1977-85. Recordings: String Quartets, Arditti String Quartet; A Symphony in Time, Danish Radio Symphony Orchestra; Movements on a Moving Line, Speculum Musicae. Honours: Carl Nielsen Prize, 1991. Memberships: Danish Music Council; Danish Arts Foundation. Address: Brokbjerggaard, DK-8752 Oestbirk, Denmark.

RASMUSSEN Paula, b. 1965, California, USA. Singer (Mezzo-soprano). Career: Concert appearances with San Francisco Symphony under Nicholas McGegan in Bach Cantatas, the Los Angeles Master Chorale in Messiah, Bruckner's Te Deum and Pergolesi's Magnificat and with José Carreras in Dublin, 1992; Opera engagements as Nancy T'ang in the Peter Sellars production of Nixon in China at Los Angeles, Paris and Frankfurt; Lola in Cavalleria Rusticana with Long Beach Opera; Nancy in Albert Herring, Hansel, Anna in Les Troyens, Hippolyta in Midsummer Night's Dream and the Composer in Ariadne auf Naxos with the Los Angeles Music Center Opera; Sang Handel's Serse at Cologne, 1996. Honours: Regional Winner, 1992 Metropolitan Opera Competition. Address: c/o IMG Artists, Media House, 3 Burlington Lane, London W4 2TH, England.

RATH John (Frédéric), b. 10 Jun 1946, Manchester, England. Opera and Concert Singer (Bass). Education: BA, Honours in Drama, Manchester University; RNCM, Opera School at Basle; Studied with Elsa Cavelti, Max Lorenz and Otakar Kraus. Debut: Ramphis in Aida, RNCM. Career includes: Appearances with: English Music Theatre Company, Glyndebourne Festival, Touring Company Royal Opera House, Covent Garden, La Fenice, Venice, Maggio Musicale in Florence; Roles include: Masetto in Don Giovanni, Argante in Handel's Rinaldo, Sparafucile in Rigoletto, Escamillo and Zuniga in Carmen; Recently in Peter Brook's La Tragèdie de Carmen in Paris, its European tour and New York as Escamillo; Kent Opera: Rocco in Fidelio; Nexus Opera: The Traveller in Britten's Curlew River at Wells Cathedral and filmed by BBC2 TV; Edinburgh Festival: Jochanaan in Salome; English Bach Festival: Charon in Handel's Alceste; Appearances at various festivals; Principal Bass with D'Oyly Carte Opera with roles including: Dick Deadeye in HMS Pinafore, 1990-92; The Mikado, Grand Inquisitor in The Gondoliers; Private Willis in Iolanthe; Concert and oratorio work throughout Europe including notable performances of Handel's Theodora in London, Spain and Italy, Bach Cantatas in NY and concert performances including Wotan in Das Rheingold and Die Walküre; Opera North: The Doctor in Berg's Wozzeck, 1993; Sarastro in Mozart's The Magic Flute, 1994; Nourabad in Bizet's Les Pêcheurs de Perles, 1995; Created a new English version of Schubert's Winter Journey with the poet Miriam Scott and performed it; Sang Herod in Stradella's San Giovanni Batista, Batignano, 1996. Recordings: The Gondoliers and Iolanthe with the D'Oyly Carte. Hobbies include: Farming. Current Management: Athole Still International Management Ltd. Address: Cwmllechwedd Fawr, Llanbister, Powys, LD1 6UH, Wales.

RATJU Adrian, b. 28 July 1928, Bucharest, Romania. Composer; Musicologist. Education: Studied harmony, counterpoint and compositions at the Bucharest Conservatory, 1950-56; Summer course at Darmstadt, Germany, 1969. Career: Professor at the Bucharest Conservatory from 1962; Executive Committee of the Union of Composers and Musicologists, Bucharest, from 1968. Compositions include: 2 String Quartets, 1956, 1988; 2 Symphonies, 1961, 1977; Concerto for oboe, bassoon and orchestra, 1963; Three Madrigals for chorus, after Shakespeare, 1964; Diptych for orchestra, 1965; Partita for wind quartet, 1966; Impressions for ensemble, 1969; Fragment of a Triumphal Arch for Beethoven for soprano, clarinet and piano, 1970; Six Images for orchestra, 1971; Transfigurations, for piano, clarinet and spring trio, 1975; Trio for flute and oboe and clarinet, 1980; Sonata a Cinque, for brass quintet, 1984; Sonata for solo violin, 1985; Trio for piano, clarinet and guitar, 1987; Piano Concerto, 1988; Echoes, for vibraphone and marimba, 1989; Violin Sonata, 1991; Convergences, for piano, clarinet and percussion, 1994; Hommage a Erik Satie, for voice and piano, 1994. Honours include: Six composition prizes from the Union of Composers and Musicologists, 1967-93. Address: c/o UCMR-ADA, Calea Victoriei 141, 71102 Bucharest, Romania.

RATTAY Evzen, b. 1945, Czechoslovakia. Cellist. Education: Studied at the Prague Academy of Arts. Career: Cellist of the Talich String Quartet from 1962; Tours to most European countries, Egypt, Iraq, North America, Japan, Indonesia; Chamber Ensemble of the Czech Philharmonic from 1975; Annual visits to France from 1976; Tours of Britain, 1990-91, with concerts at the Wigmore Hall, appearances at the Bath and Bournemouth Festivals, Elizabeth Hall and on BBC2's Late Show, with Janácek's 2nd quartet; Also played Beethoven's Quartet Opus 74, the Brahms A minor, Smetana D minor and works by Mozart in England; Festival appearances in Vienna, Besançon, Lucerne, Helsinki, Amsterdam, Prague and Salzburg; Repertoire also includes works by Debussy, Bartók (complete quartets recorded), Shostakovich, Ravel and Dvorák. Recordings include: Complete quartets of Beethoven; Albums. Honours include: Grand Prix Charles Cros. Address: c/o Clarion/Seven Muses, 64 Whitehall Park, London N19 3TN, England.

RATTI Eugenia, b. 5 Apr 1933, Genoa, Italy. Singer (Soprano). Education: Studied with her mother. Career: Concert tour with Tito Schipa, 1952; Stage debut, 1954, in Sestri Levante; La Scala Milan from 1955, as Lisa in La Sonnambula, and in the premiere of Milhaud's David, 1955, and Dialogues des Carmélites, 1957; Holland Festival, 1955, 1961, as Nannetta and Adina; Edinburgh Festival, 1957, Il Matrimonio Segreto; Holland Festival, 1970, in Haydn's La Fedeltà Premiata; Returned to Glyndebourne, 1973 and 1976, as the Italian Singer in Capriccio; Other roles include Zerlina in Don Giovanni, Susanna, Rosina, Musetta and Oscar. Recordings: Un Ballo in Maschera; Il Matrimonio Segreto; Aida; La Sonnambula; Don Giovanni, conducted by Leinsdorf. Address: c/o La Scala Opera, Via Drammetici 2, 20121 Milan, Italy.

RATTLE Simon (Sir), b. 19 Jan 1955, Liverpool, England. Conductor. 2 sons. Debut: Queen Elizabeth Hall, 1974; Royal Festival Hall, 1976; Royal Albert Hall, 1976; Glyndebourne, 1977, The Cunning Little Vixen. Career: Assistant Conductor, BBC Scottish Symphony Orchestra, 1977-80; Associate Conductor, Royal Liverpool Philharmonic Society, 1977-80; Principal Conductor, London Choral Society, 1979-84; Principal Conductor, Artistic Director, 1980-91, Music Director, 1991-97, City of Birmingham Symphony Orchestra; Principal Guest Conductor, Los Angeles Philharmonic, 1981-94, Rotterdam Philharmonic, 1981-84; Artistic Director, Aldeburgh Festival, 1982-93; Conducted Katya Kabanova, London Coliseum, 1985, Porgy and Bess, Glyndebourne, 1986; US opera debut, 1988, Wozzeck, Los Angeles; Covent Garden debut, 1990, The Cunning Little Vixen, Season 1990-91 with Berlin Philharmonic, London Philharmonic Brahms cycle, CBSO Tour, Hong Kong, Japan, Cosi fan tutte, Glyndebourne, Birmingham Symphony Hall opening, London Proms, Gubaidulina's Offertorium, Prokofiev 5th and Mahler 9th Symphonies; Season 1991-92, CBSO tours, Scandinavia, USA, appeared with Berlin, London and Rotterdam Philharmonic Orchestras; Salzburg Festival debut with City of Birmingham Symphony Orchestra, 1992; Season 1992-93 included Berlin Philharmonic at Berlin Festival, Boston Symphony, Los Angeles Philharmonic, Netherlands Opera debut (Pelléas and Mélisande) and Tanglewood; Season 1993-94 included Vienna Philharmonic and Philadelphia Orchestra debuts; Glyndebourne Festival, 1994, Don Giovanni; Season 1997 with Parsifal at Amsterdam and Towards the Millenium concerts with the CBSO. Recordings include: Recently: Mahler 1st and 7th symphonies; Szymanowski Symphony No 3 and Stabat Mater, Bartok, Elgar, Schoenberg, Liszt. Honours include: CBE, 1987, KBE, 1994; Montblanc de la Culture Award, 1993; Artist of the Year, Gramophone magazine, 1993; 3 Honorary Doctorates including University of Leeds, 1993; Chevalier des Arts et des Lettres, France, 1995. Current Management: Harold Holt Limited. Address: c/o Harold Holt Limited, 31 Sinclair Road, London W14 0NS, England.

RAUCH Wolfgang, b. 27 Jan 1957, Cologne, Germany. Singer (Baritone). Education: Studied in Cologne with Josef Metternich and in Italy with Mario del Monaco. Career: Sang with the Deutsche Oper am Rhein Dusseldorf from 1984, member of the Bayerische Staatsoper Munich from 1987; Guest appearances at La Scala Milan, the State Operas of Vienna and Hamburg and the Deutsche Oper Berlin; Sang Papageno in Mozart bicentenary performances of Die Zauberflöte at Barcelona and Bonn, 1991; Other roles include Lortzing's Tsar, Marcello, Mozart's Guglielmo and Figaro, Count Perruchetto in Haydn's La Fedeltà Premiata, Silvio, Lionel in Tchaikovsky's The Maid of Orleans, Strauss's Count in Capriccio and Harlekin and the Herald in Lohengrin; Frequent concert and broadcasting engagements. Address: Bayerische Staatsoper, Postfach 100148, 8000 Munich 1, Germany.

RAUCHS Béatrice, b. 27 July 1962, Arnsberg, Luxembourg. Concert Pianist; Conservatory Professor. m. Romain Jenn, 6 Sept 1989. Education: Graduated from Athené Grand-Ducal de Luxembourg; Conservatoire of Luxembourg with Jeanne Stein; Conservatoire of Metz with Mireille Krier; Conservatoire National Supérieur, Paris, with Aldo Ciccolini and Jean Hubeau; Solisten diplom, Music Academy of Basel, 1988, after studying with Rudolf Buchbinder. Career: Recordings for France Musique, Radio Saarbrücken, RTL and RAI; Invited to the festivals of Echternach, Paris (Chopin Festival), Nauplion and Weilburg; As soloist played with the RTL Symphony Orchestra, the Chamber Orchestra of Lithuania, Basel Symphony Orchestra and others; Repertoire includes traditional classical works (mainly Beethoven, Schumann, Brahms, Chopin, Debussy, Prokofiev), also 19th century works and contemporary music; Piano Teacher, Conservatoire de la Ville de Luxembourg, 1987-. Recordings: CD, Béatrice Rauchs plays Fanny Mendelsshon-Hensel. Honours: 1st Prize for Music and Chamber Music, Conservatoire National Supérieur, Paris, 1982, 1983; Prize Winner, International Piano Competitions: Vercelli, 1982; Finale Ligure, 1987; Senigallia, 1987; Caltanissetta, 1987; Prix de la Presse, Durlet Competition, Antwerp, 1989; Claude Kahn, Paris, 1990; Yamaha, Stresa, 1991; Semi-finalist at Queen Elisabeth Competition, Brussels. Hobbies: Movies; Reading; Cooking. Address: 17 rue Général Patton, L-4277 Esch/Alzette, Luxembourg.

RAUHE Hermann (Wilhelm), b. 6 Mar 1930, Wanna, Niederelbe, Germany. Musicologist. m. Annemarie Martin, 16 Aug 1963, 1 daughter. Education: Academy of Music and University of Hamburg, Federal Republic of Germany, 1951-55; MA, University of Hamburg, 1955; PhD, Musicology. Career: Music Teacher, Wilhelm Gymnasium, Hamburg, 1960-62; Lecturer, 1962-64, Assistant Professor of Musicology and Music Education, 1964-65, Professor, 1965-68, Dean, Department of Music Education, 1968-, Academy of Music, Hamburg; Professor of Musicology and Music Education, University of Hamburg, 1970-; President, Academy of Music and Theatre, Hamburg, 1978. Publications: Author of books including: Hören und Verstehen, 1975; Jugend zwischen Opposition und Identifikation, 1975; Musik-Intelligenz-Phantasie, 1978; Hören und Verstehen, 1986; Popmusik: Geschichte, Funktion, Wirkung and Asthetik, 1989; Musik hilft heilen, 1993; Kulturmanagement, 1994; Author, radio and TV series; Research; Numerous articles on musicology, music sociology and psychology, music education, music therapy; Editor, book series: Beitrage zur Schubmusik, 1962-; Musikalische Formen in historischen Reihen, 1962-; Schriften zur Musikpädagogik, 1975-; Editor, recorded series. Honours: Gold Medal, Society of Musicians and Music Educators, 1974. Memberships: Deutscher Musikrat; Deputation at State Department of Education and Science, Hamburg; Vice-President, Landesmusikrat Hamburg; Society of Research in Music Education, President 1971-74. Address: 18 Bredengrund, D-2104 Hamburg 92, Germany.

RAUNIG Arnold, b. 1956, Klagenfurt, Germany. Singer (Counter-tenor). Education: Member of the Vienna Boys' Choir, 1966-72, studied at the Linz Conservatoire and with Kurt Equiluz in Vienna. Career: Many appearances in Baroque music throughout Europe, notably in works by Bach, Handel and Mozart in Vienna, Berlin and Hamburg; Repertoire includes Mozart's Ascanio in Alba and Idomeneo, Handel's Radamisto and Xerxes, Cesti's Pomo d'Oro and The Fairy Queen; Wiesbaden Festival, 1992, in the premiere of Der Park by Hans Gefors. Address: c/o Wiesbaden Opera, Hessisches Staatstheater, Christian-Zais-Strasse 3-5, Pf 3247, W-6200 Wiesbaden, Germany.

RAUTAVAARA Einojuhani, b. 9 Oct 1928, Helsinki, Finland. Composer. m. Sini Koivisto, 18 Aug 1984. Education: MA, University of Helsinki; Sibelius Academy, 1950-57; Juilliard School of Music with Vincent Persichetti, NY, USA, 1955-56; Tanglewood Music Center with Aaron Copland and Roger Sessions, 1955-56; Kölner Musikhochschule with Rudolf Petzold, Germany, 1958. Career: Lecturer, Music Theory, Sibelius Academy, 1966-76; Art Professor, Finland, 1971-76; Professor of Composition, Sibelius Academy, 1976-90. Compositions: 7 Operas; 2 Choir-Operas; 7 Symphonies; Concerti for Cello, Piano, Flute, Violin, Organ, Double Bass; Cantus Arcticus concerto for Birds and Orchestra; String Quintet; 4 String Quartets; Cantatas; Chamber Music; Piano Music, Songs and other works. Recordings include: Thomas, opera; Vincent, opera; 7 Symphonies, Ondine Company; Angel of Dusk, concerto for Double Bass and Orchestra; Vigilia, orthodox Mass; Cantus Arcticus, Ondine; Bis; Piano Concertos 1 and 2, Ondine; Symphony 6, cello concerto, Ondine; Symphony 7; Organ Concerto. Publications: Libretti for operas: Kaivos, 1957; Thomas, 1983; Vincent, 1986; House of the Sun, 1990; Gift of the Magi, 1993; Alexis Kivi, 1995; Omakuva, memoirs, 1989. Honours: Sibelius Prize, 1965; Pro-Finlandia Medal, 1968; Member, Royal Swedish Academy, 1975; PhD, honoris causa, 1983; Music Prize of the State, 1985; Commander of the Finnish Lion, 1985; 15 first prizes in composition contests. Hobbies: Painting; Literature. Current Management: Edition Fazer/Warmer. Address: Bertel Jungin tie 3, Helsinki 57, Finland.

RAUTIO Nina, b. 21 Sept 1957, Bryansk, Russia. Singer (Soprano). Education: Studied at Leningrad Conservatoire. Career: Sang first at the Leningrad State Theatre, 1981-87; Bolshoi Opera from 1987; Western debut with Bolshoi Company at Metropolitan and the Edinburgh Festival 1991, as Tatiana and as Oksana in Rimsky's Christmas Eve; Season 1992, as Manon Lescaut at La Scala, conducted by Lorin Maazel, Verdi Requiem at Rome, Aida at the Savonlinna Festival and in concert performances conducted by Zubin Mehta; Sang with the Pittsburg Symphony on tour to Seville Expo 92 and as Elisabetta in Don Carlo to open the season at La Scala; Season 1993-94, as Lisa in The Queen of Spades at the Opera Bastille Paris, Ballo in Maschera and Aida at Covent Garden, Verdi Requiem at Florence and the Festival Hall, Beethoven and Mahler in Pittsburgh, Desdemona at the Orange Festival, the Glagolitic Mass at La Scala and Amelia Boccanegra at Florence; Season 1994-95, as Aida at the Staatsoper Berlin and Amelia Boccanegra at Florence and Turin; Season 1995-96 Metropolitan Opera debut as Aida; Sang Aida at the Verona Arena, 1996. Recordings: Manon Lescaut; Verdi Requiem; Guillaume Tell; Norma, Address: Allied Artists, 42 Montpelier Square, London SW7 1JZ, England.

RAWLINS Emily, b. 25 Sept 1950, Lancaster, Ohio, USA. Opera and Concert Singer. m. 18 Apr 1982. Education: BMus, Voice, Indiana University; Artist's Diploma, Curtis Institute of Music; Diploma, Hochschule für Musik, Vienna. Debut: Basel, Switzerland. Career: Basel Stadttheater, 1973-77; Deutsche Oper am Rhein, 1977-82; Debuts, Theater der Stadt Bonn, 1975, National Theater, Mannheim, 1976, Theater der Stadt Köln, 1977, Städtische Bühnen, Dortmund, 1979, Städtische Bühnen, Augsburg; San Francisco Opera, 1980; American premiere, Lear, Salzburg Festival, world premiere of Baal, 1981; Vienna Staatsoper, 1981; Teatro Nacional de Sao Carlos, Lisbon, 1982; Grand Théâtre de Génève, 1982; Houston Grand Opera, 1983; American premiere of Anna Karenina, Los Angeles Opera Theater, 1983; Appeared on television, ZDF Germany, 1981, 1982, ORF, Austria, 1981; Film appearances in Bartered Bride and Fra Diavolo, 1983, and Baal, 1984; Vienna State Opera, 1985; ORF with Wiener Symphoniker; Concert Opera Association, 1986; World premiere of Das Schloss, Opera National, Brussels, 1986. Recordings: Part of Sophie in Baal, 1985. Address: c/o California Artists' Management, 1182 Market Street, Suite 311, San Francisco, CA 94102, USA.

RAWNSLEY John, b. 14 Dec 1949, England. Singer (Baritone). Education: Royal Northern College of Music. Debut: Glyndebourne Touring Opera, 1975; Later sang Verdi's Ford and Stravinsky's Nick Shadow on tour, Mozart's Masetto, Rossini's Figaro and Puccini's Marcello at Glyndebourne; Covent Garden debut, 1979, as Schaunard in La Bohème; French debut at Nancy in 1980, as Tonio in Pagliacci; English National Opera from 1982, as Amonasro and as Rigoletto in Jonathan Miller's production of Verdi's opera; Tour to the USA, 1984; Italian debut, 1985, as Verdi's Renato in Trieste; La Scala Milan, 1987, as Tonio; Guest engagements at the Vienna Staatsoper, San Diego, Barcelona, Bilbao, Brussels and Geneva: Roles include Paolo Albiani (Simon Boccanegra), Macbeth, Papageno, Don Alfonso and Taddeo in L'Italiana in Algeri; Sang Rigoletto at Turin, 1989; Simon Boccanegra in a concert performance at the Festival Hall, 1990; Season 1992 as Rigoletto at Oslo and the Coliseum, and in The Beggar's Opera at the Aldeburgh Festival. Recordings: Rigoletto; Masetto in Don Giovanni; Videos of Così fan tutte, Il Barbiere di Siviglia, La Bohème and Rigoletto. Address: c/o Kaye Artists Management, Barratt House, 7 Chertsey Road, Woking, Surrey GU21 5AB, England.

RAXACH Enrique, b. 15 Jan 1932, Barcelona, Spain (Dutch Citizen). Composer. Education: Courses at Darmstadt with Messiaen, Boulez, Stockhausen and Maderna, 1959-66. Career: Resident in Netherlands, 1962, Citizen, 1969; Freelance Composer. Compositions include: Estudis for strings, 1952; Six Movements for orchestra, 1955; Polifonias, for strings, 1956; Metamorphose I-II for orchestra, 1956-58; Metamorphose III for 15 solo instruments, 1959; Columna de fuego for orchestra 1958; Fluxion, for 17 players, 1963; Syntagma, for orchestra, 1965; Fragmento II for soprano, flute and 2 percussionists, 1966; Textures for orchestra, 1966; Inside Outside for orchestra and tape, 1969; Paraphrase for mezzo-soprano and 11 players, 1969; 2 String Quartets, 1961, 1971; Rite of Perception, electronic tape music, 1971; Interface for chorus and orchestra, 1972; Scattertime for 6 players, 1972; Sine Nomine for soprano and orchestra, 1973; Figuren in einer Landschaft for orchestra, 1974; Chimaera for bass clarinet and tape, 1974; Erdenlicht for orchestra, 1975; Aubade for percussion quartet, 1979; The Hunting in Winter for horn and piano, 1979; Am Ende des Regenbogens, for orchestra, 1980; Careful with that.... for clarinet and percussionist, 1982; Chalumeau for clarinet quartet, 1982; Ode for flute and string trio, 1982; Vortice for 9 clarinets, 1983; ....hub of ambiguity, for soprano and 8 players, 1984; Opus Incertum for chamber orchestra, 1985; Calles y sueños, for chamber orchestra, 1986; Obsessum for bassoon and 9 accordions, 1988; Nocturno del hueco for chorus, large ensemble and tape, 1990; Danses Pythiques for harp, 1992; Decade for bass clarinet and accordion, 1992; 12 Preludes for piano, 1993; Reflections inside, electronic tape music, 1994; Piano Concertino, 1995; Neumes for percussion sextet, 1996; Nocturnal Stroll for flute orchestra, 1996; Chapter Three for orchestra, 1997. Address: c/o Vereniging Buma, PO Box 725, 1180 AS Amstelveen, The Netherlands.

RAYAM Curtis, b. 4 Feb 1951, Belleville, Florida, USA. Singer (Tenor). Education: Studied at the University of Miami with Mary Henderson Buckeley. Debut: Miami, 1971, in Manon Lescaut. Career: Appearances in Dallas, Houston and Jackson Opera South; European debut at the Wexford Festival, 1976, in Giovanni d'Arco by Verdi, returning as the Sultan in Mozart's Zaide and as Wilhelm Meister in Thomas' Mignon; Boston, 1979, as Olympion in the US premiere of Tippett's The Ice Break, conducted by Sarah Caldwell; Amsterdam, 1981, as Massenet's Werther; Further engagements at Salzburg, Paris, Frankfurt and Venice; La Scala, 1985, in Handel's Alcina, returning 1988 as Orcane in Fetonte by Jommelli; Spoleto, 1988, as Creon in Traetta's Antigone; Other roles include Rossini's Otello and Cleomene (L'Assedio di Corinto), Mozart's Idomeneo, Belmonte and Mitridate, Irus in Il Ritorno di Ulisse, Nemorino and Puccini's Pinkerton and Rodolfo. Recordings include: Treemonisha by Scott Joplin; Da-ud in Die Aegyptische Helena by Strauss. Honours include: Finalist, Metropolitan Auditions, 1972; Winner, Dallas Competition, 1974.

REA John, b. 14 Jan 1944, Toronto, Ontario, Canada. Composer. Education: Studied with John Weinzweg at University of Toronto and Milton Babbitt at Princeton. Career: Teacher at McGill University, 1973, Dean of the Faculty of Music, 1986-91; Composer-in-Residence at Mannheim, 1984; Founder Member of the Montreal music society Les Evénements du Neuf. Compositions: Music theatre pieces: Les Jours, ballet, 1969; The Prisoner's Play, opera, 1973; Hommage à Richard Wagner, 1988; Com-possession, 1980; Le Petit Livre des Ravalet, opera, 1983; Offenes Lied, operatic scenes, 1986; Operatic scenes based on Dante's Inferno and Poe's Morella, 1990-93; Orchestral: Hommage à Vasarely, 1977; Vanishing Points, 1983; Over Time, 1987; Time and Again, 1987; Chamber: Clarinet Sonatina, 1965; Sestina, 1968; Prologue, Scene and Movement for soprano, viola and 2 pianos, 1968; Tempest, 1969; What You Will for piano, 1969; La Dernière Sirène for ondes martenot, piano and percussion, 1981; Les Raison des Forces Mouvantes for flute and string quartet, 1984; Some Time Later for amplified string quartet, 1986; Vocal: Litaneia for chorus and orchestra, 1984. Address: c/o McGill University, Faculty of Music, Strathcona Music Building, 555 Sherbrooke Street West, Montreal, Quebec, Canada H3A 1E3.

READ Gardner, b. 2 Jan 1913, Evanston, Illinois, USA. Composer; University Professor. Education: BMus, 1936, MMus, 1937, Eastman School of Music; Composition with Jan Sibelius, Finland, 1939, Aaron Copland, Tanglewood, 1941, others; Piano, Organ, Conducting, Theory, various masters. Career: Teacher, Composition, Theory, 1940-; Professor, Composition, Music Theory, Composer in Residence, 1948-, Emeritus, 1978-, School of Fine and Applied Arts, Boston University; Guest Conductor, major orchestras including Boston Symphony, 1943, 1954, Philadelphia Orchestra, 1964; Originator, Host, weekly educational radio series Our American Music, 1953-60; Orchestral works performed by major orchestras, USA and abroad. Compositions: Numerous, orchestral, chamber, solo, organ, piano, choral, vocal, including Villon, opera, 1967; Many commissions such as: Passacaglia and Fugue, 1938; A Bell Overture, 1946. Recordings: Night Flight, 1942; Toccata Giocosa, 1953; Los Dioses Aztecas, 1982; De Profundis, 1985, 1991; Preludes on Old Southern Hymns, 1985, 1990; Symphony No 4, 1986; Sonata Brevis, 1986; Works for Organ, 1989; Invocation, 1991; Sonata da Chiesa, String Quartet No 1, Sononic Fantasia No 1, Fantasy-Toccata, Five Aphorisms, all 1995; Phantasmagoria, 1996; Epistle to the Corinthians; The Hidden Lute; By-Low; My Babe; Concerto for piano and orchestra, 1997. Publications include: Thesaurus of Orchestral Devices, 1969; Music Notation, 2nd edition, 1969; Contemporary Instrumental Techniques, 1976; Modern Rhythmic Notation, 1978; Style and Orchestration, 1979; Source Book of Proposed Music Notation Reforms, 1987; 20th-Century Microtonal Notation, 1990; Compendium of Modern Instrumental Techniques, 1993; Gardner Read: A Bio-Bibliography by Mary Ann Dodd and Jayson Engquist, 1995; Pictographic Score Notation, forthcoming. Contributions to: Professional journals. Honours: DMus, Doane College, Nebraska, 1962; Alumni Achievement Award, Eastman School of Music, 1982, Festival of Music by Gardner Read, Jan-Feb 1996, Eastman School of Music; Art Song Competition, National Association of Teachers of Singing, 1986. Membership: American Society of Composers, Authors and Publishers. Address: 47 Forster Road, Manchester, MA 01944, USA.

REANEY Gilbert, b. 11 Jan 1924, Sheffield, England. Professor. Education: Licentiate, Royal Academy of Music, 1946; BA 1948, BMus 1950, MA 1951, Sheffield University; Sorbonne University, Paris, France, 1950-53. Career: Performer, BBC and tours of Britain and the continent, 1952-88; Research Fellow, Reading University, 1953-56, Birmingham, 1956-59; Director of London Medieval Group, 1958-; Visiting Professor, Hamburg University, Germany, 1960; Associate Professor, University of California, Los Angeles, 1960-62, Full Professor, 1963-97. Publications: Early 15th Century Music, 7 volumes, (10 volumes for Corpus Scriptorum de Musica), 1955-83; Catalogue, Medieval Polyphonic Manuscripts to 1400, 2 volumes, 1966, 1969. Contributions to: Assistant and Co-editor of numerous articles in Musica Disciplina, 1956-97; General Editor of Corpus Scriptorum de Musica. Honour: 1st Dent Medal, Royal Musical Association, 1961. Memberships: Royal Musical Association; American Musicological Society; Plainsong and Medieval Music Society. Hobbies: Walking; Reading; Travel. Address: 1001 Third Street, Santa Monica, CA 90403, USA.

REARICK Barbara, b. 1960, USA. Singer (Mezzo-soprano). Education: Studied at Manhattan School of Music and at Britten-Pears School with Nancy Evans and Anthony Rolfe Johnson. Career: Concert and opera performances in Britain and USA; British debut, 1987, at Aldeburgh Festival as Britten's Lucretia; Sang Copland's Old American Songs with Lukas Foss, piano, at the Snape Concert Hall; Other repertoire includes Messiah, Lieder eines fahrenden Gesellen, L'Enfance du Christ and Britten's Charm of Lullabies orchestrated by Colin Matthews, all at Snape; Ravel's Chansons Madécasses, Haydn Masses with the Orchestra of St John's Smith Square and Handel's Dixit Dominus at the Norfolk and Norwich Festival, American popular songs there, 1992, with Richard Rodney Bennett; Operatic repertoire includes Meg Page, Chautauqua Opera, Suzuki in Opera Delaware and Annina in Rosenkavalier in New York City Opera; Member of the Britten-Pears Ensemble, with performances throughout Britain and USA. Address: c/o Owen-White Management, 14 Nightingale Road, London N8 7QU, England.

REASON Dana, b. 2 Jan 1968, Toronto, Canada. Pianist; Composer. Education: BMusic, McGill University, Montreal, Quebec; MA (Composition), Mills College, Oakland, California; PhD Candidate, University of California, San Diego. Debut: Deep Listening Space, Kingston, New York, 1997. Appointments: San Francisco Jazz Festival, 1995; Knitting Factory, New York City, 1997; Radio Canada, broadcast on Chants Magnetiques, 1997. Compositions: Rhizomatic Truth Table, piano solo; The Caretakers, piano, percussion and sampler. Recordings: Primal Identity, piano solo (Dana Reason) with Philip Gelb, Shakuhachi; Border Crossings, Dana Reason, piano (composer); Peter Valsamis, percussion, sampler. Honours: Scholarship, Mills College, 1995-97; Full Fellowship UCSD, 1997-98; Flora Boyd Prize for piano performance, Mills College. Memberships: American Musicological Soceity; Chamber Music America; Guild of Musicians, Quebec; Socan; International Alliance Women Musicians. Current Management: Self management. Address: 9334-H Redwood Drive, La Jolla, CA 92037, USA.

REAUX Angelina, b. 1959, Houston, Texas, USA. Singer (Soprano). Career: Sang in various New York night clubs and was discovered by Leonard Bernstein; Sang Mimi in La Bohème at Rome, 1987, and recorded the role with Bernstein; New York Academy of Music, 1989, as Dido by Purcell, Musetta at Boston and Despina at the Kentucky Opera, 1993; Other roles include Pamina, Nedda and the Woman in La Voix Humaine; Sang The Queen of Sparta in La Belle Hélène for L'Opéra Français de New York, 1996. Recordings include: La Bohème (DGG); Street Scene by Weill and Blitzstein's Regina (Decca). Address: c/o Kentucky Opera, 631 South Fifth Street, Louisville, KY 40202, USA.

REAVILLE Richard, b. 1954, England. Singer (Tenor). Career: Appearances with English National Opera, Welsh National Opera, Scottish Opera and Mid Wales Opera; Glyndebourne Festival and Tour, London Opera Players and festivals in Britain, France and Germany; Roles have included Jacquino in Fidelio, Mozart's Monostatos and Arbace, Britten's Peter Grimes and Albert Herring and Herod in Salome; Wagner's Loge, Froh and David, and Don José on tour to the Far East (1996); Concerts throughout Europe, including engagements with the BBC PO, Danish Radio SO, Belgian State Orchestra, Odense Philharmonic, Weimar Staatskapelle and various chamber ensembles; Mahler's Das Lied von der Erde with the Rander Orchestra (Denmark), Puccini's Messa di Gloria with the Ostrava PO and Ligeti's Le Grand Macabre with the Odense SO (1996-97). Address: c/o C&M Craig Services Ltd, 3 Kersley Street, London SW11 4PR, England.

REBER William (Francis), b. 3 Dec 1940, Oakland, California, USA. Conductor; Vocal Coach; Accompanist. m. Margaret Moffatt, 24 June 1986, 1 son, 1 daughter. Education: BMus magna cum laude, Theory and Composition, 1964, MMus, Conducting, 1966, University of Utah; DMA, University of Texas, Austin, 1977. Debut: Music Director and Conductor for Candide, Minnesota Opera, 1977. Career: Conductor, 17th Air Force Men's Chorus, Germany, 1969; Music Director for production of Curlew River, broadcast internationally, 'Britten in Texas'; Music Director, Minnesota Opera Company Studio, 1976-77; Conductor, University of Texas Opera Theatre, 1978-90; Conductor, Corpus Christi Ballet, Texas, 1986-; Conductor, Corpus Christi Symphony for Education Concerts, 1986-91; Music Director, Chamber Orchestra, Associate Conductor, Symphony, University of Texas; Music Director, California State University, Fullerton Symphony and Opera Theatre, 1990-91; Director, Principal Conductor, Lyric Opera Theatre, Arizona State University, 1991-; Accompanist, flute and piano recitals, Ohrid International Summer Festival and Skopje Summer Festival, 1994; Skopje American Music Festival, 1995; Also affiliated as Conductor, Vocal Coach and Accompanist with American Institute of Musical Studies, Graz, Austria, and Altenburg Musiktheater Akademie, Altenburg, Germany. Publications: The Operas of Ralph Vaughan Williams, 1977; English version of Hans Pfitzner's Das Christelflein, 1977; English translation of The Candy Tale, Dimitrije Buzarovski, composer and librettist, 1993. Honours: Cultural Travel Grantee, US Information Service, 1992, 1995. Memberships: American Symphony Orchestra League; Conductors' Guild; Opera America; National Opera Association. Hobbies: Private pilot; Chess. Address: 2025 E Campbell 331, Phoenix, AZ 85016, USA.

RECHBERGER Herman, b. 14 Feb 1947, Linz, Austria. Composer; Performer. m. (1) Ilse Maier, 1966, 1 son, 1 daughter, (2) Soili Jaatinen, 1972, 1 son, 2 daughters. Education includes: Graphic Arts, Linz, 1967; Teaching degree, Classical Guitar, Recorder, 1973, Diploma, Composition, 1976, Sibelius Academy, Helsinki. Career: Finnish citizen, 1974-; Music Teacher, Choir Conductor, 1975-79; Producer of Contemporary Music, Artistic Director of Experimental Studio, Finnish Broadcasting, 1979-84; State Grant, 1985-; Recitals of new recorder music, most European countries, Russia, Cuba, USA; Performed own works, ISCM Music Days, Helsinki and Stockholm, 1978, Athens, 1979, Warsaw, 1992, and Helsinki Biennale, 1981, 1983; Frequent performances and tours with ensembles Poor Knights and Sonores Antiqui, specialised in early music and scenic performances of contemporary music; Guest Composer for Hungarofilm at Hungarian Broadcasting Company's Electronic Music Studio, 1985, and Slovak Radio (Rustle of Spring), 1986; Currently Composer-in-Residence. Compositions include: Orchestral: Consort Music 1, 2, 4, 5; The Garden of Delights; Venezia; 3 guitar concertos; Songs from the North; Goya; Operas: The Nuns; Laurentius; Radiophonic works: The Rise of Mr Jonathan Smith; Magnus Cordius, entries in a diary; Vocal music: Vanha Linna; Hades; Dunk; Rhythm and Blues; Notturno inamorata; Seis Canciones de anochecer; Musica Picta for small children; Tape music: Cordamix; Narod; KV-622bis; Moldavia; Rustle of Spring; Multimedia: Zin Kibaru; Firenze 1582; Survol; La Folia; Chamber music: Consort Music 3 for brass nonet; El Palacio del Sonido for 3 guitars; Consort Music 6 for 12 recorders; Musical graphics and pictographic scores for educational purposes; Many arrangements and reconstructions of early music and Ancient Greek music, eg the world's first opera, Jacopo Peri's Euridice. Recordings include: The King's Hunt, Esa-Pekka Salonen, French horn; Cordamix; Rasenie järi, Rustle of Spring; The Garden of Delights, Austrian RSO, conductor Leif Segerstam; Consort Music I, Clas Pehrson, recorders, Swedish RSO, conductor Leif Segerstam. Hobbies: Graphic arts; Languages; Chinese calligraphy; Computer art. Address: Laajavuorenkuja 5 B 11, 01620 Vantaa, Finland.

RECTANUS Jans, b. 18 Feb 1935, Worms, Germany. Professor. m. Elisabeth Zilbauer, 1 son, 1 daughter. Education: Civic Music Academy and University, Frankfurt/Main; Academy of Music and Interpretive Art, University of Vienna; School for Protestant Church Music, Schlüchtern/Hesse; PhD, University of Frankfurt, 1966. Career: Teacher (Music, German Literature) for Gymnasium, 1960-63; Lecturer and Assistant, University of Frankfurt/Main, 1963-66; Lecturer, 1966-71, Professor, 1971-, Teachers' College, Heidelberg. Compositions: Edited: Hans Pfitzner String Quartet in D minor; Trio for violin, violoncello and piano. Publications: Leitmotiv und Form in den Musikdramatischen Werken Hans Pfitzners, 1967; Neue Ansätze im Musikunterricht, 1972; Hans Pfitzner, Sämtliche Lieder mit Klavierbegleitung, volume I, 1980, volume II, 1983. Contributions to: Die Musikforschung; Riemannmusiklexikon; Studien zur Musikgeschichte des 19 Jahrhundert; Mitteilungen der Hans Pfitzner-Gesellschaft; Festchrift H Osthoff; Renaissance-Studien; Zeitschrift für Musik-Pädagogik; Lexikon der Musikpädagogik; Pfitzner-Studien. Honours: Kritiker-Preis, 1956; Recipient, Music Director, Organist Prizes. Memberships: Präsidium, Hans Pfitzner Society, Munich; Society for Music Research, Cassel; Society of Professional Choirmasters. Address: Schlittweg 31, D-6905 Schriesheim/Bergstr, Germany.

REDEL Kurt, b. 8 Oct 1918, Breslau, Germany. Conductor; Flautist. Education: Studied flute, conducting and composition at the Breslau Hochschule für Musik. Career: Conductor and flute soloist from 1938; Professor at Salzburg Mozarteum, 1938; Professor at the Music Academy Detmold, 1943; Debut as flautist outside Germany at Menton, 1950; Founded the Munich Pro Arte Orchestra, 1952; Conducted at Festival de Royaumont and the Semaines Musicales in Paris, 1953; Founder and Artistic Director of the Easter Festival at Lourdes; Conductor of the Mozart Chamber Orchestra of Salzburg. Recordings include: Bach's Brandenburg Concertos, Orchestral Suites, Die Kunst der Fuge, Musikalisches Opfer, Harpsichord and Violin Concertos, Magnificat, Masses and Cantatas; Telemann Concertos for Flute, Oboe, Trumpet, Viola and Violin, St Mark Passion and St Matthew Passion; Vivaldi Four Seasons and other concertos; Concerti Grossi by Handel, Torelli, Corelli, Scarlatti, Stölzel; Music by Marais, Couperin, Caldara, Carissimi and Marcello; Mozart Symphonies, Divertimenti, and Concertante K364; Solo flautist in Mozart Sonatas, Quartets and Concertos; Schubert 4th Symphony with the Czech Philharmonic.

REDGATE Christopher (Frederick), b. 17 Sept 1956, Bolton, Lancashire, England. Musician (Oboist). m. Celia Jane Pilstow, 3 Oct 1981, 2 sons. Education: Chethams School of Music, Manchester; Royal Academy of Music, London. Career: Solo and Chamber performances, England and Europe; Performer-in-Residence, Courses for composers, York University, Aldeburgh School for Advances Musical Studies, Dartington Summer School; Artist-in-Residence, Victorian College of the Arts, Melbourne, Australia, including recitals, lectures, recordings, 1983; Toured Canada, 1985; American debut, Pittsburgh International Festival of New Music, 1986; Professor of Oboe, Darmstadt International School for Contemporary Music, 1986-94; Performed regularly with the Phoenix Wind Quintet, Krosta Trio, Exposé, Lontano; Broadcasts, radio in UK and Netherlands; television; Performed British premiere, Penderecki's Capriccio for Oboe and Strings, conducted by composer; Performed works by Strauss, Martinu, Bennett, colaborated with choreographer Ian Sping and worked for Thames Television; Lecturer on Music and Worship, London Bible College, 1994-. Contributions to: Series of articles on Woodwind instruments in Worship for Christian Music Magazine; Articles on Christianity and the Arts for Kerygma Magazine. Membership: Worship group Wellspring, 1987-; Co-ordinator, the Musician's Christian Fellowship. Hobby: Christianity. Address: 7 Glemsford Drive, Harpenden, Hertfordshire AL5 5RB, England.

REE Jean van, b. 7 Mar 1943, Kerkrade, Holland. Singer (Tenor). Education: Studied with Else Bischof-Bornes in Aachen and Franziska Martienssen-Lohmann in Dusseldorf. Debut: Mainz, 1963, in Zar und Zimmermann. Career: Sang in Basle, Augsburg and Cologne; Guest appearances in Amsterdam, Hamburg, Hanover, Salzburg and Frankfurt; Augsburg, 1971, in the premiere of Rafael Kubelik's opera on the life of Titian, Cornelia Faroli; Teatro Reggio Turin, 1983, in Lulu; Antwerp and Ghent, 1984, as Matteo in Arabella; Other roles include Don Ottavio, Hoffmann, Count Almaviva, Alfredo, and Mephistopheles in Doktor Faust by Busoni; Metropolitan Opera, 1978, as Bicias in Massenet's Thaïs; Sang Berg's Alwa at Barcelona and Vienna, 1987. Recordings include: Les Brigandes, by Offenbach. Address: c/o Staatsoper, Opernring 2, A-1010 Vienna, Austria.

REECE Arley, b. 27 Aug 1945, Yoakum, Texas, USA. Singer (Tenor). Education: Studied at North Texas State University with Eugene Conley and at Manhattan School of Music. Debut: Sang Assad in Die Königin von Saba by Goldmark with the American Opera Society at Carnegie Hall, 1970. Career: Sang with Dallas Civic Opera, Shreveport Symphony, Philadelphia Lyric Opera, Kentucky and Connecticut Opera Associations, Opera Society of Washington and at Lake George Festival; European debut in Prokofiev's The Gambler at Wexford Festival, Ireland, 1973; New York City debut, 1974, as Bacchus; European engagements in Netherlands, Belgium, France including Berlioz Festival, Germany including East and West Berlin, Spain, Italy, Austria, Poland and Switzerland; Appearances in Canada and Iran; British appearances with the Northern Ireland Trust, Scottish Opera, Welsh National Opera and at Edinburgh and Wexford Festivals; Broadcasts: Cardillac (RAI Italy), The Gambler (BBC), Oberon, Ariadne auf Naxos and Wozzeck (Radio France), Tristan und Isolde, Macbeth (Netherlands Radio), Schmidt's Das Buch mit Sieben Siegeln and Dallapiccola's Job (WDR), From the House of the Dead (CBC Canada), Turandot (Radio Warsaw), Tannhäuser (Spanish Radio, Barcelona), Wozzeck (BBC Scotland), Lohengrin (Radio Espana); TV appearances: Lohengrin (Spanish TV), Concert celebrating the 100th Anniversary of Richard Wagner (Polish TV), Das Kleine Mahagonny and Il Ritorno d'Ulisse in Patria (TV Schweiz); Season 1989-90 sang Siegmund and Siegfried in Ring cycles for Warsaw Opera, St François d'Assise for Polish Radio and TV; Lohengrin, Calaf and Samson at Wiesbaden. Other roles include Otello, Canio and Manrico; Sang Don José in Carmen for the first time at the National Theatre in Weimar in 1993; In 1995 sang Parsifal and Tenor Soloist in the Mahler 8th Symphony for the first time at the Brisbane Biennial Fesitval in Australia. Recordings include: Il Ritorno di Ulisse. Address: Martin Luther 63, 46284 Dorsten, Germany.

REED H(erbert) Owen, b. 17 June 1910, Odessa, Missouri, USA. Composer; Author; Conductor. m. (1) Esther Reed, deceased 1981, 2 daughters, (2) Mary Arwood, 12 Aug 1982. Education: University of Missouri, Columbia, 1929-33; BMus, Louisiana State University, Baton Rouge, 1934; MMus, Louisiana State University, 1936; BA, 1937; PhD, Eastman School of Music, University of Rochester, New York, 1939. Career includes: chairman of Theory and Composition, Michigan State University, 1939-67; Acting Head of Music Department, 1957-58; Chairman of Music Composition, 1967-76, Professor Emeritus, 1976-, Michigan State University; Guest Professor, Lecturer, Guest Conductor at many Universities. Compositions include: Symphony No 1, 1939; Overture, 1940; Fanfare for Remembrance, 1986; Concerto for cello and orchestra, 1949; Overture for strings, 1961; Taberbacle for the Sun, 1963; La Fiesta Mexicana for orchestra and wind ensemble, 1968; Works also recorded, kinescoped and videotaped. Recordings include: La Fiesta Mexicana, Dallas Wind Symphony conducted by Howard Dunn; La Fiesta Mexicana, Cincinnati Conservatory of Music Wind Symphony conducted by Eugene Corporon, La Fiesta Mexicana, Tokyo Kosoi Wind Orchestra conducted by Frederick Fennell. Publications include: Basic Music, 1954; Basic Music Workbook, 1954; The Materials of Musical Composition, with Robert G Sidnell, 3 volumes, volume I Fundamentals, 1978, volume II Surveying the Para; meters, 1980, volume III in preparation; Scoring for Percussion, with Joel T Leach, 1978. Honours include: Guggenheim Fellowship; Neil A Kjos Memorial Award for For The Unfortunate, 1975. Memberships: Member of professional organisations. Hobbies: Fishing. Address: c/o ASCAP, ASCAP Building, One Lincoln Plaza, New York, NY 10023, USA.

REED John, b. 30 May 1909, Aldershot, England. Broadcasting Official, BBC, retired; Writer on Music. m. Edith Marion Hampton, 30 Oct 1936, 2 s, 2 d. Education: BA, Honours, English Language and Literature, London University, 1927-30, 1934-35. Publications: Schubert: The Final Years, 1972; Schubert, Great Composer Series, 1978; The Schubert Song Companion, 1985 (Vincent H Duckles Award); Schubert, The Master Musicians Series, 1987. Contributions to: Music Critic, Guardian Newspaper, 1974-80; Musical Times; Music and Letters; Radio 3 Magazine. Memberships: Royal Musical Association; Hallé Society; Victorian Society; Ehrenmitglied, International Franz Schubert Institute of Vienna, 1989; Schubert Institute, (UK). Hobbies: Gardening; Cricket; Reference Books. Address: 130 Fog Lane, Manchester, M20 6SW, England.

REEDER Haydn Brett, b. 27 February 1944, Melbourne, Victoria, Australia. Composer; Pianist; Conductor. Education: BMus, University of Melbourne, 1965; MA, La Trobe University, 1991. Career: Editor for Universal Edition, Schott and Chestre, music publishers, 1970-82; Lecturer, La Trobe University, 1984-88; Commissions from Elision and Melbourne Windpower, 1987-88. Compositions include: Mandala Rite for clarinet and guitar, 1982; Strad Evarie, for cello and piano, 1984; Temi Distratti for trombone, cello and percussion, 1985; Sirens' Hotel, chamber opera, 1986; Masks for piano, 1986; Clashing Auras for wind octet, 1989; Dance in a Mirror of Time, for 7 instruments, 1989; Chants at Play with Solid Background, 1990; Glances Repose, for violin, 1990; Draw neat to the Bell for guitar, 1990; Piano Pieces 1-3. Honours include: Primo, Citta di Trieste Orchestral Competition. Address: c/o APRA, 1A Eden Street, Crows Nest, NSW 2065, Australia.

REES Jonathan, b. 1963, England. Violinist; Director. Education: Studied at the Yehudi Menuhin School and with Dorothy Delay at Juilliard. Career: Student engagements at the Windsor, Gstaad and Llandaff Festivals and three tours of the Netherlands; Later recitals at the Bath, City of London, Brighton, Henley and Salisbury Festivals; Concerto soloist with the Bournemouth Sinfonietta, Philharmonia, London Soloists Chamber Orchestra and the Royal Philharmonic; Concerts with the Academy of St Martin in the Fields at Carnegie Hall, the Festival Hall and at St Martin's Church; Beethoven's Concerto with the Bournemouth Sinfonietta, 1990; Director of the Scottish Ensemble: concerts in Edinburgh, elsewhere in Scotland and in Austria, Belgium, France, Germany, the Netherlands, Norway and North and Central America; Festivals include Berlin, Guelph, Prague, Sofia, Cheltenham and Edinburgh; Royal Command Performances at the Palace of Holyrood House and at Balmoral. Honours: Prize winner, 1978, BBC Young Musician of the Year Competition; 1st Prize, Royal Overseas League Competition, 1979. Address: c/o Anglo-Swiss Management, Suite 35-37 Morley House, 320 Regent Street, London W1R 5AD, England.

REEVE Stephen, b. 15 Mar 1948, London, England. Composer. Education: Composition class of Henri Pousseur, Liège Conservatoire, 1971-72. Career: Major commissions, BBC South, 1975, Institute for Research and Co-ordination in Acoustics and Music, 1980, Institute of Contemporary Arts, Londn, 1985. Compositions: The Kite's Feathers, 1969-70; Japanese Haikai for mezzo and ensemble; Colour Music for woodwind quartet, 1970; Couleurs du Spectre for orchestra with optional light projection, 1972-73; Summer Morning by a lake full of colours, an expansion of Schoenberg's Farben, for large orchestra, 1974; Aux régions éthérées for 3 chamber groups, 1975-76; Grande thèse de la petite-fille de Téthys, an ethnic encyclopaedia for solo cello, 1980-87; L'Oracle de Delphes, music-theatre for brass quintet, 1985; Strophe for solo rock and 4 classical guitars, 1985-86; Les fées dansent selon la mode double, scene for 3-5 dancer-percussionists and 6-10 or more actor extras, 1988-89; O que Zeus apparaisse à l'horizon for gamelan ensemble and tape, 1989-90. Memberships: Performing Rights Society; Association of Professional Composers. Address: 73 Knightsfield, Welwyn Garden City, Herts AL8 7JE, England.

ŘEHÁNEK František, b. 13 September 1921, Mistek, Moravia. Philologist; Musicologist; Teacher. m. MarieŘehánková-Motáčková, 17 April 1954, 1 son. Education: Philosophical Faculty, Faculty of Arts, Charles University in Prague, Czech and English Languages; Music School at Mistek, Philosophical Faculty of University in Brno/Musicology, Music Education: Gabriel Štefánek and Josef Muzika, playing on the violin. Publications include: Janáček's Teaching of Harmony, dissertation, 1965; Harmonic Thinking of Leos Janáček, 1993. Contributions include: Modality in Janáček's Music Theory, in Colloquium Probleme der Modalität, Leos Janáček heute und morgen, Brno 1988, 1994; Leos Janáček's Sonata for Violin and Piano, 1988; Modality in the Works of Vitezslav Novák, in Zprávy Spolecnosti Vitezslava Nováka 17, Brno 1990; To the Problem of Modality with Bohuslav Martinů, in Colloquium Bohuslav Martinů, His Pupils, Friends and Contemporaries, 1990, 1993; Alois Hába's Wallachian Suite/Analysis, in Zprávy Společnosti Vitězslava Nováka, 1995; The Diatonic Modes, Leos Janáček, 1994. Membership: Asociace hudebních umělcu a vědců Praha (Association of Musical Artists and Scientists), Prague. Hobbies: Chess; Touring. Address: Vlnařská 692, 460 01 Liberec VI, Czech Republic.

REICH Steve, b. 3 Oct 1936, NY, USA. Composer. m. Beryl Korot, 30 May 1976, 1 s. Education: BA, Honours, Philosophy, Cornell University, 1957; Studied composition with Hall Overton, 1957-58 and at Juilliard School of Music with William Bergsma, Vincent Persichetti, 1958-61; MA in Music, Mills College, CA, with Darius Milhaud, Luciano Berio, 1963; Studied African drumming, 1970, Balinese Gamelan Semar Pegulingan, 1974 and Hebrew Cantillation, 1976. Career: Formed own ensemble with 3 others, 1966 now with 18 or more members performing worldwide; More than 300 concerts 1971-87; Composer of music, played by major orchestras in USA and Europe also choeographed by leading dance companies. Compositions include: (recorded) Come Out, 1966; Drumming, 1971; Music for 18 musicians, 1976; Telhillim, 1981, 1982, 1994; The Desert Music, 1984; New York Counterpoint, 1985; Sextet, 1985; Three Movements, 1986; The Four Sections, 1987; Different Trains (for String Quartet and Tape), 1988; Co-Commission in 1993 by Vienna Festival, Holland Festival, Hebbel Theater, Berlin, Serious Speakout and The South Bank Centre, London, Festival d'Automne, Paris, Theatre de la Monnaie, Brussels and Brooklyn Academy of Music, Next Wave Festival for The Cave, a new form of opera with video; A collaboration with video artist Beryl Korot; City Life, 1995. Publication: Writing About Music, 1974, French edition 1981, Italian edition, 1994. Contributions to: Various journals. Honours include: Guggenheim Fellow, 1978; Many awards and grants. Memberships: American Academy of Arts and Letters, 1994; Bavarian Academy of Fine Arts, 1995; BBC Prom Concert featuring his music, 1995. Current Management: Allied Artists Management, London and Elizabeth Sobol, IMG Artists, 22 East 71st Street, NY 10021, USA. Address: c/o Allied Artists Agency, 42 Montpelier Square, London SW7 1JZ, England.

REICHERT Manfred, b. 5 May 1942, Karlsruhe, Germany. Conductor. Education: Studied at the Karlsruhe Hochschule, 1961-65; Musicology at the University of Fribourg/Breisgau, 1966-67. Career: Producer at South West German Radio, Baden-Baden, 1967-83; Founded the chamber group Ensemble 13, 1973; Directed the festivals Wintermusik and Musik auf den 49ten at Karlsruhe, 1980 and 1983; Artistic Director of the Festival of European Culture at Karlsruhe, 1983-87; Teacher at the Hochschule für Musik at Karlsruhe from 1984; Conducted the premieres of Hans-Jürgen von Böse's Variations for Strings, 1981, Wolfgang Rihm's Chiffre-Zyklus, 1988, and Gejagte Form, 1989.

REIMANN Aribert, b. 4 Mar 1936, Berlin, Germany. Composer; Pianist. Education: Berlin Hochschule für Musik with Boris Blacher (composition), Ernst Pepping (counterpoint) and Rausch (piano), 1955-59; Musicological studies, Vienna, 1958. Career: Freelance composer, notably of operas; Accompanist to Dietrich Fischer-Dieskau in Lieder recitals; London premieres, Lear and The Ghost Sonata, 1989; Opera Das Schloss premiered at the Deutsche Oper Berlin, 1992. Compositions: Operas: A Dream Play (Strindberg), 1964; Melusine, 1970; Lear (Shakespeare), 1978; The Ghost Sonata (Strindberg), 1984; Troades (Euripides), 1986; Das Schloss (Kafka), 1992; Ballet: Stoffreste, 1957, revised as Die Vogelscheuchen, 1970; Orchestral: Violin Concerto, 1959; Piano Concerto No 1, 1961, No 2, 1972; A Dream Play suite, 1965; Rondes for strings, 1968; Loqui, 1969; Variations, 1975; Sieben Fragmente, 1988; Concerto for violin, cello and orchestra, 1988-89; Vocal: Ein Totentanz, baritone, chamber orchestra, 1960; Hölderlin-Fragments, soprano, orchestra, 1963; 3 Shakespeare Sonnets, baritone, piano, 1964; Epitaph, tenor, 7 instruments, 1965; Verra la Morte, cantata, 1966; Inane, soprano, orchestra, 1968; Zyklus, baritone, orchestra, 1971; Lines, soprano, strings, 1973; Wolkenloses Christmas, Requiem for baritone, cello, orchestra, 1974; Lear, symphony for baritone, orchestra, 1980; Unrevealed, baritone, string quartet; Tre Poemi di Michelangelo, 1985; Neun Sonette der Louize Labé; Chacun sa Chimère, tenor, orchestra, 1981; Three Songs (poems by Edgar Allan Poe), 1982; Requiem, soprano, mezzo, baritone, orchestra, 1982; Apocaplytic Fragment, mezzo, piano, orchestra, 1987; Orchestration of Schumann's Gedichte der Maria Stuart, 1988; Chamber: Piano Sonata, 1958; Canzoni e Ricercare, flute, viola, cello, 1961; Cello Sonata, 1963; Reflexionen, 7 instruments, 1966; Invenzioni, 12 players, 1979; Recent works include: Ladt Lazarus, 1992; Eingedunkelt, 1992; Nightpiece (James Joyce), soprano, piano, 1992; Violin concerto, 1997. Honours include: Rome Prize, 1963; Schumann Prize, Dusseldorf, 1964; Prix de composition musicale, Fondation Prince Pierre de Monaco, 1986; Frankfurt Music Award, 1991. Current Management: B Schotts Söhne, Weihergarten 5, Postfach 3640, 6500 Mainz, Germany. Address: c/o Schott and Co Ltd, 48 Great Marlborough Street, London W1, England.

REINEMANN Udo, b. 6 Aug 1942, Lubeck, Germany. Singer (Baritone). Education: Studied at Krefeld, the Vienna Academy of Music and with Erik Werba and W Steinbruck at the Salzburg Mozarteum, 1962-67. Debut: Song recital at Bordeaux, 1967. Career: Gave more recitals, then studied further with Germaine Lubin in Paris and with Otakar Kraus in London; Many performances in Lieder, opera and oratorio; Founded a vocal quartet, 1975, with Ana-Maria Miranda, Clara Wirtz and Jean-Claude Orliac (Lieder Quartet); Sang in the premiere of Adrienne Clostre's opera Nietzsche, 1978; My Chau Trong Thuy by Dao, 1979. Recordings include: Vocal quartets by Haydn; Lieder by Clara Schumann and Richard Strauss; Posthumous Lieder by Hugo Wolf. Honours include: 1st Prize for concert singing, Vienna Academy of Music, 1967.

REINER Thomas, b. 12 August 1959, Bad Homburg, Germany (Australian resident from 1979). Composer. Education: BA, La Trobe University, 1983; Study with Hans Werner Henze, 1984-86, Barry Conyngham and Peter Tahourdin, 1987-89; MMus, University of Melbourne, 1990; PhD, University of Melbourne, 1996; Electronic and computer music studies, 1997-. Career: Staff Member, University of Melbourne, 1990-91, and Monash University, 1993-98. Compositions include: Journey and Contemplation for guitar and ensemble, 1987; Moth and Spider for alto saxophone and percussion, 1988; Paraphrase, Surge and Response, for orchestra, 1988; Bali Suite, for ensemble, 1989; Fantasy and Fugue for trombone, 1989; Kalorama Prelude for piano, 1989; Schumannianna: An Orchestration of Robert Schumann's Mondnacht, 1991; Baby Orang Utan for piano, 1991; Words for 6 solo voices, 1992; Three Sketches for cello, 1993; Construction in Time for guitar and piano, 1993; Oblique for flute, 1994; Flexious for flute and guitar, 1995-96; Septet for chamber ensemble, 1996; Grace Notes for B flat clarinet, 1997. Publications: Author of articles on musical time and electronic dance music. Honours include: Prizes in the International Witold Lutorlawrki Composers Competition, 1992; Dorian Le Gallienne Composition Award, 1994; Albert H Maggs Composition Award, 1995; International Borwil Composer's Competition, 1997. Address: c/o APRA, 1A Eden Street, Crows Nest, NSW 2065, Australia.

REINHARDT Rolf, b. 3 Feb 1927, Heidelberg, Germany. Conductor. Education: Studied piano with Kwast-Hodapp and composition with Wolfgang Fortner. Career: Conducted at the Stuttgart Opera 1945, in Heidelberg from 1946; Assistant at Bayreuth 1954-57; Conducted opera at Darmstadt, Generalmusikdirektor at the Pfaztheater Kaiserslautern 1958; Trier Opera 1959-68; Professor at the Hochschule für Musik Frankfurt from 1968. Recordings: Bach's Magnificant, Cantatas and Concertos for harpischord and violin; Haydn Sinfonia Concertante and Concertos for trumpet, Horn and oboe; Mozart Violin Concertos, Concertante K297b, Thamos King of Egypt and Litaniae Lauretanae; Handel Organ Concertos and Silete Venti; Stamitz Viola Concerto, Sinfonia Concertante; Bartók 1 and Brahms 2 Piano Concertos, with György Sandor; Mozart Bastien and Bastienne, La Finta Giardiniera; Bartók Music for Strings, Percussion and Celesta, Wooden Prince and Miraculous Mandarin; Beethoven Egmont; Schumann Cello Concerto, Violin Fantasia, Konzertstück for four horns and D minor Introduction and Allegro; Dvorak and Goldmark Violin Concertos, with Bronislav Gimpel; Lieder accompianist for Fritz Wunderlich. Address: Staatliche Hochschule für Musik, Escherheimer Landstrasse 33, Postfach 2326 Frankfurt, Germany.

REINHARDT-KISS Ursula, b. 3 Nov 1938, Letmathe, Sauerland, Germany. Soprano. Education: Studied with Ellen Bosenius in Cologne and Irma Beilke in Berlin. Debut: Saarbrücken, 1967 as Marie in Der Waffenschmied. Career: Sang in Saarbrücken until 1969 then Aachen, 1969-71; Guest appearances in Lubeck, Cologne, Zurich, Antwerp, Milan, Copenhagen and Rome; Drottningholm in 1983 in Il Fanatico Burlato by Cimarosa; Komische Oper Berlin as Susanna and Lulu, and Dresden Staatsoper as Aminta in Die schweigsame Frau; Sang at Graz in 1985, in Angelica Vincitrice di Alcina by Fux, returning in 1987 in the premiere of Der Rattenfänger by Cerha; Also sings Salomé in Hérodiade by Massenet. Recordings: Sacred Music by Mozart; Lazarus by Schubert; Epitaph For Garcia Lorca, by Nono. Address: c/o Voreinigte Bühnen, Kaiser Josef Platz 10, A-8010 Graz, Austria.

REINHART Gregory, b. 1955, USA. Singer (Bass). Career: Sang at Tourcoing, 1981, in Paisiello's Il Re Teodoro, Innsbruck, 1982 and 1987, in Cesti's Oronte and Semiramide; King of Scotland in Ariodante at Nancy (1983) and in Henze's English Cat at the Paris Opéra-Comique, 1984; Nice, 1986, as Henry VIII in Anna Bolena and at Aix-en-Provence as Ismenor in Campra's Tancrède; London concert performances of Poppea and Moses und Aron, 1988; Opera-Bastille Paris, 1990, as Panthe in Les Troyens and Santa Fe, 1992, as Mozart's Commendatore; Sang Basil Hallward in the premiere of Lowell Liebermann's The Picture of Dorian Gray, Monte Carlo, 1996; Other roles include Lord Robinson in Il Matrimonio Segreto, Monteverdi's Seneca, Huascar in Les Indes Galantes and Douglas in Rossini's Donna del Lago. Recordings: Handel's Tamerlano (CBS); Tancrède by Campra (Erato); Rameau's Zoroastre (Harmonia Mundi); Messiah (RCA). Address: c/o Santa Fe Opera, PO Box 2408, Santa Fe, NM 87504, USA.

REJSEK Radek, b. 6 July 1959, Prague, Czech Republic. Composer; Musical Editor. m. Marta Kasalova, 8 December 1984, 2 sons, 1 daughter. Education: Conservatorium, Prague; Academy of Musical Arts, Brno. Debut: Praha, 1980. Career: Music Editor, Radio Prague, 1987-; Recording Supervisor, Teacher, Musical Theory, Conservatorium of Prague, 1992-; Carillon Player, Prague's Loretto Church. Compositions: Ludus Spatic, for 2 Organs, 1991; Carmen Campanarum, 1992; Thre Pictures of Jan Zrzavy, 1992; Musica per Organum, 1997. Recordings: Music of Prague's Loretto, 1995. Publications: The Radio Project of Radio Prague: Czech Historical Organs and Bells, 1989. Contributions to: Czech Musical Magazines. Honours: 2nd Prize, Competition Musica Nova, 1992. Memberships: Czech Society of Electroaccoustic Music; Czech Society of Spiritual Music; Society of Composers Pritomnost. Hobbies: Swimming; Skiing; Tourism. Address: Badeniho 5, 160 00 Praha 6, Czech Republic.

RELTON William, b. 1 Apr 1930, Halifax, Yorkshire, England. Symphony Administrator. m. Elisa De Paola, 18 Jan 1966, 2 children. Education: Saltley College; Royal College of Music. Career: Served with the RAF, 1948-49; Freelance Trumpeter, London, 1952-55; Trumpeter, Sadler's Wells Opera, London, 1955-57, and BBC Concert Orchestra, London, 1957-60; Music Producer, 1960-70, Orchestra Manager, 1970-75, General Manager, 1975-86, BBC Symphony Orchestra; General Manager of Eastern Orchestral Board, 1986-; Assessor, Conservatoire de Lausanne, Birmingham School of Music, Royal Academy of Music, Bergen Conservatoire and National Band Festivals; Composer; International Adjudicator; Chairman, National Brass Band Championships; Composer for brass bands; Lecturer of Music in Britain. Honour: Award for Outstanding Services to Orchestral Concert Giving in England, Association of British Orchestras, 1995. Address: 23 Bark Place, London, W2 4AT.

REMEDIOS Alberto, b. 27 Feb 1935, Liverpool, England. Tenor Singer. Education: Studied in Liverpool with Edwin Francis and at The Royal College of Music. Debut: Sadler's Wells Opera, 1957 as Tinca in Il Tabarro. Career includes: Has sung at Sadler's Wells, English National Opera in many roles; Toured Australia with Joan Sutherland, 1965; At Covent Garden from 1965, as Dimitri in Boris Godunov, Erik, Florestan, Mark in The Midsummer Marriage, Siegfried, Bacchus and Max; Camden Town Hall 1968 in the British premiere of L'Arlesiana by Cilea; BBC Radio, 1970 as Huon in Oberon; Sang Mozart's Don Ottavio in South Africa, 1972; US debut as Dimitri and Don Carlos, at San Francisco; Metropolitan Opera debut in 1976 as Bacchus; Scottish Opera in 1983 as Walther in Die Meistersinger; Performances of Otello, Siemund, Florestan and Radames for Australian Opera; Sang in Schoenberg's Gurrelieder at Melbourne, 1988; Concert repertoire also includes Mahler's 8th Symphony at Promenade Concerts in London; Returned to Scotland in 1989 as Stravinsky's Oedipus; Sang in Reginald Goodall's Memorial Concert, London, 1991; Appeared in Janácek's The Excursions of Mr Broucek at London Coliseum, 1992 and sang Tristan in concert performances of Wagner's Opera at Nashville, TN, 1993. Recordings include: The Ring of the Nibelung, conducted by Reginald Goodall. Honours: Prizewinner, Sofia International Competition, 1963; CBE, 1981. Address: c/o English National Opera, St Martin's Lane, London, WC2, England.

REMEDIOS Ramon, b. 9 May 1940, Liverpool, England. Singer (Tenor). Education: Studied at the Guildhall School of Music, the National School of Opera and the London Opera Centre. Career: Has sung with Opera For All, Scottish Opera, Welsh National Opera and European companies; Notably as Alfredo, Macduff, Ismaele in Nabucco, Grigory/Dimitri, Don Ottavio, the Duke of Mantua, the Painter in Lulu, Skuratov (From the House of the Dead), Tamino and Almaviva; English National Opera: Alfredo, Rodolfo, Don José, Pinkerton, Paris in La Belle Hélène, Smith in the British premiere production of Christmas Eve (1988) and Lensky in Eugene Onegin; Covent Garden, 1990, as Uldino in a new production of Attila; Television appearances in Top C's and Tiaras, and The Word by Rick Wakeman; Season 1992 as Sir Bruno Robertson in I Puritani at Covent Garden; Concert engagements include operatic arias in Glasgow, a Viennese Evening at the Festival Hall and Verdi's Requiem (Royal Festival Hall, Mar 1991). Recordings include: The Word, with the Eton College Choir; Kalman's Countess Maritza with New Sadler's Wells Opera; A Suite of Gods, songs by Rick Wakeman. Honours: School Tenor Prize, Ricordi Prize and Countess of Munster Trust, Guildhall School of Music; Finalist, Kathleen Ferrier Competition. Address: c/o Norman McCann International Artists Ltd, The Coach House, 56 Lawrie Park Gardens, London SE26 6XJ, England.

REMENIKOVA Tanya, b. 31 Jan 1946, Moscow, USSR. Cellist (Performer and Teacher). m. Alexander Braginsky, 15 Sept 1967. Education: Moscow Conservatoire, studied with Professor Rostropovich. Career: Regular appearances in recitals and with various orchestras, including Israel Philharmonic, Orchestra National de Belgique; Foreign tours: Europe, Taiwan, People's Republic of China; New York debut, 1979; Radio: BBC, RTB (Belgium), WFMT (Chicago), WQXR (New York); North American tours: Chicago, New York, Washington DC, Minneapolis, Los Angeles, elsewhere; Professor of Cello, School of Music, University of Minnesota; Artist-in-Residence, Churchill College, Cambridge, 1981, 1986; Premieres of Stephen Paulus, American Vignettes, 1988. Recordings: Stravinsky, Suite Italienne; Shostakovich, Sonata op 40; Britten, Sonata in C. Honours: Gold Medal, Gaspar Cassado Cello Competition, 1969; Eugene Ysaye Award for Musical Contribution, Brussels, 1979. Memberships: College Music Society; American String Teachers' Association. Current Management: Richard Berg. Address: 4141 Dupont Avenue South, Minneapolis, MN 55409, USA.

REMES Vaclav, b. 1950, Czechoslovakia. Violinist. Education: Studied at the Prague Conservatory. Career: Founder member of the Prazak String Quartet, 1972; Tour of Finland, 1973, followed by appearances at competitions in Prague and Evian; Concerts in Salzburg, Munich, Paris, Rome, Berlin, Cologne and Amsterdam; Tour of Britain, 1985, including Wigmore Hall debut; Tours of Japan, the USA, Australia and New Zealand; Tour of UK, 1988, and concert at the Huddersfield Contemporary Music Festival, 1989; Recitals for the BBC, Radio France, Dutch Radio, the WDR in Cologne and Radio Prague; Appearances with the Smetana and LaSalle Quartets in Mendelssohn's Octet. Recordings: Several albums. Honours: 1st Prize, Chamber Music Competition of the Prague Conservatory, 1974; Grand Prix, International String Quartet Competition, Evian Music Festival, 1978; 1st Prize, National Competition of String Quartets in Czechoslovakia, 1978; Winner, String Quartet of the Prague Spring Festival, 1978.

REMMERT Birgit, b. 1966, Germany. Singer (Alto). Education: Studied at the Detmold Musikhochschule with Helmut Kretschmer. Career: Sang in Beethoven's Ninth under Nikolaus Harnoncourt in London, 1991, and again under Giulini in Stockholm, 1994; Further concerts include Mendelssohn's Walpurgisnacht in Graz, Biber's Requiem and Vespers under Harnoncourt in Vienna, the song cycle Sunless by Mussorgsky, in Amsterdam, and Das Lied von der Erde under Philippe Herreweghe at the Théatre des Champs-Elysées, Paris; Holland Festival 1992, as Martha in Tchaikovsky's Iolantha, Hamburg, 1993 as Erda in the Ring and Ulrica at Dresden; Zurich Opera, 1994, as Dalila, Suzuki and Third Lady in Die Zauberflote; Other repertory includes Mahler's Eighth and Das Klagende Lied (with Chailly at the Concertgebouw), Mahler 3rd Symphony with Sir Simon Rattle in Birmingham and the Nurse in Monteverdi's Poppea at Salzburg Festival. Recordings include: Beethoven's Ninth; Lieder by Brahms, Clara Schumann and Tchaikovsky; Bach Cantatas with Peter Schreier; Brüchner, Te Deum and f-moll Messe with Welser-Möst. Honours include: Lieder Prize at the Palma d'oro Competition, Ligure.

RENDALL David, b. 11 Oct 1948, London, England. Singer (Tenor). Education: Studied at the Royal Academy of Music and at the Salzburg Mozarteum, Debut: Glyndebourne Touring Company, 1975, as Ferrando in Così fan tutte. Career: Covent Garden from 1975, as the Italian Tenor in Der Rosenkavalier, Almaviva, Matteo, Rodolfo, Des Grieux in Manon and Rodrigo in a new production of La Donna del Lago by Rossini (1985); Glyndebourne Festival, 1976, Ferrando, returned as Belmonte and Tom Rakewell (1989); English National Opera from 1976, as Leicester in Mary Stuart, Rodolfo, Alfredo, Tamino and Pinkerton; European debut at Angers, 1975, as the High Priest in Idomeneo; North American debut, Ottawa, 1977, as Tamino; New York City Opera, 1978, Rodolfo and Alfredo; San Francisco debut, 1978, Don Ottavio; Metropolitan Opera from 1980, as Ottavio, Ernesto, Belmonte, Idomeneo, Lenski, Ferrando, Alfred in Die Fledermaus and Mozart's Titus; Lyon Opera, 1983, in the title role of La Damnation de Faust by Berlioz; Further engagements in Amsterdam, Berlin, Paris, Milan, Hamburg, Tel Aviv, Turin, Washington, Vienna, Dresden, Chicago, Santa Fe and Munich; Other operatic roles include Gounod's Faust (Palermo) and the Duke of Mantua; Many concert appearances in Europe and the USA; Sang the Duke of Mantua and Matteo at Covent Garden, 1989/90; Cavaradossi with English National Opera, 1990; Season 1992 as Don Antonio in the stage premiere of Gerhard's The Duenna (Madrid), Pinkerton at the Coliseum and for Welsh National Opera; Genoa 1996-97, as Hoffmann and Don José. Recordings: Maria Stuarda; Così fan tutte; Ariodante; Mozart's Requiem; Beethoven's Missa solemnis; Madama Butterfly; Bruckner's Te Deum. Honours: Young Musician of the Year Award, 1973; Gulbenkian Fellowship, 1975. Address: Portland Wallis Artists' Management, 50 Great Portland Street, London W1N 5AH, England.

RENICKE Volker, b. 3 July 1929, Bremen, Germany. Conductor; Professor. m. Rey Nishiuchi, 5 Apr 1975. Education: Nordwestdeutsche Musikakademie, Detmold, 1950-54; Accademia Chigiana, Siena, with Paul van Kempen. Career: In Korea, 1991, with Korean Symphony Orchestra in the Korean Orchestral Festival; Tokyo Mozart 200 Anniversary of Death, Idomeneo, 1991; In Seoul Opera Favorita and Fidelio at National Theatre, 1992; International Festival in Tsuyama, Japan, Mozart Tito, 1993; Salzburg Mozart Requiem, 1993; Guest conducting and concerts in England, France, Germany, Netherlands, Luxembourg, Switzerland, Italy, Yugoslavia and Korea; Concerts with Kyushu Symphony Orchestra, Yomiuri Orchestra, Tokyo Metropolitan Orchestra, Tokyo Philharmonic Orchestra, Tokyo Symphony Orchestra, Japan Philharmonic Orchestra, New Japan Philharmonic Orchestra, Shinsei Orchestra, Osaka Philharmonic Orchestra, Kansai Philharmonic Orchestra, Teleman Orchestra, Sapporo Symphony Orchestra: In Korea with Seoul Philharmonic Orchestra and Korean Symphony Orchestra; Zauberflöte and Traviata in Opernhaus Köln, 1995. Recordings: With Jörg Demus and NHK Orchestra members; Piano concertos of Bach, Haydn, Mozart, Debussy, Franck, Fauré; With Karl Suske, violin, and NHK Orchestra members; Recordings of Vivaldi and Bach; Humperdinck's Hansel and Gretel, in Japanese, with Yomiuri Orchestra. Membership: Kojimachi Rotary Club, Tokyo. Hobby: Philosophy. Current Management: Christoph Schellbach, Representation of Classical Musicians in Europa, Lutherstrasse 7, D 34117 Kassel, Germany. Address: 5-26-15 Okuzawa, Setagaya-ku, 158 Tokyo, Japan.

RENNERT Jonathan, b. 17 Mar 1952, London, England. Organist; Conductor; Writer. m. Sheralyn Ivil, 10 April 1992. Education: St Paul's School, London; Foundation Scholar, Royal College of Music; Organ Scholar, St John's College, Cambridge; Stewart of Rannoch Scholar in Sacred Music, Cambridge University; MA (Cantab); FRCO; FRCCO (hc); ARCM; LRAM. Career: Numerous organ recitals, radio and TV appearances, UK, France, Belgium, Luxembourg, Netherlands, Sweden, Denmark, Hungary, Slovakia, Germany, Switzerland, Malta, West Indies, USA, Canada, Australia, Japan; Director of Music, Holy Trinity Church, Barnes, London, 1969-71; Musical Director, Cambridge Opera, 1972-74; Director of Music, St Jude's, Courtfield Gardens, London, Conductor, American Community Choirs in London and St Jude's Singers, 1975-76; Acting Director of Music, St Matthew's, Ottawa, Canada, 1976-78; Director of Music, St Michael's, Cornhill, City of London, Musical Director, St Michael's Singers, 1979-; Musician in Residence, Grace Cathedral, San Francisco, 1982; Conductor, Elizabethan Singers, 1983-88; Conductor, English Harmony, 1988-; Moderating Examiner and Mentor, Associated Board, Royal Schools of Music, 1983-; Festival Director, Cornhill Festival of British Music, 1982-88; Administrator, International Congress of Organists, Cambridge, 1987; Course Director and Chairman, Central London Committee, Royal School of Church Music, 1995-; Director of Music, St Mary-at-Hill, City of London, 1996-; Master of Choristers, Reigate St Mary's Choir School, 1997-. Recordings: Various as solo organist, conductor, organ accompanist and harpsichord continuo player. Publications: William Crotch (1775-1847): composer, teacher, artist, 1975; George Thalben-Ball: a biography, 1979. Contributions to: The New Grove Dictionary of Music and Musicians and musical journals and publications. Address: St Michael's Vestry, Cornhill, London EC3V 9DS, England.

RENNERT Wolfgang, b. 1 Apr 1922, Cologne, Germany. Conductor. m. (1) Anny Schlem, 1958, (2) Ulla Berkewicz, 1971, div. 1975, 1 daughter. Education: Mozarteum, Salzburg, 1940-43, 1945-47. Debut: Dusseldorf Opera, 1948, Un Ballo in Maschera.

Career: Conducted Dusseldorf Opera, 1947-50, Kiel, 1950-53; Assistant Conductor, Frankfurt Opera, 1953-67; Music Director, Staatstheater am Gärtnerplatz, Munich, 1967-72; General Music Director and Opera Director, National Theatre, Mannheim, 1980-85; Conducted Mozart's Il Rè Pastore at Rome, 1988, Die Zauberflöte at Dallas; Teatro Sao Carlos, Lisbon, 1989, Die Walküre; Staatsoper, Berlin, 1990; Semperoper, Dresden, 1991; Komische Oper Berlin, 1990; Season 1992 with Arabella at Dresden. Recordings: Several labels. Current Management: Allied Artists Agency, 42 Montpelier Square, London SW7 1JZ, England.

RENTOWSKI Wieslaw (Stanislaw Vivian), b. 23 Nov 1953, Bydgoszcz, Poland. Composer; Organist. m. Magdalena Kubiak, 5 Sept 1985, 1 son. Education: MA, Psychology, University of Lodz, 1978; MA, Organ, Academy of Music, Lodz, 1985; MA, Composition, Fr Chopin Academy of Music, Warsaw, 1987; MMus, Composition, Louisiana State University School of Music, 1991. Debut: Carnegie Hall, Lagniappe for 8 instruments, 1991. Career: Compositions performed at: International Festival of Contemporary Music, Warsaw Autumn, 1984, 1986, 1987, 1989; Internationale Sinziger Orgelwoche, Bonn, 1989, 1990; Festival International de Lanaudière, Canada, 1989; International Festival of Contemporary Music, Baton Rouge, USA, 1990, 1991; Organist, many performances and recordings including solo recitals and chamber concerts in Warsaw, Banff, Toronto, Bayreuth, Baton Rouge and New Orleans. Compositions: Por dia de anos, published in 1987 and 1989; Chorea minor, published 1989. Recordings: Anagram, 1986; Wayang, 1989; Por dia de anos, 1990 11 compositions recorded by Polish National Public Radio; Anagram, 1986; Wayang, 1989. Contributions to: Intellectual music harmony, article to Ruch Muzyczny national musical magazine, Poland, 1989. Hobbies: Architecture; Historic landmarks; Swimming; Driving. Address: Louisiana State University School of Music, Baton Rouge, LA 70803, USA.

RENZETTI Donato, b. 30 Jan 1950, Milan, Italy. Conductor. Education: Studied at the Conservatorio Giuseppe Verdi, Milan. Career: Assisted Claudio Abbado in Milan, then conducted the Verdi Requiem in Salzburg; Gave Rigoletto at Verona in 1981 and has since worked at most Italian opera houses; Conducted the premiere of Corghi's Gargantua at Turin, 1984; Paris Théâtre Musical, Macbeth; Conducted La Sonnambula at the Chicago Lyric Opera, 1988, and Le nozze di Figaro at Rome, 1989; Bonn Opera and Teatro Fenice, Venice, 1990, with Il Barbiere di Siviglia and Ernani; Has given orchestral concerts in Italy and elsewhere; Conducted Turandot at the 1996 Macerata Festival. Honours include: Prize winner at the Gino Marinuzzi International Competition, 1976; Bronze Medal, Ernest Ansermet Competition at Geneva, 1978; Guido Cantelli Prize at Milan, 1980. Address: c/o Teatro dell'Opera, Piazza Beniamino Gigli 8, I-00184 Rome, Italy.

RENZI Emma, b. 8 Apr 1926, Heidelberg, Transvaal, South Africa. Singer (Soprano). Education: Studied at the College of Music in Kapstad, at the London Opera Centre, with Santo Santonocito in Catania and with Virginia Borroni in Milan. Debut: Karlsruhe, 1961, as Sieglinde. Career: Has sung in major cities worldwide including La Scala, Milan, Genoa, Lisbon, Buenos Aires, Barcelona, Edinburgh, Mexico City, Johannesburg, Naples, Rome and Munich; Italian Radio, 1977, in Parisina by Mascagni; Verona Arena, 1989; Other roles include Norma, Aida, Amelia (Un Ballo in Maschera), Tosca, Leonora (Il Trovatore), Turandot, the Duchess of Parma in Doktor Faust, Abigail, Lady Macbeth, Elisabeth, and Countess Almaviva. Address: 39 Auckland Avenue, Auckland Park, Johannesburg 2092, Gauleng, South Africa.

REPIN Vadim, b. 1974, Novosibirsk, Siberia. Concert Violinist. Career: Performances with the Royal Concertgebouw Berlin Symphonieorchester, Suddeutscher Rundfunk, Royal, Israel and St Petersburg Philharmonics, NHK and Tokyo Metropolitan, Kirov Orchestra, Hallé and Sydney Symphony; USA appearances with the Cleveland, Chicago, Minnesota Symphonies and Los Angeles Philharmonic; Season 1996-97 with the New York Philharmonic; Conductors include Menuhin, Bychkov, Gergiev, Prêtre (Orchestre de Paris), Rozhdestvensky Jansons and Boulez; Chamber Music partners include Boris Berezovsky, Bella Davidovich and Alexander Melnikov. Recordings include: Shostakovich No 1 and Prokofiev 2, with the Hallé Orchestra under Nagano; Tchaikovsky and Sibelius Concertos with the London Symphony under Krivine; Prokofiev Violin Sonatas and Five Melodies, with Berezovsky (Erato/Warner Classics). Honours include: Winner, Queen Elizabeth Competition, Brussels. Address: c/o IMG Artists, Media House, 3 Burlington Lane, London W4 2TH, England.

REPPA David, b. 2 Nov 1926, Hammond, Indiana, USA. Scenic Designer. Education: Professional training at the Metropolitan Opera, 1957-58. Debut: Designed Le Nozze di Figaro for North Shore Opera, New York, 1960. Career: Has worked with Sarah Caldwell's Opera Company of Boston and in Miami and San Francisco; Debut with the Metropolitan Opera, 1974, Duke Bluebeard's Castle and Gianni Schicchi; Other designs include Aida, 1976, Dialogues des Carmélites, 1977, and Don Carlos, 1979; As staff scenic designer has worked with most Metropolitan Opera scenic designers, supervising painting and construction of sets and adapting productions for the company's former spring tours. Address: c/o Metropolitan Opera, Lincoln Center, New York, NY 10023, USA.

REPPEL Carmen, b. 27 Apr 1941, Gummersbach, Germany. Singer (Soprano). Education: Studied at the Hamburg Musikhochschule with Erna Berger. Debut: Flensburg, 1968, as Elisabeth de Valois. Career: Has sung in Hanover, Hamburg, Frankfurt, Cologne, Mannheim, Wiesbaden and Kassel; Bayreuth Festival, 1977-80, as Freia and Gutrune, and in Die Walküre and Parsifal; Wuppertal, 1983, in a concert performance of Schwarzschwanenreich by Siegfried Wagner; San Francisco, 1983, as Ariadne auf Naxos; Sang Mozart's Electra at Stuttgart, 1985; Hamburg and Vienna, 1985, as Leonore and Chrysothemis; Munich Opera, 1986, as Andromache in the premiere of Troades by Reimann; Zurich Opera, 1986, Salome; Further appearances in Berlin, Zurich, Barcelona, Milan and Tokyo; Other roles include Fiordiligi, Donna Anna, Mélisande, Mimi, Liu, Marenka in The Bartered Bride, Violetta, Desdemona, Leonora in Il Trovatore, Ariadne, Salome, Elsa and Sieglinde; Sang in Flavio Testi's Ricardo III at La Scala, 1987; Sieglinde in Die Walküre at Bologna, 1988; Strauss's Ariadne and Salome, Turin, 1989; Salome at the Torre del Lago festival, 1989. Recordings include: Freia and Gerhilde in Der Ring des Nibelungen, from Bayreuth; Les Troyens by Berlioz; Chrysothemis in Götz Friedrich's film version of Elektra.

RESA Neithard, b. 1954, Berlin, Germany. Violist. Education: Studied in Berlin with Michel Schwalbe, Cologne with Max Rostal, USA with Michael Tree. Career: Prizewinner of German Music Foundation, 1978; Principal Viola of Berlin Philharmonic, 1978; Co-founded the Philharmonia Quartet, Berlin, giving concerts throughout Europe, USA and Japan; British debut, 1987, playing Haydn, Szymanowski and Beethoven at Wigmore Hall; Bath Festival, 1987, playing Mozart, Schumann and Beethoven; Other repertoire includes quartets by Bartók, Mendelssohn, Nicolai, Ravel and Schubert; Quintets by Brahms, Weber, Reger and Schumann. Address: Berlin Philharmonic, Philharmonie, Matthaikirchstrasse 1, D-1000 Berlin 30, Germany.

RESCIGNO Nicola, b. 28 May 1916, New York City, USA. Opera Conductor; Artistic Director. Education: Italian Jurisprudence Degree, Rome. Debut: Brooklyn New York Academy of Music, 1943. Career: Co-Founder, Artistic Director, Chicago Lyric Opera, 1954-56; Presented American Debut of Maria Callas; Co-Founder/Artistic Director, Dallas Civic Opera (currently The Dallas Opera), 1957-; Regularly presents American debuts; past debuts include, Sutherland, Vickers, Berganza, Montarsolo, Caballé, Knie, Domingo, Olivero, Dimitrova, W Meier; Instrumental in presenting baroque opera including American stage premieres of Handel's Alcina, Monteverdi's L'Incoronazione di Poppea, Samson, Giulio Cesare, and Vivaldi's Orlando Furioso; Guest Conductor: San Francisco, Metropolitan, Chicago Lyric, Cincinnati, Philadelphia, Washington, Tulsa, Houston, at the Metropolitan Opera has conducted Donizetti's Don Pasquale and L'Elisir d'Amore, Rossini's Italiana in Algeri and Verdi's La Traviata; Guest Conductor in Canada, South America, Italy, Portugal, UK, Switzerland, Austria and France; Conducted the premiere of Argento's The Aspern Papers, Dallas, 1988; Werther at Rome, 1990; Aida at the 1990 Caracalla Festival, Rome; Season 1991 with Il Barbiere di Siviglia at Philadelphia. Current Management: CAMI Conductors Division.

RESNIK Regina, b. 30 Aug 1924, New York City, New York, USA. Singer (Mezzo-soprano). m. (1) Harry W Davies, 1947, 1 son, (2) Arbit Blatas, 1975. Education: Hunter College, New York. Debut: Concert, Brooklyn Academy of Music, 1942. Career: Appeared as Leonora in Fidelio, Mexico City, 1943; With New York City Opera, 1944-45; Debut as Leonore in Il Trovatore, 1944, with company, 1946-, Metropolitan Opera, New York; Conducted seminars on opera, New School for Social Research; Subsequently sang at venues including Chicago Opera Theater and San Francisco Opera; Bayreuth debut, as Sieglinde, 1953; London debut, 1957; Has sung at Vienna, Berlin, Stuttgart, Buenos Aires, Paris, Marseilles and Salzburg; Directed Carmen, Hamburg State Opera, 1971; San Francisco, 1972, as Claire in the US premiere of Der Besuch der alten Dame by Einem; Returned, 1982, as the Countess in The Queen of Spades; Produced and acted in Falstaff, Teatr Wielki, Warsaw, Poland, 1975. Honours: President's Medal, Commandeur, Arts et Lettres, France. Address: 50 West 56th Street, New York, NY 10019, USA.

RESS Ulrich, b. 29 Oct 1958, Augsburg, Germany. Singer (Tenor). Education: Studied at Augsburg Conservatory, 1975-78, with Leonore Kirchstein from 1979. Career: Sang at Stadttheater Augsburg, 1979-84, notably as Idamante and Rossini's Almaviva; Engaged at Bayerische Staatsoper from 1984, as Mozart's Pedrillo and Monostatos, Verdi's Bardolph and Macduff, Beppe in Pagliacci and Pong in Turandot; Sang the Steersman and Strauss's Truffaldino at Munich, 1991; Guest appearances at Bayreuth and Barcelona, 1988-89, as David in Meistersinger, Strasbourg and Nice, Jacquino, 1989. Recordings: Young Servant in video of Elektra conducted by Abbado; Bardolph in Falstaff conducted by Colin Davis; Massimilia Doni by Schoeck. Address: c/o Bayerische Staatsoper, Postfach 100184, 8000 Munich 1, Germany.

RETHY Ester, b. 22 Oct 1912, Budapest, Hungary. Singer (Soprano). Education: Studied in Budapest and Vienna. Debut: Budapest, 1934, as Micaela in Carmen. Career: Sang at the Vienna Staatsoper until 1949 in operas by Mozart and Strauss; Salzburg Festival, 1937-39, as Susanna and Sophie (Der Rosenkavalier); Vienna Volksoper from 1948, notably in Der Zigeunerbaron and Eine Nacht in Venedig by Johann Strauss and in operettas by Kalman and Lehar; Returned to Salzburg, 1950 and 1952, as Donna Elvira and as Europa in the first public performance of Richard Strauss's Die Liebe der Danae; Other roles included Handel's Rodelinda and Wagner's Eva. Recordings include: Der Bettelstudent by Millöcker; Le nozze di Figaro and Die Liebe der Danae from Salzburg.

RETZEL Frank, b. 11 Aug 1948, Detroit, Michigan, USA. Composer; Organist; Conductor; Educator. m. Kathleen Buhl, 9 Aug 1975. Education: Private Studies, Organ, Piano, Counterpoint, Composition, Noel Goemanne and Lode Van Dessal, 1958-69; Studies, Palestrina Institute, 1960-63; BMus, MMus, Wayne University, Detroit, 1972, 1974; PhD, University of Chicago, 1978; Fulbright Hays Postdoctoral Fellowship, 1982-83. Career: As Composer, Performances in Major Cities of the US and Europe; Commission to Compose Opening Procession and Closing of Mass with Pope John Paul II in New York City, 1995; Participant in Gallery Exhibition, Mnemonic Conflux, Provincetown and New York City; As Organist and Music Director, Several Posts, Presently Organist and Music Director, Church of St Marys Nativity, New York City; Educator, Faculties of Catholic University of America, Brooklyn College, New York University; Professor of Music, Fordham University, New York City. Compositions: Portrait in Fantasy; Blue-Line Strophes; Summer Songs; Tamarind; Papal Music; Trinity; Daughter of Dawn; O Sons O Daughters; Sekem; Chansonnier; Horae; Line Drawings and Earthen Clay Figures; Movements; Lumen; Canticles; A Bestiary; Amber Glass; Swamp Music; Schism I; Tapestries. Recordings: Chansonnier, CD; Horae, CD; Line Drawings and Earthern Clay Figures, CD; Schism I, LP. Contributions to: Music Heritage Society Review; Notes. Memberships: American Guild of Organists; American Music Center; American Musicological Society; League of Composers/International Society of Contemporary Music, Board of Directors; Society of Composers; Music Commission, Diocese of Brooklyn, New York; New York City Speaker's Advisory Board for Music Education. Hobbies: Reading; Movies; Billiards. Address: 84-49 168 Street, Apt 6W, Jamaica Estates, NY 11432, USA.

REUTER Rolf, b. 7 Oct 1926, Leipzig, Germany. Conductor. Education: Studied at the Dresden Hochschule für Musik, 1958-61. Career: Repetiteur and conductor at Eisenach, 1951-55; Musical Director at Meinigen, 1955-61; Leipzig Opera, 1961-73 (Generalmusikdirektor from 1963); Music Director at Weimar, 1979-80, Komische Oper Berlin from 1981; Professor of Music and Conductor of the orchestra at the Hanns Eisler Hochschule, Berlin; Guest conductor in Cuba, France, Germany, Yugoslavia, Czechoslovakia, Tokyo, Houston, Rome, Buenos Aires, Copenhagen, Moscow and Prague; Gave Der Ring des Nibelungen at the Paris Opéra, 1978, and Tristan und Isolde at the Berlin Staatsoper; Gave the premieres of Guayana Johnny by Alan Bush (1966) and Judith by Siegfried Matthus (1975); Visited Covent Garden and Wiesbaden, 1989, with the company of the Komische Oper, conducting The Bartered Bride and Judith; Conducted a new production of Der Freischütz at the Komische Oper, 1989; Le nozze di Figaro for New Israeli Opera, 1992. Recordings include: Beethoven's incidental music for Egmont; Handel: Oratorio L'Allegro, il Moderato ed il Penseroso. Address: Komische Oper, Behrenstrasse 55/57, D-1080 Berlin, Germany.

REVERDY Michèle, b. 12 Dec 1943, Alexandria, Egypt. Composer. 1 daughter. Education: Literature, Sorbonne, Paris; Counterpoint with Alain Weber, Analysis with Claude Ballif, Composition with Olivier Messiaen, Paris Conservatory; Casa de Velazquez, Madrid. Career: Teaching, lycées, 1965-74; Professor of Analysis, regional and municipal conservatories, 1974-83; Producer, Radio-France, 1978-80; Professor, Class of Analysis, Paris Conservatory, 1983-. Compositions include: Kaleidoscope for harpsichord and flute, 1975; Number One for guitar, 1977; Météores for 17 instruments, 1978; L'Ile aux Lumières for solo violin and string orchestra, 1983; Scenic Railway for 16 instruments, 1983; La Nuit Qui Suivit Notre Dernier Dîner, chamber opera, 1984; Triade for guitar, 1986; Trois Fantaisies de Gaspard de la Nuit for choir or 12-voice ensemble, 1987; Sept Enluminures for soprano, clarinet, piano and percussion, 1987; Propos Félins for string orchestra and children's choir, 1988; Le

Cercle du Vent for orchestra, 1988; Vincent, opera based on the life of Vincent Van Gogh, 1984-89; Le Précepteur, opera (Jakoblent) for coloratura soprano, soprano, mezzo-soprano, contralto, 3 tenors, 2 baritones, 3 basses and 20 instruments; Recordings: CD, Michèle Reverdy (Scenic Railway, Sept Enluminures, Météores, Fugure, Kaleidoscope); Triade, CD Rafael Andia, guitar; Il Château, 1980-86, Opera for 9 singles, 2 choirs (men and children), orchestra, text from Franz Kafka. Publications: L'oeuvre pour piano d'Olivier Messiaen, 1978; Histoire de la Musique Occidentale, 1985; L'oeuvre pour orchestra d'Olivier Messiaen, 1988. Address: 75 rue des Gravilliers, 75003 Paris, France.

REY Isabel, b. 1966, Valencia, Spain. Singer (Soprano). Education: Studied at the Valencia Conservatory with Ana Luisa Chova and in Barcelona with Juan Oncina and Tatiana Menotti. Debut: Bilbao, 1987, as Amina in La Sonnambula. Career: Madrid as Ilia in Idomeneo and Vienna in Concerts of Mozart's Exultate Jubilate; Ascanio in Alba (Fauno); Handel's Saul and Beethoven's Ninth; Zurich Opera, 1991-, as Susanna in nozze di Figaro, Gilda in Rigoletto, Adina in L'elisir D'amore; Juliette in Romeo et Juliette, Marie in La Fille du Régiment; Susanna with Harnoncourt, Nederlandse Opera, 1993, 1994; Concerts with José Carreras worldwide, 1993-; Sang Susanna in a new production of Figaro at Zurich, 1996. Recordings: Nozze di Figaro, CD; Erato with José Carreras, CD; Zarzuela Arias and duets, CD. Address: Opernhaus Zurich, Falkenstrasse 1, CH-8008 Zurich, Switzerland.

REYMOND Valentin, b. 1954, Neuchâtel, Switzerland. Conductor. Education: Studied at Conservatories of Bienne and Zurich. Career: Assistant at the Grand Théâtre Geneva; Has assisted such conductors as Jean-Marie Auberson, Horst Stein, Armin Jordan and Roderick Brydon; Music Director of Opéra Décentralisé; Concert and broadcast appearances with Orchestre de la Suisse Romande amd Orchestre de la Radio Suisse Italienne, Orchestre de Chambre de Toulouse, Krasnoyarsk Symphony Orchestra (Siberia), Russian State Symphony Orchestra; Operatic appearances: Traviata (Opéra de Lucerne); Rape of Lucretia (Opéra Décentralisé and Opéra de Lausanne); Albert Herring (Bern Opera, Opéra de Lausanne and Opéra de Nantes); Les Pêcheurs de Perles (Dublin Opera); Les Mamelles de Tiresias, Das Rheingold, Die Walküre, Le Roi Malgré Lui (Opéra de Nantes); L'Etoile (Opera North); Iphigénie en Aulide for Opera North, 1996. Address: Music International, 13 Ardilaun Road, London N5 2QR, England.

REYNOLDS Anna, b. 5 June 1931, Canterbury, England. Opera and Concert Singer. Education: Royal Academy of Music (FRAM); Studied with Professoressa Debora Fambri. Career: Italy from 1958 in operas by Rossini, Donizetti and Massenet; Appearances at many international festivals including Spoleto, Edinburgh, Aix-en-Provence, Salzburg Easter Festival, Vienna, Tanglewood; Bayreuth Festival, 1970-75, as Fricka, Waltraute and Magdalena; Has sung with leading orchestras all over the world including Chicago Symphony, New York Philharmonic, Berlin Philharmonic and London Symphony; Appearances in opera performances at New York Metropolitan, La Scala Milan, Covent Garden, Bayreuth, Rome, Chicago Lyric Opera, Teatro Colon, Buenos Aires, Teatro Fenice, Venice and many others; Currently a teacher of singing. Recordings: For several labels, notably of cantatas by Bach. Hobbies: Reading; Piano; Travel; Worldwide correspondence. Address: 37 Chelwood Gardens, Richmond, Surrey TW9 4JG, England.

REYNOLDS Roger (Lee), b. 18 July 1934, Detroit, Michigan, USA. Composer. m. Karen Jeanne Hill, 11 Apr 1964, 2 daughters. Education: BSE, Physics, University of Michigan; BM, Music Literature, MM, Composition, University of Michigan. Career includes: Faculty member, University of California at San Diego, 1969-; George Miller Visiting Professor, University of Illinois, 1971; Founding Director, Center for Music Experiment, University of California at San Diego, 1972-77; Visiting Professor, Yale University, 1981; Senior Research Fellow, ISAM, Brooklyn College, 1985; Valentine Professor of Music, Amherst College, 1988; Rothschild Composer-in-Residence, Peabody Conservatory of Music, Baltimore, 1992-93. Compositions: About 85 compositions including: Dreaming, 1992; Symphony(The Stages of Life), 1991-92; The Emperor of Ice Cream, 1961-62; Visions, 1991; Transfigured Wind I-IV. 1984; Voicespace I-V, 1975-86; Odyssey, 1989-93; last things I think, to think about, 1994; The Red Act Arias, 1997. Recordings: About 45 on CD including: Whispers Out of Time; Transfigured Wind IV; Transfigured Wind II; Coconino..a shattered landscape; The Ivanov Suite; Versions/Stages/I-V; Voicespace I, III, IV, V; Variation; Archipelago; Personae; Odyssey. Publications: Mind Models: New Forms of Musical Experience, 1975; A Searcher's Path: A Composer's Ways, 1987; A Jostled Silence: Contemporary Japanese Musical Thought, 1992-93. Contributions to: The Musical Quarterly; Perspectives of New Music; The New York Times Review; Musical America; Contemporary Music Review; Inharmoniques. Honours include: Pulitzer Prize in Music, 1989; National Institute of Arts and Letters, 1971. Address: 624 Serpentine Drive, Del Mar, CA 92014, USA.

REYNOLDS Verne (Becker), b. 18 July 1926, Lyons, KS, USA. Composer; Horn Player. Education: BM, 1950, Cincinnati Conservatory of Music; MM 1951, University of Wisconsin; Further study with Herbert Howells at the Royal College of Music, London. Career: Horn player with the Cincinnati Symphony Orchestra, 1947-50, and first horn of the Rochester Philharmonic, 1959-68; Faculty Member, University of Wisconsin, 1950-53, Indiana University School of Music at Bloomington, 1954-59, and Eastman School of Music at Rochester, 1959-65. Compositions include: Violin Concerto, 1951; Saturday with Venus, overture, 1953; Serenade for 13 wind instruments, 1958; Flute sonata, 1962; String Quartet, 1967; Concertare I-V, for various instrumental combinations, 1968-76; Horn sonata, 1970; Violin's nata, 1970; Ventures for orchestra, 1975; Events for trombone choir, 1977; Scenes Revisited for wind ensemble, 1977; Festival and Memorial Music, for orchestra, 1977; Trio for horn, trombone and tuba, 1978; Fantasy-Etudes I-V for various wind instruments, 1979-92; Concerto for Band, 1980; Cello Sonata, 1983; Quintet for piano and winds, 1986; Brass Quintet, 1987; Songs of the Season for soprano, horn and piano, 1988; Trio for oboe, horn and piano, 1990; Clarinet sonata, 1994; Letter to the World for soprano and percussion, 1994; Pieces for piano. Address: c/o ASCAP, ASCAP Building, One Lincoln Plaza, New York, NY 10023, USA.

RHODES Cherry, b. 28 June 1943, Brooklyn, New York, USA. Educator; Concert Organist; Adjunct Professor. m. Professor Ladd Thomas. Education: BMus, Curtis Institute of Music, Philadelphia, Pennsylvania, 1964; HS Music, Munich, studied with Karl Richter, 1964-67; Private Study with Marie-Claire Alain and Jean Guillou, Paris, 1967-69; Summer schools, Harvard and University of Pennsylvania, 1961, 1962, 1963. Career: Soloist, Philadelphia Orchestra, South German Radio Orchestra, Chamber Orchestra of French National Radio, Pasadena Chamber Orchestra, Phoenix Symphony Orchestra; Los Angeles Philharmonic; First American to win an international organ competition, Munich; Recitals, Lincoln Center, New York City, Notre Dame, Paris, Royal Festival Hall, London, Los Angeles Music Center, Milwaukee Performing Arts Center, Meyerson Symphony Center, Dallas; Numerous appearances at national and regional conventions of AGO; Performances, several Bach festivals; International festivals Bratislava, Nuremberg, Paris, St Albans, Luxembourg and Vienna; Gave opening recital on new organ at John F Kennedy Center in Washington DC; Broadcast performances in USA, Canada and Europe; Adjudicator for national and international organ-playing competitions; Recordings: Everyone Dance, CD of music of Calvin Hampton on Pro Organ label. Address: School of Music, University of Southern California, Los Angeles, CA 90089-0851, USA.

RHODES Jane, b. 13 Mar 1929, Paris, France. Singer (Soprano). m. Roberto Benzi, 1966. Debut: Marguerite in La Damnation de Faust, Nancy, 1953. Career: Sang Renata in the first (concert) performance of The Fiery Angel by Prokofiev; Sang in the 1956 premiere of Le Fou by Landowski; Paris Opéra from 1958, as Marguerite, Carmen, Salome, and Kundry, 1974; Metropolitan Opera, 1960, Carmen; Aix-en-Provence, 1961, in L'Incoronazione di Poppea; Paris Opéra-Comique, 1968, in L'Heure Espagnole and La Voix Humaine; Also sang in Duke Bluebeard's Castle by Bartók. Recordings: Carmen; La Juive by Halévy; Mireille by Gounod; Margared in Le Roi d'Ys by Lalo; The Fiery Angel; Public Opinion in Orphée aux Enfers.

RHODES Phillip (Carl), b. 6 June 1940, Forest City, NC, USA. Composer. Education: Studied with Iain Hamilton at Duke University (BA 1962); Composition with Donald Martino and Mel Powell, theory with Gunther Schuller and George Perle at Yale Univerity (MM 1963). Career: Composer-in-residence and faculty member at Louisville, 1969-72; Composer-in-residence and Andrew W Mellon Professor of the Humanities at Carleton College, Northfield, Minnesota, from 1974; President of Carleton College Music Society, 1985-87. Compositions include: Four Movements for chamber orchestra, 1962; Remembrance for symphonic wind ensemble, 1967; About Faces, ballet, 1970; Divertimento for small orchestra, 1971; String Trio, 1973; Museum Pieces, for clarinet and string quartet, 1973; Quartet, for flute harp, violin and cello, 1975; On the Morning of Christ's Nativity, cantata, 1976; Ceremonial Fanfare and Chorale, for 2 brass choirs, 1977; Wind Songs for children's chorus and Orff instruments, 1979; In Praise of Wisdom, for chorus and brass choir, 1982; Nets to Catch the Wind, for chorus and percussion, 1986; The Gentle Boy, opera, premiered 1987; The Magic Pipe, opera, 1989; Wedding Song, for soprano, violin and organ, 1990; Reels and Reveries, variations for orchestra, 1991; Mary's Lullaby, for soprano, violin and organ, 1993; Chorale and Mediatationa (O Sacred Head Now Wounded) for women's voices and organ, 1995; Fiddle Tunes, for violin and synthesized strings, 1995; Solo instrumental pieces. Address: c/o ASCAP, ASCAP Building, One Lincoln Plaza, New York, NY 10023, USA.

RHODES Samuel, b. 13 Feb 1941, Long Beach, New York, USA. Violist. m. 30 Dec 1968, 2 daughters. Education: BA, Queens College, New York City; MFA, Princeton University. Debut: Carnegie Recital Hall, 1966. Career: Member of Juilliard String Quartet, 1969-; Appeared: Great Performances, PBS TV, 1977; Hindemith: The Viola Legacy 3 Concert Series, Carnegie Recital Hall, 1985; CBS Sunday Morning, 1986. Composition: Quintet for string quartet and viola. Recordings: Schoenberg Quartets; Complete Beethoven Quartets; Mozart-Haydn Quartets; Complete Bartók Quartets; Schubert and Dvorák Quartets; Guest Artist with Beaux Arts Trio. Honours: 3 Grammy Awards, 1971, 1976, 1985; Honorary Doctorates: Michigan State University, 1984, University of Jacksonville, 1986; Edison Award, Netherlands, 1974. Memberships: Viola Society; The Bohemians; Board Member, Chamber Music America. Hobbies: Running; Baseball. Current Management: Naomi Rhodes Associates Inc, New York City, USA; Colbert Artists Management Inc. Address: c/o The Juilliard School, Lincoln Center, 144 West 66th St, New York, NY 10023, USA.

RHYS-DAVIES Jennifer, b. 8 May 1953, Panteg, Gwent, Wales. Soprano. Education: Studied at Trinity College of Music, London. Career: Appearances with Welsh National Opera as the Forester's Wife in The Cunning Little Vixen, Fortune in Poppea, Miss Jessel in Turn of The Screw also in Dresden and Leipzig, First Lady in Die Zauberflöte and Donna Elvira; Further appearances as Constanze for Opera 80 and Donna Anna for Kent Opera on tour to Valencia; Opera North as Sandrina in La Finta Giardiniera, Aloysia in the Mozart-Griffiths pastiche; Sang Semiramide and Sieglinde at Nuremberg, Queen of Night for Dublin Grand Opera and Scottish Opera, 1993; Covent Garden and English Nationa Opera debut in 1993 as Berta in Barbiere di Siviglia and Mrs Fiorentino in Street Scene; Concert engagements in Beethoven's Mount of Olives and Haydn's Seasons at Dublin, Handel's Dixit Dominus and Poulenc's Gloria for Stuttgart Radio, Haydn's Orlando Paladino at Garsington Hall; Sang Clorinda in Cenerentola at Royal Opera House, The Duenna in Der Rosenkavalier, Amaltea in Moses, Queen of Night in Stuttgart, Lady Macbeth for WNO and Nuremberg. Recordings: As Berta in Barber of Seville; Various recordings for Opera Rara. Honours: Kennedy Scott Prize and Rowland Jones Memorial Award, Trinity College. Current Management: IMG Artists. Address: c/o IMG, Media House, 3 Burlington Lane, Chiswick, London, W4 2TH, England.

RIBARY Antal, b. 8 Jan 1924, Budapest, Hungary. Composer. Education: Diploma in Art History, Pazmany Peter University of Budapest; Diploma in Composition, Academy of Music, Budapest. Debut: 2 Michelangelo songs, 1947. Career: 6 interviews with Radio Budapest; 1 interview with Radio Bruxelles; 1 interview with Radio Stockholm; The Divorce of King Louis (1-act opera) performed at the Hungarian State Opera House, 1959. Compositions include: Pantomime Suite; Hellas Cantata; Requiem for the Lover; Six Lines from the Satyricon; Concerto Grosso; Five Quartets; Four Violin and Piano Sonatas; King Louis Divorces, opera; Two Michelangelo Songs; Five Shakespeare Sonnets; Five Villon Songs; Symphonies I-VII, 1960-84; De Profundis/Motetta; Two Poems for choirs; Rest C G Rossetti; Chant pour 8 Ligne/Baudelaire; Two Piano Concertos, 1979-80; In manuscript: Symphonies V-XII; In Memoriam Charles Beaudelaire; Six portraits imaginaires de Charles Moreas; Four Piano Concertos; Masks and Churches in Spain, suite for orchestra; Two Spanish Songs for voice and piano. Recordings: The Music of Antal Ribary, volumes 1, 2 and 3; Sonata for Alto and Piano; Six Staves from Satyricon, 1980. Publications: Music Criticism 1960-70. Hobbies: Pictures; Churches. Address: Felka 3, 1136 Budapest, Hungary.

RICCARDI Franco, b. 1921, Italy. Singer (Tenor). Debut: Naples, 1947, as Pinkerton. Career: Has sung widely in Italy, and notably at La Scala Milan from 1954, as Monostatos, Missail, Goro, Pang, and Bardolph; Rome Opera, 1963, as David in Die Meistersinger; Caracalla Festival and Verona Arena, 1968-69; Sang at Dallas Opera, 1970, Martina Franca Festival, 1982; Other roles have included Borsa in Rigoletto, Arturo in Lucia di Lammermoor, Cassio and Shuisky. Address: c/o Teatro alla Scala, Via Filodrammatici 2, 20121 Milan, Italy.

RICCI Ruggiero, b. 24 July 1918, San Francisco, California, USA. Violinist. m. (1) Ruth Rink, 1942, (2) Valma Rodriguez, 1957, (3) Julia Whitehurst Clemenceau, 1978, 2 son, 3 daughters. Education: Under Louis Persinger, Mischel Piastro, Paul Stassévitch amd Georg Kulenkampff. Debut: With Manhattan Symphony Orchestra, New York, 1929. Career: First tour of Euroipe, 1932; Served US Air Froce, 1942-46; Over 5000 concerts in 60 years worldwide; Played the first performances of the Violin concertos of Ginastera, Von Einem and Veerhoff; Specialises in violin solo literature; Professor of Violin at the Hochschule für Musik, Mozarteum, Salzburg, Austria. Recordings: 1st recording of Paganini Caprices on the Composer's violin, lent by City of Genoa; Over 500 recordings in discography. Publications: Left Hand Violin Technique, 1987. Honours: Cavaliere, Order of Merit, Italy. Current Management: Intermusica, 16 Duncan Terrace, London N1 8BZ, England. Address: c/o Hochschule für Musik Mozarteum, Mirabelplatz 1, A-5020 Salzburg, Austria.

RICCIARELLI Katia, b. 16 Jan 1946, Rovigo, Italy. Singer (Soprano). m. Pippo Baudo, 1986. Education: Studied at the Benedetto Marcello Conservatory, Venice. Debut: Mantua, 1969, as Mimi in La Bohème. Career: Sang Leonora in Il Trovatore at Parma in 1970; After winning the 1971 New Voices Competition on TV appeared throughout Italy; US debut at the Chicago Lyric Opera, 1972, as Lucrezia in I Due Foscari; Covent Garden, 1974, La Bohème and as Amelia in Un Ballo in Maschera, 1975; Metropolitan Opera from 1975, as Mimi, Micaela in Carmen, Desdemona, Luisa Miller and Amelia; Guest appearances in Moscow, Barcelona, Berlin, New Orleans and Verona; At Pesaro has sung in revivals of Rossini's Il Viaggio a Reims and Bianca e Falliero (1985-86); Other roles include Donizetti's Caterina Cornaro, Maria di Rohan, Lucrezia Borgia, Bellini's Imogene (Il Pirata) and Giulietta (I Capuleti e i Montecchi); Returned to Covent Garden, 1989, as Elisabeth de Valois in Don Carlos; Théâtre du Châtelet, Paris, 1988, as Gluck's Iphigénie en Tauride; Pesaro Festival, 1988, as Ninetta in La gazza ladra; Sang Desdemona at the Met and Covent Garden, 1990, Maria Stuarda at Reggio Emilia; Geneva, 1990, as Amenaide in Rossini's Tancredi; Season 1992/93 as Wolf-Ferrari's Susanna at Monte Carlo and Rosalinde in Fledermaus at Catania; Gave opera recital at Ljubljana, 1994; Sang Handel's Agrippina at Palermo, 1997. Recordings: Roles in Suor Angelica and Simon Boccanegra; I Due Foscari (2); Tosca; Il Battaglia di Legnano; Il Trovatore; La Bohème; Luisa Miller; Falstaff; Un Ballo in Maschera; Don Carlos; Aida; Turandot; Carmen; Il Viaggio a Reims; La Donna del Lago; I Capuleti e i Montecchi; Anacréon; Tancredi; I Lombardi; Appears as Desdemona in the video of Otello directed by Franco Zeffirelli. Address: c/o Harold Holt Ltd, 31 Sinclair Road, London W14 0NS, England.

RICH Alan, b. 17 June 1924, Boston, Massachusetts, USA. Music Critic; Editor; Author. Education: AB, Harvard University, 1945; MA, University of California, Berkeley, 1952; Studied in Vienna, Austria, 1952-53. Career: Assistant Music Critic, Boston Herald, 1944-45; New York Sun, 1947-48; Contributor, American Record Guide, 1947-61; Saturday Review, 1952-53; Musical America, 1955-61; Teacher of Music, University of California, Berkeley, 1950-58; Programme and Music Director, Pacifica Foundation FM Radio, 1953-61; Assistant Music Critic, New York Times, 1961-63; Chief Music Critic and Editor, New York-Herald Tribune, 1963-66; Music Critic and Editor, New York World-Journal-Tribune, 1966-67; Contributing Editor, Time magazine, 1967-68; Music and Drama Critic and Arts Editor, 1979-83, Contributing Editor, 1983-85; California magazine; General Editor, Newsweek magazine, 1983-87; Music Critic, Los Angeles Herald-Examiner, 1987-; Teacher, New School for Social Research, 1972-75, 1977-79; University of Southern California School of Journalism, 1980-82; California Institute of the Arts, 1982-; Artist-in-Residence, Davis Center for the Performing Arts, City University of New York, 1975-76. Publications: Careers and Opportunities in Music, 1964; Music: Mirror of the Arts, 1969; Simon & Schuster Listener's Guide to Music, 3 volumes, 1980; The Lincoln Cener Story, 1984. Contributions to: Numerous articles and reviews to various journals. Address: c/o Los Angeles Herald-Examiner, 1111 S Broadway, Los Angeles, CA 90015, USA.

RICH Elizabeth, b. 8 Feb 1931, New York City, USA. Concert Pianist. m. Joel Markowitz, 30 Jun 1952, 2 s, 1 d. Education includes: Juilliard School of Music; Scholarships at ages 7-18. Debut: New York Philharmonic Auditions, Young People's Concert, Carnegie Hall, 1949. Career: English premiere of Clara Schumann Piano Concerto, Beethoven Choral Fantasy, Queen Elizabeth Hall, London, 1985; Complete Cycle, Mozart Piano Sonatas, NY, 1984-85; Guest artist at Mt Desert Festival of Chamber Music, 1987-91, 1993, 1994 and 1995; 4th Recital, Alice Tully Hall, Lincoln Center, 1993; Mozart Concerto and Bach Concerto, St Martin's in the Field, London Chamber Soloists Orchestra, 1993. Recordings: For Dutch radio; Schumann CD for Connoisseur Society, 6 Noveletten and Carnaval, 1992; Piano Concerto, 1994; 2 Piano Concerti of Carl Maria von Weber, Clara Schumann Concerto, Little Janacek Philharmonic Orchestra, 1995. Current Management: Liegner Management. Address: c/o Liegner Management, PO Box 884, New York, NY 10023, USA.

RICHARDS Denby, b. 7 Nov 1924, London, England. Music Critic; Author; Lecturer. m. Rhondda Gillespie, 29 May 1973. Education: Regent Street Polytechnic, London; Education: Self-taught Piano and 50 years attending concerts and studying scores. Career: Early writing on Kensington News, then Music Critic to Hampstead and Highgate Express for 30 years; Contributor to Music and Musicians from first issue, 1952; Editor, 1981-84; Opera Editor, 1984-; Editor, Musical Opinion, 1987-; Many radio and TV appearances in UK, USA, Scandinavia, Australia; Lecturer including Seminar Course on History and Function of Western Musical Criticism at Yale University, USA; Programme Notes and Record Sleeves. Publication: The Music of Finland, 1966. Contributions to: Music and Musicians; Records and Recording; Musical Opinion; New Film Review; Parade; Other journals in UK and internationally. Memberships: The Critics' Circle; Royal Overseas League; Zoological Society of

London. Hobbies: Musical oddities; Puns; Exotic food; Vintage wine. Address: 2 Princes Road, St Leonards-on-Sea, East Sussex TN37 6EL, England.

RICHARDS Goff, b. 18 Aug 1944, St Minver, Cornwall, England. Composer; Arranger; Conductor; Adjudicator. m. Sue Tinkley, 2 Jun 1975, 3 s. Education: ARCM, GRSM, Royal College of Music, 1962-65; Teaching Certificate, Reading University, 1966. Career: Head of Music, Fowey School, 1966-70; Head of Music, Newquay School, 1972-75; Lecturer in Music, Salford College of Technology, 1976-81; Freelance Composer, Arranger and Conductor, 1981-; Regular contributions to BBC Radio and TV; Extensive travel including New Zealand, Norway, USA, Lithuania. Compositions include: Jaguar, 1983; Continental Caprice, 1984; Country Scene, 1985; Oceans, 1986; Cornish Fantasia, 1987; Lord Lovelace, 1987; Momentary, 1987; Homage to The Noble Grape, 1989; Cross Patonce, 1990; Counting the Days to Christmas, 1990; The Aeronauts; Saddleworth Festival Overture A; Higgyjig for E Flat Horn; Pastorale for Cornet with Piano; Rhumba for Tenor Trombone and Piano; Little Swiss Suite for 2 Cornets, E Flat Horn and Euphonium; Calling Cornwall, 1992; A Cycle Round Britain, 1992; Pilatus, 1993. Recordings: Burnished Brass, 1986; Compositions and Arrangements on many recordings by The King's Singers, leading Brass and Wind Bands and Choirs; Midnight Euphonium, 1992; Celebration, 1993. Honours: Honorary GDBM, Salford College of Technology; Director, Big Band Laureate, University College, Salford. Address: Rose Cottage, 101 Walton Road, Stockton Heath, Warrington, Cheshire, WA4 6NR, England.

RICHARDSON Carol, b. 1948, California, USA. Singer (Mezzo-soprano). Education: Studied at Occidental College, Los Angeles, with Martial Singher in Philadelphia and in New York. Debut: Klagenfurt, 1973, as Nicklausse in Hoffmann. Career: Sang at Kiel from 1975, Bayreuth Festival, 1976-81, in Parsifal; Engagements at Bern Stadttheater until 1984, Cenerentola at Bielefeld, 1988; Other roles have included Dorabella and Cherubino, Rosina, Orlofsky, Nancy in Martha, Lola and Zerlina; Further guest appearances at Hamburg, Gelsenkirchen, Karlsruhe and Hanover; Noted concert performer. Address: c/o Städtische Buhnen, Brunnerstrasse 3, 4800 Bielefeld 1, Germany.

RICHARDSON David (Vivian), b. 7 June 1941, London, England. Orchestra Manager. m. Janet Lesley Hilton, 6 July 1968, 1 son, 1 daughter. Education: BMus, Manchester University, 1964; ARMCM, 1963, GRSM, 1964, Royal Manchester College of Music; Diploma in Education, Caius College, Cambridge, 1965. Career: Professional Trumpet Player; Music Producer, BBC Manchester, 1966-70; Concerts Manager, New Philharmonia Orchestra, London, 1970-72; General Administrator, Scottish National Orchestra, 1972-80; Managing Director, St Paul Chamber Orchestra, Minnesota, USA, 1980-82; Chief Executive, Western Orchestral Society, Bournemouth, England, 1983-91; Chief Executive, Hallé Concerts Society, Manchester, 1991-94; General Manager, Eastern Orchestral Board, London, 1994-; Member, Board of Directors, 1984-94, Chairman, 1987-90, Association of British Orchestras, 1984-94; Governor, National Youth Orchestra of Great Britain, 1985-; Member, Gowrie Committee on London Music Conservatoires, 1989; Member, Arts Council Music Advisory Panel, 1995-. Honours: Winston Churchill Memorial Fellowship, 1976. Hobbies: Theatre; Photography; Paintings. Address: Eastern Orchestral Board, 10 Stratford Place, London W1N 9AE, England.

RICHARDSON Marilyn, b. 1935, Sydney, New South Wales, Australia. Singer (Soprano); Stage Director. m. (1) Peter Richardson, 1954, 3 children, (2) James Christiansen, 1974, 3 stepchildren. Education: Diplomee, New South Wales Conservatorium of Music. Debut: Schoenberg's Pierrot Lunaire, ISCM concert, Sydney, 1958. Career: Debut with Basler Theater, Switzerland, 1972, Lulu; Salome, debut with The Australian Opera, 1975, Aida; Roles and operas include Four Sopranos in Tales of Hoffmann, Marschallin, Countess, Donna Anna, Katya Kabanova, Queen of Spades, Otello, Eva, Sieglinde, Elsa, Mimi, Rosalinda, Merry Widow, Laura in Voss, Leonore (Fidelio), Isolde, 1990, and Tosca, 1992; Emilia Marty in The Makropoulos Case, 1996; Has appeared with all State Companies; The Excursions of Mr Broucek, Fiordiligi, La Traviata, Madame Butterfly, Midsummer Marriage, Desdemona, Marguerite, Mistress Ford, Senta, Alcina, Cleopatra; Soloist in a huge range of concert music, including Australian premieres of about 400 songs and vocal works; Directed Les Pêcheurs de Perles at Adelaide, 1996. Honours: Churchill Fellowship, 1969; Australian Council Creative Fellowship, 1991; Joan Hammond Award, 1993; Honorary DMus, University of Queensland, 1993. Address: Australian Opera, PO Box 291, Strawberry Hills, NSW 2012, Australia.

RICHARDSON Mark, b. England. Singer (Bass-baritone). Education: Studied at the Royal Manchester College of Music. Career: English National Opera as Lamoral in Arabella, Masetto, Colline in La Bohème and France in Reimann's Lear; Other roles in War and Peace, Der Rosenkavalier, Rimsky's Christmas Eve and The Pearl Fishers; Season 1995-96 as Bizet's Zuniga and

Nourabad; Guest appearances at Buxton, as Mustafá in L'Italiana in Algeri, Welsh National Opera (Angelotti and Rossini's Basilio) and the Bergen Festival (Sparafucile in Rigoletto). Address: c/o ENO Press Office, St Martin's Lane, London WC2N 4ES, England.

RICHARDSON Stephen, b. 1965, Liverpool, England. Singer (Bass). Education: Studied at the Royal Northern College of Music. Career: Has sung at Glyndebourne and with GTO, English and Welsh National Opera, Scottish Opera and Kent Opera; Roles have included Mozart's Osmin, Sarastro and Commendatore, Colline, Sparafucile, Silva in Ernani and Rossini's Basilio; US debut with Messiah at Carnegie Hall and other concerts with leading British orchestras Montreal Philharmonic Orchestra and Prague Symphony Orchestra; Premieres of Tavener's Eis Thanaton, Resurrection and Apocalypse, with other works by Gerald Barry, Birtwistle (Punch and Judy), Knussen, Mason and Casken; Festival appearances at Aldeburgh, BBC Proms, Vienna, Hong Kong, Boston and Brussels; Season 1996-97 with Colline and Sparafucile for Welsh National Opera, Daland with Chelsea Opera Group and Tiresias in Oedipus Rex for the BBC. Address: c/o Harrison Parrott Ltd, 12 Penzance Place, London W11 4PA, England.

RICHTER Marga, b. 21 October 1926, Reedsburg, WI, USA. Composer. Education: Juilliard School, New York, from 1943, with Rosalyn Tureck, William Bergsma and Vincent Persichetti (MS 1951). Career: Freelance Composer, with premieres of her music at Salzburg, Chicago, Cannes, Cologne, Tucson and Brooksville, NY. Compositions include: Clarinet sonata, 1948; Piano Sonata, 1955; 2 Piano Concertos, 1955, 1974; Aria and Toccata for viola and strings, 1957; String Quartet, 1958; Abyss, opera, 1964; Bird of Yearning, ballet, 1967; Requiem for piano, 1976; Blackberry Vines and Winter Fruit for orchestra, 1976; Music, for 3 quintets and orchestra, 1980; Dusseldorf Concerto for flute, viola, harp, percussion and strings, 1982; Out of Shadows and Solitude for orchestra, 1985; Quantum Quirks of a Quick Quaint Quark, I-III for orchestra, organ and piano, 1992-93; ....beside the still waters, Variations and Interludes, concerto for piano, violin, cello and orchestra, 1993; Choruses and songs. Honours include: Annua; ASCAP Awards, 1966-95. Address: c/o ASCAP, ASCAP Building, One Lincoln Plaza, New York, NY 10023, USA.

RICKARD Sylvia Carol, b. 19 May 1937, Toronto, Ontario, Canada. Composer; French Diction Teacher. 1 daughter. Education: BA, French, Russian, 1959; BC Diploma, Etudes françaises, University of Grenoble, France, 1960; BC Teachers' Certificate, Secondary School, 1969; Studies, French Literature, Stanford University Graduate School of California; Grade X, Piano Studies, Toronto Conservatory, Theory, Counterpoint, History, Harmony; Private Studies in Composition with Jean Coulthard; The Banff Centre Summer School, Alberta, Canada. Career: Appearances at major festivals including: Reunion for Cello, Piano, Percussion, Banff International Festival, 1978; Four Indian Songs for Soprano, Chamber Orchestra and Piano, Victoria Symphony Orchestra, 1986; With Every Breath You Take, for clarinet and cello; Tour of Sweden, 1993. Recordings: Songs of the Loon; Rum-Ba-Ba for 4 violas and solo contra bass; Epithalamion for soprano and violin; Gaelyne Gabora, Taras Gabora, Oberlin Conservatory, Ohio. Publications: Music of Our Time, Teachers' Manual; A Student's Guide to Musical Form, 1981; Four Indian Songs, 1989. Contributions to: Music Magazine; English and Hungarian Newspapers. Honours: 1st Prize, Okanagan Composers' Festival, 1975; 1st Prize, 1977. Memberships: Canadian Music Centre; Canadian League of Composers. Hobby: Scrabble. Address: 5373 Lochside Drive, Victoria BC, V8Y 2G8, Canada.

RICKARDS Steven, b. 1955, United States. Singer (Counter tenor); Composer; Music Educator. Education: DMA Candidate, Florida State University, Tallahassee; MM, Indiana University, Bloomington; Oberlin College Baroque Performance Institute, 1976; Bachelor of Music Education, Indiana University, Bloomington, 1979; Diploma in Singing, 1982, Diploma in Opera Performance, 1983, Guildhall School of Music and Drama, London. Career: Concert engagements with the Waverly Consort (New York), Chicago's Music of the Baroque, Concert Royal, New York, Arts Musica and Chanticleer; British appearances with the Ipswich Bach Choir and at the East Cornwall Bach Festival; Tour of Ireland with the Gabrieli Consort and worldwide recitals with lutenist Dorothy Linell; Has toured France and Michigan with Messiah 1981-82; Carnegie Hall debut 1987, with the Oratorio Society of New York; Boston Early Music Festival in Handel's Teseo and Santa Fe Opera as Ariel in the premiere of John Eaton's The Tempest (1985); Sang with the Opera Company of Philadelphia as Apollo in Death in Venice; Recent revivals of Handel's Siroe in New York, Locke's Psyche in London, Hasse's L'Olimpiade in Dresden and Mondonville's De Profundis at Harvard; Currently, teaches singing at University of Indianapolis and Butler University, USA. Compositions: A Christmas Vision; All Good Gifts; Calm on the List'ning Ear of Night; Come Let Us Sing To The Lord; Come Thou Long Expected Jesus; Little Lamb; As the Lyre to the Singer; Behold the Tabernacle of God; Breathe on Me, Breath of God; Angels Did Sing. Recordings include: Bach cantatas 106 and 131 with Joshua Rifkin; St John Passion by Bach; Gradualia by Byrd with Chanticleer; Medarse in Siroe by Handel; Mass in B Minor by Bach; Buxtehude Project Vol I Sacred Cantatas; T Campion Songs; J Dowland Songs. Honours: Fullbright Hayes Scholarship, 1981-82; Performer's Certificate, Indiana University, 1981; Royal Tunbridge Wells International Music Competition, Second Prize, 1982; Countertenor Prize, S-Hertogenbosh International Vocalisten Concourse, 1982; Rotary Scholarship, 1982-83; Ontario Society of New York, Second Prize, 1985; Music America Young Artist, 1987; Florida State University Fellowship, 1989-92. Address: 123 E Westfield Boulevard, Indianapolis, IN 46220, USA.

RICKENBACHER Karl Anton, b. 20 May 1940, Basle, Switzerland. Conductor. m. Gaye Fulton, 21 July 1973. Education: Opera and Concert Conducting Degree, Konservatorium Berlin; Studies with H v Karajan and Pierre Boulez. Debut: RIAS Berlin. Career: Assistant Conductor, Zürich Opera, 1966-69; 1st Kapellmeister Städt Bühnen Freiburg, 1969-75; Music Director of Westphalian Symphony, 1976-85; Principal Conductor of BBC Scottish Symphony, 1978-80; Featured in, Karl Anton Rickenbacher Conducts, BBC Scotland and appeared in Olivier Messiaen - Chronochromie, on Bavarian TV; Concerts for ZDF Germany and Swiss, Belgian and French TV; Since 1985, Freelance Guest Conductor in Europe, North America, Japan, Australia and Israel in opera and concert repertoire. Recordings: Over 50 titles with London Philharmonic, Bavarian Radio Symphony, Bamberg Symphony, Berlin Radio Symphony RSB, Budapest Radio Symphony. Honours: Grand Prix du Disque, for Milhaud CD, 1993; Diapason d'Or, for Messaien CD, 1994; Cannes Classical Award, for Hartmann CD, 1994. Hobbies: Fine Arts; Literature. Current Management: Valmalete, Paris; Transart, UK; Columbia Artists, USA and CH. Address: Oriole, CH-1822 Chernex-Montreux, Switzerland.

RIDDELL Alistair Matthew, b. 22 June 1955, Melbourne, Victoria, Australia. Composer; Computer Technologist. Education: BA (Hons), 1981, MA, 1989, La Trobe University (PhD 1993); Graduate Studies, Princeton University, 1989-93. Career: Fellowships at Princeton and La Trobe Universities, 1989-95. Compositions (Most with Computer-Processed Sound) include: Ligeti-Continuum, 1982; Studies in Perception, Context and Paradox: Three-Existential Constellations: Canon in 6 Voices, 1982; Bach-Inventio No 4, 1982; Atlantic Fears, 1983; Core Image (four 4), 1983; Atmisfearia, 1989; Entering 2-12, 1990; Third Hand, 1991; Idyll Moment, 1991; Heavy Mouse, 1992; Z Says, 1993; Triptychos, 1995. Recording: CD, 42, 1997. Honours include: AC Artists and New Technology Program Grant, 1987. Address: 12 Napier Street, Fitzroy, Victoria 3065, Australia.

RIDDELL David, b. 1960, Elgin, Scotland. Conductor. Education: St Andrew's University; Guildhall School, London. Career: Engagements for Den Jyske Opera, Denmark, in La Périchole, Butterfly, Cenerentola, The Pirates of Penzance, Paganini and Reesen's Farinelli (1992); Don Giovanni for Aarhus Summer Opera, 1989-90, followed by Il Barbiere di Siviglia, 1991; Die Fledermaus for Odense Symphony Orchestra, 1992; British appearances with La Forza del Destino for Scottish Opera, Eugene Onegin for Opera 80 and Rimsky's Mozart and Salieri at the Royal Scottish Academy of Music; Regular concerts at the Guildhall School; Season 1996 with Bach's Christmas Oratorio for the Randers Chamber Orchestra, and Burns International Festival Concert with the Northern Sinfonia in Scotland.

RIDDER Anton de, b. 13 Feb 1929, Amsterdam, Netherlands. Tenor. Education: Studied at the Amsterdam Conservatory with H Mulder and J Keyzer. Career: After Dutch stage debut in 1952 sang in Karlsruhe from 1956, Munich Theater am Gärtnerplatz, 1962-66, with Cologne Opera in the premiere of Zimmermann's Die Soldaten in 1965 and at the Edinburgh Festival in 1972; Guest appearances in London, East Germany and Amsterdam; Bregenz Festival in 1974 as Don José, Glyndebourne Festival in 1979 as Florestan in the Peter Hall production of Fidelio under Haitink, and Salzburg Festival in 1985 in Capriccio. Recordings: Busoni's Doktor Faust; Capriccio; La Traviata; Lucia di Lammermoor.

RIEBL Thomas, b. 1956, Vienna, Austria. Violist. Education: Studied at the Vienna Academy of Music and with Peter Schidlof and Sandor Vegh. Career: Led the violas of the World Youth Orchestra, 1972; Solo debut at the Vienna Konzerthaus in 1972 and has since appeared with leading orchestras in Europe and North America including the Chicago Symphony, Helsinki Radio, Bournemouth Symphony, Los Angeles and Vienna Chamber Orchestras; Conductors include Abbado, Walter Weller, Andrew Davis, Horst Stein, Erich Bergel and Edo de Waart; Festival appearances at Salzburg, Vienna, Aspen, Ravinia, New York, Munich, Lockenhaus and Carinthian Summer Festival; Concerts with the Juilliard Quartet, Gidon Kremer and Jessye Norman (Brahms Lieder Op 91); Founder Member of the Vienna Sextet; Professor of Viola at the Musikhochschule, Mozarteum, at Salzburg from 1983. Recordings include: Brahms Lieder Op 91 with Brigitte Fassbaender and Irwin Gage. Honours include: Prizewinner at international competitions at Budapest in 1975 and Munich in 1976; Ernst Wallfisch Memorial Award at the International Naumberg Viola Competition in New York, 1982.

RIEDEL Deborah, b. 31 July 1958, Sydney, New South Wales, Australia. Singer (Soprano). Education: Studied at the Sydney Conservatorium and in London with Audrey Langford and Paul Hamburger. Career: Sang Hansel with Western Australian Opera, 1986, followed by Meg Page and Thomas's Mignon, Mimi and Countess Moritza; The Australian Opera from 1988, as Zerlina, Micaela, Juliette, Susanna, Elvira and Violetta; Appearances with the Victorian State Opera as the Drummer in Ullmann's Emperor of Atlantis, Nayad in Ariadne auf Naxos, Leila (Les Pêcheurs de Perles), Marguerite in Faust; London engagements as Freia in Das Rheingold, Mimi and Elvira at Covent Garden; Teresa in Benvenuto Cellini at Geneva Opera, and Bastille (Paris), and Rome; Sang Elvira at Bordeaux, Violetta in the Netherlands, Amina in La Sonnambula at San Diego, California 1994, the Countess at Montpellier, Gounod's Marguerite in Faust at Geneva; Donna Anna in Munich; Concert engagements as Mariana in Il Signor Bruschino at the Festival of Flanders; Messe Solenelle - Montpelier, Messe Solonelle - Montpelier, Mozart Coronation Mass, Barcleaux, Child of Our Time with LSO; War Requiem (Britten) in London and Prague; Jemmy in Guillaume Tell and Rossini's Petite Messe Solonnelle; Scarlatti's St Cecilia Mass and frequent appearances with the Australian Pops Orchestra; Mozart's Vespers for the Rantos Collegium and Messiah for the ABC in Melbourne and Sydney; Mendelssohn's Midsummer Night's Dream and Mozart Exultate Jubilate with the Sydney Symphony Orchestra and Strauss's Four Last Songs for the Australian Ballet and ABC Perth; Season 1997 with Maria Stuarda in Sydney and Donna Anna at the Met. Honours: Winner, Australian regional final of the Metropolitan Opera Auditions; Dame Sister Mary Leo Scholarship; Dame Mabel Brookes Fellowship; Aria Award, Sydney Sun, 1986. Current Management: IMG Artists, London, England. Address: c/o IMG Artists, Media House, 3 Burlington Lane, London W4 2TH, England.

RIEGEL Kenneth, b. 19 Apr 1938, Womelsdorf, PA, USA. Opera Tenor. Education: Manhattan School of Music; Berkshire Music Center; Metropolitan Opera Studio. Debut: Santa Fe Festival in 1965 as the Alchemist in the US premiee of Henze's König Hirsch. Career: San Francisco Opera, 1971, Metropolitan Opera, NY, 1973, Vienna State Opera, 1977, Paris Opéra, 1979 as the Painter in the premiere of the 3-act version of Lulu, La Scala, 1979, Hamburg State Opera, 1981, Geneva Opera, 1981, Deutsche Opera, West Berlin, 1983, and Bonn Opera, 1983; Sang the Leper in the premiere of Messiaen's St François d'Assise, Paris in 1983, at Brussels Opera in 1984, and at Royal Opera Covent Garden, 1985 in Der Zwerg by Zemlinsky; Appeared in film, Don Giovanni, at Bavarian State Opera, Munich in 1988, and at Stuttgart in 1989 as Dionysos in The Bassarids by Henze; Season 1992 as Herod in Salome at Covent Garden and Salzburg; Season 1996 with Aegisthus at Salzburg and the Inquisitor in Dallapiccola's Prigioniero at Florence. Recordings: Der Zwerg; Damnation of Faust; Florentinische Tragoedie; Don Giovanni; Lulu; Mahler Symphony No 8; Berlioz's Requiem. Honours: Nominated for Sir Laurence Oliver Award for Best Individual Performance in an Opera, 1985. Hobbies: Cooking; Gardening. Current Management: SAFIMM Corporation. Address: c/o SAFIMM Corporation, 250 West 57th Street, Suite 1018, New York, NY 10107, USA.

RIESSAUW Anne-Marie, b. 3 July 1941, Gent, Belgium. Education: Latin-Greek Humanities; History of Art, Musicology specialisation, University of Ghent; Licentiate, 1975; Doctorate, 1978. Career: Mandatory, National Fund for Scientific Research, 1965-71; Assistant in Musicology, 1971-85, Chief Assistant, Musicology, 1985-, University of Ghent. Publication: Catalogue des oeuvres vocales écrites par des compositeurs européens sur des poèmes de Verlaine, 1980. Contributions to: Grove's Dictionary of Music and Musicians; Die Musik in Geschichte und Gegeuwort; Current Musicology; Revue Belge de Musicologie; Nationaal Biografisch Woordenboek. Memberships include: Koninklijke Vereniging voor Nederlandse Muziekgeschiedenis; Belgische Vereniging voor Muziekwetenschap; Internationale Gesellschaft für Musikwissenschaft. Hobby: Philately. Address: Cyriel Buyssestraat 5, B-9000 Gent, Belgium.

RIFKIN Joshua, b. 22 April 1944, New York, USA. Conductor; Musicologist; Composer. Education: BS, Juilliard School of Music with Persichetti, 1964; New York University with Gustave Reese, 1964-66; University of Göttingen, 1966-67; Princeton University with Lewis Lockwood, Arthur Mendel and Milton Babbitt, 1967-70. Career: Nonesuch Records, New York, 1964-75; Brandeis University, 1970-82; Visiting Lecturer to various US and Eastern Universities; As a Musicologist has researched Renaissance and Baroque music; Performances as Director of the Bach Ensemble; Guest appearances as Conductor with St Louis, San Francisco, City of Glasgow and Jerusalem Symphony Orchestras, and with the Los Angeles, St Paul, English, Scottish and Prague Chamber Orchestras; Major contribution to the revival of interest in the ragtime music of Scott Joplin; 1989 at Melbourne Summer Festival, playing Joplin and conducting Copland, Stravinsky and Weill; Conducted St John Passion by Bach at the Lufthansa Early Music Festival, London, 1991; Monteverdi's L'Orfeo at Theater Basel, 1993; St Matthew Passion by Bach at BBC Promenade Concerts, 1994; Mass in B Minor by Bach at Mostly Mozart Festival, New York, 1994, and Festival of Perth, 1997. Recordings: Bach Cantatas and Mass in B Minor in an attempt to recreate early performance practice; Music by Scott Joplin; Mozart Posthorn Serenade; Fanfares and Sonatas by Pezel and Hammerschmidt; Sonatas by Biber; Vocal Music by Busnois, Josquin, Rags and Tangos by James Scott, Joseph Lamb and Ernesto Nazareth. Publications: Articles on Haydn, Schütz, Bach and Josquin in the Musical Times, Musical Quarterly and other journals. Current Management: c/o Clarion/Seven Muses, 47 Whitehall Park, London N19 3TW, England. Address: 61 Dana Street,Cambridge, MA 02138, USA.

RIGACCI Bruno, b. 1921, Florence, Italy. Conductor; Composer; Pianist. Education: Studied conducting with Antonio Guarneri. Career includes: Early career as international pianist; Founder and later permanent conductor of Chamber Orchestra of Florence; Conductor at Royal Opera, Stockholm and permanent orchestral conductor at Accademia Chigiana in Siena; Music Director, Festival Settimane Musicali Senesi, 1966, and of Philadelphia Music Theatre, 1974; Faculty, Philadelphia Musical Academy, 1970; Appearances with major Italian orchestras in leading opera houses; Principal Conductor of San Diego Opera, 1980-84; Guest Conductor at Teatro Rossini, Lugo, 1987; Currently Artistic Director of Festival Opera at Barga, Italy; Recent engagements included Macbeth at Pittsburgh, Rossi's Orfeo at La Scala, Turandot and Semiramide at the Bilbao Festival and La Bohème at Canadian Opera in Toronto, 1989; Visiting Consultant in Italian repertoire at the Royal Opera School, Stockholm from 1988; Conducted Mascagni's Cavalleria Rusticana and Zanetto at Florence, 1996. Compositions include: Chamber music, symphonies; Ecuba; Professor Tkimg and three other operas. Recordings: La Bohème and Lucia di Lammermoor from the Maggio Musicale; Demetrio e Polibio by Rossini; Andrea Chénier; Donizetti's Pia de Tolomei and Parisina d'Este; Mascagni's I Rantzau. Honours: First Prize at the Teatro del'Opera in Rome for Ecuba; Orfeo d'Argento for Conductors. Address: Via Giambologna 3a, 50132 Firenze, Italy.

RIGAL Joel, b. 17 Aug 1950, Castres, France. Pianist; Director, Monaco Music Academy. Education: Master Degree, Musicology, University of Paris-Sorbonne; Graduate, Aix en Provence and Marseilles Conservatories; Piano and Fortepiano Studies with Pierre Barbizet and Paul Badura-Skoda, Vienna. Debut: Vienna Theatre, 1979. Career: Performances in Paris: Châtelet, 1983, Gaveau, 1987, Musée de la Villette, 1997-; Purcell Room, London, 1981-; Opera, Cairo, 1989-; Bibliotek Theatre, Rotterdam, 1991-; Budapest Strings Orchestra, Budapest, 1995; Several TV and radio appearances. Recordings: with Nadine Palmier: Mozart, Complete Works for Piano Duet and 2 Keyboards; French Music, The Golden Age; Schubert, The Final Masterpieces. Publication: Le clavier bien partagé (teaching manual), 1993. Contributions to: Marsyas. Hobbies: Jogging; Astrology. Current Management: Maurice Werner, Paris. Address: c/o Nadine Palmier, 14 rue Maitre Albert, 75005 Paris, France.

RIGBY Jean, b. 22 Dec 1954, Fleetwood, Lancashire, England. Mezzo-Soprano. m. J Hayes, producer, 1987, 3 sons. Education: Birmingham School of Music with Janet Edmunds; Royal Academy of Music with Patricia Clark; National Opera Studio, London. Career: Member of English National Opera from 1982; Roles include Mercedes in Carmen, Maddalena, Marina in Boris Godunov, Blanche in The Gambler, Britten's Lucretia and Magdalena in The Mastersingers; Octavian, Rosenkavalier; Helen, King Priam; Concert performance of Lady Essex in Gloriana with Chelsea Opera Group; Festival Hall debut in the Verdi Requiem and Covent Garden debut as Thibault in Don Carlos in 1983; Glyndebourne Festival in 1985 as Mercedes, and Zurich in 1986 as Cornelia in Handel's Giulio Cesare; Sang Penelope in The Return of Ulysses with ENO in 1989 and 1992, Ursula in Beatrice and Benedict, 1990, and at Glyndebourne in 1990 as Nancy in Albert Herring; Season 1992-93 as Amastris in Xerxes, Rossini's Isabella at Buxton and Nicklausse in Les Contes d'Hoffmann at Covent Garden and San Diego; Cenerentola, Garsington Opera; Rosina, Barber; Mahler's 2nd Symphony at the Festival Hall, 1997. Recordings include: Video of English National Opera's Rigoletto; Glyndebourne, Albert Herring/Carmen; Lucretia, Xerxes. Honours: Friends of Covent Garden Bursary; Countess of Munster Scholarship; Worshipful Company of Musicians' Medal; Royal Overseas League Competition, 1981; Young Artists Competition, ENO, 1981; ARAM, 1984; FRAM, 1989. Address: c/o Harold Holt Ltd, 31 Sinclair Road, London, W14 0NS, England.

RIGGS Krista Dyonis, b. 17 June 1977, Denver, Colorado, USA. Oboist. Education: Arizona University, 1995-96, 1997; University of Michigan, 1996-97; Studied with Martin Schuring, Harry Sargous; Interlochen Acts Camp All-State Program, 1993-94. Career: Principal Oboe, Metropolitan Youth Symphony, Phoenix, 1989-92, Arizona Regional Band, 1992-93; Assistant Principal Oboe, English Horn, Arizona All-State Orchestra, 1992-93, Indiana All-Star Orchestra, 1994, Michigan Youth Arts Festival Orchestra, 1994; Principal Oboe, Michigan Youth Band, 1993-95; Assistant Principal Oboe, English Horn, Michigan Youth Symphony Orchestra, 1993-95; Interlochen All-State Orchestra, 1994; Solo Oboist, Saline High School Orchestra, 1995; Principal Oboe, Michigan Youth Arts Festival Band, 1995; Principal Oboe, Paridise Valley Chamber Orchestra, 1995-96; Arizona State University Orchestras, 1995-96; Arizona State University Bands, 1995-96; Performer, John Mack Master Class, 1995-96; University of Michigan Orchestras, 1996-97; University of Michigan Bands, 1996-97; Performer, Kathryn Greenbank Master Class, 1997. Honours: Mountain View High School Most Outstanding Orchestral Member Award, 1993; Saline Orchestra Award, 1995. Memberships: International Double Reed Society; Chamber Music America. Address: 3684 Heron Ridge Lane, Weston, FL 33331, USA.

RIHM Wolfgang, b. 13 Mar 1952, Karlsruhe, Germany. Composer. Education: Hochschule für Musik Karlsruhe, with Eugen W Velte, 1968-72; Later studies with Stockhausen in Cologne and Klaus Huber in Freiburg. Career: Teacher at the Karlsruhe Hochschule für Musik, 1973-78; Freelance Composer; From 1985 Professor of Composition at Musikhochschule Karlsruhe, British premiere of Jakob Lenz in London in 1987, Die Eroberung von Mexiko premiered at the Hamburg Staatsoper, 1992. Compositions include: Operas: Deploration, 1974, Jakob Lenz, 1978, Oedipus, 1987; Die Eroberung von Mexico, 1992; Orchestral: Three Symphonies, 1969-76, Sub-Kontar, 1975-76, La Musique Creuse Le Ciel for 2 Pianos and Orchestra, 1979, Monodram for Cello and Orchestra, 1983, Medea-Spiel, 1988, Passion, 1989, Schwebende Begegnung, 1989, Dunkles Spiel, 1990; La lugubre gondola for orchestra, 1992; Vocal: Hervorgedunkelt for Mezzo and Ensemble, 1974, Umhergetrieben Aufgewirbelt, Nietzsche Fragments for Baritone and Mezzo, Chorus and Flute, 1981, Lowry-Lieder (Wondratschek), 1987, Song Cycles for Soprano and Orchestra, Frau, Stimme for Soprano and Orchestra, 1989, Mein Tod, Requiem In Memoriam Jane S, 1990; Chamber: Paraphrase for Cello, Percussion and Piano, 1972, Ländler for 13 Strings, 1979, 8 String Quartets, 1970-88, Gebild for Trumpet, Strings and Percussion, 1983, Duomonolog for Violin and Cello, 1989; Music for voice and piano, organ and piano. Address: c/o Universal Edition Ltd, 2 Fareham Street, London, W1, England.

RILEY Howard, b. 16 Feb 1943, Huddersfield, England. Pianist; Composer. Education: BA 1964, MA 1966, University of Wales; MMus, Indiana University, USA, 1967; MPhil, York University, England, 1970. Career: Concerts as solo or group pianist, 1967-; Broadcasts throughout Europe, USA and Canada; Festival appearances include: Berlin, Paris, New York, Debrecen, Leipzig; Creative Associate, Centre of the Creative and Performing Arts, Buffalo, NY, USA, 1976-77. Compositions include: The Contemporary Piano Collection, portfolio of piano compositions published, 1982. Recordings include: Many compositions recorded including: Angle, Zones and Trisect for 3 Pianos; 25 LP recordings of own music including: Facets, in a 3 LP box set, 1983, For Four on Two Two, 1984, In Focus, 1985, Live at the Royal Festival Hall, 1985, Feathers, 1988, Procession, 1990, The Heat of Moments, 1991, Beyond Category, 1993, and The Bern Concert, 1993. Contributions to: The Musical Times, 1966; The Music Review, 1966 and 1972; Jazz Monthly, 1969. Honour: UK/USA Bicentennial Fellowship in The Arts, 1976-77. Hobbies: Football; Walking. Address: Flat 2, 53 Tweedy Road, Bromley, Kent, BR1 3NH, England.

RILEY Terry, b. 24 Jun 1935, Colfax, CA, USA. Composer. Education: Studied at San Francisco State College, 1955-57, and the University of California, MA in 1961. Career: Member of the San Francisco Tape Music Center; Studios of the ORTF Paris, 1963; Creative Associate at the Center for Creative and Performing Arts, Buffalo, 1967; Studied Raga singing in India, 1970; Associate Professor at Mills College, 1971-80; Works include string quartets (Kronos Quartet) and Indian instruments, from 1981. Compositions include: Trio for Violin, Clarinet and Cello, 1957; Concert for 2 Pianos and Tape, 1960; String Trio, 1961; Keyboard Studies, 1963; Dorian Reeds for Ensemble, 1964; A Rainbow In The Curved Air, 1968; Persian Surgery Dervishes for Electronic Keyboard, 1971; Descending Moonshine Dervishes, 1975; Cadenza On The Right Plain for String Quartet, 1984; Works with synthesizer include Chorale Of The Blessed Day, Eastern Man, Embroidery, Song From The Old Country, G-Song, Remember This Oh Mind, Sunrise Of The Planetary Dream Collector, The Ethereal Time Shadow, Offering To Chief Crazy Horse, Rites Of The Imitators, The Medicine Wheel and Song Of The Emerald Runner, 1980-83; Do You Know How It Sounds? for Low Voice, Piano and Tabla, 1983; Cycle of five string quartets, Salome Dances for Peace, 1988. Honours include: Guggenheim Fellowship, 1979. Address: c/o ASCAP, ASCAP Building, One Lincoln Plaza, New York, NY 10023, USA.

RILEY-SCHOFIELD John, b. 1954, England. Singer (Baritone). Education: Studied at Huddersfield School of Music 1972-75 and at Royal Academy of Music 1975-78 with Raimund Herincx. Career: Sang with English National Opera 1978-85, in the chorus, many small roles; Gelsenkirchen Opera from 1986, as Germont, Mozart-Count, Giovanni and Guglielmo, the Speaker in Die Zauberflöte, the Count in Capriccio and in Matrimonio Segreto, and Mel in The Knot Garden by Tippett; Bregenz Festival 1988, in Les Contes d'Hoffmann; Further guest appearances in Cologne, Mainz, Amsterdam, New York, London, Portugal and Austria; Other roles have included Eisenstein, Wozzeck and Rossini's Figaro; German Premiere of Life with an Idiot by Schnittke; Concert repertoire includes Bach's Passions and B minor Mass, Handel's Messiah, Samson and Saul, Ein Deutsches Requiem, Haydn's Oratorios, Elijah, the Requiems of Mozart and Fauré, Carmina Burana. Address: c/o Musiktheater im Revier, Kennedyplatz, 45881 Gelsenkirchen, Germany.

RILLING Helmuth, b. 29 May 1933, Stuttgart, Germany. Conductor; Chorus Master; Organist. Education: Studied at the Musikhochschule Stuttgart, 1952-55, composition with Johann Nepomuk David; Further organ study with Fernando Germani in Rome and conducting with Bernstein in New York. Career: Founded the Gächinger Kantorei in 1954 with tours of Europe, Asia and North and South America; Organist and Choirmaster at the Gedächtniskirche, Stuttgart, 1957; Re-formed the Spandauer Kantorei while teaching at the Spandau Kirchenmusikschule, 1963-66; London debut as organist in 1963; Founded the Bach-Collegium of Stuttgart in 1965 with tours to USA, 1968, English Bach Festival, 1972 and Japan in 1974; Professor, Frankfurt Musikhochschule from 1969; Director of the Frankfurt Kanorei; Performances of works by Pepping, Bach, Handel, Verdi and Reger. Recordings: Cycle of Bach Cantatas from 1972 with the Franfurter Kantorei, the Gächinger Kantorei and the Figuralchor of Stuttgart; Motets, Lutheran Masses, Choral Preludes and Orgelbüchlein by Bach; Magnificats by Schütz, Bach, Monteverdi and Buxtehude; Carissimi's Jephte and Judicum Salomonis; Handel's Belshazzar; Telemann's Ino and Pimpinone; Mozart's Concertos K364 and K190, Mass K317 and Vesperae Solennes de Confessore; Geistliche Chormusik, St Matthew Passion, Symphoniae Sacrae and Cantiones Sacrae by Schütz; Messiaen's Cinq Rechants. Address: c/o Staatliche Hochschule für Musik, Escherheimer Landstrasse 33, Postfach 2326, Frankfurt, Germany.

RINALDI Alberto, b. 6 Jun 1939, Rome, Italy. Baritone. Education: Studied at the Accademia di Santa Cecilia, Rome. Debut: Spoleto in 1963 as Simon Boccanegra. Career: Teatro Fenice Venice in 1970 as Rossini's Figaro; Appearances in Milan, Rome, Naples, Paris, Rio de Janeiro, Ghent, Florence and Aix-en-Provence; Edinburgh Festival in 1973; Glyndebourne Festival in 1980 as Ford in Falstaff; Sang Mozart's Count on tour to Japan with the company of the Vienna Staatsoper, 1986; Sang at the Berlin Staastoper in 1987 as Dandini in La Cenerentola; Pesaro and Cologne, 1988-89 in Il Signor Bruschino and Il Cambiale di Matrimonio; Bonn Opera in 1990 as Rossini's Figaro; Sang Blansac in La Scala di Seta at the 1990 Schwetzingen Festival; Season 1992 as Blansac at Cologne and Paris; Sang Geronio in Rossini's Il Turco in Italia, Brussels, 1996. Recordings: Masetto in Don Giovanni; Il Matrimonio Segreto; Il Campanello; Pagliacci; Video of La Scala di Seta. Address: c/o Oper der Stadt Köln, Offenbachplatz, D-5000 Cologne, Germany.

RINALDI Margarita, b. 12 Jan 1933, Turin, Italy. Soprano. Education: Studied in Rovigo. Debut: Spoleto in 1958 as Lucia di Lammermoor. Career: La Scala Milan in 1959 as Siaide in Mosè by Rossini; Dublin in 1961 as Carolina in Il Matrimonio Segreto and Gilda; Verona Arena in 1962 and 1969; US debut at Dallas in 1966 as Gilda; Glyndebourne Festival in 1966 as Carolina; Bregenz Festival in 1974 and 1980 in Un Girono di Regno and as Alice Ford; Further appearances in Barcelona, Chicago, San Francisco, Wexford, Rome, Naples and Turin; Other roles include Amina, Norina, Linda di Chamounix, Marie in La Fille du Régiment, Bertha in La Prophète, Sophie, Ilia, Fiordiligi, Violetta, Oscar and the Marschallin; Maggio Musicale Florence, 1977-78 as Amenaide in Tancredi and Helena in A Midsummer Night's Dream; Retired from stage in 1981; Many concert engagements. Recordings: Lucia di Lammermoor; Rigoletto; Le Prophète; La Scala di Seta; L'Africaine; Ilia in Idomeneo.

RINGART Anna, b. 15 Jan 1937, Paris, France. Mezzo-Soprano. Education: Studied with Irene Joachim and Marguerite Liszt in Paris; Hamburg Musikhochschule with Frau Anders-Mysz-Gmeiner. Career: Sang at such German opera centres as Lubeck, Koblenz, Dusseldorf and Hamburg; Sang at the Paris Opéra from 1973 under Karl Böhm, Pierre Boulez, Seiji Ozawa and Georg Solti, in a repertoire extending from Mozart to Schoenberg's Moses und Aron; Appeared in the 1985 premiere of Docteur Faustus by Konrad Boehmer; Opéra-Comique in 1988 as the Nurse in Boris Godunov; Has sung at many festivals of contemporary music notably with the group Contrasts. Address: c/o Théâtre National de Paris, 8 Rue Scribe, F-75009 Paris, France.

RINGBORG (Hans) Patrik Erland, b. 1 Nov 1965, Stockholm, Sweden. Conductor. Education: Stockholm Institute of Music, 5 years; Royal College of Music, Stockholm, 4 years; Further studies in Vienna and London. Debuts: Ystad Summer Opera, Akhnaten by Glass, 1989; Städtische Bühnen, Freiburg, Bizet's Carmen, 1992; Royal Opera, Stockholm, triple bill with Scheherazade, 1993. Career: Conductor and Coach since 1987, Swedish Radio Choir, 1988, Sächsische Staatsoper, Dresden, 1988, Royal Opera, Stockholm, 1989-93 (including TV), Canadian Opera Company, 1992, 2nd Kapellmeister and Studienleiter, Städtische Bühnen Freiburg, 1993-95; Co 1st Kapellmeister, Städtische Bühnen Freiburg, 1995-. Honours: British Council Fellow, 1987; Major Scholarship, Royal Academy of Music, Stockholm, 1987; Music Fellowship, Swedish-American Foundation, 1990; 1st R-U, First Competition for Opera Conductors, Royal Opera, Stockholm, 1997. Current Management: Nordic Artist, Stockholm, Sweden, Künstleragentur Markow, München, Germany. Address: Hindenburgstrasse 28, D-79102 Freiburg in Breisgau, Germany.

RINGHOLZ Teresa, b. 30 Dec 1958, Rochester, NY, USA. Soprano. Education: Studied at the Eastman School, Rochester and in San Francisco. Debut: Western Opera Theatre, San Francisco in 1982 as Gilda. Career: Toured in the USA then sang in Europe from 1985 with debut at Strasbourg as Zerbinetta; Cologne Opera from 1985 as Liu, Sophie, Susanna, Despina, Pamina and Sandrina in La Finta Giardiniera; Sang at the Salzburg Festival, 1987-88 and at Tel-Aviv with the Cologne Opera Company; Further appearances in opera and concert throughout Germany, France and Switzerland; Other roles include Gretel, Oscar, Lauretta, Micaela, Marzelline and Adele in Die Fledermaus; Season 1992 as the Wife in the premiere of Schnittke's Life With an Idiot, Amsterdam, and as Fanny in Rossini's La Cambiale di Matrimonio, Paris; Most recently sang at the Kennedy Center with the Washington Opera in 1994 as Susanna in Le Nozza di Figaro; Violetta in Bogota and Fiordiligi in Barcelona, Seville and the Hamburg Staatsoper. Address: St Apernstrasse 20, 50667 Cologne, Germany.

RINKEVICIUS Gintaras, b. 20 Jan 1960, Vilnius, Lithuania. Conductor. Education: Studies at St Petersburg and Moscow Conservatoires. Career: Assistant conductor of Lithuanian Philharmonic Orchestra, 1979; Music Director of Lithuanian State Symphony Orchestra from 1988; Tours with Moscow Radio Orchestra to: Italy; Spain; Austria; Finland; Yugoslavia; Worked with such soloists as Natalia Gutman, Peter Donohoe, Oleg Kagan and Vladimir Ovchinikov; Repertoire includes music by: Dvorak, Mahler, Poulenc, Orff, Honegger, Prokoviev, Elgar and John Adams, in addition to standard works; Appearances with Lithuanian State Opera, notably conducting Nabucco in Paris, 1992; Guest engagements with Russian State Symphony, Moscow Philharmonic and St Petersburg Philharmonic Orchestras; Performed Wagner's Flying Dutchman, in Vilnius, 1995. Honours: Winner, All-Union Conducting Competition at St Petersburg Conservatoire; Third Prize, Herbert von Karajan Conducting Competition, 1985; Second Prize, in Janos Ferencsik Competition, Budapest, 1986. Address: c/o Sonata, 11 Northpark Street, Glasgow, G20 7AA, Scotland.

RINTZLER Marius, b. 14 Mar 1932, Bucharest, Rumania. Bass Singer. Education: Studied at the Bucharest Conservatory with A Alexandrescu. Debut: Bucharest in 1964 as Basilio in Il Barbiere di Siviglia. Career: Member of the Deutsche Oper am Rhein Dusseldorf; Has also sung at Covent Garden, Drottningholm, Edinburgh in Die Soldaten in 1972, and Cologne; Glyndebourne Festival, 1967-79 as the Commendatore, Enrico in Anna Bolena, Osmin, Bartolo, La Roche in Capriccio and Morosus in Die schweigsame Frau; Metropolitan Opera, 1973-74 as Alberich; Geneva in 1974 as Osmin; Further appearances in Rio de Janeiro, San Francisco, Stockholm and Oslo; Sang in the US premiere of Penderecki's Die schwarze Maske, Santa Fe, 1988; Concert engagements in sacred music by Bach. Recordings: Bruckner F minor Mass; Beethoven Mass in C; Bach Cantatas; Madama Butterfly; Shostakovich's 13th Symphony; Orlando by Handel; Tamerlano by Handel; Video of Il Barbiere di Siviglia. Address: c/o Norman McCann Artists Ltd, The Coach House, 56 Lawrie Park Gardens, London, SE26 6XJ, England.

RIPPON Michael (George), b. 10 Dec 1938, Coventry, Warwickshire, England. Bass-Baritone. Education: MA(Cantab), St John's College, Cambridge, 1957-60; Royal Academy of Music, 1960-63; ARAM. Debut: Handel Opera Society in 1963 as Nireno in Giulio Cesare. Career: Sang in the 1967 London premiere of Puccini's Edgar; Covent Garden Opera in 1969; Sang Leporello with Welsh National Opera in 1969; Glyndebourne Festival, 1970-73 in Die Zauberflöte, Le nozze di Figaro, The Queen of Spades and The Visit of The Old Lady; Has also sung with English National Opera, Scottish Opera, Handel Opera, Boston

Opera, New York City Opera and PACT, Johannesburg, and at most leading music festivals and societies in the UK and abroad; Sang in the premieres of Maxwell Davies's Martyrdom of St Magnus in 1977 and The Lighthouse in 1989, and as Merlin in Hamilton's Lancelot in 1985. Recordings: Belshazzar's Feast; Bach Cantatas and B minor Mass; Mozart's Requiem; Purcell's Ode to St Cecilia; Handel's Israel in Egypt; Schoenberg's Moses und Aron; Vaughan Williams's Hugh The Drover; Holst's The Wandering Scholar; Mathias' This Worlds Joie; Salome. Hobbies: Reading; Walking; Swimming.

RISHTON Timothy (John), b. 14 August 1960, Lancashire, England. Organist; Musicologist. m. Tracy Jane Hogg, 11 July 1987, 2 sons, 1 daughter. Education: BA Music, University of Reading; Certificate in Welsh, PhD University of Wales; MusM, University of Manchester, England; Associate, Royal College of Organists. Career: Numerous recitals worldwide including complete Stanley series, London, 1981 and complete Bach Trio Sonatas, London and Salford, 1983; Complete Bach organ works, Norway, 1988-89; Concerts in Belgium and Central Europe; 3 week tour of Arctic and Scandinavia, 1986; Subsequent tours, 1987-89 including Bodo Cathedral and Nordlands Musikkfestuke; Tours in Far East and USA; 1st performance of Smethergell Harpsichord Concerto, Tadley, 1983; Lectures, Boxhill Summer School annually since 1985, University of Oxford 1986 and 1987; University of Reading, 1988; Norwegian Music Conservatoire, Trondheim, 1993-; Many public lectures in English, Welsh and Norwegian some broadcast; Many radio and television broadcasts for HTV, 1984-87, NRK and BBC, 1989-91; College of North Wales, Bangor, Wales, 1984-87, 1989-91; Organist and Master of Choristers, Collegiate Church of St Cybi, Holyhead and Parish Churches of Holy Island, Anglesey, 1984-87. Compositions: Organ Works. Recordings: with Aled Jones, 1985; Organ Works of the Eighteenth-Century, 1986; From Many Lands, 1991. Publications: Aspects of Keyboard Music; Essays in Honour of Susi Jeans, 1986; Organist in Norway, 1989; Co-Translator of D J Grout, A History of Western Music into Welsh. Contributions to: Die Musik in Geschichte und Gegenwart; Musical Times; Music Review; The American Organist; The Organists Review; Various Newspapers. Honours: 3 Reading University Organ Playing Prizes, 1979-81; Louise Dyer Award, 1985; Robert Richards Prize, 1985; Gorsedd Beirdd Ynys Prydain, 1987. Hobbies: Walking; Welsh Literature; Typography. Address: 6386 Mandalen, Norway.

RIVA Ambroglio, b. 1951, Ignazio, Milan, Italy. Singer (Bass). Debut: Teatro Nuovo Milan, 1975, in Lucia di Lammermoor. Career: Has appeared widely in Italy, notably in La Bohème at Verona (1980) and at the Verona Arena in Aida and Carmen; Sang in Donizetti's Martyrs at Bergamo, in Anna Bolena at Brescia and Sparafucile in Rigoletto at Ferrara; Valle d'Istria Festival, 1985, as Polyphemus in Acis and Galatea; Maggio Musicale Florence, 1990, as Angelotti in Tosca; Further appearances at Salzburg, Wurzberg and Berlin. Address: c/o Teatro Comunale, Via Solferino 15, 50123 Florence, Italy.

RIVA Douglas, b. 16 August 1951, Jacksonville, Illinois, USA. Pianist. m. Karen E Riley, 9 November 1974. Education: BM 1974, MM 1975, Juilliard School; PhD, New York University, 1983. Debut: Town Hall, New York, May 1982. Career includes: World premiere, Granados Serenata for 2 violins and piano, 1987; American premiere, Scarlatti's Sonata in G major, 1987; World premiere, Granados, 15 solo piano works & duet En la Aldea, 1984; World premiere, John Corigliano's Gazebo Dances, 1984; Concerts at White House, Carnegie Hall, US National Gallery of Art, New York Museum of Modern Art, 1993; Radio Nacional de Espana, Catalunya Radio, Barcelona TV; Principal flautist, El Paso Symphony Orchestra, Texas, 1967-68; World premiere, Farfalle by Xavier Turull, Barcelona, 1991; Inaguaural Recital, Sala Fernando Coelho, Belo Horizonte, Brazil, 1992. Recordings: Centaur Records, Musical Heritage Society, Keystone Music Roll Co (Piano Roll Recordings, 1987); Documentary, Nos Dutch Television, 1991; Brazil Television, 1992. Publications: The Goyescas for Piano by Enrique Granados: A Critical Edition, 1982; The 20 Minute Piano Workout, 1987. Current Management: Conciertos Daniel, Los Madrazo 16, 28014 Madrid, Spain. Address: 200 East 36th Street, Apt. F, New York, NY 10016, USA.

RIVENQ Nicolas, b. 1958, London, England. Baritone. Education: Studied with Madame Bonnardo in Paris, at the Orleans Conservatory and with Michel Senechal at the School of The Paris Opera; Further study with Nicola Rossi-Lermeni at Indiana University. Career: Sang major roles in such operas as Boris Godunov, La Traviata and Don Giovanni at Indiana; 1984-85 season as Sulpice in La Fille du Régiment, Guglielmo, Marcello and Jupiter in Orphée aux Enfers, and Christus in Bach's St Matthew Passion; Recital in Moscow and Leningrad in 1984 and sang Bach Cantatas with English Chamber Orchestra in London and Edinburgh; Sang in Lully's Atys under William Christie at the Paris Opera in 1986 and on tour to Tourcoing, Versailles and New York, 1988; Schwetzingen and Karlsruhe Festivals in 1988 with Tarare by Salieri under Jean-Claude Malgoire, Paris Opera, 1989; Season 1989 with Rameau's Platée at Montpellier and Don Giovanni for Opera Northern Ireland; 1990-91 included Osman and Adario in Les Indes Galantes at Aix, Mozart's Count in Toulouse and performances of La Clemenza di Tito by Gluck at Tourcoing; Cherubini's Anacreon with The Orchestra of The Age of Enlightenment, 1992; Sang Sallustia in Pacini's L'Ultimo giorno di Pompei, Martina, France, 1996. Address: c/o Anglo Swiss Ltd, Suite 35-37, Morley House, 320 Regent Street, London W1R 5AD, England.

RIVERS Malcolm, b. 1940, England. Baritone. Education: Studies at Royal College of Music and is a Member of RSC. Career: Appearances with English National Opera in various roles including Alberich in The Ring, Escamillo in Carmen, and Marullo in Rigoletto; Played in Troilus and Cressida and La Fanciulla del West at Covent Garden, Germont in La Traviata and Alberich in Seattle, numerous other appearances; Sang Sullivan's Pirate King and Pooh-Bar with the D'Oyly Carte Company, 1989; Alberich in The Ring of Falstaff, Arizona, 1996. Address: c/o D'Oyly Carte Opera Company, Africa House, 64-68 Kingsway, London, WC2B 6BD, England.

RIZZI Carlo, b. 19 July 1960, Milan, Italy. Conductor. Education: Studied at the Milan Conservatoire, with Vladimir Delman in Bologna and at the Accademia Chigiana with Franco Ferrara. Debut: Milan Angelicum in 1982 in Donizetti's L'Aio nell'Imbarazzo. Career includes: Conducted Falstaff in Parma in 1985 and widely in Italy with Rigoletto, La Traviata, Tancredi, Donizetti's Torquato Tasso, Beatrice di Tenda, La Voix Humaine, Don Giovanni, L'Italiana in Algeri and Salieri's Falstaff; British debut in 1988 at Buxton Festival with Torquato Tasso; Netherlands Opera debut in 1989 with Don Pasquale and productions of Fra Diavolo and Norma at Palermo in 1989; Royal Philharmonic debut in 1989, London Philharmonic in 1990 and Philharmonia in 1991; Australian Opera, 1989-90 with Il Barbiere di Siviglia and Lucrezia Borgia; Tosca for Opera North in 1990 and La Cenerentola at Covent Garden; Concert repertoire includes symphonies by Tchaikovsky and works by Haydn, Mozart, Beethoven and French composers; Regular guest in Italy and Holland; US opera debut in 1994 with Il Barbiere di Siviglia; Season 1996 included Don Giovanni and La Bohème for WNO. Recordings: L'Italiana in Algeri; Donizetti's Il Furioso sull'Isola di San Domingo; Rossini's Ciro in Babilonia; Paisiello's La Scuffiara; Piccinni's La Pescatrice; Arias for tenor and orchestra by Rossini, with Ernesto Palacio; Schubert, Liszt and Debussy with the London Philharmonic and Philharmonia. Address: c/o Allied Artists, 42 Montpelier Square, London, SW7 1JZ, England.

RIZZI Lucia, b. 1965, Turin, Italy. Singer (Mezzo-soprano). Education: Studied architecture and music in Turin. Career: Appearances throughout Italy, in Tokyo and at the Aldeburgh Festival, under such conductors as Myung Wha Chung, Gianandrea Gavazzeni and Semyon Bychkov; Operas include Monteverdi's Poppea, Pergolesi's Frate 'nnamorato and Vivaldi's Farnace; Roles include Mozart's Fiordiligi, Dorabella and Sesto, Clarice in La Pietra del Paragone and Rossini's Roggiero (Tancredi) and Cenerentola (both at Zurich, 1996-97); Further engagements in Luisa Miller, Falstaff, Boris Godunov, Lady Macbeth of the Mtsensk District (in Florence), Stravinsky's Rossignol and Les Noces (Monte Carlo) and the Italian premiere of Tchaikovsky's Cantata Moscow, at Genoa; Other concerts in music by Vivaldi, Mahler and Schoenberg, at most Italian music centres. Recordings include: Rossini Rarities. Address: c/o Opernhaus Zurich, Falkenstrasse 1, CH-8008 Zurich, Switzerland.

RIZZO Francis, b. 8 Nov 1936, New York, NY, USA. Stage Director; Administrator. Education: BA, Hamilton College, 1958; Yale University School of Drama, 1958-60. Career: American Director, Spoleto Festival of Two Worlds, 1968-71; Artistic Administrator, Wolf Trap Farm Park for The Performing Arts, 1972-78; Artistic Director, the Washington Opera, 1977-87; As director staged productions for New York City Opera, Houston Grand Opera, Washington Opera, Wolf Trap, Opera Theater of St Louis, Santa Fe Opera, Baltimore Opera, Teatro Verdi, Trieste, Michigan Opera Theater, Théâtre Municipal, Marseilles. Contributions to: Opera News. Membership: American Guild of Musical Artists. Address: 590 West End Avenue, New York, NY 10024, USA.

ROADS Curtis (Bryant), b. 9 May 1951, Cleveland, OH, USA. Composer; Author; Producer; Editor. Education: Experimental Music Studio, University of IL, 1970-71; CA Institute of the Arts, 1972-74; University of CA, San Diego, 1974-77. Career: Associate Fellow, Center for Music Experiment, University of CA, San Diego, 1977; Editor, Computer Music Journal, The Massachusetts Institute of Technology Press, 1978-89; Co-founder, International Computer Music Association, 1979; Research Associate, Experimental Music Studio, Massachusetts Institute of Technology, 1980-86; Visiting Professor, University of Naples, 1988; Visiting Lecturer, Harvard University, 1989; Co-founder, Cahill Society, 1990; Professor, Department of Pedagogy, IRCAM, Paris, 1991-93; Currently: Professor, Les Ateliers UPIC, and Chargé de Cours, University of Paris 8. Compositions: Construction, 1976; Objet, 1977; Nscor 1980; Field, 1981; Message, 1987; Clang-tint, 1994. Recordings Music for Instruments and Computer, CD, Experimental Musi Studio, MA Institute of Technology; New Computer Music, CD Germany; Clang-tint, 1991-92. Publications: Foundations o Computer Music, 1985; Composers and The Computer, 1985 The Music Machine, 1988; Representations of Musical Signals 1991; The Computer Music Tutorial, 1995. Address: Departmen of Pedagogy, Les Ateliers UPIC, 5 Allée de Nantes, Massy France.

ROAR Leif, b. 31 Aug 1937, Copenhagen, Denmark Baritone. Education: Studied in Copenhagen. Career: Sang in Kie and Dusseldorf from 1967, at Schwetzingen Festival in 1969 ir the premiere of Klebe's Märchen von der Schönen Lilie, Munich Opera from 1971 as Wotan and Jochanaan, Salzburg Easte Festival, 1973-74 as Donner and Kurwenal, Stuttgart in 1974 as Escamillo, and Bayreuth Festival from 1976 as Telramund and Klingsor; Metropolitan Opera debut in 1982 as Pizarro in Fidelio Other roles include Mozart's Count and Don Giovanni Hindemith's Mathis, Scarpia, Nick Shadow in The Rake's Progress and Hans Sachs; Guest engagements in Moscow Milan, Buenos Aires, Hamburg, Mannheim, Bregenz and Stockholm; Sang Orestes in Elektra at Copenhagen in 1986 Wotan in the Ring at Arhus in 1987 and also heard in concerts and as oratorio singer. Recordings include: Telramund in Lohengrin, Bayreuth, 1982; Video of Die Meistersinger in a production from Royal Opera, Stockholm. Address: c/o Der Jydske Opera, Musikhuset Arhus, Thomas Jensens Alle DK-8000 Arhus, Denmark.

ROARK-STRUMMER Linda, b. 1952, Tulsa, OK, USA Soprano. Education: Studied at Tulsa University. Career: Sang Dorabella at St Louis in 1977; Engaged at Hannover, 1979-80 Linz, 1980-86 as Regina in the 1983 Austrian premiere of Lortzing's opera and in the premiere of In Seinem Garten Lieb Don Perlimpin Belinda by B Sulzer; New York City Opera in 1985 as Giselda in I Lombardi; Over 150 performances of Verdi's Abigaille, notably at the Deutsche Oper Berlin in 1987, Ravenna in 1988 and Montreal and Verona in 1992; La Scala Milan in 1988 as Lucrezia in I Due Foscari; Sang Krasava in a concer performance of Smetana's Libuse in New York; Other roles include Lina in Stiffelio, the Forza and Trovatore Leonoras Arabella, Jenufa and Antonia; Guest engagements at Hamburg Krefeld, Milwaukee and Venice; Sang Norma for Opera Hamilton at Toronto in 1991; Turandot at Portland, 1996. Address: Opera Hamilton, 2 King Street West, Hamilton, Ontario, L6P 1A1 Canada.

ROBB Anthea Jane, b. 6 June 1946, Manchester, England Opera Singer; Voice Coach. m. Robin Greaves, 19 October 1996 1 son. Education: BA, Open University; Associate, Roya Manchester College of Music. Career: Scottish Opera, 1968 Geneva Opera, 1969, 1970; Numerous Concerts Around North of England; Halle Proms. Honours: Martin Musical Scholarship, 1996; Finalist, Richard Tauber Scholarship, Wigmore Hall. Membership: ISM. Hobbies: Reading; Cooking; Dress Making. Address: 22 Market Place, Chapel en le Frith, High Peak SK23 0EN, England.

ROBBIN Catherine, b. 1950, Toronto, Canada. Mezzo-Soprano. Career: Many appearances in Baroque music; Sang in Messiah with English Baroque Soloists under Gardiner, Bach's B minor Mass with Monteverdi Choir and Handel's Orlando at the 1989 Promenade Concerts; Opera performances include Olga in Eugene Onegin at Opéra de Lyon, Purcell's Dido and Handel's Orlando, (role of Medoro) with Academy of Ancient Music and Handel's Xerxes at Carmel Bach Festival; Collaborations with Trevor Pinnock, Hogwood, Andrew Davis, John Nelson, Jukka-Peka Saraste and Charles Dutoit; Repertoire includes Les Nuits d'Été by Berlioz, Mahler's Lieder eines Fahrenden Gesellen and Rückert Lieder, Elgar's Sea Pictures and the Brahms Alto Rhapsody; Many recitals in Canada and the USA and appearances at Aldeburgh Festival and with the Songmakers' Almanac; Sang the title role in the North American premiere of Handel's Floridante in Toronto in 1990; Annius in La Clemenza di Tito at the Elizabeth hall, London in 1990; Sang in Handel's Rinaldo at Blackheath and Bromsgrove, 1996. Recordings include: Beethoven's Mass in C and Missa Solemnis; Messiah under Gardiner; Berlioz Songs, also Gardiner; Haydn's Stabat Mater with Trevor Pinnock and the English Concert; Orlando under Hogwood; Mahler Song Cycles. Honours include: Gold Award at the International Benson and Hedges Competition, Aldeburgh, England. Address: 7 Old Town, Clapham, London, SW4 0JT, England.

ROBBINS Julien, b. 14 Nov 1950, Harrisburg, Pennsylvania, USA. Singer (Bass). Education: Studied, Philadelphia Academy of Vocal Arts, and with Nicola Moscona in New York. Debut: Philadelphia 1976, in Un Ballo in Maschera. Career: Engagements at Santa Fe, Miami, Washington and Chicago; Metropolitan Opera from 1979, as Ramphis, Colline, Gremin and Don Fernando in Fidelio; Deutsche Oper Berlin 1990, as Abimelech in Samson et Dalila; Sang Masetto at the Metropolitan, 1990; World premiere, The Voyage, by Philip Glass, Metropolitan Opera (Second Mate and Space Twin), Nightwatchman in Meistersinger, 1993; Deutsche Oper Berlin, Don Giovanni, 1992, 1993, Escamillo, 1993, Turandot, (Timur), 1992; Staatsoper Berlin, Barber of Seville, Basilio, 1992; 1993 Deutsche Oper Berlin Figaro in The Marriage of Figaro; 1994 San Diego Count Rodolfo in La Sonnambala, Lisbon, Escamillo in Carmen, Dresdner Festival, Messiah; Le Comte Ory, Le Gouverneur, Glyndebourne, 1997. Recordings: Salome, First Soldier, Berlin Philharmonic, 1991; Doctor, La Traviata, Metropolitan Opera, 1992. Current Management: c/o Tony Russo, ICM Artists, 40 West 57th St, New York, NY 10019, USA. Address: 2805 Windy Hill Road, Allentown, PA 18103-4663, USA.

ROBERTI Margherita, b. 1930, Davenport, IA, USA. Soprano. Education: Studied at Hunter College and the Mannes School of Music, NY; Further study in Italy, 1956. Debut: Teatro Alfieri Turin, 1957 as Leonore in Il Trovatore. Career: Appeared at Covent Garden in 1959 as Tosca; La Scala debut in 1959 as Abigaille in Nabucco; Engagements at the Verona Arena from 1959; Metropolitan Opera debut in 1962 as Tosca; Edinburgh Festival in 1963 as Luisa Miller and Glyndebourne Festival in 1964 as Lady Macbeth; Other roles include Elisabeth de Valois, Amelia in Un Ballo in Maschera, Hélène in Les Vêpres Siciliennes and Odabella in Atilla; Guest appearances as concert artist in England and North America. Recordings include: Elena in Donizetti's Marino Faliero.

ROBERTS Brenda, b. 16 Mar 1945, Lowell, IN, USA. Soprano. Education: Studied at Northwestern University, Evanstown with Hermann Baer; Further study with Lotte Lehmann, Gerald Moore and Josef Metternich in Germany. Debut: Staatstheater Saarbrucken, 1968 as Sieglinde in Die Walküre. Career: German appearances at Dusseldorf, Essen, Frankfurt, Nuremberg, Wiesbaden and Wuppertal; Member of the Hamburg Staatsoper; Bayreuth Festival in 1974 as Brünnhilde in Siegfried; Sang Isolde at Kassel in 1983; American engagements in Baltimore, Chicago, Baltimore and San Francisco; Metropolitan Opera debut in 1982 as the Dyer's Wife in Die Frau ohne Schatten; Other roles include Salome at Vienna in 1984 and Salome at Bremmen in 1986, Wagner's Senta and Elsa, Verdi's Elisabeth de Valois, Aida, Lady Macbeth, Leonora and Violetta, Mozart's Donna Elvira and Countess, Puccini's Tosca, Giorgetta and Turandot, Santuzza and Lulu; Sang in a concert performance of Die Bakchantinnen by Egon Wellesz at Vienna in 1985; Kiel Opera in 1990 as Elektra and the title role in the premiere of Medea by Friedhelm Dohl. Address: Buhnen Landeshaupstadt, Rathausplatz, D-2300 Kiel, Germany.

ROBERTS Deborah, b. 1952, England. Soprano. Education: Studied at Nottingham University, editing and interpreting Renaissance Baroque music; Further study with Andrea von Ramm in Basle. Career: Has sung with the Tallis Scholars on tours to Europe, Australia and the USA, appearing at most major festivals; Guest concerts with the Deller Consort and the Consort of Musicke; Frequent engagements with Musica Secreta notably in the Early Music Centre Festival, the Lufthansa Festival of Baroque Music and at the National Gallery; Early Music Network tour of Britain with programme Filiae Jerusalem, sacred music for women's voices by Monteverdi, Carissimi, Cavalli, Viadana, Grandi and Marco da Gagliano; Other repertoire includes works by Marenzio, Wert, Luzzaschi, Luigi Rossi and the women composers Francesca Cacini and Barbara Strozzi; Participation in lecture-recitals and workshops on performance practice and ornamentation. Recordings: With Musica Secreta, as musical director, Luzzaschi Madrigals for 1-3 Sopranos; Ensemble Music of Barbara Strozzi, 1994; Over 30 recordings with Tallis Scholars. Honours: Prizewinner, Bruges Early Music Competition, 1981. Address: 846 Devonshire Road, London SE23 3SX, England.

ROBERTS Eric, b. 16 Oct 1944, Conway, North Wales. Singer (Baritone). Debut: Opera debut as Papageno with Welsh National Opera. Career: Has sung with various British companies as: Guglielmo; Falke; Mozart's Figaro; Count and Trinity Moses, in Mahagonny, Scottish Opera; English National Opera in Pacific Overtures and the British premiere of Rimsky's Christmas Eve, 1988; D'Oyly Carte Opera Company, 1988-90; Further appearances as: Don Alfonso for Opera North; Bartolo and Britten's Redburn for Scottish Opera; Don Isaac in the British premiere of Gerhard's The Duenna; Haly, in L'Italiana in Algeri at Dublin; Eugene Onegin, for Opera Omaha, Nebraska, 1993; Australian debut as Bartolo, Lyric Opera of Queensland, 1992; Sang Don Isaac in Gerhard's The Duenna, Leeds, 1996; Concert engagements in Britten's War Requiem at Belgrade and L'Enfant et les Sortilèges at Rotterdam. Address: c/o Athole Still International Management Ltd, Foresters Hall, 25-27 Westow Street, London, SE19 3RY, England.

ROBERTS Kathleen, b. 9 Oct 1941, Hattiesburg, MS, USA. Soprano. Education: Studied at Mississippi College, at Texas Christian University and in Zurich and Darmstadt. Debut: St Gallen in 1967 as Violetta. Career: Appearances at opera houses in Zurich, Geneva, Cologne and Frankfurt; Member of the Darmstadt Opera as Marzelline in Fidelio, Micaela, Aennchen in Der Freischütz, Mozart's Pamina, Susanna and Constanze, Gretel, Martha and Mimi; Modern repertoire has included Luise in Henze's Der Junge Lord and Laetita in The Old Maid and The Thief by Menotti; Many concert appearances; Teacher of Singing in Darmstadt and elsewhere.

ROBERTS Paul (Anthony), b. 2 Jun 1949, Beaconsfield, England. Concert Pianist. 2 sons. Education: BA, Honours, University of York, 1970; Royal Academy of Music, London. Career: Juror, International Debussy Piano Competition, France, 1982, 1984; Cycle of Complete Debussy Piano Music at Purcell Room, London in 1984; World premiere of Maurice Ohana's piano etudes in a live broadcast for Radio France, 1986; Premieres of Ohana work for BBC in 1984, 1986 and 1988; World premiere of original piano score of an unpublished opera by Debussy, Rodrigue et Chimène, BBC Radio 3 in 1988; Lecturer, Professor of Piano at Guildhall School of Music, 1985-; Director, International Piano Summer School, SW France; Music at Ladevie. Publications: Book reviews for Times Educational Supplement, Composer, and Revue Musicale, Paris. Hobbies: Theatre; Reading. Current Management: Management USA, Pat Zagelow, 3420 NE 21st Avenue, OR 97212, USA. Address: 10 Montague Road, London, E8 2HW, England.

ROBERTS Stephen (Pritchard), b. 8 Feb 1949. Singer (Baritone). Education: Scholar, Associate, 1969, Royal College of Music; Graduate, Royal Schools of Music, 1971. Career includes: Professional Lay-Cleric, Westminster Cathedral Choir, 1972-76; Sings regularly in London, UK and Europe, with all major orchestras and choral societies; Has sung in USA, Canada, Israel, Italy, Hong Kong, Paris, Poland, Spain, Singapore and South America; Opera roles include: Count in Marriage of Figaro, Falke in Die Fledermaus, Ubalde in Armide, Ramiro in Ravel's L'Heure Espagnole, Aeneas in Dido and Aeneas, Don Quixote in Master Peter's Puppet Show, Mittenhofer in Elegy for Young Lovers by Henze; Television appearances include Britten's War Requiem, Weill's Seven Deadly Sins, Delius's Sea Drift, Handel's Jephtha and Judas Maccabaeus, Penderecki's St Luke Passion at 1983 Proms, Walton's Belshazzar's Feast at 1984 Proms; Has worked with many orchestras specializing in authentic Baroque; Concert and oratorio performer singing all major baritone roles by JS Bach, Mozart, Handel, Elgar and Britten, also the choral symphonies by Mahler and Beethoven; Sang in Bach's St Matthew's Passion at the Festival Hall, 1997; Professor at Royal Schools of Music, Vocal Faculty, 1993-. Recordings include: Numerous, many with King's College and St John's College Cambridge and Bach Choir of London including: St Matthew Passion, Punch and Judy with London Sinfonietta, The Apostles with LSO, Caractacus with LSO, Requiem with RPO, Messiah, Alexander's Feast, Carmina Burana with Berlin RSO, St Luke Passion, King Priam with London Sinfonietta, and A Sea Symphony. Address: 144 Gleneagle Road, London, SW16 6BA, England.

ROBERTS Susan, b. 1960, USA. Singer - Lyric-Coloratura Soprano. m. Dimitry Sitkovetsky (qv), 26 Jul 1983. Career: Sang at first at the Frefeld Opera then in Wiesbaden and Frankfurt; Has sung Blonchen in productions of Die Entführung by Ruth Berghaus in Frankfurt, Giorgio Strehler in Bologna, Jean-Pierre Ponnelle in Cologne and Giancarlo del Monaco in Bonn; Sang Minette in the premiere of Henze's English Cat at Frankfurt and again in Edinburgh and for the BBC; Further appearances at the Bayreuth and Orange Festivals and other German theatres; Paris Opéra in 1988 in the premiere of La Celestina by Maurice Ohana; Season 1990-91 as Blondchen for Netherlands Opera and Zan in Blitzstein's Regina for Scottish Opera; Concert engagements with radio orchestras in Vienna, Turin and Berlin, the National Orchestra of Spain, Orchestre Philharmonique Paris, Orchestre de Lyon and the Dusseldorf Symphonic; Recitals at the Vassa, Lockenhaus and Schleswig-Holstein Festivals; Season 1992 as Handel's Agrippina at the Buxton Festival; Sang in Param Vir's Snatched by the Gods at the Almeida Theatre, 1996. Honours include: Martha Baird Rockefeller Foundation Grant; Laureate Winner, Concours International Musicale, Geneva. Address: Music International, 13 Ardilaun Road, London, N5 2QR, England.

ROBERTS Winifred, b. 1920, Lismore, New South Wales, Australia. Violinist. m. Geraint Jones. Education: Royal College of Music; Studied with Antonio Brosa and Albert Sammons. Career: National Gallery Concerts, England; Promenade Concerts; 3 Choirs Festival; Lake District Festival; Salisbury Festival; Manchester Festival; Soloist, Festival Hall and Queen Elizabeth Hall; Tours of Italy, Spain, USA; BBC Radio and Television appearances; Professor of Violin, Royal Academy of Music, now retired; Advanced Performers Class, Morley College, London, now retired; Private Teaching; Adjudicating and acting as Outside Examiner at Music Colleges and Schools. Recordings: History of Music; Biber Sonata; Vivaldi Double Concerto; Harpsichord and Violin Sonatas with husband. Honours: Tagore Gold Medal, 1st Prize, Violin Playing, Royal College of Music; Honorary RAM, 1983. Hobbies: Reading; Cooking; Gardening; Walking. Address: The Long House, Arkley Lane, Barnet, Hertfordshire, EN5 3JR, England.

ROBERTSON Christopher, b. 1964, USA. Singer (Baritone). Education: Studied in San Francisco (member of the 1987 Merola Opera Program). Career: Many appearances at Leading Opera Houses in North America and Europe; Metropolitan Opera, season 1992-93, as Marcello and Sharpless in Butterfly; Don Giovanni, 1995-96; European Debut as Guglielmo at Frankfurt Opera, followed by Mozart's Count at Munich, Egberto in Verdi's Aroldo at Covent Garden, and Oreste in Gluck's Iphigénie en Tauride at the Berlin Staatsoper; Prus in The Makropoulos Case at Vancouver, Germont for English National Opera (1996) & Amonasro for San Francisco Opera (1997); Further engagements as Donner in Das Rheingold at Valencia, Count Luna with Florida Grand Opera, 1997 and Rigoleto with San Francisco Opera, also in 1997, Renato in Un Ballo in Maschera Opera, Seattle for Flanders Opera, Belgium, New Orleans, Montreal, Rio de Janeiro, Madrid & Santiago. Honours include: Robert Jackson Memorial Grant, Richard Tucker Music Foundation. Address: c/o Metropolitan Opera, Lincoln Center, NY 10023, USA.

ROBERTSON Duncan, b. 1 Dec 1924, Hamilton, Scotland. Tenor. m. Mary Dawson, 24 Jun 1950, 1 s, 1 d. Education: Diploma SNAM, Gold Medal, 1945; LRAM, 1946 Royal College of Music, London; FGSM, 1975; Fellow Emeritus GSM, 1979. Career: Varied career in Oratorio including appearances in most European countries; Opera mostly at Glyndebourne and Scottish Opera, also Covent Garden, Sadler's Wells, English Opera Group, Welsh Opera, Handel Opera; Many broadcasts ranging from light music to Radio 3; Some television, recordings and recital work; Sang in Canticum Sacrum by Stravinsky, 1st performance in Britain conducted by Robert Craft, 1956; Appeared in Oedipus Rex by Stravinsky, with Jean Cocoteau as narrator and conducted by Stravinsky, 1959; Sang in Benjamin Britten's 50th Birthday Concert, 1963; Sang with Giulini conducting, performance of Schubert's Mass in E Flat, televised from the Edinburgh Festival, 1968; Professor of Singing, Guildhall School of Music and Drama, London, 1966-77; Lecturer in Singing, Royal Scottish Academy of Music and Drama, Glasgow, 1977-88. Address: 13 Priory Park, Bradford on Avon, Wiltshire, BA15 1QU, England.

ROBERTSON John, b. 20 Sep 1938, Galashiels, Scotland. Tenor. Education: Studied at Sedburgh and Edinburgh Universities. Career: Regular appearances with Scottish Opera; 850 performances in 50 roles including Ferrando, Tamino, Ottavio, Albert Herring and Almaviva; Has toured with the company to Austria, Germany, Switzerland, Yugoslavia, Poland, Portugal and Iceland in The Turn of The Screw, The Rape of Lucretia and A Midsummer Night's Dream; Appearances at Edinburgh as Tannhäuser and in Le nozze di Figaro; Has directed the Edinburgh Opera in La Traviata, L'Elisir d'Amore and La Sonnambula; Oratorio and concert work throughout Scotland and on BBC and Scottish TV; Teaches voice in Glasgow and Edinburgh and at the School of Vocal Studies at the Royal Northern College of Music, Manchester. Recordings include: Le nozze di Figaro. Address: c/o Christopher Tennant Artists Management, 11 Lawrence Street, London, SW3 5NB, England.

ROBERTSON Stewart (John), b. 22 May 1948, Glasgow, Scotland. Conductor; Pianist; Music Director. Education: Royal Scottish Academy of Music, 1965-69; Bristol University, 1969-70; Vienna Academy, 1975; Salzburg Mozarteum, 1977; Teachers: Otmar Suitner and Hans Swarowsky for conducting, and Denis Matthews for piano. Career: Assistant Chorus Master, Scottish Opera, Edinburgh Festival Chorus, 1968-69; Chorus Master, London City Singers, 1970-72; Conductor for Cologne Opera, 1972-75; Music Director, Tanz Forum, Zurich Opera, 1975-76, Scottish Opera Touring Company, 1976-79, and Hidden Valley Chamber Orchestra, CA, 1979-82; Associate Conductor and Director of Appn Artists Programme, Des Moines Metro Opera, 1980-88; Music Director, Mid-Columbus Symphony Orchestra, 1984-85, and Santa Fe Symphony Orchestra, 1986-; Assistant Conductor, Oakland Symphony Orchestra, 1985-86; Music Director and Principal Conductor, Glimmerglass Opera, NY, 1987-; Guest Conductor for SNO, and BBC Scottish Symphony Orchestra, CBSO Swiss-Italian Radio SO, San Jose Symphony Orchestra, Utah Symphony Orchestra, Britt Festival, Long Beach, Portland, Sacramento, Kentucky Opera, Arkansas Opera and Montreal Opera. Current Management: John Miller, Robert Lombardo Associates, NY, USA. Address: 81 Poppy Road, Carmel Valley, CA 93924, USA.

ROBINSON Dean, b. 20 Aug 1968, Bathurst, Australia. Singer (Bass). Education: Studied in Australia and Royal Northern College of Music, with Robert Alderson. Career: Opera engagements at Covent Garden in Don Carlos, Die Meistersinger, Lohengrin and Palestrina (also at Metropolitan Opera); Pluto in Monteverdi's Orfeo for English National Opera and Netherlands Opera; 2nd Soldier for ENO; Colline and Sparafucile for Mid

Wales Opera; Sarastro for Opera of the South; Death (Emperor of Atlantis) for Mecklenburgh Opera; Sparafucile for Scottish Opera; King of Scotland in Ariodante at Gwent Garden Festival; Concerts include Bach's St John Passion at Westminster Abbey, Beethoven's Ninth with the Northern Sinfonia and Manchester Camerata, Mozart's Requiem in Stockholm and Verdi Requiem at the Cork Festival, Ireland; Haydn's Creation in the Royal Albert Hall and L'Enfance du Christ with Kent Nagano; Season 1998 as Mr Ratcliffe and Angelotti for Welsh National Opera; Passaaf in Dr Oxis Experiment for ENO and Sarastro for Scottish Opera. Address: c/o Lies Askonas, 6 Henrietta Street, London.

ROBINSON Faye, b. 2 Nov 1943, Houston, TX, USA. Soprano. Education: Studied with Ruth Stewart at Texas Southern University and with Ellen Faull in New York. Debut: New York City Opera, 1972, as Micaela. Career: Has sung Violetta, the Queen of Shemakhan and Liu in New York; Washington Civic Opera in 1973 as Violetta and Juliette; Jackson, FL, 1974-75 as Desdemona and Adina; Aix-en-Provence in 1975 in Der Schauspieldirektor and La Serva Padrona; Engagements in Houston, Barcelona and Frankfurt; Buenos Aires in 1980 in Les Contes d'Hoffmann; Schwetzingen Festival in 1981 as Elektra in Ideomeneo; Paris Opéra and Bordeaux in 1982 as Juliette and Luisa Miller; Other roles include Constanze, Norina and Oscar; Sang in the premiere of The Mask of Time in Boston, 1984 and in the first British performance of Tippett's oratorio; Cologne in 1988 as Constanze. Recordings: Mahler's 8th Symphony; The Mask of Time. Address: c/o Oper der Stadt Köhn, Offenbachplatz, D-5000 Cologne, Germany.

ROBINSON Gail, b. 7 Aug 1946, Meridian, MS, USA. Singer (Soprano). Education: Studied at Memphis State University and with Robley Lawson. Debut: Memphis, 1967 as Lucia in Lammermoor. Career: Appearances in Berlin, Munich and Hamburg; Sang with Metropolitan Opera from 1970, in Die Zauberflöte and as Gilda, Adina, Oscar, Marie in La Fille du Régiment, Rosina and Gretel; Director, Metropolitan National Council Auditions and now Director, Metropolitan Young Artist Development Program. Honour: Winner of Metropolitan's National Council Auditions, 1966. Address: c/o Metropolitan Opera, Lincoln Center, New York, NY 10023, USA.

ROBINSON Michael (Finlay), b. 3 Mar 1933, Gloucester, England. Retired University Professor. m. Ann James, 28 Dec 1961, 2 sons. Education: BA, 1956, BMus, 1957, MA, 1960, DPhil, 1963, Oxford University. Career: Teacher, Royal Scottish Academy of Music, 1960-61; Music Lecturer, Durham University, 1961-65; Assistant Professor, 1965-67, Associate Professor, 1967-70, McGill University, Montreal, Canada; Music Lecturer, 1970-75, Senior Lecturer in Music, 1975-91, Head of Music Department, 1987-94, Professor of Music, 1991-94, Emeritus Professor of Music, 1995-, University of Wales College of Cardiff, Wales. Publications: Opera Before Mozart, 1966, 2 later editions; Naples and Neapolitan Opera, 1972, American reprint, 1984, Italian edition, 1985; Giovanni Paisiello, a thematic catalogue of his works, volume 1, 1990, Volume 2, 1993. Contributions to: Proceedings of the Royal Musical Association; New Grove; Chigiana; Studi Musicali; Soundings; Music and Letters. Honours: Recipient of numerous Research Grants from Canada Council, Ottawa, 1967-69, Leverhulme Foundation, London, 1975 and the British Academy, London, 1972. Memberships: Royal Musical Association; American Musicological Society; International Musicological Society. Hobbies: Gardening; Mountain walking; Skiing; Watercolour painting. Address: Northridge House, Usk Road, Shirenewton, Monmouthshire NP6 6RZ, Wales.

ROBINSON Paul, b. 1970, England. Singer (Baritone). Education:Chorister and Choral Scholar, Kings College, Cambridge; Royal College of Music. Career: Concerts include St John Passion at the London Bach Festival, Bach's Magnificat at Bristol Cathedral, Monteverdi Vespers in Vancouver, St Matthew Passion for Italian Radio and Schubertiade Recital at the Wigmore Hall; Mozart's Coronation Mass with the Royal Flanders Philharmonic Orchestra, Purcell's Indian Queen with the Academy of Ancient Music, Messiah with the CBSO and Haydn's Mariazeller Mass at Canterbury Cathedral; Opera Roles include The Speaker in The Magic Flute for Opera West, Mangus in Tippett's Knot Garden and Janacek's Poacher & Britten's Demetrius for the RAM; Season 1997-98 with the Brahms Requiem in London, Bach's Christmans Oratorio in Oxford, St John Passion with the Royal Liverpool Philharmonic Orchestra, Carmina Burana at Bristol and Handel's Joshua with the Academy of Ancient Music. Recordings: Many Albums with King's College Choir; Robert in Hugh the Drover by Vaughan Williams.

ROBINSON Peter, b. 1949, England. Conductor. Education: Studied music at Oxford. Career: Assistant Organist, Durham Cathedral; Associated with the Glyndebourne Festival Opera, 1971-73; Head of Music Staff and Resident Conductor, Australian Opera, 1973-80; Assistant Music Director, English National Opera, 1981-89, conducting Le nozze di Figaro, Don Giovanni, Die Zauberflöte, Così fan tutte, Otello, Rigoletto, The Mastersingers, Madame Butterfly, Orfeo, Maria Stuarda, The Mikado, Carmen, Werther, Hansel and Gretel, Simon Boccanegra and The Turn of the Screw; Appearances for Kent Opera with The Beggar's Opera and Don Giovanni, and the Scottish Opera with The Pearl Fishers; Conducted Cosi fan tutte in a production for BBC Television; Has conducted in Australia; Le nozze di Figaro, Victoria State Opera, 1987; Die Entführung VSO, 1989; Così fan tutte, The Australian Opera, 1990; Don Giovanni, State Opera of South Australia, 1991; Engagements with Opera Factory (Marriage of Figaro also for television), 1991; Symphony concerts with the London Symphony, London Mozart Players and London Sinfonietta; Concerts with the Melbourne and Sydney Symphony Orchestras, 1988-90; Sound and Video recordings with Lesley Garrett for Silva Screen Records and BBC Television; Conducted The Magic Flute for British Youth Opera, 1996. Current Management: Marks Management Limited. Address: c/o 14 New Burlington Street, London W1X 1FF, England.

ROBINSON Sharon, b. 2 Dec 1949, Houston, TX, USA. Concert Cellist. m. Jaime Laredo, 23 Nov 1976. Education: Graduated, North Carolina School of the Arts, 1968; University of Southern California, 1968-70; BM, Peabody Conservatory of Music, 1972. Debut: New York in 1974. Career: Member of Kalichstein-Laredo-Robinson Trio from 1976; Soloist at Marlboro Music Festival, Mostly Mozart Festival and South Bank Festival in London, Edinburgh Festival, Madeira Bach Festival, Helsinki Festival and Tivoli Gardens; Commissioned and premiered Ned Rorem's After Reading Shakespeare, for solo cello and premiered Alan Shulman's Kol Nidrei for cello and piano, William Bland's Rhapsody for cello and piano, and Robert Blake's Cello Sonata. Recordings: Vivaldi Sonatas; Fauré's Elegy; Debussy Sonata; Rorem's After Reading Shakespeare; Beethoven's Triple Concerto; With Kalichstein-Laredo-Robinson Trio, Mendelssohn and Brahms Trios; Duos for Violin and Cello with Jaime Laredo. Honours: Avery Fisher Award, 1979; Levintritt Award, 1975; Pro Musicis Foundation Award, 1974. Membership: Violoncello Society of America. Hobbies: Gardening; Hiking; Swimming. Current Management: Harold Shaw Concerts. Address: c/o Shaw Concerts, 1900 Broadway, New York, NY 10023, USA.

ROBINSON Timothy, b. England. Singer (Tenor). Education: Studied at New College Oxford (Choral Scholar) and with William McAlpine at the Guildhall School. Career: 1996 concerts include Mozart's Davidde Penitente at Seville, Messiah in Singapore, Weber's Euryanthe at the Elizabeth Hall, South Bank, and Proms debut as Jupiter in Semele, under William Christie; Opera roles include Kudrjash in Katya Kabanova for Glyndebourne Touring Opera, Fenton and Scaramuccio (Ariadne auf Naxos) for English National Opera and Jupiter at the Aix-en-Provence Festival (French premiere, 1996); Member of the Royal Opera, in such operas as Nabucco, Traviata and Fedora; Sang in the British premiere of Pfitzner's Palestrina, 1997; Season 1997-98 in Katya Kabanova at Glyndebourne and in Turandot at the Paris Opera; Other roles include Don Ottavio, Tamino and Alfredo, with Travelling Opera. Recordings include: Bach's Magnificat (Naxos); Vaughan Williams Serenade to Music (Decca); Beethoven Cantatas (DGG). Address: c/o Lies Askonas Ltd, 6 Henrietta St, London WC2E 8LA, England.

ROBISON Paula, b. 8 June 1941, Nashville, Tennessee, USA. Flautist. m. Scott Nickrenz, 1 daughter. Career: Founding Artist Member, Chamber Music Society of Lincoln Center; Joint Recitalist with pianist Ruth Laredo and Guitarist Eliot Fisk; Soloist, New York Philharmonic, Atlanta, American and San Francisco Symphony Orchestra; Recitalist at numerous venues including Carnegie Hall and Kennedy Center and Wigmore Hall in January 1990; Commissioned and premiered Kirchner's Music for Flute and Orchestra with the Indianapolis Symphony, Toru Takemitsu's I Hear the Water Dreaming, Robert Beaser's Song of the Bells; Numerous television appearances including Live from Lincoln Center, 1984-85; Christmas at the Kennedy Center; Sunday Morning, CBS Television; For 10 years (1978-1988) Co-Director of Chamber Music, Spoleto Festival at Charleston, South Carolina, and Spoleto, Italy; Blue Ridge Airs II, flute and orchestra, Kenneth Frazelle, 1991; Soloist, London Symphony Orchestra, Michael Tilson Thomas, 1995; I Solisti Veneti, Claudio Scimone, 1995. Recordings: Has made many recordings including, Flute Music of the Romantic Era; The Sonatas for Flute and Harpsichord by J S Bach (complete) and G F Handel (complete) with Kenneth Cooper; Release for Music Masters: American Masterworks for flute & piano; Omega, Brasileirinho, Choros of Brazil, 1993; Musicmasters, French Master pieces with Ruth Laredo, piano, 1990; Arabesque, Grieg & Anderson, 1995. Publications: The Paula Robison Flute Warmups Book, European American Publishers, 1990; The Anderson Collection, 1994; Paula Robison Flute Masterclass, Paul Hindemith, 1995. Current Management: Shaw Concerts. Address: c/o Shaw Concerts Inc, 1900 Broadway, New York, NY 10023, USA.

ROBLES Marisa, b. 4 May 1937, Madrid, Spain. Concert Harpist. m. David Bean, 29 Oct 1985, 2 sons, 1 daughter. Education: Real Conservatorio de Musica, Madrid, gaining Honours, 1953. Debut: Spain, 1954. Career: Settled in UK and appeared on many TV programmes; London concert debut, 1963; Solo recitals and major orchestral appearances in UK, Europe, Japan, Australia, Canada, USA, South America, with most London orchestras, New York Philharmonic; Professor, Real Conservatorio de Musica, Madrid, 1958-63; Professor, Royal College of Music, London, 1973-; Artistic Director: World Harp Festival, Cardiff, Wales, 1991-, World Harp Festival II, 1994. Compositions: Narnia Suite; Music for Narnia Chronicles; Irish Suite; Basque Suite for flute and harp. Recordings: For various labels. Honours: Fellow, Royal College of Music, 1983. Memberships: International Harp Association; Royal Overseas League; UK Harp Association; Vice-President, Spanish Association of Harpists. Hobbies: Gardening; Theatre. Current Management: Clarion/Seven Muses, 47 Whitehall Park, London N19 3TW, England. Address: 38 Luttrell Avenue, London SW15 6PE, England.

ROBOTHAM Barbara, b. 15 Jan 1936, Blackpool, England. Musician; Singer. m. Eric Waite, 30 Aug 1958, 1 son. Education: ARMCM TeachersDiploma with distinction, 1957, Performers Diploma with distinction, 1959, Royal Manchester College of Music. Career: Appearances with all major British Orchestras; Festival appearances include Three Choirs Festival, Cheltenham, Haydn-Mozart Festival, Gulbenkian Lisbon, and Bordeaux France; Concerts include Paris, Madrid, Barcelona, Prague, and Frankfurt; Senior Lecturer at Royal Northern College of Music and Professor of Voice at Lancaster University. Recordings: Stravinsky's Cantata on Old English Texts; Walton's Gloria. Honours: Imperial League of Opera Prize and Curtis Gold Medal, 1958; 1st Prize, Liverpool Philharmonic International Singers Competition, 1960; 2nd Prize, Concours International de Geneva, 1961; Honorary Fellowship, Royal Northern College of Music, 1992. Membership: Incorporated Society of Musicians. Hobbies: Reading; Sewing; Sailing. Address: 49 Blackpool Road North, St Annes on Sea, Lancashire, England.

ROBSON Christopher, b. 9 Dec 1953, Falkirk, Scotland. Opera and Concert Singer (Counter-Tenor). m. Laura Carin Snelling, 18 May 1974, div. 1984. Education: Cambridge College of Arts and Technology, 1970-72; Singing with James Gaddarn, Trinity College of Music, London, 1972-73; Privately with Paul Esswood and Helga Mott. Debut: Handel's Samson, Queen Elizabeth Hall, London, 1976. Career: Opera debut, Handel's Sosarme, Barber Institute, Birmingham, 1979; Principal roles, Kent Opera, Phoenix Opera, Handel Opera Society, Royal Opera Covent Garden (Semele), 1988-; English National Opera (Orfeo, Xerxes, title roles in Julius Caesar and Akhnaten, Lear), Frankfurt State Opera, Berliner Kammeroper (Orlando title role), Houston Grand Opera, New York City Opera, Opera Factory Zurich, Opera Factory-London Sinfonietta, Nancy Opera, Innsbruck Tirolertheater; Sang at major festivals, UK, France, Spain, Austria, Netherlands, USA, Switzerland, Germany, Poland, and BBC Proms; Concerts throughout UK and Europe; Broadcasts, BBC, SFB, WDR, ORF, DRS, Radio France Musique; Member: Monteverdi Choir, 1974-84; London Oratory Choir, 1974-80; The Spieglers, 1976-82; St George's Theatre Company, 1976; Westminster Cathedral Choir, 1980-85; Kings Consort, 1981-86; New London Consort, 1986-; Sang in Xerxes on ENO Russian tour, 1990; Season 1992-93, Ptolemy (Julius Caesar) for Scottish Opera, Polinesso (Ariodante) for ENO, Andronicus (Tamerlano) for Karlsruhe, Ezio title role, Berliner Kammeroper; Season 1993-94, Tamerlano title role, Opera North, Arsamenes (Xerxes), ENO, Apollo (Death in Venice), Liège, Oberon (Midsummer Night's Dream), Covent Garden Festival, Tolomeo (Giulio Cesare), Bayerische Staatsoper Munich; Season 1994-95, Oberon, ENO; Season 1995-96, Arsamenes, Chicago Lyric Opera, Vlaamse Oper Antwerp, Bayerische Staatsoper Munich, Oberon, Ravenna Festival; Season 1966-97, Didimus (Theodora), Glyndebourne Touring Opera; Season 1997-98, Orlofsky (Fledermaus), Bayerisches Staatsoper, Munich. Recordings: Numerous including: Resurrection, Maxwell Davies; Psyche, Locke; Ezio, Handel; Artaxerxes, Arne; Magnificat, Bach. Hobbies: Wine; Food. Address: c/o Music International, 13 Ardilaun Road, London N5 2QR, England.

ROBSON Elizabeth, b. 1938, Dundee, Scotland. Soprano. m. Neil Howlett. Education: Studied at Royal Scottish Academy of Music and in Florence. Debut: Sadler's Wells in 1961 as Micaela. Career: Appearances at Covent Garden throughout the 1960s as Musetta, Zdenka, Sophie, Susanna, Pamina, Marzelline and Nannetta in Falstaff; Guest appearances with Scottish Opera as Zerlina and at the 1967 Edinburgh Festival as Anne Trulove in The Rake's Progress; Sang also at Aix-en-Provence and La Scala Milan; Noted concert artist. Recordings: Marzelline in Fidelio.

ROBSON Nigel, b. 1955, Argyllshire, Scotland. Tenor. Education: Studied at the Royal Northern College of Music with Alexander Young. Career: Sang with the Glyndebourne Festival Chorus and English National Opera from 1981 as Monteverdi's Orfeo and in the premiere of Birtwistle's The Mask of Orpheus, 1986; British stage premiere of Weill's Der Protagonist; Sang Ferrando in David Freeman's production of Falstaff, in the premiere of Michael Finnissy's The Undivine Comedy and in Tippett's Songs for Dov conducted by Tippett, La Finta Giardiniera for Opera North and Don Ottavio in Don Giovanni for Opera Factory; Idomeneo at Munich (1996) and sang in new production of Monteverdi's Ulysses for Opera North, 1997 Appearances with the Monteverdi Choir and Orchestra including tours of Italy, Germany and France; Peformances of Monteverdi's Vespers in Venice and Orfeo in Spain as well as Idomeneo in Lisbon, Paris, Amsterdam and London; Sang Handel's Jephtha at the Handel Festival in Göttingen and the Holland Festival; Sang the Anonymous Voice in the British premiere of Tippett's New Year at Glyndebourne in 1990; Concerts at the Festival Hall with Janácek's Glagolitic Mass, with the Ensemble Intercontemporain in Paris and with the London Sinfonietta in Henze's Voices in 1991; Season 1992 as Claggart in Billy Budd for Scottish Opera and Nero in The Coronation of Poppea for Opera Factory. Recordings include: Handel's Tamerlano; Alexander's Feast and Jephtha; Tippett's Songs for Dov; Stravinsky's Renard; Arbace in Idomeneo. Address: c/o Ingpen and Williams Ltd, 26 Wadham Road, London SW15 2LR, England.

ROBSON Richard, b. 1964, County Durham, England. Singer (Bass). Education: Guildhall School with Otakar Kraus; Further Study with Arlene Randazzo. Debut: Badger in The Cunning Little Vixen and Antonio in Figaro, at Glyndebourne. Career: Speaker in The Magic Flute and Gremin in Eugene Onegin, for Kent Opera; Debut with Wiener Kammeroper as Rossini's Basilio, 1990; Festival Engagements at Vienna Schonbrunn, Barcelona, Brighton, Hong Kong and Edinburgh; Colline and Sparafucile in Rigoletto for Bath and Essex Opera; Wexford Festival, 1994-95, in Rubinstein's The Demon and as Il Cieco in Mascagni's Iris; Further Appearances in Iris at Rome and Munich and with the Chelsea Opera Group; Season 1996-97 with Ramfis in Aida for Norwegian Opera and return to Wexford; Concerts include Elgar's Apostles at Canterbury Cathedral, Rossini's Petite Messe in Strasbourg, Verdi Requiem in Croydon and Mozart's Requiem on Tour to Germany; Creon in Cherubini's Médée and Frederico in Verdi's Battaglia di Legnano (St John's Smith Square and Chelsea Opera Group).

ROCHAIX François, b. 2 Aug 1942, Geneva, Switzerland. Stage Director. Education: Studied at University of Geneva and at Berliner Ensemble, East Berlin. Career: Founded the Atelier de Genève, 1963, actor and director; Director of the Théâtre de Carouge, 1975-81; Produced The Turn of The Screw and Death in Venice at Geneva in 1981 and 1983, La Traviata for Opera North in 1985, Cardillac and Parsifal at Berne, 1988-89, Der Ring des Nibelungen, 1985-87, and Die Meistersinger in 1989 at Seattle; Production of Tristan und Isolde for Opera Lyon in 1990. Address: 7 Vy aux Vergnes, 1295 Mies, Switzerland.

ROCHAT Michel, b. 29 Jan 1931, Switzerland. Conductor. m. Josette-Marie Rochat, 4 Apr 1959, 2 daughters. Education: Master's degree, Clarinet, Conservatoires of Lausanne, Geneva, and Paris in class of Maestro Cahuzac; Master's degree, Conducting, Basel Musikakademie. Career: Taught Clarinet, Switzerland, 1952; Conducting, Switzerland, 1960; Played Clarinet, Basel Contemporary Music Group, 1968-72; Professor, Director, Conservatoire Supérieur, Lausanne, 1963-83; Guest Conductor, Belgium, Bulgaria, Italy, Greece, Romania, Russia, Switzerland, Venezuela, 1976-85; General Music Director, Conductor, Izmir National Symphony Orchestra, Guest Conductor, National Symphony Orchestra, Istanbul, 1982-85; Professor, National Institute of Arts and National Academy of Arts, Taiwan, 1985-; Conductor: Taiwan, Taipei City and Kaohsiung Symphony Orchestras, Taipei Bach Orchestra, Artist's Ensemble, 1985-, Hwa Shing Children's Chorus, 1989-90, Rong Shing Chorus, 1993-96, Asia International Festival for Contemporary Music, 1994, Dan Tie Orchestra, 1995-, Music Camp for Chinese Music, Ilan, 1996, Lan Yang Chinese Ensemble, performing at International Children's Festival and Taipei Chinese Music Festival, 1996, Lan Yan Chinese Ensemble, Taiwanese Opera Ilan, 1996-; Guest Conductor, Taipei Municipal Chinese Orchestra, 1993-, Experimental Chinese Orchestra, Taipei, Taichung and Kaohsiung tours, 1997. Compositions: Taiwanese operas: 7 words, Kavalan Story, Kavalan Princess, Ataya Song, 1996, 1997, 1998; Arranged Taiwanese songs. Recordings: Masterpieces of Chinese Music, 1995; Chinese Contemporary Music, 1995; Chinese Music for the Young, 1996. Publications: To Know Tonality, 1995; Clarinet for Beginners, 1996; Introduction to Conducting, 1996; Rudiments of Intervals and Notation, 1996. Honours: 1st Prize, Gold Medal, Villa-Lobos Prize, International Competition for Conductors, Rio de Janeiro, 1975; Lion's Club Award, Taiwan, 1993; Kaohsiung Mayor's Award, 1994; Ilan County President's Award, 1996. Membership: Swiss Musicians Association. Hobby: Computers. Address: Route de la Vuy 8, 1305 Penthalaz, Switzerland.

ROCHBERG George, b. 5 July 1918, Paterson, New Jersey, USA. Composer. m. Gene Rosenfeld, 18 Aug 1941, 1 son, 1 daughter. Education: BA, Montclair Teachers College, 1939; Mannes School of Music, 1939-42; BM, Curtis Institute of Music, 1948; MA, University of PA, 1949. Career: US Army, World War II, Purple Heart; Faculty, Curtis Institute; Director of Publications, Theodore Presser Company, 1951-60; Chair, Music

Department, 1960-68, Professor of Composition, 1960-79, Annenberg Professor of Humanities, 1979-, University of Pennsylvania; Work in progress: Chromaticism: Symmetry in Atonal and Tonal Music. Compositions include: 6 Symphonies; 5th Symphony commissioned for and premiered by Georg Solti and Chicago Symphony; 6th Symphony commissioned for and premiered by Lorin Maazel and Pittsburgh Symphony, also in Leningrad, Moscow and Warsaw, 1989; 7 String Quartets; Violin, Oboe and clarinet Concertos; Piano solos, trios, quartet and quintet; Various chamber works; The Confidence Man, opera, libretto by Gene Rochberg; Clarinet Concerto commissioned by the Philadelphia Orchestra, 1994-95; Circles of Fire, for 2 pianos, 1996-97. Recordings: Violin Concerto; Oboe Concerto; Black Sounds; Blake Songs; Caprice Variations; Chamber Symphony; La Bocca della Verita; Serenate d'Estate; Tableaux; 12 Bagatelles. Publication: Aesthetics of Survival, 1984. Contributions to: Critical Enquiry; New Literary History; Polarity in Music, in Proceedings of the American Philosophical Society, Philadelphia, 1997. Honours include: 1st Prize, Kennedy Friedheim Awards, 1979; Honorary Doctorates: University of Michigan; Philadelphia Musical Academy; Montclair State University; Numerous fellowships, grants and awards. Memberships: American Academies, Arts and Letters, Arts and Sciences; American Society of Composers, Authors and Publishers. Hobbies: Reading Philosophy Theory and Sciences. Address: Dunwoody Village, 3500 West Chester Pike, Newtown Square, PA 19073-4168, USA.

ROCHESTER Marc, b. 28 Apr 1954, London, England. Music Journalist; Organist; Conductor; Adjudicator. Education: BMus, MA, PhD, University of Wales, 1972-77; FTCL; ARCM; LRAM. Career: Music Critic, Western Mail, 1975-80; Correspondent, Organists review, Musical Times, 1980-89, Independent, 1987-, Gramophone, 1989; Sub-organist, Bangor Cathedral, 1978-80; Organist and Master of Choristers, Londonderry Cathedrl, 1980-82; Music Tutor, New University of Ulster, Northern Ireland, 1980-84; Solo Recitalist; Choral Conductor; Examiner, Associated Board, Royal Schools of Music, Northern Ireland Schools Examinations Council; University of London. Copositions: Hymn tunes; Various church music. Recordings: Soloist, 20th Century British Organ Music, 1983; Conductor, Hymns of C F Alexander, Derry Cathedral Choir, 1981; Accompanist, Beaufort Male Voice Choir, 1977, 1978, Leila Carewe (soprano), 1980. Publications: Frank Martin at Golgotha, 1977; Editor, catalogue, Traditional Welsh Musical Instruments. Contributions to: Articles on 20th century music. Hobbies: Croquet; Sailing; Rugby; Bus driving. Address: Bow Anchor, Squires Hill Lane, Tilford, Farnham, Surrey, England.

ROCKWELL John Sargent, b. 16 Sept 1940, Washington DC, USA. Music Critic. Education: BA, Harvard College, 1962; MA, 1964, PhD, 1972, University of California, Berkeley. Career: Music and Dance Critic for Oakland Tribune, CA, 1969, and Los Angeles Times, 1970-72; Music Critic for New York Times, 1972-. Publications: All American Music: Composition in Late 20th Century, 1983; Sinatra: An American Classic, 1984. Contributions to: Numerous books and magazines. Membership: Past Treasurer, US Music Critics' Association. Address: c/o Music Department, New York Times, 229 West 43rd Street, New York, NY 10036, USA.

RODAN Mendi, b. 17 Apr 1929, Jassy, Romania. Conductor; Professor. m. Judith Calmanovici, 2 children. Education: BMus, MA, Academy of Music, Arts Institute. Career: Permanent Conductor for Radio and TV Orchestra, Bucharest, 1953-58; Founder and Permanent Conductor of Jerusalem Chamber Orchestra; Chief Conductor, Music Director, Jerusalem Symphony, 1963-72; Music Director for Israel Sinfonietta, 1977-91; Music Director and Permanent Conductor of Orchestre National Belge, 1983-89; Music Director, IDF Educational Corp Chamber Orchestra, 1990-92; Laureate Conductor of Israel Sinfonietta, 1991-; Associate Conductor, Israel Philharmonic Orchestra, 1993-97; Guest Conductor for Israel Chamber Ensemble, Jerusalem Symphony, Israeli New Opera, Haifa Symphony; Concert tours worldwide with orchestras including Oslo Philharmonic, Vienna Symphony, Berlin Radio Symphony, London Symphony, London Philharmonia, Frankfurt Radio, Stockholm Philharmonic and Berlin Radio Symphony; Adviser at Jerusalem International Music Centre and Head of Jerusalem Academy of Music and Dance, 1985-94; Music Director and Chief Conductor, Isreal Symphony Orchestra, 1997-. Hobbies: Music; Driving; Reading. Address: 6 Shiler Street, Jerusalem 96227, Israel.

RODDE Anne-Marie, b. 21 Nov 1946, Clermont-Ferrand, France. Soprano. Education: Studied at the Conservatory of Clermont-Ferrand and at the Paris Conservatoire with Irene Joachim and Louis Nougera. Career: Sang at Aix-en-Provence in 1971 as Amor in Orfeo ed Euridice, Yniold in Pelléas et Mélisande at Paris in 1972, in Cantate Nuptial by Milhaud and The Nightingale by Stravinsky; Sang Hyppolite et Aricie at Covent Garden, Falstaff, Cherubini's Médée, and Rosenkavalier at Paris Opera House, Pelléas et Mélisande at Rome Opera House, Pearl

Fishers at Stockholm Opera, Magic Flute debut in 1991 at La Bastille Opéra, Magic Flute at Montreal and Bonn Opera; Appearances in Amsterdam in Le nozze di Figaro and at Zurich and Barcelona; Many appearances in the Baroque repertory including London Bach Festival in Les Boréades by Rameau; Other roles include Zerbinetta, Oscar, Nannetta, Ravel's Child and Dirce in Médée, Paris Opéra in 1986. Recordings: Les Indes Galantes by Rameau; Handel's Xerxes; Lully's Le Triomphe d'Alcide; Les Boréades; Honegger's Jeanne d'Arc au Bucher; Messiah; Songs by Debussy; Avietta di Camera by Rossini; Songs by Widor; Works by Bellini, Donizetti and Gluck.

RODEN Anthony, b. 19 Mar 1937, Adelaide, Australia. Tenor. m. Doreen Roden. Education: Associated Australian Insurance Institute; Licenciate, Adelaide Conservatory. Debut: Glyndebourne, England. Career: Appearances at London Opera Centre, Glyndebourne and Netherlands Festivals, English, Welsh and Scottish National Operas, Opera North, Prague National Opera, Krefeld Opera, Victorian State Opera, Covent Garden in Peter Grimes and Freiburg Opera; Numerous concerts for BBC, British, Italian and Dutch Orchestras; Sang Samson and Tannhäuser in Melbourne in 1992, Mahler's 8th Symphony, RLPO, and Florestan for Glyndebourne; Mahler, Das Lied von der Erde, Taiwan; Vitek in The Makropoulos Case at Glyndebourne, 1995; Senior Vocal Tutor, Royal Northern College of Music. Recordings: Various. Honours: John Christie Award, 1971; Opera Prize, Adelaide Conservatory. Hobbies: Antiques; Golf. Current Management: Patricia Greenan. Address: 33 Castlebar Road, Ealing, London, W5 2DJ, England.

RODERICK JONES Richard (Trevor), b. 14 Nov 1947, Newport, Gwent, Wales. Composer; Conductor; Pianist; Musicologist. m. Susan Ann Thomason, 1992. Education: Associate, Royal College of Music, 1967; Graduate, Royal Schools of Music, 1969; MMus, University of Bristol, 1989. Career: Head of Music, South Warwickshire College, Stratford-upon-Avon, 1970-79; Extramural Tutor, University of Birmingham, 1971-79; Musical Director, National Youth Theatre of Wales, 1978-87; Tutor, Welsh College of Music and Drama, 1979-93; Extramural Tutor, University College, Cardiff, 1980-93; External Tutor, University of Oxford, 1993-. Compositions: Piano concerto; 3 symphonies; 3 chamber concertos; 3 sinfoniettas; Numerous choral works including oratorio Altus Prosator; Numerous chamber works including 2 piano trios; Stage works including: Me and My Bike, opera (BBC commission); Chanticleer, church opera; Altar Fire, scenic celebration; Game Circle, scenic cantata; Over 30 scores for TV and stage. Membership: Fellow, Royal Society of Arts. Hobbies: Fishing; Reading; Walking; Record collecting. Address: 2 Primrose Court, Moreton-in-Marsh, Glos GL56 0JG, England.

RODESCU Julian, b. 1 May 1953, Bucharest, Romania. Bass Opera Singer. m. Barbara Govatos, 4 Jun 1983. Education: BMus, MMus, Juilliard School; Teachers: Giorgio Tozzi, William Glazier, Jerome Hines, Hans Hotter and Daniel Ferro. Debut: Plutone in Monteverdi's Il Ballo delle Ingrate with Brooklyn Opera, 1980. Career: Carnegie Hall debut in 1989 with Rostropovich in world premiere of Shostakovich's Rayok; Teatro alla Scala with Riccardo Muti in 1991, Boston Symphony with Seiji Ozawa in Boston Symphony Hall, Carnegie Hall and Tanglewood; Appearances with Miami Opera, New York City Opera, Knoxville Opera, Aachen Stadttheater, Kennedy Center in Washington DC, Alice Tully Hall, WHYY-TV Philadelphia, WQXR, WNCN New York, Central City Opera and Opera Delaware. Recordings: Shostakovich's Rayok; Tchaikovsky's Queen of Spades; Bortniansky's Complete Vocal Concerti. Honour: Winner of Luciano Pavarotti Competition, 1988. Hobbies: Tennis; Table Tennis; Photography; Cooking. Current Management: Ann Summers International. Address: 1420 Locust Street, Philadelphia, PA 19102, USA.

RODGERS Joan, b. 4 Nov 1956, Whitehaven, Cumbria. Soprano. m. Paul Daniel, 1988. Education: Studied at the Royal Northern College of Music with Josef Ward and with Audrey Longford. Career: Opera debut as Pamina at the 1982 Aix-en-Provence Festival; Engagements at the Ponnelle-Barenboim Mostly Mozart Festival in Paris as Zerlina, and with the English National Opera as Nannetta in Falstaff; Israel Mozart Festival as Susanna and Despina, Turin Opera as Ilia in Ideomeneo, Covent Garden debut in 1983 as the Princess in L'Enfant et les Sortilèges and has returned as Xenia in Boris Godunov, Echo in Ariadne auf Naxos, Zerlina in 1988 and Servilia in La Clemenza di Tito in 1989; Glyndebourne debut in 1989 as Susanna in an authentic version of Le nozze di Figaro under Simon Rattle; Promenade Concerts in 1989 as soloist in Mahler's 4th Symphony, featured on BBC TV's Omnibus programme; Sang at Munich Opera and Covent Garden, 1990-91 as Pamina, Mélisande in a concert performance at Madrid, Susanna and Despina at the Maggio Musicale and with the Chicago Symphony Orchestra, Mozart's Countess for English National Opera and Handel's Cleopatra for Scottish Opera in 1992; Season 1992 as Yolanta in Tchaikovsky's opera for Opera North at the Edinburgh Festival and as Susanna at Florence; Sang Mélisande for Opera

North, 1995; Many recitals and concert appearances in Britain, including Anne Trulove in The Rake's Progress at the Festival Hall, 1997; Sang Handel's Theodora at the 1997 Glyndebourne Festival. Contributions to: People, no 216, Joan Rodgers: Opera Magazine, Dec 1995 pages 1390-1398. Honours include: Kathleen Ferrier Memorial Scholarship, 1981; Peter Moores Foundation Scholarship. Address: c/o Ingpen and Williams Ltd, 26 Wadham Court, London SW15 2LR, England.

RODRIGUEZ Robert (Xavier), b. 28 June 1946, San Antonio, Texas, USA. Composer. Education: MM, University of Texas, Austin, 1969; DMA, University of California, Los Angeles, 1975; Further Study with Jakob Druckman at Tanglewood and Nadia Boulanger in Paris; Master Classes with Elliott Carter and Bruno Maderna. Career: Faculty Member, University of Southern California, 1973-75, University of Texas, Dallas, 1975-; Composer-in-Residence, Dallas Symphony Orchestra, 1982-85. Compositions include: 3 Piano Concertos, 1968, 1972, 1974; 2 Piano Trios, 1970, 1971; Cantata for Soprano, Chorus and Orchestra, 1972; Sinfonia Concertante for Saxophone, Harpsichord and Chamber Orchestra, 1974; Favola Concertante for Violin, Cello & Strings, 1975; Variations for Violin and Piano, 1975; Transfigurations Mysteria for 3 Solo Voices, Narrator, Chorus and Orchestra, 1978; Le Diable Amoureux, Opera, 1978; Frammenti Musicali for Violin and Strings, 1978; Favola Boccaccesca, 1979; Semi-Suite for Violin and Piano, 1981; Suor Isabella, Opera, 1982; Oktoechoes for Octet and Orchestra, 1983; Seven Deadly Sins for Wind Ensemble and Percussion, 1984; Tango, Chamber Opera, 1985; Monkey See, Monkey Do, Children's Opera, 1986; Invocations of Orpheus, Trumpet Concerto, 1989; Ursa: Four Seasons for Double Bass & Strings, 1990; Frida, Opera, 1990; The Old Majestic, Opera, 1991; Pinata for Orchestra, 1991; Mascaras for Cello and Orchestra, 1994; Adoracion Ambulante, Folk Mass, 1994; Scrooge, Concert Scene for Baritone, Chorus & Orchestra. Honours include: Guggenheim Fellowship, 1976. Address: c/o ASCAP, ASCAP Building, One Lincoln Plaza, NY 10023, USA.

ROESEL Peter, b. 2 Feb 1945, Dresden, Germany. Pianist. m. Heidrun Bergmann, 1 son, 1 daughter. Education: Completed study with Bazkirov and Oborin, Moscow Conservatory, 1964-69. Debut: With Berlin Symphony, 1964. Career: Regular appearances with leading European and American orchestras, 1966-; Performances at major festivals including Salzburg, Berlin, Edinburgh, Prague, London Proms, Hollywood Bowl. Recordings: Over 50 including complete concerti by Weber, Beethoven, Schumann and Rachmaninoff, complete piano works by Brahms, major piano sonatas by Mozart, Beethoven, Schubert and Schumann, various chamber music works. Honours: Prizewinner of competitions: Schumann, 1963, Tchaikovsky, 1966, Montreal, 1968; Honorary Citizen of Minnesota, USA. Memberships: Committee Member, New Saxonian Arts Association; Committee Member, Friends of Dresden Music Festival. Hobbies: Reading; Gardening. Current Management: Konzertdirektion Schmid, PF 1667, 30016 Hannover, Germany. Address: Kruegerstrasse 20, D-01326 Dresden, Germany.

ROGALA Jacek (Wojciech), b. 22 Apr 1966, Brzeg, Poland. Composer; Conductor; Journalist. Education: Diploma in Horn, State Lyceum of Music, Wroclaw; Diploma, Composition, 1990, Diploma in Conducting, 1992, Academy of Music, Wroclaw. Career: Regular performances in Poland, Germany, Spain, 1985-; Participation in summer workshops of Polish Section ISCM, 1986-89; Teacher of choirs in Wroclaw, 1988-92; Co-organizer, Young Composers' Meetings, Musica Nova in Brzeg (Poland), 1989, 1990; Journalist in Polish Radio, Wroclaw, Music Editor, 1990-91, 1990-92; Scholarship inKonservatorium Enschede, Holland, 1989; Regular concerts as a orchestra-conductor, 1990; Assistant Conductor, State Opera in Wroclaw, 1991-92; Adviser of Minister of Cultural and Fine Arts for Musical Affair, 1992-1994. Compositions: Divertimento, for strings, 1988; Litoral, for flute and piano 1988, Bassoon Concerto 1990; So-Na-Ta, for bassoon solo, 1990; Sextet Studio, for string sextet, 1991. Memberships: Youth Section, Polish Composer's Union, 1986-, Board Member 1988-90; Polish Section of ISCM, 1986-. Address: ul Trebacka 3 m 600-074 Warszawa, Poland.

ROGÉ Pascal, b. 6 Apr 1951, Paris, France. Concert Pianist. Education: Studied at the Paris Conservatoire from 1962, Piano with Lucette Descaves, Chamber Music with Pierre Pasquier; Further study with Julius Katchen, 1966-69. Career: First orchestral appearance, Paris, 1962; Many solo recitals and concerto engagements in France, elsewhere in Europe, the Far East, Australia and the USA; Noted for interpretations of Ravel, Fauré, Debussy and other French composers; Duo partnership with violinists Pierre Amoyal and Chantal Juillet. Recordings include: CDs of Satie, Poulenc and Fauré, and Brahms Piano Works; Saint-Saëns Piano Concertos, as well as Poulenc Piano Concertos and Concert Champêtre for harpsichord and orchestra, conducted by Charles Dutoit; Sonatas by Brahms, with Pierre Amoyal. Honours: Premiers Prix for Piano and Chamber Music at the Paris Conservatoire, 1966; 1st Prize, Long-Thibaud Competition, 1971; Grand Prix du Disque and Edison Award, 1984; Gramophone Award for Best Instrumental Recording, 1988 and Best Chamber Music Recording, 1997. Current Management: Balmer and Dixon, Zurich, Switzerland. Address: Balmer and Dixon Management AG, Granitweg 2, CH-8006 Zurich, Switzerland.

ROGER David, b. 1950, England. Stage Designer. Career: For Opera Factory in London has designed La Calisto, The Knot Garden, Osborne premiere of Hell's Angels, Birtwistle premiere of Yan Tan Tethera in 1986, a conflation of Gluck's Iphigenia operas, Ligeti's Adventures and Nouvelles Adventures, Mahagonny Songspiel, Cosi fan tutte, Don Giovanni, Reimann's The Ghost Sonata and The Marriage of Figaro in 1991; Other work has included La Grand Macabre by Ligeti at Freiburg, Akhnaten by Philip Glass and The Return of Ulysses at English National Opera, La Bohème for Opera North and Manon Lescault for Opéra-Comique in Paris; Has designed plays at the Traverse Theatre, Soho Polytechnic, the Royal Court, the RSC and for the Lyric Hammersmith in Faust and Morte D'Arthur. Address: c/o Opera Factory, 8a The Leather Market, Weston Street, London, SE1 3ER, England.

ROGERS Lesley-Jane, b. 25 Apr 1962, Bristol, England. Soprano. m. Robin Daniel, 3 June 1988, 1 stepson, 1 stepdaughter. Education: Royal Academy of Music, 1981-85; Harry Farjeon Prize, Harmony, 1982; LRAM (Pianoforte Teachers), 1983; Ella Mary Jacob Prize, Singing, 1983; GRSM Honours, 1984; Greta G M Parkinson Prize, Piano, 1984; LRAM (Singing Teachers), 1985. Career: Performed extensively in the fields of oratorio and solo cantatas and is also a contemporary music specialist; Particularly wide oratorio repertoire incorporating standard and unusual works; Hundreds of solo cantatas, especially Bach and Telemann; Performances of contemporary music such as Ligeti's Aventures and Nouvelles Aventures; Several world premieres, including Fédélé's La chute de la maison Usher with Ensemble InterContemporain Recordings: Handel Tamerlano (highlights), role of Asteria, European Community Baroque Orchestra (authentic instruments), director Roy Goodman, TéléDiffusion de France, live recording, 1990; Caldara Madrigals and Cantatas, Wren Baroque Soloists (authentic instruments), 1992; Caldara Motets, Wren Baroque Soloists, 1994; Peter Maxwell Davies Resurrection, role of electronic soprano, BBC Philharmonic Orchestra, conductor Davies, 1994; Peerson Private Musicke, Wren Baroque Soloists, 1994; Carl Rütti Magnificat, also Alpha et Omega (specially written for recording), BBC Symphony Chorus, conductor Stephen Jackson, 1995; George Jeffreys, Anthems, Songs and Dialogues (authentic instruments), 1995; Percy Grainger, Jungle Book, Choir and Orchestra of Polyphony Hyperion, 1996. Memberships: Life Member, National Early Music Association; British Actors' Equity Association. Hobbies: Dressmaking; Reading; Scrabble; Riding; Sports; Food and wine. Address: The Old Rectory Coach House, High Street, Bourton-on-the-Water, Gloucestershire GL54 2AP, England.

ROGERS Nigel (David), b. 21 Mar 1935, Wellington, Shropshire, England. Tenor; Conductor; Teacher. Education: Choral Scholar, King's College, Cambridge, 1953-56; BA, 1956, MA, 1960, Cantab; Private musical tuition in Rome and Milan; Hochschule für Musik, Munich, 1959-61. Career: Began professional career with quartet, Studio der Frühen Musik, 1961; Operatic debut at Amsterdam in 1969; Sang in Monteverdi's Ulisse and Orfeo under Harnoncourt at Vienna and Amsterdam, 1971, 1976, Poppea at Amsterdam under Leonhardt in 1972 and Il Combattimento at Milan under Berio in 1973; Sang in British premiere of Arden Must Die by Goehr at Sadler's Wells in 1974 and the title role in Handel's Teseo at Warsaw in 1977; Conducting from 1985; Directed and sang in the serenata La Gloria di Primavera by Alessandro Scarlatti, 1996. Recordings: About 70 recordings including Monteverdi's 1610 Vespers and Orfeo, John Dowland Lute Songs, 1988, Sigismondo d'India, 1991, Florentine Intermedi of 1589, Dido and Aeneas, Songs of Henry Lawes, 1994; Symphonie Sacrae of Schütz, 1995. Contributions to: Various magazines and academic publications; Chapter on Voice, in Companion to Baroque Music, 1991. Honour: Honorary RCM, Royal College of Music, 1980. Hobbies: Walking; Antiques; Wine; Travel. Address: Chestnut Cottage, East End, East Woodhay (Hants), Near Newbury, Berkshire, RG15 0AB, England.

ROGERS Patrick (John Francis), b. 15 Dec 1948, Eureka, CA, USA. Musicologist; Musician. m. Susan Beth Smalakis, 10 Sep 1982, 1 son. Education: BA, Humboldt State University, 1971; MA, University of California, Santa Barbara, 1977; PhD, Claremont Graduate School, 1986; University of Maryland, UCLA. Career: Director, Fiske Museum of Musical Instruments, 1986-89, Honorary Director, 1989-; Organist, St Denis Church, 1986-; Fletcher Jones Foundation Fellow, Huntington Library, 1991-92; Performed regularly with Early Music Ensemble of Los Angeles, I Cantori, Los Angeles Baroque Orchestra and Santa Barbara Chamber Orchestra, and has worked with Martial Singher and Max van Egmond; Specialist in continuo accompaniment and soloist on harpsichord, organ and clavichord. Recording: Soundtrack for the film, Foes. Publications: Continuo Realization in Handel's Vocal Music, 1989; Continuo Realizations of Baroque Cello Sonatas; American Handel Society Newsletter, Performance Practice Review, Göttinger Händel-Beiträge. Contributions to: Musical Times; Early Music; The 18th Century; American Musical Instrument Society Newsletter. Hobbies: Weight Training; Hiking; Duplicate Bridge. Address: 112 Harvard Avenue 118, Claremont, CA 91711, USA.

ROGG Lionel, b. 21 Apr 1936, Geneva, Switzerland. Organist; Composer. m. Claudine Effront, 1957, 3 sons. Education: Geneva Conservatory; Piano with Nikita Magaloff; Organ with Pierre Segond. Career includes: Complete Bach organ works in 10 recitals, Victoria Hall, Geneva, 1961; Concerts (organ, harpsichord) worldwide; Interpretative courses, USA, UK, Switzerland, Austria, Japan, Italy. Compositions include: Organ: 12 chorales; Variations, Psalm 91, 1983; Introduction, ricercare, toccata; Cantata, Geburt der Venus; Also: Face à face, 2 pianos; Missa Brevis, chorus and orchestra; Concerto for organ and orchestra, 1992. Recordings: Complete Bach organ works; Art of Fugue; Complete Buxtehude organ works; Rogg Plays Reger; Rogg Plays Rogg (organ compositions); Du Mage, Clérambault. Publication: Improvisation Course for Organists. Honours include: Grand Prix du Disque, 1970; Deutscher Schallplatten Preis, 1980; Doctor honoris causa, University of Geneva. Hobbies: Mountain climbing; Japanese culture. Address: 38A route de Troinex, CH-1234 Vessy, Geneva, Switzerland.

ROGLIANO Marco, b. 26 November 1967, Rome, Italy. Violinist. m. Ciccozzi Antonella, 1 son. Education: Conservatory Santa Cecilia, Rome; Mozarteum of Salzburg; Academy W Stauffer. Debut: Helsingborg Concert Hall Playing Sibelius Violin Concerto fo 47 with the Helsingborg Symphony Orchestra, 1989. Career: Casals Hall, Tokyo, 1991, Paris, 1993, Moscow, 1993; With the Radio Symphonic Orchestra of Moscow, 1994; Milan, 1995; Rome, 1996; Munich, 1997; Numerous Radio and Television Appearances in France, Bulgaria, Sweden. Recordings: Salvatore Sciarrino, 1947; 6 Caprieei for Solo Violin, 1976; Angelo Ragazzi; 3 Violin Concertos; Franz Adolf Berwald; The Violin Concerto. Contributions to: Musical Journals and Magazines. Address: Lorenzo il Mgnifico 15, 06162 Rome, Italy.

ROGNER Heinz, b. 1929, Leipzig, Germany. Conductor. Education: Studied composition and piano with Egon Boelsche and Hugo Steuer in Leipzig. Career: Repetiteur and Conductor at the German National Theatre in Weimar; Teacher, Leipzig Musikhochschule, 1954-58; Principal Conductor for Great Leipzig Radio Orchestra, 1959-63; General Musical Director, Deutsche Staatsoper Berlin, 1962-73; Chief Conductor of the Berlin Radio Symphony Orchestra, 1973 with tours to Eastern Europe, Austria, Sweden, France, Belgium, Switzerland, Germany and Japan; Regular Guest Conductor for Yomiuri Nippon Symphony Orchestra from 1978, Principal Conductor, 1984. Recordings: Strauss Horn Concertos; Weber's Abu Hassan and Eine Nacht in Venedig, with the Dresden Staatskapelle; Trumpet Concertos by Torelli, Grossi, Fasch and Albinoni; Schubert's 7th Symphony, arranged by Weingartner, and 9th Symphony; Reger's Romantic Suite and Symphonic Prologue; Beethoven's Cantata on the Accession of Leopold II, Die Glorreiche Augenblick and Vestas Feuer; Strauss's Duet Concertino and Preludes to Palestrina by Pfitzner. Honours: National Prize, 1975; Gerhardt Eusler Gold Plakette, 1979; Professor, 1981. Address: Norman McCann International Artists Ltd, The Coach House, 56 Lawrie Park Gardens, London, SE26 6XJ, England.

ROGOFF Ilan, b. 1950, Russia. Concert Pianist. Education: Studied with Karol Klein, Stefan Askenase, Leonard Shure and Claudio Arrau. Career: Has appeared as soloist with such conductors as Rudolf Barschai, Antal Dorati, Charles Groves, Gunther Herbig, Kurt Sanderling, Walter Weller and Zubin Mehta; Concerts with most major British orchestras including 1983 engagements with the BBC Philharmonic in Prokofiev's Third Concerto, Royal Liverpool Philharmonic and the Bournemouth Symphony; Gave the premiere of John McCabe's Third Concerto in 1978; Tours to America and the Far East, 1983-85; Performances of Beethoven's Piano Concertos directed from the keyboard in South America and Germany in 1984; Repertoire also includes Beethoven, Brahms and Liszt Sonatas, Schumann and Schubert C major Fantasies, Bach/Busoni Chaconne, Chopin Ballades and Etudes. Address: c/o Norman McCann Ltd, The Coach House, 56 Lawrie Park Gardens, London, SE26 6XJ, England.

ROHAN Jiri, b. 11 January 1965, Prague, Czech Republic. Double Bass Player. m. Dana Skrovankova, 13 June 1992, 1 daughter. Education: Conservatory, Prague; Academy of Music, Prague; 10 years Piano Studies, Art Academy, Prague; 6 years Double Bass Study, Prague Conservatory; 4 years Double Bass Studies, Academy of Music, Prague. Debut: Solo Concert with Symphony Orchestra, Prague, 1985. Career: Czech Philharmonic Orchestra, 1983-85; Suk Chamber Orchestra, 1988-91; Munich Philharmonic Orchestra, 1990; Czech String Ensemble, 1992; Prague Spirit Quintet, 1993-97; Osaka Synfoniker, 1994.

Recordings: Over 40 CD's with Several Symphonic Orchestras; Over 10 CD's with Suk Chamber Orchestra; 2 CD's with Czech String Ensemble; 3 CD's with Prague Spirit Quintet; CD with Czech Chamber Orchestra. Publications: Psychological Aspects of Music Listening, 1993; Ambient, Rythm, Industrial, 1994. Memberships: Union of Orchestral Players; Art Club of Empire Agency, Prague. Hobbies: Mountain Biking. Address: Mahenova 168/7, 150 00 Prague 5, Czech Republic.

ROHNER Ruth, b. 18 Sep 1935, Zurich, Switzerland. Soprano. Education: Studied in Winterhur and Amsterdam. Career: Sang at the Opera of Biel-Solothurn, 1960-61, Vienna Kammeroper, 1960-62 and engaged at Zurich opera from 1962 notably in the premieres of Sutermeister's Madame Bovary in 1967 and Kelterborn's Ein Engel Kommt Nach Babylon in 1977; Many performances in the lyric and coloratura repertory and in the first local performances of Burkhard's Ein Stern Geht auf Jakob and Krenek's Karl V; Guest engagements at Berne, Basle, the State Operas of Hamburg and Munich, Dusseldorf, Strasbourg, Helsinki and Châtelet Paris; Festival appearances at Lausanne, Wiesbaden and Athens; Noted concert artist in oratorio and lieder. Address: c/o Zurich Opera, CH-8008 Zurich, Switzerland.

ROHRL Manfred, b. 12 Sep 1935, Augsburg, Germany. Bass Singer. Education: Studied at the Augsburg Conservatory and with Franz Kelch and Margarethe von Winterfeld. Debut: Augsburg in 1958 as Masetto. Career: Member of the Deutsche Opera Berlin notably in the 1965 premiere of Der Junge Lord by Henze; Guest appearances in Brussels, Nancy, Dusseldorf, Geneva, Zurich, Zagreb and Edinburgh; Netherlands Opera in 1984 as Leporello; Sang Waldner in Arabella at the Deutsche Oper Berlin in 1988, and Dr Kolenaty in The Makropoulos Case in 1989; Many performances in the buffo repertory; Sang Taddeo in L'Italiana in Algeri with the Deutsche Opera in 1992; Mozart's Bartolo at Glyndebourne, 1994. Recordings: Various. Address: c/o Deutsche Oper Berlin, Richard Wagnerstrasse 10, D-1000 Berlin 1, Germany.

ROJAS Rafael, b. 15 September 1962, Guadalaja, Mexico. Singer (Tenor). Education: University of Guadalajara, Royal Scottish Academy & Northern College of Music. Career: Student roles included the Duke of Mantua, Manrico, Tamino, Rodolfo, Roberto Devereux & Ernani; Englangements in Guadalajara City & Mexico City; US Debut as Alfredo in Traviata, Seattle, Followed Rafael Ruiz in El Gato Montes for Washington Opera; Concerts include the Verdi Requiem with the Jerusalem Symphony Orchestra and the Halle Orchestra; Lambeth Palace, London, Monmouth Cathedral, and the Glasgow Mayfest; Season 1997-98 as Paco in La Vida Breve at Nice, Pinkerton for Glimmerglass Opera, USA, Werther at Boston, Rodolfo & Nemorino at Seattle & Verdi's Macduff for Houston Opera. Honours include: Domingo Prize at 1995 Placido Domingo Competition. Address: IMG Artists, Media House, 3 Burlington Lane, London W4 2TH, England.

ROLAND Claude-Robert, b. 19 Dec 1935, Pont-de-Loup, Belgium. Conductor; Organist; Composer. m. Anne-Marie Girardot, 6 Sept 1963, 1 son. Education: Athénée Royal; Academy of Music, Châtelet; Conservatories in Liege, Paris, Brussels, Messiaean and Defossez. Career includes: Organist, Notre Dame Church, Wasmes, 1955-63, and Basilica Charleroi, 1963-67; Professor, Brussels Conservatory, 1972-; Organist: Works of Hoyoul, Lohet, Dumont, Buston, Schlick, Froidebise, Guillaume, Quatrefages; Conductor: Satie, Prokofiev, Guillaume, RTBF. Compositions: Over 100 works including Demain seulement, on poems by Alain Grandbois; Preludes, piano, 1962; Rossignolet du bois, orchestra, 1971; Rondeau, organ, 1979; Thriller, trumpet and piano, 1984; Datura 281, piano, 1987; Ricordanza, bass-clarinet and piano, 1989; Music for Molière, Labiche, Turgenev and Ghelderode. Recordings: Compositeurs Liegeois, organ; Alpha; Musique Au Chateau, organ and brass; Musica Magna. Publication: Orgues en Hainaut, 1966. Contributions to: Musique Vivante; Feuillets du Spantole; Hainaut-Tourisme, UWO. Honours: Composers Prize, JMB, 1955; Prix Koopal, 1968; Prix Doehaerd, 1971. Memberships: President, Founder, Musique Vivante; Société Liégeois de Musicologie; Sabam; Cebedem; Fondatioon Claude-Robert Roland. Hobbies: Football; Martial Arts; Esoterism. Address: 59 Rue Lebeau, B-1000 Brussels, Belgium.

ROLANDI Gianna, b. 16 Aug 1952, New York, USA. Soprano. m. Andrew Davis. Education: Studied with her mother and with Ellen Faull and Max Rudolf. Debut: Sang Offenbach's Olympia in Les Contes d'Hoffmann at the New York City Opera in 1975. Career: Metropolitan Opera in 1979 as Sophie, later singing Olympia, Stravinsky's Nightingale and Zerbinetta; Glyndebourne debut in 1981 as Zerbinetta returning in 1984 as Zdenka in Arabella and Susanna; English National Opera in 1983 as Cleopatra in Giulio Cesare; San Diego in 1984 as Ophelia in Hamlet by Thomas; Sang Lucia di Lammermoor at San Francisco in 1986, and Curiazio in a performance of Cimarosa's Gli Orazi e i Curizai, to mark the 200th anniversary of the French Revolution, at Rome Opera in 1989; Other roles include Gilda, the Queen of

Night and parts in operas by Donizetti at the New York City Opera; Sang Despina at Chicago, 1993; Concert tour of the USA with the BBC Symphony Orchestra, 1996. Address: c/o Teatro dell'Opera, Piazzo Beniamino Gigli 8, I-00184 Rome, Italy.

ROLFE JOHNSON Anthony, b. 5 Nov 1940, Tackley, Oxon, England. Tenor. Education: Guildhall School of Music, London. Debut: With the English Opera Group in 1973 in Tchaikovsky's Iolanta. Career includes: European career from 1977 as Lensky and Mozart's Titus with Netherlands Opera, Hamburg State Opera, La Scala as Mozart's Lucio Silla and in Geneva and at the Edinburgh Festival as Aschenbach in Death in Venice; With English National Opera roles have included Tamino, Ferrando, Monteverdi's Ulysses, Britten's Male Chorus and Essex; Sang Jupiter in Semele at Covent Garden; US concerts with Chicago Symphony under Solti, Boston Symphony Orchestra under Ozawa, New York Philharmonic under Rostropovich and the Cleveland Orchestra under Rattle; Other conductors include Marriner, Norrington, Boulez, Haitink, and Abbado; Salzburg debut in 1987 in Schmidt's Das Buch mit Sieben Siegeln returning in 1991 in title role in Idomeneo; Season 1992-93 as Monteverdi's Ulisse and Orfeo for ENO, Lucio Silla at Salzburg, Oronte in a new production of Handel's Alcina at Covent Garden, Peter Grimes in the first season of the reopened Glyndebourne Opera and Aschenbach at the Metropolitan, 1994; Male Chorus in the Rape of Lucretia, Glyndebourne, 1996. Recordings: Handel's Acis and Galatea; Saul, Hercules, Jephtha, Alexander's Feast, Esther, Solomon, Semele and Messiah; Haydn's Il Sposo Deluso, Il Mondo della Luna and Stabat Mater; Mozart's Apollo et Hyacinthus and La Finta Semplice, from the Salzburg Mozartwoche; Bach's St John and St Matthew Passion; Mozart's Zauberflöte, La Clemenza di Tito, Idomeneo; Haydn's Creation, Seasons, Peter Grimes, Samson, Oedipus Rex, Orfeo, War Requiem. Address: c/o Lies Askonas Ltd, 6 Henrietta Street, London, WC2E 8LA, England.

ROLL Michael, b. 17 Jul 1946, Leeds, England. Pianist. m. Juliana Markova, 1 son. Education: Piano studies with Fanny Waterman. Debut: Royal Festival Hall in 1958 playing Schumann Concerto with Malcolm Sargent. Career includes: Regular appearances with major UK orchestras; Played at Hong Kong Festival with London Philharmonic and toured Japan with the BBC Symphony; Also toured Holland, Germany, Switzerland, Spain and Eastern Europe; Tours of Russia and Scandinavia in recital and with orchestra; Conductors include Boulez, Giulini, Leinsdorf, and Previn; Visits to Aldeburgh, Bath, Edinburgh, Granda and Vienna Festivals; US debut in 1974 with Boston Symphony Orchestra conducted by Colin Davis; 1987-88 season with recitals in Milan, East Berlin, Dresden, Leipzig and London; 1988-89 season with London Symphony, Scottish National, Hallé, Bournemouth Symphony, Helsinki Philharmonic and Hong Kong Philharmonic Orchestras; Recitals in London, Milan, Leipzig, Berlin and Dresden; Played concertos in the 1990 Promenade Concerts, with Kurt Masur in Leipzig and London and Valery Gergiev in Leningrad and the UK; 1991-92 season played concertos with Skrowaczewski and the Hallé, BBC Philharmonic, BBC Scottish Orchestras and Leipzig Gewandhaus, recitals in the International Piano Series at the Queen Elizabeth Hall and at the Klavierfestival Ruhr in Germany with Helsinki Philharmonic under Comissiona, for the English Chamber Orchestra at the Barbican and his New York debut recital in 1992. Address: c/o Harold Holt Ltd, 31 Sinclair Road, London, W14 0NS, England.

ROLLAND Sophie, b. 18 Jul 1963, Montreal, Canada. Solo Concert Cellist. Education: Studied with Walter Joachim, Conservatoire de Musique du Quebéc, Montreal; Further study with Nathaniel Rosen in New York, Pierre Fournier in Geneva and William Pleeth in London. Debut: Montreal Symphony Orchestra under Charles Dutoit, 1982. Career: Regular appearances throughout Canada with all major orchestras including the Montreal, Toronto and Vancouver Symphony Orchestras; Toured in USA, France, Spain, England, Wales, Germany, Switzerland, Bulgaria, Hungary, Yugoslavia, Finland and China; Frequent guest at international chamber music festivals including Kuhmo, Dubrovnik and Parry Sound; Duo partnership with pianist, Marc-Andre Hamelin since 1988; 1990-91 season includes Beethoven cycle in New York at Carnegie Hall in 1991, Washington DC, Montreal with broadcast for CBC, and in London at Wigmore Hall in 1991 and broadcast for BBC; Plays a 1674 cello by Petrus Ranta of Brescia. Honours include: Premier Prix à l'Unamanité Montreal; Study awards from the Canadian and Quebec Governments; Priz d'Europe, Canada; 1st Prize, Du Maurier Competition; Virginia P Moore Prize, Canada Arts Council, 1985. Address: 27 Cleveland Avenue, London, W4 1SN, England.

ROLNICK Neil B, b. 22 Oct 1947, Dallas, TX, USA. Composer; Professor. m. Wendy Goodale, 28 Oct 1972, 1 daughter. Education: AB, English Literature, Harvard College, 1969; San Francisco Conservatory of Music, 1973-74; Computer Music at Stanford University, summer, 1976; MA, 1976, PhD, 1980, University of California, Berkeley. Career: Researcher, IRCAM, Paris, 1977-79; Assistant Professor, 1981-86, Associate

Professor, 1986-89, Professor, 1989-, Chair, Department of the Arts, 1994-, Music, Rensselaer Polytechnic Institute, Troy, NY; Soloist on synthesizer and computer music, 1982-; Performances throughout USA and Europe. Compositions include: Screen Scenes; Requiem Songs; Home Game; HEAT: The Rise and Fall of Isabella Rico; ElectriCity; Nerve Us; A La Mode for 8 Instruments and Digital Synthesizer; Real Time for 13 Instruments and Digital Synthesizer; Wondrous Love for Trombone and Tape; Ever-Livin Rhythm for Percussion and Tape; Blowin for Solo Flute; Loopy for Solo Synclavier II; Roberet Johnson Sampler, Balkanization, What Is The Use?, Macedonian Air Drumming and Sanctus, all computer music; Drones and Dances for Chamber Orchestra and Synthesizer; I Like It for 2 Singers and Digital Processing; Vocal Chords for Voice and Digital Processing; The Original Child Bomb Song for Voices and Synthesizers. Recordings: Numerous on major labels. Honours: Grants from: Rockefeller Foundation, Asian Cultural Council, Fulbright, Cary Trust, National Endowment for the Arts, New York State Council on the Arts. Address: 3284 Route 66, Valatie, NY 12184-9633, USA.

ROLOFF Elisabeth, b. 18 Feb 1937, Bielefeld, Germany. Organist. Education: Berlin High School of Music, 1958-60; BA, Bremen Conservatory of Music, 1960-61; MA 1965, Artist's Diploma 1966, Cologne High School of Music; Royal College of Music, London, 1966-67. Career: Organist and Choirmaster, Christ Church, Hannover, Germany, 1968-74; Titular Organist, German Church, Paris, France, 1974-82; Concerts throughout Europe, Israel and USA; Faculty, Rubin Academy of Music, Jerusalem, Israel, 1983-; Titular Organist, Redeemer Church, Jerusalem, 1983-; Appearances: International Organ Festival, Soro, Denmark, Royal Festival Hall, London, King's College Chapel, Cambridge, England, St Ouen, Rouen, France, Notre Dame, Paris, Chartres Cathedral, France, Kaiser-Wilhelm-Gedächtniskirche, Berlin, Marburg University, Cathedral and St Jacobskirche, Lübeck, Liturgica, Israel, Bach Organ Festival, Israel, 1985, Tallinn, St Petersburg; Radio appearances: Belgium, Denmark, Germany, Israel, Norway and Switzerland; Festival appearances: Mexico, Kiev, Prague, Riga in Latvia, Budapest, São Paulo, Montevideo and Buenos Aires. Recordings: Musica Sacra at the Redeemer Church, Jerusalem; Organ works: Pachelbel, Buxtehude, J S Bach and Mozart; Organ Landscape Jerusalem. Honour: Decree of International Letters for Cultural Achievement, 1996. Memberships: Association Jehan Alain; Internationale Mendelssohn-Stiftung, EV. Hobby: Reading. Current Management: International Music Consultant, PO Box 45401, Tel Aviv 61453. Address: PO Box 14076, Jerusalem, Israel.

ROLOFF Roger (Raymond), b. 22 Feb 1947, Peoria, IL, USA. Baritone. m. Barbara A Petersen, 19 Mar 1982. Education: BA, magna cum laude, English, IL Wesleyan University, 1969; MA, IL State University, 1972; Graduate study in English, SUNY, Stony Brook; Private voice study with Sam Sakarian, NYC, 1975-; Vocal and Dramatic coaching with teachers including Hans Hotter. Debut: Deertrees Opera Theatre, ME, 1975. Career: Operatic roles include Wotan and Wanderer in The Ring, Jochanaan in Salome, and Ruprecht in Prokofiev's Fiery Angel; Appearances with English National Opera, Deutsche Oper Berlin, Seattle, Kentucky, Dallas, San Diego and New York City operas, Niederschsische Staatsoper Hannover, Hawaii Opera Theater, Houston Grand Opera and major orchestras in USA and Canada; Concert appearances in Milwaukee, Boston, Los Angeles, Germany and Switzerland; Sang the Dutchman in a concert performance of Der fliegende Holländer at Boston in 1990, and Telramund in Lohengrin at Nice in 1990. Contributions to: Interviews and features, Ovation Magazine. Honours: Prizes at Montreal International Competition and Awards, William M Sullivan Foundation, 1981; 1st Prize, Wagnerian Voices, Liederkranz Foundation, 1982; Richard Tucker Award, 1984. Hobbies include: Hiking; Cycling; Walking; Old Recordings; Art; Museums; Writing German Poetry. Address: International Music Consultants, PO Box 45401, Tel-Aviv 61453, Israel.

ROLTON Julian, b. 1965, England. Pianist. Career: Co-founded the Chagall Piano Trio at the Banff Centre for The Arts in Canada, currently resident artist; Debut concert at the Blackheath Concert Halls in London, 1991; Further appearances at Barbican's Prokofiev Centenary Festival, Warwick Festival and the South Place Sunday Concerts at Conway Hall in London; Purcell Room recitals in 1993 with the London premiere of Piano Trios by Tristan Keuris, Nicholas Maw and Dame Ethel Smyth, composed 1880; Premiere of Piano Trio No 2 by David Matthews at Norfolk and Norwich Festival in 1993; Engaged for Malvern Festival in 1994. Address: South Bank Centre, c/o Press Office (Pamela Chowhan Management), London, SE1, England.

ROMANENKO Yelena, b. 1951, Kharkov, Russia. Mezzo-Soprano. Education: Studied at the Institute of Arts at Kharkov. Career: Participated in the foundation of an opera programme with the State Opera Company of Kharkov; Many performances in Russia and on tour in Europe and America, as Santuzza, Azucena, Eboli, Carmen, Dalila and Marfa in

Khovanshchina; British debut on tour with the National Opera of the Ukraine in 1995, as Marina in Boris Godunov and Fenena in Nabucco; Concert recitalist in German, Czech and Russian works. Address: c/o Sonata Ltd, 11 North Park Street, Glasgow, G20 7AA, Scotland.

ROMANOVA Nina, b. 1946, Leningrad, Russia. Mezzo-Soprano. Education: Studied with Vera Sopina at Leningrad Academy of Music. Career: Performed at Pushkin Theatre in Kishinov then from 1976 member of the Maly Theatre Leningrad, now St Petersburg; Roles have included Rosina in Barber of Seville, Azucena in Verdi's Il Trovatore, Eboli in Verdi's Don Carlo, Lady Macbeth, Carmen, Olga in Tchaikovsky's Eugene Onegin, The Countess and Polina in Tchaikovsky's Queen of Spades, Marina in Mussorgsky's Boris Godunov, Marfa in Mussorgsky's Khovanshchina and Alexander Nevsky by Prokofiev also in Verona, St Matthew Passion, St John Passion, Mass in B minor by Bach, Mozart's Requiem, Verdi's Requiem, and Mahler's 2nd and 8th Symphonies; Guest performances with St Petersburg Mussorgsky State Academic Opera and Ballet Theatre, formerly Leningrad Maly Theatre, as member of the Opera Company; Sang in Italy at Palermo, Modena, Reggio, Emilia, Parma, Ferrara, Ravenna and Catania, in France at Paris, Cannes and Nantes, New York and in Japan at Tokyo, Osaka, Hiroshima and lokogama, Greece, Portugal and The Netherlands. Address: Maly Opera and Ballet Theatre, St Petersburg, Russia.

ROMANUL Myron, b. 21 Mar 1954, Baltimore, Maryland, USA. Musician; Conductor; Pianist. m. Gabriele Weber, 8 June 1990. Education: New England Conservatory of Music, Boston, 1972-75; BM, Piano, Boston University School of Music, 1978-81; Kneisel Hall, Blue Hill, Maine, 1978-79; Berkshire Music Center at Tanglewood, 1973; André Watts Piano Seminar, 1984; Conductors' Seminar. Debut: Soloist with Boston Symphony Orchestra in Weber Konzertstück as youngest winner of Harry Dubbs Memorial Award, 1965. Career: Performed and toured as Piano Soloist with Arthur Fiedler and Boston Pops and with orchestras in America and Canada, 1973-79; With three younger brothers formed Romanul Chamber Players and performed concerts, on radio and TV; Original Pianist of New England Conservatory Ragtime Ensemble, 1972-76; Performances as Pianist and Zimbalist with Boston Symphony Orchestra, Speculum Musicae and Chamber Music Society of Lincoln Center; Principal Conductor of Boston Ballet, 1984-86; Conductor and Solo Pianist with Stuttgart Ballet, 1985-90; Music Director of Fairbanks Summer Arts Festival, 1985-; 2nd Kapellmeister and Assistant Music Director at Badisches Staatstheater Karlsruhe, Germany, 1990-94; 1st Kapellmeister and Associate Music Director at Staatstheater Mainz, 1994-. Recordings: As featured Pianist and Zimbalist. Honours: Numerous honours and awards. Memberships: American Symphony Orchestra League; Conductors' Guild. Hobbies: Walking; Cooking; Travel; Magic; Chamber music. Address: Kremmlerstrasse 53, D-70597 Stuttgart, Germany.

ROMBOUT Ernest, b. 30 Aug 1959, The Netherlands. Oboe Soloist; Professor. m. Anne-Lou Langendyk, 8 Dec 1995, 1 daughter. Education: Studied with Heinz Holliger, Soloists Diploma cum laude, Staatliche Hochschule fur Musik, Freiburg, Germany, 1984. Debut: Concertgebouw, Amsterdam, 1983. Career: Played as Soloist in Major Halls in Amsterdam, Berlin, Moscow, Munich, Lisbon, Paris, Zurich; Festivals include Biennale of Venice, Donaueschinger Musiktage, Ludwigsburger Festspiele, Festival of New Music Middelburg, Takefu Festival, Japan, Summer Festival, Avignon, Summer Festival, Los Angeles; Professor of Oboe, Conservatory of Music, Utrecht, 1985-; Masterclasses and workshops, Netherlands, Austria and Liechtenstein, 1993-97. Recordings: Solo CD: Oboe Concertos, Haydn, Mozart, Theme and Variations by J N Hummel with the Concertgebouw Chamber Orchestra; Oboe Concertos by L Francesconi, D del Puerto, Qigang Chen. Honour: Prize Winner, Ancona Competition of Winds, Italy, 1979. Membership: International Double Reed Society. Hobbies: Conducting and coaching ensembles. Address: Oude Eemnesserstraat 34, 1221 HL Hilversum, The Netherlands.

ROMERO Angel, b. 17 August 1946, Malaga, Spain. Classical Guitarist; Conductor. 1 son, 2 daughters. Education: Full musical studies and only guitar training with father and master guitarist Celedonio Romero; Studied conducting with Soltan Rushnia, Eugene Ormandy, Morton Gould, Ather Fiedler. Debut: Lobero Theatre, Santa Barbara, California, 1958. Career: First classical guitarist to perform at the Hollywood Bowl at West Coast premiere of Joaquin Rodrigo's Concerto de Aranjuez with the Los Angeles Philharmonic; Performances with the Boston Symphony, Chicago Symphony, Philadelphia Orchestra, New York Philharmonic, Cleveland Orchestra, Orquesta National de Espana, Berlin Philharmonic, Concertgebouw-Amsterdam; Halls include Carnegie Hall, Musikverein-Vienna, Orchestra Hall, Chicago; Performed for both Presidents Jimmy Carter and Richard Nixon, also the Pope at the Vatican; Television appearances include the celebration of the 500th anniversary of Columbus' discovery at the United Nations with the Orquesta National de Espana, 1992; Also with Arther Fiedler and the Boston Pops; Performed with conductors including Eugene Ormandy, Raymond Leppard, Sir Neville Mariner, Jesus Lopes Cobos, Rafael Fruhbeck de Burgos, Arther Fielder, Eduardo Mata, Giuseppe Patan, Morton Gould, Andre Previn; Conducted the Academy of St Martin-in-the-Fields, Pittsburgh Symphony Orchestra, San Diego Symphony Orchestra. Composition: Movie score for Bienvenido-Welcome. Recordings: Guitar Concertos; Concerto de Aranjuez; Giuliani Guitar Concertos; Vivaldi Concertos; Villa Lobos and Schifrin Guitar Concertos; Touch of Class; Angel Romero plays Bach; Grandos 12 Spanish Dances. Honour: Mexican Academy Award (Ariel) for best original score. Address: Hans Ulrich Schmid, Postfach 16 67, 30016 Hannover, Germany.

ROMERO Patricia, b. 20 Sept 1953, Mexico City, Mexico. Concert Pianist. m. David Hanesworth, 1 son. Education: Conservatorio Nacional de Musica, Mexico City, 1965-72; Trinity College, London, 1972-76; Studies with Louis Kentner, 1976-85. Debut: Wigmore Hall, London, June 1976. Career: Performed widely in the UK, Spain, Switzerland, Italy, France, Greece and the Middle East; London appearances: Purcell Room, Wigmore Hall, Fairfield Halls, St John's Smith Square, Leighton House; Performances with Orquesta Sinfonia del Bajio, Orquesta de la Universidad de Guadalajara, Orquesta Sinfonia de Coyoacan; Radio broadcasts in Mexico City, Guadalajara and BBC; Performed complete piano works of Maurice Ravel at the Purcell Room, London, July 1994; Forthcoming tours of Australia and New Zealand. Hobbies: Archaeology; Food; Wine; Opera; Gardening. Current Management: Hanesworth Concert Management. Address: 57 Osmond Gardens, Wallington, Surrey SM6 8SX, England.

ROMERO Pepe, b. 8 Mar 1944, Malaga, Spain. Classical Guitarist. Education: Studied classical and flamenco styles with his father. Career: Moved to USA in 1958 and joined family guitar quartet, giving 3000 concerts in America, Australia, South America and Europe from 1970; Solo European tour in 1982 followed by performances in Rome, Madrid, Budapest, Stockholm, Amsterdam, Paris, Vienna, Berlin, London and Copenhagen; Festival appearances at Osaka, Bergen, Istanbul, Rome and Luxembourg; Has premiered the Concerto Andalou and the Concierto Para una Festa by Rodrigo, 1967, 1973, and the Concerto Iberico by Torroba; Professor of the Guitar Department, University of Southern California, Los Angeles, SanDiego from 1982. Recordings: Five Rodrigo Concertos with the Boccherini Guitar Quintets and the Giuliani Concerti Op 65 and Op 70; Spanish Songs with Jessye Norman. Address: c/o Anglo Swiss Ltd, Suites 35-37, Morley House, 320 Regent Street, London W1R 5AD, England.

RONCO Claudio, b. 16 Sept 1955, Torino, Italy. Cellist; Composer. m. Lone K Loëll, 17 Sept 1983, 2 sons. Education: MA in Music, Student of Anner Bijlsma and Christophe Coin, Conservatorio Music, Torino. Debut: Como with the Clemencic Consort of Vienna, 1982. Career: Soloist with the Clemencic Consort, Vienna, 1982-; Hesperion XX, Ensemble 14, for ZDF, 1991; Television programme on Jewish music and Solo recital for Radio Canada, Montreal. Compositions: Tombeau de Mr Farinelli for violin, violoncello and harpsichord, 1994; Serenata Pastorale for 3 voices, violin, violoncello, harpsichord. Recordings: Several recordings with Hesperion XX, Clemencic Consort; First recording of Veracini, Bonperti, Lanzetti; Paganini; Rolla dios and Gade, Heise trios. Hobby: Chamber music. Address: Cannaregio 3023, Venice 30121, Italy.

RONCONI Luca, b. 8 Mar 1933, Susah, Tunisia. Stage Director. Education: Graduated, Accademia d'Arte Drammatica, Rome, 1953. Career: Began as an actor then directed plays; Opera debut in 1967 with Jeanne d'Arc au Bucher by Honegger and Busoni's Arlecchino at Turin; Later work has included revivals of neglected operas by Purcell, Jommelli, Cimarosa and Rimsky-Korsakov, The Tsar's Bride; Founding Director of theatre laboratory at the Teatro Metastasio, Prato, 1977; Produced Cosi fan tutte at Teatro La Fenice, 1983, Piccinni's Iphigénie en Tauride at Bari, 1985, seen also in Paris and Rome; Teatro alla Scala with Rossi's Orfeo in 1985 and Cherubini's Lodoiska in 1990; Productions of Don Giovanni in 1990 and I Vespri Siciliani at Bologna, Rossini's Ricciardo e Zoraide at the 1990 Pesaro Festival; Staged Rossini's Otello at Brussels, 1994; Modern repertory includes stagings of works by Stockhausen, Berio and Globokar; Director of the Teatro Stabile at Turin from 1989. Address: c/o Teatro alla Scala, Via Filodrammatici 2, Milan, Italy.

RONGE Gabriela (Maria), b. 3 Jul 1957, Hanover, Germany. Soprano. Career: Sang in opera at Heidelberg from 1982, and Osnabruck from 1983 notably as Fiordiligi and Hanna Glawari; Further engagements at Hanover, 1985-87, Cologne, 1989, Frankfurt, Bonn, the Deutsche Oper Berlin and Brunswick; Bayerische Staatsoper Munich from 1987 as the Marschallin, Elsa, Eva and Agathe; Frankfurt in 1987 as Gluck's Iphigénie en Tauride, Paris Opéra in 1989 as Eva, and Isabella in Wagner's Das Liebesverbot at Palermo in 1991; Noted interpreter of Lieder. Address: c/o Bayerische Staatsoper, Postfach 100148, 8000 Munich 1, Germany.

RONI Luigi, b. 22 Feb 1942, Vergemoli, Lucca, Italy. Bass Singer. Education: Studied with Sara Sforni Corti in Milan. Debut: Spoleto in 1965 as Mephistopheles in Faust. Career: Sang in Milan, Rome, Turin, Venice, Palermo, Florence and Naples; Moscow in 1973 with the La Scala Company; Guest appearances in Vienna, Munich, Berlin, London, Paris, New York, Chicago, Dallas and Houston; Orange Festival in 1984 as the Grand Inquisitor in Don Carlos; Other roles include Mozart's Commendatore and Mussorgsky's Dosifey; La Scala in 1987 as Lodovico in Otello; Sang MacGregor in Mascagni's Guglielmo Ratcliff at Catonia, 1990, Rossini's Basilio at Bonn, and Festival d'Orange in 1990 as the Grand Inquisitor in Don Carlos. Recordings include: Aida; Don Giovanni; Fernand Cortez by Spontini; Zaira by Bellini; Otello. Address: c/o Teatro Massimo Bellini, I-95100 Catonia, Italy.

ROOCROFT Amanda, b. 9 Feb 1966, Coppull, Lancashire, England. Soprano. Education: Studied at the Royal Northern College of Music with Barbara Robotham. Career: Operatic debut as Sophie in Der Rosenkavalier with Welsh National Opera, 1990; Glyndebourne Festival debut as Fiordiligi and Covent Garden debut as Pamina, 1991; Fiordiligi in Paris, Amsterdam and Lisbon with John Eliot Gardiner, 1992; Has returned to Covent Garden for Giulietta in I Capuleti e i Montecchi, Pamina in a new Magic Flute Production, and Fiodiligli in a new Così fan tutte production; Debut at the Bayerische Staatsoper Munich as Fiordiligi, and at English National Opera as Ginevra in Ariodante, 1993; Returned to Glyndebourne Festival as Donna Elvira in 1994 and to Munich as Amelia in Simon Boccanegra, 1994; Fiordiligi at Covent Garden, 1995; Further engagements as Mimi, Handel's Cleopatra for Covent Garden, the Countess and Desdemona in Munich and Donna Elvira at the Met, New York; Sings in recitals and concert throughout Europe with many leading conductors; Song recitals include Wigmore Hall, London, 1997; Engaged as Katya Kabanova at the 1998 Glyndebourne Festival. Recordings include: Debut album, Amanda Roocroft; Mozart and his Contemporaries; Schoenberg String Quartet no 2; Così fan tutte with Gardiner; Vaughan Williams' Sea Symphony. Honours include: Various awards and prizes at RNCM; Decca-Kathleen FerrierPrize, 1988; Silver Medal of the Worshipful Company of Musicians, 1988; Charles Heidsieck Award, Royal Philharmonic Society, 1991. Current Management: Ingpen and Williams Ltd, 26 Wadham Road, London SW15 2LR, England.

ROOLEY Anthony, b. 10 June 1944, Leeds, Yorkshire, England. Musician (Lutenist); Director; Lecturer. Education: Guitar, Royal Academy of Music, 1965-68. Career: Teacher, guitar, lute, Royal Academy of Music, 1968-71; With James Tyler founded Consort of Musicke, 1969; As director and lutenist, many early music concerts, Europe, Middle East, USA; Sole director, 1971-, often giving concerts of Renaissance theme; Appearances, BBC, French and German TV and radio; International festivals, Europe, Scandinavia, USA; Concerts with sopranos Emma Kirby, Evelyn Tubb, alto Mary Nichols, tenor Andrew King, Simon Grant, Joseph Cornwell (Consort of Musicke members), bass David Thomas, tenor Paul Agnew, other early music specialists; Music-theatre includes staging of Le Veglie di Siena (music by Orazio Vecchi), Copenhagen, London, 1988; Collaboration with Italian commedia dell'arte actors La Famiglia Carrara in Marriage of Pantelone; Promenade Concert, 1988, based on settings of poet Torquato Tasso; Concerts, Tel-Aviv, New York, 1988; Co-director with Arjen Terpstra, new record label Musica Oscura; Teacher, Japan, Padova, Basle, Dartington, promoting Renaissance Attitudes to Performance; Co-director with Don Taylor, video Banquet of the Senses: Monteverdi's Madrigali Erotici. Recordings include: Madrigals by Monteverdi, de Rore, Marini, Porter, Pallavicino, Marenzio, d'India; L'anime del Purgatorio (Stradella); Madrigals and Fantasias, Psalms and Anthems (John Ward); Arie Antiche, The Mad Lover (The Orpheus Circle); The Dark is my Delight (Women in Song); Maurice Greene: Songs and Keyboard works (The Handel Circle); The Mistress, The Mantle, Orpheus, Sound the Trumpets from Shore to Shore (Purcell). Publications include: A New Varietie of Lute Lessons, record, book, 1975; The Penguin Book of Early Music, record, book, 1979; Performance: Revealing the Orpeus Within, 1990; Contributions to: Lute Society Journal; Early Music; Guitar. Memberships: Viola da Gamba Society; Galpin Society; Wine Society; Royal Society of Arts. Hobbies: Renaissance philosophy; Wine. Address: Leamington Road Villas, London W11 1HT, England.

ROOSENSCHOON Hans, b. 17 December 1952, The Hague, Netherlands (South African Citizen). Composer. Education: Pretoria Conservatory, 1969-71, 1974-75; Royal Academy of Music, London, with Paul Patterson, 1977-78; DMus, University of Cape Town, 1991. Career: Production Manager, South African Broadcasting Corporation, Johannesburg, 1980-95. Compositions: Suite for Oboe & Piano, 1973; Ekstase for Chorus & Orchestra, 1975; Cantata on Psalm 8, 1976; Tablo for Orchestra, 1976; Sinfonietta, 1976; Katutura for Orchestra, 1977;

Palette for Strings, 1977; Mosaiek for Orchestra, 1978; Ars Poetica for Baritone, Chorus & Orchestra, 1979; Psalm 23 for Choirs, 1979; Firebowl for Chorus, 1980; Ikonografie, Anagram & Architectura, all for Orchestra, 1983-86; Horizon, Night-Sky & Landscape for Strings, 1987; Chronicles for Orchestra, 1987; Clouds Clearing for Strings, 1987; Mantis, Ballet Suite, 1988; Circle of Light for Orchestra, 1989; Die Sonnevanger, for Orchestra, 1990; The Magic Marimba, 1991; Mbira for Chorus, 1994; Trombone Concerto, 1995; String Quartet, 1995; Keyboard, Organ & Electronic Music. Address: c/o SAMRO, PO Box 31609, Braamfontein 2017, Johannesburg, South Africa.

ROOT Deane (Leslie), b. 9 Aug 1947, Wausau, Wisconsin, USA. Musicologist; Museum Curator; Teacher; Librarian; Editor; Author. m. Doris J Dyen, 27 Aug 1972, 2 daughters. Education: New College, Sarasota, Florida; University of Illinois. Career: Faculty, University of Wisconsin, 1973; Editorial Staff, New Grove Dictionary of Music and Musicians, 1974-76; Research Associate, University of Illinois, 1976-80; Visiting Research Associate, Florida State University, 1981-82; Curator, Stephen Foster Memorial and Adjunct Assistant Professor in Music, University of Pittsburgh, 1982-; Heinz Chapel Administrator, University of Pittsburgh, 1983-; Director of Cultural Resources 1990, Adjunct Associate Professor 1992, University of Pittsburgh. Recordings: Proud Traditions; Musical Tribute to Pitt. Publications: American Popular Stage Music 1860-1880; Music of Florida Historic Sites; Co-Author, Resources of American Music History; Co-Editor, Music of Stephen C Foster; Series Editor, Nineteenth Century American Musical Theater, 16 vols, 1994. Contributions to: New Grove Dictionary of Music and New Grove Dictionary of American Music; American National Biography; Various journals, yearbooks, conference proceedings. Address: Centre for American Music, University of Pittsburgh, PA 15260, USA.

ROOTERING Jan-Hendrik, b. 18 Mar 1950, Wedingfeld, Nr Flensburg, Germany. Singer (Bass). Education: Studies with his father, Hendrikus Rootering, a voice teacher; Further education at Musikhochschule Hamburg. Debut: Colline in La Bohème, 1980. Career: Engagements include Conerts, Opera Performances and Lieder Recitals as well as numerous recordings with such conductors as Sawallisch, Muti, Levine, Abbado, Marriner, Davis and others; Appearances at Munich State Opera, Vienna State Opera, Berlin Deutsche Oper, Amsterdam, Geneva, Hamburg State Opera, London's Covent Garden, New York's Metropolitan Opera, Chicago's Lyric Opera, San Francisco Opera and Milan's La Scala. Recordings: Beethoven Ninth Symphony initiated and conducted by the late Leonard Bernstein, 1989; Fasolt in Das Rheingold; Sang Gurnemanz in Parsifal at the Opéra Bastille, Paris, 1997. Honours: Honorary Title of Bavarian Kammersänger, 1989; Honorary Title of Professor with the Hochschule für Musik in Munich, 1994; Principle Artist on the Grammy Award winning recording of Das Rheingold on DGG conducted by James Levine. Address: 45 West 67th Street, Apt 26C, New York, NY 10023, USA.

ROPEK Jirí, b. 1 July 1922, Prague, Czechoslovakia. Professor of Organ; Organist. m. Jirina Kupkova, 1 daughter. Education: Conservatory of Music, Prague; Charles University, Prague; Academy of Music, Prague. Career: Recitals, Czechoslovakia, 1950-, most European countries, 1960-; Regular performances, USSR, Netherlands, Germany, UK; 1st Czechoslovakian Organist to play in Royal Festival Hall, Westminster Cathedral, London; Professor of Organ, Prague Conservatory; Organist, St Jacob's Church, Prague; TV and radio appearances. Compositions include: Organ Variations on Victimae Pashali Laudes; Christmas Fantasy for choir, orchestra and organ; Toccata and Fugue for organ and Toccata for John Scott, premiered at St Paul's Cathedral, 1993, published, 1993; Music for Brass and Organ; Partita on Adoro Te Devote; Sonatas for various solo instruments, flute, trumpet, oboe, violin, with organ; Mozart: Strahover Improvisation/historical torso completed by J Ropek, 1983. Recordings: Numerous labels. Honours: Honorary FRCO, 1994. Address: U Plátenice 2, 150 00 Prague 5, Czech Republic.

ROREM Ned, b. 23 Oct 1923, Richmond, Indiana, USA. Composer. Education: American Conservatory, Chicago with Leo Sowerby; Northwestern University, 1940-42; Curtis Institute Philadelphia, 1943; Juilliard School New York, 1946; Masters Degree, Juilliard, 1948; Private studies with Thomson and Copland. Career: Lived in Morocco 1949-51, and in France, 1951-57; Composer-in-residence University of Buffalo 1959-61, University of Utah 1966-67; Curtis Institute from 1980. Compositions: 3 Symphonies, 1951, 1956, 1959; 4 String Quartets, 1948, 1950, 1990, 1994; Design for orchestra, 1953; A Childhood Miracle, opera, 1955; The Poets' Requiem, 1955; The Robbers, opera, 1958; Eleven Studies for Eleven Players, 1960; Ideas for orchestra, 1961; Lift up your Heads, for chorus and wind, 1963; Lions (A Dream) for orchestra, 1963; Miss Julie, opera, 1965; Letters from Paris for chorus and orchestra, 1966; Sun, 8 poems for high voice and orchestra; Water Music for clarinet, violin and orchestra, 1966; Bertha, 1-act opera, 1968; War Scenes for voice and piano, 1969; 3 Piano Concertos, 1950, 1951, 1969; Little Prayers for soprano, baritone and orchestra, 1973; Air Music, variations for orchestra, 1974; Serenade on Five English Poems, 1975; Hearing, 5 scenes for singers and 7 instruments, 1976; Sunday Morning for orchestra, 1977; The Nantucket Songs, 1979; Remembering Tommy, concerto for piano, cello and orchestra, 1979; After Reading Shakespeare for solo cello, 1980; The Santa Fe Songs, voice and piano quartet, 1980; After Long Silence for soprano, oboe and strings, 1982; An American Oratorio, 1983; Winter Pages, for 5 instruments, 1982; Whitman Cantata, 1983; Violin Concerto, 1984; Septet, Scenes from Childhood, 1985; Organ Concerto, 1985; End of Summer, for violin, clarinet and piano, 1985; String Symphony, 1985; Homer (Three Scenes from the Iliad) for chorus and 8 instruments, 1986; Goodbye My Fancy chorus, soloists, orchestra, 1988-89; The Auden Poems, Tenor and Piano Trio, 1989; Swords and Plowshares, 4 vocal soloists and orchestra, 1991; Piano Concerto for left-hand and orchestra, 1992; Hundreds of songs and 12 song cycles; Cor anglais concerto, 1995. Publications: Prose: Paris Diary, 1966; Music From Inside Out, 1966; New York Diary 1967; Music and People, 1968; Critical Affairs, 1970; The Later Diaries, 1974; Pure Contraption, 1974; Setting the Tone, 1980; The Nantucket Diary, 1985; Settling the Score, 1988; Knowing When to Stop, 1994; Other Entertainment, essays, 1995; Dear Paul, Dear Ned. Address: c/o ASCAP, ASCAP Building, One Lincoln Plaza, New York, NY 10023, USA.

RORHOLM Marianne, b. 1960, Denmark. Mezzo-Soprano. Education: Studied at the Opera Academy at Copenhagen. Debut: Royal Opera, Copenhagen as Cherubino. Career: Season 1984-85 sang Olga, Lola and Rosina at Copenhagen and as the Sorceress in Dido and Aeneas at Paris Opéra; Frankfurt Opera, 1985-88 as Rosina, Dorabella, Sextus in La Clemenza di Tito, Nicklausse and Octavian; Sang Cherubino with the Israel Philharmonic under Daniel Barenboim and at the 1987 Ludwigsburg Festival; Bayreuth Festival in 1988 as a Flowermaiden in Parsifal; Season 1988-89 included US debut with the Indianapolis Symphony under Raymond Leppard, a concert at Carnegie Hall, Cherubino at Glyndebourne and Isolier in Le Comte Ory for Netherlands Opera; Regular appearances with the Deutsche Oper am Rhein Dusseldorf and Basle Operas; Season 1992 as Annius in La Clemenza di Tito at Toulouse, Varvara in Katya Kabanova at Bonn, Purcell's Dido at Brussels and the Berlioz Marguerite at Amsterdam; Concert repertory includes Mahler's Das Lied von der Erde. Recordings include: Kate Pinkerton in Madame Butterfly; Salome under Giuseppe Sinopoli; Dryad in Ariadne auf Naxos; Sang Verdi's Preziosilla at Copenhagen, 1996. Honours include: Carl Neilsen Scholarship, 1984; Elisabeth Dons Memorial Prize, 1985. Address: c/o Ingpen and Williams Ltd, 14 Kensington Court, London, W11 4PA, England.

ROS MARBA Antoni, b. 2 Apr 1937, Barcelona, Spain. Conductor. Education: Barcelona Conservatory; Studied orchestral conducting with Eduard Toldra, Celibidache at Accademia Chigiana, and Jean Martinon at Dusseldorf. Debut: Barcelona in 1962. Career: Principal Conductor, 1965-68, and later as Principal Guest Conductor and Artistic Consultant for Spanish Radio and TV Orchestras, for City of Barcelona Orchestra, 1967-77, Spanish National Orchestra, 1978-81, and Netherlands Chamber Orchestra, 1979-86; Principal Guest Conductor for Netherlands Chamber Orchestra since it joined with Netherlands Philharmonic Orchestra, 1986-; Further appearances and tours worldwide including Europe, North and South America, Japan, and China and with orchestras such as Berlin Philharmonic Orchestra; Recently developed international career as an opera conductor with special success at Teatro de la Zarzuela, Madrid and Gran Teatro del Liceu, Barcelona; Appointed Musical Director at National Opera Theatre Real, Madrid, 1989; Season 1992 with the stage premiere of Gerhard's The Duenna at Madrid, repeated for Opera North; Idomeneo for Scottish Opera, 1996. Recordings include: Haydn's Seven Last Words on the Cross; Others with Victoria de Los Angeles, Teresa Berganza, English Chamber Orchestra and Netherlands Chamber Orchestra. Honours: National Music Prize of Spain, Ministry of Culture, 1989; Arthur Honegger International Recording Prize for Seven Last Words on the Cross; Cross of St Jordi Generalitat de Cataluna. Address: c/o Teatro Real, Plaza de Isabel II s/n, 28013 Madrid, Spain.

ROSAND Aaron, b. 15 Mar 1927, Hammond, IN, USA. Violinist; Teacher. Education: Studied with Marinus Paulsen, 1935-39, Leon Sameti, 1940-44, and Efrem Zimbalist, 1944-48. Debut: With the Chicago Symphony under Frederick Stock playing the Mendelssohn Concerto, 1937. Career: Played at New York Town Hall in 1948; European debut at Copenhagen in 1955; Tours of Europe, the Far East and Russia; Appearances with leading orchestras in the USA; Repertoire includes concertos by Lalo, Ries, Vieuxtemps, Joachim, Hubay and Wieniawski; Taught at the Academie Internationale d'Été in Nice from 1971, Peabody Conservatory, Baltimore and Mannes College, NY, and Curtis Institute, Philadelphia, 1981-; Plays a Guarneri del Gesu of 1741. Recordings: 15 CD recordings. Honours include: Chevalier Pour Merite Cultural et Artistique, 1965; Gold Medal of the Foundation Ysaye, Belgium, 1967. Current Management: Jacques Leiser Artist Management. Address: c/o Jacques Leiser Artist Management, The Del Prado, 666 L/Pas Street, Suite 602, San Diego, CA 92103, USA.

RÖSCHMANN Dorothea, b. 1969, Flensburg, Germany. Singer (Soprano) Education: Studied in Germany and with Vera Rozsa in London. Career: Member of the Deutsche Staatsoper Berlin, appearing as Papagena, Iris (Semele) and Sophie in Der Rosenkavalier (1997); Salzburg Festival from 1995, as Susanna and in concert; Further engagements as Zerlina at Tel Aviv, Handel's Dorinda (Orlando) at Halle, Monteverdi's Drusilla (at Munich) and Dorina in Caldara's I Disingannati at the Early Music Festival Innsbruck; Other roles include Weber's Annchen (at Berlin and Munich), Handel's Arianna (Giustino) at Göttingen and Servilia in La Clemenza di Tito, at the 1997 Salzburg Festival; Concerts at Carnegie Hall, the Vienna Musikverein, Leipzig Gewandhaus, Hamburg Musikhalle and Semperoper, Dresden. Recordings include: Pergolesi's Stabat Mater and Vivaldi's Masaniello Furioso; Messiah with Paul McCreesh and Bach's Secular Cantatas with Reinhard Goebbel (DGG); Bach's Weihnachtsoratorium and Telemann's Orpheus with René Jacobs (Harmonia Mundi). Address: c/o Lies Askonas Ltd, 6 Henrietta St, London WC2E 8LA, England.

ROSCOE Martin, b. 3 Aug 1952, Halton, Cheshire, England. Pianist. Education: Royal Manchester College of Music with Marjorie Clementi and Gordon Green. Career: Appearances at Cheltenham, Bath, Leeds, and South Bank Music Festivals; Performances at Royal Festival Hall, Queen Elizabeth Hall, Royal Albert Hall, and Wigmore Hall in London with Hallé, City of Birmingham, Royal Philharmonic, Royal Liverpool Philharmonic, Northern Sinfonia, London Mozart Players, and BBC Philharmonic Orchestras; Tours of Australia, Middle East and South America; Further appearances at Harrogate Festival with Scottish National Orchestra, BBC, and Welsh Symphony Orchestras; Played at the Promenade Concerts with BBC Symphony Orchestra in 1987, and with French Philharmonic Orchestra in 1989; Recitals with violinist Tasmin Little, notably in the Kreutzer Sonata. Recordings: Many for BBC radio 3 including Piano Concertos of Berwald, Liszt, Beethoven, Stravinsky, Fauré, Vaughan Williams, and Shostakovich; Solo works by Beethoven; Complete Sonatas of Schubert, Debussy, Liszt and Bartók; Concertos by Strauss and Szymanowski; Solo commercial recordings with music by Liszt. Honours: Davas Gold Medal, 1973; Silver Medal, Worshipful Company of Musicians, 1974; British Liszt Piano Competition, 1976; Sydney International Piano Competition, 1981. Memberships: Incorporated Society of Musicians; Musicians Union. Hobbies: Fell Walking; Reading; Cinema. Current Management: Hazard Chase Ltd, 25 City Road, Cambridge, England. Address: 225 Revidge Road, Blackburn, BB2 6DT, England.

ROSE Gregory, b. 18 Apr 1948, Beaconsfield, England. Conductor. Education: BA, Magdalen College, Oxford University, 1967-70; Trained Violinist, pianist and Singer. Career: Conductor, Founder of Singcircle, Circle, 1977-; Music Director, London Jupiter Orchestra, 1986-; Conductor, Reading Festival Chorus, 1984-88; Conductor, London Concert Choir, 1988-96; Conductor, Reading Symphony Orchestra, 1986-91; Conductor, National Youth Choir of Wales, 1986-89; Conducted BBC Concert Orchestra, Ulster Orchestra, Estonian National Symphony Orchestra, Netherlands Radio Chamber Orchestra, BBC Singers, Nederlands Kamerkoor, Groupe Vocal de France, WDR Choir, Steve Reich and Musicians, London Philharmonic, Odense Symfonieorkester and Latvian Filharmonia; Series Director, Cage at 70, Almeida Festival, 1982 and Reich at 50, Almeida Festival, 1986; Conducted Thomson's Four Saints in Three Acts, Spitalfields, 1996. Recordings: Hyperion, Mouth Music, Stockhausen's Stimmung; Wergo, Son Entero by Alejandro Viñao; Continuum, music by Simon Emmerson; October Music, music by Trevor Wishart; Chandos, music by Janácek; Numerous recordings for BBC radio and television, Channel 4, ITV and European radio stations. Publications: Various compositions. Current Management: Connaught Artists Management. Address: 57 White Horse Road, London E1 0ND, England.

ROSE John (Luke), b. 19 July 1933, Northwood Hills, Middlesex, England. Composer; Pianist; Lecturer; Teacher; Writer; Conductor. Education: University of London, Trinity College of Music, 1954-58; BMus, London, 1957; LMusTCL, 1957; PhD, Wagner's Musical Language, London, 1963. Debut: Oxford University, 1958. Career: Extension Lecturer in Music, University of Oxford, 1958-66; Lecturer, Teacher and Examiner (UK, USA, Newfoundland, Canada, Fiji, New Zealand, Australia, India), Trinity College of Music, 1960-; Part-time Teacher, St Marylebone Grammar School, 1963-66; Staff Tutor, Department of Extra-Mural Studies, University of London, 1966-84. Compositions: Symphony No 1, The Mystic, BBC Philharmonic, 1982; Piano Concerto, BBC Northern and Scottish Orchestras, 1977; Overture Macbeth, BBC Scottish Symphony Orchestra, 1977; Symphony No 2, 1985; Symphonic Dances, Hallé Orchestra; String Quartet; Part-songs; 2 Piano Sonatas; Various piano works; Blake's Songs of Innocence; The Pleasures of Youth, cantata; Hymns and Anthems; Apocalyptic Visions for piano; St Francis, musical play, 1985; Violin Concerto, BBC Philharmonic, 1987; Odysseus, opera, 1987. Publications: Wagner's Tristan and Isolde: A Landmark in Musical History, introductory essay to libretto book, English National Opera Guide No 6, 1981; Ludwig, Wagner and the Romantic View, essay and lecture, Victoria and Albert Museum Exhibition; BBC interviews. Honours: 1st British composer to win Royal Philharmonic Society Prize twice (for Symphonies 1 and 2), 1957, 1958; Honorary Fellow, Trinity College, London, 1961. Memberships: Composer's Guild of Great Britain; Society for Promotion of New Music; Association of University Tutors. Hobbies: Painting; Gardening; Tennis; Golf; Writing poetry; Vegetarianism; Health Education; Travelling. Address: Kalon, 113 Farnham Road, Guildford, Surrey GU2 5PF, England.

ROSE Jurgen, b. 25 Aug 1937, Bernburg, Germany. Stage Designer. Education: Studied acting and painting in Berlin. Career: Ballet designs for the Stuttgart Ballet, 1962-73; Collaborations with director, Otto Schenk for Don Carlos and Die Meistersinger in Vienna, Simon Boccanegra and Der Rosenkavalier at Munich and Così fan tutte in Berlin; Bayreuth Festival in 1972 and 1990 with Tannhäuser and Der fliegende Holländer, in productions by Götz Friedrich and Dieter Dorn; Salome and Die Entführung in Vienna, Lucia di Lammermoor and Lohengrin in Hamburg; Premiere of Isang Yun's Sim Tjong at Munich in 1972; Designed Die Zauberflöte for the Munich Opera and the 1981 Ludwigsburg Festival; Le nozze di Figaro for the 1997 Munich Festival. Recordings include: Video of Munich production of Die Zauberflöte. Address: c/o Bayerische Staatsoper, Postfach 100148, 8000 Munich 1, Germany.

ROSE Peter, b. 1961, Canterbury, Kent, England. Singer (Bass). Education: University of East Anglia, Guildhall School of Music with Ellis Keeler, National Opera Studio. Debut: As Commendatore in Don Giovanni with Glyndebourne Opera in Hong Kong, 1986 and on tour. Career includes: Welsh National Opera, 1986-89 as Bartolo, Basilio, Prince Gremin in Eugene Onegin, Angelotti in Tosca, Osmin, Tutor in Count Ory and Marke in Tristan; Glyndebourne Touring Opera as Don Inigo in L'Heure Espagnole, Osmin and Basilio; Maggio Musicale Florence as Commendatore; Scottish Opera as Narbal in Les Troyens; Sang in La Damnation de Faust in Chicago, BBC Proms and Salzburg Festival with Chicago Symphony under Solti; English National Opera as Angelotti and Bottom; Covent Garden debut 1988 as Lord Rochefort in Anna Bolena then Cadmus in Semele, Bonze in Madama Butterfly, Lodovico in Otello, Nightwatchman in Meistersinger; Kecal in The Bartered Bride, Chicago Lyric Opera, Commendatore, Gessler in Guillaume Tell and Basilio at San Francisco, 1991-92; Also sang Walther in Luisa Miller, Amsterdam, 1st Nazarene in Salome, Salzburg, Bottom at Aix-en-Provence, Commendatore at Covent Garden in 1993, Mustafa (Italiana), Amsterdam, Pimen in Boris Godunov at New Israeli Opera, Ramfis in Aida, Hunding in Walküre, Berlin Staatsoper, in 1994 and Dosifei in Khovanshchina, Hamburg; Other roles include Fasolt in Rheingold; Bottom at the Met; Sang in Pfitzner's Palestrina at Covent Garden, 1997. Recordings include: Nozze di Figaro with Barenboim and the Berlin Philharmonic; Video of Clemenza di Tito for Glyndebourne; Salome with Dohnányi; Seven Deadly Sins (also on video); Barber of Seville (with Peter Moores); Beatrice Cenci, Goldschmidt; Ballo in Maschera, Teldec. Current Management: IMG Artists. Address: c/o IMG Artists, 3 Burlington Lane, London, W4, England.

ROSEBERRY Eric (Norman), b. 18 Jul 1930, Sunderland, England. Musician; Writer. m. (1) Elspeth Mary Campbell, 20 Aug 1952, 4 d, (2) Frances Jill Sharp, 21 Aug, 1969. Education: BA, BMus, University of Durham; PhD, University of Bristol, 1982. Career: Director of Music, Stand Grammar School for Boys, Manchester, 1953-58; County Music Organiser, Huntingdonshire, 1958-64; Music Assistant, BBC London, 1964-69; Radcliffe Lecturer in Music, University of Sussex, 1969-72; Lecturer for University of Bristol Extra-Mural Department, 1972-; Senior Lecturer in Music, Bath College of Higher Education, 1972-85; Director of Music, Bath Symphony Orchestra, 1977-89; Founder Director of Apollo Ensemble of Bath, 1989. Publications: Faber Book of Christmas Carols and Songs, 1969; Dmitri Shostakovich: His Life and Times, 1982; Essays appearing in, Of German Music, 1976, The Britten Companion, 1984, Benjamin Britten Death in Venice, Cambridge Opera Handbooks, 1987; Shostakovich's Musical Style, USA, 1990. Contributions to: Articles and reviews in Tempo, The Listener, Music and Musicians, Music and Letters, Musical Times, CD Review; Programme Notes for BBC Symphony Concerts, Aldeburgh Festival and the Proms; Broadcast talks on BBC Radio 3. Hobbies: Gardening; Swimming; Walking; Cooking; Victorian Book Illustrations. Address: The Toll House, Marshfield, Chippenham, Wiltshire, SN14 8JN, England.

ROSELL Lars-Erik, b. 9 Aug 1944, Nybro, Sweden. Composer; Organist. Education: Organ Student, 1963-69;

Composition with Ingvar Lidholm, Stockholm Royal College of Music, 1968-72. Career: Teacher, Counterpoint, Composition, Stockholm Royal University College of Music, 1972-; Freelance Organist, Performances of Contemporary Music. Compositions include: Terry Riley for 3 Pianos, 1970; Poem in the Dark for Mezzo and Ensemble, 1972; After the Fall, Dramatic Scene Based on Arthur Miller, for Vocal Soloists and Ensemble, 1973; Visiones Prophetae, Biblical Scene, 1974; Musik for Cello and String Orchestra, 1975; Ordens källa, Scenic Cantata, 1980; Tillfälligt avbrott, Chamber Opera, 1981; Organ Concerto, 1982; Amédée, Chamber Opera, 1986; Five Aphorisms, cello solo, 1990; Fantasia Concertante for Cello and Orchestra, 1992; The Illusionist, chamber opera, 1996-; Choir music, chamber music and other stage music. Address: Gnejsstigen 2, S-19633 Kungsängen, Sweden.

ROSEN Charles, b. 5 May 1927, New York City, USA. Pianist; Writer on Music. Education: Juilliard School, 1934-38; Piano studies with Moritz Rosenthal and Hedwig Kanner-Rosenthal; Studied romance languages at Princeton, PhD, 1951. Debut: New York in 1951. Career: Recitalist and orchestral soloist in Europe and America; With Ralph Kirkpatrick premiered Elliott Carter's Double Concerto in New York, 1961; Frequent performances of Beethoven, Bach, Boulez and Debussy; Faculty, SUNY, Stony Brook, 1971-; Gave Messenger lectures at Cornell University, 1975. Recordings: First complete recording of Debussy's Etudes, 1951; Stravinsky's Movements with the composer conducting, 1961; Boulez Piano Music, volume 1. Publications: The Classical Style: Haydn, Mozart, Beethoven, 1971; Beethoven's Last 6 Sonatas, 1972; Schoenberg, 1975; Sonata Forms, 1980, revised second edition, 1988; The Romantic Century, 1995. Contributions to: New York Review of Books, and other journals. Honours include: National Book Award, 1972. Address: 101 West 78th Street, New York, NY 10024, USA.

ROSEN Jerome (William), b. 23 July 1921, Boston, MA, USA. Composer; Clarinettist; Professor of Music. m. Sylvia T Rosen, 1 son, 3 daughters. Education: MA, University of California, Berkeley, 1948; Special student at National Conservatory of Paris; Studied with Darius Milhaud, 1949-50. Career includes: Professor of Music and Director of Electronic Studio at University of California, Davis, 1963-. Compositions include: Sonata for Clarinet and Cello, 1954; 2 String Quartets, 1953 and 1965; Suite for 4 Clarinets, 1962; Three Songs for Chorus and Piano, 1968; Clarinet Concerto, 1973; Serenade for Clarinet and Violin, 1977; Calisto And Melibea, chamber opera, 1978; Campus Doorways for Chorus and Orchestra, 1978; Music for 2 Clarinets, 1980; Fantasy for Violin, 1983; Concertpiece for Clarinet and Piano, 1984. Contributions to: Various musical journals and articles in Grove's Dictionary of Music and Musicians. Honours: George Ladd Prix de Paris, 1949-51; Fromm Foundation, 1952; Guggenheim Fellowship, 1958. Memberships: American Composers' Alliance; Musicological Society. Address: Department of Music, University of California, Davis, CA 95616, USA.

ROSEN Nathaniel (Kent), b. 9 June 1948, Altadena, California, USA. Cellist. m. Margo Shohl. Education: Studied with Eleonore Schoenfeld in Pasadena and with Piatigorsky at the University of Southern California, Los Angeles. Career: Assistant to Piatigorsky, 1966-76; Solo debut with the Los Angeles Philharmonic, 1969; New York debut, 1970, Carnegie Hall; Principal Cellist, Los Angeles Chamber Orchestra, 1972-76; Pittsburgh Symphony Orchestra, 1977-79; Professor, University of Illinois at Champaign-Urbana, 1988-94; Professor, Manhattan School of Music, 1981-88, 1994-; Appearances with leading American and European Orchestras and as Recitalist and in Chamber Music. Recordings: include, Complete music for Cello and Piano by Chopin; Shostakovich Cello Concerto No 1; Brahms Sonatas; Bach Suites. Contributions to: The Strad, April 1995; American String Teacher. Honours: First Prize, Naumburg Competitions, 1977; First Prize, Tchaikovsky Competitions, Moscow, 1978. Memberships: include, New York Violoncello Society; Century Association, New York. Current Management: Gingrich Management. Address: 36 Clinton Avenue, South Nyack, New York, NY 10960, USA.

ROSEN Robert (Joseph), b. 20 May 1956, Melfort, Saskatchewan, Canada. Composer; Performer. m. Deborah Alpaugh, 18 Aug 1979, 2 sons, 1 daughter. Education: BMus, Distinction, University of Alberta, 1977; Advanced Music Studies Programme of Banff Centre, 1979-81; Darmstadt Summer Course, 1982; Studied composition with Violet Archer and Bruce Mather; Worked for short periods with John Cage, R Murray Schafer, Witold Lutoslawski, Iannis Xenakis and Morton Feldman; National Choreographic Workshop, Vancouver, 1985. Career: Broadcasts as performer on CBC National Radio; Compositions performed in Canada, Sweden, Germany, Netherlands, France, Spain, USA, Italy and Australia by such notable performers as Robert Aitken, Jean-Pierre Drouet and Alan Hacker; Founding Member of performing ensemble, Fusion 5; Created film scores for documentaries produced by Helios Pictures for the National Film Board of Canada; Assistant Director of Music Programs at

the Banff centre for The Arts from 1991; Musical Director of Kokoro Dance. Compositions: From Silence for Piano and Orchestra; String Quartet, 1979; Krikos, I, 1980, II, 1982; Enigmas From The Muse; Meditation No 1 for Flute, Violin and Cello, No 2 for Small Orchestra, No 4 for 2 Pianos, No 5, Mosaic for Flute and Piano, No 6 for Piano, No 7, Coro for 24 Voices; In Anticipation Of Beautiful Shadows for 7 Cellos; Mi Istakistsi for Flute, Percussion and String Quartet; Zero To The Power for Violin, Cello, Taiko Percussion and Electronics; Stones for 2 Sopranos, Tuba and Percussion; Canyon Shadows: Stones; Animals for 2 Sopranos, Alpenhorn and Tuba, 1993. Publications: Canadian Composers at Banff, Celebration, Canadian Music Centre. Address: PO Box 1726, Canmore, Alberta, Canada, T0L 0M0.

ROSENBAUM Victor, b. 19 Dec 1941, Philadelphia, Pennsylvania, USA. Musician (Pianist); Conductor; Administrator. 2 daughters. Education: BA (Hons), Brandeis University, 1964; MFA, Princeton University, 1967; Aspen Music School, 1957-60; Piano with Leonard Shure and Rosina Lhevinne; Composition with Roger Sessions, Earl Kim and Edward T Cone; Chamber Music with Robert Koff and Eugene Lehner. Career: Solo performances in USA, Japan, Brazil, Israel and the Soviet Union; Chamber performances with artists Leonard Rose, Laurence Lesser, Roman Totenberg, Arnold Steinhardt; Cleveland, Vermeer, New World Quartets; Tully Hall; Town Hall, New York; Jordan Hall, Boston; Conductor, Concerto Company chamber orchestra; Former Faculty Member: Eastman School of Music, Brandeis University; Faculty Member, New England Conservatory; Director, Longy School of Music, Cambridge, Massachusetts. Compositions: For voice, piano, chorus, chamber ensemble and theatre pieces. Recordings: John Harbison Trio. Contributions to: College Music Society Symposium. Honours: Young Composers' Award; Indiana Young Artists' Award. Memberships: College Music Society; Music Teachers' National Association. Address: c/o Longy School of Music, 1 Follen Street, Cambridge, MA 02138, USA.

ROSENBOOM David, b. 9 September 1947, Fairfield, Iowa, USA. Composer; Electronic Instrument Technician. Education: Studied with Gordon Binkerd, Salvatore Martirano & Kenneth Gaburro, University of Illinois, Urbana. Career: includes: Co-Founder, President, Neurona Co, New York, 1969-71; Teacher, York University, Toronto, 1972-79, Mills College, Oakland, 1979-; Head, Music Department, 1984, Darius Milhaud Chair in Music, 1988, Dean of Music, California Institute of the Arts, 1990. Compositions include: The Brandy of the Damned, music theatre, 1967; How Much Better if Plymouth Rock Had Landed on the Pilgrims, 1972; On Being Invisible, 1976; In the Beginning I-IV, for Various Instrumental Combinations, 1978-80; Future Travel for Piano, Violin & Computer Music System, 1982; Champ Vital, 1987; systems of Judgement, Tape Collage, 1987; Predictions, Confirmations & Disconfirmations, 1991; Extended Trio, 1992; It Is About To...Sound, Interactive Computer Music Installation, 1993; On Being Invisible II: Hypatia Speaks to Jefferson in a Dream, Multimedia Piece, 1995; Brave New World: Music for the Play, 1995. Publications include: Biofeedback and the Arts: Results of Early Experiments, 1975; Extended Musical Interface with the Human Nervous System: Assessment and Prospectus (study of Leonardo), 1990. Address: c/o ASCAP, ASCAP Building, One Lincoln Plaza, NY 10023, USA.

ROSENFELD Gerhard, b. 10 Feb 1931, Königsberg, Germany. Composer. Education: Studied Musicology at the Humboldt University, East Berlin and composition with Rudolf Wagner Regeny and Hanns Eisler. Career: Worked in Berlin, 1961-64, then moved to Potsdam as freelance composer. Compositions inclue: Operas: Das Autaegliche Wunder, Stralsund, 1973, Der Mantel, after Gogol, Weimar, 1978, Das Spiel von Liebe und Zufall, Potsdam, 1980, Die Verweigerung, after Gogol, Osnabruck, 1989. Address: Begasstrasse 1A, 14558 Bergholz-Rehbrück, Germany.

ROSENKRANZ Helge, b. 1962, Austria. Violinist. Career: Member of Franz Schubert Quartet, Vienna, 1989-; Many concert engagements in Europe, USA, and Australia including Amsterdam Concertgebouw, Vienna Musikverein and Kozerthaus, Salle Gaveau, Paris and Sydney Opera House; Visits to Zurich, Geneva, Basle, Hamburg, Rome, Rotterdam, Madrid and Copenhagen; Festival engagements include Salzburg, Wiener Festwochen, Prague Spring, Schubertiade at Hohenems, Schubert Festival in Washington DC, Belfast and Istanbul; Tours of Australasia, Russia and USA; Frequent concert tours to UK; Featured in Concerto by Spohr with Royal Liverpool Philharmonic, Liverpool and Festival Hall, London; Many appearances at Wigmore Hall and at Cheltenham Festival; Masterclasses at Royal Northern College of Music and Lake District Summer Music. Recordings include: Schubert's Quartet in G, 877; Complete Quartets by Dittersdorf. Address: c/o Christopher Tennant Artists Management, 11 Lawrence Street, London, SW3 5NB, England.

ROSENSHEIN Neil, b. 27 Nov 1947, New York, USA. Tenor. Education: Studied in New York. Debut: Florida Opera in

1972 as Almaviva in Il Barbiere di Siviglia. Career: Sang in Washington, Dallas, Boston and Santa Fe; European debut at Vaison-la-Romaine in 1980 as Almaviva; Further appearances in Geneva, Zurich and Paris; Covent Garden debut in 1986 as Lensky in Eugene Onegin; Chicago Lyric Opera in 1988 as Alfredo in La Traviata; Sang in the premiere of The Aspern Papers by Dominick Argento, Dallas, 1988; Berlioz Festival at Lyons in 1989 as Benvenuto Cellini; Other roles include Mozart's Tamino and Belmonte, Verdi's Fenton and Don Carlos, Massenet's Des Grieux and Werther at Turin, Sydney and Metropolitan in 1989, and Steva in Jenufa; Season 1992-93 at the Metropolitan as Faust, Werther, Alfredo in Traviata and Léon in the premiere of Corigliano's The Ghosts of Versailles; Sang the Berlioz Faust at Turin in 1992 and Peter Grimes at Sydney; Sang Cavaradossi at Santa Fe, 1994. Recording: Eugene Onegin. Address: c/o Metropolitan Opera, Lincoln Center, New York, NY 10023, USA.

ROSENTHAL Manuel, b. 18 Jun 1904, Paris, France. Conductor; Composer. m. Claudine Verneuie, 2 sons. Education: Studied with Ravel at the Paris Conservatoire, 1918-23. Career: Conducted French Radio Orchestra, 1934-47; Musical Director and Conductor for Orchestre National de Paris, 1945-48; Conducted Seattle Symphony Orchestra, 1949-51 and Royal Orchestra of Liège, Belgium, 1964-67; Composer-in-Residence, College of Puget Sound, WA, 1948-49; Guest Conductor with various orchestras in the USA; Conducted Oedipus Rex and Carmina Burana at New York City Opera in 1977; French repertory including Dialogues des Carmélites and Manon at the Metropolitan from 1981; Conducted The Ring at Seattle in 1986; Has conducted the French premieres of works by Bartók, Stravinsky, Strauss, Prokofiev and Britten. Compositions: Sonata for 2 Violins and Piano; La Fête Du Vin for Orchestra; Musique De Table for Orchestra; Magin Manhattan; Desese Deo Gratias; La Poule Noire; Les Femmes Au Tombeau. Recordings include: Violin Concertos by Saint-Saëns and Vieuxtemps, Lalo Symphonie Espagnole; Chopin 1st Concerto, Cziffra; Debussy La Demoiselle Elue. Honours: Knight, Legion of Honour; Officer of Arts and Letters. Address: c/o Seattle Opera Association, PO Box 9248, Seattle, WA 09109, USA.

ROSKELL Penelope, b. 1960, Oxford, England. Pianist. m. Richard Griffiths, 26 Oct 1985. Education: GMus (RNCM) Honours, PPRNCM, Royal Northern College of Music; Private study with Guido Agosti in Rome. Career: Solo pianist with tours worldwide at invitation of the British Council; Concerts regularly in Europe, Scandinavia, USA, Africa, Asia, Middle and Far East; Broadcasts on BBC Radio 3, WFMT Radio Chicago and British and Polish TV; Professor of Piano at London College of Music; Recitals at Wigmore Hall and Purcell Room; Concerto engagements include recording with Oxford Pro Musica; Tours with Manchester Camerata and the Bournemouth Sinfonietta under Simon Rattle. Honour: Winner of British Contemporary Piano Competition. Current Management: Helen Sykes Artists' Management. Address: c/o Helen Sykes Artists' Management, 79 Bickenhall Mansions, Bickenhall Street, London, W1, England.

ROSS Christopher, b. 1965, England. Pianist (accompanist and concert soloist). Career: Has worked as accompanist for such musicians as soprano Jennifer Smith, cellist Raphael Wallfisch, violinist Dona Lee Croft (tour of the USA), mezzo Teresa Shaw and José Carreras (2 albums); Many performances in France, Germany, Switzerland, Portugal and London's South Bank; Solo concerto repertory includes works by Brahms, Schumann, Hindemith, Ravel and Shostakovich. Honours include: Accompanist's Prize in the Richard Tauber Competition. Address: Helen Sykes Management, Fourth Floor, Parkway House, Sheen Lane, East Sheen, London, SW14 8LS, England.

ROSS Elinor, b. 1 Aug 1932, Tampa, FL, USA. Soprano. Education: Studied with Zinka Milanov in New York. Debut: Cincinnati Opera in 1958 as Leonora in Il Trovatore. Career: Guest appearances in Boston, Chicago, Baltimore and Philadelphia; Sang at Carnegie Hall in the 1968 US premiere of Verdi's Alzira; Metropolitan Opera from 1970 with debut as Turandot; European engagements at La Scala, Bologna, Palermo, Vienna, Budapest, Zagreb, Verona and Florence; Other roles include Bellini's Norma, Verdi's Aida, Elisabetta, Amelia, Lady Macbeth and Abigaille, Mozart's Donna Anna, Puccini's Tosca and Giordano's Maddalena; Sang Tosca at the Metropolitan in 1973, and the Trovatore, Leonora at Buenos Aires in 1974; Frequent concert appearances. Address: c/o Metropolitan Opera, Lincoln Center, New York, NY 10023, USA.

ROSS Elise, b. 28 Apr 1947, NY, USA. Soprano. m. Simon Rattle (divorced). Career: Sang with the Juilliard Ensemble, NY and the Los Angeles Philharmonic Orchestra from 1970; Performances of music by Berio in USA and Europe (Passagio in Rome); Tour of Europe with the London Sinfonietta and appearances at Royan and Bath Festivals and in Venice and Warsaw; Sang in Bussotti's Passion Selon Sade and Le Racine at La Scala in 1991; Concerts with the Ensemble Intercontemporain, Paris from 1976; Repertoire includes Berlin Cabaret songs, lieder by composers of the Second Viennese School, Chansons by Ravel and Debussy and lieder by Mozart, Schumann and Strauss; Shostakovich Symphony 14 with the Los Angeles Philharmonic and Ensemble Intercontemporain; Has sung Cherubino for Opera North and for Long Beach Opera; Sang Marie in Wozzeck at Los Angeles in 1989 and Mélisande with Netherlands Opera and Berlioz's Romeo and Juliette, Rotterdam, 1993. Address: c/o Harold Holt, 31 Sinclair Road, London, W14 0NS, England.

ROSS Walter, b. 3 October 1936, Lincoln, Nebraska, USA. Composer. Education: MMus, University of Nebraska, 1962; DMA, Cornell University, 1966, with Robert Palmer. Career: Music Faculty, University of Virginia, 1967-. Compositions: Concerto for Brass Quintet and Orchestra, 1966; Five Dream Sequences for Percussion Quartet and Piano, 1968; 2 Trombone Concertos, 1970, 1982; Canzona I and II for Brass Instruments, 1969, 1979; In the Penal Colony, Opera, 1972; 3 Wind Quintets, 1974, 1985, 1989; A Jefferson Symphony, for Tenor, Chorus and Orchestra, 1976; Concerto for Wind Quintet and Strings, 1977; String Trio, 1978; Nocturne for Strings, 1980; Violin Sonata, 1981; Concerto for Bassoon & Strings, 1983; Suite No 1 for Chamber Ensemble, 1983; Concerto for Oboe, Harp and Strings, 1984; 3 Brass Trios, 1985, 1986, 1986; Concerto for Flute, Guitar and Orchestra, 1987; Sinfonia Concertante for Strings, 1987; Oil of Dog, for Brass Quintet and Actor, 1988; Concerto for Euphonium, Brass and Timpani, 1988; Scherzo Festivo, for Orchestra, 1992; Summer Dances for Oboe and Marimba, 1992; Clarinet Concerto, 1994; Harlequinade for 5 Wind Instruments and Piano, 1994; Vocal Music, including Songs and Choruses. Address: c/o ASCAP, ASCAP Building, One Lincoln Plaza, New York, NY 10023, USA.

ROSSBERG Dieter, b. 1948, Hamburg, Germany. Conductor. Education: Studied at the Hamburg Academy, with Horst Stein, Gyorgy Ligeti and August Everding. Career: Principal Conductor at the Detmold Opera, 1975, Innsbruck Opera, 1983; Deputy Music Director of Kiel Opera from 1989, leading Figaro, Elektra, Rigoletto, Haydn's Orfeo, Faust, Manon Lescaut, Così fan tutte and Don Giovanni; Guest engagements at opera houses throughout Germany and in France, Japan, Russia, Italy and Austria; Led a ballet version of Mahler's Knaben Wunderhorn at Copenhagen (1994) and an arena production of Carmen at Rotterdam. Address: c/o Atholl Still Ltd, Foresters Hall, 25-27 Westow Street, London SE19 3RY, England.

RÖSSEL-MAJDAN Hildegard, b. 30 Jan 1921, Moosbierbaum, Austria. Contralto. m. Dr Karl Rossel-Majdan, 1 daughter. Education: HS for Music and Dramatic Art, Vienna. Career: Concert and oratorio singer under leading Austrian and foreign conductors, 1948-; Member of Vienna State Opera, 1951-71; Professor, University for Music and Dramatic Art, Vienna, 1971-91; Concerts, opera and oratorio in Europe, USA and Japan; Lecturer in Austrian seminaries and in Japan; President of Goetheanistic Konservatory and Waldorfpedagogical Akademy. Recordings: Various. Address: Agnesgasse 13, Vienna, Austria.

ROSSELLI John, b. 8 Jun 1927, Florence, Italy. Writer on Music. Education: Studied at Swarthmore College, PA; Research Student at Peterhouse, Cambridge. Career: Leader Writer and Deputy London Editor for The Manchester Guardian; Teacher and Reader in History at Sussex University, 1964-89. Publications include: The Opera Industry in Italy from Cimarosa to Verdi, 1984; Music and Musicians in Nineteenth Century Italy, 1991; Singers of Italian Opera; The History of a Profession, 1992. Address: c/o Cambridge University Press, Edinburgh Building, Shaftesbury Road, Cambridge, CB2 2RU, England.

ROSSI Nick, b. 14 Nov 1924, San Luis Obispo, California, USA. Opera Administrator; Author. Education: BMus, 1948, MMus, 1952, University of Southern California; PhD, Sussex College of Technology, 1971. Career: Supervisor of Music, Los Angeles City Schools, 1948-68; Senior Professor of Music, City University of New York, 1973-83; Administrative Director, 1983-91, Administrative Coordinator, 1992-, Studio Lirico, Italy; Administrative Director, Fiesta Musicale Stiana, Italy, 1985-88; Producer: 4 Saints in 3 Acts (Thomson), US West Coast premiere, 1962; Liberty? (Roy Harris), 1963; Virgil Thomson Festival, 1971; Castelnuovo-Tedesco Festival, 1974; Carmen Moore Festival, 1976; Women in Music Festival, 1978; Song of Songs (Castelnuovo-Tedesco), World premiere, 1973; L'Importanza di esser Franco (Castelnuovo-Tedesco), European premiere, 1984; Imeneo (Handel), New York premiere, 1984; Muzio Scevolo (Handel), 1985; Il principe Barba-blu (Hofmeyer), 1986; Amor soldato (Sacchini), 1987; L'impresario in angustie (Cimarosa), 1993; Il convito (Cimarosa), 1994. Recordings: As producer and author of programme notes, various labels, UK, Netherlands, USA. Publications: Music Through the Centuries, 1963; Music of Our Time, 1969; Pathways to Music, 1970; Musical Pilgrimage, 1971; Electronic Music, 1971; 20th-Century Music and Art, 1972; Hearing Music, 1981; J S Bach: Biography in Pictures, 1985; Opera in Italy, 1995; Landmarks of Twentieth-Century Music, 1995. Contributions to: Opera on Record, bi-monthly classical disc digest; Regularly to CD Classica, Italy; Italian opera critic for Opera Canada. Address: Villa Paradiso, 3404 Kennan Drive, Columbia, SC 29203, USA.

RÖSSLER Almut, b. 12 Jun 1932, Beveringen, Germany. Organist; Choral Director. Education: Studied organ with Michael Schneider at Detmold and Gaston Litaize in Paris; Piano with Hans Richter-Haaser and choral direction with Kurt Thomas. Career: Performances of music by such contemporary composers as André Jolivet, Giselher Klebe (Organ Concerto, 1980) and Olivier Messiaen; Premieres of Le Mystère de la Sainte Trinité in 1972 and Le Livre du Saint Scarement in 1986; Kantor at the Johanneskirche Dusseldorf and Professor of Organ at the Robert Schumann Conservatory; Founder and Director of the Johannes-Kantorei, giving a capella work and performing in oratorios; Director of Messiaen Festivals at Dusseldorf, 1968, 1972, 1979 and 1986; Masterclasses in Japan and at Yale University. Honours include: Organist of The Year, Yale University, 1986. Address: Staatliche Hochscule für Musik Rheinland, Robert Schumann Institut, Fischerstrasse 110, D-4000 Dusseldorf, Germany.

ROSSMANITH Gabriele, b. 1960, Stuttgart, Germany. Singer (Soprano). Education: Started Violin studies at the Staatliche Hochschule für Musik, Trossingen, finishing with an artistic examination in Violin, Music Teacher; Studies in Singing with Professor Sylvia Geszty at the Hochschule für Darstellende Kunst Stuttgart, final examination in 1985; Voice studies with Ingrid Bjoner and Judith Beckmann. Career: Sang at the Badisches Stadttheater Karlsruhe, 1985-88; Hamburg Staatsoper from 1988, notably as Susanna (Le nozze di Figaro), Sophie (Rosenkavalier), Marzelline (Fidelio), Gretel (Hänsel and Gretel), Musetta (La Bohème), Despina (Così fan tutte), Pamina (Zauberflöte), Baronin (Wildschütz) and Lauretta (Gianni Schicchi); Various performances at important opera houses in Munich, Frankfurt and Barcelona; Guest contracts with Dresdner Staatsoper (Semperoper), Opernhaus Leipzig, Théâtre Royal de la Monnaie, Brussels (Oscar, Ballo in Maschera), Komische Oper Berlin (Gilda, Rigoletto; Suer Angelilea; Schwaneuprinzassin; Zarseltan; Museka) and De Vlaamse Opera, Antwerp; Various tours including Central and South America, 1991, Japan, 1992, 1996. Recordings: Orchesterlieder of Wolf, Strauss, Schoenberg, Weill, with Radio Philharmonie Hannover des NDR and Cord Garben; TV Portrait, NDR, 1993; SDR TV recording of Das Italienische Liederbuch, with Bernd Weikel and Cord Garben, 1993; SDR film Wunderhorn, with Bernd Weikl, Helmuth Deutsch on piano, 1995; MDRTV Susanna, Nozze di Figaro, 1995; NDRTV Recording, Lauretta, Gianni Schicci, 1995. Honours include: Scholarship for study in Japan; 1st Prize, Mozartfest-Wettbewerb, Würzburg. Current Management: Artists Management Hartmut Haase, Aalgrund 8, D-31275 Lehrte, Germany. Address: c/o Staatsoper Hamburg, Grosse Theaterstrasse 34, 20354 Hamburg, Germany.

ROST Andrea, b. 1965, Hungary. Singer (Soprano). Education: Studied in Budapest until 1989. Debut: Budapest National Opera, 1989, as Gounod's Juliette. Career: Made further appearances in Hungary and sang Verdi's Nannetta at Enschede (1991), Susanna at St Gallen and Zerlina at Cologne; Vienna Staatsoper from 1991, notably as Rosina; Sang the Voice of the Falcon in Die Frau ohne Schatten at the 1992 Salzburg Festival; Covent Garden debut, 1995, in Le nozze di Figaro; Sang Mozart's Pamina at La Scala, 1996; Sang Donizetti's Linda di Chamounix at the Festival Hall, 1997. Address: c/o Staatsoper Vienna, Opernring 2, A-1010 Vienna, Austria.

ROSTROPOVICH Mstislav, b. 27 Mar 1927, Baku, Russia. Cellist; Pianist; Conductor. m. Galina Vishnevskaya, 15 May 1955, 2 daughters. Education: Moscow Conservatory. Debut: Russia in 1941, international in 1948. Career includes: Conducting debut in 1961; Professor at Moscow and Leningrad Conservatories; Music Director for National Symphony Orchestra, Washington DC, 1977; Opera engagements include The Queen of Spades at San Francisco in 1975 and Eugene Onegin at Aldeburgh in 1979, Tsar's Bride at Washington DC in 1986 and The Duenna at the Royal Academy of Music in London, 1991; Life with an Idiot, Schnittke, Netherland, 1993; Lolita, Royal Opera, Sweden, 1994; Prokofiev and Shostakovich wrote concertos for him and Britten the 3 Cello Suites and Cello Symphony; Premiered the Shostakovich Cello Sonata, concertos by Bliss, Lutoslawski, Christobal Halffter in 1986 and Panufnik in 1992; As Conductor has premiered works by Bernstein, Landowski, Mennin's 9th Symphony, Walton's Prologue and Fantasia and Penderecki's Polish Requiem; Season 1992 with the premieres of Gubaidulina's opera-oratorio-ballet, Orazione per l'era di Acquario at Genoa and Schnittke's Life With an Idiot at Amsterdam; Conducted The Golden Cockerel at the Barbican Hall in London, 1992 and the premiere of Schnittke's Gesualdo at the Vienna Staatsoper, 1995; 70th Birthday Concerts at the Barbican, and elsewhere, 1997. Recordings include: CDs of Beethovens Triple Concerto and Dvořák's Cello Concerto; Britten's Cello Symphony; Mozart Flute Quartets; Boris Godunov. Honours include: Over 30 honorary degrees; Stalin Prize; Lenin Prize; People's Artist; Commander Legion of Honour, France; Medal of Freedom from 10 countries; Fellow, Royal College of Music; KBE, 1987. Memberships include: Academy of St Cecilia, Rome; Royal Academy of Music, England. Current Management: Ronald A Wilford, Columbia Artists Management Inc. Address: 165 West 57 Street, New York, NY 10019, USA.

ROTENBERG Sheldon, b. 11 Apr 1917, Attleboro, Massachusetts, USA. Concert Violinist. m. 29 Jan 1950, 1 son, 1 daughter. Education: AB, Tufts University, 1939; Graduate School, 1940; Student of Felix Winternitz, Boston, Georges Enesco, Maurice Hewitt, Paris; Faculty, Boston University Tanglewood Institute. Debut: Boston Pops, 1939, 1941. Career: Member of Boston String Quartet, New England Conservatory; Concerts throughout New England and at Library of Congress, Washington, 1948-57; First Violin Section, Boston Symphony Orchestra, 1948-1991; Archival Consultant of the Boston Symphony. Recordings: With Library of Congress, Boston String Quartet, Mozart D Minor Quartet, Barber, op 11 Quartet, Debussy String Quartet. Honours: Cultural Exchange Representative, Boston Symphony in State Department Programme with Japan Philharmonic, Tokyo, 1969, as teacher, soloist and member of the orchestra; Occupied Kasdon-Paley Endowed Chair, Boston Symphony, 1st Violin Section. Membership: Harvard Music Association. Hobbies: Reading; Tennis. Address: 60 Browne Street, Brookline, MA 02146, USA.

ROTH Daniel, b. 31 Oct 1942, Mulhouse, France. Organist. Education: Studied at the Paris Conservatoire, 1960-70 with Maurice Durufle and Rolande Falcinelli; Further study with Marie Claire Alain. Career: Organist at Sacre-Coeur, Paris, 1963-85; Professor of Organ at Marseille Conservatoire, 1973-79, later at Strasbourg Conservatoire; Visiting Professor at the Summer Academy at Haarlem, Holland; Professor at Catholic University and Resident Artist at the National Shrine, Washington DC, 1974-76; Organist at Saint-Sulpice, Paris, since 1985; Professor at the Saarbrücken Musikhochschule, 1988; Professor of Organ, Musikhochschule, Frankfurt-am-Main. Compositions: Final Te Deum; Hommage à César Franck; Joie, Douleur et Gloire de Marie. Recordings include: C Franck: Les 12 Pièces et Pièces choisies pour orgue; C M Widor: Symphonies V and X, Symphonies III and VII, Marcel Dupré - Pièces choisies; A Guilmant, Sonatas 5 and 6 and Pièces choisies; Motett Newe-Ursina, Düsseldorf; New compositions by Leduc including: Pour la Nuit de Noël, Prelude, communion and postlude and Evocation de la Pentecôte. Honours include: Premier Prix in Harmony, Improvisation, Counterpoint, Fugue, Organ and Accompaniment at the Paris Conservatoire; SACEM Prize, Nice, 1964; Interpretation Prize at Arnhem, 1964; Improvisation and Interpretation Prize, Amis de l'Orgue, Paris, 1966; First Prize at International Competition, Chartres, 1971; Chevalier de l'ordre des Arts et des Lettres, 1986. Address: Église Saint Sulpice, F-75006 Paris, France.

ROTH David (Robert), b. 9 Mar 1936, Stockton-on-Tees, County Durham, England. Violinist. m. Ruth Elaine West, 22 July 1963, 2 sons. Education: University of Edinburgh, 1953-54; Royal Academy of Music, 1954-59; LRAM. Debut: West Linton, Peebles, Scotland, 1954. Career: With Netherlands Chamber Orchestra, Amsterdam, 1960-64; Played Bloch Sonata No 1, KOT Israel Radio, Tel Aviv, 1962; Deputy Leader, Northern Sinfinia Orchestra, Newcastle upon Tyne, 1966-68; 2nd Violin, Allegri String Quartet, 1969-. Recordings: With Allegri String Quartet for Open University; Many recordings for various labels. Honours: MMus, Hull, 1975; ARAM; DMus, Nottingham, 1994; DMus, Southampton. Memberships: Incorporated Society of Musicians; Musicians Union. Hobbies: Ancient History; Genealogy; Theatre; Reading. Address: 16 Oman Avenue, London NW2 6BG, England.

ROTHENBERGER Anneliese, b. 19 June 1924, Mannheim, Germany. Soprano. m. Gerd Dieberich, 1954. Education: Mannheim Musikhochschule with Erika Muller. Debut: Koblenz in 1943. Career: Hamburg Staatsoper, 1946-73 notably as Blonde in Die Entführung, Verdi's Oscar and Lulu; Visited Edinburgh with the company in 1952 for the British premiere of Hindemith's Mathis der Maler; Vienna Staatsoper from 1953, Salzburg from 1954 in the premiere of Liebermann's Penelope and Die Schule der Frauen; Also sang Papagena in Die Zauberflöte, Zdenka in Arabella, Sophie in Der Rosenkavalier and Flaminia in Haydn's Il Mondo della Luna; Glyndebourne, 1959-60 as Sophie; Metropolitan Opera debut in 1960 returning as Susanna, Oscar and Sophie; Zurich in 1967 in the premiere of Sutermeister's Madame Bovary; Tour of Russia in 1970. Recordings: Le nozze di Figaro; Die Fledermaus; Martha; Der Wildschütz; Die Entführung; Arabella; Gluck's Le Cadi Dupé; Sophie in 1960 film version of Der Rosenkavalier. Publication: Melodie Meines Lebens, autobiography, 1972. Address: c/o Hamburgische Staatsoper, Grosse-Theaterstrasse 34, D-2000 Hamburg 36, Germany.

ROTHSCHILD Charlotte de, b. 1958. Soprano. Education: Studied at the Salzburg Mozarteum and the Royal College of Music in London. Career: Concert repertoire ranges from Purcell to Rutter, including Mozart's Requiem in Paris and appearances with the Bach Choir; Many performances of thematically linked programmes including Family Connections, Flower Songs, Women of the Old Testament and Flowers, Dreams and Romance; Partnerships with harpist, David Watkins, and organist, David Titterington; Engagements in Japan, France, throughout Europe and Australasia. Recordings include: Family Connections; Flowers, Dreams And Romance. Address: Helen Sykes Management, Fourth Floor, Parkway House, Sheen Lane, East Sheen, London, SW14 8LS, England.

ROTZSCH Hans-Joachim, b. 25 Apr 1929, Leipzig, Germany. Tenor. Educator. Education: Institute for Church Music at the Musikhochschule Leipzig, 1949-53; Organ study with Gunter Ramin; Vocal studies with P Losse and P Polster in Leipzig. Career: Many concerts and recordings of sacred music in East and West Germany, Switzerland, Austria, Poland, Russia and Czechoslovakia; Appearances at the Leipzig Opera from 1961 and Kantor at St Thomas's School, Leipzig, from 1972; President of the Bach Committee, East Germany, 1983. Recordings: Bach Cantatas; St Luke Passion by Schütz; Dessau's Das Verhör des Lukullus; Mendelssohn's Elijah.

ROUILLON Philippe, b. 1955, Paris, France. Singer (Baritone). Education: Studied at the Conservatoire National Supérieur de Paris; Ecole d'Art Lyrique de l'Opéra de Paris. Career: Performed Golaud in Pelléas et Mélisande and High Priest of Dagon in Samson et Dalila, Vienna; Chorèbe in les Troyens, Ruprecht in L'Ange de Feu, Orest in Elektra, Renato in Un Ballo in Maschera, the High Priest of Dagon, The High Priest in Alceste and Thoas in Iphigenie en Tauride in Paris; Ruprecht, High Priest of Dagon, Gellner in La Wally and Escamillo in Carmen in Amsterdam; Jochanaan in Salome, Lisbon and Strasbourg; Guillaume Tell in Liége; Samson et Dalila and Les Contes d'Hoffmann in Zurich; Frequent appearances in Germany in a variety of leading baritone roles; Close collaborations with Festival of Bregenz, Austria; Forthcoming engagements include: Renato in Un Ballo in Maschera, Samson et Dalila in Tel Aviv, Amfortas in Parsifal, Berlin, Rigoletto in a new production with Götz Friedrich, Tonio in I Pagliacci and Alfio in Cavalleria Rusticana. Recordings include: Thaïs by Massenet; Saint François d'Assise by Messiaen with Kent Nagano; Chant de Paix by Landowski; Henry VIII by Saint-Saëns; Le Déluge by Saint-Saëns; Lélio and La Damnation de Faust by Berlioz. Honours: First Place, Prix Opéra and Prix de Public, international competition in Verviers, 1979; First Prize, Rio de Janeiro Competition, 1983. Address: 147 rue La Bruyere, F-95120 Ermont, France.

ROULEAU Joseph, b. 28 Feb 1929, Matane, Quebec, Canada. Bass Singer. Education: Montreal Conservatory with Martial Singher, Ruzena Herlinger, Albert Cornellier; Milan with Mario Basiola and Rachaele Mori. Debut: Montreal Opera Guild in 1951 in Un Ballo in Maschera. Career: Montreal in 1955 as King Philip in Don Carlos, New Orleans, 1955-56; Royal Opera House Covent Garden from 1957-92 in 624 performances of 45 operas, with debut as Colline; Sang also in the 1957 production of Les Troyens and in Turandot, Aida, Rigoletto, Simon Boccanegra, Don Giovanni and Billy Budd; Paris Opera in 1960 as Raimondo in Lucia di Lammermoor returning from 1974-79 as Titurel in Parsifal, Don Quichotte, Abimelech in Samson et Dalilah, Crespel, Contes d'Hoffman, from 1966-71 three tours of USSR singing in 12 capitals including Moscow, Leningrad; Guest appearnaces in Germany, Holland, Italy, Romania, Hungary, France, Scotland, Ireland, Argentina, Chile, Brazil, South Africa, Australia; In Toronto in 1967 premiere of Harry Summer's Louis Riel sang; Festival appearances at Edinburgh, Aldeburgh, Wexford, Paris, London and New York, Empire State Festival; Other roles include Arkel in Pelléas et Mélisande, Sarastro, Boris Godunov, Osmin in Die Entführung, Daland in Der fliegende Holländer and Oroveso in Norma, Philippe II, Don Carlo, Dosifei in Khovanshchina, Mephisto; Sang Don Marco in Menotti's The Saint of Bleecker Street at Philadelphia in 1989, Trulove in The Rake's Progress for Vancouver Opera, 1989, The Prince in Adriana Lecouvreur for L'Opéra de Montreal in 1990 and Mozart's Bartolo with Vancouver Opera, 1992; Professor, UQAM, 1980. Recordings include: Semiramide; Roméo et Juliette by Gounoud; L'Enfance du Christ; Lucia di Lammermoor; Don Carlos; Massenet's Marie-Magdalene and French Operatic arias; Metropolitan Opera, New York, 1984-88; San Francisco Opera, 1984-89. Honours include: Order of Canada, 1977; Prix du Quebec, 1990; Prix Archambault, 1967; Pantheon de l'art lyrique du Canada, 1992. Address: 32 Lakeshsore Road, Beaconsfield, Quebec H9W 4H3, Canada.

ROURKE Sean Timothy, b. 16 Sept 1960, Bradford, West Yorkshire, England. Music Marketing and Consulting. m. Julie Soraya, 8 Apr 1994, 1 daughter. Education: BA, honours, Keele University, 1979-82; MPhil, Royal Holloway College, University of London, 1996. Career: Music Promotion, Josef Weinberger Ltd, 1982-85, Novello and Co Ltd, 1985-90; Managing Director, STR Music Marketing, 1990-; Assistant Examiner, University of Cambridge; Marketing Director, Wardour Music Festival. Compositions: Bede's Death Song for unaccompanied choir; Berberis Darwinii for horn quartet, 1985; In Deed Pure Sky, Piano Solo; Nocturne, Organ. Contributions to: Musical Times; Music Teacher. Membership: PRS. Hobbies: Steam Railways; Cooking; Walking; Gardening. Address: 296 Hughenden Road, High Wycombe, Buckinghamshire HP13 5PE, England.

ROUSE Christopher (Chapman), b. 15 Feb 1949, Baltimore, Maryland, USA. Composer. m. Ann Jensen, 28 Aug 1983, 1 son, 2 daughters. Education: BMus, Oberlin Conservatory, 1971; Private study with George Crumb, 1971-73; MFA, DMA, Cornell University, 1977. Career: Assistant Professor, University of Michigan, 1978-81; Assistant Professor, 1981-85, Associate Professor, 1985-91, Professor, 1991-, Eastman School of Music; Composer-in-Residence, Indianapolis Symphony Orchestra, 1985-86; Composer-in-Residence, Baltimore Symphony Orchestra, 1986-88. Compositions: Ogoun Badagris, 1976; Ku-Ka-Ilimoku, 1978; Mitternachtslieder, 1979; Liber Daemonum, 1980; The Infernal Machine, 1981; String Quartet, 1982; Rotae Passionis, 1982; Lares Hercii, 1983; The Surma Ritornelli, 1983; Gorgon, 1984; Contrabass Concerto, 1985; Phantasmata, 1985; Phaethon, 1986; Symphony No 1, 1986; Jagannath, 1987; String Quartet No 2, 1988; Bonham, 1988; Iscariot, 1989; Concerto per corde, 1990; Karolju, 1990; Violin Concerto, 1991; Trombone Concerto, 1991; Violoncello Concerto, 1992; Flute Concerto, 1993; Symphony No 2, 1994; Envoi, 1995; Compline, 1996. Honours: Friedheim Award, Kennedy Center, 1988; Guggenheim Fellowship, 1990; Academy of of Arts and Letters Award, 1993; Pulitzer Prize, 1993.

ROUSSET Christophe, b. 12 April 1961, Avignon, France. Harpsichordist; Conductor. Education: Studies with Huguette Dreyfus, Kenneth Gilbert, Bob van Asperen and Gustav Leonhardt; Chamber Music with the Kuijken Brothers and Lucy van Dael. Career: Frequent solo appearances in France and throughout Europe with La Petite Bande, Musica Antiqua Köln, Academy of Ancient Music and Les Arts Florissants; Collaborations with such artists as William Christie, Agnes Mellon, Jean-Claude Malgoire, Wieland Kuijken and Christopher Hogwood; Conducts Les Arts Florissants, Il Seminario Musicale and other ensembles; Founded Les Talens Lyriques (title from Rameau's Les Fetes d'Hébé) 1991 giving many performances of Baroque Opera; Revival of Handel's Riccardo Primo at Fontevraud, France, 1995. Recordings include: Harpsichord Music by Bach, Rameau and Gaspard le Roux; Handel's Scipione and Riccardo Primo, Jommelli's Armida Abbandonata. Address: c/o Les Arts Florissants, 10 Rue de Florence, F-75008 Paris, France.

ROUTH Francis (John), b. 15 January 1927, Kidderminster, England. Composer; Pianist; Writer. m. (1) Virginia Anne Raphael, 1 September 1956, (2) Diana Florence Elizabeth Cardell Oliver, 1 November 1991, 2 sons, 2 daughters. Education: BA 1951, MA 1954, King's College, Cambridge; FRCO, LRAM, Royal Academy of Music; Private Study with Matyas Seiber. Career: Appeared as Pianist, occasionally Conducted in London and elsewhere, South Bank, Radio Broadcasts; Founder, Director, Redcliffe Concerts, 1963-64. Compositions: A Sacred Tetralogy, 1959-74; Dialogue for Violin and Orchestra, 1968; Double Concerto, 1970; Sonata for Solo Cello, 1971; Spring Night, 1971; Symphony, 1972; Cello Concerto, 1973; Mosaics, 1976; Oboe Quartet, 1977; Fantasy for Violin and Pf, 1978; Scenes for Orchestra, 1978; Vocalise, 1979; Concerto for Ensemble I, 1982, II 1983; Tragic Interludes for Oboe, 1984; Celebration for Piano, 1984; Elegy for Piano, 1986; Oboe Concerto, 1986; Poeme Fantastique for Piano and Orchestra, 1986-88; Four Marian Antiphons for Organ, 1988; Romance, 1989; Woefully Arranged, for Soloists, Choir and Orchestra, 1990; Fantasy Duo for Violin and Piano, 1990; Romanian Dance, 1990; Concerto for Ensemble III, 1991; Suite for String Orchestra, 1992; Clarinet Quintet, 1994; Capriccio, 1995. Recordings: A Sacred Tetralogy, Organ, Christopher Bowers-Broadbent, 1984; Celebration, Elegy, Piano, Jeffrey Jacob, 1986; Oboe Quartet, Tragic Interlude, Oboe Robin Canter with Redcliffe Ensemble, 1992; A Woman Young and Old, soprano Margaret Field, 1995; Clarinet Quintet, clarinet Nicholas Cox with Redcliffe Ensemble, 1995. Publications: The Organ, 1958; Contemporary Music, 1968; The Patronage and Presentation of Contemporary Music, 1970; Contemporary British Music, 1972; Early English Organ Music, 1973; Stravinsky, 1974. Contributions to: Various journals. Address: 68 Barrowgate Road, Chiswick, London W4 4QU, England.

ROUTLEY Nicholas, b. 26 June 1947, England. m. University Lecturer. Margo Adelson, m. 26 May 1982, 2 daughters. Education: George Heriot's and Son, Edinburgh; St John's College, Cambridge; Piano studies with Peter Feuchtwanger; Conducting with Hans Heimler, Franco Ferrara. Debut: Pianist, Wigmore Hall, 1979; Conductor, Taiwan Symphony Orchestra, 1984. Appointments: University of Cambridge, 1973-75; University of Sydney, 1975-; University of

Hong Kong, 1982-85, 1990-93. Compositions: Sicut Lilium, for choir and vibraphone, 1996; Sanctus, for choir and percussion, 1996; Like Snow, 5 songs for voice and piano, 1997; Icams For Orchestra, 1997. Recordings: The Hermit of Green Light (Australian vocal music), 1983; Monteverdi Vespers of 610, 1989; Josquin, 1994; Clare MacLean, The Complete Choral Music, 1995; Josquin, Secular Music, 1996. Publication: A Practical Guide to Musica Ficta, 1985. Contributions to: 2 articles on Debussy's Preludes in Musicology Australia, 1992, 1993. Membership: Musicological Society of Australia. Address: Department of Music, University of Sydney, NSW 2006, Australia.

ROUX Michel, b. 1 Sep 1924, Angouleme, France. Baritone. Education: Conservatoires of Bordeaux and Paris. Career: Sang in Paris from 1948 at the Opéra and Opéra-Comique; Sang in the 1950 premiere of Milhaud's Bolivar, at La Scala Milan in 1953 as Golaud in Pelléas et Mélisande, and at Glyndebourne Festival, 1956-64 as Golaud, the Count in Le nozze di Figaro and Il Segreto di Susanna, Don Alfonso and Macrobio in La Pietra del Paragone, returning in 1970 in Il Turco in Italia; Mozart performances at Aix-en-Provence; Chicago in 1959 as Athanael in Massenet's Thais; Guest appearances in Vienna, Berlin, Geneva, Brussels, Amsterdam, Barcelona and Prague. Recordings: Le Comte Ory; Thais and Werther; Pelléas et Mélisande; Rousseau's Le Devin du Village; Stravinsky's Le Rossignol.

ROVNAKOVA Magdalena, b. 5 March 1955, Skalica, Slovakia. Choir Conductor. m. Gabriel Rovnak, 22 January 1983, 1 son, 1 daughter. Education: Academy of Fine Arts, Bratislava. Debut: Missa Choralis From Franz Liszt, Slovak Philharmony Orchestra, 1984. Career: Founder, Conductor, Artistic Director, Bratislava Boys Choir, 1982-, Performed in Oratorios, Cantates, in Opera of Slovak National Theatre and Vienna State Opera. Recordings: Works of Slovak Baroque and Clasicism Period. Contributions to: Radio Programmes. Honours: Winner, International Competition of Chorals, USA, 1995; Golden Medal, President of Slovakia, 1996. Memberships: Slovak Music Society; Slovak Music Union. Hobby: Travel. Address: Balkanska 146, 851 10 Bratislava, Slovakia.

ROWLAND Christopher (Selwyn), b. 21 Dec 1946, Barnet, Hertfordshire, England. Violinist; Teacher; Quartet Leader. m. Elizabeth Attwood, 18 Dec 1982, 1 son. Education: BA, MA, Trinity College, Cambridge, 1965-68; Associate, Royal Academy of Music, 1980; DMus, Bucknell University, PA, 1981. Career: Performed live on radio throughout UK and Europe and regularly in North America; Supervisor of Chamber Music, Tutor in Violin, Royal Northern College of Music, Manchester; Violinist for contemporary music group, Lumina; Leader of Sartori Quartet, 1970-74 and Fitzwilliam Quartet, 1974-84, with tours to Russia in 1976 and 1978. Recordings: Many. Publication: Shostakovich - Man and Music, 1982. Contributions to: Music Times; Soviet Music; Berlioz Bulletin. Honours include: Numerous prizes at Royal Acadey of Music and Cambridge University; Grammy Awards and Grand Prix du Disque. Membership: Communicant Member, Church of England. Hobbies: Christianity; Soccer; Golf. Address: Fountain House, Low Street, Burton-in-Lonsdale, Via Carnforth, Lancashire, England.

ROWLAND Joan (Charlotte), b. 7 May 1930, Toronto, Canada. Pianist; Teacher. m. John Michael Thornton, 5 May 1956, 3 sons, 1 daughter. Education: BA, English, Columbia University, NY, 1970; Piano study with Mona Bates in Toronto, 1938-48, theoretical studies at Royal Conservatory of Music, 1940-46 and piano study with Eduard Steuermann at Juilliard School, NY, 1952-56. Debut: With the Toronto Symphony under Sir Ernest MacMillan in 1942; Recital debut in New York in 1948. Career: Solo recitals in Canada, USA and Europe and for Canadian Broadcasting Corporation since 1942; 2 Tours of USA and London with Columbia Canadian Trio and toured with Reginald Kell Players; Soloist for various orchestras including Toronto Symphony, Wiesbaden Orchestra, Mozarteum Orchestra, Mozart Festival Orchestra, and San Francisco and Buffalo Symphonies; Toured with Piano Duo Schnabel in USA and Europe, 1981-95. Recordings: Schubert Grand Duo and B flat Variations, Mozart Sonata in F major, Schubert E minor Sonata, Schubert Fantasy in F minor and Variations in A flat, all with Piano Duo Schnabel; Solo recording of Schumann Fantasy and Carnaval. Publication: Playing Four-Hands: A Pligrim's Progress, The Piano Quarterly, 1986-87. Honours: 1st Prize, Kranichsteiner Modern Music Competition, Darmstadt, Germany, 1954; 1st Prize, Mozarteum Piano Competition, Salzburg, 1955. Hobbies: Outdoor Sports; Swimming; Canoeing; Mountain Climbing. Address: 285 Riverside Drive No 4A, New York, NY 10025, USA.

ROWLAND-JONES (Simon) Christopher, b. 8 Sep 1950, Colchester, England. Violist; Composer. Education: Studies at The Royal College of Music. Debut: Carnegie Hall, 1979. Career: Chilingirian String Quartet, 1971-78, 1992-; Nash Ensemble, Villiers Piano Quartet; Chameleon; Arenski Ensemble; Professor and Chamber Music Coordinator, Royal College of Music. Compositions: 2 String Quartets; Piano Quartet; String Trio; Rivers Gods; Seven pieces for Solo Viola. Recordings include: Dale, Phantasy and Suite; Bloch, Suites; Schubert, Schumann and Beethoven; Bach Solo Cello Suites, volume 1, suites 1-3, after own edition/transcription. Memberships: Musicians Union; Performing Rights Society. Address: 77 The Vineyard, Richmond, Surrey, TW10 6AS, England.

ROWLANDS Carol, b. 1960, Newcastle-upon-Tyne, England. Mezzo-Soprano. Education: Studied at the Royal Northern College of Music. Career: Appeared with Scottish Opera, 1982-90 in L'Egisto, The Magic Flute, Le nozze di Figaro, Rigoletto, Il Trovatore, Lulu, Madame Butterfly and Salome; Has also understudied Mozart's Cherubino, Puck in Oberon, Wellgunde in Das Rheingold, Clairon in Capriccio, Judith in Bluebeard's Castle in 1990 and Didon in Berlioz's The Trojans for Scottish Opera; Performed Santuzza in Scottish Opera Go Round's autumn tour of Pagliacci and Cavalleria Rusticana in 1989; For University College sang Tigrana in Edgar by Puccini, also performed the title role of Regina for Scottish Opera, Santuzza in Cavalleria Rusticana for Opera South, the Mother in Amahl and the Night Visitors for Opera West, Suzuki in Madame Butterfly at Isle of Man, and concert performances in the title role of Orfeo with John Currie Singers; Season 1992-93 as Cherubino in Marriage of Figaro in Malta, Waltraute in Die Walküre for Scottish Opera, Marcellina in Marriage of Figaro for Scottish Opera, Second Lady in The Magic Flute for Scottish Opera, Marcellina for Opera Factory and the title role in Carmen for Regency Opera; Sang Mrs Grose in The Turn of the Screw for Broomhill Opera, 1996. Address: 6 Hurlingham Mansions, 218-220 New King's Road, London, SW6 4PA, England.

ROYSE Anthony, b. 18 March 1939, London, England. Teacher; Composer; Arranger. Education: Trinity College of Music, London, 1957-60. Career: Director of Music, Dragon School, Oxford, 1966-72, Appleby College, Ontario, Canada, 1972-83, Hilton College, Natal, South Africa, 1983-85. Compositions: Church Music; Carols; 3 Full Length Ballets; Choral and Orchestral Works and Chamber Pieces. Honours: Bantock Composition Prize, 1959; Amadeus Choir of Toronto Carol Competition, 1992, 1994, 1996, 1997. Address: 2 Ethel Road, Broadstairs, Kent CT10 2BE, England.

ROZARIO Patricia, b. 1960, Bombay, India. Singer (Soprano). m. Mark Troop, 1 daughter. Education: Guildhall School of Music with Walter Gruner; Pierre Bernac, St Jean de Luz; National Opera Studio; Study with Vera Rozsa from 1980. Career: Concerts with Songmakers' Almanac, including tour to USA; Solo recitals, South Bank London, elsewhere; Frequent performances of Bach, Handel, Mozart; Vaughan Williams Serenade to Music, 1988 Proms; Schumann's Paradies und der Peri at Madrid, with Gerd Albrecht; Appeared at Bath and Edinburgh Festivals; Operatic roles include Giulietta (Jommelli's La Schiava Liberata), Netherlands Opera, Gluck's Euridice for Opera North, Mozart's Bastienne and Pamina for Kent Opera, Ilia on Glyndebourne tour, Ismene in Lyon production of Mitridate and Zerlina at Aix; Statue in Rameau's Pygmalion and Purcell's Belinda for Kent Opera; Florinda in Handel's Rodrigo at Innsbruck; Nero in L'Incoronazione di Poppea and Massenet's Sophie; Concert performance, Il Re Pastore, Elizabeth Hall; World premiere of John Casken's Golem, as Miriam, Almeida Festival, London; Wexford Festival, 1989, Ismene; Created title role in premiere of Tavener's Mary of Egypt, Aldeburgh, 1992; Season 1992-93, in Monteverdi's Il Combattimento, English National Opera and Haydn's L'infedeltà delusa, Garsington Opera; 1993-94, Wexford Festival, tour of Germany with BBC Now/Otaka, Hong Kong Philharmonic, world premiere of Tavener's Apocalypse, BBC Proms, 1994-95, recital in Lebanon, Purcell Room with Nash Ensemble, Hong Kong Philharmonic; Romilda in Serse at Brussels, 1996; Sang Les Illuminations at St John's, London, 1997. Recordings: Mahler Symphony No 4, London Symphony; Songs of the Auvergne, conductor John Pritchard; Haydn Stabat Mater, conductor Trevor Pinnock; Golem; Tavener: We shall see him as he is, Mary of Egypt, To a child dancing in the wind; Spanish Songs; Britten Rape of Lucretia. Honours: British Song Prize, Barcelona; Maggie Teyte Prize; Sängerforderungspreis, Salzburg Mozarteum; Gold Medal, Guildhall School of Music; Gramophone Award, Golem, 1991. Address: c/o Harold Holt Ltd, 31 Sinclair Road, London W14 0NS, England.

ROZHDESTVENSKY Gennady (Nikolayevich), b. 4 May 1931, Moscow, Russia. Conductor. m. Viktoria Postnikova, 1969. Education: Moscow Conservatory, with Nikolay Rozhdstvensky and Lev Oborin. Debut: Bolshoy Theatre, 1951 with The Nutcracker. Career: Conducted at the Bolshoy, 1951-70 and as Principal Conductor from 1964-70, with productions including Spartacus, Prokofeiv's War and Peace and A Midsummer Night's Dream; London debut in 1956; Principal Conductor of the Symphony Orchestra of All-Union Radio and TV, 1961-; Gave works by Prokofiev, Hindemith, Berg, Martinu and Sergei Slonimsky; Conducted Boris Godunov at Covent Garden, 1970; Artistic Director of Stockholm Philharmonic Orchestra, 1974; Chief Conductor of BBC Symphony Orchestra, 1978-81, Vienna Symphony Orchestra, 1981-; Conducted the premiere of Smirnov's Jacob's Ladder at the Elizabeth Hall, 1991 with London Sinfonietta; Returned to Covent Garden in 1991 with Boris Godunov; Idomeneo at Finlandia Hall, Helsinki, 1991. Honours include: People's Artist of the RSFSR, 1966; Lenin Prize, 1970. Address: Allied Artists Agency, 42 Montpelier Square, Londn SW7 1JZ, England.

RUAN Joshua, b. 21 Feb 1964, Winnipeg, Canada. Composer. Education: Rowland School of Music, Canada; BA, Honours, Music, Composition with Dudley Hyams and Jonathan Harvey at Sussex University, England; Piano with Leslie Murchie; Postgraduate composition with Robert Saxton at Guildhall School of Music. Career: Came to England, 1975; Commissions from various ensembles including The Ensemble Notturno; Works regularly performed and broadcast in UK; His life and work featured in Kathryn Taylor's article Snakes and Ladders in several European journals. Compositions: Over 30 solo, chamber, vocal, theatrical and orchestral works including: L'Hotel Dieu for Double Bass Solo, 1986, published 1992, Serenissima Variations for Viola and Piano, 1988, published 1992, Lolita, masque in 3 acts for Piano, Actors and Dancer, 1989, Phosphate Sugar and Basses for Viola, Cello, Double Bass and Piano, 1990, published 1992, Once Five Years Pass for Solo Piano, 1991, published 1992, The Girl, The Goldwatch and Everything for 10 Instruments, 1992, Caravaggio Suite for Solo Piano, 1994, Caravaggio, 3 act opera based on life of the infamous painter, 1995, The Sleep of Apples, Solo Piano arrangement and Orchestral version from Caravaggio, 1995; Dali, a four act opera based on the painter, 1996; Dali, suite for solo piano, 1996. Honour: South East Arts Award, 1987. Memberships: Composers Guild of Great Britain; Performing Rights Society; Society for the Promotion of New Music; MCPS. Hobbies: Chess; Wine; Cooking; Collecting Paintings. Address: c/o Ricordi, The Bury, Church Street, Chesham, Buckinghamshire, HP5 1LR, England.

RUBENS Sibylla, b. 1970, Germany. Singer (Soprano). Education: Studied at Trossingen and Frankfurt Musikhochschule; Further study with Elise Cavelti in Basle. Career: Frequent Concerts with Helmuth Rilling and Bachakademie Stuttgart, including Tour of Japan, 1995 with Mozart's C Minor Mass; Bach's St John Passion under Rilling and Philippe Herreweghe, 1996; Deutsche Symphony Orchestra Berlin under Ashkenazy and Janowski, in Mendelssohn's Lobesgesang and Schumann's Scenes from Faust; Season 1997-98 with the Fauré Requiem and Poulenc's Stabat Mater at the Concertgebouw, Amsterdam, Ein Deutsches Requiem in Stuttgart and a tour of Messiah with the Windsbache Knabenchor; St John Passion under Ton Koopman, The Creation with Michael Schonwandt and tour with the group Tafelmusik; Other Engagements in Italy, France, Czech Republic, Poland and Norway; Opera includes Mozart's Pamina and Beethoven's Marzelline. Recordings include: Schubert's Lazarus, arranged by Denisov (Hanssler); Mozart's Requiem (Harmonia Mundi). Address: Kunstler Sekretariat am Gasteig, Rosenheimerstrasse 52, 81699 Munich, Germany.

RUBENSTEIN Bernard, b. 30 Oct 1937, Springfield, MO, USA. Conductor. m. Ann Warren Little, 28 Aug 1961, 1 son, 1 daughter. Education: BMus, Eastman School of Music, 1958; MMus, Yale University, 1961. Career: Assistant Conductor for Rhode Island Philharmonic Orchestra, 1961-62 and Wurttemberg State Theater, Stuttgart, 1966-68; Music Director for Santa Fe Symphony Orchestra, 1962-64, Music For Youth, Milwaukee, 1970-80 and Tulsa Philharmonic Orchestra, 1984-; Associate Professor of Conducting and Director of Orchestras for Northwestern University, 1968-80; Conductor for Greenwood Chamber Orchestra, Cummington, MA, 1968-79; Associate Conductor for Cincinnati Symphony Orchestra, 1980-86 and Guest Conductor for many orchestras in the USA and Europe. Current Management: Herbert Barrett Management, NYC, USA. Address: c/o The Tulsa Philharmonic, 2901 South Harvard, Tulsa, OK 74114, USA.

RUBIN Cristina, b. 1958, Milan, Italy. Soprano. Education: Studied at the Milan Conservatoire and the opera school of La Scala. Debut: Bergamo in 1985 as Mimi. Career: Sang Anna in Puccini's Le Villi at Torre del Lago and Trieste; Sang at Teatro Goldoni in Venice as Agata in Il Flamino by Pergolesi, Trieste in 1987 as Suzel in L'Amico Fritz, as Mimi at Zurich in 1986 and Mozart's Countess at Piacenza; Concerts with Beethoven's Missa Solemnis, Schumann's Manfred and Mendelssohn's Lobgesang Symphony. Address: c/o Teatro alla Scala, Via Filodrammatici 2, I-20121 Milan, Italy.

RUBIN Joel Edward, b. 14 Oct 1955, Los Angeles, USA. Clarinettist; Ethnomusicologist. m. Rita Ottens, 24 Apr 1990. Education: California Institute of the Arts, 1973-75; BFA, State University of New York, College of Purchase, 1978; PhD Candidate, City University, London, 1995-. Career: Leader, Joel Rubin Jewish Music Ensemble; Live National Broadcast, Deutschland Radio, 1996; World Premiere of Messianic Soundware, Collaborative Composition and Improvisation with Roberto Paci Dalo, Freunde Guter Musik, Berlin, 1995.

Recordings: Beregovski's Khasene (Beregovski's Wedding), Forgotton Instrumental Treasures From the Ukraine; Zeydes un Eyniklekh (Grandfathers and Grandsons), American-Jewish Wedding Music From the Repertoire of Dave Tarras; Bessarabian Symphony, Early Jewish Instrumental Music; Hungry Hearts, Classic Yiddish Clarinet Solos. Publications include: Back to the Future: Jewish-American Clarinet Music of the 1920s in Light of the Klezmer Revival of the Late 20th Century; Can't You Play Anything Jewish?; Mazltov!..Jewish-American Wedding Music. Honours: State University of New York, College at Purchase, Music School Award, 1978; German Record Critics' Prize, 1992, 1995; Artur Brauner Prize, 1996; Prix Europa, 1996; 18th Bavarian Film Prize, 1997. Memberships: Society for Ethnomusicology; International Council for Traditional Music; American Folklore Society. Current Management: Jewish Cultural Programming and Research. Address: Bernburger Str 18, D-10963 Berlin, Germany.

RUDAKOVA Larisa, b. 1964, Russia. Singer (Soprano). Career: Many performances in Russia and Eastern Europe in operas by Rossini (Il Barbiere di Siviglia), Donizetti (Lucia di Lammermoor), Charpentier (Louise) and Glinka (Ruslan and Ludmilla); Also sings Rossini's Bel raggio lusinghier (Semiramide); Contestant at the 1995 Cardiff Singer of the World Competition. Address: c/o Lies Askonas Ltd, 6 Henrietta Street, London WC2, England.

RUDEL Julius, b. 6 Mar 1921, Vienna, Austria. Conductor. Education: Vienna and Mannes School of Music in USA. Career: Rehearsal Pianist for New York City Opera; Conductor for Johann Strauss's The Gypsy Baron, NY, 1944, with overall command, 1957, and was responsible for many premieres of works by American and foreign composers, and for revivals of many neglected operas; Guest Conductor for La Scala Milan, Covent Garden, Teatro Colon in Buenos Aires, Vienna State Opera and the opera houses of Berlin, Munich, Paris and Hamburg; Conducted Rigoletto at the Metropolitan in 1989, Hamlet by Thomas at Chicago in 1990, and Der Rosenkavalier at Toronto in 1990; Season 1992 conducted La Bohème at Bonn, Don Carlo at Nice and Tosca at Buenos Aires; Conducted Faust at the Met, 1996. Recordings include: Julius Caesar by Handel; The Merry Widow by Lehar; Silverlake by Kurt Weill; Ginastera's Bomarzo; Works by Massenet, Donizetti, Offenbach, Verdi, Bellini, Boito and Charpentier; Many TV recordings. Honour: Julius Rudel Award established in his honour for young conductors, 1969.

RUDENKO Bela (Andreyevna), b. 18 Aug 1933, Bokovo-Antratsit, Ukraine, Russia. Soprano. Education: Studied at the Odessa Conservatory with Olga Blagovidova. Debut: Odessa in 1955 as Gilda in Rigoletto; Career: Sang at Kiev from 1965 notably as Glinka's Ludmila, Rosina in Il Barbiere di Siviglia, Lakmé and Natasha in War and Peace; Bolshoy Theatre Moscow from 1972; Also successful in operas by Ukranian composers. Recordings include: Ruslan and Ludmilla and A Life for The Tsar, by Glinka. Address: c/o TG Shevchenko Theatre, Ul Vladimirskaya 50, Kiev, Ukraine.

RUDERS Poul, b. 27 Mar 1949, Ringsted, Denmark. Composer. Education: Mainly self-taught in composition; Final degree in organ from The Royal Danish Music Academy. Career: Performances with all major Danish symphony orchestras; Performances by London Sinfonietta, Ensemble Intercontemporain, Speculum Musicae, New York Philharmonic, Philharmonia, Capricorn, Lontano; Psalmodies for Guitar and Ensemble, 1990, and frequent performances of works at several international festivals. Compositions: Major orchestral pieces: Capriccio Pian E Forte, 1978, Manhattan Abstraction, 1982, Thus Saw St John, 1984, The Drama Trilogy: Dramaphonia, Monodrama, Polydrama, 1987-88, Himmelhoch-Jauchzendzum Tode Betrübt, symphony, 1989, Violin Concerto No 2, 1991, Gong for Orchestra, 1992; Chamber works: String Quartet No 1, 1971, No 2, 1979, Four Compositions, 1980, Greeting Concertino, 1982, 4 Dances in one movement, 1983, Vox In Rama, 1983; Numerous solo pieces for various instruments; Commission from the Royal Theatre Copenhagen for opera The Handmaid's Tale, 2000. Recordings include: Four Dances, with London Sinfonietta conducted by Oliver Knussen, 1983-89; Corpus Cum Figuris, commissioned by London Sinfonietta, 1984-90; Corpus Cum Figuris: Point PCD 5084, Violin Concerto No 1 Unicorn-Kanchana, 9114, Psalmodies: Bridge 9037, Symphony: Chan 9179, commissioned by Ensemble Intercontemporain. Honours: Royal Philharmonic, London, Charles Heidsieck Prize, 1991. Membership: Danish Composers' Guild, SPNM, England. Current Management: Denmark: Edition WH; England: Chester Music; USA: Bridge Management. Address: c/o Chester Music, 8-9 Frith Stret, London, W1 5TZ, England.

RUDIAKOV Michael, b. 9 Aug 1934, Paris, France. Cellist; Conductor; Artistic Director. m. Judith Peck, 12 June 1964, 1 son, 1 daughter. Education: Studies with father, Eliahu Rudiakov; BMus, Manhattan School of Music, New York City, 1956-61. Career: Concert cellist, Solo and Chamber Music, Tours of Europe, USSR, 1972; India, 1975; Australia, 1976; Canada, Israel, China, 1981; USA; Member of Composers String Quartet, 1969-76; Guest, Fine Arts Quartet, 1977-78; Artistic Director, Chamber Music, Sarah Lawrence, 1969-80; Musical Director, Manchester Music Festival, Vermont, USA, 1983-; Television programmes for CBS and National Educational Television; Radio programme. Bern, Zurich, Paris, Rome, Jerusalem, Hamburg, Berlin, New Delhi, BBC London and Manchester; Principal Cellist, Indianapolis, 1963-65; Jerusalem Symphony, 1965-66; Faculty, Manhattan School of Music, New York City, 1981; Faculty, Lehman College, City University of New York, 1993; Founder, Manchester Festival Orchestra, 1988. Recordings: Over 25. Contributions to: Musical America, 1982. Honours: Harold Bauer Award, American Society of Composers, 1971; Grammy Nomination, 1972. Memberships: Violoncello Society of New York; Local 802 Musicians Union, New York City. Current Management: Arlisa Concerts Incorporated. Address: PO Box 682, Manchester, VT 05254, USA.

RUDOLF Max, 15 Jun 1902, Frankfurt am Main, Germany. Symphony and Opera Conductor. m. Liese Ederheimer, 4 Aug 1927, 1 son, 1 daughter. Education: Studied at Goethe-Gymnasium, Frankfurt, Hochschule Conservatory of Music, Frankfurt University and privately; DMus, Honours, Cincinnati Conservatory of Music; LHD, Honours, University of Cincinnati, 1960, Miami University, 1963, Curtis School of Music, 1972; DMus, Baldwin-Wallace College, 1973, Temple University, 1975. Career includes: Conductor for Hesse State Opera, Darmstadt, 1923-29, and German Opera, Prague, 1929-35; Guest Conductor for Gothenburg Orchestral Society also Choral Director for radio concerts for Swedish Broadcasting Corp, 1935-40; Musical Staff, 1945-58, Artistic Administrator, 1950-58, and Conductor, 1973-75, for Metropolitan Opera Association, NYC; Administrator, Kathryn Long Opera courses, Metropolitan Opera, 1949-58; Musical Director and Conductor for Cincinnati Symphony Orchestra, 1958-70 with worldwide concert tour in 1966; Distinguished Service Professor, University of Cincinnati, 1966-68; Faculty, Curtis Institute of Music, Philadelphia, 1970-73 and 1981-; Guest Conductor for symphony orchestras throughout USA and Italy and panel member for National Endowment of the Arts, WA, 1970-73; Artistic Advisor in America including Exxon/Art Endowment Conductors Programme, 1977-. Publication: Author, The Grammar of Conducting, 1950, 2nd edition, 1980. Honours include: Alice M Ditson Award, 1964; Phi Kappa Lambda. Address: 220 West Rittenhouse Square, Philadelphia, PA 19103, USA.

RUDY Mikhail, b. 3 Apr 1953, Tashkent, USSR. Concert Pianist. Education: Moscow Conservatory with Jakov Flier. Career: After winning prizes at competitions in Leipzig and Paris he made his western debut in 1977, playing Beethoven's Triple Concerto in Paris with Rostropovich and Stern; Guest appearances with the Berlin Philharmonic, Orchestre de Paris, Concertgebouw, Boston Symphony, Montreal Symphony Orchestra, London Philharmonic and Toronto Symphony; US debut 1981 with the Cleveland Orchestra conducted by Lorin Maazel; Festivals include Schleswig-Holstein, Berlin, Tanglewood, Lockenhaus and Vienna; Salzburg Eastern Festival, 1987 with Karajan; Chamber music concerts with the Amadeus Quartet until 1987, Guarneri Quartet and Vienna Philharmonic Wind Ensemble; London debut with the LSO under Michael Tilson Thomas, 1988; Promenade Concerts 1989, Prokofiev's 2nd Concerto; Subject of French television Documentary Le grand Echiquier, 1989; Debut with Dresden Staatskapelle, 1991; Season 1991-92 with concerts in Cleveland and Munich; Returned to Russia, 1990, concerts with the St Petersburg Philharmonic; Music Director, St Riquier Festival; Waldbühne Concert with Berlin Philharmonic, 1994; Janacek, Stravinsky and Schubert concert at the Wigmore Hall, London, 1997. Recordings include: Brahams and Ravel recital (EMI); Concertos by Rachmaninov and Tchaikovsky with the St Petersburg Philharmonic; Shostakovich Piano Concerto No 1 with Berlin Philharmonic. Honours include: prize winner, 1971 Bach Competition, Leipzig; First Prize, Marguerite Long Competition, Paris, 1975. Current Management: IMG Artists Europe. Address: C/O IMG Artists Europe, Media House, 3 Burlington Lane, London W4 2TH, England.

RUDZINSKI Witold, b. 14 Mar 1913, Siebiez. Composer; Musicologist; Pedagogue. m. Nina Rewienska, 26 Dec 1958. 1 son, 2 daughters. Education: Phil Mag, University of Wilno, 1936; Conservatory M Karlowicz Wilno, 1937; Studies with Nadia Boulanger and Charles Koechlin, Institut Gregorien, Paris, France, 1938-39. Debut: 1936. Career: Head, Music School Swieciany, Poland, 1937-38; Conservatory Wilno, 1939-42; Professor, Cons Lodz, 1945-47; Director of Music Department, Ministry of Culture, Warsaw, 1947-48; Academy of Music, Warsaw, 1957-. Compositions: Operas: Janko Muzykant (Janko The Fiddler), 1951; Commander of Paris, 1957; The Dismissal of Grecian Envoys, 1962; Sulamith, 1964; The Peasants, 1972; The Ring and The Rose, 1982; The Yellow Nightcap, 1969; Oratorios: The Roof of the World, 1960; Gaude mater Polonia, 1966, The Circle of Psalms 1987, Madonna 1991; Litany to the Holy Virgin of Ostra Braina, 1994; Symphonic Music: Musique Concertante for Piano and Orchestra, 1958; Pictures from Holy Cross Mountains, 1965; Concerto Grosso for Percussion and with String Orchestra, 1970; Chamber Music: Sonata for Viola and Pianoforte, 1946; Flute Quintet, 1954; Deux Portraits des Femmes for Voice and String Quartet, 1960; To Citizen John Brown, Voice and Chamber Ensemble, 1972; Duo Concertante for Percussion, 1976; Sonata Pastorale for Violin and Pianoforte, 1976; Instrumental: Variations and Fugue for Percussion, 1966; Quasi una sonata for Pianoforte, 1975; Sonata per clavicembalo, 1978; Dialogue for saxophone and piano; Pleiades, sonata for clarinet and piano, 1987; Songs: Incidental music. Recordings: Sonata for Viola and Pianoforte; Janko Muzykant Muza; Musique Concertante for Pianoforte and orchestra; The Roof of the World and Pictures from Holy Cross Mountains; Odprawa poslow greckich; Gaude mater Polonia; Children Songs. Publications: Music for Everybody, 1948, 1966; Stanislaw Moniuszko, Principal Biography in 2 volumes, 1954-61; Moniuszko's Correspondence, 1969; Moniuszko, Popular Mongr, 1978; What Is Opera? 1960; Béla Bartok Musical Technique, 1965; How to Listen to Music, 1975; Treatise on Musical Rhythm, 2 volumes, 1987. Hobbies: History; Biography. Address: PL - 02541 Warszawa, Narbutta 50 m 6, Poland.

RUDZINSKI Zbigniew, b. 23 Oct 1935, Czechowice, Poland. Composer. m. Ewa Debska, 13 July 1965, 1 daughter. Education: Warsaw University, 1956; MA, Composition Diploma with distinction, State High School for Music, Warsaw, 1956-60. Career: Professor of Composition, 1973-, Head of Composition Department, 1980-81, Rector (director), 1981-84, Academy of Music, F Chopin, Warsaw. Compositions include: Orchestral: Sonata for 2 String Quartets, Piano and Kettle Drums, 1960, Contra Fidem, 1964, Moments Musicaux I, 11, 111, 1965-68, Music By Night, 1970; Vocal/instrumental works: Four Folk Songs for soprano and piano, 1955; Sonata for clarinet and piano, 1958; Trio for 2 clarinets and bassoon, 1958; Epigrames for flute, choir and percussion, 1962; String Trio, 1964; Study for C for ensemble ad libitum, 1964; Impromptu for 2 pianos, 1968; Symphony for men's choir and orchestra, 1969; Requiem for the Victims of Wars for choir and orchestra, 1971; Tutti E Solo for soprano, flute, french horn and piano, 1973; Strings in the Earth for soprano and string orchestra, 1983; Three Romantic Portraits for 12 saxophones; Chamber: Quartet for 2 Pianos and Percussion, 1969, Sonata for Piano, 1975, Campanella for Percussion Ensemble, 1977, Tritones for Percussion Ensemble, 1979; Opera: The Mannequins, 1981, The Book Of Hours, songs for mezzo-soprano and piano trio, 1983, Das Sind Keine Träume, songs for mezzo-soprano and piano, 1986. Membership: President, Warsaw District, Polish Composers' Union, 1983-85, Secretary General, 1985-. Hobbies: Old and Folk Instruments; Musical Pictures. Address: ul Poznanska 23 m 26, 00-685 Warszawa, Poland.

RUFFINI Alessandra, b. 1961, Italy. Soprano. Education: Studied at the Milan Conservatory. Career: Sang Arianna in Vivaldi's Giustino in 1985 and appeared as Gilda at Treviso and Rovigo in 1987; Sang at Vicenza in 1988 as Elena in Gluck's Paride e Helena, Palermo in 1991 as Mariana in Wagner's Das Liebesverbot, and at Rome Opera in 1992 as Rossini's Adina and Leila in Les Pêcheurs de Perles; Other roles include Amina in La Sonnambula (Cremona, 1988) and Adina in L'Elisir d'Amore (Piacenza 1992); Sang Pauline in Donizetti's Les Martyrs, Nancy, 1996. Recordings include: Rosina in Morlacchi's Il Barbiere di Siviglia; La Locandiera by Salieri; La Cecchina by Piccinni. Address: Rome Opera, Teatro dell'Opera, Piazza B Gigli 8, 00184 Rome, Italy.

RUFO Bruno, b. 1941, Italy. Tenor. Debut: Spoleto in 1965 as Pinkerton. Career: Many appearances at La Scala Milan, Rome, Naples and as Radames in 1981 at Verona Arena; Further engagements at Bologna, Parma, Hamburg, Munich, Vienna, the Deutsche Oper Berlin and Dusseldorf; Sang Manrico at Liège, and Samson in season 1986-87; TV appearances have included Verdi's Ernani. Address: c/o Opera Royal de Wallonie, 1 Rue des Domincains, B-4000 Liège, Belgium.

RUGGEBERG Claudia, b. 1955, Hamburg, Germany. Contralto. Education: Studied in Hamburg with Judith Beckmann. Career: Many appearances throughout Germany in concerts and recitals; Guest engagements at the Hamburg and Oldenburg Operas, Bregenz Festival, 1985-86 in Die Zauberflöte, and Gelsenkirchen and Stuttgart in 1987 in La Gioconda and Die Soldaten; Sang in Eugene Onegin at Zurich in 1991 and has appeared elsewhere including Barcelona, Bologna, Cologne and Krefeld; Has sung mainly in opera houses of Hamburg, Bonn, Cologne, Stuttgart, Aalto-Theater Essen; Ring Production (Erda), Dessau, Die Verurteilung des Lukullus, Handel, Giulio Cesare, 1992-97; Teatro Liceo Barcelona: Schoenberg Moses und Aaron, Götterdämmerung, Walküre, Eugene Onegin; Teatro Communale Bologna: Walküre (Riccardo Chailly); Teatro alla Scala Milano, Elektra (Giuseppe Sinopoli), 1994; Asia-Concert tour with the Staatskapelle Dresden, Giuseppe Sinopoli: Elektra in Japan and Taiwan, 1995; Professor at the Essen Musikhochschule, 1990-. Recordings: CD's: Braunfels: Die Verkündigung, 1994. Address: Folkwang Musikhochschule, Abtei 43, 7300 Essen 16, Germany.

RUGGIERO Charles Howard, b. 19 June 1947, Bridgeport, Connecticut, USA. Composer; University Professor. m. Patricia Ann Uller, 28 June 1969, 1 son, 3 daughters. Education: BMus at New England Conservatory, 1969; MMus at Michigan State University, 1974; PhD at Michigan State University, 1979; Principal composition teachers: H Owen Reed, Jeve Hutcheson. Appointments: Jazz Percussionist, 1959-; Professor of Composition and Music Theory at Michigan State University, 1973-; Founder and Co-Director of Computer Music Studio, MSU, 1983-94; Chair of Music Theory Area, MSU, 1988-. Compositions: Three Blues for Saxophone Quartet, 1981; Interplay, for soprano saxophone and piano, 1988; From Two Ramparts, for wind symphony, 1992; Concerto for Soprano Saxophone and Orchestra, 1995. Recordings: CDs: (own composition) Three Blues for Saxophone Quartet, 1989; Aerodynamics, 1995; (own composition) Fractured Mambos; Interplay, 1997. Publications: CASAP: Computer-Assistaed Set Analysis Program for McIntosh Computer (with co-author Dr James Colman), 1990. Contributions to: ASCAP Special Awards, 1987-; National Endowment for the Arts Consortium Commissioning Grant, 1987-88. Memberships: American Musicological Society; Society for Music Theory. Address: School of Music, Michigan State University, E Lansing, MI 48824, USA.

RUK-FOCIC Bozena, b. 31 Oct 1937, Zagreb, Yugoslavia. Soprano. Education: Studied with Zlatko Sir in Zagreb. Debut: Basle in 1960 as Micaela in Carmen. Career: Member of Croatian National Opera, Zagreb; Guest appearances in Bucharest, Athens, Roma, Palermo, Napoli, Trieste, Genoa, Luxembourg, Holland, Graz, Bern, Belgrade, Vienna, Berlin, Stuttgart, Hamburg and at Covent Garden (as Eva in Die Meistersinger); La Scala as Sieglinde in Walküre in 1970 and in the Italian premiere of Dallapiccola's Ulisse; Further engagements in Kiev, Budapest, Houston, Pittsburgh, Seattle, Washington, Zurich, Geneva, Barcelona and Salzburg; Other roles include Jaroslavna in Prince Igor, Alceste, Madama Butterfly, Mozart's Countess, Verdi's Leonora and Aida, Wagner's Elsa, Elisabeth and Sieglinde, Strauss's Ariadne and Weber's Agathe, Desdemona in Otello, Tosca, Elisabetta in Don Carlos, Manon, Arabella, Ariadne, Marguerite in Faust, and Amelia in Simon Boccanegra; Many appearances as concert singer.

RUNARSDOTTIR Hildigunnur, b. 14 Mar 1964, Reykjavik, Iceland. Composer. m. Jon Larus Stefansson, 2 daughters. Education: Reykjavik College of Music, 1989; Private Studies, Hamburg and Copenhagen. Compositions: The Golden Goose, 1993; 3 Psalms for Organ. Recordings: The Golden Goose; Syngur Sumarregn; Mariuljod. Publication: Syngur Sumarregn, 1996. Memberships: Icelandic Society of Composers. Hobbies: Wine Tasting; Singing. Address: Njalsgotu 6, IS-101 Reykjavik, Iceland.

RUNDGREN Bengt, b. 21 Apr 1931, Karlskrona, Sweden. Bass-Baritone. Education: Studied with Arne Sunnegaard and Ragnar Hulten in Stockholm. Career: Sang in operetta then made opera debut as the Commendatore, Stockholm in 1962; Member of the Royal Opera, Stockholm until 1969; Sang Osmin in Die Entführung at Drottningholm, 1965-67; Member of Deutsche Oper Berlin from 1969, often being heard as Leporello in Don Giovanni; Metropolitan Opera in 1974 as Hagen repeating the role at Bayreuth in the 1976 centenary production of The Ring; Sang the Commendatore in Don Giovanni at Stockholm in 1988; Also heard as concert singer. Honours include: Swedish Court Singer, 1975. Address: Kunglica Teatern, PO Box 16094, S-10322 Stockholm, Sweden.

RUNGE Peter-Christoph, b. 12 Apr 1933, Lubeck, Germany. Baritone. Education: Studied with Lilly Schmidt di Giorgi in Hamburg. Debut: Flensburg in 1958 as Guglielmo in Cosi fan Tutte at High School. Career: Sang in Wuppertal, 1959-64, Deutsche Opera am Rhein, Düsseldorf from 1964; Roles include Mozart: Count, Alfonso, Speaker, Rossini's Cenerentola, Dandini, Strauss repertoire, Harlekin, Musiklehrer, Olivier, Barbier, Wozzeck, Beckmesser, Meistersinger; Glyndebourne Opera, 1966-73, 1982, 1983 as Papageno and Pelléas and in the Leppard/Cavalli L'Ormindo; Edinburgh Festival in 1972 in the British premiere of Zimmermann's Die Soldaten; Stocziüs Guest appearances in Vienna, Brussels, Stockholm, Amsterdam, Warsaw, Bolshoi, Berlin, Hamburg and Zurich, Bogota, Verona, Buenos Aires, Berlin, Salzburg; Sang the premieres of Goehr's Behold the Sun, Duisburg in 1985, and Reimann's Das Schloss, Dusseldorf, Berlin, 1992; Wexford Festival in 1990 as Major Max von Zastrow in The Rising of The Moon by Maw; As concert artist often heard in Bach, Schubert, Schumann, Brahms, Strauss, Mozart and Monteverdi; Oratorios include Bach Oratorio, Handel, Brahms, Mendelssohn, War Requiem by Britten, Passion Pendereck by Lucas; Teacher, Music High School, Dusseldorf and Aachen; Season 1997-98, Dresden Festival; Rossini opera, Parmenione, in L'Occasione fa il Ladro. Recordings include: L'Ormindo; Music by Monteverdi, Schitz and Bach; Auber's Manon Lescaut. Honours: Kammersänger, 1990. Current Management: Athole Still, London, England. Address: c/o Deutsche Oper am Rhein, Heinrich-Heine allee 16, D-4000 Dusseldorf, Germany.

RUNKEL Reinhild, b. 25 Dec 1943, Volkach am Main, Germany. Mezzo-Soprano. Education: Studied in Wuppertal. Career: Sang at the Nuremberg Opera, 1975-82; Guest engagements at Lisbon, Reggio Emilia, Paris and San Francisco, 1985, and Florence as Magdalene in Meistersinger in 1986; Salzburg Festival in 1987 in Moses and Aron by Schoenberg; Sang Fricka in Ring performances at Bologna, Stuttgart and Cologne, 1987-88; Appearances at the Zurich Opera from 1985 as Herodias, Fricka and Clytemnestra in a Ruth Berghaus production of Elektra in 1991; Stuttgart Staatsoper in 1992 as Begbick in Aufstieg und Fall der Stadt Mahagonny; Other roles include Erda, Waltraute, Brangaene, Lyon 1990, Jocasta in Oedipus Rex and the Nurse in Die Frau ohne Schatten; Frequent concert appearances. Recordings include: Fortune Teller in Arabella and Nurse in Die Frau ohne Schatten conducted by Solti; Beethoven's 9th. Address: c/o Zurich Opera, Falkenstrasse 1, CH-8008 Zurich, Switzerland.

RUNNICLES Donald, b. 16 Nov 1954, Edinburgh, Scotland. Conductor. Education: Studied at Edinburgh and Cambridge Universities and at the London Opera Centre. Career: Repetiteur at the Mannheim National Theatre from 1980, debut with Les Contes d'Hoffmann; Kapellmeister from 1984, conducting Fidelio, Le Nozze di Figaro, Un Ballo in Maschera, Die Walküre and Parsifal; Principal conductor at Hanover from 1987, leading Salome, Jenufa, Tosca, Don Giovanni, Werther; Regular engagements with the Hamburg Staatsoper: Turandot, The Bartered Bride, Die Zauberflöte, Manon Lescaut, Carmen, Don Carlos, Zar und Zimmermann, Il Trovatore, Il Barbiere di Siviglia, L'Elisir d'Amore, Lady Macbeth of Mtsensk; General Music Director at Freiburg from 1989: Lady Macbeth, Billy Budd, Peter Grimes; Assisted James Levine at Bayreuth, then conducted Lulu at the Metropolitan, 1988, followed by Die fliegende Holländer, 1990, and Die Zauberflöte; Conducted The Ring at San Francisco, Summer, 1990; Vienna Staatsoper from season, 1990-91, with Il Barbiere di Siviglia, Don Giovanni, Madame Butterfly, La Traviata and Prince Igor; Glyndebourne debut 1991, with Don Giovanni; Musical Director of San Francisco Opera from 1992; Season 1992-93 with Lady Macbeth of the Mtsensk District at Vienna Volksoper; The Fiery Angel, Guillaume Tell, Boris Godunov at San Francisco; Don Giovanni at Munich; Tannhäuser at Bayreuth; Der Ring des Nibelungen at Bayreuth; Other repertory includes Idomeneo at Hanover; Der Freischütz; Symphonic engagements in Darmstadt, Odensee, St Gallen, Copenhagen and with NDR Orchestra, Hamburg; Season 1997-98 at San Francisco with Death in Venice, Le nozze di Figaro, and Pelléas et Mélisande. Address: c/o Athole Still International Ltd, Foresters Hall, 25-27 Westow Street, London, SE19 3RY, England.

RUNSWICK Daryl, b. 12 Oct 1946, Leicester, England. Composer; Musician; Singer. Education: MA, hons, Music, Corpus Christi College, Cambridge, 1964-67. Career: Musical Director, Footlights Club, 1966-67; Jazz Bass Player, especially with C Laine and J Dankworth, 1968-82; Concert Bass Player, especially with London Sinfonietta, 1970-82; Session Player, bass, bass guitar, keyboards, 1970-81; Arranger, Record Producer, especially King's Singers, 1971-; Composer of Film and TV music, 1976-; Tenor Singer in Electric Phoenix, 1983-; Musical Director, Green Light Music Theatre Company, 1990-; Professor of Composition and Media Studies, Trinity College of Music, London. Compositions: Scafra Preludes; 6 Episodes forming a Threnody; Moto interrotto/Ripresso; Mouth Symphony; Four by Five; I Am A Donut; Four Nocturnes; Main-Lineing; From Two Worlds; Cool>Warm>Hot. Recordings: With Electric Pheonix including: Berio, Cage, Nordheim, Wishart; With London Sinfonietta including: Songs for Dov, Agon, King Priam; With Nash Ensemble including: The Soldier's Tale; Many Jazz records including: Cleo Laine at Carnegie Hall. Publication: Rock, Jazz and Pop Arranging, 1992. Hobbies: Touring; Cinema; Collecting Art; Visiting Gardens. Current Management: Faber Music Ltd. Address: 34A Garthorne Road, London, SE23 1EW, England.

RUOFF Axel D, b. 24 Mar 1957, Stuttgart, Germany. Composer. Education: State University for Music, Stuttgart and Academy for Music, Kassel, 1975-84; Diplomas in Piano and Music Theory, cum laude, 1979 and Diploma for Composers, 1984; National University for Fine Arts and Music, Tokyo, Japan, 1985-87. Career: Head of Department, Stuttgart Music School, 1981-88; Lecturer, State University for Music, Trossingen, 1985-87; Concurrently Guest Professor in Composition at Morioka College in 1988, selected for the Forum for Young Composers, Berlin; Fellowship from the Art Foundation of Baden, Württemberg; Fellowship from the Japanese Ministry of Culture for study at the National University for Fine Arts and Music in Tokyo; Professor at State University for Music, Stuttgart, 1992. Compositions: Prozession for Orchestra, 1983; Concerto for Flute and Orchestra, 1984; Correlations, cello solo, 1983; Jemand In Vorbeigehen for Voice and Piano, 1984; Via Dolorosa for Organ, 1985; Fassaden for Violin Solo, 1985; String Quartet, 1986; Salomo-Variations for Choir, 1986; Nacht Und Träume for Orchestra, 1987-88; String Quartet No 2, 1988; Piano Concerto, 1989. Recordings: Various records; Broadcasts for German, other European and Japanese stations. Publications: Publishing contracts with Edition Moeck, Con Brio in Berlin and Celle and Mieroprint in Münster. Honours: Valentino Bucchi, Rome, 1985, 1987; 1st Prize, ICONS, Torino, 1988; 2nd Prize, Ensemblia, Mönchengladbach, 1986; 1st Prize, Corciano, Perugia, 1991. Address: Möhringer Land Str 53, 7000 Stuttgart 80, Germany.

RUOHONEN Seppo, b. 25 Apr 1946, Turku, Finland. Tenor. Education: Studied in Helsinki, with Luigi Ricci in Rome and with Anton Dermota in Vienna. Debut: Helsinki in 1973 as Alvaro in La Forza del Destino. Career: Appearances with Finnish National Opera as Verdi's Duke and Manrico, Tchaikovsky's Lensky and Hermann, and Don Ottavio; Savonlinna in 1977 in The Last Temptations by Kokonnen, with Sallinen's The Red Line, repeated at the Metropolitan, NY in 1983; San Diego Opera as Riccardo in Un Ballo in Maschera; Returned to Savonlinna in 1983 as Don Carlos and as Erik in Der fliegende Holländer; Has sung at Frankfurt from 1978 and made guest appearances in Berlin, Dresden, Leeds, Glasgow, Stuttgart and Wiesbaden as the Duke of Parma in Doktor Faust, Puccini's Cavaradossi, Luigi and Pinkerton and Jenik in The Bartered Bride; Sang Florestan at the 1992 Savonlinna Festival; Inquisitor in Dallapiccola's Il Prigioniero for Tampere Opera, 1996. Recordings include: The Last Temptations.

RUSHBY-SMITH John, b. 28 Sept 1936, Redcar, Yorkshire, England. Record Producer; Composer; Writer. m. (1) 2 sons, (2) Margaret Field, 25 Apr 1986. Education: St Edmund Hall, Oxford. Career: Music Studio Manager, BBC, 1962-; Senior Post, 1967-, with BBC SO Broadcasts and recordings, 1971-90; Technical Director, Stockhausen Music and Machines, Barbican, 1985; Steve Reich Festival, Royal Festival Hall, 1988. Compositions: Violin Sonata; Piano duet, Aspects of Night; Syzygy for flute and piano; Piano Sonata; Saxophone Quartet; Concerto Grosso for strings; Monologue for oboe; Reverie and Valse Seriale for orchestra; Various songs. Recordings: Production of Schoenberg series for CBS; Various recordings for Erato, including Boulez series, Rameau's Nais (McGegan), Gluck's Orfeo (Leppard/Baker); Tippett's Mask of Time and Enesco's Oedipe for EMI; Further productions for Erato, Fonit, Cetra, Kiwi Pacific, Pickwick, RCA, RPO Records, Transatlantic Records and others. Contributions to: On broadcasting Wagner's Ring Cycle for Studio Sound; On broadcasting, The Proms for Proms Prospectus; The Cave of Harmony, talk for BBC Radio; Concert Hall Acoustical Design, paper for Institute of Acoustics, 1988; The Production of Enesco's Oedipe for Classic CD, 1991. Honours: Gramophone Awards: Best Contemporary Recording, 1984 for Boulez's Pli selon pli, 1987 for Tippett's Mask of Time; Prix du Disque, French Opera, 1982; Grand Prix Charles Cros, 1987 for Tippett's Mask of Time, 1991 for Enesco's Oedipe; Diapason d'or, Grand Prix du Disque, Grand Prix de la Nouvelle Academie du Disque Francaise, 1991 for Enesco's Oedipe. Memberships: Institute of Acoustics; Composers' Guild; Sonic Arts Network; PRS. Address: The Folly, Lower Soudley, Cinderford, Gloucester GL14 2UB, England.

RUSHTON Julian (Gordon), b. 22 May 1941, Cambridge, England. University Professor. m. Virginia Susan Medlycott Jones, 16 March 1968, 2 sons. Education: Studied at Trinity College, Cambridge and Magdalen College, Oxford. Career: University Lecturer, University of East Anglia, 1968-74; University of Cambridge, 1974-81; West Riding Professor and Head of Department, University of Leeds, 1982-. Publications: Berlioz: Huit Scenes de Faust, La Damnation de Faust, editions; The Musical Language of Berlioz; Classical Music: A Concise History; WA Mozart: Don Giovanni; WA Mozart: Idomeneo; Berlioz: Roméo et Juliette. Contributions to: New Grove Dictionary of Music and Musicians; Various Professional Journals; New Grove Dictionary of Opera. Honours: Honorary Professor of Music, Keele University. Memberships: Musica Britannica; President, Royal Musical Association; American Musicological Society. Hobbies: Literature; Walking. Address: Department of Music, University of Leeds, Leeds LS2 9JT, England.

RUSSELL Ken, b. 3 Jul 1927, Southampton, England. Stage Producer. Education: Nautical College, Pangbourne; Choreography with Nicolai Sergueff of the Marinsky Ballet, St Petersburg. Career: Films for BBC and ITV, 1959-70 including studies of Elgar, Debussy, Prokofiev, Delius, Vaughan Williams, Martinu and Richard Strauss; Feature films include The Music Lovers (Tchaikovsky), Mahler, and The Devils with music by Peter Maxwell Davies; First opera production was The Rake's Progress at the 1982 Maggio Musicale in Florence; Other productions include Zimmermann's Die Soldaten for Opéra de Lyon in 1983, Madama Butterfly at Spoleto in 1983, L'Italiana in Algeri at Geneva in 1984, La Bohème at Macerata Festival in 1984, Faust at Vienna in 1985 and Mefistofele at Genoa in 1987; He has directed his production of Butterfly in Houston and Melbourne, and Gilbert and Sullivan's Princess Ida at the London Coliseum in 1992. Honours include: Prix Italia for his symbolic portrait of Vaughan Williams, 1985. Address: Barratt House, 7 Chertsey Road, Woking, Surrey, GU21 5AB, England.

RUSSELL Lynda, b. 1963, Birmingham, England. Soprano. Education: Studied in London with Meriel St Clair and in Vienna with Eugene Ludwig. Career: Has sung with Glyndebourne Opera as the Queen of Night, Fortuna in Monteverdi's Ulisse and Marzelline in Fidelio; Opera engagements at Barcelona, Madrid, Nice, Venice, Vicenza, Rome, Bologna and Strasbourg; British appearances as Handel's Partenope and with Opera North and English National Opera; Trieste in 1990 as Donna Elvira; Concert showings at the festivals of Athens, Barcelona, Granada, San Sebastian, Cuence, Venice, Berne, Munich and Siena; Brahms Requiem under Jesus Lopez-Cobos and Beethoven's 9th with Walter Weller; Has sung Mozart's oratorios Davidde Penitente and Betulia Liberata in Italy; Further repertoire includes Wolf's Italienisches Liederbuch, Beethoven's Missa Solemnis under Weller, and Ah, Perfido, Mozart's Exsultate and Coronation Mass; Mozart bicentenary concerts in London, Birmingham, Winchester and Lahti in Finland in 1991; Season 1996-97 with Bach'c Jauchzet Gott in Vienna, Britten's Illuminations in Scotland, Mozart's Requiem with the Ulster Orchestra, and Handel's Samson with the Sixteen. Recording: Handel Dixit Dominus with The Sixteen.

RUSSELL William (Fletcher), b. 31 August 1950, Edinburgh, Scotland. Opera Executive; General Director, Opera/Columbus, Ohio. Education: University of California, Graduate School of Business Administration; University of Colorado, Juilliard School of Music; American Academy of Dramatic Arts. Debut: Metropolitan Opera, 1977; Washington Opera, Bars Bride, 1987; Anchorage Opera, 1991. Career: TV: Amahl and the Night Visitors; The Disappearance of Aimes; Film: Duchess and the Dirtwater Fox; TV Documentary: The Making of an Alaskan Figaro; Agri Country, on the farm with opera's Bill Russell; Administrative positions with San Francisco Opera, Washington Opera, Los Angeles Opera, Anchorage Opera. Recordings: Videos: La Gioconda, 1979; Samson et Dalila, 1981; Aida, 1982; Goya, 1987. Contributions to: National Arts Stabilization Quarterly. Honours: Emmy Award for Goya, 1988; Emmy Award, Bioconda, 1980; Peabody Award, 1980. Membership: Opera America. Hobbies: Farming; Dog Mushing. Address: Glenburnie Farms, 5003 St Rt 37 East Delaware, OH 43015, USA.

RUSSO William, b. 25 Jun 1928, Chicago, IL, USA. Composer. Education: Studied with Lenni Tristano, 1943-46, John Becker, 1953-55 and Karel Jirak, 1955-57. Career: Trombonist and Chief Composer, Arranger with the Stan Kenton Orchestra, 1950-54; Taught at the Manhattan School of Music, 1958-61 and formed and conducted the Russo Orchestra, Columbia College Chicago, 1965-67 and Antioch College, 1971-72; Founded and directed the Center for New Music and Free Theatre at Columbia College, 1965-75; Returned to teaching at Columbia in 1979. Compositions include: Operas: John Hooten, BBC, 1963, The Island, BBC, 1963, Land Of Milk And Honey, Chicago, 1967, Antigone, Chicago, 1967, A Cabaret Opera, NY, 1970, Aesop's Fables, Chicago, 1971, The Shepherds' Christmas, Chicago, 1979, Isabella's Fortune, NY, 1974, Pedrolino's Revenge, Chicago, 1974, A General Opera, Chicago, 1976, The Pay Off, Chicago, 1984, Talking To The Sun, Chicago, 1989; Ballets: The World Of Alcina, 1954, Les Deux Errants, Monte Carlo, 1956, The Golden Bird, Chicago, 1984; 2 Symphonies, 1957 and 1958; Music for Blues and Jazz Bands, Rock Cantatas and Sonata for Violin and Piano, 1986. Publications include: Composing Music: A New Approach, 1988. Address: c/o ASCAP, ASCAP Building, One Lincoln Plaza, New York, NY 10023, USA.

RUT Josef, b. 21 Nov 1926, Kutná Hora, Czechoslovakia. Violinist; Composer. m. Dr Milada Rutová, 14 Feb 1953, 1 son. Education: Studied with Professor Bedrich Voldan; State Conservatory of Music, Prague. Debut: Prague in 1951. Career: Violinist for Radio Prague Symphony Orchestra, 1953-83; Composer from 1983. Compositions: 41 Compositions based on own 12 note tonal theory. Recordings: Sonata for Double Bass and Strings; String Quartets No 1 and 2; Symphonies No 2 and 3; Sonata for Winds No 1; Wind Quintet; Concerto for Violin and Orchestra; Duo for Violin and Violoncello; Concerto for Horn and Strings; Variations for Orchestra; Sonate for Piano; Concerto for Trumpet and Strings; Sonate for Violin and Piano. Publications: Studies for Two Violins; Small Dialogues for Trumpet and Trombone; Five Little Pieces for Flute and Piano; 12 Note Tonal Theory, 1969; Die Musik und ihre Perspektive vom Gesichtspunkt der Relativitätstheorie (International Review of the Aesthetics and Sociology of Music), 1980; Manual of Rhythm, with Jan Dostal, 1979 and 1984; Beitrag zur übersichtlicheren Notierung des Rhythmus, 1982; The Relativist Theory of Musical Motion, 1990. Membership: Society of Czech Composers. Hobbies: Scoring and Revising 18th Century Music; Travelling. Address: Zborovská 40, 15000 Prague 5, Czech Republic.

RUTMAN Neil, b. 12 Jul 1953, CA, USA. Pianist. Education: BMus, San Jose State University, 1976 with Aiko Onishi; MMus, Piano Performance, Eastman School of Music, University of Rochester, 1977; Student of Cecile Genhart; DMA, Piano Performance, Peabody Institute of The Johns Hopkins University, 1983, under Ellen Mack; Private piano studies with Leon Fleisher, Frank Mannheimmer and Gaby Casadesus. Debut: US debut at Carnegie Hall in 1985; London debut at Wigmore Hall in 1985; Washington DC debut at Phillips Gallery in 1985. Career: Associate Professor of Piano at Goucher College, Baltimore, 1983-; Masterclasses on interpretation of French piano music of Fauré, Debussy, and Ravel, at Chateau de la Gesse, Toulouse, France, University of Colorado, Denver, 1986, and Wright State University, Dayton, OH, 1986; Recitalist at Chateau de la Gesse in 1985, at Cheltenham International Festival of Music in 1986 and soloist for Denver Symphony in 1986; US State Department recital tour of Yugoslavia and soloist for Metropolitan Orchestra at Carnegie Hall in 1986; Recitalist at Merkin Hall, NYC with 3 recitals of the music of Ravel, Debussy, Fauré and Poulence with American premiere each evening, 1987. Recordings: 3 Movements of Petrouchka by Stravinsky; 2 Mozart Piano Concerti, K482 and K414; Preludes Book 1 and 2 by Debussy. Current Management: Thea Dispeker, NYC, USA. Address: 20990 Valley Green Dr, Apt 700, Cupertino, CA 95014-1846, USA.

RUTTER Claire, b. 1972, South Shields, County Durham, England. Singer (Soprano). Education: Studied at the Guildhall School of Music and the National Opera Studio. Career: Sang in Birtwistle's Yan Tan Tethera for Opera Factory (1986) and Donna Anna for British Youth Opera; Violetta for Welsh National Opera (1994) and Scottish Opera from 1995, as Mozart's Countess, Terinka in The Jacobin, and Violetta; Other roles include Tatiana, Mimi and Alice Ford; Further appearances at the Buxton and Chester Festivals, at the Wigmore Hall and in South America and South Africa; Sang Mozaart's Elettra for Scottish Opera, 1996. Address: c/o Harold Holt Ltd, 31 Sinclair Road, London W14, England.

RUTTER John, b. 24 Sept 1945, London, England. Composer; Conductor. m. Joanne Redden, 1980, 2 sons, 1 daughter. Education: MA, MusB, Clare College, Cambridge. Career: Director of Music, Clare College, Cambridge, 1975-79; Lecturer, Open University, 1975-88; Honorary Fellow, Westminster Choir College, Princeton, 1980; Founder, Director, Cambridge Singers. Compositions include: The Falcon, 1969; Gloria, 1974; The Piper of Hamelin, 1980; Requiem, 1985; Magnificat, 1990; Many carols, anthems and songs; Edited and recorded original version of Fauré's Requiem, 1984. Recordings include: Many including his own Requiem with Cambridge Singers and City of London Sinfonia. Address: c/o Oxford University Press, Walton Street, Oxford OX2 6DP, England.

RUUD Ole Kristian, b. 2 Oct 1958, Oslo, Norway. Conductor. m. Karen Johnstad Ruud, 26 Mar 1988, 2 sons. Education: Norwegian Academy of Music, 1979-83; Sibelius Academy, 1984-85. Debut: Radio Concert, Oslo Philharmonic Orchestra, 1985. Career: Chief Conductor, North Norwegian Chamber Orchestra, 1986-89; Chief Conductor, Trondheim Symphony Orchestra, 1987-95, Norrkoping Symphony Orchestra, 1996-; Touring Concerts with Trondheim Symphony Orchestra, Germany, 1988, 1995, Bergen Philharmonic, Germany, 1991, Jeunesse Musicale Orchestra, Europe, 1993, Berlin, 1996, Stockholm Chamber Orchestra, Japan, 1995. Recordings: Norwegian Composers: Oslo Philharmonic, Trondheim Symphony, Stavanger Symphony Orchestra; International Composers: Swedish Radio Symphony Orchestra, Norrkoping Symphony Orchestra, Bergen Philharmonic, Trondheim Symphony. Honours: E Grieg Prize, 1992; Norwegian Newspaper Best Review Prize, 1993; Lindeman Prize, 1994; Johan Halvorsen Prize, 1996. Hobbies: Fishing; Cooking. Current Management: Van Walsum Management. Address: 4 Addison Bridge Place, London W14 8XP, England.

RUUTUNEN Esa, b. 1949, Finland. Baritone. Education: Studied at the Sibelius Academy, Helsinki, 1974-80. Career: Vicar at the Temppelaukio Church at Helsinki, 1975-84; Appearances in Lieder recitals and concerts of sacred music throughout Scandinavia and Northern Europe and in the USA; Opera engagements at Helsinki and Savonlinna as Monterone, Escamillo, Pizarro, Enrico in Lucia di Lammermoor, Klingsor and Valentin; Appeared as guest at Essen in Merikanto's Juha and at Los Angeles in 1992 in the premiere of Sallinen's Kullervo; Sang Alberich in Das Rheingold at Helsinki, 1996. Address: Finnish National Opera, Bulevardi 23-27, SF-00180 Helsinki, Finland.

RUZICKA Peter, b. 3 July 1948, Dusseldorf, Germany. Composer; Intendant. Education: Piano, Oboe and Composition, Hamburg Conservatory, 1963-68; PhD, 1977, Munich and Berlin. Career: Intendant, Berlin Radio Symphony Orchestra, 1979-87; Fellow, Bavarian Academy of Fine Arts, Munich, 1985; Free Academy of Arts, Hamburg, 1987. Compositions: Esta Noche, for the Victims of the Vietnam War, 1967; Antifone-Strofe for 25 Strings and Percussion, 1970; Elis, for Mezzo, Oboe and Orchestra, 1970; Sonata for Solo Cello, 1970; 3 String Quartets, 1970, 1970, 1992; Metastrophe for 87 Instrumentalists, 1971; Sinfonia for 25 Strings, 16 Vocalists and Percussions, 1971; Outside-Inside, Music Theatre, 1972; In Processo di Tempo for 26 Instrumentalists and Cello, 1972; Versuch, 7 Pieces for Strings, 1974; Stress for 8 Percussion Groups, 1972; Einblendungen for Orchestra, 1973-77; Feed Back for 4 Orchestral Groups, 1974; Torso for Orchestra, 1974; Emanazione Variations for Flute and 4 Orchestral Groups, 1975; Zeit for Organ, 1975; Stille for Cello, 1976; Abbruche for Orchestra, 1977; Gestalt and Abbruch for Voices, 1979; Impuls zum Weitersprechen for Viola and Orchestra, 1981; Satyagraha for Orchestra, 1985; ....der die Gesange zerschlug for Baritone and Ensemble, 1985; Metamorphosen uber ein Klangfeld von Joseph Haydn, for Orchestra, 1990; Vier Gesange nach Fragmenten von Nietzsche, for Mezzo and Piano, 1992; Klangschatten for String Quartet, 1992; Tallis, for Orchestra, 1993; ...Inseln, randlos, for Violin, Chamber Orchestra and Chorus, 1994; Music Premiered at Gottingen, Stuttgart, Berlin, Hilversum, Hamburg, Munich, Vienna & Savonlinna. Address: Alphonsstrasse 17, D-22043 Hamburg, Germany.

RUZICKA Rudolf, b. 25 Apr 1941, Brno, Czechoslovakia. Composer; Teacher. m. Bozena Ruzickova, 7 July 1967, 2 sons. Education: Composition studies, Brno Conservatory and Janácek Academy of Performing Arts. Career: Composer; Professor of Composition and Music Theory, Brno and Kromeriz Conservatories, Brno State University, Janácek Academy. Compositions: Over 100 instrumental, chamber, vocal, electroacoustic and computer compositions, including 3 cantatas, 5 symphonies, 6 concertos, 10 suites. Recordings: Approximately 60 compositions recorded for CD, gramophone, radio, TV. Publication: Use of Computers in Creating Works of Art. Contributions to: Numerous articles on music theory of computer composition and automatic notation, to various publications. Honours: Numerous honours, prizes and awards for electroacoustic and computer music. Hobbies: Theoretical research and practical composition of contemporary serious music; Electroacoustic music; Computer music and automatic note printing. Address: Serikova 32, 637 00 Brno, Czech Republic.

RUZICKOVA Zuzana, b. 14 Jan 1928, Plzen, Czechoslovakia. Harpsichordist. m. Viktor Kalabis. Education: Prague Academy of Music. Career: Has appeared widely in Europe from 1956; Co-founder with Vaclav Neumann of the Prague Chamber Soloists: performances 1962-67; Formed duo with violinist Josef Suk, 1963; Teacher at Prague Academy from 1962; Chairman International Competitions, Prague Spring Festival. Recordings: Complete keyboard works of JS Bach; Concertos by Benda; CD: Sonatas D Scarlatti, B Martinu; Concert pour Clavecin, Bach and his Predecessors; JS Bach: Concerti. Memberships: Member Directories, Neue Bachgesellshaft Leipzig; Honorary Member for Life, British National Early Music Association. Honours: Winner, Munich International Competition, 1956; Grand Prix du Disque, 1961; Supraphon Grand Prix, 1968, 1972; Artist of Merit, 1968; State Prize Czechoslovak Republic, 1970; National Artist, 1989.

RYABCHIKOV Victor, b. 13 Feb 1954, Tashkent, Uzbekistani. Pianist. m. Golovina Irina, 31 Oct 1987, 1 daughter. Education: State Music Conservatory, Tashkent, 1972-79; Moscow Conservatory, 1977-79. Career: Concert as soloist and with orchestra in various cities across Russia from 1979 and in France, Switzerland, Sweden, Holland, England from 1993; Numerous appearances on TV and radio in Russia, Sweden and Switzerland; Soloist by special request at Philips Electrics celebration of Mr Philips' 90th birthday, 1993; Artistic Director, Glinka Festival, Moscow, 1997; Vice-president, first international Glinka Society. Recordings: CD, Russian Piano Music of XIX Century, 1994; Several recordings for radio. Honours: Winner, 5th Republic Competition of Piano and Special Prize, Union of Composers, Russia, 1976; Best Pianist of the Year, APN, Moscow, 1992. Hobbies: Nature; Books; Museums. Address: Barvikha 21-7, Odinzovski R-N, Moscow 143083, Russia.

RYABETS Oleg, b. 28 June 1967, Kiev, Ukraine. Singer - Male Soprano. Education: Kiev State Conservatory and Moscow State Academy of Music, 1988-94, with Professors K Radchenko and Z Dolukhanova. Debut: Soprano part in A Shnitke's Symphony No 2 with Great Symphony Orchestra conducted by G Rozhdestvensky, Bolshoi Moscow State Conservatory Hall, 1990. Career: Professional stage performer, 1977-; Soloist, State Boys Choir and State Chapel Choir of Kiev, performing in European countries, 1977-90; Sang with Vivaldi State Chamber Orchestra in 17-19th century music programme in Russian and Italian tours, 1990-93; Soprano role in Pergolesi's Stabat Mater, Moscow and Prague, 1992-93; Amour in Gluck's Orpheus, Hermitage Theatre, St Petersburg, 1993; Concerts and recitals in Moscow and St Petersburg, including special recital dedicated to 1st and only official visit to Russia by Queen Elizabeth II, Tchaikovsky Great Concert Hall, Moscow, 17 Oct 1994; Performed in Petersbvrg's Seasons Music Festival and Ludwigsburg Festival conducted by W Gönnenwein, sang in recital at French Embassy, Vienna, and appeared as Count Myshkin in world premiere of V Kobekin's NFB at Sacro Art Festival, Loccum and Ludwigsburg, Germany, 1995; Sang in Gala dedicated to 75th birthday of HRH The Duke of Edinburgh, Britten Theatre, London, 1996; Lenin in world premiere of The Naked Revolution by D Soldier, New York, 1997; Aminta in Galuppi's Il Re Pastore, Italy, 1998. Recordings: Solo Soprano, Stabat Mater by G Pergolesi, 1993; Italian music of 17-18th centuries, Mr Soprano sings Bel Canto, 1996; King Solomon's Song, cantata composed for O Ryabets by V Kobekin. Honour: Audio tape with his voice preserved next to only recorded castrato singer Sgnr A Mareschi in British National Sound Archives, London, 1996-. Address: c/o Rare Voce Ltd, 26-6 Novy Arbat Street, Moscow 121000, Russia.

RYAN Barry, b. Australia. Singer (Tenor). Education: Graduated with Honours, the NSW Conservatorium Opera School 1981. Career: Principal tenor with Cologne Opera 1988-92; Australian Opera debut 1993, as David in die Meistersinger (returns 1998 as Laca in Jenufa, under Charles Mackerras); Season 1996-97 with Royal Opera debut, in Peter Grimes, as Armand in Henze's Boulevard Solitude at Basle and Froh in Das Rheingold at La Scala; Erik in Der fliegende Holländer for Australian Opera and as return to Covent Garden, in Elektra and Katya Kabanova; Concerts include 1988 Australian Bicentennial at Drury Lane, London, the Mozart Requiem in Bergen, Beethoven's Ninth in Tokyo and Hindemith's Cardillac at the Amsterdam Concertgebouw (1997); Further appearances at the Opéra-Comique and the Komische Oper, Berlin. Honours include: Awards at the Shell Aria, Metropolitan Opera Auditions and Marten Bequest for Singing. Address: c/o Lies Askonas Ltd, 6 Henrietta St, London WC2E 8LA, England.

RYBACH Ladislaus, b. 1 April 1935, Sopron, Hungary. Conductor. m. Ruth Kraehenbeuhl, 1 son. Education: Doctor, Natural Sciences, ETH, Zurich, Switzerland; Musical Studies with P Hindemith, University of Zurich; Conducting Classes, Zurich Conservatory & Music Academy, Basel; Masterclasses with R Kubelik and I Markevitch. Debut: Besancon Festival, France, 1965. Career: Regular Conducting of the University Choir, Zurich and Orchesterverein, Ibid. Honours: 1st Prize, International Competition for Young Conductors, Besancon, France, 1964. Membership: Association of Swiss Musicians. Address: Chrummwisstr 62, 8700 Kusnacht, Switzerland.

RYBAR Peter, b. 29 Aug 1913, Vienna, Austria. Violinist; Music Professor. m. Marcelle Daeppen, 3 Apr 1952. Education: Prague Conservatoire and with Carl Flesch in Paris and London. Career: Toured Europe as soloist, 1934-38; Concertmaster, Winterthur Symphony Orchestra; Teacher at Winterthur Conservatoire, and leader of the Winterthur Quartet, 1938-66; First Concertmaster of Orchestra Suisse Romande; Professor, Masterclass, Geneva Conservatoire, 1971-80; Many appearances as soloist at festivals in Salzburg, Montreux, Konstanz, Schaffhausen, Lucerne and Prague and recital appearances with his wife as pianist; Lecturer in Switzerland and abroad, and Judge at international competitions. Recordings: Numerous. Honours: Art Prize, Ernst Foundation; Honorary Prize, Town of Winterthur. Address: Via Stazione 57, CH-6987 Caslano, Switzerland.

RYDL Kurt, b. 8 Oct 1947, Vienna, Austria. Bass Singer. Education: Studied in Vienna and Moscow. Debut: Stuttgart in 1973 as Daland in Der fliegende Holländer. Career: Guest appearances in Venice, Barcelona and Lisbon; Sang at Bayreuth Festival in 1975; Vienna Staatsoper from 1976 as Rocco in Fidelio, Zaccaria in Nabucco, Procida in Vêpres Siciliennes, Mephistopheles in Faust, King Philip in Don Carlos, Kecal in The Bartered Bride, the Landgrave in Tannhäuser and Marke in Tristan und Isolde; Salzburg Festival in 1985 in Il Ritorno d'Ulisse by Henze/Monteverdi; Tour of Japan with Vienna Staatsoper in 1986; Sang Baron Ochs in Turin and at Monte Carlo and Florence in 1987 and 1989; Salzburg Festival, 1987-89 as Mozart's Osmin, and La Scala Milan in 1990 as Rocco; Sang Pimen at Barcelona and Rocco at the 1990 Salzburg Festival; Season 1991-92 as Titurel at La Scala, Verdi's Zaccaria at the Vienna Volksoper, Ramfis in Aida at Tel-Aviv, Padre Guardiano at Florence and the Grand Inquisitor at the Verona Arena; Sang Hagen in Götterdämmerung at Covent Garden, 1995; returned 1997, in Pfitzner's Palestrina. Recordings include: Salome; Opera scenes by Schubert; Alceste; Manon Lescaut. Address: c/o Staatsoper, Opernring 2, A-1010 Vienna, Austria.

RYHANEN Jaako, b. 2 Dec 1946, Tampere, Finland. Singer. Education: Studied in Helsinki. Career: Member of the Finnish National Opera at Helsinki from 1974; Appearances at the Savonlinna Festival and in Moscow and New York with the Helsinki Company; Further engagements in Madrid, Hamburg, Berlin, Munich, Zurich and Stuttgart; Paris Opéra in 1987 as Daland and Monte Carlo in 1988; Season 1991 as Daland at Munich, Titurel in Parsifal at Tampere and Mozart's Bartolo at Helsinki; Sang Daland at Santiago in 1992, and Sarastro at the Savonlinna Festival; Sang Fiesco in the original version of Simon Boccanegra at Covent Garden, 1997. Concerts with the Israel Philharmonic and throughout Scandinavia. Address: Finnish National Opera, Bulevardi 23-27, SF-00180 Helsinki 18, Finland.

RYPDAL Terje, b. 23 Aug 1947, Oslo, Norway. Composer; Musician. m. Elin Kristin Rypdal, 15 Jun 1988, 3 s, 1 d. Education: Grunnfag in Music at University of Oslo; Studied composition with Finn Mortensen. Career: Piano from age of 6 to 12; Electric guitar with The Vanguards, 1962-67, The Dream, 1967-69; Jan Garbarek Quartet, 1969-71; Since 1971 leader of own groups. Compositions: 6 Symphonies; 2 Operas. Recordings include: Q.E.D. Undisonus; I Mountains Could Sing, 1995; Several records on ECM. Honours: Deutscher Scallplattenpreis. Membership: Norwegian Composers Guild. Hobby: Icelandic Horses. Address: 6380 Tresfjord, Norway.

RYSANEK Leonie, b. 14 November 1926, Vienna, Austria. Singer (Soprano). m. (1) Richard Grossmann. m. (2) E L Gaussmann. Education: Vienna Conservatory with Alfred Jerger and Richard Grossmann. Debut: Innsbruck 1949, as Agathe in Der Freischütz. Career: Saarbrucken, 1950-52; Bayreuth Festival 1951-68, as Sieglinde, Elsa, Senta and Elisabeth; Bavarian State Opera from 1952; Covent Garden debut 1953, as Danae in the first British production of Strauss's Die Liebe der Danae: returned to London until 1963; Guest appearances in Paris, Berlin and Salzburg; US debut San Francisco 1956, as Senta: returned as Lady Macbeth, Turandot and the Empress in Die Frau ohne Schatten; Metropolitan Opera from 1959, as Lady Macbeth, Chrysothemis in Elektra, the Marshcallin, Tosca, Fidelio, Salome, Aida, Elisabeth de Valois and Abigaille in Nabucco; Gala concert at the Met 1984; Paris Opéra 1972, as the Empress; Orange Festival 1974, as Salome; Bayreuth 1982, as Kundry in Parsifal; Tour of Japan 1984, with the Hamburg Staatsoper; Metropolitan Opera 1986, as Ortrud in Lohengrin; Other roles include the Kostelnicka in Jenufa, Cherubini's Médée and the title role in Die Aegyptische Helena by Strauss; Paris Opera and Metropolitan, New York 1988, 1991 as the Kostelnicka; Sang in Elektra at Geneva 1990; Metropolitan, 1992; Herodias in Salome at the Deutsche Oper Berlin, 1990; Season 1992 as Clytemnestra at the Met and the Countess in The Queen of Spades at Barcelona; Last Met appearance as the Countess, 1996; Clytemnestra at Rio di Janiero, 1996. Recordings: Der fliegende Holländer; Ariadne auf Naxos; Elektra; Lohengrin; Otello; Die Walküre; Fidelio; Die Frau ohne Schatten; Video of Elektra (title role); Labels include Columbia, RCA, Deutsche Grammophon, Philips and Melodram. Address: Brahuisplatz 7/II/10a, A-1040 Wien, Austria.

RYSANEK Lotte, b. 18 Mar 1928, Vienna, Austria. Soprano. Education: Vienna Conservatory with Richard Grossman. Debut: Klagenfurt in 1950 as Massenet's Manon. Career: Member of the Vienna Staatsoper as Marzelline in Fidelio, Marguerite in Faust, Pamina, Fiordiligi, Marenka in The Bartered Bride and Donna Elvira, and parts in operas by Wagner and Verdi; Guest appearances at the Vienna Volksoper in Graz, Berlin, Dusseldorf and Hamburg; Sang at Bayreuth in 1958; Well known in operetta and as a concert singer. Recordings include: Roles in operetta. Address: c/o Staatsoper, Opernring 2, A-1010 Vienna, Austria.

RYSSOV Michail, b. 25 Aug 1955, Crimea, Russia. Singer (Bass). Career: Principal Bass at the Opera in Minsk, 1983-87, in Don Giovanni, Don Carlos, Aida, La Forza del Destino, Macbeth, Nabucco, I Vespri Siciliani, Faust, Eugene Onegin, Boris Godunov, Mefistofele; Treviso, 1989, as the Commendatore in Don Giovanni; Has recently sung Ramfis at the Deutsche Oper Berlin and at the Verona Arena; Philip II at Deutsche Oper am Rhein, Dusseldorf; Prince Gremin and The Inquisitor in Don Carlos, at La Fenice, Venice; Sang Ramfis in Aida at the 1996 Verona Arena. Honours include: Winner, Glinka Competition, 1984; International Verviers Competition, Belgium, 1987; International Ettore Bastianini Competition, Siena, 1988; International New Voice Competition in Pavia and The Toti dal Monte Competition in Treviso, 1989. Address: c/o Athole Still International Management Ltd, Foresters Hall, 25-27 Westow Street, London, SE19 3RY, England.

RZEWSKI Frederic Anthony, b. 13 Apr 1938, Westfield, MA, USA. Composer; Pianist. m. Nicole Abbeloss, 3 children. Education: BA, Harvard University, 1958, study with Thompson and Piston; MFA, Princeton University, 1960, study with Sessions and Babbitt; Italy, 1960-61 with Dallapiccola. Career: Pianist and teacher in Europe from 1962; Played in the premieres of Stockhausen's Klavierstuck X and Plus Minus; Co-founded electronic ensemble, Musica Electronica Viva, Rome, 1966; Returned to New York in 1971; Professor of Composition at the Royal Conservatory, Liege from 1977; Visiting Professor of Composition at Yale University in 1984. Compositions: For Violin, 1962; Composition for 2, 1964; Nature Morte for Instruments and Percussion, 1965; Zoologischer Garten, 1965; Spacecraft, 1967; Impersonation, audiodrama, 1967; Requiem, 1968; Symphony, 1968; Last Judgement for Trombone, 1969; Falling Music for Piano and Tape, 1971; Coming Together for Speaker and Instruments, 1972; Piano Variations On The Song No Place To Go But Around, 1974; The People United Will Never Be Defeated, 36 variations for Piano, 1975; 4 Piano Pieces, 1977; Satyrica for Jazz Band, 1983; Una Breve Storia D'Estate for 3 Flutes and Small Orchestra; A Machine for 2 Pianos, 1984; The Invincible

Persian Army for Low Voice and Prepared Piano, 1984. Recordings: As pianist, numerous items of contemporary music. Address: c/o ASCAP, ASCAP Building, One Lincoln Plaza, New York, NY 10023, USA.

S

SAARI Jouko (Erik Sakari), b. 23 Nov 1944, Stockholm, Sweden. Conductor; Musical Director. m. Raija Syvänen, 1 son, 1 daughter. Education: Sibelius Academy, 1962-68; Music Science, Helsinki University, 1965-67; Organist degree, 1966; Music Education degree, 1966; Conservatory degree in Trumpet, 1966; Conducting, Indiana University, USA, 1969-70; Music Director degree, 1966; Church Music Division degree, 1968; Conducting Diploma, 1968. Career: Musical Director, Helsinki Opera Society, 1971; Conductor, Tampere City Orchestra, 1973-74; Chorus Master, 1974-75, Conductor and Coach, 1976-78, National Opera Finland; Musical Director, Lahti Symphony Orchestra, 1978-84; Conductor, Gothenburg Opera House, Stora Teatern, 1984-85, Guest Conductor, 1985-88; Broadcast recordings with Finnish Radio Symphony Orchestra, 1971, 1973-75 and with Swedish Radio Symphony Orchestra, 1974, 1976-77; Concerts in USA, Canada, Germany, Hungary, Denmark, Sweden and Finland; Guest Conductor, Hämeenlinna Symphony Orchestra, 1989-93; Appearances on Swedish Radio and on Finnish Radio and Television; Freelance Conductor and Organist. Compositions: For Brass Band recorded with Töölö Brass Band. Hobbies: Hunting; Motor Sport. Address: Etelatie 1 D, 15610 Lahti, Finland.

SAARIAHO Kaija, b. 14 Oct 1952, Helsinki, Finland. Composer. m. Jean-Baptiste Barriere, 26 May 1984, 1 son, 1 daughter. Education: Studied at the Sibelius Academy in Helsinki and with Brian Ferneyhough and Klaus Huber at the Freiburg Hochschule für Musik. Career: Freelance Composer of orchestral and instrumental music with live electronics and computers; Music performed in most major festivals, including Salzburg Festival, 1996. Compositions: Verbledungen, 1984; Lichtbogen, 1986; Du Cristal...à la fumée, 1988-90; Graalthéatre, 1994; Château de l'âme, 1995. Recordings: for various labels. Honours include: Prix Italia, 1989; Prix Art Electronica, 1989; Suomi Prize, 1995; Chevalier de l'ordre des Arts et des Lettres, 1997. Membership: Finnish Composers Society. Address: 8 rue Bernard de Claivaux, 75003 Paris, France.

SAARINEN Eeva-Liisa, b. 1951, Finland. Mezzo-Soprano. Education: Studied at the Sibelius Academy, Helsinki, from 1972. Career: Sang throughout Northern Europe from 1981 in concerts and recitals; Stage debut at Helsinki in 1983 as Cherubino; Further roles with the Finnish National Opera have been Rosina, Cenerentola, the Composer in Ariadne auf Naxos, Marja in Merikanto's Juha and Hansel; Has sung in the premieres of Sallinen's The King Goes Forth to France at Savonlinna in 1984 and Kullervo at Los Angeles in 1992; Fricka in Das Rheingold at Helsinki, 1996. Recordings include: Kullervo Symphony by Sibelius. Address: c/o Finnish National Opera, Bulevardi 23-27, SF-00180 Helsinki, Finland.

SAARMAN Risto, b. 25 Jan 1956, Jyvaskyla, Finland. Singer (Tenor).Education: Studied at the Sibelius Academy in Helsinki, graduated 1983. Career: Finnish National Opera from 1984, at first as M Triquet in Eugene Onegin; Beppe; Borsa in Rigoletto; Don Curzio; Later sang: Tamino, Don Ottavio, Ferrando, Belmonte, Almaviva, Lensky and Albert Herring; Savonlinna Festival and Opéra de Lyon, 1987, as Tamino and Belmonte; Aix-en-Provence, 1990, as Belmonte and Almaviva; Sang Jacquino at the 1992 Savonlinna Festival; Concert engagements in the St John and St Matthew Passions; Masses by Haydn, Handel, Mozart and Beethoven; L'Enfance du Christ by Berlioz and Mendelssohn's Second Symphony; Lieder repertoire includes: Dichterliebe; Die schöne Müllerin; Songs by Strauss. Address: c/o Athole Still International Management Ltd, Foresters Hall, 25-27 Westow Street, London, SE19 3RY, England.

SABBATINI Giuseppe, b. 11 May 1957, Rome, Italy. Singer (Tenor). Education: Studied Double Bass at the Santa Cecilia Conservatory, Rome; Private study in Singing. Debut: As Opera Singer, Edgardo in Lucia di Lammermoor at Spoleto, 1987. Career: Played double bass in various Italian orchestras; Following opera debut, has sung in Faust, La Bohème, Werther, Massenet's Manon, Linda di Chamounix, Der Rosenkavalier, La Traviata, Rigoletto, I Puritani, L'elisir d'amore, Fra Diavolo, Les Pêcheurs de Perles, Eugene Onegin, Idomeneo, Maria Stuarda, Les Contes d'Hoffmann, La Favorita, Falstaff; Performances at main theatres such as Teatro alla Scala, Milan, Covent Garden, London, Vienna Staatsoper, Opéra-Bastille, Paris, Chicago Lyric Opera, Suntory Hall, Tokyo, Carnegie Hall, New York City, Hamburg Staatsoper; Sang in Massenet's Thais at Nice, 1997; Engaged as Arnold in Guillaume Tell at the Vienna Staatsoper, 1998; Concert repertoire includes: Donizetti's Requiem, Cologne, 1988, Stuttgart, 1993; Rossini's Stabat Mater, Rome, 1991, Bologna, 1992; La Damnation de Faust, Florence, 1995. Recordings include: La maga Circe; Gala Opera Concert - l'arte del belcanto, Mozart Gala - Suntory Hall, Tokyo - Simon Boccanegra; Le maschere; La Bohème; Don Giovanni; Canzone sacre; Messe Solennelle; Recital. Current Management: Stage Door SRL. Address: c/o Stage Door SRL, Via Scaglia Est 134, 41100 Modena, Italy.

SABIN Nigel, b. 25 November 1959, England (Resident in Australia from 1974). Composer; Clarinettist. Education: BMus hons, University of Adelaide; Manhattan School of Music, 1992, with David Del Tredici; Study with Richard Meale in Australia. Career: Musician-in-Residence, University of Queensland, 1988-95. Compositions: Job's Lament for Clarinet, 1984; Inner-City Counter-Points, for Clarinet, Viola, Cello and Piano, 1989; Four Studies for Flute, Clarinet, Violin and Guitar, 1990; Points of Departure for Violin, Viola, Piano and Clarinet, 1991; Time and Motion Studies: Postcards From France for Clarinet and Viola, 1991; Voyages to Arcadia for Small Orchestra, 1992; Terra Australia for Soprano & Ensemble, 1992; Another Look At Autumn, for Piano, 1993; Faint Qualm for Piano, 1993; Love Songs for Orchestra, 1993; Angel's Flight for Small Orchestra, 1994. Honours include: ASME Young Composers Award, 1981, 1984. Address: c/o APRA, 1A Eden Street, Corws Nest, NSW 2065, Australia.

SACCA Roberto, b. 12 Sep 1961, Sendehorst, Westfalen, Germany. Singer (Tenor). Education: Studied at Musikhochschule of Stuttgart and Karlsruhe. Career: Sang in Germany from 1985 and in Israel, Switzerland, France and England; Concert tour of Brazil in 1987 with appearances at Teatro Municipal Rio de Janeiro; Stadttheater Wurzburg, 1987-88, Wiesbaden from 1988; Sang at the Fermo Festival as Leandro in a 1990 revival of Paisiello's Le Due Contese; Debut at La Scala, Milan with Henze's Das Verratene Meer, 1990; Brussels and Salzburg Festival in Ulisse by Dallapiccola, 1993 and Vienna, Musikvereinsaal, 1993; Member of Zurich Opera, 1994-97; In 1994 sang Le Pêcheur in Le Rossignol at Salzburg Festival and in Mozart's Der Schauspiel direktor under Harnoncourt; Season 1994-95 as Rinuccio in Puccini's Gianni Schicchi, Vienna, title role of Orfeo, Alessandro in Mozart's Il Re Pastore, Don Ramiro in a new production of La Cenerentola, Don Ottavio in Don Giovanni and in Il Barbiere di Siviglia; Sang in Handel's Alcina at the 1997 Vienna Festival. Recordings: Handel's Messiah; Solo Recital Album; Capriccio with Vienna Philharmonic; Meistersinger von Nürnberg; Il Re Pastore. Contributions to: Openwelt, Orpheus. Honours: Winner, Opera Prize in Geneva, Switzerland, 1989. Current Management: Mag Kurt-Walther Schober. Address: c/o Mag Kurt-Walther Schober, Opernring 8-13, A-1010 Vienna, Austria.

SACCO P Peter, b. 25 Oct 1928, Albion, NY, USA. Composer; Tenor. Education: Pupil of Vivian Major and William Willett at Fredonia State University; Eastman School of Music, 1953-58 with Barlow, Rogers and Hanson; MM, 1954, DMus, 1958. Career: Studied composition with Wolfgang Niederste-Schee in Frankfurt, 1950-52; Clarinettist with 4th Division Infantry Band; Music Faculty of San Francisco State University, 1959-80; Visiting Professor at University of Hawaii, 1970-71; Concert Tenor. Compositions: Dramatic: Jesu, oratorio, 1956, Midsummer Night's Dream Night, oratorio, 1961, Mr Vinegar, chamber opera, 1967, Solomon, oratorio, 1976; Orchestral: Symphony No 1, 1955, No 2, The Symphony Of Thanksgiving, 1965-76, No 3, The Convocation Symphony, 1968, Piano Concerto, 1964, Four Sketches on Emerson Essays, 1963, 2 Piano Sonatas, 1951, 1965, Violin Concerto, 1969-74, Moab Illuminations, for Solo Piano, 1972, 5 Songs for Mezzo-Soprano and Strings; Chamber: Clarinet Quintet, 1956, String Quartet, 1966, Variations On Schubert's An Die Musik for Piano 4-Hands, 1981; 60 Solo songs, 25 choruses, 4 cantatas and 11 anthems.

SACCOMANI Lorenzo, b. 9 Jun 1938, Milan, Italy. Baritone. Education: Studied in Milan with Vladimiro Badiali and Alfonso Siliotti. Debut: Avignon in 1964 as Silvio in Pagliacci. Career: Sang the Herald in Lohengrin at Venice then appeared in many Italian houses notably La Scala Milan in operas by Puccini, Gounod, Massenet and Verdi; London in 1972 in a concert performance of Caterina Cornaro by Donizetti; US debut at Dallas in 1972 as Henry Ashton in Lucia di Lammermoor; Sang at Verona Arena in 1983, and Geneva in 1985 as Guy de Montfort in Les Vêpres Siciliennes; Further appearances in Frankfurt, New York, Chicago and Buenos Aires; Other roles include Escamillo, Zurga in Les Pêcheurs de Perles and Verdi's Nabucco, Germont, Ezio in Attila, Amonasro, Rigoletto, Luna and Francesco in I Masnadieri. Recordings include: Caterina Cornaro; Pagliacci.

SACHER Paul, b. 28 Apr 1906, Basle, Switzerland. Conductor; Music Educator. m. Maja Stehlin, 1934. Education: Conducting with Weingartner, Basle Conservatory; Musicology with Karl Nef, Basle University. Career: Founded Basle Chamber Orchestra, 1926; Commissioned many composers to write for him, such as Bartók, Hindemith, Honegger, Martin, Strauss, Stravinsky, Tippett, Britten, Henze, Birtwistle and Carter; Founded Schola Cantorum Basiliensis, 1933, for research into early music; Conducted Collegium Musicum of Zurich from 1941; Appeared regularly at Lucerne, Aix-en-Provence and Edinburgh Festivals; Glyndebourne, 1954-63, The Rake's Progress, Die Entführung and Die Zauberflöte; Formed Musikakademie der Stadt Basel, 1954, and was Principal until 1969; Conducted Bartok's 50th anniversary concert at Edinburgh, 1995. Recordings include: Brandenburg Concertos, Bach Concerto for Violin and Oboe and Violin Concerto in A minor; Mozart Cassations and Piano Concertos; Henze Double Concerto and Sonata for Strings; Moret Double Concerto for Violin, Cello and Orchestra; Concerto for cello (Rostropovitch); Hymnes de Silence; Stravinsky Concerto in D for Violin and Orchestra; Honegger Symphony No 3, Chant de Joie; Horace Victorieux. Publications: Book on Adolf Hamm; Articles in reports of Basel Chamber Orchestra. Honours: Numerous including: Honorary President, Association of Swiss Musicians, 1956; Mozart Medal, Salzburg, 1956; Honorary Member: International Society of Contemporary Music, 1971; Béla Bartók Memorial Medal, Hungary, 1981; Gold Medal for Cultural Merit, Kanton Zürich, 1981; Honorary Member, Hungarian Kodaly Society, 1990, Royal Philharmonic Society, London, 1991; Honorary Doctorates, several universities including University of Oxford, 1988; Eastman School of Music, University of Rochester, 1990; Crystal Crown Award, Birmingham Festival of Art, Alabama, 1993. Memberships: Association of Swiss Composers, Managing Committee 1931, Director 1946-55; President, Swiss Section, International Society for the Promotion of Contemporary Music, 1935-46. Hobbies: Trees; Gardening; Books. Address: Schöenberg, CH 4133 Pratteln BL, Switzerland.

SACHS (Stewart) Harvey, b. 8 June 1946, Cleveland, Ohio, USA, (Canadian citizen, 1973). Writer. m. Barbara Gogolick, 30 Sept 1967, sep, 1 son. Education: Studied Piano and Theory, Cleveland Institute of Music, 1960-64; Oberlin College Conservatory, Ohio, 1964-65; Mannes College of Music, New York, 1965-66; Conductors' Workshop, University of Toronto, 1968-71. Career: Conducting, Peterborough Symphony Orchestra, Canada, 1972-75; Guest Conductor, Pomeriggi Musicali, Milan, Italy, 1977; Angelicum, Milan, 1977; Canadian Opera Touring Company, 1979; CBC Vancouver Chamber Orchestra, 1982, 1984; Orchestre Symphonique de Québec, 1984; Toronto Chamber Players, 1984, 1985; Full-time Writer, 1985-. Publications: Toscanini, biography, 1978; Virtuoso, 1982; Music in Fascist Italy, 1987; Arturo Toscanini from 1915 to 1946: Art in the Shadow of Politics, exhibition catalogue, 1987; Reflections on Toscanini, 1991; Rubinstein: A Life, biography, 1996. Contributions to: The New Yorker; Times Literary Supplement; New York Times; Atlantic, USA; Corriere della Sera, Milan; La Stampa, Turin; Yale Review, USA; Grand Street, USA; Nouvel Observateur, Paris; Le Monde de la Musique, Paris; Neue Zeitschrift für Musik, Germany; The New Republic, USA; Southwest Review, USA; Antioch Review, USA; Amadeus, Italy; Nuova Rivista Musicale Italiana; Opera UK; Opera News, USA. Hobbies: Reading; Hiking; Travel. Current Management: Ned Leavitt Agency, 70 Wooster Street, New York, NY 10012, USA. Address: Loc Il Borro 11, 52020 San Giustino Valdarno, AR, Italy.

SACKMAN Nicholas, b. 1950, England. Composer. Education: Dulwich College, Nottingham University and Leeds University with Alexander Goehr. Career: Ensembles and Cadenzas performed in 1973 at the International Gaudaemus Week and the BBC Young Composers' Forum; A Pair of Wings for 3 Sopranos and Ensemble premiered at the 1974 ISCM Festival and Ellipsis for Piano and Ensemble premiered at Leeds Festival in 1976; Doubles for 2 Instrumental Groups and Flute Concerto commissioned by the BBC and String Quartet by the Barber Institute of Fine Arts, Birmingham; Alap for Orchestra premiered by the BBC Philharmonic Orchestra in 1983 and Hawthorn for Orchestra premiered at the 1993 London Proms. Compositions include: Simplicia, musical for schools, 1980; The World A Wonder Waking for Mezzo-Soprano and Ensemble, 1981; The Empress of Shoreditch, musical for schools, 1981; Holism for Viola and Cello, 1982; Time-Piece for Brass Quintet, 1982-83; Piano sonata, 1983-84; Corronach for Ensemble, 1985; Sonata for Trombone and Piano, 1986; Paraphrase for Wind, 1987; Flute Concerto, 1988-89; String Quartet No 2, 1990-91; Hawthorn for Orchestra, 1993, revised 1994; Address: c/o Schott and Co, 48 Great Marlborough Street, London, W1V 2BN, England.

SADAI Yizhak, b. 13 May 1935, Sofia, Bulgaria. Composer; Theorist. Education: Tel-Aviv Academy of Music with Haubenstock-Ramati and Boscovich, 1951-56. Career: Joined music staff of the University of Tel-Aviv in 1966; Professor of Music at Tel-Aviv University; Guest Professor at University of Pennsylvania, Universite de Sciences Humaines de Strasbourg, New York University, Johan-Wolfgang Goethe Universität, Frankfurt, Université de Paris Sorbonne, Hochschule für Musik und Darstellende Kunst, Frankfurst, F Liszt Academy of Music, Budapest, Conservatoire National Superieur de Musique de Paris. Compositions include: Divertimento for Flute, Viola and Piano, 1954; Ricercar Symphonique, 1957, revised 1964; Impressions D'Un Chorale for Keyboard, 1960; Interpolations Variées for String Quartet and Keyboard, 1965; Aria De Capo for 6 Instruments and Tape, 1966; Song Into The Night for Tape, 1971; Anagram for Chamber Orchestra and Tape, 1973; La Prière Interrompue for Tape, 1975; Canti Fermi for Orchestra and Synclavier. Publications: Metodologia Shel Hateoria Hamusikalit (A

Methodical Approach to Music Theory), 1965; Harmony In Its Systemic and Phemonemological Aspects, 1980, and in International Review of the Aesthetics and Sociology of Music, 1986; Analyses Musicale: Par L'Oeil ou Par L'Oreille?, in Analuse Musicale, 1, Paris, 1985; Le Modèle Syntagmatique-Paradigmatique et son Application à L'Analyse des Fonctions Harmoniques, in Analyse Musicale, 2, Paris, 1986; Die Grundlagen einer Systemischen Theorie der Tonalen Musik, in Musiktheorie, 1990-92; Various articles. Address: c/o 83 Hayarden Street, Ramat-Gan 52 256, Israel.

SADIE Julie Anne, b. 26 Jan 1948, Eugene, Oregon, USA. Musician; Lecturer and Writer on Baroque Music. m. Stanley Sadie, 1978, 1 son, 1 daughter. Education: BA, BMus, University of Oregon, 1970; MA, Cornell University, 1973; PhD, Musicology, 1978; Trained as Cellist and Viola da Gambist, later took up Baroque Cello; MA in Museum and Gallery Management, City University, 1993. Career: Taught at the Eastman School of Music, Rochester, New York, 1974-76; Freelance Musician, Lecturer and Writer on Baroque Music; Lecturer in Baroque Music, King's College, University of London, 1982; Lecturer in Early Music, Royal College of Music, London, 1986-88; Editor, The Consort: European Journal of Early Music, 1993-; Administrator of The Handel House Trust Ltd, 1994-. Recordings: As member of orchestra, with the Academy of Ancient Music in Mozart's Paris Symphony and with the English Bach Festival in Rameau's Castor et Pollux. Publications: The Bass Viol in French Baroque Chamber Music, 1980; Companion to Baroque Music (editor), 1991; The New Grove Dictionary of Women Composers (edited with Rhian Samuel), 1994. Contributions to: Gramophone; The Musical Times; Early Music; Chelys; Proceedings of the Royal Musical Association. Honours: Ford Foundation Fellowship, 1970-74. Memberships: Royal Musical Association; American Musicological Society; Viola da Gamba Society of Great Britain; American Viola da Gamba Society; Museums Association; Musical Collections Forum. Hobby: Yoga. Address: 12 Lyndhurst Road, Hampstead, London NW3 5NL, England.

SADIE Stanley, b. 30 Oct 1930, Wembley, Middlesex, England. Writer on Music. m. (1) Adèle Bloom, 10 Dec 1953, deceased 1978, 2 sons, 1 daughter, (2) Julie Anne McCormack, 18 Jul 1978, 1 son, 1 daughter. Education: St Paul's School, London, 1942-48, Gonville and Caius College, Cambridge, 1950-56; BA 1953, MusB 1953, MA 1957 and PhD 1958. Career: Professor, Trinity College of Music, 1957-65; Writer and Broadcaster, 1957-; Music Critic for The Times, 1964-81; Editor, Musical Times, 1967-87; Musical Advisor, Granada TV programme Man and Music, 1984-. Publications: Handel, 1962; Mozart, 1965; Pan Book of Opera, with A Jacobs, 1964, 1985; Beethoven, 1967, and Handel, 1968, in The Great Composers; Handel Concertos, 1972; Editor, The New Grove Dictionary of Music and Musicians, 20 volumes, 1980; Mozart, 1980; Editor, The New Grove Dictionary of Musical Instruments, 3 volumes, 1984; The Cambridge Music Guide, with A Latham, 1985; Co-editor, The New Grove Dictionary of American Music, 4 volumes, 1986; Mozart Symphonies, 1986; Stanley Sadie's Brief Music Guide, 1987; Editor, The Grove Concise Dictionary of Music, 1988, History of Opera (New Grove Handbook), 1989, Man and Music, 8 volume social history, 1989-93; Co-editor, Performance Practice (New Grove Handbook), 2 volumes, 1990; Co-editor, Music Printing and Publishing (New Grove Handbook), 1990; Editor, New Grove Dictionary of Opera, 4 volumes, 1992; New Grove Book of Opera, 1996; Grove's Dictionary of Music, 7th edition, 24 volumes, 2000. Contributions to: Many reviews and articles in Musical Times, Opera, Gramophone. Honours: Honorary RAM, 1982; Honorary LittD, 1982; CBE, 1982; FRCM, 1994. Memberships: President, Royal Musical Association, 1989-94; Critics Circle; International Musicological Society, Resident, 1992. Hobbies: Watching Cricket; Boats; Family. Address: 12 Lyndhurst Road, London, NW3 5NL, England.

SADLO Milos, b. 13 Apr 1912, Prague, Czechoslovakia. Cellist. Education: Self-taught in cello, then studied with KP Sadlo at the Prague Conservatory, 1938-40 and with Casals in 1955. Career: Member of the Prague Quartet, 1931-33, Czech Trio, 1940-56 and 1970-, Suk Trio, 1957-60, and Prague Trio, 1966-73; Soloist with the Czech Philharmonic Orchestra, 1949-; Teacher at the Prague Academy, 1950-; Has given the premieres of works by Khachaturian and other Czech composers and the first modern performances of Dvořák's early A major Concerto and Haydn's C major Concerto discovered in 1962. Honour: Artist of Merit, 1962.

SAEDEN Erik, b. 3 Sept 1924, Vanersborg, Sweden. Singer (Baritone). m. Elisabeth Murgard. Education: Studied at the Royal College of Music, Stockholm and at the Royal Opera School; Private studies with Arne Sunnegardh, Martin Ohman and W Freund. Career: Royal Opera Stockholm from 1952 as Mozart's Figaro and Count, Wagner's Sachs, Beckmesser, Pogner, Dutchman and Wolfram, Verdi's Iago, Renato, Macbeth, Germont, Ford and Nabucco; Berg's Wozzeck, Stravinsky's Nick Shadow, Tchaikovsky's Eugene Onegin, Busoni's Faust and the title role in Dallapiccola's Il Prigionierlo; created leading roles in Blomdahl's Aniara, Werle's Drommen om Therese, Berwald's Drottningen av Golconda, Dallapiccola's Ulisse, Rosenberg's Hus med Dubbel Ingang and Ligeti's Le Grand Macabre; Guest Appearances at Bayreuth, Edinburgh, Covent Garden, Montreal; Also Savonlinna as Father Henrik in Singoalla; recorded the role in complete recording of Singoalla. Recordings include: The Speaker in Bergman film version of Die Zauberflöte; Swedish Romances, Schubert's Winterreise. Honours: Swedish Court Singer; Order Litteris et Artibus. Memberships: Stockholm Academy of Music. Hobbies: Sailing; Literature. Address: Höglidsv 17 A, 182 46 Enebyberg, Sweden.

SAGAEV Dimiter, b. 27 Feb 1915, Plovdiv, Bulgaria. Composer. Education: Studied with Stoianov and Vladigerov at the Bulgarian State Conservatory, Sofia, graduated in 1940. Career: Professor at the Bulgarian State Conservatory. Compositions include: Operas: Under The Yoke, 1965, Samouil, 1975; The Madara Horseman, ballet, 1960; In The Name Of Freedom, oratorio, 1969; The Shipka Epic, cantata poem, 1977; Orchestral and instrumental: 7 String Quartets, 1945-68; Youth Suite for Orchestra, 1952, Sofia, symphonic poem, 1954, Three Bulgarian Symphonic Dances, 1956, 2 Violin Concertos, 1963, 1964, Viola Concerto, 1963, Oboe Concerto, 1964, Symphony for Narrator, Singer, 2 Female Choruses and Orchestra, 1964, Bassoon Concerto, 1973, Flute Concerto, 1974, Trio for Flute, Violin and Piano, 1975, Symphony No 2, 1977, No 3, 1979, No 4, 1980, No 5, 1981, No 6, 1982 and No 7, 1987, Orpheus, ballet, 1978, Concerto for Wind Orchestra, 1981, Valdhorn Concerto, 1986, Oboe Concerto No 2, 1991, Piano Concerto, 1992; Flute and Chamber Concerto no 2; Tuba Concerto and Chamber Orchestra; Benkovski Oratorio; Two violins concerto; Guitar Classic Concerto; Violoncello Concerto no 1, no 2; Clarinet Concerto no 1, no2; Corns Concerto; Trumpet Concerto; Voldhorn Concerto; Piano Concerto no 2. Incidental music and songs. Publications: Books: Textbook of Wind Orchestration, 1957; How To Work with Student Brass Bands, 1962; A Practical Course of Symphony and Orchestration, 1966; Autobiography, 1968; The Orchestra: Palette of Bulgarian Composers, 1969; Biography of great Bulgarian director Sasha Popov, 1987; Monograph, Gallery of Bulgarian Composers, 2 parts. Membership: Union of Bulgarian Composers. Address: KV Istok, Bl 25, et 6, App 26, Sofia 1113, Bulgaria.

SAGEMULLER Dirk, b. 30 Nov 1950, Osnabruck, Germany. Baritone. Education: Studied in Hamburg with Gisela Litz. Career: Sang at the Hamburg Staatsoper from 1978 with further appearances at Munster, Kiel, Aachen and Teatro Verdi at Trieste; Sang at the Spoleto Festival as the Father in Hansel und Gretel; Other roles have included Mozart's Count, Guglielmo, Don Giovanni and Papageno, Rossini's Figaro and Dandini, Belcore, Valentin in Faust, Marcello, Demetrius and the Secretary in Henze's Junge Lord; Guest engagements at Geneva, Dusseldorf, Mannheim, Wiesbaden and Charleston; Concert showings in works by Bach, Handel, Mozart and Orff. Recordings include: Count Ceprano in Rigoletto.

SAGER Brian, b. 5 November 1964, Madison, USA. Composer. Education: BS, University of Wisconsin, madison, 1988; PhD, Stanford University, 1994; Helen Hay Whitney Fellow, Harvard University, 1994-97; Piano Training from Age of 3 years; Course Work in Composition, Music Theory, Psychoacoustics and Computer Music, Stanford University. Compositions: Symphony #1, 1994; Symphony #2, 1998; Three Impressions for Piano, 1998. Recordings: Senses Rising, 1998. Contributions to: International Journals. Honours: Fellowship, 1988; Postdoctoral Fellow, 1994-97; National Science Foundation Predoctoral Fellow, 1988-97. Memberships: ASCAP; NACUSA; Society of Composers. Hobbies: Psychoacousticsp; Digital Recordings. Address: 12374 Melody Lane, Los Altos, CA 94022, USA.

SAHL Michael, b. 2 Sept 1934, Boston, Massachusetts, USA. Composer. Education: Studied with Israel Citkowitz, 1947-57; BA, Amherst College, 1955; MFA, Princeton University with Sessions, 1957; Berkshire Music Center and Florence in 1957 on a Fulbright Fellowship; Career: Buffalo/Lukas Foss Ensemble, 1965-66; Lincoln Centre Repertory Company, 1966; Organist, Spencer Memorial Church; Pianist/arranger for Judy Collins, 1968-69; String Quartet, 1969; Music Director, WBAI-FM, 1972-73; Music theatre works, 1975; Tango Project with William Schimmel, 1981; Film work, 1963-. Compositions include: String Quartet, 1969; Doina, violin and jazz trio, 1979; Boxes, opera, 1980; Symphony 1983, big band with electric violin, 1983; Tango from Exiles Cafe, for piano solo, 1984; Dream Beach, opera, 1987; Jungles, for electric violin, electric guitar, piano, bass and drums, 1992; John Grace Ranter, opera, 1996; Trio, violin, violincello and piano, 1997. Recordings: Tropes on the Salve Regina; A Mitzvah for the Dead; Symphony 1983; Doina; Prothalamium; Exiles Cafe Tango; New album, White Rabbit, 1997. Publication: Making Changes: A Practical Guide to Vernacular Harmony, 1977. Honours include: Prix Italia, 1980 for Civilizations And Its Discontents; Nominated for Academy Award, 1990; Seagrams Award in Opera for Boxes; Nominated for Grammy, 1982. Address: c/o ASCAP, ASCAP Building, One Lincoln Plaza, New York, NY 10023, USA.

SAINSBURY Lionel, b. 2 June 1958, Wiltshire, England. Composer. Compositions: Fiesta for two pianos performed by Doublier duo in Paris and Jonzac, 1983, by Black/Katamaya duo in Nagoya, 1988, by Claire and Antoinette Cann at St John's Smith Square, 1993, and by Filsell/Pott duo in Winchester and London, 1994; Twelve Preludes for piano premiered by Jack Gibbons at St John's Smith Square, 1987, featured in composer's own performance on Classic FM, 1993, also performed by Jeremy Filsell in London and Bath, 1996; Andalusian Fanatasy for piano premiered by Jack Gibbons, 1990; Cuban Dance No 2 for violin and piano premiered by Tasmin Little and Piers Lane, 1992, also performed by Lorraine McAslan and Nigel Clayton at Wigmore Hall, 1996; Two Nocturnes for strings premiered by William Boughton and the English String Orchestra at Malvern, 1994; Violin Concerto first broadcast by Lorraine McAslan with the BBC Concert Orchestra conducted by Barry Wordsworth, BBC Radio 3, 1995; South American Suite for piano premiered by Jack Gibbons, 1996. Honour: Mendelssohn Scholarship, 1980. Memberships: Composers Guild of Great Britain; Performing Right Society; Mechanical Copyright Protection Society. Address: Boot Cottage, Brook End, Chadlington, Chipping Norton, Oxon OX7 3NF, England.

SAINT-CLAIR Carol, b. 1951, Texas, USA. Soprano. Education: Studied at Texas State University. Career: Sang at the Gelsenkirchen Opera, 1977-82, Klagenfurt, 1982-87 and Osnabruck Opera from 1987; Guest appearances throughout Germany and South America in such roles as Mimi, Marzelline in Fidelio, Euridice, Blanche in The Carmelites, Donna Anna and Tatiana in Eugene Onegin; Frequent concert appearances. Address: c/o Osnabruck Opera, Städtische Buhnen, Osnabruck GmBH, Domhof 10-11, 4500 Osnabruck, Germany.

SAKS Gidon, b. 1960, Israel. Bass Singer. Education: Studied at Royal Northern College of Music and at University of Toronto with Patricia Kern. Debut: Stratford Festival in Canada as The Mikado. Career: Sang with Canadian Opera Company in Barbiere di Siviglia, Carmen, Les Contes d'Hoffmann, La Bohème and Anna Bolena; Gelsenkirchen Opera in Der Freischütz, Gianni Schicchi, Der Rosenkavalier, Die Zauberflöte and L'Italiana in Algeri; Member of the Bielefeld Opera and sang Colline in La Bohème for New Israel Opera; Berlin debut in Les Beatitudes by Cesar Franck, with Dietrich Fischer-Dieskau; Season 1991-92 as Seneca in L'Incoronazione di Poppea at Madrid and Leporello with Scottish Opera; Season 1992-93 as Claggart in Billy Budd for Scottish Opera followed by Achillas in a new production of Julius Caesar; Engaged as Hamilgar in the premiere of Fenelon's Salammbo, Opéra Bastille, 1998. Recordings: Zemlinsky's Der Kreidekreis; Schreker's Ferne Klang conducted by Gerd Albrecht. Address: Kaye Artists Management, Barratt House, 7 Chertsey Road, Woking, GU21 5AB, England.

SALAFF Peter, b. 1942, USA. Violinist. Career: Member of the Cleveland Quartet, 1968- with regular tours of the USA, Canada, Europe, Japan, Russia, South America, Australia, New Zealand and the Middle East; Faculty, Eastman School Rochester and in residence at the Aspen Music Festival, co-founding the Center for Advanced Quartet Studies; Tour of Russia and 5 European countries in 1988; Season 1988-89 with appearances at the Metropolitan Museum and Alice Tully, NY; Concerts in Paris, London, Bonn, Prague, Lisbon and Brussels; Appearances at Salzburg, Edinburgh and Lucerne Festivals; Many complete Beethoven Cycles and annual appearances at Lincoln Center's Mostly Mozart Festival; In addition to standard works his repertory includes performances of works by Ives, John Harbison, Sergei Slonimsky, Samuel Adler, George Perle, Christopher Rouse and Toru Takemitsu. Recordings: Repertoire from Mozart to Ravel and collaborations with Alfred Brendel in Schubert's Trout Quintet, Pinchas Zukerman and Bernard Greenhouse with Brahms's Sextets, Emmanuel Ax, Yo Yo Ma and Richard Stolzman. Address: Eastman School of Music, 26 Gibbs Street, Rochester, NY 14604, USA.

SALKELD Robert, b. 16 Apr 1920, Newcastle upon Tyne, England. Teacher; Examiner; Editor. m. (1) 2 sons, (2) 1 daughter. Education: Conservatoire of Music, Newcastle upon Tyne; ARCM, Royal College of Music, London, 1948. Career: Various teaching positions in schools, 1949-69; Head of Music Department, Collingwood School, Peckham, London, 1957-60; Tutor, Morley College, London, 1950-69; Professor, 1961-69; Examiner, 1961-82, London College of Music; Extensive work at festivals, summer schools and courses, 1949-72. Compositions: Numerous editions of recorder music including Concert Pieces and Play the Recorder Series; Many compositions and arrangements unpublished. Contributions to: Reviews, Music in Education, 1954-76. Honour: Honorary Fellow, London College of Music, 1977. Membership: Royal Musical Association. Hobby: Books. Address: Flat 11, Cossack Lane House, Lower Brook Street, Winchester, Hampshire SO23 8EG, England.

SALLINEN Aulis, b. 9 Apr 1935, Salmi, Finland. Composer. Education: Studied with Aarre Merikanto and Joonas Kokkonen, Sibelius Academy, Helsinki. Career: Teaching post, Sibelius

Academy; Administrator, Finnish Radio Symphony Orchestra, 1960-70; Board Member, Finnish National Opera; Chairman, Teosto Professor of Arts (life appointment by Finnish Government). Compositions include: Mauermusik, 1962; Elegy for Sebastian Knight, 1964; Cadenze, 1965; Quattro per Quattro, 1965; Notturno, 1966; Violin Concerto, 1968; String Quartet No 3, 1969; Chaconne, 1970; String Quartet No 4, 1971; Sonata for Solo Cello, 1971; Symphony No 1, 1971; Suite Grammaticale, 1971; Four Dream Songs, 1972; Symphony No 2, 1972; The Horseman, opera, 1973; Songs for the Sea, 1974; Symphony No 3, 1975; Chamber Music I, 1975; Chamber Music II, 1976; Cello Concerto, 1976; The Red Line, opera, 1978; Dies Irae, 1978; Symphony No 4, 1979; Song Around a Song, 1980; The Iron Age; Shadows; The King goes forth to France, 1984; Symphony No 5, 1985; Kullervo, opera, 1988; Symphony No 6, 1989; The Palace, opera, 1993. Recordings: Major works on Swedish and/or Finnish label. Honours: Wihuri International Sibelius Prize, 1983; Admitted to Membership, Royal Swedish Music Academy, 1983. Membership: Finnish Composers' Association, Secretary, Chairman. Address: TEOSTO, Lauttasaarentie 1, 00200 Helsinki 20, Finland.

SALLIS Friedemann Arthur, b. 30 Mar 1953, Kingston, Ontario, Canada. Musicologist; Professor; Choir Director. m. Christiane Parchet, 18 Feb 1980, 1 daughter. Education: BM, Queens University, Kingston, Ontario, Canada, 1976; Associate, Royal Conservatory, Toronto, 1979; MM, Université Laval, Quebec, 1983; PhD, Musicology, Technische Universität, Berlin, 1992. Debut: Choral Director, Church of Scotland, Geneva, 1978. Career: Assistant Professor, 1987-94, Associate Professor, 1995-, Université de Moncton, Canada; Visiting Professor, Universite de Genève, 1995; External Examiner, Conservatoire de Genève, 1995; Choral Director, World Premiers of Beatus Vir, 1988, Nisi Dominus, 1990, Canadian Premiers, Works by L Nono, M Ohana, I Stravinsky, F Martin and A Honegger; Numerous Concerts broadcast live and re-broadcast by CBC. Publication: An Introduction to the Early Work of György Ligeti, 1996. Contributions to: Various Journals. Honours: Doktorandenstipendium, West Berlin Senate, 1985-87; Fellowship Grants, Paul Sacher Foundation, 1994-98; Research Grant, Social Sciences and Humanities Research Council of Canada, 1997-2000. Memberships: Canadian Music Centre; Canadian University Music Society; American Musicological Society. Address: 210 Cameron Street, Moncton, NB E1C 5Z3, Canada.

SALMENHAARA Erkki, b. 12 March 1941, Helsinki, Finland. Composer; Musicologist. Education: Studies, Sibelius Academy, Helsinki with Joonas Kokkonen & Vienna with Ligeti, 1963; PhD, University of Helsinki, 1970. Career: Faculty Member, University of Helsinki, 1963-; Chairman, Society of Finnish Composers, 1974-76. Compositions: 4 Symphonies, 1962, 1963, 1963, 1972; 2 Cello Sonatas, 1960-69, 1982; Elegy for 2 String Quartets, 1963; Wind Quintet, 1964; Requiem Profanum, 1969; Quartet for Flute, Violin, Viola & Cello, 1971; Nel Mezzo Del Cammin Di Nostra Vita, for Orchestra, 1972; The Woman of Portugal, Opera, 1972 (premiered Helsinki 1976); Suomi-Finland, Unsymphonic Poem, 1967; Canzonetta per Archi, 1972; Illuminations for Orchestra, 1972; Horn Concerto, 1973; Sonatine for 2 Violins, 1973; Canzona per Piccola, Orchestra, 1974; Poema for Violin or Viola & Strings, 1976; Introduction & Chorale for Organ & Orchestra, 1978; String Quartet, 1978; Lamento per Orchrestra d'archi, 1979; Concerto for 2 Violins & Orchestra, 1980; Sonatine for Flute & Guitar, 1981; Violin Sonata, 1982; Sonatella for Piano Four Hands, 1983; Adagietto for Orchestra, 1982; Sinfonietta per archi, 1985; Introduction & Allegro for Clarinet, Cello & Piano, 1985; Cello Concerto, 1987; Isle of Bliss for Baritone, Soprano & Orchestra, 1990. Address: c/o TEOSTO, Lauttasaarentie 1, SF-00200 Helsinki, Finland.

SALMINEN Matti, b. 7 Jul 1945, Turku, Finland. Bass Singer. Education: Studied at the Sibelius Academy in Helsinki, and in Rome. Debut: Helsinki Opera in 1969 as King Philip in Don Carlos. Career: Sang in Cologne, Zurich and Berlin, 1972-76 in the principal bass parts; La Scala Milan in 1973 as Fafner and at Savonlinna Festival in 1975 as the Horseman, Sarastro, Philip, Don Carlos, Daland and Ramphis; Sang at Bayreuth from 1978 as Daland, the Landgrave, Titurel, King Mark and in The Ring operas; Metropolitan Opera from 1981 as King Mark, Rocco, Osmin, Fasolt, Fafner, Hunding and Hagen; Sang in Berlin in 1985 and Munich in 1987 as Fasolt, Hunding and Hagen, sang Prince Khovansky in 1984 at San Francisco and 1988 in Barcelona, and Boris Godunov in 1984 at Zurich and 1985 in Barcelona; Sang in Zurich in the Ponnelle productions of L'Incoronazione di Poppea, Die Zauberflöte and Die Entführung and several principal bass parts in Vienna, Hamburg, Paris, Chicago and Tokyo; Sang Hunding in Die Walküre at the Metropolitan in 1990, also televised, Rocco in Fidelio at the Los Angeles Music Center, Daland at the 1990 Savonlinna Festival; Season 1992-93 as Daland at the Metropolitan, Rocco at Zurich and Savonlinna, King Philip at the Deutsche Oper Berlin and Sarastro at the Savonlinna Festival; Sang the Landgrave in Tannhäuser at Savonlinna, 1996. Recordings: St Matthew Passion; The Landgrave in Tannhäuser; The Ring; Sallinen's The Horseman; Daland; Mozart's Requiem; Osmin; Sarastro. Address: c/o Ingpen and Williams Ltd, 26 Wadham Road, London SW15 2LR, England.

SALMON Philip, b. 1960, England. Tenor. Education: Studied at The Royal College of Music. Career: Debut recital at the City of London Festival followed by the St Matthew Passion with the Rotterdam Philharmonic, Beethoven's 9th with the Ulster Orchestra and Netherlands Philharmonic, and Mozart's Requiem with the Florida Philharmonic; Sang in Massenet's La Vierge at St Ettienne in 1991; Operatic repertoire includes Mozart's Tamino and Belmonte for Pavilion Opera and Debussy's Pelléas at Marseille and Strasbourg, 1990-91; Sang Belmonte in Die Entführung at the Buxton Festival in 1991 and Albert Herring at St Albans; Sang Tamino at the Gaiety Theatre, Dublin, 1996. Honours include: Young Musicians Recordings Prize. Address: Anglo Swiss Ltd, Suite 35-37 Morley House, 320 Regent Street, London W1R 5AD, England.

SALOMAA Petteri, b. 1961, Helsinki, Finland. Singer (Baritone). Education: Studied at the Sibelius Academy and with Hans Hotter and Kim Borg. Debut: Finnish National Opera, Helsinki 1983, as Mozart's Figaro. Career: Appeared at the Ludwigsburg and Schwetzingen Festivals, 1984; Wexford Festival 1985, as the King in Ariodante; Drottningholm from 1986, as Leporello and Nardo in La Finta Giardiniera; Geneva Opera 1987, as Papageno and Amsterdam 1988, as Masetto, conducted by Nikolaus Harnoncourt; North American debut 1988, with Messiah in San Francisco, followed by Figaro with Michigan Opera; Season 1989-90 at Freiburg Opera as Faninal, Ned Keene, the Father in Hansel and Gretel and in Purcell's King Arthur; 1989-91 at Freiburg Opera as Billy Budd, Posa, Ned Keene and Belcore, 1991 at Frankfurt Opera as Papageno and Guglielmo, 1993 as Conte Robinson in Il matrimonio Segreto; Other roles include Oreste in Iphigénie en Tauride, Posa, Billy Budd and Albert in Werther; Sang Silvio in Pagliacci with Tampere Opera, 1996. Recordings include: Beethoven's Ninth Symphony (EMI); La Finta Giardiniera (World Video); The Fiery Angel by Prokofiev, and Peer Gynt with the Berlin Philharmonic, EMI; Le nozze di Figaro (Decca); Mendelssohn Elias (Harmonia Mundi. Honours include: 1st Prize, National Singing Competition at Lappeenranta, 1981. Address: Festium Agency, Partiotic 34, 00370 Helsinki, Finland.

SALOMAN Ora (Frishberg), b. 14 Nov 1938, Brooklyn, New York, USA. Musicologist; Professor of Music. m. Dr Edward Barry Saloman, 1 July 1968. Education: PhD in Musicology, MA in Musicology, AB in Music, Columbia University, New York; Studied violin with Vladimir Graffman and Ivan Galamian, chamber music with Raphael Hillyer, Claus Adam and William Kroll. Career: Chairman, Department of Music, 1978-84, Professor of Music, Baruch College and the Graduate School, City University of New York. Publications: Beethoven's Symphonies and J S Dwight: The Birth of American Music Criticism, 1995; Essay in Music and Civilisation; Essays in Honor of Paul Henry Lang, 1984; Essay in Mainzer Studien zur Musikwissenschaft: Festschrift Walter Wiora, 1997; Essay in Music and the French Revolution. Contributions to: Acta Musicologica; Musical Quarterly, 1974, 1992, 1996; Music and Man; The Pennsylvania Magazine of History and Biography; Dallas Opera Magazine; American Music; The Journal of Musicology, 1992; International Review of the Aesthetics and Sociology of Music; The New Grove Dictionary of Opera, 1992; St James International Dictionary of Opera, 1993; American National Biography; Continental and English Foundations of J S Dwight's Early American Criticism of Beethoven's Ninth Symphony in Journal of the Royal Musical Association, 1994; Encyclopaedia of New England Culture, forthcoming; Revised New Grove Dictionary of Music and Musicians, forthcoming. Honours include: National Endowment for the Humanities Fellowship for College Teachers. 1988-89. Memberships: Editorial Board, American Music, a quarterly journal of the Sonneck Society for American Music, 1995-97; American Musicological Society; College Music Society. Address: 14 Summit Street, Englewood, NJ 07632, USA.

SALONEN Esa-Pekka, b. 30 Jun 1958, Helsinki, Finland. Conductor. Education: Qualified French Horn player by age 19. Career: Composer, 1970-; Conducting Composer, 1980; Conducted performances of Mahler's 3rd Symphony with Philharmonia Orchestra, London, 1983; Music Director, Los Angeles Philharmonic Orchestra, 1992-; Chief Conductor of Swedish Radio Symphony Orchstra, 1985; Principal Guest Conductor, Philharmonia Orchestra, London and Oslo Philharmonic Orchestra; Led first performance of Robert Saxton's The Circles of Light, 1986; Conducted Messiaen's St François d'Assise at the Salzburg Festival, 1992; Hindemith's Mathis der Maler at Covent Garden, 1995; Ligeti concerts at South Bank, London, 1997. Compositions: Horn Music I, 1976; Cello Sonata; Nachtlieder, 1978; Goodbye, 1980; Concerto for Saxophone and Orchestra; Auf der ersten Blick und ohne zu wissen; Giro; Baalal; Yta I and II; Meeting; Wind Quintet; Floof; Mimo II. Recordings include: Lutoslawski's Third Symphony; Numerous works by Stravinsky; Sibelius' Symphony No 5; Messiaen's Turangalila Symphonie; Mahler's 4th Symphony; Recordings with various orchestras including the London Sinfonietta, the Philharmonia Orchestra and the Los Angeles Philharmonic Orchestra. Current Management: Van Walsum Management. Address: c/o Van Walsum Management, 40 St Peter's Road, London W6 9BH, England.

SALTA Anita, b. 1 Sept 1937, New York, USA. Singer (Soprano). Education: Studied in New York. Debut: Jacksonville 1959, as Aida. Career: Appearances at such German Opera House Centres as Stuttgart, Wuppertal, Nuremberg, Dortmund, Cassel, Essen and Hanover; Other roles have included Gluck's Alceste, Mozart's Countess, Donna Elvira and Fiordiligi, Marquerite, the Trovatore and Forza Leonoras, Traviata, Desdemona, Helene and Elisabeth de Valois; Tatiana, Antonida in A Life for the Tsar, Marenka, Mimi, Butterfly, Santuzza, Elsa, Eva, Chrysothemis, the Marschallin and Katerina Ismailova; Many concert appearances. Address: c/o Theatre, Rolandstrasse 10, 4300 Essen, Germany.

SALTER Lionel (Paul), b. 8 Sep 1914, London, England. Musicologist; Critic; Broadcaster; Harpsichordist. m. Christine Fraser, 11 Oct 1939, 3 s. Education: BA 1935, MusB, 1936, MA, 1938, St John's College, Cambridge; London Academy of Music, 1923-31; Royal College of Music, 1931-32 and 1935-36; LRAM, 1930. Career: Pianist, Arranger, Composer in films and TV, 1936-39; During Army service was Guest Conductor for Radio France, 1943-44; Assistant Conductor, BBC Theatre Orchestra, 1945, Producer, 1946, European Music Supervisor, 1948, Artists Manager, 1954, Head of Overseas Music, 1955, Head of TV Music, 1956, Head of Opera, 1963, Assistant Controller of Music, 1967-74; Opera Coordinator and Chairman, Radio Music Group, European Broadcasting Union, 1972-75; Editor, Associated Board Examination Music, 1976-95; Performances in 17 countries as harpsichordist, pianist and conductor. Compositions: Music for radio plays, songs; Scottish Reel for 2 Pianos; Air and Scherzino for Oboe; Performing editions of operas by Cavalli and Lully and numerous 18th Century violin works. Recordings: Concertos by Haydn and Bach; Harpsichord in numerous recordings. Publications: Going to a Concert, 1950; Going to the Opera, 1955; The Musician and His World, 1963; Music and The 20th Century Media, with J Bornoff, 1972; Gramophone Guide to Classical Composers, 1978; General Editor, BBC Music Guides, 1971-75; Translations of over 110 libretti. Contributions to: Gramophone, 1948-; Listener; Musical Times; New Grove Dictionary of Opera, 4 volumes, 1992. Membership: Vice Chairman, British Federation of Music Festivals, 1985-88. Address: 26 Woodstock Road, London, NW11 8ER, England.

SALTER Richard, b. 12 Nov 1943, Hindhead, Surrey, England. Singer (Baritone). Education: Studied at Royal College of Music, London, then at the Vienna Academy of Music with Christain Moeller, Ilse Rapf and Anton Dermota. Career: Sang with King's Singers and gave concert performances; Opera debut Darmstadt 1973; Sang further in Frankfurt and at Glyndebourne; Kiel Opera 1979, as Don Giovanni; Guest appearances in Berlin and Hanover; Hamburg Staatsoper 1979, as Lenz in the premiere of Wolfgang Rihm's Jakob Lenz; Sang Beckmesser at the Paris Opera, 1988; Hamlet in Rihm's Die Hamletmaschine at Hamburg; Season 1992-93 as the Master in Höller's Meister und Margarita at Cologne and Cortez in the premiere of Rihm's Die Eroberung von Mexico at Hamburg; Sang Coupeau in the premiere of Klebe's Gervaise Macquart, Dusseldorf, 1996. Recordings: Jakob Lenz, on Harmonia Mundi. Address: c/o Hamburgische Staatsoper, Grosse Theaterstraase 34, D-2000 Hamburg 36, Germany.

SALTER Timothy, b. 15 Dec 1942, Mexborough, Yorkshire, England. Musician; Composer; Conductor; Pianist. Education: MA, St John's College, Cambridge University, 1960-64; MTC, London University, 1965, LRAM; ARCO. Career: Musical Director of the Ionian Singers; Pianist (Chamber Music) on tours in Great Britain and internationally; Conductor and Pianist on recordings and broadcasts; Professor, Royal College of Music. Compositions: Instrumental works, chamber music, songs, choral works and orchestral works. Recordings include: Many choral and piano works, 2 string quartets and other chamber music including: Fantasy on a Theme by J S Bach for Piano, String Quartets Nos 1 and 2, Abstractions for Oboe Trio, Variations 1986; English Folk Song arrangements; Katharsios for Chorus, Piano and Percussion; Perspectives, set two, for piano. Publications: Thomas Campion: Poet, Composer, Physician, with Edward Lowbury and Alison Young, 1970. Address: 26 Caterham Road, London, SE13 5AR, England.

SALVA Tadeas, b. 22 Oct 1937, Lucky Pri Ruzomberku, Slovakia. Composer. Education: Studied Composition with Alexander Moyzes and Jan Cikker in Slovakia, Szabelski and Lutoslawski in Poland. Career: Head of Music Broadcasting, Kosice Radio, 1965; Producer for Slovak TV in Bratislava, 1968; Dramaturg for the Slovak Folk Art Group. Compositions include: Operas Margita and Besna; Tears; Mechurik Koscurik and His Friends; 4 String Quartets; Symphony of Love for Narrator; Concerto for Cello and Chamber Orchestra; Music in Memoriam

Arthur Honegger for Organ, Bass Voice, Trumpet and Strings. Address: c/o SOZA, Rastislavova 3, 821 08 Bratislava, Slovakia.

SALVADORI Antonio, b. 1950, Venice, Italy. Singer (Baritone). Education: Studied at the Conservatorio Benedetto Marcello, Venice. Career: Sang first in Il Barbiere di Sivglia and Pagliacci; La Scala 1977, in Luisa Miller, with Caballé and Pavarotti; Verona Arena from 1978, notably as Amonasro (1988); Marcello and Belcore at La Scala 1987-88, tour with the company to Japan 1988; Has sung Rossini's William Tell in Milan, Linz, Nice, Zurich and New York (concert performance at Carnegie Hall); Vienna Staatsoper 1988, as Ezio in Attila; Sang Simon Boccanegra at Cremona, 1990; Other appearances at Chicago, Venice (Gerard in Andrea Chénier), Turin and Hamburg (Don Carlo in Ernani). Address: c/o Opernhaus Zurich, Falkenstrasse 1, CH-8008 Zurich, Switzerland.

SALVATORE Ramon, b. 25 Aug 1944, Oak Park, Illinois, USA. Concert Pianist; Educator. Education: BMus, Millikin University, Decatur, Illinois, 1967; MMus with honours, distinction in Piano Performance, New England Conservatory of Music, Boston, Massachusetts, 1969; Aspen School of Music, Colorado, 1970; Postgraduate study, Royal Academy of Music, London, England, 1974-77;Student of Gordon Green; Private study with William Masselos, New York City, 1985. Debut: Wigmore Hall, London, 1977; Carnegie Recital Hall, New York City, 1980; Orchestra Hall, Chicago, 1990. Career: 2 broadcasts, Capitol Radio, 1975-76; 3 Recitals, St Martin-in-the-Fields, London, 1976-78; Appearances, Purcell Room 1979, Merkin Concert Hall, New York City 1985; 2 appearances, American Music Festival at National Gallery of Art, Washington DC, live radio broadcasts, 1983, 1989; Numerous broadcasts, National Public Radio USA, 1983-; Extensive performances on university campuses nationally, USA; Performances include commissions and rarely heard US works; Faculty positions: University of Kansas, 1969-70; St Cloud State University, Minnesota, 1970-74; Ithaca College, New York, 1977-86; Charterhouse School, England, 1975-76; Three-Concert Series, American Music in the Grand Tradition, performed concurrently at the Weill Recital Hall at Carnegie Hall, New York and at the Chicago Public Library Cultural Center, 1991; Faculty, Music Center of the North Shore, Winnetka, Illinois, 186-92; Performances supported by the National Endowment for the Arts. Recordings: Music in the Grand Tradition, 1992; Music in the American Grain, 1992; Aaron Copland: Romantic and Modern, 1995; Concertos by Chicago Composers, 1996. Current Management: Beverly Wright and Associates Inc, 157 W 57th Street, New York, NY 10019, USA. Address: 5617 Capri Lane, Morton Grove, IL 60053, USA.

SALVATORI Roberto, b. Trinidad. Singer (Baritone). Education: Studied, Guildhall School, London, England and the Britten/Pears School at Aldeburgh; Master Classes with Sena Jurinac and Sherrill Milnes. Career: Roles with Pavilion Opera have included Mozart's Don Giovanni, Count and Guglielmo, Rossini's Figaro, Enrico in Lucia di Lammermoor and Donizetti's Don Pasquale and Belcore; Germont and Scarpia with European Chamber Opera, Sid in Albert Herring at Aldeburgh and Berkeley in Marschner's Vampyr for BBC TV; Principal with English National Opera from 1995, with Ping, Escamillo and Marcello (La Bohème) in first season; Stolzius in the British Company premiere of Zimmerman's Soldaten, 1996. Honours include: Scholarship from the Countess of Munster Trust. Address: c/o ENO Press Office, English National Opera, St Martin's Lane, London WC2N 4ES, England.

SALWAROWSKI Jerzy (Hubert), b. 7 Sept 1946, Krakow, Poland. Conductor; Musical Director. m. Ewa Czarniecka, 19 Sept 1976, 2 sons, 2 daughters. Education: Krakow Music High School, Conducting and Composition, Graduated 1970; Warsaw Chopin Music Academy, docent symphony and opera conducting, 1997. Career: Assistant Conductor, Krakow Philharmonic Choir, 1970-71; Second Conductor, Opole Philharmonic Orchestra, 1972-78; Second Conductor, Katowice-Silesian Philharmonic, 1978-81; Substitute Art Director, Silesian Philharmonic, 1982-84; Substitute Art Director, Polish Radio National Symphony Orchestra, 1985-; Guest Conductor, Lodz Great Opera House, tours in Europe; Artistic Director, Pomeranian Philharmonic Orchestra, 1988-90; Artistic Director, Lublin State Philharmonic Orchestra, 1991-93; Artistic Director, Szczein Symphony Orchestra and Torunn Chamber Orchestra; Tours in Europe (France, Portugal, Spain, Germany) with symphony and opera music. Compositions: Only elaboration and theatre music. Recordings: All Gershwin's Pieces for Piano and Orchestra, with A Ratusinski; All Symphonic Poems by M Karlowicz; J Sibelius: Saga and Violin Concerto, with V Brodski, for Musical Heritage Society, first digital in Poland; H Wieniawski, Violin Concerto, with V Brodski; Mozart CD, All Church Sonatas with Pomeranian Philharmonic Orchestra and Karol Golebiewski, 1988; Lessel, Grand Rondeau and Piano Concerto, with Silesian Philharmonic and Jerzy Sterczynski, 1992; Mendelssohn, Hebridean, Violin Concerto and 4th Symphony (Italian) with Krzysztof Jakowicz, 1997; Permanent Recording for Polish Radio and TV over 250 each year; TV Concerts, TV Cycles, Musical Drawing Room. Publications: New Elaborations of Karlowicz Scores in PWM Edition. Contributions to: Permanent Reviews. Honour: Gold Plate Award, for Gershwin Album, 1993. Hobbies: Yachting; Skiing; Cycling; Hunting. Address: 40-236 Katowice, VL Wietnamska 63B, Poland.

SALZEDO Leonard, b. 24 Sept 1921, London, England. Composer. Education: Royal College of Music, Violin with Isolde Menges and Composition with Herbert Howells, 1940-44. Career: Ballet, The Fugitive commissioned by Marie Rambert; Symphony premiered by Beecham at the Royal Festival Hall, 1956. Compositions: Ballets: The Fugitive, 1944; Mardi Gras, 1946; Witch Boy, 1956; The Travellers, 1963; Agriona, 1964; Realms of Choice, 1965; Hazard, 1967; Ballet Drei 1973, 1973; Orchestral: Gabble Retchit, Symphonic poem, 1955; Symphony, 1956; Rendezvous, 1960; Concerto fervido, 1964; Paean to the Sun, 1966; Toccata, 1967; Percussion Concerto, 1969; 8 String Quartets; Songs; Divertimento for Brass, 1959; Capriccio for Brass, 1978. Address: 363 Bideford Green, Leighton Buzzard, Bedford LU7 7TX, England.

SALZMAN Eric, b. 8 Sep 1933, NY, USA. Composer; Writer on Music. Education: BA, Columbia College, Columbia University, 1954; MFA, Princeton University, 1956; Teachers include Otto Luening, Ussachevsky, Jack Beeson, Roger Sessions and Milton Babbitt; Continued studies in Europe with Petrassi in Rome and Darmstadt. Career: Music critic for the New York Times, 1958-62, New York Herald Tribune, 1963-66; Teacher at Queen's College, NY, 1966-68; Director, New Images of Sounds, series of concerts at Hunter College; In 1970 founded Quog Music Theater, to explore new ideas in the performing arts; Co-founder and Artistic Director of American Music Theater Festival with Marjorie Samoff, Philadelphia, 1983-. Compositions include: String Quartet, 1955; Flute Sonata, 1956; Inventions for Orchestra, 1959; Verses and Cantos for 4 Voices, Instruments and Electronics, 1967; Larynx Music, dance piece with tape, 1968; The Conjurer, multi-media spectacle, 1975; Civilization and its Discontents, opera buffa for radio, 1977; Noah, spectacle, 1978; The Passion of Simple Simon, for performance at the Electric Circus in Greenwich Village; Variations on a Sacred Harp Tune for Harpsichord, 1982; Boxes, radio opera with Michael Sahl, 1983; Big Jim and the Small-Time Investors, music theater, 1985; Adaptation of Gershwin's Strike up The Band, 1984. Publications include: 20th Century Music: An Introduction, 1967, new edition, 1987; Civilization and Its Discontents and Making Changes, a handbook of vernacular harmony, both with Michael Sahl. Address: American Music Theater Festival, 1 Franklin Plaza, Philadelphia, PA 19103, USA.

SAMARITANI Pier Luigi, b. 29 Sept 1942, Novare, Italy. Opera Set and Costumes Designer; Director. Education: Accademia de Brera, Milan, Italy; Centre d'Art Dramatique, Paris. Debut: As Director, Werther, Florence, 1978. Career: Assisted Stage Designer, Lila de Nobili, Paris; Set Designer, Theatre du Gymnase, Paris 1962, Teatre dell'Opera, Rome 1964; Dance Design for American Ballet Theatre, 1980; Stage Designer for many companies in USA and Europe; Exhibited Stage Designs Spoleto Festival, 1972; Ernani Met/Eugene Onegin Lyric Opera of Chicago/Werther Vienna, Paris, Florence, Butterfly Berlin (1987); Season 1992 with Andrea Chenier at Florence and Turin and Die Meistersinger at Spoleto. Current Management: Herbert H Breslin Inc, New York, USA. Address: c/o Herbert H Breslin Inc, 119 West 57th Street, New York, NY 10019, USA.

SAMS Eric, b. 3 May 1926, London, England. Civil Servant (retired); Writer on Music. m. Enid Tidmarsh, 30 June 1952, 2 sons Education: Corpus Christi, Cambridge, 1947-50; BA, 1st Class Honours, 1950; PhD, 1972. Career: Army Cryptanalysis, 1947-50; Civil Service, 1950-78; Visiting Professor, McMaster University, Hamilton, Ontario, Canada, 1976-77; television film on Code and Cipher in Music, 1989. Publications: The Songs of Hugo Wolf, 1961, 2nd edition, 1983, 3rd edition, 1993; The Songs of Robert Schumann, 1969, 2nd edition, 1975, 3rd edition, 1993; Brahms Songs, 1971, French translation, 1989; The Real Shakespeare, 1995. Contributions to: New Grove Dictionary of Music and Musicians; Ballad, Cryptography, Hanslick, Lied IV, Mörike, Wolf, Schubert (work list and bibliography), Schumann (work list and bibliography); Reviews and articles in Musical Times, 1985-89; TLS, 1974-94 Honour: Honorary Member, Guildhall School of Music and Drama, 1983. Hobbies: Historical cipher and shorthand; Chess. Address: 32 Arundel Avenue, Sanderstead, Surrey CR2 8BB, Englad.

SAMSON (Thomas) James, b. 6 July 1946, Northern Ireland. University Teacher. Education: BMus, 1st Class Honours, Queen's University, Belfast, 1965-69; MMus, PhD, LRAM, University College, Cardiff, 1969-72. Career: Research Fellow in Humanities, University of Leicester, England, 1972-73; Lecturer in Music, 1973-86, Reader in Musicology, 1986-91, Professor of Musicology, 1991-94, University of Exeter; Badock Professor of Musicology, University of Bristol, 1994-. Publications: Music in Transition, 1977; The Music of Szymanowski, 1980; The Music of Chopin, 1985; Chopin Studies, 1988; Man and Music, vol 7, The Late Romantic Era, 1991; The Cambridge Companion to Chopin, 1992; Chopin: The Four Ballades, 1992; Chopin Studies 2 (with John Rink), 1994. Contributions to: Rocznik Chopinowski, Journal of the American Musicological Society, Nineteenth-Century Music, Tempo, Journal of Musicology, Music Analysis, Music and Letters, Musical Times. Honours: Szymanowski Centennial Medal, 1982; Order of Merit, Polish Ministry of Culture, 1990; Membership: Council Member, Royal Musical Association. Hobbies: Walking; Reading. Address: Music Department, University of Bristol, Royal Fort House, Tyndall Avenue, Bristol BS8 1VJ, England.

SAMUEL Gerhard, b. 20 Apr 1924, Germany. Conductor; Composer; Professor of Music. Education: BM, Eastman School of Music; MM, Yale University. Career: Conductor, Ballet Ballads on Broadway, 1947-48; Attached to Cultural Attache, American Embassy, Paris, 1948-49; Associate Conductor and Violinist, Minneapolis Symphony, 1949-59; Director and Conductor, Collegium Musicum, Minneapolis Civic Opera, 1949-59; Director and Conductor, San Francisco Composers Forum, 1959-71; Music Director Oakland Symphony Orchestra, 1959-71; Music Director/Conductor, San Francisco Ballet, 1960-70; Guest Conductor, San Francisco Opera; Conductor, Ojai Festival, 1971; Associate Conductor, Los Angeles Philharmonic Orchestra, 1970-73; Director and Conductor, Ojai Festival, 1971; Conductor of Orchestra and Opera and Director of Conducting Program, California Institute of the Arts, 1972-76; Director of Orchestral Activities, College-Conservatory of Music, University of Cincinnati, 1976-97; Conductor, Music Director, Cincinnati Chamber Orchestra, 1983-91; Guest Conductor, USA, South America, Mexico, Canada, the Philippines, England, Belgium, France, Germany, Norway, Sweden, Russia, China, Poland and Switzerland; Chief Guest Conductor, Oakland Ballet Company, 1983-86; Conducted the premiere of Harold Blumenfeld's Seasons in Hell, Cincinnati, 1996; Music Director, Cosmopolitan Orchestra, New York City, 1997-. Compositions: Over 70 including: Requiem for Survivors, Orchestral, 1973; Looking at Orpheus Looking, Orchestral, 1971; Out of Time, A Short Symphony, 1978; Chamber Concerto for Flute in the Shape of a Summer, Orchestral, 1981; Emperor and the Nightingale, Small Ensemble, 1980; Fanfare for a Pleasant Occasion, Small Ensemble, 1981; Thoughts For Sandy on His Birthday, Small Ensemble, 1983; Harlequin's Caprice, Solo Harpsichord, 1980; On the Beach at Night Alone, Orchestral, 1980; The Naumburg Cadenza, Solo Violin, 1985; Nocturne on an Impossible Dream, Small Ensemble, 1986; Nicholas and Concepcion, Orchestral, 1987; As Imperceptibly as Grief, Orchestral, 1988; Christ! What are Patterns For?, Small Ensemble, 1988; Henry's Cadenza, Solo Violin, 1989; Apollo and Hyacinth, Small Ensemble, 1989; After a Dirge, Small Ensemble, 1993; His Cincinnati Philharmonia Orchestra participated in the 1989 Mahler Cyle, Châtelet Theatre, Paris, and Festival 98 in Lisbon; In Search of Words, orchestral, 1995. Recordings include: Darrell Handel: Acquainted with the Night; Kyushu; Charles Ives/Larry Austin: Universe Symphony; Henri Lazarof: Works; Hans Rott: Symphony in E; Gerhard Samuel: Impossible Dream; String Quartets No 1 and 2, Transformations; Franz Schubert: Der Graf von Gleichen; Symphony in E; Diane Thome: The Ruins of the Heart. Honours: George Riveschl Award, 1992; Alice M Ditson Award, 1994; Numerous honorary doctorates; Professor Emeritus, University of Cincinnati. Current Management: Corbett Arts Management, San Francisco, California, USA. Address: 412 Liberty Hill 2C, Cincinnati, Ohio 45210, USA.

SAMUEL Harold, b. 12 Apr 1924, Hudson, Wiconsin, USA. Music Librarian; Musicologist. m. Hella Deffner, 2 sons, 1 daughter. Education: BA, 1949, MA, 1955, University of Minnesota; Studied Musicology with A Cherbuliez, University of Zurich, 1950-51, with Hans Heinrich Eggebrecht at University of Erlangen, 1955-57 and with Donald J Grout at Cornell University; PhD at Cornell University, 1963. Career: Music Librarian and Associate Professor of Music, Cornell University, 1957-71, Chairman of Department of Music, 1970-71; Editor-in-Chief of Notes, the quarterly journal of the Music Library Association, 1965-70; Music Librarian and Professor Music at Yale University, 1971-. Publications: The Cantata in Nuremberg during the Seventeenth Century, 1982. Contributions to: Music encyclopaedias and journals. Address: 101 Santa Fe Avenue, Hamden, CT 065717, USA.

SAMUELSON Mikael, b. 9 Mar 1951, Stockholm, Sweden. Singer (Baritone). Education: Studied with Birgit Stenberg and Erik Werba. Career: Has sung in Sweden from 1968 in opera, oratorio, music theatre and films; Royal Opera Stockholm as Rossini's Figaro; Drottningholm Theatre 1987 and 1989, as Mozart's Figaro and Papageno; Sang in Die Schöpfung 1988; Appearances with the Stockholm Music Drama Ensemble in Pagliacci, Mahagonny and Death in Venice; Television engagements in Drömmen om Thérèse by Werle and Kronbruden by Rangström; Has appeared as cabaret artist in Sweden and Finland. Address: c/o Drottningholms Slottsteater, PO Box 27050, S-102 51 Stockholm, Sweden.

SANCHEZ Ana Maria, b. 1966, Elda, Alicante, Spain. Singer (Soprano). Education: Studied at the Alicante Conservatory and in Madrid with Isabel Penagos and Miguel Zanetwi. Career: Sang in concerts and recitals in Spain, France and Germany; Stage debut as Abigaille in Nabucco at Palma (1994) followed by Donna Anna at Valencia and elsewhere; Mathilde in Guillaume Tell at Lisbon, Leonora in La Forza de destino at Barcelona and Chrysothemis in Elektra at Valencia; Sang the Trovatore Leonora at Zurich, season 1996-97, and has appeared further in Roberto Devereux and Tannhäuser in Bilbao, Salud in La Vida Breve at Malaga and in Don Giovanni at Hamburg; Engaged to return to Valencia 1998, as Gutrune in Götterdämmerung; Concerts include the Verdi Requiem and song recitals. Honours include: Prize winner in competitions at Bilbao and Enna (Italy), 1992-93. Address: c/o Opernhaus Zurich, Falkenstrasse 1, CH-8008 Zurich, Switzerland.

SAND Annemarie, b. 26 Nov 1958, Copenhagen, Denmark. Singer (Mezzo-Soprano). Education: Studied at the Royal Academy of Music and the National Opera Studio. Career: Appeared with English National Opera from 1987 as the Page in Salome, Linetta in The Love of Three Oranges, and Dryad in Ariadne auf Naxos; Welsh National Opera, 1989 as the Composer in Ariadne, conducted by Charles Mackerras; Other roles include Mother Goose in The Rake's Progress, Nancy in Albert Herring, Charlotte, Octavian, Hansel and the Mother in Amahl and the Night Visitors; Many concert appearances including Mozart's Requiem at the Teatro San Carlo, Naples, and 12 concerts in Denmark, 1989; Season 1992 as Kate Pinkerton for ENO and in Oliver's Mario and the Magician at the Almeida Theatre; Season 1993 included BBC Proms debut in The Wreckers, Ethyl Smyth. Honours include: Elena Gerhardt Lieder Prize; Minnie Hauk Prize; Clifton Prize for Best Recital. Address: c/o Marks Management Ltd, 14 New Burlington Street, London W1X 1FF, England.

SAND Malmfrid, b. 1955, Oslo, Norway. Singer (Soprano). Education: Studied in Oslo and London. Debut: Sang Pamina in Die Zauberflöte at Oslo. Career: Appearances as Fiordiligi in Brussels, London and at the Bath Festival; Irene in Tamerlano for Orpheus Opera and Isaura in Jerusalem by Verdi for BBC Radio 3; Wexford Festival 1983, as the Queen in Marschner's Hans Heiling, returning as Donna Anna in Gazzaniga's Don Giovanni and in Busoni's Turandot; Recent engagements as Electra in Idomeneo for the English Bach Festival and Manon for Dorset Opera, 1991; Concert Repertoire includes Vivaldi Gloria, Messiah, Dvorak's Requiem; Concerts and Recitals in Scandinavia, the USA and Europe, notably with the Stavanger Symphony, the Oslo NRK Symphony and the Harmonien Symphony Orchestra of Bergen; Sang Mrs Maurrant in Weill's Street Scene, Turin, 1995. Address: c/o English National Opera, St Martin's Lane, London WC2, England.

SANDER Peter, b. 9 Sept 1933, Budapest, Hungary. Composer; Arranger; Lecturer. m. Jacqueline Binns, 11 Nov 1977, 2 son, 1 daughter. Education: BA, History, University of Budapest; LGSM, Piano and Theory, Guildhall School of Music and Drama; College of Music, Debrecen, Hungary; Trinity College of Music, London; MMus, PhD, Composition, University of London, Goldsmiths College. Compositions: String Quartet Nos 1 and 2; Wind Quintet Nos 1 and 2; Brass Quintet No 1; Exploration, for Guitar; Anecdotes, Light Orchestral and Vocal Piece; Piano Pieces. Recordings: String Quartet No 1; Wind Quintet No 1; Intarsii, for Orchestra; Essay Nos 1 and 2, for Orchestra; Exploration; String Trio; Piano Trio; Wind Trio. Contributions to: Melody Maker; Music Maker; Intro Jazz. Honours: 1st Mention, French Radio and TV International Composition Competition, 1974. Memberships: Composers Guild of Great Britain; PRS; MCPS. Hobby: Reading. Address: 73 The Avenue, London NW6 7NS, England.

SANDERLING Kurt, b. 19 Sept 1912, Arys, Germany. Conductor. Education: Studied privately while working as repetiteur with the Berlin Stadtische Oper, 1931. Career: Left Germany, 1936, and was Conductor of the Moscow Radio Symphony Orchestra, 1936-41; Leningrad Philharmonic Orchestra, 1941-60; Chief Professor of conducting and orchestral classes at the Leningrad Conservatory; Berlin Symphony Orchestra, 1960-77; Dresden State Orchestra, 1964-67; Guest appearances at the Prague, Warsaw, Salzburg and Vienna Festivals; British debut, 1970, with the Leipzig Gewandhaus Orchestra; New Philharmonia Orchestra, 1972-; Recent visits to Japan, USA, Canada, Australia and New Zealand; Conducted the Los Angeles Philharmonic at Symphony Hall, Birmingham, 1991; Haydn's 39th Symphony and Shostakovich No 8. Recordings: All Beethoven's Symphonies with the Philharmonia Orchestra, 1981; Beethoven's Piano Concertos (Gilels); Complete Symphonies of Brahms and Sibelius; Prokofiev Sinfonia Concertante (Rostropovitch); Mozart Divertimento K334, Concertos K216 (Kogan) and K466 (Richter); Haydn Symphonies 88, 45, 104, 1982-87; Bruckner's 3rd Symphony and Shostakovich Nos 8, 10 and 15. Honours: Soviet Award of Honoured Artist; National Prize of the German Democratic Republic, 1962, 1974. Current Management: Norman McCann International Artists Limited, The Coach House, 56 Lawrie Park Gardens, London SE26 6XJ, England.

SANDERLING Michael, b. 1967, Berlin, Germany. Concert Cellist. Education: Studied at the Berlin Musikhochschule. Career: Principal of the Leipzig Gewandhaus Orchestra, 1987-92; Solo career from 1992, notably with the Boston Symphony Orchestra, Los Angeles Philharmonic Orchestra, Berlin and Bamberg Symphonies, Philharmonia, Royal Philharmonic Orchestra and Tonhalle Zurich; Chamber concerts with the Trio Ex Aequo at the Schleswig-Holstein, Lucerne and Salzburg Festivals. Honours: Prizewinner at the Maria-Canals Competition Barcelona, JS Bach Competition Leipzig and ARD Competition, Munich. Address: c/o Worldwide Artists, 6 Petersfield Crescent, Coulsdon, Surrey CR5 2JQ, England.

SANDERLING Thomas, b. 2 Nov 1942, Nowosibirsk, USSR. Conductor. Education: School of the Leningrad Conservatory; German High School of Music, East Berlin. Debut: Conducted Berlin Symphony Orchestra, 1962. Career: Chief Conductor, Reichenbach, 1964; Music Director, Opera and Concerts, Halle, Democratic Republic of Germany, 1966; Permanent Guest Conductor, German State Opera, East Berlin, 1978-; Moved to West Germany in 1983; Has conducted at most major centres in East and West Germany and throughout Europe including Stockholm, Oslo, Helsinki, Milan, Rome, London, Salzburg and Amsterdam; Gave the German premiere of Shostakovich's Symphonies 13 and 14 with Berlin Radio Symphony Orchestra, 1969, and A Petterson's 8th Symphony in 1979; Outstanding success with productions of Magic Flute and Marriage of Figaro at Vienna State Opera, 1979; Has worked with Rotterdam Philharmonic, Bournemouth Symphony Orchestra, Philharmonia (London), Vienna Symphony Orchestra and in Nice, Vancouver, Rochester, New Zealand, Japan, Israel and Australia, with recent productions of Figaro (Nice) and Don Giovanni (Austria and Helsinki). Recordings: Shostakovich: Michelangelo cycle (recording premiere) and Symphonies 2 and 4; Handel: Alexander's Feast and Italian Cantatas; Wolfgang Strauss: Symphony No 1; Udo Zimmermann: Ein Zeuge der liebe. Honours: Berlin Critics' Award, 1970. Current Management: Norman McCann International Artists Limited, The Coach House, 56 Lawrie Park Gardens, London SE26 6XJ, England.

SANDERS Ernest H, b. 4 Dec 1918, Hamburg, Germany. Musicologist. m. Marion Hollander, 2 Nov 1954, 1 son, 1 daughter. Education: MA, Music Historical Musicology, 1952, PhD, in the same, Columbia University, 1963. Career: Department of Music, Columbia University, Lecturer, 1954-58, Instructor, 1958-61 and 1962-63, Assistant Professor, 1963-65 and 1966-67, Associate Professor, 1967-72, Professor, 1972-86, Chairman, Department of Music, 1978-85. Publications: English Polyphony of the Thirteenth and Early 14th Centuries (Polyphonic Music of the Fourteenth Century Vol XIV, 1979); Vols XVI and XVII, co-editor. Contributions to: Numerous articles dealing with aspects of mediaeval polyphony in Journal of the American Musicological Society; The Musical Quarterly; Acta Musicologica; Archiv fur Musikwissenschaft; Music and Letters; Musica Disciplina; The New Grove Dictionary; Various Festschriften. Hobbies: Swimming; Hiking; Biking; Chamber Music. Address: 885 West End Avenue 8B, New York, NY 10025-3524, USA.

SANDISON Gordon, b. 1949, Aberdeen, Scotland. Singer (Baritone). Education: Studied at the Royal Scottish Academy. Career: Has sung with Scottish Opera from 1973 as Papageno, the Figaros of Rossini and Mozart, Malatesta, Don Giovanni, Belcore, Don Alfonso, Falstaff, Marcello; Covent Garden debut, 1984, as Fieville in Andrea Chenier, followed by Mandarin, Morales, Starveling, Montano, Masetto and the Doctor and Shepherd in Pélleas et Mélisande; Further appearances with English National Opera, Théâtre du Châtelet Paris, Opera Northern Ireland and the Glyndebourne, Wexford and Edinburgh Festivals; Sang in Carmen at Earls Court, London and on Tour to Japan; Rossini's Bartolo for ENO, 1995. Address: c/o IMG Artists, Media House, 3 Burlington Lane, London W4 2TH, England.

SANDON Nicholas (John), b. 16 Feb 1948, Faversham, Kent, England. Musicologist. m. Edith Virginia Edwards, 1 July 1975, 1 stepson, 2 stepdaughters. Education: Studied, 1967-71, BMus, 1970, University of Birmingham; PhD, University of Exeter, 1983. Career: Lecturer in Music, 1971-86, Head, Music Department, 1983-86, Professor of Music, 1993-, University of Exeter; Professor of Music, Head, Music Department, University College, Cork, Republic of Ireland, 1986-93. Publications: John Shephard's Masses, 1976; Oxford Anthology of Medieval Music, 1977; The Use of Salisbury, 1986-95; Many other editions of English church music; General Editor of Antico Edition. Contributions to: Early Music; Music and Letters; Musica Disciplina; Proceedings of the Royal Musical Association; Royal Musical Association Research Chronicle; Musical Times; Music Review; The Consort; British Broadcasting Corporation Radio 3; Journal of Theological Studies. Honours: University Scholar at Birmingham, 1967-70. Memberships: Royal Musical Associatiion; Plainsong and Medieval Society, Council Member; Henry Bradshaw Society. Hobbies: Liturgy; Cricket. Address: Department of Music, University of Exeter, Exeter EX4 4PD, England.

SANDOR György, b. 21 Sept 1912, Budapest, Hungary. Pianist; Conductor. Education: Piano Student, Liszt Academy, Budapest, Hungary; Piano Student of Bartok; Composition Student of Kodaly. Career: Appearances with the orchestras of Vienna, Baden-Baden, New York Philharmonic Orchestra and The Philadelphia Orchestra; Has performed at numerous music festivals worldwide; Concert tours, Mozarteum, Salzburg and the Assisi Festival; Gave the first performance of Bartok's 3rd Piano Concerto, Philadelphia, 1946; Judges International Piano Competitions; Holds Master Classes. Recordings: Has made numerous recordings including Bartok and the Baroque. Publication: On Piano Playing, 1981. Honour: Grand Prix du Disque.

SANDSTRÖM Sven-Erik, b. 30 Oct 1942, Motala, Sweden. Composer. m. Gudrun Sandstrom. Education: Stockholm University, 1963-67; State College of Music, 1968-72 with Lidholm; Further study with Ligeti and Norgard. Career: Joined Faculty of State College of Music Stockholm, 1980. Compositions: Stage: Strong Like Death, Church opera, 1978; Hasta O Beloved Bride, chamber opera, 1978; Emperor Jones, music drama, 1980; Incidental Music for Strindberg's Dream Play, 1980; Ballet Den elfte gryningen, 1988; Orchestral: Pictures, 1969; Intrada, 1969; In the Meantime, 1970; Around a Line, 1971; Through and Through, 1972; Con tutta Forza, 1976; Clumination, 1977; Agitato, 1978; The Rest is Dross, 1980; Guitar Concerto, 1983; Invignings fanfar, 1988; Chamber: String Quartet, 1969; Mosaic for string trio, 1970; 6 Character Pieces, 1973; Metal, Metal for 4 percussionists, 1974; Utmost, premiered by Pierre Boulez, london 1975; Within for 8 trombones and percussion, 1979; Drums for timpani and 4 percussionists, 1980; Vocal: Inventions for 16 voices, 1969; Lamento, 1971; Birgitta-Music I, 1973; Expression, 1976; A Cradle Song/The Tiger, after Blake, 1978; Requiem, for the child victims of war and racism, 1979; Agnus Dei, 1980; Piano and organ music.

SANDVE Kjell Magnus, b. 1957, Karmoy, Norway. Tenor. Education: Studied at the Oslo State Opera School, 1979-82. Career: Sang at the Nationaltheater Weimar, 1982-84 and Norwegian National Opera at Oslo from 1983, with guest appearances at Copenhagen, Opéra Bastille as Hylas in Les Troyens, the Staatsoper Berlin as Belmonte in 1989, and at Munich as Sifare in Mitridate in 1990; Other roles include Don Ottavio, Ferrando, Nemorino, Alfredo, Lensky and Nielsen's David. Recordings include: Songs by Grieg. Address: Norwegian National Opera, PO Box 8800 Youngstorget, N-0028 Oslo, Norway.

SANTE Sophia (Maris Christina) van, b. 11 Aug 1925, Zaandam, Netherlands. Singer (Mezzo-soprano). Education: Studied at the Amsterdam Muzieklyceum with van der Sluys and Ruth Horna; Further studies with Marietta Amstad in Italy. Career: Many appearances from 1960 with the Amsterdam Opera as the WOman in Schoenberg's Erwartung, Marie in Wozzeck and Judith in Duke BLuebeard's Castle; Also sang in the Dutch premieres of Henze's Der Junge Lord and Dallapiccola's Il Prigioniero. Recordings include: Der Rosenkavalier.

SANTI Nello, b. 22 Sept 1931, Adria, Rovigo, Italy. Conductor. Education: Studied at the Liceo Musicale in Padua and with Coltro and Pedrollo. Debut: Teatro Verdi, Padua, 1951, Rigoletto. Career: Conductor of the Zürich Opera from 1958; Covent Garden debut, 1960, with La Traviata; Vienna Staatsoper and Salzburg Festival debuts, 1960; Metropolitan Opera, 1962, Un Ballo in Maschera; Regular appearances from 1976; La Scala, Milan, 1971; Paris Opéra, 1974; Guest engagements in Berlin, Munich, Florence, Geneva, Lisbon and Madrid, in the operas of Rossini, Bellini, Donizetti, Verdi, Puccini and Mascagni; Orchestral concerts with L'Orchestre National, Paris; RIAS, West Berlin, and the Munich Philharmonic; New Philharmonia Orchestra and the London Symphony; Returned to Covent Garden, 1982, La Fanciulla del West; Conducted Aida in a new production by Vittorio Rossi; Conducts regularly at the Metropolitan Opera House, New York, Arena di Verona and throughout Italy and Germany; Rigoletto at Verona, 1997. Recordings: Pagliacci; L'Amore dei Tre Re; Complete Verdi tenor arias, with Carlo Bergonzi; Aria recitals with Placido Domingo; Videos of Otello, La Bohème, Nabucco, Rigoletto, Andrea Chénier, Falstaff and the Verdi Requiem. Honours: Medallion de la Cité de Zürich; Commendatore of the Republic of Italy. Address: c/o Marks Management Ltd, 14 New Burlington Street, London W1X 1FF, England.

SANTUNIONE Orianna, b. 1 Sept 1934, Sassolo, Modena, Italy. Singer (Soprano). Education: Studied in Milan with Carmen Melis and Renato Pastorino. Career: After debut as Giordano's Fedora sang in Rome, Genoa, Bologna, Trieste, Naples, Parma and Palermo; Covent Garden, London 1965, as Amelia in Un Ballo in Maschera and Elisabeth de Valois; Further appearances in Nice, Rouen, Turin, Venice, Munich, Hamburg, Amsterdam, Dallas, Philadelphia and Cincinnati; Verona Arena, 1967-77; Other roles include Desdemona, Elsa, Medea, Santuzza, Nedda, both Leonoras of Verdi, Mathilde in Guillaume Tell, Francesca da Rimini, Tosca, Madame Butterfly and Aida. Recordings include: Madame Sans-Gêne by Giordano; Pimmalione by Donizetti; Otello and Lohengrin for Italian TV. Address: c/o Arena di Verona, Piazza Bra 28, 1-37121 Verona.

SAPAROVA-FISCHEROVA Jitka, b. 7 Apr 1964, Brno, Czechoslovakia. Opera Singer (Soprano). m. Miroslav Fischer, 19 Oct 1991, 1 daughter. Education: High School of Musical Art. Debut: Mozart's Zauberflöte. Career: Soloist of Chamber Orchestre, Baroque and Renaissance Music, Musica Aeterna, 1985-86; Soloist of Slovak National Theatres Opera from 1986; Operas include: Faust; Le nozze di Figaro; Rigoletto; Suor Angelica; Carmen. Recordings: Rigoletto; La Sonnambula. Honours: 1st Prize, 1985 Competition of M Schneider Trnausee; Laureate of Singing Competition of Antonin Dvorak. Membership: Association of Slovak Theatres. Hobbies: Tourism; Folklore. Address: Dankovskeho 14, 811 03 Bratislava, Slovakia.

SARADJIAN Vagram, b. 15 July 1948, Yerevan, Armenia. Cellist. Debut: Yerevan, Armenia, 1956; US debut, Carnegie Hall, 1994. Career: Winner of Russian National Competition aged 18; Won several major contests including Tchaikovsky International Competition, 1970; Geneva International Cello Competition, 1975; Recitals performed around the world in halls including: Gaveau in Paris; La Scala in Milan, Victoria Hall in Geneva, Musikverein in Vienna, Teatro Colon in Buenos Aires, Carnegie Hall in New York, Great Hall of the Moscow Conservatory, Leningrad Philharmonic Hall; International tours playing with conductors including Gergiev, Khachaturian, Kondrashin, Svetlanov, Rostropovich, Shostakovich, Temirkanov; Premiered works by composers including Alexander Tchaikovsky, Gia Kancheli, Karen Khachaturian; Appearances include: Valery-Gergiev's Stars of the White Nights Festival in St Petersburg; Extensive tour of Argentina and Uraguay; Engaged for performances in Chicago, Los Angeles, Philadelphia, tours in Russia, Switzerland, Poland and Germany. Recordings: Karen Khachaturian Cello Concerto (USSR Symphony Orchestra); Saint-Saens, Concerto No 1; Tchaikovsky Rococo Variations; Dvorak's Concerto in B Minor, op 104 (Moscow Philharmonic); Karen Khachaturian, Sonata for Cello and Piano; Eduard Mirzoian - Sonata for Cello and Piano. Honours: Fourth Prize, Tchaikovsky International Competition, Moscow, 1970; Gold Medals, Geneva Prize Winner, Switzerland, 1975; International Music Festivals in Sofia, 1976, Prague, 1980; First Prize, Aram Khachaturian International Music Awards, New York, 1990. Address: 258 Brookside Avenue, Cresskill, NJ 07626, USA.

SARAI Tibor, b. 10 May 1919, Budapest, Hungary. Composer; Professor of Music (retired). m. Ibolya Schwoelbi, 19 Dec 1947, 1 son. Education: Academy of Music, Budapest, 1942. Career: Head of Music Department, Ministry of Culture, 1949-50; Leader of Musical Section of Hungarian Radio, 1950-53; Professor of the Béla Bartok Conservatory, Budapest, 1953-59; Professor, Franz Liszt Academy of Music, Budapest, 1959-80. Compositions: Serenade for String Orchestra, 1946; Spring Quartets, 1958, 1971, 1982; 3 Symphonies, 1967, 1973, 1987; Musica per 45 Corde, 1971; Quartet for Flute, Violin, Viola and Cello, 1962; dramma per Fiati for Wind Quintet, 1978; 2 Oratorios; 2 Cantatas; Other Orchestral, Instrumental, Choral and Chamber Music. Recordings: Spring Concerto; Serenade for String Orchestra; Symphony No 1 and No 2; Diagnosis 69 for Tenor Solo and Orchestra; String Quartets No 1 and No 2; Musica per 45 Corde. Publication: The History of Czech Music, 1959. Honours: Erkel Prize, 1959; Kossuth Prize, 1975; Merited Artist of the Hungarian People's Republic, 1988. Memberships: Executive Committee, International Music Council 1972-78, Vice President 1976-78, Re-elected 1980-85, Secretary General 1980-82; Individual Member, Executive Committee, International Music Council, 1985.

SARASTE Jukka-Pekka, b. 22 Apr 1956, Heinola, Finland. Conductor. Education: Studied Violin and Conducting at the Sibelius Academy, Helsinki. Debut: 1980 with the Helsinki Philharmonic. Career: Conductor, jointly with Okku Kamu, Helsinki Philharmonic,on 1983 tour of USA; Appointed Principal Guest Conductor of the Finnish Radio Symphony Orchestra, 1985; Principal Conductor from 1987; Principal Conductor, Scottish Chamber Orchestra, 1987-91; Music Director of the Toronto Symphony from 1994; Tours to France, Finland and the Far East; Guest Conductor with orchestras in Minnesota, Vienna, Rotterdam, Munich and Toronto; Conducted the Finnish Radio SO at the 1991 and the Scottish Chamber Orchestra at the 1992 Promenade Concerts, London. Recordings: Mozart Symphonies Nos 32, 35, 36 with the Scottish Chamber Orchestra (Virgin); Sibelius Symphonies (RCA); Debussy La Mer and Images with the Rotterdam Philharmonic, Mahler 5th Symphony with the Finnish Radio Symphony Orchestra. Address: c/o Van Walsum Management Ltd, 26 Wadham Road, London SW15 2LR, England.

SARBU Eugene, b. 1950, Bucharest, Rumania. Voilinist. Education: Following studies in Bucharest and Paris joined Curtis Institute, Philadelphia, for further study with Ivan Galamian; Later at Juilliard, New York, and with Nathan Milstein in Zurich. Career: Made first solo appearance aged 6; Won National Festival of Music Award in Bucharest, 1958; Regular solo recitals and concerts in England; Promenade Concert debut, 1982; Performances in USA, Europe, Australia and South America; Far East tour 1987-88, with the New Japan Philharmonic in Tokyo; Plays a Cremonese Violin by Tomasso Balestieri made in 1756. Recordings: Sibelius Concerto for EMI with the Hallé Orchestra, 1980; Vivaldi's Four Seasons and Mozart Concertos with European Master Orchestra, 1988. Address: c/o Anglo-Swiss Ltd, Suite 35-37, Morley House, 320 Regent Street, London W1R 5AD, England.

SARDI Ivan, b. 7 July 1930, Budapest, Hungary. Singer (Bass). Education: Studied with Antonio Mekandri at the Martini Conservatory Bologna. Debut: Brescia 1951, as Padre Guardiano in La Forza del Destino. Career: Sang in Naples, Bologna, Genoa, Trieste and Catania, as Mozart's Masetto and Bartolo and in Operas by Verdi; Glyndebourne 1956, as Don Alfonso; Further appearances in Florence, Milan and Lisbon; Staatsoper Munich, 1956-61; Member of the Deutsche Oper Berlin from 1961; Concerts in Munich, Hamburg, Vienna and elsewhere in Europe; Sang Schigolch in Lulu at Dresden, 1992. Recordings: Don Giovanni, Le nozze di Figaro, Verdi Requiem, Der junge Lord by Henze (Deutsche Grammophon); Sparafucile in Rigoletto (Philips); Guillaume Tell. Address: c/o Deutsche Oper Berlin, Richard Wagnerstrasse 10, D-100 Berlin 1, Germany.

SARDINERO Vincenzo, b. 12 Jan 1937, Barcelona, Spain. Singer (Baritone). Education: Studied at the Liceo Conservatory in Barcelona. Career: Sang first in operettas and Spanish zarzuelas; Oper debut Barcelona 1964, as Escamillo; In 1967 sang Germont in La Traviata at Barcelona and in Lucia di Lammermoor at La Scala, Milan; New York City Opera 1970, as Tonio in Pagliacci; Covent Garden debut 1976, as Marcello in La Bohème; Further appearances Lisbon, Rome, Vienna, Madrid, Lyons, Paris, Munich, Hamburg, Basle, Budapest and the Aix-en-Provence Festival; Season 1991-92 as Marcello at Barcelona and Rigoletto at Palma; Other roles include Nottingham in Roberto Devereux, Valentin (Faust), Alphonse XI (La Favorite) and Verdi's Renato, Posa and Luna. Recordings include: L'Amico Fritz, L'Atlantida, Turandot and Manon Lescaut (HMV); Lucia di Lammermoor and Un Giorno di Regno (Philips); La Navarraise by Massenet and Edgar by Puccini (CBS); La Straniera by Bellini (MRF).

SARFATY Regina, b. 1932, Rochester, New York, USA. Singer (Mezzo-soprano). Education: Studied at the Juilliard School, New York. Career: Sang with New Mexico Opera from 1948; Santa Fe Opera from 1957, notably in the 1968 US premiere of The Bassarids by Henze; New York City Opera from 1958, as Cenerentola, Maria Golovin in the opera by Menotti, Jocasta (Oedipus Rex) and Dorabella; Frankfurt Opera from 1963, as Carmen and Octavian; Sang Octavian at Glyndebourne, 1960, and returned in 1984, as Adelaide in Arabella; Sang Mme de Croissy in Dialogues des Carmélites at Baltimore, 1984; Member of the Zurich Opera, notably as the Countess Geschwitz in Lulu and in the premiere of Die Erretung Thebens by Kelterborn, 1963. Recordings: Excerpts from Die Walküre, conducted by Stokowski; The Rake's Progress, conducted by Stravinsky, and the Choral Symphony, conducted by Bernstein.

SARGON Simon A, b. 6 Apr 1938, Bombay, India. Composer; Pianist; Music Director. m. Bonnie Glasgow, 17 Nov 1961, 1 daughter. Education: BA, Brandeis University, 1959; MS, Juilliard School, 1962. Debut: Carnegie Hall, with Jennie Tourel, 1963. Career: Musical Staff, New York City Opera, 1960; Associate Conductor, Concert Opera, 1962-68; Pianist for concerts of Jennie Tourel, 1963-71; Faculty Member, Juilliard School, 1967-69; Chairman, Voice, Rubin Academy, Jerusalem, 1971-74; Faculty, Hebrew University, Jerusalem, 1973-74; Director of Music, Temple Emanu-El, 1974-; Faculty, SMU, 1983-. Compositions: Patterns in Blue, 1976; Elul: Midnight, 1980; Praise Ye the Lord, 1980; Sing His Praise, 1981; The Queen's Consort, 1982; Lord Make Me to Know My End, 1985; Voices of Change, commission, 1988; Symphony No 1, Holocaust, premiered by Dallas Symphony, 1991; Jump Back; Before the Ark. Recordings: Music for French Horn and Piano; Huntsman, What Quarry; Deep Ellum Nights. Publications: Shemà; At Grandmother's Knee, 1995; Waves of the Sea, 1995. Address: 3308 Dartmouth Avenue, Dallas, TX 75205, USA.

SARICH Paul, b. 18 September 1951, Wellington, New Zealand. Composer; Percussionist. Education: BSc, Victoria University of Wellington, 1971; Study with Leonard Salzedo and James Blades, 1981. Career: Percussionist, Various Australian Bands and Orchestras, 1973-93; Lecturer, Victoria College of the Arts, 1991-; New Notations, London, 1994-95. Compositions: Fantasia in G Minor for Violin, 1981; Sonata for Side Drum and 3 Percussion, 1981; Fantasia on a fragment of Martinu, for Orchestra, 1982; Chaconne in B Flat for Tuba, 1986; Concerto for Bass Trombone and Orchestra, 1986; Antiphons for 2 Percussions, 1986; Divertimento for Viola, cello, Double Bass and Percussion, 1986; Five in the Afternoon, Trumpet, Keyboards and Percussion, 1986; Dance Suite for 3 Tubas, 1987; Concerto da Camera, for Percussion and Strings, 1988; Music for Tubes and Sticks, 1988; Songs of Light and Shade for Soprano and Ensemble, 1989; Concerto Pieces for Timpani and Piano, 1990; Percussion Mass, 1991; The Illusionist for Bass and Piano, 1992; Fiesta, for Soprano, Timpani, 4 Percussion and Flamenco Dancers, 1993; Essay for Brass Quintet & 8 Tubas, 1993; Austranimalia for Chorus, Bass, Percussion and Piano, 1994; Invocation and Dance for Saxophone and Clarinet Trio, 1994; Three Neruda Love Songs for Soprano and Ensemble, 1994. Address: c/o APRA, 1A Eden Street, Crows Nest, NSW 2065, Australia.

SAROSI Balint, b. 1 Jan 1925, Csikrakos, Hungary. Ethnomusicologist. m. Yolande Benkö, 18 Oct 1952, 2 daughters. Education: PhD, Pazmany Peter University, Budapest; Studied Composition and Musicology, Academy of Budapest. Career: Research Fellow, 1958, Senior Member, 1971, Director, 1974, Ethnomusical Section, Institute for Musicology, Budapest; Retired, 1988-. Recordings: Hungarian Instrumental Folk Music; Folk Music collected by Béla Bartok, phonograph cylinders; Anthology of Hungarian Folk Music V and VI. Publications: Die Volksmusikinstrumente Ungarns, 1967; Gypsy Music, 1979; Folk Music, Hungarian Musical Idiom, 1986; A Hanszeres Magyar Népzene, 1996. Contributions to: Articles in Studia instrumentorum musicae popularis, Stockholm. Honours: Erkel Prize, 1976; Order of Labour, 1988; Middle Cross, Order of the Hungarian Republic, 1995. Membership: Executive Board, International Council for Traditional Music, 1972-91. Address: Alda u 11, H-1025 Budapest, Hungary.

SARROCA Suzanne, b. 21 Apr 1927, Carcassonne, France. Singer (Soprano). Education: Studied at the Toulouse Conservatoire, 1946-48. Deubt: Carcassonne 1949, as Massenet's Charlotte. Career: Sang Carmen in Brussels, 1951; Paris Opera and Opera-Comique from 1952, as Tosca, Rezia, Marina (Boris Godunov), Aida, Marguerite La Damnation de Faust, Leonore and Octavian 1957, 1966; Also sang in Les Indes Galantes by Rameau; Guest appearances in Marseille, 1961 (Donna Anna), Rome 1965 (Elisabeth de Valois) and in Buenos Aires, Geneva, New York, London, Lisbon, Strasbourg and Toulouse; Salzburg Festival 1968, in Cavalieri's La Rappresentazione di Anima e di Corpo; Further engagements in Rio de Janeiro, Hamburg and Vienna; Modern repertoire included La Voix Humaine by Poulenc and Schoenberg's Erwartung; Director of the Centre d'art Lyrique at Strasbourg, 1983-85.

SARTORETTI Christine, b. 30 Aug 1943, Sion, Switzerland. Harpsichordist. m. Jean-Pierre Girardin, 10 Jan 1976, 1 son, 1 daughter. Education: Piano studies with Pierre Cerf, Lausanne, 1968, Harpsichord with Christiane Jaccottet; Diploma, Lausanne Conservatory; Masterclasses with Gustav Leonhardt, Kenneth Gilbert and Fernando Tagliavini. Career: Soloist and continuo player at various concerts in Europe; Played with Wurttembergische Kammerorchester, 1978-81, Los Angeles Chamber Orchestra, 1980, Zurich Chamber Orchestra, 1985 and Serenata Ensemble in Geneva, 1985; Currently, Teacher of harpsichord and continuo at Lausanne Conservatory; Several performances on Swiss Radio and Swedish Radio Stockholm. Recording: Bach's Concerti for Several Harpsichords. Honour: 1st Prize, Lausanne Conservatory. Memberships: Association des Musiciens Suisses; Societé Suisse de Pedagogie Musicale. Hobbies: Playing Organ; Walking in mountains. Address: 4 Chemin de Broye, CH-1020 Renens, Switzerland.

SASAKI Ken, b. 14 Sept 1943, Sendai, Miyagi, Japan. Concert Pianist. Education: Studied at University of Arts, Tokyo and at Warsaw Conservatoire; Attended Master Classes of Vlado Periemuter in Paris and Danuta Lewandowska in Warsaw. Career: Given many concerts in France, Poland, Holland, Switzerland, Austria, Germany, Japan; British debut 1972, at the Wigmore Hall; Coast to coast tour of the USA, 1979; Queen Elizabeth Hall, London, 1986 playing Bach's 1st Partita, Gaspard de la Nuit and Chopin's 2nd Sonata; Further appearances with the Warsaw Chamber Orchestra and the Berlin Octet; Other repertory includes Concertos by Bach (D minor) and Beethoven (C minor and G major); Mozart K449 and K466; Chopin No 1 and Schumann; Ravel in G; Rachmaninov Nos 1 and 3; Mozart Sonatas K310, K311; Chopin Sonatas, Etudes Ballades, Nocturnes, Preludes and Polonaise; Schumann Fantasie Op 17, Fantasiestücke, Etudes Symphoniques and Kreisleriana; Ravel Miroirs and Le Tombeau de Couperin; Debussy Images and Suite Bergamasque; Prokofiev 3rd and 7th Sonatas and Scriabin Etudes; Scarlatti Sonatas. Recordings include: Chopin Etudes (Nimbus). Honours include: Stefanie Niekrasz Prize, 1984.

SASS Sylvia, b. 21 July 1951, Budapest, Hungary. Singer (Soprano). Education: Studied at the Liszt Academy Budapest with Ferenc Revhegyi. Debut: Budapest State Opera 1971, as

Frasquita in Carmen. Career: First major role as Gutrune, 1972; Sang Giselda in I Lombardi, 1973 and repeated the role at Covent Garden, 1976; Sofia 1972, Violetta (also at Aix-en-Provence 1976); Scottish Opera debut 1975, Desdemona; At the Budapest Opera 1977, sang in the premiere of Mozes by Zsolt Durko; Metropolitan Opera 1977, Tosca; Guest engagements at the State Operas of Hamburg and Munich and at the Paris Opéra and La Scala Milan; Other roles include Norma, Penelope (Il Ritorno d'Ulisse), Tatiana, Elvira (Ernani), Alceste, Odabella (Attila), Medea, Santuzza, Elisabeth de Valois, Lady Macbeth, Donna Elvira and Donna Anna, Countess Almaviva, Mimi, Manon Lescaut, Turandot, Adriana Lecouvreur, Nedda (Pagliacci), Juliette and Marguerite by Gounod, and Salome (Budapest 1989); Has sung Bartok's Judith on BBC television and in Montpellier and Metz, 1989; Many concert performances in music by Strauss and Wagner; Modern repertoire includes Sogno di un Tramonto d'Autumno by Malipiero; Wigmore Hall debut 1979, in songs by Strauss and Liszt; Invited to return for Andras Schiff's Beethoven-Bartok series, Sept 1990; Season 1993, as Adriana Lecouvreur at Budapest. Recordings include: Don Giovanni, Arias by Puccini and Verdi, Liszt and Bartok songs (Decca); Verdi Stiffelio, Il Trittico, Duke Bluebeard's Castle by Bartok (Philips); Wagner Wesendonck Lieder, Vier Letzte Lieder by Strauss, Medea, Ernani, I Lombardi, Macbeth, Attila, Faust, Mozes by Durko, Erkel's Hunyadi Laszlo (Hungaroton). Address: c/o Ron Gonsalves, 10 Dagnan Road, London SW12 9LQ, England.

SASSON Deborah, b. 1955, Boston, Massachusetts, USA. Singer (Soprano). m. Peter Hofmann, 1983 (divorced 1990). Education: Studied at Oberlin College with Ellen Repp and Helen Hodam; New England Conservatory, Boston with Gladys Miller. Debut: Hamburg Staatsoper 1979, as Maria in West Side Story. Career: Sang at the Stadttheater Aachen, 1979-81; Guest appearances in Hamburg, Berlin, Venice and San Francisco; Has sung at the Bayreuth Festival from 1982; Other roles include Norina, Adina, Gilda, Rosina, Despina and Zerlina. Recordings include: Arias and Duets with Peter Hofmann (CBS); Mahler's 8th Symphony, from Tanglewood (Philips). Address: c/o PO Box Bayreuther Festspiele, 8580 Bayreuth 1, Germany.

SATANOWSKI Robert (Zdzislaw), b. 20 June 1918, Lodz, Poland. Conductor; Music Director. m. 2 sons. Education: Technical University, Warsaw, 1935-39; Theory of Music and Conducting, Academy of Music, Lodz, Poland, graduated 1951. Debut: Lodz State Philharmonic, 1951. Career: Conductor, Lubin State Philharmonic, 1951-54; Artistic Director, Principal Conductor, Bydgoszcz State Philharmonic, 1954-58; General Music Director, Staedtische Oper Karl Marx Stadt/former and later Chemitz, 1960-62; General and Artistic Director, State Opera Poznan, 1962-69; Founder and Artistic Director, Poznan Chamber Orchestra, 1963-69; General Music Director, Staedtishe Buehnen Krefeld-Moenchengladbach, 1969-76, State Opera House, Cracow, 1975-77, State Opera House, Wroclaw, 1977-82, Grand Theatre Warsaw/National Opera, 1981-91; Guest Conductor, Operatic works, Staatsoper Vienna, Dresden, Berlin, Bolshoi Moscow State Opera Bucharest, Operhaus Dresden, Oslo Opera House, Opera House Seattle, USA, National Opera House Genoa, Royal Opera Liège, Zagreb Opera House, Istanbul Festival; Symphony Concerts, Paris, London, Moscow, Berlin, Dresden, Leipzig, Bucharest, Genoa, Stockholm, Gothenburg, Leningrad, Teheran, Ankara, Madrid, Vienna, Dusseldorf, Warsaw. Compositions: Symphony, Chamber and Vocal Works composed until 1958. Recordings: With National Philharmonic, Warsaw, Warsaw Grand Theatre Orchestra, State Symphony Orchestra, Poznan, Poznan Chamber Orchestra, mainly Polish, classical and contemporary, symphony and operatic works. Address: Teatr Wielki, ul Moliera 3/5, 00-950 Warsaw, Poland.

SATO Sumiko, b. 2 feb 1967, Japan. Composer; Pianist. Education: DMA, Composition, MM, Composition, University of Washington, USA. Compositions: Misthaven, for solo violin and orchestra, commissioned and premiered by Northwest Symphony Orchestra, 1996. Recording: Afterflakes, for violin, cello and harp. Publication: Morivic Improvisation: Approach and Analyses, doctoral dissertation, 1996. Honour: Rotary Foundation Scholarship, 1988-89. Membership: International Women's Association of Music. Address: 8-81-50, Kochi Ishidoriya Hienuki-Gun, Iwate 028-3101, Japan.

SATOH Somei, b. 19 January 1949, Sendai, Japan. Composer. Education: Studied in Japan. Career: Freelance Composer in Advanced Idioms, including Non-Western Techniques and Instruments; Resident in New York, 1983-84. Compositions include: Hymn for the Sun for 2 Pianos and Tape Delay, 1975; Cosmic Womb, 1975; Incarnation I and II, 1977-78; The Heavenly Spheres Are Illuminated by Light, for Soprano, Piano and Percussion, 1979; Birds in Warped Time I and II, 1980; Lyra for 2 Harps, Percussion and Strings, 1980; Sumeru I and II, 1982, 1985; A Journey Through Sacred Time, 1983; Naohi for Piano, 1983; Hikari for Trumpet and Piano, 1986; Shirasagi for String Quartet, 1987; Stabat Mater for Soprano and Chorus, 1987; A Gate into Infinity for Violin, Piano and Percussion, 1988; Homa for Soprano and String Quartet, 1988; Towards the Night for Strings, 1991; Kami No Miuri for Mezzo and 7 Instruments, 1991; Burning Meditation, for Baritone, Harp, Tubar Bells and String Quartet, 1993 (revised version, New York, 1995); Lanzarote for Soprano Saxophone and Piano, 1993. Address: c/o JASRAC, 3-6-12 Uehara, Shibuya-ku, Tokyo 151, Japan.

SATUKANGAS Arto Untamo, b. 6 Sept 1962, Espoo, Finland. Pianist. Education: Diploma, Sibelius Academy of Music, Helsinki, 1981; St Petersburg Conservatory with Professor Vladimir Nilsen, 1981-83; Private Lessons with Nikita Magaloff, Switzerland. Debut: Helsinki, 1980, Paris, 1987. Career: Concerts in Finland, Sweden, Iceland, Germany, England, France, Italy, Spain, USA, Israel, Japan and China. Recordings: Piano Music of Alexander Glazunov and Mily Balakirev; Piano Music of Ravel. Contributions to: Finnish Newspapers. Honour: 1st Prize, National Maj Lind Competition, Helsinki, 1979. Hobbies: Reading; Languages; Chess; Outdoors. Current Management: PoloArtico Oy, Helsinki. Address: Tullastrasse 76, 76131 Karlsruhe, Germany.

SAULESCO Mircea (Petre), b. 14 Sept 1926, Bucharest, Romania. Violinist. m. (1) 3 children, (2) Gunilla Sandberg-Saulesco, 1 child. Education: Bucharest Conservatory; Diploma, Bucharest Musical Academy, 1944; Studied with various masters including Iosif Dailis, Garbis Avachian, Georges Enesco and Jacques Thibaud; Studied Piano and Composition with various masters. Debut: Bucharest, 1941. Career: Member, Bucharest Radio Symphony Orchestra, 1938-50; Founder, Saulesco String Quartet, 1945; Member 1950-58, Leader 1957-58, Bucharest State Philharmonic Orchestra Georges Enesco; Numerous chamber music and solo concerts in Eastern Europe until 1958; Member and one of the Leaders, Symphony Orchestra, Swedish Broadcasting Corporation, 1958-; Founder, Swedish Saulesco Quartet, 1962; Co-Founder, Leygraf (piano) Quartet, 1965; Numerous TV and Radio appearances; Various foreign concert tours. Recordings include: Alfven Violin Sonata; Mozart Piano Quartets No 1 G minor and No 2 E flat major; Atterberg String Quartet op 11; Verdi, String Quartet E minor. Honours: Swedish Record Prize, Grammis, 1970, 1972; Austrian Mozart Prize, 1974. Memberships: Mazer Society for Chamber Music. Hobbies: Art Books; Chess; Model Railways. Address: Pepparkaksgrand 26, S-128 66 Sköndal, Sweden.

SAUNDERS Arlene, b. 5 Oct 1935, Cleveland, Ohio, USA. Soprano; Teacher. Education: Baldwin-Wallace College and New York. Debuts: Operatic, as Rosalinde with National Opera Company, 1958; New York City Opera debut as Giorgetta in Il Tabarro, 1961; European debut as Mimi, Teatro Nuovo, Milan, 1961. Career: Joined Hamburg State Opera, 1964; Also sang Pamina, Glyndebourne Festival, England, 1966 and Louise, San Francisco Opera 1967, Beatrix Cenci (world premiere) with the Washington DC Opera Society 1971, Eva, Metropolitan Opera 1976, Minnie, Royal Opera Covent Garden, London 1980; Farewell operatic appearances as the Marschallin, Teatro Colon, Buenos Aires, 1985; Other roles were Natasha (War and Peace), Nadia in The Ice Break (US premiere Boston, 1979), Mozart Donna Elvira and Fiordiligi, Wagner's Sieglinde, Elsa, Senta and Elisabeth, Tosca, Manon, Arabella and the Countess in Capriccio; Teacher, Rutgers University, New Jersey and Abraham Goodman School, New York, 1987-. Recordings: Several discs. Honours: Gold Medal, Vercelli Vocal Competition; Kammersängerin, Hamburg State Opera, 1967.

SAUNDERS Jenny, b. England. Singer (Soprano). Education: Studied with Marjorie Thomas at the Royal Academy of Music and with Mary Thomas. Career: Concerts include Mozart's C Minor Mass in Canterbury Cathedral, Mendelssohn's Elijah in Scotland, the Christmas Oratorio in Oslo and the Brahms Requiem at the St Endellion Easter Festival; Further engagements with Messiah and Carmina Burana at the Albert Hall, Gounod's St Cecilia Mass and the Fauré Requiem at the Festival Hall and Mendelssohn's Midsummer Night's Dream with the Academy of St Martin in the Fields; Appearances with the Opera Company as Helen in Mefistofele and Mozart's Barabarina and Susanna; Season 1996-97 as Zerlina for Opera East, in Dido and Aeneas at Covent Garden and The Fairy Queen on tour to Spain and Greece; Despina for Country Opera and Nannetta for Palace Opera; 1997 concerts at St John's Smith Square (Exsultate Jubilate and St Matthew Passion) St Paul's Cathedral (Vivaldi's Gloria) and Wells Cathedral (Haydn's Creation); Papagena with Opera Factory. Honours include: Winner, Soprano Section, 1992 Great Grimsby International Singers Competition. Address: c/o Hazard Chase Ltd, Richmond House, 16-20 Regent Street, Cambridge CB2 1DB, England.

SAUTER Lily, b. 16 Nov 1934, Zurich, Switzerland. Singer. Education: Studied in Milan and Zurich. Career: Sang at the Deutsche Oper am Rhein Dusseldorf, 1961-64; Zurich Opera, 1965-66; Stuttgart Staatsoper, 1964-83; Guest appearances at the State Operas of Hamburg and Munich, Berlin, Frankfurt, Barcelona, Venice, Milan, Genoa and Edinburgh; Roles have included Mozart's Susanna, Blondchen and Despina, Rosina, Martha, Norina, Adina, Marzelline, Lortzing's Gretchen and Marie, Musetta, Nannetta, Sophia in Der Rosenkavalier, Aennchen and Regina in Mathis der Maler; TV appearances in Germany and Switzerland. Address: c/o Staatsoper Stuttgart, Operer Schlossgarten 6, 7000 Stuttgart, Germany.

SAVAGE Stephen (Leon), b. 26 Apr 1942, Hertford, England. Concert Pianist; Conductor; Teacher. m. Valerie Dickson, 2 sons. Education: Vienna Akademie with Bruno Seidlhofer; Royal College of Music with Cyril Smith. Debut: Wigmore Hall, London, 1966. Career: Concerts, Radio, Television, Recordings in England, Canada, Australia, Japan; Concertos with Boult, A Davis, Zollman and others including 1st Australasian performance, Lutoslawski Concerto 1989; Director, Brisbane Tippett Festival 1990; Dedicatee of major works by Justin Connolly and Roger Smalley; Professor of Piano and co-Director, 20th Century Ensemble, Royal College of Music, 1967-81, Artistic Director, Conductor, Griffith University Ensemble, Brisbane, Australia; Frequent Residencies include, Universities of Adelaide, Toronto, Hong Kong, Guildhall School of Music; Noted for performances of classical repertoire and 20th Century Music including important first performances. Recordings: Roger Smalley, Accord for 2 Pianos with the Composer; Tippett, sonatas 1 and 3. Honours: Dannreuther Prize, 1964; Hopkinson Medal, Worshipful Company of Musicians, Medal, 1965; Recommendation of Tippett Sonatas 1 and 3 by Gramophone, 1986. Address: c/o Queensland Conservatorium of Music, Griffith University, PO Box 28, Brisbane, Albert Street, 4002 Brisbane, Australia.

SAVARY Jerome, b. 27 June 1942, Buenos Aires, Argentina. Stage Director. Education: Studied in Paris. Career: Stagings of Operettas by Offenbach and Johann Strauss at the Geneva Opera, 1982-91; La Scala Milan, 1983-92, with a Revival of Cherubini's Anacreon, the Premiere of Corghi's Blimunda, and Attila; Don Giovanni at Rome, 1984; Die Zauberflöte at Bregenz, 1985, followed by Les Contes d'Hoffmann and Carmen; Directed Le Comte Ory for the Opera de Lyons, 1988 and War and Peace for San Francisco Opera, 1991; La Cenerentola for Geneva and the Palais Garnier, Paris, 1996. Address: c/o Teatro Alla Scala, Via Filodrammatici 2, Milan, Italy.

SAVOIE Robert, b. 21 Apr 1927, Montreal, Canada. Singer (Baritone). Education: Studied with Pauline Donalda in Montreal and with Antonio Narducci in Milan. Debut: Teatro Nuovo Milan 1952, as Scarpia. Career: Sang with many seasons for L'Opéra de Montreal and made guest appearances with the Paris Opéra and the Opéra du Rhin Strasbourg; Opera houses in Nice, Toulouse, Lyon, Marseille, Dallas, Washington, Pittsburgh and London; Other roles have been Mozart's Leporello, Don Giovanni, Count Figaro and Guglielmo; Escamillo; Verdi's Iago, Amonasro and Ford in Falstaff; Puccini's Gianni Schicchi and Sharpless; Golaud in Pelléas et Mélisande, Albert in Werther and Ramiro in L'Heure Espagnole; Artistic Director, City of Lachine, Quebec, Canada, now retired; The Lachine Music Festival. Recordings include: Posa in the French version of Don Carlos. Honours: Doctorat Honoris Causa in Music, University of Moncton, Canada. Memberships: President, Founder, L'Orchestra Metropolitan of Montreal. Address: 2100 Du Calvados, St Bruno, Quebec J3V 3K2, Canada.

SAVOVA Galina, b. 1945, Sofia, Bulgaria. Singer (Soprano). Career: Sang first at the Sofia Opera before an international career at the opera houses of Rome, Naples, Karlsruhe and Bologna; Metropolitan Opera debut 1982, as Amelia in Un ballo in Maschera; Other roles include Chrysothemis (Elektra), Puccini's Minnie, Turandot and Tosca, Amelia (Simon Boccanegra), Yaroslavna in Prince Igor and Leonore; In 1989 sang Aida at the Teatro Sao Carlos, Lisbon; Chicago Lyric Opera, 1992 as Turandot. Address: c/o Teatro Sao Carlos, Rua Serpa Pinto 9, 1200 Lisbon, Portugal.

SAWALLISCH Wolfgang, b. 26 Aug 1923, Munich, Germany. Conductor; Pianist. Education: Studied at the Munich Academy. Career: Repetiteur at Augsburg; Conducted Hansel and Gretel on 1947 debut; Joint winner of prize for duos at 1949 Geneva International Competition; General Music Director at Aachen, 1953-58; Wiesbaden, 1958-60; Cologne, 1960-63; Bayreuth debut 1957, Tristan und Isolde; Later conducted Tannhäuser and Der fliegende Holländer there; London 1957, with Schwarzkopf in a Lieder programme and conducting the Philharmonia Orchestra; 1961, Principal Conductor, Vienna Symphony Orchestra and Hamburg Philharmonic Orchestra; US debut 1964; General Music Director, Bavarian State Opera Munich, 1971-92, Philadelphia Orchestra, 1993; Covent Garden debut with the Munich company 1972, conducting operas by Strauss; Lieder programmes with Dietrich Fischer-Dieskau and Hermann Prey; Solo performances as pianist in works by Mozart and Beethoven; Conducted a new production of Strauss's Friedenstag at the Munich Festival, 1988; Mathis der Maler and Dantons Tod, 1990; Arabella at La Scala, 1992; Last new production as Chief Conductor of the Bavarian State Opera, Henze's Der Prinz von Homburg, 1992. Recordings: Operas by Strauss, Mozart and Wagner (Die Meistersinger, 1994);

Orchestral music by Schubert, Mendelssohn and Beethoven; Video of The Ring, from Munich, 1989. Address: c/o Bayerische Staatsoper, Postfach 745, D-8000 Munich 1, Germany.

SAWER David, b. 14 Sept 1961, Stockport, England. Composer. Education: University of York; DPhil studies with Richard Orton; Further studies with Mauricio Kagel in Cologne. Career: Music performed by the London Sinfonietta and Music Projects, London; Commissions from Musica 1986, the Kirklees Metropolitan Council, the 1988 Almeida Festival, King's Lynn Festival, BBC Singers, 1990, and BBC Symphony Orchestra for 1992 Proms; Directed premiere productions of Kagel's Pas de Cinq and Kantrimusik (Huddersfield Festival 1983, 1984) and as Soloist in Kagel's Phonophonie at the 1987 Summerscope season on South Bank; Music for radio and theatre productions. Compositions: Solo Piano, 1983; Cat's-Eye for ensemble, 1986; Take Off for ensemble, 1987; Food of Love for actress and piano, 1988; Good Night for ensemble, 1989; Swansong for radio, 1989; Songs of Love and War, 1990, for choir SATB, 2 harp, 2 percussion; The Melancholy of Departure for piano, 1990; The Panic, a chamber opera, 4 singers and 6 instruments, 1990-91; Byrnan Wood for large orchestr, 1992; The Memory of Water for strings, 1993; Trumpet Concerto, 1994. Contributions to: Grove Dictionary of Opera, entry on Kagel. Honours: DAAD Scholarship, 1984-85; Sony Radio Award, for Swansong, 1990; Fulbright-Chester-Schirmer Fellowship in composition, 1992-93. Current Management: Unversal Edition (London) Limited. Address: c/o Universal Edition (London) Limited, 48 Great Marlborough Street, London, England.

SAWYER Philip (John), b. 3 Feb 1948, Birmingham, England. Lecturer; Organist; Continuo Player. m. Judith Susan Timbury, 9 Jan 1981. Education: Royal College of Music, 1966-68; ARCM, 1966; ARCO, 1967; Peterhouse, Cambridge, 1968-71; BA, Honours, 1971; MA, 1975; Organ study in Amsterdam with Piet Kee, 1970; MMus, 1986. Career: Assistant Director of Music, Trent College, 1971-73; Lecturer, 1975-79, Senior Lecturer, 1989-, Napier Polytechnic of Edinburgh; Organist, Choirmaster: St Cuthbert's Parish Church, Edinburgh, 1975-78, Nicolson Square Methodist Church, Edinburgh, 1978-83, Director of Music, St Andrew's and St George's Churches, Edinburgh, 1983-86; Organ recitals: Westminster Abbey, Notre Dame, Paris, Nice Cathedral, Monaco Cathedral, St Laurens, Alkmaar, St Bavo's RC Cathedral, Haarlem, Hillsborough Parish Church, N Ireland; Universities of: St Andrews, Edinburgh, Glasgow, Aberdeen; Cathedrals: Edinburgh, Glasgow, Dundee; Founder and Director, Edinburgh Organ Week; First performances of newly-commissioned organ works by Alan Ridout and others; 1st Performance of The Seven Sacraments of Poussin by John Mcleod in Edinburgh, Glasgow and London, 1992; Appearances as Continuo Player with: Scottish Chamber Orchestra, Scottish Baroque Ensemble; Head Music, Napier University, 1990-; Conductor, Scottish Chamber Choir, 1994-. Recordings: Solo Organ recitals for BBC Radio 3 and Radio Scotland; Harpsichord Continuo with Scottish Chamber Orchestra, conductor, Gibson, with music by Handel; BBC Radio Scotland recording of 1st performance of The Seven Sacraments of Poussin, Edinburgh, 1992. Contributions to: Various to journals of British Institute of Organ Studies. Address: Dept Music, Napier University, Sighthill Court, Edinburgh, EH11 4BN, Scotland.

SAXBY Joseph (Anthony), b. 3 Jan 1910, London, England. Musician; Harpsichord & Piano Player. Education: Studied Harpsichord with Arnold Dolmetsch, Piano with Herbert Fryer, Composition with Herbert Howells; Royal College of Music. Debut: Accompanist to Michael Zacharewitsch, Russian Violinist, USA Tour, 1925. Career: Farewell tour of John McCormack, Ireland; 49 overseas tours with Carl Dolmetsch, Europe, USA, Australia, New Zealand, Japan, Italy, England; Numerus radio and television appearances with Carl Dolmetsch. Compositions: Various accompaniments, from Figured Bass for Recorder Works. Recordings: Decca, EMI; Records of harpsichord recitals with Carl Dolmetsch. Contributions to: Various magazines and radio interviews. Honours: Honorary Fellow, London College of Music; Dedications in pieces for harpsichord, various artists including Arnold Cooke, Colin Hand, John Gardner. Memberships: President, haslemere & Grayshott Recorded Music Society; Incorporated Society of Musicians; Royal College of Music Union; Governor, Dolmetsch Foundation. Hobbies: Reading; Television. Address: Red Cot, Three Gates Lane, Haslemere, Surrey, England.

SAXTON Robert, b. 8 Oct 1953, London, England. Composer. Education: St Catharine's College, Cambridge; BMus, Worcester College, Oxford; Studied privately with Elisabeth Lutyens and Luciano Berio; DMus, Oxford, 1992. Career: Lecturer, Bristol University, 1984-; Currently Head of Composition, Guildhall School of Music and Drama. Compositions include: Orchestral: Ring of Eternity, 1982-83; Concerto for Orchestra, 1984; Viola Concerto, 1986; In The Beginning, 1987; Elijah's Violin, 1988; Music to Celebrate the Resurrection of Christ, 1988; Violin Concerto, 1989; Cello Concerto, 1992; Ring, Time, wind orchestra, 1994; Ensemble: Piccola Musica per Luigi Dallapiccola, 1981; Processions and Dances, 1981; Vocal: Cantata No 3, 1981; Eloge, soprano, ensemble, 1981; Chaconne, double chorus, 1981; Caritas, opera, 1991; Paraphrase on Mozart's Idomeneo, 1991; Chamber: Chiaroscuro, percussion, 1981; Piano Sonata, 1981; Fantasiestuck, accordion, 1982; The Sentinel of the Rainbow, sextet, 1984; A Yardstick to the Stars, 1994; Choral: I Will Awake The Dawn, 1987; At the Earth's Round Imagined Corners, 1992; Psalm, a song of ascents, 1992; O Sing unto the Lord a New Song, 1993; Canticum Luminis, choir, orchestra, 1994; Invocation, Dance and Meditation; A Yardstick to the Stars; Fanfare for the Golden Wedding Anniversary of Queen Elizabeth II; Songs, Dances and Ellipses. Recordings: Concerto for Orchestra; Sentinel of the Rainbow; Circles of Light; Ring of Eternity; Violin Concerto; In the Beginning; I Will Awake the Dawn; Paraphrase on Mozart's Idomeneo; Cantas, opera; At the Round Earth's Imagined Corners; Night Dance; Music to Celebrate the Resurrection of Christ; Chacony; Piano Sonata; A Yardstick to the Stars; Éloge; Processions and Dances; Invocation, Dance and Meditation. Contribution to: Where do I begin?, article, to Musical Times, Oct 1994; Reviews in Times Literary Supplement. Honours: 1st Prize, International Gaudeamus Music Week, Netherlands, 1975; Fulbright Arts Award, Visiting Fellow, Princeton University, 1986; DMus, Oxon, 1992. Memberships: Music Advisory Panel, Arts Council, 1989-93; Music Advisory Panel, South Bank Centre, 1990-; Board, South Bank, 1997-. Hobbies: Philosophy of mathematics; History; Cricket; Theatre. Current Management: Chester Music. Address: c/o Chester Music, Music Sales, 8/9 Frith Street, London W1V 5TZ, England.

SAYERS Gavin, b. 7 Jan 1962, England. Singer (Tenor). Education: Studied at the Guildhall School of Music with Johanna Peters and Maureen Morelle. Career: Sang Arturo in a concert performance of Lucia di Lammermoor, 1986; British premiere of Nino Rota's La Notte di un nevrastenico at Morley College, 1990; Concert repertoire includes Puccini's Messa di Gloria; Hiawatha's Wedding Feast by Coleridge-Taylor; Haydn's Nelson Mass and Maria Theresa Mass; Messiah and Mozart Mass in C; Hymn of Praise by Mendelssohn (2nd Symphony); Elijah (Harrow Choral Society 1990); Britten's Serenade (East Surrey Orchestra 1991); Has performed in a variety of amateur operatic performances. Address: c/o Korman International Management, Crunnells Green Cottage, Preston, Herts SG4 7UQ, England.

SAYLOR Bruce, b. 24 Apr 1946, Philadelphia, USA. Composer. Education: Studied with Hugo Weisgall and Roger Sessions; Accademia di Santa Cecilia in Rome with Petrassi and Evangelisti, CUNY Graduate School with Weisgall and George Perle. Career: Instructor, Queens College, 1970-76, NY University, 1976-79; Professor, Queens College, 1979-, Composer-in-Residence, Chicago Lyric Opera, 1992-94. Compositions include: Ballets Cycle; Inner World Out; Wildfire; Notturno for Piano and Orchestra; Woodwind Quartet; Symphony in Two Parts, Turns and Mordents for flute and orchestra; Duo for Violin and Viola; St Elmos Fire for Flute and Harp; Lyrics for Soprano and Violin; Love Play for Mezzo and Ensemble; Song from Water Street for Mezzo; See You in the Morning, Mezzo and ensemble; Orpheus Descending (Opera in two acts); My Kinsman, Major Molineux (Opera in one act); Songs from Water Street; See You in the Morning; Jessye Norman at Notre-Dame. Publications include: The Writings of Henry Cowell. Address: 318 W 85 Street, New York, NY 10024, USA.

SCALCHI Gloria, b. 1960, Trieste, Italy. Singer - Mezzo Soprano. Education: Studied with Iris Adami Corradetti and with Joseph Metternich in Munich; Seminars at the Rossini Academy in Pesaro. Career: Sang Angelina in La Cenerentola at Catania, 1988; Further appearances at the Rome Opera as Emma in Zelmira, conducted by Philip Gossett and as Andromaca in Rossini's Ermione; Concertgebouw Amsterdam as Maffio Orsini, in Lucrezia Borgia; Verona as Rosina and Angelina; Bologna as Sinaide in Mosè; Carnegie Hall, Ermione; San Francisco, Zelmira; Monte Carlo, Roberto Devereux; Paris, Rossini's Petite Messe Solonnelle and Vivaldi's Juditha Triumphans; Musikverien Vienna, Cherubini's D Minor Requiem; Rossini Festival Pesaro, 1990, as Somira in Ricciardo e Zoraide; Season 1996 as Verdi's Preziosilla at the Met and Pippo in La Gazza Ladra at Palermo. Recordings include: Juditha Triumphans. Address: c/o Athole Still International Management Ltd, Foresters Hall, 25-27 Westow Street, London, SE19 3RY, England.

SCALTRITI Roberto, b. 1969, Modena, Italy. Singer (Baritone). Debut: Philadelphia 1986, as Alcindoro in La Bohème. Career: Appearances as Schaunard in Hamburg, as Masetto at Glyndebourne and the Festival Hall (1996, under Solti), Mozart's Count in Amsterdam and at the Opéra of Nice and with Welsh National Opera, also Figaro with the Welsh National Opera, Publio in La Clemenza di Tito at the Thèatre des Champs-Elysées; Further roles in La Gazza Ladra (Nantes), Monteverdi's Orfeo (Vienna and Zurich), Cimarosa's Maestro di Cappella (Florence) and Handel's Rinaldo (Beaune Festival); Season 1996-97 with Belcore at Lyon Opera, Guglielmo and Don Giovanni in Amsterdam and Alidoro in La Cenerentola at Genoa. Recordings include: Rigoletto with Riccardo Chailly; La Traviata with Zubin Mehta; Handel's Riccardo I with Christophe Rousset; Masetto in Don Giovanni, under Solti (Decca). Honours include: Winner, 1985 Opera Company of Philadelphia Luciano Pavarotti International Voice Competition. Address: c/o Netherlands Opera, Waterloo Plein 22, 1011 Amsterdam, Netherlands.

SCANDIUZZI Roberto, b. 1955, Treviso, Italy. Singer (Bass). Debut: Sang Bartolo in Mozart's Figaro under Riccardo Muti at La Scala, 1982. Career: Appearances in Opera at Paris, Munich, Hamburg, Amsterdam, Venice, Rome, US Debut in Verdi's Requiem, 1991; Sang Fiesco in a new production of Simon Boccanegra at Covent Garden, 1991; Other conductors have included Patanè, Giulini, Colin Davis; Festival engagements 1992 at Florence as Padre Guardiano in La Forza del Destino, Ramfis at Caracalla and Philip II and Zaccaria at Verona; Other roles include Silva, Attila, Mefistofele and Don Giovani. Recordings include: Aida conducted by Mehta, I Puritani, Turandot and Simon Bocanegra; Sang Banquo in the 1847 version of Macbeth at Covent Garden, 1997.

SCARABELLI Adelina, b. 1950, Milan, Singer (Soprano). Education: Studied in Brescia. Career: Sang at the Piccola Scala, Milan from 1977; La Scala Milan from 1981, debut as Barbarina in Le nozze di Figaro; Salzburg Festival, 1984-85, as Despina and the Italian Singer in Capriccio; Florence 1988, as Lauretta in Gianni Schicchi; Rome Opera 1989, as Aminta in Mozart's Il re Pastore and as Susanna; She sang Zerlina in Don Giovanni at Parma in 1989; Other roles include Mozart's Servilia (La clemenza di Tito) and Ismene (Mitridate), Verdi's Oscar and Nannetta, Puccini's Musetta and Liu, and Micaela in Carmen; Season 1996 as Rachelina in Paisiello's La Molinara at Bologna and Olga in Fedora at La Scala. Address: c/o Teatro Dell'Opera, Piazza Beniamino Gigli 8, I-00184 Rome, Italy.

SCAUNAS MARKOS Simona, b. 12 Nov 1965, Rimnicu Vilcea, Romania. Pianist. Education: Bacalaureat Diploma, High School of Art, George Enescu, Bucharest, 1984; Conservator of Arts and Music, George Enescu, Iasi. Career: Recitals at Romanian Athene, Bucharest, 1989 and in other cities of Romania; Participant in Young Talents Piatra-Neamt; Museum of Republic, 1987-88; Concerts with: Bacau Symphony Orchestra, 1987 and Craiova Oltenia Philharmonic Orchestra, 1988; Radio appearances in musical programmes and with recitals, 1987 and 1988; Television, 1987; Participant in Young Talents Festival, 1984, 1986, 1987, 1988; Piano recitals and Chamber Music collaboration in German cities of Darmstadt, Erfurt, Freiburg, Gotha, Heiligenstadt, Nordhausen, Osnabrück, Sonderhausen, also in Poland and Italy; International Masterclasses for Pianists. Recordings: Radio appearances, 1989 and 1990. Honours: 2nd Prize, International Concours of Catanzaro, Italy; 1st Prize, Festival of Student Art and Creation, Cluj, 1989; Prize for Chamber Music Collaboration, Cluj Gheorghe Dima Concours, 1988; 3rd Prize at Gheorghe Dima, Piano Competition, Cluj, 1989. Membership: Friends of Music and Theatre Society, 1984-. Address: Morgenröte Str 7, 99734 Nordhausen, Germany.

SCHAAF Jerrold Van Der, b. 1952, Battle Creek, MI, USA. Tenor. Education: Studied at the University of Michigan. Career: Sang at the Aachen Opera, 1977-80, at Essen, 1980-83, and at Stuttgart Staatsoper, 1987-93 notably as Checchi in Henze's König Hirsch, Janácek's Steva, Tamino, Wagner's Steuermann and Don Ottavio; Guest at Frankfurt in 1983 as Hylas in Les Troyens and elsewhere in Germany in Jommelli's Fetonte; Sang at Vienna Staatsoper from 1989 notably as Tamino. Recordings include: Die Entführung; Die Soldaten. Address: c/o Staatsoper Wien, Opernring 2, A-1010 Vienna, Austria.

SCHAAF Johannes, b. 7 Apr 1933, Bad Cannstatt, Germany. Stage Director. Education: Studied Medicine. Career: Worked at the Stuttgart Schauspielhaus, then directed plays in Ulm and Bremen; Further theatre work at Munich (Twelfth Night), Vienna and Salzburg (Beaumarchais, Buchner and Lessing); Director of award winning films from 1967 (with some acting) and television programmes featuring Sviatoslav Richter, Edith Mathis, Peter Schreier and Dietrich Fischer-Dieskau; Opera productions have included Les Contes d'Hoffmann (Vienna Volksoper), Idomeneo (Vienna Staatsoper), Eugene Onegin (Geneva and Bremen) and Capriccio and Die Entführung (Salzburg); Produced Le nozze di Figaro at Covent Garden 1987 and was invited to return for Cosi fan tutte and Idomeneo (1989), Don Giovanni 1992; Also engaged for Fidelio (1989) and Die Frau ohne Schatten (1992) at Geneva Opera, The Nose by Shostakovich at Frankfurt (1990) and Schreker's Der Ferne Klang at Brussels; Engaged to produce Boris Godunov to open the New Israel Opera House, 1994; Season 1995-96 with Simon Boccanegra at Stuttgart. Contributions to: Geo, on subjects including Chinese Opera. Address: c/o Harrison/Parrott Ltd, 12 Penzance Place, London W11 4PA, England.

SCHACHTSCHNEIDER Herbert, b. 5 Feb 1919, Allenstein, Germany. Singer (Tenor). Education: Studied at the Musikhochschule Berlin. Career: Sang at the Stadttheater

Flensburg from 1953; Further engagements at Mainz and Essen; Holland Festival 1958; Cologne Opera 1959-72; Sang at the Festival Hall, London 1963, in the British premiere (concert) of Schoenberg's Von Heute auf Morgen; Roles include Florestan, Walther, Tannhäuser, Lohengrin, Parsifal, Radames, Don Carlos, Cavaradossi and Don Jose; Guest appearances in Germany and elsewhere in Europe; Professor at the Musikhochschule Saarbrücken from 1975. Address: Musikhochschule des Saarlandes, Bismarckstrasse 1, Saarbrücken, Germany.

SCHADE Michael, b. 1965, Geneva, Switzerland. Tenor. Education: Curtis Institute. Career: Early experience as Ernesto in Belgium and Rameau's Pygmalion with Opera Atelier in Toronto; Professional debut in 1990 as Jacquino with the Pacific Opera of British Columbia; Sang Tamino at Bologna, 1991; Appeared as lago in Rossini's Otello at Pesaro; Vienna Staatsoper debut in 1991 as Almaviva; Season 1991-92 as Alfred in Fledermaus at Geneva, Almaviva with Edmonton and Canadian Operas, Ernesto with Vancouver Opera and Elvino in La Sonnambula at Macerata; Season 1992-93 as Jacquino in San Francisco and the Chevalier in Dialogues des Carmelites at Geneva; Engaged by Vienna Staatsoper as Ferrando, Almaviva, Nemorino, Tamino and Nicolai's Fenton; Salzburg Festival in 1994 in a staged version of Mozart Arias; Cologne Opera as Telemaco in Monteverdi's Ulisse and Elvino at Trieste; Concert repertoire includes Beethoven's Missa Solemnis, The Creation, The Seasons and Bach's St Matthew Passion, Mozart's Requiem, Carmina Burana, Schumann's Paradies und die Peri under John Eliot Gardiner and Elijah with the Cleveland Orchestra; Sang Roderigo in Otello, 1993, Tamino, 1995, Haydn's Creation, 1995 and Fidelio, 1995; Engaged as Tamino at Salzburg (1997) and La Scala (1998); Wagner's David at Chicago, 1999. Recordings include: Haydn's Maria Theresa Mass under Trevor Pinnock; The Creation and The Seasons; St Matthew Passion under Rilling; Vogelgesang in Die Meistersinger under Sawallisch. Current Management: IMG Artists. Address: c/o IMG Artists, Media House, 3 Burlington Lane, London, W4 2TH, England.

SCHAEFER Peter, b. 14 Sept 1956, Sydney, New South Wales, Australia. Composer; Musician (Sitar). Education: BA, 1977, BMus, hons, 1984, University of Sydney; DCA, University of Wollongong, 1998; Study with Peter Sculthorpe, Barry Conyngham Ustad Ali Akbar Khan, Ashok Roy. Career: Faculty Member, New South Wales Conservatory, 1984-90; University of Wollongong, 1990-92; Founding Member of Peter Schaefer Ensemble; Performer of Indian and electroacoustic music. Compositions: Toward, for String Quartet, 1980; See, for Synthesizer and/or Computer and Digital Delay, 1983; Petal...Silence, For 2 Pianos and Tape, 1983; Chien...Still, for Orchestra, 1984; Spans, for Ensemble and Tape, 1989; Time Breathing, Dance Theatre,for Ensemble and Tape, 1990; Quartet Vibra, for String Quartet and Tape, 1991; Open/Secret, Music Theatre, for Children, 1994; Expans Series (I-VII), for Ensemble and Tape, 1990-; Tao Streams, orchestra project, 1995-. Honours: 2MBS-FM Radiophonic Tape Composition Prize, 1985. Address: c/o APRA, 1A Eden Street, NSW 2065, Australia.

SCHAEFFER Boguslaw (Julien), b. 6 June 1929, Lwow, Poland. Composer. Education: Studied Composition with Arthur Malawski in Cracow and Musicology with Jachimecki at the Jagiello University in Cracow, 1940-53; Studied further with Luigi Nono, 1959. Career: Director of the record library of Polish Radio in Cracow, 1952; Music Critic, 1953-59; Professor of Composition, Academy of Music, Cracow, from 1963; At the Hochschule für Musik und dorstellende Kunst Mozarteum, from 1985 (1989 OH Prof); Experimental Studio of Polish Radio in Warsaw, 1965-68. Compositions include: Concerto for 2 Pianos, 1951; Music for string quartet, 1954; Sonata for solo violin, 1955; Permutations for 10 instruments, 1956; 6 Models for piano, 1954-93; Extremes for 10 instruments, 1957; 4 String Quartets, 1957, 1964, 1971, 1973, 1986, 1993; Movimenti for piano and orchestra, 1957; 8 Pieces for piano, 1954-58; Monosonata for 6 string quartets, 1959; Equivalenze sonore for percussion and chamber orchestra, 1959; Concerto Breve for cello and orchestra, 1959; Concerto for string quartet, 1959; Topofonica for 40 instruments, 1960; Non-Stop for piano (8 hours playing time at premiere 1964); Musica for harpsichord and orchestra, 1961; 4 Pieces for string trio, 1962; Musical Ipsa, 1962; Expressive Aspects for soprano and flute, 1963; Collage and Form for 8 jazz musicians and orchestra, 1963; Audiences I-V for various performers, 1964; Collage for chamber orchestra, 1964; Howl, monodrama after poem by Allen Ginsburg, 1966; Decet for harp and 9 instruments, 1966; Piano Concerto, 1967; Media for voices and instruments, 1967; Jazz Concerto, 1969; Synectics for 3 performers, 1970; Algorithms for 7 performers, 1970; Thema for tape, 1970; Texts for orchestra, 1971; 15 Elements for 2 pianos, 1971; Variants for wind quintet, 1971; Confrontations, 1972; Conceptual Music, 1972; Concerto for 3 pianos, 1972; Bergsoniana for soprano and ensemble, 1972; Neues for 3 violins, 1972; Symphony in 9 movements, 1973; Tentative Music for 159 instruments, 1973; Synhistory for tape, 1973; Antiphona for tape, 1975; Missa elettronica, 1975; Iranian Set, 1976; Spnoziana, action music, 1977; Gravesono for wind instruments and percussion, 1977; Self-Expression for cello, 1977; Matan for 3 percussionists, 1978; Kesukaan for 13 strings, 1978; Miserere for soprano, choir, orchestra, organ and tape, 1978; Jangwa for double bass and orchestra, 1979; Te Deum for voices and orchestra, 1979; Maah for orchestra and tape, 1979; Berlin '80' for piano and tape, 1980; Cantata, 1980; Autogenic Composition, 1980; Introductions and an Epilogue for small orchestra, 1981; Duodrama for alto saxophone and percussion, 1981; Euphony for double bass, 1981; Stabat mater for soprano alto, descant choir, strings and organ, 1983; Organ Concerto, 1984; Miniopera, 1988; Liebesblicke, opera, 1989; Kwaiwa for violin and computer, 1986; Missa Sinfonica, 1986; Piano Concerto, 1990; 4 Sonatas for organ solo (Vier Jahreszaiten), 1985-86, Lieder for voice and orchestra 1986, Saxophone Concerto 1986, Missa Brevis for choir, 1988; Doppelhonsert for 2 violins and orchestra; Concert for percussion, piano and orchestra, 1988; Kammersymphonie, 1988; Concerto for soprano and for orchestra, 1988; Sinfonia, 1993; Violin Concerto, 1988. Publications include: Classics of Dodecaphonic Music, 1961, 1964; Lexicon of 20th Century Composers, 1963, 1965; Music of the 20th Century, 1975; History of Music, Styles and Authors, 1979; Introduction to Composition (In English), 1975. Address: A-5020, Salzburg, Plainstr 85 Top 7, Austria.

SCHÄFER Christine, b. 1964, Frankfurt, Germany. Soprano. Education: Studied at the Berlin Musikhochschule and with Arleen Auger and Aribert Reimann. Career: Has sung widely in concert from 1988, notably with such ensembles as the Windsbacher Knaben Chor and the Berlin Philharmonic Choir; Opera engagements at Brussels from 1991 as Papagena, Zerlina and Gilda; Sang title role in Berg's Lulu at Salzburg (1995) and Glyndebourne (1996). Honours include: Prizewinner at the Mozart Competitions in Vienna and Rome in 1991. Address: c/o IMS Artists, 3 Burlington Lane, London W4 2TH, England.

SCHÄFER Markus, b. 13 June 1961, Andernach am Rhein, Germany. Singer (Tenor). Education: Studied in Koblenz, Karlsruhe. Career: Sang at the Zurich Opera from 1985; Hamburg, 1986; Deutsche Oper am Rhein Dusseldorf from 1987; Sang Fenton in Die Lustige Weiber von Windsor at Duisburg, 1991; Damon in Acis and Galatea at the Elizabeth Hall; Other concerts include the Evangelist in Bach's Passions; Messiah, Elijah, St Paul, Die Schöpfung and Rossini's Stabat Mater; Opera roles include Paisiello's Almaviva, Pedrillo, Ramiro and Caramelo in Eine Nacht in Venedig. Recordings include: St Paul, Mendelssohn's Christus, Beethoven's Mass in C, Haydn's L'Infedeltà Delusa; Mozart's Mass K139. Address: c/o Deutsche Oper am Rhein, Heinrich Heine Allee 16, 4000 Dusseldorf, Germany.

SCHAFER Raymond (Murray), b. 18 July 1933, Sarnia, Ontario, Canada. Composer; Writer on Music; Educationist. Education: Studied at the Toronto Conservatory with Guerrero (piano) and Weinzweg (composition). Career: Worked freelance for the BBC in Europe, 1956-61; Founded Ten Centuries Concerts 1961, Toronto; Artist-in-Residence, Memorial University, Newfoundland, 1963-65; Simon Fraser University British Columbia, 1965; Research into acoustic ecology from 1971. Compositions: Concerto for harpsichord and 8 instruments, 1954; Minnelieder for mezzo and wind quintet, 1956; Sonatina for flute and keyboard, 1958; In Memoriam: Iberto Guerrero for strings, 1959; Protest and Incarceration for mezzo and orchestra, 1960; Brebeuf for baritone and orchestra, 1961; Canzoni for Prisoners, orchestra, 1962; Untitled Composition for orchestra, 1963; Loving/Toi, music theatre, 1963-66; Requeims for the Party Girl, 1966; Threnody, 1966; Kaleidoscope for multi-track tape, 1967; Son of Heldenleben for orchestra and tape, 1968; From the Tibetan Book of the Dead for soprano, chorus and ensemble, 1968; Yeow and Pax for chorus, organ and tape, 1969; No Longer than Ten Minutes for orchestra, 1970; Sappho for mezzo and ensemble, 1970; String Quartet, 1970; Okeanos for 4-trak tape, 1971; In Search of Zoroaster for male voice, chorus, percussion and organ, 1971; Music for the Morning for the World, 1970; Beyond the Great Gate of Light, 1972; Arcana for low voice and ensemble, 1972; East for chamber orchestra, 1972; Paria I and II music theatre, 1969-72; North White for orchestra, 1972; String Quartet No 2, Waves, 1976; Adieu Robert Schumann for alto and orchestra, 1976; Hymn to the Night for soprano and orchestra, 1976; Cortège for orchestra, 1977; Apocolypsis, music theatre, 1980; RA, multi-media pice based on the Egyptian God, 1983; Flute Concerto, 1985; String Quartet No 4, 1989. Publications include: Edition of Ezra Pound's Opera Le testament de Francois Villon, 1960; British Composers in Interview, 1963; Ezra Pound and Music, 1977; The Thinking Ear, 1986. Honours: Canada Council Grants, 1961, 1963; Ford Foundation Award, 1968; Canadian Music Council Medal, 1972; Donner Foundation Grant, 1972; Guggenheim Fellowship, 1974.

SCHAFF Gabriel (Jacob Gideon Polin), b. 9 Nov 1959, Philadelphia, Pennsylvania, USA. Violinist. m. Nancy McDill, 18 Dec 1988, 1 daughter. Education: BMus, 1981, Assistant teaching for Erick Friedman, 1979-81, Manhattan School of Music, New York City, 1981; Additional Studies, New School of Music and Temple University, Philadelphia; Studies with Norman Carol, Philadelphia Orchestra. Career: Extensive symphonic, opera, ballet and chamber music performances at Lincoln Center, Carnegie Hall and throughout Metropolitan New York City; Violin Soloist in Soviet-American Exchange Concerts organised by Claire Polin with performances in Philadelphia, New York, Moscow, Leningrad and Helsinki, 1979-88; Several commissions and premieres of works by US and Soviet composers. Recordings: Recording on numerous labels; North/South Consonance. Contributions to: reviews in Music Journal Magazine, 1983-85, including 1984 International Festival of Contemporary Music, Moscow. Honours: Artist to Watch, Music Journal Magazine, 1983; Artist Ambassador Nominee, US Information Agency, 1986. Membership: Founder, Englewood Chamber Players. Hobbies: Historical research of violins and bows with focus on the late 18th and early 19th century French and Germanbowmaker as it pertains to performance practice and compositional evolution. Address: 136 Pleasant Avenue, Englewood, NJ 07631, USA.

SCHAGIDULLIN Albert, b. Russia. Singer (Baritone). Education: Studied at the Moscow Conservatory. Career: Many concert and opera engagements throughtout Russia, notably as Tchaikovsky's Eugene Onegin, Yeletsky and Tomsky, Rangoni (Boris Godunov), Verdi's Posa and Germont, Mozart's Count and Rossini's Figaro; Debut in West as Enrico in Lucia di Lammermoor for Dublin Grand Opera, 1991; Further engagements at the Salzburg Festival (1994), Berlin Staatsoper and the Bregenz Festival (Fidelio, 1996); Season 1997-98 as Posa in Liège, Andrei in the premiere of The Three Sisters by Peter Eötvös for Lyon Opera and Figaro at Munich; Further concerts with the Oslo PO (Marcello in La Bohème) and the Vienna Philharmonic. Recordings include: Boris Godunov (Sony Classical). Honours include: Prizewinner at the 1990 Francisco Vinas Competition, Barcelona, 1991 Belvedere Competition, Vienna, and the 1992 Luciano Pavarotti International Voice Competition, Philadelphia. Address: c/o Lies Askonas Ltd, 6 Henrietta St, London, WC2E 8LA, England.

SCHARINGER Anton, b. 5 Mar 1959, Austria. Singer (Baritone). Education: Studied at Vienna Conservatory. Career: Sang with the Salzburg Landestheater, 1981-83, Vienna Volksoper from 1987; Sang Dr Falke in Fledermaus at Amsterdam, 1987; Mozart's Figaro at Ludwigsburg, 1989; Salzburg Festival, 1991; Guest appearances at Cologne, Zurich; Other roles include, Masetto and Guglielmo; Many concert engagements, notably in sacred works by Bach; Television appearances include Bass Solos in the St Matthew Passion, with the Neubeuern Choral Society and the Munich Bach Collegium. Recordings include: Die Zauberflöte with Les Arts Florissants, 1996; Masetto in Don Giovanni; Mozart's L'Oca del Cairo. Address: c/o Zurich Opera, Falkenstrasse 1, CH-8008 Zurich, Switzerland.

SCHARLEY Denise, b. 1923, France. Singer (Mezzo-soprano). Education: Studied at the Paris Conservatoire. Debut: Paris Opera Comique 1942, as Genevieve in Pelléas et Mélisande. Career: Appeared at the Opera Comique until 1947, as Carmen, Dulcineé, Charlotte and Mignon; Sang at the Théâtre de la Monnaie, Brussels, 1947-48; Sang in Rome as Carmen; Paris Opéra from 1951, as Maddalena in Rigoletto, Dalila, Amneris, Wagner's Erda, Fricka and Mary; Puck in Oberon, Bellone in Les Indes Galantes and Madame de Croissy in the local premiere of Les Dialogues des Carmélites; Guest appearances in Geneva, Lyons and Barcelona; Marseilles 1961, as the Countess in The Queen of Spades. Recordings include: Werther and Carmen; Carmélites; L'Enfant et les Sortilèges. Address: c/o Théâtre National, 8 Rue Scribe, 75009 Paris, France.

SCHÄRTEL Elisabeth, b. 6 Oct 1919, Weiden, Oberpfalz, Germany. Singer (Contralto). Education: Studied with Helma Rodgier and Wilma Kaiser and with Anna Bahr-Mildenburg in Munich; Further study with Henny Wolff in Hamburg. Career: Sang first at Regensburg, then at Freiburg; Brunswick, 1951-57; Bayreuth Festival from 1954, as Mary in Der fliegende Holländer, Erda, Magdalene and Waltraute; Cologne Opera from 1960 (sang in the premiere of Zimmermann's Die Soldaten, 1965); Appearances in Florence, Lisbon and Vienna as Adelaide in Araballa, Magdalene and Brangaene; Deutsche Oper Berlin as Kundry, Brangaene and the Kostelnicka in Jenufa; Concert Recitals, 1973. Recordings: Der fliegende Holländer (Philips); Die Zigeunerbaron (Eurodisc).

SCHASCHING Rudolf, b. 12 Apr 1957, Engelhartszell, Austria. Tenor. Education: Studied at the Vienna Musikhochschule, 1978-83. Career: Sang at the Saarbrucken Opera from 1983 as Tamino, Don Ottavio, Pinkerton, Cassio, Max, Oedipus Rex and Idomeneo; Sang Loge, Siegmund and Siegfried, 1987-90; Guest appearances at the Vienna Staatsoper as Aegisthus in 1992, Zurich and elsewhere; Concerts include Beethoven's Ninth, Bruckner's Te Deum and Haydn's Seasons. Address: c/o Staatsoper Wien, Opernring 2, A-1010 Vienna, Austria.

SCHAUERTE-MAUBOUET Helga (Elisabeth), b. 8 Mar 1957, Lennestadt, Germany. Organist. m. Philippe Maubouet, 22 July 1988, 1 daughter. Education: BA, (Abitur), St Franziskusschule, Olpe, 1976; State Examinations, Philosophy and Pedagogy, University of Cologne, 1982; Music and Artistic Maturity, 1982, Organ Playing, 1985, Musikhochschule, Cologne; Conservatory of Rueil-Malmaison, France, 1983. Debut: Public appearance as organist, aged 10; Chief Organist at local parish church, aged 13. Career: Organist, German Church, Paris, 1982-; Organ Teacher, Conservatory Paris, 9th arrondisseiment and in Andresy; Recitals, lectures, master classes, Europe and USA, including Royal Academy of Music, London, University of Michigan, USA; Radio performances, Germany, France, and Denmark; Concerts include: Performance, integral of Jehan Alain's organ works, Paris, 1986; 1st Performance, Jean Langlais' organ works, Bach and Miniature II and Mort et Resurrection. Recordings: Integral of Jehan Alain's Organ Works; Poulenc Organ Concerto; Works of Langlais, Vierne, Dupré, J S Bach, Homilius, Walther, Kittel, Kellner, Buttstett, Armsdorff, Muthel and Max Reger. Publications: Jehan Alain: Das Orgelwek, Eine monographische Studie, 1983; Jehan Alain: L'Homme et l'Oeuvre, 1985; Deutsche und französische Weihnachtslieder, 1997; Noël dans la tradition, Traditionelle Weihnacht, 1997. Contributions to: Ars Organi; Organists' Review; The American Organist L'Orgue; Musik und Gottesdienst; MGG; Rediscovered about 40 musical manuscripts as well as letters and photographs of Jehan Alain. Honours: Cultural Prize of Olpe, Germany, 1988. Memberships: SACEM; ADAMI. Hobbies: Mountain Walking; Reading; Swimming. Address: 25 rue Blanche, 75009 Paris, France.

SCHAVERNOCH Hans, b. 1955, Australia. Stage Designer. Education: Studied at the Vienna Akademie. Career: Has designed productions of Erwartung, Iphigénie en Aulide, Elektra and La Clemenza di Tito in Vienna; Tannhäuser and Werther at Hamburg, Orfeo and Die Zauberflöte at the Komische Oper Berlin; Collaborations with Producer Harry Kupfer in Berlin, at Salzburg for the premiere of Penderecki's Die schwarze Maske and the 1988 Ring des Nibelungen at Bayreuth; Metropolitan Opera with Der fliegende Holländer, Erwartung and Bluebeard's Castle; Paris Opera with Der Rosenkavalier, Il Trittico, and Katya Kabanova; Royal Opera Covent Garden designs include Ariadne auf Naxos; Followed by Così fan tutte, Idomeneo, Elektra and La Damnation de Faust; Other designs include Alceste at Versailles, Pelléas et Mélisande at Cologne, Liszt St Elisabeth in Vienna, Parsifal and the Ring at the Berlin Staatsoper and Khovanshchina in Hamburg; Rimsky's Legend of the Invisible City of Kitezh at the Bregenz Festival and Komische Oper, Berlin, 1995-96. Address: c/o Deutsche Staatsoper, Unter der Linden, Berlin, Germany.

SCHECK Marianne, b. 18 Jan 1914, Geitbau, Germany. Singer (Soprano). Education: Studied in Munich. Debut: Koblenz 1937, as Martha in Tiefland. Career: Sang at Munster, Munich, Dusseldorf and Dresden, 1937-51; Member of the Bayerische Staatsoper Munich, 1945-70; Covent Garden 1955, as Venus in Tannhäuser; Paris Opera 1957, 1960; San Francisco Opera 1959, as the Dyer's Wife in the US premiere of Die Frau ohne Schatten; Further appearances in Lisbon, Barcelona, Rio de Janeiro, Brussels, Hamburg, Stuttgart, New York and Vienna; Other roles include the Marschallin, Elsa, Senta, Chrysothemis, Pamina, and Sieglinde. Recordings: Der Rosenkavalier, Elektra, Hänsel und Gretel, Don Giovanni, Die Zauberflöte (Deutsche Grammophon); Der fliegende Holländer, conducted by Konwitschny.

SCHEIBNER Andreas, b. 18 Jan 1951, Dresden, Germany. Singer (Baritone). Education: Studied in Dresden with Gunther Leib. Debut: Gorlitz 1972, as Dr Caius in Die Lustige Weiber Von Windsor. Career: Sang at Butzen, 1974, Stralsund 1976-79, Postdam 1979-83; Engaged at the Dresden Staatsoper from 1983; Roles have included Mozart's Don Giovanni, Guglielmo, Papageno, Belcore, Eugene Onegin, Count Luna, Silvio, Marcello, Lortzing's Zar and Kilian in Der Freischütz; Concert appearances in Austria, Holland, Poland and throughout Germany. Recordings include: Der Freischütz, conducted by C Davis; Bach Cantatas. Address: c/o Semper-Oper, 8012 Dresden, Germany.

SCHEIDEGGER Hans Peter, b. 23 Feb 1953, La Bottiere, Jura, Switzerland. Singer (Bass). Education: Studied at Berne University and in Essen with Jakob Stämpfli and Paul Lohmann. Debut: Geneva Opera 1983, as Curio in Giulio Cesare, conducted by Charles Mackerras. Career: Has appeared at Lucerne and elsewhere in Switzerland as Fiesco (Simon Boccanegra), Britten's Theseus and Collatinus, Bartok's Duke Bluebeard, Zuniga, Leporello, Walter (Luisa Miller), Trulove (The Rake's Progress) and Rocco; Has sung at Karlsruhe from 1986, as King Henry (Lohengrin), Gremin, the Commendatore, Sarastro, Pogner and the Doctor in Wozzeck; Other roles include Zoroastro in Handel's Orlando, Publio in La Clemenza di Tito, and Ferrando in Il Trovatore; Sang Rocco and King Marke at Basle, 1990; Concert repertoire includes Bach Cantatas, B minor Mass, St John Passion and Christmas Oratorio; Beethoven Missa Solemnis; Dvorak Requiem, Te Deum and Mass in D; Haydn Schöpfung, Jahreszeiten, Harmonie and Nicholas Masses; Salve Regina; Handel Messiah, Saul and Hercules; Mozart Requiem and other Masses; Schubert Mass in A flat and G; Graun Der Tod Jesu; Keiser Markus Passion; Telemann Matthew and Luke Passions; Conductors have included Armin Jordan, Horst Stein, Jeffrey Tate, Roderick Brydon, Kurt Sanderling, Charles Farncombe, Wolfgang Gönnenwein and David Lloyd-Jones. Address: Badisches Staatstheater, Baumeisterstrasse 11, D-7500 Karlsruhe, Germany.

SCHEJA Steffan, b. 1950, Sweden. Concert Pianist. Education: Studied at the Stockholm College of Music, Juilliard School, New York. Debut: Concert with Swedish Radio Symphony Orchestra, 1962. Career: New York debut 1972, followed by concerts with the French Radio Symphony Orchestra, Philharmonia Hungarica, Munich Philharmonic, English Chamber Orchestra, NHK Symphony Tokyo and the major Scandinavian Orchestras; Solo Recitals and Lieder Accompanist to Håkan Hagegard, Barbara Bonney and Barbara Hendricks; Director of Chamber Music Festival at Gotland, Sweden, from 1986; Broadcasting engagements, tours of Europe, the USA and Asia; Recital programmes with Violinst Young Uck Kim. Recordings include: Albums as Concert Soloist and as Recitalist. Address: c/o Nordic Artists Management, Sveavagen 76, S-11359 Stockholm, Sweden.

SCHELE Marta, b. 1 February 1936. Singer. m. Ulf Schele, 2 sons, 2 daughters. Education: Music Conservatory, Gothenburg; Musical Academy, Stockholm. Debut: Gothenburg, 1959. Career: Tours in Scandinavia, France, Germany, Austria, Poland, Russia, The Baltic Countries; Recitals, Orchestra Concerts and Chamber Music; Radio and Television Appearances; Tutor of Masterclasses. Recordings: Swedish and French Songs, 1975; Britten, Castelnuovo Tedesco, 1975; From Solo to Quartet, 1976; Life and Death, 1987; Mélodies de la belle epoque, 1994; Flowings, 1997. Honours: Litteris et Artibus, 1990; Pro Arte et Scientia, Gothenburg University, 1994. Memberships: Royal Swedish Academy of Music, 1997-. Hobbies: Family; Sports. Address: Box 2110, 42913 Saro, Sweden.

SCHELLE Michael, b. 22 Jan 1950, Philadelphia, Pennsylvania, USA. Composer; Music Educator. m. Joyce Tucciarone, 15 Jan 1972, 1 son, 1 daughter. Education: BA, Villanova University, 1972; BM, Butler University, 1974; MM, Hartt School of Music, University of Hartford, 1976; PhD, University of Minnesota, 1980; Private study with Aaron Copland, 1976-77. Career: Teaching Assistant, hartt School of Music, University of Hartford, 1974-77; Instructor, Teaching Associate, University of Minnesota School of Music, 1977-79; Instructor, Carleton College, 19679; Instructor of Music 1979-81, Assistant Professor 1981-87, Associate Professor 1987-, Composer-in-Residence 1981-, Director, New Music Ensemble 1981-, Jordan College of Fine Arts, Butler University; Guest Composer, Lecturer, various universities and colleges, with orchestras and at festivals. Compositions: Stage: The Great Soap Opera, chamber opera, 1988; Orchestral: Lancaster Variations, 1976; Masque-A Story of Puppets, Poets, Kings and Clowns, 1977; El Medico, 1977; Pygmies for Youth Orchestra and Tape, 1982; Pygmies II for Youth Orchestra and Speaker, 1983; Golden Bells for Orchestra and Chorus, 1983; Completion of an unfinished score by N Dinerstein; Oboe Concerto, 1983; Swashbuckler!, 1984; Concerto for 2 Pianos and Orchestra, 1986; Kidspeace for Orchestra and Voices, 1987; (restless dreams before) The Big Night, 1989; Symphonic Band: King Ubu, 1980; Cliff Hanger March, 1984; Seven Steps from Hell, 1985; Chamber Music; Piano Pieces; Vocal Music includes: Swanwhite-Letters to Strindberg from Harriet Bosse, cycle for Soprano and Piano, 1980. Honours: Many composition awards and prizes, various commissions including Indianapolis Symphony Orchestra, Buffalo Philharmonic Orchestra, Kansas City Symphony. Address: 5939 N Rosslyn Ave, Indianapolis, IN 46220, USA.

SCHELLEN Nando, b. 11 Oct 1934, The Hague, Netherlands. Administrator. Career: Managing Director, Nederlandse Operastichting, Amsterdam, 1969-79; Associate General Director, 1979-87; Stage Director as of 1982; Debut Holland Festival 1982 with The Magic Flute; Debut on American Continent 1983 with Lohengrin at Toronto and Edmonton on the Occasion of the Centennial of Richard Wagner's Death; General Artistic Director of Sweelinck Conservatory of Music, 1991-93; General Artistic Director of Indianapolis Opera as of Feb 1993; Background Managerial Musical and Theatrical; 14 World Premieres during his engagement at Netherlands Opera; Initiated Major Policy Changes at Netherlands Opera including Expansion of Season from 90 to 165 Performances. Address: 250 E 38th Street, Indianapolis, IN 46205, USA.

SCHELLENBERGER Dagmar, b. 8 Jun 1958, Oschatz, Germany. Singer (Soprano). Education: Studied with Professor Ilse Hahn at Musikhochschule, Dresden. Career includes: From 1984 with Komische Oper Berlin singing: Donna Anna, in Dargomizhsky's The Stone Guest; Eurydice, in Orfeo ed Eurydice; Rosalind (1995); Guest artist in many German theatres including Dresden, as Aennchen in Freichütz and Laura in Weber's Die drei Pintos; In Leipzig as Hanna in The Merry Widow; Berlin Staatsoper as Agathe in Der Freischütz; Susanna in Le nozze di Figaro, at Hamburgische Staatsoper; United States Debut: Eurydice with Komische Oper Berlin and as Elena, in Donna del Lago, 1992; Opera of Bordeaux debut: Woglinde, in Das Rheingold; Italian Debut with RAI Roma; In France: Beethoven 9th, Bordeaux, 1992; Title role in L'incoronazione di Poppea, Opera de Marseille, 1993; Other engagements include: Countess in Le nozze di Figaro for Opera Northern Ireland; Anne in Marschner's Hans Heiling, Netherlands Opera; All four sopranos, Contes d'Hoffmann, Komische Oper Berlin; Donna Anna, in Don Giovanni, 1993; Adina, in L'Elisir d'Amore; Norina in Don Pasquale; Webern Cantatas with Beethoven Academy, Antwerp and Brussels; Brahms, Ein Deutsches Requiem with Berlin Philharmonic; Messiah with Cleveland Orchestra; Donna Anna at Strasbourg Festival. Recordings include: Mozart's Bastien et Bastienne; Hasse's Mass with Capriccio; Handel's L'Allegro, il penseroso ed il moderato; Mozart's Kleinere Kirchenwerke; Solo Recital of Mozart Arias; Marenka in The Bartered Bride. Honours: Winner, Dvorak International Voice Competition, 1982; Kammersängerin, German Government, 1988. Address: c/o Athole Still Management Ltd, Foresters Hall, 25-27 Westow Street, London, SE19 3RY, England.

SCHEMTSCHUK Ludmilla, b. 1948, Donezk, Ukraine. Singer (Mezzo-soprano). Education: Studied at the Odessa Conservatory. Career: Sang at the Minsk Opera from 1970; Bolshoi Theatre Moscow from 1978, as Pauline (The Queen of Spades), Azucena, Amneris, Eboli, Dorabella, Ortrud, Fricka, Carmen and Charlotte (Werther); Has sung at the Vienna Staatsoper from 1985 as Laura in La Gioconda, Marina (Boris Godunov), Ulrica and Marfa in Khovanshchina; Guest appearances at the Verona Arena (Azucena 1985), Munich, Hamburg, Caracalla Festival, Rome and Stuttgart (Santuzza 1987); Countess in The Queen of Spades at Buenos Aires, 1995; Concert tours of Finland, Bulgaria and Hungary. Recordings include: Video of La Gioconda with Domingo. Address: c/o Staatsoper, Opernring 2, A-1010 Vienna, Austria.

SCHENK Manfred, b. 23 Jan 1930, Stuttgart, Germany. Singer (Bass). Education: Studied at the Musikhochschule Stuttgart with Jarius. Career: Sang with the South German Radio Choir, then Solo engagements with the Frankfurt Opera from 1967; Guest appearances at Vienna and Munich in the Wagner repertory; Glynbourne 1973, as Sarastro; Bayreuth Festival 1981-86, as Pogner and Fasolt; Salzburg 1985, as Nettuno in the Henze version of Monteverdi's Il Ritorno d'Ulisse; Engagements at Covent Garden, the Metropolitan Opera, Teatro Liceo Barcelona, San Francisco Opera and in Bregenz and Rome; Other roles include Daland, Hans Sachs, Gurnemanz, Wotan, Fafner, King Marke, the Landgrave, Ramphis, Padre Guardiano, the Grand Inquisitor, Rocco and Kecal in The Bartered Bride; Bayreuth 1989, as King Heinrich and the Landgrave in Tannhäuser; Sang Fafner in Das Rheingold at Bonn, 1990; Sang Gurnemanz at the 1992 Bayreuth Festival. Recordings include: Feuersnot by Strauss (Acanta); Lulu (Decca); Bass Solo in the Choral Symphony (Denon). Address: c/o Allied Artists Agency, 42 Montpelier Square, London SW7 1JZ, England.

SCHENK Otto, b. 12 June 1930, Vienna, Austria. Opera Producer. Education: Studied acting with Max Reinhardt and production at the Unversity of Vienna. Debut: First opera production Die Zauberflöte, Salzburg Landestheater, 1957. Career: Don Pasquale at the Vienna Volksoper, 1961; Vienna Festival 1963, Dantons Tod and Lulu; Salzburg Festival 1963, Die Zauberflöte and Der Rosenkavalier; Jenufa at the Vienna Staatsoper 1964; Chief Stage Director from 1965; Further productions include Macbeth and Der Freischütz; Opera productions in Frankfurt, Berlin, Munich (Der Rosenkavalier 1975) and Stuttgart; Metropolitan Opera from 1970; Tosca, Fidelio, Tannhäuser, Les Contes d'Hoffmann, Arabella and Der Ring des Nibelungen (1986-88); La Scala Milan 1974, Le nozze di Figaro; Covent Garden 1975, Un Ballo in Maschera; Savonlinna Festival 1991, The Bartered Bride; Elektra and Die Meistersinger at the Metropolitan, 1992-93. Recordings include: Video of Der Ring des Nibelungen, from the Metropolitan. Address: c/o Bayerische Staatsoper, Postfach 745, D-8000 Munich 1, Germany.

SCHERLER Barbara, b. 10 Jan 1938, Leipzig, Germany. Singer (Contralto). Education: Studied at the Berlin Musikhochschule and with Margarete Barwinkel. Career: Sang at Frankfurt 1959-64; Cologne Opera 1964-68; Deutsche Oper Berlin from 1968, notably in the 1984 premiere of Gespenstersonate by Reimann; Guest appearances in London, Brussels, Lisbon, Mexico City, Zurich and Venice; Noted concert artist, particularly in works by Bach. Recordings: Bach Cantatas (Erato); Masses by Mozart (Electrola); Penthesilea by Schoeck (BASF).

SCHERMERHORN Kenneth (DeWitt), b. 20 Nov 1929, New York, USA. Conductor; Composer. m. (1) Lupe Servano, 1957, 2 daughters, (2) Carol Neblett, 1975, 1 son. Education: Artists Diploma; Highest Honours, New England Conservatory of Music. Career: Assistant Conductor, New York Philharmonic, 1959; Music Director, American Ballet Theatre, 1957-70; Music

Director, New Jersey Symphony, 1963-68; Music Director, Milwaukee Symphony, 1968-80; Music Director, Nashville Symphony, 1984-; Music Director, Hong Kong Philharmonic, 1985-; Guest, San Francisco Opera; Boston, Cleveland, San Francisco, Philadelphia, New York Symphonies, et al. Honours: S Koussevitsky Memorial Award; Honourary Doctorate, Ripon College. Address: 208 23rd Avenue North, Nashville, TN 37203, USA.

SCHEXNAYDER Brian, b. 18 Sept 1953, Port Arthur, Texas, USA. Singer (Baritone). Education: Studied at the Juilliard School New York. Career: Sang in Operas by Verdi and Puccini while at Juilliard; Metropolitan Opera from 1980 as Ashton (Lucia di Lammermoor), Marcello (La Bohème), Guglielmo and Lescaut in Manon Lescaut; Paris Opéra 1982-83, as Marcello; Sang Marcello at the Metropolitan 1989, Valentin in Faust, 1990. Address: c/o Metropolitan Opera, Lincoln Center, New York, NY 10023, USA.

SCHEYRER Gerda, b. 18 July 1925, Vienna, Austria. Singer (Soprano). Education: Studied at the Vienna Academy of Music. Career: Sang first at the Stadtheater Steyr, then at the Vienna Volksoper; Salzburg Festival 1955-56, in Die Zauberflöte and Ariadne auf Naxos and as Ilia in Idomeneo; Member of the Vienna Staatsoper from 1959-81; Glynbourne Festival 1961, Donna Anna; Guest appearances in Dusseldorf, Stuttgart and other German opera houses; Also heard in Oratorios. Recordings include: Die Fledermaus and Zigeunerbaron by Johann Strauss; Der Ring des Nibelungen (Electrola). Address: c/o Staatsoper, Opernring 2, A-1010 Vienna, Austria.

SCHIAVI Felice, b. 4 July 1931, Vimercate, Italy. Singer (Baritone). Education: Studied with Riccardo Malipiero in Monza and with Carlo Tagliabue, Carlo Alfieri and Enrico Pessina in Milan. Career: Has sung widely in Italy from 1955, notably at Rome, Parma, Bologna, Trieste, Naples, Milan and Venice; Verona Arena, 1977; Vienna Staatsoper 1984, as Paolo in Simon Boccanegra; Further appearances in Nice, Marseille, Edinburgh, Prague, Barcelona, Moscow, Munich, Glasgow, Cardiff and Warsaw; Other roles include Amonasro, Renato, Luna, Iago, Posa, Don Carlos (La Forza del Destino), Simon Boccanegra, Scarpia, Gerard, Barnaba and Escamillo. Address: c/o Vienna Staatsoper, Opernring 2, A-1010 Vienna, Austria.

SCHICKELE Peter, b. 17 Jul 1935, Ames, IA, USA. Musician. m. Susan Sindall, 1962, 1 son, 1 daughter. Education: MS, Juilliard School of Music, 1960; BA, Swarthmore College, 1967. Career: Composer of serious music as well as sole discoverer of works of highly figmental PDQ Bach, with public concerts of PDQ Bach's music from 1965. Compositions include: Chamber Music: Elegies, 1974, Hansel And Gretel And Ted And Alice, Howdy Symphony, Iphigenia In Brooklyn, The Abduction Of Figaro, Bestiary, 1982, Quartet, 1982, String Quartet No 1, 1983, String Quartet No 2, In Memoriam, 1987, String Quartet No 3, The Four Seasons, 1988, Concerto for Flute and Orchestra, 1990. Recordings include: An Evening with PDQ Bach; Report From Hoople: PDQ Bach On The Air; PDQ Bach's Half-Act Opera, The Stoned Guest; The Wurst of PDQ Bach; Portrait of PDQ Bach; Black Forest Bluegrass, Liebeslieder Polkas; A Little Nightmare Music; Silent Running; The Open Window; Music of Peter Schickele; 1712 Overture and Other Musical Assaults; Video: Oedipus Tex and Other Choral Calamities; The Abduction of Figaro. Publication: The Definitive Biography of PDQ Bach, 1976. Hobbies: Solving and Making Crossword Puzzles; Cinema; Tennis. Current Management: Harold Shaw, Shaw Concerts Inc. Address: c/o Shaw Concerts Inc, 1990, Broadway, New York, NY 10023, USA.

SCHIDLOWSKY Leon, b. 21 July 1931, Santiago, Chile. Composer. Education: Studies, National Conservatory, Santiago, 1940-47 & Germany, 1952-55. Career: Founded Performance Group, Agrupacion Tonus, for the Promotion of New Music; Teacher, Santaigo Music Institute, 1955-63; Professor, Composition, University of Chile, 1962-68; Emigrated to Israel, 1969; Faculty Member, Rubin Academy, Tel Aviv. Compositions: Jeremias for 8 Mixed Voices & Strings, 1966; String Quartet, 1967; Wind Quintet, 1968; Sextet, 1970; Bai Yar for Strings, Piano & Percussion, 1970; Rabbi Akiba, Scenic Fantasy, 1972; Images for Strings, 1976; Lux in Tenebris for Orchestra, 1977; Adieu for Mezzo & Chamber Orchestra, 1982; Missa in Nomine Bach for Chorus & 8 Instruments, 1984; Trilogy for Orchestra, 1986; Ballade for Violin & Orchestra, 1986; Piano Quartet, 1988; String Quartet No 2, 1988; Laudatio for Orchestra, 1988; Kaleidoscope for Orchestra, 1989; Trio In Memoriam Vruno Maderna, 1990; Sealed Room for 12 Instruments, 1991; Silvestre Revueltas, Oratorio, 1994; Am Grab Kafkas for Woman Singer Playing Crotales, 1994; I Will Lay My Hand Upon My Mouth, for Orchestra, 1994. Address: c/o SCD, Condell 346, Casilla 51270, Correo, Central Santiago, Chile.

SCHIEMER Gregory, b. 16 January 1949, Duenedoo, New South Wales, Australia. Composer; Lecturer. Education: BMus, University of Sydney, 1972; CDI Dip Computer Technology, Control Data Institute, 1976. Career: Computer Technician, 1976; Lecturer, New South Wales Conservatory, 1986. Compositions (most with interactive electronics) include: Iconophony for Piano, 1973; Ground-Harp, 1977; Karmojan Wood for 2 Marimbas, 1978; Mandala I & II, 1981-82; Porcelain Dialogue, 1982-83; Monophonic Variations, 1986; Music for Shreelata, 1986; Polyphonic Variations, 1988; Spectral Dance, 1991; Talk-Back Piano, 1991; Voltage-Control Piano Studies, 1991; Token Objects, 1993; Machine Dance, 1994. Honours include: Various Grants, University of Sydney, 1990-95. Address: c/o APRA, 1A Eden Street, Crows Nest, NSW 2065, Australia.

SCHIFF Andras, b. 21 Dec 1953, Budapest, Hungary. Pianist. m. Yuuko Shiokawa, Sept 1987. Education: Franz Liszt Academy of Music, Bucharest, with Professor Paul Kadosa and Ferenc Rados, 1975; Private Tuition, George Malcolm, London, England. Career: Regular Orchestral Engagements, New York Philharmonic, Chicago Symphony, Vienna Philharmonic, Concertgebouw, Orchestre de Paris, London Philharmonic, London Symphony, Royal Philharmonic, Israel Philharmonic, Berlin Philharmonic, Cleveland Orchestra; Artistic Director of Annual Mondsee Festival, Austria, 1989; Organised and took part in Haydn series at the Wigmore Hall, London, 1989; Bartók and Beethoven, 1990; Schubert recitals in London and elsewhere for the bicentenary, 1997. Recordings: Bach Goldberg Variations, Well-Tempered Clavier, Complete English Suites, Mendelssohn Concertos, Schumann Concerto, Chopin 2, Tchaikovsky Concerto; All Mozart Concertos and Sonatas; Brahms 1; Lieder with Peter Schreier and Robert Holl; Won a Grammy in 1990 for the Bach English Suites. Honours: Prizewinner, Tchaikovsky International Piano Competition, Mosocw, Russia, 1974; Leeds International Piano Competition, 1975; Liszt Prize Laureate; 1st Prize, Hungarian Television Talent Scouting Competition, 1968; Won RPS/Charles Heidsieck Award for best concert series of 1988-89; Instrumentalist of the Year in the First International Classical Music Awards, in 1991 was awarded the Bartok Prize, in 1989 was awarded the Wiener Flotenuhr. Hobbies: Literature; Languages; Soccer. Current Management: Terry Harrison Artists Management. Address: The Orchard, Market Street, Charlbury, Oxfordshire OX7 3PJ, England.

SCHIFF Heinrich, b. 18 Nov 1951, Gmunden, Austria. Concert Cellist; Conductor. Education: First studied piano then cello with Tobias Kuhne in Vienna and André Navarra in Detmold. Career: Prize winner at competitions in Vienna, Geneva and Warsaw; Soloist with Vienna Philharmonic, Concertgebouw, Stockholm Philharmonic, BBC Symphony and Royal Philharmonic Orchestra; Season 1988-89 with Berlin Philharmonic, Israel Philharmonic and Los Angeles Philharmonic; Conductors include Haitink, Chailly, Masur and Previn; Recent British engagements with the London Philharmonic and Academy of St Martin in the Fields at the Festival Hall; Tokyo Metropolitan Orchestra in Manchester and London playing the Elgar Concerto; Schumann Concerto with the Philharmonia Orchestra and Sinopoli; Northern Sinfonia and City of London Sinfonia as soloist and conductor; Lutoslawski Concerto with the composer conducting the Philharmonia; Artistic Director of the Northern Sinfonia, 1990-96; Has also conducted (from 1984) the Vienna Symphony Orchestra and the Stockholm and Scottish Chamber Orchestras; Played the Schubert String Quartet with the Alban Berg Quartet, London, 1997. Recordings: Deutsche Schallplatenpreis 1978, as Artist of the Year; Bach's Solo Suites (EMI); Philips contract from 1986; Schumann's Concerto with the Berlin Philharmonic and Haitink; Prokofiev's Sinfonia Concertante with the Los Angeles Philharmonic and Previn; Concertos by Vivaldi, Haydn, Dvorak and Lutoslawski. Address: c/o Van Walsum Management Ltd, 40 St Peter's Road, London W6 9BH, England.

SCHILDKNECHT Gregor, b. 18 Oct 1936, Biel, Switzerland. Singer (Baritone). Education: Studied in Vienna at the Academy of Music with Adolf Vogel, with Domgraf Fassbänder in Nuremberg and Carino in Düsseldorf. Career: Sang at the Oldenburg Opera, 1965-67, Coburg, 1968-73, Detmold, 1973-74, Krefeld, 1974-77, and Bielefeld, 1977-80; Guest engagements from 1980 at the Berlin Staatsoper, Hamburg, Düsseldorf, Karlsruhe, Geneva, Amsterdam, Brussels and Prague; Roles have included parts in operas by Mozart, Donizetti, Rossini; Verdi's Luna, Rigoletto, Germont, Macbeth, Posa, Amonasro and Carlo in La Forza del Destino; Wolfram, Scarpia, the villains in Hoffmann and Mandryka in Arabella; Concert engagement in Germany, Netherlands and Switzerland. Address: Gregor Schildknecht, CH-2555 Brügg bei Biel, Switzerland.

SCHILLER Allan, b. 18 Mar 1943, Leeds, Yorkshire, England. Concert Pianist. Education: Associate, Royal College of Music, Performance and Diploma, 1959; Moscow Conservatoire. Debut: Hallé Orchestra with Sir John Barbiroli, Leeds Town Hall, 1954. Career: Edinburgh Festival, Scotland, 1954; Promenade Concert, London, 1957; Subject of Philpott File, television documentary; Toured in Canada, Europe, Russia; Professor, Guildhall School of Music. Recordings: Recital, 1958; Chopin and Mozart; Bridge and Elgar Quintets with Coull Quartet; Complete Chopin Waltzes. Honour: Harriet Cohen Medal, 1966. Memberships: Incorporated Society of Musicians; Bristol Savages. Hobby: Walking. Address: 14 Lilymead Avenue, Knowle, Bristol 4, Avon, England.

SCHILLER Christoph, b. 17 May 1951, Zurich, Switzerland. Concert Violist of Solo and Chamber Music. m. Louise Pelerin, 29 Dec 1981, 1 s. Education: Realgymnasium Zurichberg; Matura, 1970; University of Zurich; North Carolina School of Arts, 1972-73; Accademia Chigiana, Siena, Italy; Nordwestdeutsche Musikakademie, Detmold, Germany. Career: Violist of New Zurich String Quartet, 1973-88 with tours in Europe, Israel, Scandinavia and North and South America; Viola soloist with orchestras throughout Europe; Professor at the Zurich and Basle Conservatories; Founder and Artistic Director of Ensemble Mobile, 1989-. Recordings: Charles Koechlin, Viola Sonata; Willy Burkhard, works for viola; Giacinto Scelsi, Solo and Chamber Music; String Quartets by Brahms, Mendelssohn, Debussy, Ravel, Dvorak, Grieg and Haydn; Chamber works by various Swiss composers. Honour: Soloists Prize of Swiss Musicians Association, 1976. Hobbies: Family; Hiking; Reading. Current Management: Pro Musicis, Silvia Ackermann, Rütistrasse 38, CH-8032, Zurich, Switzerland. Address: Bombachstr 21, CH-8049 Zurich, Switzerland.

SCHIML Marga, b. 29 Nov 1945, Weiden, Germany. Singer (Mezzo-soprano). m. Horst Laubenthal. Education: Studied with Hanno Blaschke in Munich and with Hartmann-Dressler in Berlin. Debut: Basle Opera 1967, in Tigrane by Hasse. Career: Has sung in Vienna, Munich, Graz, Basle and Zurich; Appearances at the Orange and Salzburg Festivals; Bayreuth Festival 1981, 1986, as Magdalene in Die Meistersinger and in Parsifal and Der Ring des Nibelungen; Sang at Turin 1986, as Fricka in Das Rheingold; Maggio Musicale Florence 1989, Annina in Der Rosenkavalier. Recordings: Puck in Oberon, La Clemenza di Tito (Deutsche Grammophon); Mozart Masses, Der Ring des Nibelungen (Philips); Choral Symphony (RCA); Masses by Weber (EMI). Address: c/o Festspielhaus, 8580 Bayreuth, Germany.

SCHIPIZKY Frederick (Alexander), b. 20 Dec 1952, Calgary, Alberta, Canada. Composer; Conductor; Bassist; Teacher. m. Ruth Fagerburg (violinist), 4 Aug 1984. Education: BMus, Composition, University of British Columbia, 1974, study with Elliot Weisgarber and Jean Coulthard; Private study with Harry Freedman and Sophie Eckhardt-Gramatte Courtenay, 1974 and with Murray Adaskin at Victoria Conservatory, 1975-76; MMus in Composition and Double Bass at Juilliard School, NY, 1976-78, with Roger Sessions, David Diamond and David Walter; DMus in Music Composition, University of Toronto, 1994, with John Beckwith and John Hawkins. Career: Appearances on CBC Radio and TV with Vancouver Symphony Orchestra, and as Composer, Conductor and Bassist; Bassist for Vancouver Symphony Orchestra; Teacher of Theory and Composition at Vancouver Academy of Music; Faculty, Courtenay Youth Music Centre, 1986; Performed with Montreal Symphony Orchestra; Faculty, Douglas College since 1989; Performed with Esprit Orchestra and Arraymusic. Compositions: Symphonic Sketches, 1977; Fanfare for The Royal Visit, 1983; Divertimento for String Orchestra, 1983; Symphony No 1, 1985, commissioned by Vancouver Symphony Orchestra for Japan tour 1985; Symphony No 2, 1988; From Under The Overture, 1990; Aurora Borealis, 1992; Concerto for Contrabass and Orchestra, 1994. Memberships: Associate Composer, Canadian Music Centre; Canadian League of Composers. Address: 5390 Larch Street, Vancouver, British Columbia, V6M 4C8, Canada.

SCHIRMER Astrid, b. 8 Nov 1942, Berlin, Germany. Singer (Soprano). Education: Studied at the Berlin Musikhochschule with Johanna Rakow and Elisabeth Grümmer. Debut: Coburg, 1967, as Senta in Der fliegende Holländer. Career: Has sung at the Hanover Opera and widely in Germany, notably in Cologne, Mannheim, Berlin, Stuttgart and Nuremberg; Guest appearances in Barcelona and Zurich; Other roles include Santuzza, Leonore, Brünnhilde, Aida, Amelia (Un Ballo in Maschera), Sieglinde, Ariadne, Arabella, Tosca, Turandot and Lady Billows in Albert Herring; Many concert appearances.

SCHIRMER Ulf, b. 1959, Germany. Conductor. Education: Studied in Bremen and in Hamburg with Horst Stein and Christoph von Dohnanyi. Career: Assistant to Lorin Maazel at the Vienna Staatsoper and from 1984 conducted Un Re in Ascolto, Erwartung, Lulu and Henze's Orpheus there; Music Consultant from 1993-95, leading Ariadne, Tannhäuser, Rosenkavalier, Fidelio, Katya Kabanova, Figaro, Parsifal and Cardillac, also Raymonda (with Rudolf Nureyev); Bregenz Festival from 1994, with Der fliegende Holländer, Nabucco and Fidelio; From 1988-91 Music Director at Wiesbaden and concerts with the Vienna Philharmonic from 1992; Engagements with the Berlin Philharmonic from 1993; Principal Conductor, Danish National Radio Symphony Orchestra, from 1995; from 1995/6 season engagements with London, Israel and Rotterdam Philharmonics and Pittsburgh, St Louis and Gothenburg Symphony Orchestras;

Nielsen's Maskarade and Berg's Lulu with the Danish Radio Symphony Orchestra; Schubert Bicentenary concert in Copenhagen, 1997; Tristan at Graz, 1997 and engaged for Rosenkavalier in Paris, 1998. Recordings include: Capriccio, with Te Kanawa (Decca). Address: c/o Harrison Parrott Ltd, 12 Penzance Place, London W11 4PA, England.

SCHLAEPFER Jean-Claude, b. 11 Jan 1961, Geneva, Switzerland. Composer; Teacher. Education: Conservatoire supérieur du Musique, Geneva; Academy of Music, Paris with Mrs Betsy Jolas, Diplomas in Musical Education and Musical Culture. Career: Composer; Professor, Department of Harmony and Analysis at the Conservatoire supérieur de Musique; Professor, Department of Musical Languages, University of Geneva. Compositions include: 3 Caprices, for violin in memory of N Paganini, 1988; 5 Pieces for Orchestra, in hommage of Anton Webern, 1988; Impressions, 1988, debut by L'Ensemble Orchestral de Geneve, under the direction of Laurent Gay, Jan 1989; Dialogues, for Violoncello, debut by Christian Secrétan, Istanbul, March 1989; Stabat Mater for Soprano, Choir and Orchestra 1990, performed by L'Orchestre de la Suisse Romande and Le Choeur de La Psalette de Genéve; Soloist, Naoko Okada, in Geneva in March 1991; 7 Preludes for two pianos, debut at Lausanne in May 1991 by Denise Duport and Gui-Michel Caillat; Motets for soprano, harp and violin, de gambe, 1992; Three Dreams on poems by Georg Trakl for narrator, soprano, alto, wind quintet, string quartet, piano, 1992; Instanes II for solo horn for the International Competition of Music in Geneva, 1993; Visibili et Invisibili, 1994; La Rose de Jérico, 1995; L'Impossible Absence, 1995. Recordings: Impressions; Stabat Mater and 7 Preludes for two pianos, Radio Suisse Romande. Honours: Prix du Conseil d'Etat de Genéve, 1986; Lauréat du Concours de Composition de Swiss Musicians Association, 1988; Prix de Composition du Conservatoire Supérieur de Musique de Genéve, 1988; Bourse de Composition de la Ville de Genéve, 1991. Memberships: SUISA; Swiss Musicians Association. Hobbies: Football; Tennis. Address: 1 Chemin de la Commanderie, 1228 Plan Les Ouates, Geneva, Switzerland.

SCHLEE Thomas (Daniel), b. 26 Oct 1957, Vienna, Austria. Composer; Organist. m. Claire Aniotz, 24 May 1986, 1 daughter. Education: Hochschule für Musik, Vienna; Composition and Organ, Conservatoire National Supérieur, Paris, France; Dr phil, Musicology, History of Arts, Theresianische Akademie Wien, University of Vienna. Career: Many organ concerts, Europe, USA and former USSR; Participant, various international festivals; Music Dramaturg, Salzburger Landestheater, 1986-89; Teacher, Wiener Musikhochschule, 1988-90; Nominated Music Director of the Brucknerhaus Linz, Upper Austria, 1990. Compositions: Organ, vocal, instrumental and orchestral music; Edited Bärenreiter, Leduc, Lemoine, Choudens, Combre, Schola Cantorum Doblinger. Recordings: Radio and TV recordings, various European countries. Contributions to: Books: Ecrivains Français et l'Opéra (Legende de Tristan, Tournemire), 1986; Studien zur Wertungsforschung 20 ('Cinq Rechants' by Messiaen), 1988; Meilensteine der Musik, 1991; Numerous music journals; Editor, Universal Organ series. Honours: Chevalier des Arts et des Lettres, 1991. Address: Prinz Eugenstrasse 44/6, A-1040 Vienna, Austria.

SCHLEMM Anny, b. 22 Feb 1929, Neu-Isenburg, Frankfurt, Germany. Singer (Mezzo-soprano). Education: Studied with Erna Westenberger in Berlin. Career: Sang at the Berlin Staatsoper and the Berlin Komische Oper from 1949; Cologne Opera 1950-51; Has sung at Frankfurt Opera from 1951; Guest appearances in Hamburg, Munich and Berlin; Glyndebourne 1954, as Zerlina; Bayreuth Festival 1978-86, as Mary in Der fliegende Holländer; Netherlands Opera Amsterdam 1978, Herodias and Clytemnestra; Cologne 1981, as the Kostelnicka in Jenufa; Covent Garden debut 1984, Madelon in a new production of Andrea Chenier; Other roles include Susanna, Desdemona, the Marschallin, Octavian and Marenka in The Bartered Bride; Sang Clytemnestra in Elektra at Stuttgart, 1989; Modern repertoire has included Miranda in Martin's The Tempest, Europera I and II by Cage (premiere at Frankfurt 1987), Mumie in Reimann's Gespenstersonate and Mother in Cerha's Baal (Vienna 1992). Recordings: Madama Butterfly, Pagliacci (Deutsche Grammophon); Hansel und Gretel; Der fliegende Holländer from Bayreuth (Philips); Video of Andrea Chénier. Address: 6078 Neeu-Isenburg, Graf-Folke-Bernasotte, Str 12, Germany.

SCHLESINGER John, b. 16 Feb 1926, London, England. Stage Director. Education: Studied at Oxford. Career: Film Actor then Director; Associate Director of the National Theatre London; Debut as Opera Producer, Les Contes d'Hoffmann at Covent Garden, 1980; Staged Der Rosenkavalier at Covent Garden, 1984; Un Ballo in Maschera at the 1989 Salzburg Festival.

SCHLICK Barbara, b. 21 July 1943, Wurzburg, Germany. Singer (Soprano). Education: Musikhochschule Wurzburg; Paul Lohmann in Wiesbaden; Further study in Essen. Career: Engaged by Adolf Scherbaum for his Baroque Ensemble in 1966; Concert engagements in Munich, Hamburg, Rome, Geneva, Paris, Prague, Leningrad and New York; Russian tour 1971 and tour of the USA and Canada with the Chamber Orchestra of Paul Kuentz in 1972; Tour of Israel and USA 1975-76 with the Monteverdi Choir under Jürgen Jürgens; Festival appearances in Aix, Paris, Berlin, Kassel and Herrenhausen; Sang at the Göttingen Handel Festival 1980, York Early Music Festival 1988, CPE Bach's Die Letzten Leiden; Further appearances at the Haydn series on South Bank with the Orchestra of the Age of Enlightenment and in Mozart's Requiem with the Amsterdam Baroque Orchestra; Repertoire includes Carissimi's Jephte; Vivaldi's Gloria; Passions and Cantatas by Bach; Handel's Messiah, Acis and Galatea and Caecilia Ode; Haydn's Creation and Last Seven Words, Mozart's Requiem and Stravinsky's Cantata; Songs by Dowland, Purcell, Handel, Scarlatti and Haydn. Recordings include: Gagliano's La Dafne (Deutsche Grammophon); Bach's St Matthew Passion (HMV); Jephtha by Reinthaler; Hasse's Piramo e Tisbe; Handel's Giulio Cesare (Harmonia Mundi). Address: Greingstrasse 9, D-8700 Wurzburg, Germany.

SCHMALFUSS Peter, b. 13 Jan 1937, Berlin, Germany. Pianist; Professor of Piano. m. Sylvia Heckendorn, 7 Mar 1966. Education: Staatliche Hochschule für Musik, Saarbrücken with Walter Gieseking, Alexander Sellier, Adrian Aeschbacher; Studied with Wilhelm Kempff, Beethoven Seminary, Positano, Italy. Career: Appearances as soloist and with orchestras in over 40 countries since 1960; Premieres of contemporary works; Many concert tours to Asia and North Africa; Concerts and participation on many Music Festivals in 4 continents, China, 1989, South America, 1990, Canada and USA, 1992, Japan, 1993. Recordings: Works of R Schumann, Grieg, Chopin, Smetana, Szymanowski, Mozart, Beethoven, Debussy. Publications: Editor of educational literature for piano. Honour: Title, Honorary Professor of the State Institute of Education, Moscow, 1993. Memberships: Chopin Society. Hobbies: Art; Nature; Travel.

SCHMID Erich, b. 1 Jan 1907, Balsthal, Switzerland. Conductor. m. Martha Stiefel, 2 sons, 1 daughter. Education: Dr Hoch's Conservatory, Frankfurt am Main, Germany, 1927-30; Master's Class, Arnold Schoenberg, Arts Academy, Berlin, 1930-31. Career: Music Director, Glarus, Switzerland, 1934-49; Chief Conductor, Tonhalle Orchestra, Zürich, 1949-57; Radio Orchestra, Beromünster, Zurich, 1957-72; Leader, Gemischter Choir, Zürich, 1949-75, Conductor's Class, Music Academy, Basle; 1960-70, Guest Conductor in many European Countries, especially England; all BBC Orchestras of the UK, 1978-82; Principal Guest Conductor CBSO Birmingham, Aldeburgh, Cambridge, Israel, Australia (Adelaide Festival), California (San Diego Brahms-Festival). Compositions include: String Quartet 1930; Widmungen for piano 1935; Kleines Haus konzert, 1937-40; Trio for flute, viola and cello, 1955. Recordings: Armin Schibler, Passacaglia op 24; Conrad Beck, Aeneas Silvius Symphony; Klaus Huber, Des Engels Anredung; Rudolf Kelterborn, Elegie; Hermann Goetz, Klavierkonzert op 18; Xavier Schnyder von Wartensee, Concerto für 2 Klarinetten und Orchester, CD grammont 33-2, Erich Schmid, and various others. Honours: Mozart Prize, Frankfurt, 1928; Arts Prize, Canton Solothurn, 1973; Honoured by the town of Zürich with the Hans Georg Nägeli-Medaille. Memberships: Swiss Artists Guild; Pro Musica Zürich (IGNM). Address: Freiestrasse 71, 8032 Zurich, Switzerland.

SCHMID Patric (James), b. 12 Apr 1944, Eagle Pass, Texas, USA. Artistic Director. Education: San Francisco State College. Career: Founded Opera Rara 1970 and has given British Premieres in Stage and Concert Performances, including Donizetti's Maria di Rudenz, Maria Padilla, Rosmonda D'Inghilterra, Le Convenieze Teatrali, Francesca di Foix and La Romanziera; Mercadante's Orazi e Curiazi and Virginia, Offenbach's Robinson Crusoe, Pacini's Maria Tudor; World Premiere of Donizetti's Gabriella di Vergy, Belfast 1978 and Offenbach pasticcio Christopher Columbus, Belfast 1976. Recordings: Donizetti Ugo, Conte di Parigi, Maria Padilla, Emilia di Liverpool, L'Assedio di Calais; Robinson Crusoe and Christopher Columbus; 100 Years of Italian Opera, Anthology. Contributions to: Opera Magazine. Honours: MRA Award; Best Opera Recording; Best Recording of the Year. Hobbies: Travel; Cooking. Address: 25 Compton Terrace, London N1 2UN, England.

SCHMIDT Andreas, b. 1960, Dusseldorf, Germany. Singer (Baritone). Education: Studied in Dusseldorf with Ingeborg Reichelt and in Berlin with Dietrich Fischer-Dieskau. Debut: Deutsche Oper Berlin 1984, as Malatesta in Don Pasquale. Career: Has sung in Berlin as Guglielmo, Lortzing's Zar, Wolfram in Tannhäuser and the title role in the premiere of Oedipus by Wolfgang Rihm, 1987; Sang in the premiere of Henze's Das verratene Meer, May 1990; Covent Garden London from 1986, as Valentin and Guglielmo; Further appearances in Munich, Vienna, Paris, New York and Hamburg; Concert appearances in Israel, Europe and North and South America under Colin Davis, Carlo Maria Giulini, Abbado, Gardiner, Barenboim, Harnoncourt, Ozawa, Mazur, Wolfgang Sawallisch, Leonard Bernstein and Giuseppe Sinopoli; Season 1989-90 sang Mephistopheles in La Damnation de Faust at the Barbican Hall; Wolfram in Hamburg and the Herald in Lohengrin at Berlin; Papageno in concert with the London Classical Players at the Proms; Oliver in Capriccio at the Salzburg Festival; Other roles include Posa, Marcello, Mozart's Count, Hindemith's Mathis, Amfortas and Don Giovanni; Brahms Centenary concert at the Wigmore Hall, London, 1997. Recordings include: Brahms and Fauré Requiems, Des Knaben Wunderhorn by Mahler, St Matthew Passion, Tannhäuser (Deutsche Grammophon); Faust (Philips); Die Frau ohne Schatten, Das Rheingold (EMI); Così fan tutte (Harmonia Mundi); Bach B minor Mass (Intercord); St Matthew Passion by CPE Bach; Hansel and Gretel; Die Zauberflöte (EMI); Schubert Lieder. Address: IMG Artists, Media House, 3 Burlington Lane, London W4 2TH, England.

SCHMIDT Annerose, b. 5 Oct 1936, Wittenberg, Germany. Pianist; Professor. Education: Studied with Hugo Steurer, Hochschule für Musik, Leipzig, 1953-58. Debut: Wittenberg, 1945. Career: Numerous engagements as Soloist with major orchestras including: Gewandhaus Orchestra, Leipzig; Dresden State Orchestra; Royal Philharmonic Orchestra, London; New Philharmonic Orchestra, London; Cleveland Orchestra; Chicago Symphony Orchestra; Tonhalle Orchestra, Zurich; Danish Radio Symphony Orchestra, Copenhagen; Concertgebouw Orchestra, Amsterdam; Residentie Orchestra, The Hague; NHK (Japan Broadcasting Orchestra) Symphony Orchestra, Tokyo; Many festival appearances including Salzburg, Holland, Prague Spring, Berlin, Dresden, Warsaw Autumn; Professor, Hochschule für Musik Berlin, 1986-. Recordings: Many as soloist with orchestra and as recitalist. Honours: Diploma, International Chopin Competition, Warsaw, 1954; 1st Prize, International Robert Schumann Competition, Zwickau, 1956; Artist's Prize, 1961; National Prize, 1965; Gold Bartók Medal, 1974. Membership: Rector, Hanns Eisler Hochschule für Musik, Berlin, 1990-. Address: Friedrich-Engels-Damm 131, Bad Saarow 75521, Germany.

SCHMIDT Carl (Brandon), b. 20 Oct 1941, Nashville, Tennessee, USA. Professor of Music; Director of Graduate Studies. m. Elizabeth Jane Kady, 25 June 1967, 2 sons, 1 daughter. Education: AB, Stanford University, 1963; AM 1967, PhD 1973, Harvard University; Diploma, Fontainebleau School of Music, 1961; Conducting with Boulanger, Solfège-Dieudonné. Debut: Conducting, Stanford, California 1963, London, 1971. Career: Assistant Professor, Wabash College, 1970-73, Bryn Mawr College 1973-79; Professor, The University of the Arts, 1978-. Publications: Antonio Cesti: Il Pomo d'oro (Music for Acts III and V from Modena, Biblioteca Estense, Ms Mus E 120), Recent Researches in the Music of The Baroque Era, Volume 42, 1982; A Catalogue raisonné of the Literary Sources for the Tragédies Lyriques of Jean-Baptiste Lully. Contributions to: Journal of the American Musicological Society; Harvard Library Bulletin; Rivista Italiana di Musicologia; Current Musicology; Recherches sur la Musique francaise classique; Dix-septieme siecle; Jean-Baptiste Lully and the Music of the French Baroque; General Editor, Jean-Baptiste Lully: The Collected Works; The Music of Francis Poulene (1899-1963): A Catalogue; Jean-Baptiste Lully: Actes du colloque/Kongressbericht; The New Grove Dictionary of Opera, 1992; Journal of Musicology. Address: 250 South Broad Street, Philadelphia, PA 19120, USA.

SCHMIDT Erika, b. 12 Jan 1913, Quirnheim, Germany. Singer (Soprano). Education: Studied in Frankfurt. Career: Sang at Frankfurt 1935-67 in operas by Mozart, Weber, Verdi, Strauss and Wagner; Guest appearances throughout Germany; Paris Opera 1941; Holland Festival 1958, Von Heute auf Morgen by Schoenberg, conducted by Hans Rosbaud; Glyndebourne Festival 1965, as the Marschallin; Lieder recitals; Oratorio performances. Address: Staatliche Hochschule für Musik, Escherheimer Landstrasse 33, Postfach 2326, Frankfurt, Germany.

SCHMIDT Hansjürgen, b. 26 Aug 1935, Jena-Burgau, Germany. Composer. m. Annemarie Illig, 11 July 1959, 2 sons. Education: Studied Philosophy at Friedrich-Schiller University, Jena; Musical Theory, Franz Liszt Hochschule Weimar, 1968; Diploma as Composer; MMus, Akademie der Künste Berlin, 1979. Career: Freelance composer in Jena from 1970; Lectureship in Theory of Music in Weimar, 1986-87; Lectureship by Volkshochschule in Erlangen since 1990. Compositions: Winterpastorale, 1976; Streichquartett II, 1979; Schwanengesang, 1983; Nachtstück and Toccata, 1987; Sinfonie III, 1989. Recordings: Nachtstück and Toccata, 1995; Chthulu Suite; Schütz-Fantasie, electronic music. Honour: Kunstpreis of the District of Gera, 1980. Membership: Union of Composers, Thüringen. Hobby: Multimedia and Electronic Arts. Address: Siedlung Sonnenblick 1, 07749 Jena, Germany.

SCHMIDT Manfred, b. 27 June 1928, Berlin, Germany. Singer (Tenor). Education: Studied with Jean Nadolovitch and with Herbert Brauer in Berlin. Career: Concert Singer from 1956; Many Radio Concerts; From the Bielefeld Opera moved to Cologne 1965, singing Ernesto, Ottavio, Tamino, Almaviva and other lyric roles; Sang at the Festivals of Salzburg, Holland, Perugia, Flanders and Prague; Guest appearances in London, Paris and Milan. Recordings include: Opera excerpts with Eurodisc, Deutsche Grammophon, Columbia, CBS and Electrola labels. Address: c/o Oper der Stadt Köln, Offenbachplatz, D-5000 Cologne, Germany.

SCHMIDT Ole, b. 14 July 1928, Copenhagen, Denmark. Conductor; Composer. Education: Royal Academy of Music, Copenhagen; Conducting studies abroad with Albert Wolff, Sergiu Celibidache, Rafael Kubelik. Career: Played jazz on leaving school; First compositions played while at university, notably ballet Behind the Curtain, Royal Theatre Copenhagen; Conductor, Royal Danish Opera and Ballet, 1959-65; Principal Conductor, Danish Radio Orchestra, 1971; Artistic Director, Principal Conductor, Aarhus Symphony Orchestra, 1979-85; Guest, major European orchestras; Often with London Symphony, notably Brian's Gothic Symphony, 1980; Prom with Philharmonia; BBC Symphony debut, 1977, since conducting all BBC regional orchestras; Royal Liverpool Philharmonic and Hallé debuts, 1978; US debut, 1980, Oakland Symphony; Many modern Danish music performances in Europe; Chief Guest Conductor, Royal Northern College of Music, 1986-89; Interim Chief Conductor, Musical Adviser, Toledo Symphony, Ohio, 1989-; 1st production in Czech in England of Janacek's From the House of the Dead, Royal Northern College of Music, 1989. Compositions: Ballets: Fever, Behind the Curtain, Ballet in D; Opera Exhibition; 2 Symphonies, 1955, 1958; Concertos, Horn, Trumpet, Trombone, Flute, Piano, Accordion, Violin, Tuba, Guitar; 6 String Quartets, 1966-97; Music for the silent film by Carl Dreyer, The Passion of Joan of Arc, 1983. Recordings: Complete symphonies of Nielsen with London Symphony Orchestra; Bentzon Symphonies 3-7, Piano Concerto No 4, Flute Concerto No 2, 5 Mobiles for orchestra; Chronicle on René Descartes; Colding Jorgensen To Love Music; Koppel Concerto for Cello and Orchestra; Gunnar Berg Essai Acoustique, Mutationen; Lovenskjold La Sylphide, complete ballet music; Sibelius Finlandia, Karelia Suite and Violin Concerto with the Hallé; Langgard Symphony No 6, 10 and Antichrist; Schmidt Concerto for brass, Symphonic Fantasy and Allegro Op 20 for accordion and chamber orchestra; Suite of the Music of Joan of Arc, 1997. Honours: Carl Nielsen and Anne Marie Carl Nielsen Prize, 1975; Gramex Prize, 1975; H C Lumbye Prize, 1988; Fellow, RNCM, 1989. Membership: Danish Composers Society. Current Management: Patrick Garvey Management, 59 Lansdowne Place, Hove, East Sussex BN3 1FL, England. Address: Mariot, Gazax et Bacarrisse, 32230 Marciac, France.

SCHMIDT Peter-Jurgen, b. 25 Jan 1941, Meiningen, Germany. Singer (Tenor). Education: Studied in Weimar. Debut: Weimar 1968, as Oberto in Alcina. Career: Sang at Weimar until 1980, Staatsoper Berlin from 1981, notably in 1989 premiere of Graf Mirabeau by Siegfried Matthus; Guest appearances in concert and opera at London, Oslo, Linz, Salzburg, Graz and Germany, Japan and Korea; Schwetzinger Festival 1989, as Bacchus in Ariadne auf Naxos; Other roles include Don José, Hoffmann, Radames, Walther Von Stolzing, Lohengrin and Laca in Jenufa. Recordings include: Levins Muhle by Udo Zimmermann and Graf Mirabeau. Address: c/o Staatsoper Berlin, Unter Den Linden 7, 1086 Berlin, Germany.

SCHMIDT Trudeliese, b. 7 Nov 1943, Saarbrucken, Germany. Singer (Mezzo-soprano). Education: Studied in Saarbrucken with Hannes Richrath and in Rome. Debut: Saabrucken 1965, as Hansel in Humperdinck's Opera. Career: Sang at the Deutsche Oper am Rhein, Dusseldorf, from 1969 and appeared widely in Germany from 1971; Holland Festival 1972, 1974; Tour of Japan with the Munich Opera 1974; Glyndebourne Festival 1976, as Dorabella in Così fan tutte; Many engagements in Italy and at the Salzburg Festival; Sang in Mozart's Coronation Mass in the 1985 concert at St Peter's Rome for the Pope (Karajan conducting); Her best roles include Cherubino in Le nozze di Figaro, the Composer in Ariadne auf Naxos, Isabella in Rossini's L'Italiana in Algeri and Octavian in Der Rosenkavalier; Sang at the Opéra-Comique Paris 1987, in Idomeneo and La Clemenza di Tito; Dusseldorf 1987, as Carlotta in Die Gezeichneten; La Scala 1989, as Fatima in Oberon; Sang Jeanne in The Devils of Loudun at Dusseldorf 1989, the composer in Aridane at Barcelona, 1990; Sang in Figaro and Giulio Cesare at the 1997 Munich Festival. Recordings: Roles in Der Barbier von Bagdad (Cornelius), Madame Butterfly, Egisto (Cavalli), Iphigenia in Aulis (Gluck), Die Lustigen Weiber von Windor (Nicolai), Mathis der Maler (Hindemith), Idomeneo, Dido and Aeneas and Monteverdi's L'Incoronazione di Poppea and Il ritorno di Ulisse; The Cunning Little Vixen. Address: c/o Lies Askonas Ltd, 6 Henrietta Street, London WC2, England.

SCHMIDT Werner Albert, b. 29 July 1925, Bad Kissingen, Germany. Composer; Educator. Education: Studied Philosophy with Ernesto Grassi; Musicology and old German Language and Literature, University of Munich, graduated 1969; Conducting and Composition under Hans Rosbaud, Joseph haas and Karl Höller, Academy of Music, Munich, 1946-50; Master Class Diploma in Composition, 1950; Pedagogic State Examination, State Academy of Music, Munich, 1972; Further studies with Carl Orff, Karl A hartmann (composition) and Kurt Eichhorn (conducting); PhD. Career: Freelance Composer in Munich (Musica Viva, Munich, 1954); Worked as Pianist with symphony and jazz orchestras; Music Teacher, Grammar School and Junior Music School in Wangen/Allgau; Head of City Orchestra; Teacher of Music Theory at State Academy of Music, Mannheim, 1975-91; Professor, 1980-. Compositions include: Kassation, for strings, 1947; Partita, for piano, 1948; Sonata per il pianoforte, 1949; Sonate, Das Ballet, for violin and piano, 1950; Tollhausballade, for speaker and chamber orchestra, 1952, new edition without speaker, 1956; Tre Pezzi drammatici per archi, 1953-54; Symphony, Aufsland der Massen (Praeludium und Toccata) for large orchestra, 1953-55; Concerto grosso, for jazz combo and wind ensemble, 1955-56; Music for Helmuth Brandt, for jazz combo, 1956; Hieroglyphik, for large orchestra, 1956-57; Faszination, music for a filmic ballet, for 2 percussionists, 1957; Positiv-Negativ-Synthesis, for 4 instrumental respect vocal groups, 1958; Apokalypsis, for large orchestra, speaker and 6 vocalists, 1982-86. Publication: Theorie der Induktion, 1974. Honours: Achievement Awards, Bavarian Academy of Fine Arts, Munich; Composition Prize, Competition of German Composers' Association. Memberships include: Several professional organizations; Deutsche Joh-Strauß Gesellschaft. Address: Herzogstr 20, 68723 Schwetzingen, Germany.

SCHMIDT Wolfgang, b. 1955, Kassel, Germany. Singer (Tenor). Education: Studied at the Frankfurt Musikochschule. Career: Sang first with the Pocket Oper Nuremburg, then at the Court Theatre Bayreuth, 1982-84; Keil 1984-86; Dortmund from 1986, notably as Otello and as Siegfried in Wagner's Opera; Appearances at the Eutin Festival 1983-87, as Tamino, Max and Huon in Oberon; Bregenz Festival 1989, as Erik in Fliegende Holländer; Bayreuth 1992, as Tannhäuser; Further engagements at Essen, Karlsruhe, Hanover, Stuttgart; Sang First Armed Man in Die Zauberflöte at the 1991 Salzburg Festival; Concert Repertoire includes the Missa Solemnis with appearances in Mexico City, Parma, Prague. Recordings include: Die Zauberflöte; Weill's Lindberghflug. Address: c/o Opernhaus Kuhstrasse 12, 4600 Dortmund, Germany.

SCHMIEGE Marilyn, b. 1955, Milwaukee, WI, USA. Singer (Mezzo- Soprano). Education: Studied at Valparaiso University, BMus; MMus at Boston University; Further study at the Zurich Opera Studio. Debut: Wuppertal as Dorabella, 1978. Career: Theater am Gärtnerplatz, Munich as Cherubino, Rosina, Hänsel, Orlovsky, 1978-82; Teatro La Fenice, Venice, 1981; Aix-en Provence as Zaide in Il Turco in Italia, 1982; Munich Radio 1982 as Dido by Jan Novák conducted by Kubelik, 1982; Düsseldorf as Cherubino, 1983; La Scala title role in Orfeo by Rossi, 1983; Vienna Staatsoper debut as Rosina, later as Octavian, The Composer, 1985; Stuttgart as Charlotte in Werther, later as Lady Macbeth of Mtensk, Marguerite in Berlioz's Damnation de Faust, 1985; Aldeburgh Festival in Das Lied von der Erde, 1985; Hamburg Staatsoper as the composer and Rosina, 1985, later as Venus in Tannhäuser; Dresden Staatsoper as the Composer, Octavian, 1986, later as Kundry; New York Philharmonic with Novák's Dido, 1986; Cologne as Lady Macbeth, 1988; Munich Staatsoper Octavian, 1988 later as Cherubino, Jeanne d'Arc, Silla in Palestrina, Dorabella, Venus, 1991; Carmen at Berlin Komische Opera, 1991; Judith in Berlin Schauspielhaus, 1993; Amsterdam as Marie in Wozzeck and at the Paris Châtelet as Waltraute in Götterdämmerung, 1994; Sang Marie in Wozzeck at Catania, 1996. Recordings include: Vivaldi's Catone in Utica, Galuppi's La Caduta d'Adamo; Haydn Cantatas and Orfeo ed Euridice; Cherubino in Mozart's Figaro, directed by Colin Davis; Dido by Novák, directed by Kubelik; Schreker Die Gezeichneten; Mélodies of Gabriel Fauré, 1994.

SCHNABEL Karl Ulrich, b. 6 August 1909, Berlin, Germany. Concert Pianist; Piano Teacher. m. Helen Fogel, deceased 1974, 1 daughter. Education: Studied with Leonid Kreutzer, State Academy of Music, Berlin, 1922-26; Studied Composition and Conducting, State Academy of Music, 1922-28. Debut: Berlin, 1926. Career: Concert tours in USA, Canada, England (83 towns), Germany, Austria, Italy, Switzerland, France, Holland, Russia, Poland, Denmark, Sweden, Norway, Brazil, Argentina, Uruguay, Chile, Australia and New Zealand; Master Classes at more than 60 Universities, Colleges, Conservatories and Music Festivals in North and South America, Europe, Japan, Israel, Australia and New Zealand; Original Compositions for one Piano Four Hands; Partners, Artur Schnabel (father) 1935-40, Helen Schnabel (wife) 1940-74, Joan Rowland since 1980. Recordings: Works for piano solo, 1 and 2 pianos four hands, pianos with orchestra and chamber music by Bach, Beethoven, Mozart, Schubert, Schumann, von Weber, Chopin, Mendelssohn, Brahms, Liszt, Dvorák, Bizet and Debussy. Publications: Modern Technique of the Pedal, published in USA, Canada, England, Italy, Germany and Japan. Hobbies: Photography; Mountain-climbing. Address: 305 West End Avenue, New York, NY 10023, USA.

SCHNAPKA Georg, b. 27 May 1932, Schlesisch Ostrau, Czechoslovakia. Singer (Bass). m. Elisabeth Schwarzenberg. Education: Studied at the Bruckner Conservatory Linz with Andreas Sotzkov. Debut: Heidelberg 1954, as Repela in Wolf's Der Corregidor. Career: Sang 1964-85 at the Vienna Volksoper in the buffo repertory, also appeared with the Vienna Staatsoper; Guest appearances in Hamburg, Munich, Stuttgart, Saarbrucken, Dusseldorf, Wuppertal, Cologne and Frankfurt; Further engagements in Florence (Maggio Musicale), Venice, Amsterdam, Strasbourg, Lisbon, Bucharest and Zurich; American centres include New York City Opera, Baltimore and Washington DC; Main roles have included Philip II in Don Carlos, Daland, Fafner, Hunding, Sarastro, Pimen, Osmin, Leporello, Nicolai's Falstaff, Baron Ochs and Rossini's Bartolo; Many concert engagements. Address: Opernhaus, Kuhstrasse 12, D-4600 Dortmund, Germany.

SCHNAUT Gabriele, b. 1951, Mannheim, Germany. Singer (Mezzo-soprano; Soprano). Education: Studied in Frankfurt with Elsa Cavelti, in Darmstadt with Aga Zah-Landzettel and in Berlin with Hanne-Lore Kuhse. Career: Sang in Stuttgart from 1976; Darmstadt, 1978-80; Member of the Mannheim Opera from 1980; Bayreuth Festival from 1977, as Waltraute, Venus and Sieglinde, Chicago 1983, as Fricka in a concert performance of Die Walküre; Dortmund 1985, as Isolde; Has sung at Stuttgart, Frankfurt, Hamburg, Barcelona, Rome and Warsaw; Covent Garden debut 1989, as Sieglinde in a new production of Die Walküre conducted by Bernard Haitink; Sang in Dusseldorf and Hamburg 1989, as Lady Macbeth and Els in Schreker's Der Schatzgräber; Brünnhilde in Die Walküre at Cologne, 1990; Bayreuth 1987-89, as Ortrud in Lohengrin; Sang Isolde at San Francisco, 1991, Elektra at the Opera Bastille, Paris, 1992; Sang the Walküre Brünnhilde at the 1997 Munich Festival, Isolde at Catania, 1996; Other roles include Octavian, Sextus (La Clemenza di Tito), Dorabella, Carmen, Brangaene, Kundry and Marie in Wozzeck. Recordings include: St Matthew Passion by Bach; Sancta Susanna and Lieder by Hindemith. Address: c/o Oper der Stadt Köln, Offenbachplatz, D-5000 Cologne, Germany.

SCHNEBEL Dieter, b. 14 Mar 1930, Lahr, Germany. Composer. Education: Studied at the Freiburg Hochschule fur Musik, at Darmstadt and the University of Thubingen, 1952-56. Career: Active in the Lutheran Church, from 1976; Professor of Experimental Music and Musicology at the Berlin Hochschule fur Musik; Work with the experimental theatre group Die Maulwerker, from 1978; Collabortions with Director Achim Freyer on Maul-werke and Cage-up. Compositions include: Music Theatre Maulwerke, 1968-74, Laut-Gesten-Laute, Zeichen-Sprache and Chili (Music and pictures on Kleist 1989-91); Orchestral, Compositio 1956, revised 1964; Webern Variations 1972; Canones, 1975; In motu proprio, 1975; Diaspason, 1977; Orchestra, 1977; Schubert-Phantasie, 1978; Wagner-Idyll, 1980; Thanatos-Eros, 1982; Sinfonie-Stucke, 1985; Beethoven-Sinfonie, 1985; Mahler Moment for Strings, 1985; Raumklang X, 1988; Chamber, Reactions, 1961; Visable Music I, 1961; Nostalgie for Conductor, 1962; Espressivo, music drama for piano, 1963; Concert sans orchestre for piano and audience, 1964; Ansclage-auschlage, 1966; Beethoven-Sonate for Percussion, 1970; Quintet, 1977; Pan for flute, 1978; Monotonien for piano and electronics, 1989; Vocal, Fur Stimmen (...missa est) for chorus, 1961; Glossolalie 61, 1961; Bach-Contrapuncti for chorus, 1976; Jowaeglili for 2 speakers, voices and chamber ensemble, 1983; Lieder ohne Worte, 1980-86; Missa Dahlemer Messe, 1984-87; Produktionprozesse series, 1968-75; Graphic works including mo-no: Musik Zum Lesen, 1969. Publications include: Study of Stockhausen's early works: Mauricio Kagel, Cologne, 1970; Denkbare Musik: Schriften 1952-72, Cologne, 1972. Address: GEMA, Postfach 80 07 67, D-81607 Munich, Germany.

SCHNEEWEISOVA Jana, b. 9 April 1940, Pribram, Czech Republic. Pianist; Teacher. Education: Private Studies Under Professor J L Stepan-Kurz, 1951-59; Prague Academy of Music, Bratislava, 1963. Career: Pianist, Teacher of Music, Interpretor; Concerts in Czech Republic, Slovakia and Abroad; Numerous Radio Appearances. Recording: A Dvorak, Concert of Minor op 33. Honours: Prize, Prague, 1984. Memberships: CHS; FS. Hobbies: Yoga; Alternative Medicine; Arts. Address: Podrouzkova 1657, 70800 Ostrava-Poruba, Czech Republic.

SCHNEIDER David E, b. 14 June 1963, Berkeley, California, USA. Musicologist; Clarinettist. m. Klára Móricz, 19 June 1994. Education: AB cum laude, Harvard University, 1985; MA, 1990, PhD, 1997, University of California at Berkeley; Private Clarinet studies with Donald Carrol, Leon Russianoff, Pasquale Cardillo, Greg Smith and Robert Marcellus; Chamber Music study with Nancy Garniez, Leon Kirchner and György Kurtag. Career: Member, Alaria Chamber Ensemble, New York City, 1986-88; Valentine Professor of Music, Amherst College, Amherst, Massachusetts, 1997-. Recording: Copland Clarinet Concerto, 1988. Publications: Bartók and Stravinsky, 1995; The Culmination Point as a Fulcrum Between Analysis and Interpretation, 1996; Expression in the Time of Objectivity: Nationality and Modernity in Five Concertos by Béla Bartók, PhD dissertation; A Context for

Béla Bartók on the Eve of World War II, 1997. Honour: American Musicological Society 50 Fellowship, 1996. Membership: American Musicological Society. Address: Amherst College, Box 2258 Music, Amherst, MA 01002-5000, USA.

SCHNEIDER Gary M, b. 1950, USA. Conductor; Composer. Career: Founder, Music Director and Principal Conductor of the Hoboken Chamber Orchestra; Debut in Europe at the International Zelt Musik Festival in Freiburg; New York debut with the American Composers Orchestra performing his Concerto for Jazz Clarinet and Orchestra; Has also conducted the Chamber Symphony of Princeton, and the New York Festival Orchestra; Artist-in-Residence at Denison University, Ohio and Composer-in-Residence at the Rockport (Massachusetts) Chamber Music Festival. Compositions include: Sonata for solo cello, 1976; String Quartet, 1977; Study for a Ballet, for piano, 1981; Piano Sonata, 1989; Nocturne for bassoon and strings, 1988; The Bremen Town Musicians, 1989; The Tell-Tale Heart and The Voice of Eternity for soloists and ensemble. Publications: Compositions have been published by Peter Southern Organization, Berben edizioni musicali and American Composers Editions. Address: c/o ASCAP, ASCAP Building, One Lincoln Plaza, New York, NY 10023, USA.

SCHNEIDER Peter, b. 26 Mar 1939, Vienna, Austria. Conductor. Education: Studied at the Academy for Music and Dramatic Art in Vienna (conducting with hans Swarowsky). Career: Sang with the Wiener Sängerknaben as a boy; Head of Studies at the Landestheater Salzburg from 1959 (conducting debut with Handel's Giulio Cesare); Principal Conductor in Heidleberg, 1961, Deutsche Oper am Rhein Dusseldorf from 1968; Performances of operas by Janacek, Berg, Wagner, Mozart, Verdi and Dallapiccola; Guest Conductor in Warsaw, Florence and Edinburgh; Music Director in Bremen 1978-85, Mannheim 1985-87; Bayreuth Festival from 1981; Der fliegende Holländer, Der Ring des Nibelungen and Lohengrin; Conducted the Vienna Opera in Der Rosenkavalier on its 1986 tour of Japan, and the Vienna Philharmonic at the Salzburg Festival; Further appearances as a Conductor of opera in Vienna, Berlin, London, Bologna, Barcelona and Madrid; Concerts in San Francisco; Die Soldaten by Zimmermann at the Vienna Staatsoper, 1990; Conducted Tristan und Isolde in Japan 1990 and San Francisco, 1991; Music Director of the Bavarian State Opera, Munich, 1993; Led Walküre and Meistersinger at the 1997 Munich Festival. Address: c/o Ingpen & Williams Ltd, 26 Wadham Road, London SW15 2LR, England.

SCHNEIDER Urs, b. 16 May 1939, St Gallen, Switzerland. Conductor; Music Director. Education: Violin Diploma, Zurich Conservatory; Conducting with Rafael Kubelik, Igor Markevitch, Otto Klemperer. Debut: With own orchestras at age 15. Career: Founder, Conductor, Artistic Director, Ostschweizer Kammerorchester, Camerata Helvetica; Guest Conductor, USA; Musical Director, Camerata Stuttgart; Musical Director, Camerata Academica Salzburg; Chief Conductor, Music Director, Haifa Symphony Orchestra; Concerts, operas, radio and TV; Guest Conductor, numerous major orchestras all over the 5 continents; Member, Jury of the Concours des Jeunes Chefs d'Orchestre, Festival International de Besançon; Jury of Conductors' Competition, Silvestri, Bucharest; Principal Conductor, Artistic Director, National Taiwan Philharmonic Orchestra; First Guest Conductor of Prague Chamber Soloists. Recordings: 50 records. Honours: Cultural Prize, City of St Gallen. Memberships: Swiss Musicians Association; Schweiz Berufsdirigenten Verband. Hobbies: Sports; Keeping fit; History; Reading; Art. Address: Gattestrasse 1B, CH-9010 St Gallen, Switzerland.

SCHNEIDER Victoria, b. 28 Oct 1952, Reading, Pennsylvania, USA. Singer (Soprano, opera and concert). m. Riccardo Malipiero, 21 Dec 1988. Education: BM, MM, Performers Certificate, Eastman School of Music, Rochester, New York. Debut: Staatsoper Stuttgart, Germany, 1981. Career: Regular collaboration with Staatsoper Stuttgart and many concert appearances throughout Germany, 1981-85; Increased activity, Italy, 1984-; Teatro alla Scala, Milan; Teatro Comunale do Bologna; Teatro dell'Opera di Roma; Teatro dell'Opera di Genova; Many concerts with major Italian Orchestras, Santa Cecilia, Rome; Radio Orchestras (RAI) of Milan, Turin, Naples, others; Festival Wien Modern, 1992; Paris Debut at Théâtre du Châtelet, 1993; Berg's Altenberg-Lieder and Der Wein with Staatsorchester Saarbrücken, 1995; Vast concert repertoire ranging from baroque to contemporary; Handel's Messiah; Beethoven's Mass in C Major and Missa Solemnis; Mozart's Requiem and Exultate Jubilate; Mahler's Kindertotenlieder; Many Strauss Orchesterlieder; Wagner's Wesendoncklieder; Berg's Sieben Frühe Lieder; Shostakovich's Seven Lyrics of Alexander Blok; Dallapiccola's An Mathilde and Commiato; Many world premieres with works by R Malipiero, S Sciarrino, Donatoni, Gentilucci, Guarnieri, others; Many concerts, Schoenberg's op 10 with Arditti String Quartet, 1989-. Recordings: Numerous radio recordings; Vara Radio, Netherlands; Suddeutsche Rundfunk, Suttgart; Bayerische Rundfunk, Munich; Radio Bremen; RSI, Lugano; Frequent

recordings, Italian National Radio RAI. Hobbies: Water-Skiing; Swimming. Address: Via Stradella 1, 20129 Milan, Italy.

SCHNEIDER-SIEMSSEN Gunther, b. 7 June 1926, Augsburg, Germany. Stage and Set Designer. m. Eva Mazar, 10 Mar 1969, 4 children. Education: Diploma, Akademie fur Kunst, Munich, 1946. Career: Film Designer, 1946-51; Head Designer, Landestheater, Salzburg, 1951-54; Head Designer, Marionetten Theater, Salzburg, 1951-; State Theater, Bremen, 1954-; Designed Der Ring des Nibelungen at Covent Garden, 1962-64; Guest Designer numerous opera houses; Professor, Stage Design, International Summer Academy Fine Arts, Salzburg, 1968-87; Designer, Salzburg Festival, 1965-89; Designer, Easter Festival, 1967-89; Notable productions include Boris Godunov, Tristan und Isolde, Die Frau ohne Schatten and Berio's Un Re in Ascolto; Designer Met Opera New York and cities in USA, including the Ring in New York (also televised and recorded 1990); Stage Director in South Africa, USA, Germany, Austria and Slovenia, 1982-. Contributions to: Professional journals. Honours: Fellow, MIT, USA, 1980-85. Memberships: President, Society of the Stage of the Future; Rotary. Address: 4 Schlickgasse, Vienna, Austria.

SCHNEIDERHAN Wolfgang, b. 28 May 1915, Vienna, Austria. Violinist; Conductor. m. Irmgaard Seefried 1948 (died 1988). Education: Studied with Sevcik in Pisek and Julius Winkler in Vienna. Career: Made public debut in 1920; Played Mendelssohn's Concerto in Copenhagen, 1926; Leader of the Vienna Symphony Orchestra, 1933-37, Vienna Philharmonic 1937-51; Led Schneiderhan Quartet, 1937-51; Teacher at the Salzburg Mozarteum, 1938-56 appointed Professor in 1937 and at the Vienna Academy of Music, 1939-50; Played in Trio with Edwin Fischer and Enrico Mainardi, 1949-60; Taught Violin at the Lucerne Conservatory from 1949 and with Rudolf Baumgartner formed the Lucerne Festival Strings, 1956; Mozart, Schubert and Beethoven have been at the centre of his repertory, also performs modern works; With Irmgaard Seefried premiered Henze's Ariosi at the 1963 Edinburgh Festival; Conducted Franz Schmidt's Notre Dame at the Vienna Volksoper in 1975. Address: c/o Harold Holt Ltd, 31 Sinclair Road, London W14 0NS, England.

SCHNEIDERMAN Helene, b. 1955, Flemington, New Jersey, USA. Singer (Mezzo-Soprano). Education: Westminster Choir College, Princeton; Artists' Diploma, University of Cincinnati College. Career: Sang at Heidelberg Opera, 1982-, Stuttgart, 1984-, with Guest Appearances at Dusseldorf, Munich, Orlando and New York City Opera; Season 1990 with the Rossini Festival at Pesaro and Smeaton in Anna Bolena at the Concertgebouw; Other Roles have included Monteverdi's Penelope Isabella, Carmen and Rosina at Stuttgart; Covent Garden Season 1995-96, as Cherubino and Dorabella; Appearances with Conductors include Bernard Haitink, Salzburg, 1993, Bernstein, Arias and Barcarolles, Bonn, Solti, and Alberto Zedda, Pesaro; Season 1998 with Cenerentola for New Israeli Opera. Recordings include: Copland's Eight Poems of Emily Dickinson. Address: c/o Robert Gilder and Co, Enterprise House, 59/65 Upper Ground, London SE1 9PQ, England.

SCHNITTKE Alfred, b. 24 Nov 1934, Engels, Russia. Composer. Education: Studied Piano with Charlotte Ruber in Vienna, 1946-48; Moscow Conservatory 1953-58, with Golubev and Rakov; Further study with Philipp Herschkowitz. Career: Began composition while in Vienna; Instrumental Teacher, Moscow Conservatory, 1969-72; Tours throughout Europe from 1967; Guest Teacher at Vienna Hochschule für Musik, 1980. Compositions: Dramatic: Labyrinths, ballet, 1971; Der Gelbe Klang, pantomime after Kandinsky, 1974; A Streetcar Named Desire, ballet, 1983; Othello, ballet, 1985; Sketches, ballet after Gogol, 1985; Peer Gynt, ballet, 1986; Life with an Idiot, opera for Netherlands Opera, 1992; Faust, opera for Hamburg, 1995; Gesualdo, opera for Vienna, 1995; Orchestral: Violin Concerto No 1 1957, rev 1962; Piano Concerto, 1960; Music for piano and chamber orchestra, 1964; Violin Concerto No 2, 1966; Pianissimo, 1968; Symphony No 1, 1969-72; Double Concerto for oboe, harp and strings, 1971; In Memoriam orchestral version of Piano Quintet, 1972-78; Requiem, after Schiller's Don Carlos, 1975; Concerto Grosso No 1, 1977; Violin Concerto No 3, 1978; Symphony No 2 St Florian for chamber chorus and orchestra, 1979; Passacaglia, 1980; Gogol Suite, after Dead Souls, 1980; Symphony No 3 1981; Concerto Grosso No 2, 1982; Seid Nuchtern und Wachet... cantata after the Faust legend, 1983; Violin Concerto No 4, 1984; Symphony No 4, 1984; Ritual, 1985; Concerto Grosso No 3, 1985; Viola Concerto, 1985; Cello Concerto, 1986; Epilogue from Peer Gynt, 1987; Trio Sonata, after the String Trio, 1987; Four Aphorisms, 1988; concerto Grosso No 4, Symphony No 5, 1988; Monologue for viola and strings, 1989; Concerto for piano, 4 hands, 1990; Cello Concerto No 2, 1990; Sutartines for percussion, organ and strings, 1991; Concerto Grosso No 5, 1991; Vocal: Three Madrigals for soprano and ensemble, 1980; Three Scenes for soprano and ensemble, 1980; Minnesang for 52 voices, 1981; Concerto for mixed chorus, 1985; Chamber: Violin Sonata No 1, 1963; Dialogue for cello and 7 instruments, 1965; String Quartet No 1, 1966; Violin Sonata No

2, 1968; Serenade for ensemble, 1968; Suite in Old Style for violin and piano, 1972; Piano Quintet, 1972-76; Hymns for cello and ensemble, 1974-79; Mozart for 2 violins, 1976; Cello Sonata, 1978; String Quartet No 2, 1980; Septet, 1982; A Paganini for solo violin, 1982; String quartet No 3, 1983; String Trio, 1985; Piano Sonata, 1988; Piano Quartet, 1988; String Quartet No 4, 1989; Aphorisms for piano, 1990; Piano Sonata No 2, 1991; Incidental music to 60 films. Publications include: Essays on Shostakovich, Stravinsky, Bartók, Berio, Webern and Ligeti. Memberships: Federation of Russian Composers, 1961-; Federation of Cinematographers in the CIS, 1970-; Akademie der Kunste of the Former German Democratic Republic, 1981-; Bayerische Akademie der Schönen Kunste, Munich, 1981-. Address: c/o Boosey & Hawkes Ltd, 295 Regent Street, London W1 8JH, England.

SCHNITZLER Michael, b. 1940, Vienna, Austria. Violinist. Education: Studied in Vienna. Career: Performances of Haydn and other composers in Vienna and elsewhere from 1968; Co-Founder, The Haydn Trio of Vienna 1968 and has performed in Brussels, Munich, Berlin, Zurich, London, Rome, Paris; New York debut 1979 and has made frequent North American appearances with concerts in 25 States; Debut tour of Japan, 1984 with further travels to the Near East, Russia, Africa, Central and South America; Series at the Vienna Konzerthaus Society from 1976, with performances of more than 100 works; Summer Festivals at Vienna, Salzburg, Axi-en-Provence, Flanders and Montreux; Master Classes at the Royal College and Royal Academy of London, Stockholm, Bloomington, Tokyo and the Salzburg Mozarteum. Recordings: Complete Piano Trios of Beethoven and Schubert, Mendelssohn D Minor, Brahams B Major, Tchaikovsky A Minor, Schubert Trout Quintet; Albums of Works by Haydn, Schumann, Dvorak and Smetana. Address: c/o Sue Lubbock Concert Management, 25 Courthorpe Road, London NW3 2LE, England.

SCHNOEBELEN Anne, b. 4 Aug 1933, Minocqua, Wisconsin, USA. Musicologist. m. John A Meixner, 7 May 1980. Education: BA, Rosary College; MMus, PhD, University of Illinois, Champaign-Urbana. Career: Professor, Shepherd School of Music, Rice University, Houston, Texas. Publications: Padre Martini's Collection of Letters, 1979; Solo Motets From the 17th Century, 10 vols, 1987-89; Seventeenth Century Italian Sacred Music: Masses, 8 vols, 1996-97. Memberships: American Musicological Society; International Musicological Society. Address: Shepherd School of Music, Rice University, 6100 South Main Street, Houston, TX 77005-1892, USA.

SCHOLL Andreas, b. 1968, Germany. Singer (Counter-Tenor). Education: Kiedriche Chorbuben, as Choir Member; Schola Cantorum Basiliensis, with René Jacobs, 1987-93. Career: Concerts include Vivaldi's Stabat Mater with Ensemble 415 of Switzerland, Messiah with Les Arts Florissanta at Aixd, Bach's Christmas Oratorio and Masses, with Philippe Herreweghe, St John Passion in Berlin and B Minor Mass with the Stuttgart Kammerchor; London Prom Concerts, 1996, with Bach Magnificat and Excerts from Handel's Julius Caesar (Collegium Vocale); Other Festival Engagements at Versailles, Saintes, Santiago, Aix and Lucerne; Season 1997-98 with recitals at the Wigmore Hall, Cologne Philharmonic, Concertgebouw Amsterdam and the Sydney Festival; Tours with La Petite Bande (Bach Cantatas) the Gabrieli Consort (Handel's Solomon) and with Collegium Vocale to Europe and Japan; Engaged as Bertarido in Handel's Rodelinda for the 1998 Glyndebourne Festival. Recordings: Messiah with William Christie, Deutsches Barocklieder, Vivaldi Stabat Mater, EnglishLute and Folksongs, Caldara Maddalena ai peide di Cristo, Bach Christmas Oratorio and Cantatas; Handel's Solomon. Honours include: Conseil de l'Europe and Foundation Claude Nicolas Ledoux, 1992. Address: c/o Harrison/Parrott Artists, 12 Penzance Place, London W11 4PA, England.

SCHOLLUM Benno, b. 1953, Klagenfurt, Austria. Singer (Baritone). Education: Studied at the Vienna Musikhochschule with Josef Greindl and with his father, Robert Schollum; Master Classes in New York and Vienna with Sena Jurinac and others. Career: Has performed in Austria and elsewhere in operettas by Lehar, Johann Strauss, Milloecker and Offenbach; Operas by Mozart, Britten, Lortzing, Mascagni; lieder by Loewe, Schubert, Wolt, Strauss, Grieg, Brahms and others; Oratorios include Schmidt's Das Buch mit Sieben Siegeln, the Brahms Requiem and Cantatas and Masses by Bach and Mozart; Festival appearances at Vienna, Antibes, Carinthian Summer and Gstaad; Guest Engagements in France, Yugoslavia, Italy, USA, South America, South Africa, Germany, Holland and Luxembourg; Berlin Philharmonic debut in Herbst by Antal Dorati; British debut, 1991 with the English Symphony Orchestra in Arias by Mozart; Stage roles include Papageno; Teacher at the Vienna Musikhochschule from 1983. Recordings: Schubert's Winterreise with Graham Johnson; Beethoven's Symphony No 9 with Yehudi Menuhin. Publications: Sprecherziehung in der Praxis der Gesangsausbildung, 1993. Honours: MA, 1993. Current Management: Eleanor Hope, London. Address: 9 Southwood Hall,

Wood Lane, London N6 5UF, England.

SCHOLZE Rainer, b. 13 May 1940, Sudetenland. Singer (Bass). Education: Studied at the Cologne Musikhochschule. Career: Sang in the Chorus of the Ludbeck Stadt Theatre, 1962-66; Discovered by Gerd Albrecht and sang small roles; Studies further and sang Solo at Ludbeck from 1966-70; Engaged at Brunswick, 1970-71; Kassel, 1971-81; Appeared at Kiel 1981-83 and made guest outings to Munich, Dresden, Hamburg; Has often appeared in operas by Mozart, Rossini, Lortzing and notably as Baron Ochs. Recordings include: Masetto in Don Giovanni; Reinmar in Tannhäuser; Larkens in Fanciulla del West.

SCHOMBERG Martin, b. 7 Nov 1944, Hoxter, Westfalen, Germany. Singer (Tenor). Education: Studied at the Hamburg Musikhochschule with Jakob Stampfli. Debut: Mainz 1972, as Lenski in Eugene Onegin. Career: Many appearances at the Opera houses of Cologne, Bssle, Hamburg, Dusseldorf; Zurich Opera in Lyric Roles and in the 1974 premiere of Ein Whrer Held by Klebe; Concert engagements at the Salzburg Festival and elsewhere; Roles have included Mozart's Belmonte, Ottavio and Tamino, Nencio in Haydn's L'Infedeltà Delusa, Florindo in Le Donne Curiose by Wolf-Ferrari, the Italian Tenor in Rosenkavalier and Alfred in Fledermaus. Address: Opernhaus Zurich, Falkenstrasse 1, CH-8008 Zurich, Switzerland.

SCHONBACH Dieter, b. 18 Feb 1931, Stolp, Pomerania, Germany. Composer. Education: Studied in Detmold and Freiburg with Gunter Bialas and Wolfgang Fortner. Career: Music Director of the Bochum Schauspielhaus, 1959-73; Has also worked at theatres in Munster and Basle. Compositions include: Die Geschichte von einem Feuer, mixed-media show with puppet, 1970; Bedrohung Und Uberleben, multi-media opera, Cologne, 1971; Hysteria-Paradies schwarz, mixed-media show after The Tempest, Wiesbaden, 1971; Hymnus II-Morgen nach dem Feuer, mixed-media show, Munich, 1972; Come S Francesco, Munster, 1979; Farben und Klange, in memory of Kandinsky for orchestra, 1958; Piano Concerto, 1958; Canticum Psalmi Resurrectionis, 1959; Kammermusik for 14 instruments, 1964; Hoquetus for 8 wind instruments, 1964. Honours include: Joint Winner, Stamitz Prize of Stuttgart, 1972. Address: GEMA, Postfach 80 07 67, D-81607 Munich, Germany.

SCHONBERG Harold (Charles), b. 29 Nov 1915, New York City, USA. Music Critic; Editor; Writer on Music. m. (1) Rosalyn Krokover, 28 Nov 1942, (2) Helene Cornell, 10 May 1975. Education: BA, Brooklyn College, 1937; MA, New York University, 1938. Career: Associate Editor, American Music Lover, 1939-41; Contributing Editor, Music Digest, 1946-48; Music Critic, New York Sun, 1946-50; Contributing Editor, Record Reviewer, Musical Courier, 1948-52; Columnist, Gramophone, 1948-60; Music Critic, Record Reviewer 1950-60, Senior Music Critic 1960-80, Cultural Correspondent 1980-85, New York Times. Publications: Chamber and Solo Instrument Music, 1955; Collector's Chopin and Schumann, 1959; Great Pianists, 1963, revised 1987; Great Conductors, 1967; Lives of Great Composers, 1970, 1981; Facing the Music, 1981; Glorious Ones: Classical Music's Legendary Performers, 1985; Horowitz. His Life and Music, 1992; Also numerous articles in various publications. Honours: 1st Music Critic to win Pulitzer Prize in Criticism, 1971. Hobbies: Drawing; Chess. Address: 160 Riverside Drive, New York, NY 10024, USA.

SCHONBERG Stig Gustav, b. 13 May 1933, Vastra Husby, Sweden. Composer; Organist. Education: Studies, Stockholm Musikhogskolan, 1953-60 (composition studies with Lars Eric Larsson and Eric Blomdahl); Organ Studies with Flor Peeters, Belgium. Career: Freelance Composer with Performances Throughout Sweden; Many Concert Tours and Church Performances Throughout Scandinavia as Organist. Compositions include: Introduction and Allegro for Strings, 1959; Concerto for Organ and Strings, 1962; Sinfonia Aperta, 1965; 3 Concertino for Strings, 1966; Madeleine and Conrad, Ballet, 1967; Fantasia for Strings, 1967; String Quartets, 1961-84; Impromptui Visionario for Orchestra, 1972; Flute Sonata, 1974; Concerto for 2 Flutes and Strings, 1976; Symphony No 2, 1977; Pastoral for Horn and Organ, 1979; Concerto for Organ and Orchestra, 1982; Missa Coralis, 1983; Missa da Pacem, 1985; Concerto for Organ and Brass Orchestra, 1987; Sonata alla ricercata for Organ and Violin, 1989; Bassoon Concerto, 1992; Gloria, 1994; Choruses; Songs. Address: c/o STIM, Sandhamnsgatan 79, PO Box 27327, S-102 54 Stockholm, Sweden.

SCHÖNE Wolfgang, b. 9 Feb 1941, Bad Gandersheim, Germany. Bass Baritone. Education: Studied with Naan Pold in Hanover and Hamburg, Diploma in 1969. Career: Winner of awards from 1966 at Bordeaux, Berlin, Stuttgart and s'Hertogenbosch; Concert tours and lieder recitals in Belgium, Netherlands, France, Denmark, USA, Mexico, Argentina and England; Appeared in film, The Chronicle of Anna Magdalena Bach; Opera career from 1970 at the State Operas of Stuttgart, Vienna and Hamburg, notably as Guglielmo, Wolfram and Count Eberbach in Der Wildschütz by Lortzing; Schwetzingen Festival 1983 as Tom, in the premiere of The English Cat by Henze; Komische Oper Berlin in 1984 as Golaud in Pelléas et Mélisande; Sang in the 1984 reopening of the Stuttgart Opera, as Don Giovanni; Season 1988-89 sang Gunther at Turin, Alidoro in Cenerentola at Salzburg and Barak at Cologne; Hamburg in 1990 as Wolfram; Sang Orestes and Pentheus in The Bassarids at Stuttgart in 1989; Sang Wolfram in Hamburg in 1990, the Count in Capriccio at 1990 Salzburg Festival, Dr Schön in Lulu at the Paris Châtelet, 1992; Amfortas in Parsifal at the Opéra Bastille, Paris, 1997. Recordings: Bach Cantatas; St Matthew Passion by Schütz; Theresienmesse by Haydn; Bach B minor Mass; Doktor und Apotheker by Dittersdorf; Giulio Cesare by Handel; Lulu; Video of Der Freischütz.

SCHONWANDT Michael, b. 10 September 1953, Copenhagen, Denmark. Conductor. m. Amalie Malling, 23 March 1991. Education: BMus, Musicology, Copenhagen University, 1975; Conducting & Compositions, Royal Academy of Music, London, England, 1975-77. Debut: Copenhagen, 1977. Career: Concerts throughout Europe, Debut Royal Danish Opera, 1979; Guest Conductor: Covent Garden, London, Paris Opéra, Stuttgart Opera; Principal Guest Conductor, Théâtre Royal de la Monnaie, Brussels, 1984-87; Principal Conductor, Collegium Musicum, Copenhagen, 1981-; Principal Guest Conductor, Nice Opera, 1987-91; Danish Radio Symphony Orchestra, 1989-; Principal Conductor, Berliner Sinfonie Orchestra, 1992; Permanent Conductor, Vienna State Opera, 1990; Conducted the BBC Symphony Orchestra at the Festival Hall, 1997. Recordings: Mozart Piano Concertos and Violin Concertos; Beethoven Piano Concertos; Niels W Gade Complete Symphonies; Kuhlau's Lulu, Complete Opera; Schoenberg and Sibelius Pelléas and Mélisande, Berlioz Requiem. Honours: Numerous Musical Prizes, Denmark. Current Management: Ingpen and Williams Limited, 14 Kensington Court, London W8, England. Address: Svalevej 24, DK 2900, Hellerup, Denmark.

SCHOPPER Michael, b. 1942, Passau, Germany. Bass-Baritone. Education: Studied at the Musikhochschule Munich with Hanno Blaschke. Debut: Sang in Bach's Christmas Oratorio with the Munich Bach Choir conducted by Karl Richter in 1968. Career: Has sung in concert in North and South America and Europe; Founded the ensemble, Musica Poetica in 1974 performing Renaissance and Baroque music; Opera appearances at the Herrenhausen Festival, in Giulio Cesare by Handel and La Clemenza di Tito by Mozart. Recordings include: Giulio Cesare; Bach Cantatas; St Matthew Passion by Bach; Masses by Mozart.

SCHOTT Howard (Mansfield), b. 17 Jun 1923, New York City, NY, USA. Musicologist; Harpsichordist. Education: BA, 1943, JD, 1948, Yale University; DPhil (Oxon), 1978; Studied Applied Music at Mannes College, NY; Musicology with Barry Brook, Emanuel Winternitz, HC Robbins Landon, City University of New York, Leo Schrade, Yale, Joseph Kerman and John Caldwell at Oxford; Keyboard with Ralph Kirkpatrick at Yale and Hans Neumann at Mannes College; Composition with Richard Donovan and Luther Noss at Yale. Career: Lecturer at New England Conservatory, Boston, MA, 1988-; Lectures at Oxford, King's College London, Harvard, Yale (Sanford Fellowship, 1979), Cornell, Paris, and City University of New York; Consultant to Boston Early Music Festival, East Nakamichi Festival, also Victoria and Albert Museum and Metropolitan Museum of Art. Publication: Playing The Harpsichord, 1971, 3rd edition, 1979, Italian edition, 1982, German edition, 1983; Oeuvres Complètes De J J Froberger, 1980-; Editor, The Historical Harpsichord Series, 1984-; Catalogue of The Musical Instruments in The Victoria and Albert Museum, I: Keyboard Instruments, 1985. Contributions to: Many articles in The New Grove Dictionary and New Harvard Dictionary of Music; Regularly to The Musical Times and to Early Music, including The Harpsichord Revival, and From Harpsichord to Pianoforte. Address: Brook House, Suite 402, 44 Washington Street, Brookline, MA 02146, USA.

SCHRADER David (Dillon), b. 15 Sep 1952, Chicago, IL, USA. Musician (Organ, Harpsichord, Fortepiano). Education: BMus, Special Honours, University of Colorado, 1974; Performers Certificate, 1975, MMus, High Distinction, 1976, DMus, Distinction, 1987, Indiana University. Career: Soloist with symphony orchestras in Chicago with Solti, Abbado, Barenboim and Leinsdorf, Milwaukee, San Francisco with Järvi, El Paso, City Musick and Music of Baroque; Engagements in Europe, Japan, Canada and Mexico; Numerous live and recorded radio broadcasts on national stations; Currently Organist at Church of Ascension, Keyboardist with City Musick, a period instrument orchestra, and Professor of Organ and Harpsichord at Chicago Musical College. Recordings: Various and with Chicago Symphony Orchestra. Contributions to: Articles in Continuo, Indiana Theory Review and Cantate Domino. Hobbies: Cooking; Physical Culture; Music. Current Management: Artra Artist Management, 555 West Madison Street, Chicago, IL 60661, USA. Address: Church of the Ascension, 1133 North Lasalle Drive, Chicago, IL 60610, USA.

SCHRANZ Karoly, b. 1950, Hungary. Violinist. Education: Studied with András Mihaly at the Franz Liszt Academy in Budapest, with members of the Amadeus Quartet and Zoltán Szekely. Career: Founder Member of the Takacs Quartet, 1975; Many concert appearances in all major centres of Europe and USA; Tours of Australia, New Zealand, Japan, South America, England, Norway, Sweden, Greece, Belgium and Ireland; Resident at the London Barbican, 1988-91, with masterclasses at the Guildhall School of Music; Visits to Japan in 1989 and 1992; Bartók Cycle for the Bartók-Solti Festival at South Bank in 1990; Great Performers Series at Lincoln Center and Mostly Mozart Festival at Alice Tully Hall, NY; Appeared at Mozart Festivals at South Bank, Wigmore Hall and Barbican Centre in 1991; Bartók Cycle at the Théâtre des Champs Elysées in 1991, and Beethoven Cycles at the Zurich Tonhalle, in Dublin, at the Wigmore Hall and in Paris, 1991-92; Plays Amati instrument made for the French Royal Family and loaned by the Corcoran Gallery, Gallery of Art, Washington DC. Recordings: Schumann Quartets, Op 41; Mozart String Quintets, with Denes Koromzay; Bartók 6 Quartets; Schubert Trout Quintet, with Zoltán Kocsis; Haydn Op 76; Brahms Op 51, Nos 1 and 2; Chausson Concerto, with Joshua Bell and Jean-Yves Thibaudet; Works by Schubert, Mozart, Dvorák and Bartók. Honours: Winner, International Quartet Competition, Evian, 1977; Winner, Portsmouth International Quartet Competition, 1979. Address: Lies Askonas Ltd, 6 Henrietta Street, Covent Garden, London, WC2, England.

SCHREIBMAYER Kurt, b. 1953, Klagenfurt, Germany. Tenor. Education: Studied at the Graz Musikhochschule. Career: Sang at Graz, 1976-78, then at the Vienna Volksoper; Further appearances at the Theater am Gartnerplatz Munich, 1987-88, Deutsche Oper am Rhein Dusseldorf from 1987, Hamburg Staatsoper and the Zurich Opera; Théâtre Royal de la Monnaie, Brussels from 1987 as Steva in Jenufa and Luka in From The House of the Dead in 1990; Bayreuth Festival engagements, 1986-90, as Froh, Walter von der Vogelweide and Parsifal; Returned to Vienna Volksoper in 1988 as Max in Der Freischütz; Has sung at Liège as Lohengrin, 1988-89; Other roles include Fra Diavalo, Babinsky in Shvanda the Bagpiper, Pedro in Tiefland, Gomez in Die drei Pintos, Wenzel in Zemlinsky's Kleider Machen Leute, and parts in operettas; Sang in Mona Lisa by Max von Schillings at the Vienna Volksoper, 1996. Address: c/o Théâtre Royal de la Monnaie, 4 Leopoldstrasse, B-1000 Brussels, Belgium.

SCHREIER Peter, b. 29 Jul 1935, Gauernitz, Near Meissen, Germany. Tenor; Conductor. Education: Sang in Dresden Kreuzchor as a child then studied with Polster in Leipzig and with Winkler at the Dresden Musikhochschule, 1956-59. Debut: Dresden Staatsoper in 1961 as First Prisoner in Fidelio. Career: Lyric tenor at the Staatsoper Berlin and in Hamburg, Vienna, London and Munich in operas by Mozart, Rossini, Weber, Wagner and Lortzing; Sang Mozart's Ferrando at Sadler's Wells Theatre, London in 1966 and Tamino at the New York Metropolitan in 1968; Also celebrated as Mozart's Belmonte and Ottavio, Tchaikovsky's Lensky, Verdi's Fenton, Wagner's David and Loge and Strauss's Leukippos; Sang at Salzburg Festival from 1967; Sang in the premiere of Orff's De Temporum Fine Comoedia in 1973 and Dessau's Einstein in 1974; Well known as the Evangelist in Bach's Passion and in concert works by Handel, Haydn, Beethoven, Berlioz and Mendelssohn; Many lieder recitals notably in song cycles by Schubert and Schumann; Debut as conductor with the Berlin Staatskapelle in 1970; First song recital at Wigmore Hall in 1989; Conducted Mozart's Mitridate at the Cuvilliés Theater in Munich, 1990; Lieder recitals for the Schubert Bicentenary, 1997. Recordings include: St Matthew Passion; Haydn's Die Jahreszeiten; CPE Bach Mark Passion; Das Buch mit Sieben Siegeln; Das Lied von der Erde; Die Zauberflöte; Così fan tutte; Der Freischütz; Lortzing's Der Wildschütz; Berlioz Requiem; Mendelssohn's Elijah; Mozart's Requiem, as conductor; Many Lieder recordings. Address: c/o Norman McCann Ltd, The Coach House, 56 Lawrie Park Gardens, London, SE26 6XJ, England.

SCHREINER Elisabeth, b. 1924, Germany. Soprano. Career: Sang in opera at Kaiserlautern, 1949-52, Coburg, 1952-55, Krefeld, 1955-59 and Mainz, 1959-65; Many appearances in operas by Wagner at Mannheim, 1966-82 and guest engagements in Germany and abroad; Vienna Staatsoper from 1970 notably as Senta and Brünnhilde, Bordeaux in 1967, Munich in 1971, Barcelona and Turin in 1972 and at Paris Opéra and Covent Garden in 1972 as Brünnhilde and Senta; Further appearances at Graz, Cologne, Nice and Vichy; Other roles include Elisabeth, Ortrud, Sieglinde, Gutrune, the Marschallin, Isolde, Ariadne, Lady Macbeth, The Countess in Capriccio, Amelia Grimaldi, Turandot, Elisabeth de Valois, Tosca and Aida; Noted concert artist. Address: c/o Staatsoper, Opernring 2, A-1010 Vienna, Austria.

SCHRÖDER Jaap, b. 31 Dec 1925, Amsterdam, Holland. Violinist. m. Agnès Jeanne Françoise Lefèvre, 3 daughters. Education: Diploma, Amsterdam Conservatory; 1st Prize, Ecole Jacques Thibaud, Paris, 1948. Debut: Holland 1949. Career:

Leader, Radio Chamber Orchestra, 1950-63; Founder, Chamber Music ensembles Quadro Amsterdam, and Concerto Amsterdam, 1962, Quartetto Esterhazy 1973-81; Smithson String Quartet, 1983; Professor of violin, Yale School of Music. Memberships: Netherlands String Quartet, 1952-69. Hobbies: French Literature. Address: Gerard Brandtstraat 18, Amsterdam, Holland.

SCHRODER-FEINEN Ursula, b. 21 July 1935, Gelsenkirchen, Germany. Singer, Soprano. Education: Studied with Maria Helm in Gelsenkirchen, then at the Folkwang School, Essen. Career: Gelsenkirchen 1961-68, debut as Aida and sang Gershwin's Bess, Handel's Cleopatra, Beethoven's Leonore and Verdi's Oscar; Deutsche Oper am Rhein, Dusseldorf, 1968-72; New York Metropolitan debut 1970, as Chrysothemis and Elektra; Bayreuth 1971, as Senta, Ortrud, Kundry and Brünnhilde; Wagner's Ortrud and Strauss's Dyer's Wife at Salzburg; British debut at the 1975 Edinburgh Festival, as Salome; Other roles include Puccini's Tosca and Turandot, Wagner's Isolde, Janacek's Jenufa, Gluck's Alceste and Strauss's Elektra. Recordings: Roles in Korngold's Violanta and Marschner's Hans Heiling.

SCHROTER Gisela, b. 19 Aug 1933, Sardenhnen, East Prussia, Germany. Singer, Mezzo-soprano. Education: Studied at the Berlin State Conservatory and with Rudolf Dittrich at the Studio of the Dresden Staatsoper. Debut: Dresden 1957, as a page in Lohengrin. Career: Sang at the Dresden Staatsoper until 1964 in the mezzo and dramatic soprano repertory, notably as the Dyer's Wife in Die Frau ohne Schatten; Bayreuth Festival 1959, as a Flowermaiden in Parsifal; Berlin Staatsoper from 1964, as Carmen, Octavian and the Composer in Ariadne; Guest appearances in Barcelona, Lausanne, Bratislava, Vienna, Hamburg, Prague, Budapest, United States and Soviet Union; Guested with the Staatsoper in North America as Sieglinde, Kundry, the Composer and Marie in Wozzeck; Sang Herodias, Salome, in Berlin 1987; Many Concert appearances. Recordings: Hansel and Gretel, Der Wildschütz; Wozzeck; Schumann's Genoveva. Address: c/o Deutsche Staatsoper, Unter den Linden 7, D-1086 Berlin, Germany.

SCHUBACK Thomas, b. 1943, Sweden. Conductor; Pianist. Education: Studied at the Stockholm College of Music. Career: Conductor, Royal Opera Stockholm from 1971; productions at the Drottningholm Theatre include L'Incoronazione di Poppea, L'Arbore di Diana by Martin y Soler, Mozart's Cosi fan tutte and Gluck's Paride ed Elena; Musical Director of Lyric Opera of Queensland from 1982; Guest Appearances with San Diego Opera and at Sydney and Copenhagen; Season 1992-93 included performances with the Drottningholm Theatre at the Barbican Centre, London; Concerts with major Swedish Orchestras and elsewhere in Scandinavia, USA and Australia; Lieder Accompanist to Gösta Winbergh, Barbara Bonney and others; Professor of Vocal Coaching, State Oper School, Stockholm. Recordings include: Electra by Haeffner. Current Management: Ulf Tornqvist Artists Management. Address: St Eriksgatan 100, S-113 31 Stockholm, Sweden.

SCHUBEL Max, b. 11 April 1932, New York, USA. Composer. Education: Graduated, New York University, 1953; Further Composition Study with Frank Martin. Career: Freelance Composer, Many Performances Throughout North America; Founded OPUS ONE, 1960, for the Recording of Unfamiliar and Electronic Music. Compositions: Insected Surfaces, Concerto for Clarinet and 4 Instruments, 1965; Exotica, for Cello and Harpsichord, 1967; 2 String Quartets, 1968, 1980; Everybody's Favourite Rag, for Piano, 1979; Divertimento for Piano, Trumpet & Chamber Orchestra, 1980; B Natural, for Prepared Piano, 1980; Guale for Orchestra, 1984; Punch and Judie, for Chamber Orchestra, 1985; The Spoors of Time for Viola and Piano, 1986; Scherzo for Orchestra, 1987; Septet, 1988; Super Scherzo, for Chamber Orchestra, 1989; String Quintet, 1989; Trio for Violin, Cello and Piano, 1989. Honours include: Residencies at the MacDowell Colony, Ossabaw Island and Wolf Trap. Address: c/o ASCAP, ASCAP Building, One Lincoln Plaza, NY 10023, USA.

SCHUDEL Thomas, b. 8 Sept 1937, Defiance, Ohio, USA (Canadian Citizen, 1974). Composer. Education: BSc, 1959, MA, 1961, Ohio University; Composition Studies with Leslie Bassett and Ross Lee Finney, University of Michigan, DMA 1971. Career: Faculty Member, University of Regina, Canada, 1964-; Bassoonist, Regina Symphony Orchestra, 1964-70. Compositions: Set No 2, for Brass and Wind Quintets, 1963; Violin Sonata, 1966; String Quartet, 1967; 2 Symphonies, 1971, 1983; Variations, for Orchestra, 1977; Winterpiece, for Chamber Orchestra and Dancers, 1979; Triptych, for Wind Ensemble, 1979; A Dream Within a Dream, for Chorus, 1985; A.C.T.S, for Narrator and Ensemble, 1986; Dialogues, for Trombone and Percussion, 1987; Concerto, for Piccolo, Strings and Percussion, 1988; Concerto, for Alto Trombone and Chamber Orchestra, 1990; An Emily Dickinson Folio, for Soprano and Ensemble, 1991; Trigon, for 2 Saxophones and Percussion, 1992; A Tangled Web, for Chamber Orchestra, 1993; The Enchanted Cat, Children's Operetta, 1993; Pick Up The Earth, Gold and Rose, and Another Love Poem, All for Chorus, 1994; Sinfonia Concertante, for Saxophone Quartet and Band, 1994. Honours include: 1st Prize, 1972 City of Trieste International Competition. Address: 149 Shannon Road, Regina, Saskatchewan S4S 5H6, Canada.

SCHULLER Gunther, b. 22 Nov 1925, NYC, NY, USA. Composer, Conductor. m. Marjorie Black, 8 June 1948, 2 sons. Education: St Thomas Choir School, NYC; Manhattan School of Music; MusDD, Northeastern University, 1967; MusD, University of Illinois, 1968; Colby College, 1969; Williams College, 1974. Career: Appeared as boy soprano, St Thomas Choir, at age 12; Teacher, Manhattan School of Music, 1950-63; Head, Composition Department, Tanglewood, 1964-84; President, New England Conservatory of Music, 1967-77; Artistic Director: Berkshire Music Center, Tanglewood, 1969-84; Festival at Sandpoint, Idaho, 1985; Founder, President: Margun Music Inc, 1975; GM Records, 1980; French Hornist, Ballet Theater, then 1st Hornist; Cincinnati Symphony Orchestra, Principal Hornist, Metropolitan Opera Orchestra, 1945-59. Compositions: Concertos: Nos 1, 2 for Horn, 1945, 1976; Concertos 1, 2, 3, Farbenspiel, for Orchestra, 1966, 1976, 1985; Violin, 1976; Contrabassoon, 1978; Trumpet, 1979; Concerto Quaternio, 1983; Other works: Quartet for Double Bass, 1947; Fantasy for Unaccompanied Cello, 1951; Recitative and Rondo for Violin and Piano, 1953; Music for Violin, Piano and Percussion, 1957; Contours, 1958; Woodwind Quintet, 1958; 7 Studies on Themes of Paul Klee, 1959; 6 Renaissance Lyrics, 1962; String Quartets Nos 1, 2, 3, 1957, 1965, 1984; Symphony, 1965; 2 Operas: The Visitation, 1966; Fisherman and His Wife, 1970; Capriccio Stravagante, 1972; The Power Within Us, 1972; 3 Invenzioni, 1972; Three Nocturnes, 1973; 4 Soundscapes, 1974; Triplum I, 1967, Triplum II 1975; Diptych, organ, 1976; Sonata Serenata, 1978; Deai, 3 orchestras, 1978; Octet, 1979; Eine Kleine Posaunenmusik, 1980; In Praise of Winds, symphony for large wing orchestra, 1981; Symphony for Organ, 1982; On Light Wings, piano quartet, 1984; Concerto for string quartet and orchestra, 1988; Flute Concerto, 1988; Chamber Symphony, 1989; Concerto for piano 3 hands and orchestra, 1990; Concertos 1 & 2 for piano, 1962, 1981. Recordings: Mozart Frau Partita, K.361; Stravinsky Octet, Sacre du Printemps, Berg Chamber Concerto, as conductor; Schuller Octet, Impromptus and Cadenzes, string quartet No 3, Troplum I, Bernstein, conductor. Publications: Early Jazz: Its Roots and Development, 1968; Musings: The Musical World of Gunther Schuller, 1985; The Weing Era: The Development of Jass, 1930-45, 1989. Honours: Branders Creative Arts Award, 1960; Guggenheim Grantee, 1962, 1963; Deems Taylor Award, 1970; Rodgers and Hammerstein Award, 1971; William Schuman Award, Columbia University, 1989; MacArthur Foundation Fellowship, 1991. Memberships: National Institute of Arts and Letters; American Academy of Arts and Sciences.Current Management: John Gingrich Management. Address: Margun Music Inc, 167 Dudley Road, Newton Centre, MA 02159, USA.

SCHULTE Eike (Wilm), b. 13 Oct 1939, Plettenberg, Germany. Singer (Baritone). Education: Studied at Cologne Musikhochschule with Joseph Metternich and at the Salzburg Mozarteum. Career includes: Member of the Deutsche Oper am Rhein Dusseldorf, 1956-69, Bielefeld Opera, 1969-73 and Hessisches Staatstheater Wiesbaden, 1973-88; Sang the Herald in Lohengrin at Bayreuth, 1988 and toured Japan with the Bayreuth Festival Company, 1989; Munich Staatsoper from 1989 as Faraone in Mosè by Rossini, the Father in Hansel and Gretel and Schtschelkalov in Boris Godunov; Baritone role in staged performances of Carmina Burana, 1990; Sang Beckmesser in Die Meistersinger at the Paris Opéra and in Munich; Guest engagements in Vienna, Hamburg, Cologne, Bonn, Trieste, Rome and Brussels, notably as Figaro and Rigoletto; Sang Kurwenal in Japan in 1990 conducted by Peter Schneider, Mahler's 8th Symphony with the London Philharmonic under Klaus Tennstedt in 1991; Season 1991-92 included: Lohengrin at Vienna State Opera, Zemlinsky, VARA Holland and Brahms Requiem with Hamburg Philharmonic; Season 1993-94 included: Hansel and Gretel, Rosenkavalier and Meistersinger in Munich, Ariadne auf Naxos in Cologne and Rigoletto in Tel Aviv; Season 1994-95 included: Gunther in a new Ring production at Paris, Tannhäuser at Bayreuth Festival and debut with the Philadelphia Orchestra in Ariadne auf Naxos in Philadelphia and Carnegie Hall, New York; Sang the Herald in Lohengrin at the Accademia di Santa Cecilia, Rome, 1996. Recordings include: Die Meistersinger conducted by Sawallisch; Video of Mahler's 8th Symphony; CDs: Berlioz's L'enfance du Christ, Wagner's Lohengrin, Beethoven's 9th, Haydn's Creation and Wagner's Das Rheingold. Address: c/o Haydn Rawstron Ltd, 36 Station Road, London SE20 7BQ, England.

SCHULTZ Andrew, b. 1960, Adelaide, South Australia. Composer; University Professor. Education: Composition studies with Colin Brumby, Composition Studies with George Crumb, Conducting with Richard Wernick, University of Pennsylvania, USA, 1983; Composition with David Lumsdaine, MMus, King's College, London, England; PhD, Queensland University. Career: Currently Head of Music Studio, Guildhall School of Music and Drama and Visiting Professor, Faculty of Creative Arts, University of Wollongong, New South Wales; Compositions performed and broadcast widely, Australia, USA, Europe; Commissions, University of Melbourne, Perihelion, Seymour Group, Elision, Flederman, Queensland Philharmonic Orchestra, Hunter Orchestra, Sydney Symphony Orchestra; 4MBS-FM, Duo Contemporain, Musica Nova; Discography includes: Garotte, 1981, on Tropic of Capricorn, Qld Symphony Orchestra, CD Cassette; Barren Grounds on Tapestry, CD; Ekstasis on Australian Vocal Music, 1992, CD; Chamber Music of Andrew Schultz, CD. Compositions: Spherics, flute, trombone, or bass clarinet, 1 percussion, synthesizer, cello, 1985; Stick Dance, clarinet, marimba, piano, 1987; Sea-Change piano, 1987; Black River, opera, 1988; Barren Grounds, clarinet, viola, cello, bass, guitar, 1990; Orchestral, choral and vocal works; Ekstasis, 1990, 6 solo voices; Calling Music, 1991, chamber orchestra; The Devil's Music, 1992, large orchestra; Diver's Lament, large orchestra, 1995. Honours: Composer Fellowship, Australia Council Music Board, 1982; Fulbright Award, Music Board Grant (Australia Council), 1983; Commonwealth Scholarship and Fellowship Plan Award for study at King's College; 2 Composer Fellowships to Young Composer Summer Schools; Australian National Composers Opera Award; Dalley-Scarlett Award; Queensland University Medal; Commenwealth Postgraduate Research Award; Albert H Maggs Composition Award; Hilda Margaret Watts Prize, Kings College, London; Composer Fellowship, Australia Council, 1990. Address: Guildhall School of Music, Silk Street, Barbican, London EC2Y 8DT, England.

SCHULTZ Robert, b. 29 September 1948, Bellefonte, Pennsylvania, USA. Composer; Arranger. m. Tina Faigen, 12 October 1997. Education: BM, Theory, Composition, 1975, MM, Composition, 1977, West Virginia University; Composition Study with Thomas Canning; Piano Study with James Miltenberger & Herman Godes. Career: Piano Arranger, 1978-81, Music Director, 1981-87, Columbia Pictures Publications; Senior Keyboard Editor, CPP/Belwin Mills Publications, 1987-90; Piano Arranger, Warner Bros Publications, 1990-. Recordings: Visions of Dunbar, Original Works & Transcriptions by Robert Schultz, 1995; Tina Faigen Plays Piano Transcriptions by Robert Schultz, 1997. Compositions: Nine Preludes, Opus 10, 1980; Fantasy Sketches, Opus 2 & Opus 12, 1981; Crystalline Miniatures, Opus 13 (flute), 1981; Winter Scenes, Opus 5, 1982; Ballet Music, Opus 15, 1983; Piano Recital Album, Opus 16, 1984; Ballade, Opus 17, 1985; Piano Recital Album, Opus 18, 1986; Schultz Piano Course, collaborated with Pamela Schultz, 1986; Montage, Opus 20, commissioned by Georgia Music Teachers Association, 1986; Three Duet Suites (1 piano-4 hands), Opus 21, 1988; Fantasy (2 pianos-4 hands), Opus 3, 1990; Five Impromptus, Opus 23, 1993; Piano Studies, Opus 28, 1997. Publications: 18 Piano Transcriptions of Major Classical Works, 1982-97. Memberships: National Academy of Recording Arts & Sciences; Music Teachers National Association; Florida Music Teachers Association; Miami Music Teachers Association, President, 1995-97. Hobbies: Bridge; Sports; Fishing. Address: 8200 SW 102 Street, Miami, FL 33156, USA.

SCHULZ Gerhard, b. 23 Sept 1951, Austria. Violinist. Education: Studied in Vienna, Dusseldorf and USA. Career: 2nd violin of the Alban Berg Quartet from 1978; Many concert engagements, including complete cycles of the Beethoven Quartets in 15 European cities 1987-88, 1988-89 seasons; Bartok-Mozart cycle in London, Vienna, Paris, Frankfurt, Munich, Geneva and Turin, 1990-91; Annual concert series at the Vienna Konzerthaus and festival engagements worldwide; Associate Artist at the South Bank Centre, London; US appearances in Washington DC, San Francisco, NY, Carnegie Hall. Recordings: Complete quartets of Beethoven, Brahms, Berg, Webern and Bartok; Late quartets of Mozart, Schubert, Haydn and Dvorak; Ravel and Debussy quartets; Live recordings from Carnegie Hall, Mozart, Schumann; Konzerthaus in Vienna, Brahms; Opera-Comique Paris, Brahms. Honours: Grand Prix du Disque; Deutsche Schallplatenpreis; Edison Prize; Japan Grand Prix; Gramophone Magazine Award. Address: Intermusica Artists' Management, 16 Duncan Terrace, London N1 8BZ, England.

SCHULZ Robert, b. 14 November 1950, temora, New South Wales, Australia. Composer; Guitarist; Mandolinist. Education: Licentiate, Guildhall School of Music, London, 1975; Conducting, Western Australia Academy of Performing Arts, 1984. Career: Director, Freemantle Music School, WA; Founded Western Australia Mandolin Orchestra, 1976; Compositions: Dance Pieces I and II for Mandolin and Orchestra, 1978; Outback for Mandolin and Orchestra, 1980; Sonata in D for Mandolin and Guitar, 1981; Three Songs From Lord of the Rings for Children's Choir and Orchestra, 1989; Eight Guitar Trios, 1989; Botany Suite for Mandolin and Orchestra, 1991; Elegy for Anne, for Flute and Cello, 1995; Six Piano Preludes, 1995; String Quartet, 1995. Address: c/o APRA, 1A Eden Street, NSW 2065, Australia.

SCHULZ Walther, b. 1940, Vienna, Austria. Cellist. Education: Studied in Vienna. Debut: NY 1979; Debut Tour of Japan 1984. Career: Performances of Haydn and Other Composers in Vienna and Elsewhere from 1968; Co Founder of the Haydn Trio of Vienna, 1968 and has performed in Brussels, Munich, Berlin, Zurich, London, Paris and Rome; Frequent North American appearances with Concerts in 25 States; Further travels to the Near East, Russia, Africa, Central and South America; Series at the Vienna Konzerthaus Society from 1976 with Performances of more than 100 works; Summer Festivals at Vienna, Salzburg, Aix en Provence, Flanders and Montreux; Master Classes at the Royal College and Royal Academy in London, Stockholm, Bloomington, Tokyo and the Salzburg Mozarteum. Recordings: Complete Piano Trios of Beethoven and Schubert, Mendelssohn D Minor, Brahms B major, Tchaikovsky A Minor, Schubert Trout Quintet; Albums of Works by Haydn, Schumann, Dvorak, Smetena. Address: c/o Sue Lubbock Concert Management, 25 Courthorpe Road, London, NW3 2LE, England.

SCHUMAN Patricia, b. 4 Feb 1954, Los Angeles, USA. Singer, (Soprano). Education: Studied at Santa Cruz University, California, USA. Career: Sang minor roles with San Francisco Opera then appeared with the Houston Opera and in a touring company; Engagements at the NYC Opera, the Paris Opera, Teatro La Fenice Venice and in Washington DC; Sang on tour with Peter Brook's version of Carmen; Théâtre de la Monnaie Brussels from 1983 as Dorabella, Zerlina, and as Angelina in La Cenerentola; St Louis 1986 and in US premiere of Il Viaggio a Reims by Rossini; Théâtre du Châtelet, Paris 1989, in the title role of L'Incoronazione di Poppea; Miami Opera and Long Beach Opera 1989, as Antonia in Les Contes d'Hoffmann and as Mozart's Countess; Seattle Opera 1990, as Blanche in Les Dialogues des Carmelites; Has also sung at the Vienna Staatsoper and in the concert hall; Metropolitan Opera debut, Donna Elvira, 1990; The Voyage, by Glass, 1996; Covent Garden debut 1992, as Donna Elvira; Salzburg Festival 1997, in La Clemenza di Tito. Recordings: Roggiero in Rossini's Tancredi; Messiah, Handel. Address: c/o Long Beach Opera, 6372 Pacific Coast Highway, Long Beach, CA 90801, USA.

SCHUNK Robert, b. 1948, Neu-Isenburg, Frankfurt, Germany. Singer, Tenor. Education: Studied with Martin Grundler at the Frankfurt Musikhochschule. Career: Sang at Karlsruhe 1973-75; Bonn Opera 1975-77; Dortmund 1977-79; Bayreuth Festival from 1977, as Siegmund, Erik and Melot; Hamburg Staatsoper 1981, as the Emperor in Die Frau ohne Schatten; Bregenz Festival 1983, Max in Der Freischutz; Engagements in Munich, Vienna, Frankfurt, London, Cologne and Berlin; Tour of Japan with the Hamburg Staatsoper 1984; Sang Florestan at the Met and Naples, 1986-87; Siegmund in NY and Munich, 1987, 1989; Emperor in Die Frau ohne Schatten and Vladimir in Prince Igor at Munich, 1989; Sang Wagner's Erik at Naples, 1992. Recordings: Erik in Der fliegende Holländer, from Bayreuth

SCHURMANN Gerard, b. 19 Jan 1924, Kertosono, Java. Composer; Conductor. m. Carolyn Nott, 26 May 1973, 1 daughter. Education: Composition with Alan Rawsthrone; Piano with Kathleen Long; Conducting with Franco Ferrara. Career: Aircrew, 320 Squadron, RAF, 1941-45; Acting Netherlands Cultural Attaché, London, 1945-47; Resident Orchestral Conductor, Radio Hilversum, 1947-50; Freelance Composer/Conductor, 1950-; Guest Conductor, France, Italy, Spain, Switzerland, Czechoslovakia, Germany, Netherlands, Scandinavia, Ireland, USA. Compositions include: Orchestral: Variants, 1970; Attack and Celebration, 1971; Piano Concerto, 1972-73; Violin Concerto, 1975-78; The Gardens of Exile, concerto, cello, orchestra, 1989-90; Man in the Sky, 1994; Concerto for Orchestra, 1994-95; Chamber, instrumental: Serenade, 1971; Contrasts, 1973; Leotaurus, 1975; Wind Quintet, flute, oboe, clarinet, horn, bassoon, 1976; 2 Ballades for piano, 1, Hukvaldy, 2, Brno, 1981; Duo, violin, piano, 1984; Quartet for Piano and Strings (violin, viola, cello, piano), 1986; Ariel, oboe, 1987; Quartet no 2 for piano and strings, 1997; Vocal, choral: Song cycle, Chuenchi, 1966; Summer is Coming, madrigal, SATB, unaccompanied, 1970; The Double Heart, cantata, SATB, unaccompanied, 1976; Piers Plowman, opera cantata, 2 acts, 1979-80; Nine Slovak folk songs, high voice, piano or orchestra, 1988; Six Songs of William Blake, 1997. Recordings: 6 Studies of Francis Bacon; Variants; Chuench'i; The Double Heart; Claretta; Piers Plowman; The Gardens of Exile; Piano Concerto; Violin Concerto; Duo for Violin and Piano; Attack and Celebration; The Film Music of Gerard Schurmann; The Gambler; Man in the Sky. Contributions to: Introductory essay to 3 volumes on Alan Rawsthorne, 1984; Essay about working on the music for the film Lawrence of Arabia, 1990. Honours: Numerous. Memberships: Performing Rights Society; American Society of Composers, Authors and Publishers; MCPS; APC; AMPAS; BAFTA; Composers' Guild of Great Britain; Phyllis Court Club. Current Management: The Marion Rosenberg Office. Address: 3700 Multiview Drive, Hollywood Hills, Los Angeles, CA 90068, USA.

SCHÜTZ Siiri, b. 26 July 1974, Berlin, Germany. Pianist. Education: Carl Phil E Bach Gymnasium, Berlin, 1985-91; Syudied with Aunerose Schmidt at the Hochschule P Musik, Berlin, 1991-96; Diploma at the Hochschule für Musik, Hanus Eisler, Berlin, 1996; Study with Leon Fleisher at the Peabody Conservatory, Baltimore, 1996-. Career: Played in a concert for the German President, Richard von Weizsäcker in Castle Bellevue; Performed in place of Claudio Arrau in the Köln Philharmony and Murray Perahia in Düsseldorf, made debut with the Berlin Philharmonic Orchestra, conducted by Claudio Abbado (this conceert was recorded and used in a film, The Year After), 1991; Further concerts include the Schleswig Holtstein Festival, the Schwetzinger Mozart Festival and the Ruhrfestspiele, with the Tonhalle Orchestra Zürich, the Bern Symphony Orchestra, and the Berlin Rundfunk Symphony Orchestra; Played chamber music during the Berliner Festwochen, 1993, and in the Faust cycle of the Philharmonic Orchestra in Berlin, 1994; Honours: First Prize in the International Piano Competition, Aussig, 1989; Jütting Award, Stendhal, Germany, 1996. Hobbies: Literature: Philosophy; Yoga. Current Management: Kowzertdirektion Hans Adler Auguste Victoriast 64 D-14199 Berlin. Address: Üderseestr 17 D-10318 Berlin, Germany.

SCHWAGER Myron (August), b. 16 Mar 1937, Pittsfield, Massachusetts, USA. Professor of Music, History and Literature. m. 1. Katharine Lake, Sept 1961, 1 son, 1 daughter. 2. Laurie Beth Lewis, June 1982. Education: Massachussetts Institute of Technology, 1955-56; BMus, Boston University, 1958; MMus, New England Conservatory of Music, 1961; MA, PhD, Harvard University, 1970. Career: Worcester Community School of the Performing Arts; Jesuit Artists Institute, Italy; Chair, Department of Music, Hartt School of Music, University of Hartford, Connecticut, 1974-; Former Principal Cellist, Springfield Symphony Orchestra; Appearances with Cambridge Society for Early Music, Boston Chamber Players, Consortium Musicale, Hawthorne Trio, Hartford Chamber Orchestra, and Karas String Quartet; Revived and reconstructed Francesco Cavalli's La Virtu de'strali d'Amore, Venice, 1642 at Wadsworth Atheneum, Hartford, 31 July-1 Aug, 1987. Contributions to: The Creative World of Beethoven, 1971; Current Musicology; Music and Letters; Early Music; Musical Quarterly. Address: 30 Hoskins Road, Bloomfield, CT 06002, USA.

SCHWANBECK Bodo, b. 20 July 1935, Scherwin, Germany. Singer, Bass-Baritone. Education: Studied with Franz-Theo Reuter in Munich and with KH Jarius in Stuttgart. Debut: Detmold 1959, as Carlaam in Boris Godunov. Career: Has sung in Frankfurt, Hamburg, Munich, Manheim, Dusseldorf, and Lisbon and at the NYC Opera, Zurich Opera 1967, in the premiere of Madame Bovary by Sutermeister; French TV as Mustafa in L'Italiana in Algeri; Théâtre de la Monnaie Brussels 1986; Sang at Madrid 1988, in Lulu; Brussels 1990, in From the House of the Dead; Covent Garden 1990, as Waldner in Arabella; Sang Antonio in Figaro with the Royal Opera on tour to Japan, 1992; Other roles include Baron Ochs, Osmin, Alfonso, Pizarro, Leporello, Mephistopheles, Nicolai's Falstaff, Don Pasquale, Dulcamara, Golaud, Don Magnifico and Wozzeck; Frequent concert appearances. Address: c/o Theatre Royal de le Monnaie, 4 Leopoldstrasse, B-1000 Brussels, Belgium.

SCHWANEWILMS Anne, b. 1965, Gelsenkirchen, Germany. Singer (Mezzo-Soprano). Education: Cologne Musikhochschule, with Hans Sotin. Career: Member, Cologne Opera Studio, 1990-92; Member, Cologne Opera, 1993-95; Freelance Engagements, 1995-; Recent engagements haver included Die Walküre in Essen and Klagenfurt, Sieglinde/Walküre in Freiburg, Die Zauberflöte in Trieste (with Arnold Östman) and Salome with the Cologne Radio Symphony Orchestra; Debut at the Bayreuth Festival in 1996 in roles of Gerhilde (Die Walküre) and Gutrune (Götterdämmerung) whilst covering the role of Kundry and has been reinvited to Bayreuth each year since; Returns to Turin in 1998 to perform Gutrune and 3 Norn in concert performances of Götterdämmerung; Recent concerts have included Zemlinsky's Der Zwerg with the Gürzenich Orchestra in Cologne, Mahler's Symphony No 8 in Udine and a concert at the Kongresshalle in Lübeck (Weber/Schubert/Rubinstein) with Erich Wächter; Further engagements with return visits to Bayreuth and concerts in Japan, Die Walküre (Gerhilde) in Hamburg, Hänsel und Gretl (Hexe) in Stuttgart, Wagner's Rienzi (Adriano) at the Komische Oper in Berlin, Die Walküre (Sieglinde) in Bonn, role of Judith in Barbe Bleu at the Brussels Opera and at the Schouwburd in Rotterdam, Beethoven's Symphony No IX in Leipzig for MDR and Wesendoncklieder (in the Mottl edition) in Freiburg. Recording: Elektra. Current Management: Haydn Rawstron Ltd, 36 Station Road, London SE20 7BQ, England.

SCHWANN William, b. 13 May 1913, Salem, IL, USA. Musician. m. Aire-Maija Kutvonen, 1 June 1959. Education: AB, University of Louisville School of Music, 1935; Graduate studies, Boston University School of Music, 1935-36; Graduate School, Harvard Music Department, 1937-39; Organ performance with E Power Biggs, 1936-38. Career: Organist, Choir Director, Louisville churches, Kentucky, 1930-35; Organ concerts and broadcasts 1930-42; Organ and Piano Teacher, Organist and Choir Director, Boston area, Massachusetts, 1935-50; Owner, The Record Shop, Cambridge, 1939-53; Complier, Publisher, 1st Long Playing Record Catalogue, now Schwann Record and Tape Guide, 1949; Compiler, Publisher, Artists Listing LP Catalogs; Schwann Children's LP Record Catalog; Basic Record Library, Basic Jazz Record Library, 1953-; Compiler, Publisher, White House Record Library Catalogs, 1973, 1980; President, Treasurer, W Schwann Incorporated, 1949-77; President, Publisher, ABC Schwann Publications, 1976-. Address: 26 Old Winter Street, Lincoln, MA 01773, USA.

SCHWANTER Joseph, b. 22 March 1943, Chicago, USA. Composer. Education: BM, American Conservatory of Music, Chicago, 1964; MM, 1966, DM, 1968, Northwestern University. Career: Faculty Member, Eastman School of Music, Rochester, 1970- (Professor of Composition, 1980); Composer-in-Residence, St Louis Symphony, 1982-85, Cabrillo Music Festival, 1992. Compositions: Chronicon, for Bassoon and Piano, 1968; Consortium I & II, for Flute and Ensemble, 1970-71; Modus Caeliestis, for Orchestra, 1973; Elixir, for Flute & 5 Players, 1975; And the Mountains Rising Nowhere, for Orchestra, 1977; Canticle of the Evening Bells, for Flute and 12 Players, 1977; Wild Angels of the Open Hills, Song Cycle, for Soprano and Ensemble, 1977; Aftertones of Infinity, for Orchestra, 1978; Sparrows, for Soprano and Chamber Ensemble, 1979; Wind Willow, Whisper, for Chamber Ensemble, 1980; Dark Millenium, for Orchestra, 1981; Through Interior Worlds, for Ensemble, 1981; Distant Runes and Incantations, for Piano and Orchestra, 1984; Someday Memories, for Orchestra, 1984; Witchnomad, Song Cycle, for Soprano and Orchestra, 1984; Dreamcaller, Song Cycle, for Soprano, Violin and Chamber Orchestra, 1984; A Sudden Rainbow, for Orchestra, 1984; Toward Light, for Orchestra, 1986; Piano Concerto, 1988; Freeflight, for Orchestra, 1989; A Play of Shadows, Fantasy, for Flute and Orchestra, 1990; Velocities, for Marimba, 1990; Percussion Concerto, 1991 (premiered 1995); Through Interior Worlds, Ballet, 1992 (concert version 1994). Honours include: Pulitzer Prize, 1979. Address: c/o ASCAP, ASCAP Building, One Lincoln Plaza, NY 10023, USA.

SCHWARTNER Dieter, b. 6 Feb 1938, Plauen, Germany. Tenor. Education: Studied in Dresden. Debut: Plauen in 1969 as the Baron in Der Wildschütz. Career: Sang at Plauen until 1972, then at Dresden, 1972-78, and Dessau, 1978-79; Member of the Leipzig Opera from 1979 singing Ligeti's Le Grand Macabre and the Duke of Parma in Busoni's Doktor Faust in 1991; Guest appearances in Dresden and at the Berlin Staatsoper; Other roles have included Tamino, Faust, Max, Lionel in Martha, Florestan, Don José, Alvaro in La Forza del Destino and Walther von Stolzing; Many concert engagements. Address: c/o Stadtische Theatre, 7010 Leipzig, Germany.

SCHWARTZ Dennis W, b. Willoughby, Ohio, USA. Musician (Viola da Gamba and Contrabass). m. Dawn Schwartz, 10 Oct 1992. Education: Principle Bassist, Northeast Ohio Regional Orchestra, 1987; BMus, Music History, 1992, MMus, 1996, Cleveland State University. Career: Foxfire, Rabbit Run Theater, on stage role, 1985; Evita, Lakeland Comm College, 1986; My Fair Lady, Richmond Heights, 1993; Tour of Germany, Odenwald Festspiele, Bassist with Cleveland Philharmonic Orchestra, 1992-94; Blossom Music Center with Cleveland State Chamber Winds, Guys and Dolls, Richmond Heights, 1994; Hermit Club, St Peter's Episcopal Church, 1995. Recordings: Recorded with Cleveland State Concert Band, 1991. Publication: Joseph Bodin de Boismortier's Diverses Pieces de Viol, 1996. Memberships: Mu Phi Epsilon; Pi Kappa Lambda; Gold Key National Honour Society; Viola da Gamba Society of America. Address: 552 Main Street, Suite C, Wadsworth, OH 44281, USA.

SCHWARTZ Elliott, b. 19 Jan 1936, Brooklyn, New York, USA. Composer; Author; Professor. m. Dorothy Feldman, 26 June 1960, 1 son, 1 daughter. Education: Studied, Columbia University, New York; Bennington Composers' Conference. Career: Professor of Music and Department Chair, Bowdoin College, Brunswick, Maine, USA, 1964-; Professor of Compositions, Ohio State University, 1985-88, 1988-; Visiting Appointment, Trinity College of Music, London, 1967-; University of California, 1973-; University of California, San Diego, 1978-79; Robinson College, Cambridge, England, 1993-94;, 1998. Recordings: Grand Concerto; Extended Piano; Mirrors; Texture for Chamber Orchestras; Concert Piece for Ten Players; Chamber Concerto; Cycles and Gongs; Extended Clarinet; Dream Music with Variations; Celebrations/Reflections for Orchestra; Memorial in Two Parts; Chiaroscuro; Elan. Publications: The Symphonies of Ralph Vaughan Williams; Contemporary Composers in Contemporary Music; Electronic Music; A Listeners Guide; Music Ways of Listening, Music since 1945. Contributions to: Contemporary music articles and essays for Music Quarterly; Musical America; Perspectives of New Music; Nordic Sounds (Denmark); Music and Musicians (UK); Nutida Musik (Sweden). Honours: Gaudeamus Prize, Netherlands, 1970; McKim Commission, Library of Congress, USA, 1983; National Endowment for the Arts, grants, 1974, 1978, 1984; Rockefeller Foundation Bellagio Centre Fellow, 1980, 1989. Membership: Former Vice President, American Music Centre; Former President, College Music Society; Former national chair, American Society of University Composers; Governing Board Member, American Composers Alliance, 1994-. Hobbies: Travel;

Baseball; Basketball; Theatre; Cooking. Address: PO Box 451, South Freeport, ME 04078, USA.

SCHWARTZ Sergiu, b. 1957, Romania (Israeli/US Citizen). Concert violinist; Conductor; Pedagogue. Education: Studied with Stefan Gheorghiu, Romania; Rami Shevelov, Rubin Academy, Tel Aviv; Yfrah Neaman, Guildhall School, London; Dorothy DeLay, Juilliard School, New York; Additional studies with Sandor Vegh, Felix Galimir, Leon Fleisher, Isaac Stern and Sergiu Celibidache. Debut: New York debut at Carnegie Recital Hall; London debut at Wigmore Hall in the Outstanding Israeli Artists series; North American debut at the Museum of Fine Arts, Montreal. Career: Soloist with leading orchestras in Europe and throughout the USA, including the Dresden Staatskapelle under Giuseppe Sinopoli, the Jerusalem Symphony under Sergiu Comissiona, the Slovak Philharmonic, the Dresden Philharmonic, the London Symphony at Barbican Hall, London Soloists at Queen Elizabeth Hall, the Bern Symphony under Peter Maag, the Polish National Radio and TV Orchestra under Antoni Wit, the Florida Philharmonic under James Judd, the Orchestra of St Luke's at New York's Lincoln Centre, the Chicago Grant Park Symphony; Soloist and Conductor with the Sarajevo Philharmonic, the Concentus Hungaricus, the European Community Chamber Orchestra, the New York Master Players; Music Advisor and Principal Guest Conductor of the Ashdod Chamber Orchestra of Israel; Recitals at major music centres throughout the US, including Carnegie's Weill Recital Hall, 92nd Street Y, Town Hall, Merkin Hall in New York; Kennedy Centre and the Library of Congress in Washington; Royce Hall (UCLA) and Ambassador Auditorium in Los Angeles; Recital and chamber music appearances at music festivals, including Newport, Rhode Island, Interlochen, Michigan, Interlaken, Switzerland, Music at La Gesse, France, Kuhmo, Finland; Broadcast recitals in Jerusalem, New York, Los Angeles, Washington, Boston, Chicago and London (BBC), including premiere of the Concerto by Samuel Coleridge-Taylor; Teaching position, artist faculty, The Harid Conservatory, USA; Master classes at music schools, colleges, universities throughout the USA including Interlochen Arts Academy, UCLA, Oberlin Conservatory and Idyllwild School of Music, Rubin Academy in Jerusalem, Franz Liszt Academy in Budapest, Rejna Sofia Academy in Madrid; Master courses in Romania, Bulgaria, Switzerland, Holland and Germany; Judge, international violin competitions in France, Italy and the USA. Recordings: Works by Sibelius with the London Symphony, Svendsen and Grieg (Vox); Works by Spohr (Arcobalen); Debussy, Schumann, R Strauss, Bloch, Enescu and Smetana. Honours: America-Isreal Cultural Foundation Award; National Endowment for the Arts Solo Recitalist Fellowship; Prizewinner, international violin competitions in the US, England, Switzerland and Chile. Address: c/o Joanne Rile Artists Management, 801 Old York Road, Noble Plaza, Suite 212, Jenkintown, PA 19046, USA.

SCHWARZ Gerard (Ralph), b. 19 Aug 1947, Weehawken, New Jersey, USA. Conductor. m. Jody Greitzer, 23 June 1984, 2 sons, 2 daughters. Education: Began Trumpet lessons, age 8; National Music Camp, Interlochen, Michigan, summers 1958-60; Studied Trumpet with William Vacchiano, 1962-68; BS, Juilliard School, 1972. Career: Trumpeter, American Brass Quintet, 1965-73; Trumpeter, American Symphony Orchestra, New York, 1966-72; Co-Principal Trumpet, New York Philharmonic Orchestra, 1972-75; Music Director, New York Chamber Symphony, 1977-; Music Director, Los Angeles Chamber Orchestra, 1978-86; Music Advisor, 1982-84, Music Director, 1984-, Mostly Mozart Festival, New York; Music Advisor, 1983-85, Principal Conductor, 1985-86, Music Director, 1986-, Seattle Symphony; Conducted Fidelio at Seattle, 1991; Artistic Advisor, Tokyo Bunkamuras Orchard Hall, Japan, 1994-; Conducted La Traviata at Seattle, 1996. Recordings include: With Seattle Symphony: Hanson's Symphonies Nos 1-7, The Four Symphonies of Schumann; Hovhaness' Symphonies Nos 1, 2, 22, 50; Shostakovich's Symphony No 11; Mozart's Piano Concertos No 21 and 24; Symphonies and other music by David Diamond; Peter Mennin's Moby Dick and Symphonies No 3 and No 7; Clarinet Concertos by Weber, Spohr and Crusell, with Emma Johnson and English Chamber Orchestra; Bach B minor Suite and Brandenburg Concertos; Schoenberg Op 16 and Op 9; Janacek's Mládi and Idyll; Mozart Symphonies K550, K551, with Los Angeles Chamber Orchestra. Honours: Honorary Doctorates: Fairleigh Dickinson University Music School, 1975-, University of Puget Sound, Seattle, and Juilliard School, 1996-; Conductor of the Year, Musical America International Directory of Performing Arts, 1994. Address: c/o Seattle Symphony, 305 Harrison Street, Seattle, WA 98109, USA.

SCHWARZ Hanna, b. 15 Aug 1943, Hamburg, Germany. Singer (Mezzo-soprano). Education: Studied in Hamburg, Hanover and Essen. Debut: Hanover 1970, as Maddalena in Rigoletto. Career: Eutin 1972, as Carmen; Member of the Hamburg Staatsoper from 1973; Guest appearances in Zurich (1975-), San Francisco (1977-), Vienna, Paris (Preziosilla 1977), Deutsche Oper Berlin (Cherubino 1978); Munich Staatsoper 1974, 1980, 1984; Bayreuth Festival 1976-85, as Fricka and Erda; sang in the first complete performance of Berg's Lulu, Paris Opéra 1979; Holland Festival 1985, as Brangaene in Tristan und Isolde; Paris 1987, as Cornelia in Giulio Cesare; Sang Fricka in Das Rheingold at Bonn and Cologne, 1990; Season 1992 as Orpheus and Fricka at Bonn; Sang Fricka at the New York Met, 1996-97; Mephistophila and Helen in the premiere of Schnittke's Historia von D Johann Fausten, Hamburg, 1995. Recordings include: Die Zauberflöte, The Queen of Spades, Lulu, Mahler's Rückert Lieder, Apollo et Hyacinthus by Mozart, Die Lustige Witwe; Les Contes d'Hoffmann, Humperdinck's Königskinder, Die Heimkehr aus der Fremde by Mendelssohn; Rhinedaughter in The Ring; Fricka in the Bayreuth Ring; Martha in Schubert's oratorio Lazarus; Mother in Hänsel und Gretel. Address: c/o Oper der Stadt Köln, Offenbachplatz, D-5000 Cologne, Germany.

SCHWARZENBERG Elisabeth, b. 23 Sept 1933, Vienna, Austria. Singer (Soprano). m. Georg Schnapka. Education: Studied in Vienna. Debut: Deutsche Oper am Rhein Dusseldorf 1956, as Eva in Die Meistersinger. Career: Sang in Munich, Paris, Brussels, Nice, Turin, Dublin, Geneva and Zurich; Many appearances at the Vienna Volksoper; Dusseldorf 1957, in the premiere of Die Räuber by Klebe; Salzburg Festival 1961, in the premiere of Das Bergwerk zu Falun by Wagner-Régeny; Bayreuth 1962-72; Teatro San Carlos Lisbon 1967; Other roles included the Marschallin and Donna Elvira. Address: c/o Volksoper, Währingerstrasse 78, A-1090 Vienna, Austria.

SCHWARZKOPF Elisabeth (Dame), b. 9 Dec 1915, Jarotschin, Poland. Singer (Soprano). m. Walter Legge 1953 (deceased 1979). Education: Studied at the Berlin Hochschule für Musik 1934; later with Maria Ivogün. Debut: Berlin Städtsiche Oper 1938 as a Flowermaiden in Parsifal; recital debut Berlin 1942; joined the Vienna Staatsoper 1944 and visited Covent Garden 1947; until 1959 sang Mozart's Pamina and Susanna, Wagner's Eva, Puccini's Mimi and Butterfly, Strauss's Sophie and Marschallin and Massenet's Manon in London; Salzburg Festival 1947-64, debut as Mozart's Susanna; Created Anne Trulove in The Rake's Progress at Venice in 1951 and sang in the premiere of Orff's Trionfi at La Scala Milan 1953; US debut San Francisco 1955, as Marenka in The Bartered Bride; appeared in operas by Mozart at the Chicago Lyric Opera in 1959; Metropolitan Opera debut 1964, as the Marschallin; other opera roles included Debussy's Mélisande, Mozart's Donna Elvira and Fiordiligi, Wagner's Elisabeth and Elsa, Gounod's Marguerite and Verdi's Gilda; Concert repertoire included Bach's Passions, oratorios by Handel and Haydn, the Requiems of Verdi and Brahms, Tippett's A Child of Our Time and the Four Last Songs of Strauss; She was particularly noted as a siger of Lieder; retired from opera 1972 and from concerts in 1975; gave master classes in Europe and America. Recordings: Many operatic roles on Columbia; also recorded for Telefunken, Electrola, Olympic, Urania and Cetra inclduing Don Giovanni; Figaro, Così fan tutte, Rosenkavalier, Capriccio, Falstaff, Turandot (as Liu), Die Meistersinger (Bayreuth 1951), St Matthew Passion (Klemperer); Les Contes d'Hoffmann (as Giulietta); Die Zauberflöte (First Lady); Die Fledermaus; Lieder recitals for EMI under the direction of Walter Legge. Honous include: Cambridge MUsD; National Socialist Party 1940, No 7548960; Grosses Verdienst-Kreuz der Bundesrepublik Deutschland; DBE, 1992.

SCHWEEN Astrid, b. 1960, NY, USA. Cellist. Education: Studied at the Juilliard School. Career: Soloist with The New York Philharmonic; Co-founder of the Lark String Quartet; Recent concert tours to: Australia; Taiwan; Hong Kong; China; Germany; Holland; US appearances at: the Lincoln Center, New York; Kennedy Center, Washington; Boston; Los Angeles; Philadelphia; St Louis; San Francisco; Repertoire includes: Quartets by Hadyn, Mozart, Beethoven, Schubert, Dvorák, Brahms, Borodin, Bartók, Debussy and Shostakovich. Honours include: Gold Medals at the 1990 Naumberg, 1991 Shostakovich Competitions; Prizewinner at the: 1990, Premio Paulio Borciani; 1990, Karl Klinger; 1991 London International String Quartet; 1991, Melbourne Chamber Music Competitions. Address: c/o Sonata (Lark Quartet), 11 Northpark Street, Glasgow, G20 7AA, Scotland.

SCHWEIKART Dieter, b. 9 Jan 1942, Iserlohn, Germany. Singer (Bass). Education: Studied in Wuppertal with Becker-Brill and with Thomas Lo Monaco in Rome. Career: Sang ion Saarbrucken from 1964; Appearances at Dusseldorf, Krefeld and Bonn; Hanover from 1976; Has sung in Dortmund, Hamburg, Frankfurt, Helsinki, Florence, Copenhagen and Cologne; Bayreuth Festival 1983-86, as Hans Foltz in Die Meistersinger and as Fafner in Der Ring des Nibelungen; Sang Daland in Der fliegende Holländer at Naples, 1992. Address: c/o PO Box 100262, Bayreuther Festspiele, 8580 Bayreuth, Germany.

SCHWEINITZ Wolfgang von, b. 7 Feb 1953, Hamburg, Germany. Composer. Education: American University in Washington, DC, 1968-69; Hamburg Hochschule fur Musik, 1971-75, with György Ligeti. Career: Center for Computer Research in Music and Acoustics, Stanford University, California, 1975-76; Resident Composer, German Academy, Rome, 1978-79; Opera 'azione musicale' Patmos Premiered at Munich, 1990; Guest Professor in composition, Weimer, 1994-96. Compositions: 2 Symphonies, 1973, 1974; Mozart Variations, for Orchestra, 1976; String Quartet, 1977; Die Brücke, for Tenor, Baritone and Chamber Orchestra, 1978; Piano Concerto, 1979; Papiersterne Song Cycle, for Mezzo and Piano, 1981; Englische Serenade, for 6 Wind Instruments, 1984; Mass, for Soloists, Chorus and Orchestra, 1984; Music for 4 Saxophones, 1984; Patmos, azione musicale, 1990; Morgenlied, for Flute, 1990; Singing Together in Harmony, for Violin, Cello and Piano, 1994; ...wir aber singen, Symphonic Cycle in 3 Parts, for Cello and Orchestra, 1992, 1995, 1996; Franz and Morton for piano trio, 1993-94; Helmholtz-Funk for 8 computer-controlled sine generators and 2 ringmodulated pianos with natural tuning, 1997. Honours include: Schneider-Schott Prize for Young Composers, 1986; Ploner-Hindemith Preis, 1988. Address: Eisenbahnstrasse 12, D-10997 Berlin, Germany.

SCHWEIZER Alfred, b. 4 Nov 1941, Sevelen, Switzerland. Composer. Education: University of Berne; Berne Conservatory; Music Academy of Basle; Swiss Centre for Computer Music. Career: Professor, Winterthur Conservatory, 1970-71; Professor, 1971-; Acting Director, 1979-80, Biel Conservtory; Manager, Classic 2000, Concerts and CD's, 1982-. Compositions include: 3 Pieces for Orchestra; Canon for open orchestra; Concertino Swiss Folk Instruments and Small Orchestra; Music for Piano No 1, 2 and 3; Music for Violin and Harpsichord; Music for Flute and Keyboard; Cosmos Nos 1, 2 and 3 for instruments and computer; Music for Guitars; Dorian Song, 1996; Music for Christian, brass and keyboards, 1997. Recordings: Orchestral Pieces Nos. 1, 2, 3; Woodwind Quintet; Piano Concerto; Mantra Avec Violin Fou; Quartet-ATON. Honours: 2nd Prize International Composers Competition, Sanremo; Recognition Prize Pro Arte Foundation Berne; Recognition Prize, Canton Berne. Memberships: Schweizerischer Tonkunstlerverein; Schweizerischer Musikpaedagogisicher Verband. Address: PO Box 17, CH-2513 Twann, Switzerland.

SCHWEIZER Daniel, b. 6 Nov 1953, Herisau, Switzerland. Conductor. m. Michiko Tsuda, 4 Oct 1980, 2 sons. Education: Zurich Konservatorium 1972-76; Cello, Musikhochschule Essen, 1976-77; Conducting, Musikhochschule Freiburg, 1979-81. Debut: With Zurich Symphony Orchestra, 23 Nov 1981; Concerts Founder, Zurich Symphony Orchestra, 1981; Concerts at festivals in Spain and Estoril, Portugal; Guest conductor, Germany, Czechoslovakia, Italy, France, Austria, Singapore, Korea, USA, Mexiko, Estonia. Recordings: Jecklin: Paul Muller, orchestral works; Motette: Marcel Dupré, Symphony G minor op 25, Dupré Concerto op 31 Demessieux op 9 Jongen Symphonie Concertante op 81, Classic 2000; Alfred Schweizer, orchestral works. Contributions to: Neue Zürcher Zeitung. Membership: Schweizerischer Tonkünstlerverein. Hobbies: Painting; Hiking. Address: Buecheneggstrasse 31, CH-8906, Bonstetten, Switzerland.

SCHWEIZER Verena, b. 9 May 1944, Solothurn, Switzerland. Singer (Soprano). Education: Studied at the Zurich Conservatory, in Frankfurt, Basle with Elsa Cavelti, in Aachen and Freiburg and in Mannheim with Anna Reynolds. Career: Sang at Aargau 1971-72, Mainz 1973-75, Dortmund 1975-83; Sang at Freiburg from 1985 and guested at Stuttgart (1986 as Jenufa, 1990 as Marenka in The Bartered Bride); Ludwigsburg 1984-89, as Fiodriligi and Mozart's Countess; Further appearances in Leeds (with the Dortmund Opera), Geneva, Cologne, Dusseldorf and Wiesbaden; Other roles include Susanna, Zerlina, Marcellina, Adina, Gilda, Micaela, Nannetta, Mimi, Sophie in Der Rosenkavalier, Anne Trulove and Desdemona; Concert engagements in Paris, Rome, Buenos Aires and Copenhagen; St Gallen 1983, in the premiere of P Huber's Te Deum. Recordings include: Christmas Oratorio by Saint-Saëns; Magnificat and other sacred music by Vivaldi (Erato); Così fan tutte (Harmonia Mundi); Hindemith's Cardillac (Wergo). Address: c/o Staatstheater Stuttgart, Oberer Schlossgarten 6, D-7000 Stuttgart, Germany.

SCHWENNIGER Aurelia, b. 1938, Austria. Mezzo-Soprano. Career: Sang at the Landestheater Linz, 1962-64, Augsburg, 1964-66 and at the Nationaltheater Mannheim, 1968-78; Roles have included Zenobia in Handel's Radamisto, Rosina, Fenena in Nabucco, Eboli, Amneris, Magdalene, the Composer in Ariadne auf Naxos, Silla in Palestrina, Janácek's Fox and Tchaikovsky's Maid of Orleans; Guest appearances at the Vienna Staatsoper, Rome and Cologne Operas and the Teatro San Carlos at Lisbon. Address: Mannheim National Theater, Nationaltheater Am Goetheplatz, 6800 Mannheim, Germany.

SCHWERTSIK Kurt, b. 25 June 1935, Vienna, Austria. Composer; Orchestra Musician (French-Horn). m. Christa, 2 children. Education: Academy of Music, Vienna, Reifeprufung. Career: Member, Nieder Osterreichesches Tonkunstler Orchester, 1955-59, 1962-68; Member, Wiener Symphoniker, 1968-; Founder with Friedrich Cerha, The Ensemble for Modern Music Die Reihe, 1959; Professor of Compositions at the Wiener Hochschule für Musik and Drammatische Kunst, 1989. Compositions include: Sonatine für Horn and Klavier, 1952-72; Trio for Violin, Horn and Piano , 1960; 5 Nocturnes for Piano,

1964; Blattause Schnecken Ohrenkreiser; Draculas Haus & Hofmusik, eine trassylvanische symphonie für Streicher, 1968; Musik vom Mutterland MU, fur 11 instruments, 1971; Entwurf for String Quartet, 1974; Der Lange Weg zur grossen Mauer, 1975; Macbeth for piano duo and percussion, 1988; Concerto for tom-tom and orchestra 1988; Double bass Concerto 1989. Recordings: Kurt Schwertsik's Musik Der Genewart Kurt Schwertsik Classic Amadeo. Membership: Internationale Gesellschaft fur Neue Musik. Hobbies: English and American Science Fiction Books; Arts and Architecture. Current Management: Boosey and Hawkes, London. Address: Hockegasse 9, A-1180 Vienna, Austria.

SCHWETS Stanislav, b. 28 Jan 1974, Ekaterinburg, Russia. Opera Singer - Bass. Education: Studied under Professors P Gluboky and V Chachava, Moscow State Conservatory, 1992-97. Debut: Banco in Verdi's Macbeth, Dublin Opera, Mar 1996. Career: Filmed in Masterclass by Galina Vishnevskaya, Moscow, 1993; Frequent broadcasts on Russian National TV; Sang Rogozhin and David in world premieres of N F B and Young David by V Kobekin, at Sacro Art Festival, Loccum, Germany, 1995, 1997; Sang in Te Deum by Handel and in Mass in B flat by Mozart, conducted by W Gönnenwein at Lüdwigsburger Festival, 1996; Sang Daland in Der fliegende Holländer by Wagner in Metz Opera, France, Oct 1997, and with Maryinsky Theatre, conducted by Valery Gergiev in Toulouse and Madrid, Nov 1997; 1988 engagements include Basilio in Rossini's Il Barbiere di Siviglia and Leporello in Mozart's Don Giovanni in Frankfurt Opera, Germany, Daland with Maryinsky Theatre conducted by V Gergiev in Lisbon, and Pimen in Boris Godunov by Musorgsky in Dublin. Has sung in concerts with V Chachava in Moscow, St Petersburg and other Russian cities; Performed in Ekaterinburg in recital by Elena Obraztsova and Vazha Chachava. Honours: Grand Prix and Special Prize, Belvedere International Singers Competition, Vienna, 1994; Prizewinner, Rimsky-Korsakov International Singers Competition, St Petersburg, 1996. Address: c/o Lies Askonas Ltd, 6 Henrietta Street, London WC2E 8LA, England.

SCHWETZ Stanislav, b. 1965, Ekaterinburg, Russia. Singer (Bass). Education: Studied at the Mussorgsky Ural State Conservatoire and the Moscow Conservatoire. Career: Has sung Sobakin in Rimsky's The Tsar's Bride at Moscow; Other roles include Verdi's Fiesco and Banquo, the Landgrave (Tannhäuser), Mozart's Leporello and Sarastro, Pimen, Daland and Basilio. Honours include: Prize winner at the 1994 Belvedere and Barcelona Vinas Competitions. Address: c/o Lies Askonas Ltd, 6 Henrietta Street, London WC2E 8LA, England.

SCHWORER-KOHL Gretel, b. 6 Sept 1951, Karlsruhe, Germany. Ethnomusicologist. m. Thomas Kohl, 1 Apr 1980, 1 son, 1 daughter. Education: Piano Studies, Musikhochschule Freiburg; Ethnomusicology, University of Hamburg and Cologne; Doctorate, 1980. Appointments: Field Research, Lecturer, University of Chiang Mai, Thailand, 1974-76; Lecturer, Ethnomusicology, University of Mainz, Frankfurt, 1993-95, University of Heidelberg, 1984-. Recordings: La Hu Nyi of Thailand; Anthology of Southeast Asian Music. Publication: Die Mundorgel Bei Den Lahu in Nord Thailand, 2 volumes, 1982. Contributions to: Grosse Brockhaus Encyclopedia, 19th Edition, 1986-94; Die Musk in Geschichte und Gegenwart. Memberships: International Council for Traditional Music; Gesellschaft fur Musikforschung; International Musicology Society; Siam Society. Address: AM Lornenberg 7, 55263 Wackernheim, Mainz, Germany.

SCIAMA Pierre, b. 1960, England. Singer (Countertenor). Education: Studied, Guildhall School with David Pollard and David Roblou, and at the GSM Early Music Course. Career: Sang Reason in Cavalieri's La Rappresentazione di Anima e di Corpo, Morley College, 1987; Purcell's Fairy Queen at the GSM conducted by William Christie; Sang in Rameau's Pygmalion at the Elizabeth Hall and in Gluck's Alceste at Covent Garden and in Monte Carlo; Acis and Galatea with Midsummer Opera in Tours and St John's Smith Square, London, 1989; Appeared in Dido and Aeneas with the Early English Opera Society as Apollo in Grabu's Albion and Albanus; Armindo in Handel's Partenope with Midsummer Opera. Address: c/o Normann McCann International Artists Ltd, The Coach House, 56 Lawrie Park Gardens, London SE26 6XJ, England.

SCIARRINO Salvatore, b. 4 Apr 1947, Palermo, Italy. Composer. Education: Studied with Tulio Belfiore, 1964 and attended electronic music sessions at the Accademia di Santa Cecilia in Rome, 1969. Career: Artistic Director of Teatro Comunale in Bologna; Teacher in Milan, Florence and Citta del Castello; Milan Conservatory from 1974. Creative Works include: Instrumental pieces; Berceuse for orchestra 1967; Quartetto 1967; Da un divertimento 1970; Sonata du camera 1971; Arabesque for 2 organs 1971; Rondo for flute and orchestra 1972; Romanza for viola d'amore and orchestra 1973; Variazioni for cello and orchestra 1974; 2 Piano Trios, 1974, 1986; 2 Quintetes, 1976, 1977; Clair de Lune for piano and orchestra 1976; Kindertotenlied for soptano.. tenor and chamber orchestra 1978; Flos Forum for chorus and orchestra 1981; Nox apud Orpheum for 2 organs and instruments 1982; String Trio 1983; 3 Piano Sonatas 1976, 1983, 1986; Violin Conceto, Allegoria nella notte 1985; Morte di Borromini for narrator and orchestra 1989; Florence, 1978; Lohengrin, 'azione invisible', Milan 1983; Perseo e Andromeda, Stuttgart 1991. Address: c/o Staatstheater Stuttgart, Oberer Schlossgarten 6, 7000 Stuttgart, Germany.

SCIMONE Claudio, b. 23 Dec 1934, Padua, Italy. Conductor;Musicologist. Career: Studied with Franco Ferrara, Dmitri Mitropoulos and Carlo Zecchi. Career: Founded the chamber ensemble I Solisti Veneti 1959; performances of 18th and 19th century Italian music, Mozart, Schoenberg and modern works (Donatoni, Bussotti, Malipiero and others); Tours of USA, Europe and Japan; wrote for La gazzetta del Veneto, 1952-57; taught at Venice Conservatory, 1961-67; Chamber Music at Verona Conservatory, 1967-74; since then Director of Padua State Conservatory of Music; Permanent Conductor and Artistic Director of the chamber orchestra, Conducted Il Barbiere di Siviglia at Caracalla, 1992 and at the Verona Arena, 1996. Recordings: More than 200 LP and CD records with I Solisti Veneti and other orchestras (London Philarmonia, Royal Philharmonic, English Chamber Orchestra, Bamberger Symphoniker, others), including L'Elisir d'Amore (Ricciarelli, Carreras); Vivaldi flute concertos and Orlando Furioso; Concerti Grossi by Albinoni, Corelli and Geminiani; Marcello La Cetra; Italian flute and oboe concertos; Rossini string sonatas and Mozart's Salzburg Divertimenti; Operas by Rossini, including Zelmira, 1990. Publications: Editions of concertos by Tartini; Complete edition of Rossini; Segno, Significato, Interpretazione 1974; Numerous articles in music journals. Honours include: Elizabeth Sprague Coolidge Memorial Medal 1969; Grammy record award (Los Angeles); several Grand Prix du Disque de l'Academie Charles Cros, Academie du Disque Lyrique and others. Address: Piazzale Pontecorvo 6, 35100 Padova, Italy.

SCIUTTI Graziella, b. 17 Apr 1927, Turin, Italy. Soprano Singer; Opera Producer. Education: Accademia di Santa Cecilia, Rome. Debut: Aix-en-Provence, 1951 as Lucy in Menotti's The Telephone. Career: Returned to Aix as Mozart's Susanna and Zerlina and in the premiere of Sauguet's Les Caprices de Marianne; Glyndebourne debut in 1954 as Rosina in Il Barbiere di Siviglia; Piccola Scala, Milan in 1955 as Carolina in Il Matrimonio Segreto; Other roles in operas by Puccini, Donizetti and Paisiello; Covent Garden debut in 1956 as Oscar in Un Ballo in Maschera; Returned to London in Mozart's Despina and Susanna and as Nannetta in Falstaff; Holland Festival 1957 as Anne Trulove in The Rake's Progress; Salzburg Festival, 1957-66, in Mozart roles and in concert; US debut in San Francisco in 1961 as Susanna; Returned to Glyndebourne in 1970 for Rossini's Il Turco in Italia and in 1977 produced Poulenc's La Voix Humaine; Other opera productions in New York, Chicago, Koblenz and Covent Garden. Recordings: Roles in Don Giovanni, Così fan tutte, Guillaume Tell, Le nozze di Figaro, Fidelio, Alcina, La Scala di Seta, La Rondine, Orlando, Donizetti's Rita, Paisiello's Barbiere di Siviglia, Pelléas et Mélisande, Il Matrimonio Segreto, L'Italiana in Algeri and Falstaff. Address: c/o New York City Opera, Lincoln Center, New York, NY 10023, USA.

SCOGNA Flavio (Emilio), b. 16 Aug 1956, Savona, Italy. Composer; Conductor. m. Fiorenza Iademarco, 1993. Education: N Paganini Conservatory, Genoa; Graduated in Music, University of Bologna, 1980; Conducting with Franco Ferrara, Rome. Career: His works performed in major international venues including Italian Radio (Rome, Naples), Centre Pompidou (Paris), Vienna Konzerthaus, and broadcast, RAI, BBC, Radio France, ORF, BRT; Many commissions, Italian Radio, Vienna Konzerthaus, Pomeriggi Musicali of Milan; Conductor, musical groups, national and international orchestras such as RAI, Radio Broadcasting of Spain, Hungarian State Symphony Orchestra; Appearances on Italian Radio, Teatro Massimo, Palermo, Teatro Opera Roma, Teatro Comunale, Firenze; Teaching, several Italian conservatories such as S Pietro a Maiella, Naples, and G Rossini, Pesaro. Compositions include: Arioso per Guillermo, 1984; Serenata, ensemble, 1984, new version, 1988; Anton, 1-act opera, 1984, new version, 1988; Incanto, string trio, 1985; Sonatina, trombone, 1985; Come un'ondo di luce, oboe, clarinet, violin, viola, cello, 1985; Canto del mare, flute, violin, cello, 1985; Cadenza seconda, piano, 1986; Sinfonia concertante, orchestra, 1986-87; Frammento, after Mario Luz's poem, soprano, piano, 1987; La mar, marimba, 1987; Concertino, 10 instruments, 1987; Tre invenzioni, piano, 1988; Risonanze, string quartet, 1988; Fluxus, orchestra, 1988; Verso, 3 winds, 3 strings, 1988; Rifrazioni, soprano, orchestra, 1989; Alternanze, piano, strings, 1989; Musica reservata, strings, orchestra, 1990; Salmo XII, violas, orchestra, 1990; Relazioni, ensemble, 1991; La memoria perduta, 2-act opera, 1991-93; Diaphonia, viola, orchestra, 1992; Trame, trumpet, 1993; Aulos, oboe, 1993. Recordings: As Conductor: Planc, chamber ensemble; Serenata; Incanto; Anton; Alternanze. Address: P 1e Ionio 13, 00141 Rome, Italy.

SCORSIN Giuseppe, b. 1961, Treviso, Italy. Singer (Bass). Education: Studied at Cremona University and the Verdi Conservatory, Milan. Debut: Treviso 1990, as Bartolo in Le nozze di Figaro. Career: Appearances at Monte Carlo in Gianni Schicchi, at Rovigo in La Bohème and La Scala in Franchetti's Cristoforo Colombo; Zurich Opera from 1992, in Semiramide, Butterfly, Lohengrin, The Rape of Lucretia, Macbeth, Salome, Otello, Roméo et Juliette and Die Zauberflöte; Lucerne Opera as Philip II in Don Carlo and at Lugarno in Mendelssohn's Die Erste Walpurgisnacht; Further roles include Bellini's Oroveso, Rossini's Don Basilio and Ferrando in Il Trovatore, Pistola in Falstaff; Season 1996 in The Gambler at La Scala, as Orbazzano in Tancredi at Winterthur, and Don Basilio throughout Italy; Zurich Opera 1997-98: Sparafucile in Rigoletto; Il Prefetto in Linda di Chamounix (also at Bologna), Raimondo in Lucia di Lammermoor; Ashby in La fanciulla del West. Honours include: Winner, 1990 Toti dal Monte Competition, Treviso. Address: c/o Opernhaus Zurich, Falkenstrasse 1, CH-8008 Zurich, Switzerland.

SCOTT John (Gavin), b. 18 June 1956, Wakefield, England. Organist; Conductor. m. Carolyn Jane Lumsden, 29 July 1979, 1 son, 1 daughter. Education: St John's College, Cambridge; BA (Cantab), 1977; MusB (Cantab), 1978; MA (Cantab), 1981; Private study with Dr P G Saunders, Jonathan Bielby, Ralph Downes, Gillian Weir. Debut: Henry Wood Promenade Concert, Royal Albert Hall, London, 1977. Career: Solo organ recitals and broadcasts, UK, Europe, USA, Australia, Far East; Organist and Assistant Conductor, The Bach Choir, 1979-92; Sub-Organist and Assistant Director of Music, 1985-90, Organist and Director of Music, 1990-, St Paul's Cathedral, London. Recordings: As Accompanist to St John's College Choir, Cambridge, and Conductor of St Paul's Cathedral Choir; Solo: Reubke - Sonata on 94th Psalm; Liszt - Fantasia and Fugue: Ad nos ad Salutarem Undam; Organ Music by Marcel Dupré; Organ Spectacular; Organ Music by Maurice Duruflé; Janácek Glagolitic Mass, with London Symphony Orchestra; Organ Music by Mendelssohn, 2 vols; Organ Music by William Mathias. Honours: ARCO, Limpus Prize, 1971; FRCO, Limpus Prize, 1973; Dr F J Read Prize, 1974; John Stewart of Rannoch Scholarship in Sacred Music, University of Cambridge, 1975; 1st Prize, Manchester International Organ Festival, 1978; 1st Prize, Leipzig International J S Bach Competition, 1984; Honorary RAM, 1990. Hobbies: Reading; Travel; Ecclesiastical architecture. Current Management: Magenta Music International Ltd. Address: 5 Amen Court, London EC4M 7BU, England.

SCOTT Stuart John, b. 29 January 1949, Stretford, Manchester, England. Teacher; Composer. m. Jane Beverley Scott, 31 August 1976, 2 daughters. Education: Stretford Technical College, 1965-67; Chorley College of Education, 1967-70; Certificate, Lancaster University; Studied Composition with Sir Lennox Berkeley, Flute with Joan Simpkin, Piano with Nancy Evans. Debut: Performer, Composer, Flute and Piano, Chorley College Concert, 1970. Career: Teacher, School Music Specialist, 1970-; BBC Broadcast of Sonata for Brass, 1973; BBC Radio Talk on Skryabin; BBC TV Advisor, Documentary on Skryabin; Music Broadcasts in England, Germany, USA, Scandinavia, Japan. Compositions: Opera (5 scenes), Jonah, Son of Mitty, Three Piano Pieces, Three Preludes Op 49 Egyptian Suite (Flute Solo); Toccatina (Guitar) Shakuhachi Suite (Flute); Cheshire Verses (soprano and piano); Songs of the Night (soprano and piano); Sonata (Solo Violin) Bagatelle (Oboe, Piano); Conversations (flute, oboe and clarinet); Intermezzo (Recorder) Sonata for Brass. Recording: Piano Preludes. Publications: The Chamber Music of John Ireland 1979-1994; Hallé Flutes, 1997. Contributions to: PAN; BFS; Composer. Honours: Wind Trio Prize, Stroud Festival International Composers Competition, 1970. Memberships: Composers Guild of Great Britain; Association of North West Composers; Association of Teachers and Lecturers. Hobbies: Egyptology; Ornithology; Woodcrafts. Address: Staverley, 6 Colville Grove, Sale, Cheshire M33 4FW, England.

SCOTTO Renata, b. 24 Feb 1933, Savona, Italy. Singer (Soprano). m. Lorenzo Anselmi. Education: Studied at the Giuseppe Verdi Conservatory, Milan, with Emilio Ghiriardini. Debut: Teatro Nuovo Milan 1953, as Violetta; Sang at La Scala from 1954 as Donizetti's Amina, Lucia and Adina and as Helena in I Vespri Siciliani; London debut Stoll Theatre 1957, as Adina, Mimi, Violetta and Donna Elvira; Edinburgh Festival 1957, as Amina in La Sonnambul; US debut Chicago 1960, Miami; Covent Garden debut 1962, as Butterfly; Metropolitan Opera from 1965, as Lucia, Verdi's Gilda, Helena, Luisa Miller, Desdemona, Elisabeth de Valois and Lady Macbeth, Norma and Adriana Lecouvreur and in Puccini's Trittico; Directed Butterfly at the Metropolitan 1986 and sang there for the last time in 1987; Returned to Edinburgh 1972, with the Palermo company in Bellini's La Straniera; Guest appearances as Anna Bolena in Dallas and in Verdi's Requiem at the Verona arena. Publication: More than a Diva, autobiography, 1984. Recordings: Roles in: Pagliacci, Cavalleria, Rusticana, Lucia di Lammermoor, La Traviata, La Bohème, Edgar, Adriana Lecouvreur, Andrea Chénier, Robert le Diable, La Straniera, I Lombardi, I Capuleti e i Montecchi, La Sonnambula; Companies include Cetra, Columbia, Ricordi and HMV 21. Address: c/o Opera Academy, Via Gentile, 25-17012 Albissola Marina, Sasvona, Italy.

SCOVOTTI Jeannette, b. 5 Dec 1933, New York City, USA. Singer (Soprano). Education: Studied at the Juilliard School, New York. Debut: Metropolitan Opera 1962, as Adele in Die Fledermaus. Career: Teatro Colon Buenos Aires 1963-65; Munich Staatsoper 1965; Sang at the Hamburg Staatsoper 1966-77, as Mozart's Zerlina and Despina, Aminta in Die schweigsame Frau, Donizetti's Lucia and Norina, and in the premiere of Krenek's Sardakai; Many engagements at opera houses elsewhere in Europe; Other roles include Olympia, Gilda, The Queen of Night, Zerlina, Aminta in Die schweigsame Frau, Zerbinetta, Constanze and Carolina in Il Matrimonio Segreto; Boston Opera 1977, in the US premiere of Ruslan and Ludmila by Glinka; Sang Costanza in a Concert performance of Vivaldi's Griselda, London, 1978. Recordings: Les Contes d'Hoffmann (Electrola); Castor et Pollux by Rameau (Telefunken); Eine Nacht in Venedig (Hungaroton); Les Huguenots; Rinaldo by Handel (CBS); Die drei Pintos by Weber/Mahler (RCA); Die schweigsame Frau (EMI). Address: c/o Hamburgische Staatsoper, Grosse Theaterstrasse 34, D-2000 Hamburg 36, Germany.

SCRIPPS Douglas Jerry, b. 25 Aug 1942, Michigan, USA. Professor; Conductor. m. Merilee Collins, 5 Apr 1975, 4 sons, 1 daughter. Education: Calvin College, 1960-65; University of Michigan, 1961-64; Eastman School of Music, 1961-62; Vienna Hochschule, 1965-66; University of Michigan, 1968-70. Career: Principal Trumpet, Grand Rapids Symphony Orchestra, 1960-65; Director, Instrumental Music, Grand Rapids City College, 1967-78; Music Director, Conductor, Lake St Clair Symphony Orchestra, 1970-72; Founder, Principal Conductor, Kent Philharmonia Orchestra, 1976-80; Associate Conductor, Resident Conductor, Grand Rapids Symphony Orchestra, 1976-85; Music Director, Grand Rapids Ballet, 1979-; Professor of Music, Conductor, Central Michigan University, 1981-85; Professor of Music, Department Chairman, Alma College, 1985-; Music Director, Conductor, Alma Symphony Orchestra, 1985-; Guest Conductor, Opera Grand Rapids, Traverse Symphony Orchestra, Interlochen Arts Center, Bay View Music Festival, Grand Rapids Summer Festival, Blue Lake Fine Arts Camp; Adjudicator in Michigan and Midwest USA. Memberships: American Symphony Orchestra League; National Association of Schools of Music; Michigan Orchestra Association; College Music Society; American Institute for Verdi Studies. Hobbies: Sailing; Reading. Address: Alma College, 614 West Superior Street, Alma, MI 48801, USA.

SCUDERI Vincenzo, b. 1961, NY, USA. Singer (Tenor). Education: Studied in New York and with Franco Corelli. Career: Long Island Opera, Pinkerton, Turiddu, Rodolfo; Appearances at Plovdiv and Zurich as Ishmaele in Nabucco and as Radames, 1987-89; Sang the Duke of Mantua on tour throughout France, 1989; Sang arias from Chenier and Fanciulla del West in Tribute Concert to Franco Corelli, Purchase, New York, 1991; Radames at the Baths of Caracalla, 1991. Address: Opera de Marseille, 2 Rue Molière, F-1321 Marseille Cedex 01, France.

SCULTHORPE Peter (Joshua), b. 29 Apr 1929, Launceston, Tasmania. Composer. Education: Melbourne University Conservatory of Music; Wadham College Oxford with Egon Wellesz and Edmund Rubbra. Career: Teacher at Syndey University from 1963; Composer in Residence Yale University, 1966; Visiting Professor, Sussex University, 1972-73. Compositions: Stage: Sun Music, ballet 1968; Rites of Passage, opera 1973; Quiros, television opera, 1982; Tatea, music theatre piece 1988; Orchestral: Irkanda IV for violin and strings, 1961; Small Town 1963-76; Sun Music I-IV 1965-67; Music for Japan, 1970; Rain 1970; Lament for strings 1976; Port Essington for string trio and strings 1977; Mangrove 1979; Guitar Concerto 1980; Piano Concerto, 1983; Little Suite for Strings, 1983; Sonata for Strings, 1983; Earth Cry, 1986; Second Sonata for Strings, 1988; At the Grave of Isaac Nathan, 1988; Instrumental: The Loneliness of Bunjil for string trio 1954; 12 String Quartets 1947-88; Sonata for viola and percussion, 1960; Tabuh Tabuhan for wind quintet and percussion 1968; How the Stars were Made for percussion ensemble, 1971; Landscape for piano quartet 1980; Songs of Sea and Sky for clarinet and piano, 1987; Vocal: Sun Music for Voices and Percussion, 1966; Love 200 for rock band 1970; Ketjak for six male voices with tape echo, 1972; The Songs of Tailitnama for high voice, 6 cellos and percussion, 1974; Child of Australia for chorus, soprano, narrator and orchestra, 1987; Piano Music; Music for the film Burke and Wills, 1985; Postcard from Nourlangie to Clapham Common, 1993; From Saibai, 1993; Memento Mori for orchestra, 1993; From Ubirr, for string quartet and didjeridoo, 1994. Honours include: Order of the British Empire, 1977; Doctor of Letters, University of Tasmania, 1980, 1985 APRA Award for his Piano Concerto. Address: c/o Faber Music Ltd, 3 Queen Square, London WC1N 3AU, England.

SEAMAN Christopher, b. 7 Mar 1942, Faversham, Kent, England. Conductor. Education: Canterbury Cathedral Choir School, 1950-55; The King's Schol Canterbury, 1955-60; ARCO, ARCM, King's College, Cambridge, 1960; MA 1963. Career: Principal Timpanist, London Philharmonic Orchestra, 1964-68; Assistant Conductor, BBC Scottish Symphony Orchestra, 1968-70; Principal Conductor, BBC Scottish Symphony Orchestra, 1971-77; Principal Conductor, Northern Sinfonia, 1973-79; Chief Guest Conductor, Utrecht Symphony Orchestra, 1979-83; Conductor-in-Residence, Baltimore Symphony Orchestra since 1987; Opened the 1995 Bergen Festival with Elgar's King of Olaf; Further concerts with the Rotterdam and Brno Philharmonics, detroit and Houston Symphony Orchestras and the CBSO. Honour: FGSM 1972. Hobbies: People; Reading; Walking; Theology. Address: Harrison/Parrott Ltd, 12 Penzance Place, London W11 4PA, England.

SEAMAN Gerald Roberts, b. 2 Feb 1934, Leamington Spa, England. Musicologist. m. Katherine Helena Fairchild, 27 Apr 1995, 1 daughter. Education: Birmingham School of Music, 1951; Oxford University, 1954-62; Leningrad Conservatory, 1960-61. Appointments: Lecturer, Music, Nottingham Teachers Training College, 1962-64; Temporary Lecturer, University of Western Australia, 1964-65; Associate Professor, University of Auckland, New Zealand, 1965-. Publications: History of Russian Music, Volume I, 1967; Rimsky-Korsakov: Garland, 1988. Honour: Senior Associate Member, St Antony's College, Oxford, 1972-. Memberships: AMS; IMS; IAML; RMA. Hobbies: Languages; Reading; Travel. Address: St Antony's College, Oxford OX2 6JF, England.

SEARS Nicholas, b. 1965, England. Singer (Tenor) Education: Studied at Trinity College, Cambridge and the Guildhall School, London. Career: As baritone, concert engagements with regular appearances at the Aldeburgh Festival and under such conductors as Simon Rattle, David Atherton and Philippe Herreweghe; With Welsh National Opera has sung Marullo in Rigoletto, Mozart's Count and Gorjanchikov in From the House of the Dead; Sang Choregos in Birtwistle's Punch and Judy at Aldeburgh, Berlin, Vienna, Malatesta for Opera 80 and Gluck's Oreste for Welsh National Opera; Appearances as Billy Budd for Opera North and in the Premiere of Jonathon Harvey's Inquest of Love for English National Opera; Made debut as tenor as the Chevalier in Poulenc's Dialogues des Carmelites at Aldeburgh and in London, 1994; Returned to Aldeburgh for Vaughan Williams's Hodie conducted by Steuart Bedford and Handel's Messiah; Sang the role of Telemachus in the Buxton Festival production of Monteverdi's Il ritorno d'Ulisse, Orfeo for the English Bach Festival in Lugano and the role of Corin in Arne's Alfred with Nicholas Kraemer and the Orchestra of the Age of Enlightenment for the BBC; Further engagements include Achilles (King Priam) for Der Vlaamse Oper in Antwerp, Dido and Aeneas at Covent Garden and the English Bach Festical, and Telemachus for Opera North, sang the High Priest in Idomeneo at Garsington, 1996, (British premiere of Strauss's Die Ägyptische Helena there, 1997). Recordings include: Captain Lillywhite in The Rising of the Moon with the Scottish Chamber Orchestra conducted by Steuart Bedford; Music by Percy Grainger with the Academy of St Martin in the Fields Chamber Ensemble; Jolivet's Suite Liturgique with the Fibonacci Sequence. Address: c/o Harold Holt Ltd, 31 Sinclair Road, London W14 0NS, England.

SEBASTIAN Bruno, b. 1947, Udine, Italy. Tenor. Education: Studied with Mario del Monaco. Debut: Venice in 1969 in Donizetti's Belisario. Career: Sang widely in Italy from 1970 notably as Arnold in Guillaume Tell at Florence, Wagner in Boito's Mefistofele at Caracalla and Radames at Verona; Sang Cavaradossi at Brussels in 1976, Otello at Basle, Manrico at Boston and the Metropolitan Opera, and Edgardo at Barcelona in 1987; Other roles include the Duke of Mantua, Macduff and Calaf (Helsinki, 1991). Address: Deutsche Oper Berlin, Bismarckstrasse 35, 1 Berlin 10, Germany.

SEBESTA Ronald, b. 22 July 1967, Senica, Slovakia. Musician (Clarinettist). Education: Diploma, Bratislava Conservatory, 1987; Studies, 1988-93, Diploma, 1993, Postgraduate study, Interpretation of Contemporary Music, 1995-, Academy of Music, Bratislava; 8 months study, Boulogne Conservatory, France, 1991-92. Career: Co-founder, VENI ensemble for contemporary music, with concerts in Bratislava (Evenings of New Music Festival), Prague, Berlin, Vienna, Perugia, Bucharest; Projects (workshops and concerts) with Younghi Pagh Paan, Siegfried Palm, Hans Deinzer, Louis Andriessen, James Tenney, Hugh Davies; Solo performance of Giacinto Scelsi's Kya, 1990; VENI ensemble recording for Die Hessische Rundfunk in Frankfurt, 1993; 1st Clarinettist, Slovak Radio Symphony Orchestra, Bratislava; Solo performance at Wien Modern Festival, 1994; Solo performance of Mozart and Brahms Clarinet Quintets, 1995; 1st Clarinet, Cappela Istropolitana, chamber orchestra, Bratislava, 1995-; Co-founder, Opera Aperta ensemble, for classical and contemporary chamber music, 1997-; Solo performances of Mozart Clarinet Concerto, 1997-; co-founder, Aerophone Group, marketing high quality woodwind instruments in Central Europe, 1997-. Recordings: 2 CDs of VENI ensemble, 1990, 1992; Third CD, VENI ensemble, with music by Daniel Matej, 1995. Publications: Clarinet quintet as a formation of chamber music and its place in the chamber music of classical-romantic tradition, diploma thesis, 1993. Membership: International Society for Contemporary Music, Slovak Section. Hobbies: History of European art; Chess; Travel. Address: Palarikova ul 303, 90501 Senica n Myjavou, Slovakia.

SEBESTYEN Janos, b. 2 Mar 1931, Budapest, Hungary. Organist; Harpsichordist. Education: Diploma, Ferenc Liszt Academy, Budapest. Career: Recitals, radio and TV in Hungary; Tours with organ and harpsichord recitals throughout Europe, USA, Japan and Philippines; Radio recordings; Founder and Leading Professor of Harpsichord Faculty, Academy of Music, Budapest, 1970-; Musical feature programme series, Radio Budapest; President of Jury, International Liszt Organ Competition, Budapest, 1983, 1988 and 1993. Recordings: Over 80 records, including Complete Organ Works of Liszt. Publications: Musical Conversations with Miklós Rózsa, 1979; ...those Radio years 1925-1995, 1995. Honours: Erkel Prize, 1967; Liszt Prize, 1974; Merited Artists, 1982; Cavaliere of the Italian Republic, 1984; Commander of the Order Infante Dom Henrique, Portugal, 1996. Current Management: Musica Sacra, Budapest. Address: Filler u 48, 1022 Budapest, Hungary.

SECUNDE Nadine, b. 21 Dec 1953, Independence, Ohio, USA. Singer (Soprano). Education: Studied at Oberlin Conservatory and at Indiana University School of Music with Margaret Harshaw; Further study in Germany on a Fulbright Scholarship. Career: Engaged first at the Hessisches Staatstheater Wiesbaden; Currently a member of the Cologne Opera, where her roles have been Katya Kabanova, Elsa, Agathe, Elisabeth, Chrysothemis and Ariadne; Vienna Staatsoper debut as Sieglinde, Hamburg Staatsoper as Katya; Bayreuth Festival debut 1987, as Elsa in a Werner Herzog production of Lohengrin: returned 1988, as Sieglinde in the Harry Kupfer production of Der Ring des Nibelungen; Covent Garden and Chicago 1988, as Elsa and Elisabeth; returned to London 1990, as Chrysothemis; Sang Elisabeth at Munich, 1994, (also televised); Concert engagements include the Choral Symphony with the Los Angeles Philharmonic, conducted by Previn, and with the Orchestre de Paris under Barenboim; Penderecki's Dies Irae with the Warsaw Philharmonic; Sang Chrysothemis at Covent Garden (1997) and in the 1997 Munich premiere of Henze's Venus and Adonis. Address: c/o Ingpen & Williams Ltd, 26 Wadham Road, London SW15 2LR, England.

SEEFEHLNER Egon (Hugo), b. 3 June 1912, Vienna, Austria. Opera Director. Education: Theresianum; University of Vienna; Konsularakademie. Career: Co-founder, General Secretary, Austrian Cultural Association, 1945; Chief Editor, Der Turm (cultural) magazine, 1945; General Secretary, Wiener Konserthausgesellschaft, 1946-61; Deputy Director, Vienna State Opera, 1954-61; Deputy General Manager, Deutsche Oper, W Berlin, 1961-72; Director General, 1972-76; Director, State Opera, Vienna, 1976-82, 1984-86. Honours: Decorated Commander's Cross, Papal Order of Silvester; Officer, Ordre des Arts et Lettres; Goldenes Ehrenzeichen fur Verdianste umidas Land Wien; Osterreichische Ehrenkreuz fur Wissenschaft und Kunst, 1st class; Clemens Krauss Silver Medal; Gold Cross of Republic of Austria. Memberships: Roman Catholic Church. Address: c/o Staatsoper, Opernring 2, Vienna, Austria.

SEEGER Horst, b. 6 Nov 1926, Erkner, Germany. Musicologist. Critic; Director of Opera. Education: Studied musicologist at the Humboldt University and the Berlin Musikhochschule with Ernest H Meyer, 1950-55. Career: Teacher 1946-50; Music critic from 1954; Established Institute of Music Education at Greifswald University 1958-59; Editor-in-Chief Musik und Gesellschaft 1959-60; Chief Dramaturg of the Berlin Komische Oper 1960-73; Intednant of the Dresden Staatsoper 1973-84: responsible for the first East European production of Schoenberg's Moses und Aron. Publications: Wolfgang Amadeus Mozart 1956; Joseph Hadyn 1961; Musiklexikon 1966; Opern-Lexikon 1978-86; Libretto for Siegfried Matthus's Opera Spanische Tugenden 1964; Translations of opera libretti include works by Verdi, Weber and Tchaikovsky. Address: Spreeufer 1, Berlin 0-10178, Germany.

SEERS Mary, b. 1958, England. Singer (Soprano). Education: Studied at Girton College, Cambridge (choral exhibitioner) and in Rome and London. Career: Appearances with the Landini Consort, the Consort of Musique, The Scholars and the Hilliard Ensemble; Festival engagements at Aix-en-Provence, Schleswig-Holstein and Greenwich; Tour of Britain and Italy 1988 with Part's St John Passion; Concerts in Sydney and Tokyo 1989 with John Eliot Gardiner and the Monteverdi Choir; Concerts: Bach B minor Mass, Wroclaw (Poland) with City of London Sinfonia; Other repertoire includes Mozart's C minor Mass, the Monteverdi Vespers (Bruges Festival), Messiah (St Martin in the Fields) and music by Finzi and Purcell); Further engagements at the Almeida, Cheltenham and Orkney Festivals and concerts with the Scottish Chamber Orchestra and the East of England Orchestra; US concerts in Chicago and New York, Pärt's St John

Passion; Opera: with Music Theatre Wales, role of Madeleine in Philip Glass, The Fall of The House of Usher; Festivals: Warsaw Contemporary Music Festival (Pärt Passio), 1992; Television: Took part in BBC 2 documentary with English Chamber Orchestra and Croydon Singers (Hyperion); Monteverdi Vespers with The Sixtenn (Hyperion). Address: Magenta Music International, 4 Highgate High Street, London N6 5JL, England.

SEGAL Uriel, b. 7 Mar 1944, Jerusalem, Israel. Conductor. m. Illana Finkelstein, 1 son, 3 daughters. Education: Studiued violin from age 7; Rubin Academy of Music, Israel; Conducting with Mendi Rodan at the Guildhall School of Music, London. Debut: With Seajillands Symphony Orchestra, Copenhagen, 1969. Career: Assistant Conductor, working with George Szell and Leonard Bernstein, New York, Philharmonic Orchestra, 1969-70; Chief Conductor, Philharmonica Hungarica, 1981-85; Principal Conductor, Bournemouth Symphony, 1980-83; Guest appearances with the Hamburg and Israel Philharmonics, Chicago Symphony, Spanish National Orchestra, London Symphony and Philharmonic, Philharmonia, French Radio Philharmonic, Montreal and New Zealand Symphony. Stuttgart Radio Symphony, RAI Rome, Hallé Orchestra, Scottish National; Chief Conductor of the Israel Chamber Orchestra from 1982; Currently Music Director of the Chautauqua Festival (New York State) and Chief Conductor of the Osaka Century Orchestra, Japan; Opera experience includes Der fliegende Holländer at Santa Fe, 1973 and Il re Pastore, Opéra de Nice; Madama Butterfly at Tel Aviv, season, 1995-96. Recordings include: Stravinsky's Firebird Suite and Symphony in C, with the Suisse Romande Orchestra; Mozart Piano Concertos with Radu Lupu and the English Chamber Orchestra; Schumann's Piano Concerto with Ashkenazy and the London Symphony; Beethoven Piano Concertos with Rudolf Firkusny and the Philharmonia. Honours: 1st Prize, Mitropoulos Conducting Competition, New York, 1969. Hobby: Reading. Current Management: Terry Harrison Artists Management. Address: c/o The Orchard, Market Street, Charlbury, Oxon OX7 3PJ, England.

SEGERSTAM Leif, b. 2 Mar 1944, Vasa, Finland. Conductor; Composer. Education: Violin, Piano, Conducting, Composition, Sibelius Academy, Helsinki until 1963; Conducting diploma, Juilliard School of Music, New York, USA, 1964; Postgraduate Diploma, 1965. Debut: Violin soloist Helsinki, 1963. Career: Conductor, Royal Opera Stockholm, 1968-72 and Musical Director, 1971-72; 1st Conductor, Deutsche Oper Berlin, 1972-73; General Manager Finnish National Opera, 1973-74; Chief Conductor ORF (Austrian Radio) Vienna 1975-82; Musical Director, Finnish Radio Symphony Orchestra, Helsinki, 1977-87: Principal Guest Conductor from 1987; General Music Director, Staatsphilharmonie Rhenland-Pfalz 1983-89; Honorary Conductor, 1989; Conductor of the Danish Radio Symphony Orchestra from 1988; Led Tannhäuser at the 1997 Savonlinna Festival and began a new Ring cycle at Stockholm with Das Rheingold. Compositions include: Divertimento for strings 1963; 6 Cello Concertos; 3 Piano Concertos; 18 Symphonies 1977-83; 8 Violin Concertos; 6 Double Concertos; Many works for orchestra under title Composed orchestral works called Thought, the most famous being, Monumental Thoughts, Martti Tavela in memorium; Orchestral Diary Sheets, 5 Songs of Experience after Blake and Auden for soprano and orchestra 1971; 27 String Quartets; 2 Piano Trios; 4 String Trios; Episodes for various instrumental combinations. Recordings: Works by Mahler, Sibelius, Brahms, Scriabin, Petterson, Schnittke, Rott, Ruders, Koechlin, Schmitt, Roussel, Caplet, Roger-Ducasse and own compositions. Honours: Second Prize with Symphony IV, Sibelius, 1991; Record of the Year, Sibelius III symphony (Chandos), 1992. Memberships: Royal Academy of Music, Sweden. Address: c/o Danish Radio Symphony Orchestra, Rosenornsallé, 22, DK-1999 Frederiksberg, Copenhagen, Denmark.

SEIFERT Gerd-Heinrich, b. 17 Oct 1931, Hamburg, Germany. Horn player. m. 29 June 1957, 3 sons, 1 daughter. Education: Music High School, Hamburg, 1944-49; Studied horn with Albert Doscher. Debut: Soloist, Horn Concerto (Strauss), 1948. Career: Substitute, Hamburg Philharmonic Orchestra, 1947-49; Solo Horn, Düsseldorfer Symphoniker, 1949-64; Solo Horn, Bayreuth Festival, 1961; Solo Horn, Berlin Philharmonic Orchestra, 1964-; Performed with Düsseldorfer Waldhorn Quartett, also 13 Bläser Philharmonic Orchestra and Philharmonic Octet, Berlin; Teacher of Horn, Music High School, Berlin, 1970-. Recordings: With Berlin Philharmonic Orchestra/Octet (Hindemith); Octet, Nonet (Spohr); Serenade for 13 Wind instruments by Mozart, and other Chamber music; Concert Piece for 4 horns (Schumann). Contributions to: Brass Bulletin. Honours: 1st Prize, ARD Competition, Munich, 1956; 125 Siegfried Calls at Bayreuth Festival since 1961; Grand Prix du Disque. Hobby: Photography. Address: Xantenerstrasse 1, 1000 Berlin 15, Germany.

SEIFERT Ingrid, b. 1952, Austria. Violinist. Education: Studied violin in Salzburg and Vienna. Career: Played with the Concentus Musicus, Vienna and studied further in Holland; With Charles Medlam co-founded London Baroque, 1978; Teaches at summer courses, notably the Innsbruck Summer Academy for Baroque Music; With London Baroque led the first performance of Scarlatti's Una Villa di Tuscolo and a revival of Gli Equivoci Sembiante, for the BBC; Season 1990-91 included: Dido and Aeneas at Paris Opéra; Music by Blow and Lully, Opéra Comique; Aci, Galatea e Polifemo in Spain, Holland and England; Cantatas by Handel and Rameau in Austria, Sweden and Germany, with Emma Kirkby; Other recent repertoire includes: Charpentier Messe de Minuit; 4 Violin music by Telemann, Vivaldi and Wassenaar; Bach Brandenburg Concertos; Monteverdi Tancredi and Clorinda; Salzburg Festival debut, 1991, with music by Mozart; Further festival engagements at Bath, Beaune, Versailles, Ansbach, Innsbruck and Utrecht. Recordings: Marais La Gamme; Theile Matthew Passion; Bach Trio Sonatas; Charpentier Theatre Music; Handel Aci, Galatea e Polifemo; Blow Venus and Adonis; Purcell Chamber Music, (Harmonia Mundi); Purcell Fantasias; Bach Violin Sonatas; Monteverdi Orfeo; Handel German Arias; A Vauxhall Gardens Entertainment; English Music of the 18th Century; François Couperin Chamber Music; Complete Trios of Handel, Purcell; Chamber Music by Lawes. Address: Brick Kiln Cottage, Hollington, Near Newbury, Berkshire, RG20 9XX, England.

SEIFFERT Peter, b. 4 Jan 1954, Dusseldorf, Germany. Singer (Tenor). m. Lucia Popp, 1986, Deceased 1993. Education: Studied at the Robert Schumann Musikhochschule Dusseldorf. Career: Sang first with the Deutsche Oper am Rhein Dusseldorf in Der Wildschütz and Fra Diavalo; Member of the Deutsche Oper Berlin from 1982, notably as Lensky, Jenik in The Bartered Bride, Huon (Oberon) and Faust; Bayerische Staatsoper Munich 1983, as Fenton in Die Lustigen Weiber von Windsor: has returned in Der Barber von Bagdad by Cornelius and as Narraboth and Lohengrin; Vienna Staatsoper and La Scala Milan debuts 1984; Covent Garden debut 1988, as Parsifal in a new production of Wagner's opera conducted by Bernard Haitink; Season 1988/89 sang Faust at the Deutsche Oper Berlin and Lohengrin in Munich (repeated 1990); Sang at Salzburg 1992, as Narraboth; Concert engagements include Mozart's Requiem with Giulini in London, and the Choral Symphony with Muti in Philadelphia; Sang Walther u Stolzing in Die Meistersinger at the 1996 Bayreuth Festival. Recordings: Elijah; Zar und Zimmerman; Matteo in Arabella, conducted by Jeffrey Tate; Die Fledermaus, conducted by Domingo; Gianni Schicchi (Patanè); Erik in Der fliegende Holländer, conducted by Pinchas Steinberg; The Choral Symphony (Muti) and Mozart's Mass in C Minor with Levine; Mendelssohn's Lobgesang and Beethoven's Symphony No 9 with Sawallisch; Solo Records of Operetta; Solo Record of Opera; Freischitz; Fidelio; Liszt, Faust Symphony, conducted by Simon Rattle. Honour: Kammersänger of the Bavarian State Opera.

SEIFRIED Reinhard, 25 July 1945, Freising. Conductor. m. Fenna Kügel, 31 Oct 1991, 2 daughters. Education: Hochschule für Musik in Munich, trade examination and master class for conducting; Assistant Conductor with Rudolf Kempe, Rafael Kudelok, Karl Richter, Leonard Bernstein. Debut: Conductor in Staatstheater am Gärtnerplatz, Munich, 1976. Career: Conductor, Nürnberg, 1986; Chief Conductor, Remscheider Symphoniker, 1991; Music Director, and Chief Conductor of Oldenburgisches Staatsorchester, 1993-; Guest Conductor, Europe, Japan and USA. Recordings: Mendelssohn-Bartholdy, all symphonies with Irish National Symphony Orchestra, Dublin; Smetana, My Home Country, with Staatl. Slowakische Philharmonie Kosice. Current Management: FAME Management, Claudius Hirt, Lucerne. Address: Oldenburgisches Staatstheater, Theaterwall 18, D-26122 Oldenburg, Germany.

SEIVEWRIGHT Robert (Peter), b. 11 July 1954, Skipton, England. Concert Pianist; Lecturer. Education: BA, 1975, MA, 1981, Worcester College, Oxford; FRCO Diploma, 1975; Royal Northern College of Music with Ryszard Bakst, 1976-79. Career: Tutor, University of Keele, 1979-83; Instructor in Music, University of Leicester, 1980-84; Lecturer in Music, Royal Scottish Academy of Music and Drama, 1984-; University Pianist, University of Strathclyde, 1990-93; Concerts throughout UK, Europe, Australia, including recitals, Huddersfield Contemporary Music Festival, 1983, 1984; Tivoli Concert Hall, Copenhagen, and Aarhus Festival, Denmark, 1986; Munch-Museum, Oslo, 1986; Danish recital tours, 1986, 1989, 1990, 1991, 1995; Performed complete Messiaen 20 Regards sur l'enfant Jésus, Dublin, Cork, Glasgow, 1988; Concertos with Hallé, Glasgow Philharmonic Pops, Northern Chamber and Bradford Chamber Orchestras, Paragon Ensemble, Scottish Sinfonietta, Strathclyde Sinfonia; Opening recital, Heilbronn International Piano Forum, Heilbronn, Germany, 1993; Australian recital tours, 1994, 1995; Recordings for BBC Radio Manchester, Radio Scotland, Radio 3, also Radio Denmark; Chamber music with violinist Peter Manning and with Edinburgh String Quartet. Compositions: Jazz Intermezzo, piano and brass band, 1973; Many Christmas music arrangements for choir and orchestra for RSAMD Carol Concerts, 1986-89; String Quartet, 1989; Trio for flute, oboe, clarinet, 1989. Recordings: Kemp's Nine Daies Wonder; Tintinnalogia; Piano Sonata; Soloist, Lambert, The Rio Grande with Scottish Sinfonietta, 1987; Contemporary British Piano Music, East Midlands Arts Association (works by Trevor Hold, Nigel Osborne, Andrew Wilson-Dickson) 1987; Contemporary Scottish Piano Music (works by Thomas Wilson, John McLeod, Rory Boyle, Judith Weir); Complete Piano Music of Carl Nielsen, 1995. Current Management: c/o Tom Kristensen, Tivoli Festival Agency, 20 H C Andersens Boulevard, Copenhagen V, Denmark. Address: The Old Joinery, Lintfieldbank, Coalburn, Lanarkshire ML11 0NJ, Scotland.

SELBY Kathryn (Shauna), b. 20 Sep 1962, Sydney, Australia. Concert Pianist. Education: Sydney Conservatorium of Music, 1975-77; BA, Bryn Mawr College, PA, 1979-83; High School Diploma and BA, Curtis Institute of Music, 1977-79, 1983-85; MM, Juilliard School of Music, 1985-86. Debut: YMCA, 92nd Street, NY, 1981; Wigmore Hall in London in 1987. Career: Appearances with Sydney Symphony Orchestra, Philadelphia Orchestra, Pittsburgh Symphony, St Louis Symphony, Cincinnati Symphony, Calgary and Erie Philharmonic, Indianapolis Symphony Orchestra, Shreveport Symphony Orchestra, among others; As Chamber Musician at Spoleto Festival, Australia in 1986, Marlboro Music Festival, Caramoor Festival, Concerto Soloists of Philadelphia, Hartford Chamber Orchestra, Kennedy Center Washington; Founding Member of Selby, Pini, Pereira Trio, Australia with appearances and tours, Musica Viva in Australia, 1985, 1987; ABC Film, Mozart in Delphi with Australian Chamber Orchestra for ABC Australia; Recitals in New York, Washington DC, Seattle, Portland, Pittsburgh, Philadelphia, Sydney, London and Munich. Hobbies: Reading; Swimming; Tennis; Embroidery. Current Management: Shaw Concerts Inc. Address: 1900 Broadway, New York, NY 10023, USA.

SELEZNEV Georgi, b. 21 Oct 1938, Tbilisi, Georgia. Singer (Bass). Education: Studied at Toilisi and the Leningrad Conservatory. Career: Bass Soloist at the Maly Opera Leningrad, 1972-78; Appearances with the Bolshoi Opera Russia, 1978-, on tour to Western Europe and USA; Solo Debut in the West as Konchak and Galitzky in Prince Igor at Trieste, 1985; Returned as Dosifei, in Khovanshchina; Title role in Salambo for RAI in Rome; Appeared in all international tours of Bolshoi Company in recent years; Engagements such as: Verdi Requiem under Chailly, with Royal Concertgebouw Orchestra in Amsterdam; Oroveso, with Joan Sutherland as Norma, at Opera Pacific and with Michigan Opera; Boris at Wiesbaden Festival; Pimen at Opéra du Rhin, Strasbourg, repeated at Bordeaux, 1993; Returned to Bordeaux as Timur, in production of Turandot, director Alain Lombard, 1994. Recordings include: Salambô; Oroveso in Norma. Honours include: Lenin Prize. Address: c/o Athole Still International Ltd, Foresters Hall, 25-27 Westow Street, London, SE19 3RY, England.

SELIG Franz-Josef, b. 11 July 1962, Germany. Singer (Bass). Education: Studied at the Cologne Musikhochschule with Claudio Nicolai. Career: Concert Tours of Italy, Germany, France, Switzerland, Holland and Turkey; Engaged at the Essen Opera from 1989, as the King in Aida, Herr Reich in Die Lustige Weiber von Windsor and Sarastro in Die Zauberflöte; Sang Mozart's Speaker at Frankfurt, 1991 and Fafner in Das Rheingold at Covent Garden; USA debut in Fidelio at San Francisco, 1995; St John Passion with Solti, 1997-98. Recordings include: Die Zauberflöte; Sacred Music by Mozart.

SELLARS Peter, b. 27 Sept 1957, Pittsburgh, Pennsylvania, USA. Opera Producer. Education: Harvard University. Career: Directed opera theatre while at Harvard; Don Giovanni for New Hampshire Symphony 1980 and Haydn's Armida; At Cambridge, Mass, directed Handel's Saul and Orlando, 1981 and at the Chicago Lyric Opera The Mikado, 1983; For the Boston Shakespeare Company produced the US premiere of The Lighthouse by Peter Maxwell Davies, 1983; British debut, Glyndebourne, 1987, with the world premiere of Nigel Osborne's The Electrication of the Soviet Union; Houston Opera 1987, with the premiere of Nixon in China by John Adams (seen at the 1988 Edinburgh Festival); Other productions include the Da Ponte operas of Mozart for the Pepsico Summerfare, New York, and Tannhäuser for the Chicago Lyric Opera, 1988; Artistic Adviser of the Boston Opera Theatre 1990; produced Die Zauberflöte at the 1990 Glyndebourne Festival; Premiere of The Death of Klinghoffer at Brussels 1991; Staged Messiaen's St Francois d'Assise, Salzburg 1992; Season 1995-96 with house premieres of Mathis der Maler at Covent Garden and Handel's Theodora at Glyndebourne; Engaged for Ligeti's Le Grand Macabre at the 1997 Salzburg Festival. Recordings include: Videos of Mozart's Da Ponte Operas (Decca). Address: c/o Harrison/Parrott Ltd, 12 Penzance Place, London W11 4PA, England.

SELLHEIM Eckart, b. 29 October 1939, Danzig. Pianist; Fortepianist; Accompanist. Education: Hamburg Conservatory; Piano, Accompanying, Musikhochschule, Cologne; Concert Diploma, 1963; Musicology, Music History, History of Art, Theatre, Cologne University. Career: Lecturer, Rheinische Musikschule, Cologne, 1963-69; Professor, Piano, Musikhochschule, Cologne, 1969-83; Piano, Piano Chamber Music, University of Michigan,

Ann Arbor, USA, 1983-89; Piano Accompanying, Director of Accompanying, Arizona State University, Tempe, 1989-; Concert tours: Germany, Austria, England, France, Spain, Italy, Poland, Netherlands, USA, Latin America, Middle East; Duo with Friedrich-Juergin Sellheim, Cello, 1965-; Several 100 Radio recordings, Germany, Europe, USA. Recordings Include: With Fr J Sellheim, Cello: Mendelssohn, 2 Cello Sonatas; 2 Variations Concertantes; Lied Ohne Worte, 1976; Brahms, 2 Cello Sonatas, 1977; Schumann, Fantasiestücke, Adagio und Allegro, Stücke im Volkston, 1978; Schubert, Arpeggione-Sonata, Brahms, Sonata, 1979, Chopin, Cello Sonata, Polonaise Brillante, Grand Duo Concertant, 1980;Piano Trio en Sol, Cello Sonata; Intermezzo for Cello and Piano; Ravel, Violin Sonata, 1985; Brahms, Transcriptions of Chopin, Bach, Weber, Gluck, Schumann, Schubert, Rakoczi March, also Brahms Transcriptions by Max Reger and Theodor Kirchner, 1990. Publications: Editor, Spielbuch fuer Klavier. Contributions to: Friedrich Gruetzmacher, 1966; Oskar von Pander, 1968; Instrumentale Ausbildung-Klavier, 1980; Die Klavierwerke W Fr Bachs, Concerto, 1984. Hobbies: Museums; Libraries; Bird-Watching. Address: 2416 West Nopal Avenue, Mesa, AZ 85202, USA.

SELLHEIM Friedrich-Juergen, b. 23 Aug 1948, Rehren, Germany. Cellist; Professor of Violoncello Performance. m. Doris M Ammann, 28 Dec 1973, 2 sons, 1 daughter. Education: NWD Musikakademie Detmold with Andre Navarra, 1967-73; Studied with Pierre Fournier in Geneva, 1971-72; Künstlerische Reifeprüfung, 1971; Konzertexamen, 1973. Career: As Soloist since 1971; Duo-Partner of his brother, pianist Eckart Sellheim and chamber musician concerts in most European and many other countries; Founder and Artistic Director of international Master Classes Porto Carras, Greece; Radio recordings for all German radio stations and many others; Professor for violoncello at the Hochschule für Musik, Hanover; Masterclasses in many countries. Recordings: Mendelssohn, complete music for cello and piano; Brahms, complete music for cello and piano; Schumann, complete music for cello and piano; Schubert, Sonata A minor, Arpeggione; Chopin, complete music for cello and piano; All recordings together with his brother, pianist Eckart Sellheim. Current Management: Konzertdirektion Drissen, Mainz. Address: Eichkatzweg 25, D-29313 Hambuehren, Germany.

SELLICK Phyllis (Doreen), b. 16 June 1911, Newbury Park, Essex. m. Cyril Smith 1937 (deceased), 1 son, 1 daughter. Education: Royal Academy of Music 1925-27. Debut: Harrogate 1933, with the Grieg Concerto. Career: Tours with husband to Portugal, Belgium, France, Middle East, India, Germany, Russia, New Zealand; TV appearances with husband This is Your Life and No Turning Back; 3 Royal Concerts. Recordings: Walton's Sinfonia Concertante, with the composer conducting; Tippett's First Sonata; 2 Piano Works and duets with husband. Honours: ARAM 1942; FRAM 1950; RCM 1960; Order of the British Empire 1971. Hobbies: Reading; Yoga.

SELTZER Dov, b. 26 Jan 1932, Iasi, Rumania. Composer; Conductor; Orchestrator; Musician. m. Grazielle Fontana, 15 May 1968, 1 stepson. Education: Piano, Theory, privately, 1944-47; Piano, General Music, Haifa and Tel-Aviv Conservatory, 1949-50; Composition with Mordecai Setter, 1950-53, with Herbert Bruen, 1952-54; Diploma, Composition, Mannes College of Music, 1958; BS, Music, State University of New York, 1960. Career: Music Director, Composer, Israel Army Nachal Theatrical Group, 1950-53; Music Teacher, Afek School, Haifa; Arranger, Music Director, Oranim Zabar Folk Singers and Theodore Bikel for Elektra, Columbia Co, USA, 1956-58; Music Teacher, Mannes College of Music, New York, 1958-60; Freelance Composer, Conductor for theatre, musicals, films, records, Israel, USA, France, Italy, England, Germany, elsewhere; Conducted Israel Philharmonic, concert of his music, 1987; Music Director, Conductor, Three Penny Opera film version, 1988;. Compositions include: 15 musicals including: The Megillah, 1966; Kazablan, 1967; I Like Mike, 1968; To Live Another Summer, 1971; Comme la neige en été, 1974; Other works: Stempeniu, symphonic poem, 1985; This Scroll, cantata for Ben Gurion centenary, 1986; Music for Thieves In The Night, German TV series, 1988; The Assisi Underground; Hassidic Rhapsody, violin solo, symphonic orchestra, 1989-90; The Gold of the Ashes, rhapsodic poem, 1991-92; Notre Dame de Paris, opera after novel by Victor Hugo, 1993-94; Film, TV, theatre and show scores; Many songs. Recordings: Tradition, as conductor and arranger with Itzhak Perlman and Israel Philharmonic Orchestra, 1986. Publications: Hassidic Rhapsody, 1992. Honours: Acum Prize, Israel Composers' Society Jury, 1984; Manger Prize, Contribution to Jewish Music and Culture, 1985; Sholom Aleichem Award, Special Contribution to Jewish Music and Culture. Hobbies: Photography; Skiing; Visual arts. Address: 19 Netiv Hamazalot, Jaffa, Israel.

SELWYN David (Morton), b. 21 Nov 1951, Bristol, England. Composer; Teacher; Lecturer; Editor. Education: BA, 1973, MMus, 1979, University of Bristol. Career: Lecturer, History and Composition, Extra Mural Department, Bristol University, 1974-; Teacher of Music and English, Bristol Grammar School, 1975-; Conductor, MD, Bristol Opera Company, 1977-90. Compositions: Operas: Conversations with Miss Brown, 1975; The Little Marchioness, 1976; The Rocking Stone, 1980; Beauty and The Beast, 1984; The Retirement of Theophrastus, 1986; Islanders, 1990; Cantatas: The Legend of St Julian; Mount Nebo; Five Songs for St Francis; Susanna and The Elders; Saint Edward; King John and The Abbot of Canterbury; The Visitation, 1991; The Colours of Mary; Harvest Work Song; Also songs, instrumental pieces and others; Libretti include: Rumpelstiltskin, Derek Bourgeois; St Patrick, Raymond Warren; Coffee Cantata, Bach. Recordings: BBC commissions: Incidental Music to The Idiot Lady, 1980; The Beatitudes, 1981. Publication: Jane Austen: Collected Poems (editor), 1996. Contributions to: Numerous reviews, articles on music, and others. Honour: Opera in Education Award for Beauty and the Beast, 1985. Memberships: Arts Club; Naval and Military Club; Composers' Guild of Great Britain; Performing Rights Society. Hobbies: Literature; Art; Travel; History. Address: 8 Barrow Court, Barrow Gurney, Bristol BS19 3RW, England.

SEMKOW Jerzy (Georges), b. 12 Oct 1928, Radomsko, Poland. Conductor. Education: 1948-51 State High School Krakow with Arthur Malawski; 1951-53 Leningrad Conservatory with Boris Khaikin; Further studies with Bruno Walter, Tullio Serafin. Career: Assistant to Mravinsky at the Leningrad Philharmonic 1954-56; Bolshoy Theatre 1056-58; 1959-62 Artistic Director and Principal Conductor of the Warsaw National Opera; 1966-76 Principal Conductor of the Danish Royal Opera, Copenhagen; US debut 1968, with the Boston Symphony Orchestra; Guest appearances with the Chicago Symphony, New York Philharmonic, Cleveland Orchestra; National Orchestra, Washington, Pittsburgh Symphony and others; UK debut 1968, with the London Philharmonic; Covent Garden 1970, Don Giovanni; Music Director St Louis Symphony 1976-79; Artistic Director RAI Rome 1979-. Recordings: Late Romantic music and contemporary Danish works; Nielsen's Helios overture and Violin Concerto (Tibor Varga); Chopin 1st Piano Concerto (Vasary); Boris Godunov and Prince Igor (EMI); Schumann Symphonies and Manfred overture (Vox); Scriabin 2nd Symphony (London Philharmonic), Mozart's Symphonies Nos 33 and 36. Hobbies: Reading; Yachting. Address: c/o ICM Artists, 40 West 57 Street, New York, NY 10019, USA.

SENATOR Ronald, b. 17 Apr 1926, London, England. Teacher; Composer. m. Miriam Brickman, 1986. Education: Hertford College, Oxford University; London University; Trinity College of Music; PhD; BMus; FTCL. Career includes: Professor, Guildhall School of Music & London University Institute of Education; Visiting Professor, Universities of Queensland & Melbourne (Australia); City of University of New York, & Massachusetts Institute of Technology (USA), Toronto & McGill Universities (Canada), Tel-Aviv University (Israel). Compositions include: Insect Play (libretto, Ursula Vaughan Williams); Echoes, Pageant of London; Trotsky (book, Anthony Burgess); Kaddish for Terezin; Basket of Eggs; Streets of London; Francis & the Wolf (libretto, Peter Porter); Mobiles; Spring Changes; My Animals; Sun's in the East. Recordings: (Counterpoint and Musica Nova label) Francis & the Wolf; Spring Changes; Mobiles; Shakespeare Sonnets; Poet to his Beloved; Delos label, Holocaust Requiem, Moscow Philharmonic. Publications: General Grammar of Music, 1975; Musicolor, 1975; Editor, review, Counterpoint, 1947-50. Address: 20 Denbigh Gardens, Richmond, Surrey TW10 6EN, England.

SENDEROVAS Anatolijus, b. 21 August 1945, Uljanovsk, Russia. Composer. 1 daughter. Education: Graduated from the Lithuanian Academy of Music (Vilnius), 1967; Post-graduate studies at the Rubin Israel Academy of Music (Tel Aviv University), 1990. Debut: International Music Festival, The Warsaw Autumn, 1978. Career: A Maiden and Death (ballet), staged at the Lithuanian Opera and Ballet Theatre, Vilnius, 1982; Mary Stewart (ballet), staged at the Vanemuine Theatre, Tartu, Estonia, 1988; Broadcast Radio 4, Amsterdam, Holland (interview and his music), 1995. Compositions: Symphony N2 (Music, St Petersburg), 1984; Der Tiefe Brunnen for voice and 5 instruments, 1993; Simeni Kahoteum al Libehe; Paratum cor Meum, Concerto for Cello, Mixed Choir, Piano (Clavinova) and Symphony Orchestra, 1995; Shme Israel (Hear O Israel) for cantor, men's and boy's choirs and symphony orchestra (Audio, Video), 1997. Recordings: Simeni Kahotam al Libehe (Set Me As A Seal Upon Your Heart) for soprano, bass, percussion solo and symphony orchestra, 1995; Two Songs of Shulamith, for voice and piano, 1996; Cantus I, Cantus II for cello solo, David Geringas, violincello, 1997. Publications: Berliner Zeitung, 1977; Ruch Muzyczny, 1978; Frankfurter Allegmeine Zeitung, 1982; Festival Zeitung, 1992. Honours: Second Prize at the International Composers Competition in Prague, 1993; Honorary Diploma at the 5th International Witold Lutoslawski; Piano Composition Contest in Kil (Sweden), 1994; Order of Lithuanian Grand Duke Gediminas. Membership: Lithuanian Composers Union. Hobbies: Swiming; Boating; Philately; Gardening. Current Management: LATGA (Agency of Lithuanian Copyright Protection). Address: Lakstingalu 5, 4031 Nemencine, Vilnius raj, Lithuania.

SENECHAL Michel, b. 11 February 1927, Tavery, France. Singer (Tenor). Education: Studies, Paris Conservatoire. Debut: Theatre de la Monnaie, Brussels, 1950. Career: Many Appearances at the Paris Opera and Opera Comique and elsewhere in France; Roles include Ferrando, Don Ottavio, Tamino, Hylas in Les Troyens, Rossini's Almaviva and Comte Ory; Successful in Such Character Roles as Rameau's Platée (Aix 1956, Brussels Opera Comique 1977), Erice in Cavalli's L'Ormindo (Glyndebourne) M. Tiquet in Eugene Onegin, Valzacchi & Scaramuccio in Ariadne auf Naxos; Glyndebourne Debut, 1966, as Gonzalve in L'Heure Espagnole; Salzburg Festival 1972-88, notably as Mozart's Basilio; Metropolitan Opera Debut 1982, as the Villains in Les Contes d'Hoffmann, returning 1997, as Basilio; Season 1985 with the Premieres of Landowski's Montsegur at Toulouse and Boehmer's Docteur Faustus at the Paris Opera; Director, Opera School at the Opera, 1980-. Address: c/o Metropolitan Opera, Lincoln Center, New York, NY 10023, USA.

SENIA Paul (Anthony), b. 26 Aug 1925, Brooklyn, New York, USA. Composer; Conductor. div., 1 son, 3 daughters. Education: MM and MA, Composition, Theory, Juilliard School of Music, 1948; DMA, Composition, Los Angeles Conservatory, 1961; PhD, Music History, Toronto, 1971. Debut: Saint-Saens Piano Concerto, Carnegie Hall, 1939. Career: Conductor, Los Angeles Conservatory Orchestra, 1960-62; Founder, Conductor, Simi Valley Symphony, 1964-67; Musical Director, Conductor: Los Angeles Civic Arts Symphony, 1964-; Los Angeles Pops Symphony, 1969-; American Theatre of the Opera, 1974-; New American Chamber Strings, 1980; UK debut, Gershwin Concerto with in F Leeds Symphony; West Coast premieres, Eugene Zador's operas Christopher Columbus, 1976, Inspector General, 1978, Jehu, 1980; Guest Conductor, US Symphony orchestra: American Korean, Philadelphia, Rochester, Utah, Detroit and Miami Philharmonic, Bank of America Radio Orchestra and Boston Pops, European Symphony, Leeds, Chesterfield, Harrogate Chamber Orchestra (England), Brussels Symphony. Compositions: Work for Piano, Strings and Vibraphone; Art Songs, 1945; 42 string quartets, 1948-60; Fisherman and the Mermaid, ballet, 1952, opera, 1954; Variety Suite for Orchestra, 1953; Piano Suite (Belle South), 1953; 3 Piano Sonatinas, 1954; Brass Processional, 1956; Choral works, 1956-70; Divertimento, Strings, 1961; Symphony No 1, based on Psalm 23, with soloists and choruses, 1966; 3 Woodwind Quintets, 1968, 1991; 2 Cello Sonatas, 1973; 3 Violin Sonatas, 1969-1972; Crystals, ballet, 1993; Triple Concerto, Violin, Viola, Cello, 1995. Address: c/o Sienna Enterprises, 5337 Northridge Drive, Palmdale, CA 93551, USA.

SENN Marta, b. 1958, Switzerland. Singer (Mezzo-Soprano). Education: Legal Training in Columbia; Musical study in USA. Career includes: Rosina and in title role of Rossi's Orfeo, at several American Opera Houses and La Scala, 1984; Charlotte in Stuttgart, Paris, Hamburg and Nantes; Giulietta in Les Contes d'Hoffmann in Madrid; Isabella in Rome; Massenet's Dulcinée at the Liceo, Barcelona; US tour with Placido Domingo; Annius in La Clemenza di Tito and Rossini's Angelina at the Saltzburg Festival, 1988; Season 1988-89, as Sara in Roberto Devereux at Naples and Meg in new production of Falstaff at Bologna; Fenena in Nabucco and Verdi's Preziosilla at Verona Arena; Carmen at Munich State Theatre; Carmen at Stuttgart State Theatre; Liceo, Barcelona, Olympics Arts Festival; Charlotte in Werther; Concerts and recording role of Salud, in La Vida Breve, Venezuela and Minnesota Orchestra, 1993; Debut role of Carmen, Paris Opera, 1994. Recordings include: Maddalena in Rigoletto, from La Scala, conducted by Riccardo Muti; Musetta, in La Bohème, at Venice; Lola in Cavalleria Rusticana; Salud in La Vida Breve, Mata conducting, 1993; El Amor Brujo, original version; Charlotte, in Lisbon and Rome; Dorabella in Toulon and Fidalma in Il Matrimonio Segreto at Bologna; Season 1996 as Charlotte at Naples. Honours include: Winner, Concours International de Paris, 1982; 1st Prize, Baltimore Opera National Auditions, 1982. Current Management: Fedeli Opera International, via Montegrappa 3, 40121 Bologna, Italy; Musicagliotz, SARL, 11 Rue La Verrier, 75006 Paris, France; Robert Lombardo Associates, 61 West 62nd St, Suite 6F, New York, NY 10023, USA. Address: c/o Athole Still International Management Ltd, Foresters Hall, 25-27, Westow Street, London, SE19 3RY, England.

SEOW Yitkin, b. 28 Mar 1955, Singapore. Pianist. Education: Yehudi Mehuhin School, 1967-72; LRSM, 1967; Royal College of Music, 1972-75. Debut: Wigmore Hall, 1968. Career: Televised, 1975-; Royal Festival Hall, Philharmonia, 1975; Berlin Radio Symphony Orchestra, Hong Kong Arts Festival, 1977; Royal Philharmonic Orchestra, London Promenade Concert, 1982; TV, BBC Scottish Orchestra, 1985; Russia Tour, BBC Welsh Orchestra, 1988. Recordings: Satie Piano Works: Janacek Piano Works; Debussy; Rachmaninov Cello Sonata; Yellow River Concerto (Gold Disc); Bartok Quartet as Violist, 1972 (with Nigel Kennedy). Honours: Winner, BBC Piano Competition, 1974; Rubinstein Prize, Tel Aviv, 1977. Membership: ISM. Hobbies:

Reading; Gardening. Address: 8 North Terrace, London SW3 2BA, England.

SEQUI Sandro, b. 10 November 1933, Rome, Italy. Stage Director. Education: Studied Literature and Philosophy at Rome University. Career: Directed La Sonnambula at the Teatro La Fenice Venice, 1961; Staging of I Puritani seen at Florence, 1971, Metropolitan 1976, Rome 1990; Guillaume Tell at Florence 1972, Les Contes d'Hoffmann at Dallas 1975; Staged the premiere production of Mannino's Il Principe Felice at La Scala, 1987; Rigoletto at the Chicago Lyric Opera, 1991; Fille du Régiment, Metropolitan, 1995-. Address: Lungotevere Sanzio 1, 00153 Rome, Italy.

SERBAN Andrei, b. 21 June 1943, Bucharest, Rumania. Opera Producer. Education: Theatre Institute, Bucharest. Career: Worked on theatre productions with Peter Brook in New York and Paris; Opera debut with Welsh National Opera, Eugene Onegin; returned for I Puritani, Rodelinda, and Norma; Produced Die Zauberflöte in Nancy, 1979; Alcina at the New York City Opera; Staging of Turandot for the Royal Opera was seen in Los Angeles and London in 1984; Premiere of The Juniper-Tree by Philip Glass for Baltimore Opera, 1985; Fidelio at Covent Garden and Prokofiev's Fiery Angel for Geneva and Los Angeles; Don Carlos in Geneva and Bologna; Permanent post with the Boston Repertory Theatre; produced Prince Igor at Covent Garden 1990; The Fiery Angel seen at the Holland Festival 1990; I Puritani in London, 1992; Tales of Hoffmann, Vienna Opera, 1993; Adriana Lecouvreur, Zurich Opera, 1994; Lucia di Lammermoor, Paris, Bastille Opera, 1995; Love of Three Oranges, Paris, Paris Conservatory, 1995; Staged Massenet's Thais at Nice, 1997. Current Management: Diana Mulgan, IMG Artists, 3 Burlington Lane, Chiswick, London W4 2TH. Address: c/o IMG, 3 Burlington Lane, Chiswick, London W4 2TH, England.

SERBO Rico, b. 9 May 1940, Stockton, CA, USA. Singer (Tenor). Education: Studied in San Francisco. Debut: San Francisco 1965 as Ramiro in Cenerentola. Career: Sang in Opera at Seattle, Santa Fe and San Francisco, Europe from 1970; Notably with Netherlands Opera and at Koblenz, Essen and the Theater am Gärtnerplatz Munich; Further engagements at San Diego, New York City Opera, Houston, Toronto and Vancouver; New Orleans, as Arvino in the US premiere of I Lombardi; Deutsche Oper and Theater des Westens Berlin, Belfast; Other roles have included Mozart's Ferrando and Tamino, Almaviva, Ernesto, Fenton, Alfredo, Tom Rakewell, Rodolfo, Boito's Faust, Lord Barrat in Der Junge Lord and Tony in Elegy for Young Lovers. Recordings include: Donizetti's L'Assedio di Calais.

SEREBRIER José, b. 3 Dec 1938, Montevideo, Uraguay. Musician; Conductor. m. Carole Farley, 29 Mar 1969, 1 daughter. Education: Diploma, National Conservatory, Montevideo, 1956; Curtis Institute of Music, USA, 1958; BA, University of MN, 1960; Studied with Aaron Copland, Antal Dorati, Pierre Monteux. Career: Apprentice Conductor, MN Orchestra, 1958-60; Associate Conductor, American Symphony Orchestra, NY, 1962-66; Music Director, American Shakespeare Festival, 1966; Composer in Residence, Cleveland Orchestra, 1968-71; Artistic Director, International Festival of Americas, Miami, 1964-; Guest Conductor of numerous orchestras including London Symphony and Philharmonic, Philadelphia and Royal Philharmonic Orchestra. Compositions include: Over 100 works including: Variations on a Theme from Childhood for Orchestra, Symphony for Percussion, for Chamber, Violin Concerto 1992; Also works for Chorus, Voice and Keyboard. Recordings include: Conductor for many recordings including: Ives 4th Symphony with London Philharmonic, RPO Tchaikovsky Works, 1993, Janácek Orchestral Works with Czech State Philharmonic, Prokofiev and Glazunov with Moscow Soloists, Beethoven Symphonies with Sydney Symphony Orchestra and Hindemith Orchestral Works with Philharmonia; Kurt Weill; Delius. Publication: Violin Concerto, 1993. Contributions to: Over 50 journals. Honours: Guggenheim Fellow, 1958-60; Rockefeller Foundation Grant, 1968-70; Ford Foundation Conductors' Award; Alice M Ditson Award, 1976; Commission Award, National Endowment for The Arts, 1978. Membership: American Symphony Orchestra League. Hobbies: Swimming; Walking; Writing Novels. Current Management: Gershunoff Inc, NY, USA. Address: 270 Riverside Drive, New York, NY 10025, USA.

SEREMBE Gilberto, b. 17 Dec 1955, Milan, Italy. Conductor; Professor of Orchestral Conducting. Education: Superior courses in Conducting, Conservatorio G Verdi, Milan, 1977, 1978, 1979, with Mario Gusella; Diploma in Composition, 1979, Conservatorio G Verdi, Milan, with Bruno Bettinelli; Diploma cum laude, Orchestral Conducting, Accademia Chigiana, Siena, 1981, with Franco Ferrara. Career: Professor of Composition, Brescia Conservatorio, 1979-81; Assistant, Teatro alla Scala, Milan, 1980; Professor of Orchestral Rehearsing: Mantova Conservatorio, 1982-83, Conservatorio G Verdi, Milan, 1984-86, Brescia Conservatorio, 1986-88, Genoa Conservatorio, 1989-97; Professor of Orchestral Conducting, International Superior courses, Accademia Musicale Pescarese, 1988-; Professor/Conductor, Orchestra of the Conservatories of Brescia, 1997-; Guest Conductor: Pomeriggi Musicali Orchestra, Milan, 1976-77, 1980-83, 1987, 1990, 1992, 1994, AIDEM Orchestra, Firenze, 1979, Angelicum Chamber Orchestra, Milan, 1980-83, San Remo Symphony Orchestra, 1980-87, Bari Symphony Orchestra, 1982-84, RAI Radio Television Symphony Orchestra, Turin, 1984, 1993; Principal Guest Conductor: International Symphony Orchestra, Jeunesses Musicales, Italian tour, 1983, International Youth Symphony Orchestra, 1984-87, Haydn Symphony Orchestra, Bozen, 1985, 1987, 1989, Teatro Massimo Symphony Orchestra, Palermo, 1986-88, Orchestra Regionale della Toscana, Florence, 1986-88, 1995, Stradivari Orchestra, Milan, 1991-92, and Hungarian tour, 1991, Teatro Regio Symphony Orchestra, Turin, 1991, Toscanini Symphony Orchestra, Parma, 1993, Brescia Symphony Orchestra, 1996, Orchestra Sinfonica Triveneta, 1997-98, Orchestra Stabile di Bergamo, 1998; Abroad: Gothenburg Symphonic Orchestra, Sweden, 1989, BRT Radio Television Symphony Orchestra, Brussels, 1991, Turku Philharmonic, Finland, 1991, Tirana Radio and Television Symphony Orchestra, Albania, 1994-95. Current Management: Via Zanella 43/1, 20133 Milan, Italy.

SERENI Mario, b. 25 Mar 1928, Perugia, Italy. Singer (Baritone). Education: Studied at the Accademia di Santa Cecilia in Rome and at the Accademia Chigiana, Siena. Debut: Florence 1953, in Lualdi's Il Diavolo nel Campanile. Career: Sang in The Stone Guest by Dargomyzhsky, Florence, 1954; Palermo 1955, as Wolfram in Tannhäuser; Metropolitan Opera from 1957: almost 400 performances in 26 roles, including Gerard, Sharpless, Germont, Amonasro, Belcore and Marcello; Vienna 1965, Verona Arena 1965-74; Further engagements in London, Chicago, Dallas, Houston, London, Milan and Buenos Aires. Recordings: Madama Butterfly, Andrea Chénier, La Bohème, Cavalleria Rusticana, Elisir d'Amore, Aida, La Traviata (EMI); Ernani, Turandot, Lucia di Lammermoor (RCA). Address: c/o Arena di Verona, Piazza Bra 28, 1-37121 Verona, Italy.

SERKIN Peter, b. 24 July 1947, New York, USA. Pianist. Education: Lessons in music and piano with Blanche Moyse and Luis Battle; Curtis Institute for six years studying with Lee Luvisi, Mieczyslaw Horszowski and his father, Rudolf Serkin; Further lessons and studies with Ernst Oster, Marcel Moyse and Karl Ulrich Schnabel. Career: Public concerts from the age of twelve; Mozart Concertos at the Marlboro Festival and concerts with Alexander Schneider; Premiered Peter Lieberson's Piano Concerto commissioned by the Boston Symphony, 1985; Seiji Ozawa, 1985; Also premiered works by Hans Werner Henze, Oliver Knussen, Toru Takemitsu, Alexander Goehr, Luciano Berio and others; Plays music by Bach, Mozart, Beethoven, Brahms, Schoenberg and Stravinsky; Teaches at the Tanglewood Music Center annually. Honour: Prize for Outstanding artistic achievement from the Premier Internazionale Accademia Musicale Chigiana. Memberships: Faculty Member of the Juilliard School of Music and the Curtis Institute of Music. Address: Shirley Kirshbaum & Associates, 711 West End Avenue, Suite 5KN, New York, NY 10025, USA.

SERMILÄ Jarmo Kalevi, b. 16 Aug 1939, Hämeenlinna, Finland. Composer. m. Ritva Vuorinen, 10 Nov 1962. Education: MA, Helsinki University, 1975; Composition Diploma, Sibelius Academy, 1975. Career: Began as Jazz Musician, then studied further, becoming a Composer; Worked as Artistic Director for Finnish Radio's Experimental Music Studio, 1973-79; President, Finnish Section, International Society for Contemporary Music, 1975-79; Composer-in-Residence, Hämeenlinna, 1977-82; Freelance Composer, 1982-; Artistic Leader, Time of Music Contemporary Music Festival, Viitasaari, 1988-. Compositions: Wolf Bride, ballet; Merlin's Mascarade, ballet; Pieces for orchestra: Mimesis 2; Manifesto; Labor Quattro rilievi; Works for instrumental solos with orchestral accompaniment: Pentagram; A Circle of the Moon; La Place Revisitée; On the Road; Numerous chamber works and electroacoustic pieces. Recordings: Quattro Rilievi; At Bizarre Exits; Random Infinities; For various labels by artists such as James McDonald, Horn, Russ Hartenberger, Percussion, The Finnish Radio Symphony conducted by Jukka-Pekka Saraste, Avanti! Ensemble conducted by Olli Pohjola, Jouko Harjanne, Trumpet, Puhallus Brass Trio, Brassologia Quintet. Publications: Various compositions published. Honours: Hämeenlinna Music Prize, 1981; Art Award, Häme Provincial Art Committee, 1988; Long-term State Grant for composition, 1990. Membership: Society of Finnish Composers, Vice-President 1981-. Address: Niittykatu 7 A 7, 13100 Hämeenlinna, Finland.

SEROV Edward, b. 9 Sept 1937, Moscow, Russia. Symphony Orchestra Conductor, m. Guenrietta Serova, 29 June 1961, 2 sons. Education: Gnessin Institute, Moscow, 1954-59; Tschaikovsky Conservatoire, Kiev, 1958-61; Rimsky-Korsakov Conservatoire, Leningrad, 1961-64. Debut: Kiev Opera, 1960. Career: Conductor, Leningrad Philharmonic Orchestra, 1961-68, 1985-90; Founder, Chief Conductor, Uljanovsk Philharmonic, 1968-77; Founder, Chief Conductor, Leningrad Chamber Orchestra, 1974-85; Founder, Chief Conductor, Volgograd Philharmonic Orchestra, 1987-; Professor, Leningrad (now St Petersburg) Conservatoire, 1987-; Chief Conductor, Odense Symphony Orchestra, Denmark, 1991-; Foreign Tours: Japan, USA, France, Germany, Austria, Spain, Sweden, Norway, Finland, Denmark, Czechoslovakia, Hungary, Yugoslavia, others. Recordings: Over 50 discs, mostly for Melodiya, including works of Webern, Tishchenko, Arensky, Mozart, Rubenstein, Tchaikovsky, Prokofiev, Sviridov, Purcell, Tartini, Bartók, Slonimski, Hindemith, Mendelssohn, Bach, Nielsen, Rossini, Ginastera, Shostakovich, Rodrigo, Elgar, Suk, Schumann, Spohr and Schubert. Contributions to: The Exploit of Service to Music; The Soviet Music Magazine, 1980; About Conductor's Art, The Soviet Music, 1980; The original Symphonic Narration, The Music Life magazine, 1984; Meditation about G Sviridov to book on Sviridov; Others. Honours: People's Artist of Russia honorary of Title, President of Russia, 1990. Hobbies: Basketball; Mountain climbing. Address: Warschawskaja str 124 kw 95, St Petersburg 196 240, Russia.

SERRA Enric, b. 1943, Barcelona, Spain. Singer (Baritone). Education: Studied in Barcelona. Debut: Teatro del Liceo Barcelona, 1986, as Morales in Carmen. Career: Has sung in Spain (Madrid, Valencia, Bilbao and Barcelona) from 1969, notably as Falstaff, Scarpia, Escamillo, Enrico, Belcore and Alcandro in Pacini's Saffo, 1987; Guest engagements in Zurich, Cologne, Nice, Tours, Naples, Venice, Bogota and Caracas, as Don Pasquale, Rossini's Figaro, Alfonso (La Favorita) and Don Carlos in La Forza del Destino; At Schwetzingen as Lescaut in Manon Lescaut and at Barcelona, 1990; Concert repertoire includes Falla's L'Atlantida (Madrid 1977). Recordings include: Madama Butterfly, with Caballé (Decca). Address: Gran Teatro del Liceo, Sant Pau I bis, 08001 Barcelona, Spain.

SERRA Luciana, b. 4 Nov 1946, Genoa, Italy. Singer (Soprano). Education: Genoa Conservatoire and with Michele Casato. Debut: Budapest Opera 1966, in Cimarosa's Il Convito. Career: Member of Teheran Opera 1969-76; Sang Gilda in Rigoletto at Genoa, 1974; Bologna 1979, in La Sonnambula; Covent Garden 1980, as Olympia in Les Contes d' Hoffmann; Rossini's Aureliano in Palmira at Genoa 1980; Hamburg 1982 and La Scala Milan 1983, as Lucia; US debut at Charleston as Violetta; Chicago Lyric Opera 1983 as Lakmé; Parma 1986 as Lucia; Rossini Opera Festival Pessaro 1987 in L'Occasione fa il ladro (Rossini); Vienna 1988 as the Queen of Night; Maggio Musicale Turin 1989, as Elvira in I Puritani; Sang Gilda at Turin 1989, Hanna Glawari at Trieste 1990; Santiago 1990, as Donizetti's Marie; Schwetzingen Festival 1990, in Fra Diavolo at La Scala and Pamira in Le Siège de Corinthe at Genoa; Sang Olympia at Genoa, 1996; Other roles include Rosina, Fiorilla; Ophelia, Philine; Bellini's Giulietta; Norina; Adina; Linda di Chamounix and Marie in La Fille du Régiment; Concert appearances in pre-classical works and music by Vivaldi, Mozart, Rossini and Rimsky-Korsakov. Recordings: Zerline in Fra Diavolo (Cetra); Torquato Tasso by Donizetti; Die Zauberflöte; Les Contes d'Hoffmann; Don Pasquale, Barbiere di Siviglia, Gianni di Parigi; Fille du Régiment; La Scala di Seta and L'Occasione fa il Ladro. Address: c/o Allied Artists Agency, 42 Montpellier Square, London SW7 1JZ, England.

SERRANO GRAMAJO Rafael, b. 11 September 1956, Guatemala, Central America. Composer. Debut: Guatemala, Central America, 1995. Career: Channel 5 Television, 1995; Television Guatemala La Cupula Theatre; Congress of FLADEM, Miami, Florida, USA, 1996; National Theatre in Guatemala, 1996. Compositions: Muier de Fugo; Cubano; Bachata; Junentud Latino; Ausencia; La Incomprendida; Lugo-Azul; Conazon de Poeta; Del Amor. Recordings: Salsu Merengue y algo mes, 1996; Romantics From Rafuel Serrano, 1996. Publications: El Primer Beso nomantica, 1997; El final, 1997; La Incomprendida, 1997; Del Amor, 1997. Contributions to: Valores de Nuestro Tiempo Channel 5. Honours: Award, Writers Guatemalan Association; Guatemalan World Culture, 1996. Memberships: Composers & Musicians of Guatemala; Writers Guatemala Association. Hobby: Basketball. Address: 28 Calle B 13-27, Zona 13 Col, Santa Fe Guatemala City, Guatemala, Central America.

SERVADEI Annette (Elizabeth), b. 16 Oct 1945, Durban, Natal. Italian Pianist. m. 1972-81, 1 son, 1 daughter. Education: Began studies with concert pianist mother, 1949; Further studies, Milan, Detmold, Salzburg, London, with Deckers, Schilde, Kabos, Zecchi, W Kempff; Also Violin and Organ studies, diploma level; LTCL (T), 1964; LRSM (P), 1965; FTCL, 1970; BMus, 1979. Debut: Wigmore Hall, London, 1972. Career: Started broadcasting at age 10; Concert debut with major orchestra, age 12; Recitals and concertos, very wide repertoire, UK, West Europe, Africa, USA; Frequent radio and TV broadcasts; University Senior Piano Tutor; Lecture recitals, master classes; Eisteddfod Adjucator; Outstanding performer of Liszt, Ravel and 20th century American music; Considered by Wilhelm Kempff as one of best Beethoven students; Played world premiere, Tavener's Palintropos, London. Recordings: Britten and Khachaturian Piano Concertos with London Philharmonic Orchestra; Recital disc of piano pieces, Mendelssohn, Schumann and Brahms; Complete piano music of

Sibelius, 5 CDs; Complete piano music of Dohnanyi, 1st CD, 1995, 4 CDs to follow; Mendelssohn, Schumann and Brahms Piano Pieces; Sibelius complete piano music, 5 volumes and continuum; Dohnanyi music volume I. Honours: Scholarships, Oppenheimer Trust and AB, 1963-70; Artist of the Year, UK Sibelius Society, 1993. Memberships: Incorporated Society of Musicians; European Piano Teachers' Association; ISSTIP. Hobbies: Dress design; Reading; Italian cooking. Current Management: Audrey Ellison International Artists. Address: 3 Bournemouth Drive, Herne Bay, Kent CT6 8HH, England.

SESTAK Zdenek, b. 10 Dec 1925, Citoliby, Czechoslovakia. Composer. m. Marie Zatecka, 2 Sep 1950, 1 s, 1 d. Education: Gymnasium, Louny, 1936-44; Conservatorium de la Musique, Prague, 1945-50; PhD, Charles University, Faculty of Philosophy, 1945-50. Career: Professor of Music, 1952-57; Freelance Composer, 1957-; Dramaturge, Centre for Symphonic Music, Radio Czechoslovakia, Prague, 1968-70. Compositions include: Symphonie II, 1970, III, 1971, IV, 1979, V Chronos, 1978 and VI L'Inquietude Eternelle du Coeur, 1979; Cycle des Cantates Spirituels sur les Textes de psaume, 1972-92; Concert for String Orchestra, 1974; String Quintet, Concentus musicus, 1975; Sonata Symphonica, 1976; Sonata da Camera, 1978; Concert for Violin: Sursum corda, 1981; Concert for Viola: Meditations de Socrates, 1982; Memoria, La Fresque Symphonique de Variation, 1983; Fatum, vocale, Symphonique Fragment d'Apres Sophocles, 1983; Concert for Violin: Jean le Violiniste, 1985; Queen Dagmar, oratorium, 1989; Les Cycles des Chants sur Vers de Villon, Michelangelo Buonarotti, Hora, Macha, Jelen, Sefl, King Salamon, Le Testament Ancien (Book of Ecclesiasticas); Evocations Paschales for Trumpet and Organ, 1992; Sonata for Trumpet and Organ, Dies Laetitiae, 1993; String Quartet VI, Variations de Mácha, 1993; String Quartet VII, Soliloquia, 1994. Publications: La Musique de Maîtres de Citoliby de 18 Siècle, 1968, 1985. Membership: Association of Music Artists Tchèques. Hobby: Cycling. Address: Pracska 2594-87, 106 00 Prague 10, Czech Republic.

SHACKLOCK Constance, b. 16 April 1913, Sherwood, Nottingham, England. Singer (Mezzo-soprano). Education: Studied at the Royal Academy of Music with Frederick Austin. Career: 1st Professional Engagement, International Ballet, singing the role of Goddess Sabrina, in Milton's Comus, London Coliseum, 1945; Sang first in Concert then joined the Covent Garden Opera Company, singing in its first production, Purcell's Fairy Queen, 1946; Guest Artist at Berlin State Opera, 1952; Remained at Covent Garden until 1956 her repertory including Carmen, Marina in Boris Godunov, Magdalene in Die Meistersinger von Nürnberg, Mrs Sedley in Peter Grimes, Brangäne in Tristan und Isolde, Azucena in Il Trovatore, Amneris in Aida, Octavian in Der Rosenkavalier, Fricka in the Ring, Herodias in Salome, Ortrud in Lohengrin and Erda in Siegfried; Has also sung in Ireland, the Netherlands, Russia and at the Teatro Colón, Buenos Aires and given many recitals, broadcasts and concerts. Recordings include: Tristan Act II duet with Flagstad and Svanholm; Messiah; Angel in Dream of Gerontius, Rome Festival, 1957, Rome Orchestra and Choir conducted by John Barbirolli. Honours: Honorary Doctor, Kingston University, 1943; OBE, 1971. Address: East Dorincourt, Kingston Vale, London SW15 3RN, England.

SHADE Ellen, b. 17 Feb 1948, New York, USA. Singer (Soprano). Education: Studied at the Juilliard Opera Center and with Cornelius Reid; Further study at the Sanata Fe Opera, 1969. Debut: Frankfurt 1972, as Liu in Turandot. Career: Sang Micaela at Pittsburgh 1972 (US debut); Further engagements in Cincinnati, Milwaukee, Dallas and New Orleans; Chicago 1976, as Emma in Khovanshchina, returning as Eve in the premiere of Penderecki's Paradise Lost, 1978; Metropolitan Opera debut, as Eva in Die Meistersinger; New York City Opera, 1981, Donna Elvira; Sang in Paradise Lost at La Scala in 1979 and has made further European appearances at Hamburg, Brussels, Vienna (Florinda in Schubert's Fierabras, conducted by Abbado), and Geneva (Katya Kabanova, 1988); Returned to the Metropolitan as Sieglinde in Die Walküre, conducted by James Levine; Season 1992 as the Empress in Die Frau ohne Schatten, at Amsterdam and Salzburg; Other roles include Verdi's Alice Ford, Wagner's Elsa and Freia, Climene in Cavalli's Egisto and Agathe in Der Freischütz; As a concert singer has appeared with the New York Philharmonic, the Chicago Symphony and the Orchestras of Boston, Cleveland, Los Angeles, Minnesota, St Louis, Pittsburgh and the National Symphony and in Europe with the Radio Orchestras of Frankfurt, Berlin, Stuttgart, Baden-Baden, Roma and Torino; Invited to teach French Art Song with the Ravinia Festival in Chicago; Revival of Die Frau Ohne Schatten in Amsterdam; Aida with the Metropolitan Opera; Sang Arabella at Covent Garden, 1996. Recordings include: Hans Pfitzner Cantata Von Deutscher Seele with the Frankfurt Radio Orchestra conducted by Horst Stein. Address: c/o Portland Wallis Management, 50 Great Portland Street, London W1N 5AH, England.

SHADE Nancy (Elizabeth), b. 31 May 1949, Rockford, Illinois, USA. Opera and Concert Singer (Soprano). Education: De Pauw University; Indiana University; Principal Voice Teacher, Vera Scammon. Debut: Kentucky Opera Theatre, 1968, as Leonora in Il Trovatore. Career: Lulu, Frankfurt Opera; Countess in Figaro, Hamburg State Opera; Manon Lescaut, Munich State Opera; Marguerite in Faust, San Francisco Opera; Madame Butterfly, New York City Opera; Marie in Die Soldaten, Lyons; Santa Fe 1984, in the US premiere of Henze's We Come to the River; Stuttgart 1988, as Marie in Die Soldaten (repeated Vienna 1990). Honours: 1st prize, National Metropolitan Auditions, 1968. Hobbies: Studying in classes with inner-development author, Vernon Howard, Boulder City, Nevada. Current Management: Thea Dispeker, 59 East 54th Street, New York, NY 10022, USA.

SHAFF Stanley M, b. 14 Feb 1929, San Francisco, California, USA. Composer; Teacher. m. Anna Gordon, 15 Dec 1967, 1 son. Education: BA Music and Education, San Francisco State College, 1946-50; MA Music, 1950-52. Career: Professional Trumpet Player, 1945-63; Compositional, 1960-64; Concerts of electronic compositions at University of California, 1960; San Francisco State College, 1962; San Francisco Musuem of Art, 1963, 1964; Creation and development of Audium, the first sound theatre for the spatial performance of electronic music, 1965-70; Re-establishment of Audium within a building designed from floor to ceiling for the special needs of spatial composition and performance, 1973-75; Weekly public performances, 1975-. Compositions: 9 music concrete works (untitled) performed at above listed institutions, 1960-64; 6 major music concrete works (untitled), various minor works composed for spatial performance at the Sound Theatre Audium, 1965-. Contributions to: Music Journal, Jan 1977. Honours: National Endowment for the Arts Grant, 1972; Six National Endowment for the Arts Grant for performance seminars series for colleges and for the creation of new compositions, 1975-81. Membership: Musicians Union. Hobby: Visual Arts. Address: c/o Audium, 1616 Bush Street, San Francisco, CA 94109, USA.

SHAGUCH Marina, b. 1964, Krasnodar, Russia. Singer (Soprano). Education: Studied at the Arts School in Maikop and at St Petersburg State Conservatoire. Career: Sang at the Kirov Opera Theatre in season 1991-92, notably in Mussorgsky's Sorochinsky Fair and Il Trovatore; Concert debuts at Grand Hall of the Moscow Conservatoire; Glinka Capella in St Petersburg; Further appearances throughout Russia, USA, Germany, Wales; Concert repertoire has included works by Handel, Mozart, Rimsky, Schumann, Schubert, Wolf, Dvorak and Brahms; Performed in The Legend of the Invisible City of Kitezh with Kirov Opera at the Barbican, 1995. Honours include: Winner, Mussorgsky All Russia and Glinka National Singing Competitions; Second Prize, Tchaikovsky International Competition. Address: c/o Sonata, 11 Northpark Street, Glasgow, G20 7AA, Scotland.

SHAHAM Gil, b. 1971, Illinois, USA. Concert Violinist. Education: Studied at the Rubin Academy in Jerusalem, in Aspen and at Juilliard with Dorothy De Lay. Debut: Concert with the Jerusalem Symphony Conducted by Alexander Schneider. Career: Appeared with the Israel Philharmonic under Zubin Mehta, 1982; Engagements with the New York Philharmonic; Season, 1987-88 with the LSO at the Barbican, Bavarian Radio Orchestra in Munich, the RAI Turin and Recitals at La Scala and in Munich; Debut with the Philadelphia Orchestra and Tour of South America, 1988; Season, 1988-89 with the Berlin Philharmonic, Orchestre de Paris, Frankfurt Symphony and the Philharmonic under Sinopoli; Bruch and Sibelius Concertos with the LSO, 1989; Recital Debut at the Wigmore Hall, London, 1990; Season 1995-96 with the Israel Philharmonic, the LSP, CBSO, Vienna Symphony Orchestra and the Philharmonic Orchestra; Recitals throughout Europe and the Far East. Honours include: First Prize, 1982 Claremont Competition, Israel. Address: c/o Harrison/Parrott Ltd, 12 Penzance Lane, London W11 4PA, England.

SHAKHOVSKOY Albert, b. 6 July 1946, Onega, Russia. Composer; Musicologist. m. Helen Shakhovskoy, 30 December 1983, 1 son, 1 daughter. Education: Composers Faculty, Conservatoire of Nijniy Novgorod. Debut: Onega, 1956. Career: Music for Show, Solitude, 1988; Music for Film, Native Land, 1989; Appearances on TV & Radio. Compositions: 121, 1956-96. Recordings: Russian Poem for Symphony Orchestra; Evening Plays for Symphony Orchestra; Homage to Mitchell for Piano; Partita for Violin Solo; Pro Memoria for Violin, Viola & Violoncello. Publications: 13 Books, 49 Articles, 10 Others. Honours: Music Festival Winner, 1987; Reward, Crossnore School, 1995; Candidate of Art Criticism, 1993; ISME Competition Winner, 1992; Honoured Science Worker, 1997. Hobby: Literary Work. Address: ul Korolenko 10 kv 25, 427600 Udmurtia, Glazov, Russia.

SHALLON David, b. 1950, Tel Aviv, Israel. Conductor. m. Tabea Zimmermann. Education: Studied in Tel Aviv and in Vienna with Hans Swarowsky. Career: Conducted the Vienna Symphony in Mahler's Third, 1980; Conducted the Bavarian Radio Symphony Orchestra from 1980 and the Berlin Philharmonic from 1986; Dusseldorf Symphony 1987-93, as Chief Conductor; Other engagements with the London Symphony and Philharmonic, San Francisco Symphony, Rotterdam and Israel Philharmonics and St Paul Chamber Orchestra; Opera appearances at the Vienna Staatsoper, Deutsche Oper am Rhein and with New Israel Opera; Has given premieres of works by Berio, Henze, Nono, Bernstein and Penderecki; Regular concerts with the Junge Deutsche Philharmonie and tours of America and Australia with the Australian Youth Orchestra; Music Director of the Jerusalem Symphony Orchestra from 1992; Season 1996-97 with the Czech, Stockholm and Royal Liverpool Philharmonias, Berlin Radio, Vienna and Barcelona Symphony Orchestras. Recordings include: Bartók, Hindemith and Schnittke viola concertos. Address: c/o Harrison Parrott Ltd, 12 Penzance Place, London W11 4PA, England.

SHAMIR Michal, b. 1960, Tel Aviv, Israel. Singer (Soprano). Education: Studied at the Rubin Academy of Music, Tel Aviv, and in London. Career: Operatic Debut at Gluck's Euridice; Followed by Cherubino and Elvira in L'Italiana in Algeri; European Debut at Hamburg as Susanna, Followed by Pamina, Gretel and Frasquita; Geneva opera 1987, as Larissa in the premiere of La Foret by Liebermann; Appearances with Frankfurt Oper as Susanna, Despina, Gilda, Marzellina and Jenny in Mahagonny; Has returned to Tel Aviv for Violetta, Nedda and Marquerite; Basle Opera in Zemlinsky's Der Zwerg, currently member of the Deutsche Oper Berlin; Concert repertoire includes Lutoslawski's Chantefleurs et Chantefables, performed with the composer in San Francisco and Helsinki; British Debut as Violetta in La Traviata with Opera North, 1994; First Tatiana in Eugene Onegin in Lausanne, Switzerland, 1994. Address: c/o IMG Artists, Media House, 3 Burlington Lane, London W4 2TH, England.

SHANAHAN Ian (Leslie), b. 13 June 1962, Sydney, New South Wales, Australia. Composer. Education: BMus, University of Sydney, 1986; Study with Eric Gross & Peter Sculthorpe. Career: Faculty Member, Department of Music, University of Sydney, 1994-; New South Wales Conservatory, 1989-94; Commissions from Roger Woodward, 1993 and others. Compositions: Echoes/Fantasies for Bass Clarinet and Percussion, 1984; Arcturus Timespace for Amplified Mandolin and Percussion, 1987; Solar Dust for Mandolin, 1988; Cycles of Vega for Clarinet & 2 Percussions, 1988-90; Lines of Light for Amplified Recorders and Percussion, 1991-93; Ritual Canons for 4 Tubas, 1982-93; Dimensions Paradisim for Alto Flute, 1993; Arc of Light, for Piano, 1993; Gate of Remembrance, for Amplified Piano, 1993. Honours include: Adolf Spivakovsky Prize, 1991. Address: c/o APRA, 1A Eden Street, Crows Nest, NSW 2065, Australia.

SHANE Rita (Frances), b. 1940, New York City, USA. Opera, Concert Singer. m. Daniel F Tritter, 1 son. Education: BA, Barnard College; Private Study, Beverly Peck Johnson, Elisabeth Schwarzkopf; Santa Fe Opera Apprentice Program; Hunter College Opera Workshop. Career: Appearances with, Metropolitan Opera, Chicago Lyric, San Francisco, New York City Opera, most American companies; La Scala, Vienna Staatsoper, Bavarian State Opera, Turin, Strasbourg, Scottish, other opera houses in Europe, South America; Orchestras of Philadelphia, Cleveland, Cincinnati, in USA, Santa Cecilia, Vienna, in Europe, Israel Philharmonic; Festivals, Salzburg, Vienna, Munich, Glyndebourne, Perugia, Aspen; Mostly Mozart, Canada; Roles at Met Opera New York include the Queen of Night, Lucia, Berthe in Le Prophète, Pamira in The Siege of Corinth, Verdi's Gilda, Oscar and Violetta; Recitals; TV, CBC Canada, Bayerische Rundfunk, Germany; Sang title role in the premiere of Argento's Miss Havisham's Fire, New York City Opera, 1979; American premieres of Henze's Elegy for Young Lovers (Hilda Mack), New York and Reimann's Lear (Regan), San Francisco. Recordings: Highlights from Handel's Athalia; Highlights from Handel's Rinaldo; Complete works of Schoenberg, volume 2; R Strauss, Brentano Songs, Op 68 with orchestra (Louisville Premiere); Various private recordings including, Les Huguenots, Die Zauberflöte; Professor of Voice, Eastman School of Music, Rochester, New York. Hobbies: Purebred Dachshunds; Floral Arrangement. Address: c/o Daniel F Tritter, 330 West 42nd Street, New York, NY 10036 USA.

SHANKAR Ravi, b. 7 Apr 1920, Varanasi, India. Musician (Sitar Player). m. Sukanya Rajan, 23 Jan 1989. Education: Studied under Ustad Allaudin Khan of solo sitarist; Former director of music, All-India Radio; Founded National Orchetra of All-India Radio; Founder/Director Kinnara School of Music, Bombay, 1962 and Los Angeles, 1967; Stage work Ghanashyam (A Broken Branch) premiered by the City of Birmingham Touring Opera, 1989. Compositions: 2 Concertos for Sitar and Orchestra, 1971, 1981; Film scores for Pather Panchali, Charlie, Chappaqua, Gandhi; Music for TV production of Alice in Wonderland; Opera-ballet Ghanashyam, 1989. Recordings: Concertos Nos 1 and 2; Several Ragas, 1981; Homage to Mahatma Gandhi 1981 West meets East, with Yehudi Menuhin, and many others. Publication: My Music, My Life, 1968. Honours: Fellow, Sangeet Natak Academy, 1976; Padma Vibhushan 1981; Elected to Rajya

Sabha (Indian Upper House) 1986; 12 Honourary Doctorates from around the world; Ramon Magsaysay Award; Grand prize, Fukuoka, Japan; Crystal Award, 'Global Ambassador', Davos, Switzerland, 1996. Address: Christopher Tennant Artists Management, Unit 10, 39 Tadema Road, London SW10 0PY, England.

SHANKS Donald, b. 5 July 1940, Brisbane, Australia. Singer (Bass-Baritone). Career: Sang first in operettas by Gilbert and Sullivan, then toured Australia with the Williamson-Sutherland Opera Company; From 1964 has sung with the Australian Opera, Sydney in over 70 roles including Boris in Boris Godunov, Don Pasquale, Phillip in Don Carlos, Baron Ochs in Rosenkavalier, Osmin, Zaccaria, Nabucco, Raimondo in Lucia di Lammermoor, Prince Gremin in Eugene Onegin, Gurnemanz, Parsifal; Sang at Covent Garden in 1974 and Paris Opera in 1976; Various roles with Queensland Lyric Opera and Victoria State Opera; Season 1996 as Rocco in Fidelio, Zaccaria in Nabucco, Daland in Der fliegende Holländer, Sarastro in The Magic Flute in Sydney for the Australian Opera. Honours: OBE, 1976; AO, 1987. Address: c/o The Australian Opera, PO Box 291, Strawberry Hills, Sydney 2012, Australia.

SHAO En, b. 1954, Tianjin, China. Conductor. Education: Piano studies from age 4, violin from 5; Peking Centre Music Conservatory and Royal Northern College of Music. Career: Deputy Principal Conductor of the Chinese Broadcasting Symphony Orchestra and Principal Guest Conductor of the Central Philharmonic Orchestra of Ogina and the National Youth Orchestra; Engagements in Europe from 1988; Associate Conductor of the BBC Philharmonic Orchestra, 1990; Principal Conductor and Artistic Advisor of the Ulster Orchestra, 1993; Guest Appearances with the Bournemouth Symphony, Northern Sinfonia, Royal Liverpool Philharmonic and other BBC orchestras; London debut 1992 with the LSO; European engagements with the Oslo Philharmonic, the Berlin Symphony and the Czech Philharmonic; Prague Autumn Festival, 1993; Concerts with the ABC Orchestras in Australia and the Hong Kong Philharmonic; North American showings with the Toronto Symphony and the Colorado and Vancouver Symphonies; Royal Philharmonic Orchestra debut, 1994; Helsinki Philharmonic. Honours: Lord Rhodes Scholarship; First Edward Van Beinum Scholarship; Winner, Sixth Hungarian Television Conductors Competition. Hobbies: Chinese cooking; Interior design; Ballet; Jazz. Current Management: IMG Artists. Address: Media House, 3 Burlington Lane, London W4 2TH, England.

SHAPERO Harold (Samuel), b. 29 Apr 1920, Lynn, Massachusetts, USA. Pianist; Teacher; Composer. Education: Studied piano with Eleanor Kerr; Composition with Nicolas Slonimsky, Malkin Conservatory, Boston 1936-37; with Ernst Krenek, 1937, with Walter Piston, Harvard University, 1938-41; With Paul Hindemith, Berkshire Music Center, Tanglewood, summers 1940, 1941; Nadia Boulanger, Longy School of Music, 1942-43. Career: Pianist; Teacher 1952-, Founder-director, electronic music studio, Brandeis University. Compositions: Orchestral: 9-minuted Overture, 1940; Serenade, 1945; Symphony for Classical Orchestra, 1947; Sinfonia: The Travelers Overture, 1948; Concerto, 1950; Credo, 1955; Lyric Dances, 1955; On Green Mountain for Jazz Ensemble, 1957; for orchestra, 1981; Partita for Piano and Small Orchestra, 1960; Chamber: String Trio, 1938; 3 Pieces for Flute, Clarinet and Bassoon, 1939; Trumpet Sonata, 1940, String Quartet, 1941; Violin Sonata, 1942; 3 Improvisations for Piano and Synthesizer, 1968; 3 Studies for Piano and Synthesizer, 1969; 4 Pieces for Piano and Synthesizer, 1969; 4 Pieces for Piano and Synthesizer, 1970; Piano: Sonata for 4-hands, 1941; 3 sonatas, all 1944; Variations, 1947; Sonata, 1948; American Variations, 1950; Vocal: 4 Baritone Songs, 1942; 2 Psalms for Chorus, 1952; Hebrew Cantata for Soprano, Alto, Tenor, Baritone, Chorus and 5 Instruments, 1954; 2 Hebrew Songs for Tenor and Piano, 1970, also for Tenor, Piano and String Orchestra, 1980. Recordings: Several compositions recorded. Honours: American Prix de Rome, 1941; Naumburg Fellowship, 1942; Guggenheim Fellowships, 1947, 1948; Fulbright Fellowship, 1948. Address: c/o Music Department, Brandeis University, MA 02254, USA.

SHAPEY Ralph, b. 12 Mar 1921, Philadelphia, Pennsylvania, USA. Composer; Conductor; Professor. m. (1) Vera Shapiro, 28 Oct 1957, 1 son, (2) Elsa Charlaton, 12 Oct 1985. Education: Violin with Emanuel Zetlim; Composition with Stefan Wolpe. Career: Assistant Conductor, Philadelphia National Youth Administration Symphony Orchestra, 1938-47; Founder-Music Director, Contemporary Chamber Players, Chicago, 1954-; Teacher, University of Pennsylvania, 1963-64; Professor of Music, University of Chicago, 1964-85, 1986-; Distinguished Professor of Music, Aaron Copland School of Music, Queens College, City University of New York, 1985-86. Compositions include: Orchestral: Double Concerto, violin, cello, orchestra, 1983; Groton: 3 movements, youth orchestra, 1984; Symphonie Concertante, 1985; Concerto, piano, cello, strings, 1986; Concerto Fantastique, symphony orchestra (Chicago Symphony/University of Chicago commission), 1989; Chamber: String Quartet No 7, 1972, No 8 (Naumburg commission for Ying Quartet), 1993, No 9 (University of Wisconsin commission for Pro Arte Quartet), 1994-95; Evocation II, cello, piano, percussion, 1979, III, viola, piano, 1981, IV, violin, cello, piano, percussion, 1994; Krosnick Soli, cello, 1983; Mann Duo, violin, piano, 1983; Concertante, trumpet, 10 players, 1984, II, alto sax, 14 players, 1987; Kroslish Sonata, cello, piano, 1985; Soli, solo percussion, 1985; Intermezzo, dulceme, piano/celesta, 1990; Duo, 6 winds, 2 players, 1991; Movement of Varied Movements for Two, flute, vibraphone, 1991; Trio 1992, violin, cello, piano, 1992; Trio Concertant, violin, piano, percussion, 1992; Constellations, Bang on Can All-stars, 1993; Dinosaur Annex, violin, vibraphone, marimba/block, 1993; Rhapsody 1993, cello, piano, 1993; Vocal: Centennial Celebration, soprano, mezzo, tenor, baritone, 12 players, 1991; Piano pieces; Sonata Appassionata for Cello and Piano, 1995; Goethe Songs, for soprano and piano, 1995; Sonata Profondo for Piano, 1995; Stony Brook Concerto for woodwind, brass, 2 percussionists, violin, cello and piano, 1996; Discourse Encore for violin, cello, clarinet and piano, 1996; Interchange in Four Movements, for percussion quartet, 1996; In Ten-Two (Between Two), for percussion duo, 1997. Recordings: Several including Arabesque Recordings, forthcoming. Honours: Elected: American Academy of Arts and Letters, 1989; American Academy of Arts and Sciences, 1994; Paul Fromm Award, Service to Contemporary Music, 1993. Current Management: Presser Publications. Address: 5532 South Shore Drive No 18D, Chicago, IL 60637, USA.

SHAPIRO Joel, b. 28 Nov 1934, Cleveland, Ohio, USA. Concert Pianist; Teacher. Education: AB, Columbia College, New York City; Private study with Beryl Rubinstein and Frank Sheridan; Brussels Royal Conservatory with Stefan Askenase; Premier Prix avec Distinction, 1959. Debut: New York City, 1963; As a Soloist with Royal Philharmonic Orchestra, 1968. Career: Extensive annual concert tours including piano recitals, concertos and chamber music in the world's leading music centres; Numerous radio and television broadcasts; Professor of Piano, University of Illinois, 1970-93; Professor of Piano and Prorektor, Staatliche Hochschule für Musik, Leipzig, 1994-. Honours: Winner, Young Concert Artists International Auditions, New York City, 1961; 1st Prize, Darche Competition, Brussels, 1962; Harriet Cohen International Bach Award, London, 1963; Awards from The International Institute, 1964 and Rockefeller Foundation, 1965. Address: Hochschule Für Musik, Grassistrasse 8, 04107 Leipzig, Germany.

SHAPIRO Michael (Jeffrey), b. 1 Feb 1951, Brooklyn, New York, USA. Composer; Pianist. m. Theresa Vorgia, 14 Aug 1975, 3 s. Education: BA, Columbia College, New York City; MM, Juilliard School, New York City. Career: Musical Assistant, International Opera Center, Zurich Opera, 1973-74; Many appearances on New York radio stations WQXR and WNYC and CBC Vancouver, KUHF Houston and National Public Radio Stations. Compositions: Orchestral: Concerto for Guitar and Strings, Lamentations, A Declaration of Independence, July 4, 1776 for Narrator and Orchestra, Sinfonia Concertante for Violin, Cello and Strings, Symphony, Pomes Penyeach, Lyric Variations, Concerto for Piano and Orchestra; Opera: The Love of Don Perlimplin and Belisa in the Garden (Federico Garcia Lorca); Chamber Music: Sonata for Violin and Piano, Sonata for Clarinet and Piano, Kaddish for Solo Flute, Shir for Flute and Piano; Variations on the Passover hymn, Eliahu Hanavi for solo violoncello; Yiddish Quartet, for string quartet; Piano Music: Five Dance Preludes, Mysteries, Songs of the Jewish Ghetto, First Sonata, Second Sonata; Vocal Music: Three Early Songs, Canciones, Songs for American Poets, Dublin Songs, Erotic Songs, Child's Garden, Wordsworth Songs; Choral Music: Three Shakespeare Madrigals (SATB), Three Psalms (SSAA), There is That in Me (SATB), Psalm 137 (SATB, Organ), Eight Medieval Lyrics (SSATB). Publications: The Jewish 100: A Ranking of the Most Influential Jews of All Time, 1994; Jewish Pride: 101 Reasons to be Proud You're Jewish, 1997. Hobbies: Home Renovations; Summer Sports. Address: 974 Hardscrabble Road, Chappaqua, NY 10514, USA.

SHAPIRRA Elyakum, b. 1926, Tel-Aviv, Israel. Conductor. Education: Studied with Bernstein and Koussevitzky at Tanglewood and the Juilliard School. Career: Assistant with the San Francisco Symphony Orchestra; Conducted the New York Philharmonic on tours to Canada and Japan, 1960-61; Associate Conductor of the Boston Symphony Orchestra 1962-67; Guest conductor with leading orchestras in England (1968) and the United States; Chief Conductor of the Malmo Symphony Orchestra, Sweden, 1969-74; Chief Conductor of the South Australian Symphony Orchestra at Adelaide, 1975; Has conducted opera in Scandinavia. Recordings include: Bruckner's F minor Symphony and G minor Overture with the London Symphony Orchestra (EMI).

SHARNINA Ljubov, b. 1962, Moscow, Russia. Soprano. Education: Studied at the Gnessin Institute, Moscow. Career: Sang at the Nemirovitsch-Danschenko Theatre Moscow from 1986, notably as Tatiana, Lisa, Iolanta, Nedda, Lisa in La Battaglia di Legnano, Zemfira in Rachmaninov's Aleko and Imogene in Bellini's Pirata; Guest engagements as Aida at Birmingham and Manchester, Desdemona at Aachen in 1990, the Trovatore Leonora at Leipzig in 1991, and Maria in Tchaikovsky's Mazeppa at Amsterdam in 1991; Many concert appearances in Cologne, Vienna, St Petersburg and North America. Address: Bolshoi Theatre, 103009 Moscow, Russia.

SHARON Jaroslav, b. 22 July 1943. Pianist; Composer; Teacher. m. Bohumila, 1 son, 1 daughter. Education: Conservatory, Prague; AMU, Music High School, Prague. Debut: 1st Symphony, 1967. Career: Professor, Prague Conservatory, 1970-82; Pianist, Czech Philharmonic Orchestra, 1976-; Senior Lecturer, docent, Music High School, Prague, 1982-. Compositions: 2 Symphonies; Suite for Strings and Tympani; Illuminations for Small Orchestra; Sonatas, Piano, Alto, Trombone; Many Songs. Recordings: As Pianist, Martinu, Double Concerto for 2 String Orchestra, Piano and Tympani. Hobby: Bee Keeping. Address: 25229 Dobrichovice 291, Czech Republic.

SHARP Norma, b. 1945, Shawnee, OK, USA. Opera Singer (Soprano). m. Jens Niggemeyer, 1 son. Education: Kansas University, USA; Hochschule für Musik, Hamburg, Cologne. Career: 1970-77 Permanent Member of the Opera Houses of Regensburg, Augsburg, Karlsruhe as Lyric Soprano; Since 1978 Freelance Opera Singer, Regular Guest at Berlin, Hamburg, Munich, Frankfurt, Cologne, Düsseldorf, Vienna; Further Guest Appearances at Dresden, Hannover, Stuttgart, Amsterdam, Antwerp, Ghent, Zurich, Basel, Bern, Geneva, Milan, Rome, Naples, Madrid, London, Glasgow, Prague, Budapest; Festivals: Bayreuth 1977-81, Glyndebourne, Vienna; Concerts throughout Europe with conductors including Pierre Boulez, Carlo Maria Giulini, Marek Janowski, Neville Marriner, Wolfgang Sawallisch, Giuseppe Sinopoli, Horst Stein; Professor of Voice, Hochschule für Musik, Hanns Eisler, Berlin, 1992-. Recordings: Tales of Hoffmann; Peer Gynt; Ring of the Nibelung; Tannhäuser. Current Management: Marquerite Kollo, Berlin. Address: Seestr 119, D-13353 Berlin, Germany.

SHAULIS Jane, b. 1950, New Jersey, USA. Singer (Mezzo-Soprano). Education: Studies, Philadelphia Academy and Curtis Institute. Career: Appearances with New York City Opera, 1977-90; Metropolitan Opera, 1990-, Notably in the Premiers of The Ghosts of Versailles by Corigliano and The Voyage by Glass; Further New York Appearances in Idomeneo, Elektra, Die Zauberflöte, The Ring, I Lombardi, Arabella and Peter Grimes; Season 1996-97 as Mozart's Marcellina, Mdme. Larina in Eugene Onegin and Marthe in Faust; Glyndebourne, 1990-, as Nan in New Year by Tippett and Ragonde in Le Comte Ory, 1997; Other Roles include Amneris at Buffalo, Azucena and Herodias for Kentucky Opera and the Countess in Andrea Chenier at Chicago; Fricka, Erda and Waltraute in The Ring at Artpark. Address: c/o New York Metropolitan Opera, Lincoln Center, New York, NY 10023, USA.

SHAVE Jacqueline, b. 1960, England. Violinist. Career: Co-Founded the Brindisi String Quartet at Aldeburgh, 1984; Wigmore Hall Debut 1984, with Peter Pears; Concerts in a wide repertory throughout Britain and in France, Germany, Spain, Italy and Switzerland; Festival Engagements at Aldeburgh, Arundel, Bath, Brighton, Huddersfield, Norwich and Warwick; First London Performance of Colin Matthews 2nd Quartet, 1990; Quartet by Mark Anthony Turnage, 1992; Many BBC Recitals and Resident Artist with the University of Ulster. Recordings include: Quartets by Britten, Bridge and Imogen Holst; Works by Piemé and Lekeu. Honours include: Prize Winner at the Third Banff International String Quartet Competition. Address: c/o Owen/White Management, 14 Nightingale Lane, London N8 7QU, England.

SHAVERZASHVILI George, b. 4 Aug 1950, Tbilisi, Georgia. Composer; Pianist. Education: State Conservatory, Tbilisi, Piano, 1973, Composition, 1984. Debut: Piano, 1970, Composer, 1980, Tbilisi. Career: Concerts at Tbilisi, Moscow, St Petersburg, Tallin, Budapest, Bratislava; Professor, State Conservatory, Tbilisi. Compositions: Quintet for Piano and String Quartet; 3 Sonatas for Piano; 2 Concerts for Piano and Orchestra, 1984, 1991; 2 Concertos for Violin, 1990, 1995; Sonata for Violin. Honours: 2nd Prize, 1972, 1985. Membership: Georgian Composers Union, 1986. Address: Mosashvili Street 8, Ap 6, 380062 Tbilisi, Georgia.

SHAW John, b. 12 Oct 1924, Newcastle, New South Wales, Australia. Singer (Baritone). Education: Studied with Henri Portnoy in Melbourne. Career: Member of the (National Theatre Movement of Victoria) Opera Company, 1951-54; Sang 15 roles with the Italian Grand Opera Company on tour of Australia 1955; Appearances with National Theatre Movement of Victoria and the Elizabethan Opera, 1956-57; Covent Garden Opera (London), 1958-74, as Rigoletto, Scarpia, Amonasro, Macbeth, Di Luna, Posa, Ford, Gunther, Telramund, Marcello, Amfortas, Ramiro in L'Heure Espagnole and Tonio in Pagliacci; Guest appearances with Welsh National Opera, Netherlands Opera (1959, Gerard), Vienna Staatsoper, (1961, Tonio) and at the Holland Festival

(1962, Don Carlo in La Forza del Destino); Australian television 1963 as Simon Boccanegra (also in London); Sang Amonasro and Scarpia at San Francisco Los Angeles and guested further at the Edinburgh Festival, Philadelphia, Toulouse, Marseille, Bordeaux, Deutsche Oper Berlin (1968), Munich, Mannheim, Scottish Opera (1966-77), Das Rheingold, Wotan, Naples, 1978; Amfortas in Parsifal, 1988; Montreal, Brussels, Geneva and Santa Fe; Aldeburgh Festival, in the premiere of The Bear, by Walton; Sang Ruprecht in the 1965 London premiere of Prokofiev's The Fiery Angel (New Opera Company) and appeared at the opening of the Sydney Opera House, 1973, in War and Peace; Sang with Australian Opera until 1989 (last role as Jack Rance); Gave 355th performance as Scarpia at Opera-in-the-Park, Adelaide, 1990. Recordings include: The Bear, and Patience (HMV). Honour: OBE, 1977, AO, 1986, Joan Hammond Opera Award, 1990. Address: c/o Sydney Opera House, Syndey, New South Wales, Australia.

SHAW Robert (Lawson), b. 30 Apr 1916, Red Bluff, CA, USA. Conductor. Education: Studied at Pomona College, Claremont, California, 1934-38. Career: Conducted Fred Waring Glee Club, 1938-45; Founded and Conducted the Collegiate Chorale in New York's 1941-54, Commissioning and Premiering Hindemith's Walt Whitman Requiem, 1946; Debut as Symphonic Conductor with the Naumburg Orchestra New York, 1946; Prepared the Chorus for Toscanini's NBC concerts and directed the Choral Departments of the Juilliard School and the Berkshire Music Center, 1946-48; Founded and Conducted the Robert Shaw Chorale, 1948-67; Conducted the San Diego Symphony, 1953-58 and was Associate Conductor to Szell at the Cleveland Orchestra, 1956-57; Music Director of the Atlanta Symphony, 1967-88; Music Director Emeritus and Conductor Laureate of the Atlanta SO, 1988. Recordings: Many albums with the Robert Shaw Chorale. Address: c/o Atlanta Symphony Orchestra, 1293 Peachtree Street North East, Suite 300, Atlanta, GA 30309, USA.

SHAW Teresa, b. 1965, England. Singer (Mezzo-soprano). Education: Studied at the Royal Academy of Music. Career: Concert appearances in Debussy's Le Martyre de Saint Sebastien with the London Philharmonic under Kurt Masur; Vivaldi's Gloria with Richard Hickox; Handel's Dixit Dominus and Haydn's Nelson Mass conducted by David Willcocks; The Dream of Gerontius at the York and Ripon Festival, 1991; The Apostles and the Glagolitic Mass at Canterbury; Operatic roles include Octavian, Third Lady in Die Zauberflöte, Dorabella (Opera Factory) and Female Chorus in Goehr's Triptych; Season 1991 included Purcell Room, Conway Hall and Wigmore Hall recitals; Premiere production of The Death of Klinghoffer by John Adams in Lyon and Vienna; Season 1992 in title role of Oliver's Beauty and the Beast, at Portsmouth; Season 1996 as the Composer in Ariadne auf Naxos for Castleward Opera. Recordings include: Sorceress in Dido and Aeneas and Brahms Liebesliederwalzer, conducted by John Eliot Gardiner. Honours: Winner, Great Grimsby International Singing Competition, 1989. Address: c/o Opera Factory, 8a The Leather Market, Weston Street, London SE1 3ER, England.

SHEBANOVA Tatiana, b. 12 Jan 1953, Moscow, USSR. Musician (Pianist). m. 18 Sept 1986, 1 son. Education: Undergraduate and Postgraduate Studies, Main Music School, Moscow Conservatory. Career: Represented Moscow Conservatory, various International competitions and meetings; Live concert performances include appearances in Czechoslovakia, Belgium, France, Germany, Switzerland, Italy, Netherlands, Greece, Portugal, Austria and many tours: Japan, Philippines, Yugoslavia, Poland, Spain; Repertoire includes about 30 recitals, about 30 piano concertos; 1st interpretation of Bach's 12 choral preludes in Feinberg's transcription, Moscow Conservatory; Currently teaching, Warsaw and Bygdoszoz Academies of Music, Poland. Recordings: Works by Tchaikovsky, Chopin (many), Szymanowski, Rachmaninov, Bach, Debussy, Brahms, on LPs and CDs for Panton, Victor, CBS-Sony, Pony Canyon, Muza PN, Melodia. Current Management: Artistic Elite, Poland. Address: Artistic Agency Elite, Aleja Ossolinskich 11, 85-903 Bydgoszcz, Poland.

SHEFFIELD Philip, b. 1960, Kenya. Singer (Tenor). Education: Studied at Cambridge University, Guildhall School and Royal College of Music; Further Study with Philip Langridge and Malcolm King. Career: Season 1989-90 in L'Incoronazione di Popea at Brussels, Hans Jurgen von Böse's 63: Dream Palace at Munich and Capriccio at Glyndebourne; Cavalli's Egisto for the Berlin Kammeroper, Scaramuccio at Antwerp and the Count in Die Tote Stadt in Holland; Other Repertoire Encludes Mozart's Ferrando and Tamino, and Agenore in Il Re Pastore; Lensky, Tamino, and Belmonte for Lucerne Opera; Recent Concert performances include Britten's Nocturne with the Berlin Symphony Orchestra in the Philharmonie, and again in Montepulciano, Haydn's L'isola disabitata in the Vienna Konzerthaus with Heinz Holliger, Alexander Goehr's Eve Dreams in Paradise with the BBC Philharmonic, Henze's Kammermusik 1958 in Amsterdam, Schreker's Der Schatzgraeber for the Dutch Radio Philharmonic Orchestra in the Amsterdam Concertgebouw,

Stravinsky's Renard with the Ensemble Modern in Frankfurt, Berlin and Vienna, Bach's St John Passion (Evangelist) with the North Netherlands Orchestra, Berio's Sinfonia in Leningrad and The Messiah in Antwerp with the Royal Flanders Philharmonic; Also many appearances throughout the UK including Monteverdi's Orfeo at the Proms, Poppea in the QEH and Bach's B Minor Mass in Canterbury, all with Roger Norrington; Sang at the Proms again The Seven Deadly Sins with the London Sinfonietta conducted by Lothar Zagrosek, since repeated at the Barbican Centre with the LSO and the Queen Elizabeth Hall with the Philharmonia; Recent operatic performances include Ferrando in Così fan tutte; Shere Khan and Harry in Baa Baa Black Sheep; Chevalier in Der Ferne Klang; Belmonte in Die Entführung; Tamino in Die Zauberflöte; Lensky in Eugene Onegin; Leading role in 63 Dream Palace; Bardolfo in Falstaff; Scaramuccio in Ariadne auf Naxos; Albert in Albert Herring and Male Chorus in The Rape of Lucretia; Sang Theseus in Goehr's Arianna at Cambridge, 1996. Recordings include: Berio's Sinfonia with Pierre Boulez; Baa Baa Black Sheep for BBC and Radio with CD to follow; Tippett's Midsummer Marriage for Thames TV and 63 Dream Palace for Bayerischer Rundfunk. Current Management: Andrew Rosner, Allied Artists. Address: c/o Anglo Swiss Ltd, Ste 35-37 Morley House, 32c Regent Street, London W1R 5AD, England.

SHELLEY Howard, b. 9 Mar 1950, London, England. Concert Pianist; Conductor. m. Hilary Macnamara, 1975, 1 s, 1 stepson. Education: Highgate School Music Scholar; Royal College of Music Foundation Scholar with Harold Craxton, Kendall Taylor, Lamar Crowson and Ilona Kabos; ARCM, Honours, 1966, ARCO, 1967. Career: First TV appearance at age 10 playing Bach and Chopin; Adult debut, Wigmore Hall, London, 1971; Televised Henry Wood Prom debut 1972; 2 Piano partnership with Hilary Macnamara, 1976-; International solo pianist; Conducting debut, 1985 with London Symphony Orchestra, Barbican Hall, London; Performed world's first cycle of complete solo piano works of Rachmaninov, Wigmore Hall, 1983; Edward Cowie, Brian Chapple and Peter Dickinson have written concertos for him; Principal Guest Conductor of the London Mozart Players, 1992-. Recordings: Complete solo piano works of Rachmaninov; Mozart Piano Concertos 21 and 24, also conducting; Chopin Recital; Concertos by Howard Ferguson and Peter Dickinson; Schubert Sonatas; Complete Concertos and 2 Piano Works by Rachmaninov; Schumann Recital; Gershwin: Piano Concerto, Rhapsody in Blue, Second Rhapsody; Hindemith's Four Temperaments; Alwyn's Piano Concerto Nos 1 and 2; Mendelssohn's Piano Concertos; Mozart's Piano Concerto Cycle: Volumes 1-5; Chopin's Scherzi; Vaughan Williams's Piano Concerto; Tippett's Piano Concerto. Honours: Chappell Gold Medal and Peter Morrison Prize, 1968; Dannreuther Concerto Prize, 1971; Silver Medal, Worshipful Company of Musicians, 1971; Honorary FRCM, 1993. Current Management: Intermusica, 16 Duncan Terrace, London, N1 8BZ. Address: 38 Cholmeley Park, London, N6 5ER, England.

SHELTON Lucy, b. 22 Feb 1954, Pomona, California, USA. Singer (Soprano). Education: Studied at Pomona College and the New England Conservatory. Career: Has performed as recitalist, soloist with orchestra and performer in opera from 1980; Sang Jenifer in Thames TV's production of Tippett's Midsummer Marriage, Jan 1989; Other operatic roles have been Euridice in Gluck's Orfeo, Salud in La Vida Breve and appearances in Deallapiccola's Il Prigioniero, Mozart's Zaide, Milhaud's Médée and John Corigliano's The Ghost of Versailles; Concert appearances throughout the US and Europe; Repertoire includes music of all periods, from Monteverdi and Bach to Boulez, and Schoenberg (Erwartung) and many first performances of works written specially for her by such composers as Carter, Goehr, Knussen, Maw and Schwantner; Has taught at the Eastman School of Music and the Cleveland Institute of Music. Honours include: Walter W Naumburg Competition (as member of the Jubal Trio) and in 1980 as winner of the International Solo Vocal Competition; National Endowment for the Arts Award. Address: c/o Ingpen and Williams Ltd, 26 Wadham Road, London SW15 2LR, England.

SHEN Bright, b. 6 December 1955, Shanghai, China. Composer. Education: Shanghai Conservatory, 1976-; Queens College, City University of New York & Columbia University, 1982-, with Chou-Wen Chung, Mario Davidovsky, George Perle & Hugo Weisgall. Career: Freelance Composer with Many Performances Throughout the USA; Commissions from Peer Serkin & Gerard Schwarz; Opera, The Song of Majnun, with Libretto by Andrew Porter, Written for the Chicago Lyric Opera, 1992 (former Composer-in-Residence); Resident, Seattle Symphony Orchestra, 1992-94. Compositions: Three Pieces, for Orchestra, 1982; Trio, for Flute, Harp & Cello, 1982; Five Pieces, for Oboe & Cello, 1983; 2 String Quartets, 1984; Suite for Piano, 1984; Four Poems From the Tang Dynasty, for Mezzo & Piano, 1984; Adagio, for Chamber Orchestra, 1987; Three Poems From the Sung Dynasty, for Soprano & Chamber Orchestra, 1987; H'UN (Lacerations): In Memoriam, 1966-76, for Orchestra, 1987; Three Pieces for Viola & Piano, 1987; MY SONG, for Piano, 1988; Three Chinese Love Songs, for Soprano, Viola & Piano,

1988; Three Chinhai Folk Songs, for Chorus, 1989; Four Movements, for Piano Trio, 1990; The Song of Majnun, Opera, 1992; Prelude, for Orchestra, 1994. Address: c/o ASCAP, ASCAP Building, One Lincoln Plaza, NY 10023, USA.

SHEPPARD Craig, b. 26 November 1947, Philadelphia, USA. Concert Pianist. Education: Studied at the Curtis Institute of Music and the Juilliard School of Music. Career: Senior Artist-in-Residence, University of Washington, Seattle; Teacher, Yehudi Menuhin School, Surrey, 1978-88; Teacher, University of Lancaster, 1979-81; Teacher, Guildhall School of Music and Drama, 1981-86; Concert Experience as Soloist in most American aand all the major British, German and Italian Orchestras; Conductors have included Georg Solti, James Levine, Leonard Slatkin, Michael Tilson Thomas, Pritchard, Neeme Järvi and Charles Mackerras; TV Appearances on PBS America and BBC England. Recordings: EMI, Liszt and Rachmaninoff; Polygram, Rossini; Sony, Jolivet. Honours: Arthur Rubinstein Prize; Silver Medal, Leeds International Pianoforte Competition; Dealey Award; Young Musicians Foundation of Los Angeles 1st Prize. Address: c/o School of Music, University of Washington, Seattle, WA 98195-3450, USA.

SHEPPARD Honor, b. 1931, Leeds, Yorkshire, England. Singer (Soprano). m. Robert Elliott, 1 son, 1 daughter. Education: Studied with Elsie Thurston and others at the Royal Manchester College of Music; FRMCM. Career: Recitalist and Oratorio singer; Appearances at major British and European Festivals; First Soprano with the Deller Consort, specialising in 17th and 18th Century Music; Extensive tours of North and South America, Canada and Europe from 1961; Many broadcasts; Tutor in vocal Studies at the Royal Manchester College of Music, since 1987. Recordings include: Belinda in Dido and Aeneas, conducted by Alfred Deller; The Fairy Queen, The Indian Queen and King Arthur; Handel's Acis and Galatea. Honours include: Curtis Gold Medal, Royal Manchester College of Music. Hobby: Gardening. Address: The Firs, 27 The Firs, Bowdon, Cheshire WA14 2TF, England.

SHEPPARD Peter, b. 1965, England. Violinist. Education: Studied at the Royal Academy with Sidney Griller and Erich Gruenberg, and in Boston with Louis Krasner. Career: Played Henze's 2nd Concerto at London's Barbican in 1991 and has performed works by Judith Weir, Dmitri Smirnov and David Matthews; Further concerts at the Wigmore Hall, Tokyo's Suntory Hall, in Istanbul and throughout Spain; Duo partnership with pianist, Aaron Shorr in works by Satie, Ustvolskaya, Berg and Bartók; Principal Lecturer at the Royal Academy of Music from 1993 and leader of the Kreutzer Quartet. Address: Manygate Management, 13 Cotswold Mews, 30 Battersea Square, London, SW11 3RA, England.

SHERE Charles, b. 20 Aug 1935, Berkeley, California, USA. Composer; Writer on Music. m. Lindsay Remolif Shere. Education: Graduated, University of California at Berkeley, 1960 and studied music at the San Francisco Conservatory. Career: Music Director at California radio stations, 1964-73; Instructor at Mills College, Oakland, 1973-84 and Critic for the Oakland Tribune, 1972-88. Compositions include: Fratture for 7 instruments, 1962; Small Concerto for piano and orchestra, 1964; Ces desirs du vent des Greogoriens for tape, 1967; Nightmusic for diminished orchestra, 1967; Handler of Gravity for organ and optional chimes, 1971; Music for Orchestra (Symphony), 1976; Tongues for poet, chamber orchestra and tape, 1978; String QuartetNo 1, 1980; The Bride Stripped Bare by Her Bachelors, Even, opera, 1981 and 1984; Certain Phenomena of Sound for soprano and violin, 1983; Concerto for Violin with Harp, Percussion and Small Orchestra, 1985; Requiem with oboe, 1985; Ladies Voice, chamber opera, 1987; Symphony in 3 Movements, 1988; I Like it to be a Play for tenor baritone, bass and string quartet, 1989; Sonata: Bachelor Machine for piano, 1989; What Happened, chamber opera after Gertrude Stein (triology with Ladies Voices and I Like it to be a Play). Contributions to: EAR (monthly new-music magazinee), which he co-founded and published. Address: c/o ASCAP, ASCAP Building, One Lincoln Plaza, New York, NY 10023, USA.

SHERLAW-JOHNSON Robert, b. 21 May 1932, Sunderland, County Durham, England. Musician. m. Rachael Marie Clarke, 28 July 1959, 3 sons, 2 daughters. Education: Associate, Piano Performance, Royal College of Music, 1950; Licentiate, Piano Teaching, 1952, Honorary Fellow, 1984, Royal Academy of Music; BA, Honours, Music, 1953, BMus, 1959, university of Durham; MA, Oxford, 1971; DMus, Leeds; DMus, Oxford, 1990; Studied with Nadia Boulanger, Olivier Messiaen and Jacques Février, Paris, France. Career: Assistant Lecturer in Music, University of Leeds, 1961-63; Director of Music, Bradford Girl's Grammar School, 1963-65; Lecturer in Music, Univerity of York, 1965-70; University Lecturer in Music, Oxford University and Fellow, Worcester College, Oxford University, 1970-. Compositions include: 3 Sonatas for Piano; 2 String Quartets; Quintet; Seven Short Pieces for piano; Asterogenesis for piano; Piano Concerto; Carmina Vernalia, soprano and chamber orchestra; Triptych, chamber ensemble; Sonata for Flute and Cello; Anglorum Feriae, choir and chamber orchestra; The Lambton Worm, opera; Projections, chamber ensemble; Sinfonietta Concertante; Solo Contata: Hymn to the Seasons; Nocturn for 2 pianos, 1992; Various choral works and song cycles and pieces for voice and tape. Recordings include: All 3 piano sonatas; Piano Music by Liszt. Publications include: Messiaen, 1974, 1989. Contributions to: Various chapters in books; Composing with Fractals, in Mathematics and Music. Honours: Charles W Black Award, 1957; Radcliffe Award for Composition, 1969. Memberships: Vice Chairman, 1979-81, Composers Guild of Great Britain; Association of University Teachers. Address: Malton Croft, Woodsland Rise, Stonesfield, Oxon OX8 8PL, England.

SHICOFF Neil, b. 2 June 1949, New York, USA. Singer (Tenor). m. Judith Haddon. Education: Studied with his father at a NY synagogue; Juilliard School with Jennie Tourel. Debut: 1975 Kennedy Center Washington as Narraboth in Salome; Metropolitan Opera 1976- as Rinuccio in Gianni Schicchi, Verdi's Duke of Mantua, Tchaikovsky's Lensky, Massenet's Werther, Offenbach's Hoffmann and Massenet's Des Grieux; European career from 1976; Don Carlos in Amsterdam, Alfredo and Cilea's Maurizio at the Munich Opera; Macduff in a BBC version of Macbeth and the Duke of Mantua at Covent Garden 1988; At La Scala he has sung Lensky and at the Paris Opéra Don Carlos; Gounod's Romeo for French TV; Chicago Lyric Opera debut 1979; San Francisco 1981; Sang Cavaradossi at Stuttgart, 1990; Debut at Barcelona as Hoffmann, 1990; Returned to Covent Garden, 1993 as Pinkerton; Don José at the Opéra Bastille, Paris, 1997. Recordings: Macduff and the Duke of Mantua for Philips; Foresto in Attila, conducted by Muti (EMI). Address: c/o Harrison/Parrott Ltd, 12 Penzance Place, London W11 4PA, England.

SHIFRIN Ken(neth Allen), b. 25 August 1952, Washington, District of Columbia, USA. Soloist; Recitalist; Tenor Trombone; Alto Trombone; Tenor Tubist; Bass Trumpeter; Music Publisher. Education: BA summa cum laude, Music and Political Science, Duke University, Durham, North Carolina, 1974; PhD candidate in Music, Oxford University, England, 1994-. Debuts: US premiere of Leopold Mozart Konzert für Posaune, 1974; World premiere of D to A for Ken Shifrin and Digital Analogue by David Maves. Career: Associate Principal Trombone, Israel Philharmonic, 1976-77; Co-Solo Trombone, Radio Sinfonie Stuttgart, 1977-78; Principal Trombone, Israel Radio Symphony, 1978-92; Principal Trombone, City of Birmingham Symphony Orchestra, 1982-95; Publisher, Director, Virgo Music, 1987-. Recordings: Featured in City of Birmingham Symphony Orchestra's recordings of Ravel's Bolero and Sibelius Symphony No 7 with Simon Rattle. Publications: Editor and compiler: Orchestral Excerpts for Alto Trombone, 1987; British Orchestra Excerpts for Trombone and Tuba, 1987; Orchestral Excerpts for Tenor Tuba and Bass Trumpet, 1995; Editor: Wolfgang Amadeus Mozart's Jener Donnerworte Kraft (for performance), 1988; Solo Baroque Trombone, vols 1 and 2, 1989; Baroque Trombone in Sonata, 1989. Honours: Phi Beta Kappa, 1973. Hobbies: Long-distance running; Ancient history. Address: 47 Colebank Road, Hall Green, Birmingham B28 8EZ, England.

SHIH Patricia, b. 1971, Canada. Concert Violinist. Education: Studied in Vancouver and with Josef Gingold at Indiana University. Career: Season 1987 with recitals in Warsaw and at the Carnegie Hall, New York; Many appearances with leading orchestras in the USA and Europe; Prokofiev's 2nd Concerto with the Toronto SO, 1994. Honours include: Prize Winner at Seattle Young Artists Festival, 1985 and Wieniawski Competition, Warsaw, 1986. Address: c/o Worldwide Artists, 6 Petersfield Crescent, Coulsdon, Surrey CR5 2JQ, England.

SHILAKADZE Shavleg, b. 21 Feb 1940, Tbilisi, Georgia. Composer; Conductor. m. Liana Shilakadze, 25 Jan 1964, 2 sons, 1 daughter. Education: Z Paliashvili Special Music School; Viola and Composition at V Saradjishvili Conservatoire, Tbilisi; Conducting at Rimsky-Korsakov State Conservatoire, Leningrad. Debuts: Composition, Tbilisi, 1959; Conducting, Tbilisi, 1967. Career: Founder, Ensemble Camerata Tbilissi; Concerts: Tbilisi, Moscow, Leningrad, Kiev, Minsk, Tallinn, Vilnius and elsewhere, 1978-85; Founder, Art Director, chamber orchestra Concertino Tbilissi, 1988-; Concerts: Tbilisi, Germany, 1990, 1991, 1993, 1995, 1996, Spain, Mar, Oct-Nov, 1993, Switzerland, 1996; Professor, Tbilisi Conservatoire. Compositions include: Sonata for viola and piano; Epitaph, chamber symphony; From Ancient Georgian Poetry, cantata; Concerto for oboe and chamber orchestra; 2 symphonies; Pages of Love, cantata; Concerto for bassoon and chamber orchestra; Concerto giocoso for 3 trumpets and percussion. Recordings: R Gabitchvadze's Chamber Symphony No 4, 1980; G Djaraidze's Chamber Symphony, 1983; Sh Shilakadze's Epitaph, 1983; Camerata Tbilissi, conductor Sh Shilakadze. Publications: Articles: About Tbilisi's musical life, 1982; The unity of creative forces, 1984. Membership: Union of Georgian Composers. Hobbies: Music; Art; Nature. Address: 20 T Tabidze st, 380079 Tbilisi, Georgia.

SHILLING Eric, b. 12 Oct 1920, London, England. Singer. m. Erica Johns, 2 children. Education: Guildhall School of Music; Royal College of Music; Further study with Walter Hyde and Frank Titterton in London. Debut: Sadler's Wells, 1945 as Marullo in Rigoletto. Career: In Operas by Smetana, Wagner, Mozart, Donizetti, Rossini and Janacek; Television apearances in Die Fledermaus, Orpheus in the Underworld, The Visitation, Trial by Jury and A Tale of Two Cities; Sang in the British Stage premiere of Prokofiev's War and Peace, London Coliseum, 1972; Further appearances in operas by Wagner, Mozart, Donizetti, Rossini, Puccini, Strauss, Prokofiev, Penderecki and Reimann; Premieres, Story of Vasco by Crosse and Clarissa by Holloway; Somarone in a new production of Beatrice and Benedict. Recordings: Has recorded for Argo, Saga, L'Orisea, Lyre, HMV, Pye, Supraphon and Charisma Labels. Honours: Opera Prize, Royal College of Music; ARCM, 1946; Worshipful Company of Musicians, Sir Charles Santley Memorial Prize, 1991. Memberships: ISM; Council Equity. Hobby: Motoring. Address: 49 Belgrave Road, Wanstead, London E11 3QP, England.

SHIMELL William, b. 23 Sept 1952, Ilford, Essex, England. Singer (Baritone). Education: Guildhall School of Music with Ellis Keeler; National Opera Studio until 1979; Debut: English National Opera 1980, as Masetto: later sang Schaunard in La Bohème, Mercutio in Romeo and Juliet, Papageno and Don Giovanni; Opera North in Le nozze di Figaro, The Cunning Little Vixen and The Rake's Progress; Scottish Opera in Cavalli's L'Egisto; Kent Opera as Guglielmo in Così fan tutte; Glyndebourne from 1983, in Cenerentola and Figaro; Welsh National Opera debut 1984, as Don Giovanni; Geneva, Vienna Staatsoper and La Scala Milan as Figaro; Paris Opera in La Gazza Ladra; San Francisco Opera as Nick Shadow; Covent Garden debut as Guglielmo, 1988; Concert appearances on South Bank and elsewhere in Britain; London Promenade Concerts 1989, as Figaro; Sang Malatesta in Don Pasquele at Amsterdam and Covent Garden, 1990; Capriccio San Francisco, 1990; Capriccio, Covent Garden, 1991; Lodoiska, La Scala, 1991; Ravenna Festival, Lodoiska, La Muette di Portici (Auber), 1991; Cosi, Covent Garden and on tour to Japan, 1992; Raimbaud in Le Comte Ory for Netherlands Opera, Marcello in London; TV engagements in L'Enfance du Christ and Mozart series with Jane Glover; Title role, Don Giovanni, Zurich Opera, 1992 and 1993; Sang in The Rake's Progress at the Festival Hall, 1997. Recordings include: Cherubini's Lodoiska, conducted by Muti; Title role: Don Giovanni, (EMI), Riccardo Muti, Vienna Philharmonic, Bach B minor Mass, Solti, Chicago Symphony. Current Management: IMG Artists, Europe. Address: c/o IMG Artists, Europe, Media House, 3 Burlington Lane, Chiswick W4 2TH, England.

SHIMIZU Takashi, b. 13 Jan 1953, Yokosuka, Japan. Violinist. m. Harue Shimizu, 18 Aug 1973, 1 son. Education: Yokosuka High School; University of Southern California, USA; Guildhall School of Music, London, England. Debut: Tokyo. Career: Performed with the Royal Philharmonic Orchestra, BBC Philharmonic Orchestra, London Mozart Players, City of Birmingham Symphony Orchestra, The Hague Philharmonic; Many TV appearances in France, Belgium, Spain, USSR and Japan. Recordings: For Adams, Japan; Polydor, Belgium; Fontec. Honours: Bronze Medal, Queen Elizabeth Competition; 2nd Prize and Beethoven Sonata Prize, Carl Flesch Competition; 1st Prize, Granada International Competition. Current Management: John Wright. Hobby: Collecting Austrian Jugendstil. Address: 18 Alyth Garden, London NW11, England.

SHIRAI Mitsuko, b. 1952, Japan. Singer (Contralto). Education: Studied in Stuttgart. Career: Appearances in Europe, Israel, Japan and USA; Recitals with piano accompanist Hartmut Holl and concerts with the Berlin Philharmonic, New Japan Philharmonic, Atlanta Symphony, Nouvel Orchestre Philharmonique de Paris and the Vienna Symphony; Conductors include Chailly, Inbal, Ahronovitch, Ferencic and Sawallisch; Repertoire includes Mahler Symphony No 8, Berlioz Les Nuits d'Été, Berg 7 Early Songs, Hindemith Das Marienleben, Complete vocal works of Webern, Schubert Winterreise and Lieder by Brahms, Wolf and Schumann; Concert performances of Mozart's Lucio Silla, Wagner's Das Liebesverbot and Ariane et Barbe-Bleue; Opened Suntory Hall Tokyo with Alexander Nevsky by Prokofiev; Stage debut Frankfurt 1987, as Despina in Così fan tutte; Master Classes with Hartmut Holl at the Savonlinna Festival, Schleswig-Holstein Festival, Aldeburgh Festival, in Switzerland and USA and at Isaac Stern's Music Centre in Jerusalem. Recordings: Mozart, Schumann and Brahms Lieder (Capriccio); Bach, Mozart and Spohr Lieder (Eurodisc); Sacred music by Mozart (Philips); Frauenliebe und-leben by Schumann; Lieder by Mendelssohn and Schumann (EMI). Honours: Winner of Competitions in Vienna, s-Hertogenbosch, Athens and Munich; Winner, Robert Schumann Prize, Zwickau, 1982. Address: c/o Städtische Bühnen, Untermainanalage 11, D-6000 Frankfurt am Main, Germany.

SHIRLEY George (Irving), b. 18 Apr 1934, Indianapolis, IN, USA. Opera Singer (Opera and Concert). m. Gladys Ishop, 24 June 1956, 1 son, 1 daughter. Education: BS, Education, Wayne State University, Detroit, Michigan, 1955. Debut: Turnau Opera Players, Woodstock, New York, 1955 (Eisenstein in Die Fledermaus). Career: Appearances: Teatro Nuovo, Milan, Italy; Teatro Della Pergola, Florence, Italy, 1960; New York City Opera, Metropolitan Opera, Santa Fe Opera, 1961; Opera Society of Washington, 1962; Teatro Colon, Buenos Aires, 1964; La Scala, Milan, 1965; Glyndebourne Festival, Sussex, England, 1966; Scottish Opera, Royal Opera, Covent Garden, 1967; Netherlands Opera, 1975; L'Opéra de Monte Carlo, 1976; San Francisco Opera, Chicago Lyric Opera, 1977; Deutsche Opera, Germany, 1983; Roles include Puccini's Rodolfo, Mozart's Ferrando, Tamino, Don Ottavio and Idomeneo, Debussy's Pelléas, Wagner's Loge and David and Donizetti's Lord Percy; Additional Festivals: Guelph, Ottawa (Canada), Berkshire, Ravinia, Saratoga Spoleto (USA and Italy), Edinburgh; Orchestras include: New York Philharmonic, Chicago, Detroit and Los Angeles Symphonies; Philadelphia Orchestra and several others; Sang Herod in Salome at Detroit, 1996. Recordings: Many recordings of Stravinsky, Mozart, Haydn; Cosi fan tutte; Pelléas et Mélisande, Oedipus Rex and Renard; Orlando Paladino and Idomeneo. Contributor to: Opera News; The Black Performer. Honours: HDH, Wilberforce University, Ohio, 1967; LLD, Montclair State College, New Jersey, 1984; First Prize, Metropolitan Opera Auditions, 1961; Distinguished Scholar-Teacher, University of Maryland, College Park, 1985-86. Memberships: National Association of Negro Musicians. Hobbies: Drawing cartoons; Tennis. Current Management: Ann Summers International. Address: c/o Ann Summers International, Box 188, Station A, Toronto, Ontario M5W 1B2, Canada.

SHIRLEY-QUIRK John, b. 28 August 1931, Liverpool, England. Concert and Opera Singer. m. Sara Van Horn Watkins, 29 December 1981, 2 sons, 3 daughters. Education: BSc, Diploma in Education, Liverpool University; Studied singing with Austen Carnegie and Roy Henderson. Career: Created roles in all Britten operas since Curlew River, notable Mr Coyle, Owen Wingrave and Traveller, Death in Venice (TV and Covent Garden, Metropolitan Opera, New York, USA); Performances with Scottish Opera and all major orchestras throughout Europe and America; Created role of Lev in The Ice Break by Tippett; Sang Folk songs by Britten at the 1991 Aldeburgh Festival; Narrator in Hans Krása's Verlobung im Traum at Washington, 1996; Sang in Vaughan Williams Five Tudor Portraits, with the LSO at the Barbican, 1997. Recordings: Numerous recordings of English songs, Lieder and especially of Britten's works for Decca; Messiah, A Child of Our Time, Die Jahreszeiten, Bach B minor Mass, Dido and Aeneas; A Village Romeo and Juliet, The Kingdom, The Pilgrim's Progress, Beethoven's Ninth. Membership: ISM. Honours: Hon RAM, 1973; CBE, 1975; Mus Doc (HC), Liverpool, 1976; D.Univ. Brunel, 1981. Hobbies: Canals; Clocks; Pottering. Current Management: Herbert Barrett, 1776 Broadway, Suite 1610, New York, NY 10019, USA. Address: 6062 Red Clover Lane, Clarksville, MD 21029-1272, USA.

SHKOSA Enkelejda, b. 29 September 1969, Tirana, Albania. Singer (Mezzo-soprano). Education: Studied at the State Conservatory, the Academy of Fine Arts, Tirana; Giuseppe Verdi Conservatory, Milan. Career: Many appearances at La Scala, Milan, Naples, Turin, Barbican Centre London (under Colin Davis), Strasbourg Cathedral (Pergolesi Stabat Mater) and the Rossini Festival, Pesaro; Season 1997-98 with Maddalena at the Opéra Bastille, Paris, Stockholm, Amsterdam, Bologna, Monte Carlo and Brussels. Honours include: Winner, Leyla Gencer Competition, Istanbul, 1995. Address: c/o Pentagramma, Via Bicetti De' Buttinoni 1, 20156 Milan, Italy.

SHMITOV Alexei, b. 1957, Moscow, Russia. Concert Organist; Pianist. Education: Studied at the Moscow Conservatoire, with Roisman and Nikolayeva. Career: Many concerts in Russia as organist and pianist; Piano concertos by Bach in Vilnius, Lithuania, and the Sonatas for Violin and Harpsichord and Violin with Viktor Pikaisen; Organ recitals in: Lithuania; Estonia; Latvia; Bach Festival in West Berlin; Recitals with the tenor Alexei Martynov in music by Bach, Handel, Scheidt, Schütz, Mendelssohn, Schumann and Verdi; Recitals at the Prokofiev Centenary Festival in Scotland, 1991; Organ Repertoire includes works by Bach, Widor, Taneyev, Liszt and Shostakovich. Honours include: 2nd Prize, Organ Competition in Dom Zu Speyer, Germany. Address: c/o Sonata, 11 Northpark Street, Glasgow, G20 7AA, Scotland.

SHOKOV Vladimir, b. 1950, Crimea, Russia. Cellist. Career: Co-founder, Rachmaninov Quartet, 1974, under auspices of the Sochi State Philharmonic Society, Crimea; Many concerts in Russia, and from season, 1975-76, tours to: Switzerland; Austria; Bulgaria; Norway; Germany; Participation in the 1976 Shostakovich Chamber Music Festival at Vilnius, and in festivals in Moscow and St Petersburg; Repertoire has included works by: Haydn, Mozart, Beethoven, Bartók, Brahms, Schnittke, Shostakovich, Tchaikovsky and Meyerovich. Honours include: Prizewinner at the first All Union Borodin String Quartet Competition. Address: c/o Sonata, 11 Northpark Street, Glasgow, G20 7AA, Scotland.

SHOOKHOFF William S, b. 9 May 1948, Brooklyn, New York, USA. Conductor; Composer; Pianist. m. Johanna Quartel, 17 May 1985, 1 daughter. Education: BMus, Distinction, Eastman School of Music, 1970. Career: Coach, University of Toronto Opera School, 1970-72; Assistant Conductor, Portland Opera Association, Oregon, USA, 1973-75; Associate Conductor, Canadian Opera Touring Company, 1975-77; Music Staff, Netherlands Opera, 1977-79; Music Director, Edmonton Opera (Canada), 1981-83, Grant McEwan Theatre Arts, Edmonton 1983-, Workshop West Theatre; Artistic Director, Opera Theatre of Alberta, Composers & Performers Festival Association of Alberta; Director, Opera Workshop, University of Alberta. Compositions: Numerous songs, incidental music, dances for stage works including: Euripides's Bacchae, 1980; Aeschylus' Oresteia, 1984; Shakespeare's Midsummer Night's Dream, 1985; Aristophanes' Birds, 1986; Original stage works: The Rich Man; Sliding for Home; Learning to Live with Personal Growth; Art of War. Recording: Monster Concert, live from Carnegie Hall. Contributions to: Music Magazine. Membership: Pi Kappa Lambda. Hobby: Swimming. Address: 11051 81st Avenue, Edmonton, Alberta, T6G 0S3, Canada.

SHORE Andrew, b. 30 Sep 1952, Oldham, Lancashire, England. Singer (Bass-Baritone). Education: Studied at Bristol University and London Opera Centre. Career: Kent Opera: Figaro, Papageno, Dr Bartolo; Opera North, from 1987: King Dodon, Le Coq D'Or; Sacristan, Tosca; Leandro, Love for Three Oranges, also at Edinburgh International Festival and recorded for television; Don Pasquale and Varlaam, Boris Godunov; King Priam, 1991; Wozzeck, 1993; Podesta in La Gazza Ladra; Varlaam; Don Jerome in La Duenna; Geronimo in Secret Marriage, 1993; Leandro, in Love for Three Oranges, 1993; Debut with English National Opera in 1988 in title role, Falstaff, then Don Alfonso, Doeg in Philip Glass's The Making of the Representative for Planet 8, and at Amsterdam; Papageno; Dr Bartolo, 1990; Frank, in Die Fledermaus, 1992; Bartolo; Don Pasquale, also in Tel Aviv; Scottish Opera: Don Alfonso; Baron in La Vie Parisienne; Mr Flint in Billy Budd; Glyndebourne Festival Opera: Falstaff; Mr Gedge in Albert Herring; Doctor Bartolo; Don Alfonso; Welsh National Opera: Bartolo; North American debut: Bartolo, Vancouver, 1991 and Ottawa, 1991; Royal Opera House, Covent Garden: Baron Tromborok in Viaggio a Rheims; French debut as Quince, in A Midsummer Night's Dream at Lyon, Opéra Comique, Paris and Montpelier; Season 1994/95 as Don Alfonso, in Così fan tutte and Bottom, A Midsummer Night's Dream, at New Israeli Opera, Tel Aviv, 1995; Falstaff in a new production of Verdi's opera for Opera North, 1997. Address: c/o Athole Still International Management Ltd, Foresters Hall, 25-27 Westow Street, London, SE19 3RY, England.

SHORE Clare, b. 18 Dec 1954, Winston-Salem, North Carolina, USA. Composer. Education: BA cum laude with honours, Music, Wake Forest University, 1976; MMus, University of Colorado, 1977; DMA, Juilliard School of Music, 1984; Studied with Annette LeSiege, Wake Forest University, Charles Eakin and Cecil Effinger, University of Colorado, David Diamond, Vincent Persichetti and Roger Sessions, Juilliard School. Career: Teaching: Fordham University, Manhattan School of Music, University of Virginia, and George Mason University, 1981-; Numerous commissions; Works performed in Carnegie Recital Hall, Alice Tully Hall, Lincoln Center, Merkin Concert Hall, Spoleto Festival, Charleston, The Barns of Wolf Trap, National Gallery of Art, throughout USA and abroad. Compositions: Early works published by Arsis Press, Plucked String, and Seesaw Music; All subsequent works published by E C Schirmer Music Co. Recordings include: July Remembrances, Owl Recordings CD-34; Nightwatch, Opus One 132; Oatlands Sketches, CRS 8842; Contemporary Records Society Grant, 1988. Hobbies: Swimming; Gardening. Current Management: E C Schirmer Music Company Inc. Address: 12329 Cliveden Street, Herndon, VA 22070, USA.

SHOSTAKOVICH Maxim, b. 10 May 1938, Leningrad, USSR. Conductor. Education: Leningrad Conservatory, 1961-62; Moscow Conservatory. Debut: London Philharmonic Orchestra, 1968. Career: Assistant Conductor, Moscow Symphony Orchestra, 1964; Moscow State Symphony Orchestra, 1966; Principal Conductor, Moscow Radio Symphony Orchestra; Toured Canada with USSR State Symphony Orchestra, 1969; Guest Conductor, Europe, North America, Japan and Australia; Pianist, including Piano Concerto No 2 by Shostakovich; Conducted New Orleans Symphony until 1991; Led Lady Macbeth of Mtsensk at Hamburg, 1990; Dmitri Shostakovich concert with the Philharmonic at the Festival Hall, London, 1997. Recordings: Father's ballet compositions, including Bolt, The Age of Gold, suites, music for films Zoya, Pirogov with Bolshoi Theatre Orchestra; Recordings EMI, Philips, including Shostakovich's Violin Concerto No 1, Shostakovich's Symphony No 5, Suites on Verses of Michelangelo, 1971, recording with Philips of Shostakovich's Cello Concerti, 1984.

SHRAPNEL Hugh (Michael), b. 18 Feb 1947, Birmingham, England. Composer. Education: Eltham College, 1960-65; Royal Academy of Music, 1966-69; Goldsmiths' College, London, 1984-88; BMus. Career: Member: Scratch Orchestra, 1969-72; Promenade Theatre Orchestra, 1970-72; People's Liberation Music, 1975-79; Co Founder of Redlands Consort, 1992 specialising in new music; Compositions widely performed in London, provinces and abroad including: Wigmore Hall, 1968; Purcell Room, 1970; San Diego, 1974; Conway Hall, 1986 and 1993; University of Redlands, Texas, 1986 and 1989; Leighton House, 1989, 1990, 1991; Slaughterhouse Gallery, 1991; Appointed Composer-in-Residence at Music Works, London. Compositions: Oakley St, 1971; Steps, 1971; 2 Pieces for Clarinet and Piano, 1986; South of the River, 1993-95; Many works for Ensemble and Piano; Educational Music. Memberships: Composer's Guild. Hobbies: Writing; Photography; Cooking; Cycling; Walking. Current Management: STR Music Marketing & Management. Address: 27A Shooters Hill Road, Blackheath, London SE3 7AS, England.

SHTOKOLOV Boris, b. 19 Mar 1930, Kuznetsk, Russia. Singer (Bass). Education: Studied at the Sverdlovsk Conservatory. Career: Joined Sverdlovsky Opera, 1951, remaining until 1959; Appearances with the Kirov Opera from 1959, as the Miller in Dargomizhsky's Russalka, Glinka's Ruslan, Dosiphey in Khovanshchina, Gremin, Rossini's Basilio and Boris Godunov; Sang Andrei Sokolov in the Premiere of Dzerzhinsky's Destiny of a Man, Moscow, 1961; Mephisto in Gounod's Faust, Galitsky in Borodin's Prince Igor, Ivan Susanin in Glinka's Life for Tsar. Recordings include: Boris Godunov and Ruslan and Ludmilla, from the Kirov; Highlights from Destiny of a Man; Burn My Star, Russian Songs and Romances (two discs album, 1984). Honours include: Peoples Artist of the USSR; Glinka Prize; State Prize of the USSR. Address: c/o Kirov Oper and Ballet Theatre, St Petersburg, Russia.

SHULMAN Andrew, b. 1960, London, England. Cellist; Conductor. Education: Studies at the RAM and the RCM (Joan Dickson and William Pleeth). Career: Principal cellist of the Philharmonia (5 years) followed by solo and conducting career; repertoire includes concertos by Dvorak, Elgar, Beethoven (Triple), Vivaldi and Haydn; Strauss's Don Quixote and Bloch's Schelomo; Founder member of the Britten Quartet, debut concert at the Wigmore Hall, 1987; Quartet in Residence at the Dartington Summer School, 1987, with quartets by Schnittke; Season 1988-89 in the Genius of Prokofiev series at Blackheath and BBC Lunchtime Series at St John's Smith Square; South Bank appearances with the Schoenberg/Handel Quartet Concerto conducted by Neville Marriner, concerts with the Hermann Prey Schubertiade and collaborations with the Alban Berg Quartet in the Beethoven Plus series; Tour of South America 1988, followed by Scandinavian debut; Season 1989-90 with debut tours of Holland, Germany, Spain, Austria, Finland; Tours from 1990 to the Far East, Malta, Sweden, Norway: Schoenberg/Handel Concerto with the Gothenburg Symphony; Festival appearances at Brighton, the City of London, Greenwich, Canterbury, Harrogate, Chester, Spitalfields and Aldeburgh; Collaborations with John Ogdon, Imogen Cooper, Thea King and Lynn Harrell; Formerly resident quartet at Liverpool University; Teaching role at Lake District Summer Music 1989; Universities of Bristol, Hong Kong 1990; Conductor of various orchestras including RCM String Ensemble, Protens Orchestra, Norfolk Youth Orchestra and Leicester Symphony Orchestra. Recordings: Beethoven Op 130 and Schnittke Quartet no 3 (Collins); Vaughan Williams On Wenlock Edge and Ravel Quartet (EMI); Britten, Prokofiev, Tippett, Elgar and Walton Quartets (Collins Classics); Exclusive contract with EMI from 1991. Honours: Piatigorsky Artist Award in Boston, USA, 1989-90. Address: c/o Fir Cottage, Kingsley, Bordon, Hampshire GU35 9NH, England.

SHUMSKY Oscar, b. 23 Mar 1917, Philadelphia, PA, USA. Violinist; Conductor. Education: Began to study the violin at the age of three; Appeared with Leopold Stokowski and The Philadelphia Orchestra at the age of seven, performing Mozart's Fifth Violin Concerto; Studied with Leopold Auer from 1925, Curtis Institute, 1928-36; Private study with Efrem Zimbalist until 1938. Debut: Conductor 1959, with the Canadian National Festival Orchestra. Career: Played in the NBC Symphony under Toscanini from 1939; Leader of the Primrose Quartet; Appeared as soloist with leading US orchestras, and on radio and TV; Musical Director of the Canadian Stratford Festivasl 1959-67; Conducted the Westchester Symphony and the Empire Sinfonietta in New York; Further conducting posts with the San Francisco Symphony, the Lincoln Center Mostly Mozart festival; The Canadian Broadcasting Symphony; Teaching posts at the Peabody Conservatory, Curtis Institute, the Juilliard School and Yale University; Ceased teaching activities 1981, resumed career as violin soloist; Engagements with the Philharmonia, London Symphony, English Chamber, City of Birmingham Orchestras, Chamber Orchestra of Europe and Rotterdam Philharmonic; Recitals in London; Stuttgart; Berlin; Naples Festival; Concerts with the Vancouver Symphony as conductor. Recordings: Mozart's Violin Sonatas with Artur Balsam; Beethoven Concerto with the Philharmonia and Andrew Davis; Concertos by Bach and Mozart with the Scottish Chamber Orchestra; Unaccompanied Sonatas by Ysaÿe; Mozart Concerto K216 and Sinfonia Concertante K364, with son Eric on viola. Address: ASV, Martin House, 179-181 North End Road, London, W14 9NL, England.

SICILIANI Alessandro, b. 5 June 1952, Florence, Italy. Conductor; Composer. Education: Studied piano, conducting and composition at the Milan Conservatoire and the Accademia Chigiana in Siena (conducting with Franco Ferrara). Career: Many appearances at leading opera centres in Italy, notably Rome, Naples, Palermo and Florence; Further engagements in Marseilles, Barcelona, Nice, Liège, New Orleans and Philadelphia; Metropolitan Opera debut 1988, with Pagliacci and Cavalleria Rusticana; Symphonic engagements throughout the USA, Far East and Europe; From 1988 principal guest conductor of the Teatro Colon, Buenos Aires, and of the Teatro Municipal, Sao Paulo; From 1992 Music Director of the Columbus, Ohio, Symphony Orchestra. Compositions include: Cantata; L'Amour peintre (ballet); Giona, oratorio. Address: Columbus Symphony Orchestra, 55 East State Street, Columbus, OH 45210, USA.

SIDLIN Murray, b. 6 May 1940, Baltimore, Maryland, USA. Conductor. Education: BA 1962, MM 1968, Peabody Conservatory, Maryland; Further study with Sergiu Celibidache at the Accademia Chigiana, Siena, 1961-62 and with Donald Grout and Karel Husa at Cornell University, 1963-65. Career: Assistant conductor at the Aspen Music Festival, 1970-71; Assistant at the Baltimore Symphony, 1971-73; Resident Conductor with the National Symphony Orchestra in Washington DC, 1973-77; Music Director of the New Haven (Connecticut) Symphony Orchestra, 1977-88; Music Director of the Tulsa Philharmonic, 1978-80 and directed the conducting fellowship programma at the Aspen Festival, 1978-93; Music Director, Long Beach, California, Symphony Orhchestra, 1980-88; Conductor of the American Music Concerts for the Chevron Corporation, 1987-92; Resident Conductor with the Oregon Symphony Orchestra, Portland, 1994-. Address: c/o Oregon Symphony Orchestra, 711 South West Adler, Suite 200, Portland, OR 97205, USA.

SIDOVSKY Janis, b. 21 January 1968, Pardubice, Czech Republic. Executive Producer; General Press Representative. Education: Charles University. Career: Dancer, Karel Gott Show; Dancer, Master, Czech Rep, 1983; General Press Representative, Westside Story, Prague, 1993, Foundation for Czech Music, 1995, Musical Dracula, 1996. Recordings: Scent of Your Skin; Garden of Wishes; Dracula. Publications: Dracula, 1997. Contributions to: Czech Professional Magazines. Honours: 2 Gold Discs, Dracula; 2 Platinum Discs; Double Platinum Disc; 2 Czech Gramy Awards. Memberships: Czech Academy of Music; Prague Convention Bureau. Hobbies: Fine Arts; Dogs; Tennis. Address: Londynska 53, CZ-120 00 Praha 2, Czech Republic.

SIEBER Gudrun, b. 1953, Germany. Singer (Soprano). Education: Studied at the Dusseldorf Opera Studio. Career: Member of the Deutsche Oper am Rhein Dusseldorf 1974-83; Deutsche Oper Berlin from 1977, notably in the 1984 premiere of Reimann's Gespenstersonate; Sang at the Bayerische Staatsoper Munich, 1978-84, in operas by Gluck, Mozart and Lortzing; Schwetzingen Festival 1980 and 1982, Salzburg Festival, 1981, 1984 and 1986 as Papagena in Die Zauberflöte; Also sang Papagena at the Théâtre des Champs-Elysées, Paris, 1987; Sang in a double bill of Il Maestro di Capella (Cimarosa) and La Serva di Padrona at the Deutsche Oper foyer, 1990; Other roles include Marie in Zar und Zimmermann; Amour in Hippolyte et Aricie and Kristen in Miss Julie by Bibalo; Many concert appearances. Recordings include: Schumann's Manfred (Schwann). Address: c/o Deutsche Oper Berlin, Richard Wagnerstrasse 10, D-1000 Berlin, Germany.

SIEBERT Isolde, b. 1960, Hunfield, Hesse, Germany. Singer (Soprano). Education: Studied at Fribourg from 1979. Career: Member of the Basle Opera, 1982-85; Sang at Darmstadt, 1985-87, debut as Zerbinetta; Hanover Opera from 1987, as Blondchen, Susanna, Gretel, Tytania in A Midsummer Night's Dream and Papagena; Bregenz Festival and Liège, 1986, 1988 as the Queen of Night in Die Zauberflöte; Sang in the 300th anniversary performance of Steffani's Enrico Leone at Hanover, 1989; Many concerts and recital appearances. Recordings include: Biblical Songs by Dvorak. Address: Niedersachsiche Staatstheater, Opernplatz 1, D-3000 Hannover, Germany.

SIEDEN Cyndia, b. 10 Sept 1954, Glendale, CA, USA. Singer (Soprano). Education: Studied at Olympia, Washington, and with Elisabeth Schwarzkopf. Career: Sang Cunegonde in Candide for New York City Opera, 1989; Sang Sifare in Mozart's Mitridate at the 1989 Wexford Festival, the Queen of Night in Toulon, Adele in Fledermaus for Scottish Opera and Offenbach's Olympia at Seattle; Salzburg Festival debut as Amor in Orfeo ed Euridice, conducted by John Eliot Gardiner; Appearances with the Bayerische Staatsoper Munich as Rosina, Helena in the premiere of Reimann's Troades, 1986, Zerbinetta and Fiakermilli in Arabella; Further engagements at Nice as Blondchen and Aminta in Die schweigsame Frau at Palermo; Sang Xenia in a concert performance of Boris Godunov conducted by Abbado, 1984,

Verdi's Oscar for Washington Opera, Donizetti's Marie with Florida Opera West, Nannetta at Omaha and Fido in the US Professional premiere of Britten's Paul Bunyan, at St Louis; Season 1990/91 as Blondchen at the Théâtre de Châtelet Paris and on tour to Amsterdam, London, Lisbon and Stuttgart; Recent appearances as the Queen of Night at the Opéra Bastille Paris and Lucia di Lammermoor at Seattle; Zerbinetta for English National Opera and at the Vienna Staatsoper, season 1992/93 with Sophie in Der Rosenkavalier at the Chatelet; Sang in Mozart's Mitridate at Salzburg, 1997; Handel's Rodelinda at Halle, 1996; Concert repertoire includes Mozart's C minor Mass (Cleveland Orchestra), Carmina Burana, Bach's St John Passion at the Concertgebouw under Frans Brüggen, and Candide at the Barbican Centre, London. Recordings include: Guardian of the Threshold in Die Frau ohne Schatten, conducted by Sawallisch (EMI); Orfeo ed Euridice (Philips); Die Entführung aus dem Serail. Address: c/o IMG Artists, Media House, Burlington Lane, London W4 2TH, England.

SIEGEL Jeffrey, b. 18 November 1942, Chicago, Illinois, USA. Concert Pianist. m. Laura Mizel, 20 May 1973, 1 son, 1 daughter. Education: DMA, Juilliard School of Music, 1971; Studies with Rudolph Ganz, Rosina Lhevinne, Franz Reizenstein, Ilona Kabos. Debut: Solist, Chicago Symphony, 1958. Career: Soloist with Orchestras of New York, Philadelphia, Boston, Cleveland, Los Angeles, London Symphony, London Philharmonic, Royal Philharmonic, Philharmonia, BBC Orchestras; NHK Orchestra of Japan; Nacionale Orchestra of Buenos Aires, Teatro Colón; Berlin Philharmonic; Recitals in Carnegie Hall, Festival Hall, Concertgebouw, Brussels, Berlin, Munich, Zurich, Tokyo, Tel Aviv, Oslo, Stockholm; TV Appearances; Frequent Radio Appearances. Compositions: Cadenza for Mozart C Minor Concerto. Recordings: Dutilleux Sonata and Hindemith Third Sonata; Gershwin Complete Works for Piano and Orchestra with St Louis Symphony, 1974; Solo works of Rachmaninov. Honours: Silver Medal, Queen Elizabeth Competition, Brussles, 1968; Honorary Doctorate, National College of Education, Evanston, Illinois, 1976. Hobbies: Cinema; Theatre; Cuisine. Current Management: ICM Artists Management. Address: c/o ICM Artists Management, 40 West 57th Street, New York City, NY 10019, USA.

SIEGEL Laurence (Gordon), b. 23 July 1931, New York City, New York, USA. Conductor. m. 15 Oct 1959, 1 daughter. Education: BA, City College of New York, 1953; MM, New England Conservatory, Boston, 1955; Studied under Boris Goldovsky and Leonard Bernstein, Berkshire Music Center, Tanglewood, 1953, 1955. Career: Conductor, NBC Symphony, Carnegie Hall concerts including tribute to Fritz Kreisler; Appeared with Honolulu Orchestra, Shreveport Festival Orchestra, Alexandria Symphony, Jacksonville Symphony and Opera Company, Connecticut Grand Opera Company; Director, Miami International Music Competition, Theater of Performing Arts, Miami Beach, 7 seasons; Worldwide conducting includes Orquesta Sinfonica del Salvador, Orquesta Sinfonica de Las Palmas, Spain, Manila Metro Philharmonic Orchestra and Opera Association, Teatro Sperimentale di Spoleto Orchestra, Belgrade Symphony, Filharmonica de Stat Oradea-Romania; Regularly conducts RAI Milan Orchestra; Music Director, Conductor, Puccini Festival Orchestra, Italy, 1984, Pan American Sinfonica, 1991-, also Festival of the Continents, Key West, Florida; Currently Music Director, North Miami Beach Orchestra; Guest Conductor, Kensington Symphony (California), Sao Paulo Symphony, Brazil, Orquesta Sinfonica Ciudad Asuncion, Paraguay (1994); Chief Conductor, Sakai City, Osaka Opera, Japan; Numerous operas include Così fan tutte, Faust, Butterfly, Tosca, La Bohème, La Traviata, Otello, Rigoletto, Die Fledermaus, Ernani, Il Trovatore, Suor Angelica, Hansel and Gretel, Samson and Delilah, La Perichole, Elisir d'Amore, Carmen (1991, 1992), Merry Widow (1992-). Recordings: Tchaikovsky Album with New Philharmonia Orchestra, London; Others with London Symphony, London Philharmonic and Royal Philharmonic Orchestras and London Festival Orchestra. Honours include: Numerous citations and medals of honour; DMus, 1993. Current Management: Pan American Sociedad de Artisias. Address: 5225 La Gorce Drive, Miami Beach, FL 33140, USA.

SIEGEL Wayne, b. 14 Feb 1953, Los Angeles, USA. Composer. m. 22 Mar 1980, 1 son. Education: BA, Music Composition, University of California, Santa Barbara, 1975; Diplomeksamen, Composition, Royal Danish Academy of Music, Aarhus. Career: Active as Composer and Performer, Europe and USA, including many radio and TV broadcasts and numerous commissions; Major performances include: Danish Radio Festival, Copenhagen, 1980; Nordic Music Days, Helsinki, 1980; German Radio, 1981; New Music America, Chicago, 1982; Warsaw Autumn, 1984; Nordic Music Days, 1984; Rostrum, Stockholm, 1988. Compositions: String Quartet, 1975-79; East LA for 4 Marimbas or 2 guitars, 1975; Narcissus ad fontem, 1976; Mosaic, 1978; Autumn Resonance, 1979; Domino Figures, 1979; Music for 21 Clarinets, 1980; Watercolor, Acrylic, Watercolor, 1981; Polyphonic Music, 1983; 42nd Street Rondo, 1984; Devil's Golf Course, 1985; Last Request, 1986; Cobra, 1988. Recordings: String Quartet and Watercolor, Acrylic, Watercolor; Autumn Resonance & Domino Figures; East LA Phase. Contributions to: Danish Music Periodical, Nutida Musik, Contemporary Music Review. Honours: Danish Art Council 3-Year Grant for Composition, 1978-81. Memberships: Administrative Director, West Jutland Symphony and Chamber Ensemble, 1984-86; Director, Danish Institute of Electroacoustic Music, 1986-. Address: DIEM, The Concert Hall Aarhus, DK 8000 Aarhus, Denmark.

SIEGELE Ulrich, b. 1 Nov 1930, Stuttgart, Germany. Musicologist. m. Dr Leonore Siegele-Wenschkewitz. Education: DPhil, Tuebingen University, 1957. Career: Lecturer in Musicology, 1965-71, Professor of Musicology, 1971-, Tuebingen University. Publications: Die Musiksammlung der Stadt Heilbronn, 1967; Kompositionsweise und Bearbeitungstechnik in der Instrumentalmusik Johann Sebastian Bachs, 1975; Bachs theologischer Formbegriff und das Duett F-Dur, 1978; Zwei Kommentare zum Marteau sans maître von Pierre Boulez, 1979; Beethoven/Formale Strategien der späten Quartette, 1990; Die Orgeln des Musikwissenschaftlichen Instituts im Pfleghof zu Tuebingen, 1992. Contributions to: Articles in periodicals, collections by several authors, and musical encyclopaedias. Address: Am Hasenborn, 61389 Schmitten, Germany.

SIEPI Cesare, b. 10 June 1923, Milan, Italy. Singer (Bass/Baritone). Education: Studied privately and at the Milan Conservatory. Debut: 1941, as Sparafucile in Rigoleto at Schio. Career: La Fenice Venice 1946 as Silva in Ernani; La Scala Milan 1946-58, notably as Donizetti's Raimondo, Verdi's Grand Inquisitor, Wagner's Pogner and as Mefistofele and Simon Mago in the 1948 Boito celebrations conducted by Toscanini; New York Metropolitan, 1950-74, principally as Mozart's Don Giovanni and Figaro; Also sang Philip II in Don Carlos, Gounod's Mephistopheles, Verdi's Padre Guardiano, Ramfis, Silva, Zacccaria and Fiesco; First Wagner role in German was Gurnemanz, 1970; Sang Don Giovanni at Salzburg in the 1950s (also filmed) and on his Covent Garden debut, 1962; Appeared as Roger in Verdi's Jerusalem at Parma in 1985. Recordings: Don Giovanni, Mefistofele and L'Amore dei tre Re (RCA); Le nozze di Figaro, Don Giovanni, La Gioconda, Rigoletto, La Forza del Destino, La Bohème, Il Barbiere di Siviglia, Lucia di Lammermoor (Decca); Faust (CBS); Boris Godunov, La Juive, Don Carlos, La Favorita, Ernani and Norma on various other labels; Five complete recordings of Don Giovanni. Address: c/o S A Gorlinsky Ltd, 33 Dover Street, London W1X 4NJ, England.

SIERRA Roberto, b. 9 Oct 1953, Vega Baja, Puerto Rico. Composer; Music Educator. Education: Puerto Rico Conservatory of Music; Graduated, University of Puerto Rico, 1976; Royal College of Music, London; University of London, 1976-78; Institute of Sonology, Utrecht, 1978; Studied with Gyorgy Ligeti, Hamburg Hochschule fur Musik, 1979-82. Career: Assistant Director, 1983-85, Director, 1985-86, Cultural Activities Department, University of Puerto Rico; Dean of Studies, 1986-87, Chancellor, 1987-, Puerto Rico Conservatory of Music. Compositions: Salsa on the C String for Cello and Piano, 1983; Salsa for Wind Quintet, 1983; Cantos Populares for Chorus, 1983; Cinco bocetos for Clarinet, 1984; El Mensajero de Plata, chamber opera, 1984; Concerto Nocturnal for Harpischord, Flute, Clarinet, Oboe, Violin and Cello, 1985; Jubilo for Orchestra, 1985; Memorias Tropicales for String Quartet, 1985; Dona Rosita for Mezzo-soprano and Wind Quintet, 1985; El sueno de Antonia for Clarinet and Percussion, 1985; Invocaciones for Voice and Percussion, 1986; Cuatro ensayos orquestales for Orchestra, 1986; Glosa a la sombra..for Mezzo-soprano, Viola, Clarinet and Piano, 1987; Essays for Wind Quintet, 1987; Mano a mano for 2 Percussionists, 1987; El Contemplado, ballet, 1987; Glosas for Piano and Orchestra, 1987; Introduccion y Descarga for Piano, Brass Quintet and Percussion, 1988; Dascarga for Chamber Ensemble or Orchestra, 1988; Entre terceras for 2 Synthesizers and Computer, 1988; Tributo for Harp, Flute, Clarinet and String Quartet, 1988; Piano Pieces; Harpischord pieces. Recordings: Number of works recorded. Honours: Several commissions; Many works performed in USA and Europe. Address: c/o Conservatorio de Musica de Puerto Rico, Apartado 41227, Minillas Station, Santurce, Puerto Rico 00940, USA.

SIEWERS Maria Isabel, b. 22 Oct 1950, Buenos Aires, Argentina. Guitarist; Professor of Guitar. m. Nicolas Pazur, 11 Aug 1973, 1 son, 1 daughter. Education: Teachers' degree, Prov Bs As Escuela Normal San Justo; Conservatorio Municipal "M de Falla"; Maria Luisa Anido (private lessons); S De Compostela (Spain), summer course with Andres Segovia; Accademia Chigiana (Siena), courses with: Oscar Ghiglia, Alain Meunier, Ruggiero Chiesa. Career: Professor, Musikhochschule Mozarteum in Salzburg; Concerts in Europe, since 1974 including: Konzerthaus Vienna, 1978 and 1996; Theatre des Champs Elysées, Paris; Wigmore Hall, London, 1983 and 1989; Carnegie Hall, New York; Latin America, Australia, New Zealand (solo and chamber music); As soloist with Philharmonic Orchestra of Krakow, Collegium Prague, RTV Symphony Zagreb, Cuban Symphony, Orquesta Sinfonica Nacional (BsAs); Recorded for BBC, Radio France, RTVE, ORF, Argentine TV. Recordings: I Siewers Plays Music From Argentina; Amigos; C Guastavino: Guitar And Chamber Music; M Pujol: Guitar And Chamber Music; A Piazzollà: Guitar and Chamber Music. Publications: Juan Carlos Zorzi, Canciones Sin Palabras, 1985; Maximo Pujol, Elegia, 1993; Maximo Pujol, Tres Piezas, 1994. Contributions to: Classical Guitar, 1984, 1985, 1988. Honour: 2nd Prize, International Guitar Competition, Paris, ORTF, 1974. Hobbies: Riding; Swimming; Yoga. Address: M H S Mozarteum, Innrain 15, A-6020 Innsbruck, Austria.

SIEWERS DE PAZUR Maria Isabel, b. 22 October 1950, Buenos Aires. Guitarist; Professor of Guitar. m. Nicolas Pazur, 11 August 1973, 1 son, 1 daughter. Education: BS, AS,Escuela Normal, San Justo; Conservatorio Municipal M De Falla, Buenos Aires; Private Study with Maria Luisa Anido; S De Compostela, Spain; Course with Andres Segovia; Accademia Chigiana; Courses with Oscar Giglia, Alain Meunier, Ruggiero Chiesa. Career: Concerts in Europe include, Wigmore Hall, 1983, 1989, Konzerthaus Vienna, 1978, 1996, Thetre des Champs Elysees, Paris, 1983, Latin America, Australia, Newzealand; As Soloist with Philarmonic Orchestra, Krakow, Collegium Prague, RTV Symphony, Zagreb, Cuban Symphony, Orchestra Sinfonica Nacional; Recorded for BBC, Radio France, RTVE, ORF, Argentine TV. Recordings: I Siewers Plays Music From Argentina; Amigos; C Guastavino: Guitar and Chamber Music; M Pujol: Guitar and Chamber Music; A Piazzolla: Guitar and Chamber Music. Publications: Juan Carloszorzi, Canciones Sin Palabras, 1985; Maximo Pujol, Elegia, 1993; Maximo Pujol, Tres Piezas, 1994. Contributions to: Classical Guitar. Honour: 2nd Prize, International Guitar Competition, Paris, 1974. Memberships: Head, Guitar Class, Musikhochschule Mozarteum, Salzburg. Hobbies: Riding; Swimming; Yoga. Address: MHS Mozarteum, Innrain 15, A6020 Innsbruck, Austria.

SIGMUNDSSON Kristinn, b. 1 May 1951, Reykjavik, Iceland. Singer (Bass-Baritone). Education: Studied at Academy of Music in Vienna and in Washington DC. Career includes: Member of Wiesbaden Opera from 1989 as Don Giovanni, the Speaker in Die Zauberflöte and Eugene Onegin; Royal Court Theatre Drottningholm, 1989-90 as Agamemnon and Thoas in Gluck's Iphigénie operas; Season 1990-91 includes: Geisterbote in Die Frau ohne Schatten at the Concertgebouw, Beethoven's 9th with the Essen Philharmonie and St John Passion in the Hague; Recital at the Stratford-upon-Avon Scandinavian Festival; Malcolm in La Donna del Lago for Vara Radio, Holland, 1992; Concert appearances with the Dutch Radio Orchestra, the Rotterdam Philharmonic and the NDR Symphony Orchestra, Hamburg; Season 1991-92 included: Don Giovanni at Stuttgart Opera, Mozart's Requiem at Drottningholm and Barber of Seville at Geneva; Season 1993-94 includes: Alidoro and Speaker in Geneva, Mathis der Maler in Barcelona and Lady Macbeth of Mtsensk at the Maggio Musicale in Florence; Sang in a new production of The Bartered Bride at the Grand Théâtre in Geneva, 1994; Sang Mephistofeles in La Damnation de Faust at the Opera National in Paris;Colline in 1996; Sang Klingsor in Parsifal at the Opéra Bastille, Paris, 1997. Recordings include: Commendatore in Don Giovanni, conducted by Arnold Östman. Honours include: Prizewinner, Belvedere Singing Competition in Vienna, 1983; Winner, Philadelphia Opera Competition, 1983. Address: c/o Haydn Rawstron Ltd, 36 Station Road, London SE20 7BQ, England.

SIGURBJORNSSON Thorkell, b. 1938, Iceland. Composer. Education: Reykjavik College of Music; Continuing Studies in USA. Career: Creative Associate, State University of New York, USA, 1973; Research Musician, Centre for Music Experiment, University of California, San Diego, 1975; Head of Theory and Composition, Reyjavik College of Music, Iceland, 1968-74; Bukolla, 1974; Wiblo, 1976; Cadensa and Dance; Seascape; Albumblatt, 1975; The Bull Man, ballet music; Caprice, 1986; Chamber Music: Differing Opinions; Intrada, 1971; For Renee, 1973; A Short Passion Story; Hasselby Icelandic Folk Songs, 1976; Ballade, 1960; Happy Music, 1971; Kissum, 1970; Copenhagen Quartet; For Better or Worse, 1975; Solstice, 1976; Auf Meinen Lieben Gott, 1981; Three Faces of Pantomine, 1982; Choir Music: Ode, 1975; Five Laudi, 1973; Beginning, 1978; Hosanna Son of David; Palm Sunday, 1978; The Artificial Flower; Seven Christmas Songs; David 121, 1984; Evening Prayers, 1983; Children's Music: Seven Songs from Apaspil; Apaspil, opera, 1966; Velferd; Four Icelandic Folk Songs; Three Songs; Gigjuleikur; The Ugly Duckling, 1981; The Last Flower, 1983; Electronic Music: La Jolla Good Friday I, 1975; La Jolla Good Friday II, 1975; fipur, 1971; Race Track, 1975. Memberships: President, Icelandic League of Composers. Address: c/o STEF, Laufasvegi 40, 101 Reykjavik, Iceland

SIKI Bela, b. 21 February 1923, Budapest, Hungary. Pianist. m. Yolande Oltramare, 18 September 1952, 1 son, 1 daughter. Education: University of Budapest; Academy Franz Liszt, Budapest; Conservatoire de Geneve, Switzerland. Career: Numerous concert tours worldwide; Appearances with major orchestras aroud the world; Extensive concert tours and master classes in Japan, Australia, USA and Canada, 1988. Recordings: Has made numerous recordings including music by Bach, Ravel, Liszt (B minor sonata), Beethoven (late sonatas) and Bartók. Publications: Piano Literature, 1982. Honours: Liszt Competition, Budapest, 1942, 1943; Concours International d'Executions Musicales, Geneva, 1948. Address: School of Music, University of Washington, Seattle, WA 98195, USA.

SIKORA Elizabeth, b. 1950, Edinburgh, Scotland. Singer (Soprano). Education: Studied at the Royal Scottish Academy and at Elsa Mayer Lismanns Opera Workshop. Career: Appearances with the Royal Opera Covent Garden in London and on Tour to Los Angeles, La Scala Milan, Japan, Korea and Greece; Solo Roles in Die Meistersinger, Butterfly, Die Frau ohne Schatten, Manon Lescaut, Parsifal, Rigoletto and Simon Boccanegra; Sang in the British premieres of Henze's Pollicino and Menotti's The Boy Who Grew Too Fast; Appearances as Carmen in Oundle and Germany with Royal Opera Education. Address: Royal Opera House, Education Department, Covent Garden, London WC2, England.

SILJA Anja, b. 17 Apr 1935, Berlin, Germany. Singer (Soprano); Director. Education: Studied with Egon van Rijn. Career: Gave concert at the Berlin Titania Palace aged 15; Stage debut Brunswick 1956, as Rosina; Stuttgart from 1958, Frankfurt from 1959; Sang the Queen of Night at Aix, 1959; Bayreuth Festival, 1960-66, as Senta, Elsa, Eva, Elisabeth, Venus and Isolde; London debut at Sadler's Wells Theatre, 1963, as Leonore; Member of the Stuttgart Staatsoper from 1965; Covent Garden debut 1969, as Leonore: returned as Cassandre in Les Troyens, Senta, and Marie in Wozzeck; Metropolitan Opera debut 1972: returned as Salome and Marie; Member of Hamburg Staatsoper from 1975; Vienna Staatsoper 1976, in the premiere of Von Einem's Kabale und Liebe; Paris Opéra 1985, as Marie; Glyndebourne Opera debut 1989, as the Kostelnicka in Jenufa; Sang the Nurse in Die Frau ohne Schatten at San Francisco, 1989; Produced Elektra at Leipzig, 1991; debut as opera producer at Brussels, 1990; Covent Garden, 1993, in Jenufa; Sang Janacek's Emilia Marty at Glyndebourne, 1995; Season 1997 in The Makropoulos Case at Glyndebourne and as Herodias at Covent Garden. Recordings: Der fliegende Holländer, Tannhäuser, Lohengrin and Parsifal from Bayreuth; Lulu and Wozzeck (Decca). Address: c/o Christoph von Dohnányi, Cleveland Orchestra, Severance Hall, 1101 Euclid Avenue, Cleveland, OH 44106, USA.

SILLA Frederick, b. 1948, Vienna, Australia. Singer (Tenor); Composer. Education: Studied at the Vienna Musikhochschule with Friedrich Cerha and Anton Dermota. Career: Sang first at the Stadttheater Krefeld, then appeared at Opera Houses in Ulm, Kiel, Munster and Gelsenkirchen; Opera Jagdszenen aus Niederbayern premiered at Karlsruhe 1979; Member of the Staatstheater am Gärtnerplatz Munich from 1985; Roles have included Mozart's Ottavio, Tamino, Ferrando and Belmonte, Nemorino and Hoffmann; Modern Repertoire includes parts in The Lighthouse by Maxwell Davies, Jakob Lenz by Wolfgang Rihm and Die Veruteilung des Lukullus by Dessau; Guest Engagements in Pisa, Venice and Madrid, Concert appearances in Germany and elsewhere. Address: c/o Staatstheater am, Gärtnerplatz, Gartnerplatz 3, 8000 Munich, Germany.

SILLS Beverly, b. 25 May 1929, Brooklyn, New York, USA. Singer (soprano); Opera Director. Education: Studied with Estelle Liebing from age 7. Career: Often sang on radio commercials as a child, with name Bubbles; Opera debut as Frasquita in Carmen, Philadelphia Civic Opera 1946; San Francisco Opera 1953, as Elena in Mefistofele; New York City Opera 1955-79 as Charpentier's Louise, Mozart's Donna Anna, Gounod's Marguerite, the heroines in Les Contes d'Hoffmann, Massenet's Manon, Donizetti's Tudor Queens and Bellini's Elvira; Success as Cleopatra in a version of Handel's Giulio Cesare led to engagements in Vienna (Mozart's Queen of Night 1967), La Scala (Pamira in Rossini's L'Assedio di Corinto 1969), and Covent Garden (Donizetti's Lucia 1970); Opera Company of Boston 1971-; Metropolitan Opera debut 1975, as Pamira; also sang Massenet's Thais, Donizetti's Norina and Violetta at the Met; Retired from opera 1979, in Menotti's La Loca; Director, New York City Opera, 1979-89; Chair of the Lincoln Center for Performing Arts, 1994. Recordings: Giulio Cesare, Lucia di Lammermoor and La Traviata (RCA), Les Contes d'Hoffmann, Manon, Thais, Maria Stuarda, Don Pasquale, Roberto Devereux, L'Assedio di Corinto, Rigoletto, I Capuleti e i Montecchi and Norma (HMV). Publication: Beverly: an Autobiography, (New York, 1988). Address: c/o New York City Opera, Lincoln Center, New York, NY 10023, USA.

SILVA Stella, b. 6 Jan 1948, Buenos Aires, Argentina. Singer (Mezzo-soprano). Education: Studied in Buenos Aires and at Vercelli, Italy. Debut: Bordeaux 1969, as Preziosilla in La Forza del Destino. Career: Many appearances in Opera Houses at Parma, Lyon, Nice, Strasbourg, Hamburg, Vienna, Berlin, Barcelona and Buenos Aires; Verona Arena, 1973-74, as Amneris; Other roles have included Carmen, Ulrica, Eboli, Azucena, Adalgisa, Charlotte, Dalila and Ortrud; Laura in La Giaconda, Leonora, Gluck's Orpheus and Holofernes in Vivaldi's Juditha Triumphans; Frequent Concert Appearances.

SILVA-MARIN Guillermo Osvaldo, b. 11 April 1944, Ponce, Puerto Rico. Singer (Tenor); Artistic Director. Education: BA, University of Puerto Rico; Diploma, Opera, University of Toronto. Career: Artistic Director, Menotti's Amahl and the Night Visitors, Merrian's The Club, Quesnel's Colas et Colinette and Gilbert and Sullivan's Iolanthe, The Pirates of Penzance and The Mikado, Metropolitan Music Theatre, Scarborough, 1976-79; Founder and Artistic Director, Toronto Operetta Theatre, 1985; Founder, Summer Opera Lyric Theatre, 1986; General Manager, Opera in Concert, 1994; Staged over 21 opera and operetta's including Donizetti's Elixir of Love, Rossini's Barber of Seville, Lehar's Land of Smiles, Offenbach's La Vie Parisienne and Strauss' Gypsy Baron with the Toronto Operetta Theatre, Summer Opera Lyric Theatre, Opera de San Juan and Sault Ste Marie Opera; 16 performances as tenor with the Canadian Opera Company, including Strauss' Ariadne auf Naxos and Leoncavallo's Pagliacci; Appearances with Opera Lyra, Cincinnati Opera Association, New York City Opera, Metropolitan Opera, Mexico State Symphony, Toronto Symphony, Edmonton Symphony, Puerto Rico Symphony, Carnegie Hall, Canadian Broadcasting Corporation, CFMX-FM include Stravinksy's Oedipus Rex, Strauss' Die Fledermaus, Zeller's The Bird Seller and Puccini's La Bohème. Recordings: Canadian Broadcasting Corporation, Classical 96 FM, WIPR Canal 6 in Puerto Rico. Honours: Floyd Chalmers Award; Canada Council Award. Memberships: Canadian Actors Equity Association. Hobbies: Travel; Films. Current Management: VKD International Artists, 9 Vernham Avenue, Willowdale, Ontario M2L 2B1, Canada.

SILVASTI Jorma, b. 9 Mar 1959, Leppavirta, Finland. Singer (Tenor). Education: Studied at Savonlinna from 1975, Sibelius Academy Helsinki, 1978-81, Frankfurt, 1981-83. Career: Appearances with the Finnish National Opera at Helsinki from 1980; Frankfurt 1981-82, Krefeld, 1982-85; Karlsruhe, 1985-88; Savonlinna Festival from 1983 as Jenik (Bartered Bride), the Steersman in Fliegende Holländer and Tamino; Premiere of Veitsi by Paavo Heikinen, 1989; Sang Ottavio at the Vienna Volksoper, 1988, Henry Morosus in Schweigsame Frau at Dresden, 1989; Further engagements at Essen, Karlsruhe and Bremen; Created Kimmo in Sallinen's Kullervo with the Company of Finnish National Opera at the Dorothy Chandler Pavilion, Los Angeles, 1992; Other roles include Ferrando, Fenton, Gluck's Pylades, Almaviva, Steva in Jenufa, Lensky, Belmonte (Vienna State Opera, 1993) Nemorino, Alfredo; Noted Concert and Oratorio Performer; Gregor in premiere of Sansibar by E Meyer at Schwetzingen with Bavarian State Opera Munich, 1994; Faust at the Dorothy Chandler Pavilion, Los Angeles; Further engagements: Stuttgart, Düsseldorf, Frankfurt, Hannover, Hamburg, Munich, Vienna State Opera; Sang Petruccio in The Palace, by Sallinen, at the 1996 Savonlinna Festival. Address: Finnish National Opera, Bulevardi 23-27, SF-00180 Helsinki, Finland.

SILVER Sheila, b. 3 October 1946, Seattle, Washington, USA. Composer. Education: Studied at the University of Washington, Seattle (1964-65) and in Paris at the Institute for European Studies, 1966-67; BA 1968 University of California at Berkeley; Stuttgart Hochschule für Musik, with Ligeti and PhD 1976 at Brandeis University (study with Alfred Berger, Lalo Schifrin and Harold Shapero); Tanglewood 1972, with Further study at Paris and London. Career: Freelance composer, with performances throughout the United states; Teacher of composition at SUNY, Stony Brook, from 1979. Compositions include: String quartet, 1977; Galixidi, for orchestra, 1977; Dynamis for horn, 1979; Canto for baritone and chamber ensemble, 1979; Chariessa for soprano and orchestra, after Sappho, 1980; Two Elizabethan Songs for chorus, 1982; Ek Ong Kar for chorus, 1983; Dance Converging, for viola, horn, piano and percussion, 1987; The Thief of Love, opera, 1987; Window Waltz for bass clarinet, horn, strings, harpischord, piano and percussion, 1988; Song for strings, 1988; Cello Sonata, 1988; Oh, Thou Beautiful One, for piano, 1989; Dance of wild Angels, for chamber orchestra, 1990. Address: c/o ASCAP, ASCAP Building, One Lincoln Plaza, New York, NY 10023, USA.

SILVERI Paolo, b. 28 Dec 1913, Ofena, Italy. Singer (Baritone). Education: Studied with Perugini in Milan and at the Accademia di Santa Cecilia in Rome with Riccardo Stracciari. Debut: Hans Schwarz in Die Meistersinger, Rome 1939. Career: Sang Germont in La Traviata at Rome, 1944; Visited Covent Garden with the company of the Naples Opera 1946, as Marcello, Scarpia and Figaro in Il Barbiere di Siviglia: returned to Covent Garden until 1952 with the resident company, and with La Scala, as Rigoletto, Count Luna, Amonasro and Iago; Edinburgh Festival with the Glyndebourne company, 1948-49, as Don Giovanni and Renato; La Scala, 1949-55; Metropolitan Opera, 1950-53, as Don Giovanni, Germont, Amonasro, Iago, Count Luna, Escamillo, Rossini's Figaro, Scarpia, Posa and Rigoletto; Sang Otello at Dublin, 1959, then reverted to baritone roles, making last engagement as Israele in Donizetti's Marino Faliero at the 1967 Camden Festival; Teacher in Rome from 1970. Recordings: Simon Boccanegra, La Gioconda, Tosca, Il Barbiere di Siviglia, Don Carlos, L'Arlesiana, Nabucco (Cetra); Il Trovatore; Alceste by Gluck. Address: c/o Conservatorio di Musica Santa Cecilia, Via Dei Greci 18, Rome, Italy.

SILVERMAN Faye-Ellen, b. 2 Oct 1947, New York, New York, USA. Composer; Pianist; Author; Educator. Education: Mannes College of Music, 1966-67; BA cum laude, Honours in Music, Barnard College, 1968; MA, Harvard University, 1971; DMA, Columbia University, 1974. Career includes: Teaching Assistant, Columbia University, 1972-74; Adjunct Assistant Professro, City University of New York, 1972-75; Assistant Professor, Goucher College, 1977-81; Graduate Facility, Department of Music History and Literature, Peabody Institute, Johns Hopkins University, 1977-85; Faculty, Center for Compositional Studies, Aspen Music Festival, 1986; Currently: Graduate and Extension Faculty at Mannes College of Music; Works performed live and/or on radio and TV in many countries. Compositions include: Kalends for Brass Quintet, 1981; Trysts for 2 Trumpets, 1982; Volcanic Songs for Harp, 1983; Restless Winds for Woodwind Quintet, 1986; Adhesions for orchestra, 1987; A Free Pen, a cantata for narrator, soloists, chorus and chamber ensemble, 1990; Journey Towards Oblivion for Soprano, Tenor and Chamber Ensemble, 1991; Azure Skies for Violin, Cello and Harp, 1993; Connections for Clarinet, Cello and Marimba, 1994; Just For Fun for Chamber Orchestra, 1994; Mariana for Mezzo-Soprano, Clarinet and Piano, 1995; At The Colour Cafe, for brass and choir, 1997; Over 55 published compositions. Recordings: LP, Oboe-sthenics; CD, Passing Fancies, Restless Winds and Speaking Alone by Aspen Music Festival Contemporary Ensemble under Stephen Mosko. Publication: 20th Century Section of the Schirmer History of Music. Contributions to: Articles in Current Musicology; The Sonneck Society Bulletin; The Goucher Quarterly; The International Women's Brass Conference Newsletter; Baltimore Sun. Hobbies: Travel; Films; Tennis; Reading. Address: 330 West 28th Street 7G, New York, NY 10001, USA.

SILVERMAN Stanley (Joel), b. 5 July 1938, New York, USA. Composer. Education: Studied at Mills College; Columbia University, 1958-59 and Berkshire Music Centre, 1961. Career: Writer of Incidental Music for Plays, Composer of Operas. Compositions include: Operas and Musical Plays, Elephant Steps, Tanglewood, 1968; Dr Selavy's Magic Theatre, Stockbridge, 1972; Hotel for Criminals, Stockbridge, 1974; Madame Adare, New York Opera, 1980; The Columbine String Quartet Tonight, Stockbridge, 1981; Up from Paradise, New York, 1983; The Golem, 1984; Africanaus Instructus, New York, 1986; A Good Life, Washington, 1986; Black Sea Follies, Stockbridge, 1986; Love and Science, 1990. Address: c/o ASCAP, ASCAP Building, One Lincoln Plaza, New York, NY 10023, USA.

SILVERSTEIN Joseph, b. 21 Mar 1932, Detroit, Michigan, USA. Violinist; Conductor. Education: Studied with Reynolds and Zimbalist, Curtis Institute of Music, Philadelphia, 1945-50; with Gingold and Mischakoff. Career: Houston Symphony Orchestra; Denver Symphony Orchestra; Philadelphia Orchestra; Member, 1955-62, Concertmaster, 1962-83, Assistant Conductor, 1971-83, Boston Symphony Orchestra; Faculty Member, Berkshire Music Center, Tanglewood; Boston University; Interim Music Director, Toledo (Ohio) Symphony Orchestra, 1979-80; Principal Guest Conductor, Baltimore Symphony Orchestra, 1981-83; Music Director, Utah Symphony Orchestra, Salt Lake City, 1983-; Chautauqua (NY) Symphony Orchestra, 1987-; Guest conductor with various orchestras. Recordings: Many discs as violinist and conductor. Honours: Winner, Queen Elisabeth of Belgium competition, 1959; Naumburg Foundation Award, 1960. Address: c/o Utah Symphony Orchestra, 123 West South Temple, Salt Lake City, UT 84101, USA.

SIMA Gabriele, b. 1955, Salzburg, Austria. Singer (Mezzo-soprano). Education: Studied at the Salzburg Mozarteum and the Vienna Musikhochschule. Career: Sang in the Baroque repertoire with the Viennese ensemble Spectaculum and studied with Nikolaus Harnoncourt from 1979; Opera Studio of the Vienna Opera, 1979-82; Has sung at the Vienna Staatsoper from 1982, Tebaldo in Don Carlos, 1989; Salzburg Festival from 1980, notably as Johanna in the premiere of Cerha's Baal, 1981 and in the 1984 premiere of Berio's Un Re in Ascolto; Guest appearances at the Hamburg Staatsoper and at Zurich, Berlin from 1988; Opera and Concert tour of Japan, 1989; Other roles include Rosina, Cherubino, Octavian, Siebel, Annio (Titus), Idamante in Idomeneo, Feodor (Boris), Dorabella (Cosi), Zerlina. Recordings: Handel's Jephtha (Telefunken); Tannhäuser, as Shepherd (Schwann); Barbiere di Siviglia, as Berta (Abbado). Address: Staatsoper, Opernring 2, A-1010 Vienna, Austria.

SIMANDY Joszef, b. 18 Sept 1918, Budapest, Hungary. Singer (Tenor). Education: Studied with Emilia Posszert in Budapest. Debut: Szeged National Theatre 1946, as Don José. Career: Sang at the Budapest Opera 1947-73, notably in the lyric tenor repertory and as Verdi's Otello and Radames and Wagner's Lohengrin and Walther; Sang as guest in Vienna and in Munich (1956-60). Recordings include: Liszt's Coronation Mass (Deutsche Grammophon); Erkel's Laszlo Hunyadi, Pagliacci, Die Meistersinger, Lohengrin (Hungaroton). Address: Magyar Allami Operahaz, Nepoztarsasag utja 22, 1061 Budapest, Hungary.

SIMCOCK Iain (Hamilton), b. 13 Mar 1965, Hemel Hempstead, England. International Concert Organist. Education: Studied at Solihull School, Christ Church Oxford and St Georges Chapel, Windsor Castle. Debut: Recitals for Major Venues all Over the UK and Europe. Career: Sub-organist of Westminster Abbey and Assistant Master of Music, Westminster Cathedral; Frequent Broadcaster for BBC Radio 3; Recitals at Notre Dame de Paris, Strasbourg Cathedral, Proms Royal Alberts Hall; Frequent Tours of Scandinavia, Germany and France. Recordings: Double CD Release of Christus; CD of Vierne Symphonies. Contributions to: Music of Louis Vierne for the Musical Times. Honours: FRCO Top Prizes for Performances & Improvisations; Second Grand Prix, Chartes International Organ Competition. Membership: Royal College of Organists. Hobbies: Cooking; Cycling. Address: 12 Vincent Square Mansions, Walcott Street, London SW1P 2NT, England.

SIMIC Goran, b. 14 Oct 1953, Belgrade, Yugoslavia. Singer (Bass). Education: Studied at the Music High School of Belgrade and Sarajevo. Career: Sang in opera at Sarajevo 1978-84; Member of the Vienna Staatsoper from 1984, notably as Wurm (Luisa Miller), Timur, Sparafucile, the Commendatore, Colline, Pimen, Titurel and Rossini's Basilio; Guest appearances in Russia, Japan, Yugoslavia and the USA; Salzburg Festival from 1986, notably as Horn in Un Ballo in Maschera, conducted by Karajan and by Solti (1990); Other roles include Padre Guardiano, Ramphis; the Grand Inquisitor, Ferrando, Kecal in The Bartered Bride, Raimondo (Lucia di Lammermoor) and Konchak in Prince Igor. Recordings include: Un Ballo in Maschera (Deutsche Grammophon); Khovanshchina conducted by Abbado; Anselmus in Schreker's Irrelohe, 1995. Honours: Prize winner in competitions at Busseto 1981, Moscow 1982 and Philadelphia 1985. Address: Staatsoper, Opernring 2, A-1010 Vienna, Austria.

SIMIĆ-MITROVIĆ Darinka, b. 19 Feb 1937, Beograd, Yugoslavia. Composer; Pianist; Writer. m. Mirosav Mitrovic, 1975, 2 daughters. Education: Elementary and high schools for music, studying piano; Piano with Emil Hajek, Composition with Predrag Milosevic, Music Academy, Beograd. Debut: Sonata in D for violin and piano, presented to Shostakovich and performed with Tripo Simonuti, 1962. Career: Music program, Radio Beograd; Editor in Chief; Manager, musical production, with symphony orchestra, choir, jazz orchestra, light music orchestra, two folk orchestras; Editor in Chief, Stereorama, classical music programme; Chamber music specialisation as both pianist and composer; Works performed at home and in Europe, and recorded and broadcast for Radio Zurich. Compositions: Sonata in D, for Violin and Piano; Give My Patch Back To Me, for 2 Voices and 6 Instruments; Plays, Variations for Bassoon and Piano; Gardener, for Voice and Piano. Publications: Sonata in D for violin, 1966; Book, Da Capo All'Infinito, 1987. Contributions to: Radio and musical magazines, reviews, journals. Honours: Annual Prize, Radio Televizija, 1987; Winner, three radio festivals in Beograd, Dubrovnik and Opatija; Other awards. Membership: Association of Composers, Serbia. Hobbies: Theatre and its history; Cats. Address: Malajnicka 3, 11000 Belgrade, Yugoslavia.

SIMIONATO Giulietta, b. 12 May 1912, Forli, Italy. Singer (Mezzo-soprano). Education: Rovigo with Ettore Locatello and Padua with Guido Palumbo. Debut: As Lola in Cavalleria Rusticana, Montagana, 1928. Career: Sang in premier of Pizzetti's Orsèolo, 1933; La Scala Milan 1936-66, notably as Thomas' Mignon, Massenet's Charlotte, Rossini's Isabella, Rosina and Cenerentola, Donizetti's Giovanna Seymour and as Valentine in Meyerbeer's Les Huguenots; Sang in premiere of Falla's L'Atlantida 1962; UK debut 1947, as Mozart's Cherubino at Edinburgh; Royal Opera House Covent Garden 1953 as Bellini's Adalgisa and Verdi's Amneris and Azucena, opposite Callas; US debut San Francisco 1953; Chicago 1954-61; Metropolitan Opera debut 1959, as Azucena; Last appearance as Servilia in La Clemenza di Tito, Piccola Scala 1966. Recordings: Il Matrimonio Segreto, Cavalleria Rusticana, La Cenerentola, Il Barbiere di Siviglia (Cetra); L'Italiana in Algeri (HMV); Il Trovatore, La Favorita, Rigoletto, La Gioconda, La Cenerentola, Falstaff, Aida, Un Ballo in Maschera (Decca); As Carmen, Gluck's Orpheus, Meyerbeer's Valentine and in partnership with Maria Callas on various minor labels. Address: 29/C Via di Villa Grazioli, Rome, Italy.

SIMKOVA Ludmila, b. 13 April 1930, Mnichovice, Czech Republic. Piano Teacher; Pianist. m. Otto Simek, 17 October 1953, 1 daughter. Education: Conservatory of Prague with Professor A Grünfeldova; Prague Academy of Performing Arts with Professor I Stepanova. Debut: J Brahms, Choice of op 118 and 119, B Smetana, Dreams, C Franck, Symphonic Variations. Career: Performances in Prague as Soloist and Accompanist. Publications: The Basis of Relation Between Tone and Motion, 1979; First Steps to Piano Playing, 1983, 1988; The Organic Piano Playing, 1995. Contributions to: Professional Journals and Magazines. Memberships: Honorary Member, EPTA, England; Czech EPTA, Brno. Address: Jeremenkova 72, Branik 147 00, Praha 4, Czech Republic.

SIMON Abbey, b. 8 Jan 1922, New York City, New York, USA. Concert Pianist. m. Dina Levinson Simon, 28 July 1942, 1 son. Education: Graduate, Curtis Institute of Music, Philadelphia, Pennsylvania. Debut: Town Hall, New York, as winner of Walter W Naumberg Award, 1940. Career: Concert tours in recital and with orchestra on six continents, 1940-; Professor of Piano, Juilliard School of Music, New York City; Cullen Chair for Distinguished Professor, University of Houston, Texas. Recordings: Complete Chopin repertoire for solo piano and orchestra; Complete Ravel repertoire for solo piano and orchestra; Rachmaninov Concerto No 2 and preludes; Many other recordings include the Piano Virtuoso and works by Schumann, Brahms and Liszt. Honours: First Prize, Walter W Naumberg Piano Competition; Best Recital of the Year, Federation of Music Clubs, New York; National Orchestral Award; Elizabeth Sprague Coolidge Medal, London; Harriet Cohen Foundation, London. Current Management: Gurtman & Murtha Associates Inc, New York City. Hobby: Tennis; Photography. Address: 45 Chemin Moise Deboule, 1209 Geneva, Switzerland.

SIMON Geoffrey, b. 3 July 1946, Adelaide, South Australia, Australia. Conductor. Education: Studied at Melbourne University, the Juilliard School and Indiana University. Career: Guest appearances with leading orchestras, 1974-; Music Director, Australian Sinfonia, London; Music Director, Albany Symphony Orchestra, New York, 1987-89; Music Director, Cala Records, London, 1991-; Artistic Advisor, 1993-94, Music Director, 1994-, Sacramento Symphony, California; Regular concerts with Te London Philharmonic, London Symphony and English Chamber Orchestras; Other engagements with the Munich, Israel and New Japan Philharmonic Orchestras, the American, City of Birmingham, Sapporo and Tokyo Metropolitan Symphonies, the Orchestras of the Australian Broadcasting Corporation and the Australian Opera; Conducted the Royal Philharmonic Orchestra in the premiere of Paul Patterson's 1st Symphony at the Cheltenham Festival. Recordings: Music by French composers of the 1920s and rare music by Respighi and Tchaikovsky; Patterson's Mass of the Sea; The Warriors and other works by Percy Grainger; Music by Debussy, Ravel, Respighi, Brahms, Borodin, Mussorgsky, Saint-Saëns and Barry Conyngham; The London Cello Sound - the 40 cellos of the London Philharmonic, Royal Philharmonic Orchestra, BBC Symphony Orchestra and the Philharmonia Orchestra, similarly, the London Violin Sound, the London Viola Sound and the London Trombone Sound. Honours: Prize Winner, John Player International Conductor's Award, 1974; Prix de la Ville de Paris, Académie du Disque Français, 1985; Gramophone Award for Respighi recordings. Membership: Vice-President, Stokowski Society, 1993-. Address: c/o Cala Records Ltd, 17 Shakespeare Gardens, London N2 9LJ, England.

SIMON Laszlo, b. 16 July 1948, Miskolc, Hungary. Pianist; Professor, 1978. Sabine Simon, 2 daughters. Education: Musica; education in Stockholm, Hannover, New York. Teachers: Hans Leygraf, Ilona Kabos, Claudio Arrau. Debut: 1966. Career: Appearances in Hamburg, Rome, Stockholm, Helsinki, Oslo, Berlin, Tokyo, Seoul, London, Porto, Professor, Karlsruhe State Academy, 1977-; Professor, Hochschule der Kunste, Berlin, 1981-; Stockholm 1988-; Master Classes at Murashino Academy in Tokyo, 1988-. Recordings: BIS: Liszt, Clementi, Kodály; Caprice: Schubert, de Frumerie, Velte, Liszt. Honours: III Prize Busoni Competition, I Prize Casagrande Competition. Hobby: Cooking. Current Management: Konsertbolaget, Stockholm. Address: Hochschule der Kunste Berlin, Fasanenstr 1, D-1000 Berlin, Germany.

SIMONEAU Leopold, b. 3 May 1928, Quebec, Canada. Tenor. m. Pierette Alarie, 1946. Education: Studied in Montreal with Salvator Issaurel and with Paul Althouse in New York. Debut: Montreal, Varietées Lyriques in 1941 as Hadji in Lakmé. Career: Sang in Montreal as Wilhelm Meister, Tamino and Ferrando, and Central City Colorado, Philadelphia and New Orleans; Sang in Paris at Opéra-Comique in 1949 in Mireille by Gounod, Aix-en-Provence in 1950 in Iphigénie en Tauride; Glyndebourne Festival, 1951-54 as Don Ottavio and Idamante; Paris in 1953 as Tom Rakewell in the French premiere of The Rake's Progress; La Scala debut in 1953, and Vienna Staatsoper in 1954; Visited London's Festival Hall with the Vienna Company in 1954; Salzburg Festival, 1956-59 as Don Ottavio and Tamino; Chicago Lyric Opera in 1959 as Alfredo; Taught in Montreal after retirement from stage; Director of the Opéra de Quebec from 1971. Recordings: Die Zauberflöte; Die Entführung; Così fan tutte; Don Giovanni; Orphée et Eurydice; Idomeneo; Iphigénie en Tauride; Berlioz's Requiem. Address: c/o San Francisco Conservatory of Music, 1201 Ortega Street, CA 94122, USA.

SIMONETTI Riccardo, b. 10 January 1970, Leigh, Lancashire, England. Singer (Baritone). Education: Royal Northern College of Music, with Robert Alderson. Career: Sang Rodimarte in Scarlatti's Il Trionfo d'Onore at Liège, Trento, Caen and Brussels; English National Opera from 1996, notably as Bill in Mahagonny (debut role) and Papageno; Ping in Turandot at Nice, Albert in Werther for English Touring Opera, Britten's Demetrius for the Broomhill Trust and Belcore for Clonter Farm Opera; Season 1997 with Mozart's Count for English Touring Opera and a principal contract with ENO; Concerts include the St Matthew Passion with the Liverpool PO, Messiah under David Willcocks and concerts with the Liverpool Philharmonic Choir. Honours include: Winner, Anne Ziegler/Esso Award, 1993. Address: c/o IMG Artists, Media House, 3 Burlington Lane, London W4 2TH, England.

SIMONOV Yuri (Ivanovich), b. 4 Mar 1941, Saratov, USSR. Conductor. Education: Studied at the Leningrad Conservatory with Kramarov (viola) and Rabinovich (conducting). Career: Debut 1953, conducting school orchestra; Led several opera productions while a student; Principal Conductor of the Kislovodsk Philharmonic 1968-69; Assistant Conductor of the Leningrad Philharmonic 1968-69; Principal Conductor of the Bolshoi Theatre, Moscow, from 1970: toured with Prince Igor to the Metropolitan Opera 1975; Premieres include Shchedrin's ballet Anna Karenina, 1972; Teacher at the Moscow Conservatory from 1975; Frequent Guest Conductor with British orchestras; Performances include: Das Rheingold, at Bolshoi Theatre, 1979; Eugen Onegin by Tchaikovsky, 1982 and La Traviata, 1986, Covent Garden; Mahler Festival in Paris with LPO, 1989; The Queen of Spades, Bastille Opera, Paris, 1993; Concert tours of Japan with NHK Orchestra, 1993-95; Der Ring des Nibelungen, Budapest Opera House, 1995-98; Shostakovich Symphony No 4, with BNO, 1996. Recordings include: Glinka, Russlan and Ludmilla, opera with the Bolshoi; Anna Karenina, ballet with the Bolshoi; Wagner, excerpts and overtures; Mahler, Symphony No 1, with RPO; Tchaikovsky, Romeo and Juliet and 1812 Overture; Prokofiev, Romeo and Juliet and Lieutenent Kije. Honours: Winner, Accademia di Santa Cecilia Competition, Rome, 1968; Artist of Merit of the USSR 1983. Address: Allied Artists Agency, 42 Montpelier Square, London SW7 1JZ, England.

SIMPSON Dudley (George), b. 4 Oct 1922, Melbourne, Victoria, Australia. Composer; Conductor; Pianist. m. Jill Yvonne Bathurst, 8 Oct 1960, 1 son, 2 daughter. Education: Studied piano with Vera Porter, Victor Stephenson, Melbourne University; Orchestration with Elford Mack, Melbourne, Dr Gordon Jacob, England; Composition with John Ingram, Australia. Debut: 1st and 2nd M D Borovansky Ballet, Royal Ballet, Covent Garden. Career: Guest Conductor, Royal Ballet, Covent Garden, 1960-62; Principal Conductor at British and European major festivals including: Monte Carlo, Nice, Athens and Middle East, 1961-63; 2 World tours with Dame Margot Fonteyn and Rudolph Nureyev, 1962-64; Conducted Tokyo Philharmonic Orchestra, Ballet Festival, 1985; Conducted premiere of own work Class, Ballet at Covent Garden, 1986. Compositions: The Winter Play, ballet, Sadler's Wells Royal Ballet; Here We Come, ballet, transcription for Orchestra, Canadian National Ballet; Ballet, Class, Royal Ballet School; Marguerite and Armand for Fonteyn and Nureyev, transcription for Orchestra; The Pastoral Symphony; Numerous TV themes and incidental music including Shakespeare Canon for BBC; A Trilogy of Psalms for Choir. Honour: Diploma of Music (Hons). Hobbies: Rotary; Gardening; Photography. Address: 6 Tristania Grove, Menai, New South Wales, 2234, Australia.

SIMS Ezra, b. 16 Jan 1928, Birmingham, Alabama, USA. Composer. Education: BA, Birmingham Southern College, 1947; BMus, Yale University School of Music, 1952; US Army Language School, 1953; MA, Mills College, 1956. Career includes: Music Director, New England Dinosaur Dance Theatre, 1968-74; Member, Theory Faculty, New England Conservatory, 1976-78; President, Dinosaur Annex Music Ensemble, 1977-81; Composer; Lecturer at Mozarteum, 1992-93. Compositions include: Twenty Years After, 1978; All Done From Memory, 1980; Ruminations, 1980; Phenomena, 1981; Sextet, 1981; Solo After Sextet, 1981; Quartet, 1982; Pictures for an Institution, 1983; String Quartet No 4, 1984; Night Unto Night, 1984; The Conversion, 1985; Solo in Four Movements, 1987; Quintet, 1987; Flight, 1989; Night Piece, 1989; Concert Piece, 1990; Duo, 1992; Invocation, 1992; Stanzas, 1995; Duo, 1996. Recordings include: Sextet; String Quartet No 2, 1962; Elegie - nach Rilke; Third Quartet; Quintet; Night Piece; Flight; Solo in Four Movements; Concert Piece. Publications: Complete works, American Composers Edition 1954-95; ..as I was saying..., Corpus Microtonole, 1987. Contributions include: Apologia pro Musica Sva, Jaarboch, 1992; Stichting Huyghaus-Fotaker; Reflections on This and That in Perspectives of New Music, volume 29 No 1; Yet Another 72-Noter, in Computer Music Journal, volume 12 No 4. Honours include: Guggenheim Foundation Fellowship, 1962; NEA Fellowships, 1976, 1978; Koussevitzky Foundation Commission, 1983; American Academy of Arts and Letters Award, 1985; Numerous other honours and awards. Memberships: American Composers Alliance; Broadcast Music Inc. Current Management: Rosalie

Calabrese, Box 20580, Park West Sta, New York, NY 10025-1521, USA. Address: 1168 Massachusetts Avenue, Cambridge, MA 02138, USA.

SIMSON Julie, b. 13 Feb 1956, Milwaukee, Wisconsin, USA. Mezzo-Soprano; Artist Performer; Assistant Professor. Education: BMusEd, Western Michigan University; MMus, University of Illinois. Career: New York recital debut, Weill Recital Hall, Carnegie Hall, 1989; Radio appearance, The Listening Room, New York Times Radio, 1989; Lyric Opera Cleveland debut, as Minerva in The Return of Ulysses, 1991; Opera Colorado debut, Emilia in Otello, 1991; Other opera appearances with Santa Fe Opera, Dallas Civic Opera, Opera Colorado, Houston Opera Association; Appeared as Soloist with symphonies, Milwaukee, Des Moines, Missoula, Denver, Cheyenne; George Crumb Festival featuring Ancient Voices of Children, Prague, Czech Republic; Gave solo recital at Prague Spring Festival, 1994; Currently Assistant Professor of Voice, University of Colorado. Recording: Horatio Parker's Hora Norissima. Honours: Mozart Prize, International Belvedere Competition, Vienna, 1985; Winner, East and West Artists International Competition for Carnegie Hall Debut; National 2nd Place Winner, NATS Artist Award. Hobby: Swimming. Address: University of Colorado-Boulder, College of Music, Campus Box 301, Boulder, CO 80309-0301, USA.

SINGER Jeanne (Walsh), b. 4 Aug 1924, New York, New York, USA. Composer; Concert Pianist; Teacher; Lecturer. m. Richard G Singer, 1945, deceased 1972, 1 son. Education: BA magna cum laude, Barnard College, Columbia University, 1944; 15 years study, piano, Nadia Reisenberg; Artist Diploma, National Guild of Piano Teachers. Career: Pianist, solo with ensembles, 30 years; Radio and TV appearances including many public performances of own compositions; Lecturer; Private Teacher; Freelance Composer, many commissions; All-Singer Concert, Boston, Massachusetts, 1979; Bogota, Colombia, South America, 1980; Performances of own compositions throughout USA, 1978-94, including Kennedy Center, Washington DC, 1988 and Lincoln Center, New York City Annual Concerts, 1983-94; Also in Toronto, Canada, 1982, Rome, Italy, 1983, Toulouse, France, 1984, Vancouver, Canada, 1984, Budapest, Hungary, 1985, Belgium, Netherlands, 1986; Recent performances of her music include Hokkaido, London, Brussels, Antwerp, Osnabruch and Bratislava; Founder and Director of The Musinger Players, vocal-chamber ensemble, 1986-97. Compositions include: Suite in Harpischord Style; A Cycle of Love; Nocturne for Clarinet; From the Green Mountains (trio); Selected Songs; Suite for Horn and Harp; Songs from Later Years; Songs of Reverence (song cycle); Composers' Prayer (choral); Mary's Boy (choral); Come Greet the Spring (choral); Five Wry Rimes (voice and clarinet); Recollections of City Island (trio); The Lost Garden (tenor, cello, piano), 1988; To Be Brave Is All, Orchestra and voice, 1993. Recordings: To Stir a Dream: American Poets in Song, CD Album of own vocal music with various artists, 1990; Suite for Horn and Harp, on CD, Horn and Harp Odyssey, 1996; A Cycle of Love, (4 songs on Long Island Composers Alliance album), 1997; To Be Brave Is All and Avenue of The Righteous, Slovak Radio Symphony Orchestra with Austin Miskell, tenor, 1998; Chamber music. Honours: 19 consecutive Annual ASCAP Awards, 1978-97; Honorary DMus, World University, 1984; Distinguished Achievement Citation, National League of American Pen Women, 1988. Memberships: ASCAP; International Alliance for Women in Music; National League of American Pen Women; The Pen and Brush Inc; National Association of Composers, USA; Long Island Composers Alliance; LPIBA; LFABI. Address: 64 Stuart Place, Manhasset, Long Island, NY 11030-2620, USA.

SINGER Malcolm (John), b. 13 July 1953, London, England. Composer; Conductor. m. Sara Catherine Nathan, 15 July 1984. Education: Magdalene College, Cambridge; Studied with Nadia Boulanger, Paris and Gyorgy Ligeti, Hamburg. Career: Teacher, Yehudi Menuhin School; Department of PCS, Guildhall School of Music and Drama; Teacher of Composition, Guildhall School of Music and Drama and The Yehudi Menuhin School. Compositions: Time Must Have a Stop for Orchestra and Piano Solo, 1976; The Icarus Toccato for Piano Duet, 1979; A Singer's Complaint, 1979; Making Music for Narrator and Orchestra, 1983; Nonet for Strings, 1984; Sonata for Piano, 1986; Yetziah, Music for Dance, 1987; Piano Quartet, 1989; York, a cantata, 1990; Kaddish for a Cappella Choir, 1991; Honk, for Ugly Culture, 1992; A Hopeful Place, for Yehudi Menuhin's 80th Birthday, 1996. Publications: Articles of self by R Rollin in Musical Quarterly and K Potter in Musical Times. Contributions to: Composer. Membership: APC; Composers Guild of Great Britain. Address: 29 Goldsmith Avenue, London, W3 6HR, England.

SINIMBERGHI Gino, b. 26 Aug 1913, Rome, Italy. Singer (Tenor). Education: Studied at the Academia di Sant Cecilia, Rome. Career: Sang at the Berlin Staatsoper, 1937-44; Italy, 1944-68 Notably as Ismaele in Nabucco; Sang in the Italian premiere of Hindemith's Long Christmas Dinner and appeared in Milan, Venice and at the Caracalla Festival; Frankfurt 1960 in Monteverdi's Orfeo, RAI Italian Radio 1970, in Rossini's La Donna del Lago. Recordings include: Massenet's Thérèse; La Donna Del Lago, Donizetti Requiem; Nabucco.

SINOPOLI Giuseppe, b. 2 Nov 1946, Venice, Italy. Conductor; Composer. Education: Benedetto Marcello Conservatory, Venice; Medical School at the University of Padua; Diploma in Medicine 1971; 1968- attended courses of Maderna and Stockhausen at Darmstadt; Conducting with Hans Swarowsky in Vienna. Career: Practised as a surgeon and psychiatrist; Faculty of Venice Conservatory 1972-; founded and conducted the Bruno Maderna Ensemble, for performances of contemporary music 1975; Opera debut Venice 1978, Aida; Concerts with the Berlin Philharmonic 1979; US debut 20 Jan 1983, with the New York Philharmonic Covent Garden debut 1983, Manon Lescaut; Principal Conductor Philharmonia Orchestra London, 1984-95; Metropolitan Opera debut 1985, Tosca; Bayreuth Festival debut 1985, Tannhäuser; Conducted Der Rosenkavalier at Berlin, 1989, Salome 1990; Music Director of the Dresden Staatskapelle from 1991; Bayreuth 1990, Der fliegende Holländer; Conducted Carmen at Munich, 1992; Parsifal at Bayreuth, 1997. Compositions: 25 Studi su tre Parametri 1969; Musica per calcolatori analogici 1969; Numquid et unum for harpischord and flute 1970; Opus Ghimal for orchestra 1971; Symphonie Imaginaire for choruses, 10 children's voices and 3 orchestras 1972-73; Requiem Hashshirim for unaccompanied voices 1976; String Quartet 1977; Lou Salomé, opera 1981. Recordings include: Madama Butterfly 1988; Aida, Salome, Tannhäuser (Deutsche Grammophon); Verdi and Puccini arias with Mirella Freni; Schubert's 8th Symphony (Philharmonia), Scriabin's 3rd (New York PO); Die Frau ohne Schatten. Address: c/o Philharmonia Orchestra, 76 Great Portland Street, London W1N 5AL, England.

SIPPOLA Ulla, b. 1959; Janakkala, Finland. Singer (Mezzo-soprano). Education: Studied at the Sibelius Academy, Helsinki. Career: Sang with the Finnish National Opera from 1985 and at Savonlinna from 1986, notably as Amneris in Aida (1990); Freiburg Opera from 1989, as Auntie in Peter Grimes, Jane Seymour in Anna Bolena and other roles; Hagen/Westfalen, 1992, in the title role of Beeson's Lizzie Borden, Deutsche Oper am Rhein as Eboli and Amneris; Many concert appearances. Address: c/o Finnish National Opera, Bulevardi 23-27, SF-00180 Helsinki, Finland.

SIRENKO Alla (Pavlovna), b. 23 June 1964, Lviv, Western Ukraine. Composer; Pianist; Organist. Education: Studied piano, Kiev Conservatory and Moscow Conservatory; Studied organ, Tallinn Conservatory, Estonia and Lviv Conservatory. Debut: Performance with Lviv Philharmonic Symphony Orchestra, Piano Concerto by Liszt, 1980. Career: Performed as Organist and Pianist throughout Western Europe, including tours in Italy, Spain and England; Frequent appearances on Radio and Television. Compositions include: Opera, Verona (Based on Shakespeare's Romeo and Juliet); Opera, Olga; Musical, The Small Prince (from the story by St Exuperi); A Cycle of Songs for mezzo soprano and piano (based on poems by Lorca); Variations for piano solo; Fly Holland Man, wind quintet with piano in five parts; Messa for string chamber orchestra (upon request of the Doppler Association of Rome); Cycle of Children's Pieces for wind instruments and piano. Honours include: Prizes for Best Performance and Best Compositions, 1982-92. Memberships: Italian Composers Society; Societa Italiana DegliAutori ed Editori. Hobbies: Theatre; Reading; Travel; Art Exhibitions. Address: The Bungalow, Dairy Cottage, Siddington, Cirencester, Glos GL7 6ET, England.

SIRKIA Raimo, b. 7 Feb 1951, Helsinki, Finland. Tenor. Education: Studied at the Sibelius Academy in Helsinki, 1977-80 and in Rome and London. Career: Has sung at the Savonlinna Festival from 1982, and Kiel Opera from 1983 as Tamino, Lionel in Martha, Pollione and Cavaradossi; Sang dramatic roles at Dortmund Opera from 1985 as Riccardo, Manrico, Otello, Alvaro, Walther, Parsifal, Don José, Bacchus, Huon in Oberon, Narraboth and Vladimir in Prince Igor; Guest appearances at the Deutsche Oper am Rhein and member since 1991, Dresden, Stuttgart, Braunschweig, Karlsruhe, Basle, Stockholm, Copenhagen, Bordeaux and the Deustche Oper Berlin (as Manrico in 1989); Hanover, Essen, Hamburg (Calaf in 1992); Member of the Finnish National Opera at Helsinki from 1989 singing Edgardo and Alfredo there and at Tallinn in 1990; Sang at Savonlinna in 1990 as Radames and as Erik in Der fliegende Holländer; Sang Idomeneo at the Finlandia Hall, Helsinki in 1991; Has appeared as a guest soloist at many important opera houses throughout Europe; Role of Canio at the Royal Opera House in Stockholm followed by new production of Pagliacci in Tampere, Finland, 1996; Debut as Tannhäuser in the Savonlinna Opera Festival's new production in 1996 and as Siegmund in the same year; Siegfried in new production of Wagner's Ring at the Finnish National Opera in 1997; Frequent concert appearances. Recordings: Jää mun lähellein, 1984; Opera Arias, 1992; Amado mio, 1994; Juha, 1995; Symphony No 8 Mahler, 1994; Der fliegender Holländer, video, 1989. Address: PO Box 176, SF 00251 Helsinki, Finland.

SISMAN Elaine (Rochelle), b. 20 Jan 1952, New York City, USA. Musicologist. m. Martin Fridson, 14 June 1981, 1 son, 1 daughter. Education: AB, Cornell University, 1972; MFA, 1974, PhD, 1978, Princeton University. Career: Instructor, 1976-79, Assistant Professor, 1979-81, University of Michigan; National Endowment for The Humanities Fellowship, 1981-82; Assistant Professor, 1982-90, Associate Professor, 1990-94; Professor, Columbia University, New York, 1995-. Publications: Haydn and The Classical Variation, 1993; Mozart's Jupiter Symphony, 1993; Haydn and His World, 1997. Contributions to: Haydn Studies, 1981; Small and Expanded Forms: Koch's Model and Haydn's Music, in Musical Quarterly, 1982; Haydn Kongress, Wien, 1982, 1986; The Orchestra: Origins and Transformations, 1986; The New Harvard Dictionary of Music, 1986; Haydn's Theater Symphonies, Journal of the American Musicological Society, 1990; Brahms and the Variation Canon, 19th Century Music, 1990; Pathos and the Pathétique, Beethoven Forum, 1994; Genre, Gesture and Meaning in Mozart's Prague Symphony, 1997; After the Heroic Style, Beethoven Forum, 1997. Address: Columbia University, Department of Music, 611 Dodge Hall, New York, NY 10027, USA.

SITKOVETSKY Dmitry, b. 27 Sep 1954, Baku, Ukraine. Violinist. m. Susan Roberts, 26 Jul 1983. Education: Moscow Central Music School, 1961-72; Moscow Conservatory, 1972-77; Artistic Diploma, Juilliard School, USA, 1977-79. Debuts: Berlin Philharmonic, 1980, Chicago Symphony, 1983, London Proms, 1986, New York Philharmonic, 1988. Career: Music Director, Korsholm Music Festival, Vaasa, Finland, 1984; Guest Soloist at Salzburg, Edinburgh, Berlin, Vienna, Ansbach, Helsinki, Istanbul, Newport, Spoleto and Mostly Mozart Festivals, with Berlin, Munich, Royal London, and Rotterdam Philharmonics, Chicago, Cincinnati, Detroit, Toronto, Montreal, London, Vienna, Munich Radio, BBC, NHK and Tokyo Symphonies and Cleveland Orchestra, Orchestre de Paris and Orchestre de la Suisse Romande; Promenade Concerts London in 1989 with concertos by Beethoven and Tchaikovsky; Played the Elgar Concerto at the 1990 Proms, and Brahms in 1991. Compositions: Transcription of Bach, Goldberg Variations for String Trio, 1984 and for String Orchestra, 1994. Recordings include: Grieg's Complete Sonatas for Violin and Piano with Bella Davidovich; Bach Sonatas and Partitas for Solo Violin, 1985; Mozart Violin Concerti with English Chamber Orchestra, 1986; Schubert Complete Piano Trios with G Oppitz and D Geringas, 1986; Brahms Complete Sonatas for Violin and Piano, 1987; Prokofiev Violin Concerti Nos 1 and 2 with London Symphony Orchestra under Colin Davis, 1988. Honours: 1st prize, Concertino Praha, 1966; 1st prize, International Fritz Kreisler Competition, Vienna, 1979; Avery Fisher Career Grant, NYC, 1983. Membership: ASCAP, 1986-. Current Management: Columbia Artists, USA; Harold Holt Ltd, London, England. Address: c/o Harolt Holt Ltd, 31 Sinclair Road, London W14 0NS, England.

SITSKY Larry, b. 10 Sept 1934, Tientsin, China. Composer; Pianist; Musicologist; Teacher; Broadcaster. m. 8 Feb 1961, 1 son, 1 daughter. Education: Graduated, 1956, Postgraduate Studies, 1956-58, New South Wales State Conservatorium, Sydney, Australia; Studied with Egon Petri, San Francisco Conservatory of Music, USA, 1959-61; Higher Doctorate in Fine Arts, Australian National University, 1997. Career: First recital aged 11; Lived Australia, 1951-; Many recitals including contemporary Australian music, USA, 1959-61; Numerous commissions; Piano Teacher, Queensland State Conservatorium of Music, Guest Lecturer, Queensland University, 1961-65; Head, Keyboard Studies, 1966-78, Department Head, Composition, Electronic Music, 1978-81, Department Head, Composition, Musicology, 1981-, Canberra School of Music, ACT; External Examiner, Composition, Piano Performance, Australian Universities and Colleges of Advanced Education; Artistic Director, Bi-Centennial Recording Project; Director, Australian Contemporary Music Ensemble; Composer-in-Residence, University of Cincinnati, USA, 1989-90; Director, Conference Music and Musicians in Australian Culture 1930-1960, Sept 1993; Promotion to Reader, 1993; Granted Personal Chair, Australian National University, 1994. Compositions: Numerous including: The Jade Flute; The Secret Doctrine: 7 Epigrams for percussion duo, 1995; Opera, The Golem, 1994; Signor Locatelli Visits Russia, for violin ensemble, 1995; Operas, Lenz, De Profundis, Fiery Tales; Concertos for various instruments; Keyboard music. Recordings: Numerous for major record labels; The Golem, 3 CD set; Piano concerto; Chamber instrumental music. Publications include: The repressed Russian Avant-Garde 1900-1929, book; Busoni and the Piano, book; Editor, Complete piano music of Roy Agnew. Contributions to: Numerous professional journals. Honours include: Critics' Circle Award, 1994; Special series of broadcasts and concerts for his 60th birthday; Awards for Piano Concerto at Paris Rostrum 1995; Biography written by Robin Holmes, 1997. Address: 29 Threlfall Street, Chifley, ACT 2606, Australia.

SIUKOLA Heikki, b. 20 Mar 1943, Finland. Singer (Tenor). Education: Studied at the Sibelius Academy, Helsinki. Career: Sang in Opera at Tempere and Helsinki; Engaged at Wuppertal

1972-79, Krefeld 1980-83; Season 1989 as Erik at Oslo, Siegmund in Naples and Tristan at Basle and Nancy; Sang Tristan at Lyon 1990, Tannhäuser at Montpellier 1991; Other roles include, Andrea Chénier, Alfredo, Cavaradossi, Don Carlos, Pinkerton, Dick Johnson, and Hoffmann; Florestan in Fidelio, Lohengrin, Parsifal and Bacchus. Recordings include: Konrad in Marschner's Hans Heiling. Address: c/o Opéra de Montpellier, 11 Boulevard Victor Hugo, F-34000 Montpellier, France.

SIXTA Jozef, b. 12 May 1940, Jicin, Czechoslovakia. Composer. Education: Bratislava Conservatory, 1955-60, High School of Music, Bratislava, 1960-64; Postgraduate studies in Paris, 1971. Career: Lecturer at University of Music and Drama, Bratislava. Compositions: Asynchronie, 1968; Noneto, 1970; Flutes Quartet 1972; Solo for Piano, 1973; Recitativo for Violin Solo, 1974; Octeto, 1977; Piano Sonata, 1985. Recordings: Variations for 13 Instruments, 1967; Asynchronie, 1968; Noneto, 1970; Punctum Contra Punctum, 1971; Flutes Quartet, 1972; Solo for Piano, 1973; Octeto, 1977; Piano Sonata, 1985. Membership: Slovak Music Union. Honours: Prague Spring Festival Composition Competition, 1966; Radio Tribune UNESCO, Paris, 1970; Haydn Festival Competition, Austria, 1987; Jan Leveslav Bella Prize, 1987 and 1990. Hobby: Travel. Address: Riazanska 68, 83102 Bratislava, Slovakia.

SJÖBERG Johan-Magnus (Göran), b. 7 June 1953, Östra Grevie, Sweden. Organist; Cantor; Composer. m. Cajsa Finnström, 4 June 1983, 1 son, 1 daughter. Education: Organist-Cantor, 1972; Music Pedagogue, 1975; Choir Pedagogue, College of Music, Malmö, 1981. Career: Music Director, Sankt Hans Church, Lund, 1974-; Performed at Poznán Spring Festival, 1989, Warsaw Autumn Festival, 1992, Festival for Contemporary Church Music, Sweden, 1993. Compositions: Face It for wind quintet and tape; Via Dolorosa for flute and tape; Windows for chamber orchestra and tape; String Quartet 1 (Reverse); Around for flute and choir; Choral works. Recordings: Composer of: Windows, Basic Music; Ave Maria Stella and Ave Maria; Five; Reverse, 1995. Honours: Culture Award, Lund, 1988. Membership: Swedish Composers' Society. Hobbies: Western riding; Cooking. Address: Flygelvägen 307, 224 72 Lund, Sweden.

SKALICKI Wolfram, b. 1938, Vienna, Austria. Amrei Skalicki. Stage Designer. Education: Studied in Austria. Career: Stage designs for San Francisco Opera from 1962, The Rake's Progress, The Ring (1967-72), Aida, Lady Macbeth of Mtsensk, L'Africaine, Andrea Chenier and Salome; Collaborations with costume designer Amrei Skalicki at the Vienna Burgtheater, Volksoper and Staatsoper; Productions in Lyon, Munich, Toronto, Buenos Aires, Hamburg, Miami, Athens and Geneva; Operas have included Lulu, Boris Godunov, Tristan und Isolde, Death in Venice, Herodiade and Giovanna d'Arco; Andrea Chenier at the Metropolitan, Boris at Pittsburgh, Falstaff for Canadian Opera, Ariadne at Los Angeles; The Queen of Spades in Santiago and Elektra for Seattle Opera; Exhibitions at Bayreuth, Vienna, Zurich, New York and San Francisco; Professor at the University for Music and the Performing Arts, Graz. Address: c/o San Francisco Opera, War Memorial House, Van Ness Avenue, San Francisco, CA 94102, USA.

SKARECKY Jana (Milena), b. 11 Nov 1957, Prague, Czechoslovakia. Composer; Teacher. m. David Colwell, 6 Aug 1983, 2 daughters. Education: BMus, Honours Composition, Wilfrid Laurier University, Ontario, Canada, 1980; ARCT, Piano Performance, Royal Conservatory of Music, Toronto, 1984; MMus, Composition, University of Sydney, Australia, 1987. Career: Composer; Teacher, piano and theory, Canada, USA, Australia, 1977-; Faculty, Piano Theory, Royal Conservatory of Music, Toronto, Canada; Co-Founder, Runningbrook Music (publishing), Mississauga, Ontario; Compositions performed in North America, Europe, Australia and Japan. Compositions include: Sea Window, brass quintet, 1983; 3 Movements on Bach Themes, trumpet and strings/trumpet and organ, 1984; Oresteia, solo double bass, 1986; Rose of Sharon, solo harp, 1985; Night Songs, 4 percussionists, 1986; The Sign of the Four, solo tenor recorder, 1986; Aquamarine, orchestra, 1986; Dayspring, mezzo-soprano, piano, 1987; Lullabies, voice, 1988; Flame of Roses, flute, cello, piano, 1989; The Living Wind, mezzo, flute, cello, harp, 1990; Consort Royal recorder quartet, 1990; Sonata for Viola and Piano, 1992; La Carona, 3 motets, 1993; Sinfonia Lauretta, string orchestra, 1994; Into the Centre of Our Heart, 1994; Numerous choral works. Recording: Flame of Roses, on Spinners of Starlight CD produced by the Ardeleana Trio. Publications include: On Her Wings, 1993, solo organ; Love Is Come Again, SATB choir, 1995. Memberships: Canadian League of Composers; Association of Canadian Women Composers; Canadian Music Centre. Address: 2318 Bonner Road, Mississauga, Ontario L5J 2C6, Canada.

SKELTON Stuart, b. 1968, Australia. Singer (Tenor). Studied in Australia, Cincinnati and San Francisco. Debut: Alfredo for Rockdale Opera Company, Australia. Career: Appearances with San Francisco Opera from 1996-, in Hamlet, Lohengrin, Carmen, Hoffman, Salome and Aida; Australian Opera debut 1993, in Die Meistersinger; Basilio and Don Curzio in Figaro for Western Opera Theater tour, 1995; Title role in Argento's The Aspern Papers for San Francisco Opera Center '96 Showcase production; Concerts include opera highlights with Louisville SO and the Verdi Requiem with the Lubbock, Texas, SO. Honours include: Winner, Marianne Mathy Award and McDonald Aria Award, Australia. Address: c/o San Francisco Opera, War Memorial House, Van Ness Avenue, San Francisco, CA 94102, USA.

SKEMPTON Howard, b. 1947, England. Composer; Accordionist; Music Publisher. Education: Studied with Cornelius Cardew, 1960s. Career: Freelance Composer; Visiting Lecturer in Composition at the University of Adelaide, South Australia, 1991; Concerto for Oboe and Accordion premiered and toured by Camerata Roman of Sweden, 1997. Compositions include: Lento for orchestra, 1990; Concerto for Hurdy Gurdy and Percussion, 1994; Gemini Dances for flute, clarinet, violin, cello, percussion and piano, 1994; Shiftwork for percussion quartet, 1994; Chamber Concerto, 1995; We Who With Songs, for chorus and organ, 1995; Winter Sunrise, string trio, 1996; Delicate, Ballet, 1996; The Flight of Song for chorus, 1996; Two Poems of Edward Thomas, for choir, 1996; Into My Heart an Air that Kills, for soprano, piano, 2 violins, viola and cello, 1996; Concerto for Oboe and Accordion, 1997; Numerous piano pieces, including Images (1989), Maestoso (1990) and Ring in the Valiant (1993). Address: c/o Promotion Department, 70 Baker Street, London W1M 7DJ, England.

SKINNER John York, b. 5 Mar 1949, York, England. Counter-Tenor. m. (1) Juanesse Adele Reeve, 15 Aug 1970, (2) Janet Lesley Budden, 16 Jan 1976, 2 daughters. Education: York Minster Song School; Colchester Institute; Royal Academy of Music in London; BMus (London); LRAM. Debut: Kassel Opera, West Germany. Career: Broadcasts on BBC, WDR, NDR, ORTF and Italian Radio; Opera appearances at Royal Opera Covent Garden, La Scala Milan, Scottish Opera, Festival Ottawa and English Music Theatre. Recordings: Works of John Dowland with Consort of Musicke; Handel's Partenope; Other Mediaeval, Renaissance and Baroque music. Honours: Honorary Member, Royal College of Music, 1982; Associate of Royal Academy of Music, 1984. Address: Denstone College, Uttoxeter, Staffordshire, ST14 5HN, England.

SKOGLUND Annika, b.. 5 Nov 1960, Vanersborg, Alvsborg, Sweden. Singer (Mezzo-Soprano). Education: Studied at Royal Academy of Music, Gothenburg and London. Career: Sang Cherubino at Drottningholm 1988, followed by Suzuki at the Royal Opera in Stockholm; Returned to Drottningholm as Ramiro in La Finta Giardiniera and made Italian debut at Venice as Isolier in Le Comte Ory; Further engagements as Cherubino at Oslo, Suzuki in Stockholm and the Countess in Maw's The Rising of the Moon at the 1990 Wexford Festival; Concert repertoire includes the Lieder eines Fahrenden Gesellen with Oregon Symphony; Songs of the Auvergne and Kindertotenlider and Das Lied Von Der Erde. Recordings include: Video of La Finta Giardiniera. Current Management: Nordic Artist AB. Address: Sveavagen 76, 113 59 Stockholm, Sweden.

SKOLOVSKY Zadel, b. 17 July 1926, Vancouver, Canada. Concert Pianist. m. Alice Glass, 29 July 1947, div 1953. Education: Piano, Conducting, Violin, various teachers including last (and youngest) student, Leopold Godowsky; Graduate Diploma, Curtis Institute of Music, Philadelphia, USA. Debut: Solo Recital as Winner, Naumburg Award, New York Town Hall; Orchestral with New York Philharmonic, Carnegie Hall. Career: Solo appearances, most great orchestras worldwide including New York Philharmonic, Philadelphia, Chicago, San Francisco, Toronto, London Philharmonic, Royal Philharmonic, BBC Symphony, French National Orchestra, Lamoureux, Israel Philharmonic, under conductors including Monteux, Munch, Bernstein, Maazel, Leinsdorf, Kubelik, Kletzki; Appearances, Mexico, South America, many world capitals; Allied Arts Piano Series, Chicago; Aaron Richmond Celebrity Series, Boston; Eaton Series, Toronto; Stage and TV; Teaching, Professor of Music, 1975-87, Professor Emeritus, 1987-, Indiana University. Recordings: Various performances, Columbia Masterworks Records, also EMI Philips. Current Management: Self. Address: 240 East 79th Street, Apt 10-A, New York, NY 10021, USA.

SKOVHUS Bo, b. 1962, Ikast, Denmark. Singer (Baritone). Education: Studied at the Aarhus Music College, the Copenhagen Royal Academy and in New York. Debut: Vienna Volksoper 1988, as Don Giovanni. Career: Many Lieder recitals in such centres as Edinburgh, Tanglewood, the Vienna Konzerthaus, Paris, Osaka, London and Amsterdam; Appearances as Don Giovanni at the Vienna Staatsoper and Schonbrunn, Deutsche Oper Berlin, 1995 Edinburgh Festival and the Hamburg Opera; Wagner's Wolfram and Olivier in Capriccio at Vienna, Mozart's Count in Munich and at San Francisco (1997), Opera de Paris, Lustige Witwe, Danilo, 1997, and Don Giovanni, forthcoming, Guglielmo at the Ravenna Festival, Wozzeck at Hamburg (season 1997-98) and concert of Mahler lieder with the Israel Philharmonic (1999); Covent Garden 1997, as Guglielmo; Concerts include Mahler's Lieder eines fahrenden Gesellen and Des Knaben Wunderhorn (Edinburgh 1995), Metropolitan, Fledermaus, Eisenstein, 1998 and Mozart's Count in 1999, Hindemith's Requiem with the Berlin Philharmonic, Mendelssohn's Walpurgisnacht at Salzburg (1992) and Elijah in Munich; Season 1997-98 with Lieder recitals in Japan, Washington DC, New York, Milan, Vienna and Amsterdam; Contract with the Vienna Staatsoper 1997-2001, for Barbier in Schweigsame Frau by Strauss, Wolfram, Mozart's Count and Don Giovanni, Danilo in Die lustige Witve, and Billy Budd. Recordings include: Fidelio under Harnoncourt and Carmina Burana under Mehta, Britten's War Requiem and Le nozze di Figaro, Don Giovanni conducted by Mackerras, Schoeck's Venus, Schwanengesang by Schubert and Schumann's Dichterliebe; Oberon; Zemlinsky, Lyric Symphony; Wolf Eichendorf Lieder; Schubert, Schöone Müllerin. Address: c/o Balmer & Dixon Management AG, 8006 Zurich, Granitweg 2, Switzerland.

SKRAM Knut, b. 18 Dec 1937, Saebo, Norway. Baritone. Education: Montana University and voice with George Buckbee; European studies with Paul Lohmann in Wiesbaden, Luige Ricci in Rome and Kristian Riis in Copenhagen. Career: Oslo Opera from 1964 with debut as Amonasro in Aida; In 1967 won first prize in Munich Radio International Competition; Sang at Glyndebourne Festival, 1969-76 as Mozart's Guglielmo, Papageno and Figaro and in Cosi fan tutte for French TV in 1977; Sang at Aix-en-Provence, 1977-, in operas by Mozart and at Spoleto Festival in Italy from 1978; Concert appearances in Europe and America with regular braodcasts on TV and radio in Scandinavia; Sang at Lyons in 1984 as Tchaikovsky's Eugene Onegin; Sang Jochanaan in Salome with the Berlin Staatsoper on tour to Japan in 1987, Amfortas, Amonasro and Kurwenal in Berlin, 1988-89 and appeared as Pizarro in Tel Aviv and Buenos Aires in 1988; Bolshoi Opera debut in 1988 as Scarpia; Season 1989-90 sang in The Makropoulos Case at the Deutsche Oper Berlin, Amfortas at the Spoleto Festival, Charleston, and Don Giovanni at Trieste; Sang Hans Sachs at Nice in 1992; Sang the Wanderer in Mike Ashman's production of Siegfried, Oslo, 1996. Recordings include: Video from Glyndebourne Festival of Le Nozze di Figaro in 1973; Many recitals of Norwegian Songs. Address: Haakon Tvetersvie 29, N-0682 Oslo 6, Norway.

SKRIPKA Sergei Ivanovich, b. 5 Oct 1949, Kharkov, Ukraine. Conductor. m. Skripka Evgenija, 11 Oct 1975, 2 daughters. Education: Graduated as Chorusmaster, Kharkov Institute of Arts, 1972; Graduated in Conducting Opera and Symphony Orchestras from Moscow State Conservatoire (studied under Professor Leo Ginzburg), 1977; Master's Degree, 1979. Debut: Zhukovsky Symphony Orchestra, 1975. Career: First performance in the USSR of R Kaiser's St Markus Passion with the Moscow Chamber Orchestra, 1982; Tour with the Zhukowsky Symphony Orchestra, 1991; Britten's War Requiem in Berlin, 1991; Mozart's Requiem and Beethoven's 9th Symphony, with the Russian State Symphony Orchestra of Cinematography, Frankfurt am Main, 1992. Recordings: Cello Concertos by Gliër and Mosolov with S Sudzilovsky (cello) and the Russian State Symphony Orchestra of Cinematography, 1996. Honours: Honourable Person in Russian Arts, 1993; Artistic Leader and Main Conductor of the Russian State Symphony Orchestra of Cinematography, Professor of the Russian Academy of Music (Gnessin's Institute), 1997. Memberships: Professional Society of Cinematography, 1988. Hobbies: Amateur radio; Photography; Wood craftsman. Address: ul Isakovskogo 1201-208, 123181 Moscow, Russia.

SKRIVAN Zvonimir, b. 12 Aug 1938, Prague, Czech Republic. ^onductor. m. 1964, 1 daughter. Education: Academy of Music Arts in Prague. Debut: Il Barbiere di Siviglia, Olomouc, 1967. Career: Albert Herring; Jakobin; Dalibor, Devil and Kate; Bartered Bride, Jenufa; Aida; Rigoletto; La Traviata; Un Ballo di Maschera; Lucia di Lammermoor; Faust; La Gioconda; Idomeneo; Cosi fan tutte; Le Nozze di Figaro; Fidelio; Other operas and ballets in the Moravian Theatre in Olomouc, 1967-97; also National Theatre, Prague; Collaboration with Moravian Filharmonia Orchestra, Olomouc. Recording: The Bell by Donizetti, Czech TV, and operas, arias and duets for Czech radio. Honours: The Prize of Oldrich Stibor, 1976, 1983; Prize of Prague Opera Festival for Lucia di Lammermoor, 1995, Idomeneo, 1997. Memberships: Association of Music Artists; Society of Music Theatre. Hobbies: Foreign languages; Bicycling; Mountain climbing; Travelling. Address: Dobnerova Str N 20, 77900 Olomouc, Czech Republic.

SKROWACZEWSKI Stanislaw, b. 3 Oct 1923, Lwow, Poland (USA 1960-). Conductor; Composer. m. Krystyna Jarosz, 6 Sept 1956, 2 sons, 1 daughter. Education: Diploma, Philosophy, University of Lwow, 1945; Diplomas, Composition, Conducting, Lwow Academy of Music, 1945, Krakow Academy 1946; LHD, Hamline University 1963, Macalester College 1972, USA. Career: Pianist 1928-, Composer 1931-, Violinist 1934-, Conductor 1939-, Guest Conductor, Europe, South Africa, USA, 1947-; Permanent Conductor, Music Director: Wroclaw Philharmonic 1946-47, Katowice National Philharmonic 1949-54, Krakow Philharmonic

1955-56, Warsaw National Philharmonic 1957-59; Minnesota Orchestra 1960-79; Principal Conductor, Musical Adviser, Hallé Orchestra, Manchester, UK, 1984-92; Musical Adviser, St Paul Chamber Orchestra, 1986-87. Compositions include: 1st symphony and overture written and played (Lwow Philharmonic), aged 8; 4 symphonies, prelude and fugue for orchestra, 1948; Overture, 1947; Cantiques des Cantiques, 1951; String Quartet, 1953; Suite Symphonique, 1954; Music at Night, 1954; Ricercari Notturni, 1978; Concerti for clarinet & orchestra, 1980; Violin Concerto, 1985; Concerto for Orchestra, 1985; Fanfare for Orchestra, 1987; Chamber Concerto, 1992; Also music for films, theatre, songs. Recordings: Numerous including Schubert 5, 8 and 9 symphonies; Chopin music for piano and orchestra (Weissenberg); Lalo and Schumann cello concertos (Starker); Beethoven 5th and Brahms 2nd piano concertos (Bachauer); Ravel orchestral works (Minnesota Orchestra); Brahms, 4 Symphonies; Bruckner, 6, 7 and 8 Symphonies; Shostakovich, No 5 and No 10 Symphonies; Stravinsky and Prokofiev, all ballets; Mahler, No 4 Symphony; Berlioz, Fantastique; Beethoven overtures and incidental music. Honours include: National prize, artistic achievement, Poland, 1953; 1st prize, St Cecilia International Concours for Conductors, Rome, 1956; Numerous awards, compositions, Poland, Belgium, USSR, USA; Honorary LHD, University of Minnesota. Memberships include: Polish and American professional associations. Address: PO Box 700, Wayzata, MN 55391, USA.

SLABBERT Wicus, b. 1941, Kroonstad, South Africa. Baritone. Education: Studied at the University of Pretoria, BA, Fine Arts; With Josef Metternich in Germany. Career: Sang in German repertory at Dusseldorf from 1968 and Italian from 1973; Appearances at Essen, 1974-79 as Germont, Don Carlo, Rigoletto, Don Giovanni, Count Almaviva in Figaro, Scapia, Jochanaan, Mandryka and Beckmesser; Staatsoper Kassel from 1979 notably as Macbeth, Iago, the Villains in Hoffmann and Dr Schön; Guest engagements at the Bregenz Festival from 1988 in Les Contes d'Hoffmann and Der fliegende Holländer, at Dusseldorf, Stuttgart, Theater am Gärtnerplatz Munich and Pretoria; Member of the Vienna Staatsoper since 1991 with performances as Boris in Lady Macbeth of Mtsensk and as Nabucco in 1992; Festival engagements at Edinburgh, Florence, Stockholm and Warsaw; Sang at Teatro Colon Buenos Aires in 1992 as Wagner's Dutchman, Alberich in the Ring and Tosca; Vienna Volksoper 1996, in Mona Lisa by Max von Schilling. Recordings include: Bohni in Zemlinsky's Kleider Machen Leute. Address: c/o Staatsoper, A-1010 Vienna, Austria.

SLADE Julian (Penkivil), b. 28 May 1930. Author; Composer. Education: Eton College; BA, Trinity College, Cambridge; Bristol Old Vic Theatre School, 1951. Career includes: Joined Bristol Old Vic Company as Musical Director, 1952; Wrote and composed, Christmas in King Street (with Dorothy Reynolds, James Cairncross), Bristol, 1952; Composed music for, Sheriden's The Duenna, Bristol, 1953; Transferred to Westminster Theatre, London, 1954; Wrote and composed, The Merry Gentlemen (with Dorothy Reynolds), Bristol, 1953; Composed incidental music for, The Merchant of Venice, 1953; Wrote musical version, The Comedy of Errors for TV, 1954 and for Arts Theatre, London, 1956; Wrote, Salad Days (with Dorothy Reynolds), Bristol, 1965, Vaudeville, London, 1954, Duke of York's, 1976; Free As Air, Savoy, London, 1957; Hooray for Daisy!, Bristol, 1959; Lyric, Hammersmith, 1960; Follow That Girl, Vaudeville, London, 1960; Wildest Dreams, 1960; Vanity Fair (with Alan Pryce-Jones, Robin Miller), Queens Theatre, London, 1962; Nutmeg and Ginger, Cheltenham, 1963; Sixty Thousand Nights (with George Rowell), Bristol, 1966; The Pursuit of Love, Bristol, 1967; Composed music for songs in: As You Like It, Bristol, 1970; A Midsummer Night's Dream and Much Ado About Nothing, Regents Park, 1970; Adapted AA Milne's Winnie The Pooh, Phoenix Theatre, 1970, 1975; music and lyrics, Trelawny, Bristol, then London West End, 1972; Out of Bounds, 1973; Wrote, Now We are Sixty (with Gyles Brandbreth), Arts Theatre, Cambridge, 1986-; Revival, Nutmeg and Ginger, New Orange Tree Theatre, Richmond, 1991; Revival, The Comedy of Errors, Grays Inn Hall, 1994. Honour: Gold Badge of Merit, BASCA, 1987. Hobbies: Drawing; Theatre; Cinema; Music. Address: 86 Beaufort Street, London, SW3 6BU, England.

SLÁMA Frantisek, b. 19 Nov 1923, Herálec. Musician (Violincello, Viola da gamba). 3 sons, 2 daughters. Education: Conservatory of Prague; Chamber of Instrumental Music (with Professor Václav Talich), Academy of Music and Dramatic Arts of Prague. Debut: R Schumann's Concerto A Minor (with Czech Philharmonic Orchestra), Rudolfinum Hall, Prague, 1952. Career: Cellist in Professor V Talich's Czech Chamber Orchestra, 1946-48; Member, Czech Philharmonic Orchestra, 1951-; Soloist and Continuo Player of two of the first European ensembles of Ancient music, Pro Arte Antiqua and Ars Rediviva, 1951-; Ars Rediviva had 45 years subscription concerts' cycle of Baroque music at Rudolfinum Hall, Prague (6 concerts annually); Repertoire of over 300 compositions of Czech and European Masters), festivals in Czechoslovakia, Germany, Spain, Italy, Austria, Sweden; Radio and television broadcasts and recordings with J P Rampal, M André, O Peter, A Adorján. Recordings: Purcell's Phantasy Upon One Note, 1959; Musical Offering, 1969, radio, 1985; Brandenburg Concertos, 1965; J D Zelenka, Lamentationes, 1970; J S Bach's Concerto G Minor For Viola da gamba, 1981; C P E Bach's Sonatas (with V Kunt), 1994; Series on viola da gamba and J Savall, for Czech Radio Prague, 1995. Hobbies: Athletics; Photography. Address: Na Šumavě 1, 150 00 Praha 5, Czech Republic.

SLATFORD Rodney (Gerald Yorke), b. 18 Jul 1944, Cuffley, Herts, England. Musician; Publisher. Education: Royal College of Music with Adrian Beers. Career: Principal Bass with Midland Sinfonia, the Academy of St Martin-in-the-Fields and English Chamber Orchestra until 1981; Edited and published 100 works for his own Yorke Edition, devoted to double bass literature; Founder member of Nash Ensemble and guest appearances with leading string quartets; Tours to Australia, New Zealand and The Far East; 1st Double Bass recital at Sydney Opera House; Lectures in USA; Professor in Residence at Kusatsu International Summer Academy in Japan, 1984; Teaching at the Toho Academy in Tokyo and at the Conservatoire in Peking; Professor at Royal College of Music, 1974-84; From 1984, Head of School of Strings at Royal Northern College of Music, Manchester; Fellow RNCM, 1987; Established teaching method for double bass, 1978; Founder of the Yorke Trust to promote the training of young bassists; Director and Founder, RNCM Junior Strings project, 1991; Chairman, European String Teachers Association, 1992; Regular Presenter of Radio 3, 1993. Recordings include: Rossini's Duetto in solo record with Academy of St Martin-in-the-Fields. Publication: The Bottom Line, 1985. Contributions to: Woman's Hour; A Word in Edgeways; One Pair of Ears; Mainly for Pleasure, Radio 3; The Strad Magazine; New Grove Dictionary of Music and Musicians, 1980. Hobby: Gardening; Address: 31 Thornhill Square, London, N1 1BQ, England.

SLATINARU Maria, b. 25 May 1938, Jassy, Romania. Soprano. Education: Studied at the Bucharest Conservatory with Arta Florescu and Aurel Alexandrescu. Debut: Bucharest in 1969 as Elisabeth de Valois. Career: Appearances as guest at Mannheim, Stuttgart, Zurich, Wiesbaden and Dusseldorf; Sang at Basle and Florence in 1983 as Giorgetta in Il Tabarro, Strasbourg n 1984 as Elisabeth in Tannhäuser and has sung Tosca in San Francisco, Dallas in 1988 and elsewhere; Other roles include Verdi's Abigaille and Amelia in Simon Boccanegra, Leonore in Fidelio, Wagner's Sieglinde, Senta and Elsa, Santuzza and Puccini's Turandot, Minnie and Manon Lescaut.

SLATKIN Leonard (Edward), b. 1 Sep 1944, Los Angeles, CA, USA. Conductor; Music Director; Pianist. m. Linda Hohenfeld, 29 Mar 1986. Education: Los Angeles City College; Juilliard School with Jean Morel; University of Indiana School of Music; Aspen Music Festival with Walter Susskind; Conducting with Felix Slatkin, Amerigo Marino, and Ingolf Dahl, piano with Victor Aller, and Selma Cramer, composition with Mario Castelnuovo-Tedesco and viola with Sol Schoenbach. Debut: Carnegie Hall, 1966. Career includes: Guest conductor with most major US orchestras and many others including Montreal, Toronto, Vienna, London Symphony, London Philharmonia, Concertgebouw, Royal Danish, English Chamber, Stockholm, Scottish National, NHK Tokyo, Israel and Berlin; Opera at Vienna State Opera, Lyric Opera of Chicago, Stuttgart Opera, Opera Theater of St Louis, and Metropolitan Opera with debut in 1991; Festivals include Tanglewood, Blossom, Mann Music Center, Mostly Mozart and Saratoga; Music Director and Conductor, 1979-96, European tour, 1985, Far East, 1986, St Louis Symphony Orchestra; Artistic Director and Conductor, Minnesota Orchestra Sommerfest, 1979-86; Music Director, National Symphony , Orchestra, 1996-; Festival Director, Cleveland Orchestra Blossom Festival, 1991-; Conducted the Philharmonic Orchestra at the Festival Hall (Principal Guest Conductor from 1997). Compositions: The Raven; Dialogue for 2 Cellos and Orchestra; 4 String Quartets; Extensions, 1-4. Recordings include: Over 100 recordings. Honours include: Numerous Honorary Doctorates; Honorary Member, Royal Academy of Music; 3 Grammy Awards; Austrian Government Declaration of Honour in Silver, 1986. Membership: Board of Governors, Chicago Chapter, National Academy of Recording Arts and Sciences. Current Management: ICM Artists Ltd; Harold Holt Ltd. Address: National Symphony Orchestra, Kennedy Center for the Performing Arts, Washington DC 20566-0002, USA.

SLAVICKY Milan, b. 7 May 1947, Prague, Czech Republic. Composer; Producer; Music Writer; Lecturer. m. Eva Hachova, 7 July 1972, 2 sons. Education: Studied at Charles University, Prague and at Janácek Academy of Music Arts, Brno. Career: Senior Music Producer of Classics, Supraphon, 1973-81; Senior music producer, 1977-; Producer of Electroacoustic Music, Radio Prague, 1981-82; Freelance composer and producer, 1982-90; Assistant Professor, Film Faculty, 1990-94; Composition, 1994-97, Academy of Music Arts; Assistant Professor, Musicology, Charles University, 1990-97; Lectures given throughout Europe, and many papers presented at congresses; Compositions performed widely at leading festivals and broadcast worldwide. Compositions: Orchestral: Hommage à Saint-Exupéry; Terre des hommes; Porta coeli; Two chapters from the Revelation, Ich dien; Synergy' Concerto: Way of the Heart, for violin, wind and percussion; Chamber: Musica lirica; Musica notturna; Brightening I-IV; Dialogues with the Silence, string quartet; Organ music and compositions for solo instruments; Vocal: Stay with Us; Sweet Loving, for soprano and ensemble; Electroacoustical: In Praise of Harpsichord; Variations on a Laser Ray; Brightening V or Prague Autumn; Adventus. Recordings: Over 400 albums as producer for many labels. Publications: Interviews from the House of the Artists; Gideon Klein: A Fragment of Life and Work. Contributions to: Reviews, criticisms and contributions to radio programmes. Honours: Carl-Maria-von Weber Prize, Dresden, 1976 and 1979; 1st Prize and Diploma, 1978; 4 times winner, Competition for Young Artists, Ostrava, 1978-81; 2nd Prize, Competition from Czech Ministry of Culture, 1980; Prize, town of Brasilia, 1985; Czech Music Critics' Award, 1992. Hobbies: History; Travel; Family Life. Address: Lukesova 39, CZ-142 00 Praha 4, Czechoslovakia.

SLAWSON A Wayne, b. 29 Dec 1932, Detroit, MI, USA. Composer; Professor of Music. Education: BA in Mathematics, 1955, MA in Music Composition, 1959, University of Michigan; PhD in Psychology, Harvard University, 1965. Career: Assistant Professor of Theory of Music, Yale School of Music, CT, 1967-72; Associate Professor, 1972-84, Chair, Department of Music, 1972-78, Professor of Music, 1984-86, University of Pittsburgh, PA; Professor of Music, University of California, Davis, 1986-. Compositions: Electronic music works: Wishful Thinking About Winter, 1966, Variations for 2 Violins, 1977, Colors, 1981, Greetings, 1985, Quatrains Miniature, 1986, If These Two Tolled, computer music, 1990, Interpolation of Dance for String Quartet, 1992, Grave Trunks for Computer Music and Video Tape, with Harvey Himelfarb, 1992, Warm Shades, an octet for Singers and Woodwinds, 1993, Match for Orchestra, 1994. Publication: Sound Color, 1985. Contributions to: Book Reviewer for Journal of Music Theory, 1986. Honours: Fellow, American Council of Learned Societies, 1978-79; Outstanding Publication Award, Society for Music Theory. Address: c/o Music Department, University of California, Davis, CA 95616, USA.

SLEZAK Pavel, b. 16 Apr 1941, Brno, Moravia, Czech Republic. Composer; Oboist. Education: Composition and oboe at Conservatoire, Brno and JAMU (Janacek's Academy of Music), Brno. Appointments: Professor for oboe, composition, psychology at conservatoire, 1963-; Teacher of composition at JAMU, 1971-73. Compositions: Ioculatores Domini, for piano; Carpatier Concerto for violin and orchestra; Eklogas and Intermezzos, for string orchestra; Porta Mortis, for orchestra; 2nd Symphony (on 21 August 1968); Meditation of S Franciscus, for ensemble; Demonologie of life and death (cantata on Buddhist text, voice, trombone, 2 percussions, piano; Ottonia, for brass ensemble; Threshold, cantata on Franz Kafka, ensemble; VVV (Wind in the Tower), for woodwind quintet. Contributions to: Hudebni rozhledy; Tvar; Ticho; Host; Perspektivy. Address: Udolni 62, 60200 Brno, Czech Republic.

SLIMACEK Jan, b. 31 Jul 1939, Kelc, Czechoslovakia. Composer. m. Marie Chvatikova, 19 Dec 1964, 2 daughters. Education: Studied at Prague Conservatory. Debut: Symfonietta for Strings, Tape Recording Czech Radio. Career: Music Director, Radio, Plzen, 1967-; Sonatina for Strings, Northern Music Festival, Ontario, 1988, Vassa, 1992; Divertimento for Flute and Piano, Inter Music Festival, Brno, 1983, Graz Wien, 1993; Quattro Intermezzi per Orchestra Gera, 1983, Musical Festival Rostow Don, 1988; Concertino for Accordion, Electravox and Orchestra Gera, 1976, Nuremberg 1982, Bern, 1983; Dramatic Picture Szczecin, Weimar, 1979; Piano Quartet, Warsaw, 1977; Three Etudes for Piano, Bristol, 1981; Professor of Music, Gymnasium Plzen, 1993-. Compositions include: Piano Quartet; Sonatina for Strings; Three Etudes for Piano; Dramatic Picture; Songs for Childrens Choir and Piano; Variations for Strings and Harpsichord. Recordings include: Quattro Intermezzi per Orchestra; The Victory Overture for Orchestra; Musica per Orchestra; Three Miniatures for Chamber Orchestra; Music per Ottoni. Honours: Audience Prize at Jihlava; Festival of Vocal Creation; Three first prizes at Olomouc Song Festival; Prize of Union of Czech Composers and Concert Artists for 3 of his compositions, 1979. Membership: Association of Musicians and Musicologists. Hobbies: Travel; Hiking. Address: Mohylová 109, Plzen 312 06, Czech Republic.

SLONIMSKY Sergey, b. 12 Aug 1932, Leningrad, Russia. Composer; Teacher. m. 1973, 1 son. Education: Graduated, Composition with Professor Evlakhov, 1955, Piano with Professor Nilsen, 1956, Postgraduate, 1957-58, Leningrad (now St Petersburg) Conservatoire. Career: Teaching Faculty, music theory and composition, 1958-, Professor, 1976-, Leningrad Conservatoire. Compositions: Wide variety of musical forms and genres including 10 symphonies, 1958-95, orchestral and vocal; Chamber works; Opera, ballet; Songs and choral pieces; Titles include: Carnival Overture, 1957; Concerto Buffa, chamber orchestra, 1966; Antiphones, string quartet, 1969; Virinea, opera, 1969; Icarus, ballet in 3 acts, 1973; Master and Margarita, chamber opera in 3 acts, 1970-85; Merry Songs, piccolo, flute and tuba, 1971; Sonata for Violoncello and Piano, 1986; Works performed widely; Opera Mary Stuart performed at 1986 Edinburgh Festival, USSR and abroad; Hamlet, opera, 1990-94; Cerch: dell'Inferno, secondo Dante, 1992; 24 Preludes and Fugues for Piano, 1994; Opera, Ivan the Terrible, 1994. Recordings: Numerous on the Melodia label. Publications: Thesis, book, Symphonies of S Prokofiev; Many works published in USSR and abroad. Honours include: Winner, M I Glinka State Prize, 1983; People's Artist of Russia, 1987. Memberships: Board, CIS Comosers' Union; Board, St Petersburg Branch, CIS Composers' Union. Address: St Petersburg Conservatoire of Music, Teatrainaya Ploshchad, St Petersburg, Russia.

SLORACH Marie, b. 8 May 1951, Glasgow, Scotland. Soprano. Education: Royal Scottish Academy of Music and Drama. Career: Member of the Scottish Opera, 1974-81 with roles including Marzelline in Fidelio, Marenka in The Bartered Bride, Zerlina in Don Giovanni, Eva in Die Meistersinger, Tatiana in Eugene Onegin, Fiordiligi in Cosi fan tutte and Jenifer in The Midsummer Marriage; Sang at Wexford Festival in Wolf-Ferrari's I Gioelli della Madonna and Smetana's The Kiss; Sang with English National Opera as Lisa in The Queen of Spades and Donna Elvira in Don Giovanni, Glyndebourne Touring Opera as Mozart's Donna Anna and Electra and Amelia in Simon Boccanegra, Opera North in Carmen, Die Meistersinger, Katya Kabanova and Così fan tutte, Dorset Opera as Gabriella di Vergy and Giovanna d'Arco and Australian Opera in Sydney as Amelia; Sang Ellen Orford in a new production of Peter Grimes for Opera North in 1989; Concert engagements with the Hallé, Liverpool Philharmonic and Scottish National Orchestras, London Mozart Players and London Sinfonietta. Address: c/o Music International, 13 Ardilaun Road, Highbury, London, N5 2QR, England.

SLOVAK Ladislav, b. 10 Sep 1919, Bratislava, Czecholsovakia. Conductor. Education: Studied at the Bratislava Conservatory, then the Academy of Music with Vaclav Talich, 1949-53, and Leningrad with Yevgeni Mravinsky, 1954-55. Career: Music Producer of the Czech Broadcasting Company at Bratislava, 1946-61; Conducted the Symphony Orchestra of Radio Bratislava, 1955-61 and Slovak Philharmonic Orchestra, 1961-81; Tours of West Germany, Britain and France; Tours with the Czech Philharmonic Orchestra to China, India, Japan, New Zealand and Russia in 1959 and the USA in 1967; Chief Conductor of the Prague Symphony Orchestra, 1972-75 and of the South Australia Symphony Orchestra at Adelaide in 1966 and 1972-73; Conducted the premieres of works by Alexander Moyzes, Eugen Suchon, Dezider Kardos and other Slovak composers; Conductor and Professor of the Academy of Music Bratislava. Recordings include: Tchaikovsky Symphonies with the Czech and Slovak Philharmonics; Shostakovich Symphonies Nos 2 and 9; Bartók Music for Strings, Percussion and Celesta; Prokofiev 5th Symphony; Music by Kubik, Ryba, Suchon, Loudova, Babusek, Cikker and Kardos; Shostakovich Complete Symphonies with the Symphony Orchestra of Radio Bratislava. Address: Banicka 3, 81104 Bratislava, Slovakia.

SLUYS Jozef, b. 22 Oct 1936, Gaasbeek, Belgium. Organist. 2 sons, 1 daughter. Education: Diploma, Lemmens Institute, Malines, at age 19; Royal Conservatoire of Music, Brussels. Career: Professor of Organ, Lemmens Institute, Louvain, to 1987; Director, Academy of Music, Schaerbeek, Brussels, 1968-95; Organist, Cathedral of SS Michael and Gudule, Brussels; Artistic Director, Cathedral Concert series and Brussels International Organ Week; Founder, Director, Historical Concerts, Church of Our Blessed Lady, Lombeek; Recitalist; Performed on radio and TV, Belgium and abroad; Appearances in many European countries; Toured former Soviet Union (1987), USA, Zaire, New Zealand, South Africa; Represented Belgium at first World Organ Festival, Cambridge, England. Recordings: On the Walcker organ in Riga, 1987; Organ works of Belgian composers A De Boeck, E Tinel, J N Lemmens, J Jongen, Flor Peeters; Chamber music of Marcel Dupré; J S Bach works on organs of Gustav Silbermann. Honours: Various 1st Prizes and Mailly and Arnold Prizes for Organ, Royal Conservatoire of Music, Brussels; Prizewinner, International J S Bach Contest, 1963; Pro Musica Medal, Belgian Ministry of National Education and Culture, 1963; Cecilia Prize, 1979; René Snepvangers Prize for recording of works of Lemmens, Belgian Musical Press Association, 1979; Commander, Order of Arts and Letters, Belgium, 1990; Cultural Ambassador, Flanders, 1996-97. Address: Domstraat 8, B-1602 Vlezenbeek, Belgium.

SMALLEY Denis (Arthur), b. 16 May 1946, Nelson, New Zealand. Composer; div, 1 son. Education: MusB, Dip Mus, University of Canterbury, 1967; BMus Honours, Victoria University of Wellington, 1969; Diplôme de Musique Electro-Acoustique et de Recherche Musicale, Paris Conservatoire, 1972; DPhil, University of York, England. Appointments: Head of Music, Wellington College, 1969-71; Northern Music Critic, The Guardian, 1972-75; Composition Fellow, 1975-76, Senior Lecturer, Music, 1976-94, University of East Anglia, Norwich, England; Professor of Music and Head of Department, City University, London, 1994. Compositions: Gradual, 1974; Pentes, 1974; Ouroboros, 1975; Pneuma, 1976; Darkness After Time's Colours, 1976; Chanson de Geste, 1978; The Pulses of Time, 1979; Word Within, 1981; Vortex, 1982; Tides, 1984; Clarinet Threads, 1985; O Vos Omnes, 1986; Wind Chimes, 1987; Piano Nets, 1990; Valley Flow, 1992; Névé, 1994;; Empty Vessels, 1997. Recordings: Gradual; Pentes; Chanson de Geste; The Pulses of Time; Pneuma; Vortex Tides; Clarinet Threads; Wind Chimes; Piano Nets; Valley Flow. Publications: Spectro-Morphology and Structuring Processes, The Language of Electro-Acoustic Music, 1986; The Listening Imagination: Listening in the Electroacoustic Era, 1992, 1996. Contributions to: Does Acousmatic Music Exist?, to Musiques et Recherches, 1991; Spatial Experience in Electroacoustic Music, to Musiques et Recherches, 1991; Defining Transformations, to Interface, 1993; Defining Timbre, Refining Timbre, to Contemporary Music Review, 1994. Honours: Fylkingen Prize, 1975; 1st Prize, Bourges Electroacoustic Awards, 1983; Special Prize, International Confederation of Electroacoustic Music, 1983; Prix Ars Electronica, 1988. Address: Music Department, City University, Northampton Square, London EC1V 0HB, England.

SMALLEY Roger, b. 26 Jul 1943, Swinton, Manchester, England. Composer; Pianist; Education: Studied at the Royal College of Music with Fricker and White; Later study with Walter Goehr at Morley College and with Stockhausen in Cologne. Career: Composer-in-Residence at King's College Cambridge, 1967; Co-founded and directed a four-man group, Intermodulation, 1970, disbanded in 1976; Has specialised as pianist in the music of Stockhausen; Appointed to University of Western Australia in 1976 as teacher, composer and performer. Compositions include: Piano Pieces I-V, 1962-65; Septet for Tenor, Soprano and Ensemble, 1963; Variations for Strings, 1964; Gloria Tibi Trinitas I for Orchestras, 1965; Missa Brevis, 1967; Missa Paraodia I for Piano, 1967; The Song Of The Highest Tower for Solo Voices, Chorus and Orchestra, 1968; Transformation I for Piano and Ring Modulator, 1969; Pulses for 5 x 4 Players, 1969; Melody Study II for 4-12 Players, 1970; Beat Music for 4 Electronic Instruments and Orchestra; Zeitenbenen for Ensemble and 4-Track Tape, 1973; Accord for 2 Pianos, 1974-75; 6 Modular Pieces for 4 Flutes, 1977; William Derrincourt, entertainment for Baritone, Male Chorus and Ensemble, 1977; String Quartet, 1979; Konzertstuck for Violin and Orchestra, 1980; Symphony, 1980-81; Movement for Flute and Piano, 1980; Piano Concerto, 1985; Strung Out for 13 Solo Strings, 1988; Ceremony I for Percussion Quartet, 1987. Publications include: Essays on Stockhausen, Debussy, Messiaen and Peter Maxwell Davies for Musical Times and Tempo. Address: c/o Music Department, University of Western Australia, Perth, Western Australia, Australia.

SMALLWOOD Robert, b. 22 July 1958, Melbourne, Australia. Composer. Education: BMus, University of Melbourne, 1980; Accademia Chigiana, Siena, 1985; Study with Barry Conyngham and Nigel Butterley. Career: Freelance Composer; Musician-in-Residence, Orange City, 1987-90. Compositions include: Trio Sonatina for 2 clarinets and piano, 1976; Discovery for orchestra, 1979; Sunshine Disaster for choir and band, 1981; Reminiscences for clarinet and percussion 1982; Kyrie, 1984; Elements for speaker, children's chorus and band, 1985; Wake up my Soul for children's and adult choirs, and orchestra, 1987; Living Land, for chorus, children's choir and ensemble, 1988; Three Little Poems for speaker, for flute, clarinet and cello, 1980; Psalm 150 for soprano, chorus, strings, piano and organ, 1991; Three Greek Dances, for flute/piccolo, clarinet and string quartet, 1993. Honours include: Twin Cities Church Musicians Competition, 1992. Address: c/o APRA, 1A Eden Street, Crows Nest, NSW 2065, Australia.

SMEDVIG Egil Steinar, b. 22 Nov 1922, Stavangar, Norway. Instrumental Music Instructor. m. Kristin Aurora Smedvig, 3 children. Education: Juilliard School, New York; BA, MA, University of Washington, 1950; Graduate, Mills College, Oakland, California. Career: District Manager, Newspaper Circulation Department, Seattle Post Intelligence; Music Performer, Composer, Arranger, Officer, US Army Band, 1942-46; Instrumental Music Instructor, John Marshall Junior High, 1951-56, Lincoln High School, 1957-63, Thomson Junior High School, 1964-80; Music Department Chairman, Nathan Hale High School, 1983. Compositions: Torque for concert band; Jubilation for symphony orchestra; Pachanga Suite. Honours include: Fine Arts Award, KING GM Rites, 1972; Thalia Award, Washington State Arts Commisssion and National Endowment for the Arts; Golden Acorn Award, Parent-Teachers Associatin, Washington State. Memberships: American Society of Composers, Authors and Publishers; American Federation of Musicians; Sons of Norway. Address: 12550-9th Avenue North West, Broadview Disitrct, Seattle, WA 98177, USA.

SMEETS Roger, b. 1959, Maastricht, Netherlands. Singer (Baritone). Education: Studied at the Maastricht Conservatory. Career: Has sung with Netherlands Opera from 1984, including the 1985 premiere of Wintercruise by Henkemans; Komische Oper Berlin as Don Giovanni, Eugene Onegin and Wagner's Dutchman; Opera Zuid in Kerkrade, Holland, from 1990, notably as Mozart's Figaro; Major roles in recent years with Netherlands Opera. Address: Netherlands Opera, Waterloodein 22, 1011 PG Amsterdam, Netherlands.

SMETANIN Michael, b. 1958, Sydney, Australia. Composer. Education: BM, Composition, New South Wales State Conservatorium of Music, 1981; Australian Broadcasting Corporation's orchestral summer schools, 1981 and 1982; Composition study with Louis Andriessen at Royal Conservatorium, The Hague. Career: Composer in Residence, Musica Viva, 1988. Compositions: Ensemble: Per Canonem, 1982, revised 1984, Lichtpunt, 1983, The Speed Of Sound, 1983, Ladder Of Escape, 1984, Track, 1985, Vault, 1986, Bellvue II, 1987, Fylgir, 1989, Spray, 1990, Strange Attractions, 1991; Orchestral: After The First Circle, 1982, Black Snow, 1987, Zyerkala, Blitz, 1989; Vocal: 3 Songs, 1981, The Skinless Kiss Of Angels, 1991; Children's music: Music for Children and Dancers, 1988; Instrumental and keyboard: Afstand, 1983, Sting, 1987, Stroke, 1988. Recordings: Works on CD; Ladder Of Escape; Spray; Sting. Address: c/o Australian Music Centre, PO Box N690, Grosvenor Street, Sydney 2000, Australia.

SMID Ilja, b. 14 February 1952, Plzen, Czech Republic. Director; Owner. m. Hana Smidova-Hulecova, 24 July 1976, 1 son, 1 daughter. Education: Czech Language, Musical Education, Faculty of Pedagogy, Plzen, 1971-75; Musicology, Faculty of Philosophy, Carol University, Prague, 1977-83; PhD, Musicology, History of Music, 1986. Career: Choirmaster, Conductor, Music and Literary Manager, Military Artistic Ensemble, Tabor, South Bohemia, 1976-82; Manager in Chief, Artistic Director, 1982-90, Artistic Ensemble, Czech Army, Prague, 1982-90; Independent Specialist, Institute of Etnography & Ethnomusicology, Czech Academy of Sciences, Prague, 1992; Editor, Publishing House, Lunarion, 1992-93; Owner, Director, Publishing House, Clarton, 1993-; Musical Manager, Director, Prague Chamber Philharmonic Orchestra, 1994-. Compositions include: Suspiria, 1973; Cekani na milého, 1974; Verbovani, 1979; Kde, lasko, kde's byla, 1986; Kone, vrany kone, 1985; Premena, 1989; Dragouni, 1989. Contributions to: Hudebni rozhledy. Memberships: Association of Musical Artists & Musicologists of Bohemia & Moravia. Hobbies: Sports; Music. Address: Bellusova 1819, 155 00 Praha 5, Czech Republic.

SMIRNOV Dmitri (Nikolayevich), b. 2 Nov 1948, Minsk, USSR. Composer. m. Elena Firsova, 19 Aug 1972, 2 children. Education: Studied with Nikolai Sidelnikov, Edison Denisov, Yuri Kholopov at Moscow Conservatoire, 1967-72; Privately with Philip Gershkovich. Career: Editor, Sovetsky Kompositor, publishing house, 1973-80; Freelance Composer, 1980-; Operas Tiriel and The Lamentations of Thel (chamber) performed in Freiburg and Almeida Theatre, London; Symphony No 1 The Seasons in Tanglewood, 1989; Oratorio A Song of Liberty premiered in Leeds, 1993; Professor, Composer-in-Residence, Keele University, 1993-. Compositions include: Violin Sonata No 2, 1979; 3 Symphonies, 1980, 1982, 1995; Songs of Fate, voice, organ, 1980; Six Poems by William Blake, voice, organ, 1981; Dirge Canons, ensemble, 1981; Serenade, ensemble, 1981; Farewell Song, viola, harp, 1982; Fantasia, saxophone quartet, 1982; The Night Rhymes, voice, orchestra; Tiriel, 1985; Partita, solo violin, 1985; String Quartets Nos 2-5, 1985, 1993 (2), 1994; The Lamentation of Thel; Mozart Variations, orchestra, 1987; The Visions of Coleridge, voice, ensemble, 1987; The Songs of Love and Madness, voice, ensemble, 1988; The Seven Angels of William Blake, piano, 1988; Blake's Pictures, visionary ballet, ensemble, 1988-92; Concerto, violin, 13 strings, 1990; From Evening to Morning, mixed chorus, 1990; Trinity Music, clarinet, violin, piano, 1990; A Song of Liberty, 1991; Three Blake's Songs, voice, ensemble, 1991; Job's Studies, solo clarinet, 1991; Wonderful Stories, voice, ensemble, 1991; The Angels of Albion, piano, 1991; Diptich, organ, 1992; Piano Sonata No 3, 1992; Piano Trio No 2, 1992; Orcades, solo flute, 1992; Piano Quintet, 1992; Cello Concerto, 1992; Ariel's Songs, voice, ensemble, 1993; Magic Music Box, piano, 1993; The Moony Space, orchestra, 1994; Dies Irae, solo recorder, 1994; The Lamb, voice, ensemble, 1995. Honours: 1st Prize for Solo for Harp, Maastricht, 1976. Address: 32 Larchwood, Keele, Newcastle, Staffs ST5 5BB, England.

SMIRNOV Oleg, b. 1950, Moscow, Russia. Cellist. Education: Studied at the Moscow Conservatoire with Professor Kosolapova. Career: Co-founder, Amisted Quartet, 1973 (now Tchaikovsky Quartet); Many concerts in Russia with a repertoire including works by: Hadyn, Mozart, Beethoven, Schubert, Brahms, Tchaikovsky, Borodin, Prokofiev, Shostakovich, Bartók, Barber, Bucchi, Golovin, Tikhomirov; Recent concert tours to: Mexico, Italy and Germany. Recordings include: Recitals for the US Russian Company Arts and Electronics. Honours include: Prizewinner at the Bela Bartók Festival and the Bucchi Competition. Address: c/o Sonata (Tchaikovsky Quartet), 11

Northpark Street, Glasgow, G20 7AA, Scotland.

SMIT Leo, b. 12 Jan 1921, Philadelphia, USA. Composer; Pianist. Education: Studied piano at the Curtis Institute, 1930-32; Composition with Nicolas Nabokov, 1935. Debut: Concert as Pianist at Carnegie Hall American Ballet Company, 1936-39. Career: Pianist with Balanchine's; Teacher at Sarah Lawrence College. 1947-49; University of California at Los Angeles, 1957-63; State University of New York at Buffalo, 1962-84; Director of Monday Evening Concerts at Los Angeles, 1957-63; Composer-in-Residence at the American Academy in Rome, 1972-73 and at Brevard Music Center, 1980; Concert Pianist; Conductor; Teacher. Compositions include: Operas The Alchemy of Love, 1969 and Magic Water, 1978; Melodrama A Mountain Eulogy, 1975; Ballets Yerma, 1946, Virginia Sampler, 1947; Orchestra: 3 Symphonies, 1956, 1965, 1981; Capriccio for Strings, 1958; Piano Concerto, 1968; Variations for piano and orchestra, 1981; The Ecstatic Pilgrimage, 1988-91; Alabaster Chambers for string orchestra, 1989; From Banja Luka, voice and orchestra, 1987; Memento '51, 1995; Petals of Amaranth, viola and piano, 1995; In Woods for oboe, harp and percussion, 1978; Sonata for solo cello, 1982; Flute of Wonder, 1983; Instruments, 1984; String Quartet, 1984; Exequy for string trio, 1985; Piano pieces, choruses, songs and Academic Graffiti for voice and ensemble to text by W H Auden, 1959. Recordings: In Woods; At The Corner of the Sky; Copernicus; Complete Piano Works. Publication Copernicus, text by Sir Fred Hoyle, 1975. Honours: Guggenheim and Fulbright Fellowships, 1950; New York Critics Award for Symphony No 1, 1958. Address: 39 Dorchester Road, Buffalo, NY 14222, USA.

SMITH Catriona, b. 1963, Scotland. Soprano. Education: Studied at the Royal Scottish Academy and the University of Toronto, Opera Division. Career: Sang Britten's Lucretia and Miss Wordsworth at the Banff Summer Arts Festival in 1988, Cathleen in Riders to the Sea at Toronto and Pamina for British Youth Opera; Wigmore Hall recital debut in 1988; Sang at Kent Opera as Juno in The Return of Ulysses; Festival engagements include Aldeburgh in Goehr's Triptych and English Bach Festival in Idomeneo; Sang Clorinda in La Cenerentola at Covent Garden in 1991 and engaged at the Stuttgart Staatsoper, 1991-95; Other roles include Mozart's Countess, Rossini's Berta, Dido, Frasquita and Susanna and Barbarina in Le nozze di Figaro; Roles in Stuttgart include Pamina, Gilda, Nyad, Sophie in Der Rosenkavalier, Erénoira (world premiere) and Zerlina; Madeline in Debussy's Fall of the House of Usher, 1996. Honours include: Winner, Maggie Teyte Competition, 1987. Address: c/o Stuttgart Staatsoper, Oberer Schlossgarten 6, 7000 Stuttgart, Germany.

SMITH Craig, b. 1960, England. Singer (Baritone). Education: Studied at the Royal Northern College of Music, with Nicholas Powell. Career: Roles at the RNCM included Sharpless, Pandolfe in Cendrillon, Zurga in Les Pêcheurs de Perles and Lionel in The Maid of Orleans by Tchaikovsky; Cecil in Jonathon Miller's production of Maria Stuarda at Buxton and Smirnov in Walton's The Bear, at Los Angeles; Zurich Opera from 1995, as Morales in Carmen, Paris in Roméo et Juliette and the Wig Maker in Ariadne auf Naxos; Other roles include Nabucco (Bad Hersfeld, 1996) and Sharpless, with the Royal Liverpool Philharmonic; Concert repertory includes CPE Bach's Magnificat, Rossini's Petite Messe Solennelle (at Winchester Cathedral), L'Enfance du Christ Queen Elizabeth Hall, London), Carmina Burana (Royal Concert Hall, Glasgow) and in Terra Pax by Frank Martin, at Schaffhausen and Ravensburg. Honours include: Peter Moores Foundation and Robert Stanley Ford Scholarships. Address: Portland Wallis Artists' Management, 50 Great Portland Street, London W1N 5AH, England.

SMITH Daniel (W), b. 11 Sept 1939, New York, New York, USA. Education: BM, Manhattan School of Music, 1961; MA, 1962, Professional Diploma, 1969, Columbia University; Doctoral studies, Mannes College of Music, 1970-73. Debut: Carnegie Recital Hall, New York; European debut, Wigmore Hall, London. Career: Soloist on recordings and in concert with English Chamber Orchestra, I Solisti di Zagreb, Royal Philharmonic Orchestra, Orchestra da Camera di Santa Cecilia, New York Virtuosi Chamber Symphony, Santa Cruz Symphony, Rome Festival Orchestra, Florida Chamber Symphony, New York String Ensemble, AIH Roma Orchestra; Recitals: BBC Concert Hall, London; Carnegie Recital Hall, New York; Wigmore Hall, London; Merkin Concert Hall, New York; Bruno Walter Auditorium, New York; Diligentia Hall, The Hague; Atalier, Belgium; Distinguished Artists Series, Long Island, New York; B'nai Brith Festival, Purcell Room, London; Premiered Contrabassoon Concerto of Gunther Schuller with Santa Cruz Symphony. Recordings: Volumes 1-6 (37 concerti), Antonio Vivaldi with English Chamber Orchestra and I Solisti di Zagreb; 3 Bassoon Concertos with English Chamber Orchestra; Bassoon Bon-Bons with Royal Philharmonic Orchestra; English Music for Bassoon and Piano with pianist Roger Vignoles; Volumes 1 and 2, 18th Century Bassoon concerti with Ravina Chamber Ensemble; Vivaldi Concerti with Ravina Chamber Ensemble; Music for Bassoon and String Quartet with Coull String Quartet; 5 Bassoon Concertos with English Chamber Orchestra.

SMITH David (Hector), b. 16 Aug 1939, Wallasey, Cheshire, England. Pianist; Piano Teacher. m. Mary Margaret Pugh, 3 Jan 1964, 1 daughter. Education: Cheshire School, England; Studied under Kendall Taylor at the Northern School of Music, Manchester, 1958-63; Diplomas in Piano Teaching and Performing and awarded the Frederick Moore Piano Prize in 1962. Career: Debut as Concerto Soloist in 1963 with the late Maurice Handford; Further concerto appearances and numerous recitals and lecturerecitals throughout England; Appointed to Piano Department at the Royal Northern College of Music, 1969 and later Senior Lecturer in Piano and Assistant to the Head of Keyboard Studies; Appointed as Examiner to the Associated Board of the Royal Schools of Music in 1976, with extensive tours in UK, Malaysia and New Zealand. Memberships: The European Piano Teachers Association. Hobbies: Foreign Travel; Reading. Address: 61 Denison Road, Hazel Grove, Stockport, SK7 6HR, England.

SMITH Donald, b. 1922, Bundaberg, Queensland, Australia. Tenor. Education: Studied in Brisbane. Debut: Brisbance in 1948 as Faust. Career: Sang with the Touring Elizabethan Opera Company's Tamino, Almaviva and Pinkerton; Guest appearances with the Italian Grand Opera throughout Australia; Sang with the Sadler's Wells Company from 1961 as Don José, the Duke of Mantua, Ramirez, Jenik, Ernani, Riccardo, Foresto in Attila and Don Alvaro; Covent Garden debut in 1965 as Calaf; Sang Corrado in Il Corsaro at Camden Festival in 1966, returning to Sydney in 1968 as Manrico, Cavaradossi, Florestan, Radames, Canio, Luigi and Carlo in I Masnadieri; Sang Erik in Der fliegende Holländer at Melbourne in 1978 and retired in 1982. Recordings include: Highlights from Rigoletto, Carmen, The Bartered Bride, all Sadler's Wells productions. Honours include: First singer to perform at the Sydney Opera House; OBE for services to music and his profession, 1973; Henry Lawson Festival Award, 1975; In honour of contributions to opera the Lyric Opera of Queensland presented a Gala Concert in 1989; Advance Australia Award, 1990; Degree of Doctor of the University, Griffith University Queensland, 1992. Address: c/o Australian Opera, PO Box 291, Strawberry Hills, New South Wales 2012, Australia.

SMITH Jennifer, b. 13 July 1945, Lisbon, Portugal. Singer (Soprano); Professor. 1 son, 1 daughter. Education: Lisbon Conservatory; Privately with Winifred Radford, London; Pierre Bernac, London and Paris; Hans Keller, London. Debut: Sang Jephtha, Carissimi, Lisbon, 1966. Career: Sang Europe before moving to England, 1971; Operatic roles have included Countess Almaviva for Welsh National, Scottish and Kent Operas; Gluck's Orfeo at the Wexford Festival; Rameau's Les Boréades and Hippolyte et Aricie at Aix-en-Provence; L'Incoronazione di Poppea conducted by Leonhardt; Aminta in Il Re Pastore, Lisbon; Cybelle in Lully's Atys at the Opéra-Comique Paris and in New York; Elektra in Mozart's Idomeneo, Lisbon, 1995; Concert repertoire includes works by Bach, Handel, Poulenc, Purcell, Britten and Berlioz (Les Nuits d'Eté); Appearances with the English Chamber Orchestra, London Bach Orchestra, the English Concert, Steinitz Bach Players and the Orchestra of the Age of Enlightenment; Conductors include Rattle, Willcocks, Leppard, Pinnock, Gardiner, Boulez, Mackerras and Kempe; Tour of Europe with the B Minor Mass, conducted by Frans Brueggen; Song recitals in Portugal, France, Germany, Switzerland, Belgium and England; TV appearances include Scarlatti's Salve Regina with George Malcolm, Handel's Judas Maccabeus conducted by Norrington and Purcell's Come, Ye Sons of Art Away and Tony Palmer's film of Purcell; Sang the Queen of Night (Mozart Experience, London) conducted by Norrington, QEH 1989; Rameau at Versailles (Flore and Nais) with the English Bach Festival, 1989; Season 1992 as Music in Monteverdi's Orfeo at ENO, Iphigénie en Tauride with the English Bach Festival at Covent Garden and in Conti's Don Chisciotte at Innsbruck; Sang the Queen of Night with Hamilton Opera, 1996. Recordings: Bach Mass in B Minor, Magnificat/Corboz, Cantata 208; Carissimi Jephte; Falla Retablo de Maese Pedro and Psyche/Rattle; Gabrieli Sacrae Symphoniae; Handel Hercules and L'Allegro/Gardiner, Il Trionfo del Tempo, Silete Venti/Pinnock, Messiah, Amadigi; Haydn Mariazeller Mass and Little Organ Mass/Guest; Lully Dies Irae, Miserere and Te Deum/Paillard; Rameau's Nais/McGegan, Castor et Pollux/Farncombe and Les Boréades/Gardiner; Purcell King Arthur, Indian Queen and Fairy Queen/Gardiner, Come Ye Sons of Art/Pinnock; Vivaldi Gloria and Kyrie/Corboz, Beatus Vir and Dixit Dominus/Cleobury; Schubert Lieder; Platée (Rameau), Titon et l'Aurore (Mondonville) Alycone (Marais) Il Trionfo del Tempo (Handel), La Resurrezione (Handel), all with Marc Minkowski; Xerxes (Handel) with Mic McGegan; Orphée aux enfers (Offenbach), with Minkowski; French Cantatas; Saudade, amor e morte, with Manuel Morais; Ottone (Handel) with Robert King. Memberships: ISM; Royal Society of Musicians. Current Management: Helen Sykes Artists. Address: 3 Gumleigh Road, London W5 4UX, England.

SMITH Lawrence (Leighton), b. 8 Apr 1936, Portland, OR, USA. Conductor; Pianist. m. (1) 2 sons, (2) Kathleen Dale, 4 Jun 1976, 1 daughter, 1 stepson, 1 stepdaughter. Education: BM, Music, Mannes College of Music, NY, 1959; Studied piano with Ariel Rubstein, Portland and Leonard Shure, NY. Career: Teacher at Mannes College of Music, 1959-62, University of Texas, 1962-63, Boston University, 1963-64, Curtis Institute of Music, 1968-69 and California Institute of The Arts, 1970-72; Professional debut as pianist in 1962; Assistant to Erich Leinsdorf, Berkshire Music Center, Tanglewood, MA, 1962-64; Assistant Conductor with Metropolitan Opera, NY, 1964-67; Music Director with Westchester Symphony Orchestra, NY, 1967-69; Principal Guest Conductor with Phoenix Symphony Orchestra, AZ, 1971-73; Music Director with Austin Symphony Orchestra, TX, 1972-73 and Oregon Symphony Orchestra, Portland, 1973-80; Artistic Adviser, Principal Guest Conductor, North Carolina Symphony Orchestra, Raleigh, 1980-81; Music Director, San Antonio Symphony Orchestra, 1980-85 and Louisville Orchestra, 1983-, and at Music Academy of the West, Santa Barbara, CA, 1985-; Guest Conductor with various orchestras in the USA and abroad. Recordings: Various. Honour: 1st Prize, Dimitri Mitropoulos International Conducting Competition, New York, 1964. Membership: American Federation of Musicians. Address: c/o Louisville Orchestra, 609 West Main Street, Louisville, KY 40202, USA.

SMITH Maureen (Felicity), b. 1940. Leeds, England. Violinist. m. Geoffrey Rivlin, 27 Aug 1974, 2 daughters. Education: Royal Manchester College of Music; Indiana University, USA. Debut: Royal Festival Hall in 1961. Career: Soloist with most leading British orchestras; Debut at London Promenade Concerts in 1965; Regular broadcasts for BBC Radio 3 and numerous TV appearances; Appearances at major festivals including Aldeburgh and Leeds, Brighton, Cheltenham, English Bach and Three Choirs. Recordings: Mendelssohn Violin Concerto; Milhaud Duos; Brahms and Mahler Piano Quartets. Honours: BBC Violin Competition, 1965; Gulbenkian Foundation Fellowship, 1966; Leverhulme Fellowship, 1966. Memberships: European String Teachers Association. Address: 8 Heath Close, London, NW11 7DX, England.

SMITH Richard Langham, b. 10 Sep 1947, London, England. Reader in Music. Education: BA, Hons, Music, University of York; Further study with Edward Lockspeiser and at Amsterdam Conservatory. Career: Harpsichordist; Musicologist, specialising in French Music; Lecturer, University of Lancaster until 1979, City University in London, until 1995; University of Exeter, 1995-. Composition: Reconstruction of Debussy's unpublished opera, Rodrigue et Chimène premiered at Opéra de Lyon in 1993. Publications: Translator and Editor, Debussy on Music, 1977; With R Nichols: Debussy, Pelléas et Mélisande, Cambridge Opera Handbook, 1989. Contributions to: Numerous articles and reviews on Debussy in journals including Music and Letters, Times Literary Supplement, 19th Century Music, Cahiers Debussy, Musical Times, The Listener, Early Music, The Strad, Frequent Broadcaster, BBC Radio 2,3 and 4, and France Musique. Hobbies: Gardening; Wine. Address: Higher Summerlands, 4 Longlands, Dawlish, Devon EX7 9NE, England.

SMITH Roger, b. 1945, England. Cellist. Career: Principal Cello with the Academy of St Martin in the Fields and member of the Academy of St Martin's Octet; Teacher at the Menuhin School; Co-Founder and Cellist of the re-constituted London String Quartet giving performances throughout Britain of English works and the recognised repertory. Address: Manygate Management, 13 Cotswold Mews, 30 Battersea Square, London, SW11 3RA, England.

SMITH Ronald, b. 3 Jan 1922, London, England. Concert Pianist. m. Anne Norman, 6 Sep 1969, 1 daughter. Education: Royal Academy of Music, London; Private studies in Paris. Debut: London Promenade Concert in 1948. Career: Sir Michael Costa Scholarship for composition to Royal Academy of Music; Continental debut with Ansermet and Swiss Romande, Geneva, 1951; Concertos with major orchestras; Specialises in works of Alkan; Tours of Australia in 1975, 1977, 1981 and 1983, the Far East in 1977, America and Canada, 1982, 1983 and 1987, and Russia in 1985; Alkan Centenary Concert at Wigmore Hall in London, 1988. Compositions: Violin Concerto; Comedy Overture. Recordings include: Boxed sets of Alkan and Chopin; Works by Beethoven, Schubert, Russian composers, and Liszt among others. Publications: Alkan: The Enigma, volume 1; Alkan: The Works, volume II, 1987. Contributions to: Articles in Musical Times, The Listener; Keyboard. Honours: FRAM, BMus (Dunelm), 1946. Memberships: President, Alkan Society, London; President, East Surrey Symphony Orchestra; Vice-President, Robert Simpson Society. Hobbies: Vegetable Gardening; Herb Growing. Current Management: Anthony Purkiss, Concert Management, 35 Fonthill Road, Hove, East Sussex, BN3 6HB, England. Address: Tanners House, School Road, Saltwood, Hythe, Kent, CT21 4PP, England.

SMITH Sidney Bertram, b. 12 Sept 1929, Corry, Pennsylvania, USA. Music Administrator; Writer. m. Beverly Smith, 1 Nov 1981, 1 son, 1 daughter. Education: Baldwin-Wallace College Conservatory, Ohio, 2 years; Longy School of Music, Cambridge, Massachusetts, 3 years; Senior Diploma, Piano, 1955; BME, MME, Boston University, 1958. Career: Teacher, Administrator, Fessenden School, Rivers Country Day School, Endicott Junior College, Beverly, Massachusetts, Head of Music, 1959-65, Holyoke Community College, Massachusetts, Second Chair of Music Department, 1966-85; Piano Accompanist, New York City Opera Singers, 1960's; Conductor and Founder, Holyoke Civic Orchestra, 1967, Plymouth Philharmonic, 1 year, Choral Groups and Choral Festivals; Teacher, Special Programs Division, College of William and Mary, Williamsburg, Virginia, 1986-94; Colonial Williamsburg Rare Music Library, 1987-94. Contributions to: Newspapers; Annotator for concert programmes. Honours: Distinguished Service Award, Holyoke Community College, 1985; Distinguished Alumnus, Longy School of Music, 1997. Hobbies: Art Galleries; Museums. Address: 27413 Detroit Road #G30, Westlake, OH 44145-2252, USA.

SMITH Trefor (Leslie), b. 4 July 1948, Aberdeen, Scotland. Pianist. Education: MA Honours, Music, Aberdeen University, 1970; BMus, Liverpool University, 1971; Associate (Performance), Royal Manchester College of Music, 1973; Concert Examination, State College of Music, Hamburg, Federal Republic of Germany; Studied with George Hadjinikos, Eliza Hansen; Further sturies with Wilhelm Kempff, Vlado Perlemuter, Paul Badura-Skoda and Hans Leygraf. Career: Numerous appearances in Germany, Great Britain, France, Italy, Spain, Norway, Republic of Ireland, Austria, USA and India; Various radio recordings; Currently Staff and Professor of Piano, Musikhochschule, Hamburg. Recordings: 2 records of Piano Music by Theodore Kirchner (1823-1903); Radio recordings for North German Radio, RTE Dublin and NRK Oslo. Memberships: Incorporated Society of Musicians; Deputy Chairman, Deutscher Tonkünstlerverband, Landesverband Hamburg.Hobbies: Foreign languages; Reading; Chess, Address: Wartenau 13, 22089 Hamburg, Germany.

SMITH Wilma, b. 1960, New Zealand. Violinist. Education: Studied at the New England Conservatory. Career: Leader of the Boston based Lydia Quartet; Co-founded the New Zealand String Quartet under the auspices of the Music Federation of New Zealand; Debut concert in Wellington in 1988; Concerts at the Tanglewood School in the USA, The Banff International Competition in Canada and performances with the Lindsay Quartet at the 1990 International Festival of The Arts; Soloist with the New Zealand Symphony Orchestra and Artist-in-Residence at Victoria University; Tour to Australia in 1990 for Music Viva Australia; Tours of New Zealand in 1992 and concerts in New York in 1993. Recordings include: Various.

SMITH BRINDLE Reginald, b. 5 Jan 1917, Bamber Bridge, Lancashire, England. Composer; Teacher. Education: Studied first as an architect then joined University College of North Wales as music student; Composition with Pizzetti and Dallapiccola in Italy. Career: Worked for Italian Radio, 1956-61; Taught at University College, Bangor, 1957-70; Professor of Music: University College of North Wales, Bangor, 1967-70, University of Surrey, 1970-85. Compositions include: Opera Antigone, 1969; Orchestral: Symphony, 1954; Epitaph for Alban Berg for Strings, 1955; Cosmos, 1959; Clarinet Concerto, 1960; Apocalypse, 1970; Fons bonitatis II, 1973; Guitar Concerto, 1977; Concerto Lirico for Guitar and Electronic Keyboard, 1991; Concerto Breve: Omnis Terra, for Guitar Orchestra. 1971; Vocal: Grafico de la Peternera for Chorus and Orchestra, 1956; Genesis Dream for Voice and Ensemble, 1962; Vivo sin Vivir for Chorus, 1968; Discoveries and Windhover for Chorus, 1970-71; Chamber: String Quartet Music, 1958; Tre dimensione for Harp, Vibraphone and Harpsichord, 1965; Tubal Cain's Legacy for Trombone and Piano, 1972; Concerto on Cum Jubilo for Brass Quintet, 1975; Music for Guitar; Electronic Music; Journey Towards Infinity, 1987; Symphony No 2 Veni Creator, 1990; Le Chant du Monde for Guitar, Orchestra and Percussion, 1984; Grande Chaconne, 1993. Publications: Serial Composition, 1966; Contemporary Percussion, 1970; The New Music, 1975; Musical Composition (OUP), 1985. Address: Fiorenza, 219 Farleigh Road, Warlingham, Surrey, CR6 9EL, England.

SMITHERS Don (Le Roy), b. 17 Feb 1933, New York, USA. Music Historian. m. (2) 1 Sep 1967, 1 daughter; 1 son and 1 daughter from previous marriage. Education: BS, Music, Physics and Philosophy, Hofstra University, 1957; Seminars in Musicology, New York University, 1957-58; Studied Renaissance and Reformation History, Columbia University, NY, 1958; PhD, History of Music, University of Oxford, England. Career includes: Associate Professor, Department of Fine Arts and School of Music, Syracuse University, 1966-75; Lectures and papers on Baroque ornament, Festival Books, the history of music and musical instruments and the history of musical performance for various groups, colleges and universities; Solo concert performances on Baroque trumpet, cornetto, and various Renaissance wind instruments; Co-founder, First Musical Director and sometime conductor of Oxford Pro Musica, Oxford, 1965-. Recordings: About 50 solo and ensemble recordings with various European and American groups including New York Pro Musica, The Leonhardt Consort, Concentus Musicus Wien and Early Music Consort of London. Publications include: The Music and History of the Baroque Trumpet Before 1721, 1973. Contributions to: Many articles to professional journals and book chapters. Honours include: Research Fellow and study with Professor Arthur Mendel, Princeton University, 1978; The Japan Foundation Grantee; ASECS/Folger Institute Fellowship, 1984. Address: 55 Van Houten Fields, West Nyack, NY 10994, USA.

SMITKOVA Jana, b. 26 Dec 1942, Prague, Czechoslovakia. Singer (Soprano). Education: Studied at the Prague Conservatory and Music Academy. Debut: Liberec, 1967, as Nancy in Martha by Flotow. Carer: Sang with the Brno Opera, 1968-70, Ceske Budejovice, 1970-73; Member of the Komische Oper Berlin from 1973, debut as Katya Kabanova; Frequent guest appearances in Dresden, notably as Agathe in Der Freischütz at the 1985 reopening of the Semper Opera House; Has also sung at the National Theatre, Prague, and in other East European centres; Sang Ludmila in Harry Kupfer's production of The Bartered Bride at Covent Garden, 1989, on visit with the company of the Komische Opera; Other roles include Pamina, Puccini's Butterly and the leading role in Die Kluge by Orff. Recordings include: Opera sets for two recording companies; Der Freischütz and Beethoven's Ninth. Honours: Prize of the Prague Spring Festival, 1963. Address: Komische Oper Berlin, Behrenstrasse 54-57, D-10117 Berlin, Germany.

SMOLKA Jaroslav, b. 8 Apr 1933, Prague, Czech Republic. Musicologist; Composer. m. Jara Popelová, 8 Sept 1956, 1 son, 1 daughter. Education: Musicology, Charles University, Prague, 1951-56; Composition, Academy of Performing Arts, Prague. Debut: Ladislav Vycpálek: Evolution as a Composer, Prague, 1960. Career: Recordings Director of LP Supraphon, 1956-62, and than Panton, 1956-62; Assistant, 1962, Docent (Assistant Professor), 1968, Professor of History and Theory of Music, 1991; Leader of Development for Theory and History of Music Academy of Performing Arts, Prague. Compositions: The Play About Teeth, chamber comic opera, 1977-78; The Cock is Sitting Over the Cloud, cycle of female choirs, 1964; Choral Overture, for orchestra, 1982; The Dialog of Forms, symphony for large orchestra, 1989; String Quartet No 2, 1963-65; Sonata for Pianoforte No 2 Kontrasty, 1978-79; The Mist of Depression, for viola solo, 1982. Publications: Ćeská hudba naseho stoleti, 1961; Ćeská kantáta a oratorium, 1970; The Fugue in the Czech Music, 1987; Smetanova vokálni tvorba (The Vocal Music by Bedrich Smetana), 1980; Smetanova Symfonická tvorba (The symphonic Music by Bedrich Smetana, 1984. Memberships: Atelier SO, The Society of Czech Musicologists. Address: Nad Bertramkou 4, 15000 Praha 5, Czech Republic.

SMOLYANINOVA Soya, b. 1960, Russia. Singer (Soprano). Education: Studied at the Gnessin Institute, Moscow. Career: Appearances at the Bolshoi Opera from 1986, as Tatiana, Lisa in The Queen of Spades, Emma (Khovanshchina), Yaroslavna (Prince Igor), the Trovatore Leonora, Tosca and Desdemona; Guest appearances at Leipzig, Dresden and the Deutsche Oper Berlin, as Amelia, Tosca and Tatiana; Soloist with the Gewandhaus Orchestra, Leipzig, and other leading orchestras; Semper Oper Dresden from 1995, as Abigaille in Nabucco, Madama Butterfly and the Forza Leonora; Season 1996 as Leonora and Tosca at Antwerp; Engaged as Turandot, 1998. Address: Athole Still Ltd, Foresters Hall, 25-27 Westow Street, London SE19 3RY, England.

SMYTHE Russell, b. 19 Dec 1949, Dublin, Ireland. Baritone. Education: Studied at Guildhall School of Music and London Opera Centre. Career: English Music Theatre Company from 1976 as: Tom Jones, Dandini and Ballad Singer in Stephen Oliver's Tom Jones, Rossini's Cenerentola and Britten's Paul Bunyan; Welsh National Opera from 1977 as Billy Budd, Onegin, Papageno, Count Almaviva and Rossini's Figaro; Covent Garden from 1983 as Malatesta in Don Pasquale, Falke in Der Fledermaus and Guglielmo; has sung with English National Opera: Pelléas, Papageno, Figaro, Tarquin, in The Rape of Lucretia, Prince Andrei in War and Peace; Hamburg Staastoper from 1980 as Tony in West Side Story, Guglielmo, Figaro, Papageno and in Ariadne and Pelléas; Vienna from 1982 as The Count in Der Wildschütz, Harlequin and Falke; Paris Opera from 1985 as Harlequin and Apollon in Alceste by Gluck; Brother in Dr Faust; North American debut 1986 as Papageno at Vancouver; Sang in Oberon at Lyon and in La Finta Giardiniera, Amsterdam, Berlin and Brussels; Buxton Festival 1988 as Donizetti's Torquato Tasso; Sang Rossini's Figaro for Opera North, 1989; Don Giovanni, Dublin, 1990; Frankfurt: Finta, 1990; Basel Opera as Orestes in Iphigénie en Tauride Germont in Traviata and Belcore in L'Elisir D'Amore, 1991; Catania: Papageno; Madrid: Ned Keene, in Peter Grimes; ENO: Albert, in Werther; Season 1992 includes Ping in Turandot, Antwerp, Eugene Onegin, Tel Aviv; Season 1993-94 Onedin, Scottish Opera; Orfeo, Monteverdi, Nancy; Season 1994-95 included Henri de Valois in Le Roi Malgré Lui for Opera North; Balstrode in Peter Grimes, Scottish Opera, The Forester, Cunning Little Vixen, Opera Zuid: (Maastricht) Sharpless in Madam Butterfly for Welsh National Opera; Season 1995-96 included Peter, Hansel and Gretel for Scottish Opera; Shishkov in House of the Dead for Opera du Rhin, Strasbourg; Concert engagements include Berlioz's L'Enfance du Christ with the Hallé Orchestra and Messiah at Valencia; Recently sang in Orfeo for English Bach Festival and Shishkov in From the House of the Dead, BBC Symphony Orchestra. Recordings: CD Edoardo III, Opera Rara; Nardo, Brussels Opera; Pantalon for BBC TV; Thésée in Hippolyte et Aricie, Rameau, Archiv; Extensive recording for Radio 3; Der Mann for WDR Cologne; Video Disc of Menotti's The Telephone. Current Management and Address: c/o Athole Still International Management Ltd, Foresters Hall, 25-27 Westow Street, London, SE19 3RY, England.

SNIPP Peter, b. 1964, London, England. Singer (Baritone). Education: Studied at the Guildhall School. Career: Appearances as Masetto with Opera North and in the title role of the premiere of Judith Weir's The Vanishing Bridegroom for Scottish Opera; Eugene Onegin for Kentish Opera and in Zaide and Les Boréades for City of Birmingham Touring Opera; Principal with English National Opera from 1994, singing Malatesta, Harlequin (Ariadne), Guglielmo and Patroclus in King Priam; Concerts include the War Requiem in Finland, Carmina Burana under Jane Glover and the Steersman in Tristan with the LPO; Sang in Henze's Prince of Homburg for ENO, 1996. Recordings include: Il Barbiere di Siviglia, with ENO. Address: Lies Askonas Ltd, 6 Henrietta Street, London WC2E 8LA, England.

SNOWMAN Nicholas, b. 18 Mar 1944, London, England. Music Administrator. m. Margo Michelle Rouard, 1983, 1 son. Education: Magdalene College, Cambridge. Career: Founder and Administrator of Cambridge University Opera Society, 1965-67; Assistant to Head of Music Staff, Glyndebourne Festival Opera, 1967-69; Co-founder and General Manager of London Sinfonietta, 1967-72; Director, Department Artistique, Institut de Recherche et de Co-ordination Acoustique-Musique (IRCAM), Paris, France, 1972-86; Co-founder and Conseiller Artistique Ensemble Inter-Contemporain, Paris, 1976-92; Member of Music Committee, Venice Biennale, 1979-86; Artistic Director, Projects, 1980, 1981, and 1983, Festival d'Automne de Paris; Initiator and Member of Steering Committee, National Studio for Electronic Music at South Bank, 1986-92; General Director, Arts, South Bank Centre, London; Responsible for the 1988-89 series, The Reluctant Revolutionary: Arnold Schoenberg His Work and His World. Publications: Co-editor, The Best of Granta, 1967; The Contemporary Composers, 1982-; Introductions and articles in Orchestre de Paris, Centre Pompidou, Festival d'Automne Programme Books. Honours: Chevalier, L'Ordre des Arts et des Lettres, 1985; Chevalier dans l'ordre National du Mérite, France, 1995. Hobbies: Films; Eating; Spy Novels. Address: South Bank Centre, Royal Festival Hall, London, SE1 8XX, England.

SNYDER Barry, b. 6 Mar 1944, Allentown, PA, USA. Concert Pianist; Teacher. Education: BM, Master's Degree, Performance and Literature, Artist Diploma in Piano, Eastman School of Music, University of Rochester. Debut: Soloist with Allentown Symphony Orchestra. Career: Has performed throughout the USA, Canada, Europe, Poland, South America and Asia; Appearances with orchestras of Montreal, Atlanta, Houston, Baltimore, National, Detroit and Cracow in Poland, with such conductors as Sixten Ehrling, David Zinman, Charles Dutoit, Robert Shaw, Leopold Stokowski; Chamber music with Jan DeGaetani, Dong-Suk Kang, Zvi Zeitlin, Ani Kavafian, Bonita Boyd, Cleveland Quartet, Composer's Quartet, Eastman Brass Quintet, New York Brass Quintet; Founding Member of Eastman Trio with tours to Europe and South America; Professor of Piano, Eastman School of Music, 1970-; Has given masterclasses with solo recitals. Recordings: Dohnányi, solo CD; Dohnányi chamber works with Cleveland Quartet; CD of complete cello music of Fauré with Steven Doone, cellist; Stephen Jaffe's Two Piano Sonata with Anton Nel. Hobbies: Weather Observation; Gardening; Socialising. Address: 166 Orchard Drive, Rochester, New York, NY 14618-2344, USA.

SOBOLEVA Galina, b. 1960, Moscow, Russia. Cellist. Education: Studied at Moscow Conservatoire with Valentin Berlinsky. Career: Member of the Prokofiev Quartet (founded at Moscow Festival of World Youth and the International Quartet Competition, Budapest); Many concerts in former Soviet Union and on tour to Czechoslovakia, Germany, Austria, USA, Canada, Spain, Japan and Italy; Repertoire includes works by Haydn, Mozart, Beethoven, Schubert, Debussy, Ravel, Tchaikovsky, Bartók and Shostakovich. Address: c/o Sonaa (Prokofiev Quartet), 11 Northgate Street, Glasgow G20 7AA, Scotland.

SOCCI Gianni, b. 19 Mar 1939, Rome, Italy. Bass Singer. Education: Studied at the Accademia di Santa Cecilia in Rome and with Franco Cavara. Debut: Piccolo Teatro Comico Rome in

1965 as Achmed in Paisiello's Il Re Teodoro in Venezia. Career: Sang in the buffo repertory at opera houses in Milan, Rome, Naples, Florence, Turin, Venice, Genoa and Trieste; Guest appearances in Brussels, Copenhagen, Toulouse, Strasbourg, Paris, Cologne, Frankfurt, Philadelphia, Montreal, Quebec, Monte Carlo and Barcelona; Many performances in operas by Mozart, Cimarosa, Rossini and Donizetti; Sang at Teatro Lirico Milan in 1975 in the premiere of Al Gran Sole Carico d'Amore by Luigi Nono; Concert engagements in Italy and elsewhere.

SÖDERSTRÖM Elisabeth (Anna), b. 7 May 1927, Sweden. Soprano Opera Singer; Administrator. m. Sverker Olow, 1950, 3 s. Education: Singing Studies, Andrejewa de Skilonz and Stockholm Opera School. Career includes: Royal Opera, Stockholm, 1950-; Appearances: Salzburg, 1955, Glyndebourne, 6 times between 1957-79 as the Composer in Ariadne, Octavian and Leonore, in Fidelio; Metropolitan Opera, NY, 8 times between 1959-87; Frequent concert and TV appearances in Europe and USA; Tour, Russia, 1966; Roles include: Fiordiligi, in Così fan tutte, Countess and Susanna, in Figaro, Countess, in Capriccio, Christine, in Intermezzo; 3 Leading roles: Der Rosenkavalier, 1959, Janácek's Emilia Marty and Jenufa, Mélisande; Sang at Dallas, 1988 in premiere of The Aspern Papers by Argento; Artistic Director, Drottningholm Court Theatre, 1993-; Member, Judging Panel, Cardiff Singer of The World, 1991; Presented, Drottningholm Theatre Saga at Barbican Hall, London, 1992. Publications: I Min Tonart, 1978; Sjung ut Elisabeth, 1986. Honours: Honorary Academician, Royal Academy of Music; Court Singer, Sweden, 1959; Order of Vasa; Stelle della Solidarieta, Italy; Prize, Best Acting, Royal Swedish Academy, 1965; Literis et Artibus Award, 1969; Commander, Order of Vasa, 1973; Commandeur des Arts et des Lettres, 1986; Commander, Order of British Empire. Hobbies: Sailing; Literature; Embroidery. Address: Drottningholms Slottsteater, Box 27050, S-10251 Stockholm, Sweden.

SOENEN Willy Julien Valentin, b. 10 Aug 1937, Menen, Belgium. Composer. m. Christiana Delobel, 21 July 1962, 2 sons. Education: Degree, Royal Conservatory of Music, Ghent, Belgium. Appointments: Trumpet Soloist; Conductor; Teacher of Trumpet and Harmony; Director, Academy of Music, Tielt, Belgium; Composer. Compositions: Concertino voor Geert; Concertino voor Henk; Paroles; Tango and Tarantella; Suite Francaise. Recordings: Concertino voor Henk, for Clarinet and Piano, also for Clarinet and Symphonic Band. Publications: De Dirigent, 1993; The Clarinet, 1993, 1994, 1995, 1996; Clarino, 1996; Conf Mus de France, 1997. Honours: Hilvarenbeek, Netherlands, 1980; Gerona, Spain, 1992; Conf Mus de France, 1995; Sabam, Belgium, 1997. Memberships: Sabam; Kon Muziekverbond, Belgium; Wasbe. Hobbies: Travel; Reading; Walking. Address: Graafschapsstraat 17, 8800 Roeselare, Belgium

SOFFEL Doris, b. 12 May 1948, Hechingen, Germany. Mezzo-Soprano. Education: Early studies as violinist, then voice with Marianne Schech in Munich, 1968-73. Career: Bayreuth Youth Festival in 1972, in Das Liebesverbot; Stuttgart State Opera, 1973-76; Sang Waltraute at Bayreuth and began career as a concert artist; Noted in Bach and other Baroque music; Sang at Bregenz Festival in 1977 as Puck in Oberon; Sang Monteverdi's Poppea in Toronto in 1983 and took part in the Hamburg premiere of JC Bach's Amadis de Gaule; Sang at Covent Garden in 1983 as Sextus in La Clemenza di Tito and Orlovsky in Die Fledermaus; Fricka (Solti/Hall), Bayreuth Festival, 1983; Mahler 3rd (Tennstedt), New York Carnegie Hall, 1983; Sang in the world premiere of Reimann's Troades in Munich, 1986; Sang Octavian in a production of Der Rosenkavalier at the renovated Brussels Opera House, and Angelina in La Cenerentola at the Berlin Staatsoper in 1987; L'Italiana in Algeri/Isabella, Schwetzingen, Zürich, Cologne, 1987; TV appearances include Das Lied von der Erde in 1988; Sang in the premiere of Penderecki's Ubu Rex at Munich in 1991; Season 1992 as Cassandra in Reimann's Troades at Frankfurt and Elizabeth in Donizetti's Maria Stuarda at Amsterdam; Verdi's Preziosilla at Munich in 1994; Bartok's Bluebeard's Castle (Judith), Deutsche Oper Berlin (Kout/Friederich), 1994; Werther (Charlotte) at Parma with Alfredo Kraus and Damnation of Faust at Munich, 1995; Returned to London 1997 for Mahler/Brahms recital at St John's Smith Square. Recordings include: Bach Cantatas and Magnificat; Flotow's Martha; Lortzing's Der Wildschütz; Haydn's St Cecilia Mass; Das Liebesverbot; Schumann's Requiem; Zemlinsky's Eine Florentinische Tragödie; Troades; Parsifal; Mahler No 2; Beethoven's Missa Solemnis; Wolf's Der Corregidor; Mahler 3; Mahler 8; Kindertotenlieder; Lieder eines fahrenden Gesellen; Mahler's Rückertlieder; Virtuoso Arias, Anna Bolena. Address: c/o Ingpen and Williams Ltd, 26 Wadham Road, London SW15 2LR, England.

SOHAL Naresh, b. 18 Sep 1939, Harsipind, Punjab, India. Composer. Education: University of Punjab; London College of Music; Leeds University. Career includes: Asht Prahar performed by London Philharmonic Orchestra under Norman del Mar at the Royal Festival Hall in 1970; BBC have commissioned four major works including The Wanderer, first performed during the 1982 Promenade Concerts, under Andrew Davis; From Gitanjali commissioned by Philharmonic Society of New York, first performed by New York Philharmonic Orchestra under Zubin Mehta in 1985; Represented the West in 2 East-West encounters in the Netherlands and Bombay in 1983; TV credits include music score for Sir William in Search of Xanadu for Scotish TV and three episodes of Granada TV's series, End of Empire, 1985; Currently member of BBC's Central Music Advisory Committee and the equivalent committee in Scotland. Compositions include: Orchestral: Indra-Dhanush, 1973, Dhyan I, 1974, Tandava Nritya, 1984; Chamber and instrumental: Shades I, 1974, Shades II, 1975, Shades III, 1978, Chakra, 1979, Shades IV, 1983, Brass Quintet No 2, 1983; Vocal and choral: Inscape, 1979, The Wanderer, 1981, From Gitanjali, 1985; Satyagraha for orchestra, 1997. Contributions to: Tempo Magazine. Membership: Society for the Promotion of New Music. Hobbies: Photography; Chess; Badminton; Cricket; Films. Address: 50 Spottiswoode Street, Edinburgh, EH9 1DG, Scotland.

SOHN Sung-Rai, b. 23 Sept 1950, Seoul, Korea. Violinist; Conductor. m. Patricia Esposito Gilleran, 6 June 1980, 1 son, 3 stepdaughters. Education: BM, Peabody Conservatory of Music (full scholarship student of Berl Senofsky), Baltimore, Maryland, USA; MFA, Sarah Lawrence College (scholarship student of Dorothy Delay); Quartet Seminar, Juilliard School of Music. Debut: As a winner of Artists International Competition and Jack Kahn Music Award, Carnegie Recital Hall, New York City, 1980. Career: Founder, Music Director/Conductor, Philharmonic Lawrencia Chamber Orchestra; Founder, 1st Violinist, Laurentian String Quartet; Appeared: Korean National TV (KBS Radio); WNYC, New York, in Rising Star, Live, and the Bosendorfer Concert Series; The Listening Room, WQXR, New York; NPR, USA; Maine TV Network; Kansas TV Network; Sendai TV Network, Japan; Toured Canada, USA, Europe, Africa, Asia. Recordings: Barber String Quartet Op 11; Rochberg String Quartet No 3; C P E Bach Concerto in A major; Ginastera Piano Quintet. Publication: Careers in Music, 1980. Current Management: Jonathan Wentworth Associates, USA; Korea Musica, Asia; USA State Department. Address: 69 Mile Road, Suffern, NY 10901, USA.

SOJAT Tiziana, b. 28 Apr 1955, Rome, Italy. Soprano. Education: Studied with her mother, Alda Noni, and Elisabeth Schwarzkopf. Debut: Dublin in 1984 as Elsa in Lohengrin. Career: Sang Mimi at Ljubljana in 1984; Concert performances of Dido and Aeneas and Gianni Schicchi at Lausanne in 1985; Sang with the company of San Carlo Naples in Pergolesi's Stabat Mater at New York; Croatian National Opera at Zagreb in 1988 as Sieglinde in Die Walküre; Marseilles in 1989 as Elena in Mefistofele; Engaged at Karlsruhe Opera from 1989, notably as Butterfly and Arabella; Concert performances at Turin, Dubrovnik, Rome and Milan; Freelance career, giving several concertts and Liederabende in Tokyo, one of which for the Richard Strauss Society of Japan, 1995-. Recordings include: Lieder by Wolf, Schumann, Liszt and Mahler; CD War Songs by Franz Lehar and Kurt Weill, 1996. Address: Badisches Staatstheater, Baumeisterstrasse 11, 7500 Karlsruhe, Germany.

SOJER Hans, b. 20 Mar 1943, Innsbruck, Austria. Tenor. Education: Studied with Franziska Lohmann. Debut: Innsbruck in 1967 as David in Meistersinger. Career: Sang at Innsbruck until 1971, Bonn, 1971-73, Wiesbaden, 1973-81, and Hanover, 1981-; Roles in operas by Rossini, Donizetti, Mozart, Wagner and Strauss, at Graz, Cologne, Mannheim, Dusseldorf, Frankfurt, Berlin, Lisbon and Karlsruhe; Sang at Bregenz and Schwetzingen Festivals; Sang the Steersman and Narraboth at Barcelona in 1988, Ernesto at Kiel and Count Riccardo in Wolf-Ferrari's Quattro Rusteghi at Hanover in 1991; Concert repertoire includes Beethoven's 9th and cantatas and Passions by Bach. Recordings include: Brighella in Ariadne auf Naxos. Address: c/o Niedersachsische Staatstheater, Opernplatz 1, 3000 Hanover, Germany.

SOKOL Ivan, b. 15 Jun 1937, Bratislava, Czechoslovakia. Organist. Education: Hochschule fur Musik, Prag Studium; Laureat Prager Frühling; Leipzig Bachwettberwerb Preisträger. Debut: Prague. Career: Concerts in Europe, Asia, USA and Mexico; Television and radio appearances; Director for International Orgelfestival Kosice, Slovakia. Recordings include: Complete works of Bach, Handel, Mendelssohn, Mozart, Brixi, Brahms, Reger-Orgelwerke, Hindemith 1, 2, 3, Sonate, Slovakische Musik, Poulenc-Concerto for Organ and Orchestra, Saint-Saëns, 3 Symphony, Janácek, Glagolitic Mass; Czech Music; French Organ Music, Franck, Mulet, Messiaen and Dupré; Romantic Organ Works: Mendelssohn-Bartholdy, Liszt and Reger. Honours: 2 Prizes, Stadt Kosice; National Prize, Verdienter Künstler. Hobbies: Literature; Art; Sport. Address: Trencianska 5, 82109 Bratislava, Slovakia.

SOKOLOV Grigory, b. 1950, Leningrad, Russia. Pianist. Education: Specialist Music School; Entered St Petersburg Conservatory, 1960. Career: First important public appearance at age 12; Toured with Moscow Philharmonic Orchestra to Italy, Portugal and Germany, then regular performances throughout Europe, North America and the Far East; Worked with Philharmonia London and Ulster Orchestra under Yan-Pascal Tortelier; Appeared with Orchestra of the Bolshoi under Alexander Lazarev at Edinburgh Festival; Has played with many foreign orchestras including Leipzig Gewandhaus, Dresden Philharmonic, Munich Philharmonic, Bamberg Symphony, Warsaw Philharmonic, Zurich Tonhalle, Vienna Symphony, Helsinki Radio Symphony, Amsterdam Concertgebouw and Philharmonic Orchestra of La Scala Milan, with such conductors as Inbal, Flor, Järvi, Stein, Saraste, Groves, Rozhdestvensky, Pinnock, Rowicki, Kondrashin, Svetlanov, Lombard, Barshai, Weller, Blomstedt and Chailly; Recitals in Paris, Vienna Musikverein, Munich, Berlin, Frankfurt, Salzburg, Helsinki, Copenhagen, Milan, Rome, New York Carnegie Hall and Tokyo; Repertoire ranges from Bach to Schoenberg including Beethoven, Brahms, Chopin, Schubert and the Russian masters. Recordings include: Beethoven Sonatas Op 90 and Op 110 and the Diabelli Variations; Chopin Preludes; Bach's The Art of Fugue and Sonatas by Prokofiev, Rachmaninov and Scriabin. Honours: First Prize, 3rd International Tchaikovsky Piano Competition, at age 16, 1966. Address: c/o Artists Management Company, Via Marconi 3, 37060 Castel d'Azzano (Vr), Italy.

SOKOLOV Ivan (Glebovitch), b. 29 Aug 1960, Russia. Composer; Solo Concert Pianist; High School Lecturer. Education: Gnesin Musical College, 1977-78; Composition with Nik Sidelnikov and piano with Lev Maumov, 1978-83; Assistant Probationer under Nik Sidelnikov, 1984-86, Moscow Conservatoire. Career: Concerts, as soloist and with others in Moscow, Leningrad, Sverdlovsk, Kharkov, Briansk, Tashkent, Alma-Ata, Lvov and Tallinn among others, 1985-; Appears at artist's shows and composer's concerts; Repertoire includes Stockhausen, Cage, Crumb, Scriabin, Shostakovich, Prokofiev, Debussy and Brahms; Festival appearances include Moscow Autumn, 1987-90, Alternative, 1988-90, Festival of Music in Russia and Germany, 1990, and Schleswig-Holstein Music Festival, Hamburg, 1991; Solo concert, playing Chopin in 1991; Teacher of Composition at Musical College, 1986-; Leader of classes in Instrumentation and Musical Score Reading at Moscow Conservatoire, 1988-. Compositions include: 10 Pieces for Flute and Piano, 1983; The Night, cantata, 1983; Rus Pevutchaya, cantata, 1985; Blazhenstvo I Beznadezhnos, vocal cycle, 1986; Volokos for Piano, 1988; Sonata for Flute and Piano, 1988; 13 Pieces for Piano, 1988; Eshtche, 7 pieces for Piano, 1989; Knigy Na Stole for Piano, 1989; Zvezda for Soprano and Piano, 1990; O, flute solo, 1990; Korably V More for 2 Pianos, 1990; Igra Bez Natchala I Konza for Percussion, 1991; Mysli O Rachmaninove for Piano, 1991. Address: uliza Staryi Gaiy, dom 1, korpus 1, Kvartira 116, 111539 Moscow, Russia.

SOKOLOV Vladimir, b. 21 Feb 1936, Uckshor, Republic of Komi, Russia. Clarinettist. m. Irina Sokolova. Education: City of Siktivkar Music School, Republic of Komi, 1950-54; Orchestra Faculty, Moscow Conservatory, 1954-59; Debut: With Moscow Conservatory Symphony Orchestra at the Grand Hall, Moscow Conservatory, 1955. Career: Clarinettist, Radio and Television Symphony Orchestra, 1960-63; Clarinettist, USSR State Symphony Orchestra, 1963-92; Clarinettist, Russian National Symphony Orchestra, 1992-94; Teacher, 1973-, Professor, 1992-, Moscow Conservatory; Teacher, Central Music School, 1977-; Professor, Korean National Institute of Arts, Seoul, 1994-. Recordings: Concertos by Mozart, Krommer and Weber; Sonatas by Brahms, Glinka, Grechaninov, Artemov, Saint-Saens, Poulenc; Works by French composers; Works by Gedike, Rakov, Svetlanov; Duets, Trios, Quartets, Quintets by Mozart, Beethoven, Brahms, Glinka, Khachaturian, Power. Honours: Silver Medal, Vienna International Competition, 1959; 1st Prize, Leningrad All-Union Competition, 1963; Honoured Artist of Russia, 1973; People's Artist of Russia, 1986; Order of Honour, 1991. Memberships: Jury Member: Geneva, Sept 1986, Sept 1990, Toulon, June 1991. Hobbies: Fishing; Swimming; Hunting. Address: Presnensky Val h 40, Apt 41, 123557 Moscow, Russia.

SOLDH Anita, b. 26 Sep 1949, Stockholm, Sweden. Soprano. Education: Studied at Stockholm University and with Erik Saéden from 1969; Further study at the Stockholm and Vienna Music Academies, 1971-75, and with Luigi Ricci in Rome. Career: Sang with Norrlands Opera, 1975-77, notably as Britten's Lucretia and Mozart's Countess, Royal Opera Stockholm from 1977 with debut as Eva in Die Meistersinger, returning as Senta, Elizabeth, Arabella, Octavian, Chrysothemis, Mozart's Countess, Elvira, Vitelia and Pamina, Tchaikovsky's Tatiana and Maid of Orleans; Concert tours of the USA, Brussels and Europe in 1984, as Cherubino; Bayreuth Festival, 1983-84 as Freia in Das Rheingold; Sang Elsa in Lohengrin at Stockholm in 1989 and First Lady in Die Zauberflöte at the Drottningholm Court Theatre, and the Queen in Vogler's Gustaf Adolf och Ebba Brahe in 1990; Season 1991-92 as Agave in the premiere of Backanterna by Daniel Börtz, production by Ingmar Bergman, and at Drottningholm in Haeffner's Electra and as Gluck's Eurydice; Concert repertoire includes Schoenberg's Erwartung, Berg's

Frühe Lieder and Haydn's Schöpfung. Recordings: Video of Idomeneo from Drottningholm as Elettra. Address: c/o Kungliga Teatern, PO Box 16094, S-10322 Stockholm, Sweden.

SOLLBERGER Harvey, b. 11 May 1938, Cedar Rapids, Iowa, USA. Composer; Conductor; Flautist. Education: BA 1960, University of Iowa; Composition with Jack Beeson and Otto Luening at Columbia University, New York (MA 1964). Career: Co-founded the Group for Contemporary Music, New York 1962; Regular tours as flautist and conductor; Faculty Member, Columbia University 1971-83, Indiana University School of Music 1983-92; Professor of Music at the University of California, San Diego, from 1992. Compositions include: Chamber Variations for 12 players, 1964; Music for Sophocle's Antigone, electronic, 1966; Musica Transalpina, 2 motets for soprano, baritone and 9 players, 1970; Folio, 11 pieces for bassoon, 1976; Sunflowers, for flute and vibraphone, 1976; Music for Prepared Dancers, 1978; Interupted Night and 5 instruments, 1983; Double Triptych for flute and percussion, 1984; Persian Golf, for strings, 1987; Aurelian Echoes for flute and alto flute, 1989; Passages, for soloists, chorus and orchestra, 1990; The Advancing Moment for flute, clarinet, violin, cello, piano and percussion, 1993; CIAO, Arcosanti for 8 instruments, 1994; In Terra Aliena for 5 soloists and orchestra, 1995. Honours include: Guggenheim Fellowships, 1969, 1973. Address: c/o ASCAP, ASCAP Building, One Lincoln Plaza, New York, NY 10023, USA.

SOLODCHIN Galina, b. 29 Apr 1944, Tientsin, China. Violinist. Education: Studied at the New South Wales Conservatorium. Career: Freelance musican, including member of Delmé Quartet from 1967; Many performances in Britain and Europe in the classical and modern repertory; Concerts at the Salzburg Festival and the Brahms Saal of the Musikverein Vienna; Season 1990 included Haydn's Last Seven Words in Italy and elsewhere, three Brahms programmes at St John's Smith Square with Iain Burnside on piano; Concerts at St David's Hall in Cardiff with Quartets by Tchaikovsky and Robert Simpson including premiere of his 13th Quartet; Appearances in Bremen, Hamburg and Trieste followed by festival engagements in 1991; Other repertory includes works by Paul Patterson, Daniel Jones, Wilfred Josephs, Iain Hamilton and Bernard Stevens. Recordings include: Haydn's Last Seven Words; Vaughan Williams's On Wenlock Edge; Gurney's Ludlow and Tame; Simpson Quartets 1-9 and String Trio; Daniel Jones 3 Quartets and Bridge No 2; Bliss's No 1 and 2; Josef Holbrooke Piano Quartet and Clarinet Quintet; Brahms Clarinet Quintet; Dvorák F major Quartet; Verdi Quartet; Strauss A major Op 2; Hummel No 1, 2 and 3; Bernard Stevens Theme and Variations and Quartet No 2 and Lyric Suite for String Trio; Beethoven Op 74 and Op 95; Favourite Encores. Address: c/o 33 Whittingstall Road, Fulham, London, SW6, England.

SOLOMON Maynard (Elliott), b. 5 Jan 1930, New York, New York, USA. Music Historian. m. Eva Georgiana Tevan, 22 Jan 1951, 2 sons, 1 daughters. Education: High School of Music and Art, New York; BA, Brooklyn College, 1950; Postgraduate studies at Columbia University, 1950-51. Career: Co-founder and Co-owner of Vanguard Recording Society Inc, New York, 1950-86; Teacher, City University of New York, 1979-81; Visiting Professor, State University of New York, Stony Brook, 1988-; Associate Editor, American Imago; Visiting Professor: Columbia University, 1989-90, Harvard University, 1991-92 and Yale University, 1994-95. Publications: Marxism and Art, 1973; Beethoven, 1977; Myth, Creativity and Psychoanalysis, 1978; Beethoven Essays, 1988; Beethoven's Tagebuch, Bonn and Mainz, 1990; Mozart: A Life, 1995. Contributions to: Articles in Beethoven Jahrbuch; Music and Letters; Musical Quarterly; 19th Century Music; Journal of The American Musicological Society. Honours: Deems Taylor Award, ASCAP, 1978, 1989, 1995; Kinkeldey Award of American Musicological Society, 1989; New York University Society of Fellows; New York Institute for the Humanities. Memberships: American Musicological Society; PEN; Phi Beta Kappa. Address: 1 West 72nd Street, New York, NY 10023, USA.

SOLOMON Yonty, b. 6 May 1938, Cape Town, South Africa. Pianist. Education: BMus, Cape Town University, 1958; Studied with Myra Hess in London and with Charles Rosen in USA. Debut: London in 1963. Career: Concert appearances with leading orchestras in Europe, USA, Canada, South Africa, Israel and Rumania; First performances of works by Bennett, Joseph, Merilaainen and Sorabji; Repertoire also includes works by Bach (Goldberg variations), Schoenberg, Albeniz, Janácek, Ives, Granados, Debussy and Shostakovich; Duos with violinist, Sylvia Rosenberg and cellist, Radu Aldulescu; Appearance on ITV programme in honour of Sorabji; Professor at the Royal College of Music; Masterclasses at Prussia Cove, Cornwall and at Nottingham University. Recordings include: Music by Sorabji; 14 Studies by Wilfred Josephs; Sonatas for Cello and Piano by Prokofiev and Fauré with Timothy Hugh for the BBC, 1991. Honours include: Beethoven International Award, 1963. Address: c/o Basil Douglas Artists Management, 8 St George's Terrace, London, NW1 8XJ, England.

SOLTESZ Stefan, b. 6 Jan 1949, Nyiregyhaza, Hungary. Conductor. Education: Studied at the Vienna Academy of Music with Dieter Weber, Hans Swarowsky, Reinhold Schmidt and Friedrich Cerha. Career: Conductor at the Theater an der Wien, Vienna, 1971-73; Coach and Conductor at Vienna Staatsoper, 1973-83; Salzburg Festivals, 1978, 1979, 1983 being assistant to Karl Böhm, Christoph von Dohnányi and Karajan; Guest Conductor of the Graz Opera, 1979-81; Permanent Conductor of the Hamburg Staatsoper, 1983-85 and Deutsche Oper Berlin since 1985; General Music Director of the State Theatre at Brunswick, 1988-93; Guest Conductor with the Opera Royale de Wallonie at Liège, Bavarian State Opera in Munich, Bonn Opera, Vlaamse Opera Antwerp, Stuttgart State Theater, Nederlandse Oper at Amsterdam, Festival de Radio France at Montpelleier, Aix-en-Provence and the Paris and Vienna State Opera; Concerts in Bologna, Hamburg, Mexico City, Naples, Paris, Salzburg, Turin, Vienna, Munich, Essen, Berlin, Karlsruhe, Hannover and Zagreb among others; Toured Japan with the German State Opera, Unter den Linden, 1990; Since season 1992-93 as Music Director of the Flanders Opera of Antwerp/Ghent, Belgium, and as Principal Guest Conductor of Leipzig Opera; Guest Conductor of Frankfurt Opera, Semper Opera, Dresden Theatre, Bellini, Catania, Hamburg Opera and Wiener Staatsoper; US debut in 1992 at Washington Opera, Kennedy Center with Otello; Deutsch Oper Berlin, 1985-97; General Director, Aalto Musiktheater in Essen and Music Director of the City of Essen, Germany, 1997. Recordings include: Swan Lake Excerpts with Vienna Symphony; La Bohème with Lucia Popp and Francisco Araiza; Opera Arias with Lucia Popp; Opera Arias with Grace Bumbry; Don Giovanni, by Giuseppe Gazzaniga with Munich Radio Orchestra; The Chalk Circle by Alexander Zemlinsky; Orchestral Songs by Hugo Wolf with Dietrich Fischer-Dieskau. Address: Aalto Musiktheater Essen, Opernplatz 10, D-45128 Essen, Germany.

SOLUM John (Henry), b. 11 May 1935, New Richmond, Wisconsin, USA. Concert Flautist; Writer; Educator. m. Millicent Hunt, 30 July 1960, 2 sons. Education: BA, Princeton University, 1957; Private Studies in flute with William Kincaid,, Philadelphia, 1953-58; Flute, Harmony, Counterpoint, Composition, Musicology, various teachers. Debut: Solo, 1953; Soloist, Philadelphia Orchestra, 1957; New York debut recital, 1959. Career: Soloist, Chamber Music Player, 37 countries on 5 continents, including Asia, 1968, 1969, 1976, Latin America, 1978, 1979, 1980; USSR, 1983 and 13 New York recitals; Guest appearances with orchestras in over 50 cities; Many Radio Broadcasts; Festivals, Europe, North America; Teacher: Vassar College, 1969-71, 1977-; Indiana University, 1973; Oberlin Conservatory, 1976; Co-Director: Bath Summer School of Baroque Music, England, 1979-89; Connecticut Early Music Festival, 1982-. Compositions: Cadenzas, Mozart's Flute Concertos. Recordings: Ibert, Jolivet, Honegger Flute Concertos, 1975; 2 Malcolm Arnold Flute Concertos, 1977; Romantic Music for Flute and Orchestra, 1978; Mozart Flute Concertos, 1980; Telemann Duets, 1981; Bach Flute Sonatas, 1988; Vivaldi Bullfinch Concerto, 1992; Bach, Handel, Telemann Trio Sonatas, 1992; Sonatas by Telemann, Handel, Vinci, Scarlatti, J C Bach, C P E Bach, Mozart, 1994; Works by Kupferman, Laderman, Beeson, Luening, Kraft and Nowak, 1994; Handel Trio Sonata in C Minor, 1995; Hummel's chamber arrangements of Mozart symphonies 35 and 36, 1997. Publications: Massenet and Delibes, 3 Original Pieces, 1978; Wilhelm Popp, Bagatelle, 1980; Wilhelm Popp, 30 Easy Studies, Op 520, 1981; J Andersen, 5 Songs Without Words, 1982; Boccherini Sextet, Op 15/6, 1990, de la Barre, Two Duets for Two Flutes, 1990; Arthur Foote, At Dusk, 1991; The Early Flute, 1992; The NFA Anthology of American Flute Music, 1993; Scarlatti, Sonata in E Minor, 1997. Contributions to: New Grove Dictionary of Musical Instruments; Revue de la Société liégeoise de musicologie. Hobby: Art collecting. Address: 10 Bobwhite Drive, Westport, CT 06880, USA.

SOLYOM-NAGY Sandor, b. 21 Dec 1934, Siklos, Hungary. Baritone. Education: Ferenc Liszt Academy of Music, Budapest, 1960. Career: Budapest State Opera, 1964-; Numerous guest performances in Berlin, Brussels, Bratislava, Prague, Cologne, Barcelona, Moscow, Leningrad, Genoa, Rome, The Hague, Rotterdam, Paris, Rio de Janeiro, Sao Paulo, Sofia, Varna and Vienna; Frequent guest appearances with Bavarian State Opera at Munich in Germany and Vienna State Opera in Austria and Japan; Regular guest artist at Bayreuth Festival from 1981 including Grail Knight in Parsifal in 1992; Sang Palatine Gara in Erkel's Hunyadi László at Budapest in 1989. Recordings: Numerous records including Liszt's Christus Oratorio, The Legend of Elisabeth, Via Crucis, The Queen of Sheba, Agamemnon in Gluck's Iphigénie en Aulide, the title role in Kodály's Háry János and in Strauss's Guntram and Respighi's La Fiamma. Honours: Liszt Prize, 1972; Merited Artist of Hungary, 1977; Hector Berlioz Prize, French Record Academy; Grand Prix, French Record Academy; Charles Cros Prize; Golden Orpheus Prize, French Record Academy. Address: c/o Budapest State Opera, Budapest, Hungary.

SOMACH Beverly, b. 17 Jan 1935, New York City, New York, USA. Violinist. m. S George Silverstein, 20 August 1959, 2 sons, 2 daughters. Education: BS, Columbia University, 1956; Certificate of Completion of Studies with Jascha Heifetz, University of California, Los Angeles, 1959. Career: Recitals, Town Hall, Carnegie Hall, Lincoln Centre, Alice Tully Hall, New York City; Recitals in London (Wigmore Hall, Purcell Room), Edinburgh, Glasgow, Stockholm, Copenagen, Zurich, Paris, Tokyo, Hong Kong, Montreal; Soloist with Orchestra: New York Philharmonic, Chicago Symphony, Los Angeles Symphony, American Symphony, Orchestra Luxembourg. Recordings: For Newport Classic, Heritage Society, Radio Free Europe, Voice of America. Conributions to: New York Times, Musical America. Current Management: Seymour F Malkin Management.

SOMARY Johannes (Felix), b. 7 Apr 1935, Zurich, Switzerland. Musician. m. Anne Van Zandt, 20 July 1963, 2 sons, 1 daughter. Education: BA, Yale University, 1957; MMus, Yale School of Music, 1959. Debut: Conducting debut with Washington Square Music Festival, New York, 1960. Career: Founder, Music Director and Conductor of Amor Artis, NYC, 1962-; Conductor for recordings with English Chamber Orchestra, London, 1968-79; Chairman, Arts and Music Department, Horace Mann School, NYC, 1971-; Conductor with Fairfield County Chorale, 1975-, Great Neck Choral Society, 1982- and Taghkanic Chorale, 1992-; Visiting Professor of Music, Yale School of Music, 1983-84; Choral Director, Madeira Bach Festival, 1984-86; Guest Conductor at Dubrovnik Music Festival, 1986, Sion Music Festival, Switzerland, 1990, and for Polish Radio and TV Orchestra, 1990, New Orleans Philharmonic, London Royal Philharmonic and for Brno State Philharmonic among others; Artist in Residence at St Jean Baptiste Church, New York; Commissioned by Jefferson Music Festival to write an oratorio for 1994. Compositions: Ballad Of God And His People, recorded; The Ultimate Quest, oratorio for Great Neck Choral Society. Recordings: Conductor for 55 recordings including Bach's St Matthew Passion; Works by Haydn, Tchaikovsky, Prokofiev and Kurt Weill; Acis and Galatea; Bach cantatas and motets; Scenes of operas by Handel with Sosarme, 1994. Honours: Certificates of Merit, Yale School of Music Alumni Association and University of Chicago; Choirmaster Certificate, American Guild of Organists; Record of Year, Stereo Review, 1969, 1970, 1975, 1978. Memberships include: Board of Directors, Friendship Ambassadors. Hobbies include: Hiking; Cycling; Reading. Address: 620 West 254 Street, Bronx, New York, NY 10471, USA.

SOMFAI László, b. 15 Aug 1934, Jászladány, Hungary. Musicologist. m. Dorrit Révész-Somfai, 1 son, 1 daughter. Education: Diploma in Musicology, Ferenc Liszt Academy of Music, Budapest, 1958; Doctor of Musicology, Hungarian Academy of Sciences, Budapest, 1982. Career: Music Librarian at National Széchényi Library, Budapest until 1962; Head of Budapest Bartók Archives, Institute for Musicology, Hungarian Academy of Sciences, 1972-; Professor of Musicology, Ferenc Liszt Academy of Music, 1980-. Publications: Co-author, Haydn als Opernkapellmeister, 1960; Joseph Haydn: Sein Leben in Zeitgenössischen Bildern, 1966, English edition, 1969; Anton Webern, 1968; The Keyboard Sonatas of Joseph Haydn, Hungarian edition, 1979, English edition, 1995; 18 Bartók Studies, 1981; Béla Bartók: Composition, Concepts and Autograph Sources, 1996; Studies on Haydn, Liszt, Stravinsky, Webern and Bartók; Critical editions in Mozart Neue Ausgabe, Gluck Neue Ausgabe, Musica Rinata; Editor, Documenta Bartókiana. Memberships: Memberships of Presidium: Zentralinstitut der Mozartforschung, Salzburg; Joseph Haydn Institut, Cologne; International Musicological Society; Corresponding Member, Hungarian Academy of Sciences; Corresponding Member, American Musicological Society; President, Hungarian Musicological Society. Address: Falk Miksa u 12, V4, H-1055 Budapest, Hungary.

SOMMER Raphael, b. 21 Jun 1937, Prague, Czechoslovakia. Cellist; Conductor. m. Geneviève Teulière, 25 Oct 1986, 2 sons. Education: Graduate, Rubin Academy of Music, Jerusalem, Israel; National Conservatory of Music, Paris, France. Career: Professor at Royal Northern College of Music, Manchester, England, 1967-; Director of first Chamber Orchestra, Royal College of Music, London, 1974-79; Profesor at Guildhall School of Music in London, 1980-. Publication: English translation of Paul Tortelier's Cello Method: How I Play, How I Teach. Honours: Winner of three international cello competitions, 1961, 1962 and 1963; 1st Prize, National Conservatory of Music, Paris. Membership: Honorary Member, Accademia Filharmonica di Musica, Bologna, Italy. Hobby: Theatre. Address: 20 Elliott Square, London, NW3, England.

SOMMER Vladimir, b. 28 Feb 1921, Dolni Jiretin, Czechoslovakia. Composer. m. 12 Feb 1983, 1 son, 1 daughter. Education: BA, 1940; School of Music, Prague, 1940-46; Graduate, School of Art and Music, Prague, 1946-50. Career: Postgradual studies, 1950-52; Radio Assistant, 1952-53; Secretary of Czech Union of Musical Composers, 1953-56; Assistant Professor at Graduate School of Art and Music, Prague, 1956-60; Professor of Theory of Music, Charles University, Prague, 1960-87. Compositions: Concerto for Violin and

Orchestra; Concerto for Violoncello and Orchestra; Overture To The Sophocles Tragedy Antigone; Vocal Symphony No 1 for Mezzo Soprano, Speaker, Chorus and Orchestra, 1965; String Quartet No 1, 1960; Seven Songs for Mezzo Soprano and Piano, 1988; String Quartet No 2, 1989. Recordings: Most works recorded by various orchestras including Czech Philharmonic Orchestra, Prague Philharmonic Orchestra, and London Symphony Orchestra. Address: Knezeveska 6, 16100 Prague 6 Ruzyne, Czech Republic.

SONDEREGGER Peter, b. 2 October 1960, St Gallen, Switzerland. Composer. Education: Konservatorium Basel, with Jacques Wildberger, 1980-85; Musikhochschule Karlsruhe, Germany, with Wolfgang Rihm, 1987-89. Compositions: Delirien I-III, Chamber Ensembles and Live Electronics, 1981-83; Piano Concerto No 1, 1985; Tombeau per tre Clarinetti, 1985; Eclairs Errants, Piano and Orchestra, 1986-87; Webern-Variations to Symphony Op 21, for Orchestra, 1987; Zeit, Verjüngendes Licht, Clarinet, Viola and Guitar, 1987-88; 73 Pezzi Degli Scrovegni, piano, 1989-90; Missa Incontri, Piano Trio, 1990-91; Auslöschung, for Panflute and Double-String Quartet, 1991; Conductus II, Violin and Organ, 1993-94; Various other compositions for Chamber Ensembles, Piano solo, Guitar Solo; Quaenam sit divina caligo, for female voices and violins, 1994; La Mallorquina, for violin and piano, 1995; Conductus IV for 2 saxophones. Recordings: Tombeau per tre Clarinetti; Zeit, Verjüngendes Licht. Honours: Scholarships: Heinrich Strobel-Stiftung des Südwestfunks, 1986, Schweizerischer Tonkünstlerverein, 1987. Address: Unterdorf 10, CH-4203 Grellingen, Switzerland.

SONDHEIM Stephen (Joshua), b. 22 Mar 1930, New York, New York, USA. Composer; Lyricist. Education: BA, Williams College, 1950. Compositions: Incidental Music: The Girls of Summer, 1956; Invitation to a March, 1961; Twigs, 1971; Lyrics: West Side Story, 1957; Gypsy, 1959; Do I Hear A Waltz?, 1965; Candide (additional lyrics), 1973; Music and Lyrics: A Funny Thing Happened on the Way to the Forum, 1962; Anyone Can Whistle, 1964; Evening Primrose, 1966; Company, 1970; Follies, 1971; A Little Night Music, 1973; The Frogs, 1974; Pacific Overtures, 1976; Sweeney Todd, 1979; Merrily We Roll Along, 1981; Sunday in the Park with George, 1984; Into the Woods, 1987; Assassins, 1991; Passion, 1994; Anthologies: Side by Side by Sondheim, 1976; Marry Me A Little, 1980; You're Gonna Love Tomorrow, 1983; Putting It Together, 1992. Film: Stavisky, 1974; Reds, 1981; Dick Tracy, 1990. Memberships: President, Dramatists Guild, 1973-81; American Academy and Institute of Arts and Letters. Address: c/o Flora Roberts Inc, 157 West 57th Street, New York, NY 10019, USA.

SONEK Frantisek, b. 12 Apr 1933, Opava, Czech Republic. Pianist; Conductor. m. Lubomíra Záškodná, 1 Aug 1959, 2 daughters. Education: Piano and conducting at Conservatory in Ostrava; Conducting at Janáček's Academy of Music Arts in Brno (JAMU). Debut: Ballet, fairy-tale about John of Oskar Nedbal in Theatre Ostrava (as conductor), Czech Republic. Career: Teacher at Conservatories of Ostrava and Brno, 1965-69; Then Janáček's Academy of Music Arts (JAMU) in Brno mainly as Pianist-Correpetitor, 1969-; Also Pianist-Correpetitor in Opera House of Opava, 1960-64: Conductor-Assistant, Janáček's Opera in Brno (music of Smetana, Dvořák, Janáček, Bizet, Moniuszko, Rimsky-Korsakov, Tchaikovsky). Recordings: Janářek's operas Jenufa and Excursions of Mr Brouček. Contributions to: JAMU: About Janáček's Glagolitic Mass and its Problems, 1972; About Work of Piano-Correpetitor, 1976. Memberships: Chief and Conductor of Amateur Symphony Orchestra of Railwaymen in Brno, 1978-. Address: Milénova 12, Brno 38, Czech Republic 63800.

SONNTAG Ulrike, b. 1959, Esslingen, Germany. Singer (Soprano). Education: Studied with Eva Sava and Dietrich Fischer-Dieskau; Hartmann-Dressler. Debut: Sang Oriane in Amadis de Gaul by J C Bach as guest with the Hamburg Staatsoper, 1983. Career: Sang at the Stadttheater Heidelberg, 1984-86; Nationaltheater Mannheim, 1986-88; Has appeared in concerts all over Europe, festivals of Salzburg, Vienna, Berlin, Frankfurt, Schweitzingen and in the USA (Los Angeles), China, Brazil, Japan; Member of the Stuttgart Opera from 1988, as Euridice, Susanna, Donna Elvira, Marcelline, Pamina, Marie, Ännchen, Micaela, Nedda, Frau Fluth, Gretel, Sophie in Der Rosenkavalier and Helena (A Midsummer Night's Dream); Sang Aennchen in Der Freischütz at the 1989 Ludwigsburg Festival; Member of Vienna State Opera for 1991-94, repertoire including Susanna, Pamina, Micaela, Zdenka, Musetta; Pamina, 1992; Freischütz production, Trieste, 1994; Wildschütz production, Cologne, 1994; Lieder tour, Moscow and St Petersburg, 1994; Guest appearances: Deutsche Oper, Berlin; Frankfurt, Belinda, Marcelline, Musetta; Monte Carlo, Ännchen, 1990; Cairo, Rosina in Haydn's La Vera Costanza, 1990; Trieste, Ännchen, 1994, Euridice, 1995; Recordings include: Bach cantatas; Bach: B minor Mass with Rilling; CD: Mignon lieder, Schubert, Schumann, Wolf; 2 CDs: Milhaud, songs and chamber music. Address: Steigstrasse 21, D-71394 Kernen, Germany.

SOOTER Edward, b. 8 Dec 1934, Salina, Kansas, USA. Singer (Tenor). Education: Studied at the Friends University in Wichita with Elsa Haury, Kansas University with Joseph Wilkins and the Hamburg Musikhochschule with Helmut Melchert. Debut: Bremerhaven, 1966, as Florestan. Career: Sang in Kiel, Karlsruhe, Wiesbaden, Munich, Frankfurt and Cologne; Metropolitan Opera from 1979, as Florestan, Tannhäuser, Otello, Aeneas in Les Troyens, Walther, Tristan and Lohengrin; Sang Siegmund in Ring cycles at Seattle; New Orleans Opera, 1992, as Florestan; Other roles include Parsifal, Don José, Canio, Aegisthus, Manrico, Ernani, Samson, and Babinsky in Schvanda the Bagpiper; Sang Siegmund at Flagstaff, 1996. Address: c/o Thea Dispeker Artist's Management, 59 E 54th, New York, NY 10021, USA.

SOPRONI Jozsef, b. 4 Oct 1930, Sopron, Hungary. Composer. Education: Studied at the Budapest Academy of Music, 1949-56. Career: Faculty Member at Bela Bartók School, Budapest, from 1957; Professor, Budapest Academy of Music, from 1977 (on faculty from 1962); Rector at Budapest Academy 1988-94. Compositions include: Concerto for Strings 1953; 10 String quartets, 1958-94; Carmina polinaesiana cantata for women's chorus and ensemble, 1963; Ovidi metamorphoses, for soprano, chorus and orchestra, 1965; 2 Cello concertos, 1967, 1984; 6 Symphonies, No 1 1975, No 2 The Seasons 1977, No 3 Sinfonia da Requiem, for soloists, chorus and orchestra, 1980, No 4 1994, No 5 1995, No 6, 1995; Horn sonata, 1976; Six Bagatelles for wind quintet, 1977; Late Summer Caprices for string trio and piano, 1978; 2 violin sonatas, 1979, 1980; Violin Concerto, 1983; Comments on a Theme by Handel, for orchestra, 1985; Antigone, opera, 1987; Three Pieces for orchestra, 1988; Magnificat for soloists, chorus and orchestra, 1989; Missa Scarbantiensis, 1991; Missa Choralis, 1992; Missa super B-A-C-H, 1992; Litaniae Omnium Sanctorum, 1993; Pslam XXIX for chorus, organ, trumpet and trombone, 1993; Missa Gurcensis for chorus and ensemble, 1994; Te Deum, for soloists, chorus and orchestra; Livre d'orgue, 9 pieces, 1994; 8 Piano sonatas, 1996-97; Piano concerto, 1997; Piano Music, songs and choruses. Address: II Pajzs-u 22/b, H-1025, Budapest, Hungary.

SORDELLO Enzo, b. 20 Apr 1927, Pievebovigliano, Macerata, Italy. Baritone. Education: Studied at the Milan Conservatory. Debut: Teatro Toselli in Cueno as Enrico in Lucia di Lammermoor, 1952. Career: La Scala, 1954-75, as Cinna in La Vestale opposite Callas; Later appeared in Milan as Belcore, Albert in Werther, Gerard in Andrea Chénier in 1955 and as Tonio; Sang at Metropolitan Opera in 1956 as Marcello, Vienna Staatsoper in 1959, Stoll Theatre in London in 1960 and Glyndebourne Festival, 1961-62 as Belcore; Frequent broadcasts on RAI. Recordings include: La Fanciulla del West; La Vestale, Pagliacci; Madama Butterfly; Lucia di Lammermoor. Address: 12018 Roccavione, Cueno, Italy.

SORENSON VON GERTTEN Iwa (Cecilia), b. 5 Sep 1946, Gothenburg, Sweden. Soprano. m. Gustf von Gertten, 5 Jul 1980, 2 sons. Education: Music Conservatory, Gothenburg, 1966-74; Staatliche Hochschule fur Musik, Cologne, 1970-71; Trained as Singer, Singing Teacher and Organist, School of Theatre and Opera, Gothenburg, 1974-75, 1976-77. Debut: Malmo, Sweden as Norina in Donizetti's Don Pasquale, 1978. Career: Opera soloist at Malmo Stadsteater, 1978-79 and Royal Opera of Stockholm, 1979-; Major roles include Rosina in The Barber of Seville, Musetta in La Bohème, Sophie in Der Rosenkavalier, Zdenka in Arabella, Fiordiligi in Così fan tutte, Susanna in The Marriage of Figaro, Blonde in The Abduction from the Seraglio, Aminta in Il Re Pastore, Violetta in La Traviata, Marguerite in Faust, and Olympia in Tales of Hoffmann; Roles in operettas include Adele in Die Fledermaus, Laura in Der Bettelstudent by Millöcker, Josephine in HMS Pinafore, and Fiametta in Boccaccio by Von Suppé; Concert repertoire includes Handel's Messiah and Judas Maccabaeus, Haydn's Creation, Mendelssohn's Elijah, and Mozart's Requiem and Mass in C minor; Recitals with piano of German Lieder, French Art Songs, Swedish repertoire and contemporary music. Recordings: Mostly 19th and 20th Century Swedish Music. Honours: 3 Gramophone Prizes, 1983, 1984, 1985. Address: Hogbergsgatan 26B, S-11620 Stockholm, Sweden.

SOROKINA Elena, b. 6 Apr 1940, Moscow, USSR. Pianist; Music Historian. m. Alexander Bakhchiev, 28 Nov 1962, 1 daughter. Education: Graduated, Central School of Music, 1958; MA, Performance, MA, History of Music, 1963, PhD, 1965, Moscow State Conservatory. Debut: Duet concert (with husband), Mozart, Schubert, Central Arts House, Moscow. Career: Professor, 1965-, Chief, Chair of Russian Music History, 1992-, Moscow State Conservatory; Regular duet performances, Beethoven, Mozart, Weber, Schumann, Schubert, Brahms, Glinka, Borodin, Rachmaninov, other Russian composers, music genres, history of Moscow Conservatory, 1969-; Series of TV programmes, chamber music concerts, 1970s; Tours lecturing on Russian music, France, Austria, Latin America; International/national festivals of music, Moscow, Leningrad (with husband); Mozart International Festival, Tokyo (1991); English tour (Cambridge, London), Soviet and British modern piano duets; Concerts with husband, Israel, Italy, Germany, USA, 1992-93; 8 programmes, all Schubert piano duets, with husband; Piano duo festivals, Novosibirsk and Ekaterinburg, 1993-95; Works dedicated to her and husband by Boyarsky, Lubovksy, Fried, Manukyan and Moore. Recordings include: Piano duets with husband: Rachmaninov; Russian Salon Piano Music; Mozart (3 discs); Schubert (2 discs); Music of France; Weber, Schumann, Mendelssohn; V Persichetti; Bartók, Lutoslawski; Enescu; Albums: Music of Old Vienna; J S Bach, his family and pupils; Music for 6 and 8 hands (with G Rozhdestvensky, V Postnikova). Publication: Piano Duet (history of genre), 1988. Honours: Honoured Artist of Russia, 1992; Kodama Prize, International Piano Duo Association, 1993. Memberships: Mozart and Schubert Societies, Moscow; Union of CIS Composers. Current Management: Vadim Dubrovitsky Producer Firm, Ramenki Gallery, Ramenki Str 6-2, 117607 Moscow, Russia. Address: 4-32 Koshkin Str, Moscow 115409, Russia.

SOTIN Hans, b. 10 Sep 1939, Dortmund, Germany. Bass Singer. Education: Studied privately with FW Hetzel; Dortmund Musikhochschule with Dieter Jacob. Debut: Essen in 1962 in Der Rosenkavalier. Career: Hamburg Staatsoper, 1964-, in the standard bass repertory and in the premieres of operas by Penderecki, Klebe, Blacher, Von Einem and Kelemen; Visits with Hamburg Company to New York, Montreal, Rome, Stockholm and Edinburgh; In 1970 sang in Beethoven's Choral Symphony at the United Nations; Glyndebourne debut in 1970 as Sarastro in Die Zauberflöte; Sang at Bayreuth Festival from 1972 as the Landgrave, Pogner, Titurel and Gurnemanz, New York Metropolitan from 1972 as Sarastro and as Hunding and Wotan in Die Walküre, Covent Garden debut in 1974 as Hunding and La Scala Milan in 1976 as Baron Ochs in Der Rosenkavalier; Sang Ochs at Covent Garden in 1986, Lodovico in Otello at the Metropolitan Opera in 1988, and Landgrave in Tannhäuser at Hamburg in 1990; Sang at Bayreuth, 1989-90 as Gurnemanz and Daland; Season 1992 as the Landgrave at Berlin and Barcelona, Gurnemanz and Daland at Bayreuth; Often heard as concert singer notably in music by Bach. Recordings include: Tannhäuser; Aida; Fidelio; Salome; Così fan tutte; Die Walküre; St Matthew Passion; Beethoven's Christ at the Mount of Olives; The Devils of Loudun; Mahler's 8th Symphony; Parsifal; Pauken Messe Haydn. Honours: Forderpreis des Landes NRW; Friedrich Oberdörfer Preis, Hamburg; Kammersänger, Hamburg. Address: c/o Lies Askonas Ltd, 6 Henrietta Street, London, WC2, England.

SOUDANT Hubert, b. 16 Mar 1946, Maastricht, Netherlands. Conductor. Education: Studied at the Maastricht Conservatory, with Franco Ferrara in Italy and at Netherlands Radio Course in Hilversum. Career: Assistant Conductor with the Hilversum Radio Orchestra, 1967-70; Has conducted the Orchestra of Radio France and the Nouvel Orchestra Philharmonique, with which he gave the French premiere of Mahler's 10th Symphony at Strasbourg in 1979; In 1980 conducted the premieres of Rene Koering's opera Elseneur and the Nana Symphonie by Marius Constant; Conductor of the Symphony Orchestra of Utrecht, 1982; Musical Director with Orchestra Sinfonica dell'Emilia Romagna Arturo Toscanini, Parma, 1988; Guest conductor in England, Germany, Belgium, Italy, Scandinavia, South Africa and Japan; Conducted Ernani at Parma in 1990 and Berlioz's Faust at Turin in 1992. Recordings: Tchaikovsky 4th and 6th Symphonies and Romeo and Juliet with the London Philharmonic; Liszt Piano Concertos with the LPO. Honours: Winner, International Competition for Young Conductors at Besançon, 1971; 2nd Prize, Herbert von Karajan International Conducting Competition, 1973; First Prize, Guido Cantelli International Conducting Competition, Milan, 1975. Address: Orchestra Sinfonica dell'Emilia Romagna, Piazzale Cesare Battisti 15, I-43100 Parma, Italy.

SOUKUPOVA Vera, b. 12 Apr 1932, Prague, Czechoslovakia. Contralto. Education: Studied in Prague with L Kaderabek and A Mustanova-Linkova. Career: Has sung in concert from 1955; Stage debut in 1957 at Pilsen; Member of the Prague National Opera from 1960; Tour of Russia in 1961 and sang Dalila in Bordeaux; Guest appearances in Vienna, France and Switzerland; Sang at State Operas of Hamburg and Berlin, 1969-71; Prague National Opera in 1983 as Radmila in Smetana's Libuse. Recordings: Erda in The Ring; Dvorák's Stabat Mater; Lieder by Mahler; Choral Symphony; Libuse; The Brandenburgers in Bohemia; The Bride of Messina by Fibich; Oedipus Rex; Janácek's Glagolitic Mass. Address: c/o National Theatre, PO Box 865, 112 30 Prague 1, Czech Republic.

SOULIOTIS Elena, b. 28 May 1943, Athens, Greece. Soprano and Mezzo-Soprano. Education: Studied in Buenos Aires with Alfedo Bonta, Jascha Galperin and Bianca Lietti, and in Milan with Mercedes Llopart. Debut: Teatro San Carlo Naples as Santuzza in 1964. Career: Sang in Italy and Spain from 1965; US debut in 1965 as Elena in Mefistofele at the Lyric Opera Chicago; In 1966 sang Anna Bolena in a concert performance of Donizetti's opera at Carnegie Hall in New York; La Scala Milan as Abigail in Nabucco, Metropolitan Opera in 1969 as Lady Macbeth and made guest appearances in Portugal, Greece, South America and Vienna; Covent Garden, 1969-73 as Santuzza, Abigail and Lady Macbeth; Other roles included Manon Lescaut, La Gioconda, Desdemona, Norma, Aida and Leonora in Il Trovatore; Sang at Florence, 1986-88 in The Gambler by Prokofiev and as the Princess in Suor Angelica; Appeared as the Nurse in Mascagni's Guglielmo Ratcliff at Catania in 1990. Recordings: Verdi's Macbeth and Nabucco; Anna Bolena; Norma. Hobbies: Country Life; Animals. Address: Villa il Poderino, Via Incontri 38, Florence, Italy.

SOUSTROT Marc, b. 15 Apr 1949, Lyon, France. Conductor. Education: Studied trombone at the Lyon Conservatoire, 1962-69, and conducting with Manuel Rosenthal at the Paris Conservatoire, 1969-76. Career: Assistant to André Previn with the London Symphony Orchestra, 1974-76; Deputy Conductor, 1976, then Musical Director of the Orchestre Philharmonique of the Loire; Artistic Director of the Nantes Opera, 1986-90; Conducted the premieres of Claude Baliff's Fantasio Grandioso in 1977, 1st Piano Concerto by Maurice Ohana in 1981, and Concerto for Orchestra by Alain Louvier, 1987; Conducted Tristan and Isolde at Nantes, 1989, Manon Lescaut, 1990, Les Contes d'Hoffmann at Geneva in 1990, and Carmen at the Bregenz Festival, Austria. Recordings: Trumpet Concertos with Maurice André; Music by Franceschini, Scarlatti, Vivaldi, Tartini and Telemann with the Monte Carlo National Opera Orchestra. Honours: Winner, Rupert Foundation Competition for Young Conductors, London, 1974; International Competition at Besançon, 1975. Address: Opera de Nantes, 1 Rue Moliere, F-44000 Nantes, France.

SOUTHGATE Sir William (David), b. 4 Aug 1941, Waipukarau, New Zealand. Conductor; Composer. Education: Studied at Otago University and the Guildhall School of Music, 1967-71. Career: Freelance Composer in London and guest musical director of the Royal Shakespeare Company; Conductor and Arranger for the Phoenix Opera Company; Musical Director of the Wellington Youth Orchestra from 1977; Musical Director of the Christchurch Symphony Orchestra from 1984; Has conducted operas by Rossini, Verdi and Johann Strauss for the Wellington and Canterbury Opera Companies; Prsenter of music programmes on New Zealand radio and television; Toured Finland as Conductor, 1986, Sweden and Finland, 1989; Debut with Honolulu Symphony, 1989; Tour of New Zealand with the Royal New Zealand Ballet Company, 1989; Premieres of children's opera Faery Tale and Cello Concerto in New Zealand, 1990; Also engaged for the Dunedin Sinfonia, New Zealand, 1991; St Matthews Chamber Orchestra, New Zealand, 1991; SWF Sinfonia Orchestra, Spohr Competition, Baden-Baden, 1991; Christchurch Symphony Orchestra, New Zealand, 1991; New Zealand Symphony Orchestra, 1992. Recordings include: Second Symphony. Honours include: Guildhall School conducting prize; 2nd prize, Besançon Conducting Competition.

SOUZA Ralph de, b. 1959, England. Violinist. Career: Founder Member and Second Violinist of the Endellion String Quartet, 1979; Many concerts in Paris, Amsterdam, Frankfurt, Munich, Salzburg and Rome; Appeared at the South Bank Haydn Festival in 1990, the Wigmore Hall Beethoven Series in 1991 and the Quartet Plus Series on South Bank in 1994; Quartet-in-Residence at Cambridge University from 1992 and Residency at MIT, United States, 1995. Recordings include: Works by Haydn, Bartók, Dvorák, Walton and Smetana. Address: Hazard Chase, Richmond House, 16-20 Regent Street, Cambridge, CB2 1DB, England.

SOUZAY Gerard, b. 8 Dec 1918, Angers, France. Baritone. Education: First Prize for Singing, and for Vocalising, at the Paris Conservatoire. Debut: Fauré's Requiem under the direction of Charles Munch, Royal Albert Hall, London, 1945. Career: Operatic repertoire includes the roles of Don Giovanni, Almaviva in Marriage of Figaro, Golaud in Pelléas et Mélisande, Mephisto in Damnation of Faust, Lescaut in Manon, Orpheus by Monteverdi and Gluck; Has appeared at the Paris Opéra and Opéra-Comique, Grand Théâtre in Geneva, Rome Opera, Munich Opera, Vienna State Opera, Glyndebourne Festival and Metropolitan Opera; Made French songs famous worldwide and sings songs by foreign composers in many languages; Appeared at many major festivals such as Salzburg, Edinburgh, Prades, Puerto Rico, Vienna, Berlin, Aix-en-Provence, Besançon, Bordeaux and Tanglewood; Sang under the direction of such conductors as Karajan, Munch, Ansermet, Maazel, Bernstein, Szell and Cluytens; Sang solo under the direction of Stravinsky at San Marco Cathedral in Venice for the first performance of Canticum Sacrum in 1956; As Professor takes classes in Holland, England, at Academie Ravel in St Jean de Luz, at Juilliard School and many American universities, in Paris and Japan. Recordings: Many. Honours: Grand Priz for records in France, Germany, Italy, America and Japan; Chevalier of French Legion d'Honneur; Commander of the Order of Merit of FRG; Officer of the French National Order of Merit. Address: 26 Rue Freycinet, Paris 75116, USA.

SOVIERO Diana, b. 1952, USA. Soprano. Career: Sang first at St Paul in 1974 appearing as Lauretta in Gianni Schicchi and as Massenet's Manon; Joined the New York City Opera in 1976 and sang further at Miami, San Francisco and Chicago; Metropolitan Opera debut in 1986 as Juliet in Roméo et Juliette; European engagements at Paris, Rome, Florence, Milan, Vienna and Hamburg; Geneva in 1988 as Gretchen in Doktor Faust by Busoni, Philadelphia and San Diego in 1988 as Margherita in Mefistofele and Marguerite in Faust; Sang Juliet and Manon at Montreal in 1989; Covent Garden debut in 1989 as Nedda; Season 1992 as Tosca with Opera Pacific at Costa Mesa, Puccini's Trittico heroines at Dallas, Manon Lescaut at Miami and Adriana Lecouvreur at Sydney; Other roles include Puccini's Butterfly and Mimi, Leila in Les Pêcheurs de Perles and Norina in Don Pasquale; Sang Maddalena in Andrea Chenier at Seattle, 1996. Address: c/o Seattle Opera Association, PO Box 9248, Seattle, WA 98109, USA.

SOYER David, b. 24 Feb 1924, Philadelphia, PA, USA. Cellist. Education: Studied with Emanuel Feurmann and Pablo Casals. Career: Played with Bach Aria Group, Guilet Quartet, New Music Quartet and Marlboro Trio; Performed in chamber music with Rudolf Serkin at Marlboro Festival and prompted by Alexander Schneider to co-found the Guarneri String Quartet in 1964; Many tours of American and Europe notably with appearances at the Spoleto Festival in 1965, to Paris with Arthur Rubinstein and London in 1970 in the complete quartets of Beethoven; Noted for performances of the Viennese Classics and works by Walton, Bartók and Stravinsky; Season 1987-88 included tour of Japan, concerts at St John's Smith Square, and Elizabeth Hall in London; Faculty at Curtis Institute, Philadelphia and the University of Maryland. Recordings include: Mozart's Quartets dedicated to Haydn; Complete Quartets of Beethoven; With Arthur Rubinstein, Piano Quintets of Schumann, Dvorák and Brahms; Piano Quartets by Fauré and Brahms. Honours include: Edison Award for Beethoven Recordings, 1971; Honorary Doctorates at University of South Florida and State University of New York; Many Grammy Awards for recordings. Address: 6 W 77th Street, New York, NY 10024, USA.

SOYER Roger, b 1 Sep 1939, Thiais, France. Bass Singer. Education: Studied at the Paris Conservatoire with Georges Daum and Georges Jouatte. Career: Sang at the Paris Opéra from 1963; Sang at La Scala Milan in 1963 as Tiresias in Les Mamelles de Tiresias by Poulenc, Aix-en-Provence Festival from 1965 as Pluto in Monteverdi's Orfeo, Don Giovanni, Don Basilio and Arkel, Paris in 1965 in Rameau's Hippolyte et Aricie, Wexford Festival in 1968 in La Jolie Fille de Perth by Bizet and US debut at Miami in 1973 as Frère Laurent in Roméo et Juliette by Gounod; Sang at Paris Opéra from 1972 in the premiere of Sud by Stanton Coe, and as Don Giovanni, Procida in Les Vêpres Siciliennes, Ferrando, Colline and Mephistopheles, Metropolitan Opera in 1972 and Edinburgh Festival in 1973 as Don Giovanni in a new production of Mozart's opera under Daniel Barenboim; Guest appearances in Cologne, Brussels, Geneva, Chicago, Lisbon, Prague, San Antonio and Salzburg; Sang Rodolfo in La Sonnambula at Geneva in 1982, Sulpice in La Fille du Régiment at Dallas in 1983 and sang in L'Heure Espagnole at Turin in 1992. Recordings: Les Troyens and Benvenuto Cellini conducted by Colin Davis; Les Pêcheurs de Perles; L'Enfance du Christ; Mozart's Requiem; Lakmé; Werther; Maria Stuarda by Donizetti; Pelléas et Mélisande; Dardanus by Rameau; David et Jonathas by Charpentier. Address: c/o Grand Théâtre de Genèva, 11 Boulevard du Théâtre, CH-1211 Geneva 11, Switzerland.

SPACAGNA Maria, b. 1951, Rhode Island, USA. Soprano. Education: Studied at the New England Conservatory. Career: Sang with Dallas Opera from 1977, New York City Opera, 1978, St Louis Opera, 1982, and Detroit, 1986; Sang Puccini's Liu at Toronto in 1983 and appeared at Santa Fe, New Orleans and Trieste in 1987; Debut at La Scala Milan in 1988 as Butterfly; Sang at Spoleto Festival in 1988 as Ismene in Traetta's Antigone, sang Mimi for New Orleans Opera in 1989, Liu and Butterfly at Costa Mesa California and Greater Miami Opera in 1990; Appearances at Memphis, the Cologne Opera and elsewhere as Violetta, Susanna, Zerlina, Norina, Gilda, Marguerite, Rusalka, Micaela, Lauretta and Mascagni's Lodoletta; Sang Madama Butterfly at Santa Fe, 1996; Active concert career. Address: c/o Greater Miami Opera Association, 1200 Coral Way, Miami, FL 33145, USA.

SPALDING Daniel, b. 20 Feb 1952, Wichita, KS, USA. Conductor. m. Gabriela Imreh, 31 Mar 1986. Education: BME, MM, Northwestern University; Salzburg Mozarteum; University of Illinois; Private study with Mircea Cristescu and John Shenant. Career: Assistant Conductor with Houston Symphony, 1986-87; Principal Guest Conductor with Transylvanian State Philharmonic, 1986-; Music Director with Trenton State College Symphony Orchestra, 1988-93; Founder and Music Director of Philadelphia Virtuosi, 1991-; Music Director of Friends of the Russian All Star Ballet, 1992-; Guest Conductor in Europe and USA including Belgrade Philharmonic, Rome Festival Orchestra, Kolozsvar Hungarian State Opera, Opera Romana, New Jersey State Opera Festival, Orchestre de Chambre, Jean-Louis Petit, Paris, Philadelphia Orchestra Society, Sacramento Symphony, and Chattanooga Symphony. Contributions to: Instrumentalist; Percussionist. Memberships: Phi Mu Alpha; Conductors Guild; Percussive Arts Society. Address: 8 Cambridge Drive, West Trenton, NJ 08628, USA.

SPARNAAY Harry (Willem), b. 14 Apr 1944, Amsterdam, Netherlands. Bass Clarinettist. m. Roswitha Sparnaay-Mol. Education: Amsterdam Conservatory. Debut: Amsterdam in 1969. Career: Performances with many leading orchestras including the BBC Symphony, Rotterdam Philharmonic, ORTF, Concertgebouw and Radio Chamber Orchestra Hilversum; Soloist at festivals of Warsaw, Zagreb, Graz, Madrid, Poitiers, Witten, Como, Paris, Naples and the ISCM World Music Days at Boston, Athens and Bonn; Concerts in Europe and America; Professor of Bass Clarinet and Contemporary Music at Sweelinck Conservatory, Amsterdam-Rotterdam Conservatory and Royal Conservatory, The Hague; Composers who have written for him include Donatoni, Ferneyhough, Bussotti, Isang Yun and Barry Anderson (premiere of ARC), 1987; Appeared at Hudderfield Festival in 1987 with Time And Motion Studies by Ferneyhough; Tour of Britain in 1989 on the Contemporary Music Network, playing Echange by Xenakis. Recordings: Bass Clarinet Identity; Harry Sparnaay/Lucien Goethals; Composers' Voice; Music by Thon Tbuynel; Music by Earle Brown; Bass Clarinet Idenitity 2; The Garden of Delight. Honours include: First Prize, Bass Clarinet Soloist, International Gaudeamus Competition, 1972. Address: Z Buiten Sparne 120, 2012 AD Haarlem, The Netherlands.

SPASOV Ivan, b. 17 Jan 1934, Sofia, Bulgaria. Composer. Education: Graduated, Sofia Conservatory, studied composition with Vladigerov, 1956, and studied further with him at Warsaw Conservatory. Compositions include: Orchestra: Sonata Concertante, 1959, 3 Symphonies, 1960-78, Micro Suite for Chamber Orchestra, 1963, Dances, 1964, Competition for 22 Winds, 1969, Cello Concerto, 1974, Piano Concerto, 1976, Firework, 1980, Violin Concerto, 1980; Vocal: Plakat, oratorio, 1958, Monodrama for Soprano and Ensemble, 1976, Canti Lamentosi for 2 Sopranos and Chamber Orchestra, 1979; Chamber: Clarinet Sonata, 1959, Viola Sonata, 1960, Episodes, 1965, Movements I and II for Strings, 1966-68, 10 Groups for Hunting Horn and Piano, 1965, String Quartet, 1973, Cello Sonata, 1980, Piano Trio, 1981; Piano Music. Address: Musicautor, 63 Tzar Assen Street, 1463 Sofia, Bulgaria.

SPEISER Elisabeth, b. 15 Oct 1940, Zurich, Switzerland. Singer (Soprano). m. Hans Jecklin, 2 children. Education: Academy of Music, Winterhur. Debut: Zurich. Career includes: Concerts in all European countries, North and South America; Guest at many festivals; Many concerts with Karl Richter; Opera debut as Pamina in Die Zauberflöte, Ludwigsburger Schloss Festspiele, 1972-73; Glyndebourne Festival, 1973; Mélisande, St Gallen, 1974; Euridice, Ludwigsburger Schloss Festspiele, 1975; Many Lieder recitals with Irwin Gage; Television and radio appearances in Germany, Italy, Switzerland; Glyndebourne Festival as Euridice, 1982. Recordings include: Secular Cantatas and Geistliche Lieder by JS Bach; Caecilien Mass by Haydn; Carissimi Cantatas; Berg/Schoenberg Lieder; Gluck's Orfeo ed Euridice; Schubert, Lieder, 1984 and 1989; Brahms, Lieder, 1985; Haydn's Arianna a Naxos and English songs, CD, 1987. Membership: Swiss Tonkunstlerverband. Address: Au Village, CH 1742 Autigny, Switzerland.

SPELINA Karel, b. 2 Nov 1936. Musician - Violist. m. Marie Husickova, 7 June 1958, 2 daughters. Education: Graduated, Technical College, 1955; Graduated, Conservatory of Music, Pilsen, 1967. Debut: With Pilsen Radio Quartet, Pilsen, 1963. Career: Principal Viola, Pilsen Radio Orchestra, 1962-70; Principal Viola, Czech Philharmonic Orchestra, 1970-; Member, Ars Rediviva Ensemble, 1970-; Member, Martinu Piano Quartet, 1979-; Professor, Prague Conservatory, 1994-; Has played concertos and orchestral works by Berlioz, J Rejcha, A Vranitzky, J V Stamitz, J K Vanhal, J S Bach, Martinu, Z Lukas, Jaroch, other composers; Sonatas and chamber music by Bach and sons, Telemann, Händel, Mendelssohn, Hindemith, Brahms, Shostakovich, Lukas, Martinu, Honegger, Milhaud, Jirak and others. Recordings: Sonatas of C P E Bach and W F Bach; Sonatas of A Honegger and D Milhaud; Sonatas of Hindemith; Concertos of Josef Rejcha; Complete Sonatas of J K Vanhel, 1st World Recording, 1997. Honour: Prize, City of Pilsen, 1968. Memberships: AHUV, Prague; Teacher, S Vegh International Chamber Music Academy. Address: Sturova 32/1153, CZ-14200 Prague 4, Czech Republic.

SPEMANN Alexander, b. 1 June 1967, Wiesbaden, Germany. Singer (Tenor); Composer. Education: Studied with Gertie Charlent at the Peter Cornelius Conservatory, Mainz and with Martin Grundler at the Frankfurt Musikhochschule. Debut: Tenor solo in Beethoven's Ninth, Milan, 1989; Stage debut as First Armed Man in Die Zauberflöte at Wiesbaden. Career: Many concert and opera appearances at Essen, Vienna, Stuttgart, Cologne, Frankfurt, Munich and Hamburg; Engaged with Bonn

Opera from 1993-97, singing Kronthal in Lortzing's Wildschütz, and making debut in a Wagner role as Erik in Der fliegende Holländer; Freelance Film and Theatre music composer, including music for the Hessiche Staatstheater, Wiesbaden; Engaged with Darmstadt since 1997 as youth heroic tenor, singing Son-Chong in Land des Ladelus, Don José in Carmen and many other roles. Recordings include: Count Rudolf in Weber's Silvana (Marco Polo); Hans in The Bartered Bride, with the orchestra of North German Radio. Honours include: Winner, Robert Stolz Competition, Hamburg 1996. Address: c/o NWB Apollon & Hermes, Kunstlergentur, Nils Management Production, 2 Bram, Im Flogerhof 12, D-53819 Neunkirchen-Wolperath, Germany.

SPENCE Patricia, b. 12 Jan 1961, Salem, Oregon, USA. Singer (Mezzo-soprano). Education: Studied in San Francisco. Debut: San Francisco Opera as Anna in L'Africaine. Career: Has performed the Princess in Suor Angelica, Mother Goose in The Rake's Progress and Meg Page in Falstaff at San Francisco; New York City debut, 1988, as Rosina; Opera Colorado, 1989 as Mistress Quickly; European debut as Edwige in Guillaume Tell at Verona followed by Mozart's Requiem at St Petersburg, Malcolm in La Donna del Lago at La Scala, 1992, and Cenerentola with Phoenix Opera, Arizona; Further engagements as Farnace in Mitridate at St Louis, Tsaura in Tancredi at La Scala, Lola at the Arena di Verona, Cenerentola at Covent Garden, (United Kingdon debut, 1993), and Ramiro in La Finta Giardinera for Welsh National Opera; recitals at Göttingen and Hesse Handel Festivals, further Handel performances with Nicholas McGegan and appearances with San Francisco, Detroit, St Louis and Sacramento Symphonies, and Fresno and Mexico City Philharmonics. Recordings include: Flora in La Traviata; Handel's La Resurrezione, Messiah and Ottone, conducted by McGegan. Honours include: Il Cenacolo Award in the 1987 Merola Opera Programme, San Francisco Opera Centre. Current Management: Neil Funkhauser. Address: c/o San Francisco Opera, War Memorial Opera House, San Francisco, CA 94102, USA.

SPENCE Toby, b. England. Singer (Tenor). Education: Choral scholar at New College, Oxford; Opera School of the Guildhall School. Debut: Barbican Hall with the Gothenburg SO in The Tempest by Sibelius. Career: Concerts with RIAS Berlin in Handel's Theodora, at the Wigmore Hall in Schubertiade series and at the Brighton Festival in the Missa Solemnis; Further concerts include the St Matthew Passion, with Frans Brueggen, Die Schopfung by Haydn and On Wenlock Edge, by Vaughan Williams (Cheltenham Festival); Other orchestras include the Bournemouth SO, Royal Philharmonic and Cleveland Orchestra; Season 1995-96 included Welsh National Opera debut, as Idamante in Idomeneo, Pane in La Calisto under René Jacobs at Brussels and in Verdi's Alzira at Covent Garden; Season 1996-97 at the Salzburg Festival in Mitridate, as Tamino at Brussels and with the Israel Philharmonic and San Francisco Symphony Orchestras. Recordings include: Albums with DGG, Decca, BMG and EMI; St Matthew Passion (Philips Classics). Address: c/o Lies Askonas Ltd, 6 Henrietta St, London WC2E 8LA, England.

SPERSKI Krzysztof, b. 11 June 1942, Cracow, Poland. Musician (Violoncellist); Teacher. m. Janina Duda, 24 June 1967, div. 1986, 1 son. Education: MA (cello class of Professor R Suchecki), Academy of Music, Gdansk, 1969; Doctorate (Adjunct qualification), Academy of Music, Poznan, 1978; Habilitation (Docent qualification), Academy of Music, Lodz, 1985. Debut: Debut recital by Association of Polish Artist Musicians, Gdansk, 1964. Career: Soloist of symphony concerts, recitals, chamber concerts in Poland and foreign concert tours, Finland, UK, Sweden, Germany, Rumania, Bulgaria, Iceland, Czechoslovakia, Austria, Greece, Italy, Switzerland, Holland, Belgium, Russia; Professor of Cello, Academy of Music, Gdansk; Guest Professor, Music Master Classes, Mynämäki, Finland, 1976, International Music Seminar, Kozani, Greece, 1990-97. Recordings: Radio and TV recordings; CD, Slavic Music, 1994; Music Treasures of Gdansk, 1997. Publications: About faults of position, left and right hand of young cellists, 1979; Characteristics of Musical Utterance, 1981; Remarks of Performing Violoncello Baroque Music in the Light of Traditions and Contemporary Requirements, 1988; Polish Violoncello Pedagogic Literature, 1988. Membership: Association of Polish Artist Musicians. Honours: Award for Polish Culture, 1979; Distinction of Merit, Town of Gdansk, 1981; Gold Cross of Merit, 1985. Hobbies: Photography; Folklore. Address: ul Goralska 55/A/9, 80-292 Gdansk, Poland.

SPICKA Daniel Hilarius, b. 5 Feb 1939, Prague, Czech Republic. Music Festival Art Director; Early Music Instrument Collector; Builder; Player. m. The Hon Victoria W Reilly, 13 Jan 1973, 2 daughters. Education: Architecture, Czech Technical University, Prague, 1956-62; Evening course in Conducting, Prague Conservatoire, 1960-63; Private studies of Piano, Viol, Classical Guitar. Debuts: With Vejvanovsky Consort, Prague, 1959; With Camerata RSX, 1977; Valtice Baroque Festival, 1989. Career: Founder, Camerata RSX, 1st authentic Renaissance Consort in Bohemia; Co-Founder of Valtice Baroque Opera Festival, South Moravia, Czech Republic; Performances on Czech and Austrian TV, BBC and Czech Radio; General Dramaturgist of Valtice Baroque Opera Festical, 1989-; Noted for introducing authentic Early Music performances to Czech music scene, by bringing books, magazines, recordings and plans of instruments from the West to former Czechoslovakia. Recordings: Gagliano - La Dafne, 1992; Monteverdi - Balli, 1994. Contributions to: Various Czech music magazines, 1982-; Articles on Valtice Festival in The Independent, 1990, Die Presse, 1990, 1992, The Times, 1992. Membership: Czech Music Society, Early Music Branch. Hobbies: Playing instruments; Riding. Current Management: Avant Promotion. Address: U Mrázovky 7, 15000 Prague 5, Czech Republic.

SPIERS Colin, b. 24 July 1957, Brisbane, Queensland, Australia. Composer; Pianist. Education: BA (Music), Queensland Conservatorium, 1978. Career: Faculty Member, University of Queensland, 1980-90; Newcastle Conservatorium, 1990-; Founding Member, Perihelion Ensemble; Solo Pianist and Recital Accompanist. Compositions include: Fantasy on Theme of Keith Jarrett, piano, 1987; Tales from Nowhere, for piano, 1988; Sonata for Solo Viola, 1988; Divertimento for strings, 1988; Day of Death and Dreams, for tenor and piano, 1989; UWJ for viola and piano, 1991; Flecks for piano, 1991; Cadenzas and Interludes for string orchestra, 1991; 4 Piano Sonatas, 1990-95: Deranged Confessions, Desperate Acts, Divine Symmetry and Delicate Games; ZYJ, for trumpet and piano, 1993; Music, Like the Dark Husk of Earth, Abiding, for string orchestra, 1994; NSJ, for clarinet, basset-horn and piano, 1995; Mutationa for piano, 1996; Five Bagatelles, for piano, 1996-97. Honours include: Medal of Excellence, Queensland Conservatorium, 1979; Jean Bogan Composition Prize, 1995. Address: c/o Newcastle Conservatorium, Auckland Street, Newcastle, NSW 2300, Australia.

SPIESS Ludovico, b. 13 May 1938, Cluj, Rumania. Tenor. Education: Studied at the Budapest Music Academy and in Milan with Antonio Narducci. Debut: Galati in 1962 as the Duke of Mantua. Career: Sang operetta at the Bucharest Operetta Theatre, 1962-64; Bucharest Opera from 1964 with debut as Cavaradossi; Sang at Salzburg Festival in 1967 as Dmitri in Boris Godunov conducted by Karajan, Vienna Staatsoper from 1968 with debut as Smetana's Dalibor, Verona Arena in 1969 as Calaf in Turandot, Covent Garden debut in 1973 as Radames, and Bregenz Festival in 1974 as Don José; Appearances at Metropolitan Opera and in Hamburg, Houston, Buenos Aires, San Francisco, Naples and Berlin; Other roles include Florestan, Rodolfo, Lohengrin and Otello. Recordings: Boris Godunov; Iphigénie en Aulide; Khovanshchina. Address: c/o Staatsoper, Opernring 2, A-1010 Vienna, Austria.

SPINK Ian, b. 29 Mar 1932, London, England. University Professor. m. 7 Children. Education: BMus, London, 1952; MA, Birmingham, 1958. Career: Lecturer, Senior Lecturer, University of Sydney, New South Wales, 1962-68; Senior Lecturer, Reader, Professor, London University (RHBNC), 1969-; Dean of Faculty of Arts, 1973-75 and 1983-85; Dean of Faculty of Music, University of London, 1974-78; Member of Senate, 1975-81. Publications include: The English Lute-Songs, volume 17, 1961, 2nd edition, 1974, volume 18, 1963, volume 19, 1966; An Historical Approach to Musical Form, 1967; Editor, English Songs 1625-1660, Musica Britannica, volume 33, 1971; English Song, Dowland to Purcell, 1974, revised edition, 1986; Editor, Arne, The Judgement of Paris, Musica Britannica, volume 42, 1979; Purcell, A Song for the Duke of Gloucester's Birthday, 1695, Purcell Society Edition, volume 4, 1990; The Seventeenth Century, Blackwell History of Music in Britain, volume 3, 1992; Purcell, Timon of Athens, volume 2, 1994; Restoration Cathedral Music, 1660-1714, OUP, 1995. Address: Royal Holloway, University of London, Egham, Surrey, TW20 0EX, England.

SPINNLER Burkhard, b. 17 Jul 1954, Goldbach, Germany. Pianist. m. Claudine Orloff, 1 Oct 1983, 2 sons. Education: Staatsexamen, Musikhochschule Wurzburg, with J von Karolyi, 1978; Diplome Superieur, Brussels Royal Conservatory, with J Cl Vanden Eynden, 1982; Ecole de Maitrise Pianistique, 1981-84; Private studies with Eduardo del Pueyo in Brussels. Debut: With University Orchestra at Wurzburg in 1978. Career: Recording for Bavarian Radio in 1979, for Belgian Radio RTB, 1984; Appearances as soloist and in chamber music in Germany, Belgium and France; Special L Godowsky commemorative programme, 1989; Regular concerts on 2 pianos with Claudine Orloff, including Musique en Sorbonne, Paris, 1991; Live radio engagement, Hommage a Milhaud, RTB Brussels in 1992; Private research of Liszt unpublished works, numerological problems in Bach's music, and 136 unedited letters of Francis Poulenc; Taught at Brussels Conservatory, 1985-90. Publication: Zur Angemessenheit Traditionelles Formbegriffe in der Analyse Mahlerscher Symphonik, in Form und Idée in G Mahler's Instrumentalmusik, 1980. Hobby: Photography. Current Management: F E de Wasseige Music Management. Address: 82 Rue des Garennes, 1170 Brussels, Belgium.

SPIROCH Pavel, b. 27 June 1949, Prague, Czech Republic. Director. m. Zlata Spirochova, 5 Sept 1978, 1 son. Education: DPhil, 1975, PhD, 1978; Faculty of Journalism, 1978, Charles University. Appointments: Musical Journalist, 1966-85; Diplomatic Service, 1985-89; General Manager, Palace of Culture, Prague, 1990-94; President, Prague Convention Bureau, 1994-96; Director, Prague Autumn International Music Festival and Music Management, 1991-. Hobby: Skiing. Address: Prague Autumn International Music Festival, Pribenicka 20, 13000 Prague 3, Czech Republic.

SPITKOVA Jela, b. 1947, Czechoslovakia. Violinist. Education: Studied at the Bratislava Conservatory and in Vienna with Riccardo Odnoposoff; Graduate, Prague College of Music; Tchaikovsky Conservatory Moscow with David and Igor Oistrakh, 1971-76. Career: Has performed with leading Czech Orchestras and in 40 other countries, including those in South and North America and Africa; Recitals in Paris, Rome, Moscow, Berlin, Prague, Amsterdam and Vienna; TV and radio recordings in Spain, Norway, Denmark, Austria, France, Finland and Russia; Leader of the Mozarteum Orchestra, 1980; Teacher at the Music Academy in Vienna; Soloist with the Slovak Philharmonic in Bratislava; Repertoire includes Concertos by Tchaikovsky, Brahms, Beethoven, Sibelius, Mendelssohn, Mozart, Bach and Haydn, Lalo Symphonie Espagnole, Sonatas by Brahms, Beethoven, Franck, Schumann, Prokofiev, Mozart, Handel, Debussy and Dvorák; Concertmaster, Mozarteum Orchestra in Salzburg, 1980-94; Teacher, violin, Music Academy, Vienna, 1985-. Recordings: Mendelssohn Violin Concerto in E Minor; Bruch Violin Concerto; Chausson, Poeme; Tchaikovsky Serenade Melancolique; Brahms Sonata no 3; Ravel's Trigane; Sibelius Violin Concerto; Suchon Sonatine op 11; Haydn Violin Concerto in C Major; Duttersdorf Violin Concerto in G Minor. Honours: 3rd Prize, National Youth Festival, Sofia, 1968; 3 Prizes in international violin competition, Tibor Varga, Switzerland, 1969; 3rd Prize, international competition, Emily Anderson, Royal Philharmonic Society, London, 1969. Address: Belopotockeho 2, SK-81105, Bratislava, Slovakia.

SPIVAKOV Vladimir, b. 12 Sep 1944, Oufa, Russia. Violinist; Conductor. Education: Studied at the Leningrad Conservatory with Sigal and at the Tchaikovsky Conservatory in Moscow with Jankelevitch. Career: Concerts in Russia and Eastern Europe followed by tour of USA in 1975; Played the Tchaikovsky Concerto in London in 1977; Founder, Leader and Conductor of the Moscow Virtuosi Orchestra, played in London and elsewhere in Europe including Promenade Concert at the Albert Hall in 1990, with Mozart's Symphony K201, Shostakovich Chamber Symphony, arranged by Barschai, and the Four Seasons; Artistic Director of Colmar International Festival, France; Co-founder of Sakharov Foundation for Human Rights at Strasbourg. Recordings include: BUG Classics, 16 CD's. Honours: 3rd Prize, Long-Thibaud Competition, 1965; Interpretation Prize at Montreal in 1968; 2nd Prize, Tchaikovsky International at Moscow, 1970. Address: Productions Internationals Albert Sarfati, 21 Rue du Pelletier, 75009 Paris, France.

SPIVAKOVSKY Tossy, b. 4 Feb 1907, Odessa, Russia. Violinist. m. Erika Lipsker, 21 Nov 1934, 1 daughter. Education: Berlin Hochschule fur Musik, studied with Professor Willy Hess and Professor Arrigo Serato. Debut: Berlin at age 10. Career: Recitals and orchestra appearances in Europe, Australia, New Zealand, Canada, South America and with every major orchestra in USA including New York Philharmonic, Boston Symphony, Philadelphia, Cleveland, Chicago, Los Angeles Philharmonic and San Francisco Symphony; Teacher at Melbourne University Conservatorium, 1933-39; Faculty, Juilliard School, New York, 1974-. Compositions: Cadenzas to Beethoven's Violin Concerto and to Mozart's Violin Concertos. Recordings: Various. Contributions to: The Music Review. Honours: Honorary DLitt, Fairfield University, USA, 1970; Honorary DMus, Cleveland Institute of Music, 1975. Membership: American Musicological Society. Address: 29 Burnham Hill, Westport, CT 06880, USA.

SPOORENBERG Erna, b. 11 Apr 1926, Yogyakarta, Java. Soprano. Education: Studied in the Netherlands with Julius Rontgen and Aaltje Noordewier-Reddingius. Debut: Hilversum concert in 1947 with Mozart's Motet Exsultate Jubilate. Career: Opera debut at the Vienna Staatsoper in 1949; Sang in Vienna, Hamburg in 1962, Dusseldorf and Amsterdam in operas by Mozart and as Debussy's Mélisande, and at Bordeaux in 1964 in La Dame Blanche by Boildieu; Concert tours of Germany, South Africa, Russia, Austria and Scandinavia; US debut at Lincoln Center in New York in 1967; Recital partnership with the pianist, Geza Frid. Recordings: Pelléas et Mélisande conducted by Ansermet; Die Schöpfung; Mahler's 8th Symphony; Bach Cantatas; Masses by Haydn.

SPOTORNO Marianangela, b. 1970, Rome. Singer (Soprano). Education: First studied cello, then singing with Magda Laszlo and Elio Battaglia. Debut: Elisabetta in Cimarosa's Il Matriomonio Segreto, for the Walton Trust at Ischia and in Scotland, 1992. Career: Sang in Offenbach's Barbe-bleue at Bologna and Messina, Mozart's Fiordiligi and Susanna at Cagliari;

Sang the title role in Manon Lescaut at the Glyndebourne Festival, 1997, and engaged 1997-98 as Antonia in L'Elisir d'Amore; Concerts include: Beethoven's Christus am Olberge, at Treviso, and opera concert with Domingo in Finland; Sang the voice of the soprano Guiditta Pasta for Italian TV film of the life of Giulio Ricordi. Address: c/o Teatro Massimo Bellini, Via Perrotta 12, 95131 Catania, Italy.

SPRATLAN Lewis, b. 5 September 1940, Miami, FL, USA. Composer. Education: Composition studies with Yehudi Wyner, Gunther Schuller and Mel Powell at Yale University (BA, 1962, MM, 1965); George Rochberg and Roger Sessions at Tanglewood, 1966. Career Faculty Member, Pennsylvania State University, 1967-70; Amherst College from 1970 (Chairman of Music Department, 1977-94, Professor from 1980). Compositions include: Missa Brevis, 1965; Cantate Domine for men's chorus, winds and tape, 1968; Serenade for 6 instruments, 1970; Moonsong for chorus and ensemble, 1970; Two Pieces for orchestra, 1971; Woodwind quintet, 1971; Fantasy for piano and chamber ensemble, 1973; Ben Jonson for soprano, violin and cello, 1974; Life is a Dream, opera, 1977; Coils for ensemble, 1980; String Quartet, 1982; When Crows Gather for 3 clarinets, violin, cello, and piano, 1986; Hung Monophonies for oboe and 11 instruments, 1990; Night Music for violin, clarinet and percussion, 1991; In Memorian for soloists, chorus and orchestra, 1993; A Barred Owl baritone and 5 instruments, 1994; Concertino for violin, cello and double baritone and 5 instruments, 1994; Concertino for violin, cello and double bass, 1995. Address: c/o ASCAP, ASCAP Building, One Lincoln Plaza, New York, NY 10023, USA.

SPRATT Geoffrey (Kenneth), b. 16 Sep 1950, London, England. Musician. m. Frances Vivien Spratt, 2 s. Education: BA, Honours with Distinction in Practical Work, 1973; PhD, University of Bristol, 1980. Career: Professional freelance flute and viola player with Cyprus Broadcasting Company Orchestras, 1969-70, and various British Orchestras, 1970-76; Part-time Tutor, Open University, 1973-76 and University of Bristol, 1974-76; Lecturer in Music, University College, Cork, Ireland, 1976-92; Founder-Conductor, UCC Choir and Orchestra, 1976-92; Conductor, UCC Choral Society, 1978-86; Director of the Cork School of Music; Founder-Conductor, Irish Youth Choir and the Fleischmann Choir of the Cork School of Music; Conductor of the Chamber Choir "Madrigal '75"; Guest Conductor: National Symphony Orchestra of Ireland, RTE Concert Orchestra, RTE Chorus, RTE Chamber Choir, Irish Chamber Orchestra and Galway Baroque Singers. Recordings: Choral music of Séamas de Barra sung by the Irish Youth Choir and Madrigal '75. Publications: Catalogue des oeuvres de Arthur Honegger, Geneva and Paris, 1986; Co-author with M Delannoy, Honegger, Geneva and Paris, 1986; The Music of Arthur Honegger, Cork, 1987. Contributions include: The New Grove Dictionary of Opera; The International Dictionary of Opera; Revue Musicale Suisse; Brio; Music Ireland; Numerous reviews; Editor of various performing editions and frequent broadcaster on music. Honour: Napier Miles Prize, Bristol University, 1972. Memberships include: Chairman, Association of Irish Choirs and Cork Orchestral Society; Council, Music Teachers' Association of Ireland, 1977-. Address: Director, Cork School of Music, Union Quay, Cork, Ireland.

SRABRAWA Daniel, b. 1948, Cracow, Poland. Violinist. Education: Studied with Z Slezer in Cracow. Career: Leader of Cracow Radio Symphony Orchestra, 1979; Joined Berlin Philharmonic Orchestra in 1983 and became leader in 1983; Co-founder of the Philharmonic Quartet Berlin giving concerts throughout Europe, USA and Japan; UK debut in 1987 playing Haydn, Szymanowski and Beethoven at Wigmore Hall; Played at Bath Festival in 1987 with Mozart, Schumann and Beethoven Op 127; Other repertoire includes quartets by Bartók, Mendelssohn, Nicolai, Ravel and Schubert, and quintets by Brahms, Weber, Reger and Schumann. Address: Anglo Swiss Management Ltd, Ste 35-37 Morley House, 320 Regent Street, London W1R 5AD, England.

SRAMEK Alfred, b. 5 Apr 1951, Nichtelbach, Vienna, Austria. Bass Singer. Education: Studied with Ludwig Weber and Hilde Zadek. Career: Has sung with the Vienna Staatsoper from 1975 in Palestrina and as Don Pasquale, Dulcamara, Beckmesser, Masetto, Leporello and Figaro; Sang at Salzburg Festival from 1976, and Bregenz Festival in 1982; Many concert appearances. Recordings: Lohengrin; Wozzeck; Don Giovanni; Ariadne auf Naxos; Die Lustigen Weiber von Windsor; Karl V by Krenek; Video of Wozzeck as First Workman conducted by Abbado. Address: c/o Staatsoper, Opernring 2, A-1010 Vienna, Austria.

ST HILL Krister, b. 1957, Sweden. Baritone. Debut: Sang Escamillo in 1982. Career: Roles in Sweden have included Sancho Panza in Massenet's Don Quichotte, Belcore and Nick Shadow in The Rake's Progress at Malmo City Theatre, Lord Sidney in Rossini's Il Viaggio a Reims, Bohème, Ned Keene, Peter Grimes, Valentin, Faust and Wolfram in Tannhäuser; Sang at Garsington Opera, Oxford as Ernesto in Haydn's Il Mondo della Luna, at Houston as Donny in the premiere of New Year by Tippett in 1989, Glyndebourne Opera in 1990 in the UK premiere of New Year and lieder recitals in Scandinavia and abroad which include Wigmore Hall recitals with Elisabeth Söderström. Recordings include: 3 solo albums; Title role in Jonny Spielt Auf by Krenek; Hindemith's Requiem. Address: Nordic Artists Management, Sveavagen 76, S-11359 Stockholm, Sweden.

STAAHLEN Torhild, b. 25 Sep 1947, Skien, Norway. Mezzo-Soprano. m. Neil Dodd, 23 Jun 1975. Education: Studied with Aase Nordmo Lovberg and Marit Isene in Oslo, Clemens Kaiser-Breme in Essen and Bayreuth, Audrey Langford in London, Hannah Ludwig in Salzburg, Ingalill Linden in Gothenburg, Ellen Sundbye in Oslo and dramatic soprano Ingrid Bjoner. Debut: Oslo in 1971 as Suzuki in Madam Butterfly. Career: Wide range of mezzo-alto repertoire including the title role in Carmen, Valencienne in The Merry Widow, Octavian in Der Rosenkavalier, Prince Orlovsky in Die Fledermaus, Olga in Eugene Onegin, Azucena, Ulrica in Un Ballo in Maschera, Amneris, Erda in Das Rheingold, Waltraute in Götterdämmerung; Frequently sings in oratorio especially with all Bach Passions and Handel's Messiah; Concert repertoire includes Brahms's Alto Rhapsody, Wagner's Wesendonck Lieder, Beethoven's 9th Symphony, Mahler's 2nd and 4th Symphonies, Elgar's Sea Pictures, Heise's Bergljot, Handel's Samson, and Pergolesi's Stabat Mater; Has sung under such conductors as Heinrich Hollreiser, Paavo Berglund, Martin Turnovsky, Jiri Starek and Maurice Handford; Frequent radio and TV appearances. Recording: Expression, 1991. Honours include: State Artist's Stipendium; Fund for Performing Artists; Rettspresident Klaestads Stipendium; Prize of Honour, Friends of Music in Telemark, 1981. Membership: Norsk Tonekunstner Samfund. Hobbies: Antiques; Dolls. Address: Munkerudveien 59c, 1165 Oslo, Norway.

STABELL Carsten, b. 5 Sep 1960, Trondheim, Norway. Bass Singer. Education: Studied at the Norwegian Opera School, Oslo. Debut: Oslo in 1984 as the King in Aida. Career: Sang at Stuttgart Opera from 1986 as Osmin, Sarastro, the Commendatore, Pietro in Simon Boccanegra and the Hermit in Der Freischütz; Sang Rustomji in Philip Glass's Satyagraha in 1990; Concert repertoire includes Bach's Magnificat and St John Passion, Messiah, Judas Maccabeus, Acis and Galatea, Die Schöpfung, the Requiems of Mozart and Verdi and Liszt's Christus; Engaged as the Commendatore at Opera Geneva and Sarastro at the Opéra de Paris Bastille in 1991, and in Perseo e Andromeda at La Scala Milan in 1992. Address: c/o Staatstheater Stuttgart, Oberer Schlossgarten 6, D-7000 Stuttgart 1, Germany.

STABLER Gerhard, b. 20 July 1949, Wilhelmsdorf, Germany. Composer. Education: Studied at Detmold Music Academy, 1968-70 and with Nicolaus Huber (composition) and Gerd Zacker (organ) at the Essen Hochschule, 1970-76; Further courses with Stockhausen, Kagel and Ligeti, at Cologne and Darmstadt. Career: Stanford University computer music centre, 1983, 1986; Faculty Member, Essen Hochschule 1989-94; Concert, lecture tours and guest professorships in Europe, Asia and North and South America from 1985. Compositions include: Drüber, for 8 screamers, cello and tape, 1972; Das Sichere ist nicht sicher, rondo for 8 instruments and tape, 1982; Schatten Wilder Schmerzen, for orchestra, 1985; Warnung mit Liebeslied for harp, accordion and percussion, 1986; .... strike the ear .... for string quartet, 1988; October for flute, violin and double bass, 1988; Den Muhlfahren von San Francisco, for 17 instruments, 1990; Ungaretti Lieder for mezzo or baritone and percussion, 1990; Sünde, Fall, Beil, opera after Catherine Howard by Dumas, 1992; Traum 1/9/92, for soprano saxophone, cello, piano and ensemble, 1992; Cassandra Complex, music theatre, 1994; Apparat, for chorus, clarinet, accordion, double bass and percussion, 1994; Karas, Krähen, for tape, 1994; Winter, Blumen, for countertenor, or solo string instruments, 1995; Internet, various works for solo instruments or chamber music ensembles, 1995-98; Spuren, for saxophone quartet, 1995; Dali, for piano solo, 1996; Poetic Arcs, for ensemble, 1996; Burning Minds, for 12 voices, 1997; Bridges, for mezzo and accordion, 1997. Honours include: Cornelius Cardew Memorial Prize, London, 1982; Fellowship in composition, Heinrich-Strobel-Stiftung, 1985-86; Niederdachsen Scholarship, 1987-88; Japa Foundation Scholarship, 1994. GEMA, Rosenheimer Str 11, 81667 Munchen, Germany.

STADELMANN Christian, b. 1958, Berlin, Germany. Violinist. Education: Studied with Charlotte Hampe and in Berlin. Career: Former Member of the Junge Deutsche Philharmonie and its Chamber Orchestra; Co-founder and second violinist of the Philharmonia Quartet Berlin, 1980; Member of the Berlin Philharmonic from 1985, leader of the 2nd violins, 1987; Annual visits to Japan from 1986; Many concerts in Europe notably at the Salzburg Festival, Bath Festival in 1990, at Wigmore Hall in London and the Berlin Festival in 1991, with works by Mozart; International career as solo violinist. Recordings include: CD of Quartets by Beethoven. Address: c/o Berlin Philharmonic, Philharmonie/Mattäukirchstrasse 1, D-1000 Berlin, Germany.

STADLER Irmgard, b. 28 Mar 1937, Michaelbeuern, Salzburg, Austria. Singer (Soprano). Education: Studied at Salzburg Mozarteum and Vienna Academy of Music. Debut: Stuttgart 1962, as Micaela. Career: Salzburg Festival 1961-62, in Idomeneo, Mozart's Requiem 1962-63; Glyndebourne Festival 1967-72 as Sicle in L'Ormindo, Donna Elvira, Juno in La Calisto and the Composer (Ariadne auf Naxos); Stuttgart 1983, as Marie in Wozzeck; Guest appearances in Vienna, Munich, Berlin, Lisbon, Venice and Rome; Other roles include Eva, Gutrune, Jenufa, Agathe, Marenka in The Bartered Bridge, Rusalka, Katya Kabonova, Jenufa, Lisa (The Queen of Spades), Tatiana, Fiordiligi, Alice, Marina, Octavian and the Marschallin; Sang in Satyagraha by Philip Glass at Stuttgart, 1990; Concert appearances in sacred music by Bach and Mozart. Address: c/o Staatstheater Stuggart, Oberer Schlossgarten 6, D-7000 Stuttgart 1, Germany.

STADLMAIR Hans, b. 3 May 1929, Neuhofen, Austria. Conductor. Education: Studied at the Vienna Academy of Music, 1946-52 with Clemens Krauss and Alfred Uhl and in Stuttgart, 1952-56 with Johann Nepomuk David. Career: Conducted the Stuttgart Chorus and became conductor of Munich Chamber Orchestra, 1956; Tours of Europe, North and South America, Asia, Africa, Canada and India; Has conducted own realisation of the Adagio from Mahler's 10th Symphony; Compositions: Concerto Profano for Violin, Cello and Orchestra; Concerto Capriccioso for two Flutes and Orchestra (composed for A Nicolet and J Pierre Rampal); Adagietto for Strings, Ecce Homo, 5 Novelletten for Strings. Sinfonia: "Da Pacem Domine" für Alphorn, Röhrenglocken and Strings, 1988; Lacrimae Metamorphosen for Strings; Essay for clarinet and strings. Recordings: W A Mozart, Piano Concertos Nr 8 KV246, Lützow and Nr 9 KV271, Jeunehomme; F Danzi: Phantasie on La ci darem la mano from Don Giovanni, C Stamitz; Concerto for Clarinet Nr 3 B flat (E Brunner - Clarinet); Haydn's Last Seven Words; Scarlatti Il Giardino di Amore; Mozart Bassoon Concerto, Clarinet Concerto and Violin Concerto K219; Vivaldi Four Seasons; CD Koch-Schwann: Hans Stadlmair, 3-1587-2 H1 CCD 215. Contributions to: Riemann Musiklexikon. Honours: Medaille: München Leuchtet, 1989; Bundesverdienstkreuz am Bande, 1989; Musikpreis der Stadt München, 1994. Current Management: MH Musik Management Kloster Schäftlarn 23, D-82067 Ebenhausen b. München, Germany. Address: Dachauerstr 175, D-80636 München, Germany.

STADLMAIR Vincent, b. 1959, Vienna, Austria. Cellist. Education: Studied at the Vienna Academy of Music. Career: Member of the Franz Schubert Quartet, Vienna from 1983; Many concert engagements in Europe, USA, and Australia including appearances at the Amsterdam Concertgebouw, the Vienna Musikverein and Konzerthaus, the Salle Gaveau Paris and the Sydney Opera House; Visits to Zurich, Geneva, Basle, Berlin, Hamburg, Rome, Rotterdam, Madrid and Copenhagen; Festival engagements include Salzburg, Wiener Festwochen, Prague, Spring Schubertiade at Hohenems, the Schubert Festival at Washington DC and the Belfast and Istanbul Festivals; Tours of Australasia, Russia and USA; Frequent concert tours of Great Britain; Featured in the Concerto by Spohr with the Liverpool Philharmonic in Liverpool at the Festival Hall; Many appearances at the Wigmore Hall and Cheltenham Festival; Teacher at the Vienna Conservatory and Graz Musikhochschule; Masterclasses at the Royal Northern College of Music, Lake District Summer Music. Recordings include: Schubert's Quartet in G, D887; Complete Quartets of Dittersdorf; Mozart's String Quartet in D, K575, and String Quartet in B flat, K589. Address: c/o Unit 2, 39 Tadema Road, London, SW10 0PY, England.

STAEHELIN Martin, b. 25 Sep 1937, Basel, Switzerland. Musicologist. m. Elisabeth Schenker. Education: Diploma, Teacher Querflöte, 1962, School Music Diploma, 1963, Music Academy, Basel; PhD, University of Basel, 1967. Career: Teacher of Latin, Greek and Music, Basel, 1963; Musicology Teacher, University of Zurich, 1971-76; Head of Beethoven Archives, Bonn, Germany, 1976-84; Teacher, 1976-77, Professor, 1977-83, University of Bonn; Professor, University of Göttingen, 1983-; Honorary Director of J S Bach Institut, Göttingen, 1992. Publications: Editor, H Isaac, Messen, 1970, 1973; Der Grüne Codex der Viadrina, 1971; Die Messen Heinrich Isaacs, 3 volumes, 1977. Contributions to: Archiv für Musikwissenschaft; Die Musikforschung; Fontes Artis Musicae; Schweizer Beiträge zur Musikwissenschaft; Tijdschrift van de Vereniging voor Nederlandse Muziekgeschiedenis; Schweizerisches Archiv für Volkskunde. Honour: Dent Medal, Royal Musical Association, 1975. Memberships: Musicological Commission, Academy of the Sciences, Mainz; Akademie der Wissenschaften, Göttingen; Academia Europaea, London. Address: Musicology Seminar of Georg August University, Kurze Geismarstraße 1, 37073 Göttingen, Germany.

STAFFORD Ashley (George), b. 3 Mar 1954, Holland, Near Oxted, Surrey, England. Counter-Tenor. m. Shauni Lee McGregor, 4 Jun 1977, 2 sons. Education: Westminster Abbey Choir School, 1963-68; Trinity School Croydon, 1968-72;

Christchurch, Oxford, Choral Award, Academical Clerkship, 1972-75; BA, Honours, 1975, MA, 1978; Certificate of Education, London, 1976; Studied with Douglas Guest, at Oxford under Simon Preston, and vocal training with Hervey Alan, 1968-72, Paul Esswood, 1972-76, Helga Mott, 1976-80, and Jessica Cash, 1980-93. Debut: Purcell Room, 1975. Career: Sang in opera at Aix-en-Provence, Lyon, Oxford and London and in concert at major festivals throughout Europe, in Sydney and Melbourne, 1989, Japan, 1987 and 1989, Taiwan in 1989, USA and Canada including Bath, Edinburgh, Three Choirs, Berlin, Rome, Venice, Madrid, Barcelona, Lisbon, New York, Boston and Ottawa, 1980-86; Sang in Judith Weir's A Night At The Chinese Opera for Kent Opera; Many appearances on Radio and on TV including Messiah in France; Visiting Professor of Voice at Royal College of Music, London in 1989. Recordings include: Purcell's Ode to St Cecilia, King Arthur, From the Nativity of Time (Songs sacred and secular); Handel's Israel in Egypt, Dettingen Te Deum; Valls's Mass Scala Aretina; Motets by Bach, Power, Dunstable and Josquin; Haydn's Nelson Mass; Scarlatti's Stabat Mater; Schütz's Muzikalisches Exequien; Handel's Alexander's Feast. Honour: Young Musician, Greater London Arts Association. Memberships: Incorporated Society of Musicians; Equity; Committee, Royal Society of Musicians. Hobbies: Gardening; Squash; Table Tennis; Computing; Cycling. Address: Fenton House, Banbury Road, Chipping Norton, Oxon, OX7 5AW, England.

STAHL David, b. 4 Nov 1949, New York, New York, USA. Symphony and Opera Conductor. m. Karen Doss Stahl, 1989, 1 son, 2 daughters. Education: Queens College of the City University of New York, BA, 1972, MA, MM, 1974. Career: Debut, Carnegie Hall, New York, 8 Dec 1973; Assistant Conductor, New York Philharmonic, 1976, and Cincinnati Symphony Orchestra, 1976-79; Music Director, St Louis Philharmonic, 1976-81; Broadway and international tour of West Side Story, 1980-82; Charleston (South Carolina) Symphony Orchestra, 1984-; Guest Conductor, Pittsburgh, Atlanta, Dallas, Indianapolis, St Louis, Buffalo, Baltimore, Long Beach, Edmonton, New World, San Jose, Winnipeg, and Louisville Symphonies; New York City Opera, Spoleto Festival, Lake George Opera, Dayton, Detroit, Hawaii and Tulsa opera companies; Overseas: RAI orchestra, Rome, Teatro Massimo, Palermo, Teatro Comunale, Geona, Festival of two worlds, Spoleto, Orchestre Colonne, Paris, Orchestra del Sodre, Montevideo and Seoul (South Korea) Philharmonic, Toronto Symphony Orchestra, Montreal Opera, Washington Opera; Stadtheater National Mannheim, Darmstadt, Bernstein Festival in the Concertgebouw, Amsterdam; Principal Guest Conductor, Bavarian Staatstheater am Gaertnerplatz; Guest Conductor: NDR Symphony, Hamburg; Bamberg Symphony; Staatskappelle Dresden; L'Orchestre National de Lyon; Helsinki Philharmonic; Dusseldorf Symphony. Recordings: Proto concertos for double bass; Portraits in Blue and Grey with Charleston Symphony; Poulenc Double Piano Concerto. Honours: ASCAP Award for Adventuresome Programming; Order of the Palmetto (highest award in South Carolina). Current Management: Colbert Artists Management Inc, 111 West 57th Street, New York, NY 10019, USA. Address: 14 George Street, Charleston, SC 29401, USA.

STAHL Volkhard, b. 19 July 1956, Hessen, Germany. Teacher; University Teacher. m. 23 June 1984, 2 sons. Education: Studies for High School Teacher, 1977-83; Studies in Music at Musikhochschule, Frankfurt-Main, Germany; Theological Studies, Goethe University, Frankfurt-Main; Studies in International Master-Classes for trumpet by Reinhold Lösch, Rolf Quinque, Edward Tarr and Bo Nilsson. Career: Recitals for Trumpet and Organ; Concerts with Different Brass Ensembles at Home and Abroad, including Radio and German TV Appearances; Teacher of Music and Religion for High School, University Teacher of Trumpet and Brass Ensemble, J W Goethe University, Frankfurt-Main, 1988-; Lectures and international brass workshops about methodical brass playng at home and abroad. Publication: Brass Professional - A Standard Work (Production) of Methodical Brass Playing. Membership: International Trumpet Guild. Address: Holzheimer Str 15, D-35510 Butzbach, Germany.

STAHLAMMER Semmy, b. 5 Mar 1954, Eskilstuna, Sweden. Musician; Violinist. Education: Soloist Diploma, Royal Music College, Stockholm, 1972; Juilliard School of Music, USA, 1972-74; BMus, Curtis Institute of Music, 1975-79; Studied with Jaime Laredo, Ivan Galamian, Felx Galimir, Isidore Cohen, Szymon Goldberg, Paul Makanowitsky, Josef Silverstein, Josef Gingold, Nathan Milstein, Isaac Stern and Henryk Szeryng. Debut: With Stockholm Philharmonic Orchestra, 1964. Career: First Concertmaster of Stockholm Royal Opera, 1979-83; Artistic Director, Chamber Music in The Mirror Hall, 1982-; Artistic Director, Chamber Music in The Parks, 1986-; Teacher at Stockholm Royal Music College, 1987-. Recordings: Collections of Swedish 20th century music; Alfred Schnittke's Labyrinths; JS Bach's Sonatas and Partitas for Solo Violin. Honour: Winner of JS Bach International Violin Competition, Washington DC, 1985. Hobbies: Violin Maker and Restorer; Sports. Address: Norr Mälarstrand 24, 112 20 Stockholm, Sweden.

STAHLMAN Sylvia, b. 5 Mar 1929, Nashville, TN, USA. Soprano. Education: Studied at the Juilliard School in New York. Career: Sang first on Broadway; Sang at Théâtre de la Monnaie in Brussels, 1951-54 with debut as Elvira in I Puritani, and at Brussels and Amsterdam as Lucia di Lammermoor and Meyerbeer's Dinorah; Engaged at the Frankfurt Opera, 1954-72; Sang at New York City Opera in 1956 as Blondchen, at Glyndebourne Festival in 1959 as Ilia in Idomeneo, Frankfurt am Main, 1959-70, Chicago in 1960, Metropolitan Opera in 1961, Santa Fe in 1964 in the US premiere of Strauss's Daphne, and Aix-en-Provence in 1967. Recordings: Un Ballo in Maschera; La Sonnambula; Mahler's 4th Symphony; Haydn's Lord Nelson Mass; Handel's Belshazzar.

STAICU Paul, b. 7 Jun 1937, Bucharest, Romania. Conductor; Professor; Horn Player. m. Irina Botez, 6 Jul 1963, 1 s. Education: Graduate Diploma in Horn, Prague Academy of Music, 1961; Graduate Diploma at Vienna Academy of Music, with conductor Hans Swarowsky. Debut: As Horn Soloist, 1954 and as Conductor, 1963, Bucharest Radio and Philharmonic Orchestra. Career: Horn Soloist, 1954-79; Solo Horn with Bucharest Philharmonic, 1961-69; Chief Conductor of Chamber Orchestra, 1966; Professor of Chamber Music, 1966-; Camerata, 1978; H von Karajan Foundation, Medal with Camerata, orchestra, 1974; Professor of Horn, 1969-89, Chief Conductor of Symphony Orchestra, Bucharest Music Academy, 1975-78; Chief Conductor, Symphony and Chamber Orchestra, Constanta Rumania, 1978-79; Professor, Conservatoire of Music, Montbeliard, France, 1990; Director, School of Music, Exincourt, France, 1990; Chief Conductor, Ensemble Orchestral Montbeliard, France, 1992; TV and Radio performances in Rumania and abroad; Summer classes at Bayreuth, Gourdon, Europe, USA and Canada tours; Membership, Munich and Prague International Music Competitions. Recordings: No 3, Beethoven Horn Sonata; Mozart and Beethoven Quintets; Mozart's Horn Concertos as Soloist and Conductor; Haydn Concertos as Conductor; Haydn Symphonies 100-103 as Conductor; Radio: Beethoven Symphony No 4, Schoenberg Verklärte Nacht and Shostakovich's Symphony No 14. Publications: Studiu introductiv si exercitii zilnice pentru corn (Introductory studies and daily exercises for horn).

STAIER Andreas, b. 13 September 1955, Göttingen, Germany. Harpsichordist; Pianist. Education: Baccalaureat in Göttingen; Studies in Piano, Harpsichord, Chamber Music in Hanover and Amsterdam. Career: Harpsichordist in Musica Antiqua, Köln, 1983-86; Professor, Schola Cantorum, Basle, Switzerland, 1987; Concerts in USA, Europe and Australia. Recordings: Haydn Piano Sonatas; J S Bach Harpsichord Works; CPE Bach Harpsichord Works; Chamber Music; Lieder; D Scarlatti; L Dussek. Current Management: Jean Michel Forest, Claudia Nitsche. Address: Rolandstr 65, D-50677 Köln 1, Germany.

STAJNC Jaroslav, b. 7 May 1943, Prague, Czechoslovakia. Bass Baritone. Education: Studied at Prague Conservatoire and Vienna Music Academy. Debut: Vienna Volksoper in 1968 as the Hermit in Der Freischütz. Career: Vienna 1968 in the premiere of Der Zerrissene by Gottfried von Einem; Member of the Deutsche Oper am Rhein, Dusseldorf and made guest appearances in Graz, Brno, Florence, Athens and Vancouver; Bregenz Festival in 1983 as Kaspar in Der Freischütz; Other roles have included Kecal in The Bartered Bride, Orestes in Elektra, Dulcamara, Dikoy in Katya Kabanova, Rossini's Basilio, Mustafà in L'Italiana in Algeri, and Tiresias in Oedipus Rex; Wagner repertoire includes Fasolt, Fafner and Hunding in Der Ring des Nibelungen; Many concert appearances. Recordings: Albums of operas by Smetana and other Czech composers; Il Lutto dell' Universo by Emperor Leopold I of Austria. Address: c/o Deutsche Oper am Rhein, Heinrich-Heine Allee 16, D-4000 Dusseldorf, Germany.

STALDER Hans Rudolf, b. 9 July 1930, Zurich, Switzerland. Clarinettist; Musician. m. Ursula Burkhard, 11 Apr 1957. Education: Konservatorium, Zurich; Bayerisches Staatskonservatorium, Wurzburg, Germany; Private studies with Louis Cahuzac, Paris. Career: International Soloist on clarinet, Bassethorn and Chalumeau, also with Chamber Music groups including: Stalder Quintet, Zurich Chamber Ensemble, Zurich Clarinet Trio; Teacher at Musik Akademie, Basle and Schola Cantorum Basiliensis. Recordings include: First recording of Mozart Clarinet Concerto in original version with Bassetclarinet, 1968; Bassethorn Concerto from A Rolla; Das Chalumeau ein Portrait. Membership: Schweizerischer Tonkunstlerverein. Address: Wengi 2, CH-8126 Zumikon, Switzerland.

STALLMAN Robert (Wooster) Jr, b. 12 June 1946, Boston, Massachusetts, USA. Flautist. m. Hannah Woods, 26 Sept 1981. Education: BMus, 1968, MMus, 1971, New England Conservatory of Music; Paris Conservatoire, France, 1968-69. Career: Major solo appearances include Library of Congress, Carnegie Hall, Weill Hall, Alice Tully Hall, Avery Fisher Hall, Symphony Hall Boston, Salle Pleyel (Paris), Suntory Hall (Tokyo), St John's Smith Square (London); Radio appearances, Boston, New York, Nationwide USA, Canada; Guest Artist appearances include American Symphony, Mostly Mozart Festival, Netherlands Chamber Orchestra, Lincoln Center Chamber Music Society, Concerto Soloists of Philadelphia, Speculum Musicae, Muir, Mendelssohn and Orion String Quartets; Festivals, Canada, Finland, France, Netherlands, Japan, USA; Founder, Artistic Director, Cambridge Chamber Players and Marblehead Music Festival, 1976-; Teaching: Aaron Copland School of Music, Queen's College, New York, 1980-; Académie Internationale d'Eté, Nice, France, 1985; Boston Conservatory, 1986-90; New England Conservatory, 1978-82; Master classes, USA, Canada, Mexico, England, France, Japan; Editor of flute repertoire, International Music Co, New York, 1984-. Recordings: Blavet Sonatas, Incantations (20th century solo flute works), Gypsy Flute, Handel Sonatas, Leclair Sonatas, Bach Sonatas; The American Flute, Schubert Sonatas, Telemann Concerti, Vivaldi Concerti; Dodgson Concerto with the Northern Sinfonia; McKinley Concerto with the Prism Orchestra. Publication: Flute Workout, 1995. Honours: Fulbright Grant, 1968-69; Chadwick Medal, 1968; Solo Recitalist Award, National Endowment for the Arts, 1983, Arcadia Foundation Grant, 1994. Address: 1530 Locust Street, #11A, Philadelphia, PA 19102, USA.

STALMAN Roger (Claude), b. 30 Jul 1927, Uxbridge, England. Bass Singer; Singing Teacher; Adjudicator. m. Jean Dorothy Kew, 1 son. Education: London University; Music studies with Eric Greene and Frederic Jackson. Debut: Concerts, opera and recitals throughout UK and Western Europe, also in Israel and Canada; 250 Performances of Handel's Messiah, including TV appearances; Sang at Berlin Festival in 1967; Papal Concert and tour of Israel in Stravinsky's Oedipus Rex, 1968. Recordings: Performances of Messiah conducted by Walter Susskind and by Frederick Jackson; Cathedral Music from Salisbury; Purcell Odes; Panufnik's Universal Prayer. Honour: ABSM, 1970. Address: Came House, Monument Lane, Chalfont St Peter, Buckinghamshire, SL9 0HY, England.

STAMENOVA Galina, b. 5 Oct 1958, Sofia, Bulgaria. Violinist. Education: Musical studies from age 5 with her mother; Studies with Dorothy Delay, Juilliard School of Music, New York. Debut: With André Previn and London Symphony Orchestra at Royal Festival Hall; American debut with Dallas Symphony in 1984. Career: Performances with most leading British orchestras, Antwerp Philharmonic and orchestras in Bulgaria; Radio and TV appearances in Bulgaria, Netherlands, UK and Belgium; Accomplished recitalist having appeared at Harrogate and Aspen Music Festivals, live on BBC and Radio VARA in The Netherlands and several other European countries. Recordings: Saint-Saëns No 3, Chausson-Poème, Sofia Radio Orchestra with Vassil Stefanov conducting. Honours include: Several first prizes for young violinists. Hobbies: Theatre; Arts; Ballet. Address: 33 Greinstraat, 2060 Antwerp, Belgium.

STAMM Harald, b. 29 Apr 1938, Frankfurt am Main, Germany. Bass Singer. Education: Studied with Franz Fehringer. Debut: Gelsenkirchen, 1968. Career: Sang at Cologne and Frankfurt, Hamburg Staatsoper, 1975, in the premiere of Der Gestiefelte Kater by Bialas; Many appearances in German opera houses and in Budapest, Venice, Rome and Nice; Metropolitan Opera from 1979; Salzburg Festival 1985, in the Henze version of Monteverdi's Ulisse; Bregenz Festival 1986, as Sarastro in Die Zauberflöte; Other roles include: Mozart's Commendatore, Beethoven's Rocco, Verdi's Grand Inquisitor and Zaccaria, Wagner's Daland, Marke, Fasolt and Hunding and Massenet's Don Quixote; Covent Garden debut in 1987 as Raimondo in Lucia di Lammermoor; Sang the King in Schreker's Der Schatzgräber at Hamburg, 1989, King Henry in Lohengrin at Brussels and Lisbon, 1990; Season 1992 as Gurnemanz at Essen; Also heard in recital and concert. Recordings: Lieder by Liszt and Franz; Vier Ernste Gesänge by Brahms; Dittersdorf's Doktor und Apotheker; Schumann's Manfred; Massimila Doni by Schoeck. Honours: Nominated Kammersänger by Hamburg Opera, 1989; Professor at Hochschule der Künste Berlin, 1993. Address: c/o Hamburgische Staatsoper, Grosse-Theaterstrasse 34, D-20354 Hamburg, Germany.

STÄMPFLI Jakob, b. 26 Oct 1934, Berne, Switzerland. Bass Singer. Education: Studied at the Berne Conservatory and in Frankfurt with Paul Lohmann. Career: Gave concerts in Germany while still a student; Sang with the Chorus of St Thomas's Leipzig, conducted by Gunter Ramin; Many performances of sacred music by Bach in Europe, USA and Japan; Sang also with the Schola Cantorum Basiliensis; Lieder recitals with music by Brahms, Schubert and Schumann; Professor at the Saarbrücken Musikhochschule from 1960 then at the Hamburg Musikhochschule. Recordings: Cantatas by Buxtehude; Bach Cantatas; Monteverdi's Orfeo; Christmas Oratorio; St Matthew Passion and Magnificat by Bach; Plutone in L'Orfeo conducted by Michel Corboz. Address: c/o Hochschule für Musik, Harvestehuderweg 12, 2000 Hamburg 13, Germany.

STANDAGE Simon, b. 8 Nov 1941, High Wycombe, Buckinghamshire, England. Violinist. m. Jennifer Ward, 15 Aug 1964, 3 sons. Education: Studied at Bryanston School and at Cambridge; Violin studies with Ivan Galamian in New York, 1967-69. Career: Associate member of the London Symphony Orchestra and deputy leader of the English Chamber Orchestra; Appointed Leader of the English Concert in 1973; Leader of the Richard Hickox Orchestra and the City of London Sinfonia; Founded the Salomon Quartet in 1981 giving performances of 18th century repertoire on original instruments; Teacher of Baroque violin at the Royal Academy of Music from 1983; Founded Collegium Musicum 90 in 1990; Associate Director of Academy of Ancient Music, 1991-95; Professor of Baroque Violin, Dresdner Akademie für Alte Musik, 1993-. Recordings: Vivaldi op 8 (including Four Seasons), op 3 (L'Estro Armonico), op 4 (La Stravaganza), op 9 (La Cetra), J S Bach Violin Concertos, Leclair complete concertos, Mozart and Haydn complete violin concertos, Mozart mature string quartets and quintets, Haydn quartets opp 17, 20, 33, 42, 50, 54/55, 64, 71/74. 77 and 103. Hobby: Crosswords. Address: 106 Hervey Road, London, SE3, England.

STANDFORD Patric, b. 5 Feb 1939, Barnsley, Yorkshire, England. Composer. m. Sarah Blyth Hilton. 2 sons, 1 daughter. Education: GGSM, London, 1963; FGSM, London, 1973; MMus, London, 1979; Studied with Rubbra, Mendelssohn Scholarship, extended studies, Malipiero in Italy; Lutoslawski in Poland; Stanley Glasser at London University. Career: Professor of Composition, Guildhall School of Music, London, 1969-80; Head of Music School, Bretton Hall College, Yorkshire, 1980-93. Compositions include: 6 symphonies, 1971-95; Cello Concerto; Violin Concerto; Christus Requiem, oratorio; Messiah Reborn, 1993; 3 string quartets; Choral and instrumental works; Villon, opera; Film and video music. Recordings: Autumn Grass; Ancient Verses; String Music. Contributions to: Musical Times; Composer; Musical Opinion; Set to Music; Yorkshire Post. Honours: Premio, Citta di Trieste, 1972; Oscar Espla, 1973; Solidarity Award, Skopje, Yugoslavia, 1974; Clements Memorial Prize, 1975; Ernest Ansermet Award, City of Geneva, 1983. Memberships: Composers' Guild of Great Britain, Chairman 1977-80, Council 1984-; Musicians' Benevolent Fund, Council; British Music Information Centre, Council Trustee 1987; Huddersfield Contemporary Music Festival, Management Committee. Current Management: RST Partnership. Address: c/o 17 Bradford Road, Wakefield, West Yorkshire WF1 2RF, England.

STANHOPE David, b. 19 December 1952, Sutton Coldfield, England (Resident in Australia from 1958). Composer; Conductor; Horn Player. Education: Studied in Melbourne. Career: 2nd Horn, Australian SO, 1970; Conductor with Australian Opera from 1986 (gave Berg's Lulu in season 1994). Compositions include: Quintet no 3 for brass quintet, 1983; The Australian Fanfare for 9 trumpets in 3 choirs, 1983; Four Concert Studies for 4 trombones, 1985; Felix Randall, for high voice and piano, 1986; Concerto for Band, 1988; Droylsden Wakes for wind or brass band, 1990; Folksongs for Band, 1990-91; Endpiece for orchestra, 1991; Three Poems for soprano and string orchestra; String Songs; Three Folksongs for brass quintet. Honours include: Prize Winner, International Horn Society Composition Contest, 1979. Address: c/o APRA, 1A Eden Street, Crows Nest, NSW 2065, Australia.

STANHOPE Paul Thomas, b. 25 November 1969, Wollongong, NSW, Australia. Composer. Education: BA (Hons), University of Sydney, 1992; MA (Hons), University of Wollongong, 1994; Study with Peter Sculthorpe, 1995-96; Career: Faculty Member, University of Wollongong, 1994-95; University of Sydney, 1995-. Compositions include: Liquid Marimba for tape, 1991; Morning Star for string quartet, 1992; Missa Brevis for chorus, 1992; The Taste of Midnight for flute, piano and clarinet, 1993; Morning Star II and III for ensemble, 1993; Kandeyala for orchestra, 1994; Satz for mandolin quartet, 1994; Rin, for tape, 1994; Snap, for clarinet, 1994; Geography Songs for chorus, 1994-95; No More than Movement.... or Stillness, for tape, 1995; Kraftwerk Overture, for string orchestra, 1995; Rain Dance for violin, 2 violas and cello, 1995; Stars Sounding for orchestra, 1996. Honours include: Australian Voices Festival Young Composers Award, 1995. Address: c/o APRA, 1A Eden Street, Crows Nest, NSW 2065, Australia.

STANICK Toni Elisabeth, b. 11 Apr 1960, Winnipeg, Canada. Pedagogue; Violin. Education: Wisconsin College Conservatory; Victoria Conservatory of Music; University of Toronto; University of British Columbia; Rotterdam Conservatory. Debut: Violin Concerto, Czech Republic, 1996. Recordings: The Spirit Emerges, Violin Concerto. Memberships: American Federation of Musicians; Pacific Chamber Music Society; Chamber Music America; Suzuki Associations of the Americas; Women in Music. Hobbies: Tennis; Gardening. Address: 3-2450 Alma Street, Vancouver BC, V6R 3R7 Canada.

STANKOV Angel (Mirchov), b. 28 Apr 1948, Sofia, Bulgaria. Concert Violinist; Violin Duo Chamber Player (with Josif Radionov). m. Meglana Stankova, 15 July 1974, 1 daughter. Education: State High School; Bulgarian State Music Academy, Sofia; Specialised in London with Professor Parikian of the Royal Academy of Music. Debut: Pleven Philharmonic Orchestra, Beethoven Concerto, 1970. Career: Regular appearances with Sofia Philharmonic Orchestra and provincial orchestras; Appearances on Bulgarian radio and television; Live recital, Hague Radio, 1991; North France and Soviet TV appearances, 1991; Foreign tours to almost all European countries and Cuba; International Music Festivals, Llandaff, UK, 1975, Brno, Czechoslovakia, 1989, Warsaw, Bydgoscz and Crete, Greece, 1983; Currently Associate Professor of Violin and Chamber Music, Sofia State Music Academy; Performer as soloist and as member of violin duo with Josif Radionov. Recordings: Bulgarian Radio and TV; BBC London; BBC Oxford; Hague Radio; Prague Radio; Discs and cassettes; Some concertos specially dedicated to the Violin Duo by outstanding Bulgarian and foreign composers, also individual pieces. Hobbies: Painting; Swimming; Antique books; Musical autographs. Address: 33 Hristo Botev Blvd, 1606 Sofia, Bulgaria.

STANZELEIT Susanne, b. 1968, Germany. Violinist. Education: Studies with Leonid Kogan and at Folkwang Hochschule in Essen (diploma 1989) and with Yfrah Neaman at the Guildhall School of Music; Masterclasses with Nathan Milstein, Sandor Vegh and György Kurtag at Prussia Cove. Career: Recitals throughout Germany, Italy, Hungary, Netherlands, Canada, USA and England; Concerto appearances with leading orchestras, leader of Werethina Quartet (Haydn, Mendelssohn and Bartók at Purcell Room, 1993) and Prometheus and Ondine Ensembles; Purcell Room Recital, 1993 with Julian Jacobson, playing Strauss, Schubert's C Major Fantasy and Beethoven, Op 96; Broadcasts with BBC Radio 3, teaching and performing with the Paxos Festival in Greece, Dartinton Summer School (1993) and International Bartók Festival in Hungary. Recordings: Bartók's music for violin and piano, Delius sonatas for violin and piano, Stanford, Bantock, Dunhill. Address: c/o Encord Concerts, Caversham Grange, The Warren, Mapledurham, Berks RG4 7TQ, England.

STAPP Olivia, b. 30 May 1940, New York, USA. Mezzo-Soprano. Education: Studied with Oren Brown in New York and Ettore Campogalliani and Rodolfo Ricci in Italy. Debut: Spoleto Festival in 1960 in L'Amico Fritz. Career: Sang in Vienna, Berlin, Wuppertal, Turin and Basle; Sang at Indiana University at Bloomington in the 1971 premiere of Eaton's Heracles; Sang at New York City Opera from 1972 notably as Carmen and Norma, Metropolitan Opera from 1982 as Lady Macbeth and Tosca, Paris Opéra in 1982, La Scala Milan, 1983-84 as Turandot and Electra in Idomeneo, and Geneva in 1985 as Elena in Les Vêpres Siciliennes; Other roles include Verdi's Ulrica and Mistress Quickly, Santuzza, Dorabella, Isabella, Rosina, Idalma in Il Matrimonio Segreto and Jocasta in Oedipus Rex; Sang Lady Macbeth at Geneva and Venice in 1986, Elektra and Abigaille at Frankfurt and Zurich, 1988-89, at Paris in 1989 in La Noche Triste by Prodomidès, and sang Shostakovich's Katherina at Hamburg in 1990. Recordings include: Cyrano de Bergerac by Alfano. Address: c/o S A Gorlinsly Ltd, 33 Dover Street, London, W1X 4NJ, England.

STAREK Jiri, b. 25 Mar 1928, Mocovice, Czechoslovakia. Conductor. m. Eva Itis, 18 Feb 1964, 1 son. Education: Studies at State Conservatory of Music, 1939-40; Private music studies, 1940-45; Graduate, Academy of Music Arts, Prague, 1950. Career includes: Conductor and Chief Conductor, Czech Radio, Prague, 1953-68; Chief Conductor and Music Director of Chamber Orchestra Collegium Musicum Pragense, 1963-68; Guest Conductor for many international symphony orchestras; Artistic Leader, Sinfonietta RIAS - Berlin, 1976-80 and Chief Conductor for Trondheim Symphony Orchestra, Norway, 1981-84; Professor and Head of Conductor's Class, Music Academy, Frankfurt am Main, 1975-97; Dean, Artisic Department, 1980-90; Principal Guest Conductor, ABC West Australia Symphony Orchestra, 1988-90; After 22 years in exile returned to Prague, conducting Czech Philharmonic Orchestra, State Philharmonic Orchestra, Brno, Janacek Philharmonic Orchestra, Ostrava, Prague Symphony Orchestra, Radio Symphony Orchestra Prague, 1990-; Chief Conductor, State Opera Prague, 1996-; Appearances at many leading international music festivals including Salzburg, Prague, Berlin, Schleswig-Holstein. Recordings: Radio and CD recordings with Prague Symphony Orchestra FOK, Radio Symphony Orchestra Prague, Sinfonietta-RIAS, Berlin, Radio Symphony Orchestra Stuttgart, Frankfurt, Munich. Honours: OIRT Award, Z Sestak: Vocal Symphony, 1964; Czech Radio Awards for operas: W Egk: Colubus, Shostakovich: The Nose, Dallapiccola: The Prisoner, 1966-67. Memberships: Czech Society of Arts and Sciences; Dvorak Society, London; Schubert Society, Prague. Hobbies: Books; Dogs. Address: Brunnenweg 18, 61352 Bad Homburg vdh, Germany.

STARER Robert, b. 8 Jan 1924, Vienna, Austria. Composer. Education: Vienna State Academy, 1937; Jerusalem Conservatory, 1938-43 with Joseph Tal and Oedeon Partos; Juilliard School, 1947; Studies with Copland at Berkshire Music Center, 1948. Career: Served as Pianist with Royal Air Force, 1943-46; Juilliard School faculty, 1949-74; Professor of Music at Brooklyn College, 1963; CBS TV commissions, 1960 and 1973; Journals of A Songmaker, commissioned by William Steinberg for the Pittsburgh Symphony; Violin Concerto written for Itzhak Perlman; Other music performed by Mitropoulos, Bernstein and Leinsdorf; Ballets for the Martha Graham Company. Compositions include: Operas: The Intruder, 1956, Apollonia, 1978; Ballets: The Story of Esther, 1960, Samson Agonistes, 1961, The Sense of Touch, 1967, Holy Jungle, 1974; Orchestral: 3 Piano Concertos, 1947, 1953, 1972, 3 Symphonies, 1950, 1951, 1969, Concerto for Violin, Cello and Orchestra, 1967, Violin Concerto, 1980, Episodes, 1992, Concerto for 2 Pianos and Orchestra, 1993, Dispositions, 1994; Vocal Music including settings of the Bible for various forces; Voices of Brooklyn, in 7 parts for Solo Voices, Chorus and Band, 1980-84; Chamber music: String Quartet, 1947, 6 Preludes for Guitar, 1984, Piano Trio, 1985, Cello Concerto, 1988, Clarinet Quintet, 1991, String Quartet No 2, 1995. Recordings: Cello Concerto with Janos Starker; CD of Chamber Music and of Vocal Music. Publications: Piano Music 1946-91, in 1 volume; Choral Music 1959-93, in 1 volume. Contributions to: Many to various journals. Membership: Elected to American Academy of Arts and Letters, 1994. Address: PO Box 946, Woodstock, NY 12498, USA.

STARK Phil, b. 30 Dec 1929, Darmstadt, Germany. Singer (Tenor). Education: Studied in Darmstadt. Debut: Heidelberg as Rossini's Almaviva, 1953. Career: Sang in opera at Solothurn-Biel, 1954-55, Dortmund, 1955-58; Appearances with Canadian Opera at Toronto, 1969-87, as Jacquino, Don Ottavio, Ferrando, Ernesto, Jenik, Rodolfo, Tom Rakewell and Turiddu; Latterly in such character roles as Monostatos, Basilio, Valzacchi in Rosenkavalier, the Captain in Wozzeck and Pang in Turandot; Guest engagements at Seattle (1970), New Orleans and Washington; Metropolitan Opera, 1973-75, as Herod, Mime and Aegisthus; European performances at Zurich, Dusseldorf, Mannheim, Karlsruhe and Cologne. Address: c/o Canadian Opera Company, 227 Front Street East, Toronto, Ontario M5A 1E8, Canada.

STARKER Janos, b. 5 July 1924, Budapest, Hungary. Educator; Cellist. m. Rae Busch, 3 daughters. Education; Franz Liszt Academy, Hungary. Career: Solo Cellist: Budapest Opera Philharmonic, 1945-46, Dallas Symphony, 1948-49, Metropolitan Opera, 1949-53, Chicago Symphony, 1953-58; Concert tours on all continents in recitals and as soloist with orchestras; Distinguished Professor of Cello, Music Department, Indiana University, Bloomington; Inventor of The Starker Bridge. Recordings: Over 120 LPs and CDs on various labels. Publications: Many articles and essays including: An Organized Method of String Playing; Bach Suites; Concerto Cadenzas; Schubert-Starker Sonatina; Bottermund-Starker Variations; Beethoven Sonatas; Beethoven Variations; Dvorák Concert; Record jacket cover notes. Honours: George Washington Award, WAshington DC, 1972; Sanford Fellow, Yale University, 1974; Herzl Award, Israel, 1978; Ed Press Award, 1983; Kodály Commemorative Medallion, New York, 1983; Arturo Toscanini Award, 1986; Tracy Sonneborn Award, Indiana University, 1986; Honorary DMus: Chicago Convs, 1961, Cornell College, 1978, East-West University, 1982, Williams College, 1983; Honorary Doctorate, Lawrence University. Memberships: Honorary Member, Royal Academy, London, England, 1981; American Federation of Musicians. Hobbies: Writing; Swimming. Current Management: Colbert Artists, 111 W 57th Street, New York, NY 10019, USA. Address: Music Department, Indiana University, Bloomington, IN 47401, USA.

STAROBIN David (Nathan), b. 27 Sep 1951, New York City, USA. Classical Guitarist. m. Rebecca Patience Askew, 22 Jun 1975, 1 son, 1 daughter. Education: BM, Peabody Conservatory, 1973; Guitar studies with Manuel Gayol, 1959-62, Abert Valdes Blain, 1963-67 and Aaren Shearer, 1967-73. Debuts: American at Carnegie Recital Hall, NY, 1978; European at Wigmore Hall, London, 1979. Career: Played the premiere performances of over 200 new compositions written for him including solo works, concerti and chamber music; Composers who have written for him include Elliott Carter, Charles Wuorinen, Barbara Kolb, David Del Tredici, William K Bland, Tod Machover, Milton Babbitt, Roger Reynolds, Robert Saxton, Mel Powell, Elisabeth Lutyens, Lukas Foss, Poul Ruders, George Crumb and Mario Davidovsky; Member of Speculum Misicae. Recordings: New Music with Guitar, volumes 1, 2, 3 and 4; A Song From The East, music from Russia and Hungary; Twentieth Century Music for Voice and Guitar. Publications: Editor: Looking for Claudio, 1978, Three Lullabies, 1980, Changes, 1984, Acrostic Song, 1983. Current Management: Bridge Records Inc. Address: c/o Bridge Records Inc, GPO Box 1864, New York, NY 10116, USA.

STARYK Steven S, b. 28 Apr 1932, Toronto, Canada. Professor; Concert Violinist; Concert Master. m. 17 May 1963, 1 daughter. Education: Royal Conservatory of Music, Toronto; Private studies in New York. Debut: Toronto. Career: Concert Master, Royal Philharmonic, London, Concertgebouw

Amsterdam, Chicago Symphony and Toronto Symphony; Professor of Violin, Amsterdam Conservatory, Oberlin Conservatory, Northwestern University, University of Victoria and Academy of Music, Vancouver; Visiting Professor at University of Ottawa and University of Western Ontario; Professor, Royal Conservatory of Music, Toronto; Faculty of Music, University of Toronto; Professor and Head String Division, University of Washington, Seattle, USA, 1987-98; Organiser of Quartet Canada; Extensive concert tours, radio and TV appearances in North America, Europe and the Far East. Recordings: 190 Compositions on 45 albums. Honours: Canada Council Arts Awards, 1967, 1975; Shevchenko Medal, 1974; Queen Elizabeth Centennial Award, 1978; Honorary DLitt, York University, Toronto, 1980; Distinguished Teaching Award, University of Washington, Seattle, 1995; Professor Emeritus, 1997. Address: 12068 E Bella Vista Cr, Scottsdale, AZ 85259, USA.

STAUFFER George (Boyer), b. 18 Feb 1947, Hershey, Pennsylvania, USA. Musicologist; Organist. m. Marie Caruso, 26 May 1985, 1 son. Education: BA, Dartmouth College, 1969; PhD, Columbia University, 1978; Organ study with John Weaver and Vernon de Tar. Career: Director of Chapel Music and Organist, Columbia University, 1977-; Adjunct Assistant Professor of Music, Yeshiva University, 1978-79; Assistant, Associate and Professor of Music, Hunter College and Graduate Center, City University of New York, 1979-. Publications: Author, Organ Preludes of J S Bach, 1980 and J S Bach: Mass in B minor, 1997; Co-editor, J S Bach as Organist, 1986; Editor, The Forkel - Hoffmeister and Kuhnel Correspondence, 1990, and Bach Perspectives 2, 1996; Co-author, Organ Technique: Modern and Early, 1992; General Editor, Monuments of Western Music series. Contributions to: Early Music; Musical Quarterly; Bach-Jahrbuch. Hobbies: Canoeing; Harpsichord Building. Address: 30 Euclid Avenue, Hastings-on-Hudson, NY 10706, USA.

STEANE J(ohn) B(arry), b. 12 Apr 1928, Coventry, England. Critic and Writer on Music. Education: Studied English at Cambridge University. Career: Teacher of English, 1952-88; Reviewer of vocal music and opera for The Gramophone from 1972; Reviews and articles in Musical Times and Opera Now, 1989- (Singers of the Century series). Publications: The Grand Tradition: Seventy Years of Singing on Record, 1974, revised 1993; Voices, Singers and Critics, 1992; Elisabeth Schwarzkopf: A career on record, with Alan Sanders, 1995. Contributions to: New Grove Dictionary of Music, 1980 and New Grove Dictionary of Opera, 1992. Address: c/o Opera Now, Rhinegold Publishing, 241 Shaftesbury Avenue, London WC2H 8EH, England.

STEBLIANKO Alexei, b. 1950, Russia. Tenor. Education: Studied at the Leningrad Conservatory. Career: Has sung at the Kirov Theatre Leningrad as Lensky (debut), Radames, Manrico, Don José, Des Grieux, Andrei in Mazeppa, Herman in The Queen of Spades, Andrei Khovansky, Dmitri in Boris Godunov, Cavaradossi, Lohengrin, Canio and Pierre Bezukhov in War and Peace; Tours of Europe with the Kirov Theatre including Covent Garden debut as Hermann in 1987; Sang at La Scala in 1982 as Aeneas in Les Troyens, and Covent Garden, 1989-90 as Jason in Médée, Vladimir in Prince Igor, both being new productions, and Manrico; Season 1992 as Otello at Reggio Emilia; Television appearances include Prince Igor, also on video; Sang Herman in The Queen of Spades at Bonn, 1996. Address: Allied Artists, 42 Montpelier Square, London, SW7 1JZ, England.

STEDRON Milos, b. 9 Feb 1942, Brno, Czechoslovakia. Composer. Education: Musicology and music theory at Brno Academy, 1965-70. Career: Researched Janácek's music and worked in administration at the Moravian Museum in Brno, 1963-72; Teacher of theory at University of Brno from 1972. Compositions include: Operas: The Apparatus, after Kafka, 1967, Culinary Cares, Brno, 1979, The Chameleon, Or Josef Fouche, Brno, 1984; Ballets: Justina, 1969, Ballet Macabre, 1986; Orchestra: Concerto for Double Bass and Strings, 1971, Diagram for Piano and Jazz Orchestra, 1971, Music for Ballet, 1972, Wheel, symphony, 1972, Cello Concerto, 1975, Sette Villanelle for Cello and Strings, 1981, Musica Concertante for Bassoon and Strings, 1986, Lammento for Viola and Orchestra, 1987; Chamber: Musica Ficta for Wind Quintet, 1968, String Quartet, 1970, Trium Vocum for Flute, Cello and Drums, 1984, Danze, Canti and Lamenti for String Quartet, 1986; Vocal: Mourning Ceremony, cantata, 1969, Vocal Symphony for Soprano, Baritone and Orchestra, 1969, Attendite, Populi, cantata for Chorus and Drums, 1982, Dolorosa Gioia Ommaggio á Gesualdo, Madrigal Cantata, 1978, Death Of Dobrovsky, cantata-oratorio, 1988; Solo instrumental music and piano pieces. Address: c/o OSA, Cs armady 20, 160-56 Prague 6 - Bubenec, Czech Republic.

STEELE-EYTLE Christopher (Michael), b. 28 May 1951, Port-of-Spain, Trinidad, West Indies. Conductor. Education: BMusEd 1975, MMus 1991, Temple University, Philadelphia, USA; Bachakademie, Oregon, USA, 1983; International Bachakademie, Stuttgart, West Germany, 1984, 1991. Career: Conductor: Southern Light Orchestra, Trinidad, 1976-78; Collegium Musicum, Trinidad, 1979-; Opera Ebony, Philadelphia,

USA, 1984; International Bachakamie, Stuttgart Federal Republic of Germany, 1984, 1991; Szombathely Symphony Orchestra, Hungary, also Hungarian Radio and TV Symphony Orchestra 1986; Music Associate 1983-85, Assistant Music Director 1985-86, Temple Opera, Philadelphia, USA; Specialist Music Teacher, School District of Philadelphia, 1986-; Solingen Stadtisches, Stuttgart, 1991; Bohuslav Martinu Philharmonic, Czech Republic, 1992; Beethoven Chamber Orchestra, Czech Republic, 1994. Honours: Sonderpreis im Wettewerb, Vienna, 1980; May Johnstone Commemoration Trophy, Trinidad, 1982; Beryl McBurnie Award, Trinidad, 1983. Memberships: Conductors' Guild; American Choral Directors Association; Music Educators' National Conference. Hobbies: Gourmet cooking; Dance; Theatre; Weights; Walking; Interior decorating; Tennis; Oil painting; Photography. Address: 4503 Chester Avenue, 2nd Floor, Philadelphia, PA 19143, USA.

STEELE-PERKINS Crispian, b. 18 Dec 1944, Exeter, England. Trumpeter. m. Jane Elisabeth Mary, 6 Apr 1995. Education: Guildhall School of Music. Career: Many appearances in the Baroque repertoire at the Barbican and Royal Festival Halls with the City of London Sinfonia and the English Chamber Orchestra; Sadlers Wells Opera, 1966-73; Royal Philharmonic, 1976-80; Played Haydn's Trumpet Concerto at the 1982 Edinburgh Festival; Performances on the Natural Trumpet with The King's Consort, The English Baroque Soloists, The Taverner Players and The Parley of Instruments; Professor of Trumpet at Guildhall School of Music, 1980; Workshops and masterclasses as preludes to concert presentations; Season 1989-90 in Boston, Tokyo, Lisbon, Stuttgart and Gstaad; British festival engagements at Edinburgh, the Proms, City of London, Cambridge, Chester, Dartington, Leeds and Glasgow; US tour in 1988 and tour of Japan in 1990; King's Consort, 1985-; Full-time Trumpet Soloist, 1990-. Recordings: Participation in over 700 recordings including 13 solo albums; Mr Purcell's Trumpeter with the City of London Sinfonia under Richard Hickox; Messiah featuring English trumpet of Handel's time; Shore's Trumpet, EMI; Let the Trumpet Sound, Carlton Classics; 6 Trumpet Concertos, Carlton Classics; 80 Film tracks. Contributions to: Articles in Historic Brass Journal. Membership: Royal Society of Musicians. Hobby: Tennis.

STEFANESCU Ana Camelia, b. 1974, Bucharest, Romania. Singer (Soprano). Education: Dinu Lipatti School, Bucharest; Cipran Porumbescu, Music Academy, Bucharest. Career: Romanian National Opera, as Lucia di Lammermoor, Rosina, the Queen of Night in Die Zauberflöte, Zerbinetta, and Zerlina; Season 1997-98 as the Queen of Night at the Teatro Comunale, Florence and at the Vienna State Opera; Deutsche Staatsoper, Berlin; Concerts and recitals in Romania, Poland, France, Holland, Luxembourg, Britain, Belgium and Switzerland. Recordings: Many recordings for Romanian radio and WDR in Cologne. Honours include: Prize Winner, Verviers International Competition and the Queen Elisabeth International Music Competition, Belgium. Address: IMG Artists, Media House, 3 Burlington Lane, London W4 2TH, England.

STEFANESCU-BARNEA Georgeta, b. 25 Apr 1934, Satu-Mare, Romania. Piano Soloist; Performer; University Reader; Diplomat in Art. m. Jean Barnea, 3 Oct 1958, 2 sons. Education: Lyceum, Cluj, 1950-52; Academy of Music, G H Dima, Cluj, 1952-55; Academy of Music, C Porumbescu, Bucharest, 1955-57; Improvement at Weimar, Germany, 1968, 1969, 1979, at Switzerland, 1970, 1972, at France, 1971. Career: Piano Teacher, Music Lyceum, 1957-60; University Lecturer, Academy of Music, C Porumbescu, Bucharest, 1960-91; University Reader, 1991-; Numerous concerts and piano recitals in Romania, Germany, Switzerland, Czechoslovakia, England, 1988; Appearances on Romania Radio and TV, Radio Weimar, Suisse Romande Radio, Geneva. Recordings: Concert for Piano and Orchestra, On Tops of Charpathians by Stan Golestan with Radio Orchestra, 1971; Piano Pieces, Carol Miculi, 1971; Sabin Dragoi Miniatures, 1982. Publications include: Mihai Burada - Homage Album, in 3 volumes, 1993; Martian Negrea - Piano Pieces, 1994; Editor, Romanian Sonatines for Piano, in 2 volumes, 1994; Many other pedagogical albums by H Herz, Schubert, Grieg, Chopin, Haydn, Mozart and Beethoven. Contributions to: Edited: Romanian Pieces for Piano of The XIXth Century, in 2 volumes, 1975, Romanian Sonatines for Piano, 1985, Lieds of Romanian Contemporary Creation, in 2 volumes, 1987, Little Pieces for Piano Four Hands, in 3 volumes, 1989; Album of Little Romanican Pieces for Piano, 1997. Honours: Commemorative Medal Woman of The Year, 1994, and 20th Century Acheievement Award, American Biographical Institute. Address: Str Compozitorilor Nr 32, Bl F8, Apt 24 Sect VI, 77353 Bucharest 66, Romania.

STEFANOWICZ Artur, b. 1968, Szczecin, Poland. Counter-Tenor. Education: Graduated from the Chopin Academy of Music, where he studied singing under Jerzy Artysz in 1991 and then continued his studies with Paul Esswood and Jadwiga Rappe. Career: Appearances from 1990 with the Warsaw Chamber Opera in Mozart's Ascanio in Alba, Apollo et Hyacinthus and Mitridate; Festival engagements at Halla, Warsaw and Bratislava and concerts with the Vienna Philharmonic, Clemencic

Consort and Ensemble Mosaique; Sang Ottone in Monteverdi's Poppea for Netherlands Opera in 1995; Various Mozart roles, including Farnace in Mitridate Re di Ponto, 1995; Recital at the Lincoln Center, New York with the Polish Chamber Orchestra, 1996 and the roles of Ottone at the Massachusetts Music Festival and Orlofsky in Austria, also in 1996. Recordings include: Mozart operatic arias for the Polskie Nagrania company, with the Warsaw Symphony Orchestra and Karol Teutsch; Stabat Mater by Pergolesi, and by Vivaldi; Recital for Polish Radio with the Hedos Ensemble, 1994. Address: Helen Sykes Management, FirstFloor, Parkway House, Sheen Lane, East Sheen, London, SW14 8LS, England.

STEFANSSON Finnur Torfi, b. 20 Mar 1947, Iceland. Composer. m. (1) 2 sons, 2 daughters, (2) Sigfridur Björnsdottir, 26 Dec 1997. Education: Cand Juris, University of Iceland, 1972; Diploma, Political Science, University of Manchester, 1974; BA, Composition, Theory, Reykjavik College of Music, 1985; MA, Composition, University of California, 1989. Career: Government and Law, Iceland; Member of Parliament, 1978; Ombudsman, Ministry of Justice, 1980; Lecturer, Reykjavik College of Music, 1991-94; Music Critic, 1991-94; Composer, 1994-. Compositions: 5 Works for Full Orchestra; The Leg and the Shell, Concerto for Violin and Orchestra; Chamber Music includes string quartets, wind quintets, solo piano; Solo songs include choir music to Icelandic and English Texts. Recordings: Piece IV for Orchestra; Chaconna for Wind Quintet; Suite From The Leg and the Shell; Concerto for Clarinet, Bassoon and Orchestra; Preludia, Toccata and Fugue for Piano. Membership: Icelandic Society of Composers. Hobby: Sailing. Current Management: Iceland Music Information Center. Address: Tungufell, 311 Borgarnes, Iceland.

STEFFEK Hanny, b. 12 Dec 1927, Biala, Poland. Soprano. Education: Studied at the Vienna Music Academy and the Salzburg Mozarteum. Career: Sang in concert from 1949 with opera debut in 1951; Sang at the Graz Opera from 1953 then the Frankfurt Opera, and at the Munich Staatsoper, 1957-72; Salzburg Festival, 1950-55 as Papagena, Ilia and Blondchen, Covent Garden in 1959 as Sophie in Der Rosenkavalier, Aix-en-Provence in 1960 and Teatro Fenice Venice in 1962; Sang at the Vienna Staatsoper, 1964-73; Sang Christine in the British premiere of Intermezzo by Strauss at Edinburgh in 1965. Recordings include: Despina in Così fan tutte; Das Buch mit Sieben Siegeln by Franz Schmidt. Address: c/o Bayerische Staatsoper, Postfach 745, D-8000 Munich 1, Germany.

STEFFENS Walter, b. 31 Oct 1934, Aachen, Germany. Professor; Composer. Education: Basic music education with Toni and Max Spindler; Conducting with Rolf Agap; Music theory and composition with Klussmann, Maler and Philipp Jarnach at Musikhochschule Hamburg; Musicology, phonetics, theology, arts and general history at University of Hamburg. Appointments: Dozent (lecturer) in Composition and Music Theory at Hamburg Conservatorium, 1962-69; Professor of Composition and Music Theory, masterclasses, Hochschule für Musik, Detmold, 1969-. Compositions: Operas: Eli, librettos by composer, after Mystery of The Sorrow of Israel by Nelly Sachs, Dortmund, 1967; Under Milk Wood, English and German versions, librettos by composer, after Dylan Thomas, Hamburg State Opera, 1973, 1977 Staastheater Kassel opening; Grabbes Leben, librettos by Peter Schütze, Landestheater Detmold, 1986, Hamburg State Opera; Der Philosoph, librettos by Schütze, Landestheater Detmold, 1990; Die Judenbuche, libretto by Schütze, after Annette von Droste-Hülshoff, Dortmund, 1993, Gelsenkirchen during the New Music Theatre Days; Bildvertonugen, over 50 individual musical settings after paintings by Bosch, Marc Chagall, Klee, Picasso, Soto and others, Kassel, 1977 and 1992; Chamber music, Lieder, Concertos, Symphonies, ballet music and oratorio. Address: Rosenstr 15, D-32756 Detmold, Germany.

STEFIUK Maria, b. 1967, Kiev, Ukraine. Soprano. Education: Studied at the Kiev State Conservatoire. Debut: Kiev Opera in 1982 as Violetta. Career: Many appearances in Kiev, Moscow and St Petersburg as Lucia, Zerlina, Marguerite de Valois, Mimi, Leila in Les Pêcheurs de Perles and Marfa in The Tsar's Bride; Guest engagements in Dresden, Madrid, Wiesbaden, London, Paris, Washington, Tokyo and Sydney, including many concert appearances; Sang at La Scala Milan in Sorochintsy Fair by Mussorgsky. Address: c/o Sonata Ltd, 11 North Park Street, Glasgow, G20 7AA, Scotland.

STEGER Ingrid, b. 27 Feb 1927, Roding, Germany. Soprano; Mezzo-Soprano. Education: Studied in Munich at the Musikhochschule. Debut: As Azucena in Passau, 1951. Career: Sang in opera at Augsburg, 1952-54, Kassel, 1954-59, Trier, 1958-60 and Oberhausen from 1960; Further engagements at Berlin Staatsoper, 1965-68, Parma and Venice, 1965 and 1968, Salzburg Easter Festival, 1967, Graz, 1974-75 and Karlsruhe, 1975-77; Sang Elektra at San Francisco in 1973 and appeared further at the state operas of Vienna, Hamburg and Stuttgart; Sang until 1986 in such roles as Rodelinda, Leonore, Senta, Elsa, Ortrud, Elisabeth, Isolde, Kundry, the Composer in Ariadne, Lady Macbeth, Amneris, Amelia in Un Ballo in Maschera, Santuzza,

Turandot, Judith in Bluebeard's Castle and Schoeck's Penthesilea. Recordings include: Die Walküre conducted by Karajan. Address: c/o Stuttgart Staatsoper, Oberer Schlossgarten 6, 7000 Stuttgart, Germany.

STEIGER Anna, b. 13 Feb 1960, Los Angeles, CA, USA. Soprano. Education: Guildhall School of Music, London; Further study with Vera Rozsa and Irmgard Seefried. Career: Associated with Glyndebourne Opera from 1983 singing Micaela on tour in 1985, Poppea at the 1986 Festival and in the 1987 premiere production of Osborne's The Electrification of the Soviet Union; Sang at Lausanne Opera in 1985 in La Cenerentola, Opera North in 1986 as Musetta, Covent Garden Opera from 1987 in Parsifal and Jenufa, English National Opera in The Makropoulos Case, and Geneva Opera as Concepcion in L'Heure Espagnole; Sang Despina in Cosi fan tutte for Netherlands Opera in 1990, and Eurydice in Milhaud's Les Malheurs d'Orphée at the Elizabeth Hall in 1990; Season 1991-92 as Despina at Stuttgart, a Hooded Figure in the premiere of Osborne's Terrible Mouth at the Almeida Theatre, and Zerlina for Netherlands Opera; Sang in Verdi's Un Giorno di Regno for Dorset Opera, 1994; Concert engagements include BBC recitals, Clarissa's Mad Scene by Holloway with the London Symphony, Les Illuminations with Bournemouth Sinfonietta and Fauré's Requiem with Scottish National Orchestra. Recording: Poème de L'Amour et de La Mer by Chausson, with the BBC Scottish Symphony Orchestra. Honours: Sir Peter Pears Award, 1982; Richard Tauber Award, 1984; John Christie Award, 1985. Address: c/o Harrison Parrott Ltd, 12 Penzance Place, London W11 4PA, England.

STEIGER Rand, b. 18 June 1957, New York, USA. Composer; Conductor. Education: New York High School of Music and Art, 1972-75; Percussion and Composition at the Manhattan School of Music (BMus 1980); California Institute of the Arts, with Brown, Subotnick and Powell (MFA 1982); Yale University with Elliott Carter, Betsy Jolas and Jakob Druckman; Further study at IRCAM, electronic music studios, Paris. Career: Faculty, University of Costa Rica, 1984-85, California Institute of the Arts, 1982-87 and University of California at San Diego, from 1987; Conductor and Director of contemporary music performances with SONOR at San Diego and with the Los Angeles Philharmonic New Music Group; From 1981 member new-music ensemble E.A.R., based at California Institute of the Arts. Compositions include: Brave New World for voices and electronics, 1980; Dialogues II for marimba and orchestra, 1980; Quintessence for 6 instruments, 1981; Currents Caprice, electronic, 1982; Kennedy Sketches for marimba and vibraphone, 1982; In Nested Symmetry for 15 instruments and electronics, 1982; Tributaries for chamber orchestra, 1986; Tribuatries for Nancarrow and double chamber orchestra, 1987; ZLoops for clarinet, piano and percussion, 1989; Mozart Tributary for clarinet quintet, 1991; The Burgess Shale for orchestra, 1991. Honours include: First Composer Fellow of the Los Angeles Philharmonic, 1987-88. Address: c/o ASCAP, ASCAP Building, One Lincoln Plaza, New York, NY 10023, USA.

STEIN Horst, b. 2 May 1928, Elberfeld, Germany. Conductor. Education: Studied at the Cologne Musikhochschule. Career: Conducted first at Wuppertal, then at the Hamburg Staatsoper, 1951-, and Berlin Staatsoper, 1955-61; Opera Director in Mannheim, 1963-70; Conducted the South American premiere of Schoenberg's Gurrelieder at Buenos Aires in 1964; Bayreuth Festival from 1969 with Parsifal and Der Ring des Nibelungen; Principal Conductor at the Vienna Staatsoper, 1970-72; Music Director at the Hamburg Staatsoper, 1972-79; Director of the Hamburg Philharmonic, 1973-76; Has conducted Tristan und Isolde in Buenos Aires, Der fliegende Holländer in Sofia and Parsifal at the Paris Opéra; Conductor of the Orchestre de la Suisse Romande, 1980-85; Director of the Bamberg Symphony from 1985, Basle Symphony from 1987; Conducted Fidelio at the 1990 Salzburg Festival; Parsifal at the Opéra Bastille, Paris, 1997; Often heard in the symphonies of Bruckner. Address: c/o Bamberger Symphoniker, Altes Rathaus, Postfach 110 146, D-8600 Bamberg, Germany.

STEIN Leon, b. 18 Sept 1910, Chicago, Illinois, USA. Musician; Educator. m. Anne Helman, 30 Oct 1937, 2 sons. Education: MusB, 1931, MusM, 1935, PhD, 1949, DePaul University. Career: Faculty, 1931-, Dean, 1966-76, Professor of Music, 1966-, Dean Emeritus, 1978-, School of Music, DePaul University, Chicago; Chairman, College of Jewish Studies, Institute of Music, 1951-57; Conducting Class, Chicago Civic Orchestra, 1937-40; Conductor, Community Symphony Orchestra, Amalgamated Chorus, Skokie Valley Symphony Orchestra, 1962-66, City Symphony, Chicago, 1963-84; Director, DePaul University Symphony Orchestra, 1965-; Founder, Conductor, DePaul University Chamber Orchestra; Guest Conductor, Illinois Symphony, Kenosha (Wisconsin) Symphony; Composer-in-residence, Ernest Bloch Composers' Symposium, Newport, Oregon, 1-10 July 1993. Compositions: 4 Symphonies; Sonatine, 2 violins, 1946; 3 Hassidic Dances, 1947: Operas: The Fisherman's Wife, 1953-54, Deirdre, 1955-56; Trio, trumpets; Quintet, saxophone, strings; Sextet, saxophone, winds; Quintet, harp, string quartet, 1977; Concerto, violoncello, orchestra, 1977; Concerto, clarinet, percussion, 1979; Suite, string trio, 1980; Nonet, winds, strings, 1982; Anthology of Musical Forms, Kaddish, tenor, string orchestra, 1984; Concerto, oboe, string orchestra, 1986; Duo Concertante, marimba, bassoon, 1993; Trio Concertante, violin, cello, piano, 1993; Quintet, clarinet, string quartet, 1993. Recordings: Numerous. Publications: Racial Thinking of Richard Wagner, 1959; Structure and Style (The Study and Analysis of Musical Forms), 1962, expanded, 1979. Contributions: Articles to music publications. Honours: American Composers' Commission Award, Triptych on 3 Poems of Walt Whitman, 1950; Symphonic Movement for Orchestra Award, Midland Music Foundation Composition Prize, 1955; Symphony No 4 won International Competition, Elkhart (Indiana) Orchestral Association, 1977-78; City of Chicago Hall of Fame, 1982; Winner, South Coast Symphony Performance Award, 1987, Address: 3405-B Calle Azul, Laguna Hills, CA 92653, USA.

STEIN Leonard, b. 1 Dec 1916, Los Angeles, CA, USA. Musicologist; Pianist. Education: Studied at University of Southern CA, 1935-36; DMA, 1965; Teaching assistant to Schoenberg at UCLA, 1939-42; BA 1939, MM, 1941. Career: Taught at Los Angeles City College, 1948-60, Pomona College, 1960-62, UCLA, 1962-64, Claremont Graduate School, 1963-67, Californian State College at Dominguez Hills, 1967-70; Music Faculty of the CA Institute of the Arts, 1970; Adjunct professor in the School of Music at University of Southern CA, 1975; Director of Arnold Schoenberg Institute, University of Southern CA, 1975-91, Director Emeritus, retired in 1991; Freelancing performer (pianist and conductor), lecturer, writing and teaching privately; Toured USA and Europe as conductor and pianist; Took part in the 1950 premiere of Schoenberg's Three Songs Op 48, 1950; Member of Editorial Board, A Schoenberg Sämtliche Werke, 1966-; Piano recitals in Mödling, Austria, 1992, Mannheim and Heidelberg, Germany in 1993, and Monday Evening Concerts, Los Angeles with Marni Nixon, soprano, 1993. Publications: Has edited and completed pedagogical works by Schoenberg; Preliminary Exercises in Counterpoint, 1963; Structural Functions of Harmony, 1969; Models for Beginners in Composition, 1972; Style and Idea: Selected Writings of Arnold Schoenberg, 1975; Editions of Schoenberg's Piano Concerto, Nachtwandler, Ode to Napolean and Brettl Lieder. Contribution to: Reflections on Performing Schoenberg in Austrian Musical Journal, 1993. Honours include: Guggenheim Fellowship, 1965-66; ASCAP Award for Style and Idea, 1976. Address: 2635 Carmen Crest Drive, Los Angeles, CA 90068, USA.

STEIN Peter, b. 1 Oct 1937, Berlin, Germany. Stage Director. Career: Worked with Munich Kammerspiele from 1964 directing Saved by Edward Bond in 1967; Directed plays by Brecht in Munich, Goethe and Schiller in Bremen; Co-founded the Berlin Schaubuhne Company in 1970 and was Artistic Director until 1985; Debut as opera director with Das Rheingold in Paris, 1976; For Welsh National Opera has directed Otello in 1986, Falstaff in 1988 and Pelléas et Mélisande in 1992; Director of Drama at Salzburg Festival, 1992-97; Staged Schoenberg's Moses und Aron at Salzburg, 1996. Recordings include: Videos of Welsh National Opera productions, as director for TV. Address: c/o Welsh National Opera, John Street, Cardiff, CF1 4SP, Wales.

STEINAUER Mathias, b. 20 Apr 1959, Basel, Switzerland. Composer. m. Elena Gianini, 3 June 1991. Education: Teaching Diploma, Piano, with P Efler, Teaching Diploma, Composition Theory, with R Moser, R Stuter, J Wildberger, Musik-Akademie, Basel, 1978-86; Private Study with G Kurtag, Budapest. Career: Various concerts of own music, radio productions, film music, 1982-; Founder, Komponisten Forum, 1982; Teacher of Music theory, Winterhur Konservatorium, 1986. Compositions include: Music for xylophone, marimba and 2 musical boxes, 1984; Musik in fünf Teilen for 3 cellists and 2 percussionists, 1985; Andante for percussion trio, 1985; Vier Klangbilder for baritone, large orchestra, female choir, 18 recorders, words by H Erni, 1986; Visions for 12 wind instruments, 2 percussionists, piano, 1987; Drei Skizzen for string quartet, 1987; Duat, 14 signs for chamber orchestra. 1988; ...wir Risse im Schatten..., concerto for flute and orchestra, 1988-89; Blutenlese for 2 choirs, soprano, children's voice, ensemble, words by 12 authors, 1990-91; Undici Duettini for violin and viola, 1991. Recordings: For various radio stations in Switzerland. Honours: 2nd Prize for Vier Klangbilder, Symphony Section, Ostschweizer Stiftung fur Musik and Theater, 1990. Address: c/o Konservatorium Winterhur, Tossertobelstrasse 1, CH 8400 Winterhur, Switzerland.

STEINBACH Heribert, b. 17 May 1937, Duisberg, Germany. Tenor. Education: Studied in Dusseldorf, and in Cologne with Clemens Glettenberg. Career: Sang at the Cologne Opera, 1964-66, and Staatstheater Karlsruhe, 1966-68; Member of the Deutsche Oper am Rhein Dusseldorf, 1968-76, and Munich Staatsoper, 1977-80; Sang at Bayreuth Festival, 1971-76 as Froh and Melot; Guest engagements at the Paris Opéra in 1976 and 1978, and Lisbon and Barcelona in 1978; Sang Loge in Das Rheingold at the 1979 Maggio Musicale Florence and again at the Teatro Colon Buenos Aires in 1982; Sang Tristan at Lausanne in 1983, Walther von Stolzing at the Metropolitan in 1985 followed by Siegfried at Kassel; Sang at Teatro Reggio Turin, 1987-88 as Siegmund in Die Walküre; At the first season of the new Musiektheater Rotterdam in 1988 sang Siegfried in Der Ring des Nibelungen; Sang Herod in Salome in 1989 at Lyric Opera of Queensland. Recordings: Pfitzner's Palestrina; Tristan und Isolde conducted by Bernstein; Die Soldaten by Zimmermann. Address: c/o Lyric Opera of Queensland, PO Box 677, South Brisbane, Queensland, 4101, Australia.

STEINBERG Pinchas, b. 12 Feb 1945, New York, USA. Conductor. Education: Studied in New York and at Tanglewood; Composition studies with Boris Blacher in Berlin. Career: Took part in the 1964 Tanglewood Festival and became Professor and Assistant at the University of Indiana; Associate Conductor at the Lyric Opera Chicago from 1967, making his debut with Don Giovanni; Conducted leading orchestras in Europe from 1972; Conducted at the Frankfurt Opera from 1979 and has led performances in Stuttgart, Hamburg and Berlin and at Covent Garden, Paris Opéra and the San Francisco Opera; Musical Director at Bremen, 1985-89, Chief Conductor at the Verona Arena in 1989 and Conductor of the Austrian Radio Symphony Orchestra notably in Janácek's Everlasting Gospel and Dvorák's Te Deum in 1990; Appeared at Bregenz Festival in 1990 with Catalani's La Wally and conducted Rossini's Tancredi at the 1992 Salzburg Festival; L'amore dei tre re at the 1994 Montpellier Festival; Further opera includes Rienzi for Radio France, Rigoletto at Orange, Nabucco at the Opéra Bastille, Tosca at Houston and Trovatore in Geneva. Honours include: Winner, Florence International Conductors' Competition, 1972. Address: c/o Austrian Radio Symphony Orchestra, Argentinerrstrasse 30, A-1040 Vienna, Austria.

STEINER Elisabeth, b. 17 Mar 1935, Berlin, Germany. Mezzo-Soprano. Education: Studied in Berlin with Frida Leider. Career: Sang at the Städtischen Oper Berlin from 1961 with debut in Blacher's Rosamunde Floris; Sang at Salzburg Festival in 1962 as Artemis in Gluck's Iphigenia in Aulis; Discovered by Rolf Liebermann and engaged for the Staatsoper Hamburg; Sang in many premieres there including Von Einem's Der Zerrissene in 1964, Penderecki's The Devils of Loudun in 1969, Kelemen's Der Belagerungszustand in 1970 and Stefen's Under Milk Wood in 1973; Appeared often at Bayreuth and in guest engagements at the Maggio Musicale Florence, Metropolitan Opera, New York and La Scala Milan; Sang at Vienna Staatsoper in 1980 in the premiere of Jesu Hochzeit by Gottfried von Einem; Sang the Countess in Lortzing's Wildschütz, Hamburg, 1994. Recordings: Roles in Tiefland, Die Fledermaus, The Devils of Loudun, Rienzi and Eine Nacht in Venedig. Address: c/o Staatsoper, Opernring 2, A-1010 Vienna, Austria.

STEINER Gitta (Hana), b. 17 Apr 1932, Prague, Czechoslovakia. Composer. Education: BM, 1967, MS, 1969, Juilliard School of Music. Career: Private Teacher of Piano, 1960-; Faculty, Brooklyn Conservatory of Music, 1963-65; Professor of Composition, 1983-; Co-Director of Composer's Group for International Performance, 1968; Performed orchestral and chamber music throughout USA and abroad. Compositions include: Suite for Flute, Clarinet and Bassoon, 1958; Suite for Orchestra, 1958; Three Songs for Medium Voice, 1960; Three Pieces for Piano, 1961; Concerto for Violin and Orchestra, 1963; Pages From A Summer Jour, 1963; String Trio, 1964; Piano Sonata, 1964; Settings for Chorus, 1970; Duo for Cello and Percussion, 1971; Percussion Music for Two, 1971; Trio for Voice, Piano and Percussion, 1971; Four Choruses, 1972; Four Settings For A Capella Chorus, 1973; New Poems for Voice and Vibes, 1974; Dream Dialogues for Voice and Percussion, 1974; Cantos, 1975; Dialogue for Two Percussions, 1975; Music for Four Players, 1976; 8 Miniatures for Vibraphone; Fantasy for Solo Percussion; Night Music for Marimba Solo, 1977; Duo for Vibe and Marimba; Duo for Trombone and Percussion, 1980; Five Pieces for Vibe and Marimba; Ten Solos for Vibe and Marimba, 1981; String Quartet, 1984; Piano Trio, 1985; Sonata for Solo Vibraphone, 1985; String Quartet, 1986; Piano Sonata, 1987; Chamber Concerto, 1988; 5 Movements for Marimba, 1988.

STEINHARDT Arnold, b. 1 Apr 1937, Los Angeles, CA, USA. Violinist. Education: Studied at the Curtis Institute, Philadelphia, with Ivan Galamian. Debut: With Los Angeles Philharmonic, 1951. Career: Assistant Concertmaster, Cleveland Orchestra under George Szell; Performed in chamber music with Rudolf Serkin at the Marlboro Festival and prompted by Alexander Schneider to co-found the Guarneri String Quartet, 1964; Many tours of America and Europe, notably in appearances at the Spoleto Festival in 1965, to Paris with Arthur Rubinstein and London in 1970, in the complete quartets of Beethoven; Noted for performances of Viennese classics, works by Walton, Bartók and Stravinsky; Season 1987-88 included opening concert in New Concert Hall at Shufmotomo Festival, Japan and British appearances at St John's Smith Square and Elizabeth Hall; Faculty Member of Curtis Institute at University of Maryland. Recordings include: Mozart's Quartets dedicated to Haydn; Complete Quartets of Beethoven; With Arthur Rubinstein, Piano

Quintets of Schumann, Dvorák and Brahms; Piano Quartets by Fauré and Brahms. Honours include: Edison Award for Beethoven recordings, 1971.

STEINSKY Ulrike, b. 21 Sep 1960, Vienna, Austria. Soprano. Education: Studied with Margaret Zimmermann, Hilde Zadek and Waldemar Kmentt in Vienna. Career: Many performances as Constanze in Die Entführung while a student; Debut at the Vienna Staatsoper in 1983 as the Queen of Night; Has also sung in Die Zauberflöte with the Cologne Opera in Tel Aviv, Covent Garden in Los Angeles in 1984 and at the 1985 Bregenz Festival; Appeared with the Bayerische Staatsoper Munich, 1984-90 and at Zurich from 1985 as Zerline in Fra Diavolo in season 1989-90; Further guest engagements at Cologne, Dortmund, Barcelona as Fiakermilli in Arabella in 1989 and at Hamburg in 1990; Season 1992 as Fiakermilli at La Scala; Other roles include Adele in Die Fledermaus, Musetta, Zerlina, Pamina, Despina, Aennchen and Papagena; Has also sung in operettas by Oscar Straus, Lehar and Millöcker; Concert performances of Cosi fan tutte, Don Giovanni and Mozart's La Finta Giardiniera. Recording: Die Fledermaus. Address: c/o Wiener Staatsoper, 1010 Vienna, Austria.

STEJSKAL Margot, b. 9 Feb 1947, Engelsdorf, Leipzig, Germany. Soprano. Education: Studied in Weimarand at Leipzig Musikhochschule with Hannelore Kuhse. Debut: Cottbus, as Musetta in 1975. Career: Sang in opera at Cottbus until 1977, Staatsoper Dresden, 1977-80, and Chemnitz, 1980-84; Sang Sophie in Der Rosenkavalier at the opening of Semper Oper Dresden, 1985; Guest appearances at Berlin Staatsoper and elsewhere in Germany; Other roles have included Blondchen, Susanna, Nannetta and Adele in Die Fledermaus; Many concert appearances. Recordings include: Der Rosenkavalier. Address: c/o Semper Oper Dresden, 8012 Dresden, Germany.

STELLA Antonietta, b. 15 Mar 1929, Perugia, Italy. Singer (Soprano). Education: Studied at the Accademia di Santa Cecilia, Rome. Debut: Leonora in Il Trovatore, Spoleto, 1950. Career: Rome debut, 1951, as Leonora in La Forza del Destino; Germany from 1951, in Stuttgart, Wiesbaden and Munich; Sang as guest all over Italy; Verona Arena and La Scala debuts, 1953; At the New York Metropolitan (debut 1956) she sang Aida, Butterfly, Tosca, Elisabeth de Valois (Don Carlos), Violetta and Amelia (Un Ballo in Maschera); At Naples in 1974 sang in the premiere of Maria Stuarda by de Bellis. Recordings: Roles in Verdi's Simon Boccanegra, Un Ballo in Maschera, Don Carlos, Il Trovatore, Aida and Il Battaglia di Legnano; Donizetti's Linda di Chamounix; Puccini's La Bohème and Tosca; Giordano's Andrea Chénier.

STENE Randi, b. Norway. Singer (Mezzo-soprano). Education: Studied at the Norwegian State Academy of Music, Oslo, and the Opera Academy, Copenhagen. Career: Salzburg Festival from 1992, in Salome and Dallapiccola's Ulisse; Premiere of Reigen by Boesmans at Brussels, 1993; Season 1993-94 as Octavian at the Thèatre du Chatelet, Paris, and Dorabella at the Royal Opera, Copenhagen; Season 1995-96 with Cherubino at Covent Garden, Olga in Eugene Onegin at the Opèra Bastille, Paris, and Carmen in Brussels; Returned to London 1997, as Silla in a new production of Palestrina by Pfitzner; Concert repertory includes Szymanowski's Stabat Mater (London Proms, 1996), Dvoráks Requiem (Edinburgh Festival, 1996), Missa Brevis by Bach (Salzburg), the Christmas Oratorio, Zemlinsky's Maeterlinck Lieder and Falla's Three Cornered Hat (with the Berlin SO); Schubert's A-flat Mass with the Oslo PO and Sibelius's Kullervo Symphony with the Stockholm PO. Recordings include: Vivaldi Cantatas (EMI); Opera Arias, with Kathleen Battle (DGG); Salome, under Christoph von Dohnanyi (Decca); Kullervo Symphony (Virgin Classics). Honours include: Finalist, 1991 Cardiff Singer of the World Competitin. Address: c/o Lies Askonas Ltd, 6 Henrietta St, London WC2E 8LA, England.

STENZ Markus, b. 28 Feb 1965, Bad Neuenahr, Germany. Conductor. Education: Studied at the Cologne Musikhochschule in Salzburg, with Gary Bertini and Noam Sheriff. Career: With Ozawa and Bernstein at Tanglewood, 1988; Association with Hans Werner Henze includes Elegy for Young Lovers at Venice, 1988, and The English Cat in Berlin, 1989; Premieres of Das Verratene Meer (Berlin, 1990) and Venus und Adonis (Munich, 1997); Musical Director of the Montepulciano Festival, 1989-92; Conducted Figaro at Los Angeles 1994 and Hamburg, 1996; English National Opera debut 1995, Don Giovanni; Principal Conductor of the London Sinfonietta from 1994, leading it at the 1994 Proms in Music by Kurtag, Ives and Xenakis; Season 1993-94 with the Berlin SO, Scottish Chamber Orchestra and BBC SO; Season 1994-95 included debuts with the Hallé Orchestra, Royal Stockholm Philharmonic, and Philharmonic of Rotterdam, Helsinki and Hamburg; Debut appearances with the Sydney and Melbourne SOs in season 1995-96 and Prom concert with Weill's Der Silbersee; Other operas include Henze's Bassarids in Hamburg (1994), Hans Zender's Stephen Climax in Brussels and Weill's Mahagonny in Stuttgart; Season 1997-98 includes debuts with the Minnesota Orchestra and the Chicago Symphony Orchestra; Chief Conductor and Artistic Director of the Melbourne SO from 1998. Address: c/o Ingpen & Williams Ltd, 26 Wadham Road, London SW15 2LR, England.

STEPHAN Erwin, b. 23 Jun 1949, Worms, Germany. Tenor. Education: Studied in Frankfurt, Osnabruck and Karlsruhe; Further study with James King. Debut: Flensburg, 1978. Career: Sang in opera at Luneburg, Coburg and Giessen; Saarbrucken, 1984-86 in debut as Florestan and sang Tannhäuser from 1985 notably at Dortmund, Bremen, Geneva and the 1986 Orange Festival; Freiburg in 1987 as Otello, Huon in Oberon at Catania and Max in Der Freischütz at Cologne; US debut in 1989 as Walther von Stolzing at Seattle; Other roles have included Don José and Ismaele in Nabucco; Opera performances at Semper Oper Dresden and concert showings in France, Austria, Switzerland, Japan and South America. Address: c/o Semper Oper Dresden, 8012 Dresden, Germany.

STEPHENSON Donald (James), b. 15 Feb 1947, Leeds, England. Tenor Opera Singer. m. 1 son, 1 daughter. Education: Royal Manchester College of Music, 1969-71; Diploma, ARCM, with Honours, Singing and Teaching, 1972; National Opera Studio, 1982-83; Diploma, ITEC, 1992. Career includes: English National Opera, 1972-75; English Opera Group, 1975; English Music Theatre, 1976-78; Freelance Opera Singer, 1978-; Festival appearances in UK and Europe; Film, Death in Venice, Benjamin Britten, English Music Theatre; Regular TV and Radio appearances; Principal Tenor, Welsh National Opera; Roles include: Radames, in Aida, Don José, in Carmen, Title role in Parsifal; Siegmund in Die Walküre, Max in Der Freischütz; Glyndebourne and Aldeburgh Festivals; Numerous British premieres; World premieres include: No 11 Bus, Peter Maxwell Davies, London, Rome and New York, 1985; Other appearances include Freiburg Opera in roles including Alwa, in Lulu, 1986, Erik, in Fliegende Holländer, 1988; Scottish Opera: Florestan, in Fidelio, 1984, Red Whiskers, in Billy Budd, 1987; Opera North: Mark, Midsummer Marriage, Tippett, 1985, Wiesbaden, 1986, Florestan, Fidelio at Regensburg and Kaiserslautern Operas, 1987-88, Hoffmann, in Tales of Hoffmann, Stockholm, 1990, First Jew, in Salome, ENO, 1991, Bob Boles in Peter Grimes, 1992; Missa Solemnis, RAH, 1992. Honour: Arts Council Scholarship to study with Otakar Kraus, 1974. Memberships: Equity; International Therapy Education Council. Hobbies: Hill Walking; Golf; Watercolour Painting. Address: Sign, Llanbadarn Fynydd, Powys LD1 6YG, Wales.

STEPHINGER Christoph, b. 4 Jun 1954, Herrshing, Germany. Bass Singer. Education: Studied at Munich Hochschule and the Opera Studio of Bayerisches Staatsoper; Further study with Kurt Moll. Career: Sang at Bielefeld Staadttheater, 1982-86, Staatstheater Hannover from 1986; Guest appearances at Dusseldorf, Dortmund, Karlsruhe, Hamburg, Berlin, Nice and Spleto; Roles have included Wagner's Guernemanz, King Henry, Pogner and Daland, Mozart's Commendatore, Osmin, Sarastro and Alfonso, Kecal in The Bartered Bride and Jim in Maschinist Hopkins by Max Brand (at Bielefeld); Concert repertoire includes Herod in L'Enfance du Christ by Berlioz, with the Gächinger Kantorei under Helmuth Rilling in 1989; Sang Fasolt and Hunding in new productions of Das Rheingold and Die Walküre at Hannover in 1992. Address: c/o Niedersachsische Staatstheater, Opernplatz 1, 30159 Hannover, Germany.

STEPTOE Roger Guy, b. 25 Jan 1953, Winchester, Hampshire, England. Composer; Pianist; Lecturer. Education: BA, Honours, Music, University of Reading, 1971-74; Royal Academy of Music, 1974-77. Debut: As composer at Purcell Room, 1977; As Pianist at Wigmore Hall, 1982. Career: Composer-in-Residence, Charterhouse, 1976-79; Professor of Composition, Royal Academy of Music, 1990-91; Administrator of Contemporary Music Projects, 1989-91, and for International Composer Festivals, 1991-93, Royal Academy of Music. Compositions include: Orchestral: Two Miniatures for Strings, 1977, Oboe Concerto, 1982, Clarinet Concerto, 1989; Choral: Two Madrigals, 1976, In Winter's Cold Embraces Dye, cantata, for Soprano, Tenor, Chorus and Chamber Orchestra, 1985; Chamber: String Quartet No 1, 1976, Four Sonnets for Brass Quintet, 1984, Piano Trio, 1993; Vocal: Aspects for High Voice and Piano, 1978, A Little Music for Baritone and Piano, 1981, The Bond Of The Sea for Bass-Baritone and Piano, 1983, Two Folksongs for baritone and Violin, 1986, Five Rondos for Soprano, Baritone and Piano, 1989, Sonnets To Delia for Baritone and Piano, 1993; Instrumental: Three Preludes for Piano, 1976, Equinox for Solo Piano, 1981, Violin Sonata No 1, 1983, No 2, 1986, In The White And The Walk Of The Morning, five poems, for 2 Guitars, 1989, Duo for Oboe and Harp, 1991. Honours: All prizes for Composition, Royal Academy of Music, ARAM 1984. Memberships: Royal Philharmonic Society; Incorporated Society of Musicians; Composers' Guild of Great Britain. Hobbies: Theatre; Travel; Cinema; Gardening; Seeing Friends. Current Management: International Artists Promotion. Address: c/o International Artists Promotion, 7 Jeffrey's Street, London, NW1 9PS, England.

STERN Isaac, b. 21 Jul 1920, Kremenets, Russia. Violinist. 2 s, 1 d. Education: San Francisco Conservatory, 1928-31; Studied with Louis Persinger and Naoum Binder, 1932-37. Debut: 1931 with San Francisco Symphony Orchestra. Career: Los Angeles Symphony, 1935 with Klemperer; Chicago Symphony, 1937 with Freidrich Stock; New York debut, 1937; Toured Australia, 1947; Appearances in Europe from 1948 at Lucerne Festival with Charles Munch; Premiered William Schuman's Concerto with Boston Symphony in 1950 and Bernstein's Serenade at Venice Festival, 1954; Played at Casals Festival Parades, 1950 and Edinburgh Festival, 1953; Toured Russia, 1956; Gave Mendelssohn's Concerto on Mount Scopus, Israel following 1967 Six-day War, conducted by Bernstein; Member of Stern-Rose-Istomin Trio, 1960-84; Formed group to save Carnegie Hall from demolition, 1960; Co-founded National Endowment for The Arts, 1964; Played on soundtrack of Fiddler on the Roof, 1971; Premiered Henri Dutilleux' Violin Concerto L'Arbre des Songes in Paris, 1985; Premiered the Violin Concerto by Peter Maxwell Davies, in Orkney, 1986. Recordings: Most major concertos from Bach to Bartók; Sibelius's Concerto conducted by Ormandy; Dutilleux and Maxwell Davies Concertos; Numerous chamber music recitals including the Complete Trios of Beethoven, Brahms and Schubert. Honours: Grammy Awards, 1971, 1973; Commander, Ordre de la Couronne, 1974; Numerous honorary doctorates. Memberships: President, Carnegie Hall Corporation; Board Chairman, American-Israel Cultural Foundation; Director, Jerusalem Music Center. Address: c/o Harold Holt Ltd, 31 Sinclair Road, London, W14 0NS, England.

STERNBERG Jonathan, b. 27 July 1919, New York, USA. Conductor. m. Ursula Hertz, 15 Oct 1957, 1 son, 1 daughter. Education: AB, Washington Square College, 1939; New York University Graduate School, 1940; Harvard Summer School, 1940; Juilliard School; Manhattan School of Music; Private studies. Debut: Vienna Symphony Orchestra, 1947. Career: Guest Conductor of major orchestras and operas worldwide, 1947-; Musical Director of Royal Flemish Opera, 1962-66, Harkness Ballet, 1966-69; Visiting Professor of Conducting, Eastman School of Music, 1969-71; Professor, Temple University College of Music, 1971-89, Professor Emeritus; Lecturer at Chestnut Hill College, 1989-; Conducted premiere performances in Europe and USA of music by Bloch, Ives, Rorem, Blackwood, Persichetti, Prokofiev, Messiaen; Faculty International Workshop for Conductors, Zlin, Czechoslovakia, 1992-. Recordings: 60 LP recordings including: several Bach Cantatas, Haydn Symphonies, and Mozart Concertos; Variations for Orchestra by Leslie Bassett, CD, Pulitzer Prize composition 1966 recorded with Zurich Radio Orchestra. Publications: Editor at Large: Journal of the Conductors' Guild, 1985- and Conductors' Guild Newsletter, 1986-. Contributions to: A Bibliography of Periodical Literature in Musicology and Allied Fields, 1940; Musical Questions and Quizzes, 1942; Author of 200 scripts for weekly music quiz programme, Symphonic Varieties, WNYC, later known as So You Think You Know Music, NBC and CBS, 1937-42. Hobbies: Tennis; Books; Travel; Visual Arts; Architecture. Address: 5 West Chestnut Hill Avenue, Philadelphia, PA 19118, USA.

STERNFIELD Frederick (William), b. 25 Sep 1914, Vienna, Austria. Educator. m. Sophia Jung. Education: Candidate Phil, Vienna University, 1937; PhD, Yale University, 1943; MA, Oxford University, England, 1956. Career: Reader, History of Music. Publications: Goethe and Music, 1954; Music in Shakespearean Tragedy, 1963; Editor: English Madrigal Verse (with Fellowes and Greer), 1967, New Oxford History of Music, volume VII (with Wellesz), 1973, and Music from the Middle Ages To the Renaissance, 1973. Contributions to: Musical Quarterly; Music and Letters; Shakespeare Quarterly; Annales Musicologiques. Memberships: Vice President, Royal Musical Association; Athenaeum. Hobbies: Swimming; Walking. Address: Sotwell Hill House, Brightwell-cum-Sotwell, Near Wallingford, OX10 0PS, England.

STERNKLAR Avraham, b. 21 Oct 1930, Trieste, Italy. Pianist; Composer; Educator. m. Evelyn Katz, 10 Jul 1953, 1 s. Education: Piano with L Kestenberg and composition with P Ben Haim, Israel; Juilliard School of Music, NY, USA, 1949-54; Piano with J Friskin and E Steuermann; Composition with V Giannini; Graduate work, chamber music. Debut: Tel Aviv, Israel. Career: Recitals, broadcasts and performances with Israel Philharmonic, Jerusalem Symphony; Music Correspondent, Israel Broadcasting Service, 1949-52; Film; Siena Pianoforte, numerous concerts throughout USA, Canada and Europe as soloist, chamber music and as soloist with orchestras; Guest performer at Festivals; Lecturer at seminars and workshops; Specialist in Contemporary Music; Premiered many works several of which are now recorded; Faculty Member, Chamber Music Workshop, sponsored by Trianing Orchestra, Long Island and NY University; Appeared in concerts with Mischa Elman, Ruggiero Ricci, Oscar Shumsky, Zvi Zeitlin, Tossy Spivakovsky, Jascha Horenstein, the Hofstra String Quartet and the Bayview Chamber Players; Associate Professor of Piano Performance at Aaron Copland School of Music, Queens College, 1992. Compositions: Educational music, piano sonatinas, violin and piano sonata, cello and piano sonata, clarinet and piano sonata, piano sonata, duo piano works, songs, chamber music, choral works, recorder works, 12 duets for 2 violins. Hobbies: Chess; Gardening; Philately; Travel. Current Management: E Florence. Address: 14 Jerold Street, Plainview, NY 11803, USA.

STEUERMAN Jean Louis, b. 16 Mar 1949, Rio de Janeiro, Brazil. Concert Pianist. m. Monica Laport, 14 Aug 1981, 2 sons. Debut: Rio de Janeiro, 1963. Career: Appearances worldwide with major orchestras with UK debut in 1976; Recent engagements with Royal Philharmonic under Menuhin, Britten's Concerto at Athens Festival, with London Symphony Orchestra under Abbado and Liverpool Philharmonic and Gewandhaus Orchestra under Masur; Played Bach's D minor Concerto at the 1985 Promenade Concerts in London; Tour of Japan in 1989 with Stuttgart Chamber Orchestra, Schumann's Concerto with the Hallé Orchestra; Season 1989-90 season included recital at Salle Gaveau in Paris, Mendelssohn's G minor Concerto with Florida Philharmonic Orchestra and Tippett's Concerto with Helsinki Philharmonic; Further tours of Switzerland, with EC Youth Orchestra under James Judd, Italy and Japan, with the Gustav Mahler Youth Orchestra of Vienna, Czechoslovakia and Ireland; Recitals in San Francisco and Scotland; Chamber music concerts with leading instrumentalists notably at the Menuhin Festival in Gstaad and Kuhmo Chamber Music Festival. Recordings include: Bach Partitas; Italian Concerto; French Overtures; Chromatic Fantasia and Fugue; Capriccio; Preludes and Fugues; Concerti; Scriabin Sonatas 3, 4 and 5. Honours include: 2nd Prize, Leipzig Bach Competition, 1972. Hobbies: Bridge; Poker. Address: c/o London Artists, 3 Wheelers Court, Stratford-upon-Avon, Warwickshire CV37 6HE, England.

STEVENS Denis (William), b. 2 Mar 1922, High Wycombe, Buckinghamshire, England. Musicologist; Conductor. m. (1) Sheila Elizabeth Holloway, 2 sons, 1 daughter, (2) Leocadia Kwasny. Education: Jesus College, Oxford with R O Morris and Egon Wellesz, 1940-42, 1946-49; MA, 1947. Career: Played violin and viola in Philharmonia Orchestra and various chamber music groups, 1946-49; BBC Music Department, 1949-54; Visiting Professor of Music, Cornell University, 1955; Columbia University, New York, 1956; Royal Academy of Music, London; Visiting Professor, University of California, Berkeley, 1962; Pennsylvania State University, 1963-64; Professor of Musicology, Columbia University, 1965-70, 1976-77; Brechemin Distinguished Chair of Music History, University of Washington, Seattle, As Conductor was Co-founder of the Ambrosian Singers and Artistic Director of Accademia Monteverdiana; Tours of Europe and USA making over 70 recordings. Publications: The Mulliner Book: A Commentary, 1952; Tudor Church Music, 1955, revised, 1973; Thomas Tomkins 1572-1656, 1957, revised, 1967; Musicology, 1980; The Letters of Claudio Monteverdi, 1995. Contributions to: Numerous articles on Music. Memberships: Honorary Member, Royal Academy of Music, 1961; Worshipful Company of Musicians, 1961. Honours: Honorary DHL, Fairfield University, Connecticut, 1967; CBE, 1984. Hobbies: Travel; Photography. Address: 3 The Quadrangle, Morden College, London SE3 0PW, England.

STEVENS Risë, b. 1 Jun 1913, NY, USA. Mezzo-Soprano. Education: Juilliard School with Anna Schoen-Rene; Study in Europe with Marie Gutheil-Schoder and Herbert Graf. Career: Sang at Prague Opera in 1936 as Mignon in Thomas's opera, as Strauss's Octavian in 1938 at the Vienna Staatsoper and at the Teatro Colon, Buenos Aires, at Glyndebourne Festival in 1939 as Dorabella and Cherubino, and at Metropolitan Opera, 1938-61 as Mignon, Carmen, Dalila, Orfeo, Ponchielli's Laura and Mussorgsky's Marina, 337 performances in New York and on tour; Sang in Chicago and San Francisco in 1940, Paris Opéra in 1949 as Octavian, and Glyndebourne in 1955 as Cherubino; Retired from stage in 1965 and became Director of the Metropolitan National Company until 1967, and President of the Mannes College of Music, 1975-78; Currently Adviser to the Metropolitan's Young Artists Development Programme. Recordings: Carmen; Le nozze di Figaro; Orpheus and Euridice; Die Fledermaus. Address: c/o Metropolitan Opera, Lincoln Center, New York, NY 10023, USA.

STEVENSON Robert (Murrell), b. 3 Jul 1916, Melrose, NM, USA. Professor of Music. Education: AB, University of Texas, 1936; Piano at Juilliard School of Music, NY; Composition and musicology at Yale University; Private lessons in composition with Stravinsky, 1939, piano with Artur Schnabel, 1940; PhD, Eastman School of Music, Rochester, NY, 1942; Theology degrees, Harvard and Princeton; BLitt, Musicology, Oxford University, UK, 1954. Career includes: Instructor at University of Texas, 1941-43, 1946; US Army Chaplain, 1942-46; Recitals as concert pianist in USA and UK, 1942-47; Lecturer of Church Music at Westminster Choir College, NJ, 1946-49; Music Faculty, 1949-, Professor of Music, 1961-, Faculty Research Lecturer, 1981-, University of California, Los Angeles; Visiting Professor to various universities. Compositions include: Orchestral: Pieces for piano, clarinet and piano, organ, mixed chorus. Publications: Prolific writings especially on Latin American, Spanish and Portuguese music, Italian Renaissance, and Baroque including Music In Mexico, Historical Survey, 1952, Patterns of Protestant Church Music, 1953, Cathedral Music in Colonial Peru, 1959, Spanish Cathedral Music in The Golden Age, 1961, Renaissance and Baroque Musical Sources in the Americas, 1970, Guide to Caribbean Music History, 1975, Antologia da Música Portuguesa 1490-1680, 1984, La Música en Las Catedrales españolas del Siglo de Oro, 1992. Contributions to: Over 400 articles in New Grove Dictionary; Numerous contributions to prestigious journals and books. Honours include: Research and teaching awards and fellowships; Honorary Degrees. Address: Department of Music, University of California, 405 Hilgard Avenue, Los Angeles, CA 90024, USA.

STEVENSON Ronald, b. 6 Mar 1928, Blackburn, Lancashire, England. Composer; Pianist; Writer on Music. m. Marjorie Spedding, 18 Aug 1952, 1 son, 2 daughters. Education: Royal Manchester College of Music, 1945-48; Accademia di Santa Cecilia, Rome, 1955. Debut: Albert Hall Proms in 1972 with own 2nd Piano Concerto. Career: Senior Lecturer in Composition at University of Cape Town, 1963-65; 12 Busoni programmes on Radio 3, 1973; Busoni documentary on BBC TV, 1974. Compositions include: Prelude, Fugue and Fantasy on Busoni's Faust for Piano, 1949-59; Harpsichord Sonata, 1968; Peter Grimes Fantasy for Piano, 1970; 9 Haiku for Soprano, Tenor and Piano, 1971; Violin Concerto, The Gypsy, 1979 commissioned by Menuhin; St Mary's May Songs, song cycle, poems by Chaucer, Tennyson, Rossetti, Joyce for Soprano and String Orchestra premiered in Edinburgh, 1988; Cello Concerto, commissioned by RSNO, 1995; Many settings for voice and piano and for chorus of Scottish folk songs; Transcriptions of works by Purcell, Bach, Chopin, Berlioz, Delius, Britten, Berg and Grainger. Recordings: Stevenson plays Stevenson piano works; Passacaglia on DSCH; Grainger's Salute to Scotland; Cathedrals in Sound; Taken into the Mountains; Piano Concertos 1 and 2; Piano Music from Scotland; The Essence of Busoni; Twentieth Century Operatic Fantasias; Busoni for Two Pianos; In memoriam John Ogdon; Essentially Scottish; In memoriam Benjamin Britten; Eurocantica; Twentieth Century Scottish Choral Music. Publications: Numerous publications for piano; Western Music: A Brief Introduction, 1971; Editor, Bernhard Ziehn: Canonical Studies, 1976; Editor, Time Remembered, a symposium for the 80th birthday of Alan Bush, 1981; The Paderewski Paradoz, 1992; Biography: Ronald Stevenson, a musical biography, by Malcolm MacDonald, 1989. Contributions to: Various publications and many learned journals. Honours: Harriet Cohen International Music Award for 1966 Busoni Centenary radio broadcasts; Fellow, RNCM, 1966; Honorary Fellow, RIAS, 1992; DUniv, Stirling, 1996; HonDMus, Aberdeen, 1998; LLD, Dundee, 1998. Memberships: Royal Society of Musicians, UK; Composers' Guild; Savile Club; Scottish Arts Club. Hobbies: Hillwalking; Reading; Poetry. Address: Townfoot House, Main Street, West Linton, Peebleshire, Scotland, EH46 7EE.

STEWART Donald (George), b. 8 Jan 1935, Sterling, Illinois, USA. Musician (Clarinettist); Composer. 1 daughter. Education: School of Jazz, 1959; BM, Indiana University, 1960; Manhattan School of Music, 1961-62; Studied with Roy Harris, Bernhard Heiden, Gunther Schuller; Clarinet with Russianoff, Cioffi and Moyse. Debut: Boehm Quintette, Carnegie Recital Hall, 1972. Career: Over 1000 chamber music concerts with Boehm Quintette and many other groups, 1955-; Tanglewood, Newport Festival, Marlboro; Composer; Copyist; Administrator; Publisher; Staff Member, New York State Council on Arts, 1970-74; Founder, 1978, Board Member, Treasurer, 1982, Chamber Music America; President, 1987-89, Board Member, 1985-95, Opera North; Founder, Trillenium Music Co, 1988-; Board Member, Vermont Symphony Orchestra, 1989-93. Compositions: August Lions for youth orchestra; Piccolo Concerto; First Blue Symphony for large orchestra; Seven Little Etudes for orchestral woodwind section; A Book of Sliding Things for 8 trombones, tuba and bass; Gesualdo Stanzas for large ensemble; 200-bar Passacaglia; 2 String quartets; Sonata No 1 for horn and piano, No 2 for wind quintet; String Quartet Nos 1 and 2; Saxophone Quartet; Brass Quintet; Duet for Flute and Bass Clarinet; Violin Sonata; Other instrumental and chamber works; Never Leave Me Blue for SSAATTBB, piano and string bass; Green Mountain Christmas Carol, opera, 1993. Recordings include: 3 records with Boehm Quintette; Marlboro Recordings; Music of Arthur Berger. Memberships: American Society of Composers, Authors and Publishers, 1974; AFM, 1951; Music Publishers Association, 1996-. Hobbies: Swimming; Tennis. Address: Box 65, Tunbridge, VT 05077, USA.

STEWART John, b. 31 Mar 1940, Cleveland, Ohio, USA. Tenor. Education: Studied at Yale and Brown Universities and with Cornelius Reid and Frederick Jagel. Debut: Sante Fe in 1968 as Pinkerton. Career: Many appearances at the opera houses of Cincinnati, Milwaukee, Pittsburgh, San Diego, San Antonio, Washington DC, Fort Worth and Philadelphia; New York engagements at the City Opera and the Metropolitan in 1974; Has sung in Europe at Amsterdam and Geneva; Ten year membership of the Frankfurt Opera; Roles have included Mozart's Don Ottavio, Ferrando and Tamino, Puccini's Rodolfo and Cavaradossi, Donizetti's Ernesto, Nemorino and Leicester in Maria Stuarda, Gounod's Romeo, and Vladimir in Prince Igor; Many appearances in concerts and oratorios. Address: c/o Städtische Buhnen, Untermainanalge 11, D-6000 Frankfurt am Main, Germany.

STEWART Murray, b. 1954, London, England. Conductor. Education: Studied at Trinity Hall, Cambridge (organ scholar) and with Daniel Roth. Career: As organist recorded works by Franck and Vierne; Artistic Director of the London Pro Arte Orchestra, conducting works by Sallinen, Szymanowski, Howells, Langlais and Ropartz; Guest engagements with the Philharmonia Orchestra, BBC Concert, Wren Orchestra, Ulster Orchestra, Bournemouth Sinfonietta and East of England Orchestra; Conductor of the East London Chorus, Bristol Choral Society and London Forest Choir; Artistic Director of the Finchley Children's Music Group. Recordings include: Albums of Jean Langlais, Maurice Duruflé and Mozart's Requiem. Address: Helen Sykes Management, Fourth Floor, Parkway House, Sheen Lane, East Sheen, London, SW14 8LS, England.

STEWART Thomas, b. 29 Aug 1926, San Saba, TX, USA. Baritone. m. Evelyn Lear, 1955. Education: Juilliard School of Music, NY, with Mack Harrell. Debut: In 1954 as La Roche in the first US performance of Strauss's Capriccio, at Juilliard. Career: Sang at New York City Opera in 1954 as the Commendatore in Don Giovanni; European career from 1956 at Berlin Städtische Opera, 1957-64; Sang at Bayreuth, 1960-72 as Amfortas, Donner, Gunther, the Dutchman and Wotan in The Ring, Covent Garden, 1960-78 as Escamillo in Carmen, Gunther, Don Giovanni and the Flying Dutchman, Metropolitan Opera, 1966- as Ford in Falstaff, Wagner's Wotan, Kurwenal and Sachs, Debussy's Golaud, Verdi's Iago, Britten's Balstrode, Almaviva and the villains in Les Contes d'Hoffmann; Sang at Santa Fe Opera as Cardillac in the first US performance of Hindemith's opera, at Washington in 1972 in A Village Romeo and Juliet, and at New York City Center in Donizetti's Maria Stuarda; Many appearances with his wife, notably at San Francisco in Eugene Onegin 1971 and Reimann's Lear in 1981; Sang at Maggio Musicale Florence in 1988 as Balstrode in Peter Grimes, Falstaff at Louisville, KY in 1988, San Francisco in 1989, and Boston Opera in 1990 as the Speaker in Die Zauberflöte. Recordings: Die Walküre; Lohengrin; Der fliegende Holländer; Götterdämmerung; Parsifal; Die Kluge; Iphigénie en Aulide; Johnny Spielt Auf; Das Rheingold. Address: c/o Ingpen and Williams Ltd, 14 Kensington Court, London, W8 5DN, England.

STICH-RANDALL Teresa, b. 24 Dec 1927, West Hartford, CT, USA. Soprano. Education: Hartford School of Music; Columbia University, NY. Career: While at college in New York created Gertrude Stein in Thomson's The Mother Of Us All in 1947 and the title role in Luening's Evangeline in 1948; Season 1949-50 sang Priestess in Aida and Nannetta in Falstaff conducted by Toscanini; European debut at Florence in 1951 as the Mermaid in Oberon; Sang at Salzburg Festival in 1952 in concert with arias by Mozart, at Vienna Staatsoper, 1952-, Aix-en-Provence Festival, 1953-71 as Mozart's Pamina, Constanze, Countess, Donna Anna and Fiordiligi; Chicago Lyric Opera debut in 1955 as Gilda; Sang at Metropolitan Opera, 1961-65 as Fiordiligi and Donna Anna; Concert performances of works by Bach and Handel, retired in 1971. Recordings: Così fan tutte; A Life for The Tsar; Falstaff; Aida; Hercules; Orpheus and Euridice; Rodelinda; Le nozze di Figaro; Don Giovanni; Beethoven's 9th Symphony; Brahms Requiem; Mozart's Coronation Mass. Honour: Austrian Kammersängerin, first American to be so honoured, 1962.

STILLER Andrew (Philip), b. 6 Dec 1946, Washington, District of Columbia. USA. Composer. m. Ernestine Steiner, 25 May 1975. Education: BA, Zoology, University of Wisconsin, 1968; MA, 1972, PhD, 1976, Composition, University of New York. Career: Center of Creative and Performing Arts, 1971-73; Decapod Wind Quintet, 1975; Age of Reason Ensemble, 1981; Buffalo New Music Ensemble, 1984-85; Network for New Music, 1986-89; Solo shows, Buffalo, 1979, 1972, 1973, 1976; Works also heard at 2nd and 3rd North American New Music Festivals, 1984, 1985; Consultant, New Grove Dictionary of Opera, 1990; Founder and Director, Kallisti Music Press, 1991-. Compositions: Orchestral: Periodic Table of Elements; Foster Song; Magnification: Procrustean Concerto, 1994; Chamber music: Numerous works including Sonata, Chamber Symphony; Also various pieces, keyboard and vocal. Recording: A Descent into the Maelstrom; The Mouse Singer; A Periodic Table of the Elements; The Water is Wide, Daisy Bell; Sonata a3 pulsatoribus. Publications: Handbook of Instrumentation, 1985; Buffalo Philharmonic Orchestra, 1985. Contributions to: Opus; Philadelphia Inquirer; Buffalo News; Revised New Grove Dictionary of Opera; New Grove Dictionary of Opera; Musical Quarterly; Musical America. Memberships: American Society of Composers, Authors and Publishers. Address: 810 South Saint Bernard Street, Philadelphia, PA 19143, USA.

STILWELL Richard (Dale), b. 6 May 1942, St Louis, MO, USA. Baritone. m. (1) Elizabeth Louise Jencks, 21 Mar 1967, (2) Kerry M McCarthy, 22 Oct 1983. Education: Anderson College, IN; BA, Indiana University School of Music, Bloomington, 1966; Studied voice with F St Leger, P Mathen and D Ferro. Debut: St Louis Grand Opera in 1962 as Silvio in Pagliacci. Career includes: First appearance as Pelléas at New York City Opera in 1970; British debut as Ulysees in Il Ritorno d'Ulisse in Patria, Glyndebourne Festival, 1973; Metropolitan Opera debut in 1975 as Guglielmo; Guest artist at Houston Grand Opera, Paris Opéra, Netherlands Opera, Chicago Lyric Opera, Washington Opera Society and Berlin Deutsche Opera; Appearances as soloist with leading US orchestras; Operatic repertory includes Don Giovanni, Don Pasquale and Eugene Onegin; Created roles in Pasatieri's The Seagull and Ines de Castro and Argento's The Aspern Papers; Sang Malatesta at Dallas in 1989, Sharpless in Madame Butterfly at Lyons in 1990 and at Chicago in 1992; Season 1992 as Mozart's Count at Dallas, Don Alfonso at Seattle and Sharpless with Opéra de Lyon at Symphony Hall, Birmingham; Sang the Doctor in Barber's Vanessa, Dallas, 1994; Washington Opera 1997, in the Ballad of Baby Doe. Recordings: Various. Honours: National Society of Arts and Letters Award, 1963; Young Artists Award, St Louis, 1963; Fisher Foundation Award, Metropolitan Opera Auditions, 1965; Honorary MusD, Knox College, 1980. Membership: American Guild of Musical Artists. Address: c/o Columbia Artists Management Inc, 165 West 57th Street, New York, NY 10019, USA.

STOCK David (Frederick), b. 3 Jun 1939, Pittsburgh, PA, USA. Composer; Conductor. m. Celia Frankel Stock, 19 Oct 1963, 1 son, 2 daughters. Education: BFA, 1962, MFA, 1963, Carnegie Mellon University; MFA, Brandeis University, 1973; Studies at Ecole Normale de Musique, Paris and Berkshire Music Centre, Tanglewood. Career: Conductor with Antioch Chamber Orchestra, 1970-74, Carnegie Symphony, 1976-82, Pittsburgh New Music Ensemble, 1975-; Associate Professor, Professor of Music at Duquesne University; Guest Conductor for Monday Evening Concerts, Res Musica Baltimore, Los Angeles Philharmonic New Music Group, Minnesota Composers Forum, American Dance Festival, American Wind Symphony, Pittsburgh Symphony, Baltimore Symphony and Chautauque Symphony. Compositions include: A Joyful Noise; American Accents; Zohar; Inner Space; Nova; The Body Electric; The Philsopher's Stone; Tekiah; Yerusha; Night Vision; Rockin Ronde; On The Shoulders Of Giants; Quick Opener; Fast Break; No Man's Land; SCAT; Triple Play; Speaking Extravagantly; October Mountain for Solo Trumpet; Wild Card for Solo Trombone; Shadow Music for 5 Percussion and Harp; Numerous other compositions including film, theatre and TV music. Recordings: Quintet for Clarinet and Strings; Inner Space; SCAT; Triple Play; The Philosopher's Stone; Serenade for 5 Instruments; The Particle Zoo, CD. Contributions to: Perspectives of New Music; Music Critic, Boston Globe, 1966-68. Hobbies: Cooking; Reading. Address: 6538 Darlington Road, Pittsburgh, PA 15217, USA.

STOCKER Markus, b. 2 Apr 1945, Basel, Switzerland. Violoncellist. m. Mei-Lee Ong, 21 Mar 1975, 2 daughters. Education: University of Basel; Teachers and soloist diplomas under August Wenzinger, Academy of Music, Basel. Debuts: At London, Paris, Vienna, Berlin, New York, Tokyo, Beijing. Career: Concerts throughout Europe, USA, Far East, Israel and Russia; Performed at Lucerne, Salzburg and Menuhin Festivals, Marlboro and Lockenhaus; Appearances with Rudolf Serkin, Martha Argerich, Sandor Vegh, Gidon Kremer; Professor at Winterhur and Zurich Conservatories; Piano Trio with violinist Wanda Wilkomirska and pianist Werner Genuit, 1985; European premiere, Cello Concerto by Oscar Morawetz, Memorial of Martin Luther King, Zürich, 1995; Professor of Cello, Queensland Conservatorium, Brisbane, 1995-. Recordings: Live recording of Bach Suites; Mendelssohn, Complete Works for Cello and Piano; Swiss composers: Martin and Honegger; Rachmaninov and Shostakovich with Victor Yampolsky, 1994. Honours: 1st Prize, Bloomington, IN, USA, 1972; Grand Prix, Maurice Marechal International Cello Competition, Paris, 1972; Soloists Prize, Association of Swiss Musicians, 1973. Memberships: Association of Swiss Musicians; Indooroopilly LC. Hobbies: Sport; Reading. Address: 11 Tarcoola Street, St Lucia, Brisbane, Qld 4067, Australia.

STOCKHAUSEN Karlheinz, b. 22 Aug 1928, Modrath, near Cologne, Germany. Composer; Teacher. Education: Piano and Theory, Cologne Musikhichschule, 1947-51; Cologne University from 1950; Composition with Frank Martin, 1950; Studied with Messiaen in Paris, 1952-53. Career: Assistant to Herbert Eimert at electronic music studio of West German Radio, Cologne, 1953; Edited Die Riehe magazine for serial music, from 1954; Head of composition courses at Darmstadt, 1957-; Lecture concerts, USA and Britain, 1958; Visiting professor, several US universities; Founded Cologne Course for New Music, 1963, teaching composition until 1968; Professor of Composition, Cologne Musikhochschule, 1971-; Dienstag aus Licht premiered at Lisbon, 1992; Freitag aus Licht at Leipzig, 1996. Compositions include: Kreuzspiel for obeo, clarinet, piano, 3 percussion, 1951; Formel for 29 instruments, 1951; Punkte for orchestra, 1952; Kontrapunkte for ensemble, 1952; Klavierstücke I-XI, 1952-56; Zeitmasze for wind quintet, 1956; Gruppen for 3 orchestras, 1957; Gesang der Jünglinge for voice and tapes, 1956; Zyklus for percussion, 1959; Refrain for ensemble; Carré for 4 choruses and 4 orchestras, 1960; Kontakte for piano, percussion, 4-track tape, 1960; Momente for soprano, 4 choruses, ensemble, 1961-64; Mikrophone I, II, for electronics, 1964-65; Mixtur for 5 orchestras, sine-wave generators, 4 ring modulators, 1964-67; Telemusik for 4-track tape, 1966; Hymnen for 4-track tape, 1967; Stimmung for voices and ensemble, 1968; Kurzwellen, for electronics and 4 short-wave radios, 1968; Auf den sieben Tagen, 15 pieces for various instrumental groups, 1968; Spiral for soloist and short-wave receiver, 1969; Stop for instrumental ensemble, 1969-73; Mantra for 2 pianos, woodblock, 2 ring modulators, 1970; Sternklang, parkmusic for 5 groups, 1971; Trans for orchestra and tape, 1971; Am Himmel wandre ich... for soprano and baritone, 1972; Intervall for piano duo, 1972; Inori for 1-2 soloists and orchestra, 1974; Atmen gibt das Leben for chorus, 1974; Herbstmusik for 4 players, 1974; Musik im Bauch for 6 percussion, 1975; Sirius for soprano, baritone, ensemble, 1977; Jubiläum for orchestra, 1977; Operas Donnerstag aus Licht, 1981, Samstag aus Licht, 1984, Montag aus Licht, 1982; Dienstag, 1992; Freitag, 1996. Publications: Texte zu eigenen Werken, zur Kunst Anderer, Aktuelles, 1963; Ein Schlüssel für Momente, 1971; Texte zur Musik 1963-70, 1971; Texte zur Musik 1970-77, 1978; Texte zur Musik, Komposition, 1977-84, 1988; Texte zur Musik 1977-84, Interpretation, 1988. Address: Kettenberg 15, D-51515 Kuerten, Germany.

STODLE Tori, b. 1 Jul 1942, Oslo, Norway. Pianist. m. Hakon Stodle, 6 Oct 1975, 1 son, 1 daughter. Education: Studied with Robert Riefling in Oslo, Jurgen Uhde in Stuttgart, and Adele Marcus in New York. Debut: Oslo in 1970 and New York in 1990. Career: Recitals in Norway, UK, Germany, Russia, Italy, Netherlands, Denmark and USA; Several TV and radio programmes for Norwegian Broadcasting; Guest artist at major music festivals including Chamber Music Festival at Tromso, Bergen Festival and North Norwegian Festival; Piano Soloist for world premieres of Ketil Vea's Piano Concertos Nos 1 and 3; Music from The Top Of The World, recital of music by 19th and 20th century Norwegian composers sponsored by various Norwegian organisations, Weill Recital Hall, Carnegie Hall, New York City, 1990; The Dream of A Sound, TV portrait, 1991; Promotes new music; Works dedicated to her by several Norwegian composers; Currently Associate Professor of Piano, North Norwegian Music Conservatory, Tromso. Recordings: Music From The North, LP; Music From The Top Of The World, CD. Honour: Northern Light Prize, 1991. Memberships: 2 Norwegian Music Associations; European Piano Teachers Association. Address: Fogd Dreyersgt 21, 9008 Tromso, Norway.

STOIANOV Konstantin, b. 1950, Russia. Violinist. Education: Studied at the Antwerp Conservatory from age 9 and in Berlin and Wurzburg. Career: Numerous solo appearances with leading orchestras; Radio broadcasts in Belgium, France and Italy; Leader of the Royal Philharmonic Orchestra of Flanders: Co-Leader of the London Philharmonic from 1990; Professor at the International Menuhin Academy at Gstaad. Hobbies: Cooking; Swimming; Walking in countryside. Address: c/o London Philharmonic Orchestra, 35 Doughty Street, London, WC1N 2AA, England.

STOJANOVIC Milka, b. 13 Jan 1937, Belgrade, Yugoslavia. Soprano. Education: Studied at the La Scala Opera School and with Zinka Milanov. Career: Sang with Belgrade National Opera from 1960, notably at Edinburgh Festival in 1962 and at Oslo and Lausanne in 1968 and 1971; Further appearances at Graz, 1962, Metropolitan Opera, 1967-68, Vienna, Bari, Munich, Cologne and Barcelona, 1970-71; Opera and concert engagements in Denmark, England, Hungary, Hamburg, Frankfurt, Dresden, West and East Berlin, Zurich, Oslo, Copenhagen, Helsinki, Rome, Venice, Bologna, Palermo, Syracuse, Valencia, Athens, Ankara, Cairo, Caracas, Petrograd, Odessa, Kiev, Baku, Perm, Sofia, Budapest, Bucharest, and Czechoslovakia; Also festival appearances at Prague Springdays and Salzburg; Roles have included Verdi's Aida, Desdemona and Amelia in Un Ballo in Maschera, Leonore, Mimi, Liu, Mozart's Countess, La Gioconda, Marenka, Santuzza and Tatiana; Verdi's Simon Boccanegra, Traviata and Vespri Siciliani, Madame Butterfly, Fidelio, Lohengrin, Tchaikovsky's Pique Dam, Borodin's Prince Igor. Recordings include: Several albums. Address: c/o Narodno Pozoriste, Francuska 3, 11000 Belgrade, Serbia.

STOJANOVIC-KUTLACA Svetlana, b. 2 May 1957, Skopje, Macedonia. Harpsichordist. m. Djuro Kutlaca, 23 Feb 1980, 1 daughter. Education: Completed Secondary Music School, 1975; BA, Piano, 1981, BA, Harpsichord, 1991, MA, Harpsichord, 1993, Faculty of Music Art, Belgrade; BSc, Electrical Engineering, Belgrade, 1982; Masterclasses with Cristine Daxelhofer, Germany, 1987, 1988, Huguette Dreyfus, France, 1989, 1990, Colin Tilney, England, 1996; Curso de perfeccionamiento with Genoveva Galvez, Madrid, 1989-90; Specialisation with Paul Simmonds, Brighton, England, 1996, 1997. Debut: Harpsichord recital, Real Conservatorio Superior da Musica, Madrid, Apr 1990. Career: Performed J S Bach's D minor Concerto, 5th Brandenburg Concerto, and Rameau's Pièces de clavecin en concerts, Belgrade, 1991; Cycle of 4 concerts and lectures on Improvisation, Folklore, Description, Polyphony, Belgrade, 1992; Over 50 harpsichord recitals, Yugoslavia, 1992-97; Harpsichord recitals, Aranjuez and Alcala de Henares, Spain, 1993, Brighton and Lewes, England, 1996; Repertoire includes works by Frescobaldi, Couperin, Rameau, Scarlatti, Soler, J S Bach, Balbastre; Teaches harpsichord, Josip Slavenski High School, Belgrade. Recordings: Vivaldi's Four Seasons, CD, 1993; Balbastre's Premier Livre de Clavecin, tape, 1994; For Radio Belgrade: Cycle of 4 concerts and lectures, Improvisation, Folklore, Description, Polyphony, 1992, Bach Goldberg Variations, 1995, Frescobaldi, Picchi, Froberger, F Couperin, D Scarlatti, M Kuzmanovic, 1997. Publication: The elements of Spanish folklore music in Domenico Scarlatti's harpsichord sonatas, MA thesis. Contributions to: Development of Harpsichord, in Continuo, 1993; Domenico Scarlatti, in Continuo, 1994. Honour: Matica Serbiana Diploma, Novi Sad, 1994. Memberships: Serbian Association of Musicians, Belgrade, 1986-; Early Music Studio, Belgrade, 1991-. Hobby: Swimming. Address: Branicevska 11, 11000 Belgrade, Yugoslavia.

STOKER Richard, b. 8 Nov 1938, Castleford, Yorkshire, England. Composer; Author; Painter; Poet. m. (2) Dr Gillian Patricia Watson, 10 July 1986. Education: Huddersfield School of Music and School of Art, 1953-58; Royal Academy of Music, with Lennox Berkeley, 1958-62; Composition with Nadia Boulanger, Paris, 1962-63; Also private study with Britten, Benjamin, Fenby and Truscott. Career: Debut with BBC Home Service 1953; Conducting debut, 1956; National and International Eisteddfords, Wales, 1955-58; Concerts as pianist at Purcell Room, Leighton House, BBC Radio 3, BBC TV, Channel 4, BBC Radio 4; Various Jazz Venues; Assistant Librarian, LSO, 1962-63; Professor of Composition, Royal Academy of Music, 1963-87; Tutor, RAM, 1969-76; Composition Teacher, St Paul's School, 1972-74; Magdalen College, Cambridge, 1974-76; Magistrate, Inner London Commission, 1995-. Compositions: Operas include: Johnson Preserv'd (3 acts), Thésèse Raquin; Piano Concerto; 3 Overtures: Antic Hay, Feast of Fools; Hergic Overture; Passacagalia, Serenade, Petite Suite; 3 String Quartets; Wind Quintet; Sextet; Nocturnal; 3 Violin Sonatas; Monologue; 2 Piano Sonatas; Partita for Clarinet and Piano; 3 Piano Trios; Festival Suite; Various Choral Works: Benedictus; Ecce Homo, Proverbs; Song Cycles: Music that Brings Sweet Sleep, Aspects of Flight, Aspects 1 in 3, Yeats Poems; Organ Works: Partita, Little Organ Book, 3 Improvisations, Symphony; Three Pieces, Contemporary Organ Technique; Two Preludes; Music for Guitar, 8 works; Chinese Canticle, The Scholars (Yeats), Piano Sonata No 2, for Eric Parkin; A York Suite, for Piano; Piano Suite; Piano Variations; Five Nocturnes; Partita for mandolin and harp; Films and theatre music. Recordings: Sonatina for Clarinet and Piano, CD, 1992; 3 String Quartets, Gaudeamas, Miniature String Trio; Sonata for Guitar Duo, Concerto for Two Guitars - Gaudeamus; Aspects of Flight, Piano Variations, Chorale for Strings; Improvisation for guitar; Song-Cycle; Featured Composer at major music festivals; Composition Teacher to Paul Patterson, q.v. Joe Jackson, Malcolm Singer, the late Paul Reade and others. Publications: Open Window-Open Door, autobiography; Words without Music (outposts); Between the Lines; Portrait of a Town, filmed 1983); Tanglewood, 1994; Diva - A Novel, 1995; Collected Short Stories, 1997; 3 plays. Contributions to: The Guardian; Records and Recording; Books and Bookmen; Performance; The Magistrate; Editor, Composer, 1969-80. Honours: Mendelssohn Scholarship, 1962; Dove Prize RAM, 1962; Associate Royal College of Music, 1962; Associate, 1965, Fellow, 1971, Royal Academy of Music; Justice of the Peace, 1995-; 3 Editor's Awards, National Library of Poetry, USA, 1995-97; Nominated Man of the Year, American Biographical Institute. Memberships: Executive Committee, Composer's Guild, 1969-74, 1974-80; Association of Professional Composers, 1977-; Royal Society; PRS, 1962-; MCPS, 1970; Founder Member, RAM Guild Committee and Treasurer; The Magistrate's Association; U3A; Founder Member, The Atlantic Council of the UK; Euro-Atlantic Group; PEN International; English PEN. Current Management: Ricordi and Co Ltd; Association of Professional Composers-Promotions Committee; RAM Guild - Executive Committee. Address: c/o Ricordi and Co Ltd, 210 New Kings Road, London SE3 9RU, England.

STOKES Eric (Norman), b. 14 Jul 1930, Haddon Heights, NJ, USA. Composer. Education: Studied at Lawrence College, New England Conservatory and with Dominick Argento at University of Minnesota, PhD 1964. Career: Teacher at University of Minnesota, 1961-88, founding an electronic music programme and Minnesota Moving and Storage Warehouse Band, 1971. Compositions include: Operas: Horpsfal, 1969, HAPP or Orpheus In Clover, 1977, The Jealous Cellist And Other Acts Of Misconduct, 1979, Itaru The Stonecutter, for children, 1982, Apollinia's Circus, 1985, We're Not Robots You Know, puppet opera, 1986, The Further Voyages Of The Santa Maria, 1990;

Orchestra: A Center Harbour Holiday, 1963, On The Badlands-Parables, 1972, The Continental Harp And Band Report, 1975, The Spirit Of Place Among The People, 1977, Captions On The War Against Earth, 1980, Prairie Drum, 1981, Concert Music for Piano and Orchestra, 1982, The Greenhouse Effect, 1983, Stages, 1988; Prophet Bird, 1992; Chamber: Trio for Clarinet, Cello and Piano, 1955, Expositions for Ensemble, 1970, Circles In A Round for Piano and Tape, 1972, Wind Quintet, 1981, Brazen Cartographies for Brass Quintet, 1988, The Lyrical Pickpocket for Ensemble, 1990; Vocal: Smoke And Steel for Tenor, Men's Chorus and Orchestra, 1958, revised, 1989, The River's Minute By The Far Brook's Year for Narrator, Chorus and Orchestra, 1981, Peppercorn Songs for Chorus, Piano and Ensemble, 1984, Firecho for Voices and Percussion, 1987, Inversnaid, acappella, 1991; Pied Beauty, chorus, 2 trumpets, 2 horns, timpani, 1997; Out of the Cradle Endlessly Rocking, chorus; Wind Symphony, soprano and baritone solos, narrator, 1997; Solo Songs. Current Management: Horspfal Music, 1611 West 32nd Street, Minneapolis, MN 55408, USA.

STOLBA K Marie, b. 22 Apr 1919, Burlington, Iowa, USA. Musicologist; Professor Emerita; Violinist; Composer. Education: AA, Burlington Junior College, Iowa; BA, Monmouth College, Illinois; MA, University of Northern Colorado, Greeley; PhD, University of Iowa; Post Doctoral studies in Russian at Fort Hays State College, Kansas, and in Violin with Robert Slaughter. Career: Professor and Coordinator of Music History, Music Literature, Musicology and Strings, Indiana University, Purdue University, Fort Wayne, Indiana; Visiting NEH Scholar, Otterbein College, 1994; Distinguished Lecturer in Music, Colorado Christian University, 1995, 1996, 1997, 1998; Lectures given in Berlin and Vienna. Compositions: And Jesus Came...for Voice and Piano; Christmas Story for Voice and Piano; Homage, choral anthem with Violin and Organ; Reflections, for voice and piano, 1996; What is Music?, chorus, flute and piano, 1997. Recordings: Edited 2 boxed sets, (13 CD recordings) to accompany The Development of Western Music: An Anthology, 2nd edition of 2 volumes, 1994; 2 boxed CD sets to accompany The Development of Western Music: An Anthology, 1997. Publications: A History of the Violin Etude to about 1800, 2 volumes, 1968, revised 1979; Translator, JS Bach: Sonaten und Partiten fur Violine Allein, 1982; Editor, A B Bruni: Caprices and Airs varies, Cinquante Etudes, 1982; The Development of Western Music: An Anthology, 3 volumes, 1990, 2nd edition, 2 volumes, 1994; The Development of Western Music: A History, 2nd edition, 1994, 3rd edition, 1997. Contributions to: Journal of the American Musicological Society; Editor, The College Music Society National Newsletter, 1994-97; Sigma Alpha Iota journal, Pan Pipes; IPFW quarterly, ArtScene. Honours: DHL, honoris causa, Monmouth College, Illinois, 1990; Hall of Achievement, Monmouth College, 1995. Memberships: The College Music Society; American Musicological Society; Sigma Alpha Iota. Address: 5621 Joyce Avenue RR12, Fort Wayne, IN 46818, USA.

STOLL David (Michael), b. 29 Dec 1948, London, England. Composer. m. Erika Eigen, 25 July 1980, 1 stepson. Education: Worcester College, Oxford, 1967-70; MA (Oxon); Royal Academy of Music, London, 1970-71. Career: Music Director, Greenwich Young People's Theatre, 1971-75; Subsequently freelance as Composer and Music Producer working in concert music, theatre and media. Compositions: Music for television, radio and film; Piano Quartet, 1987; Sonata for 2 Pianos, 1990; Piano Sonata, 1991; String Trio, 1992; Fanfares and Reflections, 1992; String Quartet, 1994; All the World's a Stage, 1994; Monument, 1995; Teller of Tales (co-composer), musical. Recordings: Innovations, 1989; Chamber Music, 1993. Honours: Hadow Open Scholarship in Composition to Worcester College, Oxford, 1967. Memberships: Association of Professional Composers; Performing Right Society; MCPS. Hobbies: Philosophy; Language; Walking. Address: 4 Cranford Avenue, London N13 4PA, England.

STOLTZMAN Richard (Leslie), b. 12 Jul 1942, Omaha, NE, USA. Clarinettist. m. Lucy Chapman. Education: BA, Ohio State University, 1964; MM, Yale University, 1967; Teachers included Donald McGinnis, Kalmen Opperman and Keith Wilson. Debut: Metropolitan Museum, NY. Career includes: Taught at the California Institute of the Arts, Valencia, 1970-75; Program Director, 1971-74, and currently Board Member of Western Region of Young Audiences; Co-founder with Peter Serkin, Ida Kavafian and Fred Sherry of chamber group, Tashi, 1973; Mozart concert debut at Carnegie Hall, 1976; Performed with Amadeus Quartet at the Aldeburgh Festival, 1978, and New York Philharmonic with James Levine, 1979; Performances with the Cleveland, Emerson, Guarneri, Tokyo and Vermeer Quartets; Concert programmes with transcriptions and commissioned pieces; Debut at the Promenade Concerts in London with Mozart's Concerto, 1989. Compositions: Edition of Schubert's Arpeggione Sonata, Sonatinas in A minor, D385 and D384; Saint-Säens's Romanza for Clarinet and Harp. Recordings include: World premiere Toru Takemitsu's Fantasma/Cantos with BBC Wales; Brahms and Weber Quintets with Tokyo Quartet; Mozart, Beethoven and Brahms Trios with Yo Yo Ma and Emmanuel Ax; Schubert and Schumann with Richard Goode; Laser Disc, Vienna Konzerthaus, 1791, 1891, 1991 - Mozart, Brahms, Takemitsu, with Rafael Frubeck de Burgos; Finzi Concerto and Bagatelles with Guildhall Concerti for Richard Stoltzman by Einar Englund, Lukas Foss, William T McKinley with Berlin Radio Orchestra under Lukas Foss. Honours: Avery Fisher Prize, 1977 and 1986; Yale University Order of Merit; Grammy Award, 1983; Emmy Award for Copland Concerto Video. Hobbies: Pastry Chef; Baseball. Address: c/o Frank Salomon Associates, 201 West 54th Street 4C, New York, USA.

STONE Carl, b. 10 February 1953, Los Angeles, USA. Composer; Electronic Music Performer. Education: Studied with Morton Subotnick at the California Institute of the Arts, Valencia (BFA 1975). Career: Music Director of KPFK Radio at Los Angeles, 1979-81; Director of Meet the Composer/Californ ia from 1985; President of the American Music Center 1992-95; Many commissions including Dance for electronics from Aichi-ken Cultural Centre, Japan, 1995; Worldwide Performer of Electronics. Compositions include: LIM, for tape, 1975; Maneeya, for tape, 1976; Thoughts in Stone, for tape, 1980; Spalding Gray's Map of LA, soundtrack, 1984; Ho Ban for piano and electronics, 1984; Samanluang, 1986; Audible Structure, 1987; Hop Ken, and Gadberry's, both for live electronics and percussion, 1991; Dur-Pars, soundtrack, 1993; Mae Ploy for string quartet and electronics, 1994; Sudi Mampir, 1995; Wei-fun, for audio samples and computer-generated images, 1996; Music for the Noh Project for electronic and Noh musicians, 1996. Address: c/o ASCAP, ASCAP Building, One Lincoln Plaza, New York, NY 10023, USA.

STONE William, b. 1944, Goldsboro, NC, USA. Baritone. Education: Studied at Duke University and University of Illinois. Career: Sang at first in concert and oratorios; Opera debut as Germont in La Traviata in 1975 at Youngstown, OH; European debut in 1977 at Spoleto Festival in Napoli Milionaria by Nino Rota, and New York City Opera debut in 1981; Sang at Lyric Opera Chicago in 1978 as Adam in the premiere of Penderecki's Paradise Lost and again at La Scala in 1979, at the Maggio Musicale Florence in 1979 as Wozzeck, as Orestes in 1981, at Opéra Comique in Paris in 1984 as Purcell's Aeneas, Aix-en-Provence in 1987 as Ford in Falstaff; Further guest engagements at Trieste, Rome, Naples and Brussels as Germont, Paolo and Simone in Simon Boccanegra; Many appearances at the New York City Opera including Mozart's Count in 1990 and sang at Santa Fe in 1980 in the US premiere of Schoenberg's Von Heute auf Morgen; Sang at Wexford Festival in 1989 as the Templar in Marschner's Der Templer und die Jüdin; Other roles include Rossini's Figaro, Enrico, Malatesta, Verdi's Ezio and Posa, Zurga, Albert in Werther, Golaud, Alfio and Eugene Onegin; Sang the title role in the US stage premiere of Busoni's Doktor Faust, New York City Opera, 1992; Sang Wozzeck at the 1994 Spoleto Festival; Concert repertoire includes the St Matthew Passion, Messiah, Missa Solemnis, Beethoven's 9th and Ein Deutsches Requiem. Recordings: Mussorgsky's Salammbo; Hindemith's Requiem; Walton's Belshazzar's Feast; Robert Ward's Arias and Songs; Bach B minor Mass; Mahler's Symphony No 8; Schubert's Mass in G; Bach's Magnificat; Mozart's C minor Mass; Video of Messiah with Robert Shaw. Address: c/o Columbia Artists Management Inc, Arbib-Treuhaft Dn, 165 West 57th Street, New York, NY 10019, USA.

STOROJEV, Nikita, b. 9 Nov 1950, Harbin, China. Singer (Bass). Education: Studied at Tchaikovsky Conservatoire, Moscow. Career: Bolshoi Theatre, Moscow, from 1978, as Pimen, Prince Igor, Gremin, Basilio and fafner; Appearances from 1983 at Vienna, Paris, Rome, Florence, Berlin, London, New York, San Francisco and Toronto; Repertoire has included Verdi's Zaccaria, Ramphis and Grand Inquisitor, Sarastro, Mephistopheles, Boris Godunov and Ivan Khovansky; Sang in Prokofiev's War and Peace at San Francisco, Rimsky's Mozart and Salieri at the Komische Oper in Berlin and Montreal, 1992; Rimsky's Ivan the Terrible at the Rome Opera, 1993, followed by Verdi Requiem at the Festival Deauville and Tchaikovsky's Iolanthe at Dresden Festiva; Song Recitals with David Ashkenazy and concert features with the Songs and Dances of Death at Festival Hall, 1991 and Gorecki's Beatus Vir at New York. Recordings include: Shostakovich 13th and 14th Symphonies; War and Peace; Gorecki's Beatus Vir and Songs of the Forest by Shostakovich; Mozart and Salieri. Honours include: Diaposon d'Or and Choc de la Musique. Address: c/o Athole Still Ltd, Foresters Hall, 25-27 Westow Street, London SE19 3RY, England.

STOTT Kathryn (Linda), b. 10 Dec 1958, Nelson, Lancashire, England. Concert Pianist. m. Michael Ardon. Education: Yehudi Menuhin School; Royal College of Music, London. Debut: Purcell Room, London, 1978. Career: Performances at the Elizabeth Hall, Wigmore Hall, and Windsor and Gstaad Festivals; Piano recital for Thames TV; Purcell Room recital (Grieg and Chopin), 1997. Recordings: For Dutch, German and BBC radio; CD of Fauré's piano works. Honours: Martin Scholarship, 1976; Churchill Scholarship, 1979; Croydon Symphony Award; Chappell Medal; Silver Medal, Royal Amateur Orchestral Society, 1979. Hobbies: Films; Riding.

STOUT Alan (Burrage), b. 26 Nov 1932, Baltimore, MD, USA. Composer; Professor. Education: BS, Johns Hopkins University, 1954; Postgraduate studies at University of Copenhagen, 1954-55; MA, Music and Swedish Language, University of Washington, 1959; Studied composition with Henry Cowell, Peabody Conservatory. Career: Teacher, 1963-76, Professor, 1976-, Northwestern University School of Music; Visiting Lecturer at Johns Hopkins University, 1968-69, Royal Academy of Music, Stockholm, 1973, Berkshire Music Center, 1974. Compositions: Orchestral: Intermezzo for English Horn, Percussion and Strings, 1954, Pieta for Strings, 1957, 4 Symphonies, 1959-71, Serenity for Solo Cello or Bassoon, Percussion and Strings, 1959, Movements for Violin and Orchestra, 1962, Fanfare For Charles Seeger, 1972, Nimbus for 18 Strings, 1979, Pilvia, 1983; Chamber: 10 String Quartets, 1952-62, Quintet for Clarinet and String Quartet, 1958, Toccata for Saxophone and Percussion, 1965, Cello Sonata, 1966, Recitative, Capriccio and Aria for Oboe, Harp and Percussion, 1970, Suite for Saxophone and Organ, 1973, Concertino for Clarinet and Chamber Group, 1978, Meditation for Tenor Saxophone and Organ, 1982, Brass Quintet, 1984; Piano pieces and vocal music. Memberships: American Composers Alliance; Arnold Schoenberg Institute; International Webern Society; Alban Berg Society; College Music Society; Sonneck Society. Address: 2309 Grey Avenue, Evanston, IL 60201, USA.

STOYANOV Boyko Stoykov, b. 4 May 1953, Sliven, Bulgaria. Composer; Conductor; Pianist; Music Teacher. m. Rikako Akatsu, dec, 2 daughters. Education: Bulgarian State Academy of Music, Sofia, 1974-75; Frederick Chopin Academy of Music, Warsaw, Poland, 1975-82; Toho Gakuen School of Music, Tokyo, Japan, 1981-82. Career: Conductor, Varna Philharmonic Orchestra, 1983-; Iwaki Symphony Orchestra, Japan, 1984-; Private music school, Iwaki Musica, 1984; Tokyo debut with Tokyo Symphony Orchestra, 1986; Conducted with Tenerife Symphony Orchestra, 1991-; Kaguyahime, opera for children, premiered in Vienna, 1993; Broadcasts on Bulgaria Radio Varna, Japan Fukushima Central Television, TV V and NHK, Radio RFC, Poland Radio, Austria Television. Honours: 1st Prize, Folk Song Section, Bulgarian National Folk Music Competition, 1959; Varna Prize for Popular Song, 1965; 2nd Prize for Conducting and Arrangement, Bulgarian National Folk Music Competition, 1972; Distinction, Wroclaw Arrangement Competition, 1979; International Composers Competition, 1985; International Electroacoustic Music Competition, 1990. Memberships: Piano Teachers National Association, Japan; Japan Computer Music Association. Address: 35 Baba, Nishiki-machi, Iwaki City, Fukushima 974, Japan.

STRAESSER Joep, b. 11 Mar 1934, Amsterdam, Netherlands. Composer. Education: Studied musicology at Amsterdam University, 1952-55, and with Ton de Leeuw at Amsterdam Conservatory. Career: Lecturer at Utrecht Conservatory, 1962-89. Compositions include: Opera, Uber Erich, performed in concert at the Royal Conservatory in The Hague, 1987; 22 Pages after John Cage for Ensemble and Voices, 1965; Summer Concerto for Oboe and Chamber Orchestra, 1967; Missa for Chorus and Wind Instruments, 1969; Enclosures for Wind and Percussion, 1970; Intersections V-2 for Bass Clarinet and Piano, 1975; Fusian A Six, symphonic music, 1980; Signals And Echoes for Bass Clarinet and Orchestra, 1982; Verzauberte Lieder for Chorus and Orchestra, 1986; Triplum for String Trio, 1986; Motetus for Chorus, 1987; Chamber Concerto I, 1991; Symphony No 3 for Orchestra, 1992; Gedanken Der Nacht (RM Rilke) for Mezzo Soprano, 1992; Chamber Concerto No 2, 1993; To The Point for 2 Marimbas, 1993; Chamber Concerto No 3, 1993. Publications: Number of essays on musical subjects among which his analyses of works of Anton Webern are prominent; Article on composer Jacques Bank, 1988-89. Honours include: Matthjs Vermeulen Prize for Uber Erich M, 1988. Address: Vereniging BUMA, PO Box 725, 1180 AS Amstelveen, Netherlands.

STRAHAN Derek, b. 28 May 1935, Penang, Malaysia. Composer. Actor. Education: BA, Cambridge University, 1956. Career: Commissions from Band Association of New South Wales, Sydney Ensemble, Sydney Youth Orchestra, and others; Writer, Director and Actor for films and television. Compositions include: Clarinet Quintet: The Princess, 1980; The Quay for orchestra, 1986; Piano Trio in F minor, 1987; Sydney 200 for orchestra, 1988; China Spring for cello and piano, 1989; Two Suites for cello, 1991; Atlantis for flute and piano, 1992; Atlantis Variations for piano, 1993; Eden in Atlantis for soprano, flute and piano, 1994; Voodoo Fire for clarinet, percussion and keyboards, 1995; String Quartet The Key. Publication: Beethoven: Sexuality of the Hero, and The Secret Life and Loves of Ludwig van Beethoven (Sydney Music Diary, and Morning Herald). Address: c/o APRA, 1A Eden Street, Crows Nest, NSW 2065, Australia.

STRAKA Peter, b. 22 Feb 1950, Zlin, Czechoslovakia. Tenor. Education: Studied in Dusseldorf, Cologne and Munich. Career: Sang at St Gallen, 1978-79, and Zurich Opera from 1979; Guest appearances at Basle, Berne, Staatsoper Berlin, Hanover, Marseilles, Volksoper Vienna, Opéra- Comique Paris, Palermo and Orange; Visits to Dresden and Lausanne and Schwetzingen Festivals with the Zurich Company; Sang in the Niklaus Harnoncourt-John Pierre Ponnelle Monteverdi cycle at Zurich and has appeared there and elsewhere as Mozart's Idamante and Tamino, Nemorino, Wagner's Froh and Steuermann, Rodolfo and Narraboth in Salome; Sang Jacquino in a concert performance of Fidelio at the Festival Hall, 1990, Alwa in Lulu at Théâtre du Châtelet in Paris, 1991; Metropolitan debut in 1991 in Katya Kabanova; Sang Sobinin in A Life for the Tsar at Zurich, 1996. Recordings include: Marzio in a video of Mozart's Mitridate conducted by Harnoncourt. Address: c/o Opernhaus Zurich, Falkenstrasse 1, CH-8008 Zurich, Switzerland.

STRATAS Teresa (Anastasia Strataki), b. 26 May 1938, Toronto, Canada. Opera Singer. m. Tony Harrison. Education: Studied with Irene Jessner, 1956-59; Graduate, Music Faculty, University of Toronto, 1959. Career: Winner, Metropolitan Opera auditions in 1959; Major roles in opera houses worldwide including Mimi in La Bohème, Tatiana in Eugene Onegin, Susanna in The Marriage of Figaro, Nedda in Pagliacci, Marenka in The Bartered Bride, Violetta in La Traviata, Rusalka, and Jennie in Mahoganny; Created the title role in the completed version of Alban Berg's Lulu at Paris Grand Opera, 1979; Recital artist and film appearances; Salome, Lulu, Paganini, Zarewitsch, Eugene Onegin, Kaiser von Atlantis, La Traviata, 1983; Sang Lulu at Brussels in 1988, Mimi at Boston in 1989, Suor Angelica, Lauretta and Giorgetta in Il Trittico at the Metropolitan in 1989, Marie Antoinette in the premiere of Corigliano's The Ghosts of Versailles at Metropolitan Opera in 1991, and Mélisande at Chicago in 1992; Double bill of Il Tabarro and Pagliacci to open the new season at the Met, 1994. Honours: Decorated Order of Canada; Named Performer of The Year, Canadian Music Council, 1979; 3 Grammy Awards with total of 7 Grammy nominations; Winner of Drama Desk Award for Leading Broadway Musical Actress, 1986; Tony Nomination for 1986. Address: c/o Metropolitan Opera Company, Lincoln Center Plaza, New York, NY 10023, USA.

STRAUCH Jacek, b. 1953, London, England. Baritone. Education: Studied at the Royal College of Music and National Opera Studio in London. Debut: Kent Opera in 1978 as Rigoletto. Career: Sang in opera at Wurzburg, 1980-82, and Saarbrucken, 1982-85; Guest appearances in Modena and Pretoria, South Africa in 1985; Berne Opera in 1987 as Wozzeck, English National Opera in 1988 as Alfio and as Jaroslav Prus in The Makropoulos Case; Season 1988-90 as Amfortas, Iago and the Hoffmann Villains at Brunswick, Kurwenal at Saarbrucken and Gunther in Götterdämmerung; Other roles include Mozart's Count; Broadcast engagements in Germany, England and Norway; Sang Pacheco in the premiere of Macmillan's Ines de Castro, Edinburgh, 1996. Honours include: Winner, Kathleen Ferrier Competition, 1978; Prizewinner, Belvedere International at Vienna, 1984. Address: c/o English National Opera, St Martin's Lane, London, WC2, England.

STRAUSSOVA Eva, b. 7 Jun 1934, Cheb, Czechoslovakia. Soprano. Education: Studied with Elisa Stunzner and with Rudolf Dittrich at the Dresden Opera Studio, 1956-59. Debut: Landestheater Dessau in 1959 as Helmwige in Die Walküre. Career: Sang at Dessau until 1963 notably as Eva in Die Meistersinger, then joined the Staatsoper Berlin in major roles including Wagner's Elisabeth and Gutrune, Amelia in Un Ballo in Maschera, Donna Anna, Turandot, Elektra, Fiordiligi, Leonore and Katerina Ismailova; Guest engagements in Zurich, Berne, West Germany, Russia and Austria; Sang Isolde at Aachen Opera. Recordings: Various albums.

STRAYER Gene Paul, b. 17 Aug 1942, York, Pennsylvania, USA. Organist; Choirmaster; Professor. Education: BA, American University, Washington, DC, 1964; AM, University of Chicago Divinity School, 1968; SMM, School of Sacred Music, Union Theological Seminary, New York City, 1972; PhD, University of Pennsylvania, 1991; Organ Studies with Ralph Scott Grover, Adam Hamme, Harlan J Laufman, Alec Wyton. Career: Chapel Organist, American University, Washington, DC, 1960-64; Organist, Choir Director, Advent Lutheran Church, New York City, 1970-72; Assistant Professor, University of Colorado, Boulder, 1972-78; Minister of Music, 1st Congregational Church, Boulder, 1973-78; Founder, Director, Boulder Bach Festival, 1974-76; Lecturer, University of Pennsylvania, 1980-86; Seminary Organist, Adjunct Professor, Lancaster Theological Seminary, Lancaster, Pennsylvania, 1986-96; Organist, Choirmaster, Trinity United Church of Christ, York, Pennsylvania, 1986-96; Minister of Music, St Rose of Lima Roman Catholic Church, York, Pennsylvania, 1996-; Founder, Director, York Ecumenical Choral Society, 1996-; Recitals: Washington National Cathedral; Cathedral of St John the Divine, New York City; New York Cultural Center, New York City; University of Colorado; Drexel University; University of Pennsylvania. Publication: The Theology of Beethoven's Masses, 1991. Contributions to: Union Theological Seminary Theological Review; New Mercersburg Review; New York Times; Chrysalis; Annual Meeting, American Academy of Religion. Honours: Appleby Fellowship, 1963-64; Ringenwald

Award, 1963; Woodrow Wilson Fellowship, 1964-65; Woodrow Wilson Teaching Internship, 1969-70; Teaching Fellowship, University of Pennsylvania, 1979-83; Dean's Award, Distinguished Teaching, University of Pennsylvania, 1981. Membership: Antiochian Orthodox Church. Address: 605 Maryland Avenue, York, PA 17404, USA.

STREATFIELD Simon, b. 3 May 1929, Windsor, Berkshire, England. Violist; Conductor. m. Elizabeth Winship, 2 daughters. Education: Eton College; Royal College of Music, London. Career: Principal Viola, Sadler's Wells Opera, 1953-55, London Symphony Orchestra, 1956-65 and Vancouver Symphony Orchestra, Canada, 1965; Assistant Conductor, 1967, Associate Conductor, 1972-77, Music Director and Conductor of the Vancouver Bach Choir, 1969-81; Season 1970-71 included concerts with the City of Birmingham Symphony, the Royal Choral Society, the BBC and with the Vancouver Bach Choir in Holland; Visiting Professor at Faculty of Music, University of West Ontario, 1977-81; Conductor, Regina Symphony Orchestra, Canada, 1981-84; Conductor, Manitoba Chamber Orchestra, 1982-; Conductor, Quebec Symphony Orchestra, 1984-; Has also conducted the National Arts Centre Orchestra in Ottawa, the Danish Radio Symphony, the Oslo Philharmonic and the Belgian Radio Symphony. Recordings include: Telemann Viola Concerto; Berlioz Harold en Italie. Hobbies: Squash; Cricket; Ornithology.

STREET Tison, b. 20 May 1943, Boston, MA, USA. Composer; Violinist. Education: Harvard University; Composition with Leon Kirchner and David Del Tredici; Violin with Einar Hansen. Career: Composer in Residence for Marlboro Music Festival, 1964-66 and 1972; Rome Prize Fellowship, 1973; National Endowment Grant to work at Experimental Music Studio, Massachusetts Institute of Technology, 1978; Associate Professor at Harvard University, 1979-82. Compositions: Adagio in Eb, 1977; Monsalvat, 1980; String Quartets 1 and 2; String Quintet; Chorals from the Northeast for Piano Solo; John Major's Medley for Guitar. Recordings: String Quartet, 1972; String Quintet, with Marcus Thompson, 1974. Honours: National Institute, American Academy of Arts and Letters Award, 1973; Brandeis Creative Arts Award, 1979. Membership: Society of Fellows, Harvard University. Address: 28 Lawrence Street, Boston, MA 02116, USA.

STREHLE Wilfried, b. 1940, Stuttgart, Germany. Violist. Education: Studied at Stuttgart and Detmold Hochschulen. Career: Violist with Sudfunk-Sinfonia-Orchester at Stuttgart; Soloist with Chamber Orchestra Tibor Varga until 1971 then Principal Violist with Berlin Philharmonic Orchestra; Co-Founded Brandis String Quartet in 1976 with chamber concerts in Paris, Munich, Hamburg, Milan, Tokyo and London, and appearances with Wiener Singverein and Berlin Philharmonic; Festival engagements at Edinburgh, Tours, Bergen, Salzburg, Lucerne, Florence and Vienna; Co-premiered the 3rd Quartets of Gottfried von Einem and Giselher Klebe in 1981 and 1983, and the Clarinet Quintet of Helmut Eder in 1984. Recordings include: Albums in the standard repertory from 1978; Recent releases of Quartets by Beethoven, Schulhoff, Weill and Hindemith, and the Schubert String Quintet. Address: c/o Berlin Philharmonie, Mattäukirchstrasse 1, D-1000 Berlin 30, Germany.

STREIT Kurt, b. 1959, Itazuke, Japan. Tenor. Education: Studied at the University of New Mexico with Marilyn Tyler. Career: Member of apprentice programmes at San Francisco and Santa Fe, also at the Texas Opera Theater; Appearances with the Milwaukee Skylight Comic Opera and in Dallas; European career with the Hamburg Staatsoper singing in operas by Mozart, Donizetti and Rossini; Guest appearances at Schwetzingen in 1987, Aix-en-Provence in 1989, Salzburg in 1989 and at Glyndebourne as Tamino in the 1990 production of Die Zauberflöte by Peter Sellars; Has also sung at opera houses in Vienna, Munich, Brussels, Leipzig, Dusseldorf and San Francisco (1990); Covent Garden debut in 1992 as Ferrando; Concert engagements with the London Symphony, Orchestre National de France, Leningrad Philharmonic, Hamburg Staatsorchester and the English Chamber Orchestra; Promenade Concerts in London in a 1990 concert performance of Die Zauberflöte; Sang Orfeo in Haydn's Orfeo ed Euridice at South Bank, London, 1997; Belmonte at Covent Garden, 1996. Recordings include: Gluck's Echo et Narcisse; Ferrando in Cosi fan tutte (also at Glyndebourne in 1990), with Daniel Barenboim and the Berlin Philharmonic; Die Entführung aus dem Serail. Address: c/o Ingpen and Williams Ltd, 26 Wadham Road, London SW15 2LR, England.

STRELLING Frank Denys, b. 9 Oct 1926, Kingston-upon-Hull, England. Teacher, Piano and Violin. Education: Associate, Guildhall School of Music. Career: Appearances with Royal Ballet and Opera, British Broadcasting Corporation Programme Monitor; Music Staff, Guildhall School of Music Junior Exhibition Scheme & Inner London Education Authority. Compositions: 2 String Quartets. Membership: Incorporated Society of Musicians. Hobbies: Photography;

Theatre; Motoring; Reading. Address: 13 Kemble Drive, Bromley Common, Bromley, Kent, England.

STRINGER Mark, b. 9 Dec 1961, Warrington, Cheshire, England. Conductor; Organist; Lecturer; Examiner in Music. Education: Chester Cathedral with Roger Fisher; Royal Northern College of Music studying with Ronald Frost, Dr Gillian Weir; Institute of Education, University of London; GMus RNCM (Hons), FTCL, ARCO (CHM), ARCM, PGCE. Debut: Conducting debut: St Martin's for Royal Gala Performance; Organ Recital Debut, Chester Cathedral. Career: Assistant Organist, St Martin-in-the-Fields, London, 1985-89; Organist and Master of the Music, St Martin-in-the-Fields, 1989-; Adjunct Professor in Music, James Madison University, Virginia, 1990-; Fellow and Examiner, Trinity College, London, 1990; Performances for television and radio. Compositions: St Martin's Service, Mass for Choir and Congregation; Were You There When They Crucified My Lord; Nocturne for piano; Exam pieces for Trinity College, London. Recordings: CD: From Darkness to Light, conducting, directing choir and choral scholars of St Martin-in-the-Fields and Solo Organ Piece. Membership: Fellow, Royal Society of Arts; National Liberal Club. Hobbies: Cricket; Food and wine; Theatre; Jazz; Country walks. Address: The Old Bakery, 1 Deweys Lane, Ludgershall, Wiltshire SP11 9QU, England.

STROHM Reinhard, b. 4 Aug 1942, Munich, Germany. Musicologist. Education: Studied musicology, Latin and Italian literature at University of Munich, Scuola Normale Superiore Pisa, and Technical University Berlin with Carl Dahlhaus; PhD, Berlin (TU), 1971. Career: Part-time work for Repertoire International des Sources Musicales, 1964-70; Editor of the Richard-Wagner-Gesamtausgabe, Munich, 1970-81; Lecturer in Music at King's College, University of London, 1975-83; Professor of Music History at Yale University, 1983-89; Reader then Professor of Historical Musicology at King's College, London, 1990; Director, Institute of Advanced Musical Studies, King's College, London, 1991-. Publications include: Italienische Opernarien des Frühen Settecento, 1976; Die Italienische Oper im 18 Jahrhundert, 1979; Music in Late Medieval Bruges, Oxford, 1985; Essays on Handel and Italian Opera, Cambridge, 1985; The Rise of European Music 1380-1500, Cambridge, 1993. Honours include: Dent Medal of the Royal Musical Association, 1977; FBA, 1993. Address: Institute of Advanced Musical Studies, King's College, Strand, London, WC2R 2LS, England.

STRUMMER Peter, b. 8 Sep 1948, Vienna, Austria. Bass-Baritone. m. Linda Roark. Education: Studied at Cleveland Institute of Music. Debut: Atlanta City in 1972 as Mozart's Antonio. Career: Opera engagements with Minnesota Opera Company and at Santa Fe and San Francisco; Sang at Heidelberg and Linz, 1978-85; Metropolitan Opera debut in 1985 as Beckmesser; US and European appearances as Don Alfonso at Miami, Mozart's Bartolo, Dulcamara, and Don Magnifico at Baltimore, and Bartolo in Il Barbiere di Siviglia at Toronto in 1992; Season 1989-90 as Baron Zeta in Die Lustige Witwe, Fabrizio in La Gazza Ladra at Philadelphia, the Music Master at Milwaukee and Faninal at Montreal; Sang at New Orleans in 1991 as Melitone in La Forza del Destino. Address: c/o Canadian Opera Company, 227 Front Street East, Toronto, Ontario, Canada, M5A 1E8.

STUART Debra, b. 1969, Scotland. Mezzo-Soprano. Education: Studied at the Royal Scottish Academy and the Guildhall School of Music. Career: Opera appearances at Covent Garden, English National Opera and with the English Touring Opera; Roles include Mozart's Annius and Dorabella, Rosina, Meg Page and Britten's Hermia; Concerts with Frans Bruggen and the Songmakers' Almanac; Sang in A Midsummer Night's Dream at Aldeburgh in 1995 and festival engagements at Aix-en-Provence and Bordeaux; Further repertoire includes Les Nuits d'Ete (BBC); Sang Luca in the premiere of Woolrich's In the House of Crossed Desires, Cheltenham, 1996. Address: c/o Ron Gonsalves Management, 7 Old Town, Clapham, London, SW4 0JT, England.

STUBBS Stephen, b. 1951, Seattle, Washington, USA. Chitarrone and Archlute Player; Ensemble Director. Career: Director of Tragicomedia, ensemble performing in the Renaissance and Baroque repertory; Concerts, Britain and leading European early music festivals; Gave Stefano Landi's La Morte d'Orfeo at the 1987 Flanders Festival; Francesca Caccini's La Liberazione di Ruggiero dall'Isola d'Alcina at the 1989 Swedish Baroque Festival, Malmö; Conducted Monteverdi's L'Incoronazione di Poppea for Norrlands Opera in Umeå, Sweden, 1993; Conducted Monetverdi's L'Orfeo at Netherlands Opera, Amsterdam, 1995. Compositions: Pegasus and the Griffin, 1-hour chamber opera for 3 singers and chamber ensemble, libretto by Peter Bockström, performed Malmö, 1994. Recordings: Solo lute recordings, David Kellner's XVI. Auserlesene Lauten-Stücke; J S Bach and S L Weis Lute Suites; With Tragicomedia, Proensa (Troubadour songs); My Mind to Me a Kingdom (Elizabethan ballads); A Musicall Dreame (duets from Robert Jones 1609 collection); Orpheus I Am (masque and theatre music by Robert Johnson and William Lawes);

Sprezzatura (Italian instrumental music); Il Ballo dell'Ingrate (and other theatrical music by Monteverdi); The Notebook of Anna Magdalena Bach; Le Canterine Romane (music for 3 sopranos by Luigi Rossi); Concert programmes including all recorded repertoire and other 17th and 18th century music including Orpheus Britannicus (best of Purcell's secular music for up to 5 singers, violins and oboes); Purcell, Songs of Welcome and Farewell, Tragicomedia, 1995. Contributions to: L'Armnonia Sonora: continuo orchestration in Monteverdi's L'Orfeo, to Early Music, 1994. Current Management: Robert White Artist Management, England. Address: Wigmore Hall (Tragicomedia), Wigmore Street, London W1, England.

STUCKY Steven, b. 7 November 1947, Hutchinson, KS, USA. Composer; Conductor. Education: BM, 1971, Baylor University; MFA, 1973, DMA, 1978, Cornell University (with Karel Husa); Conducting with Daniel Sternberg. Career: Faculty of Cornell University from 1980; Chairman of the music department at Cornell, 1991-; Composer-in-Residence with the Los Angeles Philharmonic, 1989-91. Compositions include: Four Bagatelles for string quartet, 1969; Duo for viola and cello, 1970; 4 symphonies, 1972, 1974, 1976, 1978; Two Holy Sonnets of Donne for mezzo, oboe and piano, 1982; Sappho Fragments for mezzo and ensemble, 1982; Voyages, for voice and wind orchestra, 1984; Double Concerto, for violin, oboe and chamber orchestra, 1985; Concerto for Orchestra, 1987; Threnos for wind ensemble, 1988; Son et Lumière for orchestra, 1988; Angelus for orchestra, 1989; Serenade for wind quintet, 1989; Impromptus for orchestra, 1991; Four Poems of A R Simmons for baritone and ensemble, 1992; Funeral Music for Queen Mary, arrangement of Purcell, 1992; Ancora, for orchestra, 1994; Fanfares and Arias for wind ensemble, 1994; Concerto for 2 flutes and orchestra, 1994. Publications include: Lutoslawski and his World, 1981. Honours include: Fellowship from the Guggenheim Foundation (1986) and others. Address: c/o ASCAP, ASCAP Building, One Lincoln Plaza, New York, NY 10023, USA.

STUDER Cheryl, b. 24 Oct 1955, Midland, MI, USA. Soprano. Education: Studied in USA and with Hans Hotter in Vienna. Career: Concert engagements in USA then sang with the Munich Staatsoper from 1980, notably as Marenka in The Bartered Bride; Darmstadt, 1983-85 in Mozart roles and as Bizet's Micaela, Strauss's Chrysothemis and Wagner's Irene and Eva; Berlin Deutsche Opernhaus from 1985; Bayreuth debut in 1985 as Elisabeth in Tannhäuser, returning in 1988 as Elsa in Lohengrin; Paris Opera in 1986 as Pamina in Die Zauberflöte; Covent Garden, 1987-88 as Elisabeth and Elsa; Sang Sieglinde and the Empress in Die Frau ohne Schatten at La Scala in 1987; Metropolitan debut in 1988 as Micaela; Season 1989 sang Chrysothemis at Salzburg and Vienna, Lucia at Philadelphia; Opening night of season at La Scala, 1989 as Hélène in I Vespri Siciliani; Sang Elsa at Vienna in 1990 opposite Domingo; Deutsche Oper Berlin in 1990 as Salome; Sang Mozart's Elettra at the 1990 Salzburg Festival, Donna Anna at Vienna; Season 1992-93 as Lehar's Giuditta at Vienna Volksoper, the Empress in Die Frau ohne Schatten and Madame Cortesa in Il Viaggio a Reims at Salzburg; Covent Garden in 1994 as Aida; Sang Beethoven's Leonore at the 1996 Salzburg Festival. Recordings: Zemlinsky's Der Zwerg; Sieglinde in the Haitink recording of Die Walküre; Aida and Tannhäuser; Salome; Guillaume Tell; I Vespri Siciliani; Attila; La Traviata; Die Zauberflöte; Lohengrin; Lucia di Lammermoor. Address: c/o Deutsche Oper Berlin, Richard Wagnerstrasse 10, D-1000 Berlin, Germany.

STUDER Ulrich, b. 27 August 1945, Bern, Switzerland. Singer (Baritone). Education: Studied at Bern Conservatory and Musikhochschule Munich. Career: Many appearances at Opera Houses in Italy, Netherlands (The Hague), Austria (Innsbruck), Australia and Czechoslavakia; Concert and Broadcast engagements in Switzerland, Germany and France, notably in Bach's Sacred Music and contemporary works by Burkhard, Milhaud and Huber; Recitals featuring German Lieder and French Chansons; Opera performances at Bern, 1979-83, and at Basle, Lausanne and Munich; Roles have included Morales in Carmen, Belcore, Malatesta, Valentin, Creonte in Haydn's Orfeo, Masetto, Suppé's Boccaccio and Monteverdi's Orfeo. Recordings Include: Cantatas by Bach and Charpentier; Messe des Morts by Gilles; Cantatas by Vivaldi; Elviro in Handel's Serse; Lully's Armide; Erode in Stradella's San Giovanni Battista. Address: c/o Opern-andKonzertsänger, Mittelstrasse 14-15, D-06108 Halle/Saale, Germany.

STUDNICKA Vladimir, b. 24 Aug 1935, Composer; Music Director. 2 daughters. Education: Completed Composition studies, 1957, and Classical Guitar Performance, 1966, Conservatory of Music. Debut: Suite for Orchestra performed by Janácek Philharmonic Orchestra in 1957. Career: Teacher at Music School, 1961-75; Music Director, Radio Ostrava, 1975-; Works as a Conductor; Established and conducted the Beskydska Muzika Harmonic Folk Orchestra. Compositions: All kinds especially concert pieces for harmonic orchestras, adaptations of folk songs of the Janácek region, and chamber and symphony works including: Suite for Orchestra, 1957; The May Dance, recorded, Prague Radio, 1973; The Beskydy Nocturno, Radio Ostrava, 1984; The Ondra's Dance, Radio Ostrava, 1985; Salut JV Stich-Punto for 12 Horns, Radio Ostrava, 1986. Recordings include: Radio recordings of many smaller pieces. Publications: The Round, 1985; The Song Of The Rising Sun by Wilhelm Halter, 1990; Slazsky Dance Musikvarlag Rundal, 1993. Hobbies: Tourism; Nature; Picking Mushrooms. Address: ul Prof Jana Soupala 1607, 70800 Ostrava-Poruba, Czechoslovakia.

STULBERG Neal (Howard), b. 12 Apr 1954, Detroit, MI, USA. Conductor; Pianist. m. Leah Shahmoon, 12 Jul 1987. Education: BA, Harvard College, 1976; MMus, University of Michigan, 1978; Postgraduate studies at Juilliard School, 1979-80. Career: Conductor, Massachusetts Institute of Technology Symphony Orchestra, 1980-82 and with Young Musicians' Foundation Debut Orchestra, Los Angeles, 1981-84; Exxon Arts Endowment Assistant Conductor, Los Angeles Philharmonic Orchestra, 1983-85; Music Director, New Mexico Symphony Orchestra, Albuquerque, 1985-93. Honours: Seaver - National Endowment for the Arts Conductors Award, 1988. Current Management: KMI Management, 1 Lincoln Plaza, 1900 Broadway, 2nd Floor, New York, NY 10023, USA. Address: Santa Monica, CA, USA.

STUMPF Peter Daniel, b. 16 Jan 1963, Syracuse, New York, USA. Musician (Cellist). Education: BM, Curtis Institute of Music, 1985; Artist Diploma, New England Conservatory, 1990; Teachers: David Wells, Orlando Cole, Lawrence Lesser. Debut: Boston Symphony Orchestra, Symphony Hall, Boston, 1979. Career: Participant at Marlboro Music Festival, 1985-; Tours with Music From Marlboro; Member, Philadelphia Chamber Music Society Players, 1994-; Piano Trio with Mitsoko Uchida and Mark Steinberg, 1995-; Solo recitals at the Jordan Hall, Boston, 1989-90, Phillips Collection, Washington DC, 1991, 1994, 1996, Corcoran Gallery, Washington DC, 1997; Solo appearances at: Aspen Festival, Colorado, 1984; Boston Philharmonic, 1989; Virginia Symphony, 1992; National Repertory Orchestra, 1992; Philadelphia Orchestra Chamber Music Series, 1990-; Chamber Music with Wolfgang Sawallish in Carnegie Hall and Concertgebouw; Teaching Chamber Music at the Curtis Institute of Music, 1994-. Honours: Second Prize, Evian International String Quartet Competition, 1983; First Prize, Aspen Concerto Competition for Cello, 1984; First Prize, Washington International Competition, 1991; Serving on Board of Trustees for Yellow Barn Festival, Putney, Vermont, USA, 1995-. Address: 400 South Sydenham Street, Philadelphia, PA 19146, USA.

STUR Svetozar, b. 21 February 1951, Bratislava, Slovakia. Conductor; Composer. m. Nadezda Sturova, 12 November 1977. Education: Graduate, conservatoire in Bratislava, 1972; Graduate, Academy of Music & Performing Arts, Bratislava, 1977. Debut: Conducting the Work Taras Bulba by L Janacek with the Slovak Philharmonic Orchestra, Bratislava, 1977. Career: Artistic Head of Orchestra, Slovak Folklorist Ensemble, Lucnica, 1972-77; Assistant Conductor, Slovak Philharmonic Orchestra, Bratislava, 1977-79; First Conductor, Cairo Conservatoire Orchestra, 1979-80; Conductor, Symphony Orchestra of Czech Radio, Bratislava, 1980-81; Recording Own Compositions for Films and Television with Fisyo Orchestra, Prague, 1980-; Assistant Conductor, Slovak National Theatre, Bratislava, 1980-87; Conductor, Slovak State Folk Ensemble, Bratislava, 1988-90; Freelance Composer, 1991-. Compositions: 18 Full-length Feature Films; 24 Television Feature Films; 17 Documentary Films; 13 Animated Films; 53 Television Plays; 54 Drama Plays. Recordings: 5 Records Conducting; 2 Records with Own Music; 1 Record with Own Film Music. Membership: Association of Slovak Theatre Professionals. Address: Grosslingova 28, 811 09 Bratislava, Slovakia.

STURROCK Kathron, b. 17 Jul 1948, Bournemouth, England. Pianist. Education: Studied at the Royal College of Music and with Alfred Brendel in Vienna; Further study with Mstislav Rostropovitch in Moscow. Career: Concert and TV appearances throughout Europe and in North America, India and Australia; Regular performances for the BBC and concerts in the major London halls; Founded the chamber music ensemble, The Fibonacci Sequence; Has taught at Morley College, the Royal College of Music, Royal Academy of Music and the Birmingham School of Music; Artist in Residence at the Brisbane Conservatoire, 1987; British Council tour of Oman in 1989; BBC recitals include Schubert's Wanderer Fantasy, Beethoven Op 109, and Rawsthorne Ballade; Prom debut in 1994 in Rawsthorne 2 Piano Concerto with Piers Lane. Recordings include: Bliss Viola Sonata with Emanuel Vardi; Beethoven Spring Sonata; Brahms Violin and Viola Sonatas; Cello Sonatas by Beethoven, Schnittke, Shostakovich and Kabalevsky; Songs by Rebecca Clarke with Patricia Wright. Honours: Sofia International Opera Competition, as accompanist; Martin Musical Scholarship Fund and The Countess of Munster Award, RCM. Address: 81 Lacy Road, London, SW15 1NR, England.

SUART Richard (Martin), b. 5 Sept 1951, Blackpool, England. Singer (Baritone). m. Susan Cook, 1981, 2 sons, 1 daughter. Education: Sang in choir of St John's College; Studied at Royal Academy of Music. Career: Roles in contemporary opera include Doctor in Punch and Judy, Hummel in Ghost Sonata for Opera factory; Old Man in King Priam, Astrologer in The Burning Fiery Furnace for Kent Opera; Dad, Café Manager in Greek, for English National Opera; Old Musician in Broken Strings (Param Vir) for Netherlands Opera; Chaplinoperas (Mason) in Frankfurt, Cologne and Lisbon with Ensemble Modern; Eight Songs for a Mad King, in London, Paris, Gelsenkirchen, Milan, Helsinki and Strasbourg, also televised; Stan Stock in Playing Away (Mason) for Opera North; Barabashkin in Cheryomushki for Pimlico Opera; Other roles include Frank in Die Fledermaus, Benoit and Alcindoro in La Bohème for English National Opera; Taddeo in Italian Girl for Buxton festival; Savoy Opera roles include Lord Chancellor in Iolanthe, Duke of Plaza-Toro in The Gondoliers, Major-General in The Pirates of Penzance for D'Oyly Carte; King Gama in Princess Ida, Ko-Ko in The Mikado for English National Opera; Jack Point in The Yeomen of the Guard for Welsh National Opera; Presents one-man show, As A Matter of Patter; Sang in Broken Strings by Yir at the Almeida Theatre, 1996. Recordings include: The Mikado, Pirates of Penzance and HMS Pinafore with Welsh National Opera under Charles Mackerras on Telarc label; Television appearances include The Vampyr, Greek and The Empress. Honour: ARAM, 1991. Current Management: Magenta Music International, 4 Highgate High Street, Highgate Village, London N6 5JL, England. Address: Yardley Bank, 29 Yardley Park Road, Tonbridge, Kent TN9 1NB, England.

SUBEN Joel (Eric), b. 16 May 1946, New York City, USA. Symphony Conductor; Composer; Professor. m. (1) Judith Ann Gundersheimer, 21 Oct 1979, divorced 1985, (2) Linda Rodgers, 30 Jul 1993. Education: BMus, Distinction, Eastman School of Music, 1969; MFA, 1974, PhD, 1980, Brandeis University; Hochschule Mozarteum, Salzburg; Certificate in Orchestral Conducting; Private conducting study with Jacques-Louis Monod, 1973-77. Career includes: Music Director and Permanent Conductor of Peninsula Symphony of VA, 1982-87; Guest Conductor includes: Silesian Philharmonic Orchestra, Poland, 1986 and 1994, New Jersey Composers Orchestra, 1987-, Polish Radio National Symphony Orchestra, 1993, Janacek Philharmonic Orchestra, 1994 and 1996, Slovak Radio Symphony Orchestra, Bratislava, 1995 and North Bohemian Philharmonic Orchestra, Czech Republic, 1996; Director of Orchestras, College of William and Mary, VA, 1983-92; Artistic Director, Brooklyn Heights Music Festival, 1986; Guest Lecturer, NY Philharmonic Pre-Concert Lecture Series, 1989-; Music Director, Composers Chorus, 1992-; Music Advisor, Wellesley Philharmonic, MA, 1993-. Compositions include: Gesualdo Triptych, for String Orchestra, 1984; Symphony in Old Style for Orchestra, 1987; Concerto Classico for Flute and Small Orchestra, 1991; Breve Sogno for Large Orchestra, 1993. Recordings include: Many CDs released from 1993- with one as composer in 1994. Publication: Debussy and Octatonic Pitch Structure, University Microfilms, 1980. Current Management: Linda Rodgers Associates, USA and ArsKoncert, Czech Republic. Address: c/o Linda Rodgers Associates, 628 Bloomfield Street, Hoboken, NJ 07030, USA.

SUBOTNICK Morton, b. 14 Apr 1933, Los Angeles, CA, USA. Composer; Clarinettist; Conductor; Teacher. m. Joan La Barbara, 18 Dec 1979, 1 son. Education: BA, Composition, University of Denver, 1958; MA, Mills College, 1960. Career: Various appearances as Clarinettist and Conductor; Teacher at Mills College, 1959-66 and New York University, 1966-69; Co-founder and Director of San Francisco Tape Music Center, 1961-65; Music Director for Ann Halprin Dance Company, 1961-67 and Lincoln Center Repertory Theater, 1967-68; Co-Director of Composition Program and the Center for Experiments in Art, Information and Technology at California Institute of Arts, Valencia, 1969-; Composer-in-Residence at Deutscher Akademischer Austauschdienst, West Berlin, 1979-80; Various visiting professorships. Compositions include: Orchestral: Lamination for Orchestra and Tape, 1968, Before The Butterfly, 1975, Place, 1978, Liquid Strata for Piano, Orchestra and Electronics, 1982, In Two Worlds, concerto for Saxophone, Electronic Wind Controller and Orchestra, 1987-88, All My Hummingbirds Have Alibis for Flute, Cello, Midi Piano, Midi Mallets and Computer, CD-ROM, 1991, first piece of music composed specifically for CD-ROM; Jacob's Room, chamber opera premiered at the American Music Theater Festival, Philadelphia in 1993; Various mixed-media scores; Tape Pieces; Chamber music; Vocal scores; Instrumental works with electronics; Incidental music. Recordings: Several. Honours: Fellow, Institute for Advanced Musical Studies, Princeton University, 1959, 1960; National Endowment for the Arts Grant, 1975; American Academy and Institute of Arts and Letters Award, 1979; Brandeis University Creative Arts Award, 1983; Many commissions. Address: 121 Coronado Lane, Santa Fe, NM 87501, USA.

SUBRTOVA Milada, b. 24 May 1924, Lhota, Kralovice, Czechoslovakia. Opera Singer (Dramatic Soprano). m. Jan Hus Tichy. Education: Business School, Prague; Private studies with tenor Zdenek Knittl, Prague. Debut: As Giulietta in Offenbach's

Les Contes d'Hoffmann, Theatre 5 May, Prague. Career: Opera and concerts, Czechoslovakia including National Theatre Prague and Czech Philharmonic, Prague, Italy, Poland, Rumania, Bulgaria, England, Yugoslavia, Switzerland, Spain, Iceland, Germany, Netherlands, Austria; Recitals, songs and opera arias of romantic composers, Radio Prague; Roles included: 3 female roles (Hoffmann); Norma, Dona Anna (Don Giovanni), Konstanze (Serail), Fiordiligi (Cosi fan tutte), Pamina (Die Zauberflöte), Gilda (Rigoletto), Violetta (La Traviata), Elisabeth (Don Carlo), Abigail (Nabucco), Mimi (La Bohème), Butterfly, Tosca, Turandot, Santuzza (Cavalleria), Charpentier's Louise, Marguerite (Faust), Micaela (Carmen), Woman (Poulenc's La Voix Humaine), Ännchen and Agathe (Der Freischütz), Elsa (Lohengrin), Sieglinde (Die Walküre), Tatyana (Eugene Onegin), Marenka (Bartered Bride), title roles in Libuse, Rusalka, Jenufa, many others; Concerts include Beethoven's 9th; Bach, B minor mass; Martinu, Gilgamesh; Honnegar, Jeanne d'Arc; Janácek, Glagolitic Mass; Schoenberg, Gurreleider; Mahler's 4th; Dvorák, Stabat mater; Berlioz, Damnation of Faust. Recordings: Portrait recital; Complete operas: At Well, Blodek, conductor Frantisek Skvor, 1959; Rusalka, conductor Zdenek Chalabala, 1960; The Devil's Wall, conductor Zdenek Chalabala, 1961; Libuse, conductor Jaroslav Krombholc. Honours: 1st Prize, International Vocal Competition, Prague Spring Festival, 1954. Address: Belohorska 70, 16900 Prague 6, Czech Republic.

SUHONEN Antti, b. 5 November 1956, Nurmes, Finland. Singer (Bass-Baritone). Education: Studied at Sibelius Academy and at the National Opera Studio, Helsinki and at the International Opera Studio, Zurich; Masterclasses with Charles Farncombe, Professor Herbert Brauer and Victoria de los Angeles. Career: Made debut at Zürich, 1986, engaged at Karlsruhe, 1987-91, and at Helsinki from 1991-; Made guest appearances at Dresden, Wiesbaden, Hanover and Mannheim and also at Munich State Opera, Berlin State Oera, Essen and Royal Opera in Copenhagen; Karlsruhe, 1989, in shared premiere of Graf Mirabeau by Siegfried Matthus; Appearances at Helsinki and elsewhere as Mozart's Leporello, Masetto, Figaro and Alfonso, Sparafucile, Dulcamara, Basilio, Varlaam and Rangoni in Boris Godunov, Melitone in La Forza del Destino, Méphistopélès in Gounod's Faust; Sang Klaus in premiere of Linkola's Elina, Helsinki, 1992 and Fruitseller in Bergman's The Singing Tree in Helsinki, 1995; With Berlin State Opera, Wagner's Ring, Kupfer and Barenboim, 1996; Savonlinna Festival, 1992, as Don Fernando in Fidelio; Bluebeard in Bartok's Bluebeard Castle, 1994; Alongside his opera career he frequently appears as soloist in numerous concerts. Recordings: Rautavaara: Thomas, 1986, Sampo, 1995; Mozart: Die Zauberflöte, 1988; Pacius: Kung Karls Jagd, 1991; Sang Ossip in The Palace, by Sallinen at the 1996 Savonlinna Festival. Address: c/o Finnish National Opera, Helsinginkatu 58, SF 00260 Helsinki 18, Finland.

SUITNER Otmar, b. 16 May 1922, Innsbruck, Austria. Conductor; Musical Director. m. Marita Wilckens. Education: Innsbruck Conservatory; Salzburg Mozarteum, 1940-42, under Ledwinka; Studied Conducting with Clemens Krauss. Debut: Landestheater, Innsbruck, 1942. Career: Musical Director, Remscheid, Germany, 1952-57; Musical Director of the Pfalz Orchestra, Ludwigshafen, 1957; Guest appearances in Vienna, Munich, Hamburg and Berlin; Chief Conductor of the Dresden Staatsoper and Staatskapelle, 1960; Musical Director of the Staatsoper, East Berlin, 1964-71; Conducted the premieres of Dessau's Puntilla (1966), Einstein (1974) and Leonce und Lena (1979); Tours with the Berlin company to Paris, Warsaw, Cairo and Lausanne; Bayreuth Festival, 1964-69, Der fliegende Holländer, Tannhäuser and Der Ring des Nibelungen; Engagements at the San Francisco Opera from 1969; Honorary Conductor of the Tokyo NHK Symphony Orchestra, 1973; Professor, Hochschule für Musik, Vienna, 1977-. Recordings include: Figaro, Cosi fan tutte, Salome, Die Entführung, Il Barbiere di Siviglia; Palestrina with Peter Schreier, 1989. Honours: Commendatore, Gregorius Order, 1973; Austrian Ehrenkreuz für Wissenschaft und Kunst, 1982. Address: c/o Widerhofer Platz 4/48, A-1090 Vienna, Austria.

SUK Josef, b. 8 Aug 1929, Prague, Czechoslovakia. Violinist. m. Marie Polakova. Education: Conservatory of Music in Prague; Prague Academy, 1951-53. Debut: 1940. Career: Western European engagements from 1948 in Paris and Brussels; Leader of Prague Quartet, 1951-52; Joined Suk Trio, 1952; Leader of orchestra at Prague National Theatre, 1953-55; Soloist with Czech Philharmonic Orchestra, US debut 23 Jan 1964 with the Cleveland Orchestra; British debut, 1964 at the Promenade Concerts playing Mozart and Dvorak; Formed duo with Zuzana Ruzickova in 1963 and a trio with Janos Starker and Julius Katchen, 1967-69; Duos with Jan Panenka, piano; Founded Suk Chamber Orchestra, 1974; Played at the Bath Festival, 1991. Recordings: Numerous on major record labels. Honours: Grand Prix du Disque Paris, 1960, 1966, 1968, 1974; State Prize, 1964; Artist of Merit, 1970; Edison Prize, 1972; Wiener Floteuhr, 1974; National Prize, 1977; President, Antonin Dvorak Foundation; President, Prague Spring Foundation; Golden Disco Supraphon, 1986. Memberships: Antonin Dvorak Foundation; Prague Spring Foundation; President, Castle Sirin Foundation. Address: Karlovo Manesti 5, 120 00 Prague 2, Czech Republic.

SUKARLAN Ananda, b. 10 June 1968, Jakarta, Indonesia. Pianist. m. Raquel Gomez, 28 Dec 1993. Education: Studies with Naum Grubert, Royal Conservatory of The Hague. Career: TV: Almost all TV Stations in Jakarta and VPRO Holland, Television Espanola, TV5 (France); Radio: Radio Nacional de Espana, WDR Cologne, VPRO and NCRV Holland; Festivals (Live): Holland Festival, Amsterdam, 1994, Middelburg Festival, 1994, Alicante Festival of Contemporary Music, 1995, Madrid Autumn Festival, 1996, Jakarta International Festival of Performing Arts, Barcelona Festival of 20th Century Music; With Orchestras: Berlin Symphony Orchestra, Orquesta Sinfonica de Galicia. Recordings: The Pentatonic Connection; Album de Colien (38 short pieces by 38 Spanish composers); Piano Music of Theo Loevendie; Music of HM The King of Thailand, Bhumipol Adulyadej. Honours: Cuypers Prize of Holland, 1993; First Prize, Nadia Boulanger, Orleans, 1994; First Prize, Xavier Montsalvatge, Spain, 1994; First Prize, Blanquefort International Competition, Bordeaux, 1995; First Prize, City of Ferrol, Spain. Hobbies: Gardening; Books; Films. Current Management: Marianne de Feijter, Amsterdam. Address: Avenida de Santander 57, Herrera de Camargo, 39608 Cantabria, Spain.

SULEIMANOV Stanislav, b. 1945, Baku, Russia. Singer (Bass). Education: Studied at the Baku Conservatory. Career: Sang at the Bolshoi Theatre Moscow from 1977; Since 1989 also the creator of the first Contract Musical Theatre "Forum"; Repertoire includes: Boris and Varlaam in Boris Godunov, Rimski's Salieri, Scarpia in Tosca, Malatesta in Rachmaninov's Francesca da Rimini, Boris in Lady Macbeth, Pontius Pilate in Master and Margarita by S Slonimsky; Guest appearances throughout Russia, USA, Japan, Netherlands, Belgium, Luxembourg, Italy, Spain, Greece and Germany; Concerts and Lieder recitals. Address: Halturinskaja str 4-1-58, 107392 Moscow, Russia.

SULTANOVA Razia, b. 16 June 1955, Vladivostok, Russia. Musicologist; Ethnomusicologist; Cultural Anthropologist; Pianist. m. Hamid Ismailov, 8 June 1979, 1 son, 1 daughter. Education: MA, Department of Musicology, Tashkeut Conservatoire, 1979; PhD, Moscow Conservatoire, 1988. Career: Instructor, State Conservatory, Uzbekistan, 1979-84; Editor-in-Chief, Union of Composers, 1987-89; Associate, Institute for Art Research, Moscow, 1989-92; Author, Musical Programmes, BBC World Service, 1995-; Visiting Research Fellow, Goldsmiths College, Universityof London, 1996-; Manager, International Chamber Orchestra, Tennesses Musicals, Germany, 1996-. Publications include: The Rhythm of the Vocal Parts of Sharshmagam, 1986; Song in Uzbek Riturals, 1994; Politics and Music After the October Revolution. Honours: Grants: Germany Reseach Association, 1993, Ministry of Culture, Germany, 1994, French Institute of Study of Central Asia, 1996, 1997. Memberships: British Forum of Ethnomusicology; SFE. Address: 51 Cromer Road, New Barnet, herts EN5 5HT, England.

SUMA Razvan Gabriel, b. 7 May 1977, Cluj-Napoca, Romania. Student. Education: Study with Gabriela Todor at the Music High School, Cluj-Napoca; Currently studying with Professor Marin Cazacu at the Bucharest Music Academy; Further tuition with Aurel Niculescu, Mirel Iancovivi, Radu Aldulescu, Ardo Noras and Miklos Perenyi. Debut: Concert Vivaldi No 11 with the Transylvania Philharmonic Orchestra, Cluj-Napoca, 1988. Career: Soloist with all Romanian Philharmonics, Radio Chamber Orchestra of Bucharest, Philharmonic of Sofia-Bulgaria, Orchestra of Theatre Regio Torino in Italy and the Vogtland Plauen Theatre in Germany; Performed recitals in Romania, France, Hungary, Repulic of Moldavia, Germany and Austria. Honours: 1st Prize, Cantarea Romaniei Festival, 1985, 1987, 1989; Special Prizes, Ciprian Porumbescu Interpretation Contest, Suceava, 1986, 1988; Special Prize, Constantin Silvestri International Concert Contest, Musical Youth Organisation, Romania, 1992; 1st Prize, International Jeunesse Musicale Contest, Bucharest, 1995; 1st Prize, International Contest Chisinau, Republic of Moldavia, 1997; 2nd Prize, 48th G B Viotti International Music Competition, Vercelli, Italy, 1997; 2nd Prize, Instrumental International Contest, Markneukirchen, 1997. Hobby: Sport. Address: Bd 22 Decembrie no 152, bl 2A, sc III, et 8, ap 85, 3400 Cluj-Napoca, Romania.

SUMEGI Daniel, b. 1963, Australia. Singer (Bass). Education: Studied in Australia and San Francisco. Career: Appearances with San Francisco Opera from 1992 in Andrea Chenier, Der Rosenkavalier, Die Meistersinger, Il Trovatore, Tannhäuser and Aida; La Bohème at the Golden Gate Theatre, 1997; Season 1995-96 with Ramfis and Rossini's Basilio for Australia Opera Britten's Theseus at Turin, Gremin and Mozart's Commendatore for Victorian State Opera; Seneca in Monteverdi's Poppea for Glimmerglass Opera at the Brooklyn Academy, Ratcliffe in Billy Rudd at the Opéra Bastille and Alonso in Il Guarnay for Washington Opera; Season 1996-97 with Basilio and Hunding in Die Walküre for Australian Opera, Verdi's Banquo at Houston and Sarastro in Die Zauberflöte for Bonn Opera. Honours include: Winner, 1994 Met Opera National Council Auditions; Finalist of 1992 Pavarotti and 1995 Placido Domingo Operalia Competition. Address: c/o Australian Opera, PO Box 291, Strawberry Hills, NSW 2012, Australia.

SUMMERS Hilary, b. 1965, Newport, Gwent, Wales. Contralto. Education: Studied at Reading University, Royal Academy of Music and the National Opera Studio. Career: Concert appearances at Festival Hall, Barbican Centre, Purcell Room and St John's Smith Square; Sang in The Dream of Gerontius with Liverpool Philharmonic and Henze's Novae de Infinito Laudes with London Sinfonietta; Other modern repertory includes Schoenberg's Pierrot Lunaire and works by Berio, Stravinsky, Webern, Berg, Rihm and Jonathan Harvey; Opera debut as a Valkyrie in Die Walküre for Scottish Opera in 1992; Has also sung in Die Königskinder for English National Opera and appeared as Britten's Lucretia, Ursule in Beatrice et Benedict, Cornelia in Giulo Cesare, Mercedes in Carmen, Gaea in Daphne, Martha in Mefistofele and Anna in Les Troyens; Sang Medoro in Handel's Orlando at the Brooklyn Academy of Music, 1996. Recordings include: Messiah with the King's College Choir. Honours include: The Worshipful Company of Musicians Silver Medal; Shinn Fellowship, Royal Academy of Music; Recital Diploma, Royal Academy of Music. Address: c/o Ingpen and Williams Ltd, 14 Kensington Court, London, W8 5DN, England.

SUMMERS Jonathan, b. 2 Oct 1946, Melbourne, Australia. Baritone. Education: Studied with Bettine McCaughan in Melbourne and with Otakar Kraus in London. Debut: Kent Opera in 1975 as Rigoletto. Career includes: With English National Opera has sung Posa, Renato, Rigoletto, Macbeth, Balstrode, Simon Boccanegra and Eugene Onegin; Appearances with Scottish Opera as Count Almaviva and Don Giovanni, Opera North as the High Priest, Nabucco and Onegin and at Glyndebourne as Ford; Australian Opera debut in 1981 as Germont Père, returning as Count Luna and Renato and in Les Contes d'Hoffmann; Victorian State Opera in Le nozze di Figaro and Andrea Chénier; European engagements in Hamburg as Posa, Frankfurt as Rigoletto, Munich in Le nozze di Figaro, Florence as Marcello and Sharpless, La Scala in Japan as Marcello, Avignon as Renato, Paris Opéra in La Traviata and Lohengrin and Geneva as Alceste and in Das Rheingold; Sang at Metropolitan Opera as Marcello in La Bohème under Carlos Kleiber, San Diego Opera in Il Trovatore and in debut at Lyric Opera Chicago in 1990 as Enrico in Lucia di Lammernoor; Season 1992 as Rodrigo in Don Carlos for ENO, High Priest at Covent Garden and Don Carlo in The Force of Destiny at the London Coliseum; Season 1993 included Rigoletto at the Bergen Festival, Ballo in Maschera with the Australian Opera, Sydney; Season 1994 included Père Germont, La Traviata, Australian Opera, Sydney and in Fedora with the Lyric Opera of Chicago; Season 1995 included Ford, Falstaff with Theatre du Capitole, Toulouse and Theatre Municipale, Lausanne, Marcello, La Bohème with Theatre du Capitole, Toulouse and Michele, Il Tabarro Trittico with the Australian Opera, Sydney; Debut as Mozart's Figaro 1997, for ENO. Recordings include: Peter Grimes; Samson et Dalila with Baltsa and Carreras; Videos of Samson et Dalila from Royal Opera and Il Trovatore at Australian Opera with Sutherland. Address: c/o Patricia Greenan, 19b Belsize Park, London, NW3 4DU, England.

SUMMERS Patrick, b. 1960, San Francisco, USA. Conductor. Education: Studied at Indiana University School of Music. Career: Conducted Season Preview Concerts with the San Francisco Opera, from 1989; Opera Center Showcase productions include Handel's Ariodante, Reimann's Ghost Sonata and Shield's Rosina; Projects for the Merola Opera Program include Bohème, Butterfly, Pasquale and Falstaff; Lucia di Lammermoor for the Western Opera Theater; As Music Director of the San Francisco Opera Center has led Carmen and Bohème on tour to Japan (1991, 1993) and La Fille du Régiment for the Opera Guild (1994); Performances with the San Francisco Opera include Tosca, the US premiere of Rossini's Ermione and the local premiere of his Otello; La Traviata and Cosi fan Tutte; Associated with the Shanghai Conservatory of Music in productions of Rigoletto and Don Pasquale; Asian premiere of Tosca at the Shanghai Opera House; Italian debut in season 1993-94, with Manon Lescaut for Rome Opera, and Canadian debut with Lucia di Lammermoor at Calgary; Australian debut with Cenerentola at Sydney and Melbourne, 1994; L'Incoronazione di Poppea for Dallas Opera (1995) and Tosca at Lisbon. Honours include: Named Outstanding San Franciscan by the San Francisco Chamber of Commerce, 1991. Address: c/o Lies Askonas Ltd, 6 Henrietta St, London, WC2E 8LA, England.

SUMSION Herbert (Whitton), b. 19 Jan 1899, Gloucester, England. Organist; Director of Music; Composer. m. Alice Hartley Garlich, 1927, 3 sons. Education: MusB, Durham University, 1920; DMus, Lambeth, 1947; FRCM. Career: Organist, Gloucester Cathedral, 1928-67; Director of Music, Ladies College, Cheltenham, 1935-68; Organist and Choirmaster, Christ Church, Lancaster Gate; Director of Music, Bishops Stortford College;

Assistant Instructor in Music, Morley College, London; Teacher of Harmony and Counterpoint, Curtis Institute, Philadelphia, USA, 1926-28; Conductor, Three Choirs Festival, 1928, 1931, 1934, 1937, 1947, 1950, 1953, 1956, 1959, 1962, 1965. Compositions: Introduction and Theme for Organ, 1935; Morning and Evening Service in G, 1935; Two Pieces for cello and piano, 1939 (No 1 arranged for string orchestra); Magnificat and Nunc Dimitis in G for Boys' Voices, 1953, for Men's Voices, 1953, for Boys' Voices in D, 1973; Cradle Song for organ, 1953; Benedicite in B flat, 1955; Four Carol Preludes for Organ, 1956; Festival Benedicite in D, 1971, They That Go Down to the Sea in Ships (anthem), 1979; Transposition Exercises, 1980; Piano Technique, a book of exercises, 1980; There is a Green Hill Far Away (anthem), 1981; Two Anthems for Holy Communion, 1981; In Exile (By the Waters of Babylon), (anthem), 1981. Honours: CBE, 1961; Honorary RAM, FRCO, FRSCM. Address: Church End house, Frampton-on-Severn, Glos GL2 7EH, England.

SUNDIN Nils-Göran, b. 18 May 1951, Växjö, Sweden. Music Director; Composer; Author. Education includes: Diploma, Choirmaster and Organist, Lund, 1968; Master's Degree, Musical Theory, Pedagogy of Musical Theory, Stockholm State School of Music; PhilCand, Musicology, History of Literature and Fine Arts, Stockholm University; PhD, Philosophy of Music, USA, 1988; MedCand, Lund University. Career: Lecturer in Music Theory and Interpretation at Stockholm State College of Music and Edsberg College of Music, Sollentuna, 1975-85; Lecturer in Music History at Stockholm University, 1976; Music Critic, Svenska Dagbladet, 1977-81; Executive Music Chief, Kronoberg Music Foundation, Växjö, 1987-. Compositions: Numerous for piano, chamber music, voice, choir and orchestra including: Symphony For Peace for Orchestra and Choir with poems by Dag Hammarskjöld, commissioned for The Great Peace Journey, Invitazione, Emmanuel Swedenborg In Memoriam, 1988; Concerto St George for Piano and Orchestra, 1990; Violin Concerto, 1994. Publications: Books include: Musical Interpretation in Performance, 1983, Bilder Ur Musikens Historia, 1984, Musical Interpretation Research, 1984, MIR volumes I-II, 1984, Aesthetic Criteria of Musical Interpretation in Contemporary Performance, 1994. Contributions to: About 300 articles and reviews in numerous publications including Nutida Musik, Bonniers Musiklexikon, Sohlmans Musiklexikon. Memberships: STIM; Sveriges Författaförbund; New York Academy of Sciences; International Musicological Society. Address: c/o Lorovic, Innere Ringstrasse 12, CH-3600 Thun, Switzerland.

SUNDINE Stephanie, b. 1954, Illinois, USA. Soprano. Education: Studied in Illinois and New York. Career: Sang with the New York City Opera, 1981-84 as Ariadne, Santuzza and Margherita in Boito's Mefistofeles; Sang the title roles in the US premieres of Prokofiev's Maddalena at St Louis in 1982 and Judith by Siegfried Matthus at Santa Fe in 1990; Best known as Strauss's Salome at Covent Garden (debut) in 1988, Metropolitan Opera (debut) in 1990 and Welsh National Opera in 1991; Sang Isolde at Nantes in 1989 and Fusako in the premiere production of Henze's Das Verratene Meer at the Deutsche Oper Berlin in 1990; Other roles include Janácek's Emilia Marty, Tosca, La Gioconda and Elsa; Sang the Foreign Princess in Rusalka at San Francisco, 1995. Address: c/o San Francisco Opera, War Memorial House, Van Ness Avenue, San Francisco, CA, USA.

SUNDMAN Ulf (Johan), b. 27 Feb 1929, Stockholm, Sweden. Organist; Musical Director. m. Anna-Greta Persson, 10 July 1954, 1 daughter. Education: Hogre Organistexamen, 1949; Hogre Kantorsexamen, Musiklaarexamen, 1951; Diplom Organ Playing, 1974; Royal Academy of Music, Stockholm; International Academy for Organ, Haarlem, Holland, 1967. Career: Organist, Skelleftea St Olovs Church, 1954-81; Organist, Gavle Heliga Trefaldighets Church, 1981-94; Organ concerts in Sweden, Finland, Norway, West Germany, Austria, Netherlands, Switzerland, France, Italy, Spain, East Germany, Czechoslovakia, Poland, USSR, 1974, 1976, 1979, Denmark and Belgium; Organ Music Festivals, Gottingen, West Germany, 1972, Vilinius, USSR, 1974, Madrid, 1982, Naples, Toulon, 1983, Ratzeburg, 1985, Verona and Asola, 1986, Buren 1987, Gottingen 1987, Zug 1988, Biella 1988; Concerts on Radio Sweden and Radio Netherlands. Recordings: Soviet (Melodia) Sweden (Proprius), (Opus 3). Honours: PA Berg Medal, Royal Academy of Music, Stockholm; Culture Prize of the Town of Skellftea 1972, Province of Vasterbotten 1973, Gavle 1994. Address: N Köpmangatan 22A, S-803 21 Gavle, Sweden.

SUNNEGARDH Thomas, b. 11 Jul 1949, Stockholm, Sweden. Tenor Singer. Education: Studied at The Royal School of Music in Stockholm. Career includes: Sang at Vadstena Academy, 1978-79; Appeared in Die Fledermaus and Der Vogelhändler with National Touring Company; Royal Opera Stockholm from 1982 as Albert Herring, Walther von der Vogelweide, Taverner, Ferrando, Fra Diavolo, Tamino and Steuermann in Der fliegende Holländer; Has sung Lohengrin in Stockholm, Moscow with Bolshoi, Wiesbaden and Stuttgart conducted by Silvio Varviso, 1990; Macduff at the Bergen Festival, 1988; Other roles include Florestan, Erik, Parsifal in

Denmark and Antwerp, and parts in Iphigénie en Aulide and Genoveva at Deutsche Oper am Rhein, and Die Meistersinger at Nice, 1992; Season 1991-92 sang Lohengrin at Barcelona, Parsifal at Aarhus, Die Meistersinger at Nice Opera, Der fliegende Holländer at Royal Opera Covent Garden, Das Lied von der Erde with London Philharmonic Orchestra; Season 1992-93 with Meistersinger at Brussels, Deutsche Oper Berlin, Munich, Tokyo, Stuttgart, Dutchman/Erik in Munich, Parsifal in Essen and Deutsche Oper Düsseldorf, Lohengrin in Frankfurt, Berlin, Tokyo and Toulouse; Season 1993-94 in Lohengrin in Frankfurt, Der fliegende Holländer in Munich, and Walter in Stuttgart; Season 1994-95 with Walter von Stolzing in Stuttgart, Fidelio and Lohengrin in Düsseldorf and Toulouse; Sang Paul in Korngold's Die tote Stadt at Stockholm, 1996. Recording: Role of Froh with Cleveland Orchestra under Christoph von Dohnányi, 1993. Address: c/o Haydn Rawstron Ltd, 36 Station Road, London SE20 7BQ, England.

SUNSHINE Adrian, b. 1930, New York City, USA. Conductor. m. Sheila A Genden, 1 s, 1 d. Education: San Francisco State University; University of CA, Berkeley; Private studies with Janet Hale, Georg Gruenberg, Ludwig Altman, Gabriel Sunshine, father, Herman Reinberg. Career: Appearances with: Philharmonia, London, Leningrad, Berlin, BBC, Bucharest, Cleveland, Suisse Romande, Lausanne, Holland, Denmark, Sweden, Poland, Athens, Miami, San Francisco, Rio de Janeiro, Mexico City, Buenos Aires, Caracas, Lugano, Manchester, Bournemouth, Israel, Paris, Lille, Amsterdam, Rotterdam, BBC Opera, Barcelona, Bilbao, Luxembourg, Madrid, San Sebastian Bach Festival, Maubeuge Festival, France and others; Festivals include: Blossom, Athens, Sao Paulo, Montreux-Vevey, Ascona, Cheltenham, Gulbenkian, Reims, Seville, Cluj, Romania, Lille, Chamonix and others; Founder-Conductor, San Francisco Chamber Orchestra; Chief Conductor, Gulbenkian Orchestra, Lisbon; Principal Guest Conductor, Romania; Music Director, London Chamber Players, 1979-; Principal Guest Conductor, Athens; Guest Professor, Bowling Green State University, OH; Romanian Academy of Music; Guest Lecturer, University of London Institute of Education; Conductor, Camerata Budapest, 1994-. Recordings: Works by: Shostakovitch and Schoenberg with Camerata Budapest. Publications: Articles on music and music criticism. Honours: Newhouse Foundation Scholarship. Memberships: College Music Society; Conductors' Guild. Current Management: Bureau de Concerts Camile Kiesgen, 252 Faubourg St Honore, 75008 Paris, France. Address: PO Box 84, London, NW11 8AL, England.

SUSA Conrad, b. 26 Apr 1935, Springfield, PA, USA. Composer. Education: BFA, Carnegie Institute of Technology at Pittsburgh, 1957; Juilliard School, New York, with William Bergsma and Vincent Persichetti. Career: Composer in Residence at the Old Globe Theatre, San Diego, 1959-60; Music Director of APA-Phoenix Repertory Company in New York, 1961-68, and the American Shakespeare Festival in Stratford, CT, 1969-71; Dramaturg of the Eugene O'Neill Center in Connecticut, 1986-. Compositions include: Operas: Transformations, Minneapolis, 1973, Black River: A Wisconsin Idyll, St Paul, 1975, The Love Of Don Perlimplin, Purchase, NY, 1984; A Sonnet Voyage, symphony, 1963; Choral: Dawn Greeting, 1976, The Chanticleer's Carol, 1982, Earth Song, 1988; Piano pieces. Address: c/o ASCAP, ASCAP Building, One Lincoln Center, New York, NY 10023, USA.

SUSHANSKAYA Rimma, b. 1950, Leningrad, Russia. Concert Violinist. Education: Studied at Leningrad and Moscow Conservatoires with David Oistrakh; PhD. Career: Emigrated to America in 1977 and has given many concerts there, in South America, throughout Russia and in Europe; Orchestras include Czech Philharmonic, Moscow Philharmonic, Leningrad Philharmonic Orchestras and Prague Radio Symphony Orchestra; Orchestral and recital tours of Russia, Finland and Czechoslovakia; London recital debut in 1987 at the Wigmore Hall, followed by Tchaikovsky's Concerto with the Royal Liverpool Philharmonic Orchestra and the City of Birmingham Symphony Orchestra; Based in Britain, residing in London, Stratford and New York. Honours include: First Prize, Prague International Competition; Ysaye Medal. Current Management: Stephanie Williams Artists. Address: 12 Central Chambers, Wood Street, Stratford-upon-Avon, Warwickshire CV37 6JQ, England.

SUSS Reiner, b. 2 Feb 1930, Chemnitz, Germany. Bass Singer. Education: Member of the Thomas Choir, Leipzig, 1939-48; Hochschule für Musik Leipzig, 1948-53. Career: Sang with Radio Leipzig, 1953-56 and the opera company at Bernburgan Der Saale, 1956-57 with debut in Tiefland by d'Albert; Sang at Theater der Stadt Halle, 1957-59 notably as Ochs in Der Rosenkavalier and member of the Staatsoper Berlin from 1959 as Leporello, Beckmesser, Nicolai's Falstaff, Kecal in The Bartered Bride, Varlaam and Baculus in Der Wildschütz, Dr Bartolo in Barbiere, Kovalyov in The Nose by Shostakovich, Don Pasquale, and Osmin in Entführung; Guest engagements at the Vienna Staatsoper and in Budapest, Helsinki, Lyon, Lausanne, Florence, Moscow, Prague, Warsaw and Tokyo. Recordings include:

Tannhäuser conducted by Franz Konwitschny; Tosca; Der Wildschütz; La Serva Padrona; Mozart's Zaide; Die Kluge and Der Mond by Orff; Don Pasquale. Address: c/o Deutsche Staatsoper, Unter den Linden 7, D-1086 Berlin, Germany.

SUSTIKOVA Vera, b. 9 Jan 1956, Uh Hradiste, Czech Republic. Musicologist. m. Sustik Jaroslav, 15 July 1982, 1 daughter. Education: Philosophical Faculty, Charles University in Prague, PhD, 1982; Conservatory in Brno (Guitar); Guitar-Masterclasses with Professor Cotsiolis (Greece); Musicology at the PF of Charles University in Prague. Debut: Muzeum of Czech Music in Prague. Career: 100 let spolecen pusobeni smetanova dila, 1984; Bedrich Smetana, 1824-1884, Prague, 1994; Opera and song without Singing Musical Melodram, Stamford, California, 1996; Author of major exhibitions: History of Czech Musical Culture, 1986; Smetana-Dvorak, 1988; B Smetana's Memorial in Benatky n j, 1991; Bedrich Smetana, Legend of My Country, 1994. Publications include: Bedrich Smetana - Legend of My Country, 1994; Zdenek Fibich - Master of Scenic Melodrama, 1996. Contributions to: Prodana nevesta na nekterych cizich scenach, 1985; The Path Towad, Hubicka, 1995; Fibich's Concert Melodramas in Amerika, 1996. Honours: Premiums the Czech Music Foundation, 1984, 1985, 1986, 1989. Memberships: Society of Czech Music; Bedrich Smetana's Society, Vice President; Zdenek Fibich's Society, Vice President. Hobbies: Travel; Theatre; Guitar. Address: Pstrossova 35, Prague 1, 11008, Czech Republic.

SUTCLIFFE Sidney (Clement), b. 6 Oct 1918, Edinburgh, Scotland. Musician; Oboe Player; Teacher; Conductor. m. Marion Romerts, 3 daughters. Education: George Watson's College; Royal College of Music with Leon Goossens and John Snowden. Debut: Sadler's Wells Orchestra, 1938. Career: Member of the Philharmonia Orchestra and BBC Symphony Orchestra; Professor, Royal College of Music; Woodwind Coach; Various conducting engagements. Recordings: With Philharmonia Orchestra, 1949-62, notably Mozart's Sinfonia Concertante, K297b, conducted by Karajan; Quintets By Mozart and Beethoven with Walter Gieseking, B Walton, C James and Dennis Brain. Honour: Honorary ARCM. Hobbies: Music; Golf; Swimming; Photography. Address: 94 Woodfield Lane, Ashtead, Surrey, KT21 2DP, England.

SUTER Louis-Marc, b. 2 Feb 1928, Fribourg, Switzerland. Musicologist; Emeritus Professor. m. Monique Suter, 12 Nov 1955, 4 sons. Education: Chemistry and Pedagogic Studies, University of Fribourg; Musical and Musicological Studies, Conservatory of Geneva and Berne University; PhD. Debut: 1955. Career: International Academic Orchestra, Salzburg; Lausanne Chamber Orchestra; Suisse Romande Orchestra; Professor of Musicology, University of Berne. Publications: Four concert works of Serbian composers, 1989; Norbert Moret, compositeur, 1993; Norbert Moret, compositeur, 1993; Currently completing publication of Le Langage musical de l'Europe occidentale. Contributions to: Claude Debussy: "Pour les accords", Etude No 12 pour piano, in Revue Musicale de Suisse Romande, 1983; Ronsard: "Les Amours" de 1552 mises en musique, in Actes du Colloque de Neuchâtel, 1985. Memberships: International Society for Musicology; Société Suisse de Musicologie; Association Suisse des Musiciens. Address: Route du Pré-de-L'Ile 1, CH-1752 Villars-sur-Glâne, Switzerland.

SUTHERLAND Joan (Dame), b. 7 Nov 1926, Sydney, New South Wales, Australia. Singer (Soprano). m. Richard Bonynge, 1954. Career: Came to London, 1951, to study at the Royal College of Music; Richard Bonynge became her accompanist and musical adviser; Engaged as Member of Covent Garden Opera Company, with first role as First Lady in The Magic Flute, 1952; In early years sang Amelia in A Masked Ball, Aida, Eva in The Mastersingers, Gilda in Rigoletto, Desdemona in Othello, Agathe in Der Freischütz, Olympia, Giuletta, Antonia, and Stella in Tales of Hoffmann; Sang Jenifer in the premiere of Tippett's The Midsummer Marriage, 1955; Became an international star with Covent Garden performance of Lucia di Lammermoor, 1959; Sang at Covent Garden in operas including I Puritani, Dialogues of the Carmelites, Lucia di Lammermoor, Norma; Sang in world's major opera houses including Paris, Vienna, La Scala, Hamburg, Buenos Aires, Metropolitan New York, Chicago Lyric, San Francisco, Australian Opera in Sydney, Glyndebourne, and in Edinburgh, Leeds and Florence Festivals; Specialised in bel canto operas, particularly of Rossini, Donizetti and Bellini, and operas of Handel, as well as in 19th century French repertoire; With husband was responsible for bringing back into standard repertoire previously more obscure works such as Esclarmonde, Le roi de Lahore, Semiramide, Les Huguenots, of French and Italian composers; Retired, 1990; Last operatic role Marguerite de Valois in Les Huguenots for Australian Opera, 1990; Sang as guest in Die Fledermaus at Covent Garden. Recordings: Lucia di Lammermoor, Alcina, La Sonnambula, Faust, Semiramide, I Puritani, Les Huguenots, Turandot, La Traviata, Les Contes d'Hoffmann, Don Giovanni, Don Pasquale, Adriana Lecouvreur, Le Roi de Lahore, Rodelinda, Athalia, Norma, Anna Bolena, La

Fille du Régiment. Publications include: Autobiography, 1997. Honours: Commander, Order of Australia, 1975; Dame Commander of the British Empire, 1979, and Order of Merit from H M The Queen; Commander, Ordre National du Mérit, France. Address: c/o Ingpen and Williams Ltd, 26 Wadham Road, London SW15 2LR, England.

SUTHERLAND Rosalind, b. 1963, Glasgow, Scotland. Soprano. Education: Studied at London College of Music and with Joseph Ward at Royal Northern College of Music. Career: Appearances with Royal Northern College of Music in Suor Angelica, L'Elisir d'Amore and Madama Butterfly; Sang Pamina with Liverpool Mozart Orchestra, Bournemouth Sinfonietta and Scottish National Orchestra; Recent engagements with Welsh National Opera as Madama Butterfly, Tatyana and Liu, and Mimi for New Israeli Opera; English National Opera debut season, 1993-94 as Mimi (repeated with Welsh National Opera, 1996); Sang Butterfly at Golden Gate Theatre, San Francisco, 1997. Honours include: Peter Moores Scholarship and winner of the Anne Ziegler Prize for a Singer Showing Outstanding Promise. Address: c/o Harold Holt Ltd, 31 Sinclair Road, London, W14 0NS, England.

SUTTER Ursula, b. 26 Mar 1938, Berne, Switzerland. Mezzo-Soprano. Education: Studied in Berne and Stuttgart. Career: Sang at Biel-Solothurn, 1961-63, Trier, 1963-64, Essen, 1964-66 and engaged at Stuttgart Staatsoper, 1966-85, notably in the premiere of Orff's Prometheus in 1968; Guest appearances at State Operas of Vienna, Munich and Hamburg, Cologne, Nuremburg and Dusseldorf; Further engagements at Bucharest, Lisbon, Monte Carlo, Essen and Schwetzingen Festival (premiere of Henze's The English Cat in 1983); Roles have included Dorabella, Cherubino, Rosina, Isabella, Maddalena, Preziosilla, Magdalene in Meistersinger, the Composer in Ariadne and Britten's Lucretia. Address: c/o Stuttgart Staatsoper, Oberer Schlossgarten 6, D-7000 Stuttgart, Germany.

SUTTON-ANDERSON David, b. 20 Mar 1956, London, England. Composer; Conductor; Teacher. m. Avril Anderson, 26 Aug 1980. Education: Royal College of Music; Musikhochschule, Cologne. Debut: Conducting Debut: ISCM Festival, Athens, 1979. Career: Co-Founder and Conductor of Sounds Positive; Adjunct Professor of Music, Notre Dame University, Indiana; Composition Teacher, RCM Junior Department. Compositions: Cycle, soprano and ensemble, 1984-89; Da Camera, string orchestra, 1986; Organ Concerto, 1991-93; Horizons, piano, 1995; Sephardic Songs, soprano and guitar, 1995. Recordings include: Sephardic Songs; Chant with Drone; Conductor: The Music of John Lambert. Contributions to: Boulez-Pli Selon Pli; Music and Musicians, London, 1977. Honours: Royal Philharmonic Society Prize, 1974; Gemini Fellowship, 1991-93. Memberships: PRS; SPNM; MPCS. Hobbies: Travel; Badminton. Address: 28 Cavendish Avenue, Finchley, London N3 3QN, England.

SUWANAI Akiko, b. Tokyo, Japan. Concert Violinist. Education: Studied at the Toho Gakuen School of Music College, with Dorothy DeLay at Juilliard and Cho-Liang and Cho-Liang at Columbia University, New York. Career: Many concert engagements since becoming the youngest ever winner of the Tchaikovsky Competition, Moscow; Conductor have included Bychkov, Rostropovitch, Rozhdestvensky, Ozawa, Marriner, Conlon, Previn, Svetlana and Temirkanov; Boston Symphony debut 1996, and performances with the Orchestra de Paris, Cincinnati, Pittsburgh and Seattle Symphonies and Academy of St Martin in the Fields; Ravinia and Evian Festivals, recital at the Amsterdam Concertgebouw and concert with the Toho Gakuen Orchestra at Carnegie Hall; Further engagements with the State Symphony of Russia, Russian National Orchestra and Budapest Symphony; Tours of Japan and South America. Recordings include: Concertos no 1 by Bruch and Scottish Fantasia, with Neville Marriner (Philips Classics, 1997); The Winners Gala at the Tchaikovsky Competition at Moscow; Prizewinner at the 35th International Paganini Violin Competition, the fourth International Japan Competition and the Queen Elizabeth International Competition, Belgium. Address: c/o Ingpen & Williams Ltd, 26 Wadham Road, London SW15 2LR, England.

SUZUKI Hidetaro, b. 1 June 1937, Tokyo, Japan. Violinist; Conductor. m. Zeyda Ruga, 16 May 1962, 2 sons, 1 daughter. Education: Toho School of Music, Tokyo, 1953-56; Curtis Institute of Music, Philadelphia, Pennsylvania, USA, 1956-63; Studied with Efrem Zimbalist. Debut: Tokyo, 1951. Career: Concertmaster, Quebec Symphony, Canada, 1963-78; Professor, Conservatory of Province of Quebec, 1963-79; Professor, Laval University, 1970-79; Concertmaster, Indianapolis Symphony, Indiana, USA, 1978-; Concert appearances as soloist, recitalist, conductor, Great Britain, Western Europe, Soviet Union, Central America, USA, Canada, Japan, South East Asia; Director of Chamber Music Series Suzuki and Friends, 1980. Recordings: Beethoven Sonatas; Hidetaro Suzuki Encore Album; Franck, Ravel Sonatas; Beethoven Piano Trios, Marlboro Festival. Honours: Laureat, Tchaikovsky International Competition, 1962; Laureat, Queen Elizabeth International Competition, 1963, 1967; Laureat, Montreal International Competition, 1966; Served as Jury Member, Montreal International Competition, 1979; International Violin Competition, 1982, 1986, 1990, 1994. Address: 430 West 93rd Street, Indianapolis, IN 46260, USA.

SVANIDZE Natela, b. 4 Sept 1926, Akhaltsikhe, Georgia. Composer. m. Peter Tomadze, 15 June 1952, 1 daughter. Education: Studies at Tbilisi State University, French Literature; Graduated from the Tbilisi State Conservatoire, 1951. Debut: Symphonic poem, Samgori, conducted by Odyssey Dymitriady, Tbilisi, 1951. Appointments: Improvisation, violin, piano, 1956; Fairytale, piano, Tbilisi, 1960; Kvarkvare, symphonic poem, Tbilisi, 1963; Symphony No 1, conducted G Rozdestvensky, Radio Moscow, Paris, Belgrade, 1969; Pirosmani, oratorio, conducted, Tbilisi, Moscow, Samara, 1974, 1976. Compositions: Symphony No1, for strings, piano and percussion instruments, 1967; Pirosmani, chamber oratorio, 1969; Circle, piece for prepared piano, 1972; Lamentatia Georgica, oratorio for speaker, female sextet, two choruses, instruments and tape, 1974; Symphony No 2, for big orchestra, 1983; Gaul-Gavkhe, cantata, mixed choruses, big orchestra, 1995. Honours: Honoured Art Worker of the Georgian SSR, 1981; Professor, 1991. Membership: Board member, The Georgian Composers' Union. Hobby: Modern literature. Current Management: Professor of the Institute of Theatre and Cinema, Tbilisi. Address: Griboedoff Str 4, Apt 7, 380 008, Tbilisi, Georgia.

SVATOS Vladimir, b. 19 Nov 1928, Mlada Vozice. Professor, Conservatoire Ostrava. m. 12 July 1956, 2 sons. Education: Organ at Prague Conservatory, 1947-49; AMU Prague organ by Professor Jiri Reiberger, 1949-53; JAMU Brno, Composition by Professor Vilem Petrzelka. Debut: Moods of Spring, for piano in Brno, 1953. Career: Song cycles, chamber and orchestra compositions. Compositions: Wind Quintet, 1976; Symfonietta, 1980; Concerto for Violin and Orchestra, 1981; String Quartet No 2, 1984. Recordings: Vocal Symfonia, 1984; Sonata for flute and piano, 1986; Concerto for Piano and Orchestra No 3, 1989. Honour: Chorus for Children, 1982. Memberships: Association of Czech Composers, Prague. Hobbies: Sport; Travel. Current Management: Conservatoire Ostrva. Address: Conservatoire Ostrava, Zerotínova 5, Czech Republic.

SVECENY Jaroslav, b. 8 Dec 1960, Hradec Kralove, Czechoslovakia. Concert Violinist. m. Monika Svecena. Education: Studied at the Prague Conservatoire and the Prague Academy of Arts with Vaclav Snitil; Master classes with Nathan Milstein at Zurich and Gidon Kremer at Kuhmo. Career: Concert appearances in Germany, Spain, France, Italy, Britain, Finland, Denmark, USA, Russia, Poland, Hungary and Rumania; Participated in several festivals in Berlin, Constance, Helsinki, Bilbao, Madrid, Granada, Havana, Prague, Leipzig and Palermo; Repertoire includes Concertos by Dvorák, Beethoven, Brahms, Mozart, Bach, Vivaldi, Haydn, Reicha and Martinu, Reicha Complete Works for Violin and Piano, Benda 24 Capriccios (only artist with this repertoire), and sonatas by Brahms, Beethoven, Dvorák, Benda, Handel and Ysaÿe. Recordings include: Reicha 4 Sonatas, Grand Duo Concertante and Rondo; Sonatas by Benda, Stamitz, Corelli, Handel and Tartini; Vivaldi Four Seasons. Honour: Winner, Pablo de Sarsate International Violin Competition. Address: Trojanova 18, 120 00 Prague 2, Czech Republic.

SVEINSSON Atli Heiner, b. 21 September 1938, Reykjavik, Iceland. Composer; Conductor; Administrator. Education: Studied at the Reykjavic College of Music and with Petzold and BA Zommermann at the Cologne Hochschule für Musik; Composition studies with Pousseur and Stockhausen at Darmstadt and Cologne. Career: Freelance composer and conductor throughout Iceland and Scandinavia; Chairman, Society of Icelandic Composers, 1972-83. Compositions include: Tautophony, for orchestra, 1967; Flower Shower, for orchestra, 1973; Flute Concerto, 1975; Septet, 1976; Twenty-One Sounding Minutes for flute, 1980; Bassoon Concerto, Trobar Clus, 1980; The Silken Drum, opera, 1982; Trombone Concerto, Jubilus, 1984; Recitation, for piano and orchestra, 1984; Bicentennial, for string quartet, 1984; Trio, for violin, cello and piano, 1985; The Night on our Shoulders, for soprano, alto women's chorus and orchestra, 1986; Dreamboat, concerto for violin, harpischord and orchestra, 1987; Vikivaki, TV opera, 1990; Opplaring, for soprano and wind instruments, 1991; Dernier Amour, chamber opera, 1992; Rockerauschen, Bruit des Robes for chamber orchestra, 1993. Honours include: Nordic Council Prize, 1976. Address: c/o STEF, Laufasvegi 40, 101 Reykjavik, Iceland.

SVENDEN Birgitta, b. 20 Mar 1952, Porjus, Sweden. Mezzo-Soprano. Education: Studied at the Stockholm Opera School. Career: Has sung at the Royal Opera in Stockholm as Cherubino, Orga and Erda; Sang a Rhinemaiden in The Ring under Solti at Bayreuth in 1983, at Nice Opera from 1985 in Carmen and as Meg Page and Anna in Les Troyens; Created Queen Christina in Hans Gefors' opera in 1988; Sang at Metropolitan Opera from 1988 as Erda in Das Rheingold and Siegfried and Maddalena in Rigoletto, Seattle Opera in 1989 as Magdalena in Die Meistersinger, Ravinia Festival Chicago in Mahler's 3rd Symphony under James levine, and at La Scala, Munich and San Francisco in 1990 as Magdalena, Erda and First Norn; Covent Garden debut in 1990 in a new production of Siegfried under Bernard Haitink; Sang at Théâtre du Châtelet, Paris, as Margret in a production of Wozzeck by Patrice Chéreau under Daniel Barenboim; Engaged for BBC Philharmonic in Verdi's Requiem in 1991, Gürzenich Orchestra in Mahler's 3rd in 1992, and Los Angeles Philharmonic in Mahler's 3rd; Sang in Eugene Onegin and Die Meistersinger at Metropolitan Opera in 1993; Season 1993 with Mahler's 3rd at Boston and Carnegie Hall under Ozawa, Mahler's 3rd and 8th at Rome and Rotterdam under Conlon, Missa Solemnis at Paris under Solti, and Octavian in Der Rosenkavalier at Paris Châtelet; Season 1994 with new Ring productions at Bayreuth, Covent Garden and Cologne; Season 1996-97 as Wagner's Magdalene at Bayreuth, Erda at the Met. Recordings: Das Rheingold; Mahler; Elgar; Siegfried; Zemlinsky. Honours: Royal Court Singer (Holsingrinn) 1995 by King of Sweden. Address: Artistsekretariat Ulf Törnqvist, Sankt Eriksgatan 100, 2tr, S-113 31, Stockholm, Sweden.

SVETE Tomaz, b. 29 Jan 1956, Ljubljana, Slovenia. Composer; Conductor. Education: Graduated in Composition, 1980 and Conducting, 1981, Academy of Music, Ljubljana; Studied with Professor F Cerha, Hochschule für Musik und Darstellende Kunst, Vienna, Diploma with Distinction, 1986; Studies in conducting with Otmar Suitner, Diploma 1988 and electroacoustic music with Dieter Kaufmann, Vienna; Magister Artis of the Hochschule für Musik und Darstellende Kunst, Vienna, 1989. Debut: 1st composition performance, Ljubljana, 1978. Career: Works performed in: Ljubljana, Skopje, Opatija, Zagreb-Music Biennial, Vienna, Salzburg, Prague, Brno-Moravian Autumn, Amsterdam, Rotterdam, Middleburgh, Torino, Trieste, Klagenfurt, Spittal-Drau, Tirana, Leipzig, Melk, St Pölten-Niederösterreich International; Conductor of Slovene Philharmonic and Pro Arte Orchestras, currently of Singkreis Währing, Vienna and Brno Radio Symphony Orchestra; Professor of Composition, Karl Prayner Conservatory, Vienna; Concert of own works in Brahmssaal, Musikverein, Vienna; Freelance Composer in Vienna; Currently, Docent for composition at Pedagogical Faculty, Maribor, Slovenia. Compositions include: Requiem, 1991; The Rape from Laudach Sea, opera, 1993; Isomerisms for Chamber Ensemble; Rappresentazione Sacra for Double Bass Solo and Flute Quartet, Ljubljana, 1994; Sonata Solaris for Violoncello and Piano, Salzburg, 1994; Sacrum Delirium, cantata for Soloists, Chorus, Ensembles and Orchestra (Italian Prize), 1994; Hommage à Slavko Osterc for Piano, Ljubljana, 1995; Evocazione, soprano and chamber ensemble, 1995; Concert de la Nuit, double bass, violin, harp and orchestra, 1997. Recording: Jugoton, 1986. Honours: Theodor Körner Prize, Vienna, 1992; Prize of Slovene Radiotelevision, Ljubljana, 1993; 1st Prize for cantata, Sacrum delirium, Gorizia, Italy, 1994. Memberships include: Union of Slovene Composers; ÖKB; International Society for Microtonal Music, Salzburg. Address: Prusnikova 2, S1-2000 Maribor, Slovenia.

SVETLANOV Evgeny (Fyodorovich), b. 6 Sep 1928, Moscow, Russia. Conductor; Composer; Pianist. Education: Graduated, Gnesin Institute, 1951; Moscow Conservatory, 1951-55, with Shaporin (composition) and Gauk (conducting). Career: Conducted All Union Radio Orchestra, 1953, and Bolshoy Theatre, Moscow from 1955 becoming Principal Conductor, 1962-64; Performances of operas by Tchaikovsky, Borodin, Rimsky-Korsakov and Dargomizhsky, Bartók's Bluebeard's Castle and works by other Soviet composers; Principal Conductor of the Russian State Symphony Orchestra from 1965 notably in symphonies by Myaskovsky, Tchaikovsky, Prokofiev and Shostakovich; Tours to Europe, Britain, USA and Japan; Principal Guest Conductor of the London Symphony Orchestra in 1979. Compositions: Symphony; Home Fields, cantata, 1949; Tone Poem Festival, 1950; Concerto, 1951; Daugava, 1953; Siberian Fantasy, 1953; Rhapsody, 1954; 5 Sonatinas, 50 Romances and Songs. Recordings: Tchaikovsky and Rachmaninov Complete Symphonies; Alexander Nevsky, Le Sacre du Printemps; Borodin's 2nd Symphony; Rimsky-Korsakov Overtures. Honours: People's Artist of Russia, 1968; Lenin Prize, 1972; Glinka Prize, 1975. Address: c/o Russian State Symphony Orchestra, 31 Ulitsa Gorkogo, Moscow, Russia.

SVETLEV Michail, b. 6 Mar 1943, Sofia, Bulgaria. Tenor. Education: Studied at the Sofia Conservatoire. Debut: Passau in 1971 as Manrico. Career: Appearances in Munich, Hamburg, Berlin and Vienna, and La Scala Milan in 1979; US debut as Riccardo in Un Ballo in Maschera at Washington DC in 1980; Further US appearances at Houston in 1980, San Francisco in 1980 and 1983, and Philadelphia in 1982; Sang Dmitri in Boris Godunov at Covent Garden in 1983 and has appeared elsewhere as Verdi's Radames and Gabriele Adorno, Andrea Chénier and Cavaradossi; Season 1985-86 as Hermann in The Queen of Spades at Marseilles and Lykov in Rimsky's The Tsar's Bride at Monte Carlo; Other roles include the Duke of Mantua, Don Carlos,

Bacchus, Lensky, Edgardo and the Prince in Rusalka. Address: c/o Opéra de Monte Carlo, Place du Casino, Monte Carlo.

SVOBODA Josef, b. 10 May 1920, Caslav, Czechoslovakia. Stage Designer. Education: Trained as a cabinet maker; Architectural studies 1941-43, then at Prague Art College, 1945-50. Career: Worked for an amateur theatre group in Caslav then designed for the New Group in Prague, 1943-45; Worked at the Smetana Theatre, 1945-48; From 1951, Chief Designer and Technical Director of the National Theatre Prague; Techniques of collage, mirrors, lenses and film projection seen at the premiere production of Nono's Intolleranza in Venice, 1961; Other designs for Il Trovatore in Berlin, 1966, Die Frau ohne Schatten, Pelléas et Mélisande, Nabucco and The Ring at Covent Garden, 1967-76, Oberon, Die Soldaten and Die Zauberflöte in Munich, 1968-70, Les Vepres Siciliennes in Hamburg, 1969, Wozzeck at La Scala, 1971, Carmen and The Bartered Bride at Metropolitan Opera, 1972, 1978; Czech premiere of Martinu's Ariadne at Prague in 1987; Designs for The Bartered Bride at Stuttgart in 1990, Luisa Miller at Trieste, and Salome at the Deutsche Oper Berlin, 1990; Macerata Festival in 1992 with production and designs for La Sonnambula, and designs for La Traviata; Sets for Meier's Dreyfus at Bonn, 1994; Attila at Macerata, 1996. Publications include: Designing for The Stage, in Opera Magazine, 1967. Address: c/o Deutsche Oper Berlin, Richard Wagnerstrasse 10, D-1000 Berlin 1, Germany.

SVOBODA Tomas, b. 6 Dec 1939, Paris, France. Composer; Pianist; Conductor; Professor of Music. m. Jana Demartini, 9 Oct 1965, 1 son, 1 daughter. Education: Degree in Percussion, 1956, Composition, 1958, Conducting, 1962, Conservatory of Music, Prague, Czechoslovakia; Degree in Composition, University of Southern California, USA, 1969. Debut: FOK Prague Symphony Orchestra, Symphony No 1, Op 20, 1957. Compositions: Symphonies 1-6; Overture of the Season, Op 89; Eugene Overture (Festive), Op 103; Nocturne for orchestra, Op 100; Serenade for orchestra, Op 115; Sinfonietta (à la Renaissance), Op 60; Reflections for orchestra, Op 53; Concerto for piano and orchestra, Op 71; Concerto for violin and orchestra, Op 77; Ex Libris, Op 113; Child's Dream for children's choir and orchestra, Op 66; Concerto for chamber orchestra, Op 125; Journey, cantata for mezzosoprano, baritone, choir and orchestra, Op 127; Dance Suite for orchestra, Op 128; Concerto No 2 for piano and orchestra, Op 134; Concerto for marimba and orchestra, Op 148; 72 chamber pieces and 42 keyboard compositions. Recordings: Symphony No 4 (Apocalyptic), Op 69; Ex Libris, Op 113, for orchestra; CD recording (Mirecourt Trio), Passacaglias and Fugue for piano trio, Op 87. Honours: Featured on front cover of The Piano Quarterly, summer 1981; Meet the Composer Award, American Society of Composers, Authors and Publishers Foundation, 1985; Governor's Award for the Arts, for his musical achievement, 1992. Current Management: Thomas C Stangland, Portland, USA. Hobbies: Chess; Photography; Meteorology. Address: c/o Thomas Stangland Co, PO Box 19262, Portland, OR 97219, USA.

SVORC Antonin, b. 12 Feb 1934, Jaromer, Czechoslovakia. Bass-Baritone. Education: Studied with Jan Berlik in Prague. Debut: State Theatre of Liberet as Pizarro in Fidelio, 1955. Career: Member of the National Theatre, Prague from 1958; Visited Edinburgh with the company in 1964 in the British premiere of From The House Of The Dead by Janácek; Guest appearances at the Berlin Staatsoper and in Vienna, Paris, Dresden, Cologne, Dusseldorf, Kassel, Zurich, Trieste, Venice and Barcelona; Sang in Prague in 1974 in the premiere of Cikker's Coriolanus and as Chrudos in Libuse at the 1983 re-opening of the National Opera; Sang as guest at the Paris Opéra in 1988 in From The House of the Dead. Recordings: Operas by Smetana including Dalibor and Libuse. Honours include: National Artists of Czechoslovakia, 1985. Address: c/o National Theatre, PO Box 865, 112 30 Prague 1, Czech Republic.

SWAFFORD Jan (Johnson), b. 10 Sep 1946, Chattanooga, TN, USA. Composer. Education: Harvard College; Yale School of Music; Tanglewood. Career: Teacher at: Boston University, Goddard College, Hampshire College, Amherst College, Tufts University. Compositions: Passage, 1975; Peal, 1976; Landscape With Traveller, 1981; Shore Lines, 1982; Labyrinths, 1983; Music Like Steel Like Fire, 1983; In Time Of Fear, 1984; Midsummer Variations, 1985; Chamber Sinfonietta, 1988; They Who Hunger, 1989; Requiem in Winter, 1991; Iphigenia Choruses, 1993. Recordings: Midsummer Variations; They Who Hunger, 1993. Publications: The Vintage Guide to Classical Music, 1992; A Life of Charles Ives, in progress; A Life of Brahms, in progress. Contributions to: Articles and reviews to Symphony; New England Monthly; Musical America; Yankee. Hobbies: Reading; Cooking; Hiking; Skiing. Address: 37 Magnolia Avenue 1, Cambridge, MA, USA.

SWANSTON Roderick (Brian), b. 28 Aug 1948, Gosport, England. Professor of Music Theory, Royal College of Music. Education: Music Scholar, Stowe School, 1961-66; Royal College of Music, 1966-69; Organ Scholar at Pembroke College, Cambridge, 1969-71; MA; MusB; Graduate, Royal Schools of Music; Fellow, Royal College of Organists; Licentiate of Royal Academy; Associate of Royal College of Music. Career: Organist at Christ Church, Lancaster Gate, 1972-77, and St James, Sussex Gardens, 1977-80; Conductor of Christ Church Choral Society, 1972-80; Part-Time Tutor at University of London, Department of Extra Mural Studies, 1972-; Academic Adviser in Music to Birkbeck College, University of London, Centre for Extra Mural Studies, 1987-; Visiting Lecturer for many organizations including English National Opera, Royal Opera House, Covent Garden, BBC, Oxford University and Goldsmith's College. Compositions: A Time There Was for Tenor, Choir and Strings; Let Us Gather Hand In Hand for Choir and Brass à 5, recorded by BBC. Recording: Organ recital from Framlingham Parish Church. Publication: Concise History of Music. Address: Royal College of Music, Prince Consort Road, London, SW7, England.

SWAYNE Giles, b. 30 Jun 1946, Hitchin, Hertfordshire, England. Composer. m. Camilla Brett, 1 son, 3 stepchildren. Education: Trinity College Cambridge; Royal Academy of Music; Studies with Nicholas Maw and Messiaen; Conducting course at Siena, 1968. Career: Performances at Aldeburgh and Bromsgrove Festivals and Purcell Room in London; Opera repetiteur at Wexford Festival, 1972-73 and Glyndebourne, 1973-74; Teaching Staff at Bryanston School, 1974-76; Visited West Africa in 1980 to study the music of the Jola people of Senegal and The Gambia. Compositions include: 4 Lyrical Pieces for Cello and Piano, 1970; The Good Morrow, settings for Mezzo and Piano of John Donne, 1971; Canto for Guitar, 1972; Canto for Violin, 1973; Orlando's Music for Orchestra, 1974; Duo for Violin and Piano, 1976; Pentecost-Music for Orchestra, 1976; A World Within, ballet with tape on the Bronte Sisters, 1978; Count-Down for Chorus and 2 Percussions, 1981; Le Nozze di Cherubino, opera, 1984; Missa Tiburtina, 1985; Solo for Guitar, 1986; Symphony for Small Orchestra, 1984; Tonos for 5 Players, 1987; Songlines for Flute and Guitar, 1987; The Song Of Leviathan for Chamber Orchestra, 1988; No Quiet Place for Children's Voices, String Trio and Xylophones, 1989; Circle Of Silence for Six Voices, 1991; Zebra Music, piano pieces for children, 1991; The Song Of The Tortoise for Narrator, Children's Voices, Recorders, Choir and Orchestra, 1992; The Owl And The Pussycat for Narrator and 7 Instruments, 1993; String Quartet No 3, 1993. Memberships: PRS; APC; MCPS. Address: c/o Performing Arts, 6 Windmill Street, London, W1P 1HF, England.

SWEET Sharon, b. 16 Aug 1951, New York, USA. Soprano. Education: Studied with Margaret Harshaw at the Curtis Institute, Philadelphia and with Marinka Gurewich in New York. Career: Sang in private recitals at Philadelphia then appeared in the title role in concert performance of Aida at Munich, 1985; Dortmund Opera, 1986-88, debut as Elisabeth in Tannhäuser; Deutsche Oper Berlin from 1987, notably as guest in Zurich and Japan as Elisabeth and in the Ring; Paris Opera and Hamburg, 1987 as Elisabeth de Valois; Season 1987-88 as Desdemona in Brunswick, Dvorák's Stabat Mater at the Salzburg Festival, Gurrelieder in Munich under Zubin Mehta and Wagner's Elisabeth at the Vienna Staatsoper; Norma in a concert performance of Bellini's opera at Brussels, 1988; US debut as Aida at San Francisco in 1989; Season 1992 as Aida at Dallas and Il Trovatore Leonora at Orange; Sang in the house premiere of Verdi's Stiffelio at the Metropolitan Season, 1993-94 returned 1997, as Aida; Aida at Covent Garden, 1995, returned as Turandot, 1997. Recordings include: Verdi's Requiem. Address: c/o Deutsche Oper Berlin, Richard Wagnerstrasse 10, D-1000 Berlin, Germany.

SWENSEN Joseph, b. 4 Aug 1960, New York, USA. Conductor; Violinist. Education: Studied violin at the Juilliard School with Dorothy DeLay; Conducting studies with Paavo Berglund, Jorge Mester, Otto-Werner Mueller and Lawrence Foster; Studied piano with Christian Sager and Thomas Schumacker. Career: Guest Conductor with the Jerusalem, Bournemouth and Colorado Symphonies, Aalborg Symphony in Denmark, Helsinki, Stockholm, and Israel Chamber Orchestras, Saarbrucken Radio Orchestra, Bergen Philharmonic, Spoleto Festival Orchestra, New World Symphony, Kansas City Philharmonic, and Tucson Symphony; Engagements as violin soloist with the Cleveland Orchestra, Los Angeles Philharmonic, Bavarian Radio Symphony, Leipzig Gewandhaus, Stuttgart Philharmonic, Royal Philharmonic, Philharmonia, Pittsburgh Symphony and Finnish Radio Symphony Orchestras. Recordings include: Beethoven's Violin Concerto with the Royal Philharmonic under André Previn; Complete Works of Schubert for Violin and Piano, with Jeffrey Kahane; Sibelius Violin Concerto and Humoresques with Jukka-Pekka Saraste and the Finnish Radio Symphony; Chamber Works with James Galway and Kazuhito Yamashita; Complete Works for Violin and Harpsichord by JS Bach, with John Gibbons, harpsichord and Elizabeth Anderson, cellist. Address: c/o Victoria Rowsell, Van Walsum Management Ltd, 4 Addison Bridge Place, London W1A 8XP

SWENSON Ruth-Ann, b. 1958, USA. Singer (Soprano). Career: Sang soubrette roles with the San Francisco Opera, 1983-93; Donizetti's Adina at Seattle (1984) and Despina at Geneva; Nannette at Amsterdam (1987), Mozart's Ilia at Toronto and Inez in L'Africaine at San Francisco; Metropolitan Opera debut, 1988, followed by Gilda and Zerlina; Washington Opera 1989-90, as Lucia and Rosina, Dallas 1989-92, as Norina and Susanna; Detroit 1990, as Gounod's Juliette, Cologne and Schwetzingen 1991, as Mozart's Constanze; Covent Garden debut 1996, as Handel's Semele; Sang Bellini's Elvira at the Met, 1997; Modern repertory includes Argento's The Voyage of Edgar Allan Poe (Chicago, 1990) and Moore's The Ballad of Baby Doe (Long Beach Opera, 1987). Recordings include: Video of L'Africaine (Virgin Classics). Address: c/o Lies Askonas Ltd, 6 Henrietta Street, London W1, England.

SWENSSON Evelyn (Dickenson), b. 18 Sept 1928, Woodstock, Virginia, USA. Conductor. m. Sigurd Simcox Swensson, 9 June 1949, 2 sons, 2 daughters. Education: MusM, West Chester University, 1972. Career: Conductor: Aldersgate Methodist Church, Wilmington, Delaware, 1969-; Brandywiners Ltd, Kennett Square, Pennsylvania, 1973; Conductor and Director of Education, Opera Delaware, Wilmington, 1974-; Conductor: Bi-Centennial Chorus, Wilmington, 1976; Northern Delaware Choral Society, Wilmington, 1977; Guest Conductor, Delaware Symphony Orchestra, Wilmington, 1977; Conductor: Ardensingers, Wilmington, 1978-80; Methodist Bi-Centennial in America, 1984; First State Chorus, Wilmington, 1987; Vice-President. Opera for Youth Inc, Tampa; Conductor, over 50 operas including US premieres of Sleeping Beauty (Respighi), 1977, The Zoo (Sullivan and Rowe), 1979, 1980, The Lion, the Witch and the Wardrobe (McCabe), 1990, and world premieres of The Boy Who Grew Too Fast (Menotti), 1982, Charlotte's Web (Strouse), 1989, A Wrinkle in Time (Libby Larsen), 1992; Conductor of inaugural concert for Governor P S duPont IV, Wilmington, 1977, Black History Celebrations, Wilmington, 1985, 1987; Conductor of world premieres of own compositions, The Enormous Egg, 1993, The Adventures of Beatrix Potter, 1994, The Jungle Book, 1996. Compositions include: The Phantom Tollbooth, 1995. Honours: International Reading Council Literacy Award, 1989. Address: 58A Heybrun Rd, Chadds Ford, PA 19317, USA.

SWIERCZEWSKI Michel, b. 1960, France. Conductor. Education: Studied with Jean-Claude Hartemann in Paris and Charles Mackerras at the Vienna Hochschule. Career: Made debut in 1976 and was then assistant conductor to Pierre Boulez and Peter Eötvös at the Ensemble Intercontemporain, 1983-85 and for Claudio Abbado at La Scala, including the premiere of Nono's Prometeo, 1985-86; Paris Opéra in 1986 with Georges Prêtre; Has conducted such contemporary music ensembles as Itineraire, Musique Oblique, Antidogma and New Music Ensemble, giving many premieres; Guest engagements in France, Germany, Italy, Spain, Portugal and Australia; Conducted Die Fledermaus at Lyons, 1996. Recordings: La Conference des Oiseaux by Michael Levinas; Works by Roussel with the Gulbenkian Foundation Orchestra; Complete Symphonies of Méhul. Honours: Finalist, 1984 Tanglewood International Conducting Competition; Prize, Villa Medicis Hors Les Murs. Address: Anglo Swiss Management, Ste 35-37 Morley House, 320 Regent Street, London W1R 5AD, England.

SWINGLE Ward (Lamar), b. 21 Sep 1927, Mobile, AL, USA. Choral Conductor; Composer; Arranger; Clinician. m. Françoise Demorest, 23 Sep 1952, 3 daughters. Education: BM, MM, Piano Major, Cincinnati Conservatory of Music, 1947-51; Masterclasses with Walter Gieseking at Saarbrücken, Germany, 1951-53. Career: Solo piano recitals and accompanist, 1953-55; Conductor of Ballets de Paris, France, 1955-59; Founded Swingle Singers, a worldwide touring concert group, 1963; Numerous radio and TV appearances with Swingle Singers in most major capitals and about 2000 concerts around the world, 1963-91. Compositions: Over 100 arrangements and compositions for the Swingle Singers. Recordings: About 30 with the Swingle Singers including Bach's Greatest Hits, Going Baroque, and Luciano Berio's Sinfonia. Contribution to: Article in ACDA Choral Journal, 1986. Honours: 5 Grammy Awards, 1964, 1965, 1966, 1970; Grand Priz du Disque, 1964; Edison Award, 1970. Memberships: La Societé des Auteurs, Compositeurs et Editeurs de Musique, 1963-86; Phi Mu Epsilon, 1947-51; American Choral Directors Association, 1984-89. Hobbies: Gardening; Tennis. Current Management: Piers Schmidt, 45a Chalcot Road, London, NW1 8LS, England. Address: 4 Thomas Road, Glen Gardner, NJ 08826, USA.

SYLVESTER Michael, b. 1955, Indiana, USA. Tenor. Education: Studied with Margaret Harshaw at Bloomington. Career: Sang Radames and Pinkerton at Stuttgart, 1987, at Cincinnati Opera from 1987 as Pinkerton and Sam in Floyd's Susannah, New York City Opera debut in 1987 as Rodolfo in La Bohème and further engagements at La Scala and Santiago as Pinkerton in 1990, Paris Opéra as Pollione in Norma, Hamburg Staatsoper as Rodolfo and Don José, and Vienna Staatsoper as Cavaradossi; Covent Garden debut in 1990 as Samson followed by Gabriel Adorno in a new production of Simon Boccanegra in

1991; Sang at Bregenz Festival in 1990 as Hagenbach in La Wally, and at Metropolitan Opera in debut, 1991 as Rodolfo in Luisa Miller followed by Don Carlos in 1992; Appearances as Radames at Deutsche Oper Berlin, Chicago, Orange Festival and Seattle in 1992; Further engagements at Bonn as Bacchus in 1990, San Francisco as Calaf, Venice as Don Carlos and Geneva as Foresto in Attila; Sang Radames at the Met, 1996-97. Recordings include: Title role in Oberon; Don Carlos conducted by James Levine. Address: c/o Metropolitan Opera, Lincoln Center, New York, NY 10023, USA.

SYNKOVA Milada, b. 16 May 1933, Bratislava, Czechoslovakia. Pianist; Harpsichordist; Opera Repetiteur; Tutor. Education: Conservatoire of Music, Brno; University of Bratislava, 1951-63. Debut: Slovak National Theatre, Bratislava, 1963. Career: Concerts Worldwide. Recordings: For Czechoslovak Radio, TV, Live Cycle for Slovak TV, CD. Memberships include: Bratislava City Choir; Chamber Orchestra Camerata Slovaca. Hobbies: Languages; Travel. Address: Salviova 52, 82101 Bratislava, Slovakia.

SYNOWIEC Ewa Krystyna, b. 12 April 1942, Cracow, Poland. Composer; Pianist; Teacher. Education: Diploma with honours, 1967; Studied piano with Ludwik Stefanski, Cracow Music Academy; Suzanne Roche and Vlado Perlemuter, Paris, 1967, 1968; Composition with Boguslaw Schaeffer, 1973; Adjunct Professor, Composition, 1976; Docent, 1985; Professor, 1991-. Career: Pianist, Recitals and Concerts at home and abroad, 1948-78; Exhibitions and performances in Cracow, Dublin, Edmonton (Canada), Gdansk, Katowice, London, Paris, Poznan, Salzburg, Vienna, Warsaw, Wroclaw, Zurich (Switzerland). Compositions: Over 100 works (Orchestral, Choral and Chamber Music); Over 100 Musical Graphics. Publications: Instrumental Theatre of Boguslaw Schaeffer, 1983. Memberships: Association of Polish Composers; Grupa Krakowska. Hobbies: Painting; Poetry. Address: Malczewskiego 78/92, 80-107 Gdansk, Poland.

SYRUS David, b. 1945, England. Conductor. Education: Oxford University and the London Opera Centre. Career: Repetiteur at the Royal Opera, Covent Garden, from 1971; Head of Music Staff from 1981, Head of Music and Assistant Conductor from 1993; Operas have included Ariadne auf Naxos, Die Zauberflöte, and Le nozze di Figaro; Assistant Conductor at the Bayreuth Festival for seven reasons, at Salzburg from 1991; Guest Conductor with Israeli Ballet, Garden Venture, at St John's Smith Square and the Ludlow Festival; Continuo player and an accompanist in Lieder recitals. Recordings: EMI, BMG and Phonogram. Address: Athole Still Ltd, Foresters Hall, 25-27 Westow Street, London SE19 3RY, England.

SZABO Peter, b. 1965, Rumania. Concert Cellist. Education: Studied at the Kolozsvar Academy, Budapest. Career: Played the Dvorak Concerto at Weimar 1981, with the Jena Philharmonic and is soloist with the Concentus Hungaricus and Budapest Festival Orchestra; Soloist and Chamber Musician in USA, Mexico, South Korea and throughout Europe; Recitals and recordings with pianist Denes Varjon. Recordings: Albums for Electrecord, Naxos and Hungaroton. Address: Worldwide Artists, 6 Petersfield Crescent, Coulsdon, Surrey CR5 2JQ, England.

SZABO Vilmos Imre, b. 26 May 1940, Bloske, Hungary. Tuba Player. m. Judith Andrea Fekete, 6 May 1969, 1 son, 1 daughter. Education: Artist & Teacher Diploma, Franz Liszt Acady of Music, Budapest. Career: Headmaster, Brass Teacher, Brass Band Leader, Conductor, Köszeg Music School, Hungary, 1964-66; Principal Tubist, Symphony Orchestra, Hungarian Radio & TV, 1966-; Founding Member, Hungarian Brass Septet & Pro Brass Ensemble; Concert Tours all over Europe, USA, Canada, Australia, New Zealand, japan, Korea, Taiwan. Recordings: Serenade of the Seven-Headed Dragon, Hungarian Brass; Pro Brass a la Carte; Fire Walter; Heimatlieder und Uberhaupt; Pro Brass at Abbey Road; Grad' Verkehrt; All the works of Bela Bartok, Johannes Brahms, Franz Liszt with Budapest Symphony. Honours: Hungarian Radio Niveaux Prize, 1978; 1st Prize, Premio di Ancona, Italy, 1979; Hungarian Artisjus Prize, Outstanding Interpretation of Contemporary Music, 1981; Cultural Grand Prix of the Upper Austrian Ministry of Culture, 1996. Memberships: President, Hungarian Trombone-Tuba Association; Tubists Universal Brotherhood Association; Hungarian Brass Band Association. Hobbies: Jazz; Skiing; Soccer; Jogging. Current Management: Pro Brass Ensemble, Studio fur Angewandte Musik, A-4501 Neuhofen a/d Krems, Brucknerstr 12, Austria. Address: Kerepesi ut 140-142, 1144 Budapest, Hungary.

SZAKALY Agnes, b. 14 Mar 1951, Budapest, Hungary. Cimbalom Artist; Professor. m. Gabor Baross, 23 Aug 1975. Education: Cimbalom Faculty, Ferrenc Liszt Academy of Music, Budapest, 1974; Faculty of Pedagogy, Eotvos Lorand University, 1983. Debut: Royal Opera House, Norway, Oslo, 1973. Career: Soloist, Concerts in Austria, England, Germany, Italy, Japan, Mexico, South Korea, Spain, Russia. Recordings: Bach, French Suites, 1982; Folk Arrangements, 1984; All That Music, 1986; Solo CD, Preludio, 1993; Music of 300 Years of Cimbalom, 1994;

Works for Cimbalom, 1997; J S Bach, Goldberg Variations, 1998. Honours: Artisjus Prize, 1983, 1985, 1986, 1988, 1992, 1996; Ferenc Liszt Prize, 1993. Memberships: Cimbalist Friendship Association, President; Hungarian Music Council. Current Management: Budapest Artist Management, Somloi ul 39, H-1118 Budapest, Hungary. Address: Baross u 148, H-1161 Budapest, Hungary.

SZALONEK Witold (Jozef), b. 2 Mar 1927, Czechowice, Poland. Composer. m. Beata Zygmunt, 23 Apr 1963, 2 sons. Education: Diploma of Music, Lyceum Katowice, 1949; Diploma with Distinction, MA, Composition, High School of Music, Katowice, 1956; Studied with Nadia Boulanger in Paris, 1962-63. Debut: Katowice in 1954. Career: Assistant at High School of Music, Katowice, Poland, 1956-61; Adjunct Professor, 1961-67, Profesor of Composition, 1967-75, Rector, 1972-73, Professor of Composition and Theory, High School of Arts, Berlin West, 1973-; Lecturer at universities and high schools of music in Munster, Osnabruck, Heidelberg, Mannheim, Aarhus, Helsinki, Graz, Cracow, Warsaw, Jyväskylä and Turku; Lecturer, Viitasaari. Compositions include: Pastorale for Oboe and Orchestra; Symphonic Satire; Les Sons for orchestra; Musica Concertante for Double Bass and Orchestra; Confessions for Speaker, Choir and Orchestra; Sonata for Cello and Piano; Proporzioni I for Flute, Viola and Harp; ++++ for 1-4 Instruments and Arco; Connections for Chamber Ensemble; DP's Five Ghoulish Dreams for Saxophone; Alice's Unknown Adventures In The Fairy Land Of Percussion; Nocturne for Baritone, Harp and String Orchestra; Elegy for Clarinet and Piano. Recordings: Mutanza for Piano; Improvisations Sonoristiques for Clarinet, Trombone, Cello and Piano; Piernikiana for Tuba Solo; Concertino for Flute; Les Sons; Mutazioni for Orchestra; Musica Concertante for Double Bass and Orchestra; Little B-A-C-H Symphony for Orchestra; Connections; O Pleasant Earth, cantata for Voice and Orchestra. Address: Hittorfstr 12, D-1000 Berlin 33 West, Germany.

SZEGEDI Aniko, b. 22 March 1938, Budapest, Hungary. Pianist. m. J Szavai, 20 December 1966, 1 daughter. Education: F Liszt Academy of Music, Budapest. Debut: Piano Concerto, Chopin, Budapest Academy of Music, 1961. Career: Concerts include: Budapest, 1966, Vienna Brahms Saal, 1969; Leningrad, Kiev, 1974, Dresden, London, 1974, Berlin, 1983. Recordings: Beethoven, Eroica Variations; Haydn, Sonatas, Beethoven, Piano Concerto, Triple Concerto (with D Koracs & M Pereuy). Honours: 3rd Prize, International Schumann Piano Concerts, Zwickau, 1963; F Liszt Prize, Budapest, 1973. Address: Szt Istvan krt 16, 1137 Budapest, Hungary.

SZETO Caroline, b. 15 Sept 1956, Australia. Composer. Education: BMus (Hons) 1988, MMus (Hons) 1994, University of Sydney; Study with Peter Sculthorpe, from 1985. Career: University of Sydney, 1990-91; Commissions from ABC, 1991, Sydney Metropolitan Opera, 1993, Song Company 1994, 1997; Sydney Mandolins, 1995, 1997. Compositions include: Three Pieces for Guitar, 1984; Catalogue for string quartet, 1985; C.C. 33 for concert band, 1985; Sheng for orchestra, 1986; Images of Li Po for ensemble, 1987; Missa Brevis, 1987; Energy for orchestra, 1990; Study No 1 & 2 for tuba, 1990; Moon on Night's Water for piano, 1990; Lament of the Boobook for computer-based instruments, 1991; Yunny's Treat, for piano, 1991; ABC Fanfare for orchestra, 1992; In A Garden for computer-based instruments, 1992; A Game For Violin, 1992; The Third Station of the Cross for clarinet, double bass and percussion, 1993; The Sweet Apple, for 6 vocal soloists, 1994; Energy II for orchestra, 1994; Mandolin Dance, 1995; Prelude for mandolin ensemble, 1997; Monkeys Cry for 6 vocal soloists and 2 percussionists, 1997; Cycles for guitar, 1997. Recordings: Yunny's Treat, 1993; Mandolin Dance, 1996; Energy for Orchestra, 1997; ABC Fanfare for Orchestra, 1997. Honours include: Ignaz Friedman Memorial Prize, 1985; Donald Peart Memorial Prize, 1986; 2 First Prizes, City of Sydney Eisteddfod, 1991; Composer Fellowship, Australia Council for the Arts, 1994. Address: P O Box 163, Mosman, NSW 2988, Australia.

SZILAGYI Karoly, b. 1949, Oradea Mare, Rumania. Singer (Baritone). Education: Studied at the Cluj Conservatory. Career: Sang Morales and Rigoletto at the Cluj Opera, then engaged at the Gelsenkirchen Opera 1980-85, Essen 1985-89; Guest appearances at the Vienna Staatsoper, Zurich Opera and St Gallen and throughout Germany, Hungary and Austria; Liège 1990, as Rigoletto; Also sings in operas by Donizetti and Puccini; Sang Coppelius in Les Contes d'Hoffmann at Essen, 1996. Address: c/o Essen Opera, Theater Essen, Rolandstrasse 10, W-4300 Essen 1, Germany.

SZIRMAY Marta, b. 1939, Kaposvar, Hungary. Mezzo-Soprano. Education: Studied at the Budapest Conservatory. Career: Member of the Hungarian State Opera from 1964 singing the mezzo repertory in operas by Wagner and Verdi, and Cologne Opera from 1976; Covent Garden debut in 1977 as Clytemnestra in Elektra with later London appearances as Erda in Das Rheingold and Mistress Quickly in Falstaff; Further appearances in Hamburg, Berlin, Vienna, Barcelona,

Venice and Naples; Sang at Salzburg Festival in 1985 as Ericles in Il Ritorno di Ulisse by Monteverdi, arranged by Henze; Other roles include Gaea in Daphne, Gluck's Orpheus and Brangaene in Tristan and Isolde; Season 1992 in Corghi's Blimunda at Turin. Address: c/o Oper der Stadt Köln, Offenbachplatz, D-5000 Cologne, Germany.

SZMYTKA Elzbieta, b. 1956, Prochowice, Poland. Soprano. Education: Studied in Krakow, 1975-82 with Helena Lazarska. Career: Sang at the Krakow Opera from 1978 then at Bytom and Wroclaw; Toured to West Germany and Luxembourg as Blondchen in Die Entführung; Sang widely in Western Europe from 1983 notably at Ghent, Antwerp and Brussels as Despina, Blondchen and Serpina, and as Nanetta, 1987-88; Sang at Aix-en-Provence Festival, 1987-88 as Nannetta and as Servilia in La Clemenza di Tito, Holland Festival in 1987 as Serpina in La Finta Giardiniera, at the Vienna Staatsoper in 1988 as Papagena, and in Amsterdam and Antwerp in 1989 as Gilda and Zerbinetta; Sang at Glyndebourne Festival in 1991 as Ilia in Idomeneo and Servilia in La Clemenza di Tito, Salzburg Summer Festival in 1992 as Alyeya in From the House of the Dead and Mozartwoche in 1993 as Cinna in Lucio Silla; Sang Vitellia in Gluck's La Clemenza di Tito at the Théâtre des Champs-Elysées, Paris, 1996; Other roles include Susanna, Norina and Aennchen in Der Freischütz; Engaged for Mozart's Lucio Silla and Entführung at the 1997 Salzburg Festival. Recordings include: La Finta Giardiniera; Despina in Così fan tutte; Mozart Arias; Die Entführung; Il Matrimonio Segreto; Music by Szymanowski conducted by Simon Rattle. Current Management: Harold Holt Ltd. Address: 31 Sinclair Road, London, W14 0NS, England.

SZOKOLAY Sándor, b. 30 Mar 1931, Kunágota, Hungary. Composer. m. (1) Sari Szesztay, 1952, (2) Maja Weltler, 1970, 4 sons, 1 daughter. Education: Studied with Szabo and Farkas at the Budapest Music Academy, 1950-57; Composition department graduate in 1957. Career: Music teacher, Budapest Conservatory, 1952-55; Musical Adviser and Editor at Hungarian Radio, 1955-59; Composition Teacher at Budapest Music Academy, 1959-66; Musical Adviser for Hungarian TV, 1966-. Compositions: Dramatic: The Ballad of Horror, ballet, 1961, Blood Wedding, opera, 1964, Hamlet, opera, 1968, Sacrifice, ballet, 1973, Ecce Homo, passion-opera, 1987; Margaret, Victim Sacrificed for the Country, opera, 1996; Orchestral: Concert Rondo for Piano and Strings, 1955, Violin Concerto, 1956, Piano Concerto, 1958, Trumpet Concerto, 1969, Oratorios, The Fire of March, 1958 and Isthar's Descent Into Hell, 1960, Negro Cantata, 1962, Deploration, Requiem in Memory of Poulenc, 1964, The Power of Music, choral fantasy with orchestra; Chamber: Sonata for Solo Violin, 1956, String Quartet, 1973. Honours: Erkel Prize, 1960, 1965; Kossuth Prize, 1966; Paris International Dance Festival Golden Star Prize for Best Composition, 1967; Merited Artist, 1976; Honoured Artist, 1986; Bartók-Pasztory Prize, 1987. Membership: Chairman of Hungarian Kodály Society. Hobbies: Motoring; Hiking. Current Management: Martin Perdoux, 5014 Chaparral Way, San Diego, CA 92115, USA.

SZÖLLÖSY Andras, b. 27 Feb 1921, Szaszvaros, Transylvania. Composer; Music Historian. m. Eva Kemenyfly. Education: Academy of Music, Budapest with Kodaly, 1939-44; Accademia di Santa Cecilia, Rome, with Petrassi, 1947-48; PhD, University of Budapest. Career: Academy of Music Budapest from 1950. Compositions: Ballets: Improvisations on the Fear 1963, Pantomime 1965; Sons of Fire 1977; Orchestral: Concerto for piano, brass, percussion and strings, 1957; Concerto for Strings, 1968; Trasfigurazioni, 1972; Musica concertante, 1973; Musica per orchestra, 1973; Sonorita, 1974; Concerto for harpsichord and strings, 1978; Tristia (Maros Sirato) for Strings, 1983; Concerto No V (Lehellet), 1975; Chamber Music: Pro Somno Igoris Stravinsky Quieto for small ensemble, 1978; Fragmenti for Mezzosoprano, flute and viola; Suoni di tromba for trumpet and piano, 1983; Musiche per ottoni for brass instruments, 1975; Quartetto di tromboni, 1986; Quartetto per archi, 1988; Elegy (dixtuor), 1992; Passacaglia Achatio Mathe in memoriam for string quartet and violincello solo, 1997; Choral Works: Fabula Phaedri, 1982; In Phariaeos, 1981; Plactus Mariae, 1982; Miserere, 1984. Publications: Arthur Honegger 1960, 1980; Editor of various writings by Bartok and Kodaly; Critical edition of Bartok's writings, 1967. Honours include: First Prize, UNESCO International Rostrum of Composers, Paris, 1970; Kossuth Prize, 1985; Bartok-Pasztory Prix, 1986, 1989; Commendeur de l'Ordre des Arts et Lettres, 1987. Address: Somloi ut 12, 1118 Budapest, Hungary.

SZONYI Erzsebet, b. 25 Apr 1924, Budapest, Hungary. Composer; Music Educator. Education: Budapest Music Academy, 1942-47; Paris Conservatoire, 1948 with Aubin, Messiaen and Nadia Boulanger. Career: Teacher of Music Education at Budapest Music Academy, 1948-81, prompted the Kodály Method in Hungary and elsewhere. Compositions include: Operas: Dalma, 1953, The Florentine Tragedy, Meiningen, 1960, Le Malade Imaginaire, Budapest, 1961, Joyful Lament, Budapest, 1980, Break In Transmission, Szeged, 1982, Elfrida, 1985; Other: 2 Piano Sonatinas, 1944 and 1946; 2 Divertimentos, 1948 and

1951; Piano Sonata, 1953; Organ Concerto, 1958; Trio for Oboe, Clarinet and Bassoon, 1958; Musica Festiva for Orchestra, 1964; 3 Ideas In 4 Movements for Piano and Orchestra, 1980; Sonata for Double Bass and Piano, 1982; Evocatio for Piano and Organ, 1985; Choral works. Publications include: Methods of Musical Reading and Writing, 4 volumes, Budapest, 1953-65, English translation, 1972; Study of Kodály's Teaching Methods, Budapest, 1973. Honours include: Liszt Prize, 1947; Erkel Prize, 1959. Address: c/o MASA, Nova Building, 3rd Floor, St Jean Road, Quatre-Bornes, Mauritius.

SZÖRENYI Suzana, b. 23 October 1929, Bucharest, Romania. Pianist; Lecturer. m. Corneliu Radulescu, 26 September 1968. Education: Diploma, C Porumbescu Music Academy of Bucharest, 1954; Piano Studies with Dusi Mura and Music Forms with Tudor Ciortea. Debut: Recital, Romanian Atheneum, Bucharest, 1946. Career: Currently, Professor by the Music Academy, Bucharest; Soloist, Symphony Concertos, Piano Solo Recitals, Piano Duets, Lieder, Chamber Music, Tours abroad; Recordings for Romanian Broadcasting, from Romanian and Universal repertoire; Premieres of recorded and stage performances of Romanian music by George Enescu, Constantin Silvestri, Hilda Jerea, Dan Constantinescu, and others; Premieres of works by Beethoven, Brahms, Schumann and Mendelssohn in Romania; Television films with famous pages of the pianistic literature; Participation in George Enescu International Festival, Bucharest - 11th Edition, September 1988; Tour abroad: Germany and Switzerland, with Cornelia Binonzetti (violin), 1991; Also to Austria, 1996; Participation in the Gala, first EPTA Congress in Romania, Constanto, 1992; Interpretation of Nietzsche's works; Lieder, violin, piano and four hands works. Recordings: Lieder by Brahms with Marta Kessler; Romanian Lieder with Emilia Petrecu; Romanian Dances for two Pianos by Dinu Lipatti with Hilda Jerea; Beethoven's complete works for piano - four hands; Symphony Concertante for Two Pianos and String Orchestra by Dinu Lipatti, and George Enescu's works for piano - four hands with Corneliu Radulescu; Original four-hands works by Brahms, Schumann, Mendelssohn-Bartholdy and Max Reger (with Corneliu Radulescu). Contributions to: Musica Revue; Elore, Newspapers. Hobbies: Ballet; House Plants; Domestic Animals; Swimming; Badminton. Current Management: Academia de Muzica Bucuresti, Str Stirbei Voda 33, Romania. Address: Colentina 37-VI/26, 72.245 Bucharest 10, Romania.

SZOSTTEK-RADKOVA Krystina, b. 14 Mar 1933, Katowice, Poland. Mezzo-Soprano. Education: Studied at the Katowice Conservatory with Faryaszevska and Lenczevska. Debut: Katowice in 1960 as Azucena in Il Trovatore. Career: National Opera Warsaw from 1962 as Eboli, Amneris, Ortrud, Kundry and other roles in the dramatic mezzo repertory; Guest engagements in Vienna, Hamburg, Berlin, Prague, Sofia, Belgrade, Moscow and Leningrad; Sang at Paris Opéra in 1981 as Ulrica in Un Ballo in Maschera, Grand Théâtre, Geneva in 1983 as Herodias in Salome and appeared at the Théâtre de la Monnaie Brussels and the Opéra de Lyon in operas by Verdi and Wagner; Sang Fricka in The Ring at Warsaw in 1988; Concert tours of France and South America. Recordings: Many opera albums and works by Penderecki and Tadeusz Baird. Address: Teatr Wiekli, Plac Teatrainy, 00-076 Warsaw, Poland.

SZUCS Marta, b. 1964, Hungary. Soprano. Education: Studied violin at first, then singing in Budapest. Career: Sang in concert in Hungary and abroad, 1976-78; Guest appearances at Hamburg Staatsoper and Frankfurt from 1979; Member of the Hungarian National Opera from 1981 with debut as Gilda; Further engagements at Vienna Staatsoper, La Traviata's Violetta, 1985-87, Scottish Opera as Gilda in 1984 and Anna in Anna Bolena in 1989, Liège, 1986-87 as Lucia di Lammermoor, and Monte Carlo in 1988 in Cimarosa's Il Pittore Parigino; Sang Anaide in Moise et Pharaon by Rossini at Budapest in 1992. Address: c/o Hungarian State Opera House, Nepoztarsasag utja 22, 1061 Budapest, Hungary.

T

T'HEZAN Helia, b. 23 Aug 1934, Rieumes, France. Soprano. Education: Studied at the Toulouse Conservatoire and the Musikhochschule, Berlin. Debut: Bordeaux in 1958 in Armide by Lully. Career: Sang at the Paris Opéra and the Opéra-Comique from 1959, Covent Garden in 1965 in the title role of Gluck's Iphigénie en Tauride, Glyndebourne in 1966 as Charlotte in Werther, and Monte Carlo in 1973 in the premiere of La Reine Morte by Rossellini; Has sung at Lyon, Marseille, Geneva, Rome, Trieste, Turin, Lisbon and Philadelphia; Sang at the Paris Opéra in 1988 as Juno in Orphée aux Enfers. Recordings include: Manon by Massenet. Address: Théâtre National, 8 Rue Scribe, F-75009 Paris, France.

TABACHNIK Michel, b. 10 Nov 1942, Geneva, Switzerland. Conductor; Composer. m. Sabine Tabachnik, 24 June 1981, 2 sons, 1 daughter. Education: Piano, Conducting, Writing, Composition; Assistant of Markevitch and Boulez. Debut: BBC, London; National Orchestra, Paris; Berlin Philharmonic. Career: Conducting all major orchestras including: NHK Tokyo; Orchestre de Paris; Israel Philharmonic; Berlin Philharmonic; Philharmonic, London; St Cecilia, Rome; Suisse Romande, Geneva; Concertgebouw, Amsterdam. Compositions: Cosmogonie for orchestra; Haisha for choir and orchestra; Le Pacte des Onze for choir and orchestra; L'Arch for soprano and orchestra; Concerto for Piano; Quatuor; Les Perseides for orchestra. Recordings: Schumann, Grieg, Lalo, Saint-Saëns; Xenskis. Hobbies: Mountaineering; Reading. Address: CH-1985 Villaz-La Sage, Switzerland.

TABAKOV Emil, b. 1947, Bulgaria. Conductor; Composer. Education: Bulgarian State Conservatory, degree in conducting, composition and double bass. Career: Founded and conducted the Bulgarian State Conservatoire Chamber Orchestra of Sofia, 1977; Director of the Sofia Soloists Chamber Orchestra, 1979-, touring Bulgaria, Europe, Asia, Latin America, Australia and the USA; Principal Conductor of the Sofia Philharmonic Orchestra, 1985 with tours of the USA, Japan, Hong Kong, South America and the UK; Guest Conductor in Denmark, Sweden, Germany, Poland, Brazil, Romania, Greece and France. Compositions: Concerto for Double Bass and Orchestra; Turnovgrad Velki; 1393 Cantata; Concerto for Percussion; Three Symphonies. Recordings: Mozart, The Complete Church Sonatas; Works by JS Bach, Handel, Haydn, Mendelssohn, Shostakovich, Britten and Schoenberg (with the Sofia Soloists); Complete Symphonies of Mahler, Rachmaninov and Bruckner (with the Sofia Philharmonic Orchestra). Honours: Prizewinner, Nikolai Malko International Competition for Young Conductors, Copenhagen, 1977. Address: c/o Norman McCann International Artists Ltd, The Coach House, 56 Lawrie Park Gardens, London, SE26 6XJ, England.

TADDEI Giuseppe, b. 26 Jun 1916, Genoa, Italy. Baritone. Education: Studied in Rome. Debut: Rome in 1936 as The Herald in Lohengrin. Career: Sang in Rome until 1942 as Alberich and Germont and in Dallapiccola's Volo di Notte; Sang at Vienna Staatsoper, 1946-48 as Amonasro, Rigoletto and the Figaros of Mozart and Rossini, Cambridge Theatre in London, 1947 as Scarpia and Rigoletto, Salzburg Festival in 1948 as Mozart's Figaro, and La Scala, 1948-61 as Malatesta, the villains in Les Contes d'Hoffmann and Pizarro; Sang Wagner's Dutchman, Gunther and Wolfram elsewhere in Italy, and Mozart's Papageno and Leporello; US debut at San Francisco in 1957 as Macbeth; Sang at Chicago in 1959 as Barnaba, Teatro Masimo Palermo in 1959 in Beatrice di Tenda by Bellini and Covent Garden, 1960-67 as Macbeth, Rigoletto, Iago and Scarpia; Sang at Bregenz Festival, 1968-71 as Falstaff, Dulcamara and Suplice in La Fille du Régiment, Vienna Staatsoper in 1980 in Il Tabarro, Metropolitan Opera debut in 1985 as Falstaff, Vienna Staatsoper in 1986 as Scarpia, to celebrate 70th birthday, and sang Gianni Schicchi at Torre del Lago in 1987; Appeared at Stuttgart Staatsoper in 1990 as Falstaff. Recordings: La Bohème; Ernani; Un Ballo in Maschera; Guillaume Tell; Rigoletto; Falstaff; Don Giovanni; Il Maestro di Capella; Andrea Chénier; Le nozze di Figaro; Così fan tutte; L'Elisir d'Amore; Mosè in Egitto; Linda di Chamounix; Falstaff; Tosca; Macbeth. Address: c/o Staatstheater Stuttgart, Oberer Schlossgarten 6, D-7000 Stuttgart 1, Germany.

TADDEI Ottavio, b. 15 Jul 1926, Tuscany, Italy. Tenor. Education: Studied in Siena. Debut: Sienna, as Rodolfo in La Bohème, 1953. Career: Sang the Duke of Mantua and Edgardo at Rome, 1954; Appearances at Milan, Florence, Moderna and San Jose in Costa Rica; Teatro San Carlo, Naples, 1959, as Mateo in Conchita by Zandonai; Sang at Teatro Comunale in Florence from 1960, and made tours of the Netherlands, Turkey and England; Many broadcasts for Italian radio, RAI including The Queen of Spades in 1963; Sang in Hamburg, Nuremberg and Frankfurt from 1966 notably as Pinkerton; Sang in Monteverdi's Poppea at Rome, 1966. Address: Teatro Comunale di Firenze, Via Solferino 15, 50123 Florence, Italy.

TADEO Giorgio, b. 2 Oct 1929, Verona, Italy. Bass Singer. Education: Studied in Parma with Ettore Campogalliani and at the Opera School of La Scala, Milan. Debut: Palermo in 1953 as Mephistopheles in Faust. Career: Sang at Turin, Rome, Florence and Trieste as well as La Scala; Sang at Verona Arena in 1955 and 1973-74; Covent Garden debut in 1974 as Don Pasquale; Further engagements at Buenos Aires, Mexico City, Dallas, Chicago, Paris and Salzburg. Recordings include: Tosca; Andrea Chénier conducted by Chailly; Leonore by Paer; Antonio in Le nozze di Figaro; Manon Lescaut.

TAGLIASACCI Monica, b. 1959, Turin, Italy. Singer (Mezzo-soprano). Education: Studied in Venice. Career: Sang in Rossini's Tancredi at Turin and at La Scala in Rossini's Il Viaggio a Reims, I Lombardi and Die Frau ohne Schatten; Suzuki in Butterfly at Ravenna, Verona and Zurich; Guest appearances at the Vienna Staatsoper in L'Italiana in Algeri, at Philadelphia as Dorabella and at Florence as Pantalis in Boito's Mefistofele; Bayerische Staatsoper at Munich, 1991-91; Sang Teresa in La Sonnambula at Rome, 1996. Address: c/o Bavarian State Opera, Max Joseph Platz, Pf 100148, W-8000 Munich 1, Germany.

TAGLIAVINI Franco, b. 29 Oct 1934, Novellara, Reggio Emilia, Italy. Tenor. Education: Studied at Liceo Musicale Vercelli and with Zita Fumagalli-Riva. Debut: Teatro Nuovo Milan in 1961 as Canio in Pagliacci. Career: Bologna in 1962 as Pinkerton; Sang Edgardo in Lucia di Lammermoor at Tunisia, and at Rome Opera as Dmitri in Boris Godunov, Cavaradossi and Lensky; US debut in 1964 as Ismaele in Nabucco and Calaf in Turandot at San Francisco; Sang Alfredo for Dallas Opera in 1965; La Scala debut in 1965 in Mosè by Rossini; Sang at Royal Opera House, Covent Garden, 1967-76 as Pollione, Cavaradossi, the Duke of Mantua and Macduff, and Chicago Lyric Opera, 1969-73 as Turiddu, Calaf, Pinkerton, Alfredo and Riccardo in Un Ballo in Maschera, I Due Foscari and Maria Stuarda; Appearances at the Metropolitan Opera, NY in Norma, Un Ballo in Maschera, Tosca, Vespri Siciliani and Macbeth; Guest appearances in Munich, Paris, Berlin, Vienna, Parma, Geneva, Zurich, Verona and Brussels; Other roles include Enzo in La Gioconda, Don Carlos, Don José, Des Grieux in Manon Lescaut, Paolo in Francesca da Rimini and Maurizio in Adriana Lecouvreur; Sang Rodolfo in Luisa Miller at Brussels in 1982; Retired in 1989. Recordings include: Te Deum by Berlioz; Madame Sans-Gêne by Giordano; Olympia by Spontini; Adriana Lecouvreur and Francesca da Rimini for Italian TV. Address: c/o SA Gorlinsky Ltd, 33 Dover Street, London, W1X 4NJ, England.

TAGLIAVINI Luigi (Ferdinando), b. 7 Oct 1929, Bologna, Italy. Organist; Harpsichordist; Musicologist. Education: Studied at the Conservatoires of Bologna and Paris with Marcel Dupré (organ) and Riccardo Nielsen (composition); PhD, University of Padua, 1951. Career: Teacher of Organ, 1952-54, Librarian, 1953-60, at Martini Conservatory, Bologna; Organ Professor at the Monteverdi Conservatory, Bolzano, 1954-64; Founder and Co-editor from 1960 of L'Organo; Many concert appearances in Europe and North America playing the harpsichord and organ; Visiting Professor at Cornell University, 1963 and SUNY, Buffalo, 1969; Director of the Institute of Musicology at Fribourg University, 1965, Professor from 1971; Editor of Monumenti di Musica Italiana. Recordings include: Two-Organ Works with Marie Claire Alain. Contributions to: Neue Mozart-Ausgabe, 3 volumes: Ascanio in Alba, Betulia Liberata, Mitridate Re di Ponto; Articles in L'Organo, Musik in Gesicht und Gegenwart, Ricordi, La Musica, Larousse de la Musique.

TAHOURDIN Peter, b. 1928, England. Composer. Education: Studied composition with Richard Arnell, Trinity College of Music, London, graduated in 1952; Studied at Toronto University, Canada, 1966-67. Career: Visiting Composer at University of Adelaide, 1965; Staff, Faculty of Music, University of Melbourne, 1973-88; Chairman, Composers Guild of Australia, 1978-79. Compositions: Orchestral: Sinfonietta No 1, 1952, No 2, 1959, Diversions for Orchestra, 1958-59, Symphony No 1, 1960, No 2, 1968-69, No 3, 1979, No 4, 1987, Fanfares And Variations, A Festival Overture, 1983; Solo Instrument and Orchestra: Sinfonia Concertante, 1966; Symphony No 5, 1994; Ensemble: Three Pieces for Wind Quintet, 1959, Quartet for Oboe and Strings, 1963, Celebration, 1979, Quartet for Strings, 1982, Raga Music 3 - Elision, 1988; Instrumental: Sonata for Clarinet and Piano, 1962, Dialogue No 1, 1971, No 2, 1976, No 3, 1978, No 4, 1984, Raga Music 4 for Two, 1990; Piano: Capriccio, 1963; Vocal: Raga Music 1, The Starlight Night, 1985; Exposé, 1995; Choral: Seven Gnomic Verses, 1968, King Oswald's Victory, 1970; Music Theatre: Ern Malley - A Dramatic Testament, 1975-76; Stage: Inside Information, 1 act opera, 1955, Illyria, 1 act ballet, 1965; Heloise and Abelard, chamber opera in two acts, 1991; Works for tape and education works. Memberships: Australian Performing Rights Association; Fellowship of Australian Composers. Address: c/o Australian Music Centre, PO Box N690, Grosvenor Place, New South Wales 2000, Australia.

TAILLON Jocelyne, b. 19 May 1941, Doudeville, France. Singer (Mezzo Soprano). Education: Studied with Suzanne Balguerie and Germaine Lubin at the Grenoble Conservatory. Debut: Nurse in Ariadne et Barbe-Bleue at Bordeaux, 1968. Career: Glyndebourne 1969 as Geneviève in Pelléas et Mélisande; Paris Opéra from 1973, in Pelléas, Il Trovatore, Faust and Falstaff; Geneva Opera in Macbeth by Bloch returning for season 1983-84; Guest appearances in Madrid, Brussels, Aix-en-Provence, Nantes and Marseille; Metropolitan Opera from 1979, as La Cieca in La Gioconda, Geneviève, Anna in Les Troyens, Erda and Mistress Quickly; Sang Arnalta in L'Incoronazione di Poppea at the Théâtre du Châtelet, Paris, 1989 also in Geneva, and Martha in Faust at Orange, France in 1990; Sang in Massenet's Chérubin at Monte Carlo, 1996. Recordings include: Edwige in Guillaume Tell, under Gardelli; Merope in Oedipe by Enesco under Lawrence Foster; Video of Debussy's Pelléas. Honour: Officier, des Arts et Lettres, Chevalier dans l'Ordre du Mérite. Address: 16 Avenue Franklin Roosevelt, 75008 Paris, France.

TAKACS Klara, b. 24 Apr 1945, Hungary. Mezzo-Soprano. Education: Studied at the Ferenc Liszt Academy Budapest. Career: Has sung at the Hungarian State Opera from 1973 notably as Orpheus, Adalgisa, Goldmark's Königin von Saba, Cenerentola and Cherubino; Guest appearances at Europe's leading opera houses and concert halls; Sang with the Vienna Staatsoper on a tour to Japan in 1986, Teatro Colón Buenos Aires in 1987 as Charlotte and as Eudossia in La Fiamma by Respighi and sang Mozart's Marcellina at the 1992 Salzburg Festival. Recordings: Médée by Cherubini with Sylvia Sass; Die Königin von Saba; Boito's Nerone; Hunyadi Laszlo by Erkel; Haydn's Apothecary; Mozart's Requiem; Liszt's Legend of Saint Elizabeth; Missa Solemnis by Beethoven; Mahler Lieder eines Fahreden Gesellen; Kodály's Háry János; Sacred Music by Haydn. Honours: Prizewinner, Erkel International Singing Competition, Budapest, 1975; Liszt Prize Laureate; Grand Priz de L'Accadmie du Disque, Paris, 3 times. Address: c/o Hungarian State Opera, Nepoztarsasag utja 22, 1061 Budapest, Hungary.

TAKACS Tamara, b. 1950, Hungary. Mezzo-Soprano. Education: Studied with Joszef Reti at the Ferenc Liszt Academy in Budapest until 1978. Career: Has sung at Hungarian State Opera House from 1978 as Vivaldi's Griselda, Orpheus, Mozart's 2nd Lady and Dorabella, Verdi's Azucena, Maddalena, Ulrica, Emilia, Mrs Quickly and Eboli, Wagner's Waltraute and Magdalena, Charlotte and Carmen; Sang Orzse in Kodály's Háry János in 1988; Appeared as Judit in Duke Bluebeard's Castle at Covent Garden in 1989 on a visit with the Hungarian State Opera; Season 1992 as Public Opinion in Orphée aux Enfers, at Budapest; Concert repertoire includes Purcell's Ode for St Cecilia's Day, Vivaldi's Stabat Mater, Gloria, Juditha Triumphans and Nisi Dominus, Donizetti and Verdi Requiems, Messiah and Rossini's Stabat Mater. Recordings: Numerous albums. Address: Hungarian State Opera, Nepoztarsasag utja 22, 1061 Budapest, Hungary.

TAKACS-NAGY Gabor, b. 17 Apr 1956, Budapest, Hungary. Violinist. Education: Studied with András Mihaly at the Franz Liszt Academy, Budapest, with members of the Amadeus Quartet and Zoltan Szekely. Career: Founder member of the Takacs Quartet in 1975; Many concert appearances in all major centres of Europe and USA; Tours of Australia, New Zealand, Japan, South America, England, Norway, Sweden, Greece, Belgium and Ireland; Bartók Cycle for the Bartók-Solti Festival at South Bank, 1990; Great Performers Series at Lincoln Center and Mostly Mozart Festival at Alice Tully Hall, New York; Visits to Japan in 1989 and 1992; Mozart Festivals at South Bank, Wigmore Hall and Barbican Centre in 1991; Bartók Cycle at the Théâtre des Champs Elysées in 1991; Beethoven Cycles at the Zurich Tonhalle, in Dublin, at the Wigmore Hall and in Paris, 1991-92; Resident at the University of Colorado, and at the London Barbican, 1988-91, with masterclasses at the Guildhall School of Music; Plays Amati instrument made for the French Royal Family and loaned by the Corcoran Gallery, Gallery of Art, Washington DC. Recordings: Schumann Quartets Op 41; Mozart String Quintets with Denes Koromzay; Bartók 6 Quartets; Schubert Trout Quintet with Zoltan Kocsis; Haydn Op 76; Brahms Op 51 Nos 1 and 2; Chausson Concerto with Joshua Bell and Jean-Yves Thibaudet; Works by Schubert, Mozart, Dvorák and Bartók. Honours: Winner, International Quartet Competition, Evian, 1977; Winner, Portsmouth International Quartet Competition, 1979. Address: 22 Tower Street, London, WC2H 9NS, England.

TAL Josef, b. 18 Sep 1910, Pinne, now Poland (Israeli Citizen). Composer. m. Jan 1940, 1 son. Education: Hochschule Für Musik, Berlin. Career: Director at Jerusalem Academy of Music, Israel, 1948-52 and Centre for Electronic Music, 1961; Head of Musicology Department, Incumbent Arthur Rubinstein Cathedra, Hebrew University, Jerusalem, 1965. Compositions include: Eight Operas: Saul At Ein Dor, 1957, Ammon And Tamar, 1961, Ashmedai, 1971, Massada 967, 1973, Die Versuchung, 1976, Der Turm, 1987, Der Garten, 1988, Josef, 1993; 6 Symphonies, 6 Piano Concertos and 5 Concertos for different instruments: Requiem: The Death Of Moses; Chamber Music

Works, Vocal Music, Cantatas; Psychodrama Die Hand. Recordings: Else, hommage; 3 Essays for Piano. Publication: Autobiography, 1984. Honours: 3 Engel Prizes, Tel Aviv Municipality; Unesco Fellowship, 1957; Israel State Prize, 1971; Art Prize of the City of Berlin, 1975; Wolf Prize, 1982; Verdienstkreuz 1 Klasse, BDR, 1984; Commandeur de l'Ordre des Artes et des Lettres, France, 1985. Memberships: West Berlin Academy of Arts, 1975; Honorary Member, American Academy and Institute of Arts and Letters, 1981. Hobbies: Photography; Theatre. Address: Kfar Etzion Str 39, 93392 Arnona-Jerusalem, Israel.

TALARICO Rita, b. 30 May 1941, Rome, Italy. Soprano. Education: Studied in Rome with Gabriella Besanzoni and at the Accademia di Santa Cecilia with Maria Teresa Pediconi. Debut: As Eleonora in Il Furioso all'Isola di San Domingo by Donizetti, at the 1967 Spoleto Festival. Career: Has sung at leading Italian opera houses and in Lyon, Rouen, Montreal, New York and Philadelphia; Other roles include Elvira in I Puritani, Amina in La Sonnambula, Leila in Les Pêcheurs de Perles, Mimi, Violetta, Medora in Il Corsaro, Elsa, Agathe, Donna Anna, Susanna, Countess Almaviva, Marguerite, Carolina in Il Matrimonio Segreto and Margherita in Mefistofele; Sang at La Scala in 1985 in Orfeo by Luigi Rossi. Recordings include: Il Furioso all'Isolo di San Domingo.

TALBOT Michael (Owen), b. 4 Jan 1943, Luton, England. Professor in Music. Education: BA, Honours, MusB, PhD, Clare College, Cambridge University; Royal College of Music. Career: Reader, now Professor, 1986-, in Music, Liverpool University. Compositions: Many editions, baroque music. Publications: Vivaldi, 1978, 1979-93; Albinoni, Leben und Werk, 1980; Antonio Vivaldi: A Guide To Research, 1988; Tomaso Albinoni: The Venetian Composer and His World, 1990, 1994; Benedetto Vinaccesi: A Musician in Brescia and Venice in The Age of Corelli, 1994; The Sacred Vocal Music of Antonio Vivaldi, 1995. Contributions to: Early Music; Music and Letters; Music Review; Musical Times; Soundings; The Consort; Note d'Archivio; Informazioni e Studi Vivaldiani. Honours: Cavaliere, Italy, 1980; Oldman Prize, 1990. Memberships: Historical Adviser, Vivaldi Society; Royal Musical Association; FBA, 1990. Address: Department of Music, The University, PO Box 147, Liverpool, L69 3BX, England.

TALICH Jan, b. 30 Oct 1945, Pizen, Czechoslovakia. Violist. Education: Studied at the Prague Conservatory. Career: Co-founded the Talich Quartet in 1961; After success in competitions at Kromeriz and Belgrade gained title of Laureate by the Association of International Music Festivals in Bayreuth; Moved from leader of Talich Quartet to Violist in 1972; Appearances in Europe and North America, Egypt, Iraq, Indonesia and Japan; Annual visits to France from 1976 including the complete Beethoven quartets; Engagements with festivals and music clubs in Britain; Played at Wigmore Hall in London in 1991 with the quartets of Smetana, Beethoven's Op 74, Brahms A minor and Mozart D minor, and at Bath and Bournemouth Festivals in 1991; Played at Queen Elizabeth Hall in 1991, and Janácek's 2nd Quartet for BBC 2's The Late Show. Recordings: Various albums. Address: c/o Clarion - Seven Muses, 64 Whitehall Park, London, N19 3TN, England.

TALLEY-SCHMIDT Eugene, b. 10 Feb 1932, Rome, Georgia, USA. Tenor; Professor of Voice and Chairman of Voice Department, Houston Baptist University. m. Jeanette Lombard Pecorello, 22 Nov 1960, 2 sons. Education: San Diego State College; Indiana University; Opera Arts, Atlanta, GA; Teatro dell'Opera, Rome, Italy; Diploma, Teatro Lirico, Spoleto, Italy; Voice study with Ethel Wilkerson, Rome, GA, John Walsh and Raoul Couyas, San Diego, CA. Debut: USA debut as Hans in The Bartered Bride at San Diego, CA; European debut as Fritz in L'Amico Fritz at Spoleto, Italy. Career includes: Leading Tenor with Deutsche Oper am Rhein, Dussledorf, Staatsoper Hamburg, Wuppertal and Munster Operas; Sang over 50 leading tenor roles at opera houses in USA and Europe; TV and radio performances in Europe and America; Performed at international festivals and appeared with Atlanta, Birmingham, Mobile, Miami, Palm Beach, Indianpolis, Rome, and San Diego Symphony Orchestras. Recording: Robert Schumann, Complete Duets for tenor and Soprano. Hobbies: Philately; Lapidary; Golf. Address: 3506 Oyster Cove Drive, Missouri City, TX 77459, USA.

TALMI Yoav, b. 28 Apr 1943, Kibbutz Mernavia, Israel. Conductor; Composer. m. Er'ella Talmi, 2 Sept 1964, 1 son, 1 daughter. Education: Diploma, Rubin Academy of Music, Tel-Aviv, 1961-65; Postgraduate Diploma, Juilliard School of Msic, New York, 1965-68; Summer study courses with Walter Suskind, Aspen, 1966; Bruno Maderna, Salzburg, 1967; Jean Fournet, Hilversum, 1968; Eric Leinsdorf, Tanglewood, 1969. Career: Co-Conductor, Israel Chamber Orchestra, Tel-Aviv, 1970-72; Artistic Director and Conductor, Gelders Symphony Orchestra, Arnhem, 1974-80; Principal Guest Conductor, Munich Philharmonic Orchestra, 1979-80; Music Director and Principal Conductor, Israel Chamber Orchestra, 1984-88; Music Director, New Israeli Opera, 1985-89; Music Director, San Diego Symphony, USA, 1989; Guest Conducting with the Berlin Philharmonic, Munich Philharmonic, London Symphony and Philharmonia, London Philharmonic, Royal Philharmonic, Amsterdam's Concertgebouw, Israel Philharmonic and New Japan Philharmonic, Vienna Symphony, St Petersburg and Oslo Philharmonics, Tonhalle Orchestra, Zurich, Detroit, Pittsburgh, Houston, Dallas and St Louis Symphonies; Los Angeles Chamber Orchestra; New York Chamber Symphony. Compositions: Elegy for strings, timpani and accordion; Dreams for choir a capella; Music for flute and strings; Overtur on Mexican Themes, (recorded by Louisville Orchestra); 3 monologues for flute solo, (published); Inauguration Fanfare for brass ensemble. Recordings: Bruckner: Symphony No 9, Oslo Philharmonic; Gilère: 3rd Symphony, San Diego; Brahms; Sextet-4 Serious Songs, San Diego Symphony; Tchaikovsky and Schoenberg with the Israel Chamber Orchestra; Bloch, Barber, Puccini and Grieg with the Israel Chamber Orchestra; Berlioz: Overtures; Romeo and Juliet, San Diego Symphony; Harold in Italy with San Diego Symphony. Current Management: ICM Artists Ltd, 40 W 57 Street, New York, NY 10019, USA. Address: PO Box 1384, Kfar Saba 44113, Israel.

TALVI Ilkka (Ilari), b. 22 Oct 1948, Kuusankoski, Finland. Violinist; Concertmaster. m. Marjorie Kransberg, 29 Aug 1984, 3 daughters. Education: Diploma, studied with Arno Granroth, Sibelius Academy, Helsinki, 1960-66; Studied with Jascha Heifetz, University of Southern California, USA, Ivan Galamian at Curtis Institute of Music, Riccardo Odnoposoff in Vienna, and Gabriel Bouillon at Paris. Debut: With orchestra at age 10; Recital debut at age 15, Helsinki. Career: Performances as soloist and recitalist in Europe and USA; Lecturer at Sibelius Academy, Finland, 1969-75 and at Pori School of Music, 1970-76; Concertmaster with Malmo Symphony, Sweden, 1976-77; Working in motion picture business at Los Angeles, USA, 1977-85; Principal with Los Angeles Chamber Orchestra, 1979-85; Guest Concertmaster, 1983-85, Concertmaster, 1985-, Seattle Opera; Concertmaster, Waterloo Festival, New Jersey, 1988-. Recordings include: Klami Violin Concerto; Albert Im Concordiam. Honours: Numerous honours and prizes in Finland. Hobbies: Dogs; Computers; Outdoors. Current Management: Festium, Helsinki, Finland. Address: 3456 10th Avenue West, Seattle, WA 98119, USA.

TAMAR Iano, b. 15 Oct 1963, Kashbergi, Georgia. Singer (Soprano). Education: Studied at the Tblisi Conservatory. Career: Sang at the Tblisi Opera from 1989; Best known in the title role of Rossini's Semiramide, which she has sung at the Pesaro Festival, under Alberto Zedda and at the Zurich Opera (1992); Has also sung the Rossini Stabat Mater at Dresden, Natasha in War and Peace, Mozart's Countess and Amelia (Ballo in Maschera); Sang Ottavia in Pacini's L'Ultimo giorno di Pompei, Martina Franca Festival, 1996. Address: c/o Zurich Opernhaus, Falkenstrasse 1, CH-8008 Zurich, Switzerland.

TAMASSY Eva, b. 19 Mar 1937, Budapest, Hungary. Contralto. Education: Studied with Geza Laszlo in Budapest and with Gerda Heuer and Kurt Schneider in Germany. Debut: Hungarian State Opera in 1951 as Maddalena in Rigoletto. Career: Sang at the Cologne Opera, Deutscher Oper am Rhein and the State Operas of Hamburg, Vienna, Munich and Stuttgart; Further engagements in Hanover, Nuremberg, Paris, Nancy, Nice, Lisbon, Bucharest, Prague, Rome, Venice, Naples and Berne; Other roles have been Carmen, Dalila, Verdi's Azucena, Amneris, Ulrica and Eboli, Wagner's Erda, Fricka, Waltraute and Brangaene, Konchakovna in Prince Igor and Marina in Boris Godunov, Mary Louise in Háry János, the Queen in Szokolay's Hamlet, and Clytemnestra in Elektra; Many concert appearances. Address: Caesart Str 70/A, D-50968 Cologne, Germany.

TAMAYO Arturo, b. 3 Aug 1946, Madrid, Spain. Conductor. Education: Studied at the Royal Conservatoire Madrid, harmony with A Barrera, and composition with Francisco Cales and Gerardo Gombau. Career: Gave concerts in Spain from 1967; Studied further with Pierre Boulez at Basle and at the Musikhochschule Fribourg-en-Brisgau; Studied conducting with Franc Travis, 1971-76, and composition with Wolfgang Fortner and Klaus Huber; Assisted Huber at Fribourg from 1974 and directed concerts of contemporary music; Frequent appearances at the Deutsche Oper Berlin from 1982 notably with the 1983 premiere of Wolfgang Rihm's ballet, Tutuguri; Conducted the premiere of Kelterborn's Ophelia at the 1984 Schwetzingen Festival, and Maurice Ohana's La Celestine at the Paris Opéra in 1988; Théâtre des Champs Elysées in Paris, 1990 with the local premiere of La Noche Triste by Jean Prodomidès; Graz 1996, Busoni's Doktor Faust. Address: c/o Théâtre des Champs Elysées, 15 Avenue Montaigne, F-75012 Paris, France.

TAMBERG Eino, b. 27 May 1930, Tallinn, Estonia. Composer. Education: Studied with Eugen Kapp at Tallinn Conservatory, graduated 1953. Career: Music Supervisor for Estonian Radio then Teacher at Estonian Conservatory, 1967-; Professor, 1983. Compositions include: Operas: The Iron House, 1965, Cyrano de Bergerac, 1976 and Soaring, 1983, all premiered in Tallinn; Ballets: Ballet Symphony, Schwerin, 1960, The Boy and The Butterfly, Tallinn, 1963 and Joanna Tentata, Tallinn, 1971; Orchestral: Concerto Grosso, 1956, Symphonic Dances, 1957, Toccata, 1967, Trumpet Concerto, 1972, 3 Symphonies, 1978, 1986 and 1989, Concerto for Mezzo Soprano and Orchestra, 1986, Alto Saxophone Concerto, 1987; Chamber: String Quartet, 1958, 2 Wind Quintets, 1975, 1984; Vocal: Moonlight Oratorio, 1962, Fanfares of Victory, cantata, 1975, Amores, oratorio, 1981; Songs and piano pieces. Honour: People's Artist of the Estonian SSR, 1975. Address: EE 0001 Tallinn, Lauteri 7-23, Estonia.

TAMULENAS Eva, b. 1943, Narva, Estonia. Singer (Mezzo-soprano). Education: Studied in Milwaukee and Vienna. Career: Sang at first with the Royal Opera Copenhagen and from 1977 at Gelsenkirchen; Roles have included Hansel, Rosina, Orlofsky, Olga, Maddalena and the title role in Miss Julie by Antonio Bibalo; Einem's Der Besuch der alten Dame (1991); Many concert engagements. Address: Gelsenkirchen Opera, Musiktheater im Revier, Kennedyplatz, Pf 101857, W-4650 Gelsenkirchen, Germany.

TAMULIONIS Jonas, b. 10 Jan 1949, Alytus, Lithuania. Composer. Divorced, 2 sons. Education: Graduated from the Faculty of Music of the Vilnius Pedagogical Institute, 1970; Composition with Professor Eduardos Balsys at the Lithuanian State Conservatoire, 1976. Compositions include: For string quartet: two Quartets, 1973, 1982; Diary, 1978; For string orchestras: Concertino, 1974; Toccata Diavolesca, 1988; Pastoral Suite, 1990; Three symphonies, 1976, 1978, 1986; For wind orchestra: Festive Overture, 1978; Spanish Rhapsody, 1981; Sonatas: for two guitars, 1978, two pianos, 1979, two birbynes (Lithuanian folk wind instrument), 1988; For chamber orchestra: Epitaph, 1981; Cantatas: I Sing of Lithuania, 1981; Children's Earth (verse by J Marcinkevicius), 1988; To My Motherland (verse by J Mikstas), 1989: Sinfonia Rustica, 1989; Oratorio: Six Dedications To The Town (text by various Lithunanian poets, 1985; Reminiscence for two violins and two accordions, 1989; Recollection for glass instruments, 1992; Trio for flute, viola, guitar and piano, 1993; Vocal music includes: Seven Love Elegies for soprano and chamber ensemble, 1982; Summer Psalms for soprano and piano (verse by J Marcinkevicius), 1985; Three Prayers for baritone and piano, (verse by B Brazdzionis), 1989; For Choir: Single Words, 1980; The Tears of Ablinga, 1984; Tres retratos con sombra (verse by F García Lorca), 1992; Los juegos, 1997; For accordion: Sonatina, 1978; Metamorphoses, 1984; Polyphonic Pieces, 1990; Ten Etudes, 1995; For guitar: Eleven preludes, 1982; Suite of Intervals, 1987. Recordings: CD: On The Coast, 1990; Numerations, Patterers, 1992; Ex Anima, 1994; Home Psalames, 1995; The Sea, 1996. Honours: 2nd Prize, Symphony No 1, Moscow, Russia, 1967; 1st prize, Conciones de la Tierra, Spain, 1995; 1st Prize, Oda al Atlántico, Spain, 1997; 1st Prize, Los juegos, Spain, 1997. Address: Tauro 8-11, 2001 Vilnius, Lithuania.

TAN Dun, b. 18 August 1957, Si Mao, Hunan, China. Composer. Education: Studied, Beijing Conservatory, 1978-, BA; MA. Attending lectures by Alexander Goehr, George Crumb, Hans Werner Henze, and others; Columbia University, New York, 1986. Career: Played viola in Beijing Opera Orchestra, 1976-77; Performances of music in the West from, 1983 (String Quartet, Dresden, 1983) including London Homes, 1996; Fellowship, Columbia University, 1986. Compositions include: Li Sao, symphony, 1980; Five Pieces in Human Accent for piano, 1980; Feng Ya Song, string quartet, 1982; Fu, for 2 sopranos, bass and ensemble, 1982; Piano Concerto, 1983; Symphony in Two Movements, 1985; On Taoism, for orchestra, 1985; Out of Beijing, opera for violin and orchestra, 1987; Traces, for piano, 1989; Nine Songs, ritual opera, 1989; Eight Colours, for string quartet, 1989; Silk Road, for soprano and percussion, 1989; Orchestral Theatre I: Xun (1990) II: Re (1992), III (Red) 1993; CAGE for piano, 1993; Death and Fire: Dialogue with Paul Klee, for orchestra, 1993; Circle with Four Trios, Conductor and Audience, 1993; Autumn Winds, for instruments and conductor ad lib, 1993; Memorial Nineteen, for voice, piano and double paper, 1993; Marco Polo, opera, 1994; Yi, cello concerto, 1994; Works for Asian Instruments. Address: c/o MCSC, 85 Dongsi Nan Dajie, Beijing 100703, China.

TAN Melvyn, b. 13 Oct 1956, Singapore. Musician (Harpsichord and Fortepiano). Education: Studied at the Yehudi Menuhin School, Surrey from 1968; Teachers include Vlado Perlemuter and Nadia Boulanger; Royal College of Music from 1978, where he made a special study of performing practice. Career: International appearances in the keyboard works of Baroque, Classical and early Romantic composers; Played piano until 1980 then turned to harpsichord and fortepiano; Engagements with the Academy of Ancient Music, the English Chamber Orchestra, Royal Philharmonic and London Classical Players; Tour of USA in 1985; Series of Beethoven concerts 1987 with Roger Norrington and the London Classical Players; Flanders Festival, 1988 followed by South Bank Beethoven Plus series;

Appearances during 1989 at the Bath Festival, Holland Festival, Midsummer Mozart Festival, San Francisco and the Beethoven Experience with the London Classical Players in Purchase, NY; In season 1990 visited France, Germany, Japan, Australia, San Francisco, Vancouver and New York, Carnegie Hall; Played the Schumann Concerto at the Elizabeth Hall, London, 1990; Debut at the Paris Opéra, 1991; Debut concerts as director of The New Mozart Ensemble in Britain, France, Holland and Hong Kong; Repertoire includes: Weber, Mendelssohn, Chopin and earlier music. Recordings: Beethoven's Waldstein and Appassionata Sonatas; Schubert's Impromptus; Beethoven's Concertos and Choral Fantasia conducted by Roger Norrington. Address: c/o Valerie Barber Management Ltd, Fifth Floor, 24 Chancery Lane, London, WC2A 1LS, England.

TANG Muhai, b. 10 Jul 1949, Shanghai, China. Conductor. Education: Music Conservatory at Shanghai; Music Hochschule, Munich, Germany; Masterclass Diploma. Career: Conducted the Berlin Philharmonic, London Philharmonic, Orchestre de Paris, San Francisco Symphony, Montreal Symphony, Santa Cecilia Orchestra, Rome, Tonhalle Orchestra Zurich, Helsinki Philharmonic, Hallé Orchestra, Scottish National Symphony Orchestra, National Symphony Orchestra of Spain, Mozarteum Orchestra Salzburg, Polish Chamber Orchestra, Oper Orchestra Hamburg, Frankfurt, Munich, Bonn, Monte Carlo, Radio Symphony Orchestra Munich, Berlin, Hamburg, and Cologne; Chief Conductor of Peking Central Philharmonic and Gulbenkian Orchestra of Lisbon; Classic Aid Television Gala Concert, UN Geneva, 1986. Current Management: Columbia Artists Management, NY and Harold Holt Ltd, London, England. Address: c/o Keils, Treibjagdweg 31, 1 Berlin 37, Germany.

TANGGAARD Svend Erik, b. 25 Jan 1942, Copenhagen, Denmark. Composer; Writer. m. Margit Bendtsen, 29 Feb 1980, 2 daughters. Education: Piano and Composition Studies with Helge Bonnen, Copenhagem, 1962-67; Studies in Munich, West Germany, 1968-70. Debut: Royal Academy of Fine Arts, 1962. Career: Performances of Own Works by Danish Radio Symphony Orchestra, Aalborg Symphony Orchestra, Southern Jutland Symphony Orchestra, Odense Symphony Orchestra and Moritz Fromberg Quartet; Several Transmissions on Danish Radio, NDR and Swedish Radio; Performances at the Art Association, Gronningen and Other Art Galleries. Compositions: 5 Symphonies; Concerto for Orchestra; 12 String Quartets; 3 Fuga String Quartets op 150; Piano, Violin (2), Viola, Cello, Oboe, Flute, Trumpet and Clarinet Concertos; Overtures Nos 1 and 2, for Chamber Orchestra; Concertos Nos 1, 2 & 3, for 14 Wind Instruments, 2 Double Basses and Percussion, and Concerto, for Violin and Orchestra; Vox Humana, for Orchestra, Soprano, Bass and Taperecorder; The Bells, for Orchestra and Reader; Songs, 3 Wind Quintets; 3 Solo Cello Suites; 2 Solo violin Sonatas, Piano Sonata, Day and Night; 3 Italian Prayers, for Mezzosoprano and Viola; 3 Cantatas, for Tenor and Wind Quintet; 25 Selected Songs From Omar Khayyam's Rubaiyat, for Basso and 3 Instruments; Songs for Small Ensembles. Publications: Ny Dansk Myte, 1966; Sorrig og Glaede de vandre til hobe (novel), 1986. Contributions to: Danish Music Periodical DMT. Honours: State Art Foundation Grant, 5 years; Queen Ingrid's Foundation, 5 months, 1980; Chiostra San Cataldo by Amalfi, Italy, 1978, 1984, 1994; Circolo Scandinavo per Artisti, Rome, 1988-90, 1992. Memberships: Danish Composer Society; Union of Young Composers; Danish Writers Union; Art Association Gronningen. Hobbies: Literature; Painting; Sculpture; Sponges; Travel. Address: Nikolaj Plads 7, 4, DK-1067 Copenhagen K, Denmark.

TANGUY Jean-Michel, b. 15 Nov 1944, France. Flautist. Education: French Baccalaureat, Lycee Français, Berlin; Jean-Pierre Rampal, Nice, Paris; Aurele Nicolet, Berlin; Freiburg, Breisagu Staatliche Hochschule für Musik. Debut: Orchestra der Beethovenhalle, Bonn, Germany. Career: Performances with Bonn Orchestra, Rotterdam Philharmonic, Orchestre National de Belgique, Brussels; Chargé de Cours Conservatoire Royal de Bruxelles; Professor of Flute, Hochschule für Musik, Heidelberg-Mannheim, 1992-. Recordings: Telemann Flute Concertos; Heidelberger Chamber Orchestra, JS Bach Trios, CPE Bach - Sonatas; JS Bach - Flute Sonatas; Sommermusik with Belgian Windquintett. Honours: Prize, International Music Competition, Geneva, 1973; Scholarship, DAAD; Masterclasses: Belgium, France, Italy, Germany, Vienna, Corea. Hobby: Sailing. Address: 17 rue Guimard, 1040 Bruxelles, Belgium.

TANYEL Seta, b. 1950, Istanbul. Concert Pianist. Education: Studied at Vienna Hochschule for Musik with Dieter Weber and with Louis Kentner in London. Career: Orchestral and recital debuts in New York, Philadelphia, Detroit and London in 1978; Extensive touring in Europe, the Middle East, Russia and the USA performing with such orchestras as the Vienna Symphony, Israel Philharmonic, Stuttgart Philharmonic, the Philharmonia and London Symphony Orchestra; Taught at Yehudi Menuhin School in London from 1986-1989; A pianist with an international reputation in both standard and lesser-known Romantic piano repertoire, recent performing projects include the long overdue revival in the piano music of Xaver Scharwenka. Recordings include: Shostakovich, Khachaturian, Poulenc and Bax 2-piano works (Chandos); Brahams and Beethoven solo recital; Grieg and Schumann Piano Concertos with LSO/Fruhbeck de Burgos; Brahms Piano Concerto No 1 with the Philharmonia/Vaclav Neumann; Scharwenka Piano Concerto No 1 and Chopin Piano Concerto No 1 with the Philharmonia/Rizzi; Chopin, Sharwenka and Moszkowski solo recitals; Scharwenka chamber works with piano (Complete) (Collins Classics). Honours: Prizewinner at International Beethoven Competition in Vienna in 1973, at first Arthur Rubinstein Piano Master Competition in Israel in 1974 and at Queen Elizabeth of Belgium in 1975. Address: c/o Denny Lyster Concert Management, 25 Courthorpe Road, London NW3 2LE, England.

TAPPY Eric, b. 19 May 1931, Lausanne, Switzerland. Tenor. Education: Studied with Fernando Carpi in Geneva, Ernst Reichert in Salzburg and Eva Liebenberg in Hilversum. Debut: Strasbourg in 1959 as the Evangelist in Bach's St Matthew Passion. Career: Concert performances of Milhaud's Les Malheurs d'Orphée and Martin's Le Mystère de la Nativité and Monsieur de Pourceaugnac; Sang in the premiere of Klaus Huber's Soliloquia in 1962; Stage debut at Opéra-Comique Paris in 1964 as Rameau's Zoroastre; Sang at Herrenhausen in 1966 as Monteverdi's Orfeo, Geneva Opera in 1966 in the premiere of Milhaud's La Mère Coupable, and Hanover in 1967 in L'Incoronazione di Poppea; Covent Garden debut in 1974 in the title role of La Clemenza di Tito; US debut in 1974 as Don Ottavio at San Francisco returning in Poppea and as Ideomeneo, 1977-78; Sang at Rome Opera in 1980 as Titus; Appearances in Chicago, Drottningholm, Aix-en-Provence, Salzburg as Tamino, Amsterdam, Lyon, Brussels and Lisbon; Other roles include Schoenberg's Aron, Pelléas, Lysander in A Midsummer Night's Dream, Don Ramiro, Lensky and Stravinsky's Oedipus; Concert repertoire includes music by Handel, Haydn, Campra, Carissimi, Vivaldi, Bach, Berlioz and Schütz; Retired in 1982. Recordings include: Monteverdi's Orfeo and Poppea; Zoroastre; Pelléas et Mélisande; Die Jahreszeiten by Haydn; Die Zauberflöte; La Clemenza di Tito.

TARI Lujza, b. 1 Oct 1948, Pásztó, Hungary. Ethnomusicologist. m. Gábor Mihaltz, 11 June 1971, 1 son, 1 daughter. Education: Hatvan Music School, Nagybátony, 1958; Szeged Conservatory, 1963-67; Student, 1967-72, University degree, 1972, Liszt F Zeneművészeti Főiskola, Academy of Music, Budapest. Career: Volunteer Assistant, Néprajzi Muzeum, Budapest, 1969; Folk Music Research Group, 1970-72, Research Assistant, 1972-74, Research Assistant at same institute, renamed Institute for Musicology, 1974, Senior Researcher, Institute for Musicology, 1990, Hungarian Academy of Sciences; Permanent contributor of talks, Hungarian Radio, 1969-. Recordings: Editor: Hungarian Folk Music of Kodály's Phonograph Cylinders, 1982; Anthology of Hungarian Folk Music II. The North, with László Vikár, 1986; Two folk orchestras from László Lajtha's collection, 1992. Publications: Books: Weiner Leó művészete a népzenei források tükrében Budapest, 1988; Lissznyay Julianna hangszeres gyűjteménye 1800 Budapest, 1990. Contributions to: Studia Musicologica; Magyar Zene; Ethnographia, Budapest. Honour: Prize for Paper, Weiner 100th Anniversaty Competition, 1984. Memberships: Various societies including: International Council for Traditional Music, National Representative of Hungarian National Committee 1996-; Kodály Society; Hungarian Society for Musicology; Hungarian Society of Ethnography. Hobbies: Instruments and instrumental music of the 19th century. Address: Riadó u 10a, H-1026 Budapest, Hungary.

TARLING Judith, b. 1947, England. Violinist; Violist. Career: Member of the Parley of Instruments; Frequent tours of Britain and abroad including the British Early Music Network; Performances in Spain, France, Germany, Holland, Poland and Czechoslovakia; US debut at New York in 1988; Many concerts with first modern performances of early music in new editions by Peter Holman; Numerous broadcasts on BBC Radio 3 and elsewhere; Repertoire includes Renaissance Violin Consort Music such as Christmas Music by Michael Praetorius, Peter Philips, music for Prince Charles I by Orlando Gibbons and Thomas Lupo, Baroque Consort Music by Monteverdi and Matthew Locke anthems, motets and ceremonial music, Purcell ayres for the theatre, Georg Muffat's Armonico Tributo sonatas of 1682, Heinrich Biber's Sonate tam Aris, Quam Aulis Servientes of 1676, Vivaldi sonatas and concertos for lute and mandolin, concertos for recorders, and JS Bach's Hunt Cantata, No 208; English Eighteenth Century Music such as Dr Arne at Vauxhall Gardens, William Boyce's Solomon, and John Stanley 6 Concertos in seven parts, Op 2, these works performed with Crispian Steele-Perkins on trumpet and Emma Kirkby as soprano, among others; Principal Viola of Brandenburg Consort, Director, Roy Goodman with recordings including Bach Brandenburg Concertos and Suites; Principal Viola of the Hanover Band with numerous recordings including complete symphonies of Beethoven, Schubert and Haydn. Recordings include: Numerous. Address: 3 North Street, Punnetts Town, Heathfield, East Sussex, England.

TARR Edward H(ankins), b. 15 Jun 1936, Norwich, Connecticut, USA. Trumpeter; Musicologist. Education: Studied trumpet with Roger Voisin in Boston, 1953 and with Adolph Herseth in Chicago, 1958-59; Musicology with Leo Schrade in Basle, 1959-64; DPhil, University of Hamburg, 1986. Career: Founded the Edward Tarr Brass Ensemble, 1969, giving many performances of Renaissance, Baroque and contemporary music in Europe and the United States; Early repertoire includes the trumpet works of Torelli; Modern works include Kagel's Atem and Morceau de concours and Stockhausen's Spiral, 1970; Has collaborated on the reconstruction of early instruments with the German firm Meinl and Lauber and the Swiss firm Adolf Egger and Son; Teacher of Trumpet at Rheinische Musikschule Cologne, 1968-70; Teacher of Cornett and Natural Trumpet at the Schola Cantorum Basiliensis, 1972-; Teacher of Trumpet at the Basle Conservatory, 1974-; Director of the Trumpet Museum in Bad Säckingen, Germany, 1985-. Publications include: Die Trompete, 1977; Performing editions of Baroque, Classical and Romantic Music. Address: c/o Trumpet Museum, PO Box 1143, 79702 Bad Säckingen, Germany.

TARRES Enriqueta, b. 18 Mar 1934, Barcelona, Spain. Soprano. Education: Studied at the Barcelona Conservatory with Concepcion Callao di Sanchez Parra. Debut: Valencia in 1956 as the Trovatore Leonora. Career: Sang in Spain notably at the Teatro Liceo, Barcelona, Basle and Wuppertal Opera, 1960-64, Glyndebourne in 1962 and 1964 as Ariadne and Elettra in Idomeneo, and Hamburg Staatsoper from 1964, visiting Sadler's Wells in 1966 as the Empress in the first British performance of Die Frau ohne Schatten by Strauss; Engaged with Dusseldorf, Cologne and Stuttgart Operas; Sang at Metropolitan Opera in 1973 as Mimi, Lausanne in 1983 as the Marschallin, Verona in 1984 as Carmen, and sang the Mother in Luis de Pablo's El Viajero Indiscreto at the Teatro de la Zarzuela at Madrid in 1990; Frequent concert appearances. Recordings: Falla's Atlantida; Orff's Trionfi; Les Huguenots; Idomeneo. Address: c/o Arena di Verona, Piazza Brà 28, I-37121 Verona, Italy.

TARUSKIN Richard (Filler), b. 2 Apr 1945, New York City, USA. Musicologist; Critic. Education includes: PhD, Columbia University, 1975. Career: Teacher at Columbia University, 1973-87; Professor at University of California, Berkeley, 1987; Music Critic for Opus and The New York Times. Publications include: Opera and Drama in Russia, Ann Arbor, 1981; Study of Stravinsky and articles on the 15th Century Chanson, the Early Music Movement and on Russian Music. Contributions to: Articles on Russian Composers and Operas, in New Grove Dictionary of Opera, 4 volumes, 1992. Address: University of California, Music Department, Morrison Hall, Berkeley, CA 94720, USA.

TASKOVA Slavka, b. 16 Nov 1940, Sofia, Bulgaria. Soprano. Education: Studied at the Accademia di Santa Cecilia with Gina Cigne and in Milan with Lina Pagliughi. Debut: Milan in 1966 as Rosina in Il Barbiere di Siviglia. Career: Has sung in Venice, Bologna, Berlin, Munich, Paris, Vienna, Sofia, Warsaw and Zagreb; Sang at Schwetzingen Festival in 1971 in the premiere of Reimann's Melusine, Teatro Lirico Milan in 1975 in the premiere of Nono's Al Gran Sole Carico d'Amore, and Genoa in 1983 as Violetta. Recordings include: Anacréon by Cherubini. Address: c/o Teatro Carlo Felice, I-16100 Genoa, Italy.

TATE Jeffrey, b. 28 Apr 1943, Salisbury, Wiltshire, England. Conductor. Education: Christ's College Cambridge; St Thomas' Hospital London; MA, MB, BChir, Cantab; London Opera Centre. Career includes: Assistant to Boulez at Bayreuth and Paris, 1976-80; Opera debut at Gothenburg in 1978 with Carmen; Metropolitan debut in 1980 with Lulu returning for Der Rosenkavalier, Wozzeck and Lohengrin; Covent Garden debut in 1982 in La Clemenza di Tito, becoming Principal Conductor, 1986-; Principal Guest Conductor for Geneva Opera, 1984-, Orchestre National de France, 1989-, and Royal Opera House, 1991-; Principal Conductor with English Chamber Orchestra, 1985; Conducted new production of Henze's realization of Monteverdi's Il Ritorno di Ulisse at Salzburg Festival in 1985 and the premiere of Liebermann's Le Fôret at Geneva in 1987; Works regularly with many leading orchestras including the London Symphony, Boston Symphony, and Orchestre de la Suisse Romande; Music Director for Rotterdam Philharmonic 1991-; Season 1991-92 included Mozart's Zaide in Amsterdam and at the Barbican Hall, Le nozze di Figaro and Fidelio at Covent Garden and Weill's Mahagonny at Geneva; Led new production of Parsifal for Bonn Opera, 1997. Recordings: Various with such orchestras as English Chamber, Dresden Staatskapelle and Royal Opera House. Honours: SWET Opera Award, 1984; Honorary Fellowship, Christ's College Cambridge, 1988; CBE, 1990; Chevalier des Arts et des Lettres, 1990. Hobbies: Collecting early 18th century continental porcelain; Gastronomy. Current Management: Columbia Artists Management Inc, 165 West 57th Street, New York, NY 10019, USA; Artists Management Zurich, CH-8044 Zurich Rutistrasse 52, Switzerland. Address: c/o Betty Scholar, Secretary, Royal Opera House, Covent Garden, London, WC2, England.

TATRAI Vilmos, b. 7 Oct 1912, Kispest, Hungary. Violinist. Education: Studied at the National Conservatory, Budapest with Vilmos Kladivko and Lazlo Lajtha. Career: Played in various orchestras, 1931-33, with Municipal Orchestra Budapest, 1933-36 and Radio Orchestra of Buenos Aires, 1936-37; Leader of the Hungarian State Symphony Orchestra, 1940-78; Founded the Tatrai Quartet in 1946 and has toured widely in Europe and Japan from 1955, with Festival engagements at Salzburg, Vienna, Edinburgh, Prague, Florence and Dubrovnik; Repertory of 360 compositions; 64 First performances of Hungarian composers and 54 first performances of foreign composers; Teacher of Violin and Chamber Music at the Béla Bartók Conservatory, 1947-54; Founder-Leader of the Hungarian Chamber Orchestra in 1957 and premiered Helmut Eder's 2nd Violin Concerto in 1967; Professor at the Franz Liszt Academy in Budapest, 1965. Recordings include: 130 recordings including the Complete Cycles of the Quartets by Haydn, Mozart Quintets, Bartók and Kodály. Honours: With Tatrai Quartet, Winner of Bartók Competition, 1948; Liszt Prize, 1952, 1972; Kossuth Prize, 1958; Pro Urbe, 1979; Bartók-Pasztori Grand Prize, 1985; Flag Order, 1987 and many other distinctions; Cross of Merit, 1992. Memberships: Honorary Member, F Liszt, 1992 and Kodály Associations. Address: 1136 Budapest XIII, R Wallenberg u 4, Hungary.

TATTERMUSCHOVA Helena, b. 28 Jan 1933, Prague, Czechoslovakia. Soprano. Education: Studied at the Prague Conservatory with Vlasta Linhartova. Debut: Ostrava in 1955 as Musetta. Career: National Theatre Prague from 1959; Visited Edinburgh with the company in 1964 and 1970 in the British premieres of Janácek's From The House Of The Dead and The Excursions of Mr Broucek; Guest appearances at opera houses in Barcelona, Brussels, Amsterdam, Warsaw, Naples, Venice and Sofia; Repertoire included works by Janácek, Smetana, Mozart, Puccini and Strauss; Also sang in concert. Recordings: Orfeo ed Euridice; Trionfi by Orff; The Makropoulos Case; From the House of the Dead; Glagolitic Mass; The Cunning Little Vixen. Address: c/o National Theatre, PO Box 865, 112 30 Prague 1, Czech Republic.

TATTON Thomas James, b. 14 Oct 1943. Teacher. m. Polly Tatton, 10 Aug 1996, 1 daughter. Education: California University, Northridge; BA, Emporia University, 1964-68; MMus, 1968-70, DMusArts, 1970-75, University of Illinois; Private Studies with Myron Sandler, Manual Compinsky, Guillermo Perich. Career: Multiple Appearances as Conductor of Honour Orchestras for Young Musicians; Multiple Appearances as Director of Viola Ensembles including International Viola Congresses, 1981, 1983, 1989, 1991, 1993, 1995, Lionel Tertis Competition and Workshop, 1980; Violist, Sierra String Quartet, 1981-85, Sierra Chamber Players, 1982-85; Several Lectures and Guest Appearances. Publication: Five Works for Viola Ensemble including the York Bowen Fantasie Quartet Montaine. Recording: Conversations for Viola and Piano. Honours: Outstanding Leadership, American Viola Society, 1989; Outstanding Leadership, California Unit, American String Teachers Association, 1988; Outstanding Educator of the Year, Whittier College; Performing Arts Fellowship, University of Illinois. Memberships: President, California Unit, American String Teachers Association, 1980-83; California Music Educators Association; President, California Orchestra Directors Association, 1992-94; President, American Viola Society, 1994-. Hobbies: Golf; Chess. Address: 7511 Parkwoods Drive, Stockton, CA 95207, USA.

TATUM Nancy, b. 25 Aug 1934, Memphis, TN, USA. Soprano. m. Wiley Tatum. Education: Studied with Zelma Lee Thomas in Memphis and with Samuel Margolis and Wiley Tatum in New York. Debut: Saarbrucken in 1962 as Santuzza. Career: Has sung in Paris, Geneva, Lyon, Minneapolis, Vancouver and Sofia; Member of the Deutsche Oper am Rhein Dusseldorf from 1964, and Metropolitan Opera from 1973; Further appearances in Budapest, Bucharest, Zagreb, Brussels and Amsterdam; Repertoire includes major roles in operas by Wagner and Verdi.

TAUB Robert (David), b. 25 Dec 1955, New York, USA. Concert Pianist. m. Tracy Elizabeth Milner, 27 Aug 1983. Education: AB, Princeton University, 1977; MMus, 1978, DMA, 1981, The Juilliard School. Career: Concert Pianist performing throughout the USA, Europe, Latin America and the Far East with a solo and concerto repertoire which spans from the Baroque to music of the present time. Recordings: Schumann and Liszt; Babbitt; Beethoven; Complete Sonatas of Scriabin; Perischetti Piano Concerto with the Philadelphia Orchestra under Dutoit. Contributions to: The Princeton Journal of The Arts and Sciences, 1977; The Autograph of Beethoven's Piano Trio Op 70, No 1, First Movement. Current Management: Columbia Artists Management Inc, 165 West 57th Street, New York, NY 10019, USA. Address: 185 West End Avenue, 26E, New York, NY 10023, USA.

TAUSKY Vilem, b. 20 Jul 1910, Perov, Czechoslovakia. Director of Opera; Artistic Director; Conductor; Composer. m. Margaret Helen Powell, 1948, deceased 1982. Education: University of Brno; Janácek Conservatoire, Brno; Meisterschule Prague. Career: National Opera House, Brno, Czechoslovakia, 1929-39; Military Service in France and England, 1939-45; Musical Director of Carl Rosa Opera, 1945-49; BBC Conductor, 1950-; Guest Conductor at Royal Opera House Covent Garden, 1951-, Sadler's Wells Opera, 1953-; Director of Opera, Guildhall School of Music, 1966-; Artistic Director of Phoenix Opera Company, 1967-; Conducted the first British performance of Janácek's Osud in 1972. Compositions: Czechoslovak Christmas Carols, 1942; Oboe Concerto, 1957; Concertina for Harmonica and Orchestra, 1963; Divertimento for Strings, 1966; Soho: Scherzo for Orchestra, 1966; Concert Overture for Brass Band, 1969; Cakes And Ale: Overture for Brass Band, 1971; Ballad for Cello and Piano; From Our Village, orchestral suite, 1972; Sonata for Cello and Piano, 1976; Suite for Violin and Piano, 1979; String Quartet, 1981. Publications: Vilem Tausky Tells His Story, 1979; Leos Janácek, Leaves From His Life, 1982. Contributions to: Tension in The Performance of Music, 1979; The Spectator, 1979. Honours: Czech Military Cross, 1944; Czech Order of Merit, 1945; Fellow of the Guildhall School of Music, 1968; Freeman of The City Of London, 1979; CBE, 1981. Hobby: Country Life. Address: 44 Haven Green Court, London, W5, England.

TAUTU Cornelia, b. 10 Mar 1938, Odorhei, Rumania. Composer. m. Valentin Curocichin, 6 Aug 1976, 1 daughter. Education: Ciprian Porumbescu Conservatory, Bucharest; Postgraduate studies at Long Island University, NY, USA, 1971-72. Compositions: Film Music: Tragic Holiday, Stage Music for: Prometheus (Aeschylus), La Locandiera (Goldoni), Medees (Seneca), Cherry Orchard (Chekov), The Third Stake (M Sorescu), Cold Heart (W Hauff); Symphonic: Counterpoint for String Orchestra, Segments for String Orchestra, Inventions for Piano and Orchestra, Dice, symphonic sketch, Palingenesia - Poem For 1907 for Orchestra; Engravings for Orchestra, Sinfonietta, Symphony No 1 - 1907, 1987, Concerto for Piano and Orchestra, 1989; Chamber: Concerto for 12 Instruments, Inventions for Piano, Collage for String Quartet, Carol Echoes, quintet for Flute, Oboe, Clarinet, Bassoon and Horn, Homage For Peace for String Quintet, Sonata, Trio for Flute, Piano and Harp, 8 progressive pieces for piano, 1988, Three Lieder, rhymes, by M Eminescu; Choral: Triptych. Address: Sos Stefan cel Mare, No 2 Bl 13 sc B ap 36 Sect 1, Bucharest, Rumania.

TAVENER Alan, b. 22 April 1957, Weston-Super-Mare, Avon, England. Conductor; Organist; Manager. m. Rebecca Jane Gibson, 30 August 1980. Education: Organ Scholar, Brasenose College, Oxford, 1976-79; ARCO/ARCM 1978, graduated with BA Honours, Music, 1979; Subsequently gained MA degree. Career: Director of Music, University of Strathclyde, 1980-; Founder Director, Cappella Nova, 1982-; Conducted several world premieres of new choral works, including John Tavener's Resurrection, Glasgow, 1990; and James MacMillan's Seven Last Words, Glasgow, 1994. Recordings: Robert Carver, the Complete Sacred Choral Music, 3 CD's, 1990; Scottish Medieval Plainchart, Columba, most Holy of Saints, 1992; Sacred Music for Mary Queen of Scots, 1993; Twentieth Century Scottish Choral Music, 1992. Hobbies: Architecture; Exhibitions; Scottish Country Dancing; Food and Drink. Address: Director of Music, University of Strathclyde, Livingstone Tower, Richmond Street, Glasgow G1 1XH, Scotland.

TAVENER John, b. 28 Jan 1944. Composer; Professor of Music. m. (1), div 1980, (2) Maryanna Schaefer, 1991, 2 daughters. Education: Highgate School, England; Royal Academy of Music, LRAM. Career: Professor of Music, Trinity College of Music, 1969-. Compositions: Piano Concerto; Three Holy Sonnets (Donne); Cain and Able (first prize Monaco); The Cappemakers; Three Songs of T S Eliot; Grandma's Footsteps; In Memoriam Igor Stravinsky; Responsorium in memory of Annon Lee Silver; The Whale; Introit for March 27th; Three Surrealist Songs; In Alium; Akhmatova Requiem; Ultimos Ritos, 1972; Thérèse (opera), 1972; A Gentle Spirit (opera), 1977; Kyklike Kinesis; Palin; Palintropos; Canticle of the Mother of God; Divine Liturgy of St John Chrysostum; The Immurement of Antigone; Lamentation, Last Prayer and Exaltation; Six Abbasid Songs; Greek Interlude; Sappho; Lyrical Fragments; Prayer for The World; The Great Canon of St Andrew of Crete; Trisagion; Risen!; Mandelion; The Lamb, carol; Funeral Ikos; Doxa; Lord's Prayer; Mandoodles; Towards the Son; 16 Haiku of Seferis; Ikon of Light; Orthodox Vigil Service; Two Hymns to the Mother of God; Eis Thanaton; Nativity; Angels; Love Bade Me Welcome; Panikhida, (orthodox funeral service); Ikon of St Cuthbert; Magnificat and Nunc Dimittis (Collegium Regale); Akathis of Thanksgiving; Meditation on the Light; Wedding Prayer; Many Years; Acclamation; The Protecting Veil; Ikon of St Seraphim; God is With Us; Hymn to the Holy Spirit; The Tyger; Apolytikion for St Nicholas; The Call; Let Not the Prince be Silent; Resurrection, 1989; The Hidden Treasure for String Quartet, 1989; The Repentent Thief for clarinet and strings, 1990; Mary of Egypt, chamber opera, 1991, premiere at Aldeburgh Festival in 1992; We Shall See Him as He Is, 1992; Annunciation, 1992; Theophany, 1993; The Apocalypse, 1993; Song for Athene, 1993; The World is Burning, 1993; The Myrrh-Bearer, 1993; Akhmatova Songs, 1993; Innocence, 1994; Agraphon, for soprano Patricia Rozario and string orchestra, 1995; Feast of Feasts, 1995; Prayer to the Holy Trinity, 1995; Let's Begin Again, 1995; Syvati, 1995; Vlepondas, 1996; The Hidden Face, 1996; Diodia, 1997; Fear and Rejoice, O People, 1997. Recordings: Numerous on major labels. Honours: Honorary Doctorate for Sacred Music, New Delhi, 1990; Honorary Member, Anglo-Hellenic Society; Honorary Vice President, Composers Guild; Honorary Member, Friends of Mount Athos; The Gramophone Award for Best Contemporary Recording, 1992; The Apollo Award for Contribution to Greek Culture, 1993; Honorary FRAM; Honorary FTCL; Patron of Cricklade Festival; Biography, John Tavener - Glimpses of Paradise by Geoffrey Haydon, 1995. Membership: Russian Orthodox Church. Address: c/o Chester Music Ltd, 8-9 Frith Street, London, W1V 5TZ, England.

TAYLOR Ann, b. 1966 Wrexham, North Wales. Singer (Mezzo-soprano). Education: Royal Northern College of Music, Guildhall School and the National Opera Studio. Career: Appearances with Opera North as Ramiro in La Finta Giardiniera, Feodor in Boris Godunov (also at the London Proms), Cherubino, and Donna Clara in the British premiere of Gerhard's The Duenna; Dorabella, Ramiro, Phoebe in Yeoman of the Guard and Handel's Ariodante for Welsh National Opera; Kristina in The Makropoulos Case and Oreste, La Belle Hélène for Scottish Opera, Rosina and Mozart's Annius for Glyndebourne Touring Opera; Premiere of Berkeley's Baa Baa Black Sheep at the 1993 Cheltenham Festival; Schumann's Manfred at Monnaie, Brussels and Cherubino for the Bavarian State Opera; Concerts include Chabrier's La Sulamite at the Elizabeth Hall, Schumann's Scenes from Faust at the 1994 Edinburgh Festival, Les Nuits d'Eté, and Nancy in Albert Herring under Steuart Bedford; Season 1997 with Hänsel for Opera Zuid, and Glyndebourne Festival debut, as Kate in Owen Wingrave. Recordings include: The Duenna, Baa Baa Black Sheep and Albert Herring. Address: Ingpen & Williams Ltd, 26 Wadham Road, London SW15 2LR, England.

TAYLOR Daniel, b. 1969, Canada. Counter-Tenor. Education: Studied at McGill University and at the University of Montreal. Career: Concerts with Tafelmusik, Netherlands Radio Chamber Orchestra, Dallas Symphony Orchestra, Portland Baroque, Winnipeg and Quebec Symphonies, Kammerchor Stuttgart and American Bach Soloists; Repertoire includes Messiah (at Göttingen), St Matthew Passion (Berkeley), King Arthur (with Les Violons du Roi), and Rodelinda; Sang Bertarido in Rodelinda at Broomhill and Halle, 1996. Recordings include: Jommelli La Didone Abandonata and Zelenka Missa Omnium Sanctorum. Address: c/o Ron Gonsalves Management, 7 Old Town, Clapham, London, SW4 0JT, England.

TAYLOR James, b. 1966, Dallas, TX, USA. Singer (Tenor). Education: Texas Christian University and the Munich Hochschule with Adalbert Kraus. Debut: Tony in West Side Story, with the Fort Worth SO, 1990. Career: Opera appearances in Stuttgart (Monteverdi's Ulisse and Fliegende Holländer) and the Grand Priest in Idomeneo at Brussels; Concerts include: Bach's St Matthew Passion in Munich, and the St John Passion with the Vienna Philharmonic; Beethoven's Missa Solemnis, Mendelssohn's Elijah and Bach Cantatas, conducted by Philippe Herreweghe; Season 1997 with Mozart's Requiem at Zurich and Bach's B Minor Mass with the Cleveland Orchestra under Christoph von Dohnányi. Recordings include: Orff's Catulli Carmina, Bach's Magnificat and Mass in A (with Helmuth Rilling), Missa solemnis and Mendelssohn's St Paul (Herreweghe). Address: Kunstler Sekretariat, Rosenheimerstrasse 52, 81669 Munich, Germany.

TAZZINI Rinaldo, b. 15 Feb 1942, New York City, USA. Producer; Director; Artistic Director. m. Helen Neswald, 15 Sep 1965, 1 son, 2 daughters. Education: High School of Music and Art, New York City; BA, Music, Hunter College; Mannes School of Music with Paul Berl and Carl Bamberger; Conservatorio di Cherubini with Cecilia Castelana-Zotti, Florence, Italy; Accademia di Chigiana with Gino Bechi; Accademia di Santa Cecilia with Tito Gobbi. Career includes: Sang Fanny in Cesario in 1955, Huck Finn in Tom Sawyer in 1957, sang at New York City Opera, 1971-72, Teatro dell'Opera, Rome, Italy, 1972-74, Teatro Massimo Bellini at Catania in 1974, and Teatro Lonigo in 1974; Artistic Director and Director of Productions at Brooklyn Opera Society, USA, 1977-; Madame Butterfly at Japanese Garden in New York City being the first opera for television shot on location in USA, 1980; Producer, Director of the George Gershwin Festival Tour in 1982; Creator, Director, Hot Rags Musical at Lincoln Center in 1983. Address: c/o Bernard Lewis, Director of Communications, The Brooklyn Opera Society, Borough Hall, Brooklyn, NY 11201, USA.

TCHEREPNIN Ivan (Alexandrovich), b. 5 Feb 1943, Issy-les-Moulineaux, nr Paris, France. Composer. Education: Studied with Father Alexander Tcherepnin and Academie Internationale de Musique, Nice; Further study with Randall Thompson and Leon Kirchner at Harvard; BA, 1964; MA, 1969; Electronic music with Stockhausen and Henri Pousseur in

Cologne, conducting with Pierre Boulez; Electronic music studies in Toronto. Career: Faculty of San Francisco Conservatory and at Stanford University, 1969-72 (Co-Director of New Music Ensemble, Alea II); Associate Professor and Director of the electronic music studio at Harvard University, from 1972; Performances and lectures in Shanghai and Peking, 1989. Compositions include: Wheelwinds for 9 wind instruments, 1966; Le Va et le vient for orchestra, 1978; Oboe Concerto, 1980; New Consonance for string orchestra, 1983; Solstice for chamber orchestra, 1983; Explorations for flute, clarinet, string trio, piano and electronics, 1985; Status for wind orchestra, 1986; Concerto for Two Continents for synthesizer and wind orchestra, 1989; And so it Came to Pass, cantata, 1991; Double Concerto for violin, cello and orchestra, 1995; Seven Fanfares for Three Trumpets, 1995; Further electronic pieces, including The Creative Act for 4 performers and live electronics, 1990. Honours include: Grawemeyer Award, University of Louisville, 1996. Address: Music Department, Harvard University, Cambridge, MA 02138, USA.

TCHISTJAKOVA Trina, b. 1965, Moscow, Russia. Singer (Mezzo-soprano). Education: Graduated the Gnesin Russian Academy of Music, Moscow, 1989. Career: Soloist with the Theatre Studio of the Gnesin Academy, from 1988; Principal with the Moscow Municipal Theatre, from 1990 (tour of Italy 1991, as Ratmir in Glinka's Ruslan and Ludmilla); Season 1994-95 Marina in Boris Godunov at Liège, the Verdi Requiem at Lincoln Center, New York, and Ruslan and Ludmilla at Carnegie Hall; Marfa in Khovanshcina at the Bolshoi, 1995; Season 1996-97 as Marina at Turin and Salzburg; Eugene Onegin and The Queen of Spades at Trieste; Kirov Opera St Petersburg as Cherubino, Marguerite in La Damnation de Faust, Amneris and Eboli; Concert repertory includes Skriabin's 1st Symphony (in Sweden and Germany), Beethoven's Ninth and Prokofiev's Alexander Nevsky (with the Philharmonia Orchestra). Recordings include: Verdi Arias (Capriccio); Azucena in Il Trovatore (Laserlight Classics). Honours include: Winner, Vinas Singing Competition, Barcelona, 1993. Address: c/o Lies Askonas Ltd, 6 Henrietta St, London WC2E 8LA, England.

TE KANAWA Kiri (Dame), b. 6 Mar 1944, Gisborne, New Zealand. Soprano. m. Desmond Park, 1967, divorced 1997, 2 children. Education: St Mary's College, Auckland; London Opera Centre. Debut: Royal Opera Covent Garden in 1970. Career includes: La Scala Milan debut in 1978; Sang at Salzburg Festival in 1979, with San Francisco Opera Company in 1980, and at Edinburgh and Helsinki Festivals in 1980; Operas include: Boris Godunov, Parsifal, The Marriage of Figaro, Otello, Simon Boccanegra, Carmen, Don Giovanni and as a film version in 1979, Faust, The Magic Flute, La Bohème 5 times, Eugene Onegin, Cosi fan tutte, Arabella, Die Fledermaus, La Traviata, Der Rosenkavalier, Manon Lescaut and Don Giovanni; Sang at the wedding of HRH The Prince of Wales, London in 1981; Sang the Countess in Capriccio at San Francisco in 1990 and at Covent Garden; Sang the premiere of Paul McCartney's Liverpool Oratorio, written by Carl Davis, at Liverpool Cathedral and in London, 1991; Sang Amelia in a new production of Simon Boccanegra at Covent Garden in 1991; Season 1992 with Mozart's Countess at the Metropolitan and Desdemona at Covent Garden; Sang Mozart's Countess at the Met, 1997. Recordings include: Elvira in Don Giovanni; Fiordiligi in Cosi fan Tutte; Otello; Micaela in Carmen; Mozart Vespers and C minor Mass; Pamina in The Magic Flute; The Marriage of Figaro; Hansel and Gretel; Strauss's Songs with Orchestra; Die Fledermaus; Woodbird in Siegfried; Songs of the Auvergne; La Bohème; Capriccio; Nelson Riddle's Blue Skies; Gershwin; Cole Porter; West Side Story conducted by Leonard Bernstein; Recitals records. Publications: Children's book, The Land of the Long White Cloud; Opera for Lovers, with Conrad Wilson. Honours: OBE; DBE; Honorary Degrees at Oxford, Dundee, Nottingham, Auckland, Durham and Post University in USA. Hobbies: Golf; Tennis. Current Management: Impresario AG.

TEAR Robert, b. 8 Mar 1939, Barry, South Wales. Tenor; Conductor. m. 2 daughters. Education: King's College, Cambridge. Debut: With English Opera Group, 1963. Career: Sang as Lensky in Eugene Onegin, Covent Garden; From 1970 as Dov in The Knot Garden (premiere), Lensky, Paris (King Priam), Wagner's Froh and Loge, Tom Rakewell, Admetus in Alceste, Rimbaud in Tavener's Thérèse (premiere 1979), David, Jupiter in Semele; The Director in British premiere of Berio's Un re in Ascolto, 1979, Shuisky (Boris Godunov), 1991, and the Schoolmaster (Cunning Little Vixen), 1990; Sang in world premiere of Tippett's Mask of Time with Boston Symphony Orchestras; Salzburg Festival, 1985, as Eumetus in the Henze/Monteverdi Ulisse; Season 1990-91 with the War Requiem in Detroit and The Mask of Time in London; The Turn of the Screw at Montpellier and Peter Grimes with Geneva Opera; Beethoven and Tippett in Florida and Los Angeles; Title role in premiere of Ubu Rex by Penderecki at Munich; Mephisto in the Covent Garden premiere of Prokofiev's Fiery Angel, 1992; Season 1994/95 as Janácek's Mr Broucek at Munich, Captain Vere in Billy Budd in Geneva, Figaro and The Rake's Progress at

Glyndebourne, Loge (Das Rheingold) at the Royal Opera House, Covent Garden, and Herod (Salome) at Hamburg Opera; Sang in Pfitzner's Palestrina at Covent Garden, 1997; Large repertoire in opera and lieder; Created roles in Britten's Burning Fiery Furnace and Prodigal Son; Well known Mime in Das Rheingold in London and Bayreuth; Other roles include Peter Grimes, Matteo (Arabella); Appeared in Europe at Paris Opéra including premiere of 3-act version of Berg's Lulu, La Scala Milan, and Salzburg; Regular guest of great US orchestras such as Boston, Chicago, Los Angeles and New York Philharmonic; Conducting debut in Minneapolis, 1985, subsequently conducting many orchestras including London Mozart Players, Northern Sinfonia, English Chamber Orchestra, Philharmonic, BBC Welsh Symphony, Royal Liverpool Philharmonic and Royal Scottish National Orchestra; Artistic Director, Vocal faculty of London Royal Schools of Music, 1992-94; Currently holds the Chair of International Singing at the Royal Academy of Music. Recordings: Over 250 including: Mahler (orch Schoenberg) Das Lied von der Erde, with Premiere Ensemble and Mark Wigglesworth. Honours: Honorary Fellow, King's College, Cambridge; CBE, 1984. Address: c/o Harold Holt Ltd, 31 Sinclair Road, London W14 0NS, England.

TEBALDI Renata, b. 1 Feb 1922, Pesaro, Italy. Soprano. Education: Studied at Arrigo Boito Conservatory, Parma and the Rossini Conservatory at Pesaro; Further study with Carmen Melis and Giuseppe Pais. Debut: As Elena in Mefistofele at Rovigo in 1944. Career: First sang at La Scala at post-war reopening concert under Toscanini; Stage appearances in Milan until 1955 as Marguerite (Boito and Gounod), Eva, Tatiana and Catalani's Wally; Sang at Naples from 1958 as Violetta, Elisabeth de Valois, Refice's Cecilia, Giovanna d'Arco and Amazily in Fernand Cortes by Spontini, Maggio Musicale Fiorentino, 1948-53 as Elsa, Pamira in L'Assedio di Corinto, Mathilde in Guillaume Tell and Olympie in Spontini's opera; Sang Desdemona at Covent Garden in 1950 and at Metropolitan Opera from 1955 in over 200 performances as Tosca, Mimi, La Gioconda, Desdemona, Adriana Lecouvreur, Manon Lescaut, Amelia Boccanegra, Minnie in La Fanciulla del West, Violetta, Butterfly, Leonora in La Forza del Destino and Alice Ford; Further appearances at the Chicago Lyric Opera, Vienna Staatsoper, Paris Opéra, Deutsche Oper Berlin and in Japan; Retired from opera in 1973, concerts in 1976. Recordings include: La Bohème; Tosca; Manon Lescaut; Il Trovatore; La Gioconda; Puccini's Trittico; Turandot; Otello; Un Ballo in Maschera; Don Carlos; Cavalleria Rusticana; Mefistofele; Adriana Lecouvreur; La Forza del Destino. Address: c/o SA Gorlinsky Ltd, 33 Dover Street, London, W1, England.

TEBBETT Eric William, b. 8 Sept 1951, England. Singer; Conductor; Examiner. m. Deborah Markham, 31 Dec 1997, 2 daughters. Education: Diploma, National Youth Orchestra of Great Britain, 1967-70; Royal Scottish Academy of Music and Drama, 1970-73; University of Newcastle-Upon-Tyne, 1973-74. Career: Several Appearances on Radio and TV both in England, Europe and USA; Examiner, Trinity College, London; Worked in Hong Kong, South Africa, Australia, New Zealand, Singapore, Malaysia, Spain; Chorus Director, Central Festival Opera. Honour: Hugh S Robertson Prize, Vocal Ensemble, 1973. Memberships: British Federation of Music Festivals. Hobby: Gardening. Address: Stile Cottage, School Lane, Scaldwell, Northampton NN6 9LE, England.

TEDE Margery, b. 1940, USA. Mezzo-Soprano. Education: Studied at San Francisco State College, Madrid Conservatory and the Hochschule fur Musik in Berlin. Career: Sang with the San Francisco Opera as Fricka, Amneris, Azucena, Judith in Bluebeard's Castle, Jocasta and Herodias in Salome; Sang Countess Carolina in the local premiere of Henze's Elegy for Young Lovers, conducted by Christopher Keene; Lake Tahoe Summer Music Festival as Susan B Anthony in Virgil Thomson's The Mother of Us All; Concert appearances with the San Francisco Symphony under Seiji Ozawa and in Mozart's Coronation Mass in New York; Sang in opera, concerts and recitals in Europe, Central America, Alaska and the South Pacific; Sang the world premiere of Roger Nixon's Three Transcendental Songs in New York and songs by Charles Ives in Hamburg; Now retired as singer and active as teacher. Honours include: International Scholarship from the Federation of Music Clubs. Address: Steorra Enterprises, 243 West End Avenue, Suite 907, New York, NY 10023, USA.

TEIRILÄ Tuomo Juhani, b. 22 Sept 1952, Helsinki, Finland. Composer; Teacher. m. Kielo Marjatta Alaranta, 1 son. Education: Diploma in Composition, Sibelius Academy, Helsinki, 1978. Career: Teacher of Music Theory, Sibelius Academy, 1976-; Teacher of Music Theory, Music Institute, Vantaa, 1977-. Compositions: Introitus, Kyrie and Gloria for organ, published and recorded, 1977; Oboe concerto, 1978; Concertino a quattro for organ with 9 instruments and live electronics, 1981; Four Scenes in Vantaa for orchestra, 1989; Water Music for orchestra, 1991; Night for orchestra, 1992; Die Kunst der Irre for orchestra, 1994; Birth of the Snipe for reciter and small orchestra, 1996. Address: Rakennusmestarintie 13, FIN-00680 Helsinki, Finland.

TEITELBAUM Richard (Lowe), b. 19 May 1939, New York City, USA. Composer; Performer; Teacher. Education: BA, Haverford College, 1960; MMus, Yale University School of Music, 1964; Mannes School, 1960-61; Accademia di Santa Cecilia, Rome, 1964-65; Composition with Luigi Nono in Venice, 1965-66; Wesleyan University World Music Program, 1970-71. Career: Founding Member, Musica Electronica Viva, Rome, 1966; Instructor at California Institute of the Arts, 1971-72; Founder and Director, Electronic Music Studio, Art Institute of Chicago, 1972-73; Co-Director and Visiting Professor, York University, Toronto, 1973-76; Soloist at Berlin Philharmonic Hall, Concertgebouw, Centre Pompidou, and WDR Cologne among others, 1984-86; Visiting Professor at Bard and Vassar Colleges, 1988-89. Compositions include: Intersections for Piano, 1964; In Tune for Live Electronics, 1966; Digital Piano Music, 1983; Concerto Grosso for Robotic Pianos, Winds, Trombone and Synthesizers; Iro Wa Nioedo for 20 Buddhist Monks. Recordings include: Hi Uchi Ishi, 1977; Time Zones, 1977; Concerto Grosso, 1987. Memberships: American Music Center; Composers Forum; College Music Society; International Computer Music Society. Current Management: Barbara Mayfield, New York City, USA. Address: 250 Cold Brook Road, Bearsville, NY 12409, USA.

TELLEFSEN Arve, b. 1948, Trondheim, Norway. Violinist. Education: Studied with Arne Stoltenberg, Professor Henry Holst and Professor Ivan Galamian, New York, 1960. Career: Numerous recitals and concerts in Europe; Professor of The Academy of Music in Oslo from 1973; Tour of Norway in 1985 with the RPO under Ashkenazy; Oslo Philharmonai concerts in 1987 with Mariss Jansons, Neeme Järvi and Esa-Pekka Salonen; British engagements with David Zinman, Jerzy Maksymiuk, Marek Janowski, Okko Kamu, Vernon Handley and Kurt Sanderling; Festival concerts at Schleswig-Holstein, Lockenhaus and Montreux; Founded Oslo Chamber Music Festival in 1989; Season 1997 premiered the Concerto by Nordheim, with the Oslo Philharmonic Orchestra. Recordings: Numerous discs which include concertos by Nielsen, Shostakovich, Berwald, Aulin, Valen, Sinding, Svendsen and Sibelius; Beethoven and Grieg Sonatas; Bruch and Beethoven concertos with the London Philharmonic Orchestra; Shostakovich 1 and Sibelius with the Royal Philharmonic. Honours: First Prize, Princess Astrid's Competition for Young Norwegian Artists, 1956; Harriet Cohen International Award, 1962; Awarded the prize of Bergen Festival, 1964; Grieg Prize, 1973. Address: c/o IMG Artists, Media House, 3 Burlington Lane, London WA2 2TH, England.

TEMESI Maria (Maria Toth), b. 1957, Szeged, Hungary. Soprano Singer. Education: Studied at Franz Liszt Academy; Szeged Piano, Singing Teacher, Opera Singer diplomas, Budapest; Masterclasses at Weimar Music Academy and Mozarteum, Salzburg. Debut: Budapest State Opera as Elsa, in Wagner's Lohengrin, under G Patanè, 1982. Career: Appearances: Staatsoper Hamburg, Oper der Stadt Köln, Semperoper Dresden, Staatsoper Berlin, Komische Oper Berlin, Opernhaus Zurich, Teatro Farnese Parma, Teatro de la Zarzuela Madrid, Opera de Nice, Theatre du Capitole Toulouse, Opera Company of Philadelphia, Smetana Theatre Prague, Herodes Atticus Ampthitheatre Athens, Opernhaus Graz, Montevideo Teatro Solis, Uruguay; Main Roles: Vitellia in La Clemenza di Tito, Adriana Lecouvrer, Tatiana, Lisa in The Queen of Spades, Amelia in Ballo in Maschera, Leonore in Trovatore, Elisabeth de Valois, Elena, in Vespri Siciliani, Desdemona, Alice in Falstaff, Elsa in Lohengrin, Eva in Meistersinger, Elisabeth in Tannhäuser, Estrella in Schubert's Alfonso und Estrella, Sieglinde in Die Walküre, Mimi in La Bohème and Manon in Manon Lescaut; Concert performance of Guntram by Strauss, Manhattan Cable TV, NY; Götterdämmerung (Gutrune); Mahler's 2nd Symphony under Dorati; Handel's Messiah under Gönnenwein; La Clemenza di Tito conducted by John Pritchard, Cologne; Liederabenden, Budapest Music Academy; Lisbon Fundacao Calouste Gulbenkian; Cairo Academy of Arts; Beethoven: Missa Solemnis (Milano, RAI); Verdi: Requiem; Dvorak, Requiem; Britten: War Requiem (Zagreb); Rossini: Stabat mater; Pergolesi: Stabat mater. Recordings: Liszt, Missa Choralis; Mahler, 8th Symphony. Honours include: Prizewinner in competitions in Athens, 1979, Toulouse, 1980; 1st Prize, Rio de Janeiro, 1981; Winner, Pavarotti Competition, Philadelphia, 1985; Szekely Mihaly Plaquette, Budapest, 1995. Address: Templom u 22, 1028 Budapest, Hungary.

TEMIRKANOV Yuri, b. 10 Dec 1938, Nalchik, Caucasus, Russia. Conductor. Education: Leningrad Conservatory for Talented Children, 1953-56; Leningrad Conservatory of Music, graduated as violinist in 1962 and conductor in 1965. Career: Conductor of Leningrad Opera and all major Soviet orchestras, 1968-; Director, Leningrad Symphony Orchestra, 1969 touring extensively; Artistic Director of Kirov Opera in 1977; Has conducted Berlin Philharmonic, Vienna Philharmonic, Dresden State Orchestras, and Orchestre de Paris; Following London debut with The Royal Philharmonic Orchestra in 1977 worked with Philharmonia, City of Birmingham, and Royal Liverpool Philharmonic Orchestras; Principal Guest Conductor with RPO, 1979; Conducted the BBC Symphony Orchestra in Italy and

Russia in 1987, and the Philadelphia, Boston and New York Orchestras in USA; Artistic Director of the Leningrad (now St Petersburg) Philharmonic, 1988; Conducted The Queen of Spades for RAI, Turin in 1990; Principal Conductor of the Royal Philharmonic Orchestra from 1992; Recent seasons have included Tchaikovsky Cycle with St Petersburg Philharmonic in Japan and Europe and tours of USA and Germany with the Royal Philharmonic; Engaged for Eugene Onegin at San Francisco, 1998. Honour: 1st Prize, National Conducting Competition, Russia, 1968. Current Management: IMG Artists (Europe). Address: c/o IMG Artists (Europe), Media House, 3 Burlington Lane, London, W4 2TH, England.

TEMPERLEY Nicholas, b. 7 Aug 1932, Beaconsfield, England (US citizen since 1977). Musicologist. m. Mary Dorothea Sleator, 17 Sept 1960, 1 son, 2 daughters. Education: ARCM, Royal College of Music, 1952; BA, BMus, MA, PhD, King's College, Cambridge University, 1952-59. Career: Assistant Lecturer, Music, Cambridge University and Fellow, Clare College, Cambridge, 1961-66; Assistant Professor, Musicology, Yale University, USA, 1966-67; Associate Professor 1967-72, Professor 1972-96, Professor Emeritus, 1996-, Chairman Musicology Division 1972-75, 1992-96, University of Illinois. Publications include: Critical editions, music: Raymond & Agnes, Edward J Loder, performed Cambridge, 1966; Symphonie Fantastique, Berlioz, New Berlioz Edition, 1972; English Songs 1800-60, Musica Britannica Vol 43, 1979; London Pianoforte School 1766-1860, 20 vols, Garland, 1984-87; Haydn's Creation, with authentic English text, 1987. Also: Music of English Parish Church, 2 vols, 1979; Athlone History of Music in Britain, vol 5, Romantic Age, 1981; Fuging Tunes in 18th Century, with C G Manns, 1983; The Hymn Tune Index, 4 volumes, 1997. Contributions to: Numerous musical journals; Over 100 entries, New Grove Dictionary. Honours: John Stewart of Rannoch scholarship, 1953; Otto Kinkeldey Award, American Musicological Society, 1980; University Senior Scholar, Illinois, 1986; Fellow, Guild of Church Musicians, 1990-. Memberships: Past Editor-in-Chief, offices, American Musicological Society; Past office, Hymn Society of America; Midwest Victorian Studies Association. Hobbies: Piano playing; Chamber music; Bridge; 19th century novels. Address: 805 West Indiana Street, Urbana, Illinois 61801, USA.

TENENBOM Steven, b. USA. Violist. Education: Curtis Institute of Music with Michael Tree and Karen Tuttle. Career: Soloist with the Brandenburg Ensemble and Rochester PO, Guest Artist with the Guarneri Quartet, Beaux Arts Trio and Chamber Music Society of Lincoln Center; Festival engagements at Chamber Music Northwest, Aspen, Music from Angel Fire and Bravo Colorado; Violist with the Orion String Quartet, including concerts throughout North America and in Europe; Brahms and Schubert evening in season 1996-97 at Lincoln Center, and opening night Gala in honour of Marilyn Horne; Faculty Member at Mannes College of Music and Hartt School of Music, New York. Address: Orion String Quartet, Ingpen & Williams Ltd, 26 Wadham Road, London SW15 2LR, England.

TENNFJORD Oddbjφrn, b. 1941, Oslo, Norway. Bass Singer. Education: Studied at the Bergen and Oslo Conservatories, in Essen with Clemens Kaiser-Breme, in Rome with Luigi Ricci and in London with Roy Henderson. Career: Has sung with the Norske Opera Oslo from 1971 as Osmin, Don Pasquale, Basilio, Falstaff, Pogner, Boris Godunov, Sarastro, Wotan, King Marke, Gremin and Fiesco; Concert and opera engagements for Norwegian Radio and TV, in Germany, Italy, Poland, Sweden, Denmark, Israel, Yugoslavia, France and USA; Appearances with Scottish Opera as The Commendatore, Daland, Sarastro and Fafner; Bologna in 1988 and Ravenna Festival in 1989 as the Grand Inquisitor in Don Carlos; Sang with Scottish Opera as Fafner in Das Rheingold and the Commendatore and as Daland at Oslo in 1989; Numerous guest appearances worldwide include: Baron Ochs and Daland in Montpellier, Daland in Cologne, Tokyo, Barcelona and Las Palmas, Baron Ochs in Osaka, The Grand Inquisitor in Bologna and Ravenna, Sarastro, Fafner, The Commendatore and Frank (Die Fledermaus) with the Scottish Opera; Since 1994 freelance: Gurrelieder with Mariss Jansons and the Oslo Philharmonic Orchestra, King Marke in Brussels with Antonio Pappano, Duke Bluebeard with Neeme Järvi and Gothenburg Symphony Orchestra, Vespri Siciliani, Rheingold and Die Walküre at Den Norske Opera; Season 1996-97 included Baron Ochs at Deutsche Oper, Berlin, Boris Godunov at Kungliga Operan, Stockholm, Marke and Commendatore in Brussels and Der Freidenstag and Don Giovanni at Sächsiche Staatsoper, Dresden. Address: Unit 2, 39 Tadema Road, London, SW10 0PY, England.

TENZI Fausto, b. 1 Apr 1939, Lugano, Switzerland. Tenor. Education: Studied in Milan. Career: Sang at La Scala Milan, Théâtre des Champs Elysées, Paris, Teatro Comunale, Bologna and in Florence, Lucerne, Aachen and Perugia; Engaged at Buxton Festival, England and made concert appearances in Rome, Paris, Berlin, Moscow, Leningrad and North America; Other roles include Don José, Edgardo, Manrico, Don Carlos, Pinkerton, Rodolfo, Turiddu and Ivan Khovansky in Khovanshchina. Recordings include: The Queen of Spades; Scriabin's 1st Symphony.

TERAMOTO Mariko, b. 6 June 1948, Tokyo, Japan. Musicologist. Education: BA, Musashino College of Music, Tokyo, 1971; MA, National University of Fine Arts and Music, Tokyo, 1973; PhD, University of Frankfurt am Main, 1978. Appointments: Assistant Professor, 1984-87, Professor, 1988-, Meisei University; Lecturer, Musashino College of Music, 1984-; Lecturer, National University of Fine Arts and Music, 1985-89, 1996-97. Publications: Die Psalmmotettendrucke des Johannes Petrejus in Nürnberg, 1983; Frankfurter Beiträge zur Musikwissenschaft: Katalog der Musikdrucke des Johannes Petreius in Nürnberg, 1993. Contributions to: Journal of the Japanese Musicological Society. Memberships: International Musicological Society; Gesellschaft für Musikforschung; American Musicological Society. Address: 2-10-16 Shimo-Ochiai, Shinjuku-ku, Tokyo 161-0033, Japan.

TERENTIEVA Nina, b. 1950, Russia. Singer (Mezzo-soprano). Education: Leningrad State Conservatory. Career: Sang with the Kirov Opera as Olga in Eugene Onegin, Marina (Boris Godunov) and Gounod's Siebel; Bolshoi Opera as Amneris, Marfa in Khovanshchina and Carmen; Vienna Staatsoper from 1987, as Azucena and Eboli, Azucena and Marina at La Scala, Ulrica at Munich, Berlin and Buenos Aires; Eboli in Don Carlos at Los Angeles (1990) and San Francisco (1992); Amneris in Aida at Berlin, Hamburg, Munich, and the Royal Opera Covent Garden (1996); Further appearances at the Metropolitan Opera, Washington Opera, and with the Canadian Opera Company; Season 1997 with Amneris for San Francisco Opera; Frequent concert appearances and recitals in Russia. Address: c/o Vienna State Opera, Opernring 2, A-1010 Vienna, Austria.

TEREY-SMITH Mary, b. Budapest, Hungary. Musicologist; Opera Conductor; Vocal Coach. m. C A C Smith. Education: BMus, Conducting and Composition, Liszt Academy of Music; MA, Music Literature, Univesity of Vermont, USA; PhD, Musicology, Eastman School of Music, University of Rochester. Debut: Conductor, Tatabanya Symphony Orchestra, Budapest, 1951. Career: Vocal coach, then assistant conductor, Hungarian State Opera, 1950-56; Resident conductor, Tatabanya Symphony Orchestra, 1951-56; Vocal Coach, Toronto Royal Conservatory Opera School, Canada, 1957-58; Assistant Professor, 1967-72, Associate Professor, 1972-85, Professor of Music History and Literature, 1985-, Western Washington University; Director, Opera Workshop, 1967-75, Director of the Collegium Musicum Ensemble, 1969-, Western Washington University; European tours with the Collegium Musicum Ensemble include Italy and Hungary in 1994 and Italy, Austria and Hungary in 1996. Recordings: Conductor of 2 CD's: Four Orchestral Suites from Operas by J P Rameau with the Capella Savaria Baroque Orchestra, 1996. Publications: Selection of published articles and studies: Editor, French Baroque Orchestral Dances, by Jean-Philippe Rameau, Canada 1986; Orchestral Practice in the Paris Opera, 1690-1764, and the Spread of the French influence in Europe, in Studia Musicologica xxxi, 1989; International Dictionary of Opera: Rameau: Les Boreades, essay, 1993. Contributions to: Two reviews for Music and Letters, P Brun: A History of the Double Bass, 1991; A Meyer: A Thematic Index of the Works by Johannes Sperger; New Grove Dictionary. Honours: Toured Hungary twice, 1990 and 1992 with the Collegium Musicum ensemble on the invitation of the Albert Schweitzer Chorus and Orchestra. Memberships: American Musicological Society; International Musicological Society; Early Music America. Address: 1809 Harris Avenue, Bellingham, WA 98225, USA.

TERFEL Bryn, b. 9 Nov 1965, Pwllheli, Gwynedd, Wales. Baritone. Education: Studied at the Guildhall School of Music. Debut: Welsh National Opera as Guglielmo in 1990. Career: Has sung Mozart's Figaro at Santa Fe Opera, English National Opera, Hamburg Opera in 1991; Covent Garden debut in 1992 as Masetto in Don Giovanni repeated on tour to Japan; Sang at Salzburg Festival in 1992 as the Spirit Messenger in Die Frau ohne Schatten under Solti and as Jochanaan in Salome, returning in 1994 as Leporello in Patrice Chereau's production of Don Giovanni; Further appearances at Vienna Staatsoper as Mozart's Figaro and at Chicago as Donner in Das Rheingold; Sang in the Brahms Requiem under Colin Davis and at Salzburg Easter Festival in 1993 under Abbado (Herbert von Karajan In Memoriam); Nick Shadow in The Rake's Progress for Welsh National Opera, 1996; Figaro at La Scala, 1997; Concert repertoire also includes Schubert's Schwanengesang. Recordings include: Salome conducted by Sinopoli; Figaro in version of Le nozze di Figaro under John Eliot Gardiner; Schwanengesang; Don Giovanni (1997). Honours include: Gramophone Young Artist of the Year Award, 1992; Critics' Circle Music Section Award, 1992. Address: Harlequin Agency Ltd, 203 Fidlas Road, Cardiff, CF4 5NA, Wales.

TERRACINI Lyndon, b. 1950, Australia. Baritone. Education: Studied in Australia. Debut: With Australian Opera at Sydney Opera House as Sid in Albert Herring, 1976. Career: Sang in London in 1983 as Ivan in Brian Howard's Inner Voices; Sang Daniello in the local premiere of Krenek's Jonny Spielt Auf in 1984; US debut in 1984 at the Cabrillo Music festival in Australian Folksongs; German debut in the title role in Hans Zender's Stephen Climax at Frankfurt; Italian debut as Sancio Panza in the world premiere of Henze-Paisiello Don Quischotte and Montepulciano Festival; Has sung with Opera Factory Zurich as Agamemnon and Orestes in the Iphigenias by Gluck; Sang Der Alte in Reimann's Ghost Sonata and Lansknecht in Hartmann's Simplicius Simplicissimus; Appearances in Ullmann's posthumous The Emperor of Atlantis and as Marcello in La Bohème and Bryon in the premiere of Richard Meale's La Mer de Glace at Sydney; Sang Don Giovanni in Adelaide in 1991 and appearances with Opera Factory London as Figaro on stage and on film for Channel 4 TV; Sang the title role in the premiere of Casanova Confined, by Andrew Ford, Barossa Festival, Australia, 1996. Concert repertoire includes Syringa by Elliott Carter, with Collegium Musicum, Zurich and El Cimarron by Hans Werner Henze. Address: Performing Arts, 6 Windmill Street, London, W1 1HF, England.

TERRONI Raphael, b. 6 Nov 1945, London, England. Pianist. m. 31 Jul 1971, 2 sons, 1 daughter. Education: St Ignatius College, 1956-62; Studied piano with John Vallier at London College of Music, 1965-68 and with Cyril Smith for 3 years; GLCM; ARCM (Performers). Debut: Wigmore Hall in London, 1974. Career: Performances at Festival Hall, Queen Elizabeth Hall, Purcell Room and at music clubs and festivals throughout the UK; Classical music cruises; TV appearance on BBC Pebble Mill; Head of Piano Faculty at London College of Music; Member of Terroni Piano Trio which has toured the Ukraine in 1991. Recordings: 2 with Richard Baker as Narrator; Berkeley's 80th Birthday Record of Piano Sonata; Songs of Eric Coates with singer, Brian Rayner Cook; Piano Quintets by Scott and Bridge for British Music Society. Hobbies: Golf; Watching Cricket. Current Management: Stephanie Williams Artists. Address: 4 Windsor Drive, Ramsey Fort Foot, Huntingdon, Cambridge, PE17 1XX, England.

TERZAKIS Dimitri, b. 12 March 1938, Athens, Greece. Composer. Education: Composition at the Hellenic Conservatory, Athens, 1957-64 and with Zimmermann at the Cologne Musikhochschule (Diploma 1970). Career: Co-founder of the Greek Society for Contemporary Music, 1966; Lecturer at the Robert Schumann Institute Dusseldorf from 1974; Teacher of Composition at the Dusseldorf Hochschule 1987-93; Berne Hochschule from 1990, Leipzig from 1994. Compositions include: Ikona for strings, 1963; Oboe Concerto, 1968; Okeaniden for chorus and orchestra, 1968; Ichochronos, electronic, 1968; Torquemada, opera, 1976; Circus Universal, chamber opera, 1976; 4 string quartets, 1969, 1976, 1982, 1990; Tropi for orchestra, 1976, Passionen, oratorio, 1979; Erotikon for soprano and 3 instruments, 1979; Lachesis for orchestra, 1984; Hermes, opera, 1984; Brass Quintet, 1984; Six Monologes, for soprano and orchestra, 1985; Violin Concerto, 1986; Das sechste Siegel, for chorus and ensemble, 1987; Per aspera ad Astra for orchestra, 1990; Ikaros-Daidolos for soprano quartet and brass orchestra, 1990; Der Holle Nachklang II for soprano and organ, 1993; Daphnis und Chloe for soprano and viola, 1994; Lieder ohne Worte for soprano, 1994; Alto saxophone concerto, 1995. Address: c/o AEPI, Fragoklissias & Samou Street 51, 151 25 Amaroussio, Athens, Greece.

TERZAKIS Zachos, b. 1953, Greece. Tenor. Education: Studied in Athens. Career: Sang at Athens Opera as Alfredo, Dimitri in Boris Godunov and Jim Mahoney in Mahagonny; Opera engagements at Kiel and Bielefeld from 1978 notably as Faust, the Duke of Mantua, Riccardo, Lensky, Rodolfo, the Prince in Rusalka and Guidon in The Tale of Tsar Saltan by Rimsky; Member of Nuremberg Opera from 1982; Sang at Bregenz Festival, 1987-88 as Hoffmann, Deutsche Oper Berlin and Berne Opera in 1988 as Alfredo and Werther, and Vienna Staatsoper and Bielefeld in 1991 as Mozart's Tito and as Vasco da Gama in L'Africaine; Lieder recitals and concert appearances. Address: Städtisches Buhnen, Brunnenstrasse 3, 4800 Bielefeld 1, Germany.

TERZIAN Anita, b. 12 Oct 1947, Strasbourg, France. Mezzo-Soprano. Education: Studied at the Juilliard School, New York with Jennie Tourel. Debut: Brussels in 1973 as Rosina. Career: Has appeared at many operatic centres in Europe and the USA: Opéra du Rhin, Strasbourg, Brussels, Liège and San Francisco Opera; Best known in such coloratura mezzo repertoire as Rossini's Isabella and Sinaide in Mosè, Elisetta in Il Matrimonio Segreto and Sesto in La Clemenza di Tito; Other roles include Carmen, Charlotte, Olga, Orlofsky and Konschakovna in Prince Igor; Many concert appearances. Recordings include: Title role in Handel's Serse. Address: c/o Opéra du Rhin, 19 Place Broglie, F-67008 Strasbourg Cedex, France.

TETZLAFF Christian, b. 29 Apr 1966, Hamburg, Germany. Violinist. Education: Studied at the Lubeck Conservatory with Uwe-Martin Haiberg and in Cincinnati with Walter Levine. Career: Debuts at the Berlin Festival and with the Cleveland Orchestra followed by concerts with the Berlin Philharmonic, Boston and Chicago Symphonies and Academy of St Martin in the Fields; Season 1996-97 with the Houston SO under Eschenbach and the Boston SO under Franz Welser-Möst; Brahms Double Concerto and Shostakovuch no 1 with the Bavarian Radio SO; Bach Sonatas and Partitas in Brussels and Paris 1997; Vienna Philharmonic concert at the 1997 Salzburg Festival; Chamber music series at the Vienna Konzerthaus: has collaborated with Leif Ove Andses, Yo-Yo Ma, Sabine Meyer and Heinrich Schiff. Recordings include: Bach Sonatas and Partitas; Mozart Violin Concertos, with the Deutsche Kammerphilharmonie. Address: c/o Harrison/Parrott Ltd, 12 Penzance Place, London W11 4PA, England.

TEZIER Ludovic, b. 1968, Marseilles, France. Singer (Baritone). Education: Studied in Paris and Switzerland. Career: Engagements with Lyons, Marseilles, Tours and Bordeaux Opéras; Opéra-Comique, Paris, as Don Giovanni, Marcello, Escamillo, Harlequin (Ariadne auf Naxos), Sharpless, and Britten's Demetrius; Season 1996-97 in Handel's Radamisto and as Frédéric in Lakmé at Marseilles, Guglielmo at Bordeaux; Mozart Count, Marcello and Belcore at Lyon; Season 1997-98 as Malatesta, and Mercutio in Roméo et Juliette, at Bordeux, with Escamillo, Don Giovanni and Talbot in Donizetti's Maria Stuarda at the Opéra-Comique; Glyndebourne 1997, as Comte Ory in a new production of Rossini's opera. Address: c/o Opera de Bordeaux, Grand Théâtre Municipal, Place de la Comédie, F-33074 Bordeaux, France.

THALLAUG Edith, b. 16 Jun 1929, Oslo, Norway. Mezzo-Soprano. Education: Studied with Giurgia Leppee and Joel Berglund in Stockholm. Debut: Stage debut as actress in 1952; Song recital in Oslo in 1959. Career: Stage debut as Dorabella at Gothenburg in 1960; Sang at Royal Opera Stockholm from 1964 notably as Carmen, Cherubino, Rosina, Bradamante in Alcina, Maddalena in Rigoletto, Eboli, Azucena, Amneris, Venus, Fricka, Waltraute, Octavian and The Composer in Ariadne, Judith in Bluebeard and Miss Julie; Frequent appearances at the Drottningholm Court Theatre from 1964; Sang at Glyndebourne Festival in 1971 as Dorabella, Basle in 1976 in Schoenberg's Gurrelieder and on Swedish TV as Carmen; Guest engagements in Oslo, Copenhagen, Moscow, USA, Japan, Korea, Germany, La Scala Milan, Italy, Paris, Prague and Vienna. Recordings include: CD: Songs from De Falla, Montsalvatge, Ravel and many other recordings of Scandinavian Songs; Opera Arias, Songs by Grieg, and duets with Gösta Winbergh. Honours: Critic Prizes for La Cenerentola, Oslo, 1972; Court Singer, 1976; Grieg Prize, 1978; Drottningholm Court Theater, Gold Medal, 1979; Litteris et Artibus, 1982. Address: c/o Kongliga Teatern, PO Box 16094, S-10322 Stockholm, Sweden.

THANE Amanda, b. 1960, Australia. Singer (Soprano). Education: New South Wales Conservatorium of Music, Sydney. Career: Roles with the Australian opera since 1983 include Fiordiligi, Violetta, Marzelline, Constanze, Mimi, Norina, Pamina, Mozart's Countess, Micaela, Lauretta, Antonia, Leila, Nedda, Liu, Valentine (in Joan Sutherland's farewell performance of Les Huguenots), Governess and Maria Stuarda; Additional roles ung with other Australian companies include: Gilda, Euridice, Marenka, Alice Ford, Rosalinde; Suor Angelica and Madame Butterfly; London performances include Suor Angelica, Adrianna Lecouvreur and Liu; Royal Opera House Covent Garden debut season 1991-92 as Valentine in new production of Les Huguenots and Antonia in Les Contes d'Hoffmann; European debut 1993, as Lina in Stiffelio with Opera Forum, the Netherlands; 1993 Season included new roles of Donna Elvira in Don Giovanni for Grand-Théatre de Bordeaux, Eva in Die Meistersinger and Eurydice in Gluck's Orphée for the Australian Opera; Further engagements include roles as Nedda, Liu, Gilda and Fiordiligi; Sang Micaela in Carmen at Brisbane, 1995; Many concert appearances throughout Australia, United Kingdom USA, Japan and Korea. Honours include: Prizewinner, Metropolitan Opera Auditions; Winner, ABC Instrumental and Vocal Competition; Queen Elizabeth II Silver Jubilee for Young Australians; Australian Music Foundation Award, London, Churchill Fellowship, 1990. Current Management: Athole Still International Management Limited. Address: Foresters Hall, 25-27 Westow Street, London SE19 3RY, England.

THAW David, b. 19 Jun 1928, New York, USA. Tenor. m. Claire Watson, deceased 1986. Education: Studied at Columbia University, with Giovanni Martinelli in New York and Giuseppe Pais in Milan. Debut: Vichy in 1950 as Vincent in Mireille. Career: Sang at the Theater am Gärtnerplatz Munich from 1955, with debut as the Duke of Mantua, Frankfurt am Main Opera from 1958 with debut as Lenski in Eugene Onegin and a visit to London in 1963 in Fidelio, Salome and Die Entführung, Bayreuth Festival in 1961 as Froh in Das Rheingold and member of the Bayerische Staatsoper Munich from 1963; Guest appearances in Berlin at Deutsche Opera and Staatsoper, Hanover and elsewhere; Sang at Salzburg Festival, 1964-68, and Munich in 1986 in the premiere of Belshazzar by VD Kirchner; Many appearances in musicals notably as Professor Higgins in My Fair Lady. Address: c/o Bayerische Staatsoper, Postfach 745, D-8000 Munich 1, Germany.

THEBOM Blanche, b. 19 Sep 1918, Monessen, PA, USA. Mezzo-Soprano. Education: Studied with Margharete Matzenauer and Edyth Walker in New York. Debut: Sang in concert from 1941. Career: Stage debut in 1944 at Philadelphia with the Metropolitan Opera as Brangaene; Sang in New York until 1966 as Marina, Eboli, Baba The Turk, Herodias, Orlofsky and in Wagner roles as Venus and Fricka; Sang at Chicago in 1946 as Brangaene, San Francisco Opera, 1947-59 with debut as Amneris, Glyndebourne in 1950 as Dorabella, Covent Garden in 1957 as Dido in the first British professional performance of Les Troyens and a tour of Russia in 1958; Directed the Atlanta Opera Company, 1967-68; Professor at the University of Arkansas. Recordings: Tristan und Isolde, conducted by Furtwängler; The Rake's Progress.

THEISEN Kristin, b. 13 Jan 1955, Oslo, Norway. Soprano Opera Singer. Education: Studied German, Oslo University, 1 year; Vocal Pedagogic studies, Music Conservatorium, Oslo for 4 years; Norwegian State Opera School, 3 years; Studied in Vienna, Salzburg and Bayreuth; Teachers: Erna Skaug, Ingrid Bjoner, Kim Borg, Anna Reynolds and Jean Cox. Debut: Recital, Oslo, 1979; As opera singer, Leoncavallo's Nedda, Gelsenkirchen, 1982. Career: Has appeared in Hamburg, Frankfurt, Nuremberg, Catani, Strasbourg, Eutin, Basel and Lubeck; TV, Radio and Film in Norway, Austria and Poland; Important opera roles: Agathe in Freischutz, Rezia in Oberon, Susanna in Figaro, Giulietta in Hoffmann, Ellen Orford in Peter Grimes, Euridice in Orpheus and Euridice, Sieglinde in Walküre, Senta in Holländer. Recordings: Zigeunerlieder with Audin Kayser, piano; Irmgard in Franz Schreker's opera Flammen, conducted by Frank Strobl. Membership: Leader of The Norwegian Opera Singer Society. Hobbies: Tennis; Skiing. Current Management: Kollo, Berlin and Heissler-Remy, Dusseldorf. Address: Sarbuvollveien 8A, N-1322 Hovik, Norway.

THEODOLOZ Annelise. Singer (Mezzo-soprano). Education: Violin pupil of Carl Flesch and **Tibor Varga at early age; Award-winning graduate,** Lausanne Conservatory and Guildhall School of Music and Drama, London; Masterclasses with Hugues Cuénod, Emma Kirby, Ian Partridge, Sarah Walker and Alberto Zedda. Debut: As Dorabella in Cosi fan tutte and Dalila in Samson et Dalila, National Hungarian Opera under conductor János Kovács. Career: Outstanding performances; Since her career began has performed as Soloist in major concert halls and on radio, with Orchestre de la Suisse Romande, Israel Chamber Orchestra, Bach Soloisten Amsterdam, Orchestre National de Lyon and many others all over Europe, in Middle East, Japan and Canada; Works with conductors such as Michel Corboz, Jesus Lopez-Cobos, Zoltan Nagy, Helmuth Rilling; Suited to female roles and great trouser roles such as Tancredi and Romeo; Works closely with leading artists such as Gabriel Bacquier, Christa Ludwig and Lucia Valentini-Terrani; Interprets different styles and repertoires. Honours: Award, International Competition in Lied and Oratorio, Clermont-Ferrand, 1995; Prix du Centenaire du Conservatoire de Lausanne; Stéphane Clivaz Memorial Prize. Hobby: Theatre. Current Management: Catherine Schoendorff Félix, Imprésario. Address: c/o Catherine Schoendorff Félix, Personal Manager, Avenue du Tribunal Fédéral 25, 1005 Lausanne, Switzerland.

THIBAUD Pierre, b. 22 Jun 1929, Proissans, France. Trumpeter. Education: Studied violin and trumpet at the Bordeaux Conservatoire; Premier Prix for cornet playing at the Paris Conservatoire. Career: Principal Trumpet with the Orchestre de Paris Opéra, Ensemble Ars Nova, Domaine Musicale, Musique Vivante, Musique Plus and the Chamber Orchestra Fernand Oubradous; Further experience with the Concerts Lamoureux, Concerts Colonne and Musique de la Garde Republicaine; Founded the Brass Quintet Ars Nova and collaborations with the Société des Concerts du Conservatoire and IRCAM (electronic music studios), Paris; Concert appearances with leading European orchestras in the standard classics; Also plays music by Marius Constant, Xenakis, Messaien, Varèse, Berio and Enesco; Professor of Trumpet at the Paris Conservatoire, 1975. Recordings: Brandenburg Concerto No 2; Concertos by Haydn, Hummel and Telemann. Address: Conservatoire National Superieur de Musique de Paris, 209 Avenue Jean-Jaures, 75019, Paris, France.

THIBAUDET Jean-Yves, b. 7 Sept 1961, Lyon, France. Concert Pianist. Education: Lycée Musical, Lyon; Lycée St Exupéry, Lyon; Conservatory of Music, Lyon; National Conservatory of Music, Paris. Career: Debuts and appearances throughout the world; Recitals, New York, Chicago, Washington DC, Los Angeles, San Francisco, London, Paris, Milan, Amsterdam; Played with Montreal, St-Louis National, Indianapolis, New World and Boston Symphonies, Cleveland Orchestra, Chicago Symphony, Philadelphia Orchestra, New York Philharmonic, Toronto Symphony, Los Angeles Philharmonic, Concertgebouw Orchestra, Orchestre de Paris, Ensemble Orchestral de Paris, Rotterdam Philharmonic, Stuttgart Radio Orchestra; Participated in Spoleto Festivals, USA, Italy, Australia; Regular guest, Chamber Music Society, Lincoln Center; Debut appearances at Casals and Schleswig-Holstein Festivals; Hollywood Bowl, 1989; played Debussy and Chopin at the Wigmore Hall, London, 1997. Recordings: Numerous including music by Ravel, Liszt, Chopin; Violin sonatas by Debussy, Franck, Fauré, with Joshua Bell; Chausson concerto for piano, violin and string quartet (Takacs); Ravel Trio (Bell, Isserlis); Liszt works for piano and orchestra (Montreal Symphony); Ravel: Complete solo piano works; Messiaen: Turangalila Symphony (Concertgebouw Orchestra). Hobbies: Tennis; Swimming; Riding; Water skiing; Museums; Movies; Racing cars. Address: Wigmore Hall (contracts), Wigmore Street, London WC1, England.

THIELEMANN Christian, b. 1959, Berlin, Germany. Conductor. Education: Studied piano with Helmut Roloff at the Berlin Hochschule fur Musik; Viola at the Karajan Foundation's Orchestra Academy, Berlin. Career: Musical coach in Berlin, with Karajan from 1979, at Berlin, Salzburg and Munich; Assistant to Daniel Barenboim at Paris, Berlin and Bayreuth; Principal Conductor of the Deutsche Oper am Rhein Dusseldorf, 1985; Music Director of the Nuremberg Opera, 1988-92; American debut season 1991-92, with Elektra at the San Francisco Opera; Der Rosenkavalier at the New York Met 1993, Arabella 1994; Regular concerts with the New York PO and Philadelphia and Minnesota Orchestras; British debut with Jenufa at Covent Garden 1988, returning for Elektra 1994 and the British premiere of Pfitzner's Palestrina 1997; Further opera includes Capriccio in Florence, The Makropoulos Case in Bologna, Don Giovanni in Berlin and Lohengrin on tour to Japan with the Deutsche Oper Berlin; Season 1996 with Otello in Bologna (Principal Guest Conductor), Tristan and Meistersinger with the Deutsche Opera (General Music Director from September 1997); Further concerts with the Chicago SO, Philharmonia Orchestra and the Munich PO. Recordings include: Wagner and Strauss, with René Kollo (EMI); Beethoven Cantatas, orchestral music by Wagner, Strauss and Pfitzner, Schumann 2nd Symphony Beethoven nos 5 and 7 (DGG); Video of Arabella, from the Met, with Kiri Te Kanawa. Address: Columbia Artists (Conductors Division), 165 West 57th Street, New York, NY 10019, USA.

THIEME Helga, b. 27 Feb 1937, Oberlengsfeld, Germany. Soprano. Education: Studied in Frankfurt. Career: Sang in opera at Basle, 1962-65, Bielefeld, 1965-67, Wiesbaden, 1967-68, Hamburg, 1968-83 notably in the premieres of The Devils of Loudun by Penderecki in 1969 and Josef Tal's Ashmedai in 1971, Bremen, 1974-76, St Gallen from 1980 and Zurich, 1984-85; Guest engagements at Berne, Deutsche Oper Berlin, state operas of Munich and Stuttgart, Dusseldorf, Vienna Volksoper, Barcelona and Cologne; Roles have included Susanna, Zerlina, Despina and the Queen of Night, Norina and Adina, Lortzing's Gretchen and Marie, Gilda, Aennchen, Marenka, Sophie in Der Rosenkavalier, Isotta in Die schweigsame Frau and Ida in Henze's Junge Lord. Recordings include: The Devils of Loudun. Address: c/o Opernhaus Zurich, Falkenstrasse 1, CH-8008 Zurich, Switzerland.

THIEME Ulrich, b. 5 Aug 1950, Hamm, Germany. Professor of Recorder; Musicologist. Education: State Diploma, Music Teaching, 1973; Concert Diploma, Recorder, 1974; PhD, Musicology. Career: TV appearances with broadcasts for several German stations, 1969-; Recorder Teacher at Academy of Music in Cologne, 1973-78 and Academy of Music at Hannover, 1978-; Concert tours throughout Europe, Eastern Asia and South America and 50 concerts with recorder and lute-guitar duo in Germany. Recordings: Jürg Baur's Tre Studi per Quattro; Bach's Brandenburg Concertos; Baroque Recorder Music by various composers including Delalande, Bonocini and Mancini. Publications: Studien zum Jugendwerk A Schoenbergs, 1979; Affektenlehre im Barocken Musikdenken, 1984. Contributions to: Editor of Baroque Recorder Music (Castello, Monteclair); TIBIA. Honour: 1st Prize, German Young Musicians Competition, 1967. Memberships: Vice-President, ERTA, European Recorder Teachers Association, German Section. Address: c/o Staatliche Hochschule für Musik, D-3 Hannover, Germany.

THIOLLIER Francois-Joel, b. 12 Nov 1943, Paris, France. Concert Pianist. m. Beatrice Fitch, 9 Jun 1978, 1 son. Education: Studied in Paris with Robert Casadesus, 1951-53; Juilliard Preparatory College, 1953-63. Career: Many concerts in over 30 countries including appearances with the Orchestre de Paris, Nouvel Orchestre Philharmonique, Moscow and Leningrad Philharmonic Orchestras, the Hague Residentie Orkest, Tokyo and Berlin Philharmonics and RAI in Italy; Concert halls include Amsterdam Concertgebouw, Théâtre des Champs Elysées, Teatro Real of Madrid, Accademia di Santa Cecilia, Rome, and Victoria Hall Geneva; Played the Busoni Concerto in Berlin. Recordings: Complete works of Rachmaninov and Gershwin; Beethoven Sonatas Op 27 No 2, Op 13 and Op 57; Liszt Sonata and Complete Songs for Tenor and Piano; Brahms Sonata Op 5; Paganini Variations; Mozart Sonata K330 and Quintet K452. Honours: Prizewinner at International Piano Competitions: Viotti, Casella, Busoni, Pozzoli, Montreal, Tchaikovsky Moscow, Marguerite Long, Paris, Queen Elisabeth, Brussels. Hobbies: Fishing; Snorkeling; Tennis. Address: c/o Patricia Garrasi, Via Manzoni, 20121 Milan, Italy.

THOMAS Augusta (Read), b. 24 April 1964, Glen Grove, New York, USA. Composer. Education: Studied at Northwestern University (1983-87) and with Jakob Druckman at Yale University (MM 1988); Postgraduate studies at the Royal Academy of Music, London 1988-89. Career: Freelance composer; Faculty member, Eastman School of Music, Rochester, New York. Compositions include: Glow in the Light of Darkness, for chamber orchestra, 1983; Tunnel at the End of Light for piano and orchestra, 1984; Sonnet from the Daybreak Moon, 1986; Moon and Light for trumpet and orchestra, 1987; Under the Sun, for chestra, 1987; Glass Moon for orchestra, 1989; Wind Dance, for orchestra, 1989; Haiku for violin, cello and chamber orchestra, 1990; Vigil for cello and chamber orchestra, 1992; Cathedral Summer, for violin and orchestra, 1992; Sinfonia Concertante for soprano saxophone and orchestra, 1992; Ancient Chimes, for orchestra, 1993; Night's Midsummer Blaze, concerto for flute, viola, harp and orchestra, 1993; Fantasy for piano and chamber orchestra, 1994; Ligeia, chamber opera, 1994; Nocturne for string quartet and mezzo-soprano, 1994; Echo Echo, for trombone quartet and chamber orchestra, 1995; Conquering the Fury of Oblivion, theatrical oratorio, 1995. Honours include: International Orpheus Prize for Opera, Spoleto Italy, 1994; Charles Ives Fellowship, 1994. Address: c/o ASCAP, ASCAP Building, One Lincoln Plaza, New York, NY 10023, USA.

THOMAS Caryl, b. 23 Oct 1958, Aberystwyth, Dyfed, Wales. Harpist. m. Huw Williams, 22 Oct 1985. Education: Welsh College of Music and Drama; MA, New York University, USA; Associate, Royal College of Music. Debut: Carnegie Hall, NY, 1981. Career: Freelance Harpist, concentrating on solo and concert work with great emphasis on BBC Radio 3 and Channel 4 TV broadcasting; Appearances include London debut at Wigmore Hall, concerto soloist with BBC Welsh Symphony Orchestra in 1982, and Mozarteum Orchestra at Salzburg, Austria in 1984. Recordings: Mozart Concerto for Flute and Harp with London Philharmonic Orchestra, flautist Jonathan Snowden and conducted by Andrew Litton, 1987; French Impressions with Prometheus Ensemble. Honours: 1st British Harpist to win prize at the International Harp Contest, Jerusalem, Israel, 1976; Award, Concert Artists Guild, NY, 1981; ISM and Park Lane Young Musician, 1982. Memberships: Musicians Union; UK Harpists Association. Hobbies: Cookery; Sport. Current Management: London Musicians and Harlequin, Cardiff. Address: Hendre'r Wenallt, St Athan Road, Cowbridge, South Glamorgan CF71 7LT, Wales.

THOMAS David, b. 26 Feb 1943, Orpington, Kent, England. Bass-Baritone. Education: St Paul's Cathedral Choir School; King's College, Canterbury; King's College, Cambridge. Career includes: Many concerts with the world's leading orchestras; Sang Bach Passions and B minor Mass at the 1985 International Bach Festival in Japan, under Helmuth Rilling; Oratorio and concert repertory includes works by Walton, Tippett, Britten, Stravinsky and Schoenberg; US engagements include Messiah at Lincoln Center with Academy of Ancient Music, Haydn's Creation at Boston Symphony Hall with Christopher Hogwood and Handel's Susanna with Nicholas McGegan in San Francisco; Appearances at the Tanglewood, Edinburgh, Salzburg and Lucerne Festivals and the London Promenade Concerts; Recital tours of the USA with Anthony Rooley and Emma Kirkby; Season 1990-91 included tour of Switzerland with Academy of Ancient Music, Winterresie and lectures at Tokyo University and Handel's Theodora at San Francisco; Season 1992-93 with Schubert's Winterreise at Cornell University, Handel's Susanna, Theodora and Judas Maccabaeus with Philharmonia Baroque and Nicholas McGegan; UK engagements include TV recording of Beethoven's 9th Symphony with London Classical Players and Roger Norrington, Creation with Chamber Orchestra of Europe and Frans Bruggen and Dido and Aeneas at the Barbican. Recordings include: Semele; Alceste; Bach's B minor Mass; Coffee Cantata; Mozart's Requiem; Handel's Israel in Egypt with Taverner Players. Membership: Chairman, Artistic Advisory Committee and Member of Board, Blackheath Concert Halls. Current Management: Allied Artists, 42 Montpelier Square, London, SW7 1JZ, England. Address: 74 Hyde Vale, Greenwich, London, SE10 8HP, England.

THOMAS Gwion, b. 1954, Wales. Baritone. Education: Studied at the Royal Northern College of Music. Career: Appearances with Welsh National Opera, Royal Opera Garden Venture, Kent Opera and the Aldeburgh Festival (in the title role in the premiere of Lefanu's Wildman, 1995); Other roles include Orestes, Mozart's Don Giovanni, Count and Papageno, and Britten's Tarquinius, Billy Budd and Ned Keene; TV appearances in Weir's Night at the Chinese Opera and Scipio's Dream; Concerts with the BBC Symphony Orchestra, London Philharmonic Orchestra. Address: c/o Gonsalves Artists' Management, 7 Old Town, Clapham, London, SW4 0JT, England.

THOMAS Margaret Ann, b. 12 Mar 1942, Bristol, England. Soprano. m. Reginald James Dymond, 30 Sept 1967, 1 step-daughter. Education: Royal Academy of Music, 1961-65; ARCM, 1965; FLCM, 1970. Debut: Royal Albert Hall, 1965. Career: Soloist, Throughout England; TV Documentary films; Broadcasts for radio; Teacher, Birmingham Conservatore, Clifton College. Honours: Overseas League Prize, 1965; Isabel Jay Memorial Prize, 1965. Memberships: RAM Club; ISM. Hobbies: Theatre; Cooking; Driving. Address: Barum House, 20 Kersteman Road, Bristol BS6 7BX, England.

THOMAS Matthew (Elton), b. 1963, Canada. Singer (Baritone). Career: Performances as Kuligin in Katya Kabanova for the Canadian Opera Company, and Marcello in La Bohème at Vancouver; Mozart's Count, Guglielmo and Don Giovanni at the Banff Centre of the Performing Arts; Gurrais in Gounod's Mireille and Le Conte in Massenet's Grisélidis for Opera in Concert, Toronto; British performances include Rigoletto for Clonter Opera Farm and English Touring Opera (1996); Rossini's Figaro for ETO, Belcore (L'Elisir d'amore) for Mid Wales Opera and Valentin in Faust for Dublin Grand Opera Society; Further appearances as Hercules/The Herald in Gluck's Alceste for Scottish Opera and Don Giovanni for Opera on a Shoestring, Glasgow; Concert repertoire includes Carmina Burana, Messiah, Elijah, and the Requiems of Brahms, Fauré and Duruflé. Address: c/o C&M Craig Services Ltd, 3 Kersley Street, London SW11 4PR, England.

THOMAS Michael, b. 1960, England. Violinist. Education: Studied at the Royal Northern College of Music. Career: Founder Member and Leader of the Brodsky String Quartet (his sister, Jacky Thomas plays cello in the quartet); Resident at Cambridge University for four years and later residencies at the Dartington International Summer School, Devon; Concert engagements include the Shostakovich Quartets at the Elizabeth Hall in London and performances at the Ludwigsburg and Schleswig-Holstein Festivals; New York debut at the Metropolitan Museum; Tours of Italy, North America, Australia, Poland, Czechoslovakia and Istanbul; Complete Quartets of Schoenberg for the BBC in 1992; French cncerts include visit to the Théâtre du Châtelet, Paris; Founder and Director of the Kreisler String Orchestra, 1980-90. Recordings include: Quartets of Elgar and Delius; Schubert's A minor and Beethoven's Op 74; Complete Quartets of Shostakovich. Address: c/o Harrison Parrott Ltd, 12 Penzance Place, London, W11 4PA, England.

THOMAS Michael Tilson, b. 21 Dec 1944, Los Angeles, California, USA. Conductor; Pianist. Education: Studied at University of Southern CA with Ingolf Dahl, John Crown and Alice Ehlers. Career includes: Conducted the Young Musicians Foundation Orchestra; Pianist and Conductor at Monday Evening Concerts with premieres of works by Copland, Stockhausen, Kraft, Stravinsky and Boulez and with Boston Symphony Chamber Players; Conducted Boston Symphony Orchestra from 1969, being Pricipal Guest Conductor, 1972-74; Music Director of Buffalo Philharmonic 1971-79; Directed the Young People's Concerts of the New York Philharmonic, 1971-77; Principal Guest Conductor of Los Angelos Philharmonic, 1981-85; US premiere of Berg's Lulu (3 act version) at Santa Fe, 1979; Regular Conductor of Chicago, Pittsburgh and Philadelphia Orchestras; Directed a new production of Der fliegende Holländer in France, Janácek's The Cunning Little Vixen, NY, 1980, Fidelio at Houston and Tosca at Chicgao Lyric Opera; Premiered Steve Reich's Desert Music, 1984; Engagements with various international orchestras; Principal Conductor of London Symphony Orchestra, 1988-95; BBC TV productions of "Discovery" concerts, Channel 4 BMG series of Concerto!; Founder and Music Director of New World Symphony, 1988, a national fellowship orchestra for young professionals; Music Director of San Francisco Symphony, 1995-; Conducted the London Symphony Orchestra in Debussy concert series, London Barbican, 1997; Tours with San Francisco Symphony Orchestra include USA, 1996, 1997, Europe, 1996, Japan, Hong Kong, 1997. Recordings include: 1st recording of the 4-hand version of Stravinsky's Rite of Spring with Ralph Grierson; Charles Ives's 2nd Symphony with Concertgebouw Orchestra; Complete Works of Carl Ruggles with Buffalo Philharmonic; Various musicals by Weill and Gershwin. Honours include: Koussevitzky Conducting Prize at Berkshire Music Center, 1968; Many Grammy nominations and international awards for his recordings. Address: c/o Columbia Artists Management Ltd, 28 Cheverton Road, London, N19 3AY, England.

THOMAS Nova, b. 1960, North Carolina, USA. Soprano. Education: Studied at the University of Bloomington with Eileen Farrell. Debut: Mimi in La Bohème at North Carolina. Career: Appearances at opera houses in Cologne, Hamburg, Belfast (Opera Northern Ireland), St Louis, Seattle, San Diego, Detroit and New York City Opera; Season 1991-92 in Cologne and Paris as Giulia in La Scala di Seta; Roles have included Violetta, the Four Heroines in Les Contes d'Hoffmann, the Trovatore Leonora and Anna Bolena; Further engagements as Mozart's Constanze for Cologne Opera, Norma with Seattle Opera and Hoffmann under Richard Bobynge. Recordings include: Title role in The Bohemian Girl, under Bonynge. Honours include: Winner, Metropolitan Opera National Council Auditions, 1984. Address: c/o IMG Artists, Media House, 3 Burlington Lane, London, W4 2TH, England.

THOMAS Peter, b. 1944, South Wales. Violinist. Education: Studied in England, winning the Menuhin Prize at Bath Festival, 1958. Career: Second Violinist of the Allegri Quartet, 1963-68; Co-Founder of Orion Piano Trio, becoming resident ensemble at Southampton University; Leader of BBC Welsh Symphony Orchestra, 1972, then Philharmonia; Currently leader of City of Birmingham Symphony Orchestra and Artistic Director of Birmingham Ensemble; String Adviser to Gustav Mahler Youth Orchestra, Vienna; Purcell Room, London, recital 1993, with works by Schubert, Berio (Sequenza VIII), Schoenberg and Busoni (2nd Sonata). Honours Include: With Orion Piano Trio: BBC Prize for British and Commonwealth Ensembles. Address: Camerata Artists, 4 Margaret Road, Birmingham B17 0EU, England.

THOMAS Steven (Murray), b. 26 Jun 1946, Peterborough, Ontario, Canada. Opera, Stage and TV Producer. m. Irene Wronski, 6 Jul 1985. Education: BA, English, Psychology, University of Western Ontario; Diploma in Piano, Royal Conservatory of Toronto; Private studies in brass. Debut: With New Jersey State Opera in 1976. Career: Producer, Artistic Director, Actor, Dramatic Theatre, 1964-72; Producer and Stage Director for Opera (freelance), 1972-78; Production Manager, Opera Festival at National Arts Centre, Ottawa, 1978-79; Artistic Director for Opera Hamilton, 1979-86; Producer, TV opera, CHCH-TV, Hamilton, 1979-86; Operas produced for TV include La Bohème, La Traviata, Madame Butterfly, The Barber of Seville, Rigoletto, Aida, Manon Lescaut, The Marriage of Figaro, Hansel and Gretel and Carmen. Honours: CANPRO Awards for Excellence in the Performing Arts, Canadian TV National Competition, for La Bohème, 1980, La Traviata, 1981, The Barber of Seville, 1983 and Aida, 1985; Canadian Music Council Award for TV, La Traviata, 1983; Iris Award, USA National Association of Broadcast Executives, 1st Runner-up for Madame Butterfly, 1985. Address: 226 Westmount Avenue, Toronto, Ontario, Canada, M6E 3M8.

THOMASCHKE Thomas (Michael), b. 2 Aug 1943, Pirna, Germany. Concert and Opera Singer (Bass). m. 1964, 1 son, 1 daughter. Education: Awards in Lieder, Opera and Oratorio, Dresden Hochschule für Musik, 1967; Singing Teacher's Certificate, 1970. Debut: Freiberg, Germany, in Tosca, 1963. Career: Sang in Leipzig, Dresden, and at the Komische Oper Berlin in the 1960s; La Scala, Bavarian State Opera, Glyndebourne, Covent Garden, Paris, Lisbon, Buenos Aires, Vienna, Edinburgh, Cape Town, Rome, Florence and Amsterdam; Has sung Figaro, Don Giovanni, Rocco (Fidelio), Sarastro (Magic Flute), Gurnemanz (Parsifal). Recordings include: Bach and Handel, conducted by Nikolaus Harnoncourt; Weber, Freischütz, Philips, Colin Davis; Beethoven 9th Symphony, Yehudi Menuhin. Contributions to: Opernwelt. Honours: Schumanpreis, 1966; Tschaikowskypreis, 1970; 1st Prize, Preis Hertogenbosch, 1971. Memberships: Artistic Director of Festival Mitte Europa. Hobbies: Cooking; Painting; Fine arts. Current Management: SYM Music Company Limited, 110 Gloucester Avenue, London NW1 8JA, England. Address: Fliederweg 108, D-50859 Cologne, Germany.

THOME Diane, b. 25 Jan 1942, Pearl River, NY, USA. Composer; Pianist; University Professor; Lecturer. Education: Studied piano with Dorothy Taubman, New York, composition with Robert Strassburg, Darius Milhaud at Aspen, Colorado, Roy Harris at Inter-American University, PR; PhD in Music, Princeton University, 1973; Alexander Boscovich (Israel); Milton Babbitt, Princeton. Career: Taught music at Princeton University, New Jersey, 1973-74; Taught theory and 20th century music at SUNY, Binghampton, 1974-77; Professor of Theory and Composition at University of Washington School of Music, Seattle. Compositions include: Chamber: 3 Pieces, 1958, 3 Movements, 1958, Sonatine, 1960, Suite, 1961, Quartet, 1961, Constellations, 1966; Electronic music: Le Berceau De Miel, 1968, Spectrophonie, 1969, Polyvalence, 1972, January Variations, 1973, Los Nombres, 1974, Alexander Boscovich Remembered, 1975, Anais, 1976, Sunflower Space, 1978, Winter Infinities, 1980, To Search The Spacious World, 1986, The Ruins Of The Heart for Soprano, Orchestra and Tape, 1991, Angels for Virtual Reality Artwork, 1992, The Palaces Of Memory for Large Chamber Ensemble or Chamber Orchestra and Tape, 1993; Multimedia works: In My Garden, 1956, Caprice, 1957, Night Passage, 1973; Orchestral: 3 Movements, 1962, S'Embarquement, 1971, The Golden Messengers, 1984, Lucent Flowers, 1988; Piano works: Sonatine, 1959, Pianismus; Sacred works: Three Psalms, 1979; Vocal: Ash On An Old Man's Sleeve, 1962, Spring And Fall: To A Young Child, 1962, Cantata, 1964, Songs On Chinese Verses, 1964, The Yew Tree, 1979, 3 Sonnets By Sri Aurobindo: Settings for Soprano and Orchestra, 1984. Recording: Palaces of Music, Electro-Acoustic Music. Memberships: SCI Inc; BMI; ACA; CMS.

Address: University of Washington School of Music, Box 353450, Seattle, WA 98195, USA.

THOMPSON Adrian, b. 1954, London, England. Tenor. Education: Studied at the Guildhall School of Music and Drama, London. Career: Opera engagements with the Glyndebourne Festival, Scottish Opera, Handel Opera Society and at the Buxton, Aldeburgh, Wexford, Lausanne and Göttingen Festivals; Roles include Ariodante, Snout and Flute in A Midsummer Night's Dream, Albert Herring, Podesta, Pedrillo in Die Entführung, Le nozze di Figaro, Così fan tutte, Bardolph in Falstaff, Conti's Don Quixote in Sierra Morena, the Simpleton in Boris Godunov and Nurse in L'Incoronazione di Poppea; Sang Alfred in Die Fledermaus at Belfast in 1990, the title role in Haydn's Orlando Paladino at Garsington Manor, Oxford, and Britten's Flute at Sadler's Wells in 1990 (Snout at Glyndebourne in 1989); Concert performances throughout Europe and Britain in works by Purcell, Bach, Handel, Berlioz, Schoenberg and Tippett; Britten repertoire includes Les Illuminations, The Serenade, Nocturne, Canticles and Song Cycles; Appearances with leading British orchestras, the Netherlands Chamber Orchestra, Nash Ensemble and Stockholm Bach Choir; Frequent Promenade Concerts and recitals at the Aldeburgh, Bath, Lichfield and Buxton Festivals; Has sung Schubert's Die schöne Müllerin at the Wigmore Hall and songs by Schubert and Schoenberg at South Bank; Recitals in Israel, Canada, Germany, France and Switzerland; Season 1992-93 with recitals in USA, Salome in Netherlands, Handel's Tamerlano at Karlsruhe and Irus in Monteverdi's Ulisse at the Coliseum, London; Sang Grimoaldo in Rodelinda with Broomhill Opera, 1996. Recordings include: Gurney's Ludlow and Teme; Beggar's Opera. Address: c/o Ron Gonsalves Management, 10 Dagnan Road, London, SW12 9LQ, England.

THOMPSON Arthur, b. 27 Dec 1942, New York City, USA. Baritone. Education: Studied at the Manhattan School of Music, Hartt College and the Juilliard School. Debut: Chautauqua as Papageno in 1964. Career: Performances with Metropolitan Opera Studio, 1966-71; Over 50 comprimario roles with the Metropolitan Opera, New York, from 1970 including Mandarin in Turandot in 1970; Many performances of Porgy and Bess in America and abroad; Sang at Covent Garden in 1987 as Mel in The Knot Garden. Recordings include: Four Saints in Three Acts by Virgil Thomson; Jake in Porgy and Bess conducted by Lorin Maazel. Address: c/o Royal Opera House, Covent Garden, London, WC2, England.

THOMPSON Donald (Prosser), b. 28 Feb 1928, Columbus, Ohio, USA. University Professor; Conductor; Writer. m. Ana Christina Figueroa Laugier, 23 Jan 1972, 2 sons, 1 daughter. Education: AB, University of Missouri, 1952; MA, University of Missouri, 1954; Akademie für Musik, Vienna, Austria; Eastman School of Music; PhD, University of Iowa, 1970. Career: Retired as Professor and Chair, Department of Music, University of Puerto Rico, 1956-85; Conductor, opera, music theatre, television, San Juan, Puerto Rico,1956-; Music Critic San Juan Star, 1957-60, 1975-94; Consultant in Arts Management, 1985-. Contributions to: Manual para monografias musicales, 1980; The New Grove Dictionary of Music, 1980; The New Grove Dictionary of American Music, 1986; Music Research in Puerto Rico, 1982; The Puerto Rico Symphony Orchestra, 1985; The New Grove Dictionary of Opera, 1992; El joven Tavarez; nuevos documents y nuevas perspectives, 1993; Diccionario de musica espanola e hispanoamericana, 1994. Contributions to: Revista musical chilena, 1984; African Music, 1975-76; Inter American Music review, 1989; Revista musical de Venezuela, 1989; Bibliografia musicologica latinoamericana, 1992, 1993; Latin American Music Review, 1983, 1985, 1990, 1993. Honours: Phi Beta Kappa, 1952; Professor Emeritus, University of Puerto Rico, 1995. Memberships: American Musicological Society; College Music Society, Member, Editorial Board, 1979-86; Puerto Rico Musical Society, President, 1973-77. Hobbies: Sailing; Tennis. Address: Calle Acadia N-64, Rio Piedras, Puerto Rico.

THOMPSON Kevin, b. 9 Aug 1952, England. Chief Executive; Director; Professional Trumpet Player. m. Patricia Anne Devonald, 24 July 1976. Education: GRSM ARMCM, Royal Northern College of Music, 1970-73; FTCL, Trinity College of Music, London, 1979; LRAM, Royal Academy of Music, 1976; MA, 1979-81, PhD, 1981-83, University of London. Career: Professional Trumpet Player, Director, Music, Schools and Colleges, 1974-81; Doctoral Research Student, 1981-83; Senior, Principal Lectureships, University College, Salford, 1984-87; Director of Studies, Birmingham School of Music, Birmingham Polytechnic, 1988; Principal, Birmingham Conservatoire, Dean of Music, University of Central England, Birmingham, 1989-93; Principal, Chief Executive, Dartington College of Arts Ltd, 1993-. Publications: Wind Bands and Brass Bands, 1985; An Analysis of Group Teaching, 1984; Uncle Sam's Students, Classical Music, 6 parts, 1993-94. Honours: University of London Award, Paris Conservatoire, 1983; British Association for American Studies Award, Oberlin Conservatory, 1985; Personal Professorial Chair, University of Central England, 1991; British Council Award, Royal Danish Academy of Music, Copenhagen, 1991; Winston Churchill Fellowship, 1992; Honorary Professorship, University of Plymouth, 1993; Freeman, City of London, 1993; Honorary Fellow, Trinity College, 1995. Memberships: Royal Society of Musicians; Worshipful Company of Musicians; Incorporated Society of Musicians; Royal Society of Arts; Institute of Directors. Hobbies: Arts; Skiing; Photography. Address: Oakhurst, Stratford-upon-Avon, Warwickshire CV37 6UN, England.

THOMPSON Lesleigh Karen, b. 8 Nov 1966, Bulawayo, Rhodesia (now Zimbabwe), Australian resident since 1977. Composer; Pianist. Education: BMus 1991, MMus 1994, The University of Melbourne. Career: Lecturer in Music Techniques at the University of Melbourne, 1993-96; Studied with Brenton Broadstock, 1989-93; Stephen Ingham, 1994-97; Examiner, Australian Music Examinations Board, 1997-. Compositions include: Toccata for piano, 1989; Captive, for ensemble, 1991; Enost, for string quartet, 1992; Sonata for Piano: Mad Men, Mad Times, 1992; Sphygmus for piano, 1992; Exuviae for piano, 1993; Facade for guitar, 1994; Clandestine, for orchestra, 1994; Sweet Talk, for guitar and cello, 1995; Roulette, for piano, 1996. Honours include: New Audience Award for Composition, 1990; Albert H Maggs Award, 1993. Address: c/o APRA, 1A Eden Street, Crows Nest, NSW 2065, Australia.

THOMPSON Martin, b. 1956, USA. Singer (Tenor). Career: Many appearances at leading European and American opera houses; Roles have included Werther, Hoffmann, Gounod's Roméo, Edgardo, Pinkerton, Peter Grimes, Don José, Lensky, Rodolfo, and Drombello in Bellini's Beatrice di Tenda; Concerts include Beethoven's Ninth Symphony at San Francisco, Cherubini's Mass in D Minor (Stuttgart) and Britten's War Requiem; Season 1997-98 with Covent Garden and Metropolitan Opera debuts (as the Duke of Mantua, and Pinkerton), Hoffmann in Philadelphia and Pinkerton at Santa Fe; Other repertory includes Tom Rakewell (Philadelphia, 1997), the title role in Mozart's Mitridate (Wexford Festival, 1988), Nadir in Les pêcheurs de Perles and the title role in Argento's Voyage of Edgar Allan Poe (Dallas Opera). Address: c/o Metropolitan Opera, Lincoln Center, New York, NY 10023, USA.

THOMPSON Robert (Ian), b. 5 Apr 1943, Bradford, England. Singer (Tenor); Harpsichordist; Conductor. m. Judith Welch, 18 Apr 1970. Education: Organ Scholar, Queen's College, Cambridge, 1961-64; MA, Cambridge University; ARCM; ARCO; Singing tuition with Campogalliani, Italy. Career: BBC Chorus, 1966-67; Vicar Choral, St Paul's Cathedral, London, 1967-77; Opera and Concert Singer: Kent Opera, Opera North, Debut, Royal Opera House, Covent Garden, 1993; Appearances, numerous European theatres including La Scala (Milan) and Teatro San Carlo (Naples), 1991, Châtelet (Paris), Regio (Turin), and Massimo (Palermo), 1995; Broadcasts in most European countries. Recordings: With Pro Cantione Antiqua, Early Music Consort, Società Cameristica di Lugano and Capella Clementina. Memberships: Incorporated Society of Musicians; Royal College of Organists; The Alpine Club; Amaryllis Consort. Hobbies: Alpine mountaineering; Gardening; Cooking. Current Management: Athole Still International Management; Concert Directory International. Address: Hill Top, Tearnside, Kirkby Lonsdale, Cumbria LA6 2PU, England.

THOMPSON Timothy K, b. 17 June 1936, San Francisco, California, USA. Composer. Education: BS, Meteorology; BMus, Composition, San Francisco Conservatory, 1960; Advanced Composition with Nadia Boulanger, Paris, 1963-65; MA, Music Composition, University of Illinois, 1973. Career: Orchestral music broadcast on WBAI, New York, 1978, WQXR, New York, 1978, 1981, 1982, 1986, KKHI, San Francisco, 1987, other stations including many times on KPFA, most recently Mar 1994; Many TV broadcasts of dance scores especially on PBS and many campus stations; Work of past 11 years or so nearly all related to the Earth, our habitat, the environment. Compositions: About 200 orchestral items and 13 music comedy show scores; Works include: The Circle, ballet; Duologues, piano solo, 1964-65, published 1981; Theatre Piece, 1965; Toccata Pastoral, for piano, also orchestra, 1965, published 1981; Slow Arrival Quiet Fanfares, 1966; Hymn to the Earth, orchestral-choir set of 6 works; Piano works. Recordings: Muzak Time Machine, CD; Turning Point score segments, 1977. Honours: Fellowships, Tanglewood, Massachusetts, 1960, 1968; 2 Fulbright Scholarships for study in Paris (Boulanger), 1963-65; Performances of Symphony for World Peace, United Nations, New York, 31 May and 6 Aug, 1978. Hobby: Environmental meteorology. Address: 141 Vista Grande, Greenbrae, CA 94904-1135, USA.

THOMSON Brian, b. 5 Jan 1946, Sydney, New South Wales, Australia. Stage Designer. Education: Studied architecture in Perth. Career: Designed the production of the rock-opera Tommy in Australia, Jesus Christ Superstar and The Rocky Horror Show in London, 1972-73; Designed Britten's Death In Venice for the State Opera of South Australia in 1980, and Janácek's The Makropoulos Case for Adelaide Festival of The Arts in 1982; Designs for Australian Opera have included the 1986 premiere of Voss by Richard Meale, Death in Venice in 1989 and Tristan und Isolde in 1990; Premiere of the Eighth Wonder (Sydney) 1995. Address: c/o Australian Opera, PO Box 291, Strawberry Hills, New South Wales 2012, Australia.

THOMSON Heather, b. 7 Dec 1940, Vancouver, Canada. Opera Singer (Soprano). m. Perry Price. Education: Studied at the Toronto Conservatory with Herman Geiger-Torel and Irene Jessner. Debut: Toronto in 1962 in Hansel and Gretel. Career: Debut with Sadler's Wells as Micaela followed by Mimi, Marguerite in Faust and Anne Trulove in The Rake's Progress; Canadian Opera Company roles include Manon, Rosalinda in Die Fledermaus, Donna Anna and Donna Elvira in Don Giovanni, Ellen in Peter Grimes, and world premieres of Heloise and Abelard by Wilson, and Mario and The Magician by Sommers; Has sung with Welsh National Opera and in USA; Roles with New York City Opera include Violetta, Nedda, Donna Anna and Donna Elvira, Marguerite, Rosalinda, and Agathe in Der Freischütz; 1993-94 season as Lady Macbeth in Chemnitz in Germany, Violetta in La Traviata in Toledo, Ohio, Hanna in The Merry Widow at Victoria BC and concerts in Germany and Canada. Recordings: Sang Manon for CBC-TV; Lady Billows in Albert Herring for CBC-BBC Radio; Mother in Hansel and Gretel for CBC-Radio. Contributions to: Canadian Encyclopedia of Music. Honours: Winner of CBC Talent Festival and Canadian Council Awards, 1961; Winner, Metropolitan Opera Auditions, 1961; Winner, San Francisco Opera Auditions, 1964. Memberships: AGMA; ACTRA. Current Management: Germany: Bühnen und Konzert Agentur, Marianne Böttger, Dahlmannstr 9, 1000 Berlin 12, Germany; USA: James Sardos Artists Management, 180 West End Avenue, New York, NY 10023, USA. Address: c/o Canadian Opera Company, 227 Front Street East, Toronto, Canada, M5A 1E8.

THOMSON Neil, b. 1966, London, England. Conductor. Education: Studied at the Royal Academy of Music with George Hurst and at the Royal College with Norman del Mar and Christopher Adey. Career: Director, Manson Ensemble at RAM giving many performances during the Messiaen Festival in 1987 and the Henze Festival in 1988; Conducted major orchestral and instrumental works of Paul Patterson at venues around Britain; Founded the contemporary music group, Terre Nova in 1986, with its debut at St John's Smith Square; Concerts at the Purcell Room, South Bank and the Huddersfield Contemporary Music Festival; Worked with such soloists as Christopher Bunting in Dvorák's Cello Concerto and the Brahms Double Concerto with Emanuel Hurwitz, And Suddenly It's Evening by Elisabeth Lutyens with Philip Langridge, and Philip Gammon with Saint-Saëns's 2nd Concerto; Concerts with the Royal Tunbridge Wells Symphony Orchestra; Music Director, Sadler's Wells Youth Ballet Workshop; Concerts with the Bombay Chamber Orchestra in India. Honours include: Bursary for Conductors, National Association of Youth Orchestras. Address: c/o Norman McCann International Artists Ltd, The Coach House, 56 Lawrie Park Gardens, London, SE26 6XJ, England.

THON Tomas, b. 29 April 1962, Opava, Czech Republic. Concert Organist; Professor of Music. m. Marie Thonova, 29 May 1993, 1 daughter. Education: Academy of Music & Dramatic Arts, Prague, 1980-89; Conservatory CNR Rueil-Malmaison, Paris, France. Debut: 1989. Career: Freelance Musician, 1989-93; Professor, Church Conservatory, Kromeriz, 1993-; Professor, Janacek Conservatory, Ostrava, 1993-97. Recordings: Domenico Zipoli, Sonata al Intavolatuna; Petr Eben, Job for Organ; Czech Organ Music of 18th Century. Honours: 2nd Prize, Competition for Young Organists, 1978; Prize, Czech Music Foundation for Interpretation, 1987. Memberships: Society for Ancient Music, Prague; Society of Spiritual Music, Prague. Hobbies: Nature; Sport. Address: Jureckova 16, CZ-74601 Opava, Czech Republic.

THORARINSSON Jon, b. 13 Sept 1917, Iceland. Composer; Teacher; Writer on Music. m. Sigurjona Jakobsdottir, 24 Dec 1963. Education: Graduated, Akureyri College, 1937; Reykjavik College; MMus, Yale School of Music, New Haven, Connecticut, USA; Studied with Paul Hindemith. Career: Musical Advisor, Icelandic State Radio, 1947-56; Head, Department of Theory and Composition, Reykjavik College of Music, 1947-68; Active in founding the Icelandic Symphony Orchestra in 1950 and Chairman of its first Board of Directors; Programme Director, Icelandic State TV, 1968-79; Currently engaged in writing a history of music in Iceland. Compositions: Many songs; Children's songs including 25 folk songs; Music for Organ; Sonata for Clarinet and Piano; Of Love And Death, song cycle for Baritone and Orchestra, words by C G Rossetti. Recordings: On tape for Icelandic Radio: Voluspa for Choir and Orchestra, City of Reykjavik commission for the 1100th anniversary of settlement of Iceland, 1974; Ingolfs Minni, City of Reykjavik commission for its 200th anniversary, 1986; Many songs recorded, many of the above works to be reissued on CD. Publications: Textbook in Elementary Music Theory, 1963; Pall Isolfsson, a prominent Icelandic organist and composer, 1963; Sveinbjorn Sveinbjornsson, first professional Icelandic composer, a biography, 1969; A History of Music in Iceland, forthcoming.

Contributions to: Several articles in periodicals; Numerous articles in newspapers including periodical musical criticism. Honours: Knight, 1978, Commander, 1989, Order of the Icelandic Falcon. Memberships: President, 1951-52, 1963-66, Union of Icelandic Artists; Icelandic Composers Society. Address: Aflagrandi 40, 107 Reykjavik, Iceland.

THORBURN Melissa (Rachel), b. 9 July 1956, Monmouth, Illinois, USA. Opera and Concert Singer (Mezzo-Soprano). m. Timothy Richard Sobolewski, 13 Apr 1985, 1 son. Education: BMus, Piano, 1977, BMus, Voice, 1980, Louisiana State University; Private study with Yvonne Lefebure, Paris, 1977-79; MMus, Voice, New England Conservatory, 1982. Career: Handel's Messiah with Philadelphia Orchestra, 1987-91, annually; Sang in Berlioz's L'Enfance du Christ with Seattle Symphony, WA, in 1987, Gounod's Faust as Siebel with Deutsche Oper Berlin in 1988, Pergolesi's Stabat Mater with the Puerto Rico Symphony in 1988, Mozart's Le Nozze di Figaro as Cherubino with Sarasota Opera, FL in 1988, Gilbert and Sullivan's The Yeoman of The Guard as Phoebe with Lyric Opera of Kansas City in 1990, Mozart's Requiem with Los Angeles Philharmonic conducted by Gerard Schwarz in 1991, and Handel's Messiah with National Symphony in 1992; Mozart's Requiem and Schubert's Mass in E flat with Indianapolis Symphony conducted by Richard Hickox, 1994; Bach's Mass in B Minor with Winter Park Bach Festival, Florida, 1994; Bach's Christmas Oratorio and Cantata No.78 with Baldwin-Wallace Bach Festival, Ohio, 1995; Mendelssohn's Lobgesang with Vancouver Symphony and recitals at the Bermuda Festival, 1996; Mendelssohn's A Midsummer Night's Dream with Philadelphia Orchestra conducted by Charles Dutoit, 1997, and with St Louis Symphony, 1998. Recordings: Vaughan Williams's Serenade to Music with the New York Virtuosi Chamber Symphony under Kenneth Klein; John Philip Sousa's Désirée with Pocone Pops. Current Management: Thea Dispeker Inc, Artists Representative, 59 East 54th Street, New York, NY 10022, USA. Address: c/o Music department, 222 Baird Hall, SUNY-Buffalo, NY 14260, USA.

THORN Benjamin, b. 31 January 1961, Canberra, Australia. Composer; Editor; Recorder Player. Education: BA (Hons), University of Sydney, 1983, PhD, 1989; Studied with Larry Sitsky and Donald Hollier, 1977-78. Career: University of Sydney, 1986; National Printing Industry Training Council, 1991; Performances as recorder player with the Renaissance Players, and other groups. Compositions include: Visioni di Cavoli for ensemble, 1985; Pipistrelli Gialli for bass recorder and live electronics, 1985; Chasing for 3 recorders, 1985; Croutons II for clarinet, 1985; Magnificat for chorus, 1985; The Voice of the Crocodile for bass clarinet, 1988; The Pobble for chorus, 1988; Chick Peas for two mandolins, 1990; Two Diagonals and a Squiggle for recorder and percussion, 1991; Missa Sine Verbum, 1991; Croutons III for baroque flute, 1992; Croutons IV for harpiscord, 1992; Songs for my father's wedding, bass recorder, 1995. Publications: Editor, two volumes of recorder music, Recorders at Large, Works of Sitsky, Strozzi and Castello. Honours include: Co-winner, Fellowship of Australian Composers' Competition, 1991. Address: c/o APRA, 1A Eden Street, Crows Nest, NSW 2065, Australia.

THORN Penelope, b. 19 Sept 1957, Kent, England. Singer, Soprano. Education: Studied at Guildhall School of Music and with Tito Gobbi in Italy. Career: Sang with Karlsruhe Opera from 1980 as Adriana Lecouvreur, Alice Ford, Amelia in Ballo in Maschera, Princess in Rusalka, Giorgetta in Il Tabarro, Freia, Giulietta and Armida in Handel's Rinaldo, also at Barcelona; Sang at Düsseldorf and Mannheim, then appeared at Hannover from 1985 as Tosca, Abigaille and Jenufa; Freia and Gutrune in Der Ring des Nibelungen for Deutsche Oper am Rhein; Guest appearances at Giessen in Menotti's Mara Golovin, 1986; At Bielefeld as the Forza Leonora and Asteria in Boito's Nerone; At Zürich as Freia and Gutrune; At Nice as Minnie in La Fanciulla del West; Has sung Senta at Freiburg, Lyon and Mannheim, Strauss's Empress at Karlsruhe and Bremen and Third Norn in Götterdämmerung at Munich Staatsoper; Appearances at Saarbrücken as Aida, Salome, Leonore, Butterfly and Elsa. Honours: Winner Voci Verdiane at Bussetto, 1985; Engaged as Salome at Stuttgart, 1996. Current Management: Athole Still International Management Limited. Address: Foresters Hall, 25-27 Westow Street, London SE19 3RY, England.

THORPE Marion (Stein), b. 1926, Vienna, Austria. Pianist; Writer; Musical Administrator; Teacher. m. (1) The Earl of Harewood, (2) Rt Hon Jeremy Thorpe, 3 sons, 1 stepson. Education: Private study with Franz Osborn. Career: Lectures, talks and interviews; Programme notes. Publications: Editor: Form and Performance by Erwin Stein, 1962; Classical Songs for Children, 1964; Series of 19 volumes of Piano Lessons and Pieces, The Waterman/Harewood Series, 1967-. Memberships: Aldeburgh Foundation; Co-Founder, Leeds International Pianoforte Competition; Corporation of TCM; Chairman, Britten-Pears Foundation. Hobbies: Reading; Sightseeing; Swimming. Address: 2 Orme Square, London W2 4RS, England.

THORSEN Marianne, b. 1972, Trondheim, Norway. Concert Violinist. Education: Studied in Norway, at the Suzuki Institute, London, the Purcell School, and the Royal Academy in London with György Pauk. Career: Solo performances in Berlin, with the Slovak Chamber Orchestra, Philharmonia and orchestras throughout Norway; Recitals at the Bergen International Festival; Member of the Leopold String Trio. Recordings: Svendsen's Romance with the Stavanger Symphony Orchestra; Albums with the Trondheim Soloists. Address: Manygate Management, 13 Cotswold Mews, 30 Battersea Square, London, SW11 3RA, England.

THORVALDSSON Torarne Christer, b. 9 August 1946, Arvika, Sweden. Violinist. m. Birgitta, 11 March 1978, 1 son. Education: Violin Studies, Arvika, 10 years old; Swedish Radio Music School, Edsberg Castle, Stockholm, 1964-68; Studies with Professor manoug Parikiom, London, 1971-73. Debut: Soloist with Gothenburg Symphonic Orchestra, 1975. Career: Member, Swedish Radio Symphony Orchestra, 1968-71; Co-Leader, 1973, Leader, 1976-, Gothenburg Symphony Orchestra; Performances in International Concerts; Recitals with Pianist Göran W Nilson, 1980-. Recordings: Major Sonatas and Concertos by Important Composers. Honours: 200 Years Anniversary Prize, Royal Academy of Music, 1971; Neeme Jãrui Musical Prize, 1996. Membership: Royal Swedish Academy of Music, Stockholm, 1996-. Hobby: Art. Address: Berzeliigatan 24, 41253 Goteborg, Sweden.

THUN Barbara, b. 14 December 1964. Singer. Education: Theatre Studies, UniversityMunich, 1984-89; Singing, Hochschule der Kunste, Berlin, 1994. Debut: With Rossinis Petite Messe Solenelle at Kaiser-Friedrich-Gedächtnis-Kirche, Berlin, 1992. Career: Member, Die Maulwerker Group for Experimental Music Theatre, 1993-; Festival Appearances include Denkbare Music, Groningen, 1993; Symph Intern Musica Choralis 2000, Luxemburg; Festival of Contemporary Opera, Leipzig and J Cage Symposium, Berlin, 1995; ARCHIPEL Genf and Grenzenlos Berlin-Moskau, 1996; Musik-Biennale Berlin and Vecery Novej Hudby Bratislava, 1997. Compositions: Vokalstuck 77, 1994; Stuck in drei Teilen, 1995; Hurdenlauf, 1997. Address: Menzinger Str 74, 80992 Munich, Germany.

THURMER Harvey, b. 1950, Vienna, Austria. Violinist. Education: Studied at the Vienna Academy of Music. Career: Member of the Franz Schubert Quartet, 1983-90; Many concert engagements in Europe, USA, and Australia including showings in the Amsterdam Concertgebouw, the Vienna Musikverein and Konzerthaus, the Salle Gaveau Paris and the Sydney Opera House; Visits to Zurich, Geneva, Basle, Berlin, Hamburg, Rome, Rotterdam, Madrid and Copenhagen; Festival engagements include Salzburg, Wiener Festwochen, Prague Spring Schubertiade at Hohenems, the Schubert Festival at Washington DC and Belfast and Istanbul Festivals; Tours of Russia, Australasia and USA, and frequent concert tours of Great Britain; Featured in the Concerto by Spohr with the Liverpool Philharmonic at the Liverpool Festival Hall; Wigmore Hall series includes Master Concerts, Russian Series, Summer Nights, and Coffee Concerts; Performance of Alun Hoddinott's Quartet at the 1989 Cheltenham Festival featured on BBC Welsh TV; Teacher at the Vienna Conservatory and Graz Musikhochschule; Masterclasses at the Royal Northern College of Music and at the Lake District Summer Music. Recordings include: Schubert's Quartet in G, D877; Complete Quartets of Dittersdorf. Address: c/o Christopher Tennant Management, 11 Lawrence Street, London, SW3 5NB, England.

THWAITES Penelope (Mary), b. 18 Apr 1944, Chester, England. Pianist; Composer. m. Edward Jackson CBE, 5 Dec 1981, 1 son, 1 daughter. Education: BMus, 1st class hons, Melbourne University, Australia, 1965; Postgraduate study: Piano with Albert Ferber, Composition with William Reed. Debut: Wigmore Hall, London, 1974. Career: Regular concerts and broadcasts in London; Tours on 5 continents; Concertos with leading orchestras, Australia, UK, America; Lectures, lecture recitals, radio, TV and video appearances. Compositions include: Ride! Ride!, 1976; Dancing Pieces, 1989; A Lambeth Garland, 1990; Works for organ and piano. Recordings: Australian Piano Music, 1981; Percy Grainger: complete original music for 4 hands, with John Lavender, Vol 1, 1989, Vol II, 1991, Vol III, 1993; Percy Grainger: Chosen Gems for Piano, solo disc, 1992; Her own songs recorded, 1985, 1991. Contributions to: The Singer, 1996; BBC Music Magazine, 1997. Honours: Exhibitions, Melbourne University, 1963, 1965; Medallion, International Grainger Society, 1991. Memberships: Grainger Society; Incorporated Society of Musicians; Performing Rights Society; MCPS; The Royal Philharmonic Society. Current Management: Siva Oke Music Management. Address: 23 Lyndale Avenue, Child's Hill, London NW2 2QB, England.

THYM Jürgen, b. 2 Jul 1943, Bremervörde, Germany. Musicologist. m. Peggy Dettwiler, 6 Jun 1992. Education: Diploma in School Music, Hochschule für Musik, Berlin, 1967; PhD, Musicology, Case Western Reserve University, 1974; Studies in theory and composition with Reinhard Schwarz Schilling, counterpoint with Ernst Pepping, 12-tone technique with Josef Rufer and musicology with Reinhold Brinkmann, Rudolph Stephen and Jon G Suess. Career: Visiting Instructor at Oberlin College, USA, 1973; Instructor, Assistant Professor, Associate Professor, Professor, 1973-, Chair of Musicology, 1982-, Eastman School of Music, Rochester, NY. Publications: The Solo Song Settings of Eichendorff's Poems by Schumann and Wolf, 1974; Translations of Kirnberger's The Art of Strict Musical Composition, 1982, and Schenker's Counterpoint, 1987; 100 Years of Eichendorff Songs, 1983; Schoenberg Collected Works Edition, volume XIV, 1988, volume XIII, 1993. Contributions to: Articles in Journal of Music Theory, Notes, American Choral Review, Comparative Literature, Journal of Musicological Research, Fontes Artis Musicae, Musica Realtà and Aurora, Eichendorff year book, among others; Essays on Mendelssohn and Schumann. Honours: Modern Language Association Award for Best Review, 1979 and for Best Article-Length Bibliography, 1980; Deems-Taylor Award, American Society for Composers, Authors and Publishers, 1983. Memberships: American Musicological Society; Lyrica. Hobbies: History; Travel; Chess.

TIBBELS Nicole, b. 1960, England. Singer (Soprano). Education: Sheffield University and the Guildhall School, London. Career: Sang with the Swingle Singers and has made many concert appearances in music by Berio; Other repertory includes Dies by Wolfgang Rihm, Mason's Concerto for Viola Section, Nenia by Birtwistle, and songs by Stravinsky; Opera engagements as the Queen of Night with Richard Nickox, and the European Chamber Opera, Alice Ford and Rossini's Clorinda for Pimlico Opera, Serpina in La Serva Padrona for Broomhill Opera and Mozart's Constanze for Perth Festival Opera; Royal Opera Covent Garden debut 1997, as La Comtesse in Chérubin; 1997-98 appearances as La Folie in Platée and Fido in Paul Bunyan; Premieres of works by Maxwell Davies, Bainbridge, Berio, Michael Finnissy, Jonathon Lloyd and Nigel Osborne. Recordings include: Berio's Sinfonia, and works by Bryars, Smalley, Cage and Stockhausen. Address: c/o Royal Opera House (contracts), Covent Garden, London WC2, England.

TICHOTA Jiri, b. 18 Apr 1937, Tocna, Czechoslovakia. Lutenist; Musicologist; Guitarist. m. Zdenka Tichotova, 11 Nov 1976, 1 son, 1 daughter. Education: Student, 1960-65, PhD in Musicology, 1968, Faculty of Philosophy, Charles University; Self-taught instrumentalist. Career: Director of the Spiritual Quintet Ensemble for 33 years; Lutenist and Guitarist collaborating with many soloists and orchestras and with regular appearances with Prague Madrigal Singers; Assistant Professor of Musicology, Charles University, Prague for 23 years. Recordings: About 25 of lute or guitar solos and continuo with many Czech chamber orchestras; 11 LP's and 5 CD's with Spiritual Quintet. Publications include: Francisco Tarrega: Work 1 and 2, 1959; Hudba Ceskych Loutnovych Tabulatur, 1968, 1980; Claves Musicae ad Fides Compositae Manu Nicolai Smal de Lebendorf Scriptai, 1969; Papers: Deustche Lieder in Prager Lautentabulaturen des Beginenden 17 Jahrhunderts, 1967; Die Aria Tempore Adventus Producenda, 1970; Intabulationen und Tschechischer Gemeinschaftgesang an der ende des 16 Jahrhunderts, 1970; Francouzska Loutnova Hudba v Cechach, 1973; Ceskobudejovicky Zlomek Varhanni Tabulatury, 1975; Problemes d'Edition des Tablatures de Redaction Defecteuse, 1984; Die Bohemica und das Bohmische Repertoire in den Tabulaturen für die Renaissance-Laute, 1984. Memberships: Lute Society of America; Czech Lute Society; Czech Music Society; Society of Ancient Instruments. Hobbies: Lepidopterology; Photography of Insects. Address: Vzdusna 773, 14200 Prague 4, Czech Republic.

TICHY Georg, b. 9 Jun 1944, Vienna, Austria. Baritone. Education: Studied with Hilde Zadek in Vienna. Debut: Vienna Staatsoper in 1973 in Tristan und Isolde. Career: Sang in Vienna in operas by Verdi, Rossini, Mozart, Puccini, Britten and Wagner; Sang at Maggio Musicale Florence in 1984 as Rigoletto and at Bregenz Festival in 1986 as Papageno; Sang in Schubert's Fierabras and Wagner's Lohengrin at Vienna in 1990; Sang Ned Keene in the house premiere of Peter Grimes, Vienna Staatsoper, 1996; Frequent concert appearances. Recordings: Ariadne auf Naxos; Parsifal; Alfonso und Estrella by Schubert. Address: c/o Vienna Staatoper, Opernring 1, Vienna, Austria.

TIEPPO Giorgio, b. 1953, Varese, Italy. Singer (Tenor). Education: Studied at the Giuseppe Verdi Conservatory, Milan, and with Pier Miranda Ferraro. Career: Sang in concert from 1977 and made opera debut at Pavia 1983, as Don Ruiz in Donizetti's Maria Padilla; Appeared as Don Ruiz in Parma and Ravenna and sang further in La Bohème and Lucia di Lammermoor at Bergamo; Pinkerton in Butterfly at Genoa, Bologna, Turin and New Orleans; Vienna, Mannheim and Dublin debuts as Cavaraossi; Verona Arena in Nabucco, Il Trovatore, Un Ballo in Maschera, Norma and Aida; Appearances at the Zurich Opera as Rodolfo (season 1996-97), Cavaradossi, and Luigi in Il Tabarro; Further engagements in New Yori, Dallas, Berlin, Rome and Helsinki. Honours include: Winner, Voci Nuove Verdiane

Competition, Bergamo; Voci Verdiane in Busseto. Address: c/o Opernhaus Zurich, Falkenstrasse 1, CH-8008 Zurich, Switzerland.

TIERNEY Vivian, b. 26 Nov 1957, London, England. Singer (Soprano). Career: Sang as Principal Soprano with D'Oyly Carte Opera Company; Freelance, 1982-, at first with Sadler's Wells Opera Company in Kalman's The Gypsy Princess and Lehar's The Count of Luxembourg; Edwige in Offenbach's Robinson Crusoe for Kent Opera; Hanna Glawari in Die Lustige Witwe for Opera North; English National Opera from 1987 as Frasquita, Euridice in Orpheus in the Underworld and Regan in the UK premiere of Reimann's Lear, 1989; Sang title role in world premiere of Robin Holloway's Clarissa, 1990; Has sung with Freiburg Opera as Lady Macbeth of Mtsensk, Ellen Orford and Giulietta (Les Contes d'Hoffmann); Has appeared in Handel's Alceste at Versailles; Mimi in La Bohème at Montpellier Festival; Euridice in Milhaud's Les Malheurs d'Orphée at Frankfurt; Donna Anna for Flanders Opera; Sang in Sullivan's cantata The Golden Legend for Colorado Springs orchestra; Appearance with Opera 80 as Donna Anna; Marie in Wozzeck (Almeida Festival, 1988); Other roles include the Marschallin in Der Rosenkavalier Jenny (in Mahagonny), Rosalinde in Die Fledermaus, and Malinka in The Adventures of Mr Broucek; Mimi in La Bohème for English National Opera, 1992; Gypsy Princess (Los Angeles); Sang Ellen Orford in a new production of Peter Grimes at Glyndebourne, 1992; Renata in The Fiery Angel in Freiburg, 1993; Berg's Marie for Opera North, 1993; Sang Gutrune in Götterdämmerung at Covent Garden, 1996. Current Management: Athole Still International Management Limited. Address: Foresters Hall, 25-27 Westow Street, London SW19 3RY, England.

TILLIKAINEN Sauli, b. 7 Dec 1952, Finland. Singer (Baritone). Education: Studied at the Sibelius Academy Helsinki and in Vienna with Anton Dermota and Hans Hotter. Debut: Sang in concert from 1981. Career: Sang with the Finnish National Opera from 1984 and as guest at the Moscow Bolshoi, Stockholm, Dresden and Copenhagen; Roles have included Guglielmo, Don Giovanni, Escamillo, Mozart's Count, Germont, Eugene Onegin, Ruprecht in The Fiery Angel and the title roles in Lionardo by Werle and Thomas by Rautavaara; Kennedy Center, Washington in Ein Deutsches Requiem and the Kullervo Symphony by Sibelius; Sang Valmonte in Sallinen's The Palace, Savonlinna Festival, 1996; Lieder recitals in music by Schubert and Schumann. Address: Finnish National Opera, Bulevardi 23-27, SF-00180 Helsinki 18, Finland.

TIKALOVA Drahomíra, b. 9 May 1915, Berlin, Germany. Opera Singer (Soprano). Education: Privately at Brno, Prague, Ostrava, with Professor Theodor Czernik, Ludmila Neumannová-Procházková, Rudolf Vasek. Debut: Katinka in Friml's operetta Katinka, Landstheater, Brno. Career: Landstheater, Brno, 1938-42; National Theatre, Prague, from 1942, later main member; Opera and concert activity, Czechoslovakia, including National Theatre, Prague, Czech Philharmonic Orchestra, Prague, Czech Radio, Prague; Performed in opera and concert, Belgium, Bulgaria, France, Italy, Yugoslavia, Germany, Poland, Austria, Rumania, USSR, Netherlands, Hungary; Recitals of songs and opera arias for Radio Prague, Pizen and Brno; Main theatre roles include: The Kiss, Vendulka; Bartered Bride, Marenka; The Secret, Blazenka; Blodek's At the Well, Lidunka; Carmen, Micaela; Dimitrij, Xenie; Jakobin, Julie; Masked Ball, Amelia, Don Carlo, Elisabeth; Lohengrin, Elsa; Don Giovanni, Elvira; Tannhäuser, Elisabeth; Holländer, Senta; The Queen of Spades; Lisa; Elektra, Chrysothemis; Rosenkavalier, Marschallin; Title roles: Rusalka, Jenufa, Katia Kabanova, Moniuszko's Halka, Rimsky-Korsakov's Snow Maiden, Aida, Tosca. Recordings: Bartered Bride, Marenka; Two Widows, Anezka; Katia Kabanova, title role; E Suchon's Svätopluk, Milena; Z Fibich's Spring Romance, cantata; Dvorák, Stabat mater, conductor V Talich, and The Spectre's Bride; A Fils, Missa solemnis; L Vycpálek, cantata; Complete song cycles, Dvorak, Wagner, Slavicky, Kricka, Jeremiás; Portrait recitals; Radio recordings include: Libuse, title role; Halka, title role; Anna Karenina, title role; Cavalleria Rusticana, Santuzza; Devil's Wall, Katuska. Honours: 2nd Prize, Vocal Competition, Vienna, 1938; 1st Prize, Victoria de Los Angeles, 1938. Address: Krocínova 5, 110 00 Prague, Staré mesto, Czech Republic.

TIKKA Kari (Juhani), b. 13 Apr 1946, Siilinjärvi, Finland. Conductor. m. Eeva Relander, 18 May 1979, 3 sons, 1 daughter. Education: Oboe Diploma, Conducting Diploma, Sibelius Academy, Helsinki; Private study with Arvid Jansons and Luigi Ricci. Debut: Helsinki, 1968. Career: Conductor: Tampere Theatre, 1969-70; Finnish National Opera, Helsinki, 1970-72, 1979-; Finnish Radio Symphony Orchestra, 1972-76; Royal Swedish Opera, Stockholm, 1975-77; Symphony Orchestra Vivo, Helsinki, 1986-; Guest Conductor, Scandinavia, Western and Eastern Europe, Israel. Compositions: Frieda, opera; Two Aphorisms; Due Pezzi; Many songs; Cantatas; The Prodigal Son, oratorio; Concerto for Cello; Music for choir; Chamber music. Recordings: Vivo-Tikka; Triplet; Jumala on rakkaus; Armolaulu: Armolaulu, VIVO Finlandia. Hobby: Spectator sports. Current Management: Allegro, Artist Management, Espoo, Finland. Address: Mannerheimintie 38 A 4, 00100 Helsinki, Finland.

TILLI Johann, b. 11 Nov 1967, Kerimäki, Finland. Singer (Bass). Education: Studied at the Sibelius Academy, Helsinki. Career: Appearances at the Savonlinna Festival, Finland, as Sarastro, the King in Aida, Banquo and Landgraf and other roles; National Opera, Helsinki, as Lodovico and High Priest Baal (Nabucco); Commendatore and Rossini's Basilio at Oslo, with further engagements at Amsterdam, Brussels, Tel-Aviv and Hannover; Member of the Hamburg Opera from 1990; First Bass with Düsseldorf Oper, 1996-97; Has worked with many conductors including Abbado, Cillario, de Burgos, Fricke, Harnoncourt, Steinberg, Sawallisch and Wallberg; Three Bass Concert with Matti Salminen, Jaakko Ryhänen and conductor Leif Segerstam in Helsinki, 1995. Recordings include: Gazzaniga's Don Giovanni (Sony Classics); Mahler's 8th Symphony; Schumann Genoveva; Dessau: Haggadah; Highlights from Savonlinna; Lady Macbeth of the Mtsensk District (DGG). Address: c/o Hamburg Staatsoper, Grosse Theaterstrasse 34, Pf 302448, 20354 Hamburg, Germany.

TILNEY Colin, b. 31 Oct 1933, London, England. Harpsichordist. Education: Studied harpsichord with Mary Potts at Cambridge and with Gustav Leonhardt in Amsterdam. Career: Soloist and ensemble player in Britain and Europe from the early 1960's; US debut in 1971; Repertoire has included music by Renaissance and Baroque composers; Has performed on various clavichords, harpsichords, virginals and early pianos, employing both historical instruments and modern copies. Recordings include: Parthenia, a collection of pieces by Byrd, Bull and Gibbons published in 1611; Complete Keyboard Works of Matthew Locke and the Suites of Purcell and Handel; CD of Bach's Toccatas, 1990. Publications include: Edition of the harpsichord music of Antoine Forqueray. Address: c/o Conifer Records, Horton Road, West Drayton, Middlesex, UB7 8JL, England.

TIMBRELL Charles, b. 5 May 1942, Hackettstown, New Jersey, USA. Pianist; Professor of Music. Education: BMus, Oberlin Conservatory, 1964; MMus, University of Michigan, 1967; Accademia di Santa Cecilia, Rome, 1967-68; DMA, University of Maryland, 1976; Studied piano privately in Rome and Paris. Debut: Paris, 1979; Wigmore Hall, London, 1981; Carnegie Recital Hall, New York, 1984. Career: Performed concertos, recitals; Radio broadcasts throughout the USA and Europe, including four European tours; Numerous American and European premieres (Moss, Crumb, Kirchner, Siegmeister, Corea). Recordings: American Piano Music, 1980; Songs of Walter Rummel, 1995. Publication: French Pianism, 1992. Contributions to: Over 300 articles and reviews in Music and Letters, Piano Quarterly, Fanfare, Opera News, Journal of the American Liszt Society. Honours: Haskil Prize, Oberlin, 1967; Albert Lockwood Piano Prize, Michigan, 1967; Master Teacher Certificate, MTNA, 1986. Memberships: Board of Directors, Washington Music Teachers Association; American Musicological Society; American Liszt Society. Hobbies: Travel; Swimming; Films. Address: 1824 Wyoming Avenue, NW, Washington DC, 20009, USA.

TINNEY Hugh, b. 28 Nov 1958, Dublin, Ireland. Pianist. Education: Trinity College, Dublin, 1976-79; Private piano studies with Mabel Swainson, Louis Kentner, Bryce Morrison and Maria Curcio; LRSM Diploma, 1974. Debut: Purcell Room, London in 1983. Career: Performed concertos and recitals in 30 countries in 4 continents; Radio broadcasts in 12 countries and 2 recitals for Irish TV, RTE; Concerto appearances on Irish, Italian and Spanish TV; Recitals at Queen Elizabeth Hall in London, Musikverein, Vienna, Kennedy Center, Washington; Appearances at festivals include Newport, Rhode Island, Granada, and Prague Spring Festival; Performances with Gulbenkian, Lisbon, Spanish National, Spanish Radio, and Brazil Symphony Orchestras; Proms debut in 1989 with BBC Welsh Symphony Orchestra; Other performances with British orchestras such as London Philharmonic, Philharmonia, Royal Philharmonic, Royal Liverpool Philharmonic, City of Birmingham and Royal Scottish Orchestras. Recordings: Liszt Recital - Dante Sonata, Benediction de Dieu dans La Solitude; Harmonies Poétiques et Réligieuses, Liszt, 1993. Hobbies: Tennis; Reading; Films; Swimming. Current Management: Christopher Tennant Artists Management. Address: 258b Camden Road, London, NW1 9AB, England.

TINSLEY Pauline, b. 27 Mar 1928, Wigan, England. Singer (Soprano). Education: Northern School of Music, Manchester, LRAM 1949; Opera School, London; Further study with Eva Turner and Eduardo Asquez. Career: Professional engagements in Britain from 1961 include London debut as Desdemona, Rossini's Otello; leading roles in Verdi's I Masnadieri, Ernani, Il Corsaro and Bellini's Il Pirata; Welsh National Opera from 1962 as Susanna, Elsa, Lady Macbeth, Sinaide (Rossini's Moses), Abigaille, Aida, Tosca, Turandot, Kostelnicka (Jenufa), Elektra and Dyer's Wife (Frau Ohne Schatten) 1981; Sadler's Wells/English National Opera from 1963 as Gilda, Elvira (Ernani), Fiordiligi, Queen of Night, Countess, Donna Elvira, Beethoven's Leonore and Fidelio, Leonora (Force of Destiny), Elizabeth (Mary Stuart), 1973, Mother/Witch (Hansel and Gretel), 1987, Kabanicha (Katya Kabanova), 1989; Covent Garden from 1965 as Overseer (Elektra), Amelia (Ballo in Maschera), 1971, Helmwige and 3rd Norn (The Ring), Santuzza, 1976, Mere Marie (Carmélites), 1983, Lady Billows (Albert Herring), 1989; various roles with Scottish Opera including Kostelnicka and Opera North (Fata Morgana in Love for 3 Oranges) and with Handel Opera Society; From 1966, performed abroad in Germany, Netherlands, Italy, USA, Canada, Switzerland, Czechoslovakia, Spain and Belgium; Concerts, recitals, broadcasts and television operas; Wexford Festival as Lady Jowler in The Rising of the Moon, 1990; Sang Lady Billows at Garsington, 1996. Recordings include: Electra in Idomeneo (Philips). Address: c/o Music International, 13 Ardilaun road, Highbury, London N5 2QR, England.

TINTNER George (Bernhard), b. 22 May 1917, Vienna, Austria. Conductor; Musical Director. m. 1. Rosa Muriel Norman, 1941, 3 sons, 4 daughters. 2. Cecilia Gretel Lawrence, 30 Oct 1965. 3. Tanya Ruth Buchdahl, 27 May 1978. Education: Vienna Boys' Choir; Graduate in Composition and Conducting, Vienna State Academy. Career: Resident Coach; Conductor, Wiener Volksoper, 1938; Conductor, Auckland String Players, New Zealand, 1945-54; Conductor, Elizabethan Theatre Trust, Later Australian Opera, 1954-63; Music Director, New Zealand Opera, 1964; Music Director, Cape Town Municipal Orchestra, 1967-68; Sadler's Wells, 1968-70; Music Director, West Australian Opera Company, 1971-72; Resident Conductor, Australian Opera, 1973-76; Music Director, Queensland Theatre, Philharmonic, Orchestra, 1977-87; Music Director, Resident Conductor, Symphony Nova Scotia, Canada, 1987-; Regular appearances with all Canadian, Australian and New Zealand Orchestras, including Montreal and Toronto Symphonies; Regular appearances with Canadian, Australian and New Zeland opera companies; 8 seasons with National Youth Orchestra of Canada, 1971-89; Appearances, Hong Kong Philharmonic, Singapore Symphony, Bournemouth Symphony, London Symphony Orchestra, London Mozart Players, Northern Sinfonia, many others. Recordings: Beethoven 5th Symphony and other works with Canadian Brass, principal brass of NY Philharmonic and Boston Symphony; 1st North American Performance, Bruckner 8th Symphony 1887 version, National Youth Orchestra of Canada, Jubal Records; Mozart dance music, marches; Symphony Nova Scotia, CBC Records; Music of Australia, New Zealand, Canada, Symphony Nova Scotia; Also for Festival Records, Australia, Australian Broadcasting Corp, CBC, Broadcasting Corp of New Zealand. Honours: Grosses Ehrenzeichen Officer's Cross of the Austrian Order of Merit, 1992; Commemorative Medal for the 125th Anniversay of Canadian Confederation, 1993; Doctor of Laws, honoris causa, Dalhousie University, 1989. Hobbies: Gardening; Cycling. Address: c/o Symphony Nova Scotia, 1646 Barrington Street, Suite 401, Halifax, Nova Scotia, Canada B3J 2A3.

TIPO Maria, b. 23 Dec 1931, Naples, Italy. Pianist. Education: Studied with her mother, Ersilla Cavallo. Debut: Public piano performance aged four. Career: Many solo engagements from 1949 throughout Europe, USA, Central and South America, Africa, Russia, Japan and the Middle East, including many performances in the United States after discovery by Anton Rubinstein in 1952; Teacher at the Bolzano, Florence and Geneva Conservatories; Performances of works by Clementi, Scarlatti and other Italian composers, Beethoven, Mozart, Schumann, Ravel, Debussy, Chopin, Brahms; Has performed with the Berlin Philharmonic, Vienna Philharmonic, Boston Symphony, London Philharmonic, Koninklijk Concertgebouworkest in Amsterdam, Czech Philharmonic, Orchestre de Paris, Salzburg Mozarteum, La Scala in Milan, S Cecilia in Rome and many others; Chamber music performances with the Amadeus Quartet, Salvatore Accardo and Uto Ughi; Judge at many international competitions; President, Centro Studi Musicali F Busoni. Recordings include: Piano Sonatas by Clementi; Bach's Goldberg Variations; Eighteen Scarlatti Sonatas. Honours: Many awards include: Prize winner at the 1949 Geneva and 1952 Queen Elisabeth of the Belgians Competitions; First Music Critics Prize, 1985; Gargano Award; Ernest Hemingway Award; Personality of the Year Award. Address: c/o Accademia Santa Cecilia, Via Vittoria 6, I-00187 Rome, Italy.

TIPTON Thomas, b. 18 Nov 1926, Wyandotte, MI, USA. Baritone. Education: Studied at Michigan State College with Herbert Swanson and at Ann Arbor with Chase Baromeo. Debut: New York City Opera in 1954 as Bob in The Old Maid and The Thief by Menotti. Career: Sang two seasons in New York, then visited Europe; Sang at Mannheim Opera, 1960-63, Stuttgart, 1964-66, and Bayerisches Staatsoper Munich from 1966; Guest appearances in Vienna, Berlin and Hamburg; Sang at Salzburg Festival, 1964-65, Bayreuth Festival in 1967 as Wotan and the Herald in Lohengrin, and at Covent Garden, 1972-74 as Rigoletto; Other roles included Nabucco and Macbeth; Concert appearances in North and South America. Publications: Thomas Tipton ein Leben in Bildern, Munich, 1987. Address: c/o Bayerisches Staatsoper, Postfach 745, D-8000 Munich 1, Germany.

TIRIMO Martino, b. 19 Dec 1942, Larnaca, Cyprus. Concert Pianist; Conductor. m. Mione J Teakle, 1973, 1 son, 1 daughter. Education: Royal Academy of Music, London; Vienna State Academy. Debut: Recital, Cyprus, 1949. Career: Conducted La Traviata 7 times at Cyprus Festival, 1955; London debut, 1965; Concert performances with most major orchestras, and recitals, TV and radio appearances in Britain, Europe, USA, Canada and South Africa from 1965; Gave public première of complete Schubert Sonatas, London, 1975, 1985; Public première of Beethoven concertos directing from the keyboard, Dresden and London, 1985, 1986; Gave several premières of Tippett Piano concerto since 1986. Recordings: Brahms Piano Concertos; Chopin Concertos; Tippett Piano Concerto (with composer conducting); Rachmaninov Concertos; Complete Debussy piano works; Complete Schubert Piano Sonatas; Various other solo recordings with mixed repertoire. Honours: Gold Medal, Associated Board of the Royal Schools of Music; Liszt Scholarship, Royal Academy of Music; 11 other Prizes at Royal Academy of Music including Macfarren Medal; Boise Foundation Scholarship, 1965; Gulbenkian Foundation Scholarship, 1967-69; Joint Winner, Munich International Competition, 1971; Winner, Geneva International Competition, 1972; ARAM, 1968; FRAM, 1979; Silver Disc, 1988; Gold Disc, 1994. Hobbies: Chess; Theatre; Reading; Philosophy; Badminton. Address: 2 Combemartin Road, London SW18 5PR, England.

TISHCHENKO Boris, b. 23 Mar 1939, Leningrad, USSR. Composer. m. Irene Donskaya 1977, 3 sons. Education: Leningrad with Ustvolskaya Salmanov, Voloshinov and Evlachov; with Logovinsky as a pianist; Later study with Shostakovich. Career: Freelance composer; Pianist; Teacher at Leningrad (later St Petersburg) Conservatory 1965, Assistant Professor 1980, Full Professor at Leningrad Conservatory, 1986. Compositions: Stage: The Twelve, ballet 1963; Fly-bee, ballet 1968; The Stolen Sun, opera 1968; A Cockroach, musical comedy 1968; The Eclipse (Yaroslavna), ballet 1974; Orchestral: 7 Symphonies 2nd Marina with mixed chorus to verses by Tsvetayeva, 1961-1994; 1st Violin Concerto 1958; Piano Concerto 1962; 1st Cello Concerto 1963; Sinfonia Robusta 1970; Concerto for flute, piano and strings 1972; Harp Concerto 1977; 2nd Cello Concerto, 1969; 2nd Violin Concerto 1981; Concerto allamarcia for 16 soloists, 1989; Symphony The Siege Chronicle 1984; Vocal: Lenin is Alive, cantata to verse by Mayakovsky, 1959; Requiem to text by Akhmatova 1966; To my Brother for soprano, flute and harp to verse by Lermontov "The Will", 1986; The Will for soprano, harp and organ to verse by Zabolocky, 1986; Garden of Music, cantana in 2 parts to verses by Kushner, 1987; Chamber music including 5 String Quartets 1957-84; Quintet for strings and piano 1985; 10 Piano sonatas, 1957-97; 2 sonatas for violin solo 1957, 1975; Rondo, Capriccio and Fantasy for Violin and Piano 1956, 1965, 1994; 2 sonatas for cello solo 1960, 1979; Dog Heart, novelettes for chamber ensemble, 1988; Incidental music for plays; Concerto for clarinet and piano trio, 1990; Vocal cycles, Music for films, Orchestral suites; Pieces for different instruments, songs, works for chorus a capella; Egosuite for piano, 1957; The Chelom Wise Men, a vocal instrumental quartet for violin, soprano, bass and piano, Words by O Driz, 1991; Twelve Inventions for organ, 1964; Twelve portraits for organ, 1992; The French Symphony, 1958-93; Eight Portraits for piano in 4 hands, 1996; Orchestrations: Monteverdi, Coronation of Poppea, 1967; Shostakovich, Satires, words by Chorny, 1980; Four Poems by Captain Lebjadkin, words by Dostoevsky, 1986; Antiformalistic Little Paradise, 1989; Grieg: Four Romances, 1991; Mahler: 7 songs, 1993; Prokofiev: 3 choruses, 1972. Honours: 1st prize, on the International Contest of Young Composers in Prague, 1966; State Prize of Russian Federation named by Glinka, 1978; Prize of Mayor of St Petersburg, 1995; The title, People's Artist of Russia, 1987. Membership: Union of Composers of Russian Federation. Hobbies: Reading; Travelling; Walking; Nature. Address: Rimsky-Korsakov Avenue, 79-10, St Petersburg 190121, Russia.

TISNE Antoine, b. 29 November 1932, Lourdes, France. Composer. Education: Studied at the Paris Conservatoire with Riviere and Darius Milhaud, among others. Career: Inspector of Music for the French Ministry of Culture, 1967-92; Inspector for the municipal conservatories of Paris, from 1992; Professor of compositions and orchestration at the Paris Conservatoire. Compositions include: 4 piano concertos, 1959, 1961, 1962, 1992; 4 string quartets, 1956, 1979, 1979, 1989; Cantique de Printemps, 1960; Wind Quintet, 1961; Violin Sonata, 1963; Cosmogonies for 3 orchestras, 1967; Violin Concerto, 1969; Ondes Flamboyantes, for strings, 1973; Impacts for ondes martenots and 2 string orchestras, 1973; Isle de Temps for ondes martenot sextet, 1980; La Ramasseuse de sarments, music theatre, 1982; Instant, ballet, 1985; L'Heure des Hommes, oratorio, 1985; Reliefs iradiants de New York, for orchestra, 1979; Le Chant des Yeux, oratorio, 1986; Les Voiles de la nuit, 1991; De la Nuit et L'Aurore, for oboe and strings, 1991; Le Voix d L'Ombre, for flute and string trio, 1991; Dans la lumiere d'Orcival, for chorus, 1992; Invocation, for baritone and orchestra, 1993. Honours include: Grand Prix Musical of the City of Paris, 1979. Address: c/o SACEM, 225 Avenue Charles de Gaulle, 92521 Neuilly sur Seine Cedex, France.

TITTERINGTON David Michael, b. 10 Jan 1958, Oldham, England. Concert Organist. Education: BA, Honours, 1980, Organ Scholar, 1977-81, Pembroke College, Oxford; Studied under Marie-Claire Alain, Conservatoire National de Rueil-Malmaison, Paris, 1982-85; Debut: Royal Festival Hall in 1986. Career: Recitals in cathedrals and halls throughout UK; Concert tours of Germany, Scandinavia, France, USA, Far East, New Zealand and Australia; Appearances at major international festivals at Hong Kong, Harrogate, Istanbul, Adelaide, Sydney and Brighton; Concert halls include Wigmore Hall, Royal Festival Hall, Munich, Academy for Performing Arts, Hong Kong; TV appearances on BBC 2 and Anglia TV; Professor of Organ, Royal Academy of Music, London, 1990-; Concertos with Berlin Symphony, BBC Symphony Orchestra, City of London Sinfonia and English Sinfonia; Recitals, Concertos and Masterclasses worldwide at major venues and festivals including BBC Proms, Hong Kong, Sydney, New Zealand, Tokyo. Compositions: Messiaen; La Nativite du Seigneur; Eben; Job; Eberlin; Toccatas. Recordings: Messiaen's La Nativité du Seigneur; Over 30 recordings for BBC and networks worldwide. Publications: Edited Works of Petr Eben; Editor, Organ Works. Honours: Joint Winner, Ian Fleming Music Award, 1983; Craxton Memorial Award, 1983; British Council Scholarship, 1983-84; French Government Scholarship, 1983; Arts Counil of Great Britain Bursary, 1984; Premier Prix d'Orgue, 1984; Prix d'Excellence, Conservatoire National de Rueil-Malmaison, Paris, 1985; Honorary Fellow, Bolton Institute of Higher Education, 1992; Honorary Member, Royal Academy of Music, 1994. Memberships: Royal Society of Musicians; Royal Philharmonic Society. Address: c/o Denny Lyster Concert Management, 25 Courthope Road, London NW3 2LE, England.

TITUS Alan, b. 28 Oct 1945, New York City, USA. Baritone. Education: Studied with Askel Schiotz at the Colorado School of Music and with Hans Heinz at Juilliard. Debut: Washington DC in 1969 in La Bohème. Career: Sang the Celebrant in the premiere of Bernstein's Mass at Washington DC, 1971; Sang at New York City Opera in 1972 in Summer and Smoke; European debut at Amsterdam in 1973 in Debussy's Pelléas; Sang at Metropolitan Opera in 1976 as Harlekin in Ariadne auf Naxos, Glyndebourne in 1979 as Guglielmo, Deutsche Oper am Rhein Dusseldorf in 1984 as Don Giovanni, and Santa Fe in 1985 in Strauss's Intermezzo; Engagements at Aix-en-Provence, Hamburg and Frankfurt; Sang at Maggio Musicale Florence in 1987 as Olivier in Capriccio; Sang Dandini at San Francisco in 1987, at Munich as Valentin and sang in Mathis der Maler in 1989, Bologna 1990 as Storch in the Italian premiere of Intermezzo; Sang Kovalyov in The Nose by Shostakovich at Frankfurt in 1990; Season 1992-93 in Arabella at La Scala, the title role in Donizetti's Il Duca d'Alba at Spoleto, and Hans Sachs at Frankfurt; Sang the title role in Hindemith's Mathis der Maler at Covent Garden, 1995; Engaged as Pizarro in Fidelio at Rome, 1996. Recordings include: Haydn's La Feldeltà Premiata; La Bohème; L'Elsir d'Amore; Don Giovanni; La Wally; Le nozze di Figaro; Falstaff; Paradies und die Peri; Genoveva; Carmen. Address: c/o L S Artists, Lydia Störle, Orlando Strasse 8, 8000 München 2, Germany.

TITUS Graham, b. 15 Dec 1949, Newark, Nottinghamshire, England. Baritone. Education: MA, Clare College, Cambridge University (Organ Scholar); FRCO; Cologne Musikhochschule. Debut: Purcell Room, London in 1974. Career: Appearances with New Opera Company, Handel Opera and English National Opera; Radio recitals from 1974 and appearances on Dutch Radio and TV; Concert tour of South America; Recital and oratorio work throughout Britain including the Aldeburgh Festival in 1975 and the Glyndebourne Festival in 1979 as Guglielmo. Honours: Winner of Young Musicians Competition, 1974 and s'Hertogenbosch Competition, 1977. Hobbies: Gardening; Psychic Phenomena. Address: c/o English National Opera, St Martin's Lane, London, WC2, England.

TOCZYSKA Stefania, b. 19 Feb 1943, Gdansk, Poland. Mezzo-Soprano. Education: Gdansk Conservatory with Barbara Iglikovska. Debut: Danzig in 1973 as Carmen. Career: Sang in Poland as Azucena, Leonora in La Favorite and Dalila; Western debut in 1977 as Amneris at Basle Opera; Sang at Vienna Staatsoper in 1977 as Ulrica in Un Ballo in Maschera returning as Carmen and as Verdi's Azucena, Eboli and Preziosilla; Sang at Munich and Hamburg in 1979 as Eboli in Don Carlos, San Francisco Opera as Laura in La Gioconda, Amneris and in Roberto Devereux, Royal Opera Covent Garden, 1983-84 as Azucena and Amneris, Bregenz Festival and Chicago Lyric Opera in 1986 as Giovanna Seymour in Anna Bolena, Houston Opera in 1987 as Adalgisa and Amneris, and Barcelona in 1987 and Hamburg in 1990 as Venus in Tannhäuser; Sang Laura in La Gioconda at the Metropolitan Opera in 1989, at Washington and Houston in 1990 as Amneris and Dalila and appeared in Aida at the Caracalla Festival at Rome in 1990; Season 1992 as Azucena at Munich, Massenet's Dulcinée at Toulouse, Donizetti's Maria Stuarda at Barcelona and Carmen at the Munich Festival; Sang Amneris at the Met, 1997. Address: c/o Harrison/Parrott Ltd, 12 Penzance Place, London, W11 4PA, England.

TODA Kunio, b. 11 Aug 1915, Tokyo, Japan. Composer. Education: Graduated, Tokyo University, 1938, studied composition with Saburo Moroi in Tokyo; Further study of 12-tone technique after the War. Career: Diplomat in the Far East until 1964; Professor at Toho Gakuen School of Music, 1964-76, and Senzoku Gakuen College, 1977-88. Compositions include: Operas: Akemi, Tokyo, 1956, St Paul, mystery play, Tokyo, 1973, The Story of Kyara City, Tokyo, 1973, Anna The Maid, monodrama, Tokyo, 1978, Kesa and Morito, Tokyo, 1980; Orchestra: Legend, symphonic fantasy, 1944, 2 Piano Concertos, 1944 and 1955, Symphony in G, 1953, Concerto Grosso, 1968; Chamber: Piano Trio, 1947, Violin Sonata, 1957, Bassoon Sonata, 1966; Vocal: O'Shichi The Prisoner, mono-cantata, 1981, Song Of Lute for Soprano and Piano, 1982, Song Of River for Mezzo-Soprano, Baritone and Orchestra, 1989; Piano music, choruses and songs. Address: JASRAC, Jasrac House 7-13, 1-Chome Nishishimbashi, Minato-ku, Tokyo 105, Japan.

TODISCO Nunzio, b. 1942, Italy. Tenor. Career: Has sung in Italy and at Orange, Lisbon, Rome and Zurich from 1970; US debut at San Francisco in 1978 as Pollione in Norma; Sang Loris in Fedora at the Metropolitan Opera and in Naples, 1989; Sang at Verona Arena in 1989 as Ismaele in Nabucco; Other roles include Verdi's Carlo in I Masnadieri, Foresto in Attila, Arrigo in La Battaglia di Legnano, Manrico, Ernani and Radames, Puccini's Dick Johnson, Luigi and Cavaradossi and Licinius in La Vestale by Spontini; Sang Ismaele at Verona in 1992. Address: c/o Arena di Verona, Piazza Brà 28, I-37121 Verona, Italy.

TODOROV Nedyalcho (Georgiev), b. 27 Oct 1940, Plovdiv, Bulgaria. Professor. m. Veneta Assenova Todorova, 26 Nov 1967, 1 son, 1 daughter. Education: MA, State Academy of Music, Sofia, 1964; Gnessini State Music Pedagogy Institute, Moscow, 1973-74. Career: Violin Teacher, Secondary School of Music, Plovdiv, 1964-67; Violin Professor, Deputy Rector, 1974-79, Rector, 1979-83, Academy of Music and Dance Art, Plovdiv; Concertmaster, Director, 1970-72, Concertmaster, 1976-79, Plovdiv Philharmony; 1st Violinist, Plovdiv String Quartet, 1978-; Director, Educational Department, Ministry of Culture, Sofia, 1983-91; Recitals, soloist with orchestra, chamber music concerts; Repertoire includes concertos of Bach, Mozart, Beethoven, Mendelssohn, Bruch, Hindemith, Shostakovich, V Stoyanov, sonatas, pieces, duos, trios, quartets. Recordings: Luigi Boccherini: String Quartet Op 33 No 6, A major; Quintet for oboe, violins, viola and violoncello Op 45 No 1, G major, Quintet Op 45 No 2, F major, Quintet Op 45 No 3, D major with Plovdiv String Quartet and Boryu Pamoukchiev, oboe, 1988; 4 concertos for violin, oboe and orchestra: Telemann, C minor, Fasch, D minor, Vivaldi, B flat major, Bach, D minor, soloists: self, violin, Pamoukchiev, oboe, with Jambol Chamber Orchestra, conductor N Sultanov, 1988. Publications: 1st performances, recordings, editions (pieces for violin and piano, duos for 2 violins and chamber ensembles by modern Bulgarian composers), 6 vols, 1977-88; Recordings, editions (collections of classical concertos for oboe and violin), 1990; Bulgarian Violin Literature (editor), catalogue, 1992. Address: Complex Hippodrome, Block 139, Entr A, Apt 33, 1612 Sofia, Bulgaria.

TODOROVIC Nicholas, b. 1965, Christchurch, New Zealand. Singer(Bass-Baritone). Education: University of Canterbury and Queen'sConservatorium of Music. Career: Appearances with Mercury Opera, Auckland as Hermann in The Queen of Spades and Morales in Carmen; Don Giovanni with the Lyric Opera of Queensland and Papageno with Victoria State Opera; British debut as the villains in Les Contes d'Hoffmann, for Stowe Opera; Season 1996-97 as Masetto for Victoria State Opera and Johnny Dowd in the premiere of Summer of the Seventeenth Doll by Richard Mills, at the Melbourne International Arts Festival; Masetto in Don Giovanni for Auckland Opera (with Kiri Te Kanewa) and Schaunard in La Bohème at Melbourne; Resident in Britain. Address: C&M Craig Services Ltd, 3 Kersley Street, London SW11 4PR, England.

TOFFOLUTTI Ezio, b. 1941, Venice, Italy. Stage Designer. Education: Studied set design and art at the Accademia delle Belle Arti, Venice. Career: Designer at the Volksbuhne, Berlin, 1971-79; Collaboration with such opera producers as Harry Kupfer, Johannes Schaaf and Jerome Savary (Rossini's Le Comte Ory at the 1997 Glyndebourne Festival, also televised); Engagements also include Rigoletto in Berlin, Die Meistersinger at La Scala, and Idomeneo at the Salzburg Festival; Grand Theatre, Geneva, with Così fan tutte and at the Palais Garnier, Paris; Season 1997-98 with Il Matriomonio Segreto in Vienna and Die Entführung aus dem Serail at Trieste. Address: c/o Grand Theatre de Geneve, 11 Boulevard de Theatre, CH-1211 Geneva 11, Switzerland.

TOIVANEN Heikki, b. 1947, Mikkeli, Finland. Singer (Bass). m. Ingrid Haubold. Education: Studied at the Sibelius Adacemy, Helsinki, and in Germany. Career: Sang at the Finnish National Opera, 1973-74, Wuppertal, 1974-76, and Karlsruhe, 1977-84; Bayreuth Festival, 1977-78, as Fasolt and Titurel; Guest appearances throughout Europe and in South America; Many concert engagements. Address: Staatstheater Karlsruhe, Baumeisterstrasse 11, Pf 1449, W-7500 Karlsruhe, Germany.

TOKODY Ilona, b. 27 Apr 1953, Szeged, Hungary. Soprano. Career: Has sung at the Hungarian National Opera from 1973; Engaged at Bratislava and the Vienna Staatsoper from 1978; Further appearances in Munich, Hamburg, Leningrad, Moscow, Prague, Naples, Barcelona and Cologne; Covent Garden debut in 1986 as Mimi; Sang at San Diego in 1986 as Desdemona and at Los Angeles in 1989, and Boston in 1989 as Mimi; Other roles include Violetta, Tosca, Asteria in Boito's Nerone, Rachel in La Juive, Suor Angelica, Giselda in I Lombardi, Leonora in Il Trovatore and La Forza del Destino and Puccini's Lauretta, Liu and Butterfly; Sang the Trovatore Leonora at Madrid in 1992. Recordings include: Suor Angelica; Nerone; La Fedeltà Premiata by Haydn; Strauss's Guntram; Erkel's Hunyadi Laszlo; Respighi's La Fiamma; Mascagni's Iris. Address: c/o Allied Artists, 42 Montpelier Square, London, SW7 1JZ, London, England.

TOKOS Zoltan, b. 13 November 1952, Cluj, Romania. Classical Guitarist; Professor. div, 1 son. Education: Conservatory G Dima, Cluj; Liszt Ferenc Academy, Budapest; Conservatory in Athens, Greece. Debut: Romanian Television, aged 8 years. Career: Radio and Television Appearances in Romania, Hungary, Spain, England; Concerts Worldwide. Compositions: B Bartok, Romanian Folk Dances; Turina, 5 Gipsy Dances; Milhaud, Scaramouche; Turina, Miniaturas. Recordings: The Entire Quintets of Boccherini; Music Around the World. Honours: Various 1st Prizes in Romania; Honorable Mention, Barcelona, 1981. Membership: Hungarian Musical Society. Hobbies: Flamenco; Jazz; Astronomy. Address: Bayczy Koz 3 V 1, 1065 Budapest, Hungary.

TOLL John, b. 1947, England. Conductor; Organist; Harpsichordist. Career: Keyboard Player and Repertoire Researcher for the Bournemouth Symphony Orchestra and Bournemouth Sinfonietta; Founder-Member of London Baroque visiting 20 countries; Regular appearances with the Taverner Players, London Classical Players and the Academy of Ancient Music; Director of Early Music Department, Royal Academy of Music; As member of Musica Secreta has performed at the Early Music Centre Festival, the Lufthansa Festival of Baroque Music and at the National Gallery; Early Music Network tour of Britain in 1991 with programme, Filiae Jerusalem, sacred music for women's voices by Monteverdi, Carissimi, Cavalli, Viadana, Grandi and Marco de Gagliano; Other repertoire includes works by Marenzio, Wert, Luzzaschi, Luigi Rossi and the women composers Francesca Caccini and Barbara Strozzi; Participation in lecture-recitals and workshops on performance practice and ornamentation; Conducted Kent Opera in Monteverdi's Orfeo at South Bank, London, 1997. Recordings include: 15 albums with London Baroque.

TOMAS Edward, b. 5 Apr 1960, Prague, Czechoslovakia. Singer; Composer; Vocal Arranger. 1 son. Education: Prague Conservatory; Academy of Musical Arts. Debut: Singer/Soloist, Army Artistic Group, jazz big band. Career: Performances: Music theatre, Karlin, Prague; Funny Girl; Some Like It Hot; TV Shows with DVQ, The Good Evening Quintet; Leader and Singer, 5 Vocals a cappella group. Compositions: Songs with DVQ: Smula; I'm Forgiving. Recordings: LP: ET, 1988; CDs: Manhattan Cocktail, with DVQ, 1989; J+V+W, with DVQ, 1990; Classical Music: Krystof Harant, 2 Polaio a Dezdruzie, 1993; DVQ Live, Ten Year Anniversary; Profile DVQ, 1997. Honour: Jury Prize, Vokaliza Festival, 1986. Hobbies: Sport; Cars. Current Management: Edward Tomas Productions. Address: Za'hrebska 44, 120 00 Prague, Czech Republic.

TOMASSON Tomas, b. 1968, Iceland. Singer (Bass). Education: Studied at the Reykjavik College of Music and the Royal College of Music Opera School, London. Career: Sang at first with Icelandic Opera, as Sparafucile (Rigoletto), Mozart's Sarastro and Lodovico in Otello; Further engagements as Arasse in Handel's Siroe at the RCM, the Commendatore at Valencia, Masetto at Covent Garden (1996) and in Copenhagen, Colline in La Bohème at the Royal Albert Hall (1997) and Pimen in Boris Godunov at Turin; Further Handel roles include Cadmus and Somnus in Semele at the Berlin Staatsoper, and Christian in Rinaldo at Geneva; Concerts include Haydn's Nelson Mass, Mozart's Coronation Mass and Requiem, Tippett's A Child of our Time with the Icelandic SO, Bach's St Matthew Passion at the UK Handel Festival and Verdi's Requiem at the Mayfield Festival. Address: c/o Athole Still Ltd, Foresters Hall, 25-27 Westow St, London SE19 3RY, England.

TOMASZEWSKI Rolf, b. 18 Mar 1940, Deutzen, Leipzig, Germany. Bass Singer. Education: Studied in Dresden with Johannes Kemter. Debut: Wittenberg in 1959 as Baculus in Lortzing's Der Wildschütz. Career: Teacher until 1971 then sang in opera at Dresden-Radebeul, 1971-75; Performances at the Dresden Staatsoper and elsewhere in Germany from 1975 as Sarastro, Osmin, the Commendatore, Don Alfonso, Kaspar in Der Freischütz, the Landgrave in Tannhäuser, King Henry in Lohengrin and buffo roles; Many concert appearances. Address: c/o Semper-Oper, Dresden 01067, Germany.

TOMLINSON John, b. 22 Sept 1946, Oswaldtwistle, Lancashire, England. Operatic Bass. m. Moya Joel, 1969, 1 son, 2 daughters. Education: BSc, Civil Engineering, Manchester University, England; Royal Manchester College of Music. Career: Since beginning career with Glyndebourne in 1970 has sung over 100 operatic bass roles with English National Opera and Covent Garden and in Geneva, Lisbon, Milan, Paris, Stuttgart, San Diego, Vancouver (Hagen and Hunding), San Francisco, Bordeaux, Aix-en-Provence, Avignon and Copenhagen; English National Opera from 1975 as Masetto, Wagner's Pogner, Fasolt and Mark, Bartók's Bluebeard, Rossini's Moses, Mephistopheles, Padre Guardiano and Baron Ochs; Bayreuth Festival in 1988 as Wotan in Das Rheingold and Die Walküre; Sang the Wanderer in Siegfried in 1989; Opera North in 1991 as Attila, Covent Garden in 1991 as Hagen and as the Green Knight in the premiere of Birtwistle's Gawain and sang in the Reginald Goodall Memorial Concert in London, 1991; Season 1992-93 as Boris Godunov for Opera North, Wotan and Wanderer at Bayreuth and Gurnemanz at the Berlin Staatsoper; Season 1993-94 as Hans Sachs at Covent Garden, Baron Ochs for ENO and Wotan in a new production of The Ring at Bayreuth; Videos of The Ring from Bayreuth; Returned to English National Opera for Ochs, 1997. Recordings: Roles in Donizetti's Maria Stuarda, Handel's Hercules, Rameau's Nais, Thomas' Hamlet, Martinu's Greek Passion and Verdi's Macbeth. Address: c/o Music International, 13 Ardilaun Road, Highbury, London, N5 2QR, England.

TOMOWA-SINTOW Anna, b. 22 Sept 1943, Stara Zagora, Bulgaria. Soprano. Education: Studied at the Sofia Conservatory with Zlatew Tscherkin. Debut: Stara Zagora as Tatiana in Eugene Onegin. Career: Sang at Leipzig in 1967 as Abigaille in Nabucco, Berlin in 1972 as Butterfly becoming member of the company, 1972-76; Discovered by Karajan and sang in the premiere of De Temporum Fine Comoedia by Orff at Salzburg in 1973; Appearances at Milan, Brussels, Munich, San Francisco and at Covent Garden London in her debut in 1975 as Fiordiligi; Sang at Salzburg Easter and Summer Festivals in 1976 as Elsa and Countess Almaviva, Vienna Staatsoper from 1977, Metropolitan Opera from 1978 as Donna Anna, Elsa and Aida, the Marschallin and Amelia Boccanegra, Salzburg in 1983 as the Marschallin, Paris Opéra in 1984 as Elisabeth in Tannhäuser, and Salzburg, 1987-89 as Donna Anna and Tosca; Sang in Der Rosenkavalier at Florence in 1989 and Chicago in 1990; Appeared as Yaroslavna in a new production of Prince Igor at Covent Garden in 1990; Season 1992-93 as Tosca at Helsinki and Strauss's Helen in Athens; Sang Ariadne at Lisbon, 1996. Recordings: Beethoven's 9th Symphony and Missa Solemnis; Verdi's Requiem; Ein Deutsches Requiem; De Temporum Fine Comoedia; Don Giovanni; Der Rosenkavalier; Mozart's Requiem and Coronation Mass; Bruckner's Te Deum and Lohengrin; Le nozze di Figaro; Ariadne auf Naxos; Die Frau ohne Schatten from Covent Garden, 1992; Capriccio from Salzburg, Barcelona, Berlin and Vienna, 1985, 1986, 1990; Also recordings with H von Karajan, 4 Last Songs and Capriccio by Strauss; Korngold, Das Wunder der Heliane. Honours: Prizewinner, International Competition, Sofia, 1970; Winner, Rio de Janeiro Competition, 1971; Made Kammersängerin in Berlin. Address: Teatro Nacional de Sao Carlos, Rua Serpa Pinto 9, 1200 Lisboa, Portugal

TOMTER Lars Anders, b. 30 Nov 1959. Violist. 1 daughter. Education: Piano, 5 years, Violin, 8 years, Violin and Viola, Conservatory, 13 years, Max Rostal Bern Conservatory, 3 years, Sandorvegh, Mozarteum, Salzburg, 2years. Career: Solo Performances, USA, Germany, Vienna, Scandinavia, Madrid, Budapest, Frankfurt, Cologne, Paris, London; Performer with Orchestras as Academy of St Martins-in-the-Fields, City of Birmingham Symphony Orchestra, Frankfurt Radio Symphony Orchestra, Philharmonic Orchestra of Frankfurt, Hungarian National Philharmonic Orchestra, Los Angeles Chamber Orchestra, Oslo Philharmonic Orchestra, Bergen Philharmonic Orchestra, Danish Radio Symphony Orchestra, Stockholm New Chamber Orchestra, Gavleborg Symphony, Norwegian Radio Symphony Orchestra, Trondheim Symphony Orchestra, Stavanger Symphony Orchestra; Proms debut with RPO, 1998; Artistic Director, Risar Chamber Music Festival. Recordings: Walton Concertos; Franck and Vieuxtemps Sonates; Sinfonia Concertante with Norwegian Chamber Orchestra and Jana Brown; Schumann and Brahms Sonatas with Pianist Leif Ove Andsnes. Honours: Numerous awards and prizes. Hobbies: Swimming; Reading; Cookery. Address: c/o Martin Muller, Vintrup 4, 59320 Ennigerloh Ostenfelde, Germany.

TONE Yasunao, b. 31 March 1935, Tokyo, Japan (American Citizen). Composer; Multimedia Artist. Education: Studied literature at the Japanese National University, Chiba (1957); Tokyo University of the Arts. Career: Founded performance group Ongaku at Tokyo, 1960; Wrote tape pieces Geography, and Music performed by Merle Cunningham Dance Company; Settled in New York 1972, participating in avant garde and computer music festivals in North America and Europe, FLUXUS festivals 1979-87 and Venice Biennale (1990). Compositions include: Intermedia Art Festival, 1969; Multi Performance, 1972; Voice and Phenomenon, 1976; The Wall and the Books, 1982; Word of Mouth, 1988. Publications include: Can Art be Thought, 1970. Honours include: New York Foundation for the Arts Fellowship, 1987. Address: c/o ASCAP, ASCAP Building, One Lincoln Plaza, New York, NY 10023, USA.

TOOLEY John (Sir), b. 1 Jun 1924, Rochester, Kent, England. Theatre Administrator. m. (1) Judith Craig Morris, 1951, dissolved, 1965, 3 daughters, (2) M Patricia Janet Norah Bagshawe, 1968, 1 son. Education: Repton School; Magdalene College, Cambridge. Career: Served in the Rifle Brigade, 1943-47; Secretary to the Guildhall School of Music, 1952-55; Assistant to General Administrator, 1955-60, Assistant General Administrator, 1960-70, General Administrator, 1970-80, General Director, 1980-87, Royal Opera House, Covent Garden, London; Governor, The Royal Ballet and The Royal Ballet School, also Repton School; Director, Royal Opera House Trust. Honours: Commendatore, Italian Republic, 1976; Knighted by Her Majesty in The Queen's Birthday Honours List, 1979; Honorary Fellow, Royal Academy of Music and Honorary Member, Guildhall School of Music and the Royal Northern College of Music. Memberships: Garrick Club; Arts. Hobbies: Walking; Theatre. Address: 2 Mart Street, London, WC2, England.

TOOVEY Andrew, b. 1962, England. Composer. Education: Studied at the Universities of Surrey and Sussex with Jonathan Harvey and at Dartington with Morton Feldman. Career: Music has been performed by Alan Hacker, Michael Finnissy, the Mistry Quartet and the Endimion Ensemble; Director of Ixion, founded in 1987, giving performances of works by Cage, Feldman, Ferneyhough, Finnissy, James Dillon and Xenakis. Compositions: Chamber and ensemble: Winter Solstice, 1984, String Quartet, 1985, Cantec for Viola and Piano, 1986, Ate, 1986, Shining for Violin and Cello, 1987, Shining Forth, 1987, Shimmer Bright for String Trio, 1988, White Fire, 1988, Snow Flowers, 1988, Black Light, 1989, An Die Musik, 1989, Adam, 1989; Solo instruments: Veiled Wave 1 and 2, for Flute and Clarinet, 1985, Artaud for Piano, 1986, Fragments After Artaud, 1988, Lament, Strathspey, reel for Violin, 1988, Out Jumps Jack Death and Down There By The Sea for Piano, 1989, UBU, opera in 2 acts (five scenes), 1990-92, The Juniper Tree, opera in one act (4 scenes), 1993. Recordings include: Artaud; Out Jumps Jack Death. Honours include: Tippett Prize for Untitled String Quartet; Terra Nova Prize for Ate; Bernard Shore Composition Award for Cantec; Young Concert Artists Trust Associate Composer, 1993-. Address: 57B Station Road, Willesden, London, NW10 4UX, England.

TÖPPER Hertha, b. 19 Apr 1924, Graz, Austria. Mezzo-Soprano. Education: Studied at the Graz Conservatory. Debut: Graz in 1945 as Ulrica in Un Ballo in Maschera. Career: Sang in Graz, 1945-51, at Munich Staatsoper from 1951 notably in the 1957 premiere of Hindemith's Die Harmonie der Welt, at Bayreuth Festival from 1951 as Brangaene and Fricka and visited Covent Garden with the Munich Company in 1953 as Clairon in Capriccio; Sang at San Francisco in 1960 and Metropolitan Opera in 1962 as Octavian in Der Rosenkavalier, and at Munich in 1972 in the premiere of Isang Yun's Sim Tjong; Other roles included Verdi's Eboli and Amneris, Mozart's Dorabella, Magdalena in Die Meistersinger and Nancy in Martha; Retired from stage in 1981; Often heard in sacred music by Bach; Professor at the Munich Musikhochschule from 1971. Recordings: Die Meistersinger; Bluebeard's Castle; Oedipus Rex; Schoenberg's Gurrelieder; Bach's B minor Mass; Der Rosenkavalier. Address: c/o Bayerische Staatsoper, Postfach 745, D-8000 Munich 1, Germany.

TORADZE Alexander, b. 1955, Tblisi, Georgia. Pianist. Education: Graduated the Tchaikovsky Conservatory Moscow 1978. Career: Resident in the USA from 1983, giving concerts in every major centre and appearing with such conductors as Ashkenazy, Dutoit, Eschenbach, Masur, Mehta, Ozawa and Rattle; European engagements with the Kirov Orchestra (under Valery Gergiev) Rotterdam PO, London Symphony and Philharmonic, CBSO and Philharmonia Orchestra; Season 1997 with the Los Angeles PO under Esa-Pekka Salonen, Toronto SO under Jukka-Pekka Saraste, the Orchestra National de France and the Rotterdam PO under Gergiev; Festival appearances at the London Proms, Hollywood Bowl, St Petersburg White Nights, Saratoga and Schleswig-Holstein; From 1991, Martin Endowed Professor in Piano at Indiana University South Bend. Recordings include: Prokofiev's 7th Sonata, Ravel's Miroirs, Three Movements from Petrushka, Pictures at an Exhibition, Gaspard de la Nuit (EMI/Angel); Prokofiev Concertos, with the Kirov Orchestra and Gergiev (Philips Classics). Address: c/o Lies Askonas Ltd, 6 Henrietta St, London WC2E 8LA, England.

TORCHINSKY Yuri, b. 1949, Kharkov, Ukraine. UK resident from 1991. Violinist. 1 son. Education: Tchaikovsky Conservatory Moscow, 1975-80; Postgraduate Conservatory Assistant, 1980-83. Debut: Brahms Violin Concerto with the Kharkov

Philharmonic Orchestra conducted by Vakhtang Gordania. Career: Leader of the Bolshoi Theatre in Moscow with numerous performances, concerts and tours, as soloist and orchestra leader, worldwide including the Metropolitan Opera in New York and at many opera theatres and concert halls in USA, Italy, Austria, France, Holland, Germany, Japan and elsewhere; Radio appearances with recitals in Moscow and on TV in Yugoslavia; Several appearances at the Albert Hall in London, TV and radio recordings of Promenade Concerts performance, at the Barbican Hall, Royal Festival Hall, New Symphony Hall and Town Hall in Birmingham; Many concerts and radio and CD recordings as guest leader of London Symphony Orchestra as well as tours to France, Switzerland, Austria, Portugal and Italy; Solo appearances at Royal Opera House, 1995; Guest Leader with such orchestras as BBC Welsh, Philharmonia, Royal Philharmonic, and BBC Manchester; Leader of the Royal Ballet Symphonia Orchestra of the Birmingham Royal Ballet. Contributions to: Strad, 1992; The Birmingham Post, 1992; The Guardian, 1994; The Times, 1995. Honours: First and Special Prizewinner, Vaclav Huml International Competition, Zagreb, 1981; 2nd Prize, International Competition, Tokyo, 1983. Memberships: Musicians Union. Hobbies: Snooker; Gardening. Address: 14 Ellery Road, Upper Norwood, London, SE19 3QG, England.

TORKE Michael, b. 22 Sep 1961, Milwaukee, WI, USA. Composer; Pianist. Education: Graduated from Eastman School of Music, Rochester, 1984. Career: Commissions from New York City Ballet and The Huddersfield Festival; European performances with the Danish Radio Symphony Orchestra, the Ensemble InterContemporain, London Sinfonietta and Lontano; As Pianist has recorded on several labels. Compositions: Laetus for Piano Solo, 1982; Ceremony Of Innocence for Flute, Clarinet, Violin, Cello and Piano, 1983; Ecstatic Orange for Ensemble, 1984; Vanada for Keyboards, Brass and Percussion, 1984; The Yellow Pages, 1984; Bright Blue Music for Ensemble, 1985; Verdant Music for Ensemble, 1986; The Directions, one act opera based on The Yellow Pages, 1986; Adjustable Wrench for Ensemble, 1987; Black And White for Wind Instruments, Percussion and Synthesizer, 1988; Copper for Brass Quintet and Orchestra, 1988; Ash for Orchestra or Chamber Orchestra, 1989; Slate, ballet for Concertante Group and Orchestra, 1989; Rust for Piano and Wind Instruments, 1989; Run for orchestra 1992; Four Proverbs for voice and ensemble 1993. Honours: Prix de Rome; Koussevitsky Foundation Award. Address: c/o Boosey and Hawkes Ltd, 295 Regent Street, London, W1R 8JH, England.

TORRES Jesús, b. 15 July 1965, Zaragoza, Spain. Composer. m. Eva Sanz, 24 Sept 1993. Education: Bachiller Superior; Conservatory of Madrid, completing studies in 1986; Several Musical Analysis seminars with Luis de Pablo; Composition with Francisco Guerrero, 1986-88. Career: Festival Nuove Sincronie; International Society for Contemporary Music World Music Days; Gaudeamus Music Week; Ensemblia Festival; Festival de Alicante. Compositions: Vispera de mi; Preludios; Itzal; Piano Concerto; Masques; Unidad en Ella; Trio. Honours: Premio SGAE, 1992; Gaudeamus Prize, 1995; Finalist, Nuove Sincronie, Irino Prize, Ensemblia, others. Memberships: Sociedad General de Autores. Address: Calle Oxigeno 9, 3o F, Torrejón de Ardoz 28850, Madrid, Spain.

TORRES-SANTOS Raymond, b. 19 June 1958, Puerto Rico. Composer; Arranger; Keyboardist; Conductor; Music Educator. Education: BA, Puerto Rico University and Conservatory of Music, 1980; MA 1982, PhD 1986, University of California, Los Angeles; Ferienkurse fur Neue Musik, 1982; CCRMA, Stanford University, 1985; Centro di Sonologia Computazionale, Padva University, Italy, 1988. Career: Arranger, Music Director, for best American singers and entertainers; Composer of film music, studio musician in Hollywood; Professor, California State University, San Bernardino, 1986-91; Chairman of Music Department, University of Puerto Rico, 1991-93; Chancellor, Puerto Rico Conservatory of Music, 1994-. Compositions include: Sinfonietta Concertante for Orchestra, 1980; Summertime, Clarinet Consort, 1982; Exploraciones for String Orchestra, 1982; Areytos: a Symphonic Picture, 1985; Enchanted Island, Piano and Tape, 1986; Monchin del Alma: Ballet, 1988; El Pais de los Cuatro Pisos: A Symphonic Overture, 1988; Viaggio Senza Destinazione for Tape, 1988; Danza for Orchestra, 1991; La Cancion de la Antillas: A Symphonic Poem, 1992; Fantasia Caribena, for Orchestra, 1992; Salsa y tres Sones, for piano or harp solo; Requiem for Mezzo-Soprano, Baritone, Mixed Chorus, Children's Choir and Orchestra, 1995; Concerto Grosso for clarinet, French horn, piano, percussion and strings, 1997; Performed and/or commissioned by the Casals Festival, Vienna Philharmonic, New Jersey Chamber Music Society, Continuum, Bronx Arts Ensemble, Quintet of the Americas, Paquito d'Rivera, Inter-American University, Youth Symphony of the Americas, San Juan Ballet and Pops Orchestra; Symphony Orchestra from Puerto Rico, Virginia, Pacific, Northwestern University and University of California at Los Angeles. Recordings: 25 as Arranger and/or Conductor. Address: P O Box 361743, San Juan, Puerto Rico 00936-1743, USA.

TORTELIER Yan Pascal, b. 19 Apr 1947, Paris, France. Conductor. m. Sylvie Burnet-Moret, 1970, 2 sons. Education: Paris Conservatoire, general musical studied with Nadia Boulanger; Conducting studies with Franco Ferrara. Career: Has conducted all major British orchestras and toured extensively in the USA, Canada, Japan, Australia, Scandinavia, Eastern and Western Europe; Leader and Associate Conductor, Orchestre du Capitole in Toulouse, 1974-83; Opera debut, 1978; Principal Conductor and Artist Director, Ulster Orchestra, Northern Ireland, 1989-92; Principal Conductor, BBC Philharmonic, 1992-; Conducted Stravinsky-Lutoslawski concert at York University, 1997. Recordings: Numerous including complete symphonic works of Debussy and Ravel with Ulster Orchestra and highly acclaimed series of Hindemith and Henri Dutilleux with BBC Philharmonic; Several labels. Publication: Première orchestration of Ravel's Piano Trio, 1992. Honours: Honorary Doctor of Letters, University of Ulster, 1992. Current Management: IMG, Chiswick, England. Address: c/o IMG, Media House, 3 Burlington Lane, Chiswick, London W4 2TH, England.

TORZEWSKI Marek, b. 1960, Poland. Singer (Tenor). Education: Studied at the Poznan Academy of Music. Debut: Lodz Opera 1984 as Edgardo in Lucia di Lammermoor. Career: Sang in Idomeneo at the Théatre de la Monnaie Brussels, 1984; Appearances in La Finta Giardiniera at Vienna, Salzburg, Amsterdam, Berlin and New York, 1985; Further engagements at Brussels and in Hamburg, Montpellier, Philadelphia and Lausanne; Season 1989-90 in L'Incoronazione di Poppea in Paris, Rosenkavalier, Così fan tutte and Fierabras by Schubert in Brussels, Don Ottavio at Toulouse and Glyndebourne Festival debut as Fenton in Falstaff; Season 1991-92 as Tamino at Lausanne, Alfredo for Scottish Opera and the Mozart Requiem under Muti at La Scala, Milan; Debut with the Berlin Philharmonic 1992, singing in Nono's Il Canto Sospeso, under Abbado; Opera National de Lisbon, Eugene Onegin - Lensky, Staatsoper Leipzig, Così fan Tutte - Ferrando, 1993; Théatre Municipal de Lausanne, Iphigénie en Tauride - Pylade, 1994. Recordings include: Il Canto Sospeso (Deutsche Grammophon). Address: c/o Harold Holt Ltd, 31 Sinclair Road, London W14 0NS, England.

TOSHEV Todor Stoikov, b. 24 November 1919, Popovo, Bulgaria. Musician. m. Nadejda, 22 April 1946, 1 son, 1 daughter. Education: Sofia Musical Academy, 1948; Postgraduate, Prague Academy of Music, 1950. Debut: Prague, 1951. Career: A Numer of Television Discussions and Concerts, 1971-72; Many Records in the Golden Fund of Bulgarian National Radio, Concert Kossevitsky, Botessini. Compositions: Contrabass Plays: Nokturno, Elegia, Romance, Intermezo. Recordings: Contrabass Plays: Nokturno, Elegia, Romance, Intermezo. Publications: Contrabass School for Beginners - Pt 1 & 2, 1954-92; Technical Excercises, 1954-92; Transcriptions, 1954-92. Contributions to: International Society of Bassists, USA; Finnish Double Bass Society. Honours: Highest Medal for Culture in Bulgaria, 1982; First Bassist with Academic Rank in Bulgaria. Memberships: International Society of Bassists, USA; Sibelius Academy, Finland; Honourary Member, Finnish Bass Society. Address: c/o Mladost 4, bl 468, et 2, ap 44, 1715 Sofia, Bulgaria.

TOTENBERG Roman, b. 1 Jan 1911, Lodz, Poland. Violinist; Conductor. m. 30 July 1941, 3 daughters. Education: Baccalaureat, Warsaw; Chopin School, Warsaw; Chpin School of Music Diploma, Warsaw, Gold Medal, 1929; Hochschule fur Musik with Carl Flesch, Berlin, Mendelssohn Prize, 1932; Paris Institut Instrumentale with Georges Enesco, 1933. Career: Soloist with most major orchestras, Europe, USA, South America; Formerly Director Chamber Music radio station WQXR New York and Director of Longy School, Cambridge, Massachusetts; Professor of Music, Boston University, 1962-; Summers: Kneisel Hall Blue Hill, Maine, 1975-; Formerly Music Academy of the West, Salzburg Mozarteum, Berkshire Music Centre and Aspen Festival. Recordings: Brahms and Lipinski Concertos, Titanic, 1990; Beethoven and Szymanowski Concertos, VGR, 1992; Bloch Concerto, Vanguard, 1992; All Bach Sonatas and Partitas, Schuman Sonatas, German Baroque Concerti, Musical Heritage. Contributions to: Various publications including Gustave Reese Compendium. Honours: Ysaÿe Medal, 1966; Wieniwski Medal, 1976; Artist of the Year (American String Society), 1982; Medal of Cultural Contribution to Poland, Polish Government, 1989. Membership: St Botolph Club, Boston. Hobbies: Photography; Sports; Chess. Current Management: Walter Pierce (Wang Centre), Boston, USA. Address: 329 Waverley Avenue, Newton, MA 02158, USA.

TOWER Joan (Peabody), b. 6 Sep 1938, New Rochelle, NY, USA. Composer; Pianist; Teacher. Education: BA, Bennington College, 1961; MA, 1964, DMA, 1978, Columbia University. Career: Co-founder and Pianist of Da Capo Chamber Players, NY, 1969-84; Faculty, Bard College, Annandale on Hudson, 1972-; Composer-in-Residence, St Louis Symphony Orchestra, 1985-87. Compositions include: Orchestral: Sequoia, 1980; Island Rhythms, 1985, Concerto for Flute and Orchestra, 1989, Concerto for Orchestra, 1991, Violin Concerto, 1992, Stepping Stones, ballet, 1993, Duets for Chamber Orchestra, 1995; Chamber: Percussion Quartet, 1963, revised 1969, Breakfast Rhythms I and II, 1974-75, Petroushskates, 1980, String Quartet, Night Fields, 1994, Fifth Fanfare for The Uncomman Woman for 4 Trumpets, 1994; Solo Instruments: Wings for solo clarinet, Hexachords for Solo Flute, 1972, Fantasy...Harbour Lights, for clarinet and piano, 1983, Elegy for Trombone and String Quartet, 1994, Tres Lent for Cello and Piano, 1994. Recordings include: CDs: Platinum Spirals with violinist Joel Smirnoff, Cello Concerto, with Lynn Harrell on Cello, Clarinet Concerto with Robert Spring and Eckhart Selheim, and Chamber Works, 1995; Island Rhythms with Louisville Orchestra; Clocks with Sharon Isbin on guitar; Silver Ladders, Fanfare for The Uncommon Woman with St Louis Symphony. Honours: Guggenheim Fellowship, 1976; National Endowment for the Arts Fellowships, 4 times; Koussevitzky Foundation Grant, 1982; American Academy and Institute of Arts and Letters Award, 1983; Grawemeyer Award in Composition, 1990. Address: c/o Music Department, Bard College, Annandale on Hudson, NY 12504, USA.

TOWNSEND Douglas, b. 8 Nov 1921, New York City, USA. Composer; Writer; Musicologist. Education: High School of Music and Art, New York City; Composition Teachers: Stefan Wolpe; Tibor Serly; Aaron Copland, Tanglewood, 1947; Otto Luening, Summers, 1948, 1949. Compositions include: Ballet Suite, for 3 Clarinets; Duo for Violas; 4 Fantasies on American Folk Songs; 2 Chamber Symphonies; 2 String Symphonies; 4 Chamber Concertos; Rag for Piano 4 hands and orchestra; Tower Music, for brass quintet; (Recorded): Chamber Concertos 2 & 3; Suite No 1 for Strings; Fantasy on Motives of Bacharach; Two Madrigals. Publications: Chamber Symphony No 1, Chamber Concerto No 2, 5 Madrigals, also many publications of music discovered and edited by Townsend; Hundreds of notes for record jackets including 50,000 words on Complete Piano Music of Schumann. Honours: Research Commission, New York State Bicentennial Revolution Committee, 1975; Research, New York State Council on the Arts, 1976; Composition, National Endowment on the Arts, 1981. Address: 72-28 153 St, Flushing, NY 11367, USA.

TOWSE David, b. 1956, Bridlington, England. Violinist. Education: Studied piano and violin from 1961; Royal College of Music from 1974 with Leonard Hirsch, Peter Element and Herbert Howells. Career: Leader of the East Riding County Youth Orchestra and British Youth Symphony Orchestra, 1972; Leader of the London Youth String Ensemble while at the Royal College of Music; Freelance in and around London before joining the Royal Philharmonic Orchestra in 1978 and Associate Leader, 1982; Performances of Piano Quintets and Quartets with the Forellen Ensemble (members of the RPO) at music clubs and festivals throughout Britain from 1978. Address: c/o Royal Philharmonic Orchestra, 16 Clerkenwell Green, London EC1R 0DP, England.

TOZZI Giorgio, b. 8 Jan 1923, Chicago, Illinois, USA. Singer (Bass). Education: Studied with Rosa Raisa, Giacomo Rimini and John Daggert Howell. Debut: Tarquinus in The Rape of Lucretia, on Broadway, 1948. Career: Studied further in Italy and sang Rodolfo in La Sonnambula at the Teatro Nuovo Milan, 1950; La Scala 1953, in La Wally by Catalani; Metropolitan Opera from 1955, as Alvise (La Gioconda), Sparafucile, Pimen, Boris Godonov, Mozart's Figaro, Daland, Pogner, Sachs, Rocco and Philip II; Created the Doctor in Barber's Vanessa (1958); San Francisco from 1955, as Ramfis, Calkas in Troilus and Cressida and Archibaldo (L'Amore dei tre Re); Salzburg Festival 1958, 1961 in Vanessa and as Fiesco in Simon Boccanegra; Hollywood Bowl 1956, in the US premiere of David by Milhaud; La Scala 1962, in a revival of Les Huguenots; Appearances in Florence, Palermo, Hamburg, Frankfurt, Lisbon and Munich as Sarastro, Padre Guardiano, Don Giovanni, Gurnemanz, Arkel and Gremin; Boston Opera 1977, in the US premiere of Ruslan and Ludmilla by Glinka; Active in films, television and musical comedy. Recordings: Rigoletto, Guillaume Tell (Cetra); Der fliegende Holländer, Vanessa, La Forza del Destino, Aida, La Bohème, Le nozze di Figaro, Luisa Miller (RCA); Il Trovatore, La Fanciulla del West, Rigoletto (Decca). Address: c/o Opera Company of Boston Inc, PO Box 50, Boston, MA 02112, USA.

TRACEY Edmund, b. 14 Nov 1927, Preston, England. Translator; Administrator; Librettist. Career: Music Critic for The Observer 1958-65; Sadler's Wells (later English National Opera) Director from 1965, as dramaturg and repertory planner; Translated for ENO such texts as Les contes d'Hoffmann 1970, Aida, 1978 and Manon, 1979; La Finta Giardiniera by Mozart for English Music Theatre at Sadler's Wells, 1976; Librettist for Malcolm Williamson's Lucky-Peter's Journey (after Strindberg), Sadler's Wells 1969. Address: English National Opera, St Martin's Lane, London WC2, England.

TRACK Gerhard, b. 17 Sept 1934, Vienna, Austria. Conductor; Composer. m. Micaela Maihart, 3 Aug 1958, 2 sons. Education: Music Theory, Conducting and Piano, Academy of Music and Performing Arts, Vienna, Austria; Teacher Training College, Vienna, Austria, 1953; Member, Vienna Boys Choir,

1942-48. Debut: Conductor, Vienna Boys Choir, 1953. Career: Conductor, Vienna Boys Choir, 1953-58; Music Director, St John;s Symphony Orchestra, Associate Professor, Music, St John's University, Men's Chorus, Minnesota, USA, 1958-69; Music Director, Metropolitan Youth Symphony Orchestra, Minneapolis, Minnesota, USA, 1965-69; Music Director, Pueblo Symphony Orchestra, Chorale and Youth Symphony; Founder, annual Mozart Festival, Pueblo, Colorado, USA; Thatcher Professor of Music, University of Southern Colorado, Pueblo, Colorado, 1969-86; Music Director and Conductor, Choral Society of Young Vienna (Jung-Wien), 1986-96; Orechester Pro Musica International and Vienna Serenade Orchestra, Vienna, 1986-; Teacher: Conservatory of the City Vienna and Hochschule (University) for Music and Performing Arts. Vienna, 1987-89; Director, Conservatory of the City of Vienna, 1989-; President, Austrian Composers Society, 1988-92; Music Director, Vienna Male Choral Society, 1990-; International Guest Conductor, Europe, USA, Asia and Australia; President and Founder, PMI Music Publication, California. Compositions: Over 450 compositions, orchestral works, choral compositions and arrangements, chamber music, songs, 3 operas, 6 Masses, published, published in Europe and USA. Recordings: Euro-Disc Ariola, Germany; Columbia; Polyhymnia; Rubin; Superchord; GIA; PMI. Contributions to: Sacred Music; Oesterreichische Musikzeitschrift. Hobbies: Radio work (MC, Producer); Tennis; Swimming; Cycling. Current Management: Conductors International Management (CIM), New Jersey, USA. Address: Praterstrasse 76/8, A-1020 Vienna, Austria.

TRAERUP Birthe, b. 9 Oct 1930, Kolding, Denmark. Associate Professor; Musicologist. m. Erik Elias, 1966, 1 son. Education: Ethnomusicological Studies, Yugoslavia, 1954-55, 1969; MA, Musicology, Serbocroatian Linguistics and Literature, University of Copenhagen, 1959; Short Stay Studies, Yugoslavia, Bulgaria, Albania, Greece, Poland, Czech Republic, Hungary, 1963-. Career: Research Associate, Danish Folklore Archives, Department of Ethnomusicology, Copenhagen, 1961-64, 1967-68; Consultant, South Slavic Linguistics and Literature, Royal Library, Copenhagen, 1967-86; Adjunct Professor, 1968-72, Associate Professor, Ethnomusicology, 1972-, Institute of Musicology, University of Copenhagen; Radio Programmes and lectures on music of the Balkans, Denmark, several European Countries; Research projects on songs and instrumental music in Moslem community, Gora, Kosovo, Yugoslavia, folk music of Albanian population in Yugoslavia, studies on Karol Szymanowski and Denmark. Publications include: East Macedonian Folk Songs. Contemporary Traditional Material From Malesevo, Pijanec and the Razlog District, 1970. Contributions to: Professional journals, newspapers and magazines. Honours: Study Scholarships, 1954-55, 1959-61; Order of Merit, Jugoslava Esperanto-Ligo, 1964; Honorary Member, Udruzenje Folklorista Srbije, 1972; Interval Signal Prize, Radio Denmark, 1972; Order of Merit, Ministry for Culture and Art, Poland, 1983. Address: Skovmarksvej 52, Vetterslev, 4100 Ringsted, Denmark.

TRAERUP SARK Einar, b. 27 Mar 1921, Kolding, Denmark. Composer; Organist. Education: The Royal Danish Academy of Music, Copenhagen, Denmark. Debut: Piano, 1947; Organ, 1949. Career includes: Solo performances, Radio Denmark and Radio France. Compositions: Organ works: Toccata primi toni; Dronning Dagmars Dod, stage music; The Death of Queen Dagmar, suite; Klokketaarnet i Barseback; Carillon; Toccata No 2; Bordone; Piano music: Toccata; 5 sonatinas; 3 suites; Tambutsak; Visages du Temps; La deesse du printemps; Cathedrale de verre, chaconne; La creole melancolique, nocturne; Old man goes to town; Various publications of shorter pieces; Music for 2 electric guitars; La clef inaccessible, suite; Dies irae; Church music: Motets to Danish and Swedish texts; 3 Missae Breves; Other liturgical music; Orchestral works: Capriccio; Pablo, ballet suite; 2 Suites for Chamber Orchestra; Divertimento for Chamber Ensemble; Trombone and Piano: Introduction and Carillon. Recording: Toccata primi toni, for organ. Membership: Danish Composer's Society. Address: Lyngbyvej 32 E 1 MF, DK-2100 Copenhagen O, Denmark.

TRAMA Ugo, b. 4 Aug 1932, Naples, Italy. Singer (Bass). Education: Studied with Emilia Gubitosi in Naples, at the Accademia Chigiana in Siena and at the Accademia di Santa Cecilia Rome. Debut: Spoleto Festival 1951, as Banquo in Macbeth. Career: Sang in Cairo and the Italian provinces; Holland Festival 1960, as Fiesco in Simon Bocanegra; Wexford festival 1961, as Silva in Ernani; Dallas Opera 1961; San Francisco Opera 1965; Appearances at the Maggio Musicale Florence, Teatro Liceo Barcelona and Strasbourg; Glyndebourne 1964-79, as Asdrubale in La Pietra del Paragone, Giove and Pane (Calisto), Atinoo and Tempo (Il Ritorno d'Ulisse), Bartolo (Le nozze di Figaro), Pistol (Falstaff) and Farfallo (Die schweigsame Frau). Recordings include: Ramphis in Aida; La Cenerentola (Deutsche Grammophon); Il Ritorno d'Ulisse (CBS). Address: c/o Glyndebourne Festival Opera, Lewes, Sussex.

TRAN Quang Hai, b. 13 May 1944, Vietnam. Ethnomusicologist; Educator; Musician; Composer. m. Bach-Yen

Quach, 17 June 1978, 1 daughter. Education: National Conservatory of Music, Saigon, 1961; Sorbonne, Paris, 1963; Institut d'Ethnologie, 1964; Diploma, Centre d'Etudes de Musique Orientale, Institut de Musicologie, Paris, 1969; State Diploma, Professor of Traditional Music, 1989. Career: Ethnomusicologist, Musée National des Arts et Traditions Populaires, 1968-87; Musée de l'Homme, Paris, 1968-; Professor, Centre d' Etudes de Musique Orientale, 1970-75; Lecturer, Universities of Paris X and Nanterre, 1987; Over 2000 concerts in 45 countries, 1966-; Played at many international music festivals and in films including Le chant des Harmoniques (co-author, principal actor, composer), 1989. Compositions: 300 pop songs; Ve Nguon, electroacoustical, 1975; Shaman, 1982; Nui Ngu Sông Huong, monochord, 1983; Voyage chamanique, voice, 1986; Solo Thai, zither, 1989; Tambours 89, percussion, tape, 1989; Vinh Ha Long, 1993; Hôn Viêtnam, 1993; Many others. Recordings: Numerous records on Vietnamese music. Publications: Am Nhac Viet Nam, 1989; Musique du Monde (with Michel Asselineau and Eugène Bérel), 1993, in English, 1994. Contributions to: Numerous to New Grove Dictionary of Music and Musicians, Encyclopedia Universalis, others. Address: 12 rue Gutenberg, 94450 Limeil Brevannes, France.

TRAN NGOC Stephane, b. 19 December 1965, Paris, France. Violinist. m. Arden Lambert, 25 April 1992, 2 daughters. Education: Paris Superior Conservatory; MMus, Brooklyn College Conservatory of Music, 1987. Debut: Carnegie Hall, New York, 1991. Appointments: Tours in 25 Countries. Honours: Several awards and prizes. Membership: Chamber Music America. Address: 51 Stone Avenue, Ossining, NY 10562, USA.

TRANTER John, b. 1946, Chesterfield, Derbyshire, England. Singer (Bass). Education: Studied singing with John Dethick in Sheffield; London Opera Centre. Debut: Forethcoming: Hobson in Peter Grimes, Chatalet Opera in Paris. Career: Opera for All; Kent Opera as the Commendatore in Don Giovanni and Seneca in L'Incoronazione di Poppea; English National Opera from 1976 as Sarastro, Colline, Monterone in Rigoletto, Verdi's Grand Inquisitor Opera North as Zaccaria in Nabucco, Rossini's Don Basilio, Daland in Der fliegende Holländer, Gremin in Eugene Onegin, Pogner in Die Meistersinger and Trulove in The Rake's Progress; Welsh National Opera as Wagner's Fasolt and Hagen and Grigoris in The Greek Passion; Other engagements in Nancy, Nimes, Wellington and Lausanne; Other roles include Oroveso (Norma), Ramphis (Aida), Nourabad (Les pêcheurs de Perles), Henry VIII (Anna Bolena) and Tiresias (Oedipus Rex); Fafner at Covent Garden and Pope Leone in Attila at Covent Garden, 1990; Banquo in Metz, France, and engagements in Marseille. Debut in Pittsburgh as Varlaam (Boris), Oct 1991; Season 1992 as Melchtal in Guillaume Tell at Covent Garden and Monterone for Opera North; Has sung in concert at the Royal Albert Hall, Royal Festival Hall, Canterbury Cathedral, York Minister and Leeds Town Hall; Also sung with the Scottish Opera as Gremin, King Aida, Billy Budd, Pearl Fishers; Sang Fafner in Siegfried at Santiago, 1996. Address: c/o Music International, 13 Ardilaun Road, Highbury, London N5 2QR, England.

TRAUBOTH Andrea, b. 2 Apr 1959, Seefeld, Munich, Germany. Singer (Soprano). Education: Studied in Munich. Career: Sang with the Dortmund Opera, 1983-86, Munich Staatsoper from 1986 and Cologne Opera from 1988; Dresden, 1986-87, notably as Musetta and Donna Anna; Sang Pamina at Essen, 1990, and Elsa at Kiel, 1992; Further appearances at the Komische Oper Berlin, La Scala Milan and in Madrid, as Agathe, Senta, Rusalka and Micaela; Concerts in Holland, Greece, France and England. Address: Operhause am Kleinen Kiel, Pf 1660, W-2300 Kiel, Germany.

TRAUTWEIN George, b. 5 Aug 1927, Chicago, USA. Violinist; Conductor. m. Barbara Wilson, 20 Jan 1957, 2 sons. Education: BM, Oberlin College, 1951; MM, Cleveland Institute, 1956; MusDoc, Indiana University, 1961; Fulbright Scholar, Salzburg Mozarteum, 1958. Debut: Conductor, Minneapolis Symphony Orchestra, New York, 1967. Appointments: Violinist, Indianapolis, Baltimore, Washington National, Cleveland, Mozarteum Orchestra; Associate Conductor, Dallas and Minneapolis Symphonies; Music Director, Savannah, Tucson, Piedmont Orchestras; International Congress of Strings, RIAS Ed. Network Berlin; Guest Conductor, Mexico, Puerto Rico, Germany, France, Portugal, Romania, Yugoslavia, Sweden, Hong Kong, Bombay. Publications: Toscanini, Furtwängler and Fidelio, a Comparative Study, 1961. Honours: Fulbright Grants, Salzburg Mozarteum, 1957-58; Phi Mu Alpha, 1974; Fulbright Senior Lecturer, Bombay and Goa, India, 1989-90; ASCAP Award, 1983. Memberships: Thomas Beecham Society; William Furtwängler Society; Chamber Music America. Hobbies: Art reproduction; English romantic poetry; Scandinavian cuisine. Address: Wake Forest University, Box 7411, Winston-Salem, NC 27109, USA.

TRAUX Barry, b. 10 May 1947, Chatham, Ontario, Canada. Composer. Education: Studied physics and mathematics at Queen's University Kingston, BS 1969; Electronic music at the University of British Columbia (MM 1971 and at the Institute of

Sonology, University of Utrecht, 1971-73. Career: Collaboration with Murray Schafer at World Soundscape Project in Vancouver; Director of Sonic Research Studio, and Assistant Professor in Communications Department, Simon Fraser University, 1976-83; Associate Professor at Centre for Arts. Compositions include: Hexameron, for flute, clarinet, horn, viola and piano, 1970; The Little Prince for narrator, vocal soloists and tape, 1971; From the Steppenwolf for 12 singers, 1971; Four Sonic Landscapes, 1971-79; Gilgamesh, for voices, chorus, ensemble and tape, 1974; Nautilus for percussion, 1976; East Wind for amplified recorder, 1981; Nightwatch for marimba, 1982; Etude for cello, 1983; Divan, and Wings of Nike, for computer and tape, 1985-87; Tongues of Angels for horn and oboe d'amore, 1988; Dominion for chamber ensemble and 2 digital soundtracks, 1991; Song of Songs, for oboe d'amore, 2 digital soundtracks and computer images, 1993. Publications include: Handbook for Acoustic Ecology (1978) and Acoustic Communication (1985). Address: c/o SOCAN, 41 Valleybrook Drive, Don Mills, Ontario M3B 2S6, Canada.

TRAVIS Francis Irving, b. 9 July 1921, Michigan, USA. Conductor. Education: BMus, 1943, Michigan State University; MMus, University of Michigan, 1948; PhD, Musicology, University of Zurich, 1955; Private study with Hermann Scherchen. Career: Freelance Conductor of concert, opera, radio, 1955; Professor for Orchestra Conducting, Staatliche Hochschule für Musik, Freiburg, 1964-89, concurrently with Conductor, Swiss Radio in Lugano; Frequent engagements at Dutch National Opera and appearances at international festivals such as Berliner Festwochen, Holland, Copenhagen and Lucerne Festivals; Professor for Conducting, Tokyo National, University of the Fine Arts and Music, 1990-95. Memberships: President, Swiss Section, ISCM; Honorary Member, Jean Sibelius Academi, Helsinki; Honorary Member, Richard Strauss Society, Tokyo. Hobbies: Languages; Sailing; Swimming. Address: 6-5-12 Hom-Komagome, Bunkyo-ku, Tokyo 113, Japan.

TRAVIS Roy (Elihu), b. 24 June 1922, New York, New York, USA. Composer. Education: Studied with Otto Luening at Columbia University; MA 1951; Shenkerian studies privately with Felix Salxer, 1947-59; Studied with Bernard Wagenaar at Juilliard; MS, 1950; and with Darius Milhaud in Paris, 1951-52. Career: Teacher at Columbia University, 1952-53, Mannes College of Music 1952-57 and the University of California at Los Angeles, 1957-91, Professor 1968-91. Compositions include: Symphonic Allegro 1951; First piano sonata, 1954; String Quartet 1958; African Sonata, 1966; Duo Concertante for violin and piano 1967; The Passion of Oedipus, opera, Los Angeles 1968; Collage for orchestra 1968; Piano Concerto 1969; Barma, Septet, 1968; Switched-On Ashanti for flute, piccolo and tape, 1973; Songs and Epilogues for bass and orchestra, 1975; The Black Bacchants, opera, 1982; Dover Beach for bass and piano, 1983; Concerto for violin, tabla and orchestra. 1988; Piano pieces and songs. Publications include: Toward a New Concept of Tonality, 1959; Tonal Coherence in the First Movement of Bartok's Fourth String Quartet, 1970; The Recurrent Figure in the Britten/Piper Opera Death in Venice, 1987; Traditional Ashanti Dances as a Compositional Resource: Tachema-chema and Sikyi, 1995. Honours: Gershwin Award; Martha Baird Rockefeller Award, 1968; ASCAP Standard Awards, 1969-97; Guggenheim Fellowship, 1972-73; Ford Foundation Grant, 1975; NEA Grants 1976, 1978. Address: 16680 Charmel Lane, Pacific Palisades, CA 90272, USA.

TREACHER Graham, b. 1932, England. Conductor; Composer; Lecturer. Career: Conducted the London New Music Singers 1958-63, with the first performances of works by Davies and Bennett, British premieres of works by Penderecki and Schoenberg; Tours of Europe, Henry Wood Promenade Concerts; Conductor at Morley College, London, Holst Choir and Opera Group; Director of the Thaxted Festival, Essex until 1963; Assistant Chorus Master Royal Opera House, Covent Garden 1962-64 for the British premiere of Schoenberg's Moses und Aron; Associate conductor of the BBC Scottish Symphony Orchestra and Chorus, 1964-67; Director of the Purcell School, London, 1968-70; Director of Music at the University of Warwick, 1969-70; Lecturer in Style, Interpretation and Conducting, University of York, 1972-85; Founder of the Amati Ensemble, baroque quartet, playing harpischord and chamber organ, 1978-85; Director and conductor, Northern Music Theatre 1980-84, with first performances of works by Vic Hoyland, Philip Grange and UK Premieres of Kagel and Henze; Artistic Director of the John Loosemore Early Music Centre, Devon, 1988-92. Compositions include: Music for children, vocal and instrumental music including music for Strings, Percussion and Celestine, for the 1990 Orkney Summer Festival; Choral music with settings of Chaucer and Christmas music. Publications include: Editions of Gesualdo (Cantiones Sacrae 1603) and Pallavicino's three act Carnival opera Messalina, for performance at the Vadstena International Opera Festival, Sweden; Dixit Dominus by Pallavicino. Address: Warren Cottages, Hippenscombe, Nr Marlborough, Wilts SNB 3NN, England.

TREE Michael, b. 19 Feb 1934, Newark, New Jersey, USA. Concert Violinist; Violist. m. Johanna Kreck, 1 son, 1 daughter. Education: Diploma, Curtis Institute of Music, 1955. Debut: Carnegie Hall, 1954. Career: Soloist with major American orchestras; Solo & chamber music appearances at major festivals, including Israel, Athens, Spoleto, Casals, Marlboro; Founding member, Guarneri String Quartet; Faculty member, Curtis Institute of Music University of Maryland, Rutgers University, Manhattan School of Music; Repeated appearances on the Today Show and first Telecast of Chamber Music Live from Lincoln Center. Recordings: Over 60 chamber music works on Columbia, Nonesuch, Philips and RCA labels; Complete Beethoven quartets, 10 works for piano and strings, with Artur Rubinstein; Collaborations with Emanuel Ax, Jaimie Laredo, Leonard Rose, Alexander Schneider, Rudolf Serkin and Pinchas Zuckerman. Honours: New York City Seal of Recognition, 1982; Honorary degress, Doctor of Fine Arts, University of South Florida, State University of New York at Binghampton. Memberships: President of the First American String Quartet Congress at University of Maryland and Smithsonian Institute, 1989. Hobbies: Tennis; Hiking. Current Management: Herbert Barrett Management.

TREFAS György, b. 6 Oct 1931, Budapest, Hungary. Opera Singer; Soloist; Bassist. m. Szabó Katalin, 27 Dec 1972. Education: Private education: Dr Werner Alajos, Makai Mihály, Lendvay Andor, Hetényi Kálmán. Debut: Csokonai Theatre, Debrecen, Hungary. Career: Bass characters of operas: King Philip, Don Carlos; Attila; De Silva; Ernani; Rocco, Fidelio; Duke Bluebeard, Bartók: Duke Bluebeard's Castle - radio recording, Dresden, Antwerp, Zaccaria, Nabucco, Sofia; Magdeburg, Mephisto, Faust; Ibert; Angelica; King Nero TV Film; Sarastro, Zauberflöte; Osmin, Entführung. Honours: Franz Liszt Prize, 1968; Merited Artist of the Hungarian People's Republic, 1980. Memberships: Association of Hungarian Music Artists; International Theatre Institute; Foundation Member, Hungarian Kodály Society. Hobbies: Reading; Tennis. Current Management: Interconcert, Budapest. Address: Darabos-u 6, H-4026 Debrecen, Hungary.

TREKEL Roman, b. 1962, Pirna, Saxony, Germany. Singer (Baritone). Education: Studied at the Berlin Musikhochschule 1980-86 and with Siegfried Lorenz and Hans Hotter. Career: Sang with the Berlin Staatsoper from 1986, notably in Erwin and Elmire by Reichardt 1987 and Kaiser's Emperor of Atlantis 1989; Many roles in operas by Mozart in Berlin and elsewhere; Season 1992 as Ulysees in Erendira by Violet Dinescu and as Tarquinius in the Rape of Lucretia with the Berlin Kammeroper; Concerts and Lieder recitals in Germany, Belgium, Austria, Czechoslovakia, Sweden and England. Honours include: Prize winner, Dvorak Competition, 1985; Karlovvy Vary, 1987; DDR Competition Germany; 1989 International Lieder Competition Walter Gruner in London. Address: Stuttgart Staatsoper, Oberer Schlossgarten 6, 7000 Stuttgart 1, Germany.

TREKEL-BURCKHARDT Ute, b. 3 Nov 1939, Pirna, Saxony, Germany. Singer (Mezzo-soprano). Education: Studied in Berlin with Rita Meinl-Weise. Debut: Komische Oper Berlin 1963, as the Page in Salome. Career: Sang at the Komische Oper until 1978, then joined the Staatsoper Berlin; Guest appearances in Vienna, Cologne, Brussels, Madrid and Dresden; Cologne 1984, as Renata in The Fiery Angel by Prokofiev; Nancy 1985, as The Woman in Schoenberg's Erwartung; Created Queen Marguerite in Sutermeister's Le roi Bérenger at Munich in 1985; Other roles include the Countess Geschwitz in Lulu, Mozart's Sextus and Cherubino, Verdi's Eboli, Amneris and Ulrica, Strauss's Nurse (Die Frau ohne Schatten), Composer and Octavian, and Wagner's Fricka, Kundry and Ortrud (Wiesbaden 1988); Sang Venus in Tannhäuser as guest with the Berlin Staatsoper at Las Palmas in 1986; Many concert appearances. Address: Deutsche Staatsoper, Unter den Linden 7, 1086 Berlin, Germany.

TRELEAVEN John, b. 1950, Cornwall, England. Singer (Tenor). Education: Studied in London and Naples. Career: With Welsh National Opera has sung Tamino, Alfredo (La Traviata), Pinkerton, Nadir (Les Pecheurs de Perles) and Mark in The Midsummer Marriage); At English National Opera his roles have included Don José, Cavaradossi, Faust (Berlioz), Erik in Der fliegende Holländer, the Prince in Rusalka, Hoffmann, Don Carlos and Wozzeck in a new production of Berg's Opera (1990); Royal Opera, Covent Garden, debut as Tamino, followed by Froh in Das Rheingold and Peter Grimes, 1989; Appearances with Scottish Opera have included Florestan, Jenik (The Bartered Bride), Werther and Radames; Opera North as Dick Johnson (La Fanciulla del West), Cavaradossi, Radames and Peter Grimes; Recent engagements in The Damnation of Faust at the Adelaide Festival, Pylades (Iphigénie en Tauride) at the Paris Opéra, Verdi's Attila at the Concertgebouw, Amsterdam and Prince Golitisin (Khovanshchina) at the San Francisco Opera, 1990; Concert performances include a 1981 debut at the Festival Hall in Puccini's Messa di Gloria and Rossini's Stabat Mater; Verdi Requiem under Nello Santi at the 1984 Festival de la Mediterranée; Dream of Gerontius 1989, with the Scottish National Orchestra; Concert performance of Bernstein's Candide at the Barbican in London, 1989; Season 1992 as Erik at Buenos Aires, Essex in Gloriana at Mainz (Siegmund 1993) and Weill's Jimmy Mahoney in Karlsruhe; Debut as Walther in Die Meistersinger at Mainz, 1997. Recordings include: Solo parts: Le Prophète, Meyerbeer, conducted by Henry Lewis CBS; L'Assedio di Calais, Donizetti, Opera Rara; Il Trovatore, Colin Davis, with José Carreras, Philips; Il Tabarro, Maazel with Placido Domingo, CBS; Rachmaninov Vespers, Candide, Leonard Bernstein, DGG; Videos of Rusalka for English National Opera; Richard Dauntless in Ruddigore for Brent Walker Ltd; Candide (Deutsche Grammophon). Address: c/o Athole Still, International Management Ltd, 113 Church Road, London SE19 2PR, England.

TREMBLAY Gilles L, b. 6 Sept 1932, Arvida, Quebec, Canada. Composer. Education: Conservatoire de Montréal; Conservatoire de Paris. Career: Professor of Analysis and Composition, Conservatoire de Montréal; Participation in numerous concerts as Pianist and Conductor. Compositions: Champs I, II, III Le Sifflement des Vents Porteurs de l'Amour; Soltices; Oralléluiants; Fleuves; Compostelle I, Envoi; Vêpres de la Vierge, Katadrone. Recordings: Anthology of Canadian Music; Les Vêpres de la vierge; Vers le Soleil; Triojubilus; Aubes. Publications: Champs I, II, III, 1969; Fleuves, 1976; Compostelle I, 1978; Acoustique et forme Chez Varèse, 1983; Triojubilus, 1984; L'Espace du Coeur, 1997. Honours include: First Prizes, Montréal and Paris Conservatories, 1953, 1957; Medaille du Conseil Canadien de la Musique, 1991; Chevalier dans l'orde des Arts et des Lettres, 1992. Memberships: Canadian League of Composers; Societe Francaise d'analyse Musicale; Societe de Musique Contemporaire de Quebec; SOCAN. Hobbies: Hiking; Swimming; Gardening; Socialising. Address: 439 Ouest Blvd St Joseph, Montreal, Quebec H2V 2P7, Canada.

TRETYAKOV Victor, b. 1946, Siberia, Russia. Violinist. Education: Studied at the Irkutsk Music School and the Moscow Conservatoire. Career: Many concert tours of Europe, the USA and Latin America; Leader of the State Chamber Orchestra of Moscow, from 1983; Carnegie Hall recital and appearances with the Pittsburgh, Detroit and Atlanta Symphony Orchestras; Soloist with the St Petersburg PO on tour to US, 1990; Season 1995 included concerts in Harrogate and Wiesbaden with the Oslo Philharmonic; Lucerne and Locarno Festivals with the St Petersburg PO; British tour with the Philharmonia under Mikhail Pletnev, 1996-97, and concerts with the London Philharmonic; Philharmonia and Ulster Orchestra concerts, 1997-98. Recordings include: Tchaikovsky Concerto (Olympia); Brahms Concerto (Pioneer); Bruch Double Concerto, with Yuri Bashmet (BMG). Honours include: People's Artist of the USSR. Address: c/o Lies Askonas Ltd, 6 Henrietta St, London WC2E 8LA, England.

TREW Graham (Donald), b. 18 July 1948, Epping, England. Singer (Baritone); Teacher; Adjudicator. Education: Guildhall School of Music and Drama, AGSM with distinction; MMus, University of London. Career: Performed, English Opera Group, Nottingham Music Theatre, Cockpit Opera Workshop (20 productions plus title role in video of Marriage of Figaro); Recitals, Wigmore Hall, Purcell Room, Queen Elizabeth Hall, Barbican; Oratorio and concerts throughout England, Europe, USA and Caribbean; English song recitals for Radio 3, Friday Night Is Music Night, Songs from the Shows, Melodies for You, for Radio 2; Gentleman of Her Majesty's Chapel Royal, St James's Palace, 1975-; Teaches privately; Guest Lecturer, Royal Academy of Music lieder class and Birmingham Conservatoire; Adjudicates throughout England. Recordings: English song recordings for Meridian and Hyperion with Roger Vignoles; Recordings for Priory Records and the British Music Society with John Alley; Marcello-Cantatas; Rodolophe, Florence. Honours: Gold Medal, Guildhall School of Music, 1973; Vocal Record of the Year Award for A Shropshire Lad, Gramophone Magazine, 1980. Memberships: Equity; Royal Society of Musicians; Adjudicator, British Federation of Music Festivals. Hobbies: Squash; Theatre. Current Management: Music International. Address: 61 Sydner Road, Stoke Newington, London N16 7UF, England.

TRIER Stephen (Luke), b. 13 Mar 1930, Woolton Hill, England,. Musician; Clarinettist. m. Caroline Fraser Scott 18 July 1953, 2 daughters. Education: Foundation Scholar, Royal College of Music, 1947-50. Career: Bass clarinet, clarinets, saxophones, Royal Philharmonic Orchestra, 1950-56, London Symphony Orchestra, 1956-68, London Philharmonic Orchestra, 1964-95; Clarinet, Sadler's Wells, 1953-56; Freelance appearances with various groups; Professor, saxophone and Bass Clarinet, Royal College of Music. Recordings: Many with various orchestras and groups. Publications: Essential Clarinet, Co-editor Alan Boustead, 1966; Playing the Saxophone, English Editor, 1974; 100 Classical Clarinet Studies, co-editor Gunther Joppig, 1987. Honours: Honorary Associate, Royal College of Music. Hobbies: Wine and food; Tinkering with clarinets and basset horns. Address: 6 Carthew Villas, London W6 0BS, England.

TRIMARCHI Domenico, b. 21 Dec 1940, Naples, Italy. Singer (Bass-Baritone). Education: Studied at the Naples Conservatory and with Gino Campese. Debut: Teatro La Fenice Venice 1964, as Belcore in L'Elisir d'Amore. Career: Has sung widely in Italy (Verona Arena 1975-78), Edinburgh, London, Stuttgart, Frankfurt, Chicago and Dubrovnik; Teatro Regio Parma 1987, as Falstff in the operas by Salieri and Verdi; Repertoire also includes Leporelo, Alfonso, Papageno, Arbace and Count Almaviva (Mozart); Varlaam (Mussorgsky); Germont, Paolo and Fra Melitone (Verdi); Dulcamara, Belcore, Don Pasquale, Malatesta, Enrico and Alfonso (Donizetti); Dallapiccola's Job; Marcello, Sharpless and Gianni Schicchi (Puccini); Sang Donizetti's Mamma Agata at Luga di Romagna, 1988; Marchese in Linda di Chamounix at Trieste, 1989, Leporello at Parma; Sang in Wolf-Ferrari's Quattro Rusteghi at Geneva, 1992. Recordings: Haydn's La Vera Costanza, L'Incontro Improvviso and Il Mondo della Luna, Il Barbiere di Siviglia, Vivaldi's Tito Manlio, Tosca (Philips); Elisa e Claudio by Mercadante; La Straniera by Bellini; La Cenerentola (CBS); Pimpinone by Albinoni. Address: Foresters Hall, 25-27 Westow Street, London SE19 3RY, England.

TRITT William, b. 1950, Canada. Concert Pianist. Education: Studied at the Ecole Vincent d'Indy in Montreal with Lucille Brassard and Yvonne Hubert; Further study with Yvonne Lefébure in Paris and György Sebok at Indiana University. Career: First solo appearance aged 15 with the Little Orchestra Society at Avery Fisher Hall, New York; Further engagements with the Montreal Symphony and the CBS Orchestra in Quebec; Boston Pops Orchestra and the Chicago Symphony at the Ravinia Festival; Cincinnati and Houston Symphony Orchestras; Nationwide appearances in Canada, including Toronto, Edmonton, Winnipeg and Halifax; London recital debut 1981, Wigmore Hall. Recordings include: Bach D minor Concerto; Beethoven C major Concerto and Schumann A minor; Liszt Totentanz. Honours: Winner of all major competitions in Canada, 1966-71.

TROJAHN Manfred, b. 22 Oct 1949, Cremlingen, Brunswick, Germany. Composer. Education: Studied at the Niedersächsi/sche Musikschule, Brunswick, 1966-70; Composition at the Hamburg Hochschule, 1970-77. Career: Freelance composer including Residency at the Villa Massimo in Rome, 1979-80; Teacher of composition at the Robert Schumann Hochschule, Düsseldorf, 1991. Compositions include: Opera Enrico (1991); 4 symphonies, 1973, 1978, 1985, 1992; 3 string quartets, 1976, 1980, 1983; Fünfsee Bilder für messosopran und orchester, 1979-83; Flute Concerto, 1983; Requiem, 1985; .... une campagne noire de soloeil, 7 ballet scenes for chamber ensemble, 1983-93; Sonatas for violin and cello, 1983; Variations for orchestra, 1987; Cinq Epigraphes for orchestra, 1987; Fragmente für Antigone, 6 pieces for string quartet, 1988; Transir for orchestra, 1988; Aubade for 2 sopranos, 1990; Ave Maria for chorus, 1991; Grodek for baritone and 8 instruments, 1991; Quattro Pezzi for orchestra, 1992; Divertissement for oboe and chamber orchestra, 1993; Cornisches Nachtlied for orchestra, 1994; Was ihr Wollt (As You Like It), opera, 1997-98. Address: 44 rue Dauphine, 75006 Paris, France.

TROPP Vladimir, b. 9 November 1939, Moscow, Russia. Pianist. m. Tatiana Zelikman, 30 July 1961, 1 son. Education: Ynessin's Childrens Music School; Ynessin's Specialized Music School; Ynessin's Institute. Career: Concert Tours in Russia, Holland, USA, Italy, Japan, Finland, Germany, Ireland, Consta Rica, Cuba; Masterclasses & Concerts in American Universities, Conservatories of Holland & Ireland; Numerous Chamber Music Festivals; Performances on Radio & TV in Holand, Germany, USA, Finland, Costa Rica; Recitals and Performances with Major Orchestras. Recordings: Fizma u Melodia, Scriabin, Medtner; 3 CD's. Contributions to: Several Russian Magazines. Honour: Winner, Enescu International Piano Competition, Bucharest, 1970. Hobby: Collection of Old Pianist Records. Address: Dmitry Ulianov Str 4, Block 2, Apt 251, Moscow 117333, Russia.

TROST Rainer, b. 1966, Stuttgart, Germany. Singer (Tenor). Education: Munich Hochschule, with Adalbert Kraus. Career: Member of the Hanover Staatstheater, 1991-95; Sang Ferrando in Cosí fan tutte at the Hamburg Opera 1992 and toured in Mozart's opera with the Monteverdi Choir and Orchestraa; Sang Ferrando at Munich 1993, Don Ottavio at Dresden and Vienna, Tamino in Geneva and Berlin (1994) and Eginhard in Schubert's Fierrabras at Florence (1995); Further engagements at the Cologne Opera, Opéra National de Paris, as Belmonte in Vienna and Hamburg and as Ferrando at Covent Garden, Glyndebourne, 1994 (debut role), returning 1997; Concerts include Mozart's Mass in C Minor, with the Monteverdi Choir and Orchestra; Die Schöpfung, with the Hamburg PO and the Cologne Radio SO, Bach's Christmas Oratorio (NDR SO) and the St Matthew Passion, with the Concertgebouw Orchestra. Recordings include: CD and video of Cosí fan tutte (DGG). Address: c/o Haydn Rawstron Ltd, PO Box 654, London SE26 4DZ, England.

TROTTER Thomas (Andrew), b. 4 Apr 1957, Birkenhead, England. Concert Organist. Education: ARCM, Royal College of Music, London, 1976; MA, Cambridge University, 1979; Conservatoire Rueil-Malmaison, France, 1979-81. Debut: Royal Festival Hall, 1980. Career includes: Regular broadcasts on Radio 2 and 3; Performances at festivals throughout Europe; Proms debut in 1986; Concert tours of USA, Australia and Japan; Organist for St Margaret's Church, Westminster, London, 1982-, City of Birmingham, 1983-. Recordings: The Grand Organ of Birmingham Town Hall; Liszt Organ Works and Reubke Sonata; Jehan Alain Organ Works; Charles-Marie Widor Organ Works; Antonio Soler Concertos for 2 Organs; Olivier Messiaen Organ Works; The Ride of the Valkyries: Organ Transcriptions; Liszt Organ Works volume 2; Mozart Organ Works. Honours: Scholar, RCM; Organ Scholar, St George's Chapel, Windsor and King's College, Cambridge (John Stewart of Rannock Scholarship in Sacred Music, 1979); Walford Davies Prize, RCM, 1976; 1st Prize and Bach Prize, St Alban's International Organ Competition, 1979; Prix de Virtuosite, 1981. Current Management: Karen McFarlane Artists Inc, 12429 Cedar Road, Cleveland Heights, OH 44106, USA. Address: c/o Town Hall, Birmingham, B3 3DQ, England.

TROUP Malcolm, b. 22 Feb 1930, Toronto, Canada. Concert Pianist; Professor Emeritus of Music, City University; Former Director of Music, Guildhall School of Music and Drama. m. Carmen Lamarca Bello Subercaseaux, 1 daughter. Education: DPhilMus. University of York; Associate, Royal Conservatory of Music, Toronto; FGSM; LLD, Memorial University of Newfoundland; Hon DMus, City University. Debut: With CBC Symphony Orchestra, Toronto, aged 17. Career includes: Recitals and Concertos with leading orchestras in Europe, North and South America; Premieres, important modern works; Frequent broadcaster with the BBC; External Examiner, Universities of York, Keele, London; Member of International Juries: Chopin Competition of Australia, CBC National Talent Competition, Young Musician of the Year; 1st Dvorak International Piano Competition, 1997, Rome 1997 International Piano Competition; Vice President, World Piano Competition, London. Recordings: Major record labels. Publication: Editor, The Piano Journal. Contributions to: The Messiaen Companion, 1995; Director, London International String Quartet Competition. Memberships include: Royal Society of Musicians; Royal Society of Arts and Sciences (FRSA); Worshipful Company of Musicians, Liveryman, Senior Warden, 1997; European Piano Teachers Association, Chairman, 1978-; Beethoven Piano Society of Europe, Chairman; Governor, Music Therapy Charity Trust; Trustee, Jewish Musical Heritage Trust, 1991-. Address: 86 Lexham Gardens, London W8 5JB, England.

TROWELL Brian (Lewis), b. 21 Feb 1931, Wokingham, Berkshire, England. Professor of Music. m. Rhianon James, 1958, 2 d. Education: Christ's Hospital; MA 1959, PhD 1960, Gonville and Caius College, Cambridge. Career: Assistant Lecturer later Lecturer in Music, Birmingham University, 1957-62; Freelance Scholar, Conductor, Opera Producer, Lecturer and Editor, 1962-67; Head of BBC Radio Opera, 1967-70; Regents' Professor, University of CA, Berkeley, USA, 1970; Reader in Music, 1970 then Professor of Music, 1973, KCL; Visiting Gresham Professor of Music, City University, 1971-74; King Edward Professor of Music, University of London, King's College, 1974-88; Chairman of Editorial Committee, Musica Britannica, 1983-93; Heather Professor of Music, University of Oxford, 1988-. Publications: The Early Renaissance, Pelican History of Music, volume II, 1963; Four Motets by John Plummer, 1968; Joint Editor, John Dunstable: Complete Works, Editor, M F Bukofzer, 2nd revised edition, 1970; Editor, Invitation to Medieval Music, volume 3, 1976, volume 4, 1978; Opera translations. Contributions to: Dictionaries of music and articles in books and learned journals including: Libretto II, The New Grove Dictionary of Opera, London, 1992, Acis, Galatea and Polyphemus: a serenata a tre voci?, Music and Theatre: Essays in Honour of Winton Dean, 1987, Elgar's Use of Literature in Edward Elgar Music and Literature, 1993. Hobbies: Theatre; Reading; Gardening. Address: Faculty of Music, Oxford University, St Aldate's, Oxford, OX1 1DB, England.

TRUBASHNIK Simon, b. 16 September 1939, Odessa. Oboist. divorced, 1 daughter. Education: Central Music School for Gifted Children, Moscow Conservatoire; Diploma, 1953, Graduate Diploma, Moscow Conservatorie, 1958. Debut: Solo, Youth Festival, Berlin, 1955. Career: Principal Oboe, Moscow Philharmonic Orchestra, 1955-72; Principal Oboe, Moscow Chamber Orchestra, 1958-72; Associate Principal Oboe, Israel Philharmonic Orchestra, 1972-75; Principal Oboe, Belgium National Opera, 1976-85; Principal Oboe, Halifax Symphony, Canada, 1986-87; Professor, Royal Conservatory of Music, Toronto, 1987-; Solo with Moscow Philharmonic and Moscow Chamber Orchestras (World Tours); Radio Luxenbourg Orchestra of Belgium; Mozart Chamber Orchestra, Brussels; Opera Orchestra of Ghent; Toronto Chamber Players; Kingston Philharmonic; McGill Chamber Orchestra. Recordings: Bach Concerto (with David Oistrakh) and Concertos by Mozart and Strauss with Moscow Philharmonic Orchestra; Italian Baroque Concerts with Luxembourg Radio Orchestra; 100 Orchestral Records with Moscow Philharmonic Orchestra. Honour: Gold Medal, Moscow Conservatoire, 1958. Membership: American Federation of Musicians. Current Management: Sol Hurock Management. Address: 100 Upper Madison #610, North York, Ontario M2N 6M4, Canada.

TRUDEL Alain, b. 13 June 1966, Montreal, Quebec, Canada. Trombone Soloist; Conductor; Composer. 2 sons, 1 daughter. Education: 1st Prize Diploma, Trombone, Chamber Music,Solfeggio, Musical Dictation, Conservatoire de Musique de Montréal. Debut: Ballade by Frank Martin, Orchestre Symphonique de Montréal with Charles Dutoit, at age 18. Career: Soloist with Austrian Radio Orchestra, Hong Kong Philharmonic, Tivoli Festival Orchestra, Weil Recital Hall at Carnegie Hall, Orchestre National de Radio France, Strasbourg Musica Festival and Concertgebouw; Trombone Professor, Conservatoire de Musique de Montréal. Compositions: Published: Vision for trumpet, trombone, percussion and piano; String Quartet No 2; Rose d'octobre for choir, soloists and chamber group; Yo and vita for and trombone and tape; 3 Fanfares. Recordings: Trombone Classics with Northern Symphony Orchestra, England; Power and Glory with organ; Recital with Guy Few, piano; Trombone Favourites; Tableaux de France with Guy Few, piano. Honours: 1st Brass to win 1st Prize, International Stepping Stone; 1st Brass to win 1st Prize, Orchestre Symphonique de Montréal Solo Competition; Dixon-Holmes Artist of the Year Award, 1992; Concert Hall of Joseph-François Perrault named Alain Trudel Concert Hall, 1995; Virginia Pauker Award, 1996. Memberships: International Trombone Association, Commission Committee Member; President, Foundation for the Art of Chambly. Hobbies: Badminton; Playing with my children. Current Management: Latitude 45/Arts Promotion Inc. Address: 109 Blvd St Joseph West, Montreal, Que H2T 2P7, Canada.

TRUEFITT Alison, b. 1958, England. Singer (soprano). Education: Studied at London University and the Royal Academy of Music. Debut: Sang at the Purcell Room, London, 1979. Career: Has appeared in recital with the Songmaker's Almanac and with the BBC in songs by Britten, Bartók, Fauré, Holst, Milhaud, Poulenc, and Tippett; With orchestra or ensemble in works by Gerald Finzi, Stephen Dodgson and Frank Martin; Promenade Concerts debut in La Forza del Destino; Sang Gluck's Iphigenia with Opera Factory, 1985, and created Kathe in John Metcalf's The Crossing (tours of US, UK and Canada); Sang in the British stage premiere of Schubert's Fierabras, Oxford University 1986; English National Opera 1988, as Manassah in Salome; Sang Donizetti's Rita, Madame Herz in Mozart's Impresario and Musetta with London Chamber Opera 1988; Appearances with London Chamber Opera 1988; Appearances as the Queen of Night with Birmingham Touring Opera, 1988-89; Other repertory includes Leila in Les pêcheurs de Perles, the Governess in The Turn of the Screw and Britten's Phaedra and Major Stone in Weill's Happy End; Translated Orfeo for Opera North 1990 and has provided several sets of surtitles for Covent Garden. Address: c/o Royal Opera House, Covent Garden, London WC2, England.

TRUSSEL Jacques, b. 7 Apr 1943, San Francisco, California, USA. Singer (Tenor). Education: Studied at Ball State University, Muncie, Indiana and in New York. Career: Sang at first in concert then made opera debut at the Oberlin Festival 1970, as Pinkerton; Has appeared in Boston, Dallas, Houston, Santa Fe, New Orleans, Chicago (from 1976), Pittsburgh (1979), Washington (1981) and San Francisco (Loge in Das Rheingold 1990); Sang Don José at Cincinnati 1988 and has appeared as Rodolfo, Cavaradossi, Berg's Alwa, Araquil in La Navarraise by Massenet, Steva in Jenufa, Max (Der Freischütz) and Nero in L'Incoronazione di Poppea (Geneva 1989); Sang at Houston in the title role of Hugh the Drover by Vaughan Williams (US premiere 1973) and in the 1974 word premiere of The Seagull by Pasatieri; European debut Spoleto Festival 1976, as Hermann in The Queen of Spades; Sang Alwa at Florence 1985 and at Chicago 1987; Covent Garden and Nancy 1989, as Peter Grimes and as Sergei in the French premiere of Lady Macbeth of Mtsensk by Shostakovich; Appeared with Greater Miami Opera 1990, as Pollione in Norma; London appearances 1991, as Don José; Season 1991/92 as Alexey in the US premiere of The Gambler, at Chicago; Sergei at the Opéra Bastille, Monteverdi's Nero in Florence, Don José in Birmingham and Roderick in The Fall of the House of Usher by Philip Glass at the Maggio Musicale; Sang Golitsin in Khovanschina at Brussels, 1996. Address: c/o Harold Holt, 31 Sinclair Road, London W14 0NS, England.

TRYON Valerie, b. 1934, Portsmouth, England. Pianist; Associate Professor, McMaster University, Hamilton, Ontario. Education: Studied at the Royal Academy of Music and with Jacques Fèvrier in Paris. Debut: Wigmore Hall, 1954. Career: Has appeared at the Cheltenham Festival and in all the major concert halls in Britain with leading conductors and orchestras; Recitals in Europe and Africa and in North America; Repertoire ranges from Bach to contemporary composers, with 50 concertos; Noted for playing of Chopin, Liszt and Rachmaninov; Frequent broadcasts for the BBC and other radio stations and regular chamber music concerts; Adjudicator and performer at many music festivals and competitions in Europe and North America; Fellow of the Royal Academy of Music; Associate Professor of Music at McMaster University, Hamilton, Ontario. Recordings: Albums for Pye (Virtuoso Series), BBC Enterprises, Omnibus, Argo, Lyrita, Educo and the CBC; Dorian Records: Tchaikovsky CDs; Brahms (The Rembrandt Trio); Dvorak, Trio; Bloemendaal, Tryon, Kantarjian. Honours include: Harriet Cohen Award; Ferenc Liszt Medal of Honour; Juno Award, 1994. Address: Department of Music, McMaster University, 1280 Main Street West, Hamilton, Ontario, Canada.

TRYTHALL (Harry) Gilbert, b. 28 Oct 1930, Knoxville, Tennessee, USA. Composer; Teacher. m., 2 daughters. Education: BA, University of Tennessee, 1951; MMus, Northwestern University, 1952; DMA, Cornell University, 1960; Studied with David Van Vactor, Wallingford Riegger, Robert Palmer and Donald Grout. Career: Assistant Professor of Music, Knox College, Galesburg, Illinois, 1960-64; Professor of Music Theory and Composition, 1964-75; Chairman, School of Music, George Peabody College for Teachers, Nashville, Tennessee, 1973-75; Professor of Music, 1975-, Dean, Creative Arts Center, 1975-81, Virginia University, Morgantown, West Virginia; Guest Lecturer at various universities and colleges. Compositions: Operas: The Music Lesson, 1960; The Terminal Opera, 1982, revised 1987; The Pastimes of Lord Caitanya, chamber opera, 1992; Orchestral: A solemn Chant for strings, 1955; Symphony No 1, 1958, revised 1963; Harp Concerto, 1963; Dionysia, 1964; Chroma I, 1970; Cindy the Synthe (Minnie the Moog) for synthesizer and strings, 1975; Chamber: Flute Sonata, 1964; A Vacuum Soprano for brass quintet and tape, 1966; Entropy for brass, harp, celesta, piano and tape, 1967; Echospace for brass and tape, 1973; Choral music; Piano pieces; Organ music; Electronic scores; Mixed media pieces; Film music. Publications: Principles and Practice of Electronic Music, 1974; Eighteenth Century Counterpoint, 1993; Sixteenth Century Counterpoint, 1994. Address: 41 W Main, Morgantown, WV 26505, USA.

TSCHAIKOV Basil (Nichols), b. 30 May 1925, London, England. Clarinettist. m. (1), 2 daughters, (2) Dorothy Gallon, July 1966. Education: Royal College of Music. Career: London Philharmonic Orchestra, 1943-47; Royal Philharmonic Orchestra, 1947-55; Philharmonia Orchestra, 1958-79; Visiting Lecturer, Middlesex Polytechnic, England, 1959-79; Professor, Royal College of Music, 1964-84; Director, National Centre for Orchestral Studies, London University, Goldsmiths' College, 1979-89; Artistic and Executive Director, Orchestra for Europe, 1989-90; Chairman, Music Performance Research Centre, 1987-; Editor in Chief, Musical Performance, Harwood Academic Publishers, 1993-. Compositions: First Tunes and Studies; Play the Clarinet. Recordings: Various chamber ensembles. Publications: Play the Clarinet Teachers Handbook; How to Be a Musician. Honour: Honorary RCM. Memberships: Fellow, Royal Society of Arts; Incorporated Society of Musicians; Musicians Union. Address: Hillside Cottage, Hillbrow, Liss, Hants, GU33 7PS, England.

TSCHERGOV Michail, b. 1 Oct 1928, Novo Selo, Bulgaria. Singer (Tenor and Baritone). Education: Studied in Sofia. Career: Sang with the Vraza Opera, 1952-53 (debut as Nemorino), at Rostock, 1966-68, as Max, Alvaro and Dimitri; Sang widely in Eastern Europe as Otello, Canio, Des Grieux and Pedro in Tiefland; Other roles have included Calaf, Don José, Florestan, Tannhäuser, Siegmund and Rodolfo; Sang Otello at Frankfurt, 1988, and from 1990 such baritone roles as Verdi's Rigoletto and Renato. Address: Bulgarian National Opera, Boul Dondoukov 58, 1000 Sofia, Bulgaria.

TSIOLAS Stelios, b. 28 Dec 1955, Kondea, Famagusta, Cyprus. Composer. Education: Diploma, American Academy, Larnaca, Cyprus, 1974; Diploma of Music, ACMM, Melba Memorial Conservatorium, 1978-81; BMus (Composition), University of Melbourne, 1981-83. Debut: Larnaca, Cyprus, 1976. Career: Orchestrator, Conductor, Greek Song Festival, Dallas Brooks Hall, 1983; Composer, Dollar Culture, New Audience Ensemble, Melba Hall, 1983; Composer/Musician-in-Residence, Australia Council, Carringbush Library, 1984; Orchestrator, Greek Song Festival, Dallas Brooks Hall, 1984; Composer, Musical Director, Victorian Arts Centre, 1985; Composer, Conductor, Greek Progressive Youth of Australia, 1986, 1987; Composer, Conductor, Greek Orthodox Community of South Australia, 1986; Founder, Australian-Greek Choir, 1987. Compositions include: Greek Kangaroo; Antigone; Metamorphosis; Freedom Tonight; At Dawn; A Rock Experience; Ilie, Ilie Vasilia (Sun, Sun My King); At Dawn; Musical Reflections of Composers of Diaspora; numerous songs with traditional Greek-music elements; Song-cycle of 12 poems, Thoughts from Unconjucted Colours, poetry by Anastasis Barkatsas, 1980; Song-cycle Confession, poetry by Doros Loizou, 1981; Twelve-Tone and Avant-Garde Compositions: Electronique Pieces and Musique Concrète; Short Compositions for Soloistic Use and Small Chamber Ensembles. Recordings: The Greek

Kangaroo-Children's Songs; Freedom Tonight; Ilie, Ilie Vasilia (Sun, Sun my King). Hobbies: Traveling; Learning. Address: 7 Williamstown Road, W Foostcray, 3012 Melbourne, Victoria, Australia.

TSONTAKIS George, b. 24 October 1951, New York, USA. Composer. Education: Studied with Roger Sessions (1974-79), at the Juilliard School (1978-86) and with Karlheinz Stockhausen in Rome, 1981. Career: Freelance Composer; Assistant in Electronic Music at Juilliard (1978) and Assistant Professor at the Brooklyn College Conservatory, 1986-87. Compositions include: Scenes from the Apocolypse for soloists, chorus and orchestra, 1978; The Epistle of James, Chapter I for narrator, chorus and orchestra, 1980; Erotkritos, oratorio for chorus and orchestra, 1982; Five Signs and a Fantasy for orchestra, 1985; Fantasia Habanera for orchestra, 1986; 4 string quartets, 1980, 1984, 1986, 1989; Bird-wind Quintet, 1983; Brass Quintet, 1983; Brass Quinetet, 1984; Saviours for soprano, chorus and orchestra, 1985; The Past, The Passion, for 15 players, 1987; Galway Kinnell Songs for mezzo, piano and string quartet; The the Sowers of the Seed for orchestra, 1989; Heartsounds, quintet for piano and strings, 1990; Stabat Mater, for soprano, chorus and orchestra, 1990. Honours include: Koussevitszky Foundation Commission, 1987. Address: c/o ASCAP, ASCAP Building, One Lincoln Plaza, New York, NY 10023, USA.

TSOUPAKI Calliope, b. 27 May 1963, Piraeus, Greece. Composer; Pianist. Education: Studied at the Hellinicon Conservatory, Athens and at Nikos Skalkottas Conservatory (1985); With Louis Andriessen at The Hague Royal Conservatory; Summer courses at Darmstadt with Iannis Xenakis, Olivier Messiaen and Pierre Boulez (1985-88). Career: Freelance composer and pianist; Gaudeamus International Music Week at Amsterdam, 1991 and 1993; Composer in residence at the 1993 Budapest Young Artists Foundation; Featured composer at 1995 San Francisco Other Minds Festival. Compositions include: Eclipse for orchestra, 1986; Earinon for 8 horns and percussion, 1986; Revealing Moment for alto flute, 1987; Moments I and II for piano, 1988; For Always for female voice, tape and lights, 1989; Your Thouht for voice, tape and lighting, 1989; Silver Moments for 2 pianos and 2 percussion players, 1989; Mania for amplified violin, 1989; Visions of the Night, for amplified chamber ensemble, 1989; Sappho's Tears for violin, tenor recorder, and female voice, 1990; When I was 27, for amplified viola and double bass, 1990; Song for Four, for strung quartet, 1991; Echoing Purple for violin and ensemble, 1992; Eros and Psyche, for wind octet and double bass, 1992; Orphic Fields for flute, 2 harps and 2 pianos, 1993; Phantom for tuba, 1994; Her Voice for harp, 1994; Ethra for flute, string trip and harp, 1995; Epigramma for chorus and orchestra, 1995; Lineos for chorus and ensemble, 1995.

TSUTSUMI Tsuyoshi, b. 28 July 1942, Tokyo, Japan. Recording Artist; Concert Cellist; Professor of Music. m. Harue Saji, 14 May 1978, 1 son, 1 daughter. Education: Toho Gakuen High School of Music, Tokyo, 1961; Artist Diploma, Indiana University, USA, 1965. Debut: Tokyo, Japan, 1955. Career: Soloist (Iwaki), European Tour, NHK Symphony Orchestra of Tokyo, 1960; Soloist (Ozawa), Chicago Symphony, Ravinia Festival, Ravinia Park, Chicago, Illinois, USA, 1967; Soloist (Ozawa), American and European Tour, New Japan Philharmonic, 1974; Soloist (Akiyama), American Symphony, New York City, 1978; Soloist (Ceccato), Czech Philharmonic, Prague, Czechoslovakia, 1984; Professor of Music, School of Music, University of Illinois, Urbana, Illinois, USA; Currently, Professor of Music, School of Music, Indiana University, Bloomington, Indiana, USA. Recordings: Bach, Unaccompanied Suites, complete; Beethoven, Sonatas and Variations (Turini, piano); Dvorák Concerto, Czech Philharmonic (Kosler, conductor); Haydn, Concertos, English Chamber Orchestra; Yashiro Concerto, Tokyo Symphony Orchestra, conducted by Ohtomo. Publication: An Illinois Diary (The Cello and I), 1991. Contributions to: American String Teacher, magazine, 1994. Honours: 1st Prize, Casals Cello Competition, 1963; Academy of Arts of Japan Award, 1993. Memberships: Violoncello Society of New York; President, Japan Cello Society. Current Management: John Gingrich Management, New York, USA; Kajimoto Concert Management, Tokyo, Japan. Address: 2715 Bluff Court, Bloomington, IN 47401, USA.

TSYDYPOVA Valentina, b. 1955, Buritia, Russia. Singer (Soprano). Education: Graduated the Novosibirsk Conservatory 1984. Career: Sang at the Ulan-Ude Opera Theatre 1984-89; Novosibirsk Opera Theatre 1989-92; Kirov Opera St Petersburg from 1992, notably on tour to Italy, Israel, Spain, the Met Opera in New York, France, Finland and Germany; Guest appearances as Butterfly at the Opéra Bastille, Paris (1993) and in Hamburg and Berlin, Tosca at the Savonlinna Festival and Gorislava in Ruslan and Ludmilla at San Francisco; Other roles include Tchaikovsky's Tatiana, Maria (Mazeppa) and Lisa, Elisabeth de Valois, Desdemona, Aida, Santuzza and Yaroslavna; Concerts include Wigmore Hall recital (1995) and the Verdi Requiem at the Bastille Opéra. Recordings include: Rimsky's Sadko and Glinka's Ruslan and Ludmilla, with the Kirov Opera (Philips). Honours include: People's Artist of the Buriatian Republic. Address: c/o Lies Askonas Ltd, 6 Henrietta St, London WC2E 8LA, England.

TSYPIN George, b. 1950, Russia. Set Designer. Education: Studied architecture in Moscow and set design in New York. Career: Collaborations with producer Peter Sellars include premiere of Osborne's The Electrification of the Soviet Union (1987) and Handel's Theodora (1996) at Glyndebourne; Premiere production of The Death of Klinghoffer by John Adams seen at Brussels, San Francisco, Lyon and New York, 1991; Messiaen's St Francois d'Assise (1992) and Le Grand Macabre by Ligeti (1997) at the Salzburg Festival; First staging by British company of Hindemith's Mathis der Maler, Covent Garden 1995; Further engagements with Salome and Katerina Izmailova at the Kirov, St Petersburg; The Gambler at La Scala, Die Zauberflöte in Florence and Orfeo and Euridice in Zurich; Oediupus Rex in Japan, Rigoletto for Canadian Opera with further work on Tannhäuser, Don Giovanni and Pelléas et Mélisande; Engaged for The Ring at Netherlands Opera (concluding with Götterdämmerung, 1999). Address: c/o Glyndebourne Festival Opera, Glyndebourne, Lewes, East Sussex BN8 5JJ, England.

TUCAPSKY Antonin, b. 27 Mar 1928, Opatovice, Czechoslovakia. Composer; Cnductor; Professor. m. Beryl Musgrave, 13 Oct 1972, 1 son, 1 daughter. Education: PhDr, Teacher's training College, Masaryk University, Brno; Music Education, Conducting, choral singing, composition, Janacek Academy of Music, Brno. Debut: Pstrava. Career: Conductor of various choirs, 1954-65; Children's Radio Choir, Ostrava, 1960-62; Chief Conductor, Moravian Teachers Choir, 1964-73; Appearances on Czech Radio, Supraphon Records, BBC radio and television, Belgian radio. Compositions: In Honorem Vitae; Lauds; 5 Lenten Motets, choral cycles; The Time of Christmas; the Sacrifice, cantatas; Four Dialogues, clarinet and piano; Pocket Music, wind quintet; Adieu; Moravian Polka, orchestra; Missa Serena, oratorio; Stabat Mater, oratorio; The Undertaker, opera; Triptychon, symphony orchestra, 1991; Concertino, for piano and string orchestra, 1992; Concerto, for violin and orchestra, 1993. Recordings: Choral Music; Comoedia, Cantata, Veni Sancte Spiritus, BBC Recordings. Publications: Sightreading and Sightsinging, 1969; Janacek's Male Choruses and Their Interpretation, 1971. Hobbies: Gardening; Swimming. Address: 50 Birchen Grove, Kingsbury, London NW9 8SA, England.

TUCCI Gabriella, b. 4 Aug 1929, Rome, Italy. Singer (soprano). Education: Studied at the Accademia di Santa Cecilia and with Leonardi Filoni. Debut: Teatro Giglio Lucca 1951, as Violetta. Career: Spoleto Festival 1952, as Leonora in La Forza del Destino; Florence 1953, as Cherubini's Medee; Tour of Australia 1955; La Scala Milan from 1959, as Mimi and in the Italian premiere of A Midsummer Night's Dream; Verona Arena 1959-69; US debut San Francisco 1959, as Madeleine in Andrea Chénier; Metropolitan Opera, 1960-73 as Butterfly, Aida, Euridice, Leonora in Trovatore and La Forza del Destino, Violetta and Marguerite; Covent Garden 1960, as Tosca; Appearances at Buenos Aires, Sydney, Oslo, Johannesburg, Dallas, New Orleans and Philadelphia; Other roles include Desdemona, Anaide in Mosé by Rossini, Luisa Miller, Micaela and Elvira in I Puritani; Teacher at Indiana University from 1983. Recordings: Pagliacci; Il Trovatore; Requiems by Bellini and Donizetti. Address: Music Faculty, Indiana University, Bloomington, IN 47405, USA.

TUCEK Rene, b. 8 Jan 1936, Pizen, Czechoslovakia. Singer (Baritone). Education: Studied in Pizen with M Gartnerova and in Vienna with F Schuch-Tovini. Debut: Brno 1960, as Count Luna in Il Trovatore. Career: Sang first in Brno, Pizen and Ceske Budejovice; Prague National Theatre from 1971, in the standard repertory and in operas Prokofiev, Martinu, Gershwin and Myslivicek; Guest appearances in Spain, Austria, Bulgaria, Luxembourg and Cuba; Has sung in concert and in song recitals; Teacher at the Prague Conservatory from 1973. Recordings: The Jacobin by Dvorak and operas by Smetana (Supraphon). Address: c/o National Theatre, PO Box 865, 112 30 Prague 1, Czech Republic.

TUCKER Mark, b. 10 Aug 1958, England. Singer (Tenor). Education: Studied at Cambridge and the Guildhall School of Music and Drama. Career includes: Active as concert and opera singer throughout Europe under such conductors as Michel Corboz, John Eliot Gardiner, Ton Koopman, Roger Norrington and Sigiswald Kuijken; Appearances at the Salzburg Festival in Monteverdi's Verspers of 1610 under Harnoncourt and under John Eliot Gardiner at St Mark's in Venice; Other notable concert engagements have included a tour of China with the Academy of London singing Les Illuminations, 1994; Operatic engagements include notably the title role in Monteverdi's Orfeo at the Bruges Festival, at the Arena di Verona, at the Liceu, Barcelona in 1993 and at the Palazzo Ducale, Mantua; Has also sung productions of Il ritorno di Ulisse in patria and L'incoronazione di Poppea in Amsterdam, New York, and on tour in Italy, 1993; In addition has sung numerous tenor roles, Tom Rakewell (The Rake's Progress), in a new production for Opera Factory, 1994 and recently Lysander (A Midsummer Night's Dream) in Turin, 1995; Royal Opera, Covent Garden debut in 1995 as The Novice (Billy Budd); Highlights in 1995 included Gomatz (Zaide) at La Monnaie, in Strasbourg and in Kolmar, a tour of the Netherlands with the Niuew Sinfonietta Amsterdam under Mark Wigglesworth singing Les Illuminations; 1996 included a return to Netherlands Opera (Il ritorno di Ulisse in patria), Messiah in Marseille and a performance of Elijah at the Proms; Season 1997 with Judas Maccabeas in Vienna and Ravel's L'Enfant with the London Symphony Orchestra. Recordings include: Fennimore and Gerda by Delius (1997). Address: c/o Harrison Parrott Ltd, 12 Penzance Place, London W11 4PA, England.

TUDORAN Ionel, b. 24 June 1913, Baragti de Vede, Rumania. Singer (Tenor). Education: Studied at the Conservatory of Iasi. Debut: Iasi 1936, in the operetta Die Landstreicher by Ziehrer. Career: Sang at Cluj and Timisoara 1937-48; Principal tenor at Bucharest from 1948, notably as Otello, Faust and Cavaradossi; Guest appearances in Leipzig, Dresden, Prague, Brno, Sofia, and Budapest; From 1957 sang in Russia in opera houses in Riga, Minsk, Lengingrad and Moscow; Warsaw and Poznan 1958, Belgrade, Ljubljana and Zagreb 1959; Retired 1962 and taught at the Bucharest Conservatory until 1972.

TULACEK Thomas, b. 26 April 1955, Violinist. Education: Studied at the Prague Conservatory, the Prague Academy of Musical Arts and the Guildhall School of Music. Career: First Violin Section, BBC Scottish Symphony Orchestra, 1985-89; Leader, New Chamber Orchestra, Oxford,1990-; Associate Professor, Trinity College of Music, London, 1991; Recital work has taken him to countries such as Italy, Switzerland, France, Israel and the Czech Republic and has recorded for Czech Radio and Radio Vatican; Since 1990 has been performing regularly with the English pianist Steven Wray and they have formed a piano trio with Jaroslav Ondracek; Concerto performances have included works by Prokofiev, Bruch, Haydn, Mozart and most recently Neilsen, with the Teplice Symphony Orchestra, in the Czech Republic. Address: 1 Brookes Court, Longley Road, London SW17 9LF, England.

TUMA Jaroslav, b. 1956, Czechoslovakia. Organist. Education: Studied at the Prague Academy of Arts with Milan Sleehta and with Zuzana Ruzicková; with Hans Haselböck, Summer school at Haarlem, Holland, studying improvisation, and Bach interpretation with Piet Kee. Career: Laureate of organ competitions in Prague, Linz, Leipzig, Nuremberg and Haarlem; Festival appearances by Nuremberg, Linz, Prague and Mechelen; Engagements in Europe, Japan and the USA; Concerts with Czech Philharmonic Orchestra, Three years cycle of complete organ works by J S Bach in Prague; Repertoire includes works by Bach, Franck, Liszt, Reger, Hoffhaimer, Sweelinck, Isaac and Husa; Accompanies major soloists on the harpischord. Recordings: L and H Hassler, Muffat; Handel; Series organs of Bohema I-IV, Czech compositions for harpischord. Current Management: Bohemia-Concert, PO Box 5, Prague, 100 05, Czech Republic. Address: Bohemia Concert, PO Box 5, 100 05 Prague 105, Czech Republic.

TUMAGIAN Eduard, b. 1944, Bucharest, Rumania. Singer (Baritone). Career: Sang at Bucharest from 1968 as Papageno, Alfonso, Mozart's Count, and Wolfram in Tannhäuser; Opéra du Rhin Strasbourg from 1974, as Germont, Iago, Enrico in Lucia di Lammermoor, Scarpia, Marcello, Belcore, Escamillo and Eugene Onegin; Guest appearances at Lyon, Stuttgart, Karlsruhe and Orange; Sang Rigoletto at Basle 1981 and appeared further with Welsh and English National operas, Frankfurt (Renato 1983), Nice (I Puritani and Vespri Sicilaini (Montfort), I Due Foscari and Riccardo III by Flavio Testi; Paris Opera 1985, as Germont; US debut 1986 at Pittsburgh as Don Carlo in La Forza del Destino; Carnegie Hall New York in concert peformances of Béatrice at Bénédict and Nabucco; Recent appearances at the Deutsche Oper Berlin, Staatsoper Hamburg, Vienna Staatsoper (Scarpia in season 1988-89), Toulouse (La Franciulla del West) and Oviedo Festival (Simon Boccanegra and La Favorita); Season 1991 as Nabucco at Trieste and Buenos Aires, Rigoletto at Philadelphia; Concert repertoire includes music by Bach, Handel, Beethoven, Mussorgsky, Britten and Shostakovich (14th Symphony at the 1984 Salzburg Festival). Recordings include: Miller in video of Luisa Miller from Opera de Lyon (Pioneer); Napoleon in War and Peace; Turandot.

TUMANYAN Barseg, b. 1958, Jerevan, Armenia. Singer (Bass Baritone). Education: Studied at the Komitas Conservatoire and at La Scala, Milan; Further study with Evgeny Nesterenko at the Moscow Conservatoire, 1985. Career: Sang with the Spenderian Opera (Armenia) from 1980; Performances of Basilio at the Teatro San Carlo Naples 1988; Appeared in Gala Concert for Armenia at Covent Garden 1989, and invited back to sing in La Bohème, Les Contes d'Hoffmann and Carmen; US debut with Boston Opera as Ramfis in Aida, 1989; Appearances in USA, 1989 with the Armenian State Opera; Sang Colline in La Bohème at Covent Garden and Monte Carlo, 1990; King Philip in Don Carlos at Los Angeles; Wigmore Hall recital, June 1990. Honours: Prizewinner, Bussetto Competition, 1983; 2nd Prize, Tchaikovsky

Competition, Moscow 1986; Joint First Prize, Rio de Janeiro Competition, 1987. Address: c/o 6 Lies Askonas Ltd, 6 Henrietta Street, London WC2, England.

TUNLEY David (Evatt), b. 3 May 1930, Sydney, New South Wales, Australia. Emeritus Professor of Music. m. Paula Patricia Laurantus, 26 May 1959, 1 son, 2 daughters. Education: Diploma, New South Wales State Conservatorium of Music, 1949-51; BMus, University of Durham, England, 1957; MMus, 1963, DLitt, 1970, University of Western Australia. Career: Music Master, Fort Street Boys High School, Sydney, 1952-57; University of Western Australia, 1958-; Currently Emeritus Professor of Music. Compositions: Concerto for Clarinet and Strings, recorded. Publications: Monographs: The 18th Century French Cantata, 1974; Couperin, 1982; Harmony in Action, 1984; The French Cantata Facsimile, 17 volumes, 1990-91; Romantic French Song 1830-1870, 6 volumes, 1994-95. Contributions to: New Grove Dictionary; New Oxford History of Music, vols 6 and 9. Honours: Fellow, Australian Academy of the Humanities, 1980; Chevalier, l'Ordre des Palmes Académiques, 1982; Member of the Order of Australia, 1987. Memberships: Chairman, Music Board, Australia Council, 1984-85; Past President, Musicological Society of Australia. Hobbies: Reading; Theatre; Travel. Address: 100 Dalkeith Road, Nedlands, Western Australia 6009, Australia.

TUNNELL Jonathon, b. 1955, England. Cellist. Debut: Wigmore Hall, 1984, with Peter Pears. Career: Member of the Tunnell Trio; Co-founded the Brindisi String Quintet at Aldeburgh 1984; Concerts in a wide repertory throughout Britain and in France, Germany, Spain, Italy and Switzerland; Festival engagements at Aldeburgh (residency 1990), Arundel, Bath, Brighton, Huddersfield, Norwich and Warwick; First London performance of Colin Matthews's 2nd Quartet, 1990, premiere of David Matthews's 6th Quartet 1991; Quartet by Mark-Anthony Turnage 1992; Many BBC recitals and resident artist with the University of Ulster. Recordings include: Quartets by Britten, Bridge and Imogen Holst; Works by Pierné and Lekeu. Honours include: Prize winner, Third Banff International String Quartet Competition in Canada, 1989, with Brindisi Quartet. Address: c/o Owen-White Management, 14 Nightingale Lane, London, N8 7QU, England.

TUOMELA Tapio (Juhani), b. 11 Oct 1958, Kuusamo, Finland. Composer; Conductor. m. Helena Tuovinen, 7 Sept 1985, 3 daughters. Education: Diplomas: Piano, 1982, Orchestra Conducting, 1987, Sibelius Academy, Helsinki; MMus in Composition, Eastman School of Music, Rochester, New York, USA, 1990. Debut: Concert of own compositions, Helsinki Festival, 1991. Career: Performances of own works: UNM Festivals (Young Scandinavian Composers), 1985-89; Scandinavian Music Days, 1990, 1994, 1996; Time of Music Festival, Viitasaari, 1993, 1997; Tampere Biennale, 1994, 1996; Performances in the USA, Germany, Russia, Hungary, Netherlands, all Scandinavian countries; Also active as a Conductor including numerous first performances in Scandinavia. Compositions: L'échelle de l'évasion for chamber orchestra, 1989; Symphony, 1991; The Ear's Tale, chamber opera (Finnish National Opera commission), 1993; Jokk for orchestra, 1995. Recordings: Symmetry, quintet; L'échelle de l'évasion; Conductor, world premiere recording of ballet music Maa, by K Saariaho and some late pieces for string orchestra by Sibelius, 1995. Honours: 2nd Prizes, Composition Contests on 70th and 75th Anniversary of Finnish Independence, 1987, 1992; 2 placings on UNESCO Rostrum for Composers (recommended works list). Memberships: Finnish Composers' Society, 1989-; Teosto Copyright Society, Board Member 1995-. Hobbies: Family; Fishing; Skiing. Address: Temppelikatu 14 A 12, 00100 Helsinki, Finland.

TURBAN Ingolf, b. 17 Mar 1964, Munich, Germany. Violinist. m. Barbara Meier, 28 July 1994, 1 son. Education: Studied at the Munich Musikhochschule with Gerhart Hetzel and at Aspen, Colorado with Dorothy DeLay and Jens Ellerman. debut: Munich, 1986, with the Munich Philharmonic; National Symphony Orchestra, Washington DC, USA, 1991. Career: Leader of the Munich Philharmonic, 1985-88; Solo career since 1988 in Europe, USA, Canada and Israel; Professor, Stuttgart Musikhochschule, 1995-. Compositions: Cadenzas to numerous violin concertos; Cadenza to Concerto No 2 by Paganini, 1994. Recordings: Numerous including: World premieres, Paganini Caprices with piano accompaniment by Schumann; Hartmann Solo Sonatas and Suites; Ernst Pieces; Respighi with English Chamber Orchestra; Marek with the Philharmonia, London. Current Management: Art Productions, Bertelstrasse 30, 81479 Munich, Germany. Address: Nordstrasse 4, D-82131 Stockdorf, Munich, Germany.

TURCANO Lucia, b. 1913, Bucharest. Romania. Singer (Soprano). Education: Studied at the Bucharest Conservatory with Elena Saghin and Demetru Baxiliu. Debut: Bucharest 1939, as Marguerite in Faust. Career: Sang in Bucharest until 1946 as Rachel in La Juive, Leonora (Il Trovatore), Aida and Elsa in Lohengrin; Vienna Volksoper 1942-45; La Scala Milan from 1946, notably as Abigaille in Nabucco, Gioconda and Turandot; Guest appearances in Venice, Palermo, Naples, Bologna, Trieste, Rome and Cagliari; New York City Opera 1950-60, with further appearances in Philadelphia; Returned to Rumania in 1963, gave concerts and taught.

TURCHI Guido, b. 10 Nov 1916, Rome, Italy. Composer. Education: Studied at the Rome Conservatory and with Pizzetti at the Accademia di Santa Cecilia. Career: Taught at the Rome Conservatory, Director, Parma and Florence Conservatories 1967-72; Artistic Director, Accademia Filormonica Romana 1963-66, and Teatro Comunale Bologna, 1968-70; Artistic Director, Accademia di Santa Cecilia from 1972-75; Accademia Musicale Chigiana do Siena, 1978-88. Compositions include: Opera Il buon soldato Svejk, La Scala Milan 1962; Trio for flute, clarinet and viola 1945; Invettiva for small chorus and 2 pianos 1946; Concerto for string orchestra 1948; Piccolo concerto notturno 1950; 3 Meamorfosi for orchestra 1970; Dedalo, ballet, Florence 1972; Dedica for flute 1972; Adagio for orchestra, 1983; Parabola for orchestra, 1993; Choruses, songs and incidental music. Address: Cannaregio 233, 30121 Venezia, Italy.

TURCO Enrico, b. 1962, Genoa, Italy. Singer (Bass). Education: Studied at the Accademia di Santa Cecilia, Rome. Career: Sang at first in concert and made stage debut in 1987, as King Philip in Don Carlos; Macerata Festival, 1991, as Leporello and Frankfurt Alte Oper in a concert of Franchetti's Cristoforo Colombo; Guest appearances at La Scala, Turin, Parma and the Scottish Opera. Address: c/o Teatro alla Scala, Via Filodrammatici 2, 20121 Milan, Italy.

TURECK Rosalyn, b. 14 December 1914, Chicago, Illinois, USA. Concert Artist (Pianist); Author; Editor; Professor. Education: Studied with Sophia Brilliant-Liven, Jan Chiapusso; Graduated Cum Laude, Juilliard School of Music, 1935; Studied with Olga Samaroff; Studied Electronic Instruments with Theremin. Career includes: Extensive US tours since 1937 annually; European Tours since 1947; Tours of South Africa, South America, Middle East, Far East; Experience as Conductor Soloist with London Philharmonia, 1958, New York Philharmonc, 1958, Tureck Bach Players (London) 1958, San Antonio Symphony, Oklahoma Symphony, 1962, Scottish National Symphony, Israel Philharmonic, Kol Israel Orchestra, 1963; Repeated solo appearances at major British and European Bach Festivals; Numerous TV appearances in US and England, 1963-; Numerous academic appointments. Recordings include: Numerous recordings on Decca, HMV, Brunswick, Odeon, Allegro, Capitol, Columbia; Video Teatro Colon, 1992; CDs, 1992-. Publications include: Introduction to the Performances of Bach 3 Vols, 1959-60; Tureck Bach Urtext Series: Italian Concerto, 1983, Lute Suites, E minor and C minor, edited for Classical Guitar; Italian Concerto, 2nd edition, 1991. Contributions to: Royal Institution of Great Britain, London, University of Southampton, Oxford University, All Lectures, 1993; Numerous articles in musical journals. Honours: Numerous prizes and awards in the US and Europe. Honours include: Recipient of numerous grants; Decorated Officers Cross of the Order of Merit, Germany, 1979. Memberships include: Royal Musical Association, London; American Musicological Society; Honorary Fellow, Guildhall School of Music and Drama; Royal Philharmonic Society, London; American bach Society. Century Club, New York; Oxford and Cambridge, London. Current Management: Christa Phelps, Lies Askonas Ltd. Address: c/o Christa Phelps, Lies Askonas Ltd, 6 Henrietta Street, London WC2E 8LA, England.

TURETZKY Bertram (Jay), b. 14 Feb 1933, Norwich, Connecticut, USA. Double Bass Player; Composer. Education: Studied at the Hartt School of Music (graduated 1955), at New York University (musicology with Curt Sachs) and with David Walter; Further study at the University of Hartford, MM 1965. Career: Played double bass in various orchestras and ensembles; Solo debut at Judson Hall, New York, Oct 1064, with works by Donald Erb and Barney Childs; Novel performing techniques have been exploited by such composers as Donald Martino, Richard Felciano, Paul Chihara, Kenneth Gaburro, George Perle and Ben Johnston. Compositions: Collages I-IV 1976-81; Reflections on Ives and Whittier for double bass and tape 1979-81; In memoriam Charles Mingus 1979; Baku for tape 1980. Publications include: The Contemporary Contrabass 1974; Editions of double bass studies for the American String Teachers Association; Editor of series published by the University of California Press on contemporary performance techniques. Address: ASCAP, ASCAP Building, One Lincoln Plaza, New York, NY 10023, USA.

TURKOVIC Milan, b. 14 Sept 1939, Zagreb, Yugoslavia (Austrian citizen). Bassoonist. Education: Studied in Vienna. Career: Performed with the Philharmonia Hungarica, then soloist with the Bamber Symphony and member of the Bamberg Wind Quintet; Soloist with the Vienna Symphony from 1967, with freelance concert performances from 1984; Further concerts at the Salzburg Mozarteum and with Concentus Musicus at Vienna, under Harnoncourt; Created Helmut Eder's concerto in 1968 and with Helmut and Wolfgang Schulz formed the Vienna Trio. Address: c/o Salzburg Mozarteum Orchestra, Erzbischof-Gebhardstrasse 10, A-5020 Salzburg, Austria.

TURNAGE Mark Anthony, b. 10 June 1960, Grays, Essex, England. Composer. Education: Royal College of Music, with Oliver Knussen and John Lambert; Tanglewood, USA with Henze and Gunther Schuller. Career: Commissions from the London Sinfonietta, Bath Festival, CBSO, the BBC and the Munich Biennale; Ensemble Modern; English Aldeburgh Festival; English National Opera; Radcliffe Trust Composer in Association with the City of Birmingham Symphony, 1989-93; Has been appointed Composer in Association with English National Opera, 1995-98. Compositions include: Night Dances for Orchestra, 1980-81; Entranced for Piano, 1982-86; Lament for a Hanging Man for Soprano and Ensemble, 1983; Sarabande for soprano saxophone and piano, 1985; On All Fours for chamber ensemble, 1985; Release for 8 Players, 1987; Greek Opera in 2 acts, 1987-88; Three Screaming Popes for Orchestra, 1989; Greek Suite for mezzo soprano, tenor and ensemble, 1989; Kai for solo cello and ensemble, 1989-90; Momentum for orchestra, 1990-91; Killing Time, TV scena, 1991; Drowned Out, 1992-93; Your Rockaby, saxophone concerto, 1992-93; Blood on the Floor, for large ensemble, 1994-95; Dispelling Your Fears, 1994-95; Twice Through the Heart, for mezzo and 16 players, 1997; The Country of the Blind, 1997. Recordings: Drowned Out; Kai; Momentum; Three Screaming Popes; Greek with The Greek Ensemble; Lament for a Hanging Man; On All Fours; Release; Sarabande; Sleep On. Honours: 1982 Guinness Prize for Composition and Yorkshire Arts Young Composers' Competition; Benjamin Britten Young Composers' Prize, 1983; BMW Music Theatre Prize, 1988. Current Management: Schott and Co Ltd. Address: c/o Schott and Co Ltd, 48 Great Marlborough Street, London, W1V 2BN, England.

TURNER Charles (Lloyd), b. 10 July 1948, Houston, Texas, USA. Musicologist; Bibliographer; Performer. Education: BMus, 1970; MMus, 1976; MSLS, 1979, University of Texas; DMus, Indiana University, 1986. Career: Founding Director, La Primavera, Early Music Ensemble; Concert tours of Texas, California, Southwest USA; Tour of Mexico sponsored by US State Department; Musicologist, Director of Hartt Early Music Ensemble, Hartt School, University of Hartford. Recordings: Popular Elizabethan Music; The Greater Passion Play from Carmina Burana. Publications: Bibliographer, Medieval Music, 1986; The Isorhythmic Motet in Continental Europe, Proportion and Form, 1986; Articles in Journal of the Lute Society of America, Lute Society Quarterly, Journal of the American Musicological Society and Music Analysis; Reviews in Notes. Honours: Phi Beta Kappa; Crane Award in the Arts, 1979. Memberships: American Musicological Society; Lute Society of America; Early Music America. Hobbies: Chess; Photography; Early Jazz; Pet Greyhound. Address: University of Hartford, 200 Bloomfield Avenue, West Hartford, CT 06117, USA.

TURNER Claramae, b. 28 Oct 1920, Dinuba, California, USA. Singer (Contralto). Education: Studied with Nino Comel, Armando Angini and Giacomo Spadoni at San Francisco and with Dick Marzollo in New York. Debut: San Francisco 1942, in Les Contes d'Hoffmann. Career: Sang at the Metropolitan Opera 1946-50, notably as Amneris; Sang in the premieres of Menotti's The Medium (1946), The Tender Land by Copland (1954) and Bomarzo by Ginastera (1967); Teatro Liceo Barcelona 1957-58; Chicago Lyric Opera 1956, as Azucena; Sang Diego 1967, in the US premiere of Der junge Lord by Henze; Appearances in Buenos Aires, Mexico City, Venice, Monte Carlo, Boston, Dallas, Houston, Baltimore, Philadelphia and Pittsburgh. Recordings: Un Ballo in Maschera, conducted by Toscanini (RCA); Bomarzo (CBS).

TURNER Jane, b. 1960, County Durham, England. Singer (Mezzo Soprano). Education: Guildhall School of Music; Opera Studio, London. Career: West German debut as Wellgunde and Siegrune in The Ring at Bayreuth, 1984, as a Flower Maiden and Flosshilde; UK Opera debut 1985 as Carmen with the Glyndebourne Tour; Flora in Peter Hall's production of Traviata at the Festival, 1987; Covent Garden debut 1987, as Ann Who Strips in the Hytner production of The King Goes Forth to France; returned as a Flower Maiden in Parsifal and as Flosshilde in Das Rheingold; English National Opera as Maddalena in Rigoletto and as Lola in Cavalleria Rusticana; Sang Siebel in Faust at Dublin, 1995. Current Management: IMG Artists. Address: Mary Craig Services Ltd, 3 Kersley Street, London SW1 4PR, England.

TURNER John (Brierley), b. 1 Apr 1943, Stockport, Cheshire, England. Solo Recorder Player; Composer; Editor. m. Margaret Cordall Lister, 14 Apr 1988. Education: Fitzwilliam College, Cambridge; MA; LLM; Northern School of Music; LRAM; Solicitor (Hons). Debut: Aldeburgh Festival, 1968. Career: Regular concerts and recordings with Early Music Consort of London, 1969-76; Co-Founder of Legrand Ensemble, 1968-; Duo recitals with Neil Smith on guitar and Peter Lawson on piano; 1st performances include: Leighton's Concerto, Alwyn's Seascapes, McCabe's Desert IV: Vista, Crosse's Watermusic, Burgon's Nearing the Upper Air, Pitfield's Concerto, Ball's Danserye,

Fricker's Two Dreams, Gilbert's Igorochki and Rawsthorne's Suite. Compositions: Four Diversions, 1969; A Christmas Garland, 1981; Six Bagatelles, 1983. Recordings: Brandenburg Concerto No 4 with English Chamber Orchestra, Academy of St Martin-in-the-Fields, London Philharmonic Orchestra and Virtuosi of England; Telemann Concerto for Recorder and Flute with Academy of Ancient Music; Many recordings with Early Music Consort of London; The Music of Thomas Pitfield (RNCM) 1993. Publications: Editor: A Birthday Album for Thomas Pitfield, 1983; Modern Wind Music, 6 volumes, 1984-86; A Birthday Album for the Society of Recorder Players, 1987; Pieces for Solo Recorder, 3 volumes, 1987-. Address: 40 Parsonage Road, Heaton Floor, Stockport, Cheshire, SK4 4JR, England.

TURNER Margarita, b. 11 Mar 1943, Perth, Australia. Singer (soprano). Education: Studied in London and West Germany. Debut: Krefeld 1969, as Micaela. Career: Appearances in opera at Cologne, Saarbrucken, Wiesbaden and Wuppertal; 15 year career at the Essen Opera as Fiordiligi, Pamina, Marguerite, Martha, Marenka, Violetta, Marzelline (Fidelio), Mélisande, Eva, Concepcion and Nedda; Sophie in Der Rosenkavalier, Mimi, Liu, Rosalinde and Luise in Der Junge Lord by Henze; Frequent concert engagements; Teacher at the Essen Musikhochschule. Address: c/o Theater, Rolandstrasse 10, 4300 Essen, Germany.

TURNER Paul, b. 16 April 1948, Morwell, Victoria, Australia. Composer. Education: BMus, 1977, Mus, 1980, University of Melbourne; Study with Barry Conyngham. Career includes: Composer-in-the-Community, Hamilton, Victoria, 1981; Faculty Member, University of Adelaide, 1987-92. Compositions include: Panels II for violin, clarinet and piano, 1974; Grand Pocket Sonata in B Minor for piano, 1986; Herbivores for piano, 1987; Sonata, for tape, 1994; A Spangled Pandemonium Escapes from the Zoo, for ensemble; Chronic Interludes I-III for saxophone and piano; Geraniums or Nasturtiums for saxophone and piano; Instrumental Rationality, for various combinations; Icarus Flying, for guitar or tape; Machines I-III for harp and tape; Phrygian Misery for saxophone and piano. Address: c/o APRA, 1A Eden Street, Crows Nest, NSW 2065, Australia.

TURNOVSKY Martin, b. 29 Sept 1928, Prague, Czechoslovakia. Conductor. Education: Music Academy, Prague; Studied Conducting i Dedecek, Prague Academy of Music, 1948-52; Private studiees in Conducting with Szell, 1956. Career: Conductor, Czech Army Symphony Orchestra, 1955-60; State Philharmonic Orchestra, Brno, 1960-63; Music Director, Pilsen Radio Orchestra, 1963-66; Dresden State Opera and State Orchestra, 1966-68; Guest Conductor with numerous well-known orchestras including Radio Orchestra, Berlin; Cleveland Orchestra; New York Philharmonic Orchestra; Detroit Symphony Orchestra; Toronto Symphony; Stockholm Philharmonic Orchestra; BBC Northern Orchestra, Manchester 1968; Music Director, Norwegian Opera, Oslo 1975-80; Music Director, Bonn Opera, 1979-83; Opera engagements with the Deutsche Oper Berlin, Welsh National Opera, Staatsoper Stuttgart, Royal Opera Stockholm and the Savonlinna Festival, Finland; Season 1992/93 appointed as Music Director of the Prague Symphony Orchestra and Conducted Otello and Un Ballo in Maschera at the Prague State Opera. Recordings: Has made many recordings for Supraphon including 4th Symphony of Bohuslav Martinu, Grand Prix du Disque 1968. Honours: Recipient, 1st Prize, International Competition for Conductors, Besancon, France 1958. Address: A-1190 Wien, Grinzinger Allee 39, Austria.

TUROK Paul (Harris), b. 3 Dec 1929, New York City, USA. Composer. m. Susan Kay Frucht, 24 Mar 1967. Education: BA, Queens College, 1950; MA, University of California, Berkeley, 1951; Special studies at Juilliard School of Music, 1951-53; MS, Baruch College, 1986. Career: Music Director, Experimental TV, US Army, Augusta, GA, 1954; Music Director, KPFA, Berkeley, 1955-56; Lecturer, City College of New York, 1960-63; Visiting Professor, Williams College, 1964. Compositions: Operas: Richard III, A Secular Masque, Scene Domestic; Orchestral: American Variations, Chartres West, Ultima Thule, Great Scott!, Joplin Overture, Sousa Overture, Danza Viva, Concertos for Violin, English Horn, Trombone, Cello, Oboe, Symphony; Chamber Music: 4 String Quartets, English Horn Quintet, Sonatas for Flute, Bassoon, Horn, Trumpet, Viola, Cello, Harp, Harpsichord; Numerous other works; Organ: Toccata; Piano: Passacaglia, Transcendental Etudes; Brass: Elegy, Quintet; Vocal: Lanier Songs, Evocations, To Music, Three Popular Songs. Address: c/o G Schirmer Incorporated, 24 East 22nd Street, New York, NY 10010, USA.

TURSKA Joanna (Lucja), b. 16 Oct 1958, Warsaw, Poland. Musician (Flautist). m. Roman Siczek, 28 June 1986, 1 daughter. Education: MMus, Flute Performance, Warsaw Academy of Music; Postgraduate Studies; Royal Conservatory, The Hague, Netherlands; Conservatories in Creteil and Paris, France; Teachers include E Gajewska, F Vester, A Marion (flute), S T Preston, P Sechet (baroque flute). Career: Appearances at recitals, chamber music concerts and as soloist with orchestras in Europe and America including: Germany, France, Italy, Switzerland, Austria, Netherlands, Belgium, Luxembourg, Poland, Cuba, USA; Performances at such festivls as Paris, Youth Music Festival (Bayreuth, Germany), Warsaw Autumn, New Music Festival and Early Music Festival (Chicago, USA). Recordings: Solo, chamber music and orchestral performances recorded by Polish Radio and TV, Belgian Radio, French Radio, and US Radio, TV Classical and ethnic channels; Album for winners of Premio Ancona competitions. Hobbies: Skiing; Tennis; Travel. Address: 1426 Portsmouth, Westchester, IL 60153, USA.

TUSA Andrew, b. 1966, England. Singer (Tenor). Education: New College, Oxford, Studied at the Pears-Britten School. Career: Sang in the Play of Daniel at the Elizabeth Hall 1989, followed by Asterion in Rameau's Nais for the English Bach Festival; Concert engagements include Messiah with the Leicester Bach Choir, St John Passion in Krefeld, soloist with Gothic Voices in Milan and Second Shepherd in Monteverdi's Orfeo at the 1990 Salzburg Festival; Appearances with the Gabrieli and Taverner Consorts, Christmas Oratorio under Andrew Parrott in Oslo, Masses by Mozart in Barbican Hall, 1991, St Matthew Passion with Birmingham Bach Society and Messiah with the Stavanger Symphony in Norway. Recordings include: Mozart's Salzburg Masses with the Winchester College Choir and Monteverdi Madrigals with I Fagiolini. Address: Robert Gilder & Co, Enterprise House, 59/65 Upper Ground, London SE1 9PQ, England.

TUTINO Marco, b. 30 May 1954, Milan, Italy. Composer. Education: Studied at the Giuseppe Verdi Conservatory, Milan. Career: Works performed at the 1976 Gaudeamus Festival in Amsterdam; Operas produced in Genoa, Alessandria, Livorno and Modena. Compositions: A synthesis between 19th century procedures and more modern methods. Compositions include: Operas Pinnochio, Genoa 1985; Cirano, commedia lirica, Alessandria 1987; La lupa, Livorno 1990; Le vite immaginarie, chamber opera, Modena 1990. Address: c/o Sezione Musica, Viale della Letteratura n.30, 00144 Roma (EUR), Italy.

TUVAS Linda, b. 1972, Stockholm, Sweden. Singer (Soprano). Education: Studied at Stockholm University, the Birkagarden School of Music and the Guildhall School, London. Career: Engagements as Mozart's Donna Anna and Fatma in Grétry's Zemire et Azor at Drottningholm and the Théâtre Champs-Elysées, Paris; Kate Pinkerton, Jano in Jenufa and Micaela (Carmen) for Gothenburg Opera; Further roles as Musetta for Welsh National Opera, Tatiana for British Youth Opera and the title role in Il Segretto di Susanna for Newbury Opera; Also sings Massenet's Grisélidis, Arminda in La Finta Giardiniera by Mozart, and Offenbach's Giulietta; Sang Barbarina in Le nozze de Figaro at the 1997 Glyndebourne Festival; Season 1998 as Amor in Poppea for WNO, Varvara (Katya Kabanova) for the Glyndebourne Opera. Address: c/o Welsh National Opera, John Street, Cardiff, Wales, CF1 4SP.

TWARDOWSKI Romuald, b. 17 June 1930, Wilno, Poland. Composer. m. Alice Stradczuk, 16 June 1981, 1 son. Education: Diplomas, Composition and Piano, Wilno Conservatory, 1957; Diploma, Composition, Higher School of Music, Warsaw; Postgraduate studies, Nadia Boulanger, Paris, 1963. Career: Professor, Academy of Music, Warsaw. Compositions: Operas including: Cyrano de Bergerac, 1963; Tragedy, 1969; Lord Jim, 1976; Maria Stuart, 1979; Story of St Catherine, 1985; Also numerous works for orchestra, choirs, theatre, cinema, most recent include: Old Polish Concerto for Strings, Little Concerto for Vocal Orchestra, Michelangelo Sonnets for Baritone and Piano, Lithuanian Variations for Winds/Quartet, all 1988. Recordings include: Gershwin, Variations for Symphony Orchestra, Polish Radio, Krakow, 1980; Spanish Fantasy for Cello and Orchestra, Polish Radio, Warsaw; Alleluia for mixed choir, 1990; Espressioni for violin and piano, 1990; Niggunim, chassidim tunes for violin and piano or orchestra; Numerous recordings, own compositions. Address: ul Miaczynska 54 m 61, 02-637 Warsaw, Poland.

TYL Noel, b. 31 Dec 1936, West Chester, Pennsylvania, USA. Singer (Baritone). Career: Studied with Gibner King in New York. Debut: Teatro della Pergola Florence as Basilio in Il Barbiere di Siviglia. Career: Has sung in Boston, Houston, Cincinnati, New Orleans, San Diego and New York (City Opera); Further appearances at the Vienna Staatsoper and in Dusseldorf, Munich, Barcelona and Vancouver; Other roles include Massenet's Don Quichotte, Wotan, The Golden Cockerel and Ramphis; Also sings in concert. Address: New York City Opera, Lincoln Center, New York, NY 10023, USA.

TYLER James Henry, b. 3 Aug 1940, Connecticut, USA. Lutenist; Music Director; Author; Professor. m. Joyce Geller, 7 May 1975. Education: University of Connecticut; Private study with Joseph Ladone, 1958-61. Debut: Library of Congress, Washington DC, 1962. Career includes: Member of The Early Music Consort of London, 1969-76 and Julian Bream Consort, 1975-; Founding Director, London Early Music Group, 1976-94; Tours of Australia, America, Japan, East and West Europe; Performances in festivals including those at Edinburgh, Sydney and Lucerne; Professor of Music, and Director, Early Music Performance Programme, University of Southern California, 1986-; Carnegie Hall recital, 1987. Compositions: Music for BBC TV productions of Romeo and Juliet, Measure for Measure, Henry VIII and Hamlet. Recordings include: Music of the Renaissance Virtuosi; Vivaldi's Double Concertos, Alla Rustica; Italian Airs and Dances; La Mantovana; Elizabethan Social Music; Seventeenth Century Bel Canto; Songs in Shakespeare's Plays. Publications: The Early Guitar, 1980; A Brief Tutor for The Baroque Guitar, 1984; Gasparo Zanetti: Il Scolaro 1645, 1984; The Early Mandolin, 1989. Hobbies: Collecting early instruments and early lighting. Current Management: Los Angeles Musica Viva, 2185 Las Lunas Street, Pasadena, CA 91107, USA. Address: University of Southern California, School of Music, Los Angeles, CA 90089-0851, USA.

TYLER Marilyn, b. 6 Dec 1928, New York City, USA. Singer (Soprano). Education: Studied with Friedrich Schoor in New York and with Toti dal Monte in Venice. Career: Sang first in operetta; Basle Opera 1948; Netherlands Opera 1955, as Violetta; Sang title role in Die Entführung; Bayreuth; Bayreuth 1961, Brünnhilde in Die Walküre; Appearances in Italy, Germany, North America and Israel; Teacher at the Maastricht Conservatory, Holland. Recordings include: Die Zauberflote; Die Entführung; Serse by Handel (Westminster); Stravinsky's Pulcinella (Decca). Address: c/o Conservatorium Voor Musik, Bonnerfantstraat 15, Maastricht, Holland.

TYNES Margaret, b. 11 Sept 1929, Saluda, Virginia, USA. Singer (Soprano). Education: Studied with Emil Cooper in New York and with Tullio Serafin in Italy. Debut: New York City Opera 1952, as Fata Morgana in The Love for Three Oranges. Career: Montreal 1959, as Lady Macbeth; Has sung in Spoleto (as Salome), Vienna, Budapest, Toronto, Milan, Prague, Naples and Bologna; Metropolitan Opera debut 1973, as Jenufa; Other roles have included Norma, Aida, Desdemona, Dido and Marie in Wozzeck; Many concert appearances.

TYREN Arne, b. 27 Feb 1928, Stockholm, Sweden. Singer (Bass-Baritone). Education: Studied with Ragnar Hulten at the Stockholm Opera School. Debut: Royal Opera Stockholm 1955, as Bartolo in Le Nozze di Figaro. Career: Has sung in Scandinavia as Leporello, Baron Ochs, the Grand Inquisitor, Sarastro and Wozzeck; Drottningholm Festival from 1955, as Bartolo in Paisiello's Il barbiere di Siviglia, Don Alfonso, Il Maestro di Capella, Buonafede in Haydn's Il Mondo della luna and Seneca in L'Incoronazione di Poppea; Sang at Stockholm in the premieres of Blomdahl's Aniara (1959) and Herr von Hancken (1965) and Tintomara by Werle (1973); Edinburgh Festival 1959, Wozzeck; Further engagements in Hamburg, Cologne, Turin, Lisbon and Tel Aviv; Director of the Stockholm Opera School from 1977. Recordings include: Aniara (Columbia). Honour: Swedish Court Singer 1978. Address: Opera School, Kungliga Teatern, PO Box 16094, S-10322, Stockholm, Sweden.

TYRRELL John, b. 17 Aug 1942, Salisbury, Southern Rhodesia. Musicologist. Education: BMus, University of Cape Town, 1963; Oxford. Career: Former associate editor of the Musical Times; Editorial staff, new Grove Dictionary of Music to 1980; Lecturer, Nottingham University 1976, Reader in Opera Studies 1989. Contributions to: Many learned journals, articles on Janácek and his operas in the New Grove Dictionary of Opera, 4 volumes, Cambridge 1982; Czech Opera, Cambridge 1988; Janácek's Operas: A Documentary Account, London, 1992, and Intimate Letters, 1994. Address: University of Nottingham, Department of Music, University Park, Nottingham NG7 2RD, England.

TYRRELL Lisa Jane, b. 7 June 1967, Salford. Opera Singer. Education: Chethams School of Music, Manchester: Entered as a singer aged 11 years, 2nd study, piano; Drama, Guildhall School of Music, London; Banff Centre, School of Fine Arts, Canada. Debut: Pamina in Die Zauberföte, English Touring Opera, 1990. Career: Zerlina in Don Giovanni with the English Touring Opera; Lace Seller in Death in Venice at Glyndebourne Festival Opera; Semire in Les Borades, Birmingham Touring Opera; Judith in European Story, Garden Venture (Covent Garden); Naiad in Ariadne Auf Naxos, Garsington Opera; Euridice in Orfeo, Scottish Opera-go-Round; Debut at the Welsh National Opera in The Doctor of Myddfai; as the Child, a new opera written by Peter Maxwell Davies; Debut at the Royal Opera, Covent Garden as Barbarina in the Marriage of Figaro; Concerts include: St John Passion in Salzburg, Handel's Messiah in St Johns Smith Square; Concerts with Fretwork at St John's; Monteverdi Vespers; Ariadne Auf Naxos at Endellion Festival, with Richard Hickox; Vivaldi's Gloria at St Paul's Cathedral and Brazil; Brahms's Requiem; The Fairy Queen, ENO Bayliss Programme; New commission by Peter Maxwell Davies, with Scottish Chamber Orchestra, 1997. Honours: Associate (with distinction) of G S M D, 1989; Wyburd Trust Award (for advanced lieder study), 1990; Wingate Scholar, 1996; Channel 4 at G S M D; Also BBC Film with Peter Skellern, Where Do We Go From Here, following students of Chethams. Hobbies: Swimming; Writing; Cooking. Address: 66 Princes Avenue, London, N3 2DB, England.

TYSON Alan, b. 27 Oct 1926, Glasgow, Scotland. Musicologist. Career: Fellow 1952, Senior Research Fellow, 1971- 94, All Souls College, Oxford University; Visiting Professor of Music, Columbia University, New York City, 1969; Lyell Reader in Bibliography, Oxford University, 1973-74; Ernest Bloch Professor of Music, University of California, Berkeley, 1977-78; Member of Institute for Advanced Study, Princeton, 1983-84; Visiting Professor, Graduate Center, City University of New York, 1985. Publications: The Authentic English Editions of Beethoven, 1963; English Music Publishers' Plate Numbers, with O W Neighbour, 1965; Editor, Selected Letters of Beethoven, 1967; Thematic Catalogue of The Works by Muzio Clementi, 1967; Editor, Beethoven Studies, volume 1 1973, volume 2 1977, volume 3 1982; The Beethoven Sketchbooks: History,Reconstruction, Inventory, with Douglas Johnson, Editor and Robert Winter, 1985; Mozart: Studies of the Autograph Scores, 1987; Mozart's Thematic Catalogue: A Facsimile, with A Rosenthal, 1990; Watermarks in Mozart's Autographs, published in the Neue Mozart-Ausgabe, X/33/Abteilung 2, 1992. Address: c/o D A Tyson, Stanecroft, Jarvis Lane, Steyning, Sussex BN44 3GL, England.

TZINCOCA Remus, b. 1920, Iassy, Romania. Conductor; Composer. m. Anisia Campos. Education: Diploma, Iassy Conservatory of Music; Conservatoire National Superieur de Musique de Paris; Disciple and musical assistant of George Enescu. Debut: Led Colonne Orchestra with George Enescu as soloist, Paris. Career: Conducted major orchestras in Europe and North America including: London Philharmonic, Zurich Tonhalle, Lamoureux, Pasdeloup and Colonne in Paris, Radiotelevision Francaise, New York Philharmonic, Cleveland Orchestra, CBC Orchestra, Bucharest Philharmonic; Radio TV and Bucharest Opera; Founder, Musical Director, Newport Music Festival, Rhode Island, USA; Founder, Musical Director, New York Orchestra da Camera, with concerts at Metropolitan Museum, Carnegie Hall and Town Hall; Discovered with Anisia Campos, original version, in Rumanian, of Bartok's Cantata Profana, in New York Bartok Archives and gave 1st world performance in Bucharest with the Philharmonic Orchestra, 1984. Compositions: Oratorios, symphonies, lieder, and a Byzantine Mass. Honours: 1st Prize in Conducting, Conservatoire National Superieur de Musique de Paris; Freedom Baton, Crusade for Freedom, USA, 1953; Doctor Honoris Causa, Music Academy of Cluj, Romania, 1994. Hobbies: Backgammon; Chess. Address: 632 Avenue Herve-Beaudry, Laval, Quebec H7E 2X6, Canada.

TZOUMERKA-KNOEDLER Vicky, b. 2 November 1941, Athens, Greece. Composer; Singer, Choreographer. m. W M Knoedler, 30 June 1974. Education: Piano with Dr E Snyden, Madison, Wisconsin, USA; Voice with Geneviere Gersbach; Composition with Karlo Moser, University of Wisconsin, Madison School of Music.. Debut: Dance Department Concert, University of Wisconsin. Career: Stage: Music Performed at University of Wisconsin, Madison School of Music; Several Appearances on Radio. Honours: Composition Competition, 1989; Grant, Dane County Cultural Affairs Committee. Memberships: NACUSA; Wisconsin Alliance of Composers, Madison Chapter. Hobbies: Dance; Painting; Animals; Choir Singing; Concerts; Opera. Address: 3813 South Meadow Drive, Middleton, WI 53562, USA.

U

UBANI Edurne, b. 7 Nov 1979, Puerto de la Cruz, Tenerife, Spain. Concert Pianist; Composer. Education: Purcell School of Music, Harrow, with Roshan Magub 1990-98. Debut: Pamplona, 1982. Career: Recital performances throughout Spain, Iceland, in London (Purcell Room, Buckingham Palace) and at Cliveden; Repertory includes music by Albéniz, Granados, Falla, Turina, Bach, Mozart, Beethoven, Schubert, Chopin, Grieg, Shostakovich, Rachmaninov and Ginastera. Compositions include: Serial Killer for flute, violin and cello, 1994; Dulcis Memoria for string quartet, 1995; El Niño y la Luna for woodwind quartet, piano, viola and cello, 1997; Piano trio, 1998. Honours: Second Prize, 1993 World Brain Championship, music section, Tokyo; First Prize, 1994 National Competition Pamplona. Hobbies: Painting; Photography. Address: Edificio Atlanta, c/Ramiro Campos Turmo, No 1, 20B, 29600 Marbella (Malaga), Spain.

UCHIDA Mitsuko, b. 20 Dec 1948, Tokyo, Japan. Pianist. Education: Studied at the Hochschule für Musik und Darstellende Kunst, Wien, with Professor R Hauser, 1961-68; Diploma, 1968. Debut: Vienna, 1963. Career: Extensive worldwide engagements in recitals and concerto performances with all major London orchestras, Chicago Symphony, Boston Symphony, Berlin Philharmonic Orchestras; Played and Directed the Mozart Piano Concerto Cycle (21 concertos from K175 to K595), in London with the English Chamber Orchestra in 1985-86 season; Played Beethoven's Emperor Concerto with the Houston Symphony Orchestra at the Barbican Hall, London, 1997. Recordings: Mozart Piano Sonatas, Piano Concertos with Jeffrey Tate and English Chamber Orchestra; Chopin Piano Sonatas; Debussy, 12 Etudes. Honours: 1st Prize, Beethoven Competition, Vienna, 1969; 2nd Prize, Chopin Competition, Warsaw, 1970; 2nd Prize, Leeds Competition, 1975. Hobby: Cycling. Current Management: Van Walsum Management. Address: c/o Van Walsum Management, 26 Wadham Road, London, SW15 2LR, England.

UDAGAWA Hideko b. 1960, Japan. Violinist. Education: Tokyo University of Arts; Studied with Milstein, London and Juilliard School of Music, New York. Debut: At age 15. Career: Television appearances and radio broadcasts, Europe; Concerts in USA, many European countries; Recitals, Queen Elizabeth Hall; Lincoln Center; Concerto performances with London Symphony Orchestra, the Philharmonia, the Royal Philharmonic, the London Philharmonic, the Royal Liverpool Philharmonic, the City of Birmingham Symphony, the English Chamber and the Polish Chamber Orchestras; Toured UK and Ireland with Berlin Symphony and the Bucharest Philharmonic Orchestra. Recordings: Virtuoso violin pieces for EMI Japan; Heifetz Transcriptions for ASV; Brahms and Bruch Concertos with Sir Charles Mackerras and London Symphony for Chandos. Address: c/o Normann McCann Ltd, The Coach House, 56 Lawrie Park Gardens, London SE2 6XJ, England.

UDALOVA Irina, b. 1957, Nikolajevskm, Amur, Russia. Singer (Soprano). Education: Studied at the Kischinev Conservatory. Career: Sang in opera at Aschchabad, Turkmenistan, notably as Tatiana, Iolanta, Amelia (Ballo in Maschera) and Nedda; Bolshoi Opera, Moscow, from 1985, as Militrissa in The Tale of Tsar Sultan, and Tchaikovsky's Lisa and Maid of Orleans; Guest with the Bolshoi at Glasgow 1990 and elsewhere as Voyslada in Rimsky's Mlada. Recordings include: Judith by Serov (Melodya). Address: c/o Bolshoi Theatre, 103009 Moscow, Russia, CIS.

UGHI Uto, b. 21 Jan 1944, Busto Arsizio, Italy. Violinist. Education: Studied with George Enescu, 1954. Debut: Teatro Lirico Milan, 1951, Bach's Chaconne and Paganini Caprices. Career: Performed Mendelssohn's Violin Concerto, 1954; First European Tour, 1959; Organizer, Omaggio a Venezia Festival; Collaborated with major orchestras including: Concertgebouw Orchestra; Boston Symphony Orchestra; Philadelphia Orchestra; Washington Symphony Orchestra; Santa Cecilia with major conductors; Tours of the USA, USSR, Japan, South Africa, South America, All Europe; Has appeared with such conductors as Barbirolli, Prêtre, Haitink, Cluytens, Sawallisch and Sinopoli. Recordings: Brahms Concerto; Beethoven; Mendelssohn; Bruch; Paganini; Viotti; Mozart Concertos; Beethoven Sonatas; Mozart Sonatas; Dvorak Concerto; Vivaldi, Four Seasons; Bach Sonatas and Partitas; Schumann Concerto; Vivaldi Concertos. Honour: Cavaliere di Grand Croce for artistic merit conferred by President Scalfaro, 1997. Memberships: Accademico of Santa Cecilia. Current Management: Secretary's Office, Eugenia Reato. Address: Via Marconi 1470, 45030 S Martino di Venezze RO, Italy.

UGORSKI Anatol, b. 28 Sept 1942, Leningrad, Russia. Pianist. Education: Studied at the Leningrad Conservatoire. Career: From 1962 has given many concerts and recitals, including works by Boulez, Messiaen, Berg and Schoenberg; Teacher at the Leningrad Conservatoire from 1982, Resident in Germany, 1990.

UHL Fritz, b. 2 Apr 1928, Vienna, Austria. Operatic Singer (Dramatic Tenor). 1 son. Education: State Music Academy, Vienna, 1947-52. Debut: Graz, 1952. Career includes: With Munich State Opera, 1956; Bayreuth, 1957-64, as Siegmund, Erik and Loge; Vienna State Opera, 1961-; Covent Garden, 1963, as Walther in Die Meistersinger; Festival appearances: Europe; USA; Japan; Korea; Canada; Argentina; Florestan, 1968, Drum Major in Wozzeck, 1971, 1972, Salzburg Festival; Sang at Linz in premiere of Der Aufstand by Helmut Eder, 1976; Professor, Vienna Conservatory, 1981-. Recordings include: Tristan, Flying Dutchman, Elektra, Arabella, Antigonae and Wozzeck. Honour: Bayerischer Kammersänger, 1962. Hobbies: Books; Records; Astronomy. Address: Lindauerstrasse 9, D-81735, Germany.

UHLIK Tomislav, b. 24 Oct 1956, Zagreb, Croatia. Composer; Conductor. m. Lidija, 1 son, 1 daughter. Education: Graduated in Theory of Music, 1981, Conducting, 1989, Zagreb Music Academy. Appointments: Music Director, Lado Folklore Ensemble, 1983-85; Conductor in the Komedija Theatre in Zagreb, 1992-; Regular guest conductor of the symphonic wind orchestra of the Croatian army. Compositions: Six Episodes for Wind Quintet, 1986; The Body of Our Lord (liturgical cantata for folk choir and tambouras), 1990; Divertimento for Strings, 1991; Melancholy Variations for Harp Solo, 1991; Don Quixote and Dulcinea, for cello and doublebass; Concerto for Horn and Wind Orchestra, 1997. Honours: First Prize for the Nocturne, for mixed choir acapella, Matetic Days Festival in Ronjgi, 1988; Croatian Ministry of Culture Award, for Hymne for Soprano and Orchestra. Membership: Croatian Composer's Association. Address: 10010 Zagreb, Varicakova 4, Croatia.

ULBRICH Andrea Edina, b. 1964, Budapest, Hungary. Singer (Mezzo-soprano). Education: Studied at the Budapest Music Academy. Career: Has sung with the Hungarian National Opera at Budapest from 1988, notably as Nicklausse in Les Contes d'Hoffmann, Sextus, Clemenza di Tito, Mercedes, Carmen and as Flotow's Nancy; Frankfurt, 1991, in a concert of Franchetti's Cristoforo Colombo; Guest at Ludwigshafen, 1992, as Cherubino; Dorabella (Cosi fan tutte), Olga (Onegin), Judith (Bluebeard's Castle), Octavian (Der Rosenkavalier), Rosina (Barber of Seville), Dryad (Ariadne auf Naxos), Priestess (Aida), Mirinda (Cavalli), Ormindo, Angelina (La Cenerentola), Lolette (La Rondine-Puccini) and others. Honours include: Prize winner at the Dvorak Competition, Prague and Paris competition; Belvedere Competition, Vienna; Mandi Prize Fondation from Hungarian State Opera, 1989; Grand Prix, Brussels Bel Canto competition, 1990; Bela Bartók-Pasztory Ditta Prix, 1992; Mihaly Szekely Prize, 1994; Souvenir Prix Fondation Souvenir, 1995. Address: c/o Hungarian National Opera, Népöztársaság utja 22, 1061 Budapest, Hungary.

ULFUNG Ragnar, b. 28 Feb 1927, Oslo, Norway. Singer (Tenor). Opera Producer. Education: Studied at the Oslo Conservatory and in Milan. Debut: Sang in concert from 1949; first stage role in Menotti's The Consul, Oslo, 1952; Member of Royal Opera Stockholm from 1958; Sang Gustavus in Un Ballo in Maschera at Covent Garden 1960; Sang Don Carlos at Covent Garden for two seasons, 1963-64; Returned in the premiere of Maxwell Davies's Taverner, 1972 and as Mime in the Götz Friedrich production of the Ring, 1974-6; Metropolitan Opera debut 1972, as Mime; Later sang Strauss's Herod, Wagner's Loge, Berg's Captain and Weill's Fatty in New York; Other appearances include Strauss's Liebe der Danae and Penderecki's Die schwarze Maske in Santa Fe, as Kent in Reimann's Lear in San Francisco and Tom Rakewell in The Rake's Progress; Concert performances of Messiaen's St Francois d'Assise in London and Lyon; Sang Herod in Salome at San Francisco 1986; Paris Opéra and Geneva 1988, as Shuisky (Boris Godunov) and in The Fiery Angel; Alfred in Die Fledermaus as Oslo, 1988; Festival Hall London 1989, Aegisthus in Elektra; Herod at Los Angeles; Valzacchi in Der Rosenkavalier at Santa Fe 1989; Sang Goro in Butterfly at Lyons, 1990; Season 1992 as the Witch in Hansel and Gretel at Los Angeles, Fatty in Mahagonny at Geneva and Valzacchi in Rosenkavalier at the Santa Fe Festival; Debut as stage director Santa Fe 1973, with La Bohème; Other stagings include Lulu for Santa Fe, Otello in Stockholm and Der Ring des Nibelungen in Seattle; Sang Hauk in The Makropoulos Case, Chicago, 1995. Recordings include: Monostatos in Ingmar Bergman's version of Die Zauberflöte. Address: Lies Askonas Ltd, 6 Henrietta Street, London WC2, England.

UNDERWOOD John, b. 11 Oct 1932, Luton, Bedfordshire, England. Violist. Education: Studied with Frederick Riddle at the Royal College of Music. Career: Co-principal viola of the RPO under Beecham, 1962-62; Co-founder of the Delmé Quartet 1962; Many performances in Britain and Europe in the classical and modern repertory; Concerts at the Salzburg Festival and the Brahms Saal of the Musikverein Vienna; Season 1990 included Haydn's Last Seven Words in Italy and elsewhere, three Brahms programmes at St John's Smith Square with Iain Burnside, piano; Concerts at st David's Hall Cardiff with quartets by Tchaikovsky and Robert Simpson (premiere of 13th quartet); Appearances in Bremen, Hamburg and Trieste, followed by festival engagements, 1991; Other repertory includes works by Paul Patterson, Daniel Jones, Wilfred Josephs, Iain Hamilton and Bernard Stevens. Recordings include: Haydn Last Seven Words; Vaughan Williams On Wenlock Edge and Gurney's Ludlow and Teme; Simpson quartets 1-9 and String Trio (Hyperion); Daniel Jones 3 quartets and Bridge No 2 (Chandos); Bliss Nos 1 and 2; Josef Holbrooke Piano Quartet and Clarinet Quintet (Blenheim); Brahms Clarinet Quintet and Dvorak F major (Pickwick); Verdi Quartet and Strauss A major Op 2 (Hyperion). Address: c/o J Williams, 33 Whittingstall Road, Fulham, London SW6, England.

UNG Chinary, b. 24 November 1942, Prey Lovea, Cambodia. (American Citizen). Education: Studied clarinet at the Manhattan School of Music and composition with Chou Wen-Chung at Columbia University DMA 1974. Career: Regents Professor at Arizona State University, Tempe, 1987-95; Professor of Music at University of California at San Diego, 1995-. Compositions include: Tall Wind for soprano and ensemble, after e.e. cummings, 1969; Anicca for chamber orchestra, 1970; Mohori for mezzo and ensemble, 1974; Khse Buon for cello, 1979; Child Song I-VII for various instrumental ensembles, 1979-89; Inner Voices for chamber orchestra, 1986; Grand Spiral "Desert Flowers Bloom" for orchestra, 1993; Water Rings for chamber orchestra, 1993; Antiphonal Sprials for orchestra, 1995; "...Still Life after Death" for high voice and ensemble, 1995. Honours include: First and youngest American composer to receive the Grawemeyer Award (1989) for Inner Voices; Kennedy Center Friedheim Award, 1991; Koussevitszky Foundation Commission, 1992. Address: c/o ASCAP, ASCAP Building, One Lincoln Plaza, New York, NY 10023, USA.

UNGER Gerhard, b. 26 Nov 1916, Bad Salzungen, Thuringia, Germany. Singer (Tenor). Education: Studied at Eisenach and the Berlin Musikhochschule. Career: Sang lyric roles at Weimar from 1947, Tamino, Pinkerton and Alfredo; Bayreuth Festival 1951-52 as David in Die Meistersinger; Guest appearances at the Dresden Opera as Tamino and Pinkerton; Engaged at the Berlin Staatsoper from 1952, Stuttgart from 1982; Member of the Hamburg Staatsoper 1962-73, appearing also in Vienna, Milan, Paris, Metropolitan New York and London (Alwa in Lulu at Sadler's Wells, 1966); Salzburg Festival 1961-64, as Pedrillo in Die Entführung and Brighella in Ariadne auf Naxos; Character roles later in career (Captain in Wozzeck, Mime and Shuratov in From the House of the Dead) in Europe and North and South America (Mime at Dallas 1984); Bregenz Festival 1980 as Pedrillo, Stuttgart 1987 as Mime (last major role). Recordings include: Der Waffenschmied, Steuermann in Fliegende Holländer; Die Meistersinger, Alwa in Lulu; Die Entführung, Die Meistersinger; Fidelio, Königskinder by Humperdinck, Die Zauberflöte, Carmina Burana, Elektra, Ariadne auf Naxos, Der Rosenkavalier, Tannhäuser (EMI); La Finta Giardiniera. Address: c/o Stuttgart Staatsoper, Oberer Schlossgarten 6, 7000 Stuttgart, Germany.

UNGRICHT Yvette Scharffs, b. 30 Dec 1960, Salt Lake City, Utah, USA. Pianist; Organist. m. Albert Ungricht, 6 May 1984, 1 son, 3 daughters. Education: BMus, Piano Pedagogy cum laude, 1981, MMus, Music Theory, 1983, University of Utah; Coursework, PhD, Music Theory and History, Boston University, 1983-88. Debut: University of Utah, 1981. Career: Assistant Manager, Nashville Symphony, 1984-86; Church Organist, Nashville, Boston, Salt Lake City, 1975-; Church Choir Director; Private piano and theory teacher, 1975-. Contributions to Nashville Premiere Arts Magazine; Desert News. Memberships: American Musicological Society; American Music Teachers Association; Mu Phi Epsilon; Phi Kappa Phi. Hobbies: Bonsai; Quilting; Cycling. Address: 2725 Moraine Circle, Salt Lake City, UT 84109-3576, USA.

UNGVARY Tamas, b. 12 Nov 1936, Kalosca, Hungary. Composer; Conductor; Double Bass Player; Teacher. 1 d. Education: Philosophy, Budapest; Conducting Diploma, Mozarteum at Salzburg; Double Bass at Béla Bartók Conservatory, Budapest. Career includes: Solo Double Bass, Camerata Academica, Salzburg, 1967-69; As Composer at 4 ISCM Festivals; All major European radios; Lecturer on Computer Music; Artistic Manager, EMS, Stockholm, Sweden and Director of Kineto-auditory Communication Research at Royal Institute of Technology, Stockholm. From 1992, Leader of EA-Music Courses at Vienna University of Music and Performing Arts; Associated Editor of Journal of New Music; Compositions include: Seul Traum des Einsamen; Akonel No 2 for Flute and Tape; Interaction No 2 for Organ and Tape; Ite missa est; Dis-Tanz for Ensemble and Tape; Istenem Uram! for Tape; Sentograffito, live computer music, 1993; Grattis for Tape, 1994. Recordings: Various record labels. Contributions include: Interfacing Computer Music and Computer Choreography in Neue Musik Technologie, 1993; Notes on a Prototype of human-computer interface for artistic interaction in Proceedings of SMAC 1993, Royal Academy of Music No 79

Various journals. Honours include: 1st Prize at International NEWCOMP computer music competition, 1987; Honorary Awards at the 7th and 15th International Electro-Acoustic Music Competition in Bourges, France; 2nd Prize, Ars Electronica for Realtime, 1994. Memberships: Swedish Society for Composers; Fylkingen; Swedish Section of International Society of Contemporary Music; GEM, Austria; International Computer Music Association. Address: Hagalundsgatan 31, 17151 Solna, Sweden.

UNO Koji, b. 30 Aug 1925, Tokyo, Japan. Flautist; Professor of Showa Medical College, Atsugi, Japan. m. 25 Dec 1957, 1 son, 1 daughter. Education: Diploma, National Music School of Tokyo, 1951; Corso Straordinario, Conservatorio di Musica S Cecilia, Rome, Italy, 1962-63; Studied with Severiano Gazzelloni, Rome, 1962-63. Debut: Brandenburg Concerto No 5, J S Bach, Sapporo Chamber Orchestra, Sapporo, 1950. Career: Principal Flutist, Konoe Symphony Orchestra, 1951-56; Principal Flutist, ABC Symphony Orchestra, 1956-58; Concerto in G Mozart, Sapporo Symphony Orchestra, Obihiro, 1967; 20 recitals in Tokyo, 1962-91; Molnar Harp Trio, 1959-71; Tokyo Baroque Quintet, 1964-70; Uno Quartet, 1978-89; Numerous broadcasts on radio in Japan. Recordings: Song of Londonderry, solo and chamber music, 4 track tape. Publications: Flute, Music Encyclopaedia, Heibon-sha, 1957, 1983; Knowledge for Flute, Wind Instruments Series, Ontomo-sha, 1969, 1983; 2 Flute Quartets of Mozart, Flute Club, 1965; 5 Movements by Japanese Folksongs, 1989. Contributions to: Japan Music Journal; Japan Flutists Association Journal; Showa College Bulletin. Hobby: Study of 1 Keyed Flute and 8 Keyed Flute. Current Management: Japan Concert Association, Yamanosoen 110, 3-10-6 Sendagaya, Japan. Address: 4-21-21 Nishi-Oi, Shinagawa-ku, Tokyo 140, Japan.

UNRUH Stan, b. 20 November 1938, Beaver, Oklahoma, USA. Singer (Tenor). Education: Studied at the Juilliard School, New York. Debut: Geneva 1970, as Melot in Tristan. Career: Appearances at Paris, Orange, Rouen, Bordeaux (Lohengrin 1979 and Aeneas 1980) and Toulouse; Member of the Krefeld Opera 1977-85, notably in Der Ring des Nibelungen; New York City Opera, 1976, as Erik in Der fliegende Holländer, Strasbourg 1977, as Parsifal; Further guest appearances at Barcelona, 1978, Brunswick and Innsbruck 1983, Buenos Aires, 1985 (Siegfried in Götterdämmerung) and Freiburg 1986, in the premiere of Hunger und Durst by Violeta Dinescu; Sang at the Staatstheater Kassel, 1989-90; Other roles include Wagner's Tristan, Siegmund, Loge and Walther von Stolzing, Florestan, Shuratov in From the House of the Dead, Max, Don José, Samson, Stravinsky's Oedipus and Bacchus. Address: Staatstheater, Friedrichplatz 15, 3500 Kassel, Germany.

UNWIN Nicholas, b. 1962, Cambridge, England. Concert Pianist. Education: Studied at the Royal College of Music and with Philip Fowke. Career: Played Bartók, Lambert and McCabe at the Purcell Room, London, 1986; Bartók's 2nd Concerto at St John's Smith Square (also on Radio 3); Wigmore Hall recital, 1987; BBC recital, 1989, followed by Birmingham University and Leeds Town Hall; Artist-in-residence at the King's Lynn Festival, 1989, with Nights in the Gardens of Spain and Ravel's G major Concerto; BBC documentary on Michael Tippett, 1990, playing the Second Sonata; Specialised in Spanish music, culminating in Images of Iberia at Blackheath Concert Halls; Performed Tippett in Madrid and Radio France, also at the Barbican's Tippett Festival, 1994. Recordings: Tippett Sonata 4, with Robert Saxton and Colin Matthews, 1995; Tippett Sonatas 1-3, 1995. Honours include: Chappell Gold Medal and Cyril Smith Recital Prize, Royal College of Music; Winner, Lambeth Music Award, Hastings Concerto Festival, and the Brant Piano Competition; Schott Award, 1990. Address: 95 Station Road, Impington, Cambridge CB4 4NP, England.

UPPMAN Theodor, b. 12 Jan 1920, San Jose, California, USA. Singer (Baritone). m. Jean Seward, 31 Jan 1943, 1 son, 1 daughter. Education: Curtis Institute of Music, 1939-41; Stanford University, Opera Department, 1941-42; University of Southern California, 1949-50. Debut: Pelléas with San Francisco Symphony, Monteux, 1947. Career: Title role in Billy Budd premiere, Royal Opera House, Covent Garden, 1951 and in USA premiere, NBC TV Opera, 1952; Leading Baritone at Metropolitan Opera, 1953-78 as Masetto, Papageno, Sharpless, Guglielmo, Pelléas, Paquillo in La Périchole, Taddeo, Harlekin in Ariadne auf Naxos, Kothner in Die Meistersinger, Eisenstein in Die Fledermaus; Recitals throughout USA and Canada; Sang in the premieres of Floyd's The Passion of Jonathan Wade at New York City Opera in 1962 and Yerma by Villa-Lobos in 1971; Appearances with opera companies in USA and Europe including Traveller in Death in Venice, Geneva Opera in 1983, and soloist with most major USA orchestras; Appearances on radio and television; Faculty, Manhattan School of Music, Mannes College of Music and Britten-Pears School for Advanced Musical Studies; Sang in world premiere of Bernstein's A Quiet Place, at Houston, Texas, 1983, La Scala, 1984, and Vienna Staatsoper, 1986. Recordings include: World premiere performance of Billy Budd.

Honours: Musical Prizes: Atwater Kent Auditions, Gainsborough Award; Honorary Director of Britten-Pears School for Advanced Musical Studies. Memberships: Professional Committee, Regional Auditions for Metropolitan Opera; National Association of Teachers of Singing. Address: 201 West 86th Street, New York, NY 10024, USA.

UPSHAW Dawn, b. 17 July 1960, Nashville, Tennessee, USA. Singer (Soprano). Education: Studied at the Manhattan School of Music and at the Metropolitan Opera School. Career: Sang in the 1983 US premiere of Hindemith's Sancta Susanna while at college; Metropolitan from 1985, as Countess Ceprano, Echo (Ariadne), Adina, Despina, Sophie (Werther), the Woodbird and Zerlina (1990); Salzburg Festival 1987 as Barbarina, Aix-en-Provence 1988-89, as Despina and Pamina; Sang Pamina in a concert performance at the 1990 Promenade Concerts, conducted by Roger Norrington; Other roles include Marzelline (Fidelio) and Constance in Les Dialogues des Carmélites; Season 1992 as Despina and Susanna at the Met, L'Ange in St Francois at Salzburg and Anne Trulove at Aix-en-Provence; Sang Theodora at Glyndebourne, 1996; Mozart's Cherubino at the Met, 1997; Engaged in La Finta Giardiniera for the Royal Opera at Sadlers' Wells, 1999. Recordings: Ariadne auf Naxos (Deutsche Grammophon); Mass in G by Schubert (Telarc); Gorecki's 3rd symphony; Schoenberg's 2nd Quartet. Address: c/o IMG Artisits, Media House, 3 Burlington Lane, London W4 2TH, England.

URBAIN Mady, b. 27 Apr 1946, Montegnée, Belgium. Singer (Mezzo-soprano). Education: Studied at the Liège Conservatoire and in Vienna and Salzburg. Career: Sang at the Liège Opera from 1967, and made many guest appearances elsewhere in Belgium and throughout France; Roles have included Amneris, Preziosilla, Mistress Quickly, Carmen, Marcellina, Charlotte, Puccini's Princess (Suor Angelica) and Suzuki, Strauss's Adelaide and Mère Marie in the Carmelites; Concerts include Messiah, Bach's B Minor Mass, the Verdi Requiem and Beethoven's Ninth; Professor at the Grètry Academy, Liège, from 1970. Address: c/o Opéra de Wallonie, 1 Rue des Domincains, B-4000 Liège, Belgium.

URROWS David, b. 25 Oct 1957, Honolulu, Hawaii, USA. Composer; Music Historian. Education: AB, Brandeis University, 1978; MMus, University of Edinburgh, 1980; DMA, Boston University, 1987. Career: Compositions performed, commissioned and broadcast in USA, Asia and Europe; Lecturer at several American Universities. Compositions: String Quartet, 1978; Piano Sonata, 1979; Quintet for Winds, 1981; Three Vailima Episodes, Soprano and String Orchestra, 1984; A New England Almanack, Baritone and Piano, 1985; Sonata for Oboe and Harp, 1985; Partita: Nun Komm, der Heiden Heiland, Organ, 1985; Sonata, San Angelo, 2 Violas, 1986; Ricordanza dell Umbria, Piano, 1987; Winterreise, Soprano and Chamber Orchestra, 1988; Sonata for Violin and Piano, 1991; Opera: A Midsummer Nights Dream, 1980; Oratorio: Lycidas, 1987; Epiphany Cantata, 1993; Many songs and anthems. Publications include: Sea Ballads and Songs in Whalsay, Shetland, 1983; The Choral Music of Christopher le Fleming, 1986; Randall Thompson: A Bio-Bibliography, 1991. Honours: Reiner Prize in Composition, 1978; Stratton Prize, Fellowship, 1980; ASCAP Foundation Grant, 1981; Malloy Miller Prize, 1985; Winner, National Association of Teachers of Singing Art Song Composition Contest, 1987; ASCAP Special Awards, 1987-; Ordre Royal de la Couranne de Bohème, 1995. Memberships: ASCAP; Pi Kappa Lambda; Sonneck Society for American Music; American Guild of Organists. Address: 425 Williams Place, Apt 6, San Mateo, CA 94401-2451, USA.

USTVOLSKAYA Galina, b. 17 Jun 1919, Petrograd, Russia. Composer. m. Makuhin Konstantin, 23 Dec 1966. Education: Leningrad Conservatory, 1939-47 (Rimsky Korsakov Conservatory until 1947); Postgraduate courses in composition, Leningrad Conservatory, 1947-50. Career: Tutor in Composition at Leningrad Conservatory College, 1948-77. Compositions include: Concerto for Piano, String Orchestra and Timpani, 1946; Symphony No 1, in 3 movements, for 2 boy's voices and Orchestra, 1955; Poem for Orchestra, 1958; Suite for Orchestra, 1959; Dona Nobis Pacem for Piccolo, Tuba and Piano, 1970-71; Dies Irae for 8 Double Basses, Percussion and Piano, 1972-73; Benedictus, Qui Venit for 4 Flutes, 4 Bassoons and Piano, 1974-75; Symphony No 2: True and Eternal Bliss, 1979; Bylina "Stepan Razin's Dream" for Bass and Orchestra, 1979; Symphony No 3: Jesus Messiah, Save Us!, 1983; Symphony No 4: Prayer, 1985-87; Sonata No 6 for Piano, 1988; Symphony No 5: Amen, 1989-90; Octet for 2 oboes, 7 violins, timpani and piano, 1949-50; Sonata for violin and piano, 1952; Twelve Preludes for piano, 1953; Diet for violin and piano, 1967; 6 sonatas for piano. Recordings include: 3 Sonatas, 1947, 1952 and 1957; Grand Duet for Violoncello and Piano, 1959. Honours: Heidelberger Kunstlevinnenpreis, 1992. Membership: Russian Composers Union. Hobbies: Solitude; Nature. Address: Gagarina Avenue 27-72, St Petersburg 196135, Russia.

V

VACEK Milos, b. 20 June 1928, Horni Roven, Pardubice, Czechoslovakia. Composer. Education: Studied at the Prague Conservatory, 1942-47; Academy of Musical Arts, 1947-51. Career: Freelance composer from 1954. Compositions include: Operas Jan Zelivsky, composed 1956-58, performed Olomouc 1984; Brother Zak, Ostrava, 1982; Romance of the Bugle, Ceske Budejovice 1987; Mikes the Tomcat, Brno 1986; Ballets: The Comedian's Fairytale, 1958, Wind in the Hair, 1961, The Mistress of the Seven Robbers 1966, Meteor, 1966; Lucky Sevens, 1966; Musicals: The Night is my Day (on Bessie Smith) 1962; The Emperor's New Clothes, 1962; Madame Sans Gene, 1968; Wind from Alabama, 1970; Orchestral: Sinfonietta, 1951; Spring Suite for wind instruments and strings, 1963; Serenade for Strings, 1965; May Symphony, 1974; Poem of Fallen Heroes for alto and orchestra, 1974; Olympic Flame, symphonic poem, 1975; A Solitary Seaman, symphonic picture, 1978; World's Conscience, in memory of Lidice, 1981; Chamber and piano music. Address: OSA, Cs armady 20, 160-56 Prague 6 - Bubenec, Czech Republic.

VACHHA Michel (Rumy), b. 20 Sep 1955, Bombay, India. Pianist. Education: BA, Honours, Jawahrlal Nehru University, 1976; LRSM, London, 1976; Diploma, Conservatorio di Musica Rome, 1980; Diploma, Musikhochschule, Zurich, 1984; Diploma, Conservatoire National de Paris, 1986. Debut: Rome in 1974. Career: Several solo performances and with orchestra in India, France, Austria, Yugoslavia, Switzerland, Tunisia, Kuwait and Germany; Recordings for radio and TV in India, France and Italy, and TV documentaries. Compositions: Fantasia And Fugue, 1980; Allegro Furioso for Piano and Orchestra, 1982; Sonate for Piano, 1984. Contributions to: Articles in Music World and other magazines. Membership: Accademia di Musica, Palestrina, Rome. Hobbies: Water Sports; Animals; Mountaineering; Cinema; Theatre; Skiing.

VADUVA Leontina, b. 1 Dec 1960, Rosiile, Rumania. Singer (soprano). Education: Studied with mother and at Bucharest Conservatory. Debut: Sang Manon at Toulouse 1987, conducted by Michel Plasson. Career: Appeared as Ninetta in La Gazza Ladra at the Théâtre des Champs Elysées, Paris, July 1988, followed by Manon at Covent Garden; Returned to London in a production of Rigoletto by Nuria Espert, and sang Drusilla at Théâtre du Châtelet, Paris and at the Grand Théâtre, Geneva; Engagements for season 1990-91 included appearances in Les Pêcheurs de Perles and L'Elisir d'Amore at Toulouse; Manon at Montpellier, Bordeaux, Avignon, Paris (Opéra Comique) and Vienna; Rigoletto at Bonn; Donizetti's Il Campanello di Notte at Monte Carlo; Les Contes d'Hoffmann in Paris (Théâtre du Châtelet) and London (Covent Garden); Ismene in Mitridate by Mozart at the Châtelet, conducted by Jeffrey Tate; Micaela in Carmen at Covent Garden (returned 1996, as Mimi). Recordings include: Mitridate; Le nozze di Figaro, conducted by John Eliot Gardiner (1993). Honours include: Winner, Concours de Chant, Toulouse, 1986; Winner, s'Hertogenbosch Competition, Holland, 1987; Laurence Olivier Prize, London 1989. Address: Stafford Law Associates, 6 Barham Close, Weybridge, KT13 9PR, England.

VAGGIONE Horacio, b. 21 Jan 1943, Cordoba, Argentina. Composer. Education: Composition, Arts School, National University of Cordoba. Career: Co-Founder, Experimental Music Centre, University of Cordoba, 1964-69; Alea Electronic Music Group, Madrid, Spain, 1969-74; Computer Music Project, University of Madrid, 1970-73; Guest Composer, IRCAM/Centre Georges Pompidou, 1981-85 Groupe de Musique Experimentale de Bourges, France, 1983; Technische Universität, West Berlin, 1987-88; Director, Electroacoustic Music Studio, University of Paris VIII, 1985-. Compositions: 48 including symphonic, chamber and electronic music; Performances of works at Festivals of Warsaw, Stockholm, Berlin, Kassel, Frankfurt, Amsterdam, Helsinki, Oslo, Paris, Venice, La Rochelle, Bourges, Geneva, Lausanne, Milan, Turin, Rome, Madrid, Athens and at UNESCO's Rostrum of Composers, World Music Days, Los Angeles Olympic Arts Festival, ICMC (Rochester, Illinois, The Hague, Venice, Paris, Cologne), British Arts of London, Berlin Kulturstadt Europeas 88, Darmstadt Ferienkurse für Neue Musik. Recordings: On: Compact Disk ADDA, Paris; Le Chant du Monde, Paris; WERGO, Germany. Address: Editions Salabert, 22 Rue Chauchat, 75009 Paris, France.

VAJDA Igor (Joseph Milan), b. 16 Mar 1935, Banská, Slovakia. Musicologist; Critic; Publisher. Education: MPh, Faculty of Philosophy, Comenius University, Bratislava, 1959. Career: Assistant, Slovak Academy of Sciences; Professor of Musical Theory, State Conservatory, Kosice; Dramaturgist, Opera Banská Bystrica; Editor, Slovak Music; TV broadcasts including: What is Opera? 50 Years of Slovak National Theatre, Andrej Ocenás, Eugen Suchon; Jesuit Priest, 1984, in Pastorian, 1990, Docent, 1991; Editor in Pliester, Slovak Television, 1992-93 and Editor for quarterly Viera a zivot (Belief and Life), 1994. Publications: Kantate Eugen Suchon's Zalm zeme Podkarpatskej, monograph, 1959; Sergei Prokofiev, Popular Monographie, 1964; Co-author, National Artist Eugen Suchon, 1978; Co-author, Storocnica ceského divadla, 1988; Slovak Opera, 1988; Eugen Suchon and Literature, 1993; Subjecty, Motivic, Work in Suchon's Operas, 1994. Contributions to: Musicologica Slovaca; Hudobny zivot (Musical Life); Slovenská hudba (Slovak Music); Slovenské divadlo (Slovak Theatre). Honours: Slovak Music Funde Prize, 1970; Slovak Literary Fund Prize, 1972, 1974; Union of Slovak Dramaturgist Prize, 1989; OPUS Prize, 1989. Memberships: Union of Slovak Dramatists and Musicologists. Hobby: Travel. Address: Dubnická 4, 851 02 Bratislava, Slovakia.

VAJNAR Frantisek, b. 15 Sept 1930, Strasice u Rokycan, Czechoslovakia. Conductor. Education: Studied violin and conducting at the Prague Conservatoire. Career: Played in the orchestra of the Prague National Theatre; 1950-53, conducted the ensemble of Czech Army, 1953-55; Conducted at the State Theatre of Karlina 1955-60, Ostrava 1960-62; Director of the Nejedly Theatre Usti nad Labem 1962-73, with operas by Smetana (complete), Dvorák, Janácek, Wagner, Verdi, Puccini, Strauss, Prokofiev, Henze and Hartmann; Conductor at the National Theatre Prague 1973-79, Artistic Director from 1985; Chief Conductor of the Czech Radio Symphony Orchestra 1979-85, Guest Conductor of the Czech Philharmonic; Director of the Collegium Musicum Pragense and guest conductor in Australia, Brazil, Germany, France, Greece, Italy, Japan, Poland, Scandinavia, USSR and Switzerland; Festival appearances at Salzburg, Vienna, Prague; Conducted Prokofiev's Betrothal in a Monastery at the 1979 Wexford Festival; Teacher at Prague Academy of Arts. Recordings include: Smetana The Kiss; Shostakovich 10th and 15th Symphonies (Czech Philharmonic); Beethoven Overtures; Brixi Organ Concertos; Mozart arranged Wendt Le nozze di Figaro; Dvorák's The Cunning Peasant. Address: Pragokoncert, Malterzske nam 1, 118 13 Prague 1, Czech Republic.

VAKARELIS Janis, b. 1950, Greece. Concert Pianist. Education: Studied at the Vienna Music Academy with Nikita Magaloff and Bruno Leonardo Gelber. Career: Engagements from 1979 with the Gewandhaus Orchestra, Mozarteum Orchestra of Salzburg, Zurich Chamber, Monte Carlo Philharmonic, Berlin Symphony, Stuttgart Philharmonic, Staatskapelle Dresden and BBC Symphony; Conductors have included Rattle, Weller, Masur, Kurt Sanderling, Ashkenazy, Litton and Rowicki; Recitals at the Concertgebouw in Amsterdam and the Teatro Real Madrid; Festival appearances at Spoleto and Athens, BBC Prom Concerts 1986. Recordings include: Prokofiev's 3rd Concerto and works by Brahms and Liszt; Labels include RCA, ASV and RPO. Honours include: Winner, 1979 Queens Sofia Competition, Madrid; Pan-Hellenic Piano Competition and the Prix d'Academie d'Athenes. Address: c/o Anglo Swiss Management Ltd, Suite 35-37 Morley House, 320 Regent Street, London W1R 5AD, England.

VALADE Pierre-Andre, b. 14 Oct 1959, Brive, France. Flautist; Conductor. m. 5 May 1990. Education: Michel Debost's Private Class, Paris, 1979-81; Occasional lessons from Marcel Moyse, Maxence Larrieu and Alain Marion. Debut: Paris, 1979. Career: Flautist, Numerous Stage including Ensemble, Chamber Music and Soloist appearances in repertoire from Mozart 1982-; Soloist: numerous world premieres including Eolia by Philippe Hurel, Paris, Radio-France, 1983; Jupiter by Philipe Manoury on Flute-4X, IRCAM, Paris, April 1987; ...explosante-fixe... by Pierre Boulez, for Flute, Computer and Ensemble, conducted by composer, Paris, 1991; TV-Recording for BBC Programme, Tomorrow's World, 1988; Guest Artist, Concerts, Masterclasses, Conferences, 8th Australian Flute Convention, Perth, 1991; Concerts with Ensembles: Ensemble Musique Oblique, 1983-; Co-Founder, Espace Musique Contemporary Music Ensemble, 1984; Ensemble Inter-Contemporian, 1985-90, including London Proms, 1985, US Tour with Pierre Boulez, 1986; ...explosante-fixe...Flute Concerto in New York, Carnegie Hall, with P Boulez, 1993; Co-Founder/Musical Director, Court-Circuit Ensemble, Paris, 1991-; Director, Collection Pierre-Andre Valade, Editions Henry Lemoine, Paris, 1985-; In charge of Flute 4X Research Project, 1986-90; Conductor, Festival of Perth, with West Australian Symphony Orchestra, 1995. Recordings: A Schoenberg: Pierrot Lunaire, Harmonia Mundi, 1992; Flutist, A Jolivet: The Complete Works for Flute, 1993; Conductor, T Murail: A Portrait with Ensemble Court Circuit, 1995. Publications: La Flute dans le Repertoire du XXe Siècle pour Ensemble Instrumental, 1987; Flute et Creations, 1991. Honours: Grand Prix De L'Academie Du Disque Francais. Memberships: International Contemporary Music Society. Current Management: Anne-Marie Reby, France. Address: c/o Anne-Marie Reby, 52 rue Pierre Louvrier, 92140 Clamart, France.

VALCARCEL Edgar, b. 4 Dec 1932, Puno, Peru. Musician (Pianist); Composer. m. Carmen Pollard, 1 Jan 1958, 2 sons, 2 daughters. Education: Catholic University, Lima, Peru; National Conservatory of Music, Lima; Instituto Torcuato de Tella, Buenos Aires, Argentina; Columbia Princeton University, New York, USA. Career: As Pianist: Soloist, National Symphony Orchestras of Lima, Rio de Janeiro and La Habana; As Composer: Commissions, V Inter-American Festival, Washington DC, 1971, Rochester Festival, 1972, Maracaibo Festival, Venezuela, 1977; Works premiered at Panamerican Union Peer International Corporation, 1968, Tonos, Darmstadt, 1977, Veracruz University, Mexico, 1983; Currently Head of Music Department, Newton College, Lima. Compositions: Dichotomy III, for 12 instruments, 1968; Montaje 59, for chamber ensemble, 1977; Chegan IV, for choir, 1977; Karabotasat Cutintapata, for orchestra, 1977; 4 Children's Songs, 1983. Recordings: American Contemporary Music, EDS-030-Stereo; Edul, Organization of American States; Antologia Music Peruana Siglo XX, Vol III, Edubanco. Honours: Professor honoris causa, Puno University, Peru; National Award for Composition Award, Caracas, Venezuela, 1981. Address: Avenida Angamos (Oeste) 862-C, Miraflores, Lima 18, Peru.

VALDENGO Giuseppe, b. 24 May 1914, Turin, Italy. Singer (Baritone). Education: Studied in Turin with Michele Accoriuti. Debut: Parma 1936, as Rossini's Figaro. Career: Sang at La Scala 1941-43; New York City Opera 1946, debut as Sharpless in Madama Butterfly; San Francisco 1947, as Valentin in Faust; Metropolitan Opera from 1947, as Germont, Belcore, Mozart's Almaviva, Marcello and Germont; Sang Iago, Falstaff and Amonasro, with the NBC Symphony under Toscanini, 1947-50; Covent Garden and Glyndebourne 1955, Don Giovanni and Raimbaud in Le Comte Ory; Guest appearances in Buenos Aires, Paris, Veinna, Philadelphia, Cincinnati and Rio de Janeiro. Recordings: Falstaff, Aida and Otello, conducted by Toscanini; Pagliacci; Il Segreto di Susanna; Don Pasquale. Publication: Ho cantato con Toscanini, 1962.

VALDES Maximiano, b. 17 June 1949, Santiago, Chile. Conductor. Education: Studied in Santiago, at the Santa Cecilia Rome and with Franco Ferrara. Career: Assistant conductor at La Fenice, Venice, 1976-80; Principal guest with the Spanish National Orchestra from 1984 and music director of the Buffalo Philharmonic, USA, from 1989; Guest appearances in England, Scandinavia and France (Paris Opéra). Honours include: Prize winner at the 1978 Rupert Foundation Competition, London, and the 1980 Nikolai Malko Competition, Copenhagen, Address: Buffalo Philharmonic Orchestra, PO Box 905, Buffalo, NY 14213, USA.

VALEK Jiri, b. 4 June 1940. Musician; Professor. m. Ivana Valkova, 1 son, 1 daughter. Education: Conservatoire Kromeriz; Academy of Music Arts, Praha. Career: Member, Czech Nonet, 1964-75; Professor, Conservatoire Prague, 1972-77; Member, Solo Flautist, Czech Philharmonic, 1975-; Professor of Music, Academy Prague; Wide Soloistic Activities in Concerts, Radio and CD Recordings; Chamber Music Appearances Worldwide. Compositions: 30 Jazz Compositions Performed and Recorded. Recordings: Handel Sonatas; Mozart Concerts, French Flute Works; Sonatas by Prokofiev, Hindemith, Poulenc; Compositions of J S Bach, Telemann, Martinu, Rejcha, Stamic. Honour: Golden Record of Supraphon for Handel Sonatas, 1977. Memberships: Juries at International Competitions in Geneva, 1984, 1993, Budapest, 1995, Prague, 4 times. Hobbies: Films; Garden Plants. Address: Parizska 3, 110 00 Praha 1, Czech Republic.

VALEK Vladimir, b. 1935, Czechoslovakia. Conductor. Education: Graduated, Prague Academy of Performing Arts, 1962. Career: Conductor, Czech Radio Studio Orchestra in Prague, 1965-75; Founder and Leader, Dvorák Chamber Orchestra; Conductor, Prague Symphony Orchestra, 1977-88; Chief Conductor, Prague Radio Symphony Orchestra, 1985-; Guest performances with the Czech Philharmonic in USA, Russia, Japan, Britain, Germany, Austria, Holland, Switzerland, Korea and Taiwan; Festival engagements at Lucerne, Interlaken, Montreux, Berlin, Linz, Istanbul, Prague and Bratislava. Recordings include: Bartók's Concerto for Orchestra and Prokofiev's Romeo and Juliet Ballet Suites with the Czech Philharmonic; Dvorák's Symphonies Nos 8 and 9, and Slavonic Dances, Schubert's Mass in A flat, Sibelius's Symphony No 2, Saint-Saëns's Symphony No 3, Martinu's Symphony No 6 with the Prague Radio Symphony Orchestra; Martinu's The Frescoes, Stravinsky's Petrushka and Rite of Spring, Dvorák's Symphonies Nos 5 and 7 and Suk's Symphony Asrael with the Prague Radio Symphony Orchestra, Paris. Current Management: Czech Artists Agency, Dr Bechyne, 100 00 Prague 10, Volsinách 114, Czech Republic. Address: Na Vápenném 6, 147 00 Praha 4, Czech Republic.

VALENTE Benita, b. 19 Oct 1934, Delano, California, USA. Lyric Soprano. m. Anthony Phillip Checchia, 21 Nov 1959, 1 son. Education: Graduated, Curtis Institute of Music, 1960; Studied with Chester Hayden, Martial Singher, Lotte Lehmann, Margaret Harshaw. Debut: Freiburg Opera, 1962; Metropolitan Opera, 1973, as Pamina. Career: Leading roles, Orfeo, Rigoletto, Traviata, Idomeneo, Marriage of Figaro, Faust, La Bohème, Turandot, Magic Flute, Rinaldo; Appeared throughout USA and

Europe in operas and symphonies; has sung in New York as Susanna, Ilia, Nannetta and Almirena in Rinaldo 1985; Santa Fe 1987, as Ginevra in Ariodante 1985. Recordings: Records for Columbia, Desmar, RCA, Pantheon, CRI. Honours: Winner, Metropolitan Opera Council auditions, 1960. Address: c/o Anthony P Checchia, 135 S 18th Street, Philadelphia, PA 19103, USA.

VALENTINI-TERRANI Lucia, b. 28 Aug 1946, Padua, Italy. Singer (Mezzo-soprano). Education: Studied in Padua. Debut: Padua 1969, in the title role of La Cenerentola by Rossini. Career: Sang Cenerentola, Isabella and Rosina at La Scala from 1973; Marina in Boris Godunov 1979; Metropolitan Opera 1974, as Isabella in L'Italiana in Algeri; Los Angeles 1979, in the Verdi Requiem conducted by Giulini; Guest appearances in Moscow, Paris, Vienna, Monte Carlo, Brussels, Nice, Dresden, Munich, Frankfurt and Chicago; Florence and Los Angeles 1982, as Mistress Quickly in Falstaff; Covent Garden 1987, as Rosina in Il Barbiere di Siviglia; Pesaro Festival and Vienna Staatsoper 1984 and 1988, in Il Viaggio a Reims; Pesaro 1986, in Maometto II; Naples 1988, as Gluck's Orpheus; sang Isabella in L'Italiana in Algeri at Monte Carlo, 1990 (repeated at Turin, 1992). Recordings include: La Fedeltà Premiata and Il Mondo della Luna by Haydn (Philips); Orlando Furioso by Vivaldi (RCA); L'Italiana in Algeri; Falstaff, Don Carlos, Pergolesi Stabat Mater and Il Viaggio a Reims by Rossini (Deutsche Grammophon); La Cenerentola and La Donna del Lago, by Rossini (CBS). Address: c/o Harodl Holt Ltd, 31 Sinclair Road, London W14 0NS, England.

VALJAKKA Taru, b. 16 Sept 1938, Helsinki, Finland. Singer (Soprano). Education: Studied with Antti Koskinen in Helsinki, with Gerald Moore in Stockholm and London, Erik Werba in Vienna and Conchita Badia in Santiago. Debut: Helsinki, 1964, as Donna Anna in Don Giovanni. Career: Linzer Theater, 1977; Sang in Helsinki at premiere of Sallinen's The Red Line, 1978; Budapest, Oslo, Prague and Berlin; Kiel Opera, 1980 in the German premiere of The Horseman by Sallinen; Bluthochzeit, Tannhauser, 1982; Metropolitan Opera, 1983, in The Horseman with the Helsinki Company; Savonlinna Festival Finland, 1983, as Senta in Der fliegende Holländer; Other roles include the Trovatore Leonora, Aida, Countess Almaviva, Fiordiligi, Desdemona, Pamina and Melisande; Teatro Colon Buenos Aires, 1987, as Senta; Numerous recitals in the songs of Sibelius; Singing Professor, Talkinna Music Academy, 1995-. Recordings include: Joonas Kokkonen, The Last Temptation; Lady Macbeth of Mtsensk; Paavo Heininen: Silk Trumb Finlandia; Juha by Merikanto; The Horseman. Address: Bulevardi 19A2, 00120 Helsinki, Finland.

VÄLKKI Anita, b. 25 Oct 1926, Saakmaki, Finland. Singer (Soprano). Education: Studied with Tynne Haase, Jorma Huttunen and Lea Piltti in Helsinki. Career: Performed first as an actress and sang in operettas at the theatre in Kokkola; Sang at the Helsinki National Opera from 1955; Royal Opera Stockholm from 1960, as Aida, Santuzza and Brünnhilde; Covent Garden 1961-64, as Brünnhilde; Metropolitan Opera 1962-66, Senta, Turandot, Venus, Brünnhilde, Kundry; Bayreuth Festival 1963-64; Guest appearances in Mexico City, Palermo and Philadelphia; Savonlinna Festival Finland 1983, as Mary in Der fliegende Holländer; sang at Helsinki 1986, in Juha by Merikanto. Recordings include Third Norn in Götterdämmerung, conducted by Solti (Decca); The Horseman by Sallinen. Address: c/o Finnish National Opera, Bulevardi 23-27, SF 00180 Helsinki 18, Finland.

VALLE José (Nilo), b. 20 Feb 1946, Santa Catarina State, Brazil. Conductor; Composer; Teacher. Education: Paraná Music College; School of Music, Federal University of Rio de Janeiro; MMus, DMA, University of Washington School of Music, USA. Debut: Federal University of Rio de Janeiro, 1983. Career includes: Teacher, Music Theory, Parana Music College, Curitiba, Brazil; Assistant Conductor, Federal University of Rio de Janeiro, 1981-83; Assistant Conductor, University of Washington, 1989-91; Conductor and Founder, Proconart Ensemble for Contemporary Music, University of Washington, 1989-91; Conductor, Founder, Camerata Orchestra, 1989-91; Founder, current Music Director and Conductor, St Catherine Symphony Orchestra, Florianópolis, Santa Catarina State, Brazil, 1993-. Recordings: Sparrows by Joseph Schwantner and The Yew Tree by Diane Thome. Publications include: Series of 6 Travessuras (children's plays), 1978; Language and Musical Structure, book, 1978, 1982, 1986. Honours: Best Musician, Parana Musical College, 1974. Membership: Conductors' Guild Inc, USA. Hobbies: Languages; Poetry; Literature. Address: CP 1004, 88010-970 Florianopólis, Santa Catarina State, Brazil.

VALLER Rachel, b. 14 Sept 1929, Sydney, Australia. Pianist. m. Walter Travers, 28 Feb 1965. Education: BA, 1952; DipEd, 1960; LTCL, 1947; Conservatorium of Music, Sydney; University of Sydney; Pupil of Ignaz Friedman. Debut: Sydney, 1940. Career: Soloist, Associate Artist Chamber Ensembles, ABC Radio, TV; Appearances with Sydney, Melbourne and Queensland Symphony Orchestras; Toured with Cellist André Navarra, with Violinists Wanda Wilkomirska, Stoika Milanova, Zvi Zeitlin, Erick Friedman, Erich Gruenberg, Thomas Zehetmair and Bassoonist George Zukerman. Recordings: Lesser known piano works of Beethoven issued to mark Beethoven bicentenary, 1970; Schubert's Sonatinas with violinist Susanne Lautenbacher to commemorate 150th anniversary of his death, Germany, 1978.Honours: O A M Medal of the Order of Australia, 1995. Memberships: Committee Member of Musicians for World Peace. Address: 22 Allen's Parade, Bondi Junction, New South Wales 2022, Australia.

VALLETTI Cesare, b. 18 Dec 1921, Rome, Italy. Singer (Tenor). Education: Studied with Tito Schipa. Debut: Bari 1947, as Alfredo. Career: Sang in Rome, Palermo and Naples, 1947-50, as Almaviva, Narciso in Il Turco in Italia and Elvino in La Sonnambula; Sang Fenton with La Scala company at Covent Garden, 1950; Milan from 1950, as Nemorino, Vladimir in Prince Igor and Lindoro; US debut San Francisco 1953, as Werther; Metropolitan Opera from 1953, as Don Ottavio, Almaviva, Massenet's Des Grieux, Ernesto, Ferrando and Tamino; Covent Garden 1953, as Alfredo, with Callas; Florence 1958-65, as Giacomo in La Donna del Lago, Idamante and Gianetto in La Gazza Ladra; Salzburg Festival 1960, Don Ottavio; Carramoor Festival New York, 1968, as Nero in L'Incoronazione di Poppea. Recordings: Don Pasquale, L'Elisir d'Amore, La Fille du Régiment, La Cenerentola, Il Matrimonio Segreto (Cetra); La Traviata, L'Enfance du Christ, Madama Butterfly (RCA); Linda di Chamounix (Philips); Don Giovanni, conducted by Leinsdorf.

VAN ACKERE Jules-Emile, b. 8 Feb 1914, Heule, Belgium. University Professor. m. Mady Cattebeke, 2 sons. Education: University of Ghent; Royal Conservatory, Ghent. Career: Numerous public conferences, performances; Several hundred radio lectures including complete works of Frederick Delius, P Hindemith and A Schoenberg; Professor (now Professor Emeritus), University of Antwerp. Publications include: Igor Stravinsky; Aspecten van het Melos by Ravel, 1950; Pelléas et Mélisande ou la rencontre miraculeuse d'une poésie et d'une musique, 1952; Muziek van onze eeuw 1900-1950, 1954, reprinted 1994; Maurice Ravel, 1957; Eeuwige Muziek, 1960; Claude Debussy; Debussy's Images, 1962; Schubert en de Romantiek, 1963; Meesterwerken van het Klavier, 1966; L'Age d'Or de la Musique Française, 1966; De Kamermuziek en het lied, 1967; Bartók's Concertos; Frederick Delius, Musicien Méconnu, 1968; Arnold Schoenberg en Alban Berg, 1978; Frederick Delius of de Wellust van de Klank, 1983; Van Bach tot de Jong, 1985; Ravel en zijn tijd, 1987; De Liederen van Hugo Wolf, 1991; De Vocale Muziek van Brahms, 1992. Contributions to: Numerous professional journals. Address: 38 Avenue Jean de Bologne, 1020 Brussels, Belgium.

VAN ALLAN Richard, b. 28 May 1935, Clipstone, Nottinghamshire, England. Opera Singer (Bass-Baritone). div. 2 sons, 1 daughter. Education: Dip Ed Science, Worcester College of Education; Birmingham School of Music. Debut: Glyndebourne Festival Opera,1964; sang in 1970 premiere of Maw's The Rising of the Moon: other appearances as Osmano in L'Ormindo, Leporello, Osmin, Trulove, the Speaker in Die Zauberflöte and Melibeo in La Fedeltà Premiata. Career: Welsh National Opera; English National Opera; Royal Opera House, Covent Garden, London; Scottish Opera; Paris Opéra, France; Boston, San Diego, and Miami Operas, USA; Metropolitan Opera, New York; Brussels Opera, Belgium; Buenos Aires Opera, Brazil; Director, National Opera Studio, 1986-; Sang Don Alfonso at the Metropolitan 1990, Pooh-Bah in The Mikado for ENO; Glyndebourne Festival 1990, as Budd in Albert Herring and Pistol in Falstaff; Season 1992 as Tiresias in the premiere of Buller's Bacchae at ENO and in Osborne's Terrible Mouth; Sang the Grand Inquisitor in Don Carlos for Opera North, 1993, Don Jerome in the world stage premiere of Gerhard's The Duenna (Madrid 1992); Appeared in title role of Don Quichotte by Massenet at Victoria State Opera, Melbourne, Australia, 1995 and for English National Opera, 1996. Recordings include: Phillips: Brander, La Damnation de Faust, conductor, Colin Davis; Don Alfonso, Così fan tutte, conductor, Colin Davis; EMI: Leporello, Don Giovanni, conductor, Bernard Haitink. Honours: Grand Prix du Disque, La Damnation de Faust; Grammy Award, Cosi fan tutte; Grammy Nomination, Don Giovanni; Gloriana conducted by Charles Mackerras Decca, 1992. Honours: Elected Hon RAM 1987; Fellow, Birmingham Schools of Music (FBSM), 1991. Membership: Elected to Board of Directors, English National Opera Company, 1995. Hobbies: Shooting; Tennis. Address: c/o John Coast, 31 Sinclair Road, London, W14 0NS, England.

VAN APPLEDORN Mary (Jeanne), b. 2 Oct 1927. Professor of Music; Composer. Education: BM, 1948, MMus, 1950, PhD, 1966, Eastman School of Music. Debut: Carnegie Hall, 1956. Career includes: Currently Paul Whitfield Horn Professor of Music, Texas Tech University School of Music, Lubbock, Texas, USA; Commissions, Lux Legend of Sankta Lucia for band, 1982, Concerto for Trumpet, International Trumpet Guild, 1985, New York City Ballet 40th Anniversary Festival, 1988, Terrestrial Music, 1992, Cycles of Moons and Tides, 50th Anniversary of Tau Beta Sigma, 1995. Compositions include: Passacaglia and Chorale for orchestra, 1974; Concerto for Trumpet and Band, 1977, published 1992; Set of Five for piano, published 1978; Rising Night After Night, cantata, published 1979; A Liszt Fantasie, published, 1992; Terrestrial Music, double concerto for violin, piano and string orchestra, 1992; Reeds Afire for clarinet and bassoon, 1994; Ayre for strings, published 1994; Cycles of Moons and Tides for symphonic band, 1995; Rhapsody for violin and orchestra, 1996; Passages for trombone and piano, 1996; Native American Mosaic, for Native American flute, 1997; Les Hommes vidés to French translation by Pierre Leyris of T S Eliot's 'The Hollow Men', for unaccompanied chorus, published 1997; Music of Enchantment for Native American flute and strings with percussion, 1997; Passages II, for trombone and percussion. Recordings: Rising Night After Night; Sonatine; Four Duos, Liquid Gold; Incantations, Patterns; Concerto for Trumpet and Band; Passacaglia and Chorale; A Liszt Fantasie; Atmospheres for 12 Trombones, Rhapsody for Trumpet and Harp, Sonic Mutation for Solo Harp, CD, 1995; Trio Italiano; Postcards to John; Contrasts, for piano. Publications: In Quest of the Roman Numeral, article, 1970; Cycles of Moons and Tides; Trio Italiano. Honours: Suite for Carillon, for World Carillon Federation, Dijon, 1980; Standard Panel Awards, American Society of Composers, Authors and Publishers, 1980-97; Premiere Prix, 1993; Prize, Liquid Gold, IX Premio Ancona, Italy; 1st Prize, Terrestrial Music; Utah Composers Guild Competition, 1994; Prize, Postcards to John for solo guitar, Guitar Foundation of America, 1994; Horn and Trombone Award, International Trumpet Guild, Brass Trio Competition, 1996; Reeds Afire for clarinet and bassoon, performed at 1997 International Clarinet Festival. Memberships: ASCAP; SCI. Address: PO Box 1583, Lubbock, TX 79408-1583, USA.

VAN ASPEREN Bob, b. 8 Oct 1947, Amsterdam, Netherlands. Harpsichordist. Education: Studied at the Amsterdam Conservatoire, with Gustav Leonhardt. Career: From 1971 many concerts as soloist and in concert; Appearances with La Petite Bande and Quadro Hotteterre; Founded the ensemble Melante 81, for the tercentenary of Telemann; Teacher at the Hague Conservatoire, 1973-88, Berlin Hochschule from 1987. Address: Berlin Hochschule für Musik, Ernst Reuter Platz 10, 1000 Berlin 10, Germany.

VAN BLERK Gerardus J M, b. 14 May 1924, Tilburg, The Netherlands. Concert Pianist. m. A Van den Brekel. Education: Studied Piano with Professor W Andriessen, Amsterdam Conservatory; Piano-Soloist (Prix d'excellence); Studied with Yves Nat, Paris, France 1950-52. Career: Solo concerts with Concertgebouw Orchestra, Residentie Orchestra, The Hague, Rotterdam Philharmonic Orchestra with Haitink, Jochum, Fournet; Recitals, Chamber Music, Accompaniments (instrumental and singers); Professor of Piano, Royal Conservatory, The Hague. Recordings: Hindemith, Kammermusik Number 2 Klavierkonzert, op 36 Number 1; Chopin, Grand duo Concertant, Polonaise brillante op 3, Sonata in G minor op 65 with Anner Bylsma (violoncellist); Max Reger; Sonata for Cello and Piano, Caprice and Romance with Anner Bylsma; Brahms Lieder with Jard Van Nes (Alto); French violin sonatas; works of M Ravel. Hobbies: Chess; Bridge. Current Management: Interartists, The Hague and Netherlands Impresariaat, Amsterdam. Address: Prinsengracht 1095, 1017 Amsterdam, The Netherlands.

VAN BOER Bertil (Herman) Jr, b. 2 Oct 1952, Florida, USA. Musicologist; Conductor. m. Margaret Fast, 12 June 1977. Education: PhD, Uppsala University, Sweden, 1983. Career: Musical Director, Opera Kansas, 1989-; Assistant/Associate/Full Professor, Wichita State University, 1987-; Assistant Professor of Music, Brigham Young University, UT, 1983-87; Instructor, Shasta College, 1981-83. Publications: Dramatic Cohesion in the Works of Joseph Martin Kraus, 1989; Joseph Martin Kraus: Systemtisch-thematiches Werkverzeichnis, 1988; Joseph Martin Kraus Der Tod Jesu, 1987; The Symphony: Richter, Sweden I & II, 1983-86; Gustav III and the Swedish Stage, 1993. Contributions to: Articles in Fontes, Svensk tidskrift for Musikforskning, Journal of Musicology, Journal of Musicological Research. Address: 316 S Belmont, Wichita, KS 67218, USA.

VAN BUREN John (Hidden), b. 21 Sept 1952, Portland, Oregon, USA. Dozent; Composer. m. Margret Ulrike Schaal, 9 June 1988. Education: Reed College, Portland, 1970-72; Oregon State University, 1972-74; Composition with Milko Kelemen, Piano with Edgar Trauer, Electronic Music with Erhard Karkoschka, 1973-79, Diploma, Composition, 1979, Staatliche Hochschule für Musik, Stuttgart, Germany. Career includes: His works broadcast on various German radio stations, 1974-; Other performances of his works include ZDF National TV, 1979. Städtisch Bühne Mainz Ballet, 1981, American Composers' Orchestra, in Carnegie Hall, 1987, Deutsche Sinfonie Orchester, Berlin, 1994; Interviewed on Süddeutscher Rundfunk, 1983; Organiser, new music concerts, Stuttgart, notably as Artistic Director and Manager, Musica Nova Society; Has taught music at Ludwigsburg University, John-Cranko Ballet School of Stuttgart State Opera, City School of Music, Stuttgart; Currently Dozent, Leopold-Mozart Conservatory, Augsburg. Compositions include: Streichquartett, 1981; Fünf Gesänge nach Catull, 1984-85; Les

Nuages de Magritte for violin, cello, piano, 1989 Mementos, Symphony No 1, 1989-90; Aufbruch for orchestra, 1992. Recordings: Mementos, 1994; All major works recorded by Süddeutscher, Westdeutscher, Hessischer Südwest and Sender Freies Berlin radio stations. Honours: Composition Prize, Stuttgart, 1980; Südwestfunk Stipend, 1984; Meet the Composer Stipends, New York, 1984, 1985, 1987; Stipend, State Art Foundation of Baden Württemberg, 1991. Memberships: Board Member, Composers' Association, Bavaria (Augsburg); Minnesota Composers' Forum; GEMA. Address: Daimlerstrasse 29, D-70372 Stuttgart, Germany.

VAN DAM José, b. 25 Aug 1940, Brussels, Belgium. Singer (Bass). Education: Brussels Conservatory with Frederic Anspach. Debut: Liège 1960, as Basilio. Career: Paris Opéra 1961-65, debut in Les Troyens; Geneva Opera 1965-67, taking part in the premiere of Milhaud's La mère coupable, 1966; Deutsche Oper Berlin from 1967, as Verdi's Attila, Mozart's Leporello and Don Alfonso and Paolo in Simon Boccanegra; Sang Escamillo at his US debut (Santa Fe 1967) and at Covent Garden in 1973; Salzburg from 1968, in La Rappresentazione di Anima e di Corpo by Cavalieri, as Jochanaan in Salome, the villains in Les Contes d'Hoffmann, Mozart's Figaro and Amfortas in Parsifal; Vienna Staatsoper debut 1970, as Leporello; Metropolitan Opera debut 1975, as Escamillo: returned to New York as Golaud in Pelléas et Mélisande; Berg's Wozzeck and Jochanaan; Other appearances in Venice, Stockholm, Lisbon and Munich; Salzburg Easter Festival 1982, as the Flying Dutchman; Paris Opéra 1983 as St Francis of Assisi, in the premiere of Messiaen's opera; Sang Hans Sachs in Paris, 1990, Jochanaan in Salome at Lyons; Simon Boccanegra at Brussels; Sang as Falstaff at the Salzburg Festival, 1993; Season 1992/93 as Figaro (Mozart) in Brussels, Dapertutto at the Opéra Bastille, Don Quichotte at Toulouse and Saint Francois at Salzburg; Philip II in Don Carlos, London and Paris, 1996; Wagner's Dutchman at Rome, 1997; Concert appearances in Chicago, Boston, Tokyo, Los Angeles and London. Recordings: Roles in: Carmen, Fidelio, Salome, Pelléas et Mélisande, Cosi fan tutte, Simon Boccanegra, Louise, Mireille and La jolie fille de Perth (HMV); Un Ballo in Maschera, La Damnation de Faust, Le nozze di Figaro (Decca); Parsifal, Die Zauberflöte (Deutsche Grammophon); Don Giovanni (CBS); Pénélope, Dardanus (Erato); Also heard in the Requiems of Brahms and Verdi and Bach's B Minor Mass. Address: c/o Théâtre Royal de la Monnaie, 4 Léopoldstrasse, B-000 Brussels, Belgium.

VAN DE VATE Nancy (Hayes), b. 30 Dec 1930, Plainfield, New Jersey, USA. Composer; Record Producer. m. (1) Dwight Van de Vate Jr, 9 June 1952, 1 son, 2 daughters, (2) Clyde Arnold Smith, 23 June 1979. Education: Eastman School of Music, University of Rochester, 1948-49; AB, Wellesley College, 1952; MM, University of Mississippi, 1958; DMus, Florida State University, 1968; Private piano student of Anton Rovinsky, New York City, Bruce Simmonds, New Haven, Connecticut; Postdoctoral study, electronic music, Dartmouth and University of New Hampshire, 1972. Career: Orchestral premieres: Distant Worlds, Concerto for Percussion and Orchestra, Concertpiece for Cello and Small Orchestra all premiered by Polish Radio Symphony Orchestra of Krakow, Szymon Kawalla conductor, 1987-89; Premieres, Musica Viva Festival, Munich, Aspekte, Salzburg, Poznan Spring Festival, Poland; Vice-President and Artistic Director of Vienna Modern Masters. Compositions: The Saga of Cocaine Lil, 5 singers, percussion; Teufelstanz, percussion ensemble; A Night in the Royal Ontario Musuem, soprano, tape; Pura Besakih for large orchestra; Nine Preludes for Piano; Twelve Pieces for Piano; Trio for Violin, Violoncello and Piano; Many choral, vocal, brass and solo string works; Viola Concerto; Four Sombre Songs, for mezzo and orchestra; Premieres: Katyn, 1989, Polish Radio Symphony Orchestra and Chorus, S Kawalla, Conductor; Concerto for Violin and Orchestra, 1992, Vienna Konzerthaus, Vienna Musiksommer; Operas: Nemo: Jenseits von Vulkania; In the Shadow of the Glen; All Quiet on the Western Front. Recordings: Orchestral works, Polish Radio Symphony Orchestra of Krakow; Many solo and chamber works also commercially recorded; Violin Concerto No 2, 1996; Suite from Nemo for Orchestra, 1996. Honours: Nominator for Kyoto Music Prize, 1989, 1993, 1997. Memberships: MCNA; NARAS; Austrian Composers' League; College Music Society, USA. Hobbies: Travel; Photography; Languages. Current Management: Vienna Modern Masters. Address: Margaretenstrasse 125/15, A-1050 Vienna, Austria.

VAN DEN HOEK Martijn, b. 1955, Rotterdam, Holland. Concert Pianist. Education: Studied at the Rotterdam Conservatory, in Moscow with Valeri Kastelskii, in Budapest with Pal Kadosa and in Weimar with Ludwig Hofmann; New York with Joseff Raieff and Eugene Liszt; Further study in Vienna with Paul Angerer. Career: Has performed as soloist with the Amsterdam Concertgebouw Orchestra, the Wiener String Quartet and the National Hungarian Post Orchestra; Performances in Belgium, France, Germany, Austria, Portugal, USA, Japan and Hong Kong; Recital with the BBC, London; Repertoire includes concertos by Bach Bartók, Beethoven, Chopin, Haydn, Hummel, Mozart and Schumann; Sonatas by Beethoven, Berg, Brahms, Chopin, Haydn, Mozart, Scarlatti, Schubert, Impromptus and Moments Musicaux, Schoenberg's Op 23; Schumann's Kreisleriana and Faschingsschwank aus Wien; Liszt Consolations, Sonata, Spanish Rhapsody, Valses oubliées and Opera transcriptions. Honours: Prix d'Excellence and Goethe Prize, 1978; Public Prize of the City of Amsterdam, 1981; First Prize, International Liszt Competition in Utrecht, 1986.

VAN DER ROOST Jan (Frans Joseph), b. 1 Mar 1956, Duffel, Belgium. Composer. m. Bernadette Johnson, 16 May 1980, 2 sons, 2 daughters. Education: Lemmens Institute, Leuven; Royal Academy of Music, Antwerp and Ghent; Graduated in Music Theory, Harmony, Counterpoint, Fugue, Musical History, Trombone, Choral Conducting and Composition. Compositions: Sono Aeris for Brass Quintet, 1979; Herfst (Autumn), for Mixed Choir, 1981; Divertimento, for Piano, 1982; Canzona Gothica, for Trombone and Piano, 1982; Melopee e Danza, for 2 Guitars, 1982; Per Archi, for String Orchestra, 1983; 3 Bagatels, for Flute and Piano, 1984; Rikudim, for Band or Orchestra, 1985; Van Maan en Aarde (Of the Moon and the Earth), for Mixed Choir, 1985; Mozaieken (Mosaics), for Orchestra, 1986; Concerto Grosso, for Cornet, Trombone and Brass Band, 1986; Jaargang (Turning of the Year), for Choir and Piano, 1986-87; Puszta, for Band, 1987; Excalibur, for Brass Band, 1987; Elckerlyc (Everyman), Oratorio for Soloists, Choir and Orchestra, 1987; Obsessions, for Brass Instrument and Piano, 1987-88; Arghulesques, for Clarinet Quartet, 1988; Spartacus, for Band, 1988; Symphony, for Orchestra, 1988-89; Chemical Suite, for Trombone Quartet, 1990; Amazonia, for Band, 1990; Met Annie in Toverland, for Children's Choir and Ensemble, 1990; Quattro Miniature for Woodwind Quintet, 1991; Olympica for Band, 1992; Stonehenge for Brass Band, 1992; A Year has Four Lives, for Female Choir and Guitar, 1993; Exodus, Oratorio, for soloists, choir, organ and brass band, 1994; Concierto de Homenaje for guitar and orchestra, 1995; Rhapsody for Horn, Winds and Percussion, 1995; Poème Montagnard for Band, 1996; canTUBAllada for solo tuba, 1997; Contrasto Grosso for Recorder Quartet and String Quartet, 1997. Address: Albrecht Rodenbachlaan 13, 2550 Kontich, Belgium.

VAN EEGHEN Willem, b. 12 Oct 1956, Singapore. Economist. m. Marcelle Kreuze, 1 June 1995, 1 daughter. Education: BA, MA, University of Greningen, Netherlands; Private Violin Studies; Conservatory of Arnhem; Catholic University. Career: Concert Master, Dutch National Student Orchestra; Founder, Gronings Strijkes Ensemble; Member, Grout Quartet, Sotto Voice Quartet, Envoy Quartet. Membership: Chamber Music America. Hobbies: Tennis; Soccer; String Quartets. Address: 5028 Belt Road North West, Washington, DC 20016, USA.

VAN EETVELT Francois, b. 23 May 1946, Bornem, Belgium. Bass Baritone. m. Louizette Michiels, 4 July 1970, 1 son, 1 daughter. Education: Antwerp Conservatory; Graduate of Mastersinging class, Brussels Conservatory; Voice training in Italy and Germany. Debut: Flemish Opera House, Antwerp, Belgium. Career: Engagements in Antwerp, 1976; Amfortas, R Wagner's Parsifal, Royal Flemish Opera, Antwerp, 1976; Guest appearances and concerts in Bratislava, Prague, Brussels, Mexico City, Amsterdam, Dresden, San Luis, Leipzig, Helsinki and Festival International Cervantino, Guanajuato; Regular guest, Festival of Flanders; Performances for BRT and RTB; Cast, Orfeo production during Rubensyear; Recital at Aldeburgh Festival, England; Das Schloss, (F Kafka) A Laporte, Brussels Opera, Belgium; Repertoire: Apollo in Monteverdi's Orfeo; Mozart's Don Giovanni; Amfortas in Parsifal; Donner in Rheingold, Gunther in Götterdämmerung, Wolfram in Tannhäuser, Kurwenal in Tristan and Isolde; Sharpless in Butterfly; Jochanaan in Salome; Collatinus in Benjamin Britten's The Rape of Lucretia. Honours: Winner, International Opera Belcanto Concert, Ostend, 1978. Hobbies: Walking his dog; Playing tennis. Address: Puursesteenweg 263, 2680 Bornem, Belgium.

VAN IMMERSEEL Jos, b. 2 Apr 1928, Monaco. Harpsichordist. Conductor. Education: Studied at the Anvers Conservatoire, notably with Flor Peeters and Kenneth Gilbert. Career: Professor at the Anvers Conservatoire from 1972 and Artistic Director at the Sweelinck Conservatoire Amsterdam, 1981-85; Founded the Baroque Orchestra Anima Eterna, 1985 and Professor of Piano at the Paris Conservatoire from 1992; Many recitals and concerts throughout France; Conductor of the ensemble Anime Eterna and let it in Handel's Serse for Flanders Opera, 1996. Address: Conservatoire National, 14 Rue de Madrid, F-75008 Paris, France.

VAN KEULEN Isabelle, b. 16 Dec 1966, Mijdrecht, The Netherlands. Concert Violinist and Violist. Education: Studied at the Sweelinck Conservatoire in Amsterdam and with Sandor Vegh at the Salzburg Mozarteum; Masterclassses with Max Rostal and Vladimir Spivakov. Debut: Violist, February 1992. Career: Has appeared from 1983 with Berlin Philharmonic, Vienna, Detroit, Minnesota and BBC Welsh Symphonies, NHK of Tokyo and the Concertgebouw; Conductors have included Baumgartner, Chailly, Colin Davis, Dutoit, Ehrling, Leitner, Leppard, Marriner, Neumann, de Waart and Zinman; Appearances at the Salzburg Festival and tours with the Bamberg Symphony and Gidon Kremer's Lockenhaus Soloists; BBC Proms debut 1990, in Mozart with the Rotterdam Philharmonic; Strauss's Concerto with the BBC Philharmonic and the Dutilleux Concerto with the Concertgebouw; Other repertoire includes concertos by Bach, Haydn, Henkemans, Schnittke, Spohr and Stravinsky, in addition to the standard items; As violist has collaborated with the Hagen, Orlando and Borodin Quartets. Recordings include: Saint-Saëns and Vieuxtemps Concertos, London Symphony; Schubert's Octet; Shostakovich Sonatas for Violin and Viola (Fidelio). Honours include: Silver Medal, International Yehudi Menuhin Violin Competition, 1983; Winner, Eurovision Young Musician of the Year Competition, 1984. Address: c/o Georgina Ivor Associates, 66 Alderbrook Road, London SW12 8AB, England.

VANAUD Marcel, b. 1952, Brussels, Belgium. Singer (Baritone). Education: Studied at the Brussels Conservatoire and at Liège. Career: Sang at the Liège Opera 1975-83, notably as Papageno, Escamillo, Alfonso in La Favorita, Renato and Ourrais in Mireille; Guest appearances at Pittsburgh and New Orleans 1984; New York City Opera 1985 as Zurga in Les Pêcheurs de Perles; Théâtre de la Monnaie Brussels as Raimund in Comte Ory and Mozart's Figaro; Season 1987-88 as Lescaut at Montreal, Posa in Don Carlos at Tulsa, Figaro at Santa Fe and Raimbaud at Toulouse; La Scala Milan 1989 in the premiere of Doktor Faustus by Manzoni; Returned to Liège 1992 as Mephistopheles in La Damnation de Faust and sang Germont at Los Angeles; Festival de Radio France at Montpellier 1992, as Sacchini's Oedipus and in Chateau des Carpathes by Philippe Hersant. Recordings include: Les contes d'Hoffmann and Franck's Les Beatitudes; Karnac in Le Roi d'Ys.

VANDENBURG Howard, b. 18 May 1918, Buffalo, New York, USA. Singer (Tenor). m. Anna Green. Education: Studied at the Curtis Institute Philadelphia. Debut: Philadelphia Opera Co, 1937, as Mozart's Almaviva. Career: Sang as tenor from 1951, in New York; Munich Staatsoper from 1952, as Don José, Radames, the Emperor in Die Frau Ohne Schatten, Florestan, Laca (Jenufa) and Julien in Louise; Covent Garden 1953 with the Munich company as Midas in the British premiere of Die Liebe der Danae by Strauss; Zurich 1953, Naples and Florence 1954; Guest appearances in Vienna and Germany; Sang at Dortmund 1963-72, as a baritone; Sang with the Bavarian State Opera Munich, Vienna State Opera, Royal Opera House, Covent Garden, London, La Scala, Milan, Maggio Musicale, Florence and Barcellona Licio; Numerous radio recordings with Bavarian Radio, Munich and the BBC, London. Recordings: Die Zauberflöte; Euryanthe. Honour: Awarded title of Kammersänger, following debut as Lohengrin; Deutsche Bühnen Genossenschaft. Address: Alte Hofstrasse 17, 51545 Waldbröl/Dickhausen, Germany.

VANDERSTEENE Zeger, b. 5 June 1940, Ghent, Belgium. Singer (Tenor). Career: Sang at first in concert and appeared in opera from 1980; Théâtre de la Monnaie at Brussels, 1981-84, as Evandre in Alceste and Steuermann in Fliegende Holländer; Théâtre du Châtelet, Paris, 1983, in Rameau's Les Indes Galantes; Bologna, 1987, in Gluck's La Danza; Sang Aegisthus in Elektra at Antwerp, 1990; Song recitals in works by Schubert, Schumann and Fauré. Recordings include: Castor et Pollux by Rameau (Telefunken); Armide by Lully (Erato). Address: Antwerp Opera, Ommeganchshtrasse 59, B-2018 Antwerp, Belgium.

VANDOR Ivan, b. 13 Oct 1932, Pecs, Hungary. Composer. Education: MA Ethnomusicology, UCLA, 1970. Career: Member, Musica Elettronica Viva, 1966- 68; Member, Nuova Consonanza Improvis Group, 1967-68; Research in Tibetan Budhist Music, 1970-71; Director, International Institute for comparative Music Studies, Berlin, 1977-83; Founder, Director, Scuola Interculturale di Musica, 1979-; Professor, Composition, Conservatory of Music, Bologna, 1979-. Compositions: Quartetto Perachi, 1962; Moti, 1963; Serenata, 1964; Dance Music, 1969; Winds, 1970; some short pieces for Harpischord. Publications: La Musique du Bouddhisme Tibetain, 1976; Die Musik des Tibetischen Buddhismus, 1978; Editor, The World of Music, 1975-85. Contributions to: various journals. Memberships: Italian Society for Contemporary Music; Italian Society for Ethnomusicology; Nuova Consonanza. Address: Viale Parioli 73, 00197 Rome, Italy.

VANESS Carol, b. 27 July 1952, San Diego, California. USA. Singer (Soprano). Education: Studied in California with David Scott and in 1976 won the San Francisco Opera Auditions. Career: San Francisco 1977, as Vitellia in La Clemenza di Tito; New York City Opera from 1979, as Alcina, Antonia in Les Contes d'Hoffmann, Vitelia, Flotow's Frau Fluth, Mimi, and Leila in Les pecheurs de Perles, Rigoleto (Gilda), Traviata (Violetta); Donna Anna; Glyndebourne Opera from 1982, as Donna Anna, Electra in Idomeneo, Fiordiligi and Amelia Boccanegra (1986); Covent Garden debut 1982, as Mimi: returned for Vitellia and Dalila in Handel's Samson; Countess Almaviva, 1989; Rosalinda in Der Fledermaus; Metropolitan Opera from 1984, as Armida in Rinaldo,

Fiordiligi, Electra and the Countess in Figaro, Manon; Australian Opera 1985, Amelia in Un Ballo in Maschera; Seattle Opera 1986, as Massenet's Manon; Desdemona, 1986; Violetta, 1988; Trovatore, 1989; Concert appearances in the Choral Symphony in Paris, the Verdi Requiem in Philadelphia and at the Lincoln Center New York with Pavarotti; Sang in Beethoven Missa solemnis at the Barbican Hall, London, 1989; Royal Opera, Vitellia in La Clemenza di Tito 1989; Trovatore 1990 at the Metropolitan Opera and Faust (Marguerite); Don Giovanni (Anna) at Covent Garden, 1992; Season 1992/93 as Iphigénie en Tauride at La Scala, Mathilde in Guillaume Tell at San Francisco and Olympia at the Met; Sang Desdemona at the Metropolitan, 1994; Norma at Seattle, 1994, (Amelia, Ballo in Maschera, 1995); Fiordiligi at the Met, 1997. Recordings include: Donna Anna in the Glyndebourne production of Don Giovanni conducted by Bernard Haitink; Masses by Haydn; Glyndebourne, Haitink, Cosi fan tutte; Beethoven's Ninth with Dohnányi and Cleveland Orchestra; Missa Solemnis with Tate and the ECO; Don Giovanni (Elvira), conducted by Muti, EMI; Tosca, Philips; Rossini, Stabat Mater, Philips (Bychkov). Address: c/o Herbert H Breslin, 119 West 57th Street, NY 10019, USA.

VANHULST Henri, b. 5 Dec 1943, Louvain, Belgium. Full Professor of Musicology. m. Nicole Latinne, 6 July 1968, 2 sons. Education: Licentiate in Romance Philology, 1965; Licentiate in Art History and Archaeology, 1967; Doctorate in Musicology, 1984. Career: Professor of Music History, Brussels Conservatory, 1981-90; Professor of Musicology, part-time, 1979-90, Professor of Musicology, full-time, 1991-, Free University of Brussels. Publications: Catalogue des Editions musicales de Pierre Phalèse et ses fils (Louvain, 1545-1578), 1990; Jan Evertzen van Doorn's Catalogus librorum musicorum, 1996. Contributions to: Articles in Revue Belge de Musicologie, Acta Musicologica, Tijdschrift Vereniging voor Nederlandse Muziekgeschiedenis. Honour: Prize, Royal Academy, Belgium, 1984. Membership: Secretary, Belgian Musicological Society. Address: Groene Gracht 1, B-1800 Vilvoorde, Belgium.

VANKATOVA Dagmar, b. 5 December 1963, Zatec, Czech Republic. Opera Singer (coloratura soprano). m. Josef Vankat, 2 daughters. Education: Prague Conservatory. Debut: State Opera, Prague, Köningen der Nacht in W A Mozart's Zauberflöte, 1995. Career: Concerts in France, BRD, Belgium; Opera performances: Despina in Cosi fan tutte (Mozart), France, 1989; Despina, Italy, 1989; Zauberflöte, 1991, Dortmund, 1992, Switzerland, 1995, Japan, 1996. Recordings: Czech church music, 1992; J J Ryba, Missa In B, Litaniae Lauretanae, 1992; Hieronymus Bosch (music, O Soukup), 1992; Water music for Cesky Krumlov (music, F X Thuri), 1996; Music from archives Cesky Krumlov, 1997. Honours: 2nd Prize, Dvorak's competition for singer, 1983, 1984; 3rd Prize, competition for singer in Brno, 1985; 2nd Prize, Mozart's competition for singer, 1989. Hobbies: Tourism; Literature. Address: Vesinova 8, Prague 10 - Strusnice, 100 00, Czech Republic.

VANZO Alain, b. 2 Apr 1928, Monaco. Singer (Tenor); Composer. Education: Studied with Rolande Darcouer in Paris. Debut: Paris Opera 1954, as the Pirate in Oberon. Career: Appearances in Paris as Edgardo, the Duke of Mantua, Don Ottavio, Des Grieux, Werther and Benvenuto Cellini; Covent Garden 1961-63; Appearances at the Wexford Festival, Barcelona, Lisbon, Vienna, Edinburgh, Aix-en-Provence, Montreal, San Francisco and New York (Metropolitan Opera with the company of the Paris Opéra); Sang the title role in Meyerbeer's Robert le Diable, Paris Opéra 1984; sang Faust at Philadelphia, 1984. Compositions: Operetta Le Pecheur d'etoiles (performed Lille 1972) and opera Le Chouans (performed Avignon 1982). Recordings: Lakmé, with Joan Sutherland (Decca); Mignon by Thomas, La Navarraise by Massenet (CBS); Le pêcheurs de Perles (Philips); Mireille by Gounod (EMI); Faure's Pénélope (Erato). Address: c/o Théâtre National, 8 Rue Scribe, F-75009 Paris, France.

VARADY Julia, b. 1 Sept 1941, Oradea, Rumania. Singer (Soprano). m. Dietrich Fischer-Dieskau, 1977. Education: Studied in Cluj with Emilia Popp and in Bucharest with Arta Florescu. Debut: Cluj 1962, as Fiordiligi. Career: Guest appearances at the Budapest and Bucharest Operas; Moved to Frankfurt, West Germany 1972; Sang Violetta at Cologne, 1972; Munich from 1973, as Vitellia in La Clemenza di Tito, Lady Macbeth, Butterfly, Giorgetta (Il Tabarro), Elektra in Idomeneo, Santuzza, Liu, Leonora (La Forza del Destino), Elisabeth de Valois and Cordelia in the premiere of Lear by Reimann (1978); Scottish Opera 1974, as Gluck's Alceste; Metropolitan Opera 1978, Donna Elvira; Tours of Japan, Israel and the USA; Appearances at the Berlin, Edinburgh, Munich and Salzburg Festivals and at the Promenade Concerts London; La Scala Milan 1984, in Idomeneo; Other roles include Countess Almaviva, Judith (Bluebeard's Castle), Tatiana, Desdemona and Rosalinde; Sang Wagner's Senta at Munich 1990, Covent Garden 1992; Vitella in La Clemenza di Tito at the Elizabeth Hall, 1990; Appeared as Abigaille in Nabucco at the 1990 Munich Festival; Season 1992/93 as the Trovatore Leonora at Munich, in concert performances with the Glyndebourne Company of Fidelio and Elisabeth de Valois at the Deutsche Oper Berlin; Returned to Berlin 1997, as Senta; Aida at the 1997 Munich Festival; Featured Artist (People no 181), Opera Magazine, 1992; Concert repertoire includes arias by Mozart and Beethoven, Vier Letzte Lieder by Strauss, Britten's War Requiem, the Verdi Requiem, the Faust oratorios of Schumann and Berlioz; Requiem by Reimann (premiere 1982). Recordings include: Lucio Silla by Mozart (BASF); Die Fledermaus, Il Matrimonio Segreto, Lear, Idomeneo, La Clemenza di Tito, Duke Bluebeard's Castle (Deutsche Grammophon); Gli Amori di Teolinda by Meyerbeer (Orfeo); Cavalleria Rusticana (Decca); Les Contes d'Hoffmann, Arabella (EMI); Don Giovanni (Eurodisc); Handel's Saul (Telefunken). Address: AMI, Artist Management International, 12/13 Richmond Buildings, London W1V 5AE, England.

VARCOE Stephen, b. 19 May 1949, Lostwithiel, Cornwall, England. Singer (Baritone). m. Melinda Davies, 22 Apr 1972, 3 sons, 1 deceased, 2 daughters. Education: Cathedral Choir School and King's School, Canterbury; MA, King's College, Cambridge; Guildhall School of Music, London. Career: Concerts in most major British and European festivals; Specialist in Lieder, French Mélodies and English song; Many appearances on British, French and German Radio; Sang Sarastro in Die Zauberflöte at the Mozart Experience, London, 1989; Haydn's L'Infedeltà Delusa at Antwerp in 1990; Created Zossima in the premiere of Tavener's Mary of Egypt, Aldeburgh, 1992; Peri's Eurydice in Drottningholm, 1997. Recordings: Over 95 including: Purcell's Indian Queen, Fairy Queen, King Arthur and The Tempest; Handel's Partenope, L'Allegro, Triumph of Time and Truth, Alessandro and Israel in Egypt; Bach's B Minor Mass, Masses, Cantatas and Matthew and John Passions; Fauré's Requiem; Finzi's Songs of Thomas Hardy; Rameau's Motets, French Mélodies; Britten's Cantata Misericordium and Tavener's Mary of Egypt; Schubert's Lieder, and many others. Honour: Gulbenkian Foundation Fellowship, 1977. Hobbies: Building; Gardening. Current Management: Caroline Phillips. Address: Tailor House, 63-65 High Street, Whitwell, Hertfordshire SG4 8AH, England.

VARGA Balint (Andras), b. 3 Nov 1941, Budapest, Hungary. Music Publisher; Music Interviewer. m. Katalin Zsoldos, 14 Jan 1977, 2 daughters. Education: Teacher's degree, English and Russian, University of Budapest, 1960-65; Hungarian Journalists' School, 1966-67; Studied piano privately for 13 years. Career: Regular radio programmes in Budapest, 1965-; Some foreign radio programmes; Occasional programmes on Hungarian Television; Head of Promotion, Editio Musica Budapest, 1971-; Deputy Director of the Hungarian Cultural Institute, Berlin, 1991-. Publications: Conversations with Lutoslawski, 1974; Conversations with Iannis Xenakis, 1980; Conversations with Luciano Berio, 1981; 4 other anthologies of musical interviews published in Hungarian 1972, 1974, 1979, 1986; Translated Aaron Copland's The New Music into Hungarian 1973, also two books published in English and one published in German. Contributions: Regular articles in Muzsika. Honours: Several minor prizs and decorations in Hungary. Memberships: Hungarian Journalists' Association; Hungarian Art Fund. Hobbies: Playing the Piano; Walking; Reading. Address: 1020 Berlin, Fischerinsel, 1 03 01, Germany.

VARGA Gilbert, b. 17 Jan 1952, London, England. Conductor. Education: Studied with Franco Ferrara, Sergiu Celibidache and Charles Bruck. Career: Principal Conductor, Hofer Symphoniker, 1980-85; Chief Conductor of the Philharmonia Hungarica, 1985-90; Principal Guest Conductor, Malmö Symfoniorkester, 1997-99; Music Director Orquestre Sinfonica de Euskadi, 1998-2001; Guest engagements include Orchestre de Paris, Rotterdam Philharmonic, Hallé Orchestra, City of Birmingham Symphony, BBC Philharmonic, Bavarian Radio, Gürzenich Orkester Köln, Toronto Symphony, Indianapolis Symphony, Sydney Symphony Orchestra; Yomiuri Nippon Symphony, Tokyo. Recordings include: Symphony No 6 of Anton Rubinstein and solo cello concertos with BBC Philharmonic and Rolland, and recordings with Munich Chamber Orchestra and Bamberg Symphony. Address: c/o Intermusica Artists Management Ltd, 16 Duncan Terrace, London N1 8BZ, England.

VARGA Tibor, b. 4 July 1921, Györ, Hungary. Violinist; Conductor. Education: Studied with Jeno Hubay and Carl Flesch at the Franz Liszt Academy Budapest, 1931-38. Career: Concerts worldwide 1933-, notably in the romantic repertory and with concertos by Berg, Bartók and Schoenberg; Professor of Violin at the Academy of Music Detmold 1949; Founded the Tibor Varga Chamber Orchestra 1954 conducted it until 1988; Settled in Switzerland 1955, founded the Tibor Varga Festival in Sion 1964; Masterclasses at the Salzburg Mozarteum, Switzerland; Musical Director of the Orchestre des Pays de Savoie at Annecy, 1989; Plays a Guarnerious of 1733; Repertoire has included Concertos by Bach, Beethoven, Blacher (Creation, 1950), Brahms, Bruch, Elgar, Mozart, Paganini, Sibelius, Stravinsky, Tchaikovsky; Solo sonatas by Bach, Bartók; Sonatas by Bach, Bartók, Beethoven, Brahms, Debussy, Franck, Mozart, Schubert. Honours include: Bundesverdienstkreuz 1969. Address: c/o Kammerorchester Tibor Varga, Box 528, D-4930 Detmold, Germany.

VARGAS Milagro, b. 1958, USA. Singer (Mezzo-soprano). Education: Studied at Oberlin College and the Eastman School of Music with Jan DeGaetani. Career: Member of the Stuttgart Staatsoper 1983-88, notably in the premiere of Akhnaten by Philip Glass (1984) and as Cherubino, Nancy in Albert Herring, Orlofsky, and Lybia in Jommelli's Fetonte; Komische Opera Berlin as Cherubino, Heidelberg Festival as Ramiro in La Finta Giardiniera; Sang Charlotte in Zimmermann's Die Soldaten at Strasbourg and Stuttgart, 1988; Sang Ravel's Sheherazade at the Cabrillo Festival 1986 and has appeared elsewhere in concert at the Aspen and Marlboro Festivals, with the Philadelphia Orchestra and the Rochester Philharmonic. Recordings include: Akhnaten; Die Soldaten. Address: c/o Staatsoper Stuttgart, Oberer Schlossgarten 6, 7000 Stuttgart 1, Germany.

VARGAS Ramon, b. 1959, Mexico City, Mexico. Singer (Tenor). Career: Has sung in opera a Mexico City as Fenton in Falstaff, Nemorino, Don Ottavio and Count Almaviva; Sang Gelsomino in Il Viaggio a Reims at the Vienna Staatsoper, 1987; Pesaro and Salzburg Festivals, 1987, Mexico City 1988 as Tamino: Further appearances at Lucerne 1989, Zurich 1990 as Lorenzo in Fra Diavalo and Enschede Holland, as Fenton; Season 1991-92 as Leicester in Rossini's Elisabetta at Naples, Almaviva at Rome, Rodrigo in a concert performance of La Donna del Lago at Amsterdam and Paolina in Il Matriomonio Segreto at Martina Franca; Sang Rossini's Almaviva at the Verona Arena, 1996. Address: c/o Opernhaus Zurich, Falkenstrasse 1, CH-8008 Zurich, Switzerland.

VARGYAS Lajos (Karoly), b. 1 Feb 1914, Budapest, Hungary. Musical Folklorist; Ethnographer. m. 17 Dec 1949. Education: Pupil of Kodály in Musical Folklore, Budapest University; Church Music at Budapest Music Academy, 1936-37; Doctor of Ethnography, Linguistics and Hungarian Literature, 1941; Academic DMus, 1963. Career: Assistant Professor at Budapest University, 1952-54; Director of Folk Music Research Group, Hungarian Academy, 1970-73. Recording: Mongolian Folk Music, UNESCO, 1971. Publications include: Aj falu zenei élete (The Musical Life of the Village Aj), 1941; Compiler, Kodály: A Magyar népzene; A peldatart szerkesztette Vargyas Lajos (The Hungarian Folk Music: Collection of Tune Examples by L Vargyas), 1952; A magyar vers ritmusa (The Rhythm of the Hungarian Verse), 1952; Author and Editor, Studia Memoriae Belae Bartók Sacra, 1956, 1957 and 1959; Aj falu zenei anyaga (The Tune Material of The Village Aj), 1960, 1961 and 1963; Magyar vers - Magyar Nyelv (Hungarian Verse - Hungarian Language), 1966; Researches into The Mediaeval History of Folk Ballad, 1967; Zoltan Kodály: Folk Music of Hungary, 2nd revised and enlarged edition, 1971; Balladaskonyv (Books of Ballads with their tunes), 1979; Hungarian Ballads and The European Ballad Tradition, in Hungarian, 1976, English 1983; A magyarság népzenéje (Folkmusic of the Hungarians), 1981, 1993; Keleti hagyomany - nyugati kultura, Tanulmanyok (Eastern Traditions - Western Culture, Essays), 1984; Magyar Néprajz V Népköltészet (Hungarian Ethnography Folkpoetry), 1988; Kodály hatrahagyott foljegyzesei I (Kodály's Records Left Behind), editor, 1989, 1993; Corpus Musicae Popularis Hungaricae VIII/A-B, editor, 1993; Kerítésen kivül (Emlékek életemböl) (Memoirs), 1993; Magyar népballadák (Hungarian Folkballads), 1994. Contributions to: Over 150 on musical themes and over 150 0n other themes. Honours: Erkel Prize, 1980; Széchényi Prize, 1991. Memberships: President, Committee for Scientific Classification in Musicology and Ethnography, Hungarian Academy; Music Committee, Hungarian Academy. Address: 1022 Budapest, Szemlohegy Str 4/B, Hungary.

VARNAY Astrid, b. 25 April 1918, Stockholm, Sweden. Singer (Soprano/Mezzo-Soprano). Education: Studied with Paul Altouse and Herman Weigert in New York. Debut: Metropolitan Opera 1941, as Sieglinde. Career: Sang at the Metropolitan until 1956, as Brünnhilde, Isolde, Senta, Elsa, Elisabeth, Kundry, Venus, Ortrud, the Marschallin, Amelia Boccanegra, Santuzza and Salome; Sang in the premiere of Menotti's The Island God, 1942; Chicago Opera debut 1944, Sieglinde; San Francisco Opera 1946-51, notably as Gioconda and Leonore; Mexico City 1948, as Tosca, Aida and Santuzza; Covent Garden debut 1948, as Brünnhilde in Siegfried: returned to London 1951, 1958-59 and 1968 (Kostelnicka in Jenufa); Bayreuth Festival 1951-67, as Brünnhilde, Isolde, Ortrud, Kundry and Senta; Paris Opéra and La Scala Milan as Isolde, 1956, 1957; Stuttgart 1959, as Jocasta in the premiere of Oedipus der Tyrann by Orff; Mezzo roles from 1962: Clytemnestra , Herodias and the title role in Einem's Der Besuch der Alten Dame; Salzburg Festival 1964-65, as Elektra; Professor at the Dusseldorf Musikhochschule from 1970; Returned to the Metropolitan 1974, as the Kostelnicka, then sang Herodias, Clytemnestra and Begbick in Mahagonny. Recordings: Der fliegende Holländer, Lohengrin (Decca); Oedipus der Tyrann (Deutsche Grammophon); Cavalleria Rusticana (HMV); Private recordings from Bayreuth and the Metropolitan; Der Ring des Nibelungen conducted by Clemens Krauss, Bayreuth 1953; Sang in recordings released 1984-85 by Decca: Andrea Chénier and The Rake's Progress. Address: c/o Metropolitan Opera, Lincoln Center, New York, NY 10023, USA.

VARONA Luciano, b. 14 Aug 1930, Mendoza, Argentina. Stage and Costume Designer. Education: Studied at the Escuela Superior de Bellas Artes in Buenos Aires. Debut: Colon Buenos Aires 1959 , Prokofiev's The Love for Three Oranges. Career: Collaborated with Tito Capobianco at the New York City 1966-73, with Giulio Cesare, The Golden Cockerel, Manon, Lucia di Lammermoor and Donzetti's Tudor trilogy; Handel's Ariodante for the opening of the Kennedy Center at Washington DC, 1971; San Francisco and Vancouver Opera 1972-73, with Norma and Lucrezia Borgia; Further association with Capobianco at the Deutsche Opera Berlin and the Netherlands Opera 1971-74, Attila, Aida, Rodelinda and La Traviata; Returned to the Teatro Colon 1981-88, with designs for Romeo et Juliette, Die Zauberflöte, Carmen and Die Entführung. Address: c/o Teatro Colon, Cerrito 618, 1010 Buenos Aires, Argentina.

VARVISO Silvio, b. 26 Feb 1924, Zurich, Switzerland. Conductor. Education: Studied at the Zurich Conservatory and in Vienna with Clemens Krauss. Debut: St Gallen 1944, Die Zauberflöte. Career: Assistant, then Principal Conductor of Basle Opera, 1950-62; Conducted opera in Berlin and Paris, 1958; San Francisco Opera from 1959 (US premiere of A Midsummer Night's Dream, 1960); Metropolitan Opera from 1961, Lucia di Lammermoor, Die Walküre, Die Fledermaus, Die Meistersinger, and Italian repertory; Glyndebourne and Covent Garden 1962, Le nozze di Figaro and Der Rosenkavalier; Principal Conductor of the Royal Opera, Stockholm 1965-71; Bayreuth Festival 1969-74; Die Meistersinger, Der fliegende Holländer and Lohengrin; Conducted new production of La Bohème at Covent Garden, 1974; Musical Director at Stuttgart 1972-80; has led performances of Rossini, Donizetti, Bellini, Strauss, Mozart and Wagner; Musical Director of the Paris Opéra 1980-85; Conducted Lohengrin at Stuttgart 1990, Manon Lescaut at Barcelona; Season 1992/93 with Tosca at Antwerp and Die Frau ohne Schatten in Florence; Conducted La Fanciulla del West at Ghent, 1996. Address: c/o Staatsheater Stuttgart, Oberer Schlossgarten 6, D-7000 Stuttgart 1, Germany.

VASARY Tamás, b. 11 Aug 1933, Debrecen, Hungary. Pianist; Conductor. m. Ildiko Kovacs, 15 Mar 1967. Education: Franz Liszt Music Academy, Budapest, 1951. Debut: First Concert, aged 8. Career: Performed in major music centres, worldwide; Festivals include: Salzburg, Edinburgh, Berlin; Conducting Debut in 1970; conducted over 70 orchestras; Music Director, Northern Sinfonia, 1979-83; Principal Conductor, Music Director, Bournemouth Sinfonietta, 1989-97; Musical Director of Hungarian Radio Orchestra, 1993. Recordings: Chopin; Liszt; Debussy; Brahms; Mozart; Rachmaninov. Honours: Paris, Marguerite Long, 1950; Queen Elisabeth of Belgium, 1956; Rio de Janeiro International Competition, 1956; Bach and Paderewski medals, 1960. Hobbies: Yoga; Writing. Address: 9 Village Road, London N3 1TL, England.

VASILYEVA Alla, b. 1933, Moscow, Russia. Concert Cellist. Education: Studied at the Central Music School and at the Moscow State Conservatoire, with Rostropovitch. Career: Joined the Moscow Chamber Orchestra under Rudolf Barshai 1958 and remains as principal cellist; many tours with the Moscow Chamber Orchestra and as solo recitalist, notably in modern Russian works; Plays her own arrangements of works by Resphigi and Vivaldi. Recordings: Works by Bach, Geminiani, Vivaldi, Moshei Wainberg, Boris Tchaikovsky, Khrennikov and Shostakovich (Melodiya). Address: c/o Sonata, 11 Northpark Street, Glasgow G20 7AA, Scotland.

VASSAR Frédéric, b. 1948, France. Singer (Baritone). Education: Studied at the Opera Studio of the Théatre de la Monnaie, Brussels. Career: Sang first as bass in Opera at Brussels from 1973 (Alberich), then at Ghent (Wotan, Hoffmann, Boccanegral) and for French Radio; Sang Mephistopheles in Faust at Marseilles, 1977, followed by visits to Strasbourg, Avignon, Dublin and Orange; Engagements at Liège, 1985-86 as (Escamillo, Oubbias in Mireille), Angers, Metz (Golaud), Don Giovanni and the Villains in Hoffmann; Season 1989-90, as Mephistopheles at Avignon, Lescaut at Nantes, Telramund at Limoges and Scarpia for Opera Northern Ireland in Belfast. Honours: Winner, 1976 Voix d'or Enrico Caruso and Henri Duparc, France; Winner, Toti dal Monte.

VASSILIEV Alexandre, b. 20 Mar 1970, St Petersburg, Russia. Singer (Bass). Education: Tchaikovsky Conservatory, Moscow, 1989-93, with Evgeny Nesterenko; Masterclasses with Ernst Haefliger in Moscow, Hanna Ludwig at Salzburg and Astrid Varnay at Munich. Career: Appearances at the Bavarian State Opera, Munich, 1994-95 and the Freiburg Opera 1995-97; Role have included Bottom in Britten's Midsummer Night's Dream, Alidoro in Rossini's Cenerentola and Mozart's Figaro; Achillas in Handel's Giulio Cesare for Bavarian Radio; Concerts include Bach's B Minor Mass and Mozart's Requiem under Helmuth Rilling in Moscow; Beethoven's Missa Solemnis at Landshut, Oedipus Rex at Stuttgart and Suppé's Requiem in Freiburg; Season 1997-98 includes appearances at Cologne Opera with Colline in La Boheme, Mesner in Tosca and Pistola in Falstaff; Performances of Sciarino's Die tödliche Blume at the Schwetzingen and Vienna Festivals; Concerts and recitals in Freiburg, Stuttgart, Strasbourg and Cologne. Address: c/o Haydn Rawstron Ltd, 36 Station Road, London SE20 7BQ, England.

VASSILIEVA Elena, b. 1956, France. Singer (Soprano). Education: Studied at the Paris Conservatoire. Career: Won various awards in the early 1980s and sang in Henze's Boulevard Solitude at Paris, 1984; Has sung in operas by Puccini, Massenet, Verdi, Strauss and Mozart and notably as Tatiana in Eugene Onegin; Saffi in Der Zigeunerbaron at Liège; Many concert appearances, including modern repertory and songs by Russian composers. Address: Opéra de Wallonie, 1 Rue des Domincains, B-4000 Liège, Belgium.

VAUGHAN Denis Edward, b. 6 June 1926, Melbourne, Australia. Orchestral Conductor. Education includes: MusB, University of Melbourne, 1947; Royal College of Music, London, England, 1947-50. Debut: As Conductor, Royal Festival Hall, London, 1953. Career includes: Annual harpischord concerts, Royal Festival Hall, 1948-58; Concert to honour Toscanini, with Bernstein, Klemperer, Celibidache and Maazel, Parma, 1959; Adviser to UNESCO and Berne Union on musical aspects of copyright matters, 1962-67; Music Director, Australian Elizabethan Theatre Trust, 1966; Orchestral concerts, operas in Europe, Australia, USA, Canada, 1970-89; Munich State Opera House, 1972-80; Musical Director, State Opera of South Australia, 1981-84. Recordings include: 23 with Orchestra of Naples, including complete Schubert symphonies, 12 Haydn, 11 Mozart, Re Pastore etc, RCA Victor. Publications: Le Discrepanze Nei Manoscritti Verdiani, La Scala, 1959; Preface on organ articulation and phrasing, Stanley Voluntaries, 1959; Puccini's Orchestration, Royal Musical Association, 1961. Contributions to: Opera News; High Fidelity; Journal of Sound and Vibration; Das Orchester; Musical Times; Opernwelt Jahrbuch; Studio Sound; Symphony, USA; Gramophone. Honours: Tagore Gold Medal, Royal College of Music, 1949; Silver Medal, Worshipful Company of Musicians, 1951. Hobbies: Running; Walking; Aerobic training; Theatre; Film; EAV diagnostic system; New spiritual paths; Complementary medicine; Promotion National Arts/Sports/Environment Lottery; Promotion Performing Arts Centre in Covent Garden, incorporating Opera House, Drury Lane, Coliseum and Lyceum Theatre. Current Management: Marvin Schofer (USA), Germinal Hilbert (Europe). Address: 41 Floral Street, London WC2E 9DG, England.

VAUGHAN Elizabeth, b. 12 Mar 1937, Llanfyllin, Montgomeryshire, Wales. Singer (Soprano). Education: FRAM. Debut: Welsh National Opera, 1960, as Abigaille in Nabucco. Career: Covent Garden from 1961, as Mimi, Liu (Turandot), Teresa (Benvenuto Cellini), Gayle (The Ice Break, world premiere), Andromache and Hecuba (King Priam), Mozart's Elvira and Electra, Madame Butterfly, and Verdi's Amelia, Abigaille, Alice (Boccanegra), Leonore (Trovatore), Gilda and Violetta; Opera North as Tosca, Lady Macbeth and Abigaille; Welsh National Opera as Tosca, Leonora (La Forza del Destino) and Maddalena in Andrea Chénier; English National Opera as Aida, Penelope Rich (Gloriana) and Beethoven's Leonore; Metropolitan Opera debut, 1972, as Donna Elvira; Guest engagements in Vienna, Berlin, Paris, Hamburg, Munich and Prague; Appearances in Australia, Canada, South America, Japan; Toured USA with English National Opera, 1984; Now Mezzo with major companies, roles of Herodias, Kabanicha (Katya Kabanova), and the Witch in Hansel and Gretel; Sang the Overseer in Elektra at Covent Garden, 1997; Professor, Royal Northern College of Music. Honours: Honorary DMus, University of Wales. Current Management: IMG Artists Europe, London, England. Address: c/o IMG Artists Europe, Media House, 3 Burlington Lane, Chiswick, London E4 2TH, England.

VAUGHAN Karen, b. 18 Mar 1950, Yorkshire, England. Harpist. Divorced, 1 son. Education: Royal Academy of Music, London (Baume Scholarship for Piano); Private study with Maria Korchinska. Appointments: Scottish Chamber Orchestra, 1976-78; Principal harp, Scottish National Orchestra, 1978-84; Co-principal harp, London Symphony Orchestra, 1984-. Recordings: Featured soloist in Medea in Corinto (Mayr); Numerous recordings with LSO and other London orchestras. Honours: LRAM diploma, 1969; ARAM, 1984. Memberships: United Kingdom Harp Association; American Harp Society; Royal Society of Musicians. Address: c/o London Symphony Orchestra, Barbican Centre, London EC2Y 8DS, England.

VAUGHAN WILLIAMS (Joan) Ursula (Penton), b. 15 Mar 1911, Valletta, Malta. Writer. m. (1) Michael Forrester Wood, 24 May 1933, (2) Ralph Vaughan Williams, 6 Feb 1953. Career: Writer of songs, song cycles, libretti for cantatas and opera libretti. Publications: A biography of Ralph Vaughan Williams, OM, 1964; 6 books of poems; 3 novels. Honours: FRCM; Honorary FRAM; MRNCM. Memberships Committee, Ralph Vaughan Williams Trust. Hobbies: Reading; Theatre; Films; Travel; Gardening. Address: 66 Gloucester Crescent, London NW1 7EG, England.

VAVILOV Gennadi (Alekseevich), b. 7 May 1932, Russia. Composer; Professor. m. Natalia Romanenko, 17 Mar 1971, 1 son. Education: Musical High School, 1958; Theory on Music and Composing, Leningrad Conservatory, 1966; Moscow Conservatory, 1973-83; Petrozavodsk University, 1978. Debut: Performing of Cantata for Choir and Symphony Orchestra, Moscow, 1959. Career: Composer, 1958; Teacher of Theory of Music and Composition, 1958; Professor of Theory of Music, Instruments and Scores of Symphony Orchestra, 1989; Lecturer of Music, 1982; Music Accompaniment, 1982. Compositions include: Symphony No 1, Voronexh, 1982; Philadelphia, USA, 1992; Symphony No 4, Finland, 1990; Symphony No 3, Moscow, 1973; Original musical themes, traditions of Russian classical music, intonations characteristic for Karelian and Finnish Folk Tunes. Recordings: 3 records, Symphonietta for full symphony orchestra, Sonata for piano, Karellia tunes for symphony orchestra; Songs About Karelia, 1985; More than 13 works recorded to Gold Fund of Radio Russia. Contributions to: Typical Features of Opera Orchestra by Mussorgsky, 1984; Some Problems in the Usage of Folk in Composing, 1985; Polifonia forms in the Symphony Music, 1985. Honours include: 2nd place in the competitions of Young Composers, Moscow, 1958; TV Competition of the USSR, Moscow, 1959; Honoured Composer of Karelia, 1981; Silver Medal, Soviet Fund of Peace, Moscoe, 1984; Man of the Year Gold Medal, ABI, 1996; Platinum Record for Exceptional Performance, ABI, 1996; Gold Medal, Man of the Year, ABI, 1997. Memberships: Unity of Composers of Russia; Culture Fund Bard, Karelia, Russia. Hobbies: Chess; Travel. Address: Lenin Street 13-3, 185000 Petrozavodsk, Russia.

VAVRINECZ Béla, b. 18 Nov 1925, Budapest, Hungary. Composer; Conductor. m. Amalia Endrey, 1950, 1 son, 6 daughters. Education: Diploma in Composition, 1950, Diploma in Conducting, 1952, Budapest Academy of Music. Debut: Budapest Academy of Music, 1949. Career: First Conductor, Philharmonic Orchestra, Györ, 1957-58; Chief Conductor, Ministry of Home Affairs Symphony Orchestra, Budapest, 1961-73; Artistic Director, Dance Ensemble Budapest, 1974-83; Artistic Director, Ensemble Duna Budapest, 1983-85; Works frequently performed on radio and television. Compositions: 2 operas; 2 ballets; 112 musical pieces for dance theatre; 12 incidental works; 3 oratoria; Gisela, 1991; 5 cantatas; 18 works for choir and orchestra; 20 works for symphony orchestra, including Symphonie, 1955; 6 works for chamber orchestra; 7 concerts; 45 chamber music works; Solo pieces; 33 choral works; 1 Mass; Songs; Arrangements; Music for windbands. Recordings: Numerous. Publication: Kodály Memorial Book, 1953. Contributions to: Articles in various Hungarian periodicals. Honours: 2 Prizes, World Youth Festival, 1957. Memberships: Hungarian Composers Association; Hungarian Dancers Association; Franz Liszt Society; Hungarian Kodály Society. Hobbies: Tennis; Skiing; Swimming. Address: Cinkotai utca 39, H-1141 Budapest, Hungary.

VEALE John, b. 15 June 1922, Shortlands, Kent, England. Composer. m. Diana Taylor, 26 Aug 1944, div 1971, 1 son, 2 daughters (1 dec). Education: Repton School; MA, Oxford University; Mainly self-taught musical education but some study with Thomas Armstrong, Egon Wellesz, Roger Sessions, Roy Harris. Career: Commonwealth Fellowship, USA, 1949-51; Research Fellowship, Corpus Christi College, Oxford, 1952-54; Film Correspondent, Oxford Mail, 1964-80; Copy Editor, Oxford University Press, 1968-87. Compositions: Symphonies 1 and 2; Clarinet Concerto; Violin Concerto; Panorama for Orchestra; Metropolis, Concert-Overture for orchestra; Elegy for flute, harp and strings; String Quartet; Kubla Khan for baritone solo, mixed chorus and orchestra; Song of Radha for soprano and orchestra; Demos Variations for orchestra; Apolcalypse for chorus and orchestra; Triune, for oboe/cor anglais and orchestra; Encounter, for two guitars; Three Sydney Streets, for chorus and instrumental ensemble. Contributions to: Various publications, with articles and reviews. Memberships: Performing Rights Society Limited; Composers' Guild of Great Britain; International Music Association; Royal Philharmonic Society. Hobbies: Reading; Walking; Ornithology; Astronomy. Address: 7 Nourse Close, Woodeaton, Oxford OX3 9TJ, England.

VEASEY Josephine, b. 10 July 1930, London, England. Retired Opera Singer (Mezzo-Soprano); Private Teacher; Teacher of Voice Interpretation and Production. m. dissolved, 1 son, 1 daughter. Career: Joined chorus of Royal Opera House, Covent Garden, 1949, a Principal there, 1955-82 (interval on tour in opera for Arts Council); Singer, Royal Opera House, Glyndebourne, Metropolitan (New York), La Scala and in France, Germany, Spain, Switzerland, South America; Operatic roles included: Octavian in Der Rosenkavalier; Cherubino in Figaro; Name role in Iphigénie en Tauride; Dorabella in Così fan tutte; Amneris in Aida; Fricka in Die Walküre; Fricka in Das Rheingold; Name role in Carmen; Dido and Cassandra in The Trojans; Marguerite in The Damnation of Faust; Charlotte in Werther; Eboli in Don Carlos; Name role in Gluck's Orfeo; Adalgisa in Norma; Rosina in The Barber of Seville; Kundry in Parsifal; Gertrude in Hamlet, 1980; Concerts, 1960-70; Aix Festival, 1967; Various works of Mahler; 2 tours of Israel with Solti; Sang in Los Angeles with Mehta; Handel's Messiah in England, Munich, Oporto and Lisbon; Berlioz Romeo and Juliette, London and Bergen Festival; Emperor in 1st performance of Henze's We Come to the River, Covent Garden, 1976; Final appearance at Covent Garden, 1982, as Herodias; Private Teacher, 1982-; Teacher of Voice Production and Interpretation, Royal Academy of Music, 1983-84; Voice Consultant to English National Opera, 1985-94. Recordings: Numerous: Contributions to: Time Well Spent (profile), to Opera Magazine, July 1990. Honours: CBE, 1970; Honorary RAM, 1972. Hobbies: Reading; Gardening. Address: 2 Pound Cottage, St Mary Bourne, Andover, Hampshire, England.

VEBER Petr, b. 11 November 1960, Prague, Czech Republic. Music Critic. m. Eva Veberova, 14 June 1991, 1 son. Education: Musicology, Charles University, Prague, 1984. Career: Reporter, Czech News Agency, Music Critics and Popularisation. Contributions to: Harmonie & Hudebni Rozhledy; Czech Radio; Lidové Noviny. Honour: Journalist Prize, Czech Literary Fund, 1997. Memberships: Syndicate of Czech Journalists; Association of Czech Musicians; Societas Martinu. Hobbies: Music; Travel. Address: Czech News Agency, Opletalova 5, 11144 Prague, Czech Republic.

VECCIA Angelo, b. 1963, Rome, Italy. Singer (Baritone). Education: Studied at the Santa Cecilia Academy, Rome, and the Juilliard School, New York. Debut: Sang Mozart's Figaro at Juilliard. Career: Gave concerts at the Lincoln Center, New York, and elsewhere in America, and appeared in Tosca with Placido Domingo; Appearances throughout Italy as Rossini's Figaro, Belcore, Marcello (at Verona, Venice and Florence) and Silvio; Further roles in Gluck's Iphigénie en Tauride at La Scala, Rimsky's Golden Cockerel at Rome and Schoenberg's Moses und Aron in Florence; Zurich Opera as Sharpless (Madama Butterfly), Gianni Schicchi and Marcello; Season 1997 in Bohème and Turandot at Tel Aviv, Il Barbiere di Siviglia at Zurich and Lucia di Lammermoor at La Scala; Sang as guest in Aida at Berlin and in the 1996 Christmas Concert under Riccardo Chailly at the Amsterdam Concertgebouw. Address: c/o Opernhaus Zurich, Falkenstrasse 1, CH-8008 Zurich, Switzerland.

VEDERNIKOV Alexander (Filoppovich), b. 23 Dec 1927, Mokino, nr Kirov, USSR. Singer (Bass). Education: Studied in Moscow with Alpert-Khasina. Debut: Bolshoy Theatre Moscow 1957, as Ivan Susanin in Glinka's A Life for the Tsar. Career: Appearances in Moscow, Leningrad, Tiblisi and Kiev as Boris and Varlaam in Boris Godunov, Dosifey (Khovanshchina) and Konchak in Prince Igor; Engagements with the company of the Bolshoy at Paris, New York and Milan as Philip II and the Grand Inquisitor in Don Carlos and Massimilione in Verdi's I Masnadieri; Toured West Germany with the Bolshoy 1987; Other roles include Daland in Der fliegende Holländer, Prince Gremin (Eugene Onegin), Kutuzov in War and Peace and Mephistopheles (Faust). Recordings include: The Stone Guest by Dargomizhsky; Rimsky-Korsakov's The Snow Maiden, Pimen in a video of Boris Godunov from the Bolshoy (National Video Corporation). Address: c/o Bolshoy Theatre, Pr Marxa 8/2, 103009 Moscow, Russia.

VEDERNIKOV Alexander, b. 1964, Moscow, Russia. Conductor. Education: Studied at Central Music School Moscow and at the Tchaikovsky Conservatoire with Mark Ermler. Career: Moscow Musical Theatre from 1989, conducting La Finta Giardiniera, Le nozze di Figaro, Cav and Pag, Il Barbiere di Siviglia, La Traviata, Eugene Onegin, The Queen of Spades, Boris Godunov and ballets by Tchaikovsky; Assistant Conductor at the Moscow Radio Symphony Orchestra 1990; Conductd the Junge Deutsche Philharmonie 1990, contract with the Rome Opera, 1991, debut with The Nutcracker; led the Moscow Radio Symphony at the Athens and Ankara Festivals 1992 and in Scotland, featuring music by Frank Martin, Glinka, Shostakovich and Vaughan Williams; tours to the United States and Japan in season 1992-93; Guest engagements with orchestras in the UK. Address: c/o Sonata, 11 Northpark Street, Glasgow G20 7AA, Scotland.

VEIRA Jonathan, b. 1960, England. Singer (Bass Baritone). Education: Studied at Trinity College of Music, London; The National Opera Studio. Career includes: At Glyndebourne appeared as Lemokh in the premiere of The Electrification of the Soviet Union and in Die Entführung and Capriccio; Other engagements include a tour with Opera 80, Antonio in Le nozze di Figaro at the Prom concerts and Tippett's New Year for the Glyndebourne Tour; Broadcasts of Mahagonny and Rossini's Tancredi for the BBC; Television appearances in La Traviata, The Electrification of the Soviet Union and Death in Venice; Engagements with Opera Factory, London; As a concert artist has performed at many major London venues; Has broadcast Leoncavallo's La Bohème and Königskinder for RTE Dublin; Television appearances include The Marriage of Figaro, La Traviata and Death in Venice; In 1993 he sang Falstaff to great critical acclaim and he performed his first Papageno in a new production of The Magic Flute conducted by Jane Glover at the Covent Garden Festival; Sang Bartolo (Barber of Seville) for Opera Northern Ireland and at Garsington Festival in 1994; Other performances included a premiere of a new opera by Stuart Copeland in the Barbados Festival, Bottom (A Midsummer Night's Dream) for Covent Garden Festival and Scarpia in a concert performance of Tosca for the opening of the 1994 Bournemouth International Festival; In 1995 he sang Dulcamara (L'Elisir d'amour) for Opera Northern Ireland, Dr Bartolo (The Marriage of Figaro), Melitone (La Forza del Destino) and Calchas (La Belle Helène) for Scottish Opera; Engagements in 1996 included Leporello (Don Giovanni) for Auckland Opera with Kiri Te Kanawa, Melitone with the Royal Danish Opera, Dr Bartolo for Opera de Nice; Banker (Lulu) and roles for Glyndebourne Festival Opera; 1997 Engagements include Dr Bartolo (The Barber of Seville) for Welsh National Opera. Recordings: Two solo albums; Featured soloist on recording of operatic excerpts for Opera Rara; Elgar's The Spanish Lady, CD. Honours include: Winner, Sir Peter Pears Singing Competition; Anna Instone Memorial Award. Address: Helen Sykes Artists' Management, 4th Floor, Parkway House, Sheen Lane, East Sheen, London SW14 8LS, England.

VEJZOVIC Dunja, b. 20 Oct 1943, Zagreb, Yugoslavia. Singer (Soprano). Education: Studied in Zagreb, Stuttgart, Weimar and Salzburg. Career: Sang first at Zagreb, then in Frankfurt, Dusseldorf, Vienna, Hamburg and Stuttgart; Bayreuth Festival 1978-80, as Kundry in Parsifal: also sang the role at the Salzburg Easter Festival; Metropolitan Opera 1978-79, as Venus in Tannhäuser; Paris Opéra 1982, Ortrud; Teatro Liceo Barcelona 1983 in the title role of Herodiade by Massenet; La Scala Milan 1984, as Venus; Théâtre de la Monnaie, Brussels 1984, Senta in Der fliegende Holländer; Also sings Chimène in Le Cid by Massenet; sang Ortrud at the Vienna Staatsoper, 1990; Season 1992 as Kundry in Robert Wilson's production of Parsifal at Houston. Recordings: Parsifal, conducted by Karajan (Deutsche Grammophon); Christus by Liszt; Lohengrin and Der fliegende Holländer (EMI). Address: c/o Allied Artists Agency, 42 Montpelier Square, London SW7 1JZ, England.

VELAZCO Jorge, b. 12 Jan 1942, Mexico City, Mexico. Conductor; Music Director. m. Marcia Elizabeth Yount, 25 May 1983, 3 sons. Education: General Law degree, National University of Mexico; Student of Conrado Tovar (Piano), Antonio Gomezanda (Piano, Music Theory), Rodolfo Halffter (Composition, Music Analysis), Lukas Foss, Franco Ferrara at Accademia Musicale Chigiana, Siena, Herbert von Karajan (Conducting). Career: Assistant Chairman, Mexico Federal Government's Music Department, 1972-73; Professor, National Conservatory, Mexico City, 1973-84; Chairman, Music Department, 1973-74, Vice-President for Cultural Affairs, 1974-76, Researcher in Music, 1974-, National University of Mexico; Visiting Professor, Wyoming and Michigan State Universities, Phoenix College, University of Houston, University of Oviedo (Spain), 1975-94; Associate Conductor, 1977-81, Music Director, 1985-89, UNAM Philharmonic; Assistant to Herbert von Karajan at Salzburg Easter Festival, 1977; Founder, Music Director, Minera Symphony Orchestra, 1978-84; Principal Guest Conductor, Florence Chamber Orchestra, Italy, 1990-; Director, International Studies, Texas Music Festival, Houston, 1992-; Guest Conductor, National Orchestra of Spain, Interamerican Music Festival Orchestra, several US and European orchestras. Recordings: Several with Berlin Radio Symphony Orchestra, Florence Chamber Orchestra, Berlin Symphony and Sinfonietta RIAS. Publications: Edgard Varèse, Perfil de un Revolucionario, 1975; De Música y Músicos, 1981; Dos Músicos Eslavos, 1981; El Pianismo Mexicano del Siglo XIX, 1983-84; Federico II, El Rey Músico, 1986; La Versión Original de 'Janitzio' de Silvestre Revueltas, 1986; La Música por Dentro, 1988; Antonio Gomezanda y el Nacionalismo Romántico Mexicano, 1991. Honours: Guggenheim Fellow, 1987; Wortham Chair in Performing Arts, University of Houston, 1991, 1994. Memberships: Sociedad Española de Musicologa; Royal Musical Association, London; International Musicological Society. Cedros 18, San Miguel Ajusco, Tlalpan DF, Mexico 14700.

VELIS Andrea, b. 7 June 1932, New Kensington, Pennsylvania, USA. Singer (Tenor). Education: Studied with Louise Taylor in Pittsburgh, at the Royal College of Music, London, and at the Accademia di Santa Cecilia, Rome. Debut: Pittsburgh 1954, as Goro in Madame Butterfly. Career: Appearances in Chicago, Cincinnati, Philadelphia and San Francisco; Metropolitan Opera from 1961 in 1600 performances of 50 operas, including La Fanciulla del West, Death in Venice, Hansel and Gretel, Eugene Onegin, The Ring (Mime), Les Contes d'Hoffmann, Otello, Der Rosenkavalier, Tosca and Boris Godunov; Sang Mardian in the premiere of Barber's Antony and Cleopatra, 1966. Recordings include: Tosca (HMV). Address: c/o Metropolitan Opera, Lincoln Center, New York, NY 10023, USA.

VELLA Richard, b. 1 December 1954, Melbourne, Victoria, Australia. Composer; Professor of Music. Education: BA (Hons) 1978, MA (Music) 1981, La Trobe University. Career includes: General Editor, Music Currency Press, 1989-; Professor, La Trobe University, 1996-97; Artistic Director, Calculated Risks Opera Productions, 1990-. Compositions include: Tales of Love, opera, 1990; A Piano Reminisces, 1991; Remember, Unending Love, for chorus, 1992; The Last Supper, opera, 1993; Concerto for Trombone, 1995; Commissions from Astra Choir, One Extra Dance Company, The Elizabethan Theatre Trust, and others. Honours include: Commonwealth Postgraduate Research Award, 1979. Address: P O Box N83, Grosvenor Place, Sydney 2000, NSW, Australia.

VENGEROV Maxim, b. 15 Aug 1974, Novosibirsk, Siberia. Concert Violinist. Education: Studied with Galina Turtschaninova and Zakhar Bron. Debut: Moscow 1985, playing Schubert's Rondo Brilliant. Career: Many recitals and concerts in Moscow and Leningrad; Solo debuts with the Concertgebouw Orchestra, BBC Philharmonic at Lichfield Festival, England and with the Russian State Symphony under Simonov on tour to Italy; Recital debuts at Wigmore Hall, Suntory Hall Tokyo and The Mozarteum, Salzburg; Season 1990-91 with US debut, in concert with New York Philharmonic, Israel Philharmonic at Tel-Aviv and on tour to USA under Zubin Mehta; Season 1991-92 included concerts with the Berlin Philharmonic under Abbado, LPO under Mehta, St Petersburg Philharmonic at London Proms with Sibelius Concerto, and the Salzburg Festival with the Mozarteum Orchestra and Trevor Pinnock; Season 1992-93 includes appearances with the Chicago Symphony under Barenboim, Los Angeles Philharmonic and Mehta; Prom Concerts 1993 with the BBC Symphony Orchestra, Vienna Philharmonic under Yehudi Menuhin, playing in many leading venues in 1993-94 season; Season 1994-95 playing with many major orchestras worldwide including Hallé Orchestra and Vienna Philharmonic; Barbican Hall recital 1997, with works by Mozart and Elgar. Recordings include: Sonatas by Beethoven and Brahms and Paganini 1st Concerto, 1992; Sonatas by Mozart, Beethoven and Mendelssohn, 1992; CD of virtuoso violin pieces; Bruch and Mendelssohn Violin Concertos recorded, winning 3 European music awards. Honours: Winner, Junior Wieniawski Competition, 1984; Winner, 1990 Carl Flesch International Violin Competition; Gramaphone Magazine Young Artist of the Year award, 1994. Address: c/o Lies Askonas Ltd, 6 Henrietta Street, London, WC2E 8LA, England.

VENTO Joseph, b. 16 Dec 1926, Los Angeles, California, USA. Composer; Conductor; Band Leader. Education: Composition, Film-Scoring, Psychology, University of South Califonia; Optometry, Philosophy, Fresno State College; Piano, composition, Juilliard School; Conducting, New England Conservatory of Music. Debut: Accordion Solo, Radio KFI, Los Angeles, The William Tell Overture, 10 years old, 1937. Career: Films, Counterpoint, Man's Favorite Sport, This Earth is Mine, The Competition, Guide for a Married Man, Made in Paris, Girl Happy, Those Lips Those Eyes. Compositions: The Three Suns; I Can't Forget; Our Love is Gone; City of The Angles; Sacro Sanctum; Warsaw Connection; Sarah Suite; Ole Joe, 1997; Joes Bach, 1997. Recordings: Artist of The Three Suns, Twilight Time; Joe Vento Golden Hits, volume I and II; Surfside Records; Bells of Christmas; The Best of Joe Vento; The Best of The Three Suns; Film Soundtrack, True Friends. Publications: I Can't Forget, 1939; City of the Angles, 1968; Sacro Sanctum, 1979; Love is Gon, 1995; Edulerp III, 1995. Contributions to: Midi'ing in Music Composition, Moorpark College, 1991; Nurturing Music in the Nineties. Honour: Best Accordionist Grand Prize, 1939. Memberships: ASCAP; ASMAC; AFM Local 802, New York; AFM 47, Los Angeles; NARAS; American Academy of Sciences; Disabled American Veterans, SR, CDR; Music Teachers National Association, USA. Hobbies: Oceanography; Forestry; The environment. Current Management: S V Enterprises. Address: 419 Mark Drive, Simi, CA 93065, USA.

VENTRE Carlo, b. 1965, Montevideo, Uraguay. Singer (Tenor). Education: Studied in Uraguay and in Italy (from 1991). Career: Appearances at La Scala Milan under Riccardo Muti as the Duke of Mantua, and Ismaele in Nabucco; Further engagements at Rome, Ravenna, Trieste, Athens, Tokyo and Cologne; Wexford Festival 1995, in Pacini's Saffo; Season 1996-97 included British debut, as Rodolfo with Welsh National Opera, and American debut as the Duke of Mantua for Opera Pacific; Engaged as the Duke by Michigan Opera, as Pinkerton in Trieste and Edoardo di Sanval in Un Giorno do Regno by Verdi at Parma. Recordings include: Pacini's Saffo. Honours include: Gino Becchi Prize at the 1990 Francisco Vinas Competition; Winner, 1995 Luciano Pavarotti Competition, Philadelphia. Address: c/o Harrison/Parrott Ltd, 12 Penzance Place, London W11 4PA, England.

VENTRIGLIA Franco, b. 20 Oct 1927, Fairfield, Connecticut, USA. Opera Singer (Bass). m. 12 Feb 1945. Education: American Theatre Wing, Toti Dal Monte International School of Bel Canto in Rome and Venice. Debut: Teatro Massimo Palermo, Italy, Meistersinger, Tullio Serafin, Conductor. Career: Appearances in various operas, Academia Di S Cecilia, Rome; La Scala, Vienna Staatsoper, Berlin Staatsoper; San Carlo; Reggio di Parma; Reggio di Torino; Comunale di Firenze; King's Theatre, Edinburgh; Chicago Lyric; Dallas Opera; Wexford Festival; La Fenice Venezia; Arena di Verona; Teatro de L'Opera Roma; Milwaukee; Concertgebouw, Amsterdam; Dutch Radio; Roles have included Rossini's Basilio, Raimondo, Elmiro (Otello by Rossini), Walter and Wurm in Luisa Miller, Loredano (I due Foscari), the Grand Inquistor, Alvise, Colline and Sparafucile (Rigoletto). Recordings: La Traviata, RCA; Manon Lescaut, EMI; Angelium, Vedette Records. Contributions to: Opera News. Membership: AGMA. Hobby: Musical Box Collecting. Current Management: Robert Lombardo Associates. Address: 515 Brookside Drive, Fairfield, CT 06430, USA.

VENTRIS Christopher, b. 1960, London, England. Singer (Tenor). Education: Studied at the Royal Academy of Music. Career: Joined Glyndebourne Festival Chorus, 1987; Touring opera debut, 1988 as Vanya in Katya Kabanova; Later appearances as Tom Rakewell with Glyndebourne Festival Opera and The Porter in Death in Venice, Jacquino in Fidelio, and Steva in Jenufa with GTO; Opera work with Opera North, ENO and Royal Opera; Performed in: Magic Flute, 1993 in Geneva, King Priam and Eugene Onegin, 1994 at Antwerp and Flying Dutchman, 1992 and Salome, 1995 at Leipzig; Concert work throughout Europe includes: Beethoven 9th Symphony, Mendelssohn's Second Symphony, (Lobgesang) and Elijah, and Tippett's Child of Our Time; Further engagements include: Steuermann at Amsterdam in 1995, Midsummer Marriage with Royal Opera, Title role in Parsifal at Antwerp and Boris in Katya Kabanova at Düsseldorf in 1996. Recordings: Caritas, Saxton; Blonde Eckbert, Weir. Honours include: Esso GTFO Singers Award, 1988-89; John Christie Award, Glyndebourne; Associate of Royal Academy of Music, 1993. Address: IMG Artists Europe, Media House, 3 Burlington Lane, London, W4 2TH, England.

VENZAGO Mario, b. 1 July 1948, Zurich, Switzerland. Conductor. Education: Studied at the University of Zurich and the Zurich and Vienna Conservatories, notably with Hans Swarowsky. Career: Conductor of the Collegium Musicum at Winterthur from 1977, general music director at Heidelberg from 1986, then principal conductor of the Graz Philharmonic; Further concerts with the Swiss Radio Lugano and Suisse Romande orchestras. Recordings: Works by Schumann, Janacek and others. Address: Bulmer and Dixon Ltd, Granitweg 2, CH-8002 Zurich, Switzerland.

VERA-RIVERA Santiago Oscar, b. 2 Nov 1950, Santiago, Chile. Professor; Composer. m. Maria Angelica Bustamante, 25 May 1974, 2 sons, 1 daughter. Education: University of Chile; Doctorate in Musicology, University of Oviedo, Spain, 1991. Career: Professor, University of Chile, 1974-81, University of Tarapaca, 1984; Acad Pedag Santiago, 1981-85; University Metropolitana, 1986; Escuela Moderna de Musica, 1976-87; Intern/OAS, 1984. Compositions: Choral, piano, electronic, percussion, guitar and orchestral pieces. Recordings include: Tres Temporarias, 1987; Trezs acuareskas, 1989; Chiloé, Tierre de Agua, 1989; Cirrus, 1987. Publications: Harmony for two voices, 1990; Contributor to Dictionary of Music, Hispano Americane and Espanola, 1989-92; Informusicz, Spain, 1992. Hobbies: Producing TV and radio music programmes. Address: San Juan 4967, Santiago, Chile.

VERBRUGGEN Marion, b. 2 Aug 1950, Amsterdam, Netherlands. Recorder Player; Teacher. Education: Study with Kees Otten, Amsterdam Conservatory, 1966; With Frans Bruggen, Muziek Lyceum, Amsterdam, and Royal Conservatory, The Hague, 1967; B Diploma, 1971; Solo degree cum laude, Royal Conservatory, The Hague, 1973. Career: Performances with various ensembles and solo concerts; Netherlands, USA, Canada, Japan, most European countries; Regular guest, Gustav Leonhardt, Amsterdam Baroque Orchestra, Musica Antiqua, Cologne, Tafelmusik Toronto, many others; Plays at Holland Festival of Early Music; TV appearances, Netherlands, Norway, Belgium, Italy, Federal Republic of Germany, USA; Teacher: Royal Conservatory, The Hague; Utrecht Conservatory; Guest Teacher, Malmo Conservatory, Sweden; Masterclasses and workshops, Stanford University, Toronto, Montreal, New York, Philadelphia, Malmo, Trondheim, Copenhagen, Jerusalem. Recordings: For EMI, Philips/Seon, Titanic, Hungaroton, ASV London, L'Oiseau Lyre, Monumenta Belgicae Musicae; Archiv, Harmonia Mundi. Address: Vondelstraat 99, 1054 GM Amsterdam, Netherlands.

VERCOE Elizabeth (Walton), b. 23 Apr 1941, Washington DC, USA. Composer. 1 son, 1 daughter. Education: BA in Music, Wellesley College, 1962; MMus in Composition, University of Michigan, 1963; Doctor of Musical Arts in Composition, Boston University, 1978. Career: Instructor of Musical Theory, Westminster Choir College, 1969-71; Assistant Professor of Music, Framlingham State College, Massachusetts, 1973-74; Composer, Cite Internationale des Arts, Paris, France, 1983-85 and Charles Ives Center for American Music, 1984, 1992; Co-Director of Women's Music Festival, Boston, 1985, MacDowell Colony, 1992, and St Petersburg, Russia, Spring Music Festival, 1993. Compositions include: Fantasy for Piano; Duo for Violin and Cello; Sonario for Cello; Three Studies for Piano; Irreveries from Sappho for SSA and Piano or Soprano and Piano; Herstory II for Soprano, Piano and Percussion; Herstory III; Persona for Piano; Rhapsody for Violin and Orchestra; Despite our Differences No 1 for Piano Trio, No 2 for Piano and Orchestra, 1988; Plucked String Editions: A la Fin - tout seul for Mandolin and Optional Piano; A Dangerous Man for Baritone and Piano, 1990; Changes for Chamber Orchestra, 1991; Four Humors for Cl and Pho, 1993. Recordings: Herstory III, on Owl; Herstory II; 13 Japanese Lyrics for Soprano, Piano and Percussion; Fantasy for Piano; Irreveries from Sappho for Voice and Piano. Publications: Various works published. Contributions include: The Lady Vanishes?, in Perspectives of New Music, 1982; A Composer's View, in the Journal of Early Music America, 1990. Address: 74 Judy Farm Road, Carlisle, MA 01741, USA.

VERGARA Victoria, b. 1948, Santiago, Chile. Singer (Mezzo-soprano). Education: Studied in Santiago and in New York with Nicola Moscona, and Anton Guadagno, and at the Juilliard School with Daniel Ferro and Rose Bampton. Career: Sang minor roles in the USA, before New York City Opera debut, 1977; Sang at Detroit from 1977, Santiago 1978; Houston Grand Opera from 1980; Has sung Carmen at San Francisco, Cincinnati, Zurich, Lisbon, Vancouver, Philadelphia, Seattle, New Orleans and Berlin; Chicago Lyric Opera 1982, Vienna Staatsoper 1984, as Amneris; Washington Opera 1987, as the Duchess of Alba in the premiere of Menotti's Goya, opposite Placido Domingo; Metropolitan Opera debut 1988, as Carmen; Teatro Liceo Barcelona 1989, in the premiere of Cristobal Colon by Leonardo Balada, with Caballé and Carreras; Season 1990 sang Herodias (Salome) at Santiago and at the Zarzuela Theatre Madrid in El viajero indiscreto, as Dona; Other roles include Donna Elvira, Cherubino, Frederica in Luisa Miller, Maddalena, Rosina, Dalila, Nicklausse, Charlotte and Massenet's Dulcinée. Recordings include: Maddalena in Rigoletto (Decca). Address: c/o IM Röhrich 55, 6702 Bad Dürkheim 2, Germany.

VERMEERSCH Jef, b. 7 Feb 1928, Bruges, Belgium. Singer (Baritone). Education: Studied in Bruges, Ghent and Antwerp, 1960, as Wotan in Das Rheingold; Sang at Gelsenkirchen from 1966; Member, Deutsche Oper Berlin from 1973; Guest appearances in Germany and Brussels, Amsterdam, Lyon, Venice, Lisbon, Prague, Geneva, San Francisco, Barcelona and Stockholm; Salzburg Easter Festival 1973, as Kurwenal in Tristan and Isolde, conducted by Karajan; Bayreuth Festival 1981-83, Kothner in Die Meistersinger; Other roles include Hans Sachs, Amfortas, the Dutchman, Boris Godunov, Golaud, Pizarro, Kaspar, the title role in Giulio Cesare by Handel, Leporello, Jochanaaan, Kepler in Die Harmonie der Welt, Falstaff, Amonasro and St Just in Dantons Tod; Sang Kothner at Bayreuth 1988; Kurwenal at Wuppertal 1989. Address: Wuppertal Bühnen, Spinnstrasse 4, D-5600 Wuppertal.

VERMILLION Iris, b. 1960, Bielefeld, Germany. Soprano. Education: Studied flute at first then voice with Mechthild Bohme and Judith Beckmann. Debut: Brunswick in 1986 as Zulma in L'Italiana in Algeri and as Barbara in Eine Nacht in Vendig. Career: Sang Dorabella and Octavian in Brunswick; Deutsche Oper Berlin from 1988 as a Rhinemaiden, Hansel and Cherubino; Darmstadt in 1988 as Judith in Duke Bluebeard's Castle; Sang Dorabella with Netherlands Opera in Amsterdam in 1990; Salzburg Festival in 1990 as Clairon in Capriccio; Other roles include Werther, Charlotte and Mozart's Sextus; Also sings in the St Matthew Passion and Mozart's Davidde Penitente; Sang Bianca in Zemlinsky's Florentinische Tragödie at Florence, 1995. Recordings include: Second Lady in Die Zauberflöte under Neville Marriner. Honours include: Prize Winner at Cardiff Singer of the World Competition. Address: c/o Deutsche Oper Berlin, Richard Wagnerstrasse 10, D-1000 Berlin, Germany.

VERNEROVÁ-NOVÁKOVÁ Ludmila, b. 6 Dec 1962, Prague, Czech Republic. Singer. m. Pravomil Novák, 1 daughter. Education: Academy of Musical Arts, Prague. Debut: National Theatre, Prague, 1987. Career: Bach Academy at Stuttgart, Germany, three times: - Händel, Messiah; Bach Mass in B Minor; Mozart Festival at Citta del Castello, Italy, 1991; Mozart's Missa C Major, Aria Bella mia fiamma, addio!; Sommerfestspiele at Stuttgart; Festival at Marbella, Spain, 1994; Beethoven's Missa Solemnis; Festival Prague Spring, 1995: Mozart's Concert Arias; Festival in Ludwigsburg, Germany, 1995: Mozart's Requiem; Music Festival Bratislava, Slovakia, 1997; Mozart's Missa C Minor; Festival Prague Autumn, 1997; Operas: J Myslivecek's Isaac; Purcell's Dido and Aeneas (Dido, Belinda); Britten's Bettlers Opera; Mozart's Nozze di Figaro (Contessa), Bizet's Carmen (Michaela); Sang under conductors V Neumann, H Rilling, G Deloghu, W Gönnenwein, G Albrecht, C Dohnányi and others in most European countries; Her repertoire also includes Händel's Samson, Judas Maccabäus, Rodelinde, Alcina, Jephtha, several cantatas; Beethoven's IX Symphony and Songs; Bach's Johannes Passion, Markus Passion, Messe h-moll, Magnificat, numerous cantatas; Haydn's Die Schöpfung, Stabat Mater, Vier Jahrezeiten and Masses; Schubert's Stabat Mater, Masses, Salve Regina; Brahms' Ein deutsches Requiem, Songs; Dvorak's Stabat Mater, Missa D-dur, Songs; also music by Mendelssohn, Schumann, Rameau, Pergolesi, Carissimi, Vivaldi, Zelenka, Buxtehude and others. Recordings: 42 CD's include: A Dvorák's Stabat Mater; Haydn's Nelson Mass, Stabat Mater; Schubert's Mass No 3 BFlat; Pergolesi's Stabat Mater; J S Bach's Johannes Passion; Mozart's Krönungsmesse, Vesperae Solemnes. Address: Kafkova 8, Praha 6-Dejvice, CZ 160 00.

VERNHES Alain, b. 1944, France. Singer (Baritone). Career: Sang at the Opéra de Lyon, 1969-72, and made many appearances throughout France; Opéra d'Avignon, 1982-85, with such singers as Caballé, Aragall and Bruson; Orange Festival, 1987, as Vitellius in Massenet's Herodiade, and Opéra du Rhin, Strasbourg, as Zuniga in Carmen; Avignon, 1992, as Ourrais in Gounod's Mireille; Has also sung Puccini's Marcello and Scarpia in concert performances; Sang Melitone in La Forza del destino at Orange, 1996. Address: Opéra d'Avignon, Rue Racine, F-84000 Avignon, France.

VERNON Richard, b. 1950, Memphis, Tennessee, USA. Singer (Bass). Education: Studied at Memphis State University. Debut: Memphis 1972, as Pimen in Boris Godunov. Career: Has sung with Houston Opera Studio from 1977, in operas by Verdi; Appearances with Washington Opera and Pittsburgh Opera; Metropolitan Opera from 1981, in L'Enfant et les Sortilèges, and as Titurel (Parsifal) and the Commendatore (Don Giovanni); Sang Foltz in a new Production of Die Meistersinger at the Metropolitan, 1993. Address: c/o Meistersinger at the Metropolitan, 1993. Address: c/o Metropolitan Opera, Lincoln Center, New York, NY 10023, USA.

VERONELLI Ernesto, b. 1948, Milan, Italy. Singer (Tenor). Education: Studied at the Giuseppe Verdi Conservatory, Milan. Career: Has sung in operas by Verdi, Puccini, Massenet and Giordano at Paris, Zurich, Berlin, Barcelona, Vienna and Verona; Debut with the Royal Opera Covent Garden at Manchester as Cavaradossi, 1983, later singing Chevalier Roland in Esclarmonde, opposite Joan Sutherland; Season 1985-86 sang Canio at the Metropolitan, Cavaradossi in Pretoria and Pinkerton at the Cologne Opera; Calaf in Detroit and Radames at Toronto; Other roles have been Verdi's Macduff, Carlo (Givanna d'Arco), Don Carlos and Manrico.

VERRETT Shirley, b. 31 May 1931, New Orleans, USA. Soprano; Mezzo Soprano. Education: Studied in Los Angeles with Anna Fitziu and Hall Johnson and at the Juilliard School with Madame Szekely-Freschl. Debut: Yellow Springs Ohio, 1957 as Britten's Lucretia; New York City Opera, 1958 as Irina in Lost in the Stars by Weill; European debut 1959 in Rasputins Tod by Nabokov. Career: First major success as Carmen at Spoleto in 1962, New York City Opera in 1964 and La Scala in 1966; Covent Garden from 1966 as Ulrica, Azucena, Amneris, Eboli, Carmen, Orpheus and Selika in L'Africaine; Metropolitan Opera from 1968 as Carmen, Eboli, Cassandra and Dido in Les Troyens, Judith in Bluebeard's Castle, Adalgisa, Norma, Neocle in L'Assedio di Corinto and Leonore in La Favorita; Sang at Florence in 1969 as Elisabetta in Maria Stuarda, Paris Opéra in 1983 in Moise by Rossini, and Verona Arena in 1984 as Carmen; Appearances at Salzburg, Dallas Opera, Moscow, Kiev and San Francisco; Other roles include Lady Macbeth, Tosca, Dalila and Frederica in Luisa Miller; Sang Dido in the opening production of the Bastille Opera, Paris in 1990; Season 1991-92 as Azucena at Genoa and Leonora in La Favorita at Madrid; Recital repertoire includes songs by Mahler, Brahms, Schubert and Milhaud. Recordings: Orpheus; Un Ballo in Maschera; La Forza del Destino; Luisa Miller; Lucrezia Borgia; Don Carlos; L'Africaine; Macbeth; Video of L'Africaine at San Francisco.

VERROT Pascal, b. 9 Jan 1959, Lyon, France. Conductor. Education: Studied at the Sorbonne and Conservatoire, Paris. Career: Assistant to Seiji Ozawa at the Boston Symphony, from 1985, giving concerts at Symphony Hall Boston and Tanglewood; Further concerts with the Boston Chamber Players; Guest engagements in Japan, throughout North America and France; Music director of the Quebec Symphony Orchestra from 1991. Honours include: Prize winner at the 1985 Tokyo International Competition. Address: Quebec Symphony Orchestra, 130 West Grand-Allée, Québec, Province Québec G1R, Canada.

VERROUST Denis, b. 21 Feb 1958, Vincennes, France. Flautist; Musicologist. m. Marguerite Sopinski, 27 Dec 1986. Education: Baccalaureat A, 1975; DEUG, Economics, 1979; Graduate, Saint-Maur CNR; DE, flute teacher, 1988. Career: Appearances, St Malo Festival, Brittany, 1980-; Several tours in France, Germany, Holland with Cologne Chamber Orchestra, as soloist; Radio programme for Radio-France, 1982; Invited Lecturer in several American Universities. Publications: 5 titles proposed and edited for the Billaudot Edition, Paris, 1980 and 1982; J S Bach: Sinfonia from Cantata BWV 209; 4 characteristic XIXth Century pieces by W Popp, F Doppler and A Fürstenberg; Principal editor and director of collections for the Stravaganza Edition, Paris; Mozart, Haydn, Rossini (Opera overtures for 2 flutes); A Hugot (Trios for 2 flutes and bass); Jean-Pierre Rampal, over 40 years of recordings 1946-1989; The Flute in France from Devienne to Faffanel (150 years 1770-1920) in progress; Complete Catalogue of XIXth Century Flute Literature, in progress; The Romantic Flute, in progress; Exhaustive

Researchers and Leading Authority on the Late Classical and Romantic Flute Repertoire. Contributions to: Numerous articles to professional journals. Hobby: Tennis. Address: 16 Avenue Aubert, 94300 Vincennes, France.

VERSCHRAEGEN Herman (Elie Bertha), b. 4 Apr 1936, Ghent, Belgium. Organist; Director of Music; Organ Master. m. Van Hove Genevieve, 2 July 1963, 1 son, 1 daughter. Education: Several First Prizes and Higher Diploma in Organ, Royal Conservatory of Music, Ghent, 1960; Virtuosity Prize, Organ, 1965. Debut: Ghent, 1957. Career: Organist, St Josef Church, Antwerp, 1962; Master of Music Theory and History, Music Academy of Wilrijk, 1963-73; Organ Master, Music Academy of Aalst, 1965-73 and Music Academy of Geel, 1966-73; Director, Music Academy of Wilrijk-Antwerp, 1974-; Organ Master, Royal Conservatory of Music, Brussels, 1976-; Over 700 organ concerts and recitals in Austria, Belgium, Czechoslovakia, Denmark, East and West Germany, France, Holland, Israel, Italy, Japan, Poland, South Africa, Sweden, Switzerland, England, USA, Philippines; Several seminars about C Franck and the Flemish Organ School and also masterclass in Japan; Member of Jury of International Organ Contests, Nurenberg 1970, Lokeren 1972; Recitals for International Broadcasting Corporations Belgium, Denmarks Radio, Suddeutscher Rundfunk, Hessischer Rundfunk, Bayerischer Rundfunk, Sender Freies Berlin, Sudwestfunk, Nordd Rundfunk, Czechoslovakia, Sweden, Radio Geneva, Bern, Zurich, Suisse Romande, USA, South Africa. Compositions: Fantasy for Organ. Recordings: Handel, Bach, Couperin, Van den Gheyn (Polydor). Hobby: Travel. Address: 5 Schansweg, B-2610 Wilrijk-Antwerpen, Belgium.

VERSHININA Irina, b. 24 Feb 1930, Moscow, Russia. Musicologist. div., 1 son. Education: Gnesin's Musical Academy; Institute of Art Studies, Moscow. Debut: Sowjetunion Heute, 1956. Career: Tutor, Theory of Music, Moscow Musical School; Researcher, Russia Institute of Art Studies; Senior Editor, Sovetsky Kompositor Publications (Musical Folklore of USSR). Publications: Stravinsky's Early Ballets, 1967; Contributor: 20th Century Music 1890-1917, 1976; History of Music of Peoples of USSR, 1957-67, 1974; Russian Art Culture 1907-1917, 1978; Editor: Igor Stravinsky, Vocal Music, vols 2, 1982-1988; Igor Stravinsky, Essays, Memories, Editor, 1985; Mussorgsky and Stravinsky, 1990. Contributions to: Balmont and Stravinsky; Mussorgsky as a Composer of XX Century, 1990; Zvezdoliky: one of the manuscripts, to Musical Academia, 1992. Honours: Doctor of Art Studies, 1968, Membership: Composers' Society of Russia. Hobby: History of literature. Address: Acad Scriabin Str 26-1-84, Moscow 109378, Russia.

VESKRNOVA Denisa, b. 14 May 1973, Trebic, Czech Republic. Student. Education: Classical guitar, at Conservatoire of Brno, 1987-93; Classical guitar, Performing Arts, at University Mozarteum in Salzburg and Innsbruck, Austria, 1992-. Debut: Solo performer with chamber orchestra, Brno, 1993. Career: Solo performer in Czech Republic, Austria, Germany, Bulgaria; Solo performer with chamber orchestra in Brno, 1993; Innsbruck, Austria, 1993; Gotze Deltchev, Bulgaria, 1995; Television recording, 1996, 1997. Recordings: Solo CD: Denisa in Germany recorded in 1995; CD: Antonio Vivaldi (with Mr Hudecek and Mr Brabec and Mr Stivin. 1995. Honours: Prize winner of the international guitar competition of Plovdiv, Bulgaria. Hobbies: Sport; Travelling. Address: Obráncu Míru 443, Trebic, Czech Republic 67401.

VĚŽNIK Václav, b. 1 Aug 1930, Brno, Moravia, Czech Republic. Regisseur - Stage Director. m. Helena Rozsypalova, 28 Sept 1957, 1 son, 1 daughter. Education: The Masaryk State University (Philosophy), 1949-50; The Janáček Academy of Music, 1950-54; Operatic Production, Stage Director; Private study of violin and singing. Debut: Donizetti's Don Pasquale, State Theater Brno, 1955. Career: Stage Director, State Theater, Brno, 1954; Guest Directions at all theatres in Czech and Slovak republics, 1955-97; Guest directions in Norway, Germany, Switzerland, Italy, Spain, Belgium, Austria, Yugoslavia, 1968-95: 173 operatic productions include: Janácek's The Fate (world premiere), 1958; Martinu's The Marriage (Czech premiere), 1960; Fischer's Rome, Julia and the Darkness (world premiere), 1962; Martinu's The Voice of the Forest (World Stage Production), 1964; Martinu's Alexander bis (Czech premiere), 1964; Von Einem's Dantons Tod (Czech premiere), 1966; Holoubek's Professor Mamlock (world premiere), 1966; Gershwin's Porgy and Bess (Czech premiere), 1968; Szokolay's The Blood Wedding (Czech premiere), 1971; Vacek's The Tomcat Mikes (world premiere), 1986; Television productions: Prokofiev's Duenna, Prague, 1972; Janáček's Jenufa, Brno, 1972; Rimsky-Korsakov's The Golden Cockerel, Prague, 1973; Janáček's The Excursions of Mr Broucek, Brno, 1978; Janáček's The Cunning Little Vixen, Brno, 1979; Verdi's Simone Boccanegra, Brno, 1984; Verdi's Nabucco, Brno, 1989; Vacek's The Tomcat Mikes, Brno, 1990. Contributions to: Many articles about opera productions in Program (journal of the Janáček Opera, Brno). Honours include: Bedrich Smetana Medal, 1974, Leos Janáček Medal, 1978-79, Czech Ministry of Culture. Address: Brenkova 3, Brno 613 00, Czech Republic.

VIALA Jean-Luc, b. 5 Sept 1957, Paris, France. Singer (Tenor). Education: Studied in Paris with Michel Senechal. Debut: Paris Opera-Comique 1983 in Pomme d'Apis by Offenbach. Career: Sang at the Opera-Comiq1ue in Cesar Franck's Stradella and has made many appearances at provincial French opera houses; Glydebourne Festival 1986, as the Italian Singer in Capriccio, Dublin 1987, Aix-en-Provence Festival 1989, as the Prince in the Love of Three Oranges; Recent engagements at the Opera de Lyon including Rodolfo 1990; Sang in Sacchini's Oedipe at Colone for the Festival de Radio France at de Montpellier, 1992; Other roles include Paolino in Il Matrimonio Segreto, Giannetto (La Gazza Ladra), Fenton, George Borwn in La Dame Blanche and Iopas in Les Troyens. Recordings include: Guercoeur by Magnard and Les Brigands by Offenbach; Narraboth in the French version of Salome, Osmin in Gluck's La Rencontre Imprevue and Benedict in Beatrice at Benedict, all with the Lyon Opera; The Love for Three Oranges; Engaged as Georges Brown in La Dame Blanche at St Étienne, 1996-97. Address: c/o Opera de Lyon, 9 Quai Jean Moulin, F-69001 Lyon, France.

VICAR Jan, b. 5 May 1949, Olomouc, Czech Republic. Musicologist; Composer. m. Anna Betkova, 11 August 1979, 2 sons. Education: Accordion, Conservatory in Ostrava, 1972; Music, Palacky University, Olomouc, 1972; Composition, Academy of Music & Performing Arts, Prague, 1981. Career: Lecturer, Department of Music, Palacky University, 1973-85; Editor-in-Chief, Hudebni Rozhledy, 1986-89; Senior Lecturer, Academy of Music & Performing Arts, Prague, 1985-; Professor, Head, Department of Musicology, Palacky University, 1990-. Compositions: String Quartet, 1978; Music For Strings and Timpani, 1980; The Cry, 1981; Japanese Year, 1984; Night Prayer, 1996; Instructions of Surruppak, 1996; Choruses and Songs For Children, 1997. Publications: Akordeon a Jeho Hudebni Uplatneni, 1981; Vaclav Trojan, 1989; Hudebni Kritika A Popularizace Hudby, 1997. Contributions to: The Diary of One Who Vanished, 1995; Unknown, Czech Music After 1945, 1996. Honours: Prizes, Japanese year, 1980, Hello Sea, 1983, Mickey's Ditties, 1996. Membership: Czech Music Council. Hobbies: Downhill Skiing; Swimming. Address: Malostranske Nam 1, 118 00 Praha 1, Mala Strana, Czech Republic.

VICK Graham, b. 30 Dec 1953, Liverpool, England. Opera Producer. Career includes: Productions for the ENO include Ariadne auf Naxos, the Rape of Lucretia, Madame Butterfly, Eugene Onegin, Timon of Athens by Stephen Oliver, (world premiere 1991), and the Marriage of Figaro; For Opera North, Così fan tutte, Die Zauberflöte and Katya Kabanova; For Glyndebourne Festival, Queen of Spades; Artistic Director, City of Birmingham Touring Opera; European engagements in Brussels, Bonn, Venice, Netherlands, Berlin, Paris, Italy and St Petersburg; Covent Garden debut in 1989 with the British premiere of Un Re in Ascolto by Berio, returining for Mozart's Mitridate, 1991 and Die Meistersinger, 1993, The Midsummer Marriage at Royal Opera House, 1996; Parsifal for the Opéra Bastille, Paris, 1997; Television works include Il Segreto di Susanna for Scottish TV, The Rape of Lucretia for Channel Four, a live BBC TV Broadcast of War and Peace from St Petersburg, and Queen of Spades from Glyndebourne. Honours include: Premi Abbiati Award as Best Director for Mahagonny at the Teatro Communale in Florence and a SWET Oliver Award for Mitridate at the Royal Opera, Covent Garden. Address: c/o Ingpen & Williams Ltd, 26 Wadham Road, London SW15 2LR, England.

VICKERS Jon, b. 29 Oct 1926, Prince Albert, Saskatchewan, Canada. Singer (Tenor). m. Henrietta Outerbridge, 1953, 3 sons, 2 daughters. Career: Concert and Opera Singer, Canada; Joined Royal Opera House, Covent Garden, London 1957-84 as Riccardo, Don Carlos, Radames, Florestan, Giasone (Médée), Samson (Handel and Saint-Saëns), Aeneas, Siegmund and Tristan; Sang at Bayreuth Festival, Vienna State Opera, San Francisco, Chicago Lyric Opera, Metropolitan Opera, La Scala, Milan, Paris Opera, Boston, Buenos Aires, Athens, Ottawa, Houston, Dallas, Hamburg, Berlin, Munich, Athens Festival, Salzburg Festival, Festival of Orange, Tanglewood Festival, Rio de Janeiro. Recordings: Messiah; Otello; Aida; Die Walküre, Samson and Delilah; Fidelio; Italian Arias; Verdi's Requiem; Peter Grimes; Das Lied von der Erde; Les Troyens; Tristan und Isolde; Films include, Carmen; Pagliacci; Norma; Otello; Peter Grimes. Honours: Honorary LLD, Saskatchewan; Honorary CLD, Bishop's University; Mus D, Brandon University, University of Western Ontario; LLD, University of Guelph; Civ LD, University of Laval; DMus, University of Illinois; Critics Award, London, 1978; Grammy Award, 1979. Membership: Royal Academy of Music, London. Address: c/o Metropolitan Opera, New York, NY 10029, USA.

VIERU Anatol, b. 8 June 1926, Iasi, Romania. Composer; Musicologist; Educator. m. Nina Shutikova, 29 July 1954, 1 son, 1 daughter. Education: Bucharest Conservatory; Moscow Conservatory, USSR. Debut: Enesco Composition Contest, 1946. Career: Conductor, National Theatre, Bucharest, Romania, 1947-50; Editor, Musica magazine, 1950-51; Composition Teacher, Bucharest Conservatory, 1955-86; Initiated concerts, Parallel Music, Bucharest, 1970; Doctor of Music, Cluj, 1978; Lectures: Sarah Lawrence College, Juilliard School, New York, USA, Rubin academy of Music, Jerusalem, Israel; Darmstadt International Courses, 1992-93, Composer in Residence of the New York University. Compositions include: The Feast of the Cadgers, opera, 1978-81; Concertos: For Violin, 1964; For Clarinet, 1975; For Violin and Cello, 1980; Narration II for saxophone, 1985; On records. Orchestra: Symphony 1 - Ode to Silence, 1967 on records: Symphony III - In the Memeory of an Earthquake, 1976; Symphony V with choir, 1985; Chamber Music: Mosaics, 1972; String Quartet VI, 1986; Recorded: Nocturnal Scenes, choir acappella, 1964; Jonas, opera, 1972-76; Stone Country, tape music, 1972; Orchestra: Clepsydra I and II, 1969 and 1971; Ecran, 1970; Concertos: For Orchestra, 1955; For Flute, 1958; For Cello, 1962' Jeux for piano, 1963; Museum Music for harpsichord, 1968; Narration I for Organ, 1975; Concerto for violin and cello, 1980; VII String Quartet; From Modes Toward the Musical Time; 6 symphonies, 1967-73, 1977, 1983, 1985, 1987, 1988; String Quartets, 1955-56, 1973, 1980, 1982, 1986, 1987, 1991. Address: Str Stirbei-Voda 68 ap 3, Bucharest 70734, Romania.

VIGAY Denis, b. 14 May 1926, Brixton, London, England. Cellist. m. Greta Vigay, 24 July 1952, 1 son, 2 daughters. Education: Battersea Grammar School, London; Royal Academy of Music, London. Debut: BBC, 1941. Career: Principal Cello, Royal Liverpool Philharmonic Orchestra; BBC Symphony Orchestra; Soloist, Promenade Concerts, Royal Albert Hall; Soloist, Principal Cello, Academy of St Martin-in-the-Fields. Recordings: Complete Chamber Works of Handel; Schubert Octet; Beethoven Septet; Mendelssohn Octet; Complete Boccherini Guitar Quintets; Mozart Clarinet Quintet; Mozart Oboe Quartet; Mozart Horn Quintet; Fantasia on a Theme of Corelli, Michael Tippett. Honours: FRAM, 1972. Memberships: Incorporated Society of Musicians. Hobbies: Sailing; Gardening. Address: 12 Chesterfield Road, Finchley, London N3 1PR, England.

VIGNOLES Roger (Hutton), b. 12 July 1945, England. Pianoforte Accompanist; Conductor. m. (1) Teresa Ann Elizabeth Henderson 1972, diss 1982, (2) Jessica Virginia Ford, 1982. Education: Canterbury Cathedral Choir School; Sedbergh School; BA, BMus, Magdalene College, Cambridge; Royal College of Music, London (ARCM). Career: Accompanist of national and international reputation, regularly appearing with the most distinguished international singers and instrumentalists, in London and provinces and at major music festivals including Aldeburgh, Cheltenham, Edinburgh, Brighton, Bath, Salzburg, Prague, etc; Broadcasting for BBC Radio 3 and TV; International tours include USA, Canada, Australia, New Zealand, Hong Kong, Scandinavia; Recitals at Opera Houses of Cologne, 1982; Brussels, 1983; Frankfurt, 1984; Lincoln Center, New York, 1985; San Francisco, 1986; Tokyo, 1985 and 1987; Repetiteur, Royal Opera House, Covent Garden, 1969-71; English Opera Group, 1968-74; Australian Opera Company, 1976; Professor of Accompaniment, Royal College of Music, 1974-81; Conducted Handel's Agrippina at the 1992 Buxton Festival. Recordings include: English song, various, with Graham Trew, Baritone; Lieder by Schumann and Brahms/Dvorak; Cabaret Songs by Britten, Gershwin and Dankworth with Sarah Walker, Mezzo; Premiere recording of The Voice of Love (Nicholas Maw); Franck and Grieg cello sonatas with Robert Cohen, Cello; The Sea, songs and duets with Sarah Walker and Thomas Allen, Baritone; Parry Violin Sonatas with Erich Gruenberg, Violin. Honour: Honorary RAM, 1984. Hobbies: Drawing; Painting; Looking at Pictures; Swimming; Sailing. Address: 1 Ascham Street, Kentish Town, London NW5 2PB, England.

VIHAVAINEN Ilkka, b. 18 Oct 1960, Finland. Singer (Bass-baritone). Education: Studied at the Sibelius Academy, Helsinki, 1984-87, and in Berlin and Zurich. Career: Sang with the Zurich Opera as Lord Walton in I Puritani, Belcore, Garibaldo in Rodelinda and Nick Shadow in The Rake's Progress; Royal Opera Stockholm, 1988, as the Commendatore in Don Giovanni, and the Savonlinna Festival in Sallinen's The King goes forth to France; Concert appearances in Bach, Mozart's Requiem and Haydn's Creation. Address: Finnish National Opera, Bulevardi 23-27, SF-00180 Helsinki 18, Finland.

VIHAVAINEN Satu, b. 1958, Finland. Singer (Soprano). Education: Graduated Sibelius Academy, Helsinki, 1982. Career: Sang in concert from 1981, Finnish National Opera from 1982; Roles have included Micaela, Nedda, Donna Elvira, Susanna, Mimi and Marguerite; Savonlinna Festival from 1981, as First Lady and Pamina in Zauberflöte, Priestess in Aida and Marzelline in Fidelio; Guested at Los Angeles, 1992, in premiere of Sallinen's Kullervo; Sang Freia in Das Rheingold at Helsinki, 1996; Many concert engagements. Address: Finnish National Opera, Bulevardi 23-27, SF-00180 Helsinki 18, Finland.

VIKAR Laszlo, b. 8 Jun 1929, Szombathely, Hungary. Ethnomusicologist. m. Katalin Forrai, 2 sons, 1 daughter. Education: PhD; Music Teacher and Choral Conducting Diploma; Ethnomusicology Diploma (Professor Z Kodaly). Career: Member, Institute of Musicology, Hungarian Academy of Sciences; Research: Hungary, Slovakia, Romania, China, Korea, Finland, Turkey, Bulgaria, Mongolia and especially among Finno-Ugrian and Turkic Peoples, USSR; Professor, Liszt Academy of Music. Publications: Cseremisz Népdalok, 1967; Cheremis Folksongs, 1971; Editor, Finno-Ugrian Music (record), 1972; Editor, Béla Bartok's Folk Music Research in Turkey, 1976; Editor, Music of the Tatar People (record), 1978; Chuvash Folksongs, 1978; Editor, International Kodaly Conference Budapest, 1982, 1985; Editor, Folk Music of Finno-Ugrian and Turkic Peoples (3 records), 1984; Editor, Songs of the Forest (Finno-Ugrian Song Collection), 1985; Editor, Reflections on Kodaly, 1985; Editor, Anthology of Hungarian Folk Music II (5 records), 1986; Collection of Finno-Ugrian and Turkic Folk Music in the Volga-Kama-Belaya Region, 1958-79, 1986; Votyak Folksongs, 1989; A Volga-Kamai Finnugorok és törökök dallamai, 1993. Contributions to: Studia Musicologica, Hungarian Academy of Sciences; Journal of International Council of Traditional Music. Honours: Academic Prize, 1976; Erkel Art Prize, 1977; Order of Labour, 1979; Széchenyi Prize, 1995. Membership: Hungarian National Committee, ICTM. Address: 1054 Budapest, Bajcsy 60, Hungary.

VILIMOVA Renata, b. 1 April 1959, Czech Republic. Harpenist. 1 daughter. Education: Conservatoire, Prague; Academy of Music, Prague. Debut: Prague House of Artists, 1984. Career: Solo Harpist, Royal Danish Orchestra, Copenhagen, Denmark, 1986. Conopsitions: Ravel; Debussy; Cardon. Membership: DMI. Address: Navratilova 9, 11000 Praha 1, Czech Republic.

VILJAKAINEN Raili, b. 1954, Helsinki, Finland. Singer (Soprano). Education: Studied at the Sibelius Academy, 1973-78; Further study with Luigi Ricci in Rome. Career: Has sung in Stuttgart from 1978 as Aennchen in Der Freischütz, Sophie, Pamina, Ilia, Micaela, Mimi, Liu, Eva, Freia in Das Rheingold and Countess in Figaro; Guest appearances at the Savonlinna Festival, Salzburg and the Saratoga Springs Festival; Concert appearances in works by Bach, Mozart, Beethoven, Handel and Mahler; Has sung at Carnegie Hall, NY and in Finland, throughout Germany, Austria, USA, Australia, France and Spain; Sang Pamina at the Savonlinna Festival, 1981-90, Tatiana in Eugene Onegin and Desdemona in Otello at Helsinki; Contemporary music in Paris, Biennale Helsinki, Opera in Bonn, and in Sciarrino's Lohengrin. Recording: Aennchen in Der Freischütz. Honours: 1st Prize, Timo Callio Competition at Savonlinna Festival, 1976; 1st Prize, 's Hertogenbosch Competition, Netherlands, 1977. Address: c/o Finnish National Opera, Helsinginkatu 58, SF-00260 Helsinki, Finland.

VILLA Edoardo, b. 19 Oct 1953, Los Angeles, USA. Singer (Tenor). Education: Studied at the University of Southern California and with Martial Singher, Horst Gunter and Margaret Harshaw. Career: Many appearances in opera throughout the USA and abroad; Paris Opera 1986, as Don Carlos, Houston 1988, as Don José; Sang at the Munich Staatsoper 1989 and has appeared widely in Canada; Sang Jacopo Foscari in I Due Foscari with the Opera Orchestra of New York, 1992; Other roles include Corrado in Il Corsaro, Ruggero in La Rondine, Hoffmann, the Italian Singer in Rosenkavalier and Albert Herring. Recordings include: Le Roi d'Ys by Lalo.

VILLAROEL Veronica, b. 1962, Chile. Singer (Soprano). Education: Studied in Chile and the USA. Debut: Santiago, 1988, as Marguerite in Faust. Career: Sang Antonia at the 1989 Spoleto Festival, Fiordiligi at Barcelona, 1990 (returned for Violetta 1992); Season 1991 as Nedda at Miami, Traviata at Milwaukee and Mimi at Opéra de Lyon; Los Angeles and Théâtre de Châtelet, Paris, as Violetta; Sang Nedda in Paggliacci at Los Angeles; Many concert engagements. Address: 256 West 85th Street #2C, New York, NY 10024, USA.

VILMA Michele, b. 23 Feb 1932, Rouen, France. Singer (Mezzo-soprano). Education: Studied at the Rouen Conservatoire. Debut: Sang Leonore in La Favorite at Verviers. Career: Appearances at the Rouen Opera, notably as Dalila, and elsewhere in France as Charlotte, Carmen, Herodiade, Azucena and Dulcinée in Don Quichotte by Massenet; Paris Opéra from 1970 as Eboli, Fricka and the Kostelnicka in Jenufa; Marseille Opera as Laura in La Gioconda, Fricka at Bayreuth and Brangaena at the Metropolitan; Sang Clytemnestra in Elektra at the Opéra de Toulouse. Address: c/o Opéra de Paris, Théâtre National, 8 Rue Scribe, F-75009 Paris, France.

VINCO Ivo, b. 8 Nov 1927, Verona, Italy. Singer (Bass). m. Fiorenza Cossotto. Education: Studied at the Liceo Musicale Verona and at the La Scala Opera School with Ettore Campogalliani. Debut: Verona 1954, as Ramfis in Aida. Career: Appearances at La Scala and in Rome, Naples, Bologna, Venice, Turin and Florence; Has sung at the Verona Arena almost every year from 1954; Further appearances in Vienna, Hamburg, Berlin, Buenos Aires, Paris, Lisbon, Barcelona, Monte Carlo, Moscow, Chicago, Miami and Seattle; Metropolitan Opera debut 1969; Roles include Raimondo (Lucia di Lammermoor), Alvise (La Gioconda), the Grand Inquisitor, Oroveso (Norma), Sparafucile (Rigoletto), Ferrando (Il Trovatore) and Bartolo (Le Nozze di Figaro); Sang Alvise in La Gioconda at Barcelona, 1988; Ramphis at Palma, 1992. Recordings include: Lucia di Lammermoor, Il Trovatore, Rigoletto, Don Carlos; La Gioconda, Le nozze di Figaro; Iris by Massenet; Norma. Address: c/o Arena di Verona, Piazza Bra 28, I-37121 Verona, Italy.

VINE Carl, b. 8 Oct 1954, Perth, Australia. Composer; Pianist; Conductor. Education: Studied with Stephen Doman and John Exton at the University of Western Australia. Career: Co-founder of contemporary music ensemble Flederman, 1979; Appearances as conductor and pianist in Britain, Europe and the USA; Resident Composer with the Sydney Dance Company (1979), London Contemporary Dance Theatre (1979), Australian Chamber Orchestra (1987) and Western Australia University (1989); Lecturer in Electronic Music at the Queensland Conservatorium, 1980-82. Compositions include: Cafe Concertino, 1984; Canzona, 1985; Love Song for trombone and tape, 1986; Six Symphonies (no 6 Choral Symphony), 1986-96; Defying Gravity for 4 percussion, 1987; Percussion Concerto, 1987; Piano Sonata, 1990; The Tempest, ballet, 1991; String Quartet no 3, 1993; Esperance for chamber orchestra, 1994; Five Bagatelles for piano, 1994; Inner World for cello and tape, 1994; Gaijin for koto, strings and electronics, 1994; Oboe Concerto, 1996; Flag Handover Music (for 1996 Atlanta Olympics); Metropolis, for Melbourne SO, 1997; Piano Concerto, for Sydney SO, 1997. Honours include: John Bishop Memorial, 1990. Address: Faber Music Ltd, 3 Queen Square, London WC1N 3AU, England.

VINE David, b. 1943, London, England. Conductor; Harpsichordist. Education: Royal College of Music, London, 1961-65; Studied piano with Cornelius Fischer, Bernard Roberts, Eric Harrison, piano accompaniment with Joan Trimble, harpsichord with Millicent Silver, baroque ensemble playing with Hubert Dawkes, conducting with Sir Adrian Boult; ARCM; MusB 1st Class Honours, Harpsichord Performance, Canterbury University. Career: Cellist, local youth orchestra, Northampton; Specialist Music Teacher, Inner London Education Authority; Tutored in Baroque Music, Guildhall School of Music and City Literary Institute; Founder of London Telemann Ensemble; Settled in New Zealand in 1974; Conductor of New Zealand National Youth Orchestra, Wellington Polytechnic Orchestra, Dunedin Sinfonia and Schola Cantorum, Amici Chamber Orchestra, Christchurch Symphony Orchestra, Orpheus Choir, and Cantoris; Musical Director of Gisborne Choral Society, Christchurch Operatic Society, Jubilate Singers, Perkel Opera, Academy Chamber Orchestra and Ensemble Divertimento; Orchestral keyboard: New Zealand Symphony Orchestra; Recitalist, presenter and announcer with Radio NZ's Concert FM; Currently Musical Director, Academy Opera, conducting 7 New Zealand premieres of Handel, Mozart and Puccini operas; Lectures at universities of Canterbury, Auckland and Waikato. Publications: Handel: Suite in C minor, reconstruction for 2 keyboards, 1992; A Caldara, 16 Sonatas for cello and Continue, Doblinger, Vienna, 1996-. Honours: 1st Prize, 3 times, Northampton Eisteddfod Piano Section; Acknowledged one of New Zealand's finest harpsichordists and conductors. Address: PO Box 2815, Wellington, New Zealand.

VINTON John, b. 24 Jan 1937, Cleveland, Ohio, USA. Storyteller; Compiler; Writer on Music. Education: Ohio State University, 1954-58; New York University, 1958-63; University of Southern California, 1965-66. Career: Editorial and Research Assistant, Bela Bartok Archives, New York, 1962-65; General Manager, Dance Theatre Workshop, New York, 1971-73; Assistant Music Critic, Washington Star-News, 1966-67; Left music field and specialized in story telling in literature of Adirondack mountains. Publications: Dictionary of Contemporary Music, 1974; Published in England as Dictionary of 20th Century Music; Essays after a Dictionary, 1977; A Treasury of Great Adriondack Stories, 1991. Contributions to: Music Quarterly; Music Review; Music and Letters; Journal of the American Musicological Society; Arte Musical; Studia Musicologica; Sohlmans Musiklexikon; Notes. Honours: Research on Béla Bartok won bronze medal from Hungarian Academy of Sciences, 1981. Hobbies: Mycol; Cooking; Conversation; Creative Writing; Contemporary History. Address: 167 Hicks Street, Brooklyn, NY 11201, USA.

VINZING Ute, b. 9 Sept 1936, Wuppertal, Germany. Singer (Soprano). Education: Studied with Martha Mödl. Career: Sang at Lubeck 1967-70, notably as Marenka in The Bartered Bride and Senta in Der fliegende Holländer; Wuppertal Opera 1971-76, sang Brünnhilde in Der Ring des Nibelungen; Has sung in Hamburg, Munich, Vienna, Buenos Aires, Geneva, and Seattle (as Brünnhilde); Paris Opera 1977, 1985, as Brünnhilde and Isolde; Teatro Liceo 1983; Metropolitan Opera from 1984, debut as Elektra; Other roles include Ortrud, Kundry, Leonore and the Dyer's Wife in Die Frau ohne Schatten; Teatro Colon, Buenos Aires 1987, as Elektra; Sang Isolde at Florence 1988; Elektra at Marseilles 1989; Sang Ortrud at Buenos Aires 1991. Recordings include: Elektra (Harmonia Mundi); Die Frau ohne Schatten, conducted by Sawallisch.

VIOTTI Marcello, b. 29 June 1954, Gressy (Vaud), Switzerland. Conductor. m. Marie-Laurence, 10 July 1982, 4 children. Education: Studied piano and singing, Lausanne Conservatory, Geneva. Career: Kapelllmeister for 3 years at the Opera Regio of Turin; Appointed Artistic Director of the Lucerne Opera at age 32; From 1990-93 was General Music Director of the City of Bremen and also Chief Conductor of the Symphony Orchestra of the Saarländische Rundfunk for 5 years; Currently Principal Conductor of the MDR Symphony Orchestra, Leipzig; Orchestras conducted include: Berlin Philharmonic, Vienna Symphony Orchestra, Tonhalle Orchestra, Zürich, Oslo Philharmonic, Munich Philharmonic, Japan Philharmonic, Hamberger Symphoniker, English Chamber Orchestra and all the German Radio Symphony Orchestras; In 1997 he successfully directed his first concert with the Vienna Philharmonic during the Mozart Week in Salzburg; Opera engagements include all major international opera houses such as Vienna Staatsoper, Deutsche Oper Berlin and the operas of Munich, Hamburg and Zürich; Director of numerous new productions at La Scala, Milan, Monnaie, Brussels, Paris Opera, Vienna Staatsoper, Deutsche Oper Berlin and Zurich Opera. Recordings: Numerous on major labels. Honour: 1st Prize, Gino Marinuzzi Competition, San Remo, Italy. Hobbies: Catamaran sailing; Archery. Address: c/o Hilbert Maximilianstrasse 22, D-Munich, Germany.

VIRAG Paul, b. 12 Sept 1957. Concert Piano Teacher; Accompanist; Pianist; Vocal Coach. m. 1 daughter. Education: Music School, Komarno; State Conservatorium of Music, Bratislava; Tchaikovsky Conservatorium, Moscow. Career: Professor of Piano, Chamber Music and Accompanist in Vocal, Clarinet, Violin and Violoncello Classes, State Conservatorium, Bratislava, 1983-89; Lecturer, Accompaniment in Woodwind Classes, Academy of Music and Drama, Bratislava, 1983-89; Assistant Conductor, Repetiteur, State Opera and Ballet, Izmir, Turkey, 1989-94; Freelance Concert Pianist, Accompanist, Repetiteur, Europe & Asia, 1994-96; Vocal Coach, Voice & Opera Department, University of Sydney Conservatorium of Music, 1997; Piano Teacher, Accompanist, Vocal Coach, Australian Institute of Music, Sydney, 1997. Recordings: For Slovak Television and Radio, and SBS, Sydney, Australia. Honours: Winner, State Piano Competition, Trencin, Slovak Republic, 1966; Finalist, International Young Pianists Competition, Bratislava, 1967, Virtuosi per Musica di Pianoforte, International Young Performers Competition, Usti nad Labem, Czech Republic, 1969. Address: 8/116 Victoria Avenue, Chatswood, Sydney, NSW 2067, Australia.

VIRAGH Endre, b. 23 Mar 1928, Vasvár, Hungary. Professor of Organ; Orchestra Conductor. m. Margit Piláth, 21 Sept 1958. Education: Graduated in Organ playing, Liszt Ferenc Academy of Music, Budapest, 1955; Studied with J Reinberger, Prague, 1958-59, with M Dupré, Paris, 1960, and with F Germani, Rome and Siena, 1965, 1967, 1968. Debut: Bartók Conservatoire, Miskolc, 1955; Principal Parish Church, Budapest, 1961. Career: Regularly appears as soloist at concert on Hungarian Radio and TV; Organ recitals in Brune and Siena; Permanent interpreter at prestigious organ concerts; Extensive repertoire includes all organ works of J S Bach, Liszt, and César Franck, sonatas of Mendelssohn and Hindemith, organ works by modern composers such as Dupré, Messaien, Janacek and Kodály, and organ concertos including Vivaldi's 2nd. Recordings: Video: Assisi, Italy, 1982; Castelgandolfo, Italy, 1991; Professor of Organ at Miskolc from 1955, and at Belá Bartók Conservatoire, Budapest, from 1969. Honours: Diploma of Honour, Siena, 1967; Pro-Arte Prize, 1980; Eminent Pedagogue of Organ, 1991; Rectorate Honourable Mention, 1992. Memberships: Saint Cecilia OMCE; Ferenc Liszt Society; Zoltán Kodály Society; Lajos Bardos Society. Address: Róbert-Károly krt 12 a, H-1138 Budapest, Hungary.

VIRAGOVA Silvia, b. 7 March 1959, Nove Zamky, Slovakia. Singer. m. Paul Virag, 30 January 1982, 1 daughter. Education: State Conservatorie of Music, Bratislava, 1974-78; College of Musical Arts, Bratislava, 1978-83; PhD, 1995. Debut: Opera of the Slovak National Theatre, 1984. Career: Opera of the Slovak National Theatre, 1984-86; New Scene Theatre of Operetta, Bratislava, 1986-88; Lecturer, Voice, Conservatorium of Music, Bratislava, 1988-89; Edinburgh Music Vestival, 1990; Soloist, Singing Instructor, State Opera & Ballet, Izmir, Turkey, 1990-93; Lecturer, Vocal & Opera Studies, Dokuz Eylul University Conservatorium, Izmir, Turkey, 1990-92; Freelance Artist, Europe & Asia, 1993-95; Lecturer, Voice & Opera Studies, Australian Institute of Music, 1997-. Honours include: 1st Prize, Children Vocal Competition, Bratislava, 1971; 2nd Prize, International Youth Vocalists Competition, Bratislava, 1973; Finalist, The Mikulas Schneider Trnavsky Competition, Slovakia, 1982; Semi Finalist, Belvedere International Singing Competition, Vienna,

Austria, 1991. Hobbies: Travel; Languages. Address: Kmetovo nam 2/8, 811 07 Bratislava, Slovakia.

VIRKHAUS Taavo, b. 29 June 1934, Tartu, Estonia. Symphony Orchestra Conductor. m. Nancy Ellen Herman, 29 Mar 1969. Education: BM, University of Miami, Florida, 1951-55; MM 1957, DMA 1967, Eastman School of Music, Rochester, New York; Pierre Monteux Master Class 1960 and 1961; Fulbright Grant to Cologne, Germany, 1963-64. Debut: Conducting the Miami Ballet Guild Orchestra, 1956. Career: Director of Music, University of Rochester, 1966-77; Music Director and Conductor, Duluth-Superior Symphony Orchestra, Duluth, Minnesota, 1977-94; Guest Conductor with Rochester Philharmonic; Baltimore Symphony; Estonian SSR State Symphony; Minnesota Orchestra; Music Director and Conductor of Huntsville, Alabama, Symphony Orchestra, 1990-. Compositions: 5 Symphonies, Violin Concerto. Honour: Howard Hanson Prize, 1966. Current Management: Joanne Rile Artists Management, Philadelphia, Pennsylvania, USA. Address: 111 Lake Shore Drive, Madison, AL 35758, USA.

VIRSALADZE Eliso, b. 14 Sept 1942, Russia. Concert Pianist. Education: Studied with Anastasia Virsaladze, then at Tbilsi Conservatory. Career: Since winning prizes at competitions in Moscow and Leipzig (1962, 1966) she has played all over the world, including Japan, Germany, Italy, Austria, Poland and Bulgaria; Tours of America and Europe with the Leningrad Philharmonic; British recital debut at the Elizabeth Hall 1981, followed by concerto debut with the Royal Philharmonic and Yuri Temirkanov; Season 1983-84 toured England with USSR Symphony Orchestra; Returned 1987-88 with the Bournemouth Symphony, the Royal Philharmonic under Dorati, the Royal Liverpool Philharmonic, BBC Philharmonic, City of Birmingham Symphony and the Philharmonia under Kurt Sanderling; Season 1988-89 appearances at the Berlin Festival, Prague Spring Festival and with the Cologne Radio Orchestra; Tours of the USA and Japan. Honours: Winner, Soviet Competition of Performing Musicians, 1961; Bronze Medal, Tchaikovsky Competition Moscow, 1962; Prize Winner at 1966 Schumann Competition Leipzig. Current Management: Münchner Konzertdirektion Hörtnagel Gmbh, Neufahrner Strasse 23, 8000 München 80, Germany.

VISCONTI Piero, b. 1947, Valenze, Piedmont, Italy. Singer (Tenor). Education: Studied in Rome. Debut: Naples, 1975, as Rodolfo in La Bohème. Career: Sang at Miami, 1979, Rome Opera from 1978 (debut as Ernani); Vienna Staatsoper 1980, as Edgardo, the Duke of Mantua at the 1981 Verona Arena, Barcelona and Mannheim from 1982; US appearances at Houston and Philadelphia, Verdi Requiem in London, 1985, and Sydney Opera, 1986; Other roles include Almaviva, Arturo in La Straniera, Pollione in Norma, Nemorino, Foresto, Gabriele Adorno, Pinkerton, Calaf, Enzo and Andrea Chénier. Address: Opéra de Montpellier, 11 Boulevard Victor Hugo, F-3400 Montpellier, France.

VISEK Tomás, b. 30 May 1957, Prague, Czech Republic. Pianist. Education: Music School (with Pavel Svoboda), 1965-; Prague Conservatory (with Valentina Kameníková, later Zdenik Kozina); Graduate, Prague Music Academy (with Josef Palenicek, later Zdenek Jílek), 1984; Postgraduate Studies with Zdenek Jílek), 1990-93. Career: Concerts in: Poland (also radio recordings); France including recital on Radio France, 1990; Austria including Grieg Concerto in Musikverein, Vienna, 1993; Egypt including Opera House in Cairo, 1995; Czech Republic including Prague Spring Festival, 1997; Slovakia; Hungary; Holland; Russia; Bulgaria; Slovenia; Well-known interpreter of Czech music (especially Smetana, Dvorák, Suk, Martinu, Fibich, Tomasek, Janacek) and Jewish music (Mendelssohn, Gershwin, Korngold, Tansman, Schulhoff, Ullman), unknown pieces, rarities; Television film about Schulhoff on Czech TV, 1995; Television cycle "Top of the Classics", Czech TV (Famous Piano Pieces), 1996. Recordings: CDs: Saudek's Piano Concerto; Schulhoff's Solo Piano Works (jazz-inspired works; sonatas and suites, being continued); Hába's Half-Tone Piano Works; Chamber music by Martinu, Schulhoff and others. Contributions to: Czech music magazines: Opus Musicum, 1995, Hudební Rozhledy, 1996, 1997, Harmonie, 1997; Newspapers from Poland, Gazeta Olsztynska,1993; Austria, Observer, 1993; BBC Music Magazine, 1994; Egypt, Progres, 1995. Honours: Janina Nawrocka Special Prize, Chopin, Warsaw, 1975; 2nd Prize and Smetana Award, Smetana, Hradec Králové, 1978; 2nd Prize, Vienna, 1992; 2nd Prize and Bach Award, Ragusa-Ibla, 1994; 5th Prize, Concours Milosz Magin, Paris, 1995. Memberships: Czech Music Societies of Mozart, Chopin, Smetana, Dvorák, Suk, Martinu, Fibich, Foerster. Hobbies: Swimming; Nature; Hiking; Crosswords. Current Management: Impresario Art Agency, Celetna 19, 11622, Prague 1, Czech Republic. Address: Byt c 36, 28 Pluku 12/128, 10100 Prague 10, Vrsovice, Czech Republic.

VISHNEVSKAYA Galina, b. 25 Oct 1926, Leningrad, Russia. Soprano. m. 1955, Mstislav Rostropovich, 2 daughters. Education: Studied with Vera Garina. Career: Toured with Leningrad Light Opera Company, 1944-48, with Leningrad Philharmonic Society, 1948-52; Joined Bolshoi Theatre 1952; Concert appearances in Europe and USA, 1950-; Has often sung in the 14th Symphony of Shostakovich, including first performance, 1969; First appeared at Metropolitan Opera, New York, USA, 1961; Roles included Leonora in Fidelio; Tatiana in Eugene Onegin, Iolanta; Aida; Sang in England at Festival Hall, Aldeburgh Festival, Edinburgh Festival, Covent Garden, Rostropovich Festival, Snape; Made concert tours with husband; Member of Jury, Cardiff Singer of the World, 1991. Recordings: Numerous recordings. Publications: Galina (autobiography). Address: c/o Victor Hochhauser, 4 Holland Park Avenue, London W11 3QU, England.

VISSE Dominique, b. 30 Aug 1955, Lisieux, France. Singer (Counter-Tenor). m. Angès Mellon. Education: Chorister at Notre Dame in Paris; Organ and Flute Studies at the Versailles Conservatory. Debut: Opera debut at Tourcoing 1982, in Monteverdi's Poppea; Sang Flora in the first modern performances of Vivaldi's L'Incoronazione di Dario at Grasse, 1984; Charpentier's Actéon at Edinburgh 1985, Nirenus in Nicholas Hytner's production of Giulio Ceasare at the Paris Opera 1987 and Delfa in Cavilli's Giasone at the 1988 Innsbruck Early Music Festival; Created Geronimo in the premiere of Le Rouge et Noir by Claude Prey, Aix 1989; Sang Annio in Gluck's La Clemenza di Tito at Lausanne, 1991. Career: Instrumentalist in medieval and Renaissance music; Further study with Alfred Deller, René Jacobs and Nigel Rogers, 1976-78; Founded the Ensemble Clement Janequin and sang with Les Arts Florissants under William Christie; Sang the Nurse in Monteverdi's Poppea at Buenos Aires, 1996. Recordings include: L'Incoronazione di Dario by Vivaldi; Charpentier's Acteon, Les Arts Florissants and David et Jonathas; Cavalli's Xerse and Giasone; Octavia's Nurse in L'Incoronazione di Poppea; Rameau's Anacréon and Hasse's Cleofide; Labels include Erato and Harmonia Mundi. Address: c/o Ian Malkin, 118 rue Haxo, 75019 Paris, France.

VISSER Lieuwe, b. 23 Aug 1940, Diemen, Holland. Singer (Bass). Education: Studied with Jo van de Meent in Amsterdam and at the Accademia di Santa Cecilia, Rome with Giorgio Favaretto. Debut: Netherlands Opera Amsterdam, as Don Basilio in Il Barbiere di Siviglia. Career: Has sung with Netherlands Opera in the 1974 premiere of The Picture of Dorian Gray by Kox and as Masetto, 1984; Glyndebourne Festival 1981, in A Midsummer Night's Dream; Centre France Lyrique Paris 1983, in the stage premiere of Frankenstein by Gruber. Recordings include: Lucrezia Borgia by Donizetti (Decca).

VLAD Marina Marta, b. 8 Mar 1949, Bucharest, Romania. Composer. m. Ulpiu Vlad, 15 Sept 1973, 1 son. Education: Music High School, Bucharest, 1960-65; High School, Il Caragiale, 1965-67; Graduate in Composition, The C Porumbescu Academy of Music, 1973. Career: University Assistant at the C Porumbescu Academy of Music, 1973-91; Professor at The Academy of Music, Bucharest, 1991. Compositions: Recorded at the Romanian Radio: Sonata for Violin and Piano, 1978; Rondo for Piano, 1978; Symphony Movement, 1979; Images for String Orchestra, 1980; Sonata for Piano, 1981; String Quartet No 1, 1981; String Quartet No 2, 1982; Legend and In Search of The Game for Piano, 1983; String Trio No 1, Inscriptions for Peace, 1984; String Trio No 2, Dream of Peace, 1985; String Trio No 3, 1986; This Country's Land, cantata for Solo Voice, Choir and Orchestra, a verse by Jon Brad, 1987; Light Rays, trio for Flute, Oboe and Clarinet, 1988; Thoughts for the Future, quartet for Flute, Violin, Viola and Cello, 1989; In Search of The Game No 2 for Piano, 1994. Recordings: String Quartet No 2 and Sonata for Piano, 1984. Publications: Sonata for Violin and Piano, 1982; Rondo for Piano, 1983; String Trio No 1, Inscriptions for Peace, 1986; Dream of Peace, String Trio No 2, 1988; Light Rays, trio for Flute Oboe and Clarinet, 1989; Still Life I, for Oboe solo, 1996; Still Life II, for clarinet solo, 1997. Honour: Prize granted by the Conservatory of Music, C Porumbescu for The Cantata Resonance, 1972. Membership: Union of Composers of Romania. Address: Str Andrei Popovici No 18, BL 8A, Sc c et IV, ap 39, 71254 Bucharest, Romania.

VLAD Roman, b. 29 Dec 1919, Cernauti, Romania (now Uczarna). Composer; Music Writer. Education: Studied at the Cernauti Conservatory and in Rome with Casella. Career: Active as a Pianist and Lecturer from 1939; Artistic Director of the Accademia Filarmonica in Rome, 1955-58 and 1966-69; Currently President, Accademia Filomonica, Rome; Artistic Director of the Maggio Musicale Fiorentino, 1964 and of the Teatro Comunale, Florence, 1968-72; Taught at Dartington Summer School, 1954-55; Co-Editor of the Enciclopedia dello Spettacolo, 1958-62 and the Nuova Rivista Musicale Italiana, 1967-; President of the Italian section of the ISCM, 1960-63; Professor of Composition at the Perugia Conservatory, 1968; Supervisor of the Turin Radio Symphony Orchestra, 1973-80; Artistic Adviser of the Turin Settembre Musica Festival from 1985; President of Society of Italian Authors and Publishers (SIAE) from 1987, currently Governmental Commissioner 1992-94; President of CISAC, 1982-84, 1992-96; Artistic Director, Teatro alla Scala, Milan, 1994-96. Compositions: Ballets: La Strada sul caffè, 1943; La Dama delle Camelie, 1945; Fantasia, 1948; Masques Ostendias, 1959; Die Wiederkehr, 1962; Il Gabbiano, 1968; Il Sogno, 1973; Operas: Storia di una Mamma, 1951; Il Dottore di Vetro, 1960; La Fantarca, 1967; Orchestral: Sinfonietta, 1941; Suite, 1941; Sinfonia all'antica, 1948; Variazioni Concertanti su una Serie Di 12 Note dal Don Giovanni di Mozart for Piano and Orchestra, 1955; Musica per Archi, 1957; Musica Concertata for Harp and Orchestra, 1958; Ode Super Chrysae Phorminx for Guitar and Orchestra, 1964; Divertimento Sinfonico, 1967; Vocal: 3 Cantatas, 1940-53; Lettura di Michelangelo for Chorus, 1964; Immer Wieder for Soprano and 8 Instruments, 1965; Piccolo Divertimento Corale, 1968; Lettura di Lorenzo Magnifico for Chorus, 1974; La Vespa di Toti for Boys' Voices and Instruments, 1976; Chamber: Divertimento for 11 Instruments, 1948; String Quartet, 1957; Serenata for 12 Instruments, 1959; Il Magico Flauto di Severino for Flute and Piano, 1971; Cinque elegie su testi biblici, 1990; Melodia variata, 1990; Stagioni giaponesi, 24 Haiku, 1993-94; Piano Music; Music for more than 100 films. Publications Include: Collected Essays, 1955; Luigi Dallapiccola, 1957; Storia della Dodecafonia, 1958; Strawinsky, 1958, revised 1973 and 1979; Essays on Busoni, Schoenberg and Strawinsky; Introduzione alle cultura musicale, 1988; Capire la musica, 1989. Address: Via XXIV Haggio N 51, 00187 Rome, Italy.

VLAD Ulpiu, b. 27 Jan 1945, Zarnesti, Romania. Composer. m. Marina Marta Vlad, 15 Sept 1973, 1 son. Education: Music High School, Bucharest, 1958-64; Academy of Music C Porumbescu, Bucharest, 1964-71; Seminar in Composition, Conservatory of Music, Santa Cecilia, Rome. Debut: Septet for Winds and Piano, 1970, Conservatory of Music C Porumbescu. Career includes: Researcher in Romanian Folk Music, Institut de Cercetari Etnologice si Dailectologice, Bucharest, 1977-80; Editor, 1980-84, Manager, 1984-92, Romanian Musical Publishing Company; Music Department Director, Romanian Ministry of Culture, 1992-93; Professor at The Academy of Music, Bucharest, 1990-; Romanian TV and Radio appearances. Compositions include: First Symphony Roads in The Light, 1979; Lights in The Sunset, symphonic work, 1991; The Secret of Dreams, quintet for Winds No 2, 1992; Mosaic, chamber-vocal-symphonic cycle, with unlimited possibilities of combinations between the different instruments of the orchestra and a vocal quartet, 1974-78; The Time of Dreams, quartet for Flute, Clarinet, Piano and Percussion, 1993; Suddenly Dreams, concerto for Chamber Orchestra, 1994; The Legend of Dreams, sextet for Flute, Clarinet, Piano, Percussion, Violin and Cello, 1994; Beyond Dreams, music for wind, string and keyboard, 1996; The Secret of Dreams III, septet for flute, oboe, clarinet, bassoon, horn, percussion and piano, 1996; Interlocking Dreams, for 3 flutes, oboe, clarinet, bassoon, horn, violin, viola and accordion, 1997. Recordings: Mosaic, 2 versions, 1980; The Joy of Achievement - Wedding Songs; Dreams 1. Publications include: Mosaic, 1982; 1st Symphony, Roads in The Light, 1985; 2nd Symphony, From our Hearts, 1988; Inscriptions in Hearts, 1989; Dreams II, 1992; The Spring, String Trio No 1, 1994. Honours include: Medal for Distinction in Culture, 2nd Class, 1983; Prize of the Academy of Romania, 1985; Prizes of the Union of Romanian Composers, 1987, 1991; Prize of the Union of Composers of Romania, 1995. Hobby: Mountain Climbing. Address: Andrei Popovici 18, Bl 8A, Sc c et IV Ap 39, 71254 Bucharest, Romania.

VLATKOVIC Radovan, b. 1962, Zagreb, Croatia. Horn Player. Education: Studied at the Zagreb Academy of Music and the Northwest German Music Academy at Detmold. Career: Principal of the Berlin Radio Symphony Orchestra, 1982-90; Solo engagements from 1979, notably at Salzburg 1984, the Vienna Konzerthaus, the Barbican, the Theatre de la Ville in Paris, Pushkin Museum Moscow, Metropolitan Museum New York, Orchestra Hall Chicago and Suntory Hall, Tokyo; Soloist with leading orchestras and chamber music performer with Gidon Kremer, Heinz Holliger, András Schiff and Aurèle Nicolet; Professor of Horn, Stuttgart Hochschule für Musik, 1992-. Recordings include: Mozart's Four Concertos and R Strauss Concertos with the English Chamber Orchestra conducted by Jeffrey Tate. Honours include: Prizes at the Wind Instruments Competition in Ancona, 1979; Horn Competition in Liège, 1981; 1st Prize, International ARD Competition in Munich, 1983; German Music Critics' Prize three times for recordings of solo (Mozart) and chamber music (Gubaidulina, Hindemith) Repertoire. Address: c/o Ingpen & Williams Ltd, 26 Wadham Road, London SW15 2LR, England.

VLIJMEN Jan van, b. 11 Oct 1935, Rotterdam, Netherlands. Composer; Administrator. Education: Studied composition with Kees van Baaren. Career: Director of the Amersfoort Music School, 1961-65; Lecturer in Theory at Utrecht Conservatory, 1965-67; Deputy Director of the Royal Conservatory, The Hague, 1967, Director, 1971; General Manager of Netherlands Opera, 1985-88; Director of the Holland Festival, 1991. Compositions include: Strijkkwartet No 1, 1956 and No 2, 1958 both for String Quartet; Gruppi for Orchestra, 1962, revised 1980; Sonata for Piano and Large Ensemble, 1966; Quintetto a fiati no 2 for Wind Quintet, 1972; Axel, opera with

Reinbert de Leeuw, 1977; Faithful for Viola, 1984; Nonct for Ensemble, 1985; Solo II for Clarinet, 1986; R Escher - Summer Rites at Noon for Orchestra or 2 Orchestras, 1987; Such a Day of Sweetness for Soprano and Orchestra, 1988; Un Malheureux Vêtu de Noir, opera, 1990; Concerto for Piano and Orchestra, 1991; Tombeau (Solo III), for Violoncello, 1991; Inferno (Dante), cantate for Choir and Large Ensemble, 1993; A Schönberg - 6 Kleine Klavierstücke, Op 19 arrangement for Orchestra (published), 1993. Address: Royal Conservatory of Music and Drama, Juliana van Stolberglaan 1, 2595 CA The Hague, The Netherlands.

VODICKA Leo (Marian), b. 1950, Brno, Czechoslovakia. Singer (Tenor). Education: Studied at the Janacek Academy of Arts with Josef Valek. Career: Has sung in most Czech opera houses, notably the Janacek Opera Brno and the Prague National Theatre; Guest engagements in Bologna, Rome, Milan, Geneva, Zurich, Berne, Graz, Salzburg, Cologne, Paris, Nice, Tokyo, Osaka and in Bulgaria, Hungary, the former Soviet Union and East Germany; Major roles have included Verdi's Rigoletto, Don Carlos, Manrico and Otello; Puccini's Cavaradossi, Des Grieux, Pinkerton and Rodolfo; Janacek's Laca and Boris, the Prince in Rusalka and Smetana's Jenik and Dalibor; Don José and Stravinsky's Oedipus; Concert repertoire includes Verdi Requiem; Dvorak Stabat Mater and Requiem; Janacek Amarus, Glagolitic Mass, Diary of One Who Disappeared and Everlasting Gospel; Martinu's Field Mass and Bartók's Cantata Profana; Staatsoper Vienna for role of Prince in Rusalka by Dvorak, 1990; Vienna, L Janacek-Glagolitic Mass and Osud (Fate), 1990; Solo tour in Japan/Tokyo, Koriyama, Kumamoto, Matsuyama with airs from Carmen, Andrea Chénier, La Forza del destino, Otello, Tosca, Traviata, conducted by Shigeo Genda, 1992. Recordings: Smetana The Kiss, The Secret and Libuse; Dvorák The Cunning Peasant; Foerster Eva; Janacek Amarus conducted by Charles Mackerras (Supraphon); Antonin Dvorak - Dimitrij, title role, conducted by Gerd Albrecht, Supraphon, 1989; London BBC, Diary of One Who Disappeared, with Radoslav Kvapil-piano, 1993. Current Management: Pragokoncert, Maltézské nam 1, Prague 1, Czech Republic. Address: Zlichovska 6, Prague, Czech Republic.

VOGEL Benjamin, b. 5 May 1945, Biala Woda, Russia. Musicologist; Organologist. m. (1) Lubomira Swiczeniuk, 3 Apr 1971, divorced 1990, 1 daughter, (2) Aurelia Holcman, 1 Sep 1991. Education: Walbrzych Music High School, 1968; MA, Musicology, 1973, PhD, Musicology, 1977, Qualified as Assistant Professor, 1988, Warsaw University. Career: Associate Professor of Musicology, Warsaw Institute, Warsaw University, 1978-94; Expert in Historical Music Instruments, Polish Ministry of Culture, 1978-94; Head of Warsaw University Musicological Research Station in Bydgoszcz, 1981-89; Custodian, Industrial History Museum in Opatówek n Kalisz, Piano Division, 1986-94; Associate Professor (Docent), Department of Musicology, Lund University, 1997-. Publications: Musical Instruments in Culture of The Polish Kingdom, 1980; Old Piano Collection of Pomeranian Philharmonic, 1987, 2nd edition in English; Piano Making on the Polish Soil Till World War II, 1988, 2nd extended edition, 1995; Polish Pianos 19th - 20th Century, Collection, 1994. Contributions include: Pianos and Keyboard Idiophones in The Polish Kingdom during Chopin's Younger Years, in Rocznik Chopinowski Volume 9, 1975; Der Einfluss des professionellen auf den nicht professionellen Instrumentenbau in Polen, in Studia Instrumentorum Musicae volume 6, 1979; Musica Antiqua; Muzyka; Piano as a Symbol of Burgher Culture in Nineteenth Century Warsaw, in The Galphin Society Journal volume XLVI, 1993. Honours: Gold award for Preservation of Ancient Monuments; Collective award for Preservation of Historical Musical Instruments in Poland. Memberships: Polish Composers Union; American Musical Instruments Society. Hobbies: Tinkering; Swimming; Skiing; Playing Bridge. Address: St Skarpskyttevägen 4B, S-226 42 Lund, Sweden.

VOGEL Howard (Levi), b. 21 Feb 1933, New York City, USA. Recorder Player; Bassoonist. m. Susan Bradford Walker, 7 July 1984. Education: BM, Bassoon, 1955; MM, Musicology, 1960; Manhattan School of Music; Studied Bassoon with Simon Kovar and Musicology with Joseph Braunstein; Studied Lute with Suzanne Block, Recorder with Frans Brüggen and Viol with Martha Blackman, 1958-69. Career: Bassoonist with Kansas City Philharmonic, 1956-58; Robert Shaw Chorale, New York City Opera, Metropolitan Opera and New York City Ballet, 1959-75; Recorder Soloist, New York Baroque Ensemble, 1961-81; Bassoonist and Contrabassoonist, Little Orchestra Society, New York Philharmonic and Musica Sacra, 1982; Live TV Broadcasts teaching recorder master classes and performing with New York Baroque Ensemble; School Director and Teacher of Recorder, Village Music Workshop, New York, 1965-; Assistant Professor of Music, City University, New York, 1967-75; Artist in Residence, Somerset Co College, New Jersey, 1976-79; Recorder recitals with harpsichord in Pennsylvania, New York and Massachusetts, summer 1986. Publication: On Making Baroque Music, 1975. Contributions to: Woodstock Times Music Reviews and Previews, regular columnist, 1989-. Memberships: Galpin Society; American

Lute Society; American Musical Instrumental Society; American Recorder Society; Guild of American Luthiers. Hobbies: Research into Baroque String Playing Technique especially Bowing; Baroque Recorder Playing and Ornamentation. Address: Bonna Creek Hollow, Woodstock, Mt Tremper, NY 12457, USA.

VOGEL Siegfried, b. 6 Mar 1937, Chemnitz, Germany. Singer (Bass). Education: Studied in Dresden with H Winkler and J Kemter. Debut: Dresden Staatsoper 1959, as Zizell in Si j'etais roi by Adam. Career: Sang Mozart roles in Dresden; Sarastro, Osmin and the Commendatore; Berlin Staatsoper from 1965 as Leporello, Alfonso, Hunding, Basilio, Count Almaviva, Escamillo, Kecal and Ochs; Guest appearances in Moscow, Paris, Lausanne (Hans Sachs and Baron Ochs 1983), Brussels and Vienna; Further engagements at La Scala and in Venice, Stockholm, Helsinki, Amsterdam and Cairo; Bayreuth Festival 1985-86, as Biterolf in Tannhäuser; Sang Kaspar, Rocco and the King Henry in Lohengrin, 1986 at the Berlin Staatsoper; Metropolitan debut 1986, as Hunding, sang Morosus in Die Schweigsame Frau at Palermo, 1988; Bayreuth 1989, as Fasolt, Biterolf and Titurel; Toronto Opera 1990, as the Doctor in Wozzeck; Sang the Athlete in Lulu at the Semper Oper Dresden, 1992; Concert repertoire includes sacred music by Bach and Handel; Sang Rocco in Fidelio at the 1996 Edinburgh Festival. Recordings: Der Freischütz; Ariadne auf Naxos, Die Meistersinger, Zar und Zimmermann, Genoveva, Rienzi; St Matthew Passion; Karl V by Krenek. Address: c/o Berlin Staatsoper, Unter den Linden 7, D-1086 Berlin, Germany.

VOGEL Volker, b. 13 Oct 1950, Karlsruhe, Germany. Singer (Tenor). Education: Studied at the Hanover Musikhochschule. Career: Sang at the Dortmund Opera, then at Freiburg, 1984-85, and the Vienna Volksoper, 1984-90; Zurich Opera from 1991; Guest appearances in Barcelona, Berlin, Bregenz and Verona; Vienna, 1990, in the premiere of Einem's Tuliphant; Salzburg and London, 1992, in Weill's Sieben Todsünden; Other roles include Mozart's Pedrillo and Beethoven's Jacquino. Recordings include: Zemlinsky's Kleider machen Leute (Koch); Monostatos in Die Zauberflöte (Erato). Address: Opernhaus Zurich, Falkenerstrasse 1, CH-8008 Zurich, Switzerland.

VOGEL Winston (Dan), b. 1950, Israel. Conductor. Education: Studied at the Tel Aviv Academy and at Juilliard and Mannes College, New York. Career: Appointments with Mainz Opera, Netherlands Dance Theatre, the Virginia SO and in Poland, Bulgaria, China, Japan and Israel; Tour of Europe with Kibbutz Artzi Choir. Recordings include: 18th Century Italian Symphonies. Address: c/o Donald E Scrimgeour, 49 Springcroft Avenue, London N2 93H, England.

VOGLER Jan, b. 18 Feb 1964, Berlin, Germany. Cellist. Education: Hanns Eisler Hochschule für Musik, Berlin; Basle Music Academy, Switzerland, Teachers Josef Schwab, Heinrich Schiff. Career: Concert Master, cello, Staatskapelle Dresden, 1985-; Concerts as soloist, orchestras including Berlin Radio Orchestra 1986, 1987, 1989, Staatskapelle Dresden, Berlin Chamber Orchestra, Dresden Chamber Orchestra, Virtuosi Saxoniae; US debut, Chicago 1987; Marlboro Festival, USA 1988, 1989; Numerous radio broadcasts, live recordings; Recitals, many countries. Current Management: Kunstleragentur, Krausenstrasse 9/10, GDR-1080 Berlin. Address: Bahnhofstrasse 47, GDR-1123 Berlin, Germany.

VOGT Lars, b. 8 Sept 1970, Düren, Germany. Concert Pianist. m. Tatiana Komarova. Education: Hanover Conservatoire with Professor Kämmerling. London Debut: Royal Festival Hall with London Philharmonic Orchestra. Career: Concert appearances worldwide, including Rotterdam Philharmonic and DSO Berlin, Orchestra del Maggio Musicale in Florence, and Mozarteum Orchestra, Santa Cecilia Orchestra, Rome; Leipzig Gewandhaus and Cologne Radio Orchestras; 1994, Paris debut performing the Schumann Concerto with the Orchestre National de France and Leonard Slatkin; Recital appearances include the Schleswig-Holstein Festival, London, Frankfurt, Milan, Amsterdam, Paris, Zurich and Prague, as well as tours to North Africa, the Baltic States and South East Asia; Regular Visitor to the leading UK orchestras: London Symphony Orchestra, London Philharmonic, Royal Philharmonic, Scottish Chamber Orchestra, Northern Sinfonia and Philharmonia, Royal Scottish National, Royal Liverpool Philharmonic and all the BBC orchestras including 2 performances at the BBC Proms; Plays regularly in Germany with the Trio Nova Vita and enjoys performing chamber music with colleagues such as Frank Peter Zimmermann, Christian Tetzlaff, Sabine Meyer, Heinrich Schiff, Truls Mork, Marie Luise Neunecker and Boris Pergamenschikow at a variety of festivals, including Venice, Stavanger, Davos, Berlin, Bad Kissingen, Ludwigsburg, Dresden, Schleswig-Holstein, Lockenhaus and Cologne; Collaborations with actor Klaus Maria Brandauer in programme based on Dr Faustus; Concert tour of Australia for Australian Broadcasting Corporation, 1997; Season 1997-98, London Philharmonic, Philharmonia, debuts with Orchestre Philharmonique de Paris, Oslo Philharmonic with

Paavo Berglund, Royal Concertgebouw Orchestra with Christian Thielemann; February 1998 Far East tour includes 4 concerts with NHK Symphony in Japan; Has high profile in North America and has performed 6 times with LA Philharmonic, including 2 concerts at the Hollywood Bowl with Sir Simon Rattle; Also appearances with many leading US orchestras and has given recitals in many cities; During Season 1998-99, he will return to the US and make his debut with the Atlanta and Montreal Symphony Orchestras; Broadcast on national radio and TV. Recordings: Schumann and Grieg concertos with City of Birmingham SO and Sir Simon Rattle; Beethoven concertos No 1 and 2; Varied repertoire of solo recordings of 20th century Russian works, Haydn sonatas, Schumann's Kreisleriana and Bunte Blätter and recent release of Beethoven Sonatas Op 10 No 1 and Op III; Chamber music disc; Prokofiev and Shostakovich cello sonatas with Mork. Honours: Winner of competitions in Germany, Italy and Czechoslovakia as soloist and as a member of Trio Alani; 2nd Prize, 1990 Leeds International Piano Competition, playing Schumann Concerto; Gramophone Magazine Concerto Award nomination, 1997; Diapson D'Or, for sonatas with Truls Mork. Address: Harold Holt Limited, 31 Sinclair Road, London W14 0NS, England.

VOGT Matthias (Theodor), b. 5 May 1959, Rome, Italy. Opera Director; Music Researcher. m. Tina Nelsson, 1 son. Education: Dr.Phil in Musicology, with Carl Dahlhaus, RES; Studied violoncello with Atis Teichmanis, composition with Dieter Agricola. Debut: 1979. Career: Appearances at Salzburg Festival, Vienna State Opera, Biennale di Venezia, Teatro alla Scala di Milano; 1986-89, Chief Dramaturg and Head of Press Department at Richard Wagner Festival, Bayreuth; Productions include Rigoletto at Narodni Opera, Russe, Bulgaria, 1989; Alexander Knaiffel, Kentervilskoje Prividenje, Theater Forum, Moscow, Russia, 1990; Fausto Razzi, Protocollt, Rome, Italy, 1994; Organised and directed the International Gustav Mahler Congress, Hamburg, 1989; International Merschner Congress, Zittau, Saxony, 1995; International Tannhäuser Congress, Czech Republic, 1995; Lectures on Contemporary Music Theater throughout Europe and the Far East; Head, Naumann Commission for the evaluation of Saxonian theatre and music system, 1992; Co-ordinator of Cultural Affairs, Ministry for Sciences and Art, Saxony, 1993-95. Publications include: Allan Petterson Jahrbuch (editor), 1986, 1987, 1988; Das Gustav Mahler Fest Hamburg, 1989, Kassel, 1991. Contributions to: Frankfurter Allgemeine Zeitung, Neue Zeitschrift für Musik, Cambridge Opera Journal and others; Broadcasting in France, Germany, Austria. Address: Wifardstrasse 17, 01097 Dresden, Germany.

VOICULESCU Dan, b. 20 Jul 1940, Saschiz, Sighisoara, Romania. Composer; Musicologist; Professor. Education: Diplomas in Composition (S Todutza) and Piano (M Kardos), Conservatory G Dima, Cluj, Academy of Music, 1958-64; Classes with V Mortari, Venice, Italy, 1968, K Stockhausen, Cologne, Germany, 1971-72; Doctor of Musicology, 1983. Career: Professor of Counterpoint and Composition, Academy of Music, Cluj; Editor of the Lucrari de Muzicologie (Musicological Works), Cluj, 1979-91. Compositions: Sinfonia Ostinato, 1963; Visions Comiques, 1968; Music for Strings, 1971; Pieces for Orchestra, 1973; Suite from Codex Caioni for strings, 1996; Fables, Dialogues, Sonata, Croquis, Sonantes, Spirals, 3 Toccatas for Piano Solo, 5 Sonatas, Flute Solo, Sonata for Clarinet Solo; Sketches and Sonata for oboe solo; Fiorituri for Violin and Piano; Cantata for Baritone, Choir and Orchestra, 1977; Homage to Blaga for Mixed Choir; Mass for children's choir; 4 Volumes choral music for children; Book Without End, 3 volumes of piano pieces for children; The Bald Chanteuse, chamber opera, 1993. Publications: Polyphony of Baroque in the Works of J S Bach, 1975; Polyphony of the 20th Century, 1983; Bachian Fugue, 1986. Honours: Prize, Union of Romanian Composers, 1972-1978, 1995; Prize, "G Enescu" of the Romanian Academy, 1984. Membership: Union of Romanian Composers. Address: Academy of Music, Str IC Bratianu 25, 3400 Cluj, Romania.

VOIGT Deborah, b. 4 Aug 1960, Chicago, USA. Singer, Soprano. Education: Graduate of San Francisco Opera's Merola Program. Debut: Shostakovich's 14th Symphony, San Francisco Chamber Symphony. Career: Includes: European engagements include Schubert's Fierabras at Brussels, Electra in Idomeneo for Finnish National Opera, 1991 and Elvira in Ernani for Chelsea Opera Group, 1990; Other opera performances in concert include Das Rheingold with the Minnesota Orchestra, Weber's Agathe in NY, Die Walküre, La Wally and Il Piccolo Marat for Dutch Radio; Season 1990-91, with Amelia, Ballo in Maschera, as San Francisco and Strauss's Ariadne with the Boston Lyric Opera; Metropolitan Opera debut 1991, as Amelia; Season 1992-93 included Leonora in Il trovatore with the Metropolitan Opera and as Amelia in Un ballo in maschera with the Lyric Opera of Chicago; Highlights of the 1993-94 season included her debut with the Berlin Philharmonic in Zemlinsky's Lyrische Symphonie, performances of the Verdi Requiem and her debut with the Philadelphia Orchestra in a series of highly acclaimed Wagner concerts in Philadelphia and Carnegie Hall; Made her first concert appearance with Luciano Pavarotti in Lincoln Center's Pavarotti

Plus! gala, 1994; European engagements in 1995-96 included Senta in Wagner's Der fliegende Holländer with the Vienna Staatsoper and a gala concert in Tel Aviv under Daniel Oren, and as Amelia, Covent Garden (debut), 1995; Amelia at the Metropolitan, 1997. Recordings include: Strauss's Ariadne auf Naxos; La forza del destino; Strauss's Die Frau ohne Schatten. Honours include: Prize winner, Metropolitan Opera Auditions and the Pavarotti International Competition at Philadelphia; Winner, 1989 Bussetto Verdi Competition and 1990 Tchaikovsky International at Moscow; Opera Debut of the Year, New York Times, 1991. Address: c/o Herbert H Breslin, 119 West 57th Street, New York, NY 10019, USA.

VOKETAITIS Arnold, b. 11 May 1931, New Haven, Connecticut, USA. Singer (Bass). Education: Studied in New York. Debut: New York City Opera 1958, as Vanuzzi in Die schweigsame Frau. Career: Sang in New York as Britten's Theseus, Creon in Oedipus Rex and the Father in the local premiere of Douglas Moore's Carrie Nation, 1968; Guest engagements at Houston, Miami, Pittsburgh, Mexico City, San Antonio, Montreal and Vancouver; Chicago 1968-73 in Le Rossignol, Madama Butterfly, Carmen, I Due Foscari, Werther and Billy Budd; Other roles have included Don Magnifico (Metropolitan Opera National Touring Company), Don Pasquale, Dulcamara, Basilio and John Hale in The Crucible by Robert Ward, Milwaukee 1976. Recordings: Le Cid by Massenet.

VOLDEN Torstein, b. 6 Nov 1934, Trondheim, Norway. Associate Professor in Music History; Lutenist. m. 2 sons. Education: Cand Philol, University of Oslo, 1967. Career: Concerts in Norway; Programmes for Norwegian Broadcasting Company, radio and TV, as Guitarist and Lutenist; Assistant Editor of Edvard Grieg Gesamtausgabe, 1965-69; Lecturer at Teachers' College, 1969-72; Lecturer, Senior Lecturer, Rogalund Music Conservatory, 1972-94; Senior Lecturer, Stavanger College Conservatory of Music, 1994-; Currently Associate Professor. Publications: Studies in Edvard Grieg's Haugtussen Songs, 1967. Contributions to: Riemann Musiklexicon, Personenteil, I, II, 1972, 1975. Membership: Lute Society, England; Lute Society of America. Address: Stavanger College, The Music Conservatory, PO Box 2557 Ullandhaug, N-4004 Stavangr, Norway.

VOLKERT Gudrun, b. 1942, Brno, Czeckoslovakia. Singer (Soprano). Education: Studied at the Linz Conservatory. Career: Sang dramatic roles at Klagenfurt 1966-67, Kiel 1967-74, Bielefield 1974-83; Guest appearances at Brunswick 1983-88, Kassel from 1984, Hamburg 1986 and Turin 1987; Performances as Brünnhilde in Der Ring des Nibelungen at Rotterdam, 1988, Warsaw 1988-89, and Seattle 1991; Sang Cherubini's Médée at Wuppertal 1988, followed by Isolde 1989; Metropolitan Opera 1990, as Brünnhilde; Scottish Opera 1991, as Leonore in a new production of Fidelio; Other roles include Senta, Ortrud, Salome, the Marschallin, Gioconda, Tosca, Turandot and the Countess in Die Soldaten. Address: c/o Seattle Opera Association, PO Box 9248, WA 98109, USA.

VOLLE Michael, b. 1959, Germany. Singer (Baritone). Education: Studied in Stuttgart and Trossingen with Joseph Metternich and Rudolf Piernay. Career: Sang first at Mannheim, then three seasons at Bonn as Mozart's Guglielmo, Count, Don Giovanni and Papageno, Marcello in La Bohème and Rossini's Figaro; Further engagements at Hanover, Weisbaden, Dresden, Dusseldorf, Leipzig and Paris; Season 1997-98 with Covent Garden and La Scala debuts, as the Herald in Lohengrin and the Speaker in Die Zauberflöte; Other roles include Silvio, Don Fernando (Fidelio) and Ottokar in Der Freischütz; Many concert appearances. Recordings include: Britten's War Requiem (Naxos); Schubert's Mass in A-flat and Bach's Christmas Oratorio. Honours include: Winner of numerous competitions. Address: c/o Oper der Stadt Bonn, Am Boeselaerhof 1 Pf 2440, D-5300 Bonn, Germany.

VOLZ Manfred, b. 1949, Darmstadt, Germany. Singer (Bass-baritone). Career: Sang in concert from 1972; Stage debut as Mozart's Figaro at Trier, 1980; Further appearances as Melitone in La Forza del Destino and Papageno; Engaged at Aachen 1981-83, Kassel from 1985, as Alberich, Ford, Amonasro, Mozart's Count, and Faninal; Bad Gandersheim 1986, as the King in Der Kluge by Orff; Sang Alberich in Ring cycles at Rotterdam 1988 and Dortmund 1991; Concert repertoire includes Verdi's Requiem. Address: c/o Opernhaus, Kuhstrasse 12, 4600 Dortmund, Germany.

VON MAGNUS Elisabeth, b. 1965, Vienna, Austria. Singer (Mezzo-soprano). Education: Vocal studies in Munich and Salzburg. Debut: Sang Polly to the Britten version of The Beggar's Opera, at Munich. Career: Sang Sara in Abramo ed Isaaco by Myslivicek, at Ossiach, Icaro in Testoride Argonauto by Carvalho at the Théâtre des Champs-Elysées in Paris, and appeared in Mozart's Schuldigkeit des Ersten Gebotes, at Linz; Mozart's Betulia Liberata in Cologne, and Marcellina in Figaro under Harnoncourt at Amsterdam; US debut Los Angeles 1991, in the St Matthew Passion, with the LA Philharmonic under Peter

Schreier; Other concert venues include the Barbican Hall, London, the Vienna Musikverein and Konzerthaus, the Amsterdam Concertgebouw and the Alte Oper, Frankfurt; Other conductors include Adam Fischer, Ton Koopman and Claudio Abbado; Widely admired as Rossini's Rosina and in Lieder, notably at the Schubertiade, Hohenems. Address: c/o Opernhaus Zurich, Falkenstrasse 1, CH-8008 Zurich, Switzerland.

VON PECHSTAEDT Volkmar, b. 12 Aug 1968, Germany. Lawyer; Publisher; Music Editor. Education: Franz Liszt Music Academy of Weimar; Universities of Gottingen and Burgundy at Dijon, France; Doctoral dissertation in Law, 1998. Career: Co-President, Hainholz Verlag Gottingen, 1996; Founder, Head, Franz-Danzi-Archiv, Gottingen, 1996; Editor, Veröffentlichungen des Franz-Danzi-Archivs in Göttingen, 1997-. Publications: Thematisches Verzeichnis Der Kompositionen Von Franz Danzi, 1996; Franz Danzi - Briefwechsel (1785-1826), 1997. Contributions to: Neve Schubert-Ausgabe, 1998. Membership: American Musicological Society. Address: c/o Hainholz Verlag Göttingen, Hainholzweg 32, D-37085 Göttingen, Germany.

VON STADE Frederica, b. 1 June 1945, Somerville, New Jersey, USA. Mezzo-soprano. m. Peter Elkus, 1973, 2 daughters. Education: Norton Academy; Studied with Sebastian Engelberg, Paul Berl and Otto Guth, Mannes College of Music. Career: Apprenticeship, Long Wharf Theater, New Haven, Connecticut; Metropolitan Opera debut, New York, 3rd Boy, Die Zauberflöte, 1970; Cherubino, Opera House, Versailles Palace, 1973; Covent Garden debut, London, England as Rosina, 1975; Appearances with many of the world's major opera companies; Various festival engagements; Soloist with orchestras, recitalist; Member, Chamber Music Society of Lincoln Center, New York; Operatic roles include Mozart's Idamante and Dorabella; Bellini's Adalgisa; Massenet's Charlotte; Debussy's Mélisande; Strauss's Octavian; Created roles in several operas including Nina in Pasatieri's The Seagull, 1974; Tina in Argento's The Aspern Papers, 1988; Sang Massenet's Charlotte at Milan (La Scala) and the Vienna Staatsoper, 1988; Cherubino at Los Angeles, 1990, Rosina at Chicago 1989 and at the Metropolitan, 1992; Season 1992-93 as Rosina at the Met and San Francisco; Cherubino at the Met and Mélisande at Covent Garden; Sang Offenbach's Périchole at the 1996 Metropolitan Opera gala; Appearances in many operatic films; Crossover artist, Broadway musical recordings. Recordings: For Angel-EMI; CBI; Decca-London; Deutsche Grammophon; Erato; Pantheon; Philips; RCA. Honour: Honorary DMus, Yale University, 1985. Address: c/o Columbia Artists Management Inc, 165 West 57th Street, NY 10019, USA.

VONK Hans, b. 18 June 1942, Amsterdam, Netherlands. Conductor. Education: Studied at the Amsterdam Conservatory. Career: Chief Conductor of the Netherlands Ballet, 1966; Associate Conductor of the Concertgebouw Orchestra 1969-73, and Chief Conductor of the Netherlands Radio Philharmonic, 1970; US debut 1974, with the San Francisco Symphony; British debut 1974, with the Royal Philharmonic Orchestra; Chief Conductor of Netherlands Opera 1975-85; La Scala Milan debut 1980, The Rake's Progress; Music Director of the Residentie Orchestra in the Hauge, 1980-; Tours of USA 1982, Europe and England; Tour of England with the Vienna Symphony Orchestra, 1984; Guest appearances with the Munich Philharmonic, the Philadelphia Orchestra and at La Fenice, Venice; 1992 Principal Conductor and Artist Director of the Dresden Staatskapelle and the Dresden State Opera; Toured England, Europe, Russia and USA with the Staatskapelle; Repertoire includes music by Mozart, Tchaikovsky, Bruckner and Stravinsky; 1991-92 season became Chief Conductor of the WDR Köln (West Germany Radio, Cologne); Regularly conducts in the USA with the Philadelphia Orchestra and has been a Guest Conductor with the National Symphony Orchestra (Washington DC), Pittsburgh Symphony Orchestra, Boston Symphony Orchestra, St Louis Symphony, Toronto Symphony Orchestra, Detroit Symphony Orchestra. Recordings: Extensive list of recordings with Decca and EMI; Major series of recordings for EMI with the WDR Köln Orchestra (Schumann symphonies). Address: c/o Harold Holt Ltd, 31 Sinclair Road, London W14 0NS, England.

VOSS Ealynn (Elverta Lynn), b. 10 Mar 1949, Pittsburgh, Pennsylvania, USA. Opera Singer (Soprano). Education: BS, Vocal Performance major, Oberlin Conservatory of Music, 1971. Career: Operatic appearances at various US venues, and in Canada, Australia, Spain, Japan, Netherlands and Denmark; Frequent appearances in Turandot title role include Arizona Opera (1988), Opera Carolina, 1990, Miami Opera, 1990, the Australian Opera (1991, 1994) New York City Opera (1991, 1992), Arena di Verona in Japan (1991) Baltimore Opera, 1992, San Francisco, 1993, Michigan Opera, 1994, Houston Grand Opera, 1994 and Copenhagen Opera, Denmark (1996); Sang the Foreign Princess in Rusalka at the Spoleto Festival, USA, 1988, and again at Seattle Opera, 1990; Ariadne (Ariadne auf Naxos) at Victoria State Opera, Australia, 1988, and Los Angeles Music Center Opera, 1992, where she also sang Chrysothemis in Elektra, 1991, 1994, Amelia (Un Ballo in Maschera), 1991, 1994, and Senta (Der fliegende Holländer), 1995; Manitoba Opera,

Canada, 1989, as Lady Macbeth, returning as Amelia (1992); Other appearances include Elvira (Ernani) at the Oviedo Festival, Spain, 1991, Tove in Gurre-Lieder at the Concertgebouw Amsterdam, 1995, and Brünnhilde in Götterdämmerung at the Aspen Festival; Concerts include Beethoven's 9th with Santa Barbara Symphony and Verdi's Requiem with Pasadena Symphony; Debut with the Rome Opera singing Turandot in 1996. Recording: Video, Turandot with Australian Opera, 1991. Current Management: Columbia Artists Management Inc. Address: 508 South First Avenue, Elizabeth, PA 15037-1320, USA.

VOSS Friedrich, b. 12 Dec 1930, Halberstadt, Germany. Composer. m. Erna Lewann, 10 Dec 1965, 1 son. Education: Abitur, Gymnasium Halberstadt, 1949; Studied composition & piano, Hochschule für Musik, West Berlin, 1949-54. Career: Performances with: Berlin Philharmonic Orchestra, under Karajan; Radio Symphony Orchestra, Berlin, under Maazel; Japan Philharmony Orchestra, under James Loughran; in Germany, Western Europe, USA, Australia, Asia, South Africa, Latin America; Television performances in Madrid, Johannesburg, Adelaide (Australia). Compositions include: Over 70 works: 4 symphonies; 2 violin concertos; 1 cello concerto; 1 cello concertino; 4 string quartets; 1 saxophone quartet; concertino for organ, strings and timpani; 2 works for choir; Hamlet overture; Dithyrambus for Orchestra; Metamorphosis for Orchestra; ballet, Die Nachtigall und die Rose; opera, Leonce und Lena; Cantata of Psalms for soloists, choir and orchestra. Recordings: About 100 broadcasting recordings in Germany & Western Europe; CD: CTH 2069, THOROFON (4 works). Honours: 1st place, Composers' Competition, Munich Chamber Orchestra, 1955; Stuttgart Music Prize, 1960; Berlin Art Prize (Young Generation), 1961; Düsseldorf Robert Schumann Prize, 1962; Villa Massimo Award, 1964, 1977; Johann Wenzel Stamitz Prize, Mannheim, 1985. Address: Eichertstrasse 3, D-75365 Calw/Schwarzwald, Germany.

VOSS Hermann, b. 9 July 1934, Brunen, Germany. Violist. Education: Studied in Dusseldorf with Maier and in Freiburg with Vegh. Career: Former Member of Karl Munchinger's Stuttgart Chamber Orchestra in Heibronn; Co-Founded the Melos Quartet of Stuttgart, 1965; First concert tours sponsored by the Deutsches Musikelben Foundation and represented West Germany at the Jeunesse Musicales in Paris, 1966; International concert tours from 1967; Bicentenary concerts in the Beethoven Hous at Bonn, 1970, and soon toured the USSR, Eastern Europe, Africa, North and South America, the Far East and Australia; British concerts and festival appearances from 1974; Cycle of Beethoven quartets at Edinborough Festival, 1987; Wigmore Hall, St John's Smith Square and Bath Festival, 1990; Associations with Rostropovitch in the Schubert Quintet and the Cleveland Quartet in works by Spohr and Mendelssohn; Teacher at the Stuttgart Musikhochschule. Recordings: Complete quartets of Beethoven, Schubert, Mozart and Brahms; Quintets by Boccherini with Narcisco Ypes and by Mozart with Franz Beyer. Honours: (with members of the Melos Quartet) Grand Prix de Disque and Prix Caecilia from the Academie du Disque in Brussels.

VOSTRIAKOV Alexander, b. 1948, Kurgan Region, Russia. Tenor. Education: Studied in Kursk and at the Kharkov Institute of the Arts. Career: Member of the Kharkov Opera from 1973, then Dnepropetrovsk Opera Theatre until 1983; Principal of the Kiev National Opera from 1983, notably as Lohengrin and Ismaele in Nabucco; Tour of Britain in 1996 with the Perm State Opera as Lensky in Eugene Onegin. Address: c/o Sonata Ltd, 11 North Park Street, Glasgow, G20 7AA, Scotland.

VRANA Jan, b. 6 November 1940, Ostrava. Composer and Pianist. m. Miroslava Klusova-Vranova, 1 July 1961, 2 daughters, 1 son. Education: State Conservatory in Ostrava; AMU/Academy of Arts, Praha. Debut: Concert for Piano and Orchestra No 1; Janacek's Philharmonic Ostrava and Author - Solist, 1960. Career: Concerts in Praha, Warslaw, Dresden, Moscow, Baku, Paris, Bucuresti; Festivals: Prague, 1976, 1981, 1983; Festival Estival at paris, 1977; RTV France, TV USSR and Czech Television & Radio. Compositions: Ninives' Message, 1977; Concert, for performance and string orchestra, 1981; Two Studies, for oboe and performance, 1976; Tre Invenzioni, 1976. Recordings: Piano Solo - E F Burjam: American Suite, 1976; E Satie: Jack in the Box, 1989; Zd Fibich: Moods, Impressions and Reminders, 1978; V Kapral: Sonata No 2, 1981; Chamber Music - E Suchon: Sonata. Contributions to: Special Czech Musical Magazines. Memberships: Association of Czech Composers and Concert Artist; USA (Protection Union of Artist Executive; Intergram (Association of Executive Interprets). Current Management: Prazokoncert/Praha. Address: Udolni 315, 14200 Praha 4, Czech Republic.

VRIEND Jan, b. 10 Nov 1938, Benningbroek, The Netherlands. Composer. Education: Conservatory of Amsterdam, 1960-67; Paris, 1967-68; GRM/ORTF and Schola Cantorum; Institute of Sonology, Utrecht, 1965-66; Self taught in mathematics. Career: Founder and first conductor of ASKO-Amsterdam, 1964; From 1961-70 Conductor of choirs and freelance conductor of orchestras and ensembles; Lectured on many topics concerning composition, the use of mathematics in composition and philosophy of music; Conductor of the New Stroud Orchestra, 1989-94. Compositions include: Paroesie for 10 Instruments, 1963-67; Bau for Chamber Orchestra, 1969-70; Elements of Logic for Large Wind Orchestra, 1972; Heterostase for Flute, Bass Clarinet and Piano, 1980-81; Vectorial for 6 Wind Instruments and Piano, 1983-87; Jets d'Orgue, I, II and III, 1984-91; Hallelujah I for Bass Clarinet and Large Orchestra, 1986-90; Wu Li for Cello, 1986; Hallelujah II for Large Ensemble, 1987-88; 3 Songs for Soprano and Orchestra (Paul Celan), 1991; Symbiosis for Flute, Bass Clarinet, Trombone, Piano and String Quintet, 1993. Publications: Essays on the music of Xenakis and Varèse and on musical life in Holland, published in Netherlands and France, 1977-88. Honours: 1966 Schnittger Organ Prize for Herst; Prize for Composition, Amsterdam Conservatory, 1967; First Prize, International Gaudeamus Festival for Huantan, 1969. Address: Benwell Coach House, Park Lane, South Woodchester, GL5 5HW, Scotland.

VRONSKY Petr, b. 4 Mar 1946, Prague, Czech Republic. Conductor. 1 daughter. Education: Violin, Conservatoire Plzen, Pilsen, 1967; Conducting, Academy of Music Arts, Prague, 1972. Debut: Prague, 1971. Career: Opera, Pilsen, 1971; Opera, Usti Nad Labem, Aussig, 1974; State Philharmonic Orchestra, Brno, 1979-91; Senior Lecturer, Prague, 1990; Kammeroper Wien, 1991; Dance Theatre, Haag, 1995; Guest Conductor, Czech Philharmonic Orchestra, Prague, Symphony Orchestra, Prague, National Theatre, Prague, State Opera, Prague, Metropolitan Orchestra, Tokyo, Radio Symphony Orchestra, Munchen, Philharmonic Orchestra, Dortmund. Recordings: Several. Honours: Conducting Competition Prizes, Olomouc, 1970, Besancon, 1971, Berlin, 1973. Membership: Association of Music Scientists and Musicians, Prague. Hobbies: Viniculture; Cooking. Address: Majerskeho 2049, PO Box 124, 14900 Prague 4, Czech Republic.

VROOMAN Richard van, b. 29 July 1936, Kansas City, Missouri, USA. Singer (Tenor). Education: Studied at the Kansas City Conservatorium and with Max Lorenz at the Salzburg Mozarteum. Debut: Bregenz Festival 1962, as Lorenzo in Fra Diavalo. Career: Many appearances in West Germany, Austria and Switzerland, notably at the Zurich Opera 1964-78; Guest engagements at Salzburg 1964-65, Aix-en-Provence, with the Deutsche Oper am Rhein and the Paris Opera and in Lisbon, Geneva, Frankfurt, Hamburg, Rome, Bordeaux and Marseille; Glyndebourne Festival 1968, as Belmonte in Die Entführung; Best known in operas by Mozart, Rossini and Donizetti and in the Baroque repertoire; Many concert appearances. Recordings: Wozzeck (CBS); Mozart Davidde Penitente and Handel Acis and Galatea (Schwann); Doktor und Apotheker by Dittersdorf; Cimarosa Requiem (Philips); Haydn Salve Regina (EMI). Address: c/o Opernhaus Zurich, Falkenstrass 1, CH-8008 Zurich, Switzerland.

VYZINTAS Algirdas, b. 30 July 1929, Vyzuonos, Utena Region, Lithuania. Conductor; Pedagogue. m. Lygija Vyzintiene, 5 Sept 1955, 2 sons. Education: Graduated, Department of Musical Instruments, Vilnius Conservatoire; Doctorate, 1983. Debut: Chorus Competition, 1955. Career: Conductor, all song festivals, Lithuania, 1960-; Participant, over 1000 concerts, Lithuania and abroad; Professor, Vilnius Conservatoire, 1983-; Director, Lithuanian Postgraduate Studies, Cultural Institute; Head, Department of Ethnic Culture; Head of National Musical Instruments Department of Lithuanian Academy of Music. Compositions: Published and recorded, Adaptions of Folklore Music for instrumental ensembles and orchestra. Recordings: For ITV and radio programmes. Publications: Manual for Lithuanian national instruments Birbynes, a type of clarinet, 1962; Research book about Skuduciai, 1975; Research book about Jonas Svedas, composer and founder of State Song and Dance Ensemble, 1979; Doctoral thesis about archaic Lithuanian ensembles of traditional instruments Skuduciai (type of Pan Flute) and Trumpets, their ethnogenesis, 1983; Research book, Traditional Lithuanian Instrumental Ensembles - Historical - Structural - Functional Problems, 1991. Contributions to: 200 articles in magazines. Address: Zirmunu 34-26, 2051 Vilnius, Lithuania.

W

WAAGE Lars, b. 1948, Århus, Denmark. Singer (Bass-baritone). Education: Studied at the Århus Conservatory. Career: Sang with the Lubeck Opera, 1975-80, as King Henry in Lohengrin and Wagner's Gurnemanz; Jyske Opera at Århus from 1980, notably as Wotan and Gunther in The Ring; Guest appearances as Sharpless, Iago, Pizarro, Mephistopheles and Kurwenal; Concert singer in France, Germany and Italy. Address: Århus Opera, Thomas Jensens Allee, DK-8000 Århus, Denmark.

WÄCHTER Erich, b. 3 Jul 1945, Bielefeld, Germany. Conductor. Education: Hochschule for Musik, Berlin. Career: Repetiteur at Kaiserslautern, 1969-71, Kapellmeister der Opera, 1971-74; Kapellmeister at the Saarbrucken State Opera, 1974-77; Musical Director of the Saarbrucken City Choir; Musical Assistant, Bayreuth, 1975 (and conducted Der fliegende Holländer and Die Zauberflöte at Tbilisi); Conductor at the Baden State Opera in Karlsruhe, 1977-85; Guest Conductor, Wiesbaden (with Der Rosenkavalier, Carmen and La Forza del Destino); Lecturer in Music at State Music Academy, Karlsruhe, 1980; Kappellmeister at Darmstadt, 1985-87 and National Theatre at Mannheim, 1987-90; General Music Director, Lübeck Opera, 1987-; Also engaged by the Stuttgart Opera, Vienna Volksoper, Oslo, Munich State Opera, Hamburg, Leipzig, Dresden, Stockholm and Antwerp, and Zurich Opera; Leiter des Hochschulorchesters and Leiter der Dirigierabteilung Musikhochschule Lübeck, 1993.

WADDINGTON Henry, b. 1968, Kent, England. Singer (Bass). Education: Royal Northern College of Music, with Barbara Robotham. Debut: As Bottom in A Midsummer Night's Dream, at the RNCM. Career: Glyndebourne Touring Opera from 1992, in The Rake's Progress, and in the premiere of Birtwistle's The Second Mrs Kong (1994); Appearances in Le Comte Ory and Tchaikovsky's The Enchantress for New Sussex Opera, as Colline for GTO, Farlaf in Ruslan and Ludmilla for Dorset Opera, as Falstaff for Opera North and Fiorello in Il Barbiere di Siviglia for Royal Opera House; Count Lamoral in Arabella and Mozart's Antonio at the Glyndebourne Festival, 1996-97; Concerts include: Mozart's Requiem with the English CO at the Barbican Hall, Sir John in Love for British Youth Opera, the Verdi Requiem, and The Rake's Progress with the BBC SO at the Festival Hall (1997). Address: Ingpen & Williams Ltd, 26 Wadham Road, London SW15 2LR, England.

WADE Simon, b. 28 Aug 1958, Devonport, Tasmania. Composer. Education: BA (Mus), Tasmanian Conservatory, 1979; Master of Creative Arts, Film and Communications Diplomas, 1995. Career: Tasmanian Conservatory, 1980; University of Sydney, 1988; Rare Birds Productions Co, 1993; Commissions from Tasmanian Opera Co, New England String Quartet, and others. Compositions include: Saxophone Quartet, 1984; Extracts for saxophone and piano, 1984; Songs from Shakespeare, for chorus and orchestra, 1984; Introduction to the String Quartet, 1985; The Other Meaning, song cycle for tenor and piano, 1985; Sequences for clarinet and piano, 1985; The Watching Clock, chamber opera, 1992; The Herald Angel, for alto trombone and piano, 1993; Computer generated music for film and theatre, 1993-. Address: c/o APRA, 1A Eden Street, Crows Nest, NSW 2065, Australia.

WADSWORTH Stephen, b. 3 Apr 1953, Mount Kisco, New York, USA. Stage Director; Translator; Librettist. Career: Artistic Director and Stage Director of the Skylight Opera in Milwaukee; Productions of Monteverdi's three principal operas, from 1982; Wrote libretto for Bernstein's A Quiet Place 1983 and has directed productions of it at La Scala, Milan and in Vienna; For Seattle Opera has directed Jenufa, Fliegende Holländer, and Gluck's Orphée; Handel's Xerxes at Milwaukee 1985 and Partenope at Omaha, 1988; Fidelio and La Clemenza di Tito for Scottish Opera, 1991, Die Entführung at San Francisco 1990, other productions include Le nozze di Figaro and Alcina (St Louis) and Simon Boccanegra (Netherlands Opera); Head of the Opera Program at the Manhattan School of Music, 1991; Translations of Monteverdi's Orfeo and Handel's Xerxes, Alcina and Partenope; Covent Garden debut 1992, Handel's Alcina; Staging of Xerxes seen at Santa Fe, Los Angeles and Boston (1996). Address: c/o Boston Lyric Opera, 114 State Street, Boston, MA 02109, USA

WAGENFUHRER Roland, b. 1964, Hof/Saale, Germany. Singer (Tenor). Education: Studied at the Nuremberg Conservatory, from 1982. Career: Member of the Bavarian State Opera Studio 1987-89, as Ferrando and as Chlestakov in Der Revisor; Landestheater Coburg 1989-95, as Hans in The Bartered Bride, Lensky, Don José and Wagner's Erik; Dresden Semper Oper from 1995, as Max, Laca (Jenufa), Desportes in Zimmermann's Soldaten and Dionysos in The Bassarids by Henze; Guest appearances as Florestan at the Bregenz Festival (1995-96), Tamino in Cologne, Walther von Stolzing in Lubeck and Erik at the Vienna Staatsoper; Season 1997-98 as Florestan at the Komische Oper Berlin and Hoffmann at Cologne; Engagements for 1998 in Die verkaufte Braut in Munich, Fliegender Holländer at the Bayreuth Festival and Freischütz/Max in Vienna; Forthcoming engagements in Bayreuth in Fliegende Holländer and Willy Decker in Lohengrin. Address: c/o Haydn Rawstron, 36 Station Road, London SE20 7BQ, England.

WAGNER James, b. 1949, New Orleans, Louisiana, USA. Singer (Tenor). Education: Studied at Rochester University and in Vienna. Career: Sang at the Frankfurt Opera, 1975-76, Kassel, 1976-80, New York City Opera, 1981-82, Vienna Volksoper, 1983-84; Theater am Gärtnerplatz, Munich, 1985-88, and elsewhere, as Almaviva, Xerxes, Belmonte, Giasone in Cherubini's Médée, Florestan, Edgardo, and Dionysos in Henze's Bassarids; Guest appearances in Berne, Bologne (1987), Venice (1990) and Greece. Recordings include: Amadis de Gaule by J C Bach (Hanssler). Address: Theater am Gärtnerplatz, Gärtnerplatz 3, W-8000 Munich 5, Germany.

WAGNER Sieglinde, b. 21 Apr 1921, Linz, Austria. Mezzo-Soprano. Education: Studied at the Linz Conservatory and with Luise Willer and Carl Hartmann in Munich. Debut: Linz in 1942 as Erda in Das Rheingold. Career: Sang at the Vienna Volksoper, 1947-52, and in Berlin from 1952; Appearances in Milan, Rome, Amsterdam, Madrid and Barcelona; Sang at Salzburg Festival from 1956, notably as Leda in the 1952 premiere of Die Liebe der Danae by Strauss, and in the premieres of Julietta by Erbse and Das Bergwerk zu Falun by Wagner-Régeny; Also sang at Salzburg in Romeo und Julia by Blacher, Elektra, Die Zauberflöte, Der Rosenkavalier and Le nozze di Figaro; Appeared at Bayreuth Festival from 1962, singing Mary in Der fliegende Holländer in 1971; Sang at the Deutsche Oper Berlin until 1986; Extensive concert repertoire which includes sacred music by Bach. Recordings: Christmas Oratorio by Bach; Die Zauberflöte; Der fliegende Holländer; Die Fledermaus; Solo in Beethoven's Missa Solemnis.

WAGNER Wolfgang, b. 30 Aug 1919, Bayreuth, Germany. Opera Director. m (1) Ellen Drexel, 11 Apr 1943, 1 son, 1 daughter, (2) Gudrun Armann, 1 daughter. Career: Stage Manager, Bayreuth Festival, 1940; Assistant, Preussischer Staatsoper, Berlin, 1940-44; Director, annual Wagner operatic festival, 1951-; Numerous guest appearances and international tours; Productions include, Andreasnacht, Berlin, 1944; Das Rheingold, Naples, 1952; Die Walküre, Naples, 1952 and 1953, Barcelona 1955, Venice 1957, Palermo 1962, Osaka 1967; Lohengrin, Bayreuth, 1953 and 1967; Siegfried, Naples 1953, Brussels 1954, Venice 1957, Bologna 1957; Der fliegende Holländer, Bayreuth, 1955; Dresden 1988; Tristan und Isolde, Barcelona 1955, Bayreuth 1957, Venice 1958, Palermo 1960, Osaka 1967, Milan 1978; Parsifal, Barcelona 1955, Bayreuth 1975, 1989; Don Giovanni, Brunswick, 1955; Die Meistersinger von Nuremburg, Rome 1956, Bayreuth 1968 and 1981, Dresden 1985, Der Ring des Nibelungen, Venice 1957, Bayreuth 1960 and 1970; Götterdämmerung, Venice, 1957, Tannhäuser, Bayreuth, 1985. Address: PO Box 100262 Bayreuther Festspiele, 8580 Bayreuth 1, Germany.

WAHLGREN Per-Arne, b. 1953, Sweden. Singer (Baritone). Education: Studied at the opera school of the Royal Opera Stockholm. Debut: Norrland Opera 1978, as Don Giovanni. Career: Sang at the Stora Teater Gothenburg from 1979 as Germont and Belcore; Guest appearances at the Theater an der Wien, Vienna 1980, in the premiere of Jesu Hochzeit by Gottfried von Einem; Royal Opera Stockholm from 1981, as Mozart's Count and Guglielmo, Marcello, Sharpless and Wolfram; Humbert Humbert in the premiere of Rodion Shchedrin's Lolita under the direction of M Rostropovitch, 1994; Further engagements at Nice in Tannhäuser and The Queen of Spades, at Lausanne in Dido and Aeneas and in Madrid in Mendelssohn's Elijah; Stockholm 1986 in the premiere of Christina by Hans Gefors; Drottningholm Court Theatre 1991, as Orestes in a revival of Electra by J C F Haeffner; Sang Frank in Korngold's Die tote Stadt, Stockholm, 1995. Concert repertory includes Bach's Passions, Christmas Oratorio and Cantatas, the Brahms Requiem, Messiah, Utrecht Te Deum by Handel, the Fauré Requiem, Lieder eines fahrenden Gesellen and Carmina Burana. Recordings include: Dido and Aeneas. Address: Kungliga Teatern PO Box 16094, S-10322 Stockholm, Sweden.

WAKASUGI Hiroshi, b. 31 May 1935, Tokyo, Japan. Conductor. Education: Studied conducting with Hideo Sati and Nobori Kaneko. Career: Conducted the Kyoto Symphony Orchestra from 1975; Regular concerts with the Berlin Philharmonic, Vienna Symphony, Munich Philharmonic, Toronto Symphony, Montreal Symphony, Pittsburgh Symphony, NHK Symphony, Bavarian Radio Symphony and the Frankfurt Museum Society; Chief Conductor of the Cologne Radio Symphony 1977-83; US debut 1981, with the Boston Symphony Orchestra; Music Director of the Deutsche Oper am Rhein Dusseldorf, 1981-86; Principal Guest Conductor of the Dresden State Opera and the Dresden Staatskapelle, 1982-1991; Chief Conductor, Tokyo Metropolitan Orchestra; Chief Conductor and Artistic Director of the Tonhalle Orchestra Zurich, from 1987, 1987-91; 1986-1995 Music Director and 1987-1995 Principal Conductor of Tokyo Metropolitan Symphony Orchestra; from spring 1995 Permanent Conductor of NHK Symphony Orchestra; Music Director, 1988-95 and Principal Conductor, 1987-95, of the Tokyo Metropolitan Symphony Orchestra; Has conducted first Japanese performances of Schoenberg's Gurrelieder and Pelléas und Mélisande, Wagner's Parsifal, Der fliegende Holländer, Rheingold and Siegfried, Strauss's Capriccio and Ariadne auf Naxos, and many contemporary works. Honours include: Suntory Prize, 1987. Address: c/o Astrid Schoerke, Kunstler Secretariat, Mönckebergallee 41, D-3000 Hannover, Germany.

WAKEFIELD John, b. 21 Jun 1936, Yorkshire, England. Professor of Singing. m. Rilla Welborn, 2 s, 1 d. Education: Royal Academy of Music, FRAM; Honorary FTCL. Debut: Welsh National Opera, 1960. Career: Macduff, Glyndebourne, 1964; Rinuccio at Royal Opera House, 1965; Other roles included: Fenton, Tamino, Paris, Don Ottavio, Ferrando, Belmonte, Idamante, Rodolfo, Orfeo, Ormindo, Essex and Saul. Recordings: La Traviata, Ormindo; The Mikado; Messiah. Honours: Kathleen Ferrier Scholarship, 1958; Tenor Prize, S'hertogenbusch, 1959. Memberships: Equity; NATFHE. Hobbies: Golf; Ball Games; Sport. Address: 12 Avenue Gardens, Teddington, Middlesex, TW11 0BH, England.

WALACINSKI Adam, b. 18 Sept 1928, Krakow, Poland. Composer. Education: Studied at the Krakow Conservatory, 1947-52; Further study with Boguslaw Schaffer. Career: Violinist in the Krakow Radio Orchestra, 1948-56; Teacher at the Krakow Conservatory, 1972; Member of the Grupa Krakowska, for promotion of the New Music. Compositions include: Alfa for orchestra, 1958; String Quartet, 1959; Intrada for 7 players, 1962; Canto Triodore for flute, violin and vibraphone, 1962; Horizons for chamber orchestra, 1962; A Lyric Before Falling Asleep for soprano, flute and 2 pianos, 1963; Concerto de Camera for violin and strings, 1964; Fogli volanti for string trio, 1985; Canzona for cello, piano and tape, 1966; Epigrams for chamber ensemble, 1967; Refrains and Reflections for orchestra, 1969; Notturno 70 for 24 strings, 3 flutes and percussion; Torso for orchestra, 1971; Divertimento interrotto for 13 players, 1974; Mirophonies for soprano and ensemble, 1974; Ballada for flute and piano, 1986; Little Autumn Music for flute and string trio, 1986; Drama e Burla for orchestra, 1988. Address: c/o ZAIKS, 2 rue Hipoteczna, 00 092 Warsaw, Poland.

WALBANK Jeremy (Simon), b. 10 Jan 1958, Southport, England. Organist; Composer; Writer; Producer. Education: St Mary's College, Liverpool; Bangor University; Durham University; Studied privately in Paris with Jean Langlais. Career: Performances in England including Edinburgh and City of London Festivals, Queen Elizabeth Hall; France, Germany, Malta, Russia, Menorca, Romania; TV productions for BBC, ITV, Xandir Malta, Soviet TV, has also given premiere of works by Langlais, Camilleri, McGregor, Tjeknavorian; Director of Music, St Katharine Cree Church, London; Director, Abingdon Little Arts Festival; Guest Conductor, Latvian State Opera; Visiting Teacher at Riga Conservatoire and Royal University of Malta. Compositions: Pulcinella Fantasy (organ); Seven Songs On Death; Party (chamber ensemble); Readings of Poetry; Legacy of Faritius, 1987; Tromb, 1987; Symphonic Poems, 1990; Gradualia, 1990; Recorder Music, 1991. Recordings: Pictures at An Exhibition on Phoenix Label; Pachelbel Fugues and Praetorius-Terpsichore, both on Linn Labels. Current Management: Choveaux Management, Artemis Arts Development and Tivoli Festival. Address: 35 East Saint Helen's Street, Abingdon, Oxon OX14 5EE, England.

WALDHANS Jiri, b. 17 Apr 1923, Brno, Czechoslovakia. Conductor. Education: Studied at the Brno Conservatory until 1948 and with Igor Markevitch in Salzburg. Career: Repetiteur and Chorus Master at the Ostrava Opera, 1949-51; Conducted the Brno State Philharmonic, 1951-54, Ostrava Symphony Orchestra 1955-62; Returned to the Brno State 1962-80; Janacek Academy at Brno from 1980; Guest Conductor in Czechoslovakia and elsewhere in Europe. Recordings include: Dvorak Cello Concerto with the Czech Philharmonic (Supraphon); 15 Pages after Durer's Apocolypse by Lubos Fiser; Janacek's Lachian Dances, Jealousy (Jenufa) Overture, The Fiddler's Child and The Ballad of Blanik Hill; Suites from Martinu's Ballets Istar and Spalicek; Cello Concertos by Milhaud, Beethoven's Piano Arrangement of his Violin Concerto and early Concerto in E flat 1784, with Felicia Blumenthal. Address: Slezske divadlo, Marketing Manager, Ales Waldhans, Horni Namesti 13, 749 69 Opava, Czech Republic.

WALKER David, b. 18 July 1934, Calcutta, India. Stage Designer. Education: Studied at the Central School of Arts and Crafts, London, 1952-56. Career: Designs for Joan Littlewood's Theatre from 1955; Opera designs for Werther and La Bohéme at Glyndebourne, 1966-67; Royal Opera House designs (some in collabaoration with producer John Copley), 1965-82, Suor Angelica, Cosi fan tutte, Don Giovanni and Semele; Costumes for

Carmen at the Metropolitan, 1972; Manon Lescaut at Palermao and Lucia di Lammermoor at La Fenice, Venice; Production designs for La Traviata and Der Rosenkavalier at English National Opera, 1973, 1975; Sets and costumes for Donizetti's Roberto Devereux at the Teatro dell'Opera Rome, 1988; Collaborated with John Conkin on designs for Der Rosenkavalier at Santa Fe, 1989; ENO designs for La Traviata seen at Philadelphia, 1992.

WALKER Diana, b. 1958, Salt Lake City, Utah, USA. Singer (Soprano). Career: Has sung at the New York City Opera, 1983-as Leila (Les Pêcheurs de Perles), Gilda, Adele, Micaela, Barbara (Argento's Casanova) and Ninetta (The Love of Three Oranges); Seattle Opera in the title roles of The Ballad of Baby Doe and Lucia di Lammermoor; Utah Opera as the Queen of Night; European debut as Blondchen in Die Entführung with Nice Opera; Modern repertory includes Laetitia in The Old Maid and the Thief with St Louis Opera, Abigail in The Crucible by Robert Ward and Ariel in Lee Hoiby's The Tempest (Kansas City); Performances of the ballet Alice, after Del Tredici's In Memory of a Summer Day, in Toronto, Chicago, Washington DC, Florida, California, New York (Metropolitan Opera) and London; Sang Lakmé for Chicago Opera Theatre, 1990; Premieres of Victoria Bond's Travels in Virginia, 1995; Concert repertory includes, Messiah, Handel's Joshua and Rinaldo (at Kennedy Center) and Mahler's 4th Symphony; Further roles include Donizetti's Norina, Adina and Marie; Gluck's Iphigénie; Mozart's Mme Silberklang, Blondchen and Susanna; Strauss's Sophie and Zerbinetta; Verdi's Nannetta and Ophelia in Hamlet by Thomas; Sang Carlotta/Mme Firmin in The Phantom of the Opera, Canadian National Tour, 1991-94; Guest artist with Miami Chamber Symphony, Brooklyn Symphony, New York, Utah Symphony, Kansas City Philharmonic, Roanoke, Virginia Symphony, Aspen Symphony; Special Guest in Soap Opera, Another World, as Opera Singer; Starring in: Look at Me, a National Endowment of the Arts Grant Film, 1994; Lecture concerts in USA and Canada at universities and youth leadership conventions. Recordings: Solo CD album with orchestra and chorus. Honours: 2nd Place, International American Music Competition, Carnegie Hall; Alumnus of the Year, University of Missouri, Kansas City. Current Management/Address: c/o Anthony George Management, 250 W 77th Street, No 304, New York City, NY 10024, USA.

WALKER George (Theophilus), b. 27 June 1922, Washington DC, USA. Composer; Pianist. m. Helen Siemens, 2 sons. Education: MusB, Oberlin College, 1941; Artist Diploma, Curtis Institute of Music, 1945; DMA, University of Rochester, 1957. Debut: Town Hall, New York, 1945. Career: Numerous concerts as pianist managed by Columbia Artists and National Concert Artists; Professor Emeritus, Rutgers University, 1992. Compositions include: 4 piano sonatas; Concertos for cello, trombone, violin, piano; 2 String Quartets; 2 sonatas, violin and piano; Address for Orchestra; 2 Sinfonias for Orchestra; Serenata for Chamber Orchestra; Sonata, cello and piano; Music for Brass; Mass for Chorus and Orchestra; 18 Songs for Voice and Piano, 1941-94; Arrangemnents of Spirituals for voice and piano, 1947-62; Orpheus for Chamber Orchestra, 1994; Lilacs for voice and orchestra, 1995; Pageant and Proclamation for orchestra, 1997. Recordings: Cantata for Soprano, Tenor Boys Choir and Chamber Orchestra; Concertos, Piano and Orchestra, Trombone and Orchestra; Lyric for Strings; 4 Piano Sonatas; Poem for Soprano and Chamber Ensemble; Variations for Orchestra; Antifonys for Chamber Orchestra; George Walker in Recital, 1994; George Walker, A Portrait, 1994; George Walker (Chamber Works), 1995; George Walker plays Bach, Schumann, Chopin and Poulenc, 1997; The Music of George Walker, 1997; George Walker: Works for Chamber Orchestra. Publications: Make Room for Black Classical Music, New York Times, 1992; The Lot of the Black Composer, 1992; Recordings of Solo Piano Works: George Walker in Recital, George Walker Plays Bach, Schumann, Chopin and Poulenc. Memberships: Honorary DFA, Lafayette College, 1981, Montclair State University, 1997, Bloomfield College, 1997; Pulitzer Prize in Music, 1996; Honorary Doctor of Music, Oberlin College, 1983, Curtis Institute of Music, 1997. Hobbies: Tennis; Audio. Address: 323 Grove Street, Montclair, NJ 07042, USA.

WALKER Helen, b. 1952, Tunbridge Wells, England. Singer (Soprano). Education: Guildhall School, London, with Noelle Barker. Career: Sang Verdi's Giovanna d'Arco, 1977; Glyndebourne Festival as Fiordiligi, Monterverdi's Poppea 1984, and Helena in A Midsummer Night's Dream; Glyndbourne Touring Opera as Pamina, Ann Trulove in The Rake's Progress, and Ninetta in L'Amore des Trois Oranges; Opera North as Pamina, and Fenena in Nabucco; Helena at Aldeburgh and Covent Garden; Handel roles include Polissena in Radamisto (Handel Opera Society) and Teseo, for the English Bach Festival at Sadler's Wells Theatre; Foreign engagements in Hong Kong and Nancy (with Glyndebourne Touring Opera), Montpellier and La Fenice, Venice (as Anne Trulove); Sang a Maid in Elektra at Covent Garden, 1990; Freia, Sieglinde and Gutrune in the City of Birmingham Touring Opera version of the Ring; Premiered Leaving by Turnage, Symphony Hall and Radio 3, 1992. Recordings: Dido and Aeneas (1st Witch), Philips. Honours include: Winner, Susan Longfield Competition, 1977; Ricordi Prize for Opera; Mozart Memorial Prize, 1978; South East Arts Young Musicians Platform; Glyndebourne Touring Award; Christie Award, Glyndebourne.

WALKER Jayne, b. 16 May 1958, Guiseley, Yorkshire, England. Violinist. Education: Studied with Louis Schiller followed by Herbert Whone; Studied at Royal Northern College of Music under Clifford Knowles. Debut: Recital at the Purcell Room, London Southbank, 1984. Career: Played with Royal Liverpool Philharmonic, English Northern Philharmonia, Northern Sinfonia, English Sinfonia, Glyndebourne Opera, Primavera Chamber Group, Leeds Piano Trio, London Festival Orchestra, London Mozart Players, English National Opera, London String Soloists. Recordings: Schubert Cycle with Sir Charles Groves; Mendelssohn String Symphonies; English String Music with English Sinfonia. Honour: Edward Heaton Prize for Violin, 1980. Hobbies: Reading; Photography; Walking. Address: 74 Kimbolton Crescent, Stevenage, Hertfordshire SG2 8RL, England.

WALKER John (Edward), b. 19 Aug 1933, Bushnell, Indiana. Singer (Tenor). Education: Studied at the Universities of Denver, Urbana and Bloomington. Debut: Berne 1963, as Tamino. Career: Appearances in Europe at Zurich, Cologne, Frankfurt, Stuttgart and Brussels; US engagements at San Francisco, Dallas, Santa Fe, Chicago, Seattle, San Diego, Omaha and Portland; Other roles have included Mozart's Belmonte, Don Ottavio and Ferrando, Nadir, Almaviva, Alfredo, Fenton, Ernesto, Nemorino, Werther, Lensky and Britten's Lysander; Has also sung Jenik in The Bartered Bride, Nureddin in the Barber of Bagdad, Albert Herring, and David in Die Meistersinger; Many concert and oratorio engagements. Address: c/o Staatsoper Stuttgart, Oberer Schlossgarten 6, 7000 Stuttgart 1, Germany.

WALKER Nina, b. 30 May 1926, Hyde, Cheshire, England. Pianist; Opera Coach; Chorus Master. m. Francis Barnes, 2 sons, 1 daughter. Education: Pianoforte, Composition, Royal Manchester College of Music, 1945-50; Studied with Alfred Cortot 1953, Lausanne, Bridget Wild, 1965. Career: Accompanist and Solo Pianist, Arts Council Recitals, Germany, Italy, Sweden, Greece; Solo Pianist, Marquis de Cuevas Ballet, Paris, 1957; Accompanist, Caballé, La Scala, Milan, Spain, Japan, Germany, Royal Opera House, 1975-90; Master Classes, Pavarotti, ect; Chorus Master, Royal Choral Society 1970-75, Huddersfield Choral Society 1980-83; Musical Staff, Royal Opera House, 1974-83; Chorus Master 1981-83; Founder, Director, Numbus Records, 1973. Recordings: Nimbus Records, Schubert German Song Cycles, Argentinian Songs, Raul Gimenez; Rossini, Soirees Musicales, June Anderson, Complete Schubert Piano Duets, Adrian Farmer, Fauré Duparc Songs, Shura Gehrman, Mussorgsky (Songs and Dances of Death) Songs I Love, Jenny Drivala, Soprano (Somm Records). Honours: Open Scholarship, RMCM, 1946; Hilary Haworth Memorial Prize, 1949; Edward Hecht Prize, 1949. Hobbies: Motoring; Reading. Address: 12 Ainsdale Road, Ealing, London W5 1JX, England.

WALKER Penelope, b. 12 October 1956, Manchester, England. Singer, Concert and Opera. m. Phillip Joll, 2 children. Education: GSMD, 1974-78 (AGSM and advanced studies); National Opera Studio, 1979-80. Debut: Royal Albert Hall, 1976; Prom Debut, Grimgerde in Die Walküre with Gwyneth Jones and the National Youth Orchestra, 1989; Canada with Regina Symphony Orchestra, 1993, singing Wesendonck Lieder, and Chausson's Poème de l'amour et de la mer; Royal Opera House, Covent Garden, Die Walküre, 1994. Career: BBCTV and Radio, including Elgar documentary with Simon Rattle and CBSO Operatic debut in Paris, 1982 with Opéra-Comique; London debut at Camden Festival, Maria Tudor (Pacini) Opera Rara; ENO, Siegrune (Die Walküre), Kate Pinkerton (Madame Butterfly) and Madame Sosostris (Midsummer Marriage); Opera North, Madame Sosostris; Welsh National Opera, Fricka (Das Rheingold and Die Walküre), Anna in The Trojans, Mdme Larina, Onegin, Tornrak-Main Protagonist in Metcalfe Opera; Geneviève, Pelléas; Zurich Opera, 1991, 3rd Lady; Hedwig (William Tell); Mozart Requiem; Grimgerde (Die Walküre), Chatelêt Ring, 1994; Debut at La Scala, 1994; Rossweisse, Covent Garden, 1994; Sang Handel's Riccardo Primo at the 1996 Göttingen Festival. Recordings: London Opera, Hyppolyta (Midsummer Night's Dream), Virgin, Hickox; Schwertleite (Die Walküre) C Dohnanyi, Cleveland Symphony, Decca; Flosshilde and Fricka, Das Rheingold, Operavox Animated Opera, TV; Geneviève, (Pelléas & Mélisande) WNO Video, Peter Stein production, Pierre Boulez; New Israeli Opera, Mamma Lucia (Cavalleria Rusticana). Current Management, Robert Gilder and Company. Address: Llwyni Cottage, Llandewi Rhydderch, Abergavenny, Gwent NP7 9TP, Wales.

WALKER Robert (Ernest), b. 18 Mar 1946, Northampton, England. Composer. Education: Chorister at St Matthew's Church, Northampton; Choral Scholar, Organ Scholar, at Jesus College, Cambridge. Career: Organist and Schoolmaster in Lincolnshire; Freelance Composer from 1975; Featured Composer at 1982 Greenwich Festival; Living composer, Eastern Orchestral Board 1990-91; Works performed by Royal Philharmonic Orchestra at Chichester and Exeter Festivals; Regular broadcasts on BBC Radio 3. Compositions: Orchestral, Pavan for violin and strings 1975, At Bignor Hill 1979, Chamber Symphony No 1 1981, Variations on a Theme of Elgar 1982, Charms and Exultations of Trumpets 1985, Symphony No 1 1987; Vocal, The Sun on the Celandines 1973, Psalm 150 1974, Requiem 1976, The Norwich Service 1977, Canticle of the Rose 1980, The Sun Used to Shine for tenor, harp ans strings 1983, Magnificat and Nunc Dimittis in D 1985, Missa Brevis 1985, Singer by the Yellow River for soprano, flute and harp 1985, Five Summer Madrigals 1985, Jubilate 1987, English Parody Mass for choir and organ 1988; Instrumental, String Quartet No 1 1982, Five Capriccios 1 and 2 1982-85, Piano Quintet 1984, Passacaglia for 2 pianos, Serenade for flute, harp, violin and cello, Journey into Light, A Choral Symphony 1992 and Music for BBC1, BBC2 and Channel 4. Address: c/o PO Box 46, UBVD 80571, Bali, Indonesia.

WALKER Sandra, b. 1 Oct 1948, Richmond, Virginia, USA. Singer (Mezzo-soprano). Education: Studied at the University of North Carolina and the Manhattan School of Music, New York. Debut: San Francisco 1972, as Flosshilde in Das Rheingold. Career: Sang in opera at Philadelphia, Chicago and the New York City Opera; European engagements at Gelsenkirchen, 1985 and Wiesbaden, 1987; Sang the Nurse in Ariane at Barbe Bleue at Amsterdam, 1989; San Francisco Opeera 1989 and 1992, as Bradamante in Vivaldi's Orlando Furioso and Hedwige in Guillaume Tell; Lyric Opera Chicago 1990-91, as Olga in Eugene Onegin and Marta in Mefistofele; Other roles include Carmen, Suzuki, Lola, the Marquise in La Fille du Regiment and Frugola in Il Tabarro. Address: c/o San Francisco Opera, War Memorial Opera House, San Francisco, CA 94102, USA.

WALKER Sarah, b. 11 Mar 1943, Cheltenham, England. Mezzo Soprano. m. Graham Allum. Education: Royal College of Music; Hon LRAM. Debut: Diana/Giove, Cavalli's La Calisto, Glyndebourne Festival Opera, 1971. Career: Glyndebourne, Scottish, Royal Opera House, Covent Garden, Chicago, San Francisco, Geneva, Brussels, Vienna Staatsoper; Metropolitan Opera, New York; Kent and English National Operas; Roles include: Didon, Les Troyens; Marguerite, La Damnation de Faust; Ottavia, Poppea and Penelope; Monteverdi; Maria Stuarda; Dorabella; Fricka; Herodias; Charlotte; Baba the Turk; Dejanira, Hercules; Mistress Quickly, Queen Elizabeth I, Gloriana; Frequent recitals and performances of contemporary music in Great Britain, Australia, New Zealand, USA and Europe; Concerts include appearances with Ozawa, Colin Davis, Mackerras, Bernstein, Rozdestvensky, Solti and Boulez with the Orchestre de Paris, London Symphony Orchestra, Royal Philharmonic Society; Sang Astron in The Ice Break at the 1990 Promenade concerts; Mrs Sedley in Peter Grimes at Geneva, 1991; Katisha in The Mikado for ENO, 1990; Cornelia in Giulio Cesare at the Metropolitan, 1988; Sang Stravinsky's Faun and Shepherdess and Britten's Phaedra at the Festival Hall, London, 1997. Recordings include: Voices (Henze) and Baba the Turk with the London Sinfonietta; Dejanira in Hercules, with the Monteverdi Choir and Orchestra; Numerous recital discs with Roger Vignoles and Graham Johnson including first recording of Britten's Cabaret Songs and Complete Fauré songs with Malcolm Martineau; Video recordings include Gloriana, Julius Caesar and King Priam. Honours: Recipient of various awards and honours including: FRCM, 1988; Hon GSM, 1989; CBE, 1991; President of Cheltenham Bach Choir. Membership: Incorporated Society of Musicians. Hobbies: Interior design; Reading; Watching the garden grow.

WALKER Thomas, b. 5 Nov 1936, Malden, Massachusetts, USA. Music Historian. m. Barbara Bland, 30 Jan 1965, 1 daughter. Education: AB, Harvard University, 1961; Fulbright Scholarship, Copenhagen, 1961-62; Graduate Study, University of California, Berkeley. Career: Assistant Professor, State University of New York, Buffalo, 1968-73; Lecturer, University of London King's College, 1973-80; Professor Ordinario di Storia della Musica, Universita della Calabria, 1980-81; Universita di Ferrara, 1981-. Publications: Edited to date (with Giovanni Morelli and Reinhard Strohm), 8 volumes of Drammaturgia Musicale Veneta, Milan, Ricordi, 1983-. Contributions to: Musica Disciplina, Journal of the A.M.S Musica/Realta, Rivista Italiana di Musicologia; Concert Criticism for The Times and other London newspapers, 1973-77. Memberships: Consiglio Direttivo, Societa Italiana di Musicologia; Responsible for Rivista Italiana di Musicologia. Hobby: Computer Science.

WALKER William, b. 29 Oct 1931, Waco, Texas, USA. Singer; Baritone. Education: Studied at the Texas Christian University in San Antonio. Debut: Fort Worth Opera 1955, as Schaunard in La Bohème. Career: Appearances at Opera Houses in New Orleans, Santa Fe, Milwaukee, San Antonio, Vancouver, Washington and Fort Worth; Metropolitan Opera New York from 1962, as Mozart's Guglielmo and Papageneo, Malatesta, Verdi's Germont, Ford, Amonasro and Rigoletto, Valentin, Rossini's Figaro, Marcello, Alfio, Tonio, Escamillo. Noted Concert Artist. Address: c/o Metropolitan Opera, Lincoln Centre, NY 10023, USA.

WALLACE Ian (Bryce), b. 10 July 1919, London, England. Singer; Actor. m. Patricia Gordon Black, 26 June 1948, 1 son, 1 daughter. Education: MA Law, Trinity Hall, Cambridge; Private study with Rodolfo Mele. Debut: Schaunard in Puccini's La Bohème, London, 1946. Career: 10 Glyndebourne seasons, 1948-61, as Masetto in Don Giovanni, Bartolo in Le Nozze di Figaro, Don Magnifico in La Cenerentola and Matteo in Arlecchino; Cesar in Fanny, Theatre Royal, Drury Lane, London, 1956; Berlin Festrwoche, 1954; Teatro Reale, Rome, 1955; Scottish Opera, 1966-75 (3); Panellist, My Music, radio and TV, 1966-; Porterhouse Blue, Channel 4 TV, 1987. Recordings: Ian Wallace - My Music; Your Hundred Favourite Hymns. Publications: Promise Me You'll Sing Mud, 1975; Nothing Quite Like It, 2nd volume, 1982; Reflections on Scotland, 1988. Honours: OBE, 1983; Honorary DMus, St Andrew's University, Scotland, 1991. Memberships: Honorary RAM; Honorary RCM; President, Incorporated Society of Musicians, 1979-80; Garrick Club; MCC; President, Council for Music in Hospitals, 1989-. Hobbies: Watching sport; Walking; Bowls; Birdwatching; Elementary boating. Current Management: Fraser & Dunlop Ltd, London, England. Address: Fraser & Dunlop Ltd, Fifth Floor, The Chambers, Chelsea Harbour, Lots Road, London SW10, England.

WALLAT Hans, b. 18 Oct 1929, Berlin, Germany. Conductor. Education: Studies at the Conservatory of Scherwin. Debut: Metropolitan Opera, 1971. Career: Conductor at Stendal 1950-51; Meiningen 1951-52; Schwerin Opera, 1953-56; Conductor at Leipzig Opera, 1958-61; Stuttgart, 1961-64; Deutsche Oper Berlin, 1964-65; Music Director at Bremen, 1965-70; Mannheim, 1970-80; Regular appearances at the Vienna Staatsoper from 1968; Bayreuth from 1970; Music Director at Dortmund, 1979-85; Deutsche Oper am Rhein Dusseldorf, from 1986; Conducted new production of Macbeth, 1988; Led the Company in Schreker's Die Gezeichneten at the 1989 Vienna Festival; Many engagements at the Hamburg Staatsoper. Address: c/o Deutsche Oper am Rhein, Heinrich-Heine Allee 16, D-4000 Dusseldorf, Germany.

WALLBERG Heinz, b. 16 Mar 1923, Herringen, Westphalia, Germany. Conductor. Education: Studied at Dortmund Conservatory and Hochschule für Musik in Cologne. Career includes: Played the violin and trumpet in various orchestras; Conductor at Munster, Trier, Flensburg, Hagen and Wuppertal, 1946-54; Music Director at Augsburg and Bremmen, 1955-60, Wiesbaden, 1960-74, Niederosterreichisches Tonkunstlerorchester, Vienna, 1964-75; Conductor of 450 performances at Vienna Staatsoper; Conducted Bavarian Radio Symphony Orchestra, 1975-82 and Essen Philharmonic, 1975-91; Guest appearances with leading orchestras of Vienna, Berlin, Munich, Dresden and Leipzig; Many festival engagements; Has conducted opera in Germany and at Covent Garden; Regular concerts at Vienna Musikverein and from 1970 with NHK Tokyo; US debut with National Symphony Orchestra in Washington, 1991; French debut 1992 with Orchestre National de France; Many concerts with various orchestras, 1991-92; Opened Australian Opera 1992 season with Fidelio; Engaged for: 1991-92 season with 14 orchestras worldwide, 1992-93 season with 8 orchestras worldwide, 1993-94 season with numerous orchestras worldwide; 1994-95 season for concerts with 8 orchestras worldwide. Recordings include: Opera, Hansel and Gretel; Bruckner's Symphonies 4, 8 and 9 and Te Deum; Bruch's G Minor Concerto; Haydn's Symphony 101; Has conducted 17 opera recordings and recordings with many notable soloists. Honours: Numerous including: German Grosser Verdienstkreuz, The Austrian Medal of Honour for Arts and Sciences and Gold Medal of the City of Vienna. Address: c/o Haydn Rawstron Limited, 36 Station Road, London SE20 7BQ, England.

WALLÉN Martti, b. 20 Nov 1948, Helsinki, Finland. Opera Singer (Bass). Education: Sibelius Academy, Helsinki. Debut: Helsinki. Career: Finnish National Opera, 1973-75; Principal Bass, Royal Opera, Stockholm, 1975-; Roles include Colline (Bohème), Ferrando, Philip II (Don Carlos), Sparafucile (Rigoletto), Spirit Messenger (Die Frau ohne Schatten), Dikoy (Katya Kabanova), Baron Ochs, Marke, Landgraf, Daland, Orestes, Pimen, Falstaff; Roles in Finnish modern operas such as The Last Temptations (Paavo), The Horseman (Judge); Sang Fasolt in Das Rheingold at Helsinki, 1996. Address: c/o Finnish National Opera, Bulevardi 23-27, SF00180 Helsinki 18, Finland.

WALLER Adalbert, b. 1932, Danzig, Germany. Singer; (Baritone). Education: Studied in Frankfurt. Career: Opera appearances at Bielefeld, 1958-59; Passau, 1962-65; Aachen, 1968-74, as Rigoletto, Scarpia, Alfio; Sang Telramund in Lohengrin, 1976-77; Sang Wozzeck in the Brasilian premiere of Berg's opera, Sao Paulo, Cologne, 1981, as the Dutchman; Brunswick, 1985 as Reimann's Lear and Antwerp 1982, as Dr Schön in Lulu; Further engagements as Alberich in Der Ring des Nibelungen at Buenos Aires, 1982; Kurwenal at Bologna, 1984; Other centres as Hans Sachs, Wotan, Falstaff, Count Luna; Memberships: Frankfurt Opera, from 1981. Address: c/o Städtische Buhnen, Untermainanlage 11, 6000 Frankfurt am Main, Germany.

WALLEZ Jean-Pierre, b. 18 Mar 1939, Lille, France. Conductor; Violinist. Education: Studied at the Lille and Paris Conservatories. Career: Leader of the Orchestre de Paris, 1975-77; Founder of the Ensemble Instrumental de France and director, 1968-83; Director of the Albi Festival, 1974-91, and Founder and director of the Ensemble Orchestral de Paris, 1978-86; Has premiered works by Landowski, Martinu, Jolivet and Sciortino; Professor at the Geneva Conservatory from 1987 and principal guest conductor of the Orchestra Ensemble Lanazawa, Japan, 1994-. Address: c/o Agence Artistique Monique Cazeneuve 5-7 avenue Mac Mahon, F-75017 Paris, France.

WALLFISCH Elizabeth, b. 1952 Australia. Violinist. Career: Began performing on 'modern' violin; Early professional engagements included concerto performances with orchestras in Australia and the UK, including the London Mozart Players and the Royal Liverpool Philharmonic Orchestra; Concerts, Recordings and Broadcasts, both as Concerto Soloist (often directing from the violin), and as a recitalist with the Locatelli Trio which she founded in 1989 with Paul Nicholson and Richard Tunnicliffe; Regularly leads the Orchestra of the Age of Enlightenment and the Raglan Baroque Players, director Nicholas Kraemer and, occasionally, the London Classical Players under Roger Norrington; Recent engagements performing works from the later periods include, Spohr's Concerto No 8 for the BBC with the Ulster Orchestra under Roy Goodman; the Brahms Double Concerto with her husband Raphael Wallfisch; the Viotti Concerto No 22 with the Hanover Band and the Brahms Violin Concerto with the Orchestra of the Age of Enlightenment under Charles Mackerras; Regular visits to her native Australia where, in 1992, she was welcomed as 'Artist in Residence' at Melbourne University, returned in September 1993 with the Locatelli Trio for four week tour and in 1995 toured as soloist; Since Summer of 1993 she has been a featured Soloist and led the Orchestra at the annual Carmel Bach Festival in the USA under Bruno Weil; the Locatelli Trio made USA debut at the Frick Collection in January 1994; Visited the Utrecht, Irsee and Amsterdam Locatelli Festivals, 1995. Recordings: Complete Violin Concerti by Bach (including those reconstructed from Bach's Harpsichord Concertos in D minor and G minor); Haydn, including the Sinfonia Concertante; Recently recorded a series of early Italian Violin Sonatas with the Locatelli Trio; Current releases include, Locatelli, Tartini (2 CD's) and Corelli (Double CD Set), with Albinoni and Veracini; Trio have also recorded Handel Sonatas Op 1; Locatelli Violin Concertos Op 3, 'L'Arte del Violino' performed by Elizabeth Wallfisch with Raglan Baroque Players under Nicholas Kraemer; Locatelli Concerti Grossi, also with Raglan Baroque Players, and Locatelli Opus 8 Sonatas with The Locatelli Trio; Solo recording of Bach Solo Sonatas and Partitas. Honours: Prize for most Outstanding Performance of Solo Bach, Carl Flesch Violin Competition, 1974; First Gulli Senior Prize, Accademia Chigiana, 1972; Joint First Prize in the Mozart Memorial Prize, 1972; Voted 'Best Recording: Solo with Orchestra (17th/18th Century)', Cannes, 1995. Current Management: Helen Sykes Artists' Management, Fourth Floor, Parkway House, Sheen Lane, East Sheen, London SW14 8LS, England.

WALLFISCH Lory, b. 21 Apr 1922, Ploesti, Rumania. Pianist; Harpsichordist; Professor of Music. m. Ernst Wallfisch, 12 Nov 1944 (dec. 1979), 1 son. Education: Royal Academy of Music, Bucharest; Studied with Florica Muzicescu and M Joras. Debut: Duo with Ernst Wallfisch, Bucharest, 1943. Career: Taught: Bucharest; Switzerland; Cleveland, USA; Detroit; Smith College, Northampton, Massachusetts, 1964-, currently Professor of Music; Visiting Professor, International Menuhin Music Academy, Switzerland; Masterclasses and lectures, USA and abroad; Lecture-performances on Enescu, Lipatti, other Rumanian composers; Formerly Pianist-Harpsichordist, Wallfisch Duo with violist husband; Concerts, TV appearances, radio recordings, USA, Canada, Europe, North Africa, Israel; Occasional appearances as soloist and in chamber music; Participated in music festivals, Western Europe and UK; In recent years has played in premières of Lipatti's works in Switzerland, Italy, Germany and Moscow; Member of Jury, International Piano Festival and Competition, University of Maryland, 1986. Recordings: For various labels. Honours: Iva Dee Hiatt Professor Emerita of Music, Smith College. Memberships: Co-Founder, Secretary-Treasurer, George Enescu Society of the US Inc; American Society of 18th-Century Studies; Music Teachers' National Association; Associate Member, European Piano Teachers' Association. Address: 4 Barrett Place, Northampton, MA 01060, USA.

WALLFISCH Raphael, b. 15 June 1953, London, England. Concert Cellist. Education: Studies with Amarylis Fleming; Amadeo Baldavino, in Rome; Derek Simpson at the Royal Academy; Gregory Piatigorsky, in California. Career: Since winning the 1977 Gaspar Cassado International Cello Competition in Florence, appeared widely in Europe; Australia; USA, Indianapolis Symphony Orchestra, 1988; Chamber music formerly with Heifetz in California; With Amadeus Quartet: Recitals with his father, Peter Wallfisch; Solti on TV; Piano Trio concerts with Ronald Thomas and Anthony Goldstone; Performances with most major British orchestras, including Prokofiev's Sinfonia Concertante at the Festival Hall; Promenade Concerts, London, August 1989. Recordings: Tchaikovsky's Rococo Variations, Strauss's Don Quixote and Romanze, Britten's Cello Symphony, Prokofiev's Sinfonia Concertante, Concertos by Shostakovich, Barber, Kabalevsky, Khachaturian, Finzi, Bax, Moeran, Bliss, Dvorak and Brahms on Chandos; Delius Violin and cello concerto, with Tasmin Little and Cello concerto, EMI. Address: Clarion-Seven Muses, 64 Whitehall Park, London, N19 3TN, England.

WALLIS Delia, b. 1944, Chelmsford, Essex, England. Singer, (Mezzo-Soprano). Education: Studied at the Guildhall School of Music, London. Debut: Wexford Festival, 1968, as Annius in La Clemenza di Tito. Career: Welsh National Opera from 1968, as Hansel and Cherubino, Covent Garden, from 1970; Glyndebourne, 1971-72, 1976, as Cathleen in The Rising of the Moon; Composer in Ariadne auf Naxos and Cherubino; Has sung at the Hamburg Staatsoper, from 1973. Recordings: Manon Lescaut, EMI. Address: c/o Harrison-Parrott Ltd, 12 Penzance Place, London, W11 4PA, England.

WALMSLEY-CLARK Penelope, b. 19 Feb 1949, London, England. Soprano. Career: Sang the Queen of Night in Die Zauberflöte at Covent Garden; Returned for British premiere of Berio's Un Re in Ascolto, 1989; Glyndebourne Festival in The Electrification of the Soviet Union by Nigel Osborne; Has sung the Queen of Night for Geneva Opera, and English National Opera, 1989; Ligeti's Le Grand Macabre in Vienna; Concert engagements include the Brahms Requiem at the City of London Festival; Carmina Burana with the London Symphony Orchestra; Elijah in Liverpool with Marek Janowski; Shostakovich Symphony No 14, with City of London Sinfonia; Concert performances of the operas Moses und Aron at the Festival Hall and Elegy for Young Lovers at La Fenice, Venice; Further appearances in Vienna, Berlin, Salzburg, Frankfurt, Czechoslovakia and Russia; Conductors include Birtwistle, Boulez, Colin Davis, Charles Groves, Haitink, Norrington and Leppard; Sang as Guinevere in the world premiere of Birtwistle's Gawain at Covent Garden, 1991; Donna Anna for English National Opera, 1995; Hecuba in King Priam for Flanders Opera, 1996. Address: c/o Allied Artists, 42 Monpelier Square, London, SW7 1JZ, England.

WALSH Colin (Stephen), b. 26 Jan 1955, Portsmouth, England. Organist. Education: Portsmouth Grammar School, 1966-73; Organ tuition; Nicholas Danby, Jean Langlais; Organ Scholarship, St George's Chapel, Windsor Castle, 1973-74; Organ Scholarship, Christ Church, Oxford, 1974-78; GRCO, 1976; ARCM, 1972; MA Hons, 1980. Career: Assistant Organist, Salisbury Cathedral, 1978-85; Director of Music, Salisburgh Cathedral School, 1978-85; Assistant Conductor, Salisbury Musical Society, 1978-85; Conductor, Farrant Singers, 1982-85; Organist and Master of the Music, St Albans Cathedral, St Albans, 1985-88; Conductor, St Albans Bach Choir, 1985-; Artistic Director, St Albans International Organ Festival, 1985-; Organist, Master of the choristers, Lincoln Cathedral, 1988-; Many organ recitals including Royal Festival Hall; Tours Abroad; USA; Sweden; Denmark; France; Czechoslovakia. Recordings: BBC Radio 3, regular solo organist; French Organ Music Vol I, Vol II, Salisbury Cathedral; French Organ Music, Vol III, St Albans Cathedral; Great European Organs, Lincoln Cathedral; Vierne: 24 pieces on style libre, Triptyque. Memberships: Royal College of Organists, Fellow; Franco-British Society. Hobbies: Walking; Travel; Food; Wine. Address: 12 Minster Yard, Lincoln, England.

WALSH Louise, b. 16 Mar 1966, Dublin, Ireland. Singer (Soprano). Education: Trinity College, and College of Music, Dublin; Royal Northern College of Music, and National Opera Studio, London. Career: Opera engagements as Susanna, and Le Fée in Cendrillon, for RNCM; Britten's Tytania for the Broomhill Trust, Janacek's Vixen for Opera Northern Ireland and in Handel's Tamerlano for the Covent Garden Festival; Stuttgart Opera (contract 1995-97) in Hansel and Gretel, as Serpina in La Serva Padrona, Servilia in La Clemenza di Tito, Xenia in Boris Godunov and Musetta in La Bohème; Concerts include Bach's St John Passion and Mass in B Minor, Elijah, Carmina Burana, Messiah and Mozart's Mass in C Minor; Engaged as a Flowermaiden at Brussels, 1998 (production of Parsifal). Honours include: Prizewinner, 1994 Vienna Belvedere International Singing Competition; Elizabeth Harwood Memorial Scholarship, Curtis Gold Medal for Singing and Ricordo Prize for Opera, at the RNCM. Address: 89 Ridgemount Gardens, London WC1E 7AY, England.

WALT Deon van der, b. 28 July 1958, Cape Town, South Africa. Singer, (Tenor). Education: Studied at the University of Stellenbosch. Debut: Sang Jacquino in Fidelio at the Nico Malan Opera House, Cape Town, 1981. Career: From 1982, has sung at Stuttgart, Munich, Gelsenkirchen and Hanover. Covent Garden from 1985, as Almaviva in Il barbiere di Siviglia; Hermes in King Priam; Belmonte in Die Entführung aus dem Serail; Sang in concert at Salzburg, 1985, returning 1989, as Tamino and Tonio in La fille du regiment; Metropolitan opera debut, 1995, as

Tamino; Sang Idomeneo at Florence, 1996. Recordings: Ferrando in Cosi fan tutte, from Ludwigsburg Festival, Harmonia Mundi; Massimila Doni by Schoeck, Schwann.

WALTER Bertrand, b. 17 Mar 1962, Metz, France. Violinist. Education: Studied at the Metz and Paris Conservatories. Career: After study with Franco Gulli at the University of Indiana (1985-86) became co-leader of the Orchestre Philharmonique de France; With violist Laurent Verney and cellist Dominique de Williencourt founded the string trio BWV and has given many recital concerts throughout France. Honours: Prizes at the Paris Conservatoire and the 1980 Paganini International Competition. Address: Orchestre Philharmonique de France, 116 Avenue de Pres Kennedy, F-75786 Paris, Cedex 16, France.

WALTER Horst, b. 5 Mar 1931, Hannover, Germany. Musicologist. m. Liesel Roth, 1959, 2 sons. Education: Musicology, German Philology, Philosophy, University of Cologne; DPh. Career: Scientific Co-operator, Joseph Haydn Institute, Cologne, 1962-92; Since 1992 Director of the Institute. Publications include: Music History of Lüneburg, from end 16th Century to Early 18th Century, Tutzing, 1967; Editor, Complete Haydn Edition Symphonies i/4, i/17. 1964, 1966; Baryton trios xiv/5, 1968; La Vera Costanza xxv/8, 1976; Keyboard Concertos xv/2, 1983; Accompanied Keyboard Divertimenti and Concertini xvi, 1987; Wind-band Divertimenti and Scherzandi viii/2, 1991; G van Swieten's Manuscript Notebooks of the Creation and the Seasons; Haydn Studies i/4, 1967; Haydn's Pianos, Haydn Studies, ii/4, 1970; The Biographical Relationship Between Haydn and Beethoven, Report of Bonn Conference, 1970, 1973; An Unknown Schütz Autograph in Wolfenbüttel, Festschrift K G Kellerer, 1973; The Posthorn Signal in the Works of Haydn and Other 18th Century Composers, Haydn Studies iv/1, 1976; Haydn's Pupils at the Esterhazy Court, Festschrift H Hüschen, 1980; Haydn Bibliography, 1973-83, Haydn Studies v/4, 1985; Haydn Bibliography 1984-90, Haydn Studies vi/3, 1992; String Quartets Dedicated to Haydn, Tradition and Reception, Report of the Gesellschaft für Musikforschung Köln 1982, 1985. Contributions to: Music Past and Present, MGG; New Grove Dictionary; Proceedings International Haydn Conference, Washington DC, USA 1975, 1981; International Haydn Congress, Vienna 1982, 1986. Address: Harkenfelder Weg 146, 51467 Bergisch Gladbach, Germany.

WALTER Rudolf, b. Jan 1918, Gross Wierau, Silesia. University and College Professor. m. Marianne Marx, 30 Apr 1946, 1 son, 3 daughters. Education: Universities of Breslau, Strasbourg and Mainz; Studies of Philosophy, Fine Arts, German Studies, School and Church Music and Musicology; DPhil, University of Mainz. Career: Founder and Conductor of Kissinger Kantorei and Cappella Palatina Heidelberg; Radio broadcasts in Germany, Austria, Switzerland, Czechoslovakia and France; Professor of Musicology at University of Mainz. Recordings: 12 Organ records; 1 Choral record of Monteverdi's Mass for 4 Voices. Publications include: Books: M Brosig, Dülmen, 1988, J C F Fischer, Frankfurt, 1990 and Zur Musikpflege im Schlesischen Zisterzienserkloster Grüssau, Kassel, 1995; Book articles on Southern German Organ Music; Austrian Musicology; Organs of J A Silbermann; Organs of J P H Seuffert; Sueddeutsche Orgelmeister; The Organ of O Messiaen; Max Reger's Sacred Music; Silesian Musicology. Contributions to: Editor of Sueddeutsche Orgelmeister des Barock, 20 volumes; Orgelwerke von Schlick, Tunder, Sweelinck, Reichardt, Merulo, Fasolo, Trabaci; Organum in missa cantata, 3 volumes; Sacred vocal works of German, English, French, Spanish and Italian Masters; J C F Fischer, Psalmi vespertini and J C Fischer, Litaniae Lauretanae both in Erbe Deutscher Musik; F X A Murschhauser, Vespertinus...cultus in Denkmäler der Tonkunst in Bayern; J J Fux, 8 Offertoria and 10 Offertoria in 2 volumes in Gesamtausgabe der Werke; Musik zur Verehrung der hl Hedwig aus Schlesien, Oldenburg, 1995; Die Rezeption de Kirchenmusik Carl Ditters von Dittersdorfs in Schlesien, 1997; Gregorianische Choralgesänge zur Verehrung der heiligen Hedwig, 1997; Die Vesperae chorales des Neisser Kreuzherrn Joseph Latzel un ihre historische Einordung, 1997; Noteninventar der Curatial-Kirche in Neisse von etwa 1820, 1997; Kirchen- und Schulmusik in der Bischofsstadt Neisse im 14./15. Jahrhundert, 1997. Memberships include: Johann Gottfried Herder Research Council, Marburg; Schlesisches Kulturwerk; Historische Kommission für Schlesien. Hobbies: East and West European Languages. Address: Lessing Strasse 3, D-69214 HD-Eppelheim, Germany.

WANAMI Takoyoshi, b. 1945, Tokyo, Japan. Concert Violinist. m. Mineko Tsuchiya. Education: Studied with Kichinouska Tsuji, Saburo Sumi and Toshiya Eto. Debut: Played the Glazunov Concerto with the Japan Philharmonic, 1963. Career: Performed with orchestras including the Leipzig Gewandhaus, City of Birmingham Symphony, Bournemouth Symphony, BBC Philharmonic, BBC National Orchestra of Wales, London Mozart Players, Zurich Chamber, Festival Strings Lucern, Vienna Chamber, Slovak Chamber and Boston Pops; Conductors include R Barshai, G Bertini, R Fruhbeck de Burgos, K Masur, T Otaka and S Ozawa; Collaborated with pianists including S Lorenzi, B Canino, E Lush, G Pratley and H Barth; Duo partnership with the pianist Mineko Tsuchiya since 1980; Festivals: Lucern International Music Festival 1980 and 1988; Festival Estivalde in Paris, 1981; Schaffhauson Bach Festival, 1982; Seon Bach Festival, 1984; Japan Week in Cairo, 1986; Meilingen Summer Festival, 1991; Tours: USA, 1973, 1981, 1989; Soviet Union, 1983, 1989, 1991; Egypt and Morocco, 1986; Gave numerous recitals at Queen Elizabeth Hall, Purcell Room and Wigmore Hall in London including a Solo Recital of 20th Century's Violin Music in 1987; In Tokyo, directing Izumigoh Festival Orchestra, 1991; Annual recital entitled, Christmas Bach Series, 1991-; Two performances with Academy of St Martin in the Fields under Neville Marrinner in Japan, 1994; Performed Brahms' Concerto in Budapest, 1994; Recital with Mineko Tsuchiya at St John's Smith Square in London, 1995; Fiftieth Birthday Concert in Tokyo in April 1995; Recital at St Johns, London, 1997. Recordings include: Tchaikovsky, Bruch and Mendelssohn Concertos with the Philharmonia; Bach Concertos with the London Mozart Players; Brahm and Schumann Concertos with London Philharmonic; Bach Solo Sonatas and Partitas (Complete) Ysaÿe Six Solo Sonatas; Brahms Violin Sonatas with Mineko Tsuchiya. Publications: Autobiography, The Gift of Music, 1994. Honours: Suntory Music Award, 1995; Prize Winner at the 1965 Long-Thibaud Competition and the Carl Flesch International, London 1970; Ysaÿe Medal, 1970; Mobil Music Award, 1993. Address: 61 Woodhill Crescent, Kenton, Harrow HA3 0LU, England.

WAND Gunter, b. 7 Jan 1912, Elberfeld, Germany. Conductor. Education: Studied in Wuppertal and at Cologne University with Philip Jarnach, composition; Paul Baumgartner, Piano. Debut: London Symphony at Covent Garden, 1951. Career: Worked at Wuppertal and Allenstein as repetiteur, conductor; Chief Conductor at Detmold; Conducted at the Cologne Opera, 1939-44; Musical Director, 1945-48; Director of the Gurzenich Concerts at Cologne from 1946; Works by Ligeti, Varèse, Schoenberg, Zimmermann, in addition to the Viennese Classics; Professor of Conducting at the Cologne Musikhochschule from 1948; Tours of Europe, Japan and USSR; Moved to Switzerland, 1974, conducted the Berne Symphony Orchestra; Principal Conductor of the North German Radio Symphony, Hamburg, from 1982. Recordings: Haydn Symphonies Nos. 82, 92, 103; Mozart Serenades and late Symphonies, Beethoven, Missa Solemnis; Bartók's Divertimento, Music for Strings, Percussion, Celesta; Schoenberg's Five Pieces for Orchestra; Webern's Cantata No 1; Schumann Piano Concerto, with Backhaus, Decca. Complete Symphonies of Schubert, Beethoven, Brahms and Bruckner. Address: c/o Symphonie Orcheser des Norddeutschen Rundfunks, Rothenbaum, Chausee 132-134, D-2000 Hamburg, Germany.

WANGENHEIM Volker, b. 1 July 1928, Berlin, Germany. Conductor; Composer; Professor. 1 daughter. Education: State Academy of Music, Berlin. Career: Founder, Principal Director, Berlin Mozart Orchestra, 1950-59; Conductor, Director of Studies, Mecklenburg State Opera, Schwerin, 1951-52; Conductor, orchestra, Berlin Musikfreunde, 1952-55; Conductor, Berlin Academic Orchestra, 1954-57; First concert with Berlin Philharmonic Orchestra, 1954; Guest Conductor, Germany and worldwide, 1953-; Music Director, City of Bonn, 1957; Principal Conductor, orchestras of Beethovenhalle and Philharmonic Choir, Bonn; Artistic Director, Bonn Beethoven Festival; General Music Director, 1963-78; Professor, State Academy of Music, Cologne, 1972-93; International Conducting Class; Member of Juries for international music competitions, Besançon, 1992, Copehagen, 1995, Geneva, 1996; Dean of Artistic Department, 1991-93; Co-founder, Principal Conductor, Artistic Director, German National Youth Orchestra, 1969-84. Compositions include: Sonatina for orchestra; Sinfonietta Concertante; Concerto; Sinfonia Notturna; Sinfonie, 1966; Klangspiel I and II; Mass, Stabat Mater; Psalms 70, 123, 130; Nicodemus Iesum nocte visitat; Cantus de Cognitione; German and European Folksongs, for mixed choir a cappella; Hymnus Choralis; String Quartet. Recordings: Classical; Baroque; Chamber orchestra; Symphonic and Choral. Honours: Berlin Arts Prize for Music, 1954; Federal Service Cross of Merit, 1972; Medal of Merit for Polish Arts, 1978. Memberships: German Music Council; German Society for New Music; German Heather Society. Hobbies: Heather Gardening; Astronomy; Aquatic life. Address: 12 Gerhart-Hauptmann-Strasse, 57610 Altenkirchen, Germany.

WAPP Edward, b. 19 May 1943, Winfield, Kansas, USA. Ethnomusicologist. Education: BA Music, Utah State University; MA Ethnomusicology; PhD in progress, University of Washington. Career: Instructor; Lecturer, American Indian Music; Institute of American Indian Arts, 1970-73; University of New Mexico, 1972; University of Wisconsin, Milwaukee, 1973-74; University of Minnesota, 1975-77; University of Washington, 1977; Professor of Music, Institute of American Indian Arts & Culture, 1990-; Professional performer of American Indian Courting flute and vocal music; Revival of courting flute and its music. Compositions: Music for several documentaries on the American Indian. Recordings: American Indian Flute Melodies; Flute Music of Woodland Tribes. Hobbies: American Indian traditional arts & crafts, craftman; Ethnic arts & crafts; Culinary Arts. Address: 1521 Cochiti Street, Santa Fe, New Mexico, USA.

WARCHAL Bohdan, b. 27 Jan 1930, Orlova, CSSR. Violin Soloist; Artistic Leader, Slovak Chamber Orchestra, Bratislava. m. Eva Warchalova, 3 Aug 1957, 1 son. Education: Graduated, 1948; Masaryk's Music Institute, State Conservatory, Janacek University of Music Arts in Brno, 1957. Career: First violinist, Slovak Philharmony, Bratislava, 1957; Teacher of violin, State Conservatory; Soloist of recitals & concerts; Founded, Slovak Chamber Orchestra, 1960-. Recordings: More than 80 records, CD for Opus; Supraphon. Honours: Special Award, Record Company Opus, 1989; National Artist, Czechoslavakia Socialist Republic, 1983; Professor, University of Music Arts, Bratislava. Memberships: Union of Slovak Composers. Hobbies: Collecting Old Fashioned Cameras; Photography; Tourism. Address: c/o Slovkconcert, Michalska 10, 81536 Bratislava, Slovakia.

WARD David W B, b. 28 Dec 1942, Sheffield, Yorkshire, England. Musician; Pianist; Conductor; Teacher; Lecturer. m. Elizabeth Gladstone, 1 Aug 1963, 1 s, 1 d. Education: Music Scholar at Bryanston School, Dorset, 1956-61; Music Exhibitioner, Caius College, Cambridge, 1962-63; Royal College of Music, London, 1963-67; Studied with Nadia Boulanger, Paris, 1968-69. Debut: Purcell Room, London, 1972. Career: Many concerts as soloist in London, Britain, Ireland, Holland, France, Germany, America and Australia; Conductor of La Spiritata Chamber Orchestra and others; Professor at Royal College of Music, 1969-; Well-known for interpretation of Mozart; Now playing harpsichord and more especially the fortepiano; Much recital work in UK and Holland. Recordings: Mozart Piano Music, 3 records; Tapes of Duets with Susan Rennie and Solo Works; Aslo Radio Recordings with BBC, RTE and ORTF; Mozart piano and violin sonatas with Yossi Zivoni on CD and cassette; Haydn Trios and Piano Solos with Badinage, on fortepiano and original instruments; Duets and solos by J C and C P E Bach, Haydn and first recording of a new piece by David Stoll for two fortepianos with Marejka Smit-Sibinga, Amsterdam; Mozart Keyboard Music on fortepiano; David Stoll Chamber Music, including a Piano Sonata and a two Piano Sonata with Noel Skinner. Hobbies: Philosophy, practical; Meditation; Tai Chi; Walking; Eating and Drinking; Singing. Address: 4 Patten Road, London, SE18 3RH, England.

WARD John Owen, b. 20 Sep 1919, London, England. Music Publishing Executive; Writer. Education: Dulwich College, 1933-37; MA, Oxford University, 1956; London Violoncello School. Career: Principal Cellist, Oxford University Orchestra, 1950-56; Manager, Music Department, Oxford University Press, NY, USA, 1957-72; Director of Serious Music, Boosey Hawkes, New York, 1972-79. Publications: Editor: Oxford Companion to Music, 1957-77, Junior Companion to Music; Author of Career in Music, 1968. Contributions to: New Grove Dictionary of Music; Musical America; Notes; Playboy. Memberships: Music Publishers Association, President, 1974-76; International Musicological Association; American Musicological Association; Royal Musical Association; Music Library Association. Hobby: Chamber Music. Address: 325 West 76th Street, New York, NY 10023, USA.

WARD Joseph, b. 22 May 1942, Preston, Lancashire, England. Singer (Tenor); Vocal Consultant. Education: Studied at the Royal Manchester College of Music; FRMCM; FRNCM. Debut: Royal Opera House, Covent Garden, 1962. Career: Many appearances in opera in the USA, London, Germany, Portugal, France and Austria; Formerly Head of vocal studies at the Royal Northern College of Music; Formerly Principal Tenor, Royal Opera House, Covent Garden; Consultant in Opera and Vocal Studies at the Hong Kong Academy for performing arts; Director of Opera, Freelance; Many BBC broadcasts. Recordings: Norma, Beatrice di Tenda, Montezuma, Wuthering Heights, Pilgrim's Progress and Albert Herring; Many recordings for Decca, EMI and Pye. Honours: OBE, 1991. Hobbies: Swimming; Horse Riding. Address: c/o Royal Northern College of Music, 124 Oxford Road, Manchester, M13 9RD, England.

WARD Nicholas, b. 1954, England. Violinist. Education: Studied at the Royal Northern College of Music and in Brussels. Career: Joined the Royal Philharmonic in 1977 and is currently co-leader of the City of London Sinfonia and Director of the Northern Chamber Orchestra, Manchester; Member of the Instrumental Quintet of London, with repertoire including works by Jongen, Mozart, Debussy and Villa-Lobos; Member of the Melos and Radcliffe Ensembles. Address: Upbeat Management, Sutton Business Centre, Restmor Way, Wallington, Surrey, SM6 7AH, England.

WARD Paul (Clarendon), b. 29 Aug 1918, Taunton, England. Cellist; Conductor. m. Susan Watmough, 25 Jul 1949, 1 s, 1 d. Education: St Paul's Cathedral Choir School, Haileybury College; Royal College of Music; ARCM, Cello Performance. Career: Member, Boyd Neel Orchestra, 1946-48; Sub-Principal

Cellist, Hallé Orchestra, 1948-54; Cellist, Turner Quartet, 1948-53, 1957-63; Teacher, Royal Manchester College of Music, 1948-72, Northern School of Music, 1953-72, Royal Northern College of Music, 1972-76; Founder and Conductor of Manchester Mozart Orchestra; Conductor of Northenden Choral Society, 1956-59, City of Chester Symphony Orchestra, 1966-76, Stockport Youth Orchestra, 1955-74; Cellist, Wissema Quartet, 1966-76, Brodsky Trio, 1979-81; Continuo Cellist; Various orchestral courses; Conductor, Cello Tutor, Festival Adjudicator, Lecturer. Examiner, Associated Board, Royal Schools of Music, 1978-87. Contributions to: Music Journal. Memberships: ISM; Musicians Union; Federation of Festivals; Galpin Society. Hobbies: Reading; Architecture. Address: 26 Drybridge Hill, Woodbridge, Suffolk, IP12 4HB, England.

WARD Robert (Eugene), b. 13 Sept 1917, Cleveland, Ohio, USA. Composer; Teacher; Conductor. m. Mary Raymond Benedict, 19 June 1944, 3 sons, 2 daughters. Education: BMus, Eastman School of Music, 1939; Certificate, Juilliard Graduate School, 1946; Studied Composition with Rogers, Royce, Hanson, Jacobi and Copland; Conducting with Stoessel and Schenkman. Career: Teacher, Columbia University, 1946-48; Juilliard School of Music, 1946-56; Music Director, Third Street Music Settlement, New York, 1952-55; Vice-President and Managing Editor, Galaxy Music Corporation, 1956-67; President, 1967-74, Teacher of Composition, 1967-79, North Carolina School of the Arts; Mary Duke Biddle Professor of Music, Duke University, 1979-87. Compositions include: Operas: He Who Gets Slapped, 1955; The Crucible, 1961; The Lady from Colorado, 1964, revised and retitled Lady Kate, 1981, operetta; Claudia Legare, 1971; Minutes till Midnight, 1982; Abelard and Heloise, 1981; Roman Fever, 1993; Orchestral: 6 Symphonies, 1941, 1947, 1950, 1958, 1989; Jubilation Overture, 1946; Night Music for Small Orchestra, 1949; Fantasia for Brass and Timpani, 1953; Canticles of America, 1976; Sonic Structure, 1981; Dialogues for Violin, Cello and Orchestra, 1983; Saxophone Concerto, 1984; By Way of memories, 1991; Chamber Violin Sonata, 1950; Piano Pieces; Ballet: Sacred Service: Images of God, 1989; The Scarlet Letter, 1990; Various vocal works; Cantatas; Concertos: Tenor Saxophone and Orchestra or Band, 1984, revised, 1987; Violin, 1994. Recordings: Many works recorded. Honours: Pulitzer Prize for opera, The Crucible, 1962; 3 Guggenheim Fellowships; Honorary Doctorates; Alfred I Dupont Award, 1995. Membership: American Academy of Arts and Letters; Honorary Phi Beta Kappa. Address: The Forest At Duke, 2701 Pickett Road No 4029, Durham, NC 27705, USA.

WARD-STEINMAN David, b. 6 Nov 1936, Alexandria, Louisiana, USA. Composer. m. Susan Diana Lucas, 28 Dec 1956, 1 son, 1 daughter. Education: BMus, cum laude, Florida State University, 1957; MM, University of Illinois, 1958; DMA, University of Illinois, 1961; Postdoctoral Visiting Fellow, Princeton University, 1970; National Music Camp, Interlochen, summers, 1952-53; Aspen Music School, summer, 1956; Berkshire Music Center, Tanglewood, 1957; Paris, 1958-59; Fulbright Senior Scholar in Music to Australia, 1989-90. Career: Professor of Music, San Diego State University, 1961-; Composer-in-Residence, Brevard Music Centre, North Carolina; University Research Lecturer, San Diego State University, 1986-87; Faculty, California State Summer School for the Arts, Loyola Marymount University, Los Angeles, 1988; Numerous commissions; Major orchestral Performances of his work include those by Chicago Symphony; Japan Philharmonic; New Orleans Philharmonic; San Diego Symphony; Orchestra USA; Belgrade Radio Orchestra, Yugoslavia and the Seattle Symphony; Joffrey Ballet, San Diego Ballet Company, California Ballet Co. Compositions: Major works for orchestra; ballet; band; chamber groups; vocal ensembles, over 50 works published. Recordings: Concerto No 2 for chamber orchestra; Fragments from Sappho; Duo for cello & piano; Brancusi's Brass Beds; Childs Play; 3 Songs for Clarinet & Piano; Sonata for Piano; The Tracker; Scorpio; Western Orpheus Concert Suite; Sonata for Piano Fortified, Moiré. Address: 9403 Broadmoor Place, La Mesa, CA 91942, USA.

WARFIELD Sandra, b. 6 Aug 1929, Kansas City, Missouri, USA. Singer (Mezzo-Soprano). m. James McCracken, died 1988. Education: Studied at the Kansas City Conservatory with Harold von Duze; Further study with Irran Petina, Elsa Seyfart and Joyce McClean. Debut: Metropolitan Opera, 1953, in Le Nozze di Figaro. Career: Sang in New York until 1957, as Marcellina, Madelon in Andrea Chenier, La Cieca and Ulrica, then moved to Europe; Sang at the Zurich Opera from 1959, notably in the premiere of The Greek Passion by Martinu and as Fides, Azucena, Dalila, Amneris and Leonore in La Favorita; San Francisco Opera, 1963, Dalila; Appearances in Berlin, Vienna, Perugia and elsewhere in Europe as Carmen and Fricka; Metropolitan Opera, 1972; Samson et Dalilia, with James McCracken. Recordings: Les Contes d'Hoffmann; Le nozze di Figaro.

WARFIELD William, b. 22 Jan 1920, West Helena, Alabama, USA. Singer (Bass). Education: Studied at the Eastman School; With Otto Herz; Rosa Ponselle, 1958-65. Debut: Recital at New York Town Hall, 1950. Career: Concert tours to Australia, Africa, the Middle East, Europe, Asia, Cuba, Brazil and Greece; Sang in Mozart's Requiem, conducted by Bruno Walter, New York, 1956; Concerts at the Prades Festival Puerto Rico, 1962-63; Sang in Showboat and Porgy and Bess, at the Vienna Volksoper, also New York; Repertoire also included Messiah, Operatic arias and Songs from the shows; Faculty of the University of Illinois from 1974; Professor of Music, Northwestern University, 1994-. Recording: Messiah. Honour: President of the National Association of Negro Musicians, 1984. Address: c/o Northwestern University, School of Music, Evanston, IL 60208, USA.

WARING Kate, b. 22 April 1953, Alexandria, Louisiana, USA. Composer. m. 22 May 1981, 1 son, 1 daughter. Education: BMus, Flute Performance, 1975, MMus, Composition, 1977, Louisiana State University; Doctorate Science Humaine, Sorbonne, Paris, France, 1984. Career: Solo Flute Recitals in Italy, France, Germany, USA; Original Compositions performed in USA, Italy, France, Switzerland and Germany; Radio Performances of Compositions on Swiss, German and USA Radio; Founder of annual American Music Week in Germany concert series; Appearances on American PBS and Worldnet Television. Compositions: Over 60 Works; Variations, Flute and Harpsichord, 1984; Assemblages, Soprano, Flute, Trombone, Percussion and Piano, 1977; 3 Act Ballet, Acteon, for large Orchestra, 1983; Chamber Opera, Rapunzel, 1988; Remember the Earth Whose Skin You Are, an Oratorio, 1994. Hobbies: Modern Dance. Address: Zum Kleinen Oelberg 41, 53639 Königswinter, Germany.

WARNER Keith, b. 6 Dec 1956, England. Stage Director. Education: Studied in London, at Bristol University and at Bayreuth. Career: Early work in fringe theatre; Staff Producer at English National Opera from 1981; Associate Director, 1984-89, staging Rossini's Moise, Dargomizhy's Stone Guest, Pacific Overtures and Werther; With David Pountney co-produced A Midsummer Marriage, The Flying Dutchman and The Queen of Spades; Associate Director of Scottish Opera, with Carmen, Tosca, Werther, Die Zauberflöte and Iolanthe; Handel's Flavio at Florence and Batignano; Further productions of Trovatore at Dortmund, Norma in Bielefeld and Un Ballo in Maschera with the Canadian Opera Company; Madama Butterfly and Casken's Golem at Omaha, The Queen of Spades in Madrid, Tannhäuser for the Brighton Festival, My Fair Lady for Houston: Production of Janacek's The Makropoulos Case in Oslo, 1992; Director, Designer, Der fliegende Holländer in Minneapolis, transferring to Omaha and Portland; Weill's Lost in the Stars for the Brighton Festival; Head of Productions for Omaha Fall Opera and the Omaha festival from 1992 (Eugene Onegin and Weisgall's Gardens of Adonis, 1992); Directed Tosca for English National Opera 1994; Pagliacci and Cavalleria Rusticana at the Berlin Staatsoper, 1996. Current Management: Athole Still International Management Limited. Address: Foresters Hall, 25-27 Westow Street, London SE19 3RY, England.

WARRACK John, b. 9 Feb 1928, London. Musicologist. m. Lucy Beckett, 1970, 4 sons. Education: Winchester College 1941-46; Royal College of Music, 1948-52. Career: Freelance oboist, 1951-54; Assistant Music Critic, Daily Telegraph, 1954-61; Chief Music Critic, Sunday Telegraph, 1961-72; Director, Leeds Musical Festival, 1977-83; University Lecturer in Music at Fellow St Hugh's College, Oxford, 1984-93; General Editor of series National Traditions of Opera, Cambridge; Editorial Board, Cambridge Opera Journal, Opera, New Berlioz Edition, Neue Weber Gesamtausgabe. Publications: Concise Oxford Dictionary of Opera, 1964, rev. 1979; Carl Maria von Weber, 1968, rev. 1976 and 1996; Tchaikovsky Symphonies and Concertos, 1969, rev. 1974; Tchaikovsky 1973; Tchaikovsky Ballet Music, 1979; Editor, Carl Maria von Weber, Writings on Music, 1981; Oxford Dictionary of Opera, 1992, Concise version 1996. Contributions: Musical Times; Music and Letters; Opera; Gramophone; Opera translations; Articles in the New Grove Dictionary of Music and Musicians, 1980. Honours: Colles Prize, Royal College of Music, 1951; ARCM, 1952; MA, Oxon, 1984; D.Litt, Oxon, 1989. Memberships: Royal Musical Association. Hobbies: Cooking. Address: Beck House, Rievaulx, Helmsley, Yorkshire YO6 5LB,England.

WARREN Raymond (Henry Charles), b. 7 Dec 1928, Weston-super-Mare, England. Composer; University Professor of Music. m. Roberta Smith, 9 Apr 1953, 3 sons, 1 daughter. Education: Studied at Corpus Christi College, Cambridge with robin Orr, 1949-52, then with Michael Tippett and Lennox Berkeley. Career: Teacher, Queen's University of Belfast from 1955, Professor of Composition, 1966; Professor of Music, Bristol University, 1972-94. Compositions: Incidental music for 11 plays by W B Yeats: The Lady of Ephesus, chamber opera, Belfast, 1959; Finn and the Black Hag, children's opera, Belfast, 1959; Graduation Ode, opera in 3 acts, Belfast, 1963; Church operas, Let my People Go, Liverpool, 1972, St Patrick, Liverpool, 1979, and In the Beginning, Bristol, 1982; Principal compositions include: Oratorio, The Passion, 1962, Violin Concerto, 1966, Three Symphonies, 1965, 1969, 1996, Three String Quartets, 1965, 1975 and 1977, Oratorio Continuing Cities, 1989, Violin Sonata, 1993; 6 operas. Publication: Book: Opera Workshop, 1995. Memberships: ISM; CGGB; APC. Hobby: Walking. Address: 9 Cabot Rise, Portishead, Bristol BS20 6NX, England.

WARREN-GREEN Christopher, b. 30 July 1955, Cheltenham, England. Musician (Violinist); Educator. Education: Royal Academy of Music. Debut: Solo, Berlin; London, 1984. Career: Leader, BBC Welsh Symphony Orchestra, 1977; Philharmonia Orchestra, 1980; Academy of St Martin-in-the-Fields, 1985; Music Director, London Chamber Orchestra, 1987; Tours a soloist, 1983-; Television Presenter, BBC Music & Arts; Professor, Royal Academy of Music, 1985-. Recordings: Mozart Violin concerti; Vivaldi Four Seasons; 4 records Haydn Concerti, Philharmonia; Mendelssohn Concerto; Tchaikovsky; Exclusive to Virgin Classics, 1987-; Berlin Chamber Akademie. Honour: Honorary ARAM, 1983. Address: Royal Academy of Music, Marylebone Road, London NW1 5HT, England.

WASHINGTON Daniel, b. 1955, Summerville, South Carolina, USA. Singer, (Baritone). Education: BMus, Furman University; MMus, Northwestern Univesity; International Opera Studio in Zurich. Career: Sang Marcello in La Boheme and Crown in Porgy and Bess for Zurich Opera; Sang Tarquino in Respighi's Lucrezia with the Festa Musica Pro Summer Festival; Stadttheater Luzern, 1982-87, as Don Giovanni, Simon Boccanegra, Renato, Germont, Escamillo and Guglielmo; Engagements at the International Music Festival Lucerne, the Spoleto Festival, USA; Festa Musica Riva del Garda; the Hamburg and Essen Operas; Has appeared in Porgy and Bess at the Theater des Westerns Berlin, Musikverein Vienna and Royal Liverpool Philharmonic; Sang with the Frankfurt Alte Oper and Royal Opera Liège, 1987-88; Bad Hersfeld Summer Festival, as Jochanaan in Salome; Concerts with the Milwaukee Symphony Orchestra and Austrian Television. Recordings: Respighi's Lucrezia. Honours: 1st prize, 1987, International Competition of Lyric Singing, Verviers. Address: c/o Norman McCann International Artists Ltd, The Coach House, 56 Lawrie Park Gardens, London, SE26 6XJ, England.

WASHINGTON Paolo, b. 24 May 1932, Florence, Italy. Singer (Bass). Education: Studied in Florence with Flaminio Contini and Bruno Bartoletti. Debut: Florence, 1958, as Douglas in La Donna del Lago. Career: Appearances in Parma, Palermo, Bologna, Milan, Rome and Naples; Verona Arena, 1968-86; Further engagements in Athens, Budapest, Mexico City, Brussels, Geneva, Barcelona and Edinburgh; Repertoire includes roles in operas by Rossini, Cherubini, Bellini, Donizetti and Verdi; Sang Arkel in Pelléas et Mélisande at Florence, 1989. Recordings: Requiem by Donizetti; Lucia di Lammermoor; Il Bravo by Mercadante; Zelmira and La Donna del Lago by Rossini; La Forza del Destino. Address: Teatro Comunale, Via Solferinois, I-50123 Florence, Italy.

WASSERTHAL Elfriede, b. 12 Mar 1911, Lubeck, Germany. Singer, (Soprano). Debut: Stettin 1935, as Marzelline in Fidelio. Career: Sang in Essen and Dusseldorf, then at the Deutsche Oper Berlin, Charlottenburg, debut as Fiordiligi; Sang at Dusseldorf, 1941, in the premiere of Die Hexe von Passau by Gerster; Hamburg Staatsoper 1947-64, notably as Tosca, Desdemona, Jenufa and Magda Sorel in The Consul; Visited Edinburgh Festival with the Hamburg Company 1952, for the British premiere of Mathis der Maler by Hindemith; Staatsoper Berlin 1951, as Selika in L'Africaine; Sang at Covent Garden as Eva, Sieglinde, Donna Elvira, Elsa and Marie in Wozzeck; Copenhagen, 1960; Frequent Concert Appearances.

WASSILJEV Nikolai, b. 1957, Leningrad, Russia. Singer (Tenor). Education: Studied in Leningrad. Career: Has sung with the Bolshoi Opera from 1982, with guest appearances at La Scala Milan and the Metropolitan Opera, New York; Roles have included Alfredo, Cavaradossi, Turiddu, Lensky, Guido in Rimsky's Tale of Tsar Saltan, Vladimir in Prince Igor and Dimitri in Boris Godunov; Sang in Mlada at New York, 1991. Honours include: Prize winner at the 1984 Glinka Competition and the 1986 Voci Verdiane at Busseto. Address: c/o Bolshoi Opera, 103009 Moscow, Russia, CIS.

WASSON Jeffrey, b. 24 Aug 1948, Illinois, USA. Musicologist. Education: BMus, 1970, MMus, 1973, PhD, Music History and Literature, 1987, Northwestern University; Boston College, 1989; Brandeis University, 1995. Career: Instructor, 1980-85, Visiting Associate, 1990, 1993, Northwestern University; Associate Professor of Music, Director of Music, Barat College, Lake Forest, Illinois, 1985-; Director of Music, St Mary of the Angels Church, Chicago, 1992-97; Lecturer at Universities of Yale, Michigan, Minnesota, Michigan State and Nebraska. Recordings: Jacket Annotations. Publications include: Editor, A Compendium of American Musicology: Essays in Honour of John F Ohl; Self Study Modules of History of Music in the Middle Ages and Renaissance; First Mode Gradual Salvum fac Servum: Modal

Practice Reflected in a Chant that Begins on B-Flat. Contributions to: The Hymnal, 1982; Companion. Honours: Phi Kappa Lambda; Grants from, National Endowment of the Humanities, Barat College and Northwestern University. Memberships: American Musicological Association; College Music Society; American Guild of Organists; New Music Chicago, President, 1988-92. Hobbies: Collector of Fine art and Lionel electric trains. Address: 1500 Oak Avenue, Evanston, IL 60201, USA.

WATANABE Yoko, b. 1956, Fukuoka, Japan. Singer (Soprano). m. Renato Grimaldi. Education: Studied at the University of Tokyo. Debut: Treviso, 1978, as Nedda in Pagliacci. Debut: Covent Garden, 1989, as Butterfly. Career: Has sung in Turin, Naples, Genoa, Madrid, London, Hamburg, Wien, Berlin and Chicago, New York, notably as Madama Butterfly; Further appearances in Cologne, Frankfurt and Strasbourg; in Florence as Micaela, Donna Elvira, Mimi, Liu and Suor Angelica; Los Angeles 1985; La Scala Milan, 1985; Sang Liu in Turandot; Margherita in Mefistofele at Zurich, 1988; Metropolitan Opera New York, 1986, 1987, 1990, 1992, 1993; Madame Butterfly at New Orleans, 1996. Concert repertoire includes the Choral Symphony; Stabat Mater by Rossini. Address: c/o Stafford Law Associates, 6 Barham Close, Weybridge, Surrey KT13 9PR, England.

WATERHOUSE William, b. 18 Feb 1931, London, England. Bassoonist. Education: Studied at the Royal College of Music with Archie Camden. Career: Played first with the Philharmonia Orchestra; Royal Opera House Orchestra, 1953-55; First bassoon, Italian-Swiss Radio Orchestra in Lugano, 1955-58; First bassoon, London Symphony Orchestra, 1958-64, BBC Symphony, 1964-82; Member of the Melos Ensemble from 1959, including tours of Europe and USA; Many solo appearances; Tutor in Bassoon, Royal Northern College of Music from 1966, Fellow, 1991; Visiting Faculty at Indiana University, 1972, Melbourne, 1983, Sarasota (including Faculty Artist, New College Music Festival), 1985, Banff (Faculty Artist), 1987, Victoria, 1988; Competition Juror at Munich, 1965, 1975, 1984, 1990, Prague, 1986, Eindhoven, 1988, Markneukirchen, 1990 and Victoria, British Columbia, 1993; Member of Arts Council of Great Britain Music Advisory Panel, 1983-85; Dedicatee of works by Gordon Jacob, Jean Françaix, Elliott Schwarz and other composers. Recordings: Numerous with Melos Ensemble and various orchestras. Publications: Numerous editions of wind music; Translations; Articles for Grove's Dictionary; Bibliography of Bassoon Music, 1962; Joint Editor of Universal Bassoon Edition; The New Langwill Index: Dictionary of Historical Wind Instrument Makers and Inventors, 1993. Memberships: Galpin Society, Honorary Archivist; British Double Reed Society, Chairman; International Double Reed Society, Vice-President 1987-91, Host of 18th Annual Conference (Manchester) 1989; Royal Musical Association; AMIS; CIMCIM; GeFAM; Incorporated Society of Musicians. Hobbies: Swimming; Skiing; Travel. Address: 86 Cromwell Avenue, London N6 5HQ, England.

WATERMAN David (Allen Woodrow), b. 24 Mar 1950, Leeds, England. Musician (Cellist). Education: MA, PhD in Philosophy, Trinity College, Cambridge; Musical studies with Martin Lovett, William Pleeth, Jane Cowan and with Sandor Vegh, International Musicians Seminar. Career: Cellist, Endellion Quartet (founded 1979); Appearances at Kennedy Center, Washington DC, Ambassadors Auditorium, Los Angeles, many times at London, Bath Festival, Concertgebouw, Amsterdam, Lucerne and Gstaad Festivals, Switzerland, Spoleto and Fiesole Festivals, South Bank Festival, City of London Festival, Aldeburgh Festival; Tours of USA, Australia, New Zealand and most major European centres and radio stations; Award-winning recordings of Quartetto Intimo, John Foulds. Recordings: Complete Britten Chamber Music; Haydn, Mozart, Dvorák, Smetana, Bartók, Martinu, Walton and Frank Bridge. Contributions to: European String Teachers' Association Magazine. Honours: 2nd Prize, Audience Prize, Portsmouth International String Quartet Competition, 1979; 1st Prize, British National String Quartet Competition, 1979; Winner, Young Concert Artists Awards, New York, 1981. Hobbies: Films; Reading; Dining with friends. Current Management: Hazard Chase Ltd, 25 City Road, Cambridge CB1 1DP, England. Address: 27 Lancaster Grove, London NW3 4EX, England.

WATERMAN Fanny, b. 22 Mar 1920, Leeds, England. Pianist; Teacher; Competition Chairman; Chairman of Jury. m. Geoffrey de Keyser, 1944, 2 sons. Education: Royal College of Music, London, with Tobias Matthay and Cyril Smith; FRCM, 1972. Career: Concert Pianist; Teacher of international reputation; Founded with Marion Harewood, 1961, Chairman, 1963-, Chairman of Jury, 1981-, Leeds International Pianoforte Competition; Vice-President, European Piano Teachers' Association, 1975-; Trustee, Edward Boyle Memorial Trust, 1981; Member of international juries in Austria, Italy, Germany, USA, Israel, Bulgaria, Portugal, former Soviet Union, Taiwan, Japan and China; Piano Progress series on ITV Channel 4. Publications: Series of Piano Tutors (with Marion Harewood), 1967-; Fanny Waterman on Piano Playing and Performing, 1983; Young Violinists Repertoire books (with Paul de Keyser), 1984; Music Lovers Diary, 1984-86; Merry Christmas Carols, 1986; Christmas Carol Time, 1986; Nursery Rhyme Time, 1987; Piano for Pleasure Books 1-2, 1988; Me and My Piano - duets, Books 1 and 2, 1988; Playtime Studies and Progress Studies. Honours: OBE, 1971; DMus (honoris causa), University of Leeds, 1992; Honorary Doctorate, University of York, 1995. Hobbies: Travel; Reading; Voluntary work; Cooking. Address: Woodgarth, Oakwood Grove, Leeds LS8 2PA, England.

WATERMAN Ruth (Anna), b. 14 Feb 1947, Harrogate, Yorkshire, England. Violinist. Education: Juilliard School, New York; Royal Manchester College of Music, Career: Recitals and concerts throughout Europe and USA, radio and television; Festivals include Aldeburgh, Harrogate, Montreux, Lyon, Stuttgart (complete Bach sonatas), Madeira and York; Soloist with such orchestras as London Symphony, Royal Philharmonic, BBC Symphony, BBC Scottish, English Chamber, Orpheus Chamber; Televised Prom concert, 1969; International Artists Recital at Carnegie Recital Hall, 1974; Professor, Queen's College, City University of New York; Faculty member, New York University and Royal Academy of Music. Recordings: J S Bach complete sonatas with keyboards; Bach Brandenburg Concertos. Publications: Master Classes on Bach. Contributions to: Reviews to The Strad Magazine. Membership: International Bach Society. Hobbies: Photography; Table tennis. Current Management: Del Rosenfield, New York. Address: c/o 714 Ladd Road, Riverdale, NY 10471, USA.

WATERS Susannah, b. 1965, England. Soprano Singer. Education: Studied at Guildhall School of Music and Drama, graduated 1989. Debut: Sang Belinda, in Dido and Aeneas at Symphony Place, NY, 1986. Career: The Princess in L'Enfant et les Sortilèges at 1989 Aldeburgh Festival and Louise in German production of Henze's The English Cat; Season 1990-91: Nannetta in Falstaff, Scottish Opera, Papagena at Glyndebourne, Philine in Thomas' Mignon at the Vienna Volksoper and Cherubino for Opera Factory, London, Many recital and oratorio appearances; Season 1991-92: Despina in Cosi fan tutte, Zerlina in Don Giovanni for Opera Factory, London; Martha, Sarasota Opera, USA; 1st Niece, in Peter Grimes for Glyndebourne Festival Opera; Dorlinda, in Orlando for Musica nel Chiostro, Italy; Season 1992-93: Gilda in Rigoletto for Opera Northern Ireland, Pamina in The Magic Flute, Scottish Opera, Susanna, in The Marriage of Figaro for Opera Factory, Cunegonde in Candide at Musica nel Chiostro; Season 1993-94: Fairy Godmother, in Cendrillon for Welsh National Opera,;Dalinda, in Ariodante, Welsh National Opera, Blonde, in Abduction from the Seraglio, for Sante Fe Opera; Season 1994-95: Atlanta, in Xerxes, LA Music Center Opera, Cupidon and Nereid, in King Arthur at Théâtre Musical de Châtelet, Paris and Covent Garden; Despina, Welsh National Opera; Belinda for Royal Opera of Stockholm at Drottningholm; Elizabeth, in Elegy for Young Lovers at Lausanne and on South Bank, London, 1997; Sang Salome in Stradella's San Giovanni Battista, Batignano, 1996. Recording: As Evato in King Arthur, with William Christie and Les Arts Florissants. Current Management: IMG Artists Europe, Tom Graham. Address: c/o 4 Tremadoc Road, London, SW4 7NE, England.

WATERS Willie Anthony, b. 1952, Miami, FL, USA. Conductor. Education: Studied at the University of Miami. Career includes: Assistant Conductor of the Memphis Opera, 1973-75; Music Assistant to Kurt Herbert Adler at San Francisco Opera, 1975-79; Music Director of the San Antonio Festival, 1983-84; Artistic Director of the Greater Miami Opera for whom he has conducted La Gioconda, L'Italiana in Algeri, Madama Butterfly, Ernani, 1984-85, Of Mice and Men by Floyd, Rigoletto, Cav and Pag, 1985-86, Salome, La Traviata, Hamlet, Aida, 1986-87, Bellini's Bianca e Falliero, Tosca, Otello, 1987-88, Le nozze di Figaro, Die Walküre, La Forza Del Destino, 1988-89, I Vespri Siciliani, Idomeneo, Elektra, 1989-90, Cosi fan tutte and Falstaff, 1990-91; Has also worked with the Detroit Symphony Orchestra, Fort Worth Opera, Miami City Ballet, Florida Symphony Orhestra, Cincinnati, Chautaqua and Connecticut Opera Companies, Australian Opera Sydney, Cologne Opera, Sudwestfunk Orchestra and Essen Philharmonic, debuts 1990-91; Season 1991-93 conducting Aida with Connecticut Opera, Greater Miami Opera, SWF Sinfonieorchester, Baden-Baden, Florida Philharmonic Orchestra, and Macbeth with Charlotte Opera.

WATHEY Andrew (Brian), b. 19 July 1958, Plymouth, England. Musicologist. Education: BA, St Edmund Hall, Oxford University, 1979; MA, 1983, DPhil, 1987. Career: Harmsworth Senior Scholar, 1981, Fellow of Merton (Junior Research Fellow), 1982-85, Oxford University; Research Fellow, Downing College, Cambridge University, 1985-88; Visiting Professor, Keio University, Tokyo, Japan, 1987; Lecturer in Music, University of Lancaster, 1988-89; Lecturer in Music, Royal Holloway and Bedford New College, University of London, 1989-. Recording: Broadcast radio talks for BBC Radio 3. Publication: Music in the Royal and Noble Households in Late Medieval England, 1989. Contributions to: Articles to various musicological and historical journals. Honours: J A Westrup Prize, 1986; Fellow, Royal Historical Society, 1986-; Fellow, Society of Antiquaries, London, 1989. Memberships: Royal Musical Association; American Musicological Society. Address: Department of Music, Royal Holloway and Bedford New College, Egham Hill, Egham, Surrey TW20 0EX, England.

WATKINS Glenn, b. 30 May 1927, McPherson, KS, USA. Musicologist. Education: BA 1948, MMus 1949, University of Michigan; PhD, University of Rochester, 1953; Diploma, American Conservatory, Fontainebleau, 1956. Publications: Gesualdo, Complete Works, co-editor, 1959-66; Gesualdo: The Man and His Music, 1973, 2nd edition, 1991; S D'India, Complete Works, co-editor, 1980-; Soundings Music in 20th Century, 1988; Pyramids at the Louvre, 1994. Honours: Fulbright, England, 1953-54; National Book Award Nominee, 1974; Senior Fellow, National Endowment for the Humanities, 1976-77. Address: 1336 Glendaloch Circle, Ann Arbor, MI 48104, USA.

WATKINS Michael Blake, b. 4 May 1948, Ilford, Essex, England. Composer. m. Tessa Marion Fryer, 8 Feb 1975, 2 d. Education: Studied privately, guitar and lute with Michael Jessett, 1964-67, and composition with Elisabeth Lutyens, 1966-70, and Richard Rodney Bennett, 1970-75. Career: Appointed Fellow in Television Composition with London Weekend TV, 1981-83. Compositions: Orchestral Works: Clouds and Eclipses for Guitar and Strings, 1973, Aubade for Brass Band, 1973, Horn Concerto, 1974, Violin Concerto, 1977, Etalage for Symphony Orchestra, 1979, Trumpet Concerto, 1988, Cello Concerto, 1992; Chamber works: Somnial for Guitar Solo, 1968, Solus for Guitar Solo, 1975, The Wings of Night for Solo Violin, 1975, All That We Read in Their Smiles for Tenor, Horn and Piano, 1977, The Spirit of The Universe for Soprano and Ensemble, 1978, The Spirit of The Earth for Guitar Solo, 1978, String Quartet, 1979, The Magic Shadow Show for Cello and Ensemble, 1980, Sinfonietta for 12 Instruments, 1982, Clarinet Quintet, 1984, La mort de l'aigle for Solo Trumpet, 1993; Piano quintet, 1995; The River of Time for guitar trio, 1996. Recordings: Trumpet Concerto with Håkan Hardenberger and the BBC Philharmonic Orchestra conducted by Elgar Howarth; La mort de l'aigle with trumpet played by Håkan Hardenberger. Publications: Trumpet Concerto; Violin Concerto; The Wings of Night for Solo Violin; String Quartet; Solus for Guitar Solo; The Spirit of The Earth for Guitar Solo. Honours: Menuhin Prize, 1975; Carl Flesch Composition Prize, 1976; Guinness Prize, 1978. Membership: Association of Professional Composers. Hobbies: Cinema; Cooking; Theatre. Current Management: Novello and Co, Publishers. Address: Acacia House, Uxbridge Road, Hillingdon, Middlesex, UB10 0LF, England.

WATKINS Sara (Van Horn), b. 12 Oct 1945, Chicago, Illinois, USA. Oboist; Conductor. m. John Shirley Quirk, 29 Dec 1981, 1 son, 2 daughters. Education: BMus, Oberlin Conservatory of Music, 1967; Studied with Ray Still, Marc Lifschey, Marcel Moyse; Fellowship student at Tanglewood Music Festival, 1967. Career: Principal Oboist, American National Opera Company, 1967; Honolulu Symphony Orhcestra, 1969-73; National Symphony Orchestra, 1973-81; Professor of Oboe, University of Hawaii, 1969-73; Catholic University, 1973-81; Oberlin Conservatory, 1984; In residence, Scottish Academy of Music, 1985; Oboe Soloist, Conductor, 1981-; Oboe Soloist at Aldeburgh, Sofia, Spoleto Festivals, Vienna, The Hague, Moscow, Leningrad, London, Sao Paulo, New York and other major US cities; Recent conducting appearances in Glasgow, Cambridge, London Queen Elizabeth Hall, Britten-Pears School, Snape Maltings, Paris, New York Glimmerglass Opera. Recordings: CDs: Britten Chamber Music with John Shirley-Quirk, Osian Ellis, Philip Ledger; Handel Cantatas, Arias and Sonatas with Yvonne Kenny, John Shirley-Quirk, Martin Isepp. Memberships: Musicians' Union of Chicago and London; Conductors' Guild, USA. Hobbies: Yoga; Tennis. Current Management: Columbia Artists Management. Address: 51 Wellesley Road, Twickenham, Middlesex TW2 5RX, England.

WATKINSON Andrew, b. 1955, England. Career: Founder Member and Leader of the Endellion String Quartet from 1979; Many concerts in Amsterdam, Frankfurt, Paris, Munich, Rome and Salzburg; Appeared at South Bank Haydn Festival in 1990, the Wigmore Hall Beethoven Series and the Quartet Plus Series in 1994; Quartet-in-Residence at the University of Cambridge from 1992 and Residency at MIT, United States, 1995. Recordings include: Works by Haydn, Bartók, Barber, Dvorák, Smetana and Walton. Address: Hazard Chase, Richmond House, 16-20 Regent Street, Cambridge, CB2 1DB, England.

WATKINSON Carolyn, b. 19 Mar 1949, Preston, Lancashire, England. Singer (Mezzo-soprano). Education: Royal Manchester College of Music; Muzieklyceum, The Hague, Netherlands. Career: Early specialisation in Baroque music, and sang with Syntagama Musicum, Grande Ecurie de la Chambre du Roi, with Jean-Claude Malgoire and Gächinger Kantorei, under Helmuth Rilling; Sang Phèdre in Hippolyte et Aricie at Covent Garden and Versailles, 1978, English Bach Festival; Nero in L'Incoronazione di Poppea with Netherlands Opera, 1979; Guest in Stuttgart as Rossini's Rosina and at Ludwigsburg as Mozart's

Cherubino, 1980; 1981 as Handel's Ariodante at La Scala, Milan; 1982 Edinburgh Festival, Ariodante; Glyndebourne Festival debut, 1984, as Cherubino, returned as Cenerentola; Aix-en-Provence debut, 1985, as the Messenger in Monteverdi's Orfeo; Concerts include Mahler's 3rd and 8th Symphonies, conducted by Haitink, and appearances with the Royal Liverpool Philharmonic, BBC Symphony, Scottish Chamber and National Orchestras and the Philharmonia; Sang with Boston Symphony at Tanglewood, 1985; Engagements in Paris, Vienna, San Francisco, Washington DC, Madrid, Barcelona; Toured Australia, 1987, and appeared at Sydney Opera; Sang in Gloucester Cathedral performance of St John Passion, shown by BBC TV on Good Friday, 1989; Sang Nero in L'Incoronazione di Poppea at Montpellier, 1989; Purcell's Dido conducted by John Eliot Gardiner at Salerno Cathedral, 1990; Nero at the 1990 Innsbruck Festival. Recordings: Handel Messiah (Hogwood), Rinaldo and Xerxes; Solomon (Gardiner); Mozart Requiem; Bach B Minor Mass (Schreier) and St Matthew Passion; Solo album recorded live at her debut, Wigmore Hall recital, London. Address: Lies Askonas Ltd, 6 Henrietta Street, London, WC2.

WATSON Janice, b. 1964, England. Singer (Soprano). Education: Studied at the Guildhall School, further study with Johanna Peters. Career: Concert repertory has included the Four Last Songs of Strauss, Stravinsky's Pulcinella, Les Nuits d'Eté by Berlioz, Mahler's 4th Symphony and Berio's Sinfonia (Barbican Hall, London); Has sung the Brahms Requiem with Dulwich Choral Society, Haydn's Nelson Mass and Seasons at the Usher Hall, Edinburgh; Bach's Magnificat, Christmas Oratorio and St Mark Passion on South Bank, Britten's Les Illuminations at Salisbury Cathedral; Elgar's The Spirit of England with the Hallé Orchestra; Messiah in St Alban's Cathedral and Beethoven's Missa Solemnis with the Chichester Singers; Hummel's E flat Mass and Schubert's Stabat Mater at the Elizabeth Hall; Mendelssohn's Elijah with the Bristol Bach Choir; Further repertory includes Handel's Saul, Mendelssohn's Hymn of Praise (2nd Symphony), Vaughan Williams's Pastoral Symphony and Beethoven's Mass in C (Barcelona Palace of Music); Recitals with the Songmakers' Almanac and in the crush bar at Covent Garden; Opera engagements at Glyndebourne, in Monteverdi's L'Incoronazione di Poppea at the City of London Festival and Musetta in La Bohème at Covent Garden (1990); With Welsh National Opera has sung Musetta, Fiordiligi, Micaela, Adèle in Le Comte Ory, Pamina and Rosalinde (Die Fledermaus); US and Canadian debuts in Messiah, conducted by Trevor Pinnock, 1990; Eugene Onegin for Welsh National Opera and recently Lucia di Lammermoor, Daphne for San Francisco Opera and as Santa Fe (1996), Les Illuminations by Benjamin Britten in the Proms, Messiah at the Barbican with Richard Hickox; Engaged as Pamina at the Berlin Staatsoper and Arabella at San Francisco, 1998. Address: Lies Askonas, 6 Henrietta Street, London WC2 8LA, England.

WATSON Lillian, b. 4 Dec 1947, London, England. Singer (Soprano). Education: Studied at the Guildhall School of Music and the London Opera Center. Career: Sang first at the Wexford Festival, then with the Welsh National Opera; Glyndebourne from 1976, as Susanna, Despina, Sophie, Titania in A Midsummer Night's Dream and Blondchen (1988); Covent Garden debut, 1971, as Barbarina in Le nozze de Figaro; Appearances in die Entführung, Der Rosenkavalier and Arabella; Guest engagements with English National Opera and Scottish Opera and in Munich, Paris, Rouen, Marseilles and Bordeaux; Salzburg Festival, 1982, as Marzelline in Fidelio; Vienna Staatsoper in Le nozze of Figaro; Sang Strauss's Sophie at the Théâtre des Champs-Elysées, 1989; Norina in Don Pasquale at Amsterdam; Title role in The Cunning Little Vixen at Covent Garden, 1990; Sadler's Wells Theatre, 1990, as Britten's Tytania; TV engagements in Don Pasquale and Orpheus in the Underworld. Sang Fairy Godmother in Massenet's Cendrillon for Welsh National Opera, 1993; Bella in The Midsummer Marriage at Covent Garden, 1996; Despina, 1997. Recordings: Carmen; Le nozze di Figaro; Monteverdi Madrigals and Handel's Israel in Egypt; Die Entführung aus dem Serail; The Cunning Little Vixen; Così fan tutte; Britten's A Midsummer Night's Dream. Address: IMG Artists, Media House, 3 Burlington Lane, London W4 2TH, England.

WATTS André, b. 20 June 1946, Nuremberg, Germany. Pianist. Education: Studied with Genia Robiner, Doris Bawden and Clement Petrillo, Philadelphia Musical Academy; Artist's Diploma, Peabody Conservatory of Music, Baltimore, 1972, and with Leon Fleisher. Debut: Soloist, Haydn's Concerto in D Major, Philadelphia Orchestra Children's Concert, 1955. Career: Soloist, Franck's Symphonic Variations, Philadelphia Orchestra, 1960; Soloist, Liszt's Concerto No 1, with Bernstein and New York Philharmonic Orchestra, 1963; European debut, London Symphony Orchestra, 1966; New York recital debut, 1966; World tour, 1967; First pianist to play a recital on live network television in USA, New York, 1976; Celebrated 25th anniversary of debut as soloist with New York Philharmonic Orchestra, Liszt Concerto No 1, the Beethoven Concerto No 2 and Rachmaninov Concerto No 2 telecast nationwide, 1988. Recordings: Various. Honours: Honorary Doctorates from Yale University, 1973, Albright College, 1975; Film documentary of his career; Avery Fisher Prize, 1988. Address: c/o Columbia Artists' Management Inc, 165 West 57th Street, New York, NY 10019, USA.

WATTS Helen, b. 9 Dec 1927, Milford Haven, Wales. Singer (Contralto). Education: Studied at the Royal Academy of Music with Caroline Hatchard and Frederick Jackson. Career: Sang in the BBC Chorus; Solo engagements from 1953, including Gluck's Orpheus; Promenade Concerts, 1955, singing Bach Arias with Malcolm Sargent; Sang with Handel Opera Society from 1958, as Didymus in Theodora, Ino and Juno in Semele and Rinaldo; Toured with the English Opera Group to Russia, 1964, performing Britten's Lucretia under the composer; Covent Garden, 1965-71, as First Norn in Götterdämmerung, Erda and Sosostris in The Midsummer Marriage; Welsh National Opera, 1969, as Mistress Quickly; US debut, New York Philharmonic Hall, 1966, in A Mass of Life, by Delius; Carnegie Hall, 1970, in Kindertotenlieder by Mahler with the Chicago Symphony under Solti; Repertoire included music by Strauss, Schoenberg, Stravinsky, Mendelssohn, Elgar and Berlioz. Recordings: Handel's Sosarme and Semele; Bach B Minor Mass; First Norn in Götterdämmerung; A Midsummer Night's Dream; Béatrice et Bénédict; Messiah; St Matthew Passion; The Apostles by Elgar; Handel's Samson. Honours include: Commander of the British Empire, 1976. Address: c/o Harold Holt Ltd, 31 Sinclair Road, London W14 0NS, England.

WAYENBERG Daniel (Ernest Joseph Carel), b. 11 Oct 1929, Paris, France. Pianist; Composer. Education: Studied with his mother and with Marguerite Long. Career: Played in private houses, 1939-46; Public debut, Paris, 1949; Opening recital of the Chopin Centenary Festival, Florence, 1949; Besançon Festival, 1951; US debut, Carnegie Hall, 1953, conducted by Mitropoulos; Numerous concerto appearances throughout the world (tours of USA and Indonesia, 1955); Repertoire centres on 19th century classics but also plays Haydn and Stockhausen; Teacher at Conservatory of Rotterdam. Compositions: Ballet Solstice, 1955; Sonata for violin and piano; Concerto for 5 wind instruments and orchestra; Capella, symphony; Concerto for 3 pianos and orchestra, 1975. Recordings: Numerous concertos including Brahms, Tchaikovsky, Beethoven, Gershwin and Rachmaninov. Hobbies: Computer chess; Building miniature railways; Swimming. Current Management: Concert Director, Samama 8C, Netherlands. Address: 17 rue Thibault, 94520 Mandres-Les Roses, France.

WEALE Malcolm (Angus), b. 11 Mar 1947, London, England. Professor of Music. m. Janet Kerr Corbett, 27 Mar 1971, 2 daughters. Education: Graduate, 1968; Licentiate in Trumpet, Royal Academy of Music; Licentiate in Trumpet, Guildhall School of Music; Associate in Pianoforte, London College of Music. Debut: London Symphony Orchestra, 1968. Career: Principal Trumpet for Bolshoi and Kirov Ballet Companies, UK tour, 1969, Bournemouth Symphony and Sinfonietta Orchestras, 1969-81; Appearances on British and German TV on Music in Camera series, BBC Radio 3 as soloist and performer; Conductor, adjudicator, teacher, and lecturer at Bournemouth and Poole Colleges of Further Education and Crickland College, Andover; Professor of Music, Ministry of Defence, 1983-; Examiner for Associated Board, Royal Schools of Music. Recordings: Manfredini Double Trumpet Concerto, 1979; Bournemouth Symphony; Bournemouth Sinfonietta; London Symphony Orchestra; Scottish National Orchestra. Contributions to: Music Lover's Guide to Instruments of the Orchestra; British Musical Directory; Music and Musicians (biographies). Membership: Incorporated Society of Musicians. Hobbies: Travel; Sport; Reading. Address: 73 Beaufoys Avenue, Ferndown, Wimborne, Dorset, BH22 9RN, England.

WEATHERS Felicia, b. 13 Aug 1937, St Louis, MO, USA. Soprano. Education: Studied at Lincoln University in Jefferson City and Indiana University with Frank St Leger; Further study with Charles Kullman and Dorothea Manski. Career: Sang in Kansas City, Chicago and Detroit and at Kiel Opera in Germany from 1961; Member of the Hamburg Staatsoper, 1963-70; Metropolitan Opera debut in 1965 as Lisa in The Queen of Spades; Appeared at Lisbon in 1968 and Chicago Lyric Opera in 1968 as Salome; Appearances in Sweden, Yugoslavia, Germany and North America; Other roles include Aida, Leonora, Tosca and Ariadna Lecouvreur; Often heard in Negro spirituals. Address: c/o Hamburgische Staatsoper, Grosse Theaterstrasse 34, D-2000 Hamburg 36, Germany.

WEAVER James (Merle), b. 25 Sep 1937, Champaign, IL, USA. Harpsichordist; Pianist; Fortepianist. Education: BA, 1961, MM, 1963, University of Illinois, Urbana-Champaign; Studied with Gustav Leonhardt, Sweelinck Conservatory, Amsterdam, 1957-59. Career: Many appearances as keyboard artist; Curator of historic instruments at the Smithsonian Institution, Washington DC, USA, 1967; Co-founder of Smithsonian Chamber Players, 1976; Teacher, Cornell University and American University; Various masterclasses in 18th century performance practice. Recordings include: Smithsonian Collection. Address: c/o Smithsonian Chamber Players, Smithsonian Institution, Washington DC 20560, USA.

WEAVING John (Weymouth), b. 23 Feb 1936, Melbourne, Australia. Tenor. Education: Studied with Browning Mummery in Melbourne, Audrey Langford in London and Ken Neate in Munich. Debut: Sadler's Wells in 1960 as Eisenstein in Die Fledermaus. Career: Has sung in operas by Wagner with the English National Opera; Engagements at opera houses in Kiel, Essen, Hanover, Lyon, Wiesbaden and Munich; Other roles included Florestan, Huon in Oberon, Alvaro in La Forza del Destino, Otello, Don José, Bacchus, Herman in The Queen of Spades, and Sali in A Village Romeo and Juliet; Many concert appearances. Address: c/o English National Opera, St Martin's Lane, London, WC2, England.

WEBB Peter, b. 29 Feb 1948, Melbourne, Victoria, Australia. Composer; Conductor. Education: BA, University of Melbourne, and Teaching Certificate, 1970. Career: Oboe and Cor Anglais in the Adelaide Symphony Orchestra, 1975-95; Conductor and Teacher; Commissions from ABC, Adelaide Harmony Choir, Unley Chamber Orchestra, and others. Compositions include: Songs of the Wind, song cycle for soprano and orchestra, 1978; Quintet for Brass, 1980; Sonata for Clarinet and Piano, 1981; Songs of the Shadows, song cycle for mezzosoprano and orchestra, 1985; The Christmas Kangaroo for narrator and orchestra, 1986; Sextet for pairs of horns, clarinets and bassoons, 1987; Sonata for bassoon and piano, 1987; Five Blake Songs for chorus and orchestra, 1988; Trio for clarinet, bassoon and piano, 1989; Sinfonietta for orchestra, 1990; Trio for 2 oboes and piano, 1992; Trio for flute, oboe and piano, 1992; Sonata for Cor Anglais and piano, 1995. Address: c/o APRA, 1A Eden Street, Crows Nest, NSW 2065, Australia.

WEBER Margit, b. 24 Feb 1924, Ebnat-Kappel, St Gallen, Switzerland. Pianist. Education: Studied organ with Heinrich Funk in Zurich and piano with Max Egger and Walter Lang at the Zurich Conservatory. Career: Frequent concert tours of the USA and Europe; Festival appearances at Lucerne, Munich, Venice, Berlin and Vienna; Has given the premieres of Martinu's Fantasia Concertant, 1958, Stravinsky's Movements in 1960, and Tcherepnin's Bagatelles and 5th Piano Concerto; Has performed Moeschinger's Piano Concerto in 1962, Schibler's Ballade for Piano and Strings in 1963, Fortner's Epigrams for Piano in 1964, Vogel's Horformen for Piano and Strings in 1972; Concert classes at the Zurich Musikhochschule from 1971. Recordings include: Mozart Concerto K414 under Baumgartner; Nights in the Gardens Of Spain; Franck Symphonic Variations; Weber's Konzertstück; Stravinsky's Movements with the Berlin Radio Symphony Orchestra under Fricsay. Honour: Hans Georg Nägeli Medal of Zurich, 1971.

WEBER Peter, b. 1955, Vienna, Austria. Baritone. Education: Diploma, Hochschule für Musik, Vienna. Career: Engaged by the Studio of the Vienna Staatsoper, 1976; Member of ensemble of the Vienna Staatsoper, 1978; Engaged at the Nuremberg Opera in 1980 and Hanover Staatsoper in 1982; Regular appearances at the Salzburg Festival and the Vienna Festwochen from 1977; Appeared at Glyndebourne Festival 1985-89 as Mandryka in Arabella and Olivier in Capriccio; Debut at the Teatro Colón in Buenos Aires in 1986 as Mozart's Count; Debuts at the Teatro Liceo Barcelona and the Teatro dell'Opera Rome in 1988; Guest engagements in Hamburg, Dusseldorf, Geneva, Paris and Milan; Sang Mandryka at Covent Garden in 1990; USA debut as Amonasro at Dallas Opera in 1991; Contracted to Vienna State Opera in 1992; Other roles include Silvio, Sharpless, Malatesta, Falke and the Secretary in Der Junge Lord by Henze, Don Giovanni, Don Alfonso, Telramund, Pizarro, Amfortas, Eisenstein, Onegin; Debuts as Wagner's Gunther and Strauss's Barak at Hanover in 1993; Concerts and recitals in Europe and the USA; Radio and TV appearances; Engaged as the Count in Capriccio, Vienna 1996-97. Recordings: Ariadne auf Naxos; Un Ballo in Maschera; Die Frau ohne Schatten; Die Zauberflöte; Schoeck Penthesilea; Schubert Alfonso und Estrella; Haydn's Die Feuerbrunst. Honours: Prize winner, Hugo Wolf Competition in Salzburg in 1976; Interpretation Prize from the Mozartgemeinde Vienna in 1976; International Schubert-Wolf Competition, Vienna in 1978. Address: c/o Vienna State Opera, Ringstrasse, Vienna, Austria.

WEBSTER Beveridge, b. 30 May 1908, Pittsburgh, USA. Pianist. Education: Studied at the Pittsburgh Conservatory and with Isidor Philipp at the Paris Conservatoire; Graduated in 1926; Further study with Artur Schnabel. Career: Many solo, orchestral and recital engagements in USA and abroad; Associated with Ravel and performed Tzigane in 1924; US debut in 1934 in MacDowell's 2nd Concerto with New York Philharmonic; Many appearances with Curtis, Juilliard, Kolisch, Fine Arts and Pro Arte String Quartets; Often heard in modern American music and works by Debussy and Ravel; Jury member for numerous important competitions and awards; Gives lecture-concerts and masterclasses at leading colleges and universities throughout USA; Teacher at New England Conservatory, 1940-46; Professor of Piano at the Juilliard School from 1946; Music Editor for

International Music Co; Gave recital at Juilliard in 1978 to celebrate 70th birthday. Recordings: For various labels. Honours: 1st Prize in Piano at the Paris Conservatoire; NAAAC Award for Outstanding Services to American Music; Honorary DMus, University of New Hampshire in 1962. Membership: National Society of Literature and Arts, 1975-. Address: Juilliard School of Music, Piano Faculty, Lincoln Center Plaza, New York, NY 10023, USA.

WEBSTER Gillian, b. 2 May 1964, Scotland. Singer (Soprano). m. Brain Kay. Education: Studied at the Royal Northern College of Music, graduate, 1987; National Opera Studio. Career: Appearances with the English Bach festival, Scottish Opera, Glyndebourne Festival and English National Opera; Roles include Micaela, Pamina, Agilea (Handel's Teseo) and Ilia in Idomeneo; Sang Klim (debut) in The Making of the Representative from Planet 8 by Philip Glass for ENO; Covent Garden from 1988 as Servilia in La Clemenza di Tito and in Rigoletto, Peter Grimes, Médée, Elektra and Prince Igor; Other Royal Opera roles include Micaela and Euridice; Sang Micaela with Welsh National Opera, 1990; Television appearances include Gluck's Euridice at Covent Garden; Engaged as Mozart's Countess with the Royal Opera at the Shaftesbury Theatre, 1998. Honours include: John Noble Award from Scottish Opera, 1986. Address: c/o Athole Still Ltd, Foresters Hall, 25-27 Westow Street, London SE19 3RY, England.

WEGELIN Arthur (Willem), b. 5 Mar 1908, Nijmegen, Netherlands. Violin Teacher; Chamber Music Player; Orchestral Violinist; Composer; Theorist; Educator; Director of Conservatory of Music; Professor; Music Department Head; Researcher. m. (1) Sophia Betsy Hiebendaal, (2) Wytske Johanna Zoetelief Tromp, 1 son, 1 daughter. Education: BMus, MMus, UNISA, Pretoria; FTCL. Career: Violinist, Utrechtsch Stedelijk Orchestra and various Dutch chamber orchestras; Violin Teacher, Netherlands; Lecturer, Potchefstroom University, South Africa; Director and Founder, Conservatoire and Department of Music, University of Port Elizabeth. Compositions: Works for piano, for violin, for organ, for woodwind, for choir unaccompanied and with orchestra, for voice and orchestra, for string orchestra and symphony orchestra, including: Violin Concerto; Harp Concerto; Lieder; Sonatas; Piano Trios; String Quartets; Wind Quartet; Educational series; Old Man's Diary I, II, III; Numerous commissions. Publications: Gevorderde Harmonie, 1968; Junior and Senior Musical Aptitude Tests, 1977. Contributions to: Newspapers; Journals; Encyclopaedia. Memberships: Number of professional organisations. Hobby: Poetry. Address: Zoetelief, Kruinsingel, Montagu 6720, South Africa.

WEGENER Margaret Rosalind, b. 10 Apr 1920, Hendon, London, England. Composer; Teacher. m. Hans Bernhard Wegemer, 30 Oct 1947, 1 daughter. Education: 1st Class Certificate, NFF, 1945; Self-taught, Composition; Music Studies, College. Career: Director of Music, several schools; Conductor, many choirs and orchestras. Compositions: Overture Rennaissance; Mass of St Oswald; Intro, Fantasia and Passacaglia; Three Carols; Anthems, Songs and Carols. Recordings: Intro Fantasia and Passacaglia, 1997. Publications: Carols, 1951; Mass of St Oswald, 1989. Honours: 2nd Prize, EPSS, 1994; 2nd Prize, Song, EPSS, 1995. Memberships: Composers Guild of England; Northwest Composers Association; Women in Music. Hobbies: Reading; Crosswords. Current Management: Musica Ariosa. Address: Fron Llwyd, Glyn Ceiriog, Llangollen LL20 7DB, North Wales.

WEHOFSCHITZ Kurt, b. 3 May 1923, Vienna, Austria. Tenor. Education: Studied at the Vienna Music Academy. Debut: Linz in 1948 as Wilhelm Meister. Career: Sang at Kiel, 1953-54, Munich, 1956-59 notably as Ulrich Greiner-Mars in the premiere of Hindemith's Harmonie der Welt in 1957; Sang at Dusseldorf, 1959-64, Frankfurt, 1964-66 notably in The Photo of the Colonel by Humphrey Searle, Dusseldorf in 1960 as Creon in the German premiere of Edipo Re by Enescu; Guest appearances at Zurich, Lisbon, Rio de Janeiro and the Vienna Staatsoper; Sang at the Vienna Volksoper until 1980; Other roles have included Mozart's Belmont and Basilio, Leandro in Haydn's Mondo della Luna, Strauss's Leukippos and Flamand, Alfredo, Germont, Don Carlos, Riccardo and Tom Rakewell. Recordings include: Carmen.

WEIDENAAR Reynold (Henry), b. 25 Sep 1945, East Grand Rapids, MI, USA. Composer; Video Artist. Education: BMus, Composition, Cleveland Institute of Music, 1973; MA, 1980, PhD, 1989, Composition, New York University; Studied composition with Donald Erb and Brian Fennelly. Compositions include: Between The Motion And The Act Falls The Shadow: Love Of Line, Of Light And Shadow, The Brooklyn Bridge; The Stillness; Night Flame Ritual; The Thundering Scream Of The Seraphim's Delight; Long River, 1993; Long into the Night, Heavenly Music FLowed Out Of the Street, 1995. Recordings: The Tinsel Chicken Coop, 1978, 1982; Twilight Flight, 1986; Harmony, 1986; Imprint: Footfalls To Return, 1986; Night Flame Ritual, 1986. Publication: Magic Music From The Telharmonium, 1995. Contributions to: New Music America: A Moveable Fest, in The Independent, 1984; Down Memory Lane: Forerunners of Music and The Moving Image and So You Want to Compose for The Moving Image, in Ear Magazine, 1985; Live Music and Moving Images: Composing and Producting The Concert Video, in Perspectives of New Music, 1986; The Alternators of the Telharmonium, 1906, in Proceedings of the International Computer Music Conference, 1991; Editor: Sci Online News, 1993. Hobbies: Jogging; Cooking. Address: William Paterson College, Department of Communication, Wayne, NJ 07470, USA.

WEIDINGER Christine, b. 31 Mar 1946, Springville, NY, USA. Opera Singer (Dramatic Coloratura). m. Kenneth Smith, 7 Jul 1976. Education: BA, Music, Grand Canyon College, Phoenix; Studied singing with Marlene Delavan, Phoenix, 1967-70, Adrian de Peyer, Wuppertal, and Dean Verhines in Los Angeles. Debut: Musetta in La Bohème at the Metropolitan in 1972. Career: Sang at Metropolitan Opera, 1972-76, Stuttgart and Bielefeld Operas, Germany, 1981-; Guest Artist at La Scala, State Opera, Vienna, Barcelona, Venice, Bologna, West Berlin and others; Regular Guest in Marseille; Specialist for bel-canto roles of Bellini and Donizetti; Interpreter of Constanze in Abduction from the Seraglio; Repertoire includes: Norma, Donna Anna, Electra in Idomeneo, Queen Elizabeth in Roberto Devereux, Gilda, Leonora in Trovatore, Mimi, Liu; Sang Constanze at Monte Carlo in 1988, Adèle in Le Comte Ory at Montreal in 1989, and Vitellia in La Clemenza di Tito at La Scala in 1990; Appeared at Cincinnati Opera in 1990 as Lucia di Lammermoor; Sang Violetta for San Diego Opera in 1991. Recordings: Handel's Rinaldo with Marilyn Horne; L'Africaine with Caballé and Domingo; Die Freunde von Salamanka by Schubert; Medea with Caballé and Lima; Mitridate by Mozart. Honour: National 1st Prize, Metropolitan Opera Auditions, 1972. Hobbies: Yoga; Jogging; Electric Trains. Current Management: Robert Lombardo Associates. Address: c/o Robert Lombardo, 1 Harkness Plaza, 61 West 62nd Street, Suite 6F, New York 10023, USA.

WEIGLE Jorg-Peter, b. 1953, Greifswald, Germany. Conductor. Education: Studied at the Thomasschule, Leipzig, 1963-71; Hochschule für Musik, East Berlin from 1973. Career: First kapellmeister at the State Symphony Orchestra of Neubrandenburg, 1978-80; Conductor of the Leipzig Radio Chorus, 1980; Currently, Chief Conductor of the Dresden Philharmonic Orchestra; Repertoire has included Bach's Christmas Oratorio, St John Passion and B Minor Mass, symphonies by Beethoven, Haydn, Mozart, Shostakovich and Schubert, and Janácek's Sinfonietta; Visited Wales and the West Country with the Dresden Philharmonic in 1989, with works by Beethoven, Brahms, Weber and Tchaikovsky, Hamburg and Spain in 1989 and Czechoslovakia in 1990; Season 1990-91 included Mahler's Das Klagende Lied, Haydn's Symphony No 92, Mozart's Requiem and Concertante K364, Sibelius's Symphonies 2, 3 and 7, Brahms's 2nd Symphony and D Minor Concerto, Berg's Violin Concerto; Concert performance of Meyerbeer's Il Crociato in Egitto, to celebrate the bicentenary of the composer's birth. Recordings: Albeniz' Iberia Suite; Falla's Three Cornered Hat; Mozart's Horn Concertos, Arias and Duets; Ravel's Rhapsodie Espagnole; Reger's Böcklin Tone Pictures and Mozart Variations. Address: Dresden Philharmonic Orchestra, Kulturpalast am Altmarkt, D-8012 Dresden, Germany.

WEIKERT Ralf, b. 10 Nov 1940, St Florian, Linz, Austria. Conductor. Education: Studied at the Bruckner Conservatory Linz, the State Academy Vienna with Hans Swarowsky. Career: Coach, Conductor at the Landestheater Salzburg 1963; Concerts in Austria, Scandinavia from 1965; Conductor at the Bonn Opera 1966, Music Director 1968; Salzburg Festival (concert) 1971; Guest Conductor, Royal Opera Copenhagen, 1972; with works by Mozart, Verdi, Stravinsky; Hamburg Staatsoper from 1975, with Don Quichotte, works by Mozart, Puccini and Donizetti; Vienna Staatsoper debut 1974, Il Trovatore; Zurich Opera 1976-80, with Le nozze di Figaro, Arabella, Fidelio, La Cenerantola and Il Barbiere di Siviglia; Deutsche Oper Berlin 1978-80, Figaro and Don Pasquale; US debut 1980, with the City Opera's Giulio Cesare in New York and Los Angeles; Teatro La Fenice Venice 1981, Tancredi by Rossini; Further engagements in Barcelona, Munich, Vienna, 1968-88, Rosenkavalier, Carmen, Die Entführung and L'Elisir d'Amore; Metropolitan Opera 1987-90, Elisir, Barbiere and Bohème; Concert engagements with leading orchestras in Berlin, Vienna, Scandinavia, Paris, Hungary, West Germany, Britain (English Chamber Orchestra); Festival appearances at Salzburg (Mozart Matinées, Serenades and Cenerentola), Aix-en-Provence, Orange, Bregenz and Lucerne; Conducted Offenbach's Barbe Bleue at Stuttgart, 1996. Recordings: Rossini Tancredi (CBS Masterworks) Schoeck Lebendig Begraben; James Morris Recital (EMI); Love Duets Araiza-Lind (Philips); Video-tape and laser disc; Barbiere di Siviglia, Metropolitan Opera (Deutsche Grammophon). Address: Neubruchstrasse 5, CH-8127 Zurich, Switzerland.

WEIKL Bernd, b. 29 Jul 1942, Vienna, Austria. Baritone. Education: Hannover Musikhochschule. Career: Sang Ottokar in Der Freischütz, Hannover, 1968; Appeared at Deutsche Oper am Rhein, Dusseldorf, 1970-73, Bayreuth Festival from 1972, as Wolfram, Amfortas and Hans Sachs, more than 160 performances in all; Member of Deutsche Oper Berlin from 1974, debut as Eugene Onegin; Covent Garden debut in 1975 as Rossini's Figaro; Later sang Giordano's Gerard and Strauss's Mandryka in London; Sang at Vienna Staatsoper in 1976 at premiere of Von Einem's Kabale und Liebe; Metropolitan Opera debut in 1977 as Wolfram with later New York appearances as Mandryka, Jokanaan in Salome and Beethoven's Don Fernando; Guest engagements at La Scala Milan, Bavarian State Opera, Hamburg State Opera and Salzburg Festival; Further appearances as Hans Sachs under Sawallisch at La Scala and under Dohnányi at Covent Garden in 1990; Sang Iago at Stuttgart in 1990, Boaccanegra at Hamburg in 1991 and Dutchman at Bayreuth in 1990; Sang Sachs in a new production of Die Meistersinger at the Metropolitan in 1993; Jochanaan at San Francisco, 1997. Also sings lieder and oratorio; TV appearances include Mendelssohn's Elijah, from Israel, 1983. Recordings: Opera sets include L'Elisir d'Amore, Tristan und Isolde, Palestrina, Der Freischütz, Don Giovanni, Alceste, and Lohengrin; Solo in Ein Deutsches Requiem by Brahms. Address: c/o Lies Askonas Ltd, 6 Hennrietta St, London, WC2, England.

WEIL Bruno, b. 1949, Hahnstatten, Germany. Conductor. Education: Studied with Franco Ferrara in Italy and with Hans Swarowsky in Vienna. Career: Conducted at the opera houses of Wiesbaden and Brunswick; Debut with the Berlin Radio Symphony Orchestra in 1977; Concerts with the Berlin Philharmonic from 1979; Music Director of Augsburg Opera, 1979-89; Debut at the Deutsche Opera Berlin in 1980 with Weill's Die Sieben Todsünden; Salzburg Festival from 1982 including Don Giovanni at the 1988 Festival; Conducted Fidelio for Radio France in Paris, 1984, and led the Yomiuri Nippon Symphony Orchestra in Japan; In 1985 conducted Aida at the Vienna Staatsoper and Ariadne auf Naxos at Bordeaux, and in 1986 Le nozze di Figaro at Trieste; Initiated series of Mozart operas in joint production with the Vienna Volksoper and Austrian TV, 1987; Conducted Die Entführung aus dem Serail in Bonn and Die Zauberflöte in Karlsruhe, 1987; US debut in 1988 in a Schubertiade in New York; Concerts in Holland with the Residentie Orchestra and Rotterdam Philharmonic; Concerts with the Los Angeles Philharmonic and the BBC Scottish Symphony from season 1988-90; Tour of Germany with the English Chamber Orchestra; Season 1990-91 with the Orchestre National de France and the Montreal Symphony; Conducted Brahms with the Orchestra of the Age of Enlightenment, London, 1997. Recordings: Various albums with the Deutsche Philharmonie. Honours include: Second Prize, Herbert von Karajan Conductors' Competition in 1979. Address: c/o Ingpen and Williams Ltd, 26 Wadham Road, London SW15 2LR, England.

WEIL Tibor V, b. 16 May 1942, Hungary. Baritone Singer; Pianist; Cellist; Impressario; Economist. Education: Economist, Mackenzie University, Sao Paulo, Brazil; MA, New York University, USA; Pianist and cellist, Budapest Music High School, Salvador Music High School, Pro Arte Music High School. Debut: Piano and Cello in 1960. Career: Concerts, TV appearances in Sao Paulo, Rio de Janeiro, and Salvador, 1958-; Regular chamber music performances; Frequent concerts as lieder and light opera singer, sacred music and requiems, 1989-. Honours: Viscua Konservatoire Scholarship, 1956; Pro Arte Scholarship, 1959. Memberships: Pro Arte, Sao Paulo; Managing Advisor, Centro de Musica Brasiliera. Hobbies: Travel; Sports. Current Management: TAW Promotions SP. Address: Rua Angatuba 80, Bairro, Pacaembu, CEP 01247 Sao Paulo SP, Brazil.

WEILAND Frederik (Christoffel), b. 14 Sept 1933, Bilthoven, Netherlands. Composer; Film Maker; Musicologist. Education: BA, Higher School for Radio Engineering, Hague, 1957; Physics of Architecture, Delft Technical University; Hilversum School of Music, 1957-59; MA, Royal Academy of Music, Hague, 1966. Career: Recording Engineer, radiophonic experiments, Radio Nederland, 1957-59; Video Editor, Nederlandse TV Stichting, 1959-61; Studio for Electronic Music, 1961-67, Institute of Sonology, 1967-86, University of Utrecht; Lecturer, Researcher, Sonology Department, Royal Conservatory, Hague, 1986-; Guest Lecturer, Amsterdam Film and Television Academy; Musical Adviser, Stedelijk Museum, Amsterdam, Utrecht Music Centre. Compositions include: Etude, 1959; A City Awakes, 1959; Filmproject 1, 1969; Play Without Words, music for Beckett TV production, 1970; 4 American Pieces, 1982-83; Art Of Flying, 1984; Never Mon Amour, 1985; Music For Mesa, 1986. Recordings: Several for major labels. Publications: International Electronic Music Discography, book, 1979; Stockhausen in The Hague, book, 1983; Co-editor, Interface, journal of new music research. Honours: Composition grants, film subsidies, Dutch Ministry of Culture, Amsterdam Foundation for the Arts. Memberships: Society of Dutch Composers; Confederation International de Musique Electroacoustique. Address: Wagenmakerssteeg 2, 1211 Hilversum,The Netherlands.

WEILERSTEIN Donald, b. 14 Mar 1940, Washington DC, USA. Violinist. Education: BS; MS, Julliard School of Music, 1966.

Debut: New York, 1963. Career: Founding First Violinist, Cleveland Quartet, 1969-89; Professor of Violin and Chamber Music; Cleveland Institute of Music, 1967-71, 1989-, SUNY at Buffalo, 1971-76, Eastman School of Music, NY, 1976-89. Recordings: Complete Brahms Quartets; Complete Beethoven Quartets; Schubert 2 cello Quintet; Schubert Trout Quintet; Mendelssohn and Schubert Octets; Complete Violin and Piano and Solo Violin Works of Ernest Bloch; Sonatas of Dohnanyi and Janacek; The Complete Sonatas of Robert Schumann with pianist Ulvian Hornik Weilerstein, 1995. Honours: NEA Grant; Grammy nominations for recorded works; Prize winner, Munich Competition for violin and piano duo. Memberships: American String Teachers' Association. Hobbies: Reading; swimming; Hiking; Basketball; Sport. Current Management: Deborah Fleischman. Address: 2645 Fairmount Blvd, Cleveland Heights, OH 44106, USA.

WEIN Erika, b. 2 Sep 1928, Vienna, Austria. Mezzo-Soprano. Education: Studied at the Vienna Music Academy with Erik Werba. Career: Sang at the Vienna Volksoper, 1952-53, Bremen, 1953-59, and Dusseldorf, 1959-64; Engagements at the Zurich Opera, 1964-80, notably in the premieres of Sutermeister's Madame Bovary in 1967, and Kelterborn's Ein Engel Kommt nach Babylon, 1977; Guest appearances in Berlin, the State Operas of Munich, Hamburg, Stuttgart, Frankfurt and Cologne, at the Holland Festival, Florence, Lyon, Buenos Aires, Paris, San Francsico and Turin; Roles included: Carmen, Azucena, Amneris, Eboli, Ulrica, Ortud, Fricka, Brangane, Venus, Orpheus, Marina in Boris Godunov, Clytemnestra and Berg's Marie; Concert showings in works by Bach, Beethoven and Brahms; Lieder recitals and concerts in Germany, Switzerland, Spain and Austria. Recordings include: Highlights from Rigoletto and Nabucco. Address: c/o Opernhaus Zurich, Falkenstrasse 1, CH-8008 Zurich, Switzerland.

WEINGARTNER Elisabeth, b. 23 Jan 1938, Sissach, Switzerland. Singer (Mezzo-Soprano). Education: Studied in Basle and with Res Fischer in Stuttgart. Career: Sang at the Basle Opera, 1973-81 and made guest appearances at Nantes, Paris, Trier and Cannes; Roles have included Dorabella in Così fan tutte by Mozart, Carmen by Bizet, Isabella in L'Italiana in Algeri, Idamantes in Idomeneo, Geneviève in Pelléas, Annina, and the Hostess in Boris Godunov; Sang at Strasbourg in 1984 in the premiere of H H Ulysse by Prodromides; Concert and lieder engagements in France and Switzerland and at Liège, Stuttgart and Vienna; Sang in Verdi's Requiem in Paris with Orchestra Lamoureux and Dvorák's Requiem at San Sebastian in Spain. Recordings include: H H Ulysse. Address: Opéra du Rhin, 19 Place Brogile, F-67008 Strasbourg Cedex, France.

WEINSCHENK Hans-Jorg, b. 14 Nov 1955, Stuttgart, Germany. Tenor. Career: Sang in Opera at Heidelberg, 1974-76, and Wuppertal, 1976-80; Member of the Zurich Opera, 1981-85, and Theater am Gärtnerplatz Munich from 1984; Guest appearances at Lausanne in 1985, and the Grand Opera Paris in 1986; Sang in the premiere of Der Meister und Margarita by Kunad, Karlsruhe, 1986; Roles have included such buffo and character repertory as Pedrillo, the Witch in Hansel and Gretel, Monostatos, David in Die Meistersinger and the Steuermann in Fliegende Holländer; Frequent concert engagements; Sang in The Cunning Little Vixen at Karlsruhe, 1996. Address: c/o Badische Staatstheater Karlsruhe, Baumersterstrasse,11, Pf 1449, W-7500 Karlsruhe, Germany.

WEIR Gillian (Constance), (Dame) b. 17 Jan 1941, New Zealand. Concert Organist. m. Lawrence I Phelps, 4 Aug 1972. Education: Royal College of Music, London; Further studies with Nadia Boulanger, Marie-Claire Alain and Anton Heiller. Debut: Royal Festival Hall, 1965. Career: Concerto appearances with leading British and foreign orchestras; Regular appearances at international festivals in Edinburgh, Aldeburgh, Proms, and Europalia, performing at the Royal Festival and Albert Halls, Lincoln and Kennedy Centers, Palais des Beaux Arts and Sydney Opera House; Frequent Radio and TV appearances worldwide including the BBC programme The King of Instruments, as presenter and performer, 1989; Adjudicator at international competitions; Artist in Residence at several universities, giving lectures and masterclasses internationally. Recordings include: Poulenc Concerto, 1990-96; Complete Organ Works of Olivier Messiaen, 1994, Cesar Franck, 1997. Contributions to: Chapter on organ works of Messiaen: The Messiaen Companion, 1996; Professional journals. Honours include: Honorary FRCO, 1975; Honorary FRCCO, Canada, 1983; CBE, 1989; DBE, 1996; Honorary Member of RAM; President, Incorporated Association of Organists, 1982-84; Honorary DMus, University of Victoria, Wellington, 1983; President, Incorporated Society of Musicians, 1992-93; President, Royal College of Organists, 1994-96; Council Member, Royal Philharmonic Society, 1996-; Honorary DLitt, University of Huddersfield, 1997. Memberships: Incorporated Society of Musicians; Royal College of Organists; Incorporated Association of Organists; Royal Philharmonic Society, Council Member, 1996-; Royal Society of Musicians. Hobbies: Reading; Theatre. Current Management: Karen McFarlane Artists Inc, USA; Denny Lyster Artists Management, UK. Address: Karen McFarlane Artists Inc, 12429 Cedar Road, Suite 29, Cleveland Heights, OH 44106, USA.

WEIR Judith, b. 11 May 1954, Cambridge, England. Composer. Education: Studied composition with John Tavener; King's College, Cambridge, 1973-76 with Robin Holloway; Tanglewood, 1975 with Gunther Schuller. Career: Southern Arts Association's Composer-in-Residence, 1976-79; Music Department, Glasgow University, 1979-82; Creative Arts Fellowship at Trinity College, Cambridge, 1983-85; Composer-in-Residence, Royal Scottish Academy of Music and Drama, 1988-91; Fairbairn Composer in Association with The City of Birmingham Symphony Orchestra, 1995-97. Compositions: Stage: The Black Spider, opera in 3 acts, 1984, The Consolations of Scholarship, musical drama, 1985, A Night at The Chinese Opera, opera in 3 acts, 1986, The Vanishing Bridegroom, opera, 1990, Blond Eckbert, opera, 1993; Orchestral: Music Untangled, 1991-92, Heroic Strokes of The Bow, 1992, Moon and Star, 1995; Vocal: King Harald's Saga, 1979, Missa del Cid, 1988, Heaven Ablaze in His Breast, for Voices, 2 Pianos and 8 Dancers, 1989. Honour: Critics' Circle Award for the Most Outstanding Contribution to British Musical Life, 1994. Address: c/o Chester Music, 8-9 Frith Street, London, W1V 5TZ, England.

WEIR Kenneth Ross, b. 23 May 1938, Dunblane, Scotland. Pianist; Teacher. Education: Otago University, New Zealand; BA, BMus, New Zealand; MMus, Indiana; AMusD, Michigan; Studied with Jorge Bolet, Marie-Claire Alain and Cyril Smith. Career: Concert Organist, BBC, ABC (Australia) and Radio New Zealand; Lecturer, Piano, University of Canterbury, Christchurch, New Zealand, 1973-75; Teacher, University of Melbourne and Western Australia Conservatorium of Music; Appearances as Solo Pianist and Chamber Musician Throughout Australia and New Zealand; Teacher, Sherborne School, Dorset, England; Piano Concerts in England, Scotland, Asia and Australia. Recordings: Piano: Debussy, Ginastera, Granados, Scriabin; Organ: Clerambault, Alain, Messiaen; Live Recording of Recital at Kings College, Cambridge, 1978. Publications include: Aspects of Rhythm in the Organ and Piano Music of Jehan Alain. Honours: Prize, International Organ Competition, St Albans, England, 1967; Highest Distinction Award in Piano, Indiana University, 1972. Membership: Incorporated Society of Musicians. Hobbies: Travel; Thai language. Address: 1 St Nicholas Mews, Church Walk, Thames Ditton, Surrey KT7 0NP, England.

WEIR Scot, b. 1954, New Mexico, USA. Singer (Tenor). Education: Studied at Colorado University and in Graz. Career: Sang at the Gelsenkirchen Opera, 1981-85, notably as Don Ottavio, Lenski and Xerxes; Wiesbaden Opera, 1985-89, as Almaviva, Medro in Haydn's Orlando Paladino, Belfiore in La finta giardiniera, and Veit in Lortzing's Undine; Sang Hylas in Les Troyens at Brussels (1992) and has appeared as guest in Canada, Israel, Japan and the USA. Recordings include: Franck's Les Béatitudes (EMI); Mozart C minor Mass (Hanssler). Address: Théâtre Royale de la Monnaie, 4 Leopoldstrasse, B-1000 Brussels, Belgium.

WEISBERG Arthur, b. 4 Apr 1931, New York City, USA. Bassoonist; Conductor; Teacher. Education: Studied bassoon with Simon Kovar, conducting with Jean Morel, Juilliard School of Music, New York. Career: Bassoonist with Houston Symphony Orchestra, Baltimore Symphony Orchestra, and Cleveland Orchestra; Member of New York Woodwind Quintet, 1956-70; Founder-Director of Contemporary Chamber Ensemble, NY, 1969-; Chief Conductor, Iceland Symphony Orchestra, Reykjavik, 1987-88; Guest Conductor with various orchestras including New York Philharmonic, 1983, 1984; Teacher, Juilliard School of Music, 1960-68, State University of New York, Stony Brook, 1971-89, Yale University, 1975-89. Recordings: Several discs. Publication: The Art of Wind Playing, 1973. Address: 12008 South 35th Ct, Phoenix, AZ 85044, USA.

WEISBROD Annette, b. 9 Dec 1937, Blackburn, Lancashire, England. Pianist. m. Charles Kirmess, 21 Jan 1967. Education: Teaching Diploma, Chamber Music Diploma, Zurich Conservatory; Soloist and Concert Diploma, Basle Conservatoire. Debut: Wigmore Hall in London, 1960. Career: Concert appearances worldwide; Radio and TV appearances in Switzerland, Germany, England, France, the former Yugoslavia and China; Professor at Berne Conservatoire. Recordings: Over 40 LPs and CDs including: Haydn Trios with the Swiss Festival Trio; Complete Works for Piano and Cello by Beethoven; Several piano concertos and many piano works. Memberships: Swiss Tonkünstler Verein; Swiss Musikpädagogischer Verein; International Piano Teachers Association. Hobbies: Walking; Cooking. Address: Heuelstr 33, CH-8032 Zurich, Switzerland.

WEISE Klaus, b. 30 Jan 1936, Kolpin, Poland. Conductor. Education: Studied at Berlin, Dresden and Leipzig. Career: Conducted first at Wuppertal, then principal conductor of the Essen Opera; Musical director at Fribourg Opera, 1978-81, Kiel, 1981-85, and Dortmund, 1985-90; Director of the Nice Opera and Philharmonic Orchestra, from 1990. Address: Théâtre de l'Opéra de Nice, 4 and 6 Rue St François de Paule, F-06300 Nice, France.

WEISEL-CAPSOUTO Robin, b. 1952, USA. Soprano Singer. Education: Studied at Oberlin College, The University of Illinois, with Jean Tourel in Jerusalem and with Heather Harper in London. Debut: Sang Vivaldi's Gloria with the Jerusalem Symphony Orchestra in 1974. Career: Sang in Mahler's 4th with Israel Philharmonic, 1976; Opera engagements in USA and Israel as Gluck's Amor, Lucy in The Beggar's Opera, and in La Voix Humaine, Le Roi David, Bacchus and Ariadne by Thomas Arne and Rameau's Les Fêtes d'Hébé; Sang Zerlina with New England Opera Company in 1984, and The Governess in The Turn of The Screw for New Israeli Opera in 1992; Concert repertoire includes Bach's B minor Mass, Carissimi's Jephte, Solomon and other oratorios by Handel.

WEISGARBER Elliot, b. 5 Dec 1919, Pittsfield, Massachusetts, USA. Composer; Conductor; Researcher; Performer of Japanese Music. m. Bethiah Setter, 21 Dec 1943, 1 daughter. Education: BMus, MMus, Performer's Certificate, Eastman School of Music, University of Rochester; Studies in clarinet, chamber music, composition and Japanese Music. Career includes: Instructor to Professor, 1960-85, Emeritus Professor, 1985-, University of British Columbia, Canada. Compositions include: Kyoto Landscapes: Lyrical Evocations for Orchestra, 1979; Night for Baritone; Chorus and String Quartet; Concerto for Violin and Orchestra, 1974; Pacific Triology for Full Orchestra; Fantasia A Tre for Horn, Violin and Piano; Illusions Of Immortality, song cycle for Soprano and Piano, poems by Clive Simpson; Crown Of Fire, film music; Music For Morning Of World for Wind and Percussion; Quintet for Flute, Oboe, Clarinet, Horn and Bassoon; Fantasia, Eclogue and Rondo for Clarinet and Piano, 1982; Epigrams for Flute and Piano; Songs Of 1000 Autumns, commissioned by New Vancouver Music Society, 1984; 32 Concert etudes for solo clarinet, 1985-86; Quintet for Clarinet and Strings, 1988; Music In Memory Of Andrei Sakharov, commissioned by Augustine's Artists, Anchorage, 1990; Sonata Piacevole for Clarinet and Piano, 1990; Adaptations for Clarinet and Piano; Claude Debussy Sonate for Violin and Piano, 1991; Claude Debussy L'Isle Joyeuse; Claude Debussy 12 Preludes under title of Paysages Intimes, 1992; Claude Debussy Suite Bergamasque, 1993; Omnia Exeunt in Misterium, Poems by George Sterling (1869-1926) for soprano and orchestra, 1993; Trio, for violin, violoncello and piano, 1993; Ama Dablam: A Soliloquy, for piano, 1994; Fuyu-hi-no-tabi (A Day's Journey in Winter), for soprano, cor anglais (or alto flute) and harp, 1995; Vier Lieder (Rilke), 1995; Fuji-daké no kei, (Views of Mount Fuji), six miniatures for violin and harp, 1995; Canciones del sur, Amor y el Mar, settings in Spanish of poetry by Pablo Neruda, 1996; Fantasia on Down Ampney, flute and double string orchestra, 1996; Divine Immanence: 3 Poems by Robinson Jeffers (Gray landmarks of an end, Continents, End, Tor House), voice and piano, 1997; Colloquies for Flute and Orchestra, 1997. Recordings: Night with Vancouver Chamber Choir, Jon Washburn and Bruce Pullen, Baritone; Purcell String Quartet with Wilmer Fawcett, double bass. Publications: Miyako Sketches, Flute and Piano, 1996; Fantasia on Down Ampney, flute and organ, 1996; A Japanese Miscellany, vol 1, Piano Solo, 1997; Concert Etudes for Solo Clarinet. Address: 4042 West 33rd Avenue, Vancouver, British Columbia V6N 2J1, Canada.

WEISS Ferdinand, b. 6 June 1933, Vienna, Austria. Composer; Educator. m. Ingeborg Scheibenreiter, 16 Sept 1967, 2 sons. Education: Diplomas: Music, 1958, Composition (prize) 1960, Conducting (prize) 1961, Flute, Viennese Academy of Music. Debut: As Composer, Eisenstadt, 1957. Career: Freelance composer, private teacher of music theory, conductor and orchestra musician, 1960-; Music Master, Vienna Conservatory and Baden Pedagogische Academie; Manager, Concert Chamber Ensemble, Lower Austria Composer's Society; President of Inoek. Compositions: About 205 works including: 3 Symphonies, Concertos for Flute, Oboe, Clarinet, Trumpet and Trombone, Chamber music, Lieder; About 700 performances, concerts and radio in Austria, USA, Italy, Argentina, Germany, France, Netherlands, Hungary, Belgium, Portugal, Spain, Norway, Poland, England, Switzerland, Finland, Australia and Japan; Quattrofonia for Saxophone Quartet at Carnegie Hall; 5 Scènes pour Quatuor De Guitares in Paris. Recordings: Konzert-Stueck for Oboe and String Orchestra; Flute en Miniature, Die Fliege, Ragtime, Trio Infernale (CD Turning Pro); Trio for Mandolin and Harp; Relazioni Variabili. Publications: Pedagogical works. Contributions to: Bildung und Kulturakuell. Hobbies: Photography; Sport; Travel. Address: Christalnigg-Gasse 11, A-2500 Baden, Austria.

WEISS Howard A, b. 1938 Chicago, Illinois, USA. Violinist; Conductor; Concertmaster; Educator. Education: BM, 1960, MM, honours, 1966, Chicago Musical College, Roosevelt University. Career: Founder, Music Director, Conductor, Rochester Philharmonic Youth Orchestra, 1970-89, with 12 tours including England, Scotland, 1984, Germany, Austria, Switzerland, 1986, Dominican Republic, 1987, Alaska, 1988; Jamaica, 1989, also on

Voice of America; Advisory Board, Young Audiences of Rochester, 1975-; Rochester Chamber Orchestra, 1981-; Professor, Violin: Eastman School of Music, Rochester, 1981-, Nazareth College, Rochester, 1983-85; Concertmaster: Chicago Chamber Orchestra, 1962-70, San Francisco Ballet Orchestra, 1962, Virginia Symphony, 1964, Rochester Philharmonic, 1967-87 (Concertmaster Emeritus, 1987-), Eastern Music Festival, Greensboro, North Carolina, 1976-80, Grand Teton Music Festival Seminar, Jackson Hole, Wyoming, 1983-86, Rochester Oratorio Society, 1987-, Bear Lake Music Festival, Utah, 1992-93; 1st Violinist, Cleveland Orchestra, 1965-67; Violin Soloist, over 45 concerti with Cleveland Orchestra, Rochester and New Orleans Philharmonics, Chicago Grant Park Symphony, Cincinnati, Chicago and Rochester Chamber Orchestras; Violin soloist with conductors James Levine, David Zinman, Alexander Schneider, Walter Hendl and Gerard Schwarz; Soloist, complete concerti for violin and orchestra of J S Bach (5), Rochester Bach Festival, of Haydn (3), Rochester Chamber Orchestra; Violinist of Brockport Piano Trio, 1971-74; Leader, Hartwell String Quartet, 1975-78; Participant, Casals Festival, Puerto Rico, 1975-80; Chamber music with Misha Dichter, Leonard Rose, Lynn Harrell, Yo-Yo Ma; Elly Ameling, Jaime Laredo, Walter Trampler, Lillian Fuchs, James Buswell, Gary Karr, Alan Civil, Lukas Foss. Recordings: Amram Elegy for Violin and Orchestra, David Zinman, Rochester Philharmonic; Music Director, Conductor, Rochester Philharmonic Youth Orchestra, 21 LPs. Honours: Outstanding Graduate of 1966, Roosevelt University, 1973; Monroe County (New York) Medallion, 1986. Address: 228 Castlebar Road, Rochester, NY 14610, USA.

WEISS Susan (Forscher), b. 22 Jul 1944, New York, USA. Professor; Musicologist. m. James L Weiss, 23 Jul 1967, 1 son, 1 daughter. Education: BA, Goucher College, 1965; MA, Smith College, 1967; PhD, University of Maryland, 1985; Further studies at Juilliard School of Music, 1957-61, Aspen Music Festival, 1960-61, Ecoles d'Art Américaines, 1962, New York University, 1967-68, and University of Michigan, 1968-70. Career: Chairman, Music Department, The Garrison Forest School, MD, 1973-; Lecturer in Music, Goucher College, Towson, MD, 1985-87; Assistant Professor, Music History, Peabody Conservatory of the Johns Hopkins University, 1987-. Publications: Dissertation: The Manuscript Bologna Q18: A Bolognese Instrumental Collection of the Early Cinquecento, 1985; Bologna Q18: Some Reflection on Content and Context, The Journal of the American Musicological Society, 1988; Musical Patronage of the Bentivoglio Signoria 1465-1512; Atti del XIV Congresso della Società Internazionale de Musicologica, Trasmissione e recezione delle forme di cultura musicale, Bologna, 1987, volume III. Contributions to: Journal of the American Musicological Society; Acta Musicologica. Address: 8302 Tally Ho Road, Lutherville, MD 21093, USA.

WEISSENBERG Alexis, b. 26 Jul 1929, Sofia, Bulgaria. Pianist. Education: Piano and composition studies with Pancho Viadiguerov at age 3, Olga Samarov, Juilliard School of Music, New York, USA, 1946. Debut: Concert with New York Philharmonic under George Szell at Carnegie Hall, New York. Career: 1st orchestral concert in Israel in 1944; Concert tour to South Africa in 1944; USA coast to coast tour and concerts in Paris, Vienna, Madrid, Milan, with Philadelphia Orchestra under Eugene Ormandy in 1951; Soloist playing Tchaikovsky's 1st Piano Concerto with Berlin Philharmonic Orchestra under Herbert von Karajan in 1966; Invited performer for many leading conductors and orchestras worldwide including Abbado, Bernstein, Karajan and Ormandy, 1967-; Played at Royal Festival Hall in London in 1974; Various world tours with New Philharmonic Orchestra under Maazel. Recordings include: Music by Beethoven, Chopin, Tchaikovsky, Rachmaninov, Bach and Schumann. Address: c/o Michal Schmidt, Thea Dispeker Inc, 59 East 54th Street, New York, NY 10022, USA.

WEITHAAS Antje, b. 1966, Germany. Concert Violinist. Education: Hanns Eisler Hochschule, Berlin. Career: Frequent concerts with the Deutsches SO and Vladimir Ashkenazy, Leipzig Gewandhaus Orchestre, Suisse Romande and Acadamy of St Martin in the Fields; Los Angeles PO, Boston SO and Minneapolis Orchestra; Philharmonia, BBC SO, Dresdner Staatskapelle and Scottish Chamber Orchestra; Season 1995-96 with recitals at the Bath Festival and Wigmore Hall, London, San Francisco SO Debut Series and in Toronto; Season 1996-97 with the Orchestre de Paris, Zurich Tonhalle, Gothenburg SO, BBC SO, and tour of Germany with the Bournemouth SO; Repertory includes works by Schnittke, Gubaidulina and Tippett; Chamber music with the Ex Aequo Trio; Chamber concerts at the Paris Châtelet and Berlin Konzerthaus, 1997; Plays Matteo Goffriller violin (1700). Honours include: Winner of Wieniawski and Kreisler Competitions, and 1991 Joseph Joachim Competition. Address: Harrison/Parrott Ltd, 12 Penzance Place, London W11 4PA, England.

WELBORN Tracey, b. 1967, Stoneville, North Carolina, USA. Singer (Tenor). Education: Curtis Institute of Music, Philadelphia. Career: School teacher until 1989; Opera engagements with Lausanne Opera, Boston Lyric Opera, Spoleto USA, Opera Co of Philadelphia and Portland Opera; Season 1993-94 with Rossini's Lindoro for Utah Opera, Ernesto and Tamino for Canadian Opera and Gluck's Pylade at Strasbourg; Season 1994-95; Season 1995 with Paris in La Belle Hélène for Scottish Opera, Ferrando at Pittsburgh and Jupiter in Semele at Spoleto, Italy; Concerts include Candide with the San Francisco SO, Messiah with the Baltimore SO, Honegger's King David, and Mozart's Requiem; Phoenix SO in Bach's St Matthew Passion; Season 1997 with Mozart's Belmonte at Edmonton, Don Ottavio at Costa Mesa and in Prokoviev's The Duenna at Geneva title role in Rossini's Le Comte Ory, at Glyndebourne. Recordings include: Paolo in Il Matrimonio Segreto. Honours include: Winner, Washington International Competition and Mario Lanza Competition. Address: c/o Allied Artists, 42 Montpellier Square, London SW7 1JZ, England.

WELCHER Dan, b. 2 Mar 1948, Rochester, New York, USA. Composer; Conductor. Education: BMus, 1969, Eastman School at Rochester (composition with Samuel Adler); MM, 1972, Manhattan School of Music and postgraduate studies in electronic music at the Aspen Music School, 1972. Career: Bassoonist with the Rochester PO, 1968-69, and US Military Band at West Point, 1969-72; Louisville Orchestra, 1972-78; Assistant Conductor with the Austin, Texas, SO (1980-90); Faculty of University of Texas 1978, Full Professor from 1989; Faculty of Aspen Music Festival, 1976-93. Compositions include: Flute Concerto, 1974; 2 Wind Quintets, 1972, 1977; Concerto da Camera for bassoon and chamber orchestra, 1975; Trio for violin, cello and piano, 1976; The Visions of Merlin for orchestra, 1980; Partita for horn, violin and piano, 1980; Vox Femina for soprano and ensemble, 1984; Quintet for clarinet and strings, 1984; Prairie Light for orchestra, 1985; Arches: An Impression for concert band, 1985; Evening Scenes: Three Poems of James Agee, 1985; Della's Gift, opera, 1986; The Yellowstone Fires for wind ensemble, 1988; Clarinet Concerto, 1989; Bridges, 5 pieces for strings, 1989; 2 string quartets, 1987, 1992; 2 symphonies, 1992, 1994; Violin Concerto, 1993; Piano Concerto, Shiva's Drum, 1994; Zion for wind ensemble, 1994; Bright Wings, for orchestra, 1996. Honours include: Residencies, MacDowell Colony, 1989, and Bellagio, 1997; Composer-in-Residence with the Honolulu SO, 1990-93; Guggenheim Fellowship, 1997; 3 National Endowment for the Arts awards. Address: c/o Theodore Presser Co, 1 Presser Place, Bryn Mawr, PA 19010, USA.

WELKER Hartmut, b. 27 Oct 1941, Velbert, Rhineland, Germany. Opera Singer (Bass-Baritone). m. Edeltraut, 2 July 1982, 1 son, 1 daughter. Education: Studied for technical career, took up singing, 1972. Debut: Opera, Aachen, 1974; UK debut, Edinburgh Festival with LSO/Abbado, 1983. Career: Aachen Opera, 1974-80; Since then has had 3-year contract with Karlsruhe Opera; Sang at La Scala (Lohengrin with Abbado), Geneva, Paris (Khovanshchina); Sang Don Pizarro (Fidelio), Madrid and at Maggio Musicale, FLorence, Italy and for scottish Opera, 1984; Appeared in Hamburg, Munich and Stuttgart; Boris Godunov in North America with Chicago Symphony Orchestra/Abbado; Vienna State Opera, Berlin and Hamburg in productions of Fidelio, Flying Dutchman, Salome, Lohengrin; Covent Garden debut. Fidelio, 1986; Sang also with Philharmonia Orchestra/Muti, also at Turin, Vienna, Madrid, Bologna, Naples, Tokyo, Chicago; Season 1988 included appearances in San Francisco, Berlin, Geneva, with further visits to La Scala, Covent Garden and Salzburg; Sang in London, 1986-89, as Pizarro and Kaspar; Theater an der Wien and Turin, 1989 in Schubert's Fierabras and as Wozzeck; Telramund in Lohengrin at the Vienna Staatsoper and the Deutsche Opera Berlin, 1990; Other roles include Kurwenal, Klingsor, Macbeth, Carlos in La Forza del destino; Amonasro, Barnaba and Scarpia; Sang Pizarro in Fidelio at the Metropolitan, 1991; Sang Wozzeck at Catania, 1996. Recordings include: Der Traumgörge as Kaspar/Hans; Notre Dame as Archidiakonus; Fierabras, Brutamonte, 1992, Fidelio (Pizarro), Lohengrin (Telramund); Das Wunder der Heliane, Korngold, 1992. Address: Frühlingstrasse 10, D-76327 Pfintzal/Wöschbach, Germany.

WELLEJUS Henning, b. 23 Aug 1919, Roskilde, Denmark. Composer. m. Inge Osterby, 2 children. Education: Studied with composer Svend Erik Tarp and conductor Giovanni Di Bella; University of Copenhagen. Debut: Copenhagen. Compositions include: 3 Symphonies; 4 Concerts for violin and orchestra, oboe and orchestra, cello and orchestra, and piano and orchestra; Symphonic Fantasies: The History of the Year, Nina; Our Childhood's Friends and from Hans Christian Anderson's picturebook, 2 suites from ballet, The Swan; Wind Quintet; Flute Serenade Just for Fun, for flute, violin, viola and cello; 2 String Quartets; Several Songs; Trio for clarinet, viola and piano; The Dream, ballet; Passacaglia for orchestra; A Freedom Overture; Copenhagen Rhapsody; A Danish Summer Pastorale; Grates Nune Omnes Reddamus Domini, for soprano, chorus and orchestra; A Danish Requiem for soprano, baritone and orchestra; A Trio for Piano, Violin and Oboe; 3 Symphonic Fantasies, Dionysia, A Summer Morning in Hornbiek and the Distant Morningsong of the Stars; a Trio for Violin, Viola and Cello; Operas; The Changed Bridegroom and Barbara; Several songs and numerous other works. Recordings: CD of music of his concert for violin and orchestra; CD of orchestra music. Honours include: Lange-Müller Stipendich, 1956; Aksel Agerbys Mindelegat, 1957; Det Anckerske Legat, 1958; Aügüst and Theodore Kassels Familie-og, Künstnerlegat, 1987; Cross, Order of Knighthood, Denmark. Memberships include: Danish Composers Society. Address: Godthaabsvej 99, 2000 Frederiksberg, Denmark.

WELLER Dieter, b. 25 May 1937, Essen, Germany. Singer (Bass Baritone). m. Dorte Fischer. Education: Studied with Erwin Rottgen in Essen; Further study in Cologne. Career: Debut at Bremerhaven, 1963-66 as Padre Guardiano in La Forza del Destino; Member of the Frankfurt Opera from 1966; Appeared in San Francisco in 1974 as Wurm in Luisa Miller; Further appearances in Berlin, Dusseldorf, Hamburg, Brussels and Edinburgh; Sang at Teatro Regio Turin in 1983 in Berg's Lulu, at Metropolitan Opera in 1985 as the Music Master in Ariadne auf Naxos; Many appearances in operas by Rossini, Lortzing, Weber, Smetana, Wagner and Wolf-Ferrari; Frequent concert engagements. Recordings: Der Freischütz and Martha; Der Zwerg by Zemlinsky.

WELLER Walter, b. 30 Nov 1939, Vienna, Austria. Conductor; Violinist. m. Elisabeth Samohyl, 1966, 1 son. Education: Studied violin at High School for Music and Dramatic Art, Vienna. Career: Member, 1946-, Soloist, 1951-, Violinist, Concertmaster, 1956-69, Vienna Philharmonic Orchestra; Founder and Director of Weller Quartet touring Europe, Asia and North America; Conductor, Vienna State Opera, 1969-, touring USA, Scandinavia, Israel, Italy, Netherlands, Spain, Switzerland, Belgium and France; Principal Conductor, Artistic Advisor, Royal Liverpool Philharmonic Orchestra, 1977-80; Principal Conductor, Royal Philharmonic Orchestra, London, 1980-85; President of the Rodewald Concert Society in England, 1984-, touring Japan, Germany, Scotland, Hong Kong, and Russia; Chief Guest Conductor of Royal Philharmonic Orchestra, London, 1985-; Conductor Laureate of the Royal Philharmonic Orchestra, Liverpool, 1980-; Chief Guest Conductor, National Orchestra of Spain, 1987-; Conducted Prince Igor at the Deutsche Staatsoper, Berlin, 1989; Principal Guest Conductor of the Royal Flanders Philharmonic Orchestra in Belgium, 1990; Music Director and Chief Conducter of the Basle Theatre and Symphony Orchestra from 1994. Has conducted Fidelio and Der Rosenkavalier for Scottish Opera, Der fliegende Holländer and Ariadne auf Naxos for English National Opera, and Der Freischütz at Bologna and Holländer at La Scala, Milan; Die Zauberflöte at Basle, 1996. Recordings: Numerous. Honours: Grand Prix du Discque Charles Cros; Beethoven Gold Medal; Mozart Interpretation Prize; Medal of Arts and Science, Austria, 1968. Address: c/o Harrison/Parrott Ltd, 12 Penzance Place, London W11 4PA, England.

WELLINGTON Christopher (Ramsay), b. 5 Feb 1930, London, England. Viola and Viola d'Amore Player. m. (1) Joanna Donat, 30 Oct 1954, 1 s, 1 d, (2) Eileen Darlow, 1 Jul 1988. Education: MA, Oxford University, 1953; ARCM, Royal College of Music, 1954. Career: Sadler's Wells Opera Orchestra, 1954-58; Philharmonia Orchestra, 1958-65; Principal Viola, London Bach Orchestra, Philomusica of London, Tilford Bach Orchestra; Currently Principal Viola of Southern Pro Musica, English Baroque Orchestra; Viola player of Zorian String Quartet, Amici String Quartet, Nemet Piano Quartet, Music Group of London, Rasumovsky String Quartet; Frequent soloist at Queen Elizabeth Hall; Professor of Viola, Royal College of Music. Recordings: Elegiac Meditation by Robin Milford; Works of Haydn, Rubbra, Charles Ives, Shostakovich with Amici Quartet; Works by Elgar, Vaughan Williams, Frank Bridge, Schubert with Music Group of London. Membership: Warden, Solo Performers Section, 1986-87, Incorporated Society of Musicians. Hobby: Sailing. Address: 13 Cambridge Road, New Malden, Surrey, KT3 3QE, England.

WELSBY Norman, b. 7 Feb 1939, Warrington, Cheshire, England. Singer (Baritone). Education: Studied at the Royal College of Music in Manchester and with Gwilym Jones and Otakar Kraus in London. Debut: Sadler's Wells Opera, London in 1968 as Masetto. Career: Many appearances at Covent Garden and with English National Opera in the standard repertoire and in modern works; Sang Gunther in The Ring, under Reginald Goodall, 1973-74; Sang in the premiere of The Magic Fountain by Delius, BBC 1977; Sang Pentheus in the British premiere of The Bassarids in 1974 and The General in the premiere of We Come to The River, at Covent Garden in 1976; Many concert appearances. Recordings include: The Ring of the Nibelung conducted by Reginald Goodall; The Magic Fountain. Address: c/o English National Opera, London Coliseum, St Martin's Lane, London, WC2, England.

WELSER-MÖST Franz, b. 16 Aug 1960, Linz, Austria. Conductor. Education: Completed music studies with Professor Balduin Sulzer. Career: Principal Conductor of the Austrian Youth Orchestra until 1985; Mahler's 1st Symphony and Bruckner's 5th Symphony in the Musikverein, live recording with the London Philharmonic Orchestra; Salzburg Festival debut, 1985; British debut, 1986 with the London Philharmonic; European tour with the orchestra to Vienna, Berlin and Amsterdam; Guest engagements with the Zurich Tonhalle, Vienna Symphony, New York Philharmonic, Boston Symphony, Philadelphia Orchestra, Chicago Symphony, Cleveland, St Louis and Los Angeles Philharmonic, Bayerischer Rundfunk, Berlin Philharmonic; 2 tours to South Africa with the London Philharmonic Orchestra, 1983, 1994; Opera debut in October 1987 with a new production of L'Italiana in Algeri at the Vienna State Opera; Cosi fan Tutte at the Deutsche Oper, Berlin; Formerly Chief Conductor in Norrkoeping and Winterthur; London Philharmonic Orchestra, 1990; Season 1991-92 with La Clemenza di Tito at the Deutsche Oper Berlin and Rosenkavalier at Zurich; Season 1993-94 with Tristan und Isolde at the Festival Hall, London and Peter Grimes at Glyndebourne; Music Director, Zurich Opera, September 1995-; Music Director, London Philharmonic Orchestra, 1990-96; Elektra at Linz; Die Lustige Witwe, Glyndebourne Company at the Festival Hall; Die Fledermaus, Un Ballo in Maschera and Dvorak's Rusalka at Zurich; Glyndebourne Festival 1996, Cosi fan Tutte. Recordings include: Lehar's Die Lustige Witwe, 1994; Bruckner's Symphony No 5; Beethoven's Symphony No 5; Mozart's C Minor Mass. Current Management: IMG Artists Europe. Address: c/o Media House, 3 Burlington Lane, Chiswick, London W4 2TH, England.

WELSH Moray, b. 1 Mar 1947, Haddington, Scotland. Cellist. m. Melissa Phelps, 13 Oct 1984. Education: York University; Moscow Conservatoire. Debut: Wigmore Hall, 1972. Career: Concerts with London Symphony Orchestra, Royal Philharmonic Orchestra, Philharmonic, BBC Symphony; Tours to Scandinavia, USA, Russia, Europe; Principal Cellist, London Symphony Orchestra, 1992-; Played in the Brahms Double Concerto, Barbican, 1997. Recordings: Concertos by Boccherini, Vivaldi, Hugh Wood (Sunday Times Record of the Year), Alexander Goehr, as well as chamber music. Honours: British Council Awards, 1969; Gulbenkian Fellowship, 1972-74. Hobbies: Skiing; Walking; Gardening; Instrument making. Address: 28 Summerfield Avenue, Queens Park, London NW6 6JY, England.

WELTING Ruth, b. 11 May 1949, Memphis, TN, USA. Singer (Soprano). m. Edo de Waart. Education: Studied with Daniel Ferro in New York, Luigi Ricci in Rome and Jeanne Reiss in Paris. Debut: New York City Opera in 1970 as Blondchen in Die Entführung. Career: Has sung at opera houses in Dallas, Houston, San Antonio, Santa Fe and San Francisco; Sang at Covent Garden and Metropolitan Opera, 1975-76 as Zerbinetta in Ariadne auf Naxos, Ottawa and Washington, 1979-80 as the Fairy Godmother in Cendrillon by Massenet, and Teatro Liceo Barcelona in 1984 as Marie in La Fille du Régiment; Sang Lucia di Lammermoor at Cincinnati in 1985, and Rosina in 1987; Sang at Teatro Regio Parma in 1985 as Olympia in Les Contes d'Hoffmann, Chicago Lyric Opera in 1990 as Ophelia in Hamlet, and Olympia at Barcelona in 1990; Other roles include Zerlina, the Princess in L'Enfant et les Sortilèges, Norina, Gilda and Adele in Die Fledermaus; Many Lieder recitals. Recordings: Sophie in Der Rosenkavalier; Der Schauspieldirektor; Mignon by Thomas; Hansel and Gretel. Address: c/o Lyric Opera of Chicago, 20 North Wacker Drive, Chicago, IL 60606, USA.

WEN De-Qing, b. 10 July 1958, Jian Yang, Fujian, China. Composer. Education: Art Department, Fujian Normal University, 1978-82; China Conservatory of Music, Beijing, 1988-90; Conservatoire de Musique de Genève, Switzerland, 1992-96; Conservatoire National Supérieur de Musique de Lyon, France, 1993-94. Debut: Composer, Ningxia Ensemble, China, 1984. Career: Concert Portrait performed by Ningxia Ensemble, Xining, 1986; Music for Fan Jun's film Tong Nian Zai, Ruijing, 1990; Concert Portrait performed by Ensemble Contrechamps and Ensemble CIP, Geneva, 1995. Compositions: Ji I and Ji II for piano, 1992-93; Complainte for 1 speaker of Beijing Opera and 3 percussionists, 1994; Le souffle for 6 instruments, 1994; String Quartet No 1, 1995; Spring, River, Flowers, Moon, Night for 12 women's voices, 1995; Traces II for 9 instruments, 1996; Divination for 6 instrumentalists, 1997. Recordings: CD: Deqing Wen, Ensemble Contrechamps and CIP, Quatuor du Temps, recorded for Radio Suisse Romande, Espace 2, 1996. Publications: Musical Works, China, 1997, Switzerland, 1998, France, 1998. Honours: 1st Prize for Composition, Ningxia, China, 1986, 1988; Prix du Conseil d'Etat, Geneva, 1993; 1st Prize for Composition, Neuchâtel, Switzerland, 1996. Memberships: Association Suisse des Musiciens; Société Suisse pour les Droits des Auteurs d'Oeuvres Musicales. Hobby: Chinese violin. Address: 36 Avenue de la Roseraie, 1205 Geneva, Switzerland.

WENDELBURG Norma (Ruth), b. 26 Mar 1918, Stafford, Kansas, USA. Musician (Composer-Performer). Education: BM, Music and General, Bethany College, Lindsborg, Kansas, 1943; MMus, Music Education, Composition, Piano, University of Michigan, Ann Arbor, 1947; MMus, Composition, Piano, 1951, PhD, Composition, 1969, Eastman School of Music, Rochester, New York; Fulbright Award to Mozarteum, Salzburg, and State Academy of Music, Vienna, Austra, 1953-55. Career: Teaching: Head of Graduate Department, Hardin Simmons University, Abilene, Texas, 1958-63; Theory, Composition, Piano, Head of Theory and Composition, SW Texas State University, San Marcos, 1969-72; Also served at Dallas Baptist College, Texas, and Friends College, Haviland, Kansas; Performance of original works in USA and Europe; Performer-Pianist. Compositions include: Published choral music. Recordings: Own compositions: Suite No 2 for Violin and Piano, 1989; Fantasy for trumpet and piano, 1990; Sonata for clarinet and piano, 1992; Sinfonietta for large orchestra, performed by St Petersburg Orchestra; Clarinet Concerto, Warsaw, Poland, 1996; London Rhapsody composed for the London Philharmonic Orchestra, 1997. Contributions to: 4 articles to Challenge Magazine, 1988-91. Honours: American Society of Composers, Authors and Publishers Awards, each year from 1988; Fulbright Award, 2 years; Numerous fellowships and scholarships; Meet the Composer Awards; Numerous performances in music centresl Memberships include: American Society of Composers, Authors and Publishers; Sigma Alpha Iota; American Music Centre; MacDowell Colonists. Hobbies: Travel; Photography; Gardening. Address: 2206 Van Buren, Hutchinson, KS 67502, USA.

WENKEL Ortrun, b. 25 Oct 1942, Buttstadt, Thuringia, Germany. Singer (Mezzo Soprano and Alto). m. Dr Peter Rothe, 7 Jun 1966. Education: Franz Liszt Hochschule Weimar, Hochschule für Musik, Frankfurt; Lohmann Masterclass and operatic studies with Cavelti. Debut: Concert, as student, in London, 1964; Opera in Heidelberg, 1971. Career: Performed at opera houses throughout Europe including Milan Scala, Covent Garden, Bayerische Staatsoper, Hamburg, with appearances at the Salzburg Festival, Munich Opera Festival and festivals of Schwetzingen, Edinburgh, Berlin and Vienna, notably as Penelope in the Zurich production of the Monteverdi Cycle; Has given numerous lieder recitals and made guest appearances with symphony orchestras in New York, London, Berlin, Vienna, Paris, Bayreuth, Amsterdam, Buenos Aires and Rio de Janeiro among others. Recordings include: Boulez Bayreuth Centenary Ring, The Ring with Dresdner Staatskapelle; Mahler's 3rd Symphony and 8th Symphony; Mozart's Requiem; The Magic Flute; Schoenberg's Jacob's Ladder; Dvořák's Stabat Mater; Handel's Xerxes; Solo recitals of Italian Baroque Music; St Matthew Passion by Bach and several of his cantatas; Zemlinsky Lieder, Schreker and Shostakovich Lieder; Henze's The Bassarids. Honours: Grammy for Wagner's Ring des Nibelungen, principal soloist, 1982; Deutscher Schallplattenpreis for Mozart's Requiem, 1983. Hobbies: Gardening; Birds. Address: Eichendorffstrasse 25, D-69493 Hirschberg-Leutershausen, Germany.

WENKOFF Spas, b. 23 Sep 1928, Tirnovo, Bulgaria. Singer (Tenor). Education: Studied with J Jossifov in Sofia, Madame Saffiriva in Russe and Johannes Kemter in Dresden. Debut: Tirnovo 1954, in Keto and Kote by Dolidse. Career: Sang in Russe, Bulgaria, 1962-65, East Germany from 1965, Dobben, Madgeburg, Halle and the Staatsoper Berlin; Sang Tristan at Dresden Staatsoper in 1975, and Tristan and Tannhäuser at Bayreuth Festival, 1976-83; Has sung roles in operas by Verdi and Puccini as well as leading parts in operas by Wagner; Sang Tannhäuser at Vienna Staatsoper in 1982; Further appearances at the Deutsche Oper Berlin in 1984, Munich and Cologne; Sang Tannhäuser at Berne in 1987. Address: c/o SA Gorlinsky Ltd, 33 Dover Street, London, W1X 4NJ, England.

WENNBERG Siv (Anna Margareta), b. 18 Sept 1944, Timrå, Sweden. Dramatic Soprano. Education: Ingesunds Musikskola, Sweden; Musikaliska Akademien Stockholm; Qualified Pianist, Organist and Music Director. Debut: Royal Opera House, Stockholm in 1972. Career includes: Opera performances from 1972 throughout Europe; Extensive concert appearances with roles including Brünnhilde in Siegfried and Valkyrie, Empress in Die Frau ohne Schatten (TV), Amelia in Ballo in Maschera (TV), Alice in Falstaff, Puccini's Tosca, Leonora in Fidelio, Mozart's Donna Elvira, Daisy Doody in Aniara, Euridice in Orpheus in the Underworld and Beatrice in von Suppé's Boccaccio; TV and Radio appearances in Sweden, throughout Europe and the USA; Permanent member of the Royal Opera Stockholm; Sang Verdi: title role, Aïda and Lady Macbeth; Wagner: Senta, Elisabeth, Elsa and Sieglinde; Strauss: Elektra, Salome, Ariadne. Recordings: Scandinavian Songs with Geoffrey Parsons; Wagner's Rienzi, Irene, with Dresden Staatskapelle; Royal Opera Stockholm Gala excerpt from Aïda, 1995; Schubert and Strauss songs with Jan Eyron, 1997. Honours: First prizes at Jussi Björling Competition and Scandinavian Singing Contest, 1971; Swedish Opera Prize for Wagner's Isolde, 1988; Appointed Court Singer by King Carl Gustaf XVI of Sweden, 1994. Hobby: Classical Music. Current Management: Svenska Konsertbyrån, Jungfrugatan 45, SE-11444, Stockholm, Sweden. Address: Odengatan 32, S-11351 Stockholm, Sweden.

WENZINGER August, b. 14 Nov 1905, Basle, Switzerland. Cellist; Conductor; Educator. m. Ilse Hartmann. Education: Studied cello at the Basle Conservatory, 1915-27; Studied in Cologne with Jarnach and Grummer, 1927-29. Career: First Cellist of the Bremen Orchestra, 1929-34, Basle Allgemeine Musikgesellschaft, 1936-70; Cellist in the Basle String Quartet, 1933-47; Co-founded the Schola Cantorum Basiliensis in 1933, teaching viola da gamba, ensemble and ornamentation there; Co-leader, Kammermusikkreis Scheck-Wenzinger, 1936-43; Lectured at Harvard University on performance practice and viola da gamba playing, 1953; Directed the Capella Coloniensis for West German Radio in Cologne, 1954-58; Directed performances of baroque operas at Herrenhausen, 1958-66; Founded the viola da gamba trio of the Schola Cantorum Basiliensis, 1968; Musical Director of Baroque concerts at Oberlin, OH; Guest Professor for Viola Da Gamba at the Hochschule für Musik, Vienna, 1976-; Concert tours of Europe, Asia and the USA; Gave the premieres of Martin's Ballade for Cello and Schoeck's Cello Concerto. Publications include: Bach Solo Suites for Cello; JCF Bach Sonata in A; Monteverdi's Orfeo, 1955. Honours include: Honorary DMus, University of Basle, 1960; Fellow, Royal Swedish Academy of Music, 1965; Honorary DMus, Berlin College, 1981. Address: 3 Zehntenfreistrasse, CH-4103 Bottmingen, Switzerland.

WERDER Felix, b. 24 February 1922, Berlin, Germany. Australian Citizen. Education: Studied in Germany before moving to England, 1934; Settled Australia, 1941. Career includes: Adult Education Class Music Lecturer, 1956-; Music Critic, The Age, Melbourne, 1960-77. Compositions include: Kisses for a Quid, opera, 1960; En Passant, ballet, 1964; The General, opera, 1966; Agamemnon, opera, 1967; The Affair, opera, 1969; The Vicious Square, opera, 1971; The Conversation, opera, 1973; Banker, music theatre, 1973; La Belle Dame sans Merci, ballet, 1973; Quantum, ballet, 1973; Cranach's Hunt, horn concerto, 1974; Six Symphonies, 1948-79; Sans souci, flute concerto, 1974; Synorgy for synthesizer, winds and organ, 1974; The Tempest, electronic music for V100, 1974; Index for chamber ensemble, 1976; Bellyful, music theatre, 1976; The Director, music theatre, 1980; Board Music, for piano, 1983; The Medea, opera, 1985; Opening for contrabass and flute, 1987; Concerto for Orchestra, 1987; Concert Music for bass clarinet and orchestra, 1987; Renunciation for viola and orchestra, 1987; Business Day, music theatre, 1988; Two Fantasias for string trio, 1988; Saxophone Quintet, 1988; Belzaser, choral cantata, 1988; Off Beat for cello and piano, 1990; Four Violin Sonatas, 1958-88; Los Dramas, for soprano and chamber ensemble, 1990; The Wenzel Connection, clarinet concerto, 1990; Music for a While, for chamber orchestra, 1991; Taffelmusik, for clarinet, cello and piano, 1991. Honours include: The Sir Zelman Cowan Medal, 1991. Address: c/o APRA, 1A Eden Street, Crows Nest, NSW 2065, Australia.

WERLE Lars Johan, b. 23 Jun 1926, Gavle, Sweden. Composer. Education: Studied musicology with Moberg at Upsala University, counterpoint with Sven-Erik Back. Career: Music Producer for Swedish Radio, 1958; Teacher at the National School for Music and Drama in Stockholm; Opera Drömmen om Therese performed at the 1974 Edinburgh Festival and elsewhere; Resan commissioned by the Hamburg Staatsoper; Tintomara premiered for the bicentenary of the Stockholm Opera House. Compositions: Operas and musicals: Drömmen om Therese, 1960-64, Resan, 1969, Tintomara, 1973, En Saga Om Sinnen, TV opera, 1971, Medusan Och Djaavulen, 1973, A Midsummer Night's Dream, 1985, Lionardo, 1988; Orchestral and instrumental: Pentagram for String Quartet, 1959-60, Sinfonia Da Campa, 1961, Summer Music for Strings and Piano, 1965, Attitudes for Piano, 1965, Zodiak, ballet, 1966, Varieté for String Quartet, 1971, Det Himelska Djuret for Tape, 1975, Vaggsang for Jorden, 1977; Film music for Bergman's Persona; Vocal: Canzone 126 Di Francesco Petraca for Chorus, 1967, Sound Of M4b, Nautical Preludes, 1970, Now All The Fingers Of This Tree (Cummings) for Soprano and Ensemble, 1971, Chants For Dark Hours for Mezzo, Flute, Guitar and Percussion, 1972, Night Hunt for Mezzo and Piano, 1973, Turned Away Songs, 1973, Fabel for 5 Voices, 1974, Flower Power for 6 or more Voices and Instruments, 1974, En Hog Visa for Baritone and Piano, 1975. Address: c/o STIM, Sandhamnsgatan 79, PO Box 27327, S-102 54 Stockholm, Sweden.

WERNER Regina, b. 9 Apr 1950, Zwickau, Germany. Soprano. Education: Studied at the Thomasschule and the Musikhochschule, Leipzig. Career: Sang in sacred concerts at Leipzig, 1974-87; Engagements at the Komische Opera Berlin, 1975-77 and 1989, Halle from 1979, Leipzig and Chemnitz Operas from 1986; Guest appearances throughout Eastern Europe, Korea, Holland, Belgium, Switzerland, Portugal, Japan, Germany and Austria; Roles have included Mozart's Susanna, Bastienne and the Queen of Night, Marzeline, Gilda, Adele in Die Fledermaus and Sophie; Concert repertoire includes music by Bach, Handel, Haydn, the Requiems of Brahms, Mozart and Dvořák, Mahler's Knaben Wunderhorn and Carmina Burana; Professor at the Leipzig Musikhochschule from 1987. Address: c/o Komische Opera Berlin, Behrenstrasse 55-57, 1086 Berlin, Germany.

WERNICKE Herbert, b. 24 Mar 1946, Auggen, Germany. Stage Director and Designer. Education: Studied at the Brunswick Musikhochschule and at the Munich Kunstakademie. Career: Designs for the theatre at Landshut and Wuppertal; Staged Handel's oratorios, Belshazzar at Darmstadt, 1978, and Judas

Maccabeus at the Bayerische Staatsoper; Rameau's Hippolyte et Aricie at the Deutsche Staatsoper Berlin and the 1980 Schwetzingen Festival; Other work includes Fliegende Holländer at Munich and Die Meistersinger at Hamburg; Completed a production of Der Ring des Nibelungen at the Théâtre de la Monnaie, Brussels, 1991; Engaged at Basle Opera for Simon Boccanegra, followed by Don Giovanni, Così fan tutte and Die Fledermaus, 1991-92; Directed Fidelio for the 1996 Salzburg Festival. Address: Theater Basel, Theaterstrasse 7, CH-4010 Basel, Switzerland.

WERRES Elisabeth, b. 1954, Germany. Singer (Soprano). m. Anthony Bramall. Education: Studied in Chicago and Cologne Conservatory. Career: While student sang small roles at Cologne Opera for one season; Engaged at Staatstheater Karlsruhe, 1978-80; Roles including Rosina, Marguerite in Gounod's Faust, Adele and the European Premiere of Argento's Postcard from Morocco; Engaged at Dortmund Opera, 1980-82, as Gilda, Nedda, Musetta, Susanna, Adina; From 1982 Guest Engagements at Staatsoper Hamburg, Staatsoper Munich, Deutsche Oper Berlin, Düsseldorf, Essen, Leipzig, Zürich, Vienna Volksoper, Mannheim; Roles include Rosalinde, The Merry Widow, Martha, Aminta, Euridice, Marenka in The Bartered Bride; Recordings and Broadcast Concerts followed with Westdeutscher Rundfunk, Südwestfunk, Sender Freies Berlin, ORF, Norddeutscher Rundfunk; Television appearances as well as concerts in Chicago, Tokyo, Barcelona, Vienna and throughout Germany; Engaged at the Staatsoper Hannover, 1989-97, gradual transition from the lyric to the jugendlich-dramatische "Fach"; Tatjana in Eugen Onegin, Rosalinde, Freia in Das Rheingold, Frieda in Aribert Reimann's Das Schloss; More recent debuts include the Feldmarschallin in Der Rosenkavalier, The Countess in The Marriage of Figaro and Marie in Alban Berg's Wozzeck. Recordings: CD's, live recording of the Offenbachiade for the opening of the Cologne Philharmonic; Laura in the first complete recording of Hindemith's comic opera Neues Von Tage. Address: Brucknerallee 127, D-41236 Mönchengladbach, Germany.

WERTHEN Rudolf, b. 16 July 1946, Malines, Belgium. Violinist; Conductor. Education: Studied at the Gand and Brussels Conservatories, with André Gertler. Career: Soloist with the NDR Symphony Orchestra at Hamburg and professor at the Robert Schumann Institute, Detmold; Flanders Chamber Orchestra from 1977 and musical director of Flanders Opera at Anvers, from 1992; Has rediscovered and premiered the 7th Concerto of Vieuxtemps and the Russian Concerto of Lalo. Honour: Prizewinner of competitions at Vienna, Amsterdam and Brussels. Address: Robert Schumann Institute & Hochschule für Musik, Allee 22, 4930 Detmold, Germany.

WESLEY-SMITH Martin, b. 1945, Adelaide, Australia. Composer. Education: Studied composition at University of Adelaide and York, England; DPhil. Career: Senior Lecturer in Composition and Electronic Music, New South Wales State Conservatorium of Music, Sydney; Established, First Computer Music Studio, Central Conservatory of Music, Peking, China, 1986. Compositions: Orchestral Works: Interval Piece, 1970, Hansard Music, 1970, Sh..., 1973; Ensemble Works: Snark-Hunting, 1984, White Knight, 1984; Instrumental Works: Improvisations, 1966, Piano Piece, 1968, Small Bitonal Study, 1968, Tiger, Tiger, 1970, Guitar Music 1, 1973; Vocal Works: Gum Tears Of An Arabian Tree, 1966, To Noddy-Man, 1969, Doublets 2(b), 1975; Choral Works: Three Shakespearean Songs, 1965-87, Who Killed Cock Robin, 1979, Lost In Space, 1982, Songs For Snark-Hunters, from Boojum!, 1985; Stage Works: The Wild West Show, 1971, Machine, 1972, Boojum!, 1985-86; Works for Tape: Vietnam Image, 1970, Media Music 1, 1971, 2, 1973, Kdadalak, For the Children of Timor, 1977, Japanese Pictures, 1981, Echoes And Star Tides, 1981, Electronic Study 37(b), 1982, Dah Dit Dah Dah, from Night Satellite, 1983, Wattamolla Red, 1983, Music Box Music, 1984, Venceremos!, 1984, Tango, 1984, Snark-Huntingdon 2, from Boojum!, 1986. Honours: Recipient of numerous awards including Don Banks Composer Fellowship, Australian Council, 1987.

WESSELY Othmar, b. 31 Oct 1922, Linz, Upper Austria. Professor of Musicology. m. Helen Kropik, 19 Sep 1951. Education: Academy of Music and Dramatic Art, Vienna, 1940-42; PhD, University of Vienna, 1947. Career: Archivist, State Opera, Vienna, 1948-49; Secretary for Publishing Society of Monuments of Music in Austria, 1949; Assistant, 1950-63, Lecturer, 1958-63, Musicology, University of Vienna; Professor of Musicology, University of Graz, 1963-71, University of Vienna, 1971-. Publications: Musik in Oberoesterreich, 1951; Die Musikinstrumentensammlung des Oberoesterreichischen Landesmuseums, 1952; Johannes Brassanicus: Ausgewaehile Werke, 1954; Arnold von Bruck: Sämtliche Lateinische Motetten, 1961; Die Grossen Darstellungen de Musikgeschichte in Barock und Aufklaerung, 1964-; E L Gerbers Tonkuenstlerlexika, 1966-77; Fruemeister des stile nuovo in Oesterreich, 1974; Musik, 1973; Philippus de Monte, Madrigals for Five Voices, 1977-82. Contributions to: Numerous national and international scientific journals. Honour: Honorary Member, Johann Joseph Fux Society, Graz, 1978-. Memberships: President, Publishing Society for Monuments of Music in Austria, 1974-91; Academy of Sciences, Austria, 1982-; Head, Commission for Musicology, Austrian Academy of Sciences and Head for Commission for Science of Sound; Trustee, Istituto Storico Austriaco, Rome, Italy. Address: Universitaestrasse 7, A-1010 Vienna, Austria.

WEST Ewan (Donald), b. 9 Aug 1960, Cheltenham, Gloucestershire, England. Music Writer. Education: BA, 1st Class Honours, 1981, MA, 1985, DPhil, 1992, Exeter College, University of Oxford. Career: Lecturer, History of Music, Worcester College, Oxford, 1986-94; Junior Research Fellow, Mansfield College, Oxford, 1988-92; Director of Studies in Music, Somerville College, Oxford, 1989-94. Publications: The Hamlyn Dictionary of Music, 1982; The Oxford Dictionary of Opera, with John Warrack, 1992; The Concise Oxford Dictionary of Opera, 3rd edition, with John Warrack, 1996. Contributions to: Music and Letters; Austrian Studies. Honour: James Ingham Halstead Scholar, University of Oxford, 1985-87. Memberships: American Musicological Society; Royal Musical Association. Hobbies: Reading; Food; Wine. Address: 8 Drakes Place, Malvern, Cheltenham, Glos GL50 2JF, England.

WEST John, b. 25 Oct 1938, Cleveland, OH, USA. Bass Singer. Education: Studied with Martial Singher at the Curtis Institute and with Beverley Johnson in New York. Debut: San Francisco in 1963 as Sarastro. Career: Many appearances at US opera centres including Houston, Philadelphia, Seattle, Santa Fe, Portland, San Francisco, Washington and Fort Worth; Guest engagements at Vancouver, Mexico City, Hanover and Spoleto; Other roles have included Don Alfonso, Oroveso in Norma, Basilio, Mephistopheles of Gounod and Berlioz, Boris Godunov, Ramphis, Arkel, Ochs, La Roche in Capriccio, Hunding and Tiresias; Frequent concert engagements. Address: c/o San Francisco Opera, War Memorial Opera House, San Francisco, CA 94102, USA.

WEST Kevin, b. 1960, England. Tenor. Education: Studied at the Guildhall School with Walter Gruner. Career: Sang first with the D'Oyly Carte Opera Company; Appearances with Opera 80 as Sellem in The Rake's Progress and Don Ottavio, and Britten's Peter Quint for Music Theatre Wales; Engagements with Opera Restor'd in English Baroque Music and throughout Britain; Sang Monteverdi's Orfeo at the Prom Concerts in London; English National Opera debut, 1989 as David in The Mastersingers; Has also sung with English National Contemporary Opera Studio, Opera Factory as Trimalchio in Maderna's Satyricon in 1990 and the Montepulciano Festival in The English Cat in 1990; Appeared with Opera Northern Ireland in 1991 as Mozart's Don Basilio (repeated for Opera North, 1996); Concert repertoire includes Bach's St John Passion and Easter Oratorio, works by Handel, Mozart and Schubert and Tippett's A Child Of Our Time at South Bank in London. Address: c/o Anglo Swiss Ltd, Suite 35-37 Morley House, 320 Regent Street, London W1R 5AD, England

WESTENBURG Richard, b. 26 Apr 1932, Minneapolis, USA. Conductor. Education: Studied at Lawrence University and MA, 1956, at the University of Minnesota; Further study in Paris with Nadia Boulanger and Pierre Cochereau; Postgraduate study at Theological Seminary School of Sacred Music in New York, 1960-66. Career: Teacher at University of Montana, 1956-60; Director of Music at the First Unitarian Church in Worcester, MA, 1960-62; Organist and Choirmaster of the Central Presbyterian Church, New York, 1964-74; Music Director of Musica Sacra from 1968 giving five concert winter season and six concert Bach Festival, annually at Avery Fisher Hall; Frequent guest conductor of choruses and orchestras throughout the USA; Music Director of Collegiate Choral, 1973-79; Head of Choral Department at the Juilliard School of Music, 1977-; Visiting Professor, Rutgers University, 1986-87. Honours include: Honorary DFA, Lawrence University, 1980. Address: 2 Strawberry Hill Avenue, 2-F, Stamford, CT 06902, USA.

WESTERGAARD Peter, b. 28 May 1931, Champaign, Illinois, USA. Composer; Professor of Music. Education: AB, Magna cum Laude, Harvard College, 1953; MFA, Princeton University, 1956; Studied Composition with Walter Piston, Darius Milhaud, Roger Sessions, and Wolfgang Fortner. Career: Assistant, Salzburg Seminar in American Studies, Summer Session 1953; Assistant in Instruction, Princeton University, 1955-56; Assistant to Professor, Wolfgang Fortner, Staatliche Hochschule für Musik, Freiburg, Germany, 1957; Fulbright Guest Lecturer, Staatliche Hochscule für Musik, Freiburg, Germany, 1958; Instructor in Music, 1958-63, Assistant Professor 1963-66, Columbia College; Visiting Lecturer with rank of Associate Professor, Princeton University, 1966-67; Associate Professor, Amherst College, 1967-68; Princeton University, 1968-71; Professor, Princeton University, 1971-; Chairman, Department of Music, Princeton University, 1974-78, 1983-86; Director, Princeton University Orchestra, 1968-73; Board of Directors: American Music Centre, 1969-72; International Society for Contemporary Music, 1970-74; Director, Princeton University Opera Theatre, 1970-; Executive Board, 1977-81; Programme Committee, 1983-84; Society for Music Theory, Publicatio Awards Committee, 1987-91; Chairman, 1988-89; Director, Ju Opera Festival of New Jersey, 1983-86; Visiting Profess University of British Columbia, 1987; Lecturer, International Mu Seminar, University of Bahia, Brazil, 1992; Interdepartmen Committee for the Program in Musical Performance, Princet University, 1992-93; William Shubael Conant Professor of Mus Princeton University, 1995-. Compositions include: 5 Movemer for Small Orchestra, 1959; Cantata II, 1959, III, 1966; Quartet Violin, Vibraphone, Clarinet and Violoncello, 1961; Variations 6 Players, 1967; Mr and Mrs Discobbolos, 1967; Divertimento Discobbolic Fragments, 1967; Noises, Sounds and Sweet Ai 1968; Tuckets and Sennets, 1969; Cantata I, 1956; Two Rhym for soprano and violin, 1979, 1997; Ariel Music, 1987; Ode, 19 The Tempest, Opera in Three Acts after William Shakespea 1990; Ringing Changes, 1996; All 4s, 1996; anyone lived in pretty how town, 1996; Byzantium for baritone and percussi quartet on poems by Yeats, 1997; Chicken Little, an opera children, 1997; Singing Translations of following operas: T Magic Flute, Don Giovanni, Der Freischütz, Fidelio (origir version of 1805), Cosi fan Tutte, The Marriage of Figaro a Cinderella. Recordings: Mr and Mrs Discobbolos; Ariel Mus Divertimento on Discobbolic Fragments, 1995. Honou Commissioned to celebrate 250th anniversary of Princet University, 1994; Keynote Speaker, SMT Annual Conventic 1994; Endowed Professorship, University of Alabar January-February 1995. Address: 40 Pine Street, Princeton, 08542, USA.

WESTERLINCK Wilfried A M, b. 3 Oct 1945, Leuve Belgium. Musician; Composer. Education: Royal Conservatory Brussels and Antwerp. Career: Professor of Music Analysis a Composition, Antwerp 1971-83; BRTN Producer, Belgian Rad 1972. Compositions: Metamorfose for Orchestra; 3 Stri Quartets, 1978, 1984 and 1994; Lanscapes I to V; Sonate 1-3 Piano Solo; Variations on a Theme of Paganini for Piar Sinfonietta; Solo works for Guitar, Cello, Flute, Harp, Harpsicho bass-clarinet, Marimba, 1991 and Songs. Honours: Tenuto Pri for Metamorfose, 1972; Composition Prize of Antwerp, 1977; Baie Prize, 1985; J Van Hoof Prize for song cycle, 19 Composition Prize, Town of Mechelen for Bells, 1986; Adam O Prize for Symphonic work, 1987. Memberships: SABAM; Boa Belgian Composers Society; Flemish Composers R CeBeDeM. Hobbies: Walking; Cooking; Reading. Addre Potvlietaan 1-106 app 15a, B-2600 Antwerpen, Belgium.

WESTERN Hilary, b. 1948, Cardiff, Wales. Sopra Education: Studied at the Royal Academy of Music and t London Opera Centre. Career: Sang at the Wexford a Glyndebourne Festivals and in Angers as Mimi and Toulouse Frasquita; Appearances as Fiordiligi in Grenoble, Anchorage a Britain; Sang Mimi, Papagena and Diana for Opera Nor Ariadne, Louise, Micaela, Christine in Blake's Toussaint, Muse and Diana; Sang at Almeida Festival in 1990 in the wo premiere of Europeras III and IV by John Cage; Performances Birtwistle's Punch and Judy, The Beggar's Opera and Orfeo w Opera Factory; Schoenberg's Pierrot Lunaire for Ballet Rambe Has sung in the musicals, Chess and A Little Night Music, in t West End and at the Chichester Festival in Born Again. Honou include: Arts Council Award, to study with Martin Isepp in N York. Address: c/o Korman International Management, Crunne Green Cottage, Preston, Hertfordshire, SG4 7UQ, England.

WESTLAKE Nigel, b. 6 September 1958, Perth, Weste Australia. Composer; Clarinettist. Education: Clarinet with D Westlake, 1970-78; Bass Clarinet with Harry Sparnay, 19 Composition self taught. Career includes: Freelance clarinet from 1975; Principal of Australia Ensemble, 1987-92, with to throughout Australia and abroad; Tour of Australai and Engla 1992, with John Williams' group, Attaca; Film and televisi music. Compositions include: Onomatopoeia for bass clarinet a digital delay, 1984; Omphalo Centric Lecture, for 4 percussi 1984; Entomology, for chamber ensemble and tape, 19 Refractions at Summercloud Bay, for bass clarinet, flute a string trio, 1989; Malachite Glass, for bass clarinet and percussi quartet, 1990; Antarctica Suite, for guitar and orchestra (from t film score), 1992; Tall Tales But True, for 2 guitars and ensemb 1992; Songs from the Forest, for guitar duo, 1994; High Tensi Wires, for string quartet, 1994; Invocations, concerto for ba clarinet and orchestra, 1995; Babe: orchestral excerpts from t film, 1996; Piano Sonata, 1997. Honours include: Gold Med New York radio festival, 1987; APRA Award, Babe, Best Fi Score, 1996. Address: c/o APRA, P O Box 576, Crows Ne NSW 2065, Australia.

WETHERELL Eric (David), b. 30 Dec 1925, Tynemou Northumbria, England. Musician. m. (1) Jean Bettany, 4 J 1949, 1 son, 1 daughter, (2) Elizabeth Major, 16 Jan 1976, daughters. Education: BA, BMus, The Queen's College, Oxfo 1945-47; Royal College of Music, 1948-49. Career: Horn Play 1949-59; Repetiteur, Royal Opera House, Covent Gard 1960-63; Assistant Music Director, Welsh National Ope 1963-69; Music Director, HTV, 1969-76; Chief Conductor, B

Northern Ireland Orchestra, 1976-81. Compositions: Choral, Solo Songs, Orchestral including Airs and Graces and Welsh Dresser for Orchestra, Bristol Quay for String Orchestra, Your Gift to Man for Chorus; Music for TV plays and films. Publications: Life of Gordon Jacob, 1995; Arnold Cooke, 1996; Patrick Hadley, 1997. Membership: ISM. Hobbies: Jazz; Filmmaking. Address: 24 The Crescent, Henleaze, Bristol, BS9 4RW, England.

WETHERILL Linda, b. 1950, USA. Flautist. Career: Recital and concerto Soloist in major cities of Europe, Canada, USA; Principal Flautist with the orchestras of Hessischer Rundfunk Frankfurt and of Pierre Boulez's IRCAM at Pompidou Centre, Paris, France; Repertoire includes Baroque, Classic, Romantic and Impressionist works; Performed and premiered the flute music of Luciano Berio, Pierre Boulez, Elliott Carter, Olivier Messiaen, Goffredo Petrassi and Karl-Heinz Stockhausen; Taught master classes in English, French, German, Spanish and American Conservatories. Recordings: Numerous for DTR and Deutsche Grammophon. Honours: Won New York Young Artists debut, 1979; First American and first flautist to be featured artist, 35 year running World Peace Festival, Llangollen, Wales, 1982; Selected by West German Broadcasting Association for a 10 country European Concerto debut, 1975. Address: c/o Norman McCann Limited, The Coach House, 56 Lawne Park Gardens, London SE26 6XJ, England.

WETTSTEIN Peter, b. 15 Sept 1939, Zurich, Switzerland. Composer; Conductor; Violinist. m. Elisabeth Wille, 2 sons. Education: Violin Teacher's Diploma, Zurich Music Academy, 1969; Composer's Diploma, 1964; Conductor;s Exam, 1965, Detmold Music Academy, Germany. Career: Theory teacher, Zurich Music Academy, 1965; Lehrauftrag (akustik, analysis), Zurich University, 1973; Vice-Director, Conservatory and Music High School, Zurich, 1976-. Compositions: Works for choir and orchestra; Chamber music. Publication: Akustik und instrumentenkunde, 1976. Memberships: Schweizerische Tonkunstlerverein; Schweizerischer Musikpadagogischer Verband; President, Schweizer Musikinstitut. Address: Seestrasse 146, CH-8700 Kusnacht, Switzerland.

WEWEL Gunter, b. 29 November 1934, Arnsberg, Sauerland, Germany. Singer (Bass). Education: Studied with Johannes Kobeck in Vienna, Rudolf Watzke in Dortmund, Emmi Muller in Krefeld. Career: Member of the Dortmund Opera from 1963; Guest appearances in Dusseldorf, Cologne, Karlsruhe, Hanover, Budapest, Paris, Zurich, Salzburg, Munich; Radio and Television engagements in Germany, France; Roles include Wagner's Daland, Titurel, Fafner, King Mark, Landgrave and King Heinrich; Philip II in Don Carlos, Gremin in Eugene Onegin and Beethoven's Rocco; Mozart's Sarastro, Osmin and Commendatore; Nicolai's Falstaff and Rossini's Bartolo. Recordings Include: Die Zauberflöte conducted by Sawallisch; Schumann's Paradies und die Peri under Henryk Czyz; Suppé's Boccaccio with Willi Boskovsky; Die Königskinder, Mendelssohn's Die Beiden Pädagogen, Les Contes d'Hoffmann and Millöcker's Gasparone, conducted by Heinz Wallberg; La Vie Parisienne, with Willy Mattes.

WHEATLEY Patrick, b. 1950, Hinckley, Leicestershire, England. Singer (Baritone). Education: Studied at London Opera Centre, 1973. Career: Appeared with English National Opera, 1974-80, as Germont Amonasro, Marcello, Sharpless, Donner, Gunther, De Bretigny (Manon), Albert (Werther), Schelkalov (Boris Godunov) and the King in Dalibor; Guest appearances as Escamillo, Kothner, Hans Sachs and Talbot and Cecil in Maria Stuarda; Other roles include Renato (Northern Ireland Opera Trust); Ezio in Attila (University College Opera); Falstaff and Papageno (City of Birmingham Touring Opera); Zurga in Les Pêcheurs de Perles (Scottish Opera); Jochanaan, and Yeletsky in The Queen of Spades (Chelsea Opera Group); Nabucco (Opera West); Mercutio in Roméo et Juliette (Las Palmas); Don Pasquale (Neath Opera); Rigoletto (Welsh National Opera); Sang Wotan and the Wanderer in a version of Wagner's Ring for the City of Birmingham Touring Opera, 1990-91; Concert engagements in Italy, Belgium and Spain and at the Promenade Concerts, London. Address: Music International, 13 Ardilaun Road, London N5 2QR, England.

WHEELER Antony, b. 9 August 1958, Dunedin, New Zealand. Composer; Instrumentalist. Education: BMus, Queensland Conservatory, 1982; Certificate of Post-Graduate studies, Shanghai Conservatory, 1987; MPhil, Hong Kong University, 1991; Study with Ann Boyd, 1987-90. Career: Clarinettist with Queensland SO and PO 1980-82, ABC Sinfonia 1983-85, Sydney SO 1983-85; Freelance Teacher and Performer, 1987-95; Lane Cove Public School, 1992-98; Trinity Grammar School, 1996-98; Australian Institute of Music, 1992-98. Compositions (many for Chinese instruments) include: Piano Variations, 1982; Incidental Music for Ubu the King, for ensemble, 1983; Sarabande and Fugue, brass quintet, 1984; Winter, 1986; Bodhisattva of the Silk Road, 1986; Cold Moon Shines South of the River, 1987; Approach to Peace, for Chinese orchestra, 1988; Snake, 1988; Wind Quintet in Five Movements, 1988; Love Songs of the Grasslands for chorus and string orchestra, 1989; Rising, for Chinese orchestra, 1990; Hearing Thunder on the Fishing Boat, for Chinese percussion ensemble, 1990; Back to the Bush for clarinet, saxophone and piano, 1990; Birthday Variations, wind quintet, 1991; Now Close the Windows, for tenor and piano, 1991. Address: c/o APRA, 1A Eden Street, Crows Nest, NSW 2065, Australia.

WHEELOCK Donald (Franklin), b. 17 Jun 1940, Stamford, CT, USA. Composer; College Teacher. 1 s, 2 d. Education: AB Union College, Schenectady, NY, 1962; MM, Yale School of Music, New Haven, 1964. Career: Works performed by Rochester and Hartford Symphonies, Boston Musica Viva, Lennox Quartet and others; Teacher at Colgate University and Amherst College; Currently, Professor of Music at Smith College, Northampton, MA. Compositions: 11 works for orchestra, including voices and orchestra; 4 String quartets; Many ensemble pieces; Works for piano solo, solo cello, solo flute; Many vocal and choral compositions using own texts; 10 Bagatelles for Oboe and String Quartet; Sonata for Solo Flute; String Quartets Nos 3 and 4, Ciompi String Quartet; Partita for Solo Violin, Veronica Kadlubkiewicz. Recording: Dreams Before a Sacrifice, a dramatic monologue for Mezzo Soprano and Orchestra. Address: Department of Music, Smith College, Northampton, MA 01063, USA.

WHELAN Paul, b. 1966, New Zealand. Singer (Baritone). Education: Studied at the Wellington Conservatoire and the Royal Northern College of Music. Career: Concerts and Recitals in New Zealand, the USA and Europe; Nielsen's 3rd Symphony under Simon Rattle, Messiah in Russia with Yehudi Menuhin and in London with the London Mozart Players; Vaughan Williams's Five Mystical Songs and Sea Symphony, Messiah at the Albert Hall under Charles Farncombe; Opera engagements include roles in Death in Venice for Glyndebourne Opera, Schaunard in La Bohème at Stuttgart, Masetto in Bordeaux, 1993, Britten's Demetrius for Australian Opera and on tour in France and Guglielmo for Dublin Grand Opera; Welsh National and Scottish Opera debuts 1994, as Timur in Turandot and Mozart's Figaro; Messiah with Hallé Orchestra, conductor Roger Vignoles; Verdi, Requiem, Budapest Symphony Orchestra, conductor Paolo Olmi; Recitals at Blackheath and Wigmore Halls, London; Sang Demetrius at the Edinburgh Festival, 1994 and Schaunard for Netherlands Opera; Covent Garden debut 1996, as Schaunard. Honours Include: Brigitte Fassbaender Award for Lieder. Address: c/o IMG Artists, Media House, 3 Burlington Lane, London W4 2TH, England.

WHETTAM Graham Dudley, b. 7 September 1927, Swindon, Wiltshire, England. Composer. m. (1) Rosemary B Atkinson, 20 November 1948. m. (2) Janet Rosemary Lawrence, 31 March 1959, 4 sons, 1 daughter. Education: Self-taught Composer. Concert Debut: C.B.S.O., Birmingham, 1950; Radio Debut: BBC 3rd Programme, 1951. Career: Works in Concert and Broadcast in Britain and abroad; Has withdrawn recognition of works written mostly prior to 1959. Compositions Include: Orchestra: Clarinet Concertos No 1, 1959, No 2, 1982; Introduction and Scherzo Impetuoso, 1960; Sinfonia Contra Timore, 1962; Cello Concerto, 1962; Sinfonia Intrepida, 1976; Sinfonia Drammatica, 1978; Hymnos for Strings, 1978; Sumphonic Prelude, 1985; Ballade for Violin & Orchestra, 1988; Choral: The Wounded Surgeon Plies the Steel, 1960; Magnificat and Nunc Dimmitis, 1962; Do Not Go Gentle Into That Good Night, 1965; Consecration, 1982; A Mass for Canterbury, 1986; Chamber Music: 3 String Quartets, 1967, 1978, 1980; Sextet for Wind and Piano, 1970; Quintetto Concertato, Wind Quintet, 1979; Percussion Partita for Six Players, 1985; Quartet for Four Horns, 1986; Piano, Prelude, Scherzo and Elegy, 1964, revised 1986; Prelude and Scherzo Impetuso, 1967; Night Music, 1969; Solo Violin Sonatas No 1, 1957, revised 1987, No 2, 1972; Solo Violin Sonata No 3, 1989; Suite for Timpani, 1982; Solo Cello Sonata, 1990; Andromeda for Percussion Quartet, 1990; Concerto Ardente for Horn and Strings, 1992; Les Roseaux au Vent for Two Oboes, Cor Anglais and Strings, 1993; Romanza for Solo Violin (also arr. for Solo Viola and Solo Cello), 1993; Les Roseaux au Ventr, for 2 oboes, bassoon and strings, 1993; Concert for Brass Quintet, 1993; Three Shakespearian Elegies, 1994. Recordings: Quartet for Four Horns, 1989. Contributions to: Listener; Times Educational Supplement; Guardian. Honours: Gregynog Arts Fellowship, Welsh Arts Council and University of Wales, 1978. Memberships: Chairman 1971 and 1983-86, Composers' Guild of Great Britain; Vice-Chairman, 1972-85, 1987-94, British Copyright Council; Director, Mechanical Copyright Protection Society Limited, 1984-; Director, National Discography Limited, 1985-93; Director, The Performing Right Society Limited, 1988-94; Royal Society of Musicians. Address: Meriden Music, The Studio Barn, Silverwood House, Woolaston, Nr Lydney, Gloucestershire GL15 6PJ, England.

WHITE (Edwin) Chappell, b. 16 Sept 1920, Georgia, USA. Educator; Musicologist. m. Barbara Tyler, 22 Aug 1959, 1 son, 2 daughters. Education: BA, Emory University, 1940; BMus, Westminster Choir College, 1947; MFA, 1950, PhD, 1957, Princeton University. Career: Instructor, Agnes Scott College, 1950-52; Instructor and Associate Professor, Emory University, 1952-74; Professor, Kansas State University, 1974-91 now retired; Violist with Atlanta Symphony, 1950-57; Music Critic, Atlanta Journal, 1959-72; Visiting Professor, University of Georgia, 1970-71, Indiana University, 1972-73; Brown Foundation Fellow, University of the South, 1993. Publications: G B Viotti: A Thematic Catalogue of His Works, 1985; Intro to Life and Works of R Wagner, 1969; Editor, 4 Concertos by G B Viotti, 1976, and 3 Concertos by J Myslivecek, 1994; From Vivaldi to Viotti: A History of The Classical Violin Concerto, 1992. Contributions to: 15 articles in New Grove Dictionary, 1980; Journal of American Musicological Society; Fontes Artis Musiche; Musical Quarterly. Honour: Research Grant, NEH, 1982-83. Memberships: College Music Society, President, 1979-80; American Musicological Society. Hobby: Golf. Address: 150 Bobtown Circle, Sewanee, TN 37375, USA.

WHITE David (Ashley), b. 11 December 1944, San Antonio, Texas, USA. Composer; Professor. Education: BMus, MMus, University of Houston; DMA, University of Texas, 1978. Career: Professor of Composition and Theory, Director of Graduate Studies, University of Houston, School of Music. Compositions: Elegy and Exaltation, Violin, Cello, Piano; Homages, Mezzo-Soprano, Viola, Piano; This Bitterly Beautiful Land, Cantata for Mixed Chorus, Soloists, and Chamber Ensemble; The Ruins of Missolonghi, Orchestra; Evening Service, Mixed Chorus a Cappella, Manus. Publications Include: Elegy and Exaltation, Homages, The Ruins of Missolonghi; The Lord Is King; The David Ashley White Hymnary, 1993; Hymns included in Worship Songs Ancient and Modern, 1992. Honours: Composer in Residence, Houston Chapter, American Guild of Organists, 1992-94. Memberships: Association of Anglican Musicians; Texas Composers Forum; American Guild of Organists. Hobbies: Walking; Cooking; Travel. Address: School of Music, University of Houston, Texas, TX 77204-4893, USA.

WHITE Emily, b. 15 Dec 1962, Port Chester, New York, USA. Concert Pianist. Education: BMus, summa cum laude with High Honours in Music, University of MD; MMus, The Juilliard School; Recital Diploma, 1st Class Honours, Royal Academy of Music; Doctor of Musical Arts, Manhattan School of Music; Studies with Sascha Gorodnitzki, Christopher Elton, Nelita True, Solomon Mikowsky, Donn-Alexandre Feder; Teaching Fellowships at The Juilliard School and Royal Academy of Music; Coaching Fellowship at Juilliard Opera Center. Career: New York debut in all-Chopin programme; Weill Recital Hall, Carnegie Hall, 1988; Recitals and concerts throughout the US and Great Britain, also in Switzerland, Belgium, Italy and Canada; Masterclasses in USA and UK; Recital broadcasts on WQXR New York and WFLN Philadelphia as well as National Public Radio and Italian national television. Recordings: MacDowell's Woodland Sketches, 1993; Piano works of Ray Green, 1997. Publication: Featured in Piano and Keyboard Magazine, 1997; Doctoral thesis on Vladimir Sofronitsky, 1995. Honours include: Top Prizes at International Mozart Competition, Salzburg, Bergen Philharmonic Competition; Sigma Alpha Iota Graduate Performance Awards, Manhattan School of Music Concerto Competition. Memberships: Sigma Alpha Iota; Phi Kappa Phi; Omicron Delta Kappa; Steinway Artist; Faculty Member, Juilliard Evening Division; Chair, Piano Department, Brooklyn College Preparatory Center. Current Management: Ellison International. Address: 825 West 187th Street, Apt 1C, New York, NY 10033, USA.

WHITE Frances, b. 30 August 1960, Philadelphia, USA. Composer. Education: BMus, University of Maryland, 1981; MA, Princeton University, 1990. Career: Technical Assistant to John Cage 1985-87, collaborating on works for computer-generated tape; Resident in Princeton, as freelance composer. Compositions include: Ogni pensiero vola, for tape, 1985; Chiaroscura, for percussion and tape, 1986; Design for an Invisible City for tape, 1987; Valdrada, 1988; Still Life with Piano, for piano and tape, 1989; Resonant Landscape, interactive computer-music, 1990; Trees for 2 violins, viola and tape, 1992; Nocturne, 1992; Walks Through Resonant Landscapes 1-5 for tape, 1992; Winter Aconites (commission from ASCAP in memory of John Cage) for clarinet and ensemble, 1993. Honours include: First Prize, programme music category, 18th Bourges International Electro-Acoustic Music Competition, 1990; ASCAP Awards, 1990, 1993, 1994. Address: c/o ASCAP, One Lincoln Plaza, New York, NY 10023, USA.

WHITE Harry, b. 4 July 1958, Dublin, Republic of Ireland. University Professor of Music. m. Eithne Graham, 11 June 1980, 2 sons. Education: University College, Dublin; University of Toronto; Trinity College, Dublin. Career: Part-time Lectureship, 1984-85, Assistant Lectureship in Music, 1985-88, St Patrick's College; College Lectureship in Music, 1988-93, Professor of Music, 1993-, University College, Dublin; Director, Irish Opera Theatre Company, 1987-. Publications: J J Fux, Il Trionfo della Fede; Irish Musical Studies I: Musicology in Ireland; Irish Musical Studies II: Music and The Church; Johann Joseph Fux and the Music of the Austro-Italian Baroque (editor). Contributions to: Acta

Musicologica; Fontes Artis Musicae; Bach; Kirchenmusikalisches Jahrbuch; International Review of the Aesthetics and Sociology of Music; Journal of American Studies; Musik und Kirche; Hermathena; Modern Drama; Journal of Musicology; The Irish Review; The Irish University Review; 18th-Century Ireland; Canadian Journal of Irish Studies. Honours: Open Fellowship; E J Pratt Medal for Poetry. Memberships: Royal Musicological Association; International Musicological Society; 18th Century Ireland Society. Hobbies: Canadiana; Walking. Address: Department of Music, University College, Dublin, Republic of Ireland.

WHITE Jeremy, b. 1953, Liverpool, England. Singer (Bass-Baritone). Education: Studied at Queen's College and Christ Church, Oxford; Singing Studies with David Johnston, Elisabeth Fleming. Career: Many performances with early music ensembles in Britain and Europe; Acis and Galatea for Swiss Television, debut at the Amsterdam Concertgebouw in Bach cantatas under Ton Koopman; Performances in Vienna, Budapest and Turku (Finland); Bach's St John Passion in England and Spain with The Sixteen; CPE Bach's Oratorio Auferstehung und Himmelfahrt Jesu, in Munich; Bach's Magnificat and Christmas Oratorio in Oxford and London with King's College Choir and English Chamber Orchestra; Handel/Mozart Messiah in Paris and Lucerne; Bach's Passions in English Cathedrals; Modern concert repertoire includes Abraham and Isaac by Stravinsky, and music by Berio and Taverner; Has sung in The Lighthouse by Maxwell Davies, Walton's The Bear (title role), Pfitzner's Palestrina (Cardinal Morone), Les Troyens and Der Rosenkavalier (the Notary, Aix-en-Provence Festival); Roles in operas by Mozart and Rossini; Recent engagements 1993: Tour of Verdi's Requiem, including Paris and the Flanders Festival; Series of performances of Arvo Pärt's Passio in Jerusalem, Seville and throughout Poland and Finland, Berio in Helsinki conducted by the composer and Beethoven's Ninth Symphony for Swiss Radio; Sang Don Prudenzio in Rossini's Il Viaggio a Reims, Covent Garden; Sang Webern's Second Cantata with Pierre Boulez in a broadcast from Birmingham Symphony Hall; Season 1993-94: Contemporary Music Network tour as Peter in Jonathan Harvey's Passion and Resurrection, followed by a return to the Royal Opera to sing Benoit in La Bohème; Visit to Brazil with the Scottish Chamber Orchestra; Return to Swiss Radio in Lugano; Concert appearances with The Sixteen and The Taverner Players in Beethoven and Schütz in Germany, Norway and Switzerland, and Handel's La Resurrezione in Paris and Bourges; Concerts in London and the provinces; Sang in Pfitzner's Palestrina at Covent Garden, 1997. Recordings Include: John Tavener's Great Canon of St Andrews; Monteverdi's Vespers, with The Sixteen; Handel Israel in Egypt conducted by Andrew Parrott. Current Management: (Opera and Concerts): Magenta Music International; (Concerts only): Musicmakers, Little Easthall Farmhouse, St Paul's Walden, Nr Hitchin, Herts SG4 8DH. Address: c/o Royal Opera, Covent Garden, London WC2, England.

WHITE John, b. 28 May 1938, Leeds, Yorkshire, England. Musician; Professor of Viola. m. Carol Susan Shaw, 29 August 1964, 1 son, 1 daughter. Education: Charles Oldham Scholar, 1959-63, Royal Academy of Music; Huddersfield Technical College, Music Department, 1953-57. Career includes: Member, Alberni String Quartet, 1960-67, Stadler Trio 1967-76; Senior Lecturer, Hockerill College of Education, 1970-78; Tutor, RNCM, 1974, BSM, Colchester Institute; Conductor and Tutor at various music courses; Artistic Director, Annual Viola Festival, Harlow; Professor of Viola, 1976-, and Former Head of Instrumental Studies, Royal Academy of Music, 1984-90; Host Chairman for the 1978, 1984 and 1994 International Viola Congress'; Jury Member, William Primrose International Viola Competition, USA, 1991; Jury Member, Lionel Tertis International Viola Competition, 1994; External String Examiner, RSAMD, 1993-. Recordings: Haydn String Quartets; Rawsthorne String Quartets. Publications include: Editor, Sonatina for Viola and Piano by Alan Bush; (Richard Schaeur), Three Miniature String Quartets by Richard Stoker (Hinniksen); Ballade for Viola and Piano, Minna Keal; Scales and Arpeggios for viola players, Watson Forbes (ed John White); Sonata Impromtu Violin and Viola by William Alwyn; Pastoral Fantasia Viola and Strings (piano) William Alwyn; Nocturne Viola and Cello, Gordon Jacob; In preparation, An Anthology of British Viola Players by John White; Sussex Lullaby, Autumn Sketches, Intrada, Rhapsody Alan Richardson. Honours: FRAM; ARAM; ARCM. Memberships: Royal Society of Musicians; British Federation of Music Festivals. Address: c/o British Music Information Centre, 11 Stratford Place, London W1N 9AE, England.

WHITE John, b. 5 April 1936, Berlin, Germany. Composer. Education: Studied with Elisabeth Lutyens at the Royal College of Music, 1954-57. Career: Music Director of the Western Theatre Ballet, 1959-60; Teacher of Composition at the Royal College of Music, 1961-66; Tuba Player with the London Gabrieli Brass Ensemble, 1971-72. Compositions Include: 119 Piano Sonatas; 21 Symphonies; 30 Ballets; Music for Films and Television; Operas Stanley and the Monkey King, London 1975, and the Trial; Orpheus: Eurydice, London 1976; Music Theatre Man-Machine Interface. Address: c/o PRS Limited, Member Registration, 29-33 Berners Street, London W1P 4AA, England.

WHITE John (David), b. 28 Nov 1931, Rochester, Minnesota, USA. Composer; Cellist. m. Marjorie Manuel, 27 Dec 1952, 2 sons, 1 daughter. Education: BA, University of Minnesota 1953; MA 1954; PhD 1960; Eastman School of Music, University of Rochester, 1960. Career: University of Wisconsin, Kent State University, Music Department, Chair, Whitman College, 1978-80; Dean, School of Music, Ithaca College 1973-75; Professor and Head of Composition and Theory, University of Florida 1980-; Active Cellist in recital and chamber music; Soloist with Atlanta, Rochester, Madison and Akron Orchestras; Composer of 50 works, performances by Cleveland, Atlanta, Rochester, Madison and Akron Orchestras; Music published by G Schirmer, Galaxy, Carl Fischer, Lawson-Gould; Author of Five Books; Taught at University of Michigan. Compositions: Symphony No 2, 1960; Symphony No 3; Legend of Sleepy Hollow, 1962; 3 Choruses from Goethe's Faust; 3 Madrigals for Chorus and Orchestra; Numerous choral works, 1960-87; Variations for Clarinet and Piano; Zodiac, Chorus and Piano; Music for Oriana, 1979 (for Violin, Cello and Piano); Pied Beauty, Chorus and Piano; Eiseleic Madrigals; Sonata for Cello and Piano, 1982; Music for Violin and Piano, 1983; Concerto for Flute and Wind Ensemble, 1984; Symphony for Wind Band, 1985; Dialogues for Trombone and Piano, 1984; Symphony for A Saint, 1987; Songs of the Shulamite, 1988; Mirrors for Piano and Orchestra, 1990. Recordings: Variations for Clarinet and Piano, Advent 5005. Publications: Understanding and Enjoying Music, 1968; Music in Western Culture, 1972; Guidelines for College Teaching of Music Theory, 1981; The Analysis of Music, 2nd Edition, 1984. Contributions to: Journal of Music Theory; Journal for Musicological Research; Music and Man. Hobbies: Tennis; Skiing. Address: 5715 NW 62nd Court, Gainesville, FL 32606, USA.

WHITE Willard, b. 10 October 1948, St Catherine, Jamaica. Singer (Bass). Education: Juilliard School of Music, New York, with Beverley Johnson, Giorgio Tozzi and Erik Thorendahl. Debut: New York City Opera 1974, as Colline in La Bohème: later sang Giorgio in I Puritani, Creon in Médée and Osmin in Die Entführung; Washington Opera as Trulove in The Rake's Progress; Houston Opera in Scott Joplin's Treemonisha; European debut 1976 with Welsh National Opera, as Osmin; English National Opera 1976, as Seneca in L'Incoronazione di Poppea: Hunding in Die Walküre 1983; Glyndebourne 1978-, as The Speaker in Die Zauberflöte, the King in Love for Three Oranges, and Gershwin's Porgy, 1986; Guest appearances with Netherlands Opera (Oroveso in Norma), Bavarian State Opera (Munich) and in Florence; Covent Garden debut 1980, as Don Diego in L'Africaine: returned as Klingsor (Parsifal), Fafner (Das Rheingold) and the Grand Inquisitor (Don Carlos, 1989); Also heard in concert, notably in the 14th Symphony of Shostakovich; Sang Wotan in Act III of Die Walküre at the Festival Hall, 1990; Ferrando in Il Trovatore and Fafner in Siegfried at Covent Garden, 1990; Teatro de la Zarzuela, Madrid, 1990, in Il Turco in Italia; Sang Wotan for Scottish Opera, 1991, Porgy at Covent Garden, 1992; Sang in Ligeti's Le Grand Macabre at the Paris Châtelet and Salzburg Festival, 1997; English National Opera as Mephistopheles in The Damnation of Faust and Boris Godunov in Mussorgsky's opera, 1998. Recordings: Porgy and Bess; Die Aegyptische Helena; Acis and Galatea. Address: c/o Harrison Parrott Limited, 12 Penzance Place, London W11 4PA, England.

WHITEHEAD Gillian, b. 23 April 1941, Whangarei, New Zealand. Composer. Education: University of Auckland; BMus, University of Wellington; MMus, University of Sydney, New South Wales; Studied with Peter Maxwell Davies in Adelaide, then in Britain. Career: Lived in UK and Europe, 1967-81; Appointed 1st Composer-in-Residence, Northern Arts, Newcastle-upon-Tyne, England, 1978; Lecturer in Composition, Sydney Conservatorium of Music, New South Wales, Australia, 1981; Various commissions funded by Music Board of Australia Council, Arts Council of Great Britain, New Zealand Arts Council. Compositions: Published and/or Recorded: Missa Brevis, 1963; Qui Natus Est, Carol, 1966; Fantasia on Three Notes, Piano Solo, 1966; Whakatau-Ki, Chamber Music with Voice, 1970; La Cadenza Sia Corta, Piano Solo, 1974; Tristan and Iseult, for 4 Singers, Mimes and Puppets, Instrumental Ensemble, 1975; Voices of Tane, Piano Solo, 1976; At Night the Garden Was Full of Flowers, for 4 Recorders, 1977; The Tinker's Curse, Children's Opera, 1979; Requiem, for Male Soprano and Organ (Dance Score), 1981. Honours: Recipient of numerous grants including New Zealand Queen Elizabeth II Arts Council and Vaughan Williams Trust. Current Management: Helen Lewis. Address: c/o Helen Lewis, 10 John Street, Woollahra, New South Wales 2025, Australia.

WHITELEY John (Scott), b. 1 January 1950, Leicester, England. Cathedral Organist. m. Hilary Elizabeth Holte Cox, 3 August 1974, 2 sons. Education: BSc, London University, 1971; PhD Candidate, Leeds University; Associate, Royal College of Music; Fellow, Royal College of Organists. Debut: Royal Festival Hall, London, March 1983. Career: Radio appearances on Choral Evensong, 1978, 1979, 1983-93; Record Review, 1979; Choirs of Britain, 1983-84; Sunday Half Hour; Songs of Praise; Sub-Organist, St Edmundsbury Cathedral, 1973-75; Assistant Organist, York Minster, 1975-; Organ Tutor, Hull University, 1978-; Formed York Piano Duo, 1982; 1st Concert Tour of North America, May and June 1985; Concert tour of Australia, 1988. Compositions: Anthem, Jesu Redemptor Omnium, 1983; Magnificat & Nunc Dimittis (York Service), 1984, published Banks; 2 Anthems, 1991; Complete Organ Works of Joseph Jongen (Volumes I and II), 1990-92. Recordings: The Organ at York Minster, Volumes 1 and 2; Several Records with the Choir of York Minster; Great Romantic Organ Music, 1986; Cathedral Windows (The Organ of York Minster), 1987; Haarlem Grote Kerk, 1988; Hadersiev, DK 1989, Music of Prague and Vienna. Publications: Editor, For Manuals Only (8 pieces for organ), 1982; Jongen J Petit Prelude, 1973, Jongen J Four Pieces, 1983; Editor, Jongen: Mass Op. 130, 1990. Contributions to: Musical Times; Organists Review; Magazine of AGO, USA. Honours: Studies with Fernando Germani and Flor Peeters; Turpin Prize of Royal College of Organists; Studies with Ralph Downes. Address: 1 Chapter House, York, North Yorkshire, YO1 2JH, England.

WHITFIELD John (Peter), b. 21 Mar 1957, Darlington, County Durham, England. Conductor; Musical Director; Bassoonist. Education: Chetham's School of Music, 1973-75; Kebie College, Oxford, 1975-78; National Youth Orchestra, 1973-77; European Community Youth Orchestra, 1978; International Youth Orchestra; Bassoon Studies with Charles Cracknell, Martin Gatt and Mordechai Rechtmann, Tel Aviv. Debut: South Bank Conducting Debut, 27 March 1983. Career: Israel Chamber Orchestra; City of London Sinfonia; English Baroque Orchestra; London Sinfonietta; London Symphony Orchestra, also tours; LSO Israel Chamber Orchestra; Founder and Musical Director of Endymion Ensemble; Many concerts in London and UK festivals as bassoonist, conductor, with soloists; commissioned and conducted premieres of works by David Bedford, Dominic Muldowney, Nigel Osborne, Michael Nyman, Giles Swayne, Anthony Payne; Assistant Conductor for Spitalfields Festival Production and EMI recording of Armide (Gluck) with Felicity Palmer in title role; Assistant to Richard Hickox; Stage Debut as Conductor of Birtwistle's Down by the Greenwood Side at the Bath Festival, also broadcast by Radio 3. Recordings: Stravinsky record including Symphonies of Wind and Dumbarton Oaks and Britten Record with Gomez and Palmer on EMI. Current Management: Music & Musicians Artists Management, London. Address: 45 Chalcot Road, London NW1 8lS, England.

WHITICKER Michael, b. 1954, Gundagai, New South Wales, Australia. Composer. Education: Degree, Composition, New South Wales Conservatorium of Music, 1982; Studied with Richard Troop; Postgraduate Composition Studies, West Germany with Isang Yun and Witold Szalonek. Compositions: Orchestral Works: Ad Marginem, 1986; Tartengk, 1985; Tya, 1984; Works for the Stage: The Bamboo Flute, 1982; Gesualdo, 1987; Ensemble Works: Hunufcu, 1979; Korokon, 1983; Quidong, 1983; Kwa, 1986; Winamin, 1986; Orpheus and Persephone, 1987; Plangge, 1987; Venus Asleep, 1987; Min-amé, 1988; Ad Parnassum, 1989; Redror, 1989; Solo Instrumental Works: Vibitqi, 1980; Tulku, 1982; If Buifs, 1981; Kiah, 1986; The Hands, The Dream, 1987; In Prison Air, 1988; On Slanting Ground, 1988; Vocal Works: A Voice Alone, 1982; Night Swimming, 1984; Sheaf Tosser, 1984; As Water Bears Salt, 1989; Works for Students: Boinko the Billio, 1979; Hommage to Alban Berg, 1980; Liexliu, 1980; Introduction for Concert Band, 1985; Karobaan, 1985; Taldree, 1985; The Bankstown Pageant, 1985; The Hollow Crown, 1985; The Serpent Beguiles, 12985; Three Episodes, 1985; Works for Tape Alone: Cement Mounted Inlays, 1981; Model Sequence II, 1981; Slid PC, 1982; Ballets: Factor X, 1980; Passion, 1989; Film Scores: Atlantis, 1981; Conferenceville, 1982; The Bus Trip, 1982; Man, The Skin Cancer of the Earth, 1991 for Three Voices, Sax, Percussion and Tape; Jellingroo, 1990 for Didjeridoo, Flute and Cello; Encircled by Lillies, 1991, for Soprano, Tenor and Piano. Address: c/o Australian Music Centre, P O Box 49, Broadway 2007, Australia.

WHITTLESEY Christine, b. 12 January 1950, New York City, USA. Singer (Soprano). Education: Studied in Boston. Career: Sang with opera companies in Boston, Washington and Santa Fe; Concerts with the New York Pro Musica Antique and other Chamber Ensembles; Resident in Europe from 1981: Concert engagements with the Sudwestfunk and Austrian Radio, conducted by Boulez and Michael Gielen; Tours of Russia and South America with Ensemble Modern; Ensemble InterContemporain in Paris and Ensemble Kontrapunkte in Vienna; Debut with the BBC Symphony 1988, in Pli selon Pli under Boulez; Sang in Dallapiccola's Ulisse with the BBC Symphony Orchestra under Andrew Davis and appeared at the Henze Festival at the Barbican Centre, London, 1991, with the BBC Philharmonic and the Scottish Chamber Orchestra; Further concerts in Berlin, Salzburg, Strasbourg and Warsaw: Season

1992-93 with Debussy's Damoiselle Elue in the Netherlands and Russian songs in Paris. Recordings Include: Hommage to T S Eliot by Gubaidulina and albums for Harmonia Mundi, Bridge Records and Intercord. Address: c/o Ingpen & Williams Limited, 26 Wadham Road, London SW15 2LR, England.

WHITWORTH-JONES Anthony, b. 1945, England. Administrator. Education: Qualified as Chartered Accountant. Career: Administrative Director of London Sinfonietta, 1972-80, including Schoenberg/Gerhard series, Webern and Stravinsky festivals and tours of Europe, Australasia and North America; Opera Manager of Glyndebourne Festival and Administrator of Glyndebourne Touring Opera, 1981-88; General Director, Glyndebourne Festival Opera, 1989-97; From 1983 responsible for new opera policy, introducing such works as Knussen/Sendak double bill: Where the Wild Things Are and Higglety Pigglety Pop!, 1985, Osborne's Electrification of the Soviet Union (1987), Tippett's New Year (British premiere, 1990) and Birtwistle's The Second Mrs Kong (1994); Presided over rebuilding of Festival Theatre, 1993-94. Address: c/o Glyndebourne Festival Opera, Lewes, East Sussex BN8 5UU, England.

WHYTE George. Education: Piano and composition. Career: Exective posts, arts-related, 1952-72; Founder member, Arthur Rubinstein Piano Competition; Chairman and Board Member, many music festivals; Chairman, British National Export Council Arts Committee; Producer, Holocaust Concert, Royal Opera House; Adviser, opera and dance productions in Berlin, Vienna, Washington and New York; Research and authorship of Dreyfus Trilogy, with associated lectures and interviews throughout Europe; Subject of television documentary, Odyssey of George Whyte, Germany, Hungary and Sweden; Exhibition, J'Accuse, throughout Germany and in New York. Compositions: Dreyfus - Die Affäre, opera; Dreyfus - J'Accuse, dance-drama; Rage and Outrage, musical satire; Works in progress include: Dreyfus Fragments for soprano, tenor, violin, viola and chamber orchestra; Madeleine, music-drama; My burning protest for speaker and percussion; Cabaret in Exile. Publications: Set for Enterprise, study for the Royal Opera House; The Accused: Dreyfus Trilogy, 1994; L'Affaire en Chansons, 1994; La Chanson, Musée d'Histoire Contemporaine, 1994; Is Dreyfus Free?, forthcoming. Address: c/o Sara Nathan-Davis, Coda Editions, Suite 23a, 78 Buckingham Gate, London SW1E 6PD, England.

WIBAUT Frank, b. 10 November 1945, London, England. Concert Pianist. m. Kay Alexander. Education: Studied at the Royal College of Music; ARCM. Debut: Wigmore Hall, London, 1969. Career: Concert performances in Holland, Belgium, Denmark, Germany, Ireland, Spain and Malta; Frequent broadcaster on Radio and TV; Member, The Camirilla Ensemble. Recordings: The Romantic Chopin; Favourite Piano Classics; Elgar's From the Bavarian Highlands (in original form); Piano Quintets by Elgar, Suk and others. Honours: Senior Foundation Scholarship, Leverhulme Scholarship and Countess of Munster Award, Royal College of Music; 1st Prize, Chopin Competition, London; Chappell Gold Medal; BBC Piano Competition, 1968. Memberships: Musicians Union; Incorporated Society of Musicians. Address: Highfield Lodge, 68 Harborne Road, Edgbaston, Birmingham B15 3HE, England.

WICH Gunther, b. 23 May 1928, Bamberg, Germany. Conductor. Education: Studied in Freiburg, 1948-52. Career: Conducted at the Freiburg Town Theatre, 1952-59; Opera Director at Graz, 1959-61; General Music Director at Hanover, 1961-65; Conducted the first production of Schoenburg's three one-act operas as a triple bill, 1963; General Music Director, Deutsche Oper am Rhien, Dusseldorf/Duisburg, 1965-87; Took the Company to Edinburgh, 1972, for the French premiere of Zimmermann's Die Soldaten; Covent Garden debut 1968, Die Zauberflöte; Professor of Conducting, Musikhochschule, Würzburg, 1982-94; Guest Conductor with major orchestras in Europe, Japan and the USA; Has led the Capella Colonsiensis on tours to North and South America. Recordings include: Handel's Concerti Grossi Op 3 and Alexander's Feast; Haydn's Symphonies Nos 82 and 85; Serenades by Dvorak, Mozart and Tchaikovsky; Early Mozart Piano Concertos with Martin Galling; Pfitzner's Violin Concerto with Susanne Lautenbacher, 21. Address: c/p Spitalrain 10, 97234 Reichenberg, Germany.

WICK Tilman (Eugen), b. 6 October 1959, Ludwigshafen, Germany. Solo Concert Cellist. Education: Architecture, University of Munich, 1980-81; Concert Artist Diploma with distinction, Northwest German Music Academy, Detmold, 1987. Debut: Soloist with Osnabruck Symphony Orchestra, 1976. Career: Principal Cellist, Chamber Orchestra of Europe, conductors Claudio Abbado and Sir Georg Solti, 1981-84; Worldwide tours, 1985-; Highlights include: Debut at Carnegie Hall, New York, Tonhalle, Zurich, Alte Oper, Frankfurt, Montreal, Santiago, Melbourne, Seoul, Brussels, London, Boston, Washington DC and appearances at the Berlin Festival, 1986, St Moritz Musiktreffen, 1987, Ludwigsburg Festival, 1988, Salzburg Festival, 1989, with the Hallé Orchestra in Manchester, with the Bavarian State Orchestra under Wolfgang Sawallisch in Munich, 1990, at the Spanish Festival Quincena Musical, 1991, with the MDR Symphony Orchestra Leipzig, 1991, 1992; Many appearances on radio and television in over 20 countries; Performed in Chamber Music Concerts with Shlomo Mintz and Rudolf Buchbinder; Conducted master classes in Canada, Italy, Seoul and Melbourne, 1986-. Recordings: MD&G and EMI/Electrola: Schubert, Mendelssohn, Schumann with Koko Sakoda, Piano, 1984; Mozart piano quartets with Frank Peter Zimmermann, Tabea Zimmermann, Christian Zacharias, 1988; Miaskovsky, Carter, Poulenc with Heasock Rhee, piano, 1991. Hobbies: Writing; Chess; Cabinetmaking; Free Climbing; Astrology. Address: c/o LS Artists Management, Orlandostrasse 8, D-8000 Munich 2, Germany.

WICKS Camilla, b. 1925, USA. Concert Violinist; Professor of Violin. m. 5 children. Education: Fellowship to Juilliard School aged 10. Debut: New York Town Hall aged 13. Career: Solo appearances with the Hollywood Bowl Orchestra, the Los Angeles and New York Philharmonic Orchestras and the Chicago Symphony; Many concerts with European Orchestras from age 18; Played the Sibelius Concerto before the composer in Helsinki and has also featured the Bloch Concerto in addition to the standard repertory; Frequent engagements in Norway and elsewhere in Scandinavia; Teaching appointments 1960's-; notably faculties of North Texas State University, California State College at Fullerton, San Francisco Conservatory of Music, Banff Centre for the Performing Arts, University of Washington and University of Southern California; Professor and Head of the String Department, Royal Academy of Music, Oslo; Professor of Violin, University of Michigan School of Music, 1984; Shepherd School of Music at Rice University, Houston, Texas, 1988-; Continuing performances in recital and as orchestral soloist and in Chamber Music Concerts. Recordings: Albums for Capitol, Philips and HMV, including the Sibelius Concerto. Address: Shepherd School of Music, Rice University, Houston, Texas, USA.

WICKS Dennis, b. 6 October 1928, Ringmer, Sussex. Singer (Bass). Education: Studied with Jani Strasser and David Franklin. Career: Sang at Glyndebourne from 1950 as Antonio (Le nozze di Figaro), Alcade in La Forza del Destino, Doctor (Macbeth), Keeper of the Madhouse and Trulove (The Rake's Progress), Lictor (L'Incoronazione di Poppea), Truffaldino (Ariadne), Priest and Man in Armour (Die Zauberflöte) and Voice of Neptune (Idomeneo); Sang in the British premiere of Rossini's La Pietra del Paragone, Camden Festival 1963; Police Commissioner in a new production of Der Rosenkavalier for Welsh National Opera, 1990; Sang with the English National Opera and in Cardiff and Glasgow; US appearances with the Chicago Opera; Many performances in operas by Verdi, Mozart, Beethoven, Smetana, Wagner and Strauss at the Royal Opera House, Covent Garden. Address: c/o Royal Opera House, Covent Garden, London WC2, England.

WIDDICOMBE Gillian, b. 11 June 1943, Aldham, Suffolk, England. Music Critic; Journalist. m. Jeremy Isaacs, 1988. Education: Studied at the Royal Academy of Music and Gloucester Cathedral. Career: Music Division, BBC, 1966; Glyndebourne Festival Opera, 1969; Critic and Journalist, various publications including Financial Times, 1970-76; The Observer, 1977-93; Sub-titles for TV Opera productions; Opera Consultant, Channel Four TV, 1983-88; Arts Editor, The Observer, 1988-93; Feature Writer, The Independent, 1993-95. Honours: ARAM. Address: 80 New Concordia Wharf, Mill Street, Bermondsey, London SE1 2BB, England.

WIDÉN Anne Kristiina, b. 24 July 1972, Turku, Finland. Pianist. Education: Postgraduate, Trinity College of Music, London, Royal Academy of Music, London; Graduate, Piano Performance and Piano Teaching, Turku Conservatory, Finland, 1996; MMus, London, 1997. Career: Several recitals and concerts in Finland and London; Chamber Musician, Accompanist, Orchestral Piano Player; Fortepianoist and Harpsichordist. Honours: Award, Turku Conservatory Piano Competition, 1990, 1992; Turku Conservatory Scholarship Prize for Achievement, 1996; Scholarship, Finnish Wihuri Fund, 1996. Membership: Finnish Wagner Society. Hobbies: Reading; Theatre; Early Recordings; Opera. Address: Queen Alexandra's House, Bremner Road, Kensington Gore, London SW7 2QT, England.

WIDMANN Jörg, b. 19 June 1973, Munich, Germany. Composer; Clarinettist. Education: Studied clarinet with Professor Gerd Starke at the Hochschule für Musik and with Charles Neidich at the Juilliard School, New York; Studied composition with Hans Werner Henze, Wilfried Hiller and Wolfgang Rihm. Debut: As soloist in Mozart's Clarinet Concerto with members of Munich Philharmonic on a tour of Japan (aged 12). Career: Soloist with orchestras including: Münchener Rundfunkorchester, Sinfonia Varsovia, Capella Istropolitana. Compositions include: Absences, 1990; La Verrière Lilas, 1991; Jardin du Luxembourg, 1992; Carillon, 1992-93; Kreisleriana, 1993; 180 Beats per minute, 1993; Tränen der Musen, 1993; Stimmbruch, 1994; Nickel List, 1994; Badinerie, 1994; Wunder Verwirklichen, 1995; Knastgesänge, 1995; Trauergesang und Frühlingsmusik, 1995-96; Three Rilke Fragments, 1996; Beitrage, Lea and Rachel, Lilith, 1996; Fleurs du Mal, 1996-97; Fünf Bruchstücke, 1997; Mullewapp, 1997; Sieben Abesänge Auf Eine Tote Linde, 1997; Insel der Sirenen, premiere, with Isabelle Faust on violin in Warsaw Autumn, 1997; Kleine Morgenstern-Szene for Soprano, rusiches Cymbalon und Schlagzeug, 1997; Werk für Klarinette, Streichquartett und Klavier, 1997; Sieben Miniaturen; Pas de deux, Ritual, für zwei Flöten und Orchester, 1997. Recordings: As composer and clarinettist, Honours: Kulturfördpreis of city of Munich, 1996; 1st Prize, Wettwerb deutscher Musikhochschulen, Berlin, 1996; 1st Prize, Carl Maria Von Weber Competition, Munich, 1996; Bavarian State Prize for Young Artists, 1997. Address: Barerst 3, 80333 München, Germany.

WIDMER Oliver, b. 1965, Zurich, Switzerland. Singer (Baritone). Education: Studied at the Basle Music Academy with Kurt Widmer; Masterclasses with Fischer-Dieskau in Berlin, 1986 and 1989. Career: Concert appearances at the Salzburg Festival, Festival de Musique de Strasbourg, the Vienna Musikverein, the San Francisco Symphony Hall and the Leipzig Gewendhaus; Recitals at the Schubertiade in Hohenems, the Wigmore Hall, London, the Residenz in Munich, Alte Oper Frankfurt, Fêtes Musicales de Touraine, Louvre de Paris, the Vienna Konzerthaus and the 1992 Aldeburgh Festival; Zurich Opera from 1991 as Mozart's Papageno and Guglielmo, Olivier in Capriccio and Harlequin in Ariadne auf Nazos; Salzburg Festival 1993, conducted by Harnoncourt. Recordings: Die Zauberflöte and Schreker's Die Gezeichneten. Honours: Prizewinner at ARD Competition Munich, Hugo Wolf International Competitions Stuttgart and the Othmar Schoeck Competition in Lucerne. Address: c/o IMG Artists, Media House, 3 Burlington Lane, London W4 2TH, England.

WIEDSTRUCK Yvonne, b. 1960, Potsdam, Germany. Singer (Soprano). Education: Studied in Germany. Career: Sang first at Altenburg, in Rusalka, Hansel und Gretel, La Bohème and Faust; Komische Oper Berlin as Despina, Zerlina, Euridice, Susanna, Micaela, the Daughter in Hindemith's Cardillac and Stella in Goldschmidt's Der Gewaltige Hahnrei; Schwetzingen Festival, 1992, in the premiere of Desdemona und ihre Schwestern, by Siegfried Matthus; Appearances as Octavian in Der Rosenkavalier at the Deutsche Oper Berlin and Covent Garden (1995); La Scala debut 1996, in Das Rheingold under Riccardo Muti, and debut as Beethoven's Leonore at Essen Opera, 1997; Engaged as the Composer in Ariadne auf Naxos, Bayerische Staatsoper Munich, 1998; Resident artist at the Deutsche Oper Berlin from 1996; Concert repertory includes Bach's St Matthew Passion (under Kurt Masur), Schubert's E-flat Mass, Pergolesi's Stabat Mater and Les Illuminations by Britten; Pfitzner's choral fanatasia Das Dunkle Reich under Rolf Reuter. Recordings include: Songs by Shostakovich. Address: c/o Lies Askonas Ltd, 6 Henrietta Street, London WC2E 8LA, England.

WIEGOLD Peter (John), b. 29 Aug 1949, Ilford, Essex, England. Composer; Conductor; Teacher. Education: BMus, MMus, University College of Wales, Aberystwyth; PhD, University of Durham. Career: Director of Gemini, regular tours of Britain including many broadcasts; Many residencies involving local participance in shared concerts; Artistic Director, Performance and Communication Skills Project, Guildhall School of Music; Has directed many workshops in music and music theatre including those with London Sinfonietta, Royal Opera House, English National Opera, Scottish Chamber Orchestra and City of London Sinfonia; Junge Deutsche Philharmonie in Greece, Canada, Spain and Sweden; London Symphony Orchestra. Compositions include: Gemini; Sing Lullaby; The Flowers Appear on the Earth; Preludes I-V; The Dancing Day; Songs from Grimm; Half-hour opera commissioned by the Royal Opera House, performed 1989. Honours: Several Arts Council awards. Membership: Past Member, Council and Executive Committee of SPNM. Hobbies; Buddhism; Cycling; Football. Address: 82 Lordship Park, London N16 5UA, England.

WIENER Otto, b. 13 February 1913, Vienna, Austria. Singer (Baritone). Education: Studied in Vienna with Kuper and Hans Duhan. Career: Sang in Concert from 1939; Stage debut Graz 1953, as Simon Boccanegra; Sang at the Salzburg Festival from 1952; in Pfitzner's Palestrina 1955 and in the stage premier of La Mystère de la Nativité by Martin, 1960; Deutsche Oper am Rhein Dusseldorf, 1956-59; Bayreuth Festival from 1957, as Hans Sachs, Gunther and the Dutchman; Member of the Vienna Staatsoper from 1957, Munich Staatsoper, 1960-70; Guest appearances in Paris, London, Rome and Brussels, often in operas by Wagner; Glyndebourne Festival 1964, as La Roche in Capriccio; Retired from stage 1976 and led an Opera School at the Vienna Staatsoper. Recordings Include: Missa Solemnis, conducted by Klemperer; Faninal in Der Rosenkavalier; Lohengrin; St Matthew Passion. Address: c/o Staatsoper, Opernring 2, A-1010 Vienna, Austria.

WIENS Edith, b. 1954, Canada. Singer (Soprano). Career: Concert engagements with orchestras in Berlin, London, Israel,

Munich and New York (Philharmonic); Cleveland, Philadelphia, San Francisco, Montreal and London Symphony Orchestras; Bavarian Radio, Dresden Staatskapelle, Leipzig Gewandhaus Orchestra; Conductors include Barenboim, Georg Solti, Colin Davis, Haitink, Kurt Masur, Marriner, Sawallisch and Tennstedt; Salzburg debut 1984, with the Boston Symphony under Ozawa with whom she has also sung Mozart's Ilia in Japan; Other operatic roles include Donna Anna (at Glyndebourne under Haitink, in Paris and at Amsterdam under Harnoncourt) and Mozart's Countess (Buenos Aires); St Matthew Passion in Paris and Salzburg under Masur with whom she also appeared in Mendelssohn's Elijah in New York; L'Enfant et les Sortilèges at Carnegie Hall; Mahler's 4th Symphony in Munich; Recitals in Paris, Vienna, Florence, Buenos Aires, New York and Montreal; Concertgebouw, Amsterdam, and the Pushkin Museum, Moscow. Recordings include: Schubert, Schumann, Strauss and Zemlinsky Lieder, the title role in Schumann's Das Paradies und die Peri, which won a Grammy in 1990, and the Maurice Fleuret (Paris) Prize in 1991; Flowermaiden in Parsifal, conducted by Barenboim; Albums for Philips, Erato, Teldec and EMI (Mahler's 8th Symphony, conducted by Tennstedt), as well as Haydn's Creation, conducted by Neville Marriner. Address: George Schuster, Str 10, 82152 Krailling, Germany.

WIESE Henrik, b. 22 July 1971, Vienna, Austria. Flautist. Education: Studied with Ingrid Koch, Roswitha Staege and Paul Meisen at Musikhochschule Hamburg and Musikhochschule Munich. Career: Engaged as 1st Principal Flautist, Bavarian State Opera, Munich, 1995-; Solo concerts with Berlin Radio Symphony Orchestra, Orchestra of the Beethovenhalle in Bonn, Polish Chamber Philharmonic, others. Recordings: Mozart, Flute Quartets and Ouvertures arranged for flute and string quartet, with Artemis. Publication: Mozart, Flute Quartets, 1998. Contributions to Mozart-Jahrbuch, 1997. Honours: Prize, German Music Competition, 1995; 3rd Prize, Kobe International Flute Competition, 1997. Address: Franziskanerstrasse 16/909, 81669 Munich, Germany.

WIGGLESWORTH Mark, b. 19 July 1964, Sussex, England. Music Director; Conductor. Career: Music Director, Première Ensemble, 1989-; Associate Conductor of the BBC Symphony Orchestra, 1991-93; Music Director, Opera Factory, 1991-94; Music Director, BBC National Orchestra of Wales, 1996-; Has worked in the United Kingdom with the BBC Symphony, BBC Scottish Symphony, London Philharmonic, London Symphony, Bournemouth Symphony, the English and Scottish Chamber Orchestras, the Royal Scottish National Orchestra and the European Community Youth Orchestra; Conducted both the Premiere Ensemble annd the BBC National Orchestra of Wales in the Centenary Season of the BBC Proms; Guest Conducting in Europe has included the Berlin Philharmonic at the Philharmonie and the Deutsches Symphonie-Orchester Berlin; Conducted the BBC National Orchestra of Wales in the Mahler Festival at the Concertgebouw, Amsterdam, 1995 (10th Symphony); In the Netherlands has also worked with the Royal Concertgebouw, Rotterdam Philharmonic, Residentie Orchestra, Radio Philharmonic and the Netherlands Wind Ensemble; Further European engagements have included the Oslo Philharmonic, Swedish Radio Orchestra, Deutsche Kammerphilharmonie and Mozarteum Orchestra at the Salzburg Festival; In North America he has worked with the Chicago, Philadelphia, Minnesota, Los Angeles Philharmonic, St Louis and San Francisco Symphony Orchestras and at the Hollywood Bowl; Plans include debuts with the Israel Philharmonic, Cleveland, Santa Cecilia and Sydney Symphony Orchestras. Recordings: Schoenberg's arrangement of Mahaler's Das Lied von der Erde, with the Premiere Ensemble. Honours: First Prize, International Kondrashin Competition, Netherlands, 1989; Technics sponsored Gramophone magazine award. Address: Harold Holt Limited, 31 Sinclair Road, London W14 0NS, England.

WILBRAHAM John, b. 15 April 1944, Bournemouth, England. Trumpet Player. m. Susan Drake. Education: Royal Academy of Music, London; LRAM; ARCM. Career: New Philharmonia Orchestra, 1966-68; Royal Philharmonic Orchestra, 1968-72; BBC Symphony Orchestra from 1972. Recordings Include: Concertos by Haydn, Hummel, Mozart, Telemann and Torelli. Memberships: Savage Club; ISM. Honour: Silver Medal, Worshipful Company of Musicians, 1965. Hobby: Cooking. Address: 14b Elizabeth Mews, London NW3, England.

WILBRINK Hans, b. 1933, Holland. Singer (Baritone). Education: Studied in Utrecht and Amsterdam. Debut: Amsterdam 1956, in Beethoven's Ninth. Career: Amsterdam 1958, in the premiere of François Villon by Sam Dresden; Member of the Frankfurt Opera, 1959-66, notably in the 1964 premiere of Wimberger's Dame Kobold; Sang at the Bayerische Staatsoper Munich, 1966-86, including the premieres of Aucassin und Nicolette by Bialas, 1969, Der Versuchung by Josef Tal, 1976 and Belshazar by V D Kirchner, 1986; Guest appearances in Paris 1962, Glyndebourne 1963 (Pelléas), Cologne and Vienna; Other roles have included Henze's Prinz von Homburg, Stolzius in Die Soldaten, Mozart's Figaro, Papageno and Guglielmo, Malatesta, Strauss's Olivier and Britten's Oberon. Recordings Include: Masses by Mozart and Schubert; Reimann's Lear. Address: c/o Bayerische Staatsoper, Postfach 100148, 80539 Munich, Germany.

WILBY Philip, b. 1949, Pontefract. Composer. Education: Leeds Grammar School, with Herbert Howells and at Keble College, Oxford. Career: Violinist with the Covent Garden Orchestra and City of Birmingham Symphony Orchestra; Senior Lecturer at Leeds University from 1972. Compositions: Orchestral Sunstudy; The Wings of Morning, 1988; Vocal: Et Surrexit Christus for 3 Sopranos and Ensemble, 1979; Ten Songs of Paul Verliane for Baritone and Piano, 1983; The Temptations of Christ for Soprano and Ensemble, 1983; Winter Portrait in Grey and Gold for Voice and Ensemble, 1977-85; Cantiones Sacrae: In Darkness Shine, 1987; Magnificat and Nunc Dimittis, 1988; Easter Wings for Soprano and Ensemble, 1989; Chamber: Little Symphony for Brass, 1985; The Night and All The Stars, Horn Quintet, 1985; Sonata Sacra: In Darkness Shine for Clarinet, Viola and Piano, 1986; And I Move Around The Cross for Double Wind Quintet, 1985; Two Concert Studies for Violin and Piano, 1986; Capricorn Suite for 4 Trombones, 1987; Parables for Cello and Piano, 1988; Classic Images, Partita for Brass Quintet, 1988; Concertmusic for Winds, 1988; Green Man Dancing, Wind Quintet, 1988; Breakdance for Recorder and Tape, 1988; Wind Band: Firestar, 1983; Symphonia Sacra: In Darkness Shine, 1986; Catcher of Shadows, 1988; Keyboard: Roses for the Queen of Heaven, 1982; Two Preludes on English Tunes, 1987; Lifescape-Mountains, 1987; ...Aunque es de Noche, 1989; Mozart Reconstructions include Concerto for Violin and Piano K315f and Concerto for Violin, Viola, Cello and Orchestra K320e, for the Philips Mozart Edition; Commissions include Symphony for the BBC Philharmonic. Address: c/o Chester Music, 8/9 Frith Street, London W1V 5TZ, England.

WILD Earl, b. 26 Nov 1915, Pittsburgh, Pennsylvania, USA. Pianist; Composer; Teacher. Education: Carnegie Technical College, 1930-34; Studied Piano with Egon Petri, Selmar Jansen, Paul Doguereau. Debut: New York City, 1934. Appointments: Pianist, KOKA Radio, Pittsburgh, 1930-35; Pianist, NBC Symphony Orchestra, under Toscanini, 1937-44; Soloist with Toscanini and NBC Symphony, 1942; Staff Pianist, Composer, Conductor, ABC TV, New York City, 1945-68; Teacher, Juilliard School of Music, 1977-; Teacher, Manhattan School of Music, 1981-83. Compositions: 14 Rachmaninoff song transcriptions; 7 Gershwin song transcriptions, Porgy and Bess Fantasy; Dance of the Four Swans, Tchaikovsky's Swan Lake. Recordings: Liszt the Virtuoso, Transcriber and Poet; Beethoven Sonatas Op 22, Op 31 No 3; Rachmaninoff Concertos; Fauré Cello Sonatas Nos 1 and 2; Chopin Record. Publications: 2 volumes of Liszt Piano Music, 1986. Honours: Performed for US Presidents Hoover, Roosevelt, Truman, Eisenhower and Kennedy; Performed for Kennedy at his inauguration, 1961. Current Management: Judd Concert Bureau, New York City, USA.

WILDE David (Clark), b. 25 Feb 1935, Manchester, England. Pianist; Composer; Conductor; Professor of Piano. m. (1) Jeanne Lukey, 23 May 1956, 1 son, 1 daughter, (2) Jane Heller, 14 June 1984. Education: Privately, Solomon/Reizenstein, 1945-47; Royal Manchester College of Music, Piano (Elinson), Composing (Hall), Conducting (Cohen), 1948-53; Nadia Boulanger, privately and American Conservatoire, Fontainebleau; Caird Foundation Scholar, 1963-64. Career: Concerts, USA, Canada, Australia, New Zealand, India, Brazil, France, Belgium, Holland, Spain, Germany, Hungary, Russia; International recording and concert artist for BBC, 1961-; Henry Wood Proms from 1961; Soloist, Royal concert in HM the Queen's presence, Royal Festival Hall, and at BBC TV2 inaugural concert, Manchester (Hallé Orchestra, Barbirolli), 1962; Edinburgh, Cheltenham, Three Choirs, Perth (Australia) festivals; Tours, all leading British orchestras; Conductor, Worthing Symphony, season 1967-68; Writer, narrator, pianist, BBC TV Liszt and Bartók documentary programmes, 1972-73; Guest Conductor, Royal Philharmonic, 1975; Liszt in Weimar, film, Granada TV, 1986; Soloist, Tippett's Concerto, BBC Philharmonic, conducted Tippett (Manchester), Edward Downes (London Proms), 1988. Compositions: Love, song for baritone and cello, 1981; Jens, Heidi und die Schneekönigin, 1984; Vocalise, mezzo soprano, guitar; Die Jahreszeiten, song cycle, 1986; Mandala, solo viola, 1986; Piano trio, 1987-88; String quartet, 1991; The Cellist of Sarajevo, solo cello, 1992; Suite, Cry Bosnia-Herzogovina, violin, piano, 1993. Recordings include: Schumann Fantasie; Liszt Sonata; Complete Beethoven Sonatas with Gruenberg, violin. Publications: Transcriptions for piano, chapter in Franz Liszt, The Man and His Music, 1970; Liszt's Consolations, complete (editor), 1978. Address: c/o J Audrey Ellison International Artists' Management, 135 Stevenage Road, Fulham, London SW6 6PB, England.

WILDING Simon, b. 1970, Leigh, Lancashire, England. Singer (Bass). Education: Studied with Robert Alderson at the Royal Northern College of Music, from 1992. Career: Sang with the Bayreuth Festival Chorus, from 1989; Britten's Quince, and Walter Raleigh in Donizetti's Roberto Devereux withe the RNCM; Luka in Walton's The Bear at Manchester and the UK/LA Festival at Los Angeles; Count Ceprano in Rigoletto for English National Opera and Giove in La Calisto for the Batignano Festival and engagements in Lohengrin, Salome and Die Meistersinger at Covent Garden, 1997; Concerts include Bach Cantatas at the Aldeburgh Festival, Salome with the Bournemouth SO at the Barbican, the Verdi Requiem at Liverpool and Die Schöpfung at Warwick University. Address: c/o IMG Artists, Media House, 3 Burlington Lane, London W1 2TH, England.

WILDING-WHITE Raymond, b. 9 October 1922, Caterham, Sutrey, England. Composer; Teacher. Education: Studied at the Juilliard School (1947-49), New England Conservatory (MM 1953) with Copland and Dallapiccola at Tanglewood (1949-51) and at Boston University with Gardner Read (DMA 1962). Career: Teacher at Case Institute of Technology, Cleveland, 1961-67 and De Paul University, Chicago (1967-88); Founder and Director of the Loop ensemble, 1969-89, for the performance of contemporary music; Many music education broadcasts on WFMT-FM, Chicago, including series Our American Music, 1976, and a memorial tribute to John Cage (1992). Compositions include: Piano Concerto, 1949; The Tub, chamber opera, 1952; The Selfish Giant, TV fable, 1952; Even Now for baritone and orchestra, 1954; Paraphernalia for chorus and five instruments, 1959; The Lonesome Valley, ballet, 1960; Yerma, opera, 1962; Concertante for viola, violin, horns and strings, 1963; Bandmusic, 1966; Encounters, ballet, 1967; 6 string quartets, 1948-88; Violin Concerto, 1978; Beth, musical, 1989 (renamed Trio 1994); Gifts, liturgical drama, 1993; Symphony of Symphonies, 1995. Address: c/o ASCAP, ASCAP Building, One Lincoln Plaza, New York, NY 10023, USA.

WILKE Elisabeth, b. 19 May 1952, Dresden, Germany. Singer (Mezzo-Soprano). Education: Studied at the Musikhochschule Dresden. Debut: Dresden 1974, as Hansel. Career: Appearances with the Dresden Staatsoper-Semper Oper in Germany and on tour as Dorabella, Amastris in Handel's Serse, Olga (Eugene Onegin) and Tisbe in Cenerentola, 1992; Sang Veronika in the premiere of Der Goldene Topf by E Mayer, 1989. Recordings include: Symphoniae Sacrae by Schütz (Capriccio); Saint-Saëns Christmas Oratorio; Missa Brevis by C P E Bach; J S Bach's St Matthew Passion. Address: c/o Semper Oper, 8012 Dresden, Germany.

WILKENS Anne, b. 1948, England. Singer (Mezzo-Soprano). Education: Guildhall School of Music; London Opera Centre; Further Study with Dame Eva Turner. Career: Sang in Verdi's Ernani at the Festival Hall, 1972; The Nose by Shostakovich for the New Opera Company, 1973; Sang with English Opera Group in operas by Britten, in Aldeburgh, Venice and Brussels; Sang in world premieres of Death in Venice, 1973, and Musgrave's The Voice of Ariadne, 1974; Member of the Royal Opera Company, Covent Garden, 1974-78, as Olga in Eugene Onegin, Maddalena in Rigoletto, and in the world premiere of Henze's We Come to the River, 1976; Appearances with Handel Opera Society: Handel roles include Julius Caesar, Dejanaira (Hercules) and Ezio; Welsh National Opera 1979, as Brangaene in Tristan und Isolde; Guest appearances in Frankfurt (Azucena), Marseille and Stuttgart (Brangaene); Bayreuth 1983, in the Solti/Hall production of The Ring; Karlsruhe from 1983, as Eboli in Don Carlos and as Wagner's Venus, Fricka, Ortrud and Waltraute; Sang in the premiere of Der Meister und Margarita by Kunaud, Karlsruhe, 1986; Sang Neris in Cherubini's Médée for Opera North, 1996. Concert engagements with the London Symphony Orchestra, Hallé Orchestra, Bournemouth Symphony and in Holland, Spain, Brussels and Stockholm. Recordings Include: Tristan und Isolde, conducted by Reginald Goodall. Address: c/o Music International, 13 Ardilaun Road, Highbury, London N5 2QR, England.

WILKINS Caroline, b. 31 July 1953, Somerset, England. Composer. Education: BMus, Royal College of Music, London, 1975; Cologne Music Academy, with Mauricio Kagel, 1987-88. Career: Composer and performer with new music projects in Australia, 1984-86; Freelance composer in Germany, 1989-; Commissions from Ensemble Köln (1991), the Hilliard Ensemble (1994) and others; Festival Participation at Darmstadt, Rheinland, Zurich and Witten, 1990-94. Compositions include: Piece for Accordion and Phonograph, 1988; Piece for Accordion with Screens, 1988; Arias for Phonograph and Singers, 1988; Piece for 17 Tones, for 2 pianos, 1990; Piece for Player Piano and Piano, 1990; Loquela, for 1 to 8 female voices, 1991; Automatophone, for ensemble, 1991; The Bird Organ is Made of Wood for Percussion, 1991; Camera Aeolia for organ, 1992; Auroram Lucifer for chorus, 1993; For These My Friends and Yours for 4 male voices, 1994. Honours include: First Prize, Frauenmusik-Forum, Berne, 1992. Address: c/o HUG Music Publishers, Limmatquai 28-30, CH 8022, Zürich, Switzerland.

WILKINS Margaret (Lucy), b. 13 Nov 1939, Kingston upon Thames, England. Composer; Music Educator. m. Nigel E Wilkins, 11 Aug 1962 (divorced 1977), 2 d. Education: Trinity

College of Music, London, 1952-57; BMus, University of Nottingham, 1960; LRAM, 1960. Debut: BBC. Career: Works performed worldwide, South Bank, and Wigmore Hall, London, England, Scotland, Canada, Germany, Italy, Switzerland, Austria, Holland, America, Spain and Poland; Commissions: BBC SSO, University of St Andrews, New Music Group of Scotland, William Byrd Singers, John Turner, Julie Wilson, Goldberg Ensemble, Kirklees Cultural Services; Festivals: Durham, Edinburgh, Huddersfield, Nottingham, Donne in Musica, Llangollen Eistedfodd, ISCM, World Music Days, Poland, Middelburg, Netherlands; Member of Scottish Early Music Consort, 1970-76; Senior Lecturer, Music, University of Huddersfield, 1976-; Artistic Director, Polyphonia, 1989-; Maude Clarke Visiting Professor at Queen's University, Belfast, 1995. Compositions include: Struwwelpeter, 1973; Etude, 1974; Circus, 1975; Gitanjali, 1981; Aspects of Night, 1981; Epistola da San Marco, 1987; Réve, Réveil, Révélations, Réverbérations, 1988; Revelations of the Seven Angels, 1988; Symphony, 1989; Kanal, 1990; Musica Angelorum, 1991; Stringsing, 1992; L'Attente, 1994. Recordings: Study in Black and White Nos 1 and 2, Ananda Sukarlan, solo piano. Publications: Composer, volume 58, 1976; Contact 32, 1988; British Journal of Music Education, volume 10, No 3, 1993. Honours include: Cappiani Prize for Women Composers, 1971; Hinrichsen Foundation Award, 1979; Arts Council of Great Britain Bursary for Composers, 1981-82. Memberships include: Executive Committee, Composers' Guild of Great Britain, 1972-78, 1986-92; Council, 1980-86, Reader, 1995, SPNM; Women in Music. Address: 4 Church Street, Golcar, Huddersfield, HD7 4AH, West Yorkshire, England.

WILKINSON Katie, b. 1960, England. Violist. Debut: Wigmore Hall 1984, with Peter Pears. Career: Co-Founded the Brindisi String Quartet at Aldeburgh, 1984; Concerts in a wide repertory throughout Britain and in France, Germany, Spain, Italy and Switzerland; Festival engagements at Aldeburgh (residency 1990), Arundel, Bath, Brighton, Huddersfield, Norwich and Warwick; First London Performance of Colin Matthews's 2nd Quartet 1990, premiere of David Matthews's 6th Quartet, 1991; Quartet by Mark-Anthony Turnage, 1992; Many BBC recitals and Resident Artist with the University of Ulster. Recordings Include: Quartets by Britten, Bridge and Imogen Holst; Works by Pierné and Lekeu. Honours Include: (with Brindisi Quartet) Prize winner at the Third Banff International String Quartet Competition in Canada, 1989. Address: c/o Owen-White Management, 14 Nightingale Lane, London N8 7QU, England.

WILKOMIRSKA Wanda, b. 11 January 1929, Warsaw, Poland. Violinist. m. 2 sons. Education: Studied with Irena Dubiska, Lodz Conservatory; Studied with Ede Zathureczky, Budapest, Hungary; Studied with Henryk Szeryng, Paris, France. Debut: Age 7; With orchestra, Cracow, Poland, age 15. Career: Appears frequently with most major orchestras throughout the world; Defected whilst on tour of Federal Republic of Germany, 1982. Recordings: Numerous. Honours Include: Polish State Prize, 1952 and 1964; Several Foreign prizes including Bach Competition Award; Officer's Cross of Polonia Restituta, 1958; Order of Banner of Labour 2nd Class 1959, 1st Class 1964; Minister of Culture and Arts Prize, Polish Musicians' Association, 1979. Hobbies: Theatre; Literature; Sports.

WILKOMIRSKI Jozef, b. 15 May 1926, Kalisz, Poland. Conductor; Composer; Broadcaster; Lecturer; Freelance Journalist. m. Margaret Zasinska, 16 Aug 1980, 1 daughter. Education: Diploma, Warsaw Music High School; MA, 1950. Debut: Warsaw Philharmonic, 1950. Career: Assistant Conductor, Krakow Philharmonic, 1950-51; Conductor, Poznan Philharmonic, 1954-57; Director and Chief Conductor of State Philharmonic at Szczecin, 1957-71; Chief Manager and Artistic Director of Sudettic Philharmonic at Walbrzych, 1978-; Guest Conductor of numerous countries in Europe, Asia and America. Compositions: 2 Sinfoniettas; Symphonic Poems; Symphonic Suite, Royal Castle in Warsaw; Sonatas for Violin, Cello, and Double Bass; Harp Concerto; Concerto for Violin and Cello; Trio; Songs. Recordings: Various broadcasting companies in Poland, Ireland and Luxembourg. Honours: Pomeranian Gryphon Medal, 1960; Musical Prize, 1961; Cavalry Cross, 1963; Officer's Cross, 1979; Order of Polonia Restituta; Medal, Cultural Merit, 1967; Prize, Public Cultivation of Music, 1970; Order of Labour Flag, 1st class, 1986; Cross of Warwaw Insurrection, 1986; Cross of Home Army, 1995. Hobbies: Literature; History; Psychology. Address: Sudettic Philharmony, ul Slowackiego 4, 58-300 Walbrzych, Poland.

WILL Jacob, b. 8 June 1957, Hartsville, South Carolina, USA. Singer (Bass). Education: Studied at the Cincinnati Conservatory and at San Francisco Opera Studio. Career: Sang Masetto at San Francisco, followed by appearances with Long Beach and Anchorage Operas, as Basilio in Il Barbiere di Siviglia; Carmel Beach Festival as Mozart's Figaro; Appearances throughout the USA as Don Giovanni, Frank in Die Fledermaus, and Dulcamara; Sang in Europe from 1986, Zurich Opera from 1988 as Basilio and Melcthal in Guillaume Tell; St Gallen as Sparafucile and Raimondo in Lucia di Lammermoor, Barnaba in Andrea Chenier, 1989; Vancouver 1990, as Oroveso, Bregenz Festival 1992, as Zuniga in Carmen; Concert engagements include Rossini's Petite Messe Solonelle, Lincoln Center, 1989. Recordings include: Zemlinsky's Kleider Machen Leute. Address: c/o Opernhaus Zurich, Falkenstrasse 1, CH-8008 Zurich, Switzerland.

WILLCOCK Christopher John, b. 8 Feb 1947, Sydney, New South Wales, Australia. Composer. Education: BMus (Hons), University of Sydney, 1974; Theological Doctorates at Paris, 1987. Career includes: Trinity Mass for Cantor, chorus, congregation and organ, 1977; Psalms for Feasts and Seasons, 1977; Convict and the Lady, for chorus and chamber ensemble, 1978; Lines from Little Gidding for chorus and organ, 1978; Friday 3.30 for chorus and string orchestra, 1986; Easter Moon for chorus and brass instruments, 1988; Two Pastorals for voice and harpsichord, 1990; Duo for Oboe and Harpsichord, 1992; Plaint Over Dili for oboe and harpsichord, 1992; The Frilled Lizard for viola and harp, 1993; Here be Dragons, for harpsichord, 1994. Honours include: Dr Percy Jones Award for Outstanding Services to Liturgical Music, 1993. Address: c/o APRA, 1A East Street, Crows Nest, NSW 2065, Australia.

WILLCOCKS David (Sir), b. 30 Dec 1919, Newquay, Cornwall, England. Conductor. m. Rachel Blyth, 8 Nov 1947, 2 s (1 deceased), 2 d. Education: Chorister at Westminster Abbey; King's College, Cambridge; Royal College of Music. Career: Organist, Salisbury Cathedral, 1947-50; Organist, Worcester Cathedral, 1950-57; Conductor, City of Birmingham Choir, 1950-57; Fellow and Organist, King's College, Cambridge, 1957-73; University Lecturer, 1957-74, Organist, 1958-74, Cambridge; Conductor, Cambridge University Musical Society, 1958-73; Musical Director, The Bach Choir, 1960-; Annual performances of the St Matthew Passion at the Royal Festival Hall; Director, The Royal College of Music, 1974-84. Compositions: Ceremony of Psalms; Carols for Choirs in 4 volumes, joint editor. Recordings: Many with The Bach Choir, Royal College of Music Chamber Choir, Choir of King's College, Cambridge and the principal London orchestras. Honours: MC, 1944; CBE, 1971; Knight Bachelor, 1977; Honorary MA, Bradford, 1973; Honorary DMus, Exeter, 1976, Leicester, 1977, Westminster Choir College, Princeton, 1980, Bristol, 1981, St Olaf College, 1991; Honorary DLitt, Sussex, 1982; Honorary Doctor of Sacred Letters, Trinity College, University of Toronto, 1985; Freeman, City of London, 1981. Memberships: President: RCO, 1966-68, ISM, 1978-79, NFMS, 1980-89, Association of British Choral Directors, 1993-. Address: 13 Grange Road, Cambridge, CB3 9AS, England.

WILLEN Niklas Olov, b. 30 Mar 1961, Stockholm, Sweden. Conductor. m. Anna Schulze, 26 July 1997, 2 sons, 1 daughter. Education: Royal College of Music, Stockholm. Debut: Gavleborg Symphony Orchestra, Sweden, 1988. Career: Royal Opera, Stockholm; Gothenburg Opera; Principal Conductor, The Sundsvall Chamber Orchestra, Sweden, 1993-97; Principal Guest Conductor, Royal Stockholm Philharmonic Orchestra, 1993-96; Guest Appearances in Norway, Finland, Denmark, Germany, England, Scotland, Ireland. Compositions: Lux Aeterna for Choir, 1983; Bassoon Concerto, 1988; Wind Quintet, 1993. Honour: 2nd Prize, Nordic Competition, 1990. Membership: Swedish Society of Musical Artists. Current Management: Patrick Garvey Management. Address: Top Floor, 59 Lansdowne Place, Hove, East Sussex BN3 1FL, England.

WILLI Herbert, b. 7 Jan 1956. Composer. Education: Abitur; MPhil, University of Innsbruck; Diploma in Composition and MA, Mozarteum, Salzburg; Studies with Helmut Eder and Boguslav Schaeffer. Compositions: Opera Schlafes Bruder (libretto by Robert Schneider); Orchestral works: Der Froschmäusekrieg - for sprechgesang, 3 orchestral groups and tape, 1989; Räume für Orchester, 1991; Konzert für Orchester, 1991-92; Flötenkonzert, 1993; Chamber music: Stück für Flöte solo, 1985, 1986; Streichquartett, 1986; Trio für Violine, Horn und Klavier, 1992; Performances of his works: New York (Carnegie Hall), London (Royal Albert Hall), Vienna (Konzerthaus/Musikverein), Salzburg Festival (Grosses Festspielhaus), Berlin Philharmonic Hall, performed by International orchestras Vienna Philharmonic, Berlin Philharmonic, Cleveland Orchestra, conducted by Claudio Abbado and Christoph von Dohnányi. Honours: Prize of the Rep of Austria, 1986; Rome Prize, 1987, 1988; Rolf Liebermann Scholarship, 1990; Ernst-von-Siemens Prize, 1991; Composer in Residence, Salzburg Festival, 1992. Current Management: Schott Musik International.

WILLIAM Louis (Hagen), b. 1950, New Orleans, USA. Singer (Bass-Baritone). Education: Studied at University of Los Angeles Opera Workshop and at Paris Conservatoire. Career: With Lyons Opera sang Sarastro, Daland and the Langrave in Tannhäuser, Paris Opera Company in Turandot and L'Heure Espagnole; Other roles include Mephistopheles, Nilakanta in Lakmé, Rossini's Bartolo and the villians in Les Contes d'Hoffmann; Has sung in various versions of Porgy and Bess with the Royal Liverpool Philharmonic, the Scottish Chamber Orchestra under Carl Davis, the Ulster Orchestra under Yan Pascal Tortelier, and the Hallé and Royal Philharmonic Orchestras; Has also sung in Handel's Judas Maccabeus and on French Radio and Television. Recordings include: Negro Spitituals (Quantum) and Mozart Concert Arias. Honours: First Prizes for Opera and Concert Singing at the Paris Conservatoire. Address: c/o Norman McCann International Artists Limited, 56 Lawrie Park Gardens, London SE26 6XJ, England.

WILLIAMS Adrian b. 30 April 1956, Watford, Hertfordshire, England. Composer; Pianist. m. Tijana Miletic, 7 Nov 1992. Education: Royal College of Music, London. Career: Composer-in-Residence, Charterhouse, 1980-82; Founder Director, Presteigne International Festival, 1983-92. Compositions: Sonata for Solo Cello, 1977; String Quartet No 2, 1981; Tess, Orchestral Poem, 1982; Cantata: September Sky, 1985; Mass, 1986; Chaconne for Guitar, 1986; Images of a Mind, Cello and Piano, 1986; Cantata: Not Yet Born, 1986; Leaves from the Lost Book, 1987; Dies Irae, 1988; Music for the Film Gernika, 1987; Cantata: The Ways of Going, 1990; String Quartet No 3, 1991; The King of Britain's Daughter, 1993. Honours: Menuhin Prize, 1978; Guinness Prize, 1986. Memberships: Composers' Guild of Great Britain. Hobbies: Walking; Railways; Gardening; Cooking. Address: Llwynbedw, Llanwrtyd Wells, Powys LD5 4SY, Wales.

WILLIAMS Bradley, b. 1965, Texas, Singer (Tenor). Education: University of Texas and Cincinnati Conservatory of Music. Debut: As Ernesto with the Metropolitan Opera Guild, 1991. Career: Sang with the Santa Fe Opera, then with New York City Opera in Zimmermann's Soldaten and Korngold's Tote Stadt; Uberto in La Donna del Lago and George in La Dame Blanche, at New York concerts; Fenton for Long Beach Opera and Ernesto at Edmonton; European debut in the professional premiere production of Bellini's Adelson e Salvini, Catania; Season 1993 with La Gazza Ladra at Barcelona, Arturo in I Puritani at Malaga and Alfonse in Herold's Zampa at the Wexford Festival; Further engagements as Lindoro in L'Italiana in Algeri at Florence, Rossini's Almaviva at Copenhagen and the premiere of Harvey Milk in Houston and New York; Season 1997 with Tonio in Cenerentola at Genoa; Other roles include Don Ottavio (Florence) and Tebaldo in Bellini's Gapuleti e i Montecchi (Turin). Address: Athole Still Ltd, 25-27 Westow Street, London SE19 3RY, England.

WILLIAMS Camilla, b. 8 Oct 1922, Danville, Virginia, USA. Concert Singer; Professor of Voice, Indiana University. m. Charles T Beavers, 28 Aug 1950. Education: Honour Graduate, Virginia State College; Studied Music under Madame Marion Szekely-Freschl. Career: Sang role of Madame Butterfly as first black singer, New York City Centre, 1946; Created first Aida, New York City Centre, 1948; First New York Performance of Mozart's Idomeneo, Little Orchestra Society, 1950; First Tour of Alaska, 1950; First European Tour (London), 1954; First Viennese Performance of Menotti's Saint of Bleecker Street, 1955; American Festival, Belgium, 1955; First African Tour for US State Department (14 countries), 1958-59; First Tour of Israel, 1959; Guest of President Eisenhower, Concert for Crown Prince of Japan, 1960; Tour of Formosa, Australia, New Zealand, Korea, Japan, Philippines, Laos, South Vietnam, 1962; First New York Performance of Handel's Orlando, 1971; First Tour of Poland, 1974; Appearances with Orchestra's such as the Royal Philharmonic, Vienna Symphony, Zurich, Tonhalle; Berlin Philharmonic; New York Philharmonic, Chicago Symphony; Philadelphia Orchestra; BBC Orchestras and Stuttgart Orchestra; Geneva; Belgium; Professor of Voice, Brooklyn College, 1970-73; Professor of Voice, Bronx College, 1970-; Professor of Voice, Queens College, 1974-; First Black Professor of Voice, Indiana University, Bloomington, Indiana, 1977-. Address: Professor of Voice, School of Music-Studio MU104B, Indiana University, Bloomington, IN 47405, USA.

WILLIAMS David Russell, b. 21 Oct 1932, Indianapolis, Indiana, USA. Educator. m. Elsa Buehlmann Williams, 30 Jan 1960. Education: BA, MA, Columbia University; PhD, Music Composition, Eastman School of Music, University of Rochester, 1965; Composition with Howard Hanson, Otto Luening, Henry Cowell. Appointments: Associate Professor of Music, Eastman School of Music, Rochester, 1965-80; Chairman, Department of Music, 1980-87, Professor of Music Theory, 1980-, University of Memphis. Compositions: Five States of Mind; 9 x 9 Variations on a Theme by Howard Hanson; Suite, for Oboe, Clarinet and Piano. Recordings: Producter, Highwater Records Album 8201: John Stover, Classical Guitar. Publications: Bibliography of the History of Music Theory, 1971; Conversations With Howard Hanson, 1988; Music Theory From Zarlino to Schenker: A Bibliography and Guide, 1990. Contributions to: Editor, Theory Column, Quarterly Newsletter, New York Music Teachers Association, 1970-74. Honours: Winner, Edward Benjamin Contest for Tranquil Music, Eastman School, 1963; Eastman School of Music Publication Award, 1970. Memberships: Phi Beta Kappa; Pi Kappa Lambda; College Music Society; National Academy of Recordings Arts and Science; National Association of Schools of Music; Tennessee Association of Music Executives in College and University. Hobbies: Word Puzzles; Languages. Address: 273 Central Park West #1, Memphis, TN 38111-4570, USA.

WILLIAMS Edgar Warren, b. 12 June 1949, Orlando, Florida, USA. Professor; Composer; Conductor. m. Christine Anderson, 19 June 1971, 1 son, 1 daughter. Education: BA, Duke University, 1971; MA, Columbia University, 1973; MFA 1977; PhD 1982, Princeton University. Career: Teaching Assistant, Columbia University, 1972-73; Assistant in Instruction, Princeton University, 1977-78; Visiting Lecturer in Music, University of California, Davis, 1978-79; Assistant Professor, The College of William and Mary, Williamsburg, Virginia, 1979-82; Associate Professor, 1982; Guest Conductor with orchestras including Bennington Composers Conference Ensemble, 1969-70 and Columbia Composers Ensemble, 1973; Conductor, William and Mary Orchestra, 1979-82. Compositions: Numerous published including: Three Songs, 1977; Across a Bridge of Dreams, 1979-80; Amoretti, 1980; Some Music for Merry Wives, 1982; Landscapes With Figure, 1983; Now Showing, for wind and percussion, 1993; Pentimenti, for chamber orchestra, 1993; String Quartet II, 1996; String Quartet III, 1997. Publications: Harmony and Voice Leading, with Taylor and Miller, 1993; Introduction to Music, 1993. Contributions to: In Theory Only; 19th Century Music. Honour: Prize Winner for Amoretti, East and West Artists Sixth Annual Composition Contest. Current Management: Broadcast Music Incorporated; Mobart Music Publications, Hilsdale, New York. Address: Department of Music, College of William and Mary, Williamsburg, VA 23185, USA.

WILLIAMS Elvira, b. 25 February 1923, Brighton, Sussex, England. Performer; Teacher of Piano. m. Alan Leonard Martin, 14 April 1947, 2 daughters. Education: LRAM, ARCM, Royal College of Music, 1942-46. Debut: Wigmore Hall, London. Career: Recitals in Italy; Concert Broadcasts; Piano Teacher. Honours: Open Scholarship, Royal College of Music; Marmaduke Barton Prize. Membership: Incorporated Society of Musicians. Address: 42 The Vineries, Nizells Avenue, Hove, East Sussex BN3 1PY, England.

WILLIAMS Hermine (Weigel), b. 4 Feb 1933, Sellersville, Pennsylvania, USA. Teacher; Writer; Editor; Musician. m. Jay Gomer Williams, 9 Sept 1956, 2 sons, 2 daughters. Education: PhD, Musicology. Columbia University, 1964; Private study with Grete Sultan. Career: Teacher, Vassar College, 1954-59; Hamilton College, 1964-65, 1972-92; Scholar-in-Residence, Hamilton College, 1994-; Assistant to General editor of The Operas of Alessandro Scarlatti; Associate Editor, The Facts Behind the Songs; A Handbook of Popular American Music; Member of Editorial Board for complete works edition of Giovanni Pergolesi; Professional Accompanist; Organist and Choral Director in area churches; Organ Soloist with Utica Symphony; Solo and Ensemble Recitals; Freelance Writer and Opera Consultant. Compositions: Piano vocal score of A Scarlatti's The Triumph of Honour 1718, 1984 and La Caduta Dei Decemviri 1697, 1980. Publications: The Operas of Alessandro Scarlatti, volume 6, 1980; The Symphony 1720-1840, 1983; A Short History of Opera, 1988; Giovanni Battista Pergolesi: A Guide to Research, 1989. Contributions to: Current Musicology; New Grove Italian Baroque Opera; New Grove Dictionaries of Music and Musicians and of Opera; Studi Pergolesiani; Music and Civilization; Facts Behind the Songs; The History of European Ideas. Honours: Maarston Fellowship; Theodore Presser Award in Composition; Commission from San Francisco Opera, 1982; Fulbright Lecturer in Musicology, New Zealand, 1987. Memberships: American Musicological Society; American Handel Society. Hobby: Swimming. Address: 300 College Hill Road, Clinton, NY 13323, USA.

WILLIAMS Howard, b. 25 Apr 1947, Hemel Hempstead, Hertfordshire, England. Conductor. m. Juliet Solomon, 24 Dec 1977, 1 s, 1 d. Education: King's School, Canterbury; BA, New College, Oxford; BMus, Liverpool University; Advanced conducting course, Guildhall School of Music and Drama. Career: Conducted over 40 opera productions with English National Opera and elsewhere, including Punch and Judy and The Knot Garden for Channel 4 TV; Other modern repertory includes the premieres of Holloway's Liederkreis and Concertino No 1, Hamilton's Anna Karenina, and Cowie's Choral Symphony and Concerto for Orchestra; Many productions with Royal Ballet at Covent Garden and abroad; Regular Guest Conductor with BBC Symphony Orchestra, BBC Welsh Orchestra; Regular appearances with Royal Philharmonic, Scottish National, Bournemouth Symphony, Northern Sinfonia, English Chamber, London Sinfonietta and Royal Liverpool Philharmonic; Regular visitor overseas to orchestras in France, Belgium, Netherlands, Sweden and Hungary; Principal Conductor, Pècs Symphony Orchestra, Hungary, 1989-, being first British conductor to hold appointment in Hungary. Composition: Shadowdance, 1991. Recordings include: 3 Discs of music by Frank Bridge including his opera The Christmas Rose; Premiere pressing of Bizet's Ivan The Terrible. Honours: Artisjus Award, Hungarian Performing Rights Society, 1991; Pro Civitate Medal, City of Pècs. Membership: Royal Philharmonic Society. Current Management: Christopher Tennant Artists. Address: c/o Christopher Tennant Artists, Unit 2, 39 Tadema Road, London, SW10 0PY, England.

WILLIAMS John, b. 24 Apr 1941, Melbourne, Victoria, Australia. Guitarist. Education: Taught guitar by father from age 4; Studied with Segovia, London, 1952; Later study, Accademia Musicale, Chigiana, Siena, and Royal College of Music, London. Career: Toured USSR, 1962, Japan, USA, 1963; Regular tours, USA, Australia, Far East, South America, Europe; Frequent TV appearances; With 4 others played in group SKY; Many concerts with group John Williams and Friends, including Italian tour, 1987; Has appeared at Ronnie Scotts Club; Has performed with: Academy of St-Martin-in-the-Fields, City of Birmingham Symphony Orchestra, English Chamber Orchestra, London Symphony Orchestra; Performed with National Youth Jazz Orchestra at 1988 Proms; Composers who have written for him include Takemitsu, Leo Brouwer, Stephen Dodgson, André Previn, Peter Sculthorpe (concerto) and Nigel Westlake (concerto); Artistic Director of South Bank Summer Music Festival, 2 years, Melbourne Arts Festival, 1987; Premiered Played Brouwer's 4th Concerto in Toronto, 1987; US tour, 1989, and recital at South Bank Latin America Festival; Premiered Sculthorpe's works in Australia, 1989, Nigel Westlake's Antarctica with London Symphony, autumn 1992; Attacca tour, UK, Australia, 1992; Solo tours, UK, 1992, 1993; Documentary film The Seville Concert for Sony/LWT South Bank Show, 1993; Wigmore Hall series, US tour, Barcelona, Prague Spring Festival, 1994; Japan, Australia and European recitals, 1995; Concerts in Chicago and the Lincoln Center, New York, and in China, Greece and Scandinavia, 1997; Also played Takemitsu and the London premiere of Richard Harvey's Concerto Antico at the Barbican with the LSO conducted by Daniel Harding, followed by tours of UK, Ireland and Australia in recital with Timothy Kain; Solo recital at the Royal Festival Hall, followed by a recital of the UK and a trip to the Melbourne Festival, 1997. Recordings: Classical and popular works; Vivaldi Concertos; Australian Album; Music of Agustin Barrios Mangoré; John Williams Plays the Movies. Address: c/o Harold Holt Ltd, 31 Sinclair Road, London W14 0NS, England.

WILLIAMS John, b. 8 February 1932, New York, USA. Composer; Arranger; Conductor; Pianist. Education: Studied with Bobby Van Eps in Los Angeles with Rosina Lhevinne at the Juilliard School and Castelnuovo-Tedesco at University of California at Los Angeles. Career: Orchestrated for and Conducted USF bands; Wrote music for feature films and for television, including the Kraft Theatre Series; Pianist, Arranger and Conductor for Columbia Records, with collaborations with André Previn; Film music association with Steven Spielburg and other leading directors; Conductor of the Boston Pops Orchestra from 1980; Guest Conductor with orchestras in London, Canada and most American cities. Compositions: Film scores include The Towering Inferno, 1974; Jaws, 1975; Close Encounters of the Third Kind, 1977; Star Wars, 1977; Superman, 1978; Raiders of the Lost Ark, ET 1982; Indiana Jones and the Temple of Doom, 1984; Symphony, 1966; Essay for Strings, 1966; Violin Concerto, 1974; Flute Concerto, 1980; Pops on the March, 1982; Olympic Fanfare and Themes, 1984. Address: c/o ASCAP, ASCAP Building, One Lincoln Plaza, New York, NY 10023, USA.

WILLIAMS Julius (Penson), b. 22 June 1954, Bronx, New York, USA. Composer; Conductor. m. Lenora B Williams, 7 Aug 1977, 1 son, 1 daughter. Education: Music major, Andrew Jackson High School, 1972; BS, Herbert H Lehman College, City University of New York, 1977; MM, Hartt School of Music, 1980; Aspen Music School, 1984; Professional Fellow, Aspen, 1985. Debut: Premiere of A Norman Overture, New York Philharmonic and Zubin Mehta, 1985. Career: Music Director, CPTV, 1984-85; Arts Award Guest Conductor, Connecticut Opera, 1983, Dallas Symphony, 1986, Savannah Symphony, 1987; Assistant Conductor, Aspen Music Festival, 1985; Conductor, Composer-in-Residence, Nutmeg Ballet, Connecticut, 1986-88; Guest Conductor, New Haven Symphony, May 1987; Guest Conductor, Amor Artist Chamber Orchestra, 1987; Artistic Director, New York State Summer School of the Arts (Choral Studies), 1988-; Principal Guest, School of Orchestral Studies; Associate Professor, University of Vermont; Artist-in-Residence, Saratoga Arts Festival, Aug 1988; National TV, CBS Sunday Morning with Charles Kuralf, 11 Sept 1988. Compositions: A Norman Overture; Toccatina for Strings; Incommendation of Music; The Spring; Rise Up Shepherd and Follow; Vermont's Escape; Alison's Dream; The Fall, Summers Good Ecelin. Contributions to: American Choral Directors' Journal Choral Review, 1982. Current Management: Euphonia Artist Management, PO Box 809, Cambridge, MA 02238, USA. Address: Henderson, 7th Ave, Apt 4K, New York, NY 10026-2231, USA.

WILLIAMS Laverne, b. 1935, San Francisco, California, USA. Singer (Tenor). Education: Master's Degree, University of California; Alfred Hertz Memorial Scholarship and Rockefeller Foundation Scholarship for studies in Europe. Career: Concerts and Opera appearances ranging from Baroque to Contemporary; L'Incoronazione di Poppea, Salome, Idomeneo and Porgy and Bess, Switzerland; Appeared with Jessye Norman in Great Day in the Morning, Paris; Porgy and Bess, Glagolitic Mass and Jenufa under Simon Rattle, UK; Appearances with most major orchestras in London and UK including London Symphony, Royal Philharmonic and the Royal Liverpool Philharmonic Orchestra; Directed and sung in an experimental evening of spirituals, Almeida Theatre; Performed Virgil Thomson's Four Saints in Three Acts, Almeida Theatre; European Opera appearances include Zurich, Lyon and Brussels operas; Television and Radio appearances include: Gershwin's Blue Monday in Switzerland; Hermann Prey Show for German television; Here Comes the Classics and excerpts from Carmen Jones, BBC Television; Club Mix, Channel 4; Leading role, European premiere of Carmen Jones; Weber's Oberon, Edinburgh Festival, Tanglewood and Frankfurt, 1986. Recordings: Great Day in the Morning, with Jessye Norman. Honours: Competition successes in S'Hertogenbosch, Rio de Janeiro and Barcelona. Hobbies: Tennis, Squash, Art work of all kinds; Pottery.

WILLIAMS Louise, b. 23 Sept 1955, England. Violinist and Violist. Career: Co-founder and second violinist Endellion Quartet, 1979-83; Violist of the Chilingirian Quartet joined 1987-92; Resident Quartet of Royal College of Music; Annual series of concerts at the Elizabeth Hall and the Wigmore Hall and the Wigmore Hall; Performances at the Edinburgh, Bath, Aldeburgh Festivals; Munich Herkulessaal, Amsterdam Concertgebouw, Zurich Tonhalle, Vienna Konzerthaus, Stockholm Konserthuset; New York debut 1976; Annual coast-to-coast tours of the USA and Canada; Represented Britain at the New York International Festival quartet series; Tours of Australia, New Zealand, South America, the Far East; Television and radio throughout Europe, National Public Radio in the USA, the BBC; Presently, Freelance Chamber Musician and Soloist, Violin and Viola. Recordings: Complete Quartets of Bartok and Dvorak; Bartok Piano Quintet; Mozart Flute Quartets; Beethoven Serenade; Labels include Chandos. Address: The Top, Exbury House, Exbury, Southampton S045 1AF, England.

WILLIAMS Peter (Fredric), b. 14 May 1937, Wolverhampton, Staffordshire, England. University Professor; Organ and Harpsichord Recitalist. m. Rosemary Seymour, 10 June 1982, 3 sons, 1 daughter. Education: Birmingham Institute; St John's College, Cambridge, 1955-62. Career: Lecturer, 1962, Reader, 1972, Professor, 1982, Dean, 1984, University of Edinburgh, Scotland; Director, Russell College of Harpsichords, Edinburgh, 1969; Distinguished Professor and University Organist, Duke University, North Carolina, USA, 1985. Recordings: Several including editions: Bach, Musical Offering and Art of Fugue; Handel Op IV and VII; Handel Organ Concertos; Handel Harpsichord Music, 4 volumes; Miscellaneous organ music; Projected Bach organ music. Publications: The European Organ, 1966; Figured Bass Accompaniment, 2 volumes, 1970; Bach Organ Music, 1972; New History of the Organ, 1980; The Organ Music of J S Bach, 3 volumes, 1980-84; The Organ: New Grove Instrument Series, 1988; Playing the Organ Music of Bach, 1988; The Chromatic Fourth, 1995; Venta/Peeters The Organ of the Netherlands (translator), 1971; Editor: Tercentenary Essays, 1985; The Organ in Western Culture, 1993; The King of Instruments: How Do Churches Come to Have Organs?, 1993; Series editor: Cambridge Studies in Performance Practice, 4 volumes, by 1995. Contributions to: Essays to virtually all serious journals; Editor, series Biblioteca Organologica, 80 volumes, 1966-; Editor, The Organ Yearbook, Amsterdam, 1969-. Honours: LittD (Cambridge), 1981; Honorary FRCO, 1982; Honorary FRSA, 1985. Address: St Cecilia's Hall, University of Edinburgh, Edinburgh, Scotland.

WILLIAMS Sioned, b. 1 July 1953, Mancot, Clwyd, North Wales. Harpist. m. Kim A L Sargeant, 6 August 1977. Education: Welsh College of Music and Drama, 1971-74; Recital Diploma, Royal Academy of Music. Debut: Purcell Room, Park Lane Group Young Artists/20th Century Music, 1977; Carnegie Hall, New York, USA (Concert Artists Guild Award), 1980. Career: Appearances worldwide with London Symphony Orchestra, Philharmonia, London Philharmonic Orchestra, RPO, BBC Symphony Orchestra, BBC Philharmonic, CBSO, Royal Ballet, London Sinfonietta, Royal Opera House, ENO, WNO, SNO; Solo and Concerto performances, premiering over 80 works; Chamber Music with Uroboros, Gemini, Spectrum, Endymion, Divertimenti, Koenig, Grosvenor, Circle; Theatre, Radio, TV and Festival appearances; Professor of Harp, Royal College of Music Junior Department, 1976-85; Royal Academy of Music, 1983-84; London College of Music, 1985-86; Trinity College of Music, 1986-; Adjudicator at major Welsh Eisteddfods, 1981-. Compositions: Cyfres i'r Delyn, 1973 (special prize, 17th International Harp Week); Serenata e Danza, 1983. Recordings: Harp Music, John Thomas; Harp Music, John Parry; Spun Gold for Flute and Harpa; Ceremony of Carols, Britten; Nielsen with James Galway. Publications: Editor, John Parry: Four Sonatas, 1982; Four Sonatas, 1982; J S Bach: Suite BMV1006a, 1986. Honours: Numerous Prizes, Awards and Scholarships including Bursary, Arts Council Advanced Training Scheme, 1982. Memberships:

Telynores Garmon in Bardic Circle; Incorporated Society of Musicians; United Kingdom Harpists Association; World Harp Congress; American Harp Society; Cymdeithas Cerdd Dant; Guild for the Promotion of Welsh Music. Hobbies: Embroidery; Reading. Address: 181 Gloucester Road, Cheltenham, Gloucester, GL51 8NQ, England.

WILLIAMS Wayne, b. Cleveland, Ohio, USA. Singer (Tenor). Education: Studied at the Cleveland Music Settlement and with Gerard Souzay in Geneva. Career: Concert appearances with the Suisse Romande, Chamber Orchestra of Lausanne, Berne Symphony, Tonhalle Zurich, YMSO (London), Orchestra Haydn (Italy) and the Shanghai Symphony (China); Conductors have included Armin Jordan, Peter Maag, Horst Stein, Lopez-Cobos, James Blair, Paul Angerer and Herbert Handt; Recitals throughout the USA and Europe with Dalton Baldwin; Appearances in Paris in Dvorak's Requiem and Stabat Mater, Switzerland in The Creation and St Matthew Passion; Opera repertoire includes Schubert's Fierabras, L'Elisir d'Amore, La Traviata and A Midsummer Night's Dream. Recordings include: Poulenc Gloria; Great Day in the Morning, with Jessye Norman; Dvorak Stabat Mater. Address: c/o Anglo Swiss Limited, Suite 35-37 Morley House, 320 Regent Street, London W1R 5AD, England.

WILLIAMS-KING Anne, b. 1960, Wrexham, Wales. Soprano. Education: Studied at the Royal Northern College of Music and the National Opera Studio in London. Career: Sang with the Welsh National Opera as Lenio in The Greek Passion by Martinu, Mimi, Gilda, Fiordiligi, Marzelline in Fidelio and Micaela; Covent Garden debut in 1988 as Freia in Das Rheingold; Appearances with Opera North as Mimi and in Rebecca by Josephs and A Village Romeo and Juliet by Delius; Scottish Opera as Freia and Violetta, invited to return as Jenufa, Madama Butterfly and Mimi; Foreign engagements include Anne Trulove in The Rake's Progress at Berne; Frequent concert appearances with leading British Orchestras and on TV; Sang Butterfly with Scottish Opera at Edinburgh, 1990. Address: c/o Stafford Law Associates, 6 Barham Close, Weybridge, Surrey, England.

WILLIAMSON Malcolm (Benjamin Graham Christopher), b. 21 Nov 1931, Sydney, Australia. Composer; Pianist; Organist. m. Dolores Irene Daniel, 9 Jan 1960, 1 son, 1 daughter. Education: Studied at the Sydney Conservatory with Eugene Goossens and in London with Elisabeth Lutyens and Erwin Stein. Debut: Organ in London, 1966. Career: Soloist with numerous orchestras including London Philharmonic, Hallé, Vienna, Melbourne and Sydney Symphonies; Lecturer in Music, Central School of Speech and Drama, 1961-62; Composer-in-Residence, Westminster Choir College, Princeton, 1970-71, and Florida State University, USA, 1975; Visiting Professor at Strathclyde University, 1983-86; Myth Of The Cave premiered at the 1991 Promenade Concerts, London; A Year of Birds premiered 1995. Compositions include: Operas: Our Man In Havana, 1963, The Happy Prince, 1965, The Violins Of St Jacques, 1966, The Growing Castle, 1968, The Red Sea, 1972; Ballets: The Display, 1964, BigfellaTootsSquoodge And Nora, 1967; Orchestral: 7 Symphonies, 1956-84, Sinfonietta, 1967, Fiesta, 1978, Organ Concerto, 1961, Concerto for 2 Pianos and Strings, 1972, Myth Of The Cave, 1991, Ode To Music, 1972, Mass Of Christ The King for Soloists, Chorus and Orchestra, 1978, Unaccompanied Works for Chorus; A Year of Birds for Soprano and Orchestra, 1995; Chamber music, brass band music, organ music; Now Is The Singing Day, 1981, The True Endeavour, 1988, Our Church Lives, 1989, Requiem For A Tribe Brother, 1992. Honours include: Sir Arnold Bax Memorial Prize, 1963; DMus, Westminster Choir College, Princeton, NJ, 1971; Creative Arts Fellowship, Australian National University, Canberra, 1973; Master of the Queen's Music, 1975; CBE, 1976; AO, 1987. Hobby: Literature. Address: c/o Campion Press, Sandon, Buntingford, Hertfordshire, SG9 0QW, England.

WILLIS Helen, b. 25 Jul 1959, Newport, Gwent, Wales. Mezzo-Soprano. m. Robert Venn, 17 Dec 1983. Education: Diploma, Royal Academy of Music, 1977-83. Debut: Wigmore Hall, London, 1983. Career: Member of Glyndebourne Festival Chorus, 1983-85; Solo Operatic debut with Welsh National Opera as Siegrune in Die Walküre in 1984; Concerts and recitals throughout UK and abroad; Broadcasts include Sea Pictures and Wesendonk Lieder with BBC Welsh Symphony Orchestra. Honours: Triennial Young Welsh Singer of the Year, 1982. Hobbies: Food and Cooking; Walking.

WILLIS Nuala, b. 1950, England. Singer (Mezzo-soprano). Career: Worked as Designer and Costumier and as Actress in England in North America; Sang with Opera Studio in Brussels and small roles with the Glyndebourne Tour; Aldenburgh Festival in Eugene Onegin and A Midsummer Night's Dream; Guest appearances at Nancy, Metz, Marseilles (Herodias in Salome), Geneva (Larina in Eugene Onegin), Marseilles (Jezibab in Rusalka) and Zurich (The Hostess in Boris Godunov); At Covent Garden appeared in A Midsummer Night's Dream, Eugene Onegin and Faust as Martha; In Ireland has sung Widow Bebick (Mahagonny) at Wexford and Clytemnestra in Elektra conducted by Janos Fürst, in Dublin; Season 1989-90 included Herodias in the Swedish Folkopera's Salome at the Edinburgh Festival; Ulrica in Un Ballo in Maschera for Canadian Opera in Toronto; Royal National Theatre in Sondheim's Sunday in the Park with George; Engagements still with the D'Oyly Carte Opera; Sang the Elephant in Paran Vir's Broken Strings at the Almeida Theatre, 1996. Current Management: Athole Still International Management Limited. Address: Foresters Hall, 25-27 Westow Street, London SE19 3RY, England.

WILLS Arthur, b. 19 September 1926, Coventry, England. Composer; Cathedral Organist. m. Mary Elizabeth Titterton, 14 November 1953, 1 son, 1 daughter. Education: St John's School, Coventry; St Nicholas College, Canterbury; FRCO, 1948; ADCM, 1951; BMus, 1952; DMus, 1958; Hon RAM, 1974; FRSCM, 1977. Career: Organist, Ely Cathedral, 1958-90; Professor, Royal Academy of Music, 1964-92; Organ Recitals in Europe, USA, Australia and New Zealand. Compositions: Organ Concerto, 1970; An English Requiem, 1971; Guitar Sonata, 1974; Three Poems of EE Cummings for Tenor, Oboe and Piano, 1974; Love's Torment (Four Elizabethan Love Songs) for Alto and Piano, 1975; The Fenlands (Symphonic Suite for Brass Band and Organ), 1981; Overture: A Muse of Fire for Brass Band, 1983; Concerto Lirico for Guitar Quartet, 1987; When the Spirit Comes (Four Poems of Emily Brontë for Mezzo Soprano and Piano), 1985; Piano Sonata "1984"; The Dark Lady (Eight Sonnets of Shakespeare for Baritone and Piano), 1986; Sacrae Symphonia: Veni Creator Spiritus, 1987; Choral Concerto: The Gods of Music, 1992; Eternity's Sunrise, Three Poems by William Blake, 1992; A Toccata of Galuppi's Scena for Countertenor and String Quartet, 1993. Recordings: Mussorgsky: Pictures at an Exhibition (transcribed Wills), Hyperion; Bach at Ely: Nine transcriptions (Wills), Hyperion; Christmas Eve at Ely (Priory); The Music of Arthur Wills (Priory); Symphonic Suite: The Fenlands for Organ and Brass Band, Hyperion. Publications: Organ, Menuhin Music Guide Series, 1984 and 1993. Contributions to: Musical Times. Honours: OBE, 1990. Memberships: Royal Academy of Music. Hobbies: Reading. Address: Paradise House, 26 New Barns Road, Ely, Cambridgeshire CB7 4PN, England.

WILSON Catherine, b. 1936, Glasgow, Scotland. Soprano. Education: Royal Manchester College of Music with Elsie Thurston; Further study with Ruth Packer in London and Maria Carpi in Geneva. Debut: Sadler's Wells, London in 1960 as Angelina in La Cenerentola. Career: Glyndebourne in 1960 in Die Zauberflöte; Sadler's Wells in 1965 in the premiere of Bennett's The Mines Of Sulphur; Scottish Opera in the 1977 Edinburgh Festival, title role in Thea Musgraves Mary Queen of Scots; Scottish Opera in 1974 in the premiere of Hamilton's The Catiline Conspiracy; Guest appearances in Aldeburgh, Cologne, Geneva, Boston, Houston, Louisville and English National Opera in London, and Santa Fe; Often heard in operas by Mozart, Rossini, Puccini, Strauss and Britten and as a concert singer; Teacher at Royal Northern College of Music, 1980-91; Performance Coach, William Walton Trust, 1990-95. Recordings include: Albert Herring by Britten; The Merry Widow; Dido and Aeneas. Honour: Fellow, Royal Manchester College of Music. Hobbies: Gardening; Cooking. Address: 18 St Mary's Grove, London, N1, England.

WILSON Charles, b. 8 May 1931, Toronto, Canada. Composer. Education: Studied with Godfrey Ridout at the Toronto Conservatory; DMus, Toronto University in 1956; Further study with Lukas Foss and Carlos Chavez at the Berkshire Music Center. Career: Head of the Music Department at Guelph Collegiate Institute, 1962-70; Composer-in-Residence at Canadian Opera Company from 1972, and at the University of Guelph in Ontario. Compositions include: 3 String Quartets, 1950, 1968, 1975; The Strolling Clerk From Paradise, chamber opera, 1952; Symphony in A, 1954; Sonata de Chiesa for Oboe and Strings, 1960; String Trio, 1963; The Angels Of The Earth, oratorio, 1966; En Guise for Baritone and Strings, 1968; Concert 5x4x3 for String Quintet, Woodwind Quartet and Brass Trio, 1970; Johnny Fibber, operetta, 1970; Phrases From Orpheus, multi media opera, 1971; The Summoning Of Everyman, church opera, 1973; Heloise And Abelard, opera in 3 acts, 1973; The Selfish Giant, children's opera, 1973; Sinfonia for Double Orchestra, 1973; Image Out Of Season for Chorus and Brass Quintet, 1973; Christo Paremus Canticum for Chorus and Orchestra, 1973; Symphonic Perspectives: Kingsmere for Orchestra, 1974; Missa Brevis for Chorus and Organ, 1975; Psycho Red, opera in 2 acts, 1978; Kamouraska, opera in 3 acts, 1979. Address: SOCAN, 41 Valleybrook Drive, Don Mills, Ontario M3B 2S6, Canada.

WILSON Christopher, b. 1951, England. Lutenist; Vihuela Player. Education: Studied the lute at the Royal College of Music with Diana Poulton. Career: Has specialised in the performance of Renaissance music throughout Britain; Concert tours of Europe, Scandinavia, USA, the Baltic States, Russia and the Far East; As well as working with his own group Kithara, interest in the lute song repertoire has led him to work with such song recitalists as counter tenor Michael Chance and the tenor Rufus Müller; He also performs with Fretwork, Gothic Voices, the Consort of Musicke and the English Baroque Soloists; Concerts 1993-94 include tours to Sweden, Hong Kong and Japan, Poland and Taiwan. Recordings: Has appeared on over 50 recordings and on solo recordings.

WILSON David Fenwick, b. 31 Aug 1929, Pittsburgh, Pennsylvania, USA. Educator; Organist; Choir Director. m. Barbara Thompson, 20 Feb 1982, 2 stepsons, 1 stepdaughter. Education: BFA, Carnegie Institute of Technology, 1950; MMus, Eastman School of Music, 1955; PhD in Musicology, Case Western Reserve University, 1977. Career: Founding Chairman, Department of Music, 1962, Professor of Musicology and Director of Early Music Ensembles and Baroque Opera, Dalhousie University, Canada, retiring in 1993; Founder, Early Music Society of Nova Scotia, 1980; Founding President, Music Royale Summer Festival of Early Music, 1983; Music Director, Halifax Baroque Ensemble, 1986-; Organist and Choir Master, St James Anglican Church, 1993-. Publications: Music in the Middle Ages: Style and Structure, 1990; Music in the Middle Ages - An Anthology, 1990. Honours: Certificate of Merit, Cultural Federations of Nova Scotia, 1992. Memberships: American Musicological Society; Early Music Society of Nova Scotia; Royal Canadian College of Organists; Organ Historical Society; International Federation for Choral Music. Address: 15 Bayview Road, Halifax, Nova Scotia, Canada B3M 1N8.

WILSON Elisa, b. 1965, Perth, Western Australia. Singer (Soprano). Education: Australian Conservatorium, Perth. Career: Engagements throughout Australia, notably for Western Australia Opera Company, as Pamina, Donna Elvira, Micaela, Leila (Pêcheurs de Perles), Norina (Don Pasquale), Nannetta and Musetta; Sang in Sydney and Melbourne at the finals of the Covent Garden and Metropolitan Opera Competitions; Sang Helena in A Midsummer Night's Dream with Australian Opera at the 1994 Edinburgh Festival and Sydney 1996; Other roles include Gilda, Adina (L'Elisir d'Amore), Alice Ford (Falstaff), Handel's Alcina, and Rosalinda in Die Fledermaus (Australian Opera, 1997). Honours include: Armstrong-Martin Award, WA Opera; Dame Mabel Brookes Award, 1992; ABC Prize, 1992. Address: C&M Craig Services Ltd, 3 Kersley Street, London SW11 4PR, England.

WILSON Fredric (Woodbridge), b. 8 Sept 1947, Point Pleasant, New Jersey, USA. Musicologist. Education: BA, Music, Lehigh University, Bethlehem, Pennsylvania, 1969; MA, Musicology, New York University, 1977. Career: Director, The Wall Choirs, New Jersey, 1969-81; Editor, Allaire Music Publications, 1980-; Curator, The Pierpont Morgan Library, New York City, 1981; Professor of Museum Studies, Graduate School of Arts and Science, New York University, 1994-; Musical and Textual Consultant to opera companies. Compositions: More than 50 musical editions published, including motets by Gallus, Charpentier, mass by Lotti. Publications: Introduction to the Gilbert and Sullivan Operas, 1989; Index to the Opus Musicum of Jacob Handl, 1992; General Editor, The W S Gilbert Edition, 1986-; Complete Savoy Opera Libretti, Folio Society, 1994. Contributions to: New Grove Dictionary of Opera; Many papers and articles to various publications; Organised conferences in English Opera, New York, 1985, Gilbert and Sullivan, New York, 1989, Purchase College, 1994; Organised exhibitions at Pierpont Morgan Library, 1985, 1989, Kentucky Center for the Arts, 1987, 1988, Purchase College, 1994. Address: Pierpoint Morgan Library, 29E 36th Street, New York, NY 10016, USA.

WILSON Gordon, b. 1968, Scotland. Tenor. Education: Studied at the Royal Scottish Academy. Career: Appearances at Covent Garden, Glyndebourne, Scottish Opera, Opera North and the Buxton Festival; Sang Philidor's Tom Jones at Drottningholm and in Massenet's Chérubin at Covent Garden; Roles have included Nathaniel in Hoffmann, Alfredo, the Duke of Mantua, Riccardo in Oberto, Jenik in The Bartered Bride and Walton's Troilus; Concerts with the Ulster Orchestra, Northern Sinfonia and Manchester Camerata. Address: c/o Ron Gonsalves Management, 7 Old Town, Clapham, London, SW4 0JT, England.

WILSON James, b. 27 Sept 1922, London, England. Composer. Education: Studied at Trinity College of Music, London. Career: Resident in Ireland from 1948; Freelance Composer of music for stage and other works. Compositions: The Hunting of the Snark, children's opera, 1965; Twelfth Night, opera in 3 acts, 1969; Letters to Theo, opera in one act, 1984; Grinning at the Devil, opera in 2 acts, 1989; The King of the Golden River, 1990; A Passionate Man, Opera in 2 acts, 1995; Numerous concerti including those for viola, violin, harpsichord; Chamber music; Choral works; Numerous song cycles. Address: 10a Wyvern, Killiney Hill, Co Dublin, Ireland.

WILSON Neil, b. 4 Jun 1956, Lubbock, TX, USA. Tenor. Education: Studied at Dallas and Oklahoma Universities and in New York. Debut: Wolf Trap Washington in 1980 as Verdi's Fenton. Career: Sang with the Houston Opera and appeared with Stuttgart Opera from 1985 with debut as Werther; Further appearances in Munich, Vienna, Hamburg, Bologna, Los Angeles and Cologne (as Duke of Mantua in 1987); Sang at Washington Opera in 1987 as Gounod's Romeo, New York Metropolitan in 1988 as Macduff, sang Boito's Faust at the Zurich Opera, 1989-90, and at Glyndebourne Festival in 1986 as Monteverdi's Nero; Sang Rodolfo with Florentine Opera at the Performing Arts Center in Milwaukee in 1992; Other roles include Alfredo, Giasone in Médée, Nemorino, Lensky, Don Ottavio, Tamino and Pelléas; Concert repertoire includes Verdi's Requiem in Israel in 1986. Address: c/o Zurich Opera, Falkenstrasse 1, CH-8008 Zurich, Switzerland.

WILSON Paul, b. 1952, Gloucester, England. Tenor. Education: Studied at Jesus College Oxford and at the Royal College of Music. Career: British appearances with English National, Welsh National and Scottish Opera companies, Kent Opera, Glyndebourne Festival, Chelsea Opera and Opera North; Foreign engagements with the Opera Factory Zurich, Pocket Opera Nürnberg and Nairobi Opera; Roles include Tom Rakewell, Andrea Chénier, Bacchus, Mark in The Wreckers, and Don José; Royal Opera Covent Garden in Handel's Samson, Ariadne auf Naxos, King Priam and Der Rosenkavalier; Welsh National Opera debut in 1987 as Florestan, and English National Opera debut in 1988 as Monostatos; Sang in the world premieres of Golem by John Casken and Cage's Europeras III and IV (Almeida Festival, 1989-90) and Oliver's Timon of Athens (ENO, 1991); Opera North from 1990 in Gianni Schicchi and L'Heure Espagnole; Sang Siegmund and Siegfried in Birmingham Touring Opera's truncated Ring performances in Britain, 1990-91; Concert repertory includes The Dream of Gerontius, the Glagolitic Mass, Verdi's Requiem and Beethoven's 9th Symphony, conducted by Roger Norrington; Performance of Stravinsky's Les Noces with the National Youth Orchestra of Spain; Aldeburgh Festival in 1990 in Goehr's Triptych; Garsington Manor Opera in Ariadne auf Naxos in 1993; Kong in Harrison Birtwistle's The Second Mrs Kong, Glyndebourne, 1995. Recordings: Golem, John Gasken, 1991; Caritas, Robert Saxton, 1992. Honours include: First Wagner Society Bayreuth Bursary, 1983; Arts Council Bursary.Address: 94 Earlsfield Road, London, SW18 3DP, England.

WILSON Richard E, b. 15 May 1941, Cleveland, Ohio, USA. Composer; Pianist; Professor of Music. m. Adene Stevenson Green, 15 May 1971, 1 son, 1 daughter. Education: AB, Harvard University, 1963; Cello studies with Ernst Silberstein, piano with Leonard Shure, composition with Robert Moevs. Career: Works performed in New York including Tully Hall, 1991, London, Tokyo, San Francisco, Los Angeles, Bogata, Stockholm, Aspen, Boston, Chicago; Assistant Professor, 1966, Associate Professor, 1970, Professor, 1976-, Vassar College, Poughkeepsie, New York; Composer in Residence, American Symphony, 1992-. Compositions include: Quartet 3, Eclogue for Piano; The Ballad of Longwood Glen; Concert Piece for Violin and Piano; Music Solo for Flute; Music for Violin and Cello; Aethelred the Unready, opera in 1 act, 1994; Agitations for Full Orchestra, 1994; Transfigured Goat, 1996; String Quartet No 4, 1997. Recordings: Concerto for Piano and Orchestra; Concerto for Bassoon and Chamber Orchestra; Persuasions; Lord Chesterfield. Publications include: Sour Flowers; Profound Utterances; A Dissolve; Light in Spring Poplars; Home From the Range; Soaking; Fixations, 1991; Intercalations, 1991; Eight Comic Songs, 1995. Honours: Stoeger Prize for Chamber Music Composition, 1994; Commissions from the Chicago String Quartet and the Koussevitzky Music Foundation. Address: c/o Department of Music, Vassar College, Poughkeepsie, NY 12601, USA.

WILSON Robert, b. 4 Oct 1941, Waco, TX, USA. Playwright; Stage Director; Designer. Education: University of Texas, 1959-65; BFA, Architecture, Pratt Institute, NY. Career: Produced plays from 1969, firstly in New York then in Europe including the 12 hour play, The Life and Times of Joseph Stalin at Copenhagen in 1973; Collaboration with Philip Glass in Einstein On The Beach, premiered at Avignon in 1976 and repeated at the Metropolitan Opera; Further music theatre work with Glass and Gavin Bryars on Civil Wars in 1984; Directed Charpentier's Médée and Medea by Bryars, at Lyons in 1984; Designed the opening concert of the Opéra de Bastille in Paris, 1989; Premiere of Louis Andriessen's Die Materie at Amsterdam, 1989; Produced and designed Gluck's Alceste, for Chicago Lyric Opera in 1990 with Jessye Norman, Lohengrin for Zurich Opera in 1991, Palace of Arabian Nights with music by Philip Glass, produced at Lisbon and the Seville World Fair in 1992, and Parsifal at Houston in 1992; Directed Nono's Prometeo at Brussels, 1997; Engaged for The Ring at Bayreuth, 2000. Address: c/o Lyric Opera of Chicago, 20 North Wacker Drive, Chicago, IL 60606, USA.

WILSON Thomas (Brendan), b. 10 Oct 1927, Trinidad, Colorado, USA. Composer; Professor. m. Margaret Rayner, 20 Sept 1952, 3 sons. Education: MA, 1951, BMus, 1954, University of Glasgow; ARCM, Royal College of Music, 1954. Career: Freelance Composer; Royal College of Organists commission for Centenary, performed by St Paul's Cathedral Choir, brass ensemble and organ, London, 1993. Compositions: 4 symphonies, other orchestral music including: Piano Concerto, orchestra and triple wind, 1985; Willow Branches, 1986; Chamber music including: Chamber Concerto, 1986; St Kentigern Suite, string orchestra, 1986; Much music for films, TV and radio including Splendid Silent Sun, Voyage of St Brendan and Music for Sunset Song, Cloud Howe, Grey Granite; Numerous commissions including: 1-act opera, for BBC TV; 3-act opera, for Scottish Opera; Ballet, for Scottish Ballet; Te Deum, Edinburgh International Festival; Symphony No 3, 1978; Symphony No 4, for Scottish National Orchestra, 1989; Cantigas Para Semana Santa, 1991; Violin Concerto (National Youth Orchestra of Scotland commission), 1993; Confitemini Domino, 3 anthems (Royal College of Organists commission), 1993; Numerous vocal works, choral pieces, instrumental and band music. Recordings: Piano Concerto, Introit, David Wilde, Bryden Thomson, Scottish National Orchestra; Chamber Symphony; Violin Concerto; Piano Sonata, St Kentigern Suite; CD, Royal Albert Hall performance; Violin Concerto, National Youth Orchestra of Scotland with Ernst Kovacic and Christopher Seaman, 1993. Honours: CBE, 1990; Honorary DMus, Glasgow, 1991; FRSAMD, 1991; Elected Fellow of the Royal Society (Edinburgh), 1992. Memberships: Chairman, Composers' Guild of Great Britain; President, Scottish Society of Composers. Hobbies: Golf; Talking shop with like-minded friends.Address: 120 Dowanhill Street, Glasgow G12 9DN, Scotland.

WILSON Timothy, b. 18 Jul 1961, England. Counter Tenor. Education: Studied at the Royal Academy of Music. Career: Operatic engagements include Handel's Orlando and Britten's Death in Venice for Scottish Opera, Dido and Aeneas in Frankfurt, Gluck's Orfeo in Kassel, L'Incoronazione di Poppea in Gelsenkirchen, The Fairy Queen in Florence, A Midsummer Night's Dream in Kentucky, the modern premiere of Cesti's Il Pomo d'Oro in Vienna, and the world premieres of Maxwell Davies's Resurrection in Darmstadt, and Luis de Pablo's El Viajero Indiscreto in Madrid; Season 1990-91 with Vivaldi in Prague, Messiah in Valencia, Bach in the Philippines and the title role in Handel's Xerxes at Innsbruck; Covent Garden debut in 1992 as Oberon in A Midsummer Night's Dream; Sang in Agrippina at Buxton Festival, Alcina at the Halle Festival and Giulio Cesare at Ludwigshafen, 1992-93; Further concert appearances with Mackerras, Hickox, Pinnock, Herreweghe, Leonhardt, Norrington and Parrott; Venues include Holland, France, Germany, Austria, Spain, Italy and Britain including the Promenade Concerts. Recordings include: Alcina, Purcell's Come Ye Sons of Art Away and Handel's Israel in Egypt.

WILSON-JOHNSON David, b. 16 Nov 1950, Northampton, England. Singer (Baritone). Education: St Catharine's College, Cambridge; Royal Academy of Music, London. Career includes: Royal Opera House, Covent Garden from 1976 in Le Rossignol, L'Enfant et les Sortilèges, Boris Godunov, Die Zauberflöte, Werther, Turandot, Roméo et Juliette; Appearances with Welsh National Opera and Opera North, in operas by Delius, Rossini and Mozart; Concerts under Boulez, Giulini, Harnoncourt, Masur and Mehta; Sang title part in the first British performance of Messiaen's St François d'Assise, Royal Festival Hall, 1988; King Fisher in a televised production of Tippett's A Midsummer Marriage, 1989; Tours with David Owen Norris in Schubert's Winterreise; Lev in The Ice Break at the 1990 Promenade Concerts; Sang Choregos in Birtwistle's Punch and Judy for Netherlands Opera, 1993; Billy Budd, Arianna at Royal Opera House; Albert Herring, Billy Budd and Peter Grimes with Geneva Opera; Die Glückliche Hand and Von Heute auf Morgen by Schoenberg with the Netherlands Opera, 1995; Sang in Pfitzner's Palestrina at Covent Garden, 1997. Recordings: Over 100 including: Mozart Masses; Winterreise; Tippett's King Priam; Birtwistle's Punch and Judy; Walton's Belshazzar's Feast; B Minor Mass; Von Heute auf Morgen. Address: Lies Askonas Ltd, 6 Henrietta Street, Covent Garden, London WC2E 8LA, England.

WIMBERGER Peter, b. 14 May 1940, Vienna, Austria. Singer, Bass-Baritone. Education: Studied at the Vienna Music Academy with Paul Schoffler and Adolf Vogel. Debut: Dortmund 1963, as Pietro in Simon Boccanegra. Career: Appearances in the opera houses of Frankfurt, Karlsruhe, Kassel, Dusseldorf, Munich, Warsaw and Copenhagen; Barcelona 1985, as the Wanderer in Siegfried; Festivals of Bregenz and Florence; Repertoire includes principal roles in operas by Mussorgsky, Mozart, Wagner, Rossini, Verdi and Strauss; Sang at Palermo and Naples, 1988, as Amfortas; Rangoni at the Vienna Staatsoper, 1988; Kuno in Der Freischütz, 1996. Recordings: Haydn's Harmoniemesse; Spirit Messenger in Die Frau ohne Schatten by Strauss. Memberships: Vienna Staatsoper from 1968. Address: c/o Landestheater, Promenade 39, A 4010 Linz, Austria.

WINBECK Heinz, b. 11 February 1946, Piflas, Landshut, Germany. Composer; Teacher. Education: Studied piano and conducting at the Munich Richard Strauss Conservatory, 1964-67; Composition with Harald Genzmer and Gunter Bialas at the Munich Hochschule, 1963-73. Career: Conductor and Composer at Ingolstadt and Wunsiedel, 1974-78; Teacher at the Munich Hochschule 1980-88, Professor of Composition at the Wurzburg Hochschule, from 1988; Composer in Residence at the Cabrillo, California, Music Festival, 1985. Compositions include: In Memorian Paul Celan, for soprano, flute, piano and percussion, 1970; Sie Tanzt for baritone and ensemble, 1971; Sonosillent, for cello and strings, 1971; Musik for wind quintet, 1971; Espaces, for 4 percussionists, piano and flute, 1972; Nocturne I for chamber ensemble, 1972; Lenau-Fantasien for cello and chamber orchestra, 1979; 3 String Quartets, 1979, 1980, 1984; Chansons a Temps, for women's voices and 13 instruments, 1979; 4 Symphonies, 1983, 1987, 1988, 1993; Blick in den Strom, for String Quintet, 1993. Honours include: Music Prize of the Akademie der Schonen Kunste, Berlin, 1985. Address: c/o GEMA, Rosenheimer Str 11, 81667 Munchen, Germany.

WINBERGH Gösta, b. 30 Dec 1943, Stockholm, Sweden. Singer, Tenor. m. Elena Jungholm 1967, 1 son, 1 daughter. Education: Music Academy of Stockholm, vocal studies with Eric Saeden; Stockholm Opera School. Debut: Gothenburg 1971, as Rodolfo in La Bohème. Career: Principal tenor, Royal Opera, Stockholm, 1973-80; Joined Zurich Opera Company 1981; Guest appearances in Geneva, Berlin, Hamburg, Munich, Stuttgart, Amsterdam, Paris, Madrid, London and New York; Glyndebourne 1980, as Belmonte in Die Entführung; Salzburg Easter Festival and Vienna Staatsoper 1983; Drottningholm Opera 1984, as Ferrando in Così fan tutte; La Scala Milan 1985, as Tamino in Die Zauberflote; Sang in Mozart's Coronation Mass at St Peter's Rome 1985; Other roles include Mozart's Mitridate and Don Ottavio, Lensky in Eugene Onegin, Gennaro in Lucrezia Borgia and Donizetti's Dom Sebastian, Gluck's Admetus and Narraboth in Salome; Sang Ottavio at Barcelona 1986; Salzburg Festival 1987-88, as Ottavio and Titus; Houston Opera 1988, as Des Grieux in Manon; Tito at Chicago 1989, and La Scala, 1990; Covent Garden debut 1993, as Walther in a new production of Die Meistersinger; Sang Lohengrin at Covent Garden, 1997; Appearances in numerous concerts. Recordings: Don Pasquale; Liszt's Faust Symphony; Laertes in Hamlet by Thomas; Le Roi Arthus by Chausson; Bruckner's Te Deum. Hobbies: Golf; Sailing; Skiing. Address: Hilbert Agency, Maximilianstrasse 22, D 80539 Munich, Germany.

WINCENC Carol, b. 29 June 1949, Buffalo, New York, USA. Flautist; Teacher. Education: Studied in Italy with Severino Gazzeloni (Chigiana Academy 1966-67) and Santa Cecilani, Rome, 1967-68); Oberlin Ohio College Conservatory, 1967-69; BMus, Manhattan School of Music 1971, MM Juilliard School, 1972. Career: Flautist with National Orchestral Association, NY, 1970-71, Aspen Colorado Festival Chamber Orchestral, 1970-72 and St Paul's, Minnesota, Chamber Orchestra, 1972-77; New York recital debut at Carnegie Hall 1972, with many appearances nationwide as chamber orchestral soloist; Founder, Artistic-Director of the International Flute Festival at St Paul's (1985-87); Teacher at the Manhattan School of Music 1980-86; Indiana University Music School at Bloomington, 1986-88 and the Juilliard School, New York, from 1988; Many performances of contemporary composers, including Henryk Gorecki, Lukas Foss and John Tower. Address: c/o Wind Music Faculty, Juilliard School of Music, Lincoln Center, New York, NY 10023, USA.

WINDMULLER Yaron, b. 1956, Israel. Singer (Baritone). Education: Studied in Tel Aviv, Munich with Ernst Haefliger and in Vicenza with Malcolm King; Further study at the Opera Studio of the Bayerische Staatsoper. Debut: City of London Festival in 1982, in Gluck's Armide. Career: Sang as soloist with the Israel Philharmonic, and as member of Theater am Gärtnerplatz, Munich from 1986, as Purcell's Aeneas, Mozart's Count, Guglielmo, Don Giovanni and Papageno, Wolfram, Marcello, Hans Jurgen von Böse's Werther and Kaspar in Der Zaubergeige by Werner Egk; Sang Trinity Moses in Weill's Mahagonny at Frankfurt in 1990; Many concert appearances and Lieder recitals. Address: c/o Staatstheater am Gärtnerplatz, Gartnerplatz 3, 8000 Munich 1, Germany.

WINKLER Hermann, b. 3 Mar 1924, Duisburg, Germany. Tenor. Education: Studied at the Hanover Conservatory. Career: Has sung at the Bayreuth Festival from 1957, notably as the Steersman in Der fliegende Holländer in 1965 and Parsifal, 1976-77; Member of the Zurich Opera from 1970; Frankfurt Opera, 1970 as Lohengrin and Florestan; Munich in 1972 as Mozart's Don Ottavio and Idomeneo; Salzburg Festival and Deutsche Oper Berlin, 1976, 1981 in Idomeneo; USA debut in 1980 as Don Ottavio; Sang Florestan in USA and Japan in 1981; Covent Garden debut in 1984 as the Captain in Wozzeck; Zurich Opera in 1985 as the Emperor in Die Frau ohne Schatten; Guest appearances in Vienna and Hamburg; Sang Herod in Salome at La Scala, 1987, and Loge at Bologna; Season 1987-88 at the Teatro Real Madrid in Wozzeck and Lulu; Marseilles and Barcelona in 1989 as Aegisthus in Elektra; Sang in Peter Grimes at Zurich in 1989; Many appearances in the concert hall, often in Das Lied von der Erde by Mahler. Recordings: Arabella; Mahler's 8th Symphony; Idomeneo; Drum Major in Wozzeck.

WINKLER Peter, b. 26 January 1943, Los Angeles, USA. Composer; Editor. Education: BA 1960, University of California at Berkeley (study with Andrew Imbrie and Lalo Schifrin); MFA 1967,

Princeton University (study with Milton Rabbitt and Earl Kim). Career: Teacher at State University of New York, Stony Brook, from 1971; Editor of Journal of Popular Music Studies, 1992-. Compositions include: String Quartet, 1967; Praise of Silence for soprano, chorus, Renaissance ensemble and tape, 1969; Symphony, 1971-78; Clarinet Bouquet; Four Concert Rags, 1976-80; No Condition is Permanent, for flute and piano, 1990; Waterborne, for violin and tape, 1991; Sing Out the Old Sing in The New for men's chorus, tuba and violin, 1992; Saboreando el Gusto Cubano, for violin, piano and percussion, 1994; One Light, for men's chorus, piano and percussion, 1994; Tingle-Tangle: A Wedekind Cabaret, collaboration with William Bolcom and A Black, 1994. Honours include: MacDowell Colony Fellowship, 1971. Address: c/o ASCAP, ASCAP Building, One Lincoln Plaza, New York, NY 10023, USA.

WINSCHERMANN Helmut, b. 22 Mar 1920, Munich, Germany. Oboist; Conductor. Education: Studied in Essen and Paris. Career: Principal with the Frankfurt Radio Symphony Orchestra, 1945-51; Co-founded Collegium Instrumental Detmold, 1954, and became professor at the Detmold Academy, 1956; Appearances with the Capella Coloniensis and Stuttgart Chamber Orchestra; Founded the Deutsche Bachsolisten, giving many performances throughout Europe and elsewhere; Premiered La tomba di Igor Stravinsky by Giselher Klebe, 1979. Address: Detmold Hochschule für Musik, Allee 22, 4930 Detmold, Germany.

WINSLADE Glenn, b. 1958, Australia. Tenor Singer. Education: Studied at the New South Wales Conservatorium and at Vienna Conservatory. Career: Has sung with English National Opera as Ferrando, Victoria State Opera as Belmonte, Walter von der Vogelweide and Don Ottavio, Scottish Opera as Mozart's Titus and Australian Opera as Oronte in Alcina; Covent Garden debut in 1990 as Vogelgesang in Die Meistersinger; Further appearances with Glyndebourne Festival and Touring Opera, New Sadler's Wells Opera in Merry Widow, Freiburg Opera, Semper Oper Dresden as Belmonte, Stuttgart Opera and the Netherlands Opera in Idomeneo; Other roles include Tamino, The Prince in The Love of Three Oranges, Stroh (Intermezzo), Elemer in Arabella, Amenophis in Mosè, Ernesto and Nemorino, Fracasso in La Finta Semplice, Lindoro and Alfredo, Jacquino in Fidelio, Steuermann in Der fliegende Holländer and Jason in Cherubini's Médée; Engaged as Wagner's Rienzi at the Vienna Staatsoper, 1998; Concert engagements with the Musica Antiqua Vienna, Duke University, NC, RAI Milan and The BBC. Recordings include: Messiah with the Scottish Chamber Orchestra; Merry Widow. Honours: Winner, Australian Opera Auditions, Esso/Glyndebourne Touring and John Christie Glyndebourne Awards. Current Management: Lies Askonas. Address: c/o Lies Askonas, 6 Henrietta Street, London WC2, England.

WINSTEAD William (Owen), b. 11 Dec 1942, Hopkinsville, Kentucky, USA. Bassoonist; Composer. Education: BM, Bassoon, Curtis Institute of Music, 1964; MM, Composition, West Virginia University, 1965. Career: Principal Bassoon, Marlboro Festival Orchestra, 1965-71; Marlboro Music Festival, 1994-; Professor of Music, West Virginia University, 1965-78; Principal Bassoon, Fort Wayne, Indiana Philharmonic, 1977-78; Professor of Music, Florida State University, 1979-87; Principal Bassoon, Cincinnati Symphony Orchestra, 1986-; Faculty, Sarasota Music Festival, 1987-; Professor of Bassoon, Oberlin College Conservatory, 1988-89; Professor of BSN, Cincinnati College Conservatory of Music, 1989-; Solo Recitalist in USA and Europe; Faculty, Aspen Music Festival, 1996. Composition: The Moon Singer for Narrator and Orchestra. Recordings: With Marlboro Festival Orchestra under Pablo Casals, and with Cincinnati Symphony Orchestra for various labels; Chamber music recordings. Publications: Co-Editor, Ten Vivaldi Concerti; Co-Editor, Program Solos for The Bassoon. Membership: Former President, International Double Reed Society. Address: 4663 Glenway Avenue, Cincinnati, OH 45238, USA.

WINTER Louise, b. 29 Nov 1959, Preston, Lancashire, England. Mezzo-Soprano. m. Gerald Finley. Education: Studied at Chethams School of Music and at the Royal College of Music with Frederick Cox. Career: With Glyndebourne Touring Opera (from 1982) has sung Tisbe in La Cenerentola, Dorabella in Cosi fan tutte and Mercedes in Carmen; Sang Zerlina on Glyndebourne's tour to Hong Kong, Nancy in Albert Herring at the 1986 summer festival and in the Ravel double bill in 1987-88; Covent Garden debut in 1988 as a Flowermaiden in Parsifal; Has sung Janácek's Varvara and Ravel's Concepcion for Opera North; Netherlands Opera as Rosina in Il Barbiere di Siviglia and Second Lady in Die Zauberflöte; Glyndebourne Festival, 1988-90, in Katya Kabanova, Il Barbiere di Siviglia and the Ravel double bill; Appearances with the Canadian Opera Company in Eugene Onegin and as Dorabella in Cosi fan tutte in 1991; Concert engagements with the König Ensemble and in the Choral Symphony conducted by Simon Rattle; Season 1997 with Carmen and the Berlioz Marguerite for English National Opera and Jocasta in Oedipus Rex at the Festival Hall. Address: c/o Harrison Parrott Ltd, 12 Penzance Place, London, W11 4PA, England.

WINTER Quade, b. 1950, Oregon, USA. Composer; Tenor. Debut: Sang Max in Der Freischütz at San Francisco. Career: Has sung the Duke of Mantua for Eugene Opera, Canio at Anchorage, Don Ottavio at the Carmel Bach Festival and Ishmael in Nabucco for San Francisco Opera; Appeared in US premiere of The Excursions of Mr Broucek, with the Berkeley Symphony; Concerts have included Beethoven's Ninth with the Stockton Symphony and the Verdi Requiem at the San Francisco Festival of Masses, conducted by Robert Shaw; European debut as Hermann in The Queen of Spades with Graz Opera in 1982; La Scala Milan in 1982 as Cherubini's Anacréon; Roles with the Stadtheater Wurzburg have included Don Carlos, Lensky, Herod, Rodolfo and Canio; Has sung Parsifal at Graz and Herod in Heidelberg and Seattle; Scottish Opera debut as Mark in The Midsummer Marriage, in 1989; Music for Gilbert and Sullivan's Thespis performed by Ohio Light Opera, 1996. Address: Music International, 13 Ardilaun Road, London, N5 2QR, England.

WINTER Sidonie, b. 1965, England. Singer (Soprano). Education: University of East Anglia, Royal Academy of Music and Brereton International Summer School. Career: Frequent concerts throughout Britain, including Wigmore Hall, St John's Smith Square and South Bank; Royal Albert Hall debut as Lady Angela in Patience; Other concerts include Messiah and Handel's Dixit Dominus, the Missa solemnis in D Minor by Hadyn, Beethoven's Mass in C and Elgar's Apostles; Opera debut as Leila in Iolanthe for D'Oyly Carte Opera; Other roles include Siebel in Faust, Elena (Aroldo), Sofia (Lombardi) and Priestess (Aida, Covent Garden, 1996); Fiordiligi at Ischia for the Walton Trust, Geisha in Iris for Chelsea Opera Group Group, Mozart's Countess and Donna Elvira at Aldeburgh. Address: C&M Craig Services Ltd, 3 Kersley Street, London SW11 4PR, England.

WIORDA Walter, b. 30 Dec 1906, Katowice, Poland. Professor Emeritus; Musicologist. m. Dr Christa Wiora-von Hertzberg. Education: Hochschule fur Musik and University, Berlin, with Blume, Gurlitt and Schering; PhD, University of Freiburg, 1937. Career: Archivist, Deutsches Volkslied Archiv, 1937-57; Lecturer, University of Freiburg, 1940; Full Professor, Universities of Kiel, 1958-64, SaarbrÜcken, 1964-73; Visiting Professor, Columbia University, New York, USA, 1962-63. Publications: Das Deutsche Volkslied und der Osten, 1940; Zur Fruheschichte der Musik in den Alpenländern, 1949; Das echte Volkslied, 1950; Europäischer Volksgesang, 1952; Biography of Bruckner, 1952; Europäische Volksmusik und abendländische Tonkunst, 1957; Die Vier Weltalter der Musik, 1961, 1988; Das deutsche Lied, 1971; Ideen zur Geschichte der Musik, 1980; Das musikalische Kunstwerk, 1983. Honours: Honorary Member, deutsche Musikrat und Gesellschaft Musikforschung; Festschriften, 1967, 1979, 1988. Memberships: Bayerische Akademie der Schönen Kunste; International Musicological Society; Gesellschaft fur Musikforschung; International Council for Traditional Music. Address: D-82327 Tutzing, Oberes Vocherl, Germany.

WIRKKALA Merja, b. 7 Oct 1954, Kaustinen, Finland. Singer (Soprano). Education: Studied at the Sibelius Academy, Helsinki. Career: Sang with the Helsinki Opera from 1976, notably as Nannetta, Zerlina, Despina, Susanna, Kaisa in Merikanto's Juha, and Siebel; Sang Marzelline in Fidelio at the Vienna Staatsoper (1980), Zerlina at Covent Garden, 1981, and the title role in the premiere of Elina by Liukolas at Helsinki, 1992; Guest in Juha at the Edinburgh Festival, 1987. Address: Finnish National Opera, Bulevardi 23-27, SF-00180 Helsinki 18, Finland.

WIRTZ Dorothea, b. 13 Mar 1953, Tuttlingen, Germany. Soprano. Education: Studied in Berlin with Hugo Diez and in Munich with Hanno Blaschke. Career: Sang at the Munich Staatsoper, 1979-80, Kassel, 1980-84; Member of the Zurich Opera from 1984; Guest appearances in Dusseldorf, Venice, Naples, Lisbon, Bologna, Berlin, Cologne, Wiesbaden, Florence and Strasbourg; Roles include Olympia in Les Contes d'Hoffmann, Blondchen, the Queen of Night, Zerlina, Despina, Ilia in Idomeneo, Rosina, Sophie in Der Rosenkavalier, Zerbinetta, Norina, Adina, Marzelline and the Woodbird in Siegfried; Sang Blondchen at Buenos Aires in 1987; Concert Repertoire includes works by Handel, Mozart, Bach and Schumann including Paradies und die Peri. Recordings include: Strauss's Daphne. Address: c/o Operhaus Zurich, Falkerstrasse 1, CH-8008 Zurich, Switzerland.

WISE Patricia, b. 31 Jul 1944, Wichita, Kansas, USA. Soprano. Education: Studied at Kansas University, Santa Fe, and in New York with Margaret Harshaw. Debut: Susanna in Mozart's Marriage of Figaro, Kansas City in 1966. Career: Appearances at the Houston Opera, New York City Opera, New Orleans, Philadelphia, Chicago, San Francisco, Washington, Miami, Baltimore, San Antonio and Pittsburgh; Carnegie Hall, New York in 1971 in Handel's Ariodante, Covent Garden, London in 1971 as Rosina in Rossini's Barber of Seville with New York City Opera; Glyndebourne in 1972 as Zerbinetta in Ariadne auf Naxos; Vienna Staatsoper in 1983 as Pamina, Nannetta and Sophie; Sang at the 1984 Salzburg Festival in the premiere of Un Re in Ascolto by Berio; 1st appearance in Geneva in 1985 as Lulu; Repertoire includes roles in operas by Donizetti, Gounod, Gluck, and Verdi's Gilda; Sang with the Vienna Staatsoper, 1976-91 in 300 performances, many of which were Strauss or Mozart operas; Since 1985 has appeared in five other productions of Berg's 3 act Lulu, from Berlin to Paris; Sang Lulu at Madrid in 1987, Sophie in Der Rosenkavalier at Budapest, 1989, Gilda in Rigoletto at Madrid, 1989, Fiordiligi in Mozart's Così fan tutte, and Violetta in Verdi's Traviata, 1990; Guest appearances in European opera houses including La Scala, Munich, Berlin, Hamburg, Barcelona, Geneva, Glyndebourne and at Salzburg Festival. Honours include: Kammersängerin, Vienna Staatsoper, 1996. Address: c/o Harold Holt, 31 Sinclair Road, London, W14 0NS, England.

WISHART Trevor, b. 11 Oct 1946, Leeds, England. Composer. m. Jacqueline Joan Everett, 2 d. Education: BA Music, Oxford University; MA, Analysis of Contemporary Music, Nottingham University; DPhil, Composition, York University. Career: Foreign tours: Scandinavia, Australia, Japan, USA, Netherlands, Spain, Germany, IRCAM commission, Vox-5, 1986; Vox cycle performed at London Proms, 1988; Sound Designer, Jorvik Viking Centre Museum, York; Special Professor of Music, University of Nottingham, 1990-92; Visiting Fellow, Bretton Hall College of the University of Leeds, 1994-. Composition: Red Bird; Anticredos; The Vox Cycle; Pastorale - Walden 2; Beach Singularity; Tongues of Fire, 1994. Recordings: Vox; Vox 5; Red Bird; Anticredos; October Music; Audible Design, 1994. Publications: Sounds Fun, educational music games, 1974 also in Japanese; On Sonic Art, 1985; Audible Design, 1994; Sun, Creativity and Environment; Sun-2, A Creative Philosophy; Whose Music, A Sociology of Musical Language. Contributions to: Contact; Musics; Ear Magazine, New York; Interface, Utrecht; Computer Music Journal, USA; Musica Realta, Milan. Honours: Prizewinner: Bourges International Electro-Accoustic Music Festival, 1978, Gaudeamus International Festival, Netherlands, 1979, Linz Ars Electronica, 1985, 1995. Memberships: Chair, Sonic Arts Network, 1990-92; Founder, Composers Desktop Project. Hobbies: Philsophy of Science; Mathematics; Fell Walking.

WISLOCKI Leszek, b. 15 Dec 1931, Chorzow, Poland. Composer; Pianist. m. Renata Krumpholz, 9 July 1968, 2 sons. Education: Piano, 1955, Composition, 1957, Conducting, 1962, Academy of Music, Wroclaw. Career: Concerts as Pianist and Composer, Polish Radio and TV. Compositions: Andante and Presto for xylophone and piano; Two Miniatures for violin and cello; Sonata for oboe and cello; Ostinato and Toccatina for piano solo; Polonaise for piano solo; Suita Lubuska for wind orchestra; Songs for choir a cappella (male and female). Recordings: Many tapes, Radio-Wroclaw; Andante and Presto for xylophone and piano. Honours: Prize, Ministers of Culture and Art, 1973; Prize, City of Wroclaw, 1977; Honorary Diploma, Ministers of Culture and Art. Memberships: Polish Composers' Society; President, Lower Silesian Musical Society. Hobbies: Collecting old instruments and antiques. Address: ul Komandorska 48-8, 53-343 Wroclaw, Poland.

WISLOCKI Stanislaw, b. 7 July 1921, Rzeszow, Poland. Conductor; Composer; Pianist. m. 31 Dec 1944. Education: Academy of Music, Timisoara, 1942. Debut: As Pianist, 1941; As Conductor and Composer, 1944. Career: Chief Conductor, Warsaw Chamber Orchestra, 1945-47, Philharmonic Orchestra, Poznan, Poland, 1947-58; Conductor, National Philharmonic, Warsaw, 1961-66; Art Director, Chief Conductor, Polish Radio and TV National Symphony Orchestra, Katowice, 1978-82; Musical Director, Philharmonic Orchestra, Teatro Colon, Buenos Aires, 1981; Concerts in Europe, Japan, USA, Latin America; Lecturer, Opera High School, Poznan, 1948; Lecturer, 1949-55, Junior Lecturer, 1955-58, Poznan Conservatoire; Junior Lecturer, Warsaw Conservatoire, 1955-65; Professor, Academy of Music, Warsaw, 1965-. Compositions: Symphony of Dance; Concerto for Piano and Orchestra; Overture; Ballade for Orchestra; Chamber music; Music for film and theatre. Address: ul Zdrojowa 55, 02 927 Warsaw, Poland.

WISSMER Pierre, b. 30 Oct 1915, Geneva, Switzerland. Composer. m. Laure-Anne Etienne, 6 Feb 1948. Career: Professor of Composition, Geneva Conservatoire; Music Critic, La Suisse Journal, Music Department, Radio-Geneve, 1944-48; Director, Radio Luxembourg, 1951-57; Director, Schola Cantorum, Paris, 1957-63; Director, L'Ecole Nationale de Musique du Mans, 1969-81; Professor of Composition and Orchestration, Geneva Conservatoire, 1973-86. Compositions include: 3 Operas, 4 ballets, 9 symphonies, 3 oratorios, 12 concertos and numerous other compositions. Recordings: 6th Symphonie; 2eme Quatuor A Cordes; Sonatine for Flute and Guitar; Prestique De Votre Discotheque; Trois Silhouettes for Piano; Reflexions Et Variations Sur Un Noel Imaginaire for Organ; Partita for Guitar; Prestilagoyana for 2 Guitars; CD, Piano Concerto and Symphonique Suite Que Alerte. Honours: Grand Priz Suisse de la Radio, 1950; Prix Lyrique, Societe des Auteurs et Compositeur Dramatiques, 1956; Grand Prix Paul Gilson, Communauté Radiophonique, 1965; Grand Prix Musical, Ville de Paris, 1967; Grand Prix Musical, Ville de Geneve, 1983; Chevalier, Ordre des Arts et des Lettres, France, 1988. Memberships: SACEM; SACD, France. Hobby: Skiing. Address: 9 Square de Mondori, F-78150 Le Chesnay, France.

WIT Antoni, b.7 Feb 1944, Krakow, Poland. Conductor. m. Zofia Cwikilewicz, 12 Oct 1977. Education: Law, Jagiellonian University, Krakow, 1969; Conducting, Krakow Academy of Music, 1967, Composition, 1969. Debut: Concert with Krakow Philharmonic Orchestra, 1964. Career: Assistant Conductor, National Philharmonic, Warsaw, 1967-70; Engagements at the Grand Theatre, Warsaw, 1970-80; Conductor, Poznan Philharmonic, 1970-72; Artistic Director, Principal Conductor, Pomeranien Philharmonic in Bydgoszcz, 1974-77; Artistic Director, Principal Conductor, Krakow Radio Symphony and Choir, 1977-83; Artistic Director, Principal Conductor, Polish Radio National Symphony Orchestra, Katowice, 1983-; Artistic Director, later Principal Guest Conductor, Philharmonic Orchestra, Gran Canaria, 1987-91. Recordings: Over 80 CD's. Honours: 2nd Prize, Herbert von Karajan Competition, Berlin, 1971; Diapason d'or and the Grand Prix du Disque 92 for Piano Concertos No 1-5 by Prokofiev Recorded for Naxos, 1993. Hobbies: Cycling; Travel; Foreign Languages. Current Management: Konzertdirektion Hans Adler, Berlin; Musicaglotz, Paris; Worldwide Artists, London. Address: ul Klonowa 34a/3, 40-168 Katowice, Poland.

WITTE Erich, b. 19 Mar 1911, Graudenz, Bremen, Germany. Tenor; Producer. Education: Studied at the Bremen Conservatory with P Kraus. Debut: In Bremen in 1930 as Nando in Tiefland. Career: Sang at Bremen until 1937, then at Wiesbaden and Breslau, 1937-42; Metropolitan Opera, 1938-39 as Froh, Mime and the Simpleton in Boris Godunov; Bayreuth Festival, 1943-44 as David in Die Meistersinger; Sang at the Berlin Staatsoper from 1941, Städtische Oper Berlin in 1947, in Peter Grimes, and Bayreuth, 1952-53 as Loge; Sang Loge at Covent Garden in the 1950s, and Walther in Die Meistersinger in 1957; Chief Opera Producer at Frankfurt from 1961, and Staatsoper Berlin from 1964; Lecturer at the Berlin Musikhochschule.

WITZENMANN Wolfgang, b. 26 Nov 1937, Munich, Germany. Musician. m. Renata Di Salvo, 5 Mar 1977, 1 son, 1 daughter. Education: Privatmusiklehrer Diplom, Musikhochschule Stuttgart, 1960; DPhil History of Music, Universitaet Tübingen, 1965. Career: As composer: Gaudeamus-Festival, Netherlands, 1967, 1968, 1970 and 1971; Internationale Ferienkurse für Neue Musik, Darmstadt, Federal Republic of Germany, 1969; Autunno Musicale, Como, Italy, 1975; Festival Internazionale Nuova Consonanza, Rome, 1985; Festival Internazionale Terenzio Gargiulo, Naples, 1986. Compositions: Choirs; Oden I-V for voice and piano; 6 cycles of Lieder; Operas Nivasio and Mary; Eigenklänge, Natur, Deutschland-Lieder for orchestra; Sinfonia 1 and 2 for orchestra; Violin Concerto; Antiphonales Konzert, for trumpet and orchestra; Piano and organ music, chamber music, and music for early instruments. Recordings: Monographic disc, EDI-PAN, Rome, 1989. Publication: Domenico Mazzocchi (1592-1665), Dokumente und Interpretationen, 1970. Contributions to: Analecta Musicologica; Acta Musicologica; Die Musikforschung; Rivista Italiana di Musicologica; Studi Musicali. Hobbies: Hiking; Swimming; Skiing. Address: Via Licinio Calvo 14, I-00136, Rome, Italy.

WIXELL Ingvar, b. 7 May 1931, Lulea, Sweden. Baritone. Education: Studied in Stockholm with Dagmar Gustavson. Debut: Sang at Gavle in 1952. Career: Stockholm in 1955 as Papageno; Member of The Royal Opera Stockholm from 1956; Appeared with the company in Alcina at Covent Garden in 1960; Glyndebourne Festival in 1962 as Guglielmo in Così fan Tutte; US debut at Chicago Lyric Opera in 1967 as Belcore in L'Elisir d'Amore; Salzburg Festival 1966-69, as Count Almaviva and Pizarro; Hamburg Staatsoper in 1970 as Rigoletto and Scarpia; Covent Garden, 1972-77 as Simon Boccanegra, Scarpia, Belcore and Mandryka in Arabella; Metropolitan Opera from 1973 as Rigoletto, Germont, Amonasro, Marcello and Renato in Un Ballo in Maschera; Other roles include Don Carlo in La Forza del Destino, Count Luna, Posa and Pentheus in The Bassarids by Henze; Sang Amonasro at Houston in 1987; Covent Garden, 1987-90 as Rigoletto and Belcore; Stuttgart Staatsoper, 1990 as Scarpia; Sang in Tosca at Earl's Court in London, 1991. Recordings: Le nozze di Figaro, Don Giovanni, Zaide, La Bohème, Un Ballo in Maschera, Tosca, Un Giorno di Regno, Il Trovatore, L'Elisir d'Amore; Video of Tosca. Address: c/o Harold Holt Ltd, 31 Sinclair Road, London, W14 0NS, England.

WLASCHIHA Ekkerhard, b. 28 May 1938, Pirna, Germany. Baritone. Education: Studied at the Franz Liszt Musikhochschule in Leipzig and with Helene Jung. Debut: Gera in 1961 as Don Fernando in Fidelio. Career: Sang in Dresden and Weimar, 1964-70; Leipzig Opera from 1970 as Scarpia, Pizarro, Alfio, Tonio, Dr Coppelius, and Jochanaan in Salome; Sang in the premieres of Greek Wedding by Hannell in 1969 and The Shadow by Fritz Geissler in 1975; Lausanne Opera and Staatsoper Berlin in 1983 as Kurwenal and Telramund; Sang Kaspar in Der Freischütz at the reopening of the Semper Opera House in Dresden, 1985; Bayreuth Festival in 1986 as Kurwenal; Appeared on Russian TV in Fidelio by Beethoven; Sang Telramund at the Berlin Staatsoper in 1990, and Alberich in a new production of Siegfried at Covent Garden in 1990; Returned to London 1997, as Bishop Ercole in Pfitzner's Palestrina. Address: c/o Allied Artists Agency, 42 Montpellier Square, London, SW7 1JZ, England.

WOHLERS Rudiger, b. 4 May 1943, Hamburg, Germany. Tenor. Education: Studied at the Hamburg Musikhochschule. Career: Sang at Darmstadt, 1968-71; Sang at Zurich, 1971-74 as Mozart's Belmonte, Ferrando, Tamino and Don Ottavio; Sang at Stuttgart from 1974 and has made guest appearances in Hamburg, Munich, Vienna and Frankfurt; Schwetzingen Festival in 1975 as Belmonte; Deutsche Oper Berlin from 1977; Sang Tamino at the 1981 Salzburg Festival; La Scala Milan in 1983 as Ferrando in Cosi fan Tutte; Sang in Cavalli's L'Ormindo at the Hamburg Staatsoper in 1984 and toured with the company to Japan; Stuttgart in 1984 as Don Ottavio in the newly restored opera house; Other roles include Fenton in Die Lustigen Weiber von Windsor, Lionel in Martha, Nemorino, Lensky and Almaviva in Il Barbiere di Siviglia; Many concert engagements and lieder recitals; Sang Idomeneo with the English Bach Festival at Covent Garden in 1990. Recordings: Jacquino in Fidelio; Cantatas by Bach, Fux and Scarlatti; Die Schöpfung by Haydn. Address: c/o Hamburgische Staatsoper, Grosse Theaterstrasse 34, D-2000 Hamburg 36, Germany.

WOHLHAUSER René (Claude), b. 24 Mar 1954, Zürich, Switzerland. Composer. m. Eva Ruth Sieber, 29 Feb 1980, 2 sons, 2 daughters. Education: Diploma as Teacher of Music Theory, Basel Conservatory, 1975-79; Composition courses with Kazimierz Serocki, Mauricio Kagel, Herbert Brün and Heinz Holliger; Study with Klaus Huber, Staatliche Musikhochschule, Freiburg, 1980-81; Composition with Brian Ferneyhough, 1982-87. Career includes: Works played by Arditti String Quartet, Basel, Biel and Luzern Symphony Orchestras, also at 4 Schweizer Tonkünstlerfeste and 4 International Darmstädter Ferienkurse für Neue Musik, Notre Dame de Paris, Toronto, New Castle, Baku, Klangforum Wien and Schauspielhaus Berlin; Portraits and works on radio programmes; Lectures on musical and philosophical aspects of his works at Darmstädt, Winterthur and Basel; Founder, Komponistenforum Basel and Co-founder of Adesso, contemporary music of independently published composers. Compositions include: Duometrie, for flute and bass clarinet, 1985-86; Adagio assai for String Quartet, 1982-88; In statu mutandi, for orchestra, 1991-93; Vocis Imago for Flute, Clarinet, Percussion, Piano, Violin and Cello, 1993-95. Recordings: Wer den Gesang nicht kennt, CD; Drei Stücke für Klavier, CD; Portrait, CD. Contributions include: Ueber kompositorische, ästhetische und philosophische Aspekte eigener Werke, in Musik Texte, Köln, 1990 and in Darmstädter Beiträge zur Neuen Musik, volume XX, 1994. Honours include: Prizes at many international composers competitions, 1978-92. Memberships include: Schweizerischer Tonkünstlerverein, Switzerland. Address: Schillerstrasse 5, CH-4053 Basel, Switzerland.

WOHLLEBEN Rosemarie, b. 27 Aug 1938, Bremerhaven, Germany. Piano Teacher; Choir Leader; Author. m. Rudolf Wohlleben, 21 Dec 1982, 1 son, 1 daughter. Education: Volksschule Bremerhaven, 1944-48; Realschule B, 1948-54; Musikhochschule Hannover, 1961-67; Musikhochschule Koeln, 1986-88. Debut: Piano, Bremerhaven, 1954. Compositions: Reise ins Klaraffia-Land, pre-school piano tutor. Recording: LP with Children Choir. Memberships: Gesellschaft deutscher und oesterreichischer Kunstlerinnen; Ges Beethoven-Haus, Bonn; Ges Schumann-Haus, Bonn. Hobbies: Painting; Folk-dancing. Address: Am Bogen 9, D 53125 Bonn-Roettgen, Germany.

WOLANSKY Raymond, b. 15 Feb 1926, Cleveland, Ohio, USA. Baritone. Education: Studied in Cleveland. Career: Sang at the Stuttgart State Opera from 1952; Rio de Janeiro in 1959 as Count Almaviva; Teatro San Carlos Lisbon in 1961 in Iphigénie en Tauride; Sang at the Hamburg Staatsoper from 1960, visiting Edinburgh in 1966; Glyndebourne Festival, 1963-64 as Olivier in Capriccio; Sang at San Francisco in 1972 in the US premiere of The Visit of The Old Lady by Von Einem; Covent Garden in 1973 as Mandryka in Arabella; Sang at La Scala in 1976 as Faninal in Der Rosenkavalier; Repertoire includes roles in operas by Wagner, Verdi, Puccini and Bizet; Many concert appearances. Recordings: Excerpts from Il Trovatore; Carmina Burana. Address: c/o Hamburgische Staatsoper, Grosse Theaterstrasse 34, D-2000 Hamburg 36, Germany.

WOLF Gerd, b. 18 Apr 1940, Floha, Saxony, Germany. Bass Singer. Education: Studied at the Berlin Musikhochschule. Debut: Dresden Radesbeul in 1970 as the Hermit in Der Freischütz. Career: Sang at Dresden and elsewhere in East Germany until 1982, Berlin Staatsoper from then as Mozart's Osmin, Leporello and Bartolo, Nicolai's Falstaff, Bett in Zar und Zimmerman, Geronimo in Il Matrimonio Segreto and the Doctor in Wozzeck; Guest appearances in Leipzig, Karlsruhe and with the Berlin Staatsoper company at Naples, Messina, Prague, Bratislava, Japan and Holland. Recordings include: Pfitzner's Palestrina; Graf Mirabeau by Siegfried Matthus; Ariadne auf Naxos. Address: Deutsche Staatsoper Berlin, Unter den Linden 7, 1086 Berlin, Germany.

WOLF Harold, b. 15 May 1921, Berkeley, California, USA. Violinist; Conductor. m. Katherine Steve, 1 May 1944, 1 daughter. Education: Pierre Monteaux School for Conductors; Curtis Institute of Music; Juilliard School of Music; Further studies with Mishel Piastro. Debut: Violin, 1940; Conducting, 1953. Career: Los Angeles Philharmonic Symphony 1948-52; 1st Violin, Utah String Quartet, 1952-66; Concertmaster, Utah Symphony, 1952-66; Lecturer, University of Utah, 1953-66; Concertmaster, Alabama Symphony, 1968-74; San Diego Symphony, 1974-76; Recording Musician, motion picture and TV soundtracks in Hollywood, 1974-93; Concertmaster, Los Angeles Civic Light Opera Orchestra, 1976-81; Member, Los Angeles Chamber Orchestra, 1983-88; Concertmaster, Portland Chamber Orchestra, Portland, Oregon, 1995. Compositions: Three Cadenzas for the Mozart Violin Concerto No 5, 1983; Cadenza for the Brahms Violin Concerto, 1990. Recordings: Gordon Ramsey, String Quartet, 4 descriptive pieces for violin and viola, flute quartet, violin and piano sonata. Honours: Scholarships: Curtis Institute of Music, 1930; New York Philharmonic, 1932; Juilliard School of Music, 1936. Memberships: Life Member, American Federation of Musicians, Los Angeles; Portland Youth Philharmonic Search Committee, 1995. Hobbies: Flying; Golf; Model building; Reading; Collecting records. Address: 1-Jefferson Parkway No 180, Lake Oswego, OR 97035, USA.

WOLF Markus, b. 28 May 1962, Vienna, Austria. Violinist. 2 sons. Education: Violin studies at Wiener Musikhochschule with Edith Bertschinger and Guenter Pichler, 1968-83; Diploma with Honours, 1983; Further studies with Max Rostal, Klagenfurt and Bern; Masterclasses with Nathan Milstein and Oscar Shumsky. Debut: Wiener Musikverein, 1976, Wigmore Hall, London, 1987, Suntory Hall, Tokyo, 1990. Career: Violist, String trio with brothers Reinhold and Peter Wolf, 1973-; Appearances with the Alban Berg Quartet, 1986; Violinist, Assistant of Guenter Pichler, Wiener Musikhochschule, 1983-89; Principal Concertmaster, Wiener Symphoniker, 1987-88; Principal Concertmaster, Bavarian State Opera in Munich, 1989-; Guest Leader, London Symphopny Orchestra, 1997-; Co-Founder of Beethoven Trio Wien in 1985 with the pianist Christiane Karajeva and cellist Yves Savary. Recordings: Mozart with Alban Berg Quartet; Tchaikovsky, Beethoven, Mendelssohn, Mozart, Schubert; Dvorak, Smetana and Suk with Beethoven Trio, Vienna. Honours: Winner, Austrian Youth Competition, "Jugend musiziert" and Special Prize, "Jeunesses Musicales", 1973; Winner, Stefanie-Hohl-Violin Competition, Wiener Musikhochschule, 1982. Memberships: European String Teachers Association, 1981-; Musikalische Akademie des Bayerischen Staatsorchesters Muenchen, 1990-. Current Management: Robert Friedman Presents, San Francisco.. Address: Bayerisches Staatsorchester München, Max Joseph Platz 2, D-80539 Münich, Germany.

WOLF R Peter, b. 5 Dec 1942, Washington DC, USA. Musicologist; Harpsichordist. Education: AB, Harvard University, 1965; MPhil, 1969; PhD, 1977, Yale University; Studied harpsichord with Gustav Leonhardt at Amsterdam Conservatorium, 1965-66 and with Ralph Kirkpatrick at Yale School of Music, 1966-70. Debut: Carnegie Recital Hall, NY, 1975. Career: Numerous concerts as harpsichord soloist and continuo player; Musician-in-Residence, NC State University, Raleigh; 2 TV shows, NC Educational Network, 1972; Instructor in Music, SUNY, Stony Brook, 1972-78; Assistant Professor of Music, University of Utah, 1978-80, and at Rutgers University, 1980-85; Editor, Brouda Brothers Ltd, 1985-89; Director of Development, Hoboken Chamber Orchestra, 1989-; Member of Bowers-Wolf Duo, Salt Lake Chamber Ensemble, Apollo's Banquet, and New York Baroque. Recordings: Telemann's Instrumental Chamber Music with Concertmasters Ensemble; Private recording of works by Rameau, JS Bach, CPE Bach; Violin Sonatas by Biber, 1681, with Sonya Monosoff and Judith Davidoff. Publications include: Joint Editor, ms Bauyn, New York; Editor, Rameau, Les Paladins, New York and Paris; Editor, facsimile edition of Rameau, Les Paladins, 1986. Contributions to: The Scriblerian; Actes; Colloque International Rameau, Dijon, 1983; The Musical Quarterly; Journal of The American Musical Instrument Society; Recherches; Early Music; Journal of The American Musicological Society. Address: 37A Phelps Avenue, New Brunswick, NJ 08901, USA.

WOLF Reinhold (Michael), b. 23 May 1956, Vienna, Austria. Violinist. Education: Piano lessons at age 6; 1st Violin instruction at Wiener Musikakademie at age 8, later chamber music lessons with Alban Berg Quartet; Kuenstlerische Diplompruefung mit Auszeichnung, 1976; Violin studies with G

Poulet in Paris and M Rostal in Cologne; Chamber music with Amadeus Quartet; Konzert-Examen mit Auszeichnung Cologne, 1981. Career: Established the Wolf Trio with brothers Markus on Viola and Peter on Violoncello; Concertmaster, World Youth Orchestra with L Bernstein at Tanglewood, USA at age 18; Concertmaster, Orchestra of the Deutsche Oper Berlin, 1982-; Soloist with various European orchestras; Appeared as Double Concerto partner of H Szeryng with Vienna Symphony Orchestra; Established ensemble, Contraste in Berlin, 1989. Honours: Special Prize, Jeunesse Musicales Austria for the Wolf Trio, 1973; 1st Prize as Soloist, Jugend Musiziert Competition, Austria, 1975. Address: c/o Deutsche Oper Berlin, Orchesterdirektion, Richard Wagnerstrasse 10, D-10585 Berlin, Germany.

WOLF Sally, b. 1957, USA. Singer (Soprano). Career: Santa Fe Opera from 1982, as the Queen of Night, in the premiere of Eaton's The Tempest (1985) and in Sallinen's The King goes forth to France; Has sung the Queen of Night throughout North America, at Covent Garden (1986) and with Opera North at Leeds (1987); Seattle Opera, 1992, as Lucia di Lammermoor, Netherlands Opera, 1990, as Constanze, and San Francisco, 1991, as Giunia in Mozart's Lucio Silla; Other roles include Eternita in La Calisto (at Santa Fe), Gilda, Violetta and Oscar; Sang Donna Anna at the 1996 Munich Festival. Address: Santa Fe Opera, PO Box 2408, Santa Fe, NM 87504, USA.

WOLFE Marguerite, b. 1930, London, England. Concert Pianist. m. Derrick Moss (dec), 2 daughters. Education: FTCL, Royal Academy of Music. Career: Soloist, London Symphony Orchestra, Royal Philharmonic Orchestra, Philharmonia, Bournemouth and Birmingham Orchestras; Radio and TV broadcasts with major orchestras; Toured USA, Europe and Far East; 9 tours of Far East (Nepal, Delhi, Bombay, Calcutta, Malaysia, Indonesia, Singapore, Hong Kong), East Africa, Mexico, Peru and North America; 10 tours of South America. Recordings: Bliss Piano Sonata; Liszt Society recording Lizt; Liszt recording, Wright Society. Honours: Incorporated Society of Music Winner, International Bambridge Competition. Memberships: Women's University Club, Councillor, Liszt Society; Royal Society of Musicians; Royal Philharmonic Society; Chopin Society. Hobbies: Reading; Walking. Current Management: Classical Company. Address: Chandos House, 17A Chester Street, Belgravia, London SW1, England.

WOLFF Beverly, b. 6 Nov 1928, Atlanta, GA, USA. Mezzo-Soprano. Education: Studied with Sidney Dietch and Vera McIntyre at The Academy of Vocal Arts in Philadelphia. Debut: Sang Dinah in a TV production of Bernstein's Trouble In Tahiti, 1952. Career: Has sung with the New York City Opera from 1958, with debut as Dinah; Appeared on NBC TV in the premiere of Menotti's Labyrinth, 1963; Stage engagements in Mexico City, Cincinnati, Boston, Houston, Washington and San Francisco as Carmen, Adalgisa, Cherubino, Kabanichka in Katya Kabanova, Radamisto, Dalila and Sesto in Handel's Giulio Cesare; Concert appearances as Dalila and Sesto; Sang in the Premieres of Douglas Moore's Carrie Nation in 1966 and Menotti's The Most Important Man in 1971; Concert appearances with leading American orchestras. Recordings: Roberto Devereux by Donizetti; Rossini's La Pietra del Paragone; Giulio Cesare. Honours include: Winner, Youth Auditions, Philadelphia, 1952.

WOLFF Christian, b. 8 Mar 1934, Nice, France. Composer. Education: Influenced by John Cage, Morton Feldman and Earle Brown after moving to the USA; Studied classics at Harvard, PhD in 1963. Career: Taught at Harvard University, 1962-76; Teacher of Classics and Music at Dartmouth College from 1976. Compositions include: Nine for Ensemble, 1951; Suite for Prepared Piano, 1954; Duo for Pianists I and II, 1957-58; Music For Merce Cunningham, 1959; Duo for Violin and Piano, 1961; Summer for String Quartet, 1961; In Between Pieces for 3 players, 1963; Septet, 1964; Quartet for 4 Horns, 1966; Elec Spring I-III, 1966-67; Toss for 8 or more players, 1968; Snowdrop for Harpsichord, 1970; Burdocks for 1 or more Orchestras or 5 or more Players, 1971; Accompaniments, 1972; Lines for String Quartet, 1972; Changing The System, 1973; Exercises 1-24, 1973-84; Wobbly Music for Mixed Chorus and Instruments, 1976; Bread And Roses for Piano and for Violin, 1976; Dark As A Dungeon for Clarinet, 1977, for Trombone and Double Bass, 1977; The Death Of Mother Jones for Violin, 1977; Stardust Pieces for Cello and Piano, 1979; Isn't This A Time for Saxophone, 1981; Eisler Ensemble Pieces, 1983; Piano Song - I Am A Dangerous Woman, 1983; Peace March 1-3, 1983-84; I Like To Think Of Harriet Tubman for Female Voice, Treble and Alto, 1984. Address: 104 South Main Street, Hanover, NH 03755, USA.

WOLFF Hugh (MacPherson), b. 21 Oct 1953, Paris, France. Conductor. Education: Piano lessons from Fleisher and Shure; Studied composition with Crumb Kirchner; BA, Harvard University, 1975; Studied composition with Messiaen; Piano with Sancan; Conducting with Bruck; MM, Piano, 1977, MM, Conducting, 1978, Peabody Institute. Career: Exxon/Arts Endowment Conductor, 1979-82, Associate Conductor, 1982-85, National Symphony Orchestra, Washington DC; Music Director, Northeastern Pennsylvania Philharmonic Orchestra, 1981-86; European debut with London Philharmonic Orchestra in 1982; Music Director, New Jersey Symphony Orchestra, Newark, 1985-; Principal Conductor, St Paul Chamber Orchestra, Minn, 1988-; Guest Conductor with various North American and European orchestras. Honours: Frank Huntington Beebe Fellow, 1975-76; Annette Kade Fellow, 1978; Co-Recipient, Affiliate Artist's Seaver Conducting Award, 1985. Address: c/o ICM Artists Ltd, 40 West 57th Street, New York, NY 10019, USA.

WOLFF Jean-Claude, b. Oct 1946, Paris, France. Composer. Education: Studied Composition, Analysis, History of Music, at L'Ecole Normale de Musique de Paris, then at Conservatoire National Supérieur de Musique de Paris with Henri Dutilleux, Jean-Pierre Guezec, Michel Philippot, Ivo Malec; Electro-acoustic classes with Jean-Etienne Marie, Centre International de Recherches Musicales; Spent 3 summers following Composition courses with Franco Donatoni, Accademia Chigiana, Siena, Italy; Laureate, Académie de France, Rome (Villa Medici), 1978-80. Compositions include: About 40 works performed at various festivals and concerts of contemporary music in France (Radio-France, International Musical Weeks in Orleans, Angers Music Festival, Contemporary Music Meetings at Metz) and abroad in Italy, Switzerland, Denmark, Spain, Netherlands; For several years has concentrated mainly on chamber music; Currently working on four pieces for piano solo or with violin or violoncello; Next project: a symphony for voices and large orchestra. Honours: 1st Prize, Vienna Modern Masters, 1991. Address: 39 rue Bouret, 75019 Paris, France.

WOLOVSKY Leonardo, b. 1922, York, Pennsylvania, USA. Singer (Bass-Baritone). Education: Studied at Oberlin College, Ohio. Career: Sang at first in concert then appeared with Maria Callas in Norma at Catanua, 1952; Engaged at Wiesbaden Opera, 1953-57, Nuremberg, 1957-73; Guest appearances at Frankfurt, 1959-73, Bayerische Staatsoper Munich, 1961-69, Hanover, 1961-73, Hamburg, 1956-60; Sang also at Graz, Essen, Amsterdam, Zurich, Paris, Barcelona and Athens; Bielefeld 1988, as Simon Mago in Nerone by Boito; Other roles have included Enrico (Lucia di Lammermoor); Oroveso, King Philip, Nabucco, the Dutchman, Hans Sachs, the Wanderer in Siegfried and Boris Godunov; Concert repertoire included Beethoven's Ninth, the Verdi Requiem and Bach's Christmas Oratorio. Address: Städtische Buhnen, Brunnenstrasse 3, 48000 Berlin 1, Germany.

WONG On-Yuen, b. 16 Nov 1945, Chong Ging, China. Conductor. m. Chi-Hung Chan, 1 Feb 1973, 2 sons. Education: Central Conservatory of Music, Beijing; China Competition of Music, Beijing. Career: Music Instructor, Chinese University of Hong Kong, Hong Kong Academy of Performing Arts; Consultant, Council for the Performing Arts of Hong Kong; Currently, Concert Master and Assistant Conductor, Hong Kong Chinese Orchestra. Compositions: Autumn Harvest; The Happy Peasant; The Train Entering Tung Village. Recordings: 21 Solo and Concerto recordings including The World of Wong On-Yuen's Hu-Qin Music, The Song Of Wine, Wong On-Yuen and 12 Kinds Of Hu-Qins, The Butterfly Lover Concerto. Honours: Golden Tripod Award, 1984, 1987; One Of Ten Outstanding Young Persons, 1985; Music Performer of The Year, 1989; Most Outstanding Asian Artist Award, 1991. Memberships: Hong Kong Outstanding Persons Association; Executive Member, Chinese Folk Symphonic Music Society. Hobbies: Sport; Photography. Address: Room 2201, Block B, Parkway Court, 4 Park Road, Hong Kong.

WOOD Hugh, b. 27 Jun 1932, Parbold, Lancashire, England. Composer. Education: Studied at Oxford University and in London with W S Lloyd Webber; Further study with Anthony Milner, Iain Hamilton and Matyas Seiber. Career: Professor of Harmony at the Royal Academy of Music, 1962-65; Teacher at Morley College, 1958-67; Research Fellow in Composition, Glasgow University, 1966-70; Lecturer in Music, Liverpool University, 1971-73 and at Cambridge University from 1976; Talks on BBC Radio 3; Piano Concerto premiered at the 1991 Promenade Concerts. Compositions: Songs For Springtime for Chorus and Piano, 1954; Suite for Piano, 1956; String Quartet, 1957; Variations for Viola and Piano, 1958; Laurie Lee Songs, 1959; Songs To Poems By Christopher Logue, 1961; Trio for Flute, Viola and Piano, 1961; String Quartet No 1, 1962; Scenes From Comus for Soprano, Tenor and Chorus, 1965; 3 Choruses, 1966; Songs To Poems By D H Lawrence, 1966; Capriccio for Organ, 1967; Quintet for Clarinet, Horn and Piano Trio, 1967; The Horses, song cycle, 1967; The Rider Victory, song cycle, 1968; Cello Concerto, 1969; String Quartet No 2, 1970; Chamber Concerto, 1971; Violin Concerto, 1972; 2 Choruses, 1973; Songs To Poems By Robert Graves, 1973; Songs To Poems By Pablo Neruda for High Voice and Chamber Orchestra, 1973; String Quartet No 3, 1978; Symphony, 1979-82; Piano Trio, 1984; Comus Quadrilles, 1988; Horn Trio, 1987-89; Cantata for Chorus and Orchestra, 1989; Marina for High Voice and Ensemble, 1989; Piano Concerto, 1990; Funeral Music (brass quintet), 1992; String Quartet No 3, 1993; Poem, for violin and piano, 1993; The Kingdom of God, anthem, 1994. Address: c/o Churchill College, Cambridge, CB3 0DS, England.

WOOD James (Peter), b. 27 May 1953, Barton-on-Sea, Hampshire, England. Composer; Conductor; Percussionist. m. Penny Irish, 25 Jun 1977, 1 son, 1 daughter. Education: Radley College, 1966-71; ARCO, 1969; FRCO, 1971; Sidney Sussex College, Cambridge, 1972-75; BA, Music, 1975; Studied with Nadia Boulanger in Paris, 1971-72; RAM, 1975-76. Career: Conductor, Schola Cantorum of Oxford, 1977-81; Founder and Conductor of New London Chamber Choir, 1981; Professor of Percussion, Internationale Ferienkurse, Darmstadt, 1982-; Regular Radio and TV appearances; Artistic Advisor to Percussion Foundation and Percussion 88 and 90 Festivals; Founder and Director, Centre for Microtonal Music, 1990-; Director of Barbican's Annual Weekend of Microtonal Music. Compositions include: Phaedrus; Oreion, BBC SO commission, premiered at 1989 Promenade Concerts; Stoicheia, Darmstadt commission; Ho Shang Yao; T'ien Chung Yao; Choroi Kaithaliai; Spirit Festival With Lamentations; Village Burial With Fire; Incantamenta. Recordings include: Stoicheia; Music for Percussion and Voices; Stravinsky's Les Noces and other choral works; Bergman's Choral Works; 15th Century Flemish Choral Works, 2 records. Contributions to: A New System for Quarter-Tone Percussion, in Musical Times and Percussive Notes. Honours: Lili Boulanger Prize, 1975; Lili Boulanger Memorial Award, 1980. Current Management: Colin Boyle. Address: Bancroft, Rectory Lane, Fringford, Bicester, Oxfordshire, OX6 9DX, England.

WOOD Jeffrey (Neal), b. 3 Oct 1954, Allentown, PA, USA. Composer; University Professor. 1 son. Education: BMus, Oberlin College Conservatory of Music, 1976; MMus, 1978, MA, 1980, PhD, 1982, State University of New York, Stony Brook. Career: Visiting Lecturer, University of New Mexico, Albuquerque, New Mexico Institute of Mining and Technology, 1983-84, Austin Peay State University, Clarksville, TN, 1984-. Compositions: Duo for Cello and Piano, 1982 (recorded); In Memoriam Magistri for Brass Quintet, 1982; Sonata for Cello and Piano, 1984; String Quartet No 2, 1985; MCMXIV for Tenor and Piano, 1985; Now The Most High Is Born, 1985; Trio-Sonata for Cello, Piano and Percussion, 1986; The Dream Of The Rood for Tenor Solo, Chorus and Organ, 1986; Swifts for Violin and Cello, 1986; First Essay for Orchestra, 1986; Music for Concert Band, 1987; Comedies for Woodwind Quintet, 1988; Quartet for Flute, Violin, Cello and Piano, 1988; Lay Your Sleeping Head My Love for Soprano, Tenor and Piano, 1987; Kreigeslieder for Mezzo-Soprano and Piano, 1988; Time Let Me Hail And Climb for Chorus, Brass Quintet and Piano, 1990; The Killing for Tenor and Piano, 1989; Four Deadly Serious Songs for Baritone and Piano, 1990; Ballads For The Goodly Fere for Voice and Piano, 1991; Dances for 2 Pianos, 1992; Preludes for Piano Solo, 1992; Ghosts for Clarinet, Viola and Piano, 1993. Recordings: Comedies, by Quintet of the Americas, 1991. Contributions to: In Theory Only, volume 7, 1983. Hobby: Calligraphy. Current Management: Broadcast Music Inc. Address: Department of Music, Austin Peay State University, Clarksville, TN 37044, USA.

WOODLAND Rae, b. 1930, Nottingham, England. Singer (Soprano); International Adjudicator and Examiner. m. Denis Stanley. Education: Private studies with Roy Henderson, Joan Cross and Vittorio Gui. Debut: Sadler's Wells Theatre. Career: Performances with opera companies in United Kingdom, and as guest throughout Europe, Mauritius and Russia, also radio and TV appearances; Roles include: Queen of Night, Magic Flute; Luisa in Luisa Miller, Fiordiligi in Cosi, Constanze in Enführung; Donna Elvira in Don Giovanni, Alice Ford in Falstaff, Mimi in La Bohème, Electra in Idomeneo; Aida, Verdi; Odabella in Attila; Marguerite in Mefistofele, Leonora in Trovatore, Venus in Tannhäuser, Naiade in Ariadne, Marguerite in Faust and Lady Jowler in Rising of the Moon by Maw at Glyndebourne, among others; Professor of Singing, Royal Academy of Music, London; Vocal Consultant, Britten Pears School, Snape; International Adjudicator and Examiner; Advisor to Arts Council of Great Britain; Principal, Benjamin Britten's English Opera Group, Roles include: Lady Billows, Miss Jessel, Turn of the Screw, Female Chorus in The Rape of Lucretia and Solo Soprano in the War Requiem. Recordings include: Messiah, John Tobin-Handel Society; Arthur Bliss's Birthday; Midsummer Night's Dream, Haitink; Montezuma, Bonynge; Idomeneo, Davis; Mahler No 2, Stokowski; Glyndebourne, Macbeth and Ritorno d'Ulisse; Queen of the Night, BBC Prom, Glyndebourne. Honour: Classics Prize, Hon Professor of Singing, RAM. Memberships: Music Panel of English Speaking Union; Life Member, British Actors Society; FRSA; Women of the Year Association; Erin Arts Trust; Association of Teachers of Singing; RAM Guild; ISM; President, Aldeburgh Music Club. Hobbies: Gardening; Cooking. Address: Brackendale, Priory Lane, Snape, Saxmundham, Suffolk IP17 1SD, England.

WOODLEY Ronald, b. 24 Jun 1953, Kingston-upon-Thames, England. University Lecturer in Music. Education: University of Manchester, 1971-75; Royal Northern College of Music, 1971-75; MusB, 1st Class Honours; GRNCM and Associate, Royal Northern College of Music, 1975; University of Oxford, Keble College and Christ Church, 1975-79; MA, 1979; DPhil, 1982. Career: TV and Radio appearances as clarinet and chalumeau player and as 15th century musicologist, 1970-; Lecturer in Music, Christ Church, Oxford, 1979-81, University of Liverpool, 1981-84, and at University of Newcastle Upon Tyne, 1984-; Professor of Music Techniques, Royal Academy of Music, 1982-83. Recordings: BBC recordings as clarinettist, pianist and chalumeau player and as musicologist, 1970-. Publications: Articles on the 15th century musical theorist, Johannes Tinctoris, and Steve Reich among others; Books on Tinctoris and Reich. Contributions to: Journal of The American Musicological Society; Early Music History; Early Music; Music and Letters; Renaissance Studies. Honours: Hargreaves Musical Scholarship, University of Manchester, 1972; Rothwell Prize, University of Manchester, 1973; PJ Leonard Prize for Composition, University of Manchester, 1975. Memberships: Royal Musical Association; American Musicological Society. Hobbies: Chamber Music; Food; Snooker. Address: Department of Music, Univesity of Newcastle Upon Tyne, Newcastle Upon Tyne, NE2 7RU, England.

WOODROW Alan, b. 1952, Toronto, Canada. Singer (Tenor). Education: Studied at the Royal Conservatory in Toronto and at the London Opera Centre. Career: From 1976 sang with English National Opera as Pedrillo, Don Ottavio, Froh (Das Rheingold), Lindoro, Vasek, Monostatos, Canio, Hermann, Don José, Edmund in Reimann's Lear and Walther von Stolzing; Recent London appearances as the Prince in The Love of Three Oranges, the Captain in Wozzeck, Herod in Salome and Siegmund in Die Walküre, season 1992-93; Has also sung Sergei in Lady Macbeth of Mtsensk at La Scala and the Bastille, Paris; Concert engagements in Canada with the Mozart and Verdi Requiems; the Choral Symphony and Mahler's Eighth; A Mass of Life by Delius; Kodály's Psalmus Hungaricus. Current Management: Athole Still International Management Limited. Address: Foresters Hall, 25-27 Westow Street, London SW19 3RY, England.

WOODS Elaine, b. 1958, Lancashire, England. Soprano. Education: Studied at Oxford University and at the Royal Manchester College of Music with Elsie Thurston; Further study with Marjorie Thomas. Debut: With Kent Opera as Violetta in 1979 at the Edinburgh Festival. Career: Sang in Handel's Tolomeo at the Batigniano Festival in Italy, 1980; German debut in 1981 as Mimi in Mannheim; Bremen Opera from 1982 as Fiordigili, Tatiana, Eva, Liu and the Countess in Capriccio; In 1983 sang in JC Bach's Lucio Silla in Frankfurt and Acis and Galatea at Karlsruhe; Appeared as Pamina at the 1986 Bregenz Festival and sang Belinda in a new production of Dido and Aeneas at Frankfurt; With Welsh National Opera has sung Donna Elvira, Fiordigili and Mozart's Countess; Concert repertoire includes the Verdi and Mozart Requiems, Haydn's Creation and Seasons, Messiah and Beethoven's Missa Solemnis and Ninth Symphony. Honours include: Prizewinner at the 1978 s'Hertogenbosch Competition. Address: c/o Ingpen and Williams Ltd, 26 Wadham Road, London SW15 2LR, England.

WOODS Thomas, b. Tanzania (Australian citizen). Conductor. Education: Studied at the Western Australian Conservatorium, Perth and with Vladimir Ponkin at the Gnessin Institute, Moscow. Career: From 1982 Assistant Conductor with West Australian Opera Company for productions of Don Pasquale and Madam Butterfly; Assistant Chorus Master and Conducter at the Australian Opera, from 1994, leading Il Barbiere di Siviglia, A Midsummer Night's Dream, La Traviata and The Gondoliers; Season 1997 with La Fille du Régiment in Sydney, Il Barbiere in Sydney and La Traviata in Perth. Honours include: Cultural Exchange Scholarship, 1989. Address: c/o Magenta Music International, 4 Highgate High Street, London N6 5JL, England.

WOODWARD Donna, b. 2 Jun 1946, Baltimore, MD, USA. Soprano. Education: Studied in Cincinnati and Europe. Career: Sang in opera at Lucerne, 1970-71, Darmstadt, 1971-73, and Heidelberg, 1973-75; Engaged at the Nationaltheater at Mannheim, 1975-86; Guest appearances in Germany, France, Switzerland and Belgium; Roles have included Blondchen, Adele, Aennchen in Der Freischütz, Sophie in Rosenkavalier, Rosina and Musetta. Recordings include: Dittersdorf's Doktor und Apotheker. Address: c/o Nationaltheater, Am Goetheplatz, 6800 Mannheim, Germany.

WOODWARD Roger (Robert), b. 20 Dec 1942, Sydney, Australia. Conductor; Composer; Pianist. 1 son, 1 daughter. Education: DSCM, Sydney Conservatory of Music; Warsaw Academy, Poland. Debut: Royal Festival Hall in London, 1970. Career: His career has been closely associated with leading composers including Xenakis, Boulez, Stockhausen, Takemitsu, Bussotti, Berio, and Cage with works specially written for him by many others; Has worked with many leading conductors including Boulez, Leinsdorf, Masur and Mehta; Has performed throughout Europe, USA and Australia and has appeared at international festivals and with major orchestras worldwide; Founder Member of contemporary music series in London in 1972 and in Australia in 1975; Performed historic series of 16 concerts presenting the complete works of Chopin in 1985; World premiere of Xenakis' Keqrops, conceived for him with New York Philharmonic under Mehta, 1986; Music Director, Xenakis' ballet, Kraanerg, by Sydney Dance Company, 1988. Recordings include: Rachmaninov Preludes; Australian Contemporary Music; Barraqué Sonata by Bussotti; Werder 3rd Sonata, 1969; 2 Beethoven Sonatas; Shostakovich's 24 Preludes and Fugues, double album; Liszt's transcription of Beethoven's Eroica; Brahms's 1st Piano Concerto under Masur. Honours: Fellow, Chopin Institute, Warsaw, 1976; OBE, 1980; KT (Breffni), 1985. Current Management: Norman Lawrence Artist Management. Address: c/o Norman Lawrence Artist Management, 35 Britannia Row, London, N1 8QH, England.

WOOF Barbara, b. 2 September 1958, Sydney, New South Wales, Australia. Composer. Education: BMus (Hons), University of Sydney, 1981; Royal Conservatory, The Hague; Study with Peter Sculthorpe and Jan van Vlijman. Career includes: Faculty Member, Utrecht School of Arts, the Netherlands, 1988-; Resident Composer with the Sydney SO, 1992. Compositions include: Homage à Odilon Redon, for orchestra, 1982; Maldoror, for violin, 1983; Schiamachy for 2 guitars, 1985; Caoine, for alto saxophone, 1985; Star-Streams, for harpsichord, 1987; Hymns and Melodies, for saxophone quartet, 1989; Soundings, for gamelan, 1990; Banshee's Dance, for orchestra, 1992; Night Crossing, for orchestra, 1993; Odile, for bass clarinet and marimba, 1994; Matador, for flute, bass clarinet and piano, 1995; Amber, for string trio. Honours include: Winner, Martin Codex Composition Competition, Spain, 1985. Address: c/o DONEMUS, Paulus Potterstraat 16, 1016-CZ-Amsterdam, The Netherlands.

WOOLFENDEN Guy (Anthony), b. 12 July 1937, Ipswich, England. Composer; Conductor. m. Jane Aldrick, 29 September 1962, 3 sons. Education: Westminster Abbey Choir School; Whitgift School; Christ's College, Cambridge; MA (Cantab); LGSM. Career: Head of Music, Royal Shakespeare Company, Stratford-upon-Avon and London, composed more than 150 scores for this company; Also Composed scores for Burgtheater, Vienna; Comèdie Française, Paris; Teatro di Stabile, Genoa and National Theatre, Norway; Also for Films, Radio, TV; Conducted concerts with most British Symphony Orchestras; Conducted concerts and ballet in Canada, Germany, Japan, USA, Hong Kong, and France; Conducted opera for BBC Radio, TV and 3 productions with Scottish Opera; Conductor of Birmingham Conservatoire Wind Orchestra; Arranged and composed music for four full-length ballets by choreographer André Prokovsky: Anna Karenina, The Three Musketeers, La Traviata and The Queen of Spades, all now in the repertory of the world's major companies; Conducted Russian premiere of Anna Karenina with Kirov Ballet in St Petersburg, 1993; Artistic Director, Cambridge Festival, 1986-91. Compositions: composed 3 musicals; Comedy of Errors for RSC; A Children's Opera, The Last Wild Wood Sector 88 with Adrian Mitchell; Works for the Concert Hall include: Concertos, Chamber Music and Several works for Symphonic Band. Recordings: Music for Royal Shakespeare Company; Music for The Winter's Tale; Songs of Ariel; Gallimaufry featuring the wind music of Guy Woolfenden; Sweet Swan of Avon; Video: The Comedy of Errors, Antony and Cleopatra, Macbeth. Honours: PRS Ivor Novello Award for Best British Musical, 1976-77; Society of West End Theatre Award for Best British Musical, 1977 (both for The Comedy of Errors); FBSM (for services to music in the Midlands), 1991. Memberships: NCA; APC; Composers Guild of Great Britain; Performing Rights Society; MCPS; Musicians Union, SPNM. Current Management: Stephannie Williams Artists. Address: Malvern House, Sibford Ferris, Banbury, Oxon OX15 5RG, England.

WOOLLAM Kenneth (Geoffrey), b. 16 Jan 1937, Chester, England. Opera Singer. m. Phoebe Elizabeth Scrivenor, 4 d. Education: Chester Cathedral Choir School; Royal College of Music. Debut: Sadler's Wells, London, 1972. Career: Appearances with; Royal Opera Copenhagen, Saul and David, David; Florestan in Frankfurt; English National Opera roles include: Rienzi, Radames, Aida; Sang with Scottish Opera, Royal Opera, Ghent, Opera du Nord, Warsaw Philharmonic Orchestra in various roles including: Walther in Die Meistersinger, Siegfried in The Ring, Laca in Jenufa; Sang Husband in world premiere of John Tavener's Gentle Spirit at Bath; 3 Films as: Canio, Alfredo and Hoffmann; Concerts and oratorios with leading societies; Sang in the premieres of Hamilton's Royal Hunt of The Sun and Blake's Toussaint L'Ouverture, 1977; Covent Garden debut 1988, as Aegisthus; Professor of Singing at Royal College of Music; Vocal Consultant to David Puttnam's Film, Meeting Venus, 1990; Appointed Vocal Consultant to DeVlaamse Opera in Antwerp and Ghent, Belgium, 1995; Pierre (War and Peace, Prokofiev); Tristan. Recordings: Delius's Margot-La-Rouge; Berlioz's La Mort d'Orphée, conductor Jean Fournet, 1987; TV, Songfest by Bernstein; BBC TV, Elgar's Gerontius, conducted by Vernon Handley, 1987; Gurre-Lieder, Bergen International Festival, televised; Herod in Salome at Edinburgh Festival, 1989. Honours: Honorary Member, Royal College of Music, 1992. Memberships: Incorporaated Society of Musicians; Savage Club; Glass Circle. Hobby: Antique Glass. Address: 33 Blenheim Road, Bedford Park, Chiswick, London, W4 1ET, England.

WOOLLETT Elizabeth, b. 13 Mar 1959, Hillingdon, Middlesex, England. Singer (Soprano). Education: Studied at Royal Academy of Music from 1977. Career: Sang Magda in La Rondine and Irene in Donizetti's Belisario at the RAM; Opera North from 1984, as the Owl in The Cunning Little Vixen, Papagena, Kate Pinkerton, Mermaid in Oberon at Le Fenice, Venice, Anna in Intermezzo and Second Maid in the British premiere of Strauss's Daphne; Scottish Opera debut 1989, as Mozart's Susanna; Buxton festival, 1990, as Amenaide in Tancredi; Debut, Royal Opera House, Covent Garden, 1991, as Clorinda in La Cenerentola; Other roles include Adina (L'Elisir d'Amore), Cherubino, Micaela, Bella (The Midsummer Marriage) and Despina; Isabella in L'Assedio di Calais by Donizetti for the Wexford Festival, 1991; Sang Weber's Agathe for Chelsea Opera Group, South Bank, 1997; Has also sung for the BBC Radio 3 and has recorded works by Gilbert and Sullivan for TER records. Honours include: Alec Redshaw Memorial Award. Grimsby, 1986. Current Management: Musicmakers, Hertfordshire, England. Address: Little Easthall, St Paul's Warden, Hertfordshire SG4 8DH, England.

WOOLLEY Robert, b. 1954, England. Harpsichordist; Organist. Career: Harpsichordist, Organist, Member of the Purcell Quartet, debut concert at St John's Smith Square, London in 1984; Professor, The Royal College of Music; Extensive tours and broadcasts in France, Belgium, Holland, Germany, Austria, Switzerland, Italy and Spain; British appearances include four Purcell concerts at the Wigmore Hall, 1987, later broadcast on Radio 3; Tours of USA and Japan, 1991-92; Repertoire includes music on the La Folia theme by Vivaldi, Corelli, CPE Bach, Marais, Scarlatti, Vitali and Geminiani, instrumental songs by Purcell, music by Matthew Locke, John Blow and fantasias and airs by William Lawes, 17th century virtuoso Italian music by Marini, Buonamente, Gabrieli, Fontana, Stradella and Lonati, JS Bach and his forerunners Biber, Scheidt, Schenk, Reinken and Buxtehude; Many Concerts with other ensembles and as soloist. Recordings include: Complete Keyboard works of Henry Purcell; Solo recordings of Bach, Scarlatti, Frescobaldi, Couperin and Gibbons. Address: 11 Sterry Drive, Thames Ditton, Surrey KT7 0YN, England.

WOOLRICH John, b. 1954, England. Composer. Education: English at Manchester University; Composition with Edward Cowie at Lancaster University. Career: Northern Arts Fellow in Composition at Durham University, 1982-85; Composer-in-Residence, National Centre for Orchestral Studies, 1985-86; Animateur of various educational and music-theatre projects; Visiting Lecturer and Composer-in-Residence, Goldsmiths College, London, 1987-88; Artistic Director, Composers Ensemble, 1989-; Tutor at Guildhall School of Music, 1990-91; Composition Teacher, Dartington Summer School, 1991-93; Professor, Stage Internacional de Musica de Cambra, 1992; Visiting Lecturer, Reading University, 1993. Compositions include: Four Songs After Hoffmann for Soprano and Clarinet, 1981; Spalanzani's Daughter for Instrumental Ensemble, 1983; Black Riddle for Soprano and Chamber Orchestra, 1984; The Barber's Timepiece for Orchestra, 1986; Dartington Doubles for Chamber Ensemble, 1988; Night Machines for Instrumental Ensemble, 1988; The Turkish Mouse for Soprano and Ensemble, 1988; Barcarolle for 6 Players, 1989; Lending Wings, 1989; The Ghost In The Machine, 1990; Berceuse, 1990; Quicksteps, 1990; The Death Of King Renaud, 1991; The Theatre Represents A Garden: Night, 1991; It Is Midnight, Dr Schweitzer, 1992; A Farewell, 1992; String Quartet, 1995; In the House of Crossed Desires, opera, 1996; Oboe concerto, 1996; String Trio, 1996. Address: c/o Faber Music Ltd, 3 Queen Sqaure, London, WC1N 3AU, England.

WORDSWORTH Barry, b. 1948, England. Conductor. Education: Studied at the Royal College of Music, London; Conducting with Adrian Boult in London and harpsichord with Gustav Leonhardt in Amsterdam. Debut: Soloist in Frank Martin's Harpsichord Concerto at the Royal Opera House, for Kenneth Macmillan's ballet, Las Hermanas. Career: Freelance conductor with the Royal Ballet, the Australian Ballet and the National Ballet of Canada (including performances at the Metropolitan, New York); Music Director of the BBC Concert Orchestra and the Brighton Philharmonic in 1989; Music Director of the Royal Ballet and the Birmingham Royal Ballet in 1991; Debut with the Royal Opera at Covent Garden with Carmen in 1991; Conducted the BBC Concert Orchestra at the 1991 Promenade Concerts; Piano Concerto by Bliss, Malcolm Arnold's Guitar Concerto, Vaughan Williams's 8th Symphony, and Act 3 of Sleeping Beauty; Conducted Last Night of The Proms, with the BBC Symphony Orchestra in 1993; Conducted New Queen's Hall Orchestra at the 1995 Proms; Raymond Gubay's Carmen at the Albert Hall, 1997. Recordings include: Series of British music with the BBC Concert Orchestra, 1990-91. Hobbies: Walking; Cooking; Photography; Swimming; Tennis. Address: ICM Artists, Oxford House, 76 Oxford Street, London, W1R 1RB, England.

WORKMAN William, b. 4 Feb 1940, Valdosta, GA, USA. Baritone. Education: Studied at Davidson College, at the Curtis Institute in Philadelphia, Music Academy of the West, California, and with Martial Singher. Debut: Hamburg in 1965 in Fidelio. Career: Many performances at the Hamburg Staatsoper, notably in the premieres of Help, Help The Globolinks by Menotti in 1967, and The Devils of Loudun by Penderecki in 1969; Member of the Frankfurt Opera from 1972; Further appearances in Amsterdam, Paris, Strasbourg, Vienna, Geneva, Santa Fe and Dallas; German TV as Papageno in Die Zauberflöte; Season 1987-88, sang in Die schweigsame Frau at Santa Fe, Ping in Pittsburgh and in Schreker's Der Ferne Klang at Brussels. Recordings include: Zoroastre by Rameau. Address: c/o Théâtre Royal de la Monnaie, 4 Léopoldstrasse, B-1000 Brussels, Belgium.

WORLEY Larry Daryle, b. 8 Dec 1931, Baltimore, Maryland, USA. Assistant Professor. m. Lois Cox, 30 Aug 1957, 1 son, 1 daughter. Education: BA, Toccoa Falls College; BM, 1959, MM, 1960, Virginia Commonwealth University; Postgraduate Study, Indiana University, Wittenberg University, Chadek Conservatory, University of Tennessee, Akron University, University of Georgia. Career: Numerous Oratorio Performances; Performed 15 Operatic Roles; Guest Conductor, All State Christian School, Ohio, North Georgia Choral Festival; Performed with Chattanooga, Tennessee, Springfield, Ohio and Richmond Opera Society. Honours: Certificate of Merit, Bryan College, 1968 and Toccoa Falls College. Memberships: American Musicological Society; National Association of Teachers and Singing; American Choral Directors Association. Hobbies: Jogging; Gardening; Cabinet Making. Address: 8830 Scenic Drive, Toccoa, GA 30577, USA.

WORTON-STEWARD Andrew, b. 20 Feb 1948, Kent, England. Course Tutor and Lecturer, Open University; Composer; Organist. Education: BA, Honours, DMus, Cincinnati Conservatory, USA, 1976; Diploma of Education; LLCM; ARCO. Career: Performances of own music worldwide including New York, Long Island, Milan, London, Manchester, Sydney, and Australia; Music Adviser for Somerset University, England; Recital tour on organ, Texas Gulf, USA in 1985, and New York in 1986; Concert of choral works in New York, 1986; BBC Radio broadcast, 1987; Concert in Paris in 1987 and at Purcell Room in 1987; Organist at Holy Trinity in New York, 1987-88; Commissions for Chichester Cathedral, 1987, Hove Festival, 1987 and Hanover, 1988; Choral masterclass at Tallahassee, FL, USA, 1988; Organ recitals at St Thomas, and St James in New York, 1988; TVS documentary, Requiem, in the series, Music Makers in 1989. Compositions: (recorded) Chamber Music, 1978; Soli 3, 1980; Via Crucis, 1983; My Eyes For Beauty Pine; Oecumuse. Publications: Piano music published. Address: c/o White Lodge, 105 Pembroke Crescent, Hove, Sussex, England.

WOSNITZA Cornelia, b. 28 Nov 1960, Dresden, Germany. Singer (Soprano). Education: Studied at the Dresden Musikhochschule. Career: Sang Yniold in Pelléas and the Shepherd Boy in Tannhäuser at Dresden, 1979; Has appeared throughout Germany and in Russia, Amsterdam and elsewhere as Aennchen, Gretel, Blondchen, Norina, Susanna, Zerlina, Papagena and Musetta; Concert appearances in works by Bach, Handel, Mozart, Schumann, Strauss and Orff (Carmina Burana). Honours include: Prizewinner at the 1981 Robert Schumann Competition at Zwickau and the 1985 Mozart Competition at Salzburg. Address: Dresden Staatsoper, Theaterplatz 2, O-8010 Dresden, Germany.

WRAY Steven (Donald), b. 10 Jun 1959, Bolton, Lancashire, England. Pianist. Education: BA, Honours, Queen's College, Oxford, 1976-79; Private studies with Dorothea Law and Ruth Nye; International Summer Musical Academy at Salzburg, masterclasses with Hans Graf and Carmen Graf-Adnet, 1985-86; Further studies at Hochschule für Musik und Darstellende Kunst, Vienna. Career: Live Music Now! solo artist, 1985; Solo recital, Park Lane Group, Young Artists and Twentieth Century Music series, Purcell Room in London, 1988; Formation of duo with Czech violinist Tomas Tulacek in 1990; Concert and festival appearances, solo and duo recitals, and ensemble and concerto engagements in Austria, Czechoslovakia, Slovenia, Britain, Israel and Portugal. Hobbies: Walking; Cycling; Theatre; Reading; Languages. Current Management: Chameleon Arts Management. Address: 1 Brookes Court, Longley Road, London, SW17 9LF, England.

WRIGHT Brian (James), b. 4 Aug 1946, Tonbridge, Kent, England. Conductor. Education: Gulbenkian Scholar, Guildhall School of Music; Guildhall School of Music; Studieds with George Hurst and Jascha Horenstein; Munich Music Academy, Germany. Debut: Royal Festival Hall, London, 1972 (Messiah). Career: Professional singer (Tenor) with English Opera Group; Recitals Wigmore Hall 1971, Purcell Room 1972; Associate Conductor Goldsmith's Choral Union 1972; Musical Director 1973; Conductor Highgate Choral Society 1972; Assistant Conductor London Symphony Orchestra 1974-75; Conductor BBC Symphony Orchestra Chorus 1976-84; Berlioz Requiem 1982; Liszt's Christus, 1985- Guest Conductor with UK orchestras: London Symphony (Mendelssohn 3, Sibelius 2); Philharmonia (Beethoven 6); Hallé (Brahms 2); Bournemouth Symphony (A Child of our Time, Verdi Requiem); Scottish National (Dvorak Requiem); Royal Liverpool Philharmonic (Hugh Wood Symphony); World and UK premieres of works by Robert Simpson, Wilfred Josephs, Penderecki and Lutoslawski; First complete performance of Furtwängler's 3rd Symphony; Season 1988-89 conducted Tippett's Mask of Time on South Bank and Stravinsky's Pulcinella for BBC TV; Season 1990 with the Bach B Minor Mass at the Barbican the Verdi Requiem at the Festival Hall, and concerts with the RPO, BBC and BBC Welsh Symphony Orchestras. Honours include: Silver Medal, Guido Cantelli Competition, Milan 1975. Membership: ISM. Hobbies: Singing; Reading; DIY. Current Management: Worldwide Artists. Address: c/o Worldwide Artists, 6 Petersfield Crescent, Coulsdon, Surrey CR5 2JQ, England.

WRIGHT Christopher George, b. 30 Apr 1954, Ipswich, Suffolk, England. Composer. m. Ruth, 23 Oct 1993. Education: Colchester Institute, 1971-76; BA, honours, Anglia Polytechnic University, 1994-96; MA; Studied Composition with Richard Arnell, Stanley Glasser and Alan Bullard. Career: Music Teacher, Various Posts, 1977-93. Compositions: Wind Quintet; 2 String Quartets; Concertino, for 3 Violins and Piano; Anthems; Part Songs; Solo Voice/Instrument Piano; Brass Band; Symphonic Orchestral include The Lost City, Symphony, Brass Quintet. Memberships: Composers Guild; Performing Right Society; Society for the Promotion of New Music. Hobbies: DIY; Reading; Church Work. Address: Greenways, 46 Dukes Drive, Halesworth, Suffolk IP19 8DR, England.

WRIGHT Gordon (Brooks), b. 31 Dec 1934, New York City, USA. Symphony Conductor.m. 2 sons, 1 daughter. Education: BMus, College of Wooster, 1957; MA, University of Wisconsin, Madison. Career: Founder and Music Director, Madison Summer Orchestra (now Wisconsin Chamber Orchestra), 1960-69; Musical Director, Fairbanks Light Opera Theatre, 1975, 1980, 1988; Musical Director, University of Alaska Opera Workshop, 1969, 1971, 1974, 1977; Orchestral Conductor, Western Opera of San Francisco, 1974, 1978, 1980; Guest Conductor of numerous orchestras; Music Director and Conductor, Fairbanks Symphonyu Orchestra, 1969-89; Founder and Conductor, Arctic Chamber Orchestra, 1970-89; Professor of Music, University of Alaska Fairbanks, 1969-89; Founder and Executive Director, Reznicek Society, 1982-; Professor Emeritus, University of Alaska, 1989; Music Director Emeritus, Fairbanks Symphony Orchestra, 198. Compositions: Suite of Netherlands Dances, 1966; Six Alaskan Tone Poems, 1976; Transitional Metamorphoses, 1976; Symphony in Ursa Major, 1978; Heigh Ho, to the Greenwood!, 1982; Grumbling Old Man, 1982; Freest Fancy, 1982; Canzona (G Gabrieli), 1983; Sally Gardens, 1984; 1984 Overture, 1984; Suite for Piano and Orchestra (Scott Joplin), 1987; Toccata Festiva, 1992. Contributions to: Beato Music Incorporated, Japan; Elsewhere, Turnagain Music, Indian, Alaska, USA. Hobbies: Hiking; Kayaking; Photography. Address: HC 52 Box 8899, India, AK 99540, USA.

WRIGHT Rosemarie, b. 12 Dec 1931, Chorley, Lancashire, England. Concert Pianist. m. Michel Brandt, 28 Oct 1961, 2 sons. Education: Royal Academy of Music, London; Staatsakademie, Vienna; Master classes with Edwin Fischer, Pablo Casals and Wilhelm Kempff. Debut: Grosser Musikvereinssaal, Vienna, 1960. Career: Concerts throughout Europe, USA, Far East, Australasia; Broadcasts worldwide; Concertos with London Philharmonic, Philharmonia, English Chamber Orchestra, London Mozart Players, BBC Orchestras, Vienna Symphony Orchestra, and Danish and French Radio; Professor of Piano: Royal Northern College of Music, Manchester, 1973-78, Royal Academy of Music, London, 1978-; Pianist-in-Residence, Southampton University, 1972-80. Recordings: Piano Music by Edward Macdowell; Volumes 1, 2 and 3, and Double CD of Haydn Sonatas on 1799 Broadwood Fortepiano. Honours: Chappell Silver Medal, 1953; Tobias Matthay Fellowship, 1954; Haydn Prize, Vienna, 1959; Bosendorfer Prize, 1960. Membership: British Federation of Festivals for Music, Dance and Speech, Adjudicator. Hobbies: Flowers; 19th-century painting; Literature. Address: 84 Filsham Road, Hastings, East Sussex TN38 0PG, England.

WROBLEWSKI Patryk, b. 4 Dec 1956, Mishawaka, Indiana, USA. Singer (Baritone). Debut: Sang Malatesta at the 1980 Blossom Festival. Career: Recent appearances as Fernando in La Gazza Ladra at Philadelphia, Silvio, Valentin and Monteverdi's Orfeo at Dallas; Lyric Opera of Chicago as Germont and Marcello and in Satyagraha by Glass; Opera Grand Rapids as Don Giovanni; Season 1991-92 with debut at New York City Opera as Zurga in Les pêcheurs de perles and as Silvio; Puccini's Lescaut with Greater Miami Opera and Silvio at the Munich Staatsoper (European stage debut); Season 1992-93 as Zurga in Holland, Taddeo in L'Italiana in Algeri at Dublin, and Marcello and Rossini's Figaro for the New Israel Opera; Concert appearances with the Chicago Symphony under Leppard and the Grant Park Concerts under Leonard Slatkin; Santa Fe Opera in Henze's Young Lord; Weill, The Protagonist; Dublin Grand Opera, Marcello in La Bohème; Manitoba Opera, Zurga, Canada. Honours include: Grand Prize, 1984 Rosa Ponselle International Competition; Winner, Luciano Pavarotti Competition, 1985. Address: 1723 W Montrose 2W, Chicago, IL 60613, USA.

WU Mary Mei-Loc, b. 22 Dec 1964, Hong Kong. Pianist. m. James Wong, 4 July 1992. Education: Yehudi Menuhin School, 1976-83; Performer's Diploma of Royal College of Music, London, 1983-87; Banff Center of Fine Arts, Winter School Diploma, Canada, 1987-88; Master of Music, 1988-89, Doctorate of Musical Arts, 1989-92, State University of New York at Stony Brook, USA. Debut: Queen Elizabeth Hall, London, 1979. Career: Beethoven Sonata with Lord Yehudi Menuhin in Germany, 1985; Bach Double Concerto with Vlado Perlemuter, London South Bank, 1986; Solo Recital, Wigmore Hall, London, 1994; Artist-in-Residence, Chinese University, Hong Kong, 1997. Recordings: Fantasias; Chinese Contemporary Piano Music; Piano Classico. Honours: First Prize Winner, Overseas Section, Royal Overseas League Competition, London, 1983; Clavichord Competition, 1984, Harpsichord Competition, 1984, Chappell Gold Medal, 1985, Royal College of Music; Mozart Bicentenary International Competition of Asia, 1992. Hobbies: Sports; Reading. Current Management: J Audrey Ellison, International Artists Management. Address: 135 Stevenage Road, Fulham, London SW6 6PB, England.

WU Zuqiang, b. 24 Jul 1927, Peking, China. Professor. m. Zheng Liqin, 29 Jan 1953, 1 s, 1 d. Education: Graduate in Composition, China's Central Conservatory of Music, 1952; Graduate, Tchaikovsky Music Conservatory, Moscow, 1958. Career: Teacher, 1952, Senior Lecturer, 1962, Associate Professor, 1978, Deputy President, 1978-81, President, 1982-88, Professor, 1983-, Supervisor of Doctoral Work, 1986-, Central Conservatory of Music; Head of Composition Section, China's Central Philharmonic Orchestra, 1972-75; Vice-Executive Chairman, China Federation of Literary and Art Circles, 1988-; Board of Directors, China's Copyright Agency Corporation, 1988-; Advisor, Chinese Music Copyright Association, 1993-; Adjudicator of many Chinese and foreign music competitions. Compositions: String Quartet, 1957; The Mermaid, dance drama, 1958; Red Woman's Detachment, ballet, 1964; Moon Reflected in the Erquan Pool for String Orchestra, 1976; Young Sisters of the Grassland, pipa concerto, 1973-76. Publication: Analysis of Music Form and Composition, textbook. Honour: Excellent Textbook Prize, National Universities and Colleges, 1987. Memberships: Vice-President, Chinese Musicians Association, 1985-; Executive Vice-Chairman, China Symphony Development Foundation, 1994-. Hobbies: Literature; Fine Arts; Travel. Address: Central Conservatory of Music, 43 Baojia Street, Beijing 100031, China.

WULSTAN David, b. 18 Jan 1937, Birmingham, England. Professor of Music. m. Susan Nelson Graham, 9 Oct 1967, 1 son. Education: BSc, College of Technology, Birmingham; BA, 1st Class, Music, 1963, Fellow, 1964, MA, 1966, Magdalen College, Oxford. Career: Founder and Director, The Clerkes of Oxenford, 1961-; Numerous appearances on BBC TV and Radio 3, Thames TV, NWDR, BRT, Cheltenham, York, Bologna, Holland and Flowers Festivals, Proms and various films; Visiting Professor, University of California, Berkeley, 1977; Professor of Music, University College, Cork, 1980; Professor of Music, University College, Aberystwyth, Wales, 1983-90; Research Professor, 1991-. Compositions: Various Christmas carols, and film music. Recordings: Tallis; Sheppard; Gibbons's Play of Daniel; Robert White. Publications include: Early English Church Music, volume 3, 1964, volume 27, 1979; Anthology of Carols, 1968; Anthology of English Church Music, 1971; Play of Daniel, 1976; Coverdale Chant Book, 1978; Complete Works, 1979-; Tudor Music, 1984. Contributions to: Journal of Theological Studies; Journal of the American Oriental Society; Music and Letters; Galpin Society Journal; Musical Times. Membership: Council, Plainsong and Medieval Music Society. Hobbies: Cooking and Eating; Tennis; Badminton; Semitic Philology. Address: Ty Isaf, Lianilar, Aberystwyth, Wales, SY23 4NP.

WUORINEN Charles, b. 9 June 1938, New York City, USA. Composer. Education: Attended Columbia University, BA 1961, MA 1963. Career: Founded the Group for Contemporary Music 1962; Teacher at Columbia University 1964-71; Visiting lecturer at Princeton University, 1969-71; New England Conservatory, 1968-71; Manhattan School of Music from 1971-79; Professor of Music, Rutgers University, 1984-; Visiting Professor, New York University, 1990; Visiting Professor, State University of New York at Buffalo, 1989-94; Visiting Professor, Yale University, 1991 and 1983; Composer-in-residence at: Ojai Festival, 1975, Universities of Iowa, South Florida, the Berkshire Music Center, the Chamber Music Northwest, 1978, Grand Teton Music Festival, 1979 and 1980, San Francisco Symphony (and New Music Adviser to Music Director Herbert Blomstedt), 1985-89; American Academy in Rome, 1990; Santa Fe Chamber Music Festival, 1993. Compositions include: Stage: The Politics of Harmony 1968 and The W of Babylon; Orchestral: Music for orchestra 1956; Orchestral and Electronic Exchanges 1965; 3 Piano Concertos 1966, 1975, 1984; Contrafactum 1969; Grand Bamboula 1971;

Concerto for amplified violin and orchestra 1972; The Magic Art: An Instrumental Masque, after Purcell, 1978; On Alligators, for 8 players, 1972; Short Suite, 1981; Crossfire, 1984; Movers and Shakers, 1984; Rhapsody for violin and orchestra, 1984; Electronic piece Time's Encomium, 1970, not for orchestra (purely electronic); Concerto for Saxophone Quartet and Orchestra, 1993; The Mission of Virgil, for orchestra, 1993; Chamber Music includes 3 String Quartets, 1971, 1979, 1987; Horn Trio, 1981 & 1985; Vocal Music includes: Genesis for chorus and orchestra, The Celestial Sphere, oratorio, 1980; Mass for soprano, chorus, violin 3 trombones and organ; Piano and Organ music; Many keyboard works including 3 Sonatas; A Winter's Tale (2 versions), soprano and chamber and w/piano, 1991, 1992. Publications: Charles Wuorinen, a Bio-Bibliography by Richard Burbank. Honours include: Joseph Bearns Prize 1958, and Letters Award 1967; Guggenheim Fellowship, 1968-72; Pulitzer Prize for Time's Encomium, 1970; Rockefeller Foundation Fellowship, 1979, 1981, 1982; American Academy of Arts & Letters, 1985; MacArthur Foundation Fellowship, 1986-91. Current Management: c/o Howard Stokar Management. Address: c/o Howard Stokar Management, 870 West End Avenue, New York, NY 10025, USA.

WÜTHRICH Hans, b. 3 Aug 1937, Aeschi, Switzerland. Composer. m. Beatrice Mathez, 6 May 1977, 1 daughter. Education: Piano and Violin studies at Conservatory of Music, Berne, 1957-62; Studies of composition with Klaus Huber, Academy of Music, 1968-74; Doctor's Degree, University of Zurich, 1973. Career: Lecturer of Linguistics, Zurich University, 1971-85, and Teacher, Winterhur Conservatory, 1985-; Performances of compositions in Donaueschingen, 1978, 1985, at ISCM World Music Festival, Bonn in 1977 and at Athens in 1979. Compositions: Kommunikationsspiele, 1973; Das Glashaus, 1974-75; Netz-Werke I, II, 1983-85; Annaeherungen an Gegenwart, 1986-87; Procuste Deux Etoiles, 1980-81; Supplement: Netz-Werk III, 1987-89; Chopin Im TGV Basel-Paris, 1989; Wörter Bilder Dinge, 1990-91; Leve, 1992; Ah! Vous voila!, 1994; Happy Hour, 1995-97. Recordings: Procuste Deux Etoiles, 1980-81; Annäherungen an Gegenwart, 1986-87; Chopan im TGV Basel-Paris, 1989; Wörter Bilder Dinge, 1990-91.Contributions to: Interface, volume 12, 1983; Musiktheorie, 1987. Honours: Prize, Composers Competition, Zurich, 1972; Prize, International Composers Competition, Boswil, 1974, 1976, 1978; Grand Prix Paul Gibson de la CRPLF, 1984; Cultural Prize of Canton Basel-Landschaft, Switzerland, 1991. Address: Kirchgasse 4, CH-4144 Arlesheim, Switzerland.

WYN DAVIES Catrin, b. England. Singer (Soprano). Education: Studied at the Guildhall School of Music. Career: Roles with Welsh National Opera (1994-96) have included Mozart's Ilie, Zerlina and Susanna, and Anne Truelove in The Rake's Progress; Season 1996-97 with Gilda for WNO, First Flower Maiden in Parsifal at the Paris Châtelet and Handel's Acis and Galatea with the English Concert; Concerts have included Soprano Solo in Schoenberg's Moses und Aron with the Philharmonia (1996), Handel's Orlando, Elijah with David Willcocks and Bach's Christmas Oratorio with René Jacobs on tour to Europe; Wigmore Hall debut recital 1994; Further opera roles include Kristine in The Makropoulos Case and Monteverdi's Poppea (for WNO). Recordings include: Sacred music by Vivaldi with the King's Consort; Weill's Der Silbersee under Marcus Stenz; Beethoven Folk Songs, with Malcolm Martineau. Honours include: Decca Award at the 1994 Kathleen Ferrier Awards. Address: Harrison/Parrott Ltd, 12 Penzance Place, London W11 4PA, England.

WYN-ROGERS Catherine, b. 1958, England. Contralto. Education: Studied at the Royal College of Music with Meriel St Clair and later with Ellis Keeler and Diane Forlano. Career: Regular concerts with the Bach Choir under David Willcocks in London and abroad; Frequent appearances with Britain's major orchestras; Tours with English Concert and Trevor Pinnock including Messiah in Germany and Vivaldi's Gloria in Rome for TV/Deutsche Grammophon recording; Appearances at the Proms with the Sixteen, the National Youth Orchestra and the English Concert Opera including Il Ritorno d'Ulisse for English National Opera and Stuttgart, Rigoletto in Nantes, La Gioconda for Opera North, Die Zauberflöte for the ROH and Salzburg Festival; Sang First Norn in Götterdämmerung at Covent Garden, 1995; Sang in Palestrina and Pfitzner recital at Covent Garden, 1997. Recordings: Vaughan Williams's Serenade To Music and Magnificat with Matthew Best; Teixera Te Deum and Bach's Christmas Oratorio with the Sixteen; Elgar's Dream of Gerontius with Vernon Handley and the Royal Liverpool Philharmonic. Honours include: College Song Recital Prize; Dame Clara Butt Award; Grantee, Countess of Munster Trust, RCM. Current Management: Lies Askonas Ltd. Address: c/o Lies Askonas Ltd, 6 Henrietta Street, London, WC2, England.

WYNER Susan (Davenny), b. 17 Oct 1945, New Haven, CT, USA. Soprano. Education: Graduated from Cornell University, 1965; Vocal studies with Herta Glaz, 1969-75. Debut: Carnegie Hall recital in 1972. Career: Alice Tully Hall recital in 1973; Orchestral debut with the Boston Symphony in 1974;

Engagements with all leading orchestras in USA and Canada and with Israel Philharmonic and London Symphony; Repertoire includes Baroque and contemporary works; Operatic debut as Monteverdi's Poppea, New York City Opera, 1977; Metropolitan Opera in 1982 as Woglinde in Das Rheingold; Has sung in the premieres of Del Tredici's Adventures Underground in 1975 and Carter's A Mirror On Which To Dwell in 1965, and in the premieres of Memorial Music and Fragments from Antiquity by Yehudi Wyner; Also sings works by Rochberg (Quartet No 2) and Reimann (Inane).

WYNER Yehudi, b. 1 Jun 1929, Calgary, Alberta, Canada. Composer; Pianist; Conductor. m. Susan Davenny Wyner. Education: Studied at the Juilliard School then at Yale University with Paul Hindemith gaining BMus in 1951 and MMus in 1953; Further study with Walter Piston at Harvard University gaining MA in 1952. Career: American Academy in Rome, 1953-56; Performed and recorded contemporary music in New York; Directed the Turnau Opera; Teacher at Yale School of Music from 1963, Chairman of Composition, 1969-73; Music Director of the New Haven Opera Society and keyboard player with the Bach Aria Group; Berkshire Music Center, 1975; Professor of Music at State University of New York, Purchase, 1978, Dean of Music, 1978-82. Compositions include: Piano Sonata, 1954; 3 Informal Pieces for Violin and Piano, 1961; Torah Service, 1966; Cadenza for Clarinet and Harpsichord, 1969; Canto Cantabile for Soprano and Band, 1972; Memorial Music for Soprano and 3 Flutes, 1971-73; Intermedio for Soprano and Strings, 1974; Fragments From Antiquity for Soprano and Orchestra, 1978-81; Romances for Piano Quartet, 1980; On This Most Voluptuous Night for Soprano and 7 Instruments, 1982; Wind Quintet, 1984; String Quartet, 1985; Toward The Center for Piano, 1988; Il Cane Minore for 2 Clarinets and Bassoon, 1992; Concerto for Cello and Orchestra, 1994. Honours include: Guggenheim Fellowship, 1958-59, 1977-78; NEA Grant, 1976; Commissions from the Ford Foundation, Delos String Quartet and the Aeolian Chamber Players. Address: c/o ASCAP, ASCAP Building, One Lincoln Plaza, New York, NY 10023, USA.

WYZNER Franz, b. 1932, Vienna, Austria. Bass Singer. Education: Studied in Vienna. Career: Sang at the Landestheater in Salzburg, 1958-59, Gelsenkirchen, 1959-64, Wuppertal, 1964-65, notably in the German premiere of Crime and Punishment by Petrovic, 1971, and the first performance of The Gamblers by Shostakovich in the arrangement by K Meyer, 1986; Guest appearances at the Schwetzingen Festival, 1970, Vienna Volksoper in the Austrian premiere of The Burning Fiery Furnace by Britten in 1977, Salzburg Festival in Dantons Tod, 1983, Buenos Aires in Alberich in 1983, and Cologne in 1985; Other roles have included Mozart's Leporello, Figaro, Papageno and Alfonso, Kaspar in Der Freischütz, Don Magnifico, Mephistopheles, the Doctor in Wozzeck, and Kecal in The Bartered Bride. Recordings include: Dantons Tod, Orfeo. Address: Theater am Gärtnerplatz, Gärtnerplatz 3, 8000 Munich 1, Germany.

X

XENAKIS I, b. 29 May 1922, Braila, Romania. Composer; Architect; Civil Engineer. m. Francoise Gargouil, 3 Dec 1953, 1 daughter. Education: Polytechnic School, Athens, Greece; Ecole Normale Musique, Paris, France; Paris Conservatoire; Composition with Hermann Scherchen, Olivier Messiaen, Darius Milhaud, France and Switzerland. Career: Architectual collaborator with Le Corbusier, Paris, France, 12 years; Designs include Philips Pavilion, Brussels World Fair, Belgium, 1958, Polytope French pavilion, Montreal, Canada, 1967, Persepolis, 1971, and Polytope de Cluny, Paris, France, 1972-74; Director, Founder, Centre d'Etudes de Mathematique et Automatique Musicales, Paris, 1966-, and Centre for Mathematics and Automated Music, Indiana University, USA, 1967-72; The Bacchae premiered by Opera Factory, London 1993. Compositions: 63 compositions for all media including: ST/10- 1,080262 for 10 instruments, 1957-62; Achorripsis for chamber orchestra, 1958; Syrmos for chamber orchestra, 1959; Analogiques for instruments and tape, 1959; Atrees (Hommage a Pascal) for 10 instruments, 1962; Bohor, 8 track electroacoustic music, 1962; Strategie for orchestra and 2 conductors, 1962; Duet for 54 instruments and 2 conductors, 1963; Nuits for 12 voices, 1968; Momos Gammas, 1968; Persephassa, 1969; Hibiki-Hana-Ma (12 tapes distributed kinematically over 800 speakers), 1970; Antikhthon, 1971; Aroura, 1971; Linaia-Agon, 1972; Bridanos, 1973; Cendrees, 1974; Erikhthon, 1974; Gmeeoorh, 1974; Noomena, 1974; Empreintes, 1975; Phlegra, 1975; Psappha, 1975; N'Shima, 1975; Khoai, 1976; Epei, 1976; Dmaathen, 1976; Kottos, 1977; Akanthas, 1977; á Hélène,1977; La Légende d'Er, 1977; á Colone, 1977; Jonchaies, 1977; Diatope, 1978; Polytope at Mycenae, 1978; Pleiades, 1978; Ais, 1980; Nekuia, 1981; Palimpsest for piano and ensemble, 1982; Keqrops for piano and orchestra, 1986; Alax for 3 instrumental ensembles, 1985; Thallein for 14 instruments 1985; Idmen A for chorus and 4 percussionists, 1985; Akea for piano and sting quartet 1986; Horos for orchestra 1986; Jalons for 15 instruments 1986; Tracées for orchestra, 1987; Ata for orchestra, 1987; Waarg for 13 instruments, 1989; Voyage vers And omède 1989; Epicyles for cello and 12 instruments, 1989; Knephas for chorus, 1990; Tuorakemsu for orchestra, 1990; Kyania for orchestra; Tetora for string quartet, 1990; Doxorkh for violin and orchestra 1991; Music for The Bacchae by Euripides, 1992. Publications: Musiques Formelles, 1963; Musique-Architecture, 1970; Formalized music, 1971. Contributions to: Professional journals. Honours: Maurice Ravel Gold Medal, 1974; Honorary Member, American Academy of Arts and Letters, National Institute of Arts and Letters. Address: 9 rue Chaptal, 75009 Paris, France.

XIA Liping, b. Feb 1935, China. Music Educator. m. Mar 1963, 3 sons. Education: Music Institute of China, graduated 1958. Career: Music Editor, radio station of Hainan, China; Leader, music group at radio station, Guangdong, China; Professor of Music Education for 17 years. Publication; Research in Chinese Classical Music, 1993. Contributions to: Chief Editor, University Music Education, Guangdong. Honours: Broadcasting Award, honoured for Excellent Programme, China, 1980's; Honoured, Excellent Education Award, numerous times, China, 1980's. Memberships: ICIM; Deputy Director, National Music Education Association, China. Address: 388-5 Dong-Hua Doag Road Rm# 703, Guangzhou, China.

Y

YAHIA Mino, b. 1928, Alexandria, Egypt. Bass-Baritone. Education: Studied in New York and Europe. Career: Sang at the Heidelberg Stadttheater, 1955-56, Kiel, 1956-57, and Nuremberg, 1957-60; Appearances at the Bayerische Staatsoper Munich from 1960, notably in the 1963 premiere of Die Verlobung by Werner Egk, in San Domingo; Salzburg Festival in 1961 in the premiere of Das Bergwerk zu Falun by Wagner-Régeny; Further guest appearances at the Vienna Staatsoper as Hunding in Die Walküre, Buenos Aires in Strauss' Barak in 1965, Hanover and with the New York Concert Opera in the local premiere of Die Frau ohne Schatten; Other roles have included Wagner's Daland, King Henry, Marke, Pogner, Fafner and Hagen, Ariodate in Handel's Xerxes, Publio in La Clemenza di Tito, Verdi's Zaccaria and Sparafucile, and Gremin in Eugene Onegin. Address: c/o Bayerische Staatsoper, Postfach 100148, 8000 Munich 1, Germany.

YAHR Carol, b. 1959, USA. Singer (Mezzo-soprano). Career: Sang at the Cologne Opera, 1987, as Venus in Tannhäuser, Théâtre des Champs-Elysées, 1988, as Fricka in The Ring; Nice Opera, 1988-89, as Genevieve in Pelleas and Dido in Les Troyens; Seattle, 1989, as Wagner's Eva, Leonore at Innsbruck, 1990, and with Glyndebourne Tour; Scottish Opera and Innsbruck, 1991, as Sieglinde and Elisabeth; Sang the Walküre Brünnhilde at Wiesbaden, 1993; Sang Brunnhilde in The Ring for Norwegian Opera, 1996. Address: c/o Der Norske Opera, P O Box 8800, Youngstorget, N0028 Oslo, Norway.

YAKAR Rachel, b. 3 Mar 1938, Lyon, France. Soprano. Education: Studied at the Paris Conservatoire and with Germaine Lubin. Career includes: Sang with Deutsche Oper am Rhein, Dusseldorf from 1964 in roles including Antonia in Les Contes d'Hoffmann; Sang at Aix-en-Provence in 1966 in Ariadne auf Naxos, Strasbourg Opera in 1967 in a new production of Der Junge Lord by Henze, Amsterdam, 1968-69 as Cleopatra in Giulio Cesare and as Marguerite, at Messiaen Festival, Dusseldorf in 1969, and Paris Opéra in 1970 as Gilda and Micaela; Baroque repertoire from 1971 includes Deidamia by Handel; Munich Festival in 1974 as Donna Elvira, Bayreuth Festival in 1976 as Freia and Gerhilde in Patrice Chéreau's centenary production of Der Ring des Nibelungen, Glyndebourne Festival, 1977, 1980 as Donna Elvira and the Marschalin, Strasbourg and Dusseldorf in 1978 as Mélisabde; Sang Cycle of operas by Monteverdi at Zurich in 1978; Geneva Opera in 1981 as Janácek's Jenufa; Guest appearances in San Francisco, East Berlin, Edinburgh, Lausanne, Monte Carlo and Santiago; Other roles include Mozart's Ilia and Fiordigili; Sang Madame Lidoine in Dialogues des Carmélites at Lyons, 1990. Recordings include: Rameau's Les Indes Galantes, and Pygmalion; Idomeneo; Monteverdi's Orfeo; Dido and Aeneas; Bach B minor Mass; Lully's Armide; Schütz's Christmas Story and Magnificat; Fux's and Scalatti's Baroque Cantatas; Die Zauberflöte, from the Salzburg Festival conducted by James Levine.

YANAGIDA Takayoshi, b. 27 Mar 1948, Sapporo, Hokkaido, Japan. Composer. m. Keiko Tsuhako, 16 May 1973, 1 son, 1 daughter. Education: Advanced Degree, Graduate School of Musashino Music College; Studied with Professor Klaus Pringsheim at Musashino Music College; Studied with Professor Harald Genzmer at Musik Hochschule in München. Debut: Iino Hall, Tokyo, 1969. Career: Professor of Music, Bunkyo University; Composer for the Music of NHK Educational Program. Compositions: Mixed Chorus Suite, Kitano-kawa, MCS Pony of Stars (Kawai edition); Seen in the Twilight, for flute, violin and piano (JFC edition); Beside a Stream, for piano (JFC). Recordings: Concert Tableau for wind orchestra; Johi-haku-un. Publications: Orchestra Project '93; Libretto on a Dreamy Vision for flute and orchestra (recorded and sent on the air by NHK), 1993. Honours: 1st Prize in the 38th Japan Music Competition, Composition Division, 1969. Memberships: ISME; JSCM; JFC. Hobby Igo. Address: 913-4 Ohmaki Urawa-shi, Saitama-ken 336, Japan.

YANAGITA Masako, b. 30 Mar 1944, Tokyo, Japan. Violinist. m. Abba Bogin. Education: Artist Diploma, Mannes College of Music, New York City, USA; Studied with Eijin Tanaka, Louis Graeler, William Kroll. Debut: Tokyo, 1966. Career: Concert appearances throughout USA, Europe, Near and Far East; Soloist, orchestras in Japan, UK, Germany, Philippines, USA; 1st Violinist, toured with Vieuxtemps String Quartet; Faculty Member, Mannes College of Music. Recordings: Schubert. Honours: Silverstein Prize, Berkshire Music Center, Massachusetts, 1966; Carl Flesch Competition, London, England, 1968; Paganini Competition, Genoa, Italy, 1968; Munich International Competition, 1969. Current Management: Raymond Weiss Artists Management, New York City, USA. Address: 838 West End Avenue, New York, NY 10025, USA.

YANG Liqing, b. 30 April 1942, Sichuan, China. Composer. Education: BA, 1970, Shenyang Conservatory, MA, 1980, Shanghai Conservatory; Further study at the Hanover Musikhochschule (PhD in composition, 1983). Career: Faculty Member of Shanghai Conservatory from 1983 (Professor, 1991-); Guest Professor at Salzburg Mozarteum, 1990; Research in USA, 1995. Compositions include: Violin Concerto for violin and piano, 1970; The Night of a Festival for dancer and chamber orchestra, 1973; Dujuan Mountain Suite for vocal soloists and ensemble, 1974; The Sun, ballet music for soprano chorus and orchestra, 1976; Mister O, incidental music, 1977; Festival by Hailan River, for orchestra, 1978; Mountain Song and Work Song, for piano 4 hands, 1980; Three Lorca Songs for mezzo, flute, cello and piano, 1982; Yi, for orchestra, 1983; Chamber Music for Ten, 1983; The Story about the Birth of Tao, for chorus, 1983; The Monument Without Inscription, dance drama, 1989; Ode to Apollo, for orchestra, 1991; Two Folksongs for piano and orchestra, 1993; Concerto for Zheng, 1994; Costs of Peace for orchestra, 1995. Publications include: The Compositional Techniques of Olivier Messiaen, 1989. Address: c/o MCSC, 85 Dongsi Nan Dajie, Beijing 100703, China.

YANG Sungsic, b. 1966, Korea. Concert Violinist. Education: Studied at the Paris Conservatoire and with Yfrah Neaman at the Guildhall School of Music, 1987. Debut: Recital in Seoul in 1977. Career: Solo appearances throughout Europe including tour with the Seoul Philharmonic; Tchaikovsky and Mendelssohn Concertos with the Moscow Philharmonic at Seoul for the Olympic Festival in 1988; Paris concerto debut with Orchestre National de France, conducted by Lorin Maazel, 1988; BBC Radio recording, 1988; Appearances with National Symphony Orchestra, RTE, Dublin, and Gävleborgs Symfoniorkester, Sweden, 1991; Plays a Joseph Guarneri del Gesu of 1720; Repertoire also includes concertos by Bach, Brahms, Bruch, Beethoven, Mozart, Prokofiev, Saint-Saëns, Sibelius and Wieniawski; Solo works by Bach, sonatas by Brahms, Beethoven, Debussy, Fauré, Franck, Tartini and Ysaÿe, and Stravinsky's Suite Italienne. Honours: Prizewinner in Paganini Competition, Genoa, Long-Thibaud Paris, and Indianapolis, USA; 1st Prize, Carl Flesch Competition, London, 1988.

YANNAY Yehuda, b. 26 May 1937, Timisora, Rumania. Composer. Education: Graduated Rubin Academy of Music, Tel Aviv, 1964; MFA, Brandeis University, USA, 1966 (study with Berger, Shapero and Krenek); DMA University of Illinois at Urbana, 1974. Career: Resident in Israel from 1951; Teacher of theory and composition at University of Wisconsin, Milwaukee, 1970-; Music from Almost Yesterday concert series, 1971-. Compositions include: Spheres for soprano and 10 instruments, 1963; Two Fragments for violin and piano, 1966; Wraphap, theatre music, 1969; Coloring Book from the Harpist, 1969; Concert for Audience and orchestra, 1971; The Hidden Melody for cello and horn, 1977; Concertino for violin and chamber orchestra, 1980; Celan Ensembles: Augentanz and Galgenlied for tenor and instruments, 1986-; In Madness There is Order for voice, projections and synthesizers, 1988-92; The Oranur Experiment, music video, Part 1, Journey to Orgonon for actor, projections and synthesizer, 1991; Five Pieces for Three Players for soprano saxophone, clarinet and marimba, 1994. Address: c/o ASCAP, One Lincoln Plaza, New York, NY 10023, USA.

YARBOROUGH William, b. 3 Jan 1926, Wilmington, North Carolina, USA. Symphony Conductor. m. Ruth M Feldt, 29 Jan 1955. Education: BM, Chicago Musical College and University of Chicago; MM, Indiana University; Studied with Frank Gittelson, Nadia Boulanger, Vittorio Rieti and Serge Koussevitsky; Studied at Peabody Conservatory and Berkshire Music Center. Debut: As Conductor, aged 19, American Symphony in Paris; As Concert Violinist, aged 8. Career: Music Director and Conductor, American Symphony Orchestra, Paris, France, Richmond Philharmonic Orchestra, Richmond, Virginia; CBS Radio broadcasts; Music Director at Michigan's Bach-Mozart Festival; Music Director, Conductor, Michigan Bach-Mozart Festival; Performances with Touring American Opera Company and American Chamber Orchestra at present; Music Director, Conductor, American Chamber Orchestra, Washington DC since 1980; Guest Conductor of many of the major symphonies in Europe and USA including Royal Philharmonic, Vienna Symphony, St Cecilia Orchestra in Rome, Boston Symphony and Philadelphia Orchestra; Numerous radio and television appearances; Speaker, Chicago Adult Education Council; Music Advisor, Old Dominion Symphony Council. Contributions to: Journal of the American Musicological Society. Hobbies: Golf; Travel; People. Address: American Chamber Orchestra Society, 4201 Cathedral Avenue NW, Suite 706-E, Washington DC 20016, USA.

YARON Gilah, b. 1941, Tel-Aviv, Israel. Soprano. Education: Studied in Tel-Aviv with Tuerk Bernstein and with Gunter Reich, George London and Elisabeth Schwarzkopf. Career: Sang with the Israel Philharmonic and other orchestras from 1970; Israel Festival in 1972 in Bach's Magnificat; Sang in Switzerland and other European centres from 1975 including concert at Berlin Festival with works by Hindemith and Webern; Guest appearances in Austria, Belgium, Holland, Italy, Denmark and England; Sang Psaumes Hebraiques by Markevitch and Poèmes pour Mi by Messiaen; Other repertoire includes Penderecki's St Luke Passion, Mahler's 2nd Symphony and Mendelssohn's music for A Midsummer Night's Dream; Singing Teacher at The Rubin Academy of Music and Dance, Jerusalem, 1982-. Address: c/o PO Box 2179, Bat Yam 59121, Israel.

YASSA Ramzi, b. 15 Mar 1948, Cairo, Egypt. Pianist. m. Brigitte Chevrot, 7 Jun 1978, 1 son, 1 daughter. Education: Lycee of Heliopolis; Diploma, Cairo Conservatory, 1968; Tchaikovsky Conservatory, Moscow, 1969-74; FTCL, 1972; Licence de Concert, Ecole Normale, Paris, 1977. Career: Appearances at The Barbican in London with Royal Philharmonic Orchestra, conductor Sir Charles Groves, Kennedy Center, Mann Auditorium with IPO, conductor Zubin Mehta, Musikverien, Palau, Barcelona, Théâtre des Champs Elysees and South Bank, London; TV Mondovision with Zubin Mehta in 1987; Inaugural concert, Cairo Opera House, 1988; BBC recordings and live broadcasts; Adjudicator for international piano competitions; Appearances with Yehudi Menuhin as conductor. Recordings: Tchaikovsky's The Seasons, Ades, France; Prokofiev's Cinderella, 2nd Sonata, Belgium; Chopin's Ballades and Opus 22, Belgium. Honours: Prizewinner of Marguerite Long Competition, 1971 and G B Viotti Competition, 1972; Certificate of Honour, Tchaikovsky Competition, 1974; 1st Grand Prix, Paloma O'Shea International Competition, Santander, Spain, 1977; Recipient, Franz Liszt Centenary Commemorative Medal. Address: 14 Rue Sainte Cecile, 75009 Paris, France.

YASUNAGA Toru, b. 14 Nov 1951, Fukuoka, Japan. Violinist. Education: Studied at the Toho Music Academy, Tokyo, and with Michael Schwalbe in Berlin. Career: Many appearances in Europe and the Far East as recitalist and in concert; Joined Berlin Philharmonic Orchestra, 1977, and became leader. Honours include: Winner, Leu Cadia prize at the All Japan Music Competition, 1971. Address: c/o Berlin Philharmonic Orchestra, Philharmonie, Matthaikirchestrasse 1, W-10785 Berlin, Germany.

YATES Martin, b. 1 July 1958, London, England. Conductor; Composer. Education: Royal College of Music, 1976-77; Trinity College of Music, 1977-79; Studied Composition with Richard Arnell and John Tavener, Conducting with Bernard Keeffe, Piano with Ian Lake and Jacob Kaletsky. Debut: Israel National Opera, 1982. Career: Guest Conductor, Israel National Opera, 1982-84; Music Director, Phantom of the Opera, Miss Saigon, Carousel, Sunset Boulevard, 1989-95; Principal Conductor, National Symphony Orchestra, 1994-; Numerous guest conducting appearances with Royal Scottish National Orchestra, Royal Philharmonic, Philharmonia, Royal Ballet Sinfonia, Wren Orchestra, others. Compositions: Symphony; 4 string quartets; Concertos for horn, flute and harp, organ; Sonata for flute and piano; Sonata for flute and harp; Sonatinas for flute and piano, harpsichord; At the Sea's Edge, text by John Addey; The Soap Opera, musical; Nothing Doing Tonight, musical, lyrics by Dudley Stevens; Wuthering Heights, opera, libretto by Steve Devereaux. Recordings: Over 30 including: Eternal Caballé, Monseratt Caballé, with Philharmonia; The Phantom of the Opera; Jesus Christ Superstar; Nick and Nora; Carousel; Seven Brides for Seven Brothers; New Symphony Orchestra Classics. Membership: Noble Baron, Wine Order of Klosterneuberg, Austria. Hobbies: Reading; Travel; 2nd World War history. Current Management: Janet Glass, Eric Glass Ltd, London, England. Address: c/o Janet Glass, Eric Glass Ltd, 28 Berkeley Square, London W1X 6HD, England.

YAUGER Margaret, b. 1947, Birmingham, Alabama, USA. Mezzo-Soprano. m. Malcolm Smith, 4 Oct 1975. Education: BM, Converse College; MM, New England Conservatory of Music; Special studies at American Opera Centre, Juilliard School of Music, New York City, and Goldovsky Opera Studio. Debut: American National Opera Company, Sarah Caldwell, Conductor. Career: Performances with New York City Opera, 1973-75, Lake George Opera Festival, 1972-74, Central City Opera Festival, 1973-76, Boris Goldovsky Opera Tour, 1973-74, Mexico City Opera, Teatro Regio Turin, Italy; Sang at Knoxville with Tennessee Opera, Birmingham Alabama Civic Opera, Fort Worth, Texas Opera; Deutsch Oper am Rhein, Dusseldorf, Germany, 1977-86; Sang at Krefeld, Hanover, Karlsruhe, Freiburg, Wiesbaden and Gelsenkirchen Opera Houses and with Solingen, Duisburg, Münchengladbach- Krefeld, and Trier Symphonies; Appearances on East Berlin Radio and with Dresden Philharmonic; Sang Fricka in Das Rheingold, Washington National Symphony, Margret in Wozzeck, with Boston Symphony Orchestra, 3rd Magd, Elektra with London Symphony Orchestra; Heidelberg Schloss, Festspiele, 1992; Sang in Verdi Requiem, Delaware Symphony Orchestra, 1993; Mahler Symphony No 2, Roanoke Symphony, 1994; Choral Arts Society of Washington tour of France, 1996; Youngstown Symphony, 1996; Cincinnati Opera, 1996. Recordings: Beethoven Symphony No 9, alto part, with Mexico City Symphony; Live recording of Rigoletto, New York City Opera. Honours: Miss Alabama Competition Scholarship; 3 Scholarships, William Mathis Sullivan Foundation.

Membership: AGMA. Current Management: Thea Dispecker, Artists' Representative, 59 East 54th Street, New York, NY 10022, USA. Address: Markgrafenstr 10, 40545 Düsseldorf, Germany.

YEEND Frances, b. 28 Jan 1918, Vancouver, WA, USA. Soprano. Education: Studied at Washington State University. Career: From 1943 sang in musicals and on the radio; Concert tour of USA in 1944; Sang Ellen Orford in the US premiere of Peter Grimes, at Tanglewood in 1946; World tour in 1947 with Mario Lanza and George London, as Bel Canto Trio; New York City Opera, 1948-65, as Violetta, Eva in Die Meistersinger, Micaela, Mozart's Countess and Marguerite; Metropolitan Opera, 1961-64, as Chrysothemis in Elektra and Gutrune in Götterdämmerung; European engagements in Barcelona, Edinburgh in 1951, London in Mimi in 1953, Munich, Verona in Turandot in 1958, and Vienna. Recordings include: Micaela in Carmen; Ein Deustches Requiem by Brahms.

YELLIN Victor (Fell), b. 14 Dec 1924, Boston, MA, USA. Professor. m. Isabel S Joseph, 26 May 1948, 1 son. Education: New England Conservatory of Music, 1942-43; BA, cum laude, Harvard College, 1949; AM, 1952, PhD, 1957, Harvard University. Compositions: Abaylar, opera; Passacaglia for Strings; Sonata for Violoncello and Piano. Recordings: Victor Fell Yellin Restoration Of 2 Early American Operas, Rayner Taylor's The Ethiop and John Bray's The Indian Princess. Publications: The Operas of Virgil Thomson (American music since 1910), 1970; Preface to How Music Works, 1981; Chadwick, Yankee Composer, Washington and London, 1990. Contributions to: Musical Quarterly; American Music; Grove VI. Honour: Grantee, National Endowment for the Humanities. Memberships: American Musicological Society; Sonneck Society. Hobby: Collecting Cameras. Address: 52 Washington Mews, New York, NY 10003, USA.

YEN Wen (Hsiung), b. 26 June 1934, Taiwan, US citizen since 1986. Professor of Music. m. Yuan Yuan Yen, 6 Jan 1961, 3 sons. Education: BA, National Taiwan Norman University, 1956-60; MA, 1962-64, PhD Candidate, 1965-68, Chinese Culture University; MA, University of California, Los Angeles, 1969-71; PhD Candidate, University of Maryland, 1982-83; Cultural Doctorate, Philosophy of Music; Degree, Candidate, Philosophy in Ethnomusicology, 1995. Career: Instructor, Taiwan Provincial Taichung Teacher College, 1961-62; Professor, Chinese Culture University, 1964-69; Founder and Music Director, Chinese Music Orchestra of Southern California, 1974-; Founder Chinese Culture School, Los Angeles, 1976-; Lecturer, West Los Angeles College, 1978-82; Faculty, Department of Music, University of Maryland, 1982-83; Instructor, Los Angeles City College and California State University, Los Angeles, 1984-; Instructor, California State University, Northridge and Santa Monica City College, 1986-; Founder and President of The Chinese Musicians Association of Southern California, 1990-; Conducted the orchestra for the Dragon Boat Festival, at the Chinese Cultural Center in Los Angeles' Chinatown in 1993, and for the opening ceremony of the annual Chinese Writer's Association of Southern California Conference, 1993. Publications: Taiwan Folk Songs, 1967, volume 2, 1968; Co-author, A Dictionary of Chinese Musicians, 1967; A Collection of Wen-hsiung Yen's Songs, 1968, volume 2, 1987; Chinese Musical Culture and Folk Songs, written in Chinese with article, A Study of Si Xiang Qi in English, 1989. Honours: Award, Associates of Ethnic Arts At UCLA; Fellowship, UCLA. Memberships: Society for Ethnomusicology; International Council for Traditional Music; Society for Asian Music. Hobbies: Walking; Table Tennis; Tai Chi Chuan. Address: 1116 Drake Road, Arcadia, CA 91007, USA.

YERNA Alexise, b. 1959, Belgium. Singer (Mezzo-soprano). Education: Studied at the Brussels Conservatoire with Jules Bastin. Career: Sang in operas by Handel, Chabrier and Puccini at the Brussels opera studio; Opéra Wallonie at Liège from 1982, as Orlofsky and in operettas by Offenbach; Has appeared throughout Belgium and France at Lola, Pepa in Goyescas, Fenena (Nabucco) and the Priestess in Aida; Many concert engagements. Address: c/o Opéra de Wallonie, 1 Rue des Domincains, B-4000 Liège, Belgium.

YEROFEEVA Yelena, b. 1960, Moscow, Russia. Cellist. Education: Studied at the Moscow Conservatoire with Alexei Shislov. Career: Co-founded the Glazunov Quartet 1985; Many concerts in the former Soviet Union and recent appearances in Greece, Poland, Belgium, Germany and Italy; Works by Beethoven and Schumann at the Beethoven Haus in Bonn; Further engagements in Canada and Holland; Teacher at the Moscow State Conservatoire and Resident at the Tchaikovsky Conservatoire; Repertoire includes works by Borodin, Shostakovich and Tchaikovsky, in addition to the standard works. Recordings includes: CDs of the six quartets of Glazunov. Honours include: (with the Glazunov Quartet) Prizewinner of the Borodin Quartet and Shozstakovich Chamber Music Competitions. Address: c/o Sonata (Glazunov Quartet), 11 Northpark Street, Glasgow G20 7AA, Scotland.

YEUNG Angela Chiu-Wah, b. 8 Nov 1960, Hong Kong. Music Director; Baroque and Modern Cellist; Music Theorist. Education: Hon BMus, Cello Performance, Wilfrid Laurier University, Canada; MA, Music Theory, McGill University, Canada; PhD, Music Theory, Columbia University, USA; Concert Diploma with Distinction, McGill University. Career: President, Co-Director, Orvieto Musica Inc, Annual International Summer chamber music workshop, Orvieto, Italy; Artistic Director, Early Music at Saint Peter's Church, New York, Concert Series; Faculty, University of San Diego, California; Featured in New York's Sino Radio Broadcast Production VIP, 1990; Frequent Presenter, Lecturer, Universities in USA and Hong Kong; Solo Recitals & Chamber Music Concerts on Both Coasts of Canada and USA, in many countries in Europe and Hong Kong. Address: Department of Fine Arts, University of San Diego, 5998 Alcalá Park, San Diego, CA 92110, USA.

YI Suk Won, b. 6 Feb 1959, Seoul, Korea. Professor; Director. m. Sukhee Cho, 4 June 1983, 2 daughters. Education: BA, Composition, Seoul National University; MA, PhD, Systematic Musicology, University of California, Los Angeles. Career: Chairman, 5th International Conference on Music Perception, 1998; Professor, Director, Western Music Research Institute, College of Music, Seoul National University. Publications: A Theory of Melodic Contour, 1990; Psychology of Music, 1994; Modern Music, 1997; Cognitive Musicology (forthcoming). Contributions to: Journal of the Musicological Society of Korea; Music, Mind and Science. Memberships: International Musicological Society; American Musicological Society; Musicological Society of Korea; European Society for the Cognitive Sciences of Music. Address: College of Music, Seoul National University, Seoul 151-742, Korea.

YIM Jay (Alan), b. 24 Apr 1958, St Louis, MO, USA. Composer. Education: BA, University of California, 1980; MMus, Royal College of Music, London, England, 1981; Studied at Dartington, England, 1985, and Tanglewood in 1986; Currently pursuing PhD at Harvard University. Career: Lecturer, Director of Electronic Music Studio, University of California, Santa Barbara, 1978-80; Composer-in-Residence, Cummington School of the Arts, 1984; Major festival performances at Huddersfield, 1982, International Computer Music Conference, 1985, Tanglewood in 1986 and 1987, and Gaudeamus in 1987. Compositions: Orchestral: Askesis, 1980-81, Eastern Windows, 1981, Karénas, 1986; Chamber: Palimpsest, 1979, Piak, 1981, Autumn Rhythm, 1984-85, Moments Of Rising Mist, 1986, Mille Graces, 1986, Geometry And Delirium, 1987; Solo instrument: Timescreen for Pianoforte No 1, 1984, No 2, 1983, Furiosamente for Piccolo, 1985, Más Furiosamente for Flute, 1985; Electronic: Kinkakuji, 1984, Shiosai, 1984. Address: c/o ASCAP, ASCAP Building, One Lincoln Plaza, New York, NY 10023, USA.

YOES Janice, b. 1947, USA. Soprano. Debut: New York City Opera in 1973 as Santuzza. Career: Sang at the Augsburg Opera, 1975-77, Saarbrucken, 1976-77, and Karlsruhe, 1977-78; Engaged at Nuremberg, 1978-84, with guest appearances at Graz, 1980-83; Sang Strauss's Elektra at the Vienna Staatsoper, Marseilles, Madrid, the Deutsche Oper Berlin, Seattle and Santiago in 1984; Bregenz Festival in 1977 as Reiza in Oberon; Appearances as Brünnhilde in Der Ring de Nibelungen at Naples, Lisbon and Seattle, 1982-86; Further engagements at Basle, Trieste, Brunswick and Pretoria, 1987-88; Other roles have included Isolde, Salome and Lady Macbeth. Address: Opera of the Performing Arts Council, Transvaal PO Box 566, Pretoria 0001 Transvaal, South Africa.

YORDANOV Luben, b. 6 Dec 1926, Sofia, Bulgaria. Violinist. Education: Studied at the Paris Conservatoire, with Pierre Pasquier. Career: Has performed throughout Europe as concert soloist from 1951; Leader of the orchestra of the Monte Carlo Opera, 1958-67; Orchestre de Paris, 1967-91; Premiered the Concerto by André Jolivet, 1973, and became professor of chamber music at the Paris Conservatoire, 1987. Address: Conservatoire National Superieur de Musique et de Danse de Paris, 209 Avenue Jean-Jaures, Paris 75019, France.

YORK David (Stanley), b. 25 June 1920, West Hartford, Connecticut, USA. College Professor; Church Organist; Composer. m. (1) Marian Paquin, 8 June 1946, 2 sons, (2) Joyce Van Nest Billhardt, 20 Feb 1976, 1 son, 4 daughters. Education: BM, Theory major, Yale University, 1944; MM Composition, Westminister Choir College, 1946; Additional Study: With Oliver Strunk, Princeton University; With Willi Apel and Bernard Heidan, Indiana University; With Robert Morgan, Temple University. Career: Organist-Director of Churches, Hartford, Connecticut 1940-44, Philadelphia, Pennsylvania 1944-46, Trenton-Princeton, New Jersey 1946-63, Chatham 1963-; Professor of Music Theory, twice Head of Theory Department at Westminster Choir College, 1946-85; Affiliate Professor of Music Theory at Temple University, 1988-; Adjunct Professor, Raritan Valley Community College, 1995-; Editor with Theodore Presser, Westminster Series, 1963-75; Editor with Hinshaw Music, 1987-90; Editor Music Series with National Music, 1990-95. Compositions: 44 anthems and 1 organ selection, with Theodore Presser, Carl Fisher, Harold Flammer, Golden Music, Lorenz and National Music. Honour: 2nd Prize for Divinum Mysterium for Organ and Bells, Schulmerich Contest, 1947. Membership: American Guild of Organists. Hobbies: Swimming; Beach walking. Address: 746 Old Farm Road, Bridgewater, NJ 08807, USA.

YORK Deborah, b. 9 Nov 1964, Sheffield, Yorkshire, England. Education: Manchester University and the Guildhall School of Music, with Laura Sarti; Further study with Janice Chapman. Career: Opera engagements with Glyndebourne Touring Opera as Servilia in La Clemenza di Tito, Mirror in Birrtwistle's The Second Mrs Kong; Emilia in Handel's Flavio for Dublin Touring Opera; Mozart's Barbarina at Covent Garden and Fortuna in Monteverdi's Poppea for Netherlands Opera (1995-96); Concerts include Pergolesi's Stabat Mater under Marc Minkowski, Purcell's Tempest with Ivor Bolton, Handel's Israel in Egypt with the Brandenburg Consort and Dixit Dominus with the Halle Orchestra; Purcell's King Arthur with the King's Singers in Italy and with the English Concert at the 1995 London Proms; Other broadcasts include music by Purcell with the King's Consort for the BBC, and with the Gabrieli Players in France; Music for the Mona Lisa on Radio 3; Season 1997-98 with Gianetta in L'Elisir d'amore at Covent Garden, Semele at Berlin, Anne Trulove in concert with the LSO and Handel's Jephtha at the 1997 London Proms; Acis and Galatea in Spain and the St John Passion at Montpellier. Address: c/o IMG Artists Media House, 3 Burlington Lane, London W4 2TH, England.

YORK John, b. 20 Mar 1949, Eastbourne, England. Pianist. m. Fiona Osborne, 5 Sept 1981, 1 son, 1 daughter. Education: AGSM Diploma, Guildhall School of Music and Drama, London, 1971; Studied in Paris with Jacques Février, 1971-72; Vienna Hochschule with Dieter Weber, 1972-74. Debut: Wigmore Hall, 1974. Career: Recitals and concerts in UK, Ireland, France, throughout Europe, USA, Canada, Brazil, Bermuda, Singapore, Malaysia; Partner to Raphael Wallfisch, cello; Member of York Trio of London and York 2 Piano Duo; Classic FM, BBC Radio, and CBC TV and Radio. Recordings: Many albums on several labels including: 3 albums of York Trio; Eminence with Raphael Wallfisch. Publications: Selector and assistant in new issue of Mikrokosmos (Bartók); Fingers and Thumbs, 1993. Contributions to: Reviewer for Classical Piano, The Strad. Honours: Debussy Prize, Paris, 1973. Memberships: Member-Adjudicator, British Federation of Music Festivals; MENSA. Hobbies: Train travel and time-tables; Winemaking. Current Management: Clarion/Seven Muses, London, England. Address: 38 Caterham Road, Lewisham, London SE13 5AR, England.

YOSHINO Naoko, b. 1967, London, England. Harpist. Education: Studied with Susan McDonald of Indiana University from 1974. Career: Soloist with leading orchestras from 1977, notably the Israel Philharmonic under Mehta in 1985, the Philadelphia Orchestra under Frühbeck de Burgos in 1987, and in Japan with Seiji Ozawa and Wolfgang Sawallisch; New York recital debut at Merkin Hall in 1987 and chamber concert with members of the Berlin Philharmonic; Soloist with the Berlin Philharmonic under Ozawa in 1988; Classic Aid concerts with Lorin Maazel in Paris, 1988, and Yehudi Menuhin at Gstaad Festival in 1988; London debut with James Galway in Mozart's Concerto K299 in 1990; London recital debuts in 1990; English Chamber Orchestra at the Barbican under Menuhin in 1990; Played at the World Harp Festival at Cardiff in 1991. Recording: Album with the English Chamber Orchestra under Menuhin; 5 Other albums recorded: 3 as solo artist, 1 with flute and 1 concerto album. Honours include: Second Prize, First International Harp Contest, Santa Cecilia Academy in Rome, 1981; 1st Prize, 9th International Harp Contest in Israel, 1985. Current Management: Kajimoto Concert Management Ltd, Kahoku Building 8-6-25 Ginza, Chuo-Ku, Tokyo, Japan.

YOST Ricardo, b. 1943, Chile. Singer (Bass-baritone). Education: Studied in Santiago. Career: Sang at the Teatro Colon Buenos Aires from 1973, notably as Guglielmo, Rigoletto, Amonasro, Iago, Renato, Malatesta, Escamillo and Napoleon in Prokofiev's War and Peace; Has appeared throughout South America and in bass roles such as Mephistopheles and Rossini's Basilio; Sang Amonasro at Buenos Aires, 1996. Address: Teatro Colon, Cerrito 618, 1010 Buenos Aires, Argentina.

YOUNG Alexander, b. 18 Oct 1920, London, England. Concert and Opera Singer (Tenor); Educator. m. Jean Anne Prewett, 1 son, 1 daughter. Education: Royal College of Music; Studied with Professor Stefan Pollmann, London. Debut: As Scaramuccio in Ariadne auf Naxos, Glyndebourne Company, Edinburgh, 1950. Career includes: Numerous appearances in opera and oratorio, UK and abroad; Sang title role in Stravinsky's The Rake's Progress, 1953; Sang at Covent Garden, 1955-70, as Lysander and Matteo, and at Sadler's Wells as Almaviva, Count Ory, Orpheus by Gluck and Monteverdi, in Xerxes, and as Belmonte; Sang in premiere (BBC) of Henze's Bassarids, 1968, and Hamilton's Catiline Conspiracy, 1974; Many recitals with accompanists Rex Stephens, Harold Lester and Keith Swallow;

Regular broadcasts for BBC; Also broadcast for Dutch and German radios and European Broadcasting Union; Head, School of Vocal Studies, Royal Northern College of Music, Manchester, 1973-86; Has made over 50 recordings of opera, oratorio, song recitals, notably The Rake's Progress; Now retired. Honours: Fellow, Royal Northern College of Music, 1977. Membership: British Actors' Equity. Hobbies: Choral conducting; Railway modelling; Stamp collecting. Address: Treetops, Eccles Road, Whaley Bridge, via Stockport, Cheshire SK12 7EL, England.

YOUNG Douglas, b. 18 Jun 1947, London, England. Composer; Pianist; Conductor; Writer; Broadcaster. m. Susan Anne Devlin, 22 Nov 1980, 1 daughter. Education: Trinity College of Music, Junior Exhibitioner, 1957-66; ATCL, Piano Performance, 1963; BMus, London Royal College of Music, 1969. Debut: As Pianist, Royal Festival Hall, London, 1970. Career includes: Works with Ronald Hynd, choreographer for Royal Ballet and München Staatsoper Ballet, 1970-; Fellow, Commoner in The Creative Arts, Trinity College, Cambridge, 1973-75; Composer-in-Residence, Leicester Education Authority, 1975-77; Founded internationally renowned ensemble, Dreamtiger, 1975. Compositions include: Works in all genres including several inspired by Apollinaire, Lewis Carroll, Joyce, Virginia Woolf and Borges; Series of Concerti, Night Journeys Under The Sea; Ludwig - Fragments Eines Ratsels, ballet in 2 acts, 1986. Recordings include: Virages - Region One for Cello and Large Orchestra; Trajet, Inter Lignes, 1980; The Hunting Of The Snark, 1982; Third Night Journey Under The Sea, 1980-82; Rain, Steam And Speed, 1982; Dreamlandscapes, Portrait Of Apollinaire, 1983; Dreamlandscapes Book II, 1986. Contributions to: Tempo; Music Teacher; Composer. Honours: Cobbett Prize for Chamber Music, 1968; Karl Rankl Prize for Orchestral Composition, Musica Nova, 1970-71. Memberships: Trustee, LAMA; SPNM; BMIC. Hobbies: Reading; Visual Arts; Travel; Wine. Address: c/o Ricordi (London) Ltd, The Bury, Church Street, Chesham, Buckinghamshire, HP5 1JG, England.

YOUNG Josephine, b. 1960, Auckland, New Zealand. Cellist. Education: Studied at the New England Conservatory, and in London with Christopher Bunting. Debut: Concert in Wellington, 1988. Career: Chamber musician and soloist in New Zealand; Co-founder of the New Zealand String Quartet in 1987 under the auspices of the Music Federation of New Zealand; Concerts at the Tanglewood School in USA, the Banff International Competition in Canada and performances with the Lindsay Quartet at the 1990 International Festival of the Arts, Wellington; Soloist with the New Zealand Symphony Orchestra and artist-in-residence at Victoria University, Wellington; Tour to Australia in 1990 for Musica Viva Australia; Tours of New Zealand in 1992 and concerts in New York, 1993. Recordings: Various albums.

YOUNG La Monte (Thornton), b. 14 Oct 1935, Bern, ID, USA. Composer; Performer. m. Marian Zazeela, 1963. Education: Studied at Los Angeles City College, 1953-56, Los Angeles State College, 1956-57 and UCLA with Robert Stevenson; Further study with Andrew Imbrie at the Stockhausen masterclasses at Darmstadt and electronic music at the New School for Social Research, NY. Career: Performed and taught Kirana style of North Indian classical vocal music, with Pran Nath; Collaborations with Marian Zazeela; Associations with the Fluxus and Minimalist movements of artistic endeavour; Returned to California in 1959 and became Music Director of the Ann Halprin Dance Company, 1959-60; With Marian Zazeela made tours of USA and Europe with the Theatre of Eternal Music, 1969-75; Director of the Kirana Center for Indian Classical Music, 1971; Dream House maintained by the Dia Art Foundation's programme at Harrison Street, NY, 1979-85. Compositions include: Various pieces for electronic and mixed-media forces, 1959-67; Trio for Strings, 1958; Studies I-III, 1959; Arabic Numeral, 1960; Death Chant for Male Voices and Carillon, 1961; The Well-Tuned Piano, on-going series of pieces for Prepared Piano. Publications include: An Anthology, 1963, revised, 1970; Selected Writings, 1969. Honours include: Woodrow Wilson Fellowship, 1959; Guggenheim Fellowship, 1966; Creative Arts Public Service Grants; Commission from the Dia Art Foundation, 1975-85. Address: c/o ASCAP, ASCAP Building, One Lincoln Plaza, New York, NY 10023, USA.

YOUNG Lesley (Margaret), b. 3 March 1954, Mossman, Queensland, Australia. Concert Pianist; Lecturer. Education: Queensland Conservatorium of Music, Brisbane, 1970-75; Royal Northern College of Music, Manchester, England, 1976-78; Royal College of Music, London, 1989-90; MMus in Performance Studies, Royal College of Music; BMus; ARCM; LMusA; AMusA. Debut: Wigmore Hall, 1977. Career: Australian National Music Camp and Music Rostrum, Australia, 1975; Radio Broadcasts for ABC including being featured in Pianists of Brisbane recital/broadcast series, 1974; Television appearances in Australia; Concerto performances with Queensland Symphony Orchestra, Sydney Symphony Orchestra, Melbourne Symphony Orchestra, QCM Chamber Orchestra, Royal Northern College of Music Symphony Orchestra, Queensland Youth Orchestra, Merseyside Youth Orchestra, Orchestra da Camera; Recitals for Queensland Conservatorium of Music, Royal Northern College of Music, Australian Society for Keyboard Music, International Society for Contemporary Music, Incorporated Society of Musicians, Manchester Midday Concerts Society, Australian Musical Association, London; Lecturer in Piano, James Cook University, 1991-92; Head of Keyboard Studies, School of Music, Colchester Institute, 1995-. Address: c/o School of Music, Colchester Institute, Sheepen Road, Colchester, Essex CO3 3LL, England.

YOUNG Percy (Marshall), b. 17 May 1912, Northwich, Cheshire, England. Writer on Music; Music Educationist. Education: Christ's Hospital, 1926-30; Organ scholar at Selwyn College, Cambridge, BA, 1933, MusB, 1934; MusD, Trinity College, Dublin, 1937; DMus, HC, Birmingham, 1985; Honorary Fellow, Institute for Advanced Research in the Humanities, Birmingham University. Career: Director of Music at Stranmillis Teachers Training College, Belfast, 1934-37; Music Adviser to Stoke on Trent, 1937-44; Director of Music at Wolverhampton College of Technology, 1944-65; Choral Director, with performances of music by Handel; Visiting scholar and lecturer to USA, 1971-72. Compositions: Over 30 published reconstructions, orchestrations and accompaniments including Elgar's The Spanish Lady (Premiered at Cambridge in 1994); Over 20 published works including Fugal Concerto in G minor, 1954 and Festival Te Deum, 1961. Publications include: Samuel Pepys' Music Book, 1942; The Oratorios of Handel, 1949; Messiah: A Study in Interpretation, 1951; Elgar, O M, 1955, revised, 1973; Tragic Muse: The Life and Music of Robert Schumann, 1957, revised, 1961; The Choral Tradition, 1962; A History of British Music, 1967; The Bachs 1500-1850, 1970; Sir Arthur Sullivan, 1972; Beethoven: A Victorian Tribute, 1976; George Grove, 1980; The Spanish Lady: Unfinished Opera by Percy M Young: Critical Edition, 1991; Elgar, Newman and The Dream of Gerontius, 1995. Honour: Honorary Fellow, University of Wolverhampton, 1992. Hobbies: Sport; Gardening. Address: 72 Clark Road, Wolverhampton, WV3 9PA, England.

YOUNG Richard, b. 1945, USA. Violist. Education: Studied at Indiana University and Catholic University; Teachers included Josef Gingold, Aaron Rosand and William Primrose. Career: Performed at Queen Elisabeth of Belium Competition aged 13; Member of Faculty at Oberlin Conservatory of Music, 1972-84; Performances with the Rogeri Trio and the Hungarian Quartet in the USA, Europe, South America, Africa and Australia; Member of the Vermeer Quartet from 1985; Performances at all major US centres and in Europe, Israel and Australia; Festival engagements at Tanglewood, Aspen, Spoleto, Edinburgh, Mostly Mozart in New York, Aldeburgh, South Bank, Santa Fe, Chamber Music West and the Casals Festival; Resident quartet for Chamber Music Chicago; Annual masterclasses at the Royal Northern College of Music, Manchester; Member of the Resident Artists Faculty of Northern Illinois University. Recordings include: Quartets by Beethoven, Dvořák, Verdi and Schubert; Brahms Clarinet Quintet with Karl Leister. Address: Allied Artists, 42 Montpellier Square, London, SW7 1JZ, England.

YTTREHUS Rolv, b. 12 March 1926, Duluth, USA. Composer. Education: BS in music at University of Minnesota, 1950; MM with Ross Lee Finney, at University of Michigan, 1955; Further study with Brustad in Oslo, Boulanger in Paris, Sessions at Princeton (1957-60) and Petrassi in Rome, 1960-61. Career: Teacher at the University of Wisconsin, Oshkosh, 1969-77; State University of New Jersey, Rutgers, from 1977. Compositions include: Six Haiku for flute, cello and harp, 1959; Music for Winds, Percussion and Viola, 1961; Expression for orchestra, 1962; Sextet for 6 instruments, 1969; Music for winds, percussion, cello and voices, 1969; Angstwagen for soprano and percussion, 1971; Quintet, for flute, violin, clarinet, cello and piano, 1973; Gradus ad Parnassum, for soprano and chamber orchestra, after Nietzsche and Fux, 1979; Explorations for piano, 1985; Cello Sonata, 1988; Raritan Variation for piano, 1989; Symphony, 1995. Address: c/o ASCAP, One Lincoln Plaza, New York, NY 10023, USA.

YU Chun Yee, b. 12 July 1936, Shanghai, China. Pianist. m. (1) Isabella Miao, Dec 1963, 2 sons, (2) Jung Chang, Jun 1982. Education: Royal College of Music, England under Kendall Taylor; Agostic, Italy; Tagliaferro, France. Career: Examiner to the Associated Board of Royal School of Music; Professor of Piano, Royal College of Music; Represented Singapore at the First Asian Music Festival in Hong Kong; First appeared at the Royal Festival Hall in 1963 as soloist with London Philharmonic Orchestra; Has played extensively in the Far East and throughout Britain; Recently toured Taiwan and China. Honours: Recordi Prize for Conducting; Prize Winner, International Piano Competition; Scholarship to study in Siena under Agosti. Hobbies: Bridge; Sport; Motoring. Address: c/o Royal College of Music, London, SW7, England.

YU Julian Jing-Jun, b. 2 Sept 1957, Beijing, China. Composer. m. Marion Hazel Gray, 9 Nov 1984. Education: Diploma of Music, Central Conservatory of Music, Beijing, 1977; Postgraduate Diploma in Composition, Tokyo College of Music, 1982; Graduate Diploma in Music, Queensland Conservatorium of Music, 1987; MA, Music (Composition), La Trobe University, Melbourne, 1994. Career: Emigrated to Australia in 1985; Tanglewood Fellow, 1988; Victorian Ministry for The Arts Music Advisory Panel, 1991-93 and 1995-96; Work commissioned by Hans Werner Henze; Jury Member for BMW Music Theatre Prize at 3rd Munich Biennale, 1992; Works performed at ISCM World Music Days in Zurich, 1991 and New Mexico in 1993. Compositions: Wu-Yu for Orchestra, 1987; Great Ornamented Fuga Canonica, 1988; Reclaimed Prefu, 1989; Hsiang-Wen (Filigree Clouds), for orchestra, 1991; Philopentatonia for chamber orchestra, 1994; Three Symphonic Poems, 1994; Sinfonia Passacaglissima, 1995; Scintillation I, II and III, 1997; Recordings: Vienna Modern Masters; Scintillation II; Wu-Yu; Jangled Bells; Scintillation III; Impromptu (Tall Poppies); Trio for violin, cello and piano. Publications include: Wu-Yu; Hsiang-Wen; Hsiang-Chi; Great Ornamented Fuga Canonica; Scintillation I, II and III; Reclaimed Prefu I and II; The White Snake; Medium Ornamented Fuga Canonica; In The Sunshine of Bach; Impromptu; First Australian Suite. Contributions to: Journal of The Central Conservatory of Music in China and Sounds Australian. Honours: 56th Japan Music Concours Award, 1987; International New Music Composers' Competition Award, 1988, 1989-90; 35th Premio Musicale, Citta di Trieste, 1988; Koussevitzky Composition Prize, Tanglewood, 1988; 10th Irino Prize, 1989; Inaugural and 2nd Paul Lowin Orchestral Awards, 1991 and 1994; Vienna Modern Masters Recording Award, 1992; A H Maggs Composition Award, University of Melbourne, 1992; Spivakovsky Composition Award, 1992; Jean Bogan Memorial Prize for Piano Composition, 1993. Memberships include: Australian Music Centre; Australian Performing Right Society. Address: 6 Kelvin Road, Alphington, Victoria 3078, Australia.

YURISICH Gregory, b. 13 Oct 1951, Mount Lawley, Western Australia, Australia. Singer (Baritone). Education: Studied in Perth. Debut: Paolo in Simon Boccanegra for Australian Opera at Sydney, 1978. Career: Roles in Australia have included Mozart's Masetto and Don Alfonso, Verdi's Germont and Melitone, Alberich in The Ring, Varlaam in Boris Godunov, Beethoven's Pizarro and Wagner's Dutchman; European debut, Frankfurt, 1989, as Bottom in A Midsummer Night's Dream; Covent Garden debut, 1990, as William Tell, returning as Dr Bartolo, the villains in Les Contes d'Hoffmann, Don Profondo in a new production of Il Viaggio a Reims, 1992; Pizarro in Fidelio and Scarpia in Tosca; For English National Opera has sung in two world premieres: Alcibiades in Timon of Athens by Stephen Oliver, 1991, and Cadmus in Bakxai by John Buller, 1992; Sang Stankar in a new production of Verdi's Stiffelio at Covent Garden, 1993; Other roles include Escamillo, Leporello (Glyndebourne 1991), King Henry in Anna Bolena, and Verdi's Iago, Simon Boccanegra, Rigoletto and Nabucco; Further engagements incude: San Francisco and Geneva (Germont Père in La Traviata); Covent Garden (title role in Nabucco); Australia (title role in Falstaff); Vienna (Balstrode in Peter Grimes and title role in Rigoletto); Munich (title role in Nabucco); Sang in opening gala concert of Belfast Concert Hall, 1997. Recording: Leporello with Roger Norrington. Address: c/o IMG Artists, Media House, 3 Burlington Lane, London W4 2TH, England.

Z

ZABARA Maksim, b. 12 April 1957, Minsk, Belarus. Bassoonist. Education: Belorus Lyceum of Music, 1982-91; Kiev Special Music School Lisenko, 1991-94; National Academy of Music, Ukraine, 1994-97. Career: Many recital and concert appearances in Belarus, Ukraine, Germany, The Netherlands and Canada. Repertory includes CP Bach Sonatas, Concertos by Devienne, Francaix, Hummel, Mozart, Vivaldi and Weber; Sonatas by Glinka, Saint-Saëns and Schubert (arrangement of Arpeggione Sonata); Beethoven's Trio op 11 (arranged), Kreutzer's Trio op 43 and the Trio Pathétique by Glinka. Honours include: Second Prize, Belarus Youth Woodwind Competition, 1991; Diploma of the International Woodwind Competition, Minsk, 1994. Address: c/o NWB Apollon & Hermes, Künstleragentur Management Production, Im Flögerhof 12, D-53819 Neunkirchen-Wolperath, Germany.

ZABILIASTA Lydia, b. 1959, Oleno-Koshorivka, Kirovgrad, Ukraine. Soprano. Education: Studied in Kirovgrad and at the Kiev State Conservatoire; Further study with Giulietta Simionato at La Scala. Career: Principal at the National Opera in Kiev from 1982, with such roles as Elsa, Tatiana, Nedda, Xenia in Boris Godunov and Mimi; Tours to North and South America, Japan, Australia and Britain (with Perm Opera, 1996), adding roles of Abigaille in Nabucco and Madama Butterfly. Honours include: Gold Medal, Tchaikovsky Singing Competition, Moscow, 1982. Address: c/o Sonata Ltd, 11 North Park Street, Glasgow, G20 7AA, Scotland.

ZABLOCKI Jerzy, b. 25 Jul 1928, Lublin, Poland. Conductor. m. 4 Jan 1968, 1 son. Education: Studied Musicology at University of Wroclaw, conducting at Faculty of Composition, Theory and Conducting, Academy of Music, Wroclaw, 1955. Career: Teacher in schools, college and at Academy of Music since 1948; Conductor, Polish Radio Orchestra; Over 400 pieces performed and recorded including 120 own compositions and arrangements for orchestra and choir with orchestra, 1953-58; Operetta Theatre, Wroclaw, 1959-62; Conductor, Wroclaw State Opera, 1970-77, Bydgoszcz State Opera, 1981-82 and Warsaw Operetta, 1982-84; Recently Professor in Warsaw Academy of Music and Bydgoszcz Academy of Music, Director of postgraduated study for choir conductors; Other positions have included chairman, music critic and journalist. Compositions: 120 recorded works including 20 folk songs of Lower Silesia and 50 Polish folk songs and dances. Recordings: 400 Pieces, Polish Radio and TV. Publications: In Polish: About the Techniques of Conducting, 1972, and About Chorus Conducting, 1978. Contributions to: Methodological articles, Poradnik Muzyczny; Lodz; Music Critiques, Gazeta Robotnicza. Honours: Ministry of Culture Prizes Grades I and II, 1967, 1972, 1978; Town of Legnica, 1972; Wroclaw City, 1976; Board Chief, Polish Music Artists Society. Memberships: Polish Music Artists Society; Honorary Member, Lower Silesian Music Society. Hobbies: Photography; Painting; Linguistics. Address: Marszalkowska 68-70 m6, Warsaw, Poland.

ZABRACK Harold A, b. 30 June 1928, St Louis, Missouri, USA. Pianist; Composer; Pedagogue; Professor of Piano. Education: BM, Piano, 1949, MM, Piano and Composition, 1951, Doctoral study, Indiana University and Washington University; Fulbright Award to Germany, 1955; Study with Nadia Boulanger, France, 1962. Debut: Soloist with St Louis Symphony, Grieg Piano Concerto, 1944. Career: US State Department tour of Germany, 1955-56; Recital of original piano music, Carnegie Hall, Apr 1982; Soloist, 1st Piano concerto, with St Louis Symphony, 1965, with Baton Rouge Symphony, 1982; Soloist, Milwaukee Symphony with own Symphonic Variations for piano and orchestra, 1977; Lecture-Recital on Debussy Préludes, Carnegie Recital Hall, 1987; AIDS Benefit concert featuring music of Brahms and Zabrack, Carnegie Recital Hall, 1988; TV appearances on New Jersey Cable Channel 34; Piano series in Vancouver, British Columbia, Canada, July 1989. Compositions: Published: Scherzo; Hommage à Prokofiev; Two Piano Sonatas; Eight Contours; Three Etudes; Six Preludes; Variations for Piano; Twilight for Piano commissioned by Yorktown Press, Jan 1986. Recordings include: Original piano works as well as those by Beethoven, Debussy, Kabalevsky and Bartók. Publications: Creative Musical Encounters, 1978. Contributions to: Clavier; American Music; Teacher. Hobbies: Psychology; Philosophy.

ZACCARIA Nicola, b. 9 Mar 1923, Athens, Greece. Bass Singer. Education: Studied at the Royal Conservatory, Athens. Debut: Athens in 1949 as Raimondo in Lucia di Lammermoor. Career: Has sung at many Italian centres; La Scala debut in 1953 as Sparafucile in Rigoletto; Sang in Milan in the standard bass repertory until1974, and created the Third Knight in the premiere of Pizzetti's Assassino nella Cattedrale, 1958; Vienna Staatsoper from 1956; Salzburg Festival from 1957 as the Minister in Fidelio, the Monk in Don Carlos, the Commendatore in Don Giovanni and Ferrando in Il Trovatore; Covent Garden in 1957 and 1959, as Oroveso in Norma, and Creon in Médée, both with Maria Callas; Further appearances in Brussels, Cologne, Geneva, Moscow, Rio di Janiero, Mexico City, Berlin, Monte Carlo, Edinburgh, Aix and Orange; Dallas in 1976 as King Marke in Tristan and Isolde; Sang Colline in La Bohème at Macerata in 1982; Other roles included Verdi's Zaccaria in Nabucco and Silva in Ernani, Rodolfo in La Sonnambula and Sarastro in Die Zauberflöte. Recordings include: Norma; Aida; Un Ballo in Maschera; Il Trovatore; La Sonnambula; Rigoletto; Turandot; Barbiere di Siviglia; La Bohème; Falstaff; L'Italiana in Algeri; La Navarraise; Orlando Furioso; Mignon by Thomas; Beethoven's Missa Solemnis.

ZACH Miriam Susan, b. 2 October 1954, Muscatine, Iowa, USA. Musicologist; Organist; Harpsichordist. Education: BS, Northwestern University, Evanston, Illinois, 1976; MA, Univeristy of Chicago, 1980; PhD, University of Florida, 1993. Career: Performer and organizer, International Festivals of Women Composers, University of Florida, 1989, 1997; Messiaen's Les Corps Glorieux in Paris, France and Lemgo, Germany, 1990; Organ Music by Women Composers, Princeton University Chapel, 1993-97; Messiaen's La Nativité, Lemgo, Germany, 1993. Publications: Deconstructing The Metaphysics of Love, in Seminar, 1991; Choral Music of Ernst Toch, PhD dissertation, 1993; Palimpsest, Florida Harn Museum of Art, 1996. Honours: International Woman of the Year, for distinguished service to music, from International Biographical Centre, 1992. Memberhips: American Musicological Society; College Music Society; American Guild of Organists; Mensa. Hobbies: Travel; Gardening. Address: Founding Director, International Women Composers Library, PO Box 5566, Gainesville, FL 32627-5566, USA.

ZACHARIAS Christian, b. 27 Apr 1950, Tamshedpur, India. Pianist. Education: Moved to West Germany aged 2 and studied with Irene Slavin in Karlsruhe, then with Vlado Perlemuter in Paris. Career: Won prizes in Geneva in 1969 and in the Van Cliburn Competition, won the 1975 European Broadcasting Union's Ravel Prize; Appears in USA with the Boston Symphony, Cleveland Orchestra and New York Philharmonic, and in Canada with the Montreal Symphony; Regular appearances in UK including the Edinburgh Festival in 1985 with the Polish Chamber Orchestra and Jerzy Maksymiuk; Engagements at major European festivals include Salzburg and the piano festival at La Roque d'Antheron; Chamber concerts with the violinist Ulf Hoelscher, the cellist Heinrich Schiff and the Alban Berg Quartet; British concerts include appearances with the London Symphony Orchestra, BBC Welsh Symphony and Royal Liverpool Philharmonic. Recordings: Schubert, Scarlatti and Mozart Sonatas, and Concertos by Beethoven with the Dresden Staatskapelle. Address: c/o Harold Holt Ltd, 31 Sinclair Road, London, W14 0NS, England.

ZACHARIASSEN Mathias, b. 1968, Stockholm, Sweden, Singer (Tenor). Education: Stockholm College of Opera, with Nicolai Gedda. Debut: Eurimedes in Telemann's Orfeo, at the Staatsoper Berlin and Innsbruck Festival of Early Music, 1994. Career: Opera engagements as the Singer in Der Rosenkavalier at Stockholm and Oslo, Mozart's Ferrando and Idamante at Brussels, Lenski and Elemer in Arabella at the 1996 Glyndebourne Festival; Season 1996-97 with Ferrando and Tamino at Graz, Don Ottavio in Oslo; Concerts have included Mozart's C Minor Mass in Oslo and Gothenburg, the Requiem with the Danish Radio SO and Schubert's A-flat Mass; Verdi Requiem at Norrkoping; Further concerts in Helsinki, Trondheim, Bad Kissingen and Amsterdam. Address: c/o IMG Artists, Media House, 3 Burlington Lane, London W4 2TH, England.

ZACHER Gerd, b. 6 July 1929, Meppen, Germany. Concert Organist. Eduction: Studied at Detmold with Gunter Bialas and in Hamburg. Career: Worked at the German Church, Santiago, before position as organist at the Lutheran Church, Hamburg Wellingsbutel, 1957-70; Director of the Church Music Institute at the Essen Hochschule and interpreter of many modern works; Has premiered music by John Cage (Variations, 1963), Mauricio Kagel (Phantasie, 1967), Ligeti (Two Studies, 1967) and Isang Yun (Fragment, 1975); Also a noted performer of works by Bach, Frescobaldi, Liszt and Cabezon.

ZADEK Hilde, b. 15 Dec 1917, Bromberg, Bydgoszcz, Austria. Soprano; Teacher. Education: Studied with Rose Pauly in Jerusalem and with Ria Ginster in Zurich. Debut: Vienna Staatsoper in 1947 as Aida. Career: Salzburg Festival from 1948 as Brangaene in Tristan und Isolde, Ariadne, Vitelia in La Clemenza di Tito, and in the premiere of Orff's Antigonae; Glyndebourne Festival in 1950 and 1951 as Ariadne and Donna Anna; Covent Garden in 1950 as Lisa in The Queen of Spades and Tosca; Further appearances in Edinburgh, Lisbon, Buenos Aires, Paris, Brussels, Amsterdam, New York, Rome and San Francisco; Professor at the Vienna Music Academy from 1967; Led masterclasses at Riva del Garda in Italy, 1990. Recordings include: Donna Anna in Don Giovanni, under Rudolf Moralt; Excerpts from Der Vogelhändler, Die Zigeunerbaron and Aida.

ZAGORZANKA Barbara, b. 31 Jul 1938, Kazimierzow, Poland. Soprano. Career: Sang at the Bydgoszcz Opera, 1960-67 as Butterfly, Gilda, Tosca and Tatiana, Poznan from 1967 as Halka, Micaela, Elisabeth de Valois, Marguerite, Odabella in Attila, Mozart's Countess and Fiordiligi, and Lucia, and Warsaw Opera from 1967 as Aida, Liu, Leonore, Norma, Abigaille, Sieglinde and Roxana in Szymanowski's King Roger; Has sung Halka on tour to the USA and Roxana in Vienna in 1989; Concert of Penderecki's Utrenja at Frankfurt in 1992; Further guest appearances in Paris including Lisa in The Queen of Spades, and Wiesbaden. Address: Polish National Opera, Grand Theatre, Plac Teatrainy 1, 00-950 Warsaw, Poland.

ZAGROSEK Lothar, b. 13 Nov 1942, Waging, Germany. Conductor; Composer. Education: Studied in Vienna with Hans Swarowsky and with Karajan and Bruno Maderna. Career: Appointments at opera houses in Salzburg, Kiel and Darmstadt, 1967-73; Frequent appearances with the London Sinfonietta from 1978, conducting music by Weill, Ligeti, Messiaen and Stravinsky; Engagements in USA, notably San Diego and Seattle, from 1984; Guest Conductor for BBC Symphony Orchestra; Musical Director, Paris Opera, 1986-88; Glyndebourne debut in 1987 with Cosi fan tutte; Conducted the premiere of Krenek's oratorio, Symeon Stylites at the 1988 Salzburg Festival; Conducted the Paris Opéra Orchestra in York Höller's Der Meister und Margarita in 1989, the last new production at the Paris Opéra, Palais Garnier, before the opening of the Opéra de la Bastille; Conducted the BBC Symphony Orchestra at the 1989 Promenade Concerts in music by Markevitch, Mozart, Mendelssohn, Kodály and Brahms's Ein Deutsches Requiem; Conducted Peter Sellars production of Die Zauberflöte at Glyndebourne in 1990; Promenade Concerts in 1991; Recordings include: Jonny spielt auf (Krenek), Goldschmidt's Der gewaltige Hahnrei and Die Vögel by Braunfels, Gruber's Cello Concerto, Schnittke's Piano Concerto, Haydn's 47th Symphony, Brahms No 1 and Mendelssohn's Violin Concerto; Appointed Music Director at the Stuttgart State Opera, 1996; Currently Chief Conductor of the Städtische Theater, Leipzig; Led the premiere of Das Mädchen by Lachenmann, Hamburg, 1997.

ZAHORTSEV Volodymr (Mykolayovych), b. 27 Oct 1944, Kiev, Ukraine. Composer. Education: Graduated from Tchaikovsky Conservatory, Kiev in 1968. Career: Joined avant-garde group of post-Stalinist composers in Kiev. Compositions include: Priskaski, song cycle, 1963; Violin Sonata, 1964; String Quartet, 1964; Sizes for 5 Instruments, 1965; Graduations for Chamber Group, 1966; Games for Chamber Orchestra, 1968; Symphony No 1, 1968; Music for 4 Strings, 1968; Sonata for Strings, Piano and Percussion, 1969; Rhythms for Piano, 1970; Symphony No 2 for Soprano, Tenor and Orchestra, 1978; Oboe Sonata, 1978; Music for 4 Strings, No 2, 1978; A Day In Pereyaslavl for Soloists, Chorus and Orchestra, 1979; In The Children's Room, cantata, 1979; Maty (Mother), Lvov, opera, 1985. Address: c/o Music Information of the Composers Union of the Ukraine, Ul Sofiuska 16/16, 252001 Kiev 1, Ukraine.

ZAIDEL Nahum, b. 20 Sep 1933, Russia. Musician; Conductor. m. 30 Aug 1976. Education: Graduated as Orchestra Soloist, Chamber Music Performer, and Teacher, P I Tchaikovsky State Conservtoire, Moscow, 1957; Studied in conducting with Professor Igor Markevitch and Professor Genady Rozhdestvensky, 1963-66. Career: Solo Flautist, Moscow Chamber Orchestra under Rudolf Barschai, 1957-58, Moscow Radio Symphony Orchestra under Genady Rozhdestvensky, 1959-72, and Jerusalem Symphony Orchestra, Israel, 1972-; Professor, Rubin Music Academy, Jerusalem, 1972-; Masterclasses for flute and appearances as guest conductor. Recordings: Works by Handel, Bach, Beethoven, Gluck, Hindemith, Prokofiev, Doppler, Vivaldi, Stamitz, Cimarosa, Salieri, Chaminade, Bloch, Dvorák, Stravinsky and Kurt Weill, for record and radio. Honour: 1st Prize for Flute, International Competition in Moscow, 1957. Hobbies: Chess; Photography. Address: Haviv Avshalom 4-7, Jerusalem 93802, Israel.

ZAJICK Dolora, b. 1960, Nevada, USA. Mezzo-Soprano. Education: Studied at the University of Nevada with Ted Puffer and at the Manhattan School of Music with Helen Vanni and Lou Galtiero; Further study with Donald Hall. Debut: San Francisco Opera in 1986 as Azucena. Career includes: Metropolitan Opera debut in 1988 as Azucena; Season 1988-89 with further debuts at Lyric Opera of Chicago, Vienna Staatsoper, Rome's Caracalla Festival and the Arena of Verona; Sang Rossini's Stabat Mater at the Cincinnati May Festival and Mahler's 8th Symphony at Washington DC under Rostropovich, Verdi's Requiem at Carnegie Hall and in Paris and London, Mahler's 2nd Symphony in Paris under Lorin Maazel; Season 1989-90 as Amneris and Azucena at the Metropolitan, Tchaikovsky's Maid of Orleans at Carnegie Hall, Il Trovatore in Toulouse and Florence, Aida in Reno, the Arena di Verona and at the Carcalla Festival, as Marfa in Khovanschina at San Francisco Opera, 1990, Eboli in Don Carlo at the Metropolitan, La Scala and in Reno, 1990; Sang Principessa in Adriana Lecouvreur at San Carlo, Naples, 1992, and Jezibaba in

Rusalka at the Metropolitan in 1993; Other opera houses include Barcelona, Houston, Florence, Orange Festival, and Covent Garden with debut in 1994; Sang Amneris at the Verona Arena, 1996; Sang in Cav and Pag double bill, Met 1997. Recordings include: La Forza del Destino and Verdi Requiem under Muti; Aida; Il Trovatore, 1991; Don Carlo, under Levine; Alexander Nevsky, under Rostropovich. Honour: Bronze Medal, Tchaikovsky International Competition, Moscow, 1982. Address: Edgar Vincent-Patrick Farrell Associates, 157 West 57th Street, Suite 502, New York, NY 10019, USA.

ZAK Jerzy, b. 31 Mar 1954, Lodz, Poland. Performer; Musicologist; Specialist in Historical Plucked Instruments, lute and guitar. m. Malgorzata Wojciechowska, 22 Sep 1984. Education: MA, Higher School of Music, Lodz, 1979; Conservatorio Superior de Musica, Alicante; Early Music Centre, London; ARCM, Royal College of Music, London, 1983. Career includes: Recitals in Poland, Greece, Hungary, France and UK; Chamber Musician and Basso Continuo Player on lute, theorbo and guitar; Several broadcasts on Polish Radio, and TV appearances, 1980-; Assistant, Academy of Music, Lodz, 1983-; Artistic Director, Days of Guitar Music, International Festival, Lodz, 1984, 1986; Consultant, Akademie Weiss-Institute for Lute Studies, Parc de Schoppenwihr, France, 1992-; Researcher, chamber music with plucked instruments. Honours: 2nd Prize, Polish Guitar Competition in 1976; 1st Prize, Guitar Competition, Hungary, 1977; Distinction and Prize, Volo Guitar Festival, Greece, 1979; 1st Prize, Early Music Competition, Manchester, UK, 1983. Address: Piotrkowska 145 m 21, 90-434 Lodz, Poland.

ZAKAI Mira, b. 1952, Jerusalem. Contralto. Education: Studied in Tel-Aviv with Jennie Tourel. Debut: Vienna in 1976 with Mahler's Rückert Lieder. Career: Further concerts with the Philharmonia Orchestra, Berlin Philharmonic (Mahler No 2 under Abbado), in New York (Bach B minor Mass), and throughout Germany (Das Lied von der Erde and Mahler No 3, 1987); Sang with Israel National Opera from 1990 in The Medium and Hansel and Gretel; Sang at Bonn in 1992 in Beethoven's Ninth; Opera includes Gluck's Orpheus with Scottish Opera, and Anne in Les Troyens with Opéra de Lyon. Recordings include: Mahler 2nd Symphony. Address: New Israeli Opera, 7-9 Jerusalem Boulevard, 68114 Tel-Aviv, Israel.

ZALEWSKI Wlodzimerz, b. 1949, Poland. Bass-Baritone. Career: Sang at the Lodz Opera, 1975-82 and Gelsenkirchen from 1982; Bregenz Festival in 1978 as the Dutchman, and Philadelphia in 1988 as Don Alfonso in Cosi fan Tutte; Professor at the Lodz Music Academy from 1981; Sang in the 1989 premiere of Michael Kohlhaas by Karl Kogler at the Landestheater, Linz; Appearances at Lodz and elsewhere as Boris Godunov; Other roles have included Hindemith's Cardillac, Kaspar in Der Freischütz, Basilio, Mustafa, Wotan and Scarpia; Frequent concert appearances.

ZAMBELLI Marco, b. 1965, Genoa, Italy. Conductor. Education: Studied at the Geneva Conservatoire (organ and composition). Career: Chorus Master at the Grasse Boys Choir, 1988-89, Opera de Lyon 1989-92 (including the premiere of Debussy's Rodrigue et Chimène); Other repertory includes all major operas of Mozart, L'Elisir d'amore, La Bohème, Butterfly, Poppea, Orfeo and Il Trovatore; Assistant with such conductors as John Eliot Gardiner (Manon Lescaut at Glyndebourne and other repertory with Monteverdi/EBS), Luciano Berio and Woldemar Nelsson; Season 1996-97 with Pergolesi/Cimarosa double bill at Messina, La Cenerentola at Ascoli and Don Giovanni for Opera Zuid; Haydn's Creation in Cogliou I, 1996; Butterfly, 1996, and Don Pasquale and Rigolette, 1997, at the Tenerife Opera Festival; Luisa Miller and Butterfly for Opera North and Manon Lescaut at the 1997 Glyndebourne Festival; Così fan tutte. Address: c/o Music Hall, 6 Windmill Street, London W1P 1HF, England.

ZAMBELLO Francesca, b. 24 Aug 1956, New York, USA. Producer; Artistic Director. Education: American School of Paris, 1974; BA, Colgate University, 1978. Career: Assistant Director, Lyric Opera of Chicago, 1981-82, and San Francisco Opera, 1983-84; Artistic Director, Skylight Music Theater, 1984-; Guest Producer, San Francisco Opera, Teatro La Fenice, Savonlinna Festival, Houston Grand Opera, National Opera of Iceland, Seattle Opera, San Diego Opera, Wolftrap Farm Park, Greater Miami Opera, Pesaro Festival, Opera Theatre of St Louis, Rome Opera, Théâtre Municipal de Lausanne, Teatro Regio, Parma, and Wexford Festival, 1988-89, The Devil and Kate and Der Templer und die Jüdin; Produced Mussorgsky's Khovanshchina for English National Opera and the premiere of Goehr's Arianna at Covent Garden, 1994-95; Staged Gluck's Iphigénie en Tauride for the 1997 Glimmerglass Festival. Honours: National Opera Institute Grant for 1 Year Apprenticeship in Stage Direction. Current Management: Columbia Artists. Address: c/o Columbia Artists, 165 West 57th Street, New York, NY 10019, USA.

ZAMBON Amadeo, b. 19 Jul 1934, Fontana, Villorba, Venice, Italy. Tenor Singer. Education: Studied with Marcello del Monaco. Career: Sang in La Bohème at the Teatro la Fenice in 1961; Istanbul, 1962-65 as Rodolfo, Cavaradossi, Calaf and Radames; Appearances in Milan, Naples, Palermo, Vienna, Paris, Monte Carlo, Stockholm and Frankfurt; Verona Arena in 1967; Sang in concert performances of Bellini's Il Pirata and La Straniera at New York in 1969 with Montserrat Caballé; Sang in Cairo in 1970 as Radames and Torre Del Lago in 1976 as Calaf in a performance of Turandot marking the 50th anniversary of Puccini's death; La Scala in 1977 in Giordano's Siberia and La Cena delle Beffe; Sang Verdi's Otello at Berne in 1985; Other roles in operas by Rossini, Mercadante, Donizetti and Mascagni.

ZAMBORSKY Stanislav, b. 12 April 1946, Kosice. Professor. m. Zlata Olachova, 8 July 1972, 2 daughters. Education: Konservatorium Kosice; Academy of Music & Dramatic Arts, Bratislava; Franz Liszt Academy, Budapest; Doctor Degree, Academy of Arts, Bratislava. Debut: Bratislava Music Festival. Career: Many Concerts with Orchestra and Recitals in Netherlands, France, Bulgaria, Poland, Soviet Union, Germany, Italy, Sweden, Spain, Belgium, Kuwait, Cuba, Korea, Jerusalem. Recordings: Mozart, Haydn Concerts; Mozart Piano Sonatas; Grieg Piano Concerto, Donau; Schuman, Sonata G-mol; Liszt, Dreams of Love, Au bord d une source, Death of Isolde. Honours: 2nd Prize, Prague, 1968; 4th Prize, Utrecht, 1969; Frico Kafenda Prize, Excellent Interpretation, Slovak Music, Bratislava, 1995. Address: Bieloruska 52, 821 06 Bratislava, Slovakia.

ZAMECNIK Evzen, b. 5 Feb 1939, Frydek Mistek, Czechoslovakia. Composer. Education: Studied in Brno at the Conservatory and the Janácek Academy of Musical Arts, 1963-68; Music Hochschule with Gunter Bialas, 1968-70, and in Prague at the Academy of Musical Arts. Career: Played violin in various Czech orchestras, 1963-81. Compositions include: A Farce About The Tub, opera, 1968; Ferda The Ant, stage piece for children and adults, 1977; Baggy The Beetle, Smetana Theatre, 1988. Address: c/o Cs armady 20, 160-56 Prague 6 - Bubenec, Czech Republic.

ZAMIR, b. 1953, USA. High Tenor. Education: Universities of Massachusetts at Amherst, and Maine at Portland-Gorham, and Chicago and San Francisco Conservatories of Music. Career: Has appeared since 1985 in major cities of Israel, USA, Iceland, Germany, England and Cyprus in wide range of concert and operatic music; Conductors include Marc Minkowski, Christopher Hogwood, Nicholas McGegan, and Richard Westenberg; Has performed as Male Soprano, Countertenor and Baritone as well as Tenor, currently specialising as high tenor, Tenore di Grazia; Has sung in Die Fledermaus in 1977, Cendrillon in 1986, A Midsummer Night's Dream in 1987, La Bohème in 1988, Lucia di Lammermoor, Mefistofele, Attila, Platée and Cavalleria Rusticana in 1988, La Clemenza di Tito and Alcina in 1990, and Riccardo Primo at Covent Garden in 1991.

ZAMPIERI Maria, b. 24 May 1951, Padua, Italy. Soprano. Education: Studied at the Padua Conservatory. Debut: Pavia in 1972. Career: La Scala Milan from 1977 as Amalia in I Masnadieri, Leonora in Il Trovatore and Elisabeth de Valois; Trieste as Elvira in Ernani; Lisbon as Amelia Boccanegra; Vienna Staatsopers from 1979 in Il Giuramento, Attila and Macbeth; Deutsche Oper Berlin and Verona Arena as Aida; Covent Garden debut in 1984 as Tosca; Other engagements in Munich, Buenos Aires, San Francisco, Bregenz, Bonn and Frankfurt; Sang Francesca da Rimini at Karlsruhe in 1986; Season 1987-88 as Norma at Nimes and Lady Macbeth at Spoleto; Stuttgart Staatsoper in 1990 as Tosca, Bregenz Festival in 1990 in the title role of La Wally; Debut as Salome at Vienna, 1991; Sang Suor Angelica at Zurich, 1996. Recordings include: Il Giuramento; Attila; Belisario; Macbeth. Address: Allied Artists, 42 Montpellier Square, London, SW7 1JZ, England.

ZANABONI Giuseppe, b. 25 Nov 1926, Pontelagoscuro, Italy. Organist; Conductor; Composer. m. Clelia Losi, 12 Sep 1951, 1 son, 1 daughter. Education: Accountancy studies; Organ Diploma in 1945; Composition diploma in 1949; Choral Music and Conducting in 1949. Debut: 1945. Career: Major solo organ concerts worldwide; Masterclasses in Europe and America; Chamber and Symphonic Orchestra Conductor in Italy; Director of State Music Conservatorium, Piacenza, 1968-89; Artistic Director, V L Ciampi instrumental group for diffusion of ancient music; Founder and Director, Gruppe V Legrenzio Ciampi, chamber music ensemble in Piacenza. Compositions include: Cantatas: Cantata a Roma, 1950, I Bambini di Terezin, 1991; Chamber Music: Quartetto, 1949, Liric Opera Myrica, 1949, Casello 83, 1956, Toccata for Organ, 1966, Meditazione per Archi and Organ, 1968, Luna Park, 1968, Profilo Di Un Organo, 2nd Suite, 1988, Quatuor Per Archi, 1988, Pinocchio In Fantasia, 1990, Studio Per Fagotto, 1992, Impressioni Sinfoniche, 1992; Choral Music: La Fravezzosa - Carme Madricalis, 1984. Recordings: 10 Records of organ music in series, Antichi Organi Italiani, and instrumental music recorded. Publications: Ciampi, 30 anni di musica a Piacenza, 1987. Hobby: Photography. Address: Via Giulio Alberoni 33, 29100 Piacenzo, Italy.

ZANASI Mario, b. 8 Jan 1927, Bologna, Italy. Baritone. Education: Studied at the Conservatorio Martini, Bologna; La Scala Opera School. Debut: Cesena in 1954 in Lohengrin. Career: Sang widely in Italy and at opera houses in Portugal, France, Belgium and Germany; Metropolitan Opera from 1958 as Sharpless in Butterfly, Escamillo, Marcello in La Bohème, Amonasro and Enrico in Lucia di Lammermoor; Sang at Covent Garden in 1958 and Verona Arena, 1957-72; Further appearances in Paris, Vienna, Chicago, Dallas, Miami, San Francisco and Munich. Recordings: Giuletta e Romeo by Zandonai; Madame Sans-Gêne by Giordano; Madama Butterfly; Maria di Rohan by Donizetti.

ZANAZZO Alfredo, b. 14 Oct 1946, Imperia, Italy. Bass Singer. Education: Studied with Tancredi Pasero. Debut: Verona Arena in 1981 as the King in Aida. Career: Verona Arena, 1982-89, as Ramphis and Timur; Sang Wagner's Dutchman at Treviso in 1981, La Scala Milan in 1982 as Narbal in Les Troyens, and the King of Scotland in Ariodante; Season 1986-87 as Colline in La Bohème at the Paris Opera, Padre Guardiano at Rome, Zaccaria and Masetto at Turin and Ramphis at the Metropolitan; Appearances at Luxor and the Vienna Staatsoper as Ramphis, Macerata Festival as Raimondo in Lucia di Lammermoor; Zurich Opera in 1988 as Banquo and Walter Furst in Guillaume Tell; Further engagements at the Geneva Opera as Pluto in Monteverdi's Orfeo, at Frankfurt as Raimondo, in Toronto as Procida in Les Vêpres Siciliennes and at Las Palmas as Alvise in La Gioconda; Teatro Margherita Genoa in 1991 as Roucher in La Gioconda; Sang Pagano in i Lombardi at Piacenza, 1995. Address: c/o Opernhaus Zurich, Falkenstrasse 1, CH-8008 Zurich, Switzerland.

ZANCANARO Giorgio, b. 9 May 1939, Verona, Italy. Baritone. Debut: Teatro Nuovo Milan in I Puritani. Career: Sang widely in Italy from 1971; International career from 1977, notably in London, Frankfurt, Rome, Hamburg, Paris and Zurich; Milan La Scala debut in 1981 as Ford in Falstaff; Metropolitan Opera debut in 1982 as Renato in Un Ballo in Maschera; Macerata Festival in 1983 as Posa in Don Carlos; Florence, 1984-85 as Germont and Posa; Covent Garden in 1985 as Gerard in Andrea Chénier; Other roles include Verdi's Rigoletto, Luna and Ezio in Attila, Escamillo, Tonio in Pagliacci and Albert in Werther; Hamburg and La Scala in 1988 as Count Luna and William Tell; Sang Ezio in Attila at Covent Garden in 1990, and in Donizetti's Parisina d'Este in Florence in 1990; Sang Michele in Il Tabarro at Zurich, 1996. Recordings include: Il Trovatore, conducted by Giulini. Address: c/o Stafford Law Associates, 6 Barham Close, Weybridge, Surrey, KT13 9PR, England.

ZANDER Benjamin, b. England. Conductor. Education: Studied with Benjamin Britten and Imogen Holst at Aldeburgh; At Florence with cellist Gaspar Cassado, at the Academica Chigiana in Siena, the State Conservatory Cologne and London University; Graduate work at Harvard and in New York. Career: Faculty member of the New England Conservatory from 1968, conducting the Youth Philharmonic Orchestra and the Conservatory's SO; Ten International tours with the Youth PO, including South America, 1995; Artistic Director of the New England Conservatory at Walnut Hill School, 1986-; Guest conductor with American orchestras and in the Far East, Russia, Italy, Germany and Israel; Founding Director with the Boston Philharmonic, leading it in many concerts; Debut with the London Philharmonic Orchestra, January 1995, with Mahler's Sixth, returning for the Ninth Symphony. Recordings include: Mahler's 6th Symphony, Beethoven's Ninth and The Rite of Spring, with the Boston PO. Address: c/o Boston Philharmonic Orchestra, P O Box 3000, Cambridge, MA 02238, USA.

ZANETTOVICH Renato, b. 28 July 1921, Trieste, Italy. Violinist. m. Bianca Negri, 28 June 1947, 3 sons. Education: Violin Diploma. Debut: With the Trio Di Trieste in 1933. Career: Concerts and records with Trio Di Trieste worldwide; Violin Teacher at Conservatories of Bolzano, 1950-55, Trieste, 1955-70 and Venice, 1970-86. Recordings: Numerous recordings. Publications: Revision of Etudes by Kayser Op 20, Mazas Op 36, Dont Op 37, Sitt Op 32; Scale and Arpeggio Exercises, 5 books. Honours: Accademico di S Cecilia; Grande Ufficiale dell'Ordine Al Merito della Repubblica Italiana. Membership: Rotary Club, Trieste. Address: Via Catraro 9, Trieste, Italy.

ZANGERLE Helmut, b. 6 Mar 1930, Lermoos, Tyrol, Austria. Musician (Flautist). m. Annemarie Zatschek, 21 June 1960, 1 son, 1 daughter. Education: Innsbruck Conservatory; Scholarship, Paris Conservatory; Studied with Gaston Crunelle (Diploma, 1954), André Jaunet, Zurich, and Réné Le Roy, Paris. Debut: Soloist, 1954. Career: Co-Principal Flute Player, Innsbruck Symphony, 1957-93; Member, Principal Flautist, Mozarteum Orchestra, Salzburg; Soloist with orchestras in Europe, Asia and Africa; Duo with harpist Annemarie Zatschek, numerous concert tours; Also with Quintet, flute, violin, viola, violoncello and harp; Flute Teacher, Mozarteum Conservatory, Salzburg, 1962-86; Member of Jury, national and international competitions. Honours: Diploma, International Competition, Munich, 1956. Memberships:

National Flute Association Inc, USA; World Institute of Achievement, USA. Address: Tiefenbachstrasse 19, A-5161 Elixhausen, Salzburg, Austria.

ZANNINI Laura, b. 4 Apr 1937, Trieste, Italy. Mezzo-Soprano. Education: Studied at the Conservatorio Benedetto Marcell in Venice, with Gilda dalla Rizza, and with Bruno Maderna. Debut: Spoleto in 1955 as Isabella in L'Italiana in Algeri. Career: Sang leading roles at La Scala Milan, Genoa, Palermo, Naples, Parma, Venice, Turin and Trieste; Sang at Verona Arena in 1957, 1967, 1979-80, 1986, and Piccola Scala in 1966 in the premiere of Flavio Testi's Albergi dei Poveri; Further appearances at the Maggio Musicale Fiorentino, the State Operas of Vienna and Munich, the Paris Opera, Brussels, Bordeaux, Wiesbaden, Copenhagen, London, Edinburgh, Moscow and Budapest; Sang Alisa in Lucia di Lammermoor at Bari and Tisbe in La Cenerentola at Glyndebourne, 1983; Also sang in operas by Henze, Britten, Menotti, Poulenc, Stravinsky, Schoenberg and Zandonai; Sang Caterina in L'Amico Fritz at Livorno, 1996. Recordings: Tisbe in La Cenerentola; Flora in La Traviata with Callas; Mascagni's Isabeau.

ZANOLLI Silvana, b. 14 Oct 1928, Fiume, Italy. Soprano. m. Otello Borgonova. Education: Studied at the Milan Opera School and with Luciano Tomerilli and Tomaso Japelli. Debut: La Scala Milan in 1951 in La Buona Figiuola, by Piccinni. Career: Appearances in leading roles at Rome, Palermo, Bologna, Parma, Turin, Trieste, Naples and Venice; Festival engagements at Florence and Rome with guest showings at Buenos Aires, the State Operas of Vienna, Stuttgart and Munich, at Brussels, Cologne, Rio de Janeiro, Geneva, Barcelona, Lisbon and London Covent Garden; Verona Arena, 1957-58 and Glyndebourne, 1959-60 as Clorinda in La Cenerentola; Also sang in Mexico City, Monte Carlo and New York at Metropolitan Opera. Recordings: Amelia al Ballo by Menotti; Cimarosa's Il Matrimonio Segreto; Il Campiello by Wolf-Ferrari.

ZANOTELLI Hans, b. 1927, Wuppertal, Germany. Conductor. m. Ingeborg Schlosser. Education: Student in Cologne. Career: Choirmaster, Solingen, 1945; Conductor, Wuppertal in 1950, Dusseldorf, 1951-54, Bonn, 1954-55, Hamburg State Opera, 1955-57; General Music Director, Darmstadt, 1957-63, Augsburg, 1963-72; Chief Conductor, Stuttgart Philharmonic Orchestra, 1971-; Guest Conductor, Dresden Staatskapelle, 1964-67, Bavarian State Opera, 1968-71, Wurttemberg State Opera; Tours of many European countries; Leader, Der Rosenkavalier at Dresden for 300th anniversary; Leader, Verdi's Requiem at Dresden for anniversary of destruction of city in World War II. Recordings: Many. Address: Stuttgarter Philharmoniker, Leonhardplatz 28, D-7000 Stuttgart, Germany.

ZARITZKAYA Irina, b. 1940, Kiev, Ukraine. Concert Pianist. Career: Appearances in Eastern Europe from 1960, notably with the Russian State Orchestra and the Moscow, Warsaw and Kiev Philharmonics; Conductors included Kondrashin, Barshai, Ahronovitch and Natan Rachlin; Broadcasting engagements in Poland and Russia; Emigrated to Israel in 1972, becoming Senior Lecturer at the Rubin Academy; Recitals at the South Bank in London and concerts with the LSO, Royal Philharmonic and City of Birmingham Symphony; Tours to France, Spain, USA, Argentina, Colombia, Brazil, Italy, Hong Kong and Taiwan; Duo recitals with violinist Boris Belkin; Currently resident in London and is Professor at the Royal College of Music; Recitals with cellist Natalia Gutman and performances throughout Western Europe. Honours include: Second Prize, Chopin Competition in Warsaw, 1960; Honorary Member, Royal College of Music, 1980. Address: Robert Gilder and Co, Enterprise House, 59-65 Upper Ground, London, SE1 1PQ, England.

ZAROU Jeannette, b. 1942, Ramallah, Palestine. Soprano. Education: Studied at The Royal Conservatory of Music in Toronto with Irene Jessner, Halina Wyszkowski and Herman Geiger-Torel. Debut: Priestess in Aida with Canadian Opera at Toronto, 1964. Career: Sang Liu in Turandot for Canadian Opera in 1965; Member of the Deutsche Oper am Rhein Dusseldorf from 1967; Guest appearances in Toronto, Deutsche Oper Berlin, Hamburg and Munich State Opera, Cologne, Frankfurt, Karlsruhe, Nuremberg, Bordeaux and Rouen; Other roles have included Mimi, Marguerite, Ilia in Idomeneo, Pamina, and Sophie in Rosenkavalier; Modern repertoire has included Miss Wordsworth in Albert Herring and Blanche in Dialogues des Carmélites; Many concert appearances. Recordings include: Requiem by Draeske.

ZAWADZKA-GOLOSZ Anna, b. 1 Dec 1955, Krakow, Poland. Composer. m. Jerry Golosz, 6 Jul 1986. Education: Diploma in Theory of Music, Academy of Music, Krakow, 1981; Studies in composition at the Academy of Music, Krakow under Krystyna Moszumanska-Nazar; Diploma, Academy of Music, Krakow and at the Hochschule für Musik, Theater und Tanz in Essen under Wolfgang Hufschmidt. Career: Teacher of Theory of Music, 1981-; Assistant at Academy of Music in Krakow; Performances in Poland and abroad including Warsaw Autumn - International Festival of Contemporary Music, 1986. Compositions: A Duo for Double Bass and Tape, 1980; Esoterikos for Soprano and Oboe Quartet, 1984; Senza for Double Bass, 1984; Girare for Percussion and Tape, 1986; Obraz w Pieciu Ujeciach (The Picture In Five Aspects), 1987; Vitrail II for Clarinet, Cello, Accordion and Vibraphone, 1988. Membership: Polish Section of ISCM. Address: ul Basztowa 5-28, 31-134 Krakow, Poland.

ZAZOFSKY Peter, b. 1955, Boston, USA. Concert Violinist. Education: Studied with Joseph Silverstein, Dorothy DeLay and Ivan Galamian and at the Curtis Institute of Music. Career: Frequent appearances from 1977 with such orchestras as the Berlin and Rotterdam Philharmonics, the Vienna Symphony and the Amsterdam Concertgebouw Orchestra; North American engagements at Atlanta, Baltimore, Boston, Minnesota, Montreal, Philadelphia, San Francisco, Toronto and Vancouver; Tour of the USA with the Danish Radio Orchestra and recitals at the Kennedy Center and New York's Carnegie Hall; Further concerts in Israel and throughout Europe with such conductors as Dutoit, Zinman, Ormany, Tennstedt and Ozawa; 1978 recital tour of South America; Season 1995-96 with concertos by Bartók and Mendelssohn in Germany and Belgium; Also plays Nielsen and Bernstein (Serenade). Honours: Prize winner at the 1977 Wieniawski Competition, 1978 Montreal International and 1980 Queen Elisabeth of the Belgians Competition, Brussels; Avery Fisher Career Grant, 1985. Address: c/o Künstler Sekretariat am Gasteig, Rosenheimerstr 52, 81669 Munich, Germany.

ZAZZO Lawrence, b. 1970, Philadelphia, USA. Singer (Counter-tenor). Education: King's College, Cambridge, and Royal College of Music, with David Lowe. Career: Concerts include Bach Cantatas at the 1997 Lufthansa Festival, London, Vivaldi, Nisi Dominus and Handel's Messiah with the Israel Camerata, Season 1996-97; Opera debut as Oberon in A Midsummer Night's Dream at the RAM, London, 1996; Title role in Handel's Arminio and Alessandro Severo for the London Handel Festival, Bacco in Goehr's Arianna at Cambridge, 1996, Athamas in Semele at Santa Fe Opera; 1998 season includes Unulfo in Rodelinda at the Karlsruhe Handel Festival and with the Glyndebourne Touring Opera, title role in Cavalli's Giasone at the Spoleto Festival in Charleston, South Carolina. Recordings include: Purcell's Jubilate, Britten's Rejoice in the Lamb, Bernstein's Chichester Psalms and Pergolesi's Stabat Mater. Address: c/o Portland Wallis, 50 Great Portland Street, London W1N 5AH, England.

ZEANI Virginia, b. 21 Oct 1925, Solovastru, Rumania. Singer (Soprano). m. Nicola Rossi-Lemeni, 1957 (dec. 1991). Education: Studied in Bucharest with Lucia Angel and Lydia Lipkovska, and with Aureliano Pertile in Milan. Debut: Bologna, 1948, as Violetta. Career: London debut, Stoll Theatre, 1953, as Violetta; La Scala, 1956, as Cleopatra in Giulio Cesare; Sang Blanche in premiere of Dialogues des Carmélites, 1957; Vienna and Paris debuts, 1957; Verona Arena, 1956-63; Took part in revivals of Donizetti's Maria di Rohan (Naples 1965), Rossini's Otello (Rome 1968), Verdi's Alzira (Rome 1970); Further appearances at Covent Garden, 1959, Metropolitan, 1966, and Budapest, Bucharest, Mexico City, Rio de Janeiro, Zurich, Amsterdam, Belgrade, Moscow, Madrid; Other roles include Aida, Desdemona, Tosca, Manon and Manon Lescaut, Lucia di Lammermoor, Elvira (I Puritani), Magda Sorel in The Consul (Menotti); Further engagements, Barcelona, Lisbon, Leningrad, Houston, Philadelphia, Berlin and New Orleans, 1966; Sang at Barcelona, 1977-78, as Giordano's Fedora; Sang 67 roles, 648 times Traviata around the world; Professor of Voice, 1980-, Distinguished Professor, 1994-, Emeritus Professor, 1995-, Indiana University School of Music, USA. Recordings: La Traviata; Rossini's Otello; Elisa e Claudio by Mercadante; Rossini's Zelmira; Alzira; Le Serva Padrona. Honours: 34 awards including: Gold Medal, Egypt, 1951; Gold Medal, Barcelona, 1963; Maschera d'Argento, 1965-70; Arena d'Oro, 1966; Diapason d'Oro, 1968. Memberships: Accademia Tiberina-Roma; Commendatore of Italian Republic; Soroptimist Club of Rome. Address: 2616 Robins Bow, Bloomington, IN 47401, USA.

ZEAVIN Carol, b. 2 May 1948, San Bernardino, CA, USA. Violinist. Education: Studied in New York. Career: Co-Founder of Columbia String Quartet, 1977, initially called Schoenberg String Quartet; Many performances in the standard and modern repertory, including the premieres of Wuorinen's Archangel and Second Quartet, 1978, 1980, Roussaki's Ephermeris, 1979, and quartets by Morton Feldman, 1980, Wayne Peterson, 1984, and Larry Bell, 1985; In 1979 at Abraham Goodman House, NY, played in the premiere of Berg's Lyric Suite with recently discovered vocal finale. Recordings include: String Quartet No 3 by Lukas Foss and Ned Rorem's Mourning Song.

ZEBAIDA Robin, b. London, England. Pianist. Education: St Paul's School; Music Exhibitioner at New College, Oxford, MA; Studied privately with Ann Driver, Miles Coverdale, Leslie Howard and as postgraduate at Royal College of Music. Debut: Queen Elizabeth Hall, 1992. Career: Resident in Hong Kong, 1987-89; Taught privately and at Academy for Performing Arts; Masterclasses/lecture recitals in Europe and Overseas for British Council; International radio and TV broadcasts for various networks including BBC, HTV, RTHK and European Stations; Concertos and solo recitals in UK, USA, Europe and Far East. Compositions: March for HMS Invincible, for wind band; Suite Orientale, for piano solo. Contributions to: Music reviews and interviews for BBC World Service; RTHK; Musical Opinion; Classical Music; Classical Piano. Hobbies: Backgammon; Table tennis; Modern Languages. Address: c/o Maureen Lunn, Top Farm, Parish Lane, Hedgerley, Bucks SL2 3JH, England.

ZECCHILLO Giuseppe, b. 18 Dec 1929, Sao Paulo, Brazil. Baritone. Education: Studied at the Conservatorio Giuseppe Verdi at Milan and with Aureloano Pertile and Carlo Taglibus. Debut: Teatro Nuovo Milan in 1953 as Germont in La Traviata. Career: Leading roles at La Scala, Rome, Bologna, Naples, Palermo, Parma, Turin, Trieste and Venice; Festival engagements at Caracalla, Verona, 1972-85, as Sharpless in Butterfly in 1983 and Florence, Maggio Musicale; Further appearances at the New York City Opera and in San Francisco and Monte Carlo; Distinguished in contemporary as well as standard repertory. Recordings include: Nina by Paisiello.

ZECHBERGER Gunther, b. 24 Apr 1951, Zams, Tyrol, Austria. Composer; Conductor. Education: Studied at the Innsbruck Conservatory, 1968-74 and at University of Innsbruck with Witold Rowicki and Boguslaw Schaeffer. Career: Founder and Conductor of the Tyroler Ensemble für Neue Musik, 1984. Compositions include: Trio for Clarinet, Horn and Bassoon, 1973; Trio for Violins, 1975; Das Neue Preislied for Women's Chorus and Speaker, 1975; Schlus Stuck for Mixed Chorus and Orchestra, 1979; Mass for Mixed Chorus and Orchestra, 1979; Trombone Quartet, 1980; Stabat Mater for Mixed Chorus, 1981; Im Nebel for Mezzo and Orchestra, 1982; Study for 12 Strings, 1983; Hendekegon for 26 Instruments, 1984; Tieferschuttert for Mezzo, Trombone and Guitar, 1984; String Quartet, 1985; Chorus for 5 Musicians, 1985; Stabat Mater II for Mezzo and Ensemble, 1985-88; Kammermusik for Conductor and 5 Musicians, 1986; Dear Mr J, 1987; Interview for Tape, 1987; Guitar Concerto, 1988; Duet for Guitars, 1988. Address: c/o AKM, III Baumanstrasse 8-10, Postfach 334-338, 1031 Vienna, Austria.

ZECHLIN Ruth, b. 22 Jun 1926, Grosshartmannsdorf, Germany. Composer; Harpsichordist. Education: Studied composition with Johann Nepomuk David, organ with Karl Straube and Gunther Ramin, 1943-49. Career: Lecturer in Music from 1950 and Professor of Composition from 1969 at the Berlin Musikhochschule; Member of the Akademie der Künste Berlin in 1970. Compositions include: Reineke Fuchs, opera for actors, 1967; Ballet, La Vita, 1983; Opera Die Salamandrin und Die Bildsäule, 1989; Opera Die Reise, 1991; Orchestral: 2 Violin Concertos, 1963, 1990, 3 Symphonies, 1965, 1966, 1971, 19 Great Mixed Chamber Music, 1966-93, 2 Chamber Symphonies, 1967, 1973, Piano Concerto, 1974; 4 Organ Concertos, 1974, 1975, 1980, 1984; 2 Harpsichord Concertos, 1975, 1986, Briefe, 1978, Situationen, 1980, Musik für Orchester, 1980, Metamorphosen, 1982, Musik Zu Bach, 1983, Kristallisation, 1987, Stufen, 1993; Chamber: 6 String Quartets, 1959-77, Reflexionen for 14 Strings, 1979, Konstellationen for 10 Winds, 1985, Akzente Und Flächen for 5 Percussions, 1993, Circulations for 8 Percussions, 1994; Vocal: Lidice Kantante, 1958, Canzoni Notte for Baritone and Orchestra, 1974, Der Sieg Von Guernica for 4 Voices, 1975, Das Hohelied for Tenor and Orchestra, 1979, Das A Und Das O for Mezzo Solo, 1990; Piano, harpsichord and organ music. Honours: Gothepreis Berlin, 1962; Kunstpreis, 1965; Hanns-Eisler-Preis, 1968; Nationalpreis der DDR, 1975, 1982; Heidelberger Künstlerinnenpreis, 1996; Verdienstkreuz 1st class; BRD. Memberships: Akademie der Künste Berlin; Freie Akademi der Künste Mannheim. Address: Waldeckstrasse 14, D-94086 Griesbach, IR, Germany.

ZEDDA Alberto, b. 2 Jan 1928, Milan, Italy. Conductor; Musicologist. Education: Studied at the Milan Conservatory with Galliera, Fait, Votto and Giulini. Debut: Conducted the Polytechnic Chamber Group of Milan, 1956. Career: Taught at the Cincinnati College of Music, 1957-59; Coached winners of American vocal competitions, 1959-61; Conducted Italian operas at the Deutsche Oper Berlin, 1961-63, and New York City Opera from 1963; Guest Conductor with leading orchestras and opera companies in the USA, Israel and Europe; Covent Garden debut in 1975 with Il Barbiere di Siviglia; Co-editor with Philip Gossett of the complete edition of Rossini's works, Rossini Foundation; Conducted Il Barbiere with the company of Cologne Opera at Hong Kong, 1989, Il Turco in Italia at the Teatro de la Zarzuela, Madrid, 1990, La Scala di seta at the 1990 Pesaro Festival, Semiramide, 1992; Conducted La Cenerentola at Parma, 1996. Publications: Critical edition of Il Barbiere Di Siviglia, 1969; Further editions of Torvaldo e Dorliska and La Gazza Ladra by Rossini. Address: c/o Philip Gossett, Department of Music, University of Chicago, 5345 Ellis Avenue, IL 60637, USA.

ZEDNIK Heinz, b. 21 Feb 1940, Vienna, Austria. Tenor. Education: Studied with Marga Wissmann and at the Vienna Conservatory. Debut: Graz in 1964 in La Forza del Destino. Career: Vienna Staatsoper from 1964, notably in the 1976 premiere of Von Einem's Kabale und Liebe; Guest appearances in Nice, Moscow, Montreal and Baden; Bayreuth Festival from 1970 as David, the Steersman, Mime and Loge; Salzburg Festival in 1984 in the premiere of Berio's Un Re in Ascolto; Other roles include Mozart's Pedrillo and Monostatos, Beethoven's Jacquino and Peter the Great in Zar und Zimmermann; Salzburg Festival in 1986 in the premiere of Penderecki's Die schwarze Maske; Pedrillo, 1987-89; Mime at New York Metropolitan, 1989-90, also televised; Sang Baron Laur in Weill's Silbersee at the 1996 London Proms. Recordings: Parsifal; Lustige Weiber Von Windsor; Le nozze di Figaro; Wozzeck; Salome; Wiener Blut; Die Zauberflöte; Das Rheingold and Siegfried from Bayreuth. Address: c/o Allied Artists, 42 Montpellier Square, London, SW7 1JZ, England.

ZEFFIRELLI (G) Franco (Corsi), b. 12 Feb 1923, Florence, Italy. Opera, Film and Theatrical Producer. Career: Early career as actor, under Visconti; Began opera in 1948; Producer and Designer of La Cenerentola, La Scala Milan in 1953; Responsible for many famous productions including Maria Callas in Tosca, and Joan Sutherland in Lucia di Lammermoor; Designs for opening production of Metropolitan Opera at Lincoln Center in 1966 of Barber's Antony and Cleopatra; Films of operas include La Bohème, Cavalleria Rusticana, Pagliacci, Carmen, Tosca, La Traviata and Otello; Numerous other non-operatic subjects; Producer and Designer of La Traviata and Don Giovanni at the Metropolitan, 1989-90, and Don Carlos for the opening of the 1992-93 season at La Scala; Il Trovatore in 1998. Address: c/o Metropolitan Opera, One Lincoln Plaza, New York, NY 10023, USA.

ZEHETMAIR Thomas, b. 23 Nov 1961, Salzburg, Austria. Concert Violinist. Education: Studied at the Salzburg Mozarteum; Masterclasses with Max Rostal and Nathan Milstein. Career: Concert appearances with the Boston, Chicago, Cleveland, Minnesota and San Francisco Orchestras, Philharmonia, English and Scottish Chamber, BBC Symphony, City of Birmingham, Rotterdam Philharmonic and Concertgebouw, Stockholm Philharmonic and Leipzig Gewandhaus; Conductors have included Blomstedt, Eschenbach, Harnoncourt, Horst Stein, Sawallisch, Leppard, Dohnanyi, Marriner, Rattle and Norrington; Guest engagements at international music festivals; Chamber music with Gidon Kremer at Lockenhaus; London recital debut at Wigmore Hall in 1993; Concerto engagements with the BBC Philharmonic, Bournemouth Symphony, Northern Sinfonia and Scottish Chamber Orchestra, 1993; Edinburgh Festival, 1995 with Bach's works for solo violin; Berlioz Harold in Italy, London Proms, 1997; Repertoire includes concertos by Szymanowski, Bach, Bartok, Henze, Berg and Prokofiev, in addition to the standard works; Founder of the Zehetmair Quartet. Recordings: Beethoven's Kreutzer and Spring Sonatas, Concertos by Brahms, Joseph and Michael Haydn, Mendelssohn, Mozart, Schumann and Sibelius; Berg's Chamber Concerto and Schoenberg's Violin Concerto under Heinz Holliger; Szymanowski, Concertos no 1 and 2 with Sir Simon Rattle; Bartok Concertos no 1 and 2 with Ivan Fischer. Address: c/o Sue Lubbock Concert Management, 25 Courthope Road, London NW3 2LE, England.

ZEITLIN Zvi, b. 21 Feb 1923, Dubrovna, USSR. Concert Violinist; Professor of Violin. m. Marianne Langner, 1 son, 1 daughter. Education: Juilliard School of Music; Hebrew University, Jerusalem. Debut: New York, 1951. Career: Professor, Eastman School of Music, University of Rochester, New York; Head of Violin Department, Music Academy of the West, Santa Barbara, California; Concert tours worldwide; Appearances with leading world symphony orchestras; Broadcasts on radio and TV; Editor, newly discovered Nardini Concerto, 1958; Currently working on 6 other Nardini concertos. Recordings: Schoenberg Violin Concerto; Rochberg Variations; Schumann Sonatas; Schubert Trios with Eastman Trio. Honours: American Israel Society Award for furthering cultural relations between USA and Israel, 1957; Commission of violin concerto by Gunther Schuller by Eastman School of Music and National Endowment of the Arts; Commission of violin concerto by Carlos Surinach by Music Academy of the West Summer Festival; Commission of Paul Ben Haim Violin Concerto for Zeitlin, American Israel Cultural Foundation; 1st Kilbourn Professor, Eastman School of Music. Memberships: The Bohemians, New York; University of Rochester Faculty Club; New York State Teachers' Association; American Federation of Musicians. Current Management: Thea Dispeker, New York City, USA. Address: 204 Warren Avenue, Rochester, NY 14618, USA.

ZELJENKA Ilja, b. 21 Dec 1932, Bratislava, Czechoslovakia. Composer. m. Maria Kimlickova, 13 Apr 1957, 1 daughter. Education: Gymnasium 1943-51; Compositions studies at Academy of Music and Drama, Bratislava, 1951-56. Debut: 1956. Career: Dramaturgist of the Slovak Philharmony, 1957-61; With Slovak Radio, 1961-68; Freelance Composer, 1968-90; Chairman of the Slovak Music Union, 1990-91; President of the International Festival of Contemporary Music, Melos-Ethos, 1991. Compositions: 5 Symphonies, 6 string quartets, 4 piano sonatas, 2 piano concertos, clarinet concerto, violin concerto, Dualogues for Violoncello and Chamber String Orchestra, Oswienczym Cantata, 2 piano quartets, Polymetric Music for 4 String Quintets, music for clarinet, piano and percussion, Metamorphoses XV for Chamber Ensemble and Reciter, Galgenlieder for Soprano, String Quartet, Clarinet, Flute and Piano, Mutations for Soprano, Bass, Wind Quintet and Percussion, Astecian Songs for Soprano, Piano and Percussion, and Plays for 13 Singers and Percussion. Hobbies: Astronomy; Biology. Address: 11A Zeljenka, Slavicie udolie 14, 81102 Bratislava, Slovakia.

ZELTSER Mark, b. 3 Apr 1947, Kischiniev, Russia. Concert Pianist. Education: Graduated Moscow Conservatory, 1971. Career: Resident in USA from 1976; Played at the 1977 Salzburg Festival under Karajan and performed in Berlin with the Philharmonic in 1979; Debut with the New York Philharmonic, 1980; Further appearances with leading orchestras in Europe and America. Address: c/o Berlin Philharmonic Orchestra, Philharmonie, Matthaikirchstrasse 1, W-1000 Berlin, Germany.

ZELTER Sandra, b. 1972, Paris, France. Singer (Soprano). Education: Graduated the Paris Conservatoire 1994 (study with Christine Eda-Pierre), Guildhall School, London, 1996. Career: Covent Garden recital 1995, with appearances in Cosi fan tutte and Elektra 1997; Further engagements at Tatiana at the Paris Conservatoire, Linda di Chamounix at the Guildhall, Micaela for Mid Wales Opera and Bizet's Leila for English Touring Opera; Arminda, La Finta Giardiniera for Opera Zurich in the Netherlands; Concerts include Gounod's Requiem in France and recitals in Oxford and at the Wigmore Hall, London. Honours include: 1994 James Gulliver Prize; Bourse Lavoisier Scholarship; Prize Winner at the 1995 Maggie Teyte Competition. Address: Ingpen & Williams Ltd, 26 Wadham Road, London SW15 2LR, England.

ZEMTSOVSKY Izaly (Iosifovich), b. 22 Feb 1936, Leningrad, Russia. Ethnomusicologist. m. Alma Kunanbay, 29 Jan 1982. Education: MA, Philology, University of Leningrad, 1958; Diploma, Russian Folklore, Musicology and Composition, 1955-60, 1961; Leningrad Conservatoire; MA, PhD. Debut: 1958. Career: Senior Research Fellow, Head of Folklore Department, Leningrad State Institute of Theatre, Music and Cinema (now Russian Institute of History of the Arts, 1990-), 1960-; Head, Department of Traditional Culture, Russian Pedagogic University; Vice-President, Jewish Musical Society of St Petersburg, 1992; Vice President, International Delphic Council, 1994; President, Delphic Movement in Russia, 1995; Fellow, Institute for Research in the Humanities, University of Wisconsin-Madison, 1995-. Publications include: Russian Folk Song, 1964; The Russian Song, 1967; Songs of Toropets: Songs of The Homeland of Moussorgsky, 1967; Song Hunters, 1967; The Poetry of Peasant Holidays, 1970; The Melodics of Calendar Songs, 1975; Folklore and The Composer, 1978; Tracing the Melody Vesnianka from P Tchaikovsky's Piano Concerto: The Historical Morphology of the Folk Songs, 1987; Russian Folk Music, in Grove's Dictionary of Music and Musicians, 1980; Boris Assaf'yev on Folk Music, 1987; Jewish Folk Songs: An Anthology, 1994. Address: Folklore Department, Institute of History of the Arts, 190000 St Petersburg, Isaakievskaja pl 5, Russia.

ZENATY Ivan, b. 1960, Czechoslovakia. Concert Violinist. Education: Studied at the Prague Conservatoire and the Academy of Arts, Weimar with Andre Gertler, Zurich with Nathan Milstein. Career: Solo appearances with all leading Czech orchestras in Austria, Bulgaria, England, Finland, Holland, Italy, Poland, Spain, Russia, Switzerland and Yugoslavia; Festival engagements in Prague, Dubrovnik, Moscow, Sofia, Berlin and Havana; Repertoire includes concertos by Bach, Haydn, Mozart, Vivaldi, Myslivicek, Sibelius, Dvorák, Vieuxtemps and Kalabis, Bach solo sonatas and Telemann solo fantasies, sonatas by Mozart, Beethoven, Vanhal, Schubert, Schumann, Brahms, Prokofiev, Dvorák, Janácek and Martinu. Recordings: Various albums. Honours include: First Prize, Prague Spring Festival Competition, 1987. Address: Pragokoncert, Maltezske nam 1, 118 13 Prague 1, Czech Republic.

ZENDER J(ohannes) W(olfgang) Hans, b. 22 Nov 1936, Wiesbaden, Germany. Composer; Conductor. m. Gertrud Achenbach. Education: Diplomas in Conducting, Piano and Composition, Academy of Music, Freiburg. Career: Conductor, Freiburg, 1959; Principal Conductor, Bonn, 1964; General Music Director, City of Kiel, 1969; Principal Conductor, Saar Broadcasting, 1971-83; Chief Conductor, Hamburg State Opera House, 1984-87Guest Conductor for Berlin Philharmonic, London Symphony Orchestra, BBC, Residentie-Orkest, ORF Vienna, Tonhalle Zurich, Opera Houses of Munich, and Bayreuth (Parsifal); Chief Guest Conductor of the National Opera Orchestra, Brussels with Fidelio, 1989; Professor of Composition, Musikhochschule, Frankfurt, 1988-; Guest Conductor, SWF Symphony Orchestra, until 1999. Compositions include: Vexilla Regis; Quartet for Flute, Cello, Piano and Percussion; Trifolium for Flute, Cello and Piano; Les Sirènes Chantent for Soprano and Instruments; Muji No Kyo for Trio and Instruments; Bremen Wodu, electronic; Schachspiel for Orchestra; Zeitstrome for Orchestra; Cantos I-V for Voices and Instruments; Hölderlin Lesen for String Quartet and Voice; Modelle I-XII for Orchestral Groups; Loshu I-VII for Flute and Instruments; Dialog Mit Haydn; Stephen Climax, 1979-84; Hölderlin II, for viola and electronics; Hölderlin Lesen III for string quartet and gramophone; Jours de Silence for baritone and orchestra; Furin No Kyo, for soprano and ensemble; Animula for female choir, instruments and electronics; Schumann-Fantasiecs for large orchestra; Römer VIII for Soprano, alto and organ; Joh III for a cappella choir. Recordings include: Elemente; Litanei; Mondschrift; Cantos I, II, V, VI, VIII; Dialogue with Haydn; Furin No Kyo; Zeitströme; Stephen Climax; Shuberts Winterreise; Hölderlin Lesen I-III. Contributions to include: Neue Zeitschrift für Musik; Frankfurter Allgemeine Zeitung; Die Zeit; Frankfurter Rundschau Hörspiel: Nanzen und die Katze. Honours: Kunstpreis des Saarlandes; Musikpreis der Stadt Frankfurt; Goethepreis der Stadt Frankfurt. Memberships: GEMA; International Society for Contemporary Music; Freie Akademie der Künste Berlin; Bayerische Akademie der Künste München. Hobbies: Arts; Literature. Current Management: Astrid Schoerke. Address: Astrid Schoerke, Moenckebergallee 41, D-30453 Hannover, Germany.

ZENTAI Csilla, b. 23 May 1940, Mako, Hungary. Soprano. Education: Studied at Szeged and Budapest, and with Lore Fischer and Hubert Giessen in Stuttgart. Debut: Stuttgart Opera School, 1969, in Ibert's Angelique. Career: Sang at Ulm Opera, 1969-72, Bremen, 1973-79, Deutsche Oper am Rhein from 1979; Guest appearances at the State Operas of Stuttgart, Hamburg and Munich, Vienna Staatsoper as Mozart's Countess and Fiordigili, Zurich as the Marschallin, Deutsche Oper Berlin as Elvira and Blumenmädchen 1, and Cologne Opera as Fiordigili, Agathe, Butterfly and Marenka; Further engagements at Bordeaux, Brussels, Salzburg as Donna Anna in concert performance of Don Giovanni, and Moscow; Other roles have included Violetta, Composer, Jenufa, Pamina, Rosalinde, Marguerite and Amaranta in La Fedeltà Premiata by Haydn; Concert appearances in Germany, Holland, Belgium, Italy, Spain, Mexico and Hungary; Title of Kammersängerin of the Deutsche Oper am Rhein, 1990-; Professor, Folkwang Musikhochschule, 1991-. Address: c/o Deutsche Oper am Rhein, Heinrich Heine Allee 16, 40667 Dusseldorf, Germany.

ZENZIPER Arkadi, b. 10 Apr 1958, Leningrad, Russia. Pianist. m. Tatjana Zenziper, 10 Aug 1990, 3 sons, 2 daughters. Education: Specialised Music School at Leningrad Conservatory, with T Orlovsky; Final Examination with distinction, Leningrad Conservatory, 1981, after studying with N Perlmann and G Sokolov; Master's degree, 1984. Debut: TV piano recital in Vilnius, Lithuania, 1982. Career: Major concerts with orchestras: Berlin Symphonic Orchestra, 1990, Munich Klaviersommer, 1994, Ljubljana Festival, 1994; Major chamber music concerts: Schleswig-Holstein Music Festival, 1989, 1990, Lucerne Festival, 1989, Concertgebouw, Amsterdam, 1990, 1991, Berlin Philharmonic Hall, 1992, and frequently at Berlin Konzerthaus; Radio performance of Prokofiev 4th and 5th Piano Concertos with Berlin Radio Orchestra, 1992; TV portrait and recording of Rachmaninov with Staatskapelle Dresden; Chamber music: Rheingau Festival, 1996; Dresdner Musikfestspiele, 1996; Tibor Varga Festival Sion, 1997; Beethovenhaus Bonn, 1997; Hitzacker-Festival, 1997. Appointed regular Professor, Dresden Musikhochschule, 1993. Recordings: Radio recordings of chamber music with RIAS-Berlin, Hessischer Rundfunk, South German Radio, Deutschland Radio; 9 CDs. Hobbies: Gardening; Railways. Current Management: Secretariat WIESE, Zurich. Address: Amtshof, D-29493 Schnackenburg, Germany.

ZERBINI Antonio, b. 1928, Italy. Bass Singer. Debut: Sang in La Forza del Destino at Spoleto in 1952. Career: Sang at the Verona Arena, 1958-71 with debut as Ramphis in Aida; Further appearances at La Scala Milan, Moscow, Buenos Aires and the Paris Opéra; Théâtre de la Monnaie Brussels, 1960, 1962, 1969, and 1979 as the King in Aida, Mozart's Commendatore, Angelotti in Tosca, Timur in Turandot and Padre Guardiano in La Forza del Destino; Also sang in Nice and Monte Carlo in 1979; Verona Arena in 1981 as Sparafucile in Rigoletto; Sang Hieros in a revival of L'Assedio di Corinto by Rossini at Florence in 1982. Recordings: Tosca; Aida; Don Giovanni; L'Arlesiana; Donizetti's Maria Stuarda; I Lombardi; La Forza del Destino; Manon; Lucia di Lammermoor.

ZERVA-KONSTANTOPOULOU Aspasia, b. 10 July 1940, Filipiada, Greece. Pianist; Conductor; Composer. m. Pantelis Zervas, 2 July 1961, 2 sons. Education: National Conservatory in Athens, Diplomas in Piano, Conducting, Composition; Mozarteum Summer Academy, Piano Lessons with Dr Scholz. Career: Musical Producer, Greek Radio-Television, 1971-76; Soloist with the State Philharmonic of Athens; Artisitc Director of Epirotic Conservatory, Tsakalof and three more conservatories; Founder of the World famous Tsakalof Youth Symphony Orchestra. Compositions: The Power of Creation, symphonic poem; Greek Danses, suite; Variations on Folk Themes for piano; Yiannena, for orchestra and choir. Recordings: Yiannena, Collector's CD for the VE-Day. Publication: Harmony and 450 exercises. Honours: National Technical University of Athens, 1993; Conservatory of Corfu, 1994; Municipality of Ioannina, 1995. Memberships: Incorporated Society of Musicians; Vice President, Soroptimist. Address: Platia G Stavrou 5, 45444 Ioannina, Greece.

ZETCHEVITCH Xenia, b. 16 Feb 1956, Zadar, Croatia, formerly Yugoslavia. Education: BA, Composition, Piano, MA, Piano, Academy of Music, University of Belgrade; Specialisation, Antwerp, Belgium, Paris, France. Debuts: Piano, 1963, Composition, 1965, Pula, Istria. Career: 1st work, age 5, played in Pula, 1965; Concerts include Zagreb, 1967, 1969, Antwerp, 1975, Belgrade, 1971, 1973, 1975, 1977, 1981 - Rachmaninov Concerto No 3, D flat; Played own works at piano concerts including Belgrade, 1977, 1986, 1989, Novi Sad, 1987, Nis, 1987, Budva Summer Festival, 1989, Pula, 1989, Tel Aviv, 1990; Works recorded for Yugoslav TV and radio, performed Opetija Tribune, 1980, Zagreb Biennial, 1981, Dubravnik Summer Festival, 1983, UK TV and Carnegie Hall, New York, 1988, Tel Aviv, 1990. Compositions include: Lento, Scherzo, Rondo estatico, piano, 1971; Suite, flute, piano, 1973; Powder, Trace, To You, triptych, chorus, percussions, 1978; Concerto, chorus, piano, orchestra, 1981; Requiem for End of the 20th Century, 1984; Prayer of the Lust, symphonic poem, 1985; Prayer for Casualties of the Banjica Lager, 1986; Cantata for Slaughtered in Kragujevac, 1987; String quartet, 1988; A Blind Glance of God, 2 violins, synthesizers, 1988; Requiem aeternam per mio nonno Ferdinando Gherghetta....; 2 cycles: Lilith, 1989; Before the Mind and Before the Dawn, 1991; Theatre and film music. Recordings: The Book of Secrets, 1986; Music from musical Peter Pan, 1992; Music from film Some Birds Can't Fly, 1997; The Return to Southern Mountains. Publication: The Book of the Defeated, poems, 1991. Contributions to: Regular music essays and reviews in magazines. Honours: 1st Prizes, piano contests, Zagreb, 1967, 1969, Belgrade, 1971; 1st Prize, Theatre Festival of Bosnia and Herzegovina, 1990; Awards, Best Original Film Music, Belgrade Festival, 1978, 1991, 1995, Herzeg Novi Film Festival, 1994, 1997, Mojkovac Film Festival, 1997; Crystal Prize, Best Yugoslav Film Music in 1994. Memberships: Association of Composers of Serbia and Yugoslavia; Music Association. Address: Komnen Barjaktara 6, 11000 Belgrade, Yugoslavia.

ZETTERSTROM Rune, b. 1936, Vasteras, Sweden. Bass Singer. Education: Studied at the opera school of the Stora Teatern, Gothenburg, 1963-66. Debut: Gothenburg 1966, as Mozart's Bartolo. Career: Guest engagements: Oslo, 1970, Bergen, 1972, 1975, Copenhagen, 1976, London, 1977; Major roles have been: Seneca, in L'Incoronazione di Poppea, Rossini's Basilio, Verdi's Anckarström, in Tintomara by Werle, Timur in Turandot, Puccini's Colline; Sang the Lion in Werle's Animalen with the Stora Teatern at the Wiesbaden Festival, 1981; Recent roles include: Mozart's Figaro, Sarastro, Leporello, Osmin, Philip, in Don Carlos; Guest engagements, in Semperopera in Dresden, 1988 with Osmin; Sang Leporello at Stockholm, 1996. Recordings include: Tintomara. Address: Stora Teatern, PO Box 53116, S-40015 Goteborg, Sweden.

ZHADKO Victoria, b. 1967, Kiev, Ukraine. Conductor. Education: Studied at the Kiev Conservatoire. Career: Deputy Conductor of the Kiev Radio Symphony Orchestra in 1993; Performances of Ukrainian music with the St Petersburg Philharmonic and guest engagements with the Rotterdam Philharmonic, Netherlands Radio, Helsinki, Wroclaw and Poznan Philharmonics; Repertoire includes the Viennese classics, Strauss, Tchaikovsky, Brahms, Liszt and Ravel; Teacher at the Kiev School of Arts and Odessa Conservatoire. Address: c/o Sonata Ltd, 11 North Park Street, Glasgow, G20 7AA, Scotland.

ZHANG Dinghe, b. 1916, Shanghai, China. Composer. Education: Graduate, Music Department, Hsin-hua School of Fine Arts; Music Theory, Composition, National Conservatory of Music, Shanghai, 1933-37. Career: Teacher, National Musical Drama School; Researcher, Teacher, Composer, Central Academy of Drama, National Opera, Dance Drama Troupe, 1950-. Compositions: 29 plays, 11 modern Chinese operas, 7 traditional Chinese operas, 5 motion pictures, 3 radio plays, 1 puppet play, 160 songs, 30 instrumental pieces, including: Bush Cherry Flowers, 1941; Peach Blossom Fan; Princess Wencheng; Love Under the Scholartree; The Great Wind; Dancers on the Bronze Phoenix Terrace; Fifteen Strings of Coins; A Second Blossom of Plums. Honours: Several National 1st Class Awards for Composition. Address: 2 Nanhua East Street, Beijing 100050, China.

ZHANG Lei, b. 15 April 1958, China. Mucia and Film Director. m. 20 December 1985, 1 son, 1 daughter. Education: Graduate, Shanyang Music University, 1982; Kobe University, 1993; Osaka University, 1996. Career: Actor in Dubbing Films; Actor, Producer, Player of Bamboo Pipe; Appeared in Over 100 Programs in China and 150 in Japan; Over 350 Instrumental Concerts in Japan. Compositions: The Dream of Emperor; Chinese Living in Japan; Nhkty. Recordings: CD of Bamboo Pipe Music, 1995; The Sun of Kobe, 1996; Roman Holidays; Yotsuya Ghost Story. Publications: Yao mi wu li, 1995; A Sahi, 1995; Mayiniqi, 1995. Contributions to: Osaka of Japan Newspaper; Engish Newspaper of Japan. Honours: 1st Prize, Chinese Movie Writers Organization, 1981; 1st Prize, Chinese Central Broadcasting Station Western Wind Cup, 1988. Membership: Picture Writer Society of Japan. Hobby: Sports. Address: Kitaougi 2, Qiaomei 2-3-103, Higaxi Nadaku, Kobei Xi Hiyougoken, Japan.

ZHISLIN Grigory, b. 7 May 1945, St Petersburg, Russia. Violinist; Violist. Education: Studied at the Central Music School and the State Conservatoire in Moscow. Career: Many appearances with such leading ensembles as the Leipzig Gewandhaus, Dresden Staatskapelle, Vienna Symphony, Warsaw National Philharmonic, Bergin Philharmonic and all the major Russian orchestras: Conductors have included Moshe Atzmon, Neeme Järvi, Herbert Blomstedt, Mariss Jansons, Leif Segerstram Kurt Sanderling, Kyrill Kondrashin and Yuri Temirkanov; Concerts at such festival at the Warsaw Autumn, Prague Spring, Maggio Musicale, Istanbul, Bergen and Kuhmo; Performances of such contemporary composers as Schnittke, Gubaidulina, Denisov and Penderecki (tours with the Krakow Philharmonic to Britain and Europe 1990, playing the Penderecki Violin and Viola concertos which were written for him); Assistant Professor at the Moscow Conservatoire 1969-71; Teacher at the Gnessin Institute, Moscow, and masterclasses in Krakow, Oslo, Montreal and Genoa (students have included Dimitri Sitkovetsky); Professor of Violin and Viola at the Royal Academy of Music, London from 1991. Honours: Gold Medal of the International Paganini Competition at Genoa, 1967; Silver Medal at the Queen Elisabeth Competition in Brussels, 1968. Current Management: Georgina McIvor Associates. Address: c/o Sonata, 11 Northgate Street, Glasgow G20 7AA, Scotland.

ZHOU Long, b. 8 July 1953, Beijing, China. m. Chen Yi. Education: Dr of Musical Arts, Columbia University in the City of New York, USA, 1993; BA, Central Conservatory of Music, Beijing, China, 1983; Studied composition with Chou Wen-chung, Mario Davidovsky, George Edwards and Su Xia. Career: Music Director, Music from China, New York City, 1989-; Composer-in-Residence, China Broadcasting Symphony, Beijing, 1983-85, New Music Consort, 1995-, Brooklyn Philharmonic, 1998-. Recordings: For various labels. Honours include: New York State Council on the Arts Commissions, 1986-94; ASCAP Composers Awards, 1987-; Winner, Ensemblia Composition Competition, Monchengladbach, Germany, 1990; Winner, The Dr Rapaport Prize, Columbia University, 1991; Winner, 5th International Composition Competition, d'Avray, France, 1991; Pittsburgh New Music Ensemble commission, 1992; Kronos Quartet commission, 1992; Koussevitzky Music Foundation in the Library of Congress (USA) Commission Award, 1993; Meet the Composer Commission Awards, 1993; Fromm Music Foundation Commission Award, Harvard University, 1993; Rockefeller Foundation Fellowship, 1994; Winner, 4th (1985), 13th (1994), Chinese National Composition Competition, Beijing; Winner, Barlow International Competition, 1994; John Simon Guggenheim Foundation Fellowship, 1994; Brooklyn Philharmonic commissions, 1995-98 (concerto for Yo-Yo Ma); National Endowment for the Arts (USA) Fellowships, 1993-96; Mary Cary Trust and Aaron Copland Fund for Music Recording Grants, 1994-97; American Academy of Arts and Letters Fellowship, 1997. Address: 728 41st St 4E, Brooklyn, NY 11232, USA.

ZHU Ai-La, b. 1957, Nanking, China. Soprano. Education: Studied in Peking and Berlin. Career: Sang first with the Peking Central Opera notably as Butterfly, Violetta and Mimi; Studied further at the Hartt School of Music and sang Micaela with Texas Opera, Mimi and Marguerite with Virginia Opera and Xola in the premiere of Under The Double Moon by A Davis, with the St Louis Opera; Appeared at Pepsicosummerfare as Zerlina in the Peter Sellars production of Don Giovanni; Season 1990-92 as Violetta at Boston, Gilda at Philadelphia and Leila with Minnesota Opera; Sang at Glyndebourne Festival, 1990-91 as Pamina; Also features in Lieder recitals. Address: c/o Glyndebourne Festival Opera, Lewes, East Sussex, BN8 5UU, England.

ZHU Hong, b. 1 Mar 1960, Guiyang, China. Violinist; Assistant Professor. m. Lu Deng, 24 Oct 1988, 1 daughter. Education: DMA, MM, Michigan University; BA, Central Conservatory of Music, Beijing. Debut: 15 years old, Guiyang, China. Career: Assistant Professor, Violin and Chamber Music, Central Conservatory of Music, Beijing, 1982-87; Visiting Scholar, Violin, Michigan University, 1987-88; Adjunct Instructor, Violin, University of Michigan, 1991-93; Instructor, Violin, Flint Institute of Music, 1989-94; Lecturer, Violin, Murray University, 1994-96; Instructor, Violin and Chamber Music, Colorado Music Festival String Camp, University of Southern Colorado, 1996; Assistant Professor, Violin, University of Central Oklahoma, 1996-; Musical Career: Chinese Youth String Quartet, Central Conservatory of Music, Beijing, 1980-87; Continental String Quartet, Michigan University, 1987-94; Murray String Quartet, Murray University, 1994-96; UCO Faculty String Quartet, University of Central Oklahoma, 1996-. Honours: Yehudi Menuhin Prize, Portsmouth International String Quartet Competition, England, 1982; Champion, Beijing National String Quartet Competition, 1982; Distinguished Artist Award, Beijing, 1985. Memberships: Chamber Music America; American Federation of Musicians. Hobby: Tennis. Address: 1125 Bradford Place, Edmond, OK 73003, USA.

ZHU Jian-er, b. 18 Oct 1922, Tianjin, China. Composer; Professor of Composition. m. Qun Shu, 1949, 2 sons, 1 daughter. Education: Graduated, Moscow State Conservatory, 1960; Studied with Professor Sergey Balasanian. Career: Composer, Art Troupe, New 4th Army, 1945-49; Conductor, Brass Band, 1946-49; Composer, Shanghai and Peking Film Studios, 1949-63; Shanghai Opera House, 1963-75; Shanghai Symphony Orchestra, 1975-; Professor of Composition, Shanghai Conservatory of Music. Compositions: Main Works: Orchestral: Festival Overture, 1958; In Memorian, for Strings, 1978; Symphonic Fantasia, 1980; Sketches in Mountains of Guizhou, 1982; The Butterfly Fountain for Er-hu and Orchestra, 1983; A Wonder of Naxi, 1984; Symphonies No 1, 1986; No 2, 1987; No 3 Tibet, 1988; No 4, 1990; No 5, 1991; No 6, 1994; No 7, 1994; No 8, 1994; Sinfonietta, 1994; Concerto for Sona and Orchestra, 1989; Choral: Salute 1946, 1945; Gada-meilin, 1958; Symphony-Cantata Heroic Poems, 1960; A Cappella Cycle The Green, Green Water Village, 1981; Piano: Preludes, 1955; Theme and Var, 1956; Ballade, 1958; Five Yunnan Folk Songs, 1962; Quintet, 1992; Folk Instrumental Ensemble Day of Liberation, 1953; Song of the Spring, for Oboe and Piano, 1956; Numerous Songs. Recordings: Numerous. Publications: Numerous. Contributions to: Author of more than 50 Articles to Professional Journals. Honours: China State Prizes for Symphony Works, 1981, 1994; Prizes in Music Festival Spring in Shanghai; Musical Prize, Shanghai Federation of Culture and Arts, 1984-85; State Prizes for Songs, 1951, 1952, 1982-83; The Queen Marie José Prize for Musical Composition, 1990 (Symphony No 4); 1st Shanghai City Award, Distinguished Achievements, 1989-90. Address: 105 Hu Nan Road, Shanghai Symphony Orchestra, Shanghai 200031, China.

ZHUKOV Sergei, b. 30 August 1951, Zhitomir, Ukraine. Composer. m. Natalia Zhukova, 4 March 1982, 2 daughters. Education: Musical College, Zhitomir, 1973-; Graduated, Department of Composition, 1978, Postgraduate Course, 1980, Moscow State Conservatory. Debut: Chamber Music Concert, Maliy Hall, Moscow Conservatory, 1973. Career: Participated, All-Union and International Concerts, Festivals, Symposia, including: Moscow Autumn Musical Festival, 1981, 1982, 1983, 1984; Warsaw Autumn, 1988; International Musical Festival, Leningrad, 1989; Charles Ives Festival, USA, 1990; Week Van de Hedendaagse Musiek, Belgium, 1991; Works performed on ITV, Radio: Symphony, All-Union Radio, 1987; Moments, running in succession, oratorio, All-Union TV, 1987; Partita for violin solo, Donderdag, Dutch Radio, 1990; Landscape for Clarinet Solo, BRT-3, Belgium Radio; Solaris, fantasic ballet, Ukrainian TV recording, 1991; Teaching, Department of Theory and Composition, Moscow State Conservatory, 1991. Compositions: Spivanochcki, Chamber Cantata to Traditional Words, 1975, published 1983; Partita for Violin Solo, 1983, published 1986; Refracted Sounds, Wind Quintet, 1984; Symphony, 1985; Sonata-Bussanda for Piano, 1988; Concerto for Orchestra and Solo Percussions, 1990; Image and Transfiouration, for Organ, 1991; Concerto-Partes for String Orchestra, 1992; Lot of Nemisida, Choreographic Composition for Clarinetist, Dancer, Magnetic Tape, 1993; Concerto-Mystery for Piano, Violin, Violoncello and Orchestra, 1994. Contributions to: Some aspects of Creation of Musical Compositions, article, 1980; Series of Articles for The Musical Encyclopedia, 1991. Memberships: Union of Composers of Russia, 1980. Hobbies: Cars; Travel; Nature. Address: Studencheskaja Str 44-28, Apt 128, 121165 Moscow, Russia.

ZIDEK Ivo, b. 4 Jun 1926, Kravare, Opava, Czechoslovakia. Tenor; Administrator. Education: Studied with Rudolf Vasek in Ostrava. Debut: Ostrava in 1945 as Massenet's Werther. Career Sang at the Prague National Theatre from 1948, notably as Smetana's Jenik and Ladislav in The Two Widows, Steva and Laca in Jenufa, Mozart's Tamino, Ferrando and Ottavio, and Michel in Martinu's Julietta; Guest singer with the Vienna Staatsoper in 1957 with visit to Barcelona in 1958; Holland Festival in 1960 and 1963; Edinburgh Festival 1964 and 1970 with the Prague National Theatre in the British premieres of Janácek's From the House of the Dead and The Excursions of Mr Broucek; Sang at New York in 1966 in a concert performance of Jenufa; Also appeared at the Berlin Staatsoper, 1963-68, Moscow, Stuttgart, Venice and the Teatro Colon, Buenos Aires; Intendant of the National Theatre Prague from 1990; Concert repertory has included Les Noces by Stravinsky, Oedipus Rex, sacred works by Dvorák and Janácek's Diary of One Who Disappeared. Recordings: The Bartered Bride; Libuse; The Two Widows; The Excursions of Mr Broucek; The Makropoulos Case; From the

House of the Dead; Jenufa; Julietta; The Bride of Messina by Fibich; Les Noces; Dvorák's Stabat Mater; Jenufa. Honours: Artist of Merit, 1958; National Artist, 1976. Address: National Theatre, PO Box 865, 112 30 Prague 1, Czech Republic.

ZIEGLER Delores, b. 4 Sep 1951, Atlanta, GA, USA. Mezzo-Soprano. Education: Studied at the University of Tennessee. Career: Sang at first in concert then made stage debut as Flora in Traviata at Knoxville, TN, 1978; Sang Maddalena in Rigoletto at St Louis in 1979; Bonn Opera from 1981 as Emilia in Otello, Dorabella and Octavian; Member of the Cologne Opera from 1982, notably as Cherubino, Orlofsky and Octavian; La Scala Milan, 1984-87 in Bellini's Romeo; Guest engagements in Munich, Oslo, San Diego, Toronto, Hamburg and at the Glyndebourne Fesival as Dorabella in 1984; Maggio Musicale Florence in 1989 as Idamantes; Salzburg Festival in 1988 as Mozart's Sextus; Metropolitan Opera, 1989-91 as Siebel and Octavian; Sang in Der Rosenkavalier with the Canadian Opera Company at Toronto, 1990; Sang Dorabella at Washington DC, 1996; Many concert engagements. Recordings include: Bach's B minor Mass; Così fan tutte; Mozart's Mass in C; Second Lady in Die Zauberflöte; Le Roi d'Ys by Lalo. Address: c/o Cote Artists Management, 150 West 57th Street, Suite 803, New York, NY 10019, USA.

ZIELINSKA Lidia, b. 30 Oct 1953, Poznan, Poland. Composer. m. Zygmunt Zielinski, 3 Aug 1974, 1 daughter. Education: MA, State Higher School of Music, Poznan; Studied composition with Andrzej Koszewski. Career: Collaborated in Electronics Music Studio in Crakow, 1978-; Composers Workshops in Poland, Holland, France and Switzerland, 1979-87; Polish Radio Experimental Studio, 1980-81, 1986- and Studio IPEM, Ghent, 1985; Polish Center of Art for Children and Youth, Artistic Group, Artificial Cult; Co-organised Multimedia Art Meetings, Obecnosc, Poznan; Festivals, Young Polish Music, Szczecin; Concerts and performances in Europe, Asia and USA; Assistant Professor, Academy of Music, Poznan, 1983-. Compositions include: Violin Concerto, 1979; Farewell Mr Toorop for Orchestra, 1981; Lullaby Gagaku for Double Bass, 1984; Sonnet On The Tatras for 4 Musicians, 1985; Music For Stanislaw Wyspianski for Tape, 1985; Glossa for Viola or Violin, 1986; Polish Dances for Tape after Father Baka, 1986; Pleonasmus for Oboe, Violin and String Orchestra, 1986; Kaleidoscope, Passacaglia for Percussion, Slides and Clapping Hands, for children, 1987; Concrete Music for Choir and Orchestra, 1987; The Same, 1988; Little Atrophic Symphony, 1988; Musica Humana Or How Symphonies Are Born, radio piece, 1989; Jacquard Loom for 15 Musicians, 1991; Fago for Bassoon, Double Bass and Accordion or Electronic Keyboard, 1992. Recordings: Numerous. Address: ul Poplinskich 7-9, 61-573 Poznan, Poland.

ZIELINSKI Andrzej (Sylwester), b. 26 Nov 1937, Wagrowiec, Poland. Musician; Cellist. Education: MA, Music, State Higher School of Music, Cracow, 1962; Postgraduate studies in Cello, Tchaikovsky Conservatoire, Moscow, 1966. Debut: With Poznan Symphony Orchestra in 1953. Career: Cello Soloist with Cracow, Poznan and National Philharmonic Orchestras, chamber orchestras include Iranian Radio and TV and Polish Radio and TV orchestras; Appearances with Sinfonia Varsovia, Swedish Radio and TV orchestras in Stockholm; Professor of Cello, Warsaw Academy of Music; Vice-Rector, Frédéric Chopin Academy of Music, Warsaw; Lecturer, International music courses, Lancut, Poland, 1990-91; Juror for national competitions and Consultant to music schools. Recordings: Various records, radio and TV recordings including 1st performance and recording of I J Pleyel's Cello Concerto in C major. Publications: Elaboration of I J Pleyel's Cello Concerto in C major, 1991. Honours: Golden Cross of Merit, 1987; Minister of Culture Award, 1990. Membership: Association of Polish Musicians. Hobbies: Sailing; Cycling; Driving. Address: ul Koszykowa 70 m, 00-671 Warsaw, Poland.

ZIESAK Ruth, b. 1963, Hofheim, Taunus, Germany. Soprano. Education: Studied with Christoph Pregardien, at the Frankfurt Musikhochschule with Elsa Cavelti, and at the Frankfurt Opera School. Debut: Heidelberg in 1988 as Valencienne in Die Lustige Witwe. Career: Sang at Heidelberg as Pamina, Gilda, Sesto in Giulio Cesare and Despina; Deutsche Oper am Rhein in 1989 as Marzelline; Tour of Tokyo, Osaka and Kyoto with the Ludwigsburg Festival Ensemble, singing in Messiah and Mozart's Requiem, 1989; Sang Susanna at the Opera Bastille Paris and Pamina, 1991, and at the Salzburg Festival, 1993; Season 1993-94 as Sophie in Rosenkavalier at the Deutsche Oper Berlin, 1993; Sang Ighino in Pfitzner's Palestrina at Covent Garden, 1997. Recordings include: Servilia in La Clemenza di Tito, under Harnoncourt. Address: IMG Artists, Media House, 3 Burlington Lane, London W4 2TH, England.

ZIESE Christa-Maria, b. 13 Jul 1924, Aschersleben, Germany. Soprano. m. Rainer Ludeke. Education: Studied with Gottlieb Zeithammer and Josef-Maria Hausschild in Leipzig. Debut: Leipzig in 1947 as Gretel. Career: Sang at the Leipzig Stadtische Theater, 1951-77 notably as Fidelio, Santuzza, Tosca, Salome, Aida, Carmen, Turandot, Senta, Isolde and Venus; Guest appearances in Weimar, 1951-54, Dresden, Komische Oper Berlin, Moscow Bolshoi, Dusseldorf, Hamburg, Nice, Zurich and Brno; Many concert appearances. Recordings: Many. Honours: Bach Competition Dresden and International Competition in Prague, 1949.

ZIKMUNDOVÁ Eva, b. 4 May 1932, Kroměříž, Czechoslovakia. Soprano Opera Singer. Divorced, 1 son. Education: State Conservatory, Brno; Music Academy, Prague. Debut: Opera House, Ostrava. Career: Member of Opera Company of National Theatre, Prague, 1958-92; Assistant Producer, State Opera, Prague, 1992-; Guest appearances at State Opera, Berlin, Hannover, Mannheim, Germany, Venice, Genoa, Naples, Italy, Lausanne, Switzerland, Vienna, Austria, Edinburgh, Scotland, Amsterdam, Holland, Warsaw, Poland, Budapest, Hungary, Sofia, Bulgaria, and Brussels, Belgium; Recitals for Czech Radio and Television; Professor of Singing at State Conservatory, Teplice. Recordings: Dvořák's St Ludmila and Moravian duets; Janáček's The Cunning Little Vixen; Numerous recordings of arias and duets. Publications: Translations into Czech of: Martienssen-Lohmann, Der wissende Sänger and Das bewusste Singen, 1994. Honours: Supraphon Annual Award for Cunning Little Vixen, 1974; Merited Member of The National Theatre, Ministry of Culture. Current Management: Pragokoncert, Prague 1, Czech Republic. Address: Mánesova 23, Prague 2, Czech Republic.

ZILBERSTEIN Lilya, b. 19 Apr 1965, Moscow, Russia. Concert Pianist. m. Alexander Gerzenberg, 27 Aug 1988, 2 sons. Education: Moscow Gnessin Special Music School with Ada Traub, 1972-83; Gnessin Music Pedagogical Institute, with Alexander Satz, 1983-90. Career: St Louis Symphony, Chicago Symphony, Berlin Philharmonic, London Symphony, Royal Philharmonic, Dresden Staatskapelle, Moscow Philharmonic, Finnish Radio. Recordings: 8 CDs, 6 Recitals. Honours: 1st Prize, Busoni International Piano Competition, 1987. Hobbies: Family; Children. Address: TransArt (UK) Ltd, 8 Bristol Gardens, London W9 2JC, England.

ZILIO Elena, b. 1941, Bolzano, Italy. Soprano. m. Sttilo Burchiellaro. Education: Studied at the Conservatorio Monteverdi in Bolzano, at the Accademia Chigiana in Siena and the Accademia di Santa Cecilia, Rome. Debut: At Spoleto in 1963 as Sofia in Rossini's Il Signor Bruschino. Career: Has sung at La Scala Milan, Rome, Genoa, Palarmo, Naples, Turin, Trieste, Venice and Verona Arena in 1970, 1973, 1976; Festivals at Caracalla and Florence; Sang Lisa in La Sonnambula at Geneva in 1982; Chicago Opera in 1983 as Susuki in Madama Butterfly; Milan at La Scala and Piccola Scala in 1983 as Amore in Cherubini's Anacréon and Dardane in Le Rencontre Imprévue by Gluck; Sang Smeaton in Anna Bolena at Bergamo in 1983 returning in 1988 as the Page in Donizetti's Gianni di Parigi; With the company of the San Carlo Naples sang Giustinio in Pergolesi's Flaminio at Versailles and Spoleto, USA, 1983 and Wiesbaden in 1985; Cologne Opera in 1984 as Pippo in La Gazza Ladra; Returned to La Scala in 1985 in a revival of Rossi's Orfeo; Further appearances in Brussels, at Paris Opéra, in Boston, San Antonio, Montreal, Bregenz and Dubrovnik; Sang Elena in La Gazza Ladra at Palermo, 1996. Recordings: La Buona Figliola by Piccinni; La Straniera by Bellini; Un Giorno di Regno by Verdi. Address: c/o Teatro alla Scala, Via Filodrammatici, I-20121 Milan, Italy.

ZIMANSKY Robert, b. 20 Apr 1948, Iowa City, USA. Violinist. m. Lucia Borsatti, 9 Apr 1979. Education: University of Iowa, 1960-66; Juilliard School of Music, 1966-71; Masterclasses with various teachers, 1970-74. Debut: Orchestra Hall, Chicago with Civic Symphony Orchestra. Career includes: Resident Europe, 1972-; Leader of Symphonie-Orchester Graunke, 1972-73, Suddeutsche Rundfunk, 1974, and Orchestre de la Suisse Romande, 1975-; Professor of Advanced Classes, Geneva Conservatory, 1980-; Soloist with Wolfgang Sawallisch, Horst Stein, Charles Dutoit, Leif Segerstam, David Zinman, George Cleve and Herbert Blomstedt. Recordings: X and P Scharwenka Violin Sonatas; Bach 5th Brandenberg; Albéric Magnard Sonata; Schumann 3 Sonatas (award); Reger, Sonatas op 72 and 84; Schubert, Octet and Janácek complete violin works. Honour: Grand Priz du Disque, Academie Charles Cros, 1986. Membership: Board of Directors, Association des Musiciens Suisses. Current Management: Wismer- Casetti, 30, CH Du Vieux-Vesenaz, CH-1222 Vesenaz. Address: 6 Tour de Champel, 1206 Geneva, Switzerland.

ZIMERMAN Krystian, b. 5 Dec 1956, Zabrze, Poland. Concert Pianist. m. 1 son, 1 daughter. Education: Studied at the Music Academy in Katowice. Career: Concerts in Vienna and all world's music centres; Concets and recordings with such conductors as Bernstein, Giulini and Karajan, and more recently Witold Lutoslawski dedicated his Piano Concerto to Zimerman who gave its premiere in 1989; Repertoire extends through solo piano music, concertos and chamber music. Recordings include: Beethoven No 1-5, Piano Concertos; Brahms Piano Concertos No 1 and 2; Liszt B minor Sonata. Honours include: Youngest ever winner of the Chopin Piano Competition, Warsaw, 1975; Grammy Award; Gramophone Award. Address: Kernmattstr 8B, CH-4102 Binningen, Switzerland.

ZIMMER Ján, b. 16 May 1926, Ruzomberok, Czechoslovakia. Composer; Pianist. Divorced, 1 son. Education: Class 4, Gymnasium; Studied organ, piano and composition at State Conservatory, Bratislava; Composition, High School of Music at Budapest and at Salzburg Seminar in American Studies. Career: Music Director, Broadcasting Corporation, Bratislava, 1945-48; Professor of Piano and Composition, State Conservatory, Bratislava, 1948-52; Freelance Composer and Pianist, 1952-. Compositions include: Operas: Oedipus Rex, 1963, The Broken Time, 1977; Music for films, 1946-52 and piano music for children; 12 Symphonies, 1955-86 and 7 Concertos for Piano and Orchestra; Chamber Works: Sonata for Organ, Op 65, 1970, Poetical Sonata for Violin and Piano, Op 85, 1976, Trio for Flute, Violin and Piano, Op 93, 1979; Vocal Works: Spring In The Valley, cycle of songs for Soprano and Piano, 1947, Songs of Spring for Tenor and Piano, Op 67, 1970, Concerto Poliphonier for Organ and Orchestra, Op 108. Hobbies: Sports; Swimming; Motoring; Travel. Address: Letecká 10, 831-03 Bratislava, Slovakia.

ZIMMERLIN Alfred (Peter), b. 12 Apr 1955, Zurich, Switzerland. Musician; Composer; Improvising Musician. m. Claudia Ulla Binder, 14 Feb 1986, 1 daughter. Education: Mayura Type B, Kantonsschule Aarau, 1975; Lic Phil I, University of Zurich, 1981; Studied composition with H Wüthrich-Mathez and H U Lehmann; Violoncello with A Zürcher. Career: Performances in Europe and USA and at festivals. Compositions: Etüdens über ein Thema Von Friedrich Nietzsche, 1976-78; 5 Preludes, Klavierstück 1, 1980-81; Duett II, 1983; Sätze, aug einen text von Elisabeth Wandeler-Deck, 1984; Zeile (aus einem Gedicht von Wyston Hugh Auden), 1984-86; Klavierstück 2, 1985; Toute L'Étendue Ne Vaut Pas Un Cri, 1985; Brechungen, 1986; From Alabama From Anywhere, 1986; Fünf Stücke Für Acht Flöten, 1986-87; Wahrnehmungsschwäche Für Das Tempo Der Zerstörung, 1987; L'Espace Tout A Coup M'Irrite, 1987; Gänge, 1988; Knotting, 1988; Klavierstück 3, 1988; 3 Mal 3, 1989; Wortstücke, 1988-89. Recordings: Numerous. Honours: Werkjahr des Aargauischen Kuratoriums, 1983, 1985; Musikpreis der C F Meyer-Stiftung, 1986; Komponistenwerkjahr der Stadt Zürich, 1988. Address: Mohrlistrasse 17, CH-8006 Zürich, Switzerland.

ZIMMERMAN Christopher, b. 1957, England. Conductor. Education: Studied at Yale and the University of Michigan; Further study with Nadia Boulanger and at the Pierre Monteux School of Conducting, Maine. Career: Music Director of the Yale Bach Society, 1980; Conducted the Michigan University Symphony Orchestra in the USA and Europe; Worked with the Toronto Symphony, the the Czech Philharmonic, 1983-85; London 1985, leading concerts with the Royal Philharmonic and the London Symphony Orchestras; Appearancs with the Royal Liverpool Philharmonic and at the Concertgebouw in Amsterdam; Prague 1987, with the Prague Symphony Orchestra; Conducted the Seoul Philharmonic in Korea, 1989; Guest Music Director at Mexico City Opera; Music Director, City of London Chamber Orchestra, 1988-93; Most recent Guest Engagements: Edmonton Symphony Orchestra, 1993, Waterbury Symphony Orchestra, 1994; Upcoming engagements in Finland and Venezuela; Currently Music Director, Bangor Symphony Orchestra, Bangor Maine, and Music Director, Concert Orchestra, Cincinnati College Conservatory of Music, Cincinnati, Ohio, USA. Memberships: A S O L. Current Management: Kenneth Wentworth, Jonathan Wentworth & Associates Limited. Address: Artist Management, Suite 503, 100 Stevens Avenue, Mount Vernon, New York 10550, USA.

ZIMMERMAN Franklin B, b. 20 Jun 1923, Wanneta, KS, USA. Musician; Conductor; Musicologist. m. 8 Aug 1988, 1 son, 5 daughters. Education: Studied at the University of Southern California, PhD in 1958; BLitt, Oxford University, 1956; Studied French Horn with Audrey Brain, 1954-56, conducting with Ernest Read, 1955-58 and orchestration with Leon Kirchner and Ingolf Dahl. Debut: London in 1957. Career: Founder and Director, Pennsylvania Pro Musica playing over 520 concerts. Recording: Handel L'Allegro ed Il Penseroso, 1981. Publications: Henry Purcell: Analytical Catalog, 1963; Henry Purcell: Life and Times, 1967, 1983; Henry Purcell: Thematic Index, 1973; Words to Music, 1965; Facsimile Editions: An Introduction to the Skill of Musick by John Playford, 12th edition corrected and amended by Henry Purcell, with index, introduction and glossary, 1972; The Gostling Manuscript, compiled by John Gostling, Foreword by Franklin B Zimmerman, 1977. Contributions to: Numerous articles and monographs. Honours: Arnold Bax Medal for Musicology, 1958. Memberships: AMS; IMS. Hobbies: Tennis; Hiking; Swimming; Deep Sea Fishing. Address: 225 South 42nd Street, Philadelphia, PA 19104, USA.

ZIMMERMAN Willi, b. 1955, Switzerland. Violinist. Education: Studied with the Alban Berg Quartet in Vienna. Career: Leader, Amati String Quartet, 1981-; Further study with members of the Amadeus and Bartók Quartets, and with Walter Levin; Many performances in Switzerland, USA and elsewhere in the classical repertoire, and in works by Szymanowski, Tailleferre, Cui, Steuermann, Vladimir Vogel, Kelterborn and Robert Suter; Recitals at Basle in 1986 and tours of Britain, 1990-91; Menuhin Festival at Gstaad in 1991; Recitals with Bruno Canino, Malcolm Frager, Bruno Giuranna, Karl Leister among others. Honours: With Amati Quartet: Grand Priz, Concours International at Evian, 1982, Art Prize of the Lions Club in 1985, and 1st Prize, Karl Klinger Competition in Munich, 1986. Address: c/o Anglo-Swiss Management, Suite 35-37 Morley House, 320 Regent Street, London W1R 5AD, England.

ZIMMERMANN Frank Peter, b. 27 Feb 1965, Duisburg, Germany. Concert Violinist. Education: Studied with Valery Gradov at Folkwang Musikhochschule Essen, Staatliche Hochschule Berlin with Saschko Gawrillof and from 1980 with Hermann Krebbers in Amsterdam. Debut: Duisburg in 1975 playing Mozart's Concerto K216. Career includes: Appearances with many international orchestras including Vienna Philharmonic, London Symphony Orchestra, English Chamber Orchestra, Boston Symphony, under such conductors as Maazel, Barenboim, Haitink, Sanderling, Sawallisch, and Ozawa; Festival engagements include Lucerne, 1979, and Salzburg, from 1983; USA debut in 1984 with the Pittsburgh Symphony; Tour of USA with Chamber Orchestra of Europe under Lorin Maazel, 1986; Performed at the Mostly Mozart in New York, Tanglewood and Ravinia Festivals in 1987; Season 1988-89 playing at Germany, London, Boston, Munich, Milan and Oslo with tour of Australia in 1989; Sibelius Concerto at the Helsinki Festival and the Beethoven Concerto with the Berlin Philharmonic; Season 1990-91 included concerts with the Philharmonia Orchestra, the Chicago Symphony and the Royal Concertgebouw; Invited for the Leipzig Gewandhaus 150th anniversary season, 1992; Highlights during 1993-94 included extensive tours sin Japan and Australia, concerts with the Berlin Philharmonic Orchestra and Bernard Haitink, Munich Philharmonic and Christoph von Dohnanyi and the orchestra of the NDR Hamburg and Jukka-Pekka Saraste; Furthur engagements include the Vienna Philharmonic Orchestra and Lorin Maazel, the Gustav Mahler Jugend Orchester and Bernard Haitink, the Tonhalle Orchestra Zürich and Claus Peter Flor and the Rotterdam Philharmonic Orchestra. Recordings include: Tchaikovsky Concerto with the Berlin Philharmonic and Concertos by Prokofiev, Beethoven, Mendelssohn, Bach and Sibelius; Brahms Concerto with the Berlin Philharmonic and Sawallisch; Sonatas by Mozart and Prokofiev, with pianist Alexander Lonquich. Address: c/o Intermusica Artists Management, 16 Duncan Terrace, London, N1 8BZ, England.

ZIMMERMANN Margarita, b. Aug 1942, Buenos Aires, Argentina. Mezzo-Soprano. Education: Studied in Buenos Aires. Debut: Teatro Colon Buenos Aires, as Orpheus in the opera by Gluck, 1977. Career: European debut at the Landestheater in Salzburg, as Carmen and Ulrica in Un Ballo in Maschera; Covent Garden debut in 1980 as Cherubino; US appearances at Miami as Dalila in 1979 and San Francisco as Rosina in 1982; Further engagements at Naples, Bologna, Venice, Rome, Lyons, Geneva and Paris; Further roles include Mozart's Sextus, Idamante and Zerlina, Handel's Guilio Cesare and Agrippina, Juno in Cavalli's Ercole Amante and Wagner's Fricka; In 1988 sang at Piacenza and Madrid as Massenet's Charlotte and as Andromache in Rossini's Ermione; Appeared as Thérèse in the opera by Massenet at Opéra de Monte Carlo, 1989. Recordings include: the Singer in Manon Lescaut.

ZIMMERMANN Margrit, b. 7 Aug 1927, Bern, Switzerland. Composer. Education: Studied piano and theory with Jeanne Bovet and Walter Furrer in Bern, with Denise Bidal in Lausanne, and masterclasses with Alfred Cortot; Diploma in Pianoforte; Composition studies under Arthur Honegger, Ecole Normale de Musique de Paris; Study as conductor with Ewald Korner, Municipal Theatre of Bern; International masterclasses with Igor Markevitch, Monte Carlo and Hans Swarowsky, Ossiach; Diploma in Composition, Giuseppe Verdi Conservatorium, Milan. Career: Music teacher, Bern; Composer. Compositions: Numerous including symphonic and scenic works, chamber music for a wide range of instruments, vocal and solo works for piano, strings, wind, percussion and guitar; Works include Panta Rhei, Op 39, 1987, Cloccachorda, Op 40, 1987, Die Gestundete Zeit, Op 52, 1987; Piano Time, Op 46, 1987; Quadriga, Op 51, 1987; Murooji, Op 57, for Guitar Solo; Trptychon, Op 58; Pianorama, Op 59; In Urbis Honorem, symphony for Orchestra and Choir; Jubilation, concert for Orchestra. Recordings: Cloccachordia; Piano Time; Quadriga; Pensieri; Orphische Taenze; Quartetto d'Archi. Address: Ostermundigenstrasse 22, CH-3006 Bern, Switzerland.

ZIMMERMANN Tabea, b. 8 Oct 1968, Lahr, Germany. Concert Violist. Education: Studied with Ulrich Koch and Sandor Vegh. Career: Frequent concerts with such soloists as Gidon Kremer, Heinz Holliger, Thomas Zehetmair, Steven Isserlis and Heinrich Schiff; Appearances at Prades, Schleswig-Holstein, Lockenhaus, Marlboro and other chamber music festivals; Regular recitals with pianist Hartmut Holl; Concert engagements include Mozart's Sinfonia Concertante in Amsterdam, at the Salzburg Festival and at Buckingham Palace for Prince Charles; Has also performed with the Bamberg Symphony under Christoph Eschenbach, at Frankfurt with Gary Bertini, Penderecki's Concerto with the composer conducting the Munich Philharmonic and concerts in Hamburg, Tokyo, Rome, Copenhagen, Helsinki and Israel; Gave the world premieres of concertos by Mark Koptyman and Volker David Kirchner in 1992; Premiere of Ligeti's Viola Sonata at Cologne in 1993; Alexander Goehr's Schlussgesang at the 1997 Aldeburgh Festival and Berio's Concerto for Clarinet and Viola (1996) with Paul Meyer. Recordings: Mozart's Concertante K364; Bach Trio Sonatas; Gubaidulina Hommage; Chamber works by Bruch, Mozart and Schumann; The Concerto in Europe; Double Concertos and works by Penderecki. Honours include: First Prize at competitions in Geneva, Budapest and awarded the Vatelot Viola at Paris. Address: c/o Harrison Parrott Ltd, 12 Penzance Place, London, W11 4PA, England.

ZIMMERMANN Udo, b. 6 Oct 1943, Dresden, Germany. Composer; Conductor. Education: Studied composition with J P Thilman at the Dresden Musikhochschule, 1962-68; Masterclasses at the Akademie der Kunste East Berlin, 1968-70. Career: Composer and Producer at the Dresden State Opera, 1970; Founded the Studio for New Music in Dresden, 1974; Professor of Composition at the Dresden Hochschule für Musik, 1978; Professor of Experimental Music Theatre at Dresden, 1982; Conducted the Bavarian Radio SO in the premiere of Hartmann's Sinfonia Tragica, Munich, 1989; Premiere of Bernhard Jesl's Opera Der König Stirbt at Bonn in 1990; Intendant of the Leipzig State Opera from 1990. Compositions include: Operas: Die Weisse Rose, 1967, Levins Muhle, 1973, Die Wundersame Schusterfrau, 1982; 5 Songs for Baritone and Orchestra, 1964; Musik für Streicher, 1967; String Quartet, 1967; Sieh, Meine Augen for Chamber Orchestra, 1970; Mutazioni for Orchestra, 1972; Choreographien Nach Edgar Degas for 21 Instruments, 1974; Hymnus An Die Sonne, after Kleist, for Soprano, Flute and Harpsichord, 1976; Pax Questuosa for 5 Soloists, 3 Choirs and Orchestra, 1980. Address: c/o AWA, Storkower Strasse 134, 1055 Berlin, Germany.

ZIMMERMANN Walter, b. 15 Apr 1949, Schwabach, Germany. Composer. Education: Studied piano, violin and oboe; Composition with Werner Heider and Otto Laske at Utrecht; Ethnological Centre Jaap Kunst in Amsterdam, 1970-73; Computer music in the USA, 1974. Career: Pianist in the Ars-Nova Ensemble of Nuremberg, 1968-70; Founded Beginner Studio at Cologne, 1977; Lecturer at Darmstadt, 1982, and Liege Conservatory from 1982; Professor of Composition, HDK Berlin. Compositions include: Lokale Musik, 15 works for various forces, 1977-81; Uber Die Dörfer, dramatic song for Soprano, Chorus and Orchestra, 1986; Fragmente der Liebe for Saxophone and String Quartet, 1987; Beginners Mind for piano, 1975; Wüstenwanderung for piano, 1986; Festina lente for string quartet; Diastasis/Diastema for 2 orchestras without conductor, 1992; Distentio for string trio, 1990; Affektenlehre for ensemble, 1995-. Address: c/o GEMA, Postfach 80 07 67, D-81607 Munich, Germany.

ZIMMERMANN Wolfram, b. 17 Apr 1920, Stuttgart, Germany. Bass-Baritone. Education: Studied with his father, at the Stuttgart and Vienna Academies and with Anna Bahr-Mildenburg. Debut: Stuttgart in 1947 as Rossini's Basilio. Career: Radio broadcasts in Germany and Austria; Sang Beckmesser in Die Meistersinger, under Furtwängler, at La Scala, 1952; Created title role in Titus Feuerfuchs by Heinrich Sutermeister for TV in Austria, 1959; Vienna Staatsoper 1958-63, notably as Leporello, Mozart's Papageno and the Doctor in Wozzeck by Berg; Rome Opera in 1956, Graz in 1958, Barcelona, 1958-63, and Mexico City in 1966 as Beckmesser; Other roles include the title roles in Mozart's Figaro, Gounod's Mephistopheles and Donizetti's Don Pasquale. Recordings: Zar und Zimmermann by Lortzing; Tannhäuser by Wagner. Contributions to: TV magazines in Austria and Germany, also Spain and Italy; Frankfurter Allgemeine; Suddeutsche Zeitung, Munich. Honours: Diploma, International Song, Geneva, 1949; Bach Prize, Leipzig, 1950; Gold Medal, Accademia Italia, 1980. Membership: Honorary Cavalier, Deutscherm-Ritterbund Norimberga. Hobbies: Tennis; Mountaineering. Address: Erbisleiten 6, D-91227 Weissenbrunn, Gemeinde Leinburg, Germany.

ZIMMERSCHIED Dieter, b. 1 Jul 1934, Danzig (now Gdansk), Poland. Professor of Music Education. m. Christa Brauch, 1 d. Education: Abitur, 1954; Various studies including School Music and Research, 1954-58, Staats Examen; Musikerzieher am Schlossgymnasium Mainz, Germany, 1960-76; Promotion, 1967. Career: Leader of Music Cultural Commission, 1970-73; Music Adviser to Ministry of Culture, Rheinland-Pfalz, 1969-76; Professor of Music Pedagogy, 1976-, Leader of School Music Section, 1977-, Musikhochschule, Stuttgart; Team Member, Funk-Kolleg Musik, 1976-78. Publications include: Die Kammermusik Johann Nepomuk Hummels, 1967; Perspektiven Neuer Musik, 1974; Tendenzen der Musikdidaktik, 1978; Operette - Phänomen und Entwicklung, 1988; Kinder Singen Überall - Lieder Aus Aller Welt, 1992. Contributions to: Musik und Bildung, bi-monthly, Mainz. Memberships: Chairman, Verband Deutscher Schulmusiker E V; Bundeshauptausschuß Jugend Musiziert; Vice Chairman, Arbeitsgemeinschaft Musikerziehung und Musikpflege im Deutschen Musikrat; Board, European Association for Music in Schools, 1995. Address: Weidmannstrasse 43, D-55131 Mainz, Germany.

ZINKLER Christiane, b. 23 Nov 1947, Coburg, Germany. Mezzo-Soprano. Education: Studied with Willi Domgraf-Fassbaender in Nuremberg and with Clemens Kaiser-Breme in Essen. Debut: Deutsche Oper am Rhein Dusseldorf in 1968 as Messenger in Dallapiccola's Job. Career: Member of the Dortmund Opera notably as Gluck's Orpheus, Erda and Fricka in Der Ring des Nibelungen, Ulrica, Hansel, Monteverdi's Poppea, Anina in Der Rosenkavalier, Cherubino and Dorabella; Guest appearances in Hamburg, Essen, Copenhagen, Wiesbaden and Florence; Many concert appearances. Address: c/o Opernhaus, Kuhstrasse 12, D-4600 Dortmund, Germany.

ZINMAN David (Joel), b. 9 Jul 1936, New York City, USA. Conductor. m. Mary Ingham. Education: Violin at Oberlin Conservatory, 1954-58; MA, Composition, University of Minnesota; Pierre Monteux's assistant at his summer school in Maine, 1961-63. Debut: Holland Festival in 1963; Philadelphia Orchestra, 1967. Career: Music Director, Netherlands Chamber Orchestra, 1964-77, Rotterdam Philharmonic Orchestra, 1979-82, Rochester Philharmonic Orchestra, 1974-85 and Baltimore Symphony Orchestra, 1985-; Music Director of the Tonhalle Orchestra, Zurich, 1995-; Music Director of the Aspen Music Festival and School, 1998-. Recordings: About 40 albums including Janácek's Sinfonietta, Chopin's Les Sylphides, Tchaikovsky's Serenade for String, Grieg's Holberg Suite, CPE Bach's Complete Flute Concerti, JC Bach's Symphonies, Chopin's Concerto No 2 in F minor for Piano and Orchestra, Mozart's Piano Concerto No 12 in A, K414, Dvorák's Legends, Op 59, Berlioz's Overture to Benvenuto Cellini, Love Scene from Roméo et Juliette, Three Excerpts from La Damnation de Faust, Minuet of the Will-o-the-Wisps, Dance of the Sylphs, Rákóczy March, Le Corsaire Overture, Trojan March, Royal Hunt and Storm from Les Troyens, La Marseillaise; Masterworks - Britten's Symphony for Cello and Orchestra, Op 68; Barber's Concerto for Cello and Orchestra, Op 22; Roussel's Symphony No 1; Mozart's Piano Concerto No 22, K482, and No 23, K488. Honours: Named by Time Magazine as One of the Five For the Future, 1982; 2 Grand Prix du Disque Awards; Edison Prize. Current Management: ICM Artists Ltd, 40 West 57th Street, New York, NY 10019, USA. Address: Harrison/Parrott Ltd, 12 Penzance Place, London W11 4PA, England.

ZINN William, b. 19 Nov 1924, New York City, USA. Violinist; Composer; Author; Professor; Business Executive; Humanitarian. m. Sophie Kalish, 11 Jul 1948, 1 son, 1 daughter. Education: Violin with Raphael Bronstein, 1942-43. Career includes: Baltimore Symphony, 1944-45, Indianapolis Symphony, 1945-46, Fort Wayne Philharmonic, 1946-47, Pittsburgh Symphony, 1947-49, and Minneapolis Symphony, 1950-51; Concertmaster for New Britain Symphony, CT, 1968-, Queen's Symphony, 1969-71, Ridgefield Symphony, CT, 1973-76, and Chappagua Symphony, NY, 1976; Soloist with various orchestras on records, radio and in recitals; Founder of Masterwork Piano Trio, Masterwork Piano Quartet, Classical String Quartet, Zinn's Ragtime String Quartet, Excelsior String Quartet, and Queen's Festival Orchestra, Bayside, NY, 1965; Associacion Musical William Zinn, Caracas, Venezuela, 1968; Vitametrics of America, 1976; International Symphony for World Peace, 1978; Big Apple Chamber Pops, 1983; Excelsior Composer's Festival Competition, 1984; Professor of Music, New York University, 1987-. Compositions: Published over 300 works for string quartet or string orchestra. Recording: Zinn's Ragtime String Quartet, 1974. Publications include: Co-author, Themography, dictionary of musical themes, 1947; The Mystery of the Lost Chord, 1987. Hobbies: Painting; Carving; Inventing.

ZINOVENKO Yuri, b. 1955, Simferopol, Ukraine. Singer (Bass). Education: Studied in Tashkent. Career: Sang first at the Kirov Opera St Petersburg; Croatian National Opera, Zagreb, 1981-87; Further engagements at the Frankfurt Opera and the Staatstheater, Darmstadt; Guest appearances in Italy, Israel, Austria, Russia and the USA; Roles have included the Hermit in Der Freischütz, Water Sprite in Rusalka, Prince Gremin (Eugene Onegin), and Kochubey in Tchaikovsky's Mazeppa; Verdi roles include Zaccaria and Lodovico; Sang The Prophet in the first production this century of Zenlinsky's first opera, Sarema (Trier Opera, 1996); Concerts include Mozart's Requiem and Shostakovich's 13th Symphony, Babi-Yar. Recordings include: Sarema (Koch International). Address: c/o Theater der Stadt Trier, Am Augustinerhof, D-5500 Trier, Germany.

ZINSSTAG Gérard, b. 9 May 1941, Geneva, Switzerland. Composer. m. 29 Feb 1984, 1 son, 1 daughter. Education: CNSM Paris and Chigiana Academy Siena, 1961-63; Studied composition with H U Lehmann, Musikhochschule, Zurich, 1973-75; Studied composition with Helmut Lachenmann, Stuttgart and Hanover, 1975-77; Composer-in-Residence, Berlin, 1981 (DAAD); IRCAM, Paris, 1982. Career: Orchestral musician touring Europe, 1964-67; Solo Flute, Orchestra of Zurich, Tonhalle, 1967-75; Participation in summer course, Darmstadt, 1976-78; Visitied San Francisco, New York for seminar at University of California, Berkeley, 1979; Founder of Festival of Zurich, Tage für neue Musik Zurich, 1986-; Tour of Russia, Moscow and Baku, 1990. Compositions: Dements; Wenn Zum Biespiel; Tatastenfelder; Suono Reale; Innanzi; Foris; Perforation; Altération; Trauma; Edition, Modern Munich; Cut Sounds; Incalzando, 1981; Artifices, 1982-83; Sept Fragments, 1982-83; Stimuli, 1984; Tempi Inquieti, 1984-86; Eden Jeden, 1987; Artifices II, 1988. Recordings: Ahaphoren, 1989, Radio France; Many radio station recordings. Publications: Pro Musica, 1988; Revue Musicale Suisse, 1979-80. Memberships: Suisa; Composers' Forum, New York; ISCM. Address: Froschaugasse 2, CH-8001 Zurich, Switzerland.

ZITEK Vaclav, b. 24 Mar 1932, Tisa, Czechoslovakia. Baritone. Education: Studied in Prague with Adrian Levicky. Debut: Prague Opera Studio in 1957 as Germont in La Traviata. Career includes: Member of the National Theatre, Prague, in operas by Mozart, Verdi, Tchaikovsky, Smetana, Dvorák, Martinu, Puccini, Strauss and Prokofiev; Guest appearances at the Bolshoi Theatre Moscow, the Staatsoper and Komische Oper Berlin, National Opera in Bucharest and the Bordeaux Opera; Sang at Prague National Theatre in 1983 as Premysl in Smetana's Libuse; Frequent concert and oratorio engagements. Recordings: Operas by Smetana, Dvorák's Jacobin and Sarka by Fibich; Siskov in From the House of the Dead, and Jenufa with the Vienna Philharmonic conducted by Charles Mackerras; Don Giovanni, Don Carlos, Trovatore, Pelléas et Mélisande, Faust, Macbeth, The Queen of Spades, Pagliacci; Smetana/Dalibor, Libuse, The Kiss, The Secret, The Devil's Wall; The Makropulos Affair; From the House of the Dead; Jenufa; The Cunning Little Vixen; Don Giovanni; Luisa Miller. Honours: Laureate of the State Prize, 1981; National Artist of Czechoslovakia, 1985; Prize of the National Academy of Recording and Science, Siskov, in Janacek's From the House of the Dead, with the Vienna Philharmonic conducted by Charles Mackerras, 1981. Address: Ke skalkam 2450, 106 00 Praha 10, Czech Republic.

ZIVONI Yossi, b. 2 Dec 1939, Tel-Aviv, Israel. Violinist. m. Jeanne, 21 Mar 1962, 1 daughter. Education: Graduate, Israel Academy of Music, Tel-Aviv, 1958; Graduate, Conservatoire Royal de Musique de Bruxelles, Belgium, 1962. Debut: Amsterdam, The Netherlands, 1964. Career: Concert Tours in Europe, Israel, Australia, Canada, Far East and South America. Recordings: Mozart Sonatas (Meridian); Bach: Sonatas and Partitas, Mendelssohn: Sonatas, (Meridian); Artistic Director, International Music Festival of Entrecasteaux, Provence, France; Principal Tutor, Royal Northern College of Music. Honours: Prizes: Paganini International Competition, 1960; Bavarian Radio International Competition, Munich, Federal Republic of Germany, 1961; Queen Elisabeth International Competition, Brussels, Belgium, 1963; Fellow, Royal Northern College of Music. Memberships: Royal Society of Musicians of Great Britain. Current Management: Anglo-Swiss Management. Address: 18 Midholm, London NW11, England.

ZLATKOVA Sonia, b. 1963, Tolbuchin, Bulgaria. Soprano. Education: Studied in Varna and Sofia. Career: Sang in concert in France in 1988 and made her stage debut at Ruse in 1989 as Despina; Sang at Bulgarian National Opera at Sofia from 1989 as Gilda, Lucia, the Queen of Night and Rosina; Guest appearances at Bregenz in 1991 as Frasquita, at St Gallen as Oscar and at Kaiserslautern as the Queen of Night; Sang Pamina at Schönbrunn, Vienna, 1996. Address: Bulgarian National Opera, Boulevard Dondoukov 58, 1000 Sofia, Bulgaria.

ZMRZLY Karel, b. 5 July 1936, Brno, Czech Republic. 1 son, 1 daughter. Education: Drama Academy of Musical Arts, Prague. Debut: Scenography for a Chinese Story, Drama Academy of Musical Arts, Prague, 1958. Career: Chief Scenographer of Theatres, Sumperk, 1959-62; Hradec Kralove, 1962-80, Brno DBM, 1980-88, State Theatre, Brno, 1988-91; Many Exhibitions of Czech Scenography at Home and Abroad. Memberships: International Theatre Institute; OISTT. Hobby: Painting. Address: H Malirove 5, 600 00 Brno-Lesna, Czech Republic.

ZOBEL Ingeborg, b. 31 Jul 1928, Gorlitz, Schlesien, Germany. Soprano. Education: Studied at the Dresden State Music Academy with Eduard Plate. Debut: As Amelia in Un Ballo in Maschera, Cottbus, 1952. Career: Sang in Schwerin, 1955-57, Rostock, 1957-66, and Weimar, 1966-72. Dresden Staatsoper from 1972, notably as Wagner's Brünnhilde, Isolde and Ortrud, the Marschallin, Tosca, Santuzza, Lady Macbeth and Leonore in

Fidelio; Guest appearances in Leningrad, Barcelona, Budapest, Wiesbaden, Prague, Belgrade and Sofia; Teacher at the Franz Liszt Musikhochschule in Weimar. Recordings: Various albums. Address: c/o Dresden Staatsoper, D-8012 Dresden, Germany.

ZOGHBY Linda, b. 17 Aug 1949, Mobile, AL, USA. Soprano. Education: Studied at Florida State University and with Elena Nikolaii. Career: Sang at first in concert; Stage debut at Houston in 1974 as Donna Elvira in Don Giovanni; Dallas Opera in 1976 as Giulietta in I Capuleti e i Montecchi; Glyndebourne Festival from 1978 as Mimi and in Haydn's La Fedeltà Premiata; Metropolitan Opera in 1982 and 1986 as Mimi and as Ilia in Idomeneo; Other roles include Mozart's Fiordigili and Pamina. Recordings: Haydn's L'Isola Disabitata and L'Incontro Improvviso.

ZOLLER Karlheinz, b. 24 Aug 1928, Hohr-Grenzhausen, Germany. Flautist. Education: Studied at the Detmold and Frankfurt Musikhochschule. Career: Many performances as concert soloist and chamber musician from 1950; Soloist with the Berlin Philharmonic, 1960-69, and teacher at the Berlin Musikhochschule; Professor at Hamburg before returning to Berlin; Has premiered the Double Concerto by Ligeti (1972) and the flute concerto by Isang Yun (1977). Address: Berlin Philharmonic Orchestra, Philharmonie, Matthaikirchstrasse, W-1000 Berlin, Germany.

ZOLLMAN Ronald, b. 8 Apr 1950, Antwerp, Belgium. Conductor. m. Dominique G Mols. Education: Diploma in Conducting, Brussels Conservatoire; Diploma, Academy Chigiana. Career: Has conducted throughout Europe, North and South America, and in Australia; Head of Conducting Faculty at the Royal Brussels Conservatory of Music; Musical Director of the Philharmonic Orchestra of UNAM, Mexico. Recordings: Belgian Music for Ministry of Culture, Brussels; Various recordings with the National Orchestra of Belgium, the World Orchestra and the London Sinfonietta. Honour: Premio Firenze for Conductors, 1972. Current Management: Konsertbolaget, Kungsgatan 32, S-11132, Stockholm, Sweden. Address: Rue Général de Gaulle 36, 1310 La Hulpe, Belgium.

ZOUBEK Bohus, b. 16 Nov 1942, Brno, Czech Republic. Director. 2 sons. Education: Brno Conservatory, 6 years; Janacek Academy of Music and Dramatic Arts, 4 years. Career: Approximately 60 radio appearances and 10 television, with Quintet and French Horn Quartet. Recordings: 2 recordings with Wind Quintet Q Moravi; Approximately 100 recordings as First French Horn with Czech Symphonic Orchestra of Brno. Contributions to: Hornforum. Honours: Honorable Mention, International French Horn Competition, Prague Spring Festival, 1968. Memberships: The Horn Call; Czech Horn Society; Hornforum. Hobbies: Tennis; Jogging; Hiking. Address: Ant Macka 6, 61200 Brno, Czech Republic.

ZOUHAR Vit, b. 13 Mar 1966, Brno, Czech Republic. Composer; Musicologist. m. Karla Zemanová, 28 June 1997. Education: Master, 1989, Postgraduate degree, 1993, Composition, Janácek University of Music and Dramatic Arts, Brno; Composition, University of Music and Dramatic Arts, Graz, Accademia Chigiana, Siena; Master, Musicology, Masaryk University, Brno, 1996. Career: Teacher, Musical Theory, State Conservatory, Brno, 1989; Assistant, Palacky University, Olomouc, 1992-; Teacher, 1992-, Guest Composer, 1993, Institute of Electronic Music, Graz, Austria; Guest Composer, Werkstadt Graz, 1994; Co-Founder, Teacher, Computer Music Study Room, Ostrava University, 1996; Works performed by State Philharmonic Orchestra Brno, Moravian Symphony Orchestra, DAMA DAMA percussion ensemble, Sonata a Tre, also many concerts, festivals, radio, TV, including: Hörgänge Wien; Experimental Music Festival, Prague; IST alles, ballet, Czech TV, 1992; The Garden, Forfest Music Festival, 1995; Like Water Is, ballet, Janácek Theatre, Brno, National Theatre, Prague, 1996; Wide Crossing, ballet, Graz Opernhaus, 1997. Compositions include: Le Vedute di Bruna, string quartet, 1985; Agastia, large orchestra, 1988; The Sun Gate, 4 percussionists, large orchestra, 1989; Es scheint mir aber immer, violin, clarinet, piano, 1992; Ist alles, 2 guitarists, 1992; Close Encounters of Those Wild at Heart, stereo-orchestra, 1993; Like Water Is, clarinet, fagot, piano, 1994; Wide Crossing, 1994. Recordings: The Sun Gate; Wide Crossing; Close Encounters; Je Vsechno; Es scheint mir aber immer. Publications: Postmoderní tendence a funkení rozruznenost hudby 80.let dvacátého století, 1993; Vít Zouhar: Texte, 1994; Arvo Pärt: Passio, 1996. Honours: Czech Music Fund Award, 1988, 1989, 1994; City of Graz Scholarship, 1991; Prize, Generace Composition Competition, yearly 1992-95; OSA Foundation Award, 1994; Musica Nova Prize, 1994. Memberships: Bohuslan Martinu Foundation; Society of Electronic Music; Q Society; Artistic Association. Address: CZ-67907 Kotvrdovice 175, Czech Republic.

ZOUHAR Zdenek, b. 8 Feb 1927, Kotvrdovice, Czechoslovakia. Composer; Musicologist. Education: PhD, Brno University, 1967; Studied at Brno Academy. Career: Head of Music Section at Brno University Library, 1953-61; Editor for

Czech Radio, 1961-70; Professor at Brno Janáfek Academy, 1962-. Compositions include: Sonatina for Piano, 1948; Spring Suite for 3 Violins, 1949; Partita for Organ, 1956; Midnight Mass, 1957; "151" Music for Wind Quintet, 1958; Trio for Flute, Contralto and Bass Clarinet, 1961; Divertimento I for 4 Winds and Percussion, 1965; Music for Strings, 1966; 2 String Quartets, 1966, 1983; Symphonic Triptych, 1967; Music for Wind Quintet II, 1982; Triple Concerto for Clarinet, Trumpet, Trombone and Orchestra, 1970; Chamber radio opera, Metamorphosis, 1971; Variations On A Theme By B Martinu for Symphonic Orchestra, 1979; Musica Giocosa Per Archi, 1981; Brass Quintet, 1985; Comic opera, A Great Love, 1986; Oratorio, The Flames Of Constance, 1988; Divertimento III for Brno Brass Band, 1993. Address: c/o OSA, Cs armady 20, 160-56 Prague 6 - Bubenec, Czech Republic.

ZSAPKOVA Dagmar, b. 24 June 1956, Bratislava, Slovakia. Musician (Flute). m. Jozef Zsapka, 24 Oct 1981, 1 son. Education: Music Conservatory in Bratislava; Music Academy in Bratislava. Debut: Jacques Ibert's Concerto, State Philharmonic Orchestra, Kosice, 1979. Career: Member of duo with guitarist Jozef Zsapka from 1979-; Performed as duo worldwide including Japan, USA, Australia, England, Spain, France, Luxemburg, Switzerland, Lichtenstein, Germany, Italy, Austria, Sweden, Greece, Turkey, Jugoslavia, Hungary, Poland, Ukraine, Rusland, Cuba; Repertoire as duo includes Bach, Baron, Quantz, Vivaldi, Popper, Giuliani, Coste, Borne, Bozza, Ibert, Dodgson, Duarte, Castelnuovo-Tedesco, Rodrigo, Gnattali, Piazzolla, Babcock, Martincek, Rak, Ginalis, Domeniconi, Pujol; Also plays flute with renowned symphonic and chamber ensembles; Invited to lead international master classes in Spain, France, Italy, Lichtenstein, Austria, Slovak Republic; Regularly records for broadcasting and televison studios; Currently Professor at the Conservatoire in Bratislava. Recordings: As flute and guitar duo with Jozef Zsapka: Bonjour Monsieur; Dedication; Dagmar and Jozef Zsapka; J J Quantz, Sonata D dur (with Dagmar & Jozef Zsapka). Honour: 1st Prize in Flute Competition of Slovakia, 1980. Current Management: Interartists; Bajzova 4, Bratislava. Address: Jégého 5, 82108 Bratislava, Slovak Republic.

ZSCHAU Marilyn, b. 9 Feb 1944, Chicago, Ilinois, USA. Soprano. Education: Juilliard School of Music, 1961-65; Further study with John Lester in Montana. Career: Toured with Metropolitan National Company, 1965-66; Debut at Vienna Volksoper as Marietta in Die Tote Stadt, 1967; Vienna Staatsoper in 1971 as the Composer in Ariadne auf Naxos; New York City Opera from 1978, as Puccini's Minnie and Butterfly, Odabella in Attila, and Maddalena in Andrea Chénier; Metropolitan Opera debut in 1985 as Musetta in La Bohème; La Scala debut in 1986 as the Dyer's Wife in Die Frau ohne Schatten; Appearances worldwide in operatic roles including Aida, Leonora, Desdemona, Butterfly, Brünnhilde in Die Walküre and Götterdämmerung, Salome, Elektra, Prokofiev's Renata in The Fiery Angel, Shostakovich's Katerina in Lady Macbeth of Mtsensk, Santuzza and Manon Lescaut; Sang Puccini's Minnie at Reggio Emilia and Chicago in 1990, and The Fiery Angel at the 1990 Holland Festival; Other roles include: Janácek's Vixen and Kostelnicka in Jenufa, the Marschallin and Octavian in Der Rosenkavalier, Mozart's Fiordigili, Countess and Pamina, Lucille in Dantons Tod, and Tatiana in Eugene Onegin; Sang Elektra at Buenos Aires, 1996. Recordings include: Video of Covent Garden performance of La Bohème. Honours: Martha Baird Rockefeller Foundation Scholarships, 1962, 1963. Hobbies: Drawing; Painting; Reading New Age Publications; Walking; Hiking. Address: c/o Janine Meyer and Associates, Suite 1C, 201 West 54th Street, New York, NY 10019, USA.

ZSIGMONDY Denes, b. 9 Apr 1922, Budapest, Hungary. Violinist. m. Anneliese Nissen, pianist, Aug 1947, 2 daughters. Education: Baccalaureat, University of Budapest; Franz Liszt Academy, Budapest; Studied with Geza de Kresz, Leo Weiner, Imre Waldbauer and others. Career: Soloist with Vienna and Berlin Symphonies, Tokyo, Budapest and Munich Philharmonies, Radio Orchestras ABC Sydney, Melbourne and Munich, Stuttgart Chamber Orchestra, and Salzburg Camerata; Performed with BBC Radio London, NHK Tokyo, Radio Paris and others; World premieres of works by Bialas, Eder, Genzmer, Rozsa and others; Professor, University of Washington, Seattle, USA, 1971-; Occasional masterclasses including New England Conservatory; Established annual Holzenhausen Festival in Ammerland, Bavaria with concerts and violin courses, 1978-; Visiting Professor, Boston University, 1981-82; Courses at the Summer Academy, Salzburg-Mozarteum, Austria and in Germany, Italy, Hungary, Poland and others, 1986-. Recordings include: The Virtuoso Violin; The Romantic Violin; Zsigmondy Plays Bartók, volumes 1 and 2; Sonatas by Beethoven, Brahms, Grieg, Franck, Debussy and all Mozart and Schubert violin-piano music. Hobbies: Tennis; Gardening. Address: Bonselweg 10, 8193 Ambach, Bavaria, Germany.

ZUKERMAN Eugenia, b. 25 Sep 1944, Cambridge, MA, USA. Flautist. m. (1) Pinchas Zukerman, divorced, (2) David Seltzer, 1988. Education: Juilliard School, New York with Julius

Baker. Debut: New York Town Hall in 1971. Career: Has played with most major orchestras in the USA and Canada; Tour of US with English Chamber Orchestra; European performances with the Royal Philharmonic, Israel Chamber Orchestra and the Hamburg Bach Solisten; Participation in Festival of Two Worlds at Spoleto, London's South Bank Festival and the Edinburgh Festival; Collaborations with Jean-Pierre Rampal at Carnegie Hall in 1976, and James Galway; Music Commentator on CBS News's Sunday Morning. Recordings: Many discs recorded. Address: c/o ICM Artists, Oxford House, 6 Oxford Street, London W1N 0AX, England.

ZUKERMAN Pinchas, b. 16 Jul 1948, Tel-Aviv, Israel. Conductor; Violist; Violinist; Teacher. m.(1) Eugenia Zukerman, divorced, (2) Tuesday Weld, 2 d. Education: Israel Conservatory and Academy of Music, 1956; Juilliard School, NY, 1961 with Ivan Galamian. Career: Won 1967 Leventritt Competition and soon appeared with most of the world's leading orchestras in the standard repertoire; 1969 with New York Philharmonic and at Brighton Festival; Debut as conductor in London, 1970; Guest appearances include English Chamber Orchestra, Philadelphia Orchestra, Boston Symphony and Israel Philharmonic; Artistic Director, South Bank Summer Music, London, 1978-80; Music Director of St Paul Chamber Orchestra, 1980-86, conducting in the stage premiere of Oliver Knussen's Where the Wild Things Are at Minnesota Opera, 1985; Principal Guest Conductor of Dallas International Music Festival, 1990-; Assumed post of Principal Guest Conductor of Dallas Symphony, 1993; Noted in chamber music repertory in which he also plays viola; Concerts with Daniel Barenboim, the late Jacqueline du Pré, Isaac Stern, Yo-Yo Ma, Itzhak Perlman and Jean-Pierre Rampal; Participant in many TV specials including Alexander's Bachtime Band, with Stern and Alexander Schneider; Premieres of Boulez, Kraft, Lutoslawski, Neikrug, Takemitsu and Picker. Recordings include: Over 90 recordings including, Bach with English Chamber Orchestra as director and soloist, Beethoven and Mozart Sonatas with Marc Neikrug, Mozart Quintets with Tokyo String Quartet. Honours: Numerous including, Doctorate of Brown University, Achievement Award from International Centre, NY, and Medal of Arts Award presented by President Regan, 1983. Address: c/o Harold Holt Ltd, 31 Sinclair Road, London, W14 0NS, England.

ZUKOFSKY Paul, b. 22 Oct 1943, Brooklyn, NY, USA. Violinist; Conductor. Education: BM, 1964, MS, 1964, Juilliard School of Music. Career includes: Creative Associate, SUNY, Buffalo, 1964-65; Various positions as violinist, and violin teacher, 1965-75; President, Musical Observations Inc, 1975-; Principal Investigator, Project Director, Limits, 1976-82; Conductor with various orchestras, 1977-79; Programme Coordinator, American Portraits, concert series at John F Kennedy Center, 1980-; Conductor, Contemporary Chamber Ensemble at Juilliard School of Music, 1984-; Founder, Principal Conductor, Sinfoniuhljomsveit Aeskunnar, 1985-; Director of Chamber Music Activities, The Juilliard School, 1987-89; Artistic Director, Summer Garden Concert Series, Museum of Modern Art, NYC, 1987-. Recordings include: As conductor: Various Icelandic Orchestral Works, 1987, Sixteen Dances by Cage, 1984; As violinist: Penderecki's Capriccio for Violin and Orchestra, 1968, Babbitt and Milton Sextets, 1972, Glass's Strung Out, 1977, Cage's Cheap Imitation, 1981, Sonata for Solo Violin, 1983, For John Cage, Feldman, Morton, 1984. Contributions to: Articles in professional journals including The Psychology of Music, with Sternberg and Knoll. Honours include: Nominee for Grammy Awards, 1972; Pick of the Pack, Time Magazine, 1975; ASCAP Community Orchestra Award, 1979; ASCAP Citation, 1979; Guggenheim Fellowship, 1983-84; National Endowment for The Arts Fellowship, 1983; Knight's Cross, Icelandic Order of the Falcon. Address: c/o The Juilliard School of Music (Violin Faculty), Lincoln Plaza, New York, NY 10023, USA.

ZUPKO Ramon, b. 14 November 1932, Pittsburgh, PA, USA. Composer. Education: Studied with Vincent Persichetti at Juilliard (BS 1956, MS 1957) and with Schiske at the Vienna Academy of Music, 1958-59; Electronic music at Columbia University, and with Koenig at the University of Utrecht. Career: Teacher of Theory and Director of Electronic Music at the Chicago Musical College of Roosevelt University, 1967-71; Professor of Composition and Director of Electronic Music at Western Michigan University, Kalamazoo, from 1971; Gilmore Foundation Commission, 1990. Compositions include: Variations for orchestra, 1961; Violin Concerto, 1962; Transluscents, for strings, 1967; Tangents, for 18 bass instruments, 1967; Radiants, for orchestra, 1971; Proud Music of the Storm, multi-media theatre, 1976; Wind Song, piano concerto, 1979; Life Dances, for orchestra, 1981; Where the Mountain Crosses, song cycle for mezzo and piano, 1982; Canti Terrae, for orchestra, 1982; 2 Symphonies, 1984, 1986; Series of ten Chamber Pieces, Fluxus, for various instrumental combinations (1977-94); Vox Naturae, Concerto for Brass Quintet and Orchestra, 1992; Chaconne for piano, 1995. Honours include: NEA Grants, Koussevitzky Foundation Award and Guggenheim Fellowship (1981-82). Address: c/o ASCAP, One Lincoln Plaza, New York, NY 10023, USA.

ZUR Menachem, b. 6 Mar 1942, Tel Aviv, Israel. Composer; Teacher of Theory and Composition. Education: Teacher's Diploma, College for Teachers of Music, Jerusalem, 1964; Diploma, Rubin Academy of Music, 1967; BMus, Mannes College of Music, NY, USA, 1971; MFA, Sarah Lawrence College, 1972; DMusA, Columbia University, 1975. Career: Musical Advisor to the Israel Museum, Jerusalem; Chairman of the Music Education Department of the Rubin Academy of Music, 1991; Chairperson, Israeli Composers' League, 1992-94. Compositions include: Fantasy for Piano; Sonata for Cello and Piano; Several works for Tape; Prisma for two pianos; Double Concerto for Bassoon, French Horn and Chamber Orchestra; Clarinet Quintet; Piano Concerto; Tuba Concerto; Violin Concerto, Concerto Grosso; Centres, string quartet; Pygmalion, chamber opera; Sonata for Violin and Piano; 3 Symphonies; Prelude for Band; The Golem for 11 Instruments and Baritone Solo; Horn Trio; 2 Sonatas for Cello and Piano; Fantasy for Brass Quintet; Circles of Time for Piano Solo; Pieces for Choir: Hallelujah, Kedushah, Shiluvium, A Tale of Two Sandles. Recordings include: Chants and Horizons for Magnetic Tape; Sonata No 1 for Cello and Piano; Clarinet Quintet, electroacoustic music. Publications: Keyboard Harmony, co-author, 1980. Contributions to: Musical Quarterly. Address: Rubin Academy of Music, Givat-Ram, Jerusalem, Israel.

ZVETANOV Boiko, b. 14 Jun 1955, Sofia, Bulgaria. Tenor. Education: Studied at the Sofia Conservatory. Career includes: Sang with the Bulgarian National Opera from 1982 as the Duke of Mantua, Foresto in Attila, Fernando in La Favorita, Pollione and Radames; Concerts in Russia, Czechoslovakia and France (Verdi's Requiem at Paris), and the Italian Singer in Der Rosenkavalier at the Vienna Staatsoper; Sang at St Gallen in 1991 as Riccardo in Un Ballo in Maschera, Opernhaus Zurich as Lensky, Alvaro in Forza del Destino, Arnold in Guillaume Tell and Rodolfo; 1992 included Capriccio, Wiener Staatsoper, La forza del destino in Zurich, Gugielmo Tell, La Bohème and Il Pirata in Zurich; 1993 included Herodiade in Zurich, Cavalleria rusticana in Wiesbaden and Capriccio in Dresden; La Forza del destino in Karlsruhe in 1993-94; Season 1994-95 included Rosenkavalier and Ballo in Maschera with Deutsche Oper Berlin; Lucia di Lammermoor in Teatro Principal in Valencia with L Alberti, 1995; Rosenkavalier, Oper der Stadt Bonn director Spiros Argiris, 1995. Recordings: CDs of arias and duets from Verdi's operas. Address: Opernhaus Zurich, Falkenstrasse 1, CH-8008 Zurich, Switzerland.

ZWIAUER Florian, b. 1954, Vienna, Austria. Violinist. Education: Studied at the Vienna Academy of Music. Career: Co-founded the Franz Schubert Quartet, 1974; Won the European Broadcasting Union's International String Quartet Competition in Stockholm, 1974; Appearances at Amsterdam Concertgebouw, Vienna Musikverein and Konzerthaus, the Salle Gaveau, Paris, and Sydney Opera House; Visits to Zurich, Geneva, Basle, Berlin, Hamburg, Rome, Rotterdam, Madrid, Copenhagen, Stockholm, Dublin, Manchester, Munich, Lisbon and many more; Festival engagements include Salzburg, Wiener Festwochen, Prague Spring, Bregenz Gestival, Schubertiade at Hohenems, the Schubert Festival at Washington DC and the Belfast and Istanbul Festivals; Tours of Australasia, USSR and USA; British debut at the Queen Elizabeth Hall, 1979; Frequent appearances at Wigmore Hall and Cheltenham Festival; 1st Leader of Vienna Symphony Orchestra, 1989-; Teacher at the Vienna Conservatory and Graz Musikhochschule; Masterclasses at the Royal Northern College of Music and at the Lake District Summer Music. Recordings include: Schubert's Quartet in G, D877; Complete quartets of Dittersdorf; Haydn's 3 Last String Quartets; The 10 late Mozart String Quartets; Complete Tchaikovsky string chamber music; Complete string quartets of Franz Schmidt, Erich Wolfgang Korngold; Complete string quartets of Hans Pfitzner. Honours: As Soloist won 2nd Prize at the W A Mozart International Violin Competition in Salzburg, 1978. Current Management: Christopher Tennant Artists Management, Unit 2, 39 Tadema Road, London SW10 0PY, England. Address: Alszeile 15/14, A-1170 Vienna, Austria.

ZWILICH Ellen Taaffe, b. 30 Apr 1939, Miami, FL, USA. Composer. m. Joseph Zwilich, 22 Jun 1969, deceased 1979. Education: MusB, 1960, MusM, 1962, Florida State University; DMA, Juilliard School of Music, 1975; Other study with various teachers. Career: Violinist with American Symphony, NY, 1965-73; Freelance Composer, 1973-, works performed include: Premier Symposium for Orchestra, Pierre Boulez, NYC, 1975, Chamber Symphony and Passages, Boston Musica Viva, 1979, 1982, Symphony No 1, Gunther Schuller, American Composers Orchestra, 1982. Compositions include: Orchestral and Chamber Music includes: Sonata In 3 Movements, 1973-74, Chamber Symphony, 1979, String Trio, 1982, Cello Symphony, 1985, Concerto Grosso, 1985, Images for 2 Pianos and Orchestra, 1987, Piano Trio, 1987, Symbolon for Orchestra, 1987, Trombone Concerto, 1988, Flute Concerto, 1990, Oboe Concerto, 1990. Honours: Numerous honours and awards including: Elizabeth S Coolidge Chamber Music Prize, 1974, Viotti Gold Medal, Italy, 1975, Pulitzer Prize, 1983, Award, National Institute of Arts and Letters, 1984, Arturo Toscanini Music Critics Award, 1987,

Honorary MusD, Oberlin College, 1987. Memberships: Honorary Life Member, American Federation of Musicians; Past Board, Past Vice President, American Music Centre; International League of Women Composers. Current Management: Music Associates of America, 224 King Street, Englewood, NJ 07631, USA. Address: Hainburger Strasse 47, A-1030 Wien, Austria.

ZYKAN Otto M, b. 29 April 1935. Vienna, Austria. Composer; Pianist. Education: Studied piano & Composition at the Vienna Academy of Music. Career: Many concert appearances, performing contemporary works. Compositions: Opera, Auszahireim, 1986; Sonata for cello & piano, 1958; String Quartet, 1958; Piano Concerto, 1958; Kyryptomnemie for winds, percussion, piano, 1963; Schon der Reihe ballet, 1966; Kurze Anweisung for orchestra, 1969; Miles Smiles, chamber music theatre, 1974; Symphonie der heilen welt, scenic concerto, 1977; Trio for violin, 1977; Ausgesucht Freundliches, concerto for 2 soloists, chorus, orchestra, 1979; Kunst Kommt von Gonnon, opera, 1980; Cello concerto, 1982. Honours: Winner, Darmstadt Competition for pianist, 1958. Address: c/o AKM, III Baumanstrasse 8-10, Postfach 334-338, 1031 Vienna, Austria.

ZYLIS-GARA Teresa, b. 23 Jan 1935, Landvarov, Vilna, Poland. Singer, (Soprano). Education: Studied at the Lodz Academy with Olga Ogina. Debut: Cracow, 1957, as Halka in Moniusko's opera and Violetta. Career: Sang in Oberhausen, Dortmund, Dusseldorf, 1960-70. Glyndebourne Festival, 1965, 1967 as Octavian and Donna Elvira; Covent Garden, from 1968; Salzburg Festival, 1968; Metropolitan Opera, from 1968, as Mozart's Elvira and Fiordiligi, Verdi's Desdemona, Wagner's Elisabeth and Elsa, Strauss's Marschallin, Puccini's Suor Angelica and Manon Lescaut and Tatiana in Eugene Onegin; Vienna Staatsoper, from 1972; Barcelona, 1973-74; Orange Festival, 1979, as Liu in Turandot; Guest engagements in Hamburg, Paris, Berlin and Warsaw; Concert appearances in Bach, Chopin, Handel, Mozart and Brahms; Sang at the Hamburg Staatsoper, 1988, as Desdemona. Recordings: Mosè in Egitto by Rossini; Songs by Chopin; Il Giuramento by Mercadante; Bach's Easter and Christmas Oratorios, St Matthew Passion, Cavalieri's Rappresentazione di Anima e di Corpo, Mozart's Requiem; Ariadne auf Naxos, Electrola. Honours: Winner, International Singing Competition, Munich, 1960; Mozart Gold Medal, Mexico City; Polish National Award, great distinction of aristic achievement. Address: Hamburg State Opera, Grosse Theaterstasse 34, D-2000 Hamburg 36, Germany.

ZYSSET Martin, b. 1965, Solothurn, Switzerland. Singer (Tenor). Education: Studied at the Berne Conservatory and with Ernst Haefliger, Edith Mathis and Roland Hermann. Debut: Selzach Summer Festival, 1992, as Pedrillo in Die Entführung. Career: Appearances at the Zurich Opera, 1992-, as Scaramuccio in Ariadne aur Naxos, Monostatos in Die Zauberflöte, Count Hohenzollern (Henze's Der Prinz von Homburg), Cassio, Jacquino and Tamino; Vienna Festival, 1994, in the premiere of Ein Narrenparadies by Ofer Ben-Amots; Further engagements with the Radio della Svizzera Italiana, in Antwerp and in Luxembourg (concert performance of Fidelio, under Leopold Hager); Other roles include Don Ottavio, Goro in Butterfly and Spoletta in Tosca. Honours include: Prize winner at the 1990 Pro Arte Lyrica Competition, Lausanne. Address: c/o Opernhaus Zurich, Falkenstrasse 1, CH-8008 Zurich, Switzerland.

APPENDIX A
ORCHESTRAS

ARGENTINA

Buenos Aires: Orquesta Filarmónica de Buenos Aires, Cerrito 618, 0101 Buenos Aires. Tel: 54 1 383 5199; Fax: 54 1 383 6167/382 2389
Orquesta Sinfónica Nacional, Córdoba 1155, 1055 Buenos Aires. Tel: 54 1 45 4252

ARMENIA

Yerevan: Armenian Philharmonic Orchestra, Mashtotz 46, 375019 Yerevan. Tel: 37 885 256 4965; Fax: 37 885 258 1142
Music Director: Loris Tjeknavorian; Manager: George Avedissian

AUSTRALIA

AUSTRALIAN CAPITAL TERRITORY

Canberra: Canberra Symphony Orchestra, GPO Box 1919, Canberra, ACT 2601. Tel: 61 6 247 9191; Fax: 61 6 247 9026
General Manager: Jane Woodley

NEW SOUTH WALES

Sydney: Sydney Symphony Orchestra, Australian Broadcasting Corporation, GPO Box 9994, Sydney, NSW 2001. Tel: 61 2 9334 4644; Fax: 61 2 9334 4646
Music Director: Edo de Waart; General Manager: Mary Vallentine

QUEENSLAND
Brisbane: Queensland Symphony Orchestra, Australian Broadcasting Corporation, GPO Box 9994, Brisbane, QLD 4001. Tel: 61 7 3377 5000; Fax: 61 7 3377 5001 *Chief Conductor: Muhai Tang; General Manager: Mary Lyons*

SOUTH AUSTRALIA

Adelaide: Adelaide Symphony Orchestra, Australian Broadcasting Corporation, GPO Box 9994, Adelaide, SA 5001. Tel: 61 8 8343 4820; Fax: 61 8 8343 4808
Chief Conductor: David Porcelijn; General Manager: Michael Elwood

TASMANIA

Hobart: Tasmanian Symphony Orchestra, Australian Broadcasting Corporation, GPO Box 9994, Hobart, TAS 7001. Tel: 61 03 6235 3646; Fax: 61 03 6235 3651 *General Manager: Julie Warn*

VICTORIA

Melbourne: Melbourne Symphony Orchestra, GPO Box 994, Melbourne, VIC 3001. Tel: 61 3 9626 1110; Fax: 61 3 9626 1101
Conductor Laureate: Hiroyuki Iwaki; General Manager: Steven Porter
State Orchestra of Victoria, 100 St Kilda Road, Melbourne, VIC 3004. Tel: 61 3 9281 8000; Fax: 61 3 9281 8282
Administrator: Pamela Foulkes
Victorian Concert Orchestra, 1 Treasury Place, 3rd Floor, Melbourne, VIC 3002
Music Director: Martin Rutherford

WESTERN AUSTRALIA

Perth: West Australian Symphony Orchestra, GPO Box 9994, Perth, WA 6848. Tel: 61 8 9326 0054 / Fax: 61 8 9220 2551
Music Director: Vernon Handley; General Manager: Henk Smit

AUSTRIA

Graz: Grazer Philharmonisches Orchester, Kaiser-Josef-Platz 10, A-8010 Graz
Manager: Dr Gerhard Brunner
Linz: Bruckner-Orchester, Promenade 39, A-4020 Linz. Tel: 43 70 761 1195; Fax: 43 70 761 1315
Chief Conductor: Martin Sieghart; Manager: C-F Steiner
Salzburg: Mozarteum Orchester, Erzbischof-Gebhyardstrasse 10, A-5020 Salzburg
Music Director: Hubert Soudant; Executive Director: Dr Peter Ramsauer
Vienna: Austro-Hungarian Haydn Orchestra, Raffaelgasse 20/1/32, A-1200 Vienna. Tel/Fax: 43 1 334 6356
Director: Adam Fischer
Niederösterreichisches Tonkünstler-Orchester, Elisabethstrasse 22/9, A-1010 Vienna
Chief Conductor: Fabio Luisi; General Manager: Peter Roczek
Orchester "Pro Musica International", Praterstrasse 76/8, A-1020 Vienna
Music Director: Gerhard Track; Manager: Joanna Lewis
Österreichisches Rundfunk Symphonie Orchester, Argentinierstrasse 30, A-1040 Vienna
Chief Conductor: Pinchas Steinberg; Director of Music: Andrea Seebohm
Wiener Kammerorchester, Schachnerstrasse 32, A-1220 Vienna. Tel 43 1 203 6357; Fax 43 1 203 7483
Chief Conductor: Philippe Entremont; General Manager: Christian Buchmann
Wiener Musica Antiqua Ensemble, Minoritenplatz 2, Arkadentrakt, A-1010 Vienna *Music Director: Bernhard Kiebel*
Wiener Philharmoniker, Bösendorferstrasse 12, A-1010 Vienna. Tel: 43 1 505 6525
Manager: Walter Blovsky
Wiener Symphoniker, Lehargasse II, A-1060 Vienna. Tel: 43 1 591 8916
Chief Conductor: Rafael Frühbeck de Burgos; Manager: Rainer Bischof

AZERBAIJAN

Baku: Azerbaijan Symphony Orchestra, Baku

BELGIUM

Antwerp: Koninklijk Filharmonisch Orkest van Vlaanderen, Britselei 80, B-2000 Antwerp. Tel: 32 3 231 3737; Fax: 32 2 231 9126
Music Director: Grant Llewellyn
La Petit Bande, Terlinckstr 16, B-2600 Antwerp
Music Director: Sigiswald Kuijken
Philharmonische Vereniging van Antwerpen, De Boeystraat 6, B-2018 Antwerp
Manager: Albrecht Klora

Brussels: Filharmonisch Orkest van der BRT, Magdalenazaal Duquesnoystr. 14, B-1000 Brussels
Music Director: Alexander Rahbari; Manager: André Laporte
Orchestre National de Belgique, 23 rue Ravenstein, B-1000 Brussels. Tel: 32 2 552 0464; Fax: 32 2 552 0468
Orchestre Symphonique de la RTBF, Place Eugène Flagey18, B-1050 Brussels
Orchestre Symphonique du Théâtre Royal de la Monnaie, 4 Rue Leopold, B-1000 Brussels. Tel: 32 2 229 1218; Fax: 32 2 229 1386
Conductor: Antonio Pappano; Manager: Bernt Sandstad

Leuven: Het Nieuw Belgisch Kamerorkest, Bondgenteniaan 114, B-3000 Leuven
Music Director: Jan Caeyers; Manager: Jan Roekens

Liège: Ensemble Musique Nouvelle, Place de Vingt Août 16, B-4000 Liège
Music Director: Patrick Davin; Manager: Michel Schoonbrood
Orchestre Philharmonique de Liège et de la Communauté Française, 11 Rue Forgeur, B-4000 Liège. Tel: 31 41 236360; Fax: 32 41 237065
Music Director: Pierre Bartholomée; Manager: Roger Pernay

Mons: Orchestre Royal de Chambre de Wallonie et de la Communauté Française, Rue Neuve 5, B-7000 Mons
Music Director: Georges Octors; Manager: Robert Leleu

St-Martens-Latem: I Fiamminghi: The Belgian Chamber Orchestra, Buizenbergstrasse 1, B-9830, St-Martens-Latem
Conductor: Rudolf Werthen; Manager: Dries Sel

BOSNIA AND HERZEGOVINA

Sarajevo: Sarajevo Philharmonic Orchestra, Obala 9, 71000 Sarajevo
Sarajevo Radio and Television Symphony Orchestra, Sarajevo Radio and Television, 71000 Sarajevo

BRAZIL

Brasilia: Orquestra Sinfônica do Teatro Nacional de Brasilia, Av N2, Anexo do Teatro Nacional de Brasilia, 70000 Brasilia
Conductor: Silvio Barbato

Rio de Janeiro: Orquestra Filharmônica do Rio de Janeiro, Rua das Marrecas 25, Sala 901, Centro, 20031 Rio de Janeiro. Tel: 55 21 240 7354; Fax: 55 21 262 4269
Music Director: Florentino Dias
Orquestra Sinfônica Brasileira, Av Rio Branco 135, Room 918, 20040 Rio de Janeiro. Tel: 55 21 222 5842/4592; Fax: 55 21 242 5754
Music Director: Isaac Karabtchevsky

BULGARIA

Sofia: Bulgarian Radio and Television Symphony Orchestra, 4 Dragan Tsankov Boulevard, Sofia. Tel/Fax: 359 2 661812
Sofia Philharmonic Orchestra, Benkovski str 1, 1000 Sofia
Music Director: Emil Tabakov; Administrator: Vassil Kostov

CANADA

ALBERTA

Calgary: Calgary Philharmonic Orchestra, 205 Eighth Avenue, Calgary, Alberta T2G 0K9. Tel: 1 403 571 0270; Fax: 1 403 294 7424
Music Director: Hans Graf

Edmonton: Edmonton Symphony Orchestra, Winspear Centre, Winston Churchill Sq NW, Edmonton, AB T5J 4X8. Tel: 1 403 428 1108; Fax: 1 403 425 1067
Music Director: Gregorz Nowak; Managing Director: W R McPhee

BRITISH COLUMBIA

Vancouver: Vancouver Symphony Orchestra, 601 Smithe Street, Vancouver, British Columbia V6B 5G1. Tel: 1 604 684 9100; Fax: 1 604 684 9264
Music Director: Sergiu Comissiona

Victoria: Victoria Symphony Orchestra, 846 Broughton Street, Victoria, British Columbia V8W 1E4. Tel: 1 604 385 9711; Fax: 1 604 385 7767
Music Director: Peter McCoppin; General Manager: C Stephen Smith

MANITOBA

Winnipeg: Winnipeg Symphony Orchestra, Centennial Concert Hall, 555 Main Street, Room 101, Winnipeg, Manitoba R3B 1C3. Tel: 1 204 949 3950; Fax: 1 204 956 4271 *Artistic Director: Bramwell Tovey; Executive Director: Barry McArton*

NOVA SCOTIA

Halifax: Symphony Nova Scotia, 1646 Barrington Street, Suite 401, Halifax, Nova Scotia B3J 2A3
Music Director: Leslie B Dunner; General Manager: Jody Wood

ONTARIO

Hamilton   Hamilton Philharmonic Orchestra, PO Box 2080, Station A, Hamilton, Ontario L8N 3Y7
Music Director: Akira Endo; General Manager: John Shaw

Kitchener   Kitchener-Waterloo Symphony Orchestra, 101 Queens Street North, Kitchener, Ontario N2H 6P7. Tel: 1 519 745 4711; Fax: 1 519 745 4474
Music Director: Chosi Komatsu; Managing Director: Barry Cole

London: Orchestra London Canada, 520 Wellington Street, London, Ontario N6A 3P9. Tel: 1 519 679 8558; Fax: 1 519 679 8914
Principal Conductor: Uri Mayer; General Manager: John Melnyk

Ottawa: National Arts Centre Orchestra, PO Box 1534, Station B, Ottawa, Ontario K1P 5W1. Tel: 1 613 996 5051; Fax: 1 613 943 1400
Managing Director: J M Mills

Thunder Bay   Thunder Bay Symphony Orchestra, PO Box 2004, Thunder Bay, Ontario P7B 5E7
Music Director: Glenn Mossop; General Manager: Erik Perth

Toronto: Toronto Symphony, Suite 550, 212 King Street West, Toronto, Ontario M5H 1K5. Tel: 1 416 593 7769; Fax: 1 416 593 6788
Music Director: Jukka-Pekka Saraste; Managing Director: Max Tapper

Windsor: Windsor Symphony Orchestra, 174-198 Pitt Street West, Windsor, Ontario N9A 5L4
Music Director: Susan Haig; General Manager: Judith Brander

QUÉBEC

Montréal: Orchestre Symphonique de Montréal, 85 Ste-Catherine W, Suite 900, Montréal, PQ H2X 3P4. Tel: 1 514 842 3402; Fax: 1 514 842 0728
Music Director: Charles Dutoit; Managing Director: Robert Spickler

Québec   Orchestre Symphonique de Québec, 130 Grande Alleé Ouest, Québec, PQ G1R 2G7. Tel: 1 418 643 5598; Fax: 1 418 646 9665
Music Director: Pascal Verrot; Manager: Louis Laplante

SASKATCHEWAN

Regina: Regina Symphony Orchestra, 200 Lakeshire Drive, Regina, Saskatchewan S4P 3V7
Music Director: Vladimir Conta; Executive Director: Pat Middleton

Saskatoon: Saskatoon Symphony Orchestra, PO Box 1361, Saskatoon, Saskatchewan S7K 3N9
Music Director: Dennis Simons; General Manager: Shirley Spafford

CHILE

Santiago: Orquesta Filarmónica de Santiago, San Antonio 149, PO Box 18, Santiago. Tl: 56 2 638 1515; Fax: 56 2 633 7214
Manager: Andrés Pinto

CHINA

Beijing: Central Philharmonic Orchestra, Beijing
Shanghai: Shanghai Symphony Orchestra, 105 Hunan Lu, Shanghai 200031. tel/Fax: 86 21 6433 3752
Conductor: Chen Xie-Yang; General Manager: Cao Yiji

COLOMBIA

Bogotá: Orquesta Filarmónica de Bogotá, Calle 39A, No 14-57, Apdo Aereo 16034, Bogotá. Tel: 57 1 288 3466/4453; Fax: 51 1 288 3162/245 6150
Music Director: Francisco Rettig; Executive Director: Maria Cristina Sánchez
Orquesta Sinfónica de Colombia, Teatro Colón, Calle 10, No 5-32, Bogotá. Tel: 57 243 5316; Fax: 57 820 854
Music Director: Federico Garcia Vigil; Manager: Blanca Cecilia Carreno

COSTA RICA

San José: Orquesta Sinfónica Nacional, PO Box 1035, San José 1000
Music Director: Irwin Hoffman; General Manager: Gloria Waissbluth

CROATIA

Zagreb: Croatian Radio and Television Symphony Orchestra, Dezmanova 10, 41000 Zagreb
Zagreb Philharmonic Orchestra, Trg S Radica 4, Zagreb. Tel: 385 1 539699/539339; Fax: 385 1 539933

CZECH REPUBLIC

Brno: Brno State Philharmonic Orchestra, Komenského nám 8, 602 00 Brno. Tel/Fax: 420 5 4221 2300/8284
Conductor: Aldo Ceccato

Česke Budějovice: South Bohemian State Orchestra, Ceská ul 1, 370 21 Česke Budějovice
Chief Conductor: Ondřej Kukal; Director: Milan Kraus

Hradec Králové: Hradec Králové State Symphony Orchestra, Nábřeží Eliščino 777, 500 70 Hradec Králové
Chief Conductor: František Vajnar; Manager: Radomir Malý

Karlovy Vary: Karlovy Vary Symphony Orchestra, Nábřeží CSP 1, 360 01 Karlovy Vary
Music Director: Bostock Douglas; Manager: Peter Kuliš

Košice: Košice State Philharmonic Orchestra, Dom umenia, Moyzesova 66, 041 23 Košice
Mariánské Lázně: West Bohemian Symphony Orchestra, Třída Odborářu 51, 353 21 Mariánské Lazně. Tel: 420 165 2141/2567; Fax: 420 68 5228 511
Music Director: Radomil Eliška; Manager: Naděžda Domanjová

Olomouc: Moravian Philharmonic Orchestra, Horni náměsti 23, 772 00 Olomouc. Tel: 420 6 5228 971/5225 302; Fax: 420 68 5228 51
Ostrava: Janáček Philharmonic Orchestra, Michálkovická 181, 710 08 Ostrava 2. Tel: 420 69 622 6144; Fax: 420 69 222 886
Music Director: Dennis Burkh; Manager: Miroslav Snyrich

Plzeň: Plzeň Radio Symphony Orchestra, náměsti Miru 4, 320 70 Plzeň. Tel/Fax: 420 19 272254
Chief Conductor: Alexander Apolin

Prague: Czech Philharmonic Orchestra, Alsovo Nábrezi 12, 110 00 Pargue 1. Tel: 420 2 248 93201; Fax: 420 2231 9051
Manager: Ladislov Kantor

Prague Chamber Orchestra, Maltčzské náměsti 1, 118 00 Prague 1
Artistic Director: Jan Opsitos
Prague Radio Symphony Orchestra, Vinohradská 12, 120 99 Prague 2
Chief Conductor: Vladimir Válek; Manager: Dr Vlastimil Neklapil
Prague Symphony Orchestra (FOK), Obecni dum, náměstí Republiky 5, 110 00 Prague 1. Tel: 420 2 231 5981/200 2425; Fax: 420 2 231 0784
Chief Conductor: Gaetano Delogu; Manger: Roman Bělor

DENMARK

Ålborg: Ålborg Symphony Orchestra, Kjellerupsgade 14, DK-9000 Ålborg. Tel: 45 98 131955; Fax: 45 98 130378
Music Director: Owain Arwel Hughes

Århus Århus Symphony Orchestra, Musikhuset Århus,Thomas Jensens Allé, DK-8000 Århus C. 45 89 318280; Fax: 45 86 127466
Music Chief: Joern Baerentzen

Copenhagen: Danish National Radio Symphony Orchestra, Rosenornsallé 22, DK-1999 Copenhagen. Tel: 45 35 203040; Fax: 45 35 206121
Chief Conductor: Ulf Schirmer; Manager: Per Erik Veng
Royal Danish Orchestra, Box 2185, DK-1017 Copenhagen. Tel: 45 33 096701; Fax: 45 33 696767
Sjaellands Symphony Orchestra, Bernstorffsgade 9, DK-1577 Copenhagen V
Manager: Maria Sørensen
Tivoli Symphony Orchestra, Tivoli, Vesterbrogade 3, DK-1620 Copenhagen V

Esbjerg: West Jutland Symphony Orchestra, Islandsgade 50, DK-6700 Esbjerg. tel: 45 75 139339; Fax: 45 75 133242
Administrative Director: Leif Pedersen

Odense: Odense Symphony Orchestra, Claus Bergsgade 9, DK-5000 Odense C. Tel: 45 66 129357; Fax: 45 65 910047
Music Director: Edward Serov; Manager: Per Holst

Sønderborg: South Jutland Symphony Orchestra, Skovvej 16, DK-6400 Sønderborg. Tel: 45 74 426161; Fax: 45 74 426106
Manager: Jytte Rasmussen

DOMINICAN REPUBLIC

Santo Domingo: Orquesta Sinfónica Nacional, Palacio de Bellas Artes, Santo Domingo
Music Director: Carlos Piantini; Manager: Sofia de Sturla

ECUADOR

Quito: Orquesta Sinfónica Nacional, Casilla 2844, Calle Venezuela 666, Quito
Music Director: Alvaro Manzano; Manager: G Sáenz

EGYPT

Cairo: Cairo Symphony Orchestra, c/o Egyptian Opera House, Geziro, Cairo. eTel: 202 342 0601/02/03; Fax: 202 342 0599
Music Director: Ahmed Elsaedi

EIRE

Dublin: Irish Chamber Orchestra, 18 Kildare Street, Dublin 2
Artistic Director and Principal Conductor: Stephen Kovacevich; Manager: Gerard Kennan
National Symphony Orchestra of Ireland, National Concert Hall, Earlsfort Terrace, Dublin 2
Radio Telefis Eireann Concert Orchestra, RTE Donnybrook, Dublin 4
Principal Conductor: Proinnsias Duinn; Manager: Sam Ellis

EL SALVADOR

San Salvador: Orquesta Sinfónica de El Salvador, Apartdao Postal 3150, Correro Central, San Salvador
Music Director: German Cáceres; Manager: Alfredo Iraheta

ESTONIA

Tallin: Estonian State Symphony Orchestra, Lomonossovi 21, 200100 Tallin

FINLAND

Helsinki: Helsinki Philharmonic Orchestra, Finlandia-talo, Karamzininkatu 4, 00 100 Helsinki. tel: 358 9 40241; Fax: 358 9 406484
Chief Conductor: Leif Segerstam; Manager: Helena Ahonen
Finnish Radio Symphony Orchestra, PO Box 14, 00 024 Yleisradio, Helsinki. Tel: 358 9 1480 4366; Fax: 358 9 1480 3551
Chief Conductor: Jukka-Pekka Saraste; Manager: Helena Hiilivirta

Tampere: Tampere Philharmonic Orchestra, PL 16, 31 101 Tampere. Tel: 358 3 243 4411; Fax: 358 3 243 4400
Artistic Director: Eri Klas; General Manager: Maritta Hirvonen

Turku: Turku Philharmonic Orchestra, Sibeliuksenkatu 2 B, 20 110 Turku. Tel: 358 21 2314 577; Fax: 358 21 2328 231
Music Director: Jacques Mercier; Manager: Kalevi Kuosa

FRANCE

Angers: Orchestre Philharmonique des Pays de la Loire, 25 Avenue Montaigne, BP 2157, F-49000 Angers Cédex. Tel: 33 41 24 11 24;
Fax: 33 41 87 80 52 *Music Director: Marc Soustrot; General Administrator; Maryvonne Lavigne*

Avignon: Orchestre Lyrique de Région Avignon Provence, 250 Rue des Rémouleurs, ZI de Courtine, BP 260, F-84011 Avignon Cédex
Music Director: François Bilger

Bordeaux: Orchestre National Bordeaux-Aquitaine, BP 95, F-33025 Bordeaux. Tel: 33 56 44 70 71; Fax: 33 56 44 64 85
Administrator: Daniel Dourneau-Gabory

Cachan: Orchestre National d'Ile de France, 8 Rue Marcel Bonnet, F-94230 Cachan
Music Director: Jacques Mercier; General Administrator: Phillippe Fanjas

Caen: Orchestre de Caen, F-14027 Caen Cédex
Music Director: Jean-Marc Laureau; Manager: Delphine Chevallier

Cannes: Orchestre Régional de Cannes-Provence Alpes Côte d'Azur, 104 Avenue Francis Tonner, BP 46, F-06321 Cannes La Bocca Cédex
Director: Philippe Bender; Manager: Catherine Morschel

Chambéry: Orchestre des Pays de Savoie, 67 Carre Curial, F-73000 Chambéry
Music Director: Tibor Varga; Manager: Sylvain Gautier

Clermont-Ferrand Orchestre D'Auvergne, 2 Rue Urbain II, F-63000 Clermont-Ferrand
Music Director: Jean-Jacques Kantorow; Manager: Anne Bertet

Grenoble: Ensemble Instrumental de Grenoble, 1 Rue du Vieux Temple, F-38000 Grenoble
Director: Marc Tardue; Manager: Jean-Peter Roeber

Lille: Orchestre National de Lille, 30 Place Mendès-France, BP 119, F-59027 Lille Cédex. Tel: 33 3 20 12 8240; Fax: 33 3 20 78 29
Music Director: Jean-Claude Casadesus; Manager: Jacqueline Brochen

Lyon: Orchestre National de Lyon, 82 Rue de Bonnel, F-69431 Lyon Cédex. Tel: 33 4 78 95 95 00; Fax: 33 4 78 60 13 08
Music Director: Emmanuel Krivine; Director General: Patrice Armengau

Marseille: Société des Concerts du Conservatoire, 1 Rue de la Bibliothéque, F-13000 Marseille

Metz: Orchestre Philharmonique de Lorraine, 25 Avenue Robert Schumann, F-57000 Metz
Music Director: Jacques Houtmann; Manager: Pascal Schwan

Montpellier: Orchestre Philharmonique de Montpellier, Le Corum, BP 9056, F34041Montpellier. Tel: 33 67 61 67 21; Fax: 33 67 61 67 20
Music Director: Friedemann Layer; Director General: René Koering; Administrator: Dominique Stobinsky

Mulhouse: Orchestre Symphonique de Rhin-Mulhouse, 38 Passage du Théâtre, F-68100 Mulhouse
Music Director: Luca Pfaff; Manager: Jean-Luc Fischer

Nancy: Orchestre Symphonique et Lyrique de Nancy, 1 Rue Sainte Catherine, F-54000 Nancy. Tel: 33 83 85 33 20; Fax: 33 83 85 30 66
Music Director: Jérome Kaltenbach; Manager: Astrid Chepfer

Nice: Orchestre Philharmonique de Nice, 9 Rue de la Terrasse, F-06300 Nice. Tel: 33 93 80 59 83; Fax: 33 93 80 34 83
Music Director: Klaus Weise; Manager: Pierre Medecin

Noisy le Grand: La Grande Ecurie et la Chambre du Roy, 9 Place des Federées, F-93160 Noisy le Grand
Music Director: Jean-Claude Malgoire

Paris: Association des Concerts Colonne, 2 Rue Edouard Colonne, F-75001 Paris
Music Director: Antonello Allemandi; General Manger: Guy Arnaud
Association des Concerts Lamoureux, 252 Rue de Faubourg St-Honoré, F-75008 Paris. Tel: 33 1 45 63 44 34/6062; Fax: 33 1 45 62 05 41
Manager: Annie Foultier
Association des Concerts Pasdeloup, 18 Rue de Berne, F-75008 Paris
Manager: Roger Landy
Ensemble Ars Antiqua de Paris, 167 Rue de Flandre, F-75019 Paris
Music Director: Joseph Sage
Ensemble Ars Nova, 16 Rue des Fossés St Jacques, F-75005 Paris
Music Director: Marius Constant
Ensemble InterContemporain, 9 Rue de 'Echelle, F-75001 Paris
Music Director: David Robertson; Manager: Claude Le Cleach
Ensemble Orchestral de Paris, Salle Pleyel, 252 Rue du Faubourg St Honoré, F-75008 Paris
Conductor: Jean-Jacques Kantorow; Manager: Alain Guillon
Ensemble Orchestral Harmonia Nova, 74 Rue de Faubourg St Denis, F-75010 Paris
Music Director: Didier Bouture; Manager: Daniel Gutenberg
La Chapelle Royale, 10 Rue Coquilliere, F-75001 Paris. Tel: 33 1 40 26 58 00; Fax: 33 1 40 26 38 37
Music Director: Philippe Herreweghe
Les Arts Florissants, 10 Rue de Florence, F-75008 Paris
Music Director: William Christie; Administrative Manager: Bruno Schuster
Nouvel Orchestre Philharmonique, Radio France, 116 Avenue du Président Kennedy, F-75786 Paris Cédex 16. Tel: 33 1 42 30 36 30; Fax: 33 1 42 30 47 48 *Music Director: Marek Janowski; Artistic Director: Yvon Kapp*
Orchestre de Chambre Jean-François Paillard, 50 Rue Laborde, F-75008 Paris
Music Director: Jean-François Paillard; Administrator: Richard Siegel
Orchestre de Chambre Paul Kuentz, 144 Rue du Faubourg St Antoine, F-75012 Paris
Music Director: Paul Kuentz
Orchestre de Paris, Salle Pleyel, 252 Rue du Faubourg St Honoré, F-75008 Paris. Tel: 33 1 45 61 65 60; Fax: 33 1 42 89 24 49
Music Director: Semyon Bychkov; General Director: Stéphane Lissner
Orchestre Française des jeunes, 39 Rue Censier, F-75005 Paris
Music Director: Emmanuel Krivine; Manager: Aude le Clech
Orchestre National de France, Radio France, 116 Avenue du Président Kennedy, F-75786 Paris Cédex 16. Tel: 33 1 42 30 26 03; Fax: 33 1 42 30 43 33 *Music Director: Charles Dutoit; General Manager: Patrice d'Ollone*
Orchestre Symphonique de la Garde Républicaine, 12 Boulevard Henri IV, F-75004 Paris
Music Director: Roger Boutry

Poitiers: Orchestre Régional Poitou-Charentes, 3 Place Prosper Mérimée, BP 422, F-86011 Poitiers Cédex
Director: Charles Frey

Rennes: Orchestre de Bretagne, 42A Rue St-Melaine, F-35000 Rennes
Director: Claude Schnitzler; Manager: Jean-François Jeandet

Rouen: Ensemble Orchestral de Haute-Normandie, 50 Avenue de la Porte des Champs, F-76000 Rouen
Music Director: Jean-Pierre Berlingen; Administrator: Jean-Michel Bernard

Strasbourg: Orchestre Philharmonique de Strasbourg, Palais de la Musique et des Congrès, Avenue Schutzenberger, F-67082 Strasbourg Cédex.
Tel: 33 03 88 15 09 00; Fax: 33 03 88 15 09 01 *Music Director: Theodor Guschlbauer; General Manager: Albert-Michel Moritz*

Sèvres:	Orchestre de Chambre de Versailles, 3 Rue Descartes, F-92310 Sèvres
	Music Director: M B Wahl
Toulouse:	Orchestre de Chambre National de Toulouse, 76 Allée Jean-Jaurès, F-31071 Toulouse
	Director: Alain Moglia; Manager: Jean-Pierre Paragon
	Orchestre National du Capitole de Toulouse, Halle aux Grains, Place Dupuy, F-31000 Toulouse. Tel: 33 61 23 21 35; Fax: 33 61 62 10 48
	Music Director: Michel Plasson; Manager: George Schneider
Versailles:	Orchestre Jean-François Gonzales, 32 Rue du Marechal Joffre, Residence 7, F-78000 Versailles
	Music Director: J-F Gonzales-Hamilton; Manager: Lenore Gouyet
Ville d'Avray:	Orchestre de Chambre Jean-Louis Petit, 34 Rue Corot, F-92410 Ville d'Avray
	Music Director: Jean-Louis Petit

GERMANY

Aachen:	Städtisches Orchester Aachen, Stadttheater, 5100 Aachen
	Music Director: Yukio Kitahara; Manager: Julian Sieben
Augsburg:	Philharmonisches Orchester der Stadt Augsburg, Kasernstrasse 4, Pf 111949, D-86044 Augsburg. Tel: 49 821 324 4903; Fax: 49 821 324 4935
	General Music Director: Peter Leouard; Manager: Andreas Finke
Baden-Baden:	SWF-Sinfonieorchester Baden-Baden, Hans-Bredow-Strasse, 7570 Baden-Baden
	Chief Conductor: Michael Gielen; Manager: Mathias Weigmann
Bamberg:	Bamberger Symphoniker, Mussstrasse 1, D-96047 Bamberg. Tel: 49 951 964 7100; Fax: 49 951 964 7123
	Music Director and Manager: Francis Hunter
Berlin:	Berliner Barock-Orchester, Arnold-Knoblauch-Ring, 64, Pf 173, 1000 Berlin
	Music Director: Konrad Latte
	Berliner Philharmonisches Orchester, Philharmonie, Matthäikirchstrasse 1, D-14057 Berlin. Tel: 49 30 254 880; Fax: 49 30 261 4887
	Artistic Director: Claudio Abbado; Manager: Elmar Weingarten
	Berliner Sinfonie-Orchester, Gendarmenmarkt, 1086 Berlin
	Music Director: Michael Schønwandt; Manager: Frank Schneider
	Berliner Symphoniker, Charlotten Stre 56, D-14057 Berlin. Tel: 49 30 209 02002; Fax: 49 30 229 1818
	Music Director: Alun Francis; Manager: Jochen Thärichen
	Deutsches Kammerorchester, Lietzenburger Strasse 51, 1000 Berlin
	Music Director: Fritz Weisse
	Deutsches Symphonie Orchester Berlin, Charlottenstrasse 56, D-10117 Berlin
	Chief Conductor: Vladimir Ashkenazy
	Freies Kammerorchester Berlin e V, Antonstrasse 25, 1000 Berlin
	Music Director: Christoph Hagel
	Orchester der Deutschen Oper Berlin, Richard-Wagner-Strasse 10, D-10585 Berlin. Tel: 49 30 34381; Fax: 49 30 348 8232
	General Music Director: Rafael Frühbeck de Burgos
	Orchester der Komischen Oper Berlin, Behrenstrasse 55-57, 1086 Berlin
	General Music Director: Yakov Kreizberg
	Orchester des Friedrichstadtpalastes Berlin, Friedrichstrasse 107, 1040 Berlin
	Music Director: Detlef Klemm; Manager: Julian Herrey
	Orchester des Metropol-Theaters, Friedrichstrasse 101/102, Pf 1302, 1086 Berlin
	General Music Director: Günter Joseck
	Orchester des Theaters des Westens, Kantstrasse 12, 1000 Berlin 12
	Music Director: Peter Keuschnig
	Rundfunk-Sinfonieorchester Berlin, Napelstrasse 18-50, 1160 Berlin
	Chief Conductor: Rafael Frühbeck de Burgos
	Staatskapelle Berlin, Unter den Linden 7, 1086 Berlin
	General Music Director: Daniel Barenboim
Bielefeld:	Philharmonisches Orchester der Stadt Bielefeld, Brunnenstrasse 3, 4800 Bielefeld 1
	General Music Director: Rainer Koch
Blankenburg:	Telemann-Kammerorchester Sachsen-Anhalt, Institut für Auffuhrungspraxis Michaelstein, Pf 24, 3720 Blankenburg
	Music Director: Eitelfriedrich Thom
Bochum:	Bochumer Symphoniker, Prinz-Regent-Strasse 50-60, 4630 Bochum
	General Music Director: Steven Sloane
Bonn:	Deutsche Bachsolisten, Goddardstrasse 28, 5300 Bonn
	Music Director: Helmut Winschermann
	Klassische Philharmonie Telekom Bonn, Theaterstrasse 10, 5300 Bonn 1
	Music Director: Heribert Beissel
	Orchester der Beethovenhall Bonn, Verwaltung, Wachsbleiche 2, 5300 Bonn 1
Brandenburg:	Brandenburger Symphoniker, Grabenstrasse 14, 1800 Brandenburg
	Music Director: Heiko Mathias Förster
Braunschweig:	Staatsorchester Braunschweig, Staatstheater Braunschweig, Pf 4539, 3300 Braunschweig
	General Music Director: Stefan Soltesz
Bremen:	Philharmonisches Staatsorchester der Freien Hansestadt Bremen, Wüste Stätte 11, 2800 Bremen
	General Music Director: Marcello Viotti
Bremerhaven:	Städtisches Orchester Bremerhaven, Theodor-Heuss-Platz, Pf 12051, 2850 Bremerhaven
	General Music Director: Leo Plettner
Chemnitz:	Robert-Schumann-Philharmonie, Städtische Theater Chemnitz, Theaterplatz 2, Pf 756, 9001 Chemnitz
	General Music Director: Dieter Gerhardt Worm
	Staatliches Orchester Sächsen, Chemnitzer Strasse 46, 9125 Grüna
	Music Director: Manfred Grafe
Coburg:	Landestheaterorchester Coburg, Coburger Landestheater, Schlossplatz, 8630 Coburg
	General Music Director: Christian Fröhlich

Cologne: Gürzenich-Orchester, Bischofsgartenstrasse 1, Pf 180241, 5000 Cologne 1
                     General Music Director: James Conlon
                     Kölner Kammerorchester e V, Schlosstrasse 2, 5040 Bruhl
                     Music Director: Helmut Müller-Bruhl
                     Kölner Rundfunk-Sinfonie-Orchester, Appellhofplatz 1, D-50600
                     Chief Conductor: Hans Vonk; Director of Music Programming: Hermann Lang
                     Rheinisches Kammerorchester Köln, Steinfelder Gasse 11, 5000 Cologne 1
                     Music Director: Jan Corazolla
                     Sinfonietta Köln, Auf der Kuhle 11, 5250 Engelskirchen
                     Music Director: Cornelius Frowein
Cottbus: Brandenburgisches Kammerorchester e V, A Thiemig, Schopenhauerstrasse 9, 7513 Cottbus
                     Music Director: Bernhard Schleinitz
                     Philharmonisches Orchester der Staatstheaters Cottbus, Karl-Liebknecht-Strasse 136, 7500 Cottbus
                     General Music Director: Frank Morgenstern
Darmstadt: Kammerorchester Merck, Stefan Reinhardt, Pf 4119, 6100 Darmstadt
                     Orchester des Staatstheaters Darmstadt, Auf dem Marienplatz, 6100 Darmstadt
Dessau: Orchester des Landestheaters Dessau, Fritz-Hesse-Platz 1, 4500 Dessau
                     General Music Director: Daniel Lipton
Detmold: Detmolder Kammerorchester e V, Bruchstrasse 25, Pf 1404, 4930 Detmold
                     Music Director: Christoph Poppen
                     Orchester des Landestheaters Detmold, Landestheater Detmold, Theaterplatz, 4930 Detmold1
Dortmund: Philharmonisches Orchester der Stadt Dortmund, Kuhstrasse 12, 4600 Dortmund 1
                     General Music Director: Moshe Atzmon
Dresden: Dresdner Kammerorchester, c/o Sächsische Staatskapelle Dresden, Theaterplatz 2, 8010 Dresden
                     Dresdner Philharmonie, Kulturpalast am Altmarkt, Pf 120424, D-01005 Dresden. Tel: 49 351 486 6282; Fax: 49 351 486 6283
                     General Music Director: Michel Plasson; Artist Manager: Dr Olivier von Winterstein
                     Orchester der Staatsoperette, Pirnaer Landstrasse 131, 8045 Dresden
                     Music Director: Volker Munch
                     Robert Schuman Philharmonie, Pf 120368, Kulturpalast am Altmarkt, D-01005 Dresden. Tel: 49 351 486 6282; Fax: 49 351 486 6283
                     Music Director: John Carewe
                     Sächsische Staatskapelle Dresden, Theaterplatz 2, 8010 Dresden
                     Chief Conductor: Giuseppe Sinopoli
                     Virtuosi Saxoniae, Welterstrasse 16, 8029 Dresden
                     Music Director: Ludwig Güttler
Duisburg: Duisburger Sinfoniker, Beckarstrasse 1, 4100 Duisburg 1
                     General Music Director: Bruno Weil
Düsseldorf: Düsseldorfer Symphoniker, Ehrenhof 1, D-40479 Düsseldorf. Tel: 49 211 899 3606; Fax: 49 211 892 9143
                     Music Director: Salvador Mas Conde; Manager: Freimut Richter-Hansen
                     Robert-Schumann-Kammerorchester Düsseldorf, Kronerweg 34, D-40479 Düsseldorf
                     Music Director: Jürgen Kussmaul
Erfurt: Erfurter Kammerorchester, Strasse der Einheit 12, 5082 Erfurt
                     Music Director: Margit Borner
                     Philharmonisches Orchester Erfurt, Gorkistrasse 1, 5020 Erfurt
                     General Music Director: Wolfgang Rögner
Essen: Folkwang Kammerorchester Essen e V, Hollestrasse Ig, D-45128 Essen
                     Music Director: Karl-Heinz Bloemeke
                     Philharmonic Essen, Rolandstrasse 10, D-45128 Essen
                     General Music Director: Wolf-Dieter Hauschild
Flensburg: Schleswig-Holsteinisches Sinfonieorchester, Rathausstrasse 22, 2390 Flensburg
                     General Music Director: Gerhard Schneider
Frankfurt am Main: Concerto Grosso Frankfurt e V, Ludwigstrasse 66, 6050 Offenbach
                     Music Director: Irina Edelstein
                     Deutsche Kammerphilharmonie, Schwedlerstrasse 2-4, D-60320 Frankfurt am Main 1
                     Deutsches Kammerorchester Frankfurt am Main, Carl-von-Ossietzky-Strasse 56, 6200 Wiesbaden
                     Opernhaus-und Museumsorchester Frankfurt am Main, Untermainanlage 11, D-60320 Frankfurt am Main
                     General Music Director: Sylvain Cambreling
                     Radio-Sinfonie-Orchester Frankfurt, Hessischer Rundfunk, Bertramstrasse 8, D-60320 Frankfurt am Main 1. Tel: 49 69 155 2071;
                     Fax: 49 69 155 2720 *Orchestra Manager: Medi Gasteiner-Girth*
                     Rundfunkorchester des Hessischen Rundfunks, Bertramstrasse 8, D-60320 Frankfurt am Main 1
                     Music Director: Peter Falk; Director of Music Programing: Leo Karl Gerhartz
Frankfurt   Philharmonisches Orchester Frankfurt an der Oder, Collegienstrasse 7, 1200 Frankfurt an der an Oder
der Oder: *General Music Director: Nikos Athinãos*
Freiburg im   Collgium Aureum, Nordstrasse 2, 7800 Freiburg im Breisgau
Breisgau: *Music Director: Franzjosef Maier*
                     Philharmonisches Orchester der Stadt Freiburg, Bertoldstrasse 46, 7800 Freiburg im Breisgau
                     General Music Director: Donald Runnicles
Gelsenkirchen: Philharmonisches Orchester der Stadt Gelsenkirchen, Musiktheater im Revier, 4650 Gelsenkirchen
                     General Music Director: Neil Varon
Gera: Philharmonisches Orchester Gera, Bühnen der Stadt Gera, Küchengartenalle 2, 6500 Gera
                     Music Director: Wolfgang Wappler
                     Reussisches Kammerorchester, Bühnen der Stadt Gera, Küchengartenalle 2, 6500 Gera
                     Music Director: Herbert Voigt
Gotha: Landessinfonieorchester Thüringen-Gotha, Reinhardsbrunner Strasse 23, 5800 Gotha
                     Music Director: Hermann Breuer
Göttingen: Göttinger Symphonie-Orchester, Godehardstrasse 19-21, 3400 Göttingen
                     Music Director: Christian Simonis

Hagen: Philharmonisches Orchester Hagen, Elberfelder Strasse 65, 5800 Hagen 1
General Music Director: Gerhard Markson
Halle an der Saale: Händelfestspielorchester, Universitätsring 24, D-06108 Halle an der Saale. Tel: 49 345 511 10300; Fax: 49 345 511 0303
Music Director: Roger Epple
Kammerorchester "musica juventa" Halle, Hegelstrasse 9, D-06108 Halle an der Saale
Music Director: Matthias Erben
Philharmonisches Staatsorchester Halle, Kleine Brauhausstrasse 26, D-06108 Halle an der Saale. Tel: 49 345 202 4754; Fax: 49 345 202 3278
General Music Director: Herbert Beissel
Hamburg: Akademie Hamburger Solisten, Seilerstrasse 41, D-20355 Hamburg
Music Director: Joachim Kerwin
Hamburger Mozart-Orchester, Helgolandstrasse 12, 2000 Wedel
Music Director: Robert Stehli
Hamburger Symphoniker, Dammtorwall 46, D-20355 Hamburg. Tel: 49 40 344851; Fax: 49 40 353788
Music Director: Miguel Gómez Martínez
NDR-Sinfonieorchester, Norddeutscher Rundfunk Hamburg, Rothenbaumchaussee 132, D-20355 Hamburg
Chief Conductor: Herbert Blomstedt; Director of Music Programming: Bernhard Hansen
Philharminisches Kammerorchester Hamburg e V, Musikhalle, Karl-Muck-Platz, D-20355 Hamburg
Music Director: Wilfried Laatz
Philharmonisches Staatsorchester Hamburg, Grosse Theaterstrasse 34, D-20355 Hamburg
General Music Director: Gerd Albrecht; Manager: Peter Ruzicka
Radiokammerorchester Hamburg, Zum Forellenback 11, 2000 Oststeinbek
Music Director: Karl Henke
Hannover: Niedersächsisches Staatsorchester, Opernplatz 1, 3000 Hannover 1
General Music Director: Christof Prick
Rundfunkorchester Hannover, Rudolf-von-Benningsen-Ufer 22, 3000 Hannover
Chief Conductor: Bernhard Klee
Heidelberg: Orchester der Stadt Heidelberg, Friedrichstrasse 5, 6900 Heidelberg 1
General Music Director: Anton Marik
Heilbronn: Württembergisches Kammerorchester Heilbronn, Pf 3830, 7100 Heilbronn
Music Director: Jörg Faerber
Herford: Nordwestdeutsche Philharmonie, Stiftbergstrasse 2, 4900 Herford
Music Director: Michail Jurowski
Hilchenbach: Südwestfälische Philharmonie, Im Langen Feld 2, Pf 1320, 5912 Hilchenbach
Music Director: Hiroshi Kodama; Manager: Volker Mattern
Hof: Hofer Symphoniker, Klosterstrasse 9-11, D-95028 Hof. Tel: 48 09281 720015; Fax: 49 09281 720072
Intendant: Wilfried Anton
Jena: Jenaer Philharmonie, August-Babel-Strasse 4, 6900 Jena
General Music Director: Andreas S Weiser
Kaiserslautern: Orchester des Pfalztheaters Kaiserslautern, Fruchthallstrasse, 6750 Kaiserslautern
General Music Director: Lior Shambadal
Rundfunkorchester des Südwestfunks, Fliegerstrasse 36, 6750 Kaiserslautern
Music Director: Klaus Arp; Director of Music Programming: Dr Reimund Hess
Karlsruhe: Badische Staatskapelle Karlsruhe, Baumeisterstrasse 11, 7500 Karlsruhe
General Music Director: Günter Neuhold
Kassel: Orchester des Staatstheaters Kassel, Staatstheater Kassel, Friedrichsplatz 15, 3500 Kassel
General Music Director: Georg Schmöhe
Kiel: Philharmonisches Orchester der Landeshauptstadt Kiel, Rathausplatz, D-24103 Kiel. Tel: 49 431 901 2895/2853; Fax: 49 431 901 2889
General Music Director: Klauspeter Seibel
Koblenz: Staatsorchester Rheinische Philharmonie, Eltzerhostrasse 6a, 5400 Koblenz
General Music Director: Christian Klutting; Manager: Hans Richard Stracke
Konstanz: Südwestdeutsche Philharmonie Konstanz, Spanierstrasse 3, 7750 Konstanz
General Music Director: Petr Altrichter
Leipzig: Gewandhausorchester zu Leipzig, Augustusplatz 8, D-04109 Leipzig. Tel: 49 341 1270; Fax: 49 341 12 70200
Music Director: Kurt Masur
Leipziger Kammerorchester, Schorlemmerstrasse 3, 7022 Leipzig
Music Director: Otto-Georg Moosdorf
Orchester der Musikalischen Komödie Leipzig, Dreilindenstrasse 30, 7033 Leipzig
Music Director: Roland Seiffarth
Sinfonieorchester des Mitteldeutschen Rundfunks, Springerstrasse 22-24, D-04105 Leipzig. Tel: 49 341 300 5505; Fax: 49 341 5532
Chief Conductor: Daniel Nazareth; Director of Music Programming: Hubertus Franzen
Leverkusen: Westdeutsche Sinfonia, Am Kreispark 32, Pf 310154, 5090 Leverkusen
Music Director: Dirk Joeres
Lübeck: Orchester der Hansestadt Lübeck, Fischergrube 5/21, 2400 Lübeck
General Music Director: Erich Wächter
Ludwigshafen: Staatsphilharmonie Rheinland-Pfalz, Heinigstrasse 40, D-67059 Ludwigshafen. Tel: 49 621 524025; Fax: 49 621 623467
Music Director: Bernhard Klee; Manager: Raimund Gress
Magdeburg: Magdeburgische Philharmonie, Theater der Landeshauptstadt Magdeburg, Pf 1240, 3010 Magdeburg
General Music Director: Mathias Husmann
Mainz: Mainzer Kammerorchester e V, Sertoriusring 56, 6500 Mainz 21
Philharmonisches Orchester des Staatstheaters Mainz GmbH, Gutenbergplatz 7, 6500 Mainz 1
General Music Director: Peter Erckens
Mannheim: Kürpfalzisches Kammerorchester, D 6, 2, 6800 Mannheim 1
Music Director: Jiří Malát
Nationaltheater-Orchester Mannheim, Mozartstrasse 9, 6800 Mannheim 1
Marl: Philharmonia Hungarica, Am Theater 1, 4370 Marl
General Music Director: Jun Märkl

Meiningen: Orchester des Meininger Theaters, Bernhardstrasse 5, 6100 Meiningen
  Music Director: Wolfgang Hocke
Mönchengladbach: Niederrheinische Sinfoniker, Opernhaus, Odenkirchener Strasse 78, 4050 Mönchengladbach
  General Music Director: Yakov Kreizberg
Munich: • Bach Collegium München e V, Elisabethstrasse 9, 8000 Munich
  Music Director: Florian Sonnleitner
  Bayerisches Staatsorchester, Max-Joseph-Platz 2, D-80539 Munich. Tel: 49 89 218501; Fax: 49 89 2185 1003
  Musical Director: Zubin Meha
  Münchener Kammerorchester e V, Wittelsbacherplatz 2, 8000 Munich
  Music Director: Christoph Poppen
  Münchner Philharmoniker, Gasteig Kulturzentrum, Kellerstrasse 4/III, D-81667 Munich. Tel: 49 89 4809 8509; Fax: 49 89 4809 8513
  General Music Director: James Levine; Manager: Norbert Thomas
  Münchner Symphoniker e V, Drachslstrasse 14, 8000 Munich
  Music Director: Christoph Stepp
  Orchester des Staatstheaters am Gärtnerplatz, Gärtnerplatz 3, 8000 Munich
  Music Director: Reinhard Schwarz
  Philharmonisches Kammerorchester München e V, Connolly-Strasse 15, 8000 Munich
  Music Director: Michael Helmrath
  Rundfunkorchester des Bayerischen Rundfunks, Rundfunkplatz 1, 8000 Munich
  Music Director: Roberto Abbado
  Symphonieorchester des Bayerischen Rundfunks, Rundfunkplatz 1, 8000 Munich
  Chief Conductor: Zubin Mehta (from 1998)
Münster: Symphonieorchester des Stadt Münster, Neubrückenstrasse 63, 4400 Münster
  General Music Director: Will Humburg
Neubrandenburg: Neubrandenburger Philharmonie, Friedrich-Engels-Ring 52, 2000 Neubrandenburg
  Music Director: Romely Pfund
Neustrelitz: Orchester des Landestheaters Mecklenburg, Friedrich-Ludwig-Jahn-Strasse, 2080 Neustrelitz
  Music Director: Golo Berg
Neuss: Deutsche Kammeradademie, Oberstrasse 17, Pf 101452, 4040 Neuss 1
  Music Director: Johannes Goritzki
Nordhausen: Orchester des Theaters Nordhausen, Kathe-Kollwitz-Strasse 15, 5500 Nordhausen
  Music Director: Kurt Schafer
Nürnberg: Nürnberger Symphoniker, Bayernstrasse 100, 8500 Nürnberg
  Manager: Günter Einhaus
  Philharmonisches Orchester der Stadt Nürnberg, Städtische Bühnen Nürnberg, Musiktheater, Richard-Wagner-Platz 2-10, Nürnberg.
  General Music Director: Eberhard Kloke
Oldenburg: Oldenburgisches Staatsorchester, Theaterwall 18, 2900 Oldenburg
  General Music Director: Kurt Mahike
Osnabrück: Osnabrücker Symphonieorchester, Städtische Bühnen Osnabrück, Musikbüro, Domhof 10/11, 4500 Osnabrück
  General Music Director: Jean-François Monnard
Pforzheim: Südwestdeutsches Kammerorchester Pforzheim, Westliche 257A, 7530 Pforzheim
  Music Director: Vladislav Czarnecki
Plauen: Orchester des Vogtland-Theaters Plauen, Theaterplatz 1-3, 9900 Plauen
  Music Director: Paul Theissen
Potsdam: Brandenburgische Philharmonie, Zimmerstrasse 10, 1570 Potsdam
  Music Director: Stefan Sanderling
Radebeul: Orchester der Landesbühnen Sachsen, Meissner Strasse 152, 8122 Radebeul
  Music Director: Joachim Widlak; Manager: Christian Schmidt
Recklinghausen: Westfälisches Sinfonieorchester, Dorstener Strasse 16, D-45657 Recklinghausen. Tel: 49 236 150 1961; Fax: 49 236 123687
  General Music Director: Walter Gillessen
Regensburg: Philharmonisches Orchester Regensburg, Bismarckplatz 7, 8400 Regensburg
  General Music Director: Hilary Griffiths
Reichenbach: Vogtlandphilharmonie, Weinholdstrasse 7, 9800 Reichenbach
  Music Director: Stefan Fraas
Remscheid: Remscheider Symphoniker, Stadt Remscheid, Kulturverwaltungsamt, Konrad-Adenauer-Strasse 31/33, 5630 Remscheid
  General Music Director: Reinhard Seifried
Reutlingen: Württembergische Philharmonie Reutlingen, Wilhelmstrasse 69, 7410 Reutlingen
  General Music Director: Roberto Paternostro
Rostock: Norddeutsche Philharmonie Rostock, Patriotischer Weg 33, 2500 Rostock
  General Music Director: Michael Zilm
Rudolstadt: Thüringer Symphoniker Saalfeld/Rudolstadt, Thüringer Landestheater Rudolstadt, Anger 1, 6820 Rudolstadt
  Music Director: Konrad Bach
Saarbrücken: Rundfunk-Sinfonieorchester Saarbrücken, Funkhaus Halberg, Pf 1050, 6600 Saarbrücken
  Chief Conductor: Marcello Viotti; Director of Music Programming: Dr Peter Rocholl
  Saarländisches Staatsorchester Saarbrücken, Schillerplatz, 6600 Saarbrücken
  General Music Director: Jun Märkl
Schwerin: Mecklenburgische Staatskapelle, Alter Garten, 2750 Schwein
Senftenberg: Theaterorchester Senftenberg, Rathenaustrasse 6/8, 7840 Senftenberg
  Music Director: Michael Keschke
Solingen: Symphonieorchester der Stadt Solingen, Konrad-Adenauer-Strasse 71, 5650 Solingen
  General Music Director: Christian Süss
Stendal: Orchester des Theaters der Altmark-Landestheater Sachsen-Anhalt Nord, Karlstrasse 4-6, 3500 Stendal
  Music Director: Frank Jaremko
Stralsund: Sinfonieorchester des Theaters der Hansestadt Stralsund, Olaf-Palme-Platz, 2300 Stralsund
  Music Director: Daniel Kleiner

Stuttgart: Kammerorchester Arcata Stuttgart e V, Heumadener Strasse 23, 7302 Ostfidern
Music Director: Patrick Strub
Radio-Sinfonieorchester Stuttgart, Neckarstrasse 230, D-70190 Stuttgart. Tel: 49 711 929 2590; Fax: 49 711 268 7051
Chief Conductor: Gianluigi Gelmetti; Manager: Hermann Funfgeld
Staatsorchester Stuttgart, Oberer Schlossgarten 6, 7000 Stuttgart
General Music Director: Gabriele Ferro
Stuttgarter Kammerorchester e V, Johann-Sebastian-Bach-Platz, 7000 Stuttgart
Music Director: Dennis Russell Davies
Stuttgarter Philharmoniker, Schickhardstrasse 5, 7000 Stuttgart
General Music Director: Jörg-Peter Weigle
Suhl: Thüringen Philharmonie suhl, Bahnhofstrasse 8-10, Pf 306, 6000 Suhl
General Music Director: Olaf Koch
Trier: Städtisches Orchester Trier, Am Augustinerhof, 5500 Trier
General Music Director: Reinhard Petersen
Ulm: Orchester der Stadt Ulm, Ulmer Theater, Olgastrasse 73, 7900 Ulm
General Music Director: Alicja Mounk
Waiblingen: Waiblinger Kammerorchester e V, Friedemann Enssle, Lindauer Strasse 40, 7150 Backnang
Music Director: Gerd Budday
Weimar: Staatskapelle Weimar, Theaterplatz, 5300 Weimar
General Music Director: Hans-Peter Frank
Thüringisches Kammerorchester Weimar, Theaterplatz 2, 5300 Weimar
Conductors: Max Pommer and Claus Gebauer
Werneck: Kammerorchester Schloss Werneck e V, Balthasar-Neumann-Platz 8, Pf 65, 8727 Werneck
Music Director: Ulf Klausenitzer
Wernigerode: Kammerorchester Wernigerode, Bahnhofstrasse 16, 3700 Wernigerode
Music Director: Thomas Brezinka
Wiesbaden: Orchester des Hessischen Staatstheater Wiesbaden, Christian-Zais-Strasse, 6200 Wiesbaden
General Music Director: Oleg Caetani
Pro Arte Ensemble Mainz e V, Werderstrasse 8, 6200 Wiesbaden
Music Director: Juan Levy
Wittenberg: Orchester der Elbe-Saale Bühnen, Thomas-Müntzer-Strasse 14/15, 4600 Wittenberg
Music Director: Klaus Hofmann
Würzburg: Städtisches Philharmonisches Orchester Würzburg, Theaterstrasse 21, 8700 Würzburg
General Music Director: Jonathan Seers
Wuppertal: Sinfonieorchester Wuppertal, Spinnstrasse 4, 5600 Wuppertal
General Music Director: Peter Gülke
Zwickau: Orchester des Theaters Zwickau, Gewandhausstrasse 7, Pf 308, 9541 Zwickau
Music Director: Welisar Gentscheff

GREECE

Athens: Athens Radio Symphony Orchestra, 432 Messioghion Street, 15310 Athens. Tel: 30 1 639 2721; Fax: 30 1 639 6012
Director: Mrs Karmiadaki; Chairman: Mikis Theodorakis
Athens State Orchestra, 2 Kapodistriou Street, 10682 Athens
Ioannina: Tsakalof Symphony Orchestra and Opera, Platia G, Stavrou 5, 45444 Ioannina.
Principal Conductor: George Chlitsios; Generl Director: Aspasia Zerva.
Thessaloniki: Thessaloniki Orchestra, 21 Ippodromiou Street, 54621 Thessaloniki. Tel: 30 31 221185; Fax: 30 31 260620

GUATEMALA

Guatemala City: Orquesta Sinfónica Nacional, 3a Ave 4-61, Zona 1, Guatemala City

HONDURAS

Tegucigalpa: Orquesta Sinfonica Nacional, PO Box 2298, Tegucigalpa
Music Director: Ramiro Soriano-Arce; Manager: David Vides

HONG KONG

Kowloon: Hong Kong Philharmonic Orchestra, Level 8, Administration Building, Hong Kong Cultural Centre,Tsimshatsui. Kowloon.
Tel: 852 2721 2030; Fax: 852 2311 6229 *Music Director: David Atherton; General Manager: Edith Lei*

HUNGARY

Budapest: Budapest Chamber Orchestra "Franz Liszt", Sxecheny emlekut 23, H-1121 Budapest
Director: János Rolla
Budapest Concert Orchestra MAV, Muzeum utca 11, H-1088 Budapest. Tel: 36 1 138 2664; Fax: 36 1 138 4085
Music Director: Tamás Gál; Managing Director: Géza Kovécs
Budapest Festival Orchestra, V Vörösmarty tér 1, H-1369 Budapest
Music Directors: Ivan Fischer and Zoltán Kocsis; Manager: Ildikó Gedényi
Budapest Philharmonic Orchestra, Hajos u 8, H-1065 Budapest. Tel: 36 1 131 9817; Fax: 36 1 138 8910
Music Director: Rico Saccani
Hungarian Radio and Television Symphony Orchestra, Bródy Sándor utca 5-7, H-1800 Budapest
Music Director: Tamás Vásáry

Hungarian State Symphony Orchestra, Vörösmarty tér 1, H-1364 Budapest
Music Director: Ken-Ichiro Kobayashi

Debrecen: Debrecen Philharmonic Orchestra, Simonffy utca 1/c, H-4025 Debrecen
Music Director: László Szabó

Gyór: Gyór Philharmonic Orchestra, Bajcsy Zsilinszky u 36, H-9021 Gyór. Tel/Fax: 36 96 312 452
Music Director: Tamas Koncz; Manager: Gabor Baross

Miskolc: Nord Hungarian Symphony Orchestra Miskolc, Fábián u 6a, H-3525 Miskolc. Tel: 36 46 323488; Fax: 36 46 351497
Music Director: László Kovács; Manager: László Sir

Pécs: Pécs Symphony Orchestra, Kossuth Lajos u 19, H-7621 Pécs
Music Director: Nicolas Pasquet; Administrator: Péter Szkladányi

Szeged: Szeged Symphony Orchestra, Festó utca 6, H-6721 Szeged
Music Director: Ervin Acél; Manager: István Szelezsan

Szombathely: Savaria Symphony Orchestra, Thököly u 14, H-9700 Szombathely
Music Director: Robert Houlihan, Manager: Tibor Menyhárt

ICELAND

Reykjavík: Iceland Symphony Orchestra, Háskólabió v/Hagatorg, PO Box 7052, IS-127 Reykjavík. Tel: 354 562 2255; Fax: 354 562 4475
Music Director: Petri Sakari; Manager: Runólfur Birgir Leifsson
Reykjavík Chamber Orchestra, Hauhlid 14, IS-105 Reykjavík
Manager: Rut Ingolfsdottir

INDIA

Calcutta: Calcutta Symphony Orchestra, 6B Sunny Park, Calcutta 700019
New Delhi: Delhi Symphony Orchestra, Humayun Road, New Delhi 110003

ISRAEL

Beer Sheva: Israel Sinfonietta, Derech Hameshachrerim 12, 84299 Beer Sheva
Artistic Director: Uri Mayer; Manager: Misha Grass

Haifa: Haifa Symphony Orchestra, PO Box 5210, 50 Pevsner Street, 33134 Haifa. Tel: 972 4 862 0741; Fax: 972 4 862 0342
Music Director: Stanley Sperber; Director General: Ben-Ami Einav
Israel Pro-Musica Orchestra, PO Box 7191, 31071 Haifa
Music Director: Dalia Atlas
Technion Symphony Orchestra, Churchill Auditorium, 32000 Haifa
Music Director: Dalia Atlas

Jerusalem: Jerusalem Symphony Orchestra, PO Box 4640, 91040 Jerusalem. Tel: 972 2 660211; Fax: 972 2 669117
Music Director: David Shallon; Managing Director: Zusia Rodan; Artistic Director: Gideon Paz

Netanya: Netanya Orchestra, PO Box 464, 42103 Netanya
Music Director: Samuel Lewis; General Manager: Yafe Duek

Ramat Gan: Ramat Gan Chamber Orchestra, PO Box 138, 13 Hertzel Street, Ramat Gan
Music Director: Zeev Steinberg; Manager: Sarah Lash-Yolowitz

Rishon Le-Zion: Rishon Le-Zion Symphony Orchestra, 5 Habanim Street, 75254 Rishon Le-Zion
Music Director: Asher Fisch; General Director: Menachem Shai; Assistant Conductor: Ilan Schul

Shefayim: Israel Kibbutz Orchestra (formerly Kibbutz Chamber Orchestra), 60990 Shefayim. Tel: 972 9 9503715; Fax: 972 9 9523643
Music Director: Noam Yeny; Manager: Aharon Kidron

Tel Aviv: Israel Chamber Orchestra, Amot Mishpat House, 8 Shaul Ha'melech Blvd, 64733 Tel Aviv. Tel: 972 3 696 1167; Fax: 972 3 691 0104
Conductor: Philippe Entremont; Managing Director: Eli Doron
Israel Philharmonic Orchestra, PO Box 11292, 1 Huberman Street, 61112 Tel Aviv. Tel: 972 3 528 8660; Fax: 972 3 290 097
Music Director: Zubin Mehta; General Secretary: Avi Shoshani
Young Israel Philharmonic, PO Box 11292, 1 Huberman Street, 61112 Tel Aviv
Music Director: Ze-ev Dorman; Administrative Director: Yaffa Sharett

ITALY

Bolzano: Orchestra Sinfonica Haydn di Bolzano e Trento, Piazza dei Domenicani 19, 39100 Bolzano
Artistic Director: Hubert Stuppner

Florence: Orchestra della Toscana, Via del Benci 20, 50122 Florence. Tel: 39 55 242767; Fax: 39 55 248 0511
Artistic Director: Aldo Bennici; Principal Conductor: Lü Jia

Milan: Orchestra da Camera dell'Angelicum, Piazza S Angelo 2, 20121 Milan
Orchestra Sinfonica di Milano della Radiotelevisione Italiana, Via Conservatorio 12, 21011 Milan
Artistic Director: Mario Messinis

Naples: Orchestra Alessandro Scarlatti di Napoli della Radiotelevisione Italiana, Via Marconi 5, 80125 Naples
Artistic Director: Massimo Fargnoli

Padua: Orchestra da Camera di Padova e del Veneto, Via Marsilio da Padova 19, 35139 Padua
Principal Conductor: Peter Maag
I Solisti Veneti, Piazzale Pontecorvo 6, 35100 Padua
Conductor: Claudio Scimone; Manager: Mirella Gualandi

Palermo: Orchestra Sinfonica Siciliana, Via G La Farina 29, 90141 Palermo. Tel: 39 91 300609; Fax: 39 91 300155
Artistic Director: Roberto Pagano; Conductor: Gabriele Ferro

Parma: Orchestra Sinfonico dell'Emilia Romagna Arturo Toscanini, Via G Tartini 13, 43100 Parma. Tel: 39 521 2741/274417/274418;
Fax: 39 251 272134/785257 *Principal Conductor: Gianandrea Gavazzeni*

Rome:	Orchestra Sinfonica dell'Accademia Nazionale de Santa Cecilia, Via Vittoria 6, 00187 Rome
	Music Director: Daniele Gatti
	Orchestra Sinfonica di Roma della Radiotelevisione Italiana, Foro Italico, Piazza L de Bosis 5, 00196 Rome. Tel: 39 6 322 6941;
	Fax: 39 6 322 7951 *Artistic Director: Michelangelo Zurletti*
San Remo:	Orchestra Sinfonica di San Remo, Corso Cavallotti 51, 18038 San Remo
	Artiistic Director: Giovanni Guglielmo
Turin:	Orchestra Sinfonica di Torino della Radiotelevisione Italiana, Piazza F lli Rossaro 15, 10124 Turin. Tel: 39 11 812 3424; Fax: 39 11 817 7410
	Artistic Director: Sergio Sablich; Orchestral Manager: Carla Bosco

JAPAN

Fukuoka-shi:	Kyushu Symphony Orchestra, 1-11-50 NoNaKuma, Jonan-ku, Fukuoka-shi 814-01
	Music Director: Kazuhiro Koisumi; Chairman: Kenzou Tanaka
Hiroshima:	Hiroshima Symphony Orchestra, 7-4 Hatchobori, Naka-ku, Hiroshima 730. Tel: 81 82 222 8448
	Music Director: Naohiro Totsuka
Kanazawa:	Orchestra Esemble Kanazawa, Hirosaka 1-7-1, Kanazawa 920
	Music Director: Hiroyuki Iwqki; Managing Director: Masayuki Yamada
Kobe-shi:	Kobe Philharmonic Orchestra, 1-9-1 San-no-miya-cho, Chuo-ku, Kobe-shi 650
	Conductor: Chitaru Asahina
Kyoto:	Kyoto Symphony Orchestra, 103 Izumojitatemoto-cho, Kita-ku, Kyoto 603. Tel: 81 75 222 0331
	Music Director: Michiyoshi Inoue; Manager: Yoshiyuki Murano
Nagoya:	Nagoya Philharmonic Orchestra, 1-5-1 Kanayama, Naka-ku, Nagoya 460. Tel: 81 52 322 2775; Fax: 81 52 322 3066
	Manager: Susumu Nonoyama
Osaka:	Kansai Philharmonic Orchestra, Diahatsu Building, 40-2-2 Katmachi, Miyakozima-ku, Osaka
	Conductor: Hideomi Kuroiwa
	Osaka Philharmonic Orchestra, Shirakabe Building, 7F, 1-14-7 Shibata, Kita-ku, Osaka 530. Tel: 81 6 665 7711; Fax: 81 6 656 7714
	Music Director: Takashi Asahina; Secretary General: Toshio Myazawa
	Osaka Symphony Orchestra, 4-3-9 203 Tezukayama naka, Sumiyoshi-ku, Osaka 558
	Music Director: Thomas Sanderling; General Manager: Tetsuo Shikishima
Sapporo:	Sapporo Symphony Orchestra, c/o Kyoiku Bunka Kaikan, Nishi 13-chome, Kita 1-jo, Chuo-ku, Sapporo 060
	Conductor: Kazuyoshi Akiyama; President: Hideji Kitagawa
Tokyo:	Japan Philharmonic Symphony Orchestra, 1-6-1 Umezato, Suginami-ku, Tokyo 166. Tel: 81 3 5378 6311; Fax: 81 3 5378 6161
	Music Director: Kenichiro Kobayashi; General Manager: Minoru Tanabe
	Kunaicho Gakuba (Imperial Court Orchestra), Imperial Palace, Tokyo 100
	NHK (Japan Broadcasting Corporation) Symphony Orchestra, 2-16-49 Takanawa, Minato-ku, Tokyo 108. Tel: 81 3 3443 0271; Fax: 81 3 3443 0278
	Music Director: Charles Dutoit; Executive Director: Takeshi Hara
	New Japan Philharmonic Orchestra, Towa Building, 5th Floor, 3-16-3 Shibuya-ku, Tokyo 150
	Honorary Artistic Director: Seiji Ozawa; Manager: Chiyoshige Matsubara
	Shinsei Nihon Symphony Orchestra, Maruishi Building, 3-16-4 Nishi Ikebukuro, Toshima-ku, Tokyo 171
	Music Director: Ryusuke Numjiri; Executive Director: Saburo Kurematsu
	Tokyo City Philharmonic Orchestra, 20-14 Daikanyama-cho, Shibuya-ku, Tokyo 150
	Music Director: Naohiro Totsuka; Executive Director: Tatatsugu Kuwahata
	Tokyo Metropolitan Symphony Orchestra, c/o Tokyo Bunkakaikan, 5-45 Ueno Park, Taito-ku, Tokyo 110. Tel: 81 3 3822 0727
	Music Director: Hiroshi Wakasugi; Executive Director: Hiroshi Kainuma
	Tokyo Philharmonic Symphony Orchestra, Eiritsu Building, 3-3 Kanda Kajicho, Chiyoda-ku, Tokyo 10. Tel: 81 3 3256 9696; Fax: 81 3 3256 9698
	Conductor: Kazushi Ohno; Director: Shogo Matsuki
	Tokyo Symphony Orchestra, 2-23-5 Hyakunin-cho, Shinjuku-ku, Tokyo 160
	Music Director: Kazuyoshi Akiyama; General Manager: Shigteto Kanayama
	Yomiuri Nippon Symphony Orchestra, Yomiuri Shimbun, 1-7-1 Ohtemachi, Chiyoda-ku, Tokyo 100
	Principal Conductor: Tadaaki Otaka; General Manager: Akira Takasaki
Yokohama:	Kanagawa Philharmonic Orchestra, Hanami-dai 110, Hodogaya-ku, Yokohama 240. tel: 81 45 331 4001; Fax: 81 45 331 4022
	Music Director: Yuzo Toyama; Executive Director: Yutaka Ueno

KOREA (SOUTH)

Seoul:	KBS (Korean Broadcasting System) Symphony Orchestra, 18 Yoido-dong, Youngdungpo-gu, Seoul 150-790
	Chief Conductor: Othmar Maga
	Seoul Philharmonic Orchestra, 81-3 Sejong-Ro, Chong Ro-Gu, Seoul 110-050. Tel: 82 2 736 2721; Fax: 82 2 738 0948
	Music Director: Kyung-Soo Won

LATVIA

Riga:	Latvian National Symphony Orchestra, 6 Amatu Street, 226350 Riga. Tel: 371 7 224 850/229537; Fax: 371 7 224850
	Music Director: Terje Mikkelsen
	Latvian Radio and Television Symphony Orchestra, c/o Latvian Radio and Television, Riga
	Riga Chamber Orchestra, Kalku Street 11a, 226350 Riga

LITHUANIA

Vilnius:	Lithuanian State Symphony Orchestra, Zygimantu 6, 2600 Vilnius. Tel: 370 2 628127; Fax: 370 2 220966
	Chief Conductor: Juozas Domarkas; General Director: Gintautas Kevisas

LUXEMBURG

Luxembourg: Orchestre Philharmonique du Luxembourg, Villa Louvigny, BP 2243, L-1022 Luxembourg. Tel: 352 22 99 01205; Fax: 352 22 99 98
Chief Conductor: David Shallon
Orchestre Symphonique de Radio Luxembourg, Villa Louvigny, L-1022 Luxembourg
Chief Conductor: Leopold Hager; Manager: Jacques Mauroy

MEXICO

Guadalajara: Orquesta Filarmónica de Jalisco, Teatro Degollado, 44100 Guadalajara, Jalisco. Tel: 52 658 3812/3819; Fax: 52 614 9366/658 3820
Music Director: José Guadalupe Flores; Manager: Silvia Susana Hernandez Huerta
Mexico City: Orquesta de Cámera de Bellas Artes, Extemplo de Santa Teresa La Antigua, Lic Verdad No 8
and Moneda, Centro, 06060 Mexico City, DF
Music Director: Ildefonso Cedillo; Manager: Maricarmen Guerrero Meneses
Orquesta del Teatro de Bellas Artes, Regina 52, Centro 06050 Mexico City, DF
Music Director: Enrique Barrios; Manager: José Lopez
Orquesta Filarmónica de la Ciudad de Mexico, Periférico Sur 5141, Sala Ollin Yoliztli, 14030 Mexico City, DF. Tel: 52 905 606 8933; Fax: 52 905 606 8401 *Principal Conductor: Luis Herrera de la Fuente*
Orquesta Filarmónica de la Universidad Autónoma de México, Av Insurgentes Sur 3000. Sala Nezahualcóyotl, 04510 Mexico City, DF, Coyoacán
Music Director: Ronald Zollman; General Manager: Maricarmen Costero
Toluca: Orquesta Sinfónica del Estado de Mexico, Plaza Fray Andrés de Castro, Edif 'C', Primer Piso, 50000 Toluca. Tel: 52 72 44 5219; Fax: 52 72 45 6216
Music Director: Enrique Bátiz; General Manager: Maria Dolores Castillo

MONACO

Monte Carlo: Orchestre Philharmonique de Monte Carlo, Casino, BP 139, 98007 Monte Carlo Cédex. Tel: 33 93 92 16 2121; Fax: 33 93 93 15 0871
Music Director: James DePreist; Director: René Croesi

NETHERLANDS

Amsterdam: Koninklijk (Royal) Concertgebouworkest, Jacob Obrechtstraat 51, 1071 KJ Amsterdam. Tel: 31 20 20 679 2211; Fax: 31 20 676 3331
Chief Conductor: Riccardo Chailly
Nederlands Philharmonisch Orkest, Beurs van Berlage, Damrak 213, 1012 ZH Amsterdam. Tel: 31 20 627 1161; Fax: 31 20 622 9939
Music Director: Hartmut Haenchen; Manager: Dr J W Loot
Arnhem: Het Gelders Orkest, Velperbuitensingel 12, 6828 CV Arnhem. Tel: 31 26 442 2632; Fax: 31 26 443 9966
Principal Conductor: Roberto Benzi; General Administrator: H Hierck
Bussum: Amsterdam Baroque Orchestra, Meerwag 23, 1405 BC Bussum
Music Director: Ton Koopman; General Manager: Hans Meijer
Eindhoven: Brabants Philharmonisch Orkest, PO Box 230, 5600 AE Eindhoven. Tel: 31 40 265 5699; Fax: 31 40 246 3459
Managing Director: Huber van Wekhoven
Enschede: Forum Filharmonisch, PO Box 1321, 7500 BH Enschede
General Manager: J M Bal
Groningen: Noord-Nederlands Orkest, PO Box 818, 9700 AV Groningen. Tel: 31 35 6714 140; Fax: 31 35 6714 171
Manager: A L E Verberne
Haarlem: Noordhollands Philharmonisch Orkest, Klokhuisplein 2 A, 2011 HK Haarlem. Tel: 31 235 319248; Fax: 31 235 32 8533
Music Director: Lucas Vis; Manager: Casper Vogel
The Hague: Residentie Orkest, PO Box 11543, 2502 AM The Hague. Tel/Fax: 31 70 360 7925
Chief Conductor: Evgeny Svetlanov; Manager: H Van den Akker
Hilversum: Metropole Orkest, PO Box 10, 1200 JB Hilversum
Music Director: Dick Bakker; Manager: Fred Dekker
Radio Filharmonisch Orkest, PO Box 10, 1200 JB Hilversum. Tel: 31 35 6714 130; Fax: 31 35 6714 171
Chief Conductor: Edo de Waart; Manager: Rob Overman
Radio Kamerorkest, Postbus 125, 1200 JB Hilversum. Tel: 31 35 6714150; Fax: 31 35 6714171
Conductor: Frans Bruggen; Manager: Ferdinand L J Vrijma
Radio Symphonie Orkest, PO Box 10, 1200 JB Hilversum
Chief Conductor: Kees Bakels
Leeuwarden: Frysk Orkest, PO Box 666, 8901 BL Leeuwarden
Maastricht: Limburgs Symphonie Orkest, PO Box 482, 6200 AL Maastricht. Tel: 31 43 350 7000; Fax: 31 30 404 8023
Manager: Dr H P van de Braak
Rotterdam: Rotterdams Philharmonisch Orkest, de Doelen, Kruisstraat 2, 3012 CT Rotterdam
Chief Conductor: Valery Gergiev; Manager: P P F M Zeegers

NEW ZEALAND

Auckland: Auckland Philharmonic Orchestra, PO Box 56-024, Auckland. Tel: 64 9 638 7073; Fax: 64 9 630 9687
General Manager: Paul McLaren
Christchurch: Christchurch Symphony Orchestra, PO Box 3260, Christchurch 8000. Tel:64 3 379 3886; Fax: 64 3 379 3861
Artistic Director: Iola Shelley; General Manager: A H Kunowski
Dunedin: Dunedin Sinfonia, PO Box 5571, Dunedin
Wellington: New Zealand Chamber Orchestra, PO Box 11263, Wellington
Music Director: Donald Armstrong; Manager: Dr Allan Badley
New Zealand Symphony Orchestra, PO Box 6640, Wellington 6035. Tel: 64 4 3851 735; Fax: 64 4 3842 824
Chief Conductor: Franz-Paul Decker; Chief Executive: Mark Keyworth

Wellington Regional Orchestra, PO Box 6314, Te Aro, Wellington
Manager: Brian Budd

NORWAY

Bergen: Bergen Filharmoniske Orkester, Grieghallen, Lars Hilles Gata 3a, N-5000 Bergen. Tel: 47 5521 6100; fax: 47 5531 8534
Music Director: Dmitri Kitayenko; Manager: Jostein Osnes
Oslo: Norsk Kammerorkester, Grev Wedels Plass 2, N-0151 Oslo 1
Artistic Director: Iona Brown
Oslo Filharmoniske Orkester, PO Box 1607 Vika, Konserhuset, Munkedamsveien 14, N-0119 Oslo 1. Tel: 47 2201 4900; Fax: 47 2201 4901
Chief Conductor: Mariss Jansons; Manager: Trond Okkelmo
Stavanger: Stavanger Symfoniorkester, Bjergsted, N-4007 Stavanger. Tel: 47 5150 8830; Fax: 47 5150 8839
Managing Director: Anna-Marie Antonius; General Manager: Erik Landmark
Trondheim: Trondheim Symfoniorkester, PO Box 764, N-7001 Trondheim. Tel: 47 7353 0760; Fax: 47 7351 4888
Artistic Director: Ole Kristian Ruud

PANAMA

Panama City: Orquesta Sinfónica Nacional, Apto 9190, Panama City 6
Conductor: Eduardo Charpentier de Castro

PARAGUAY

Asunción: Orquesta Sinfónica de la Ciudad de Asunción, Luis A de Herrea 364, Asunción
Director: Luis Szarán

PERU

Lima: Orquesta Sinfónica Nacional, Avda Javier Prado Este 2465, Lima 41. Tel/Fax: 51 37 7633
Artistic Director: José Carlos Santos

PHILIPPINES

Manila: Manila Symphony Orchestra, Manila Metropolitan Theater, Liwasang Bonifacio, PO Box 664, Manila
Music Director: Alfredo Buenaventura
National Philharmonic Orchestra, PO Box 1721, Manila. Tel: 63 817 2601/815 2651; Fax: 63 815 3483
Music Director: Redentor Romero
Philippine Philharmonic Orchestra, Cultural Center of the Philippines, Roxas Boulevard, Manila. Tel: 63 2 832 1125; Fax: 63 2 832 3683
Music Director: Oscar Yatco; Executive Director: Amelita Guevara

POLAND

Bialystok: Bialystok State Philharmonic Orchestra, Podlesna 2, 15-227 Bialystok
Music Director: Miroslaw Blaszczyk
Bydgoszcz: Pomeranian State Philharmonic Orchestra "Ignacy Paderewski", Libelta 16, 85-080 Bydgoszcz
Czestochowa: Czestochowa State Philharmonic Orchestra, Kakielów 16, 42-2000 Czestochowa
Music Director and Director: Jerzy Kosek
Gdańsk: Baltic State Philharmonic Orchestra, Aleja Zwycięstwa 15, 80-219 Gdańsk
Jelenia Gora: Jelenia Gora State Philharmonic Orchestra, ul 22-go Lipca 60, 58-500 Jelenia Gora
Music Director: Tadeusz Wicherek; Director: Zuzanna Dziedzic
Katowice: Polish Radio National Symphony Orchestra, PL Sojmu Slaskiego 2, 40-032 Katowice. Tel: 48 32 518903; Fax: 48 32 571384
Music Director: Antoni Wit; Manager: Irena Siodmok
Silesian State Philharmonic Orchestra, Sokolska 2, 40-084 Katowice. Tel: 48 32 597571/598679/598621; Fax: 48 32 589885
Music Director: Jerzy Swoboda
Kraków: Chopin Chamber Orchestra, 25/54 ul Gabrieli Zapolskiej, 30-126 Kraków
Music Director and Manager: Boguslaw Dawidów
Kraków State Philharminic Orchestra "Karol Szymanowski", Zwierzyniecka 1, 31-103 Kraków. tel/Fax: 48 12 224312
Chief Conductor: Marek Pljarowski; Manager: Joanna Vnuk-Nazarowa
Łodz: Łodz State Philharmonic Orchestra "Artur Rubinstein", Piotrkowska 243, 90-456 Łodz
Music Director: Ilya Stupel; General Manager: Jan Wolański
Olsztyn: Olsztyn State Philharmonic Orchestra "Feliks Nowowiejski", Kościuszki 39, 10-503 Olsztyn. tel: 48 81 24421
Music Director: Piotr Borkowski
Poznań: Poznań State Philharmonic Orchestra, ul Sw Marcina 81, 61-808Poznań. Tel/Fax: 48 61 523451
Artistic Director: Andrey Boreyko; General Director: Jerzy Laskowski
Rzeszów: Rzeszów State Philharmonic Orchestra "Artur Malawski", Chopina 30, 35-055 Rzeszów
Music Director: Adam Natanek
Szczecin: Szczecin State Philharmonic Orchestra "Mieczyslaw Karlowicz", Dzierzyńskiego 1, 70-455 Szczecin
Music Director: Stefan Marczyk; Manager: Jadwiga Igiel
Walbrzych: Sudettic Philharmonic Orchestra, Slowackiego 4, 58-3000 Walbrzych
Music Director and Manager: Jozef Wilkomirski
Warsaw: New Polish Radio Orchestra, J P Woronicza 17, 00-950 Warsaw
Artistic Director and Principal Conductor: Tadeusz Strugala
Polish Chamber Orchestra, Centrum Sztuki "Studio", Palac Kultury i Nauki, 00-901 Warsaw
Music Director: Franciszek Wybrańczyk

Sinfonia Varsovia, Centrum Sztuki "Studio", Palac Kultury i Nauki, 00-901 Warsaw
Music Director and Manager: Franciszek Wybrańczyk
Warsaw Chamber Orchestra, ul Freta 28/8, 00-227 Warsaw
Artistic Director: Marek Sewen
Warsaw National Philharmonic Orchestra, Jasna 5, 00-950 Warsaw
Chief Conductor: Kazimierz Kord; Manager: Borys Frydrychowicz

Wroclaw: Wroclaw State Philharmonic Orchestra,ul Pilsudskiego 19, 50-044 Wroclaw. Tel: 48 71 342 2001; Fax: 4871 342 8980
Artistic Director and Manager: Merek Pijarowski

Zielona Góra: Zielona Góra State Philharmonic Orchestra, Plac Powstańców Wielkopolskich 10, 65-075 Zielona Góra
Music Director: Czeslaw Grabowski

PORTUGAL

Lisbon: Orquestra Gulbenkian, Fundaçao Calouste Gulbenkian, Avda de Berna 45, 1093 Lisbon. Tel: 351 1 793 5131 Fax: 351 1 793 5139
Principal Conductor: Muhai Tang; Manager: Dr Luis Pereira Leal
Orquestra Sinfónica Portuguesa, Rua Serpa Pinto 9, 1200 Lisbon. Tel: 351 1 343 1734; Fax: 351 1 343 1735
Chief Conductor: Alvaro Cassuto

Porto: Orquesta Sinfónica do Porto, Radiodifusao Portuguesa, Rua Candido Reis 74/10, 4000 Porto
Music Director: Gunther Arglebe

ROMANIA

Bucharest: Bucharest Chamber Orchestra, Allée Ioanid 4, Bucharest 70259
Music Director: Ion Voicu; Manager: Madeleine Cretu
Rumanian Radio and Television Symphony Orchestra, Str Nuferilor 62-64, 79756 Bucharest
Bucharest State Philharmonic Orchestra "George Enescu", Ateneul Roman, Franklin Str 1, Bucharest

Iasi: Iasi Philharmonic, Str Cuza Voda 29, 6600 Iasi. Tel: 40 32 114601/112100/212620; Fax: 40 32 214160

RUSSIA

Moscow: Bolshoi Symphony Orchestra, Bolshoi Theater, Petrovka Street 1, Moscow. Tel: 7 095 292 6570; Fax: 7 095 292 9032
Ensemble XXI Moscow (Moscow International Chamber Orchestra), Ul Ostozhenka 12, Apt 1, Moscow
Conductor: Lygia O'Riordan
Moscow Chamber Orchestra, Ul Gorkogo 37, Moscow
Moscow Philharmonic Orchestra, Ul Gorkogo 37, Moscow
Chief Conductor: Vassily Sinaisky
Moscow Radio and Television Symphony Orchestra, Ul Piatnitskaya 25, Moscow
Chief Conductor: Vladimir Fedoseyev
Moscow Symphony Orchestra, Moscow
Chief Conductor: Antonio de Almeida
Russian National Symphony Orchestra, Studio Moscow, Alexeya Tolstovo St 26-33, 103001 Moscow. Tel: 7 095 290 6262;
Fax: 7 095 292 6511 *Conductor: Mikhail Pletnev*
State Symphonic Kapelle of Moscow
Chief Conductor: Gennady Rozhdestvensky
State Symphony Orchestra of Russia, Arbat 35, 121835 Moscow
Chief Conductor: Evgeny Svetlanov

St Petersburg: St Petersburg Chamber Orchestra, Ul Brodskogo 2, St Petersburg
St Petersburg Philharmonic Orchestra, Mikhailovskaya St 2, 219011 St Petersburg. Tel: 7 812 311 7331; Fax: 7 812 311 2126
Chief Conductor: Yuri Temirkanov

SINGAPORE

Singapore: Singapore Symphony Orchestra, Victoria Concert Hall, Empress Place, Singapore 179558. Tel: 65 336 4417; Fax: 65 336 6382
Music Director: Choo Hoey; General Manager: Tisa Ng

SLOVAK REPUBLIC

Bratislava: Capella Istropolitna, Schillerove 23, 811 04 Bratislava
Music Director: Ewald Daniel; Manager: Karol Kopernický
Musica Aeterna, Fučikova 3, 816 01 Bratislava
Chief Conductor: Peter Zajiček
Slovak Chamber Orchestra, Fučikova 3, 816 01 Bratislava
Chief Conductor: Bohdan Warchal
Slovak Philharmonic Orchestra, Fučikova 3, 816 01 Bratislava
Chief Conductor: Ondrej Lenárd
Symphony Orchestra of the Slovak Radio, Mýtna 1, 812 90 Bratislava. Tel: 421 1 11162; Fax: 42 117 393947
Chief Conductor: Robert Stanovsky

SLOVENIA

Ljubljana: Slovenian Philharmonic Orchestra, Kongresni trg 10, 61000 Ljubljana. Tel: 386 61 213554; Fax: 386 61 213640
Slovenian Radio and Television Symphony Orchestra, Tavcarjeva 17, 61000 Ljubljana

SOUTH AFRICA

Cape Town:	Cape Town Symphony Orchestra, City Hall, Darling Street, Cape Town 8001
Durban:	Natal Philharmonic Orchestra, PO Box 5353, Durban 4000. Tel: 27 31 9555/9437/9438; Fax: 27 31 306 2166
	Principal; Conductor: Johann Zietsman
Johannesburg:	National Symphony Orchestra, South African Broadcasting Corporation, PO Box 4559, Johannesburg 2000
Pretoria:	The National Orchestra, PO Box 566, Pretoria 0001
	Principal Conductor: Carlo Franci; General Manager: Stephen Wikner
	New Arts Philharmonic Orchestra (NAPOP), PO Box 566, Pretoria 0001. Tel: 27 12 322 1665; Fax: 27 12 322 3913

SPAIN

Barcelona:	Orquesta Ciudad de Barcelona, Via Laietan a 41, pral, 08003 Barcelona
	Music Director: Garcia Navarro; Manager: Jaume Masferrer
	Orquesta Sinfónica de barcelona i Nacional de Catalunya (OBC), Via Laietana 41, 08003 Barcelona. Tel: 34 3 317 1096; Fax: 34 3 317 5439
	Artistic Director: Lawrence Foster
Madrid:	Joven Orquesta Nacional de España, Principe de Vergara, 28002 Madrid
	Principal Conductor: Edmon Colomer; Manager: Juanm Wesolowski y Fernández-Heredia
	Orquesta Nacional de España, Principe de Vergara 146, 28002 Madrid
	Principal Conductor: Aldo Ceccato; Managing Director: Tomas Marco
	Orquesta Sinfónica de Radiotelevision Española, Sor Angela de la Cruz 2, 7th floor, 28020 Madrid
	Chief Conductor: Sergiu Comissiona
Málaga:	Orquesta Sinfónica de Málaga, C Ramos Marin s/n, 29012 Málaga
	Music Director: Octav Calleya
Oviedo:	Orquesta del Principado de Asturias, Corrado del Obispo, s/n Edif, del conservatorio de Musica
	"Eduardo Martinez Torner", 33003 Oviedo
	Music Director: Maximiano Valdes
Palma:	Orquesta Sinfónica de Balears, Vicente Juan Rossello Ribas 22-B, 07013 Palma. Tel: 34 71 287 565; Fax: 34 71 287 758
	Music Director: Luis Remartinez Gomez; Manager: Pere Esterlrich 1 Massuti
Pamplona:	Orquesta Santa Cecilia de Pamplona, Padre Moret s/n, 31002 Pamplona
	Artistic Director: Jacques Bodmer; Manager: José Maria Montes Navio
San Sebastian:	Orquesta Sinfónica de Euskaki, Paseo de Miramon 124, 20011 San Sebastian. tel: 34 43 451 1022; Fax: 34 43 470 999
	Music Director: Miguel Gomez Martinez; General Director: Jesús Maria Aguirre Lazcano
Santa Cruz	Orquesta Sinfónica de Tenerife, Plaza Espana 1, 38001 Santa Cruz de Tenerife
de Tenerife:	*Music Director: Victor Pablo Pérez; General Manager: Enrique Rojas*
Seville:	Orquesta Sinfónica de Sevilla, Cerrajeri 10, Sgdo Izda, 41004 Seville
	Music Director: Vjekoslav Sutej; General Manager: Francisco José Senra Lazo

SRI LANKA

Colombo:	Tamil Service Orchestra, c/o Sri Lanka Broadcasting Corp, Torrington Square, Colombo 7

SWEDEN

Gävle:	Gävleborgs Symfoniorkester, Staketgatan 37, S-803 21 Gävle
	Music Director: Hannu Koivula
Göteborg:	Göteborgs Symfoniker, Konserthuset, Stenhammarsgatan 1, S-412 56 Göteborg
	Music Director: Neeme Järvi; Manager: Sture Carlsson
Hälsingborg:	Hälsingborgs Symfoniorkester, Konserthuset, S-252 21 Hälsingborg
	Music Director: Okko Kamu; Manager: Lennart Stenkvist
Malmö:	Malmö Symfonie Orkester, S-205 80 Malmö
	Music Director: James DePreist; Manager: Gunilla von Bahr
Norrköping:	Norrköpings Symfoniorkester, Box 2144, S-600 02 Norrköping
	Music Director: Jun'ichi Hirokami; General Manager: Anders Franzén
Orebro:	Orebro Symphony Orchestra and Swedish Chamber Orchestra, Konserthuset, Farriksgatan 2, S-702 10 Orebro
	Music Director: Goran Nilson; Manager: Karl Friman
Stockholm:	Royal Swedish Chamber Orchestra, The Royal Palace, S-111 30 Stockholm
	Music Director: Mats Liljefors
	Stockholms Filharmoniska Orkester, PO Box 7083, S-103 87 Stockholm. tel: 46 8 221 800; Fax: 46 8 791 7330
	Chief Conductor: Gennady Rozhdestvensky; Executive and Artistic Director: Ake Holmquist
	Sveriges (Swedish) Radios Symfoniorkester, Sveriges Radio, S-105 10 Stockholm
	General Manager: Trygve Nordwall
Uppsala:	Uppsala Kammarorkester, Box 1510, S-751 45 Uppsala
	Music Director: Kjell Söderqvist; Manager: Nils-Olof Sondell
Västeras:	Västeras Musiksällskap, Sangargatan 3, S-722 20 Västeras
	Manager: Ulf Stenberg

SWITZERLAND

Basel:	Basler Kammerorchester, Postfach 4001, CH-4051 Basel
	Conductor: Paul Sacher
	Basler-Sinfonie-Orchester, Freie Strasse 52, CH-4001 Basel. Tel: 41 61 269 9595; Fax: 41 61 269 9599
	Chief Conductor: Walter Weller

	Radio-Sinfonie-Orchester, Münsterplatz 18, CH-4051 Basel
	Chief Conductor: Nello Santi
Bern:	Berner Symphonieorchester, Münzgraben 2, CH-3011 Bern: Tel: 41 31 328 2424; Fax: 41 31 328 2425
	Chief Conductor: Dmitri Kitaenko; Manager: Margrit Lenz
	Camerata Bern, Mayweg 4, CH-3007 Bern
	Conductor: Thomas Füri; General Secretary: Rose Brügger
Geneva:	Collegium Academicum de Genève, Casa Postale 539, CH-1211 Geneva 4
	Music Director: Thierry Fischer; Manager: Janine Mariz
	Orchestre de la Suisse Romande, Promenade du Pin 3, CH-1211 Geneva. tel: 41 22 311 2511; Fax: 41 22 310 1789
	Chief Conductor: Armin Jordan; Secretary General: Ron Golan
Grüt:	Sinfonietta Wetzikon, Lindenhofstr 12a, CH-8624 Grüt. Tel: 41 1 972 1898; Fax: 41 1 972 1897
	Artistic Directors: Werner Bärtsch, Matthias Ziegler; Secretary: Pauline d'Hooghe
Lausanne:	Orchestre de Chambre dé Lausanne, Chemin du Devin 72, CH-1010 Lausanne
	Music Director: Jesús López-Cobos; Chairman: Jean-Jacques Rapin
Lucerne:	Festival Strings Lucerne, Klusstrasse 8, CH-8032 Zürich
	Music Director: Matthias Bamert; Manager: Rita Dahinden
	Sinfonieorchester der Allgemeinen Musikgesellschaft Luzern, Moosstrasse 15, CH-6003
	Music Director: Olaf Henzold; Manager: Peter Keller
Lugano:	The Masterplayers, Via Losanna 12, CH-6900 Lugano
	Conductor: Richard Schumacher; Manager: Dr D V Zschinsky
	Orchestra della Radiotelevisione della Svizzera Italiana, Casella Postale, CH-6903 Lugano
St Gallen:	Stadtisches Orchester St Gallen, Museumstrasse 1, CH-9004 St Gallen
	Music Director: John Neschling; Manager: Marc Walter Haefelin
Winterthur:	Stadtorchester Winterthur, Musikkollegium Winterthur, Rychenbgergstrasse 94, CH-8400 Winterthur
	Music Director: János Fürst
Zürich:	Camerata Zürich, Bergstrasse 50-G, CH-8712 Stáfa
	Conductor: Räto Tschupp; Secretary: Rosemarie Kleinert
	Collegium Musicum Zürich, Konzertgesellschaft, Steinwiesstrasse 2, CH-8032 Zürich
	Music Director: Paul Sacher; Manager: Barbara Oehninger
	Symphonisches Orchester Zürich, Postfach 1016, CH-8021 Zürich
	Music Director: Daniel Schweizer; Manager: Paul Trachsel
	Tonhalle-Orchester Zürich, Gotthardstrasse 5, CH-8002 Zürich. Tel: 41 1 206 3440; Fax: 41 1 206 3436
	Music Director: David Zinman; Managing Director: Richard Bächi
	Zürciher Kammerorchester, Kreuzstrasse 55, PO Box 244, CH-8032 Zürich
	Music Director: Edmond de Stoutz; Manager: Nelly Eschke

TAIWAN

Taipei:	Taipei City Symphony Orchestra, 25 Pa Teh Road, Sec 3, Taipei 10560. Tel: 886 2 752 3731; Fax: 886 2 751 8244
	Music Director: Chen Chiu-sen
Wu Feng, T'ai-chung:	Taiwan Symphony Orchestra, Ming-Sheng Road, No 292, Wu Feng, T'ai-chung
	Conductor: Tze-shiou Liu; Manager: Po-chou Chang

THAILAND

Bangkok:	Bangkok Symphony Orchestra, Tejapaibil Building, 5th Floor,16 Plubplachai Road, Bangkok. Tel: 66 2 252 1772; Fax: 66 2 255 3947
	Music Director: John Georgiadis; General Manger: Witaya Tumornsoontorn

TURKEY

Ankara:	Presidential Symphony Orchestra, Talatpasa Bulvari 38/A, 06330 Ankara. Tel: 90 312 309 1348; Fax: 90 312 311 7548
	Music Director: Gürer Aykal
Istanbul:	Istanbul State Symphony Orchestra, Atatürk Kültür Merkezi-Taksim, Istanbul. Tel: 90 212 243 1068; Fax: 90 212 251 0507
	Music Director: Alexander Schwinck; Manager: Ozer Sezgin
Izmir:	Izmir State Symphony Orchestra, Büro SSK Ishani C Blok 4, Kat Konak, 352260 Izmir. Tel: 90 232 484 8343; Fax: 90 232 484 5172
	Music Director: Iosif Conta; Director: Numan Pekdemir

UK

Altrincham:	Northern Chamber Orchestra, 16 Rilway Street, Altrincham, Ceshire WA14 2RE
	Music Director: Nicholas Ward; Artistic Director: David Ellis
Barnet:	London Concert Orchestra, 176a High Street, Barnet, Hertfordshire EN4 5SZ
	Administrator: Raymond Gubbay
Beaconsfield:	Sinfonia of London, 27 Grove Road, Beaconsfield, Buckinghamshire HP9 1UR. Tel: 44 1494 677934; Fax: 44 1494 670433
	Musical Director: Bruce Broughton; Director and General Manager: Peter Willison
Beckenham:	Musiciens du Roi, 6 Aldersmead Road, Beckenham, Kent BR3 1NA
	Director: Lionel Sawkins
Belfast:	Ulster Orchestra, Elmwood Hall at Queen's, 89 University Road, Belfast BT7 1NF. Tel: 44 1232 664535; Fax 44 1232 662761
	General Manager: Roger Lloyd
Biggleswade:	New English Concert Orchestra, 23 Hitchin Street, Biggleswade, Bedfordshire SG18 8AX
	Music Director: Douglas Coombes
Birmingham:	Birmingham Sinfonietta, 41 St Agnes Road, Birmingham B13 9PJ
	Music Director: Jeremy Ballard; Manager: Susan Savage
	City of Birmingham Symphony Orchestra, Paradise Place, Birmingham B3 3RP. Tel: 44 121 236 1555; Fax: 44 121 233 2423

	Principal Conductor: Sakari Oramo; Chief Executive: Edward Smith
Bournemouth:	Basildon Symphony Orchestra, 101 Queeens Park Avenue, Bournemouth BH8 9LJ
	Conductor/Artistic Director: Richard Studt
	Bournemouth Sinfonietta, 2 Seldown Lane, Poole, Dorset BH15 1UF
	Principal Conductor: Alexander Polianichko; Chief Executive: David Richardson
	Bournemouth Symphony Orchestra, 2 Seldown Lane, Poole, Dorset BH15 1UF. Tel: 44 1202 670611; Fax: 44 1202 687235
	Principal Conductor: Yakov Kreizberg; Principal Guest Conductor: Kees Bakels; Chief Executive: David Richardson
	London Camerata, 60 Strouden Avenue, Bournemouth BH8 9HX
	Conductor: Paul Hilliam
Bradford:	English Camerata, Bradford Catherdal, 1 Stott Hill, Bradford BD3 4EH
	Music Director: Elizabeth Altman
Bridgend:	Welsh Chamber Orchestra, 100 Ystrad Fawr, Bridgend, Mid-Glamorgan CF31 4HW
Brighton:	Brighton Philharmonic Orchestra, 50 Grand Parade, Brighton, East Sussex BN2 2QA
	Principal Conductor: Barry Wordsworth; General Manger: Tony Woodhouse
Bristol:	Philharmonia of Bristol, 11 Windsor Court, Bristol BS8 4LJ
	Artistic Director: Dr Derek Bourgeois; General Manager: Kenneth H Gibbs
Cambridge:	The Academy of Ancient Music, 10 Brookside, Cambridge CB2 1JE. Tel: 44 1223 301509; Fax: 44 1223 327377
	Director: Christopher Hogwood
	The Britten Sinfonia, 6-8 Hills Road, Cambridge CB2 1JP
	Artistic Director: Nicholas Cleobury
Cardiff:	BBC National Orchestra of Wales, Broadcasting House, Landaff, Cardiff CF5 2YQ. Tel: 44 1222 572524; Fax: 44 1222 322575
	Principal Conductor: Tadaaki Otaka; Manager: Bryon Jenkins
	Orchestra of Welsh National Opera, c/o Welsh National Opera Ltd, John Street, Cardiff CF1 2SP
	Music Director: Carlo Rizzi
Cheltenham:	New Cheltenham Chamber Orchestra, 27 Merestones Drive, The Park, Cheltenham, Gloucestershire GL50 2SU
	Music Director: Robin Proctor
Chesham:	Kreisler String Orchestra, 57 Sunnyside Road, Chesham, Buckinghamshire HP5 2AR . Tel/Fax: 44 1494 792572.
	Manager: Robert Woollard
Colchester:	Belmont Ensemble of London, The Old School House, St Mary's Road, Angers Greens, Great Bentley, Colchester, Essex CO7 8NF
	Music Director: Peter Gilbert-Dyson; Manager: Rebekah Gilbert-Dyson
Colyton:	European Community Chamber Orchestra, Fermain House, Dolphin Street, Colyton, Devon EX13 6LU
Derby:	East of England Orchestra, Derby College at Wilmorton, Pentagon Centre, Beaufort Street, Derby
Edinburgh:	Scottish Chamber Orchestra, 4 Royal Terrace, Edinburgh EH7 5AB. Tel: 44 131 557 6800; Fax: 44 131 557 6933
	Principal Conductor: Jospeh Swensen; Managing Director: Roy McEwen
Farnham:	National Chamber Orchestra, Fir Tree Lodge, Jumps Rd, Churt, Nr Farnham, Surrey GU10 2JY
	National Symphony Orchestra, Fir Tree Lodge, Jumps Rd, Churt, Nr Farnham, Surrey GU10 2JY
Glasgow:	BBC Scottish Symphony Orchestra, Broadcasting House, Queen Margaret Drive, Glasgow G12 8DG. Tel: 44 141 338 2606; Fax: 44 141 307 4312 *Chief Conductor: Osmo Vänskä*
	Royal Scottish National Orchestra, 73 Claremont Street, Glasgow G3 7HA. Tel: 44 141 226 3868; Fax: 44 141 221 4317
	Music Director: Walter Weller; Chief Executive: Paul Hughes
Guildford:	Guildford Philharmonic Orchestra, Millmead House, Millmead, Guilford, Surrey GU2 5BB
	Principal Conductor: En Shao
	Langham Chamber Orchestra, 9 Weylea Avenue, Burpham, Guildford, Surrey GU4 7YN
	Orchestra Manager: Peter Holt
Hove:	The Hanover Band, 45 Portland Road, Hove , East Sussex BN3 5DQ. Tel: 44 1273 206978; Fax: 44 1273 329636
Inkpen:	London Baroque Players, Weavers House, Inkpen, Buckinghamshire RG17 9DN (also London Classical Players)
	Music Director: Roger Norrington; Managing Director: Kay Lawrence
Ipswich:	London City Chamber Orchestra, 3/5 Bridge Street, Hadleigh, Ipswich, Suffolk IP7 6BY. Tel: 44 1473 822596; Fax: 44 1473 824175
	Conductor: Thomas McIntosh; General Manager: M H V Reckitt
Kenilworth:	Orchestra de Camera, 41 Fishponds Road, Kenilworth, Warwickshire CV8 1EY. Tel/Fax: 44 1926 858187
	Music Director: Kenneth Page
Leeds:	English Northern Philharmonia, Opera North, Grand Theatre, Leeds LS1 6NU
	Principal Conductor: Paul Daniel; Orchestra Manager: Richard Mantle
Liverpool:	Liverpool Sinfonietta, 40 Caulfield Drive, Greasby, Wirral, Merseyside L49 1SW
	Music Director: Anthony Ridley
	Royal Liverpool Philharmonic Orchestra, Philharmonic Hall, Hope Street, Liverpool L1 9BP
	Principal Conductor: Libor Pešek; Music Director elect: Petr Altrichter; Chief Executive: Robert Creech
London:	Academy of London, Studio 26, Building 56, Magnet Road, GEC East Lane Estate, Wembley, Middlesex HA9 7RG
	Conductor: Richard Stamp; General Manager: Elaine Baines
	Academy of St Martin-in-the-Fields, Raine House, Raine Street, Wapping, London E1 9RG. Tel: 44 171 702 1377; Fax: 44 171 481 0228
	Artistic Director: Neville Marriner; Manager: Gillian Brierley
	All Souls Orchestra, All Souls Music Office, St Paul's Church, Robert Adam Street, London W1M 5AH
	Principal Conductor: Noël Tredinnick
	Ambache Chamber Orchestra, 9 Beversbrook Road, London N19 4QG. Tel: 44 171 263 4027; Fax 44 171 281 7880
	Music Director: Diana Ambache
	Barbican Chamber Orchestra, 10 Acacia Road, London E17 8BW
	Principal Conductor: Gregory Rose; Manager: Paul Thomas
	BBC Concert Orchestra, BBC Hippodrome, North End Road, London NW11 7RP. Tel: 44 171 765 4010; fax: 44 171 765 4929
	Principal Conductor: Barry Wordsworth; Manager: Adrian Evett
	BBC Radio Orchestra, Maida Vale Studios, Delaware Road, London W9 2LG
	Manager: David Williams
	BBC Symphony Orchestra, Maida Vale Studios, Delaware Road, London W9 2LG. Tel: 44 171 765 5751
	Ben Uri Chamber Orchestra, 5 Bradby House, Carlton Hill, London NW8 9XE
	Conductor: Sydney Fixman
	Cantelli Chamber Orchestra, 13 Cotswold Mews, 12-16 Battersea High Street, London SW11 3JB

Cantelli Chamber Orchestra, 13 Cotswold Mews, 12-16 Battersea High Street, London SW11 3JB
Conductor: Philip Ellis; Manager: Alexander Waugh
Chamber Orchestra of Europe, 8 Southampton Place, London WC1A 2EA. Tel: 44 171 831 2326; Fax: 44 171 831 8248
Artistic Advisor: Claudio Abbado; General Manager: June Megennis
City of London Sinfonia, 11 Drum Street, London E1 1LH. Tel: 44 171 480 7743; Fax: 44 171 488 2700
Music Director: Richard Hickox; General Manager: Stephen Carpenter
Collegium Musicum 90, 71 Priory Rd, Kew, Surrey TW9 3DH. Tel: 44 181 940 7086; Fax: 44 181 332 0879
Music Directors: Richard Hickox & Simon Standage
Consort of London, 36 Minsterley Avenue, Shepperton TW17 8QT
Music Director: Robert Haydon Clarke
English Bach Festival Orchestra and English Bach Festival Baroque Orchestra, 15 South Eaton
Place, London SW1W 9ER.
Tel: 44 171 730 5925; Fax: 44 171 730 1456
Director: Lina Lalandi; Manager: Pippa Thynne
English Baroque Orchestra, 57 Kingswood Road, London SW19 3ND
Music Director: Leon Lovett; Manager: Robert Porter
English Baroque Soloists, PO Box 145, Tower Place, London EC3P 3BE. Tel: 44 171 480 5183; Fax: 44 171 480 5185
Music Director: John Eliot Gardiner; General Manager: Michael B MacLeod
English Chamber Orchestra, 2 Coningsby Road, London W5 4HR. Tel: 44 181 840 6565; Fax: 44 181 567 7198
Principal Conductor: Jeffrey Tate; Managing Director: Quintin Ballardie
The English Concert, 8 St George's Terrace, London NW1 8XJ. Tel: 44 171 911 0905; Fax: 44 171 911 0904
Artistic Director: Trevor Pinnock; Manager: Felix Warnock
English Festival Orchestra, 151 Mount View Road, London N4 4JT. Tel: 44 181 341 6408; Fax: 44 181 340 0021
General Manager: Trevor Ford
English National Opera Orchestra, London Coliseum, St Martin's Lane, London WC2N 4ES. Tel: 44 171 836 011; Fax: 44 171 836 8379
Orchestra Manager: Richard Smith; Music Director: Paul Daniel
Esterhazy Orchestra, 278 Kew Road, Richmond, Surrey TW9 3EE. Tel: 44 181 948 6140
European Community Youth Orchestra, 53 Sloane Street, London SW1X 8SW
Music Director: Claudio Abbado; General Manager: Helen Skerratt
Fine Arts Chamber Orchestra and Viennese Orchestra of London, 12 Tiverton Road, London NW10 3HL
Artistic Director: Jack Rothstein
Gabrieli Consort and Players, Foresters Hall, 25-27 Westow Street, London SE19 3RY. Tel: 44 181 771 7974; Fax: 44 181 771 7973
Director: Paul McCreesh; Administrator: Nicholas Morrison
Guildhall String Ensemble, 2 Highgate Spinney, Crescent Road, London N8 8AR
Director: Robert Salter
Haydn Orchestra, c/o NFMS, Francis House, Francis Street, London SW1P 1DE
Conductor: Harry Newstone; Administrator: Russell Jones
Henry Wood Chamber Orchestra, 64 Ashley Gardens, Ambrosden Avenue, London SW1P 1QG
Music Director: John Landor; Administrator: William Corke
The King's Consort, 34 St Mary's Grove, London W4 3LN. Tel: 44 181 995 9994; Fax: 44 181 995 2115
Director: Robert King
Little Symphony of London, 14 Beaumont Road, Purley, Surrey CR8 2EG. Tel/Fax: 44 181 668 5883
Artistic Director: Darrell Davison
London Chamber Orchestra, c/o The London Chamber Society Ltd, 6 Hambalt Road, London SW4 9EB. Tel: 44 181 772 9741; Fax: 44 181 772 9742 *Music Director: Christopher Warren-Green; Manager: Step Parikian*
London Chamber Players, PO Box 84, London NW11 8AL. Tel/Fax: 44 181 455 6799
Conductor: Adrian Sunshine; Manager: Sheila Genden
London Chamber Symphony, Toynbee Studios, 28 Commercial Street, London E1 6LS. Tel: 44 171 247 2950
Conductor: Odalaine de la Martinez; Co-Director: Sophie Langdon
London Festival Orchestra, 13 Theed Street, London SE1 8ST. Tel: 44 171 928 9251; Fax: 44 171 928 9252
Music and Artistic Director: Ross Pople; Manager: Anne Storrs
London Handel Orchestra, 32 Wolverton Gardens, London W6 7DX. Tel: 44 181 563 0618; Fax: 44 181 741 5233
Musical Director: Denys Darlow; Administrator: Joya Logan
London Jupiter Orchestra, 57 White Horse Road, London E1 0ND. Tel: 44 171 790 5883; Fax: 44 171 265 970
Conductor: Gregory Rose
London Mozart Players, 92 Chatsworth Road, Croydon CR0 1HB. Tel: 44 181 686 1966; Fax: 44 181 686 2187
Music Director: Matthias Bamert; Principal Guest Conductor: Howard Shelley
London Philharmonic Orchestra, 35 Doughty Street, London WC1N 2AA. Tel: 44 171 546 1600; Fax: 44 171 546 1601
Artistic Director: Serge Dorny
London Pro Arte Orchestra, 121 Addiscombe Court Road, Croydon, Surrey CR0 6TX. Tel: 44 181 655 3950; Fax: 44 181 654 9137
Music Director: Murray Stewart; General Manager: Kerstin Stolte
London Repertoire Orchestra & Chamber Orchestra, 56 Alexandra Road, Croydon, Surrey CR0 6EU
Conductor: Francis Griffin
London Sinfonietta, Clove Building, 4 Maguire St, London SE1 2NQ. Tel: 44 171 378 8123; Fax: 44 171 378 0937
Principal Conductor: Markus Stenz
London Soloists' Chamber Orchestra, 76 Sloane Street, London SW1
Director: David Josefowitz
London Symphony Orchestra, Barbican Centre, Silk Street, London EC2Y 8DS. Tel: 44 171 588 1116; Fax: 44 171 374 0127
Principal Conductor: Colin Davis; Managing Director: Clive Gillinson
Melos Ensemble, 35 Doughty Street, London WC1N 2AA
Monteverdi Orchestra, PO Box 145, Tower Place, London EC3P 3BE
Artistic Director: John Eliot Gardiner; General Manager: Michael MacLeod
National Philharmonic Orchestra, 7 Lowlands, Eton Avenue, Hampstead, London NW3 3EJ
Managing Director: Sidney Sax
New London Orchestra, 4 Lower Belgrave St, London SW1 0LJ. Tel: 44 171 823 5523; Fax: 44 171 823 6373
Music Director: Ronald Corp

New Queen's Hall Orchestra, c/o Manygate Management, 13 Cotswold Mews, 30 Battersea Square, London SW11 3RA. Tel: 44 171 223 7265; Fax: 44 171 585 2830. 1*Artistic Director: John Boyden; General Administrator: James Thomson*

New Wind Symphony Orchestra, 119 Woolstone Road, Forest Hill, London SE23 2TQ. Tel: 44 181 699 1101; Fax: 44 181 699 2219
Music Director: Catherine Pluygers; Manager: Jonathan Lindridge

Orchestra of St John's Smith Square, Clove Building, Maguire Street, London SE1 2NQ. Tel: 44 171 378 1358; Fax: 44 171 403 5620
Artistic Director: John Lubbock; Manager: Emma Abel

Orchestra of the Age of Enlightenment, 5th Floor, Westcombe House, 56-58 Whitcomb Street, London WC2H 7DN. Tel: 44 171 930 0646; Fax: 44 1717 930 0626. *Manager: David Pickard*

Orchestra of the Royal Opera House, Covent Garden, London WC2E 9DD. Tel: 44 171 240 1200; Fax: 44 171 836 1762
Music Director: Bernard Haitink

Orchestra of Sadler's Wells Royal Ballet, Sadler's Wells Theatre, Rosebery Avenue, London EC1R 4TN
Manager: Wendy Hacker

Orchestre Revolutionnaire et Romantique, PO Box 145, Tower Place, London EC3P 3BE. Tel: 44 171 480 5183; Fax: 44 171 480 5185
Music Director: John Eliot Gardiner; General Manager: Michael MacLeod

Park Lane Music Players, Bedford Chambers, Covent Garden Piazza, London WC2E 8HA
Administrator: John Woolf

Per Musica Chamber Orchestra, 50 Cranfield Court, Homer Street, London W1
Music Director: Julian Reynolds; Administrator: Joan Cruickshank

Philharmonia Orchestra, 76 Great Portland Street, London W1N 5AL. Tel: 44 171 580 9961; Fax: 44 1717 436 5517
Principal Conductor: Christoph von Dohnányi; Managing Director: David Whelton

Philomusica of London, 24 Stormont Road, London N6 4NP. Tel: 44 181 340 9729/0270
Conductors: Neville Dilkes and David Littaur; Administrator: Joyce Fox

Purcell Orchestra, 86 Park Hill, Carshalton Beeches, Surrey SM5 3RZ. Tel: 44 181 669 4358
Artistic Director: Robin Page; Administrator: Fiona Fairbairn

Raglan Baroque Players, 140 Muswell Hill Road, London N10 3JD. Tel: 44 181 444 2507; Fax: 44 181 444 1795
Music Director: Nicholas Kraemer

Regent Sinfonia of London, 17 Parliament Hill, London NW3 2TA
Artistic Director: George Vass

Rosebery Orchestra, 51 Stradella Road, London SE24 9HL
Orchestra Manager: Clarissa Melville

Rossini Chamber Orchestra, 10a Radipole Road, London SW6 5DL
Conductor: Alexander Bryett; Secretary: John Biggin

Royal Philharmonic Orchestra, 16 Clerkenwell Green, London EC1R 0DP. Tel: 44 171 608 2381; Fax: 44 171 608 1226
Music Director: Daniele Gatti; Managing Director: Ian Maclay

Sinfonia 21, Office Unit 2, Free Trade Wharf, 350 The Highway, London E1 9HU. Tel: 44 171 780 9434; Fax: 44 171 780 9379

St James's Baroque Players, 200 Broomwood Road, London SW11 6JY. Tel: 44 171 228 6388; Fax: 44 171 736 1706
Music Director: Ivor Bolton; Manager: Delia Pye

Taverner Players, Ibex House, 42-46 Minories, London EC3N 1DY. Tel: 44 1717 481 2103; Fax: 44 171 481 2865
Conductor: Andrew Parrott; Administrator: Victoria Newbert

Tilford Bach Orchestra, 31 Davies Street, London W1Y 1FH
Conductor: Denys Darlow; Administrator: Joya Logan

Wren Orchestra of London, c/o Capital Radio, Euston Tower, Euston Road, London NW1 3DR
Principal Conductor: Hilary Davan Wetton; General Manager: Kevin Appleby

Manchester: BBC Philharmonic Orchestra, New Broadcasting House, Oxford Road, Manchester M60 1SJ. Tel: 44 161 244 4005; Fax: 44 161 244 4010
Chief Conductor: Yan Pascal Tortelier; Manager: Peter Marchbank

Hallé Orchestra, The Bridgewater Hall, Manchester M2 3WS. Tel: 44 161 237 7000; Fax 44 161 237 7029
Music Director: Kent Nagano; Chief Executive: David Richardson

London Bach Orchestra, c/o Goldberg Ensemble, 1 Rowsley Avenue, West Didsbury, Manchester M20 2XD
Artistic Director: Nicholas Kraemer

Manchester Camerata, The Bridgewater Hall, Manchester M2 3WS. Tel: 44 161 237 7012; Fax: 44 161 237 7014
Principal Conductor: Sachio Fujioka

Manchester Mozart Orchestra, 30 Derby Road, Fallowfield, Manchester M24 6UW
Manager: John Whibley

Mertsham: Virtuosi of England, Glencairn, Shepherd's Hill, Mertsham, Surrey RH1 3AD
Artistic Director: Arthur Davison

Milton Keynes: Milton Keynes City Orchestra, Acorn House, 369 Midsummer Boulevard, Central Milton Keynes MK9 3HP. Tel: 44 1908 692777; Fax: 44 1908 230099. *Music Director: Hilary Davan Wetton; General Manager: Nicholas Bamford*

Newcastle upon Tyne: Northern Sinfonia of England, The Sinfonia Center, 41 Jesmond Vale, Newcastle upon Tyne NE1 1PG
Artistic Director: Heinrich Schiff; Chief Executive: John Summers

Northampton: Corelli Strings, Billing Arbours House, Heather Lane, Northampton NN3 4EY
Director: Kenneth Sillito; Director: Susan Brown

Midland Philharmonic Orchestra, Ridgway House, Great Brington, Northampton NN7 4JA
Artistic Director: John Gale; Administrator: Trisha Shoebridge

Oxford: City of Oxford Orchestra, Bury Knowle House, North Place, Headington, Oxford OX3 9HY
Chief Conductor: Marios Papadopoulos; Managing Director: John King

European Community Baroque Orchestra, 6a Cumnor Hill, Oxford OX2 9HA
Music Director: Roy Goodman; General Administrator: Paul James

Potters Bar: Vivaldi Concertante, 35 Laurel Avenue, Potters Bar, Hertfordshire EN6 2AB
Conductor: Joseph Pilberty

Reading: The Brandenburg Consort, 97 Mill Lane, Lower Earley, Reading, Berkshire RG6 3UH. Tel: 44 118 935 2595; Fax: 44 118 935 2627
Music Director: Roy Goodman

Royston: English Sinfonietta, The Barn, Layston Park, Royston, Hertfordshire SG8 9DS. Tel: 44 1763 2424847; Fax: 44 1763 248048
Principal Conductor: Steuart Bedford; General Manager: Graham Pfaff

Salford: Northern Chamber Orchestra, Jubilee House, Acton Square, The Crescent, Salford M5 4WX
Artistic Director: Nicholas Ward

Sheffield: South Yorkshire Symphony Orchestra, 35 Grove Road, Totley, Sheffield S17 4DJ
Music Director: Paul Scott

Stevenage: English Sinfonia, 1 Wedgewood Court, Stevenage, Hertfordshire GG1 4QR. Tel: 44 1438 350990; Fax: 44 1438 350930
General Manager: Graham Pfaff

Tadworth: English Classical Players Ltd, 25 Epsom Lane South, Tadworth, Surrey KT20 5TA. Tel: 44 1737 813273; Fax: 44 1737 215676
Artistic Director: Jonathan Brett

Tamworth: London String Orchestra, 37 St Davids Road, Clifton Campville, nr Tamworth, Staffordshire B79 0BA
Conductor: James Maddocks

Tring: Divertimenti, 1 Pendley Bridge, Tring Station, Tring, Herts HP23 5QU

Uckfield: London Chanticleer Orchestra, Tickerage Castle, Pound Lane, Framfield, Uckfield, East Sussex TN22 5RT. Tel: 44 1825 890348
Music Director: Ruth Gipps; Secretary: H J Graty

Wakefield: Yorkshire Philharmonic Orchestras, Torridon House, 104 Bradford Road, Wrenthorpe, Wakefield,
West Yorkshire WF1 2AH. Tel: 44 1924 371496
General Manager: Brian Greensmith

Waltham Abbey: New Symphony Orchestra, 19 Broomstick Hall Road, Waltham Abbey, Essex EN9 1LN
General Manager: Julian J Smyth

**Welwyn Garden
City:** Amici Chamber Orchestra, 55 Rosedale, Welwyn Garden City, Hertfordshire AL7 1DP
Conductor: Nigel Springthorpe

Wigan: Orchestra of The Mill, Trencherfield Mill, Wallgate, Wigan WN3 4EF
Music Director: Peter Donohoe; Manager: Christopher Robins

Wolverhampton: English Philharmonic Orchestra, Sounds Music Ltd. 70 Lea Road, Pennfields, Wolverhampton WV3 0LW
Music Director: Neil Moore; Managing Director: Mark Jarvis

Worcester: English Symphony Orchestra and English String Orchestra, Rockliffe House, 40 Church Street, Malvern, Worcestershire WR1 2AZ..
Tel: 44 1684 560696; Fax: 44 1684 560656. *Artistic Director: William Boughton; Administrator: Margaret MackSmith*
New English Orchestra,141 Woodbine Road, Barbourne, Worcester WR1 3JB
Principal Conductor: Nigel Swinford; Administrator: Alison Hawcutt

Worthing: Worthing Symphony Orchestra, Town Hall, Worthing, West Sussex BN11 1HQ

UKRAINE

Kiev: Kiev Chamber Orchestra, Vladirmirsky Spusk 2, 252001 Kiev
Ukrainian State Symphony Orchestra, Vladimirsky Spusk 2, 252001 Kiev
Music Director: Igor Blazhkov

Odessa: Odessa Chamber Orchestra, 15 R Louxembourg Street, Odessa
Odessa Philharmonic Orchestra, 15 R Louxembourg Street, 270026 Odessa. Tel/Fax: 7 048 222 6349

Yalta: Crimean State Philharmonic, 13 Litkens Street, 334200 Yalta

USA

ALABAMA

Huntsville: Huntsville Symphony Orchestra, PO Box 2400, Huntsville, AL 35804
Music Director: Taavo Virkhaus; Executive Director: Samuel Woodward

ALASKA

Anchorage: Anchorage Symphony Orchestra, 524 West Fourth Avenue, Suite 205, Anchorage, AK 99501
Music Director: George Hanson; Executive Director: Sherri Reddick

Fairbanks: Fairbanks Symphony Orchestra, PO Box 82104, Fairbanks, AK 99708
Music Director: Madeline Schatz; Executive Director: Jane Aspnes

ARIZONA

Phoenix: Phoenix Symphony Orchestra, 3707 North Seventh Street, Phoenix, AZ 85014. Tel: 1 602 277 7291; Fax: 1 602 277 7517
Principal Guest Conductor: Hermann Michael; President and Chief Executive Officer: Conrad Kloh; Music Director: James Sedares

Tucson: Tucson Symphony Orchestra, 443 South Stone Avenue, Tucson, AZ 85701
Music Director: Robert Bernhardt; Executive Director: Eric G Meyer

ARKANSAS

Little Rock: Arkansas Symphony Orchestra, PO Box 7328, 2417 North Tyler, Little Rock, AR 72217. Tel: 1 501 666 1761; Fax: 1 501 666 3193
Music Director: David Itkin; Executive Director: JoAnn Greene

CALIFORNIA

Berkeley: Berkeley Symphony Orchestra, 2322 Shattuck Avenue, Berkeley, CA 94704
Music Director: Kent Nagano; Executive Director: Kelly Johnson

Fresno: Fresno Philharmonic Orchestra, 2610 West Shaw Avenue, Suite 103, Fresno, CA 93711
Music Director: Raymond Harvey; General Manager: Irene Klug Nielson

Glendale: Glendale Symphony Orchestra, 401 North Brand Boulevard, Suite 520, Glendale, CA 91203
Music Director: Lalo Schifrin

Long Beach: Long Beach Symphony Orchestra, 555 East Ocean Boulevard, No 106, Long Beach, CA 90802
Music Director: JoAnn Falletta; General Manager: Mary Newkirk

Los Angeles: Los Angeles Chamber Orchestra, 315 West Ninth Street, Suite 801, Los Angeles, CA 90015
Artistic Advisor: Christof Perick; Executive Director: Erich Vollmer
Los Angeles Philharmonic Orchestra, 135 North Grand Avenue, Los Angeles, CA 90012. Tel: 1 213 972 7300; Fax: 1 213 617 3065
Music Director: Esa-Pekka Salonen

Oakland: Oakland East Bay Symphony Orchestra, 1999 Harrison Street, Suite 2030, Oakland, CA 94612
Music Director: Michael Morgan

Pasadena: Pasadena Symphony Orchestra, 117 East Colorado Boulevard, No 375, Pasadena, CA 91105
Music Director: Jorge Mester; Executive Director: Wayne Shilkret
Sacramento: Sacramento Symphony Orchestra, 77 Cadillac Drive, Sutie 101, Sacramento, CA 95825
Music Director: Geoffrey Simon
San Francisco: Philharmonia Baroque Orchestra, 57 Post Street, Suite 705, San Francisco, CA 94104
Music Director: Nicholas McGegan; Executive Director: George Gelles
The Women's Philharmonic, 330 Townsend Street, Suite 218, San Francisco, CA 94107
Executive Director: Shira Cion
San Francisco Symphony, Louise M Davies Symphony Hall, San Francisco, CA 94102. Tel 1 415 552 8000; Fax: 1 415 431 6857
Music Director: Michael Tilson Thomas; Executive Director: Peter Pastreich
San Jose: San Jose Symphony Orchestra, 99 Almaden Boulevard, Suite 400, San Jose, CA 95113. Tel: 1 408 287 7383; Fax: 1 408 286 6391
Music Director: Leonid Grin
Santa Ana: Pacific Symphony Orchestra, 1231 E Dyer Road, Suite 200, Santa Ana, CA 92705-5606. Tel: 1 714 755 5788; Fax: 1 714 755 5789
Music Director: Carl St Clair; Executive Director: Louis G Spisto
Santa Barbara: Music Academy of the West Summer Festival Orchestra, 1070 Fairway Road, Santa Barbara, CA 93108
Music Director: Lawrence Leighton Smith; Artistic Operations Manager: Carleen Landes
Santa Barbara Symphony Orchestra, 214 Easr Victoria Street, Santa Barbara, CA 93101
Music Director: Gisèle Ben-Dor; General Manager: James L Wright
Stockton: Stockton Symphony Orchestra, 37 West Yokuts, C-4, Stockton, CA 95207
Music Director: Peter Jaffe; Executive Director: George A Sinclair

COLORADO

Aspen: Aspen Festival Orchestra and Chamber Symphony, PO Box AA, Aspen, CO 81612
General Manager: Thomas Eirman
Colorado Springs: Colorado Springs Symphony Orchestra, PO Box 1692, Colorado Springs, CO 80901
Music Director: Christopher Wilkins
Denver: Colorado Symphony Orchestra, 821 17th Street, Suite 700, Denver, CO 80202. Tel: 1 303 292 5566; Fax: 1 303 293 2649.
Music Director: Marin Alsop; Artistic Administrator: David T Abosch
Denver Chamber Orchestra, 1616 Glenarm Place. Suite 1360, Denver, CO 80202
Music Director: Paul Lustig Dunkel; Executive Director: Lynn Case
Keystone: National Repertory Orchestra, PO Box 38, Keystone, CO 80435
Conductor: Carl Topilow

CONNECTICUT

Bridgeport: Greater Bridgeport Symphony Orchestra, 446 University Avenue, Bridgeport, CT 06604
Music Director: Gustav Meier; General Manager: Jena Maric
Hartford: Hartford Symphony Orchestra, 228 Farmington Avenue, Hartford, CT 06105
Music Director: Michael Lankester
New Haven: New Haven Symphony Orchestra, 33 Whitney Avenue, New Haven, CT 06510
Music Director: Michael Palmer; General Manager: Catherine Weiskel

DELAWARE

Wilmington: Delaware Symphony Orchestra, PO Box 1870, Wilmington, DE 19899
Music Director: Stephen Gunzenhauser; Executive Director: Curtis Long

DISTRICT OF COLUMBIA

Washington: National Gallery Orchestra, Sixth Street and Constitution Avenue North West, Washington, DC 20565
Music Director: George Manos
National Symphony Orchestra, John F Kennedy Center for the Performing Arts, Washington, DC 20566. Tel: 1 202 416 8100; Fax: 1 202 416 8105
Music Director: Leonard Slatkin; General Manager: Richard Hancock
Theater Chamber Players of Kennedy Center, John F Kennedy Center for the Perfoming Arts,
Washington, DC 20566. *Directors: Leon Fleisher and Dina Koston*

FLORIDA

Boca Raton: Florida Symphonic Pops, 120 North East First Avenue, Boca Raton, FL 33432
Artistic Director: Derek Stannard; Executive Vice President: Carol Simmons
Fort Lauderdale: Florida Philharmonic Orchestra, 3401 North West Ninth Avenue, Fort Lauderdale, FL 33309. Tel: 1 305 561 2997; Fax: 1 305 561 1390
Music Director: James Judd; Executive Director: John Graham
Jacksonville: Jacksonville Symphony Orchestra, 33 South Hogan Street, Jacksonville, FL 32202. Tel: 1 904 354 5479; Fax: 1 904 354 9238
Music Director: Roger Nierenberg; Executive Director: David Pierson
Miami Beach: New World Symphony, 541 Lincoln Road, 3rd Floor, Miami Beach, FL 33139. Tel: 1 305 673 3330; Fax: 1 305 673 6749
Artistic Director: Michael Tilson Thomas; Artistic Administrator: John Duffy
Naples: Naples Philharmonic, 5833 Pelican Bay Boulevard, Naples, FL 33963
Music Director: Christopher Seaman; President and Chief Executive Officer: Myra Janco Daniels
Sarasota: Florida West Coast Symphony Orchestra, 709 N Tamiami Trail, Sarasota, FL 34236. Tel: 1 941 953 4252; Fax: 1 941 953 3059
Music Director: Paul Wolfe; Executive Director: Gretchen Serrie
Tampa: Florida Orchestra, 5670 West Cyprus Street, Suite C, Tampa, FL 33607. Tel: 1 813 286 1170; Fax: 1 813 286 2316
Music Director: Jahja Ling; Executive Director: Kathryn Holm

GEORGIA

Atlanta: Atlanta Symphony Orchestra, 1293 Peachtree Street North East, Sutie 300, Atlanta, GA 30309. Tel: 1 404 733 4900; Fax: 1 404 733 4901
Music Director: Yoel Levi; President: Allison Vulgamore
Savannah: Savannah Symphony Orchestra, PO Box 9505, Savannah, GA 31412
Music Director: Philip Greenberg; General Manager: Gregg W Gustafson

HAWAII

ORCHESTRAS

Honolulu: Honolulu Symphony Orchestra, 677 Ala Moana Blvd, Suite 615, Honolulu, HI 96813. Tel: 1 808 524 0815; Fax: 1 808 524 1507

IDAHO

Boise: Boise Philharmonic, 205 North 10th, Suite 617, Boise, ID 83702
Music Director: James Ogle; General Manager: Margie Stoy

ILLINOIS

Chicago: Chicago Chamber Orchestra, 410 South Michigan Avenue, Suite 631, Chicago, IL 60605
Music Director: Dieter Kober; General Manager: Magdalene Lornez
Chicago Symphony Orchestra, Orchestra Hall, 220 South Michigan Avenue, Chicago, IL 60604. Tel: 1 312 435 8122; Fax: 1 213 786 1207
Music Director: Daniel Barenboim; Executive Director: Henry Fogel
Grant Park Symphony Orchestra, 425 East McFetridge Drive, Chicago, IL 60605
Principal Conductor: Hugh Wolff
Music of the Baroque Orchestra, 343 South Dearborn, Sutie 1716, Chicago, IL 60604
Music Director: Thomas Wikman

INDIANA

Fort Wayne: Fort Wayne Philharmonic Orchestra, 222 West Berry Street, Fort Wayne, IN 46802
Music Director: Edvard Tchivzhei; General Manager: Christopher D Guerin
Indianapolis: Indianapolis Chamber Orchestra, 4600 Sunset Avenue, Indianapolis, IN 46208
Music Director: Kirk Trevor; Administrative Director: Charles Manning
Indianapolis Symphony Orchestra, Circle Theatre, 45 Monument Circle, Indianapolis, IN 46204. Tel: 1 317 262 1100; Fax: 1 317 637 1917
Music Director: Raymond Leppard; President: Robert C Jones

IOWA

Cedar Rapids: Cedar Rapids Symphony Orchestra, 205 Second Avenue, South East, Cedar Rapids, IA 52401
Music Director: Christian Tiemeyer; Executive Director: Kathy Hall

KANSAS

Wichita: Wichita Symphony Orchestra, 225 West Douglas, Suite 207, Wichita, KS 67202. Tel: 1 316 267 8259; Fax: 1 316 267 1937
Music Director: Zuohuang Chen; General Manager: Mitchell A Berman

KENTUCKY

Louisville: Louisville Orchestra, 611 West Main Street, Louisville, KY 40202. Tel: 1 502 587 8681; Fax: 1 502 589 7870
Music Director: Max Bragado-Darman; Executive Director: Wayne S Brown

LOUISIANA

New Orleans: Louisiana Philharmonic Orchestra, 305 Baronne Street, Suite 600, New Orleans, LA 70112. Tel: 1 504 523 6530; Fax: 1 504 595 8468
Music Director: Klauspeter Seibel; Executive Director: Robert Stiles

MAINE:

Portland: Portland Symphony Orchestra, 30 Myrtle Street, Portland, ME 04101
Music Director: Toshiyuki Shimada; Executive Director: Jane E Hunter

MARYLAND:

Baltimore: Baltimore Symphony Orchestra, 1212 Cathedral Street, Baltimore, MD 21201. Tel: 1 410 783 8100; Fax: 1 410 783 8077
Music Director: David Zinman; Executive Director: John Gidwitz
Hagerstown: Maryland Symphony Orchestra, 12 Rochester Place, Hagerstown, MD 21740
Music Director: Barry Tuckwell; Managing Director: Cassandra H Wantz

MASSACHUSETTS

Boston: Boston Symphony Orchestra, Symphony Hall, 301 Massachusetts Avenue, Boston, MA 02115. Tel: 1 617 266 1492; Fax: 1 617 638 9367
Music Director: Seiji Ozawa; Managing Director: Kenneth Haas
Handel & Haydn Society, Symphony Hall, 301 Massachusetts Avenue, Boston, MA 02115
Artistic Director: Christopher Hogwood; Executive Director: Mary Deissler
Springfield: Springfield Symphony Orchestra, 1391 Main Street, Suite 1006, Springfield, MA 01103
Music Director: Mark Russell Smith; Executive Director: Susan Davison

MICHIGAN

Ann Arbor: Ann Arbor Symphony Orchestra, PO Box 1412, Ann Arbor, MI 48106
Music Director: Samuel Wong; Executive Director: Mary Blaske
Detroit: Detroit Symphony Orchestra, 3711 Woodward Avenue, Detroit, MI 48201. Tel: 1 313 833 3362; Fax: 1 313 833 3047
Music Director: Neeme Järvi; Executive Director: Mark Volpe
Michigan Chamber Orchestra, 60 Farnsworth, Detroit, MI 48202
Principal Conductor: Andrew Massey; General Manager: Virginia Catanese
Grand Rapids: Grand Rapids Symphony Orchestra, 220 Lyon North West, Suite 415, Grand Rapids, MI 49503. Tel: 1 616 454 9451; Fax: 1 616 454 7477
Music Director: Catherine Comet; Executive Director: Peter W Smith
Kalamazoo: Kalamazoo Symphony Orchestra, 426 South Park Street, Kalamazoo, MI 49007
Music Director: Yoshimi Takeda; General Manager: John Forsyte

MINNESOTA

Minneapolis: Minnesota Orchestra, 1111 Nicollet Mall, Minneapolis, MN 55403. Tel: 612 371 5600; Fax: 1 612 371 0838
Music Director: Eiji Oue; President: David J Hyslop
St Paul: St Paul Chamber Orchestra, 408 St Peter Street, Suite 500, St Paul, MN 55102. Tel: 1 612 292 3248; Fax: 1 612 292 3281
Music Director: Hugh Wolff; President and Managing Director: Brent Assink

MISSISSIPPI

Jackson: Mississippi Symphony Orchestra, PO Box 2052, Jackson, MS 39225
Music Director: Colman Pearce; Executive Director: Philip K Messner

MISSOURI

Kansas City: Kansas City Symphony Orchestra, 1020 Central, Suite 300, Kansas City, MO 64105. Tel: 1 816 471 1100; Fax: 1 816 471 0976
Music Director: William McGlaughlin; General Manager: Susan Franano

St Louis: St Louis Symphony Orchestra, Powell Symphony Hall, 718 North Grand Boulevard, St Louis, MO 63103. Tel: 1 314 533 2500; Fax: 1 314 286 4142
Music Director: Hans Vonk; Executive Director: Bruce Coppock

NEBRASKA

Omaha: Omaha Symphony Orchestra, 1615 Howard Street, Suite 310, Omaha, NE 68102
Music Director: Bruce Hangen; Executive Director: Roland Valliere

NEW HAMPSHIRE

Manchester: New Hampshire Symphony Orchestra, PO Box 1298, Manchester, NH 03105
Music Director: James Bolle; General Manager: David A Ball

NEW JERSEY

Newark: New Jersey Symphony Orchestra, 2 Central Avenue, Newark, NJ 07102. Tel: 1 201 624 3713; Fax: 1 201 624 2115
Music Director: Zdenek Macal; Executive Director: Lawrence Tamburri

Trenton: Greater Trenton Symphony Orchestra, 28 West State Street, Suite 201, Trenton, NJ 08608
Executive Director and Principal Conductor: John Peter Holly

NEW MEXICO

Albuquerque: New Mexico Symphony Orchestra, 220 Gold South West, Albuquerque, NM 87102
Music Director: David Lockington; Executive Director: Paul Bunker

NEW YORK

Albany: Albany Symphony Orchestra, 19 Clinton Avenue, Albany, NY 12207
Music Director: David Alan Miller

Brooklyn: Brooklyn Philharmonic Symphony Orchestra, 30 Lafayette Avenue, Brooklyn, NY 11217
Music Director: Robert Spano; Executive Director: Joseph Horowitz

Buffalo: Buffalo Philharmonic Orchestra, PO Box 905, Buffalo, NY 14213. Tel: 1 716 885 0331; Fax: 1 716 885 9372
Music Director: Maximiano Valdes; Executive Director: John Bauser

Chautauqua: Chautauqua Symphony Orchestra, Chautauqua, NY 14722
Music Director: Uriel Segal; General Manager: Marty W Merkley

Dobbs Ferry: Philharmonia Virtuosi, 145 Palisade Street, Sutie 341, Dobbs Ferry, NY 10522
Music Director: Richard Kapp; General Manager: Sally Forrest

Greenvale: New York Virtuosi Chamber Symphony, C W Post College, Greenvale, NY 11548
Music Director: Kenneth Klein; Executive Director: Yolanda Padula

Melville: Long Island Philharmonic Orchestra, 1 Hungtington Quadrangel, Suite LL 09, Melville, NY 11747
Executive Director: Camille Reed

New York: American Composers Orchestra, 37 West 65th Street, 6th Floor, New York, NY 10023
Music Director: Dennis Russell Davies; Executive Director: Jesse Rosen
American Symphony Orchestra, 850 Seventh Avenue, Suite 1106, New York, NY 10019
Music Director: Leon Botstein; Executive Director: Eugene Carr
New York Chamber Symphony, 92nd Street Y, 1395 Lexington Avenue, New York, NY 10128
Music Director: Gerard Schwarz; Manager: Tom Gaitens
New York Philharmonic Orchestra, 10 Lincoln Center Plaza, Lincoln Center for the Performing Arts,
Broadway at 65th Street, New York, NY 10023. Tel: 1 212 875 5000; Fax: 1 212 875 5717
Music Director: Kurt Masur; Managing Director: Deborah Borda
Orchestra of St Luke's, 130 West 42nd Street, Suite 804, New York, NY 10036
Executive Director: Marianne Lockwood
Orpheus Chamber Orchestra, 490 Riverside Drive, New York, NY 10027
Executive Director: Julian Fifer

Poughkeepsie: Hudson Valley Philharmonic Orchestra, PO Box 191, Poughkeepsie, NY 12602
Music Director: Randall Fleischer; Managing Director: Karen Deschere

Rochester: Rochester Philharmonic Orchestra, 108 East Avenue, Rochester, NY 14604. 1 716 454 2620; Fax: 1 716 423 2256
Principal Conductor: Robert Bernhardt; President: Nan Haman

Syracuse: Syracuse Symphony Orchestra, 411 Montgomery Street, Sryacuse, NY 13202. Tel: 1 315 424 8222; Fax: 1 315 424 1131
Music Director: Fabio Mechetti; Executive Director: David Worters

NORTH CAROLINA

Charlotte: Charlotte Symphony Orchestra, 211 N College Street, Suite 202, Charlotte, NC 28202. Tel: 1 704 332 0468; Fax: 1 704 332 1963
Music Director: Peter McCoppin; President and Executive Director: William Lester

Greensboro: Eastern Philharmonic Orchestra, PO Box 22026, Greensboro, NC 27420
Music Director: Sheldon Morgenstern

Raleigh: North Carolina Symphony Orchestra, 2 E South Street, Raleigh, NC 27601. Tel: 1 919 733 2750; Fax: 1 919 733 9920
Music Director: Gerhardt Zimmerman; Executive Director: Banks C Talley Jnr

OHIO

Cincinnati: Cincinnati Symphony Orchestra, 1241 Elm Street, Cincinnati, OH 45210. Tel: 1 513 621 1919; Fax: 513 621 2132
Musix Director: Jesús López-Cobos; Executive Director: Steven I Monder

Cleveland Cleveland Orchestra, Severance Hall, 11001 Euclid Avenue, Cleveland, OH 44106. Tel:1 216 231 7300; Fax: 1 216 231 0202
Music Director: Christoph von Dohnányi; Executive Director: Thomas W Morris

Columbus: Columbus Symphony Orchestra, 55 East State Street, Columbus, OH 43215. Tel: 1 614 224 5381; Fax: 1 614 224 7273
                 Music Director: Alessandro Siciliani; Executive Director: Susan Franano
Dayton: Dayton Philharmonic Orchestra, 125 East First Street, Dayton, OH 45422
                 Music Director: Isaiah Jackson; Executive Director: Curtis Long
Toledo: Toledo Symphony Orchestra, 2 Maritime Plaza, Toledo, OH 43604. Tel: 1 419 241 1272; Fax: 1 419 321 0890
                 Music Director: Andrew Massey; Managing Director: Robert Bell

OKLAHOMA

Oklahoma City: Oklahoma City Philharmonic Orchestra, 428 West California, Suite 210, Oklahoma City, OK 73102
                     Music Director: Joel Levine; General Manager: Alan D Valentine
Tulsa: Tulsa Philharmonic Orchestra, 2901 South Harvard, Tulsa, OK 74114
                     Music Director: Bernard Rubenstein; General Manager: William Schmieding

OREGON

Eugene: Eugene Symphony Orchestra, 45 West Broadway, Suite 201, Eugene, OR 97401
                 Music Director: Marin Alsop; Executive Director: Stuart Weiser
Portland: Oregon Symphony Orchestra, 711 South West Alder, Suite 200, Portland, OR 97205. Tel: 1 503 228 4294; Fax: 1 503 228 4150
                 Music Director: James DePreist; President: Don Roth

PENNSYLVANIA

Philadelphia: Philadelphia Orchestra, Academy of Music, 1420 Locust Street, Suite 400, Philadelphia, PA 19102. Tel: 1 215 893 1900; Fax: 1 215 893 1948
                   Music Director: Wolfgang Sawallisch; President and Chief Operating Officer: Joseph H Kluger
Pittsburgh: Pittsburgh Symphony Orchestra, Heinz Hall, 600 Penn Avenue, Pittsburgh, PA 15222. Tel: 1 412 392 4800; Fax: 1 412 392 4909
                   Music Director: Mariss Jansons; Vice President and Managing Director: Gideon Toeplitz

PUERTO RICO

Santurce: Puerto Rico Symphony Orchestra, Box 41227, Minillas Station, Santurce, PR 00940
                 Music Director: Eugene Kohn; General Director: Félix Rosas Crespo

RHODE ISLAND

Providence: Rhode Island Philharmonic Orchestra, 222 Richmond Street, Providence, RI 02903
                 Music Director: Zuohuang Chen; Executive Director: Karen Dobbs

SOUTH CAROLINA

Chareston: Charleston Symphony Orchestra, 14 George Street, Charleston, SC 29401
                 Music Director: David Stahl; Executive Director: Darrell G Edwards

SOUTH DAKOTA

Sioux Falls: South Dakota Symphony Orchestra, 300 North Dakota Avenue, No 405, Sioux Falls, SD 57102
                  Music Director: Henry Charles Smith; Executive Director: Wimack Richardson

TENNESSEE

Knoxville: Knoxville Symphony Orchestra, 623 Market Street, Suite 600, Knoxville, TN 37902. Tel: 1 423 523 1178; Fax: 1 423 546 3766
                 Music Director: Kirk Trevor; Executive Director: Constance Harrison
Memphis: Memphis Symphony Orchestra, 3100 Walnut Grove, Suite 501, Memphis, TN 38111
                 Music Director: Alan Balter; Executive Director: Martha Maxwell
Nashville: Nashville Symphony Orchestra, 209 10th Avenue South, Suite 448, Nashville, TN 37203. Tel: 1 615 255 5600; Fax: 1 615 255 5656
                 Music Director: Kenneth Schemerhorn; Executive Director: Stephen R Vann

TEXAS

Austin: Austin Symphony Orchestra, Symphony Square, 1101 Red River, Austin, TX 78701
                 Music Director: Sung Kwak; Executive Director: Kenneth K Caswell
Dallas: Dallas Symphony Orchestra, 2301 Flora Street, Suite 300, Dallas, TX 75201. Tel: 1 214 871 4000; Fax: 1 214 871 4049
                 Music Director: Andrew Litton; Executive Director: Eugene Bonelli
Fort Worth: Fort Worth Symphony Orchestra, 4401 Trail Lake Drive, Fort Worth, TX 76109. Tel: 1 817 921 2676; Fax: 1 817 921 9795
                 Music Director: John Giordano; Excutive Director: Ann Koonsman
Houston: Houston Symphony Orchestra, 615 Louisiana Street, Houston, TX 77002. Tel 1 713 224 4240; Fax: 1 713 222 7024
                 Music Director: Christoph Eschenbach; Executive Director: David M Wax
San Antonio: San Antonio Symphony Orchestra, 220 E Houston Street, Suite 200, San Antonio, TX 78205. Tel: 1 210 554 1000; Fax: 1 210 554 1008
                 Music Director: Christopher Wilkins; Executive Director: David Schillhammer

UTAH

Salt lake City: Utah Symphony Orchestra, 123 West South Temple, Salt Lake City, UT 84101. Tel: 1 801 533 5266; Fax: 1 801 521 6634
                     Music Director: Joseph Silverstein; Artistic Administrator: Cecil Cole

VIRGINIA

Norfolk: Virginia Symphony Orchestra, PO Box 26, Norfolk, VA 23501. Tel: 1 804 623 8590; Fax: 1 804 623 7068
                 Music Director: JoAnn Falletta; Executive Director: Daniel Hart

Richmond: Richmond Symphony Orchestra, The Berkshire, 300 West Franklin Street, Richmond, VA 23220
                 Music Director: George Manahan; Executive Director: Catherine Wichterman
Roanoke: Roanoke Symphony Orchestra, PO Box 2433, Roanoke, VA 24010
                 Executive Director: Patricia Avise

WASHINGTON

Seattle: Seattle Symphony Orchestra, 305 Harrison Street, Seattle, WA 98109. Tel: 1 206 215 4700; Fax: 1 206 215 4701
Music Director: Gerard Schwarz; Executive Director: Deborah Card
Spokane: Spokane Symphony Orchestra, 621 Mallon, Suite 203, Spokane, WA 99201
Music Director: Fabio Mechetti; Executive Director: Richard Early

WEST VIRGINIA

Charleston: West Virginia Symphony Orchestra, PO Box 2292, Charleston, WV 24328
Music Director: Thomas Conlin; Manager: Shirley Furry

WISCONSIN

Milwaukee: Milwaukee Symphony Orchestra, 330 E Kilbourn Avenue, Suite 900, Milwaukee, WI 53202. Tel: 1 414 291 6010; Fax: 1 414 291 7610
Artistic Advisor: Stanislaw Skrowaczewski; Executive Director: Joan Squire

URUGUAY

Montevideo: Orquesta Sinfónia del SODR E, CAlle Sarandi 450, Montevideo 1100
Music Director: Robeeto Montenegro; President: Escribano Ramiro Llana

VENEZUELA

Caracas: Orquesta Sinfónica Municipal de Caracas, Apdo 17390, Parque Central, Caracas 1015-A
Director: Carlos Riazuelo
Simon Bolivar Symphony Orchestra of Venezuela, Torre Oeste, Piso 1, Parque Central, Caracas
Music Director: José Antonio Abreu

YUGOSLAVIA

Belgrade: Belgrade Philharmonic Orchestra, Studentski Trg 11, 11000 Belgrade
Belgrade Radio and Television Symphony Orchestra, Hilendarska 2, 11000 Belgrade

APPENDIX B
OPERA COMPANIES

ARGENTINA

Buenos Aires: Teatro Colón, Cerrito 618, 1010 Buenos Aires. Tel: 54 1 382 8924/2389; Fax: 54 1 111232
General Director: Klve Staiff

AUSTRALIA

NEW SOUTH WALES

Strawberry Hills: Australian Opera, PO Box 291, Strawberry Hills, NSW 2012. Tel: 61 2 9699 1099; Fax: 61 2 9699 3184
General Manager: Donald McDonald; Artistic Director: Moffat Oxenbould

QUEENSLAND

Brisbane: Opera Queensland, PO Box 3677, South Brisbane, QLD 4101. Tel: 61 7 3875 3030; Fax: 61 7 3844 5352
General Manager: Suzannah Conway

SOUTH AUSTRALIA

Adelaide: State Opera of South Australia, PO Box 211, Marleston BC, SA 5033. Tel: 61 8 226 4790; Fax: 61 8 226 4791
Artistic Director: Bill Gillespie; General Director: Stephen Philips

VICTORIA

Melbourne: Victoria State Opera, 77 Southbank Boulevard, Melbourne, VIC 3205
General Manager: Ken Mackenzie-Forbes; Artistic Administrator: Kate Stevenson

WESTERN AUSTRALIA

Perth: West Australian Opera, 3rd Floor, His Majesty's Theatre, 825 Hay Street, Perth, WA
General Manager: Lisa Shilton

AUSTRIA

Bad Ischl: Sommertheater, Wiesingerstrasse 7, A-4820 Bad Ischl
Music Director: Eduard Macku; Manager: Silvia Müller
Baden bei Wien: Stadttheater, Theaterplatz 7, A-2500 Baden bei Wien
Director: Helmuth Brandstätter
Graz: Vereinigte Bühnen, Kaiser Josef Platz 10, A-8010 Graz. Tel: 43 316 8000; Fax: 43 316 8565
Director: Gerhard Brunner
Innsbruck: Tiroler Landerstheater, Rennweg 2, A-6020 Innsbruck. Tel: 43 512 520744; Fax: 43 512 52074333
Director: Dominique Mentha
Klagenfurt: Stadtheater, Theaterplatz 4, A-9020 Klagenfurt
Director: Dietmar Pflegerl
Linz: Landestheater, Promenade 39, A-4010 Linz. Tel: 43 732 761 1100; Fax: 43 732 761 1105
Director: Roman Zeilinger
St Pölten: Stadttheater, Rathausplatz 11, A-3100 St Pölten
Director: Perter Wolsdorff
Salzburg: Landestheater, Schwarstrasse 22, A-5020 Salzburg. Tel: 43 662 871512; Fax: 43 662 87151213
Director: Lutz Hochstraate
Vienna: Raimund Theater, Wallgasse 18-20, A-1060 Vienna
Staatsoper, Opernring 2, A-1010 Vienna. Tel: 43 1 514440; Fax: 43 1 514 442330
Director: Ioan Holender
Vereinigte Bühnen Wien GmbH (Theater an der Wien), Linke Wienzeile 6, A-1060 Vienna
Volksoper, Währingerstrasse 78, A-1090 Vienna. Tel: 43 1 514 443318
Director: Ioan Holender
Wiener Kammeroper, Fleischmarkt 24, A-1010 Vienna. Tel: 43 1 512 0100; Fax: 43 1 512 010010
Artistic and General Manager: Hans Gabor

BELGIUM

Antwerp: Vlaamse Kameropera, Ommeganchstrasse 59, B-2018 Antwerp
Brussels: Théâtre Royal de la Monnaie, 4 Léopoldstrasse, B-1000 Brussels. Tel: 32 2 229 1200; Fax: 32 2 229 1380
Director: Bernard Foccroulle; Musical Director: Antonio Pappano
Ghent: Opera voor Vlaanderen, Schouwburgstrasse 3, B-9000 Ghent. Tel: 32 9 225 2425
Music Director: Marc Minkowski; General Manager: Marc Clémeur
Liège: Opéra Royal de Wallonie, 1 Rue des Domincains, B-4000 Liège. Tel: 32 4 221 4720; Fax: 32 4 221 0201

BOSNIA AND HERZEGOVINA

Sarajevo: National Theater Opera, Obala 9, 71000 Sarajevo

BULGARIA

Bourgas: Bourgas State Opera, K1, Ohridski St 2, 8000 Bourgas
Plovdiv: Plovdiv State Opera, 4000 Plovdiv
Sofia: Sofia State Opera, Boul Dondoukov 58, 1000 Sofia. Tel: 359 2 877 011
Stefan Makedonski Musical Theater, 3P Volov St, 1500 Sofia
Stara Zagora: Stara Zagora State Opera, 6000 Stara Zagora
Varna: Varna State Opera, 9000 Varna

CANADA

ALBERTA

Calgary: Calgary Opera, #601 237-8 Avenue SE, Calgary, Alberta T2G 5C3. Tel: 1 403 262 7286; Fax: 1 403 263 5428
General Director: David Speers
Edmonton: Edmonton Opera Association, 320-10232 112th Street, Edmonton, Alberta T5K 1M4. Tel: 1 403 423 424 4040/1000; Fax: 1 403 423 429 0600
General Director: Richard Mantle

BRITISH COLUMBIA

Vancouver: Vancouver Opera, Suite 500, 845 Cambie Street,Vancouver, British Columbia V6B 4Z9. Tel: 1 604 682 2871; Fax: 1 604 682 3981
Music Director: David Agler; General Director: Robert J Hallam
Victoria: Pacific Opera Victoria, 1316B Government Street, Victoria, British Columbia V8W 1YB. Tel: 1 250 385 0222; Fax: 1 250 382 4944
General Manager: Marcus Handman

MANITOBA

Winnipeg: Manitoba Opera Association, PO Box 31027, 393 Portage Avenue, 3rd Floor, Winnipeg, Manitoba R3B 3K9. Tel: 1 204 92 7479;
Fax: 1 204 949 0377 *Artistic Director: Irving Guttman; Executive Director: Joann Alexander Smith*

ONTARIO

Hamilton: Opera Hamilton, 2 King Street West, Hamilton, Ontario L8P 1A1
Artistic Director: Daniel Lipton
Ottawa: Opera Lyra, Arts Court, 110-12 Daly Avenue, Ottawa, Ontario K1N 6E2. Tel: 1 613 233 9200; Fax: 1 613 233 5431
Artistic Director: Jeannette Aster; General Manager: Maria Hansen
Toronto: Canadian Opera Company, 227 Front Street East, Toronto, Ontario M5A 1E8. Tel: 1 416 363 6671; Fax: 1 416 363 5584
Chief Conductor: Richard Bradshaw

QUÉBEC

Montréal: L'Opera de Montréal, 260 de Maisonneuve Boulevard West, Montréal, Québec H2X 1Y9. Tel: 1 418 529 4142; Fax: 1 418 529 3735
Artistic and General Director: Bernard Uzan
Québec: Opéra de Québec, 1220 Avenue Taché, Québec, Province Québec G1R 3B4
Artistic Director: Bernard Labadie; Administrative Director: Grégoire Legendre

CHILE

Santiago: Opera del Teatro Municipal, San Antonio 149, Santiago Centro. Tel: 56 2 638 1515; Fax: 56 2 633 7214
General Director: Andrés Rodriguez

CHINA

Beijing: Central Opera Theater, Dongzhimenwai, Zuojiazhuang, Beijing 100028. Tel: 86 465 2317
Director: Wang Shi-guang
China Peking Opera Theater, Beijing
President: Zhang Dong-Chuan
Shanghai: Shanghai Opera House, Lane 100, Changshu Road, Shanghai 200040. Tel: 86 216 248 5359; FaxL 86 216 249 8127

COLOMBIA

Bogotá: Compania Nacional de Opera, Teatro Colón, Celle 10, No 5-32, Bogotá

COSTA RICA

San José: Compania Lirica Nacional, PO Box 1035, San José 1000
Director: Gloria Waissbluth

CROATIA

Zagreb: Croatian National Theatre, 41000 Zagreb

CZECH REPUBLIC

Brno: National Theatre, Dvořákova 11, 657 70 Brno. Tel: 420 5 4232 1285; Fax: 420 5 4221 3746
Košice: Košice State Theatre Opera, Šrobárova 14, PO Box E-47, 042 77 Košice
Olomouc: Moravian State Theatre, Tr Svobdy 33, 771 07 Olomouc. Tel: 420 68 522 5727; Fax: 420 68 522 5781
Opava: Silesian Theatre, Horní námésti 13, 74669 Opava

Ostrava: Ostrava State Theatre, Pabla Nerudy 14, 701 04 Ostrava
Pizeň: J K Tyl Theatre, Prokopova 14, 304 11 Pizeň
Prague: National Theatre, PO Box 865, 112 30 Prague 1. Tel: 420 2 24 910312/901227; Fax: 420 2 24 911524
Ustí nad Labem: Z nejedlý State Theatre, Kralova Výšina 10, 400 00 Ustí nad Labem

DENMARK

Århus: Den jyske Opera, Thomas Jensens Alle, DK-8000 Århus
Administrator: Tony Borup Mortenson
Copenhagen: Det kongelige Teater, Box 2185, DK-1017 Copenhagen K. Tel: 45 33 696701; Fax: 45 33 696767
Artistic Director: Elaine Padmore; Manager: Michael Christiansen
Musikdramatisk Teater, Ernst Meyersgade 8, DK-1772 Copenhagen V

EIRE

Dublin: Dublin Grand Opera Society, John Player Theatre, 276-288 Circular Road, Dublin 8
Administrator: David Collopy
Opera Theatre Company, 18 St Andrew Street, Dublin 2. Tel: 353 1 679 4962; Fax: 353 1 679 4963
Director: James Conway

ESTONIA

Tallinn: Estonian State Opera and Ballet, Estonia Boulevard 4, EE-0105 Tallinn. Tel: 372 626 0201; Fax: 372 6 313080
Chief Conductor: Eri Klas

FINLAND

Helsinki: Finnish National Opera, PO Box 176, Helsingkatu 58, 002 51 Helsinki. Tel: 358 9 403021; Fax: 358 9 40302305
Music Director: Miguel Gómez-Martínez; Artistic Director: Walton Grönroos

FRANCE

Angers: Théâtre Musical d'Angers, 7 Rue Duboys, F-49100 Angers.
Avignon: Opéra d'Avignon, Regie Municpale, BP 111, F-84007 Avignon. Tel: 33 90 82 42 42; Fax: 33 90 85 04 23
Bordeaux: Grand Théâtre Municipal, Place de la Comédie, F-33074 Bordeaux Cédex. Tel: 33 56 00 85 0; Fax: 33 56 81 93 66
Administrator: Daniel Doumeau-Gabory
Caen: Théâtre de Caen Atelier/Lyrique de Caen, BP 217, F-14007 Caen Cédex
Director: Jean Malraye
Colmar: Atelier du Rhin, 6 Route d'Ingersheim, BP 593, F-68008 Colmar
Director: Pierre Barrat
Dijon: L'Opéra de Dijon, Service Location, 2 Rue Longpierre, F-21000 Dijon. Tel: 33 80 67 23 23
Director: Pierre Filippi
Lille: Opéra de Lille, Théâtre de l'Opéra, 2 Rue des Bons Enfants, F-59800 Lille. 33 3 20 14 99 20; Fax: 33 3 20 14 99 27
Artistic Director: Ricardo Szwarcer; Administrator: Michel Default
Lyon: Opéra de Lyon, 1 Place de la Coméde. F-69001 Lyon. Tel: 33 72 00 45 00; Fax: 33 72 00 45 01
Music Director: Kent Nagano; Administrator: Jacques Hedouin
Marseille: Opéra de Marseille, 2 Rue Molière, F-1321 Marseille Cédex 01. Tel: 33 4 91 55 21 12
Metz: Théâtre Municipal de Metz, 5 Place de la Comédie, F-57000 Metz. Tel: 33 87 55 51 87
Administrator: Daniel Lucas
Montpellier: Opéra de Montpellier, 11 Boulevard Victor Hugo, F-34000 Montpellier. Tel: 33 4 67 60 19 80/99; Fax: 33 4 67 60 19 90
General Director: Henri Maier; Administrator: Renée Panabière
Nancy: Opéra de Nancy et de Lorraine, 1 Rue Ste Catherine, F-54000 Nancy. Tel: 33 83 85 33 20; Fax: 33 83 85 30 66
Director: Antoine Bourseiller; Administrator: Christophe Bezzone
Nantes: Opéra de Nantes, 1 Rue Molière, F-44000 Nantes. Tel: 33 40 41 90 60; Fax: 33 40 41 90 77
Director: Philippe Goderfroid; Administrator: Serge Cochelin
Nice: Théâtre de l'Opéra de Nice, 4 and 6 Rue St François de Paule, F-06300 Nice. Tel: 33 93 80 59 83; Fax: 33 93 80 34 83
General Director: Jean Albert Cartier.
Orange: Chorégies d'Orange, BP 205, F-84107 Orange Cedex.
Paris: Châtelet Théâtre Musical, 2 Rue Edouard Colonne, F-75001 Paris.
Ecole 'Art Lyrique de l'Opéra, 5 Rue Favart, F-75009 Paris
Director: Michel Sénéchal; Administrator: Francis Meunier
L'Opéra Comique, 5 Rue Favart, F-75002 Paris.
Opéra de La Bastille, 120 Rue de Lyon, F-75012 Paris. Tel: 33 1 40 01 17 89; Fax: 33 1 44 73 13 00
Conductor: James Conlon; General Administrator: Hugues Gall
Théâtre des Champs-Elysées, 15 Avenue Montaigne, F-75008 Paris. Tel: 33 1 49 52 50 00; Fax: 33 1 49 52 07 41
General Director: Alain Durel; Administrator: Francis Lepigeon
Théâtre National de l'Opéra de Paris, 8 Rue Scribe, F-75009 Paris
Reims: Grand Théâtre de Reims, 9 Rue Chanzy, F-51100 Reims
Rouen: Théâtre des Arts, F-76177 Rouen Cédex
Director: Marc Adam
Strasbourg: Opéra du Rhin, 19 Place Broglie, F-67008 Strasbourg Cédex. Tel: 33 3 88 75 48 23; Fax: 33 3 88 24 09 34
General Director: Laurent Spielmann; Administrator: Lucien Colinet
Toulouse: Théâtre du Capitole, Place du Capitole, F-31000 Toulouse. Tel: 33 61 23 21 35
Artistic Director: Nicolas Joel; Administrator: Robert Gouaze

Tourcoing:	Atelier Lyrique de Tourcoing, 82 Boulevard Gambetta, F-59200 Tourcoing. Tel: 33 20 26 66 03 *General Director: Jean-Claude Malgoire; General Administrator: Catherine Noel*
Tours:	Centre Lyrique de Tours, Grand Théâtre, Rue de la Scellerie, F-37000 Tours. Tel: 33 47 05 33 47; Fax: 33 47 05 37 87 *Director: Michel Jarry; Administrator: Michel Berthon*

GERMANY

Aachen:	Stadttheater Aachen, Theaterplatz, 5100 Aachen *Music Director: Stefan Lano; General Manager: Elmar Ottenthal*
Altenburg:	Landestheater Altenburg, Theaterplatz 19, 7400 Altenburg *Manager: Georg Mittendrein*
Annaberg-Buchholz:	Eduard-von-Winterstein-Theater, Buchholzer Strasse 67, 9300 Annaberg-Buchholz *Music Director: Ulrich Sprenger; Manager: Hans-Hermann Krug*
Augsburg:	Städtische Bühnen Augsburg, Kasernstrasse 4-6, Pf 111949, D-86044 Augsburg. Tel: 49 821 324 3933; Fax: 49 821 324 4544 *General Music Director: Michael Luig; Manager: Peter Baumgardt*
Bautzen:	Deutsch-Sorbisches Volkstheater Bautzen, Seminarstrasse 12, 8600 Bautzen *Music Director: Dieter Kempe; Manager: Michael Grosse* Sorbisches National-Ensemble Bautzen, Aussere Lauenstrasse 2, 8600 Bautzen *Music Director: Jan Bulank; Manager: Detlef Kobjela*
Berlin:	Berliner Kammeroper e V, Kottbusser Damm 79, D-10967 Berlin. Tel: 49 30 693 1054; Fax: 49 30 692 5201 *Music Director: Brynmor Llewelyn Jones; Artistic Director: Henry Akina* Deutsche Oper Berlin, Richard Wagner Str 10, D-10585 Berlin. Tel: 49 30 343 8401; Fax: 49 30 343 84232 *General Music Director: Christian Thielemann; General Manager: Götz Friedrich* Deutsche Staatsoper Berlin, Unter den Linden 7, 1060 Berlin. Tel: 49 30 20 354555; Fax: 49 30 20 354481 *General Music Director: Daniel Barenboim; Manager: Georg Quander* Komische Oper Berlin, Behrenstrasse 55-57, D-10117 Berlin. Tel: 49 30 20 2600; Fax: 49 30 20 260405 *General Music Director: Yakov Kreizberg; Manager: Werner Rackwitz* Metropol-Theater Berlin, Friedrichstrasse 101/102, 1986 Berlin *General Music Director: Günter Joseck; Manager: Werner P Seiferth* Neuköllner Oper e V, 1000 Berlin *Artistic Director: Winfried Radeke* Theater des Westens Berlin, Kantstrasse 12, 1000 Berlin *Music Director: Peter Keuschnig; Manager: Helmut Baumann*
Bielefeld:	Bühnen der Stadt Bielefeld, Brunhenstrasse 3-9, Pf 220, 4800 Bielefeld. Tel: 49 521512502; Fax: 49 521 513430 *General Music Director: Rainer Koch; Manager: Heiner Bruns*
Bochum:	Starlighttheater Bochum, Stadionring 24, 4630 Bochum *Music Director: Phil Edwards*
Bonn:	Oper der Stadt Bonn, Am Boeselagerhof 1, Pf 2440, D-53111 Bonn. Tel: 49 228 7281; Fax: 49 228 728371 *Manager: Gian-Carlo del Monaco*
Brandenburg:	Brandenburg Theater, Grabenstrasse 14, 1800 Brandenburg *Music Director: Heiko Mathias Förster; Manager: Ekkehard Phophet*
Braunschweig:	Staatstheater Braunschweig, Postfach 4539, D-38100 Braunschweig. Tel: 49 531 484 2700; Fax: 49 531 484 2727 *General Music Director: Stefan Soltesz; General Manager: Jürgen Flügge*
Bremen:	Bremen Theater, Pf 101046, 2800 Bremen
Bremerhaven:	Stadttheater Bremerhaven, Theodor-Heuss-Platz, Pf 120541, D-27519 Bremerhaven. Tel: 49 471 482 0645; Fax: 49 471 482 0682 *General Music Director: Leo Plettner; Manager: Dirk Böttger*
Chemnitz:	Städtische Theater Chemnitz, Theaterplatz 2, 9001 Chemnitz *General Music Director: Dieter-Gerhardt Worm; General Manager: Jörg Liljeberg*
Coburg:	Landestheater Coburg, Schlossplatz 6, 8630 Coburg *General Music Director: Christian Fröhlich; Manager: Ernö Weil*
Cologne:	Offenbach-Theater Köln, Vietorstrasse 70, 5000 Cologne 91 *Director: Karl-Wolfgang Saalmann* Oper der Stadt Köln, Offenbachplatz, Pf 180241, D-50505 Cologne. Tel: 49 221 221 8282/8400 *General Music Director: James Conlon; Manager: Michael Hampe*
Cottbus:	Staatstheater Cottbus, Karl-Liebknecht-Strasse 136, 7500 Cottbus *General Music Director: Frank Morgenstern; Manager: Johannes Steurich*
Darmstadt:	Staatstheater Darmstadt, Postfach 111432, D-64229 Darmstadt. Tel: 49 6151 28111; Fax: 49 6151 281 1226 *Manager: Peter Girth*
Dessau:	Landestheater Dessau, Fritz-Hesse-Platz 1, 4500 Dessau *Manager: Johannes Felsenstein*
Detmold:	Landestheater Detmold, Theaterplatz 1, 4930 Detmold *Manager: Ulf Reiher*
Döbein:	Stadttheater Döbein, Theaterstrasse, 7300 Döbein *Music Director: Harald Weigel; Manager: Wolfram Jacobi*
Dortmund:	Städtische Bühnen Dortmund, Kuhstrasse 12, 4600 Dortmund *General Music Director: Moshe Atzmon; General Manager: Horst Fechner*
Dresden:	Landesbühnen Sachsen, Meissner Strasse 152, D-01445 Dresden. Tel: 49 351 704; Fax: 49 351 704201 *Music Director: Joachim Widlak; Manager: Christian Schmidt* Sächsische Staatsoper Dresden (Semperoper), Theaterplatz 2, D-01067 Dresden. Tel: 49 351 49110; Fax: 49 351 491 1691 *Music Director: Giuseppe Sinopoli; Manager: Christoph Albrecht* Staatsoperette Dresden, Pirnaer Landstrasse 131, 8045 Dresden *Music Director: Volker Münch; Manager: Elke Schneider*
Düsseldorf:	Deutsche Oper am Rhein, Theatergemeinschaft Düsseldorf-Duisburg, Opernhaus Düsseldorf Heinrich-Heine-Alle 16a, D-40213 Düsseldorf . Tel: 49 211 89080; Fax: 49 211 890 8389 *General Music Director: Zoltan Pesko; General Manager: Kurt Horres*

Eggenfelden: Theater an der Rott, Pfarrkirchener Strasse 70, 8330 Eggenfelden
Music Director: Lutz Teschendorf; Manager: Adi Fischer

Eisenach: Landestheater und Landeskapelle Eisenach, Theaterplatz 4-7, 5900 Eisenach
General Music Director: Harke de Roos; Manager: Jürgen Fabritius

Eisleben: Landesbühne Sachsen-Anhalt Lutherstadt Eisleben, An der Landwehr 5, 4250 Eisleben
Music Director: Paul Sergiou; Manager: Frank Hofmann

Erfurt: Städtische Bühnen Erfurt, Dalbergsweg 2, D-99084 Erfurt. Tel: 49 361 562 6267
General Music Director: Wolfgang Rögner; General Manager: Dietrich Traube

Eschwege: Minipolitan-Eschweges Kleine Schaubühne e V, Niederhoner Strasse 2, 3440 Eschwege
Conductors: Andreas Paetzold and Andreas Worm

Essen: Theater und Philharmonie Essen, Rolandstrasse 10, 4300 Essen 1
General Music Director: Wolf-Dieter Hauschild

Flensburg: Schleswig-Holsteinisches Landestheater und Sinfonieorchester, Rathausstrasse 22, 2390 Flensburg
General Music Director: Gerhard Schneider; General Manager: Dr Horst Mesalla

Frankfurt am Main: Die Theater der Stadt Frankfurt, Untermainanlage 11, 6000 Frankfurt am Main. Tel: 49 69 21202; Fax: 49 69 212 37565
General Music Director: Sylvain Cambreling
Kammeroper Frankfurt, Nordenstrasse 60, 6000 Frankfurt am Main. Tel/Fax: 49 69 55 6189
Music Director: Martin Krähe; Artistic Director: Rainer Pudenz

Frankfurt an der Oder: Kleist-Theater, Gerhart-Hauptmann-Strasse, 1200 Frankfurt an der Oder
General Music Director: Nikos Athinäos; Maria-Luise Preuss

Freiberg: Stadttheater Freiberg, Borngasse 1, 9200 Freiberg
Music Director: Jany Renz; Manager: Rüdiger Bloch

Freiburg im Breisgau: Städtische Bühnen Freiburg, Bertoldstrasse 46, D-78000 Freiburg im Breisgau. Tel: 49 761 34874/94
General Music Director: Johannes Fritzsh

Gelsenkirchen: Musiktheater im Revier, Kennedyplatz, Pf 101854, 4650 Gelsenkirchen
General Music Director: Neil Varon; General Manager: Ludwig Baum

Gera: Bühnen der Stadt Gera, Küchengartenalle 2, 6500 Gera
Music Director: Wolfgang Wappler; Manager: Eberhard Kneipel

Giessen: Stadttheater Giessen GmbH, Berliner Platz, 6300 Giessen
General Music Director: David de Villiers; Manager: Jost Miehlbradt

Görlitz: Musiktheater der Stadt Görlitz, Demianiplatz 2, Pf 661, 8900 Görlitz
Music Director: Reinhard Seehafer; Manager: Wolf-Dieter Ludwig

Greifswald: Theater Greifswald, Anklamer Strasse 106, 2200 Greifswald
Chief Conductor: Ekkehard Klemm; Manager: Dieter Wagner

Gummersbach: Theater der Stadt Gummersbach, Reininghause Strasse, 5270 Gummersbach
Music Director and Manager: Gus Anton

Hagen: Theater Hagen, Elberfelder Strasse 65, 5800 Hagen
General Music Director: Gerhard Markson; Manager: Peter Pietzsch

Halberstadt: Theater Halberstadt, Spiegelstrasse 20a, 3600 Halberstadt
Music Director: Christian Hammer; Manager: Gero Hammer

Halle an der Saale: Opernhaus Halle, Universitätsring 24, 4020 Halle an der Saale
Music Director: Wolfgang Balzer; Manager: Klaus Froboese

Hamburg: Hamburgische Staatsoper, Grosse Theaterstrasse 34, D-20354 Hamburg. Tel: 49 35 680; Fax: 49 30 356 8456
General Music Director: Gerd Albrecht; State Opera Manager: Peter Ruzicka
Neue Flora, Stresemannstrasse 159a, 2000 Hamburg 50
Music Director: David Caddick
Operettenhaus Hamburg, Spielbudenplatz 1, 2000 Hamburg 36
Music Director: Koen Schoots

Hannover: Niedersächsische Staatstheater Hannover, Opernhaus, Opernplatz 1, D-30159 Hannover. Tel: 49 511168 6161; Fax: 49 511 368 1768/363
General Music Director: Christof Prick; Manager: Hans-Peter Lehmann
Operetten-Tournee-Theater Hannover, Auf dem Lärchenberge 18, 3000 Hannover 1
Music Director: Katalin Doman; Artistic Director: Wolfgang Pose

Heidelberg: Theater der Stadt Heidelberg, Friedrichstrasse 5, D-69117 Heidelberg. Tel: 49 6221 583502; Fax: 49 6221 583599
General Music Director: Anton Marik; Manager: Peter Stoltzenberg

Hildesheim: Stadttheater Hildesheim GmbH, Theaterstrasse 6, 3200 Hildesheim
Music Director: Werner Seitzer; Manager: Klaus Engeroff

Hof an der Saale: Städtebundtheater, Schützenstrasse 8, 8670 Hof an der Saale
Music Director: Klaus Straube; Manager: Reinhold Röttger

Kaiserslautern: Pfalztheater Kaiserslautern, 6750 Kaiserslautern
General Music Director: Lior Shambadal; Manager: Pavel Fieber

Karlsruhe: Badisches Staatstheater Karlsruhe, Baumeisterstrasse 11, Pf 1449, 7500 Karlsruhe
General Music Director: Günter Neuhold; General Manager: Günter Könemann

Kassel: Staatstheater Kassel, Friedrichsplatz 15, 3500 Kassel
General Music Director: Georg Schmöhe; Manager: Michael Leinert

Kiel: Bühnen der Landeshauptstadt Kiel, Rathausplatz 4, D-24103 Kiel. Tel: 49 431 901 2880; Fax: 49 431 901 2838
General Music Director: Klauspeter Seibel; General Manager: Peter Dannenberg

Koblenz: Theater der Stadt Koblenz, Clemensstrasse 1, 5400 Koblenz 1
General Music Director: Christian Klutting; Manager: Hannes Houska

Langenhagen: Kammeroper-Niedersachsen, Eibenstrasse 5c, 3012 Langenhagen
Music Director: Wolfgang M Sieben; Manager: Helmut M Erlwein

Leipzig: Oper Leipzig-Musikalische Komödie, Dreilindenstrasse 30, D-04109 Leipzig. Tel: 49 341 12610; Fax: 49 341 12 61387
Music Director: Roland Seiffarth; Manager: Udo Zimmermann
Oper Leipzig-Opernhaus, Augustusplatz 12, 7010 Leipzig
Manager: Udo Zimmermann

Lübeck: Bühnen der Hansestadt Lübeck, Fischergrube 5-21, 2400 Lübeck
General Music Director: Erich Wächter; General Manager: Dietrich von Oertsen

Lüneburg: Stadttheater Lüneburg, An den Reeperbahnen 3, 2120 Lüneburg
Music Director: Michael Dixon; Manager: Jan Aust

Magdeburg: Theater der Landeshauptstadt Magdeburg, Universitätsplatz 13, Pf 1240, 3010 Magdeburg
General Music Director: Mathias Husmann; General Manager: Max K Hoffmann

Mainz: Staatstheater Mainz, Gutenbergplatz 7, 6500 Mainz
General Music Director: Peter Erckens; Manager: Dr Peter Brenner

Mannheim: Nationaltheater Mannheim, Mozartstr. 9, D-68161 Mannheim. Tel: 49 621 16800; Fax: 49 621 21540
Chief Conductor: Jun Märkl; Manager: Klaus Schultz

Meiningen: Das Meininger Theater, Bernhardstrasse 5, 6100 Meiningen
Music Director: Wolfgang Hocke; Manager: Ulrich Burkhard

Mönchengladbach: Vereingte Städtische Bühnen Krefeld und Mönchengladbach, Opernhaus, Stadthalle Rheydt,
Odenkirchener Strasse 78, 4050 Mönchengladbach 2
General Music Director: Neville Dove; General Manager: Wolfgang Gropper

Munich: Bayerische Staatsoper-Nationaltheater, Max-Joseph-Platz, D-80539 Munich. Tel: 49 89 2185 01; Fax: 49 89 2185 1003
General Music Director: Zubin Mehta; Manager: Peter Jonas
Big Bang Theater München, Dachauer Strasse 192, 8000 Munich 50
Music Director: Walter Waidosch
Comédia Opera Instabile, Holzstrasse 11, 8000 Munich 5
Münchner Opernbühne (Deutsches-Tourneetheater), Damborstrasse 11, 8900 Augsburg
Conductors: Paul Popescu and Tams Sulyok; Manager: Kurt Rösler
ppp-musiktheater (Pianopianissimo-Musiktheater), Lierstrasse 31, 8000 Munich 19
Music Director: Frank Strobel; Manager: Peter P Pachl
Staatstheater am Gärtnerplatz 3, 8000 Munich 5
Music Director: Reinhard Schwarz; Manager: Hellmuth Matiasek

Münster: Städtische Bühnen Münster, Neubrückenstrasse 63, 4400 Münster
General Music Director: Will Humburg; General Manager: Achim Thorwald

Neuburg/Donau: Neuburger Kammeroper, Willstätter Strasse 18, 8070 Ingolstadt

Neustrelitz: Landestheater Mecklenburg, Friedrich-Ludwig-Jahn-Strasse, 2080 Neustrelitz
Music Director: Golo Berg; Manager: Manfred Straube

Nordhausen: Theater Nordhausen, Käthe-Kollwitz-Strasse 15, Pf 109, 5500 Nordhausen
Manager: Hubert Kross

Nürnberg: Pocket Opera Company Nürnberg, Gertrudstrasse 21, 8500 Nürnberg 80
Artistic Director: Peter B Wyrsch
Städtische Bühnen Nürnberg, Richard-Wagner-Platz 2-10, D-90443 Nürnberg. Tel: 49 911 231 3808; Fax: 49 911 231 3534
General Manager: Lew Bogdan

Oldenburg: Oldenburgisches Staatstheater, Theaterwall 18, 2900 Oldenburg
General Music Director: Knut Mahike; General Manager; Hans Häckermann

Osnabrück: Städtische Bühnen Osnabrück GmbH, Domhof 110-1, 4500 Osnabrück
General Music Director: Jean-François Monnard; Manager: Norbert Kleine-Borgmann

Passau: Südostbayerisches Städtetheater (Fürstbischöfliches Opernhaus), Gottfried-Schäffer-Strasse
2, 8390 Passau
Music Director: Jeanpierre Faber; Manager: Klaus Schlette

Pforzheim: Stadttheater Pforzheim, Am Waisenhausplatz 5, 7530 Pforzheim
General Music Director: Klaus Eisenmann; Manager: Manfred Berben

Plauen: Vogtland-Theater Plauen, Theaterstrasse 1-3, 9900 Plauen
Music Director: Paul Theissen; Manager: Dieter Roth

Potsdam: Hans-Otto-Theater Potsdam, Zimmerstrasse 10, 1570 Potsdam
Music Director: Stefan Sanderling; Manager: Guido Huonder

Regensburg: Städtische Bühnen Regensburg, Bismarckplatz 7, D-93047 Regensburg. Tel: 49 941 507 1422 Fax: 49 941 507 4429
General Music Director: Hilary Griffiths; Manager: Marietheres List

Rostock: Volkstheater Rostock, Patriotischer Weg 33, 2500 Rostock
General Music Director: Michael Zilm; General Manager: Berndt Renne

Rudolstadt: Thüringer Landestheater, Anger 1, 6820 Rudolstadt
Music Director: Konrad Bach; Manager: Peter P Pachl

Saarbrücken: Saarländisches Staatstheater, Schillerplatz, D-66111 Saarbrücken. Tel: 49 681 30920; Fax: 49 681 309 2325

Schwerin: Mecklenburgisches Staatstheater Schwerin, Alter Garten, 2751 Schwerin

Stendal: Theater der Altmark Stendal, Karlsstrasse 4-6, 3500 Stendal
Music Director: Frank Jaremko; Manager: Erdmut Christian August

Stralsund: Theater der Hansestadt Stralsund, Olof-Palmer-Platz, 2300 Stralsund
Music Director: Daniel Kleiner; Manager: Thomas Bayer

Stuttgart: Staatstheater Stuttgart, Oberer Schlossgarten 6, D-70173 Stuttgart. Tel: 49 711 203 2520; Fax: 49 711 203 2514
Music Director: Gabriele Ferro

Trier: Theater der Stadt Trier, Am Augustinerhof, 5500 Trier
General Music Director: Reinhard Petersen

Ulm: Süddeutsche Kammeroper, Am Eselsberg 10-12, 7900 Ulm
Ulmer Theater, Olgastrasse 73, 7900 Ulm
General Music Director: Alicja Mounk; Manager: Dr Bernd Wilms

Veitshöchheim: Bayerische Kammeroper, Rathaus, Gemeinde Veitshöchheim, 8707 Veitshöchheim
Music Director: Siegfried Köhler; Manager: Blagoy Apostolov

Weimar: Deutsches Nationaltheater Weimar, Theaterplatz 2, D-99401 Weimar. Tel: 49 3643 755334; Fax: 49 3643 755 307
General Music Director: Hans-Peter Frank; General Manager: Fritz Wendrich

Wiesbaden: Hessisches Staatstheater, Christian-Zais-Strasse 3-5, Pf 3247, 6200 Wiesbaden
General Music Director: Oleg Caetani; Manager: Claus Leininger

Wittenberg: Elbe-Saale-Bühnen Wittenberg-Bernburg, Thomas-Müntzer-Strasse 14/15, 4600 Wittenberg
Music Director: Klaus Hofmann; Manager: Helmut Blass

Wuppertal: Schillertheater NRW Opernhaus, Spinnstrasse 4, D-42283 Wuppertal. Tel: 49 202 563 4230; Fax 49 202 563 8078
General Music Director: Peter Gülke; General Manager: Holk Freytag

Würzburg: Städttheater Würzburg, Theaterstrasse 21, 8700 Würzburg
General Music Director: Jonathan Seers; Manager: Dr Tebbe Harms Kleen

Zeitz: Theater Zeitz, August-Bebel-Strasse 2, 4900 Zeitz
Music Director: Hans-Frieder Liebmann; Manager: Wolfgang Eysold

Zwickau: Theater Zwickau, Gewandhausstrasse 7, Pf 308, 9541 Zwickau
Music Director: Albrecht Hofmann; Manager: Horst-Dieter Brand

GREECE

Athens: National Opera of Greece, 18-A Harilaou Trikoupi Street, GR-106 79 Athens

HUNGARY

Budapest: Magyar Allami Operaház (Hungarian State Opera House), Népöztársaság utja 22, 1061 Budapest. Tel: 36 1131 2550; Fax: 36 1332 7331

Debrecen: Csokonai Szinház (Csokonai Theatre), PO Box 79, 4001 Debrecen

Pécs: Pécsi Nemzeti Szinhás (Pécs National Theatre), PO Box 126, 7601 Pécs

Szeged: Szegedi Nemzeti Szinház (Szeged National Theatre), PO Box 69, 6701 Szeged

ICELAND

Reykjavík: The Icelandic Opera, PO Box 1416, 121 Reykjavík. Tel: 354 56 21 077; Fax: 354 55 27 384
Director: Olöf Kolbrun Hardardottir

ISRAEL

Tel Aviv: New Israeli Opera, 28 Leonardo da Vinci St, PO Box 3321, Tel Aviv 61332. Tel: 972 692 7707; Fax: 972 696 6606
Music Director: Gary Bertini

ITALY

Bari: Teatro Petruzzelli, Via Cognetti 26, 70100 Bari

Bergamo: Teatro Donizetti, Piazza Cavour 14, 24100 Bergamo

Bologna: Teatro Comunale di Bologna, Largo Respighi 1, 40126 Bologna. Tel: 39 51 52 9901; Fax: 39 51 52 9934

Brescia: Teatro Grande, Via Paganora 19, 25100 Brescia

Cagliari: Teatro Lirico "G Pierluigi da Palestrina" di Cagliari, Viale Regina Margherita 6, 09100 Cagliari

Catania: Teatro Massimo Bellini, Via perrotta 12, 95131 Catania

Como: Teatro Sociale, Via Bellini 3, 22100 Como

Cremona: Teatro Comunale, Corso Vittorio Emanuele 52, 26100 Cremona

Ferrara: Teatro Comunale, Rotonda Foschini 4, 44100 Ferrara

Florence: Teatro Comunale di Firenze, Via Solferino 15, 50123 Florence. Tel: 39 55 27791; Fax: 39 55 239 6954

Genoa: Teatro Comunale dell'Opera de Genova,Passo Al Teatro 4, 16121 Genoa. Tel: 39 10 53811.

Jesi: Teatro Comunale "G B Pergolesi", Piazza della Repubblica, 60035 Jesi. Tel: 39 731 59788

Lecce: Teatro Politearna Greco, Via XXV Luglio 30, 73100 Lecce

Lucca: Teatro Comunale del Giglio, Piazza del Giglio, 55100 Lucca

Macerata: Teatro Arena Sferisterio, Piazza Mazzini 10, 62100 Macerata. Tel: 39 733 26 1335; Fax: 39 733 26 1449

Mantua: Teatro Sociale, Piazza Cavollotti, 46100 Mantua

Milan: Teatro all Scala di Milano, Via Filodrammatici 2, 20121 Milan. Tel: 39 2 88 791; Fax: 39 2 887 9331
Artistic Director: Roman Vlad; Musical Director: Riccardo Muti

Modena: Teatro Comunale, Via del Teatro 8, 41100 Modena

Naples: Teatro San Carlo di Napoli, Via S Carlo, 80132 Naples. Tel: 39 81 797 2111; Fax: 39 81 797 2309
Artistic Director: Salvatore Accardo

Novara: Teatro Coccia, Via Fratelli Resselli 4, 28100 Novara

Palermo: Teatro Massimo di Palermo, Via R Wagner 2, 90139 Palermo. Tel: 39 91 605 3111; Fax: 39 91 605 3324/5

Parma: Teatro Regio, Via Garibaldi 16, 43100 Parma. 39 521 218912; Fax: 39 521 206156

Piacenza: Teatro Municipale, Via Verdi 41, 29100 Piacenza. Tel: 39 523 49 2254

Pisa: Teatro Comunale "G Verdi", Via Palestro 40, 56200 Pisa

Ravenna: Teatro Alighieri, Piazza Garibaldi 5, 48100 Ravenna

Reggio Emilia: Teatro Municipale "Romolo Valli", Piazza Martiri 7 Luglio, 42100 Reggio Emilia. Tel: 39 522 434244

Rome: Teatro dell'Opera di Roma, Piazza B Gigli 8, 00184 Rome. Tel: 39 648 81601; Fax: 39 6 488 1253

Rovigo: Teatro Sociale, Piazza Garibaldi 14, 45100 Rovigo

Treviso: Teatro Comunale, Corso del Popolo 31, 31100 Treviso. Tel: 39 422 410130

Trieste: Teatro Comunale, "G Verdi" di Trieste, Riva Novembre 1, 34121 Trieste. Tel: 39 40 6722111; Fax: 39 40 6722 249

Turin: Teatro Regio di Torino, Piazza Castello 215, 10124 Turin

Venice: Teatro La Fenice di Venezia (Theatre destroyed by fire, 1996), Campo S Fantin 2519, 30100 Venice

Verona: Arena di Verona, Piazza Bra 28, 37121 Verona. Tel: 39 45 590109; Fax: 39 45 590201/8011566

JAPAN

Osaka: Kansai Nikkai Opera Company, 3-3-9 Bingo-cho, Chyno-ku, Osaka
Director: Makoto Kikawada
Kansai Opera Group, 3-57 Kyobashi, Higashi-ku, Osaka
Director: Takashi Asahina

Tokyo:	Mio Nagato, 2-21-12 Daita, Setagaya-ku, Tokyo 155
	Nihon Opera Shinkokai (Japanese Opera Foundation), Nishiazabu 28, Mori Building, 4-16-13 Nishiazabu, Minato-ku,Tokyo 106. Tel: 81 3 5466 3181; Fax 813 5466 3186 *Chairman: Seiya Matsumoto*

KOREA (SOUTH)

Seoul: National Opera Group, c/o The National Theatre, Jangchoong-dong, Choong-ku, Seoul

LATVIA

Riga: Latvian National Opera, 3 Aspazijas Blvd, 1050 Riga. Tel: 371 722 3436; Fax: 371 722 8930
Chief Conductor: Alexander Vilumanis

LITHUANIA

Vilnius: Lithuanian State Opera and Ballet Theatre, Vienuolio 1, 232600 Vilnius. Tel: 370 2 620093; Fax: 370 2 623503
Chief Conductor: Rimas Geniušas; Administrator: Zigmas Piečaitis

LUXEMBOURG

Luxembourg: Théâtre Municipal, 2525 Luxembourg
Director: Jeannot Comes

MEXICO

México City: Opera de Bellas Artes, Avenida Hidalgo 1, tercer piso, Centro, México City, DF 06050. Tel: 525 905 521 3688
General Director: Gerardo Kleinburg

MONACO

Monte Carlo: Opera de Monte Carlo, Place du Casino, Monte Carlo. Tel: 377 92 162318; Fax: 377 93 30 0757
Director: John Mordler

NETHERLANDS

Amsterdam: De Nederlandse Opera, Waterlooplein 22, 1011 PG Amsterdam. Tel: 31 20 551 8922; Fax: 3120 551 8311
Artistic Director: Pierre Audi; General Administrator: Truze Lodder

NEW ZEALAND

Auckland:	Auckland Opera Company, PO Box 77066, Mount Albert, Auckland 1. Tel: 64 9846 7433; Fax: 64 9846 7141
	General Manager: Stephen Dee
Christchurch:	Canterbury Regional Opera Trust, PO Box 176, Christchurch 1
	Chairman: Lewis Brown
Dunedin:	Dunedin Opera Company, PO Box 533, Dunedin
	Chairman: Ian Page
Wellington:	Wellington City Opera, PO Box 6588, Te Aro, Wellington. Tel: 64 4 384 4434; Fax: 64 4 384 3333
	Manager: Patricia Hurley

NORWAY

Bergen:	Opera Bergen, Komediebakken 9, N-5016 Bergen. Tel: 47 55 32 3856; Fax: 47 55 32 2435
	Artistic Director: Anne Randine Øverby
Kristiansund:	Operaen i Kristiansund, PO Box 401, N-6501 Kristiansund N. Tel: 47 71 677733; Fax: 47 71 676657
Oslo:	Den Norske Opera, PO Box 8800 Youngstorget, N-0028 Oslo. Tel: 47 22 42 9475; Fax: 47 22 33 4027
	Artistic Director and General Manager: Sven Olof Eliasson
Trondheim:	Trondheim Opera, Kongsgårdsgt 2, N-7013 Trondheim. Tel: 47 73 52 56 65

POLAND

Bydgoszcz:	Bydgoszcz Opera, Al 1 Maja 20, 85-006 Bydgoszcz
Bytom:	Silesian Opera, Moniuszki 21, 41-902 Bytom
Gdańsk:	Baltic Opera, Al Zwyciêstwa 15, 80-219 Gdańsk
Kraków:	Kraków Music Theatre, Senacka 6, 31-002 Kraków
Łódź:	Łódź Grand Theatre, Plac Dâbrowskiego, 90-249 Łódź
Poznán:	Poznán Grand Theatre, Fredry 9, 60-967 Poznán
Warsaw:	Warsaw Chamber Opera, Nowogrodzka 49, 00-695 Warsaw. Tel: 48 22 826 28 3096; Fax: 48 22 31 4764
	The National, Plac Teatrainy 1, 00-950 Warsaw. Tel: 48 22 826 3289/1620; Fax:48 22 826 0423/5012
Wroclaw:	Wroclaw State Opera, Swidnicka 35, 50-066 Wroclaw

PORTUGAL

Lisbon: Companhia de Opera do Teatro Nacional Sao Carlos, Rua Serpa Pinto 9, 1200 Lisbon. tel: 35 1 346 8408

ROMANIA

Bucharest: Bucharest State Operetta, Str Operetei 4, Bucharest
     Rumanian State Opera, Boulevard Mihail Kogainiceanu 70-72, 70609 Bucharest
Cluj-Napoca: Cluj-Napoca Hungarian Opera, Str 1 Mai 26-28, Cluj-Napoca
     Cluj-Napoca Rumanian Opera, Piata Stefan cel Mare 24, 3400 Cluj-Napoca
Iasi: Iasi Musical Theatre, Str 9 Mai nr 18, 6600 Iasi
Timişoara: Timişoara State Opera, Str Mărăsesti 2, Timişoara

RUSSIA

Moscow: Bolshoi Theatre, 103009 Moscow
St Petersburg: Kirov Opera, 1 Theatre Square, St Petersburg. Tel: 7 812 314 9083
     Chief Conductor: Valery Gergiev
     Maly Opera, St Petersburg

SLOVAK REPUBLIC

Bratislava: Bratislava Chamber Opera, Fučikova 3, 816 01 Bratislava
     Slovak National Theatre Opera, Gorkého 4, 815 06 Bratislava. Tel: 421 7 533 5085; Fax: 421 7 533 5072

SLOVENIA

Ljubljana: Slovenian National Theatre Opera, Zupanciceva 1, 61000 Ljubljana

SOUTH AFRICA

Bloemfontein: Opera of the Orange Free State Performing Arts Council, PO Box 1292, Bloemfontein 9300
     General Director: Fred Sharp
Cape Town: Opera of the Cape Performing Arts Board, PO Box 4107, Cape Town 8000. Tel: 27 21 215470; Fax: 27 21 215 448
Durban: Opera of the Natal Performing Arts Council, PO Box 5353, Durban 4000, Natal
Johannesburg: Johannesburg Operatic and Dramatic Society, PO Box 7010, Johannesburg 2000, Transvaal
Pretoria: Opera of the Performing Arts Council, Transvaal, PO Box 566, Pretoria 0001, Transvaal
     General Manager: Johan Maré

SPAIN

Barcelona: Gran Teatre del Liceu, Rambla dels Capuxins 61, 08001 Barcelona. Tel: 34 3 318 9122/412 3532; Fax: 34 3 412 1198
Bilbao: Bilbao Opera, Bilbao
Madrid: Madrid Opera, Madrid
Oviedo: Oviedo Opera, Oviedo

SWEDEN

Göteborg: Göteborgs Operan, Christina Nilssons Gatan, S-411 04 Göteborg. Tel: 46 31 1080; Fax: 46 31 1080 30
     Managing Director: Dag Hallberg
Malmö: Malmö Stadsteater, Box 17520, S-200 10 Malmö
     Director: Lars Rudolfsson
Stockholm: Drottningholms Slottsteater, PO Box 270505, S-102 51 Stockholm. Tel: 46 8 665 1400; Fax: 46 8 665 1473
     Artistic Director: Elisabeth Söderström
     Folkoperan, Hornsgatan 72, S-117 21 Stockholm. Tel: 46 8 616 0750/0700; Fax: 46 8 44146
     Music Director: Kerstin Nerbe
     Kungliga Teatern, PO Box 16094, S-103 22 Stockholm. Tel: 46 8 791 4300; Fax: 46 8 791 4444
     General Manager: Eskil Hemberg
Umea: Norriandsoperan, PO Box 360, S-901 08 Umea
     Director: Per-Erik Ohrn

SWITZERLAND

Basel: Theater Basel, Elisabethenstrasse 16, CH-4010 Basel. Tel: 41 61 295 1100; Fax: 41 61 295 1200
     Music Director: Walter Weller
Bern: Stadttheater Bern, Nägeligasse 1, CH-3011 Bern
     Administrator: Ernst Gosteli
Biel: Stadttheater Biel, Burggasse 19, CH-2502 Biel
     Administrator: Mario Bettoli
Geneva: Grand Théâtre de Genève, 11 Boulevard du Théâtre, CH-1211 Geneva 11. Tel: 41 22 418 3000; Fax: 41 22 418 3001
     General Director: Renée Auphan
Lausanne: Opéra de Lausanne, PO Box 3972, CH-1002 Lausanne. Tel: 41 21 310 1616/1600; Fax: 341 21 310 1690

Lucerne: Stadttheater Lucerne, Theaterstrasse 2, CH-6002 Lucerne
Director: Horst Statkus

St Gallen: Stadttheater St Gallen, Museumstrasse 24, CH-9000 St Gallen. Tel: 41 71 242 0505; Fax: 41 71 242 0506
Director: Werner Signer

Zürich: Opernhaus Zürich, Falkenstrasse 1, CH-8008 Zürich. Tel: 41 1 268 6400/6666; Fax: 41 1 268 6401/6555
Chief Conductor: Franz Welser-Möst

TURKEY

Ankara: Turkish State Opera and Ballet, Opera Binasi, Ankara
Istanbul: Istanbul State Opera and Ballet, Atatürk Merkezi, Taksim, 80124 Istanbul
Izmir: Izmir State Opera and Ballet, Izmir

UK

Belfast: Opera Northern Ireland, 35 Talbot Street, Belfast, Northern Ireland BT1 2LD. Tel: 44 1232 322538; Fax: 44 1232 32291
Artistic Director: Stephen Barlow; General Manager: Tim Kerr

Birmingham: City of Birmingham Touring Opera, 205 The Argent Centre, 60 Frederick Street, Birmingham B1 3HS. Tel: 44 121 246 6644; Fax: 44 121 246 6633
Administrator: Andrew Bennett; Artistic Director: Graham Vick

Bristol: Wessex Opera, 11 Luccombe Hill, Redland, Bristol BS6 6SN
Music Director: Paul Webster; General Manager: Richard Evans

Buxton: Buxton Festival Opera, 1 Crescent View, Hall Bank, Buxton, Derbyshire SK17 6EN
Artistic Director: Anthony Hose; General Manager: Gordon Monsen

Cardiff: Music Theatre Wales, 5 Llandaff Road, Cardiff CF1 9NF. Tel: Tel: 44 1222 230 833; Fax: 44 1222 342046.
Music Director: Michael Rafferty
Welsh National Opera, John Street, Cardiff CF1 4SP. Tel: 44 1222 464666; Fax: 44 1222 483050.
Music Director: Carlo Rizzi; General Director: Anthony Freud

Epsom: London Opera Group, 14 Downs Way, Downs Road, Epsom, Surrey KT18 5LU

Glasgow: Scottish Opera, 39 Elmbank Crescent, Glasgow G2 4PT. Tel: 44 141 248 4567; Fax: 44 141 221 8812.
Music Director: Richard Armstrong; General Director: Ruth Mackenzie.

Hatfield: Opera East, Hatfield Polytechnic, PO Box 109, Hatfield, Hertfordshire AL10 9AB
Artistic Director: Howard Burrell; Administrator: Anne Lee

Hungerford: Early Opera Project, 112b High Street, Hungerford, Berkshire RG17 0NB
Musical Directors: Roger Norrington and Kay Lawrence

Leeds: Opera North, Grand Theatre, 46 New Briggate, Leeds, Yorkshire LS1 6NU. Tel: 44 113 243 9999; Fax: 44 113 244 0418.
General Director: Richard Mantle; Controller of Planning: Christine Chibnall

Lewes: Glyndebourne Festival Opera, Glyndebourne, Lewes, East Sussex BN8 5UU. Tel: 44 1273 812321; Fax: 44 1273 812783
Music Director: Andrew Davis; Director of
Productions: Graham Vick
Glyndebourne Touring Opera, Glyndebourne, Lewes, East Sussex BN8 5UU. Tel: 44 1273 812321; Fax: 44 1273 812783
Music Director: Louis Langrée; Administrator: Sarah Playfair
New Sussex Opera, 22 Bradford Road, Lewes, East Sussex BN7 1RB. Tel: 44 1273 471851.
Director of Planning: David James; Music Director:David Angus; Director of Productions: John Lloyd Davies

Lincoln: Pavilion Opera Company, Thorpe Tilney Hall, Thorpe Tilney, nr Lincoln LN4 3SL. Tel: 44 1526 378231; Fax: 44 1526 378315.
Music Director: Lesley-Anne Sammons; General Manager: Freddie Stockdale

London: Abbey Opera, 68 Queens Gardens, London W2 3AH. Tel: 44 171 262 9023.
Conductor: Antony Shelley; Artistic Director: Mary Hill
British Opera Company, The Coach House, 56 Lawrie Park Gardens, London SE26 6XJ
Director: Norman McCann
English National Opera, London Coliseum, St Martin's Lane, London WC2N 4ES. Tel: 44 171 836 0111; Fax: 44 171 836 8379.
General Director: Nicholas Payne; Music Director: Paul Daniel
English Touring Opera, W121 West Block, Westminster Business Square, Durham Street, London SE11 5JH. Tel: 44 171 820 1131/1141;
Fax: 44 171 735 7008 *Music Director: Andrew Greenwood; Chief Executive: Katharine Herbert*
London Chamber Opera, 82 Redcliffe Gardens, London SW10 9HE. Tel: 44 171 373 8535.
Music Director: David Wordsworth
Midsummer Opera, 90 Grange Road, London W5 3PJ. Tel: 44 181 579 7477/840 9560.
Music Director: David Roblou; Producer: Alan Privett; Chairman: David Skewes
Modern Music Theatre Troupe, 65 Hydethorpe Road, London SW12 0JE. Tel: 44 181 675 5365; Fax: 44 181 675 5365
Artistic Director: Caroline Sharman
Musica nel Chiostro, 377 Liverpool Road, London N1
Director: Adam Pollock
New Sadler's Wells Opera, Sadler's Wells Theatre, Roseberry Avenue, London EC1R 4TN
Director: Joseph Karaviotis
Nexus Opera, 16 Kennington Park Road, London SE11 4AS. Tel: 44 171 582 0980; Fax: 44 171 582 1444.
Artistic Director: Delia Lindon; Music Director: Lionel Friend
Opera Factory, 9 The Leathermarket, Weston Street, London SE1 3ER. Tel: 44 171 378 1029; Fax: 44 171 378 0185.
Artistic Director: David Freeman; Administrator: Jane Hellings
Opera London, 45 Chalcot Road, London NW1 8LS
General Director: Jonathan Balkind; Music Director: Richard Hickox
Opera Rara Ltd, 134-146 Curtain Road, London EC2A 3AR. Tel: 44 171 613 2858; Fax: 44 171 613 2261.
Artistic Director: Patric Schmid
Opera Restor'd, 54 Astonville Street, London SW18 5AJ. Tel: 44 181 870 7649; Fax: 44 181 672 6540.
Administrator: Caroline Anderson; Music Director: Peter Holman; Stage Director: Jack Edwards
Opera on the Move, 47 Queen's Drive, London N4 2SZ
Directors: Odaline de la Martinez and Linda Hirst

Pisa Opera Group, Flat 2, 79 Linden Gardens, London W2 4EU. Tel: 44 171 229 7060.
Director: Stella J Wright
The Royal Opera, Royal Opera House, Covent Garden, London WC2E 9DD. Tel: 44 171 212 9502; Fax: 44 171 212 9502.
Music Director: Bernard Haitink; General Director: Colin Southgate
Telemann Opera, 1a Warwick Chambers, Pater Street, London W6 6EN
Artistic Director: Jill Watt

Market Harborough: Travelling Opera, 114 St Mary's Road, Market Harborough, Leicestershire LE16 7DT. Tel: 44 1858 434677; Fax: 1858 463617.
Artistic Director: Peter Knapp

Walton-on-Thames: Opera Brava, 28 Annett Road, Walton-on-Thames, Surrey KT12 2JR. Tel: 44 1932 248874.
Artistic Director: Bronek Pomorski; Music Director: Susan Grahm Smith

Windsor: Thameside Opera, Hatch House, Oakley Green, Windsor, Berkshire SL4 5UD
Music Director: George Badacsonyi; Administrator: Maurice Maggs

Wolverhampton: D'Oyly Carte Opera Company, Valley Park, Cromer Gardens, Wolverhampton WV6 0UA. Tel: 44 1902 744555/744414; Fax: 44 1902 744333.
General Manager: Ray Brown; Musical Director: John Owen Edwards.

Yeovil: Dorset Opera, 26 Central Acre, Yeovil, Somerset BA20 1NU. Tel: 44 1935 479297; Fax: 44 1935 412210.
Music Director: Patrick Shelley; Administrator: Joy Liddiard

USA

ALABAMA

Birmingham: Birmingham Opera Theater, 1 Commerce Center, Suite 1, Birmingham, AL 35203
Executive Director: Howard Burkett

Mobile: Mobile Opera Inc, PO Box 8366, Mobile, AL 36689
General Manager: Pelham G Pearce Jr

ALASKA

Anchorage: Anchorage Opera Company Inc, 1507 Spar Avenue, Achorage, AK 99501
Director: Peter H Brown

ARIZONA

Phoenix: Arizona Opera Company, 3501 North Mountain Avenue, Phoenix, AZ 85719. Tel: 1 520 293 4336; Fax: 1 520 293 5097
General Director: Clynn Ross

ARKANSAS

Little Rock: Opera Theatre at Wildwood, PO Box 25202, Little Rock, AR 72221
Artistic Director: Ann Chotard

CALIFORNIA

Berkeley: Berkeley Opera, 715 Arlington, Berkeley, CA 94707
General Director: Richard Goodman

Beverly Hills: Los Angeles Concert Opera, 2250 Gloaming Way, Beverly Hills, CA 90210
General Director: Loren L Zachary

Fullerton: Fullerton Civic Light Opera, 218 West Commonwealth, Fullerton, CA 92632
General Manager: Griff Duncan

Hollywood: Casa Italiana Opera Company, 5959 Franklin Avenue, Sutie 212, Hollywood, CA 90028
General Director: Mario E Leonetti

Irvine: Opera Pacific, 9 Executive Circle, Suite 190, Irvine, CA 92714
General Director: David DiChiera

Long Beach: Long Beach Civic Light Opera, Box 20280, Long Beach, CA 90801
Executive Director: J Phillip Keene III
Long Beach Opera, 6372 Pacific Coast Highway, Long Beach, CA 90803
General Director: Michael Milenski

Los Angeles: Los Angeles Music Center Opera, 135 North Grand Avenue, Los Angeles, CA 90012. Tel: 1 213 972 7219; Fax: 1 213 687 3490
General Director: Peter Hemmings

Oakland: Oakland Lyric Opera, PO Box 20209, Oakland, CA 94620
General Director: Marilyn Kosinski

Palo Alto: West Bay Opera, PO Box 1714, Palo Alto, CA 94302
General Director: Maria Holt

Palm Desert: West Coast Opera Theatre, PO Box 166, Palm Desert, CA 92661
General Director: Josephine Lombardo

Sacramento: Sacramento Opera Company, PO Box 161027, Sacramento, CA 95816. Tel: 1 916 264 5181; Fax: 1 916 442 4254
General Director: Marianne Oaks

San Bernardino: San Barnardino Civic Light Opera Association, Box 606, San Bernardino, CA 92402
General Manager: Keith Stava

San Diego: San Diego Civic Light Opera Association, "Starlight", PO Box 3519, San Diego, CA 92103
Executive Director: Leon Drew
San Diego Comic Opera Company, 545 Market Street, Box 1726, San Diego, CA 92101
Managing Director: Kathleen Switzer
San Diego Opera, PO Box 988, San Diego, CA 92112. Tel: 1 619 232 7636; Fax: 1 619 231 6915
General Director: Ian D Campbell

San Francisco: San Francisco Opera, War Memorial Opera House, San Francisco, CA 94102. Tel: 1 415 565 6431/864 3300; Fax: 1 415 621 7508
Music Director: Donald Runnicles; General Director: Lotfi Mansouri
Western Opera Theater, War Memorial Opera House, San Francisco, CA 94102
Director: Christopher Hahn

San Jose: Opera San Jose, 12 South First Street, Suite 207, San Jose, CA 95113
General Director: Irene Dalis
San Jose Civic Light Opera, 4 North Second, No 100, San Jose, CA 95113
Artistic Director: Dianna Shuster
Stockton: Stockton Opera, PO Box 7883, Stockton, CA 95267
Artistic Director: George Buckbee

COLORADO

Aspen: Aspen Music Festival, PO Box AA, Aspen, CO 81612. Tel: 1 970 925 3254; Fax: 1 970 925 3802
Music Director: Lawrence Foster; President and Chief Executive Officer: Robert Harth
Denver: Central City Opera House Association, 621 17th Street, No 1601, Denver, CO 80293. Tel: 1 303 292 6700; Fax: 1 303 292 4958
General Manager: Daniel R Rule
Opera Colorado, 695 South Colorado Boulevard, Suite 20, Denver, CO 80222. Tel: 1 303 986 8742; Fax: 1 303 436 1286
President and General Director: Nathaniel Merrill

CONNECTICUT

Clinton: Opera Theater of Connecticut, PO Box 733, Clinton, CT 06413
Administrative Director: Kate A Ford
Darien: New England Lyric Operetta Inc, Box 79, Darien, CT 06820
President and Artistic Director: William H Edgerton
Hartford: Connecticut Opera Association, 226 Farmington Avenue, Hartford, CT 06105. Tel: 1 203 953 3517/27; Fax: 1 203 293 1715
General Director: George D Osborne
Stamford: Connecticut Grand Opera, 61 Atlantic Street, Stamford, CT 06901
Artistic Director: Laurence Gilgore

DELAWARE

Wilmington: Opera Delaware Inc, 4 South Poplar Street, Wilmington, DE 19801. Tel: 1 302 658 8063; Fax: 1 302 658 4991
General Director: Leland Kimball, III

DISTRICT OF COLUMBIA

Washington: National Lyric Opera Company, 5332 Sherrier Place North West, Washington, DC 20016
General Manager: Nikita Wells
Summer Opera Theatre Company, c/o Benjamin T Rome School of Music, 620 Michigan
General Manager: Elaine R Walter
Washington Concert Opera, 1690 36th Street North West, Suite 411, Washington, DC 20007
General Manager: Stephen Crout
Washington Opera, John F Kennedy Center for the Performing Arts, Washington, DC 20566. Tel: 1 202 416 7890; Fax: 1 202 298 6008
Artistic Director: Placido Domingo; General Director: Martin Feinstein

FLORIDA

Clearwater: Tampa Bay Opera, 2035 Arbor Drive, Clearwater, FL 34620
Artistic Director: Mario Laurenti; General Manager: Cynthia Youkon
Miami: Florida Grand Opera, 1200 Coral Way, Miami, FL 33145. Tel: 1 305 854 1643; Fax: 1 305 856 1042
Artistic Director: James Judd; General Manager: Robert M Heuer
Miami Beach: North Miami Beach Opera, 5225 La Gorce Drive, Miami Beach, FL 33140
Music Director: Laurence Siegal
Orlando: Orlando Opera Company Inc, c/o Dr Phillips Center for Performing Arts, 1111 North Orange Avenue, Orlando, FL 32804
General Director: Robert Swedberg
Palm Beach: Palm Beach Opera Inc, 415 South Olive Avenue, West Palm Beach, FL 33401. tel: 1 407 833 7888; Fax: 1 561 833 8294
Artistic Director: Anton Guadagno; General Director: Herbert P Benn
St Petersburg: Florida Lyric Opera Association/Lyric Opera Theater, 1185-D 85 Terace North, St Petersburg, FL 33702
General Director: Rosalia Maresca
Sarasota: Sarasota Opera Association, 61 North Pineapple Avenue, Sarasota, FL 34236. Tel: 1 941 366 8450; Fax: 1 941 955 5571
Artistic Director: Victor De Renzi; Executive Director: Deane C Allyn
Tampa: Spanish Lyric Theatre, 1032 Coral Street, Tampa, FL 33602
Artistic Director: Rene Gonzalez

GEORGIA

Atlanta: Atlanta Opera, 1800 Peachtree Street North West, Suite 620, Atlanta, GA 30309. Tel: 1 404 355 3311; Fax: 1 404 355 3529
Artistic Director: William Fred Scott; General Manager: Alfred D Kennedy
Augusta: Augusta Opera Company, PO Box 3865, Hill Station, Augusta, GA 30904
General Director: Edward Bradberry

HAWAII

Honolulu: Hawaii Opera Theater, 987 Waimanu Street, Honolulu, HI 96814
General Director: J Mario Ramos

IDAHO

Boise: Boise Opera Inc, 516 South 9th Street, Suite B, Boise, ID 83702

ILLINOIS

Chicago: Chicago Opera Repertory Theater, PO Box 921, Chicago, IL 60690
Executive Director: Bruce Kamsler
Chicago Opera Theater, 20 East Jackson Boulevard, Sutie 1400, Chicago, IL 60604
Lincoln Opera, 2456 North Surrey Court, Chicago, IL 60614
Artistic Director: Norma M Williams

Lyric Opera of Chicago, 20 North Wacker Drive, Chicago, IL 60606. Tel: 1 312 332 2244; Fax: 1 312 419 8345
General Director: Ardis Krainik
The Opera Factory, 6161 North Hamilton, Chicago, IL 60659
Executive Director: Blanche Artis Lewis

Evanston: Light Opera Works, 927 Noyes Street, Evanston, IL 60201
Artistic Director: Philip A Kraus

Peoria: Peoria Civic Opera, PO Box 120198, Peoria, IL 61614
Artistic Director: F Contino

INDIANA

Bloomington: Indiana University Opera Theater, School of Music, Indiana University, Bloomington, IN 47405
Indianapolis: Indiana Opera Theater, 7515 East 30th Street, Indianapolis, IN 46219
Executive/Artistic Director: Elaine Morgan Bookwalter
Indianapolis Opera, 250 East 38th Street, Indianapolis, IN 46205. Tel: 1 317 921 6444; Fax: 1 317 923 5611

Richmond: Whitewater Opera Company Inc, PO Box 633, 805 Promenade, Richmond, IN 47375
Artistic Director and General Manager: Charles Combopiano

IOWA

Indianola: Des Moines Metro Opera Inc, 106 West Boston Avenue, Indianola, IA 50125. Tel: 1 515 961 6221; Fax: 1 515 961 2994
Artistic Director: Robert L Larsen

KENTUCKY

Louisville: Kentucky Opera, 101 South 8th Street, Louisville, KY 40202. Tel: 1 502 584 4500; Fax: 1 502 584 7484
General Director: Thomson Smillie

LOUISIANA

Baton Rouge: Baton Rouge Opera Inc, PO Box 2269, Baton Rouge, LA 70821
Artistic Director: Marioara Trifan

New Orleans: New Orleans Opera Association, 305 Baronne Street, Suite 500, New Orleans, LA 70130. Tel: 1 504 529 2278; Fax: 1 504 529 7668
General Director: Arthur Cosenza

Shreveport: Shreveport Opera, 212 Texas Street, Suite 101, Shreveport, LA 71101. Tel: 1 318 227 9503; Fax: 1 318 227 9518
General Director: Robert Murray

MARYLAND

Annapolis: Annapolis Opera Inc, PO Box 24, Annapolis, MD 21201
Music Director: Ava Shields

Baltimore: Baltimore Opera Company Inc, 1202 Maryland Avenue, Baltimore, MD 21201. Tel: 1 410 727 6000; Fax: 1 410 727 7854
General Director: Michael Harrison

MASSACHUSETTS

Boston: Boston Lyric Opera Company, 114 State Street, Boston, MA 02109. Tel: 1 617 248 8660; Fax: 1 617 248 8810
General Director: Janice DelSesto
Opera Company of Boston Inc, PO Box 50, Boston, MA 02112
Artistic Director: Sarah Caldwell

Lee: Berkshire Opera Company, PO Box 598, 17 Main Street, Lee, MA 01238
Artistic Director: Joel Revzen

Northampton: Commonwealth Opera, 160 Main Street, Northampton, MA 01060
Artistic Director and Principal Conductor: Richard R Rescia

MICHIGAN

Detroit: Michigan Opera Theater, Lothrop Landing. 104 Lothrop, Detroit, MI 48202. Tel: 1 313 874 7850; Fax: 1 313 871 7213
General Director: David DiChiera

Grand Rapids: Opera Grand Rapids, 161 Ottawa NW, Suite 205-B, Grand Rapids, MI 49503
General Director: Robert Lyall

Lansing: Opera Company of Mid-Michigan, 300 South Washington, Suite 410, Lansing, MI 48933
Executive Director: Theresa Weller

MINNESOTA

Minneapolis: Minnesota Opera, 620 North First Street, Minneapolis, MN 55401. Tel: 1 612 333 2700; Fax: 1 612 333 0869
President and General Director: Kevin Smith

St Paul: North Star Opera, 1863 Eleanor Avenue, St Paul, MN 55116
Administrative Director: Irma Wachtler

MISSISSIPPI

Gulfport: Gulf Coast Opera Theatre Inc, PO Box 7067, Gulfport, MS 39501
President: Dr Laurence M Oden

Jackson: Mississippi Opera, PO Box 1551, Jackson, MS 39217. Tel: 1 601 960 1528
Artistic Director: Carroll Freeman

MISSOURI

Kansas City: Lyric Opera of Kansas City, 1029 Central, Kansas City, MO 64105. Tel: 1 816 471 7344
General Artistic Director: Russell Patterson

St Louis: Opera Theater of Saint Louis, PO Box 191910, St Louis, MO 63119. Tel: 1 314 961 0171/0644; Fax: 1 314 961 7463
General Director: Charles MacKay

Springfield: Springfield Regional Opera, 109 Park Central Square, Springfield, MO 65806
Managing Artistic Director: James Billings

NEBRASKA

Omaha: Opera/Omaha Inc, 1613 Farnam, Suite 200, Omaha, NE 68101. Tel: 1 402 346 4398/0357; Fax: 1 402 346 7323
General Director: Mary Robert

NEVADA

Reno: Nevada Opera Association, PO Box 3256, Reno, NV 89505. tel: 1 702 786 4046; Fax: 1 702 786 4063
Artistic Director: Ted Puffer

NEW JERSEY

Allenhurst: Metro Lyric Opera, 40 Ocean Avenue, Allenhurst, NJ 07711
General and Artistic Director: Erq M Tognoli
Newark: New Jersey State Opera, 1020 Broad Street, Newark, NJ 07102
General Director: Alfredo Silipigni

NEW MEXICO

Albuquerque: Albuquerque Civic Light Opera Association, 4201 Ellison North East, Albuquerque, NM 87109
Executive Director: Linda E McVey
Opera Southwest, 515 15th Street North West, Albuquerque, NM 87104
Artistic and Music Director: Richard Boldrey
Santa Fe: Santa Fe Opera, PO Box 2408, Santa Fe, NM 87504. Tel: 1 505 986 5955; Fax: 1 505 986 5999
General Director: John Crosby

NEW YORK

Binghamton: Tri-Cities Opera Inc, 315 Clinton Street, Binghamton, NY 13905. Tel: 1 607 772 0400; Fax: 1 607 797 6344
Artistic Directors: Carmen Savoca and Peyton Hibbitt; Executive Director: Edward Cordick
Bronx: Bronx Opera Company, 5 Minerva Place, Bronx, NY 10468
Artistic Director: Michael Spierman
Queens Opera Association Inc, PO Box 140066, Brooklyn, NY 11214
General Director: Joe Messina
Buffalo: Greater Buffalo Opera Company, 24 Linwood Avenue, Buffalo, NY 14309. Tel: 1 716 447 7000; Fax: 1 716 447 7004
Artistic Director: Gary Burgess
Chautauqua: Chautauqua Opera, Chautauqua Institution, Chautauqua, NY 14722. Tel: 1 716 357 6200; Fax: 1 716 357 9014
General Director: Linda Jackson
Cooperstown: Glimmerglass Opera, PO Box 191, Cooperstown, NY 13326. Tel: 1 607 547 2255; Fax: 1 607 547 1257
General Director: Paul Kellogg
Garden City: National Grand Opera Inc, 231 Washington Avenue, 2nd Floor, Garden City, NY 11530
General Director: Linda Holgers
Glens Falls: Lake George Opera Festival, PO Box 2172, Glens Falls, NY 12801
Artistic Director: Joseph Illick
Ithaca: Ithaca Opera, 109 East Seneca Street, Ithaca, NY 14850
New York: American Chamber Opera, PO Box 909, New York, NY 10023
Executive Director: Doug Anderson
The Juilliard Opera Center, The Juilliard School, Lincoln Center for the Performing Arts, New York, NY 10023
Artistic Director: Frank Corsaro
Manhattan Opera Association, PO Box 475, Planetarium Station, New York, NY 10024
Artistic Director and President: Barbara Norcia
Metropolitan Opera, Lincoln Center for the Performing Arts, New York, NY 10023. Tel: 1 212 799 3100/362 6000; Fax: 1 212 874 2569
Artistic Director: James Levine; General Director: Joseph Volpe
New York City Opera, New York State Theater, Lincoln Center for the Performing Arts, New York, NY 10023. Tel: 1 212 870 5633/5600
Music Director: George Manahan
New York Gilbert and Sullivan Players Inc, 251 West 91st Street, No 4C, New York, NY 10024
Artistic Director: Albert Bergeret
New York Grand Opera, 154 West 57th Street, Suite 125, New York, NY 10019
Artistic Director: Vincent LaSelva
Opera Northeast, 530 East 89th Street, New York, NY 10128
Artistic Director: Donald Westwood
Opera Orchestra of New York, 239 West 72nd Street, No 2R, New York, NY 10023
Music Director: Eve Queler; Manager: Alix Barthelmes
Operaworks Ltd, 170 West 73rd Street, New York, NY 10023
Director: Joel P Casey
Rochester: Opera Theatre of Rochester, 494 East Avenue, Rochester, NY 14607
Executive Director: Glenn A West
Syracuse: Syracuse Opera Company, PO Box 6904, Syracuse, NY 13217
Artistic Director: Richard McKee

NORTH CAROLINA

Charlotte: Opera Carolina, 345 North College Street, Suite 409, Charlotte, NC 28205. Tel: 1 704 332 7177/372 1000; Fax: 1 704 332 6448/1154
General Director: James W Wright
Durham: Triangle Opera Theater Association, 120 Morris Street, Durham, NC 27701
General Manager: Rebecca Siegel
Greensboro: Greensboro Opera Company, PO Box 29031, Greensboro, NC 27429
Conductor: Norman Johnson
Raleigh: National Opera Company, PO Box 12800, Raleigh, NC 27605
Artistic Director: Don Wilder

Winston-Salem: Piedmont Opera Theater Inc, 7990 North Point Boulevard, Suite 109, Winston-Salem, NC 27106. Tel: 1 910 759 2277; Fax: 1 910 759 7722
                       General Director: Norman Johnson

NORTH DAKOTA

Fargo: Fargo-Moorhead Civic Opera Company, 806 NP Avenue, Fargo, ND 58102
                       Artistic Director: David F Martin

OHIO

Cincinnati: CCM Opera/Musical Theater, University of Cincinnati College - Conservatory of Music, Cincinnati, OH 45221
                       Artistic Director: Malcolm Fraser
                       Cincinnati Opera Association, Music Hall, 1241 Elm Street, Cincinnati, OH 45210. Tel: 1 513 621 1919/241 2742; Fax: 1 513 621 4310
                       Artistic Director: James de Blasis
Cleveland: Cleveland Opera, 1422 Euclid Avenue, Sutie 1052, Cleveland, OH 44115. tel: 1 216 575 0903; Fax: 1 216 575 1918
                       General Director: David Bamberger
                       Lyric Opera Cleveland, PO Box 06198, Cleveland, OH 44106
                       Executive Director: Michael McConnell
Columbus: Opera/Columbus, 177 Naghten, Columbus, OH 43215
                       General Director: William F Russell
Dayton: Dayton Opera Association, 125 East First Street, Dayton, OH 45402
                       General Director: Jane Nelson
Middletown: Sorg Opera Company, PO Box 906, Middletown, OH 45042
                       Artistic Director and General Manager: Charles Combopiano
Toledo: Toledo Opera Association, 406 Adams Street, Toledo, OH 43604
                       Artistic Director: James Meena

OKLAHOMA

Oklahoma City: Lyric Theater of Oklahoma, 2501 North Blackwelder, Oklahoma City, OK 73106
                       General Manger: Gayle Pearson
Tulsa: Tulsa Opera, 1610 South Boulder Avenue, Tulsa, OH 74119
                       Executive Director: Gayle Pearson

OREGON

Eugene: Eugene Opera, PO Box 11200, Eugene, OR 97440
                       Artistic Director: Francis Graffeo
Portland: Portland Opera Association Inc, 1516 South West Alder Street, Portland, OR 97205
                       General Director: Robert Bailey

PENNSYLVANIA

Lancaster: Lancaster Opera Company, Box 8382, Lancaster, PA 17604
                       Artistic Director: Dorothy Rose Smith
Philadelphia: Opera Company of Philadelphia, 510 Walnut Street, Suite 1600, Philadelphia, PA 19106
                       General Director: Robert Driver
Pittsburgh: Pittsburgh Opera Inc, 711 Penn Avenue, 8th Floor, Pittsburgh, PA 15222
                       General Director: Tito Capobianco
                       Opera Theater of Pittsburgh, PO Box 110108, Pittsburgh, PA 15232
                       Artistic Director: Gary Race

PUERTO RICO

Santurce: Teatro de la Opera Inc, PO Box 40734, Minillas Station, Santurce, PR 09940
                       Artistic Director: Alberto Esteves

TENNESSEE

Chattanooga: Chattanooga Opera, 630 Chestnut Street, Chattanooga, TN 37402
                       Managing Director: Donal L Andrews
Knoxville: Knoxville Opera Company, PO Box 16, Knoxville, TN 37901
                       General Director: Robert Lyall
Memphis: Opera Memphis, Memphis State University, South Campus, Building 47, Memphis, TN 38152
                       Artistic Director: Michael Ching
Nashville: Nashville Opera, 1900 Belmont Boulevard, Fidelity Hall, Suite 405, Nashville, TN 37212
                       Executive Director: Carol Penterman
                       Tennessee Opera Theatre, 5924 Sedberry Road, Nashville, TN 37205
                       Artistic Director: Daniel Killman

TEXAS

Abilene: Abilene Opera Association, PO Box 6611, Abilene, TX 79608
Austin: Austin Lyric Opera, PO Box 984, Austin, TX 78767
                       General Director: Joseph McClain
Beaumont: Beaumont Civic Opera, 1030 Harriot Street, Beaumont, TX 77705
                       Conductor: L Randolph Babin; Business Manager: Delores Black
Dallas: Dallas Opera, The Centrum, 3102 Oak Lawn Avenue, Sutie 450, LB-130, Dallas, TX 75219
                       Music Director: Graeme Jenkins; General Director: Plato Karayanis
                       Lyric Opera of Dallas, 8111 Preston Boulevard, No 818, Dallas, TX 75225
                       General Director: Charles Kuba
Fort Worth: Fort Worth Opera, 3505 West Lancaster, Fort Worth, TX 76107
                       General Director: William Walker

Houston:	Houston Grand Opera Association, 510 Preston Avenue, Houston, TX 77002 *General Director: R David Gockley*

UTAH

Salt Lake City:	Salt Lake Opera Theatre, 44 West 3000 South American Towers, No 8075, Salt Lake City, UT 84101 *General Director: Robert Zabriskie* Utah Opera Company, 50 West Second South, Salt Lake City, UT 84101 *General Director: Anne Ewers*

VIRGINIA

Arlington:	Opera Theatre of Northern Virginia, 2700 South Lang Street, Arlington, VA 22206 *Artistic Director: John Edward Niles* Potomac Valley Opera Company, 2218 North Kensington Street, Arlington, VA 22205 *Director: Richard Wilmer*
Charlottesville:	Ash Lawn-Highland Opera Company, Route 6, Box 37, Charlottesville, VA 22901 *General Manager: Judith H Walker*
Norfolk:	Virginia Opera, PO Box 2580, Norfolk, VA 23501 *General Director: Peter Mark*
Roanoke:	Opera Roanoke, Box 1014, Roanoke, VA 24005 *Executive Director: Judith Clark*
Vienna:	Wolf Trap Opera Company, 1624 Trap Road, Vienna, VA 22182 *Administrative Director: Peter Russell*

WASHINGTON

Seattle:	Seattle Opera Association, PO Box 9248, Seattle, WA 98109 *General Director: Speight Jenkins*
Tacoma:	Tacoma Opera, PO Box 7468, Tacoma, WA 98407 *Executive Director: Ann Farrell*

WISCONSIN

Green Bay:	Pamiro Opera Company, 115 South Jefferson Street, No 301-A, Green Bay, WI 54301 *Artistic and Music Director: Miroslav Pansky*
Madison:	Madison Opera, 458 Charles Lane, Madison, WI 53711 *Music Director: Roland Johnson; Manager: Ann Stanke*
Milwaukee:	Florentine Opera Company, 735 North Water Street, Suite 1315, Milwaukee, WI 53202 *General Director: Dennis Hanthorn* Milwaukee Opera Company, 820 East Knapp Street, Milwaukee, WI 53202 *Executive Director: Josephine Busalacchi* Skylight Opera Theatre, 158 North Broadway, Milwaukee, WI 53202

UKRAINE

Kiev:	Ukrainian National Opera, Kiev
Odessa:	Odessa State Opera, Odessa

VENEZUELA

Caracas:	Opera de Caracas, Museo del Teclado, Parque Central, Edif, Tacaqua, Mezzanina, Caracas 1010 *Director: Josélgnacio Cabrujas*

YUGOSLAVIA

Belgrade:	Narodno Pozoriste, Francuska 3, 11000 Belgrade

APPENDIX C
FESTIVALS

ARGENTINA

Festival Internacional de Musica de San Juan	*25 de Mayo & Urquiza*	5400 San Juan

AUSTRALIA

Adelaide Festival of Arts	*February-March*	GPO Box 1269, Adelaide, SA 5001
Australian Festival of Chamber Music	*July*	James Cook University of North Queensland, Townsville, QLD 4811
Brisbane Warana Festival	*September-October*	PO Box 3611, South Brisbane, QLD 4101
Festival of Perth	*February-March*	University of Western Australia, Nedlands, WA 6009
Festival of Sydney	*January*	Level 11, 31 Market Street, Sydney, NSW
Melbourne International Festival of Organ and Harpsichord	*Easter Week*	PO Box 92, Parkville, VIC 3052
Melbourne International Festival of the Arts	*September*	35 City Road, Melbourne, VIC 3205
Musica Nova	*August*	GPO Box 9994, Brisbane, QLD 4001

AUSTRIA

Ars Electonica	*June*	Untere Donaulände, 7, A-4010 Linz
Aspekte Salzburg	*June*	Lasserstrasse 6, A-5020 Salzburg
Bregenz Festival	*July-August*	Postfach 311, A-6901 Bregenz
Carinthian Summer	*June-August*	A-9570 Ossiach
Chamber Music Festival Austria	*August-September*	Germergasse 16, A-2500 Baden
Easter Festival Salzburg		Herbert von Karajan Platz, A-5010 Salzburg
Festival Wien Modern	*October-November*	Lothringerstrasse 20, A-1030 Vienna
Fedtival Wiener Klassik	*April, July, & December*	Preindlgasse 1, A-1130 Vienna
Haydnfestival	*September*	Schloss Esterhazy, A-7000 Eisenstadt
Innsbruck Festival of Early Music	*June-September*	Haspingerstrasse 1, A-6020 Innsbruck
International Competition of Choral Singing	*July*	Burgplatz 1, A-9800 Spittal an der Drau
International Cultural Days and Symposium	*July-August*	Postfach 18, A-8692 Neuberg an der Mürz
International Youth and Music Festival	*July*	Kongresszentrum, A-1014 Vienna
Internationale Brucknerfest Linz	*September-October*	Untere Donaulände 7, A-4010 Linz
Internationale Musikwochen Millstatt	*May-October*	Postfach 27, A-9872 Millstatt/See
Kitzbüheler Sommerkonzerte	*July-August*	Stadtgemeinde, A-6730 Kitzbühel
Mozart Festival Week	*January*	Getreidegasse 14/2, A-5020 Salzburg
Operetta Weeks	*July-August*	Wiesingerstrasse 7, A-4820 bad Ischl
Salzburg Easter Festival	*July-August*	PO Box 140, A-5010 Salzburg
Salzburg Festival	*Easter*	Herbert von Karajan Pla 9, A-5020 Salzburg
Salzburg Palace Concerts	*January-December*	Makartplatz 9, A-5020 Salzburg
Salzburger Kulturtage	*October*	PO Box 42, Waagplatz 1a, A-5010 Salzburg
Salzburger Operetten Konzerte	*May-October*	Lerchenstrasse 33, A-5023 Salzburg
Schubertiade Feldkirch	*June-July*	Schubertplatz 1, Postfach 625, A-6803 Feldkirch
Seefestspiele Mörbisch	*June-August*	Schloss Esterhazy, A-7000 Eisenstadt
Styrian Autumn	*October*	Sackstrasse 17/1, A-8010 Graz
Styriarte Graz	*June-July*	Sachstrasse 17, A-8010 Graz
Szene: International Theatre and Dance Festival		Anton Neumayr-Platz 2, A-5020 Salzburg
Vienna Festival	*May-June*	Lehargasse 11, A-1060 Vienna
Vienna Music Summer	*June-September*	Laudongasse 29, A-1080 Vienna

BELGIUM

Ars Musica: The Spring of Contemporary Music	*March-April*	18 Pl Eugène Flageyplein 18, Rm 245, B-1050 Brussels
Europalia	*September-December of odd-numbered years*	10 Rue Royale, B-1000 Brussels
Festival de Wallonie	*June-November*	29 Rue du Jardin Botanique, B-4000 Liège
Festival van Vlaanderen-Antwerpen	*August-September*	Stadhuis, Grote Markt, B-2000 Antwerp
Festival van Vlaanderen	*April-October*	Flageyplein 18, B-1050 Brussels
Week of Contemporary Music	*February*	Muzikon vzw, Hoogpoort 64, B-9000 Ghent

BERMUDA

Bermuda Festival	*January-February*	PO Box HM 297, Hamilton, HM AX

BRAZIL

Bienal de Música Contemporânes Brasileira	*November*	Sala Cecilia Meireles, Largo da Lapa 47, Lapa, 20021 Rio de Janeiro
Festival Música Nova de Santos		Sociedade Ars Viva, Rua Barâo de Paranapiacaba 31, 11050Santos

Festival Villa-Lobos	November	Rua Sorocaba 200, 22271 Rio de Janeiro
Petrópolis Summer Festival and	January-February	Rua Franio Peixoto 134, Bingen, 25600
Winter Festivals	June-August	Petrópolis

BULGARIA

Apollonia	April, September and October	54/B Korab Planina Street, 1125 Sofia
March Music Days, Sofia Music Weeks	May-June	PO Box 387, 1090 Sofia
Chamber Music Festival	June	PO Box 387, 1090 Sofia
Varna Summer	June-July	Municpal Council BG, 9000 Varna

CANADA

Banff Festival of the Arts	June-August	Box 1020, Station 28, Banff, Alta, T0L 0C0
Calgary International Organ Festival	October	237 Eighth Avenue South East, No 315, Calgary Alta, T2G 5C3
Charlottetown Festival	June-October	PO Box 848, Charlottetown, PEI, C1A 7L9
Festival International de Lanaudière	June-August	1500 Base-de-Roc Boulevard, Joliette, PQ J6E 3Z1
Festival International de Musique Baroque	July	PO Box 644, Lameque, NB E0B 1V0
Festival of the Sound	July-August	PO Box 750, Parry Sound, Ontario, P2A 2Z1
Guelph Spring Festival	May	PO Box 1718, Guelph, Ontario, N1H 6Z9
International Choral Festival	May-June	70 York Street, 3rd Floor, Toronto, Ontario, M5J 1S9
Scotia Festival of Music	May-June	1541 Barrington Street, Suite 317, Halifax, NS, B3J 1Z5
Shaw Festival	April-November	PO Box 774, Niagara-on-the-Lake, Ont L0S 1J0
Vancouver Early Music Summer Festival	July-August	1254 West Seventh Avenue, Vancouver, BC V6H 1B6
Victoria International Festival	July-August	3400 Richmond Road, Victoria, BC, V8P 4P5

CROATIA

| Zagreb Musical Biennale - International Festival of Contemporary Music | | HD Skladatelja, Berislaviceva, HR-1000 Zagreb |

CZECH REPUBLIC

Brno International Music Festival	September-October	Vvoz 39, 602 00 Brno
Prague Autumn Festival		Sekaninova 26, 120 00 Prague 2
Prague Cultural Summer	June-September	nam Republiky 5, 110 00 Prague 1
Prague Easter Festival		Sonus Pod Smukýřkou 1049, 150 00 Prague 5
Prague Festival	September-October	Sonus Pod Smukýřkou 1049, 150 00 Prague 5
Prague Spring International Music Festival	May-June	Hellichova 18, 118 00 Prague 1

DENMARK

Århus Festival	September	Vester Allé 3, DK-8000 Århus
Fanø Music Festival	June, July & August	Toftestein 21, Sønderho, DK-6720 Fanø
Lerchenborg Music Days	July-August	Tuborgvej 99, DK-2900 Hellerup
Royal Danish Ballet and Opera Festival		PO Box 2185, DK-1017 Copenhagen

EIRE

Adare Festival	July	Adare Manor, Adare, County Limerick
Cork International Choral Festival	April	PO Box 68, Cork
Dublin International Organ and Choral Festival	September	City Hall, Dublin 2
Galway Arts Festival	July	The Cornstone, Galway
Kilkenny Arts Week	August	22 Rosehill Court, Kilkenny
Waterford International Festival of Light Opera	September-October	60 Morrissons Avenue, Waterford
Wexford Festival Opera	October-November	Theatre Royal, Wexford

ESTONIA

| Tallinn International Organ Festival | July-August | Niguliste Str, 13, EE-0001 Tallinn |

FINLAND

Finland Festivals	year-round	PO Box 56, SF-00101 Helsinki
Helsinki Festival	August-September	Rauhankatu 7E, SF-00100 Helsinki
Joensuu Song Festival	June	Koskikatu 1, SF-80100 Joensuu
Jyväskylä Arts Festival	June	Kauppakatu 14 A 4, SF-40100 Jyväskylä
Kangasniemi Music Festival	June-July	Kulttuuritoimisto, SF-51200 Kangasniemi

Karjaa Music Festival	June-July	Rantatie 1, SF-10300 Karjaa
Korsholm Music Festival	June-July	Festival Office, SF-65610 Korsholm
Kuhmo Chamber Music Festival	July-August	Torikatu 39, SF-88900 Helsinki 10
Lahti Organ Festival	August	Kirkkokatu 5, SF-15110 Lahti 11
Oulu Music Festival	January-May	Lintulammentie 1 K, SF-90140 Oulu
Naantali Music Festival	June	PO Box 46, SF-21101 Naantali
Savonlinna Opera Festival	June-July	Olavinkatu 35, SF-57130 Savonlinna
Suvisoitto-Porvoo Summer Sounds	June-July	Erottajankatu 19 D 21, SF-00130 Helsinki
Tampere Biennale	April	Tullikamarinaukio 2, SF-33100 Tampere
Time of Music	July	Kunnantalo, SF-44500 Vitasaari
Turku Music Festival	August	Uudenmaankatu 1 A SF-20500 Turku

FRANCE

Academie internationale d'Art Musicale: Festival Semaines Musicales de Tours	July	17 Rue des Ursulines, F-37000 Tours
Avignon Festival	July-August	8 bis Rue de Mons, F-84000 Avignon
Biennale de la Musique Française	September of odd-numbered years	Masion de Lyon, Place Bellecour, F-69002 Lyon
Chorégies d'Orange	July-August	18 Place Silvain, BP 205, F-84107 Orange Cédex
Festival d'Aix		Palais de l'Ancien Archevêché, F-13100 Aix-en-Provence
Festival d'Art Sacré de la Ville de Paris	October-December	17 Rue de l'Arbe Sec, F-75001 Paris
Festival d'Automné à Paris	September-December	156 Rue de Rivoli, F-75001 Paris
Festival de Chartres/Grandes Orgues de Chartres	July and September	75 Rue de Grenelle, F-75007 Paris
Festival de Colmar	July	4 Rue des Unterlinden, F-68000 Colmar
Festival del la Rochelle	June-July	26 Rue Washinton, F-75008 Paris
Festival de L'Ile de France	September-October	26 Rue de Gramont, F-75002 Paris
Festival de Paris	May-June	2 Rue Edouard Colonne, F-75001 Paris
Festival de Prades	July-August	Rue Victor Hugo, F-66500 Prades
Festival de Versailles	May-June	Maire de Versailles, RP 144, F-78011 Versailles
Festival de Ville d'Avray	May-June	10 Rue de Marnes, F-92410 Ville d'Avray
Festival des instruments Anciens	March-April	58 Rue Viollet-la-Duc, F-94210 St Maur La Varenne
Festival des Nations europeennes	July	BP 60, F-68140 Munster
Festival du Comminges	July-August	Academie Internationale, F-31260 Mazeres-sur-Salat
Festival Estival de Paris	July-September	20 Rue Geoffroy l'Asnier, F-75004 Paris
Festival international Atlantique	June-August	7 quai de Versailles, F-44000 Nantes Cédex
Festival international d'Art Lyrique et de Musique	July-August	Palais de l'Ancien Archevêché, F-13100 Aix-en-Provence
Festival international d'Eté de Nantes	July	Porte St Pierre, Rue de l'Evêché, F-44000 Nantes
Festival international de Besançon et Franche-Comte	August-September	2d Rue Isenbart, F-25000 Besançon
Festival international de Carpentras	July-August	La Charité, Rue Cottier, BP 113, F-84204 Carpentras Cédex
Festival international de Chant Choral	May	5 Square Gandjean, F-54220 Malzeville
Festival international de Musique Sacrée de Lourdes	Easter	Place du Champ Commun, F-65100 Lourdes
Festival international de Musique de Toulon	May-June	Palais de la Bourse, Avenue Jean-Moulin, D-83000 Toulon
Festival international des Musiques d'Aujourd'hui de Strasbourg	September-October	9 Rue de Général Frère, F-67000 Strasbourg
Festival J S Bach	July-August	Palais Delphinal, F-26260 Saint-Donat-sur-Berbasse
Festival Mediterranéen	June-August	BP 4, F-13129 Salin de Giraud
Festival Musique en Sorbonne	June-July	2 Rue Francis de Croisset, F-75018 Paris
Fêtes Musicales en Touraine	June	Hôtel de Ville, F-37032 Tours Cédex
Lille Festival	October-December	64 Avenue President J F Kennedy, F-59800 Lille
Mai Musical de Bordeaux	May	Grand Théâtre, Place de la Comédie, F-33074 Bordeaux Cédex
Musique Action	May	BP 126, Centre Cultural André Malraux, F-54504 Vandoevre-les-Nancy Cédex
Nuits de la Fondation Maeght	July	Fondation Maeght, F-06570 St Paul-de-Vence
Recontres d'Eté de la Chartreuse	July	La Chartreuse, BP 30, F-30400 Villeneuve-les-Avignon
Recontres internationales de la Guitare	July	Hôtel de Ville, BP 114, F-65013 Tarbes Cédex
Recontres Musicales d'Evian	May	Château de Blonay, F-74500 Evain les Bains
Strasbourg International Festival	June-July	Wolf Musique, 24 Rue de la Mésange, F-67000 Strasbourg

GERMANY

Augsburger Mozart-Sommer	August-September	Kulturamt, Maximilianstrasse 36, 8900 Augsburg
Bachfest der Neuen Bachgesellschaft	June-July	Johann Sebastian bach Platz, 7000 Stuttgart
Bach Festival Berlin	July	Bismarckstrasse 73, 1000 Berlin 12
Bach Week	June	Rathaus, 2120 Lüneburg
Bachwoche Ansbach	July-August of odd-numbered years	Postfach 1741, 8800 Ansbach
Bad Hersfeld Festival Concerts and Opera	June-August	Nachtigallenstrasse 9, 6430 Bad Hersfeld
Berliner Festwochen	September	Budapeststasse 50, 1000 Berlin 30
Beyreuth Festival	July-August	PO Box 100262, 8580 Bayreuth 2
Bodensee Festival	May-June	Spanierstrasse 3, 7750 Konstanz
Bonner Herbst	October-November	Wachsbleiche 21, 5300 Bonn 1
Brahms Days	May of odd-numbered years	PO Box 1609, 7560 Gaggenau
Brühler Schlosskonzerte eV	May-September	Schlosstrasse 2, 5040 Brühl

Cloister Concerts	June-August	Kurverwaltung Alpirsbach, 7297 Alpirsbach
Collegium Musicum Schloss Pommersfelden	July-August	Austrasse 10, 8501 Burgthann/Dörlbach
Corveyer Musikwochen	May-June	Stadtverwaltung/Stadthaus am Petritor, 3470 Höxter 1
Das Treffen	August	PO Box 100642, 8580 Bayreuth
Deutsches Mozartfest Augsburg	September	Deutsche Mozart Gesellschaft eV, Karlstrasse 6, 8900 Augsburg
Dollart Festival		Postfach 1580, 2960 Aurich 1
Donaueschingen Festival of Contemporary Music	October	Südwestfunk Baden-Baden, PO Box 820, 7570 Baden-Baden
Dresdner Musikfestspiele	May-June	Postfach 20723, D-01193 Dresden
Dresdner Tage der Zeitgenössischen Musik	October	Schevenstrasse 17/150-05, 8054 Dresden
Ettingen Schloss-Festspiele	June-August	Postfach 0762, 7505 Ettingen
European Festival	June-July	Dr Hans Kaptingerstrasse 22, 8390 Passau
Festliche Sommer in der Wies	June-August	Bahnhofstrasse 44, 8920 Schongau
Festspiele am Roten Tor	July	Kasernstrasse 4-6, 8900 Augsburg
Feuchtwangen Kreuzgangspiele	June-August	Markplatz, 8805 Feuchtwangen
Gandersheimer Donfestspiele	June-August	Barfüsserkloster 15, 3353 Bad Gandersheim
Gewandhaus-Festtage Leipzig	June	Augustusplatz 8, 7010 Leipzig
Göttingen Handel Festival	June	Hainholzweg 3-5, 3400 Göttingen
Händelfestspiele in Halle	June	Gorsse Nikolaistrasse 5, D-06108 Halle
Heidelberg Castle Festival	July-August	Friedrichstrasse 5, 6900 Heidelberg
Herbstliche Musiktage Bad Urach	September-October	Postfach 1240, 7432 Bad Urach
Hitzacker Summer Music Festival	July-August	Barkhausenweg 12, 2000 Hamburg
International Castle Concerts	April-October	Schloss, 8851 Leitheim bei Donauwörth
International May Festival	May	Postfach 3247, 6200 Wiesbaden
International Organ Festival	October of odd-numbered years	Jacobikirchof 3, 3400 Göttingen
Internationale Orgelwoche Nürnberg-Music Sacra	June-July	Bismarckstrasse 46, 8500 Nürnberg
Internationales Beethovenfest Bonn	triennial	Wachsbleiche 21, 5300 Bonn
Kassel Music Festival	October	Friedrich Ebertstrasse 159, 3500 Kassel
Kissinger Sommer Music Festival	June-July	Postfach 2260, 8730 Bad Kissingen
Leitheim Schloss Concerts	May-October	Schloss Leitheim, 8851 Kaisheim
Limburger Organ Vespers	April-August	Städtisches Verkehrsamt, 6250 Limburg an der Lahn
Ludwigsburger Schlossfestspiele/Internationale Festspiele Baden-Württemberg	May-September	Postfach 1022, 7140 Ludwigsburg
Münchener Biennale	April	Rindermarkt 3-4, 8000 Munich 2
Munich Opera Festival	July-August	Bayerische Staatsoper, Max Jospeh Platz 2, D-80539 Munich
Music in the 20th Century	May	Postfach 1050, 6600 Saarbrücken
Musica Bayreuth	May	Ludwigstrasse 26, 8580 Bayreuth
Musik-Biennale Berlin	March	Budapesterstrasse 50, 1000 Berlin 30
Musikfest Hamburg	September	Grosse Theaterstrasse 34, 2000 Hamburg 36
Musiksommer Obermain	May-December	Bambergerstrasse 25, 8623 Staffelstein
Nymphenburg Summer Festival		Zuccalistrasse 21, 8000 Munich 19
Opera Festival Eutiner Sommerspiele GmbH	July-August	Postfach 112, 2420 Eutin/Holstein
Palace Courtyard Serenade Concerts	June-July	Friedrichstrasse 5, 6900 Heidelberg
Pro Musica Nova	May	Heinrich-Hertzstrasse 13, 2800 Bremen
Ruhrfestival-Europäisches Festival	May-June	Otto Burrmeister Alle 1, 4350 Recklinghausen
Schleswig-Holstein Music Festival	June-August	Postfach 2655, D-23514 Lubeck
Schloss Elmau		Schloss Elmau, 8101 Klais/Oberbayern
Schwetzingen Festival	April-June	Postfach 106040, D-70049 Stuttgart
Tage Alter Musik	June	Postfach 100830, 8400 Regensburg
Tage für Neue Musik	October-November	Kornbergstrasse 32, 7000 Stuttgart 1
Tage Neuer Kammermusik Braunschweig	November-December	Steintorwall 3, 3300 Braunschweig
Telemann-Festtage	March	Liebigstrasse 10,. 3010 Magdeburg
Witten Festival of Contemporary Chamber Music	April	Bergerstrasse 25, 5810 Witten
Würzburg Bach Festival	November	Hofstallstrasse 5, 8700 Würzburg
Würzburg Mozart Festival	June	Haus zum Falken, 8700 Würzburg
Zelt Music Festival Freiburg	June	10 Haslacherstrasse, 7800 Freiburg

GREECE

Athens Festival	June-September	1 Voukourestiou Street, 10564 Athens
Iraklion Summer Festival		71202 Iraklion, Crete
Patras International Festival	June-August	PO Box 1184, 26110 Patras

HONG KONG

Hong Kong Arts Festival	January-February	GPO Box 2547, Hong Kong; International Programme Office, 35 Little Russell St, London W1A 2HH, England

HUNGARY

Beethoven Concerts	June-August	Vörösmarty tér 1, 1364 Budapest
Budapest Arts Festival	September-October	Vörösmarty tér 1, 1051 Budapest
Budapest Autumn Festival	September-October	PO Box 95, Rákóczi u. 65, VI 66, H-1081 Budapest
Esztergom International Guitar Festival	August	PO Box 38, H-2501 Esztergom
Open Air Theatre-Summer Festival	June-August	Pf 95, H-1525 Budapest

Sopron Early Music Days	*June*	PO Box 80, 1366 Budapest

ICELAND

Dark Music Days	*January-February*	Laufásvegur 40, 101 Reykjavík
Reykjavík Arts Festival	*June*	PO Box 88, 121 Reykjavík

ISRAEL

Ein Gev Music Festival	*Passover*	Ein Gev, 14940 Kibbutz Ein Gev
Israel Festival	*May-June*	Jerusalem Theatre, PO Box 4409, 91040 Jerusalem
Kol-Israel, Upper Galliee Chamber Music Days	*July-August*	Hakirya, 61070 Tel Aviv
Vocalisa 90	*April*	PO Box 515, 20101 Carmiel

ITALY

Antidogma Musica Festival	*September-October*	Via Alberto Nota 3, 10122 Turin
Aterforum	*June-July*	Piazetta Sant'Anna 3, Int 8, 44100 Ferrara
Autunno Musicale a Como	*September-October*	Via Cantoni 1, 22100 Como
Batignano Musica nel Chiostro		Santa Croce, Comune di Grosseto, 58041 Batignano
Biennale di Venezia, Festival Internazionale di Musica Contemporanea	*September-October*	Ca'Giustinian, S Marco, 30100 Venice
Canto delle Pietro-Musiche Sacre e Spiritual nel Monumenti Romantici Lombardi	*April-June*	Via Cantoni 1, 22100 Como
Ente Autonomo Spettacoli Lirici Arena di Verona	*July-August*	Piazza Bra 28, 37121 Verona
Estate Maceratese	*July*	Arena Sferisterio, 62100 Macerata
Festa Musica Pro Mundo Uno	*July-August*	Via di Villa Maggiorani 20,. 00168 Rome
Festival Barocco	*May and September*	Corso Massimo d'Azeglio, 10126 Turin
Festival dell'Opera Siciliana e Taormina	*October*	Via Cavour 117, 90133 Palermo
Festival dell'organo/Festival delclavicembalo		Via dei Banchi Vecchi 61, 00153 Rome
Festival di Musica Antica	*July*	Via Zeffirino Re 2, 47023 Cesena
Festival di Musica Contemporanea "900 Musicale Europeo"	*October*	Via Capodimonte 23, 80131 Naples
Festival di Musica Sacra		Villa Igea, 90142 Palermo
Festival de Opera Barga	*July-August*	Via della Fornacetta 11, 55051 Barga Lucca
Festival Internazionale di Musica Antica	*July*	Via f Confalonieri 5, 00195 Rome
Festival Internazionale di Musica Classica e Contemporanea	*June-July*	PO Box N95, 16038 Santa Margherita Ligure
Festival Mozart in Lombardia	*September-November*	Via Cantoni 1, 22100 Como
Festival of Contemporary Music "Nuovi Spazi Musicali"	*June*	Via Divisione Torin 139, 00143 Rome
Festival of Two Worlds	*June-July*	Via Cesare Beccaria 18, 00196 Rome
Festival Pontino	*June-July*	Viale le Corbusier 379, 04100 Latina
Festival Romaeuropa	*May-July*	Via Sistina 48, 00187 Rome
Festival Spaziomusica	*October-November*	Via Liguria 60, 09127 Cagliari
Gli Incontri Musicale Romani		Largo Nazzareno 8, 00187 Rome
Gubbio Festival	*July-August*	Corso Garibaldi 88, 06024 Gubbio
Incontri con La Nuova Musica	*November-December*	PO Box 196, 25100 Brescia
International Chamber Music Festival of Asolo	*August-September*	Via Browning 141, 31011 Asolo
Lucca in Villa Festival	*August*	Via Turati 31, 55049 Viareggio, Lucca
Maggio Musicale Fiorentino	*April-July*	Via Solferino 15, 50123 Florence
Musica 2000 Festival	*April*	8 Via Alpi, 60131 Ancona
Musica Verticale Festival	*October-November*	Via Lamarmora 18, 00185 Rome
Puccini Festival	*July-August*	Piazza Belvedere Puccini 4, 55048 Lucca
Rassegna di Nuova Musica	*May-June*	Arena Sferisterio, CP 92, 62100 Macerata
Ravenna Festival	*June-July*	Via Dante Alighieri 1, 48100 Ravenna
Rome Festival	*May-August and October-November*	Via Francesco Duodo 49, 00136 Rome
Rossini Opera Festival	*August*	Via Rossini 37, 61100 Pesaro
Sagra Musical al Tempio Maiatestiano	*September*	47037 Rimini
Sagra Musicale Umbra	*October*	Cas Post No 341, 06100 Perugia
Settembre Musica	*August-September*	Piazza S Carlo 161, 10123 Turin
Settimane Musicali di Stresa	*August-September*	Via R Bonghi 4, 28049 Stresa
Settimane Musicali Senese	*July*	Via di Città 89, 53100 Siena
I Suoni del Tempo	*July*	Via Zeffirino Re 2, 47023 Cesena
Taormina Arte	*July-September*	Via Pirandello 31, 98039 Taormina
Triest Prima, Incontri internazionale con la Musica Contemporanea	*September*	Via Settefontane 30, 34141 Trieste
Veneto Festival	*May-July*	Piazzale Pontecorvo 4a, 35100 Padua
Verdi Festival	*September*	Via Farini 34, 43100 Parma
Verona Festival	*July-September*	Piazza Brà 28, 37121 Verona

JAPAN

Japan International Chamber Music Festival	*April-May*	32-11-411 Kamikitazawa 4-chome, Setagaya-ku, Tokyo
Kusutsu International Summer Music Academy and Festival in Gumma-ken	*August*	Aoyama Ten-X 8F, 5-50-6, Jingumae, Shibuya-ku, Tokyo 150

Min-On Contemporary Music Festival	June	1-32-13 Kita-Shinjuku, Shinjuku-ku, Tokyo 169
National Arts Festival	October-November	Ministry of Education, Tokyo 100
Osaka International Festival Society	April	New Asahi Building, Nakanoshima 2-3-18, Kita-ku, Osaka 530
Pacific Music Festival	July-August	c/o Sapporo Concert Hall, 1-15 Nakajima-Koen, Chuo-ku, Sapporo 064
Tokyo City Arts Festival	January-March	3-5 Marunouchi, Chiyoda-ku, Tokyo
Tokyo Summer Festival	July	Copacabana Building, 5F, 3-6-4 Akasaka, Minato-ku, Tokyo 107

KOREA SOUTH

| Autumn Music Festival in Seoul | October-November | Dong-Hwa Building, Suite 210, 43-1, Pil-Dong 1-Ga, Choong-gu, Seoul 100-271 |
| Seoul International Music Festival | October-November | Korean Broadcasting System, 18 Yoido-dong, Youngdungpo-gu, Seoul 150-790 |

LITHUANIA

| Baltic Music Festival | October | Mickevičiaus 29, 2600 Vilnius |

LUXEMBOURG

| Festival Européen de Wiltz-Luxembourg | July | Château de Wiltz, 9516 Wiltz |
| Festival International Echternach Luxembourg | May-June | Parvis de la Basilique 9, 6486 Echternach |

MACAO

| International Music Festival of Macao | October | Avda Aviso Goncalves Zarco, s/n, 1st Floor, Macao |

MEXICO

Festival de Música de Cámara de San Miguel de Allende	July-August	Calle Hernádez Macias 75, San Miguel de Allende
Festival de San Miguel de Allende	December	Hospicio 48, San Miguel de Allende
Festival Internacional Cervantino	October	Alvaro Obregón 273, 06700 Mexico, DF
Gran Festival Ciudad de Mexico	July	Alvaro Obregón 73, 06700 Mexico, DF

MONACO

| Printemps des Arts de Monte Carlo | April-May | Rue Louis Notari, MC 98000 Monaco |

NETHERLANDS

Festival Amsterdam Chamber Music Society	March and November	Ceintuurbaan 376, 1073 EM Amsterdam
Festival Nieuwe Muziek	June-July	Postbox 15, 4330 AA Middleburg
Haarlem Organ Festival	July	Postbus 3333, 2011Haarlem
Holland Festival	June	Kleine-Gartmanplantsoen 21, 1071 RP Amsterdam
Holland Festival Early Music Utrecht	August-September	PO Box 734, 3500 AS Utrecht
International Choir Festival	June	Plompetorengracht 3, 3512 CA Utrecht
International Gaudeamus Music Week	September	Swammerdamstr 38, 1090 RV Amsterdam
New Music Festival Maastricht	September	St Maartenspoort 23, 6221 BA Maastricht

NEW ZEALAND

| New Zealand International Festival of the Arts | February-March | PO Box 10113, Wellington 6036 |

NORWAY

Bergen International Festival	June	Strandgt 18, PO Box 183, N-5001 Bergen
Elverum Festival	August	PO Box 313, N-2401 Elverum
Northern Norway Festival	June	Box 901, N-9401 Harstad
Oslo Sommeropera	June	Grev Wedels Plass 2, N-0151 Oslo
St Olav Festival of Trondheim	July-August	PO Box 2045, N-7001 Trondheim
Stord International Choir Festival	June	Box 433, N-5401 Stord

PHILIPPINES

| Philippine Music Festival | October-November | NAMCYA-FAT, CCP Complex, Roxas Boulevard, Manila |

POLAND

| Festival of Early Music of Central and Eastern Europe | September | Libelta 16, 85-080 Bydgoszcz |
| Henryk Wieniawski Days | June | Tadeusza Kościuszki nr 19, 58-310 Szczawno-Zdrój |

International Music and Arts Festival	*September*	Rynek-Ratusz 24, 50-1010 Wroclaw
Music in Old Kraków	*August*	ul Zwierzyniecka 1, 31-103 Kraków
Polish and International Music Festival	*May*	Chopina 30, 35-055 Rzeszów
Warsaw Autumn-International Festival of Contemporary Music	*September*	Rynek Starego Miasta 27, 00-272, Warsaw

PORTUGAL

Encontros de Música Contemporanes	*May*	Avda de Berna 45, 1093 Lisbon Codex

ROMANIA

Cluj-Napoca Musical Autumn	*October*	Str E de Martonne 1, 3400 Cluj-Napoca
George Enescu International Festival	*September*	Artexim, Calea Victoriei 155, Bl.D1, Sc.8 et.2, 71012 Bucharest
Tirgu Mures Musical Days	*May*	2 Enescu Street, 4300 Tirgu Mures

RUSSIA

December Nights	*December*	Volkhona 12, 121019 Moscow
International Music Festival St Petersburg Spring	*April*	Herzena 45, 190000 St Petersburg
Festival Moscow	*July-August*	Ul Kalantchovskaya 15, Moscow
Moscow International Music Festival	*May*	RosInterFest, 12 Sadovaya Triumfalnaya Str, 103006Moscow
St Petersburg Palaces International Chamber Music Festival	*June*	c/o M & N Artists Ltd, 400 West 43rd Street # 19A, New York, NY 10036, USA
White Nights	*June*	Fontanki 41, St Petersburg

SINGAPORE

Singapore Festival of Arts	*June of even-numbered years*	PSA Building, 35th Storey, 460 Alexandria Road, Singapore 0511

SLOVAK REPUBLIC

Bratislava Cultural Summer	*July-August*	Suché Mýto 17, 812 93 Bratislava
Bratislava Music Festival	*October*	Michalská 10, 815 36 Bratislava
Evenings of New Music	*June*	Fučikova 29, 811 02 Bratislava

SLOVENIA

Ljubljana Festival	*July-August*	Trg Francoske Revolucije 1-2, 61000 Ljubljana

SPAIN

Curso de Música Barroca y Rococo	*August*	Acuerdo 17-1° A, 28015 Madrid
Festival de Música de Canarias	*January-February*	Leon y Castillo 427-3°, 35007 Las Palmas de Gran Canaria
Festival internacional de Guitarra "Andres Segovia"	*November*	Ramon Llull 2, 07001 Palma de Mallorca
Festival internacional de Música & Danza de Granada	*June-July*	PO Box 64, 18080 Granada
Festival internactional de Música Castell de Peralada	*July-August*	Pere de Moncada 1, 08034 Barcelona
Festival internacional de Música Contemporanea de Alicante	*September*	Piaza del Ayuntamiento, 03001 Alicante
Festival internacional de Música de Barcelona		Via Laietana, 41 pral, 08003 Barcelona
Festival internacional de Organo	*September-October*	Calle La Paloma 7, 24003 Leon
Festival internacional de Santander	*July-September*	Avda Calvo Sotelo 15, 5th Floor, 39002 Santandar
Semana de Música de Cámara Festival internacional de Segovia	*July*	San Facundo 5, Segovia
Serenatas Musicales de Valencia	*July*	Avellanas 603a, 46003 Valencia

SWEDEN

Drottningholm Court Thetare Festival	*May-September*	PO Box 27050, S-10251 Stockholm
Electro-Acoustic Music Festival	*June*	Box 101, S-739 22 Skinnskatteberg
Helsingborg Summerfestival	*August*	Konserthuset, S-252 21 Helsingborg
Royal Palace Music Festival	*July-August*	Royal Palace, S-111 30 Stockholm
Stockholm New Music	*March*	Box 1225, S-111 82 Stockholm
Umeå International Festival of Chamber Music	*June*	S-901 78 Umeå
Visby Festival	*July-August*	Tranhusgatan 47, S-621 55 Visby

SWITZERLAND

Estate Musicale internazionale de Lugano	*August*	Via Losanna, CH-6900 Lugano
European International Festival	*May-July*	10 Rue des Eaux-Vives, CH-1207 Geneva
Festival "Ars et Musica" Aranno	*July-August*	Gatterstrasse 1b, CH-9010 St Gallen
Festival de Musique Sacrée de Friboug	*July*	Case Postale 292, CH-1701 Fribourg
Festival d'Eté-"A Swiss Summer"	*July-August*	PO Box 10, CH-1211 Geneva
Festival of Music Tibor Varga Sion/Valais	*July-September*	PO Box 954, CH-1951 Sion
Interlakner Festwochen	*August*	Postfach, CH-3800 Interlaken

FESTIVALS

International Bach Festival	May	Stadthaus, CH-8201 Schaffhausen
International Choral Festival	April	PO Box 97, CH-1820 Montreux
International Festival of Music Lucerne	August-September	Hirschmattstrasse 13, Postfach, CH-6002 Lucerne
International Festival of Organ Music	June-July	Ente Turistico del Gambarogno, CH-6574 Vira
Montreux-Vevey Music Festival	August-October	Rue du Théâtre 5, Case Postale 162, CH-1820 Montreux
Settimane Musicale d'Ascona	August-October	Via Lido 24, CH-6612 Ascona
Tage für Neue Musik Zürich	November	Hegibachstrasse 38, CH-8032 Zürich

TAIWAN

Taipei Music Festival	September-October	25 Pa Teh Road, Sec 3, 10560 Taipei

TURKEY

Ankara International Festival	April	Tunali Hilmi Cad 114/43, 06700 Kavaklidere/Ankara
Istanbul International Festival	June-July	Istiklal Caddesi 146, Luvr Apt, Beyoglu, 80070 Istanbul
Izmire International Festival	June-July	1442 Sok No 4/6, 35220 Alsancak, Izmir

UK

Aberdeen International Youth Festival	August	Town House, Aberdeen, Scotland AB9 1AQ
Aberystwyth International MusicFest	July-August	Aberystwyth Arts Centre, Penglais, Aberystwyth, Dyfed SY23 3DE
Aldeburgh Early Music Festival	March	Aldeburgh Foundation, High Street, Aldeburgh, Suffolk IP15 5AX
Aldeburgh Festival of Music and the Arts	June	Aldeburgh Foundation, High Street, Aldeburgh, Suffolk IP15 5AX
Almeida Opera	June-July	Almeida Street, London N1 1TA
Bath International Festival of Music and the Arts	May-June	Bath Festivals Trust, 2 Midland Bridge Road, Bath, Avon BA2 3EQ
Bath Mozartfest	November	110 Gloucester Avenue, London NW1 8JA
BBC Henry Wood Promenade Concerts	July-September	16 Langham Street, Room 425, London W1A 1AA
Belfast Festival at Queen's	November	25 College Gardens, Belfast, Northern Ireland BT9 6BS
Beverly Early Music Festival	May	Register Square, Beverley HU17 9AU
Birmingham Early Music Festival	July	42 Beech Avenue, Worcester WR3 8PY
Bournemouth International Festival	June	Digby Chambers, Suite 2, Post Office Road, Bournemouth BH1 1BA
Bournemouth Musicmakers Festival	June-July	Westover Road, Bournemouth BH1 2BU
Brighton Festival	May	54 Old Steine, Brighton, Sussex BN1 1EQ
Bromsgrove Festival	April-May	10 Evertons Close, Droitwich, Worcestershire WR9 8AE
Buxton International Festival	July-August	1 Crescent View, Hall Bank, Buxton, Derbyshire SK17 6EN
Cambridge Festival	July	10 Gurney Way, Cambridge CB7 2ED
Canterbury Festival	October	59 Ivy Lane, Canterbury, Kent CT1 1TU
Cardiff Festival of Music	September-October	St David's Hall, The Hayes, Cardiff, Wales CF1 2SH
Chard Festival of Women in Music	May	6 Gables, Otterford, Chard, Somerset TA20 3QS
Cheltenham International Festival of Music	July	Town Hall, Imperial Square, Cheltenham, Gloucestershire GL50 1QA
Chester Summer Music Festival	July	8 Abbey Square, Chester CH1 2HU
Chichester Festivities	July	Canon Gate House, South Street, Chicester, Sussex PO19 1PU
Dartington International Summer School	July-August	Dartington Hall, Totnes, Devon TQ9 6DE
City of Leeds College of Music Festival	February-March	Cookridge Street, Leeds, Yorkshire LS2 8B
City of London Festival	July	Bishopsgate Hall, 230 Bishopsgate, London EC2M 4QH
East Anglia Summer Music Festival	July-August	The Old School, Bridge Street, Hadleigh, Suffolk IP7 6BY
Edinburgh International Festival	August	21 Market Street, Edinburgh, Scotland EH1 1BW
Exeter Festival	July	Dix's Field, Room G2A, Exeter EX1 1JN
Fishguard Music Festival	July	Fishguard, Pembrokeshire, Wales SA65 9BJ
Garsington Opera Festival	June-July	Garsington Opera, Garsington, Oxon
Glasgow International Early Music Festival	August of even-numbered years	22 Falkland Street, Glasgow, Scotland G12 9PR
Glyndebourne Festival Opera	May-August	Glynedbourne, Lewes, Sussex BN8 5UU
Greenwich Festival	June	151 Powis Street, London SE18 6JL
Handel in Oxford Festival	July	Cumnor Hill, Oxford OX2 9HA
Harrogate International Festival	July-August	Royal Baths, Harrogate, Yorkshire HG1 2RR
Haslemere Festival	July	Jesses, Grayswood Road, Haslemere, Surrey GU27 2BS
Henley Festival of Music and the Arts	July	Festival Yard, 42 Bell Street, Henley-on-Thames RG9 2BG
Huddersfield Contemporary Music Festival	November	University of Huddersfield, Queensgate, Huddersfield HD1 3DH
International Covent Gardens Art Festival	September of even-numbered years	42 Central Avenue, London WC2 8RF
International Organ Festival	July	PO Box 80, St Albans AL3 4HR
King's Lynn Festival	July	29 King Street, King's Lynn, Norfolk PE30 1HA
Lake District Summer Music	August	68 Grosvenor Street, Manchester M1 7EW
Lichfield Festival	July	7 The Close, Lichfield, Staffordshire WS13 7LD
Llandaff Summer Festival	May-July	1 St Mary's, Cardiff, Wales CF5 2EB
Lufthansa Festival of Baroque Music	May-June	4 Bennett Park, London SE3 9RB
Malvern Festival	May-June	Rockliffe House, 40 Church Street, Malvern, Worcs WR14 2AZ
Mananan International Festival of Music and the Arts	June-July	Port Erin, Isle of Man, UK
Manchester-Hallé Proms Festival	June-July	Hallé Concerts Society, Heron House, Albert Sq., Manchester M2 5HD
Mayfest	April-May	18 Albion Street, Glasgow, Scotland G1 1LH
Newbury Spring Festival	May	1 Bridge Street, Newbury, Berks RG14 5BE
Norfolk and Norwich Festival	October	16 Princes Street, Norwich NR3 1AE
North Wales Music Festival	September	High St, St Asaph, Clwyd, North Wales LL17 0RD

FESTIVALS

Perkshore Festival	June-July	Manor House Barn, Fladbury, Pershore, Worcs WR10 2QN
Perth Festival of the Arts	May	2 High Street, Perth, Scotland
Peterborough Cathedral Festival	July	The Cathedral Shop, 24 Minster Precincts, Peterborough PE1 1XZ
Royal National Eisteddfod of Wales	August	40 Parc Ty Glas, Llansihen, Cardiff, Wales CF4 5WU
Salisbury Festival	September	75 New Street, Salisbury SP1 2PH
Sheffield Chamber Music Festival	May	65 Rawcliffe Lane, Clifton, York YO3 6SJ
South Bank Summer Festival	July-September	Royal Festival Hall, Belvedere Road, London SE1 8XX
Stratford-upon-Avon Festival	July-August	2 Chestnut Walk, Stratford-upon-Avon, Warwickshire CV37 6HG
Swansea Festival of Music and the Arts	September-November	The Guildhall, Swansea SA1 4PE
Tilford Bach Festival	May	Old Quarry House, Seale, Farnham, Surrey GU10 1LD
Three Choirs Festival	August	Comunity House, College Green, Gloucester GL1 2LZ
Vale of Glamorgan Festival	August	St Donat's Castle, Llantwit Major, Wales CF6 9WF
Walsingham Variations	August	The Grove, 61 Bracondale, Norwich, Norfolk NR1 2AT
Warwick Festival	June-July	Northgate, Warwick CV34 4JL
Windsor Festival	September-October	Dial House, Englefield Green, Egham, Surrey TW20 0DU
York Early Music Festival	July	PO Box 226, York YO3 6ZU

USA

ARIZONA

Grand Canyon Chamber Music Festival	September	PO Box 1332, Grand Canyon, AZ 86023
Flagstaff Festival of the Arts	July-August	PO Box 1607, Flagstaff, AZ 86002

ARKANSAS

Music Festival of Arkansas	June	PO Box 1243, Fayetteville, AR 72702

CALIFORNIA

Berkeley Festival and Exhibition	June	101 Zellerbach Hall, Univ.of California at Berkeley, Berkeley, CA 94720
Cabrillo Music Festival	July-August	104 Walnut Lane, Suite 206, Santa Cruz, CA 95060
Carmel Bach Festival	July-August	PO Box 575, Carmel-by-the-Sea, CA 93921
Hollywood Bowl Summer Festival	June-September	PO Box 1951, 2301 N Highlands Avenue, Hollywood, CA 90078
La Jolla Chamber Music Society	August	PO Box 2168, La Jolla, CA 92038
Los Angeles Festival	September	PO Box 5210, Los Angeles, CA 90055
Mendocino Music Festival	July	PO Box 1808, Mendocino, CA 95460
Midsummer Mozart Festival	July-August	World Trade Center, No 280, San Francisco, CA 94111
Music Academy of the West Summer Concert Season	June-August	1070 Fairway Road, Santa Barbara, CA 93108
Music in the Mountains	June-July	401 Spring St, No 101, Nevada City, CA 95959
Ojai Festival	June	PO Box 185, Ojai, CA 93024
Redlands Bowl Summer Music Festival	June-August	PO box 466, Redlands, CA 92373
San Luis Obispo Mozart Festival	July-August	PO Box 311, San Luis Obispo, CA 93406
Stern Grove Midsummer Music Festival	June-August	44 Page St, Suite 604-D, San Francisco, CA 94102

COLORADO

Aspen Music Festival	June-August	2 Music School Road, Aspen, CO 81611
Bravo! Colorado Music Festival at Vail, Beaver Creek	July-August	953 South Frontage Road, Suite 104, Vail, CO 81657
Central City Opera House	June-August	621 17th Street, Suite 1601, Denver, CO 80293
Colorado Music Festival	June-August	1035 Pearl St, Suite 303, Boulder, CO 80302

CONNECTICUT

Connecticut Early Music Festival	June	PO Box 329, New London, CT 06320
Norfolk Chamber Music Festival	June-August	135 College Street, New Haven, CT 06520
Summer Music at Harkness Park	July-August	300 Captain's Walk, Room 503, New London, CT 06320

DISTRICT OF COUMBIA

American Music Festival	April-May	National Gallery of Art, Sixth St & Constitution Ave NW, Washington, DC 20565
Library of Congress Summer Chamber Festival	June	Library of Congress, Washington, DC 20540
National Symphony Orchestra: Concerts at the Capitol	Memorial Day weekend, Fourth of July,and Labor Day weekend	John F Kennedy Center for the Performing Arts, Washington, DC 20566

FLORIDA

Festival Miami	September-October	University of Miami School of Music, PO Box 248165, Coral Gables, FL 33124
Florida International Festival	August	PO Box 1310, Daytona Beach, FL 32115-1310
Sarasota Music Festival	May-June	709 North Tamiami Trail, Sarasota, FL 34236
Winter Park Bach Festival	February-March	Rollins College, Box 2763, Winter Park, FL 32789

GEORGIA

Arts Festival of Atlanta	September	999 Peachtree St, Ste 140, Atlanta, GA 30309
Atlanta Symphony Orchestra: Summer Concerts	June-August	1293 Peachtree Street, North East, Suite 300, Atlanta, GA 30309
Southeastern Music Center	July	PO Box 8348, Columbus, GA 31908

IDAHO

Festival at Sandpoint	July-August	Box 695, Sandpoint, ID 83864
Sun Valley Music Festival	July-August	PO Box 656, Sun Valley, ID 83353

ILLINOIS

Grant Park Music Festival	June-August	Chicago Park District Admin Bldg, 425 E. McFetridge Drive, Chicago, IL 60605
Ravinia Festival	June-September	1575 Oakwood Avenue, Highland Park, IL 60035
Woodstock Mozart Festival	JUly-August	PO Box 734, Woodstock, IL 60098

INDIANA

Festival Music Society of Indiana	June-July	6471 Central Avenue, Indianapolis, IN 46220
Firefly Festival for the Performing Arts	June-August	202 South Michigan Street, Suite 845, South Bend, IN 46601
Indiana University School of Music Summer Festival	June-August	Indiana University School of Music, Bloomington, IN 47405
Indianapolis Symphony Orchestra-Symphony on the Prairie	July-August	45 Monument Circle, Indianapolis, IN 46204

IOWA

Ames Festival		PO Box 1243, Ames, IA 50010
Des Moines Metro Opera	June-July	106 West Boston Avenue, Indianola, IA 50125

LOUISIANA

FANFARE	October	Southeastern Louisiana University, Box 797, Hammond, LA 70402

MAINE

Bay Chamber Concerts	July-August	Box 191, Camden, ME, 04843

MARYLAND

Baltimore Symphony Orchestra Summerfest! and Oregon Ridge Concert Series	July June-August	1212 Cathedral Street, Baltimore, MD 21201
Columbia Festival of the Arts	June	10221 Wincopin Circle, Columbia, MD 21044
Maryland Handel Festival	November	Univ of MD, Tawes Fine Arts Bldg, Ste 2140, College Park, MD 20742

MASSACHUSETTS

Aston Magna Festival	July-August	PO Box 1035, Great Barrington, MA 01230
Berkshire Choral Festival	July-August	Route 41, Sheffield, MA 01257
Boston Early Music Festival and Exhibition	June	PO Box 2632, Cambridge, MA 02238
Boston Pops	May-June	Symphony Hall, 301 Massachusetts Avenue, Boston, MA 02115
Boston Symphony Orchestra-Tanglewood Festival	June-August	Lenox, MA 01240
Castle Hill Festival	July-September	PO Box 563, Ipswich, MA 01938
Great Woods Center for the Performing Arts	June-September	PO Box 810, Mansfield, MA 02048
Rockport Chamber Music Festival	June	PO Box 312, Rockport, MA 01966
Worcester Music Festival		Memorial Auditorium, Worcester, MA 01608

MICHIGAN

Ann Arbor May Festival	May	Burton Memorial Tower, Suite 100, Ann Arbor, MI 48109
Ann Arbor Summer Festival	June-July	PO Box 4070, Ann Arbor, MI 48106
Interlochen Arts Festival	June-August	PO Box 199, Interlochen, MI 49643
Irving S Gilmore International Keyboard Festival	January	Kalamazoo Center, 100 West Michigan, Kalamazoo, MI 49007
Michigan Bach Festival	March-April	400 Town Center Drive, Suite 300, Dearbon, MI 48126

MINNESOTA

Minnesota Orchestra Viennese Sommerfest	July-August	1111 Nicollet Mall, Minneapolis, MN 55403

MISSOURI

Missouri River Festival of the Arts	August	PO Box 1776, Boonville, MO 65233
Opera Theatre of St Louis	May-June	PO Box 191910, St Louis, MO 63119
Saint Louis Symphony Orchestra Queeny Pops	July-August	718 North Grand Boulevard, St Louis, MO 63103

MONTANA

Big Sky Arts Festival	July	Box 160308, Big Sky, MT 59716
Flathead Music Festival	July	PO Box 1780, Whitefish, MT 59937

NEW HAMPSHIRE

Monadnock Music	July-August	PO Box 255, Peterborough, NH 03458
New Hampshire Music Festival		88 Belknap Mountain Road, Gilford, NH 03246
North County Chamber Players Summer Festival	July-August	PO Box 99, Franconia, NH 03580

NEW JERSEY

Cape May Music Festival	May-June	PO Box 340, Cape May, NJ 08204
Garden State Arts Center	June-September	PO Box 116, Holmdel, NJ 0733
New Jersey Festival of American Music Theatre	June-August	1650 Broadway, New York, NY 10019
Opera Festival of New Jersey	June-July	55 Princeton-Highstown Road, Princeton Junction, NJ 08550

FESTIVALS

Rutgers SummerFest	*June-July*	Rutgers Arts Center, New Brunswick, NJ 08903
Waterloo Festival	*July-August*	Village of Waterloo, Stanhope, NJ 07874

NEW MEXICO

Music From Angel Fire	*August-September*	PO Box 502, Angel Fire, NM 87710
Santa Fe Chamber Music Festival	*July-August*	PO Box 853, Santa Fe, NM 87504
Santa Fe Opera Festival		PO Box 2408, Santa Fe, NM 87504-2408

NEW YORK

Artpark	*May-September*	Box 371, Lewiston, NY 14092
Bach Aria Festival and Institute	*June*	PO Box 997, Stony Brook, NY 11790
Bard Music Festival	*August*	Bard College, Annandale-on-Hudson, NY 12504
Binghamton Summer Music Festival	*July-August*	PO Box 112, Binghamton, NY 13903
Caramoor Festival	*June-August*	PO Box R, Katonah, NY 10536
Chautauqua Institution	*June-August*	Chautauqua Institution, Chautauqua, NY 14722
Glimmerglass Opera	*July-August*	PO Box 191, Cooperstown, NY 13326
Huntington Summer Arts Festival	*June-August*	213 Main Street, Huntington, NY 11743
Lake George Opera Festival	*July-August*	PO Box 2172, Glen Falls, NY 12801
Lincoln Center Out-of-Doors	*August*	70 Lincoln Center Plaza, 9th Floor, New York, NY 10023
Mostly Mozart Festival	*July-August*	70 Lincoln Center Plaza, 9th Floor, New York, NY 10023
New York Festival of American Music Theatre	*July-August*	1650 Broadway, New York, NY 10019
Saratoga Performing Arts Center	*June-September*	Saratoga Springs, NY 12866

NORTH CAROLINA

An Appalachian Summer	*July*	801 Rivers Street, Boone, NC 28608
Brevard Music Festival	*July-August*	PO Box 592, Brevard, NC 28712
Eastern Music Festival	*June-August*	PO Box 22026, Greensboro, NC 27420

OHIO

Art Song Festival	*May*	11021 East Boulevard, Cleveland, OH 44106
Cincinnati May Festival	*May-June*	Music Hall, 1241 Elm Street, Cincinnati, OH 45210
Cincinnati Opera Association Summer Festival	*June-July*	1241 Elm Street, Cincinnati, OH 45210
Cincinnati Symphony and Pops Orchestras at Riverbend	*June-August*	1241 Elmstreet, Cincinnati, OH 45210
Cleveland Orchestra at the Blossom Music Center	*May-September*	PO Box 1000, Cuyahoga Falls, OH 44223
Kent/Blossom Music	*July-August*	Kent State University, E101 M&S, Kent, OH 44242
Lakeside Summer Festival	*June-September*	236 Walnut Avenue, Lakeside, OH 43440
Lancaster Festival	*July*	PO Box 1452, Lancaster, OH 43130
Ohio Light Opera	*June-August*	College of Wooster, Wooster, OH 44691

OKLAHOMA

OK Mozart International Festival	*June*	PO Box 2344, Bartlesville, OK 74005

OREGON

Britt Festivals, Music and Performing Arts Festivals	*June-September*	PO Box 1124, Medford, OR 97501
Chamber Music Northwest	*June-July*	522 South West Fifth Avenue, Sutie 725, Portland, OR 97204
Oregon Bach Festival	*June-July*	University of Oregon School of Music, Eugene, OR 97403

PENNSYLVANIA

Bethlehem Musikfest Association	*August*	22 Bethlehem Plaza, Bethlehem, PA 18018
Hartwood Music and Dance Festival	*May-September*	1520 Penn Avenue, Pittsburgh, PA 15222
Mann Music Center	*June-September*	1617 J F Kennedy Boulevard, Philadelphia, PA 19103
Three Rivers Arts Festival	*June*	207 Sweetbriar Street, Pittsburgh, PA 15211

PUERTO RICO

Festival Casals	*June*	PO Box 41227, Minillas Station, Santurce, PR 09940
Festival of Young Orchestras of the Americas	*June*	PO Box 41227, Minillas Station, Santurce, PR 00940
Inter-American Festival of the Arts	*September-October*	PO Box 41227, Minillas Station, Santurce, PR 00940

RHODE ISLAND

Newport Music Festival	*July*	PO Box 3300, Newport, RI 02840

SOUTH CAROLINA

Spoleto Festival USA	*May-June*	PO Box 157, Charleston, SC 29402

TENNESSEE

Riverbend Festival	*June*	PO Box 886, Chattanooga, TN 37401

TEXAS

Dallas Symphony Orchestra EDS International Summer Music Festival	*June-July*	2301 Flora Street, Dallas, TX 75201
Houston International Festival	*April*	1100 Louisiana, Sutie 1275, Houston, TX 77002
Rio Grande Valley International Music Festival	*February*	PO Box 2315, McAllen, TX 78502
Round Top Festival	*June-July*	PO Box 89, Round Top, TX 78954

FESTIVALS

SMU Conservatory Summer Music Festival	*June*	Southern Methodist University, Dallas, TX 75275
Texas Music Festival	*June-July*	University of Houston School of Music, Houston, TX 77204

UTAH

Gina Bachauer International Piano Festival	*June*	PO Box 11664, Salt Lake City, UT 84147

VERMONT

Manchester Music Festival	*July-August*	Box 735, Manchester, VT 05254
Marlboro Music Festival	*July-August*	Marlboro, VT 05344
New England Bach Festival	*September-October*	15 Walnut Street, Brattleboro, VT 05301
Vermont Music Festival	*July-August*	PO Box 512, Burlington, VT 05402

VIRGINIA

Wolf Trap Foundation	*May-September*	1624 Trap Road, Vienna, VA 22182

WASHINGTON

Seattle Chamber Music Festival	*June-July*	2618 Eastlake Avenue East, Seattle, WA 98102
Seattle Opera Summer Festival	*July-August*	PO Box 9248, Seattle, WA 98109

WYOMING

Grand Teton Music Festival	*June-August*	PO Box 490, Teton Village, WY 83025

YUGOSLAVIA

Belgrade Music Festival	*October*	Terazije 41, 11000 Belgrade

APPENDIX D
MUSIC ORGANIZATIONS

ALBANIA

Albanian National Music Committee, Lidya e Shrkrimtare de Artistere,R Kavojes Nr4, Tirana. *Contact: Dr Vasil S. Tob.* Tel / Fax: 355 42 274 71

ARGENTINA

Asociacion Argentina de Interpretes (SADEM), Av. Belgrano 3655, 1210 Buenos Aires.
Consejo Argentino de la Musica, Casilla de Correo 5532, Correo Central, 1000 Buenos Aires.
Fundacion Encuentros Internacionales de Musica Contemporanea, Casilla de Correo 1008, Correo Central, 100 Buenos Aires.
Sociedad Argentina de Autores y Compositores de Musicia, Lavalle 1547, 1048 Buenos Aires

AUSTRALIA

Australasian Mechanical Copyright Owners Society Ltd, 56 Berry Street, 14th Floor, North Sydney, NSW 2060.
Australasian Performing Right Association (APRA), Locked Bag 3665, St Leonards, NSW 2065.
Australia Council, 181 Lawson Street, Redfern, NSW 2060.
Australian Copyright Council, 3/245 Chalmers Street, Redfern, NSW 2016.
Australian Music Centre, Ltd, trading as Sounds Australian, PO Box 690, Sydney, NSW 2000.
Australian Music Publishers Association, Ltd, 56 Berry Street, 14th Floor, North Sydney, NSW 2060.
Australian Record Industry Association (ARIA), 263 Clarence Street, 9th Floor, Sydney, NSW 2000.
Australian Society for Keyboard Music, 9 Glenroy Avenue, Middle Cove, NSW 2068.
Confederation of Australasian Performing Arts Presenters, GPO Box 4274, Sydney, NSW 2001.
International Society for Contemporary Music (Australian Section), c/o University of Sydney Music Department, Sydney, NSW 2006.
Musica Viva Australia, PO Box 49, Railway Square, NSW 2000.
Phonographic Performance Company of Australia, Ltd. (PPCA), 263 Clarence Street, 9th Floor, Sydney, NSW 2000.
Youth Music Australia, PO Box 160, Rozelle, NSW 2039.

AUSTRIA

Austro-Mechana (Gesellschaft zur Wahrnehmung mechanisch-musikalischer Urheberrechte GmbH), Baumannstrasse 10, A-1031 Vienna.
Gesellschaft der Musikfreunde in Wien, Bösendorferstrasse 12, A-101 Vienna.
Gesellchaft für Forschungen zur Aufführungspraxis, Zuckerkanlg 14 A, A-1190 Vienna.
Gewekschaft Kunst, Medien, Freie Berufe, Sektion Musiker, Maria Theresienstrasse 11, A-1090 Vienna.
I F D I Landesgruppe Österreich, Habsburgergasse 6-8/18, A-1010 Vienna.
International Music Centre Vienna (IMZ), Lothringerstrasse 20, A-1030 Vienna.
Internationale Bruckner Gesellschaft, Rathausplatz 3, A-1010 Vienna.
Internationale Gesellschaft für Neue Musik, Ungargasse 9/3, A-1030 Vienna.
Internationale Gustav Mahler Gesellschaft, Wiedner guertel 6/2, A-1040 Vienna.
Internationale Hugo Wolf Gesellschaft, Latschkagasse 4, A-1090 Vienna.
Internationale Schönberg Gesellschaft, Bernhardgasse 6, A-2340 Mödling.
Literar-Mechana (Wahrnemungsgesellschaft für Urheberrechte), Linke Wienzelle 18, A-1060 Vienna.
Musikalische Jugend Österreichs (Jeunesses Musicales), Bösendorferstrasse 12, A-1010 Vienna.
Musikverleger Union Österreich, Baumannstrasse 10, A-1030 Vienna.
Österreichischer Komponistenbund (OKB), Ungargasse 9/3, A-1030 Vienna.
Staatlich genehmigte Gesellschaft der Autoren, Komponisten, und Musikverleger (AKM), Baumannstrasse 8-10, A-1030 Vienna.

BELGIUM

Association des Arts et de la Culture rue royale 10, 1000 Brussels.
Association dese Artistes professionnels de Belgique, Rue Paul Lauters 1, 1050 Brussels.
Association Internationale du Théâtre Lyrique, Rue des Dominicains 1, 4000 Liège.
Association pour la Diffusion de la musique Belge, Rue d'Arlon 75-77, 1040 Brussels.
Atelier créatif de Musique électroacoustique, Avenue du Cor de Chasse 99, 1040 Brussels.
Centre belge de Documentatyion musicale, Rue d'Arlon 75-77, 1040 Brussels.
Centre International d'Echanges Musicaux, Rue des Patriotes 60, 1040 Brussels.
Chambre Syndicale des Agents Artistiques et Impresario de Belgique, Rue Rogier 3, 6040 Charleroi.
Confédération muscale de Belgique, Rue du Loncin 22, 4430 Alleur. *President: S Coucke.*
Conseil de la Musique de la Communauté française de Belgique, Boulevard Reyers 52, 1040 Brussels. *President: Dr Robert Wangermée.*
Fondation pour la Promotion des Arts, Rue aux Choux 47, 1000 Brussels.
Jeunesses musicales de la Communaute française de Belgique, Rue Royale 10, 1000 Brussels.
Promotion artisque belge, Rue d'Arlon 75-77, 1040 Brussels.
Royale Union Artistique et Littéraire, Rue du Tombeux 52A, 1801 Stembert.
Société belge de musicologie, Rue de la Régence 30, 1000 Brussels. *Contact: Dr Robert Wangermée.*
Société belge des Auteurs, Compositeurs et Editeurs, Rue d'Arlon 75-77, 1040 Brussels.
Société Cesar Franck de Belgique, Rue des Foulons 11, 400 Liège.
Société culturell d'Arts dramatique et musical, Rue F Ferrer 37, 1360 Tubize.
Société des Auteurs et Compositeurs Dramatiques, Avenue Jeanne 29, 1050 Brussels.
Société liégoise de Musicologie, Les Enclos 13, 4080 Werbomont.

Société wallonne de Recherche et d'Expansion du Marché de Spectacle et de l'Audio-visuel, Rue P.-E Janson 9, 1050 Brussels.
Union de la Presse musicale belge, Avenue C. Woeste 140, 1090 Brussels.
Union des Artistes, Rue du Marché aux Herbes 105, 1000 Brussels.
Union des Compositeurs Belges, Rue d'Arlon 75-77, 100 Brussels.
Union Royale Belge des Éditeurs de Musique, Rue F. Neuray 8, 1060 Brussels.
Union wallonne des Organistes, Rue Romainville 25a, 5228 Bas-Oha/Wanze.

BOLIVIA

Sociedad Boliviana de Autores & Compositores de Música, Figueroa 788, Depto 1, 2nd Floor, La Paz.

BRAZIL

Associacao Brasileira dos Produtores de Discos, Rua Sao josé 90, Gr 1406/10, 22021 Rio de Janeiro, R J.
Associacao de Canto Coral, Rua das Marrecas 40, 9th Floor, 20080-010 Rio de Janeiro, R J.
Fundaçao de Educaçao Artistica, Rua Gonçalves Dias 320, 30000 Belo Horizonte, M G.
Instituto Brasileiro de Arte e Cultura, Rua de Imprensa 16, 20030 Rio de janeiro, R J.
Juventude Musical do Brasil, Caixa Postal 62626, 22257 Rio de Janeiro, R J.
Sindicato dos Músicos Profissionals do Estado de Sao Paulo, Largo Paissandu, Sao Paulo.
Sindicato dos Músicos Profissionals do Estado do Estado do Rio de Janeiro, Rua Alvaro Alvim 24, Grupo 401, 20031 Rio de Janeiro, R J.
Sociedada Brasileira de Autores Teatrais, Av Almirante Barroso 97, 3rd Floor, PO Box 1503, 20031-002 Rio de Janeiro, R J.
Sociedada Brasileira de Música Contemporânea, SQS 105, Bloco B, Ap 506, 70344-020 Brasili, D F.
Sociedada Brasileira de Realizçoes Artistico-Culturais, Av Franklin Roosevelt 23, Room 310, 20021 Rio de Janeiro, R J.
Sociedad de Cultura Artistica, Rua Nestor Pestana 196, CEP 01303 Sao Paulo.
Sociedada independente de Compositores & Autores Musicals, Largo Paissandú 51, 10th, 11th, and 16th floors, 01034 Sao Paulo.
Uniao Brasileira de Compositores, Rua Visconde de Inhaúma 107, 20091 Rio de Janeiro, R J.
Uniao dos Músicos do Brasil, Av Rio Branco 185, Rio de Janeiro, R J.

BULGARIA

Jeunesses Musicales de Bulgarie, 56 Rue Alabine, PO Box 387, 1040 Sofia.
Union of Bulgarian Composers, 2 Ivan Vazoz Str, 1000 Sofia.
Union of Bulgarian Musicians and Dancers, 14 Serdica Str, Sofia.

CANADA

Alliance for Canadian New Music Projects, 9 St Joseph Street, Suite 303, Toronto, Ontario M4Y 1J6. *President: Janet Fothergill.*
American Federation of Musicians of the United States and Canada, Canadaian Office, 75 The Donway West, Suite 1010, Don Mills, Ontario M3C 2E9. *Vice President from Canada: Ray Petch.*
Association of Canadian Orchestras, 56 The Esplanade, Suite 311, Toronto, Ontario M5E 1A7. Executive Director: Elizabeth Webster.
Association of Canadian Women Composers, 20 St Joseph Street, Toronto, Ontario M4Y 1J9. *Chairerson: Lorraine Johnson.*
Association of Cultural Executives, 720 Bathurst Street, Suite 503, Toronto, Ontario M5S 2R4.
C(anadian) A(mateur) M(usicians) M(usiciens) A(mateurs du) C(anada), PO Box 353, Westmount, PQ H3Z 2T5. *Director General: Barry Crago.*
Canada Council/Conseil des Arts du Canada, PO Box 1047, 99 Metcalfe Street, Ottawa, Ontario K1P 5V8. *Director: Roch Carrier.*
Canadian Association of Artists Managers, 117 Ava Road, Toronto, Ont M6C 1W2.
Canadian Association of Arts Administration Educators, Simon Fraser University, 515 West Hastings Street, Vancouver, BC V6B 5K3. *President: Letia Richardson.*
Canadian Bureau for the Advancement of Music, Exhibition Place, Toronto, Ontario M6K 3C3.
Canadian Conference of the Arts, 189 Laurier Avenue East, Ottawa, Ont K1N 6P1. *Director: Keith Kelly.*
Canadian Independent Record Production Association, 144 Front Street West, Suite 202, Toronto, Ontario M5J 2L7. Executive Director: Brian Chater.
Canadian League of Composers, Chalmers House, 20 St Joseph Street, Toronto, Ontario, M4Y 1J9. *President: Patrick Cardy.*
Canadian Music Centre/Centre de musique canadienne, 20 St Joseph Street, Toronto, Ont M4Y 1J9. *Executive Director: Simone Auger.*
Canadian Music Educators Association, 16 Royaleigh Avenue, Etobicoke, Ontario M9P 2J5. *President: Rodger Beatty.*
Canadian Music Publishers Association, 56 Wellesley Street West, Suitye 320, Toronto, Ontario M5S 2S4. *President: Mark Altman.*
Canadian Musical Reproduction Rights Agency, Ltd, 56 Wellesley Street West, Suite 320, Toronto, Ontario M5S 2S4. *General Manager: David A Basskin.*
Canadian Recording Industry Association, 1255 Yonge Strret, Suite 300, Toronto, Ontario M4T 1W6. *President: Brian Robertson.*
Canadian Resource Centre for Career Performing Artists, Box 188, Station A, Toronto, Ontario M5W 1B2. *President: Ann Summers.*
Canadian University Music Society, University of Calgary, 2500 University Drive, Calgary, Alberta T2N 1N4. *President: Dr Eugene Cramer.*
Jeunesses Musicales du Canada/Youth and Music Canada, 305 Mont-Royal East, Montréal, PQ H2T 1P8. *General Director: Nicolas Desjardins.*
Ontario Choral Federation, 20 St Joseph Street, Toronto, Ontario M4Y 1J9. *Executive Director: Bev Jahnke.*
Organization of Canadian Symphony Musicians, 455 Gérard Morisset, No 6, Québec, PQ G1S 4V5. *Chairman: Evelyne Robitaille.*
Society of Composers, Authors and Music Publishers of Canada, SOCAN, 41 Vallyeybrrok Drive, Don Mills, Ontario M3B 2S6. *General Manager; Michael Rock.*

CHILE

Asociación Nacional de Compositores, Almirante Moritt 453, Santiago.
Instituto de Música, Universidad Católica de Chile, Jaime Guzman E 3 300, Santiago.
Juventudes Musicales, Universidad de Chile, Facultad de Artes, Compania 1264, 4 to piso, Santiago.
Sociedad Chilena del Derecho de Autor, San Antonio 427, 2nd Floor, Santiago.
Sociedad de Autores Teatrales de Chile, San Diego 246, Santiago.

CHINA

Association of Chinese Musicians, Nong zhanguan Nan Li, No 10, Beijing 100026.

COLOMBIA

Asociación, Colombiana de Músicos Profesionales, Calles 17, No 10-16, Of 607, Bogotá, D E.
Asociación des Artistas de Colombia, Calle 13, No 9-63, Interior 104, Apdo Aéreo 24627, Bogotá, D E.
Centro de Documentación Musical-Instituto Colombiano de Cultura, Calle 11, No 5-51, 2nd Floor, Bogotá, D E.
Instituto Colombiano de Cultura-Colcultura, Calle 11, No 5-51, 2nd Floor, Santafé de Bogotá, D C.
Juventudes Musicales de Colombia, Apartado Aereo 089436, Cra 16A No 202, Bogotá 8.
Sociedad de Autores y Compositores de Colmbia, Carrera 19, No 40-=72, Apdo Aéreo 6482, Santafé de Bogotá, DC ZP1.

COSTA RICA

Juventudes Musicales de Costa Rica, Apartado 1035, San José 1000.

CUBA

Centro de Información y Promoción de la Música Cubana "Odilio Urfé", Calle 17 esq. a E, Vedado, Havana.
Centro de Investigación y Desarrollo de la Música Cubana, Calle G, No 505 e/21 y 23, Vedado, Havana.
Centro Nacional de Derecho de Autor, Calle Línea No 365 (altos), esp a G, Vedado, Havana.
Centro Nacional de Música de Concierto, Calle Línea No 365, esq a G, Vedado, Havana.
Centro Nacional de Música Popular, Avenida 1 ra. e/10 y 12, Playa, Havana.
Editora Musical de Cuba, San Rafael No 104, esq a Consulado, Centro Habana, Havana.
Empresa de Grabaciones y Ediciones Musicales, Campanario No 315, e/Neptuno y San Miguel, Centro Habana, Havana.
Instituto Cubano de la Música, Calle 15 No 452, esq a F Vedado, Havana.
Unión de Escritores y Artistas de Cuba (Music Section), Calle 17 No 351, esq a H, Vedado, Havana.

CZECH REPUBLIC

Association of Musicians and Musicologists, Maltézské nám. 1, 118 00 Prague 1.
Authors Association of Protection for rights on Musical Works, Čs. armády 20, 160 56 Prague 6.
Confederation of Arts and Culture, Gorkého nám. 23, 116 13 Prague 1.
Czech Music Association (includes the Dvořák Society, Janáček Society, Martinů Society, Smetana Society, Society for Contemporary Music, Society for Early Music, Society for Jazz, and Society for Music Education), Janáčkovo nábř. 59, 150 00 Prague 5.
Czech Music Fund, Besedbí 3, 118 00 Prague 1.
Czech Society for Chamber Music, Korunní 98, 101 00 Prague 10.
International Federation of Phonogram and Videogram Producers (Czechoslovak Section), Gorkého nam. 23, 112 82 Prague 1.
International Music Council (National Committee), Valdstejnske nám. 1, Prague 1.
International Society for Contemporary Music (Czechoslovak Section), Na Březince 22, 150 00 Prague 5.
Music Information Centre of the Czech Music Fund, Besední 3, 118 00 Prague 1.
Union of Authors and Interpreters, Škroupova nám 9, 130 00 Prague 3.

DENMARK

Choir Conductors' Society, Astrugårdsvej 12, 2650 Hvidovre.
Danish Choral Association, Slagelsegade 9, 2100 Copenhagen O.
Danish Composers' Society, Valkendorfsgade 3, 1151 Copenhagen K.
Danish Cultural Insititute, Kultorvet 2, 1175 Copenhagen K.
Danish Jazz Center, Boripvej 66, 4683 Rønnede.
Danish Music Information Centre, 48 Vimmelskaftet, 1161 Copenhagen K.
Danish Musicians' Union, Vendersgade 25, 1363 Copenhagen K.
Danish Musicological Society, Abenrå 34, 1124 Copenhagen K.
Danish Organ Society, Dønnerupvej 2, 2720 Vanløse.
Danish Organists' and Precentors' Society, Flegmade 14, 7100 Vejle.
Danish Society of Composers, Authors, and Editors, Maltegårdsvej 24, 2820 Gentofte.
Danish Society of Jazz, Rock, and Folk Composers, Klerkegade 19, 1308 Copenhagen K.
Danish Soloists' Association, Sundholmsvej 49, 2300 Copenhagen S.
Dansk Arbeider Sanger-og Musikforbund, Skovgade 6, 5500 Middelfart.
Dansk kapelmesterforening, Rosenvangsvej 47, 2670 Greve Strand.
International Society for Contemporary Music (Danish Section), Valkendorfsgade 3, 1151 copenhagen K.
Samrået for Musikundervisning, Vallerod-skolen, Stadion Allé, 2960 Rungsted Kyst.
Society of Danish Church Singing, Hoyrups Allé 7, 2900 Hellerup.
Society for Publishing Danish Music, Valkendorfsgade 3, 1151 Copenhagen K.
State Music Council, Vesterbrodgade 24, 1620 Copenhagen V.
Union of Danish Singers, Norre Sovej 26 A, 8800 Viborg.

DOMINICAN REPUBLIC

Juventudes Musicales Dominicanas, Apartado Postal 21920, Santo Domingo.

ECUADOR

Juventudes Musicales, Casilla Correo, 8162, Sucursal 8, Quito.

EIRE

Arts Council, 70 Merrion Square, Dublin 2.
Contemporary Music Centre, 95 Lower Baggot Street, Dublin 2.
International Songwriters Association, Ltd, Raheen, Limerick City.
Irish Composers Centre, Liberty Hall, Room 804, Dublin 1.
Irish Federation of Musicians and Associated Professions, 63 Lower Gardiner Street, Dublin 1.
Irish Music Rights Organization (IMRO), 15 Herbert Street, Dublin 2.
Mechanical Copyright Society, Ltd (MCPS), 15 Herbert Street, Dublin 2.

EL SALVADOR

Centro Nacional de Artes, 2a Avenida Norte Pje. Contreras, No 145, San Salvador.

ESTONIA

Jeunesses Musicales Eestis, Estonia pst 4 tuba 410, 200105 Tallinn.

FINLAND

Association of Finnish Conservatories, Fredrikinkati 34 B, SF-00100 Helsinki.
Association of Finnish Music Schools, Urho Kekkosen katu 8C 30, SF-00100 Helsinki.
Association of Finnish Operas, Iso-Roobertinkatu 20-22 A 76, SF-00120 Helsinki.
Association of Finnish Soloists, Museokatu 3 B 12, SF-00100 Helsinki.
Association of Finnish Symphony Orchestras, Aninkaistenkatu 3 B, SF-20110 Turku.
Association of Military Conductors, Helsingin varuskuntasoittokunta, PL 13, SF-00251 Helsinki.
Association of Music Libraries in Finland (Finnish Section, International Association of Music Libraries), PO Box 148, SF-01301 Vantaa.
Association of Swedish Speaking Church Musicians, SF-10210 Ingå.
Concert Centre, Urho Kekkosen katu 8 C 30, SF-00100 Helsinki.
Federation for Church Music in Finalnd, Tollinpolku 1 C, SF-00410 Helsinki.
Federation for Finnish Traditional Music, Raumantie 1, SF-00350 Helsinki.
Federation of Music Teachers in Finland, Asemamiehenkatu 4, SF-00520 Helsinki.
Finland Festivals, PO Box 56, SF-00100 Helsinki.
Finlands svenska sång-och musikförbund r.f., Handelsespladen 23 B, SF-65100 Vasa.
Finnish Composers' Copyright Bureau, Lauttasaarentie 1, SF-00200 Helsinki.
Finnish Jazz Federation, PO Box 54, SF-00101 Helsinki.
Finnish Music Information Centre, Runeberginkatu 15 A, SF-00100 Helsinki.
Finnish Music Publishers' Association, Runeberginkatu 15 A 12, SF-00100 Helsinki.
Finnish Musicians' Union, Udenlaankatu 36 D 21, SF-00120 Helsinki.
Finnish Society for Ethnomusicology, Mannerheimintie 40 C 69, SF-00100 Helsinki.
Folk Music Institute, SF-69600 Kaustinen.
Foundation for the Promotion of Finnish Music, Runeberginkatu 15 A 6, SF-00100 Helsinki.
Guild of Light Music Composers and Authors in Finalnd, Runeberginkatu 15 A 11, SF-00100 Helsinki.
Head Organization of Finnish Traditional Music, SF-39170 Jumesniemi.
IFPI (Finnish National Group), Runeberginkatu 15 A 12, SF-00100 Helsinki.
International Music Council (Finnish Section), Ukonkivenpolku 4 D 28, SF-01610 Vantaa.
Institute of Accordion Music in Finland, Kvrösselänkatu 3, SF-39599 Ikaalinen.
Korvat Auki r.y. (Society for Young Contemporary Composers), Kurkisuontie 12 D 35, SF-00940 Helsinki.
Music Artists Organization, Kuususaarenkuia 9, SF-00340 Helsinki.
Musicological Society of Finland, Töölönkatu 28, SF-00260 Helsinki.
Performing Music Promotion Centre, Hietaniemenkatu 2, SF-00100 Helsinki.
Society of Finnish Composers, Runeberginkatu 15 A 11, SF-00100 Helsinki.
SULASOL (Federation of Amateur Musicians in Finland), Fredrikinkatu 61, SF-00100 Helsinki.
Workers' Institute of Music, Mannerheimintie 40 C 74, SF-00100 Helsinki.
Workers' Musical Organization in Finalnd, Hämeenpuisto 33 B 25, SF-33200 Tampere.

FRANCE

Académie du Disque Français et du Film musical, 68 Boulevard de Courcelles, F-75017 Paris.
American Center, 51 Rue de Bercy, F-75592 Paris Cédex 12.
Association des Festivals Internationaux de France, 16 Place du Havre, F-75009 Paris.
Association Nationale de Diffusion Culturelle, 5 Rue Bellart, F-75015 Paris.
Association pour le Developpement des Echanges Artistique et Culturels (ADEAC), 101 Boulevard Raspail, F-75006 Paris.
Bibliothèque internationale de Musique Contemporaine (BIMC), 52 Rue de l'Hotel de Ville, F-75004 Paris.
Bibliothèque Musicale Gustav Mahler, 11 bis Rue de Vézelay, F-75008 Paris.
Bibliothèque-Musée de l'Opera de Paris, 8 Rue Scribe, F-75009 Paris.
Bureau International des Sociétés Gerant les Droits d'Enregistrement et de Reproduction Méchanique (BIEM), 56 Avenue Kléber, F-75116 Paris.
Centre de Documentation de la Musique Contemporaine, 225 Avenue Charles de Gaulle, F-92521 Neuilly-sur-Seine Cédex. *Director: Marianne Lyon.*
Centre de Documentation de Musique internationale, 116 Avenue du Président Kennedy, F-75016 Paris.
Centre Européen de Documentation et d'information des Maitrises d'Enfants (CEDIME), BP 143, F-06130 Grasse. *Director: Jacques Menet.*
Chambre Syndicale de l'Edition Musicale (CSDEM), 62 Rue Blanche, F-75009 Paris. *President: Jean Devoust.*
Chambre Syndicale de la Facture instrumentale, 62 Rue Blanche, F-75009 Paris. *President: Bernard Maillot.*
Chambre Syndicale des Editeurs de Musique, Editions Choudens, 38 Rue Jean Mermoz, F-75008 Paris.
Comite National de la Musique (CNM) (French section of the International Music Council-UNESCO), 252 Rue de Faubourg St. Honoré, Salle Pleyel, F-75008 Paris.

General Manager: Jacques Masson-Forestier.
Commission d'Attribution de la Carte de Critique, 6 bis Rue Gabriel Laumain, F-75010 Paris.
Confédération internationales des Sociétés d'Auteurs et Compositeurs (CISAC), 11 Rue Keppler, F-75116 Paris.
Fédération Nationale de la Musique, 62 Rue Blanche, F-75009 Paris. *President: Pierre Henry.*
Groupe de l'Edition Audiovisuelle et Electronique (HAVE), 35 Rue Gregoire de Tours, F-75006 Paris.
Groupment des industries Electroniques (GIEL), 11 Rue Hamelin, F-75783 Paris Cédex 16.
Institute de Recherche et Coordination Acoustique/Musique, 31 Rue Saint-Merri, F-75004 Paris. *Director: Laurent Bayle; Honorary Director: Pierre Boulez.*
International Music Council (UNESCO), 1 Rue Miollis, F-75732 Paris Cédex 15. *Secretary-Gerneral: Guy Huot.*
International Music Critics Association, 11 Avenue d-Iena, F-75016 Paris.
Jeunesses musicales de France, 20 Rue Geoffroy l'Asnier, F-75004 Paris. *Director: Robert Berthier.*
Musicora: Salon de la Musique, 62 Rue de Miromesnil, F-75008 Paris.
Réunion des Théâtres Lyriques de France, Délégation Permanente in Paris, 7 Rie du Helder, F-75009 Paris.
Société Alkan, Rue de Saussure, F-75017 Paris. *Chief Officer: Laurent Martin.*
Société des Auteurs et Compositeurs Dramatiques (SACD), 11 bis Rue Ballu, F-75009 Paris. *Chief Officer; Jean-Jacques Plantin.*
Société des Auteurs, Compositeurs et Editeurs (SACE), 62 Rue Blanche, F-75009 Paris. *President: Wladimir Walberg.*
Société des Auteurs, Compsituers et Editeurs de Musqiue (SACEM), 225 Avenue Charles de Gaulle, F 92521 Neuilly-sur-Seine Cédex.
Director-General: Jean-Loup Tournier.
Société pour l'Administration de Droit de Reproduction Méchanique des Auteurs, Compositeurs et Editeurs (SDRM), 225 Avenue de Charles de Gaulle, F-92521 Neuilly-sur-Seine Cédex.
Syndicat des Artistes de Variétés-Syndicat des Artistes Lyriques, 29 Rue Jean Jacques Rousseau, F-75001 Paris.
Syndicat des Artistes Musiciens Professionnels de Paris et de la Région Parisienne (SAMUP), 14-16 Rue des Lilas, F-75019 Paris.
Secretary-General: François Nowak.
Syndicat des industries de Materiels Audiovisuels Electroniques (SIMAVELEC), 11 Rue Hamelin, F-75783 Paris Cédex 16.
Syndicat Francais des Artistes interprétes (SFA), 21 bis Rue Victor Massé, F-75009 Paris.
Syndicat National des Agents Artistiques et Litteraires (SNAAL), 17 tRue Brey, F-75017 Paris. *President: Roland Bertin.*
Syndicat National des Artistes Musiciens de France (SNAM), 14-16 Rue des Lilas, F-75019 Paris. *Secretary-General: François Nowak.*
Syndicat National des Auteurs et des Compositeurs de Musique 80 Rue Taitbout, F-75442 Paris Cédex 09.
Syndicat National des Chefs d'Orchestre, 3 Rue Chateau d'Eau, F-75010 Paris.
Union des Artistes, 21 bis Rue Victor Massé, F-75009 Paris.

GERMANY

Akademie der Künste Berlin, Hanseatenweg 10, W-1000 Berlin 21. *President: Prof Dr Walter Jens.*
Allgemeiner Cäcilien-Verband für Deutschland (ACV Dautschland), Andreasstrasse 9, W-8400 Regensburg. *President: Dr Wolfgang Bretschneider.*
Arbeitsgemeinschaft der Leiter musikpädagogischer Studiengänge in der Bundesrepublik Deutschland (ALMS/BRD), Hochschule der Künste Berlin, Fachbereichb 8/KWE 2, Fasanenstrasse 1, W-1000 Berlin 12. *Speaker: Prof Dr Ulrich Mahlert.*
Arbeitsgemeinschaft der Leidermacherinnen und Liedermacher aus der Bundesrepublik Deutschland (AG Song), Mailänder Strasse 14/92, Frankfurt am Main.
Contact: Stephan Rögner.
Arbeitsgemeinschaft der Musikakademien, Konservatorien und Hochschulinstitute, Städtische Akademie für Tonkunst, Ludwigshöhstrasse 120, Darmstadt.
Chairman: Hartmut Gerhold.
Arbeitgemeinschaft der Volksmusikverbände e.V. (AVV), Rudolf-Maschke-Platz 6, W-7218 Trossingen. *President: Dr Johann Bauer.*
Arbeitsgemeinschaft Deutsche Saxophonisten e.V. (ARDESA), Rötenäckrtstrasse 2, W-8500 Nürnberg 90. *Chairman: Günter Priesner.*
Arbeitsgemeinschaft Deutscher Chorverbände (ADC), Adersheimer Strasse 60, W-3340 Wolfenbüttel. *Chairman: Lore Auerbach.*
Arbeitsgemeinschaft Deutscher Studentenorchester, Wilhelmstrasse 30, W-7400 Tübingen. *Chairman: Helmut Calgéer.*
Arbeitsgemeinschaft Deutscher Zupfinstrumenten-Verbände (AZV), Rissweg 22, W-7507 Pfinztal 2. *Chairman: Adolf Mössner.*
Arbeitsgemeinschaft freikirchlicher Chorwerke in Europa (AFC), Westfalenweg 207, W-5600 Wuppertal 1. *Chairman: Pastoe Frieder Ringeis.*
Arbeitsgemeinschaft für mittelrheinische Musikgeschichte e V, Musikwissenschaftliches Institut der Universität Mainz,
Arbeitsstelle für landeskundliche Musikforschung, Welderweg 18, Pf 3980, W-6500 Mainz. *Chairman: Prof Dr Christoph-Hellmut Mahling.*
Arbeitsgemeinschaft für rheinische Musikgeschichte e V, Musikwissenschaftliches Institut der Universität Köln, Albertus-Magnus-Platz, W-5000 Cologne.
Chairman: Prof Dr Siegfried Kross.
Arbeitsgemeinschaft Musik in der Evangelischen Jugend e. V. (AG Musik), Dorfstrasse 4, W-2309 Löptin. *Chairman: Carl-Walter Petersen.*
Arbeitsgemeinschaft Schulmusik an den Hochschulen für Msuik in der Bundesrepublik Deutschland, Musikhochschule Lübeck, Grosse Peters-grube 17-29,
W-2400 Lübeck. *Chairman: Prof Dr Wilfried Ribke.*
Arbeitsgemeinschaft zur Talentförderung in der Popularmusik und Unterhaltung, Rosenheimer Strasse 11, W-8000 Munich 80. *Director: Prof Hr h.c. Erich Schulze.*
Arbeitskreis der Musikbildungsstatten in der Bundesrepublik Deutschland, Landesakademie für die musikierende Jugend in Baden-Wüttemberg, Dr Hans-Bruno Ernst, Schlossbezirk 6, Pf. 1180, W-7955, Ochsenhausen.
Arbeitskreis der Orgelsachverständigen, Hohenstrasse 19, W-7541 Straubenhardt 6 (Langenalb). *Chairman: KMD Heinrich R Trötschel.*
Arbeitskreis für Schulmusik und allgemeine Musikpädagogik e.V. (AFS), Gründgensstrasse 16, W-2000 Hamburg 60. *Chairman: Prof Dr Volker Schütz.*
Arbeitskreis Musik in der Jugend e.V. (AMJ) (Deutsche Foderation junger Chore und Intrumentalgruppen), Adersheimer Strasse 60, W-3340 Wolfenbüttel.
Chairman: Lore Auerbach.
Arbeitskreis Musikpädagogische Forschung e.V. (AMPF), Nycolaystrasse, W-4790 Paderborn-Dahl. *Chairman: Dr Georg Maas.*
Arbeitskreis sorbischer Musikschaffender (ASM) beim sorbischen Künstlerbund e.V., Postplatz 2, 0-8600 Bautzen. *Chairman: Merko Solta-Scholze.*
A rbeitskreis Studium Populärer Musik e.V., Alenka Barber-Kersovan, Ahornweg 154, W-2083 Halstenbek.**Bayerische Akademie der Schönen Künste,** Max-Joseph-Platz, W-8000 Munich 22. *President: Heinz Friedrich.*
Bayerischer Landesverein für Heimatpflege e.V. Beratungsstelle für Volksmusik, Ludwigstrasse 23, Rgb., W-8000 Munich 22. *1st Chairman: Max Streibl.*
Bayerischer Musiklehrer-Verband e.V., Willibaldstrasse 49, W-8000 Munich 21. *Chairman: Roland Sieber.*
Beethoven-Gesellschaft München e.V., Karwendelstrasse 6, W-8011 Poring. *President: Dr Rüdiger V Canal.*
Berufsverband der Musiktherapeuten Deutschlands e.V. (BMD), Waldhüterofad 38, W-1999 Berlin 37. *Chairman: Herbert Lunkenheimer.*
Berusfverband für Kunst-, Musik-und Tanztherapie: Europäischer Dachverband für kunstlerische Therapien e.V., Grüner Hang 16, W-4400 Münster.
Chairman: Prof Dr Georg Hörmann.
Berufsverband klinischer Musiktherapeuten in der Bundesrepublik Deutschland e.V., Stader Weg 31, W-2800 Bremen. *Chairman: Ilse Wolfram.*
Bildungswerk Rhythmik e.V. (BWR), Kalscheurer Weg S Nr. 12, W-5000 Cologne 1. *Chairman: Christine Humpert.*
Bogenforschungsgesellscaft: Förderverein zur Darstellung und Entwicklung von Bogenformen für Musikinstrumente e.V., Ankerstrasse 34, W-5205 Sankt Augustin. *Chairman: Rudolf Gahler.*
Brahmsgellschaft Baden-Baden e.V., Pf. 1609, W-1609, W-7560 Gaggenau. *Chairman: Dr Werner Hoppe.*

Brandenburgiaches Colloquiem für Neue Musik e V, Clara-Zetkin-Strasse 1, 0-1276 Buckow.

Bruder-Busch-Gesellschaft e V, Untere Wiesenstrasse 33, W-5912 Hilchenbach. *Business Manager: Wolfgang Burbcah.*

Bund Christlicher Posaunenchöre Deutschlands e V (BCPD), Sophienstrasse 21 D, W-7000 Stuttgart 1. *Chairman: Pastor Reiner Haidle*

Bund der Theatergemeinden e V, Bonner Talweg 10, W-5300 Bonn 1. *President: Friedrich von Kekulé*

Bund Deutscher Blasmusikverbände e V (BDB), Am Märzengraben 6, W-7800 Freiburg im Breisgau. *1st President: Dr Norbert Nothhelfer*

Bund Deutscher Klavierbauer e V, Frankenwert 35, W-5000 Cologne 1. *Chairman: Udo Schmidt*

Bund Deutscher Liebhaberorchester e V (BDLO), Schlegelstrasse 14, W-8500 Nürnberg. *Chairman: Dr Joachim Conradi.*

Bund Deutscher Orgelbaumeister e v (BDO), Frankfurter Ring 243, W-8000 Munich 40. *1st Chairman: Hans-Gerd Klais*

Bund Deutscher Zupfmusiker e V (BDZ), Huulkamp 26, W-2000 Hamburg 65. *Chairman: Rüdiger Grambow.*

Bund sorbischer Gesangsvereine: Zwjazk serbskich spewarskich towarstwow, Haus der Sorben, Referat Kultur, Postplatz 2, 0-8600 Bautzen. *Chairman: Achim Brankatschk.*

Bundes-Eltern-Vertretung e V der Musikschulen des VdM, Ossietzkkyring 55, W-3000 Hanhover 91. *1st Chairman: Dieter Fröhling*

Bundesfachgruppe Musikpädagogik e V (Bfg), Eosanderstrasse 24, W-1000 Berlin 10. *Chairman: Prof Dr Thomas Ott.*

Bundesinnungverband für das Musikinstrumenten-Handwerk (BIV), Kreishandwerkerschaft Köln, Frankenwerft 35, Cologne. *Chairman: Johann Scholtz.*

Bundesverband der Deutschen Musikinstrumenten-Hersteller e V (BdMH), Hildastrasse 5, W-6200 Wiesbaden. *1st Managing Director: Winfried Baumbach.*

Bundesverband der deutschen Volksbühnen-Vereine e V, Am Handelshof 9, W-4300 Essen 1. *Chairman: Axel Wolters.*

Bundesverband der Jugendkunstschulen und kulturpädagogischer Einrichtungen e V (BJKE), Luisenstrasse 22, W-4750 Unna. *Chairman: Peter Vermeulen.*

Bundesverband der Phonographischen Wirtschaft e V (Bundesverband Phono), Greickstrasse 36, W-2000 Hamburg 54. *Chairman: Thomas M Stein.*

Bundesverband Deutscher Gesangspädagogen e V (BDG), Waldeck 7, W-4930 Detmold. *President: Professor Helmut Kretschmar.*

Bundesverband für Tanztherapie Deutschland e V, Hostrasse 16, Marienburg, W-4019 Monheim. *1st Chairman: Wally Kaechele.*

Bundesverband Rhythmische Erziehung e V (BRE), Akademie Remscheid, Küppelstein 34, W-5630 Remscheid 1. *Chairman: Prof Brigitte Steinmann.*

Bundesverband Studentische Kulturarbeit e V (BSK), Kaiserstrasse 32, W-5300 Bonn 1.

Bundesvereinigung der Musikveranstalter e V, Kronprinzenstrasse 46, W-5300 Bonn 2. *President: Leo Imhoff.*

Bundesvereinigung Deutscher Blas-und Volksmusikverbände e V (BDBV), König-Karl-Strasse 13, W-7000 Stuttgart 50. *President: Minister Gerhard Weiser.*

Bundesvereinigung Deutscher Laienmusikverbande (BDLV), Arbeitsgemeinschaft der Volksmusikverbande, Rudolf-Maschke-Platz 6, W-7218 Trossingen.

Bundesvereinigung Kulturelle Jugendbildung e V (BKJ), Küppelstein 34, W-5630 Remscheid. *Chairman: Prof Bruno Tetzner.*

BVT-Bundesverband Ton der Film-Tonmeister in der Bundesrepublik Deutschland e V, Jenfelder Allee 80, W-2000 Hamburg 70.

Carl-Orff-Stiftung, Königinstrasse 25, W-8000 Munich 22. *Chairman: Liselotte Orff.*

Chopin-Gesellschaft in der Bundesrepublik Deutschland e V, Kasinostrasse 3 (J F Kenedy-Haus), W-6100 Darmstadt 11. *President: Maciej Lukasz*

Christlicher Sängerbund e V (CS), Westfalenweg 207, W-5600 Wuppertal 1.

Club Deutscher Drehorgelfreunde e V, Wilfried Hömmerich, Brusseler Strasse 20, Pf 170103, W-5300 Bonn 1. *Chairman: Wilfried Hömmerich.*

Confédération des Associations des Facteurs d'Instruments de Musique de la CEE (CAFIM), Hildstrasse 5, W-6200 Wiesbaden. *President: Bernard Mailot.*

Deutsche Angestellten-Gewerkschaft (DAG), Karl-Marx-Platz 1, Pf 301230, Hamburg.

Deutsche Arbeitsgemeinschaft für Akustik (DAGA), Hauptstrasse 5, W-5340 Bad Honnef 1. *Chairman: Prof Dr H Kuttruff.*

Deutsche Disc-Jockey-Organization (DDO), Kaiser-Friedrich-Alle 1-3, W-5100 Aachen. *Contact: Klaus Quirini.*

Deutsche Forschungsgemeinschaft e V (DFG), Kennedyalle 40 Pf 205004, W-5300 Bonn 2. *President: Prof Dr Wolfgang Fruhwald.*

Deutsche Frank-Martin-Gesellschaft e V, Hochschule für Musik Köln, Dagobertstrasse 38, W-5000 Cologne 1. *President: Dirk Schortemeier.*

Deutsche Gesellschaft für Flote e V, Eschenheimer Anlage 30, W-6000 Frankfurt am Main 1. *President: András Adorján.*

Deutsche Gesellschaft für Musik bei Behinderten e V (DGMB), Frangenheimstrasse 4, W-5000 Cologne 41. *Chairman: Prof Dr Helmut Moog.*

Deutsche Gesellschaft für Musikpsychologie e V (DGfM), Meisenweg 7, W-3008 Garbsen 1. *Chairman: Prof Dr Klaus-Ernst Behne.*

Deutsche für Musiktherapie e V, (DGMT), Collinistrasse 22, Pf 100738, W-6800 Mannheim 1. *1st Chairman: Franz Mecklenbeck.*

Deutsche Gesellschaft für Volkstanz e V (DGV), Anni Herrmann, Paul-Lincke-Ufer 25, W-1000 Berlin 36. *Chairman: Gerhard Palmer.*

Deutsche Glockenspiel-Vereinigung e V, Dr K F Waack, Stedebring 7, W-3000 Hannover 71. *Chairman: Dr Karl-Friedrich Waack.*

Deutsche Johann-Strauss-Gesellschaft e V, Untere Anlage 2, W-8630 Coburg. *Chairman: Arthur Kulling.*

Deutsche Mozart-Gesellschaft e V (DMG), Karlstrasse 6, W-8900 Augsburg.

Deutsche Musikinstrumentenstiftung, Emil-Nolde-Weg 29, W-3400 Göttingen. *Chairman: Prof Dr Jürgen Costede.*

Deutsche Orchestervereinigung e V in der DAG (DOV), Heimhuder Strasse 5, W-2000 Hamburg 13. *Chairman: Dr Rolf Dünnwald.*

Deutsche Phono-Akademie e V (DPhA), Grelckstrasse 36, W-2000 Hamburg 54. *Chairman: Gerd Gebhardt.*

Deutsche Richard-Wagner-Gesellschaft e V, Schlosstrasse 9a, W-1000 Berlin 28. *1st Chairman: Prof Uwe Faerber.*

Deutsche Rossini-Gesellschaft e V, Hohenheimerstrasse 84, W-7000 Stuttgart 1. *1st Chairman: Gustav Kuhn.*

Deutsche Sängerschaft (Weimarer CC), Cranachweg 9, W-7320 Göppingen. *Chairman: Franz Jedlitschka.*

Deutsche Schubert-Gesellschaft e V (DSG), Handelstrasse 6, W-4100 Duisburg 14 (Rheinhausen). *Chairman: Günter Berns.*

Deutsche Sektion der Internationalen Gesellschaft für Elektroakustische Musik e V (DecimE), Treuchtlinger Strasse 8, Berlin. *Chairman: Folkmar Hein.*

Deutsche Stiftung Musikleben (DSM), Herrengraben 3, W-2000 Hamburg 11. *President: Erhard Bouillons.*

Deutsche Suzuki Gesellschaft e V, Ankerstrasse 34, W-5205 Sankt Augustin 1. *1st Chairman: Rudolf Gahler.*

Deutscher Akkordeonlehrer-Verband e V (DALV), Kapfstrasse 68, W-7218 Trossingen 1. *Chairman: Wolfgang Eschenbacher.*

Deutscher Allgemeiner Sängerbund e V (DAS), Dohlenstrasse 11, W-4600 Dortmund 15. *President: Fritz Neuhaus.*

Deutscher Berufsverband für Tanzpadagogik e V, Hollestrasse 1g, W-4300 Essen 1. *1st Chairman: Ulrich Roehm.*

Deutscher Bühnenverein-Bundesverband deutscher Theater e V (DBV), Quatermarkt 5, W-5000 Cologne 1. *Contact: Rolf Golwin.*

Deutscher Bundesverband der Spielmanns-, Fanfaren-, Hörner-und Musikzüge e V, Haupstrasse 61, W-3300 Braunschweig. *President: Paul Mittag.*

Deutscher Bundesverband Tanz e V (DBT), Küppelstein 34, W-5630 Remscheid. *Chairman: Annmargret Pretz.*

Deutscher Chorverband Pueri Cantores, Zwölfling 12, W-4300 Essen 1. *President: Georg Sump.*

Deutscher Feuerwehrverband e V: Fachgebiet Musik, Koblenzer Strasse 133, W-5300 Bonn 2. *President: Hinrich Struve.*

Deutscher Harmonika-Verband e V (DHV), Rudolf-Maschke-Platz 6, Pf 1150, W-7218 Trossingen 1. *President: Ernst Pfister.*

Deutscher Hotel-und Gaststättenverband (DEHOGA), Fachabteilung musikveranstaltende Betriebe, Kronprinzenstr. 46, Bonn. *Chairman: Otto Manfred Lamm.*

Deutscher Komponisten-Verband e V (DKV), Beuckestrasse 26, W-1000 Berlin 37. *President: Karl Heinz Wahren.*

Deutscher Kulturrat, Adenaueralle 7, W-5300 Bonn 1.

Deutscher Musikrat e V (DMR), Nationalkomitee der Bundesrepublik Deutschaland im Internationalen Musikrat, Am Michaelshof 4a, W-5300 Bonn 2. *President: Prof Dr Franz Müller-Heuser.*

Deutscher Musikverleger-Verband e V (DMV), Friedrich-Wilhelm-Strasse 31, W-5300 Bonn 1. *General Manager: Dr H H Wittgen.*

Deutscher Rockmusiker-Verband e V, Kolbergerstrasse 30, W-2120 Lüneburg. *Chairman: Ole Seelenmeyer.*

Deutscher Sängerbund e V (DSB), Bernhardstrasse 166, Pf 510628, W-5000 Cologne 51. *President: Dr Heinz Eyrich.*

Deutscher Schützenbund e V, Fachgruppe Musik, Niedersächsischer Sportschützenverband, Wunstorfer Lanndstrasse 57, W-3000 Hannover 91.

Deutscher Tanzrat/Deutscher ballettrat e V, Bonner Künstlerhaus, Graurheindorfer Strasse 23, W-5300 Bonn 1. *Chairman: Iskra Zankova.*

Deutscher Textdichter-Verband e V, Dohlenweg 5, W-5020 Frechen. *President: Heinz Korn.*

Deutscher Tonkünstlerverband e V, Verband deutscher Musikerzieher und konzertierender Künstler (VDMK), Landsberger Str 425, Munich. *President: Prof Dr Inka Stampfl.*

Deutscher Turner-Bund e V, Fachgebiet Musik und Spielmannswesen, Bernhard Lott, Ellernstrasse 20, W-3000 Hannover 1. *President: Prof Dr Jürgen Dieckert.*

Deutscher Zithermusik-bund e V (DZB), Ulrich Oesterle, Steigäcker 4, W-7140 Ludwigsburg.

Deutsches High-Fidelity Institu e V (DHFI), Karlstrasse 19-21, W-6000 Frankfurt am Main 1. *Chairman: Karl Breh.*

Deutsches Tubaforum e V, Saarbrückener Stasse 26, W-3000 Hannover 71. *Chairman: Prof Klemens Propper.*

Die Kunstlergilde e V, Hafenmarkt 2, W-7300 Esslingen/Neckar. *Chairman: Albrecht Baehr.*

Dr Hanns-Simon-Stiftung, Bedaplatz, W-5520 Bitburg.

Dramatiker-Union e V (DU), Bismarckstrasse 107, W-1000 Berlin 12. *President: Prof Giselher Klebe.*

Dramaturgische Gesellschaft e V, Tempelhofer Ufer 22, W-1000 Berlin 61. *Chairman: Dr Klaus Pierwoss.*

Dresdner Zentrum für zeitgenössische Musik, Schevenstrasse 17/150-05, 0-8054 Dresden. *Director: Prof Udo Zimmermann.*

Emil-Berliner-Stiftung in der Deutschen Phono-Akademie e V, Grelckstrasse 36, W-2000 Hamburg 54. *Chairman: Richard Busch.*

EPTA-Gesellschaft der Padagogik für Tasteninstrumente e V, Bult 6, W-4590 Cloppenburg. *Chairman: Prof Edith Picht-Axenfeld.*

Ernst-Pepping-Gesellschaft e V, Jebensstrasse 3, W-1000 Berlin 12. *Chairman: Prof Dr Heinrich Poos.*

E T A-Hoffmann-Gesellschaft e V, Dr Georg Wirth, Wetzelstrasse 19, W-8600 Bamberg. *1st Chairman: Dr Georg Wirth.*

Ernst-von-Siemens-Stiftung, Zug (Schweiz), Wittelsbacherplatz 2, W-8000 Munich 2.

Eugen-Jochum-Gesellschaft e V, Marktplatz 14, Kulturamt, W-8942 Ottobeuren. *President: Dr Georg Simnacher.*

Europa Cantat-Europäische Föderation Junger Chöre e V (EC-EFJC), Grosser Hillen 38, W-3000 Hannover 71. *Secretary-General: Hans Dieter Reinecke.*

Europäische Arbeitsgemeinschaft Schulmusik (EAS) (European Alliance for School Music), Bundesgeschaftsstelle VDS, Weihergarten 5, Mainz.

Europäische Union der Musikwettbewerbe für die Jugend-European Union of Music Competitions for Youth (EMCY), Herzog-Johann-Strasse 10, W-8000 Munich 60. *Contact: Dr Eckart Rohlfs.*

European Guitar Teachers Association (EGTA), Haslei 40, W-4780 Lippstadt. *1st chairmen: Reinhard Froese and Michael Koch.*

European String Teachers Association (ESTA)-Union der Bundesrepublik Deutschland e V, Dagmar klevenhusen, Friedenweg 6, W-2807 Achim.

Evangelischer Sängerbund e V (ESB), Bremer Strasse 2, W-5600 Wuppertal 1. *Chairman: Rudolf Steege.*

Fachverband Deutsche Klavierindustrie e V (FDK), Friedrich-Wilhelm-Strasse 31, W-5300 Bonn 1. *General Manager: Dr Hans-Henning Wittgen.*

Fachverbad Deutscher Berufscholeiter e V (FDB), Unkenweg 19, W-4330 Müllheim/Ruhr.

Fachverband Historische Tasteninstrumente e V (FHT), Untermarkt 40, W-8190 Wolfratshausen. *Chairman: Reinhard Hoppe.*

Fachverband Unterhaltungselektronik im Zentralverband Elektrotechnik-und Elektroniindustrie e V, Stresemannallee 19, W-6000 Frankfurt am Main 70. *Chairman: Wilhelm Kahle.*

Ferenc-Fricsay Gesellschaft e V (FFG), Heerstrasse 70, W-1000 Berlin 19. *Chairman: Prof Dr Wolfgang Geisler.*

Förderkreis Hugo Herrmann e V, Ringinger Tal 26, W-7453 Burladingen. *Chairman: Werner Zintgraf.*

Förderkreis Instrumentales Musizieren e V, Friedrich-Wilhelm-Strasse 31, W-5300 Bonn 1. *Chairman: Alfred Döll.*

Förderkreis Unterhaltungsmusik e V (FKU), Ringstrasse 4, W-4223 Voerde 1. *Chairman: Kurt Althans.*

Förderverein der Klassischen Gesangskunst in Deutschland e V, Pf. 101516, W-7000 Stuttgart 10. *Chairman: Prof Sylvia Geszty.*

Fonds Darstellende Künste e V, Am Handelshof 9, W-4300 Essen 1. *Chairman: Prof Dr Jürgen-Dieter Waidelich.*

Fonds Soziokultur e V, Stirnband 10, W-5800 Hagen 1. *Chairman: Dr Olaf Schwencke.*

Forschungsgemeinschaft Musikinstrumente e V (FG), Hildastrasse 5, W-6200 Wiesbaden. *Chairman: Hugo Schreiber.*

Franz-Grothe-Stiftung, Rosenheimer Strasse 11, W-8000 Munich 80. *Chairman: Hans Schröpf.*

Franz-Liszt-Gesellschaft e V Weimar, Platz der Demokratie 2/3, 0-5300 Weimar. *President: Prof Dr Detlef Altenburg.*

Franz-Wirth-Gedächtnis-Stiftung zur Förderung der musikalischen Nachwuchses, Spitalerstrasse 28, W-2000 Hamburg 1. *Chairman: Margot Brandes.*

Frau und Musik-Internationaler Arbeitkreis e V Geschäftsstelle, Adelheid Klammt, Vogesort 8 F, W-3000 Hannover 91. *Chairman: Prof Siegrid Ernst.*

Freie Akademie der Künste Hamburg, Ferdinandstor la, W-2000 Hamburg. *President: Prof Armin Sandig.*

Freunde der Querflöte e V Gevelsberg-Gemeinrütziger Verein zur Erforschung und Förderung des Querflötenspeils (fdq), Körnerstrasse 51, W-5820 Gevelsberg. *Chairman: Elli Edler-Busch.*

Freunde der Tonkunst und Musikerziehung e V, Landsberger Strasse 425, W-8000 Munich 60. *1st Chairman: Dr Rüdiger von Canal.*

Freidich-Kiel-Gesellschaft e V, Ithstrasse 20, W-3256 Coppenbrügge 1. *1st Chairman: Dr Jürgen Böhme.*

Fritz-Büchtger-Kuratorium, Musica Sacra Viva, Pf. 750202, W-8000 Munich 75. *Chairman: Andreas Weymann.*

GEDOK-Verband der Gemeinschaften der Künstlerinnen und Kunstfreunde e V, Einern 29, W-5600 Wuppertal 2. *President: Dr Renate Massmann.*

GEMA-Stiftung, Rosenheimer Strasse 11, W-8000 Munich 80. *Chairman: Prof Dr Reinhold Kreile.*

Genossenshaft Deutscher Bühnenangehöriger (GDBA) in der DAG, Feldbrunnenstrasse 74, W-2000 Hamburg 13. *President: Hans Herdlein.*

Georg Hesse Stiftung, Am Brühl 13, W-7825 Lenzkirch 3 (Kappel). *Chairman: Hannelore Hesse-Mange.*

Georg-Friedrich-Händel-Gesellschaft-Internationale Vereinigung e V, Händelhaus, Grosse Nikolaistr. 5/6, Halle an der Saale. *President: Prof Dr Bernd Baselt.*

Gesamtverband Deutscher Muskfachgeschäfte e V (GDM), Friedrich-Wilhelm-Strasse 31, W-5300 Bonn 1. *General Manager: Dr H H Wittgen.*

Gesellschaft der Orgelfreunde e V (GdO), Josestrasse 6, W-6642 Mettlach 1. *Chairman: Prof Alfred Reichling.*

Gesellschaft für Alte Musik e V (GAM), Birkenstrasse 18, W-7218 Trossingen. *Chairman: Prof Dr Ludger Lohmann.*

Gesellschaft für Bayerische Musikgeschichte e V, Pf 100611, W-8000 Munich 1. *Chairman: Prof Dr Theodor Göllner.*

Gesellschaft für Musikforschung (GfM), Heinrich-Schüz-Allee, W-3500 Kassel. *President: Prof Dr Klaus W Niemöller.*

Gesellschaft für Musikpädagogik e V (GMP), Von-der-Tann-Strasse 38, W-8400 Regensburg. *Chairman: Prof Dr Reinhard Schneider.*

Gesellschaft für Musikwissenschaft e V, Akademie der Künste, Luisenstrasse 58-60, 0-0140 Berlin. *President: Dr Klaus Mehner.*

Gesellschaft für Neue Musik e V (GNM)-Sektion Bundesrepublik Deutschland der Internationalen Gesellschaft für Neue Musik (IGNM), Schwedlerstrasse 2-4, W-6000 Frankfurt am Main 1. *President: Friedrich Goldmann.*

Gesellschaft für Selbstspielende Musikinstrumente e V, Heiligenstock 46, W-5060 Bergisch Gladbach 2. *Chairman: Dr Jürgen Hocker.*

Gesellschaft für Theatergeschichte e V, Mecklenburgische Strasse 56, W-1000 Berlin 33. *Chairman: Prof Dr Peter Spengel.*

Gesellschaft zur Förderung der Berufsbildung junger Künstler e V (GFBK), Eichkatzweg 25, W-3107 Hambuhren.

Gesellschaft zur Förderung der Westfalischen Kulturarbeit e V, Landschaftsverband Westfalen-Lippe, Warendorfer Str 14, Münster. *Chairman: Reinhold Brauner.*

Gottfried-Silbermann-Gesellschaft e V, Beethovenstrasse 7, 0-9200 Freiberg/Sachsen. *President: Hans Otto.*

Gotthard-Schierse-Stiftung, Bundesallee 1-12, W-1000 Berlin 15. *Chairman: Horst Göbel.*

Günter Henle Stiftung München, G Henle Verlag, Forstenrieder Allee 122, Pf 710466, W-8000 Munich 71. *Chairman: Anne Liese Henle.*

Günter-Neumann-Stiftung, Schlüterstrasse 36, W-1000 Berlin 12. *Chairman: Dr Hans Peter Wüst.*

Hamburger Bach-Gesellschaft e V, Internationaler Verëin für die Musik der Bach-Sohne (HBG), Durchschnitt 25, Hamburg. *Chairman: Prof Edith Picht-Axenfeld.*

Hamburger Telemann-Gesellschaft e V, Haus der Patriotischen Gesellschaft, Trostbrücke 4, W-2000 Hamburg 11. *Chairman: Eckart Klessmann.*

Hamburgische Kulturstiftung, Chilehaus C, Burckardplatz 13, W-2000 Hamburg 1.

Hans-Breuer-Stiftung zur Pflege und Förderung des deutschen Liedgutes e V, Hochschule für Musik and Theater, Harvestehuder Weg 10-12, W-2000 Hamburg 13. *Chairman: Prof Dr Hermann Rauhe.*

Hans-Pfitzner-Gesellschaft e V, Mauerkircher Strasse 8, W-8000 Munich 80. *Chairman: General Music Director Prof Rolf Reuter.*

Heinrich-Heine-Gesellschaft e V (HHG), Bolkerstrasse 53, Pf 1120, W-4000 Düsseldorf 1. *Chairman: Gerd Högener.*

Heinrich-Kaminski-Gesellschaft e V, Storchen-Apotheke, Hauptstrasse 20, W-7890 Waldshut-Tiengen 2. *1st Chairman: Jürgen Klein.*

Herbert von Karajan Stifung, Prof Peter Csobádi, Seestrasse 13, A-5322 Hof bei Salzburg.

Industriegewerkschaft Medien-Druck und Papier, Publizistik und Kunst (IG Medien), Friedrichstrasse 15, Pf 102451, Stuttgart. *Chairman: Erwin Ferlemann.*

Institut für Bildung und Kultur e V (IBK), Küppelstein 34, W-5630 Remscheid. *Chairman: Prof Bruno Tetzner.*

Institut für Neue Musik und Musikerziehung e V, Grafenstrasse 35, W-6100 Darmstadt. *Chairman: Dr Susanne Liegler.*

Institut für Studien der Musikkultur des Portugiesischen Sprachraumes, An Der Münze 1, D-50668 Cologne. *Contact: Dr Harald Hülskath*

Interessenverband Deutscher Komponisten e V (IDK), Willinghusener Landstrasse 70, W-2000 Barsbüttel. *Chairman: Gustav Kneip.*

Interessenverband Deutscher Konzertveranstaler und Künstlervermittler e V (IDKV) Lenhartstrasse 15, W-2000 Hamburg 20. *President: Jens Michow.*

International Council for Traditional Music (ICTM)-Nationalkomitee der Bundeserpublik Deutschland, Otto-Friedrich-Universität Bamberg-Volksmusik, Feldkirchenstrasse 21, W-8600 Bamberg. *President: Prof Dr Marianne Bröcker.*

International Federation of the Phonographic Industry (IFPI)-Deutsche Landesgruppe, Grelckstrasse 36, W-2000 Hamburg 54. *Chairman: Helmut Fest.*

Internationale Andreas-Werckmeister-Gesellschaft e V, Kulturamt der Stadt Halberstadt, Dominikanerstrasse 16, Halberstad. *President: Dr Rüdiger Pfeiffer.*

Internationale Arbeitsgemeinschaft der Theaterbesucherorganisationen (IATO), Am Handelshof 9, Essen. *President: Prof Dr Jurgen-Dieter Waidelich.*

International Carl-Maria-von-Weber-Gesellschaft e V, Staatsbibliothek zu Berlin (Preussischer Kulturbsitz), Musikabteilung, Unter den Linden 8, Pf 1312, 0-1086 Berlin. *Chairman: Dr Ute Schwab.*

Internationale Discotheken Organisationen, Deutsche Diskotheken-Unternehmer, Kaiser-Friedrich-Allee 1-3, W-5100 Aachen. *Contact: Halga Quirini.*

Internationale Draeseke-Gesellschaft e V, Matthias-Grünewald-Strasse 5, W-6720 Speyer. *1st Chairman: Dr Helmut Loos.*

Internationale Fasch-Gesellschaft e V, Franciceum Zerbst, Weinberg 1, 0-3400 Zerbst. *President: Dr Rüdiger Pfeiffer.*

Internationale Föderation für Chormusik-International Federation for Choral Music (IFCM), Burgstrasse 33, Bonn. *President: Dr H Royce Saltzmann.*

Internationale Gesellschaft für Musik in der Medisin e V (ISFMIM), Paulmannshöher Strasse 17, W-5880 Ludenscheid. *Chairman: Dr Roland Droh.*

Internationale Gesellschaft für Musikerziehung (ISME), Deutsche Sektion, Deutscher Musikrat/AGMM, Am Michaelsahof 4 a, W-5300 Bonn 2.

Internationale Gesellschaft für musikpädagogische Fortbildung e V (IGMF) Pf 1443, W-5920 Bad Berleburg. *Chairman: Prof Dr Hans-Walter Berg.*

Internationale Gesellschaft für Urheberrecht e V (INTERGU), Rosenheimer Strasse 11, W-8000 Munich 80.

Internationale Gitarristische Vereinigung Freiburg e V (IGVF), Lessingstrasse 4, W-7800 Freiburg im Breisgau. *Chairman: Jörg Sommermeyer.*

Internationale Heinrich-Schütz-Gesellschaft e V (ISG), Heinrich-Schütz-Allee 35, W-5300 Kassel. *Chairman: Prof Dr Arno Forchert.*

Internationale Hugo-Wolf-Akademie für Gesang-Dichtung-Liedkunst e V, Neckarstrasse 86, W-7000 Stuttgart 1. *Chairman: Dr Rainer Wilhelm.*

Internationale Johann-Nepomuk-David-Gesellschaft E V (IDG), Fichenstrasse 19, W-7336 Uhingen. *Chairman: Wolfgang Dallmann.*

Internationale Joseph-Martin-Kraus-Gesellschaft e V, Kellereistrasse 25, Pf 1422, W-6967 Buchen 1. *Chairman: Prof Dr Friedrich W Riedel.*

Internationale Louis Spohr Gesellschaft e V, Schöne Aussicht 2, W-3500 Kassel. *President: Wolfgang Windführ.*

Internationale Meyerbeer-Gesellschaft e V, Tristanstrasse 10, W-8034 Germering. *Chairman: Karl Zelenka.*

Internationale Posaunenvereinigung (IPV)-Sektion Deutschland, Launhardt, Hahnenstrasse 18, W-5024 Pulheim. *President: Prof Johannes Doms.*

Internationale Trompetergilde e V, Europäische Sektion (Euro-ITG), Pf 1143, Bad Sackingen. *Chairmen: Dr Edward H Tarr and Prof Max Sommerhalders.*

Internationale vereinigung der Musikbibliotheken, Musikarchive und Musikdokumentationszentren (AIBM) Gruppe Bundesrepublik Deutschland, Dr Bettina Seyfried, Gärtnerstrasse 25-32, Pf-450229, W-12207 Berlin. *President: Dr Joachim Jaenecke.*

Internationale Viola-Gesellschaft-Sektion Bundesrepublik Deutschland e V, Ahornweg 9, W-5308 Rheinbach. *1st Chairman: Prof Barbara Westphal.*

Internationaler Arbeitskreis für Musik e V (IAM), Heinrich-Schütz-Allee 29, W-3500 Kassel. *Chairman: Adolf Lang.*

Internationaler Verein Freund behinderter Tonkünstler e V, Melchiorstrasse 74, W-8000 Munich 71. *Chairman: Elisabeth Stöcklein-Weiss.*

Internationales Forum Junge Chormusik Rotenburg (Wümme), e V, Rathaus, Grosse Strasse 1, Rotenburg/Wümme. *President: Prof Dr Guy Maneveau.*

Jacques-Offenbach-Gesellschaft e V Bad Ems (JOG), Dr Günther Obst, Waldstrasse 3, W-5427 Bad Ems. *Dr Günther Obst.*

Jean Sibelius Gesellschaft Deutschland e V, Trivstrasse 19, W-8000 Munich 19. *President: Prof August Everding.*

Johann Adolph Hasse-Gesellschaft München e V, Ursula Biehl, Landsberger Strasse 55, W-8080 Fürstenfeldbruck. *Chairman: Ursula Biehl.*

Johannes-Brahms-Gesellschaft Internationale e V, Trostbrücke 4, W-2000 Hamburg 11. *President: Detlef Kraus.*

Jospeh-Haas-Gesellschaft e V (JHG), Veroneserstrasse 4, W-8000 Munich 90. *President: Prof Dr Siegfried Gmeinwieser.*

Jospeh-Suder-Gesellschaft e V, Grünwalderstrasse 250, W-8000 Munich 90. *Chairman: Reinhold Pfandzelter.*

Jürgen Ponto-Stiftung zur Förderung junger Künstler, Jürgen-Ponto-Platz 1, W-6000 Frankfurt am Main 11. *Chairman: Wolfgang Röller.*

Karg-Elert-Gesellschaft e V (KEG), Lortzingstrasse 11, W-7980 Ravensburg. *Chairmen: Prof Dr Wolfgang Stockmeier and Johannes Michel.*

Karl-Klingler-Stiftung e V, Siemens AG, Dr Rüdiger v Canal, Wittelsbacherplatz 2, W-8000 Munich 2.

Kodály-Gesellschaft e V, Conrad W Mayer, Grabenstrasse 22, W-7812 Bad Krozingen.

Körber-Stiftung, Kampchaussee 10, Pf 800660, W-2050 Hamburg 80. *Chairman: Ulrich Voswinckel.*

Konferenz der Leiter der kirchlinchen und der staatslichen Ausbildungsstatten für Kirchenmusik und der Landeskirchenmusikdirektorn in der Evangelischen Kirche in Deutschland (EKD), Miquelallee 7, W-6000 Frankfurt am Main. *President: LKMD Dr Dietrich Schuberth.*

Konferenz der Leiter katholishcer kirchenmusikalischer Ausbildungsstatten Deutschlands, Amt für Kirchenmusik, Schoferstrasse 4, W-7800 Freiburg im Breisgau. *Chairman: Prof Matthias Kreuels.*

Kulturinstitut Kompoistinnen gestern-heute e V, Theaterstrasse 11, W-6900 Heidelberg. *Chairman: Roswitha Sperber.*

Kulturkreis im Bundesverband der Deutschen Industrie e V, Gustav-Heinemann-Ufer 84-88, W-5000 Cologne 51. *Chairman: Dr Arend Oetker.*

Kulturpolitische Gesellschaft e V, Stirnband 8-10, W-5800 Hagen 1. *President: Dr Olaf Schwencke.*

Kulturstiftung des Landes Schleswig-Holstein, Ministerium für Bildung, Wissenschaft, Jugend und Kultur, Gartenstrasse 6, W-2300 Kiel 1. *Chairman: Staatssekretar Dr Peter Joachim Kreyenberg.*

Kunststiftung Baden-Württemberg GmbH, Gerokstrasse 37, W-7000 Stuttgart 1. *Chairman: Dr Christof Müller-Wirth.*

Kurt-Weill-Vereinigung Dessau, Stadtverwaltung Dessau, Dezernat IV, Kulturamt, Zerbster Strasse 1, 0-4500 Dessau. *Chairman: Dr Jürgen Schebera.*

Landgraf-Moritz-Stiftung (LMST), Heinrich-Schütz-Allee 35, Pf 100329, W-3500 Kassel. *Chairman: Walter Olbrich.*

Lehrervereinigung Schlaffhorst-Andersen-Berufsverband der Atem-, Sprech- und Stimmlehrer e V, Schule Schlaffhorst-Andersen, Bornstrasse 20, W-3052 Bad Nenndorf. *1st Chairman: Ingeborg Rinke.*

Lohmann-Stiftung Wiesbaden e V, Prinz-Nikolas-Strasse 26, W-6200 Wiesbaden. *1st Chairman: Prof Hildegund Lohmann-Becker.*

Medizinische Gesellschaft für Kunstschaffende-Musikkorthopädie und Kunstmedizin-e v, Universität Ulm, Am Hochstrasse 8, Pf 4066, Ulm. *Dr A Lahme.*

Mendelssohn-Gesellschaft e V, Zerbster Strasse 59, W-1000 Berlin 45. *Chairman: Ernst Thamm.*

Motivgruppe Musik e V, Arbeitsgemeinschaft im Bund deutscher Philatelisten e V, H J Kaufmann, Am Birkenhain 6, Voerde. *Chairman: H J Kaufmann.*

Musica Reanimata, Förderverein zur Wiederentdeckung NS-verfolgter Komponisten und ihrer Werke e V, Heidi Tamar Hoffmann, Johannisberger Strasse 12A, W-1000 Berlin 33. *Chairman: Dr Albrecht Dümling.*

Musik + Tanz + Erziehung, Orff-Schulwerk-Gesellschaft Deutschland e V, Hermann-Hummel-Strasse 25, W-8032 Lochham. *Chairman: Gerhard Kuhn.*

Musikalische Jugend Deutschlands e V (MJD)-Sektion Bundesrepublik Deutschland der Féderation Internationale des Jeunesses Musicales, Marktplatz 12, W-6992 Weikersheim. *Chairman: Dr Michael Jenne.*

Musikfonds für Musikurheber e V, Adenauerallee 134, W-5300 Bonn 1. *Chairman: Prof Dr Peter Ruzicka.*

Musiktherapie e V, Von-Esmarch Strasse 111, W-4400 Münster. *Chairman: Prof Dr Karl Hörmann.*

Neue Bachgesellschaft e V (NBG) Internationale Vereinigung, Hauptgeschäftsstelle Leipzig, Thomaskirchhof 16, Pf 727, Leipzig. *Chairman: Prof Dr h c Helmuth Rilling.*

Neue Deutsche Händel-Gesellschaft e V, Im Brögen 4 b, W-5204 Lohmar 21. *President: Prof Dr Albert Scheibler.*

Neue Zentralstelle der Bühnenautoren und Bühnenverleger GmbH, Bismarckstrasse 107, W-1000 Berlin 12. *Chairman: Dr Maria Müller-Sommer.*

NRW Zentrum für Popularmusik und Kommunikationstechnologie, Rottscheidter Strasse 6, Pf 201414, W-5600 Wuppertal 11. *Contact: Dieter Gorny.*

ORPLID internationale Gesellschaft für Musiktheater und Architektur e V, Hohenheimer Strasse 84, W-7000 Stuttgart . *Chairman: Wilhelm Keitel.*

Oscar-und-Vera-Ritter-Stiftung, Bundesstrasse 4, W-2000 Hamburg 13. *Chairman: Jürgen Wittekind.*

Otto-Jägermeier-Gedächtnisstifting, Postfach, W-5562 Manderscheid. *President: Dr Hinrich Brecht-Jägermeier.*

PE-Förderkreis für Studierende der Musik e V, Dr Ralph Landsittel, Otto-Back-Strasse 46, W-6800 Mannheim 1. *Chairman: Angelika Milos-Engelhorn.*

Percussion Creativ e V, Am Katharinenkloster 6, W-8500 Nürnberg 1. *Chairman: Prof Werner Thärichen.*

Posaunenwerk in der Evangelischen Kirche in Deutschland e V, Hinter der Grambker Kirche 5, W-2820 Bremen 77. *Chairman: Günther Schulz.*

Pro Musica Viva-Maria Strecker-Daelon-Stiftung (PMV), Pf 3146, W-6500 Mainz 1.

ProFolk, Dachverband für Folkmusik e V, Brigitte Kempe, Oberachernerstrasse 93, W-7590 Achern 2. *1st Chairman: Jens Peter Müller.*

Rachmaninoff-Gesellschaft e V Wiesbaden, Richard Henger, Pf 4853, W-6200 Wiesbaden. *President: Richard Henger.*

Ralph-Vaughan-Williams-Gesellschaft e V, Jugendmusik-u Kunstuschule, Elberfelder Strasse 20, W-5630 Remscheid. *Chairman: Dr Lutz-Werner Hesse.*

Rektorenkonferenz der Musikhochschulen in der Bundesrepublik Deutschland, Hochschule für Musik Köln, Dagobertstr 38, Cologne. *Contact: Isabel Pfeiffer-Poensgen.*

Richard-Strauss-Gesellschaft München e V, Viktualienmarkt 3, W-8000 Munich 2. *Chairman: Prof Wolfgang Sawallisch.*

Richard-Wagner-Verband International e V (RWVI), Salzstrasse 11, W-7800 Freiburg im Breisgau. *Chairman: Josef Lienhart.*

Robert-Schumann-Gesellschaft e V, Bilker Strasse 4-6, W-4000 Düsseldorf 1. *Chairman: Dr Herbert Zapp.*

Robert-Schumann-Gesellschaft Zwickau e V, Robert-Schumann-Haus, Hauptmarkt 5, 0-8540 Zwizkau. *Chairman: Dr Martin Schoppe.*

Robert-Stolz-Stiftung e V, Steinhauser-Strasse 3, W-8000 Munich 80. *Chairman: Thomas M Stein.*

Rudolf Eberle-Stiftung, Schloss Solitude, Haus 3, W-7000 Stuttgart 1. *Chairman: Hans-Jürgen Müller-Arens.*

Sängerbund der Deutschen Polizei e V (SbdDP), Rosenfelder Strasse 20, W-2300 Kiel 14. *Chairman: Werner Busche.*

Schostakowitsch-Gesellschaft e V, Klaustalerstrasse 2, 0-1100 Berlin. *Chairman: Hilmar Schmalenberg.*

Schütz-Akademie e V, Heinrich-Schütz-Strasse 1, Pf 22, 0-6514 Bad Kostritz. *Chairman: Prof Dr Silke Leopold.*

Sinfonima-Stiftung, Mannheimer Versicherung AG, Augsaanlage 66, Pf 102161, W-6800 Mannheim 1.

Sonderhauser Verband akademisch-musikalishcer Verbindungen (SV), Hilger Schallen, Bahnweg 85, W-6500 Mainz 42. *Chairman: Gerhard Seher.*

Spitzenverband Deutsche Musik e V (SPIDEM), Adenauerallee 134, W-5300 Bonn 1. *President: Prof Dr hc Erich Schulze.*

Stiftung Bayerischer Musikfonds, Salvatorstrasse 2, W-8000 Munich 2.

Stiftung 100 Jahre Yamaha-Verein zur Popularisierung der Musik, Siemensstrasse 22-34, W-2084 Rellingen. *Chairman: Kyoji Ogawa.*

Stiftung fur Kutturell Weiterbildung und Kulturberatung, Jägerstrasse 51m 0-1080 Berlin. *Chairman: Prof Dr Hermann Glaser.*

Stiftung Kulturfonds, Molkenmarkt 1-3, Pf 240, 0-1020 Berlin.

Stiftung Kunst und Kultur des landes Nordrhein-Westfalen, Haus der Stiftungen in NRW, Rossstrasse 133, W-4000 Düsseldorf 30. *Chairman: Minister President Johannes Rau.*

Stiftung Kuratoren-Konseil zur Förderung der Tätigkeit russischer Komponisten und Musiker, Burgmauer 68, Cologne. *Chairman: Serge Tcherepnin.*

Stiftung Ostdeutscher kulturrat (OKR), Kaiserstrasse 113, W-5300 Bonn 1. *President: Dr Herbert Hupka.*

Stiftung Preussischer Kulturbesitz, Von-der-Heydt-Strasse 16-18, W-1000 Berlin 30. *President: Prof Dr Werner Knopp.*

Stiftung Rheinland-Pfalz für Kultur, Ministerium für Bildung und Kulter, Mittlere Bleiche, W-6500 Mainz 1. *Chairman: Minister President Rudolf Scharping.*

Stiftung Volkslied (STV), Heinrich-Shütz-Allee 33, W-3500 Kassel. *Chairman: Alfred Peters.*

Sudetendeutscher Sängerbund e V (SDS), Hans-Schitzer-Weg 19, W-8960 Kempten. *Chairman: Gunther Wohlrab.*

Telemann-Gesellschaft e V Internationale Vereinigung, Liebigstrasse 10, 0-3010 Magdeburg. *President: Prof Dr Martin Ruhnke.*

Union Deutscher Jazz-Musiker e V (UDJ), Am Michaelshof 4a, W-5300 Bonn 2. *1st Chairman: Prof Joe Viera.*

Verband der Deutschen Konzertdirektionen e V, Liebigstrasse 39, W-8000 Munich 22. *President: Michael Russ.*

Verband der deutschen Kritiker e V, Andreas Richter, Prinz-Fr-Leopold Strasse 34a, W-1000 Berlin 38. *Chairman: Hartmut Krug.*

Verband der Musikpädagogen e V (VMP), Von-der-Tann-Strasse 38, W-8400 Regensburg. *Chairman: Dr Lothar Schubert.*

Verband der Vertriebe von Musikinstrumenten und Musikelektronik in Deutschland e V (VVMD), Heinstrasse 169, Stuttgart. *Chairman: Werner Sonderwald.*

Verband Deutscher Bühnenverleger e V, Bismarckstrasse 107, W-1000 Berlin 12. *Chairman: Stefani Cremer-Hunzinger.*

Verband Deutscher Geigenbauer e V (VDG), Hohenzollernstrasse 16, W-7000 Stuttgart 1. *Chairman: Hieronymus Köstler.*

Verband Deutscher Komponisten, An der Kolonnade 15, 0-1080 Berlin. *Chairman: Hans J Wenzel.*

Verband Deutscher KonzertChöre e V (VDKC), Kempener Strasse 5, W-4060 Viersen 12. *President: Hans-Heinrich Grosse-Brockhoff.*

Verband Deutscher Musikschaffender (VDM), Kaiser-Friedrich-Allee 1-3, W-5100 Aachen. *President: Klaus Quirini.*

Verband Deutscher Musikschulen e V (VDM), Plittersdorfer Strasse 93, W-5300 Bonn 2. *Chairman: Reinhart von Gutzeit.*

Verband Deutscher Schulmusiker (VDS), Weihergarten 5, Pf 3640, W-6500 Mainz. *Chairman: Prof Dr Dieter Zimmerzchied.*

Verband Deutscher Tonmeister e V (VDT), Masurenallee 8-14, W-1000 Berlin 19. *President: Günter Griewisch.*

Verband evangelischer Kirchenchöre Deutschlands e V (VEK), Hasenburger Weg 67, W-2120 Lüneburg. *President: Dr Hans-Christian Drömann.*

Verband evangelischer Kirchenmusiker Deutschlands (VeM), Domplatz 5, W-6720 Speyer. *President: KMD Prof Hermann Rau.*

Verein Arbeitsgemeinschaft Deutsche Musikwettbewerbe, Rosenheimer Strasse 11, W-8000 Munich 80. *Chairman: Prof Dr h c Erich Schulze.*

Verein für musikalische Archiv-Forschung e V, Grossh-Friedrich-Strasse 62, W-7640 Kehl. *Chairman: Prof Dr Werner Unger.*

Verein zur Förderung der Nordoff/Robbins Musiktherapie e V, Beckweg 4, W-5804 Herdecke. *Chairman: Prof Dr Eduard David.*

Verein zur Förderung des musikalischen Schaffens des Komponisten Waldemar Edler von Bausznern, Haus Nr 31, Kludenbach. *Chairman: Horst Gehann.*

Verein zur Förderung Historischer Harfen e V, Rainer m Thurau, Helenenstrasse 10, W-6200 Wiesbaden. *Chairman: Elena Polonska.*

Vereinigung deutscher Harfenisten e V, Vera Munkel-Remann, Goldammerweg 183, W-5000 Cologne 30. *Chairman: Therese Reichling.*

Vereinigung Deutscher Musik-Bearbeiter e V, Kiesstrasse 44a, W-1000 Berlin 45.

Vereinigung Deutscher Opernchöre und Bühnentanzer e V in der DAG (VdO/DAG), Bismarchstrasse 14-16, W-5000 Cologne 1. *Chairman: Heinz Mersch.*

Villa Musica, Stiftung zur Förderung der Musik, Auf der Bastei, W-6500 Mainz. *Chairman: Mindirig Ernst Maurer.*

Walcker-Stiftung für orgelwissenschaftliche Forschung, Pf 1128, W-6601 Kleinblittersdorf 2. *Chairman: Klaus Walcker.*

Walter Kaminsky-Stiftung, Kösener Strasse 4, W-1000 Berlin 33.

Walther-Hensel-Gesellschaft e V ,München, Ob dem Staffele 2, W-7057 Winnenden. *Chairman: Herbert Preisenhammer.*

Werkgemeinschaaft Musik e V, Carl-Mosterts-Platz 1, W-4000 Düsseldorf 30. *Chairman: Prof Karl Berg.*

Wilhelm-Furtwängler-Gesellschaft e V, Schwelmer Strasse 4, W-1000 Berlin 45. *Chairman: Dr FriedhelmSchöning.*

Wilhelm-Petersen-Gesellschaft e V, Brahmsweg 4, W-6100 Darmstadt.

Wissenschaftliche Sozietät Musikpädagogik e V (WSMP), Fachbereich Erziehungswissenschaft, Insitut für Musikpadagogik, Von-Melle-Park 8, W-2000 Hamburg 13. *Chairman: Prof Dr Hermann J Kaiser.*

Xaver & Philipp Scharwenka-Gesellschaft e V, Prasseekstrasse 5, W-2400 Lübeck. *1st Chairman: Prof Evelinde Trekner.*

Zentralverband katholischer Kirchenangestellter Deutschlands e V (ZKD), Am Kielshof 2, Pf 990125, W-5000 Cologne 91. *Chairman: Franz Kopecky.*

Zentrum Bundesrepublik Deutschland des Internationalen Theaterinstituts e V (ITI), Bismarckstrasse 107, W-100 Berlin 12. *President: Prof August Everding.*

Zentrum für Kunst und Medientechnologie Karlsruhe (ZKM), Institut für Musik und Akustik, Ritterstrasse 42, Karlsruhe. *Director: Prof Dr Heinrich Klotz.*

GREECE

International Music Council (Greek Section), 38 Mitropleos Street, 105 63 Athens. *General Secretary: Apostolos Kositios.*
Jeunesses Musicales de Grece/Musique Pour l'Enfant, Stratigou Kallari 52, Psychico, 154 52 Athens. *President: Domini Sarris.*
Société Hellenique pour la Protection de la Proprieté intellectuelle, 14 Delighianni Street, 106 83 Athens. *Managing Director: George Galanakis.*
Tsakalof Cultural Centre, Platia G, Stavrou5, 45444 Ioannina. *President: Aspasia Zerva.*

GUATEMALA

Asociacion Guatemalteca de Autores y Compositores (AGAYC), 14 Calle 11-42, Zona 1, 01001 Guatemala City.
Juventudes Musicales de Guatemala, Diagonal 6, Calle Real de la villa 13-46, Zona 10, Guatemala City. *President: Francisco Saravia.*

HONG KONG

Hong Kong Arts Administrators Association Ltd, c/o ARIC, Room 301, 3/F Hong Kong Arts Centre, 2 Harbour Road, Wanchai.
Hong Kong Government Music Office, 25/F Wanchai Tower One, 12 Harbour Road, Wanchai.

HUNGARY

Artisjus Hungarian Office for Copyright Protection, PO Box 67, 1364 Budapest, Vörösmarty tér, 1051 Budapest.
President: Kamilló Lendvay; General Director: Dr György Boytha.
Association of Hungarian Musicians, PO Box 47, 1364 Budapest; Vörösmarty tér 1, 1051 Budapest.
Council of Hungarian Choirs, PO Box 345, 1370 Budapest, Vörösmarty tér 1, 1051 Budapest.
Hungarian Arts Foundation, Music Department, Báthori-utca 10, 1054 Budapest. *Director of the Music Department: Kálmán Strém.*
Hungarian ISME Committee, PO Box 47, 1364 Budapest; Vörösmarty tér 1, 1051 Budapest.
Hungarian Music Society, Vörösmarty tér 1, 1051 Budapest. *Honorary President: Prof Ferenc Farkas: President: Zsolt Durkó.*
Interart Festival Center, National Center of International Music Competitions and Festivals, PO Box 80, 1366 Budapest, Vörösmarty tér 1, 1051 Budapest.
Director: Tamás Klenjánszky.
Institute for Musicology of the Hungarian Academy of Sciences/Bartók Archives, Táncsics Mihály u.7, 1014 Budapest.
Director: Dr Zoltán Falvy; Head of the Bartók Archives: Prof Dr Lázló Somfai.
International Jazz Federation/Hungarian Section,PO Box 47, 1364 Budapest; Vörösmarty tér 1, 1051 Budapest.
International Kodály Society, PO Box 8, 1502 Budapest.
International Music Council, PO Box 47, 1364 Budapest; Vörösmarty tér 1, 1051 Budapest.
 International Society for Contemporary Music, PO Box 47, 1364 Budapest; Vörösmarty tér 1, 1051 Budapest.
Jeunesses Musicales of Hungary, PO Box 80, 1366 Budapest, Vörösmarty tér 1, 1051 Budapest. *Secretary General: Beáta Schanda.*
Liszt Ferenc Társaság (Ferenc Liszt Society), Vörösmarty u 35, 1064 Budapest.
 Music Information Center, PO Box 47, 1364 Budapest Vörösmarty tér 1, 1051 Budapest.
Trade Union of Hungarian Musicians, Gorkij Fasor 38, 1068 Budapest.

ICELAND

Association of Icelandic Composers, Laufásvegi 40, Reykjavík.
Association of Light Composers and Songwriters, Háteigsvegur 28, 105 Reykiavik.
Association of Music School Directors, Kennarasamband Islands, Grettisgata 89, 105 Reykjavík.
Association of Music School Teachers, Kennarasamband Islands, Grettisgata 89, 105 Reykjavík.
Iceland Music Information Centre, Freyjugata 1, PO Box 978, 121 Reykjavík. *Director: Bergljót Jónsdóttir.*
Icelandic Musicians' Union, Laufásvegur 40, Reykjavík.
International Society for Contemporary Music, Icelandic Section, Tonskaldafelag Islands, Laufásvegur 40, Reykjavík.
Reykjavík Music Society, Garoastraeti 17, 101 Reykjaík.
Society of Icelandic Musicians, Dalsel 8, Reykjavík.
Union of Authors and Copyright Owners, Laufásvegur 40, 101 Reykjavík.

INDIA

Inter-National Cultural Centre, 205 Tansen Marg, New Delhi 1.
National Centre for the Performing Arts. Nariman Point, Bombay 400021.

ISRAEL

Independent Musicians Union, 6 Malkei Yisrael Square, 64591 Tel Aviv. *Chairman: Dany Gottfried.*
International Music Council (Israeli Section), Ministry of Education and Culture, Devora Hanaviah Street 2, 91911 Jerusalem.
Chief Officer: Raaya Zimran.
International Society for Contemporary Music (Israeli Section), c/o Israel Composers' League, PO Box 45068, 61450 Tel Aviv.
Israel Composers'League, PO Box 45068, 61450 Tel Aviv. *Chairman: Manachem Zur.*
Israel Music Institute (IMI), PO Box 3004, 61030 Tel Aviv. *Director: Paul Landau.*
Israel Musicians Union, Histradut Building, 93 Arlozorof Street, 62098 Tel Aviv. *General Secretary: Aryeh Levanon.*
Jerusalem Music Centre, Mishkanot Sha'ananim, Jerusalem. *Director: Benny Gal-Ed.*
Jeunesses Musicales d'Israel, 8 Sderot Chen, 64071 Tel Aviv.
Music Information Centre of Israel, PO Box 3004, 61030 Tel Aviv. *Director: Paul Landau.*
National Council for Culture and Arts, 16 Hanatziv Street, 67018 Tel Aviv. *Chief Officer: David Sinai.*
Society of Authors, Composers, and Music Publishers in Israel (ACUM), 118 Rothschild Boulevard, 61110 Tel Aviv. *Chairman: Shlomo Tanny.*

ITALY

Accademia Luigi Boccherini, piazza Insurrezione 10, 35129 Padua.

Accademia Tartiniana, piazzale Pnotecorvo 4/A, 35121 Padua.

Associazione "Antiquae Musicae Italicae Studiosi", via Remorsella 5/A, 40125 Bologna.

Associazione Centro Studi Carusiani, via Omboni 1, 20129 Milan.

Associazione dei Fonografici Italiani (AFI), via Vittor Pisani 10, 20124 Milan.

Associazione dei Rappresentanti Italiani di Artisti di Concerti e Spettacoli (ARIACA), via Cappuccio 11, 20123 Milan.

Associazione di Informatica Musicale Italiana (AIMI), c/o La Biennale di Venezia, Settore Musica, San Marco, Ca Giustinian, 30124 Venice.

Associazione Festival Teatrali, Musicali e Cinematografici (Federfestival), c/o AGIS, via di Villa Patrizi 10, 00161 Rome.

Associazione Generale Italiana dello Spettacolo (AGIS), via di Villa Patrizi 10, 00161 Rome.

Associazione Internazionale Biblioteche Musicali (AIBM), Italian Section, c/o Conservatorio "Giuseppe Verdi", vai Conservatorio 12, 20111 Milan.

Associazione Internazionale Studi di Canto Gergoriano, via Battaglione 58, 26100 Cremona.

Associazione Italiana Archivi Sonori e Audiovisivi, c/o Insituto di Ricereca per il Teatro Musicale, Via dei Delfini 16, 00186 Rome.

Associazione Italiana Biblioteche (AIB), c/o Biblioteca Nazionale, via le Castro Pretorio 105, 00186 Rome.

Associazione Italiana Degli Editori di Musica (AIDEM), via Enrico Tito 4, 20123 Milan.

Associazione Italiana delle Scuole di Musica, Villa La Torraccia, via delle Fontanelle 24, 50016 San Domenico di Fiesole (FI).

Associazione Italiana di Acustica (AIA), via Cassia 1216, 00189 Rome.

Associazione Italiana Operatori Musicali (ASSIOM), c/o Centro di Ricerca e Sperimentazione per la Didattica Musicale, Villa La Torraccia, via delle Fontanelle 24, 50016 San Domenico di Fiesolo (FI).

Associazione Italiana per la Musica Sacra "S Cecilia" (AISC), piazza S Apollinare 49, 00186 Rome.

Associazione Italiana Studi di Musicoterapia (AISMt), via Brignole De Ferrari 6, 16122 Genoa.

Associazione Liutariana Italiana (ALI), piazza Cavour 5, 26100 Cremona.

Associazione Nazionale Agenti Teatrali (ANAT), via Assietta , 00141 Rome.

Associazione Nazionale Artisti Lirici Primarii Italiani (ANALPI), corso Venezia 61, 20121 Milan.

Associazione Nazionale Bande Italiane Musicali (AMBIMA), via Marianna Dionigi 43, 00193 Rome.

Associazione Nazionale Critici Musicali, via Cardinale Mimmi 32, 70124 Bari.

Associazione Nazionale delle Cooperative Culturali, via dei Alpi 32, 00198 Rome.

Associazione Nazionale Insegnanti di Danza (ANID), via A Gramsci 36, 00197 Rome.

Associazione Nazionale Liuteria Artistica Italiana (ANLAI), piazza Venezia 11, 00187 Rome.

Associazione Nazionale Musicisti di Jazz (AMJ), via Vallerozzi 77, 53100 Siena.

Associazione Pro Musica Studium, via Ferdinando Martini 23/8, 00137 Rome.

Centre International de Recherches sur la Presse Musicale (CIRPEM), via del Conservatorio 31/B, 43100 Parma.

Centro di Sonologia Computazionale, c/o Uniersità di Padova, via San Francesco 11, 35121 Padua.

Centro di Studi Donizettiani, c/o Ateneo di Scienze, Lettre ed Arti, via Torquato Tasso 4, 24121 Bergamo.

Centro di Studi Musicali Ferruccio Busoni, piazza della Vittoria 16, 50053 Empoli (F1).

Centro Internazionale per la Divulgazione della Musica Italiana, via Sistina 48, 00187 Rome.

Centro Internazionale per la Ricerca Strumentale, Cannaregio 3099, 30121 Venice.

Centro Studi Giovanni Paisiello, via Euclide 15, 74100 Taranto.

Centro Studi Rinascimento Musicale, Villa Medicea "La Ferdinanda", 50040 Artimino (F1).

Centro di Studi Spontiniani, c/o Comune, via Spontini, 60030 Maiolati Spontini (AN).

CIDIM-National Music Committee of Italy (IMC-UNESCO), via Vittoria Colonna 18, 00193 Rome.

Civico Instituto di Studi Paganiani, Palazzo Tursi, via Garibaldi, 16124 Genoa.

Editori Muscali Associati (EMA), piazza Liberty 2, 20121 Milan.

Ente Nazionale Previdenza e Assistenza per i Lavatori dello Spettacolo (ENPALS), viale Regina Margherita 206, 00198 Rome.

Federazione Industria Musicale Italiana (FIMI), via Vittor Pisani 10, 20124 Milan.

Federazione Informazione Spettacolo (FIS)CISL), via Boncompagni 19, 00187 Rome.

Federazione Italiana dei Compositori de Musica Contemporanea, via Cavalieri di Vittorio Veneto 34, 56121 Cascina (PI).

Federazione Italiana della Musica (FEDERMUSICA), via Vittor Piasni 10, 20124 Milan.

Federazione Italiana Lavatori informazione e Spettacolo (FILISCGIL), piazza Sallustio 24, 00187 Rome.

Federazione Italiana Lavoratori Stampa, Spettacolo, Informazione e Cultura (FILSIC-UIL), via Belisario 7, 00187 Rome.

Federazione Italiana Tradizioni Popolari (FITP), via E Gattamelata 25, 00176 Rome.

Federazione Nazionale delle Cooperative Culturali, piazza della Libertà, 00192 Rome.

Federazione Nazionale Italiana delle Associazioni Regionali Corali (FENIARCO), via Castellana 44, 30174 Venezia Mestre.

Federazione Nazionale Lavoratori Spettacolo (CISNAL), via Principe Amedeo 42, 00185 Rome.

Fondazione Claudio Monteverdi, via Ugolani Dati 4, 26100 Cremona.

Fondazione Giacomo Puccini, c/o Teatro del Giglio, corte San Lorenzo, corte San Lorenzo 9, 55100 Lucca.

Fondazione Giorgio Cini, Instituti per la Musica, Isola di San Giorgio Maggiore, 30124 Venice.

Fondazione Giovanni Pierluigi da Palestrina, vicolo Pierluigi 3, 0036 Palestrina (Rome).

Fondazione Rossini, piazza Olivieri 5, 61100 Pesaro.

Fondazione Ugo e Olga Levi, Centro di Cultura Musicale Superiore, palazzo Giustinian-Lolin, San Marco 2893, 30124 Venice.

Fondazione Vincenzo Bellini, c/o Università delgi Studi di Catania, via Biblioteca 13, 95124 Catania.

Fondo Ottorino Respighi, c/o Fondazione Giorgio Cini, Isola San Giorgio Maggiore, 30124 Venice.

International Association for the Study of Popular Music (IASPM), Italian Section, Il Giornale della Musica, corso Vittorio Emanuelle II n 198bis, 10138 Turin.

International Center of New Musical Sources, via Alberto Nota 3, 10122 Turin.

International Dance Organization (IDO), via Bronzino 117, 50142 Florence.

Instituto di Bibliografia Musicale, c/o Biblioteca Nazionale, viale Casteo Pretoria 105, 00185 Rome.

Instituto di Paleografia Musicale, circonvallazione Casilini 122, 00176 Rome.

Instituto di Ricerca per il Teatro Musicale, via Francesco tamagno 65, 00168 Rome.

Instituto di Studi Organologici, via monte Zebio 33, 00195 Rome.

Instituto di Studi Rinascimentali, Palazzo Paradiso, via delle Scienze 17, 44100 Ferrrara.

Instituto Interzionale Luigi Cherubini, via Giovanni Secchi 3, 00136 Rome.

Instituto Italiana Antonio Vivaldi, /o Fondazione Giorgio Cini, Isola di San Giorgio Maggiore, 30124 Venice.

Instituto Italiano per la Storia della Musica, via Vittoria 6, 00187 Rome.

Instituto Mutualistico tra Artisti Interpreti Esecutori (IMAIE), Piazza Sonnio 37, 00153 Rome.

Instituto Nazionale di Studi Verdiani, strada della Repubblica 56, 43100 Parma.
Instituto di Studi Pucciniani, piazza Buonarroti 29, 20149 Milan.
Pontificio Instituto Ambrosiano di Musica Sacra, viala Gorizia 5, 20144 Milan.
Pontificio Instituto di Musica Sacra, via di Torre Rossa 21, 001165 Rome.
Sindacato Musicisti Italiani (SMI), via Goito 39, 00185 Rome.
Sindacato Nazionale Autonomo, Telecomunicazioni Radiotelevisione Italcable-Telespazio Società Consociate della Pubblicità e dello Spettacolo (SNATER), via Dardanelli 13, 00185 Rome.
Sindacato Nazionale Instruzione Artistica, via Antonio Pio 40, 00145 Rome.
Sindacato Nazionale Musicisti (SNM), via Pinelli 100, 10144 Turin.
Società Italiana degli Autori ed Editori (SIAE), via le della Letteratura 30, 00144 Rome.
Società Italiana della Viola da Gamba, via dei Servi 51, 50122 Florence.
Società Italiana di Etnomusicologia (SIE), c/o Centro Flog Tradizioni Popolari, via Maestri del Lavoro 1, 50134 Florence.
Società Italiana di Musicologia (SIdM), via Galliera 3, 40125 Bologna.
Società Italiana Musica Contemporanea (SIMC), via F Juvara 11, 21029 Milan.
Società Italiana per l'Educazione Musicale (SIEM), via Guerrazzi 20, 40125 Bologna.
UNION-Operatori Indipendenti, c/o "I Soluzionisti", via Trionfale 85, 00136 Rome.
Unione Folclorica Italiana (UFI), via Mazzini 22, 33081 Aviano (PN).
Unione Nazionale Arte Musica Spettacolo (UNAMS), viale delle Provincie 18, 00162 Rome.
Unione Nazionale Editori di Musica Italiani (UNEMI), via Teulada 52, 00195 Rome.

JAPAN

Concert Managers Association of Japan, Mitoko Building, 6-2-4 Akasaka, Minato-ku, Tokyo 107. *Chairman: Naoyasu Kajimoto.*
Electronic Industries Association of Japan, Tokyo Shoko Kaigisho Building, 3-2-2 Marunouchi, Chiyoda-ku, Tokyo 100. *Chairman: Dr Tadahiro Sekimoto.*
Japan Audio Society, Mori Building, 1-14-34 Jingumae, Tokyo 150. *Secretary-General: Sho Nagasawa.*
Japan Conductors Association, 4-18-20 Ogikubo Suginami-ku, Tokyo 167. *President: Takashi Asahina.*
Japan International League of Artists, 2-3-16-607 Shinjuku, Shinjuku-ku, Tokyo 160. *Chief Officer: Kazuhiko Hattori.*
Japanese Composers Society, Ogawa Building, 3-7-15 Akasaka, Minatoku, Tokyo 107.
Japanese Society for Rights of Authors, Composers, and Publishers, 1-7-13 Nishishimbashi, Minato-ku, Tokyo 105.
Music for Youth, Inc, Kowa Building, No 24, 3-1-1 Roppongi, Minato-ku, Tokyo 106. *President: Eloise Cunningham.*
Recording Industry Association of Japan, 2-8-9 Tsukiji, Chuo-ku, Tokyo 104.

KOREA (SOUTH)

Asian Composers League (Korean Committee), KPO Box 874, Seoul 110-062. *Director: Sung-Jae Lee.*
Federation of Artistic and Cultural Organisations of Korea, 1-117 Dongsoong-dong, Chongro-ku, Seoul.
Jeunesses Musicales of Korea, PO Box 10980, Seoul.
Korean Cultural Foundation , Inc, 25 Neung-Dong, Sung-ku, Seoul 133-180. *Director: No Hi Pak.*
Music Association of Korea, 1-117 Dongsoong-dong, Chongro-ku, Seoul. *President: Sang-Hyun Cho.*

LUXEMBURG

Jeunesses Musicales de Luxembourg, 18 A rue de la Poste, L-2346 Luxembourg.
Luxemburger Gesellschaft für Neue Musik (International Society for Contemporary Music, Luxembourg Section), BP 828, L-2018 Luxembourg. *President: Marcel Wengler.*
Union Grand-Duc Adolphe, 2 rue Sosthène Weis, L-2722 Luxembourg.

MACAO

Instituto Cultural de Macau, Rua Pedro Coutinho 27, 3rd Floor, Macao.

MEXICO

Asociación Mexicana de Productores de Fonogramas y Videogramas AC (Amprofon), Francisco Petrarca 223-503, Chapultepec Morales, 11560 México.
Juventudes Musicales de México, Santisimo 25, San Angel, 01000 México 20, DF.
Sociedad de Autores y Compositores de Música S de A (SACM), San Felipe 143, Col General Anaya, 03330 México, DF.

NETHERLANDS

Association for the Performing Arts in the Netherlands, herengracht 122, 1015 BT Amsterdam. *General Secretary: J Rudolf Wolfensberger.*
BUMA (Composers Rights Society), Prof E M Meijerslaan 3, 1183 AV Amsterdam. *Chief Officer: G P Willemsen.*
CNM (Center for Netherlands Music), PO Box 1634, 1200 PB Hilversum. *Chief Officer: J W ten Broeke.*
Contactorgaan van Nederlandse Orkesten (Association of Netherlands Orchestras), Herengracht 122, 1015 BT Amsterdam. *Executive Director: J Rudolf Wolfensberger.*
Donemus (Publishing House and Library of Contemporary Dutch Music), Paulus Potterstraat 14, 1071 CZ Amsterdam.
Foundation Gaudeamus (Center of Contemporary Music), Swammerdamstraast 38, 1091 RV Amsterdam. *Director: Henk Heuvelmans.*
Gentootschap van Nederlandse (Society of Netherlands Composers), Prof E M Meijerslaan 3, 1183 AV Amsterdam. *President: Gilius van Bergejik.*
International Society for Contemporary Music (Netherlands Section), Swammerdamstraat 38, 1091 RV Amsterdam. *President: H Reiziger.*
Jeugd en Musiek Nederland, Roemer Visscherstraat 42, 1054 EZ Amsterdam. *President: Jur Naessens.*
Jeunesses Musicales, Amstel 177, 1018 ES Amsterdam.
KDOV (Katholieke Dirigenten en Organisten Vereniging), Koningen Wilhelmialaan 532, 2274 BM Voorburg. *Secreatry: Dr T van Eck.*
Koninklijke Nederlandse Toonkunstenaars Vereniging (Royal Netherlands Musicans Society), Keizersgracht 480, 1017 EG Amsterdam. *Chief Officer: H Luif.*
NTB (Nederlandse Toonkunstenaars Bond), Herengracht 272, 1016 BW Amsterdam.

Nederlandse Vereniging van Grammofoondetallhandelaren (NVGD), Die Noord 3, 1452 PS Ilpendam. *Chairman: J F T Hotzenbosch.*
Netherlands Committee of the International Music Council, Rubenslaan 200, 3582 JJ Utrecht.
Netherlands Theater Institute, PO Box 19304, 1000 GH Amsterdam. *Chief Officer: Ton Offerman.*
STEMRA (Mechanical Rights Society), Prof E M Meijerslaan 3, 1183 AV Amsterdam. *Chief Officer: G P Willemsem.*
Stichting Contactorgaan Electronische Muziek, Swammerdamstraat 38, 1091 RV Amsterdam. *Chief Officer: Henk Heuvelmans.*
Stichting voor Kamermuziek, Sijzenlaan 6, 2566 WG The Hague.
Vereniging voor Nederlandse Muziekgeschiedenis (Society for Netherlands Music History), Postbus 1514, 3500 BM Utrecht.

NEW ZEALAND

Australasian Performing Right Association Ltd (APRA), PO Box 5028, Wellington. *General Manager: Bernie Darby.*
Composers Association of New Zealand, PO Box 4065, Wellington. *President: Denise Hulford.*
Music for Youth, 26 Patanga Crescent, Wellington 6001. *Chairperson: Beverley Wakem.*
Music Trades Association (NZ) Inc, Box 386, Auckland. *Executive Officer: Dean Reynolds.*
New Zealand Composers Foundation, PO Box 633, Wellington. *Chairman: Ashley Heenan.*
New Zealand Music Centre Ltd, trading as SOUNZ New Zealand, PO Box 102, The Terrace, Wellington. *Executive Director: Nicholas McBryde.*
New Zealand Opera Society Inc, PO Box 44-022, VIC, Lower Huttl. *President Sam Robinson.*
Phonographic Performances (New Zealand) Ltd, PO Box 9241, Wellington. *General Manager: Tony Chance.*
Queen Elizabeth II Arts Council of New Zealand, PO Box 3806, Welington. *Director: Peter Quin.*
Recording Industry Association of New Zealand Inc, PO Box 9241, Wellington. *Chief Executive: Tony Chance.*
Service Workers Union, Musicians Division, Private Bag 68-914, Newton, Auckland. *Secretary: Peter Shannon.*

NORWAY

International Music Council (National Committee), c/o Statens Musikkrad, Toftesgate 69, N-0552 Oslo.
International Society for Contemporary Music (Norwegian Section), c/o Ny Musikk, Toftesgate 69, N-0552 Oslo.
Jeunesses Musicales (Norwegian Section), c/o Landslaget Musikk i Skolen, Toftesgate 69, N-0552 Oslo.
Landslaget Musikk i Skolen (Youth & Music), Toftesgate 69, 0552 Oslo.
New Music (Ny Musikk), Toftesgate 69, N-0552 Oslo.
NASOL (Norwegian Association of Symphony Orchestras), Toftesgate 69, N-0552 Oslo.
NOPA (Norwegian Society of Popular Composers, Authors and Arrangers), PO Box 9171, Gronland, N-0134 Oslo.
Norsk Tonekunstnersamfund (Norwegian Association of Musical Artists), Bogstadvn 66, N-0366 Oslo.
Norwegian Archives for Folk and Popular Songs, Toftesgate 69, N-0552 Oslo.
Norwegian Cultural Council, Militaerhospitalet, PO Box 101, Sentrum, N-0102 Oslo.
Norwegian Music Information Centre, Toftesgate 69, N-0552 Oslo. *Manager: Jostein Simble.*
Norwegian Musicians' Union, Youngsgate 11, N-0181 Oslo. *President: Tore Nordvik.*
Norwegian Song and Music Council, Toftesgate 69, N-0552 Oslo.
Rikskonsertene (Norwegian State Travelling Concerts Organization), PO Box 7613, Skillebekk, N-0205, Oslo.
Society of Norwegian Composers, PO Box 9171, Grønland, N-0134 Oslo.

PARAGUAY

Juventudes Musicales, c/o Saul Gaona, RI 3 Corrales 516, Asuncion.

PERU

Asociación Peruana de Autores y Compositores (APDAYC), Jiron Ica 559, Lima 1.
Juventudes Musicales, Garcilaso de la Vega 1746, Lima 14. *President: Oscar Zamora.*

PHILIPPINES

Andres Bobifacio Music Foundation, Union Village, Tandang Sora, Quezon City.
Choral Conductors Association of the Philippines, c/o University of the Philippines, College of Music, Quezon City.
Eliseo Pajaro Foundation Inc, c/o Cultural Center of the Philippines, Roxas Boulevard, Manila.
Filipino Society of Composers, Authors and Publishers (FILSCAP), 308 RCBC Building, Buendia Extension, Makati, Metro Manila.
Kodály Society of the Philippines, c/o St Paul's College, Herran Street, Manila.
League of Filipino Composers, c/o Cultural Center of the Philippines, Roxas Boulevard, Manila.
Music Theater Foundation, c/o University of the Philippines, College of Music, Diliman, Quezon City.
Musika, 9-A Manga Road, New Manila, Quezon City.
National Music Council of the Philippines, c/o University of the Philippines, College of Music, Diliman, Quezon City.
Organisasyon ng Pilipinong Mang-aawit (OPM), Zeta Building, Suite 65, 191 Salcedo Street, Legaspi Village, Makati, Metro Manila.
Piano Teachers' Guild of the Philippines, c/o St Scholasticas's College, Leon Guinto, Malate, Manila.
Philippine Musicians Guild, 409 Unlad Condominium, Taft Avenue and General Malvar Street, Malate, Manila.
Philippine Society for Music Education, c/o Philippine Normal College, Music and Arts Department, Taft Avenue, Manila.
Samahan ng mga Manunuri at Manunulat ng Musika sa Pilipinas (SAMMPI), Aurora Pijuan St, Bl. 5, Lot 1, BF Resort Village, Pamplona, Las Pinas, Metro Manila.
University of the Philippines Musical Arts and Research Management Inc, University of the Philippines, College of Music, Abelardo Hall, Diliman, Quezon City.

POLAND

Association of Polish Violin Makers, Krakowskie Przedmieście 16/18, 00-325 Warsaw.
Chopin Society of Music, Okólnik 1, 00-368 Warsaw.
Jeunesses Musicales de Pologne, Lwowska 13, 00-660 Warsaw.
Polish Composers' Union, Rynek Starego Miasta 27, 00-272 Warsaw. *President: Andrzej Chodkowski.*
Polish Composers' Union, Musicological Section, Rynek Starego Miasta 27, 00-272 Warsaw. *President: Maciej Malecki.*

Polish Music Centre, Fredry 8, 00-097 Warsaw. *Manager: Barbara Zwolska-Steszewska.*
Polish Music Council, Fredry 8, 00-097 Warsaw.
Society of Authors "ZAIKS", Hipoteczna 2, 00-092 Warsaw. *General Manager: Witold Kolodziejski.*
Society of Music Education, Koszykowa 24/7a, 00-553 Warsaw. *President: Adrianna Poniecka-Piekutowska.*
Society of Polish Librarians, Music Libraries Section, c/o Warszawskie Towarzystwo Muzyczne, Bibliotéka Zakroczymska 2, 00-225 Warsaw.
Society of Polish Musicians, Krucza 24-26, 00-526 Warsaw.
Szymanowski Society of Music, Kasprusie 19, willa "Atma", 34-500 Zakopane.
Union of Polish Lyric Writers and Composers of Light Music "ZAKR", Hipoteczna 2, 00-092 Warsaw.
Warsaw Music Society, Morskie Oko 2, 02-511 Warsaw.
Wieniawski Society of Music, Sweitosławska 7, 61-840 Poznań.

PORTUGAL

Fundacâo Calouste Gulbenkian, Servico de Musica, Av de berna 45, 1093 Lisbon Codex.
Juventude Musical Portuguesa, Rua Rosa Araujo 6, 3rd Floor, 1200 Lisbon. *President: Miguel Henriques.*
Sindicato dos Músicos, Av D Carlos I 72, 2nd Floor, 1200 Lisbon.
Sociedade Portuguesa de Autores (SPA), Avda Dugue de Louié 31, 1098 Lisbon Codex. *President: Luis Francisco Rebelo.*

ROMANIA

Jeunesses Musicales, Str Lipscani 53, Bucharest.
Union of Rumanian Composers, Calea Victoriei 141, 70149 Bucharest.

RUSSIA

Intercultcentre (International Center for Festivals, Competitions and Intergovernmental Cooperation), Arbat Str 35, 121835 Moscow. *Director General: Suren Shaumian.*
International Union of Musicians, ul Gertsena 14/2, 103009 Moscow. *President: Irina Arkhipova.*
Union of Composers of Russia, ul Nezhdanovoi 8/10, 103009 Moscow K-9. *Chairman: V Kazenin.*
VAAP (Russian Copyright Agency), ul Bolshaia Bronnais 6-A, GSP K 104, 103670

SINGAPORE

Musicians and Singers Association, Block 3, 03-628, Rochor Centre, Rochor Road, Singapore 0718. *Chief Officer: Stephen Gomez.*
National Arts Council, PSA Building, 35th Storey, 460 Alexandria Road, Singapore 0511.

SLOVAK REPUBLIC

Music Information Centre of the Slovak Music Fund, Fučikova 29, 811 02 Bratislava.
Slovak Music Association, Šafárikova nám 4, 811 02 Bratislava.
Slovak Music Fund, Fučikova 29, 811 02 Bratislava.
Slovak Music Union (includes the Club of Concert Artists, Club of Music Folklorists, Club of Slovak Composers, and Slovak Musicologists' Association), Michalská 10, 815 36 Bratislava.
Slovkoncert (Slovak Artistic and Publicity Agency), Michalská 10, 815 36 Bratislava.
Study S (Agency for Theatre and Music), nám 1 mája, 815 36 Bratislava.

SOUTH AFRICA

Association of the South African Music Industry, PO Box 367, Randburg 2125, Johannesburg. *Chief Executive: Des Dubery.*
Dramatic, Artistic, and Literary Rights Organization Ltd (DALRO), PO Box 9292, Johannesburg. *Managing Director: Gideon Ross.*
Foundation for the Creative Arts, PO Box 91122, Auckland Park 2006. *Executive Manager: Herman Van Niekerk.*
South African Music Rights Organization Ltd (SAMRO), PO Box 9292, Johannesburg 2000. *Managing Director: Gideon Ross.*
South African Musicians Union, PO Box 5837, Johannesburg 2000.
South African Recording Rights Association Ltd (SARRAL), PO Box 4378, Johannesburg 2000. *Chief Officer: George Hardie.*
South African Society of Music Teachers, PO Box 5318, Walmer 6065.

SPAIN

Asociación Cultural Laboratorio de Interpretacion Musical (LIM), Seco 12, 28007 Madrid. *President: Jesús Villa Rojo.*
Asociación de Musica en Compostela, Pablo Aranda 6, 28006 Madrid. *President: Margarita Pastor Zacharias.*
Centro Para la Difusion de la Musica Contemporanea, Santa Isabel 52, 28012 Madrid. *Director: Tomas Marco.*
Direccion General de Musica y Teatro, Ministerio de Cultura, Psza del Rey 1, 28071 Madrid.
International Society for Contemporary Music (Spanish Section), Avda de America 58-5, 28028 Madrid. *Chief Officer: Luis de Pablo.*
Instituto de Bibliografica Musical, penulas 12, 12p 28071 Madrid. *President: Jacinto Torres Mulas.*
Joventuts Musical de Barcelona, Pau Claris 139, 4th Floor, 1a, 08009 Barcelona.
Juventudes Musicales, Girona 10, 3, Barcelona.
Sociedad de Conciertos, Atlamira 3, 03002 Alicante. *Director: Margarita Berenger.*
Sociedad Española de Musicologica (SEM), Canos del Peral 7, 28013 Madrid. *President: Ismael Fernandez de la Cuesta.*
Sociedad General de Autores de España (SGAE), Fernando VI 4, 28004 Madrid. *President: Manuel Gutierrez Aragón.*

SWEDEN

Association of Swedish Symphony Orchestras, Schönfeldts gränd 1, 111 27 Stockholm.
International Music Council, Swedish National Committee, c/o Royal Swedish Academy of Music, Blasieholmstorg 8, 111 48 Stockholm.
International Society for Contemporary Music (Swedish Section), c/o FST, Box 27327, 102 54 Stockholm.
Society of Music Teachers in Sweden, c/o Nordstedt, Otroftagatan 37, 216 20 Malmö.
Society of Swedish Church Musicians, c/o S Henriksson, Storgatan 36, 520 40 Floby.
Society of Swedish Composers, Box 27327, 102 54 Stockholm. *Chairman: Thomas Jennefelt.*
Swedish Artists and Musicians Interest Organization, Mosebacke Torg 16, 116 20 Stockholm.
Swedish Choral Association, Box 38014, 100 64 Stockholm.
Swedish Music Information Center, Box 27327, 102 54 Stockholm. *Director: Roland Sandberg.*
Swedish Musicians Union, Box 43, 101 20 Stockholm. *Chairman: Roland Almlén.*
Swedish Performing Rights Society, Box 27327, 102 54 Stockholm. *Director: Gunnar Petri.*
Swedish Piano TeaChers Association, Solbacken 9, 131 42 Nacka.
Swedish Society for Musicology, c/o Statens Musiksamlingar, Box 16326, 103 26 Stockholm.
Swedish Society of Light Music Composers, Box 27327, 102 54 Stockholm.
Swedish Union of Professional Musicians, Drottninggatan 55, 111 21 Stockholm.

SWITZERLAND

Association of Concert Giving Societies of Switzerland, Münsterplatz 18, 4051 Basel.
Association of Swiss Musicians, Avenue du Grammont 11 bis, Case postale 177, 1000 Lausanne 13. *General Secretary: Hélène Petitpierre.*
European Association of Amateur Orchestras, Heimstrasse 24, 3018 Bern. *Secretary General: J Nyffenegger.*
European Association of Music Festivals, c/o Centre Européen de la Culture Villa Moynier, 122 rue de Lausanne, 1211 Geneva. *Secretary: Dr Henry Siegwart.*
Federation of International Music Competitions, 104 rue de Carouge, 1205 Geneva.
Gesellschaft der Freunde alter Musikinstrumente, Mühlebachstrasse 174, 8008 Zürich.
Goethe Foundation of Arts and Sciences, Münstergasse 9, 8001 Zürich.
International Federation of Musicians, Hofackerstrasse 7, 8032 Zürich.
International Music Council (National Committee), Bahnhofstrasse 78, 5000 Aarau.
International Musicological Society, PO Box 1561, 4001 Basel.
International Society for Contemporary Music, Association of Swiss Musicians, Ave du Grammont 11 bis, Case postale 177, 1000 Lausanne 13.
Jeunesses Musicales de Suisse, Case postale 233, 1211 Geneva 8.
National Association of Orchestras, Wattenwylweg 30, 3006 Bern.
National Association of Singers, Burgstrasse 1, 4143 Dornach.
National Music Association, 3946 Turtmann.
Performing Right Society of Switzerland, SUISA, Bellariastrasse 82, 8038 Zürich.
Romand Centre of Sacred Music, PO Box 204, Champel, 1211 Geneva.
Schweiz Chorvereinigung, Scheuchzerstrasse 14, 8006 Zürich.
SUISA Music Foundation (Music Information Centre), Passage Maxmililien-de-Meuron 4, PO Box 409, 2001 Neuchâtel. *Managing Director: P Liechti.*
Swiss Association for Concert Managers, 7 rue do la Fontaine, 1204 Geneva. *Secretary and President: Jack Yfar.*
Swiss Association for Church Singing, Hirschengraben 7, 8001 Zürich.
Swiss Association of Mixed Choirs, Rainallee 68, 4125 Riehen.
Swiss Association of Professional Conductors, Stutzstrasse 9, 8834 Schindellegi.
Swiss Association of Professional Musicians, Elisabethenstrasse 2, 4051 Basel.
Swiss Music Education Association, Forchstrasse 376, 8008 Zürich.
Swiss Music Interpreters Society, Mittelstrasse 49, 8008 Zürich.
Swiss Music Teachers Association, Forchstrasse 376, 8008 Zürich.
Swiss Society of Music Teachers, Alpstrasse 34, 6020 Emmenbrücke.
Swiss Society for Musical Research, PO Box 231, 4020 Basel.
Swiss Society for Popular Music, c/o SUISA, Bellariastrasse 82, 8038 Zürich.
Swiss Workers' Music Association, PO Box 29, 3000 Bern 9.

UK

Alkan Society, 21 Heronswood, Salisbury, Wiltshire SP2 8DH. *Honorary Secretary: Peter Grove.*
Amateur Music Association, Medlock School, Wadeson Road, Manchester M13 9UR. *General Secretary: Ian Clarke.*
Arts Council of Great Britain, 14 Great Peter Street, London SW1P 3NQ. *Secretary-General: Anthony Everitt.*
Association for the Advancement of Teacher Education in Music, 16 Ullswater Avenue, Cardiff CF2 5PT. *Chairman: Dr William Salaman.*
Association of British Choral Directors, 6 Hillside Road, Leighton Buzzard, BedsLU7 8BU. *General Secretary: Anthony Philpott.*
Association for British Music, 2 Union Place, Boston, Lincs PE21 6PS. *Honorary Secretary: Estelle Stiles.*
Association of British Orchestras, Francis House, Francis Street, London SW1P 1DE. *General Administrator: Libby MacNamara.*
Association for Business Support of the Arts, 2 Chester Street, London SW1X 7BB. *Director: Colin Tweedy.*
Association of Entertainment and Arts Management, 3a-5a Stanley Street, Southport, Merseyside PR9 0BY. *General Secretary: J B A Sharples.*
Association of Professional Composers, 34 Hanway Street, London W1P 7DE. *Administrator: Rosemary Dixson.*
Association of Teachers of Singing, 146 Greenstead Road, Colchester, Essex CO1 2SN. *General Secretary: Colin J Schooling.*
Association of University Teachers, 1 Pembridge Road, London W11 3HJ. *General Secretary: Laurie Sapper.*
Association of Woodwind Teachers, 100 Common Road, Chatham, Kent ME5 9RG. *Secretary: Bernard Parris.*
Audio Engineering Society Ltd (British Section), PO Box 645, Slough SL1 8BJ.
Bantock Society, 54 Clarendon Road, Bristol BS6 7ET. *Honorary Secretary: Ron Bleach.*
Barbirolli Society, 8 Tunnel Road, Retford, Notts DN22 7TA. *Chairman: Pauline Pickering.*
Beecham Trust, Denton House, Denton, Harleston, Norfolk IP20 0AA. *Trustee: Shirley, Lady Beecham.*
Benslow Association, Little Benslow Hills, Ibberson Way, Benslow Lane, Hitchin, Herts SG4 9RB. *Secretary: Katharine Bramley.*

Benslow Music Trust, Little Benslow Hills, Ibberson Way, Benslow Lane, Hitchin, Herts SG4 9RB. *Director: Michael Procter.*

Boughton Trust, 4 Church Street, W Liss, Hants.

Bowen Society, Cairnbield, Gordon, Berwickshire. *Chairman: John Lindsay.*

Brian Society, 17 Ash Tree Dell, London NW9 0AG. *Secretary: David Brown.*

Bridge Trust, 14 Barlby Road, London W10 6AR. *Secretary: John Bishop.*

British Academy of Songwriters, Composers and Authors, 34 Hanway Street, London W1P 9DE. *Chairman: Guy Fletcher.*

British-American Arts Association, 116 Commercial Street, London E1 6NF. *Director: Jennifer Williams.*

British Arts Festivals Association, 3rd Floor, Whitechapel Library, 77 Whitechapel High Street, London E1 7QX. *Co-ordinator: Gwyn Rhydderch.*

British Association of Concert Agents, 26 Wadham Road, London SW15 2LR. *President: David Sigall.*

British Association of Symphonic Bands and Wind Ensembles, 3 Northbrook Road, Solihull, West Midlands B90 3NT. *Secretary: Tony Veal.*

British Broadcasting Corporation, Broadcasting House, London W1A 1AA.

British Copyright Council, 29 Berners Street, London W1P 4AA. *Secretary: Geoffrey Adams.*

British Council, Arts Division, 10 Spring Gardens, London SW1A 2BN. *Department of Music Director: John Acton.*

British Federation of Brass Bands, 4 Kingsway Park, Davyhulme, Urmston, Manchester M31 2FB. *Publicity Officer: Gary Newborough.*

British Federation of Music Festivals, Festivals House, 198 Park Lane, Macclesfield, Cheshire SK11 6UD. *Secretary: Eileen Craine.*

British Flute Society, 65 Marlborough Place, London NW8 0PT. *Secretary: John Francis.*

British Horn Society, c/o Paxman Ltd, 116 Long Acre, London WC2E 9PA.

British Institute of Organ Studies, c/o University of Reading, Department of Music, 35 Upper Redlands Road, Reading, Berks RG1 5JE. *Secretary: Dr Christopher Kent.*

British Kodály Society, 31 Woodlands Road, London SW13 0JZ.

British Music Information Centre, 10 Stratford Place, London W1N 9AE. *Manager: Elizabeth Yeoman.*

British Music Society, 30 High Beeches, Gerards Cross, Bucks SL9 7HX. *President: John McCabe.*

British Phonographic Industry Ltd, 25 Saville Row, London W1X 1AA. *Director General: John Deacon.*

British Society for Electronic Music, 277 Putney Bridge Road, London SW15 2PT. *Secretary: Dr Peter Zinovieff.*

British Suzuki Institute, The Old School, Brewhouse Hill, Wheathampstead, Herts AL4 8AN. *Administrator: Miss B S Breslin.*

Cathedral Organists' Association, c/o Royal School of Church Music, Addington Palace, Croydon CR9 5AD. *Secretary: Dr Lionel Dakers.*

Choir Schools' Association, Westminster Cathedral Choir School, Ambrosden Avenue, London SW1P 1QH. *Honorary Secretary: P Hannigan.*

City of London Society of Organists, Hill House, 17 Hans Place, London SW1X 0EP. *Chairman and Secretary: Richard Townend.*

Clarinet and Saxophone Society of Great Britain, 43 Keward Avenue, Wells, Somerset BA5 1TS. *Membership Secretary: Susan Moss.*

Composers' Guild of Great Britain, 34 Hanway Street, London W1P 9DE. *Secretary: Elizabeth Yeoman.*

Computer Arts Society, 50-51 Russell Square, London WC1B 4JP. *Secretary: John Lansdown.*

Concert Artistes' Association, 20 Bedford Street, London WC2E 9HP. *Secretary: Jo Palmer.*

Critics' Circle, 47 Bermondsey Street, London SE1 3XT. *Secretary: Peter Hepple.*

Crotch Society, 74 Pembroke Road, London W8 6NX. *Secretary: Jonathan Rennert.*

Dalcroze Society Inc, 26 Bullfinch Road, Selsdon Vale, South Croydon CR2 8PW. *Chairman: Ruth Stewart.*

Delius Society, 28 Emscote Street South, Bell Hall, Halifax, West Yorks HX1 3AN. *Secretary: Diane Eastwood.*

Delius Trust, 16 Ogle Street, London W1P 7LG. *Chairman: Norman K Millar.*

Dolmetsch Foundation, High Pines, Wood Road, Hindhead, Surrey GU6 6PT. *Secretary: Pat Dutton.*

Donizetti Society, 56 Harbut Road, LondonSW11 2RB. *Honorary Secretary: J R Carter.*

Dvořák Society, 162 Frant Road, Thornton Heath, Surrey CR4 7JW. *Chairman: Mark Todd.*

Early Music Centre Ltd, Charles Clore House, 17 Russell Square, London WC1B 5DR. *Administrator: Frederik Martin.*

Electro-Acoustic Music Association of Great Britain, 10 Stratford Place, London W1N 9AE. *Administrator: Charol Butler.*

Elgar Society, 20 Geraldine Road, Malvern, Worcs WR14 3PA.

English Folk Dance and Song Society, 2 Regents Park Road, London NW1 7AY. *Managing Director: Brenda Godrich.*

European Piano Teachers' Association, 28 Emperor's Gate, London SW7 4HS. *Chairman: John Bigg.*

European String Teachers' Association, 5 Neville Avenue, New Malden, Surrey KT3 4SN. *Organizing Secretary: Nannie Jamieson.*

Federation of British Audio, 19 Charing Cross Road, London WC2H 0ES. *Chairman: N J Crocker.*

Federation of Master Organ Builders, Petersfield GU32 3AT. *Secretary: D M van Heck.*

Federation of Music Industries, 24 Fairlawn Grove, Chiswick, London W4 5EH. *General Secretary/Administrator: Arthur Spencer-Bolland.*

Federation of Recorded Music Societies Ltd, c/o The Secretary, Mrs M Williamson, 67 Galleys Bank, Whitehill, Kidsgrove, Staffs ST7 4DE.

Fellowship of Makers & Researchers of Historical Instruments, c/o St Aldate's Faculty of Music, Oxford OX1 1DB. *Honorary Secretary: Jeremy Montagu.*

Galpin Society, 38 Eastfield Road, Western Park, Leicester LE3 6FE. *Secretary: Pauline Holden.*

Gilbert and Sullivan Society, 273 Northfield Avenue, London W5 4UA.

Grainger Society, 6 Fairfax Crescent, Aylesbury, Bucks HP20 2ES. *Secretary: Barry P Ould.*

Guild of Professional Musicians, 48 Chalcot Road, London NW1 8LS. *Administrator: Ian Bonner.*

Guild for the Promotion of Welsh Music, 94 Walter Road, Swansea SA1 5QA. *Honorary Secretary: Geraint W Walters.*

Haydn Society of Great Britain, c/o University of Lancaster, Department of Music, Bailrigg, Lancaster LA1 4YW. *Director: Denis McCaldin.*

Hazard Chase Ltd, Richmond House, 16-20 Regent Street, Cambridge CB2 1DB. *Tel: 44 1223 312400; Fax: 44 1223 460827.*

Hymn Society of Great Britain and Ireland, The Vicarage, 51 Overgreen Drive, Kinghurst, Birmingham B37 6EY. *Secretary: Rev Michael Garland.*

Incorporated Association of Organists, 11 Stonehill Drive, Bromyard, Herefordshire HR7 4XB. *General Secretary: Roger Bishton.*

Incorporated Society of Musicians, 10 Stratford Place, London W1N 9Ae. *General Secretary: David Padgett-Chandler.*

Incorporated Society of Organ Builders, Petersfield GU32 3AT. *Secretary: D M van Heck.*

Institute of Musical Instrument Technology, 8 Chester Court, Albnay Street, London NW1 4BU. *Secretary: Frank Fowler.*

International Association of Music Libraries, Archives and Documentation Centres, c/o Royal Northern College of Music Library, 124 Oxford Road, Manchester M13 9RD. *General Secretary: Anna Smart.*

International Council for Traditional Music, Flat 1, 30 Holland Park, London W11 3TA. *Secretary: Philippa Heale.*

International Federation of Musicians, 29 Catherine Place, Buckingham Gate, London SW1E 6EH.

International Federation of Phonogram and Videogram Producers, 54 Regent Street, London W1R 5PJ.

International Society for Contemporary Music, British Section, c/o West Heath Studios 174 Mill Lane, London NW6 1TB. *Administrator: Richard Steele.*

International Society for Music Education, ISME International Office, ICRME, University of Reading, Bulmershe Court, Reading, Berks RG6 1HX. *Secretary General: Ronald Smith.*

Ireland Trust, 35 St Mary's Mansions, St Mary's Terrace, London W2 1SQ.

Kempe Society, 135 Stevenage Road, London SW6 6PB. *Treasurer-Secretary: J Audrey Ellison.*

Korngold Society, 12 Townhead Terrace, Paisley, Renfrewshire PA1 2AX. *Secretary: Konrad Hopkins.*

Liszt Society Ltd, 135 Stevenage Road, London SW6 6PB. *Secretary: Audrey Ellison.*

Lute Society, 26B Hindes Road, Harrow, Middlesex HA1 1SL.

Massenet Society, Flat 2, 79 Linden Gardens, London W2 4EU. *Director: Stella J Wright.*
Mechanical Copyright Protection Society Ltd, 41 Streatham High Road, London SW16 1Er. *Managing Director: Frans J P De Wit.*
Music Advisers' National Association, Education Department, Avon House North, St James Barton, Bristol BS99 7EB. *Secretary: Carl Sidgreaves.*
Music Industries Association, 7 The Avenue, Datchet, Slough, Berks SL3 9DH. *Secretary: J A Fox.*
Music Masters' and Mistresses' Association, Steepcot, Bedales School, Petersfield, Hants GU32 2DG. *Honorary Secretary: Jonathan Willcocks.*
Music Publishers' Association Ltd, Strandgate, 3rd Floor, 18-20 York Buildings, London WC2N 6JU. *Secretary: Peter Dadswell.*
Music Retailers Association, PO Box 249, London W4 5EX. *Secretary: Arthur Spencer-Bolland.*
Music for Youth. 4 Blade Mews, Deodar Road, London SW15 2NN. *Director: Larry Westland.*
Musicians' Union, 60-62 Clapham Road, London SW9 0JJ. *General Secretary: Dennis Scard.*
National Association of Art Centres, The Arts Centre, Room 110, Vane Terrace, Darlington DL3 7AX.
National Association for Education in the Arts, c/o University of Exeter, School of Education, St Luke's, Exeter EX1 2LU. *Secretary: Beryl Phillips.*
National Association of Teachers in Further and Higher Education, 27 Britannia Street, London WC1X 9JP.
National Association of Youth Orchestras, 11 St Colme Street, Edinburgh EH3 6AG. *Secretary: Carol Main.*
National Campaign for the Arts, Francis House, Francis Street, London SW1P 1DE. *Director: Simon Mundy.*
National Early Music Association, 39 Chapel Road, London E7 0JP.
National Federation of Gramophone Societies, Withyfeld, 192c Woodrow Forest, Melksham, Wilts SN12 7RF. *Chairman: J R Shaw.*
National Federation of Music Societies, Francis House, Francis Street, London SW1P 1DE. *Administrator: Russell Jones.*
National Operatic and Dramatic Association, 1 Crestfield Street, London WC1H 8AU.
National School Band Association, East Cliffe, Side Cliff Road, Roker, Sunderland SR6 9PX. *Secretary: Alan Winwood.*
National Union of Musical Instrument Makers, c/o Furniture, Timber and Allied Trades Union, Fairfields, Roe Green, Kingsbury, London NW9 0PT. *General Secretary: Colin Christopher.*
Open University Arts Faculty, Walton Hall, Milton Keynes MK7 6AA. Tel: 44 1908 653280. *Contact: Prof D Burrows / Prof T Herbert*
Orff Society, 7 Rothesay Avenue, Richmond, Surrey TW10 5EB. *Secretary: Margaret Murray.*
Organ Club, 10 Roxburgh Court, 69 Melrose Road, London SW18 1PG. *General Secretary: Adrian Mumford.*
Performing Right Society Ltd, 29-33 Berners Street, London W1P 4AA. *Chief Executive: M J Freegard.*
Personal Managers' Association, c/o Rooke Holt & Co, 83 Elbury Street, London SW1. *Chairman: Peter Dunlop.*
Plainsong and Mediaeval Music Society, 72 Brewery Road, London N7 9NE. *Secretary: Catherine Harbor.*
Pro Corda, Leiston Abbey House, Leiston, Suffolk IP16 4TB. *Directors: Pamela Spofforth and Elizabeth Hewlin.*
Rawsthorne Society, c/o Royal Northern College of Music Library, 124 Oxford Road, Manchester M13 9RD. *Secretary: Tony Hodges.*
Robert Farnon Society, 'Stone Gables', Upton Lane, Searington St Michael, Ilminster, Somerset, TA19 0PZ.
Royal College of Organists, Kensington Gore, London SW7 2QS. *Honorary Secretary: Stephen Cleobury.*
Royal Musical Association, St Aldates, Faculty of Music, Oxford OX1 1DB. *Secretary: Dr Ewan West.*
Royal Philharmonic Society, 10 Stratford Place, London W1N 9AE. *Honorary Secretary: Eric Thompson.*
Royal School of Church Music, Addington Palace, Croydon CR9 5AD. *Director: Dr Lionel Dakers.*
Royal Society of Musicians of Great Britain, 10 Stratford Place, London W1N 9AE. *Secretary: Marjorie Gleed.*
Schools Music Association, Town Hall, Education Office, Friern Barnet, London N11 3DL. *Honorary Secretary: Maxwell Pryce.*
Schubert Society of Great Britain, Garden Flat, 125 Grosvenor Avenue, London N5 2NL. *Secretary: Alan Tabelin.*
Scottish Arts Council, 12 Manor Place, Edinburgh EH3 7DD. *Music Director: Christie Duncan.*
Scottish Music Information Centre, 1 Bowmont Gardens, Galsgow G12 9LR.
Simpson Society, 3 Engle Park, London NW7 2HE. *Secretaries: John and Sylvia Brooks.*
Society for the Promotion of New Music, West Heath Studios, 174 Mill Lane, London NW6 1TB. *Administrator: Richard Steele.*
Society for the Research in the Psychology of Music and Music Education, Westminster College, N Hinksey, Oxford OX2 9AT. *Secretary: Dr Janet Mills.*
Spohr Society of Great Britain, 123 Mount View Road, Sheffield S8 8PJ.
Stokowski Society, 7 Priestfields, Rochester, Kent ME1 3AG. *Secretary: Andrew Barker.*
Sullivan Society, 51 Nowton Road, Bury St Edmunds, Suffolk IP33 2BU. *Secretary: Stephen Turnbull.*
UK Council for Music Education and Training, 13 Black Lane, South Luffenham, Oakham, Leics LE15 8NQ. *Secretary: Linda Cummins.*
United Kingdom Harpists Association, 39 Villiers Clo, Surbiton, Surrey KT5 8DN. *Secretary: Angela Moore.*
Viola d'Amore Society, 1 Parkside Avenue, Wimbledon Common, London SW19 5ES.
Viola da Gamba Society, 93A Sutton Road, London N10 1HH. *Administrator: Caroline Wood.*
Visiting Orchestras' Consultative Association, 10 Stratford Place, London W1N 9AE. *Secretary: Hilary Ougham.*
Wagner Society, 15 David Avenue, Wickford, Essex SS11 7BG. *Secretary: Dr J J Pritchard.*
Warlock Society, 32a Chipperfield House, Cale Street, London SW3 2SA. *Secretary: Malcolm Rudland.*
Welsh Arts Council, 9 Museum Place, Cardiff CF1 3NX. *Music Director: Roy Bohana.*
Welsh Music Information Centre, PO Box 78, University College, Cardiff, S Glam CF1 1XL. *Director: A J Howard Rees.*
Workers' Music Association, 17 Prideaux House, Prideaux Place, London WC1. *Secretary: Anne Gilman.*
Worshipful Company of Musicians, 2nd Floor, St Dunstan's House, 2-4 Carey Lane, London EC2V 8AA. *Clerk: W R I Crewdson.*

USA

Amateur Chamber Music Players Inc, 545 Eighth Avenue, 9th Floor, New York, NY 10018. *Chief Officer: Cecilia Drinker Saltonstall.*
American Academy and Institute of Arts and Letters, 633 West 155th Street, New York, NY 10032. *Executive Director: Virginia Dajani.*
American Academy of Teachers of Singing, Hotel Ansonia, Studio No 5-517, 2109 Broadway, New York, NY 10023. *Chairman: Donald Read.*
American Accordionists' Association Inc, PO Box616, Mineola, NY 11501. *Presidnet: Faithe Deffner.*
American Arts Aliance, 1319 F Street North West, Suite 500, Washington, DC 20004.
American Association for Music Therapy, PO Box 80012, Valley Forge, PA 19484.
American Beethoven Society, San Jose State University, 1 Washington Square, Ira F Brilliant Center for Beethoven Studies, San Jose, CA 95192. *Contact: William Meredith.*
American Berlin Opera Foundation Inc, 666 Fifth Avenue, 21st Floor, New York, NY 10103. *Chief Officer: Christa Drechsler.*
American Brahms Society, University of Washington, School of Music, Box 353450, Seattle, WA 98195-3450. *Executive Director: George S Bozarth.*
American Cello Council Inc, 340 West 55th Street, New York, NY 10019. *Administrator and Treasurer: Esther Prince.*
American Choral Directors' Association, PO Box 6310, Lawton, OK 73506. *Executive Director: Gene Brooks.*
American College of Musicians, PO Box 1807, 808 Rio Grande, Austin, TX 78767. *President: Richard Allison.*
American Composes Alliance and Edition, 170 West 74th Street, New York, NY 10023. *President: Richard Brooks.*
American Federation of Musicians, 1501 Broadway, Suite 600, New York, NY 10036. *President: Mark Tully Massagli.*

MUSIC ORGANIZATIONS

American Federation of Television and Radio Artists (AFTRA), 260 Madison Avenue, New York, NY 10016. *Executive Director: Bruce A York.*
American Federation of Violin and Bow Makers Inc, 33 North "B" Street, No 8, San Mateo, CA 94401.
American Guild of Music, 5354 Washington Street, Downers Grove, IL 60515. *Registered Agent: E D Herrick.*
American Guild of Musical Artists, 1727 Broadway, New York, NY 10019. *Executive Secretary: Louise Gillmore.*
American Guild of Organists, 475 Riverside Drive, Sutie 1260, New York, NY 10115. *Executive Director: Daniel N Colburn.*
American Harp Society Inc, 6331 Quebec Drive, Los Angeles, CA 90068. *President: Molly Hahn.*
American Liszt Society Inc, 210 Devonshire Drive, Rochester, NY 14625. *President: Fernando Laires.*
American Matthay Association, 46 Popular Street, Pittsburgh, PA 15205. *President: Thomas C Davis.*
American Mechanical Rights Agency Inc (AMRA), 333 South Tamiami Trail, Suite 295, Venice, FL 34285. *Chief Officer: Patricia Bente.*
American Music Center Inc, 30 West 26th Street, Sutie 1001, New York, NY 10010. *Executive Director: Nancy C Clarke.*
American Music Conference, 5140 Avenida Encinas, Carlsbad, CA 92008. *Executive Director: Robert Morrison.*
American Musical Instrument Society, c/o Shrine to Music Museum, 414 East Clark Street, Vermilliom, SD 57069.
American Musicians Union, 8 Tobin Court, Dumont, NJ 07628. *President: Ben Intorre.*
American Musicological Society, 201 South 34th Street, Philadelphia, PA 19104. *Executive Director: Ruth Steiner.*
American New Music Consortium, 87-27 Santiago Street, Holliswood, NY 11423. *Executive Director: Dinu Ghezzo.*
American Orff-Schulwerk Association, PO Box 391089, Cleveland, OH 44139.
American Recorder Society, 236 West County Line Road, Jackson, NJ 08527. *President: Constance Primus.*
American Society of Composers, Authors and Publishers (ASCAP), 1 Lincoln Plaza, New York, NY 10023. *President: Marilyn Bergman.*
American String Teachers Association Inc, 1806 Robert Fulton Drive, Suite 300, Reston, VA 22091. *Executive Administrator: Galen Wixson.*
American Symphony Orchestra League, 777 14th Street North West, Suite 500, Washington, DC 20005. *Chief Executive Officer: Catherine French.*
American Viola Society, 24833 Sage Crest Road, Newhall, CA 91321. *President: Alan de Veritch.*
American Women Composers Inc, George Washington University, Washington, DC 20052. *President: Stephania de Kenessey.*
Arts International Program, Institute of International Education, 809 UN Plaza, New York, NY 10017. *Director: Jane M Gullong.*
The Asia Society, 725 Park Avenue, New York, NY 10021. *Director: Rhoda Grauer.*
Associated Male Choruses of America Inc, PO Pox 771, Brainerd, MN 56401. *Executive Secretary: Forbes H Martinson.*
Association for Recorded Sound Collections Inc, PO Box 10162, Silver Spring, MD 20904. *Executive Director: Peter Shambarger.*
Association of Arts Administration Educators Inc, c/o American Council for the Artis, 1 East 53rd Street, New York, NY 10022. *President: J Dennis Rich.*
Association of Performing Arts Presenters, 1112 16th Street North West, Suite 400, Washington, DC 20036. *Executive Director: Susan Farr.*
Audio Engineering Society Inc, 60 East 42nd Street, Lincoln Building, Room 2520, New York, NY 10165. *Executive Director: Donald J Plunkett.*
B(roadcast) M(usic) I(nc), 320 West 57th Street, New York, NY 10019. *President and Chief Executive Officer: Frances W Preston.*
Box Office Management International, 333 East 46th Street, Suite 1B, New York, NY 10017. *President: Patricia Spira.*
Bruckner Society of America Inc, 2150 Dubuque Road, Iowa City, IA 52240. *President: Charles L Eble.*
Business Committee for the Arts Inc, 1775 Broadway, Suite 510, New York, NY 10019. *President: Judith A Jedlicka.*
Chamber Music America, 545 Eighth Avenue, New York, NY 10018. *President: Bonnie Hampton.*
Chopin Foundation of the United States, 1440 79th Street Causeway, Miami, FL 33141.
Choristers Guild, 2834 West Kingsley Road, Garland, TX 75041. *Executive Director: Patricia M Evans.*
Chorus America: Association of Professional Vocal Ensembles, 2111 Sansom Street, Philadelphia, PA 19103. *Executive Director: Kenneth Garner.*
College Band Directors National Association, University of Texas, Box 8028, Austin, TX 78713. *Secretary-Treasurer: Richard L Floyd.*
The College Music Society Inc, 202 West Spruce Street, Missoula, MT 59802. *Executive Director: Robby D Gunstream.*
Composers' Forum Inc, 73 Spring Street, Suite 506, New York, NY 10012.
Composers Guild, Box 586, Farmington, UT 84025. *President: Ruth Gatrell.*
Composers' Resources Inc, PO Box 19935, Atlanta, GA 30325. *President: Howard Weshil.*
Concert Music Broadcasters Association, Hotel St Francis, 335 Powell Street, San Francisco, CA 94102.
Conductors' Guild Inc, PO Box 3361, West Chester, PA 19381. *Executive Secretary: Judy Ann Voois.*
Creative Audio and Music Electronics Organization, 7753 State Boulevard Ext, Meridan, MS 39305. *President: Larry Blakely.*
Delta Omicron (International Music Fraternity), 841 W Cherokee Drive, Jefferson City, TN 37760.
Early Music America, 30 West 26th Street, Suite 1001, New York, NY 10010.
George Enescu Society of the United States Inc, 4 Barrett Place, Northampton, MA 01060.
Guitar Foundation of America, Box 1240, Claremont, CA 91711. *General Manager: Gunnar Eisel.*
The Hymn Society in the United States and Canada, Texas Christian University, Box 30854, Fort Worth, TX 76129. *Executive Director: W Thomas Smith.*
Independent Composers Association, Box 45134, Los Angeles, CA 90045. *President: Burt Goldstein.*
Institute for Music, Health and Education, PO Box 4179, Boulder, CO 80306. *Director: Don G Campbell.*
Institute of Audio Research, School of Audio and Video Technology, 64 University Place, Greenwich Village, New York, NY 10003. *Director: Miriam Friedman.*
International Association of Auditorium Managers, 4425 West Airport Freeway, Suite 590, Irving, TX 75062. *Executive Director: John S Swinburn.*
International Computer Music Association, 2040 Polk Street, Suite 330, San Francisco, CA 94109. *President: Allen Strang.*
International Double Reed Society, University of North Texas, School of Music, Denton, TX 76203. *President: Charles Veazey.*
International Federation of Festival Organizations, 4230 Stansbury Avenue, No 105 Sherman Oaks, CA 91423. *Secretary General: Armando Moreno.*
International Horn Society, 2220 North 1400 East, Provo, UT 84604. *Executive Secretary: Ellen Powley.*
International League of Women Composers, Abilene Christian University, ACU Box 8274, Abilene, TX 76999.
International Society of Bassists, 4020 McEwen, Suite 105, Dallas, TX 75244. *General Manager: Madeleine Crouch.*
International Society of Performing Arts Administrators, 2920 Fuller Avenue, NE, Suite 205, Grand Rapids, MI 49505. *Executive Director: Michael C Hardy.*
International Teleproduction Society Inc, 350 Fifth Avenue, Suite 2400, New York, NY 10118. *Executive Director: Janet Luhrs.*
Jeunesses Musicales of the USA, c/o Trinity University, 715 Stadium Drive, San Antonio, TX 78284. *Director: Gerald Benjamin.*
Keyboard Teachers Association International Inc, 361 Pin Oak Lane, Westbury, NY 11590. *President: Albert DeVito.*
League of Composers, International Society of Contemporary Music, 30 W 26th St #1001, New York, NY 10010. *Executive Director: Geoffrey Kidde.*
Leschetizky Association, 105 West 72nd Street, New York, NY 10023. *President: Genia Robinor.*
Lute Society of America, PO Box 1328, Lexington, VA 24450.
Gustav Mahler Society USA, 1616 N Sierra Bonita Avenue, Los Angeles, CA 90046.
The Masterwork Music and Art Foundation Inc, Morristown, NJ 07962. *Executive Director: Shirley S May.*
Moravian Music Foundation Inc, 20 Cascade Avenue, Winston-Salem, NC 27127. *President: M Keith Kapp.*
Mu Phi Epsilon, 2212 Mary Hills Drive, Minneapolis, MN 55422. *President: Katherine Doepke.*
Music Association of America, 224 King Street, Englewood, NJ 07631. *Executive Director: George Sturm.*
Music Critics Association Inc, 7 Pine Court, Westfield, NJ 07090. *Manager: Albert H Cohen.*
Music Educators National Conference, 1806 Robert Fulton Drive, Reston, VA 22091.
Music Library Association Inc, PO Box 487, Canton, MA 02021.
Music Publishers' Association of the United States, 711 Third Avenue, New York, NY 10017.

Music Teachers National Association Inc, 441 Vine Street, Suite 505, Cincinnati, OH 45202.
National Academy of Recording Arts and Sciences Inc, 3402 Pico Boulevard, Santa Monica, CA 90405. *President: Michael Greene.*
National Assembly of Local Arts Agencies, 927 15th Street NW, 12th Floor, Washington, DC 20005. *President/Chief Executive Officer: Robert Lynch.*
National Assembly of State Arts Agencies, 1010 Vermont Avenue NW, Suite 920, Washington, DC 20005. *Executive Director: Jonathan Katz.*
National Association for Music Therapy Inc, 8455 Colesville Road, Suite 930, Silver Spring, MD 20910.
National Association of Broadcasters, 1771 N Street North West, Washington, DC 20036. *President and Chief Executive Officer: Edward Fritts.*
National Association of Composers, USA, PO Box 49652, Barrington Station, Los Angeles, CA 90049. *President: Marshall H Bialosky.*
National Association of Negro Musicians, 11551 S Laflin Street, Chicago, IL 60643. *Executive Secretary: Ona Campbell.*
National Association of Pastoral Musicians, 225 Sheridan Street North West, Washington DC 20011. *President: Virgil C Funk.*
National Association of Performing Arts Managers and Agents Inc, 137 East 30th Street, Suite 3-B, New York, NY 10016.
National Association of Recording Merchandisers Inc, 9 Eves Drive, Suite 120, Mariton, NJ 08053. *Executive Vice President: Pam Horovitz.*
National Association of Schools of Music, 11250 Roger Bacon Drive, Suite 21, Reston, VA 22090. *Executive Director: Samuel Hope.*
National Association of Teachers of Singing Inc, 2800 University Boulevard North, Jacksonville, FL 32211.
National Choral Council, 1650 Broadway, New York, NY 10019. *Executive Director: Martin Josman.*
National Council of Acoustical Consultants, PO Box 359, Springfield, NJ 07081. *Executive Secretary: Virginia Marguire.*
National Federation of Music Clubs, 1336 North Delaware Street, Indianapolis, IN 46202. *Chief Officer: Mrs D Clifford Allison.*
National Foundation for Advancement in the Arts, 800 Brickell Avenue, Suite 500, Miami, FL 33131. *President: William H Banchs.*
National Guild of Community Schools of the Arts Inc, PO Box 8018, Englewood, NJ 07631. *Executive Director: Lolita Mayadas.*
National Music Council, 711 Third Avenue, 8th Floor, New York, NY 10017.
National Music Publishers' Association Inc, 205 East 42nd Street, 18th Floor, New York, NY 10017. *President: Edward P Murphy.*
National Opera Association, Northwestern University, School of Music, 711 Elgin Road, Evanston, IL 60208.
National Orchestral Association, 245 Park Avenue, 15th Floor, New York, NY 10167.
National School Orchestra Association, PO Box 1087, Mill Valley, CA 94942.
National Women Composers Resource Center, 330 Townsend Street, Sutie 218, San Francisco, CA 94107.
Network for New Music, PO Box 29550, Philadelphia, PA 19144. *Artistic Director: Linda Reichert.*
New Music Alliance, 508 Woodland Terrace, Philadelphia, PA 19104. *President: Tina Davidson.*
New York Consortium for New Music, 215 West 90th Street, New York, NY 10024. *President: Patricia Spencer.*
OPERA America Inc, 777 14th Street North West, Suite 520, Washington DC 20005. *Excutive Vice President and Chief Executive Officer: Marc A Scorca.*
Percussive Arts Society, Box 25, Lawton, OK 73502. *Administrative Manager: Steve Beck.*
Phi Beta National Professional Fraternity for Creative and Performing Arts, 801 N Thompson Drive, No 109, Madison, WI 53704. *President: Sarah Whelan.*
Piano Manufacturers Association International, National Piano Foundation, 4020 McEwen, Suite 105, Dallas, TX 75244. *Executive Director: Donald W Dillon.*
Piano Technicians Guild Inc, 3930 Washinton, Kansas City, MO 64111. *Executive Director: Larry Goldsmith.*
Recording Industry Association of America, 1020 19th Street North West, Suite 200, Washington, DC 20036. *President: Jason S Berman.*
SESAC Inc, 55 Music Square East, Nashville, TN 37203.
Society for Ethnomusicology Inc, Indiana University, Morrison Hall 005, Bloomington, IN 47405.
Society of Composers Inc, PO Box 296, Old Chelsea Station, New York, NY 10011.
Songwriters Guild of America, 1500 Harbor Boulevard, Weehawken, NJ 07087. *President: George David Weiss.*
Sonneck Society for American Music, PO Box 476, Canton, MA 02021.
Suzuki Association of the Americas Inc, PO Box 17310, Boulder, CO 80308. *President: Jeffrey Cox.*
Theatre Communications Group Inc, 355 Lexington Avenue, New York, NY 10017. *Director: Peter Zeisler.*
Tubists Universal Brotherhood Association, University of Texas at Austin, Austin, TX 78712.
United States Information Agency, Arts America Program, 301 Fourth Street South West, Washington, DC 20547.
Viola da Gamba Society of America, University of Colorado, Department of Music, Boulder, CO 80302. *President: Gordon Sandford.*
Violin Society of America, 8507 Abingdon Road, Kew Gardens, NY 11415. *President: Hans E Tausig.*
Violoncello Society Inc, 127 West 72nd Street, No 2R, New York, NY 10023. *Executive Administrator: Esther Prince.*
Kurt Weill Foundation for Music Inc, 7 East 20th Street, 3rd Floor, New York, NY 10003. *President: Kim H Kowalke.*
Young Audiences Inc, 115 East 92nd Street, New York, NY 10128. *Executive Director: Richard Bell.*

URUGUAY

Asociación General de Autores del Uruguay, Canelones 1122, PZ 11100 Montevideo. *President: Antonio Italiano.*
Asociación, Uruguay de Musicos, Calle Maldonado 983, CP 11100 Montevideo. *President: Alfonson Coronel.*
Centro Cultural de la Música, Apdo 5, Av 18 de Julio 1006, 6th Floor, Montevideo. *Director: Jorge Calvetti.*
Juventudes Muscales del Uruguay, Sarandi 444, 1st Floor, Edif, SODRE, Montevideo. *President: Maria Tania Siver.*
Sociedad Uruguay de interpretes, Canelones 1090, Montevideo. *President: José Maria Lorenzo.*
Sociedad Uruguay de Música Contemporánea, Casilla de Correo 1328, Montevideo. *President: Diego Legrand.*

VENEZUELA

Juventudes Musicales, Apartado 51441, Caracas 1050.
Sociedad de Autores y Compositores de Venezuela, Edif Vam, entrade Oeste, 9th Floor, Avda, Andrés Bello, Caracas 1050. *President: Guillermo Carrasco.Moscow.*

YUGOSLAVIA

International Society for Contemporary Music (Yugoslav section), PO Box 213, 11000 Belgrade.
Union of Yugoslav Composers, Misarska 12-14, 11000 Belgrade.

APPENDIX E
MAJOR COMPETITIONS AND AWARDS

of awards, restrictions on entrants, dates, etc, may vary from year to year and interested readers are advised to contact the sponsoring organizations directly for complete nation. It should also be noted that many institutions listed in Appendix F also maintain competitions, awards, and scholarship programmes.

AUSTRALIA

ralian Broadcasting Corporation Young Performers' Awards.
Box 9994, Sydney, NSW 2001.
al awards for singers and instrumentalists to the age of 30 who have been in continuous residence in Australia for one year. Must compete in state of residence. Award of 00 plus concert engagements. Next competition 1998.

ralian Singing Competition.
ridiger & Co, Solicitors, 67 Castlereagh Street, Sydney, NSW 2000.
al awards for operatic and classical singers. Must be an Australian or New Zealand citizen under the age of 26 for classical singers and under the age of 35 for operatic rs. Mathy and Opera Awards totalling $100,000.

ey International Piano Competition of Australia.
ox 420, Double Bay, Sydney, NSW 2028.
rennial competition open to pianists of all nationalities between the ages of 18 and 32. Prizes include 1st prize of $15,000 and various other prizes totalling $60,000. Next etition in 1998.

AUSTRIA

ig van Beethoven International Piano Competition.
ingerstrasse 18, A-1010 Vienna.
rennial competition open to pianists of all nationalities between the ages of 17 and 32. Prizes include 1st prize of 80,000 schillings, a Bösendorfer piano, and concert gements, 2nd prize of 60,000 schillings, 3rd prize of 50,000 schillings, and 3 other prizes of 20,000 schillings. Next competition in 1998.

national Anton Bruckner Organ Competition.
re Donaulande7, A-4010 Linz.
rennial competition open to organists of all nationalities to the age of 35. Prizes include 1 st prize of 50,000 schillings, 2nd prize of 40,000 schillings, and 3rd prize of 30,000 ings. Next competition in 1998.

national Belvedere Competition for Opera Singers.
hmarkt 24, A-1010 Vienna.
al competition for singers to the age of 35. Cash prizes (ATS 50, 000).

national Fritz Kreisler Competition.
artstalstrasse 8/19, A-1160 Vienna.
rennial competition for violin and viola. Prizes include 1st prize of 150,000 schillings, 2nd prize of 125,000 schillings, and 3rd prize of 100,000 schillings. Next competition 00.

national Mozart Competition of the Hochschule "Mozarteum".
ellplatz 1, A-5020 Salzburg.
rennial competition open to musicians of all nationalities, singers born after Jan 15 1957, and pianists and violinists born after Jan 15 1959. Prizes include the Mozart Prize the Austrian Ministry of Science and Research, as well as other prizes and concert engagements. Next competition in 1998. First prize ATS 120, 000 in each category.

nationaler Chorwettberwerb.
rreferat der Stadtgemeinde, A-9800 Spittal.
al competition for Choirs. Prizes include money and documents.

Ars Electronica.
ckstrasse 2a, A-4010 Linz.
al competition for the computer arts open to individuals, groups, and organizations. Prizes include money and awards.

na International Competition for Composers.
nos Austria, Dr Karl-Lueger Ring 14, A-1015 Vienna.
al competition open to composers to the age of 40, who submit a composition not previously accepted for performance, or performed in public, or awarded a prize in another etition.

na Modern Masters Annual Orchestral Recording Award.
aretenstrasse 125/15, A-1050 Vienna.
al competition open to all composers of orchestral music.

BELGIUM

ours International de Chant de Verviers.
des Dominicains 1, B-4000 Liège.
nial competition open to singers of all nationalities.

ours International de Guitare.
e Printemps de la Guitare asbl, Place du Chef Lieu 9, B-6040 Charleroi.
nial competition open to solo classical guitarists of all nationalities to the age of 32. Prizes include 1st prize of 200,000 Belgian francs, 2nd prize of 150,000 Belgian francs, rize of 100,000 Belgian francs, and 4th prize of 75,000 Belgian francs. Next competition in 1998.

Festival of Flanders Bruges Musica Antiqua Contest.
Collaert Mansionstraat 30, B-8000 Bruges.
Annual competition open to solo singers, solo instrumentalists, and Baroque ensembles with categories rotating annually on a triennial schedule. Prizes total over 600,000 B francs.

Queen Elisabeth International Music Competition of Belgium.
20 Rue Aus Laines, B-1000 Brussels.
Competition for Composition and Piano in 1999, Singing in 2000, and Violin in 2001. First prize of 500,000 BF.

BULGARIA

International Competition for Young Opera Singers.
56 Rue Alabin, 1000 Sofia.
Quadrennial competition open to men up to the age of 35 and to women up to the age of 33. Prizes include a Grand Prize, 1st prize, 2nd prize, 3rd prize, medals, and diple Next competition in 2000.

CANADA

Banff International String Quartet Competition.
c/o Banff Centre School of Fine Arts, PO Box 1020, Banff, Alberta T0L 0C0.
Triennial competition open to quartets whose members are under 35 years of age at the time of the competition. Prizes include $20,000, $12,000, $8,000, $5,000, $500, bows, Canadian tour, and Banff Centre residency. Next competition in 1998.

Canada Council/Conseil des Arts du Canada Grants and Awards.
PO Box 1047, 99 Metcalfe Street, Ottawa, Ont K1P 5V8.
Grants and awards to artists of Canadian citizenship and to non-profit arts organizations.

Canadian Music Competitions.
1030 St Alexandre, Suite 306, Montréal, PQ H2Z 1P5.
Annual competition for pianists, string players, wind players, and singers open to Canadian citizens or those holding a Landed Immigrant Certificate or those studying Canadian teacher for the last three years between the age of 7 and 31.

Concours Orchestre Symphonique de Montréal.
85 St Catherine West, Montréal, PQ H2X 3P4.
Annual competition open to Canadian citizens or those holding a Landed Immigrant Certificate featuring piano and voice one year and strings and wind the following year; p category A for between the ages of 18 and 25 and category B for those 17 and under; voice - for those between the ages of 18 and 30; strings - category A for those be the ages of 18 and 25 and category B for those 17 and under; winds - for those between the ages of 16 and 25. Prizes totalling $15,500 and an appearance on the re subscriptions series of the Orchestre Symphonique de Montréal.

Eckhardt-Gramatté National Music Competition for the Performance of Canadian Music.
Queen Elizabeth II Building, Room 211, 270-18 Street, Brandon, Man R7A 6A9.
Annual competition open to Canadian citizens or Canadian residents alternating annually between voice, strings, and piano. Prizes include 1st prize of $5,000 and a concer 2nd prize of $3,000, and 3rd prize of $2,000.

Glenn Gould Prize.
Canada Council, 350 Albert Street, PO Box 1047, Ottawa, Ont D1P 5V8.
Triennial prize open to individuals of all nationalities who have made a exceptional contribution to music and its communication through the use of any of the communica technologies. Candidates must be nominated by three specialists in the nominee's field or a related field. Next prize awarded in 1999.

Kamloops Symphony Orchestra New Celebrity Competition.
PO Box 57, Kamloops, BC V2C 5K3.
Annual competition open to Canadian citizens or those holding a Landed Immigrant Certificate. Prizes include 1st prize of $1,000 and 2nd prize of $500, with the two fir appearing in concert with the Kamloops Symphony Orchestra.

Montréal International Music Competition.
Place des Arts, 1501 Jeanne-Mance Street, Montréal PQ H2X 1Z9.
Competition for violin (1995), piano (1996), and voice (1997) with a recess (1998) before pursuing the cycle again; violin and piano for those between the ages of 16 and 3 voice for those between the ages of 20 and 35. Prizes totalling $40,500.

CZECH REPUBLIC

Czech Music Competition of the Czech Ministry of Culture.
Malézské nám 1, 118 00 Prague 1.
Annual competition with categories changing annually.

Prague Spring International Music Competition.
Hellichova 18, CS-118 00 Prague 1.
Annual competition open to performers of all nationalities with categories changing annually in five-year cycles. Prizes include money and an appearance at the Prague S International Music Festival. Piano and String Quartet, 1998; Organ and Harpsichord, 1999; Conducting and Cello, 2000.

DENMARK

International Carl Nielsen Violin Competition.
Claus Bergsgade 9, DK-5000 Odense C.
Quadrennial competition open to violinists of all nationalities to the age of 29. Prizes include a minimum of 300,000 kroner. Next competition in 2000.

national Organ Competition, Odense.
soegade 74, DK-5230 Odense M.
nial competition open to organists of all nationalities to the age of 34. Prizes include 1st prize of 20,000 kroner, 2nd prize of 15,000 kroner, and 3rd prize of 10,000 kroner.
competition in 1998.

ai Malko International Competition for Young Conductors.
anmarks Radio, Rosenoerns Alle 22, DK-1999 Frederiksberg C.
nial competition open to conductors between the ages of 20 and 31. Prizes include cash. Next competition in 1998.

EIRE

Dublin International Piano Competition.
ity Hall, Dublin 2.
nial competition open to pianists between the ages of 17 and 30. Prizes include 1st prize of 10,000 Irish pounds, debut recitals in London, Vienna, Paris, and New York,
concert engagements with major international orchestras, 2nd prize of 7,500 Irish pounds, 3rd prize of 5,000 Irish pounds, and lesser prizes. Next competition in 2000.

FINLAND

m Helin International Singing Competition.
innish Cultural Foundation, PB 203, SF-00121 Helsinki 12.
quennial competition open to singers of all nationalities, women born after 1 Jan 1968, and men born after 1 Jan 1966. Prizes separate for men and women including 4 prizes
totalling $120,00. Next competition in 1999.

national Jean Sibelius Violin Competition.
31, SF-00100 Helsinki 10.
quennial competition for violinists. Prizes totalling about $34,000. Next competition in 2000.

o Cello Competition.
ox 782. SF-00101 Naantali.
quennial competition for cellists of all nationalities born between 1963 and 1980. Prizes include cash. Next competition in 2001.

FRANCE

cours International d'Ensembles de Musique de Chambre de Colmar.
ervice des Activités Culturelles, Hôtel de Ville, F-68000 Colmar.
nial competition for chamber music ensembles for performers to the age of 35 Prizes include 30,000 francs, 15,000 francs, and 10,000 francs. Next competition in 1998.

cours International d'Orgue "Grand Prix de Chartres".
ue de Grenelle, F-75007 Paris.
nial competition open to all organists born after 1 Jan 1961. Prizes include two grand prizes of 20,000 francs each, one for interpretation and one for improvisation, and two
prizes of 5,000 francs each, one for interpretation and one for improvisation. Next competition in 1998.

cours International de Chant de La Ville de Toulouse.
héâtre du Capitole, F-31000 Toulouse.
al competition open to singers between the ages of 18 and 33. Prizes totalling 135,000 francs.

cours International de Chant de Paris.
ue du Dôme, F-75016.
nial competition open to singers, women to the age of 32 and men to the age of 34. Prizes include 120,000 francs and concert engagements. Next competition in 1998.

cours International de Chant Offenbach.
ue Jouffroy, F-75017 Paris.
nial competition open to singers of all nationalities and all ages. Prizes include appearances in European theaters and festivals. Next competition in 1998.

cours International de Clavecin.
estival Estival de Paris, 20 Rue Geoffroy l'Asnier, F-75004 Paris.
nial competition open to harpsichordists to the age of 32. Prizes include cash. Next competition in 1999.

cours International de Flute Jean-Pierre Rampal.
e Bellart, F-75015.
competition tentatively set for 1999.

cours International de Guitare.
adio France, 116 Avenue du President Kennedy, F-75786 Paris Cédex 16.
al competition open to classical guitarists of all nationalities to the ages of 30 and biennial competition open to composers of all nationalities. Prizes include cash and concerts
itals.

cours International de Jeunes Chefs d'Orchestre.
Rue Isenbart, F-25000 Besançon.
al competition open to conductors under the age of 35. Prizes include Emile Vuillermoz Prize and others.

cours International de Musique de Chambre.
de Dôme 10, F-75116 Paris.
nial competition open to instrumentalists and singers to the age of 35. Prizes include 62,500 francs. Next competition in 1998.

cours International de Musique Electroacoustique.
B, Place André Malraux, BP 39, F-18000 Bourges.
al competition for electroacoustic music, music for performer(s) and tape, electroacoustic program music, and live electroacoustic music.

cours International de Trompette "Maurice André".
e Bellart, F-75015 Paris.
petition for young trumpeters. Prizes include four grand prizes. Next competition tentatively set for 2000.

Concours International de Violon "Yehudi Menuhin".
5 Rue Bellart, F-75015 Paris.
Competition for young violinists. Prizes include a grand prize and three other prizes. Next competition in 1998.

Concours International de Violoncelle "Rostropovich".
146 Rue de Rennes, F-75006 Paris.
Competition for cellists of all nationalities to the age of 33. Prizes include cash and public performances. Next competition in 1998.

Concours International du Festival de Musique de Toulon.
Palais de la Bourse, Avenue jean-Moulin, F-83000 Toulon.
Annual competition open to instrumentalists between the ages of 18 and 30 with categories rotating on annual schedule. Prizes include 1st prize of 20,000 francs, 2nd pr *12,000 francs, and 3rd prize of 8,000 francs.*

Concours International Marguerite Long-Jacques Thibaud.
32 Avenue Matignon, F-75008 Paris.
Triennial competition open to pianists and violinists between the ages of 16 and 30. Prizes include 250,000 francs for winners in each category. Next competition for pian *1998 and for violinists in 1999.*

Florilège Vocal de Tours.
BP 1452, F-37014 Tours Cédex.
Annual competition open to choral and vocal performers and composeres. Prizes include 18 prizes totalling 100,000 francs.

Fondation des Etats-Unis Harriet Hale Woolley Scholarships.
15 Boulevard Jourdan, F-75690 Paris Cédex 14.
Annual scholarships open to single American instrumentalists or artists between the ages of 21 and 30 for study in Paris. Scholarships include from four to five $8,500 aw

International Rostroprovitch Cello Competition.
c/o Association Acanthes, 3 Rue des Couronnes, F-75020 Paris.

Yvonne Lefébure International Piano Competition.
c/o Association Acanthes, 146 Rue de Rennes, F-75006 Paris.
Biennial competition open to pianists of all nationalities to the age of 35. Prizes include cash and public performances. Next competition in 1998.

Prix Musical International Arthur Honegger.
c/o Fondation de France, 40 Avenue Hoche, F-75008 Paris.
Biennial competition open to all composers. Prizes include 50,000 francs. Next competition in 1998.

Rencontres Musicales d'Evian International String Quartet Competition.
6 Rue Téhéran, F-75008 Paris or Château de Blonay, F-74500 Evian les Bains.
Biennial competition open to string quartets of all nationalities whose average age does not exceed 33 years of age. Prizes include over 500,000 francs. Next competition in

World Music Masters International Piano Competition.
Salle Gaveau, 45 Rue La Boétie, F-75008 Paris.
Annual competition open only to pianists who have been finalists in other international competitions. Prizes include $30,000 and concert engagements.

GERMANY

Hannover International Violin Competition.
Stiftung Niedersachsen , Ferdinandstrasse 4, D-30175 Hannover.
Triennial competition open to violinists of all nationalities between the ages of 16 and 30. Prizes include cash, a recording, and concert engagements. Next competition in

International Johann Sebastian Bach Competition.
Thomaskirchhof 16, D-04109 Leipzig.
Quadrennial competition open to pianists, organists, violinists, harpsichordists, and singers of all nationalities born after 31 Dec 1966. Prizes include cash. Next competit *2000.*

International Kuhlau Wettbewerb für Flotisten.
Herzogenplatz 5, Postfach 2061, D-29510 Uelzen.
Triennial competition for solo flute and flute with piano, two flutes or two flutes with piano, or three or four flutes. Next competition in 1998.

International Music Competition of the Broadcasting Corporations of Germany.
c/o Bayerischer Rundfunk, Rundfunkplatz 1, D-80300 Munich.
Annual competition open to solo instrumentalists, string quartets, and singers with categories changing annually.

International Piano Competition of Cologne.
c/o Foundation Tomassoni, Dagobertstrasse 38, D-50668 Cologne.
Triennial competition open to pianists of all nationalists between the ages of 18 and 29. Prizes include 1st prize of 15,000 marks, 2nd prize of 10,000 marks, and 3rd prize of 5 *marks. Next competition in 1999.*

International Robert Schumann Contest.
Muenzstrasse 12, 9540 Zwickau.
Quadrennial competition open to pianists to the age of 25 and to singers to the age of 32. Prizes include cash. Next competition in 2001.

International Violin Competition Louis Spohr.
Burgunderstrasse 4, D-79104 Freiburg.
Triennial competition open to violinists of all nationalities to the age of 32. Prizes include 1st prize of 12,000 marks, 2nd prize of 8,000 marks, and 3rd prize of 5,000 marks. *competition in 2000.*

Internationaler Wettbewerb für Junge Painisten Ettingen.
Pforzheimerstrasse 25a, D-76275 Ettlingen.
Biennial competition open to pianists of all nationalities; category A for those born on or after 7 August 1984, or category B for those born on or after 7 August 1979. *competition in 1998.*

nationaler Wettbewerb für Komponistinnen.
ɔethstrasse 5, Mannheim.
drennial competition open to women composers of all nationalities. Prizes include cash. Next competition in 1998.

nationaler Wettbewerb für Streichquartett Karl Klingler-Preis.
schule für Musik, Charlottenstr. 55, D-10117 Berlin.
nial competition open to string quartets whose total age is 128 years with no members over the age of 37. Prizes include cash. Next competition in 1998.

GREECE

ris Mitropoulos International Competition
ex Soutaou, GR-10671 Athens
al competition.

national Music Competition Maria Callas.
rikis Street 8, 10671 Athens.
nial competition open to singers (opera, oratorio, lieder) and pianists with the categories alternating annually. Prizes include cash. Next competition for piano in 19968and
ice in 1999.

HUNGARY

pest International Music Competition.
terArt Festivalcenter, PO Box 80, H-1366 Budapest.
al competition with categories changing annually.

national Conductors Competition of the Hungarian Television.
ox 80, Vorasmarty tér 1, H-1366 Budapest
nial competition open to conductors of all nationalities under the age of 35. Next competition in 1998.

ISRAEL

national Harp Contest.
aronowitz Street, 63566 Tel Aviv.
nial competition open to harpists of all nationalities. Prizes include 1st prize of a Lyon and Healy concert grand harp, 2nd prize of $5,000, and 3rd prize of $3,000. Next
petition in 2000.

ard Bernstein Jerusalem International Music Competition.
vka Street, PO Box 10185, 91101 Jerusalem.
al competition open to all musicians between the ages of 24 and 37 and all composers between the ages of 22 and 50 rotating in three-year cycles. Prize of $25,000 to all
ers.

ur Rubinstein International Piano Master Competition.
ox 6018, 61060 Tel Aviv.
nial competition open to pianists of all nationalities between the ages of 18 and 32. Prizes include 1st prize of the Arthur Rubinstein Award Gold Medla and $10,000, 2nd
of the Silver Medal and $5,000, 3rd prize of the Bronze Medal and $3,000, and 4th, 5th, and 6th prizes of $1,000 each. Next competition in 1998.

ITALY

ociazione Concorisi & Rassegno Musicali (ACERM) Concorso Internazionale per Complessi da Camera Città di Firenze "Premio Vittorio Gui".
o Albizi, I-50122 Florence.
ual competition open to chamber music instrumnetalists to the age of 32. Prizes totalling some 30,000,000 lire.

entino Bucchi" Competition.
Jbaldino Peruzzi 20, I-00139 Rome.
al competition open to performers and composers. Prizes totalling some 100,000,000 lire.

co Caruso International Competition for Young Tenors.
ssociazione Enrico Caruso, Via Degli Omenoni 2, I-20121 Milan.
nial competition open to tenors between the ages of 18 and 28.

sandro Casagrande Concorso Pianistico Internazionale.
une de Terni, Vico S Lorenzo 1, I-05100 Terni.
nial competition open to pianists born after 1 January 1966. Prizes include 1st prize of 12,000,000 lire, 2nd prize of 8,000,000 lire, and 3rd prize of 5,000,000 lire. Next
petition in 1998.

ar Cassadó International Cello Competition.
olferino 15, I-50123 Florence.
nial competition open to cellists. Next competition in 1998.

corso Internazionale di Chitarra Classica "Città di Alessandria".
za Garibaldi 16, I-15100 Alessandria.
ual competition open to solo classical guitarists of all nationalities. Prizes include cash.

corso Internazionale di Composizione "Camilo Togni".
ssociazione Nuovi Spazi Sonori, Casella Postale 196, I-25100 Brescia.
nial competition open to composers of all nationalities born after 31 December 1956. Prizes include 1st prize of 10,000,000 lire, plus publication and performance of winning
osition.

Concorso Internazionale di Composizione "Goffredo Petrassi".
Piazzale Cesare Battisti 15, I-43100 Parma.
Biennial competition open to composers of all nationalities for an unpublished symphonic composition not exceeding 30 minutes in length. Prizes include 1st prize of 15,00
lire. Next competition in 1998.

Concorso Internazionale di Composizione "Guido d'Arezzo" Fondazione.
Corso Italia 102, I-52100 Arezzo.
Annual competition for polyvocal composition which has never been published or performed, the duration of which lasts more than 5 minutes.

Concorso Internazionale di Direzione d'Orchestra "Arturo Toscanini".
Via G Tartini 13, I-43100 Parma.
Triennial competition open to conductors of all nationalities to the age of 32. Prizes include 1st prize of 15,000,000 lire, 2nd prize of 10,000,000 lire, and 3rd prize of 6,00
lire. Next competition in 2000.

Concorso Internazionale di Violino "Alberto Curci".
Via Nardones 8, I-80132 Naples.
Competition open to violinists to the age of 32.

Concorso Internazionale "Luigi Russolo" per Giovani Compositori di Musica Elettroacustica Analogica E Digitale.
c/o Fondazione "Russolo-Pratella", Via G Bagaini 6, I-21100 Varese.
Annual competition open to composers of all nationalities to the age of 35 for electroacoustic, analog, and digital music compositions.

Concorso Internazionale per Contrabasso Giovanni Bottesini.
c/o Conservatorio di Musica "Arrigo Boito", Via del Conservatorio 27, I-43100 Parma.
Triennial competition open to double bass players of all nationalities between the ages of 16 and 32. Prizes include 1st prize of 10,000,000 lire, 2nd prize of 6,000,000 lir
3rd prize of 4,000,000 lire. Next competition in 1998.

Concorso Internazionale per La Conquista Della chitarra Classica.
CP 10673, I-20125 Milan.
Annual competition open to classical guitarists of all ages. Prizes include cash, gold medals, and guitars.

Concorso Internazionale per Quartetto d'Archi Premio "Paolo Borciani".
c/o Teatro Municipale Romolo Valli, Piazza Martini 7 Luglio, I-42100 Reggio Emilia.
Triennial competition open to string quartets of all nationalities whose members were born after 20 June 1962. Prizes include 1st prize of 30,000,000 lire and 2nd pr
20,000,000 lire. Next competition in 2000.

Concorso Internazionale per "Voci Verdiane".
Coumne di Busseto, Piazza Giuseppe Verdi 10, I-43011 Busseto (Parma)

Concorso Internazionale Pianistico "Ettore Pozzoli".
Segreteria, Piazza 34, I-20038 Seregno.
Biennial competition open to pianists of all nationalities born after 1 January 1965. Prizes include 1st prize of 15,000,000 lire and recitals, 2nd prize of 8,000,000 lire and a r
3rd prize of 5,000,000 lire and a recital, 4th prize of 3,000,000 lire, 5th prize of 2,000,000 lire, and 6th prize of 1,000,000 lire. Next competition in 1999.

Concorso Internazionale Pianistico "Liszt" Premio Mario Zanfi.
c/o Conservatorio di Musica "Arrigo Boito", Via del Conservatorio 27, I-43100 Parma.
Triennial competition open to pianists of all nationalities between the ages of 16 and 32. Prizes include 1st prize of 10,000,000 lire, 2nd prize of 6,000,000 lire, and 3rd pr
4,000,000 lire. Next competition in 1998.

Concorso Pianistico Internazionale "Alfredo Casella".
Via del Parco Margherita 49, pal 5, I-80121 Naples.
Biennial competition open to pianists of all nationalities.

Concorso Pianistico Internazionale Ferruccio Busoni.
c/o Conservatorio Statale di Musica "Claudio Monteverdi", Piazza Domenicani 19, I-39100 Bolzano.
Annual competition open to pianists of all nationalities between the ages of 15 and 32. Prizes include 1st prize of 15,000,000 lire and concert engagements, 2nd prize of 9,00
lire, 3rd prize of 7,000,000 lire, 4th prize of 6,000,000 lire, 5th prize of 5,000,000 lire, and 6th prize of 4,000,000 lire.

International Competition of the Teatro Alla Scala: Dino Ciani Prize.
c/o Teatro all Scala, Via Filodrammatici 2, I-20121 Milan.
Triennial competition open to pianists of all nationalities born after 31 December 1969. Prizes include 1st prize of 20,000,000 lire, 2nd prize of 8,000,000 lire, and 3rd pr
3,000,000 lire, with medals and performances for each. Next competition in 1999.

Rodolfo Lipizer International Violin Contest.
Via Don Giovanni Bosco 91, I-34170 Gorizia.
Annual competition open to violinists of all nationalities born after 17 September 1962. Prizes include cash and concert appearances.

"Niccolò Paganini" Premio Internazionale di Violino.
Palazzo Doria, Via Garibaldi 9, I-16124 Genoa.
Annual competition open to violinists of all nationalities under the age of 35. Prizes include 1st prize of 20,000,000 lire, 2nd prize of 10,000,000 lire, 3rd prize of 6,000,00
4th prize of 4,000,000 lire, 5th prize of 3,000,000 lire, and 6th prize of 2,000,000 lire.

"Antonio Pedrotti" International Competition for Orchestra Conductors.
Via San Croce 67, I-38100 Trento.
Biennial competition open to conductors between the ages of 18 and 33. Prizes include 1st prize of 10,000,000 lire and engagements with Italian Orchestras, 2nd prize of 7,00
lire, and 3rd prize of 5,000,000 lire. Next competition in 1999.

"Premio Ancona" Concorso Internazionale di Esecuzione & Composizione & Musicale per Strumenti a Fiato.
Assissorato Cultura, Comune di Ancona, I-60100 Ancona.
Annual competition open to instrumentalists and composers of wind music.

Premio Musicale Città di Trieste: Concorso Internazionale di Composizione Sinfonica.
Palazzo Municipale, Piazza dell'Unità d'Italia 4, I-34121 Trieste.
Biennial competition open to composers of all nationalities. Prizes include 1st prize of 5,000,000 lire and performance of composition, 2nd prize of 2,500,000 lire, and 3rd
of 1,500,000 lire. Next competition in 1999.

segna della Canzone d'Autore-Premio Tenco.
Meridiana 7, I-18038 San Remo.
ual competition open to singers who are lyricists and composers by invitation only.

dal Monte International Singing Competition.
Teatro Comunale, Corso del Popolo 31, Via Diaz 7, I-31100 Treviso.

B Viotti" Concorso Internazionale di Musicale.
ella Postale 127, I-13100 Vercelli.
ual competition for singers and instrumentalists.

orio Gui International Chamber Music Competition.
RM, Borgo degli Albizi 15, I-50122 Florence.

JAPAN

rnational Music Competition of Japan.
st Park Builing 4F, 1-10-16, Ebisunhishi, Sibuya-ku, Tokyo 150.
nnial competition open to instrumentalists of all nationalities betwen the ages of 17 and 32. Prizes include 1st of money, medal, and concert appearances. Next competition
998.

o Prize Foundation.
JML Seminar, Yoshiro Irino Institute of Music, 5-22-2 Matsubara, Setagaya-ku, Tokyo 156.
ual prize open to composers of all nationalities under the age of 40 rotating annually between an orchestral and a chamber music composition. Prizes include 650,00 yen
an orchestral composition and 200,000 yen for a chamber music composition.

yo International Competition for Chamber Music Composition.
Japan International Artists, 2-3-16-607 Shinjuku, Shinjuku, Tokyo.
npetition open to composers of chamber music of all ages and nationalities Prizes include 1st prize of 300,000 yen, 2nd prize of 150,000 yen, and 3rd prize of 100,000. Next
petition in 1998.

yo International Music Competition.
-13 Kita-Shinjuku, Shinjuku-ku, Tokyo 169.
ual competition open to performers of all nationalities with categories changing annually. Prizes include 1st prize of 1,000,000 yen and a medal, 2nd prize of 700,000 yen
a medal, 3rd prize of 500,000 yen and a medal, and a certificate of honorable mention, 4th prize of 200,000 yen, and a medal.

MONACO

de Composition Musicale Prince Pierre de Monaco.
tre Administratif, Rue Louis Notari, MC098000 Monaco.
ual prize awarded to the best musical composition of the year prize of 50,000 French francs.

NETHERLANDS

S-Hertogenbosch International Singing Competition.
Box 1225, 5200 BG's-Hertogenbosch.
ual competition open to singers. Prizes include cash.

ar Franck Organ Competition.
ghwaterstraat 14, 2012 GD Haarlem.

t Chamber Music Festival.
af Willemlaan 52, 1181 EH Amstelveen. Tel: 31 20 643 2043; Fax: 31 20 640 3961

F International Choir Festival.
23, 3512 BR Utrecht.
drennial prizes awarded to choirs. Next prizes given in 1999.

rnational Competition for Early Music Ensembles.
gel 308-sous, 1016 AE Amsterdam.
ual competition open to young professional early music ensembles consisting of two to eight performers.

rnational Competition for Organ Improvisation.
tbus 3333, 2001 DH Haarlem.
ual competition open to concert organists experienced in improvisation. Prizes include cash.

rnational Franz Liszt Piano Competition.
ziekcentrum Vredenburg, PO Box 550, 3500 AN Utrecht.
nnial competition open to pianists of all nationalities between the ages of 16 and 30. Prizes include cash and engagements for the 1st prize winner. Next competition in 1999.

rnational Gaudeamus Composers Competition.
deamus Foundation, Swammerdamstraat 38, 1091 RV Amsterdam.
ual competition open to composers to the age of 30. Prizes include cash.

rnational Gaudeamus Interpreters Competition.
ammerdamstraat 38, 1091 RV Amsterdam.
ual competition open to instrumentalists and singers of contemporary music. Prizes include cash, with a first prize of DFL 10,000.

rnational Kirill Kondrashin Competition for Young Conductors.
Box 444, 1200 JJ Hilversum.
nquennial competition open to conductors to the age of 36. Prizes include guest conducting engagements with major orchestras. Next competition in 1999.

Scheveningen International Music Competition.
Gevers Deynootweg 970 Z, 2586 BW Scheveningen.
Annual competition open to instrumentalists to the age of 30. Prizes include cash.

NEW ZEALAND

Lexus New Zealand International Violin Competition.
PO Box 10-113, Wellington.
Quadrennial competition open to violinists of all nationalities between the ages of 18 and 28. Prizes include cash. Next competition in 2000.

NORWAY

Queen Sonja International Music Competition.
PO Box 1568 Vika, N-0116 Oslo 1.
Triennial competition open to instrumentalists or singers. Prizes include cash and concert engagements. Next competition in 1998.

POLAND

Fryderyk Chopin International Piano Competition.
ul Okólnik 1, PL-00-368 Warsaw.
Quinquennial competition open to pianists of all nationalities born between 1 October 1970 and 1 October 1982. Prizes include 1st prize of $11,000 and a gold medal, 2nd of $7,142 and a silver medal, 3rd prize of $5,357 and a bronze medal, and three other cash prizes. Next competition in 2000.

Grzegorz Fitelberg International Competition for Conductors.
Sokolska 2, 40-048 Katowice.
Quadrenial competition open to conductors to the age of 35. Prizes include cash and medals. Next competition in 1999.

International Composer's Competition "Kasimierz Serocki".
ul Mazowiecka 11, 00-052 Warsaw.
Triennial competition open to composers of all nationalities. Prizes include cash. Next competition in 1998.

International Henryk Wieniawski Competition for Violinists, Composers, and Violin Makers.
Swietoslawska St 7, 61-840 Poznań.
Quinquennial competition open to violinists of all nationalities to the age of 30. Prizes include cash. Next competition in 2000.

International Stanislaw Moniuszko Competition for Young Vocalists.
c/o Warsaw Philharmonic, ul Jasna 5, 00-950 Warsaw.
Triennial competition open to young vocalists. Prizes include cash. Next competition in 1998.

International Witold Lutoslawski Composers Competition.
c/o Warsaw Philharmonic, ul Jasna 5, 00-950 Warsaw.
Biennial competition open to composers of all nationalities and all ages. Prizes include cash and performances by the Warsaw Philharmonic. Next competition in 1998.

PORTUGAL

Porto International Music Competiton.
Rua Azevedo Coutinho 195, 4100 Porto.
Annual competition.

ROMANIA

George Enescu International Piano, Violin and Singing Competiton.
Calea Victoriei 155, Bl. D1, sc.8, et.2, 71012 Bucharest.

RUSSIA

International Tchaikovsky Competition.
15 Neglinnaya Street, Moscow.
Quadrennial competition open to pianists, violinists, cellists, and singers of all nationalities. Prizes include cash and medals. Next competition in 1998.

SINGAPORE

Rolex Music Performance Awards.
The Rolex Centre, 302 Orchard Road, 01-01 Tong Builidng, Singapore 0923.
Biennial competition open to pianists and violinists who are citizens or permanent residents of Singapore, Malaysia, Brunei, Indonesia, Thailand, the Philippines and Hong K Prizes include cash. Next competition in 1999.

SPAIN

Concurso Internacional de Canto Julián Gayarre.
c/o Festival de Navarra, Ansoieaga 10, 31001 Pamplona.
Biennial competition open to singers of all nationalities, women between the ages of 18 and 32, and men between the ages of 20 and 35. Prizes include cash. Next compe in 1998.

Concurso Internacional de Ejecución Musical Maria Canals de Barcelona.
Gran Via de les Corts Catalanes 654, pral, 08010 Barcelona.
Annual competiton open to instrumentalists between the ages of 18 and 32. Prizes include cash.

urso Internacional de Piano "Frederic Chopin".
ervatorio Professional de Musica de Baleares, Calle Hospital 4, 07012 Palma de Mallorca.
ial competition open to pianists of all nationalitites to the age of 35. Prizes include 1st prize of 1,000,000 pesetas and recitals, 2nd prize of 500,000 pesetas, and 3rd prize
),000 pesetas. Next competition in 1998.

urso Internacional de Piano "José Iturbi".
, de Manises 4, 46003 Valencia.
ial competition open to pianists of all nationalities under the age of 32. Prizes include 1st prize of 1,000,000 pesetas, 2nd prize of 750,000 pesetas, 3rd prize of 500,000
as, and 4th prize of 300,000 pesetas, with recitals for each category. Next competition in 1998.

urso Internacional de Piano Premio "Jaén".
stituto de Estudios Giennenses, 23002 Jaén.
al competition open to pianists of all nationalities, winners of the Jaén Prize excepted. Prizes include 1st prize of 2,000,000 pesetas, a gold medal, and concert engagements,
rize of 1,000,000 pesetas, 3rd prize of 400,000 pesetas, and the Rose Sabater Prize of 500,000 pesetas for the best interpreter of Spanish music.

io Internacional de Canto Fundación Guerrero.
Via 78, 28013 Madrid.
ial competition open to singers of all nationalities and ages. Prizes include 1st prize of 2,500,000 pesetas and a prize of 600,000 pesetas for the best interpreter of the music
cinto e Inocencio Guerrero. Next competition in 1999.

io Internacional de Piano Fundación Guerrero.
Via 78, 28013 Madrid.
ial competition open to pianists of all nationalities and ages. Prizes include 1st prize of 2,500,000 pesetas. Next competition in 1997.

ander International Piano Competition.
án Cortés 3, 39003 Santander.
nial competition open to pianists of all nationalities between the ages of 17 and 30. Prizes totalling 15,000,000 pesetas, recordings, concerts, travel grants etc. Next
etition in 1998.

Sarasata International Violin Competition.
Ansoleaga 10, 31001 Pamplona.
ial competition open to violinists. Next competition in 1999.

cisco Viñas International Singing Contest.
125, 08037 Barcelona.
al competition open to singers, women between the ages of 18 and 32, and men between the ages of 20 and 35. Prizes for both include 1st prize of 1,350,000 pesetas, 2nd
of 800,000 pesetas, and 3rd prize of 400,000 pesetas , plus medals and special prizes.

SWEDEN

i Björling Tenor Competition.
nge Kommun 781, 81 Borlänge, Höbergstatan 76B, S-118 56 Stockholm

SWITZERLAND

cours Géza Anda.
herweg 18, CH-8002 Zürich.
nial competition open to pianists to the age of 32. Prizes include cash and major concert engagements. Next competition in 2000.

cours International d'Execution Musicale.
Rue de Carouge, CH-1205 Geneva.
al competition open to performers of all nationalities with categories changing annually. Prizes totalling 130,000 francs.

cours Suisse de l'Orgue.
e du Prieur, CH-1323 Romainmôtier.
al competition open to organists of all nationalities and ages.

Haskil Piano Competition.
ue du Simplon, PO Box 234, CH-1800 Vevey.
nial competition open to pianists to the age of 30. Prizes include 20,000 Swiss francs and concert engagements. Next competition in 1999.

national Competition in Composition of Sacred Music.
ox 292, CH-1701 Fribourg.
nial competition open to composers of all nationalities and ages. Prizes include 10,000 Swiss francs and the premiere of the winning work at the Fribourg Festival of Sacred
c. Next competition in 1999.

erplayers International Music and Conductors Competition.
lasterplayers International Music Academy, Via Losanna 12, CH-6900 Lugano.
al competition open to performers. Prizes include various awards and concert engagements.

cal Prize Contest Queen Marie-José.
Postale 19, CH-1252 Meinier/Geneva.
nial competition open to composers of all nationalities and ages who submit an unpublished composition. Prizes include 10,000 francs. Next competition in 1998.

s Organ Competition.
e du Prieur, CH-1323 Romainmôtier.

r Varga International Competition for Violinists.
ureau du Festival, PO Box 954, CH-1951 Sion.
al competition open to violinists between the ages of 15 and 32. Prizes totalling 30,000 Swiss francs.

UK

British Broadcasting Corporation Television Young Musician of the Year Competition.
c/o BBC-TV, Kensington House, Richmond Way, London W14 0AX.
Biennial televised competition open to British resident performers to age 18 and composers to age 21. Prizes totalling £32,000. Next competition in 1998.

Cardiff Singer of the World Competition.
c/o BBC Wales, Music Department, Broadcasting House, Llandaff, Cardiff, Wales CF5 2YQ.
Biennial competition open to singers 18 years of age or older. Prizes include £5,000 and concert engagements. Next competition in 1999.

City of London Carl Flesch International Violon Competition.
c/o City Arts Trust, Bishopsgate Hall, 230 Bishopsgate, London EC2M 4QH.
Biennial competition open to violinists of all nationalitites under the age of 28. Prizes include 1st prize of £6,000, 2nd prize of £4,000, 3rd prize of £3,000, 4th prize of £1,75 prize of £1,250, and 6th prize of £750, with five additional prizes of £500 each. Next competition in 1998.

City of London Walter Gruner International Lieder Competition.
c/o City Arts Trust, Bishopsgate Hall, 230 Bishopsgate, London EC2M 4QH.
Biennial competition open to singers to the age of 28. Prizes include 1st prize of £3,500 and a debut recital in London, 2nd prize of £2,250, 3rd prize of £1,250, and 4th pr £750, with an accompanists' prize of £1,250. Next competition in 1999.

Donatella Flick Conducting Competition.
47 Brunswick Gardens, London W8 4AW.
Biennial competiton open to European Community nationals under 35. Next competition 1998.

Folkestone Menuhin International Violin Competition.
72 Leopold Road, Londo SW19 7JQ.
Biennial competition open to violinists prizes totalling £15,700. Next competition in 1999.

Great Grimsby International Competition for Singers.
23 Enfield Avenue, New Waltham, Great Grimsby, South Humberside DN36 5RD.
Triennial competition open to singers between the ages of 20 and 30 with accompanists to age 26. Prizes include 1st prize of £2,000, 2nd prize of £1,000, and 3rd prize of with an accompanists' prize of £500. Next competition in 1998.

Harveys Leeds International Pianoforte Competition.
c/o University of Leeds, Leeds, Yorkshire LS2 9JT.
Triennial competition open to professional pianists under the age of 30. Prizes totalling £57,600 and concert engagements worldwide. Next competition in 1999.

International Young Concert Artists Competition of Royal Tunbridge Wells.
Paddock Wood, Kent TN12 6PA.
Biennial competition open to performers to the age of 25. Prizes totalling £9,000. Next competition in 1999.

Kathleen Ferrier Awards.
K. Ferrier Memorial Scholarship Fund, 52 Rosebank, Holyport Road, London SW6 6LR.
Annual competition open to British and Commonwealth singers aged 21-28, First prize £10,000 and Wigmore Hall recital.

London International String Quartet Competition.
62 High Street, Fareham, Hampshire PO16 7BG.
Triennial competition open to string quartets whose aggregate ages do not exceed 120 years. Prizes include 1st prize of £8,000 and the Amadeus Trophy, 2nd prize of £4 3rd prize of £3,200, 4th prize of £2,400, and 5th prize of £1,600, with the Menuhin Prize of £750 and the Audience Prize of £500. Next competition in 2000.

National Power World Piano Competition London.
26 Wallace Road, London N1 2PG.
Triennial competition open to pianists of all nationalities to the age of 29. Prizes include prizes totalling £30,000 concert engagements, and scholarships. Next competition in 2

Newport International Competition for Young Pianists.
Civic Centre, Newport, Gwent NP9 4UR.
Triennial competition open to pianists to the age of 25. Prizes include cash and concerts. Next competition in 2000.

Performing Right Society E-A Composition Prize.
c/o Electro-Acoustic Music Association of Great Britain, 10 Stratford Place, London W1N 9AE.
Biennial competition open to composers. Next competition in 1998.

Royal Over-Seas League of Music Competition.
Over-Seas House, Park Place, St James's Street, London SW1A 1LR.
Annual competition open to Commonwealth and former Commonwealth citizens, for instrumentalists to the age of 28 and for singers to the age of 30. Various prizes.

Scottish International Piano Competition.
c/o Royal Scottish Academy of Music and Drama, 100 Renfrew Street, Glasgow, Scotland G2 2BS.
Triennial competition open to pianists of all nationalities to the age of 32. Prizes include £8,000. Next competition in 1998.

USA

ALEA International Competition Prize.
c/o Boston University School of Music, 855 Commonwealth Avenue, Boston, MA 02215.
Annual competition open to composers of all nationalities born after 1955; submitted compostition must not have been published, publicly performed, or awarded any pri

ASCAP Foundation Grants to Young Composers.
1 Lincoln Plaza, New York, NY 10023.
Annual cash grants to composers who are citizens or permanent residents of the US and have not reached their 30th birthday by 15 March.

American Academy and Institute of Arts and Letters.
633 West 155th Street, New York, NY 10032.
Various awards are given in the field of music.

erican Academy in Rome.
Park Avenue, New York, NY 10017.
ual residents program to support distinguished artists and scholars as residents at the academy for a year and annual Rome Prize Fellowships for American composers to
*y at the academy.

erican Berlin Opera Foundation Inc.
Fifth Avenue, 21st Floor, New York, NY 10103.
ual scholarships for American singers who are citizens or permanent residents between the ages of 18 and 32 to study at the Deutsche Oper Berlin. Prizes include a
*larship of $15,000 and a round trip flight.

erican Guild of Organists/National Young Artists Competition in Organ Performance.
Riverside Drive, Suite 1260, New York, NY 10115.
*nial competition open to organists between the ages of 22 and 32. Next competition in 1998.

erican Musicological Society Inc.
South 34th Street, Philadelphia, PA 19104.
h Greenberg Award up to $2,000 for a distinguished contribution to the study and/or performance of music prior to 1700. Otto Kinkeldey Award of $400 and a scroll to a US
*anadian writer of the most notable full-length study in musicology. Alfred Einstein Award of $400 to a young scholar who has published an articles on a musicological subject
*e preceeding year.

erican Pianists Association National Fellowship Piano Auditions.
ves Memorial Hall, Butler University, 4600 Sunset Avenue, Indianapolis, IN 46208.
*nial fellowships open to American classical pianists between the ages of 18 and 30. Prizes include three-year fellowship, $10,000, sponsorship at an international competition,
US concert engagements. Next competition in 1999.

ian Anderson Award.
Ives Center, PO Box 2957, Danbury, Connecticut.
*gnificant financial award to an American singer of concert and opera by recommendation.

sts International's Annual New York Debut Award Auditions.
Fifth Avenue, Suite 1700, New York, NY 10017.
ual auditions open to performers of all nationalities who have not given a New York recital debut or who have not received a New York review for a solo recital. Prizes include
*/ York recital debut at Carnegie Recital Hall, or Merkin Concert Hall, or Alice Tully Hall at Lincoln Center.

sts International's Distinguished Artists Award Auditions.
Fifth Avenue, Suite 1700, New York, NY 10017.
ual auditions open to soloists or chamber groups who have received at least one review from a major New York publication and have no management. Prizes include recital
*agement in New York.

badcast) M(usic) I(nc) Student Composers Awards.
West 57th Street, New York, NY 10019.
*ual awards open to student composers who are citizens or permanent residents of a country in the Western Hemisphere to the age of 25. Prizes totalling $16,000.

ann Sebastian Bach International Competition.
1 Potomac Street North West, Washington, DC 20007.
*npetition open to performers of the works of J S Bach between the ages of 20 and 40. Prizes include cash and concert engagements.

a Bachauer International Piano Competition.
Box 1164, Salt Lake City, UT 84147.
*nnial competition open to pianists between the ages of 19 and 32. Prizes include 1st prize of a grand piano and New York and Los Angeles debut concerts; other prizes include
*d, Silver, and Bronze medals, cash prizes, concerts and recitals, with finalists appearing with the Utah Symphony Orchestra. Also a junior section for pianists between the
*s of 8 and 18. Next competition in 2000.

timore Opera Vocal Competition for American Operatic Artists.
West Read Street, Suite 605, Baltimore, MD 21201.
ual competition open to operatic singers between the ages of 20 and 35. Prizes include 1st prize of $10,000, 2nd prize of $8,000, 3rd prize of $4,500, 4th prize of $2,500,
*prize of $2,000, 6th prize of $1,200, and 7th prize of $1,000 with additional prize of $1,000, with additional prize of $1,000 awarded by the audience.

low International Competition.
Brigham Young University, Harris Fine Arts Center, Provo, UT 84602.
*ual competition open to composers of all nationalities; composition must not have won any other competition. Prizes totalling $10,000.

eph H Bearns Prize in Music.
Columbia University, Department of Music, 703 Dodge Hall, New York, NY 10027.
*ual competition open to American composers between the ages of 18 and 25. Prizes include cash awards.

nk Huntington Beebe Fund for Musicians.
Huntington Avenue, Boston, MA 02115.
*ual scholarships open to American post-graduate music students for study abroad.

one Belsky Music Award Competition.
North Street, PO Box 1112, Litchfield, CT 06759.
*nnial competition open to pianists 30 years old or older. Prizes include 1st prize of $1,500 and concert engagements. Next competition in 1999.

ston Classical Orchestra Youth Competition.
Tremont Street, Boston, MA 02116.
*ual competition open to high school seniors in New England and New York who wish to pursue a career as an instrumentalist. Prizes include a four-year merit scholarship
*ne Boston University School of Music and an appearance as soloist with the Boston Classical Orchestra at a youth concert.

ndeis University Creative Arts Awards.
*ndeis University, PO Box 9110, Waltham, MA 02254.
*ual prizes open to established artists in various fields, including music. Prizes include a medal and an honourarium.

Benjamin Britten Memorial Fund.
135 East 83rd Street, Suite 4/5-C, New York, NY 10028.
Annual scholarships open to American students for study at the Britten-Pears School for Advanced Musical Studies in Aldeburgh, Suffolk, England.

Bryan International String Competition.
North Carolina Symphony Orchestra, PO Box 28026, Raleigh, NC 27611.
Quadrennial competition open to violinists, violists, and cellists between the ages of 18 and 30. Prizes include 1st prize of $12,000, 2nd prize of $6,000, and 3rd prize of $3
Next competition in 2000.

Grace Bumbry Student Assistance Award.
c/o AGMA Relief Fund, 1727 Broadway, New York, NY 10019.
Study grant for American classical singers between the ages of 18 and 25. Prizes include 1st prize of $2,000.

William C Byrd Young Artist Competition.
c/o Flint Institute of Music, 1025 East Kearsley Street, Flint, MI 48503.
Annual competition open to performers with categories changing annually. Prizes include 1st prize of $2,500 and an appearance with the Flint Symphony Orchestra.

CRS National Festival for the Performing Arts.
724 Winchester Road, Broomall, PA 19008.
Annual competition with prizes including fellowships, recording contracts, national appearances, and artist representation.

Carmel Chamber Music Competition.
PO Box 6283, Carmel, CA 93921.
Annual competition open to non-professional chamber groups of three to six players averaging under the age of 26. Prizes include cash.

Carmel Music Society Competition.
PO Box 1144, Carmel, CA 93921.
Annual competition open to musicians who are residents or full-time students in California. Prizes include cash and an appearance at a Carmel Chamber Music concert

Center for Contemporary Opera International Opera Singers Competition.
PO Box 1350, Gracie Station, New York, NY 10028.
Annual competition open to singers who have not attained a major operatic career. Prizes include cash.

Chamber Music America.
Commissioning Program, 305 Seventh Avenue, 5th Floor, New York, NY 10001-6008.
Annual ASCAP Awards for various activities devoted to the performance and promotion of chamber music.

Chopin Foundation of the United States National Chopin Piano Competition of the United States.
1440 79th Street Causeway, Miami, FL 33141.
Quinquennial competition open to American pianists between the ages of 16 and 18, to enable them to participate in the International Chopin Piano Competition in Warsaw. .
include 1st prize of $15,000, 2nd prize of $9,000, 3rd prize of $6,000, 4th prize of $3,500, 5th prize of $2,500, and 6th prize of $2,000. Next competition in 2000.

Civic Orchestra of Chicago Soloist Competition.
220 South Michigan Avenue, Chicago, IL 60604.
Annual competition open to soloists between the ages of 19 and 30. Prizes include $1,000 and concert engagements.

Cleveland International Piano Competition.
11021 East Boulevard, Clevelenad, OH 44106.
Biennial competition open to pianists between the ages of 17 and 32. Prizes include cash and concert engagements. Next competition in 1999.

Van Cliburn International Piano Competition.
2525 Ridgmar Boulevard, Suite 307, Fort Worth, TX 76116.
Quadrennial piano competition open to pianists between the ages 18 and 30. Prizes include 1st prize of $15,000, Carnegie Hall recital and orchestral debuts, US recit
orchestral tour, and European recital and orchestral tour, 2nd prize of $10,000, New York debut, and US tour, 3rd prize of $7,5000 and US tour, 4th prize of $5,000, 5th p
$3,500, and 6th prize of $2,000. Next competition in 2001.

Coleman Chamber Ensemble Competition.
202 South Lake Avenue, No 201, Pasadena, CA 91101.
Annual competition open to non-professional chamber ensembles with members under the age of 27 and prepared by a coach. Prizes include $3,000, $3,000, $1,800, $
and $50 for coaches.

Composers Guild Annual Competition Contest.
40 North 100 West, Box 586, Farmington, UT 84025.
Annual competition open to composers. Prizes include cash.

Concert Artists Guild International New York Competition.
850 Seventh Avenue, Suite 1205, New York, NY 10019.
Annual competition open to instrumentalists, chamber ensembles, and singers. Prizes include cash, concert engagements, recordings, free management services, etc.

Concerto Competition of the Rome Festival Orchestra.
Empire State Builidng, Suite 3304, New York, NY 10118.
Annual competition open to North American performers of violin, viola, cello, double bass, oboe, and horn. Prizes include five tuition fellowships and solo appearance in F

Aaron Copland Competition for Young Composers.
25 Ria Drive, White Plains, NY 10605.
Biennial competition open to composers between the ages of 5 and 15 for a composition lasting at least three minutes. Prizes include cash.

Corporation of Yaddo.
PO Box 395, Union Avenue, Saratoga Springs, NY 12866.
Room, board, and studio for professional composers of all nationalities. Residency up to two months.

Council for International Exchange for Scholars-Fulbright Scholar Program: Research and Lecturing Grants for Faculty and Professionals.
3007 Tilden Street North West, Suite 5M, Washington, DC 20008.
Annual grants for university lecturing and/or advanced research abroad by Americans, including several in the field of music.

...gelo Young Artist Competition.
...Mercyhurst College, 501 East 38th Street, Erie, PA 16546.
...ual competition open to performers under the age of 35 with categories rotating annually. Prizes include 1st prize of $10,000 and concert engagements, 2nd prize of $5,000, ...3rd prize of $3,000, with $1,000 to all finalists.

...neth Davenport National Competition for Orchestral Works.
...State University of New York, College of New Paltz, New Paltz, NY 12561.
...ual competition open to composers who are American citizens or permanent residents. Prizes include $1,500 and performance of composition.

...us Composition Contest.
...Jacksonville University, College of Fina Arts, Jacksonville, FL 32211.

...ual competition open to composers. Prizes include 1st prize of $500, $100 for the best vocal, keyboard, and instrumental composition, and high school composition category ...st prize of $200 and 2nd prize of $100.

...a Omicron International Music Fraternity Triennial Composition Competition.
...) Volk Drive, Dayton, OH 45415.
...nnial competition open to American composers of college age or older. Prizes include $500 and premiere of composition. Next competition in 2000.

...oit Symphony Orchestra Fellowship Program.
...Buhl Building, 535 Griswold Street, Detroit, MI 48226.
...-year residency for African-American orchestral players with the Detroit Symphony Orchestra.

...ray Dranoff International Two Piano Competition.
...North East 72nd Street, Miami, FL 33138.
...nial competition open to duo pianists between the ages of 18 and 35. Prizes include 1st prize of $10,000, 2nd prize of $5,000, and 3rd prize of $2,000, plus concert ...agements. Next competition in 1999.

...t and West Artists International Auditions for New York Debut.
...Riverside Drive, No 313, New York, NY 10025.
...ual competition open to performers who have not given a New York debut recital. Prizes include debut at Weill Recital Hall at Carnegie Hall, cash, radio and concert ...agements.

...hoff National Chamber Music Competition.
...Box 1303, South Bend, IN 46624.
...ual competition open to instrumental ensembles of three to five members to the age of 18. Prizes include cash.

...ry Fischer Artist Program.
...oln Center, 140 West 65th Street, New York, NY 10023.
...eer grants open to American instrumental soloists by a recommendation board and chosen by the executive committee. No applications accepted. Prizes include Avery Fischer ...eer Grant of $10,000 and Avery Fischer Prize of $25,000.

...t Collins Symphony Association Young Artists Competition.
...Box 1963, Fort Collins, CO 80522.
...ual competition open to instrumentalists. Prizes include $2,000 Adeline Rosenberg Memorial Prize.

...t Smith Symphony Association Young Artist Competition.
...Box 3151, Fort Smith, AR 72913.
...ual competition open to string, brass, and woodwind players to the age of 18. Prizes include 1st prize of $1,000 and an apppearance with the Fort Smith Symphony Orchestra.

...mm Music Foundation at Harvard University.
...Harvard University, Department of Music, Cambridge, MA 02138.
...nsorship of composers, performers, and concerts of contemporary music.

...vey Gaul Composition Contest.
...Duquesne University, School of Music, Pittsburgh, PA 15282.
...nnial competition open to American composers of unpublished and unperformed compositions. Prizes include $3,000 and performance of composition. Next competition in ...8.

...rida Grand Opera Young Artist/Technical/Apprentice Programs.
...0 Coral Way, Miami, FL 33145.
...ual seven-month program (October-April) open to singers to work with the Greater Miami Opera.

...rles Tomlinson Griffes American Music Composers Competition.
...oseph Wallace Drive, Croton-on-Hudson, NY 10521.
...ual competition open to American or permanent resident composers between the ages of 12 and 18 whose submitted composition has not won any other competition. Prizes ...ude cash and performance of composition.

...n Simon Guggenheim Memorial Foundation.
...Park Avenue, New York, NY 10016.
...ual fellowships in music open to composers and scholars who have demonstrated previous outstanding ability. Fellowships in two categories: For citizens or permanent ...dnets of the US and Canada, and for citizens or permanent residents of Latin America and the Caribbean.

...ddonfield Symphony Young Instrumentalists Solo Competition.
...Box 212, Haddonfield, NJ 08033.
...ual competition open to solo instrumentalists resident in one of the eleven Northeastern states or the District of Columbia between the ages of 16 and 25. Prizes include 1st ...e of $2,500 and an appearance with the Haddonfield Symphony, and 2nd prize of $750.

...in Harp Competition.
...Greater Trenton Symphony Orchestra Foundation, 28 West State Street, Suite 201, Trenton, NJ 08608.
...ual competition open to American harpists who are college students. Prizes include 1st prize of $1,600.

Joanna Hodges International Piano Competition.
c/o College of the Desert, 43500 Monterey Avenue, Palm Desert, CA 92260.
Biennial competition open to pianists to the age of 35. Prizes include cash, scholarships, concert, radio, and television appearances. Next competition in 1999.

Ima Hogg National Young Artist Audition.
c/o Houston Symphony Orchestra, 615 Louisiana Street, Houston, TX 77002.
Annual competition open to instrumentalists between the ages of 19 and 27. Prizes include 1st prize of $5,000 and an appearance with the Houston Symphony, 2nd prize of
and an appearance with the Houston Symphony, and 3rd prize of $1,000.

Henry Holt Memorial Scholarship.
PO box 1714, Palo Alto, CA 94302.
Annual scholarship open to singers between the ages of 18 and 26. Prizes include 1st prize of $1,000 and 2nd prize of $500.

Holtkamp/American Guild of Organists Award in Organ Composition.
475 Riverside Drive, Suite 1260, New York, NY 10115.
Biennial competition open to composers of organ compositions. Prizes include $2,000, publication and performance of composition. Next competition in 1999.

Houston Opera Studio Auditions.
c/o Houston Grand Opera, 510 Preston, Houston, TX 77002.
Annual auditions open to performers to work with the Houston Opera Studio.

Indiana State University Contemporary Music Festival Competition.
c/o Louisville Orchestra, 609 West Main Street, Louisville, KY 40202.
Annual competition open to composers who have not won the competition within the previous five years.

Institute of International Education/Fulbright and Other Graduate Study Scholarships.
809 United nations Plaza, New York, NY 10017.
Annual scholarships open to Americans with a BA or equivalent for graduate study abroad.

International Horn Society Composition Contest.
c/o University of Missouri at Kansas City, Conservatory of Music, 4949 Cherry, Kansas City, MO 64110.
Annual competition open to composers. Prizes include cash.

International Trombone Association Ensemble Composition Contest.
c/o University of North Texas, School of Music, Denton, TX 76203.
Biennial competition open to composers. Prizes include $1,000. Next competition in 1999.

International Violin Competition of Indianapolis.
47 South Pennsylvania Street, Suite 401, Indianapolis, IN 46204.
Quadrennial competition open to violinists of all nationalities between the ages of 18 and 30. Prizes totalling more than $200,000 in money, medals, concert engagements in
America and Europe, and recordings. Next competition in 1998.

Ivo Pogorelich International Solo Piano Competition (USA).
c/o Kantor Concert Management, 67 Teignmouth Road, London NW2 4EA, England.
Open to prizewinners and finalists in any previous international competition. First prize $100,000. Next competition 1999.

Kennedy Center Friedheim Awards.
John F Kennedy Center for the Performing Arts, Washington, DC 20566.
Annual award to a living American composer of orchestral or chamber music. Prizes include 1st prize of $5,000, 2nd prize of $2,500, 3rd prize of $1,000, and 4th prize of

Kingsville International Young Performers' Competition.
PO Box 2873, Kingsville, TX 78363.
Annual competition open to pianists and orchestral instrumentalists to the age of 26. Prizes totalling more than $20,000, with highest ranking winner receiving a minimum of $
and an appearance with the Corpus Christi Symphony.

Kate Neal Kinley Memorial Fellowship.
c/o University of Illinois, 110 Architecture Building, 608 East Lorado Taft Drive, Champaign, IL 61820.
Annual fellowship open to graduates under the age of 25 for advanced study in the US or abroad. Fellowship of $7,000.

Irving M Klein International String Competition.
c/o San Francisco State University, Department of Music, 1600 Holloway Avenue, San Francisco, CA 94132.
Annual competition open to string players between the ages of 15 and 23. Prizes include 1st rpize of $10,000 and appearances with the Peninsula and Santa Cruz Sym
orchestras, and other prizes.

Kosciuszko Foundation Chopin Piano Competition.
15 East 65th Street, New York, NY 10021.
Annual competition open to pianists who are American citizens or permanent residents of the US or full-time foreign students with valid visa between the ages of 17 and 23.
include $2,500, $1,500, and $1,000.

Olga Koussevitsky Young Artist Awards Competition.
165 West 66th Street, New York, NY 10023.
Annual competition open to performers between the ages of 16 and 26 with categories rotating annually. Prizes totalling $3,500, concert egagements, and auditions.

Eleanor Lieber Awards for Young Singers.
1516 South West Alder, Portland, OR 97205.
Biennial awards open to singers who are residents of Oregon, Washington, Idaho, Montana, and Alaska between the ages of 20 and 31. Prizes include cash. Next awards in

Liederkranz Foundation Scholarship Awards.
6 East 87th Street, New York, NY 10128.
Annual awards open to singers and pianists. Prizes totalling some $35,000.

Luciano Pavarotti International Voice Competition.
1616 Walnut Street, Suite 2115, Philadelphia, PA 19103.
Triennial competition.

allister Award for Opera Singers.
ndiana Opera Theatre, 7515 East 30th Street, Indianapolis, IN 46219.
ual audition open to opera singers. Prizes include 1st prize of $10,000, 2nd prize of $5,000, 3rd prize of $3,000, 4th prize of $1,500, and 5th prize of $1,000.

Dowell Colony Inc.
High Street, Peterborough, NH 03458.
rds residency fellowships for composers and other creative artists.

ato Maganini Award in Composition.
alley View Road, Norwalk, CT 06851.
nial competition open to American composers of orchestral music not publicly performed. Prizes include $2,500 and premiere by the Norwalk Symphony Orchestra. Next
petition in 1998.

guerite McCammon Voice Competition.
Coombs Creek Drive, Dallas, TX 75211.
nial competition open to singers between the ages of 21 and 32. Prizes include 1st prize of $3,000 and operatic engagements. Next competition in 1999.

ise D McMahon International Music Competition.
School of Fine Arts, Cameron University, 2800 West Gore Boulevard, Lawton, OK 73505.
petition open to instrumentalists and singers 25 years old or older. Prizes include cash and solo performance with orchestra.

dows Foundation Young Artists Auditions Competition.
ake Road, Somerset, NJ 08873.
ual competition open to performers in three divisions:- Junior Division (Junior High School), High School Division, and Senior Division (to the age of 35). Prizes include cash,
als, concert, and chamber music engagements.

ropolitan Opera National Council Auditions.
oln Center, New York, NY 10023.
ual competitive auditions open to singers. Prizes include cash and study grants.

land-Odessa Symphony and Chorale Inc, National Young Artist Competition.
Box 60658, Midland, TX 79711.
nial competition open to performers. Prizes include cash and appearances with the Midland-Odessa Symphony and Chorale. Next competition in 1999.

souri Southern International Piano Competition.
souri Southern State College, 3950 Newman Road, Joplin, MO 64801.
nial competition open to pianists of all nationalities to the age of 30. Prizes include 1st prize of $5,000 and appearance at Carnegie Recital Hall. Next competition in 1998.

Phi Epsilon International Competition.
8 stallcup Drive, Mesquite, TX 75150.
nnial competition open to members of Mu Phi Epsilon who have appeared in recital and/or as soloist with orchestra but not under contract to a professional management.
es include two-year concert engagements. Next competition in 1999.

eum in the Community Composer's Award.
Box 251, Scott Depot, WV 25560.
nial competition open to American composers of a composition for string quartet not previously performed in public. Prizes include $5,000 and performance of composition.
t competition in 1999.

ic Teachers National Association-CCP/ Belwin Student Composition Competition.
Eastman School of Music, 26 Gibbs Street, Rochester, NY 14604.
ual competition open to American composers who are in college, high school, junior high school, and elementary school who are studying with an active member of the Music
chers National Association. Prizes include cash.

zger Young Artists Auditions and Music Awards.
Wichita Symphony Society, 225 West Douglas, Suite 207, Wichita, KS 67202.
ual competition open to instrumentalists between the ages of 18 and 26 and to singers between the ages of 20 and 28. Prizes include $5,000 Naftzger Young Artist Award
$2,000 each in various categories.

onal Association of Composers, USA.
Cresta Verde Drive, Rolling Hills Estate, CA 90274.
ual competition open to composers between the ages of 18 and 30 with 1st prize of $200 and Los Angeles performance of composition. Competition open to performers of
erican music between the ages of 10 and 30 with prizes of $500 and concert engagements.

ional Association of Teachers of Singing Artist Award Competition.
Jacksonville University, Department of Music, Jacksonville, FL 32211.
npetition held every 18 months open to singers between the ages of 21 and 35 whose most recent teacher has been a member of the National Association of Teachers of
ging. Prizes include 1st prize of $10,000, and Carnegie Hall concert, and AIMS scholarship, and 2nd prize of $2,500.

onal Competition for Performing Artists.
Contemporary Recording Society, 724 Winchester Road, Broomall, PA 19008.
ual competition open to performers. Prizes include recording.

ional Endowment for the Arts, Music Program Office.
0 Pennsylvania Avenue North West, Washington, DC 20506.
ds organizational assistance to professional music organizations and gives fellowships to composers, performers, etc.

ional Endowment for the Humanities.
Pennsylvania Avenue North West, Washington, DC 20506.
rds fellowships and grants for various projects in the field of music.

ional Federation of Music Clubs.
6 North Delaware Street, Indianapolis, IN 46202.
vides various annual awards and fellowships.

National Symphony Orchestra Young Soloists' Competition, College Division.
5931 Oakdale Road, McLean, VA 22101.
Annual competition open to high school graduates studying music in the Washington metropolitan area or Washington residents studying elsewhere. Prizes include ca
appearances with the National Symphony Orchestra.

Walter W Naumburg Foundation International Competition.
60 Lincoln Center Plaza, New York, NY 10023.
Annual competition open to performers of all nationalities with categories rotating annually. Prizes include 1st prize of $5,000, concert engagements, and a recording, 2n
of $2,500, and 3rd prize of $1,000.

New Jersey Symphony Orchestra Young Artists Auditions.
Robert Treat Center, 11th Floor, 50 Park Place, Newark, NJ 07102.
Annual competition open to New Jersey residents who are instrumentalists under the age of 20. Prizes include top prize of an appearance with the New Jersey Sym
Orchestra; cash prizes range from $500 to $3,000.

New York Foundation for the Arts Artists' Fellowship Program.
155 Avenue of the Americas, New York, NY 10013.
Biennial fellowships for non-students of two or more years residency in New York State. Prizes include grants. Next fellowships awarded in 1999.

Omaha Symphony Guild New Music Competition.
8723 North 57th Street, Omaha, NE 68152.
Annual competition open to composers of chamber orchestra compositions. Prizes include $2,000.

Opera at Florham Guild Vocal Competition.
Box 343, Convent Station, NJ 07961
Competition open to all singers between the ages of 18 and 35. Prizes include 1st prize of $3,000 and a recital.

Opera/Columbus Vocal Competition.
177 Naghten, Columbus, OH 43215.
Competition open to singers who are residents of Ohio. Prizes for senior level (ages 24 to 35) include 1st prize of $2,000 and a scholarship to the American Institute of M
Studies in Graz, Austria.

Oratorio Society of New York Solo Competition.
Carnegie Hall, Suite 504, 881 Seventh Avenue, New York, NY 10019.
Annual competition open to solo oratorio singers under the age of 40. Prizes include $10,000.

Palm Beach Invitational International Piano Competition.
PO Box 3094, Palm Beach, FL 33480.
Annual competition open to 25 young pianists, each from a different nation and each the winner of an international competition. Prizes totalling $50,000, including 1st p
$15,000 and a concert at Alice Tully Hall in New York.

Palm Beach Opera Vocal Competition.
415 South Olive Avenue, West Palm Beach, FL 33401.
Annual competition open to singers with Junior Division between the ages of 18 and 23 and Senior Division between the ages of 24 and 30. Prizes totalling $43,0
performances.

Performing Arts Assistance Corporation.
PO Box 1296, Ansonia Station, New York, NY 10023.
Gives seminars for performers.

Gregor Piatigorsky Seminar for Cello.
c/o University of Southern California School of Music, Los Angeles, CA 90089.
Seminar open to cellists.

Rosa Ponselle International Vocal Competition for the Vocal Arts.
"Windsor", Stevenson, MD 21153.
Biennial competition open to singers to the age of 25. Prizes include study grants between $20,000 and $25,000, medallions, and training in Italy and France. Next comp
in 1999.

Pro Musicis International Award.
140 West 79th Street, No 9F, New York, NY 10024.
Annual career development award. Prizes include major recitals in New York, Los Angeles, Washington DC, Boston, Paris, and Rome.

Pulitzer Prize in Music.
c/o Columbia University, 702 Journalism Building, New York, NY 10027.
Annual prize of $3,000 to an American composer for a major composition premiered in the US during the year.

Queens Opera Vocal Competition.
313 Bay 14 Street, Brooklyn, NY 11214.
Annual competition open to singers who have appeared in one opera performance. Prizes include 1st prize of cash and an appearance in a full opera performance.

Rome Prize Fellowships of the American Academy in Rome.
41 East 65th Street, New York, NY 10021.
Annual fellowships for American composers with a BA or equivalent degree. Fellowships include one year residency at the American Academy in Rome, stipend, and
allowance.

San Antonio International Keyboard Competition.
PO Box 39636, San Antonio, TX 78218.
Triennial competition open to pianists between the ages of 20 and 32. Prizes include 1st prize of $5,000 and gold medal, 2nd prize of $2,500 and silver medal, 3rd prize of $
and bronze medal, and 4th prize of $500. Next competition in 2000.

San Francisco Opera Center National Auditions.
c/o War Memorial Opera House, San Francisco, CA 94102.
Annual competitive auditions for singers, sopranos between the ages of 20 and 30 and all other singers between 20 and 34. Prizes include awards given in the Merola
Program totalling $28,000. Participants may also apply for the Adler Fellowship Program.

Jose Symphony Young Pianist Concerto Competition.
maden Boulevard, Suite 400, San Jose, CA 95113.
al competition open to pianists to the age of 30. Prizes include grand prize of $5,000 and an appearance with the San Jose Symphony.

a Barbara Symphony and the Esperia Foundation Young Artists' Competition.
East Victoria Street, Santa Barbara, CA 93101.
petition open to string players and pianist alternating between instruments every even year. Prizes include cash and an appearance with the Santa Barbara Symphony. Next petition in 1998.

rich Schorr Memorial Performance Prize in Voice.
South Madison Street, Adrian, MI 49221.
al competition open to all professional singers. Prizes include $10,000 in performance awards/stipends.

anee Music Festival International Scholarships.
University Avenue, Sewanee, TN 37375.
al scholarships for musicians of all nationalities between the ages of 16 and 25.

veport Symphony/Nena Plant Wideman Annual Piano Competition.
Box 205, Shreveport, LA 71162.
al competition open to pianists between the ages of 18 and 28. Prizes include 1st prize of $2,500, 2nd prize of $1,000, and 3rd prize of $500.

onia Foundation.
hi Mus Alpha Sinfonia Fraternity, 10600 Old State Road, Evansville, IN 47711.
missions to composers and annual research grants for scholarly research on music in America or American music.

ntin Young Artists Award.
Box 5922, San Angelo, TX 76902.
competition 1998.

nd Research Residencies.
*e*llow Springs Institute for Contemporary Studies and the Arts, 1645 Art School Road, Chester Springs, PA 19425.
al ten-day residency for composers with at least three years of professional experience.

thwestern Youth Music Festival Competition.
Box 41104, Los Angeles, CA 90041.
al competition open to pianists to the age of 18 whose teacher must become a member of the festival. Prizes include $10,000 and orchestral appearances.

es Spencer Memorial Performance Prize in Composition.
South Madison Street, Adrian, MI 49221.
es open to American composers. Prizes include travel and housing allowance, lecture stipend, and performance and recording by the Adrian Symphony Orchestra.

ey International Performance Competition.
ton State College, Morrow, GA 30260.
al competition for performers. Prizes include 1st prize of $5,000.

art Awards National Operatic Voice Competition.
Box 18321, Oklahoma City, OK 73154.
nial competition open to American singers between the ages of 20 and 32. Prizes include cash totalling $14,000. Next competition in 1998.

vinsky Awards International Piano Competition for Children and Young Adults.
West Church Street, Champaign, IL 61821.
nial competition open to pianists of all nationalities in age divisions ranging from small children to the age of 22. Prizes include various cash awards. Next competition in 1999.

us Stulberg International String Competition.
Box 107, Kalamazoo, MI 49005.
al competition open to string players to the age of 19. Prizes include cash and performances.

is and Virginia Sudler International Wind Band Composition Contest.
US Marine Bane, Eighth and 1 Streets South East, Washington, DC 20390.
nial competition open to composers of wind music. Prizes include 1st prize of $12,000. Next competition in 1997.

am Matheus Sullivan Musical Foundation Inc.
West 89th Street, Suite 10-B, New York, NY 10024.
al assistance program for professional young singers.

as Institute Scholarships.
Sunset Boulevard, No 1180, Hollywood, CA 90028.
al scholarships for educational opportunities in the music business and the recording arts and sciences.

ard Tucker Music Foundation.
Broadway, Suite 715, New York, NY 10019.
al awards to American singers by recommendation. Prizes include the Richard Tucker Award of $30,000, four career grants of $6,500, and other grants.

International Harp Competition.
Box 2718, Bloomington, IN 47402.
nial competition open to harpists of all nationalities born in 1966 through 1982. Prizes include 8 awards. Next competition in 1998.

sys African-American Composers Forum and Symposium.
H Education Department, 400 Buhl Building, 535 Griswold Street, Detroit, MI 48226.
ourages performances of orchestral compositions by African-American composers by major professional symphony orchestras.

ed States Information Agency Artistic Ambassador Program.
Fourth Street, South West, Room 216, Washington, DC 20547.
al program for American musicians at least 21 years old to serve as Artistic Ambassadors abroad at government expense for four to six weeks.

University of Louisville Grawemeyer Award for Music Composition.
c/o University of Louisville, School of Music, Grawemeyer Music Award Committee, Louisville, KY 40292.
Annual award for outstanding achievement by a composer. Compositions may not be submitted by the composer but must be sponsored by a professional music organ
or individual. Award totalling $150,000, paid in five annual instalments of $30,000.

University of Maryland International Competitions (William Kapell, Leonard Rose and Marian Anderson)
c/o University of Maryland, College Park, MD 20742.
Annual competition open to pianists, cellist, and singers of all nationalities. Prizes include 1st prize of $20,000 and concert engagements, 2nd prize of $10,000, and 3rd p
$5,000.

Elizabeth Harper Vaughan Concerto Competition.
1200 East Center Street, Kingsport, TN 37600.
Annual competition open to performers of classical music to the age of 26. Prizes include $1,000 and an appearance with the Kingsport Symphony Orchestra.

WAMSO (Women's Association of the Minnesota Orchestra) Young Artist Competition.
c/o Minnesota Orchestra, 1111 Nicollet Mall, Minneapolis, MN 55403.
Annual competition open to instrumentalists to the age of 25. Various prizes.

Washington International Competition.
4530 Connecticut Avenue, Apt 704, Washington, DC 20008.
Annual competition open to performers between the ages of 18 and 32 with categories rotating annually. Prizes include cash.

Abby Whiteside Foundation Inc.
8 East 83rd Street, No 8-E, New York, NY 10028.
To encourage the study, education, and performance of piano music.

Andrew Wolf Chamber Music Award.
PO Box 191, Camden, ME 04843 or Newton Music School, 321 Chestnut Street, West Newton, MA 02165.
Biennial award given to an American chamber music pianist under the age of 40. Award includes $10,000 and concert appearances. Next competition in 1999.

Young Concert Artists International Auditions.
250 West 57th Street, Suite 921, New York, NY 10019.
Annual auditions for solo performers and string quartets.

Loren L Zachary Society Opera Awards National Vocal Competition.
2250 Gloaming Way, Beverly Hills, CA 90210.
Annual competition open to professional opera singers seeking contracts for leading roles in European opera houses; for women between the ages of 21 and 33 and fe
between the ages of 21 and 35. Prizes totalling about $25,000 and a round trip flight to Europe for auditioning purposes.

URUGUAY

Concurso Internacional de Piano "Ciudad de Montevideo".
Santiago Vásquez, Montevideo.
Triennial competition open to pianists to the age of 32. Next competition in 1997.

APPENDIX F
MUSIC LIBRARIES

AFGHANISTAN

Kabul Public Library, Kabul.

ALBANIA

Biblioteka Kombetare (National Library), Tirana.

ALGERIA

Bibliothèque nationale, Avenue Frantz Fanor, Algiers.
Bibliothèque Universitarie, Lrue Didouche Mourad, Algiers.

ARGENTINA

Academia Nacional de Bellas Artes, Biblioteca, Sanchez de Bustamante 2663, 1425 Buenos Aires.
Bibliteca Nacional, México 564, 1097 Buenos Aires.
Fondo Nacional de Las Artes, Biblioteca, Alsina 673, 1087 Buenos Aires.

AUSTRALIA

AUSTRALIAN CAPITAL TERRITORY

National Library of Australia, Music Division, Parkes Place, Canberra, ACT 2600.

NEW SOUTH WALES

Australia Music Centre Ltd Library, 1st Floor, Argyle Centre, 18 Argyle Street, The Rocks, NSW 2000.
City of Sydney Public Library, Music Division, 473 George Street, Sydney, NSW 2000.
Dennis Wolanski Library, Sydney Opera House, Bennelona Point, GPO Box 4274, Sydney, NSW 2000.
Federal Music Library, Australian Broadcasting Corporation, GPO Box 9994, Sydney, NSW 2001.
State Library of New South Wales, Music Division, Macquarie Street, Sydney, NSW 2000.

QUEENSLAND

State Library of Queensland, Music Division, William Street, Brisbane, QLD 4000.

SOUTH AUSTRALIA

State Library of South Australia, Music Division, North Terrace, GPO Box 419, Adelaide, SA 5001.

TASMANIA

State Library of Tasmania, Music Division, 91 Murray Street, Hobart, TAS 7000.

VICTORIA

State Library of Victoria, Music Division, 328 Swanston St, Melbourne, VIC 3000.

WESTERN AUSTRALIA

State Library of Western Australia, Music Division, Alexander Library Building, Perth Cultural Centre, Perth, WA 6000.

AUSTRIA

Burgenländische Landesbibliothek, Landhaus Freiheitsplatz 1, 7001 Eisenstadt.
Stadbücherien, Landhausgasse 2, 8010 Graz.
Kammer für Arbeiter und Angestelle, Volksbüchereien, Bahnhofplatz 3, 9021 Klagenfurt.
Büchereien der Stadt Linz, Zentrale und Hauptbücherei, Museumstrasse 15, 4020 Linz.
Stadbücherei, Schloss Mirabell, 5020 Salzburg.
Gesellschaft der Musikfreunde in Wien, Archiv und Bibliothek, Bösendorferstrasse 12, 1010 Vienna.
Haus des Buches, Hauptbücherei, Skodagasse 20, 1080 Vienna.
Musik Informations Zentrum Österreich (MICA), Stiftgasse 29, A-1070 Vienna.
Österreichische Akademie der Wissenschaften, Bibliothek, Dr Ignaz Seipelplatz 2, 1010 Vienna 1.
Österreichische Gesellschaft für Musik, Bibliothek, Hanuschgasse 3, A-1010 Vienna.
Österreichische Nationalbibliothek, Josefplatz 1, 1015 Vienna.
Österreichische Gewerkschaftsbund, Bibliothek, Grillparzerstrasse 14, 1010 Vienna.
Stadtbücherei, Herzog Leopoldstrasse 21, 2700 Wiener Neustadt.
Wiener Stadt-und Landesbibliothek, Rathaus, 1082 Vienna.

BELGIUM

Stadsbibliotheek, Hendrik Conscienceplein 4, 2000 Antwerp.
Academie royale des sciences, des lettres et des beaux arts de Belgique, Bibliothèque, 1 Rue Ducale, Palais des academies, 1000 Brussels.

Bibliothèque royale Albert Ier, Boulevard de l"Empereur 4, 1000 Brussels.
Koninklijke Academie voor Wetenschappen, Letteren en schone Kunsten van Belgie, Hetogsstraat 1, Paleis der Academien, 1000 Brussels.
Bibliothèque centrale, En Hors Chateau 31, 4000 Liège.
Bibliothèque provinciale du degré moyen, Rue des Croisiers 15, 4000 Liège.

BOLIVIA

Biblioteca y Archivo Nacional de Bolivia, C Espana 25, Casilla 338, Sucre.

BRAZIL

Biblioteca Nacional, Fundaçao Nacional Pro-Memoria, Avenida Rio branco 219-239, 20042 Rio de Janeiro.

BULGARIA

Nacionalna Biblioteka, "Kiril i Metodij", F Tolbuhin 11, 1504 Sofia.
Union of Bulgarian Composers, Iv Vazov 2, 1000 Sofia.

CAMBODIA

Bibliothèque nationale, 4, Phnom Penh.

CANADA

ALBERTA

Calgary Public Library, Music Division, 616 Macleod Trail South East, Calgary, AB T2G 2M2.
Edmonton Public Library, Music Division, 7 Sir Winston Churchill Square, Edmonton, AB T5J 2V4.

BRITISH COLUMBIA

Vancouver Public Library, Music Division, 750 Burrard St, Vancouver, BC V6 1X5.
Greater Victoria Public Library, Music Division, 735 Broughton St, Victoria, BC V8W 3H2.

MANITOBA

Winnipeg Public Library, Music Division, 251 Donald St, Winnipeg, MN R3C 3P5.

NOVA SCOTIA

Halifax City Regional Library, Music Division, 5381 Spring Garden Road, Halifax, NS B3J 1E9.

ONTARIO

Guelph Public Library, Music Division, 100 Norfolk Street, Guelph, ON N1H 4S6.
Hamilton Public Library, Music Division, 55 York Blvd, Hamilton, ON L8R 3K1.
Kingston Public Library, Music Division, 130 Johnson Street East, Kingston, ON K7L 1X8.
Kitchener Public Library, Music Division, 85 Queen St N, Kitchener, ON N2H 2H1.
National Library of Canada, Music Division, 395 Wellington Street, Ottawa, ON K1A 0N4.
Ottawa Public Library, 120 Metcalfe Street, Ottawa, ON K1P 5M2.
Canadian Music Centre, 20 St Joseph Street, Toronto, ON M4Y 1J9.
Toronto Public Library, Music Division, 40 St George St, Toronto, ON M5S 2E4.
Windsor Public Library, Music Division, 850 Quellette Ave, Windsor, ON N9A 4M9.

QUÈBEC

Bibliothèque municipale de Montréal, 1210 Sheerbrooke St East, Montréal, PQ H2L 1L9.
Bibliothèque nationale du Quèbec, 1700 St Denis Street, Montréal, PQH2X 3K6.
Bibliothèque municipale de Quèbec, 37 Rue Sainte-Angéle, Quèbec, PQ G1R 4G5.

SASKATCHEWAN

Regina Public Library, Music Division, 2311 12th Ave, PO Box 2311, Regina, SK S4P 3Z5.
Saskatoon Public Library, Music Division, 311 23rd St Et, Saskatoon, SK S7K 0J6.

CHILE

Biblioteca Nacional, Avenida Bernardo O'Higgins 651, Santiago.

CHINA

National Library of China, 39 Baishiqiao Road, Haidian District, Beijing 100 081.

COLOMBIA

Biblioteca Nacional de Columbia, C24, 5-60, Apdo 27600 Bogotá.

COSTA RICA

Biblioteca Nacional, C 15-17, Av 3Y 3b, Apdo 10008, San José.

CUBA

Biblioteca Nacional "José Marti", Apdo oficial No 3, Avenida de Independencia 3/20 de Mayo y Arangusen, Plaza de la Revolucion José Marti, Havana.

CZECH REPUBLIC

Městská knihovna v Praze (City Library of Prague), Knhovna Bedřicha Smetany (Bedrich Smetana Library), Dr V Vacka 1, 115 72 Prague.
Music Information Centre, Besední 3, 118 00 Prague 1.
Státni knihovna (State Library), Klementinum 190, 110 01 Prague 1.

DENMARK

Danish Music Informationa Centre, 48 Vimmelskaftet, 1161 Copenhagen K.
Det Kongelige Bibliotek (Royal Library), Christians Brygge 8, 1219 Copenhagen K.
Musikhistorisk Museum and Carl Claudius' Samling, Bibliotek, Åbenrå 30, 1124 Copenhagen K.

DOMINICAN REPUBLIC

Biblioteca Nacional, César Nicolás Penson 91, Plaza de la Cultura, Santo Domingo.

ECUADOR

Biblioteca Nacional de Ecuador, 12 de Octubre 555, Apdo 67, Quito.

EGYPT

Egyptian National Library, Sharia Corniche El-Nil, Bulaq, Cairo.

EIRE

National Library of Ireland, Kildare Street, Dublin 2.

EL SALVADOR

Biblioteca National, 8A Avenida Norte Calle Delgado, San Salvador.

ETHIOPIA

National Library and Archives of Ethiopia, PO Box 1907, Addis Ababa.

FINLAND

Finnish Music Information Centre, Lauttasaarenti 1, 00120 Helsinki.

FRANCE

Bibliothèque centrale de prêt du Pas-de-Calais, 13 Pl. Guy Mollet, 62000 Arras.
Bibliothèque centrale de prêt du Boubs et du Territorie de Belfort, 24 Avenue de l'Observatorie, 25000 Besançon.
Bibliothèque municipale classée, 3 Rue Mably, 33075 Bordeaux, Cédex.
Bibliothèque de la ville de Caen, Place Guillouard, 14027 Caen Cédex.
Bibliothèque municipale d'étude et d'information, Boulevard Maréchal-Lyautey, BP 1095 RP, 38021 Grenoble Cédex.
Bibliothèque municipale, 32-34 Rue Edouard-Delesalle, 59043 Lille Cédex.
Bibliothèque municipale, 30 Boulevard Vivier-Merle, 69431 Lyon Cédex 03.
Bibliothèque municipale, 38 Rue du 141e RIA, 13001 Marseille Cédex 3.
Bibliothèque municipale, 1 Cour Elie Fleur, 57000 Metz.
Bibliothèque de la ville et du musée Fabre, 37 Blvd Bonnes-Nouvelles, 34000 Montepellier.
Bibliothèque municipale, 19 Grand Rue, 68090 Mulhouse Cédex.
Bibliothèque municipale, 43 Rue Stanislas, 54000 Nancy.
Bibliothèque municipale, 37 Rue Gambetta, 44041 Nantes Cédex.
Bibliothèque municipale d'études, 21 bis Blvd Dubouchage, 06047 Nice Cédex.
Bibliothèque municipale, 1 Rue Dupanloup, 45043 Orléans Cédex.
Bibliothèque-Musée de l'Opera, Place Charles Garnier, 75009 Paris.
Bibliothèque Musicale Gustav Mahler, 11 bis rue Vézelay, 75008 Paris.
Bibliothèque nationale, Department de la musique, 2 Rue Louvois, 75084 Paris.
Bibliothèque municipale classée, 43 Place Charles-de-Gaulle, 86000 Poitiers.
Bibliothèque municipale classée, 2 Place Carnegie, 51095 Reims Cédex.
Bibliothèque municipale, 1 Rue de La Borderie, 35042 Rennes Cédex.
Bibliothèque municipale, e Rue Jacques Villon, 76043 Rouen Cédex.

Bibliothèque municipale, 3 Rue Kuhn, 67000 Strasbourg Cédex.
Bibliothèque municipale, 1 Rue de Périgord, 31070 Toulouse.
Bibliothèque municipale, 2 bis Quai d'Orléans, 37042 Tours Cédex.
Bibliothèque municipale, 5 Rue de l'indépendence américaine, 78000 Versailles.
Institut de France: Acádemie des Beaux-Arts, 23 Quai de Conti, 75006 Paris.

GERMANY

Öffentliceh Bibliothek der Stadt Aachen, Couvenstrasse 15, Pf 1210, Aachen.
Staats-und Stadtbibliothek, Schaezlerstrasse 25, Postfach 111909, Augusburg.
Stadtbücherei, Gutenbergstrasse 2, Augsburg.
Stadtbibliothek, Luisenstrasse 34, Baden-Baden.
Staatsbibliothek, Neue Residenz, Domplatz 8, Bamberg.
Stadtbücherei, Friedrichstrasse 2, Bamberg.
Statsbibliothek, Luitpoldplatz 7, Postfach 2840, Bayreuth.
Akademie der Kunste, Robert-Koch-Platz 7, Berlin.
Deutsche Staatsbibliothek, Unter den Linden 8, Berlin.
Staatsbibliothek, 24 Berlin-Preussischen Kulturbesitz, Musikabteilung, Pf 1312 Berlin.
Stadtbibliothek, Wilhelmstrasse 3, Postfach 181, Bielefeld.
Stadtbücherei, Rathausplatz 2-6, Postfach 102269-2270, Bochum.
Stadtarchiv und Wissenschaftliche Stadtbibliothek, Berliner Platz 2, Bonn.
Stadtbücherei Bonn, Bottlerplatz 1, Bonn.
Stadtbibliothek, Schusterstrasse 7, Brandenburg.
Offentliche Bücherei, Hintern Brudern 23, Braunschweig.
Stadtbibliothek, Steintorwall 15, Postfach 3309, Braunschweig.
Staats-und Universitätsbibliothek, Bibliothekstrasse, Postfach 330160, Bremen.
Stadtbibliothek, Schwachhauser Heerstrasse 30, Bremen.
Stadt-und Bezirksbibliothek, Haus am Schillerplatz, Chemnitz.
Landesbibliothek, Schlossplatz 1 Schloss Ehrenburg, Coburg.
Stadtbücherei Köln, Zentralbibliothek, Josef-Haubrich-Hof 1, Pf 108020, Cologne.
Hessische Landes-und Hochschulbibliothek, Schloss 6, Darmstadt.
Stadtbibliothek, Stasse d DSF 10, Dessau.
Lippische Landesbibliothek, Hornschestrasse 41, Detmold.
Stadt-und Landesbibliothek, Hansaplatz, Postfach 907, Dortmund.
Stadtbücherei, Markt 12, Postfach 907, Dortmund.
Sächsische Landesbibliothek, Marienalle 12, Dresden.
Stadtbibliothek, Düsseldorfer Stasse 5-7, Postfach 100991, Duisburg.
Stadtbüchereien, Berliner Alle 59, Postfach 1120, Düsseldorf.
Stadt-und Kreisbibliothek, Johannisplatz 18-20, Eisenach.
Stadtbücherei, Marktplatz 1, Postfach 3160, Erlangen.
Stadtbibliothek, Hinderburgstrasse 25-27, Essen.
Deutsche Bibliothek, Zeppelinalle 8, Frankfurt am Main.
Stadt-und Universitätsbibliothek, Bockenheimer Landstr. 134-138, Frankfurt .
Stadtbücherei, Zentralbibliothek, Zeil 17-19, Postfach 102113, Frankfurt am Main.
Stadtbibliothek, Münsterplatz 17, Freiburg.
Stadtbücherei, Ebertstrasse 19, Gelsenkirchen.
Stadbibliothek, Jochmannstrasse 2-3, Görlitz.
Stadt-und Kreisbibliothek "Heinrich Heine", Orangerie, Gotha.
Stadtbibliothek, Gotmarstrasse 8, Postfach 3842, Göttingen.
Stadt-und Bezirksbibliothek, Salzgrafenstrasse 2, Halle.
Hamburger Öffentliche Bücherhallen, Grosse Bleichen 23-27, Hamburg.
Stadtbibliothek, Hildesheimer Strasse 12, Postfach 125, Hannover.
Stadtbücherei, Deutschordenshof, Kirchburnnenstrasse, Heilbronn.
Stadtarchiv und Stadtbibliothek, Am Steine 7, Hildesheim.
Stadtbucherei, Hallstrasse 2-4, Ingolstadt.
Stadtbibliothek, Stadtverwaltung, St-Martins-Platza 3, Pf 1320, Kaiserslautern.
Stadtbibliothek, Zähringerstrasse 96-98, Postfach 6260, Karlsruhe.
Stadtbibliothek, Rathaus, Kassel.
Stadtbücherei, Holstenbrücke 1, Postfach 4140, Kiel.
Stadtbibliothek, Kornpforstrasse 15, Postfach 2064, Koblenz.
Deutsche Bücherei, Deutscher Platz, Leipzig.
Kreisbibliothek, Leipzig-Land, Karl-Rothe-Strasse 13, Leipzig.
Musikbibliothek de Stadt Leipzig, Ferdinand-Lassale-Strasse 21, Leipzig.
Stadt-und Bezirksbibliothek, Mozartstrasse 1, Leipzig.
Bibliothek der Hansestadt Lübeck, Hundestrasse 5-17, Lübeck.
Stadtbibliothek, Bismarckstrasse 44-48, Postfach 212125, Ludwigshafen.
Stadt-und Kreisbibliothek, Strasse d DSF 8, Ludwigslust.
Ratsbücherei, Am Marienplatas 3, Postfach 2540, Lüneburg.
Stadt-und Bezirksbibliothek, Weitlingstrasse 1a, Magdeburg.
Stadtbibliothek, Rheinalle 3b, Mainz.
Stadtbücherei, N 3, 4 (Dalberghaus), Postfach 5868, Mannheim.
Stadt-und Kreisbibliothek, Ernestiner Strasse 38, Meiningen.
Stadbibliothek, Blücherstrasse 6, Postfach 85, Mönchengladbach.
Stadt-und Kreisbibliothek, Mühlhausen.
Stadtbücherei, Friedrich-Ebert-Strasse 47, Postfach 011620, Mülheim.

Bayerische Staatsbibliothek, Ludwigstrasse 16, Munich.
Münchner Städtische Bibliotheken, Rosenheimerstrasse 5, Munich.
Stadtbücherei, Alter Steinweg 7, Postfach 5909, Münster.
Stadtbibliothek, Zentralbibliothek, Egidienplatz 23, Nuremberg.
Stadtbücherei, Langemarkstrasse 19-21, Oberhausen.
Stadt-und Kreisbibliothek, Strasse d Friedens 54, Oranienburg.
Stadt-und Kreisbibliothek, August-Wolf-Strasse 10, Quedlinburg.
Bischöfliche Zentralbibliothek, St Petersweg 11-13, Regensburg.
Stadtbücherei, Haidplatz 8, Regensburg.
Stadt-und Berzirksbibliothek, Kröpeliner Strasse 82, Rostock.
Stadt-und Kreisbibliothek, Schulplatz 13, Rudolstadt.
Stadtbibliothek, Nauwieser Strasse 5, Saarbrücken.
Kreisbibliothek Schwerin-Land, Wismarsche Strasse 144, Schwerin.
Stadt-und Kreisbibliothek, Schloss Sondershausen.
Stadtbücherei, Konrad-Ademauer-Strasse 2, Stuttgart.
Stadtbücherei, Bunnenstrasse 3, Tübingen.
Stadtbibliothek, Weinhof 12, Ulm.
Stadtbibliothek, Steubenstrasse 1, Weimer.
Stadtbibliothek, Rathauspassage, Wiesbaden.
Stadtbibliothek, Kolpingstrasse 8, Wuppertal.
Städtbucherei, Max-Heim-Bücherei, Haus zum Falken, Würzburg.
Stadtbibliothek, Zwickau.

GHANA

Central Reference and Research Library, PO Box M 32, Accra.

GREECE

Ethnike Bibliotheke tes Hellados, Odos Venizelou 32, 106 79 Athens.

GUATEMALA

Biblioteca Nacional de Guatemala, 5a Avenida 7-26, Guatemala City.

HAITI

Bibliothèque Nationale d'Haiti, 193 Rue du Centre, Port-au-Prince.

HONDURAS

Biblioteca Nacional de Honduras, 6a Avenida Salvador Mendieta, Tegucigalpa.

HUNGARY

Állami Gorkij Könyvtar (Gorky State Library), Molnár u 11, 1056 Budapest.
Magyar tudományos Akadémia Zenetudományi Intézete (Institute for Musicology of the Hungarian Academy of Sciences), Táncsis M u 7, 1014 Budapest.
Magyar Zeneműveszek Szövetsége (Association of Hungarian Composers), Vörösmarty tér 1 1364, PO Box 47, 1051 Budapest.
Országos Széchémyi Könyvtar (National Széchémyi Library), 1 Budavári Palota F-épület, 1827 Budapest.

ICELAND

Landsbokasafn Islands (National Library of Iceland), Reykjavík.

INDIA

National Library, Belvedere, Calcutta 700027.

INDONESIA

Perpustakaan Nasional (National Library of Indonesia), J1 Salemba Raya 28, PO Box 3624, Jakarta 10002.

IRAN

National Library of Iran, 30 Tir Street, Tehran 11363.

IRAQ

National Library, Bab-el-Muaddum, Baghdad.

ISRAEL

AMLI Library of Music, 23 Arlosoroff Street, Haifa.
Jewish National and University Library, PO Box 503, 91004 Jerusalem.
AMLI Central Library for Music and Dance, 26 Bialik Street, 65241 Tel Aviv.

ITALY

Biblioteca Civica, Via Tripoli 16, 15100 Alessandria.
Associazione Culturale Archivi del Sud, Via Giovanni Spano 5, 07041 Alghero.
Archivio di Stato di Ancona, Via Maggini 80, 60127 Ancona.
Biblioteca Comunale Luciano Benincasa, Via Bernabel 32, 60121 Ancona.
Biblioteca della Città di Arezzo, Via dei Pileati-Palazzo Pretorio, 52100 Arezzo.
Archivio di Stato de Bari, Via Pasubio 137, 70124 Bari.
Biblioteca nazionale "Sagarriga-Visconti-Volpi", Palazzo Ateneo, Piazza Umberto, 70100 Bari.
Biblioteca Civica A Mai, Piazza Vecchia 15, 24100 Bergamo.
Archivio di Stato di Bologna, Piazza dei Celestini 4, 40123 Bologna.
Universitaria di Bologna Biblioteca, Via Zamboni 35, 40126 Bologna.
Civica Biblioteca Queriniana, Via Mazzini 1, 25100 Brescia.
Archivio di Stato di Cagliari, Via Gallura 2, 09125 Cagliari.
Biblioteca Universitaria, Via Università32A, 09100 Cagliari.
Archivio di Stato di Cantania, Via Vittorio Emanuele 156, 95131 Catania.
Biblioteca Regionale Universitaria, Piazza Università 2, 95124 Catania.
Biblioteca Riunite Civica e A Ursino Recupero, Via Biblioteca 13, 95124 Catania.
Biblioteca Comunale, Via Indipendenza 87, 22100 Como.
Biblioteca Statale e Libreria Civica, Via Ugolani Dati 4, 26100 Cremona.
Biblioteca Comunale Arisotea, Via Scienze 17, 44100 Ferrara.
Archivio di Stato di Firenze, Loggiato degli riffizi, 50100 Florence.
Biblioteca Medicea-Laurenziana, Piazza S Lorenso 9, 50100 Florence.
Biblioteca Nazionale Centrale, Piazza Cavalleggeri 1B, 50122 Florence.
Biblioteca Comunale "A Saffi", Corso della Repubblica 72, 47100 Forli.
Archivio di Stato di Genova, Via Teatro Regio 14, 16123 Genoa.
Biblioteca Durazzo Giustiniani, Via Balbi 1, 16126 Genoa.
Biblioteca Comunale "Labronica" Francesco Domenico Guerrazzi, Villa Fabbricotti, Viale della Libertà 30, 57100 Livorno.
Biblioteca Statale di Lucca, Via S Maria Corteorlandini 12, 55100 Lucca.
Biblioteca Comunale, Via Roberto Ardigò 13, 46100 Mantua.
Biblioteca Regionale, Via dei Verdi 71, 98122 Messina.
Archivio de Stato di Milano, Via Senato 10, 20121 Milan.
Biblioteca Comunale, Palazzo Sormani, Corso di Porta Vittoria 32, 20133 Milan.
Raccolte storiche del Comune di Milano, Biblioteca e Archivio, Palazzo De Marchi, Via Borgonuovo 23, 20121 Milan.
Biblioteca Estense, Palazzo dei Musei, Piazzo S Agostino 309, 41100 Modena.
Archivio di Stato di Napoli, Piazzetta Grande Archivio 5, 80138 Naples.
Biblioteca nazionale "Vittorio Emanuele III", Palazzo Reale, 80133 Naples.
Biblioteca Civica, Via Arto Botanico 5, 35123 Padua.
Archivio di Stato di Palermo, Corso Vittorio Emanuele 31, 90133 Palermo.
Biblioteca Centrale della Regione Siciliana, Corso Vittorio Emanuele 429-431, 90134 Palermo.
Biblioteca Comunale, Piazza Brunaccini, 90100 Palermo.
Biblioteca Palatina, Palazzo della Pilotta, 4300 Parma.
Instituto Nazionale di Studi Verdiani, Strada della Repubblica 56, 43100 Parma.
Biblioteca Civica, Piazza, Petrarca 2, 27100 Pavia.
Biblioteca Universitaria, Palazzo dell'Università, 27100 Pavia.
Biblioteca Augusta del Domune di Perugia, Palazzo Conestabile della Staffa, Via delle Prome 15, 06100 Perugia.
Biblioteca Comunale Passerini Landi, Via Neve 3, 29100 Piacenza.
Biblioteca Universitaria, Via Curtatone e Montanara 15, 56100 Pisa.
Biblioteca Comunale Forteguerriana, Piazza della Sapienza 1, PO Box 177, Pistoia.
Biblioteca Comunale Classense, Via Baccarini 3, 48100 Ravenna.
Biblioteca Municipale "A Panizzi", Via Farini 3, 42100 Reggio Emilia.
Biblioteca Civica Gambalunga, Via Gambalunga 27, Rimini.
Archivio Centrale dello Stato, Piazzale degli Archivi, EUR, 00144 Rome.
Biblioteca Comunale degli Intronati, Via della Sapienza 5, 53100 Siena.
Biblioteca dell'Archivio di Stato di Trento, Via Rome 51, Trento.
Biblioteca Comunale, Via Roma 51, 38100 Trento.
Biblioteca Comunale, Borgo Cavour 18, 31100 Treviso.
Archivio di Stato di Trieste, Via Lamarmora 17, 34139 Trieste.
Archivio de Stato di Torino, 10100 Turin Centro.
Biblioteca Reale, Piazzo Castello 191, 10100 Turin.
Biblioteca Civiche e Raccolte Storiche, Via Cittadella 5, 10122 Turin.
Biblioteca Comunale Joppi, Piazza Marconi 8, 33100 Udine.
Biblioteca Universitaria, Via Aurelio Saffi 2, 61029 Urbino.
Biblioteca del Civico Museo Correr, Piazza San Marco 52, Procuratie Nuove, 30100 Venice.
Biblioteca Nazionale Marciana, Palazzi della libreria Vecchia e della Zecca, San Marco 7, 30124 Venice.
Biblioteca Civica, Via Cappello 43, 37121 Verona.
Biblioteca Civica Bertoliana, Via Riale 5-13, 36100 Vicenza.

JAMAICA

Institute of Jamaica Library, 12-16 East Street, Kingston.

JAPAN

Hiroshima Prefectural, 2020 Kami-Nobori-machi, Hiroshima.
Kyoto Prefectural Library, Okazaki Park, Kyoto Shi, Kyoto.
Osaka Prefectural Nakanoshima Library, 1-2-10 Nakanoshima, Kita-ku, Osaka.
Documentation Centre of Modern Japanese Music, 8-14 Azaudai 1-chome, Minato-ku, Tokyo 106.
National Diet (Parliament) Library, 10-1 Nagatacho 1-chome, Chiyoda-ku, Tokyo 100.
Tokyo Metropolitan Central Library, 5-7-13 Minami-Azabu, Monato-ku, Tokyo 106.

JORDAN

Greater Amman Public Library, PO Box 182181, Amman.

KENYA

Central Government Archives, PO Box 30050, Nairobi.
Kenya National Archives, PO Box 49210, Moi Avenue, Nairobi.

KOREA (NORTH)

Grand People's Study House (National Library), PO Box 200, Pyongyang.

KOREA (SOUTH)

National Central Library, 60-1, Panpo-Dong, Seocho-Gu, Seoul.

LAOS

Bibliothèque Nationale, BP 704, Vientiane.

LEBANON

Bibliothèque Nationale du Liban, Place de l'Etoile, Beirut.

LIBYA

National Library of Libya, PO Box 9127, Benghazi.

LUXEMBURG

Bibliothèque Nationale, 37 Boulevard F D Roosevelt, 2450 Luxembourg.

MALAYSIA

Perpustakaan Negara Malaysia (National Library of Malaysia), Wisma-Thakurdas/Sachdev, Jl Raja Laut, 50572 Kuala.

MEXICO

Asociacion Musical Manuel M Ponce, AC, Bucareli No 12, Desp 411, Mexico City.
Biblioteca Nacional de México, Insurgentes Sur s/n, Centro Cultural, Ciudad Universitaria, Del Coyoacán, 04510.

MONACO

Bibliothèque Louis Notari, 8 Rue Louis Notari, Monte Carlo.

MOROCCO

Bibliothèque Générale et Archives, BP 1003, Avenue ibn Battouta, Rabat.

MYANMAR

National Library, Town Hall, Rangoon.

NETHERLANDS

Maatschappij tot Bevordering der Toonkunst (Society for the Advancement of Music), le jac Van Campenstraat 59, 1072 BD Amsterdam.

Openbare Bibliotheken (Public Library), Centraale Bibliotheek, Prinsengracht 587, 1016 HT Amsterdam.
Stichting Arnhemse Openbare en Gelderse Wilenschappelijke Bibliotheek (Arnhem Public and Learned Library of Gelderland), Koningstaat 26 681 DG, PO Box 1168, 6810 ML Arnhem.
Stichting Samenwerkende Openbare Biblitheken, Kruissstraat 71, 2611 ML Delft.
Openbare Bibliotheek, Brink 70, 7411 BW Deventer.
Gemeenschappelijke Openbare Bibliotheek, Piazza 201, 5611 AG Eindhoven.
Openbare Bibliotheek, H B Blijdensteinstichting, Pijpennstraat 15, 7511 GM Enschede.
Stichting Openbare Bibliotheek, Postbus 30004, 9700 RE Groningen.
Openbare Bibliotheek, Doelenplein 1, 2011 XR Haarlem.
Koninklijke Bibliothek (Royal Library), PO Box 90407, Prins Willen-Alexanderhof 5, 2509 LK, The Hague.
Openbare Bibliotheek, Bilderdijkstraat 103, 2513 CM The Hague.
Stichting Openbare Bibliotheek, Hinthamerstraat 72, 5211 MR's-Hertogenbosch.
Stichting Openbare Biblitheken, 's-Gravelandseweg 55, 1217 EH Hilversum.
Stichting Centrale Bibliotheekdienst voor Friesland, Zuiderkruisweg 2, Postbus 530, 8901 BH Leeuwarden.
Stadsbibliotheek, Nieuwenhofstraat 1, 6211 KG Maastricht.
Gemeenschappelijke Openbare Bibliotheek, Ridderstraat 29, 6511 TM Nijmegen.
Gemeentebibliothek, Hoogstraat 110, 3011 PV Rotterdam.
Rotterdamsch Leeskabinet, Bibliotheek, Burg Oudlaan 50(16), Postbus 1738, 3000 DR Rotterdam.
Openbare Bibliotheek, Koningsplein 1, 5038 WG Tilburg.
Gemeentelijke Utrechtse Openbare Bibliotheek, Oude Gracht 167, 3511 AL Utrecht.

NEW ZEALAND

Auckland Public Library, Lorne Street, PO Box 4138, Auckland 1.
Canterbury Public Library, Orford Terrace and Gloucester Street, PO Box 1466, Christchurch. 1.
Dunedin Public Library, Moray Place, PO Box 5542, Dunedin.
Centre for New Zealand Music Ltd (SOUNZ New Zealand), PO Box 10 042, Level 3, 15 Brandon Street, Wellington.
National Library of New Zealand, 44 The Terrace, Private Bag, Wellington 1.
Wellington Public Library, Mercer Street, PO Box 1992, Wellington 1.

NICARAGUA

Biblioteca nacional, C del Triunfo 302, Apdo 101, Managua.

NIGERIA

National Library of Nigeria, 4 Wesley Street, Private Mail Bag, 12626, Lagos.

NORWAY

Bergen offentlige bibliotek, Hordaland fylkesbibliotek, Strømgaten 6, 5000 Bergen.
Drammen folkebibliotek, Gamle Kirke Plass 7, Postboks 1136, 3001 Drammen.
Kristiansands folkebibliotek, Radhusgate 11, Postboks 476, 4601 Kristiansand.
Deichmanske Bibliotek, Henrik Ibsensgate 1, 0179 Oslo 1.
Norweigan Music Information Centre, 28 Tollbugate, 10157 Oslo.
Universitetsbiblioteket og Norges Nasjonalbiblioteket, Drammensun 42, 0255 Oslo.
Rogaland fylkesbibliotek, Haakon VII's gate 11, Postboks 310/320, 4001 Stavanger.
Sør-Trøndelag folkebibliotek, Søndregate 5 og Kongensgate 2, Postboks 926, 7001 Trondheim.

PAKISTAN

National Library of Pakistan, Constitution Avenue, PO Box 1982, Islamabad.
Punjab Public Library, Library Road, Lahore 1884.

PANAMA

Biblioteca Nacional, Apdo 2444, Panama City 1892.

PARAGUAY

Biblioteca y Archivo Nacionales, Mariscal Estigarriba 95, Asuncion.

PERU

Biblioteca Nacional del Perú, Avenida Abancay S/N, Apdo 2335, Lima.

PHILIPPINES

National Library, Ermita, T M Kalaw Street, Naila.

POLAND

Biblioteka Slaska (Silesian Library), ul Francuska 12, 529, 40956 Katowice.
Wojewódzka i Miejska Biblioteka Publiczna (District and City Library), ul Warszawska 45, 40010 Katowice.
Biblioteka w Krakowie PAN (Library of the Polish Academy of Sciences), ul Slawkowska17, 31016 Krakow.
Miejska Biblioteka Publiczna (City Library), ul Franciskanska 1, 31004 Krakow.
Miejska Biblioteka Publiczna im L Warynskiego, Gdańska 102, 90508 Łódź.
Wojewodzka i Miejska Biblioteka Publiczna im H Lopacinskiego, ul Narutowicza 4, 20950 Lublin.
Miejska Biblioteka Publiczna im Edwards Rqaczynskiego, Pl Wolnosci 19, 60967 Poznań.
Wojewodzka i Miejska Biblioteka Publiczna im St Staszica, ul Podgórna 15, 70952 Szczecin.
Wojewodzka Biblioteca Publiczna i Ksiaeznica miejska, ul J Slowackiego 8, 87100 Toruń.
Biblioteka Narodowa, Centraina Biblioteka Państwa, Hankiewicza 1, 00973 Warsaw.
Biblioteka Publiczna m st Warszawy, ul Koszykowa 26, 00950 Warsaw.
Towarzystwo im Fryderyka Chopina (Frederic Chopin Society), Ostrogski Palais, Okólnik 1, 00368 Warsaw.
Wojewodzka i Miejska Biblioteka Publiczna im T Mikulskiego, Rynek 58, 50116 Wroclaw.

PORTUGAL

Biblioteca Municipal Central, Largo do Campo Pequeno, Palácio Galveias, 1000 Lisbon.
Biblioteca Nacional, Rua Ocidental do Campo Grande 83, 1751 Lisbon.

ROMANIA

Academia România Library, Calea Victoriei 125, Sect 1, 71102 Bucharest.
Biblioteca centrală de stat, str Ion Ghica 4, Bucharest.

RUSSIA

Moscow State Library, Vozdvizhenka 3, 101000 Moscow.
St Petersburg State Library, St Petersburg.

SINGAPORE

National Library, Stamford Road, Singapore 0617.

SLOVAK REPUBLIC

Matica slovenska Kniğica (Slovak National Library), Hostihora, 03652 Martin.

SOUTH AFRICA

Cape Town City Libraries, Mayor's Garden, Longmarket Street, PO Box 4728, Cape Town 8000.
South African Library, Queen Victoria Street, Cape Town 8001.
Durban Municipal Library, Smith Street, City Hall, PO Box 917, Durban 4000.
Johannesburg Public Library, Market Square, Johannesburg 2001.
Pretoria Public Library, 159 Andries Street, Pretoria 0002.
State Library, 239 Vermeulen Street, PO Box 397, Pretoria 0001.

SPAIN

Biblioteca Pública, "F Bonnemaison de Verdaguer i Callis", Baja de San Pedro 7, Barcelona.
Biblioteca Pública Provincial, Plaza de San Juan, Burgos.
Biblioteca Pública Provincial, Avda Ramón Carranza 16, Cádiz.
Biblioteca Pública del Estado, Jardines del Salón, s/n, Apdo Oficial, Granada.
Biblioteca Pública del Estado, Santa Nonia 5, Casa de Cultura, León.
Biblioteca del Ministerio de Cultura, Calle San Marcos 40, 5A, 28004 Madrid.
Biblioteca Municipal del Ayuntamiento, Fuencarral 78, Madrid 4.
Biblioteca Nacional, Paseo de Recoletos 20, 28001 Madrid.
Centro de Documentación Musica y de la Danza, Torregalindo 10, 28016 Madrid.
Real Academia de Bellas Artes de San Fernando, Biblioteca, Alcala 13, 28014 Madrid.
Biblioteca Pública, Ramón Llull 3, Palma de Mallorca.
Biblioteca Pública e Archivo Distrital de Ponta Delgada, Rua Ernest do Canto, Ponta Delgada, San Miguel.
Biblioteca de Menéndez Pelayo, Rubio 6, Santander.
Biblioteca Pública del Estado, Alfonso XII 19, 41001 Seville.
Biblioteca Provincial, Paseo del Misadero, Toledo.
Biblioteca Pública Provincial, Paseo de la Florida 9, Victoria.
Biblioteca Púlica de la Ciudad, Plaza de los Sitios 5, Zaragoza.

SRI LANKA

National Museum Libary, Sr Marcus Fernando Mawatha, PO Box 854, Colombo 7.

SWEDEN

Gävle stadsbibliotek, Södra Strandgatan 6, Box 801, 80130 Gävle.
Göteborgs stadsbibliotek, Box 5404, 40229 Göteborg.
Helsingborgs stadsbibliotek, Bolbrogatan, S-25225 Helsingborg.
Malmö stadsbibliotek, Regementsgatan 3, 21142 Malmö.
Norrköpings stadsbibliotek, Södra Promenaden 105, 60181 Norrköping.
Örebros stadsbibliotek, Nabbtorgsgatan 12, 70114 Örebro.
Kungliga Biblioteket (Royal Library), Humlegården, Box 5039, 10241 Stockholm.
Kungliga Musikaliska adademien (Royal Academy of Music Library), Blasieholmstorg 8, 11148 Stockholm.
Swedish Music Information Centre, Box 27327, 79 Sandhamnsgatan, S-102 54 Stockholm.
Uppsala stadsbibliotek, Östra Ågatan 19, Box 643, 75127 Uppsala.
Västeräs stadsbibliotek, Biskopsgatan 2, Box 717, 72120 Västerås.

SWITZERLAND

Allgemeine Bibliotheken der GGG, Rümelinsplatz 6, Postfach, 4051 Basel.
Berner Volksbücherie, Monbijoustrasse 45a, Postfach 2267, 3001 Bern.
Stadtbibliothek, Dufourstrasse 26, 2502 Biel.
Bibliothèques municipales, 16 Place de la Madeleine, 1204 Geneva.
Bibliothèque municipale, 11 Place Chauderon, 1003 Lausanne.
Stadtbibliothek, Kauffmannweg 4, 6003 Lucerne.
Biblithèque publique et universitarie, 3 Place Numa-Droz, 2000 Neuchâtel.
Stadtbibliothek, Hauptgasse 12, 4600 Olten.
Stadtbibliothek, Goldsteinstrasse 15, Postfach 91, 82025 Schaffhausen.
Stadtbibliothek, Museumstrasse 52, 8401 Winterthur.
Pestalozzi-Bibliothek, Zahingerstrasse 17, 8001 Zürich.

SYRIA

Al Maktabah Al Wataniah (National Library), Bab El-Faradj, Aleppo.
Al Zahiriah National Library, Bab el Barid, Damascus.

THAILAND

Ho Samut Haeng Chat (National Library of Thailand), Samsen Road, Bangkok 10300.

TUNISIA

Dar al-Katub Al-Wataniyya/Bibliothèque Nationale, Ministere des Affaires Culturelles, 20 souk El Attarine, 1008 Tunis.

TURKEY

Milli Kütüphane (National Library), Bahçelievier, Ankara.
Beyazit Deviet Kütüyshanesi (Beyazit State Library), Imaret Sok 18, Istanbul.

UK

Aberdeen Central Library, Rosemount Viaduct, Aberdeen, Scotland AB9 1GU.
National Library of Wales, Aberystwyth, Wales SY23 3BU.
Belfast Public Library, Royal Avenue, Belfast, Northern Ireland BT1 1EK.
Birmingham Central Library, Chamberlain Square, Birmingham B3 3HQ.
University of Birmingham, Department of Music, Barber Institute, Edgbaston, Birmingham B15 2TT
Bristol Central Library, College Green, Bristol BS1 5TL.
Cardiff Central Library, The Hayes, Cardiff, Wales CF1 2QU.
Carmarthen Public Library, St Peter's Street, Carmarthen, Wales SA31 1LN.
Dundee Central Library, The Wellgate, Dundee, Scotland DD1 1DB.
Edinburgh Central Library, George IV Bridge, Edinburgh, Scotland EG1 1EG.
National Library of Scotland, George IV Bridge, Edinburgh, Scotland EH1 1EW.
Mitchell Library, North Street, Glasgow, Scotland G3 7DN.
Leeds Central Library, Calverley Street, Municipal Building, Leeds LS1 3AB.
Liverpool Central Library, William Brown Street, Liverpool L3 8EW.
British Library, Music Library, Reference Division, Great Russell Street, London WC1B 3DG.
British Music Information Centre, 10 Stratford Place, London W1N 9AE.
English Folk Dance and Song Society, Cecil Sharp House, Library, 2 Regent's Park Road, London NW1 7AY.
Manchester Central Library, St Peter's Square, Manchester M4 5PD.
Newcastle upon Tyne Central Library, Princess Square, Newcastle upon Tyne NE99 1MC.

USA

ALABAMA

Birmingham Public Library, 2100 Park Place, Birmingham, AL 35203.

ARIZONA

City of Phoemix Public Library, 12 East McDowell Road, Phoenix, AZ 85004.

CALIFORNIA

Los Angeles Public Library, 630 West 5th Street, Los Angeles, CA 90071.
California State Library, PO Box 942837, Sacramento, CA 94237.
Sacramento Public Library, 1010 8th Street, Sacramento, Ca 95814.
San Diego Public Library, 820 E Street, San Diego, CA 92101.
San Francisco Public Library, San Francisco, CA 94102.

COLORADO

Denver Public Library, 1357 Broadway, Denver, CO 80203.

CONNECTICUT

Connecticut State Library, 231 Capitol Avenue, Hartford, CT 06106.

DISTRICT OF COLUMBIA

Library of Congress, Music Division, Washington, DC 20540.

FLORIDA

Miami-Dade Public Library, 101 West Flagler Street, Miami, FL 33130.

GEORGIA

Atlanta-Fulton Public Library, 1 Margaret Mitchell Square, North West, Atlanta, GA 30303.

ILLINOIS

Chicago Public Library, 425 North Michigan Avenue, Chaicago, IL 60611.
Illinois State Library, Springfield, IL 62756.

INDIANA

Indiana State Library, 140 North Senate Avenue, Indianapolis, IN 46204.
Indianapolis-Marion County Public Library, 40 East St Clair Street, PO Box 211, Indianapolis, IN 46406.

KENTUCKY

Louisville Free Public Library, 301 York Street, Louisville, KY 40203.

LOUISANA

New Orleans Public Library, 219 Loyola Avenue, New Orleans, LA 70140.

MARYLAND

Enoch Pratt Free Library, 400 Cathedral Street, Baltimore, MD 21201.

MASSACHUSETTS

Boston Public Library, Copley Square, Boston, MA 02117.
State Library of Massachusetts, 341 State House, Boston, MA 02133.

MICHIGAN

Detroit Public Library, 5201 Woodward Avenue, Detroit, MI 48202.
Library of Michigan, 735 East Michigan Avenue, PO Box 30007, Lansing, MI 48909.

MINNESOTA

Minneapolis Public Library, 300 Nicollet Mall, Minneapolis, MN 55401.
St Paul Public Library, 90 West 4th Street, St Paul, MN 55102.

MISSOURI

Missouri State Library, 2002 Missouri Boulevard, Jefferson City, MO 65102.
Kansas City Public Library, 311 East 12th Street, Kansas City, MO 64106.
St Louis Public Library, 1301 Olive Street, St Louis, MO 63103.

NEW HAMPSHIRE

New Hampshire State Library, 20 Park Street, Concord, NH 03301.

NEW JERSEY

Newark Public Library, PO Box 630, Newark, NJ 07101.
New Jersey State Library, 185 West State Street, Trenton, NJ 08625.

NEW MEXICO

New Mexico State Library, 325 Don Gaspar, Santa Fe, NM 87503.

NEW YORK

American Music Center, 30 West 26th Street, Suite 1001, New York, NY 10010-2011.
New York State Library, Albany, NY 12230.
Buffalo and Erie County Public Library, Lafayette Square, Buffalo, NY 14203.
New York Public Library, Fifth Avenue and 42nd Street, New York, NY 10018.
Rochester Public Library, 115 South Avenue, Rochester, NY 14604.

OHIO

Public Library of Cincinnati and Hamilton County, 800 Vine Street, Library Square, Cincinnati, OH 45202.
Cleveland Public Library, 325 Superior Avenue, Cleveland, OH 44114.
Columbus Metropolitan Library, 28 South Hamilton Road, Columbus, OH 43213.
State Library of Ohio, 65 South Front Street, Columbus, OH 43215.

OREGON

Oregon State Library, State Library Building, Salem, OR 97310.

PENNSYLVANIA

State Library of Pennsylvania, PO Box 1601, Harrisburg, PA 17105.
Free Library of Philadelphia, Logan Square, Philadelphia, PA 19103.
Carnegie Library of Pittsburgh, 4400 Forbes Avenue, Pittsburgh, PA 15213.

RHODE ISLAND

Providence Public Library, 225 Washington Street, Providence, RI 02903.

TENNESSEE

Memphis and Shelby County Public Library, 1850 Peabody Avenue, Memphis, TN 38104.

TEXAS

Austin Public Library, 800 Guadalupe Street, Box 2287, Austin, TX 78768.
Dallas Public Library, 1515 Young Street, Dallas, TX 75201.
Houston Public Library, 500 McKinney Avenue, Houston, TX 77002.

VIRGINIA

Richmond Public Library, 101 East Franklin Street, Richmond, VA 23219.
Virginia State Library, 11th Street at Capitol Square, Richmond, VA 23219.

WASHINGTON

United States Information Agency, Arts America Program, 301 Fourth Street Room 568, Washngton, DC 20547.
Washington State Library, Olympia, WA 98504.
Seattle Public Library, 1000 4th Avenue, Seattle, WA 98104.

WISCONSIN

Milwaukee Public Library, 814 West Wisconsin Avenue, Milwaukee, WI 53233.

URUGUAY

Biblioteca Nacional del Uruguay, 18 de Julio 1790, Casilla 452, Montevideo.

VENEZUELA

Biblioteca Nacional, Bolsa a San Francisco, Apdo 68350, Caracas 106.

VIETNAM

National Library, 31 Rue Trang-Thi, Hanoi 1918.
National Library II, 69 Gia-Long Street, Ho Chi Minh City 1976.

APPENDIX G
MUSIC CONSERVATOIRES

ARGENTINA

Buenos Aires: Conservatorio Provincial de Música de Bahla Blanca, Belgrano 446, 800 Bahla Blanca, Provincia de Buenos Aires.
Conservatorio de Música "Julián Aguirre", Gral Rodriguez 7672, Banfield, Provincia de Buenos Aires.
Conservatorio Municipal de Música "Manuel de Falla", Sarmiento 1551, 1042 Buenos Aires.
Conservatorio Nacional de Música, "Carlos Lopez Buchardo", Callao 1521, 1024 Buenos Aires.
Pontificia Universidad Católica Argentiń "Santa Maria de los Buenos Aires", Faculty of Arts and Music, Juncal 1912, Buenos Aires 1116.

AUSTRALIA

AUSTRALIAN CAPITAL TERRITORY

Canberra: Canberra School of Music, GPO Box 804, ACT 2603.

NEW SOUTH WALES

Newcastle: Newcastle Conservatorium of Music, Acukland Street, Newcastle, NSW 2300.
Sydney: New South Wales State Conservatorium of Music, Macquarie Street, Sydney, NSW 2000.
University of Sydney, Department of Music, Sydney, NSW 2006.
Wollongong: Wollongong Conservatorium "Gleniffer Brae", Murphries Road, Wollongong, NSW 2500.

QUEENSLAND

Brisbane: Queensland Conservatorium of Music, 259 Vulture Street, South Brisbane, Queensland 4101.
St Lucia: University of Queensland, Faculty of Music, St Lucia, Queensland 4067.

SOUTH AUSTRALIA

Adelaide: University of Adelaide, Elder Conservatorium of Music, GPO Box 498, Adelaide, SA 5001.

TASMANIA

Hobart: Tasmanian Conservatorium of Music, GPO Box 252 C, Hobart, Tasmania 7001.

VICTORIA

Melbourne: Victorian College of Arts, 234 St Kilda Road, Melbourne, Victoria 3004.
Parkville: University of Melbourne, Faculty of Music, Parkville, Victoria 3052.

WESTERN AUSTRALIA

Nedlands: University of Western Australia, Department of Music, Nedlands, WA 6009.

AUSTRIA

Graz: Hochschule für Musik und Darstellande Kunst, Leonhardstrasse 15, A-8010 Graz.
Innsbruck: Konservatorium der Stadt Innsbruck, Museumstrasse 17a, 6020 Innsbruck.
Klagenfurt: Kärntner Landeskonservatorium, Miesstalerstrasse 8, A-9021 Klagenfurt.
Linz: Bruckner-Konservatorium des Landes Oberösterreich, Postfach 95, 4041 Linz.
Salzburg: Hochschule für Musik und Darstellande Kunst "Mozarteum", Mirabellplatz 1, A-5020 Salzburg.
Vienna: Hochschule für Musik und Darstellende Kunst, Lothringerstrasse 18, Postfach 146, A-1037 Vienna III.
Horak-Konservatorium für Musik und Darstellende Kunst, Hegelgasse 3, A-1010 Vienna.
Konservatorium für Musik und Dramatische Kunst, Mühlgasse 28-30, A-1040 Vienna.
Konservatorium der Stadt Wien, Johannesgasse 4a, A-1010 Vienna 1.

BELGIUM

Antwerp: Koninklijk Vlaams Conservatorium van Antwerpen, Desguinler 25, B-2018 Antwerp.
Argenteuil-Waterloo: Chapelle Musicale Reine Elisabeth, Chaussée de Tervuren 445, B-1410 Argenteuil-Waterloo.
Bruges: Stedelijk Muziekconservatorium, Sint-Jacobsstratt 23, B-8000 Bruges.
Brussels: Conservatoire Royal de Musique de Bruxelles, 30 Rue de la Régence, B-1000 Brussels.
Koninklijk Muziekconservatorium van Brussel, Regentschapsraat 30, B-1000 brussels.
Charleroi: Conservatoire de Musique de Charleroi, 1 Rue Adolphe Biarrent, B-6000 Charleroi.
Ghent: Conservatoire de Musique de Grand, 54 Rue de la Hoogpoort, B-9000 Ghent.
Koninklijk Muziekconservatorium van Gent, Hoogpoort 64, B-9000 Ghent.
Huy: Conservatoire de Musique de Huy, 11-13 Rue du Palais de Justice, B-5200 Huy.
Liège: Conservatoire Royal de Musique de Liège, 14 Rue Forgeur, B-4000 Liège.
Louvain: Stedelijk Muziekconservatorium, Koning Albertaan 50-52, B-3000 Louvain.
Mechelen: Koninklijk Beiaardschool Jef Denyn, Fredrik de Mersdestraat 63, B-2800 Mechelen.
Stedelijk Muziekconservatorium, Melaan 3-5, B-2800 Mechelen.
Mons: Conservatoire Royal de Musique de Mons, 7 Rue de Nimy, B-7000 Mons.
Namur: Conservatoire de Musicque, Chaussée de Louvain 121, B-5000 Namur.
Institute de Musique Sacrée, 28 Rue Juppin, B-5000 Namur.
Ostende: Conservatoire de Musique de Ostende, 36 Rue de Rome, B-8400 Ostend.
Tournai: Conservatoire de Musique de Tournai, 2 Place Raine Astrid, B-7500 Tournai.

Verviers: Conservatoire de Musique de Verviers, 6 Rue Chapuis, B-4800 Verviers.

BOLIVIA

La Paz: Academia de Música Hohner, Calle Goitia 162, La Paz.
Conservatorio Nacional de Música, Avenida 6 de Agosto, No 2092, La Paz.
Escuela Superior de Bellas Artes, Calle Rosendo Gutierrez 323, La Paz.

BRAZIL

Bahia: Instituto de Música de Bahia, Universidade Catolica de Salvador, Rua Carlos Gomes 400, Centro, 4000 Salvador, Bahia.
Universidade Federal de Bahia, Escola de Música, Parque Universitario Edgard Santos, Canela, 40140, Salvador, Bahia.

Belo Horizonte: Escola de Música-Minas Gerais, Rue Santa Catarina 466, 30000 Belo Horizonte, Mina Gerais.
Universidade Federal de Minas Gerais, Escola de Música, Avenida Antônio Carlos 6627, Pampulha, 3000 Belo Horizonte, Minas Gerais.

Brasilia: Fundaçao Universidade de Brasilia, Institute of Arts and Communication, Campus Universitário, Asa Norte, 70910 Brasilia, DF.

Paraiba: Universidade Federal de Paraiba, Department of Music, Cidade Universitária, 5800 Joao Pessôa, Paraiba.

Paraná: Escola de Música e Belas Artes do Paraná, Rue Emilian Perneta 179, 80000 Curitiba, Paraná.
Faculdade de Música Mae de Deus, Avenida Sao Paulo 651, CP106, 86100 Londrina, Paraná.

Petotas: Instituto de Letras a Artes, Rua Marechal Floriano 179, 96100 Pelotas, RS.

Rio de Janeiro: Conservatorio Brasileiro de Música, Avenida Graça Aranha 57, No 12, 20000 Rio de Janeiro.
Universidade do Rio de Janeiro, Leters and Arts Center, Avenida Pasteur 296, 22290 Rio de Janeiro.
Universidade Federal do Rio de Janeiro, Escola de Música, Rua do Passeio 98, Rio de Janeiro.

São Paulo: Conservatorio Dramático e Musical de Sao Paulo, Avenida Sao Joao 269, São Paulo.
Faculdade de Música "Sagrado Coracao de Jesus", Rua Caraibas 882, CP 8383, Villa Pompéia, São Paulo.
Faculdade Santa Marcelina, Rua Dr Emilio Ribas 89, 05006 São Paulo.
UNESP-Universidade Estadual Júlio de Mesquita Filho, Instituto do Artes do Planalto, Dept of Music, Rua Dom Luis Lasagna 400, São Paulo.
Universidade de Sao Paulo, Department of Music, Cidade Universitaria, Butanta, 05508 São Paulo.

BULGARIA

Plovdiv: Viss Musikalno-Pedagogiceski, Ul Todor Samodumov 2, Plovidiv 4025.

Sofia: Conservatoire Bulgare d'Etat, Sofia 1505.

CANADA

ALBERTA

Banff: Banff Centre, School of Fine Arts, Box 1020, Banff, Alberta T0L 0C0.

Calgary: University of Calgary, Department of Music, 2500 University Drive, N W Calgary, Alberta T2N 1NF.

Edmonton: University of Alberta, Department of Music, Edmonton, Alberta t6G 2C9.

Lethbridge: University of Lethbridge, Department of Music, 4401 University Drive, Lethbridge, Alberta T1K 3M4.

BRITISH COLUMBIA

Burnaby: Simon Fraser University, Centre for the Arts, Burnaby, British Columbia V5A 1S6.

Vancouver: University of British Columbia, School of Music, 6361 Memorial Road, Vancouver, British Columbia V6T 1W5.
Vancouver Academy of Music, Music Centre, Vanier Park, 1270 Chestnut Street, Vancouver, British Coumbia V6J 4R9.

Victoria: University of Victoria, School of Music, PO Box 1700, Victoria, British Columbia V8W 2Y2.
Victoria Conservatory of Music, 839 Academy Close, Victoria, British Columbia V8X 3Y1.

MANITOBA

Brandon: Brandon University, School of Music, Brandon, Manitoba R7A 6A9.

Winnipeg: University of Manitoba, School of Music, 65 Dafoe Road, Winnipeg, Manitoba R3T 2N2.

NEW BRUNSWICK

Moncton: Université de Moncton, Department of Music, Moncton, New Brunswick E1A 3E9.

Sackville: Mount Allison University, Department of Music, Sackville, New Brunswick E0A 3C0.

NOVA SCOTIA

Antigonish: St Francis Xavier University, Department of Music, Box 108, Antigonish, Nova Scotia B2G 1C0.

Halifax: Dalhousie University, Department of Music, Arts Centre, Room 514, Halifax, Nova Scotia B3H 3J5.
Maritime Conservatory of Music, 5820 Spring Garden Road, Halifax, Nova Scotia B3H 1X8.

Wolfville: Acadia University, School of Music, Wolfville, Nova Scotia B0P 1X0.

ONTARIO

Gueiph: University of Guelph, College of Arts, Department of Music, Room 207, Guelph, Ontario N1G 2W1.

Hamilton: McMaster University, Department of Music, 1280 Main Street West, Hamilton, Ontario L8S 4M2.

Kingston: Queen's University, School of Music, Kingston, Ontario K7L 3N6.

London: University of Western Ontario, Faculty of Music, London, Ontario N6A 3K7.

North York: York University, Department of Music, 4700 Keele Street, North York, Ontario M3J 1P3.

Ottawa: Carleton University, Department of Music, Colonel By Drive, Ottawa, Ontario K1S 5B6.
University of Ottawa, Department of Music, Ottawa, Ontario K1N 6N5.

Toronto: Royal Conservatory of Music, 273 Bloor Street West, Toronto, Ontario M5S 1W2.
University of Toronto, Faculty of Music, Edward Johnson Building, Room 238, 80 Queen's Park Circle, Toronto, Ontario M5S 1A1.

Waterloo: Wilfrid Laurier University, Faculty of Music, 75 University Avenue West, Waterloo, Ontario N2L 3C5.

Windsor: University of Windsor, School of Music, 401 Sunset Avenue, Windsor, Ontario N9B 3P4.

QUÉBEC

Montréal: Concordia University, Department of Music, 7141 Sherbrooke Street West, Montréal, Québec H4B 1R6.
McGill University, Faculty of Music, Strathcona Music Building, 555 Sherbrooke Street West, Montréal, Québec H3A 1E3.
Université de Montréal, Faculty of Music, 2900 Boulevard Edouard-Montpetit, Montréal, Québec H3C 3J7.
Québec: Conservatoire de Musique de Québec, 270 St Amable, Québec G1R 5G1.
Université Laval, Ecole de Musique, Cité Universitaire, Québec G1K 7P4.

SASKATCHEWAN

Regina: University of Regina, Department of Music, Regina, Saskatchewan S4S 0A2.
Saskatoon: University of Saskatchewan, Department of Music, Saskatoon S7N 0W0.

CHILE

Santiago: Conservatorio Nacional de Música, Compania, 1264, Santiago.
Pontificia Universidad Católica de Chile, Faculty of Architecture and Fine Arts, Avenida Alameda 340, Casilla 114-D, Santiago.
Universidad de Chile, Faculty of Fine Arts, Avenida Bernardo O'Higgins 1058, Casilla 10-D, Santiago.
Valparaiso: Universidad Católica de Valparaiso, Caonservatorio de Música, Avenida Brasil 2950, Valparaiso.

CHINA

Beijing: Central Conservatory of Music, 43 Baojiajie, Beijing.
Conservatory of Chinese Music, 17 Qianhaixijie, Beijing.
Chengdu: Sichuan Conservatory Of Music, Xinnanmenwai, Chengdu.
Guangzhou: Guangzhou Xinghai Conservatory of Music, 48 Xianliedonghenglu, Guangzhou.
Harbin: Harbin Normal University, Department of Music, Harbin.
Lanzhou: Northwest Teacher's College, Department of Music, Lanzhou.
Nanjing: Nanjing Arts College, 15 Hujubeilu, Nanjing.
Shandong: Shandong Academy of Arts, Music Division, Shandong.
Shanghai: Shanghai Conservatory of Music, 20 Fen Yang Road, Shanghai 200031.
Shengyang: Shengyang Conservatory of Music, No 1, Section 2, San Hao Street, Peace District, Shengyang.
Tianjin: Tianjin Conservatory of Music, 5, 11th Meridian Road, Tianjin.
Wuhan: Wuhan Conservatory of Music, 255 Jiefanglu, Wuchang District, Wuhan.
Xian: Xian Conservatory of Music, 118 Changanzhonglu, Xian 710061.

COLOMBIA

Barranquilla: Universidad del Atlántico, Conservatorio de Música, Carrera 43, Nos 50-53, Apartado Nacional 148, Aéreo 1890, Barranquilla.
Bogotá: Conservatorio Nacional de Música, Departmento de Música, Facultad de Artes, Universidad Nacional, Bogotá.

COSTA RICA

San José: Universidad de Costa Rica, School of Fine Arts, San José.

CUBA

Havana: Instituto Superior de Arte, Facultad de Música, Calle 120, No 1110, Havana.

CZECH REPUBLIC

Brno: Janáčkova Akademie Mûzických Umeni (Janáček Academy of Music and Dramatic Arts), Komenskeho nam 6, 662 15 Brno.
Konservatoř v Brne (Brno Conservatory), Trida Kpt Jarose 43-45, Brno.
Ostrava: Konservatoř v Otrave (Ostrava Conservatory), Hrabakova 1, Ostrava.
Prague: Konservatoř v Praza (Prague Conservatory), Na Rejdišti 1, 110 00 Prague.
Vysoká Skola Mûzických Umeni v Praha (Academy of Music and Dramatic Arts Prague), Dům umělců, Alsovo nábřeží 12, 1101 00 Prague 1.

DENMARK

Alborg: Nordjysk Musikkonservatorium (North Jutland Conservatory of Music), Ryesgade 52, 9000 Alborg.
Århus: Det Jydske Musikkonservatorium (The Royal Conservatory of Music), Fuglesangsalle 26, DK-8210 Århus V.
Copenhagen: Det Kongelige Danske Musikkonservatorium (The Royal Danish Conservatory of Music), Niels Brocksgade 7, 1574 Copenhagen V.
University of Copenhagen, Department of Music, Frue Plads, DK-1168 Copenhagen K.
Esbjerg: Vestjysk Musikkonservatorium (West Jutland Conservatory of Music), Islandsgade 50, DK-6700 Esbjerg.
Odense: Det Fynske Musikkonservatorium (The Funen Conservatory of Music), Islandsgade 2, DK-5000 Odense C.

DOMINICAN REPUBLIC

Santo Domingo: Conservatorio Nacional de Música, Cesar Nicolas Penson, Santo Domingo.

ECUADOR

Quito: Conservatorio Nacional de Música-Quito, Madrid 11-59, Quito.

EGYPT

Cairo: Cairo Conservatory of Music, Academy of Arts, Avenue of the Pyramids, Al Jizah.

EIRE

Dublin: College of Music, Adelaide Road, Dublin 2.
Royal Irish Academy of Music, 36-38 Westland Row, Dublin 2.

EL SALVADOR

San Salvador: Centro Nacional de Artes "CENAR", Department of Music, 6A Avenida Norte 319, San Salvador.

ESTONIA

Tallinn: Tallinn State Conservatory, Vabaduse Pst 130, 200015 Tallinn.

FINLAND

Åbo: Sibeliusmuseum Misikvetenskapliga Institutionen vid Åbo Akademi (Sibelius Museum, Musicological Institution at Åbo Academy), Biskopsgatan 17 20500, Åbo 50.
Helsinki: Helsingin Konservatorio, Fredrikinkatu 34 B, SF-00100 Helsinki.
Sibelius Academy of Music, Töölönkatu 28, SF-00260 Helsinki 26.
Jyväskylä: Keski-Suomen Konservatorio, Pitkäkatu 18-22, SF-40700 Jyväskylä.
Kuopio: Kuopion Konservatorio, Kuopionlahdenkatu 23 C, SF-70200 Kuopio.
Lahti: Paijat-Hameen Konservatorio, Sibeliuksenkatu 8, SF-15110 Lahti.
Oulu: Oulun Kaupungin Konservatorio, Lintulammentie 1 K, SF-90140 Oulu.
Tampere: Tampereen Konservatorio, F E Sillanpään Katu 9, 33230 Tampere.

FRANCE

Bordeaux: Conservatorie National de Région, Bordeaux, 22 Quai Saint Croix, F-33800 Bordeaux.
Dijon: Conservatoire National de Région, Dijon, 24 Boulevard Clemenceau, F-21000 Dijon.
Grenoble: Conservatorie National de Région, Grenoble, 6 Chemin de Gordes, F-38100 Grenoble.
Lille: Conservatorie National de Région, Lille, 48 Place du Concert, F-59800 Lille.
Limoges: Conservatorie National de Région, Limoges, 9 Rue Fritz-James, F-87000 Limoges.
Lyon: Conservatorie National Supérieur de Musique de Lyon, 3 Rue de l'Angile, 69005 Lyon.
Marseille: Conservatorie National de Région, Marseille, 2 Place Carli, F-13001 Marseille.
Metz: Conservatorie National de Région, Metz, 2 Rue Paradis, F-57036 Metz.
Montpellier: Conservatorie National de Région, Montpellier, 14 Rue Eugene Lisbonne, F-34000 Montpellier.
Nancy: Conservatorie National de Région, Nancy, 3 Rue Michel Ney, F-54000 Nancy.
Nantes: Conservatorie National de Région, Nantes, Rue Gaëtan Rondeau Ile Beaulieu, F-44200 Nantes.
Nice: Conservatorie National de Région, Nice, 24 Boulevard de Cimiez, F-06000 Nice.
Paris: Conservatoire National Supérieur de Musique, 14 Rue de Madrid, F-75008 Paris.
École Normale de Musique, 114 bis Boulevard Malesherbes, F-75017 Paris.
Schola Cantorum, École Supérieure de Musique, de Danse et d'Art Dramatique, 269 RueSt Jacques, Paris.
Poitiers: Conservatorie National de Région, Poitiers, 5 Rue Franklin, F-86000 Poitiers.
Reims: Conservatorie National de Région, Reims, 14 Rue Carnot, F-51100 Reims.
Rennes: Conservatorie National de Région, Rennes, 26 Rue Hoche, F-35000 Rennes.
Rouen: Conservatorie National de Région, Rouen, 50 Avenue de la Porte des Champs, F-76000 Rouen.
Rueil-Malmaison: Conservatorie National de Région, Tueil-Malmaison, 182 Avenue Paul Doumer, F-92500 Rueil-Malmaison.
Strasbourg: Conservatorie National de Région, Strasbourg, 2 Avenue de la Marseillaise, F-67000 Strasbourg.
Toulouse: Conservatorie National de Région, Toulouse, 3 Rue Labéda, F-31000 Toulouse.
Tours: Conservatorie National de Région, Tours, 17 Rue des Ursulines, F-37000 Tours.
Versailles: Conservatorie National de Région, Versailles, 24 Rue de la Chancellerie, F-78000 Versailles.

GERMANY

Aachen: Staatliche Hochschule für Musik Rheinland, Aachen, Grenzland-Institut, Aachen, Theaterstrasse 2-4, D-52062, Aachen.
Augsburg: Leopold-Mozart-Konservatorium, Augsburg, Maximilianstrasse 59, D-86150 Augsburg.
Berlin: Hochschule der Künste, Berlin, Ernst-Feuter-Platz 10, D-10587 Berlin.
Hochschule für Musik "Hanns Eisler", Charlottenstrasse 55, D-10117 Berlin.
Cologne: Staatliche Hochschule für Musik Rheinland, Köln, Dagobertstrasse 38, D-50668 Cologne.
Detmold: Staatliche Hochschule für Musik Westfalen-Lippe, Allee 22, D-32756 Detmold.
Dortmund: Staatliche Hochschule für Musik Westfalen-Lippe, Institut Dortmund, Hanastrasse 7, Dortmund.
Dresden: Hochschule für Musik "Carl Maria von Weber", Blochmannstrasse 2-4, D-01001 Dresden.
Düsseldorf: Staatliche Hochschule für Musik Rheinland, Düsseldorf, Robert-Schumann-Institut, Fischerstrasse 110, D-40416 Düsseldorf.
Frankfurt am Main: Hochschule für Musik und Darstellende Kunst, Frankfurt am Main, Eschersheimer Landstrasse 29-39, D-60322 Frankfurt am Main.
Freiburg im Breisgau: Staatliche Hochschule für Musik, Freiburg im Breisgau, Schwarzwaldstrasse 141, D-79102 Freiburg im Breisgau.
Hamburg: Hochschule für Musik und Darstellende Kunst, Hamburg, Harvestehuder Weg 12, D-20148 Hamburg.
Hannover: Hochschule für Musik und Theater, Hannover, Emmichplatz 1, D-70175 Hannover.
Heidelberg: Staatliche Hochschule für Musik, Heidelberg-Mannheim, Friedrich-Ebert-Anlage 62, Heidelberg.
Karlsruhe: Staatliche Hochschule für Musik, Karlsruhe, Wolfartsueiesstrasse 7, D-76131 Karlsruhe.

Leipzig:	Hochschule für Musik "Felix Mendelssohn-Bartholdy", Leipzig, Grassistrasse 8, D-04107 Leipzig.
Lübeck:	Musikhochschule, Lübeck, Grosse Petersgrube 17-29, D-23552 Lübeck.
Munich:	Richard-Strauss-Konservatorium, Ismaningerstrasse 29, D-81667 Munich.
	Hochschule für Musik, München Arcisstrasse 12, D-80333 Munich 2.
Nürnberg:	Konservatorium der Stadt Nürnberg, Fachakademie für Musik, Am Katharininkloster 6, D-90403 Nürnberg.
Saarbrücken:	Musikhochschule des Saarlandes, Bismarckstrasse 1, D-66111 Saarbrücken.
Stuttgart:	Staatliche Hochschule für Musik und Darstellende Kunst, Urbanplatz 2, D-20182 Stuttgart.
Trossingen:	Staatliche Hochschule für Musik, Trossingen, Schultheiss-Koch-Platz 3, D-78647 Trossingen.
Weimar:	Hochschule für Musik "Franz Liszt", Platz der Demokratie 2-3, Weimar.
Wiesbaden:	Wiesbadener Musikakademie, Bodenstedtstrasse 2, D-65189 Wiesbaden.
Wuppertal:	Staatliche Hochschule für Musik Rheinland, Wuppertal, Institut Wuppertal, Friedrich-Ebert-Strasse 141, Wuppertal.
Würzburg:	Bayerisches Staatskonservatorium für Musik, Mergentheimerstrasse 76, Würzburg.

GREECE

Athens:	Odeion Athenon, Odos Rigillis and Vassileos Georgiou 17-19, Athens.
	Odeion Ethnikon, Odos Maizonos 8, 108 Athens.
	Odeion Hellenikon, Odos Phidiou 3, Athens.
	Skalkotas Conservatory, Agias Lavras 78, Ano Patisia, 11141 Athens.
Ioannina:	Epirotic Conservatory Tsakalof, Platia G, Stavrou 5, 45444 Ioannina.
Thessaloniki:	Kratikon Odeion Thessaloniki, Leondos Sofou 16, 54625 Thessaloniki.

GUATEMALA

Guatemala City:	Conservatorio Nacional de Música, 3a Avenida 4-61, Zona 1, Guatemala City.

HONDURAS

Tegucigalpa:	Escuela Nacional de Música, 2a Avda, 307, Tegucigalpa.

HONG KONG

Hong Kong:	Hong Kong Academy for Performing Arts, School of Music, 1 Gloucester Road, Wanchai, Hong Kong.
	University of Hong Kong, Faculty of Music, Pokfulam Road, Hong Kong.

HUNGARY

Budapest:	Liszt Ferenc Zeneműves-zeti Föiskola (Franz Liszt Academy of Music), PO Box 206, Liszt Ference tér 8, H-1391 Budapest VI.

ICELAND

Reykjavík:	Tónlistarskólinn i Rekyavík (Reykjavík College of Music), Skipholti 33, 105 Reykjavík.

INDIA

Bombay:	Bhavan's Bharatiya Sangeet and Nartan Skikshapeeth (Academy of Music and Drama), Cahupatty Road, Bombay 4000007.
Calcutta:	Rabindra Bharati University, Department of Music, 6-4 Dwarakanath Tagore Lane, Calcutta 700007.
Khairagarth:	Indira Kala Sangit Vishwavidyalaya (University of Music and Fine Arts), Khairagarth, Madhya Pradesh 491881.
Madras:	Kalakshetra, Tiruvanmiyur, Madras 600041.
	Music Academy, Teachers' College of Music, 306 T T K Road, Madras 600041.
	University of Madras, Department of Indian Music, University Centernary Building, Chepauk, Triplicane, PO, Tamil Nadu, Madras 600005.
New Delhi:	Delhi School of Music, 8 Nyaya Marg, new Delhi 110021.
	Sangeet Natak Akademi (National Academy of Music, Dance and Drama), Rabindra Bhavan, Feroze Shah Road, New Delhi 11001.

INDONESIA

Bandung:	Academi Seni Tari Indonesia, Jl Buahbatu 212, Bandung.
Jakarta:	Institute Kesenian Jakarta, Taman Ismial Marzuki, Jalan Cikini, Jakarta.

ISRAEL

Haifa:	Samuel Rubin Conservatory of Music, 9 Haparsim Street, Haifa.
Jerusalem:	Jerusalem Rubin Academy of Music and Dance, Givat-Ram Campus, 91904 Jerusalem.
Tel Aviv:	Israel Conservatory of Music, 19 Shtriker Street, Tel Aviv.
	Levinsky Teachers College, Music Teachers Seminary, 15 Shoshana Persitz Street North, PO Box 48130, Tel Aviv.
	University of Tel Aviv, Faculty of Fine Arts, Rubin Academy of Music, PO Box 39040, Ramat Aviv, Tel Aviv.

ITALY

Alessandria:	Conservatorio Statale di Musica "Antonio Vivaldi", Via Parma 1, Alessandria.
Bari:	Conservatorio Statale di Musica "Niccolo Piccinni", Via Brigata Bari 26, I-70124 Bari.
Bologna:	Conservatorio Statale di Musica "Giovanni Battista Martini", Piazza Rossini 2, I-40126 Bologna.

Bolzano:	Conservatorio Statale di Musica "Claudio Monteverdi", Piazza Domenicani 19, I-39100 Bolzano.
Cagliari:	Conservatorio Statale di Musica "Giovanni Pierluigi da Palestrina", Via Bacaredda, I-09100 Cagliari.
Florence:	Conservatorio Statale di Musica "Luigi Cherubini", Piazza Belle Arti 2, I-50122 Florence.
Genoa:	Conservatorio Statale di Musica "Niccòlo Paganini", Via Albaro 38, I-16145 Genoa.
L'Aquila:	Conservatorio Statale di Musica "Girolamo Frescobaldi", Via Previati 22, L'Aquila.
Lucca:	Istituto Musicale Pareggiato "Luigi Boccherini", Piazza S Ponziano, I-55100 Lucca.
Messina:	Conservatorio Statale di Musica "Arcangleo Corelli", Via Laudamo 9-11, I-98100 Messina.
Milan:	Accademia Musicale di Milano, Viale dei Mille 17, Milan.
	Conservatorio Statale di Musica "Giuseppe Verdi", Via del Conservatorio 12, I-20122 Milan.
Naples:	Accademia Musicale Napoletana, Via del Parco Margherita 49, pal 5, I-80121 Naples.
	Conservatorio Statale di Musica "San Pietro a Majella", Via San Pietro a Majella 35, I-80138 Naples.
Padua:	Conservatorio Statale di Musica "Cesare Pollini", Via Eremitani 6, I-35121 Padua.
Palermo:	Conservatorio Statale di Musica "Vincenzo Bellini", Via Squarcialupo 45, I-90133 Palermo.
Parma:	Conservatorio Statale di Musica "Arrigo Boito", Via del Conservatorio 27, I-43100 Parma.
Perugia:	Conservatorio Statale di Musica "Francesco Morlacchi", Piazza Mariotti 2, I-06100 Perugia.
Pesaro:	Conservatorio Statale di Muscia "Gioachino Rossini", Piazza Olivieri 5, I-61100 Pesaro.
Rome:	Accademia Nazionale di Santa Cecilia, Via Vittoria 6, I-00187 Rome.
	Conservatorio Statale di Musica "Santa Cecilia", Via del Greci 18, I-00187 Rome.
	Pontificïo Istituto di Musica Sacra, Via di Torre Rossa 21, I-00165 Rome.
Siena:	Accademia Musicale Chigiana, Via di Citta 89, I-53100 Siena.
Trieste:	Conservatorio Statale di Musica "Giuseppe Tartini", Via Carlo Ghega 12, I-34132 Trieste.
Turin:	Conservatorio Statale di Musica "Giuseppe Verdi", Via Mazzini 11, Piazza Bodoni, I-10123 Turin.
Venice:	Conservatorio Statale di Musica "Benedetto Marcello", Palazzo Pisani, San Marco 2809, I-30124 Venice.
Vercelli:	Liceo Musicale "Giovanni Battista Viotti", Casella Postale 127, I-13100 Vercelli 39.

JAPAN

Hiroshima:	Elizabeth University of Music, 4-15 Nobori-cho, Naka-ku, Hiroshima 730.
Kyoto:	Kyoto City University of Fine Arts and Music, 13-6 Ohe Kutsukake-cho, Nishikyo-ku, Kyoto 610-11.
Osaka:	Osaka College of Arts, 469 Higashiyama, Kanan-cho, Minamilawachi-gun, Osaka 561.
	Osaka Ongaku Daigaku (Osaka College of Music), 1-1-8 Saiwaimachi, Shonai, Toyonaka, Osaka 561.
Tokyo:	Kunitachi College of Music, 5-5-1 Kashiwa-cho, Tachikawa-shi, Tokyo 190.
	Musashino Ongaku Daigaku (Musashino College of Music), 1-13-1 Hazawa, Nerima-ku, Tokyo 176.
	Toho Gakuen School of Music, 1-41-1 Wakaba-cho, Chofu-shi, Tokyo 182.
	Tokyo College of Music, 3-4-5 Minami-Ikebukuro, Toshima-ku, Tokyo 171.
	Tokyo Daigaku (University of Tokyo), Faculty of Musicology, 7-3-1 Hongo, Bungyo-ku, Tokyo 113.
	Tokyo Geijutsu Daigaku (Tokyo University of Fine Arts and Music), 12-8 Ueno-koch, Taito-kut, Tokyo 110.
	Ueno Gakuen College, Department of Music, 4-24-12 Higashiueno, Taito-ku, Tokyo 110.

KOREA (SOUTH)

Seoul:	Korean Union College, Department of Music, Cheongryang, PO Box 18, Seoul.
	Korea University, 1 5-KA, Anamdong, Sungbukku, Seoul 136-701.
	Kyung Hee University, College of Music, 1 Hoegi-dong, Tongadaemun-gu Seoul 131.
	National Academy of Arts, Department of Music, 1 Sejongno, Chongno-gu, Seoul.
	Seoul National University, College of Music, San 56-1, Shinrim-dong, Kwanak-gu, Seoul 151.
	Yongsei University, College of Music, 134 Shinchon-dong, Sodaemun-gu, Seoul 120.

LATVIA

Riga:	Latvian Y Vitol State Conservatory, Ul Krisyana Barona 1, 226050 Riga.

LITHUANIA

Vilnius:	Lithuanian State Conservatory, 232001 Vilnius.

LUXEMBOURG

Esch-sur-Alzette:	Conservatoire de Musique d'Esch-sur-Alzette, 10 Rue de l'Eglise, BP 145, 4002 Esch-sur-Alzette.
Luxembourg:	Conservatoire de Musique de la Ville de Luxembourg, 33 Rue Charles Martel, 2134 Luxembourg.

MEXICO

Mexico City:	Conservatorio Nacional de Música de México, Avenida Presidente Masaryk 582, Mexico City 5, DF.
	Universidad Nacional Autónoma de México, Escuela Nacional de Música, Xicotencat 126, Coyoacán, Mexico City 04100, DF.
Veracruz:	Facultad de Música, Universidad Veracruzana, Barragán No.32, Xalapa Veracruz CP 91000.

MONACO

Monte Carlo:	Académie de Musique Prince Rainier III de Monaco, 1 Boulevard Albert, 98000 Monte Carlo.

MOROCCO

Casablanca:	Ecole Nationale de Musique, 133 Avenue Ziraoui, Casablanca.
Marrakesh:	Conservatorie de Musique, Marrakesh.
Meknes:	Ecole Nationale de Musique, 22 Rue Marrakchia, Kaa Ouarda, Meknes.
Rabat:	Conservatoire National de Musique, de Danse, et d'Art Dramatique, Rabat.
Tangier:	Conservatoire de Tangier, Tangier.

NETHERLANDS

Amsterdam:	Stichting Sweelinck Conservatorium, Van Baerlestraat 27, 1071 AN Amsterdam.
Arnhem:	Hogeschool Voor de Kunsten Arnhem, Fakulteit Muziek, Weverstraat 40, 6811 EM Arnhem.
Enschede:	Hogeschool Enschede sector Conservatorium, Van Essengaarde 10, 7511 PN Enschede.
Groningen:	Rijkshogeschool Groningen sector Kunstvakopleidingen afdeling Conservatorium, Veemarkstraat 76, 9724 GA Groningen.
The Hague:	Koninklijk Conservatorium voor Muziek en Dans, Juliana van Stolberglaan 1, 2595 CA The Hague.
Hilversum:	Akademie voor Muziek, Koninginneweg 25, 1217 KR Hilversum.
	Hilversums Conservatorium, Snelliuslaan 10, 1222 TE Hilversum.
Leeuwarden:	Stedelijke Muziekpedagogische Akademie, Eewal 56-58, Leeuwarden.
Maastricht:	Rijkshgeschool Maastricht, Subfaculteit Conservatorium, Bonnefanten 15, 6211 KL Maastricht.
Rotterdam:	Rotterdams Conservatorium, Pieter de Hooghweg 122, 3024 BJ Rotterdam.
	Toonkunst Conservatorium, Mathenesserlaan 219, Rotterdam.
Tilburg:	Brabants Conservatorium voor Muziek en Dans, Kempenbaan 27, 5022 KC Tilburg.
Utrecht:	Utrechts Conservatorium, Mariaplaats 28, 3511 LL Utrecht.
Zwolle:	Christelijke Hogeschool voor de Kunsten "Constantijn Huygens", Aan de Stadsmuur 88, 8011 VD Zwolle.

NEW ZEALAND

Auckland:	University of Auckland, Faculty of Music, Private Bag, Auckland.
Christchurch:	University of Canterbury, Faculty of Music, Christchurch.
Dunedin:	University of Otago, Arts and Music, PO Box 56, Dunedin.
Wellington:	Victoria University of Wellington, Faculty of Music, PO Box 600 Wellington.

NICARAGUA

Managua:	Escuela Nacional de Musica, Antigua Hacienda el Retiro, Managua.

NORWAY

Bergen:	Bergen Musikkonservatorium, Lars Hilles Gate 3, N-5015 Bergen.
Oslo:	Østlandets Musikkonservatorium, Vetlandsveien 45, N-0685 Oslo 6.
	Statens Operahøgskole, Tjuvholmen, bygning B, N-0250 Oslo 2.
Stavanger:	Rogaland Musikkonservatorium, Bjergsted, N-4007 Stavanger.
Trondheim:	Trondelag Musikkonservatorium, Homebergvn 1, N-7038 Trondheim.

PANAMA

Panama City:	Escuela Nacional de Música, Apartado 1414, Panama City.

PARAGUAY

Asunción:	Conservatorio Municipal de Música, Mcal Estigarribia, E-Pai Perez y Curupayty, Asunción.
	Escuela Municipal de Canto, Dr Eduardo Victor Haedo 682, Asunción.

PERU

Lima:	Conservatorio Nacional de Música, Avenida Emancipatión 180, Lima 1.

PHILIPPINES

Iloilo City:	University of San Augustin, Conservatory of Music, General Luna Street, Iloilo City 5901.
Manila:	St Paul College, College of Music, 680 Pedro Gil Street, Malate, Manila.
	St Scholastica's College, School of Music, 2560 Leon Guinto Sr Street, Malate, Manila.
	University of Santo Tomas, Conservatory of Music, Espana, Manila.

POLAND

Bydgoszcz:	Akademia Muzyczna im Feliksa Nowowiejskiego w Bydgoszczy, Ul J Slowackiego 7, 85-008 Bydgoszcz.
Gdańsk:	Akademia Muzyczna im Stanislaw Moniuszko w Gdańsku, Lagiewniki 3, 80-847 Gdańsk.
Katowice:	Akademia Muzyczna im Karola Szymanowskiego w Katowice, UL Zacisze 3, Katowice.
Kraków:	Akademia Muzyczna w Krakówie, Ul Bohaterów Stalingradu 3, 31-038 Kraków.

Lódź:	Akademia Muzyczna w Lódź, Ul Gdańska 32, 90-716 Lódź.
Poznań:	Akademia Muzyczna Poznańiu, Ul Czerwonej Armii 87, 61-808 Poznań.
Warsaw:	Akademia Muzyczna im Fryderyka Chopina w Warzawie, Ul Okólnik 2, 00-368 Warsaw.
Wroclaw:	Akademia Muzyczna Wroclawiu, Ul Powstancow Ślaskich 204, 53-140 Wroclaw.

PORTUGAL

Coimbra:	Conservatório Regional de Coimbra, Rua do Brasil, 3000 Coimbra.
Lisbon:	Academia de Amadores de Musica, R Nova da Trindade 18, 2nd Floor, E, 1200 Lisbon.
	Escola Superior de Musica, Conservatório Nacional, Rua dos Caetanos 29, 1200 Lisbon.
Oporto:	Conservatório de Musica, Rua de Maternidade 13, 4000 Oporto.

ROMANIA

Bucharest:	Conservatorul de Muzică Ciprian Porumbescu, Str Stirbei Voda 33, 70732 Bucharest.
Cluj-Napoca:	Conservatorul de Muzică Gheorghe Dima, Str 23 August 25, 3400 Cluj-Napoca.
Iasi:	Conservatorul de Muzică Georges Enescu, Str Closca 9, 6600 Iasi.

RUSSIA

Moscow:	Moscow Conservatory, Ul Gertzena 13, 103009 Moscow.
St Petersburg:	St Petersburg Conservatory, Teatralnaya Pl 3, 192041 St Petersburg.

SINGAPORE

Singapore:	School of Arts and Language, 469 Bukit Gimah Road, Singapore 1025.

SLOVAK REPUBLIC

Bratislava:	Bratislava Konzervatorium, Tolstého 11, 811 06 Bratislava.
	Vysoká Skola Mǔzických Umeni v Bratisaave (Academy of Music and Dramatic Arts Bratislava), Jiráskova 3, 813 01 Bratislava.

SOUTH AFRICA

Bloemfontein:	University of the Orange Free State, Department of Music, PO Box 339, Bloemfontein 9300.
Cape Town:	University of Cape Town, College of Music, Private bag, Rondebosch 7700, Cape Town.
Durban:	University of Natal, Department of Music, King George V Avenue, Durban 4001.
Johannesburg:	University of the Witwatersrand, Wits School of Music, Jan Smuts Avenue, Johannesburg 2001.
Pretoria:	University of Pretoria, Department of Music, Pretoria 0002.
	University of South Africa, Department of Music, PO Box 392, Pretoria 0001.
Stellenbosch:	University of Stellenbosch, Department of Music, Stellenbosch 7600.

SPAIN

Barcelona:	Conservatorio Superior de Música de Barcelona, Calle Bruche 112, Barcelona 9.
Cadiz:	Conservatorio de Música "Manuel de Falla", Calle del Tinte 1, Cadiz.
Cordoba:	Conservatorio Superior de Música y Escuela de arte Dramatico y Danza, Calle Angel de Saavedra 1, Cordoba.
Madrid:	Escuela Superior de Música Sagrada y de Pedagogia Musical Escolar, Victor Pradera 65 bis, Madrid 8.
	Real Conservatorio Nacional de Música y Declamacion, San Bernardo 44, Madrid.
	Real Conservatorio Superior de Música, Plaza de Isabell II, S-N, Madrid 28013.
San Sebastian:	Conservatorio Superior de Música, Easo 39, San Sebastian 20006.
Seville:	Conservatorio Superior de Música y Escuela de Arte Dramatico, Calle Jesus del Gran Poder 49, Seville 41002.
Valencia:	Conservatorio Superior de Música y Escuela de Arte Dramatico y Danza, Plaza San Esteban 3, Valencia.

SRI LANKA

Colombo:	Institute of Aesthetic Studies, 21 Albert Crescent, Colombo 7.

SWEDEN

Göteborg:	Göteborgs Universitet, Musikhögskolan, Box 3174, S-400 10 Göteborg.
Malmö:	Musikhögskolan och teaterhögskolan, Box 13515, Ystadvägen 25, S-200 44 Malmö.
Stockholm:	Musikhögskolan, Valhallavägen 103-109, S-115 31 Stockholm.

SWITZERLAND

Basel:	Musik-Akademie der Stadt Basel, Leonhardsstrasse 6, CH-4501 Basel.
Bern:	Konservatorium für Musik und Theater, Kramgasse 36, CH-3011 Bern.
Biel:	Stadtische Musikschule und Konservatorium, Ring 12, CH-2500 Biel.
Fribourg:	Conservatoire et Académie de Musique, 228-A Rue Pierre Aeby, CH-1700 Friboug.
Geneva:	Conservatoire de Musicque de Genève, Place Neuve, CH-1204 Geneva.
	Institute jaques-Dalcroze, 11 Rue Sillem, CH-1207 Geneva.

La Chaux-de-Fonds:	Conservatoire de Musique de La Chaux-de-Fonds-Le Locie, Avenue Léopold-Robert 34, CH-2300 La Chaux-de-Fonds.
Lausanne:	Conservatoire de Musique de Lausanne, 6 Rue du Midi, CH-1002 Lausanne.
Lucerne:	Konservatorium Luzern, Dreilindenstrasse 93, CH-6006 Lucern.
Neuchâtel:	Conservatoire de Musique de Neuchâtel, 106 Faubourg de l'Hopital, CH-2000 Neuchâtel.
Olten:	Stadtische Musikschule, CH-4600 Olten.
Schaffhausen:	Musikschule und Konservatorium Schaffhausen, Rosengasse 16, CH-8200 Schaffhausen.
Vevey:	Conservatoire de Musique de Vevey, 4 Rue des Communaux, CH-1800 Vevey.
Winterthur:	Musikschuel und Konservatorium Winterthur, Tössertobelstrasse 1, CH-8400 Winterthur.
Zürich:	Konservatorium und Musikhochschule Zürich, Birchstrasse 95, CH-8050 Zürich.
	Musikakademie Zürich, Florastrasse 52, CH-8008 Zürich.

TAIWAN

Taipei:	National Institute of the Arts, Music Department, 172 Chung Cheng Road, Ru Chow, Taipei.
	National Taiwan Academy of Arts, 59, Section 1, Ta Kuan Road, Pan-Chiao Park, Taipei.

TUNISIA

Tunis:	Conservatoire de Musique, 5 Rue Zarkoun, Tunis.
	Institut Superieure de Musique, 20 Avenue de Paris, Tunis.

TURKEY

Ankara:	Hacettepe Üniversitesi, Ankara State Conservatory, Hacetlepe Parki, Ankara.
Istanbul:	Mimar Sinan Üniversitesi, Istanbul State Conservatory of Music, Findikli, Istanbul.
	Istanbul Teknik Üniversitesi, Turkish Conservatory of Music, Ayazaga, Istanbul.

UK

Bangor:	University College of North Wales, Department of Music, Bangor, Wales LL57 2DG.
Barnet:	Middlesex Polytechnic School of Music, Trent Park, Cockfosters Road, Barnet, Herts EN4 0PT.
Belfast:	City of Belfast School of Music, 99 Donegal Pass, Belfast, Northern Ireland BT7 1DR.
	Queen's University of Belfast, Department of Music, University Road, Belfast, Northern Ireland BT7 1NN.
Birmingham:	Birmingham Conservatoire, Paradise Place, Birmingham B3 3HG.
	Birmingham School of Music, Paradise Circus, Birmingham B3 3HG.
	Department of Music,The University of Birmingham, Barber Institute, Edgbaston, Birmngham B15 2TT
Brighton:	University of Sussex, Department of Music, Arts Building, Falmer, Brighton, East Sussex BN1 9QN.
Cambridge:	University of Cambridge, School of Music, 11 West Road, Cambridge CB3 9DP.
Cardiff:	University of Wales, College of Cardiff, Department of Music, Corbett Road, Cardiff, Wales CF1 3EB.
	Welsh College of Music and Drama, Castle Grounds, Cathays Park, Cardiff, Wales CF1 3ER.
Cobham:	Yehudi Menuhin School, Stoke D'Abernon, Cobham, Surrey KT11 3QQ.
Croydon:	Royal School of Church Music, Addinton Palace, Croydon CR9 5AD.
Edimburgh:	St Mary's Music School, Old Coates House, Manor Place, Edinburgh, Scotland EH3 7EB.
	University of Edinburgh, Faculty of Music, Edinburgh, Scotland EH8 9YL.
Egham:	Royal Holloway and Bedford College, Department of Music, Egham, Surrey TW20 0EX.
Exeter:	University of Exeter, Department of Music, Exeter EX4 4QJ.
Fife:	University of St Andrews, Department of Music, Fife, Scotland.
Glasgow:	Royal Scottish Academy of Music and Drama, St George's Place, Glasgow, Scotland G2 1BS.
	University of Glasgow, Department of Music, Glasgow, Scotland G12 8QH.
Harrow-on-the-Hill:	Purcell School, Mount Park Road, Harrow-on-the-Hill, Middlesex HA1 3JS.
Hull:	University of Hull, Department of Music, Cottingham Road, Hull HU6 7RX.
Lancaster:	University of Lancaster, Department of Music, Lancaster LA1 4YW.
Leeds:	City of Leeds College of Music, Cookridge Street, Leeds LS2 8BH.
	University of Leeds, Department of Music, Leeds LS2 9JT.
Leicester:	University of Leicester, Department of Music, University Road, Leicester LE1 7RH.
Liverpool:	University of Liverpool, Department of Music, PO Box 147, Liverpool L69 3BX.
London:	Guildhall School of Music and Drama, Barbican, London EC2Y 8DT.
	King's College, Department of Music, Strand, London WC1.
	London-City University, Department of Music, Northampton Square, London EC1V 0HB.
	London College of Music, c/o Polytechnic of London, St Mary's Road, London W5 5RF.
	Royal Academy of Music, Marylebone Road, London NW1 5HT.
	Royal College of Music, Prince Consort Road, London SW7 2BS.
	Trinity College of Music, 11 Mandeville Place, London W1M 6AQ.
	University of London, Department of Muisc, Senate House, London WC1E 7AU.
Manchester:	Chetham's School of Music, Long Millgate, Manchester M3 1SB.
	Royal Northern College of Music, 124 Oxford Road, Manchester M13 9RD.
	Salford College of Technology, Adelphi, Peru Street, Salford, Manchester M3 6EQ.
	University of Manchester, Department of Music, Denmark Road, Manchester M15 6FY.
Oxford:	University of Ozford, Faculty of Music, St Aldate's, Oxford OX1 1DB.
Reading:	University of Reading, Department of Music, 35 Upper Redlands Road, Reading RG1 5JE.
Southampton:	University of Southampton, Department of Music, Highfield, Southampton SO9 5NH.
Totnes:	Dartington College of Arts, Department of Music, Totnes, Devon TQ9 6EJ.

| Twickenham: | Royal Military School of Music, Kneller Hall, Twickenham, Middlesex TW2 7DU. |
| York: | University of York, Department of Music, Heslington, York YO1 5DD. |

USA

ALABAMA

Auburn:	Auburn University, Department of Music, Auburn, AL 36849.
Birmingham	Samford University, School of Music, 800 South Lakeshore Drive, Birmingham, AL 35229.
	University of Alabama at Birmingham, Department of Music, 401 Humanities Building, Birmingham, AL 35294.
Jacksonville:	Jacksonville State University, Department of Music, Mason Hall, Jacksonville, AL 36265.
Mobile:	University of South Alabama, Department of Music, 9 Faculty Court E, Mobile, AL 36688.
Montevallo:	University of Montevallo, College of Fine Arts, Station 6670, Montevallo, AL 35115.
Montgomery:	Alabama State University, School of Music, 915 South Jackson Street, Montgomery, AL 36195.
Troy:	Troy State University, School of Fine Arts, Music Department, Long Hall, Troy, AL 36082.
Tuscaloosa:	University of Alabama, School of Music, PO Box 2876, Tuscaloosa, AL 35487.

ALASKA

| Anchorage: | University of Alaska, Anchorage, Music Department, 3211 Providence Drive, Achorage, AK 99508. |
| Fairbanks: | University of Alaska, Fairbanks, Music Department, 301 Fine Arts Complex, Fairbanks, AK 99775. |

ARIZONA

Flagstaff:	Northern Arizona University, Music Department, PO Box 6040, Flagstaff, AZ 86011.
Phoenix:	Arizona State University, Interdisciplinary Fine Arts Department, 4701 W Thunderbird Road, Phoenix, AZ 85069.
Tempe:	Arizona State University, School of Music, Tempe, AZ 85287.
Tucson:	University of Arizona, School of Music, Tucson, AZ 85721.

ARKANSAS

Arkadelphia:	Henderson State University, Department of Music, 1100 Henderson Street, Arkadelphia, AR 71923.
	Quachita Baptist University, School of Music, Box 37771, Arkadelphia, AR 71923.
Conway:	University of Central Arkansas, Department of Music, Box 1726, Conway, AR 72032.
Fayetteville:	University of Arkansas, Department of Music, 201A Music Building, Fayetteville, AR 72701.
Little Rock:	University of Arkansas at Little Rock, Department of Music, 2801 South University, Little Rock, AR 72204.
Russellville:	Arkansas Tech University, Department of Music, Russellville, AR 72801.
State University:	Arkansas State University, Department of Music, Box 779, State University, AR 72467.

CALIFORNIA

Azusa:	Azusa Pacific University, School of Music, Citrus and Alosta, Azusa, CA 91702.
Bakersfield:	California State University, Bakersfield, Fine Arts Department, 9001 Stockdale Highway, Bakersfield, CA 93311.
Berkeley:	University of California, Berkeley, Department of Music, Morrison Hall, Berkeley, CA 94720.
Carson:	California State University, Dominguez Hills, Department of Music, 1000 E Victoria, Carson, CA 90747.
Chico:	California State University, Chico, Department of Music, Chico, CA 95929.
Claremont:	The Claremont Graduate School, Department of Music, 150 East 20th Street, Claremont, CA 91711.
	Pomona College, Department of Music, Thatcher Music Building, Claremont, CA 91711.
Davis:	University of California, Davis, Department of Music, 112 Music Building, Davis, CA 95616.
Fresno:	California State University, Fresno, Department of Music, Maple and Shaw Avenue, Fresno, CA 93740.
Fullerton:	California State University, Fullerton, Department of Music, 800 North State College Boulevard, Fullerton, CA 92634.
Hayward:	California State University, Hayward, Department of Music, Hayward, CA 94542.
Hollywood:	Musicians Institute, 1655 McCadden Place, Hollywood, CA 90028.
Irvine:	University of California, Irvine, School of Fine Arts, Department of Music, Irvine, CA 92717.
La Jolla:	University of California, San Diego, Department of Music, B-026, La Jolla, CA 92093.
La Mirada:	Biola University, Department of Music, 13800 Biola Avenue, La Mirada, CA 90639.
Long Beach:	California State University, Long Beach, Department of Music, 1250 Bellflower Boulevard, Long Beach, CA 90840.
Los Angeles:	California State University, Los Angeles, Department of Music, 5151 State University Drive, Los Angeles, CA 90032.
	Los Angeles City College, Department of Music, 855 N Vermont Avenue, Los Angeles, CA 90020.
	University of California, Los Angeles, Department of Music, 405 Hilgard Avenue, Los Angeles, CA 90024.
	University of Southern California, School of Music, University Park, Los Angeles, CA 90089.
Northridge:	California State University, Northridge, Department of Music, 18111 Nordhoff Street, Northridge, CA 91330.
Oakland:	Mills College, Music Department, 5000 MacArthur Boulevard, Oakland, CA 94613.
Pasadena:	Pasadena Conservatory of Music, PO Box 91533, 1815 Queensberry Road, Pasadena, CA 91109.
Pomona:	California State Polytechnic University, Department of Music, 3801 West Temple Avenue, Pomona, CA 91768.
Redlands:	University of Redlands, School of Music, PO Box 3080, Redlands, CA 92373.
Riverside:	University of California, Riverside, Department of Music, 900 University Avenue, Riverside, CA 92521.
Sacramento:	California State University, Sacramento, Department of Music, 6000 Jay Avenue, Sacramento, CA 95819.
San Diego:	San Diego State University, Department of Music, 5300 Campanile Drive, San Diego, CA 92182.
San Francisco:	Music and Arts Institute of San Francisco, 2622 Jackson Street, San Francisco, CA 94115.
	San Francisco Conservatory of Music, 1201 Ortega Street, San Francisco, CA 94122.
	San Francisco State University, Department of Music, 1600 Holloway Avenue, San Francisco, CA 94132.
San Jose:	San Jose State University, Department of Music, 1 Washington Square, San Jose, CA 95192.
Santa Barbara:	Music Academy of the West, 1070 Fairway Road, Santa Barbara, CA 93108.
	University of California, Santa Barbara, Department of Music, Santa Barbara, CA 93106.
Santa Cruz:	University of California, Santa Cruz, Department of Music, Porter College, Santa Cruz, CA 95064.
Stanford:	Stanford University, Department of Music, Stanford, CA 94305.
Stockton:	University of the Pacific, Conservatory of Music, 3601 Pacific Avenue, Stockton, CA 95211.
Turlock:	California State University, Stanislaus, Department of Music, 801 Monte Vista Avenue, Turlock, CA 95380.
Valencia:	California Institute of the Arts, School of Music, 24700 McBean Parkway, Valencia, CA 91355.

COLORADO

Aspen:	Aspen Music School, PO Box AA, Aspen, CO 81612.
Boulder:	University of Colorado, College of Music, Box 301, Boulder, CO 80309.
Colorado Springs:	Colordado College, Department of Music, Packard Hall, Colorado Springs, CO 80903.
Denver:	Metropolitan State College, Department of Music, 1006 11th Street, Box 58, Denver, CO 80204.
	University of Denver, Lamont School of Music, 7111 Mountview, Denver, CO 80220.
Fort Collins:	Colorado State University, Department of Music, Fort Collins, CO 80523.
Greeley:	University of Northern Colorado, School of Music, Greeley, CO 80639.
Pueblo:	University of Southern Colorado, Department of Music, 2200 Bonforte Boulevard, Pueblo, CO 81001.

CONNECTICUT

Bridgeport:	University of Bridgeport, Department of Music, Arnold Bernhard Arts-Humanities Center, Bridgeport, CT 06602.
Danbury:	Western Connecticut State University, Department of Music, 181 White Street, Danbury, CT 06810.
Hartford:	University of Hartford, Hartt School of Music, 200 Bloomfield Avenue, Hartford, CT 06117.
Middletown:	Wesleyan University, Department of Music, Middletown, CT 06457.
New Haven:	Yale University, School of Music, Box 2104A, Yate Station, New Haven, CT 06520.
Storrs:	University of Connecticut, Department of Music, Box U-12, Room 228, 876 Coventry Road, Storrs, CT 06269.

DELAWARE

Milford:	Delaware Music School, PO Box 442, Milford, DE 19963.
Newark:	University of Delaware, Department of Music, Newark, DE 19716.
Wilmington:	Wilmington Music School, 4101 Washington Street, Wilmington, DE 19802.

DISTRICT OF COLUMBIA

Washington:	American University, Department of Performing Arts, Kreeger Building, No 200, Washington, DC 20016.
	The Catholic University of America, Benjamin T Rome School of Music, 620 Michigan Avenue North East, Washington, DC 20064.
	George Washington University, Department of Music, B-144 Academic Center, Washington, DC 20052.
	Howard University, College of Fine Arts, Sixth and Fairmont Streets North West, Washington, DC 20059.
	Levine School of Music, 1690 36th Street North West, Washington, DC 20007.

FLORIDA

Boca Raton:	Florida Atlantic University, Conservatory of Music, College of Liberal Arts, 2912 College Avenue, Boca Raton, FL 33314.
Coral Gables:	University of Miami, School of Music, PO Box 248165, Coral Gables, FL 33124.
De Land:	Stetson University, School of Music, De Land, FL 32720.
Gainsville:	University of Florida, Department of Music, 130 MUB, Gainesville, FL 32611.
Jacksonville:	Jacksonville University, College of Fine Arts, Division of Music, Jacksonville, FL 32211.
Miami:	Florida International University, Department of Music, University Park Campus, Miami, FL 33199.
Orlando:	University of Central Florida, Department of Music, Orlando, FL 32816.
Pensacola:	University of West Florida, Department of Music, Pensacola, FL 32514.
Tallahassee:	Florida Agricultural and Mechanical University, Department of Music, Tallahassee, FL 32307.
	Florida State University, School of Music, Tallahassee, FL 32306.
Tampa:	University of South Florida, Department of Music, Tampa, FL 33620.
	University of Tampa, Music Division, 401 West J F Kennedy Boulevard, Tampa, FL 33606.

GEORGIA

Athens:	University of Georgia, School of Music, 203 Fine Arts Building, Athens, GA 30602.
Atlanta:	Emory University, Department of Music, Humanities Building, Room 101, Atlanta, GA 30322.
	Georgia State University, School of Muisc, University Plaza, Atlanta, GA 30303.
	Spelman College, Department of Music, 350 Spelman Lane South West, Atlanta, GA 30314.
Carrolton:	West Georgia College, Department of Music, Carrolton, GA 30118.
Columbus:	Columbus College, Schwob Music Department, Columbus, GA 31993.
Rome:	Shorter College, Fine Arts Division, Box 8, Rome, GA 30161.
Statesboro:	Georgia Southern College, Department of Music, Landrum Box 8052, Statesboro, GA 30460.
Valdosta:	Valdosta State College, Department of Music, North Patterson Street, Valdosta, GA 31698.

HAWAII

Honolulu:	University of Hawaii, Department of Music, 2411 Dole Street, Honolulu, HI 96822.

IDAHO

Boise:	Boise State University, Department of Music, 1910 University Drive, Boise, ID 83725.
Moscow:	University of Idaho, Lionel Hampton School of Music, Moscow, ID 83843.
Pocatello:	Idaho State University, Department of Music, PO Box 8099, Pocatello, ID 83209.
Rexburg:	Ricks College, Department of Music, Rexburg, ID 83440.

ILLINOIS

Bloomington:	Illinois Wesleyan University, School of Music, Presser Hall, Bloomington, IL 61702.
Carbondale:	Southern Illinois University at Carbondale, School of Music, Carbondale, IL 62901.
Charleston:	Eastern Illinois University, Department of Music, Charleston, IL 61920.
Chicago:	American Conservatory of Music, 16 North Wabash Avenue, Suite 1850, Chicago, IL 60602.
	Chicago Musical College of Roosevelt University, 430 South Michigan Avenue, Chicago, IL 60605.
	Chicago State University, 95 State and King Drive, Chicago, IL 60628.
	De Paul University, School of Music, 804 West Belden, Chicago, IL 60614.
	Moody Bible Institute, Department of Music, 820 North LaSalle Drive, Chicago, IL 60610.
	North Park College, Department of Music, 3225 West Foster, Chicago, IL 60625.
	The People's Music School, 4750 North Sheridan, Suite 340, Chicago, IL 60640.

	Sherwood Conservatory of Music, 1014 South Michigan Avenue, Chicago, IL 60605.
	University of Chicago, Department of Music, 5845 South Ellis Avenue, Chicago, IL 60637.
	University of Illinois at Chicago, Department of Music, PO Box 4348, Chicago, IL 60680.
	VanderCook College of Music, 3209 South Michigan Avenue, Chicago, IL 60616.
Decatur:	Millikin University, School of Music, 1184 West Main Street, Decatur, IL 62522.
DeKalb:	Northern Illinois University, School of Music, Music Building 140, DeKalb, IL 60115.
Edwardsville:	Southern Illinois University at Edwardsville, Department of Music, Box 1771, Edwardsville, IL 62026.
Evanston:	Northwestern University, School of Music, 711 Elgin Road, Evanston, IL 60208.
Macomb:	Western Illinois University, Department of Music, 122 Browne Hall, Macomb, IL 61455.
Normal:	Illinois State University, Department of Music, Normal, IL 61761.
Peoria:	Bradley University, Division of Music and Theater Arts, Peoria, IL 61625.
Urbana:	The Conservatory of Central Illinois, 312 West Green, Urbana, IL 61801.
	University of Illinois, School of Music, 1114 West Nevada Street, Urbana, IL 60801.
Wheaton:	Wheaton College, Conservatory of Music, Wheaton, IL 60187.

INDIANA

Anderson:	Anderson University, Department of Music, 110 East Fifth Street, Anderson, IN 46012.
Bloomington:	Indiana University, School of Music, Music Building, Bloomington, IN 47405.
Evansville:	University of Evansville, Department of Music, 1800 Lincoln Avenue, Evansville, IN 47722.
Greencastle:	DePauw University, School of Music, Performing Arts Center, Greencastle, IN 46135.
Hanover:	Hanover College, Department of Music, Hanover, IN 47243.
Indianapolis:	Butler University, Jordan College of Fine Arts, 4600 Sunset Avenue, Indianapolis, IN 46208.
	Indiana University-Purdue University at Indianapolis, Department of Music, 525 North Blackford Street, Room 010, Indianapolis, IN 46202.
	University of Indianapolis, 1400 East Hanna, Indianapolis, IN 46227.
Muncie:	Ball State University, School of Music, Muncie, IN 47306.
North Manchester:	Manchester College, Department of Music, College Avenue, North Manchester, IN 46962.
Notre Dame:	Saint Mary's College, Department of Music, Notre Dame, IN 46556.
	University of Notre Dame, Department of Music, Crowley Hall of Music, Notre Dame, IN 46556.
Saint Mary-of-the-Woods:	Saint Mary-of-the-Woods College, Department of Music, Saint Mary-of-the-Woods, IN 47876.
Terre Haute:	Indiana State University, Department of Music, 217 North Sixth Street, Terre Haute, IN 47809.
Upland:	Taylor University, Department of Music, Upland, IN 46989.
Valparaiso:	Valparaiso University, Department of Music, Valparaiso, IN 46383.
West Lafayette:	Purdue University, Department of Music, 135 Hall of Music, West Lafayette, IN 47907.

IOWA

Ames:	Iowa State University, Department of Music, 149 Music Hall, Ames, IA 50011.
Cedar Falls:	University of Northern Iowa, School of Music, Cedar Falls, IA 50614.
Cedar Rapids:	Coe College, Department of Music, 1220 First Avenue North East, Cedar Rapids, IA 52402.
Decorah:	Luther College, Department of Music, Decorah, IA 52101.
Des Moines:	Drake University, School of Fine Arts, Des Moines, IA 50311.
Indianola:	Simpson College, Department of Music, Army Robertson Music Center, Indianola, IA 50125.
Iowa City:	Preucil School of Music, 524 North Johnson, Iowa City, IA 52245.
	University of Iowa, School of Music, Iowa City, IA 52242.
Mount Vernon:	Cornell College, Department of Music, Mount Vernon, IA 52314.
Sioux City:	Morningside College, 1501 Morningside Avenue, Sioux City, IA 51106.
Waverly:	Wartburg College, Department of Music, PO Box 1003, 222 Ninth Street North West, Waverly, IA 50677.

KANSAS

Emporia:	Emporia State University, Division of Music, 1200 Commercial Street, Emporia, KS 66801.
Hays:	Fort Hays State University, Department of Music, 600 Park Street, Hays, KS 67601.
Lawrence:	University of Kansas, School of Fine Arts, 452 Murphy Street, Lawrence, KS 66045.
Lindsborg:	Bethany College, Department of Music, 421 North First Street, Lindsborg, KS 67456.
Manhattan:	Kansas State University, Department of Music, McCain Auditorium, Room 109, Manhattan, KS 66506.
North Newton:	Bethel College, Department of Music, Drawer A, North Newton, KS 67117.
Pittsburg:	Pittsburg State University, Department of Music, 1701 South Broadway, Pittsburg, KS 66762.
Topeka:	Washburn University, Department of Music, 17 and College, Topeka, KS 66621.
Wichita:	Friends University, Fine Arts Division, 2100 University, Wichita, KS 67213.
	Wichita State University, School of Music, 1845 Fairmont, Wichita, KS 67208.

KENTUCKY

Berea:	Berea College, Department of Music, CPO 1127, Berea, KY 40404.
Bowling Green:	Western Kentucky University, Department of Music, 351 Fine Arts Center, Bowling Green, KY 42101.
Frankfort:	Kentucky State University, Fine Arts Division, Frankfort, KY 40601.
Lexington:	University of Kentucky, School of Music, 105 Fine Arts Building, Lexington, KY 40506.
Louisville:	Southern Baptist Theological Seminary, School of Church Music, 2825 Lexington Road, Louisville, KY 40280.
	University of Louisville, School of Music, Louisville, KY 40292.
Morehead:	Morehead State University, Department of Music, Baird Music Hall, Room 106, Morehead, KY 40351.
Murray:	Murray State University, Department of Music, University Station, Murray, KY 42071.
Richmond:	Eastern Kentucky University, Department of Music, Richmond, NY 40475.
Williamsburg:	Cumberland College, Department of Music, PO Box 7525, Williamsburg, KY 40769.

LOUISIANA

Baton Rouge:	Louisiana State University, School of Music, Baton Rouge, LA 70803.
	Southern Univesity, Deparment of Music, PO Box 10215, Baton Rouge, LA 70813.
Grambling:	Grambling State University, Department of Music, Grambling, LA 71245.

Hammond:	Southeastern Louisiana University, Department of Music, Box 815, University Station, Hammond, LA 70402.
Lafayette:	University of Southwestern Louisiana, School of Music, PO Box 41207, Lafayette, LA 70505.
Lake Charles:	NcNeese State University, College of Liberal Arts, Department of Music, Ryan Street, Lake Charles, LA 70609.
Monroe:	Northeast Louisiana University, School of Music, 700 University, Monroe, LA 71209.
Natchitoches:	Northwestern State University of Louisiana, Department of Music, College Avenue, Natchitoches, LA 71497.
New Orleans:	Loyola University, College of Music, 6363 St Charles Avenue, New Orleans, LA 70118.
	New Orleans Baptist Theological Seminary, Church Music Ministries Division, 3939 Gentilly Boulevard, New Orleans, LA 70126.
	Tulane University-Newcomb College, Department of Music, Dixon Hall, New Orleans, LA 70118.
	University of New Orleans, Department of Music, Lakefront, New Orleans, LA 70148.
	Xavier University of Louisiana, Department of Music, 7352 Palmetto Street, New Orleans, LA 70125.
Pineville:	Louisiana College, Department of Music, College Station, Pineville, LA 71359.
Ruston:	Louisiana Tech University, School of Performing Arts, PO Box 8608, Ruston, LA 71272.
Shreveport:	Centenary College of Louisiana, Hurley School of Music, Shreveport, LA 71134.

MAINE

Brunswick:	Bowdoin College, Department of Music, Gibson Hall, Brunswick, ME 04011.
Gorham:	University of Southern Maine, Department of Music, College Avenue, 102A Corthell Hall, Gorham, ME 04038.
Lewiston:	Bates College, Department of Music, Lewiston, ME 04240.
Orono:	University of Maine, Department of Music, 123 Lord Hall, Orono, ME 04469.

MARYLAND

Baltimore:	Morgan State University, Department of Music, Coldspring and Hillen Roads, Baltimore, MD 21239.
	Peabody Institute of the Johns Hopkins University, 1 East Mount Vernon Place, Baltimore, MD 21202.
	Towson State University, Department of Music, Baltimore, MD 21204.
College Park:	University of Maryland, Department of Music, Tawes Fine Arts Building, College Park, MD 20742.
Princess Anne:	University of Maryland Eastern Shore, Fine Arts Department, Music Division, Princess Anne, MD 21853.
Rockville:	Montgomery College, Department of Music, 51 Mannakee Street, Rockville, MD 20850.
Saint Mary's City:	Saint Mary's College of Maryland, Arts and Letters Division, Saint Mary's City, MD 20686.
Towson:	Goucher College, Department of Music, 1021 Dulaney Valley Road, Towson, MD 21204.

MASSACHUSETTS

Amherst:	Amherst College, Department of Music, Amherst, MA 01022.
	University of Massachusetts, Music and Dance Department, Fine Arts Center, Amherst, MA 01003.
Boston:	Berklee College of Music, 1140 Boylston Street, Boston, MA 02215.
	Boston Conservatory, Music Division, 8 The Fenway, Boston, MA 02215.
	Boston University, School of Music, 855 Commonwealth Avenue, Boston, MA 02215.
	New England Conservatory of Music, 290 Huntington Avenue, Boston, MA 02115.
	Northeastern University, Department of Music, 360 Huntington Avenue, Boston, MA 02115.
	Tanglewood Music Center, c/o Symphony Hall, Boston, MA 02115.
	University of Massachusetts at Boston, Department of Music, Harbor Campus, Boston, MA 02125.
Cambridge:	Harvard University, Department of Music, Music Building, Cambridge, MA 02138.
	Longy School of Music Inc, 1 Follen Street, Cambridge, MA 02138.
	New School of Music, 25 Lowell Street, Cambridge, MA 02138.
Great Barrington:	Aston Magna Performance Practice Institute, PO Box 28, Great Barrington, MA 01230.
Lowell:	University of Lowell, College of Music, 1 University Avenue, Lowell, MA 01854.
Medford:	Tufts University, Department of Music, 20 Professors Row, Medford, MA 02155.
Northampton:	Smith College, Department of Music, Northampton, MA 01063.
Waltham:	Bradeis University, Department of Music, South Street, Waltham, MA 02254.
Williamstown:	Williams College, Department of Music, Bernhard Music Center, Williamstown, MA 01267.

MICHIGAN

Albion:	Albion College, Department of Music, Albion, MI 49224.
Allendale:	Grand Valley State University, Department of Music, Allendale, Mi 49401.
Ann Arbor:	University of Michigan, School of Music, Ann Arbor, MI 48109.
Berrien Springs:	Andrews University, Department of Music, Berrien Springs, MI 49104.
Detroit:	Center for Creative Studies - Institute of Music and Dance, 200 East Kirby, Detroit, MI 48202.
	Wayne State University, Department of Music, 5451 Cass Avenue, Room 105 Music, Detroit, MI 48202.
East Lansing:	Michigan State University, School of Music, Music Building, East Lansing, MI 48824.
Flint:	Flint School of Performing Arts, Dort Music Center, 1025 East Kearsley, Flint, MI 48503.
Grand Rapids:	Calvin College, Department of Music, Fine Arts Center, 3215 Burton Street South East, Grand Rapids, MI 49506.
Holland:	Hope College, Department of Music, Holland, Mi 49423.
Interlochen:	Interlochen Arts Academy, Department of Music, Interlochen, MI 49643.
Kalamazoo:	Kalamazoo College, Department of Music, 1200 Academy Street, Kalamazoo, MI 49007.
	Western Michigan University, School of Music, Kalamazoo, MI 49008.
Marquette:	Northern Michigan University, Department of Music, Fine Arts Building, C-130, Marquette, MI 49855.
Mount Pleasant:	Central Michigan University, Department of Music, Powers Music Building, No 102, Mount Pleasant, MI 48859.
Rochester:	Oakland University, Music, Theatre, and Dance Department, Rochester, MI 48309.
Ypsilanti:	Eastern Michigan University, Department of Music, N101 Alexander Music Building, Ypsilanti, MI 48197.

MINNESOTA

Bemidji:	Bemidji State University, Department of Music, PO Box 53, 1500 Birchmont Drive North East, No 53, Bemidji, MN 56601.
Collegeville:	St John's University, Department of Music, Collegeville, MN 56321.
Duluth:	University of Minnesota, Duluth, Department of Music, 10 University Drive, Duluth, MN 55812.
Mankato:	Mankato State University, Department of Music, Box 5, Mankato, MN 56002.
Minneapolis:	Augsburg College, Department of Music, 731 21st Avenue South, Minneapolis, MN 55454.
	University of Minnesota, Minneapolis, School of Music, 2106 Fourth Street South, Minneapolis, MN 55455.

Moorhead:	Concordia College, Department of Music, Moorhead, MN 56560.
	Moorhead State University, Department of Music, 1104 Seventh Avenue South, Moorhead, MN 56560.
Northfield:	Carleton College, Department of Music, 1 North College Street, Northfield, MN 55057.
	St Olaf College, Department of Music, Northfield, MN 55057.
St Cloud:	St Cloud State University, Department of Music, Performing Arts Center, Room 240, St Cloud, MN 56301.
St Joseph:	College of St Benedict, Department of Music, St Joseph, MN 56374.
St Paul:	Bethel College, Department of Music, 3900 Bethel Drive, St Paul, MN 55112.
	College of St Catherine, Department of Music, 2004 Randolph Avenue, St Paul, MN 55105.
	College of St Thomas, Department of Music, 2115 Summit Avenue, St Paul, NB 55105.
	Hamline University, Department of Music, Hewitt Avenue at Snelling, St Paul, MN 55104.
	Macalester College, Department of Music, 1600 Grand Avenue, St Paul, MN 55105.
St Peter:	Gustavus Adolphus College, Department of Music, St Peter, MN 56082.
Winona:	Winona State University, Department of Music, 145 Performing Arts Center, Winona, MN 55987.

MISSISSIPPI

Cleveland:	Delta State University, Department of Music, PO Box 3256, Cleveland, MS 38733.
Clinton:	Mississippi College, Department of Music, Box 4206, Clinton, MS 39058.
Hattiesburg:	University of Southern Mississippi, School of Music, Box 5081, Southern Station, Hattiesburg, MS 39406.
	William Carey College, Winters School of Music, Tuscan Avenue, Hattiesburg, MS 39401.
Jackson:	Jackson State University, Department of Music, PO Box 17055, Jackson, MS 39217.
Lorman:	Alcorn State University, Fine Arts Department, PO Box 29, Lorman, MS 39096.
Mississippi State:	Mississippi State University, Department of Music Education, Drawer F, Mississippi State, MS 39762.
University:	University of Mississippi, Department of Music, 132 Meek Hall, University, MS 38677.

MISSOURI

Bolivar:	Southwest Baptist University, School of Fine Arts, 1601 South Springfield Street, Bolivar, MO 65613.
Cape Girardeau:	Southeast Missouri State University, Department of Music, Brandt Music Hall, Cape Girardeau, MO 63701.
Columbia:	University of Missouri at Columbia, Department of Music, 140 Fine Arts Center, Columbia, MO 65211.
Fayette:	Central Methodist College, Swinney Conservatory of Music, 411 CMC Square, Fayette, MO 65248.
Independence:	Music/Arts Institute, 1010 South Pearl, PO Box 1141, Independence, MO 64051.
Joplin:	Missouri Southern State College, Department of Music, Newman and Duquesne Roads, Joplin, MO 64801.
Kansas City:	Park College, Department of Music, Parkville, Kansas City, MO 64152.
	University of Missouri at Kansas City, Conservatory of Music, 4949 Cherry, Kansas City, MO 64110.
Kirksville:	Northeast Missouri State University, Fine Arts Division, Kirksville, MO 63501.
Liberty:	William Jewell College, Department of Music, Liberty, MO 64068.
Maryville:	Northwest Missouri State University, Department of Music, DeLuce Fine Arts Building, Maryville, MO 64468.
Springfield:	Evangel College, Department of Music, 1111 N Glenstone, Springfield, MO 65802.
	Southwest Missouri State University, Department of Music, 901 South National, Springfield, MO 65804.
St Joseph:	Missouri Western State College, Department of Music, 4525 Downs Drive, St Joseph, MO 64507.
St Louis:	Saint Louis Conservatory and Schools for the Arts, 560 Trinity at Delmar, St Louis, MO 63130.
	Saint Louis University, Department of Music, 221 North Grand Boulevard, St Louis, MO 63103.
	University of Missouri a t St Louis, Department of Music, 8001 Natural Bridge, St Louis, MO 63121.
	Washington University, Department of Music, Campus Box 1032, 1 Brookings Drive, St Louis, MO 63130.
	Webster University, Department of Music, 470 East Lockwoof, St Louis, Mo 63119.
Warrensburg:	Central Missouri State University, Department of Music, Warrensburg, MO 64093.

MONTANA

Billings:	Eastern Montana College, Department of Music, 1500 North 30th, Billings, MT 59101.
Bozeman:	Montana State University, Department of Music, Bozeman, MT 59717.
Missoula:	University of Montana, Department of Music, Missoula, MT 59812.

NEBRASKA

Hastings:	Hastings College, Department of Music, Seventh and Turner, Hastings, NE 68901.
Kearney:	Kearney State College, Department of Musicm Kearney, NE 68847.
Lincoln:	Nebraska Wesleyan University, Department of Music, 50 and St Paul Street, Lincoln, NE 68504.
	University of Nebraska at Lincoln, School of Music, Westbrook Music Building 120, Lincoln, NE 68588.
Omaha:	University of Nebraska at Omaha, Department of Music, College of Fine Arts, 60 and Dodge Street, Omaha, NE 68182.
Seward:	Concordia College, Music Division, 800 North Columbia Street, Seward, NE 68434.

NEVADA

Las Vegas:	University of Nevada, Las Vegas, Department of Music, 4505 South Maryland Parkway, Las Vegas, NV 89154.
Reno:	University of Nevada, Reno, Department of Music, Reno, NV 89557.

NEW HAMPSHIRE

Durham:	University of New Hampshire, Department of Music, Durham, NH 03824.
Hanover:	Dartmouth College, Department of Music, Hopkins Center, Hanover, NH 03755.
Plymouth:	Plymouth State College, Department of Music, Plymouth, NH 03264.

NEW JERSEY

Glassboro:	Glassboro State College, Department of Music, Glassboro, NJ 08028.
Haddonfield:	Haddonfield School of Creative and Performing Arts, Box 383, Haddonfield, NJ 08033.
Jersey:	Jersey City State College, Music, Dance, and Theatre Department, 2039 Kennedy Boulevard, Jersey City, NJ 07305.
Little Silver:	Monmouth Conservatory of Music, 2 Cross Street, Little Silver, NJ 07739.
Newark:	Rutgers University, Faculty of Arts and Sciences, Department of Music, Newark, NJ 07102.
New Brunswick:	Mason Gross School of the Arts of Rutgers University, Old Music Building, Douglass Campus, PO Box 270, New Brunswick, NJ 08903.
Princeton:	Princeton University, Department of Music, Woolworth Center, Princeton, NJ 08544.

MUSIC CONSERVATOIRES

	Westminster Choir College, Hamilton and Walnut, Princeton, NJ 08540.
Rutherford:	Fairleigh Dicksnson University, Fine Arts Department, 223 Montross Avenue, Rutherford, NJ 07070.
	Garden State Academy of Music, 88 Park Avenue, Rutherford, NJ 07070.
Trenton:	Trenton State College, Department of Music, Hillwood Lakes, CN4700, Trenton, NJ 08650.
Upper Montclair:	Montclair State College, School of Fine and Performing Arts, Valley Road, Upper Montclair, NJ 07043.
Wayne:	William Paterson College of New Jersey, Department of Music, 300 Pompton Road, Wayne, NJ 07470.

NEW MEXICO

Albuquerque:	University of New Mexico, Department of Music, College of Fine Arts, Albuquerque, NM 87131.
Las Cruces:	New Mexico State University, Department of Music, Box 30001, Las Cruces, NM 88003.
Las Vegas:	New Mexico Highlands University, Creative and Performing Arts Department, Las Vegas, NM 87701.
Portales:	Eastern New Mexico University, School of Music, Station 16, Portales, NM 88130.

NEW YORK

Albany:	State University of New York at Albany, Department of Music, 1400 Washington Avenue, Albany, NY 12222.
Binghamton:	State University of New York at Binghamton, Department of Music, Vestal Parkway, Binghamton, NY 13901.
Brockport:	State University of New York, College at Brockport, Music and Theatre Department, Tower Fine Arts Center, Holley Street, Brockport, NY 14420.
Bronx:	Herbert H Lehman College, City University of New York, Department of Music, Bedford Park Boulevard West, Bronx, NY 10468.
Bronxville:	Sarah Lawrence College, Department of Music, 1 Meadway, Bronxville, NY 10708.
Brooklyn:	Brooklyn College, Conservatory of Music, Bedford Avenue and Avenue H, Brooklyn, NY 11210.
	Brooklyn Conservatory of Music, 58 Seventh Avenue, Brooklyn, NY 11217.
Buffalo:	State University of New York at Buffalo, Department of Music, Baird Hall, Room 226, Amherst Campus, Buffalo, NY 14260.
	State University of New York, College at Buffalo, Performing Arts Department, 1300 Elmwood Avenue, Buffalo, NY 14222.
Chautauqua:	Chautauqua Institution Summer School of Music, Box 1098, Chautauqua, NY 14722.
Cortland:	State University of New York, College at Cortland, Department of Music, Box 2000, Cortland, NY 13045.
Flushing:	Queens College, City University of New York, Aaron Copland School of Music, 65-30 Kissena Boulevard, Flushing, NY 11367.
Fredonia:	State University of New York, College at Fredonia, School of Music, Mason Hall, Fredonia, NY 14063.
Garden City:	Adelphi University, Department of Music, Post Hall, Garden City, NY 11530.
Geneseo:	State University of New York, College at Geneseo, Department of Music, Geneseo, NY 14454.
Hamilton:	Colgate University, Department of Music, Dana Arts Center, Hamilton, NY 13346.
Hempstead:	Hofstra University, Department of Music, 1000 Fulton Avenue, Hempstead, NY 11550.
Houghton:	Houghton College, School of Music, Houghton, NY 14744.
Ithaca:	Cornell University, Department of Music, Lincoln Hall, Ithaca, NY 14853.
	Ithaca College, School of Music, Ithaca, NY 14850.
New Paltz:	State University of New York, College at New Paltz, Department of Music, New Paltz, NY 12561.
New York:	Baruch College, City University of New York, Department of Music, 17 Lexington Avenue, New York, NY 10010.
	Cantors Institute-Seminary College of Jewish Music of the Jewish Theological Seminary of America, 3080 Broadway, New York, NY 10027.
	City College of New York, Department of Music, West 138th Street and Convent Avenue, New York, NY 10031.
	Columbia University, Department of Music, 703 Dodge, New York, NY 10027.
	Dalcroze School of Music, 161 East 73rd Street, New York, NY 10021.
	Diller-Quaile School of Music Inc, 24 East 95th Street, New York, NY 10128.
	Harlem School of the Arts Inc, 645 St Nicholas Avenue, New York, NY 10030.
	Hebrew Union College, Jewish Institute of Religion, School of Sacred Music, 1 West Fourth Street, New York, NY 10012.
	Hunter College, City University of New York, Department of Music, 695 Park Avenue, New York, NY 10021.
	Julliard School, Lincoln Center Plaza, New York, NY 10023.
	Manhattan School of Music, 120 Claremont Avenue, New York, NY 10027.
	Mannes College of Music, 150 West 85th Street, New York, NY 10024.
	New School for Social Research, Department of Music, 66 West 12th Street, New York, NY 10011.
	New York University, Tisch School of the Arts, 721 Broadway, 4th Floor, New York, NY 10003.
	92nd Street Y School of Music, 1395 Lexington Avenue, New York, Ny 10128.
Nyack:	Nyack College, Music and Fine Arts Department, Nyack, NY 10960.
Oneonta:	State University of New York, College at Oneonta, Fine Arts Center, Oneonta, NY 13820.
Oswego:	State University of New York, College at Oswego, Department of Music, Tyler Hall, Oswego, NY 13126.
Potsdam:	State University of New York, College at Potsdam, Crane School of Music, Pierrepont Avenue, Potsdam, NY 13676.
Poughkeepsie:	Vassar College, Department of Music, Raymond Avenue, Poughkeepsie, NY 12601.
Purchase:	Manhattanville College, Department of Music, Purchase, NY 10577.
	State University of New York, College at Purchase, Music Division, Purchase, NY 10577.
Rochester:	Eastman School of Music, University of Rochester, 26 Gibbs Street, Rochester, NY 14604.
	Hochstein Memorial Music School, 50 North Plymouth Avenue, Rochester, NY 14614.
	Roberts Wesleyan College, Fine Arts Division, 2301 Westside Drive, Rochester, NY 14624.
Saratoga Springs:	Skidmore College, Department of Music, Saratoga Springs, NY 12866.
Scarsdale:	Hoff-Barthelson Music School, 25 School Lane, Scarsdale, NY 10583.
Staten Island:	College of Staten Island, City University of New York, Department of Music, 130 Stuyvesant Place, Staten Island, NY 10301.
	Wagner College, Department of Music, 631 Howard Avenue, Staten Island, NY 10301.
Stony Brook:	State University of New York at Stony Brook, Department of Music, Stony Brook, L I, NY 11794.
Syracuse:	Syracuse University, School of Music, 215 Crouse College, Syracuse, NY 13244.
White Plains:	Westchester Conservatory of Music, 20 Soundview Avenue, White Plains, NY 10606.

NORTH CAROLINA

Boiling Springs:	Gardner-Webb College, Fine Arts Department, Boiling Springs, NC 28017.
Boone:	Appalachian State University, School of Music, Broyhill Music Center, Boone, NC 28608.
Brevard:	Brevard College, Fine Arts Division, North Broad Street, Brevard, NC 28712.
Buies Creek:	Campbell University, Fine Arts Division, Buies Creek, NC 27506.
Chapel Hill:	University of North Carolina at Chapel Hill, Department of Music, Hill Hall CB3320, Chapel Hill, NC 27599.
Charlotte:	Community School of the Arts, 200 West Trade Street, Charlotte, NC 28202.
	Queens College, Fine Arts Division and Music Department, 1900 Selwyn Avenue, Charlotte, NC 28274.

	University of North Carolina at Charlotte, Performing Arts Department, Charlotte, NC 28223.
Cullowhee:	Western Carolina University, Department of Music, Cullowhee, NC 28723.
Davidson:	Davidson College, Department of Music, Box 358, Davidson, NC 28036.
Durham:	North Carolina Central University, Department of Music, Box 19405, Durham, NC 27707.
	Duke University, Department of Music, PO Box 6695, College Station, Durham, NC 27708.
Elizabeth City:	Elizabeth City State University, Department of Music, Box 820, Elizabeth City, NC 27909.
Greensboro:	North Carolina Agricultural and Technical State University, Department of Music, 1601 East Market Street, Greensboro, NC 27411.
	University of North Carolina at Greensboro, School of Music, Greensboro, NC 27412.
Hickory:	Lenoir-Rhyne College, Department of Music, Box 7355, Hickory, NC 28603.
Mars Hill:	Mars Hill College, Fine Arts Division, PO Box 530, Mars Hill, NC 28754.
Misenheimer:	Pfeiffer College, Fine Arts Department, Misenheimer, NC 28109.
Pembroke:	Pembroke State University, Department of Music, Pembroke, NC 28372,
Raleigh:	Meredith College, 3800 Hillsborough Street, Raleigh, NC 27607.
Salisbury:	Catawba College, Department of Music, 2300 West Innes Street, Salisbury, NC 28144.
Wilmington:	University of North Carolina at Wilmington, Creative Arts Department, 601 South College Road, Wilmington, NC 28403.
Wilson:	Atlantic Christian College, Fine Arts Department, Wilson, NC 27893.
Wingate:	Wingate College, Fine Arts Department, Wingate, NC 28174.
Winston-Salem:	North Carolina School of the Arts, School of Music, 200 Waughtown Street, Winston-Salem, NC 27117.
	Salem College, School of Music, Winston-Salem, NC 27108.
	Wake Forest University, Department of Music, 7345 Reynolds Station, Winston-Salem, NC 27109.
	Winston-Salem State University, Department of Music, PO Box 13176, Winston-Salem, NC 27101.

NORTH DAKOTA

Fargo:	North Dakota State University, Music and Visual Arts Department, Box 5691, Fargo, ND 58105.
Grand Forks:	University of North Dakota, Department of Music, Box 8124, Grand Forks, ND 58202.
Mayville;	Mayville State University, Humanities and Social Science Division, Mayville, ND 58257.
Minot:	Minot State University, Music Division, 500 Ninth Avenue North West, Minot, ND 58701.
Valley City:	Valley City State University, Department of Music, Valley City, ND 58072.

OHIO

Ada:	Ohio Northern University, Department of Music, 525 South Main Street, Ada, OH 45810.
Akron:	University of Akron, School of Music, 302 East Buchtel, Akron, OH 44325.
Alliance:	Mount Union College, Department of Music, 1972 Clark Avenue, Alliance, OH 44601.
Ashland:	Ashland University, Department of Music, 401 College Avenue, Ashland, OH 44805.
Athens:	Ohio University, School of Music, Athens, OH 45701.
Berea:	Baldwin-Wallace College, Conservatory of Music, Berea, OH 44017.
Bluffton:	Bluffton College, Department of Music, Bluffton, OH 45817.
Bowling Green:	Bowling Green State University, College of Musical Arts, Bowling Green, OH 43403.
Canton:	Malone College, Fine Arts Department, 515 25th Street North West, Canton, OH 44709.
Cincinnati:	University of Cincinnati, College-Conservatory of Music, Cincinnati, OH 45221.
	Xavier University, Department of Music, 3800 Victory Parkway, Cincinnati, OH 45207.
Cleveland:	Case Western Reserve University, Department of Music, Haydn Hall, Cleveland, OH 44106.
	Cleveland Institute of Music, 11021 East Boulevard, Cleveland, OHN 44106.
	Cleveland Music School Settlement, 11125 Magnolia Drive, Cleveland, OH 44106.
	Cleveland State University, Department of Music, Cleveland, OH 44115.
Columbus:	Capital University, Conservatory of Music, 2199 East Main Street, Columbus, OH 43209.
	Ohio State University, School of Music, 1866 College Road, Columbus, OH 43210.
Dayton:	University of Dayton, Music Division, 300 College Park Drive, Dayton, OH 45469.
	Wright State University, Department of Music, Dayton, OH 45435.
Delaware:	Ohio Wesleyan University, Department of Music, Delaware, OH 43015.
Granville:	Denison University, Department of Music, Granville, OH 43023.
Hiram:	Hiram College, Department of Music, Hiram, OHN 44234.
Kent:	Kent State University, School of Music, Kent, OH 44242.
Marietta:	Marietta College, Edward E MacTaggart Department of Music, Marietta, OH 45750.
Mount St Joseph:	College of Mount St Joseph, Department of Music, Delhi and Neeb Roads, Mount St Joseph, OH 45051.
New Concord:	Muskingum College, Department of Music, New Concord, OH 43762.
Oberlin:	Oberlin College Conservatory of Music, Oberlin, OH 44074.
Oxford:	Miami University, Department of Music, 121 Center for Performing Arts, Oxford, OH 45056.
Springfield:	Wittenberg University, Department of Music, Springfield, OH 45501.
Toledo:	University of Toledo, Department of Music, 2801 West Bancroft Street, Toledo, OH 43606.
Westerville:	Otterbein College, Department of Music, Battelle Fine Arts Center, Westerville, OH 43081.
Wilberforce:	Central State University, Department of Music, Paul Robeson Cultural and Performing Arts Center, Room 218, Wilberforce, OH 45384.
Wooster:	College of Wooster, Department of Music, Wooster, OH 44691.
Youngstown:	Youngstown State University, Dana School of Music, 410 Wick Avenue, Youngstown, OH 44555.

OKLAHOMA

Bethany:	Southern Nazarene University, School of Music, 6729 North West 39 Expressway, Bethany, OK 73008.
Chickasha:	University of Sciences and Arts of Oklahoma, Box 3388, Chickasha, OK 73018.
Durant:	Southeastern Oklahoma State University, Department of Music, Box 4173, Station A, Durant, OK 74701.
Edmond:	Central State University, Department of Music, 100 North University Drive, Edmond, OK 73034.
Enid:	Philips University, Department of Music, Division of Fine Arts, PO Box 2000, University Station, Enid, OK 73702.
Lawton:	Cameron University, Department of Music, Lawton, OK 73505.
Norman:	University of Oklahoma, School of Music, 560 Parrington Oval, No 109A, Norman, OK 73019.
Oklahoma:	Guy Fraser Harrison Academy for the Performing Arts, Box 60408, Oklahoma City, OK 73146.
	Oklahoma City University, School of Music and Performing Arts, 2501 North Blackwelder, Oklahoma City, OK 73106.
Shawnee:	Oklahoma Baptist University, Warren M Angell College of Fine Arts, 500 West University, Shawnee, OK 74801.

MUSIC CONSERVATOIRES

Stillwater:	Oklahoma State University, Department of Music, 132 Seretean Center, Stillwater, OK 74078.
Tahlequah:	Northeastern State University, College of Arts and Letters, Tahlequah, OK 74464.
Tulsa:	Oral Roberts University, Fine Arts Department, Tulsa, OK 74171.
	University of Tulsa, Department of Music, 600 South College, Tulsa, OK 74104.

OREGON

Ashland:	Southern Oregon State College, Department of Music, 1250 Siskiyou Boulevard, Ashland, OR 97520.
Corvallis:	Oregon State University, Department of Music, Benton 101, Corvallis, OR 97331.
Eugene:	University of Oregon, School of Music, Eugene, OR 97403.
Forest Grove:	Pacific University, Department of Music, Forest Grove, OR 97116.
Marylhurst:	Marylhurst College, Department of Music, Marylhurst, OR 97036.
Monmouth	Western Oregon State College, Creative Arts Division, Monmouth, OR 97361.
Portland:	Lewis and Clark College, Department of Music, 0615 South West Palatine Hill Road, Portland, OR 97219.
	Portland State University, Department of Music, PO Box 751, Portland, OR 97207.
	University of Portland, Performing and Fine Arts Department, 5000 North Williamette Boulevard, Portland, OR 97203.
Salem:	Willamette University, Department of Music, 900 State Street, Salem, OR 97301.

PENNSYLVANIA

Annville:	Lebanon Valley College, Department of Music, Blair Music Center, Annville, PA 17003.
Edinboro:	Edinboro University of Pennsylvania, Department of Music, Heather Hall Music Building, Edinboro, PA 16444.
Elizabethtown:	Elizabethtown College, Fine and Performing Arts Department, Rider Hall, 1 Alpha Drive, Elizabethtown, PA 17022.
Erie:	Mercyhurst College, D'Angelo School of Music, Glenwood Hills, Erie, PA 16546.
Gettysburg:	Gettysburg College, Department of Music, Gettysburg, PA 17325.
Grantham:	Messiah College, Department of Music, Grantham, PA 17027.
Greensburg:	Seton Hill College, Department of Music, Greensburg, PA 15601.
Immaculate:	Immaculate College, Department of Music, Immaculate, PA 19345.
Indiana:	Indiana University of Pennsylvania, Department of Music, 101 Cogswell Hall, Indiana, PA 15705.
Lewisburg:	Bucknell University, Department of Music, Lewisburg, PA 17837.
Mansfield:	Mansfield University, Department of Music, Butler Music Center, Mansfield, PA 16933.
Meadville:	Allegheny College, Department of Music, 520 North Main Street, Meadville, PA 16335.
Millersville:	Millersville University of Pennsylvania, Department of Music, Northumberland House, Millersville, PA 17551.
New Wilmington:	Westminster College, Department of Music, New Wilmington, PA 16172.
Philadelphia:	Academy of Vocal Arts, 1920 Spruce Street, Philadelphia, PA 19103.
	Curtis Institute of Music, 1726 Locust Street, Philadelphia, PA 19103.
	Drexel University, Performing Arts Department, 32 and Chestnut Streets, Philadelphia, PA 19104.
	La Salle University, Fine Arts Department, Philadelphia, PA 19141.
	Philadelphia College of Performing Arts, The University of the Arts - The School of Music, 250 South Broad Street, Philadelphia, PA 19102.
	Settlement Music School, 416 Queen Street, Philadelphia, PA 19147.
	Temple University, Esther Boyer College of Music, 13th and Norris Streets, Philadelphia, PA 19122.
	University of Pennsylvania, Department of Music, 201 South 34th Street, Philadelphia, PA 19104.
Pittsburgh:	Carnegie Mellon University, Department of Music, 5000 Forbes Avenue, Pittsburgh, PA 15213.
	Duquesne University, School of Music, 600 Forbes Avenue, Pittsburgh, PA 15282.
	University of Pittsburgh, Department of Music, 110 Music Building, Pittsburgh, PA 15260.
Scranton:	Marywood College, Department of Music, 2300 Adams Avenue, Scranton, PA 18509.
Selinsgrove:	Susquehanna University, Department of Music, Selinsgrove, PA 17870.
Slippery Rock:	Slippery Rock University, Department of Music, Slippery Rock, PA 16057.
University Park:	Pennsylvania State University, School of Muisc, 232 Music Building, University Park, PA 16802.
Wawa:	Darlington Fine Arts Center, Baltimore Pike, Wawa, PA 19063.

PUERTO RICO

Rio Piedras:	University of Puerto Rico, Department of Music, Box 23335, Rio Piedras, PR 00931.
San Germán:	Interamerican University of Puerto Rico, Department of Music, Wilson Cottage, Call Box 5100, San Germán, PR 00735.
Santurce:	Conservatory of Music of Puerto Rico, PO Box 41227, Minillas Station, Santurce, PR 00940.

RHODE ISLAND

Kingston:	University of Rhode Island, Department of Musc, Fine Arts Center, Kingston, RI 02881.
Providence:	Brown University, Department of Music, Box 1924, 1 Young Orchard Avenue, Providence, RI 02912.
	The Music School, 75 John Street, Providence, RI 02906.
	Providence College, Department of Music, River Avenue and Easton Street, Providence, RI 02918.
	Rhode Island College, Department of Music, 600 Mount Pleasant Avenue, Providence, RI 02908.
Westerly:	Center School for the Arts, 116 High Street, Westerly, RI 02891.

SOUTH CAROLINA

Anderson:	Anderson College, Department of Music, 316 Boulevard, Anderson, SC 29621.
Charleston:	Baptist College at Charleston, Department of Music, PO Box 10087, Charleston, SC 29411.
Clemson:	Clemson University, Performing Arts Department, Clemson, SC 29634.
Columbia;	Columbia College, Department of Music, Columbia, SC 29203.
	University of South Carolina, School of Music, Columbia, SC 29208.
Gaffney:	Limestone College, Fine Arts Division, 115 College Drive, Gaffney, SC 29340.
Greenville:	Bob Jones University, Music Division, Box 34533, Greenville, SC 29614.
	Furman University, Department of Music, Greenville, SC 29613.
Hartsville:	Coker College, Department of Music, Hartsville, SC 29550.
Newberry:	Newberry College, Department of Music, Newberry, SC 29108.
Orangeburg:	South Carolina State College, Department of Music, Box 1917, Orangeburg, SC 29117.
Rock Hill:	Winthrop College, Department of Music, 112 Conservatory of Music, Rock Hill, SC 29733.
Spartanburg:	Converse College, School of Music, Spartanburg, SC 29301.

SOUTH DAKOTA

Aberdeen:	Northern State College, School of Fine Arts, Aberdeen, SD 57401.
Brookings:	South Dakota State University, Department of Music, Brookings, SD 57007.
Sioux Falls:	Augustana College, Department of Music, Sioux Falls, SD 57197.
	Sioux Falls College, Fine Arts Division, 1501 South Prairie Avenue, Sioux Falls, SD 57105.
Spearfish:	Black Hills State University, School of Arts and Humanities, PO Box 9003, Spearfish, SD 57783.
Vermllion:	University of South Dakota, Department of Music, Vermillion, SD 57069.

TENNESSEE

Athens:	Tennessee Wesleyan College, Department of Music, PO box 40, Athens, TN 37303.
Chattanooga:	Tennessee Temple University, Department of Music, 1815 Union Avenue, Chattanooga, TN 37404.
	University of Tennessee at Chattanooga, Cadek Department of Music, 308 Fine Arts Center, Chattanooga, TN 37403.
Clarksville:	Austin Peay state University, Department of Music, Box 4625, Clarksville, TN 37044.
Cookeville:	Tennessee Technological University, Department of Music, Box 5045, Cookeville, TN 38505.
Jackson:	Union University, Department of Music, 2447 Highway 45 Bypass, Jackson, TN 38305.
Jefferson City:	Carson-Newman College, Music Division, Box 1839, Jefferson City, TN 37760.
Johnson City:	East Tennessee State University, Department of Music, Box 22330A, Johnson City, TN 37614.
Knoxville:	University of Tennessee at Knoxville, Department of Music, 1741 Volunteer Boulevard, Knoxville, TN 37996.
Martin:	University of Tennessee at Martin, Department of Music, 232 Fine Arts Building, Martin, TN 38238.
Maryville:	Maryville College, Fine Arts Department, Box 2805, Maryville, TN 37801.
Memphis:	Memphis State University, Department of Music, Memphis, TN 38152.
	Rhodes College, Department of Music, 2000 North Parkway, Memphis, TN 38112.
Murfreesboro:	Middle Tennessee State University, Department of Music, Box 47, Murfreesboro, TN 37132.
Nashville:	Belmont College, School of Music, 1900 Belmont Boulevard, Nashville, TN 37212.
	Fish University, Department of Music, 1000 17th Avenue North, Nashville, TN 37208.
	Tennessee State University, Department of Music, 3500 John A Merritt Boulevard, Nashville, TN 37203.
	Vanderbilt University, Blair School of Music, 2400 Blakemore Avenue, Nashville, TN 37212.

TEXAS

Abilene:	Abilene Christian University, Department of Music, Box 8274, Abilene, TX 79699.
	Hardin-Simmons University, School of Music, Drawer J Abilene, TX 79698.
Alpine:	Sul Ross State University, Department of Music, Alpine, TX 79832.
Amarillo:	Amarillo College, Department of Music, Box 447, Amarillo, TX 79178.
Arlington:	University of Texas at Arlington, Department of Music, Box 19105, Arlington, TX 76019.
Austin:	University of Texas at Austin, Department of Music, Austin, TX 78712.
Beaumont:	Lamar University, Department of Music, PO Box 10044, Beaumont, TX 77710.
Brownwood:	Howard Payne University, School of Music, Brownwood, TX 76801.
Canyon:	West Texas State University, Music and Dance Department, PO Box 870, Canyon, TX 79016.
Commerce:	East Texas State University, Department of Music, Commerce, TX 75428.
Corpus Christi:	Corpus Christi State University, Visual and Performing Arts Department, 6300 Ocean Drive, Corpus Christi, TX 78412.
Dallas:	Richland College, Humanities Division, 12800 Abrams Road, Dallas, TX 75243.
	Southern Methodist University, Meadows School of the Arts, Owen Arts Center, Dallas, TX 75275.
Denton:	Texas Woman's University, Performing Arts Department, PO Box 23865, Denton, TX 76204.
	University of North Texas, School of Music, PO Box 13887, Denton, TX 76203.
Edinburg:	Pan American University, Department of Music, Edinburg, TX 78539.
El Paso:	University of Texas at El Paso, Department of Music, University Avenue at Hawthorne, El Paso, TX 79968.
Fort Worth:	Southwestern Baptist Theological Seminary, School of Church Music, PO Box 22000, Fort Worth, TX 76122.
	Texas Christian University, Department of Music, Box 32887, Fort Worth, TX 76129.
	Texas Wesleyan University, School of Fine Arts, Fort Worth, TX 76105.
Georgetown:	Southwestern University, School of Fine Arts, Georgetown, TX 78626.
Houston:	Houston Baptist University, College of Fine Arts, 7502 Fondren Road, Houston, TX 77074.
	Rice University, Shepherd School of Music, PO Box 1892, Houston, TX 77251.
	San Jacinto College North, Fine Arts Division, 5800 Uvalde Road, Houston, TX 77049.
	University of Houston, School of Music, 4800 Calhoun, Houston, TX 77204.
Huntsville:	Sam Houston State University, Department of Music, Huntsville, TX 77341.
Kingsville:	Texas A & I University, Department of Music, Box 174, Kingsville, TX 78363.
Lubbock:	Texas Tech University, School of Music, PO Box 4239, Lubbock, TX 79409.
Marshall:	East Texas Baptist University, Department of Music, 1209 North Grove, Marshall, TX 75670.
Nacogdoches:	Stephen F Austin State University, Department of Music, Box 13043, Nacogdoches, TX 75962.
Odessa:	Odessa College, Department of Music, 201 West University Boulevard, Odessa, TX 79764.
San Angelo:	Angelo State University, Department of Music, San Angelo, TX 76909.
San Antonio:	Incarnate Word College, Department of Music, 4301 Broadway, San Antonio, TX 78209.
	St Mary's University of San Antonio, Department of Music, 1 Camino Santa Maria, San Antonio, TX 78284.
	Trinity University, Department of Music, 715 Stadium Drive, San Antonio, TX 78284.
	University of Texas at San Antonio, Music Division, San Antonio, TX 78285.
San Marcos:	Southwest Texas State University, Department of Music, San Marcos, TX 78666.
Sherman:	Austin College, Department of Music, PO Box 1177, Sherman, TX 75091.
Texarkana:	Texarkana College, Department of Music, Texarkana, TX 75501.
Waco:	Baylor University, School of Music, Box 7408, Waco, TX 76798.
Wichita Falls:	Midwestern State University, Department of Music, 3400 Taft, Wichita Falls, TX 76308.

UTAH

Logan:	Utah State Univesity, Department of Music, Logan, UT 84322.
Ogden:	Weber State College, Performing Arts Department, 3750 Harrison Boulevard, Odgen, UT 84408.
Provo:	Brigham Young University, Department of Music, C-550 Harris Fine Arts Center, Provo, UT 84602.

Salt Lake City:	University of Utah, Department of Music, 204 Gardner Hall, Salt Lake City, UT 84112.

VERMONT

Bennington:	Bennington College, Department of Music, Jennings Hall, Bennington, VT 05201.
Brattleboro:	Music School of Brattleboro Music Center, 15 walnut Street, Brattleboro, VT 05301.
Burlington:	University of Vermont, Department of Music, Music Building, Redstone Campus, Bulington, VT 05405.
Middlebury:	Middlebury College, Department of Music, 326 Johnson Building, Middlebury, VT 05753.
Winooski:	St Micael's College, Fine Arts Department, 56 College Farkway, Winooski, VT 05404.

VIRGINIA

Blacksburg:	Virginia Polytechnic Institute and State University, Department of Music, 256 Lane, Blacksburg, VA 24061.
Charlottsville:	University of Virginia, Department of Music, 112 Old Cabell Hall, Charlottesville, VA 22903.
Fairfax:	George Mason University, Department of Music, 4400 University Drive, Fairfax, VA 22030.
Farmville:	Longwood College, Department of Music, Farmville, VA 23901.
Fredericksburg:	Mary Washington College, Department of Music, Fredericksburg, VA 22401.
Hampton:	Hampton University, Department of Music, Hampton, VA 23668.
Harrisonburg:	James Madison University, Department of Music, Harrisonburg, VA 22807.
Lynchburg:	Liberty University, Department of Music, Box 20000, Lynchburg, VA 24506.
	Virginia School of the Arts, Department of Music, 2240 Rivermont Avenue, Lynchburg, VA 24503.
Newport News:	Christopher Newport College, Department of Music, 50 Shoe Lane, Newport News, VA 23606.
Norfolk:	Norfolk State University, Department of Music, 2401 Corprew Avenue, Norfolk, VA 23504.
	Old Dominion University, Department of Music, Norfolk, VA 23508.
Petersburg:	Virginia State University, Department of Music, Box 7, Petersburg, VA 23803.
Radford:	Radford University, Department of Music, East Norwood Street, Radford, VA 24142.
Richmond:	University of Richmond, Department of Music, Richmond, VA 23173.
	Virginia Commonwealth University, Department of Music, 922 Park Avenue, Richmond, VA 23284.
Roanoke:	Hollins College, Department of Music, PO Box 9642, Roanoke, VA 24020.
Salem:	Roanoke College, Fine Arts Department, Olin Hall Center for Arts and Humanities, Salem, VA 24153.
Sweet Briar:	Sweet Briar College, Department of Music, Sweet Briar, VA 24595.
Williamsburg:	College of William and Mary, Department of Music, Williamsburg, VA 23185.
Winchester:	Shenandoah College and Conservatory, Winchester, VA 22601.

WASHINGTON

Bellingham:	Western Washington University, Department of Music, PA 273, Bellingham, WA 98225.
Cheney:	Eastern Washington University, Department of Music, Cheney, WA 99004.
College Place:	Walla Walla College, Department of Music, College Place, WA 99324.
Ellensburg:	Central Washington University, Department of Music, Ellensburg, WA 98926.
Pullman:	Washington State University, School of Music, Kimbrough Music Building, Pullman, WA 99164.
Seattle:	Cornish College of Arts, Department of Music, 710 East Roy Street, Seattle, WA 98102.
	Seattle Pacific University, School of Fine and Performing Arts, 3307 Third Avenue West, Seattle, WA 98119.
	University of Washington, School of Music, DN-10, Seattle, WA 98195.
Spokane:	Whitworth College, Department of Music, Spokane, WA 99251.
Tacoma:	Pacific Lutheran University, Department of Music, Tacoma, WA 98447.
	University of Puget, School of Music, 1500 North Warner, Tacoma, WA 98416.
Walla Walla:	Whitman College, School of Music, 345 Boyer, Walla Walla, WA 99362.

WEST VIRGINIA

Buckhannon:	West Virginia Wesleyan College, Department of Music, Box 40, Buckhannon, WV 26201.
Fairmont:	Fairmont State College, Fine Arts Division, Fairmont, WV 26554.
Huntington:	Marshall University, Department of Music, Huntington, WV 25701.
Institute:	West Virginia State College, Department of Music, Box 4, Institute, WV 25112.
Morgantown:	West Virginia University, Department of Music, Creative Arts Center, Morgantown, WV 26506.
Philippi:	Alderson-Broaddus College, Department of Music, College Hill, Philippi, WV 25416.
West Liberty:	West Liberty State College, Department of Music, Hall of Fine Arts, West Liberty, WV 26074.

WISCONSIN

Appleton:	Lawrence University, Conservatory of Music, PO Box 599, Appleton WI 54912.
Beloit:	Beloit College, Department of Music, Beloit, WI 53511.
De Pere:	St Norbert College, Department of Music, De Pere, WI 54115.
Eau Claire:	University of Wisconsin, Eau Claire, Department of Music, Fine Arts Center, Eau Claire, WI 54701.
Green Bay:	University of Wisconsin, Green Bay, Department of Music, Green Bay, WI 54301.
Kenosha:	Carthage College, Department of Music, Kenosha, WI 53141.
	University of Wisconsin, Parkside, Department of Music, 285 Communication Arts Building, Kenosha, WI 53141.
La Crosse:	University of Wisconsin, La Crosse, Department of Music, 234 Fine Arts Building, La Crosse, WI 54601.
	Viterbo College, Department of Music, 815 South Ninth Street, La Crosse, WI 54601.
Madison:	University of Wisconsin, Madison, School of Music, 455 Park Street, Madison, WI 53706.
Manitowoc:	Silver Lake College, Department of Music, 2406 Alverne Road, Manitowoc, WI 54220.
Milwaukee:	Alverno College, Department of Music, 3401 South 39th Street, Milwaukee, WI 53215.
	University of Wisconsin, Milwaukee, Department of Music, PO Box 413, Milwaukee, WI 53201.
	Wisconsin Conservatory of Music, 1584 North Prospect Avenue, Milwaukee, WI 53202.
Oshkosh:	University of Wisconsin, Oshkosh, Department of Music, Arts and Communication Center, 800 Algoma Boulevard, Oshkosh, WI 54901.
Platteville:	University of Wisconsin, Platteville, Department of Music, 1 University Plaza, Platteville, WI 53818.
Ripon:	Ripon College, Department of Music, 300 Seward Street, Box 248, Ripon, WI 54971.
River Falls:	University of Wisconsin, River Falls, Department of Music, River Falls, Wi 54022.
Stevens Point:	University of Wisconsin, Stevens Point, Department of Music, Stevens Point, WI 54481.
Superior:	University of Wisconsin, Superior, Department of Music, Superior, WI 54880.

Waukesha:	Carroll College, Department of Music, 100 North East Avenue, Waukesha, WI 53186.
Wausau:	Wausau Conservatory of Music, 404 Seymour Street, PO Box 606, Wausau, WI 54402.
Whitewater:	University of Wisconsin, Whitewater, Department of Music, 800 West Main Street, Whitewater, WI 53190.

WYOMING

Laramie:	University of Wyoming, Department of Music, Box 3037, University Station, Laramie, WY 82071.

URUGUAY

Montevideo:	Conservatorio Falleri-Balzo, Avenida Uruguay 994, Montevideo.
	Conservatorio Nacional de Música, 25 De Mayo 692, Montevideo.
	Escuela Universitaria de Música, Paysandu 843, Montevideo.

VENEZUELA

Caracas:	Academia de Música Fischer, Edificio Léon de San Marco, Avenida Ciencias y Calle Risques, Los Chaguaramos, Caracas.
	Academia de Música Padre Sojo, 4A Avenida Trans, 8AY9A, Apdo 60479 Este, Caracas.
	Conservatorio Nacional de Música, "Juan José Landeata", Urbanización Campo Alegre, 4A Avenida, Caracas.
	Conservatorio Italiano de Música, Calle Montesacro, Colinas de Bello Monte, Caracas.
	Escuela de Música Lino Gallardo, Avenida Principal de la Castellana, Entre 21 y 3a Transversales, Quinta Yudith, Caracas.
	Escuela de Música Prudencio Esás, Avenida Principal El Paraiso, Quina Villa Helena, Caracas.
	Escuela Nacional de Música "Jose Angel Lamas", Veroes a Santa Capilla, Avenida Urdaneta, Caracas.
	Escuela Nacional de Opera, Este 2 con Sur 25, El Conde, Los Caobos, Caracus.

APPENDIX H
MASTERS OF THE KING'S/QUEEN'S MUSIC

It has long been the tradition for the Kings and Queens of England to retain a band of musicians as part of their household.

In 1660 Charles II established a band of performers of stringed instruments popularly known as the 'four and twenty fiddlers'. After the death of Charles the band was kept up but no longer consisted exclusively of stringed instruments. Its duties were mainly those of entertaining the King, playing in the royal chapel and the performance of music composed annually for the King's birthday and New Year's Day.

The holder of Master of the Music is now honorary and it is usual, though not obligatory, for the holder of the post to compose on important state occasions.

The following is the succession of the Masters of the King's/Queen's Music from the Restoration onwards. Unfortunately, complete records has not always been kept so there is some doubt concerning some of the dates:

Nicholas Lanier:	*1660.*
Louis Grabu:	*1666.*
Nicholas Staggins:	*1674.*
John Eccles:	*1700.*
Maurice Greene:	*1735(?).*
William Boyce:	*1755.*
John Stanley:	*1779.*
Sir William Parsons:	*1786.*
William Shield:	*1817.*
Christian Kramer:	*1834.*
George Frederick Anderson:	*1848.*
Sir William George Cusins:	*1870.*
Sir Walter Parratt:	*1893.*
Sir Edward Elgar:	*1924.*
Sir Walford Davies:	*1934.*
Sir Arnold Bax:	*1941.*
Sir Arthur Bliss:	*1953.*
Malcolm Williamson:	*1975.*

APPENDIX H

MASTERS OF THE KING'S/QUEEN'S MUSIC

It has long been the practice for the Kings and Queens of England to retain a band of musicians as a part of their household.

Until Charles I established a band of performers of stringed instruments popularly known as the 'twenty-four fiddlers', after the death of Charles the band was kept up but no longer consisted exclusively of stringed instruments. In earlier years many 'Odes' of entertaining the king, playing on the royal chapel and the performance of music composed annually for the King's birthday and the New Year's Day.

The title of Master of the Music is now honorary and titular, though not obligatory, but the period for the post is regulated on a permanent stipend or salary.

The following is the appointees of the Masters of the King's/Queen's Music from the first establishment, although, unfortunately, complete records has not always been kept so that the dates given below containing some of the dates.

Nicholas Lanier	1660?
Louis Grabu	1666
Nicholas Staggins	1674
John Eccles	1700
Maurice Greene	1735
William Boyce	1755
John Stanley	1779
Sir William Parsons	1786
William Shield	1817
Christian Kramer	1834
George Frederick Anderson	1848
Sir William George Cusins	1870
Sir Walter Parratt	1893
Sir Edward Elgar	1924
Sir Walford Davies	1934
Sir Arnold Bax	1941
Sir Arthur Bliss	1953
Malcolm Williamson	1975

*For Product Safety Concerns and Information please contact
our EU representative GPSR@taylorandfrancis.com Taylor & Francis
Verlag GmbH, Kaufingerstraße 24, 80331 München, Germany*

T - #0065 - 270225 - C0 - 280/208/40 [42] - CB - 9780948875922 - Gloss Lamination